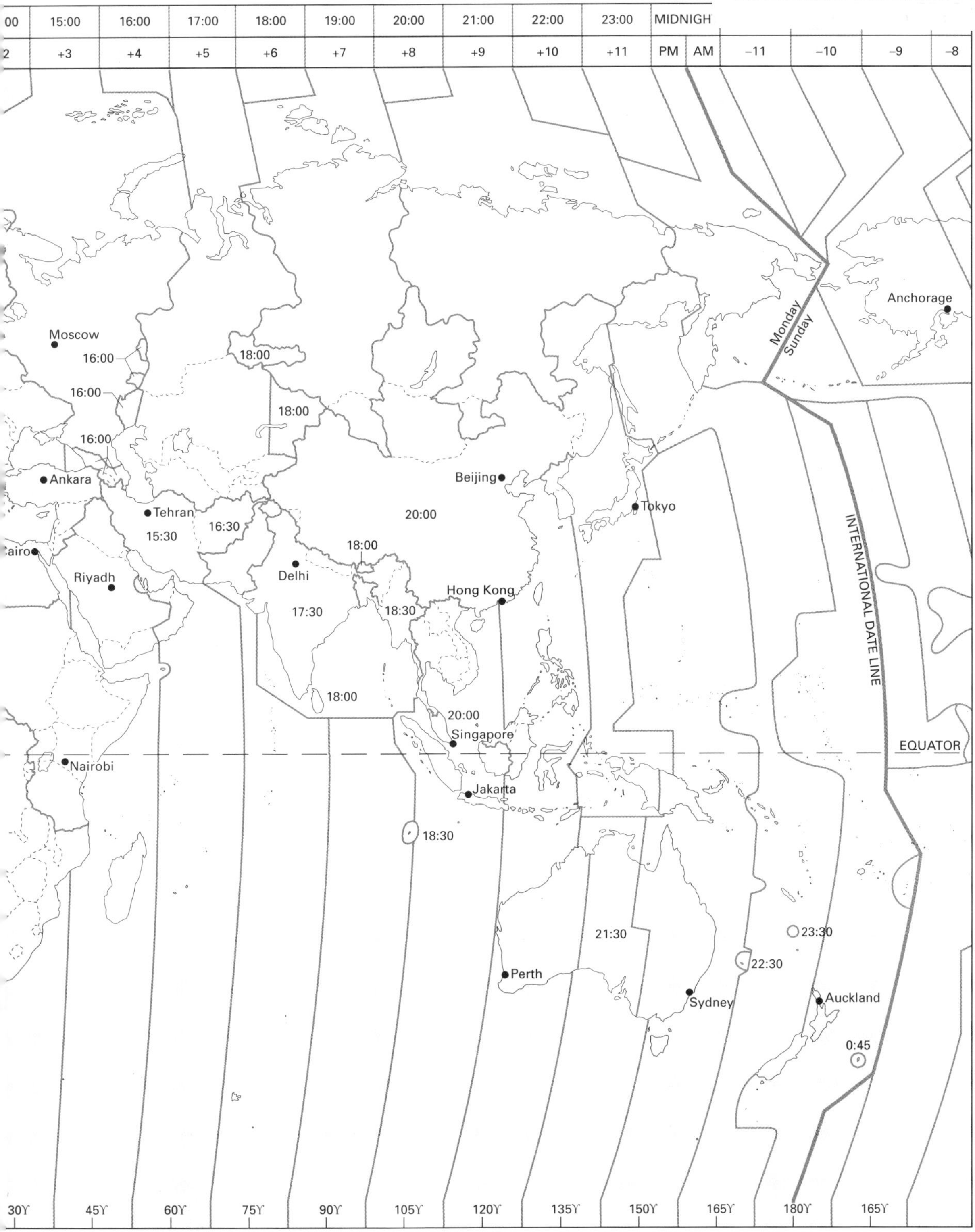
00
15:00
16:00
17:00
18:00
19:00
20:00
21:00
22:00
23:00
MIDNIGH
2
+3
+4
+5
+6
+7
+8
+9
+10
+11
PM
AM
–11
–10
–9
–8
Moscow
16:00
16:00
16:00
18:00
18:00
Ankara
Tehran
15:30
16:30
airo
Riyadh
Delhi
17:30
18:00
18:30
18:00
20:00
Beijing
Tokyo
Hong Kong
20:00
Singapore
Nairobi
Jakarta
18:30
Monday
Sunday
Anchorage
INTERNATIONAL DATE LINE
EQUATOR
21:30
Perth
Sydney
22:30
23:30
Auckland
0:45
30°
45°
60°
75°
90°
105°
120°
135°
150°
165°
180°
165°

THE STATESMAN'S YEARBOOK

2011

'Common sense is the best distributed commodity in the world, for every man is convinced that he is well supplied with it.'

René Descartes (1596–1650)

Editors

Frederick Martin	1864–1883
Sir John Scott-Keltie	1883–1926
Mortimer Epstein	1927–1946
S. H. Steinberg	1946–1969
John Paxton	1969–1990
Brian Hunter	1990–1997
Barry Turner	1997–

Credits

Publisher	Hazel Woodbridge (London) Airie Stuart (New York)
Editor	Barry Turner
Editorial Assistant	Jill Fenner
Senior Research Editor	Nicholas Heath-Brown
Research	Judith Frazer Jack Yuille Daniel Smith Richard German Saif Ullah Ingeborg Farstad Robert McGowan Ben Eastham James Wilson Justine Foong Liane Jones Matthew Lane Sharita Oomeer Martha Nyman
Index	Richard German
Print Production	Phillipa Davidson-Blake Michael Card
Design	Jim Weaver
Online Production	Semantico
Technical Support	Chetan Babu ERK
Marketing	Charley Holyhead (London) Denise De La Rosa (New York)

email: sybcomments@palgrave.com

THE STATESMAN'S YEARBOOK

THE POLITICS, CULTURES AND ECONOMIES OF THE WORLD

2011

Edited by
BARRY TURNER

palgrave
macmillan

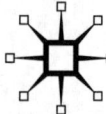

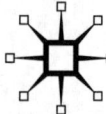

Published annually since 1864

This edition published 2010 by
PALGRAVE MACMILLAN

Palgrave Macmillan in the UK is an imprint of Macmillan Publishers Limited, registered in England, company number 785998, of Houndmills, Basingstoke, Hampshire RG21 6XS

Palgrave Macmillan in the US is a division of St Martin's Press LLC, 175 Fifth Avenue, New York, N. Y. 10010

Palgrave Macmillan is the global academic imprint of the above companies and has companies and representatives throughout the world.

Palgrave® and Macmillan® are registered trademarks in the United States, the United Kingdom, Europe and other countries.

ISBN 978-0-230-20603-8
ISSN 0081-4601

This book is printed on paper suitable for recycling and made from fully managed and sustained forest sources. Logging, pulping and manufacturing processes are expected to conform to the environmental regulations of the country of origin.

A catalogue record for this book is available from the British Library.

A catalog record for this book is available from the Library of Congress.

10 9 8 7 6 5 4 3 2 1
19 18 17 16 15 14 13 12 11 10

Printed in China

PREFACE

Every year the last few days before sending the book to press are particularly busy at *The Statesman's Yearbook* office, as, inevitably, new world events take place just at this critical time and need to be included. This year was no exception, and it means that the *Yearbook* can be relied upon to be as comprehensive as possible.

The Statesman's Yearbook is also available online as a dynamic resource. Institutions and organizations wanting a reliable online source of political, economic and social information on every country in the world can subscribe to www.statesmansyearbook.com. It is regularly updated and contains even more information than we are able to include in the printed book including a detailed week-by-week chronology of world events since the year 2000, fact sheets, city profiles, detailed biographical profiles of major post-WWII leaders, and the complete 146-year archive of previous editions. For more information and to arrange a free trial contact onlinesales@palgrave-usa.com (the Americas) or onlinesales@palgrave.com (rest of world).

If you have any comments or suggestions to help improve *The Statesman's Yearbook* we'd love to hear from you; please email us at sybcomments@palgrave.com or write to *The Statesman's Yearbook* team, Palgrave Macmillan, Houndmills, Basingstoke RG21 6XS, UK.

Hazel Woodbridge
Publisher, *The Statesman's Yearbook*

CONTENTS

Part I: International Organizations

Part II: Countries of the World A–Z

KEEPING UP WITH THE NEWS

Online competition is putting newspapers at risk—should we care?

Asked to lead a university seminar on careers in the media, a journalist friend spoke about his life in newspapers and the role of the press in a functioning democracy. He invited comments. Silence. To provoke discussion, he put a question. How many of you take a daily paper? No hands went up. Weekly? No hands went up. Now and then? A few, a very few hands were lifted. It dawned on my friend that instead of talking about the future of his industry he had instead given a history lesson.

That newspapers are in trouble no one can doubt. On both sides of the Atlantic they are either shutting down or cutting back on costs to a point where the value of the product risks being fatally undermined. We all know why this is happening. Online competition is taking away readers and advertisers, each accelerating the decline of the other. The question is, does it matter?

There are those who argue that newspapers, their owners and the journalists they employ, had it coming to them; that in their pursuit of the trivial and artificial, their dependence on a celebrity culture ('An individual emptiness gawped at by a collective emptiness ... a manifestation of the cretinisation of our culture'.[1]) they are all culpable. It is surely no coincidence that journalists rival politicians for the lowest rank in public esteem.

There is, however, a strong counter argument, put succinctly by the philosopher A. C. Grayling who asserts that a free press 'although it always abuses its freedom in the hunt for profit, is necessary with all its warts, as one of the two essential estates of a free society, the other being an independent judiciary'.[2] For all the miles of column inches devoted to mindless, often degrading, ephemera, the press is the first line of defence against the political, doctrinal and commercial manipulators who try to work the system in defiance of the public interest. Television has its role but traditionally, the BBC excepted, it depends on the press for its lead as do the online bloggers and twitterers. Though opinion is unfettered it is diminished if not supported by serious and costly investigative journalism.

Cost. It always comes back to that economic imperative. Newspapers have not done themselves any favours by making much of their content available online free of charge. This apparently loony business model was based on the assumption that internet users would be so inspired as to rush out to buy the print version or become so hooked on the online service that, eventually, they would be happy to pay for access.

The strategy has foundered on the popular conception of the net as a benevolent information provider unencumbered by the profit motive. Specialist services such as those provided by the *Wall Street Journal* and the *Financial Times* can sustain a substantial price tag but general news, by definition short-lived and easily discarded, has yet to find a profitable niche.

As the mightiest media mogul of them all, Rupert Murdoch is characteristically robust, predicting that 'newspapers will reach new heights in the 21st century'. The form of delivery may change but 'the potential audience for our content will multiply many times over. Our real business isn't printing on dead trees. It is giving our readers great journalism and great judgement'.[3]

No one would argue with that though there might be disagreement on what constitutes great journalism and great judgement. In a vigorous attack on the BBC for trying to dominate the market with 'state-sponsored news', James Murdoch, Rupert's heir apparent, claims that 'the ability to generate a profitable return is fundamental to media quality, plurality and independence'.[4]

But while the BBC has its faults, the denigration of public service broadcasting would be more convincing if the privately owned media was shown to be genuinely independent. Even if we have moved a long way from the dictum of Lord Beaverbrook, creator of the mass circulation Express group, who told a Royal Commission on the press that he owned newspapers not for profit but for disseminating political propaganda, it is still true that press freedom often translates into the freedom of newspaper owners to promote causes they hold most dear. Editorial judgement is only free within the parameters set by those who hold the purse strings. Readers know this. It is not surprising to find that public broadcasting has the higher trust rating.

Even if the BBC cuts back on activities that threaten open competition, it is not about to abandon its online ventures. Indeed, non-profit online services are set to increase as wealthy foundations, mostly in the US, are persuaded to back independent investigative reporting.

The success of free newspapers which account for 7 percent of global circulation, 8 percent in the US and 23 percent of circulation in Europe alone, suggests that advertisers are by no means convinced that only paying readers make the best customers.

That said, subscriptions, if they can be made to work, are unarguably the best guarantee of newspaper survival. In Japan, where 90 percent of newspapers are sold on monthly subscriptions with a guarantee of home delivery, circulations are holding up remarkably well. The challenge for the American and European press is to hold together on the need for subscriptions. It takes only one major paper to offer free journalism for a potentially devastating circulation war to break out. If this happens, and it is a distinct probability, the paying option will have to be made more enticing by newspapers creating their own distinctive websites. It will not be enough simply to reproduce hard print onscreen. There has to be more must-read content with more inside information on high value subjects.

Leading the way is the *New York Times* with a digital edition that is awash with videos, charts and specialist blogs, all calculated to entice the reader to sign on for the long term. The *NYT* will charge for full access to its website from 2011. But it is still to be seen whether this editorial profusion will generate sufficient income to support worldwide news gathering of the quality traditionally associated with America's top newspaper.

Meanwhile, the search is on for ways in which powerful brands (which is what newspapers with instantly recognizable names really are) can be used to generate revenue from add-on services and products. The Murdoch papers already have this well in hand with enterprises ranging from fantasy football associated with the tabloid *Sun* to a wine club promoted by the upmarket *Sunday Times*. The full potential of branding has still to be realized as the digital guru Chris Anderson points out; there might even be a case for reassessing free online access since 'companies ought to be able to make huge amounts of money around the thing being given away as Google gives away its search and email and makes its money on advertising'.[5] One possibility for Murdoch with his multimedia interests is to bundle print and television together in a one for all subscription. Equally, stand alone newspapers might forge strategic partnerships with parallel media.

Another option to be taken seriously, though up to now entirely foreign to the private enterprise instinct of the Anglo-American press barons, is state subsidy. Put baldly, the acceptance of government help would seem to place at risk the first requirement of a free press, that it should be immune to political interference. But no one is suggesting an all-embracing subsidy which shifts the balance of ownership.

In Sweden, financial support for the press is largely in the form of a grant-aided national system of early morning delivery.

There are also easy term loans to encourage the updating of print technology. France has a novel scheme whereby eighteenth birthdays are marked by the gift of a newspaper subscription, compliments of the government. Press subsidies in one form or another are common in Austria, Norway and Spain where they are judged to be essential to the diversity of the press, particularly at regional and local level.

The formula is attracting interest in the US where Leonard Downie, a vice president and former executive editor of *The Washington Post*, has put his name to a report advocating a national fund for local news with money collected from a federal tax on telecom users, broadcast licensees and internet service providers. Grants would be made by independent local news fund councils for innovative reporting and support services.[6]

But whether by self help or state help, newspapers can only meet the online challenge by reinventing the ways they do business and the ways they serve their readers. The accountants' knee jerk solution to a deficit, to fire expensive front line journalists, is to accelerate the downward spiral—falling circulations following superficiality. Swamped by gossip served up as information, readers of hard print as much as those seduced by online, will need more guidance on finding a way through the maze of irrelevancy. That means hiring top rank journalists who combine inquiring minds with the ability to communicate clearly and persuasively. Such paragons do not come cheaply.

Time is short. Even if all that needs to be done is done, it may not be enough. Waiting in the wings are Google, Microsoft and the other internet giants who must see news gathering as one of the next big things in their business plans. The media revolution is only just beginning.

Barry Turner

[1] Raymond Tallis, *The Times*. October 14th, 2009
[2] A. C. Grayling, *Liberty in the Age of Terror*. Bloomsbury, 2009
[3] Boyer Lectures. ABC Radio National. November 16th, 2008
[4] MacTaggart Lecture. Edinburgh International Television Festival. August 28th, 2009
[5] Chris Anderson, *Free: The Future of a Radical Price*. 2009
[6] *Financial Times*. October 21st, 2009

NEWS MEDIA FACT SHEET

• Number of people globally who read a paid-for newspaper daily (2008)	1·9bn.
• Number of paid-for daily newspapers around the world (2008)	12,000
• Estimated total value of newspaper publishing market (2007)	US$191·5bn.
• Top three highest circulation paid-for daily papers	Yomiuri Shimbun (Japan; 10·0m.); The Asahi Shimbun (Japan; 8·0m.); Mainichi Shimbun (Japan; 3·9m.)
• Free daily paper with largest circulation	Metro (UK; 1·4m.)
• Countries with highest circulation of daily newspapers (2007)	China (108m.); India (99m.); Japan (69m.); USA (54m.)
• Country with the largest uptake of paid-for daily newspaper (copies per 1,000 adults)	Liechtenstein (714)
• OECD country with the largest uptake of paid-for daily newspaper (copies per 1,000 adults)	Japan (612)
• Country reporting highest daily newspaper reach	Costa Rica (92·8%)
• Country with highest news media-based advertising revenues	USA
• Value of advertising revenues of US paid-for dailies in 2007	US$42·2bn.
• Value of advertising revenues of US paid-for dailies in 2008	US$34·7bn.
• % decline of advertising revenues of US paid-for dailies, 2004–08	–25·62%
• Number of daily newspaper websites in the USA (2006)	1,674
• US internet advertising expenditure (2007)	US$16·1bn.
• % increase of US internet advertising revenues, 2004–08	124·67%
• World's largest multi media news organization by market capitalization	Thomson Reuters (US$20·7bn.)
• World's oldest newspaper still in existence (online only since 2007)	Post- och Inrikes Tidningar (Sweden, 1645)
• World's oldest newspaper still in print	Opregte Haarlemsche Courant (Netherlands, 1656)
• % of world's nations with Press Freedom designation of 'free' (2009)	36%
• % of world's nations with Press Freedom designation of 'partly free' (2009)	31%
• % of world's nations with Press Freedom designation of 'not free' (2009)	33%
• Countries with highest Press Freedom rating (2009; Freedom House)	Iceland, Finland, Norway
• Countries with lowest Press Freedom rating (2009; Freedom House)	North Korea, Turkmenistan, Myanmar
• Number of journalists killed in 2009	71

Sources: Committee to Protect Journalists, Forbes.com, Freedom House, World Press Trends 2009 (World Association of Newspapers)

HAITI IN PERSPECTIVE: A TIMELINE OF NATURAL DISASTERS

December 2004–January 2010

At least 36 million people were displaced by sudden-onset natural disasters in 2008 according to the Internal Displacement Monitoring Centre. A new report by the Norwegian Refugee Council/Internal Displacement Monitoring Centre and the Office for the Coordination of Humanitarian Affairs adds that of this total, over 20 million were displaced by climate-related, sudden-onset disasters. 4·6 million people were displaced during the year by conflict and violence. A 2009 World Bank report showed that the number of natural disasters has significantly increased over the past decades. In the 1970s there were on average 78 disasters a year. Between 2000 and 2006 this had increased to an average of 351 a year, with the most marked rise among hydro-meteorological disasters. Since 2000 disaster-related damages have averaged US$83bn., up from an average US$12bn. in the 1970s (in constant 2005 US dollars).

Certain natural disasters can be determined by location and season. Although globally Sept. is the month most affected by hurricanes and May the least, storm seasons vary. Officially, the Atlantic season runs from 1 June to 30 Nov. with a peak in activity in late Aug. to Sept. and the Northeast Pacific basin follows a similar pattern. In the Northwest Pacific basin, peak season occurs in early Sept. while the North Indian basin has two peaks in May and Nov. The Southwest Indian and Australian/Southeast Indian seasons begin in late Oct. or early Nov. and have a double peak of activity in mid-Jan. and mid-Feb. to early March. The Australian/Southwest Pacific season starts around late Oct. or early Nov., peaks in late Feb. and finishes at the beginning of May.

Monsoons affect half of the tropics or a quarter of the globe's surface area. They are caused by the wind reversing direction owing to differences of temperature between land and sea. The major monsoon systems are the West African and Asia-Australian monsoons. The monsoon season runs between mid-June and Oct. in western sub-saharan Africa. In Asia, the Southwest Monsoon begins in June and lasts until Sept. affecting Bangladesh, India, Nepal, Pakistan and Sri Lanka and the Northeast Monsoon or Retreating Monsoon occurs between Dec. and early March. The East Asia Monsoon runs between May and Aug. and the Indo-Australian Monsoon between Sept. and Feb.

2010

12 Jan. – An earthquake measuring 7·0 in magnitude struck Haiti some 16 km (10 miles) west of the capital Port-au-Prince in the region's strongest quake since 1770. Some 3m. people were affected with at least 230,000 killed and 1·5m. left homeless.

4 Jan. – Around 70,000 people in the east and northeast of drought-ridden Kenya were affected by landslides and flooding caused by heavy rains attributed to the El Niño climate pattern. 30,000 required emergency aid relief.

2009

Nov. – In El Salvador, a national emergency was declared after 200 people lost their lives in mudslides and floods affecting the capital San Salvador and the central San Vicente province. Victims numbered around 75,000.

28 Oct. – Torrential rain causing flash floods in southwest Somalia forced over 15,000 people to flee their homes.

Sept.–Oct. – The Philippines experienced its worst typhoon season in decades. Typhoon Parma and tropical storm Ketsana caused the most destruction leaving around 900 dead and affecting over 4·5m. In an average year the Philippines is hit by 20 typhoons.

30 Sept. – A 7·6 magnitude earthquake off the coast of Sumatra in Indonesia killed more than 1,100 people and left 135,000 houses severely damaged.

8 Aug. – Northern Taiwan was struck by Typhoon Morakot that left over 600 dead.

9 July – 300 people were injured and over 10,000 houses collapsed after an earthquake measuring 6·0 hit China's Yunnan province.

25 May – Cyclone Aila, which hit India and Bangladesh affecting much of West Bengal, left 190 dead and over 7,000 injured. Some 323,000 acres of crops were damaged and 600,000 houses destroyed.

April–May – Torrential rain in Brazil caused the worst flooding and mudslides in over 20 years in its northeastern states. Around 270,000 people were made homeless.

6 April – L'Aquila, the capital of the Abruzzo region in central Italy, experienced a 6·2 magnitude earthquake that left 307 dead.

March – Angola, Namibia and Zambia experienced their worst flooding in 40 years with the River Zambezi swollen to record levels. Around 400,000 people were affected and food stocks and road infrastructure were badly damaged.

16 Feb. – 44,000 people, mainly in the department of Nariño in Colombia, were badly affected when intense rainfall caused the River Mira to flood.

7 Feb.–14 March – In Australia, 173 people died in the 'Black Saturday' Bush Fires in Victoria making them the most deadly in the country's history. Over 450,000 ha. (1·1m. acres) were burnt, 2,000 homes destroyed and 500 people injured.

Feb. – Floods in Queensland, Australia following torrential rain affected over 1m. sq. km (400,000 sq. miles) of land causing around US$70m. worth of damage.

Feb. – Northeast China suffered a drought that began in Nov. and affected some 9·73m. ha. (24·04m. acres) of cropland (29% severely). Nearly 4m. people and 2m. livestock faced drinking water shortages.

Jan. – 285,000 people were left homeless in Mozambique after heavy rains in Malaŵi and Zambia caused severe floods.

2008

29 Oct. – The province of Balochistan in Pakistan was hit by an earthquake measuring 6·4 in magnitude some 60 km (40 miles) to the north of Quetta leaving more than 200 dead.

Aug.–Sept. – Hurricane Hanna swept across the Caribbean and the east coast of the USA. Haiti suffered the majority of the casualties with around 530 dead in floods brought on by torrential rain. Combined with the victims of the preceding Tropical Storm Fay and Hurricane Gustav in Aug. and the ensuing Hurricane Ike later in Sept., the country's hurricane death toll for 2008 totalled approximately 800. 60% of the food harvest was also destroyed. In the wake of the disaster, then prime minister Michèle Pierre-Louis said 'We cannot keep going on like this. We are going to disappear one day. There will not be 400, 500 or 1,000 deaths. There are going to be a million deaths.'

July – Several states of India, notably Maharashtra, Bihar and Andhra Pradesh, were affected by flooding caused by heavy monsoon rains. The death toll numbered over 2,400.

17–26 June – Typhoon Fengshen (Frank) struck the Philippines with winds of up to 160 km/h (100 mph) and heavy rain causing flash floods, storm surges and landslides. Over 550 people were reported dead on land and an estimated 2·4m. were displaced. In addition 856 people lost their lives when the Princess of the Stars, a ferry going from Manila to Cebu, capsized and sank.

June – 11m. people were affected by floods in the US states of Illinois, Indiana, Iowa, Michigan, Minnesota, Missouri and Wisconsin. Damage costs were an estimated US$10bn.

June–Aug. – California experienced its worst wildfires in decades when freak dry lightning storms sparked as many as 2,000 fires across the north of the state. 530,000 ha. (1·3m. acres) and 2,219 structures were burned resulting in approximately US$2bn. worth of damage.

12 May – An earthquake struck China's southwestern Sichuan province, measuring 7·9 in magnitude. With an estimated death toll of 87,000, it was the deadliest Chinese earthquake since the 1976 Tangshan quake. On 6 Nov. the government announced a 1trn. yuan (US$146bn.) three-year reconstruction plan making the earthquake the most costly natural disaster in the country's history.

2 May – Cyclone Nargis swept through the Irrawaddy Delta and southern Yangon in Myanmar leaving nearly 140,000 dead and many more missing. A total of 2·4m. people were severely affected and around 42% of food stocks destroyed.

Feb. – In Afghanistan, temperatures fell to –30°C (–22°F) during their coldest winter on record. Blizzard conditions resulted in over 1,300 deaths and more than 700 homes were destroyed in avalanches.

Jan.–Feb. – Extreme winter temperatures across 21 of the 31 provincial divisions of China affected 77m. people. Among the hardest hit were Anhui, Henan, Hubei, Hunan, Jiangsu, Shandong and the municipality of Shanghai. A total of 485,000 homes were destroyed in snow storms and an estimated 1·66m. people displaced.

2007

11–16 Nov. – Cyclone Sidr formed in the Bay of Bengal and struck Bangladesh. Official government figures suggested 3,363 died as a result of the storm but humanitarian organizations claimed that the death toll was higher. Coming at the end of the monsoon season, flooding was exacerbated and infrastructure badly affected. 1·5m. houses and 1m. ha. (2·5m. acres) of crops were damaged and 4m. trees destroyed.

Oct.–Nov. – Following a week's heavy rain, the southeastern Mexican states of Chiapas and Tabasco experienced severe flooding that left up to 800,000 people homeless.

15 Aug. – 519 people died as a result of an 8·0 magnitude earthquake that struck off the coast of Peru around 145 km (90 miles) south-southeast of Lima affecting the Ica Region and the Lima Province. Over 35,500 buildings were destroyed and the road infrastructure, including the Pan American Highway, badly damaged.

July–Oct. – Floods across south Asia were described as 'the worst in living memory' by UNICEF. Around 112,000 houses were damaged or destroyed in the northern Indian states of Bihar and Uttar Pradesh and 270,000 people were displaced in Nepal. In east Asia at least 600 died in North Korea in Aug. and 100,000 were left homeless as a result of floods and landslides. Bangladesh, Pakistan and Vietnam were also badly affected.

July – A heatwave across central and southern Europe brought record temperatures of 41·9°C (107·4°F) to Hungary where some 500 people died as a result.

July – In China, a tenth of the population (some 119m. people) were affected by heavy rains. Deaths caused by floods and landslides totalled 700.

16 July – An earthquake measuring 6·6 struck the Niigata and Nagano prefectures in central Japan. Although fatalities were minimal, more than 1,000 people were injured and it was estimated to be the costliest natural disaster of the year with damages amounting to US$12·5bn.

March – Freak flash floods brought on by torrential rain and fast-melting snow affected a third of Afghanistan's provinces. More than 80 people were thought to have been killed. Further flooding in June in the Panjshir and Kapisa regions left some 100 dead and destroyed much farmland and livestock.

9–15 March – Madagascar was buffeted by winds up to 245 km/h (150 mph) when Cyclone Indlala struck. 150 people died and 188,300 lost their homes according to the national disaster management agency.

Feb.–March – Bolivia experienced its worst flooding in 25 years, which was attributed to the El Niño effect. The northeastern department of Beni was almost entirely covered by water.

2006

Nov.–Dec. – Typhoon Durian struck the Philippines triggering flooding and mudslides that claimed the lives of some 1,400 people.

Aug.–Oct. – In Ethiopia, the rivers Omo, Awash and Blue Nile all experienced flash flooding as a result of unprecedented heavy seasonal rain. Over 700 people were killed and 240,000 displaced.

Aug. – The Barmer district of drought-prone Rajasthan, India experienced devastating flash floods owing to southwestern monsoon rains. The worst in 200 years, the floods left 800,000 people without homes.

Aug. – Almost 500 people died after Typhoon Saomai struck Taiwan and the east coast of China.

July–Aug. – A heatwave across most of the USA and parts of southern Canada saw record temperatures in many states. There were an estimated 130 deaths in California alone but subsequent research suggested figures closer to 350–450. 2006 was the second hottest year in the USA since records began in 1895 and only marginally cooler than the record average temperature of 1998. South Dakota had its hottest temperature on record on 15 July when it reached 49°C (120°F) at Usta.

14–15 July – The North Korean provinces of Kangwon, North Hwanghae, South Hamgyong and South Pyongan were severely affected by flooding caused by high winds and torrential rain. Country officials reported around 550 dead and 300 missing but aid agency reports suggested that the true figure could be in the tens of thousands.

July – More than 3,000 deaths were caused by a heatwave across western Europe.

17 July – At least 600 people were killed when the southern coast of the Indonesian island of Java was hit by a tsunami caused by a 7·7 magnitude undersea earthquake.

July – Tropical storm Bilis swept through China, Taiwan and the Philippines. The death toll mounted to 843, over 500 of which occurred in the Chinese province of Hunan. Damage costs amounted to 34·82bn. yuan (US$4·3bn.).

27 May – A 6·3 magnitude earthquake struck the region of Yogyakarta on the Indonesian island of Java killing some 6,000 people and leaving around 50,000 injured. An estimated 127,000 buildings were completely destroyed and 1·17m. people were made homeless.

17 Feb. – In Southern Leyte in the Philippines, the village of Guinsaugon was submerged by a mudslide caused by rains from Typhoon Chanchu. 1,126 people were killed and around 8,000 affected.

Jan.–Feb. – An anticyclone bringing extreme cold weather extended across central and eastern Europe. Some 750 Ukrainians died as a result of the cold according to the country's ministry of health.

2005

20 Nov. – In Honduras, 30,000 people were left homeless in the wake of Tropical Storm Gamma and another 60,000 were affected.

8 Oct. – An earthquake measuring 7·6 in magnitude struck northern Pakistan and Kashmir leaving millions homeless. Pakistan suffered the most fatalities with 73,300 people killed. In India the death toll came to 1,300.

1–5 Oct. – Flooding and mudslides in Central America caused by Hurricane Stan claimed over 2,000 lives. Southwestern Guatemala was one of the worst affected areas with whole villages swept away by mud, notably Panabaj near Lake Atitlán.

Sept.–Oct. – 600,000 people were evacuated from the Vietnamese provinces of Thanh Hoa, Ninh Binh and Nam Dinh to escape Typhoon Damrey. 130,000 ha. (320,000 acres) of rice fields ready for harvest were submerged under water and 200,000 people faced food shortages. China and the Philippines were also affected.

Aug.–Sept. – The eastern Chinese provinces of Anhui, Fujian, Henan, Hubei, Jiangxi, Shanghai Municipality and Zhejiang were severely affected by Typhoons Talim and Khanun. The former resulted in the evacuation of some 1·84m. people according to the ministry of civil affairs, and some 102,000 houses were destroyed. The State Flood Control and Drought Relief headquarters reported that Typhoon Khanun had affected 5·5m. people and 2·25m. ha. (5·56m. acres) of cropland.

Aug. – The US states of Louisiana, Mississippi and Alabama were hit by Hurricane Katrina, estimated to be costliest hurricane in US history and the third deadliest. 80% of New Orleans was flooded. The official death toll mounted to 1,836 with several hundred others missing. Damages totalled an estimated US$110bn.

July–Aug. – Heavy monsoon rains caused flooding and landslides in the Indian states of Goa and Maharashtra. The city of Mumbai was particularly badly affected—of the 1,094 recorded deaths, 447 occurred there.

28 March – In Indonesia, at least 900 people lost their lives when an 8·7 magnitude earthquake struck off the coast of the island of Nias, west of Sumatra.

22 Feb. – An earthquake measuring 6·4 on the Richter scale hit the Kerman province of Iran near the city of Zarand. Four villages were completely destroyed and there were an estimated 600–700 fatalities.

Jan.–Feb. – Nearly 500 people were killed after three weeks of heavy rain and snow fell across Pakistan with Balochistan, the North-West Frontier Province and the Federally Administered Tribal Areas suffering the brunt of the damage.

2004

26 Dec. – An underwater earthquake measuring 9·3 in magnitude struck west of northern Sumatra triggering a tsunami. It was the second largest earthquake ever recorded. The damage and destruction affected at least 5m. people and 1·8m. people were left homeless. The estimated total death toll exceeded 225,000 with Indonesia (165,700 deaths), Sri Lanka (35,400), India (16,400) and Thailand (8,300) the worst afflicted countries. Bangladesh, Kenya, Malaysia, the Maldives, Myanmar, the Seychelles, Somalia, South Africa, Tanzania and Yemen also experienced casualties.

Countries with the highest level of disaster-related displacement in 2008

Country	*Total displaced and evacuated (in 1,000)*
China	19,979
India	6,705
Philippines	2,736
USA	2,014
Cuba	980
Myanmar	800
Indonesia	401
Brazil	381
Mozambique	289
Thailand	203

Findings of a study by the United Nations Office for the Coordination of Humanitarian Affairs and the Internal Displacement Monitoring Centre published in Sept. 2009.

KEY WORLD FACTS

• World population in 2010	6,909 million (3,483 million males and 3,426 million females)
• World population under 30 in 2010	3,634 million
• World population over 60 in 2010	759 million
• World population over 100 in 2010	492,000
• Number of births worldwide every day	373,000
• Number of deaths worldwide every day	156,000
• World economic growth rate in 2008	3·4% (5·2% in 2007)
• Number of illiterate adults	774 million
• Number of unemployed people	190 million
• Average world life expectancy	69·8 years for females; 65·4 years for males
• Annual world population increase	79·30 million people
• Number of people living outside country of birth	191 million, or nearly 3% of the world's population
• Fertility rate	2·6 births per woman
• Urban population	49·9% of total population
• World trade in 2008	US$32·5 billion
• World defence expenditure	US$1,500 billion
• Number of TV sets	1·4 billion
• Number of radio receivers	2·2 billion
• Number of cigarettes smoked	5,600 billion a year
• Number of Internet users	1·8 billion
• Number of mobile phone users	4·1 billion
• Number of motor vehicles on the road	790 million
• Number of people who cross international borders every day	2 million
• Number of people living in extreme poverty	1·4 billion
• Number of people living in urban slums	828 million
• Number of undernourished people	1,020 million
• Number of overweight adults	1·6 billion
• Number of obese adults	400 million
• Number of people dying of starvation	24,000 every day
• Number of people lacking clean drinking water	880 million
• Number of people lacking adequate sanitation	2·7 billion
• Number of recorded executions in 2008	2,390
• Number of people worldwide exposed to indoor air pollution that exceeds WHO guidelines	1 billion
• Annual carbon dioxide emissions	7·7 billion tonnes of carbon equivalent

WORLD POPULATION DEVELOPMENTS

1950		
1.	China	554,951,000
2.	India	371,857,000
3.	USSR	180,980,000
4.	USA	157,813,000
5.	Japan	82,824,000
6.	Indonesia	77,152,000
7.	Brazil	53,975,000
8.	UK	50,616,000
9.	West Germany	49,986,000
10.	Italy	46,376,000

2010		
1.	China	1,354,146,000
2.	India	1,214,464,000
3.	USA	317,641,000
4.	Indonesia	232,517,000
5.	Brazil	195,423,000
6.	Pakistan	184,753,000
7.	Bangladesh	164,425,000
8.	Nigeria	158,259,000
9.	Russia	140,367,000
10.	Japan	126,995,000

2050		
1.	India	1,613,800,000
2.	China	1,417,054,000
3.	USA	403,932,000
4.	Pakistan	335,195,000
5.	Nigeria	289,083,000
6.	Indonesia	288,110,000
7.	Bangladesh	222,495,000
8.	Brazil	218,512,000
9.	Ethiopia	173,811,000
10.	Congo (Democratic Republic of)	147,512,000

Source: United Nations World Population Prospects (2008 Revision)

LARGEST URBAN AGGLOMERATIONS

1950		
1.	New York-Newark, USA	12,338,000
2.	Tokyo, Japan	11,275,000
3.	London, United Kingdom	8,361,000
4.	Paris, France	6,522,000
5.	Shanghai, China	6,066,000
6.	Moscow, USSR	5,356,000
7.	Buenos Aires, Argentina	5,098,000
8.	Chicago, USA	4,999,000
9.	Calcutta, India	4,513,000
10.	Beijing, China	4,331,000

2010		
1.	Tokyo, Japan	36,094,000
2.	Mumbai (Bombay), India	20,072,000
3.	São Paulo, Brazil	19,582,000
4.	Mexico City, Mexico	19,485,000
5.	New York-Newark, USA	19,441,000
6.	Delhi, India	17,015,000
7.	Shanghai, China	15,789,000
8.	Kolkata (Calcutta), India	15,577,000
9.	Dhaka, Bangladesh	14,796,000
10.	Buenos Aires, Argentina	13,089,000

2025		
1	Tokyo, Japan	36,400,000
2.	Mumbai (Bombay), India	26,385,000
3.	Delhi, India	22,498,000
4.	Dhaka, Bangladesh	22,015,000
5.	São Paulo, Brazil	21,428,000
6.	Mexico City, Mexico	21,009,000
7.	New York-Newark, USA	20,628,000
8.	Kolkata (Calcutta), India	20,560,000
9.	Shanghai, China	19,412,000
10.	Karachi, Pakistan	19,095,000

Source: United Nations Department of Economic and Social Affairs/Population Division, World Urbanization Prospects (2007 Revision)

CHRONOLOGY

April 2009–March 2010

Week beginning 5 April 2009

Lars Løkke Rasmussen succeeded Anders Fogh Rasmussen as prime minister of Denmark following the latter's appointment as NATO secretary general.

In Moldova's parliamentary elections, the ruling Party of Communists of the Republic of Moldova (PCRM) won 61 seats, the Liberal Party 15, the Liberal Democratic Party of Moldova 14 and the Party Alliance Our Moldova 11. Turnout was 59·5%.

Elena Salgado was appointed finance minister in a cabinet reshuffle in Spain.

Incumbent Abdelaziz Bouteflika dominated Algeria's presidential elections winning 90·2% of the vote to claim a third term of office.

The court of appeals in the Fiji Islands ruled that prime minister Frank Bainimarama's government was illegal, forcing him to stand down. However, president Ratu Josefa Iloilo disbanded the court and restored Bainimarama to power. Ratu Epeli Nailatikau was appointed vice president.

The Democratic Party won 148 of 560 seats in Indonesia's parliamentary elections, the Party of the Functional Groups (Golkar) 108, the Indonesian Democratic Party-Struggle 93, the Prosperous Justice Party 59, the National Mandate Party 42, the United Development Party 39, the Great Indonesia Movement Party 30, the National Awakening Party 26 and the People's Conscience Party 15.

Sanoussi Touré was appointed finance minister in a cabinet reshuffle in Mali.

Week beginning 12 April 2009

In Hungary, a vote of no confidence resulted in Ferenc Gyurcsány being replaced as prime minister by Gordon Bajnai. Péter Balázs was named foreign minister and Péter Oszkó finance minister.

Gen. Mohamed Ould Abdel Aziz resigned as head of state to run in upcoming presidential elections in Mauritania. Ba Mamadou Mbaré became interim head of state.

Week beginning 19 April 2009

The African National Congress won 264 seats in South Africa's presidential elections followed by the Democratic Alliance with 67, Congress of the People with 30 and Inkatha Freedom Party with 18.

Said Sammur was named Syria's interior minister in a cabinet reshuffle.

In Iceland's parliamentary election the Social Democratic Alliance won 20 of the 63 seats, the Independence Party 16, the Left-Green Movement 14, the Progressive Party 9 and the Citizens' Movement 4.

Week beginning 26 April 2009

Following the Social Democratic Party's victory in Andorra's legislative elections with 14 of 28 seats, Jaume Bartumeu became president-delegate.

Incumbent Rafael Vicente Correa Delgado won 51·9% of the vote against 27·9% for Lucio Edwin Gutiérrez Borbúa in Ecuador's presidential elections.

Héctor Lacognata became Paraguay's foreign minister.

Senegalese prime minister Cheikh Hadjibou Soumaré resigned for personal reasons. He was succeeded by Souleymane Ndéné Ndiaye who made no major changes to the cabinet.

The UK's military mission in Iraq was ended.

Tonga's prime minister Fred Sevele added foreign affairs and defence to his portfolio following a cabinet reshuffle.

In Turkey, Mehmet Şimşek was named finance minister, Ali Babacan economy minister and Ahmet Davutoğlu foreign minister in a major cabinet reshuffle.

Week beginning 3 May 2009

In Nepal, the summary dismissal of the head of the army by prime minister Pushpa Kamal Dahal led the ministers of the Communist Party of Nepal (Unified Marxist-Leninist) including home minister Bamdev Gautam to resign. President Ram Baran Yadav reinstated the army chief, in turn prompting the resignation of prime minister Pushpa Kamal Dahal.

Ricardo Martinelli won 60·3% of the vote in Panama's presidential elections against 37·3% for Balbina Herrera of the ruling Revolutionary Democratic Party.

Moldovan prime minister Zinaida Greceanîi's government resigned before the first meeting of the new parliament. The cabinet, reappointed with no changes to key positions, was scheduled to hold office until parliamentary elections could be called.

In the Czech Republic, Jan Fischer took over as prime minister of a caretaker government that included Jan Kohout as deputy prime minister and foreign minister, Martin Barták as deputy prime minister and defence minister, Eduard Janota as finance minister and Martin Pecina as interior minister.

Peter Tom succeeded James Tora as home minister of the Solomon Islands.

The South African parliament elected Jacob Zuma president. He appointed Lindiwe Sisulu defence minister, Pravin Gordhan finance minister, Nkosazana Dlamini-Zuma home minister and Maite Nkoana-Mashabane international relations minister.

The Dhivehi Rayyithunge Party won 28 of 77 seats in the Maldives' parliamentary elections and the Maldivian Democratic Party 26.

Week beginning 10 May 2009

In Iceland, prime minister Jóhanna Sigurðardóttir's government was re-elected with no key changes.

Gjorgje Ivanov was sworn in as president of Macedonia.

The Indian National Congress (INC) and its allies won 262 of 543 seats in India's parliamentary elections, with the INC claiming 206 seats. The National Democratic Alliance won 159, the Bharatiya Janata Party 116, the Third Front 79 and the Fourth Front 27. Manmohan Singh was reappointed prime minister while Pranab Mukherjee became finance minister and S. M. Krishna foreign minister. The defence and home affairs portfolios remained unchanged.

In Kuwait's parliamentary elections, independents claimed the majority of seats taking 21 out of 50, followed by Sunni Islamists with 13, Liberals (7), Shia Islamists (6) and the popular Bloc (3). Sheikh Nasser Muhammad Al-Ahmad Al-Sabah regained his position as prime minister and reappointed his former cabinet with no changes in key portfolios.

Week beginning 17 May 2009

Dalia Grybauskaitė won Lithuania's presidential election with 69·1% of the vote, ahead of Algirdas Butkevičius with 11·8%.

In Colombia, Juan Manuel Santos resigned as defence minister. He was succeeded by the commander of the armed forces, Gen. Freddy Padilla de León.

Incumbent Malaŵian president Bingu wa Mutharika won a second term in office after he gained 66·0% of the vote against 30·7% for John Tembo in presidential elections although Tembo contested the results. Mutharika's party also achieved success in parliamentary elections winning 114 of 193 seats.

Salam Fayyad was reappointed prime minister of the Palestinian Authority by president Mahmoud Abbas. Hamas refused to recognize the new Fatah-dominated coalition government.

Estonia's prime minister, Andrus Ansip, fired three Social Democratic ministers, including finance minister Ivari Padar and interior minister Jüri Pihl, following disputes over economic policy. Agriculture minister Helir-Valdor Seeder was temporarily given the finance portfolio and justice minister Rein Lang the interior portfolio before they were later transferred to Jürgen Ligi and to Marko Pomerants respectively.

Horst Köhler was re-elected president of Germany.

Week beginning 24 May 2009

In Mongolia's presidential election Tsakhiagiin Elbegdorj of the Democratic Party won 51·2% of the vote against 47·4% for the incumbent Nambaryn Enkhbayar.

Madhav Kumar Nepal was sworn in as prime minister of Nepal. Bidhya Bhandari was appointed defence minister and Surendra Pande finance minister.

Turkmenistan's interior minister, Orazgendy Amanmyradov, was dismissed for his reported failure to lower the country's crime rates and levels of corruption. Isgender Mulikov succeeded him.

Week beginning 31 May 2009

Mauricio Funes took office as president of El Salvador. His cabinet included Hugo Martínez as foreign minister, David Munguía Payes as defence minister, Carlos Cáceres as finance minister and Humberto Centeno as interior minister.

In the Maldives, Mohamed Shihab became home minister.

The resignations of home secretary Jacqui Smith and defence secretary John Hutton prompted a cabinet reshuffle in the UK. Alan Johnson became home secretary and Bob Ainsworth defence secretary.

In Andorra, parliament elected Jaume Bartumeu president. His new government included Xavier Espot Miró as foreign minister, Pere López as finance minister and Víctor Naudi as interior minister.

Australia's defence minister Joel Fitzgibbon resigned amidst allegations of ministerial misconduct. He was succeeded by John Faulkner.

In Nepal, Sujata Koirala was appointed foreign minister.

Ukraine's defence minister Yuriy Yekhanurov was ousted after losing a parliamentary vote by 363 votes to 18. Valeriy Ivashchenko became acting defence minister.

Week beginning 7 June 2009

In European Parliament elections the European People's Party took 265 of 736 seats, Progressive Alliance of Socialists and Democrats 184, Alliance of Liberals and Democrats for Europe 84, Greens/European Free Alliance 55, European Conservatives and Reformists 54, European United Left/Nordic Green Left 35, Europe of Freedom and Democracy 32 and non-attached members 27.

The anti-Syrian opposition won 71 of 128 seats in Lebanon's parliamentary elections while Hizbollah and its allies took 29 and the Free Patriotic Movement and its allies 28.

In Luxembourg, the Christian Social Party won 26 of 60 seats in parliamentary elections, the Socialist Workers' Party 13, the Democratic Party 9, the Greens 7, the Alternative Democratic Reform Party 4 and the Left 1.

Following the death of Gabon's president Omar Bongo Ondimba, Rose Francine Rogombé became interim president. Jean François Ndongou was appointed interior minister in a subsequent cabinet reshuffle.

Gambia's finance minister, Musa Gibril Balal Gaye, was sacked. He was succeeded by Abdou Kolley.

Montenegro's new cabinet, including Ivan Brajović as interior minister and Branko Vujović as economy minister, was approved by parliament.

Idrissou Daouda was named finance minister of Benin.

Incumbent Iranian president Mahmoud Ahmadinejad gained 62·6% of the vote in presidential elections ahead of Mir-Hossein Mousavi with 33·8%. The official results were widely disputed, sparking opposition protests across the country.

In Japan, Kunio Hatoyama resigned as interior minister following a dispute with prime minister Taro Aso. He was succeeded by Tsutomu Sato.

Week beginning 14 June 2009

The Solomon Islands' parliament elected Frank Kabui governor-general.

Vanuatu's prime minister Edward Natapei defeated a parliamentary vote of no-confidence. He appointed Joe Natuman foreign minister in a subsequent cabinet reshuffle.

In Kazakhstan, the defence minister Daniyal Akhmetov was sacked over corruption allegations. Adilbek Dzhaksybekov succeeded him.

Following a major cabinet reshuffle in Malaŵi, Joyce Banda became vice-preisdent, Ken Kandodo finance minister, Etta Banda foreign minister and Aaron Sangala interior minister.

Tsakhiagiin Elbegdorj took office as prime minister of Mongolia.

Week beginning 21 June 2009

A cabinet reshuffle in France saw Brice Hortefeux become interior minister.

President Manuel Zelaya's attempt to seek re-election in Honduras led to the resignation of defence minister Edmundo Orellana. Shorty afterwards, the president was overthrown by the military and sent into exile in Costa Rica. Roberto Micheletti became interim president, appointing Adolfo Lionel Sevilla defence minister, Gabriela Núñez finance minister and Enrique Ortez Colindres foreign minister.

In Mauritania, before ousted president Mohmed Ould Cheikh Abdallahi resigned officially, he appointed a new cabinet that included Yedali Ould Cheikh as defence minister, Mohamed Ould R'Zeyzim as interior minister and Sidi Ould Salem as finance minister.

Week beginning 28 June 2009

In the first round of Guinea-Bissau's presidential elections, Malam Bacaï Sanhá took 39·6% of votes cast, ahead of former president Mohamed Ialá Embaló with 29·4% and former interim president Henrique Rosa with 24·2%.

Philémon Yang became prime minister of Cameroon, appointing Edgard Alain Mebe Ngo'o defence minister.

In Lithuania, finance minister Algirdas Šemeta stepped down to become a European Union commissioner.

Croatia's prime minister Ivo Sanader resigned. He was succeeded by Jadranka Kosor.

Ricardo Martinelli took office as president of Panama. His cabinet included Juan Carlos Varela Rodríguez as vice-president and foreign minister, José Raúl Mulino as government and justice minister and Alberto Vallarino Clément as finance minister.

Week beginning 5 July 2009

Citizens for the European Development of Bulgaria won 116 of 240 seats in Bulgaria's legislative elections followed by the Coalition for Bulgaria (headed by the Bulgarian Socialist Party) with 40 seats, the Movement for Rights and Freedoms with 38, the Attack coalition with 21, the Blue Coalition with 15 and Order, Law and Justice with 10.

Željko Komšić took over Bosnia and Herzegovina's rotating presidency.

In a cabinet reshuffle in Argentina, Aníbal Fernández was appointed chief of the cabinet and Amado Boudou economy and public finance minister.

Ingrida Šimonytė was sworn in as Lithuania's finance minister.

In the Solomon Islands, Frank Kabui took office as governor-general.

Zambia's defence minister George Mpombo resigned on personal grounds. In a subsequent reshuffle, home affairs minister Kalombo Mwansa was appointed defence minister and Lameck Mangani home affairs minister.

Honduras' foreign minister Enrique Ortez Colindres was moved to the interior ministry after attracting criticism for his remarks about US president Barack Obama. He resigned shortly afterwards. Carlos López Contreras took over as foreign minister.

In Indonesia's presidential election, incumbent Susilo Bambang Yudhoyono won 60·8% of the vote against 26·8% for former president Megawati Sukarnoputri.

Peru's president Alan García appointed a new cabinet that included Ángel Javier Velásquez Quesquén as prime minister, Rafael Rey Rey as defence minister and Octavio Edilberto Salazar Miranda as interior minister.

Week beginning 12 July 2009

In elections in the Republic of the Congo, incumbent president Denis Sassou-Nguesso was re-elected with 78·6% of the vote.

Dalia Grybauskaitė took office as president of Lithuania.

Japan's prime minister Taro Aso defeated a parliamentary vote of no confidence by 333 votes to 139. He later dissolved parliament in preparation for a general election to be held in August.

Former Polish prime minister Jerzy Buzek was elected president of the European Parliament.

In Gabon, Jean Eyeghe Ndong resigned as prime minister. Interim president Rose Francine Rogombé appointed Paul Biyoghé Mba his successor. There were no major changes in the new cabinet.

In a cabinet reshuffle in Belgium, Yves Leterme became foreign minister and Annemie Turtelboom interior minister.

Mohamed Ould Abdel Aziz, leader of the 2008 coup, won Mauritania's presidential election with 52·6% of the vote against 16·3% for Messaoud Ould Boulkheir and 13·7% for Ahmed Ould Daddah.

Week beginning 19 July 2009

Kyrgyzstan's incumbent president Kurmanbek Bakiyev was re-elected with 76·1% of the vote in presidential elections although the results were disputed by several opposition candidates.

Ratu Inoke Kubuabola was appointed foreign minister in the Fiji Islands' cabinet.

Week beginning 26 July 2009

Malam Bacaï Sanhá claimed victory in the second round of Guinea-Bissau's presidential elections, with 63·3% of the vote against 36·7% for Mohamed Ialá Embaló.

In the Fiji Islands, Ratu Josefa Iloilo stepped down as president. Vice president Ratu Epeli Nailatikau succeeded him on an interim basis.

In Moldova's parliamentary elections the ruling Party of Communists of the Republic of Moldova won 48 seats, the Liberal Democratic Party of Moldova 18, the Liberal Party 15, the Democratic Party 13 and the Party Alliance Our Moldova 7.

Former Danish prime minister Anders Fogh Rasmussen took office as secretary general of NATO.

Week beginning 2 August 2009

Costa Rican finance minister Guillermo Zúñiga resigned to work on the National Liberation Party's presidential campaign. He was succeeded by Jenny Phillips.

Mohamed Ould Abdel Aziz took office as president of Mauritania. His cabinet appointments included Naha Mint Mouknass as foreign minister, Hamadi Ould Hamadi as defence minister, Mohamed Ould Boilil as interior minister and Kane Ousmane as finance minister. Moulaye Ould Mohamed Laghdaf remained prime minister.

Week beginning 9 August 2009

Gabon's defence minister Ali Bongo Ondimba stood down to run for president. Jean-François Ndongou succeeded him.

Week beginning 16 August 2009

In Vanuatu, after president Kalkot Mataskelekele Mauliliu reached the end of his term of office, speaker Maxime Carlot Korman became acting president.

Louis B. Susman took up his duties as United States ambassador to the UK.

Niger's cabinet resigned, allowing a constitutional amendment to be passed that extended president Tandja Mamadou's term by three years. The cabinet was reappointed with no changes.

Ali Jama Ahmed Jengeli was appointed foreign minister and Abdalla Bos defence minister following a cabinet reshuffle in Somalia.

In Iran, president Mahmoud Ahmadinejad named Ahmad Vahidi defence minister and Mostafa Mohammad Najjar interior minister in his new cabinet while Manouchehr Mottaki and Shamseddin Hosseini remained as foreign and economy and finance minister respectively.

In the first round of Afghanistan's presidential election, initial counts suggested that Hamid Karzai would be re-elected president with 54% of the vote compared to his closest rival Abdullah Abdullah's 28%. However, doubt as to the validity of the elections was widespread at home and abroad with all candidates accused of ballot-rigging.

Week beginning 23 August 2009

Following July's election, Moldova's cabinet headed by prime minister Zinaida Greceanîi resigned after Greceanîi declared that she was unable to serve as prime minister while remaining a member of parliament.

Bacho Akhalaia was appointed defence minister of Georgia in a cabinet reshuffle.

Week beginning 30 August 2009

In Gabon, the late president's son Ali Bongo Ondimba won the presidential election with 41·7% of votes cast against 25·9% for Andre Mba Obame and 25·2% for Pierre Mamboundou.

Legislative elections in Japan resulted in the ruling Liberal Democratic Party being ousted after winning only 119 seats compared to the Democratic Party of Japan's 308.

In a cabinet reshuffle in Uruguay, Pedro Vaz was appointed foreign minister and Gonzalo Fernández defence minister.

Iolu Abil was elected president of Vanuatu in the third round of parliamentary voting.

Moldovan president Vladimir Voronin announced his resignation in the wake of the Communist Party defeat at legislative elections. He appointed Vitalie Pirlog as acting prime minister.

In Albania, a coalition government was formed between the Democratic Party and the Socialist Movement for Integration. Sali Berisha remained prime minister while Ilir Meta was named foreign minister.

Chung Un-chan was named prime minister of South Korea and Gen. Kim Tae-young defence minister in a cabinet reshuffle.

Week beginning 6 September 2009

Following criticism of his government's handling of the recent Typhoon Morakot, Taiwanese prime minister Liu Chao-shiuan announced his resignation and that of his cabinet. He was succeeded by Wu Den-yih. The new cabinet comprised Timothy Yang as foreign minister, Kao Hua-chu as defence minister and Jiang Yi-huah as interior minister.

Malam Bacaï Sanhá took office as president of Guinea-Bissau.

In Madagascar's latest cabinet reshuffle, Hery Rajaonarimampianina was named finance and budget minister and Cécile Manorohanta interior minister.

Saad al-Hariri stood down as prime minister-designate of Lebanon after Hizbollah politicians rejected his choice of cabinet ministers. However, he was reappointed by parliamentary vote shortly afterwards.

Week beginning 13 September 2009

In Norway's parliamentary elections the ruling Labour Party won 64 out of 169 seats ahead of the Progress Party with 41 and the Conservative Party with 30.

Following his re-election, president of the Republic of the Congo Denis Sassou-Nguesso abolished the post of prime minister and reshuffled his cabinet. Gilbert Ondongo was appointed finance minister and Charles Zacharie Bowao defence minister.

José Manuel Barroso was re-elected president of the European Commission by 382 votes to 219. There were 117 abstentions.

Yukio Hatoyama took office as prime minister of Japan. His cabinet included Katsuya Okada as foreign minister, Toshimi Kitazawa as defence minister, Hirohisa Fujii as finance minister and Kazuhiro Haraguchi as internal affairs minister.

In Switzerland, Didier Burkhalter was named interior minister.

Week beginning 20 September 2009

The prime minister of Niger, Seyni Oumarou, resigned to run in October's presidential election. He was replaced temporarily by interior minister Albadé Abouba before Ali Badjo Gamatié took over the post on a permanent basis.

Week beginning 27 September 2009

In Germany's Bundestag elections the Christian Democratic Union/Christian Social Union won 239 seats; the Social Democratic Party, 146; the Free Democratic Party, 93; the Left, 76; and the Greens, 68.

The ruling Socialist Party retained power in Portugal's legislative elections winning 96 seats; the Social Democratic Party won 78; the Popular Party, 21; the Left Bloc, 16; and the Communist Party/Green Party coalition, 15.

In Romania, prime minister Emil Boc dismissed interior minister Dan Nica who had suggested that forthcoming presidential elections would be marred by fraud. This prompted the resignation of Nica's fellow Social Democratic Party members, resulting in the collapse of the coalition government. Vasile Blaga was appointed acting interior minister and justice minister Cătălin Predoiu took over as acting foreign minister.

Canadian prime minister Stephen Harper's government survived a parliamentary vote of no-confidence by 144 votes to 117.

A no-confidence motion brought against the prime minister of Finland, Matti Vanhanen, was dismissed by 117 votes to 27.

Francesco Mussoni and Stefano Palmieri were sworn in as captains-regent of San Marino.

In a cabinet reshuffle in Senegal, foreign minister Cheikh Tidiane Gadio lost his post to Madické Niang.

The new Supreme Court came into existence in the United Kingdom, replacing the Appellate Committee of the House of Lords as the highest court in the country.

Week beginning 4 October 2009

In Greece's parliamentary elections the opposition Pasok won 160 seats, the ruling New Democracy 91, the Communist Party 21, the Popular Orthodox Rally 15 and the Coalition of the Radical Left 13. Georgios Papandreou was sworn in as prime minister and foreign minister and appointed Evangelos Venizelos defence minister, Yiannis Ragoussis interior minister and Georgios Papaconstantinou finance minister. The government won a parliamentary vote of confidence shortly afterwards.

Gold prices hit a record high at US$1,040 an ounce.

Eugène Mangalaza was designated prime minister of a unity government in Madagascar after months of political upheaval. However, power-sharing collapsed when former president Marc Ravalomanana refused to recognize president Andry Rajoelina and prime minister Monja Roindefo refused to stand down. Mangalaza's appointment was then suspended by the State Council. Cécile Manorohanta was made acting prime minister.

Poland's deputy prime minister and interior minister Grzegorz Schetyna and justice minister Andrzej Czuma resigned after they were allegedly involved in a gambling scandal. Economy minister Waldemar Pawlak became deputy prime minister and Jerzy Miller interior minister.

US president Barack Obama was awarded the Nobel Peace Prize for his 'extraordinary efforts to strengthen international diplomacy and co-operation between peoples'.

Petro Poroshenko was appointed foreign minister in the Ukrainian cabinet, filling a post that had been vacant since March.

Turkey and Armenia signed an agreement to normalize ties and establish diplomatic relations.

Week beginning 11 October 2009

The government of Timor-Leste led by prime minister Xanana Gusmão survived a parliamentary vote of no-confidence by 38 votes to 25.

In Portugal, prime minister José Sócrates appointed a new cabinet including Augusto Santos Silva as defence minister.

Abdoulaye Baldé was appointed defence minister and Bécaye Diop interior minister following a cabinet reshuffle in Senegal.

In Botswana's parliamentary elections the ruling Botswana Democratic Party gained 45 seats, ahead of the Botswana National Front with 6 and the Botswana Congress Party with 4.

Ali Bongo Ondimba was sworn in as Gabon's president. In the new cabinet Paul Biyoghé Mba remained prime minister while Angélique Ngoma was made defence minister.

Week beginning 18 October 2009

After Afghanistan's Independent Election Commission found that Hamid Karzai had not won a 50% majority as initially declared in August's presidential election, a second round runoff between Karzai and Abdullah Abdullah was announced.

In Kyrgyzstan, prime minister Igor Chudinov resigned along with his cabinet to make way for government reforms sought by president Kurmanbek Bakiyev. Daniyar Usenov succeeded Chudinov as prime minister.

The National Movement for the Development of Society dominated parliamentary elections in Niger, winning 76 seats against 15 for the Social Democratic Rally and 7 for the Rally for Democracy and Progress. Opposition parties boycotted the election.

Norwegian prime minister Jens Stoltenberg's new cabinet was sworn in following September's parliamentary elections with Grete Faremo as defence minister and Sigbjørn Johnsen as finance minister.

In Indonesia's new cabinet Marty Natalegawa was made foreign minister, Purnomo Yusgiantoro defence minister and Gamawan Fauzi home affairs minister.

After losing a parliamentary vote of no-confidence, the president of the Marshall Islands Litokwa Tomeing was succeeded by Ruben Zackhras on a temporary basis before speaker Jurelang Zedkaia was elected the new president by parliament.

German chancellor Angela Merkel's new cabinet comprised Guido Westerwelle as foreign minister, Karl-Theodor Freiherr zu Guttenberg as defence minister, Thomas de Maizière as interior minister and Wolfgang Schäuble as finance minister.

Week beginning 25 October 2009

Presidential elections in Tunisia resulted in president Zine El Abidine Ben Ali being re-elected by 89·6% of votes cast. In the parliamentary elections the ruling RCD won 161 of 214 available National Assembly seats, ahead of the Movement of Social Democrats with 16 and the Popular Unity Party with 12.

In Uruguay's presidential election a runoff was scheduled to be held between José Alberto Mujica Cordano who received 48·0% of the vote and Luis Alberto Lacalle de Herrera who received 29·1%. In the General Assembly elections the Broad Front won 50 seats in the Chamber of Deputies (16 in the senate), the National Party 30 (9 in the senate), the Colorado Party 17 (5 in the senate) and the Independent Party 2.

The prime minister of Mongolia, Sanj Bayar, resigned because of health problems. He was succeeded by foreign affairs minister Sukhbaataryn Batbold.

Incumbent Armando Guebuza won 75·0% of the vote against 16·4% for Afonso Marceta Macacho Dhlakama of the Mozambican National Resistance (RENAMO) in Mozambique's presidential election.

Following a cabinet reshuffle in Guinea-Bissau, Aristides Ocante da Silva was appointed defence minister, Adelino Mano Quetá foreign minister and José Mário Vaz finance minister.

The US Department of Commerce announced that the economy was out of recession. Third quarter growth, initially put at 3·5%, was revised down to 2·2% in Dec.

Week beginning 1 November 2009

A second round runoff between the incumbent president Hamid Karzai and Abdullah Abdullah in Afghanistan's presidential elections was cancelled after Abdullah pulled out, questioning the impartiality of the Afghani Independent Electoral Commission. Karzai was duly elected.

Jurelang Zedkaia was sworn in as president of the Marshall Islands.

In Romania, parliament failed to endorse Lucian Croitoru as prime minister. Liviu Negoiţă was nominated prime minister by president Băsescu.

The Fiji Islands' president, Ratu Epeli Nailatikau, was sworn in having served in an interim capacity since July.

Week beginning 8 November 2009

The Lebanese prime minister Saad al-Hariri took office. Ali Shami was appointed foreign minister and Raya al-Haffar al-Hassan finance minister while Elias al-Murr remained defence minister and Ziad Baroud interior minister

Marian Lupu failed to win the majority in a parliamentary vote to become president of Moldova. A new election was scheduled to be held within 30 days.

In Haiti, Jean-Max Bellerive was sworn in as prime minister. His cabinet included Marie-Michèle Rey as foreign minister and Ronald Baudin as finance minister while Paul Antoine Bien-Aimé remained interior minister.

Gombojav Zandanshatar became foreign minister of Mongolia.

Eugène Mangalaza was sworn in as prime minister of Madagascar, having been appointed five weeks earlier.

Week beginning 15 November 2009

In a cabinet reshuffle in Vanuatu, Moana Carcasses Kalosil was appointed internal affairs minister.

The Belgian prime minister Herman Van Rompuy was named the first president of the European Council.

In Afghanistan, Hamid Karzai was sworn for a second term as president.

Week beginning 22 November 2009

In the first round of Romania's presidential elections, incumbent Traian Băsescu of the Democratic Liberal Party won 32·4% of the vote, followed by Mircea Geoană (Social Democratic Party) with 31·2%, Crin Antonescu (National Liberal Party) with 20·0% and Corneliu Vadim Tudor (Greater Romania Party) 5·6%.

In Belgium, Yves Leterme was nominated by King Albert to replace Herman Van Rompuy as prime minister after the latter was made president of the European Council. Steven Vanackere replaced Leterme as foreign minister but otherwise key cabinet positions remained unchanged.

Vanuatu's prime minister Edward Natapei lost his seat after he failed to attend parliament on three consecutive occasions. He launched a legal appeal against the ruling and was scheduled to remain in office until after the announcement of the court's decision in Dec.

Incumbent president Hifikepunye Pohamba of the South West Africa People's Organization won presidential elections in Namibia with 75·3% of votes cast. In parliamentary elections held on the same day the South West Africa People's Organization won 54 of 72 seats, Rally for Democracy and Progress 8 and the Democratic Turnhalle Alliance, National Unity Democratic Organization and United Democratic Front 2 each.

Week beginning 29 November 2009

President Nguema Mbasogo was re-elected with 95·4% of votes cast in presidential elections in Equatorial Guinea. The opposition accused Mbasogo of electoral fraud.

Presidential and parliamentary elections took place in Honduras. Early results indicated that Porfirio Lobo Sosa of the National Party had won 56% of votes cast against 38% for Elvin Santos of the Liberal Party.

In Uruguay's presidential election runoff, José Alberto Mujica Cordano gained 54·8% of the vote to Luis Alberto Lacalle's 45·2%.

Yukiya Amano of Japan succeeded Dr Mohamed ElBaradei as head of the International Atomic Energy Agency.

Switzerland's vice president and minister of economic affairs, Doris Leuthard, was elected president for 2010. Moritz Leuenberger was named vice president.

Louise Mushikiwabo was named foreign minister and John Rwangombwa finance minister in a cabinet reshuffle in Rwanda.

Yury Zhadobin wass appointed defence minister of Belarus.

In Vanuatu, prime minister Edward Natapei retained his seat in parliament after the chief justice ruled that it was unconstitutional to exclude him for lack of attendance. Natapei subsequently survived a parliamentary no-confidence motion by 36 votes to 11.

Week beginning 6 December 2009

In Bolivia's presidential election Evo Morales Ayma (Movement Towards Socialism) won 64·1% of votes cast against 26·6% for Manfred Reyes Villa (Progress Plan for Bolivia). The Movement Towards Socialism claimed 88 of 130 seats in elections to the Chamber of Deputies, Progress Plan for Bolivia 37, the National Unity Front 3 and the Social Alliance 2.

The pro-presidential party and its allies won 20 of 24 elected seats in the Comoros' parliamentary election while the opposition took four.

In the second round run-off in Romania's presidential election incumbent Traian Băsescu retained the presidency with 50·3% of the vote against 49·7% for Mircea Geoană. The opposition contested the results and accused Băsescu of ballot-rigging.

The 15th United Nations Climate Change Summit began in Copenhagen.

In the second round of Moldova's indirect presidential elections, Marian Lupu of the Liberal Democratic Party of Moldova failed to gain sufficient votes to secure the presidency.

Jordan's prime minister, Nader Dahabi, resigned along with his cabinet after King Abdullah dissolved parliament in late Nov. Samir Zaid al-Rifai succeeded Dahabi as prime minister and defence minister. He appointed Mohammad Abu Hammour finance minister.

Week beginning 13 December 2009

In the first round of Chile's presidential election, Eduardo Frei Ruiz-Tagle of the Christian Democratic Party took 44·1% of the vote against 29·6% for Sebastián Piñera Echineque of National Renewal.

The ruling Dominica Labour Party won 18 of 21 elected seats in Dominica's parliamentary elections with three seats going to the United Workers Party.

In Madagascar, president Andry Rajoelina dismissed prime minister Eugène Mangalaza. Acting prime minister Cécile Manorohanta succeeded him but shortly afterwards Rajoelina appointed Col. Albert Camille Vital in her place.

Week beginning 20 December 2009

Peru's finance minister Luis Carranza resigned. He was succeeded by Mercedes Rosalba Aráoz Fernández.

Week beginning 27 December 2009

Ivo Josipović of the Social Democratic Party of Croatia won the first round of Croatia's presidential elections with 32·4% of the vote, followed by 14·8% for Milan Bandić (ind.), 12·0% for Andrija Hebrang (Croatian Democratic Union) and 11·3% for Nadan Vidošević (ind.).

Herman Van Rompuy was sworn in as president of the European Union.

Doris Leuthard took over the Swiss presidency.

Afghanistan's parliament rejected the majority of president Hamid Karzai's cabinet nominations excepting the unchanged defence, finance and interior portfolios.

Week beginning 3 January 2010

In Dominica, a new cabinet took office with prime minister Roosevelt Skerrit as foreign and finance minister and Charles Savarin as national security minister.

Taib Cherkaoui became Morocco's interior minister in a cabinet reshuffle.

Japan's finance minister, Hirohisa Fujii, resigned owing to ill health and purported disagreements with Democratic Party leader Ichiro Ozawa. He was succeeded by Naoto Kan.

A cabinet reshuffle in São Tomé e Príncipe saw António Paquete become interior minister.

Week beginning 10 January 2010

In the second round runoff of Croatia's presidential elections, Ivo Josipović received 60·3% of votes cast against 39·7% for Milan Bandić.

In Uzbekistan's parliamentary elections, the Liberal-Democratic Party won 53 seats, the People's Democratic Party 32, the National Revival Democratic Party 31 and the Justice Social Democratic Party 19.

Ecuador's foreign minister, Fander Falconí, resigned after disagreements with president Rafael Correa over oil exploitation negotiations. Ricardo Patiño succeeded him.

In Equatorial Guinea, prime minister Ignacio Milam Tang and his cabinet resigned in order to fulfil a legal requirement following the re-election of president Brig.-Gen. Teodoro Obiang Nguema Mbasogo in Dec. They were reappointed later the same day with no changes in key cabinet positions.

Kamel Morjane became Tunisian foreign minister, Ridha Grira defence minister and Mohamed Ridha Chalghoum finance minister in a cabinet reshuffle.

In Venezuela, Jorge Giordani headed the newly-merged finance and planning ministries.

Aires Bonifácio Ali took office as prime minister of Mozambique.

Week beginning 17 January 2010

Bulgaria's defence minister, Nikolai Mladenov, took over the foreign affairs portfolio. Anyu Angelov became defence minister.

Following the resignation of Lithuania's foreign minister, Vygaudas Ušackas, over disagreements with president Dalia Grybauskaitė, Audronius Ažubalis was appointed to the ministry.

Week beginning 24 January 2010

Bolivia's new cabinet included Rubén Saavedra Soto as defence minister and Sacha Sergio Llorenti as finance minister.

Venezuela's vice-president and defence minister, Ramón Carrizales, resigned. Elías Jaua was appointed new vice-president and Carlos Mata defence minister.

Mohamed Abdul Quasim al-Zwai replaced Imbarek Shamekh as secretary general of Libya's General People's Congress.

Jean-Marie Doré took office as prime minister of Guinea.

The incumbent president Mahinda Rajapaksa won Sri Lanka's presidential elections with 57·9% of the vote against 40·2% for Sarath Fonseka.

Porfirio Lobo Sosa took office as president of Honduras. Mario Canahuati was named foreign minister, África Madrid interior minister and William Chong Wong finance minister.

Despite dismissal by parliamentary vote, Ukrainian interior minister Yuriy Lutsenko was reappointed to the ministry in an acting capacity by prime minister Yuliya Tymoshenko.

Week beginning 31 January 2010

In Greece, parliament re-elected president Karolos Papoulias by a large majority.

Angola's new constitution took effect replacing the office of prime minister with that of vice-president. Fernando Dias dos Santos became the country's first vice-president. Carlos Alberto Lopes was appointed finance minister.

Week beginning 7 February 2010

Laura Chinchilla of the National Liberation Party (PLN) won Costa Rica's presidential elections with 46·8% of the vote against 25·2% for Ottón Solís of the Citizens' Action Party (PAC) and 20·8% for Otto Guevara of the Libertarian Movement (ML). In parliamentary elections, the PLN took 24 of 57 seats, the PAC 11, the ML 9, the Social Christian Unity Party 6 and the Accessibility Without Exclusion Party 4, with the remaining seats going to minor parties.

St Kitts and Nevis' new government was sworn in. Prime minister Denzil Douglas took on the finance portfolio while the foreign affairs and national security ministries went to deputy prime minister Sam Condor.

The second round of presidential elections in Ukraine saw Viktor Yanukovych retain his first round majority against Yuliya Tymoshenko. He won 49·0% of the vote against her 45·5% although Tymoshenko challenged the results.

Nigeria's vice president, Goodluck Jonathan, was confirmed as acting president by the senate, having assumed power in Jan. after president Umaru Yar'Adua was incapacitated by ill health.

Madagascar's vice prime minister and foreign minister, Ny Hasina Andriamanjato, resigned over disagreements with the interim president, Andry Rajoelina. He was succeeded as foreign minister by Hyppolite Ramaroson.

In a dispute over preparations for long-postponed elections in Côte d'Ivoire, president Laurent Gbagbo dissolved the cabinet and the Independent Electoral Commission. He immediately reappointed prime minister Guillaume Soro who formed a new government. Michel Amani N'Guessan remained defence minister but Désiré Tagro took over as interior minister and Charles Diby Koffi as finance minister.

Week beginning 14 February 2010

The cabinet of Guinea's new prime minister, Jean-Marie Doré, included Bakary Fofana as foreign minister, Kerfala Yansané as economy and finance minister and Gen. Mamadouba Toto Camara as security minister.

Nauru's president, Marcus Stephen, defeated a parliamentary vote of no-confidence.

In Croatia, Ivo Josipović took office as president.

The Irish defence minister, Willie O'Dea, resigned after a defamation case concerning a political rival. Prime minister Brian Cowen took over the defence portfolio.

Following a military coup in Niger, power went to a new political organization called the Supreme Council for the Restoration of Democracy headed by Salou Djibo. Mahamadou Danda was appointed interim prime minister.

Adolphe Mulenda Bwana Sefu became interior minister and Matata Mponyo Mapon finance minister in a cabinet reshuffle in the Democratic Republic of the Congo.

The Labour Party withdrew from the Dutch coalition government after disputes over the Netherlands' military presence in Afghanistan. Subsequently, prime minister Jan Peter Balkenende tendered the government's resignation. A caretaker government of the remaining coalition partners headed by Balkenende with Jan Kees de Jager as finance minister and Ernst Hirsch Ballin as interior minister agreed to serve until elections scheduled for June 2010.

Week beginning 21 February 2010

A major cabinet reshuffle in Denmark resulted in Lene Espersen becoming foreign minister, Gitte Lillelund Bech defence minister and Bertel Haarder interior and health minister.

Pakistan's finance minister Shaukat Tarin resigned citing personal reasons.

In Honduras, Marlon Pascua was sworn in as defence minister.

Week beginning 28 February 2010

The People's Democratic Party won Takjikistan's parliamentary elections, taking 54 of 63 seats.

Niger's post-coup transitional government was sworn in. It included Touré Aminatou as foreign minister, Gen. Mamadou Ousseini as defence minister, Cissé Ousmane as interior minister and Anou Badamassi as economy and finance minister.

José Alberto Mujica took office as president of Uruguay. His cabinet included Luis Almagro as foreign minister, Fernando Lorenzo as finance minister, Eduardo Bonomi as interior minister and Luis Rosadilla as defence minister.

The Ukrainian prime minister, Yuliya Tymoshenko, was ousted after losing a parliamentary vote of confidence. Oleksandr Turchynov succeeded her in an acting capacity.

In Côte d'Ivoire, Jean-Marie Kacou Gervais was appointed foreign minister.

Faure Gnassingbé of the Rally for the Togolese People won Togo's presidential elections with 60·9% of the vote against 33·9% for his nearest rival, Jean-Pierre Fabre of the Union for the Forces of Change.

Chad's prime minister, Youssouf Saleh Abbas, resigned after cabinet ministers were connected to an embezzlement scandal. He was succeeded by Emmanuel Nadingar. There were no changes to key ministries.

In Bosnia and Herzegovinia, Haris Silajdžić took over the rotating chairmanship of the presidency from Željko Komšić.

Week beginning 7 March 2010

The Iraqi National Movement coalition won 91 of 325 seats in Iraq's parliamentary elections, the State of Law Coalition 89, the National Iraqi Alliance 70, the Kurdistan List 43 and the Movement for Change 8.

In Chile, Sebastián Piñera took office as president. Alfredo Moreno was appointed foreign minister.

Week beginning 14 March 2010

Nigeria's acting president, Goodluck Jonathan, dissolved the cabinet. He subsequently named Adetokunbo Kayode defence minister, Olusegun Olutoyin Aganga finance minister, Henry Odein Ajumogobia foreign minister and Emmanuel Iheanacho interior minister.

In Palau, Victor Yano was named Sandra Pierantozzi's successor as secretary of state.

Week beginning 21 March 2010

A new Namibian cabinet, including Utoni Nujoma as foreign minister, was sworn in.

In Latvia, disagreements over economic policy caused the People's Party to withdraw from the coalition government. Four cabinet ministers resigned including the foreign minister, Māris Riekstiņš, although he agreed to remain in office until a replacement could be appointed.

Tony Killeen was appointed Ireland's defence minister.

Week beginning 28 March 2010

In a cabinet reshuffle, Ahmed Ould Moualaye Ahmed took over Mauritania's finance ministry.

In San Marino, Marco Conti and Glauco Sansovini were sworn in as captains-regent.

As we go to press

All dates are 2010

BAHAMAS. Sir Arthur Foulkes was sworn in as Governor-General on 14 April.

CANADA. On 10 May a cabinet reshuffle in New Brunswick resulted in Bernard LeBlanc becoming Minister for Justice and Consumer Affairs and Donald Arsenault, the Minister for Post-Secondary Education, Training and Labour, taking on the additional role of Deputy Prime Minister. In Alberta, Donald Ethell took office as Lieutenant-Governor replacing Norman Kwong on 11 May.

COSTA RICA. President Laura Chinchilla's cabinet was sworn in on 8 May and included René Castro as Foreign Minister, Fernando Herrero as Finance Minister, José María Tijerino as Public Security Minister and Hernando París as Justice Minister.

ESTONIA. On 11 May the European Commission announced that Estonia would adopt the euro on 1 Jan. 2011 making it the 17th country to do so.

GERMANY. In elections held on 9 May in North Rhine-Westphalia the Christian Democratic Union took 67 seats, the Social Democratic Party also 67, the Green Party 23, the Free Democratic Party 13 and the Left 11.

INDIA. The Chief Minister of Meghalaya, D. D. Lapang, resigned on 19 April. He was succeeded by Mukul Sangma on 20 April. The Governor of Rajasthan, Prabha Rau, died on 26 April. On 28 April the Governor of Punjab and Administrator of Chandigarh Shivraj Patil added the governorship of Rajasthan to his responsibilities.

MAURITIUS. In the parliamentary election of 5 May, the ruling coalition of the Mauritius Labour Party, the Militant Socialist Movement and the Mauritian Social Democrat Party won 41 of 62 available seats, followed by the Mauritian Militant Movement-led coalition with 18, the Rodrigues Movement with two and the Mauritian Solidarity Front with one. Estimated turnout was

78%. Prime Minister Navin Ramgoolam's new cabinet took office on 11 May. Ahmed Rashid Beebeejaun remained Deputy Prime Minister and Arvin Boolell Foreign Affairs Minister. Newcomers included Xavier-Luc Duvai and Pravind Jugnauth as Deputy Prime Ministers, the latter also responsible for finance and economic development.

NAURU. In parliamentary elections on 24 April, President Marcus Stephen's supporters won 9 of the 18 seats allowing him to continue to head a caretaker government.

NIGERIA. President Umaru Yar'Adua died on 5 May. He was succeeded by Acting President Goodluck Jonathan.

PANAMA. Following the split of the justice and government ministry in a cabinet reshuffle on 15 April, Roxana Méndez became Interior Minister and José Raúl Mulino Public Security Minister.

PHILIPPINES. Initial results of the presidential election held on 10 May suggested that Benigno Aquino III was set for victory by a large margin over his nearest rival, former President Joseph Estrada.

RUSSIA. In Kalmykia, Oleg Kichikov became acting Prime Minister on 28 April prior to be being sworn in on 4 May.

SOLOMON ISLANDS. Several cabinet ministers were sacked on 21 April including Finance Minister Snyder Rini. Francis Billy Hilly was appointed his successor in a subsequent reshuffle.

UK—FALKLAND ISLANDS. A British company announced the discovery of oil in the North Falkland Basin on 6 May.

USA. A merger between Continental Airlines and United Airlines announced on 3 May created the world's largest carrier.

INTERNATIONAL ORGANIZATIONS

OECD. Chile became a full member of the OECD on 7 May. Estonia, Israel and Slovenia were invited to join the organization on 10 May.

PART I

INTERNATIONAL ORGANIZATIONS

United Nations (UN)

Origin and Aims. The United Nations is an association of states, or intergovernmental organizations, pledged to maintain international peace and security and to co-operate in solving international political, economic, social, cultural and humanitarian problems. The name 'United Nations' was devised by US President Franklin D. Roosevelt and was first used in the Declaration by United Nations of 1 Jan. 1942, during the Second World War, when 26 nations pledged to continue fighting the Axis Powers.

The United Nations Charter was drawn up by the representatives of 50 countries at the United Nations Conference on International Organization, which met in San Francisco from 25 April to 26 June 1945. Delegates started with proposals worked out by the representatives of China, the Soviet Union, the United Kingdom and the United States at Dumbarton Oaks (Washington, D.C.) from 21 Aug. to 28 Sept. 1944. The Charter was signed on 26 June 1945 by the representatives of the 50 countries. Poland, which was not represented at the Conference, signed later and became one of the original 51 member states. The United Nations came into existence officially on 24 Oct. 1945, with the deposit of the requisite number of ratifications of the Charter with the US Department of State. United Nations Day is celebrated on 24 Oct.

In recent years, most of the UN's work has been devoted to helping developing countries. Major goals include the protection of human rights; saving children from starvation and disease; providing relief assistance to refugees and disaster victims; countering global crime, drugs and disease; and assisting countries devastated by war and the long-term threat of landmines.

Members. New member states are admitted by the General Assembly on the recommendation of the Security Council. The Charter provides for the suspension or expulsion of a member for violation of its principles, but no such action has ever been taken. The UN has 192 member states, comprising every internationally recognized sovereign state, with the exception of the Holy See. (For a list of these, see below.)

Finance. Contributions from member states constitute the main source of funds. These are in accordance with a scale specified by the Assembly, and determined primarily by the country's share of the world economy and ability to pay, in the range 22%–0·001%. The Organization is prohibited by law from borrowing from commercial institutions.

A Working Group on the Financial Situation of the United Nations was established in 1994 to address the long-standing financial crisis caused by non-payment of assessed dues by many member states. As of 30 Nov. 2009 member states owed the UN a total of US$3,021m., of which the USA owed US$1,411m. (47%). Total regular budget debts as of 30 Nov. 2009 were US$823m., of which the USA's share was US$771m. (94%).

Official languages: Arabic, Chinese, English, French, Russian and Spanish.

Structure. The UN has six principal organs established by the founding Charter. All have their headquarters in New York except the International Court of Justice, which has its seat in The Hague. These core bodies work through dozens of related agencies, operational programmes and funds, and through special agreements with separate, autonomous, intergovernmental agencies, known as Specialized Agencies, to provide a programme of action in the fields of peace and security, justice and human rights, humanitarian assistance, and social and economic development. The six principal UN organs are:

1. **The General Assembly**, composed of all members, with each member having one vote. Meeting once a year, proceedings begin on the Tuesday of the third week of Sept. The 64th Session opened on 15 Sept. 2009.

At least three months before the start of each session, the Assembly elects a new President, 21 vice-presidents and the chairs of its six main committees, listed below. To ensure equitable geographical representation, the presidency of the Assembly rotates each year among the five geographical groups of states: Africa, Asia, Eastern Europe, Latin America and the Caribbean, and Western Europe and other States. Special sessions may be convoked by the Secretary-General if requested by the Security Council, by a majority of members, or by one member if the majority of the members concur. Emergency sessions may be called within 24 hours at the request of the Security Council on the vote of any nine Council members, or a majority of United Nations members, or one member if the majority of members concur. Decisions on important questions, such as peace and security, new membership and budgetary matters, require a two-thirds majority; other questions require a simple majority of members present and voting.

The work of the General Assembly is divided between six Main Committees, on which every member state is represented: the Disarmament and International Security Committee (First Committee); the Economic and Financial Committee (Second Committee); the Social, Humanitarian and Cultural Committee (Third Committee); the Special Political and Decolonization Committee (Fourth Committee); the Administrative and Budgetary Committee (Fifth Committee); and the Legal Committee (Sixth Committee).

There is also a General Committee charged with the task of co-ordinating the proceedings of the Assembly and its Committees, and a Credentials Committee, which examines the credentials of representatives of Member States. The General Committee consists of 28 members: the president and 21 vice-presidents of the General Assembly and the chairs of the six main committees. The Credentials Committee consists of nine members appointed by the Assembly on the proposal of the President at each session. In addition, the Assembly has two standing committees—an Advisory Committee on Administrative and Budgetary Questions and a Committee on Contributions—and may establish subsidiary and *ad hoc* bodies when necessary to deal with specific matters. These include the Special Committee on Peacekeeping Operations (144 members), the Human Rights Council (47 members), the Committee on the Peaceful Uses of Outer Space (69 members), the Committee on the Exercise of the Inalienable Rights of the Palestinian People (23 members), the Conference on Disarmament (65 members), the International Law Commission (34 independent members), the Scientific Committee on the Effects of Atomic Radiation (21 members), the Special Committee on the Situation with Regard to the Implementation of the Declaration on the Granting of Independence to Colonial Countries and Peoples (known as the Special Committee of 24 on Decolonization; 28 members), and the Commission on International Trade Law (60 members).

The General Assembly has the right to discuss any matters within the scope of the Charter and, with the exception of any situation or dispute on the agenda of the Security Council, may make recommendations accordingly. Occupying a central position in the UN, the Assembly receives reports from other organs, admits new members, directs activities for development, sets policies and determines programmes for the Secretariat and approves the UN budget. The Assembly appoints the Secretary-General, who reports annually to it on the work of the Organization.

Under the 'Uniting For Peace' resolution (377) adopted by the General Assembly in Nov. 1950, the Assembly is also empowered to take action if the Security Council, because of a lack of unanimity of its permanent members, fails to exercise its primary responsibility for the maintenance of international peace and security in any case where there appears to be a threat to the peace, breach of the peace or act of aggression. In this event, the General Assembly may consider the matter immediately with a view to making appropriate recommendations to members for collective measures, including, in the case of a breach of the peace or act of aggression, the use of armed force to maintain or restore international peace and security.

The first Emergency Special Session of the Assembly was called in 1956 during the Suez Crisis by Yugoslavia, which cited Resolution 377; demands were made for the withdrawal of British, French and Israeli troops from Egypt. On the Assembly's recommendations, the United Nations Emergency Force (UNEF1) was formed as the UN's first peacekeeping force.

Website: http://www.un.org/ga

President: Ali Treki (Libya) was elected President for the Sixty-Fourth Session in 2009.

2. **The Security Council** has primary responsibility for the maintenance of international peace and security. Under the Charter, the Security Council alone has the power to take decisions that member states are obligated to carry out. A representative of each of its members must be present at all times at UN Headquarters, but it may meet elsewhere as best facilitates its work.

The Presidency of the Council rotates monthly, according to the English alphabetical order of members' names. The Council consists of 15 members: five permanent and ten non-permanent elected for a two-year term by a two-thirds majority of the General Assembly. Each member has one vote. Retiring members are not eligible for immediate re-election. Any other member of the United Nations may participate without a vote in the discussion of questions specially affecting its interests.

Decisions on procedural questions are made by an affirmative vote of at least nine members. On all other matters, the affirmative vote of nine members must include the concurring votes of all permanent members (subject to the provision that when the Council is considering methods for the peaceful settlement of a dispute, parties to the dispute abstain from voting). Consequently, a negative vote from a permanent member has the power of veto. If a permanent member does not support a decision but does not wish to veto it, it may abstain. From 1945–91 the USSR employed its veto 119 times, the USA 69 times, the UK 32 times, France 18 times and China three times. From 1992–2009 the USA vetoed 13 resolutions, Russian Federation six and China four; France and the UK did not veto any resolutions.

The Council has three standing committees—the Committee of Experts, the Committee on the Admission of New Members and the Committee on Council Meetings away from Headquarters. It may establish *ad hoc* committees and commissions, which include all Council members. Currently they include: the Governing Council of the United Nations Compensation Commission, established in 1991 by Security Council Resolution 692 to compensate for losses related to the Iraqi invasion of Kuwait; the Counter-Terrorism Committee, established pursuant to Resolution 1373 (2001); and the 1540 Committee, established pursuant to Resolution 1540 (2004).

When a threat to peace is brought before the Council, it may undertake mediation, setting out principles for a settlement, and may take measures to enforce its decisions by ceasefire directives, economic sanctions, peacekeeping missions or, in some cases, by collective military action. For the maintenance of international peace and security, the Council can, subject to special agreements, call on the armed forces, assistance and facilities of the member states. It is assisted by a Military Staff Committee consisting of the Chiefs of Staff of the permanent members of the Council or their representatives.

The Council also makes recommendations to the Assembly on the appointment of the Secretary-General and, with the Assembly, elects the judges of the International Court of Justice.

Peacekeeping. The Charter contains no explicit provisions for peacekeeping operations (PKOs), yet they have the highest profile of all the UN's operations. PKOs are associated with humanitarian intervention though their emergence was primarily a result of the failure of the Charter's collective security system during the Cold War and the absence of a UN Force. The end of the Cold War and the rise of intra-state conflict led to a proliferation of PKOs from the late 1980s and a greater proportion of armed missions. However, notable failures in the early and mid-1990s, such as the missions to Somalia in 1993 and to Rwanda in 1994, account for a drop in PKOs and shorter mandates. In 1992 Secretary-General Boutros Boutros-Ghali presented the 'Agenda for Peace', which laid out four phases to prevent or end conflict: preventative diplomacy; peacemaking with civilian and military means; peacekeeping, in its traditional sense of operations in the field; and post-conflict peace-building, an area seen as comparatively neglected in previous missions. Secretary-General Kofi Annan presented a report aimed at conflict prevention in July 2001 emphasizing inter-agency co-operation and long-term strategies to prevent regional instability.

Recent History. In Nov. 2002 the Security Council adopted Resolution 1441, holding Iraq in 'material breach' of disarmament obligations. Weapons inspectors, led by Hans Blix (Sweden), returned to Iraq four years after their last inspections but US and British suspicion that the Iraq regime was failing to comply led to increasing tension. The USA, the UK and Spain reserved the right to disarm Iraq without the need for a further Security Council resolution. Other Council members, notably China, France, Germany and Russia, opposed such action. On 20 March 2003 US forces, supported by the UK, launched attacks on Iraq, bringing an end to Saddam Hussein's rule. In May 2003 the Council adopted Resolution 1483, empowering the occupying coalition as an interim authority and peacekeeping force. The Resolution recognized a transitional Iraqi governing council and withdrew all previous sanctions against Iraq. Resolution 1483 did not address the legality of the invasion, treating the USA and the UK as *de facto* occupying powers. Resolution 1546, approved in June 2004, recognized the transfer of sovereignty to the interim government of Iraq.

Reform. The composition of the Security Council, with its five permanent members having qualified as the principal Second World War victors, has been subject to intense debate in recent years. The lack of permanent representation from Latin America and the Caribbean or from Africa and the Islamic World is frequently cited to demonstrate that the Council is unrepresentative. However, reform is in the hands of the permanent members and a unanimous agreement has proved elusive. In Sept. 2004 Brazil, Germany, India and Japan (the G4) launched a joint bid for permanent membership, along with a seat for an African state. In March 2005 Secretary-General Annan proposed either six new permanent members and three new non-permanent members or the election of a new type of member, eight of which would be elected for a four-year period. The World Summit in Sept. 2005 failed to agree on Security Council reform but pledged to continue negotiations.

Permanent Members. China, France, Russian Federation, UK, USA (Russian Federation took over the seat of the former USSR in Dec. 1991).

Non-Permanent Members. Austria, Japan, Mexico, Turkey and Uganda (until 31 Dec. 2010); Bosnia and Herzegovina, Brazil, Gabon, Lebanon and Nigeria (until 31 Dec. 2011).

Finance. The budget for UN peacekeeping operations in 2009–10 was US$7·8bn. The estimated total cost of operations between 1948 and mid-2009 was US$61bn. In June 2009 outstanding contributions to peacekeeping totalled US$1·6bn.

3. **The Economic and Social Council (ECOSOC)** is responsible under the General Assembly for co-ordinating international economic, social, cultural, educational, health and related matters.

The Council consists of 54 member states elected by a two-thirds majority of the General Assembly for a three-year term. Members are elected according to the following geographic distribution: Africa, 14 members; Asia, 11; Eastern Europe, 6; Latin America and Caribbean, 10; Western Europe and other States, 13. A third of the members retire each year. Retiring members are eligible for immediate re-election. Each member has one vote. Decisions are made by a majority of the members present and voting.

The Council holds one five-week substantive session a year, alternating between New York and Geneva, and one organizational session in New York. The substantive session includes a high-level meeting attended by Ministers, to discuss economic and social issues. Special sessions may be held if required. The President is elected for one year and is eligible for immediate re-election.

The subsidiary machinery of ECOSOC includes:
Nine Functional Commissions. Statistical Commission; Commission on Population and Development; Commission for Social Development; Commission on the Status of Women; Commission on Narcotic Drugs (and Subcommission on Illicit Drug Traffic and Related Matters in the Near and Middle East); Commission on Science and Technology for Development; Commission on Crime Prevention and Criminal Justice; Commission on Sustainable Development; United Nations Forum on Forests.

Five Regional Economic Commissions. ECA (Economic Commission for Africa, Addis Ababa, Ethiopia); ESCAP (Economic and Social Commission for Asia and the Pacific, Bangkok, Thailand); ECE (Economic Commission for Europe, Geneva, Switzerland); ECLAC (Economic Commission for Latin America and the Caribbean, Santiago, Chile); ESCWA (Economic Commission for Western Asia, Beirut, Lebanon).

Three Standing Committees. Committee for Programme and Co-ordination; Commission on Non-Governmental Organizations; Committee on Negotiations with Intergovernmental Agencies.

Other related operational programmes, funds and special bodies reporting to ECOSOC (and/or the General Assembly) include: the United Nations Children's Fund (UNICEF); Office of the United Nations High Commissioner for Refugees (UNHCR); United Nations Conference on Trade and Development (UNCTAD); United Nations Development Programme (UNDP) and Population Fund (UNFPA); United Nations Environment Programme (UNEP); World Food Programme (WFP); International Research and Training Institute for the Advancement of Women (INSTRAW); United Nations Office on Drugs and Crime (UNODC).

In addition, the Council may consult international non-governmental organizations (NGOs) and, after consultation with the member concerned, with national organizations. Over 3,000 organizations have consultative status. NGOs may send observers to ECOSOC's public meetings and those of its subsidiary bodies, and may submit written statements relevant to its work. They may also consult with the UN Secretariat on matters of mutual concern. The term of office of the members listed below expires on 31 Dec. of each year.

Members. Argentina (2012), Bahamas (2012), Bangladesh (2012), Belgium (2012), Brazil (2010), Cameroon (2010), Canada (2012), Chile (2012), China (2010), Comoros (2012), Republic of the Congo (2010), Côte d'Ivoire (2011), Egypt (2012), Estonia (2011), France (2011), Germany (2011), Ghana (2012), Greece (2011), Guatemala (2011), Guinea-Bissau (2011), India (2011), Iraq (2012), Italy (2012), Japan (2011), South Korea (2010), Liechtenstein (2011), Malaysia (2010), Mauritius (2011), Moldova (2010), Mongolia (2012), Morocco (2011), Mozambique (2010), Namibia (2011), New Zealand (2010), Niger (2010), Norway (2010), Pakistan (2010), Peru (2011), Philippines (2012), Poland (2010), Portugal (2011), Russia (2010), Rwanda (2012), St Kitts and Nevis (2011), St Lucia (2010), Saudi Arabia (2011), Slovakia (2012), Sweden (2010), Ukraine (2012), United Kingdom (2010), United States of America (2012), Uruguay (2010), Venezuela (2011), Zambia (2012).

Finance. In 2006, US$14,527m. in socio-economic development assistance grants was provided through the organizations of the UN system.

4. **The Trusteeship Council** was established to ensure that Governments responsible for administering Trust Territories take adequate steps to prepare them for self-government or independence. It consists of the five permanent members of the Security Council. The task of decolonization was completed in 1994, when the Security Council terminated the Trusteeship Agreement for the last of the original UN Trusteeships (Palau), administered by the USA. All Trust Territories attained self-government or independence either as separate States or by joining neighbouring independent countries. The Council formally suspended operations on 1 Nov. 1994 following Palau's independence. By a resolution adopted on 25 May 1994 the Council amended its rules of procedure to drop the obligation to meet annually and agreed to meet as occasion required.

The proposal from then Secretary-General Kofi Annan, in the second part of his reform programme, in July 1997, was that it should be used as a forum to exercise their 'trusteeship' for the global commons, environment and resource systems. However, in his 2005 report, *In Larger Freedom*, Annan called for the deletion of the Council from the UN Charter.

Members. China, France, Russia, UK, USA.

5. **The International Court of Justice** is the principal judicial organ of the UN. It has a dual role: to settle in accordance with international law the legal disputes submitted to it by States; and to give opinions on legal questions referred to it by authorized international organs and agencies.

The Court operates under a Statute of the United Nations Charter. Only States may apply to and appear before the court. The Court is composed of 15 judges, each of a different nationality, elected by an absolute majority by the General Assembly and the Security Council to nine-year terms of office. The composition of the Court must reflect the main forms of civilization and principal legal systems of the world. Elections are held every three years for one-third of the seats; retiring judges may be re-elected. Judges do not represent their respective governments but sit as independent magistrates. They must have the qualifications required in their respective countries for appointment to the highest judicial offices, or be jurists of recognized competence in international law. Candidates are nominated by the national panels of jurists in the Permanent Court of Arbitration established by The Hague Conventions of 1899 and 1907. The Court elects its own President and Vice-President for a three-year term, and is permanently in session.

Decisions are taken by a majority of judges present, subject to a quorum of nine members, with the President having a casting vote. Judgment is final and without appeal, but a revision may be applied for within ten years from the date of the judgment on the ground of new decisive evidence. When the Court does not include a judge of the nationality of a State party to a case, that State has the right to appoint a judge *ad hoc* for that case. While the Court normally sits in plenary session, it can form chambers of three or more judges to deal with specific matters. Judgments by chambers are considered as rendered by the full Court. In 1993, in view of the global expansion of environmental law and protection, the Court formed a seven-member Chamber for Environmental Matters.

Judges. The nine-year terms of office of the judges currently serving end on 5 Feb. of each year indicated: Hishashi Owada, President (Japan) (2012), Peter Tomka, Vice-President (Slovakia) (2012), Shi Jiuyong (China) (2012), Bruno Simma (Germany) (2012), Abdul G. Koroma (Sierra Leone) (2012), Bernardo Sepúlveda Amor (Mexico) (2015), Mohamed Bennouna (Morocco) (2015), Kenneth Keith (New Zealand) (2015), Leonid Skotnikov (Russian Federation) (2015), Thomas Buergenthal (USA) (2015), Antônio Augusto Cançado Trindade (Brazil) (2018), Ronny Abraham (France) (2018), Awn Shawkat Al-Khasawneh (Jordan) (2018), Abdulqawi Yusuf (Somalia) (2018), Sir Christopher Greenwood (UK) (2018).

Competence and Jurisdiction. In contentious cases, only States may apply to or appear before the Court. The conditions under which the Court will be open to non-member states are laid down by the Security Council. The jurisdiction of the Court covers all matters that parties refer to it and all matters provided for in the Charter or in treaties and conventions in force. Disputes concerning the jurisdiction of the Court are settled by the Court's own decision. The Court may apply in its decision:

(a) international conventions;
(b) international custom;
(c) the general principles of law recognized by civilized nations;
(d) as subsidiary means for the determination of the rules of law, judicial decisions and the teachings of highly qualified publicists. If the parties agree, the Court may decide a case *ex aequo et bono*.

Since 1946 the Court has delivered 102 judgments on disputes concerning *inter alia* land frontiers and maritime boundaries, territorial sovereignty, the use of force, interference in the internal affairs of States, diplomatic relations, hostage-taking, the right of asylum, nationality, guardianship, rights of passage and economic rights.

The Court may also give advisory opinions on legal questions to the General Assembly, the Security Council, certain other organs of the UN and 16 agencies of the UN family.

Since 1946 the Court has given 24 advisory opinions, concerning *inter alia* admission to United Nations membership, reparation for injuries suffered in the service of the United Nations, the territorial status of South-West Africa (Namibia) and Western Sahara, expenses of certain United Nations operations, the status of human rights informers, the threat or use of nuclear weapons and legal consequences of the construction of a wall in the Occupied Palestinian Territory.

Finance. The expenses of the Court are borne by the UN. No court fees are paid by parties to the Statute.

Official languages: English, French.
Headquarters: The Peace Palace, 2517 KJ The Hague, Netherlands.
Website: http://www.icj-cij.org
Registrar: Philippe Couvreur (Belgium).

6. **The Secretariat** services the other five organs of the UN, carrying out their programmes, providing administrative support and information. It has a staff of 8,900 at the UN Headquarters in New York and around the world. At its head is the Secretary-General, appointed by the General Assembly on the recommendation of the Security Council for a five-year, renewable term. The Secretary-General acts as chief administrative officer in all meetings of the General Assembly, Security Council, Economic and Social Council and Trusteeship Council. An Office of Internal Oversight, established in 1994 under the tenure of former Secretary-General Boutros Boutros-Ghali (Egypt), pursues a cost-saving mandate to investigate and eliminate waste, fraud and mismanagement within the system. The Secretary-General is assisted by Under-Secretaries-General and Assistant Secretaries-General. A new position of Deputy Secretary-General was agreed by the General Assembly in Dec. 1997 to assist in the running of the Secretariat and to raise the economic, social and development profile of the UN. Peacekeeping operations (PKOs) are chiefly run by Secretariat officials, who present a report to, and are authorized by, the Security Council.

Finance. The financial year coincides with the calendar year. The budget for the two-year period 2010–11 is US$5,156,029,100, compared to US$4,171,359,700 for 2008–09.

Headquarters: United Nations Plaza, New York, NY 10017, USA.
Website: http://www.un.org
Secretary-General: Ban Ki-moon (sworn in 1 Jan. 2007, South Korea). *Deputy Secretary-General:* Asha-Rose Migiro (appointed 5 Jan. 2007, Tanzania).

Secretaries-General since 1945

1945–46	UK	Gladwyn Jebb (acting)
1946–52	Norway	Trygve Halvdan Lie
1953–61	Sweden	Dag Hammarskjöld
1961–71	Burma	Sithu U Thant
1972–81	Austria	Kurt Waldheim
1982–91	Peru	Javier Pérez de Cuéllar
1992–96	Egypt	Boutros Boutros-Ghali
1997–2006	Ghana	Kofi Atta Annan
2007–	South Korea	Ban Ki-moon

Current Leaders

Ban Ki-moon

Position
Secretary-General

Introduction
A career diplomat and politician, Ban Ki-moon served as South Korea's foreign minister before becoming the eighth UN Secretary-General in Jan. 2007. He has a reputation as a mediator and administrator, and has prioritized UN structural reform to deliver operations more effectively. He is the first Asian to head the UN since 1971.

Early Life
Ban Ki-moon was born on 13 June 1944 in Chungju, Chungcheongnam province, South Korea. After graduating in international relations from Seoul University in 1970, he joined the ministry of foreign affairs and in 1972 was posted to New Delhi. In the early 1980s he studied at the Kennedy School of Government at Harvard University, gaining a masters degree in public affairs in 1984. He joined the South Korean permanent observer mission at the UN in New York and rose to become first secretary.

From July 1987–May 1990 Ban was posted to the Korean embassy in Washington, becoming director-general of American affairs in 1990. In 1992, after South and North Korea adopted the joint declaration on the denuclearization of the Korean peninsula, Ban was vice chairman of the South-North joint nuclear control commission. He was made deputy minister for policy planning and international organizations in 1995 and in 1996 became national security adviser to the president.

Ban was appointed ambassador to Vienna in May 1998, where he resumed his involvement in nuclear control issues as chairman of the preparatory commission for the comprehensive nuclear-test-ban treaty in 1999. From Jan. 2000–March 2001 he served as Korea's vice minister of foreign affairs. When South Korea took the presidency of the 56th UN General Assembly in 2001, he worked as chef de cabinet to the president of the assembly.

In Feb. 2003 Ban became foreign policy adviser to the then South Korean president, taking over the foreign affairs portfolio the following year and leading negotiations on the North Korean nuclear issue.

Ban declared his candidacy for the post of UN Secretary-General in Feb. 2006. He was considered an experienced diplomat with a non-confrontational style, although some critics suggested that his low-key manner might prove a weakness. In the last round of voting his rivals withdrew and he was formally appointed on 13 Oct. 2006, taking office on 1 Jan. 2007.

Career in Office

With UN peacekeeping activities at an unprecedented high, Ban has prioritized more effective operational delivery, although some of his plans have met with resistance. He has supported the principle of reforming the UN structure.

Regarding North Korea, Ban has favoured negotiations alongside sanctions rather than the more punitive US approach. Other ongoing challenges include Iran's defiance of the UN over its nuclear programme, the conflict in the western Sudanese province of Darfur and the long-running division of Cyprus. Ban has also presided over progress in the global approach to climate change at international conferences in Indonesia in Dec. 2007 and Denmark in Dec. 2009.

In Jan. 2009 Ban was the first international leader to visit the Palestinian Gaza Strip for several years. He expressed his concern over Israeli attacks on a UN compound in Gaza during a month-long military offensive and called on Israel to lift its blockade of the territory. At the same time, he criticized indiscriminate rocket attacks by the Islamist Hamas movement on Israeli towns.

Also in Jan. 2009, Ban visited Afghanistan and declared that delivering peace and security to the war-torn country was a UN priority. In Jan. 2010 he stressed the need to strengthen the Afghan government and to co-ordinate more effective international civilian efforts under the UN umbrella to spur economic and social development.

In Feb. 2010 he said that global food and energy crises and climate change, coupled with the economic downturn, had eroded advances made in Africa over the previous decade and he called for a stronger partnership for African development.

Member States of the UN

The 192 member states, with percentage scale of contributions to the Regular Budget in 2009 and year of admission:

	% contribution	*Year of admission*		% contribution	*Year of admission*		% contribution	*Year of admission*
Afghanistan	0·001	1946	Djibouti	0·001	1977	Liberia[1]	0·001	1945
Albania	0·006	1955	Dominica	0·001	1978	Libya	0·062	1955
Algeria	0·085	1962	Dominican Republic[1]	0·024	1945	Liechtenstein	0·010	1990
Andorra	0·008	1993	Ecuador[1]	0·021	1945	Lithuania	0·031	1991
Angola	0·003	1976	Egypt[1,2]	0·088	1945	Luxembourg[1]	0·085	1945
Antigua and Barbuda	0·002	1981	El Salvador[1]	0·020	1945	Macedonia[3]	0·005	1993
Argentina[1]	0·325	1945	Equatorial Guinea	0·002	1968	Madagascar	0·002	1960
Armenia	0·002	1992	Eritrea	0·001	1993	Malaŵi	0·001	1964
Australia[1]	1·787	1945	Estonia	0·016	1991	Malaysia[4]	0·190	1957
Austria	0·887	1955	Ethiopia[1]	0·003	1945	Maldives	0·001	1965
Azerbaijan	0·005	1992	Fiji Islands	0·003	1970	Mali	0·001	1960
Bahamas	0·016	1973	Finland	0·564	1955	Malta	0·017	1964
Bahrain	0·033	1971	France[1]	6·301	1945	Marshall Islands	0·001	1991
Bangladesh	0·010	1974	Gabon	0·008	1960	Mauritania	0·001	1961
Barbados	0·009	1966	Gambia	0·001	1965	Mauritius	0·011	1968
Belarus[1,5]	0·020	1945	Georgia	0·003	1992	Mexico[1]	2·257	1945
Belgium[1]	1·102	1945	Germany[6]	8·577	1973	Micronesia	0·001	1991
Belize	0·001	1981	Ghana	0·004	1957	Moldova	0·001	1992
Benin	0·001	1960	Greece[1]	0·596	1945	Monaco	0·003	1993
Bhutan	0·001	1971	Grenada	0·001	1974	Mongolia	0·001	1961
Bolivia[1]	0·006	1945	Guatemala[1]	0·032	1945	Montenegro	0·001	2006
Bosnia and			Guinea	0·001	1958	Morocco	0·042	1956
Herzegovina	0·006	1992	Guinea-Bissau	0·001	1974	Mozambique	0·001	1975
Botswana	0·014	1966	Guyana	0·001	1966	Myanmar[7]	0·005	1948
Brazil[1]	0·876	1945	Haiti[1]	0·002	1945	Namibia	0·006	1990
Brunei	0·026	1984	Honduras[1]	0·005	1945	Nauru	0·001	1999
Bulgaria	0·020	1955	Hungary	0·244	1955	Nepal	0·003	1955
Burkina Faso	0·002	1960	Iceland	0·037	1946	Netherlands[1]	1·873	1945
Burundi	0·001	1962	India[1]	0·450	1945	New Zealand[1]	0·256	1945
Cambodia	0·001	1955	Indonesia[8]	0·161	1950	Nicaragua[1]	0·002	1945
Cameroon	0·009	1960	Iran[1]	0·180	1945	Niger	0·001	1960
Canada[1]	2·977	1945	Iraq[1]	0·015	1945	Nigeria	0·048	1960
Cape Verde	0·001	1975	Ireland, Rep. of	0·445	1955	Norway[1]	0·782	1945
Central African Rep.	0·001	1960	Israel	0·419	1949	Oman	0·073	1971
Chad	0·001	1960	Italy	5·079	1955	Pakistan	0·059	1947
Chile[1]	0·161	1945	Jamaica	0·010	1962	Palau	0·001	1994
China[1]	2·667	1945	Japan	16·624	1956	Panama[1]	0·023	1945
Colombia[1]	0·105	1945	Jordan	0·012	1955	Papua New Guinea	0·002	1975
Comoros	0·001	1975	Kazakhstan	0·029	1992	Paraguay[1]	0·005	1945
Congo,			Kenya	0·010	1963	Peru[1]	0·078	1945
Dem. Rep. of the[9]	0·003	1960	Kiribati	0·001	1999	Philippines[1]	0·078	1945
Congo, Rep. of the	0·001	1960	Korea, North	0·007	1991	Poland[1]	0·501	1945
Costa Rica[1]	0·032	1945	Korea, South	2·173	1991	Portugal	0·527	1955
Côte d'Ivoire	0·009	1960	Kuwait	0·182	1963	Qatar	0·085	1971
Croatia	0·050	1992	Kyrgyzstan	0·001	1992	Romania	0·070	1955
Cuba[1]	0·054	1945	Laos	0·001	1955	Russia[1,10]	1·200	1945
Cyprus	0·044	1960	Latvia	0·018	1991	Rwanda	0·001	1962
Czech Republic[11]	0·281	1993	Lebanon[1]	0·034	1945	St Kitts and Nevis	0·001	1983
Denmark[1]	0·739	1945	Lesotho	0·001	1966	St Lucia	0·001	1979

	% contribution	Year of admission		% contribution	Year of admission		% contribution	Year of admission
St Vincent and the Grenadines	0·001	1980	Spain	2·968	1955	Turkey[1]	0·381	1945
Samoa	0·001	1976	Sri Lanka	0·016	1955	Turkmenistan	0·006	1992
San Marino	0·003	1992	Sudan	0·010	1956	Tuvalu	0·001	2000
São Tomé e Príncipe	0·001	1975	Suriname	0·001	1975	Uganda	0·003	1962
Saudi Arabia[1]	0·748	1945	Swaziland	0·002	1968	Ukraine[1]	0·045	1945
Senegal	0·004	1960	Sweden	1·071	1946	United Arab Emirates	0·302	1971
Serbia[1, 12, 13]	0·021	1945	Switzerland	1·216	2002	UK[1]	6·642	1945
Seychelles	0·002	1976	Syria[1, 14]	0·016	1945	USA[1]	22·000	1945
Sierra Leone	0·001	1961	Tajikistan	0·001	1992	Uruguay[1]	0·027	1945
Singapore[16]	0·347	1965	Tanzania[15]	0·006	1961	Uzbekistan	0·008	1992
Slovakia[11]	0·063	1993	Thailand	0·186	1946	Vanuatu	0·001	1981
Slovenia	0·096	1992	Timor-Leste	0·001	2002	Venezuela[1]	0·200	1945
Solomon Islands	0·001	1978	Togo	0·001	1960	Vietnam	0·024	1977
Somalia	0·001	1960	Tonga	0·001	1999	Yemen[17]	0·007	1947
South Africa[1]	0·290	1945	Trinidad and Tobago	0·027	1962	Zambia	0·001	1964
			Tunisia	0·031	1956	Zimbabwe	0·008	1980

[1]Original member. [2]As United Arab Republic, 1958–71, following union with Syria (1958–61). [3]Pre-independence (1992), as part of Yugoslavia, which was an original member. [4]As the Federation of Malaya till 1963, when the new federation of Malaysia (including Singapore, Sarawak and Sabah) was formed. [5]As Byelorussia, 1945–91. [6]Pre-unification (1990) as two states: the Federal Republic of Germany and the German Democratic Republic. [7]As Burma, 1948–89. [8]Withdrew temporarily, 1965–66. [9]As Zaïre, 1960–97. [10]As USSR, 1945–91. [11]Pre-partition Czechoslovakia (1945–92) was an original member. [12]As Yugoslavia, 1945–2003, and Serbia and Montenegro, 2003–06. [13]Excluded from the General Assembly in 1992; readmitted in Nov. 2000. [14]As United Arab Republic, by union with Egypt, 1958–61. [15]As two states: Tanganyika, 1961–64, and Zanzibar, 1963–64, prior to union as one republic under new name. [16]As part of Malaysia, 1963–65. [17]As Yemen, 1947–90, and Democratic Yemen, 1967–90, prior to merger of the two.

The USA is the leading contributor to the Peacekeeping Operations Budget, with 25·9624% of the total in 2009, followed by Japan (16·6240%), Germany (8·5770%), UK (7·8383%), France (7·4359%), Italy (5·0790%), China (3·1474%), Canada (2·9770%), Spain (2·9680%) and South Korea (2·1730%). All other countries contribute less than 2%.

Publications. Yearbook of the United Nations. New York, 1947 ff.—*United Nations Chronicle. Quarterly.—Monthly Bulletin of Statistics.—General Assembly: Official Records: Resolutions.—Reports of the Secretary-General of the United Nations on the Work of the Organization.* 1946 ff.—*Charter of the United Nations and Statute of the International Court of Justice.—Official Records of the Security Council, the Economic and Social Council, Trusteeship Council and the Disarmament Commission.—Demographic Yearbook.* New York.—*The United Nations Today.* New York, 2008.—*Statistical Yearbook.* New York, 1947 ff.—*Yearbook of International Statistics.* New York, 1950 ff.—*World Economic Survey.* New York, 1947 ff.—*Economic Survey of Asia and the Far East.* New York, 1946 ff.—*Economic Survey of Latin America.* New York, 1948 ff.—*Economic Survey of Europe.* New York, 1948 ff.—*Economic Survey of Africa.* New York, 1960 ff.—*United Nations Reference Guide in the Field of Human Rights.* UN Centre for Human Rights, 1993.

Further Reading

Arnold, G., *World Government by Stealth: The Future of the United Nations.* 1998

Baehr, Peter R. and Gordenker, Leon, *The United Nations: Reality and Ideal.* 2005

Bailey, S. D. and Daws, S., *The United Nations: a Concise Political Guide.* 3rd ed. 1994

Beigbeder, Y., *The Internal Management of United Nations Organizations: the Long Quest for Reform.* 1996

Carnegie Commission on Preventing Deadly Conflict, Preventing Deadly Conflict: Final Report. 1997

Cortright, D. and Lopez, G. A., *The Sanctions Decade: Assessing UN Strategies in the 1990s.* 2000

Durch, W. J., *The Evolution of UN Peacekeeping: Case Studies and Comparative Analysis.* 1993

Gareis, S. B. and Varwick, J., *The United Nations: An Introduction.* 2005

Ginifer, J. (ed.) *Development Within UN Peace Missions.* 1997

Hoopes, T., and Brinkley, D., *FDR and the Creation of the UN.* 1998

Kennedy, Paul, *The Parliament of Man: The Past, Present, and Future of the United Nations.* 2006

Knight, W. Andy, *Adapting the United Nations to a Postmodern Era.* 2nd ed. 2005

Meisler, S., *United Nations: The First Fifty Years.* 1998

New Zealand Ministry of Foreign Affairs and Trade, *United Nations Handbook 2009/10.* 2009

Parsons, A., *From Cold War to Hot Peace: UN Interventions, 1947–94.* 1995

Price, Richard and Zacher, Mark W., *United Nations and Global Security.* 2004

Pugh, M., *The UN, Peace and Force.* 1997

Ratner, S. R., *The New UN Peacekeeping: Building Peace in Lands of Conflict after the Cold War.* 1995

Simma, B. (ed.) *The Charter of the United Nations: a Commentary.* 1995

Universal Declaration of Human Rights

On 10 Dec. 1948 the General Assembly of the United Nations adopted and proclaimed the Universal Declaration of Human Rights.

Preamble

Whereas recognition of the inherent dignity and of the equal and inalienable rights of all members of the human family is the foundation of freedom, justice and peace in the world,

Whereas disregard and contempt for human rights have resulted in barbarous acts which have outraged the conscience of mankind, and the advent of a world in which human beings shall enjoy freedom of speech and belief and freedom from fear and want has been proclaimed as the highest aspiration of the common people,

Whereas it is essential, if man is not to be compelled to have recourse, as a last resort, to rebellion against tyranny and oppression, that human rights should be protected by the rule of law,

Whereas it is essential to promote the development of friendly relations between nations,

Whereas the peoples of the United Nations have in the Charter reaffirmed their faith in fundamental human rights, in the dignity and worth of the human person and in the equal rights of men and women and have determined to promote social progress and better standards of life in larger freedom,

Whereas Member States have pledged themselves to achieve, in co-operation with the United Nations, the promotion of universal respect for and observance of human rights and fundamental freedoms,

Whereas a common understanding of these rights and freedoms is of the greatest importance for the full realization of this pledge,

Now, Therefore **THE GENERAL ASSEMBLY proclaims THIS UNIVERSAL DECLARATION OF HUMAN RIGHTS** as a common standard of achievement for all peoples and all nations, to the end that every individual and every organ of society, keeping this Declaration constantly in mind, shall strive by teaching and education to promote respect for these rights and freedoms and by progressive measures, national and international, to secure their universal and effective recognition and observance, both among the peoples of Member States themselves and among the peoples of territories under their jurisdiction.

Article 1. All human beings are born free and equal in dignity and rights. They are endowed with reason and conscience and should act towards one another in a spirit of brotherhood.

Article 2. Everyone is entitled to all the rights and freedoms set forth in this Declaration, without distinction of any kind, such as race, colour, sex, language, religion, political or other opinion, national or social origin, property, birth or other status. Furthermore, no distinction shall be made on the basis of the political, jurisdictional or international status of the country or territory to which a person belongs, whether it be independent, trust, non-self-governing or under any other limitation of sovereignty.

Article 3. Everyone has the right to life, liberty and security of person.

Article 4. No one shall be held in slavery or servitude; slavery and the slave trade shall be prohibited in all their forms.

Article 5. No one shall be subjected to torture or to cruel, inhuman or degrading treatment or punishment.

Article 6. Everyone has the right to recognition everywhere as a person before the law.

Article 7. All are equal before the law and are entitled without any discrimination to equal protection of the law. All are entitled to equal protection against any discrimination in violation of this Declaration and against any incitement to such discrimination.

Article 8. Everyone has the right to an effective remedy by the competent national tribunals for acts violating the fundamental rights granted him by the constitution or by law.

Article 9. No one shall be subjected to arbitrary arrest, detention or exile.

Article 10. Everyone is entitled in full equality to a fair and public hearing by an independent and impartial tribunal, in the determination of his rights and obligations and of any criminal charge against him.

Article 11. (1) Everyone charged with a penal offence has the right to be presumed innocent until proved guilty according to law in a public trial at which he has had all the guarantees necessary for his defence.

(2) No one shall be held guilty of any penal offence on account of any act or omission which did not constitute a penal offence, under national or international law, at the time when it was committed. Nor shall a heavier penalty be imposed than the one that was applicable at the time the penal offence was committed.

Article 12. No one shall be subjected to arbitrary interference with his privacy, family, home or correspondence, nor to attacks upon his honour and reputation. Everyone has the right to the protection of the law against such interference or attacks.

Article 13. (1) Everyone has the right to freedom of movement and residence within the borders of each state.

(2) Everyone has the right to leave any country, including his own, and to return to his country.

Article 14. (1) Everyone has the right to seek and enjoy in other countries asylum from persecution.

(2) This right may not be invoked in the case of prosecutions genuinely arising from non-political crimes or from acts contrary to the purposes and principles of the United Nations.

Article 15. (1) Everyone has the right to a nationality.

(2) No one shall be arbitrarily deprived of his nationality nor denied the right to change his nationality.

Article 16. (1) Men and women of full age, without any limitation due to race, nationality or religion, have the right to marry and to found a family. They are entitled to equal rights as to marriage, during marriage and at its dissolution.

(2) Marriage shall be entered into only with the free and full consent of the intending spouses.

(3) The family is the natural and fundamental group unit of society and is entitled to protection by society and the State.

Article 17. (1) Everyone has the right to own property alone as well as in association with others.

(2) No one shall be arbitrarily deprived of his property.

Article 18. Everyone has the right to freedom of thought, conscience and religion; this right includes freedom to change his religion or belief, and freedom, either alone or in community with others and in public or private, to manifest his religion or belief in teaching, practice, worship and observance.

Article 19. Everyone has the right to freedom of opinion and expression; this right includes freedom to hold opinions without interference and to seek, receive and impart information and ideas through any media and regardless of frontiers.

Article 20. (1) Everyone has the right to freedom of peaceful assembly and association.

(2) No one may be compelled to belong to an association.

Article 21. (1) Everyone has the right to take part in the government of his country, directly or through freely chosen representatives.

(2) Everyone has the right of equal access to public service in his country.

(3) The will of the people shall be the basis of the authority of government; this will shall be expressed in periodic and genuine elections which shall be by universal and equal suffrage and shall be held by secret vote or by equivalent free voting procedures.

Article 22. Everyone, as a member of society, has the right to social security and is entitled to realization, through national effort and international co-operation and in accordance with the organization and resources of the State, of the economic, social and cultural rights indispensable for his dignity and the free development of his personality.

Article 23. (1) Everyone has the right to work, to free choice of employment, to just and favourable conditions of work and to protection against unemployment.

(2) Everyone, without any discrimination, has the right to equal pay for equal work.

(3) Everyone who works has the right to just and favourable remuneration ensuring for himself and his family an existence worthy of human dignity, and supplemented, if necessary, by other means of social protection.

(4) Everyone has the right to form and to join trade unions for the protection of his interests.

Article 24. Everyone has the right to rest and leisure, including reasonable limitation of working hours and periodic holidays with pay.

Article 25. (1) Everyone has the right to a standard of living adequate for the health and well-being of himself and his family, including food, clothing, housing and medical care and necessary social services, and the right to security in the event of unemployment, sickness, disability, widowhood, old age or other lack of livelihood in circumstances beyond his control.

(2) Motherhood and childhood are entitled to special care and assistance. All children, whether born in or out of wedlock, shall enjoy the same social protection.

Article 26. (1) Everyone has the right to education. Education shall be free, at least in the elementary and fundamental stages. Elementary education shall be compulsory. Technical and professional education shall be made generally available and higher education shall be equally accessible to all on the basis of merit.

(2) Education shall be directed to the full development of the human personality and to the strengthening of respect for human rights and fundamental freedoms. It shall promote understanding, tolerance and friendship among all nations, racial or religious groups, and shall further the activities of the United Nations for the maintenance of peace.

(3) Parents have a prior right to choose the kind of education that shall be given to their children.

Article 27. (1) Everyone has the right freely to participate in the cultural life of the community, to enjoy the arts and to share in scientific advancement and its benefits.

(2) Everyone has the right to the protection of the moral and material interests resulting from any scientific, literary or artistic production of which he is the author.

Article 28. Everyone is entitled to a social and international order in which the rights and freedoms set forth in this Declaration can be fully realized.

Article 29. (1) Everyone has duties to the community in which alone the free and full development of his personality is possible.

(2) In the exercise of his rights and freedoms, everyone shall be subject only to such limitations as are determined by law solely for the purpose of securing due recognition and respect for the rights and freedoms of others and of meeting the just requirements of morality, public order and the general welfare in a democratic society.

(3) These rights and freedoms may in no case be exercised contrary to the purposes and principles of the United Nations.

Article 30. Nothing in this Declaration may be interpreted as implying for any State, group or person any right to engage in any activity or to perform any act aimed at the destruction of any of the rights and freedoms set forth herein.

Nobel Peace Prize Winners: 1985–2009

When the scientist, industrialist and inventor Alfred Nobel died in 1896, he made provision in his will for his fortune to be used for prizes in Physics, Chemistry, Physiology or Medicine, Literature and Peace. A prize for Economics was added later. The Norwegian Nobel Committee awards the Nobel Peace Prize, and the Nobel Foundation in Stockholm (founded 1900; Mailing address: Box 5232, SE-10245, Stockholm, Sweden) awards the other five prizes. The Prize Awarding Ceremony takes place on 10 Dec., the anniversary of Nobel's death. The last 25 recipients of the Nobel Peace Prize, worth 10m. Sw. kr. in 2009, are:

2009 – Barack Obama (USA) for his extraordinary efforts to strengthen international diplomacy and co-operation between peoples.

2008 – Martti Ahtisaari (Finland) for his important efforts, on several continents and over more than three decades, to resolve international conflicts.

2007 – the Intergovernmental Panel on Climate Change and Al Gore for their efforts to build up and disseminate greater knowledge about man-made climate change.

2006 – Muhammad Yunus and Grameen Bank of Bangladesh for their efforts to create economic and social development from below.

2005 – Mohamed ElBaradei and the IAEA for their efforts to prevent nuclear energy from being used for military purposes and to ensure that nuclear energy for peaceful purposes is used in the safest possible way.

2004 – Wangari Maathai (Kenya) for her contribution to sustainable development, democracy and peace.

2003 – Shirin Ebadi (Iran) for her work fighting for democracy and the rights of women and children.

2002 – Jimmy Carter (USA) for his decades of untiring effort to find peaceful solutions to international conflicts, to advance democracy and human rights, and to promote economic and social development.

2001 – the United Nations and Kofi Annan for a better organized and more peaceful world.

2000 – Kim Dae-jung for his work for democracy and human rights in South Korea and in East Asia in general, and for peace and reconciliation with North Korea in particular.

1999 – *Médecins Sans Frontières* (Doctors Without Borders) in recognition of the organization's pioneering humanitarian work on several continents.

1998 – John Hume and David Trimble for their efforts to find a peaceful solution to the conflict in Northern Ireland.

1997 – ICBL (*International Campaign to Ban Landmines*) and Jody Williams for their work for the banning and clearing of anti-personnel mines.

1996 – Carlos Felipe Ximenes Belo and José Ramos-Horta for their work towards a just and peaceful solution to the conflict in Timor-Leste.

1995 – Joseph Rotblat and the *Pugwash Conferences on Science and World Affairs* for their efforts to diminish the part played by nuclear arms in international politics and eventually to eliminate such arms.

1994 – Yasser Arafat (Chairman of the Executive Committee of the PLO, President of the Palestinian National Authority), Shimon Peres (Foreign Minister of Israel) and Yitzhak Rabin (Prime Minister of Israel) for their efforts to create peace in the Middle East.

1993 – Nelson Mandela (Leader of the ANC) and Fredrik Willem De Klerk (President of the Republic of South Africa).

1992 – Rigoberta Menchú Tum (Guatemala) for his campaign work for human rights, especially for indigenous peoples.

1991 – Aung San Suu Kyi (Myanmar), opposition leader and human rights advocate.

1990 – Mikhail Sergeyevich Gorbachev (president of the USSR) for helping bring the Cold War to an end.

1989 – The 14th Dalai Lama (Tenzin Gyatso) for his religious and political leadership of the Tibetan people.

1988 – *The United Nations Peace-Keeping Forces.*

1987 – Oscar Arias Sánchez (President of Costa Rica) for initiating peace negotiations in Central America.

1986 – Elie Wiesel (USA), author and humanitarian.

1985 – *International Physicians for the Prevention of Nuclear War*, Boston, USA.

Norwegian Nobel Committee Headquarters: Det Norske Nobelinstitutt, Henrik Ibsens gate 51, N-0255 Oslo, Norway.
Website: http://www.nobel.no/

United Nations System

Programmes and Funds. Social and economic development, aimed at achieving a better life for people everywhere, is a major part of the UN system of organizations. At the forefront of efforts to bring about such progress is the United Nations Development Programme (UNDP), the UN's global development network, advocating for change and connecting countries to knowledge, experience and resources to help people build a better life. In 2006 UNDP helped people in 174 countries and territories, supporting programmes and projects that focus on democratic governance, poverty reduction, crisis prevention and recovery, environment and energy, HIV/AIDS and women's empowerment.

UNDP assistance is provided only at the request of governments and in response to their priority needs, integrated into overall national and regional plans. Its activities are funded mainly by voluntary contributions outside the regular UN budget. More than 80% of the UNDP's core programme funds go to countries with an annual per capita GNP of US$750 or less, which are home to 90% of the world's poorest peoples. Headquartered in New York, the UNDP is governed by a 36-member Executive Board, representing both developing and developed countries.

In addition to its regular programmes, UNDP administers various special-purpose funds, such as the *UN Capital Development Fund (UNCDF)*, which offers a unique combination of investment capital, capacity building and technical advisory services to promote microfinance and local development in the Least Developed Countries (LDCs), the *United Nations Volunteers (UNV)*, which is the UN focal point for promoting and harnessing volunteerism for effective development, and the *UN Development Fund for Women (UNIFEM)*, whose mission is the empowerment of women and gender equality in all levels of development planning and practice. Together with the World Bank and the United Nations Environment Programme (UNEP), UNDP is one of the three implementing agencies of the Global Environment Facility (GEF), the world's largest fund for protecting the environment.

UNDP is on the ground in 166 countries, working with governments and local communities on their own solutions to global and national development challenges. In each country office, the UNDP Resident Representative normally also serves as the Resident Coordinator of development activities for the UN system as a whole.

Administrator: Helen Clark (New Zealand).

United Nations development agencies include the *United Nations Children's Fund (UNICEF)*. It was established in 1946 by the United Nations General Assembly as the United Nations International Children's Emergency Fund, to meet the emergency needs of children of post-war Europe. In 1953 the organization became a permanent part of the UN and its mandate was expanded to carry out long-term programmes to benefit children worldwide. Guided by the Convention on the Rights of the Child and its Optional Protocols, UNICEF supports low-cost community-based programmes in immunization, nutrition, education, HIV/AIDS, water supply, environmental sanitation, gender issues and development, and child protection in more than 158 countries and territories. In 2001, with the assistance of UNICEF, WHO and other key partners, a record 575m. children were vaccinated against polio. UNICEF is the largest supplier of vaccines to developing countries, providing 40% of the world's doses of vaccine for children. UNICEF also provides relief and rehabilitation assistance in emergencies.

UNICEF served as the substantive secretariat for the UN General Assembly Special Session on Children held in New York from 8–10 May 2002, and supported a wide range of consultations and events around the world to ensure that children and young people had a voice in the process and in the Session itself. The Special Session adopted the outcome document, 'A World Fit For Children', setting 21 concrete time-bound goals for children on four key priorities: promoting healthy lives; providing quality education for all; protecting children against abuse, exploitation and violence; and combating HIV/AIDS.

In 2003 UNICEF intensified its '25 by 2005' campaign to accelerate progress in 25 countries where girls fall behind boys in enrolment, and where intensified actions would make the greatest impact.

UNICEF works towards eliminating the worst forms of child labour, protecting children affected by armed conflict and, in 2003, also supported programmes for children orphaned by HIV/AIDS in 38 countries in sub-Saharan Africa.

Executive Director: Ann Veneman (USA).

The United Nations Population Fund (UNFPA) was established in 1969 and is the world's largest multilateral source of population assistance. About a quarter of all population assistance from donor nations to developing countries is channeled through UNFPA. The fund extends assistance to developing countries at their request to help them address reproductive health and population issues, and raises awareness of these issues in all countries.

In 2005 UNFPA provided assistance to some 146 developing nations, with special emphasis on increasing the quality of reproductive health services, ending gender discrimination and violence, formulating effective population policies and reducing the spread of HIV/AIDS.

UNFPA's main objectives are to expand access to comprehensive reproductive health care, including family planning and sexual health, skilled birth attendance, and emergency obstetric care, to all couples and individuals in or before the year 2015. It also supports population and development strategies that enable capacity-building in population programming. UNFPA's strategy focuses on helping to meet the needs of individual women and men. Key to this approach is providing women with more choices through expanded access to education, health services and employment opportunities, and promoting the equal rights of women all over the world. UNFPA's *The State of World Population* report is published annually.

Executive Director: Thoraya Obaid (Saudi Arabia).

The United Nations Environment Programme (UNEP), established in 1972, works to encourage sustainable development through sound environmental practices everywhere. UNEP has its headquarters in Nairobi, Kenya and other offices in Paris, Geneva, Bangkok, Washington, D.C., New York, Osaka, Manama and Mexico City. Its activities cover a wide range of issues, from atmosphere and terrestrial ecosystems, to the promotion of environmental science and information, to an early warning and emergency response capacity to deal with environmental disasters and emergencies. UNEP's present priorities include: environmental information, assessment and research; enhanced co-ordination of environmental conventions and development of policy instruments; fresh water; technology transfer and industry; and support to Africa. Information networks and monitoring systems established by the UNEP include: the Global Environment Information Exchange Network (INFOTERRA); Global Resource Information Database (GRID); the International Register of Potentially Toxic Chemicals (IRPTC); and the recent UNEP.net, a web-based interactive catalogue and multifaceted portal that offers access to environmentally relevant geographic, textual and pictorial information. In June 2000 the World Conservation and Monitoring Centre (WCMC) based in Cambridge, UK became UNEP's key biodiversity assessment centre. UNEP's latest state-of-the-environment report is the *UNEP Year Book* 2010.

Executive Director: Achim Steiner (Germany).

Other UN programmes working for development include: the *UN Conference on Trade and Development (UNCTAD)*, which promotes international trade, particularly by developing countries, in an attempt to increase their participation in the global economy; and the *World Food Programme (WFP)*, the world's largest international food aid organization, which is dedicated to both emergency relief and development programmes.

The United Nations Human Settlements Programme (UN-Habitat), which assists over 600m. people living in health-threatening housing conditions, was established in 1978. The 58-member *UN Commission on Human Settlements (UNCHS)*, Habitat's governing body, meets every two years. The Centre serves as the focal point for human settlements action and the co-ordination of activities within the UN system.

The United Nations Office on Drugs and Crime (UNODC) educates the world about the dangers of drug abuse; strengthens international action against drug production, trafficking and drug related crime; promotes efforts to reduce drug abuse, particularly among the young and vulnerable; builds local, national and international partnerships to address drug issues; provides information, analysis and expertise on the drug issue; promotes international co-operation in crime prevention and control; supports the development of criminal justice systems; and assists member states in addressing the challenges and threats posed by the changing nature of transnational organized crime.

Executive Director: Antonio Maria Costa (Italy).

The UN work in crime prevention and criminal justice aims to lessen the human and material costs of crime and its impact on socio-economic development. The UN Congress on the Prevention of Crime and Treatment of Offenders has convened every five years since 1955 and provides a forum for the presentation of policies and progress. The Eleventh Crime Congress (Bangkok, 2005) discussed global co-operation in combating transnational organized crime and terrorism, and also decisive action against new manifestations of evil such as cybercrime. The *Commission on Crime Prevention and Criminal Justice*, a functional body of ECOSOC, established in 1992, seeks to strengthen UN activities in the field, and meets annually in Vienna. The interregional research and training arm of the UN crime and criminal justice programme is the *United Nations Interregional Crime and Justice Research Institute (UNICRI)* in Rome.

Humanitarian assistance to refugees and victims of natural and man-made disasters is also an important function of the UN system. The main refugee organizations within the system are the *Office of the United Nations High Commissioner for Refugees (UNHCR)* and the *United Nations Relief and Works Agency for Palestine Refugees in the Near East (UNRWA)*.

UNHCR was created in 1951 to resettle 1·2m. European refugees left homeless in the aftermath of the Second World War. It was initially envisioned as a temporary office with a projected lifespan of three years. However, in 2003, in a move to strengthen UNHCR's capacity to carry out its work more effectively, the General Assembly removed the time limitation on the organization's mandate and extended it indefinitely, until 'the refugee problem is solved'. Today, with some 20·8m. persons of concern across the globe, UNHCR has become one of the world's principal humanitarian agencies. Its Executive Committee currently comprises 70 member states. With its Headquarters in Geneva, UNHCR has some 6,600 staff, including short-term contract staff, 84% of whom work in field locations in 116 countries across the globe. The organization has twice been awarded the Nobel Peace Prize. UNHCR is a subsidiary organ of the United Nations General Assembly.

The work of UNHCR is humanitarian and non-political. International protection is its primary function. Its main objective is to promote and safeguard the rights and interests of refugees. In so doing UNHCR devotes special attention to promoting access to asylum and seeks to improve the legal, material and physical safety of refugees in their country of residence. Crucial to this status is the principle of *non-refoulement*, which prohibits the expulsion from or forcible return of refugees to a country where they may have reason to fear persecution. UNHCR pursues its objectives in the field of protection by encouraging the conclusion of intergovernmental legal instruments in favour of refugees, by supervising the implementation of their provisions and by encouraging governments to adopt legislation and administrative procedures for the benefit of refugees. UNHCR is often called upon to provide material assistance (e.g. the provision of food, shelter, medical care and essential supplies) while durable solutions are being sought. Durable solutions generally take one of three forms: voluntary repatriation, local integration or resettlement in another country.

UNHCR co-operates both multilaterally and bilaterally with a wide range of partners in order to fulfil its mandate for refugees and other people of concern to the Office. Partners include UN co-ordination bodies, other UN agencies and departments, intergovernmental organizations, non-governmental organizations (NGOs), universities and research institutes, regional organizations, foundations and corporate entities from the private sector, as well as governments, host communities and refugee and other displaced population representatives. In response to calls by the international community to improve the global humanitarian response capacity, today UNHCR is playing an active role in the inter-agency 'cluster leadership approach' with respect to protecting and assisting internally displaced persons. UNHCR's involvement is focused on conflict-generated situations of internal displacement, where it leads the protection 'cluster', the camp co-ordination and camp management 'cluster' and the emergency shelter 'cluster'. At present, UNHCR is funded almost entirely by voluntary contributions. In 2008 UNHCR's expenditure amounted to approximately US$1·6bn.

High Commissioner: António Guterres (Portugal).

UNRWA was created by the General Assembly in 1949 as a temporary, non-political agency to provide relief to the nearly 750,000 people who became refugees as a result of the disturbances during and after the creation of the State of Israel in the former British Mandate territory of Palestine. 'Palestine refugees', as defined by UNRWA's mandate, are persons or descendants of persons whose normal residence was Palestine for at least two years prior to the 1948 conflict and who, as a result of the conflict, lost their homes and means of livelihood. UNRWA has also been called upon to help persons displaced by renewed hostilities in the Middle East in 1967. The situation of Palestine refugees in south Lebanon, affected in the aftermath of the 1982 Israeli invasion of Lebanon, was of special concern to the Agency in 1984. UNRWA provides education, health, relief and social services to eligible refugees among the 4·5m. registered Palestine refugees in its five fields of operation: Jordan, Lebanon, Syria, the West Bank and the Gaza Strip. Its mandate is renewed at intervals by the UN General Assembly, and has most recently been extended until 30 June 2011. The total budget for 2009 amounted to US$1·2bn.

Commissioner-General: Karen AbuZayd (USA).

Research and Training Institutes. There are five research and training institutes within the UN, all of them autonomous.

United Nations Institute for Disarmament Research (UNIDIR). Established in 1980 to undertake research on disarmament and security with the aim of assisting the international community in their disarmament thinking, decisions and efforts. Through its research projects, publications, small meetings and expert networks, UNIDIR promotes creative thinking and dialogue on both current and future security issues, through examination of topics as varied as tactical nuclear weapons, refugee security, computer warfare, regional confidence-building measures and small arms.

Address: Palais des Nations, 1211 Geneva 10, Switzerland.
Website: http://www.unidir.org

United Nations Institute for Training and Research (UNITAR). Founded in 1965, UNITAR is the leading UN institute offering training on global and strategic challenges. As an autonomous body within the UN system, UNITAR is led by an Executive Director, governed by a Board of Trustees and is supported by voluntary contributions from governments, intergovernmental organizations, foundations and the private sector. With 80,000 beneficiaries in 2008–09 the Institute provides short executive training to national and local government officials of UN member states and civil society representatives around the world. UNITAR aims to meet the growing demand, especially from the least developed countries, for capacity development in the fields of environment, peace, security and diplomacy, and governance.

Address: Palais des Nations, 1211 Geneva 10, Switzerland.
Website: http://www.unitar.org

United Nations International Research and Training Institute for the Advancement of Women (INSTRAW). Established by ECOSOC and endorsed by the General Assembly in 1976, INSTRAW provides training, conducts research, and collects and disseminates information to promote gender equality and stimulate and assist women's advancement. Its ten-member Board of Trustees, which reports to ECOSOC, meets annually to review its programme and to formulate the principles and guidelines for INSTRAW's activities.

Address: POB 21747, Santo Domingo, Dominican Republic.
Website: http://www.un-instraw.org

United Nations Interregional Crime and Justice Research Institute (UNICRI). Established in 1967 to support countries worldwide in crime prevention and criminal justice, UNICRI offers technical co-operation, research and training at various levels for governments and the international community as a whole. The institute particularly focuses on security and counter-terrorism, counter-trafficking and preventing money laundering.

Address: 10 Viale Maestri del Lavoro, 10127 Turin, Italy.
Website: http://www.unicri.it

United Nations Research Institute for Social Development (UNRISD). Established in 1963 to conduct multidisciplinary research into the social dimensions of contemporary problems affecting development, it aims to provide governments, development agencies, grassroots organizations and scholars with a better understanding of how development policies and processes of economic, social and environmental change affect different social groups.

Address: Palais des Nations, 1211 Geneva 10, Switzerland.
Website: http://www.unrisd.org

Other UN Entities. In addition to the operational programmes and funds and the research and training institutes there are a number of other entities that fall within the UN system.

Joint UN Programme on HIV/AIDS (UNAIDS). In 1996 the Assembly reviewed implementation of the global strategy for the prevention and control of AIDS, and progress of the Joint UN Programme on HIV/AIDS (UNAIDS), which became operational in 1996. The impact of the HIV/AIDS epidemic is seen to be expanding and intensifying, particularly in developing countries, and new resource mobilization mechanisms were called for to support countries in combating HIV/AIDS. UNAIDS brings together the HIV/AIDS responses of ten co-sponsor UN agencies, providing an overall framework for action and ensuring better co-ordination between its members. The co-sponsor agencies are: International Labour Organization (ILO), Office of the United Nations High Commissioner for Refugees (UNHCR), United Nations Children's Fund (UNICEF), United Nations Development Programme (UNDP), United Nations Educational, Scientific and Cultural Organization (UNESCO), United Nations Office on Drugs and Crime (UNODC), United Nations Population Fund (UNFPA), World Bank, World Food Programme (WFP) and World Health Organization (WHO). The proposed budget for 2008–09 amounted to US$468·8m.

Address: 20 avenue Appia, 1211 Geneva 27, Switzerland.
Website: http://www.unaids.org

Office of the High Commissioner for Human Rights (OHCHR). The UN's activities in the field of human rights are the primary responsibility of the High Commissioner for Human Rights, a post established in 1993 under the direction and authority of the Secretary-General. The High Commissioner is nominated by the Secretary-General for a four-year term, renewable once. The principal co-ordinating human rights organ of the UN was until mid-2006 the 53-member Commission on Human Rights, set up by ECOSOC in 1946. On 15 March 2006 the UN General Assembly voted overwhelmingly to abolish the Commission after it was criticized for having member countries with poor human rights records. A new 47-member *Human Rights Council* was established as its successor and held its first session in June 2006.

Address: Palais des Nations, 1211 Geneva 10, Switzerland.
Website: http://www.ohchr.org

UN Office for Project Services (UNOPS). Established in 1995, the self-funding unit provides a range of services for other organizations in the UN system, the private sector, NGOs and academic institutions. Services offered include procurement, recruitment and human resources, and loan supervision.

Address: Midtermolen 3, PO Box 2695, 2100 Copenhagen, Denmark.
Website: http://www.unops.org

United Nations University (UNU). Sponsored jointly by the UN and UNESCO, UNU is guaranteed academic freedom by a charter approved by the General Assembly in 1973. It is governed by a 28-member Council of scholars and scientists, of whom 24 are appointed by the Secretary-General of the UN and the Director-General of UNESCO. Unlike a traditional university with a campus, students and faculty, it works through networks of collaborating institutions and individuals to undertake multidisciplinary research on problems of human survival, development and welfare; and to strengthen research and training capabilities in developing countries. It also provides postgraduate fellowships and PhD internships to scholars and scientists from developing countries. The University focuses its work within two programme areas: peace and governance, and environment and development.

Address: 53–70 Jingumae 5-chome, Shibuya-ku, Tokyo 150-8925, Japan.
Website: http://www.unu.edu

Information. *The UN Statistics Division* in New York provides a wide range of statistical outputs and services for producers and users of statistics worldwide, facilitating national and international policy formulation, implementation and monitoring. It produces printed publications of statistics and statistical methods in the fields of international merchandise trade, national accounts, demography and population, gender, industry, energy, environment, human settlements and disability, as well as general statistics compendiums including the *Statistical Yearbook* and *World Statistics Pocketbook*. Many of its databases are available on CD-ROM and the internet.

Website: http://unstats.un.org

UN Information Centre. Public Inquiries Unit, Department of Public Information, Room GA-57, United Nations Plaza, New York, NY 10017. There are also 63 UN Information Centres in other parts of the world.

Website: http://www.un.org

Specialized Agencies of the UN

The intergovernmental agencies related to the UN by special agreements are separate autonomous organizations which work with the UN and each other through the co-ordinating machinery of the Economic and Social Council. Of these, 19 are 'Specialized Agencies' within the terms of the UN Charter, and report annually to ECOSOC.

Food and Agriculture Organization of the United Nations (FAO)

Origin. In 1943 the International Conference on Food and Agriculture, at Hot Springs, Virginia, set up an Interim Commission, based in Washington, with a remit to establish an organization. Its Constitution was signed on 16 Oct. 1945 in Quebec City. Today, membership totals 192 countries. The European Union was made a member as a 'regional economic integration organization' in 1991.

Aims and Activities. The aims of FAO are to raise levels of nutrition and standards of living; to improve the production and distribution of all food and agricultural products from farms, forests and fisheries; to improve the living conditions of rural populations; and, by these means, to eliminate hunger. Its priority objectives are to encourage sustainable agriculture and rural development as part of a long-term strategy for the conservation and management of natural resources; and to ensure the availability of adequate food supplies, by maximizing stability in the flow of supplies and securing access to food by the poor.

In carrying out these aims, FAO promotes investment in agriculture, better soil and water management, improved yields of crops and livestock, agricultural research and the transfer of technology to developing countries; and encourages the conservation of natural resources and rational use of fertilizers and pesticides; the development and sustainable utilization of marine and inland fisheries; the sustainable management of forest resources and the combating of animal disease. Technical assistance is provided in all of these fields, and in nutrition, agricultural engineering, agrarian reform, development communications, remote sensing for climate and vegetation, and the prevention of post-harvest food losses. In addition, FAO works to maintain global biodiversity with the emphasis on the genetic diversity of crop plants and domesticated animals; and plays a major role in the collection, analysis and dissemination of information on agricultural production and commodities. Finally, FAO acts as a neutral forum for the discussion of issues, and advises governments on policy, through international conferences like the 1996 World Food Summit in Rome and the World Food Summit: five years later, held in Rome in 2002.

Special FAO programmes help countries prepare for, and provide relief in the event of, emergency food situations, in particular through the rehabilitation of agriculture after disasters. The *Special Programme for Food Security*, launched in 1994, is designed to assist target countries to increase food production and productivity as rapidly as possible, primarily through the widespread adoption by farmers of available improved production technologies, with the emphasis on high-potential areas. FAO provides support for the global co-ordination of the programme and helps attract funds. The *Emergency Prevention System for Transboundary Animal and Plant Pests and Diseases (EMPRES)*, established in 1994, strengthens FAO's existing contribution to the prevention, control and eradication of diseases and pests before they compromise food security, with locusts and rinderpest among its priorities. The *Global Information and Early Warning System (GIEWS)* provides current information on the world food situation and identifies countries threatened by shortages to guide potential donors. The interagency Food Insecurity and Vulnerability Information and Mapping System initiative (FIVIMS) was established in 1997, with FAO as its secretariat. More than 60 countries have nominated national focal points to co-ordinate efforts to collect and use statistics related to food insecurity more efficiently. Together with the UN, FAO sponsors the *World Food Programme (WFP)*.

Finance. The budget for the 2008–09 biennium was US$929·8m. FAO's Regular Programme budget, financed by contributions from member governments, covers the cost of its secretariat and Technical Co-operation Programme (TCP), and part of the costs of several special programmes.

FAO continues to provide technical advice and support through its field programmes in all areas of food and agriculture, fisheries, forestry and rural development. In 2007 expenditures in the field totalled US$473m. for both development and emergency operations with money provided by donor agencies and governments. In addition, FAO spent US$31·9m. from its regular budget on its field programme. The FAO Investment Centre organizes more than 600 field missions for 140 investment projects in around 100 countries.

Organization. The FAO Conference, composed of all members, meets every other year to determine policy and approve the FAO's budget and programme. The 49-member Council, elected by the Conference, serves as FAO's governing body between conference sessions. Much of its work is carried out by dozens of regional or specialist commissions, such as the Asia-Pacific Fishery Commission, the European Commission on Agriculture and the Commission on Plant Genetic Resources. The Director-General is elected for a renewable six-year term.

Headquarters: Viale delle Terme di Caracalla, 00153 Rome, Italy.
Website: http://www.fao.org
Director-General: Jacques Diouf (Senegal).

Publications. *Unasylva* (quarterly), 1947 ff.; *The State of Food and Agriculture* (annual), 1947 ff.; *Animal Health Yearbook* (annual), 1957 ff.; *Statistical Yearbook* (annual), 2004 ff.; *FAO Commodity Review* (annual), 1961 ff.; *Yearbook of Forest Products* (annual), 1947 ff.; *Yearbook of Fishery Statistics* (in two volumes); *FAO Plant Protection Bulletin* (quarterly); *Environment and Energy Bulletin; Food Outlook* (monthly); *The State of World Fisheries and Aquaculture* (annual); *The State of the World's Forests; World Watch List for Domestic Animal Diversity; The State of Food Insecurity in the World.*

International Bank for Reconstruction and Development (IBRD) — The World Bank

Origin. Conceived at the UN Monetary and Financial Conference at Bretton Woods (New Hampshire, USA) in July 1944, the IBRD, frequently called the World Bank, began operations in June 1946, its purpose being to provide funds, policy guidance and technical assistance to facilitate economic development in its poorer member countries. The Group comprises four other organizations (see below).

Activities. The Bank obtains its funds from the following sources: capital paid in by member countries; sales of its own securities; sales of parts of its loans; repayments; and net earnings. A resolution of the Board of Governors of 27 April 1988 provides that the paid-in portion of the shares authorized to be subscribed under it will be 3%.

The Bank is self-supporting, raising most of its money on the world's financial markets. In the fiscal year ending 30 June 2008 it achieved an operating income of US$2,271m. Income totalled US$6,863m. and expenditure US$4,592m.

In the fiscal year 2008 the Bank lent US$13·5bn. for 99 new operations. Cumulative lending had totalled US$446bn. by June 2008. 89% of borrowers took advantage of the new single-currency loans which became available in June 1996 to provide borrowers with the flexibility to select IBRD loan terms that are consistent with their debt-managing strategy and suited to their debt-servicing capacity. In order to eliminate wasteful overlapping of development assistance and to ensure that the funds available are used to the best possible effect, the Bank has organized consortia or consultative groups of aid-giving nations for many countries. These include Bangladesh, Belarus, Bolivia, Bulgaria, Egypt, Ethiopia, Jordan, Kazakhstan, Kenya, Kyrgyzstan, Macedonia, Malaŵi, Mauritania, Moldova, Mozambique, Nicaragua, Pakistan,

Peru, Romania, Sierra Leone, Tanzania, the [Palestinian] West Bank and Gaza Strip, Zambia, Zimbabwe and the Caribbean Group for Co-operation in Economic Development.

For the purposes of its analytical and operational work, in 2008 the IBRD characterized economies as follows: low income (average annual *per capita* gross national income of $975 or less); lower middle income (between $976 and $3,855); upper middle income (between $3,856 and $11,905); and high income ($11,906 or more).

A wide variety of technical assistance is at the core of IBRD's activities. It acts as executing agency for a number of pre-investment surveys financed by the UN Development Programme. Resident missions have been established in 64 developing member countries and there are regional offices for East and West Africa, the Baltic States and South-East Asia which assist in the preparation and implementation of projects. The Bank maintains a staff college, the *Economic Development Institute* in Washington, D.C., for senior officials of member countries.

The Strategic Compact. Unanimously approved by the Executive Board in March 1997, the Strategic Compact set out a plan for fundamental reform to make the Bank more effective in delivering its regional programme and in achieving its basic mission of reducing poverty. Decentralizing the Bank's relationships with borrower countries is central to the reforms. The effectiveness of devolved country management and the bank's promotion of good governance and anti-corruption measures to developing countries are likely to be key policies of the new strategy.

Organization. As of Feb. 2010 the Bank had 186 members, each with voting power in the institution, based on shareholding which in turn is based on a country's economic growth. The president is selected by the Bank's Board of Executive Directors. The Articles of Agreement do not specify the nationality of the president but by custom the US Executive Director makes a nomination, and by a long-standing, informal agreement, the president is a US national (while the managing director of the IMF is European). The initial term is five years, with a second of five years or less.

European office: 66 avenue d'Iéna, 75116 Paris, France. *London office:* New Zealand House, Haymarket, London SW1Y 4TE, England. *Tokyo office:* Kokusai Building, 1–1, Marunouchi 3-chome, Chiyoda-ku, Tokyo 100, Japan.

Headquarters: 1818 H St., NW, Washington, D.C., 20433, USA.
Website: http://www.worldbank.org
President: Robert Zoellick (USA).

Publications. World Bank Annual Report; Summary Proceedings of Annual Meetings; The World Bank and International Finance Company, 1986; *The World Bank Atlas* (annual); *Catalog of Publications,* 1986 ff.; *World Development Report* (annual); *World Bank Economic Review* (thrice yearly); *World Bank and the Environment* (annual); *World Bank News* (weekly); *World Bank Research Observer; World Tables* (annual); *Social Indicators of Development* (annual); *ICSID Annual Report; ICSID Review: Foreign Investment Law Journal* (twice yearly); *Research News* (quarterly).

Current Leaders

Robert Zoellick

Position
President

Introduction
Following a career in international trade, finance and diplomacy, Robert Zoellick was appointed president of the World Bank in July 2007.

Early Life
Robert Bruce Zoellick was born on 25 July 1953 in Naperville, Illinois. He attended Naperville Central High School and Swarthmore College in Pennsylvania, graduating in 1975. He went on to Harvard Law School and earned a masters in public policy from Harvard University's John F. Kennedy School of Government in 1981.

Zoellick then worked in the US Court of Appeals for the District of Columbia circuit before moving to the Federal National Mortgage Association. He also held various posts at the US Treasury department. From 1989–92 he served as under-secretary of state for economic and agricultural affairs and as counselor for the department of state, during which time he was involved in negotiations for the reunification of Germany.

From 1992–93 he was deputy chief of staff at the White House. In 1993 he returned to the Federal National Mortgage Association, serving as executive vice-president until 1997. From 1997–98 Zoellick was Olin Professor of National Security at the US Naval Academy and from 1999–2000 sat on the board of the German Marshall Fund of the United States. He then served as the US trade representative until 2005, when he was sworn in as deputy secretary of state. From 2006 until joining the World Bank he held an executive position with Goldman Sachs.

Zoellick is a free-trade enthusiast who argued the connection between global trading alliances and US security long before the attacks of 11 Sept. 2001. In 1998 he was a signatory (along with 17 others) of a letter to then president Bill Clinton calling for the ousting of Saddam Hussein. Zoellick was also one of the so-called 'Vulcans', an informal group who advised George W. Bush when running for office in the 2000 election.

Career in Office
Zoellick succeeded Paul Wolfowitz to become the eleventh president of the World Bank on 1 July 2007. In the shadow of the global financial crisis, in Jan. 2009 he called on the developed world to contribute to a vulnerability fund to assist developing countries. Then, in Sept., he warned that the US dollar would likely be usurped as the world's reserve currency as US dominance waned, maintaining that it was time for decision-making to be shared between the older powers and developing countries such as China and India. He also welcomed the expanded role of the G20 group of nations. In Feb. 2010 the World Bank said that it might need to restrict lending as the recession pushed requests for loans to a record level and that it was negotiating a capital increase.

International Development Association (IDA)

A lending agency established in 1960 and administered by the IBRD to provide assistance on concessional terms to the poorest developing countries. Its resources consist of subscriptions and general replenishments from its more industrialized and developed members, special contributions, and transfers from the net earnings of IBRD. Officers and staff of the IBRD serve concurrently as officers and staff of the IDA at the World Bank headquarters.

In fiscal year 2008 IDA commitments totalled US$11·2bn.; new commitments totalled 199 new operations. Since 1960 IDA has lent US$193bn. to 108 countries.

Headquarters: 1818 H St., NW, Washington, D.C., 20433, USA.
Website: http://www.worldbank.org/ida
President: Robert Zoellick (USA).

International Finance Corporation (IFC)

Established in 1956 to help strengthen the private sector in developing countries, through the provision of long-term loans, equity investments, quasi-equity instruments, standby financing, and structured finance and risk management products. It helps to finance new ventures and assist established enterprises as they expand, upgrade or diversify. In partnership with other donors, it provides a variety of technical assistance and advisory services to public and private sector clients. To be eligible for financing, projects must be profitable for investors, must benefit the economy of the country concerned, and must comply with IFC's environmental and social guidelines.

The majority of its funds are borrowed from the international financial markets through public bond issues or private placements. Its authorized capital is US$2·45bn.; total capital at 30 June 2008 was US$18·3bn. IFC committed US$16·1bn. in total financing in fiscal year 2008 and committed 372 projects in 85 countries. It has 182 members.

Headquarters: 2121 Pennsylvania Ave., NW, Washington, D.C., 20433, USA.
Website: http://www.ifc.org
President: Robert Zoellick (USA).

Publications. Annual Reports; Lessons of Experience (series); *Paths Out of Poverty.*

Multilateral Investment Guarantee Agency (MIGA)

Established in 1988 to encourage the flow of foreign direct investment to, and among, developing member countries, MIGA is the insurance arm of the World Bank. It provides investors with investment guarantees against non-commercial risk, such as expropriation and war, and gives advice to governments on improving climate for foreign investment. It may insure up to 90% of an investment, with a current limit of US$50m. per project. In March 1999 the Council of Governors adopted a resolution for a capital increase for the Agency of approximately US$850m. In addition US$150m. was transferred to MIGA by the World Bank as operating capital. In Feb. 2010 it had 175 member countries. It is located at the World Bank headquarters (see above).

Headquarters: 1818 H Street, NW, Washington, D.C., 20433, USA.
Website: http://www.miga.org

International Centre for Settlement of Investment Disputes (ICSID)

Founded in 1966 to promote increased flows of international investment by providing facilities for the conciliation and arbitration of disputes between governments and foreign investors. The Centre does not engage in such conciliation or arbitration. This is the task of conciliators and arbitrators appointed by the contracting parties, or as otherwise provided for in the Convention. Recourse to conciliation and arbitration by members is entirely voluntary.

In Feb. 2010 its Convention had been signed by 155 countries. 181 cases had been concluded by it and 127 were pending. Disputes involved a variety of investment sectors: agriculture, banking, construction, energy, health, industrial, mining and tourism.

ICSID also undertakes research, publishing and advisory activities in the field of foreign investment law. Like IDA, IFC and MIGA, it is located at the World Bank headquarters in Washington (see above).

Website: http://www.worldbank.org/icsid
Secretary-General: Meg Kinnear (Canada).

Publications. ICSID Annual Report; News from ICSID; ICSID Review: Foreign Investment Law Journal; Investment Laws of the World; Investment Treaties.

Further Reading

Miller-Adams, M., *The World Bank: New Agendas in a Changing World.* 1999
Stone, D. L. and Wright, C., *The World Bank and Governance.* 2006
Woods, N., *The Globalizers: The IMF, the World Bank and Their Borrowers.* 2007

International Civil Aviation Organization (ICAO)

Origin. The Convention providing for the establishment of the ICAO was drawn up by the International Civil Aviation Conference held in Chicago in 1944. A Provisional International Civil Aviation Organization (PICAO) operated for 20 months until the formal establishment of ICAO on 4 April 1947. The Convention on International Civil Aviation superseded the provisions of the Paris Convention of 1919 and the Pan American Convention on Air Navigation of 1928.

Functions. It assists international civil aviation by establishing technical standards for safety and efficiency of air navigation and promoting simpler procedures at borders; develops regional plans for ground facilities and services needed for international flying; disseminates air-transport statistics and prepares studies on aviation economics; fosters the development of air law conventions and provides technical assistance to states in developing civil aviation programmes.

Organization. The principal organs of ICAO are an Assembly, consisting of all members of the Organization, and a Council, which is composed of 36 states elected by the Assembly for three years, which meets in virtually continuous session. In electing these states, the Assembly must give adequate representation to: (1) states of major importance in air transport; (2) states which make the largest contribution to the provision of facilities for the international civil air navigation; and (3) those states not otherwise included whose election would ensure that all major geographical areas of the world were represented. The budget approved for 2010 was $85·5m. CDN.

Headquarters: 999 University St., Montreal, PQ, Canada H3C 5H7.
Website: http://www.icao.int
President of the Council: Roberto Kobeh González (Mexico).
Secretary-General: Raymond Benjamin (France).

Publications. Annual Report of the Council; ICAO Journal (six yearly; quarterly in Russian); *ICAO Training Manual; Aircraft Accident Digest; Procedures for Air Navigation Services.*

International Fund for Agricultural Development (IFAD)

The idea for an International Fund for Agricultural Development arose at the 1974 World Food Conference. An agreement to establish IFAD entered into force on 30 Nov. 1977, and the agency began its operations the following month. IFAD is an international financial institution and a United Nations specialized agency dedicated to eradicating rural poverty in developing countries. It mobilizes resources from its 165 member countries to provide low-interest loans and grants to help middle and low-income member countries fight poverty in their poor rural communities. IFAD works with national partners to design and implement innovative initiatives that fit within national policies and systems. These enable poor rural people to access the assets, services, knowledge, skills and opportunities they need to overcome poverty. Since starting operations in 1978, IFAD has invested more than US$11·3bn. in 829 projects and programmes that have reached some 350m. people.

Organization. The highest body is the Governing Council, on which all 165 member countries are represented. Operations are overseen by an 18-member Executive Board (with 18 alternate members), which is responsible to the Governing Council. The Fund works with many partner institutions, including the World Bank, regional development banks and financial agencies, and other UN agencies; many of these co-finance IFAD programmes and projects.

Headquarters: Via Paolo di Dono 44, 00142 Rome, Italy.
Website: http://www.ifad.org
President: Kanayo F. Nwanze (Nigeria).

Publications. Annual Report; Polishing the Stone; What Meets the Eye: Images of Rural Poverty.

International Labour Organization (ILO)

Origin. The ILO was established in 1919 under the Treaty of Versailles as an autonomous institution associated with the League of Nations. An agreement establishing its relationship with the UN was approved in 1946, making the ILO the first Specialized Agency to be associated with the UN. An intergovernmental agency with a tripartite structure, in which representatives of governments, employers and workers participate, it seeks through international action to improve labour and living conditions, to promote productive employment and social justice for working people everywhere. On its fiftieth anniversary in 1969 it was awarded the Nobel Peace Prize. In Feb. 2010 it numbered 183 members.

Functions. One of the ILO's principal functions is the formulation of international standards in the form of International Labour Conventions and Recommendations. Member countries are required to submit Conventions to their competent national authorities with a view to ratification. If a country ratifies a Convention it agrees to bring its laws into line with its terms and to report periodically how these regulations are being applied. More than 7,500 ratifications of 188 Conventions had been deposited by 30 June 2007. Procedures are in place to ascertain whether Conventions thus ratified are effectively applied. Recommendations do not require ratification, but member states are obliged to consider them with a view to giving effect to their provisions by legislation or other action. By 30 June 2007 the International Labour Conference had adopted 199 Recommendations.

The ILO's programme and budget set out four strategic objectives for the Organization at the turn of the century: i) to promote and realize fundamental principles and rights at work; ii) to create greater opportunities for women and men to secure decent employment and income; iii) to enhance the coverage and effectiveness of social protection for all; iv) to strengthen tripartism and social dialogue.

Activities. In addition to its research and advisory activities, the ILO extends technical co-operation to governments under its regular budget and under the UN Development Programme and Funds-in-Trust in the fields of employment promotion, human resources development (including vocational and management training), development of social institutions, small-scale industries, rural development, social security, industrial safety and hygiene, productivity, etc. Technical co-operation also includes expert missions and a fellowship programme.

In 1994 the technical services offered by the ILO to its tripartite constituents came under scrutiny leading to a reaffirmation of technical co-operation as one of the principal means of ILO action. Since 1994 the process of implementing the new Active Partnership Policy made significant progress and today 16 multidisciplinary advisory teams are engaged in a dialogue with ILO constituents centred on the identification of Country Objectives to form the basis of the ILO's contribution.

In June 1998 delegates to the 86th International Labour Conference adopted a solemn ILO Declaration in Fundamental Principles and Rights at Work, committing the Organization's member states to respect the principles inherent in a number of core labour standards: the right of workers and employers to freedom of association and the effective right to collective bargaining, and to work toward the elimination of all forms of forced or compulsory labour, the effective abolition of child labour and the elimination of discrimination in respect of employment and occupation.

In June 1999 delegates to the 87th International Labour Conference adopted a new Convention banning the worst forms of child labour. The International Labour Conference 2009 adopted a budget of US$726·7m. for the 2010–11 biennium.

Field Activities. The ILO's *International Institute for Labour Studies* promotes the study and discussion of policy issues. The core theme of its activities is the interaction between labour institutions, development and civil society in a global economy. It identifies emerging social and labour issues by opening up new areas for research and action; and encourages systematic dialogue on social policy between the tripartite constituency of the ILO and the international academic community, and other public opinion-makers.

The *International Training Centre* of the ILO, in Turin, was set up in 1965 to lead the training programmes implemented by the ILO as part of its technical co-operation activities. Member states and the UN system also call on its resources and experience, and a UN Staff College was established on the Turin Campus in 1996.

Organization. The International Labour Conference is the supreme deliberative organ of the ILO; it meets annually in Geneva. National delegations are composed of two government delegates, one employers' delegate and one workers' delegate. The Governing Body, elected by the Conference, is the Executive Council. It is composed of 28 government members, 14 workers' members and 14 employers' members. Ten governments of countries of industrial importance hold permanent seats on the Governing Body. These are: Brazil, China, Germany, France, India, Italy, Japan, Russia, UK and USA. The remaining 18 government members are elected every three years. Workers' and employers' representatives are elected as individuals, not as national candidates. The ILO has 52 branch offices throughout the world.

Headquarters: International Labour Office, CH-1211 Geneva 22, Switzerland.
Website: http://www.ilo.org
Director-General: Juan Somavia (Chile).
Governing Body Chairman: Dayan Jayatilleka (Sri Lanka).

Publications (available in English, French and Spanish) include: *International Labour Review; Bulletin of Labour Statistics; Official Bulletin* and *Labour Education; Yearbook of Labour Statistics* (annual); *World Labour Report* (annual); *World Employment Report* (annual); *Encyclopaedia of Occupational Health and Safety; Key Indicators of the Labour Market* (*KILM*); *World of Work* (3 a year).

International Maritime Organization (IMO)

Origin. The International Maritime Organization (formerly the InterGovernmental Maritime Consultative Organization) was established as a specialized agency of the UN by a convention drafted in 1948 at a UN maritime conference in Geneva. The Convention became effective on 17 March 1958 when it had been ratified by 21 countries, including seven with at least 1m. gross tons of shipping each. The IMCO started operations in 1959 and changed its name to the IMO in 1982.

Functions. To facilitate co-operation among governments on technical matters affecting merchant shipping, especially concerning safety and security at sea; to prevent and control marine pollution caused by ships; to facilitate international maritime traffic. The IMO is responsible for convening international maritime conferences and for drafting international maritime conventions. It also provides technical assistance to countries wishing to develop their maritime activities, and acts as a depositary authority for international conventions regulating maritime affairs. The *World Maritime University (WMU)*, at Malmö, Sweden, was established in 1983; the *IMO International*

Maritime Law Institute (IMLI), at Valletta, Malta and the *IMO International Maritime Academy*, at Trieste, Italy, both in 1989.

Organization. The IMO has 169 members and three associate members. The Assembly, composed of all member states, normally meets every two years. The 40-member Council acts as governing body between sessions. There are four principal committees (on maritime safety, legal matters, marine environment protection and technical co-operation), which submit reports or recommendations to the Assembly through the Council, and a Secretariat. The budget for 2008–09 amounted to £49,827,300.

Headquarters: 4 Albert Embankment, London SE1 7SR, UK.
Website: http://www.imo.org
Email: info@imo.org
Secretary-General: Efthimios Mitropoulos (Greece).

Publication. IMO News.

International Monetary Fund (IMF)

Established in 1945 as an independent organization, the International Monetary Fund began financial operations on 1 March 1947. An agreement of mutual co-operation with the UN came into force on 15 Nov. 1947. The first amendment to the Articles of Agreement, creating the special drawing right (SDR), the IMF's reserve asset, took effect on 28 July 1969. The second amendment took effect on 1 April 1978, and established a new code of conduct for exchange arrangements in the wake of the collapse of the par value system. The third amendment came into force on 11 Nov. 1992; it allows for the suspension of voting and related rights of any member that fails to settle its outstanding obligations to the IMF. The fourth Amendment, which came into force on 10 Aug. 2009, provides for a special one-time allocation of SDRs.

Aims. To promote international monetary co-operation, the expansion of international trade and exchange rate stability; to assist in the removal of exchange restrictions and the establishment of a multilateral system of payments; and to alleviate any serious disequilibrium in members' international balance of payments by making the financial resources of the IMF available to them, usually subject to economic policy conditions.

Activities. The IMF is mandated to oversee the international monetary system and monitor the economic and financial policies of its member countries. The IMF highlights possible risks to domestic and external stability and advises on policy adjustments.

Lending. A core responsibility of the IMF is to provide loans to member countries experiencing balance of payments problems. This financial assistance enables countries to rebuild their international reserves, stabilize their currencies, continue paying for imports and restore conditions for strong economic growth, while undertaking policies to correct underlying problems. Unlike development banks, the IMF does not lend for specific projects.

The IMF has various loan instruments, or 'facilities', that are tailored to address the specific circumstances of its diverse membership. Nonconcessional loans are provided mainly through Stand-By Arrangements (SBAs) and the Extended Fund Facility (which is useful primarily for longer-term needs). The Flexible Credit Line (FCL) was introduced in 2009, for countries with very strong fundamentals, policies and track records of policy implementation.

The IMF also offers special financing facilities for low-income countries. A new Poverty Reduction and Growth Trust, expected to become effective in the course of 2010, incorporates: the Extended Credit Facility, which provides flexible medium-term support; the Standby Credit Facility, which addresses short-term and precautionary needs; and the Rapid Credit Facility, which offers emergency support with limited conditionality. The IMF also provides emergency assistance to support recovery from natural disasters and conflicts, in some cases at concessional interest rates.

A major reform of the IMF's lending facilities took place in March 2009. Conditions linked to IMF loan disbursements are to be better focused and more adequately tailored to the varying strengths of countries' policies and fundamentals. The flexibility of the SBA has been enhanced. In addition, access limits have been doubled, the cost and maturity structure of the Fund's lending has been simplified and its lending facilities have been streamlined.

Technical assistance. The IMF provides technical assistance in its areas of core expertise: macroeconomic policy, tax policy and revenue administration, expenditure management, monetary policy, the exchange rate system, financial sector sustainability, and macroeconomic and financial statistics. About 90% of IMF technical assistance goes to low and lower-middle income countries. The IMF operates seven regional technical assistance centres: in the Pacific (Fiji Islands), the Caribbean (Barbados), three in Africa (Gabon, Mali and Tanzania), the Middle East (Lebanon) and Central America (Guatemala).

Finances. Quota subscriptions from member countries are the IMF's main source of financing. A member's quota is largely determined by its economic position relative to other members; it is also linked to their drawing rights on the IMF, their voting power and their share of SDR allocations. Quotas are reviewed at least every five years, with the next review to be completed by Jan. 2011. The IMF can supplement its resources through borrowing if it believes that resources might fall short of members' needs.

The General Arrangements to Borrow (GAB) and New Arrangements to Borrow (NAB) are credit arrangements between the IMF and a group of member countries and institutions to provide supplementary resources to the IMF to deal with an exceptional situation that poses a threat to the stability of that system. The GAB, established in 1962, enables the IMF to borrow specified amounts of currencies from 11 industrial countries (or their central banks) under certain circumstances, at market-related rates of interest. The potential credit available to the IMF under the GAB totals SDR 17bn., with an additional SDR 1·5bn. available under an associated arrangement with Saudi Arabia. The NAB, which came into effect in 1998, is a set of credit arrangements between the IMF and 26 member countries and institutions. Importantly, the NAB is the facility of first and principal recourse vis-à-vis the GAB. The maximum amount of resources available to the IMF under the NAB and GAB is SDR 34bn.

In April 2009 the G20 agreed to increase the lending resources available to the IMF by up to US$500bn., thereby tripling total pre-crisis lending resources. The increase was to be made through immediate bilateral financing from IMF member countries and by subsequently incorporating this financing into an expanded and more flexible NAB increased by up to US$500bn. This objective was achieved by Sept. 2009.

Bilateral loans. Under such an agreement, the member normally commits to allow the Fund to make drawings up to a specified ceiling during the period for which drawings can be made. In 2009 the IMF signed a number of bilateral loan agreements.

IMF notes. Some official creditors may prefer to invest in paper or notes issued by the IMF. In 2009 the IMF's Executive Board approved a new framework for issuing notes to the official sector. China was the first country to have signed such a note purchase agreement.

SDR allocations. The IMF may allocate SDRs to members in proportion to their IMF quotas. Such an allocation provides each member with a costless asset. There have been three general

SDR allocations, made in response to a long-term global need for reserve assets: (i) SDR 9·3bn., distributed in 1970–72; (ii) SDR 12·3bn., distributed in 1979–81; and (iii) SDR 162·1bn., distributed in Aug. 2009. A special one-off allocation of SDRs amounting to SDR 21·4bn. was implemented on 9 Sept. 2009. This allocation was for those countries that joined the Fund after 1981—more than one fifth of the IMF membership—and had never received an SDR allocation.

Governance Reform. Implemented on 28 April 2008 this reform aims to make quotas more responsive to economic realities by increasing the representation of fast-growing economies while at the same time giving low-income countries more say in the IMF's decision making. The reform builds on an initial step agreed by the IMF's membership in Sept. 2006 to have *ad hoc* quota increases for four countries—China, South Korea, Mexico and Turkey. In Oct. 2009 the IMF membership supported a shift in quota share to dynamic emerging markets and developing countries of at least 5% using the current quota formula as the basis. This shift is expected to take place by Jan. 2011.

Organization. The highest authority is the Board of Governors; each member government is represented. The Board of Governors has delegated many of its powers to the 24 executive directors in Washington, D.C., who are appointed or elected by individual member countries or groups of countries. The managing director is selected by the executive directors and serves as chairman of the Executive Board, but may not vote except in case of a tie. The term of office is for five years, but may be extended or terminated at the discretion of the executive directors. The managing director is responsible for the ordinary business of the IMF, under the direction of the executive directors, and supervises a staff of about 2,400. There are three deputy managing directors. As of Feb. 2010 the IMF had 186 members.

The IMF Institute is a specialized department providing training in macroeconomic analysis and policy, and related subjects, for officials of member countries. In addition to training offered in Washington, D.C., the IMF also offers training for country officials through a network of seven regional training institutes and programmes. These are: the IMF-Singapore Regional Training Institute; the Joint Africa Institute (in Tunisia); the Joint China-IMF Training Program (in Dalian, China); the Joint IMF-Arab Monetary Fund Regional Training Program (in the United Arab Emirates); the Joint India-IMF Training Program (in Pune, India); the Joint Regional Training Center for Latin America (in Brazil); and the Joint Vienna Institute (in Austria).

Headquarters: 700 19th St. NW, Washington, D.C., 20431, USA. European office in Paris and regional offices in Tokyo and Warsaw.
Website: http://www.imf.org
Managing Director: Dominique Strauss-Kahn (France).

Publications. Annual Report of the Executive Board; Annual Report on Exchange Arrangements and Exchange Restrictions; International Financial Statistics (monthly); *IMF Survey* (online); *IMF Economic Review; World Economic Outlook; Global Financial Stability Report*; and *Finance & Development.* More publications information may be found online at: http://www.imf.org/external/pubind.htm.

Current Leaders

Dominique Strauss-Kahn

Position
Managing Director

Introduction
A former French minister of finance, Strauss-Kahn became managing director of the IMF in Nov. 2007. He took office promising reforms to increase the influence of developing nations.

Early Life
Strauss-Kahn was born on 25 April 1948 to a Jewish family in Neuilly-sur-Seine, France. Schooled in France, Morocco and Monaco, he studied economics and political science at the Institut d'Études Politiques in Paris. He went on to study law and business administration before beginning an academic career and winning an economics professorship in 1977. An active member of the French Socialist Party (PS) in the 1970s, in 1981 he founded the Socialisme et Judaisme (Socialism and Judaism) organization. From 1981–86 he was deputy commissioner of the Economic Planning Agency.

Strauss-Kahn was elected to the National Assembly in 1986. From 1991–93 he served as minister of industry and international trade, participating in the Uruguay Round of trade negotiations. Following a period in the private sector as a corporate lawyer and lobbyist he returned to government in 1997 as minister of economy, finance and industry. He managed the launch of the euro, implemented privatization reform and championed the reforming wing of the PS. He resigned in 1999 when he was linked to a financial scandal but was re-elected to the National Assembly after his acquittal in 2001.

Following the PS' electoral defeat in 2003, Strauss-Kahn took control of party strategy for the 2007 presidential election. He co-founded a think tank—To The Left in Europe—and campaigned unsuccessfully for a 'yes' vote in the referendum to establish a European constitution. Having stood unsuccessfully for nomination in 2006 as the PS' presidential candidate, he was appointed managing director of the IMF in July 2007 by its board of directors.

Career in Office
Strauss-Kahn took office on 1 Nov. 2007 aiming to rebuild the Fund's legitimacy and relevance to developing nations. However, the global credit crisis has since dominated the financial landscape. In Jan. 2009 he stressed that monetary and fiscal stimulus alone would not be enough to counter the recessionary slide. He maintained that a restructuring of the banking system through strong public intervention was necessary to rebuild economic confidence and fix the underlying causes of the crisis. In Nov. he warned that the nascent economic recovery was uneven and that governments should avoid withdrawing stimulus measures too soon. He also called on China to let its undervalued currency rise to help development and ease global imbalances.

Further Reading

Humphreys, N. K., *Historical Dictionary of the International Monetary Fund.* 1994

James, H., *International Monetary Cooperation since Bretton Woods.* 1996

Samans, Richard, Uzan, Marc and Lopez-Claros, Augusto, *The International Monetary System, the IMF, and the G-20: A Great Transformation in the Making?* 2007

Woods, N., *The Globalizers: The IMF, the World Bank and Their Borrowers.* 2007

International Telecommunication Union (ITU)

Origin. Founded in Paris in 1865 as the International Telegraph Union, the International Telecommunication Union took its present name in 1934 and became a specialized agency of the United Nations in 1947. Therefore, the ITU is the world's oldest intergovernmental body.

Functions. To maintain and extend international co-operation for the improvement and rational use of telecommunications of all kinds, and promote and offer technical assistance to developing countries in the field of telecommunications; to promote the development of technical facilities and their most efficient operation to improve the efficiency of telecommunication services, increasing their usefulness and making them, so far as possible, generally available to the public; to harmonize the actions of nations in the attainment of these ends.

Organization. The supreme organ of the ITU is the Plenipotentiary Conference, which normally meets every four years. A 46-member Council, elected by the Conference, meets annually in Geneva and is responsible for ensuring the co-ordination of the four permanent organs at ITU headquarters: the General Secretariat; Radiocommunication Sector; Telecommunication Standardization Sector; and Telecommunication Development Sector. The Secretary-General is also elected by the Conference. ITU has 191 member countries; a further 697 scientific and technical companies, public and private operators, broadcasters and other organizations are also ITU members.

Headquarters: Place des Nations, CH-1211 Geneva 20, Switzerland.
Website: http://www.itu.int
Secretary-General: Hamadoun Touré (Mali).

United Nations Educational, Scientific and Cultural Organization (UNESCO)

Origin. UNESCO's Constitution was signed in London on 16 Nov. 1945 by 37 countries and the Organization came into being in Nov. 1946 on the premise that: 'Since wars begin in the minds of men, it is in the minds of men that the defences of peace must be constructed'. In Feb. 2010 UNESCO had 193 members including the UK, which rejoined in 1997 having left in 1985, and the USA, which rejoined in 2003 having left in 1984. There are also seven associate members which are not members of the UN (Aruba, British Virgin Islands, Cayman Islands, the Faroe Islands, Macao, Netherlands Antilles, Tokelau).

Aims and Activities. UNESCO's primary objective is to contribute to peace and security in the world by promoting collaboration among the nations through education, science, communication, culture and the social and human sciences in order to further universal respect for justice, democracy, the rule of the law, human rights and fundamental freedoms, affirmed for all peoples by the UN Charter.

Education. Various activities support and foster national projects to renovate education systems and develop alternative educational strategies towards a goal of lifelong education for all. The World Development Forum in Dakar in 2000 set an agenda for progress towards this aim expressed as six goals. Two of these, attaining universal primary education by 2015 and gender parity in schooling by 2005, were also UN Millennium Development Goals. Three elements define the context for pursuing this purpose: promoting education as a fundamental right, improving the quality of education and stimulating experimentation, innovation and policy dialogue.

Science. UNESCO seeks to promote international scientific co-operation and encourages scientific research designed to improve living conditions and to protect ecosystems. Several international programmes to better understand the Earth's resources towards the advancement of sustainable development have been initiated, including the Man and the Biosphere (MAB) programme, the International Hydrological Programme (IHP), the Intergovernmental Oceanographic Commission (IOC) and the International Geoscience Programme (IGCP).

Culture. Promoting cultural diversity and intercultural dialogue is the principal priority of UNESCO's cultural programmes. The World Heritage Centre, with its World Heritage List now covering 890 sites around the world, promotes the preservation of monuments and natural sites.

Communication. Activities are geared to promoting the free flow of information, freedom of expression, press freedom, media independence and pluralism. Another priority is to bridge the digital divide and help disadvantaged groups in North and South participate in the knowledge societies created through the information and communication technologies. To this end, UNESCO promotes access to public domain information and free software, as well as encouraging the creation of local content.

Social and Human Sciences. UNESCO works to advance knowledge and intellectual co-operation in order to facilitate social transformations conducive to justice, freedom, peace and human dignity. It seeks to identify evolving social trends and develops and promotes principles and standards based on universal values and ethics, such as the *Universal Declaration on the Human Genome and Human Rights* (1997) and the *International Declaration on Human Genetic Data* (2003).

Organization. The General Conference, composed of representatives from each member state, meets biennially to decide policy, programme and budget. A 58-member Executive Board elected by the Conference meets twice a year and there is a Secretariat. In addition, national commissions act as liaison groups between UNESCO and the educational, scientific and cultural life of their own countries. The budget for the biennium 2008–09 was US$631m.

There are also 11 separate UNESCO institutes and centres: the International Bureau of Education (IBE), in Geneva; the UNESCO Institute for Lifelong Learning (UIL), in Hamburg; the International Institute for Educational Planning (IIEP), in Paris; the International Institute for Capacity Building in Africa (IICBA), in Addis Ababa; the International Institute for Higher Education in Latin America and the Caribbean (IESALC), in Caracas; the Institute for Information Technologies in Education (IITE), in Moscow; the UNESCO Institute for Statistics (UIS), in Montreal; the UNESCO International Centre for Technical and Vocational Education and Training (UNEVOC), in Bonn; the European Centre for Higher Education (CEPES), in Bucharest; the UNESCO-IHE Institute for Water Education (UNESCO-IHE), in Delft; and the International Centre for Theoretical Physics (ICTP), in Trieste.

Headquarters: UNESCO House, 7 Place de Fontenoy, 75352 Paris 07 SP, France.
Website: http://www.unesco.org
Director-General: Irina Bokova (Bulgaria).

Periodicals (published quarterly). *Museum International; International Social Science Journal; The UNESCO Courier; Prospects; Copyright Bulletin; World Heritage Review.*

United Nations Industrial Development Organization (UNIDO)

Origin. UNIDO was established by the UN General Assembly in 1966 and became a UN specialized agency in 1985.

Aims. UNIDO helps developing countries, and countries with economies in transition, in their fight against marginalization and poverty in today's globalized world. It mobilizes knowledge, skills, information and technology to promote productive employment, a competitive economy and a sound environment. UNIDO focuses its efforts on relieving poverty by fostering productivity growth and economic development.

Activities. As a global forum, UNIDO generates and disseminates knowledge relating to industrial matters and provides a platform for the various actors—decision makers in the public and private sectors, civil society organizations and the policy-making community in general—to enhance co-operation, establish dialogue and develop partnerships in order to address the challenges ahead. As a technical co-operation agency, UNIDO designs and implements programmes to support the industrial development efforts of its clients. It also offers tailor-made specialized support for programme development. The two core functions are both complementary and mutually supportive. On the one hand, experience gained in the technical co-operation work of UNIDO can be shared with policy makers; on the other, the Organization's analytical work shows where technical co-operation will have the greatest impact by helping to define priorities.

Organization. As part of the United Nations common system, UNIDO has the responsibility for promoting industrialization throughout the developing world, in co-operation with its 173 member states. Its headquarters are in Vienna, Austria, and with 47 smaller country and regional offices, 18 investment and technology promotion offices and a number of offices related to specific aspects of its work, UNIDO maintains an active presence in the field. The General Conference meets every two years to determine policy and approve the budget. The 53-member Industrial Development Board (membership according to constitutional lists) is elected by the General Conference. The General Conference also elects a 27-member Programme and Budget Committee for two years and appoints a Director-General for four years.

Finance. UNIDO's financial resources come from the regular and operational budgets, as well as voluntary contributions, budgeted for 2008–09 at €154·6m., €22·1m. and €204·9m. respectively, totalling €381·6m. The regular budget derives from assessed contributions from member states.

Technical co-operation is funded mainly from voluntary contributions from donor countries and institutions as well as UNDP, the Multilateral Fund for the Implementation of the Montreal Protocol, the Global Environment Facility and the Common Fund for Communities.

Headquarters: Vienna International Centre, POB 300, A-1400 Vienna, Austria.
Website: http://www.unido.org
Director-General: Kandeh Yumkella (Sierra Leone).

Publications. UNIDOScope (weekly internet newspaper); *UNIDO Annual Report; Industry for Growth into the New Millennium, African Industry 2000: The Challenge of Going Global; Using Statistics for Process Control and Improvement: An Introduction to Basic Concepts and Techniques; Guidelines for Project Evaluation; Practical Appraisal for Industrial Project Applications—Application of Social Cost-Benefit Analysis in Pakistan; Manual for the Evaluation of Industrial Projects; Guide to Practical Project Appraisal—Social Benefit-Cost Analysis in Developing Countries; Manual for Small Industrial Businesses: Project Design and Appraisal; Manual for the Preparation of Industrial Feasibility Studies; Manual on Technology Transfer Negotiations; Guidelines for Infrastructure Development Through Build-Operate-Transfer (BOT) Projects; Gearing up for a New Development Agenda; Reforming the UN System: UNIDO's Need-Driven Model; World Directory of Industrial Information Sources; Woodworking Machinery: A Manual on Selection Options; Competition and the World Economy; The International Yearbook of Industrial Statistics 2010; Industrial Development Report 2009.*

Universal Postal Union (UPU)

Origin. The UPU was established in 1875, when the Universal Postal Convention adopted by the Postal Congress of Berne on 9 Oct. 1874 came into force. It has 191 member countries.

Functions. The UPU provides co-operation between postal services and helps to ensure a universal network of up-to-date products and services. To this end, UPU members are united in a single postal territory for the reciprocal exchange of correspondence. A Specialized Agency of the UN since 1948, the UPU is governed by its Constitution, adopted in 1964 (Vienna), and subsequent protocol amendments (1969, Tokyo; 1974, Lausanne; 1979, Rio de Janeiro; 1984, Hamburg; 1989, Washington; 1994, Seoul; 1999, Beijing; 2004, Bucharest; 2008, Geneva).

Organization. It is composed of a Universal Postal Congress which meets every four years; a 41-member Council of Administration, which meets annually and is responsible for supervising the affairs of the UPU between Congresses; a 40-member Postal Operations Council; and an International Bureau which functions as the permanent secretariat, responsible for strategic planning and programme budgeting. A new UPU body, the Consultative Committee, was created at the Bucharest Congress. This committee represents the external shareholders of the postal sector as well as UPU member countries. The budget for the biennial period 2007–08 was 71·4m. Swiss francs.

Headquarters: Weltpoststrasse 4, 3000 Berne 15, Switzerland.
Website: http://www.upu.int
Director-General: Edouard Dayan (France).

Publications. Bucharest World Postal Strategy (2004), *Postal Statistics* (annual), *Postal Market 2004: Review and Outlook, Post 2005—Follow-up and Trends* (2000), *Union Postale* (quarterly), *POST*Code* (also in CD-ROM).

World Health Organization (WHO)

Origin. An International Conference convened by the UN Economic and Social Council to consider a single health organization resulted in the adoption on 22 July 1946 of the Constitution of the World Health Organization, which came into force on 7 April 1948.

Functions. WHO's objective, as stated in the first article of the Constitution, is 'the attainment by all peoples of the highest possible level of health'. As the directing and co-ordinating authority on international health, it establishes and maintains collaboration with the UN, specialized agencies, governments, health administrations, professional and other groups concerned with health. The Constitution also directs WHO to assist governments to strengthen their health services; to stimulate and advance work to eradicate diseases; to promote maternal and child health, mental health, medical research and the prevention of accidents; to improve standards of teaching and training in the health professions, and of nutrition, housing, sanitation, working conditions and other aspects of environmental health. The Organization is also empowered to propose conventions, agreements and regulations, and make recommendations about international health matters; to develop, establish and promote international standards concerning foods, biological, pharmaceutical and similar substances; to revise the international nomenclature of diseases, causes of death and public health practices.

Methods of work. Co-operation in country projects is undertaken only on the request of the government concerned, through the six regional offices of the Organization. Worldwide technical services are made available by headquarters. Expert committees, chosen from the 55 advisory panels of experts, meet to advise the Director-General on a given subject. Scientific groups and consultative meetings are called for similar purposes. To further the education of health personnel of all categories, seminars, technical conferences and training courses are organized, and advisors, consultants and lecturers are provided. WHO awards fellowships for study to nationals of member countries.

Activities. The main thrust of WHO's activities in recent years has been towards promoting national, regional and global strategies for the attainment of the main social target of the member states: 'Health for All in the 21st Century', or the attainment by all citizens of the world of a level of health that will permit them to lead a socially and economically productive life. Almost all countries indicated a high level of political commitment to this goal; and guiding principles for formulating corresponding strategies and plans of action were subsequently prepared.

The WHO has organized its responsibilities into four priorities: enhancing global health security, which includes preventing, detecting and containing disease outbreaks, preparing the world for controlling pandemic influenza, combating new diseases such as SARS, preparing for emergencies and responding quickly to minimize death and suffering; accelerating progress on the Millennium Development Goals (MDGs) by reducing maternal and child mortality, tackling the global epidemics of HIV/AIDS, tuberculosis and malaria, promoting safe drinking water and sanitation, promoting gender equality and increasing access to essential medicines; responding to non-communicable disease such as cardiovascular diseases, diabetes and cancers by reducing smoking, promoting a healthy diet and physical activity and reducing violence and road traffic crashes; promoting equity in health through strengthening health systems to reach everyone, particularly the most vulnerable people.

World Health Day is observed on 7 April every year. The 2010 theme for World Health Day was 'Be part of a global movement to make cities healthier'; the theme for 2009 was 'Save lives. Make hospitals safe in emergencies'. World No-Tobacco Day is held on 31 May each year; International Day Against Drug Abuse on 26 June; World AIDS Day on 1 Dec.

The 50th World Health Assembly which met in 1997 adopted numerous resolutions on public health issues. *The World Health Report, 1997: Conquering suffering, enriching humanity* focused on 'non-communicable diseases'. It warned that the human and social costs of cancer, heart disease and other chronic diseases will rise unless confronted now.

The number of cancer cases was expected to double in most countries by 2020. The incidence of lung cancers in women and prostate cancers in men in the Western world is becoming far more prevalent. The incidence of other cancers is also rising rapidly, especially in developing countries. Heart disease and stroke, the leading causes of death in richer nations, will become more common in poorer countries. Globally, diabetes will more than double by 2025, with the number of people affected rising from about 135m. to 300m. By 2006 the number of people living with diabetes had reached 180m. There is likely to be a huge rise in some mental and neurological disorders, especially dementias and particularly Alzheimer's disease. In 1997 an estimated 29m. people suffered from dementia, and at least 400m. suffered from other mental disorders ranging from mood and personality disorders to neurological conditions like epilepsy, which affected some 40m. worldwide.

These projected increases are reported to be owing to a combination of factors, not least population ageing and the rising prevalence of unhealthy lifestyles. Average life expectancy at birth globally reached 65 years in 1996. It is now well over 70 years in many countries and exceeds 80 years in some. In 1997 there were an estimated 380m. people over 65 years. By 2020 that number is expected to rise to more than 690m.

The ten leading killer diseases in the world according to *The World Health Report, 2004* are: coronary heart disease, 7·2m. deaths annually; cancer (all sites), 7·1m.; cerebrovascular disease, 5·5m.; acute lower respiratory infection, 3·9m.; HIV/AIDS, 2·8m.; chronic obstructive pulmonary disease, 2·7m.; perinatal conditions, 2·5m.; diarrhoeal diseases, 1·8m.; tuberculosis, 1·6m.; malaria, 1·3m. Tobacco-related deaths, primarily from lung cancer and circulatory disease, amount to 4·9m. a year. Smoking accounts for one in seven cancer cases worldwide, and if the trend of increasing consumption in many countries continues, the epidemic has many more decades to run.

In response, WHO has called for an intensified and sustained global campaign to encourage healthy lifestyles and attack the main risk factors responsible for many of these diseases: unhealthy diet, inadequate physical activity, smoking and obesity.

The WHO Framework Convention on Tobacco Control (WHO FCTC) was developed in response to the globalization of the tobacco epidemic, and is the first global health treaty negotiated under the auspices of the World Health Organization. The provisions in the Treaty require countries to ban tobacco advertising, sponsorship and promotion; establish new packaging and labelling of tobacco products with prominent health warnings; establish smoking bans in public places, increase price and tax on tobacco products; and strengthen legislation to clamp down on tobacco smuggling, among other measures.

World Health Report, 2008: Primary Health Care – Now More Than Ever assesses the way that health care is organized, financed and delivered in rich and poor countries around the world. Its publication marks the 30th anniversary of the Alma-Ata International Conference on Primary Health Care, which was credited with putting issues of health equity on the international political agenda. Nonetheless, the 2008 report concludes that health systems remain 'unfair, disjointed, inefficient and less effective than they could be'.

The report recommends that countries make health system and health development system decisions on the basis of four broad, interlinked policy directions: universal coverage—for fair and efficient systems, all people must have access to health care according to need and regardless of ability to pay; people-centred services—health systems can be reorientated to better respond to people's needs through delivery points embedded in communities; healthy public policies—ministries of trade, environment, education and others all have their impact on health, and yet little attention is generally paid to decisions in these ministries that have health impacts; leadership—existing health systems will not naturally gravitate towards more fair, efficient and effective models. So, rather than command and control, leadership has to negotiate and steer.

Organization. The principal organs of WHO are the World Health Assembly, the Executive Board and the Secretariat. Each of the 193 member states has the right to be represented at the Assembly, which meets annually in Geneva. The 32-member Executive Board is composed of technically qualified health experts designated by as many member states as elected by the Assembly. The Secretariat consists of technical and administrative staff headed by a Director-General, who is appointed for not more than two five-year terms. Health activities in member countries are carried out through regional organizations which have been established in Africa (Brazzaville), South-East Asia (New Delhi), Europe (Copenhagen), Eastern Mediterranean (Cairo) and Western Pacific (Manila). The Pan American Sanitary Bureau in Washington serves as the regional office of WHO for the Americas. It is the oldest international health agency in the world and is the secretariat of the Pan American Health Organization (PAHO). Co-operation in country projects is undertaken only at the request of the government concerned, through the six regional offices.

Finance. The total two-year budget planned for 2008–09 was US$4·2bn.

Headquarters: 20 avenue Appia, CH-1211 Geneva 27, Switzerland.
Website: http://www.who.int
Director-General: Dr Margaret Chan Fung Fu-chun (China).

Publications. Annual Report on World Health; Bulletin of WHO (6 issues a year); *International Digest of Health Legislation* (quarterly); *Health and Safety Guides; International Statistical Classification of Diseases and Related Health Problems; WHO Technical Report Series; WHO AIDS Series; Public Health Papers; World Health Statistics Annual; Weekly Epidemiological Record; WHO Drug Information* (quarterly).

Current Leaders

Margaret Chan Fung Fu-chun

Position

Director-General

Introduction

Dr Margaret Chan was appointed Director-General of the WHO on 9 Nov. 2006. She is serving a scheduled five-year term from 4 Jan. 2007 to 30 June 2012.

Early Life
Chan was born in 1947 in Hong Kong. She graduated in medicine from the University of Western Ontario, Canada in 1977, and joined the Hong Kong department of health as a medical officer in Dec. 1978. In 1985 she gained an MSc. in public health from the National University of Singapore. In June 1994 she became the health department's first female director. Her nine-year tenure was marked by outbreaks of H5N1 avian influenza in 1997 and SARS in 2003.

In 2003 Chan joined the WHO as director of the department for protection of the human environment. She was promoted to director of communicable diseases surveillance and response in June 2005 and also became the representative of the director-general for pandemic influenza. In Sept. that year she was appointed assistant director-general for communicable diseases. When Dr Lee Jong-wook died in May 2006, Chan was nominated by China to succeed him as Director-General.

Career in Office
Chan identified improvements in health of women and in Africa as key to her term. However, she courted early controversy when, in Feb. 2007, she was accused of favouring pharmaceutical companies over the sick in developing countries by humanitarian groups lobbying for cheaper generic drugs. Then in April she was criticized for her defence of the WHO's refusal to extend membership to Taiwan. In June 2007 new international health regulations obliged governments to report potential pandemics to Chan as WHO Director-General immediately. In June 2009 the WHO declared a global swine flu pandemic. The outbreak, first detected in March, had seemingly peaked in many countries by the end of the year, but Chan warned against complacency in tracking the evolution of the virus.

World Intellectual Property Organization (WIPO)

Origin. The roots of the World Intellectual Property Organization go back to the Paris Convention for the Protection of Industrial Property, adopted in 1883, and the Berne Convention for the Protection of Literary and Artistic Works (adopted 1886). The Convention establishing WIPO was signed at Stockholm in 1967 by 51 countries, and entered into force in April 1970. WIPO became a UN specialized agency in 1974.

Aims. To promote the protection of intellectual property throughout the world through co-operation among member states; and to ensure administrative co-operation among the intellectual property unions created by the Paris and Berne Conventions.

Intellectual property comprises two main branches: industrial property (inventions, trademarks and industrial designs) and copyright and neighbouring rights (literary, musical, artistic, photographic and audiovisual works).

Activities. There are three principal areas of activity: the progressive development of international intellectual property law; global protection systems and services; and co-operation for development. WIPO seeks to harmonize national intellectual property legislation and procedures; provide services for international applications for industrial property rights; exchange intellectual property information; provide training and legal and technical assistance to developing and other countries; facilitate the resolution of private intellectual property disputes; and marshal information technology as a tool for storing, accessing and using valuable intellectual property information. World Intellectual Property Day is held annually on 26 April.

New approaches to the progressive development of international intellectual property law. The development and application of international norms and standards is a fundamental part of WIPO's activities. It administers 23 treaties (15 on industrial property, eight on copyright). The Organization plays an increasing role in making national and regional systems for the registration of intellectual property more user-friendly by harmonizing and simplifying procedures.

Global protection systems and services. The most successful and widely used treaty is the Patent Co-operation Treaty (PCT), which implements the concept of a single international patent application that is valid in many countries. Once such application is filed, an applicant has time to decide in which countries to pursue the application, thereby streamlining procedures and reducing costs. In 2004 the PCT system recorded over 120,000 applications.

The treaties dealing with the international registration of marks and industrial designs are, respectively, the Madrid Agreement (and its Protocol) and the Hague Agreement. In 2004 there were 29,482 registrations of marks under the Madrid System. By the end of 2004 WIPO had registered nearly 35,000 international deposits of industrial designs.

Co-operation for development. On 1 Jan. 2000 many developing and other countries, as members of the World Trade Organization, brought their national legislative and administrative structures into conformity with the Agreement on Trade-Related Aspects of Intellectual Property Rights (TRIPS). WIPO and WTO agreed, in the framework of a Co-operation Agreement which entered into force on 1 Jan. 1996, and a Joint Initiative launched in July 1998, on a joint technical co-operation initiative to provide assistance to developing countries to meet their obligations to comply with the TRIPS Agreement. This represented a major step in the international harmonization of the scope, standards and enforcement of Intellectual Property rights.

The WIPO Worldwide Academy, created in 1998, co-ordinates training activities, originates new approaches and methods to expand the scope, impact and accessibility of WIPO programmes, and creates more effective training tailored for diverse-user groups. The Academy has also launched an internet-based distance-learning programme.

Impact of digital technology on intellectual property law. WIPO takes a range of initiatives to tackle the implications of modern digital and communications technology for copyright and industrial property law, and in electronic commerce transcending national jurisdictions. The WIPO Arbitration and Mediation Centre was established in 1994 to provide online dispute-resolution services. The Centre developed an operational and legal framework for the administration of disputes, including those relating to new technologies such as internet domain name disputes.

Organization. WIPO has three governing bodies: the General Assembly, the Conference and the Co-ordination Committee. Each treaty administered by WIPO has one or more Governing Bodies of its own, composed of representatives of the respective member states. In addition, the Paris and Berne Unions have Assemblies and Executive Committees. The executive head of WIPO is the Director-General, who is elected by the General Assembly. In Feb. 2010 WIPO had 184 member states, with an international staff of around 850 from 86 countries. The approved budget for 2008–09 was 628m. Swiss francs, the majority of which was covered by revenue earned by the Organization's international registration and publication activities.

Official languages: Arabic, Chinese, English, French, Russian and Spanish.
Headquarters: 34 chemin des Colombettes, 1211 Geneva 20, Switzerland.
Website: http://www.wipo.int
Director-General: Francis Gurry (Australia).

Periodicals. Industrial Property and Copyright (monthly, bi-monthly, in Spanish); *PCT Gazette* (weekly); *PCT Newsletter* (monthly); *International*

Designs Bulletin (monthly); *WIPO Gazette of International Marks* (fortnightly); *Intellectual Property in Asia and the Pacific* (quarterly).

World Meteorological Organization (WMO)

Origin. A 1947 (Washington) Conference of Directors of the International Meteorological Organization (est. 1873) adopted a Convention creating the World Meteorological Organization. The WMO Convention became effective on 23 March 1950 and WMO was formally established. It was recognized as a Specialized Agency of the UN in 1951.

Functions. (1) To facilitate worldwide co-operation in the establishment of networks of stations for the making of meteorological observations as well as hydrological or other geophysical observations related to meteorology, and to promote the establishment and maintenance of meteorological centres charged with the provision of meteorological and related services; (2) to promote the establishment and maintenance of systems for the rapid exchange of meteorological and related information; (3) to promote standardization of meteorological and related observations and ensure the uniform publication of observations and statistics; (4) to further the application of meteorology to aviation, shipping, water problems, agriculture and other human activities; (5) to promote activities in operational hydrology and to further close co-operation between meteorological and hydrological services; and (6) to encourage research and training in meteorology and, as appropriate, to assist in co-ordinating the international aspects of such research and training.

Organization. WMO has 183 member states and six member territories responsible for the operation of their own meteorological services. Congress, which is its supreme body, meets every four years to approve policy, programme and budget, and adopt regulations. The Executive Council meets at least once a year to prepare studies and recommendations for Congress, and supervises the implementation of Congress resolutions and regulations. It has 37 members, comprising the President and three Vice-Presidents, as well as the Presidents of the six Regional Associations (Africa, Asia, South America, North America, Central America and the Caribbean, South-West Pacific, Europe), whose task is to co-ordinate meteorological activity within their regions, and 27 members elected in their personal capacity. There are eight Technical Commissions composed of experts nominated by members of WMO, whose remit includes the following areas: basic systems, climatology, instruments and methods of observation, atmospheric sciences, aeronautical meteorology, agricultural meteorology, hydrology, oceanography and marine meteorology. A permanent Secretariat is maintained in Geneva. There are three regional offices for Africa, Asia and the Pacific, and the Americas. The budget for 2008–11 is 269·8m. Swiss francs.

Headquarters: 7 bis, avenue de la Paix, Case Postale 2300, CH-1211 Geneva 2, Switzerland.
Website: http://www.wmo.int
Email: wmo@wmo.int
Secretary-General: Michel Jarraud (France).

Publications. WMO Bulletin (quarterly); *WMO Annual Report.*

World Tourism Organization (UNWTO)

Origin. Established in 1925 in The Hague as the International Congress of Official Tourist Traffic Associations. Renamed the International Union for Official Tourism Organizations after the Second World War when it moved to Geneva, it was renamed the World Tourism Organization in 1975 and moved its headquarters to Madrid the following year.

The World Tourism Organization became an executing agency of the United Nations Development Programme in 1976 and in 1977 a formal co-operation agreement was signed with the UN itself. With a UN resolution on 23 Dec. 2003 the World Tourism Organization became a specialized agency of the United Nations.

Aims. The World Tourism Organization exists to help nations throughout the world maximize the positive impacts of tourism, such as job creation, new infrastructure and foreign exchange earnings, while at the same time minimizing negative environmental or social impacts.

Membership. The World Tourism Organization has three categories of membership: full membership which is open to all sovereign states; associate membership which is open to all territories not responsible for their external relations; and affiliate membership which comprises a wide range of organizations and companies working either directly in travel and tourism or in related sectors. In Feb. 2010 the World Tourism Organization had 154 full members, seven associate members and more than 400 affiliate members.

Organization. The General Assembly meets every two years to approve the budget and programme of work and to debate topics of vital importance to the tourism sector. The Executive Council is the governing board, responsible for ensuring that the organization carries out its work and keeps within its budget. The World Tourism Organization has six regional commissions—Africa, the Americas, East Asia and the Pacific, Europe, the Middle East and South Asia—which meet at least once a year. Specialized committees of World Tourism Organization members advise on management and programme content.

Headquarters: Capitán Haya 42, 28020 Madrid, Spain.
Website: http://www.unwto.org
Secretary-General: Dr Taleb Rifai (Jordan).

Publications. Yearbook of Tourism Statistics (annual); *Compendium of Tourism Statistics* (annual); *Travel and Tourism Barometer* (3 per year); *UNWTO News* (4 per year); *various others* (about 100 a year).

Other Organs Related to the UN

International Atomic Energy Agency (IAEA)

Origin. An intergovernmental agency, the IAEA was established in 1957 under the aegis of the UN and reports annually to the General Assembly. Its Statute was approved on 26 Oct. 1956 at a conference at UN Headquarters.

Functions. To accelerate and enlarge the contribution of atomic energy to peace, health and prosperity throughout the world; and to ensure that assistance provided by it or at its request or under its supervision or control is not used in such a way as to further any military purpose. In addition, under the terms of the Non-Proliferation Treaty, the Treaty of Tlatelolco, the Treaty of Rarotonga, the Pelindaba Treaty and the Bangkok Treaty: to verify states' obligation to prevent diversion of nuclear fissionable material from peaceful uses to nuclear weapons or other nuclear explosive devices.

Activities. The IAEA gives advice and technical assistance to developing countries on nuclear power development, nuclear safety and security, radioactive waste management, legal aspects of atomic energy use, and prospecting for and exploiting nuclear raw materials. In addition, it promotes the use of radiation and isotopes in agriculture, industry, medicine and hydrology through expert services, training courses and fellowships, grants of equipment and supplies, research contracts, scientific meetings and publications. During 2007 support for operational projects for technical co-operation involved 3,546 expert and lecturer assignments, 4,149 meeting and workshop participants, 2,287 participants in training courses and 1,661 fellows and visiting scientists.

Safeguards are the technical means applied by the IAEA to verify that nuclear equipment or materials are used exclusively for peaceful purposes. IAEA safeguards cover more than 95% of civilian nuclear installations outside the five nuclear-weapon states (China, France, Russia, UK and USA). These five nuclear-weapon states have concluded agreements with the Agency which permit the application of IAEA safeguards to all their civil nuclear activities. A total of 237 safeguards agreements in force in 163 states involved 2,122 safeguard inspections performed in 2007. Safeguards activities are applied routinely at over 900 facilities in 71 countries. A programme designed to prevent and combat illicit trafficking of nuclear weapons came into force in April 1996.

Organization. The Statute provides for an annual General Conference, a 35-member Board of Governors and a Secretariat headed by a Director-General. The IAEA had 151 member states in Feb. 2010.

There are also research laboratories in Austria and Monaco. *The International Centre for Theoretical Physics* was established in Trieste, in 1964, and is operated jointly by UNESCO and the IAEA.

Headquarters: PO Box 100, Wagramer Strasse 5, A-1400 Vienna, Austria.
Website: http://www.iaea.org
Director-General: Yukiya Amano (Japan).

Publications. Annual Report; IAEA Bulletin (quarterly); *IAEA Yearbook; INIS Reference Series; Legal Series; Nuclear Fusion* (monthly); *Nuclear Safety Review* (annual); *INIS Atomindex* (CD-Rom); *Technical Directories; Technical Reports Series.*

World Trade Organization (WTO)

Origin. The WTO is founded on the General Agreement on Tariffs and Trade (GATT), which entered into force on 1 Jan. 1948. Its 23 original signatories were members of a Preparatory Committee appointed by the UN Economic and Social Council to draft the charter for a proposed International Trade Organization. Since this charter was never ratified, the General Agreement remained the only international instrument laying down trade rules. In Dec. 1993 there were 111 contracting parties, and a further 22 countries applying GATT rules on a *de facto* basis. On 15 April 1994 trade ministers of 123 countries signed the Final Act of the GATT Uruguay Round of negotiations at Marrakesh, bringing the WTO into being on 1 Jan. 1995. As of Feb. 2010 the WTO had 153 members.

The object of the Act is the liberalization of world trade. By it, member countries undertake to apply fair trade rules covering commodities, services and intellectual property. It provides for the lowering of tariffs on industrial goods and tropical products; the abolition of import duties on a variety of items; the progressive abolition of quotas on garments and textiles; the gradual reduction of trade-distorting subsidies and import barriers; and agreements on intellectual property and trade in services. Members are required to accept the results of the Uruguay Round talks in their entirety, and subscribe to all the WTO's agreements and disciplines. There are no enforcement procedures, however; decisions are ultimately reached by consensus.

Functions. The WTO is the legal and institutional foundation of the multilateral trading system. Surveillance of national trade policies is an important part of its work. At the centre of this is the *Trade Policy Review Mechanism (TPRM)*, agreed by Ministers in 1994 (Article III of the Marrakesh Agreement). The TPRM was broadened in 1995 when the WTO came into being, to cover services trade and intellectual property. Its principal objective is to facilitate the smooth functioning of the multilateral trading system by enhancing the transparency of members' trade policies. All members are subject to review under the TPRM, which mandates that four members with the largest share of world trade (European Union, USA, Japan, Canada) be reviewed every two years; the next 16, every four years; and others every six, with a longer period able to be fixed for the least-developed members. Also, in 1994, flexibility of up to six months was introduced into the review cycles, and in 1996, it was agreed that every second review of each of the first four trading entities should be an interim review. Reviews are conducted by the Trade Policy Review Body (TPRB) on the basis of a policy statement by the member under review and a report by economists in the Secretariat's Trade Policy Review Division.

The *International Trade Centre* (since 1968 operated jointly with the United Nations through UNCTAD) was established by GATT in 1964 to provide information and training on export markets and marketing techniques, and thereby to assist the trade of developing countries. In 1984 the Centre became an executing agency of the UN Development Programme, responsible for carrying out UNDP-financed projects related to trade promotion.

Organization. A two-yearly ministerial meeting is the ultimate policy-making body. The 150-member General Council has some 30 subordinate councils and committees. The *Dispute Settlement Body* was set up to deal with disputes between countries. Appeals against its verdicts are heard by a seven-member *Appellate Body*. In Feb. 2010 it was composed of representatives of Belgium, China, Japan, Mexico, Philippines, South Africa and USA. Dispute panels may be set up *ad hoc*, and objectors to their ruling may appeal to the Appellate Body whose decision is binding. Refusal to comply at this stage can result in the application of trade sanctions. Each appeal is heard by three of the Appellate Body members. Before cases are heard by dispute panels, there is a 60-day consultation period. The previous GATT Secretariat now serves the WTO, which has no resources of its own other than its operating budget. The budget for 2009 was 189,257,600 Swiss francs.

Headquarters: Centre William Rappard, 154 rue de Lausanne, CH-1211 Geneva 21, Switzerland.
Website: http://www.wto.org
Email: enquiries@wto.org
Director-General: Pascal Lamy (France).

Publications. Annual Report; International Trade: Trends and Statistics (annual); *WTO Focus* (10 a year).

Further Reading

Croome, J., *Reshaping the World Trading System.* 1996
Fulton, Richard and Buterbaugh, Kevin, *The WTO Primer: Tracing Trade's Visible Hand through Case Studies.* 2008
Preeg, E., *Traders in a Brave New World.* 1996

Preparatory Commission for the Comprehensive Nuclear-Test-Ban Treaty Organization (CTBTO)

The Preparatory Commission for the Comprehensive Nuclear-Test-Ban Treaty Organization (CTBTO Preparatory Commission) is an international organization established by the States Signatories to the Treaty on 19 Nov. 1996. It carries out the necessary preparations for the effective implementation of the Treaty, and prepares for the first session of the Conference of the States Parties to the Treaty.

The Preparatory Commission consists of a plenary body composed of all the States Signatories, and the Provisional Technical Secretariat (PTS). Upon signing the Treaty a state becomes a member of the Commission. Member states oversee the work of the Preparatory Commission and fund its activities. The Commission's main task is the establishment of the 337 facility International Monitoring System and the International Data Centre, its provisional operation and the development of operational manuals. The Comprehensive Nuclear-Test-Ban Treaty prohibits any nuclear weapon test explosion or any other nuclear explosion anywhere in the world. As of Feb. 2010 the Treaty had 182 States Signatories and 151 ratifications.

Headquarters: Vienna International Centre, PO Box 1200, A-1400 Vienna, Austria.
Website: http://www.ctbto.org
Executive Secretary: Tibor Tóth (Hungary).

Organization for the Prohibition of Chemical Weapons (OPCW)

The OPCW is responsible for the implementation of the Chemical Weapons Convention (CWC), which became effective on 29 April 1997. The principal organ of the OPCW is the Conference of the States Parties, composed of all the members of the Organization.

Given the relative simplicity of producing chemical warfare agents, the verification provisions of the CWC are far-reaching. The routine monitoring regime involves submission by States Parties of initial and annual declarations to the OPCW and initial visits and systematic inspections of declared weapons storage, production and destruction facilities. Verification is also applied to chemical industry facilities which produce, process or consume dual-use chemicals listed in the convention. The OPCW also when requested by any State Party conducts short-notice challenge inspections at any location under its jurisdiction or control of any other State Party.

The OPCW also co-ordinates assistance to any State Party that falls victim of chemical warfare as it fosters international co-operation in the peaceful application of chemistry.

By Feb. 2010 a total of 188 countries and territories were States Parties to the Chemical Weapons Convention.

Headquarters: Johan de Wittlaan 32, 2517 JR The Hague, Netherlands.
Website: http://www.opcw.org
Director General: Rogelio Pfirter (Argentina).

European Union (EU)

Origin. The Union is founded on the existing European communities set up by the Treaties of Paris (1951) and Rome (1957), supplemented by revisions, the Single European Act in 1986, the Maastricht Treaty on European Union in 1992, the Treaty of Amsterdam in 1997, the Treaty of Nice in 2000 and the Treaty of Lisbon in 2009.

Members. (27). Austria, Belgium, Bulgaria, Cyprus (Greek-Cypriot sector only), the Czech Republic, Denmark, Estonia, Finland, France, Germany, Greece, Hungary, Ireland, Italy, Latvia, Lithuania, Luxembourg, Malta, the Netherlands, Poland, Portugal, Romania, Slovakia, Slovenia, Spain, Sweden and the UK.

History. European disillusionment with nationalism after the Second World War fostered a desire to bind key European states—France and (West) Germany—to each other and prevent future conflict. In 1946 Winston Churchill called for a moral union in the form of a 'united states of Europe'. Unsupported by the British Government, Churchill chaired the 1948 European Congress of The Hague, a meeting of 800 Europeanists that resulted in the creation of the *Council of Europe*, a European assembly of nations whose aim (Art. 1 of the Statute) was: 'to achieve a greater unity between its members for the purpose of safeguarding and realizing the ideals and principles which are their common heritage'.

The formation of the *Benelux Economic Union* in 1948 provided a model for a regional customs union; the free movement of goods, people, capital and services was achieved by 1960. Further European integration and the eradication of tariff trade barriers were encouraged by the US-financed European Recovery Program (Marshall Plan) and the *Organisation for European Economic Co-operation* (later the *OECD*). Western European co-operation was also spurred on by distrust of Soviet power in the East, leading to the Brussels Treaty of 1948; the collective defence pact that established the *Western European Union (WEU)*. The North Atlantic Treaty of 1949 cemented Western European (and American) security co-operation.

Jean Monnet, a French economic advisor, suggested joint development to solve Franco-German tensions over the industrial power of the Ruhr and Saarland. Monnet's plan was championed by the French foreign minister, Robert Schuman, whose Declaration of 9 May 1950 (now celebrated as Europe Day) proposed the pooling of coal and steel production. Belgium, France, the Federal Republic of Germany, Italy, Luxembourg and the Netherlands signed the Treaty of Paris establishing the *European Coal and Steel Community (ECSC)*, regarded as a first step towards a united Europe. However, the *European Defence Community (EDC)* of 1952 was rejected by the French Parliament, ending hopes for a *European Political Community*. Encouraged by the success of the ECSC, European integrationists pressed for further economic co-operation. The *European Economic Community (EEC)* and the *European Atomic Energy Community* (*EAEC* or *Euratom*) were subsequently created under separate treaties signed in Rome on 25 March 1957. The treaties provided for the establishment by stages of a common market with a customs union at its core, the development of common transport and agricultural policies, and the promotion of growth and research in the nuclear industries for peaceful purposes. Euratom was awarded monopoly powers of acquisition of fissile materials for civil purposes (it is not concerned with the military uses of nuclear power).

The executives of the three communities (ECSC, Euratom, EEC) were amalgamated by a treaty signed in Brussels in 1965, forming a single Council and single Commission of the European Communities, today the core of the EU. The Commission is advised on matters relating to Euratom by a Scientific and Technical Committee.

Enlargement. On 30 June 1970 membership negotiations began between the European Community and the UK, Denmark, Ireland and Norway. On 22 Jan. 1972 all four countries signed a Treaty of Accession but Norway rejected membership in a referendum in Nov. The UK, Denmark and Ireland became full members on 1 Jan. 1973 (though Greenland exercised its autonomy under the Danish Crown to secede in 1985). Greece joined on 1 Jan. 1981; Spain and Portugal on 1 Jan. 1986. The former German Democratic Republic entered into full membership on reunification with Federal Germany in Oct. 1990 and, following referenda in favour, Austria, Finland and Sweden became members on 1 Jan. 1995. In a referendum in Nov. 1994 Norway again rejected membership. On 1 May 2004 a further ten countries became members—Cyprus, the Czech Republic, Estonia, Hungary, Latvia, Lithuania, Malta, Poland, Slovakia and Slovenia. On 1 Jan. 2007 Bulgaria and Romania also became members.

Single European Act. The enlarging of the Community resulted in renewed efforts to promote European integration, culminating in the signing in 1986 of the Single European Act. The SEA represented the first major revision of the Treaty of Rome. It provided for greater involvement of the European Parliament in the decision-making process and it extended Qualified Majority Voting (QMV). The SEA also removed barriers within the EEC to movement and transnational business.

Maastricht Treaty on European Union. Following German reunification, closer European integration was pursued in the political as well as economic spheres. The Maastricht Summit of Dec. 1991 produced a new framework—a European Union based on three 'pillars': a central pillar of the existing European Communities and two supporting pillars based on formal intergovernmental co-operation. One pillar comprised a Common Foreign and Security Policy (CFSP) and the other focused on justice and home affairs, including policing, immigration and law enforcement. Signed in Feb. 1992, the Treaty on European Union laid down a timetable for the creation of a common currency (subject to specific conditions, including an opt-out clause for the UK). The Community Charter of Fundamental Social Rights for Workers, signed in 1989 by all members except the UK, was strengthened by a protocol, allowing member states to use EC institutions to co-ordinate social policy. The UK agreed to abide to the protocol in 1998. Ratification by member states of the Maastricht Treaty proved controversial. In June 1992 it was rejected in a Danish referendum but approved in a second referendum in May 1993. Ratification was finally completed during 1993, with the UK ratifying on 2 Aug. The European Union (EU) came into being officially on 1 Nov. that year.

Treaty of Amsterdam. The Turin Inter-Governmental Conference (IGC) of 1996 failed to advance the reform programme, in part because of the British Conservative Government's opposition to extending EU powers. The election in 1997 of a more Europeanist Labour Government led to the adoption of most of the IGC's proposals at the Amsterdam summit in 1997. Designed to further political integration, the Treaty did little more than adjust the institutions to prepare for EU enlargement. Strengthened policies included police co-operation, freedom of movement and the promotion of employment. Elements of the justice and home affairs 'pillar' were transferred to the Communities. The treaty also allows for member states to progress with selected areas of policy at different rates.

Treaty of Nice. Many of the problems unanswered at Amsterdam were left until the Dec. 2000 IGC at Nice. However, the tense summit failed to find consensus on key institutional reforms. The Treaty included a reweighting of votes in the Council of Ministers, adjustments to the composition of the Commission and several extensions to QMV. Ireland rejected the Treaty in a referendum in June 2001; this was reversed in the referendum in Oct. 2002. The Treaty came into effect on 1 Feb. 2003.

Charter of Fundamental Rights. The Charter, based on the Universal Declaration of Human Rights (UDHR), contains several provisions such as workers' rights and the right to good administration that are not included in the political and civil rights of the European Convention on Human Rights (ECHR). The Treaty was proclaimed by the European Parliament, the Commission and the Council—at the Nice IGC in 2000—but was not incorporated in the Treaty of Nice.

European Convention. In Dec. 2001 the Laeken European Conference adopted the Declaration on the Future of the European Union, committing the EU to becoming more democratic, transparent and effective, while opening the way to a constitution for the people of Europe. The European Council set up a convention, comprising 105 members—chaired by Valéry Giscard d'Estaing, a former French president—to draft the Treaty establishing a Constitution for Europe (the EU constitution), to be ratified by all member states. The Treaty was to confer legal personality on the European Union, giving it the right to represent itself as a single body under international law. The constitution included provision for a President of the European Council, to replace the current six-month rotating presidency, to be elected by member states for 2½-year terms. The European Parliament was to be granted co-legislative powers in all policy areas with the Council. A new position of Union Minister of Foreign Affairs would have merged the responsibilities of the external relations Commissioner and the High Representative for the CFSP. The constitution incorporated the Charter of Fundamental Rights. Member states would have had reduced powers of veto, although the veto was to have remained in key areas including taxation, defence and foreign policy. Plans for the new constitution to be ready for EU governments to sign after the ten new members joined on 1 May 2004 were dropped when the Brussels summit of Dec. 2003 ended in stalemate over the weighting of voting rights in the Council of Ministers. On 29 Oct. 2004 the Treaty was approved for ratification by the 25 member countries, either by referendum or parliamentary vote. On 29 May 2005, after nine countries had ratified the Treaty, France became the first to reject it; the Netherlands followed suit three days later. Subsequently a further seven countries ratified the Treaty. In addition, Bulgaria and Romania ratified the constitution as part of their preparations for joining the EU. With ratification in the Czech Republic, Denmark, Ireland, Poland, Portugal, Sweden and the UK delayed indefinitely, the treaty's progress stalled.

In June 2007 the European Council initiated talks on a replacement Reform Treaty (the Treaty of Lisbon). Drafting was completed in Oct. 2007, with the intention that the treaty should be signed and ratified by all member governments in time for the European parliamentary elections of June 2009. The treaty removes much of the constitutional terminology in the draft constitution text, reduces the reach of the European charter of human rights and allows for individual states to opt out of certain legislative areas. It does, nonetheless, retain many of the draft constitution's provisions, including a reformed EU presidency, a representative for EU foreign affairs and security and the recognition of the EU as a full legal personality. The treaty was subject to ratification in the parliaments of member countries. There were calls in several countries for the reform to be put to a public vote, but only Ireland was required by its constitution to hold a referendum. The treaty was rejected in the Irish referendum held on 13 June 2008 but accepted in a second referendum on 2 Oct. 2009. On 3 Nov. 2009 the Czech Republic was the final nation to ratify the treaty, which came into effect on 1 Dec. 2009. On 1 Jan. 2010 Herman Van Rompuy, formerly Belgium's prime minister, was sworn in as the first president of the European Council. On 1 Dec. 2009 Catherine Ashton, a British politician, became high representative of the Union for foreign affairs and security policy.

Recent and Future Enlargement. On 15 July 1997 the European Commission adopted *Agenda 2000*, which included a detailed strategy for consolidating the Union through enlargement as far eastwards as Ukraine, Belarus and Moldova. It recommended the early start of accession negotiations with the Czech Republic, Estonia, Hungary, Poland and Slovenia under the provision of Article O of the Maastricht Treaty, whereby 'any European State may apply to become a member of the Union' (subject to the Copenhagen Criteria set by the European Council at its summit in 1993).

In 2002 it was announced that ten countries would be ready to join in 2004: Cyprus, the Czech Republic, Estonia, Hungary, Latvia, Lithuania, Malta, Poland, Slovakia and Slovenia. Following a series of referenda held in 2003 they all became members on 1 May 2004. Bulgaria and Romania signed an accession treaty in April 2005 and became members on 1 Jan. 2007. Entry talks with Croatia began in Oct. 2005—it was recognized as an official candidate country in June 2004—in response to greater co-operation with the International Criminal Tribunal for the former Yugoslavia. Turkey is also hoping to join, but talks on membership which also began in Oct. 2005 may take up to 15 years. Switzerland applied for membership in May 1992 but this was rejected by a Swiss referendum later that year. The first Switzerland-EU summit, in 2004, brought Switzerland closer to the EU with a series of bilateral agreements. A referendum in

June 2005 approved joining the Schengen Accord (see below). The former Yugoslav Republic of Macedonia (FYROM) applied for membership in March 2004; in Dec. 2005 it was recognized as an official candidate country. Montenegro applied for membership in Dec. 2008, as did Albania in April 2009, Iceland in July 2009 and Serbia in Dec. 2009. Croatia is expected to be the next country to join the EU, probably in 2012. Iceland, although not yet an official candidate country, may also become a member in 2012.

Objectives. The Maastricht Treaty claimed the ultimate goal of the EU is 'an ever closer union among the peoples of Europe, in which decisions are taken as closely as possible to the citizen'. However, there are competing views over what that 'union' should be: political confederation or federation or primarily economic union. Priorities include: economic and monetary union; further expansion of the scope of the Communities; implementation of a common foreign and security policy; and development in the fields of justice and home affairs. The Lisbon Strategy, presented in 2000, strives to turn the EU into 'the most competitive and dynamic knowledge-based economy in the world'. Yet tensions remain over how to balance economic growth measures and social welfare provisions.

Structure. The EU's main institutions are: the European Commission, an independent policy-making executive with powers of proposal; the Council of the European Union (known informally as the Council of Ministers), a decision-making body drawn from the national Governments (headed by a permanent president since ratification of the Treaty of Lisbon); the European Parliament, which has joint legislative powers in most policy areas and final say over the EU budget; the European Court of Justice, the EU's supreme court; and the Court of Auditors, which checks the financing of the EU's activities.

Defence. At the 1999 Helsinki European Conference plans were drawn up for the formation of a rapid response capability that could be deployed at short notice. The success of Operation Artemis in 2003 (when an EU peacekeeping force, spearheaded by France, intervened in the humanitarian crisis in the Democratic Republic of the Congo) led to the statement at the Franco-British summit in Nov. 2003 that the EU should be able and willing to deploy forces within 15 days in response to a UN request. The 'EU Battlegroup Concept' was approved in 2004, reached its initial operational capability in Jan. 2005 and its full operational capability in Jan. 2007. The battlegroups are considered to be the smallest self-sufficient military unit capable of stand-alone operations or deployment in the initial phase of larger operations. The battlegroups are particularly suited for tasks such as conflict prevention, evacuation and humanitarian operations; however, they have yet to be deployed. There are currently 18 battlegroups, typically consisting of around 1,500 personnel. Two battlegroups remain on standby at any one time, rotating every six months. The European Union's first ever peacekeeping force (EUFOR) officially started work in Macedonia on 1 April 2003.

The European Union Institute for Security Studies (EUISS) was created by a Council Joint Action in July 2001 with the status of an autonomous agency. It contributes to the development of the Common Foreign and Security Policy (CFSP) through research and debate on major security and defence issues. The European Defence Agency, headed by Javier Solana, the EU's High Representative, was founded by the Council in July 2004 to improve defence co-ordination, especially crisis management.

Major Policy Areas. The major policy areas of the EU were laid down in the 1957 Treaty of Rome, which guaranteed certain rights to the citizens of all member states. Economic discrimination by nationality was outlawed, and member states were bound to apply 'the principle that men and women should receive equal pay for equal work'.

The Single Internal Market. The core of the process of economic integration is characterized by the removal of obstacles to the four fundamental freedoms of movement for persons, goods, capital and services. Under the Treaty, individuals or companies from one member state may establish themselves in another country (for the purposes of economic activity) or sell goods or services there on the same basis as nationals of that country. With a few exceptions, restrictions on the movement of capital have also been ended. Under the Single European Act the member states bound themselves to achieve the suppression of all barriers to free movement of persons, goods and services by 31 Dec. 1992. Since then the economies of the member states have expanded to such an extent that in 2007 the EU replaced the USA as the world's largest economy.

The *Schengen Accord* abolished border controls on persons and goods between certain EU states plus Norway and Iceland. It came into effect on 26 March 1995 and was signed by Austria, Belgium, Denmark, Finland, France, Germany, Greece, Iceland, Italy, Luxembourg, the Netherlands, Norway, Portugal, Spain and Sweden. The ten countries that joined the EU in 2004 signed the treaty, which came into force in nine of the countries (the Czech Republic, Estonia, Hungary, Latvia, Lithuania, Malta, Poland, Slovakia and Slovenia) on 21 Dec. 2007. Only Cyprus has yet to implement it. Switzerland became the 25th country to join the Schengen area on 12 Dec. 2008. Other signatory countries still to implement it are Bulgaria and Romania, which signed as part of their accession terms.

Economic and Monetary Union. The establishment of the single market provided for the next phase of integration: economic and monetary union. The *European Monetary System (EMS)* was founded in March 1979 to control inflation, protect European trade from international disturbances and ultimately promote convergence between the European economies. At its heart was the *Exchange Rate Mechanism (ERM).* The ERM is run by the finance ministries and central banks of the EU countries on a day-to-day basis; monthly reviews are carried out by the EU Monetary Committee (finance ministries) and the EU Committee of Central Bankers. Sweden is not in the ERM; the UK suspended its membership on 17 Sept. 1992. In Jan. 1995 Austria joined the ERM. Finland followed in 1996, and in Nov. that year the Italian lira, which had been temporarily suspended, was readmitted.

With the introduction of the euro, exchange rates have been fixed for all member countries. The member countries are Austria, Belgium, Cyprus, Finland, France, Germany, Greece, Ireland, Italy, Luxembourg, Malta, the Netherlands, Portugal, Slovakia, Slovenia and Spain.

European Monetary Union (EMU). The single European currency with 11 member states came into operation in Jan. 1999, although it was not until 2002 that the currency came into general circulation. Greece subsequently joined in Jan. 2001, Slovenia in Jan. 2007, Cyprus and Malta in Jan. 2008 and Slovakia in Jan. 2009. The euro became legal tender from 1 Jan. 2002 across the region (apart from in Cyprus, Malta, Slovakia and Slovenia). National currencies were phased out in the 12 countries that were using the euro from 1 Jan. 2002 by the end of Feb. 2002. The euro zone is the world's second largest economy after the USA in terms of output and the largest in terms of trade. EMU currency consists of the euro of 100 cents. EU member countries not in EMU will select a central rate for their currency in consultation with members of the euro bloc and the European Central Bank. The rate is set according to an assessment of each country's chances of joining the euro zone.

An agreement on the legal status of the euro and currency discipline, the Stability and Growth Pact, was reached by all member states at the Dublin summit on 13 Dec. 1996. Financial penalties are meant to be applied to member states running a GDP deficit (negative growth) of up to 0·75%. If GDP falls between 0·75% and 2%, EU finance ministers have discretion as to whether to apply penalties. France and Germany have exceeded their deficit limits repeatedly, despite the efforts of the Commission to penalize them. However, the Council of Ministers has decided to suspend penalties. Members running an excessive deficit are automatically exempt from penalties in the event of a natural disaster or if the fall in GDP is at least 2% over one year.

Environment. The Single European Act made the protection of the environment an integral part of economic and social policies. Public support for EU environmental activism is strong, as evinced by the success of Green parties in the parliamentary elections. Community policy aims to prevent pollution (the Prevention Principle), rectify pollution at source, impose the costs of prevention or rectification on the polluters themselves (the Polluter Pays Principle), and promote sustainable development. Water pollution policy covers quality standards for drinking, bathing and aquaculture and binds EU members to international waterway conventions. The European Environment Agency (see below) was established to ensure that policy was based on reliable scientific data.

In March 2002 the 15 EU member states agreed to the 1997 Kyoto Protocol to the United Nations Framework on Climate Change, which commits the EU to reduce its emissions of greenhouse gases by 8% of 1990 levels between 2008–12.

The Common Agricultural Policy (CAP). The objectives set out in the Treaty of Rome are to increase agricultural productivity, to ensure a fair standard of living for the agricultural community, to stabilize markets, to assure supplies, and to ensure reasonable consumer prices. In Dec. 1960 the Council laid down the fundamental principles on which the CAP is based: a single market, which calls for common prices, stable currency parities and the harmonizing of health and veterinary legislation; Community preference, which protects the single Community market from imports; common financing which seeks to improve agriculture and to stabilize markets against world price fluctuations through market intervention, with levies and refunds on exports. The CAP has made the EU virtually self-sufficient in food.

Following the disappearance of stable currency parities, artificial currency levels have been applied in the CAP. This factor, together with over-production owing to high producer prices, meant that the CAP consumed about two-thirds of the Community budget. In May 1992 it was agreed to reform CAP and to control over-production by reducing the price supports to farmers by 29% for cereals, 15% for beef and 5% for dairy products. In June 1995 the guaranteed intervention price for beef was decreased by 5%. In July 1996 agriculture ministers agreed a reduction in the set-aside rate for cereals from 10% to 5%. Fruit and vegetable production subsidies were fixed at no more than 4% of the value of total marketed production, rising to 4·5% in 1999. Compensatory grants are made available to farmers who remove land from production or take early retirement. The CAP reform aims to make the agricultural sector more responsive to supply and demand.

Customs Union and External Trade Relations. Goods or services originating in one member state have free circulation within the EU, which implies common arrangements for trade with the rest of the world. Member states can no longer make bilateral trade agreements with third countries; this power has been ceded to the EU. The Customs Union was achieved in July 1968.

In Oct. 1991 a treaty forming the *European Economic Area (EEA)* was approved by the member states of the then EC and European Free Trade Association (EFTA). The EEA consists of the 27 EU members plus Iceland, Liechtenstein and Norway; a Swiss referendum rejected ratification of the EEA in Dec. 1992. Association agreements, which could lead to customs union, have been made with Israel and Morocco. The customs union with Turkey came into force on 1 Jan. 1996. Commercial, industrial, technical and financial aid agreements have been made with a number of countries, including Algeria, Egypt, Jordan, Lebanon, Morocco, Russia, Syria and Tunisia. In 1976 Canada signed a framework agreement for co-operation in industrial trade, science and natural resources, and a transatlantic pact was signed with the USA in Dec. 1995. Co-operation agreements also exist with a number of Latin American countries and groupings, and with Arab and Asian countries, and an economic and commercial agreement has been signed with the Association of South East Asian Nations (ASEAN). Partnership and co-operation agreements exist with a number of eastern European and central Asian countries. In the Development Aid sector, the EU has an agreement (the Cotonou Agreement, signed in 2000, the successor of the Lomé Convention, originally signed in 1975 but renewed and enlarged in 1979, 1984 and 1989) with 77 African, Caribbean and Pacific (ACP) countries that removes customs duties without reciprocal arrangements for most of their imports to the Community. Since 2002, under the terms of the Cotonou Agreement, the EU and all participating ACP nations have been in talks to establish Economic Partnership Agreements (EPAs) designed to end non-reciprocal trade agreements that conflict with WTO rules. The EPAs were scheduled to come into force before the end of 2008 but by Feb. 2010 the only signatories to a formal (as opposed to interim) agreement were 14 Caribbean nations.

The application of common duties has been conducted mainly within the framework of the *General Agreement on Tariffs and Trade (GATT)*, which was succeeded in 1995 by the establishment of the World Trade Organization.

Fisheries. The Common Fisheries Policy (CFP) came into effect in Jan. 1983. All EU fishermen have equal access to the waters of member countries (a zone extending up to 200 nautical miles from the shore), with the total allowable catch for each species being set and shared out between member countries according to pre-established quotas. In some cases 'historic rights' apply, as well as special rules to preserve marine biodiversity and ensure sustainable fishing.

A number of agreements are operating with third countries (with ten African countries, the Faroe Islands, Greenland, Iceland, Kiribati, Micronesia, Norway, the Seychelles and the Solomon Islands) allowing reciprocal fishing rights. When Greenland withdrew from the Community in 1985 EU boats retained their fishing rights subject to quotas and limits, which were revised in 1995 owing to concern about the overfishing of Greenland halibut. An agreement was initialled with Argentina in 1992.

Transport. Failure to create a common transport policy, as expected by the Treaty of Rome, led in 1982 to parliamentary proceedings against the Council at the Court of Justice. Under the Maastricht Treaty, the Community must contribute to the establishment and development of Trans-European Networks (TENs) in the areas of transport, telecommunications and energy infrastructures. The TEN budget for 2000–06 was €4·6bn. Enlargement into Central and Eastern Europe necessitates a much larger budget; for 2007–13, €8·0bn. has been allocated. Common transport policy includes safety agreements, such as lorry weight and driver hours limits, the easing of border crossings for commercial vehicles and progress towards a common transport market. Rail plans include a 35,000 km high-speed train (HST) network, incorporating France's TGV and Germany's ICE networks.

Competition. The Competition (anti-trust) law of the EU is based on two principles: that businesses should not seek to nullify the creation of the common market by the erection of artificial national (or other) barriers to the free movement of goods; and that there should not be any abuse of dominant positions in any market. These two principles have led to the outlawing of prohibitions on exports to other member states, of price-fixing agreements and of refusal to supply; and to the refusal by the Commission to allow mergers or takeovers by dominant undertakings in specific cases. Increasingly heavy fines are imposed on offenders.

Funds. There are two Structural Funds: the European Regional Development Fund (promoting economic and social cohesion through the reduction of imbalances between regions or social groups) and the European Social Fund (combating unemployment, developing human resources and promoting integration into the labour market). These Structural Funds along with the Cohesion Fund are the financial instruments of EU regional policy, which is intended to narrow the development disparities among regions and member states.

Finances. Around 35% of the EU budget for the period 2007–13 (€348bn.) has been allocated to regional policy; comprising €278bn. for the Structural Funds and €70bn. for the Cohesion Fund (which provides assistance in the fields of the environment and trans-European transport networks to member states with a gross national income below 90% of the EU average).

EU revenue in €1m.:

	Financial year 2008
Agricultural duties	1,703·5
Customs duties	20,396·6
VAT-based resource	19,007·7
GNI-based resource	74,477·3
Miscellaneous	5,650·6
Total	121,235·7

Expenditure for the financial year 2007 was €105,299·5m., of which the expenditure on agriculture markets accounted for €41,859·3m. (39·8% of the total).

The resources of the Community (the levies and duties mentioned above, and up to a 1·4% VAT charge) have been agreed by Treaty. The Budget is made by the Council and the Parliament acting jointly as the Budgetary Authority. The Parliament has control, within a certain margin, of non-obligatory expenditure (where the amount to be spent is not set out in the legislation concerned), and can also reject the Budget. Otherwise, the Council decides.

Official languages: Bulgarian, Czech, Danish, Dutch, English, Estonian, Finnish, French, German, Greek, Hungarian, Irish, Italian, Latvian, Lithuanian, Maltese, Polish, Portuguese, Romanian, Slovak, Slovenian, Spanish and Swedish.

Website: http://www.europa.eu

EU Institutions

European Commission

The European Commission consists of 27 members. The Commission President is selected by a consensus of member state heads of government and serves a five-year term. The Commission acts as the EU executive body and as guardian of the Treaties. In this it has the right of initiative (putting proposals to the Council of Ministers for action) and of execution (once the Council has decided). It can take the other institutions or individual countries before the European Court of Justice should any of these fail to comply with European Law. Decisions on legislative proposals made by the Commission are taken in the Council of the European Union. Members of the Commission swear an oath of independence, distancing themselves from partisan influence from any source. The Commission operates through 41 Directorates-General and services.

At the European Summit held in Nice in Dec. 2000 it was decided that from 2005 each EU member state would have one commissioner until there are 27 members (which there have now been since 1 Jan. 2007). According to the Treaty of Lisbon, in 2014 the Commission will comprise representatives from two-thirds of the member states at the time on a rotating basis. However, in Dec. 2008 it was agreed that if the Treaty of Lisbon enters force (which it did on 1 Dec. 2009) a decision will be taken to allow the Commission to retain one national from each member state.

The current Commission took office in Feb. 2010. Members, their nationality and political affiliation (S-Socialist/Social Democrat; C-Christian Democrat/Conservative; L-Liberal; G-Green; Ind-Independent) in Feb. 2010 were as follows:

President: José Manuel Barroso (Portugal, S).

The commissioners are:

Vice-president: Catherine Ashton (UK, S); high representative of the Union for foreign affairs and security policy.

Vice-president: Viviane Reding (Luxembourg, C); responsible for justice, fundamental rights and citizenship.

Vice-president: Joaquín Almunia (Spain, S); responsible for competition.

Vice-president: Siim Kallas (Estonia, L); responsible for transport.

Vice-president: Neelie Kroes (Netherlands, L); responsible for digital agenda.

Vice-president: Antonio Tajani (Italy, C); responsible for industry and entrepreneurship.

Vice-president: Maroš Šefčovič (Slovakia, Ind); responsible for inter-institutional relations and administration.

Agriculture and Rural Development: Dacian Cioloş (Romania, C).

Climate Action: Connie Hedegaard (Denmark, C).

Development: Andris Piebalgs (Latvia, L).

Economic and Monetary Affairs: Olli Rehn (Finland, L).

Education, Culture, Multilingualism and Youth: Androulla Vassiliou (Cyprus, L).

Employment, Social Affairs and Inclusion: László Andor (Hungary, Ind).

Energy: Günther Oettinger (Germany, C).

Enlargement and European Neighbourhood Policy: Štefan Füle (Czech Republic, Ind).

Environment: Janez Potočnik (Slovenia, Ind).

Financial Programming and Budget: Janusz Lewandowski (Poland, C).

Fisheries and Maritime Affairs: Maria Damanaki (Greece, S).

Health and Consumer Policy: John Dalli (Malta, C).

Home Affairs: Cecilia Malmström (Sweden, L).

Internal Market and Services: Michel Barnier (France, C).

International Co-operation, Humanitarian Aid and Crisis Response: Kristalina Georgieva (Bulgaria, C).

Regional Policy: Johannes Hahn (Austria, C).

Research and Innovation: Máire Geoghegan-Quinn (Ireland, L).

Taxation and Customs Union, Audit and Anti-Fraud: Algirdas Šemeta (Lithuania, C).

Trade: Karel De Gucht (Belgium, L).

Headquarters: 200 rue de la Loi/Wetstraat, B-1049 Brussels, Belgium.

Secretary-General: Catherine Day (Ireland).

Current Leaders

José Manuel Barroso

Position

President of the European Commission

Introduction

Former prime minister of Portugal and leader of the right-wing Partido Social Democrata (Social Democrats, PSD), José Manuel

Barroso was nominated in June 2004 to succeed Romano Prodi as president of the European Commission and his appointment was approved by the European Parliament. Since taking up office on 23 Nov. 2004 he has been confronted with controversial EU constitutional and membership issues and the fall-out from the global financial crisis.

Early Life

Born on 23 March 1956, Barroso studied law at the Universidade de Lisboa and gained a masters degree in political science from the Université de Genève. He lectured at universities in Geneva and the USA, as well as working for the department of international relations at Universidade Lusíada, Lisbon.

In 1980 Barroso joined the PSD and was elected as a parliamentary deputy from 1985. In the 1990s he held foreign ministry posts before his election in 1999 as PSD leader. In elections that year the Socialist Party under incumbent prime minister António Guterres retained power, while the PSD came second. Two years later, with increasing criticism of the government's heavy public spending, the PSD made significant gains in local elections. Guterres resigned and elections were brought forward to March 2002. The PSD won a narrow victory and Barroso was appointed prime minister.

He reduced public spending, which affected local authorities' budgets and civil service recruitment, and plans were made to streamline or dissolve numerous state bodies. He also planned to accelerate privatization and introduce labour reforms and imposed an unpopular wage freeze.

In Jan. 2003 Barroso was one of eight European leaders to issue a combined declaration of support for the efforts of the United States to disarm Iraq, while making it clear that Portugal would not take part in military action.

After dropping earlier reservations concerning the European Commission's next president, Spain and France joined the other members in June 2004 to invite Barroso to succeed the incumbent, Romano Prodi. Following his appointment, Barroso resigned as prime minister of Portugal.

Career in Office

Barroso was quickly embroiled in controversy as a row broke out in the European Parliament over several contentious Commission nominees. The controversial candidates were replaced and in Nov. 2004 the Parliament approved a new team of commissioners (three weeks later than planned).

Rejection of the proposed new EU constitution in mid-2005 by the French and Dutch electorates in referendums posed a Union-wide dilemma. Barroso sought, particularly in 2007, to reopen the debate in language more acceptable to national sensibilities. As a result of further negotiations, EU leaders reached an outline agreement in June that year on streamlining the institutional structure and operation of the enlarged Union and gathered in Lisbon in Dec. to sign a new treaty. However, in June 2008 the treaty was rejected by voters in a referendum in Ireland, which again threw the future of the agreement into question. Eventually the Lisbon treaty was endorsed in a second Irish referendum in Oct. 2009 and entered into force on 1 Dec.

Meanwhile, Turkey's EU membership aspirations have also generated controversy, with accession negotiations hampered by Turkey's attitude to the issue of Cypriot sovereignty.

Since the second half of 2008 European attention has been focused increasingly on combating the global financial crisis and ensuing economic downturn. In Nov. that year the Commission unveiled proposals for a co-ordinated fiscal stimulus across the EU worth €200bn.

In Sept. 2009 the European Parliament re-elected Barroso for a second five-year term as Commission president, but wrangling over the finalization of the Lisbon treaty and a disputed nomination meant that the other members of the new Commission were not endorsed by the Parliament until Feb. 2010.

Council of the European Union (Council of Ministers)

The Council of Ministers consists of ministers from the 27 national governments and is the only institution which directly represents the member states' national interests. It is the Union's principal decision-making body. Here, members legislate for the Union, set its political objectives, co-ordinate their national policies and resolve differences between themselves and other institutions. The presidency rotates every six months. Spain had the presidency during the first half of 2010 and Belgium has the presidency during the second half of 2010; Hungary will have it during the first half of 2011 and Poland during the second half of 2011. Spain, Belgium and Hungary are co-operating in a triple presidency over an 18-month period. There is only one Council, but it meets in different configurations depending on the items on the agenda. The meetings are held in Brussels, except in April, June and Oct. when all meetings are in Luxembourg. Around 100 formal ministerial sessions are held each year.

Decisions are taken either by qualified majority vote or by unanimity. Since the entry into force of the Single European Act in 1987 an increasing number of decisions are by majority vote, although some areas such as taxation and social security, immigration and border controls are reserved to unanimity. At the Nice Summit in Dec. 2000 agreement was reached that a further 39 articles of the EU's treaties would move to qualified majority voting. 26 votes were then needed to veto a decision (blocking minority), and member states were allocated the following number of votes: France, Germany, Italy and the UK, 10; Spain, 8; Belgium, Greece, the Netherlands and Portugal, 5; Austria and Sweden, 4; Denmark, Finland and the Republic of Ireland, 3; Luxembourg, 2. During a six-month transitional period that followed the accession of the ten new member states on 1 May 2004 these vote weightings remained unchanged, while the new members were allocated the following number of votes: Poland, 8; Czech Republic and Hungary, 5; Estonia, Latvia, Lithuania, Slovakia and Slovenia, 3; Cyprus and Malta, 2. Since Bulgaria and Romania joined the EU on 1 Jan. 2007 the allocation of vote weightings has been: France, Germany, Italy and the UK, 29; Poland and Spain, 27; Romania, 14; the Netherlands, 13; Belgium, the Czech Republic, Greece, Hungary and Portugal, 12; Austria, Bulgaria and Sweden, 10; Denmark, Finland, the Republic of Ireland, Lithuania and Slovakia, 7; Cyprus, Estonia, Latvia, Luxembourg and Slovenia, 4; Malta 3. A qualified majority will be reached if a majority of member states approve a proposal, the countries supporting the proposal represent at least 62% of the EU's population and a minimum of 255 votes is cast in favour of the proposal. Each member state has a national delegation in Brussels known as the Permanent Representation, headed by Permanent Representatives, senior diplomats whose committee (Coreper) prepares ministerial sessions. Coreper meets weekly and its main task is to ensure that only the most difficult and sensitive issues are dealt with at ministerial level.

The General Secretariat of the Council provides the practical infrastructure of the Council at all levels and prepares the meetings of the Council and the European Council by advising the Presidency and assisting the Coreper and the various committees and working groups of the Council.

Legislation. The Community's legislative process starts with a proposal from the Commission (either at the suggestion of its services or in pursuit of its declared political aims) to the Council, or in the case of co-decision, to both the Council and the European Parliament. The Council generally seeks the views of the European Parliament on the proposal, and the Parliament adopts a formal Opinion after consideration of the matter by its specialist Committees. The Council may also (and in some cases is obliged to) consult the Economic and Social Committee and the Committee of the Regions which similarly deliver an opinion.

When these opinions have been received, the Council will decide. Most decisions are taken on a majority basis, but will take account of reservations expressed by individual member states. The text eventually approved may differ substantially from the original Commission proposal.

Provisions of the Treaties and secondary legislation may be either directly applicable in member states or only applicable after member states have enacted their own implementing legislation. Community law, adopted by the Council (or by Parliament and the Council in the framework of the co-decision procedure) may take the following forms: (1) *Regulations*, which are of general application and binding in their entirety and directly applicable in all member states; (2) *Directives*, which are binding upon each member state as to the result to be achieved within a given time, but leave to the national authorities the choice of form and method of achieving this result; and (3) *Decisions*, which are binding in their entirety on their addressees. In addition the Council and Commission can issue recommendations, opinions, resolutions and conclusions which are essentially political acts and not legally binding.

Transparency. In order to make its decision-making process more transparent to the European citizens, the Council has, together with the European Parliament and the Commission, introduced a set of rules concerning public access to the documents of the three institutions. A considerable number of Council documents can be accessed electronically via the Council's public register of documents, whereas other documents which may not be directly accessible can be released to the public upon request. With a view to ensure the widest possible access to its decision-making process, some Council debates and deliberations are open to the public. The Council systematically publishes votes and explanations of votes and minutes of its meetings when it is acting as legislator.

Headquarters: 175 rue de la Loi, B-1048 Brussels, Belgium.
Website: http://www.consilium.eu.int
Secretary-General and High Representative for the Common Foreign and Security Policy of the European Union: Dr Javier Solana Madariaga (Spain).

The European Council

Since 1974 Heads of State or Government have met at least twice a year (until the end of 2002 in the capital of the member state currently exercising the presidency of the Council of European Union, since 2003 primarily in Brussels) in the form of the European Council or European Summit as it is commonly known. Its membership includes the President of the European Commission, and the President of the European Parliament is invited to make a presentation at the opening session. The European Council has become an increasingly important element of the Union, setting priorities, giving political direction, providing the impetus for its development and resolving contentious issues that prove too difficult for the Council of the European Union. It has a direct role to play in the context of the Common Foreign and Security Policy (CFSP) when deciding upon common strategies, and at a more general level, when deciding upon the establishing of closer co-operation between member states within certain policy areas covered by the EU-treaties. Moreover, during recent years, the European Council has played a preponderant role in defining the general political guidelines within key policy areas with a bearing on growth and employment and in the context of the strengthening of the EU as an area of freedom, security and justice. With the entry into force of the Treaty of Lisbon on 1 Dec. 2009, it has become a full EU institution.

Headquarters: 175 rue de la Loi, B-1048 Brussels, Belgium.
Website: http://www.european-council.europa.eu
President: Herman Van Rompuy (Belgium).

Current Leaders

Herman Van Rompuy

Position
President of the European Council

Introduction
Former Belgian Prime Minister Herman Van Rompuy became the first permanent president of the European Council in Nov. 2009, a post created by the Treaty of Lisbon. His tenure is scheduled to last until May 2012. Van Rompuy overcame a long list of rival candidates, including Tony Blair, to secure the consensus of the 27 member states.

Early Life
Van Rompuy was born in Oct. 1947 in Etterbeek, in the Brussels-Capital Region. In 1968 he graduated in philosophy from the Catholic University of Leuven before studying for a masters in economic science.

He began his political career as vice-president of the Young Christian People's Party after two years at the Belgian Central Bank. In 1978 he joined the national bureau of the Christian People's Party (CVP). By the end of the 1970s he was serving in the cabinet of Léo Tindemans and in 1980 was appointed director of the CVP Study Centre. In 1988 he was elected to the Senate and became president of the CVP, serving until his promotion to minister for the budget and deputy prime minister in 1993. During six years as budget minister Van Rompuy significantly reduced the national debt, which had stood at 130% of GDP when he took office. In 1995 he left the Senate to take up a seat in the Chamber of Representatives.

The heavy defeat of the CVP at the 1999 election, which followed a scandal concerning the contamination of feedstock with dioxins, precipitated a party crisis that saw it renamed as the Christian Democratic and Flemish (CD&V). After eight years out of power, the 2007 general election returned the CD&V to government, with Van Rompuy as speaker of the Chamber.

On 19 Dec. 2008 the Supreme Court announced 'strong indications' that the government had attempted to influence a court decision on the break-up of the Fortis financial group. King Albert accepted the resignation of Prime Minister Yves Leterme's administration and on 28 Dec. asked Van Rompuy to form a government. Van Rompuy was reportedly reluctant to assume the premiership but bowed to pressure from colleagues eager to prevent the return of ex-prime minister Guy Verhofstadt.

Van Rompuy sought to rebuild confidence in the political system, while confronting the financial crisis and attempting to diffuse tensions between the Dutch- and French-speaking communities. In Nov. 2009 he was selected for the post of president of the European Council, taking office in Jan. 2010.

Career in Office
On assuming the presidency Van Rompuy emphasized his consensus-building objectives. His first meeting with the Council on 11 Feb. 2010 was dominated by the Greek financial crisis. Despite opposition Van Rompuy managed to secure agreement on the possibility of an EU bail-out.

European Parliament

The European Parliament consists of 736 members (785 prior to the elections that took place in June 2009). All EU citizens may stand or vote in their adoptive country of residence. Germany returned 99 members in 2009 (and returned 99 in 2004), France, Italy and the UK 72 each (78 each in 2004), Poland and Spain 50 each (54 each in 2004), the Netherlands 25 (27 in 2004), Belgium, Czech Republic, Greece, Hungary and Portugal 22 each (24 each in 2004), Sweden 18 (19 in 2004), Austria 17 (18 in 2004), Denmark, Finland and Slovakia 13 each (14 each in 2004), Ireland

and Lithuania 12 each (13 each in 2004), Latvia 8 (9 in 2004), Slovenia 7 (7 in 2004), Cyprus, Estonia and Luxembourg 6 each (6 each in 2004) and Malta 5 (5 in 2004). Romania and Bulgaria only joined the European Union in 2007; they did not vote in the 2004 elections. Romania returned 33 members in 2009 (35 in 2007) and Bulgaria 17 (18 in 2007).

Political groupings. Following the 2009 elections to the European Parliament the European People's Party (EPP) had 265 seats, Progressive Alliance of Socialists and Democrats (S&D) 184, Alliance of Liberals and Democrats for Europe (ALDE) 84, Greens/European Free Alliance (Greens/EFA) 55, European Conservatives and Reformists (ECR) 54, European United Left/Nordic Green Left (EUL/NGL) 35, Europe of Freedom and Democracy (EFD) 32, Non-attached members (NI) 27.

The Parliament has a right to be consulted on a wide range of legislative proposals and forms one arm of the Community's Budgetary Authority. Under the Single European Act, it gained greater authority in legislation through the 'concertation' procedure under which it can reject certain Council drafts in a second reading procedure. Under the Maastricht Treaty, it gained the right of 'co-decision' on legislation with the Council of Ministers on a restricted range of domestic matters. The President of the European Council must report to the Parliament on progress in the development of foreign and security policy. It also plays an important role in appointing the President and members of the Commission. It can hold individual commissioners to account and can pass a motion of censure on the entire Commission, a prospect that was realized in March 1999 when the Commission, including the President, Jacques Santer, was forced to resign following an investigation into mismanagement and corruption. Parliament's seat is in Strasbourg where the one-week plenary sessions are held each month. In the Chamber, members sit in political groups, not as national delegations. All the activities of the Parliament and its bodies are the responsibility of the Bureau, consisting of the President and 14 Vice-Presidents elected for a two-and-a-half year period.

Location: Brussels, but meets at least once a month in Strasbourg.
Website: http://www.europarl.europa.eu
President: Jerzy Buzek (Poland, EPP).

Court of Justice of the European Communities

The Court of Justice of the European Communities is composed of 27 judges and eight advocates general. It is responsible for the adjudication of disputes arising out of the application of the treaties, and its findings are enforceable in all member countries. A Court of First Instance (est. 1989) handles certain categories of cases, particularly actions brought by private individuals, companies and some organizations, and cases relating to competition law.

Address: Court of Justice of the European Communities, L-2925 Luxembourg.
President of the Court of Justice: Vassilios Skouris (Greece).
President of the Court of First Instance: Marc Jaeger (Luxembourg).

European Court of Auditors

The European Court of Auditors was established by a treaty of 22 July 1975 which took effect on 1 June 1977. It consists of 27 members (one from each member state) and was raised to the status of a full EU institution by the 1993 Maastricht Treaty. It audits the accounts and verifies the implementation of the budget of the EU.

Address: 12, rue Alcide De Gasperi, L-1615 Luxembourg.
Website: http://eca.europa.eu
Email: euraud@eca.europa.eu
President: Vítor Caldeira (Portugal).

European Central Bank

The European System of Central Banks (ESCB) is composed of the European Central Bank (ECB) and 27 National Central Banks (NCBs). The NCBs of the member states not participating in the euro area are members with special status; while they are allowed to conduct their respective national monetary policies, they do not take part in decision-making regarding the single monetary policy for the euro area and the implementation of these policies. The Governing Council of the ECB makes a distinction between the ESCB and the 'Eurosystem' which is composed of the ECB and the 16 fully participating NCBs.

Members. The 16 fully participating National Central Banks are from: Austria, Belgium, Cyprus, Finland, France, Germany, Greece, Ireland, Italy, Luxembourg, Malta, Netherlands, Portugal, Slovakia, Slovenia and Spain. The other 11 EU members (those which do not use the euro as their currency) have special status.

Functions. The primary objective of the ESCB is to maintain price stability. Without prejudice to this, the ESCB supports general economic policies in the Community with a view to contributing to the achievement of the objectives of the Community. Tasks to be carried out include: i) defining and implementing the monetary policy of the Community; ii) conducting foreign exchange operations; iii) holding and managing the official foreign reserves of the participating member states; iv) promoting the smooth operation of payment systems; v) supporting the policies of the competent authorities relating to the prudential supervision of credit institutions and the stability of the financial system.

The ECB has the exclusive right to issue banknotes within the Community.

Organization. The ESCB is governed by the decision-making bodies of the ECB: the Governing Council and the Executive Board. The Governing Council is the supreme decision-making body and comprises all members of the Executive Board plus the governors of the NCBs forming the Eurosystem. The Executive Board comprises the president, vice-president and four other members, appointed by common accord of the heads of state and government of the participating member states. There is also a General Council which will exist while there remain members with special status.

Address: Kaiserstrasse 29, 60311 Frankfurt am Main, Germany.
Website: http://www.ecb.int
President: Jean-Claude Trichet (France).

Other EU Structures

European Investment Bank (EIB)

The EIB is the financing institution of the European Union, created by the Treaty of Rome in 1958 as an autonomous body set up to finance capital investment furthering European integration. To this end, the Bank raises its resources on the world's capital markets where it mobilizes significant volumes of funds on favourable terms. It directs these funds towards capital projects promoting EU economic policies. Outside the Union the EIB implements the financial components of agreements concluded under European Union development aid and co-operation policies. The members of the EIB are the member states of the

European Union, who have all subscribed to the Bank's capital. Its governing body is its Board of Governors consisting of the ministers designated by each of the member states, usually the finance ministers.

Address: 100 Bd Konrad Adenauer, L-2950 Luxembourg.
Website: http://www.eib.org
President and Chairman of the Board: Philippe Maystadt (Belgium).

European Investment Fund Founded in 1994 as a subsidiary of the European Investment Bank and the European Union's specialized financial institution. It has a dual mission that combines the pursuit of objectives such as innovation, the creation of employment and regional development with maintaining a commercial approach to investments. It particularly provides venture capital and guarantee instruments for the growth of small and medium-sized enterprises (SMEs). In 2002 it began advising entities in the setting up of financial enterprise and venture capital and SME guarantee schemes. A team has been created to structure and expand its advisory services.

Address: 43 avenue J. F. Kennedy, L-2968 Luxembourg.

European Data Protection Supervisor

The European Data Protection Supervisor protects those individuals whose data are processed by the EU institutions and bodies by advising on new legislation and implications, processing and investigating complaints, and promoting a 'data protection culture' and awareness. The present incumbent is Peter Hustinx (Netherlands).

Address: Rue Wiertz, 60-MO 63, B-1047 Brussels, Belgium.
Website: http://www.edps.europa.eu
Email: edps@edps.europa.eu

European Ombudsman

The Ombudsman was inaugurated in 1995 and deals with complaints from citizens, companies and organizations concerning maladministration in the activities of the institutions and bodies of the European Union. The present incumbent is P. Nikiforos Diamandouros (Greece).

Address: 1 avenue du Président Robert Schuman, B.P. 403, F-67001 Strasbourg Cedex, France.
Website: http://www.ombudsman.europa.eu

Advisory Bodies There are two main consultative committees whose members are appointed in a personal capacity and are not bound by any mandatory instruction.

1. *European Economic and Social Committee.* The 344-member committee is consulted by the Council of Ministers or by the European Commission, particularly with regard to agriculture, free movement of workers, harmonization of laws and transport. It is served by a permanent and independent General Secretariat, headed by a Secretary-General.

Secretary-General: Martin Westlake (UK).

2. *Committee of the Regions.* A political assembly which provides representatives of local, regional and city authorities with a voice at the heart of the European Union. Established by the Maastricht Treaty, the Committee consists of 344 full members and an equal number of alternates appointed for a four-year term. It must be consulted by the European Commission and Council of Ministers whenever legislative proposals are made in areas which have repercussions at the regional or local level. The Committee can also draw up opinions on its own initiative, which enables it to put issues on the EU agenda.

President: Luc Van den Brande (Belgium).

Main EU Community Agencies

Community Fisheries Control Agency

Established in 2005 to oversee compliance with the 2002 reforms of the common fisheries policy.

Address: Community Fisheries Control Agency, Rue de la Loi 56, B-1049 Brussels, Belgium.

Community Plant Variety Office

Launched in 1995 to administer a system of plant variety rights. The system allows Community Plant Variety Rights (CPVRs), valid throughout the European Union, to be granted for new plant varieties as sole and exclusive form of Community intellectual property rights.

Address: PO Box 2141-3, Boulevard Maréchal Foch, F-49021 Angers Cédex 02, France.

European Agency for Safety and Health at Work

Founded in 1996 in order to serve the information needs of people with an interest in occupational safety and health.

Address: Gran Via 33, E-48009 Bilbao, Spain.

European Agency for the Management of Operational Cooperation at the External Borders

Established in 2004 to facilitate co-operation between member states in managing external borders. It assists in the training of national border guards, provides risk analyses and where necessary offers technical and operational assistance at external borders. It works in conjunction with other relevant EU partners, such as EUROPOL.

Address: Blue Point, Al. Stanów Zjednoczonych 61A, 04-028 Warsaw, Poland.

European Aviation Safety Agency

Established in 2002 to establish and maintain a high uniform level of civil aviation safety in Europe. It offers technical expertise to the European Commission, such as assisting in the drafting of aviation safety regulations, and carries out executive tasks including the certification of aeronautical products and organizations involved in their design, production and maintenance.

Address: Ottoplatz 1, D-50679 Cologne, Germany.

European Centre for Disease Prevention and Control

Established in 2004 to help strengthen Europe's defences against infectious diseases, such as influenza, SARS and HIV/AIDS. It co-operates with a network of partners across the EU and the EEA/EFTA member states to strengthen and develop continent-wide disease surveillance and early warning systems. By pooling Europe's health knowledge, it provides analyses of risks posed by new and emerging infectious diseases.

Address: Tomtebodavägen 11A, Solna, Sweden.

European Centre for the Development of Vocational Training

Generally known as 'Cedefop', it was set up to help policy-makers and practitioners of the European Commission, the member states and social partner organizations across Europe make informed choices about vocational training policy.

Address: PO Box 22427, Thessaloniki 55102, Greece.

European Chemicals Agency

Established in 2007 to manage the Registration, Evaluation, Authorisation and Restriction of Chemicals (REACH) system of the EU. There is a staff of around 200.

Address: PO Box 400, 00121 Helsinki, Finland.

European Environment Agency

Launched in 1993 to orchestrate and put to strategic use information of relevance to the protection and improvement of Europe's environment. It has a mandate to ensure objective, reliable and comprehensive information on the environment at European level. The Agency carries out its tasks through the European Information and Observation Network (EIONET). Membership is open to countries outside the EU and currently includes all EU countries, Iceland, Liechtenstein, Norway, Switzerland and Turkey.

Address: Kongens Nytorv 6, 1050 Copenhagen K, Denmark.

European Food Safety Authority

Founded in 2002 to provide independent scientific advice on all matters with a direct or indirect impact on food safety.

Address: Rue de Genève 1, B-1140 Brussels, Belgium.

European Foundation for the Improvement of Living and Working Conditions

Launched in 1975 to contribute to the planning and establishment of better living and working conditions. The Foundation's role is to provide findings, knowledge and advice from comparative research managed in a European perspective, which respond to the needs of the key parties at the EU level.

Address: Wyatville Road, Loughlinstown, Dublin 18, Ireland.

European GNSS Supervisory Authority

Established in 2007 to manage the public interests related to and to be the regulatory authority for the European global navigation satellite system, taking over tasks previously assigned to the Galileo Joint Undertaking.

Address: Rue de la Loi, 56, 1049 Brussels, Belgium.

European Maritime Safety Agency

Established in 2003 to enhance the EU's pre-existing range of legal tools to deal with incidents resulting in serious casualties or pollution in European waters and coastlines. The agency gives advice to member states and offers support to the directorate-general of energy and transport. As well as the 27 member states, it also covers Norway and Iceland. The Agency is active across issues including maritime safety controls, classification societies and port reception facilities for hazardous substances. It plays a major role in harmonizing member states' methodologies in post-accident investigations.

Address: Av. Dom João II, Lote 1.06.2.5, 1998-001 Lisbon, Portugal.

European Medicines Agency

Founded in 1995 (as European Agency for the Evaluation of Medicinal Products) to evaluate the quality and effectiveness of health products for human and veterinary use.

Address: 7 Westferry Circus, Canary Wharf, London E14 4HB, UK.

European Monitoring Centre for Drugs and Drug Addiction

Established in 1993 to provide the European Union and its member states with objective, reliable and comparable information on a European level concerning drugs and drug addiction and their consequences.

Address: Rua da Cruz de Santa Apolónia 23–25, PT-1149-045 Lisbon, Portugal.

European Network and Information Security Agency

Established in 2004 to serve as a centre of expertise on the digital economy, providing advice to member states and EU institutions in matters of network and information security.

Address: Science and Technology Park of Crete (ITE), Vassilika Vouton, 700 13 Heraklion, Greece.

European Railway Agency

Established in 2004 to reinforce safety and interoperability of railways throughout Europe. It has a staff of 100, most of whom come from the European railway sector.

Address: 160 Boulevard Henri Harpignies, 59300 Valenciennes, France.

European Training Foundation

Launched in 1995 to contribute to the process of vocational education and training reform that is currently taking place within the EU's partner countries and territories.

Address: Villa Gualino, viale Settimio Severo 65, I-10133 Turin, Italy.

European Union Agency for Fundamental Rights

In 2007 the FRA succeeded the European Monitoring Centre on Racism and Xenophobia, which was established in 1997. It seeks to provide assistance and expertise to relevant institutions and authorities in relation to fundamental rights when implementing Community law.

Address: Rahlgasse 3, A–1060 Vienna, Austria.

Europol

Founded in 1994 to exchange criminal intelligence between EU countries. Its precursor was the Europol Drug Unit; Europol took up its activities in 1999. Europol's current mandate includes the prevention and combat of illicit drug trafficking, illegal immigration networks, vehicle trafficking, trafficking in human beings including child pornography, forgery of money, terrorism and associated money laundering activities. There are about 600 staff members from all member states. Of these, 105 are Europol

Liaison Officers working for their national police, gendarmerie, customs or immigration services. The 2010 budget is €80·1m.

Address: Raamweg 47, The Hague, Netherlands.

Office for Harmonization in the Internal Market

The Office was established in 1994, and is responsible for registering Community trade marks and designs. Both Community trade marks and Community designs confer their proprietors a uniform right, which covers all member states of the EU by means of one single application and one single registration procedure.

Address: Avenida de Europa 4, Apartado de Correos 77, E-03080 Alicante, Spain.

Translation Centre for Bodies of the European Union

Established in 1994, the Translation Centre's mission is to meet the translation needs of the other decentralized Community agencies. It also participates in the Interinstitutional Committee for Translation and Interpretation.

Address: Bâtiment Nouvel Hémicycle 1, rue du Fort Thüngen, L-1499 Luxembourg Kirchberg, Luxembourg.

Statistical Office of the European Communities (EUROSTAT)

Eurostat's mission is to provide the EU with a high-quality statistical service. It receives data collected according to uniform rules from the national statistical institutes of member states, then consolidates and harmonizes the data, before making them available to the public. The data are available from the Eurostat website.

Address: Jean Monnet Building, L-2920 Luxembourg.
Website: http://www.europa.eu

EU general information. The Office for Official Publications of the European Communities is the publishing house of the institutions and other bodies of the European Union. It is responsible for producing and distributing EU publications on all media and by all means.

Address: 2 rue Mercier, L-2985 Luxembourg.
Website: http://publications.eu.int

Further Reading

Official Journal of the European Communities.—General Report on the Activities of the European Communities (annual, from 1967).—*The Agricultural Situation in the Community* (annual).—*The Social Situation in the Community* (annual).—*Report on Competition Policy in the European Community* (annual).—*Bulletin of the European Community* (monthly).—*Register of Current Community Legal Instruments* (biannual).

Chang, Michele, *Monetary Integration in the European Union.* 2009

Christiansen, Thomas and Reh, Christine, *Constitutionalizing the European Union.* 2009

Cini, Michelle and McGowan, Lee, *Competition Policy in the European Union.* 2nd ed. 2008

Cowles, M. G. and Dinan, D., *Developments in the European Union 2.* 2004

Davies, N., *Europe: A History.* 1997

Déloye, Yves and Bruter, Michael, (eds.) *Encyclopaedia of European Elections.* 2007

Dinan, D., *The Encyclopaedia of the European Union.* 2000.—*Europe Recast: A History of European Union.* 2004.—*Ever Closer Union? An Introduction to the European Union.* 3rd ed. 2005

Dod's European Companion. Occasional

Gänzle, Stefan and Sens, Allen G. (eds.) *The Changing Politics of European Security: Europe Alone?* 2007

Grabbe, Heather, *The EU's Transformative Power: Europeanization through Conditionality in Central and Eastern Europe.* 2005

Greenwood, Justin, *Interest Representation in the European Union.* 2nd ed. 2007

Hantrais, Linda, *Social Policy in the European Union.* 2007

Hitiris, T., *European Community Economics: a Modern Introduction.* 1991

Howorth, Jolyon, *Security and Defence Policy in the European Union.* 2007

Judge, David and Earnshaw, David, *The European Parliament.* 2nd ed. 2008

Keukeleire, Stephan and MacNaughtan, Jennifer, *The Foreign Policy of the European Union.* 2008

Lea, Ruth, *The Essential Guide to the European Union.* 2004

Lewis, D. W. P., *The Road to Europe: History, Institutions and Prospects of European Integration, 1945–1993.* 1994

Mancini, Judge G. F., *Democracy and Constitutionalism in the European Union.* 2000

Mazower, M., *Dark Continent: Europe's 20th Century.* 1998

McCormick, John, *Understanding the European Union.* 4th ed. 2008.—*The European Superpower.* 2006

McGuire, Steven and Smith, Michael, *The European Union and the United States: Competition and Convergence in the Global Arena.* 2008

Menon, Anand, *Europe: the State of the Union.* 2008

Nugent, N., *The European Commission.* 2000.—*European Union Enlargement.* 2004.—*The Government and Politics of the European Union.* 6th ed. 2006

Wallace, Helen, Wallace, William and Pollack, Mark, (eds.) *Policy-Making in the European Union.* 5th ed. 2005

Council of Europe

Origin and Membership. In 1948 the Congress of Europe, bringing together at The Hague nearly 1,000 influential Europeans from 26 countries, called for the creation of a united Europe, including a European Assembly. This proposal, examined first by the Ministerial Council of the Brussels Treaty Organization, then by a conference of ambassadors, was at the origin of the Council of Europe, which is, with its 46 member States, the widest organization bringing together all European democracies. The Statute of the Council was signed at London on 5 May 1949 and came into force two months later.

The founder members were Belgium, Denmark, France, Ireland, Italy, Luxembourg, the Netherlands, Norway, Sweden and the UK. Turkey and Greece joined in 1949, Iceland in 1950, the Federal Republic of Germany in 1951 (having been an associate since 1950), Austria in 1956, Cyprus in 1961, Switzerland in 1963, Malta in 1965, Portugal in 1976, Spain in 1977, Liechtenstein in 1978, San Marino in 1988, Finland in 1989, Hungary in 1990, Czechoslovakia (after partitioning, the Czech Republic and Slovakia rejoined in 1993) and Poland in 1991, Bulgaria in 1992, Estonia, Lithuania, Romania and Slovenia in 1993, Andorra in 1994, Albania, Latvia, Macedonia, Moldova and Ukraine in 1995, Croatia and Russia in 1996, Georgia in 1999, Armenia and Azerbaijan in 2001, Bosnia and Herzegovina in 2002, Serbia in 2003 (as Serbia and Montenegro until 2006), Monaco in 2004 and Montenegro in 2007.

Membership is limited to European states which 'accept the principles of the rule of law and of the enjoyment by all persons within [their] jurisdiction of human rights and fundamental freedoms'. The Statute provides for both withdrawal (Article 7) and suspension (Articles 8 and 9). Greece withdrew during 1969–74.

Aims and Achievements. Article 1 of the Statute states that the Council's aim is 'to achieve a greater unity between its members for the purpose of safeguarding and realizing the ideals and principles which are their common heritage and facilitating their economic and social progress'; 'this aim shall be pursued ... by discussion of questions of common concern and by agreements and common action'. The only limitation is provided by Article 1 (d), which excludes 'matters relating to national defence'.

The main areas of the Council's activity are: human rights, the media, social and socio-economic questions, education, culture and sport, youth, public health, heritage and environment, local and regional government, and legal co-operation. 198 Conventions and Agreements have been concluded covering such matters as social security, cultural affairs, conservation of European wildlife and natural habitats, protection of archaeological heritage, extradition, medical treatment, equivalence of degrees and diplomas, the protection of television broadcasts, adoption of children and transportation of animals.

Treaties in the legal field include the adoption of the European Convention on the Suppression of Terrorism, the European Convention on the Legal Status of Migrant Workers and the Transfer of Sentenced Persons. The Committee of Ministers adopted a European Convention for the protection of individuals with regard to the automatic processing of personal data (1981), a Convention on the compensation of victims of violent crimes (1983), a Convention on spectator violence and misbehaviour at sports events and in particular at football matches (1985), the European Charter of Local Government (1985), and a Convention for the Prevention of Torture and Inhuman or Degrading Treatment or Punishment (1987). The European Social Charter of 1961 sets out the social and economic rights which all member governments agree to guarantee to their citizens.

European Social Charter. The Charter defines the rights and principles which are the basis of the Council's social policy, and guarantees a number of social and economic rights to the citizen, including the right to work, the right to form workers' organizations, the right to social security and assistance, the right of the family to protection and the right of migrant workers to protection and assistance. Two committees, comprising independent and government experts, supervise the parties' compliance with their obligations under the Charter. A revised charter, incorporating new rights such as protection for those without jobs and opportunities for workers with family responsibilities, was opened for signature on 3 May 1996 and entered into force on 1 July 1999.

Human rights. The promotion and development of human rights is one of the major tasks of the Council of Europe. The European Convention on Human Rights, signed in 1950, set up special machinery to guarantee internationally fundamental rights and freedoms. The European Commission of Human Rights which was set up has now been abolished and has been replaced by the new European Court of Human Rights, which came into operation on 1 Nov. 1998. The European Court of Human Rights in Strasbourg, set up under the European Convention on Human Rights as amended, is composed of a number of judges equal to that of the Contracting States (currently 46). There is no restriction on the number of judges of the same nationality. Judges are elected by the Parliamentary Assembly of the Council of Europe for a term of six years. The terms of office of one half of the judges elected at the first election expired after three years, so as to ensure that the terms of office of one half of the judges are renewed every three years. Any Contracting State (State application) or individual claiming to be a victim of a violation of the Convention (individual application) may lodge directly with the Court in Strasbourg an application alleging a breach by a Contracting State of one of the Convention rights.

President of the European Court of Human Rights: Jean Paul Costa (France).

The Development Bank, formerly the Social Development Fund, was created in 1956. The main purpose of the Bank is to give financial aid in the spheres of housing, vocational training, regional planning and development.

The *European Youth Foundation* provides money to subsidize activities by European youth organizations in their own countries.

Structure. Under the Statute, two organs were set up: an intergovernmental *Committee of [Foreign] Ministers* with powers of decision and recommendation to governments, and an interparliamentary deliberative body, the *Parliamentary Assembly* (referred to in the Statute as the Consultative Assembly)—both served by the Secretariat. A Joint Committee acts as an organ of co-ordination and liaison between the two and gives members an opportunity to exchange views on matters of important European interest. In addition, a number of committees of experts have been established. On municipal matters the Committee of Ministers receives recommendations from the Congress of Local and Regional Authorities of Europe. The Committee meets at ministerial level once a year; the ministers' deputies meet once a week. The chairmanship of the Committee is rotated on a six-monthly basis.

The *Parliamentary Assembly* consists of 318 parliamentarians elected or appointed by their national parliaments (Albania 4, Andorra 2, Armenia 4, Austria 6, Azerbaijan 6, Belgium 7, Bosnia and Herzegovina 5, Bulgaria 6, Croatia 5, Cyprus 3, the Czech Republic 7, Denmark 5, Estonia 3, Finland 5, France 18, Georgia 5, Germany 18, Greece 7, Hungary 7, Iceland 3, Ireland 4, Italy 18, Latvia 3, Liechtenstein 2, Lithuania 4, Luxembourg 3, Macedonia 3, Malta 3, Moldova 5, Monaco 2, Montenegro 3, Netherlands 7, Norway 5, Poland 12, Portugal 7, Romania 10, Russia 18, San Marino 2, Serbia 7, Slovakia 5, Slovenia 3, Spain 12, Sweden 6, Switzerland 6, Turkey 12, Ukraine 12, UK 18). It meets three times a year for approximately a week. The work of the Assembly is prepared by parliamentary committees. Since June 1989 representatives of a number of central and East European countries have been permitted to attend as non-voting members ('special guests'). Armenia and Azerbaijan have subsequently become full members.

Although without legislative powers, the Assembly acts as the powerhouse of the Council, initiating European action in key areas by making recommendations to the Committee of Ministers. As the widest parliamentary forum in Western Europe, the Assembly also acts as the conscience of the area by voicing its opinions on important current issues. These are embodied in Resolutions. The Ministers' role is to translate the Assembly's recommendations into action, particularly as regards lowering the barriers between the European countries, harmonizing their legislation or introducing, where possible, common European laws, abolishing discrimination on grounds of nationality, and undertaking certain tasks on a joint European basis.

Official languages: English and French.
Headquarters: Council of Europe, F-67075 Strasbourg Cedex, France.
Website: http://www.coe.int
Email: infopoint@coe.int
Secretary-General: Thorbjørn Jagland (Norway).

Publications. European Yearbook, The Hague; *Yearbook on the Convention on Human Rights,* Strasbourg; *Catalogue of Publications* (annual); *Activities Report* (annual). Information on other bulletins and documents is available on the Council of Europe's website.

Further Reading

Cook, C. and Paxton, J., *European Political Facts of the Twentieth Century.* 2000

Western European Union (WEU)

Origin. In March 1948 the signing of the Brussels Treaty of Economic, Social and Cultural Collaboration and Collective Defence by Belgium, France, Luxembourg, the Netherlands and the UK opened the way for the establishment of Western

European Union. The Paris Agreements were signed in Oct. 1954, amending the Brussels Treaty and giving birth to WEU as a new international organization; they also provided for the Federal Republic of Germany and Italy to join. WEU came into being in 1955. Today, as an international defence and security organization, it brings together 28 nations encompassing four types of status: member state, associate member, observer and associate partner. Only the ten member states are signatories to the modified Brussels Treaty and have full decision making rights in WEU. The other 18 countries have been increasingly associated with WEU's activities. WEU's role and operational capabilities developed considerably after 1991. This development was based on close co-operation with the European Union and NATO. WEU acquired the necessary instruments to undertake any European-led crisis management operations and worked to develop them further as preparation for the establishment within the European Union of a crisis management capability in accordance with the decisions taken at the Cologne European Council in June 1999. Following decisions taken by the European Council since its meeting in Cologne to strengthen the European Security and Defence Policy within the EU, WEU relinquished its crisis management functions to the EU on 1 July 2001.

Member states. Belgium, France, Germany, Greece, Italy, Luxembourg, the Netherlands, Portugal, Spain and the UK. *Associate members:* Czech Republic, Hungary, Iceland, Norway, Poland and Turkey. *Observers:* Austria, Denmark, Finland, Ireland and Sweden. *Associate partners:* Bulgaria, Estonia, Latvia, Lithuania, Romania, Slovakia and Slovenia.

Reform. At the Alliance Summit of Jan. 1994 NATO leaders gave their full support to the development of a European Security and Defence Identity (ESDI) and to the strengthening of WEU. They declared their readiness to make collective assets of the Alliance available for WEU operations. The Alliance leaders also endorsed the concept of Combined Joint Task Forces (CJTFs) with the objective not only of adapting Alliance structures to NATO's new missions but also of improving co-operation with WEU, and in order to reflect the emerging ESDI. Work on the CJTF concept came to fruition at the NATO Ministerial meeting in Berlin in June 1996. One of the fundamental objectives of the Alliance adaptation process identified by NATO Ministers in Berlin was the development of the European Security and Defence Identity within the Alliance.

With the agreement on the Treaty of Amsterdam revising the Treaty on European Union, WEU has drawn closer to the EU. In particular, the European Council's guidelines for the Common Foreign Security Policy (CFSP) 'shall obtain in respect of WEU for those matters for which the Union avails itself of the WEU'; and the Petersberg tasks have been incorporated into the EU Treaty. It is stated that WEU is an integral part of the development of the European Union, giving the Union access to an operational capability, notably in the context of the Petersberg tasks. In the WEU Ministerial Declaration of 22 July 1997 responding to the Treaty of Amsterdam, WEU confirmed its readiness to develop WEU's relations with the EU and work out arrangements for enhanced co-operation.

Operations. In the context of the conflict in the former Yugoslavia, WEU undertook three operations, two of them to help in the enforcement of sanctions imposed by the UN Security Council and one to assist in the European Union administration of the town of Mostar. From 1997 to 2001 WEU deployed a Multinational Advisory Police Element (MAPE) in Albania to assist in the reorganization of the Albanian Police. A WEU Demining Assistance Mission to Croatia (WEUDAM), operating from 1999 to 2001, provided advice, technical expertise and training support to the Croatian Mine Action Centre.

Organization. WEU comprises an intergovernmental policy-making council and an assembly of parliamentary representatives, together with a number of subsidiary bodies set up by the council to facilitate its work. Since the 1984 reforms, the Council, supreme authority of the WEU, meets twice a year at ministerial level (foreign and defence) in the capital of the presiding country. The presidency rotates biannually. The Permanent Council, chaired by the Secretary-General, meets whenever necessary at ambassadorial level, at the WEU headquarters in Brussels. The WEU Assembly, located in Paris, comprises 400 representatives of member states and meets twice a year, in plenary sessions in Paris. There are Permanent Committees on: defence questions and armaments; political affairs; technological and aerospace questions; budgetary affairs and administration; rules of procedure and privileges; and parliamentary and public relations.

Headquarters: WEU, Rue de l'Association 15, B-1000 Brussels, Belgium.
Website: http://www.weu.int
Secretary-General: Dr Javier Solana Madariaga (Spain).

Organization for Security and Co-operation in Europe (OSCE)

The OSCE is a pan-European security organization of 56 participating states. It has been recognized under the UN Charter as a primary instrument in its region for early warning, conflict prevention, crisis management and post-conflict rehabilitation.

Origin. Initiatives from both NATO and the Warsaw Pact culminated in the first summit Conference on Security and Co-operation in Europe (CSCE) attended by heads of state and government in Helsinki on 30 July–1 Aug. 1975. It adopted the *Helsinki Final Act* laying down ten principles governing the behaviour of States towards their citizens and each other, concerning human rights, self-determination and the interrelations of the participant states. The CSCE was to serve as a multilateral forum for dialogue and negotiations between East and West.

The Helsinki Final Act comprised three main sections: 1) politico-military aspects of security: principles guiding relations between and among participating States and military confidence-building measures; 2) co-operation in the fields of economics, science and technology and the environment; 3) co-operation in humanitarian and other fields.

From CSCE to OSCE. The Paris Summit of Nov. 1990 set the CSCE on a new course. In the Charter of Paris for a New Europe, the CSCE was called upon to contribute to managing the historic change in Europe and respond to the new challenges of the post-Cold War period. At the meeting, members of NATO and the Warsaw Pact signed an important Treaty on Conventional Armed Forces in Europe (CFE) and a declaration that they were 'no longer adversaries' and did not intend to 'use force against the territorial integrity or political independence of any state'. All 34 participants adopted the Vienna Document comprising Confidence and Security-Building Measures (CSBMs), which pertain to the exchange of military information, verification of military installations, objection to unusual military activities etc., and signed the Charter of Paris. The Charter sets out principles of human rights, democracy and the rule of law to which all the signatories undertake to adhere, and lays down the basis for East-West co-operation and other future action. The 1994 Budapest Summit recognized that the CSCE was no longer a conference and on 1 Jan. 1995 the CSCE changed its name to the Organization for Security and Co-operation in Europe (OSCE). The 1996 Lisbon

Summit elaborated the OSCE's key role in fostering security and stability in all their dimensions. It also stimulated the development of an OSCE Document-Charter on European Security.

Members. Albania, Andorra, Armenia, Austria, Azerbaijan, Belarus, Belgium, Bosnia and Herzegovina, Bulgaria, Canada, Croatia, Cyprus, the Czech Republic, Denmark, Estonia, Finland, France, Georgia, Germany, Greece, Holy See, Hungary, Iceland, Ireland, Italy, Kazakhstan, Kyrgyzstan, Latvia, Liechtenstein, Lithuania, Luxembourg, Macedonia, Malta, Moldova, Monaco, Montenegro, Netherlands, Norway, Poland, Portugal, Romania, Russian Federation, San Marino, Serbia, Slovak Republic, Slovenia, Spain, Sweden, Switzerland, Tajikistan, Turkey, Turkmenistan, Ukraine, UK, USA and Uzbekistan. *Partners for co-operation:* Afghanistan, Japan, Mongolia, South Korea and Thailand. *Mediterranean partners for co-operation:* Algeria, Egypt, Israel, Jordan, Morocco, Tunisia.

Organization. The OSCE's regular body for political consultation and decision-making is the Permanent Council. Its members, the Permanent Representatives of the OSCE participating States, meet weekly in the Hofburg Congress Center in Vienna to discuss and take decisions on all issues pertinent to the OSCE. The Forum for Security Co-operation (FSC), which deals with arms control and confidence- and security-building measures, also meets weekly in Vienna. Summits—periodic meetings of Heads of State or Government of OSCE participating States—set priorities and provide orientation at the highest political level. In the years between these summits, decision-making and governing power lies with the *Ministerial Council*, which is made up of the Foreign Ministers of the OSCE participating States. In addition, a Senior Council also meets once a year in special session as the Economic Forum. The Chairman-in-Office has overall responsibility for executive action and agenda-setting. The Chair rotates annually. The Secretary-General acts as representative of the Chairman-in-Office and manages OSCE structures and operations.

The Secretariat is based in Vienna and includes a *Conflict Prevention Centre* which provides operational support for OSCE field missions. There are some 400 staff employed in OSCE institutions, and about 1,000 professionals, seconded by OSCE-participating states, work at OSCE missions and other field operations, together with another 2,500 local staff.

The *Office for Democratic Institutions and Human Rights* is located in Warsaw. It is active in monitoring elections and developing national electoral and human rights institutions, providing technical assistance to national legal institutions, and promoting the development of the rule of law and civil society.

The *Office of the Representative on Freedom of the Media* is located in Vienna. Its main function is to observe relevant media developments in OSCE participating States with a view to providing an early warning on violations of freedom of expression.

The *Office of the High Commissioner on National Minorities* is located in The Hague. Its function is to identify and seek early resolution of ethnic tensions that might endanger peace, stability or friendly relations between the participating States of the OSCE.

The budget for 2008 was €164m.

Headquarters: Wallnerstrasse 6, A-1010 Vienna, Austria.
Website: http://www.osce.org
Chairman-in-Office: Kanat Saudabayev (Kazakhstan).
Secretary-General: Marc Perrin de Brichambaut (France).

Further Reading

Freeman, J., *Security and the CSCE Process: the Stockholm Conference and Beyond.* 1991

European Bank for Reconstruction and Development (EBRD)

History. The European Bank for Reconstruction and Development was established in 1991 when communism was collapsing in central and eastern Europe and ex-Soviet countries needed support to nurture a new private sector in a democratic environment.

Activities. The EBRD is the largest single investor in the region and mobilizes significant foreign direct investment beyond its own financing. It is owned by 61 countries and two intergovernmental institutions. But despite its public sector shareholders, it invests mainly in private enterprises, usually together with commercial partners. Today the EBRD uses the tools of investment to help build market economies and democracies in 30 countries from Central Europe to Central Asia.

It provides project financing for banks, industries and businesses, for both new ventures and investments in existing companies. It also works with publicly-owned companies, to support privatization, restructuring of state-owned firms and improvement of municipal services. The EBRD uses its close relationship with governments in the region to promote policies that will bolster the business environment.

The mandate of the EBRD stipulates that it must only work in countries that are committed to democratic principles. Respect for the environment is part of the strong corporate governance attached to all EBRD investments.

Organization. All the powers of the EBRD are vested in a Board of Governors, to which each member appoints a governor, generally the minister of finance or an equivalent. The Board of Governors delegates powers to the Board of Directors, which is responsible for the direction of the EBRD's general operations and policies. The President is elected by the Board of Governors and is the legal representative of the EBRD. The President conducts the current business of the Bank under the guidance of the Board of Directors.

Headquarters: One Exchange Square, London EC2A 2JN, UK.
Website: http://www.ebrd.com
President: Thomas Mirow (Germany).
Secretary-General: Enzo Quattrociocche (Italy).

European Free Trade Association (EFTA)

History and Membership. The Stockholm Convention establishing the Association entered into force on 3 May 1960. Founder members were Austria, Denmark, Norway, Portugal, Sweden, Switzerland and the UK. With the accession of Austria, Denmark, Finland, Portugal, Sweden and the UK to the EU, EFTA was reduced to four member countries: Iceland, Liechtenstein, Norway and Switzerland. In June 2001 the Vaduz Convention was signed. It liberalizes trade further among the four EFTA States in order to reflect the Swiss–EU bilateral agreements.

Activities. Free trade in industrial goods among EFTA members was achieved by 1966. Co-operation with the EU began in 1972 with the signing of free trade agreements and culminated in the establishment of a *European Economic Area (EEA)*, encompassing the free movement of goods, services, capital and labour throughout EFTA and the EU member countries. The Agreement was signed by all members of the EU and EFTA on 2 May 1992, but was rejected by Switzerland in a referendum on 6 Dec. 1992. The agreement came into force on 1 Jan. 1994.

The main provisions of the EEA Agreement are: free movement of products within the EEA from 1993 (with special arrangements to cover food, energy, coal and steel); EFTA to assume EU rules on company law, consumer protection, education, the environment, research and development, and social policy; EFTA to adopt EU competition rules on anti-trust matters, abuse of a dominant position, public procurement, mergers and state aid; EFTA to create an EFTA Surveillance Authority and an EFTA Court; individuals to be free to live, work and offer services throughout the EEA, with mutual recognition of professional qualifications; capital movements to be free with some restrictions on investments; EFTA countries not to be bound by the Common Agricultural Policy (CAP) or Common Fisheries Policy (CFP).

The EEA-EFTA states have established a Surveillance Authority and a Court to ensure implementation of the Agreement among the EFTA-EEA states. Political direction is given by the EEA Council which meets twice a year at ministerial level, while ongoing operation of the Agreement is overseen by the EEA Joint Committee. Legislative power remains with national governments and parliaments.

EFTA has formal relations with several other states. Free trade agreements have been signed with Turkey (1991), Israel and Czechoslovakia (1992, with protocols on succession with the Czech Republic and Slovakia in 1993), Poland and Romania (1992), Bulgaria and Hungary (1993), Estonia, Latvia, Lithuania and Slovenia (1995), Morocco (1997), the Palestine Liberation Organization on behalf of the Palestinian Authority (1998), the former Yugoslav Republic of Macedonia and Mexico (2000), Jordan and Croatia (2001), Singapore (2002), Chile (2003), Lebanon and Tunisia (2004), South Korea (2005), the Southern African Customs Union (2006), Egypt (2007), Canada and Colombia (2008), Albania, the Gulf Co-operation Council and Serbia (2009). Negotiations on free trade agreements are ongoing with Algeria, Hong Kong, India, Peru, Thailand and Ukraine. There are currently Joint Declarations on Co-operation with Mercosur and Ukraine (2000), Algeria (2002), Peru (2006), Mongolia (2007) and Mauritius (2009).

Organization. The operation of the free trade area among the EFTA states is the responsibility of the EFTA Council which meets regularly at ambassadorial level in Geneva. The Council is assisted by a Secretariat and standing committees. Each EFTA country holds the chairmanship of the Council for six months. For EEA matters there is a separate committee structure.

Brussels Office (EEA matters, press and information): 12–16 Rue Joseph II, B-1000 Brussels.

Headquarters: 9–11 rue de Varembé, 1211 Geneva 20, Switzerland.
Website: http://www.efta.int
Email: mail.gva@efta.int
Secretary-General: Kåre Bryn (Norway).

Publications. Convention Establishing the European Free Trade Association; EFTA Annual Report; EFTA Fact Sheets: Information Papers on Aspects of the EEA; EFTA Bulletin.

European Space Agency (ESA)

History. Established in 1975, replacing the European Space Research Organization (ESRO) and the European Launcher Development Organization (ELDO).

Members. Austria, Belgium, Czech Republic, Denmark, Finland, France, Germany, Greece, Ireland, Italy, Luxembourg, the Netherlands, Norway, Portugal, Spain, Sweden, Switzerland, United Kingdom. Canada takes part in some projects under a co-operation agreement.

Activities. ESA is the intergovernmental agency in Europe responsible for the exploitation of space science, research and technology for exclusively peaceful purposes. Its aim is to define and put into effect a long-term European space policy that allows Europe to remain competitive in the field of space technology. It has a policy of co-operation with various partners on the basis that pooling resources and sharing work will boost the effectiveness of its programmes. Its space plan covers the fields of science, Earth observation, telecommunications, navigation, space segment technologies, ground infrastructures, space transport systems and microgravity research.

Headquarters: 8–10 rue Mario Nikis, 75738 Paris Cedex 15, France.
Website: http://www.esa.int
Director-General: Jean-Jacques Dordain (France).

CERN – The European Organization for Nuclear Research

Founded in 1954, CERN is the world's leading particle physics research centre. By studying the behaviour of nature's fundamental particles, CERN aims to find out what our Universe is made of and how it works. CERN's biggest accelerator, the Large Hadron Collider (LHC), became operational in Sept. 2008. One of the beneficial byproducts of CERN activity is the Worldwide Web, developed at CERN to give particle physicists easy access to shared data. One of Europe's first joint ventures, CERN now has a membership of 20 member states: Austria, Belgium, Bulgaria, Czech Republic, Denmark, Finland, France, Germany, Greece, Hungary, Italy, the Netherlands, Norway, Poland, Portugal, Slovak Republic, Spain, Sweden, Switzerland, United Kingdom. Some 6,500 scientists, half of the world's particle physicists, use CERN's facilities. They represent 500 institutions and 85 nationalities.

Address: CH-1211 Geneva 23, Switzerland.
Website: http://www.cern.ch
Director-General: Rolf-Dieter Heuer (Germany).

Central European Initiative (CEI)

In Nov. 1989 Austria, Hungary, Italy and Yugoslavia met on Italy's initiative to form an economic and political co-operation group in the region.

Members. Albania, Austria, Belarus, Bosnia and Herzegovina, Bulgaria, Croatia, Czech Republic, Hungary, Italy, Macedonia, Moldova, Montenegro, Poland, Romania, Serbia, Slovakia, Slovenia, Ukraine.

Address: Executive Secretariat, Via Genova 9, 34132 Trieste, Italy.
Website: http://www.ceinet.org
Email: cei-es@cei-es.org

Nordic Council

Founded in 1952 as a co-operative link between the parliaments and governments of the Nordic states. The co-operation focuses on Intra-Nordic co-operation, co-operation with Europe/EU/EEA and co-operation with the adjacent areas. The Council consists of 87 elected MPs and the committees meet several times a year, as required. Every year the Nordic Council grants prizes for literature, music, nature and environment.

Members. Denmark (including the Faroe Islands and Greenland), Finland (including Åland), Iceland, Norway, Sweden.

Address: Store Strandstræde 18, DK-1255 Copenhagen K, Denmark.
Website: http://www.norden.org
Email: nordisk-rad@norden.org
President: Helgi Hjörvar (Iceland).

Nordic Development Fund (NDF)

NDF is a multilateral development finance institution established by the five Nordic countries, Denmark, Finland, Iceland, Norway and Sweden. Since operations started in 1989, the Fund has provided soft loans to 190 projects of Nordic interest in developing countries. It entered a new phase in 2009 and changed its focus to grant aid for climate change related projects.

Address: Fabianinkatu 34, PO Box 185, FIN-00171 Helsinki, Finland.
Website: http://www.ndf.fi
Email: info.ndf@ndf.fi
Managing Director: Helge Semb (Norway).

Nordic Investment Bank (NIB)

The Nordic Investment Bank, which commenced operations in Aug. 1976, is a multilateral financial institution owned by Denmark, Estonia, Finland, Iceland, Latvia, Lithuania, Norway and Sweden. It finances public and private projects both within and outside the Nordic area. Priority is given to projects furthering economic co-operation between the member countries or improving the environment. Focal points include the neighbouring areas of the member countries.

Address: Fabianinkatu 34, PO Box 249, FI-00171 Helsinki, Finland.
Website: http://www.nib.int
Email: info@nib.int
President: Johnny Åkerholm (Finland).

Council of the Baltic Sea States

Established in 1992 in Copenhagen following a conference of ministers of foreign affairs.

Members. Denmark, Estonia, Finland, Germany, Iceland, Latvia, Lithuania, Norway, Poland, Russia, Sweden and the European Commission.

Aims. To promote co-operation in the Baltic Sea region in the field of trade, investment and economic exchanges, combating organized crime, civil security, culture and education, transport and communication, energy and environment, human rights and assistance to democratic institutions.

The Council meets at ministerial level once a year, chaired by rotating foreign ministers; it is the supreme decision-making body. Between annual sessions the Committee of Senior Officials and three working groups meet at regular intervals. In Oct. 1999 ministers of energy of the CBSS member states agreed to achieve the goal of creating effective, economically and environmentally sound and more integrated energy systems in the Baltic Sea region. Seven summits at the level of heads of government of CBSS member states and the President of the European Commission have taken place; in 1996, 1998, 2000, 2002, 2004, 2006 and 2008. The Baltic Sea Region Energy Cooperation (BASREC) is made up of energy ministers from the region and is chaired by the energy minister from the chair country of the CBSS.

Official language: English.
CBSS Secretariat: Strömsborg, PO Box 2010, S-103 11 Stockholm, Sweden.
Website: http://www.cbss.st
Director of the Secretariat: Vacant.

European Broadcasting Union (EBU)

Founded in 1950 by western European radio and television broadcasters, the EBU is the world's largest professional association of national broadcasters, with 75 active members in 56 countries of Europe, North Africa and the Middle East, and 43 associate members worldwide.

The EBU merged with the OIRT, its counterpart in eastern Europe, in 1993. The EBU's Eurovision Operations Department has a permanent network offering 50 digital channels on five satellites. Two satellite channels also relay radio concerts, operas, sports fixtures and major news events for Euroradio.

Headquarters: Ancienne Route 17, CH-1218 Grand-Saconnex, Geneva, Switzerland.
Website: http://www.ebu.ch
Email: ebu@ebu.ch
Director-General: Jean Réveillon (France).

Black Sea Economic Cooperation (BSEC)

Founded in 1992 to promote economic co-operation in the Black Sea region. Priority areas of interest include: trade and economic development; banking and finance; communications; energy; transport; agriculture and agro-industry; healthcare and pharmaceutics; environmental protection; tourism; science and technology; exchange of statistical data and economic information; combating organized crime, illicit trafficking of drugs, weapons and radioactive materials, all acts of terrorism and illegal immigration.

Members. Albania, Armenia, Azerbaijan, Bulgaria, Georgia, Greece, Moldova, Romania, Russia, Serbia, Turkey, Ukraine.

Observers. Austria, Belarus, Black Sea Commission, Commission of the European Communities, Croatia, Czech Republic, Egypt, Energy Charter Secretariat, France, Germany, International Black Sea Club, Israel, Italy, Poland, Slovakia, Tunisia, USA.

The *Parliamentary Assembly of the Black Sea Economic Cooperation* is the BSEC parliamentary dimension. The *BSEC Business Council* is composed of representatives from the business circles of the member states. The *Black Sea Trade and Development Bank* is considered as the financial pillar of the BSEC. There is also an *International Center for Black Sea Studies* and a *Coordination Center for the Exchange of Statistical Data and Economic Information.*

Headquarters: Sakıp Sabancı Caddesi, Müşir Fuad Paşa Yalısı, Eski Tersane 34460, İstanbul, Turkey.
Website: http://www.bsec-organization.org
Secretary-General: Leonidas Chrysanthopolous (Greece).

Danube Commission

History and Membership. The Danube Commission was constituted in 1949 according to the Convention regarding the regime of navigation on the Danube signed in Belgrade on 18 Aug. 1948. The Belgrade Convention, amended by the Additional Protocol of 26 March 1998, declares that navigation on the Danube from Kelheim to the Black Sea (with access to the sea through the Sulina arm and the Sulina Canal) is equally free and open to the nationals, merchant shipping and merchandise of all states as to harbour and navigation fees as well as conditions of merchant navigation. The Commission holds annual sessions and is composed of one representative from each of its 11 member countries: Austria, Bulgaria, Croatia, Germany, Hungary, Moldova, Romania, Russia, Serbia, Slovakia and Ukraine.

Functions. To ensure that the provisions of the Belgrade Convention are carried out; to establish a uniform buoying system on all navigable waterways; to establish the basic regulations for navigation on the river and ensure facilities for shipping; to co-ordinate the regulations for river, customs and sanitation control as well as the hydrometeorological service; to collect relevant statistical data concerning navigation on the Danube; to propose measures for the prevention of pollution of the Danube caused by navigation; and to update its recommendations regularly with a view to bringing them in line with European Union regulations on inland waterway navigation.

Official languages: German, French, Russian.
Headquarters: Benczúr utca 25, H-1068 Budapest, Hungary.
Website: http://www.danubecommission.org
Email: secretariat@danubecom-intern.org
President: Aleksandr Tolkach (Russia).
Director-General: István Valkár (Hungary).

European Trade Union Confederation (ETUC)

Established in 1973, the ETUC is recognized by the EU, the Council of Europe and EFTA as the only representative cross-sectoral trade union organization at a European level. It has grown steadily with a membership of 82 National Trade Union Confederations from 36 countries and 12 European Industry Federations with a total of 60m. members. The Congress meets every four years; the 11th Statutory Congress took place in Seville in May 2007.

Address: 5 Boulevard Roi Albert II, B-1210 Brussels, Belgium.
Website: http://www.etuc.org
Email: etuc@etuc.org
General Secretary: John Monks (UK).

Amnesty International (AI)

Origin. Founded in 1961 by British lawyer Peter Benenson as a one-year campaign for the release of prisoners of conscience, Amnesty International has grown to become a worldwide organization, winning the Nobel Peace Prize in 1977.

Activities. AI is a worldwide movement of people campaigning for human rights. It acts independently and impartially to promote respect for internationally recognized human rights standards.

Historically, the focus of AI's campaigning has been: to free all prisoners of conscience (a term coined by Peter Benenson); to ensure a prompt and fair trial for all political prisoners; to abolish the death penalty, torture and other cruel, inhuman or degrading punishments; to end extrajudicial executions and 'disappearances'; to fight impunity by working to ensure perpetrators of such abuses are brought to justice. AI is independent of any government or political ideology, and neither supports nor opposes the views of the victim it seeks to protect.

AI has over 2·8m. members, subscribers and regular donors in more than 150 countries. Major policy decisions are taken by an International Council comprising representatives from all national sections. AI's national sections, members and supporters are primarily responsible for funding the movement. During the financial year 1 April 2007–31 March 2008 AI's total income was £35,224,000.

Every year AI produces a global report detailing human rights violations in all regions of the world.

International Secretariat: Peter Benenson House, 1 Easton Street, London WC1X 0DW, UK.
Website: http://www.amnesty.org
Secretary-General (acting): Claudio Cordone (Italy).

Bank for International Settlements (BIS)

Origin. Founded on 17 May 1930, the Bank for International Settlements fosters international monetary and financial co-operation and serves as a bank for central banks.

Aims. The BIS fulfils its mandate by acting as: a forum to promote discussion and facilitate decision-making processes among central banks and within the international financial community; a centre for economic and monetary research; a prime counterparty for central banks in their financial transactions; and an agent or trustee in connection with international financial operations.

Finance. As of 31 March 2007 some 130 central banks and other official monetary authorities, as well as a number of international institutions, made active use of BIS financial services. Total currency deposits amounted to SDR 222bn., representing around 6% of world foreign exchange reserves.

Organization and Membership. There are 55 member central banks. These are the central banks or monetary authorities of Algeria, Argentina, Australia, Austria, Belgium, Bosnia and Herzegovina, Brazil, Bulgaria, Canada, Chile, China, Croatia, the Czech Republic, Denmark, Estonia, Finland, France, Germany, Greece, Hong Kong, Hungary, Iceland, India, Indonesia, Ireland, Israel, Italy, Japan, South Korea, Latvia, Lithuania, Macedonia, Malaysia, Mexico, the Netherlands, New Zealand, Norway, Philippines, Poland, Portugal, Romania, Russia, Saudi Arabia,

Singapore, Slovakia, Slovenia, South Africa, Spain, Sweden, Switzerland, Thailand, Turkey, UK and USA, as well as the European Central Bank.

The BIS is administered by a Board of Directors, which is comprised of the governors of the central banks of Belgium, France, Germany, Italy and the UK and the Chairman of the Board of Governors of the US Federal Reserve System as *ex officio* members, each of whom appoints another member of the same nationality. The Statutes also provide for the election to the Board of not more than nine Governors of other member central banks. The Governors of the central banks of Canada, China, Japan, Mexico, the Netherlands, Sweden, Switzerland and the President of the European Central Bank are currently elected members of the Board.

Headquarters: Centralbahnplatz 2, CH-Basle, Switzerland.
Website: http://www.bis.org
Email: email@bis.org
Chairman of the Board of Directors: Guillermo Ortiz (Mexico).
Representative Office for Asia and the Pacific: 78th Floor, Two International Finance Centre, 8 Finance Street, Central, Hong Kong SAR, People's Republic of China.
Representative Office for the Americas: Torre Chapultepec, Rubén Dario 281, Col. Bosque de Chapultepec, 11580 México, D. F., Mexico.

Further Reading

Deane, M. and Pringle, R., *The Central Banks.* 1995
Goodhart, C. A. E., *The Central Bank and the Financial System.* 1995
Who's Who in Central Banking. 2002

Commonwealth

The Commonwealth is a free association of sovereign independent states. It numbered 54 members in Feb. 2010. With a membership of over 2bn. people, it represents around 30% of the world's population. There is no charter, treaty or constitution; the association is expressed in co-operation, consultation and mutual assistance for which the Commonwealth Secretariat is the central co-ordinating body.

Origin. The Commonwealth was first defined by the Imperial Conference of 1926 as a group of 'autonomous Communities within the British Empire, equal in status, in no way subordinate one to another in any aspect of their domestic or external affairs, though united by a common allegiance to the Crown, and freely associated as members of the British Commonwealth of Nations'. The basis of the association changed from one owing allegiance to a common Crown, and the modern Commonwealth was born in 1949 when the member countries accepted India's intention of becoming a republic at the same time as continuing 'her full membership of the Commonwealth of Nations and her acceptance of the King as the symbol of the free association of its independent member nations and as such the Head of the Commonwealth'. In Feb. 2010 the Commonwealth consisted of 33 republics and 21 monarchies, of which 16 are Queen's realms. All acknowledge the Queen symbolically as Head of the Commonwealth. The Queen's legal title rests on the statute of 12 and 13 Will. III, c. 3, by which the succession to the Crown of Great Britain and Ireland was settled on the Princess Sophia of Hanover and the 'heirs of her body being Protestants'.

A number of territories, formerly under British jurisdiction or mandate, did not join the Commonwealth: Egypt, Iraq, Transjordan, Burma (now Myanmar), Palestine, Sudan, British Somaliland and Aden. Five countries, Ireland in 1948, South Africa in 1961, Pakistan in 1972, Fiji (now Fiji Islands) in 1987 and Zimbabwe in 2003 have left the Commonwealth. Pakistan was readmitted to the Commonwealth in 1989, South Africa in 1994, Fiji Islands in 1997. Nigeria was fully suspended in 1995 for violation of human rights but was fully reinstated on 29 May 1999. Pakistan was suspended from the Commonwealth's councils following a coup in Oct. 1999 but was readmitted in May 2004. It was again suspended in Nov. 2007 after President Musharraf declared emergency rule but was readmitted in May 2008. The Fiji Islands were suspended from the Commonwealth's councils in June 2000 following a coup there but were readmitted in Dec. 2001 following the restoration of democracy. They were again suspended from the councils following the coup of Dec. 2006 and fully suspended from membership in Sept. 2009. Zimbabwe was suspended from the Commonwealth's councils for a year on 19 March 2002 for a 'high level of politically motivated violence' during the vote that saw President Robert Mugabe re-elected. In March 2003 it was suspended for a further nine months. The suspension was extended at the Abuja meeting in Dec. 2003. Mugabe responded by withdrawing Zimbabwe from the Commonwealth. Mozambique, admitted in Nov. 1995, was the first member state not to have been a member of the former British Commonwealth or Empire.

Member States of the Commonwealth

The 54 member states, with year of admission:

	Year of admission		*Year of admission*
Antigua and Barbuda	1981	Namibia	1990
Australia[1]	1931	Nauru[2]	1968
Bahamas	1973	New Zealand[1]	1931
Bangladesh	1972	Nigeria[3]	1960
Barbados	1966	Pakistan[4]	1989
Belize	1981	Papua New Guinea	1975
Botswana	1966	Rwanda	2009
Brunei[5]	1984	St Kitts and Nevis	1983
Cameroon	1995	St Lucia	1979
Canada[1]	1931	St Vincent and	
Cyprus	1961	Grenadines	1979
Dominica	1978	Samoa	1970
Fiji Islands[6]	1997	Seychelles	1976
Gambia	1965	Sierra Leone	1961
Ghana	1957	Singapore	1965
Grenada	1974	Solomon Islands	1978
Guyana	1966	South Africa[7]	1994
India	1947	Sri Lanka	1948
Jamaica	1962	Swaziland	1968
Kenya	1963	Tanzania	1961
Kiribati	1979	Tonga[5]	1970
Lesotho	1966	Trinidad and Tobago	1962
Malaŵi	1964	Tuvalu	1978
Malaysia	1957	Uganda	1982
Maldives	1982	United Kingdom	1931
Malta	1964	Vanuatu	1980
Mauritius	1968	Zambia	1964
Mozambique	1995		

[1]Independence given legal effect by the Statute of Westminster 1931.
[2]Nauru joined as a special member on independence in 1968. It became a full member in 1999 but its status was changed back to that of a special member in 2006.
[3]Nigeria was suspended in 1995 but readmitted as a full member in 1999.
[4]Left 1972, rejoined 1989.
[5]Brunei and Tonga had been sovereign states in treaty relationship with Britain.
[6]Fiji left in 1987 but rejoined in 1997. It changed its name to Fiji Islands in 1998. The Fiji Islands were suspended in Sept. 2009 although technically they remain a member.
[7]Left 1961, rejoined 1994.

Aims and Conditions of Membership. Membership involves acceptance of certain core principles, as set out in the Harare

Declaration of 1991, and is subject to the approval of other member states. The Harare Declaration charted a course to take the Commonwealth into the 21st century affirming members' continued commitment to the Singapore Declaration of 1971, by which members committed themselves to the pursuit of world peace and support of the UN.

The core principles defined by the Harare Declaration are: political democracy, human rights, good governance and the rule of law, and the protection of the environment through sustainable development. Commitment to these principles was made binding as a condition of membership at the 1993 Heads of Government meeting in Cyprus.

The Millbrook Action Programme of 1995 aims to support countries in implementing the Harare Declaration, providing assistance in constitutional and judicial matters, running elections, training and technical advice. Violations of the Harare Declaration will provoke a series of measures by the Commonwealth Secretariat, including: expression of disapproval, encouragement of bilateral actions by member states, appointment of fact-finders and mediators, stipulation of a period for the restoration of democracy, exclusion from ministerial meetings, suspension of all participation and aid and finally punitive measures including trade sanctions. A nine-member *Commonwealth Ministerial Action Group on the Harare Declaration (CMAG)* may be convened by the Secretary-General as and when necessary to deal with violations. The Group held its first meeting in Dec. 1995. Its terms of reference are as set out in the Millbrook Action Programme.

The *Commonwealth Parliamentary Association* was founded in 1911. As defined by its constitution, its objectives are to 'promote knowledge of the constitutional, legislative, economic, social and cultural aspects of parliamentary democracy'. It meets these objectives by organizing conferences, meetings and seminars for members, arranging exchange visits between members, publishing books, newsletters, reports, studies and a quarterly journal and providing an information service. Its principal governing body is the General Assembly, which meets annually during the Commonwealth Parliamentary Conference and is composed of members attending that Conference as delegates. The Association elects an Executive Committee comprising a Chair, President, Vice-President, Treasurer and 27 regional representatives, which meets twice a year. The Chair is elected for three-year terms.

Commonwealth Secretariat. The Commonwealth Secretariat is an international body at the service of all 54 member countries. It provides the central organization for joint consultation and co-operation in many fields. It was established in 1965 by Commonwealth Heads of Government as a 'visible symbol of the spirit of co-operation which animates the Commonwealth', and has observer status at the UN General Assembly.

The Secretariat disseminates information on matters of common concern, organizes and services meetings and conferences, co-ordinates many Commonwealth activities, and provides expert technical assistance for economic and social development through the multilateral Commonwealth Fund for Technical Co-operation. The Secretariat is organized in divisions and sections which correspond to its main areas of operation: political affairs, economic affairs, human rights, gender affairs, youth affairs, education, information, law, health and a range of technical assistance and advisory services. Within this structure the Secretariat organizes the biennial meetings of Commonwealth Heads of Government (CHOGMs), annual meetings of Finance Ministers of member countries, and regular meetings of Ministers of Education, Law, Health, Gender Affairs and others as appropriate. To emphasize the multilateral nature of the association, meetings are held in different cities and regions within the Commonwealth. Heads of Government decided that the Secretariat should work from London as it has the widest range of communications of any Commonwealth city, as well as the largest assembly of diplomatic missions from Commonwealth member countries.

Commonwealth Heads of Government Meetings (CHOGMs). Outside the UN, the CHOGM remains the largest inter-governmental conference in the world. Meetings are held every two years. The 2002 CHOGM in Coolum, Australia, scheduled for Oct. 2001 but postponed following the attacks on the United States of 11 Sept. 2001, was dominated by the Zimbabwe issue, as was the meeting held in Abuja, Nigeria in Dec. 2003. The last meeting was held in Nov. 2007 in Uganda. The next CHOGM is scheduled to be held in Australia in Nov. 2011. A host of Commonwealth organizations and agencies are dedicated to enhancing inter-Commonwealth relations and the development of the potential of Commonwealth citizens. They are listed in the Commonwealth Yearbook which is published by the Secretariat.

Commonwealth Day is celebrated on the second Monday in March each year. The theme for 2010 was 'Science, Technology and Society'.

Overseas Territories and Associated States. There are 14 United Kingdom overseas territories (see pages 1329–44), six Australian external territories (see pages 147–50), two New Zealand dependent territories and two New Zealand associated states (see pages 932–5). A dependent territory is a territory belonging by settlement, conquest or annexation to the British, Australian or New Zealand Crown.

United Kingdom Overseas Territories administered through the Foreign and Commonwealth Office comprise, in the Indian Ocean: British Indian Ocean Territory; in the Mediterranean: Gibraltar, the Sovereign Base Areas of Akrotiri and Dhekelia in Cyprus; in the Atlantic Ocean: Bermuda, Falkland Islands, South Georgia and South Sandwich Islands, British Antarctic Territory, St Helena and Dependencies (Ascension and Tristan da Cunha); in the Caribbean: Montserrat, British Virgin Islands, Cayman Islands, Turks and Caicos Islands, Anguilla; in the Western Pacific: Pitcairn Group of Islands.

The Australian external territories are: Ashmore and Cartier Islands, Australian Antarctic Territory, Christmas Island, Cocos (Keeling) Islands, Coral Sea Islands, Heard and McDonald Islands and Norfolk Island. The New Zealand external territories are: Tokelau Islands and the Ross Dependency. The New Zealand associated states are: Cook Islands and Niue.

Headquarters: Marlborough House, Pall Mall, London SW1Y 5HX, UK.
Website: http://www.thecommonwealth.org
Secretary-General: Kamalesh Sharma (India).

Selected publications. Commonwealth Yearbook; Commonwealth Today (biannual); *The Commonwealth at the Summit: Communiqués of Commonwealth Heads of Government Meetings.*

Further Reading

The Cambridge History of the British Empire. 8 vols. 1929 ff.
Chan, S., *Twelve Years of Commonwealth Diplomatic History: Summit Meetings, 1979–1991.* 1992
Judd, D. and Slinn, P., *The Evolution of the Modern Commonwealth.* 1982
Keeton, G. W. (ed.) *The British Commonwealth: Its Laws and Constitutions.* 9 vols. 1951 ff.
Madden, F. and Fieldhouse, D., (eds.) *Selected Documents on the Constitutional History of the British Empire and Commonwealth.* 1994
Mansergh, N., *The Commonwealth Experience.* 1982
McIntyre, W. D., *The Significance of the Commonwealth, 1965–90.* 1991
Moore, R. J., *Making the New Commonwealth.* 1987

Commonwealth of Independent States (CIS)

The Commonwealth of Independent States, founded on 8 Dec. 1991 in Viskuli, a government villa in Belarus, is a community of independent states which proclaimed itself the successor to the Union of Soviet Socialist Republics in some aspects of international law and affairs. The member states are the founders, Russia, Belarus and Ukraine, and seven subsequent adherents: Armenia, Azerbaijan, Kazakhstan, Kyrgyzstan, Moldova, Tajikistan and Uzbekistan. Turkmenistan withdrew its permanent member status on 26 Aug. 2005 and became an associate member. Georgia withdrew on 18 Aug. 2008, with effect from 17 Aug. 2009.

History. Extended negotiations in the Union of Soviet Socialist Republics (USSR) in 1990 and 1991 sought to establish a 'renewed federation' or, subsequently, to conclude a new union treaty that would embrace all the 15 constituent republics of the USSR at that date. In Sept. 1991 the three Baltic republics—Estonia, Latvia and Lithuania—were recognized as independent states by the USSR State Council, and subsequently by the international community. Most of the remaining republics reached agreement on the broad outlines of a new 'union of sovereign states' in Nov. 1991, which would have retained a directly elected President and an all-union legislature, but which would have limited central authority to those powers specifically delegated to it by the members of the union.

A referendum in Ukraine in Dec. 1991, however, showed overwhelming support for full independence, and following this Russia, Belarus and Ukraine concluded the Minsk Agreement on 8 Dec. 1991, establishing a Commonwealth of Independent States (CIS), headquartered in Minsk. Each of the three republics individually renounced the 1922 treaty through which the USSR had been established.

In Dec. 1991 a further declaration was signed with eight other republics: Armenia, Azerbaijan, Kazakhstan, Kyrgyzstan, Moldova, Tajikistan, Turkmenistan and Uzbekistan. The declaration committed signatories to recognize the independence and sovereignty of other members, to respect human rights including those of national minorities, and to the observance of existing boundaries. Relations among the members of the CIS were to be conducted on an equal, multilateral, interstate basis, but it was agreed to endorse the principle of unitary control of strategic nuclear arms and the concept of a 'single economic space'. In a separate agreement the heads of member states agreed that Russia should take up the seat at the United Nations formerly occupied by the USSR, and a framework of interstate and intergovernment consultation was established. On 26 Dec. the USSR Supreme Soviet voted a formal end to the 1922 Treaty of Union, and dissolved itself. Georgia decided to join on 9 Dec. 1993 and on 1 March 1994 the national parliament ratified the act.

The Charter, adopted on 22 Jan. 1993 in Minsk, proclaims that the Commonwealth is based on the principles of the sovereign equality of all members. It is not a state and does not have supranational authority.

Activities and Institutions. The principal organs of the CIS, according to the agreement concluded in Alma-Ata on 21 Dec. 1991, are the *Council of Heads of States*, which meets twice a year, and the *Council of Heads of Government*, which meets every three months. Both councils may convene extraordinary sessions, and may hold joint sittings. There is also a *Council of Defence Ministers*, established in Feb. 1992, and a *Council of Foreign Ministers* (Dec. 1993). The Secretariat is the standing working organ.

At a summit meeting of heads of states (with the exception of Azerbaijan) in July 1992, agreements were reached on a way to divide former USSR assets abroad; on the legal cessionary of state archives of former Soviet states; on the status of an Economic Court; and on collective security. In 1992 an *Inter-Parliamentary Assembly* was established by seven member states (Armenia, Belarus, Kazakhstan, Kyrgyzstan, Russia, Tajikistan and Uzbekistan).

At a subsequent meeting in Jan. 1993 Armenia, Belarus, Kazakhstan, Kyrgyzstan, Russia, Tajikistan and Uzbekistan agreed on a charter to implement co-operation in political, economic, ecological, humanitarian, cultural and other spheres; thorough and balanced economic and social development within the common economic space; interstate co-operation and integration; and to ensure human rights and freedoms. Heads of State established an *Inter-State Bank* and adopted a Provision on it. Its charter was signed by ten Heads of State (Armenia, Belarus, Kazakhstan, Kyrgyzstan, Moldova, Russia, Tajikistan, Turkmenistan, Ukraine, Uzbekistan) on 22 Dec. 1993.

In accordance with the Agreement on Armed Forces and Border Troops, concluded on 30 Dec. 1991, it was decided to consider and solve the issue on the transference of the management of the General-Purpose Armed Forces in accordance with the national legislation of member states. On 14 Feb. 1992 the *Council of Defence Ministers* was established. In 1993 the Office of Commander-in- Chief of CIS Joint Armed Forces was reorganized in a Staff for Coordinating Military Co-operation. Its Chief of Staff is appointed by the Council of Heads of State.

On 24 Sept. 1993 Armenia, Azerbaijan, Belarus, Kazakhstan, Kyrgyzstan, Moldova, Russia, Tajikistan and Uzbekistan signed an agreement to form an *Economic Union*. Georgia and Turkmenistan signed later (14 and 23 Jan. 1994). Ukraine became an associated member on 15 April 1994. In Oct. 1994 a summit meeting established the *Inter-State Economic Committee (MEK)* to be based in Moscow. Members include all CIS states except Turkmenistan. The Committee's decisions are binding if voted by 80% of the membership. Russia commands 50% of the voting power; Ukraine 14%. The Committee's remit is to co-ordinate energy, transport and communications policies. A *Customs Union* to regulate payments between member states with nonconvertible independent currencies and a regulatory *Economic Court* have also been established.

On 29 March 1996 Belarus, Kazakhstan, Kyrgyzstan and Russia signed an agreement increasing their mutual economic and social integration by creating a *Community of Integrated States* (Tajikistan signed in 1998). The agreement established a Supreme Inter-Governmental Council comprising heads of state and government and foreign ministers, with, an integration committee of Ministers and an Inter-Parliamentary Committee. On 2 April 1996 the Presidents of Belarus and Russia signed a treaty providing for political, economic and military integration, creating the nucleus of a *Community of Russia and Belarus*. A further treaty was signed on 22 May 1997, instituting common citizenship, common deployment of military forces and the harmonization of the two economies with a view to the creation of a common currency. The Community was later renamed the *Union of Belarus and Russia* and signed subsequent agreements on equal rights for its citizens and equal conditions for state and private entrepreneurship. In March 1994 the CIS was accorded observer status in the UN.

Headquarters: 220000 Minsk, Kirova 17, Belarus.
Website: http://www.cis.minsk.by
Executive Secretary: Sergei Lebedev (Russia).

Further Reading

Brzezinski, Z. and Sullivan, P. (eds.) *Russia and the Commonwealth of Independent States: Documents, Data and Analysis.* 1996

International Air Transport Association (IATA)

Founded in 1945 for inter-airline co-operation in promoting safe, reliable, secure and economical air services, IATA has approximately 230 members from 115 nations worldwide. IATA is the successor to the International Air Traffic Association, founded in The Hague in 1919, the year of the world's first international scheduled services.

Main offices: IATA Centre, Route de l'Aéroport 33, PO Box 416, CH-1215 Geneva, Switzerland. 800 Place Victoria, PO Box 113, Montreal, Quebec, Canada H4Z 1M1. 111 Somerset Road, #14-05 Somerset Wing, Singapore 238164.
Website: http://www.iata.org
Director-General: Giovanni Bisignani (Italy).

International Committee of the Red Cross (ICRC)

The International Committee of the Red Cross (ICRC) is an impartial, neutral and independent organization whose exclusively humanitarian mission is to protect the lives and dignity of victims of armed conflict and other situations of violence and to provide them with assistance.

Established in 1863, the ICRC is at the origin of the International Red Cross and Red Crescent Movement and of international humanitarian law, notably the Geneva Conventions. As the promoter and guardian of international humanitarian law, the ICRC must encourage respect for the law. It does so by spreading knowledge of the humanitarian rules and by reminding parties to conflicts of their obligations.

The ICRC has a permanent mandate under international law to take impartial action for prisoners, the wounded and sick, and civilians affected by conflict.

With its HQ in Geneva, Switzerland, the ICRC is based in around 80 countries and has a total of more than 12,000 staff.

In situations of conflict the ICRC co-ordinates the response by national Red Cross and Red Crescent societies and the International Federation of Red Cross and Red Crescent Societies. It acts in consultation with all other organizations involved in humanitarian work.

The ICRC relies for its financing on voluntary contributions from States signatories to the Geneva Conventions, organizations such as the European Union, and public and private sources.

In 2007 ICRC delegates visited more than 510,000 people deprived of their freedom in some 80 countries. ICRC water, sanitation and construction projects catered for the needs of around 14m. people. The ICRC supported hospitals and health care facilities serving some 2·9m. people. It also provided essential household goods to more than 3·9m. people, food aid to 2·5m. people and assistance to another 2·7m. people in the form of sustainable food production and micro-economic initiatives.

Headquarters: 19 Avenue de la Paix, 1202 Geneva, Switzerland.
Website: http://www.icrc.org
President: Jakob Kellenberger (Switzerland).

Further Reading

Moorehead, Caroline, *Dunant's Dream: War, Switzerland and the History of the Red Cross.* 1998

International Criminal Court (ICC)

Origin. As far back as 1946 an international congress called for the adoption of an international criminal code prohibiting crimes against humanity and the prompt establishment of an international criminal court, but for more than 40 years little progress was made. In 1989 the end of the Cold War brought a dramatic increase in the number of UN peacekeeping operations and a world where the idea of establishing an International Criminal Court became more viable. The United Nations Conference of Plenipotentiaries on the Establishment of an International Criminal Court took place from 15 June–17 July 1998 in Rome, Italy.

Aims and Activities. The International Criminal Court is a permanent court for trying individuals who have been accused of committing genocide, war crimes and crimes against humanity, and is thus a successor to the *ad hoc* tribunals set up by the UN Security Council to try those responsible for atrocities in the former Yugoslavia and Rwanda. Ratification by 60 countries was required to bring the statute into effect. The court began operations on 1 July 2002 with 139 signatories and after ratification by 76 countries. By Feb. 2010 the number of ratifications had increased to 110. Its first trial, with Thomas Lubanga facing war crimes charges for his role in the Democratic Republic of the Congo's civil war, opened on 26 Jan. 2009.

Judges. The International Criminal Court's first 18 judges were elected in Feb. 2003, with six serving for three years, six for six years and six for nine years. Every three years six new judges will be elected. At present the 18 judges, with the year in which their term of office is scheduled to end, are: Joyce Aluoch (Kenya, 2018); Bruno Cotte (France, 2012); Fatoumata Dembele Diarra (Mali, 2012); Silvia Fernández de Gurmendi (Argentina, 2018); Sir Adrian Fulford (United Kingdom, 2012); Hans-Peter Kaul (Germany, 2015); Erkki Kourula (Finland, 2015); Akua Kuenyehia (Ghana, 2015); Sanji Mmasenono Monageng (Botswana, 2018); Daniel David Ntanda Nsereko (Uganda, 2012); Elizabeth Odio Benito (Costa Rica, 2012); Kuniko Ozaki (Japan, 2018); Song Sang-hyun (South Korea, 2015); Sylvia Helena de Figueiredo Steiner (Brazil, 2012); Cuno Tarfusser (Italy, 2018); Ekaterina Trendafilova (Bulgaria, 2015); Anita Ušacka (Latvia, 2015); Christine Van Den Wyngaert (Belgium, 2018). René Blattmann (Bolivia), whose term ended in March 2009, will continue to serve for the duration of the Lubanga trial (*see* above).

Prosecutor. Luis Moreno-Ocampo (Argentina) was elected the first prosecutor of the Court on 21 April 2003.

Headquarters: Maanweg 174, 2516 AB The Hague, Netherlands.
Website: http://www.icc-cpi.int
President: Song Sang-hyun (South Korea).

Further Reading

Macedo, Stephen, (ed.) *Universal Jurisdiction: National Courts and the Prosecution of Serious Crimes Under International Law.* 2003
Reydams, Luc, *Universal Jurisdiction: International and Municipal Perspectives.* 2003
Struett, Michael J., *The Politics of Constructing the International Criminal Court: NGOs, Discourse, and Agency.* 2008

International Institute for Democracy and Electoral Assistance (IDEA)

Created in 1995, International IDEA is an intergovernmental organization that supports sustainable democratic change through providing comparative knowledge, assisting in democratic reform, and influencing policies and politics. International IDEA focuses on the ability of democratic institutions to deliver a political system marked by public participation and inclusion, representative and accountable government, responsiveness to citizens' needs and aspirations, and the rule of law and equal rights for all citizens.

Aims and Activities. International IDEA undertakes work through three activity areas: providing comparative knowledge derived from practical experience on democracy-building processes—elections and referendums, constitutions, political parties, women's political empowerment and democracy self-assessments—from diverse contexts around the world; assisting political actors in reforming democratic institutions and processes, and engaging in political processes when invited to do so; influencing democracy-building policies and assistance to political actors.

Membership. The International IDEA had 25 full member states and one observer state in Feb. 2010.

Organization. IDEA has regional operations in Latin America, Africa, the Middle East, Asia and the Pacific, and has a staff of over 70 worldwide.

Headquarters: Strömsborg, 103 34 Stockholm, Sweden.
Website: http://www.idea.int
Secretary-General: Vidar Helgesen (Norway).

International Mobile Satellite Organization (IMSO)

Founded in 1979 as the International Maritime Satellite Organization (Inmarsat) to establish a satellite system to improve maritime communications for distress and safety and commercial applications. Its competence was subsequently expanded to include aeronautical and land mobile communications. Privatization, which was completed in April 1999, transferred the business to a newly created company and the Organization remains as a regulator to ensure that the company fulfils its public services obligations. The company has taken the Inmarsat name and the Organization uses the acronym IMSO. In Feb. 2010 the Organization had 94 member parties.

Organization. The Assembly of all Parties to the Convention meets every two years.

Headquarters: 99 City Road, London EC1Y 1AX, UK.
IMSO Website: http://www.imso.org
Email: info@imso.org
Inmarsat Website: http://www.inmarsat.com
Director of the Secretariat, IMSO: Esteban Pachá Vicente (Spain).
Chief Executive, Inmarsat Ltd: Andrew Sukawaty (USA).

International Olympic Committee (IOC)

Founded in 1894 by French educator Baron Pierre de Coubertin, the International Olympic Committee is an international non-governmental, non-profit organization whose members act as the IOC's representatives in their respective countries, not as delegates of their countries within the IOC. The Committee's main responsibility is to supervise the organization of the summer and winter Olympic Games. It owns all rights to the Olympic symbols, flag, motto, anthem and Olympic Games.

Aims. 'To contribute to building a peaceful and better world by educating youth through sport, practised without discrimination of any kind and in the Olympic Spirit, which requires mutual understanding with a spirit of friendship, solidarity and fair play.'

Finances. The IOC receives no public funding. Its only source of funding is from private sectors, with the substantial part of these revenues coming from television broadcasters and sponsors.

Address: Château de Vidy, Case Postale 356, CH–1007 Lausanne, Switzerland.
Website: http://www.olympic.org
President: Jacques Rogge (Belgium).

International Organization for Migration (IOM)

Established in 1951, the International Organization for Migration (IOM) is dedicated to promoting humane and orderly migration. It does so by providing services and advice to governments and migrants.

Members (127 as of Feb. 2010). Afghanistan, Albania, Algeria, Angola, Argentina, Armenia, Australia, Austria, Azerbaijan, Bahamas, Bangladesh, Belarus, Belgium, Belize, Benin, Bolivia, Bosnia and Herzegovina, Brazil, Bulgaria, Burkina Faso, Burundi, Cambodia, Cameroon, Canada, Cape Verde, Chile, Colombia, Democratic Republic of the Congo, Republic of the Congo, Costa Rica, Côte d'Ivoire, Croatia, Cyprus, Czech Republic, Denmark, Dominican Republic, Ecuador, Egypt, El Salvador, Estonia, Finland, France, Gabon, Gambia, Georgia, Germany, Ghana, Greece, Guatemala, Guinea, Guinea-Bissau, Haiti, Honduras, Hungary, India, Iran, Ireland, Israel, Italy, Jamaica, Japan, Jordan, Kazakhstan, Kenya, South Korea, Kyrgyzstan, Latvia, Liberia, Libya, Lithuania, Luxembourg, Madagascar, Mali, Malta, Mauritania, Mauritius, Mexico, Moldova, Mongolia, Montenegro, Morocco, Namibia, Nepal, Netherlands, New Zealand, Nicaragua, Niger, Nigeria, Norway, Pakistan, Panama, Paraguay, Peru, Philippines, Poland, Portugal, Romania, Rwanda, Senegal, Serbia, Sierra Leone, Slovakia, Slovenia, Somalia, South Africa, Spain, Sri Lanka, Sudan, Sweden, Switzerland, Tajikistan, United Republic of Tanzania, Thailand, Togo, Trinidad and Tobago, Tunisia, Turkey, Uganda, Ukraine, UK, USA, Uruguay, Venezuela, Vietnam, Yemen, Zambia and Zimbabwe. 17 countries and a large number of government agencies and NGOs have observer status.

Activities. IOM assists refugee populations during and after emergencies and facilitates their resettlement. IOM also helps find solutions for internally displaced persons (IDPs), former combatants, victims of ethnic engineering, and populations in transition or recovery environments. IOM activities that cut across these areas include the promotion of international migration law, the protection of migrants' rights, policy debate and guidance, migration health and the gender dimension of migration. Since 1952 IOM has directly assisted some 13m. migrants. In 2005 IOM launched its largest ever emergency response following the Indian Ocean tsunami in Dec. 2004. IOM's programme budget for 2008 exceeded US$1bn., funding over 2,030 active programmes and more than 6,690 staff members serving in over 440 field offices in more than 100 countries.

Official languages: English, French, Spanish.
Headquarters: Route des Morillons 17, POB 71, 1211 Geneva 19, Switzerland.
Website: http://www.iom.int
Director-General: William Lacy Swing (USA).

International Organization for Standardization (ISO)

Established in 1947, the International Organization for Standardization is a non-governmental federation of national standards bodies from 157 countries worldwide, one from each country. ISO's work results in international agreements which are published as International Standards. The first ISO standard was published in 1951 with the title 'Standard reference temperature for industrial length measurement'.

Some 15,400 ISO International Standards are available on subjects in such diverse fields as information technology, textiles, packaging, distribution of goods, energy production and utilization, building, banking and financial services. ISO standardization activities include the widely recognized ISO 9000 family of quality management system and standards and the ISO 14000 series of environmental management system standards. Standardization programmes are now being developed in completely new fields, such as food safety, security, social responsibility and the service sector.

Mission. To promote the development of standardization and related activities in the world with a view to facilitating the international exchange of goods and services, and to developing co-operation in the spheres of intellectual, scientific, technological and economic activity.

Headquarters: 1 chemin de la Voie-Creuse, Case postale 56, CH-1211 Geneva 20, Switzerland.
Website: http://www.iso.org
Secretary-General: Rob Steele (New Zealand).

International Organization of the Francophonie

The International Organization of the Francophonie represents 70 countries and provinces/regions (including 14 with observer status) using French as an official language. Objectives include the promotion of peace, democracy, and economic and social development, through political and technical co-operation. The Secretary-General is based in Paris.

Members. Albania, Andorra, Belgium, Benin, Bulgaria, Burkina Faso, Burundi, Cambodia, Cameroon, Canada, Canada–New Brunswick, Canada–Quebec, Cape Verde, Central African Republic, Chad, Comoros, Democratic Republic of the Congo, Republic of the Congo, Côte d'Ivoire, Djibouti, Dominica, Egypt, Equatorial Guinea, France, French Community of Belgium, Gabon, Greece, Guinea, Guinea-Bissau, Haiti, Laos, Lebanon, Luxembourg, Macedonia, Madagascar, Mali, Mauritania, Mauritius, Moldova, Monaco, Morocco, Niger, Romania, Rwanda, St Lucia, São Tomé e Príncipe, Senegal, Seychelles, Switzerland, Togo, Tunisia, Vanuatu, Vietnam. *Associate Members.* Armenia, Cyprus, Ghana. *Observers.* Austria, Croatia, Czech Republic, Georgia, Hungary, Latvia, Lithuania, Mozambique, Poland, Serbia, Slovakia, Slovenia, Thailand, Ukraine.

Headquarters: 28 rue de Bourgogne, 75007 Paris, France.
Website: http://www.francophonie.org (limited English)
Secretary-General: Abdou Diouf (Senegal).

International Road Federation (IRF)

The IRF is a non-profit, non-political service organization whose purpose is to encourage better road and transportation systems worldwide and to help apply technology and management practices to give maximum economic and social returns from national road investments.

Founded following the Second World War, over the years the IRF has led major global road infrastructure developments, including achieving 1,000 km of new roads in Mexico in the 1950s, and promoting the Pan-American Highway linking North and South America. It publishes *World Road Statistics*, as well as road research studies, including a 140-country inventory of road and transport research in co-operation with the US Bureau of Public Roads.

Headquarters: 2 chemin de Blandonnet, CH-1214 Vernier/GE, Switzerland.
Website: http://www.irfnet.org
Director-General (Brussels): Christophe Nicodème (Belgium).
Director-General (Geneva): Sibylle Rupprecht (Switzerland).
Director-General (Washington, D.C.): C. Patrick Sankey (USA).

International Seabed Authority (ISA)

The ISA is an autonomous international organization established under the UN Convention on the Law of the Sea (UNCLOS) of 1982 and the 1994 Agreement relating to the implementation of Part XI of the UNCLOS. It came into existence on 16 Nov. 1994 and became fully operational in June 1996.

The administrative expenses are met from assessed contributions from its members. Membership numbered 160 in Feb. 2010; the budget for the biennium 2007–08 was US$11,782,400.

The UNCLOS covers almost all ocean space and its uses: navigation and overflight, resource exploration and exploitation, conservation and pollution, fishing and shipping. It entitles coastal states and inhabitable islands to proclaim a 12-mile territorial sea, a contiguous zone, a 200-mile exclusive economic zone and an extended continental shelf (in some cases). Its 320 Articles and nine Annexes constitute a guide for behaviour by states in the world's oceans, defining maritime zones, laying down rules for drawing sea boundaries, assigning legal rights, duties and responsibilities to States, and providing machinery for the settlement of disputes.

Organization. The Assembly, consisting of representatives from all member states, is the supreme organ. The 36-member Council, elected by the Assembly, includes the four largest importers or consumers of seabed minerals, four largest investors in seabed minerals, four major exporters of the same, six developing countries representing special interests and 18 members from all the geographical regions. The Council is the executive organ of the Authority. There are also two subsidiary bodies: the Legal and Technical Commission (currently 25 experts) and the Finance Committee (currently 15 experts). The Secretariat serves all the bodies of the Authority and under the 1994 Agreement is performing functions of the Enterprise (until such time as it starts to operate independently of the Secretariat). The Enterprise is the organ through which the ISA carries out deep seabed activities directly or through joint ventures.

Activities. In July 2000 the ISA adopted the Regulations for Prospecting and Exploration for Polymetallic Nodules in the

Area. Pursuant thereto, it signed exploration contracts with eight contractors who have submitted plans of work for deep seabed exploration. These are: Institut Français de Recherche pour l'Exploitation de la Mer (IFREMER) and Association Française pour l'Etude de la Recherche des Nodules (AFERNOD), France; Deep Ocean Resources Development Co. Ltd (DORD), Japan; State Enterprise Yuzhmorgeologiya, Russian Federation; China Ocean Minerals Research and Development Association (COMRA); Interoceanmetal Joint Organization (IOM), a consortium sponsored by Bulgaria, Cuba, Czech Republic, Poland, Russia and Slovakia; the government of the Republic of Korea; the Republic of India; and the Federal Institute for Geosciences and Natural Resources, Germany.

Between 1998 and 2007 the ISA organized nine workshops on a range of topics, including: the development of guidelines for the assessment of the possible environmental impacts arising from exploration for polymetallic nodules; a standardized system of data interpretation; and prospects for international collaboration in marine environmental research. While continuing to develop a database on polymetallic nodules (POLYDAT), the Authority has also made significant progress towards the establishment of a central data repository for all marine minerals in the deep seabed.

Headquarters: 14–20 Port Royal St., Kingston, Jamaica.
Website: http://www.isa.org.jm
Secretary-General: Nii Allotey Odunton (Ghana).

Publications. Handbook 2009; Selected Decisions and Documents from the Authority's Sessions; various others.

International Telecommunications Satellite Organization (ITSO)

Founded in 1964 as Intelsat, the organization was the world's first commercial communications satellite operator. Today, with capacity on a fleet of geostationary satellites and expanding terrestrial network assets, Intelsat continues to provide connectivity for telephony, corporate network, broadcast and internet services.

Organization. In 2001 the member states of the organization implemented restructuring by transferring certain assets to Intelsat Ltd, a new Bermuda-based commercial company under the supervision of the International Telecommunications Satellite Organization, now known as ITSO. The Intelsat Global Service Corporation is located in Washington, D.C., and Intelsat Global Services & Marketing Ltd, the sales arm of the international firm, has its headquarters in London. Intelsat also has offices in Australia, Brazil, China, France, Germany, Hawaii, India, Peru and South Africa. There were 150 member countries in Feb. 2010.

Headquarters: 3400 International Drive, NW, Washington, D.C., 20008–3006, USA.
Website: http://www.itso.int
Director-General: José Manuel Toscano (Portugal).

International Trade Union Confederation (ITUC)

Origin. Founded in Nov. 2006, the ITUC was formed after the merging of the International Confederation of Free Trade Unions (ICFTU) and the World Confederation of Labour (WCL). The WCL was established in 1920 as the International Federation of Christian Trade Unions, but went briefly out of existence in 1940 owing to the suppression of affiliated unions by the Nazi and Fascist regimes. Declining to merge with the World Federation of Trade Unions (WFTU) or ICFTU, it reconstituted in 1945 and became the WCL in 1968. The founding congress of the ICFTU took place in London in Dec. 1949 following the withdrawal of some Western trade unions from the WFTU, which had come under Communist control.

By Feb. 2010 the ITUC represented 175m. members of 311 affiliates in 155 countries and territories, consisting of the former affiliates of the WCL and ICFTU and a number of other national organizations.

Aims. The ITUC aims to defend and promote the rights of workers, particularly the right to union organization and collective bargaining; to combat discrimination at work and in society; to ensure that social concerns are put at the centre of global economic, trade and finance policies; to support young people's rights at work; and to promote the involvement of women in trade unions. In 2006 it also ran campaigns against child labour and to promote the prevention of HIV/AIDS.

Organization. The Congress meets every four years to set policies and to elect the General Secretary and the General Council, composed of 70 members, which is the main decision-making body between congresses. The President and Deputy Presidents are appointed by the General Council. The Founding Congress was held in Vienna in Nov. 2006.

The ITUC has offices which deal with the International Labour Organization (Geneva), the United Nations (New York) and the World Bank and International Monetary Fund (Washington, D.C.). There are also offices in Amman, Moscow, Sarajevo and Vilnius. The ITUC is a member of the Global Unions Council and the Trade Union Advisory Committee to the OECD.

Headquarters: Bd du Roi Albert II, N°5, bte 1, Brussels 1210, Belgium.
Website: http://www.ituc-csi.org
General Secretary: Guy Ryder (UK).
President: Sharan Burrow (Australia).

International Tribunal for the Law of the Sea (ITLOS)

The International Tribunal for the Law of the Sea (ITLOS), founded in Oct. 1996 and based in Hamburg, adjudicates on disputes relating to the interpretation and application of the United Nations Convention on the Law of the Sea. The Convention gives the Tribunal jurisdiction to resolve a variety of international law of the sea disputes such as the delimitation of maritime zones, fisheries, navigation and the protection of the marine environment. Its Seabed Disputes Chamber has compulsory jurisdiction to resolve disputes amongst States, the International Seabed Authority, companies and private individuals, arising out of the exploitation of the deep seabed. The Tribunal also has compulsory jurisdiction in certain instances to protect the rights of parties to a dispute or to prevent serious harm to the marine environment, and over the prompt release of arrested vessels and their crews upon the deposit of a security. The jurisdiction of the Tribunal also extends to all matters specifically provided for in any other agreement which confers jurisdiction on the Tribunal. The Tribunal is composed of 21 judges, elected by signatories from five world regional blocs: five each from Africa and Asia; four from Western Europe and other States; four from Latin America and the Caribbean; and three from Eastern Europe. The judges serve a term of nine years, with one third of the judges' terms expiring every three years.

Headquarters: Am Internationalen Seegerichtshof 1, D-22609 Hamburg, Germany.
Website: http://www.itlos.org
Registrar: Philippe Gautier (Belgium).

International Union Against Cancer (UICC)

Founded in 1933, the UICC is an international non-governmental association of 353 member organizations in 112 countries.

Objectives. The UICC is the only non-governmental organization dedicated exclusively to the global control of cancer. Its objectives are to advance scientific and medical knowledge in research, diagnosis, treatment and prevention of cancer, and to promote all other aspects of the campaign against cancer throughout the world. Particular emphasis is placed on professional and public education.

Membership. The UICC is made up of voluntary cancer leagues, patient organizations, associations and societies as well as cancer research and treatment centres and, in some countries, ministries of health.

Activities. The UICC creates and carries out programmes around the world in collaboration with several hundred volunteer experts, most of whom are professionally active in UICC member organizations. It promotes co-operation between cancer organizations, researchers, scientists, health professionals and cancer experts, with a focus in four key areas: building and enhancing cancer control capacity, tobacco control, population-based cancer prevention and control, and transfer of cancer knowledge and dissemination. The next UICC World Cancer Congress is scheduled to take place in Montreal, Canada in 2012.

Address: 62 route de Frontenex, 1207 Geneva, Switzerland.
Website: http://www.uicc.org
President: Dr David Hill (Australia).
Executive Director: Cary Adams (UK).

Inter-Parliamentary Union (IPU)

Founded in 1889 by William Randal Cremer (UK) and Frédéric Passy (France), the Inter-Parliamentary Union was the first permanent forum for political multilateral negotiations. The Union is a centre for dialogue and parliamentary diplomacy among legislators representing every political system and all the main political leanings in the world. It was instrumental in setting up what is now the Permanent Court of Arbitration in The Hague.

Activities. The IPU fosters contacts, co-ordination and the exchange of experience among parliaments and parliamentarians of all countries; considers questions of international interest and concern, and expresses its views on such issues in order to bring about action by parliaments and parliamentarians; contributes to the defence and promotion of human rights—an essential factor of parliamentary democracy and development; contributes to better knowledge of the working and development of representative institutions and to the strengthening of representative democracy.

Membership. The IPU had 151 members and eight associate members in Feb. 2010.

Headquarters: Chemin du Pommier 5, C.P. 330, 1218 Le Grand Saconnex, Geneva 19, Switzerland.
Website: http://www.ipu.org
President: Theo-Ben Gurirab (Namibia).
Secretary-General: Anders B. Johnsson (Sweden).

Interpol (International Criminal Police Organization)

Organization. Interpol was founded in 1923, disbanded in 1938 and reconstituted in 1946. The International Criminal Police Organization—Interpol was founded to ensure and promote the widest possible mutual assistance between all criminal police authorities within the limits of the law existing in the different countries worldwide and the spirit of the Universal Declaration of Human Rights, and to establish and develop all institutions likely to contribute effectively to the prevention and suppression of ordinary law crimes.

Aims. Interpol provides a co-ordination centre (General Secretariat) for its 188 member countries. Its priority areas of activity concern criminal organizations, public safety and terrorism, drug-related crimes, financial crime and high-tech crime, trafficking in human beings and tracking fugitives from justice. Interpol centralizes records and information on international offenders; it operates a worldwide communication network.

Interpol's General Assembly is held annually. The General Assembly is the body of supreme authority in the organization. It is composed of delegates appointed by the members of the organization.

Interpol's Executive Committee, which meets four times a year, supervises the execution of the decisions of the General Assembly. The Executive Committee is composed of the president of the organization, the three vice-presidents and nine delegates.

Interpol's General Secretariat is the centre for co-ordinating the fight against international crime. Its activities, undertaken in response to requests from the police services and judicial authorities in its member countries, focus on crime prevention and law enforcement.

As of Feb. 2010 Interpol's Sub-Regional Bureaus were located in Abidjan, Buenos Aires, Harare, Nairobi, San Salvador and Yaoundé. Interpol's Liaison Office for Asia is located in Bangkok.

Headquarters: 200 Quai Charles de Gaulle, 69006 Lyon, France.
Website: http://www.interpol.int
President: Khoo Boon Hui (Singapore).

Islamic Development Bank

The Agreement establishing the IDB (Banque islamique de développement) was adopted at the Second Islamic Finance Ministers' Conference held in Jeddah, Saudi Arabia in Aug. 1974. The Bank, which is open to all member countries of the Organization of the Islamic Conference, commenced operations in 1975. Its main objective is to foster economic development and social progress of member countries and Muslim communities individually as well as jointly in accordance with the principles of the Sharia. It is active in the promotion of trade and the flow of investments among member countries, and maintains a Special Assistance Fund for member countries suffering natural calamities. The Fund is also used to finance health and educational projects aimed at improving the socio-economic conditions of Muslim communities in non-member countries. A US$1·5bn. IDB Infrastructure Fund was launched in 1998 to invest in projects such as power, telecommunications, transportation, energy, natural resources, petro-chemical and other infrastructure-related sectors in member countries.

Members (56 as of Feb. 2010). Afghanistan, Albania, Algeria, Azerbaijan, Bahrain, Bangladesh, Benin, Brunei, Burkina Faso, Cameroon, Chad, Comoros, Côte d'Ivoire, Djibouti, Egypt, Gabon, The Gambia, Guinea, Guinea-Bissau, Indonesia, Iran, Iraq, Jordan, Kazakhstan, Kuwait, Kyrgyzstan, Lebanon, Libya, Malaysia, Maldives, Mali, Mauritania, Morocco, Mozambique, Niger, Nigeria, Oman, Pakistan, Palestine, Qatar, Saudi Arabia, Senegal, Sierra Leone, Somalia, Sudan, Suriname, Syria, Tajikistan, Togo, Tunisia, Turkey, Turkmenistan, Uganda, United Arab Emirates, Uzbekistan, Yemen.

Official language: Arabic. *Working languages:* English, French.
Headquarters: PO Box 5925, Jeddah 21432, Saudi Arabia.
Website: http://www.isdb.org
President: Ahmed Mohamed Ali (Saudi Arabia).

Médecins Sans Frontières (MSF)

Origin. Médecins sans Frontières was founded in 1971 by a small group of doctors and journalists who believed that all people have a right to emergency relief.

Functions. MSF was one of the first non-governmental organizations to provide both urgently needed medical assistance and to publicly bear witness to the plight of the people it helps. Today MSF is an international medical humanitarian movement with branch offices in 19 countries. In 2008 MSF volunteer doctors, nurses, other medical professionals, logistical experts, water and sanitation engineers, and administrators departed on more than 4,600 missions and joined more than 23,900 locally hired staff to provide medical aid in over 65 countries. MSF was awarded the 1999 Nobel Peace Prize.

Headquarters: MSF International Office, Rue de Lausanne 78, CH-1211 Geneva 21, Switzerland.
Website: http://www.msf.org
Secretary-General: Christopher Stokes (France/UK).
International Council President: Dr Christophe Fournier (France).

North Atlantic Treaty Organization (NATO)

Origin. On 4 April 1949 the foreign ministers of Belgium, Canada, Denmark, France, Iceland, Italy, Luxembourg, the Netherlands, Norway, Portugal, the UK and the USA signed the North Atlantic Treaty, establishing the *North Atlantic Alliance.* In 1952 Greece and Turkey acceded to the Treaty; in 1955 the Federal Republic of Germany; in 1982 Spain; in 1999 the Czech Republic, Hungary and Poland; in 2004 Bulgaria, Estonia, Latvia, Lithuania, Romania, Slovakia and Slovenia; and in 2009 Albania and Croatia, bringing the total to 28 member countries.

Functions. The Alliance was established as a defensive political and military alliance of independent countries in accordance with the terms of the UN Charter. Its fundamental role is to safeguard the freedom and security of its members by political and military means. It also encourages consultation and co-operation with non-NATO countries in a wide range of security-related areas to help prevent conflicts within and beyond the frontiers of its member countries. NATO promotes democratic values and is committed to the peaceful resolution of disputes. If diplomatic efforts fail, it has the military capacity needed to undertake crisis-management operations alone or in co-operation with other countries and international organizations.

Reform and Transformation of the Alliance. Following the demise of the Warsaw Pact in 1991, and the improved relations with Russia, NATO established security dialogue and co-operation with the states of Central and Eastern Europe and those of the former USSR. These changes were reflected in the publication in 1991 of a new Strategic Concept for the Alliance outlining NATO's enduring purpose and nature, and its fundamental security tasks. Further changes in the security environment during the 1990s led to the development of the current Strategic Concept, published in 1999 to address new risks such as terrorism, ethnic conflict, human rights abuses, political instability, economic fragility, and the spread of nuclear, biological and chemical weapons and their means of delivery. A new Strategic Concept, which will reflect new and emerging security threats, is currently being discussed and is expected to be published at a NATO summit meeting in late 2010.

The Euro-Atlantic Partnership. In 1991 the North Atlantic Co-operation Council (NACC) was established as a forum for dialogue with former Warsaw Pact countries. The NACC was replaced in 1997 by the Euro-Atlantic Partnership Council (EAPC), which brings together all 50 NATO and partner countries in the Euro-Atlantic area for dialogue and consultation on political and security-related issues. It provides the overall political framework for NATO's co-operation with partner countries and the bilateral relationships developed between NATO and individual partner countries under the Partnership for Peace (PfP) programme, which was launched in 1994.

Since its launch, the PfP programme has been adapted to expand and intensify political and military co-operation throughout Europe. Core objectives are: the facilitation of transparency in national defence planning and budgeting processes; democratic control of defence forces; members' maintenance of capability and readiness to contribute to operations under the authority of the UN; development of co-operative military relations with NATO (joint planning, training and exercises) in order to strengthen participants' ability to undertake missions in the fields of peacekeeping, search and rescue, and humanitarian operations; development, over the longer term, of forces better able to operate with those of NATO member forces. NATO will consult with any active partner which perceives a direct threat to its territorial integrity, political independence or security.

One of the most tangible aspects of co-operation between partner countries and NATO has been their individual participation in NATO-led peace-support operations. PfP has done much to facilitate this and has also been a key factor in promoting a spirit of practical co-operation and commitment to the democratic principles that underpin the Alliance. In Feb. 2010 NATO had 22 PfP partners: Armenia, Austria, Azerbaijan, Belarus, Bosnia and Herzegovina, Finland, Georgia, Ireland, Kazakhstan, Kyrgyzstan, the former Yugoslav Republic of Macedonia, Malta, Moldova, Montenegro, Russia, Serbia,

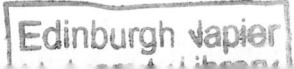

Sweden, Switzerland, Tajikistan, Turkmenistan, Ukraine and Uzbekistan. Many of these countries have accepted the Alliance's invitation to send liaison officers to permanent facilities at NATO Headquarters in Brussels and to the Partnership Co-ordination Cell in Mons, Belgium, where the Supreme Headquarters Allied Powers Europe (SHAPE) is located.

Country Relations. On 27 May 1997 in Paris, NATO and Russia signed the Founding Act on Mutual Relations, Co-operation and Security, committing themselves to build together a lasting peace in the Euro-Atlantic area, and establishing a new forum for consultation and co-operation called the NATO-Russia Permanent Joint Council. In May 2002 the Permanent Joint Council was replaced by a new NATO-Russia Council which brings together all NATO member countries and Russia in a forum in which they work as equal partners, identifying and pursuing opportunities for joint action in areas of common concern.

At the meeting in Sintra, Portugal in May 1997 a NATO-Ukraine Charter on a Distinctive Partnership was drawn up and signed in Madrid in July, establishing the NATO-Ukraine Commission (NUC). Dialogue and co-operation has become well-established with NATO and individual allies supporting Ukraine's ongoing reform efforts, particularly in the defence and security sectors.

NATO launched the Mediterranean Dialogue with six countries of the Mediterranean (Egypt, Israel, Jordan, Mauritania, Morocco and Tunisia) in 1995. In 1997 allied foreign ministers agreed to enhance the Dialogue. A new committee, the Mediterranean Co-operation Group, was established to take the Mediterranean Dialogue forward and Algeria joined in March 2000. Later, in 2004, NATO also launched the İstanbul Co-operation Initiative that aims to develop bilateral co-operation with countries in the broader Middle East. Bahrain, Kuwait, Qatar and the United Arab Emirates have since joined the Initiative.

Relations with other international organizations. NATO is gradually developing a strategic partnership with the European Union. Efforts to strengthen the security and defence role of NATO's European allies were initially organized through the Western European Union (WEU) during the 1990s, when there was a growing realization of the need for European countries to further develop defence capabilities and to assume greater responsibility for their common security. In 2000 the crisis management responsibilities of the WEU were increasingly assumed by the EU. Institutionalized relations between NATO and the EU were launched in 2001. The political principles underlying the NATO-EU relationship were set out in the Dec. 2002 NATO-EU Declaration on ESDP (European Security and Defence Policy). These decisions paved the way for the two organizations to work out the modalities for the transfer of responsibilities to the EU for the NATO-led military operations in the former Yugoslav Republic of Macedonia in 2003 and, from Dec. 2004, in Bosnia and Herzegovina.

NATO and the UN share a commitment to maintaining international peace and security and have been co-operating in this area since the early 1990s with consultations established between NATO and UN specialized bodies on a range of issues including crisis management, combating human trafficking, mine action and the fight against terrorism.

NATO and the OSCE work together to build security and promote stability in the Euro-Atlantic area, co-operating at both the political and the operational level in areas such as conflict prevention, crisis management and addressing new security threats.

Operations. One of the most significant aspects of NATO's transformation has been the decision to undertake peace-support and crisis-management operations in the Euro-Atlantic area and further afield.

In the wake of the disintegration of the former Yugoslavia, the Alliance has focused much of its attention on the Balkans. NATO first committed itself to peacekeeping in Bosnia and Herzegovina in Dec. 1995, through the NATO-led Implementation Force (IFOR), which was replaced by the Stabilization Force (SFOR) in 1996. Improvements in the security situation allowed NATO to hand over its operation to the EU in Dec. 2004.

Since 1999, following a 78-day air campaign against the Yugoslav regime to bring an end to the violent repression of ethnic Albanians, NATO has led a peacekeeping mission in Kosovo (the Kosovo Force, or KFOR). NATO also intervened in the former Yugoslav Republic of Macedonia at the request of the government to help avoid a civil war in 2001, and maintained a small peacekeeping presence there until March 2003, when the operation was handed over to the EU.

Following the attacks on New York and Washington, D.C. on 11 Sept. 2001, NATO invoked article five of the Washington Treaty (the collective defence clause) for the first time in its history, declaring it considered the attack on the USA as an attack against all members of the Alliance. It subsequently launched a series of initiatives aimed at curtailing terrorist activity. Operation Active Endeavour is a maritime operation led by NATO's naval forces to detect and deter terrorist activity in the Mediterranean. Operation Eagle Assist was one of the measures requested by the USA in the aftermath of the attacks in Sept. 2001. Aircraft from NATO's Airborne Warning and Control System (AWACS) patrolled American airspace from mid-Oct. 2001 to mid-May 2002.

In Aug. 2003 NATO took over responsibility for the International Security Assistance Force (ISAF) in Afghanistan. Currently NATO's largest and most robust peace-support operation, ISAF's presence was gradually expanded out from the capital Kabul into the provinces, covering the entire country by Oct. 2006. Provincial Reconstruction Teams, combining both civilian and military personnel, have been set up to help provide security and promote reconstruction and development. ISAF is also assisting the Afghan government in developing reliable security structures and training Afghan security forces.

NATO is also helping train Iraqi military personnel and supporting the development of security institutions in Iraq, as well as providing logistical support to the African Union's mission in Darfur, Sudan.

Since late 2008 NATO has been conducting counter-piracy operations in the Gulf of Aden and off the Horn of Africa, where piracy is threatening to undermine international humanitarian efforts in Africa, as well as the safety of commercial maritime routes and international navigation.

Since the establishment in 1998 of the Euro-Atlantic Disaster Response Co-ordination Centre to serve as a focal point for co-ordinating the disaster-relief efforts of NATO member states and partner countries, NATO plays an increasingly important role in humanitarian relief. Most notably, in 2005 some NATO capabilities and forces were deployed to support relief efforts following Hurricane Katrina in the USA and the devastating earthquake in Pakistan.

Defence capabilities. This widened scope of NATO military operations is radically transforming the military requirements of the Alliance. The large defence forces of the past are being replaced by more flexible, mobile forces which are able to deploy at significant distances from their normal operating bases and to engage in the full range of missions, ranging from high-intensity combat to humanitarian support. A modernization process was launched at the Prague Summit in 2002 to ensure that NATO could effectively deal with the security challenges of the 21st century and measures to enhance the Alliance's military operational capabilities were agreed. A new capabilities initiative (the Prague Capabilities Commitment) and a NATO Response Force were created and the Alliance's military command structure streamlined. In addition, steps were taken to increase efforts in the areas of intelligence sharing and crisis response arrangements, as well as greater co-operation with partner countries. Five nuclear, biological and chemical (NBC) weapons defence initiatives were also endorsed, as well as the creation of a multinational chemical, biological, radiological and nuclear battalion. At subsequent NATO summit meetings in İstanbul in 2004 and Riga in 2006, further initiatives were taken to promote the Alliance's ongoing transformation.

Organization. The North Atlantic Council (NAC) is the highest decision-making body and forum for consultation within the Atlantic Alliance. Composed of Permanent Representatives of all the member countries, it meets at least once a week and also meets at higher levels involving foreign ministers, defence ministers or heads of state or government. The authority and powers of decision-making and status and validity of its decisions remain the same at whatever level it meets. All decisions are taken on the basis of consensus, reflecting the collective will of all member governments. The NAC is the only body within the Atlantic Alliance which derives its authority explicitly from the North Atlantic Treaty.

The Military Committee is responsible for making recommendations to the NAC and the Defence Planning Committee on military matters and for supplying guidance to the Allied Commanders. Composed of the Chiefs-of-Staff of member countries (Iceland, which has no military forces, may be represented by a civilian), the Committee is assisted by an International Military Staff. It meets at Chiefs-of-Staff level at least twice a year but remains in permanent session at the level of national military representatives. The military command structure of the Alliance is divided into two strategic commands, one based in Europe and the other based in the USA.

Finance. The greater part of each member country's contribution to NATO, in terms of resources, comes indirectly through its expenditure on its own national armed forces and on its efforts to make them interoperable with those of other members so that they can participate in multinational operations. Member countries usually incur the deployment costs involved whenever they volunteer forces to participate in NATO-led operations, although in 2006 agreement was reached on using common funding for some aspects of deployments on a trial basis.

Member countries make direct contributions to three budgets managed directly by NATO: namely the Civil Budget, the Military Budget and the Security Investment Programme. Member countries pay contributions to each of these budgets in accordance with agreed cost-sharing formulae broadly calculated in relation to their ability to pay.

Under the terms of the Partnership for Peace strategy, partner countries undertake to make available the necessary personnel, assets, facilities and capabilities to participate in the programme, and share the financial cost of any military exercises in which they participate.

Headquarters: NATO, 1110 Brussels, Belgium.
Website: http://www.nato.int
Secretary General: Anders Fogh Rasmussen (Denmark)

Publications. For a full list of NATO publications, visit the website: http://www.nato.int/cps/en/natolive/publications.htm.

Current Leaders

Anders Fogh Rasmussen

Position

Secretary General

Introduction

Anders Fogh Rasmussen took office as Secretary General on 1 Aug. 2009, having served as prime minister of Denmark for the preceding eight years. Fogh Rasmussen is the highest-ranked official to be appointed Secretary General.

Early Life

Fogh Rasmussen was born on 26 Jan. 1953 in Ginnerup, Jutland. He joined the Young Liberals (Venstres Ungdom) in 1970 and stood unsuccessfully as the Liberal parliamentary candidate for Viborg in Jan. 1973. In 1978 he graduated with a masters degree in economics from Aarhus University. In the same year he joined the Folketing as a replacement member for Viborg County.

From 1981–86 Fogh Rasmussen was vice chairman of the Folketing's housing committee and in 1985 was appointed deputy chairman of the Liberal Party (Venstre, or V). After re-election at the 1987 general election he became taxation minister, adding the role of finance minister in 1990. In April 1998 he was elected Liberal chairman. Following the attacks on the USA in Sept. 2001, the incumbent Social Democrat prime minister, Poul Nyrup Rasmussen, called a snap election. The election campaign was fought largely on the issue of immigration, with Fogh Rasmussen gaining popular support for his proposed hard line. Having defeated the Social Democrats he took office on 27 Nov. 2001 but needed to form a coalition with the Conservatives. Although espousing a centre-right line, his government was also supported by the far-right Danish People's Party. Following the 2005 and 2007 general elections, he became the first Liberal leader to win a second, and then a third, consecutive term of office.

In opposition to public opinion Fogh Rasmussen supported the USA's invasion of Iraq, pledging 500 troops to the war effort. In early 2006 the republication in western European newspapers of cartoon caricatures of the Prophet Muhammad, which first appeared in Denmark in Sept. 2005, sparked mass protests and unofficial boycotts of Danish exports across the Muslim world. While arguing that the issue was one of freedom of expression, Fogh Rasmussen's government sought more effective engagement with Islamic opinion.

Fogh Rasmussen resigned as prime minister shortly after his appointment as NATO Secretary General was announced on 4 April 2009.

Career in Office

Despite having the backing of the major NATO members, the appointment of Fogh Rasmussen as Secretary General was controversial following his role in the Danish cartoon affair. His selection was contested by Turkey, which relented after the personal intervention of President Barack Obama at the NATO summit in Strasbourg in April 2009.

He came to power at a difficult time for the alliance as the situation in Afghanistan deteriorated. In July 2009, the month preceding his assumption of the post, NATO suffered record casualties in Afghanistan. Nevertheless, Fogh Rasmussen was quick to call for a greater commitment to the war effort by European states. On 4 Dec. 2009, a week after Obama had announced the deployment of a further 30,000 US troops to Afghanistan, Fogh Rasmussen declared that NATO would commit an extra 7,000 troops to the country.

He has made clear his determination to reform the internal workings of the organization to reduce bureaucracy and speed up decision-making. He has described his mission as being to 'modernize, transform and reform so that NATO adapts to the security environment for the 21st century'.

Further Reading

Carr, F. and Infantis, K., *NATO in the New European Order.* 1996
Cook, D., *The Forging of an Alliance.* 1989
Cottey, Andrew, *Security in the New Europe.* 2007
Heller, F. H. and Gillingham, J. R. (eds.) *NATO: the Founding of the Atlantic Alliance and the Integration of Europe.* 1992
Rupp, Richard E., *NATO after 9/11: An Alliance in Continuing Decline.* 2006
Smith, J. (ed.) *The Origins of NATO.* 1990
Yost, David S., *NATO Transformed: The Alliance's New Roles in International Security.* 1999

Organisation for Economic Co-operation and Development (OECD)

Origin. Founded in 1961 to replace the Organisation for European Economic Co-operation (OEEC), which was established in 1948 and linked to the Marshall Plan. The change of title marks the Organisation's altered status and functions: it ceased to be a European body with the accession of Canada and USA as full members and became a forum of global influence adding development to its list of core priorities. The Organisation aims to promote policies designed to achieve the highest sustainable economic growth and employment, as well as raising standards of living in member countries, while maintaining financial stability, thereby contributing to the development of the world economy; to contribute to sound economic expansion in member as well as non-member economies in the process of economic development; and to contribute to the expansion of world trade on a multilateral, non-discriminatory basis in accordance with international obligations.

Members. Australia, Austria, Belgium, Canada, Czech Republic, Denmark, Finland, France, Germany, Greece, Hungary, Iceland, Ireland, Italy, Japan, South Korea, Luxembourg, Mexico, Netherlands, New Zealand, Norway, Poland, Portugal, Slovakia, Spain, Sweden, Switzerland, Turkey, UK and USA. An accession agreement with Chile was signed in Jan. 2010. It will become a member once parliament ratifies the OECD's convention. Discussions that began in May 2007 on the possible future accession of Estonia, Israel, Russia and Slovenia are ongoing.

Activities. The OECD's main fields of work are: economic policy; statistics; energy; development co-operation; sustainable development; public governance and territorial development; international trade; financial and enterprise affairs; tax policy and administration; food, agriculture and fisheries; environment; science, technology and industry; biotechnology and biodiversity; education; employment, labour and social affairs; entrepreneurship, small and middle-sized enterprises; and local development.

Relations with non-members. In order to ensure its continuing relevance as a hub for dialogue and action on globally significant policy issues, the OECD has developed an active global relations strategy and maintains co-operative relations with many economies outside the OECD. Officials from non-member economies increasingly discuss policy with their counterparts from member countries and conduct peer assessments while sharing each other's policy experiences. In 2007 the OECD launched a process of enhanced engagement with five countries whose engagement in the work of the OECD is particularly important for the fulfilment of the Organisation's mandate to promote policy convergence and global economic development: Brazil, China, India, Indonesia and South Africa. It aims to bring these countries closer to the OECD by engaging them actively in the OECD's analytical and policy development work, while supporting their own reform processes.

Other activities with non-OECD members are grouped around Global Forums in 12 policy areas. Created by Committees as stable, active networks of policy makers in OECD member and non-member economies, as well as other stakeholders, the Global Forums focus on: agriculture, biotechnology, competition, development, education, environment, finance, international investment, the knowledge economy, public governance, taxation and trade. A regional approach provides for targeted co-operation with non-OECD economies in Europe, Asia, Latin America, the Middle East and Northern Africa (MENA), and in Africa more generally, where the OECD supports the objectives of the New Partnership for Africa's Development (NEPAD) and the initiatives of the African Partnership Forum. The Centre for Co-operation with Non-Members develops the overall architecture of co-operation and general liaison with non-members, while the substantive directorates implement the programmes and activities in each policy area.

Relations with developing countries. Developing countries participate in many of the OECD's above-mentioned activities with non-members. The principal body dealing with issues related to development co-operation is the Development Assistance Committee (DAC). Its 23 members are major aid donors, collectively accounting for over 90% of total official development assistance (ODA) worldwide amounting to approximately US$120bn. in 2008. The DAC largely focuses on how to spend and invest this aid so as to help its partners achieve the Millennium Development Goals and produces analysis and guidance on a range of topics, including aid for trade, aid effectiveness, capacity development, poverty reduction, environment, conflict and fragility, gender equality, good governance, evaluation and aid architecture.

The OECD Development Centre links OECD member countries and developing countries in Africa, Asia and Latin America by helping policy makers in OECD and developing countries find solutions to the challenges of development, poverty alleviation and the curbing of inequality through recommendations designed to promote constructive policy change. Annual publications include the *Latin American Economic Outlook* and, jointly with the African Development Bank, the *African Economic Outlook*.

The OECD's policy dialogue is also developing at a regional level, particularly through the work of the Sahel and West Africa Club (SWAC) which acts as an interface between West African actors and OECD member countries. Administratively attached to the OECD, the SWAC is led by a secretariat based in Paris and combines direct field involvement with analyses of West African realities. The SWAC works with regional institutions, governments, business and civil society organizations to promote the regional dimension of development, support the formulation and implementation of joint or intergovernmental policies and thereby contribute to mobilizing and strengthening West African capacities.

Relations with other international organizations. Under a protocol signed at the same time as the OECD Convention, the European Commission takes part in the work of the OECD. EFTA may also send representatives to attend OECD meetings. Formal relations also exist with the Asian Development Bank, Inter-American Development Bank, World Bank, IMF, UNCTAD, WHO and the Parliamentary Assemblies of the Council of Europe and NATO.

Relations with civil society. Consultations with civil society organizations (CSOs) take place across the whole range of the OECD's work. The Business and Industry Advisory Committee to the OECD (BIAC) and the Trade Union Advisory Committee to the OECD (TUAC) have consultative status enabling them to discuss subjects of common interest and be consulted in a particular field by the relevant OECD Committee or its officers. Individual committees are in direct dialogue with CSOs interested in following their areas of work and establish modalities for consultations, and in some exceptional cases CSOs have expert status. Since 2000 the OECD has organized the annual OECD Forum, an international public conference offering business, labour and civil society the opportunity to discuss key issues of the 21st century with government ministers and leaders of international organizations.

Organization. The governing body of the OECD is the Council, comprising representatives of each member country and in which the European Commission participates. It usually meets once a year at the level of government ministers, with a rotating chairmanship at ministerial level among member governments. The Council also meets regularly, under the chairmanship of the Secretary-General at the level of Permanent Representatives to OECD (ambassadors who head resident diplomatic missions). It is responsible for all questions of general policy and may establish subsidiary bodies as required to achieve the aims of the Organisation. Decisions and recommendations of the Council are adopted by consensus of all its members.

An Executive Committee, a Budget Committee and an External Relations Committee assist the Council although they have limited decision-making power within their fields of competence. In addition, the Executive Committee in Special Session meets, usually twice a year, and is attended by senior government officials. Most of the work of the OECD is prepared and carried out by about 250 specialized bodies (Committees, Working Parties, etc.). All members are normally represented on these bodies, except a few which have a more restricted membership. Delegates are usually officials from either the capitals of member states or the Permanent Delegations to the OECD. Funding is by member state contributions based on a formula related to their size and economy.

The International Energy Agency (IEA) and the Nuclear Energy Agency (NEA) are also part of the OECD system.

Headquarters: 2 rue André Pascal, 75775 Paris Cedex 16, France.
Website: http://www.oecd.org
Secretary-General: Angel Gurría (Mexico).
Deputy Secretaries-General: Aart de Geus (Netherlands), Pier Carlo Padoan (Italy), Mario Amano (Japan), Richard A. Boucher (USA).

Publications include: *OECD Factbook; Economic, Environmental and Social Statistics* (annual); *OECD Policy Briefs* (20 a year); *OECD Economic Surveys* (by country); *Environmental Performance Reviews* (by country); *OECD Economic Outlook* (twice a year); *Economic Policy Reform: Going for Growth* (annual); *OECD-FAO Agricultural Outlook* (annual); *Education at a Glance* (annual); *OECD Employment Outlook* (annual); *OECD Science, Technology and Industry Outlook* (biennial); *International Migration Outlook* (annual); *Health at a Glance* (biennial); *Society at a Glance* (biennial); *OECD Health Data* (CD-ROM; annual); *Financial Market Trends* (twice a year); *Statistics of International Trade* (monthly); *International Trade by Commodity Statistics* (annual); *Main Economic Indicators* (monthly); *Energy Balances* (annual); *World Energy Outlook* (annual); *National Accounts* (quarterly and annual); *African Economic Outlook* (annual); *OECD Observer* (6 a year); *Quarterly Labour Force Statistics; Model Tax Convention; Development Co-operation Report* (annual); *Development Centre Policy Briefs*. For a full list of OECD publications, visit the website: http://www.oecdbookshop.org.

Organization of the Islamic Conference (OIC)

Founded in 1969, the objectives of the OIC are to promote Islamic solidarity among member states; to consolidate co-operation among member states in the economic, social, cultural, scientific and other vital fields of activities, and to carry out consultations among member states in international organizations; to endeavour to eliminate racial segregation, discrimination and to eradicate colonialism in all its forms; to take the necessary measures to support international peace and security founded on justice; to strengthen the struggle of all Muslim peoples with a view to safeguarding their dignity, independence and national rights; to create a suitable atmosphere for the promotion of co-operation and understanding among member states and other countries.

Members (57 as of Feb. 2010). Afghanistan, Albania, Algeria, Azerbaijan, Bahrain, Bangladesh, Benin, Brunei, Burkina Faso, Cameroon, Chad, Comoros, Côte d'Ivoire, Djibouti, Egypt, Gabon, The Gambia, Guinea, Guinea-Bissau, Guyana, Indonesia, Iran, Iraq, Jordan, Kazakhstan, Kuwait, Kyrgyzstan, Lebanon, Libya, Malaysia, Maldives, Mali, Mauritania, Morocco, Mozambique, Niger, Nigeria, Oman, Pakistan, Palestine, Qatar, Saudi Arabia, Senegal, Sierra Leone, Somalia, Sudan, Suriname, Syria, Tajikistan, Togo, Tunisia, Turkey, Turkmenistan, Uganda, United Arab Emirates, Uzbekistan, Yemen. *Observers.* Bosnia and Herzegovina, Central African Republic, Russia, Thailand, Turkish Republic of Northern Cyprus.

Headquarters: PO Box 178, Jeddah 21411, Saudi Arabia.
Website: http://www.oic-oci.org
Secretary-General: Dr Ekmeleddin İhsanoğlu (Turkey).

Unrepresented Nations and Peoples Organization (UNPO)

UNPO is an international organization created by nations and peoples around the world who are not represented in the world's principal international organizations, such as the UN. Founded in 1991, UNPO now has 69 members representing over 100m. people worldwide.

Membership. Open to all nations and peoples unrepresented, subject to adherence to the five principles which form the basis of UNPO's charter: equal right to self-determination of all nations and peoples; adherence to internationally accepted human rights standards; to the principles of democracy; promotion of non-violence; and protection of the environment. Applicants must show that they constitute a 'nation or people' as defined in the Covenant.

Functions and Activities. UNPO offers an international forum for occupied nations, indigenous peoples, minorities and oppressed majorities, who struggle to regain their lost countries, preserve their cultural identities, protect their basic human and economic rights, and safeguard their environment.

It does not represent those peoples; rather it assists and empowers them to represent themselves more effectively. To this end, it provides professional services and facilities as well as education and training in the fields of diplomacy, human rights law, democratic processes, conflict resolution and environmental protection. Members, private foundations and voluntary contributions fund the Organization.

In total six former members of UNPO (Armenia, Belau, Estonia, Georgia, Latvia and Timor-Leste) subsequently achieved full independence and gained representation in the UN. Belau is now called Palau. Current members Bougainville and Kosovo have achieved a degree of political autonomy. Kosovo has declared itself an independent state, although both Serbia and Russia oppose its sovereignty.

Headquarters: Laan van Meerdervoort 70, 2517 AN The Hague, Netherlands.
Website: http://www.unpo.org
General Secretary: Marino Busdachin (Italy).

Publication. UNPO News (quarterly).

World Council of Churches

The World Council of Churches was formally constituted on 23 Aug. 1948 in Amsterdam. In Feb. 2010 member churches numbered 349 from more than 110 countries.

Origin. The World Council was founded by the coming together of Christian movements, including the overseas mission groups gathered from 1921 in the International Missionary Council, the Faith and Order Movement, and the Life and Work Movement. On 13 May 1938, at Utrecht, a provisional committee was appointed to prepare for the formation of a World Council of Churches.

Membership. The basis of membership (1975) states: 'The World Council of Churches is a fellowship of Churches which confess the Lord Jesus Christ as God and Saviour according to the Scriptures and therefore seek to fulfil together their common calling to the glory of the one God, Father, Son and Holy Spirit.' Membership is open to Churches which express their agreement with this basis and satisfy such criteria as the Assembly or Central Committee may prescribe. Today, more than 340 Churches of Protestant, Anglican, Orthodox, Old Catholic and Pentecostal confessions belong to this fellowship. The Roman Catholic Church is not a member of the WCC but works closely with it.

Activities. The WCC's Central Committee comprises the Programme Committee and the Finance Committee. Within the Programme Committee there are advisory groups on issues relating to communication, women, justice, peace and creation, youth, ecumenical relations and inter-religious relations. Following the WCC's 8th General Assembly in Harare, Zimbabwe in 1998 the work of the WCC was restructured. Activities were grouped into four 'clusters'—Relationships; Issues and Themes; Communication; and Finance, Services and Administration. The Relationships cluster comprises four teams (Church and Ecumenical Relations, Regional Relations and Ecumenical Sharing, Inter-Religious Relations and International Relations), as well as two programmes (Action by Churches Together and the Ecumenical Church Loan Fund). The Issues and Themes cluster comprises four teams (Faith and Order; Mission and Evangelism; Justice, Peace and Creation; and Education and Ecumenical Formation).

In Aug. 1997 the WCC launched a Peace to the City campaign, as the initial focus of a programme to overcome violence in troubled cities. The Decade to Overcome Violence was launched in Feb. 2001 during the meeting of the WCC Central Committee in Berlin.

Organization. The governing body of the World Council, consisting of delegates specially appointed by the member Churches, is the Assembly, which meets every seven or eight years to frame policy. It has no legislative powers and depends for the implementation of its decisions upon the action of member Churches. The 9th General Assembly, held in Porto Alegre, Brazil in Feb. 2006, had as its theme 'God, in your grace, transform the world'. A 154-member Central Committee meets annually to carry out the Assembly mandate, with a smaller 25-member Executive Committee meeting twice a year.

Headquarters: PO Box 2100, 150 route de Ferney, 1211 Geneva 2, Switzerland.
Website: http://www.oikoumene.org
General Secretary: Rev. Dr Olav Fykse Tveit (Norway).

Publications. Annual Reports; Dictionary of the Ecumenical Movement, Geneva, 1991; *Directory of Christian Councils,* 1985; *A History of the Ecumenical Movement,* Geneva, 1993; *Ecumenical Review* (quarterly); *Ecumenical News International* (weekly); *International Review of Mission* (quarterly).

Further Reading

Castro, E., *A Passion for Unity.* 1992
Raiser, K., *Ecumenism in Transition.* 1994
Van Elderen, M. and Conway, M., *Introducing the World Council of Churches revised and enlarged edition.* 1991

World Customs Organization

Established in 1952 as the Customs Co-operation Council, the World Customs Organization is an intergovernmental body with worldwide membership, whose mission it is to enhance the effectiveness and efficiency of customs administrations throughout the world. It has 176 member countries or territories.

Headquarters: Rue du Marché, 30, B-1210 Brussels, Belgium.
Website: http://www.wcoomd.org
Secretary-General: Kunio Mikuriya (Japan).

World Federation of Trade Unions (WFTU)

Origin and History. The WFTU was founded on a worldwide basis in 1945 at the international trade union conferences held in London and Paris, with the participation of all the trade union centres in the countries of the anti-Hitler coalition. The aim was to reunite the world trade union movement at the end of the Second World War. The acute political differences among affiliates, especially the east–west confrontation in Europe on ideological lines, led to a split. A number of affiliated organizations withdrew in 1949 and established the ICFTU. The WFTU now draws its membership from the industrially developing countries like India, Vietnam and other Asian countries, Brazil, Peru, Cuba and other Latin American countries, Syria, Lebanon, Kuwait and other Arab countries, and it has affiliates and associates in more than 20 European countries. It has close relations with the International Confederation of Arab Trade Unions, the Organization of African Trade Union Unity as well as the All-China Federation of Trade Unions. The 15th Congress was held in Havana, Cuba in Dec. 2005 and used the slogan 'The working people of the world against globalization and exploitation. For social justice, full employment, solidarity and peace'. Its Trade Unions Internationals (TUIs) have affiliates in Russia, the Czech Republic, Poland and other East European countries, Portugal, France, Spain, Japan and other OECD countries.

The headquarters of the TUIs are situated in Helsinki, New Delhi, Budapest, Mexico, Paris and Moscow. The WFTU and its TUIs have 130m. members, organized in 92 affiliated or associated national federations and six Trade Unions Internationals, in 130 countries. It has regional offices in New Delhi, Havana, Dakar, Damascus, Moscow and Nicosia and Permanent Representatives accredited to the UN in New York, Geneva, Paris and Rome.

Headquarters: 40 Zan Moreas St., 117 45 Athens, Greece.
Website: http://www.wftucentral.org
Email: info@wftucentral.org
President: Mohammad Assouz (Syria).
General Secretary: George Mavrikos (Greece).

Publications. Flashes From the Trade Unions (fortnightly, published in English, French, Spanish and Arabic), reports of Congresses, etc.

World Wide Fund for Nature (WWF)

Origin. WWF was officially formed and registered as a charity on 11 Sept. 1961. The first National Appeal was launched in the

United Kingdom on 23 Nov. 1961, shortly followed by the United States and Switzerland.

Organization. WWF is the world's largest and most experienced independent conservation organization with over 4·7m. supporters and a global network of 27 National Organizations, five Associates and 24 Programme Offices.

The National Organizations carry out conservation activities in their own countries and contribute technical expertise and funding to WWF's international conservation programme. The Programme Offices implement WWF's fieldwork, advise national and local governments, and raise public understanding of conservation issues.

Mission. WWF has as its mission preserving genetic, species and ecosystem diversity; ensuring that the use of renewable natural resources is sustainable now and in the longer term, for the benefit of all life on Earth; promoting actions to reduce to a minimum pollution and the wasteful exploitation and consumption of resources and energy. WWF's ultimate goal is to stop, and eventually reverse, the accelerating degradation of our planet's natural environment, and to help build a future in which humans live in harmony with nature.

Address: Avenue du Mont-Blanc, CH–1196 Gland, Switzerland.
Website: http://www.panda.org
Director General: James P. Leape (USA).
President Emeritus: HRH The Prince Philip, Duke of Edinburgh.
President: Yolanda Kakabadse (Ecuador).

African Development Bank

Established in 1964 to promote economic and social development in Africa.

Regional Members. (53) Algeria, Angola, Benin, Botswana, Burkina Faso, Burundi, Cameroon, Cape Verde, Central African Republic, Chad, Comoros, Democratic Republic of the Congo, Republic of the Congo, Côte d'Ivoire, Djibouti, Egypt, Equatorial Guinea, Eritrea, Ethiopia, Gabon, The Gambia, Ghana, Guinea, Guinea-Bissau, Kenya, Lesotho, Liberia, Libya, Madagascar, Malaŵi, Mali, Mauritania, Mauritius, Morocco, Mozambique, Namibia, Niger, Nigeria, Rwanda, São Tomé e Príncipe, Senegal, Seychelles, Sierra Leone, Somalia, South Africa (Rep. of), Sudan, Swaziland, Tanzania, Togo, Tunisia, Uganda, Zambia, Zimbabwe.

Non-regional Members. (24) Argentina, Austria, Belgium, Brazil, Canada, China, Denmark, Finland, France, Germany, India, Italy, Japan, South Korea, Kuwait, Netherlands, Norway, Portugal, Saudi Arabia, Spain, Sweden, Switzerland, UK, USA.

Within the ADB Group are the African Development Fund (ADF) and the Nigerian Trust Fund (NTF). The ADF, established in 1972, provides development finance on concessional terms to low-income Regional Member Countries which are unable to borrow on the non-concessional terms of the African Development Bank. Membership of the Fund is made up of 24 non-African State Participants and the African Development Bank. The NTF is a special ADB fund created in 1976 by agreement between the Bank Group and the Government of the Federal Republic of Nigeria. Its objective is to assist the development efforts of low-income Regional Member Countries whose economic and social conditions and prospects require concessional financing.

Official languages: English, French.
Headquarters: 01 BP 1387, Abidjan 01, Côte d'Ivoire.
Website: http://www.afdb.org
President: Donald Kaberuka (Rwanda).

African Export–Import Bank (Afreximbank)

Established in 1987 under the auspices of the African Development Bank to facilitate, promote and expand intra-African and extra-African trade. Membership is made up of three categories of shareholders: Class 'A' Shareholders consisting of African governments, African central banks and sub-regional and regional financial institutions and economic organizations; Class 'B' Shareholders consisting of African public and private financial institutions; and Class 'C' Shareholders consisting of international financial institutions, economic organizations and non-African states, banks, financial institutions and public and private investors.

Official languages: English, French, Arabic, Portuguese.
Headquarters: World Trade Center, 1191 Corniche El-Nil, Cairo 11221, Egypt.
Website: http://www.afreximbank.com
President and Chairman of the Board: Jean-Louis Ekra (Côte d'Ivoire).

African Union (AU)

History. The Fourth Extraordinary Session of the Assembly of the Heads of State and Government of the Organization of African Unity (OAU) held in Sirté, Libya on 9 Sept. 1999 decided to establish an African Union. At Lomé, Togo on 11 July 2000 the OAU Assembly of the Heads of State and Government adopted the Constitutive Act of the African Union, which was later ratified by the required two-thirds of the member states of the Organization of African Unity (OAU); it came into force on 26 May 2001. The Lusaka Summit, in July 2001, gave a mandate to translate the transformation of the Organization of African Unity into the African Union, and on 9 July 2002 the Durban Summit, in South Africa, formally launched the African Union.

Members. Algeria, Angola, Benin, Botswana, Burkina Faso, Burundi, Cameroon, Cape Verde, Central African Republic, Chad, Comoros, Democratic Republic of the Congo, Republic of the Congo, Côte d'Ivoire, Djibouti, Egypt, Equatorial Guinea, Eritrea, Ethiopia, Gabon, Gambia, Ghana, Guinea*, Guinea-Bissau, Kenya, Lesotho, Liberia, Libya, Madagascar**, Malaŵi, Mali, Mauritania, Mauritius, Mozambique, Namibia, Niger***, Nigeria, Rwanda, Sahrawi Arab Democratic Republic (Western Sahara), São Tomé e Príncipe, Senegal, Seychelles, Sierra Leone, Somalia, South Africa, Sudan, Swaziland, Tanzania, Togo, Tunisia, Uganda, Zambia, Zimbabwe. *Membership suspended since the coup of Dec. 2008. **Membership suspended since the change of government in March 2009. ***Membership suspended since the coup of Feb. 2010.

Aims. The African Union aims to promote unity, solidarity, cohesion and co-operation among the peoples of Africa and African states, and at the same time to co-ordinate efforts by African people to realize their goals of achieving economic, political and social integration.

Activities. The African Union became fully operational in July 2002, and is working towards establishing the organs stipulated in the constitutive act. These include a Pan-African parliament, an Economic, Social and Cultural Council (ECOSOCC) and a Peace and Security Council (which have now been inaugurated), plus a Central Bank and a Court of Justice.

Official languages: Arabic, English, French, Ki-Swahili, Portuguese and Spanish.
Headquarters: POB 3243, Addis Ababa, Ethiopia.
Website: http://www.africa-union.org
Chairman: Bingu wa Mutharika (Malaŵi).

Bank of Central African States (BEAC)

The Bank of Central African States (Banque des Etats de l'Afrique Centrale) was established in 1973 when a new Convention of Monetary Co-operation with France was signed. The five original members, Cameroon, Central African Republic, Chad, Republic of the Congo and Gabon, were joined by Equatorial Guinea in 1985. Under its Convention and statutes, the BEAC is declared a 'Multinational African institution in the management and control of which France participates in return for the guarantee she provides for its currency'.

Official language: French.
Headquarters: Avenue Monseigneur Vogt, Yaoundé, Cameroon.
Website: http://www.beac.int (French only)
Governor: Philibert Andzembe (Gabon).

Publications. Etudes et Statistiques (monthly bulletins); *Annual Report*; *Directory of Banks and Financial Establishments of BEAC Monetary Area* (annual); *Bulletin du Marché Monétaire* (monthly bulletins); *Annual Report of the Banking Commission.*

Central Bank of West African States (BCEAO)

Established in 1962, the Central Bank of West African States (Banque Centrale des Etats de l'Afrique de l'Ouest) is the common central bank of the eight member states which form the West African Monetary Union (WAMU). It has the sole right of currency issue throughout the Union territory and is responsible for the pooling of the Union's foreign exchange reserve; the management of the monetary policy of the member states; the keeping of the accounts of the member states treasury; and the definition of the banking law applicable to banks and financial establishments.

Members. Benin, Burkina Faso, Côte d'Ivoire, Guinea-Bissau, Mali, Niger, Senegal, Togo.

Official language: French.
Headquarters: Avenue Abdoulaye Fadiga, Dakar, Senegal.
Website: http://www.bceao.int
Governor: Philippe-Henri Dacoury-Tabley (Côte d'Ivoire).

Publications. Rapport annuel (annual); *Annuaire des Banques* (annual); *Bilan des Banques U.M.O.A.* (annual); *Notes d'information et statistiques* (monthly bulletin).

Common Market for Eastern and Southern Africa (COMESA)

COMESA is an African economic grouping of 19 member states who are committed to the creation of a Common Market for Eastern and Southern Africa. It was established in 1994 as a building block for the African Economic Community and replaced the Preferential Trade Area for Eastern and Southern Africa, which had been in existence since 1981.

Members. Burundi, Comoros, Democratic Republic of the Congo, Djibouti, Egypt, Eritrea, Ethiopia, Kenya, Libya, Madagascar, Malaŵi, Mauritius, Rwanda, Seychelles, Sudan, Swaziland, Uganda, Zambia and Zimbabwe.

Objectives. To facilitate the removal of the structural and institutional weaknesses of member states so that they are able to attain collective and sustainable development.

Activities. COMESA's Free Trade Area (FTA) was launched on 31 Oct. 2000 at a Summit of Heads of States and Government in Lusaka, Zambia. The FTA participating states have zero tariff on goods and services produced in these countries.

In addition to creating the policy environment for freeing trade, COMESA has also created specialized institutions like the Eastern and Southern African Trade and Development Bank (PTA Bank), the PTA Reinsurance Company (ZEP-RE), the Clearing House and the COMESA Court of Justice, to provide the required financial infrastructure and service support. COMESA has also promoted a political risk guarantee scheme, the Africa Trade Insurance Agency (ATI), a Leather and Leather Products Institute (LLPI), as well as a cross-border insurance scheme, the COMESA Yellow Card.

Official languages: English, French, Portuguese.
Headquarters: COMESA Secretariat, COMESA Centre, Ben Bella Road, PO Box 30051, 10101 Lusaka, Zambia.
Website: http://www.comesa.int
Secretary General: Sindiso Ngwenya (Zimbabwe).

East African Community (EAC)

The East African Community (EAC) was formally established on 30 Nov. 1999 with the signing in Arusha, Tanzania of the Treaty for the Establishment of the East African Community. The Treaty envisaged the establishment of a Customs Union, as the entry point of the Community, a Common Market, subsequently a Monetary Union and ultimately a Political Federation of the East African States. In Nov. 2003 the EAC partner states signed a Protocol on the Establishment of the East African Customs Union, which came into force on 1 Jan. 2005. The Common Market was scheduled to come into force on 1 July 2010.

Members. Burundi, Kenya, Rwanda, Tanzania, Uganda.

Headquarters: PO Box 1096, Arusha, Tanzania.
Website: http://www.eac.int
Secretary General: Juma Mwapachu (Tanzania).

East African Development Bank (EADB)

Established originally under the Treaty for East African Co-operation in 1967 with Kenya, Tanzania and Uganda as signatories, a new Charter for the Bank (with the same signatories) came into force in 1980. Under the original Treaty the Bank was confined to the provision of financial and technical assistance for the promotion of industrial development in member states but with the new Charter its remit was broadened to include involvement in agriculture, forestry, tourism, transport and the development of infrastructure, with preference for projects which promote regional co-operation.

Official language: English.
Headquarters: 4 Nile Avenue, Kampala, Uganda.
Website: http://www.eadb.org
Chairman of the Board: Ezra Suruma (Uganda).

Economic Community of Central African States (CEEAC)

The Economic Community of Central African States (Communauté Economique des Etats de l'Afrique Centrale) was established in 1983 to promote regional economic co-operation and to establish a Central African Common Market. There are plans for both a common market and a single currency.

Members. Angola, Burundi, Cameroon, Central African Republic, Chad, Democratic Republic of the Congo, Republic of the Congo, Equatorial Guinea, Gabon, São Tomé e Príncipe.

Headquarters: BP 2112, Libreville, Gabon.
Website: http://www.ceeac-eccas.org
President: Joseph Kabila (Democratic Republic of the Congo).
Secretary General: Louis Sylvain-Goma (Republic of the Congo).

Economic Community of West African States (ECOWAS)

Founded in 1975 as a regional common market, and now planning to introduce a single currency, the eco, by 2020, ECOWAS later also became a political forum involved in the promotion of a democratic environment and the pursuit of fundamental human rights. In July 1993 it revised its treaty to assume responsibility for the regulation of regional armed conflicts, acknowledging the inextricable link between development and peace and security. Thus it now has a new role in conflict management and prevention through its Mediation and Security Council, which monitors the moratorium on the export, import and manufacture of light weapons and ammunition. However, it still retains a military arm, ECOMOG. It is also involved in the war against drug abuse and illicit drug trafficking.

Members. Benin, Burkina Faso, Cape Verde, Côte d'Ivoire, The Gambia, Ghana, Guinea, Guinea-Bissau, Liberia, Mali, Niger (suspended since Oct. 2009), Nigeria, Senegal, Sierra Leone, Togo.

Organization. It meets at yearly summits which rotate in the different capitals of member states. The institution is governed by the Council of Ministers, and has a secretariat in Abuja which is run by an Executive Secretary.

Official languages: English, French, Portuguese.
Headquarters: 101 Yakubu Gowon Crescent, Asokoro, Abuja, Nigeria.
Website: http://www.ecowas.int
Email: info@ecowas.int
Executive Secretary: Dr Mohamed Ibn Chambas (Ghana).

Intergovernmental Authority on Development

The Intergovernmental Authority on Development was created on 21 March 1996 and has its origins in the Intergovernmental Authority on Drought and Development, which had been established in 1986. It has three priority areas of co-operation: conflict prevention, management and humanitarian affairs; infrastructure development; food security and environment protection.

Members. Djibouti, Ethiopia, Kenya, Somalia, Sudan, Uganda. Eritrea was formerly a member but withdrew in April 2007.

Headquarters: PO Box 2653, Djibouti, Republic of Djibouti.
Website: http://www.igad.org
Executive Secretary: Mahboub Maalim (Kenya).

Lake Chad Basin Commission

Established by a Convention and Statute signed on 22 May 1964 by Cameroon, Chad, Niger and Nigeria, and later by the Central African Republic, to regulate and control utilization of the water and other natural resources in the Basin (Sudan has also been admitted as an observer); to initiate, promote and co-ordinate natural resources development projects and research within the Basin area; and to examine complaints and promote settlement of disputes, with a view to promoting regional co-operation.

In Dec. 1977, at Enugu in Nigeria, the 3rd summit of heads of state of the commission signed the protocol for the Harmonization of the Regulations Relating to Fauna and Flora in member countries, and adopted plans for the multi-donor approach towards major integrated development for the conventional basin. An international campaign to save Lake Chad following a report on the environmental degradation of the conventional basin was launched by heads of state at the 8th summit of the Commission in Abuja in March 1994. The 10th summit, held in N'Djaména in 2000, saw agreement on a US$1m. inter-basin water transfer project.

The Commission operates an annual budget of 1bn. francs CFA, and receives assistance from various international and donor agencies including the FAO, and UN Development and Environment Programmes.

Official languages: English, French.
Headquarters: BP 727, N'Djaména, Chad.
Executive Secretary: Abdullahi Umar Ganduje (Nigeria).

Niger Basin Authority

As a result of a special meeting of the Niger River Commission (established in 1964), to discuss the revitalizing and restructuring of the organization to improve its efficiency, the Niger Basin Authority was established in 1980. Its responsibilities cover the harmonization and co-ordination of national development policies; the formulation of the general development policy of the Basin; the elaboration and implementation of an integrated development plan of the Basin; the initiation and monitoring of an orderly and rational regional policy for the utilization of the waters of the Niger River; the design and conduct of studies, researches and surveys; the formulation of plans, the construction, exploitation and maintenance of structure, and the elaboration of projects.

Members. Benin, Burkina Faso, Cameroon, Chad, Côte d'Ivoire, Guinea, Mali, Niger, Nigeria.

Official languages: English, French.
Headquarters: BP 729, Niamey, Niger.
Website: http://www.abn.ne
Executive Secretary: Oyewole Ogunmola (Nigeria).

Southern African Customs Union (SACU)

Established by the Customs Union Convention between the British Colony of Cape of Good Hope and the Orange Free State Boer Republic in 1889, the Southern African Customs Union was extended in 1910 to include the then Union of South Africa and British High Commission Territories in Africa and remained unchanged after these countries gained independence. South Africa was the dominant member with sole-decision making power over customs and excise policies until the 2002 SACU Agreement which created a permanent Secretariat, a Council of Ministers headed by a minister from one of the member states on a rotational basis, a Customs Union Commission, Technical Liaison Committees, a SACU tribunal and a SACU tariff board.

Members. Botswana, Lesotho, Namibia, South Africa, Swaziland.

Aims. To promote economic development through regional co-ordination of trade.

Headquarters: Private Bag 132845, Windhoek, Namibia.
Website: http://www.sacu.int
Email: info@sacu.int
Executive Secretary: Tswelopele Cornelia Moremi (Botswana).

Southern African Development Community (SADC)

The Southern African Development Co-ordination Conference (SADCC), the precursor of the Southern African Development Community (SADC), was formed in Lusaka, Zambia on 1 April 1980, following the adoption of the Lusaka Declaration—*Southern Africa: Towards Economic Liberation*—by the nine founding member states.

Members. The nine founder member countries were Angola, Botswana, Lesotho, Malaŵi, Mozambique, Swaziland, Tanzania, Zambia and Zimbabwe. The Democratic Republic of the Congo, Madagascar, Mauritius, Namibia, the Seychelles and South Africa have since joined. The Seychelles left in July 2004 but rejoined in Aug. 2007. As a result there are now 15 members.

Aims and Activities. SADC's Common Agenda includes the following: the promotion of sustainable and equitable economic growth and socio-economic development that will ensure poverty alleviation with the ultimate objective of its eradication; the promotion of common political values, systems and other shared values that are transmitted through institutions that are democratic, legitimate and effective; and the consolidation and maintenance of democracy, peace and security.

In contrast to the country-based co-ordination of sectoral activities and programmes, SADC has now adopted a more centralized approach through which the 21 sectoral programmes are grouped into four clusters; namely: Trade, Industry, Finance and Investment; Infrastructure and Services; Food, Agriculture and Natural Resources; Social and Human Development and Special Programmes.

SADC has made significant progress in implementing its integration agenda since the 1992 Treaty came into force. Since then, more than 20 Protocols to spearhead the sectoral programmes and activities have been signed. Those Protocols that have entered into force include: Immunities and Privileges; Combating Illicit Drugs; Energy; Transport, Communications and Meteorology; Shared Watercourse Systems; Mining; Trade; Education and Training; Tourism; and Health.

Official languages: English, French, Portuguese.
Headquarters: Private Bag 0095, Gaborone, Botswana.
Website: http://www.sadc.int
Email: registry@sadc.int
Executive Secretary: Tomaz Augusto Salomão (Mozambique).

West African Development Bank (BOAD)

The West African Development Bank (Banque Ouest Africaine de Développement) was established in Nov. 1973 by an Agreement signed by the member states of the West African Monetary Union (UMOA), now the West African Economic and Monetary Union (UEMOA).

Aims. To promote balanced development of the States of the Union and to achieve West African economic integration.

Members. Benin, Burkina Faso, Côte d'Ivoire, Guinea-Bissau, Mali, Niger, Senegal, Togo.

Official language: French.
Headquarters: 68 Avenue de la Libération, Lomé, Togo.
Website: http://www.boad.org (French only)
Email: boadsiege@boad.org
President: Abdoulaye Bio-Tchané (Benin).

West African Economic and Monetary Union (UEMOA)

Founded in 1994, the UEMOA (Union Economique et Monétaire Ouest Africaine) aims to reinforce the competitiveness of the economic and financial activities of member states in the context of an open and rival market and a rationalized and harmonized juridical environment; to ensure the convergence of the macro-economic performances and policies of member states; to create a common market among member states; to co-ordinate the national sector-based policies; and to harmonize the legislation, especially the fiscal system, of the member states.

Members. Benin, Burkina Faso, Côte d'Ivoire, Guinea-Bissau, Mali, Niger, Senegal, Togo.

Headquarters: 01 B.P. 543, Ouagadougou 01, Burkina Faso.
Website: http://www.uemoa.int
Email: commission@uemoa.int
President: Soumaïla Cisse (Mali).

Agency for the Prohibition of Nuclear Weapons in Latin America and the Caribbean (OPANAL)

The Agency (Organismo para la Proscripción de las Armas Nucleares en la América Latina y el Caribe) was established following the Cuban missile crisis to guarantee implementation of the world's first Nuclear-Weapon-Free-Zone (NWFZ) in the region. Created by the Treaty of Tlatelolco (1967), OPANAL is an inter-governmental agency responsible for ensuring that the requirements of the Treaty are enforced. OPANAL has played a major role in establishing other NWFZs throughout the world.

Organization. The Agency consists of three main bodies: the General Conference which meets for biennial sessions and special sessions when deemed necessary; the Council of OPANAL consisting of five member states which meet every two months plus special meetings when necessary; and the Secretariat General.

Members of the Treaty. Antigua and Barbuda, Argentina, Bahamas, Barbados, Belize, Bolivia, Brazil, Chile, Colombia, Costa Rica, Cuba, Dominica, Dominican Republic, Ecuador, El Salvador, Grenada, Guatemala, Guyana, Haiti, Honduras, Jamaica, Mexico, Nicaragua, Panama, Paraguay, Peru, St Kitts and Nevis, St Lucia, St Vincent and the Grenadines, Suriname, Trinidad and Tobago, Uruguay, Venezuela.

Headquarters: Schiller No. 326, 5th Floor, Col. Chapultepec Morales, México, D. F. 11570, Mexico.
Website: http://www.opanal.org
Email: info@opanal.org
Secretary-General: Edmundo Vargas Carreño (Chile).

Andean Community

On 26 May 1969 an agreement was signed by Bolivia, Chile, Colombia, Ecuador and Peru establishing the Cartagena Agreement (also referred to as the Andean Pact or the Andean Group). Chile withdrew from the Group in 1976. Venezuela, which was actively involved, did not sign the agreement until 1973. In 1997 Peru announced its withdrawal for five years. In 2006 Venezuela left as a result of Colombia and Peru signing bilateral trade agreements with the USA.

The Andean Free Trade Area came into effect on 1 Feb. 1993 as the first step towards the creation of a common market. Bolivia, Colombia, Ecuador and Peru have fully liberalized their trade. A Common External Tariff for imports from third countries has been in effect since 1 Feb. 1995.

In March 1996 at the Group's 8th summit in Trujillo in Peru, the then member countries (Bolivia, Colombia, Ecuador, Peru, Venezuela) set up the Andean Community, to promote greater economic, commercial and political integration between member countries under a new Andean Integration System (SAI).

The member countries and bodies of the Andean Integration System are working to establish an Andean Common Market and to implement a Common Foreign Policy, a social agenda, a Community policy on border integration, and policies for achieving joint macroeconomic targets.

Organization. The Andean Presidential Council, composed of the presidents of the member states, is the highest-level body of the Andean Integration System (SAI). The Commission and the Andean Council of Foreign Ministers are legislative bodies. The General Secretariat is the executive body and the Andean Parliament is the deliberative body of the SAI. The Court of Justice, which began operating in 1984, resolves disputes between members and interprets legislation. The SAI has other institutions: Andean Development Corporation (CAF), Latin American Reserve Fund (FLAR), Simon Bolivar Andean University, Andean Business Advisory Council, Andean Labour Advisory Council and various Social Agreements.

Further to the treaty signed by 12 South American countries in May 2008, it is anticipated that the Andean Community will gradually be integrated into the new Union of South American Nations.

Official language: Spanish.
Headquarters: Avda Paseo de la República 3895, San Isidro, Lima 17, Peru.
Website: http://www.comunidadandina.org
Email: contacto@comunidadandina.org
Secretary-General: Freddy Ehlers (Ecuador).

Association of Caribbean States (ACS)

The Convention establishing the ACS was signed on 24 July 1994 in Cartagena de Indias, Colombia, with the aim of promoting consultation, co-operation and concerted action among all the countries of the Caribbean, comprising 25 full member states and three associate members. A total of eight other non-independent Caribbean countries are eligible for associate membership.

Members. Antigua and Barbuda, Bahamas, Barbados, Belize, Colombia, Costa Rica, Cuba, Dominica, Dominican Republic, El Salvador, Grenada, Guatemala, Guyana, Haiti, Honduras, Jamaica, Mexico, Nicaragua, Panama, St Kitts and Nevis, St Lucia, St Vincent and the Grenadines, Suriname, Trinidad and Tobago, Venezuela.

Associate members. Aruba, France (on behalf of French Guiana, Guadeloupe and Martinique), the Netherlands Antilles and the Turks and Caicos Islands.

The CARICOM Secretariat, the Latin American Economic System (SELA), the Central American Integration System (SICA) and the Permanent Secretariat of the General Treaty on Central American Economic Integration (SIECA) were declared Founding Observers of the ACS in 1996. The United Nations Economic Commission for Latin America and the Caribbean (ECLAC) and the Caribbean Tourism Organization (CTO) were admitted as Founding Observers in 2000 and 2001 respectively.

Functions. The objectives of the ACS are enshrined in the Convention and are based on the following: the strengthening of the regional co-operation and integration process, with a view to creating an enhanced economic space in the region; preserving the environmental integrity of the Caribbean Sea which is regarded as the common patrimony of the peoples of the region; and promoting the sustainable development of the Greater Caribbean. Its current focal areas are trade, transport, sustainable tourism and natural disasters.

Organization. The main organs of the Association are the Ministerial Council and the Secretariat. There are Special Committees on: Trade Development and External Economic Relations; Sustainable Tourism; Transport; Natural Disasters; Budget and Administration. There is also a Council of National Representatives of the Special Fund responsible for overseeing resource mobilization efforts and project development.

Headquarters: ACS Secretariat, 5–7 Sweet Briar Road, St Clair, PO Box 660, Port of Spain, Trinidad and Tobago.
Website: http://www.acs-aec.org
Email: mail@acs-aec.org
Secretary-General: Luis Fernando Andrade Falla (Guatemala).

Caribbean Community (CARICOM)

Origin. The Treaty of Chaguaramas establishing the Caribbean Community and Common Market was signed by the prime ministers of Barbados, Guyana, Jamaica and Trinidad and Tobago at Chaguaramas, Trinidad, on 4 July 1973.

Six additional countries and territories (Belize, Dominica, Grenada, St Lucia, St Vincent and the Grenadines, Montserrat) signed the Treaty on 17 April 1974, and the Treaty came into effect for those countries on 1 May 1974. Antigua acceded to membership on 4 July that year; St Kitts and Nevis on 26 July; the Bahamas on 4 July 1983 (not Common Market); Suriname on 4 July 1995.

Members. Antigua and Barbuda, Bahamas, Barbados, Belize, Dominica, Grenada, Guyana, Haiti, Jamaica, Montserrat, St Kitts and Nevis, St Lucia, St Vincent and the Grenadines, Suriname, and Trinidad and Tobago. Anguilla, Bermuda, the British Virgin Islands, Cayman Islands and Turks and Caicos Islands are associate members.

Objectives. The Caribbean Community has the following objectives: improved standards of living and work; full employment of labour and other factors of production; accelerated, co-ordinated and sustained economic development and convergence; expansion of trade and economic relations with third States; enhanced levels of international competitiveness; organization for increased production and productivity; the achievement of a greater measure of economic leverage and effectiveness of member states in dealing with third States, groups of States and entities of any description; enhanced co-ordination of member states' foreign and foreign economic policies; enhanced functional co-operation.

At its 20th Meeting in July 1999 the Conference of Heads of Government of the Caribbean Community approved for signature the agreement establishing the Caribbean Court of Justice. They mandated the establishment of a Preparatory Committee comprising the Attorneys General of Barbados, Guyana, Jamaica, St Kitts and Nevis, St Lucia and Trinidad and Tobago assisted by other officials, to develop and implement a programme of public education within the Caribbean Community and to make appropriate arrangements for the inauguration of the Caribbean Court of Justice prior to the establishment of the CARICOM Single Market and Economy. To this end at its 23rd Meeting in July 2002 the Heads of Government agreed on immediate measures to inaugurate the Court by the second half of 2003, although delays meant it was not inaugurated until April 2005. Among the measures adopted was the establishment of a Trust Fund with a one-time settlement of US$100m. to finance the Court. The President of the Caribbean Development Bank was authorized to raise the funds on international capital markets, so that member states could access these funds to meet their assessed contributions towards the financing of the Court. The agreement establishing the Regional Justice Protection Programme was also approved for signature.

Structure. The Conference of Heads of Government is the principal organ of the Community, and its primary responsibility is to determine and provide the policy direction for the Community. It is the final authority on behalf of the Community for the conclusion of treaties and for entering into relationships between the Community and international organizations and States. It is responsible for financial arrangements to meet the expenses of the Community.

The Community Council of Ministers is the second highest organ of the Community and consists of Ministers of Government responsible for Community Affairs. The Community Council has primary responsibility for the development of Community strategic planning and co-ordination in the areas of economic integration, functional co-operation and external relations.

The Secretariat is the principal administrative organ of the Community. The Secretary-General is appointed by the Conference (on the recommendation of the Community Council) for a term not exceeding five years, and may be reappointed. The Secretary-General is the Chief Executive Officer of the Community and acts in that capacity at all meetings of the Community Organs.

Associate Institutions. Caribbean Development Bank (CDB); University of Guyana (UG); University of the West Indies (UWI); Caribbean Law Institute (CLI)/Caribbean Law Institute Centre (CLIC); Organisation of Eastern Caribbean States; Anton de Kom University of Suriname.

Official language: English.
Headquarters: Bank of Guyana Building, PO Box 10827, Georgetown, Guyana.
Website: http://www.caricom.org
Secretary-General: Edwin W. Carrington (Trinidad and Tobago).

Publications. CARICOM Perspective (annual); *Annual Report; Treaty Establishing the Caribbean Community; Caribbean Trade and Investment Report 2005.*

Further Reading

Parry, J. H., *et al. A Short History of the West Indies.* Rev. ed. 1987

Caribbean Development Bank (CDB)

Established in 1969 by 16 regional and two non-regional members. Membership is open to all states and territories of the region and to non-regional states which are members of the UN or its Specialized Agencies or of the International Atomic Energy Agency.

Members—regional countries and territories: Anguilla, Antigua and Barbuda, Bahamas, Barbados, Belize, British Virgin Islands, Cayman Islands, Dominica, Grenada, Guyana, Haiti, Jamaica, Montserrat, St Kitts and Nevis, St Lucia, St Vincent and the Grenadines, Trinidad and Tobago, Turks and Caicos Islands. *Other regional countries:* Colombia, Mexico, Venezuela. *Non-regional countries:* Canada, China, Germany, Italy, United Kingdom.

Function. To contribute to the economic growth and development of the member countries of the Caribbean and promote economic co-operation and integration among them, with particular regard to the needs of the less developed countries.

Headquarters: PO Box 408, Wildey, St Michael, Barbados.
Website: http://www.caribank.org
Email: info@caribank.org
President: Dr Compton Bourne (Guyana).

Publications. Annual Report; Basic Information; Caribbean Development Bank: Its Purpose, Role and Functions; Summary of Proceedings of Annual Meetings of Board of Governors; Statements by the President; Financial Policies; Guidelines for Procurement; Procedures for the Selection and Engagement of Consultants by Recipients of CDB Financing; Special Development Fund Rules; Sector Policy Papers; CDB News (newsletter).

Central American Bank for Economic Integration (CABEI)

Established in 1960, the Bank is the financial institution created by the Central American Economic Integration Treaty and aims to implement the economic integration and balanced economic growth of the member states.

Members. (Regional) Costa Rica, El Salvador, Guatemala, Honduras, Nicaragua. (Non-regional) Argentina, Colombia, Dominican Republic, Mexico, Panama, Spain, Taiwan.

Official languages: Spanish, English.
Headquarters: Apartado Postal 772, Tegucigalpa, DC, Honduras.
Website: http://www.bcie.org
President: Nick Rischbieth (Honduras).

Central American Common Market (CACM)

In Dec. 1960 El Salvador, Guatemala, Honduras and Nicaragua concluded the General Treaty on Central American Economic Integration under the auspices of the Organization of Central American States (ODECA) in Managua. Long-standing political and social conflicts in the area have repeatedly dogged efforts to establish integration towards the establishment of a common market.

Members. Costa Rica, El Salvador, Guatemala, Honduras and Nicaragua.

A protocol to the 1960 General Treaty signed by all five members and Panama in Oct. 1993 reaffirmed an eventual commitment to full economic integration with a common external tariff of 20% to be introduced only voluntarily and gradually.

A Treaty on Democratic Security in Central America was signed by all five members plus Panama at San Pedro Sula, Honduras in Dec. 1995, with a view to achieving a proper 'balance of forces' in the region, intensifying the fight against trafficking of drugs and arms, and reintegrating refugees and displaced persons.

In addition, the CACM countries signed a new framework co-operation agreement with the EC in Feb. 1993, revising the previous (1985) failing agreement between them, to provide support to CACM's integration plans.

Headquarters: 4a Avenida 10–25, Zona 14, Ciudad de Guatemala, Guatemala.
Secretary-General: Alfonso Pimentel Rodríguez (Guatemala).

Eastern Caribbean Central Bank (ECCB)

The Eastern Caribbean Central Bank was established in 1983, replacing the East Caribbean Currency Authority (ECCA). Its purpose is to regulate the availability of money and credit; to promote and maintain monetary stability; to promote credit and exchange conditions and a sound financial structure conducive to the balanced growth and development of the economies of the territories of the participating Governments; and to actively promote, through means consistent with its other objectives, the economic development of the territories of the participating Governments.

Members. Anguilla, Antigua and Barbuda, Dominica, Grenada, Montserrat, St Kitts and Nevis, St Lucia, St Vincent and the Grenadines.

Official language: English.
Headquarters: PO Box 89, Bird Rock, Basseterre, St Kitts and Nevis.
Website: http://www.eccb-centralbank.org
Email: info@eccb-centralbank.org
Governor: Sir Dwight Venner (St Vincent and the Grenadines).

Inter-American Development Bank (IDB)

The IDB, the oldest and largest regional multilateral development institution, was established in 1959 to help accelerate economic and social development in Latin America and the Caribbean. The Bank's original membership included 19 Latin American and Caribbean countries and the USA. Today, membership totals 48 nations, including non-regional members.

Members. Argentina, Austria, Bahamas, Barbados, Belgium, Belize, Bolivia, Brazil, Canada, Chile, China, Colombia, Costa Rica, Croatia, Denmark, Dominican Republic, Ecuador, El Salvador, Finland, France, Germany, Guatemala, Guyana, Haiti, Honduras, Israel, Italy, Jamaica, Japan, South Korea, Mexico, the Netherlands, Nicaragua, Norway, Panama, Paraguay, Peru, Portugal, Slovenia, Spain, Suriname, Sweden, Switzerland, Trinidad and Tobago, UK, USA, Uruguay, Venezuela.

The Bank's total lending up to 2007 has been US$156bn. for projects with a total cost of over US$353bn. Its lending has increased dramatically from the US$294m. approved in 1961 to US$8,970m. in 2007.

Current lending priorities include poverty reduction and social equity, modernization and integration, and the environment. The Bank has a Fund for Special Operations for lending on concessional terms for projects in countries classified as economically less developed. An additional facility, the Multilateral Investment Fund (MIF), was created in 1992 to help promote and accelerate investment reforms and private-sector development throughout the region.

The Board of Governors is the Bank's highest authority. Governors are usually Ministers of Finance, Presidents of Central Banks or officers of comparable rank. The IDB has country offices in each of its borrowing countries, and in Paris and Tokyo.

Official languages: English, French, Portuguese, Spanish.
Headquarters: 1300 New York Avenue, NW, Washington, D.C., 20577, USA.
Website: http://www.iadb.org
President: Luis Alberto Moreno (Colombia).

Latin American Economic System (SELA)

Established in 1975 by the Panama Convention, SELA (Sistema Económico Latinoamericano) promotes co-ordination on economic issues and social development among the countries of Latin America and the Caribbean.

Members. Argentina, Bahamas, Barbados, Belize, Bolivia, Brazil, Chile, Colombia, Costa Rica, Cuba, Dominican Republic, Ecuador, Grenada, Guatemala, Guyana, Haiti, Honduras, Jamaica, Mexico, Nicaragua, Panama, Paraguay, Peru, Suriname, Trinidad and Tobago, Uruguay, Venezuela.

Official languages: English, French, Portuguese, Spanish.
Headquarters: Av. Francisco de Miranda, Torre Europa, Piso 4, Urb. Campo Alegre, Caracas 1060, Venezuela.
Website: http://www.sela.org
Email: difusion@sela.org
Permanent Secretary: José Rivera Banuet (Mexico).

Publications. Capitulos (in Spanish and English, published thrice yearly); *SELA Antenna in the United States* (quarterly bulletin); *Integration Bulletin on Latin America and the Caribbean* (monthly).

Latin American Integration Association (ALADI/LAIA)

The ALADI was established to promote freer trade among member countries in the region.

Members. (12) Argentina, Bolivia, Brazil, Chile, Colombia, Cuba, Ecuador, Mexico, Paraguay, Peru, Uruguay and Venezuela.

Observers. (28) Andean Development Corporation (CAF), China, Commission of the European Communities, Costa Rica, Dominican Republic, El Salvador, Guatemala, Honduras, Ibero-American General Secretariat (SEGIB), Inter-American Development Bank, Inter-American Institute for Cooperation on Agriculture (IICA), Italy, Japan, South Korea, Latin American Economic System (SELA), Nicaragua, Organization of American States (OAS), Pan American Health Organization (PAHO), Panama, Portugal, Romania, Russia, Spain, Switzerland, Ukraine, UN Development Programme, UN Economic Commission for Latin America and the Caribbean (ECLAC), World Health Organization (WHO).

Official languages: Portuguese, Spanish.
Headquarters: Calle Cebollatí 1461, Casilla de Correos 20005, 11200 Montevideo, Uruguay.
Website: http://www.aladi.org
Secretary-General: Hugo Saguier Caballero (Paraguay).

Latin American Reserve Fund

Established in 1991 as successor to the Andean Reserve Fund, the Latin American Reserve Fund assists in correcting payment imbalances through loans with terms of up to four years and guarantees extended to members, to co-ordinate their monetary, exchange and financial policies and to promote the liberalization of trade and payments in the Andean sub-region.

Members. Bolivia, Colombia, Costa Rica, Ecuador, Peru, Uruguay, Venezuela.

Official language: Spanish.
Headquarters: Edificio Banco de Occidente, Carrera 13, No. 27–47, Piso 10, Santafe de Bogota, DC, Colombia.
Website: http://www.flar.net
Executive President: Rodrigo Bolaños (Costa Rica).

Organisation of Eastern Caribbean States (OECS)

Founded in 1981 when seven eastern Caribbean states signed the Treaty of Basseterre agreeing to co-operate with each other to promote unity and solidarity among the members.

Members. Antigua and Barbuda, Dominica, Grenada, Montserrat, St Kitts and Nevis, St Lucia, St Vincent and the Grenadines. The British Virgin Islands and Anguilla have associate membership.

Functions. As set out in the Treaty of Basseterre: to promote co-operation among the member states and to defend their sovereignty and independence; to assist member states in the realization of their obligations and responsibilities to the international community with due regard to the role of international law as a standard of conduct in their relationships; to assist member states in the realization of their obligations and responsibilities to the international community with due regard to the role of international issues; to establish and maintain, where possible, arrangements for joint overseas representation and common services; to pursue these through its respective institutions by discussion of questions of common concern and by agreement on common action.

OECS' work is carried out through the office of the Director General which encompasses: the Legal Unit, Research and Communication Information Services, Functional Co-operation Services, Overseas Diplomatic Mission, Social and Sustainable Development Division, Economic Affairs Division and Corporate Service Division. These oversee the work of a number of specialized institutions, work units and projects in four countries. There is an OECS secretariat in St Lucia, which is comprised of several operating units, responsible for the following functions: Education and Human Resource Development, Export Development Unit, Legal Unit, Environment and Sustainable Development Unit, Pharmaceutical Procurement Service, Social Development Unit and OECS Sports Desk.

Official language: English.
Headquarters: Morne Fortune, PO Box 179, Castries, St Lucia.
Website: http://www.oecs.org
Email: oesec@oecs.org
Director-General: Dr Len Ishmael (St Lucia).

Organization of American States (OAS)

Origin. On 14 April 1890 representatives of the American republics, meeting in Washington at the First International Conference of American States, established an International Union of American Republics and, as its central office, a Commercial Bureau of American Republics, which later became the Pan-American Union. This international organization's object was to foster mutual understanding and co-operation among the nations of the western hemisphere. This led to the adoption on 30 April 1948 by the Ninth International Conference of American States, at Bogotá, Colombia, of the Charter of the Organization of American States. This co-ordinated the work of all the former independent official entities in the inter-American system and defined their mutual relationships. The Charter of 1948 was subsequently amended by the Protocol of Buenos Aires (1967) and the Protocol of Cartagena de Indias (1985).

Members. Antigua and Barbuda, Argentina, Bahamas, Barbados, Belize, Bolivia, Brazil, Canada, Chile, Colombia, Costa Rica, Cuba (suspended 1962*), Dominica, Dominican Republic, Ecuador, El Salvador, Grenada, Guatemala, Guyana, Haiti, Honduras (suspended since the coup of July 2009), Jamaica, Mexico, Nicaragua, Panama, Paraguay, Peru, St Kitts and Nevis, St Lucia, St Vincent and the Grenadines, Suriname, Trinidad and Tobago, USA, Uruguay, Venezuela. *In June 2009 the OAS voted to lift Cuba's suspension, although Cuba had stated that it did not wish to rejoin the organization.

Permanent Observers. Algeria, Angola, Armenia, Austria, Azerbaijan, Belgium, Benin, Bosnia and Herzegovina, Bulgaria, China, Croatia, Cyprus, Czech Republic, Denmark, Egypt, Equatorial Guinea, Estonia, EU, Finland, France, Georgia, Germany, Ghana, Greece, Holy See, Hungary, Iceland, India, Ireland, Israel, Italy, Japan, Kazakhstan, South Korea, Latvia, Lebanon, Luxembourg, Morocco, the Netherlands, Nigeria, Norway, Pakistan, Philippines, Poland, Portugal, Qatar, Romania, Russia, Saudi Arabia, Serbia, Slovakia, Slovenia, Spain, Sri Lanka, Sweden, Switzerland, Thailand, Tunisia, Turkey, UK, Ukraine, Vanuatu, Yemen.

Aims and Activities. To strengthen the peace and security of the continent; promote and consolidate representative democracy; promote by co-operative action economic, social and cultural development; and achieve an effective limitation of conventional weapons.

In Sept. 2001 an Inter-American Democratic Charter was adopted, declaring: 'The peoples of the Americas have a right to democracy and their governments have an obligation to promote and defend it.' The Charter compels the OAS to take action against any member state that disrupts its own democratic institutions.

Organization. Under its Charter the OAS accomplishes its purposes by means of:

(a) The General Assembly, which meets annually. The Secretary-General is elected by the General Assembly for five-year terms. The General Assembly approves the annual budget which is financed by quotas contributed by the member governments. The budget in 2009 amounted to US$96·12m.

(b) The Meeting of Consultation of Ministers of Foreign Affairs, held to consider problems of an urgent nature and of common interest.

(c) The Councils: The Permanent Council, which meets on a permanent basis at OAS headquarters and carries out decisions of the General Assembly, assists the member states in the peaceful settlement of disputes, acts as the Preparatory Committee of that Assembly, submits recommendations with regard to the functioning of the Organization, and considers the reports to the Assembly of the other organs. The Inter-American Council for Integral Development (CIDI) directs and monitors OAS technical co-operation programmes.

(d) The Inter-American Juridical Committee which acts as an advisory body to the OAS on juridical matters and promotes the development and codification of international law. 11 jurists, elected for four-year terms by the General Assembly, represent all the American States.

(e) The Inter-American Commission on Human Rights which oversees the observance and protection of human rights. Seven members elected for four-year terms by the General Assembly represent all the OAS member states.

(f) The General Secretariat, which is the central and permanent organ of the OAS.

(g) The Specialized Conferences, meeting to deal with special technical matters or to develop specific aspects of inter-American co-operation.

(h) The Specialized Organizations, intergovernmental organizations established by multilateral agreements to discharge specific functions in their respective fields of action, such as women's affairs, agriculture, child welfare, Indian affairs, geography and history, and health.

Headquarters: 17th Street and Constitution Avenue, NW, Washington, D.C., 20006, USA.
Website: http://www.oas.org
Secretary-General: José Miguel Insulza (Chile).

Publications. Charter of the Organization of American States. 1948.—*As Amended by the Protocol of Buenos Aires in 1967 and the Protocol of Cartagena de Indias in 1985; The OAS and the Evolution of the Inter-American System; Annual Report of the Secretary-General; Status of Inter-American Treaties and Conventions* (annual).

Secretariat for Central American Economic Integration (SIECA)

SIECA (Secretaría de Integración Económica Centroamericana) was created by the General Treaty on Central American Economic Integration in Dec. 1960. The General Treaty incorporates the Agreement on the Regime for Central American Integration Industries. In Oct. 1993 the Protocol to the General Treaty on Central Economic Integration, known as the Guatemala Protocol, was signed.

Members. Costa Rica, El Salvador, Guatemala, Honduras, Nicaragua. *Observer:* Panama.

Official language: Spanish.
Headquarters: 4a Avenida 10–25, Zona 14, Ciudad de Guatemala, Guatemala.
Website: http://www.sieca.org.gt
Secretary-General: Yolanda Mayora de Gavidia (El Salvador).

Southern Common Market (MERCOSUR)

Founded in March 1991 by the Treaty of Asunción between Argentina, Brazil, Paraguay and Uruguay, MERCOSUR committed the signatories to the progressive reduction of tariffs culminating in the formation of a common market on 1 Jan. 1995. This duly came into effect as a free trade zone affecting 90% of commodities. A common external tariff averaging 14% applies to 80% of trade with countries outside MERCOSUR. Details were agreed at foreign minister level by the Protocol of Ouro Preto signed on 17 Dec. 1994.

In 1996 Chile negotiated a free-trade agreement with MERCOSUR which came into effect on 1 Oct. Subsequently Bolivia, Chile, Colombia, Ecuador and Peru have all been granted associate member status. Mexico has observer status. Venezuela, which had associate membership between 2004 and 2006, became the fifth member of MERCOSUR in July 2006, although it was only scheduled to have full voting rights in mid-2010.

Organization. The member states' foreign ministers form a Council responsible for leading the integration process, the chairmanship of which rotates every six months. The permanent executive body is the Common Market Group of member states, which takes decisions by consensus. There is a Trade Commission and Joint Parliamentary Commission, an arbitration tribunal whose decisions are binding on member countries, and a secretariat in Montevideo.

Further to the treaty signed by 12 South American countries in May 2008, it is anticipated that Mercosur will gradually be integrated into the new Union of South American Nations.

Headquarters: Dr Luis Piera 1992, Piso 1, 11200 Montevideo, Uruguay.
Website: http://www.mercosur.org.uy (Spanish and Portuguese only)
Administrative Secretary: Agustín Colombo Sierra (Argentina).

Union of South American Nations (UNASUR)

History. Established in May 2008 in Brazil, it is anticipated that the Union of South American Nations will eventually supersede Mercosur and the Andean Community, creating an enlarged customs union with a single market, parliament, secretariat and central bank, based on the European Union structure. UNASUR is the successor body to the now defunct South American Community of Nations (CSN/SACN), founded in 2004. However, insufficiently defined goals and ongoing disputes between members of the already-existing blocs may hamper development, as may the growing US military presence in Colombia and future bilateral trade negotiations with the USA.

Members. Argentina, Bolivia, Brazil, Chile, Colombia, Ecuador, Guyana, Paraguay, Peru, Suriname, Uruguay, Venezuela.

Asian Development Bank

A multilateral development finance institution established in 1966 to promote economic and social progress in the Asian and Pacific region, the Bank's strategic objectives are to foster economic growth, reduce poverty, improve the status of women, support human development (including population planning) and protect the environment.

The bank's capital stock is owned by 67 member countries, 48 regional and 19 non-regional. The bank makes loans and equity investments, and provides technical assistance grants for the preparation and execution of development projects and programmes; promotes investment of public and private capital for development purposes; and assists in co-ordinating development policies and plans in its developing member countries (DMCs).

The bank gives special attention to the needs of smaller or less developed countries, giving priority to projects that contribute to the economic growth of the region and promote regional co-operation. Loans from ordinary capital resources on non-concessional terms account for about 80% of cumulative lending. Loans from the bank's principal special fund, the Asian Development Fund, are made on highly concessional terms almost exclusively to the poorest borrowing countries.

Regional members. Afghanistan, Armenia, Australia, Azerbaijan, Bangladesh, Bhutan, Brunei, Cambodia, China, Cook Islands, Fiji Islands, Georgia, Hong Kong, India, Indonesia, Japan, Kazakhstan, Kiribati, South Korea, Kyrgyzstan, Laos, Malaysia, Maldives, Marshall Islands, Micronesia, Mongolia, Myanmar, Nauru, Nepal, New Zealand, Pakistan, Palau, Papua New Guinea, Philippines, Samoa, Singapore, Solomon Islands, Sri Lanka, Taiwan, Tajikistan, Thailand, Timor-Leste, Tonga, Turkmenistan, Tuvalu, Uzbekistan, Vanuatu and Vietnam.

Non-regional members. Austria, Belgium, Canada, Denmark, Finland, France, Germany, Ireland, Italy, Luxembourg, Netherlands, Norway, Portugal, Spain, Sweden, Switzerland, Turkey, UK, USA.

Organization. The bank's highest policy-making body is its Board of Governors, which meets annually. Its executive body is the 12-member Board of Directors (each with an alternate), eight from the regional members and four non-regional.

The ADB also has resident missions: in Afghanistan, Armenia, Azerbaijan, Bangladesh, Cambodia, China, India, Indonesia, Kazakhstan, Kyrgyzstan, Laos, Mongolia, Nepal, Pakistan, Papua New Guinea, Sri Lanka, Tajikistan, Thailand, Uzbekistan, Vietnam; a Pacific Liaison and Co-ordination Office in Sydney; and a South Pacific Subregional Office in Suva, Fiji Islands. There are also three representative offices: in Tokyo, Frankfurt and Washington, D.C.

Official language: English.
Headquarters: 6 ADB Avenue, Mandaluyong, Metro Manila, Philippines.
Website: http://www.adb.org
President: Haruhiko Kuroda (Japan).

Asia-Pacific Economic Co-operation (APEC)

Origin and Aims. APEC was originally established in 1989 to take advantage of the interdependence among Asia-Pacific economies, by facilitating economic growth for all participants and enhancing a sense of community in the region. APEC is now the premier forum for facilitating economic growth, co-operation, trade and investment in the Asia-Pacific region. APEC has a membership of 21 economic jurisdictions, a population of over 2·5bn. and a combined GDP of US$19trn. accounting for 47% of world trade. APEC is working to achieve what are referred to as the 'Bogor Goals' of free and open trade and investment in the Asia-Pacific area.

Members. Australia, Brunei, Canada, Chile, China, Hong Kong, Indonesia, Japan, South Korea, Malaysia, Mexico, New Zealand, Papua New Guinea, Peru, Philippines, Russia, Singapore, Taiwan, Thailand, USA and Vietnam.

Activities. APEC works in three broad areas to meet the Bogor Goals. These three broad work areas, known as APEC's 'Three Pillars', are: Trade and Investment Liberalization—reducing and eliminating tariff and non-tariff barriers to trade and investment, and opening markets; Business Facilitation—reducing the costs of business transactions, improving access to trade information and co-ordinating policy and business strategies to facilitate growth, and free and open trade; Economic and Technical Co-operation—assisting member economies build the necessary capacities to take advantage of global trade and the new economy. The 20th APEC Ministerial Meeting, held in Lima, Peru in Nov. 2008, had as its theme 'A New Commitment to Asia-Pacific Development'

Official language: English.
Headquarters: 35 Heng Mui Keng Terrace, Singapore 119616.
Website: http://www.apecsec.org.sg
Executive Director: Muhamad Noor Yacob (Malaysia).

Association of South East Asian Nations (ASEAN)

History and Membership. ASEAN is a regional intergovernmental organization formed by the governments of Indonesia, Malaysia, the Philippines, Singapore and Thailand through the Bangkok Declaration which was signed by their foreign ministers on 8 Aug. 1967. Brunei joined in 1984, Vietnam in 1995, Laos and Myanmar in 1997 and Cambodia in 1999. Papua New Guinea also has observer status. The ASEAN Charter, signed in Nov. 2007, established the group as a legal entity and created permanent representation for members at its secretariat in Jakarta.

Objectives. The main objectives are to accelerate economic growth, social progress and cultural development, to promote active collaboration and mutual assistance in matters of common interest, to ensure the political and economic stability of the South East Asian region, and to maintain close co-operation with existing international and regional organizations with similar aims.

Activities. Principal projects concern economic co-operation and development, with the intensification of intra-ASEAN and global trade; joint research and technological programmes; co-operation in transportation and communications; promotion of tourism, South East Asian studies, cultural, scientific, educational and administrative exchanges. An *ASEAN Free Trade Area (AFTA),* aiming to reduce trade tariffs in the region and attract investment, became operational for its first six signatories—namely Brunei, Indonesia, Malaysia, Philippines, Singapore and Thailand—in 2003. The four other members are set to join in 2012. The ASEAN Charter of 2007 established a schedule for the elimination of non-tariff barriers and other restrictions on trade. On 1 Jan. 2010 ASEAN signed a free trade agreement with China, creating the world's largest free trade area by population (encompassing 1·9bn. people) and the third largest by economic value.

Heads of government who met in Bangkok in Dec. 1995 established a South-East Asia Nuclear-Free Zone, which was extended to cover offshore economic exclusion zones. Individual signatories were to decide whether to allow port visits or transportation of nuclear weapons by foreign powers through territorial waters. The first formal meeting of the *ASEAN Regional Forum (ARF)* to discuss security issues in the region took place in July 1994 and was attended by the then six members (Brunei, Indonesia, Malaysia, Philippines, Singapore and Thailand). Also in attendance were ASEAN's dialogue partners (Australia, Canada, the EU, Japan, South Korea, New Zealand and the USA), consultative partners (China and Russia) and observers (Laos, Papua New Guinea and Vietnam). In 2009 the participants in the ARF were the ten ASEAN members, Australia, Bangladesh, Canada, China, the EU, India, Japan, North Korea, South Korea, Mongolia, New Zealand, Pakistan, Papua New Guinea, Russia, Sri Lanka, Timor-Leste and the USA.

ASEAN is committed to resolving the dispute over sovereignty of the Spratly Islands, a group of more than 100 small islands and reefs in the South China Sea. Some or all of the largely uninhabited islands have been claimed by Brunei, China, Malaysia, the Philippines, Taiwan and Vietnam. The disputed areas have oil and gas resources.

Organization. The highest authority is the meeting of Heads of Government, which takes place twice annually. The highest policy-making body is the annual Meeting of Foreign Ministers, commonly known as AMM, the ASEAN Ministerial Meeting, which convenes in each of the member countries on a rotational basis in alphabetical order. The AEM (ASEAN Economic Meeting) meets each year to direct ASEAN economic co-operation. The AEM and AMM report jointly to the heads of government at summit meetings. Each capital has its own national secretariat. The central secretariat in Jakarta is headed by the Secretary-General, a post that revolves among the member states in alphabetical order every five years.

Official language: English.
Headquarters: POB 2072, Jakarta 12110, Indonesia.
Website: http://www.aseansec.org
Secretary-General: Surin Pitsuwan (Thailand).

ASEAN-Mekong Basin Development Co-operation (Mekong Group)

The ministers and representatives of Brunei, Cambodia, China, Indonesia, Laos, Malaysia, Myanmar, Philippines, Singapore, Thailand and Vietnam met in Kuala Lumpur on 17 June 1996 and agreed the following objectives for the Group: to co-operate in the economic and social development of the Mekong Basin area and strengthen the link between it and ASEAN member countries, through a process of dialogue and common project identification.

Priorities include: development of infrastructure capacities in the fields of transport, telecommunications, irrigation and energy; development of trade and investment-generating activities; development of the agricultural sector to enhance production; sustainable development of forestry resources and development of mineral resources; development of the industrial sector, especially small to medium enterprises; development of tourism; human resource development and support for training; co-operation in the fields of science and technology.

Further Reading

Beeson, Mark, *Regionalism & Globalization in East Asia: Politics, Security & Economic Development.* 2006.—*Contemporary Southeast Asia.* 2nd ed. 2008

Broinowski, A., *Understanding ASEAN.* 1982.—(ed.) *ASEAN into the 1990s.* 1990

Van Hoa, Tran, (ed.) *Economic Developments and Prospects in the ASEAN.* 1997

Wawn, B., *The Economics of the ASEAN Countries.* 1982

Colombo Plan

History. Founded in 1950 to promote the development of newly independent Asian member countries, the Colombo Plan has grown from a group of seven Commonwealth nations into an organization of 25 countries. Originally the Plan was conceived for a period of six years but the Consultative Committee gave the Plan an indefinite life span in 1980.

Members. Afghanistan, Australia, Bangladesh, Bhutan, Fiji Islands, India, Indonesia, Islamic Republic of Iran, Japan, South Korea, Lao People's Democratic Republic, Malaysia, Maldives, Mongolia, Myanmar, Nepal, New Zealand, Pakistan, Papua New Guinea, Philippines, Singapore, Sri Lanka, Thailand, USA and Vietnam. *(Provisional member country)* Brunei.

Aims. The aims of the Colombo Plan are: (1) to provide a forum for discussion, at local level, of development needs; (2) to facilitate development assistance by encouraging members to participate as donors and recipients of technical co-operation; and (3) to execute programmes to advance development within member countries. The Plan currently has the following programmes: Programme for Public Administration (PPA); South-South Technical Co-operation Data Bank Programme (SSTC/DB); Drug Advisory Programme (DAP); Programme for Private Sector Development (PPSD); Colombo Plan Staff College for Technician Education (CPSC).

Structure. The Consultative Committee is the principal policy-making body of the Colombo Plan. Consisting of all member countries, it meets every two years to review the economic and social progress of members, exchange views on technical co-operation programmes and review the Plan's activities. The Colombo Plan Council represents each member government and meets several times a year to identify development issues, recommend measures to be taken and ensure implementation.

Headquarters: PO Box 596, 31 Wijerama Road, Colombo 7, Sri Lanka.
Website: http://www.colombo-plan.org
Email: info@colombo-plan.org
Secretary-General: Patricia Yoon-Moi Chia (Malaysia).

Publications. *Consultative Committee Meeting—Proceedings and Conclusions* (biennial); *Report of the Colombo Plan Council* (annual); *The Colombo Plan Brochure* (annual); *The Colombo Plan Focus* (quarterly newsletter); *South-South Technical Co-operation in Selected Member Countries.*

Economic Co-operation Organization (ECO)

The Economic Co-operation Organization (ECO) is an intergovernmental regional organization established in 1985 by Iran, Pakistan and Turkey and the successor of the Regional Co-operation for Development (RCD). ECO was expanded in 1992 to include seven new members: Afghanistan, Azerbaijan, Kazakhstan, Kyrgyzstan, Tajikistan, Turkmenistan and Uzbekistan. The organization's objectives, stipulated in its Charter, the Treaty of Izmir, include the promotion of conditions for sustained economic growth in the region. Transport and communications, trade and investment, and energy are the high priority areas in ECO's scheme of work although industry, agriculture, health, science and education, drug control and human development are also on the agenda.

The Council of Ministers (COM) remains the highest policy and decision-making body of the organization, meeting at least once a year and chaired by rotation among the member states.

ECO Summits were instituted with the First Summit held in Tehran in 1992; the Second Summit was held in İstanbul in 1993, the Third in Islamabad in 1995, the Fourth in Ashgabat in 1996, the Fifth in Almaty in May 1999, the Sixth in Tehran in 2000, the Seventh in İstanbul in 2002, the Eighth in Dushanbe in 2004, the Ninth in Baku in 2006 and the Tenth in Tehran in 2009.

The long-term perspectives and priorities of ECO are defined in the form of two Action Plans: the Quetta Plan of Action and the İstanbul Declaration and Economic Co-operation Strategy.

ECO enjoys observer status with the United Nations, World Trade Organization and the Organization of Islamic Conference.

Headquarters: 1 Goulbou Alley, Kamranieh, PO Box 14155-6176, Tehran, Islamic Republic of Iran.
Website: http://www.ecosecretariat.org
Email: registry@ecosecretariat.org
Secretary-General: Mohammed Yahya Maroofi (Afghanistan).

Pacific Islands Forum (PIF)

In Oct. 2000 the South Pacific Forum changed its name to the Pacific Islands Forum. As the South Pacific Forum it held its first meeting of Heads of Government in New Zealand in 1971. The Agreement Establishing the Forum Secretariat defines the membership of the Forum and the Secretariat. Decisions are reached by consensus. The administrative arm of the Forum, known officially as the Pacific Islands Forum Secretariat, is based in Suva, Fiji Islands. In Oct. 1994 the Forum was granted observer status to the UN.

Members. Australia, Cook Islands, Fiji Islands*, Kiribati, Marshall Islands, Micronesia, Nauru, New Zealand, Niue, Palau, Papua New Guinea, Samoa, Solomon Islands, Tonga, Tuvalu and Vanuatu. Associate Members. French Polynesia, New Caledonia. *Observers.* Asian Development Bank, the Commonwealth, Timor-Leste, Tokelau, Wallis and Futuna. *Membership suspended since May 2009 after calls for fresh elections by a set date were ignored.

Functions. The Secretariat's mission is to provide policy options to the Pacific Islands Forum, and to promote Forum decisions and regional and international co-operation. The organization seeks to promote political stability and regional security; enhance the management of economies and the development process; improve trade and investment; and efficiently manage the resources of the Secretariat.

Activities. The Secretariat has four core divisions: Trade and Investment; Political and International Affairs; Development and Economic Policy; Corporate Services. It provides policy advice to members on social, economic and political issues. Since 1989 the Forum has held Post Forum Dialogues with key dialogue partners at ministerial level. There are currently twelve partners: Canada, China, EU, France, India, Indonesia, Japan, South Korea, Malaysia, the Philippines, the United Kingdom and the United States.

Organization. Established in 1972, the South Pacific Bureau for Economic Co-operation (SPEC) began as a trade bureau and was, before being reorganized as the South Pacific Forum Secretariat in 1988. The Secretariat is headed by a Secretary-General and Deputy Secretary-General who form the Executive. The governing body is the Forum Officials Committee, which acts as an intermediary between the Secretariat and the Forum. The Secretariat operates four Trade Offices in Auckland, Beijing, Sydney and Tokyo.

The Secretary-General is the permanent Chair of the Council of Regional Organisations in the Pacific (CROP), which brings together ten main regional organizations in the Pacific region: Fiji School of Medicine (FSM); Forum Fisheries Agency (FFA); Pacific Islands Development Programme (PIDP); Pacific Islands Forum Secretariat (PIFS); Secretariat for the Pacific Community (SPC); South Pacific Applied Geoscience Commission (SOPAC); South Pacific Board for Educational Assessment (SPBEA); South Pacific Regional Environment Programme (SPREP); South Pacific Tourism Organisation (SPTO); and the University of the South Pacific (USP).

Official language: English.
Headquarters: Ratu Sukuna Road, Suva, Fiji Islands.
Website: http://www.forumsec.org.fj
Secretary-General: Tuiloma Neroni Slade (Samoa).

Secretariat of the Pacific Community (SPC)

Until Feb. 1998 known as the South Pacific Commission, this is a regional intergovernmental organization founded in 1947 under an Agreement commonly referred to as the Canberra Agreement. It is funded by assessed contributions from its 26 members and by voluntary contributions from member and non-member countries, international organizations and other sources.

Members. American Samoa, Australia, Cook Islands, Fiji Islands, France, French Polynesia, Guam, Kiribati, Marshall Islands, Federated States of Micronesia, Nauru, New Caledonia, New Zealand, Niue, Northern Mariana Islands, Palau, Papua New Guinea, Pitcairn Islands, Samoa, Solomon Islands, Tokelau, Tonga, Tuvalu, USA, Vanuatu, and Wallis and Futuna.

Functions. The SPC has three main areas of work: land resources, marine resources and social resources. It conducts research and provides technical assistance and training in these areas to member Pacific Island countries and territories of the Pacific.

Organization. The Conference of the Pacific Community is the governing body of the Community. Its key focus is to appoint the Director-General, to consider major national or regional policy issues and to note changes to the Financial and Staff Regulations approved by the CRGA, the Committee of Representatives of Governments and Administrations. It meets every two years. The CRGA meets once a year and is the principal decision-making organ of the Community. There are also regional offices in the Fiji Islands and Micronesia.

Headquarters: BP D5, 98848 Nouméa Cedex, New Caledonia.
Website: http://www.spc.int
Email: spc@spc.int
Director-General: Dr Jimmie Rodgers (Solomon Islands).

South Asian Association for Regional Co-operation (SAARC)

SAARC was established to accelerate the process of economic and social development in member states. The foreign ministers of the seven member countries met for the first time in New Delhi in Aug. 1983 and adopted the Declaration on South Asian Regional Co-operation whereby an Integrated Programme of Action (IPA) was launched. The charter establishing SAARC was adopted at the first summit meeting in Dhaka in Dec. 1985.

Members. Afghanistan, Bangladesh, Bhutan, India, Maldives, Nepal, Pakistan, Sri Lanka. *Observers.* Australia, China, EU, Iran, Japan, South Korea, Mauritius, Myanmar, USA.

Objectives. To promote the welfare of the peoples of South Asia; to accelerate economic growth, social progress and cultural development; to promote and strengthen collective self-reliance among members; to promote active collaboration and mutual assistance in the economic, social, cultural, technical and scientific fields; to strengthen co-operation with other developing countries and among themselves. Co-operation within the framework is based on respect for the principles of sovereign equality, territorial integrity, political independence, non-interference in the internal affairs of other states and mutual benefit. Agreed areas of co-operation under the *Integrated Programme of Action (IPA)* include agriculture and rural development; human resource development; environment, meteorology and forestry; science and technology; transport and communications; energy; and social development.

A SAARC Preferential Trading Arrangement (SAPTA) designed to reduce trade tariffs between SAARC member states was signed in April 1993, entering into force in Dec. 1995. In 1998 at the Tenth Summit in Colombo, the importance of achieving a South Asian Free Trade Area (SAFTA) as mandated by the Malé Summit in 1997 was reiterated and it was decided to set up a Committee of Experts to work on drafting a comprehensive treaty regime for creating a free trade area. The Colombo Summit agreed that the text of this regulatory framework would be finalized by 2001.

Organization. The highest authority of the Association rests with the heads of state or government, who meet annually at Summit level. The Council of Foreign Ministers, which meets twice a year, formulates policy, reviews progress and decides on new areas of co-operation. The Council is supported by a Standing Committee of Foreign Secretaries, by the Programming Committee and by 11 Technical Committees which are responsible for individual areas of SAARC's activities. There is a secretariat in Kathmandu, headed by a Secretary-General, who is assisted in his work by seven Directors, appointed by the Secretary-General upon nomination by member states for a period of three years which may in special circumstances be extended.

Official language: English.
Headquarters: PO Box 4222, Kathmandu, Nepal.
Website: http://www.saarc-sec.org
Secretary-General: Dr Sheel Kant Sharma (India).

Arab Fund for Economic and Social Development (AFESD)

Established in 1968, the Fund commenced operations in 1974.

Functions. AFESD is an Arab regional financial institution that assists the economic and social development of Arab countries through: financing development projects, with preference given to overall Arab development and to joint Arab projects; encouraging the investment of private and public funds in Arab projects; and providing technical assistance services for Arab economic and social development.

Members. Algeria, Bahrain, Comoros, Djibouti, Egypt, Iraq, Jordan, Kuwait, Lebanon, Libya, Mauritania, Morocco, Oman, Palestine, Qatar, Saudi Arabia, Somalia, Sudan, Syria, Tunisia, United Arab Emirates, Republic of Yemen.

Headquarters: PO Box 21923, Safat 13080, Kuwait.
Website: http://www.arabfund.org
Director General and Chairman of the Board of Directors: Abdulatif Y. Al Hamad (Kuwait).

Publications. Annual Report; Joint Arab Economic Report.

Arab Monetary Fund (AMF)

Origin. The Agreement establishing the Arab Monetary Fund was approved by the Economic Council of the League of Arab States in April 1976 and the first meeting of the Board of Governors was held on 19 April 1977.

Aims. To assist member countries in eliminating payments and trade restrictions, in achieving exchange rate stability, in developing capital markets and in correcting payments imbalances through the extension of short- and medium-term loans; the co-ordination of monetary policies of member countries; and the liberalization and promotion of trade and payments, as well as the encouragement of capital flows among member countries.

Members. Algeria, Bahrain, Comoros, Djibouti, Egypt, Iraq, Jordan, Kuwait, Lebanon, Libya, Mauritania, Morocco, Oman, Palestine, Qatar, Saudi Arabia, Somalia, Sudan, Syria, Tunisia, United Arab Emirates, Republic of Yemen.

Headquarters: PO Box 2818, Abu Dhabi, United Arab Emirates.
Website: http://www.amf.org.ae
Director General and Chairman of the Board of Directors: Jassim A. Al-Mannai (Bahrain).

Publications (in English and Arabic): *Annual Report; The Articles of Agreement of the Arab Monetary Fund; Money and Credit in Arab Countries* (annual); *National Accounts of Arab Countries* (annual); *Foreign Trade of Arab Countries* (annual); *Cross Exchange Rates of Arab Currencies* (annual); *Arab Countries: Economic Indicators* (annual); *Balance of Payments and External Public Debt of Arab Countries* (annual); *AMF Publications Catalogue* (annual). (In Arabic only): *The Joint Arabic Economic Report* (annual); *AMF Economic Bulletin; Developments in Arab Capital Markets* (quarterly).

Arab Organization for Agricultural Development (AOAD)

The AOAD was established in 1970 and commenced operations in 1972. Its aims are to develop natural and human resources in the agricultural sector and improve the means and methods of exploiting these resources on scientific bases; to increase agricultural productive efficiency and achieve agricultural integration between the Arab States and countries; to increase agricultural production with a view to achieving a higher degree of self-sufficiency; to facilitate the exchange of agricultural products between the Arab States and countries; to enhance the establishment of agricultural ventures and industries; and to increase the standards of living of the labour force engaged in the agricultural sector.

Organization. The structure comprises a General Assembly consisting of ministers of agriculture of the member states, an Executive Council, a Secretariat General, seven technical departments—Food Security, Human Resources Development, Water Resources, Studies and Research, Projects Execution, Technical Scientific Co-operation, and Financial Administrative Department—and two centres—the Arab Center for Agricultural Information and Documentation, and the Arab Bureau for Consultation and Implementation of Agricultural Projects.

Members. Algeria, Bahrain, Comoros, Djibouti, Egypt, Iraq, Jordan, Kuwait, Lebanon, Libya, Mauritania, Morocco, Oman, Palestine, Qatar, Saudi Arabia, Somalia, Sudan, Syria, Tunisia, United Arab Emirates, Republic of Yemen.

Official languages: Arabic (English and French used in translated documents and correspondence).
Headquarters: Street No. 7, Al-Amarat, Khartoum, Sudan.
Website: http://www.aoad.org
Director General: Dr Tariq Moosa Al-Zadjali.

Gulf Co-operation Council (GCC)

Origin. Also referred to as the Co-operation Council for the Arab States of the Gulf (CCASG), the Council was established on 25 May 1981 on signature of the Charter by Bahrain, Kuwait, Oman, Qatar, Saudi Arabia and the United Arab Emirates.

Aims. To assure security and stability of the region through economic and political co-operation; promote, expand and enhance economic ties on solid foundations, in the best interests of the people; co-ordinate and unify economic, financial and monetary policies, as well as commercial and industrial legislation and customs regulations; achieve self-sufficiency in basic foodstuffs.

Organization. The Supreme Council formed by the heads of member states is the highest authority. Its presidency rotates, based on the alphabetical order of the names of the member states. It holds one regular annual session in addition to a mid-year consultation session. Attached to the Supreme Council are the Commission for the Settlement of Disputes and the Consultative Commission. The Ministerial Council is formed of the Foreign Ministers of the member states or other delegated ministers and meets quarterly. The Secretariat-General is composed of Secretary-General, Assistant Secretaries-General and a number of staff as required. The Secretariat consists of the following sectors: Political Affairs, Military Affairs, Legal Affairs, Human and Environment Affairs, Information Centre, Media Department, Gulf Standardization Organization (GSO), GCC Patent Office, Secretary-General's Office, GCC Delegation in Brussels, Technical Telecommunications Bureau in Bahrain. In Jan. 2003 it launched a customs union, introducing a 5% duty on foreign imports across the trade bloc.

Finance. The annual budget of the GCC Secretariat is shared equally by the six member states.

Headquarters: PO Box 7153, Riyadh-11462, Saudi Arabia.
Website: http://www.GCC-SG.org
Secretary-General: Abdul Rahman bin Hamad Al-Attiyah (Qatar).

Publications. Attaawun (quarterly, in Arabic); *GCC Economic Bulletin* (annual); *Statistical Bulletin* (annual); *Legal Bulletin* (quarterly, in Arabic).

Further Reading

Twinam, J. W., *The Gulf, Co-operation and the Council: an American Perspective.* 1992

League of Arab States

Origin. The League of Arab States is a voluntary association of sovereign Arab states, established by a Pact signed in Cairo on 22 March 1945 by the representatives of Egypt, Iraq, Saudi Arabia, Syria, Lebanon, Jordan and Yemen. It seeks to promote closer ties among member states and to co-ordinate their economic, cultural and security policies with a view to developing collective co-operation, protecting national security and maintaining the independence and sovereignty of member states, in order to enhance the potential for joint Arab action across all fields.

Members. Algeria, Bahrain, Comoros, Djibouti, Egypt, Iraq, Jordan, Kuwait, Lebanon, Libya, Mauritania, Morocco, Oman, Palestine, Qatar, Saudi Arabia, Somalia, Sudan, Syria, Tunisia, United Arab Emirates and Republic of Yemen. *Observers.* Eritrea, India and Venezuela.

Joint Action. In the political field, the League is entrusted with defending the supreme interests and national causes of the Arab world through the implementation of joint action plans at regional and international levels. It examines any disputes that may arise between member states with a view to finding a peaceful resolution. The Joint Defence and Economic Co-operation Treaty signed in 1950 provided for the establishment of a Joint Defence Council as well as an Economic Council (renamed the Economic and Social Council in 1977). Economic, social and cultural activities constitute principal and vital elements of the joint action initiative.

Arab Common Market. An Arab Common Market came into operation on 1 Jan. 1965. Initial plans to abolish customs duties on agricultural products, natural resources and industrial products by incremental reductions never came to fruition although the concept remains an ambition shared by many people in the Arab world.

Organization. The machinery of the League consists of a Council, 11 specialized ministerial committees entrusted with drawing up common policies for the regulation and advancement of co-operation in their fields (information, internal affairs, justice, housing, transport, social affairs, youth and sports, health, environment, telecommunications and electricity), and a permanent secretariat.

The League is considered to be a regional organization within the framework of the United Nations at which its Secretary-General is an observer. It has permanent delegations in New York and Geneva for the UN and in Addis Ababa for the African Union (AU), as well as offices in a number of cities throughout the world.

Headquarters: Al Tahrir Square, Cairo, Egypt.
Website: http://www.arableagueonline.org (Arabic only)
Secretary-General: Amr Moussa (Egypt).

Further Reading

Gomaa, A. M., *The Foundation of the League of Arab States.* 1977

Organization of Arab Petroleum Exporting Countries (OAPEC)

Established in 1968 to promote co-operation and close ties between member states in economic activities related to the oil industry; to determine ways of safeguarding their legitimate interests, both individual and collective, in the oil industry; to unite their efforts so as to ensure the flow of oil to consumer markets on equitable and reasonable terms; and to create a favourable climate for the investment of capital and expertise in their petroleum industries.

Members. Algeria, Bahrain, Egypt, Iraq, Kuwait, Libya, Qatar, Saudi Arabia, Syria, Tunisia*, United Arab Emirates. *Tunisia's membership was made inactive in 1986.

Headquarters: PO Box 20501, Safat 13066, Kuwait.
Website: http://www.oapecorg.org
Secretary-General: Abbas Ali Naqi (Kuwait).

Publications. Secretary General's Annual Report (Arabic and English editions); *Oil and Arab Co-operation* (quarterly; Arabic with English abstracts and bibliography); *OAPEC Monthly Bulletin* (Arabic and English editions); *Energy Resources Monitor* (Arabic); *OAPEC Annual Statistical Report* (Arabic/English).

Organization of the Petroleum Exporting Countries (OPEC)

Origin and Aims. Founded in Baghdad in 1960 by Iran, Iraq, Kuwait, Saudi Arabia and Venezuela. The principal aims are: to unify the petroleum policies of member countries and determine the best means for safeguarding their interests, individually and collectively; to devise ways and means of ensuring the stabilization of prices in international oil markets with a view to eliminating harmful and unnecessary fluctuations; and to secure a steady income for the producing countries, an efficient, economic and regular supply of petroleum to consuming nations, and a fair return on their capital to those investing in the petroleum industry. It is estimated that OPEC members possess 75% of the world's known reserves of crude petroleum, of which about two-thirds are in the Middle East. OPEC countries account for about 43% of world oil production (55% in the mid-1970s).

Members. (Feb. 2010) Algeria, Angola, Ecuador, Iran, Iraq, Kuwait, Libya, Nigeria, Qatar, Saudi Arabia, United Arab Emirates and Venezuela. Membership applications may be made by any other country having substantial net exports of crude petroleum, which has fundamentally similar interests to those of member countries. Gabon became an associated member in 1973 and a full member in 1975, but in 1996 withdrew owing to difficulty in meeting its percentage contribution. Ecuador joined the Organization in 1973 but left in 1992; it then rejoined in Oct. 2007. Indonesia joined in 1962 but left in 2008 as it had ceased to be an oil exporter.

Organization. The main organs are the Conference, the Board of Governors and the Secretariat. The Conference, which is the supreme authority meeting at least twice a year, consists of delegations from each member country, normally headed by the respective minister of oil, mines or energy. All decisions, other than those concerning procedural matters, must be adopted unanimously.

Headquarters: Helferstorferstrasse 17, A-1010 Vienna, Austria.
Website: http://www.opec.org
Secretary-General: Abdullah Salem al-Badri (Libya).

Publications. Annual Statistical Bulletin; Annual Report; OPEC Bulletin (monthly); *OPEC Review* (quarterly); *OPEC General Information; Monthly Oil Market Report*; OPEC Statute.

Further Reading

Al-Chalabi, F., *OPEC at the Crossroads.* 1989
Skeet, I., *OPEC: 25 Years of Prices and Policies.* 1988

OPEC Fund for International Development

The OPEC Fund for International Development was established in 1976 as the OPEC Special Fund, with the aim of providing financial aid on advantageous terms to developing countries (other than OPEC members) and international development agencies whose beneficiaries are developing countries. In 1980 the Fund was transformed into a permanent autonomous international agency and renamed the OPEC Fund for International Development. It is administered by a Ministerial Council and a Governing Board. Each member country is represented on the Council by its finance minister.

The initial endowment of the fund amounted to US$800m. At the start of 2004 pledged contributions totalled US$3,435m., and the Fund had extended 1,024 loans totalling US$5,845·7m. including US$4,582·6m. for project financing, US$724·2m. for balance-of-payments support, US$314·8m. for programme funding and US$174·0m. for debt relief within the context of the Highly Indebted Poor Countries Initiative. In addition, and through its private sector window, the Fund had approved financing worth a total of US$335·4m. in 67 operations in support of private sector entities in Africa, Asia, Latin America, the Caribbean and Europe. Through its grant programme the Fund had also committed a total of US$321·7m. in support of a wide range of initiatives, ranging from technical assistance, research and emergency aid to dedicated operations to combat HIV/AIDS and relief hardship in Palestine.

Headquarters: POB 995, A-1011 Vienna, Austria.
Website: http://www.ofid.org
Email: info@ofid.org
Director-General: Suleiman Jasir al-Herbish (Saudi Arabia).

Antarctic Treaty

Antarctica is an island continent some 15·5m. sq. km in area which lies almost entirely within the Antarctic Circle. Its surface is composed of an ice sheet over rock, and it is uninhabited except for research and other workers in the course of duty. It is in general ownerless: for countries with territorial claims, see ARGENTINA; AUSTRALIA: Australian Antarctic Territory; CHILE; FRANCE: Southern and Antarctic Territories; NEW ZEALAND: Ross Dependency; NORWAY: Queen Maud Land; UNITED KINGDOM: British Antarctic Territory.

12 countries which had maintained research stations in Antarctica during International Geophysical Year, 1957–58 (Argentina, Australia, Belgium, Chile, France, Japan, New Zealand, Norway, South Africa, the USSR, the UK and the USA) signed the Antarctic Treaty (Washington Treaty) on 1 Dec. 1959. Austria, Belarus, Brazil, Bulgaria, Canada, China, Colombia, Cuba, Czech Republic, Denmark, Ecuador, Estonia, Finland, Germany, Greece, Guatemala, Hungary, India, Italy, North Korea,

South Korea, Monaco, the Netherlands, Papua New Guinea, Peru, Poland, Romania, Slovakia, Spain, Sweden, Switzerland, Turkey, Ukraine, Uruguay and Venezuela subsequently acceded to the Treaty. The Treaty reserves the Antarctic area south of 60° S. lat. for peaceful purposes, provides for international co-operation in scientific investigation and research, and preserves, for the duration of the Treaty, the status quo with regard to territorial sovereignty, rights and claims. The Treaty entered into force on 23 June 1961. The 47 nations party to the Treaty (28 full voting signatories and 19 adherents) meet biennially.

An agreement reached in Madrid in April 1991 and signed by all 39 parties in Oct. imposes a ban on mineral exploitation in Antarctica for 50 years, at the end of which any one of the 28 voting parties may request a review conference. After this the ban may be lifted by agreement of three quarters of the nations then voting, which must include the present 28.

Headquarters: Av. Leandro Alem 884–4° Piso, C1001AAQ, Buenos Aires, Argentina.
Website: http://www.ats.aq
Email: secret@ats.aq
Executive Secretary: Manfred Reinke (Germany).

Further Reading

Elliott, L. M., *International Environmental Politics: Protecting the Antarctic.* 1994
Jørgensen-Dahl, A. and Østreng, W., *The Antarctic Treaty System in World Politics.* 1991

United Nations Framework Convention on Climate Change

The convention was produced at the 1992 UN Conference on Environment and Development with the stated aim of reducing global greenhouse gas emissions to 'a level that would prevent dangerous anthropogenic (human induced) interference with the climate system'. Signatories agreed to take account of climate change in their domestic policy and to develop national programmes that would slow its progress. However, no mandatory targets were established for the reduction of emissions so the treaty remained legally non-binding. Instead it operates as a 'framework' document, with provisions for regular updates and amendments.

The first of these additions was the Kyoto Protocol in 1997. Under the protocol, 36 developed countries are committed to reducing their collective emissions of six greenhouse gases to at least 5% below 1990 levels. These targets are scheduled to be met in the period 2008–12. By Feb. 2010, 189 countries plus the European Union had signed and ratified the treaty. The USA has not ratified the protocol. China and India, also amongst the world's top five producers of emissions, are exempt from the protocol's constraints by virtue of their status as developing countries.

The members of the UNFCCC meet on an annual basis. The conference in Indonesia in Dec. 2007 led to the creation of the 'Bali Roadmap', which timetables negotiations for a protocol to succeed Kyoto. This process was continued at the 2008 conference in Poland with the aim of agreeing an international response to climate change at the next UNFCCC conference, which took place in Copenhagen, Denmark in Dec. 2009. The resulting Copenhagen Accord was not legally binding and failed to set out concrete measures for tackling climate change. The 16th conference is scheduled to be held in Nov.–Dec. 2010 in Cancún, Mexico.

Headquarters: United Nations Framework Convention on Climate Change, Haus Carstanjen, Martin-Luther-King-Strasse 8, D-53175 Bonn, Germany.
Website: http://unfccc.int
Email: secretariat@unfccc.int
Executive Secretary: Vacant.

PART II

COUNTRIES OF THE WORLD A—Z

AFGHANISTAN

Da Afganistan Islami Jomhoriyat—
Jamhuri-ye Islami-ye Afganistan
(Islamic Republic of Afghanistan)

Capital: Kabul
Population estimate, 2010: 29·12m.
GDP per capita: not available
GNI per capita, 2007: US$385
HDI/world rank: 0·352/181

KEY HISTORICAL EVENTS

Excavations near Kandahar in southern Afghanistan have revealed Neolithic settlements dating to 5000 BC. Subsequent settlements bear witness to trade links with cities in the Indus Valley and Mesopotamia. Aryan tribes settled in modern Afghanistan's northern plains near Balkh (Bactria) from around 1500 BC, controlling the region until it came under successive Persian dynasties, including the Acaemanid Empire (550 BC–330 BC) ruled by Darius the Great from Persepolis after 515 BC.

Alexander the Great conquered Bactria in 328 BC but his rule was short-lived and the region fell first to the Seleucid, then to the Parthian empires. Buddhism was spread by the Yuechi, who invaded from the northeast and established the Kushan dynasty at Peshawar in around 200 BC. The famous Buddha statues at Bamiyan, destroyed in 2001 by the Taliban, dated from the 3rd and 5th centuries AD. Invasions by Scythians, White Huns and Turkish Tu-Kuie took place in the first half of the first millennium. The Muslim conquest of Afghanistan began with the arrival of Arab settlers in 642 AD, although the region became a thriving cultural centre only during the reign of Mahmud of Ghazni (998–1030). Mahmud was succeeded by various smaller dynasties, all of which fell to Genghis Khan's Mongol invasion in 1219.

Following Genghis Khan's death in 1227, a succession of chiefs and princes vied for supremacy until one of his descendants, Timur-i Lang, incorporated Afghanistan into his central Asian empire late in the 14th century. Babur, a descendant of Timur and founder of India's Moghul dynasty at the beginning of the 16th century, made Kabul his capital, although power later transferred to Delhi and Agra. The early sixteenth century also saw the rise of the Safavid dynasty in Iran, which ruled over western Afghanistan, while the Shaibanid Uzbeks controlled northern Afghanistan and territory stretching northward across central Asia.

The early 18th century was marked by Afghan tribes revolting against foreign occupation. Ahmad Shah Durrani, a Pashtun, became the founder of modern Afghanistan following the death of the Persian ruler, Nadir Shah, in 1747. The subsequent rule by Dost Muhammad, who became Amir in 1826, was overshadowed by the power struggle between Britain, dominant in India, and the expanding Russian empire. The British attempt to oust Dost Muhammad sparked the first Afghan War (1838–42), during which the British were forced to retreat by an armed rebellion in Kabul in 1841.

Dost Muhammad returned from exile and governed for the next 20 years. British attempts to delineate India's northwest frontier and prevent Russian advances led to another invasion of Afghanistan in 1878, when British-Indian troops seized the Khyber Pass. Abd Ar-Rahman Khan, who became the Amir of Afghanistan in 1880, abolished the traditional regional centres of power and consolidated his government in Kabul. Border treaties were signed with Russia and British India. Following the Anglo-Russian agreement of 1907 Afghanistan's independence was guaranteed, although foreign affairs remained under British control until the 1919 Treaty of Rawalpindi. King Amanullah ushered in Western-style reforms in the 1920s but development was restricted by tribal wars and banditry.

Záhir Shah took power in 1933 and ruled for 40 years, bringing stability and the expansion of education. In 1964 he established parliamentary democracy. In 1973 his cousin and brother-in-law, and a former prime minister, Mohammed Daoud, led a military coup and abolished the constitution to declare a republic. In April 1978 President Daoud was killed in a further coup, which installed a pro-Soviet government. The new president, Noor Mohammad Taraki, was overthrown in Sept. 1979, whereupon the USSR invaded in Dec. to install Babrak Karmal in power.

In Dec. 1986 Sayid Mohammed Najibullah became president amid continuing civil war between government and rebel Muslim forces. The USSR provided military support and aid to the authorities while the USA extended limited support to the rebels. In the mid-1980s the UN began negotiating the withdrawal of Soviet troops and the establishment of a national unity government. Soviet troops began withdrawing in early 1988. After talks in Nov. 1991 with Afghan opposition movements ('mujahideen'), the USSR transferred its support from the Najibullah regime to an 'Islamic Interim Government'. As mujahideen insurgents closed in on Kabul on 16 April 1992 President Najibullah stepped down but fighting continued.

In 1994 a newly-formed militant Islamic movement, the 'Taliban' ('students of religion'), took Kabul, apparently with Pakistani support. The Taliban, most of whose leaders were Pashtuns, were in turn defeated by the troops of President Rabbani. However, in Sept. 1996 Taliban forces recaptured Kabul and set up an interim government under Mohamed Rabbani. Afghanistan was declared an Islamic state under Sharia law. Government forces counter-attacked but a new Taliban offensive, launched in Dec. 1996, took most of the country. The opposition Northern Alliance controlled the northeast of the country. Under the Taliban, irregular forces were disarmed and roads cleared of bandits. Rebuilding of towns and villages started. Only three countries—Pakistan, Saudi Arabia and the United Arab Emirates—recognized the Taliban as the legal government.

In March 2001 Afghanistan was widely condemned for destroying the ancient Buddha statues at Bamiyan. In May 2001 the Taliban refused to extradite Osama bin Laden, a Saudi militant, to the USA to face charges connected to the bombing of American embassies in Kenya and Tanzania in 1998. In Sept. 2001 Ahmed Shah Masood, leader of the Northern Alliance, was killed by two suicide bombers.

Following the attacks on the USA on 11 Sept. 2001, Saudi Arabia and the United Arab Emirates broke off relations with Afghanistan and the USA unsuccessfully put pressure on the Taliban to hand over bin Laden. Consequently the USA launched air strikes on 7 Oct. On 13 Nov. the Northern Alliance took the capital Kabul, effectively bringing an end to Taliban rule. With the surrender of Kandahar the Taliban lost control of their last stronghold. On 27 Nov. representatives of rival factions, but excluding the Taliban, joined UN-sponsored talks on Afghanistan's future. Hamid Karzai, a Pashtun tribal leader, was chosen to head an interim power-sharing council which took office in Dec. He was appointed president of the transitional government in June 2002. In Sept. 2002 he survived an assassination attempt.

Since Aug. 2003 the government has attempted to assert its authority with the help of the NATO-controlled International Security Assistance Force (ISAF), operating under a UN mandate. The 50,000-strong international force is battling a resurgent Taliban, who are supported by around a quarter of the population in the south of the country. The International Red Cross reported in June 2007 that violence had intensified in the previous year in the south and east of the country, resulting in a growing humanitarian crisis.

TERRITORY AND POPULATION

Afghanistan is bounded in the north by Turkmenistan, Uzbekistan and Tajikistan, east by China, east and south by Pakistan and west by Iran.

The area is 645,807 sq. km (249,346 sq. miles). The last census was in 1979. In 2001 an estimated 22·3% of the population lived in urban areas.

The UN gives an estimated population for 2010 of 29·12m.; density, 45 per sq. km.

According to humanitarian agencies in Jan. 2002 there were almost 1·2m. internally displaced persons in Afghanistan. An estimated 4m. sought asylum outside Afghanistan including 2m. in Pakistan, 1·5m. in Iran, 26,000 in Turkmenistan, Tajikistan and Uzbekistan, and several hundred thousand in western European countries, Australia and North America. Approximately half of the internally displaced persons in Afghanistan moved prior to the events of Sept. 2001, for reasons such as drought and food scarcity. As a consequence of the US war in Afghanistan, numbers of refugees to Pakistan and Iran increased dramatically. Pakistan took more than 70,000 Afghan refugees in the months following 11 Sept. 2001 while Iran admitted some 60,000. In the meantime more than 1·6m. Afghans have returned to their country since a UN-sponsored programme began in early 2002, and in Dec. 2002 Pakistan and Afghanistan agreed to repatriate the remaining refugees, lodged in various camps in Pakistan, within three years.

The country is divided into 34 regions *(velayat)*. Area and estimated population in 2006:

Region	*Area (sq. km)*	*Population (1,000)*	*Region*	*Area (sq. km)*	*Population (1,000)*
Badakhshan	44,059	823	Kabul	4,462	3,138
Badghis	20,591	430	Kandahar	54,022	1,012
Baghlan	21,118	779	Kapisa	1,842	383
Balkh	17,249	1,096	Khost	4,152	498
Bamyan	14,175	387	Konar	4,942	390
Daikondi	—[1]	400	Kondoz	8,040	851
Farah	48,471	438	Laghman	3,843	386
Faryab	20,293	859	Logar	3,880	340
Ghazni	22,915	1,063	Nangarhar	7,727	1,289
Ghowr	36,479	599	Nimroz	41,005	141
Helmand	58,584	799	Nurestan	9,225	128
Herat	54,778	1,578	Paktika	19,482	377
Jawzjan	11,798	462	Paktiya	6,432	478
Panjshir	3,610	133	Takhar	12,333	845
Parwan	5,974	573	Uruzgan	—[1]	304
Samangan	11,262	335	Vardak	8,938	517
Saripul	15,999	483	Zabul	17,343	263

[1]Daikondi split from Uruzgan in 2004; the combined area of the two regions is 30,784 sq. km.

The capital, Kabul, had a population of 2·54m. in 2006. Other towns (with population estimates, 2002): Herat (349,000), Kandahar (324,800), Mazar i Sharif (300,600), Jalalabad (168,600).

Main ethnic groups: Pashtuns, 38%; Tajiks, 25%; Hazaras, 19%; Uzbeks, 6%; others, 12%. The official languages are Pashto and Dari.

SOCIAL STATISTICS

Based on 2001 estimates: birth rate, 41 per 1,000 population; death rate, 18 per 1,000. Infant mortality (2005), 165 per 1,000 live births. Life expectancy at birth, 2007, was 43·5 years for women and 43·6 years for men (the lowest life expectancy for females and the second lowest overall, ahead of only Zimbabwe). Fertility rate, 2004, 7·4 births per woman.

The maternal mortality rate is among the highest in the world with some 16,000 pregnancy-related deaths every year.

CLIMATE

The climate is arid, with a big annual range of temperature and very little rain, apart from the period Jan. to April. Winters are very cold, with considerable snowfall, which may last the year round on mountain summits. Kabul, Jan. 27°F (–2·8°C), July 76°F (24·4°C). Annual rainfall 13" (338 mm).

CONSTITUTION AND GOVERNMENT

Following UN-sponsored talks in Bonn, Germany in Nov. 2001, on 22 Dec. 2001 power was handed over to an Afghan Interim Authority, designed to oversee the restructuring of the country until a second stage of government, the Transitional Authority, could be put into power. This second stage resulted from a *Loya Jirga* (Grand Council), which convened between 10–16 June 2002. The Loya Jirga established the Transitional Islamic State of Afghanistan. A constitutional commission was established, with UN assistance, to help the Constitutional Loya Jirga prepare a new constitution. A draft constitution was produced for public scrutiny in Nov. 2003 and was approved by Afghanistan's *Loya Jirga* on 4 Jan. 2004. The new constitution creates a strong presidential system, providing for a *President* and two *Vice-Presidents*, and a bicameral parliament. The lower house is the 249-member House of the People (*Wolesi Jirga*), directly elected for a five-year term, and the upper house the 102-member House of Elders (*Meshrano Jirga*). The upper house is elected in three divisions. The provincial councils elect one third of its members for a four-year term. The district councils elect the second third of the members for a three-year term. The President appoints the remaining third for a five-year term. At least one woman is elected to the *Wolesi Jirga* from each of the country's 32 regions, and half of the president's appointments to the *Meshrano Jirga* must be women. The constitution reserves 25% of the seats in the *Wolesi Jirga* for women. The president appoints ministers, the attorney general and central bank governor with the approval of the *Wolesi Jirga*. Cabinet ministers must be university graduates. Presidential and parliamentary elections, the first in 25 years, were scheduled for June 2004 but were put back to Oct. 2004. The parliamentary elections were subsequently delayed again and were set to be held in April 2005, but were postponed a further time until Sept. 2005. In Dec. 2005 an elected parliament sat for the first time since 1973.

National Anthem

'Daa watan Afghanistan di' ('This land is Afghanistan'); words by Abdul Bari Jahani' tune by Babrak Wassa.

RECENT ELECTIONS

In presidential elections held on 20 Aug. 2009 initial counts suggested that Hamid Karzai would be re-elected president with 54% of the vote compared to his closest rival Abdullah Abdullah's 28%. However, doubt as to the integrity of the elections was widespread in both the local and international communities with all candidates accused of ballot-rigging. A second round run-off was scheduled for 7 Nov. after Afghanistan's Independent Election Commission (IEC) found that Karzai had not obtained a 50% majority and only took 48·2% of the vote. On 2 Nov. Abdullah pulled out of the second round after calling for the resignation of the head of the IEC and disputing its impartiality. The run-off was subsequently cancelled and Karzai declared the winner. He was sworn in on 19 Nov. 2009 although legal experts questioned the legitimacy of his re-election.

Although not staged on a party political basis, delayed national elections for a new 249-member parliament took place on 18 Sept. 2005. Turnout was about 50%. Of the 249 non-partisans elected, former warlords and their followers gained the majority of seats.

Parliamentary elections are scheduled to take place on 18 Sept. 2010.

CURRENT ADMINISTRATION

In March 2010 the government was composed as follows:

President: Hamid Karzai; b. 1957 (Pashtun; sworn in 19 June 2002 and re-elected 2 Nov. 2009).

Vice Presidents: Mohammad Qasim Fahim (Tajik); Karim Khalili (Hazara Shia).

Minister of Agriculture: Mohammad Asif Rahimi. *Anti-Narcotics:* Zarar Ahmad Moqbel. *Defence:* Abdul Rahim Wardak. *Economy:* Abdul Hadi Arghandiwal. *Education:* Ghulam Farooq Wardak. *Finance:* Omar Zakhilwal. *Foreign Affairs:* Zalmai Rasul. *Hajj (Pilgrimage) and Awqaf:* Mohammad Yousuf Neyazi. *Information and Culture:* Sayed Makhdum Rahin. *Interior:* Mohammad Hanif Atmar. *Justice:* Habibullah Ghaleb. *Labour, Social Affairs, Disabled and Martyrs:* Amina Afzali. *Mines:* Wahidullah Sharani. *Rural Rehabilitation and Development:* Jarullah Mansoori.

Government Website: http://www.afghangovernment.com

CURRENT LEADERS

Hamid Karzai

Position
President

Introduction
Hamid Karzai was sworn in as chairman of the interim government of Afghanistan in Dec. 2001 at a conference in Bonn, Germany before taking the position permanently in June 2002. He was appointed by the United Nations in consultation with the Northern Alliance and the *Loya Jirga*, a group of elected delegates. His main aim has been to try and bring stability to the country, but there has been a resurgence of resistance by the Taliban since 2006 particularly in the south and east. His other major challenges have been tackling widespread corruption and drug-trafficking. He was re-elected controversially in autumn 2009.

Early Life
Karzai was born on 24 Dec. 1957 into the Popolzai tribe, one of Southern Afghanistan's most powerful factions. His father, who was chief of the Popolzai clan, was assassinated in 1999 in what was widely believed to be a Taliban attack.

Karzai believes in a system of broad-based government called the *Loya Jirga*, with an integrated approach intended to reduce violence between tribal warlords. He first entered politics in the early 1980s during the Soviet invasion and organized the Pashtun Popolzai against Moscow. He spent time in Pakistan, during which time he developed his nationalist philosophy. Karzai returned to Afghanistan in 1992 and linked up with the leader of the Northern Alliance, Burhanuddin Rabbani. When Rabbani formed the first mujahideen government, Karzai served as the deputy foreign minister, but left the government because of infighting.

Karzai initially supported the Taliban when it was created in 1994 but in 1995 he rejected a government post, disillusioned by increasing foreign interference. Karzai left the country in 1996 but secretly re-entered in 2001 during the USA's post-11 Sept. air strikes. He co-ordinated Pashtun resistance to the Taliban and only narrowly evaded capture.

Career in Office
Hamid Karzai was sworn in as chairman of the interim administration in Dec. 2001, taking the title of president in June 2002. In his first speech as president, he vowed to resign if he failed to introduce 'forceful Islamic government'. He has since enjoyed the support of a majority of the main tribal leaders. However, his lack of military strength has required him to maintain alliances with armed regional factions and his rule has remained tenuous outside the capital. In Sept. 2002 he survived an assassination attempt in Kandahar, two months after his vice president Haji Abdul Qadir had been assassinated by two unidentified gunmen. Despite the precarious security situation throughout Afghanistan, Karzai won outright the country's first-ever democratic presidential election on 9 Oct. 2004 with 55·4% of votes cast. He was inaugurated on 7 Dec. that year.

In May–June 2006 Afghanistan experienced the worst insurgent violence and casualties since the US invasion and toppling of the Taliban in 2001. Having taken over the leadership of military operations in the south from July 2006, NATO then assumed responsibility for security across the whole of the country from Oct., taking command in the east from a US-led coalition force. NATO and Afghan forces have since sought to contain a Taliban resurgence. Karzai has meanwhile expressed his increasing concern over ongoing civilian casualties in military operations. In Nov. 2008 Karzai pledged protection for the leader of the Taliban if he agreed to enter into peace negotiations with the Afghan government, but this offer was rejected. In Feb. 2009 US President Barack Obama announced that a further 17,000 US troops would be deployed to Afghanistan, partly to train and support the Afghan army and police service, and in July NATO and Afghan forces pursued a new operation against Taliban strongholds in Helmand province. In Dec. 2009 Obama ordered a further deployment over six months of 30,000 US troops and other NATO members promised to provide another 7,000. This policy of reinforcement heralded the launch in Feb. 2010, again in Helmand, of the biggest coalition offensive in the country since the defeat of Taliban government in 2001.

On the political front, Karzai meanwhile sought re-election as president in a campaign tainted by widespread alleged fraud. In the first round of voting in Aug. 2009 Karzai claimed to be ahead of rival candidate Abdullah Abdullah with 54% of the vote. In the face of domestic and international concern over the evidential scale of vote-rigging, Karzai subsequently conceded that the elections should go to a second round which was scheduled for early Nov. However, Abdullah Abdullah then withdrew his candidacy and Karzai was declared the winner as the only remaining contender. The president subsequently struggled in Jan. and Feb. 2010 to form a new government as a hostile parliament rejected many of his nominees for cabinet posts. He also remained under pressure from the international community to confront Afghanistan's pervasive corruption. In late Feb. Karzai provoked further criticism when he assumed exclusive power to appoint all five members of the independent Electoral Complaints Commission (three of whom had previously been UN nominees) which had earlier rejected his claims to a first-round victory in the 2009 presidential elections.

DEFENCE

In 2006 military expenditure totalled US$143m. (US$5 per capita), representing 1·7% of GDP.

A UN-mandated international force, ISAF, assists the government in the maintenance of security throughout the country. It has been led by NATO since Aug. 2003 and comprises approximately 71,000 troops from 43 countries (of which 34,800 from the USA).

Army

The decimation of the Taliban's armed forces left Afghanistan without an army. A multi-ethnic Afghan National Army, under the command of President Hamid Karzai, has been established, currently numbering 94,000 (up from 12,000 in 2004) but ultimately with a strength of 134,000.

Air Force

Afghanistan's air forces were severely damaged with all planes destroyed by US military operations in 2001, but the Afghan National Army Air Corps is being rebuilt with a planned strength of 7,400.

INTERNATIONAL RELATIONS

UN sanctions were imposed in 1999 but were withdrawn following the collapse of the Taliban regime.

Afghanistan is a member of the UN, World Bank, IMF and several other UN specialized agencies, IOM, Islamic Development Bank, OIC, Asian Development Bank, Colombo Plan, ECO and SAARC. In April 2003 the transitional government applied for membership of the WTO although membership negotiations are expected to take several years.

ECONOMY

In 2007 agriculture accounted for 37% of GDP, industry 25% and services 38%.

Afghanistan featured among the ten most corrupt countries in the world in a 2009 survey of 180 countries carried out by the anti-corruption organization *Transparency International*.

Overview

Reconstruction started at the end of 2001 when the economy was in an impoverished state after more than 20 years of conflict, exacerbated by periodic earthquakes and drought. Problems included largely defunct government and financial institutions, weak administrative capacity and a devastated infrastructure. Social indicators are among the worst in the world.

Progress has been made in rebuilding institutions and in the implementation of sound economic policies. There has been a strong commitment to fiscal discipline. A new currency was launched in late 2002 and monetary policy has been restrained since then, prompting significant recovery. Real GDP, excluding opium production, is estimated to have grown on average by almost 17% per year between 2002 and 2005, driven by the end of a prolonged drought and by donor assistance. Opium production accounts for about half of overall GDP. Following the US-led military campaign in Afghanistan, pledges of economic aid worth US$4·5bn. came from the international community, with the USA accounting for US$1·8bn. Large scale US economic aid continues, as does assistance from the World Bank and the IMF's Poverty Reduction and Growth Facility.

Currency

The *afghani* (AFN) was introduced in Oct. 2002 with one of the new notes worth 1,000 old *afghani* (AFA). The old *afghani* had been trading at around 46,000 to the US$. Inflation was 13·0% in 2007, rising to 26·8% in 2008.

Budget

The fiscal year begins on 21 March. Revenues in 2005–06 were 67,531m. afghani and expenditures 91,417m. afghani.

Performance

Real GDP growth was 12·1% in 2007 and 3·4% in 2008. Average annual per capita income has risen from US$180 in 2001 to US$355 in 2006. Total GDP in 2007 was US$11·6bn.

Banking and Finance

Da Afghanistan Bank undertakes the functions of a central bank, holding the exclusive right of note issue. Founded in 1939, its *Governor* is Abdul Qadeer Fitrat. The banking sector has undergone major reconstruction since the removal of the Taliban government in 2001, with a number of new private banks having opened in the meantime.

Weights and Measures

The metric system is in increasingly common use. Local units include: one *khurd* = 0·11 kg; one *pao* = four khurds; one *charak* = four paos; one *sere* = four charaks; one *kharwar* = 580 kg or 16 maunds of 36·25 kg each; one *gaz* = 101·6 cm; one *jarib* = 60 x 60 kabuli yd or 0·202 ha.; one *kulba* = 40 jaribs (area in which 2½ kharwars of seed can be sown); one jarib yd = 73·66 cm.

ENERGY AND NATURAL RESOURCES

Environment

Carbon dioxide emissions from the consumption and flaring of fossil fuels were the equivalent of less than 0·1 tonnes per capita in 2008.

Electricity

Installed capacity was an estimated 0·43m. kW in 2004. Production was 779m. kWh in 2004 with consumption per capita 38 kWh.

Oil and Gas

Proven natural gas reserves were 50bn. cu. metres in 2007. Production in 2004 was 3m. cu. metres.

Minerals

There are deposits of coal, copper, barite, lapis lazuli, emerald, talc and salt. Mining, particularly of copper, is considered to be the country's best prospect for economic growth. In spite of the instability, Afghanistan is still one of the world's leading producers of lapis lazuli.

Agriculture

The greater part of Afghanistan is mountainous but there are many fertile plains and valleys. In 2007 there were an estimated 8·53m. ha. of arable land and 0·13m. ha. of permanent cropland; 2·25m. ha. were irrigated in 2007. The agricultural population was approximately 16·0m. in 2007, of whom around 5·08m. were economically active.

Output, 2003, in 1,000 tonnes: wheat, 4,361; rice, 433; barley, 410; grapes, 365; maize, 310; potatoes, 240. Opium production in 2001 was just 185 tonnes (down from 4,565 tonnes in 1999), but in 2002 it went up to 3,400 tonnes, and further to 3,600 tonnes in 2003 and 4,200 tonnes in 2004. There was a slight decline in 2005, to 4,100 tonnes, but production then rose to 6,100 tonnes in 2006 and reached a record 8,200 tonnes in 2007. The area under cultivation in 2007 was a record high of 193,000 ha., up from 165,000 ha. in 2006. It had been just 7,606 ha. in 2001. Afghanistan accounts for more than 90% of the world's opium. In Feb. 2001 the United Nations Drug Control Programme reported that opium production had been almost totally eradicated after the Taliban outlawed the cultivation of poppies. As a result in 2001 Myanmar became the largest producer of opium, but since then Afghanistan has again been the leading producer.

Livestock (2003): cattle, 3·7m.; sheep, 8·8m.; goats, 7·3m.; asses, 920,000; camels, 175,000; horses, 104,000; chickens, 6m.

Forestry

In 2005 forests covered 0·87m. ha., or 1·3% of the total land area. Timber production in 2007 was 3·29m. cu. metres.

Fisheries

In 2005 the total catch was estimated to be 1,000 tonnes, exclusively from inland waters.

INDUSTRY

Major industries include natural gas, fertilizers, cement, coalmining, small vehicle assembly plants, building, carpet weaving, cotton textiles, clothing and footwear, leather tanning and fruit canning.

Labour

The workforce was 9,800,500 in 2002. In 1995 the unemployment rate was estimated at 8%.

INTERNATIONAL TRADE

Imports and Exports

Total imports (2005), US$2,218m.; exports US$365m. Main imports: foodstuffs and live animals, beverages and tobacco, mineral fuels, manufactured goods, chemicals and related products, machinery and transport equipment. Main exported products: opium (illegal trade), non-edible crude materials (excluding fuels), manufactured goods (raw material intensive), machinery and transport equipment, fruits, nuts, hand-woven carpets, wool, hides, precious and semi-precious gems. The illegal trade in opium is the largest source of export earnings and accounts for half of Afghanistan's GDP. Main import sources in 2005 were Japan (18·7%), Pakistan (17·8%), China (14·3%) and Russia (10·2%). The leading export destination was Pakistan (81·6%), followed by India (6·3%) and Russia (3·6%).

Imports and exports were largely unaffected by the sanctions imposed during the Taliban regime.

COMMUNICATIONS

Roads

There were 34,782 km of roads in 2004, of which 23·7% were paved. A large part of the road network is in a poor state of repair as a result of military action, but rebuilding is under way. In Jan. 2003 women regained the right to drive after a ten-year ban. 431,600 passenger cars (15 per 1,000 inhabitants in 2007) and 153,600 lorries and vans were in use in 2008.

Rail

There are two short stretches of railway in the country, extensions of the Uzbek and Turkmen networks. A Trans-Afghan Railway was proposed in an Afghan-Pakistan-Turkmen agreement of 1994.

Civil Aviation

There is an international airport at Kabul (Khwaja Rawash Airport). The national carrier is Ariana Afghan Airlines, which in 2003 operated direct flights from Kabul to Amritsar, Delhi, Dubai, Frankfurt, Islamabad, İstanbul, Sharjah and Tehran. In 1999 scheduled airline traffic of Afghanistan-based carriers flew 2·7m. km, carrying 140,000 passengers (36,000 on international flights). The UN sanctions imposed on 14 Nov. 1999 included the cutting off of Afghanistan's air links to the outside world. In Jan. 2002 Ariana Afghan Airlines resumed services and Kabul airport was reopened. The airport was heavily bombed during the US campaign and although it is now functioning with some civilian flights it is still being used extensively by the military authorities. Afghanistan's first private airline, Kam Air, was launched in Nov. 2003.

Shipping

There are practically no navigable rivers. A port has been built at Qizil Qala on the Oxus and there are three river ports on the Amu Darya, linked by road to Kabul. The container port at Kheyrabad on the Amu Darya river has rail connections to Uzbekistan.

Telecommunications

In 2005 there were 1,300,000 telephone subscribers, or 43·5 per 1,000 inhabitants. There were 1,200,000 mobile phone subscribers in 2005 and 30,000 internet users.

Postal Services

In 2003 there were 313 post offices.

SOCIAL INSTITUTIONS

Justice

A Supreme Court was established in June 1978. It retained its authority under the Taliban regime.

Under the Taliban, a strict form of Sharia law was followed. This law, which was enforced by armed police, included prohibitions on alcohol, television broadcasts, internet use and photography, yet received its widest condemnation for its treatment of women. Public executions and amputations were widely used as punishment under the regime.

The Judicial Reform Commission is in the process of establishing a civil justice system in accordance with Islamic principles, international standards, the rule of law and Afghan legal traditions. The death penalty is still in force. In 2008 there were nine confirmed executions (although none in 2009).

Education

Adult literacy was 28·1% in 2004.

In 2007 there were 4,718,077 pupils at primary schools (37% female) with 110,312 teaching staff and 1,035,782 at secondary schools (26% female) with 32,817 teaching staff. There were around 9,000 schools in 2008. Schools are often burned down and insurgents have attacked both teachers and pupils.

In 2006 there were 13 universities, 19 institutions of higher education and six pedagogical institutes. In 2004 there were 27,648 students (20% female) in tertiary education and 1,781 academic staff. Kabul University had some 8,000 students in 2006. Formerly one of Asia's finest educational institutes, Kabul University lost many of its staff during the Taliban regime, and following the US bombing attacks it was closed down, although it has since reopened.

In areas controlled by the Taliban education was forbidden for girls. Boys' schools taught only religious education and military training. Female teachers and pupils have now returned to education after five years of exclusion.

Health

Afghanistan is one of the least successful countries in the battle against undernourishment. Between 1980 and 2000 the proportion of undernourished people rose from 33% of the population to 70%. Half of all Afghan children suffer from chronic malnutrition. One in four children die before reaching the age of five, largely as a result of diarrhoea, pneumonia, measles and other similar illnesses.

The bombing of Afghanistan beginning in Oct. 2001 severely disrupted the supply of aid to the country and left much of the population exposed to starvation.

In 2001 there were 4,104 physicians, 630 dentists (1999), 4,752 nurses and 525 pharmacists (1999) in Afghanistan.

In 2000 only 13% of the population had access to safe drinking water (the lowest percentage of any country).

RELIGION

The predominant religion is Islam. An estimated 86% of the population are Sunni Muslims and 9% Shias.

The Taliban provoked international censure in May 2001 by forcing the minority population of Afghan Hindus and Sikhs to wear yellow identification badges.

CULTURE

World Heritage Sites

There are two UNESCO sites in Afghanistan: the Minaret and Archaeological Remains of Jam (inscribed in 2002), a 12th century minaret; the Cultural Landscape and Archaeological Remains of the Bamiyan Valley (2003), including the monumental Buddha statues destroyed by the Taliban in 2001.

Broadcasting

Under Taliban Rule, broadcasting was banned with the exception of Radio Afghanistan, which was renamed Voice of Sharia and used for official propaganda purposes and religious sermons. Since the collapse of the regime, Radio-Television Afghanistan has resumed services as the state broadcasting outlet. Private television and radio networks have also been established, including Tolo TV, Ariana TV, Radio Arman and Radio Killid. Relays of foreign radio services are available in Kabul. In 2003 there were 312,000 television receivers (colour by PAL).

Cinema

Cinemas were banned under the Taliban but have since reopened. The Afghan Film Institute is responsible for censorship.

Press

Afghanistan had approximately 300 publications in 2004. The main dailies were Hewad, Anis and the English language publications Daily Arman and Kabul Times.

Tourism

In 1998 there were 4,000 foreign tourists bringing in receipts of US$1m.

Calendar

In 2002 the Afghan Interim Authority replaced the lunar calendar with the traditional Afghan solar calendar. The solar calendar had previously been used in Afghanistan until 1999 when it was changed by the Taliban authorities who wanted the country to adopt the system used in Saudi Arabia. The change back to the solar calendar means the current year is 1389.

DIPLOMATIC REPRESENTATIVES

Of Afghanistan in the United Kingdom (31 Prince's Gate, London, SW7 1QQ)
Ambassador: Homayoun Tandar.

Of the United Kingdom in Afghanistan (15th St., Roundabout Wazir Akbar Khan, PO Box 334, Kabul)
Ambassador: Vacant.
Chargé d'Affaires a.i.: Tom Dodd.

Of Afghanistan in the USA (2341 Wyoming Ave., NW, Washington, D.C., 20008)
Ambassador: Said Tayeb Jawad.

Of the USA in Afghanistan (Great Masood Rd between Radio Afghanistan and Ministry of Public Health, Kabul)
Ambassador: Karl W. Eikenberry.

Of Afghanistan to the United Nations
Ambassador: Zahir Tanin.

Of Afghanistan to the European Union
Ambassador: Zia Nezam.

FURTHER READING

Amin, S. H., *Law, Reform and Revolution in Afghanistan.* 1991
Arney, G., *Afghanistan.* 1990
Edwards, David B., *Before Taliban: Genealogies of the Afghan Jihad.* 2002
Ewans, Martin, *Afghanistan, A New History.* 2001
Goodson, Larry, *Afghanistan's Endless War: State Failure, Regional Politics and the Rise of the Taliban.* 2001
Griffiths, John, *Afghanistan: A History of Conflict.* 2001
Hyman, A., *Afghanistan under Soviet Domination, 1964–1991.* 3rd ed. 1992
Magnus, Ralph H. and Naby, Eden, *Afghanistan: Mullah, Marx and Mujahid.* Revised ed. 2002
Maley, William, *The Afghanistan Wars.* 2002
Margolis, Eric, *War at the Top of the World: The Struggle for Afghanistan, Kashmir and Tibet.* 2001
Montgomery, John Dickey D. and Rondinelli, Dennis A., (eds.) *Beyond Reconstruction in Afghanistan: Lessons from Development Experience.* 2004
Nojumi, Neamatollah, *The Rise of the Taliban in Afghanistan.* 2001
Roy, O., *Islam and Resistance in Afghanistan.* 2nd ed. 1990
Rubin, B. R., *The Fragmentation of Afghanistan: State Formation and Collapse in the International System.* 1995.—*The Search for Peace in Afghanistan: from Buffer State to Failed State.* 1996
Smith, Mary, *Before the Taliban: Living with War, Hoping for Peace.* 2002
Vogelsang, Willem, *The Afghans.* 2002

National Statistical Office: Central Statistics Office, Ansar-i-Watt, Kabul.
Website: http://www.cso.gov.af

ALBANIA

Republika e Shqipërisë
(Republic of Albania)

Capital: Tirana
Population estimate, 2010: 3·17m.
GDP per capita, 2007: (PPP$) 7,041
HDI/world rank: 0·818/70

KEY HISTORICAL EVENTS

Albania was originally part of Illyria which stretched along the eastern coastal region of the Adriatic. By 168 BC the Romans, having conquered Illyria, administered it as a province (Illyricum) of their empire. From AD 395 Illyria became part of the eastern Byzantine empire, the decline of which over the following centuries encouraged waves of Slavic invasions across the region. During the middle ages the name Albania began to be increasingly applied to the modern day region, possibly deriving from Albanoi, the name of an Illyrian tribe. Ottoman intrusion began in the 14th century and, despite years of resistance under the leadership of national hero Gjergj Kastrioti, Turkish suzerainty was imposed from 1478. During the 15th and 16th centuries, many Albanians fled to southern Italy to escape Ottoman rule and conversion to Islam. After the Russo-Turkish war of 1877–78 there were demands for independence from Turkey. With the defeat of Turkey in the Balkan war of 1912, Albanian nationalists proclaimed independence and set up a provisional government.

During the First World War Albania became a battlefield for warring occupation forces. Albania was admitted to the League of Nations on 20 Dec. 1920. In Nov. 1921 the conference of ambassadors confirmed its 1913 frontiers with minor alterations. Although declared a republic in 1925, Albania then became a monarchy from 1928 until April 1939 when Italy's dictator, Mussolini, invaded and set up a puppet state. During the Second World War Albania suffered first Italian and then German occupation. Resistance was led by royalist, nationalist republican and Communist movements, often at odds with each other. The Communists enjoyed the support of Tito's partisans, who were instrumental in forming the Albanian Communist Party on 8 Nov. 1941. Communists dominated the Anti-Fascist National Liberation Committee which became the Provisional Democratic Government on 22 Oct. 1944 after the German withdrawal, with Enver Hoxha, a French-educated school teacher and member of the Communist Party Central Committee, at its head. Large estates were broken up and the land distributed, although full collectivization was not brought in until 1955–59. Close ties were forged with the USSR. However, following Khrushchev's reconciliation with Tito in 1956, China replaced the Soviet Union as Albania's powerful patron from 1961 until the end of the Maoist phase in 1977. The regime then adopted a policy of 'revolutionary self-sufficiency'.

Following the collapse of the USSR, the People's Assembly legalized opposition parties. The Communists won the first multi-party elections in April 1991, but soon resigned from office following a general strike. They were replaced firstly by a coalition government, which collapsed in Dec. 1991, and then by an interim technocratic administration. A new, non-Communist government was elected in March 1992.

In 1997 Albania was disrupted by financial crises caused by the collapse of fraudulent pyramid finance schemes. A period of violent anarchy led to the fall of the administration and to fresh elections which returned a Socialist-led government. A UN peacekeeping force withdrew in Aug. 1997, but sporadic violence continued.

In April 1999 the Kosovo crisis which led to NATO air attacks on Yugoslavian military targets set off a flood of refugees into Albania.

Having won a decisive victory in the 2001 elections, the ruling Socialist Party lost power to the opposition Democratic Party in the July 2005 polling, the results of which were only confirmed in Sept. following a lengthy appeals process and reruns in three constituencies.

TERRITORY AND POPULATION

Albania is bounded in the north by Montenegro and Serbia, east by Macedonia, south by Greece and west by the Adriatic. The area is 28,748 sq. km (11,100 sq. miles). At the census of April 2001 the population was 3,069,275; density, 107 per sq. km.

The UN gives an estimated population for 2010 of 3·17m.

In 2005, 54·6% of the population lived in rural areas. The capital is Tirana (population in 2003, 555,565); other large towns (population in 2003) are Elbasan (226,670), Durrës (209,289), Fier (201,397), Shkodër (184,989), Vlorë (148,821), Lushnjë (145,762), Korçë (144,439), Berat (126,608), Kavajë (81,145) and Gjirokastër (Argyrocastro) (56,664).

The country is administratively divided into 12 prefectures, 36 districts, 306 communes and 65 municipalities.

Districts	Area (sq. km)	Population (2003)	Districts	Area (sq. km)	Population (2003)
Berat	939	126,608	Lezhë	479	72,001
Bulqizë	469	38,105	Librazhd	1,023	70,045
Delvinë	348	11,628	Lushnjë	712	145,762
Devoll	429	34,951	Malësi e Madhe	555	37,232
Dibër	1,088	79,582	Mallakastër	393	38,458
Durrës	433	209,989	Mat	1,029	58,391
Elbasan	1,372	226,670	Mirditë	867	34,202
Fier	785	201,397	Peqin	109	32,777
Gjirokastër	1,137	56,664	Përmet	930	23,777
Gramsh	695	31,852	Pogradec	725	71,738
Has	393	19,360	Pukë	1,034	33,444
Kavajë	414	81,145	Sarandë	749	40,398
Kolonjë	805	16,316	Shkodër	1,973	184,989
Korçë	1,752	144,439	Skrapar	775	25,093
Krujë	333	66,084	Tepelenë	817	30,189
Kuçovë	84	35,557	Tirana	1,238	555,565
Kukës	938	62,778	Tropojë	1,043	24,270
Kurbin	273	54,886	Vlorë	1,609	148,821

In most cases districts are named after their capitals. Exceptions are: Devoll, capital—Bilisht; Dibër—Peshkopi; Has—Krumë; Kolonjë—Ersekë; Kurbin—Laç; Mallakastër—Ballsh; Malësi e Madhe—Koplik; Mat—Burrel; Mirditë—Rrëshen; Skrapar—Çorovodë; Tropojë—Bajram Curri.

Albanians account for 91·7% of the population, Aromanians 3·6%, Greeks 2·3% and others 2·4%.

The official language is Albanian.

SOCIAL STATISTICS

2003: births, 47,012; deaths, 17,967. Rates in 2003 (per 1,000): births, 14·8; deaths, 5·7. Infant mortality, 2005, was 16 per 1,000 live births. Fertility rate (number of births per woman), 2·2 in 2004. Annual population growth rate, 2000–05, 0·5%. Life expectancy at birth, 2007, was 73·4 years for men and 79·8 years for women. Abortion was legalized in 1991.

CLIMATE

Mediterranean-type, with rainfall mainly in winter, but thunderstorms are frequent and severe in the great heat of the plains in summer. Winters in the highlands can be severe, with much snow. Tirana, Jan. 44°F (6·8°C), July 75°F (23·9°C). Annual rainfall 54" (1,353 mm). Shkodër, Jan. 39°F (3·9°C), July 77°F (25°C). Annual rainfall 57" (1,425 mm).

CONSTITUTION AND GOVERNMENT

A new constitution was adopted on 28 Nov. 1998. The supreme legislative body is the single-chamber *People's Assembly* of 140 deputies. As from April 2009 all members are elected through proportional representation, for four-year terms. Where no candidate wins an absolute majority, a run-off election is held. The *President* is elected by parliament for a five-year term.

National Anthem

'Rreth Flamurit të përbashkuar' ('The flag that united us in the struggle'); words by A. S. Drenova, tune by C. Porumbescu.

RECENT ELECTIONS

Parliamentary elections took place on 28 June 2009. The Democratic Party of Albania (PD) won 68 of the 140 seats with 40·0% of votes cast, the Socialist Party of Albania 65 with 40·8%, the Socialist Movement for Integration 4 with 4·8%. Three other parties won one seat each. The PD and its allies received a total of 70 seats, one short of a majority, and the Socialist Party and its allies 66. Turnout was an estimated 50%. The Socialist Movement for Integration joined the PD and its allies to form a working coalition in Sept. 2009.

Parliament elected Bamir Topi (ind.) president on 20 July 2007 in a fourth round after votes on 8, 10 and 14 July had failed to result in the required three-fifths majority.

CURRENT ADMINISTRATION

President: Bamir Topi; b. 1957 (in office since 24 July 2007).

The government is formed by a coalition of the Democratic Party of Albania (PD), the Socialist Movement for Integration (LSI), the Republican Party of Albania (PR) and the Party for Justice and Integration (PDI). In March 2010 the cabinet was composed as follows:

Prime Minister: Sali Berisha; b. 1944 (Democratic Party of Albania; sworn in 11 Sept. 2005, having previously been president from April 1992–July 1997).

Deputy Prime Minister and Minister for Foreign Affairs: Ilir Meta.

Minister for Agriculture, Food and Consumer Protection: Genc Ruli. *Defence:* Arben Imami. *Economy, Trade and Energy:* Dritan Prifti. *Education and Science:* Myqerem Tafaj. *Environment:* Fatmir Mediu. *European Integration:* Majlinda Bregu. *Finance:* Ridvan Bode. *Health:* Petrit Vasili. *Interior:* Lulëzim Basha. *Justice:* Bujar Nishani. *Labour, Social Affairs and Equal Opportunities:* Spiro Ksera. *Public Works, Transportation and Telecommunications:* Sokol Olldashi. *Tourism, Culture, Youth and Sports:* Ferdinand Xhaferri. *Minister of State:* Genc Pollo.

Albanian Parliament: http://www.parlament.al

CURRENT LEADERS

Bamir Topi

Position
President

Introduction
Bamir Myrteza Topi was sworn in as president in July 2007 after four rounds of voting, succeeding the Socialist Party's Alfred Moisiu. A former minister of agriculture and chairman of the Democratic Party of Albania parliamentary group, Topi is no longer formally linked to any political party.

Early Life
Topi was born in April 1957 in Tirana. After graduating in veterinary medicine at the Tirana Agricultural University, he moved to the neighbouring town of Petrela to continue studies in toxicology and pharmacology. In 1984 he took up a position as a researcher at the Institute of Veterinary Studies. From 1987–90 he left the Institute for Italy, where he completed a doctorate in molecular biology. His return to Albania coincided with the first large scale anti-communist protests. Topi became the Veterinary Institute's director, lecturing in toxicology and pharmacology until 1995 when he was conferred a professorship.

Topi entered professional politics in 1996, winning an Assembly seat as a PD candidate before being appointed minister of food and agriculture. In 1997 accusations of fraud and civil unrest briefly forced the PD, led by Sali Berisha, out of power. Topi remained loyal to Berisha and in July 2001 was elected PD candidate for Tirana and appointed to lead the PD caucus in parliament. In Dec. he was appointed party vice president.

In March 2007 Topi was announced as the PD candidate for the presidential election later in the year. While attracting support from the Christian Democrat and Republican parties, he faced fierce opposition from the Socialists. After failing to achieve the required three-fifths majority in three successive polls, the Assembly elected Topi president on 20 July 2007 in the penultimate round of scheduled voting. Topi resigned his party affiliation before being sworn in on 24 July.

Career in Office
Chief among Topi's objectives has been driving forward Albania's campaign to join the European Union and NATO. In 2006 the

government had signed a Stabilization and Association Agreement with the EU, and Topi subsequently negotiated a relaxation of the EU's visa conditions for Albania from Jan. 2008. Albania secured an invitation to membership of NATO in April 2008 and became a member in April 2009. In the same month Albania's application to join the EU was submitted. The issue of the independence of predominantly Albanian Kosovo has also taken centre stage, with Topi maintaining a supportive stance for the province's unilateral declaration of separation from Serbia in Feb. 2008.

At the domestic level, with the EU pushing for a tougher line on corruption, Topi was confronted in Oct. 2007 with a corruption scandal when several ministers were arrested on charges of embezzlement.

Sali Berisha

Position
Prime Minister

Introduction
Dr Sali Berisha returned as prime minister on 11 Sept. 2005 after eight years in opposition. He was a leading opponent of the communist regime in the late 1980s and served as Albania's first elected post-communist president from 1992–97. Breathing life into Albania's ailing economy, reforming its institutions and tackling corruption and organized crime have remained his policy priorities. Following parliamentary elections in June 2009, Berisha retained the premiership at the head of a new coalition formed in Sept. between his Democratic Party of Albania and its allies and the Socialist Movement for Integration.

Early Life
Sali Ram Berisha was born in Vuçidol in northern Albania on 15 Oct. 1944, the year in which the communist leader, Enver Hoxha, seized power and established a hard-line Stalinist regime. Berisha graduated in medicine from the University of Tirana in 1967, subsequently specializing in cardiology and publishing numerous textbooks and scientific papers. He joined the communist Party of Labour in 1971.

In the late 1980s Berisha was one of a group of intellectuals who called for democratic reforms. Following student protests at the University of Tirana in early Dec. 1990, he founded the PD and was elected a member of parliament in the country's first multi-party elections on 31 March 1991. During the PD's first Congress in Sept. 1991 Berisha was voted chairman and led the party to victory in the general election of 22 March 1992. Elected president of Albania on 9 April 1992, he set out to open up the economy, promote foreign investment and reform the country's institutions. However, the administration was marred by corruption and Albania remained mired in poverty. Tens of thousands emigrated and Berisha faced growing opposition to his increasingly authoritarian rule, particularly in the south of the country.

Support for Berisha was further eroded by the collapse of various pyramid investment schemes in 1997. An uprising in the south threatened to spill over into civil war and tensions remained high when Berisha refused to step down after the electoral victory of a socialist-led coalition in June 1997. He eventually resigned under international pressure on 23 July 1997, to be replaced by the head of the Socialist Party, Rexhep Meidani. Fatos Nano, a fellow socialist and arch-rival of Berisha, became prime minister.

Tensions between the two main parties remained. Berisha accused Fatos Nano's administration of corruption and incompetence and withdrew from parliament between 1998 and early 2002. The arrival of hundreds of thousands of ethnic Albanian refugees from Kosovo in 1999 placed further strain on the faltering economy and infrastructure. Berisha fought the general election on 3 July 2005 on an anti-corruption platform and the PD claimed victory, although foreign monitors criticized the vote as falling short of international standards. Having formed a coalition with other centre-right groups to take control of 81 of the 140 seats in the legislature, Berisha was sworn in as prime minister on 11 Sept. 2005.

Career in Office
Berisha promised to build a 'social state' by streamlining the government and purging it of corrupt elements, reducing taxes and enabling private enterprise to flourish. He also declared his aim of eventual Albanian membership of NATO and the EU. In June 2006 his government signed a Stabilization and Association Agreement with the EU after three years of negotiations, and in April 2009 Albania joined NATO and applied for EU membership.

Berisha has presided over an improvement in the economy, a revival of agriculture and the attraction of greater foreign investment. However, Albania's reputation for lawlessness has endured and criticisms of the country's ineffective judicial system remain. In March 2008 Berisha removed the defence minister, Fatmir Mediu, from office following a series of explosions at an ammunition depot near Tirana airport which killed 26 people and injured 250 more. A new coalition government comprising the PD, the Republican Party of Albania, the Party for Justice and Integration and the Socialist Movement for Integration, with Berisha retaining the premiership, was sworn in on 17 Sept. 2009 following earlier parliamentary elections.

DEFENCE

Since 1 Jan. 2010 Albania has had an all-volunteer professional army. In 2006 defence expenditure totalled US$141m. (US$39 per capita), representing 1·5% of GDP.

Army
Strength of the Land Forces (Army) Command in 2007 was 6,200. There is an internal security force, and frontier guards number 500.

Navy
Navy Forces Command personnel in 2007 totalled 1,100. The fleet comprises 35 vessels including five torpedo craft. There are naval bases at Durrës and Vlorë.

Air Force
In 2007 the Air Forces Command had 1,370 personnel and operated 13 helicopters (including seven Agusta Bell 206s).

INTERNATIONAL RELATIONS

Albania is a member of the UN, World Bank, IMF and several other UN specialized agencies, WTO, Council of Europe, OSCE, Central European Initiative, BSEC, IOM, Islamic Development Bank, NATO and OIC. It applied to join the EU in April 2009, although membership is not expected until 2015 at the earliest.

ECONOMY

In 2007 agriculture accounted for 21% of GDP, industry 20% and services 59%.

Overview
Albania is a low middle income county and one of the poorest countries in Europe. Despite efforts to support macroeconomic stability and economic growth, 20% of the population is in poverty and 3% are unable to meet basic food needs.

The economy collapsed following the dissolution of the USSR in 1990. Unemployment rose to 30% and by 1992 industrial production had fallen by almost half. With the help of the World Bank and the IMF, the government embarked on a programme of privatization and economic liberalization. Privatization of land, small businesses and housing was achieved between 1991–93 and a privatization programme for large enterprises was initiated in 1995 under the aegis of the National Privatization Agency. The

Tirana Stock Exchange was established in 1996 during a period of strong growth, with GDP annual growth averaging 9% between 1993–95. However, the absence of banking sector reform led to informal credit arrangements such as pyramid schemes, many of which collapsed to devastating effect in 1997, sparking widespread social unrest and the downfall of the government.

The agricultural sector remains important, although its share of GDP had dropped from around 35% in 1990 to 23% in 2005 despite some revival under private ownership from 2002. Recent economic growth has been stimulated chiefly by the manufacturing and service sectors, especially construction. The industrial sector shrank from 44% to 19% of GDP between 1990 and 2002. Economic growth declined slightly in 2006 owing to unreliable electricity supply and slowing activity in construction and export production.

Currency

The monetary unit is the *lek* (ALL), notionally of 100 *qindars*. In Sept. 1991 the lek (plural, *lekë* or leks) was pegged to the ecu at a rate of 30 leks = one ecu. In June 1992 it was devalued from 50 to 110 to US$1. There was inflation of 2·9% in 2007 and 3·4% in 2008, extending the economic stabilization that followed several years of high inflation (225% in 1992).

Foreign exchange reserves were US$1,180m. in July 2005, total money supply was 184,249m. leks and gold reserves totalled 69,000 troy oz.

Budget

The fiscal year is the calendar year. In 2004 budgetary central government revenue was 150,231m. leks and expenditure 134,009m. leks.

Principal sources of revenue in 2004 were: taxes on goods and services, 89,354m. leks; taxes on income, profits and capital gains, 27,220m. leks; taxes on international trade and transactions, 13,880m. leks. Main items of expenditure by economic type in 2004 were: compensation of employees, 48,998m. leks; interest, 28,423m. leks; use of goods and services, 19,251m. leks.

VAT is 20%.

Performance

Total GDP in 2008 was US$12·3bn. After the economy contracted by 10·5% in 1997 following the collapse of pyramid finance schemes, real GDP growth averaged 6·9% from 1998 to 2006. The economy grew by 6·3% in 2007 and 6·8% in 2008.

Banking and Finance

The central bank and bank of issue is the Bank of Albania, founded in 1925 with Italian aid as the Albanian State Bank and renamed in 1993. Its *Governor* is Ardian Fullani. The Savings Bank of Albania, which serves around 75% of the Albanian market, was sold by the government to Raiffeisen Zentralbank Österreich AG in Dec. 2003. In 2002 it had total assets of US$1·4bn., approximately 60% of the total assets of the Albanian banking sector. In 2002 there were six other banks: American Bank of Albania; Arab-Albanian Islamic Bank; Fefad Bank; Italian-Albanian Bank; National Commercial Bank of Albania; and Tirana Bank SA.

A stock exchange opened in Tirana in 1996.

ENERGY AND NATURAL RESOURCES

Environment

Albania's carbon dioxide emissions from the consumption and flaring of fossil fuels in 2008 were the equivalent of 1·3 tonnes per capita (compared to the European average of 7·8 tonnes per capita).

Electricity

Albania is rich in hydro-electric potential. Although virtually all of the electricity is generated by hydro-electric power plants only 30% of potential hydro-electric sources are currently being used. Power cuts are common. Electricity capacity was an estimated 1·72m. kW in 2004. Production was 5·56bn. kWh in 2004 and consumption per capita 1,847 kWh. Albania imported 477m. kWh of electricity in 2004 and exported 274m. kWh.

Oil and Gas

Offshore exploration began in 1991. Oil has been produced onshore since 1920. Oil reserves in 2007 were 165m. bbls. Crude oil production in 2004, 2·8m. bbls. Natural gas is extracted. Reserves in 2007 totalled 2bn. cu. metres; output in 2007 was 11m. cu. metres.

Minerals

Mineral wealth is considerable and includes lignite, chromium, copper and nickel. Output (in 1,000 tonnes): lignite (2004), 109; copper ore (2005), 73; chromite (2005), 66. Nickel reserves are 60m. tonnes of iron containing 1m. tonnes of nickel, but extraction had virtually ceased by 1996. A consortium of British and Italian companies is modernizing the chrome industry with the aim of making Albania the leading supplier of ferrochrome to European stainless steel producers.

Agriculture

In 2007 the agricultural population was an estimated 1·37m., of whom around 620,000 were economically active. The country is mountainous, except for the Adriatic littoral and the Korçë Basin, which are fertile. Only 24% of the land area is suitable for cultivation; 15% of Albania is used for pasture. In 2007 there were 578,000 ha. of arable land and 120,000 ha. of permanent cropland. 106,530 ha. were irrigated in 2007.

A law of Aug. 1991 privatized co-operatives' land. Families received allocations, according to their size, from village committees. In 2007 there were 369,598 agricultural holdings. Since 1995 owners have been permitted to buy and sell agricultural land. In 2007 there were 10,833 tractors in use and 1,643 harvester-threshers.

Production (in 1,000 tonnes), 2007: total grains, 494 (including wheat 250 and maize 216); watermelons, 190; tomatoes, 160; potatoes, 155; grapes, 147; onions, 73; cucumbers and gherkins, 50.

Livestock, 2007: sheep, 1,853,000; goats, 876,000; cattle, 577,000; pigs, 147,000; horses, 46,000; chickens, 4,712,000.

Livestock products, 2007 (in 1,000 tonnes): beef, 83; mutton, lamb and goat, 46; pork, 16; poultry, 13; milk, 1,016; eggs, 736m. units.

Forestry

Forests covered 1,455,000 ha. in 2003 (36·9% of the total land area), mainly oak, elm, pine and birch. Timber production in 2007 was 296,000 cu. metres.

Fisheries

The total catch in 2005 amounted to 3,802 tonnes (2,065 tonnes from sea fishing).

INDUSTRY

Output is small, and the principal industries are agricultural product processing, textiles, oil products and cement. Closures of loss-making plants in the chemical and engineering industries built up in the Communist era led to a 60% decline in production by 1993. Output in 2004 (in 1,000 tonnes): distillate fuel oil, 73; residual fuel oil, 67; petrol, 35; cement (2001), 30; rolled steel (1994), 17; beer (2003), 39·0m. litres; wine (2003), 9·2m. litres; 40m. bricks (1994); 126m. cigarettes (2001).

Labour

In 2003 the workforce was 1,089,000, of which 926,000 were employed (745,000 in the private sector). Unemployment was 15·0% at the end of 2003.

The average monthly wage in 2007 was 27,350 leks; the official minimum wage in 2007 was 16,100 leks. Minimum wages may not fall below one-third of maximum.

Trade Unions

Independent trade unions became legal in Feb. 1991.

INTERNATIONAL TRADE

Foreign investment was legalized in Nov. 1990. Foreign debt was US$1,839m. in 2005.

Imports and Exports

Foreign trade (in US$1m.):

	2002	2003	2004	2005	2006
Imports	1,485·4	1,783·5	2,194·9	2,477·6	2,915·6
Exports	330·2	447·2	603·3	656·3	792·9

Principal imports in 2004: transport and machinery equipment, 23·7%; food and livestock, 14·5%; chemicals and related products, 7·9%; apparel and clothing, 6·3%. Leading exports in 2004: clothing and apparel, 32·9%; footwear, 27·7%; iron and steel, 5·2%; manufactures of metal, 4·7%.

Main import suppliers, 2004 (% of total trade): Italy, 32·6%; Greece, 18·5%; Turkey, 7·1%. Main export markets, 2004: Italy, 73·1%; Greece, 12·0%; Germany, 3·1%.

COMMUNICATIONS

Roads

In 2002 there were 3,220 km of main roads, 4,300 km of secondary roads and 10,480 km of other roads. There were 237,932 passenger cars in 2007, as well as 29,506 buses and coaches and 59,645 lorries and vans. There were 384 fatalities in road accidents in 2007.

Rail

Total length in operation in 2005 was 447 km. Passenger-km travelled in 2003 came to 105m. and freight tonne-km to 18m. In Aug. 2003 the government announced plans to re-establish rail links with Montenegro and the European network and construct a railway to Macedonia with the financial assistance of the World Bank.

Civil Aviation

The national carrier is Albanian Airlines, a joint venture with a Kuwaiti firm. It began operations in Oct. 1995. In 2002 it flew services to Bologna, Frankfurt, İstanbul, Priština and Rome. Air civil transportation is carried out by 12 airlines, of which ten are foreign airlines and two are joint ventures. In 2003 scheduled airline traffic of Albania-based carriers flew 2m. km, carrying 159,000 passengers (all on international flights). The main airport is Mother Teresa International Airport at Rinas, 25 km from Tirana, which handled 906,103 passengers in 2006.

Shipping

In 2002 merchant shipping totalled 49,000 GRT. The main port is Durrës, with secondary ports being Vlorë, Sarandë and Shëngjin.

Telecommunications

In 2005 there were 354,000 telephone main lines. A state-owned mobile telephone network was set up in 1996, initially serving 8,000 subscribers. By 2005 there were 1·53m. mobile subscribers. There were 54,000 PCs in use in 2005 (17·4 for every 1,000 persons). Albania had 75,000 internet users in 2004.

Postal Services

In 2003 there were 565 post offices. A total of 6·6m. pieces of mail were processed in 2004.

SOCIAL INSTITUTIONS

Justice

A new criminal code was introduced in June 1995. The administration of justice (made up of First Instance Courts, The Courts of Appeal and the Supreme Court) is presided over by the *Council of Justice*, chaired by the President of the Republic, which appoints judges to courts. A Ministry of Justice was re-established in 1990 and a Bar Council set up. In Nov. 1993 the number of capital offences was reduced from 13 to six and the death penalty was abolished for women. In 2000 the death penalty was abolished for peacetime offences; it was abolished for all crimes in 2007. The prison population in Nov. 2005 was 3,491 (111 per 100,000 of national population).

Education

Primary education is free and compulsory from six to 14 years. Secondary education is also free and lasts four years. Pupils who fail exams at 14 are required to remain in school until the age of 16. Secondary education is divided into three categories: general; technical and professional; vocational. There were, in 2003–04, 1,763 nursery schools with 79,905 pupils and 3,770 teachers; 27,248 primary school teachers with 505,141 pupils; and 142,402 pupils and 6,873 teachers at secondary schools. In 2000–01 there were five universities, one agricultural university, one technological university, one polytechnic, one academy of fine arts and one higher institute of physical education. There were 53,255 university students registered and 1,750 academic staff in 2003–04; Tirana is the largest university, with 12,190 students in 2003–04. Adult literacy in 2003 was 98·7% (99·2% among males and 98·3% among females).

In 2004 total expenditure on education came to 3% of GNP.

Health

Medical services are free, though medicines are charged for. In 2003 there were 50 hospitals, 4,100 doctors and 11,470 nurses or midwives. In 2003 there were 9,514 hospital beds. The expenditure on health in 2003 was 15,698m. leks (7·8% of total government expenditure).

Welfare

The retirement age was 60 (men) or 55 (women) until 2002, since when the ages have been rising by six months annually until they become 65 (men) and 60 (women) in July 2011; to be eligible for a state pension contributions over 35 years are required. Old-age benefits consist of a basic pension and an earnings-related increment. The basic pension is indexed according to price changes of selected commodities.

Unemployment benefit was 5,240 leks per month as of 2007.

RELIGION

In 2001, 39% of the population were Muslims, mainly Sunni with some Bektashi, 17% Roman Catholic, 10% Albanian Orthodox and the remainder other religions or atheist. The Albanian Orthodox Church is autocephalous; it is headed by an Exarch, Anastasios, Archbishop of Tirana, Durrës and All Albania, and three metropolitans. In 2001 there were 118 priests. The Roman Catholic cathedral in Shkodër has been restored and the cathedral in Tirana has been rebuilt, opening in 2002. In 2000 there were one Roman Catholic archbishop and three bishops.

CULTURE

World Heritage Sites

In 1992 Butrint was added to the UNESCO World Heritage List (reinscribed in 1999 and 2007). Butrint is a settlement in the southwest of the country, near the port of Sarandë, which was inhabited from 800 BC and is now a major site of archaeological investigation. The site was extended for protection after looting in 1997. The historic town of Gjirokastër was added in 2005 (reinscribed in 2008) and is a rare example of a well-preserved Ottoman town built around the 13th century.

Broadcasting
Broadcasting is regulated by the National Council for Radio-Television (NCRT). In Dec. 2000 the NCRT licensed two national television stations, 31 local radio stations and one national radio station. The public national broadcaster is Radiotelevizioni Shqiptar. In 2005, 669,000 households were equipped with televisions (colour by SECAM H).

Cinema
In 2002 there were 25 cinemas, compared to 65 in 1991.

Press
In 2006 there were 28 paid-for dailies (combined circulation of 65,000).

Tourism
In 2004, 645,000 foreign tourists visited Albania (including 610,000 from other European countries and 26,000 from the Americas). There were 199 hotels in 2004.

Libraries
The National Library in Tirana contains over 1m. items.

Theatre and Opera
The National Albanian Theatre, Tirana, is the most prestigious, with a capacity of 540. The Opera and Ballet Theatre, Tirana, is the home of the Albanian Philharmonic Orchestra.

Museums and Galleries
The largest museum is the National Historical Museum in Tirana.

DIPLOMATIC REPRESENTATIVES
Of Albania in the United Kingdom (2nd Floor, 24 Buckingham Gate, London, SW1E 6LB)
Ambassador: Zef Mazi.

Of the United Kingdom in Albania (Rruga Skenderbeg 12, Tirana)
Ambassador: Fiona McIlwham.

Of Albania in the USA (2100 S St., NW, Washington, D.C., 20008)
Ambassador: Aleksandër Sallabanda.

Of the USA in Albania (Tirana Rruga Elbasanit 103, Tirana)
Ambassador: John Withers II.

Of Albania to the United Nations
Ambassador: Ferit Hoxha.

Of Albania to the European Union
Ambassador: Mimoza Halimi.

FURTHER READING
Fischer, Bernd, *Albania at War 1939–45.* 1999
Hutchings, R., *Historical Dictionary of Albania.* 1997
Sjoberg, O., *Rural Change and Development in Albania.* 1992
Vickers, M., *The Albanians: a Modern History.* 1997
Vickers, M. and Pettifer, J., *Albania: from Anarchy to a Balkan Identity.* 1997
Winnifrith, T. (ed.) *Perspectives on Albania.* 1992

National Statistical Office: Albanian Institute of Statistics, Rr. 'Lek Dukagjini', Nr 5, Tirana. *Director General:* Ines Nurja.
Website: http://www.instat.gov.al

ALGERIA

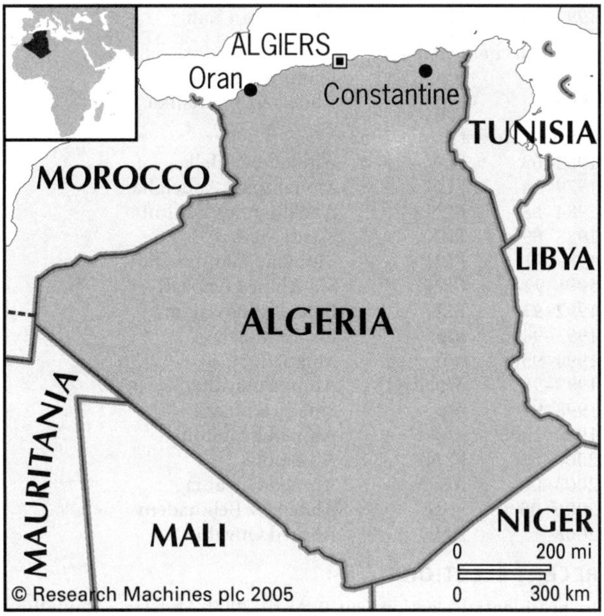

Jumhuriya al-Jazairiya ad-Dimuqratiya ash-Shabiya (People's Democratic Republic of Algeria)

Capital: Algiers
Population estimate, 2010: 35·42m.
GDP per capita, 2007: (PPP$) 7,740
HDI/world rank: 0·754/104

KEY HISTORICAL EVENTS

Algeria came under French control in the 1850s. French settlers developed political and economic power at the expense of the indigenous Muslim population. In Nov. 1954 the *Front de Libération Nationale* (FLN), representing the Muslim majority, declared open warfare against the French administration. There was extensive loss of life and property during the fighting which continued unabated until March 1962 when a ceasefire was agreed between the French government and the nationalists. Against the wishes of the French in Algeria, Gen. de Gaulle conceded Algerian independence on 3 July 1962.

The Political Bureau of the FLN took over the functions of government, a National Constituent Assembly was elected and the Republic was declared on 25 Sept. 1962. One of the founders of the FLN, Ahmed Ben Bella, became prime minister, and president the following year. On 15 June 1965 the government was overthrown by a junta of army officers, who established a Revolutionary Council under Col. Houari Boumedienne. After ten years of rule, Boumedienne proposed elections for a president and a National Assembly. A new constitution was accepted in a referendum in Nov. 1976 and Boumedienne was elected president unopposed. With all parties except the FLN banned from participating, a National Assembly was elected in Feb. 1977.

On the death of the president in Dec. 1978 the Revolutionary Council again took over the government. A state of emergency was declared in Feb. 1992 that remains in place. The Islamic Salvation Front (FIS) was banned in March 1992. The head of state, Mohamed Boudiaf, was assassinated on 29 July 1992 and a campaign of terrorism by fundamentalists has continued to the present day. It is estimated that over 100,000 lives have been lost, although Algeria has emerged from the worst of the war, with most of the guerrilla activity now restricted to the countryside. Unrest among Berbers, Algeria's main ethnic community, erupted into violence in May 2001, resulting in 60 deaths in the Berber region of Kabylie. In March 2002 President Bouteflika agreed to grant the Berber language official status alongside Arabic.

TERRITORY AND POPULATION

Algeria is bounded in the west by Morocco and Western Sahara, southwest by Mauritania and Mali, southeast by Niger, east by Libya and Tunisia, and north by the Mediterranean Sea. It has an area of 2,381,741 sq. km (919,595 sq. miles). Population (census 2008, provisional) 34,459,729; density, 14·5 per sq. km. In 2005, 63·3% of the population lived in urban areas.

The UN gives an estimated population for 2010 of 35·42m.

2·5m. Algerians live in France.

86% of the population speak Arabic, 14% Berber; French is widely spoken. A law of Dec. 1996 made Arabic the sole official language, but in March 2002 Tamazight, the Berber language, was given official status and also made a national language.

The 2008 census populations (provisional) of the 48 *wilayat* (provincial councils) were as follows:

Adrar	402,197	Laghouat	477,328
Aïn Defla	771,890	Mascara	780,959
Aïn Témouchent	368,713	Médéa	830,943
Algiers (El Djazaïr)	2,947,461	Mila	768,419
Annaba	640,050	Mostaganem	746,947
Batna	1,128,030	M'Sila	991,846
Béchar	274,866	Naâma	209,470
Béjaia	915,835	Oran (Ouahran)	1,443,052
Biskra	730,262	Ouargla	552,539
Blida	1,009,892	Oum El Bouaghi	644,364
Bordj Bou Arreridj	634,396	Relizane	733,060
Bouira	694,750	Saida	328,685
Boumerdès	795,019	Sétif	1,496,150
Chlef	1,013,718	Sidi-bel-Abbès	603,369
Constantine (Qacentina)	943,112	Skikda	904,195
Djelfa	1,223,223	Souk Ahras	440,299
El Bayadh	262,187	Tamanrasset	198,691
El Oued	673,934	Tébessa	657,227
El Tarf	411,783	Tiaret	842,060
Ghardaia	375,988	Tindouf	58,193[1]
Guelma	482,261	Tipaza	617,661
Illizi	54,490	Tissemsilt	296,366
Jijel	634,412	Tizi-Ouzou	1,119,646
Khenchela	384,268	Tlemcen	945,525

[1]Excluding Saharawi refugees in camps.

The capital is Algiers (1998 population, 1,519,570). Other major towns (with 1998 census populations): Oran, 655,852; Constantine, 462,187; Batna, 242,514; Annaba, 215,083; Sétif, 211,859; Sidi-bel-Abbès, 180,260; Biskra, 170,956; Djelfa, 154,265; Tébassa, 153,246; Blida, 153,083; Skikda, 152,335; Béjaia, 147,076; Tiaret, 145,332; Chlef, 133,874; al-Buni, 133,471; Béchar, 131,010.

SOCIAL STATISTICS

2007 estimates: births, 783,000; deaths, 149,000; marriages, 325,000. Rates (2007 estimates): births, 23·0 per 1,000; deaths, 4·4 per 1,000. Infant mortality in 2005 was 34 per 1,000 live births. Expectation of life (2007), 73·6 years for females and 70·8 years for males. Annual population growth rate, 2000–04, 1·6%. Fertility rate, 2004, 2·5 births per woman.

CLIMATE

Coastal areas have a warm temperate climate, with most rain in winter, which is mild, while summers are hot and dry. Inland, conditions become more arid beyond the Atlas Mountains. Algiers, Jan. 54°F (12·2°C), July 76°F (24·4°C). Annual rainfall 30" (762 mm). Biskra, Jan. 52°F (11·1°C), July 93°F (33·9°C). Annual rainfall 6" (158 mm). Oran, Jan. 54°F (12·2°C), July 76°F (24·4°C). Annual rainfall 15" (376 mm).

CONSTITUTION AND GOVERNMENT

A referendum was held on 28 Nov. 1996. The electorate was 16,434,527; turnout was 79·6%. The electorate approved by 85·8% of votes cast a new constitution which defines the fundamental components of the Algerian people as Islam, Arab identity and Berber identity. It was signed into law on 7 Dec. 1996. Political parties are permitted, but not if based on a separatist feature such as race, religion, sex, language or region. There is no limit to the number of presidential terms after parliament voted in favour of abolishing the two-term limit in Nov. 2008, allowing the current president, Abdelaziz Bouteflika, to run for a third term. The President appoints the prime minister and cabinet ministers. Parliament is bicameral: a 389-member *National Assembly* elected by direct universal suffrage using proportional representation, and a 144-member *Council of the Nation*, one-third nominated by the President and two-thirds indirectly elected by the 48 local authorities. The Council of the Nation debates bills passed by the National Assembly which become law if a three-quarters majority is in favour.

In a referendum on 16 Sept. 1999 voters were asked 'Do you agree with the president's approach to restore peace and civilian concord?' Turnout was 85·1% and 98·6% of the votes cast were in favour.

National Anthem

'Qassaman bin nazilat Il-mahiqat' ('We swear by the lightning that destroys'); words by M. Zakaria, tune by Mohamed Fawzi.

GOVERNMENT CHRONOLOGY

(FLN = National Liberation Front; PRS = Revolutionary Socialist Party; RND = National Rally for Democracy; n/p = non-partisan)

Heads of State since 1962.

President of the Provisional Executive

1962	FLN	Abderrahmane Farès

Chairman of the National Constituent Assembly

1962	FLN	Ferhat Abbas

President of the Republic

1962–65	FLN	Ahmed Ben Bella

Chairman of the Revolutionary Council

1965–76	military/FLN	Houari Boumedienne

Presidents of the Republic

1976–78	FLN	Houari Boumedienne
1979–92	FLN	Chadli Bendjedid

Chairman of the Constitutional Council

1992	FLN	Abdelmélik Benhabilès

High Council of State (HCE) (collective presidency)

1992	military	Gen. Khaled Nezzar
	FLN	Ali Hussain Kafi
	FLN	Ali Haroun
	n/p	El-Tidjani Haddam

Chairman of the HCE

1992	PRS	Mohamed Boudiaf

High Council of State (HCE) (collective presidency)

1992	n/p	Redha Malek
	military	Gen. Khaled Nezzar
	FLN	Ali Hussain Kafi
	FLN	Ali Haroun
	n/p	El-Tidjani Haddam

Chairman of the HCE

1992–94	FLN	Ali Hussain Kafi

Presidents of the Republic

1994–99	n/p, RND	Liamine Zéroual
1999–	n/p	Abdelaziz Bouteflika

Prime Ministers since 1962.

1962–63	FLN	Ahmed Ben Bella
1979–84	FLN	Mohammed Abdelghani
1984–88	FLN	Abdelhamid Brahimi
1988–89	FLN	Kasdi Merbah
1989–91	FLN	Mouloud Hamrouche
1991–92	FLN	Sid Ahmed Ghozali
1992–93	FLN	Belaid Abdessalam
1993–94	n/p	Redha Malek
1994–95	n/p	Mokdad Sifi
1995–98	n/p, RND	Ahmed Ouyahia
1998–99	n/p	Smail Hamdani
1999–2000	n/p	Ahmed Benbitour
2000–03	FLN	Ali Benflis
2003–06	RND	Ahmed Ouyahia
2006–08	FLN	Abdelaziz Belkhadem
2008–	RND	Ahmed Ouyahia

RECENT ELECTIONS

In presidential elections on 9 April 2009 Abdelaziz Bouteflika won a third term of office, gaining 90·2% of the votes cast; Louisa Hanoune (Parti du Travail/Workers' Party) received 4·5% of votes cast; Moussa Touati (Front National Algérien/Algerian National Front), 2·0%; Djahid Younsi, 1·5%; Ali Fawzi Rebaine, 0·9%; and Mohammed Said, 0·9%. Turnout was 74·6%.

Parliamentary elections were held on 17 May 2007. The ruling coalition won 249 out of 389 seats (consisting of the Front pour la Libération Nationale/National Liberation Front, 136 with 23·0% of votes cast; Rassemblement National Démocratique/National Rally for Democracy, 61 and 10·3%; and Mouvement de la Société pour la Paix/Movement of the Society for Peace, 52 and 9·6%); Parti du Travail/Workers' Party, 26 with 5·1%; and Rassemblement pour la Culture et la Démocratie/Rally for Culture and Democracy, 19 with 3·4%. The remaining seats went to minor parties and independents. Turnout was 35·6%.

CURRENT ADMINISTRATION

President and Minister of Defence: Abdelaziz Bouteflika; b. 1937 (ind.; sworn in 27 April 1999; re-elected 8 April 2004 and 9 April 2009). In March 2010 the government comprised:

Prime Minister: Ahmed Ouyahia; b. 1952 (Rassemblement National Démocratique; sworn in 23 June 2008, having previously been prime minister from 1995–98 and 2003–06).

Minister of State, Interior and Local Communities: Noureddine Yazid Zerhouni. *Minister of State representing the Presidential Staff:* Abdelaziz Belkhadem.

Minister of Agriculture and Rural Development: Rachid Benaïssa. *Commerce:* El-Hachemi Djaaboub. *Communication:* Abderrachid Boukerzaza. *Culture:* Khalida Toumi. *Energy and Mines:* Chakib Khelil. *Finance:* Karim Djoudi. *Fisheries and Marine Resources:* Smaïl Mimoune. *Foreign Affairs:* Mourad Medelci. *Health, Population and Hospital Reform:* Saïd Barkat. *Higher Education and Scientific Research:* Rachid Harraoubia. *Housing and Urban Planning:* Noureddine Moussa. *Industry and Promotion of Investments:* Abdelhamid Temmar. *Justice and Keeper of the Seals:* Tayeb Bélaïz. *Labour, Employment and Social Security:* Tayeb Louh. *Land Management, Environment and Tourism:* Chérif Rahmani. *Moudjahidine (War Veterans):* Mohamed Chérif Abbes. *National Education:* Boubekeur

Benbouzid. *National Solidarity, Families and National Community Abroad:* Djamel Ould Abbas. *Postal Services, and Information and Communication Technologies:* Hamid Bessalah. *Public Works:* Omar Ghoul. *Relations with Parliament:* Mahmoud Khedri. *Religious Affairs:* Bouabdellah Ghlamallah. *Small and Medium-Sized Businesses, and Handicrafts:* Mustapha Benbada. *Transport:* Amar Tou. *Vocational and Educational Training:* El-Hadi Khaldi. *Water Resources:* Abdelmalek Sellal. *Youth and Sports:* Hachemi Djiar.

President's Website (Arabic and French only):
http://www.elmouradia.dz

CURRENT LEADERS

Abdelaziz Bouteflika

Position
President

Introduction
Abdelaziz Bouteflika became president in April 1999 following disputed elections, vowing to improve Algeria's weak economy and end civil discord. Improvements in the economy and state reform have since been slow. However, the significant reduction in Islamist rebel violence following an amnesty in 1999 was a key factor in Bouteflika's re-election in 2004, making him the first Algerian leader to be returned to power in a democratic vote since the country's independence. His charter for peace and national reconciliation was approved in a national referendum in Sept. 2005. He won a further term in the election of April 2009, having secured earlier parliamentary approval in Nov. 2008 of constitutional changes allowing him to run for a third consecutive term of office.

Early Life
Bouteflika was born on 2 March 1937 in Morocco. In 1956 he joined the Armée de Libération Nationale—a wing of the Front de Libération Nationale (FLN; National Liberation Front). Stationed in southern Algeria in 1960, he was involved in secret talks with the French authorities, which eventually led to Algerian independence two years later.

Bouteflika joined the government of Ahmed Ben Bella as minister of youth, sport and tourism and was appointed foreign minister in 1963. He retained the position in the government of Houari Boumedienne. Having failed to secure military support to succeed Boumedienne, he was pushed out of the political mainstream. In 1981 he was charged with corruption and forced into exile for seven years. With the charges dropped, he re-entered Algeria in Jan. 1987.

In Oct. 1988 he protested against human rights violations by government troops against young demonstrators. He rejoined the FLN congress the following year and was elected to the central committee. In Dec. 1998 he announced his intention to contest the presidency. At the elections, he won almost three quarters of the vote after his six opponents all stood down from the race the day before polling, accusing him of vote rigging.

Career in Office
Having become president and commanding army support, Bouteflika declared that his primary aim was to end Algeria's many years of civil unrest. In July 1999 parliament passed the National Harmony Law, which offered an amnesty to all rebels who had not been directly responsible for loss of life. The Islamic Salvation Army declared a ceasefire, although a radical wing—the Armed Islamic Group—continued its campaign along with elements of other groups. A national referendum in Sept. 1999 approved the amnesty scheme, with nearly 99% in favour. Violence continued, but at a greatly reduced rate.

In order to alleviate Algeria's widespread poverty, Bouteflika has pursued the exploitation of the country's large oil and gas reserves. In foreign policy, he has striven to improve relations with Morocco, declaring a period of public mourning on the death of King Hassan in 1999 and leaving the resolution of the thorny question of Western Sahara to the UN (although he opposed proposals for autonomy for the disputed territory made by UN Special Envoy James Baker in 2001, arguing that the envisaged referendum would deprive the Sahrawis of their right to self-determination).

In 2000 he made the first state visit by an Algerian leader to Europe since the civil war. His visit to Paris, although historic, failed to win concessions, such as the resumption of Air France flights to Algiers. However, large debt repayment reductions and visa concessions were promised by the French government.

Violence in Algeria increased in 2001, including car bombs in major urban areas. Attempts to wipe out the Islamist rebel insurgency increased in 2003. Particular attention was paid to the Salafist Group for Preaching and Combat (GSPC), which had drawn international media attention following the capture of 32 tourists in the Algerian Sahara. Over 150 GSPC rebels were reported killed after raids in northeastern Algeria in Sept. 2003. The following month the GSPC voiced its support for al-Qaeda in jihad against the USA.

Bouteflika's relations with his prime ministers have been turbulent. Ahmed Benbitour, prime minister from Dec. 1999 to Aug. 2000, resigned over divergent attitudes on economic recovery. His successor, Ali Benflis, was a personal friend and the leader of the largest party, the FLN. However, Benflis' reformist agenda was too radical for Bouteflika, who feared violent insurrection. Since Benflis' resignation in May 2003, the two have been at political loggerheads. Bouteflika appointed Ahmed Ouyahia to succeed Benflis.

Benflis refused to support the president's bid for re-election in 2004, instead announcing his own candidacy, supported by the FLN, in Oct. 2003. However, Bouteflika's bid was supported by a coalition of the Rassemblement National Démocratique (RND; National Rally for Democracy), the Islamic Mouvement de la Société pour la Paix (MSP; Movement of the Society for Peace) and also renegade members of the FLN. The elections on 8 April 2004 gave Bouteflika a resounding victory with 85% of the vote in a 58% turnout—against just 6% for Benflis. International observers declared the elections free and fair, despite opposition claims of electoral fraud. His dramatic win was ascribed to the much improved security situation and a steadily growing economy, even though unemployment remained around 30%.

Bouteflika pledged to investigate the disappearance of around 7,000 Algerians, allegedly killed or imprisoned by the security forces during the 1990s. Improving relations with the Berber community was also a priority (election disturbances in 2004 having been mainly limited to the Berber Kabylie region), and he promised reform of Algeria's family law, which he described as unfair to women. In Sept. 2005 his charter for peace and national reconciliation to end 13 years of civil war, envisaging a limited amnesty and compensation for some victims of violence, was approved in a national referendum. A six-month amnesty from March–Aug. 2006 resulted in the release of some 2,200 Islamist militants (except those accused of the most serious crimes) from prison. However, incidents of terrorism have since increased again, particularly in Aug. 2008 when almost 60 people were killed in a series of bombings in towns to the east of Algiers.

In May 2006 Bouteflika appointed Abdelaziz Belkhadem as prime minister in place of Ahmed Ouyahia, but reinstated the latter in June 2008. In Nov. Algeria's parliament overwhelmingly approved constitutional amendments (by 500 votes to 12, with eight abstentions) that abolish presidential term limits, paving the way for Bouteflika to retain the presidency in the election held on 9 April 2009.

Ahmed Ouyahia

Position
Prime Minister

Introduction
Ahmed Ouyahia was appointed prime minister in June 2008, having previously served two terms from Dec. 1995 to Dec. 1998 and from May 2003 to May 2006. He is the head of the Rassemblement National Démocratique (RND; National Rally for Democracy). A hard-line technocrat, he is widely regarded as President Bouteflika's *sale boulot* ('dirty work') aide.

Early Life
Ouyahia was born at Bouadnane in the Berber Kabylie region of Eastern Algeria in 1952. Ouyahia studied in the diplomatic section of the École Nationale d'Administration (ENA) and subsequently gained a political sciences diploma from the University of Algiers. In 1975 he was recruited by the ministry of foreign affairs, where he held a variety of posts until his appointment as ambassador to Mali in Sept. 1992. A year later he joined Redha Malek's government as secretary of state for Maghrebi co-operation and affairs.

Career in Office
President Liamine Zéroual appointed Ouyahia prime minister on 31 Dec. 1995. His first term in office was dominated by austerity measures taken to reduce inflation and create a free-market economy. About 500,000 people lost their jobs but inflation was reduced to 5% and foreign currency reserves were replenished. Nonetheless, the measures were extremely unpopular.

Ouyahia resigned on 15 Dec. 1998 after widespread criticism of his economic programme and allegations of vote-rigging. In Jan. 1999 he replaced Tahar Benbaibeche as secretary general of the RND and supported Abdelaziz Bouteflika (seen as the army's choice) in the presidential elections of April 1999.

Ouyahia was appointed minister of justice in Dec. 1999 in the government of Prime Minister Ahmed Benbitour. President Bouteflika used Ouyahia as a roving ambassador and he was sent to mediate OAU-sponsored peace talks between Ethiopia and Eritrea during their long-running border war. As minister of justice, Ouyahia promoted a penal code amendment to curb the freedom of the press in April 2001.

The parliamentary elections of May 2002 were a triumph for Prime Minister Ali Benflis' FLN party, relegating the RND to opposition. However, having refused to support Bouteflika for the 2004 presidential elections, Benflis was sacked on 5 May 2003. The appointment of Ouyahia as his successor was particularly controversial because the constitution demands that the prime minister be chosen from the majority party in parliament (at that point the FLN).

Bouteflika was re-elected in April 2004 and Ouyahia was confirmed as prime minister in May, with a reform agenda focusing on justice, education and women's rights. Ouyahia resigned on 24 May 2006 after ongoing disputes between the RND and the FLN. In June 2008 he was returned to power by Bouteflika. On 12 Nov. 2008 Ouyahia oversaw parliamentary approval of a constitutional amendment allowing the incumbent president to run for a third term in 2009. Following the presidential election in April 2009, Ouyahia was reappointed prime minister with an almost unchanged cabinet.

DEFENCE

Conscription is for 18 months (six months basic training and 12 months civilian tasks).

Military expenditure totalled an estimated US$5,172m. in 2008 (up by 18% in real terms on 2007), representing 20% of Africa's total military spending. In 2006 defence spending amounted to US$94 per capita (equivalent to 2·7% of GDP).

Army

There are six military regions. The Army had a strength of 127,000 (approximately 80,000 conscripts) in 2007. The Directorate of National Security maintains National Security Forces of 16,000. The Republican Guard numbers 1,200 personnel and the Gendarmerie 20,000. There were in addition legitimate defence groups (self-defence militia and communal guards) numbering around 150,000.

Navy

Naval personnel in 2007 totalled about 6,000. The Navy's 44 vessels included two submarines and three frigates. There are naval bases at Algiers, Annaba, Jijel and Mers el Kebir.

Air Force

The Air Force in 2007 had some 14,000 personnel; equipment included 141 combat capable aircraft and 33 attack helicopters.

INTERNATIONAL RELATIONS

Algeria is a member of the UN, World Bank, IMF and several other UN specialized agencies, IOM, Islamic Development Bank, OIC, African Development Bank, African Union, League of Arab States and OPEC.

ECONOMY

In 2008 agriculture accounted for 9% of GDP, industry 69% and services 23%.

Overview

The economy is heavily dependent on the sale of oil and gas. Following the collapse of oil prices in 1986 the government negotiated heavy loans that became unmanageable. In 1994 an IMF-sponsored programme for economic reconstruction was implemented. Austerity measures to reduce inflation and create a free-market economy lifted the country's debt burden but also generated large-scale unemployment. Privatization policy got off the ground in 1994, as demanded by the IMF, but failed to make significant strides until 2003. The government privatized 270 enterprises in the period 2003–05.

The economy has achieved growth in every year since 1995, averaging 4·5% annually from 2000–05. Rising oil prices enabled more robust growth in 2003, 2004 and 2005. The hydrocarbon sector has continued to lead growth but in more recent years other sectors, particularly services and construction, have made a stronger contribution. Unemployment is considerably lower than its peak of 27% at the beginning of the decade, falling to 12·3% in 2006 as a result of government initiatives implemented since 2001. The economy is well positioned to reduce unemployment and achieve high growth while maintaining macroeconomic stability. The IMF emphasizes the need for sound management of hydrocarbon resources together with structural reforms to improve the business climate and increase productivity.

Currency

The unit of currency is the *Algerian dinar* (DZD) of 100 *centimes*. Foreign exchange reserves were US$146,130m. in Sept. 2009, with gold reserves 5·58m. troy oz. Total money supply was 4,071·5bn. dinars in June 2009. Inflation rates (based on IMF statistics):

1999	*2000*	*2001*	*2002*	*2003*	*2004*	*2005*	*2006*	*2007*	*2008*
2·6%	0·3%	4·2%	1·4%	2·6%	3·6%	1·6%	2·5%	3·6%	4·5%

The dinar was devalued by 40% in April 1994.

Budget

The fiscal year starts on 1 Jan. In 2005 budgetary central government revenue totalled 3,112,700m. dinars and expenditure 1,292,900m. dinars.

VAT is 17%.

Performance
Real GDP growth rates (based on IMF statistics):

1999	2000	2001	2002	2003	2004	2005	2006	2007	2008
3·2%	2·2%	2·7%	4·7%	6·9%	5·2%	5·1%	2·0%	3·0%	3·0%

Total GDP was US$173·9bn. in 2008.

Banking and Finance
The central bank and bank of issue is the Banque d'Algérie. The *Governor* is Mohammed Laksaci. In 2002 it had total reserves of US$23·5bn. Private banking recommenced in Sept. 1995. In 2002 there were five state-owned commercial banks, four development banks, nine private banks and two foreign banks.

ENERGY AND NATURAL RESOURCES

Environment
Algeria's carbon dioxide emissions from the consumption and flaring of fossil fuels in 2008 were the equivalent of 3·1 tonnes per capita.

Electricity
Installed capacity was 7·2m. kW in 2004 (4·0% is hydro-electric). Production in 2004 was 31·25bn. kWh, with consumption per capita 889 kWh.

Oil and Gas
A law of Nov. 1991 permits foreign companies to acquire up to 49% of known oil and gas reserves. Oil and gas production accounted for 48·0% of GDP in 2007. Oil production in 2008 was 85·6m. tonnes; oil reserves (2008) totalled 12·2bn. bbls. Production of natural gas in 2008 was 86·5bn. cu. metres (the sixth highest in the world); proven reserves in 2008 were 4,500bn. cu. metres.

Minerals
Output in 2004 unless otherwise indicated (in 1,000 tonnes): iron ore, 1,554; gypsum, 1,058; phosphate rock, 1,017; salt, 183; lead (2002), 1·1. There are also deposits of mercury, silver, gold, copper, antimony, kaolin, marble, onyx, salt and coal.

Agriculture
Much of the land is unsuitable for agriculture. The northern mountains provide grazing. There were 7·47m. ha. of arable land in 2007 and 0·92m. ha. of permanent crops. 0·91m. ha. were irrigated in 2007. In 1987 the government sold back to the private sector land which had been nationalized on the declaration of independence in 1962; a further 0·5m. ha., expropriated in 1973, were returned to some 30,000 small landowners in 1990. In 2007 the agricultural population was an estimated 7·41m. There were 135 tractors and 11 harvester-threshers per 10,000 ha. in 2006.

The chief crops in 2003 were (in 1,000 tonnes): wheat, 2,970; potatoes, 1,300; barley, 1,220; tomatoes, 820; melons and watermelons, 465; onions, 450; dates, 420; oranges, 360; olives, 300; grapes, 230; chillies and green peppers, 165; carrots, 158.

Livestock, 2003: sheep, 17·3m.; goats, 3·2m.; cattle, 1·5m.; camels, 245,000; asses, 170,000; horses, 44,000; mules, 43,000; chickens, 115m. Livestock products, 2003 (in 1,000 tonnes): poultry meat, 244; lamb and mutton, 165; beef and veal, 121; eggs, 110; cow's milk, 1,160; sheep's milk, 200; goat's milk, 155.

Forestry
Forests covered 2·28m. ha. in 2005, or 1·0% of the total land area. The greater part of the state forests are brushwood, but there are large areas with cork-oak trees, Aleppo pine, evergreen oak and cedar. The dwarf-palm is grown on the plains, alfalfa on the tableland. Timber is cut for firewood and industrial purposes, and bark for tanning. Timber production in 2007 was 7·97m. cu. metres.

Fisheries
There are extensive fisheries for sardines, anchovies, sprats, tuna and shellfish. The total catch in 2005 amounted to 126,259 tonnes, exclusively from marine waters.

INDUSTRY
Output (in 1,000 tonnes): cement (2007), 15,886; distillate fuel oil (2004), 6,340; residual fuel oil (2004), 5,560; petrol (2004), 1,925; crude steel (2007), 1,278; pig iron (2007), 1,193; jet fuel (2004), 986; rolled steel (1997), 439; phosphate fertilizers (2001), 254; ammonitrates (1992), 193; concrete bars (1992), 134; steel tubes (2001), 62; bricks (2007), 122,000 cu. metres. Production in units: TV sets (2001), 245,000; lorries (2001), 2,811 (assembled); tractors (2001), 2,105.

Labour
In 2005 there were 6,889,000 employed persons. The main areas of activity were: community, social and personal services, 1,826,000; agriculture, forestry and fishing, 1,440,000; transport, storage and communications, 1,268,000; construction, 902,000; manufacturing, 772,000. In 2006 unemployment was 17·3%.

INTERNATIONAL TRADE
Foreign debt was US$16,879m. in 2005. Foreign investors are permitted to hold 100% of the equity of companies, and to repatriate all profits.

Imports and Exports
In 2006 imports were valued at US$21,456m. and exports at US$54,613m. Main import suppliers in 2006: France, 20·3%; Italy, 8·8%; China, 8·0%; Germany, 6·9%; USA, 6·6%; Spain, 4·8%. Main export markets, 2006: USA, 27·2%; Italy, 17·1%; Spain, 11·0%; France, 8·4%; Canada, 6·6%; Netherlands, 5·2%. Main imports in 2006: machinery and transport equipment, 37·5%; manufactured goods, 22·6%; food and live animals, 16·9%. Main exports, 2006: petroleum and petroleum products, 63·0%; natural and manufactured gas, 35·1%.

COMMUNICATIONS

Roads
There were, in 2004, 108,302 km of roads including 645 km of motorways. There were 2,042,800 passenger cars (58 cars per 1,000 inhabitants in 2005) and 1,166,200 lorries and vans in use in 2006.

Rail
In 2005 there were 2,889 km of 1,435 mm route (283 km electrified) and 1,085 km of 1,055 mm gauge. The railways carried 8·3m. tonnes of freight and 27·3m. passengers in 2004.

A metro system is scheduled to open in Algiers during 2010, 27 years after work on the project first began.

Civil Aviation
The main airport is Algiers International, which opened a new terminal in July 2006 to allow for more international air traffic; some international services also use Annaba, Constantine and Oran. The national carrier is the state-owned Air Algérie which in 2003 operated direct flights to Frankfurt, Geneva and London. There were direct international flights in 2003 with other airlines to Barcelona, Cairo, Casablanca, Damascus, İstanbul, Lille, Lyon, Malaga, Marseille, Milan, Montpellier, Munich, Nantes, Nice, Palma de Mallorca, Paris, Rome, Strasbourg, Toulouse, Tripoli and Tunis. In 2001 Houari Boumedienne International Airport handled 3,397,867 passengers (1,871,052 on domestic flights) and 16,191 tonnes of freight. In 2005 scheduled airline traffic of Algerian-based carriers flew 30·4m. km, carrying 2,760,700 passengers.

Shipping
In 2001 vessels totalling 118,994,000 GRT entered ports and vessels totalling 119,074,000 GRT cleared. The state shipping

line, Compagnie Nationale Algérienne de Navigation, owned 47 vessels in 2001. The merchant shipping fleet totalled 936,000 GRT in 2002, including oil tankers 19,000 GRT.

Telecommunications

In 2008 there were 3,314,000 main (fixed) telephone lines. In the same year mobile phone subscribers numbered 31,871,000 (927·2 per 1,000 persons). There were 350,000 PCs in use in 2005 and 4·1m. internet users in 2008.

Government plans to privatize Algérie Télécom, the major state-owned telecommunications company, were rejected in Feb. 2009.

Postal Services

There were 3,272 post offices in 2002.

SOCIAL INSTITUTIONS

Justice

The judiciary is constitutionally independent. Judges are appointed by the Supreme Council of Magistrature chaired by the President of the Republic. Criminal justice is organized as in France. The Supreme Court is at the same time Council of State and High Court of Appeal. The death penalty is in force for terrorism.

The population in penal institutions in Dec. 2005 was 42,000 (127 per 100,000 of national population).

Education

Adult literacy in 2003 was 69·8% (79·5% among males and 60·1% among females). In 2007 there were 171,000 children in pre-primary education. There were 4,078,954 pupils with 170,207 teaching staff in primary schools in 2007, and 3,677,107 pupils with 176,375 teaching staff in secondary schools in 2004.

The leading institute of higher education is the University of Algiers, founded in 1909 although Algerians were not admitted until 1946. In 2007 there were 901,562 students in tertiary education and 31,683 academic staff.

In 1996 expenditure on education came to 5·1% of GNP and represented 16·4% of total government expenditure.

Health

In 2002 there were 28,642 physicians, 8,662 dentists and 5,198 pharmacists. There were 185 government hospitals, 1,252 health centres, 497 polyclinics and 3,964 care centres in 2000.

Welfare

Welfare payments to 7·4m. beneficiaries on low incomes were introduced in March 1992.

RELIGION

The 1996 constitution made Islam the state religion, established a consultative *High Islamic Council*, and forbids practices 'contrary to Islamic morality'. Over 99% of the population are Sunni Muslims. There are also around 180,000 Ibadiyah Muslims and 90,000 others. The Armed Islamic Group (GIA) vowed in 1994 to kill 'Jews, Christians and polytheists' in Algeria. Hundreds of foreign nationals, including priests and nuns, have since been killed. Signalling an increasing tolerance amongst the Muslim community, the Missionaries of Africa's house at Ghardaia Oasis was reopened in 2000.

CULTURE

World Heritage Sites

There are seven UNESCO sites in Algeria: Al Qal'a of Beni Hammad (inscribed in 1980), the 11th century ruined capital of the Hammadid emirs; Tassili n'Ajjer (1982), a group of over 15,000 prehistoric cave drawings; the M'zab Valley (1982), a tenth century community settlement of the Ibadites; Djémila (1982), or Cuicul, a mountainous Roman town; Tipasa (1982), an ancient Carthaginian port; Timgad (1982), a military colony founded by the Roman emperor Trajan in AD 100; the Kasbah of Algiers (1992), the medina of Algiers.

Broadcasting

The state-controlled Radiodiffusion Algérienne and Entreprise Nationale de Télévision broadcast home services in Arabic, Kabyle (Berber) and French. Radio Algérie Internationale is an external service. Satellite television from Europe and particularly France has become popular. There were 6·4m. TV sets in 2006 (colour by PAL).

Press

Algeria had 48 daily newspapers in 2006, with a combined circulation of 960,000.

Tourism

In 2005 there were 1,443,090 non-resident visitors; receipts totalled US$184m.

DIPLOMATIC REPRESENTATIVES

Of Algeria in the United Kingdom (54 Holland Park, London, W11 3RS)
Ambassador: Mohammed Salah Dembri.

Of the United Kingdom in Algeria (3 Chemin Capitaine Hocine Slimane [ex Chemin des Glycines], Hydra, Algiers)
Ambassador: Andrew Henderson.

Of Algeria in the USA (2118 Kalorama Rd, NW, Washington, D.C., 20008)
Ambassador: Abdallah Baali.

Of the USA in Algeria (5 Chemin Cheich Bachir Ibrahimi, Algiers)
Ambassador: David D. Pearce.

Of Algeria to the United Nations
Ambassador: Mourad Benmehidi.

Of Algeria to the European Union
Ambassador: Halim Benattallah.

FURTHER READING

Ageron, C.-R., *Modern Algeria: a History from 1830 to the Present*. 1991
Eveno, P., *L'Algérie*. 1994
Heggoy, A. A. and Crout, R. R., *Historical Dictionary of Algeria*. 1995
Roberts, Hugh, *The Battlefield: Algeria 1998–2002, Studies in a Broken Polity*. 2003
Ruedy, J., *Modern Algeria: the Origins and Development of a Nation*. 1992
Stone, M., *The Agony of Algeria*. 1997
Stora, B., *Histoire de l'Algérie depuis l'Indépendance*. 1994
Volpi, Frédéric, *Islam and Democracy: The Failure of Dialogue in Algeria, 1998–2001*. 2003
Willis, M., *The Islamist Challenge in Algeria: A Political History*. 1997

National Statistical Office: Office National des Statistiques, 8–10 rue des Moussebilines, Algiers.
Website (French only): http://www.ons.dz

ANDORRA

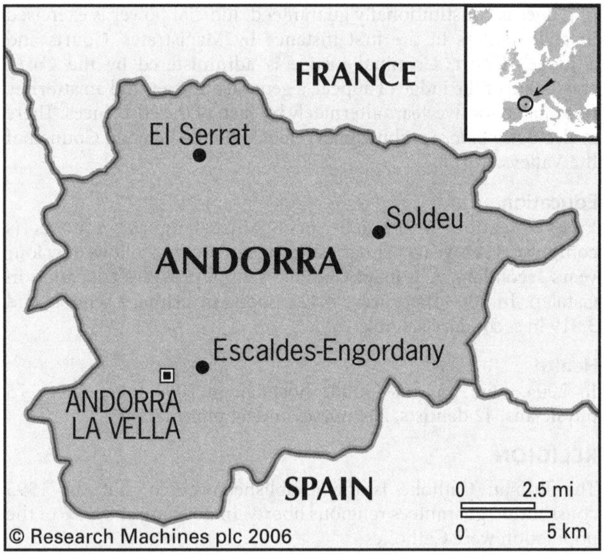

Principat d'Andorra
(Principality of Andorra)

Capital: Andorra la Vella
Population, 2007: 83,000
GDP per capita, 2007: (PPP$) 41,235
HDI/world rank: 0·934/28

KEY HISTORICAL EVENTS

The Andosini, a tribe subdued by Hannibal in 218 BC, are the first recorded inhabitants of the Pyreneean state of Andorra. In the 9th century the Holy Roman Emperor, Charles II, reputedly made the bishop of Seo de Urgel the overlord of Andorra. The *Paréage* of 1278 placed Andorra under the joint suzerainty of the bishop of Seo de Urgel and the Comte de Foix. The rights vested in the house of Foix passed by marriage to that of Bearn and, on the accession of Henri IV, to the French crown. In the 19th century the *Consell General* (parliament) was strengthened, but the constitution remained traditional and unwritten until 8 Sept. 1993, when political parties and labour unions were legalized and Andorra joined the UN.

TERRITORY AND POPULATION

The co-principality of Andorra is situated in the eastern Pyrenees on the French–Spanish border. The country is mountainous and has an average altitude of 1,996 metres. Area, 464 sq. km. In lieu of a census, a register of population is kept. The estimated population in 2007 was 83,137; density, 179 per sq. km.

In 2003, 93% of the population lived in urban areas.

The chief towns are Andorra la Vella, the capital (estimated population, 21,556 in 2007) and Escaldes-Engordany (16,475). In 2004, 35·7% of the residential population were Andorran, 37·4% Spanish, 13·0% Portuguese and 6·6% French. Catalan is the official language, but Spanish and French are widely spoken.

SOCIAL STATISTICS

Births in 2006 numbered 843 (rate of 10·4 per 1,000 inhabitants) and deaths 260 (3·2 per 1,000 inhabitants). Life expectancy (2006): males, 78 years; females, 85 years. Annual population growth rate, 2000–05, 3·5%. Fertility rate, 2004, 1·3 births per woman.

CLIMATE

Escaldes-Engordany, Jan. 35·8°F (2·1°C), July 65·8°F (18·8°C). Annual rainfall 34·9" (886 mm).

CONSTITUTION AND GOVERNMENT

The joint heads of state are the co-princes—the President of the French Republic and the Bishop of Urgel.

A new democratic constitution was approved by 74·2% of votes cast at a referendum on 14 March 1993. The electorate was 9,123; turnout was 75·7%. The new Constitution, which came into force on 4 May 1993, makes the co-princes a single constitutional monarch and provides for a parliament, the unicameral *General Council of the Valleys*, with 28 members, two from each of the seven parishes and 14 elected by proportional representation from the single national constituency, for four years. In 1982 an *Executive Council* was appointed and legislative and executive powers were separated. The General Council elects the President of the Executive Council, who is the head of the government.

There is a *Constitutional Court* of four members who hold office for eight-year terms, renewable once.

National Anthem

'El Gran Carlemany, mon pare' ('Great Charlemagne, my father'); words by D. J. Benlloch i Vivò, tune by Enric Marfany Bons.

RECENT ELECTIONS

Elections to the General Council were held on 26 April 2009. The Social Democratic Party (PS) won 14 seats (45·0% of the vote), the Reformist Coalition (CR, including the ruling Liberal Party of Andorra) 11 (32·3%) and Andorra for Change (ApC) 3 (18·9%). Turnout was 75·3%.

CURRENT ADMINISTRATION

In March 2010 the government comprised:

President, Executive Council: Jaume Bartumeu Cassany; b. 1954 (Social Democratic Party; sworn in 5 June 2009).

Minister for Economy and Finance: Pere López Agràs. *Education, Culture and Youth:* Susanna Vela Palomares. *Foreign Affairs and Institutional Relations:* Xavier Espot Miró. *Health, Wellbeing and Employment:* Cristina Rodríguez Galan. *Interior and Justice:* Víctor Naudi Zamora. *Land Management, Environment and Agriculture:* Vicenç Alay Ferrer.

Government Website (Catalan only): http://www.govern.ad

CURRENT LEADERS

Jaume Bartumeu Cassany

Position
President, Executive Council

Introduction
Jaume Bartumeu Cassany took office on 5 June 2009 after his Partit Socialdemòcrata won the April 2009 parliamentary elections with 14 of the 28 General Council seats.

Early Life
Jaume Bartumeu was born in Andorra la Vella on 10 Nov. 1954. He graduated in law from the Universitat de Barcelona in Spain having also attended the Université de Toulouse in France.

A practising lawyer from 1982, Bartumeu was appointed minister of finance, trade and industry in 1990, serving until 1992. In that year he was elected to parliament, retaining his seat in all subsequent elections. From 1995–2008 he was a member of the Andorran delegation to the parliamentary assembly of the Council of Europe. In 2000 he helped establish Partit Socialdemòcrata, serving first as party secretary and then as leader of the opposition from 2005–09. He was confirmed as head of the government with 14 of 28 available votes on 3 June 2009.

Career in Office
Bartumeu is expected to pursue a traditional social democratic centre-left agenda.

INTERNATIONAL RELATIONS

The 1993 constitution empowers Andorra to conduct its own foreign affairs, with consultation on matters affecting France or Spain.

Andorra is a member of the UN, UNESCO, WIPO, Council of Europe, OSCE and International Organization of the Francophonie.

ECONOMY

Currency

Since 1 Jan. 2002 Andorra has been using the euro (EUR). Inflation was 2·8% in 2001, rising to 3·4% in 2002.

Budget

In 2005 central government revenue was €516,000,000 and expenditure €484,900,000.

Performance

Real GDP growth was 3·8% in 2000.

Banking and Finance

The banking sector, with its tax-haven status, contributes substantially to the economy. Leading banks include: Andbanc-Grup Agricol Reig; Banc Internacional d'Andorra SA; Banca Mora SA; Banca Privada d'Andorra SA; CaixaBank SA; and Crèdit Andorrà.

ENERGY AND NATURAL RESOURCES

Electricity

Installed capacity was 26,500 kW in 2000. Production in 1998 was 116m. kWh. 60% of Andorra's electricity comes from Spain.

Agriculture

In 2001 there were some 1,000 ha. of arable land (2% of total) and 1,000 ha. of permanent crops. Tobacco and potatoes are principal crops. The principal livestock activity is sheep raising.

INDUSTRY

Labour

Only 1% of the workforce is employed in agriculture, the rest in tourism, commerce, services and light industry. Manufacturing consists mainly of cigarettes, cigars and furniture.

INTERNATIONAL TRADE

Andorra is a member of the EU Customs Union for industrial goods, but is a third country for agricultural produce. There is a free economic zone.

Imports and Exports

2004 imports (c.i.f.), US$1,762m.; exports (f.o.b.), US$123m. Leading import suppliers (2003): Spain, 54·1%; France, 25·7%. Main export markets (2003): Spain, 55·7%; France, 19·2%.

COMMUNICATIONS

Roads

In 1994 there were 269 km of roads (198 km paved). Motor vehicles (2000) totalled 60,287, including 46,421 cars and 6,029 trucks and vans.

Civil Aviation

There is an airport at Seo de Urgel.

Telecommunications

In 2004 there were 97,600 telephone subscribers, or 1,457·3 per 1,000 inhabitants. There were 62,600 mobile phone subscribers in 2004 and 21,900 internet users in 2005.

SOCIAL INSTITUTIONS

Justice

Justice is administered by the High Council of Justice, comprising five members appointed for single six-year terms. The independence of judges is constitutionally guaranteed. Judicial power is exercised in civil matters in the first instance by Magistrates' Courts and a Judge's Court. Criminal justice is administered by the *Corts*, consisting of the judge of appeal, a general attorney and an attorney nominated for five years alternately by each of the co-princes. There is also a *raonador* (ombudsman) elected by the General Council of the Valleys.

Education

Free education in French- or Spanish-language schools is compulsory: six years primary starting at six years, followed by four years secondary. A Roman Catholic school provides education in Catalan. In 2007 there were 4,427 pupils in primary schools and 3,819 in secondary schools.

Health

In 2004 there was one public hospital; in 2001 there were 175 physicians, 42 dentists, 204 nurses and 64 pharmacists.

RELIGION

The Roman Catholic is the established church, but the 1993 constitution guarantees religious liberty. In 2001 around 88% of the population were Catholics.

CULTURE

World Heritage Sites

There is one UNESCO site in Andorra: Madriu-Perafita-Claror Valley (entered on the list in 2004 and 2006).

Broadcasting

Ràdio i Televisió d'Andorra is the public broadcaster. There are also private radio stations. There were 16,000 TV sets in 2001 (colour by PAL).

Press

In 2006 there were three daily newspapers with a combined circulation of about 32,000.

Tourism

Tourism is the main industry, averaging 11m. visitors a year and accounting for 80% of GDP.

DIPLOMATIC REPRESENTATIVES

Of Andorra in the United Kingdom (63 Westover Rd, London, SW18 2RF)
Ambassador: Vacant.
Chargé d'Affaires a.i.: Eva Descarrega Garcia.

Of the United Kingdom in Andorra
Ambassador: Giles Paxman, LVO (resides in Madrid).

Of Andorra in the USA (2 United Nations Plaza, 25th Floor, N.Y. 10017)
Ambassador: Narcís Casal de Fonsdeviela.

Of USA in Andorra
Ambassador: Alan D. Solomont (resides in Madrid).

Of Andorra to the United Nations
Ambassador: Narcís Casal de Fonsdeviela.

Of Andorra to the European Union
Ambassador: Imma Tor Faus.

FURTHER READING

A Strategic Assessment of Andorra. 2000

National Statistical Office: Servie d'Estudis, Ministeri de Finances, c/Doctor Vilanova, núm. 13, Edifici Davi, Esc. c, 5è, Andorra la Vella.
Website: http://www.estadistica.ad

ANGOLA

República de Angola
(Republic of Angola)

Capital: Luanda
Population estimate, 2010: 18·99m.
GDP per capita, 2007: (PPP$) 5,385
HDI/world rank: 0·564/143

KEY HISTORICAL EVENTS

The Portuguese were dominant from the late 19th century. Angola remained a Portuguese colony until 11 June 1951, when it became an Overseas Province of Portugal.

A guerrilla war broke out in 1961 when the People's Movement for the Liberation of Angola launched an offensive to end colonial rule. After the coup d'état in Portugal in April 1974, negotiations with Portugal, the MPLA (Popular Movement for the Liberation of Angola), the FNLA (National Front for the Liberation of Angola) and UNITA (National Union for the Total Liberation of Angola) led to independence on 11 Nov. 1975. The FNLA tried to seize power by force but was driven out of the capital. As independence approached, invasion from the north was combined with a South African invasion in support of UNITA. The MPLA declared independence and subsequently, with the help of Cuban troops, defeated the FNLA in the north and drove the invading South African army out of the country. South African invasions and the occupation of large areas of Angola continued until the signing of the New York Agreement in Dec. 1988, when South Africa agreed to withdraw its forces from Angola and Namibia (and grant independence to Namibia), while Angola and Cuba agreed to the phased withdrawal of Cuban troops.

After abortive attempts to end the conflict with UNITA, a peace agreement was signed on 31 May 1991. A national army was to be formed and multi-party elections held. In Sept. 1992 the MPLA won the elections and José Eduardo dos Santos was re-elected president, defeating UNITA leader Jonas Savimbi. But the latter rejected the election results, withdrew his generals from the unified army and went back to war, seizing an estimated 70% of the country.

On 20 Nov. 1994 a peace agreement was signed in Lusaka, allowing for UNITA to share in government.

In Jan. 1998 Jonas Savimbi, UNITA's leader, met with President dos Santos but talks soon foundered and serious fighting resumed in the north, raising fears of a major new offensive by the Angolan Armed Forces against the UNITA rebels. Meanwhile, Angolan troops fought in the Democratic Republic of the Congo alongside the forces of President Kabila in his efforts to quash a Rwandan-backed rebellion in the east of his country. They remained after the assassination of Kabila in Jan. 2001 but renewed hopes of peace resulted in their withdrawal in Jan. 2002. In Feb. 2002 Jonas Savimbi was killed in fighting with government troops. On 4 April 2002 commanders of the Angolan army and UNITA signed a ceasefire agreement. More than half a million Angolans died in the civil unrest that plagued the country for over a quarter of a century.

TERRITORY AND POPULATION

Angola is bounded in the north by the Republic of the Congo, north and northeast by the Democratic Republic of the Congo, east by Zambia, south by Namibia and west by the Atlantic Ocean. The area is 1,246,600 sq. km (481,324 sq. miles) including the province of Cabinda, an exclave of territory separated by 30 sq. km of the Democratic Republic of the Congo's territory. The population at census, 1970, was 5,646,166, of whom 14% were urban. In 2005, 53·3% of the population were living in urban areas. Population figures are rough estimates because the civil war led to huge movements of population. More than 300,000 Angolan refugees have returned to the country since the civil war ended in 2002.

There were 0·3m. Angolan refugees in the Democratic Republic of the Congo, Zambia and the Republic of the Congo in 1995.

The UN gives an estimated population for 2010 of 18·99m.; density, 15 per sq. km.

Area, population and chief towns of the provinces:

Province	*Area (in sq. km)*	*Population estimate, 1995 (in 1,000)*	*Chief town*
Bengo	31,371	184	Caxito
Benguela	31,788	702	Benguela
Bié	70,314	1,246	Kuito
Cabinda	7,270	185	Cabinda
Cunene	88,342	245	Ondjiva
Huambo	34,274	1,687	Huambo
Huíla	75,002	948	Lubango
Kuando-Kubango	199,049	137	Menongue
Kwanza Norte	24,110	412	Ndalatando
Kwanza Sul	55,660	688	Sumbe
Luanda	2,418	2,002	Luanda
Lunda Norte	102,783	311	Lucapa
Lunda Sul	56,985	160	Saurimo
Malanje	87,246	975	Malanje
Moxico	223,023	349	Luena
Namibe	58,137	135	Namibe
Uíge	58,698	948	Uíge
Zaire	40,130	247	Mbanza Congo

The most important towns are Luanda, the capital (2000 population, 2·34m.), Huambo, Lobito, Benguela, Kuito, Lubango, Malanje and Namibe.

The main ethnic groups are Umbundo (Ovimbundo), Kimbundo, Bakongo, Chokwe, Ganguela, Luvale and Kwanyama.

Portuguese is the official language. Bantu and other African languages are also spoken.

SOCIAL STATISTICS

Life expectancy at birth, 2007, 44·6 years for males and 48·5 years for females. 2001 births (estimates), 656,000; deaths, 246,000. Estimated birth rate in 2001 was 51·2 per 1,000 population; estimated death rate, 19·2. Annual population growth rate, 1992–2002, 2·9%. Fertility rate, 2004, 6·7 births per woman; infant mortality, 2005, 154 per 1,000 live births.

CLIMATE

The climate is tropical, with low rainfall in the west but increasing inland. Temperatures are constant over the year and most rain falls in March and April. Luanda, Jan. 78°F (25·6°C), July 69°F (20·6°C). Annual rainfall 13" (323 mm). Lobito, Jan. 77°F (25°C), July 68°F (20°C). Annual rainfall 14" (353 mm).

CONSTITUTION AND GOVERNMENT

Under the Constitution adopted at independence, the sole legal party was the MPLA. In Dec. 1990, however, the MPLA announced that the Constitution would be revised to permit opposition parties. The supreme organ of state is the 220-member *National Assembly*. For the 2008 elections 30% of seats were guaranteed for women. There is an executive *President*, elected for renewable terms of five years, who appoints a *Council of Ministers*.

In Dec. 2002 Angola's ruling party and the UNITA party of former rebels agreed on a new constitution. The president would keep key powers, including the power to name and to remove the prime minister. The president will also appoint provincial governors, rather than letting voters elect them, but the governor must be from the party that received a majority of votes in that province. A draft constitution was submitted to the constitutional commission of the Angolan parliament for consideration in Jan. 2004.

A new constitution was adopted on 21 Jan. 2010 and came into effect on 5 Feb. although the opposition party UNITA boycotted the vote. Direct presidential elections were abolished. Instead the party with the majority in parliament will choose the president. A two-term limit was introduced although it is not scheduled to take effect until after the 2012 parliamentary elections. The president was also made responsible for judicial appointments while the office of prime minister was replaced by that of a vice-president to be appointed by the president.

National Anthem

'O Pátria, nunca mais esqueceremos' ('Oh Fatherland, never shall we forget'); words by M. R. Alves Monteiro, tune by R. A. Dias Mingas.

GOVERNMENT CHRONOLOGY

Presidents since 1975. (MPLA = Popular Movement for the Liberation of Angola)

1975–79	MPLA	António Agostinho Neto
1979–	MPLA	José Eduardo dos Santos

RECENT ELECTIONS

At the presidential elections of 29–30 Sept. 1992 the electorate was 4,862,748. Turnout was about 90%. José Eduardo dos Santos (Popular Movement for the Liberation of Angola/MPLA) was re-elected as president with 49·5% of votes cast against 40·5% for his single opponent, Jonas Savimbi (National Union for the Total Independence of Angola/UNITA). The latter refused to accept the result.

In parliamentary elections held on 5–6 Sept. 2008, the first since 1992, the electorate was 7,213,281. Turnout was 87·4%. The MPLA gained 191 seats in the National Assembly with 81·6% of votes cast, UNITA 16 with 10·4%, Social Renewal Party 8 with 3·2%, National Front for the Liberation of Angola 3 with 1·1% and New Democracy Electoral Union 2 with 1·2%.

CURRENT ADMINISTRATION

President: José Eduardo dos Santos; b. 1943 (MPLA; since 10 Sept. 1979; re-elected 9 Dec. 1985 and 29–30 Sept. 1992).

Prime Minister: António Paulo Kassoma; b. 1951 (MPLA; since 30 Sept. 2008).

In March 2010 the government comprised:

Vice-president: Fernando da Piedade Dias dos Santos.

Minister for Agriculture, Rural Development and Fisheries: Afonso Pedro Canga. *Commerce and Tourism:* Maria Idalina de Oliveira Valente. *Culture:* Rosa Maria Martins da Cruz e Silva. *Economy:* Manuel Nunes Júnior. *Education:* M'pinda Simão. *Energy and Water:* Emanuela Afonso Viera Lopes. *Environment:* Maria de Fátima Monteiro Jardim. *Family and Women's Affairs:* Genoveva da Conceição Lino. *Finance:* Carlos Alberto Lopes. *Foreign Affairs:* Assunção Afonso dos Anjos. *Geology, Mines and Industry:* Joaquim Duarte da Costa David. *Health:* José Vieira Dias Van-Dúnem. *Interior:* Roberto Leal Monteiro. *Justice:* Guilhermina Contreiras da Costa Prata. *National Defence:* Gen. Candido Pereira dos Santos Van-Dúnem. *Oil:* José Maria Botelho de Vasconcelos. *Parliamentary Affairs:* Norberto Fernando dos Santos. *Planning:* Ana Dias Lourenço. *Public Administration, Employment and Social Security:* António Domingos Pitra da Costa Neto. *Science and Technology:* Maria Cândida Teixeira. *Social Communication:* Carolina Cerqueira. *Social Welfare:* João Baptista Kussumua. *Telecommunications and Information Technology:* José Carvalho da Rocha. *Territorial Administration:* Bornito de Sousa Baltazar Diogo. *Transport:* Augusto da Silva Tomás. *Urban Development and Housing:* José dos Santos da Silva Ferreira. *War Veterans:* Kundi Paihama. *Youth and Sports:* Gonçalves Manuel Muandumba.

Government Website (Portuguese only):
http://www.angola-portal.ao/PortaldoGoverno

CURRENT LEADERS

José Eduardo dos Santos

Position
President

Introduction
José Eduardo dos Santos, one of Africa's longest-serving leaders, has been president of Angola since the death of the country's first post-colonial president Agostinho Neto in 1979. He is also head of the ruling Movimento Popular de Libertação de Angola (MPLA; Popular Movement for the Liberation of Angola), and was prime minister from 1999–2002. He has said that he will stand down at the next presidential elections, which have been on hold as Angola has sought to recover from the years of civil war with UNITA rebels led by Jonas Savimbi.

Early Life
Dos Santos was born on 28 Aug. 1942 in Luanda. In 1961 he joined Neto's MPLA rebel movement, fighting for Angolan independence. The movement was forced into exile in neighbouring Zaïre (now the Democratic Republic of the Congo). As his party standing increased, dos Santos founded the MPLA youth movement before being sent to Moscow to study telecommunications and petroleum engineering. He returned to fight for Angolan independence, which finally came in 1975. Under Neto's presidency, dos Santos served first as prime minister (1975–78) and then planning minister (1978–79). After Neto's death in Sept 1979, dos Santos assumed the leadership as Angola's second post-independence president.

Career in Office
During the first ten years dos Santos upheld the MPLA's traditional Marxist doctrine and the government's single party rule while continuing the war against the UNITA rebels begun under his predecessor. The government received Cuban military help in the conflict and the Soviet Union supplied funds. The USA and South Africa meanwhile backed UNITA's leader Jonas Savimbi.

A rapprochement began in 1988 when both Cuba and South Africa withdrew their forces. In 1990, following the collapse of communism, dos Santos moved away from Marxism to adopt 'democratic socialism'. This allowed for the introduction of a free market economy and multi-party elections. The following year, a peace agreement signed in Lisbon culminated in Angola's first nationwide elections in 1992. In a turnout of 91% of registered voters, the MPLA won 54% compared to UNITA's 34%. In the presidential poll dos Santos secured 49·6%, while Savimbi polled 40·7%. Before a second round run-off, Savimbi rejected the election, claiming the first round results had been fraudulent. The civil war resumed and elections scheduled for 1997 were postponed indefinitely.

Attempts to resolve the conflict through amnesties, military action and peace talks all failed. In 1999 dos Santos assumed the role of prime minister and took over control of the armed forces. In Feb. 2002 Savimbi was killed by government soldiers and two months later a ceasefire was signed between the government and the rebels. In 2001 dos Santos announced his intention to step down from the presidency at the next elections, although these would not take place until there was free movement of people and goods in the country and the many Angolans displaced by the conflict had returned home. Since the end of hostilities in most of the country in 2002, his government has committed substantial resources, financed by oil exports and diamonds, to reconstruction. Nevertheless, much of the population still lives in extreme poverty. Also, it was not until Aug. 2006 that a ceasefire agreement was achieved with separatists fighting for independence of the northern enclave of Cabinda, where much of Angola's oil wealth lies. The final stage of a United Nations refugee repatriation scheme, involving some 60,000 Angolans, began in Oct. 2006.

In Jan. 2007 dos Santos oversaw Angola's accession to the Organization of the Petroleum Exporting Countries (OPEC), and in Feb. he declared that parliamentary elections would be held in 2008 and presidential polls in 2009. The parliamentary polls took place in Sept. and resulted in a landslide victory for the ruling MPLA. Despite some criticisms of the poll by an observer mission from the European Union and the rejection of opposition demands for a rerun of voting in the capital Luanda, UNITA leader Isaias Samakuva accepted his party's defeat. In mid-2009 presidential elections scheduled for Sept. were postponed, reportedly to allow more time for the drafting of a new constitution.

DEFENCE

Conscription is for two years. Defence expenditure totalled US$1,588m. in 2006 (US$132 per capita), representing 4·7% of GDP.

Army

In 2007 the Army had 42 regiments. Total strength was 100,000. In addition the paramilitary Rapid Reaction Police numbered 10,000.

Navy

Naval personnel in 2007 totalled about 1,000 with nine operational vessels. There is a naval base at Luanda.

Air Force

The Angolan People's Air Force (FAPA) was formed in 1976 and has 6,000 personnel. In 2007 there were 90 combat capable aircraft and 16 attack helicopters.

INTERNATIONAL RELATIONS

Angola is a member of the UN, World Bank, IMF and several other UN specialized agencies, WTO, IOM, African Development Bank, African Union, CEEAC, SADC, OPEC and is an ACP member state of the ACP-EU relationship.

ECONOMY

In 2006 agriculture accounted for 8·9% of GDP, industry 69·7% and services 21·4%.

Overview

Since 2000 the government has operated under reform programmes from the IMF and World Bank. Increased oil production produced average growth of more than 15% per year between 2004–07. Angola is one of Africa's major oil exporters, joining OPEC in 2007, and an important diamond exporter.

Improved economic performance has allowed for the rebuilding of the infrastructure destroyed during the civil war. The agricultural and construction sectors have benefited particularly and have returned high rates of growth. Other major industries include coffee, fish and timber. The country's rich natural resources offer great potential.

Angola adopted an anti-inflation policy in 2003 that reduced inflation from around 100% to 12% by the end of 2006. However, despite an improving outlook, Angola continues to suffer from poverty, unequal income distribution and the effects of years of war. The global economic crisis has presented additional problems, with slower growth rates and an increase in inflation, down in part to higher food prices.

Currency

The unit of currency is the *kwanza* (AOA), introduced in Dec. 1999, replacing the *readjusted kwanza* at a rate of 1 kwanza = 1m. readjusted kwanzas. Foreign exchange reserves were US$2,017m. in July 2005 and money supply was 103,304m. kwanzas. Inflation, which reached 4,146% in 1996, was 12·2% in 2007 and 12·5% in 2008.

Budget

Revenues in 2004 were 602·2bn. kwanzas and expenditures 592·0bn. kwanzas

Performance

Total GDP was US$83·4bn. in 2008. The civil war meant GDP growth in 1993 was negative, at –24·0%, but a recovery followed and in 2007 and 2008 it was 20·3% and 13·2% respectively, mainly thanks to booming diamond exports and post-war rebuilding. Angola's growth in both 2007 and 2008 was amongst the highest in the world.

Banking and Finance

The Banco Nacional de Angola is the central bank and bank of issue (*Governor*, Abraão Pio do Amaral Gourgel). All banks were state-owned until the sector was reopened to commercial competition in 1991. In 2002 there were three commercial banks, one development bank, one investment bank and three foreign banks.

Angola received US$1·4bn. in foreign direct investment in 2004 (US$3·5bn. in 2003).

ENERGY AND NATURAL RESOURCES

Environment

In 2008 Angola's carbon dioxide emissions from the consumption and flaring of fossil fuels were the equivalent of 1·9 tonnes per capita. An *Environmental Performance Index* compiled in 2008 ranked Angola 148th in the world out of 149 countries analysed, with 39·5%. The index examined various factors in six areas—air pollution, biodiversity and habitat, climate change, environmental health, productive natural resources and water resources.

Electricity

Installed capacity was an estimated 0·5m. kW in 2004. Production in 2004 was 2·34bn. kWh, with consumption per capita 205 kWh.

Oil and Gas

Oil is produced mainly offshore and in the Cabinda exclave. Oil production and supporting activities contribute more than half of Angolan GDP and provide the government with 80% of revenues. The oil industry is expected to invest US$3·5bn. a year in offshore Angola in the early part of the 21st century. Angola's oil production ranks among the fastest-growing in the world. There are plans for a new US$8bn. oil refinery near Lobito which is scheduled to be completed by 2011. Only Nigeria among sub-Saharan African countries produces more oil. It is believed that there are huge oil resources yet to be discovered. Proven oil reserves in 2008 were 13·5bn. bbls. Total production (2008) 92·2m. tonnes. Proven natural gas reserves (2007) 57bn. cu. metres; production, 2004, 730m. cu. metres.

Minerals

Mineral production in Angola is dominated by diamonds and 90% of all workers in the mining sector work in the diamond industry. Production in 2006 was an estimated 9·2m. carats. Angola has billions of dollars worth of unexploited diamond fields. In 2000 the government regained control of the nation's richest diamond provinces from UNITA rebels. Other minerals produced (2006 estimates) include granite, 1·5m. cu. metres; marble, 100,000 cu. metres; salt, 35,000 tonnes. Iron ore, phosphate, manganese and copper deposits exist.

Agriculture

In 2007 there were an estimated 3·3m. ha. of arable land and 0·3m. ha. of permanent crops. 75,000 ha. were irrigated in 2002. The agricultural population in 2007 was approximately 12·29m., of whom an estimated 5·41m. were economically active. Although more than 70% of the economically active population are engaged in agriculture it only accounts for 8% of GDP. There were 31 tractors per 10,000 ha. of arable land in 2006. Principal crops (with 2003 production, in 1,000 tonnes): cassava (5,699); maize (545); sweet potatoes (439); sugarcane (360); bananas (300); millet (97); citrus fruits (78); dry beans (66).

Livestock (2003): 4·1m. cattle, 340,000 sheep, 2·05m. goats, 780,000 pigs.

Forestry

In 2005, 59·10m. ha., or 47·4% of the total land area, was covered by forests, including mahogany and other hardwoods. Timber production in 2007 was 4·84m. cu. metres.

Fisheries

Total catch in 2004 came to 240,005 tonnes, mainly from sea fishing.

INDUSTRY

The principal manufacturing branches are foodstuffs, textiles and oil refining. Output, 2004 (in 1,000 tonnes): distillate fuel oil, 669; residual fuel oil, 604; jet fuel, 302; cement (1997), 301; flour (1998), 172; petrol, 96; beer (2003), 160m. litres; 33,000 TV sets (1992); 29,000 radio sets (1992).

Labour

In 1996 the total labour force numbered 5,144,000 (54% males).

INTERNATIONAL TRADE

In 2005 total foreign debt was US$11,755m.

Imports and Exports

In 2007 imports (c.i.f.) totalled US$15,048m. (US$9,586m. in 2006); exports (f.o.b.), US$38,997m. (US$31,862m. in 2006).

Main exports, 2007 (in US$1m.): crude oil, 36,417; diamonds, 1,552; manufactures, 359. Chief import suppliers (2003): Portugal (18·1%); USA (12·1%); South Africa (12·3%); Netherlands (11·6%). Chief export markets (2003): USA (47·1%); China (23·1%); Taiwan (8·7%); France (7·3%).

COMMUNICATIONS

Roads

There were 51,429 km of roads in 2001 (7,944 km highways; 10·4% of all roads surfaced) and 671,100 vehicles in use in 2007. Many roads remain mined as a result of the civil war; a programme of de-mining and rehabilitation is under way.

Rail

Prior to the civil war there was in excess of 2,900 km of railway (predominantly 1,067 mm gauge track), but much of the network was damaged during the war. However, restoration and redevelopment of the network is now under way, notably the Benguela Railway, linking the port city of Lobito with Huambo in Angola's rich farmlands and neighbouring Democratic Republic of the Congo and Zambia.

Civil Aviation

There is an international airport at Luanda (Fourth of February). The national carrier is Linhas Aéreas de Angola (TAAG), which operated direct flights in 2003 to Johannesburg, Kinshasa, Paris, Pointe-Noire, Rio de Janeiro, São Tomé and Windhoek. There were direct flights in 2003 with other airlines to Addis Ababa, Brussels, Libreville, Lisbon, London and Moscow. In 2003 scheduled airline traffic of Angola-based carriers flew 5m. km, carrying 198,000 passengers (99,000 on international flights).

Shipping

There are ports at Luanda, Lobito and Namibe, and oil terminals at Malongo, Lobito and Soyo. In 2002 the merchant fleet totalled 55,000 GRT, including oil tankers 3,000 GRT.

Telecommunications

There were 1,188,400 telephone subscribers in 2005, or 74·5 per 1,000 inhabitants. Mobile phone subscribers numbered 1,094,100 in 2005 and internet users 172,000 in 2004.

Postal Services

In 2003 there were 55 post offices, or one for every 248,000 persons.

SOCIAL INSTITUTIONS

Justice

The Supreme Court and Court of Appeal are in Luanda. The death penalty was abolished in 1992. In 2002–03 the US government's Agency for International Development assisted in the modernization of the judicial system. Measures including the introduction of a court case numbering system were intended to reduce legal costs and attract foreign investment.

The population in penal institutions in 2002 was 4,975 (36 per 100,000 of national population).

Education

The education system provides three levels of general education totalling eight years, followed by schools for technical training, teacher training or pre-university studies. In 2000–01 there were 1,178,485 pupils and 33,478 teachers at primary schools, 399,712 pupils and 19,798 teachers at secondary schools and (1999–2000) 7,845 students with 796 academic staff in tertiary education institutions. There is one university. Private schools have been permitted since 1991. The University of Luanda has campuses at Luanda, Huambo and Lubango. It had 8,954 students in 1991–92. The adult literacy rate was 66·8% in 2003 (82·1% among males and 53·8% among females).

In 2000–01 expenditure on education came to 3·4% of GNP.

Health

In 1997 there were 736 physicians, 10,942 nurses and 411 midwives. In 1990 there were 266 hospitals and health centres with 11,857 beds. There were 1,339 medical posts.

In 2000 only 38% of the population had access to safe drinking water. It was estimated that 60% of the 3·9m. displaced people were suffering from malnutrition in 2000.

RELIGION

In 2001 there were 6·44m. Roman Catholics, 1·55m. Protestants and 710,000 African Christians, and most of the remainder follow traditional animist religions. In Feb. 2010 there was one cardinal.

CULTURE

Broadcasting

There were 582,000 TV receivers in Angola in 2003 (colour by PAL). Rádio Nacional de Angola (RNA) and Televisão Pública de Angola (TPA) are state-controlled broadcasters. RNA includes programmes in indigenous languages in its services. There are private radio stations in the main cities, and some pay-TV services carrying Portuguese and Brazilian channels.

Press

The government-owned Jornal de Angola (circulation of 41,000) was the only daily newspaper in 2006. The Diário da República is the official gazette. There are 12 private weekly publications and four smaller regional weeklies.

Tourism

In 2004 there were 194,000 foreign tourists (including 101,000 from European countries and 42,000 from other African countries), bringing revenue of US$82m.

DIPLOMATIC REPRESENTATIVES

Of Angola in the United Kingdom (22 Dorset St., London, W1U 6QY)
Ambassador: Ana Maria Teles Carreira.

Of the United Kingdom in Angola (Rua Diogo Cão 4, Caixa Postal 1244, Luanda)
Ambassador: Vacant.
Chargé d'Affaires a.i.: Angela Trott.

Of Angola in the USA (2108 16th St., NW, Washington, D.C., 20009)
Ambassador: Josefina Pitra Diakite.

Of the USA in Angola (32 rua Houari Boumedienne, Miramar, Luanda)
Ambassador: Dan W. Mozena.

Of Angola to the United Nations
Ambassador: Ismael Gaspar Martins.

Of Angola to the European Union
Ambassador: Toko Diakenga Serão.

FURTHER READING

Anstee, M. J., *Orphan of the Cold War: the Inside Story of the Collapse of the Angolan Peace Process, 1992–93.* 1996
Brittain, Victoria, *Death of Dignity: Angola's Civil War.* 1999
Guimarães, Fernando Andersen, *The Origins of the Angolan Civil War: Foreign Intervention and Domestic Political Conflict.* 2001
Hodges, Tony, *Angola: Anatomy of an Oil State.* 2004
James, W. M., *Political History of the War in Angola.* 1991

National Statistical Office: Instituto Nacional de Estatística, Luanda.

ANTIGUA AND BARBUDA

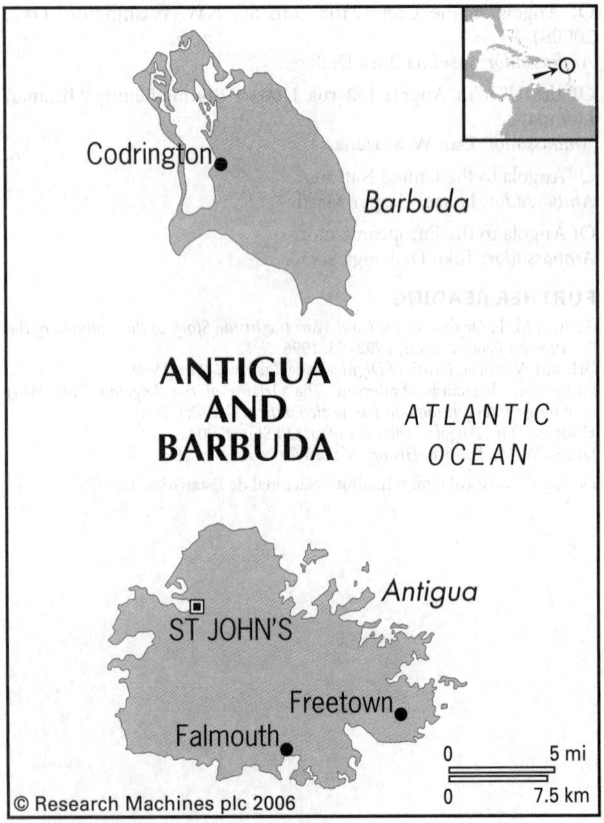

Capital: St John's
Population, 2002: 67,000
GDP per capita, 2007: (PPP$) 18,691
HDI/world rank: 0·868/47

KEY HISTORICAL EVENTS

Antigua and Barbuda were populated by Arawak-speaking people from at least 1000 BC. By 1493, when Columbus passed Antigua, it was occupied by Carib Indians. English settlers arrived in 1632. Sugar plantations, using slave labour, appeared in the 1650s. As British colonies, Antigua and Barbuda formed part of the Leeward Islands Federation from 1871 until 1956 when they became a separate Crown Colony. This was merged into the West Indies Federation from Jan. 1958 until May 1962 and became an Associated State of the UK on 27 Feb. 1967. Antigua and Barbuda gained independence on 1 Nov. 1981.

TERRITORY AND POPULATION

Antigua and Barbuda comprises three islands of the Lesser Antilles situated in the eastern Caribbean with a total land area of 442 sq. km (171 sq. miles); it consists of Antigua (280 sq. km), Barbuda, 40 km to the north (161 sq. km) and uninhabited Redonda, 40 km to the southwest (one sq. km). The population in July 2002 was 67,400 (1,400 on Barbuda); density, 153 per sq. km. In 2005, 60·9% of the population lived in rural areas.

The chief town is St John's, the capital, on Antigua (24,451 inhabitants in 2001). Codrington (914) is the only settlement on Barbuda.

English is the official language; local dialects are also spoken.

SOCIAL STATISTICS

Expectation of life, 2003: males, 70·0 years, females, 75·0. Annual population growth rate, 2000–05, 2·7%. Births, 2003, 1,241; deaths, 2003, 454. Infant mortality in 2005 was 11 per 1,000 live births; fertility rate, 2004, 2·3 births per woman.

CLIMATE

A tropical climate, but drier than most West Indies islands. The hot season is from May to Nov., when rainfall is greater. Mean annual rainfall is 40" (1,000 mm).

CONSTITUTION AND GOVERNMENT

H.M. Queen Elizabeth, as Head of State, is represented by a Governor-General appointed by her on the advice of the Prime Minister. There is a bicameral legislature, comprising a 17-member Senate appointed by the Governor-General and a 17-member House of Representatives elected by universal suffrage for a five-year term. The Governor-General appoints a Prime Minister and, on the latter's advice, other members of the Cabinet.

Barbuda is administered by a nine-member directly-elected council.

National Anthem

'Fair Antigua and Barbuda'; words by N. H. Richards, tune by W. G. Chambers.

RECENT ELECTIONS

At the elections to the House of Representatives of 12 March 2009 the United Progressive Party (UPP) won 9 seats, the Antigua Labour Party (ALP) 7 and the Barbuda People's Movement (BPM) 1.

CURRENT ADMINISTRATION

General: Louise Lake-Tack, GCMG; b. 1944 (in office since 17 July 2007).

In March 2010 the UPP government comprised:

Prime Minister and Minister of Foreign Affairs: Baldwin Spencer; b. 1948 (UPP; in office since 24 March 2004).

Deputy Prime Minister and Minister of Health, Social Transformation and Consumer Affairs: Wilmoth Daniel. *Attorney General and Legal Affairs:* Justin Simon. *National Security:* Errol Cort. *Finance, the Economy and Public Administration:* Harold Lovell. *Agriculture, Lands, Housing and the Environment:* Hilson Baptiste. *Education, Sports, Youth and Gender Affairs:* Jacqui Quinn-Leandro. *Tourism, Civil Aviation and Culture:* John Maginley. *Works, Transport and Labour:* Trevor Walker.

Government Website: http://www.ab.gov.ag

CURRENT LEADERS

Baldwin Spencer

Position
Prime Minister

Introduction
Baldwin Spencer is leader of the United Progressive Party (UPP) and took office as prime minister in March 2004, defeating the Antigua Labour Party (ALP), which had held power continuously since 1976.

Early Life
Baldwin Spencer was born on 8 Oct. 1948 in Grays Green, Antigua. After secondary school, he studied social leadership at St Francis Xavier University's Coady International Institute in Nova Scotia. He also obtained a diploma in labour and economic studies from

Ruskin College (at Oxford in the UK) and in labour and industrial relations from Oslo University.

In the 1970s Spencer worked as a trade unionist, serving as vice-president and, later, assistant general secretary of the Antigua and Barbuda Workers' Union (AWU). He also served as president of the Caribbean Maritime and Aviation Council.

In 1989 Spencer entered parliament as the United Democratic Party (UNDP) representative for St John's Rural West constituency. In 1991 he became leader of the UNDP and, as leader of the opposition in parliament, formed an alliance with the two other main opposition parties, the Antigua Caribbean Liberation Movement and the Progressive Labour Movement. They merged in 1992 to form the UPP.

During the 1990s Spencer regularly accused Prime Minister Vere Bird, Sr and his ALP of corruption. The campaign helped exploit rifts within the government and Bird's own son, Lester Bird, called for his father's resignation. Lester Bird took over as prime minister shortly before the general election of March 2004. Spencer led the UPP into the election promising more transparent government, and the party won 12 of 17 seats.

Career in Office

Spencer vowed to combat corruption, develop tourism and foster economic co-operation with other countries. In the first year he introduced legislation to improve government accountability and took steps to de-politicize the government-owned media. However, corruption investigations were hampered by the loss of government files and in 2005 Spencer set up a task-force to tackle organized crime and corruption among officials.

In Oct. 2004 an IMF report concluded that Antigua and Barbuda's economy suffered from high levels of public debt and over-reliance on the government for jobs (accounting for 40% of total employment). Spencer responded in 2005 by launching a drive to expand the tourism industry, taking measures to cut the public service salary bill, and reintroducing income tax. The tourism drive was undermined, however, in July 2008 by the murder of a visiting British couple. Spencer's UPP won a second term by taking 9 of the 17 seats in the parliamentary elections of March 2009.

He has pursued closer ties with Brazil, China, India, Russia and neighbouring Caribbean countries (serving as chair of CARICOM in 2004).

DEFENCE

The Antigua and Barbuda Defence Force numbers 170. There are some 75 reserves. A coastguard service has been formed.

In 2006 defence expenditure totalled US$5m. (US$70 per capita), representing 0·5% of GDP.

Army

The strength of the Army section of the Defence Force was 125 in 2007.

Navy

There was a naval force of 45 operating three patrol craft in 2007.

INTERNATIONAL RELATIONS

Antigua and Barbuda is a member of the UN, World Bank, IMF and several other UN specialized agencies, WTO, Commonwealth, ACS, CARICOM, OECS, OAS and is an ACP member state of the ACP-EU relationship.

ECONOMY

In 2005 agriculture accounted for 4% of GDP, industry 23% and services 74%.

Currency

The unit of currency is the *East Caribbean dollar* (XCD), issued by the Eastern Caribbean Central Bank. Foreign exchange reserves in July 2005 were US$122m. and total money supply was EC$573m. Inflation was 1·4% in 2007, rising to 5·3% in 2008.

Budget

In 2007 revenues totalled EC$718·3m. and expenditures EC$923·8m. Tax revenue accounted for 91·4% of revenues in 2007; current expenditure accounted for 78·3% of expenditures.

Performance

Real GDP growth was 6·9% in 2007 and 2·8% in 2008. Total GDP was US$1·2bn. in 2008.

Banking and Finance

The East Caribbean Central Bank based in St Kitts functions as a central bank. The *Governor* is Sir Dwight Venner. In 2002, nine commercial banks were operating (four foreign). Total national savings were EC$1,357m. in Dec. 2001.

In 1981 Antigua established an offshore banking sector which in 2002 had 21 banks registered and operating. The offshore sector is regulated by the Financial Services Regulatory Commission, a statutory body.

ENERGY AND NATURAL RESOURCES

Environment

In 2008 Antigua and Barbuda's carbon dioxide emissions from the consumption and flaring of fossil fuels were the equivalent of 8·1 tonnes per capita.

Electricity

Capacity in 2004 was 27,000 kW. Production was estimated at 109m. kWh in 2004 and consumption per capita about 1,595 kWh.

Water

There is a desalination plant with a capacity of 0·6m. gallons per day, sufficient to meet the needs of the country.

Agriculture

In 2007 there were around 8,000 ha. of arable land and 1,000 ha. of permanent crops. Production (2003) of fruits and vegetables, 13,000 tonnes (notably melons and mangoes).

Livestock (2003): goats, 36,000; sheep, 19,000; cattle, 14,000; pigs, 6,000.

Forestry

Forests covered 9,000 ha., or 21·4% of the total land area, in 2005.

Fisheries

Total catch in 2005 came to 2,999 tonnes, exclusively from sea fishing.

INDUSTRY

Manufactures include beer, cement, toilet tissue, stoves, refrigerators, blenders, fans, garments and rum (molasses imported from Guyana).

Labour

The unemployment rate in 1998 was the lowest in the Caribbean, at 4·5%. Between 1994 and 1998, 2,543 jobs were created. The average annual salary in 1998 was US$8,345 per head of population.

INTERNATIONAL TRADE

Imports and Exports

Imports in 2005 totalled US$390m. and exports US$82m. The main trading partners were CARICOM, the USA, the UK and Canada.

COMMUNICATIONS

Roads

In 2002 there were 1,165 km of roads of which 33·0% were paved. 23,700 passenger cars and 5,200 commercial vehicles were in use in 2002. More than EC$64m. was spent to rebuild major roads and highways in the three years following damage caused by hurricanes Luis and Marilyn in 1995.

Civil Aviation

V. C. Bird International Airport is near St John's. There were flights in 2003 to Anguilla, Barbados, Dominica, Dominican Republic, Georgetown, Grenada, Kingston, London, Milan, Montego Bay, New York, Paris, Philadelphia, Puerto Rico, St Croix, St Kitts and Nevis, St Lucia, St Maarten, St Vincent, Tampa, Toronto, Trinidad and Tobago and the British and US Virgin Islands. A domestic flight links the airports on Antigua and Barbuda.

Shipping

The main port is St John's Harbour. The merchant shipping fleet of 762 vessels totalled 4,541,940 GRT in Dec. 2001. In 1997 vessels totalling 94,907,000 NRT entered ports and vessels totalling 667,126,000 NRT cleared.

Telecommunications

There were 92,000 telephone subscribers in 2004, or 1,142·6 per 1,000 inhabitants, with 54,000 mobile phone subscribers. There were 20,000 internet users in 2004.

Postal Services

The main post office is located in St John's. In 2003 there were 13 post offices in total.

SOCIAL INSTITUTIONS

Justice

Law is based on UK common law as exercised by the Eastern Caribbean Supreme Court (ECSC) on St Lucia. There are Magistrates' Courts and a Court of Summary Jurisdiction. Appeals lie to the Court of Appeal of ECSC, or ultimately to the UK Privy Council. Antigua and Barbuda was one of ten countries to sign an agreement in Feb. 2001 establishing a Caribbean Court of Justice to replace the British Privy Council as the highest civil and criminal court. In the meantime the number of signatories has risen to twelve. The court was inaugurated at Port-of-Spain, Trinidad on 16 April 2005.

The population in penal institutions in Jan. 2005 was 184 (equivalent to 269 per 100,000 of national population).

Education

Adult literacy was 95% in 1998. In 2007 there were 11,569 pupils at primary schools and 7,838 pupils at secondary schools. In 1992–93 there were 72 government primary and secondary schools. Other schools were run by religious organizations. The Antigua State College offers technical and teacher training. Antigua is a partner in the regional University of the West Indies.

In 2002 public expenditure on education came to 4·1% of GNI.

Health

There is one general hospital, a private clinic, seven health centres and 17 associated clinics. A new medical centre at Mount St John's opened in Feb. 2009. In 1996 there were 75 physicians, 12 dentists, 187 nurses and 13 pharmacists.

Welfare

The state operates a Medical Benefits Scheme providing free medical attention, and a Social Security Scheme, providing age and disability pensions and sickness benefits.

RELIGION

In 2001 there were 30,000 Protestants, 23,000 Anglicans and 8,000 Roman Catholics.

CULTURE

Broadcasting

Radio and television services are operated mainly by the government-owned Antigua and Barbuda Broadcasting Service (ABS). Private stations include Observer Radio, Caribbean Radio Lighthouse (Baptist Mission) and Crusader Radio (launched in 2003 and owned by the United Progressive Party).

Press

The main newspapers are *The Antigua Sun* and *The Daily Observer*, with a combined circulation of 9,000 in 2006.

Tourism

Tourism is the main industry, contributing about 70% of GDP and 80% of foreign exchange earnings and related activities. In 2005 there were 261,000 foreign tourists. Tourist expenditure (excluding passenger transport) amounted to US$327m. in 2005.

Festivals

Of particular interest are the International Sailing Week (April–May); Annual Tennis Championship (May); Mid-Summer Carnival (July–Aug.).

Museums and Galleries

The main attractions are the Museum of Antigua and Barbuda; Coates Cottage; Aiton Place; Harmony Hall; Cedars Pottery; SOFA (Sculpture Objects Functional Art); Pigeon Point Pottery; Harbour Art Gallery; Nelson's Dockyard; Shirley Heights.

DIPLOMATIC REPRESENTATIVES

Of Antigua and Barbuda in the United Kingdom (2nd Floor, 45 Crawford Place, London, W1H 4LP)
High Commissioner: Carl Roberts.

Of the United Kingdom in Antigua and Barbuda
High Commissioner: Paul Brummell (resides in Bridgetown, Barbados).

Of Antigua and Barbuda in the USA (3216 New Mexico Ave., NW, Washington, D.C., 20016)
Ambassador: Deborah Mae Lovell.

Of the USA in Antigua and Barbuda
Ambassador: Vacant (resides in Bridgetown, Barbados).
Chargé d'Affaires a.i.: D. Brendt Hardt.

Of Antigua and Barbuda to the United Nations
Ambassador: John W. Ashe.

Of Antigua and Barbuda to the European Union
Ambassador: Vacant.

FURTHER READING

Dyde, Brian, *The Unsuspected Isle: A History of Antigua.* 2000
Nicholson, Desmond, *Antigua, Barbuda and Redonda: A Historical Sketch.* 1991

ARGENTINA

República Argentina
(Argentine Republic)

Capital: Buenos Aires
Population estimate, 2010: 40·67m.
GDP per capita, 2007: (PPP$) 13,238
HDI/world rank: 0·866/49

KEY HISTORICAL EVENTS

Before European colonization two main indigenous American groups and numerous nomadic tribes peopled the region that is now Argentina, probably constituting a population of some 300,000. Both groups—the Diaguita people in the northwest, and the Guarani people in the south and east—created the basis for a permanent agricultural civilization. The Diaguita also prevented the powerful Inca from expanding their empire from Bolivia into Argentina.

Europeans first came to Argentina in the early 16th century and a series of expeditions and attempts at colonization followed. The explorer Sebastian Cabot established the first Spanish settlement in 1526, abandoned just three years later following attacks by natives. He reported Argentina's natural silver resources, possibly inspiring the name *Argentina* ('of silver'). Ten years later Pedro de Mendoza founded Buenos Aires; however, it was not until its re-establishment in 1580 that the region's indigenous peoples, weakened by European diseases as much as European military campaigns, were finally defeated and Spanish rule established.

Largely neglected as Spain looked instead to the riches of Peru, the majority of settlers in Argentina hailed from the neighbouring colonies of Chile, Peru and Paraguay. Missions established by the Roman Catholic Church played an important part in the colonizing process.

In 1776 Buenos Aires, known throughout the 18th century as a smuggler's haunt, was made a free port at the centre of a viceroyalty comprising Argentina, Uruguay, Paraguay and Bolivia. As trade with Europe became increasingly important, Buenos Aires adopted the ideas of the European enlightenment and was seen as more cosmopolitan than its rivals.

When Spain came under Napoleonic control the British attacked Buenos Aires, first in 1806 and then again in 1807. On both occasions the city was able to repel the invasions without any help from Spanish forces, and the event in part helped to trigger the independence movement.

Independence

Having separated from Paraguay in 1814, Argentina gained its independence from Spain in 1816. Unable to control its outlying regions, it lost Bolivia in 1825 and Uruguay in 1828. During the early years of independence, the country was embroiled in bitter internal struggles between the Unitarists and the Federalists. Unitarists wanted a strong central government, particularly as Britain agreed to recognize Argentinian independence only if it could devise a government representing the whole country. Federalists, on the other hand, advocated regional control, as each province had formed its own political regime, based on local interests and reinforced by the leadership of military powers dominant since the war.

In 1827 Argentinians joined forces with Uruguay to repel a Brazilian invasion, thereby securing independence for Uruguay and encouraging Argentinian unification. From 1835–52, the Federalists held power under Gen. Juan Manuel de Rosas, an important landowner and commander of a rural militia. Governor of Buenos Aires from 1829, Rosas proved a formidable leader who used a secret police force, the Mazorca, to defeat his opponents. He also consolidated church support, compelling priests to display his portrait at the altar.

Britain seized the Falkland Islands (Islas Malvinas) in 1833, while Bolivia, Paraguay and Uruguay continued to isolate the federation. In 1838, following a trade dispute with Uruguay, Argentinian political exiles gained French support in an attempt to overthrow Rosas. But he remained in power until 1853 when he was ousted by Gen. Justo José de Urquiza. The Unitarists were then able to inaugurate a new constitution and achieve a more stable government, although Urquiza's overthrow by Santiago Derquai led to another civil war. An agreement between Urquiza and Gen. Bartolomé Mitre, governor of Buenos Aires, saw a return of stability, and established the city as the seat of government.

The next 50 years saw a steady period of presidential succession along with impressive economic growth. In the period 1862–80 schools were built, public works started, and liberal reforms instituted. From 1865–70 Argentina was also involved in the War of the Triple Alliance, joining with Uruguay and Brazil in a campaign against Paraguay. This ultimately strengthened the newly centralized Argentina.

From 1880–86 Argentina thrived under the leadership of Gen. Julio Roca. A Federalist, Roca nevertheless retained Buenos Aires as the capital. During his second term of office, Roca restored peace with Chile after years of dispute over territory.

Argentina became a magnet for European immigration, putting pressure on the political system to broaden its representation. The immigrants, mainly Italian and Spanish, established the new Socialist, Anarchist and Unión Cívica Radical parties. This latter group became the main political force and under the leadership of Hipólito Irigoyen won their first presidential election in 1916, following Roque Sáenz Peña's electoral reforms of 1910–14. The conservatives regained power in 1930, supported by the military, and the activities of radicals were restricted, until Gen. Augustín Pedro Justin, heading a coalition of conservatives, radicals and independent socialists, was elected in 1931. A succession of leaders regime instigated controversial political and economic reforms, resulting in agreements with Britain over trade and a gradual improvement in the economy.

Perón

Although Argentina remained neutral at the outbreak of the Second World War, another coup in 1943 brought Gen. Juan Domingo Perón to power. He chose to side with the allies and declared war on the axis powers.

A strong leader, Perón led a regime that was autocratic but populist and nationalistic, winning presidential elections in 1946 and 1951 with the support of the urban working class that industrialization had created. His political success was reinforced by his second wife Eva Duarte de Perón, 'Evita'. Acting as *de facto* minister of health and labour, she awarded wage increases that led to inflation. In 1952 her death, caused by cancer, combined with Perón's increasing authoritarianism and his excommunication from the church, led to a fall in his popularity. In 1955 a coup by the armed forces sent him into exile.

In 1957 Argentina reverted to the constitution of 1853, and a year later Dr Arturo Frondizi was elected president. With US financial aid, Frondizi attempted to stabilize the economy, but faced heavy criticism from left-wing parties and from the Peronists, the political party that had established itself around the Peróns. Frondizi also fell out of favour with the military, whose intervention continued to overshadow Argentinian politics throughout the period. The Peronists achieved the highest number of votes in elections in 1962 prompting the military to take control and ban the Peronists, along with the Communist party, before elections in 1963. Dr Arturo Illia, a moderate liberal, was elected and many political prisoners were released. An attempted return by Perón in 1964 drove the military to install Gen. Carlos Onganía as president. Responding to popular resistance, the military eventually allowed the re-election of Perón in 1973.

After Perón's death in 1974 his third wife, María Estela Martínez de Perón, 'Isabelita', succeeded him, becoming the Americas' first woman chief of state. She was deposed by military coup two years later and the army's commander-in-chief, Gen. Jorge Videla, became president. Once in power, Videla dissolved Congress, banned trade unions, and imposed military control. Censorship and military curfews were imposed and the secret police was used extensively. His savagely repressive regime implemented what became known as the 'Dirty War'. Playing on the fears of the Argentinian people, Videla justified the 'disappearance' of 13,000–15,000 countrymen, many believed to have been tortured and executed, claiming that they threatened to undermine the government.

Falklands War

Videla was eventually succeeded by Gen. Leopoldo Galtieri, the army commander-in-chief. In April 1982 Galtieri, in an effort to distract attention from internal tension, invaded the Falkland Islands. The subsequent military defeat helped to precipitate Galtieri's fall in July 1982. The war in the Falklands exacerbated the country's problems. Decades of state intervention, regulation, inward looking policies and special interest subsidies had caused economic chaos. Presidential elections were held in Oct. 1983 and civilian rule was restored under Raúl Alfonsín, leader of the middle-class Unión Cívica Radical. Despite attempting to redress the finances of the bloated public sector, growing unemployment and four-figure inflation led to a Peronist victory in the 1989 elections and Carlos Menem, a Peronist, became Argentina's new president.

After an attempted military coup in Dec. 1990, Menem responded to allegations of corruption in the country's privatization programme by reshuffling his government. Economy Minister Domingo Cavallo's plan to stabilize the economy allowed Menem to alter the constitution in 1994 to permit his re-election for a second term.

By 1999, with economic recession in South America and high unemployment, Menem's popularity had plummeted. In the election that year Fernando de la Rúa of the centrist Alliance became the first president in a decade from outside of the Peronist party. Menem was later accused of illegal arms deals, but was released by a federal court and announced his intention to return to politics.

A state of emergency was introduced in Dec. 2001 as Argentina verged on bankruptcy. De la Rúa resigned on 20 Dec. 2001 after days of rioting and looting. Three interim presidents held power over a period of just 11 days before Eduardo Duhalde was elected president by Congress. With the economy still in crisis, Duhalde held office until the election of Peronist Néstor Kirchner in May 2003. The economy subsequently recovered as the world recession receded.

TERRITORY AND POPULATION

The second largest country in South America, the Argentine Republic is bounded in the north by Bolivia, in the northeast by Paraguay, in the east by Brazil, Uruguay and the Atlantic Ocean, and the west by Chile. The republic consists of 23 provinces and one federal district with the following areas and populations in 2001 (in 1,000):

Provinces	*Area (sq. km)*	*Population (census 2001)*	*Capital*	*Population (census 2001)*
Buenos Aires	307,571	13,827	La Plata	564
Catamarca	102,602	335	Catamarca	141
Chaco	99,633	984	Resistencia	274
Chubut	224,686	413	Rawson	22
Córdoba	165,321	3,067	Córdoba	1,268
Corrientes	88,199	931	Corrientes	315
Entre Ríos	78,781	1,158	Paraná	236
Formosa	72,066	487	Formosa	198
Jujuy	53,219	612	San Salvador de Jujuy	231
La Pampa	143,440	299	Santa Rosa	94
La Rioja	89,680	290	La Rioja	144
Mendoza	148,827	1,580	Mendoza	111
Misiones	29,801	966	Posadas	253
Neuquén	94,078	474	Neuquén	202
Río Negro	203,013	553	Viedma	47
Salta	155,488	1,079	Salta	462
San Juan	89,651	620	San Juan	113
San Luis	76,748	368	San Luis	153
Santa Cruz	243,943	197	Río Gallegos	79
Santa Fé	133,007	3,001	Santa Fé	369

Provinces	Area (sq. km)	Population (census 2001)	Capital	Population (census 2001)
Santiago del Estero	136,351	804	Santiago del Estero	231
Tierra del Fuego	21,571	101	Ushuaia	45
Tucumán	22,524	1,339	San Miguel de Tucumán	527
Federal Capital	200	2,776	Buenos Aires	2,776

Argentina also claims territory in Antarctica.

The area is 2,780,400 sq. km excluding the claimed Antarctic territory, and the population at the 2001 census was 36,260,130, giving a density of 13 per sq. km.

The UN gives an estimated population for 2010 of 40·67m.

In 2005, 90·1% of the population were urban.

In April 1990 the National Congress declared that the Falklands and other British-held islands in the South Atlantic were part of the new province of Tierra del Fuego formed from the former National Territory of the same name. The 1994 constitution reaffirms Argentine sovereignty over the Falkland Islands.

The population of the main metropolitan areas in 2001 was: Buenos Aires, 12,046,799; Córdoba, 1,368,301; Rosario, 1,161,188; Mendoza, 848,660; Tucumán, 738,479; La Plata, 694,253.

97% speak the national language, Spanish, while 2% speak Italian and 1% other languages. In 2002, 10,395 immigrants were granted permanent residency, down from 19,916 in 2001.

SOCIAL STATISTICS

2005 births, 712,220; deaths, 293,529. Rates, 2005 (per 1,000 population): birth, 18·5; death, 7·6. Infant mortality, 2005, 14 per 1,000 live births. Life expectancy at birth, 2007, 71·5 years for males and 79·0 years for females. Annual population growth rate, 2000–05, 1·0%; fertility rate, 2004, 2·3 births per woman.

CLIMATE

The climate is warm temperate over the pampas, where rainfall occurs in all seasons, but diminishes towards the west. In the north and west, the climate is more arid, with high summer temperatures, while in the extreme south conditions are also dry, but much cooler. Buenos Aires, Jan. 74°F (23·3°C), July 50°F (10°C). Annual rainfall 37" (950 mm). Bahía Blanca, Jan. 74°F (23·3°C), July 48°F (8·9°C). Annual rainfall 21" (523 mm). Mendoza, Jan. 75°F (23·9°C), July 47°F (8·3°C). Annual rainfall 8" (190 mm). Rosario, Jan. 76°F (24·4°C), July 51°F (10·6°C). Annual rainfall 35" (869 mm). San Juan, Jan. 78°F (25·6°C), July 50°F (10°C). Annual rainfall 4" (89 mm). San Miguel de Tucumán, Jan. 79°F (26·1°C), July 56°F (13·3°C). Annual rainfall 38" (970 mm). Ushuaia, Jan. 50°F (10°C), July 34°F (1·1°C). Annual rainfall 19" (475 mm).

CONSTITUTION AND GOVERNMENT

On 10 April 1994 elections were held for a 230-member constituent assembly to reform the 1853 constitution. The Justicialist National Movement (Peronist) gained 39% of votes cast and the Radical Union 20%. On 22 Aug. 1994 this assembly unanimously adopted a new constitution. This reduces the presidential term of office from six to four years, but permits the President to stand for two terms. The President is no longer elected by an electoral college, but directly by universal suffrage. A presidential candidate is elected with more than 45% of votes cast, or 40% if at least 10% ahead of an opponent; otherwise there is a second round. The Constitution reduces the President's powers by instituting a *Chief of Cabinet.* The bicameral *National Congress* consists of a Senate and a Chamber of Deputies. The Senate comprises 72 members (one-third of the members elected every two years to six-year terms). The Chamber of Deputies comprises 257 members (one-half of the members elected every two years to four-year terms) directly elected by universal suffrage (at age 18).

National Anthem

'Oíd, mortales, el grito sagrado: Libertad' ('Hear, mortals, the sacred cry of Liberty'); words by V. López y Planes, 1813; tune by J. Blas Parera.

GOVERNMENT CHRONOLOGY

Presidents since 1944. (FREJULI = Justicialista Liberation Front; FV = Front for Victory; PJ = Justicialist Party; PL = Labour Party; PP = Peronist Party; UCR = Radical Civic Union; UCRI = Radical Intransigent Civic Union; UCRP = People's Radical Civic Union)

1944–46	military	Edelmiro Julián Farrell Plaul
1946–55	military/PL/PP	Juan Domingo Perón Sosa
1955	military	Eduardo A. Lonardi Doucet
1955–58	military	Pedro Eugenio Aramburu Cilveti
1958–62	UCRI	Arturo Frondizi Ercoli
1962–63	UCRI	José María Guido
1963–66	UCRP	Arturo Umberto Illia Francesconi
1966–70	military	Juan Carlos Onganía Carballo
1970–71	military	Roberto Marcelo Levingston Laborda
1971–73	military	Alejandro Agustín Lanusse Gelly
1973	FREJULI	Héctor José Cámpora Demaestre
1973	FREJULI	Raúl Alberto Lastiri
1973–74	PJ	Juan Domingo Perón Sosa
1974–76	PJ	María Estela Martínez de Perón
1976–81	military	Jorge Rafael Videla
1981	military	Roberto Eduardo Viola
1981–82	military	Leopoldo Fortunato Galtieri
1982–83	military	Reynaldo Benito Bignone
1983–89	UCR	Raúl Ricardo Alfonsín
1989–99	PJ	Carlos Saúl Menem
1999–2001	UCR	Fernando de la Rúa
2003–07	PJ	Néstor Carlos Kirchner
2007–	FV	Cristina Fernández de Kirchner

RECENT ELECTIONS

In the presidential elections held on 28 Oct. 2007 Cristina Fernández de Kirchner (Front for Victory) won 44·9% of the vote, followed by Elisa Carrió (Civic Coalition Confederation) with 22·9%, Roberto Lavagna (An Advanced Nation) with 16·9% and Adolfo Rodríguez Saá (Justice, Union, and Liberty Front Alliance) with 7·7%. There were ten other candidates. Turnout was 74·1%.

In the elections to the Chamber of Deputies held on 28 Oct. 2007 for 130 seats, the Front for Victory won 78 seats, the Civic Coalition Confederation won 19, the Radical Civic Union 14 and others 19. Elections for the 127 seats not contested at the 2007 elections were scheduled for Oct. 2009 but were brought forward to 28 June 2009 by President Kirchner. The Justicialist Party and its allies won 47 seats (of which the Justicialist Party won 19 and the Front for Victory 14), the Social and Civic Agreement and its allies 41 (of which the Social and Civic Agreement won 28), the Republican Proposal 20 and others 19.

CURRENT ADMINISTRATION

President: Cristina Fernández de Kirchner; b. 1953 (Front for Victory; sworn in 10 Dec. 2007).

Vice-President: Julio Cobos.

In March 2010 the cabinet comprised:

Chief of the Cabinet: Aníbal Fernández. *Minister of Agriculture:* Julián Domínguez. *Defence:* Nilda Garré. *Economy and Public Finance:* Amado Boudou. *Education:* Alberto Sileoni. *Federal Planning, Public Investment and Services:* Julio De Vido. *Foreign Affairs, International Trade and Worship:* Jorge Taiana. *Health:* Juan Luis Manzur. *Interior:* Florencio Randazzo. *Justice, Security and Human Rights:* Julio Alak. *Labour, Employment and Social Security:* Carlos Tomada. *Production:* Débora Giorgi. *Science, Technology and Innovative Production:* Lino Barañao. *Social Development:* Alicia Kirchner.

Office of the President (limited English):
http://www.presidencia.gov.ar

CURRENT LEADERS

Cristina Fernández de Kirchner

Position
President

Introduction
Cristina Fernández de Kirchner was sworn in as president on 10 Dec. 2007, representing the ruling Front for Victory party (FV). She succeeded her husband, Néstor Kirchner, and is the first elected female president of Argentina, though not the first female president.

Early Life
Cristina Kirchner, also called Fernández, was born in 1953 in the La Plata region of Buenos Aires. Her father was a businessman and unionist of Spanish heritage. Her mother was a civil servant in the ministry for the economy and member of the Peronistas of German decent. Fernández was educated at secondary level in Buenos Aires and at the Colegio Nuestra Señora de la Misericordia, a private college run by nuns.

During the 1970s she studied at La Plata National University, reading psychology before converting to law. In 1974 she met Néstor Kirchner, a law student, and they married after six months. Both were members of the Tendencia Revolucionaria faction of the Peronist Justicialista Party (PJ). In 1975, following Juan Perón's death, the Kirchners moved to Rio Gallegos, the capital of Santa Cruz. They set up a law practice and distanced themselves from politics while the military junta that had ended the Peronista government in 1976 with a coup d'état held power until 1983. Whether Fernández completed her law degree remains disputed.

Her political career began shortly after her husband's. In 1985 she became a member of the PJ and was elected provincial representative of Santa Cruz in 1989, 1993 and 1995. Her husband became mayor of Rio Gallegos in 1987 and governor of Santa Cruz in 1991. In 1995 Fernández resigned from provincial politics to represent Santa Cruz in the Senate, where she built her national profile. In 1997 and 2001 she was elected to represent Santa Cruz in the Chamber of Deputies. In 2003 she helped her husband win the presidential election and became first lady. Two years later she secured the senatorship for Buenos Aires, representing the FV. In 2007, despite good poll ratings, Néstor Kirchner decided not to run for re-election as president and Fernández was elected in his place.

Career in Office
Fernández pledged to further her husband's economic policies. However, in the early stages of her tenure she faced budget restrictions and other challenges, including an energy shortage, rising inflation, large public debt and dependency on GM soya exports. She also faced accusations from the IMF that the national statistics institute manipulated official inflation figures. In July 2008, in a politically damaging defeat, Fernández cancelled tax increases on agricultural exports that had provoked months of protests by farmers. This was followed by another controversial government plan to nationalize private pension funds, ostensibly to protect pensioners' assets during the erupting global financial crisis, which was approved by parliament in Nov. As the economy deteriorated rapidly from late 2008 and her popularity slumped, Fernández brought forward partial congressional elections from Oct. 2009 to June. However, her party supporters still lost their absolute majorities in both parliamentary houses in the polling and her husband failed to gain election to the Chamber of Deputies.

In Oct. 2009 the government indicated its willingness to negotiate with holders of US$20bn. of bonds (on which Argentina had defaulted in 2001) in a debt restructuring initiative aimed at restoring the country's access to international credit. Meanwhile, Fernández's public announcement in Sept. 2008 that Argentina would repay US$6·7bn. in overdue loans to the Paris Club of creditors had yet to be honoured.

Internationally, Fernández has sought to raise Argentina's profile. Talks began with Brazil and Bolivia on a regional gas deal, but diplomatic relations with Uruguay have remained strained over the environmental risks linked to a paper pulping plant. She has represented Argentina at the G20 forum of wealthy nations.

DEFENCE

Conscription was abolished in 1994. In 2006 defence expenditure totalled US$1,873m. (US$47 per capita), representing 0·9% of GDP (compared to over 8% in 1981).

Army

In 2007 the Army was 41,400 strong. There are no reserves formally established or trained.

There is a paramilitary gendarmerie of 18,000 run by the Ministry of Interior.

Navy

In 2007 the Argentinian Navy included three diesel submarines, five destroyers and nine frigates. Total personnel was 20,000 including 2,000 in Naval Aviation and 2,500 marines. Main bases are at Puerto Belgrano, Mar del Plata and Ushuaia.

The Naval Aviation Service had 28 combat capable aircraft in 2007, including Super-Etendard strike aircraft, and 19 helicopters, including Agusta/Sikorsky ASH-3H Sea Kings.

Air Force

The Air Force is organized into Air Operations, Air Regions, Logistics and Personnel Commands. There were (2007) 14,600 personnel and 119 combat capable aircraft including A-4 Skyhawk, Mirage 5 and Mirage III jet fighters.

INTERNATIONAL RELATIONS

Argentina is a member of the UN, World Bank, IMF and several other UN specialized agencies, WTO, BIS, IOM, Inter-American Development Bank, SELA, LAIA, OAS, MERCOSUR, UNASUR and Antarctic Treaty. Diplomatic relations with Britain, broken since the 1982 Falklands War, were reopened in 1990.

In Jan. 2006 the government repaid the country's entire US$9·57bn. debt to the IMF ahead of schedule.

ECONOMY

Agriculture contributed 8·4% of GDP in 2006, industry 35·6% and services 56·0%.

Overview

By the late 1980s macroeconomic mismanagement in Argentina had caused hyperinflation. The economy contracted at an average annual rate of 0·7% over the decade. Structural reforms and a 1991 convertibility plan—establishing a currency peg to the US dollar—helped stabilize the economy for most of the 1990s. Between 1991 and 1997 GDP grew by 6·2% per year on average. The fixed exchange-rate regime survived the Mexican and Asian financial crises but the balance of payments was unable to withstand the pressure caused by subsequent shocks. By the fourth quarter of 1998 the economy was in recession which, combined with a low fiscal surplus and weak restraint in the provinces, threatened the country's ability to pay its foreign debt. The growing strength of the US dollar and the devaluation of the Brazilian *real* in 1999 increased pressure on the pegged peso.

The slowdown of the global economy in 2001 added to Argentina's economic plight. In Dec. 2001 it recorded the largest sovereign debt default in history and in Jan. 2002 abandoned convertibility. From 1999–2002 the economy contracted by 18·4% and poverty grew dramatically. Strong recovery between 2003 and 2007 was underpinned by a firm fiscal policy, successful debt restructuring and favourable international market conditions including high commodity prices, low interest rates and strong world growth. Unemployment fell and the urban poverty rate dropped from 48% in 2003 to 27% in 2007.

Economic well-being is threatened by energy shortages resulting from underinvestment in utilities after the country's default. Inflationary pressures have mounted although official statistics downplay this threat, claiming an inflation rate for 2008 of 7·2%. More objective estimates suggest a rate of 20–25%. Investor confidence has suffered as a consequence.

There were signs of recession in 2008. Real GDP had fallen by 6·5% by the end of Sept. 2008 and annual economic growth was down to 7·1%, with decreasing industrial activity resulting from low external demand. Consumer confidence declined sharply and a 47% fall in automotive output exacerbated the growing trade deficit.

Currency

The monetary unit is the *peso* (ARS), which replaced the austral on 1 Jan. 1992 at a rate of one peso = 10,000 australs. For nearly a decade the peso was pegged at parity with the US dollar, but it was devalued by nearly 30% in Jan. 2002 and floated in Feb. 2002. Inflation rates (based on IMF statistics):

1999	*2000*	*2001*	*2002*	*2003*	*2004*	*2005*	*2006*	*2007*	*2008*
−1·2%	−0·9%	−1·1%	25·9%	13·4%	4·4%	9·6%	10·9%	8·8%	8·6%

Gold reserves were 1·76m. troy oz in Sept. 2009; foreign exchange reserves were US$43,111m. Total money supply was 107,615m. pesos in Aug. 2009.

Budget

Central government revenue and expenditure (in 1m. pesos):

	2002	*2003*	*2004*
Revenue	44,015	64,711	81,428
Expenditure	61,507	74,570	81,870

VAT is 21% (reduced rate, 10·5%).

Performance

Real GDP growth rates (based on IMF statistics):

1999	*2000*	*2001*	*2002*	*2003*	*2004*	*2005*	*2006*	*2007*	*2008*
−3·4%	−0·8%	−4·4%	−10·9%	8·8%	9·0%	9·2%	8·5%	8·7%	6·8%

The economy grew in 1998 by 3·8% but shrank by 3·4% and 0·8% in 1999 and 2000 respectively, mainly as a result of the recession in Brazil, which started in 1998, and the devaluation of the Brazilian *real* in Jan. 1999. Total GDP was US$328·4bn. in 2008.

In March 2001 the economy minister, José Luis Machinea, resigned after a turbulent 15 months in which he had failed to revive a stagnant economy. As the economic situation deteriorated Argentina had a further five economy ministers in the space of just over a year. In Nov. 2001 the government tried to persuade creditors to accept a restructuring of the US$132bn. public debt, but on 23 Dec. 2001 interim President Adolfo Rodríguez Saá announced that Argentina would default on the debt payments—the biggest debt default in history.

Banking and Finance

The total assets of the Argentine Central Bank (BCRA) in Dec. 2007 were 228·92bn. pesos. The *President* of the Central Bank is Mercedes Marcó del Pont. In early 2002 banks and financial markets were temporarily closed as an emergency measure in response to the economic crisis that made the country virtually bankrupt. In 2002 there were 16 government banks, 24 private commercial banks, four co-operative banks, one other national bank (Banco Hipotecario Nacional) and 17 foreign banks.

There is a main stock exchange at Buenos Aires and there are others in Córdoba, Rosario, Mendoza and La Plata.

ENERGY AND NATURAL RESOURCES

Environment

Argentina's carbon dioxide emissions from the consumption and flaring of fossil fuels in 2008 were the equivalent of 4·3 tonnes per capita. An *Environmental Performance Index* compiled in 2008 ranked Argentina 38th in the world, with 81·8%. The index examined various factors in six areas—air pollution, biodiversity and habitat, climate change, environmental health, productive natural resources and water resources.

Electricity

Installed capacity in 2004 was 30·7m. kW. Electric power production (2004) was 100,260m. kWh; consumption per capita in 2004 was 2,714 kWh. In 2003 there were two nuclear reactors.

Oil and Gas

Oil production (2008) was 34·1m. tonnes. Reserves were 2·6bn. bbls in 2008. The oil industry was privatized in 1993. Natural gas extraction in 2008 was 44·1bn. cu. metres. Reserves were 440bn. cu. metres in 2008. The main area in production is the Neuquen basin in western Argentina, with over 40% of the total oil reserves and nearly half the gas reserves. Natural gas accounts for approximately 45% of all the energy consumed in Argentina. In 2004 Argentina exported 17% of the natural gas produced.

Minerals

Minerals (with production in 2005) include clays (6·4m. tonnes), salt (1·8m. tonnes), borates (632,792 tonnes), aluminium (270,714 tonnes), bentonite (247,101 tonnes), copper (187,317 tonnes), coal (51,000 tonnes in 2004), zinc (30,227 tonnes of metal), lead (10,683 tonnes of metal), silver (264 tonnes), gold (27,904 kg), granite, marble and tungsten. Production from the US$1·1bn. Alumbrera copper and gold mine, the country's biggest mining project, in Catamarca province in the northwest, started in late 1997. In 1993 the mining laws were reformed and state regulation was swept away, creating a more stable tax regime for investors. In Dec. 1997 Argentina and Chile signed a treaty laying the legal and tax framework for mining operations straddling the 5,000 km border, allowing mining products to be transported out through both countries.

Agriculture

In 2007 there were around 32·5m. ha. of arable land and 1·0m. ha. of permanent crops. The agricultural population was 3·45m. in 2004, of whom 1·46m. were economically active. 1·56m. ha. were irrigated in 2002. In 2003 organic crops were grown in an area covering 2·96m. ha. (the second largest area after Australia), representing 1·7% of all farmland.

Livestock (2002): cattle, 48,539,000; sheep, 12,559,000; goats, 4,061,000; pigs, 2,185,000; horses, 1,517,000. In 2000 wool production was 38,892 tonnes; milk (in 2007), 9,527m. litres; eggs (in 2007), 696m. dozen.

Crop production (in 1,000 tonnes) in 2006–07: soybeans, 47,500; maize, 21,800; sugarcane (1998–99), 18,193; wheat, 14,500; sunflower seeds, 3,500; potatoes (1997–98), 3,412. Cotton, vine, citrus fruit, olives and *yerba maté* (Paraguayan tea) are also cultivated. Argentina is the world's leading producer of sunflower seeds, and is now the fifth largest wine producer (15,396,000 hectolitres in 2006) after France, Italy, Spain and the USA; it ranked seventh in the world in 2004 for wine consumption and 11th for wine exports.

Forestry

The forest area was 33·02m. ha., or 12·1% of the total land area, in 2005. Production in 2006 included 1·75m. cu. metres of sawn wood, 8·80m. tonnes of rough timber, 1·43m. tonnes of paper and cardboard and 585,000 cu. metres of chipboard.

Fisheries
Fish landings in 2005 amounted to 931,472 tonnes, almost exclusively from sea fishing. Hake and squid are the most common catches.

INDUSTRY
Production, (in 1,000 tonnes): distillate fuel oil (2004), 10,590; cement (2007), 9,602; crude steel (2007), 5,388; pig iron (2007), 4,389; petrol (2004), 4,018; residual fuel oil (2004), 2,368; sugar (2006), 2,312; paper (2006), 1,721; jet fuel (2004), 1,209; polyethylene (2007), 575; synthetic rubber (2007), 54. Motor vehicles produced in 2003 totalled 109,364; tyres, 9,578,000; motorcycles, 11,430.

Labour
In 2005 the economically active population totalled 15·79m., of which 12·55m. were employed and 3·24m. were unemployed. The urban unemployment rate, which had been 12·9% in 1998, rose to a record 21·5% by May 2002 at the height of the economic crisis before falling to 15·6% in May 2003.

INTERNATIONAL TRADE
External debt was US$114,335m. in 2005.

Imports and Exports
Imports (c.i.f.) in 2007 totalled US$44,707m. (US$34,154m. in 2006); exports (f.o.b.), US$55,780m. (US$46,546m. in 2006).

Principal imports in 2007 (in US$1m.) were machinery and transport equipment (21,201); chemicals and related products (8,252); petroleum and petroleum products (1,835); iron and steel (1,498). Principal exports in 2007 (in US$1m.) were food and livestock (18,270); machinery and transport equipment (7,656); fixed vegetable fats and oils (5,208); petroleum and petroleum products (4,699).

In 2005 imports (in US$1m.) were mainly from Brazil (10,625); USA (4,532); China (1,529); Germany (1,335); Italy (766). Exports went mainly to Brazil (6,328); USA (4,570); Chile (4,497); China (3,154); Spain (1,565).

COMMUNICATIONS

Roads
In 2003 there were 231,374 km of roads, of which 30·0% were paved. The four main roads constituting Argentina's portion of the Pan-American Highway were opened in 1942. Vehicles in use in 2007 totalled 12,399,900. In 2005, 3,443 people were killed in road accidents.

Rail
Much of the 33,000 km state-owned network (on 1,000 mm, 1,435 mm and 1,676 mm gauges; 210 km electrified) was privatized in 1993–94. 30-year concessions were awarded to five freight operators; long-distance passenger services are run by contractors to the requirements of local authorities. Metro, light rail and suburban railway services are also operated by concessionaires.

In 2002 railways carried 17,469,000 tonnes of freight and 355,420,000 passengers. There were 37,856 km of track in 2002.

The metro and light rail network in Buenos Aires extended to 75 km in 2005.

Civil Aviation
The main international airport is Buenos Aires Ezeiza, which handled 5,958,649 passengers on international flights out of a total of 6,140,790 passengers in 2005. The second busiest airport is Buenos Aires Aeroparque, which handled 5,780,695 passengers in 2005. It is much more important as a domestic airport, with only 498,237 passengers on international flights in 2005. The national carrier, Aerolíneas Argentinas, was privatized in 1990 but renationalized in Sept. 2008. In 2003 it operated direct flights to Asunción, Auckland, Caracas, Florianópolis, Lima, London, Madrid, Miami, Montevideo, New York, Paris, Pôrto Alegre, Rio de Janeiro, Rome, Santa Cruz, Santiago, São Paulo and Sydney. There were direct flights in 2003 with other airlines to Barcelona, Bogotá, Cancún, Cape Town, Chicago, Cochabamba, Colonia, Dallas, Fortaleza, Frankfurt, Guayaquil, Havana, Johannesburg, Kuala Lumpur, La Paz, Los Angeles, Mexico City, Milan, the Netherlands Antilles, Panama City, Puerto Montt, Punta Cana, Punta del Este, Quito, Puerto Rico, Salvador, Varadero and Zürich.

In 2003 scheduled airline traffic of Argentinian-based carriers flew 104m. km, carrying 5,946,000 passengers (1,709,000 on international flights).

Shipping
The merchant shipping fleet totalled 423,000 GRT in 2002, including oil tankers totalling 51,000 GRT.

Telecommunications
The telephone service Entel was privatized in 1990. The sell-off split Argentina into two monopolies, operated by Telefónica Internacional de España, and a holding controlled by France Télécom and Telecom Italia. In Nov. 2000 the industry was opened to unrestricted competition. In 2008 there were 9·7m. main (fixed) telephone lines. In the same year mobile phone subscribers numbered 46·5m. (1,166·1 per 1,000 persons). There were 3·5m. PCs in use in 2005 and 11·2m. internet users in 2008.

Postal Services
In 2003 there were 5,724 post offices. In 2002, 5·3m. telegrams were sent.

SOCIAL INSTITUTIONS

Justice
Justice is administered by federal and provincial courts. The former deal only with cases of a national character, or those in which different provinces or inhabitants of different provinces are parties. The chief federal court is the Supreme Court, with five judges whose appointment is approved by the Senate. Other federal courts are the appeal courts, at Buenos Aires, Bahía Blanca, La Plata, Córdoba, Mendoza, Tucumán and Resistencia. Each province has its own judicial system, with a Supreme Court (generally so designated) and several minor chambers. The death penalty was reintroduced in 1976—for the killing of government, military police and judicial officials, and for participation in terrorist activities—but was abolished in 2008. The population in penal institutions in Dec. 2002 was 56,313 (148 per 100,000 of national population). In 2002 there were 1,340,529 crimes reported; and 23,538 guilty verdicts were passed.

The police force is centralized under the Federal Security Council.

Education
Adult literacy was 97·2% in 2003 (97·2% for both males and females). In 2005, 1,324,529 children attended pre-school institutions, 6,510,382 pupils were in basic general education, 1,545,992 in 'multimodal' secondary schooling and 509,134 in higher non-universities.

In 2006, in the public sector, there were 39 universities (including one technical university and one art institute) and university institutes of aeronautics, military studies, naval and maritime studies, and police studies. In the private sector, there were 40 universities (including seven Roman Catholic universities) and ten university institutes. In 2006 there were 1,304,003 students attending public universities and 279,373 at private universities.

In 2004 public expenditure on education came to 3·8% of GDP and 13·1% of total government spending.

Health
Free medical attention is obtainable from public hospitals. In 2001 there were 7,833 public health care institutions which had an average of 75,075 available beds. In 2002 there were 99,400 physicians.

Welfare

Until the end of 1996 trade unions had a monopoly in the handling of the compulsory social security contributions of employees, but private insurance agencies are now permitted to function alongside them.

Unique Social Security System Expenditure (in 1m. pesos):

	1999	*2000*
Retirement and pensions	17,508	17,386
Healthcare assistance and other forms of social insurance	5,249	5,440
Family allowances	1,879	1,920
Unemployment insurance, employment and training programmes	519	484
Work risks insurance	323	367
Other	2,201	2,361
Total	27,679	27,958

RELIGION

The Roman Catholic religion is supported by the State; affiliation numbered 29·92m. in 2001. There were four cardinals in Feb. 2010. There were 2·04m. Protestants of various denominations in 2001, 730,000 Muslims and 500,000 Jews. There were 275,000 Latter-day Saints (Mormons) in 1998.

CULTURE

World Heritage Sites

Argentina's heritage sites as classified by UNESCO (with year entered on list) are: Los Glaciares national park (1981), the Iguazu National Park (1984), and the Ischigualasto and Talampaya Natural Parks (2000). The Cueva de las Manos (Cave of Hands, 1999), in Patagonia, contains cave art that is between 1,000 and 10,000 years old. The Península Valdés (1999) in Patagonia protects several endangered species of marine mammal. The Jesuit Block and Estancias of Córdoba (2000) are the principal buildings of the Jesuit community from the 17th and 18th century. The Quebrada de Humahuaca (2003) is a valley on the Camino Inca trade route. Shared with Brazil, the Jesuit Missions of the Guaranis (1984) encompasses the ruins of five Jesuit missions.

Broadcasting

Broadcasting is overseen by the Comisión Nacional de Comunicaciones, the Comité Federal de Radiodifusión and the Asociación de Teleradiodifusoras Argentinas. There is a multiplicity of commercial radio and television stations, mainly owned by large conglomerates, and cable TV is widely available. Public broadcasting is limited: Canal 7 TV and Radio Nacional are nationwide state-operated services. There were 12·6m. TV receivers (colour by PAL N) in 2005.

Cinema

In 2006 there were 978 cinema screens with an audience of 35·4m. In 2005, 65 Argentinian films were released.

Press

In 2006 there were 184 daily newspapers with a combined circulation of 1·5m. The main newspapers are Clarin, La Nación and Crónica. In 2002 a total of 15,137 book titles were published.

Tourism

In 2005, 3,823,000 tourists visited Argentina (3,457,000 in 2004). Receipts in 2005 totalled US$2·7bn.

DIPLOMATIC REPRESENTATIVES

Of Argentina in the United Kingdom (65 Brook St., London, W1K 4AH)
Ambassador: Vacant.
Chargé d'Affaires a.i.: Osvaldo Mársico.

Of the United Kingdom in Argentina (Dr Luis Agote 2412, 1425 Buenos Aires)
Ambassador: Shan Morgan.

Of Argentina in the USA (1600 New Hampshire Ave., NW, Washington, D.C., 20009)
Ambassador: Héctor Timerman.

Of the USA in Argentina (Av. Colombia 4300, 1425 Buenos Aires)
Ambassador: Vilma S. Martinez.

Of Argentina to the United Nations
Ambassador: Jorge Argüello.

Of Argentina to the European Union
Ambassador: Jorge Remes Lenicov.

FURTHER READING

Bethell, L. (ed.) *Argentina since Independence.* 1994

Levitsky, Steven, *Argentine Democracy: The Politics of Institutional Weakness.* 2006

Lewis, P., *The Crisis of Argentine Capitalism.* 1990

Manzetti, L., *Institutions, Parties and Coalitions in Argentine Politics.* 1994

Pion-Berlin, David, *Broken Promises? The Argentine Crisis and Argentine Democracy.* 2006

Powers, Nancy R., *Grassroots Expectations of Democracy and Economy: Argentina in Comparative Perspective.* 2001

Romero, Luis Alberto, *A History of Argentina in the Twentieth Century;* translated from Spanish. 2002

Shumway, N., *The Invention of Argentina.* 1992

Wynia, G. W., *Argentina: Illusions and Realities.* 2nd ed. 1993

National Statistical Office: Instituto Nacional de Estadística y Censos (INDEC). Av. Julio A. Roca 615, PB (1067) Buenos Aires. *Director:* Ana María Edwin.

Website: http://www.indec.gov.ar

ARMENIA

Hayastani Hanrapetoutiun
(Republic of Armenia)

Capital: Yerevan
Population estimate, 2010: 3·09m.
GDP per capita, 2007: (PPP$) 5,693
HDI/world rank: 0·798/84

KEY HISTORICAL EVENTS

According to tradition, the kingdom was founded in the region of Lake Van by Haig, or Haik, a descendant of Noah. Historically, the region and former kingdom that was Greater Armenia lay east of the Euphrates River; Little, or Lesser, Armenia was west of the river. In 189 BC the Armenians split from the Syrians to found a native dynasty, the Artashesids. The imperialistic ambitions of King Tigranes led to war with Rome and defeated Armenia became a tributary kingdom. In the 3rd century AD it was overrun by Sassanian Persia. Armenia was the first country to adopt Christianity as its state religion, in the early 4th century. The persecution of Christians under Persian rule kindled nationalism, particularly after the partition in AD 387 of the kingdom between Persia and Rome. However, because of its strategic location, attempts at independence were short-lived, as Armenia was the constant prey of the Persians, Byzantines and Arabs, and later of the Turkish and Russian Empires.

In the early part of the 20th century the Armenians under Turkish rule suffered brutal persecution. An estimated 1·75m. were massacred or deported to present-day Syria from their homeland in Anatolia. Armenia enjoyed a brief period of independence after the First World War but in 1920 the country was proclaimed a Soviet Socialist Republic. After the collapse of Communism, 99% of voters supported a breakaway from the Soviet Union. A declaration of independence in Sept. 1991 was followed by presidential elections after which President Levon Ter-Petrosyan came to an agreement on economic co-operation with the other Soviet republics and joined the CIS. A new constitution adopted in July 1995 led to National Assembly elections. President Ter-Petrosyan was re-elected in Sept. 1996. OSCE observers noted 'very serious irregularities' in the conduct of the election and there were demonstrations in Yerevan, leading to several deaths.

Hostilities with Azerbaijan over the enclave of Nagorno-Karabakh were brought to an end with a 1994 ceasefire. Resigning over Nagorno-Karabakh in Feb. 1998, President Ter-Petrosyan was succeeded by Robert Kocharian, who was sworn in as president in April 1998. On 27 Oct. 1999, five men burst into the parliamentary chamber, killing the Prime Minister, Vazgen Sarkisian, and seven other officials. Aram Sarkisian, brother of the slain prime minister, was named as his successor. In April 2001 a first round of high-level talks on the settlement of the Nagorno-Karabakh conflict was held in Florida. Armenia and Azerbaijan agreed, in principle, to continue talks.

TERRITORY AND POPULATION

Armenia covers an area of 29,743 sq. km (11,484 sq. miles). It is bounded in the north by Georgia, in the east by Azerbaijan and in the south and west by Iran and Turkey.

The 2001 census population was 3,213,011 (53·1% females); population density, 108 per sq. km. The United Nations population estimate for 2001 was 3,065,000. Armenians account for 97·9%, Kurds 1·3% and Russians 0·5%—in 1989, prior to the Nagorno-Karabakh conflict, 2·6% of the population were Azeris. 64·1% lived in urban areas in 2007.

The UN gives an estimated population for 2010 of 3·09m.

According to the Second Armenia-Diaspora Conference in May 2002 there are approximately 10m. Armenians worldwide.

The capital is Yerevan (1,103,488 population in 2001). Other large towns are Gyumri (formerly Leninakan) (150,917 in 2001) and Vanadzor (formerly Kirovakan) (107,394 in 2001).

The official language is Armenian.

SOCIAL STATISTICS

2005 births, 37,499; deaths, 26,379; marriages, 16,624; divorces, 2,466. Rates, 2005 (per 1,000 population): birth, 11·7; death, 8·2; marriage, 5·2; divorce, 0·8. Infant mortality, 2005, 26 per 1,000 live births. Annual population growth rate, 2000–05, 0·0%. Life expectancy at birth, 2007, 70·1 years for men and 76·7 years for women; fertility rate, 2004, 1·3 births per woman.

CLIMATE

Summers are very dry and hot although nights can be cold. Winters are very cold, often with heavy snowfall. Yerevan, Jan. –9°C, July 28°C. Annual rainfall 318 mm.

CONSTITUTION AND GOVERNMENT

The constitution was adopted by a nationwide referendum on 5 July 1995. The head of state is the *President*, directly elected for five-year terms. Parliament is a 131-member *Azgayin Zhoghov* (National Assembly), with 90 deputies elected by party list and 41 chosen by direct election. The government is nominated by the President.

National Anthem

'Mer Hayrenik, azat ankakh' ('Land of our fathers, free and independent'); words by M. Nalbandyan, tune by B. Kanachyan.

RECENT ELECTIONS

In presidential elections held on 19 Feb. 2008 incumbent prime minister Serzh Sargsyan received 52·8% of votes cast, ahead of

Levon Ter-Petrosyan (the president from 1991–98) with 21·5%, Artur Baghdasarian with 17·7% and six other candidates. Turnout was 72·1%. Although the OSCE commended the conduct of the election, there was subsequently a series of protests against alleged electoral fraud held in Yerevan organized by supporters of Ter-Petrosyan.

Elections to the National Assembly were held on 12 May 2007. The Republican Party of Armenia (HHK) won 64 seats with 32·8% of the vote; Prosperous Armenia (BHK), 24 seats (14·7%); Armenian Revolutionary Federation (HHD), 16 (12·7%); Rule of Law (OE), 9 (6·8%); Heritage Party (Z) 6 (5·8%). The remaining seats went to smaller parties. Turnout was 60·0%.

CURRENT ADMINISTRATION

President: Serzh Sargsyan; b. 1954 (HHK; in office since 9 April 2008).

In March 2010 the government comprised:

Prime Minister: Tigran Sargsyan; b. 1960 (ind.; appointed 9 April 2008).

Deputy Prime Minister and Minister of Territorial Administration: Armen Gevorgyan.

Minister of Foreign Affairs: Edvard Nalbandyan. *Defence:* Seyran Ohanyan. *Justice:* Gevorg Danielyan. *Education and Science:* Armen Ashotyan. *Health:* Harutiun Kushkyan. *Culture:* Hasmik Poghosyan. *Transportation and Communications:* Gurgen Sargsyan. *Agriculture:* Gerasim Alaverdyan. *Environmental Protection:* Aram Harutyunyan. *Economy:* Nerces Yeritzyan. *Finance:* Tigran Davtyan. *Energy and Natural Resources:* Armen Movsissyan. *Urban Development:* Vardan Vardanyan. *Labour and Social Affairs:* Mkhitar Mnatsakanyan. *Sport and Youth Affairs:* Arthur Petrosyan. *Emergency Situations:* Mher Shahgeldyan. *Diaspora Affairs:* Hranush Hacobyan.

Government Website: http://www.gov.am

CURRENT LEADERS

Serzh Sargsyan

Position
President

Introduction
Serzh Sargsyan was sworn into office on 9 April 2008, nearly two months after he was declared the winner of the disputed presidential election. Although said to be fair by international observers, the election sparked violent clashes with police. A 20-day state of emergency was declared by the government before Sargsyan took office.

Early Life
Sargsyan was born on 30 June 1954 in Stepanakert, the capital of the Nagorno-Karabakh region. He enrolled at Yerevan State University in 1971 but served in the Soviet armed forces from 1972–74. He then worked as a metal turner from 1975–79 before graduating from the philological department of Yerevan State University in 1979. In the same year he became the divisional head of the Young Communist Union for Stepanakert.

Rising through the ranks of the Communist Party, Sargsyan was the leader of the Nagorno-Karabakh Republic self-defence forces committee during the Nagorno-Karabakh conflict of 1989–93, masterminding many battles. From 1993–95 he served as the Armenian minister of defence and was appointed head of the state security department in 1995. He was later promoted to minister of national security. In 1996 he took over the ministry of interior portfolio when it merged with the ministry of national security. When the offices separated in 1999, Sargsyan retained the ministry of national security. In the same year he joined the president's office as chief of staff and was selected as secretary of Armenia's national security council. In 2000 he returned to the defence ministry, where he served until 2007.

Sargsyan joined the conservative Republican Party of Armenia (HHK) in 2006 and from July 2006 to Nov. 2007 chaired the party council. He became party chairman in Nov. 2007. On 4 April 2007 President Robert Kocharian appointed Sargsyan prime minister after the sudden death of incumbent Andranik Margaryan. On 19 Feb. 2008 Sargsyan won the presidential election by a landslide.

Career in Office
Responding to the violent protests that followed his election victory, Sargsyan called for unity and co-operation among all political factions. He appointed the non-partisan Tigran Sargsyan, former chairman of the central bank, as prime minister. Serzh Sargsyan has aimed to raise living standards and promote economic growth. He has also sought to improve international relations, especially with Armenia's neighbours. Turkey's rejection of charges of genocide in Armenia during the First World War has previously posed a stumbling block to bilateral reconciliation, but in Oct. 2009 the two governments agreed on a framework to normalize relations, subject to parliamentary ratification by both sides. Meanwhile, Azerbaijan refuses to concede its claim on Nagorno-Karabakh, although at a Russian-hosted meeting in Nov. 2008 Sargsyan and the Azeri president agreed to intensify their efforts to find a political settlement over the territory.

DEFENCE

There is conscription for 24 months. Total active forces numbered 42,080 in 2007, including 25,105 conscripts.

Defence expenditure in 2006 totalled US$184m. (US$62 per capita), representing 2·9% of GDP.

There is a Russian military base in Armenia with 3,170 personnel in 2007.

Army

Current troop levels are 38,950, plus air and defence aviation forces of 2,220, air/air defence joint command forces of 915 and paramilitary forces of 4,750. There are approximately 210,000 Armenians who have received some kind of military service experience within the last 15 years.

INTERNATIONAL RELATIONS

There is a dispute over the mainly Armenian-populated enclave of Nagorno-Karabakh, which lies within Azerbaijan's borders—Armenia and Azerbaijan are technically still at war.

Armenia is a member of the UN, World Bank, IMF and several other UN specialized agencies, WTO, Council of Europe, OSCE, BSEC, CIS, IOM, NATO Partnership for Peace and Asian Development Bank. It is among biggest recipients of US government aid.

ECONOMY

In 2006 agriculture contributed 19·6% of GDP, industry 43·6% and services 36·8%.

Overview

After independence in 1991 most agricultural land was privatized. By the end of 2000, with support from the IMF and the World Bank, over 80% of medium and large enterprises and 90% of small enterprises had been privatized. Following reforms in 2001 to strengthen the business environment and promote exports and investment, the economy experienced five consecutive years of double-digit growth. It has also benefited from grants from foreign countries and the Armenian diaspora. The construction sector's share in GDP has expanded considerably, whilst reliance on agriculture and manufacturing has declined. There is potential for tourism, with visitor numbers growing consistently. However, despite an overall reduction, poverty levels remain high.

Currency

In Nov. 1993 a new currency unit, the *dram* (AMD) of 100 *lumma*, was introduced to replace the rouble. Inflation, which had been

5,273% in 1994, was 4·4% in 2007 and 9·0% in 2008. Foreign exchange reserves were US$658m. in July 2005 and total money supply was 164,589m. drams.

Budget

In 2004 total revenue was 302,249m. drams and total expenditure 333,970m. drams.

VAT is 20%.

Performance

Real GDP growth was 13·2% in 2006, 13·7% in 2007 and 6·8% in 2008. Total GDP in 2008 was US$11·9bn.

Banking and Finance

The *Chairman* of the Central Bank (founded in 1993) is Arthur Javadyan. In 2008 there were 22 commercial banks. There are commodity and stock exchanges in Yerevan and Gyumri.

ENERGY AND NATURAL RESOURCES

Environment

Armenia's carbon dioxide emissions from the consumption and flaring of fossil fuels in 2008 were the equivalent of 3·7 tonnes per capita.

Electricity

Output of electricity in 2004 was 6·03bn. kWh. Capacity was estimated at 3·3m. kW in 2004. Consumption per capita was 1,744 kWh in 2004. A nuclear plant closed in 1989 was reopened in 1995 because of the blockade of the electricity supply by Azerbaijan.

Minerals

There are deposits of copper, zinc, aluminium, molybdenum, marble, gold and granite.

Agriculture

The chief agricultural area is the valley of the Arax and the area round Yerevan. Here there are cotton plantations, orchards and vineyards. Almonds, olives and figs are also grown. In the mountainous areas the chief pursuit is livestock raising. In 2007 there were an estimated 406,000 ha. of arable land and 54,000 ha. of permanent crops Major agricultural production (in tonnes in 2003): potatoes, 508,000; tomatoes, 226,000; wheat, 217,000; cabbage, 98,000; grapes, 82,000; barley, 68,000. Livestock (2003): sheep, 553,000; cattle, 514,000; pigs, 111,000; goats, 50,000; chickens, 3m.

Forestry

In 2005 forests covered 283,000 ha., or 10·0% of the total land area. Timber production in 2007 was 44,000 cu. metres.

Fisheries

Total catch in 2004 came to 218 tonnes, exclusively from inland waters.

INDUSTRY

Among the chief industries are chemicals, producing mainly synthetic rubber and fertilizers, the extraction and processing of building materials, ginning- and textile-mills, carpet weaving, and food processing (including wine-making).

Labour

In 2006 the population of working age was 2·04m., of whom 1·09m. were employed: 46% in agriculture, hunting and forestry, 10% in manufacturing. The registered unemployment rate was 7·4% of the workforce in 2006. The average monthly salary in 2008 was 92,759 drams.

INTERNATIONAL TRADE

External debt was US$1,861m. in 2005.

Imports and Exports

Imports and exports for calendar years in US$1m.:

	2002	2003	2004	2005	2006
Imports f.o.b.	882·5	1,130·2	1,196·3	1,592·8	1,921·3
Exports f.o.b.	513·8	696·1	738·3	1,004·9	1,018·6

The main import suppliers in 2004 were Russia (13·3%), Belgium (8·3%), United Kingdom (8·2%) and USA (7·7%). Principal export markets were Belgium (15·2%), Israel (13·8%), Germany (11·6%) and Russia (10·6%). Manufactured goods account for 27% of Armenia's imports, food and live animals 16%, and mineral fuels and lubricants also 16%. Manufactured goods (in particular diamonds) account for 52% of Armenia's exports, crude materials (excluding fuels) 14%, and beverages and tobacco 9%.

COMMUNICATIONS

Roads

There were 7,515 km of road network in 2007, of which 89·8% were paved. In 1996 there were 5,760 passenger cars, buses, coaches, lorries and vans as well as 7,200 motorcycles and mopeds. There were 371 fatalities as a result of road accidents in 2007.

Rail

Total length in 2005 was 845 km of 1,520 mm gauge. Passenger-km travelled in 2003 came to 47m. and freight tonne-km to 354m.

There is a metro and a tramway in Yerevan.

Civil Aviation

There is an international airport at Yerevan (Zvartnots). The main Armenian carrier is Armavia. In 2003 there were direct flights from Yerevan to 34 international destinations. In 2005 scheduled airline traffic of Armenian-based carriers carried 264,000 passengers.

Telecommunications

Telephone subscribers numbered 785,800 in 2004 (259·7 per 1,000 inhabitants), of which 203,300 were mobile phone subscribers. There were 200,000 PCs in use (66·1 for every 1,000 persons) in 2004 and 150,000 internet users.

Postal Services

In 2002 there were 943 post offices.

SOCIAL INSTITUTIONS

Justice

In 2006, 9,757 crimes were reported, including 96 murders or attempted murders. The population in penal institutions in Jan. 2007 was 3,520 (109 per 100,000 of national population). The death penalty was abolished in 2003.

Education

Armenia's literacy rate was 99·4% in 2003 (99·7% among males and 99·2% among females). In 2007, 48,015 children attended pre-school institutions. There were 127,546 pupils in primary schools with 6,606 teaching staff; and 336,877 pupils in secondary schools with 43,372 teaching staff. At the tertiary level there were 107,398 students in 2007 and 12,521 academic staff. The National Academy of Sciences of the Republic of Armenia (NAS RA), located in Yerevan, comprises more than 50 institutions and organizations with a staff of over 3,700.

Public expenditure on education in 2006 came to 2·6% of GNI.

Health

In 2006 there were 12,388 physicians, 18,574 paramedics and 140 hospitals with 14,276 beds.

Welfare

In 2008 there were 523,839 pensioners. The average monthly pension was 21,370 drams in 2008.

RELIGION

Armenia adopted Christianity in AD 301, thus becoming the first Christian nation in the world. The Armenian Apostolic Church is headed by its Catholicos (Karekin II, b. 1951) whose seat is at Echmiatsin, and who is head of all the Armenian (Gregorian) communities throughout the world. In 1995 it numbered 7m. adherents (4m. in diaspora). The Catholicos is elected by representatives of parishes. The Catholicos of Cilicia is Aram I (b. 1947), with seat at Antelias. In 2001, 65% of the population belonged to the Armenian Apostolic Church.

CULTURE

World Heritage Sites

There are three UNESCO sites in Armenia: the Monasteries of Haghpat and Sanahin (inscribed in 1996 and 2000); the Monastery of Geghard and the Upper Azat Valley (2000); the Cathedral and Churches of Echmiatsin and the Archaeological Site of Zvartnots (2000).

Broadcasting

Public TV of Armenia and Public Radio of Armenia are the state-run national broadcasters. There are more than 40 private television stations, the largest of which is Armenia TV. Russian television channels can also be received. Public Radio of Armenia runs two national radio services and the Voice of Armenia external service. There are some private radio stations. There were 762,000 television-equipped households in 2005 (colour by SECAM H).

Press

In 2006 there were eight daily newspapers and 46 non-dailies with a combined circulation of 84,000.

Tourism

In 2005 there were 319,000 foreign tourists bringing in receipts of US$161m.

Libraries

There were 1,045 libraries in 2006, which lent 12·1m. items.

Theatre and Opera

380,000 people attended 26 theatres in 2006.

Museums and Galleries

In 2006 there were 96 museums with 878,000 visitors.

DIPLOMATIC REPRESENTATIVES

Of Armenia in the United Kingdom (25A Cheniston Gdns, London, W8 6TG)
Ambassador: Vahe Gabrielyan.

Of the United Kingdom in Armenia (34 Baghramyan Ave., Yerevan 375019)
Ambassador: Charles Lonsdale.

Of Armenia in the USA (2225 R St., NW, Washington, D.C., 20008)
Ambassador: Tatoul Markarian.

Of the USA in Armenia (1 American Ave., Yerevan 375082)
Ambassador: Marie Yovanovitch.

Of Armenia to the United Nations
Ambassador: Garen Nazarian.

Of Armenia to the European Union
Ambassador: Avet Adonts.

FURTHER READING

Brook, S., *Claws of the Crab: Georgia and Armenia in Crisis.* 1992
De Waal, Thomas, *Black Garden: Armenia and Azerbaijan Through Peace and War.* 2003
Hovannisian, R. G., *The Republic of Armenia.* 4 vols. 1996
Libaridian, Gerard J., *The Challenge of Statehood: Armenian Political Thinking Since Independence.* 1999
Malkasian, M., *Gha-Ra-Bagh: the Emergence of the National Democratic Movement in Armenia.* 1996
Masih, Joseph, *Armenia: At the Crossroads.* 1998
Walker, C. J., *Armenia: The Survival of a Nation.* 1990

National Statistical Office: National Statistical Service of the Republic of Armenia, Republic Square, 3 Government House, Yerevan 375010. *President:* Stepan L. Mnatsakanyan.
Website: http://www.armstat.am

AUSTRALIA

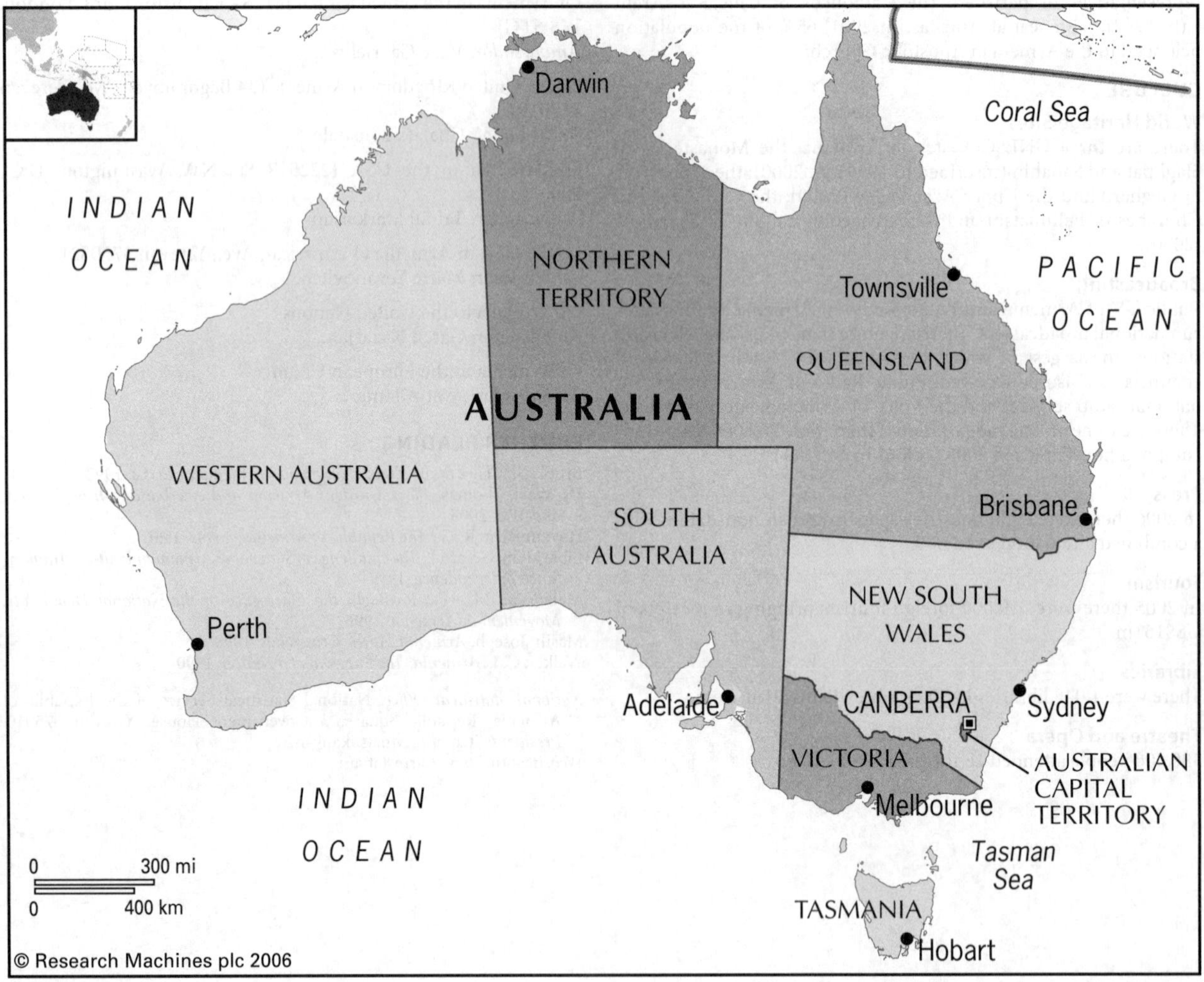

Commonwealth of Australia

Capital: Canberra
Population estimate, 2010: 21·51m.
GDP per capita, 2007: (PPP$) 34,923
HDI/world rank: 0·970/2

KEY HISTORICAL EVENTS

The Australian landmass, reaching northwards to Papua New Guinea and including Tasmania in the south, was inhabited in prehistoric times until adverse climatic conditions led to a population exodus between 15,000 and 25,000 years ago. A population using stone tools was in evidence by 2000–1000 BC.

The Aboriginal society was composed of extended family groups. At maximum there were 1m. Aborigines, using 200 different languages. By the early 18th century there was contact with traders from the area of modern Indonesia and Papua New Guinea.

Various dates are given for the European discovery of Australia but the north coast was explored by traders from the South long before any Europeans ventured into the area. Australia was sighted in 1522 by compatriot explorers of the Portuguese Ferdinand Magellan and in 1642 the Dutch explorer Abel Tasman mapped what is now Tasmania and part of New Zealand's east coast. By the middle of the century the Dutch had charted the western part of Australia, calling it New Holland.

But while the Dutch, Portuguese and Spanish made the early running in charting the continent, it was the discovery of the east coast by Capt. James Cook in 1770 that prompted colonization. Over the course of several voyages he charted the Torres Strait and 8,000 kilometres of coastline. Having lost their penal settlements in the American War of Independence, the British decided to send convicts to Australia. Botany Bay was selected as the first settlement.

By 1800 the colony was self-sufficient in food and convicts had established legal rights as crown subjects. Many freed men were able to make a successful living. However, there were several uprisings against penal rule culminating in the Rum Rebellion of 1808, in which John Macarthur led a troop of New South Wales officers against Gov. William Bligh. The response of the British government was to appoint Lachlan Macquarie, who promoted reform.

His tenure began a period of development in which Australia ceased to be primarily a penal settlement. The crossing of the Blue Mountains in 1813 was the first of many expeditions which led to discovery of vast areas of good grazing land, although sealing and whaling were more important than agriculture until the 1830s. Macquarie's benevolent despotism rewarded freed men and several of the more talented were appointed to official posts. He did much to develop Sydney, instigating public works and establishing a bank and currency. His policies caused concern in London and by 1815 his costs were spiralling. In 1822 he was forced to resign.

The Aboriginal question remained unresolved throughout the early 19th century. The early assumption that the Aboriginal people were nomadic meant that Britain had claimed much of the Australian land without an agreement of purchase from the natives. There was some peaceful interaction with the Aborigines but resentment grew as British encroachment damaged Aboriginal culture. Diseases brought in by the colonists decimated the Aboriginal population. By the late 18th century there was widespread and persistent conflict. The most notable Aboriginal resistance leader was Pemulwuy (killed in 1802) who fought battles at Hawkesbury and Parramatta. Between 1820–50 the indigenous population fell from 600,000 to 300,000.

Trade and Prosperity

The wool trade took off in the middle of the 19th century. The introduction of the Merino sheep meant that between 1830–50 Australia's share of the British wool market rose from 10% to 50%, accounting for 90% of all Australia's exports. The pastoral economy boomed and from the 1830s the population was swelled by 'free immigrants' from Britain. A settler population of 30,000 in 1820 grew to over 1·1m. in 1860. The economy was further boosted by the discovery of copper and gold in several locations and by 1850 Victoria accounted for one third of the world's gold supply. The gold rushes attracted prospectors from Britain, the USA, Western and Central Europe and China.

Sydney, Melbourne, Adelaide and Perth all grew during these boom decades, developing their own institutions and gradually attaining a degree of self-rule. New South Wales, Tasmania and Victoria were granted full parliamentary control of their own affairs in 1855, with South Australia and the newly formed Queensland following in the next five years. However, the UK government retained control of foreign policy and kept a power of veto.

By the 1860s there was a culture of bushranging as epitomized by Ned Kelly. Bad relations between settlers, immigrant workers and the Aboriginal population persisted. The population passed 3m. in 1888. In the 1890s recession the economy shrank by 30%. Unemployment among skilled workers stood at 30% in 1893 and was higher among unskilled workers, for whom records were not kept. Problems were exacerbated by a severe drought in the east of the country.

Social and Constitutional Reform

Trade unionism grew from the 1870s, gaining strength in the 1890s. Between 1899, when a first Labor government took power in Queensland, and the outbreak of the First World War, Labor was in government in every state. Union membership included a third of all workers. The 1890s witnessed the emergence of the federalist movement, with Sydney hosting conventions in 1891 and 1897–98. On 1 Jan. 1901 the six separately constituted colonies of New South Wales, Victoria, Queensland, South Australia, Western Australia and Tasmania were federated under the name of the Commonwealth of Australia, the designation of 'colonies' being at the same time changed into that of 'states'—except in the case of Northern Territory, which was transferred from South Australia to the Commonwealth as a 'territory' on 1 Jan. 1911. A bicameral parliament was established while the states retained certain powers. Foreign policy continued to be guided by London and in 1907 Australia gained dominion status. By the following year there was female suffrage for the national and all state legislatives.

The Labor party formed its first national government in 1904 and their old allies in the protectionist parties forged an alliance with free trade parties, forming the Liberal party to challenge Labor's growth. A period in which the government switched between Labor and the Liberals saw pension and welfare reforms. The growing fear of an Asian (and especially Japanese) threat—Britain was reluctant to keep a strong military presence in the Pacific—led to the development of the army and navy.

In 1911 a site in New South Wales was designated the Australian capital, to be known as Canberra. Construction began in 1923 and the Federal Parliament was opened in Canberra in 1927. With the outbreak of the First World War Australia rallied to the British cause but at significant cost. Around 330,000 Australian troops served in the war—60,000 died and over 150,000 were wounded. Such losses caused unrest and conscription was rejected by referendum in 1916. In addition Australia lost its markets in France, Belgium and Germany, which together accounted for 30% of its exports. The economy contracted by 10% in 1914 and unemployment soared.

The Labor party, in power at the start of the war, gave way to a national government. The effect of the war years kept Labor out of power until 1929. The early 1920s was a period of recovery, assisted by an influx of 200,000 immigrants from Britain. Sydney and Melbourne expanded to a point where they accounted for a third of the Australian population. However, the economy (with the notable exception of the wool industry) relied on government subsidy, leaving it exposed in the depression which followed the 1929 Wall Street Crash. Under Labor public spending was cut, a 10% reduction in wages imposed and the currency devalued by 25%. Unemployment approached 30%. The government collapsed but the depression had the long-term effect of radicalizing the trade unions.

Jo Lyons and the recently formed United Australia Party took over the government. Lyons was succeeded by Robert Menzies in 1939. The late 1930s saw deteriorating relations with Japan but broad support for the policy of appeasement of Nazi Germany. However, when war became inevitable, Australia again rallied to the imperial cause. 100,000 Australian troops were killed or wounded. Fear of Japan escalated after Pearl Harbor and Darwin was attacked in 1942. These events marked a watershed in foreign relations, with the Labor prime minister, John Curtin, commenting that 'Australia looks to America, free from any pangs about our traditional links of friendship to Britain.'

Post-War Recovery

The war encouraged the rapid expansion of Australian industry and the 1950s and 1960s were something of a golden age. Robert Menzies led successive Liberal governments from 1949–66. The population nearly doubled as immigration from Britain and continental Europe was encouraged. Unemployment was consistently low and the economy tripled in size during the two decades. Aware of its 'junior partner' status in the relationship with America, Australia undertook nuclear development with Britain. In 1951 it entered the ANZUS group with New Zealand and the USA and three years later joined the South-East Asian Treaty Organization. Australia's new found confidence was reflected in the success of the 1956 Melbourne Olympics.

The growing number of non-English speaking immigrants accentuated racial problems, with a succession of governments holding to a monocultural policy. The future of the Aboriginal population was one of assimilation. The movement for Aboriginal rights grew after the war, with a strike by Aboriginal workers at Pilbara in 1946 marking a new phase in the conflict. It climaxed in 1966 when an Aboriginal demand for equal pay in Northern

Australia turned into demands for land. There was a swathe of moderate reforms favouring the Aboriginal population between 1959–67 but at the same time the assimilation policy allowed for the forced removal of large numbers of children from their families. The last of the Aboriginal reserves was taken over in the 1960s. The policy of forced removal of children did not prompt an apology until the 1980s.

When Menzies retired in 1966 he was followed by a succession of leaders who weakened the standing of the Liberals. Australia's participation in the Vietnam War also drew criticism. Gough Whitlam led the Labor party to power in 1972 and oversaw a radical administration. He withdrew Australian forces from Vietnam, set about modernizing the education and health programmes and funded extensive urban renewal. Government expenditure doubled over his three years in office and Australia was ill-prepared when the global oil crisis struck in 1974.

Whitlam's Liberal opponents, many of whom regarded him as a dangerous maverick, led a parliamentary revolt. A failure to win approval for the national budget led to a constitutional crisis in which the Governor-General John Kerr (himself recommended for the post by Whitlam) dismissed the prime minister and invited Malcolm Fraser to form an administration. Fraser believed that Australian society had become overly dependent on the state. He authorized cuts in public spending but was unable to counter rising unemployment and inflation and was voted out of government in 1983.

Free Market Politics

Bob Hawke took power at the head of a Labor government, assisted by his finance minister (and successor as prime minister), Paul Keating. Their terms of office, spanning 1983–96, saw a shift in Labor's stance on state control and economic planning to allow for an ambitious programme of privatization and financial deregulation. Trade with Asia took on increasing importance and Hawke stood fully behind US foreign policy. In March 1986 the Australia Act abolished the remaining legislative, executive and judicial controls of the British Parliament. By the end of the decade unemployment stood at a respectable 6% but the Australian dollar had suffered a 40% loss of value in 1986 and foreign debt stood at around 30% of GNP. Keating described the recession of the late 1980s as 'necessary'.

Keating took over the premiership in 1991 and mounted a programme of economic reform. He was replaced in 1996 by the Liberal, John Howard, who pressed on with economic reforms and won re-election two years later. The Aboriginal question continued to test every government. There were some symbolic gestures such as the return of Ayers Rock (with its Aboriginal name Uluru restored) in 1988. The High Court's Mabo ruling of 1992, which overturned a previous ruling that the Aboriginal title to land had not survived British settlement, raised expectations. Keating officially acknowledged injustices to the Aboriginal population when the 'Native Title' legislation was passed in Dec. 1993. Howard's tenure, however, saw disputes over indigenous land rights following a 1996 court ruling against Aboriginal access to cultural sites owned by non-Aboriginals.

A referendum to decide if Australia should become a republic was held on 6 Nov. 1999. 54·87% of votes cast were in favour of the monarchy with Queen Elizabeth II as head of state, against 45·13% for a republic with a president chosen by parliament. In foreign policy Howard agreed to military involvement in UN peacekeeping in Timor-Leste and NATO action against Serbia. His government's approach to immigration came under the spotlight in July 2001, when a refugee-laden Norwegian cargo ship was caught in a diplomatic gridlock between Australia, the UN and Norway. Its passengers were eventually diverted to Papua New Guinea, with Howard assuming a firm and populist stance against asylum seekers. He won a further term of office at the elections of Nov. 2001. The Liberals also won the elections of Oct. 2004. Howard pursued an interventionist foreign policy in the Pacific region—with notable success in the peacekeeping mission to the Solomon Islands—and committed Australia to the US-led war in Iraq in 2003. Labor returned to power with victory in the elections of Nov. 2007.

TERRITORY AND POPULATION

Australia, excluding external territories, covers a land area of 7,703,354 sq. km, extending from Cape York (10° 41' S) in the north some 3,680 km to South East Cape, Tasmania (43° 39' S), and from Cape Byron, New South Wales (153° 39' E) in the east some 4,000 km west to Steep Point, Western Australia (113° 9' E). External territories under the administration of Australia comprise the Ashmore and Cartier Islands, Australian Antarctic Territory, Christmas Island, the Cocos (Keeling) Islands, the Coral Sea Islands, the Heard and McDonald Islands and Norfolk Island. For these *see below.*

Growth in census population has been:

1901	3,774,310	1966	11,599,498	1991	16,852,258
1911	4,455,005	1971	12,755,638	1996	17,752,829
1921	5,435,734	1976	13,915,500	2001	18,769,249
1947	7,579,358	1981	15,053,600	2006	19,855,288
1961	10,508,186	1986	15,763,000		

Population (preliminary estimate) at 31 March 2009 was 21,779,100.

The UN gives an estimated population for 2010 of 21·51m.

At the census of 8 Aug. 2006 density was 2·6 per sq. km. In 2005, 88·2% of the population lived in urban areas.

Areas and populations of the States and Territories at the 2006 census:

States and Territories	*Area (sq. km)*	*Population*	*Per sq. km*
New South Wales (NSW)	801,352	6,549,177	8·2
Victoria (Vic.)	227,590	4,932,422	21·7
Queensland (Qld.)	1,734,190	3,904,532	2·3
South Australia (SA)	985,324	1,514,337	1·5
Western Australia (WA)	2,532,422	1,959,088	0·8
Tasmania (Tas.)	67,914	476,481	7·0
Northern Territory (NT)	1,352,212	192,898	0·1
Australian Capital Territory (ACT)	2,349	324,034	137·9

Resident population in capitals and other statistical districts with more than 150,000 population (2006 census figures):

Capital	*State*	*Population*	*Capital*	*State*	*Population*
Canberra	ACT	323,056	Darwin	NT	105,991
Sydney	NSW	4,119,190	*Statistical district*		
Melbourne	Vic.	3,592,591	Newcastle	NSW	493,467
Brisbane	Qld.	1,763,131	Gold Coast[1]	Qld.	541,675
Adelaide	SA	1,105,839	Wollongong	NSW	263,535
Perth	WA	1,445,078	Sunshine Coast[2]	Qld.	209,578
Hobart	Tas.	200,525	Geelong	Vic.	160,992

[1]Includes part of Tweed Shire (in NSW).
[2]Includes Caloundra, Maroochy and Noosa.

The median age of the 2006 census population was 37 years.

Australians born overseas (census 2006), 4,416,037 (22·2%—one of the highest proportions in the industrialized world), of whom 856,939 (4·3%) were from England.

Aboriginals have been included in population statistics only since 1967. At the 2006 census 455,031 people identified themselves as being of indigenous origin (2·3% of the total population). A 1992 High Court ruling that the Meriam people of the Murray Islands had land rights before the European settlement reversed the previous assumption that Australia was *terra nullius* before that settlement. The Native Title Act setting up a system for deciding claims by Aborigines came into effect on 1 Jan. 1994.

Overseas arrivals and departures:

	Settler arrival numbers[1]	Permanent departure numbers	Net permanent migration
2001–02	84,400	45,900	38,500
2002–03	89,400	48,100	41,300
2003–04	111,600	59,100	52,500
2004–05	123,400	62,600	60,800

[1]Equals the total number of people entitled to permanent residence actually arriving.

The Migration Act of Dec. 1989 sought to curb illegal entry and ensure that annual immigrant intakes were met but not exceeded. Provisions for temporary visitors to become permanent were restricted. According to the 2006 census, 73% of the population born overseas have become Australian citizens. In May 2008 the government announced that 190,300 immigrants would be admitted in 2008–09.

The national language is English.

SOCIAL STATISTICS

Life expectancy at birth, 2007, 79·0 years for males and 83·7 years for females.

Statistics for years ended 30 June:

	Births	Deaths	Marriages	Divorces
2003	251,161	132,292	106,394	53,145
2004	254,246	132,508	110,958	52,747
2005	259,791	130,707	109,323	52,399
2006	265,949	133,739	114,222	51,375
2007	285,200	137,854	116,322	47,963

In 2007 the median age for marrying was 31·6 years for males and 29·3 for females. Infant mortality, 2007, was 4·2 per 1,000 live births. Population growth rate in the year ended 31 March 2008, 1·6%; fertility rate, 2007, 1·9 births per woman.

Suicide rates (per 100,000 population, 2005): 10·3 (men, 16·4; women, 4·3).

A UNICEF report published in 2005 showed that 14·7% of children in Australia live in poverty (in households with income below 50% of the national median), compared to just 2·4% in Denmark.

In the Human Development Index, or HDI (measuring progress in countries in longevity, knowledge and standard of living), Australia was ranked second (behind Norway) in the 2007 rankings published in the annual Human Development Report.

CLIMATE

Over most of the continent, four seasons may be recognized. Spring is from Sept. to Nov., summer from Dec. to Feb., autumn from March to May and winter from June to Aug., but because of its great size there are climates that range from tropical monsoon to cool temperate, with large areas of desert as well. In northern Australia there are only two seasons, the wet one lasting from Nov. to March, but rainfall amounts diminish markedly from the coast to the interior. Central and southern Queensland are subtropical, north and central New South Wales are warm temperate, as are parts of Victoria, Western Australia and Tasmania, where most rain falls in winter. Canberra, Jan. 68°F (20°C), July 42°F (5·6°C). Annual rainfall 25" (635 mm). Adelaide, Jan. 73°F (22·8°C), July 52°F (11·1°C). Annual rainfall 21" (528 mm). Brisbane, Jan. 77°F (25°C), July 58°F (14·4°C). Annual rainfall 45" (1,153 mm). Darwin, Jan. 83°F (28·3°C), July 77°F (25°C). Annual rainfall 59" (1,536 mm). Hobart, Jan. 62°F (16·7°C), July 46°F (7·8°C). Annual rainfall 23" (584 mm). Melbourne, Jan. 67°F (19·4°C), July 49°F (9·4°C). Annual rainfall 26" (659 mm). Perth, Jan. 74°F (23·3°C), July 55°F (12·8°C). Annual rainfall 35" (873 mm). Sydney, Jan. 71°F (21·7°C), July 53°F (11·7°C). Annual rainfall 47" (1,215 mm).

CONSTITUTION AND GOVERNMENT

Federal Government

Under the Constitution legislative power is vested in a Federal Parliament, consisting of the Queen, represented by a Governor-General, a Senate and a House of Representatives. Under the terms of the constitution there must be a session of parliament at least once a year.

The Senate (Upper House) comprises 76 Senators (12 for each State voting as one electorate and, as from Aug. 1974, two Senators respectively for the Australian Capital Territory and the Northern Territory). Senators representing the States are chosen for six years. The terms of Senators representing the Territories expire at the close of the day next preceding the polling day for the general elections of the House of Representatives. In general, the Senate is renewed to the extent of one-half every three years, but in case of disagreement with the House of Representatives, it, together with the House of Representatives, may be dissolved, and an entirely new Senate elected. Elections to the Senate are on the single transferable vote system; voters list candidates in order of preference. A candidate must reach a quota to be elected, otherwise the lowest-placed candidate drops out and his or her votes are transferred to other candidates.

The *House of Representatives* (Lower House) consists, as nearly as practicable, of twice as many Members as there are Senators, the numbers chosen in the several States being in proportion to population as shown by the latest statistics, but not less than five for any original State. The 150 membership is made up as follows: New South Wales, 50; Victoria, 37; Queensland, 27; South Australia, 12; Western Australia, 15; Tasmania, 5; ACT, 2; Northern Territory, 2. Elections to the House of Representatives are on the alternative vote system; voters list candidates in order of preference, and if no one candidate wins an overall majority, the lowest-placed drops out and his or her votes are transferred. The first Member for the Australian Capital Territory was given full voting rights as from the Parliament elected in Nov. 1966. The first Member for the Northern Territory was given full voting rights in 1968. The House of Representatives continues for three years from the date of its first meeting, unless sooner dissolved.

Every Senator or Member of the House of Representatives must be a subject of the Queen, be of full age, possess electoral qualifications and have resided for three years within Australia. The franchise for both Houses is the same and is based on universal (males and females aged 18 years) suffrage. Compulsory voting was introduced in 1925. If a Member of a State Parliament wishes to be a candidate in a federal election, he must first resign his State seat.

Executive power is vested in the *Governor-General*, advised by an Executive Council. The Governor-General presides over the Council, and its members hold office at his pleasure. All Ministers of State, who are members of the party or parties commanding a majority in the lower House, are members of the Executive Council under summons. A record of proceedings of meetings is kept by the Secretary to the Council. At Executive Council meetings the decisions of the Cabinet are (where necessary) given legal form, appointments made, resignations accepted, proclamations, regulations and the like made.

The policy of a ministry is, in practice, determined by the Ministers of State meeting without the Governor-General under the chairmanship of the Prime Minister. This group is known as the *Cabinet*. There are 11 Standing Committees of the Cabinet comprising varying numbers of Cabinet and non-Cabinet Ministers. In Labor governments all Ministers have been members of Cabinet; in Liberal and National Country Party governments, only the senior ministers. Cabinet meetings are private and deliberative, and records of meetings are not made public. The Cabinet does not form part of the legal mechanisms of government; the decisions it takes have, in themselves, no legal effect. The Cabinet substantially controls, in ordinary circumstances, not only the general legislative programme of Parliament but the whole course of Parliamentary proceedings. In effect, though not in form, the Cabinet, by reason of the fact that all Ministers are members of the Executive Council, is also the dominant element in the executive government of the country.

The legislative powers of the Federal Parliament embrace trade and commerce, shipping, etc.; taxation, finance, banking, currency, bills of exchange, bankruptcy, insurance, defence, external affairs, naturalization and aliens, quarantine, immigration and emigration; the people of any race for whom it is deemed necessary to make special laws; postal, telegraph and like services; census and statistics; weights and measures; astronomical and meteorological observations; copyrights; railways; conciliation and arbitration in disputes extending beyond the limits of any one State; social services; marriage, divorce, etc.; service and execution of the civil and criminal process; recognition of the laws, Acts and records, and judicial proceedings of the States. The Senate may not originate or amend money bills. Disagreement with the House of Representatives may result in dissolution and, in the last resort, a joint sitting of the two Houses. The Federal Parliament has limited and enumerated powers, the several State parliaments retaining the residuary power of government over their respective territories. If a State law is inconsistent with a Commonwealth law, the latter prevails.

The Constitution also provides for the admission or creation of new States. Proposed laws for the alteration of the Constitution must be submitted to the electors, and they can be enacted only if approved by a majority of the States and by a majority of all the electors voting.

The Australia Acts 1986 removed residual powers of the British government to intervene in the government of Australia or the individual states.

In Feb. 1998 an Australian Constitutional Convention voted for Australia to become a republic. In a national referendum, held on 6 Nov. 1999, 54·9% voted against Australia becoming a republic.

State Government

In each of the six States (New South Wales, Victoria, Queensland, South Australia, Western Australia, Tasmania) there is a State government whose constitution, powers and laws continue, subject to changes embodied in the Australian Constitution and subsequent alterations and agreements, as they were before federation. The system of government is basically the same as that described above for the Commonwealth—i.e. the Sovereign, her representative (in this case a Governor), an upper and lower house of Parliament (except in Queensland, where the upper house was abolished in 1922), a cabinet led by the Premier and an Executive Council. Among the more important functions of the State governments are those relating to education, health, hospitals and charities, law, order and public safety, business undertakings such as railways and tramways, and public utilities such as water supply and sewerage. In the domains of education, hospitals, justice, the police, penal establishments, and railway and tramway operation, State government activity predominates. Care of the public health and recreative activities are shared with local government authorities and the Federal government; social services other than those referred to above are now primarily the concern of the Federal government; the operation of public utilities is shared with local and semi-government authorities.

Administration of Territories

Since 1911 responsibility for administration and development of the Australian Capital Territory (ACT) has been vested in Federal Ministers and Departments. The ACT became self-governing on 11 May 1989. The ACT House of Assembly has been accorded the forms of a legislature, but continues to perform an advisory function for the Minister for the Capital Territory.

On 1 July 1978 the Northern Territory of Australia became a self-governing Territory with expenditure responsibilities and revenue-raising powers broadly approximating those of a State.

National Anthem

'Advance Australia Fair' (adopted 19 April 1984; words and tune by P. D. McCormick). The 'Royal Anthem' (i.e. 'God Save the Queen') is used in the presence of the Royal Family.

GOVERNMENT CHRONOLOGY

Prime Ministers since 1945. (ALP = Australian Labor Party; LP = Liberal Party; CP = Australian Country Party)

1945	ALP	Francis Michael (Frank) Forde
1945–49	ALP	Joseph Benedict (Ben) Chifley
1949–66	LP	Robert Gordon Menzies
1966–67	LP	Harold Edward Holt
1967–68	CP	John (Jack) McEwen (acting)
1968–71	LP	John Grey Gorton
1971–72	LP	William (Bill) McMahon
1972–75	ALP	(Edward) Gough Whitlam
1975–83	LP	(John) Malcolm Fraser
1983–91	ALP	Robert James Lee (Bob) Hawke
1991–96	ALP	Paul John Keating
1996–2007	LP	John Winston Howard
2007–	ALP	Kevin Michael Rudd

RECENT ELECTIONS

The 42nd Parliament was elected on 24 Nov. 2007.

House of Representatives

Australian Labor Party (ALP), 83 seats and 43·4% of votes cast; Liberal Party (LP), 55 seats and 36·3% of votes cast; National Party of Australia (NP), 10 (5·5%); ind., 2 (2·2%). The Greens received 7·8% of the vote but did not win any seats.

Senate

As at March 2010 the make-up of the Senate was Australian Labor Party, 32; Liberal Party, 32; Greens, 5; National Party of Australia, 4; Northern Territory Country Liberal Party, 1; Family First, 1; Independent, 1.

CURRENT ADMINISTRATION

Governor-General: Quentin Bryce, AC, b. 1942 (took office on 5 Sept. 2008).

Following the 2007 general election the first Labor government since 1996 was formed. In March 2010 the cabinet comprised:

Prime Minister: Kevin Michael Rudd; b. 1957 (ALP; in office since 3 Dec. 2007).

Deputy Prime Minister and Minister for Education, Employment and Workplace Relations, and Social Inclusion: Julia Gillard. *Treasurer:* Wayne Swan. *Agriculture, Fisheries and Forestry:* Tony Burke. *Broadband, Communications and Digital Economy:* Stephen Conroy. *Climate Change, Energy Efficiency and Water:* Penny Wong. *Defence:* John Faulkner. *Environment Protection, Heritage and the Arts:* Peter Garrett. *Families, Housing, Community Services and Indigenous Affairs:* Jenny Macklin. *Finance and Deregulation:* Lindsay Tanner. *Financial Services, Superannuation and Corporate Law, and Human Services:* Chris Bowen. *Foreign Affairs:* Stephen Smith. *Health and Ageing:* Nicola Roxon. *Immigration and Citizenship:* Chris Evans. *Infrastructure, Transport, Regional Development and Local Government:* Anthony Albanese. *Innovation, Industry, Science and Research:* Kim Carr. *Resources and Energy, and Tourism:* Martin Ferguson. *Trade:* Simon Crean. *Cabinet Secretary and Special Minister of State:* Joe Ludwig. *Attorney General:* Robert McClelland.

The *Speaker* is Harry Jenkins (ALP).

The *President* of the Senate is John Hogg (ALP).

Leader of the Opposition: Tony Abbott (LP).

Government: http://www.gov.au

CURRENT LEADERS

Kevin Rudd

Position
Prime Minister

Introduction
Having defeated Kim Beazley to become leader of the Australian Labor Party (ALP) in Dec. 2006, Kevin Rudd maintained his political momentum into the Nov. 2007 general election in which he ousted Prime Minister John Howard's centre-right government from power. Meanwhile, he has sought to modernize the ALP—out of power for more than a decade—but has faced opposition from trade unions (over proposed changes to industrial relations laws) and from within the party. Although his fiscal policy plans have been deflected by the effects of the global financial crisis, he has maintained a high voter approval rating as a capable leader and economic manager.

Early Life
Kevin Rudd was born on 21 Sept. 1957 in Queensland, the son of a dairy farmer who died after a car accident when Kevin was just 11. At 15 Rudd joined the Labor Party. In 1981 he graduated in Chinese language and history from Australian National University. His fluency in Mandarin led to a role as a diplomat, working at embassies in Beijing and Stockholm before moving to the Department of Foreign Affairs and Trade's Policy Planning Bureau.

In 1988 Rudd moved into state politics, becoming chief of staff to the then Queensland opposition leader Wayne Goss. The ALP came to power the following year after 32 years in opposition. Rudd was appointed director general of the Office of the Cabinet in Goss' government, during which time he earned a reputation for overseeing public service cutbacks. In 1996 Rudd stood for election to the federal House of Representatives. However, the ALP suffered heavy losses at both state and federal levels and he was unsuccessful. He left politics immediately after, becoming a business consultant and adjunct professor of Asian languages at the University of Queensland.

In 1998 Rudd secured election to the federal parliamentary seat of Griffith, Brisbane, although the ALP failed to dislodge the ruling Liberal-National coalition from power. He was promoted to opposition spokesman on foreign affairs, trade and national security and led criticism of Howard's handling of the 2003 Iraq war, calling for an inquiry into intelligence failures. His political rise was nevertheless controversial; he was accused of self-promotion in 2003 when he greeted Hu Jintao, the Chinese president, in Mandarin and was attacked ferociously by a former ALP leader, Mark Latham, in his autobiography.

In Nov. 2006 Rudd declared that he would challenge Kim Beazley for the leadership of the ALP, pledging a new style of politics. He won by 49 votes to 39 and was officially announced as leader on 4 Dec. 2006.

Career in Office
Following the ALP's election victory, Rudd was sworn in on 3 Dec. 2007. He promised the staged withdrawal of Australian combat troops from Iraq (achieved by mid-2008) and a 'three pillars' approach to foreign policy through closer engagement with the UN, Asia and the US-led coalition. He also pledged substantial extra investment in health and education, despite some concerns over a faltering economy. On taking office he immediately reversed the Howard government's refusal to ratify the Kyoto protocol on climate change and its decision to sell uranium to India (which is not a signatory of the Nuclear Non-Proliferation Treaty).

In Feb. 2008 Rudd made a formal apology in parliament for past injustices by the state against the indigenous population, and in July he reversed the long-standing policy of detaining all asylum seekers upon arrival until their cases are heard. Meanwhile, on his return from an overseas tour of the USA, Europe and China, he announced the appointment in April of human rights lawyer Quentin Bryce as Australia's first female Governor-General.

His government's first budget, presented in May 2008, sought to address rising inflation while earmarking anticipated budget surplus funds for infrastructure, education and health service investment. However, in response to the effects of the worsening global financial crisis, Rudd announced in Oct. a $A10·4bn. stimulus package to boost the economy, support families and households, and create jobs. Further government funding to help the ailing Australian motor industry followed in Nov. The next budget, delivered in May 2009, revealed a deficit of nearly 5% of GDP (one of the largest ever), underlining the economy's fragility. Rudd nevertheless used the budget to invest further in infrastructure and clean energy projects while cutting forms of middle class tax breaks. Also in May 2009, the government published a defence White Paper envisaging weapons modernization and procurement costing about US$70bn.

In Nov. 2009 Rudd offered a formal apology to surviving British children who had been forcibly shipped to Australian orphanages and other institutions and suffered abuse and neglect between 1930 and 1970.

DEFENCE

The Minister for Defence has responsibility under legislation for the control and administration of the Defence Force. The Chief of Defence Force Staff is vested with command of the Defence Force. He is the principal military adviser to the Minister. The Chief of Naval Staff, the Chief of the General Staff and the Chief of the Air Staff command the Navy, Army and Air Force respectively. They have delegated authority from the Chief of Defence Force Staff and the Secretary to administer matters relating to their particular Service. Conscription was abolished in 1972.

2008 defence expenditure was US$18,399m., amounting to US$876 per capita. In 2007 defence spending represented 1·9% of GDP.

Having contributed to the 2003 US-led invasion of Iraq, the last Australian troops left the country in July 2009. There were 1,350 Australian troops serving with the International Security Assistance Force (ISAF) in Afghanistan in Oct. 2009.

Army

The strength of the Army was 25,259 in 2007. The effective strength of the Army Reserve was 17,200.

Women have been eligible for combat duties since 1993.

Navy

The all-volunteer Navy had 12,784 personnel in 2007, with a reserve of 1,850. Equipment in 2007 included six diesel-powered submarines and 12 frigates.

The main naval bases are at Sydney and Perth with further bases at Cairns and Darwin.

Air Force

The Royal Australian Air Force (RAAF) operated 120 combat capable aircraft including F-111s and F-18 'Hornets' in 2007. Personnel in 2007 numbered 13,250. There is also an Australian Air Force Reserve, 2,400-strong.

INTERNATIONAL RELATIONS

Australia is a member of the UN, World Bank, IMF and several other UN specialized agencies, WTO, BIS, Commonwealth, IOM, OECD, Asian Development Bank, APEC, Colombo Plan, the Pacific Islands Forum, SPC and Antarctic Treaty.

Australia gave US$2·7bn. in international aid in 2007, equivalent to 0·32% of GNI (compared to the UN target of 0·7%).

ECONOMY

In the year ended 30 June 2004 service industries accounted for almost 56% of GDP and manufacturing 10·9%.

According to the anti-corruption organization *Transparency International*, Australia ranked equal eighth in the world in a 2009 survey of the countries with the least corruption in business and government. It received 8·7 out of 10 in the annual index.

Overview

In 15 continuous years of strong economic expansion, the economy has grown at an average annual rate of 3·6%, more than 1% higher than the OECD average. Reforms in the 1980s and early 1990s liberalized the previously heavily-protected and regulated economy. Increased competition and technological advances have helped drive productivity gains. The Economist Intelligence Unit estimates that average annual total factor productivity growth over the period 1991–2000 was 1·67%, six times greater than the previous decade's average. The OECD has stressed the importance of sound macroeconomic policies backed by a framework emphasizing transparency and accountability. Reform and good management facilitated growth even in the face of global economic crises such as the Asian crisis of 1997–98 and the US downturn of 2001–02.

The buoyant domestic economy withstood the impact of a severe drought in 2003 and a global slowdown. A fall in the housing market from its 2004 peak brought down growth rates but a commodities boom helped cushion the economy. The terms of trade improved by 30% between 2005–08 to register their highest level for over 50 years. A position of near full employment in 2007 saw unemployment at its lowest since the mid-1970s. Per capita GDP compares favourably with that of Western European countries and services account for the majority of output. Australia has promoted itself to global and regional businesses (especially in the financial sector) as an ideal location for back office operations. Its location in the Asia-Pacific region adds to its business attractiveness, although labour shortages, infrastructure deficiencies and limited port capacity are obstacles to commercial development. According to the World Bank, Australia ranks 9th out of 183 economies for the ease of doing business. The export sector is driven by mining and agriculture although there are concerns about the long-term revenue dependency on natural resources.

The global financial crisis starting in 2007 hit the economy but owing to its limited higher-tech manufacturing, robust commodity exports and an effective policy response, real activity has not suffered as much as in other advanced nations. Government response has been strong, with two fiscal stimulus packages to support domestic demand and interest rates reduced by 425 basis points between Sept. 2008 and Jan. 2010. The banking sector remains sound and has adjusted its funding structure. With the lower risk of serious economic contraction, the Reserve Bank of Australia has adopted a tighter monetary policy with interest rates back on the rise. The OECD forecasts a positive recovery in the short-term, with growth set to reach 2·5% in 2010 and unemployment likely to peak at around 6% before moderating. However, the IMF suggests high household debt (at 150% of disposable income in 2008) and short-term external borrowing make the near-term outlook uncertain. Long term, the National Reform Agenda's focus on increasing worker participation and labour productivity may ease the impact of an ageing population.

Currency

On 14 Feb. 1966 Australia adopted a system of decimal currency. The currency unit, the Australian dollar (AUD), is divided into 100 *cents*.

Foreign exchange reserves were US$34,857m. in Sept. 2009 and gold reserves 2·57m. troy oz. Total money supply was $A376·5bn. in July 2009.

Inflation rates (based on OECD statistics):

1999	*2000*	*2001*	*2002*	*2003*	*2004*	*2005*	*2006*	*2007*	*2008*
1·5%	4·5%	4·4%	3·0%	2·8%	2·3%	2·7%	3·5%	2·3%	4·4%

Budget

The fiscal year is 1 July–30 June. In Aug. 1998 the Commonwealth government introduced a tax reform package including, from 2000, the introduction of a Goods and Services Tax (GST) at a 10% rate, with all the revenues going to the states in return for the abolition of a range of other indirect taxes; the abolition of Financial Assistance Grants to states; the abolition of wholesale sales tax (which is levied by the Commonwealth government); cuts in personal income tax; and increases in social security benefits, especially for families. In the 2007–08 Mid-Year Economic and Fiscal Outlook an underlying cash surplus of $A14·8bn. (1·3% of GDP) was anticipated in 2007–08, an increase of $A4·2bn. since the 2007–08 budget.

The Australian Government levies income taxes. State expenditure is backed by federal grants. Australian Government General Government Sector expenses and revenue outcomes (in $A1m.):

	2006–07	*2007–08*[1]
Total expenses (by function)	219,362	235,410
including		
General public services	14,615	15,774
Defence	16,854	19,243
Public order and safety	3,318	3,772
Education	16,898	17,386
Health	39,948	43,357
Social security and welfare	92,075	95,132
Housing and community amenities	2,909	3,345
Recreation and culture	2,561	2,861
Fuel and energy	4,635	5,310
Agriculture, fisheries and forestry	2,831	3,685
Mining, manufacturing and construction	1,920	2,046
Transport and communication	3,296	4,484
Other economic affairs	5,165	6,123
Other purposes	12,338	12,893
Total revenue (by source)	237,008	251,885
including		
Income tax		
Individuals and other witholding	117,614	121,650
Fringe benefits tax	3,754	3,970
Superannuation funds	7,879	10,130
Company tax	58,538	65,250
Petroleum resource rent tax	1,594	2,060
Indirect tax		
Excise duty—Petroleum products and crude oil	16,479	14,830
Other excise	6,255	8,260
Total excise duty	22,734	23,090
Customs duty	5,644	6,010
Other taxes	3,748	3,710
Non-tax revenue	15,504	16,013

[1]Estimate.

Performance

Real GDP growth rates (based on OECD statistics):

1999	*2000*	*2001*	*2002*	*2003*	*2004*	*2005*	*2006*	*2007*	*2008*
4·5%	3·5%	2·1%	4·0%	3·4%	3·2%	3·1%	2·6%	4·2%	2·3%

In fiscal year 2009 (July 2008–June 2009) the GDP growth rate was 1·1%. The current account deficit was expected to widen to 6·25% of GDP in 2006–07 reflecting increasing world interest rates and a higher stock of net foreign debt. During much of the 1990s the real GDP growth rate, along with lower inflation, made the Australian economic performance one of the best in the OECD area. In 2008 total GDP was US$1,015·2bn.

Banking and Finance

From 1 July 1998 a new financial regulatory framework based on three agencies was introduced by the Australian government, following recommendations by the Financial System Inquiry. The framework included changes in the role of the Reserve Bank of Australia and creation of the Australian Prudential Regulation Authority (APRA) with responsibility for the supervision of deposit-taking institutions (comprising banks, building societies and credit unions), friendly societies, life and general insurance companies and superannuation funds. It further involved replacement of the Australian Securities Commission with the Australian Securities and Investments Commission (ASIC) with responsibility for the regulation of financial services and Australia's 1·2m. companies.

The banking system comprises:

(a) The Reserve Bank of Australia is the central bank. It has two broad responsibilities—monetary policy and the maintenance of financial stability, including stability of the payments system. It also issues Australia's currency notes and provides selected banking and registry services to Commonwealth Government customers and some overseas official institutions. Within the Reserve Bank there are two Boards: the Reserve Bank Board and the Payments System Board; the *Governor* (present incumbent, Glenn Stevens) is the Chairman of each.

At 30 June 2006 total assets of the Reserve Bank of Australia were $A109,932m., including gold and foreign exchange, $A76,889m.; and Australian dollar securities, $A31,102m. At 30 June 2006 capital and reserves were $A6,325m. and main liabilities were Australian notes on issue, $A38,069m.; and deposits, $A46,212m.

A wholly owned subsidiary of the Reserve Bank (Note Printing Australia Limited) manufactures currency notes and other security documents for Australia and for export.

(b) Four major banks: (i) The Commonwealth Bank of Australia; (ii) the Australia and New Zealand Banking Group Ltd; (iii) Westpac Banking Corporation; (iv) National Australia Bank.

(c) The Commonwealth Bank of Australia has a subsidiary—Commonwealth Development Bank. There are nine other Australian-owned banks—Adelaide Bank Ltd, AMP Bank Ltd, Bank of Queensland Ltd, Bendigo Bank Ltd, Elders Rural Bank (50% owned by Bendigo Bank Ltd), Macquarie Bank Ltd, Members Equity Pty Ltd, St George Bank Ltd and Suncorp-Metway Ltd.

(d) There are ten banks incorporated in Australia which are owned by foreign banks and 30 branches of foreign banks (these figures include five foreign banks which have both a subsidiary and a branch presence in Australia).

(e) According to the Australian Prudential Regulation Authority (APRA), as at 30 June 2006 there were 52 authorized banks with Australian banking assets of $A1,363·5bn., with 5,147 branches, 24,616 reported ATMs and 540,189 reported EFTPOS terminals. As at 30 June 2006 there were 14 building societies with assets of $A17·9bn. and 144 credit unions with assets of $A35·7bn.

There is an Australian Stock Exchange (ASX) in Sydney.

ENERGY AND NATURAL RESOURCES

Environment

Australia's carbon dioxide emissions from the consumption and flaring of fossil fuels were the equivalent of 20·8 tonnes per capita in 2008. An *Environmental Performance Index* compiled in 2008 ranked Australia 46th in the world, with 79·8%. The index examined various factors in six areas—air pollution, biodiversity and habitat, climate change, environmental health, productive natural resources and water resources.

With only 0·003% of the world's population, Australia emits 1·4% of the world's greenhouse gases, making the country the largest generator of greenhouse gases per capita. However, in 2004 the government launched a $A1·8bn. Climate Change Strategy. A centrepiece of the government's Energy White Paper is a $A500m. Low Emissions Technology Demonstration Fund.

Electricity

Electricity supply is the responsibility of the State governments. 2007–08 total production was 228,600m. kWh (5·2% hydro-electric). In 2007–08 consumption stood at 201,307m. kWh including 57,868m. kWh by residential customers.

Oil and Gas

The main fields are located in the Gippsland Basin (Vic.) and the North West Shelf (WA). In 2006, three new offshore fields (Enfield, Vincent and Stybarrow) in the Carnarvon Basin (WA) were expected to supply about 280,000 bbls of crude oil production per day. Crude oil and condensate production was 25,870m. litres in 2007–08, a reduction of 7·2% over the previous year. The ex-mine value of oil and natural gas production in 2004–05 totalled $A14·33bn. Oil reserves at the end of 2008 totalled 4·2bn. bbls and natural gas reserves 2,510bn. cu. metres. Natural gas production (2007–08) was 39·3bn. cu. metres.

Minerals

Australia is the world's largest producer of bauxite and alumina. It is the world's largest producer of diamonds, ranking first for industrial-grade diamonds and second for gem-grade diamonds, after Botswana. It is also the third largest gold and uranium producer. Black coal is Australia's major source of energy. Reserves are large (2005: 39·2bn. economically recoverable tonnes) and easily worked. The main fields are in New South Wales and Queensland. Brown coal (lignite) reserves are mined principally in Victoria and South Australia. In 2005–06 raw coal production was 398m. tonnes; lignite production, 71m. tonnes; and iron ore and concentrates, 250m. tonnes.

Estimated production of other major minerals in 2005–06 (in tonnes): bauxite, 61m.; alumina (2005), 17·7m.; salt, 11·8m.; manganese, 4·1m.; zinc, 1·4m.; nickel, 183,000; uranium, 9,974; silver, 2,218; gold, 250. Diamond production, 2005–06: 25·4m. carats.

Agriculture

At 30 June 2005 there were an estimated 129,934 establishments mainly engaged in agriculture; the estimated total area of land under agricultural use was 445·1m. ha. (about 57% of total land area). Gross value of agricultural production in 2004–05, $A36·2bn., including (in $A1bn.) cattle and calves slaughtering, 7·3; sheep and lamb slaughtering, 1·7; wheat, 4·3; wool, 2·2; milk, 3·2. In year ending 30 June 2005 there were 24·8m. ha. of crops. An estimated 2·41m. ha. of crops and pastures were irrigated in 2004–05. Important crops (2004–05): wheat (22·6m. tonnes from 13·8m. ha.); barley (7·7m. tonnes from 4·6m. ha.); grain sorghum (2·2m. tonnes from 0·81m. ha.); oats (1·3m. tonnes from 0·89m. ha.); canola (1·5m. tonnes from 1·4m. ha.); sugarcane (37·5m. tonnes from 0·44m. ha.). Severe drought in recent years has held back the production of wheat, Australia's most important crop. In the year ended 30 June 2007 an estimated 1·53m. tonnes of grapes were harvested from 173,776 ha. of vines.

Beef cattle farming represents the largest sector, accounting for 25% of farming establishments. Livestock totals at June 2005: beef cattle and calves, 24·7m.; dairy cattle, 3·0m.; sheep and lambs, 102·7m.; pigs, 2·5m. Livestock products (in 1,000 tonnes) in 2004–05: beef and veal, 2,162; lamb and mutton, 591; pigmeat, 389; poultry meat, 792; wool, 525. Milk in the same year, 10,125m. litres.

Estimated fruit and vegetable production in 2004–05 (in 1,000 tonnes): potatoes, 1,288; oranges, 498; tomatoes, 408; apples, 327; carrots, 316; bananas, 266; onions, 256.

Wine production (2006): 14,263,000 hectolitres. Australia was the sixth largest wine producer in the world in 2006 (5·0% of the global total) and the fourth largest wine exporter (9·1% of the global total).

In 2003 organic crops were grown in an area covering 10m. ha. (the largest area of any country in the world), representing 2·2% of all farmland.

Australia is the world's leading wool producer; only China has more sheep.

Forestry

The Federal government is responsible for forestry at the national level. Each State is responsible for the management of publicly owned forests. Estimated total native forest cover was 164·5m. ha. at June 2006 (approximately 21·4% of Australia's land area), made up of (in 1,000 ha.): public forest, 121·6m.; privately owned, 38·9m. The major part of wood supplies derives from coniferous plantations, of which there were 1,001,100 ha. in 2006. Australia also had 807,400 ha. of broadleaved plantation in 2006. Timber production in 2007 was 32·26m. cu. metres.

Fisheries

The Australian Fishing Zone covers an area 16% larger than the Australian land mass and is the third largest fishing zone in the world, but fish production is insignificant by world standards owing to low productivity of the oceans. The major commercially exploited species are prawns, rock lobster, abalone, tuna, other fin fish, scallops, oysters and pearls. Estimated total fisheries production in 2005–06 came to 240,988 tonnes with a gross value of $A2·13bn. In the same year aquaculture production was an estimated 54,076 tonnes with a gross value of $A748·32m., which represented 35% of the total value of fisheries production.

INDUSTRY

The leading companies by market capitalization as at March 2009 were: BHP Billiton Ltd (Australian/British), a resources company (US$118·2bn.); Rio Tinto (Australian/British), a mining company (US$51·6bn.); and Westpac Banking (US$38·6bn.).

Manufacturing industry in 2004–05 contributed almost 11% to Australia's GDP. In May 2006 almost 1·1m. people were employed, 10% of Australia's total employed.

Manufacturing by sector in the year ended 30 June 2005:

	Labour costs in $A1m.	*Total income in $A1m.*
Food, beverages and tobacco	8,764	71,996
Textiles, clothing, footwear and leather products	1,656	9,501
Wood and paper products	3,020	18,499
Printing, publishing and recorded media	5,101	22,300
Chemical, petroleum, coal and associated products	5,646	59,504
Non-metallic mineral products	2,250	14,304
Metal products	8,347	64,897
Machinery and equipment	11,254	63,467
Other manufacturing	2,325	13,025

Manufactured products in 2004–05 included: clay bricks, 1,704m.; portland cement, 8·9m. tonnes; ready-mixed concrete, 23m. cu. metres; tobacco and cigarettes (2003–04), 18,785 tonnes; newsprint (2003–04), 421m. tonnes; pig iron, 6·5m. tonnes; aviation turbine fuel, 5,325m. litres; beer, 1,686m. litres.

According to the World Bank's *Doing Business 2010* Australia is the third easiest country in which to start a business, after New Zealand and Canada.

Labour

In 2005–06 the total labour force (persons aged 15 and over) numbered 10,605,300 (4,770,700 females). In 2005–06 there were 10,065,800 employed persons (44·9% females) with 2,885,400 in part-time employment (72% females). The majority of wage and salary earners have had their minimum wages and conditions of work prescribed in awards by the Industrial Relations Commission. In Oct. 1991 the Commission decided to allow direct employer-employee wage bargaining, provided agreements reached are endorsed by the Commission. In some States, some conditions of work (e.g. weekly hours of work, leave) are set down in State legislation. Average weekly wage, May 2006, $A1,041·60 (men, $A1,101·20; women, $A932·90). Average weekly hours worked by full-time employed person, 2004–05: 40·7 hours. Four weeks annual leave is standard. In 2004–05 part-time work accounted for 29% of all employment in Australia and persons born overseas made up 25% of the total labour force.

Employees in all States are covered by workers' compensation legislation and by certain industrial award provisions relating to work injuries.

In 2005 there were 472 industrial disputes recorded which accounted for 228,300 working days lost (379,800 in 2004). In these disputes 241,000 workers were involved.

In 2004–05 retail trade (15% of employed persons) and property and business services (12%) were the largest employers, ahead of the manufacturing industry (11%). Health and community services employ 10%.

In Aug. 2005, 1,581,600 (19%) wage and salary earners worked in the public sector and 6,945,900 (81%) in the private sector.

The following table shows the percentage distribution of employed persons in 2004–05 according to the *Australian Standard Classification of Occupations:*

	Employed persons (%)
Professionals	18·7
Intermediate clerical, sales and service workers	16·6
Tradespersons and related workers	12·6
Associate professionals	12·6
Elementary clerical, sales and service workers	9·9
Labourers and related workers	9·0
Intermediate production and transport workers	8·4
Managers and administrators	8·3
Advanced clerical and service workers	3·7

In 2005–06, 539,500 persons were unemployed, of whom 17·9% had been unemployed for more than one year. The unemployment rate in Dec. 2009 was 5·5% (compared to 4·2% in 2008 as a whole).

Trade Unions

In Aug. 2006, 1·79m. employees were members of a trade union representing 20·0% of all full-time employees (19·3% females). Many of the larger trade unions are affiliated with central labour organizations, the oldest and by far the largest being the Australian Council of Trade Unions (ACTU) formed in 1927. In 2002, 46 unions were affiliated to ACTU, representing approximately 1·8m. workers. In July 1992 the Industrial Relations Legislation Amendment Act freed the way for employers and employees to negotiate enterprise-based awards and agreements.

INTERNATIONAL TRADE

In 1990 Australia and New Zealand completed a Closer Economic Relations agreement (initiated in 1983) which establishes free trade in goods. Net foreign debt was $A359·0bn. as at 30 June 2003 (an increase of 9·0% on the previous year). In 1998 the effect of the Asian meltdown on exports resulted increasingly in shipments of commodities and exports of manufactures and some services being redirected to other destinations, notably the USA and Europe. Merchandise exports decreased by 5% in 2002–03 against the previous year while imports rose by 11%.

Imports and Exports

Merchandise imports and exports for years ending 30 June (in $A1m.):

	Imports	*Exports*
2001–02	119,649	121,108
2002–03	133,129	115,479
2003–04	130,997	109,049
2004–05	149,520	126,719

The Australian customs tariff provides for preferences to goods produced in and shipped from certain countries as a result of reciprocal trade agreements. These include the UK, New Zealand, Canada and Ireland.

Most valuable commodity imports, 2004–05 (in $A1m.): passenger motor vehicles, 11,597; crude petroleum oils,

9,703; computing equipment, 5,792; medicaments, 5,719; telecommunications equipment, 5,031; petroleum oils, oils from bituminous minerals (not crude), 4,861. Most valuable commodity exports, 2004–05 (in $A1m.): coal, 17,117; iron ore, 8,084; crude petroleum products, 5,692; gold (non-monetary), 5,643; bovine meat, 4,878; aluminium ores and concentrates (including alumina), 4,432; aluminium, 4,127.

Australia is the world's largest exporter of iron ore, black coal, bauxite, lead, diamonds, alumina, beef, barley and wool.

Trade by bloc or country in 2004–05 (in $A1m.):

	Imports	*Exports*
APEC	103,758	92,913
ASEAN	25,196	14,952
EU	35,085	13,804
OECD	88,895	70,125
China	19,812	12,980
Indonesia	3,318	3,410
Japan	17,157	24,917
South Korea	5,004	9,701
Malaysia	5,920	2,582
New Zealand	5,340	9,160
Singapore	7,280	3,344
Taiwan	3,612	4,883
Germany	8,644	1,315
UK	5,934	4,813
USA	21,273	9,434

China has in the meantime surpassed Japan as Australia's leading trading partner.

COMMUNICATIONS

Roads

At 30 June 2004 there was a total of 741,621 km of roads, of which 57·8% were paved.

As at 31 March 2006 registration totals were: 11,101,441 passenger vehicles, 2,114,333 light commercial vehicles, 475,519 trucks, 75,375 buses, 41,520 campervans and 463,057 motorcycles.

In 2005, 1,636 persons were killed in road accidents (1,583 in 2004).

Rail

Privatization of government railways began in Victoria in 1994 with West Coast Railway and Hoys Transport being granted seven-year franchises. Specialised Container Transport (SCT) won the first private rail freight franchise in 1995 followed by TNT (now Toll Holdings). Australian National Railway Commission was sold by the Commonwealth Government in Nov. 1997 and in Feb. 1999 V/Line Freight Corporation, owned by the Victorian Government, was sold to Freight Australia. Rail passenger services in Victoria were franchised in mid-1999. The Australian Railroad Group acquired Western Australia's government rail freight operation, Westrail, in Nov. 2000. In Jan. 2002 Toll Holdings and Lang acquired the rolling stock of the National Rail Corporation (NRC) and New South Wales freight carrier, FreightCorp. These two sales leave QR as the only government-owned rail freight operator in Australia.

At 30 June 2003 the total length of track was 4,150 km (broad gauge, 1,600 mm); 17,720 km (standard, 1,435 mm); 15,160 km (narrow, 1,067 mm); 4,150 km (narrow, 610 mm gauge); and 281 km (dual gauge). In 2002–03 a total of 598·6m. tonnes of freight were carried; passengers carried totalled 586m. urban (including train and tram); 9m. non-urban.

Under various Commonwealth–State standardization agreements, all the State capitals are now linked by standard gauge track. The 'AustralAsia Rail Project', which involved the construction of 1,420 km standard gauge railway between Alice Springs and Darwin, has been completed and passenger services from Adelaide through Alice Springs and on to Darwin commenced on 1 Feb. 2004.

There are also private industrial and tourist railways, and tramways in Adelaide, Melbourne and Sydney. In the latter two cities there are also metro systems.

Civil Aviation

Qantas Airways is Australia's principal international airline. In 1992 Qantas merged with Australian Airlines, and in 1993, 25% of the company was purchased by British Airways. The remainder is government-owned. A total of 49 international airlines operated scheduled air services to and from Australia in 2004. There are 13 international airports, the main ones being Adelaide, Brisbane, Cairns, Darwin, Melbourne, Perth and Sydney. In 2003–04 international passenger traffic increased by 12·6% to 18·1m.; international freight decreased by 1·3% to 627,002 tonnes; mail increased by 3·0% to 28,444 tonnes.

Sydney (Kingsford Smith) handled the most traffic (29·5%) in Australia in 2003–04 (26,072,647 passengers, of which 15,817,603 on domestic flights), followed by Melbourne International (21·1%) and Brisbane (15·6%).

Internal airlines (domestic and regional) carried 43·7m. passengers in the year ended 31 July 2006. Domestic airlines were deregulated in Oct. 1990.

In 2003–04 there were 256 licensed, registered and certified aerodromes in Australia and its external territories. At 31 Dec. 2004 there were 17,841 registered aircraft.

Shipping

The chief ports are Brisbane, Dampier, Fremantle, Gladstone, Hay Point, Melbourne, Newcastle, Port Hedland, Port Kembla, Port Walcott, Sydney and Weipa. Dampier, Australia's busiest port, handled 100,213,978 tonnes of cargo in 2003–04. As at 30 June 2004 the trading fleet comprised 82 vessels totalling 2,052,795 DWT, 1,643,709 GRT.

Coastal cargo handled at Australian ports in 2003–04 (in gross weight tonnes): loaded, 53·2m.; unloaded, 55·1m. International trade loaded, 558·0m. tonnes; unloaded, 64·0m. tonnes. Calls to ports made by commercial ships in 2003–04 totalled 23,436 with 791 made by passenger vessels.

Telecommunications

In 1989 the domestic market became a regulated monopoly with Telstra as the government-owned company providing all services and, in 1991, a duopoly (with Optus) in fixed network services. In 1993 Vodafone joined Telstra and Optus in the provision of mobile phone services. A new regulatory regime was created by the introduction of the Telecommunications Act 1997 and both markets were opened to wholesale and retail competition. There is no limit to the number of carriers that can hold licences under the new arrangements and by June 2002 a total of 83 licences had been issued. The Australian Communications and Media Authority (ACMA) and the Australian Competition and Consumer Commission (ACCC) are the primary regulators with responsibility for the industry's development. The privatization of Telstra was completed in Nov. 2006.

In 2008 there were 9,370,000 main (fixed) telephone lines, down from 10,460,000 in 2003. Mobile phone subscribers numbered 22,120,000 in 2008 (1,049·6 per 1,000 persons). There were 13,720,000 PCs in use in 2004 (689·0 per 1,000 persons) and 15,170,000 internet users in 2008. The broadband penetration rate in June 2008 was 23·5 subscribers per 100 inhabitants.

Three telecommunications satellites are in orbit covering the entire continent.

Postal Services

Postal services are operated by Australia Post, operating under the Australian Postal Corporation Act 1989 as a government business enterprise. In the year ended 30 June 2006 revenue was $A4,530·1m., expenditure $A4,014·5m. There were 4,474 corporate outlets, licensed post offices and other agencies at 30 June 2006; in 2005–06, 5,418·1m. mail items were handled.

SOCIAL INSTITUTIONS

Justice

The judicial power of the Commonwealth of Australia is vested in the High Court of Australia (the Federal Supreme Court), in the Federal courts created by the Federal Parliament (the Federal Court of Australia and the Family Court of Australia) and in the State courts invested by Parliament with Federal jurisdiction.

High Court

The High Court consists of a Chief Justice and six other Justices, appointed by the Governor-General in Council. The Constitution confers on the High Court original jurisdiction, *inter alia*, in all matters arising under treaties or affecting consuls or other foreign representatives, matters between the States of the Commonwealth, matters to which the Commonwealth is a party and matters between residents of different States. Federal Parliament may make laws conferring original jurisdiction on the High Court, *inter alia*, in matters arising under the Constitution or under any laws made by the Parliament. It has in fact conferred jurisdiction on the High Court in matters arising under the Constitution and in matters arising under certain laws made by Parliament.

The High Court may hear and determine appeals from its own Justices exercising original jurisdiction, from any other Federal Court, from a Court exercising Federal jurisdiction and from the Supreme Courts of the States. It also has jurisdiction to hear and determine appeals from the Supreme Courts of the Territories. The right of appeal from the High Court to the Privy Council in London was abolished in 1986.

Other Federal Courts

Since 1924, four other Federal courts have been created to exercise special Federal jurisdiction, i.e. the Federal Court of Australia, the Family Court of Australia, the Australian Industrial Court and the Federal Court of Bankruptcy. The Federal Court of Australia was created by the Federal Court of Australia Act 1976 and began to exercise jurisdiction on 1 Feb. 1977. It exercises such original jurisdiction as is invested in it by laws made by the Federal Parliament including jurisdiction formerly exercised by the Australian Industrial Court and the Federal Court of Bankruptcy, and in some matters previously invested in either the High Court or State and Territory Supreme Courts. The Federal Court also acts as a court of appeal from State and Territory courts in relation to Federal matters. Appeal from the Federal Court to the High Court will be by way of special leave only. The State Supreme Courts have also been invested with Federal jurisdiction in bankruptcy.

At 30 June 2006 the prison population was 25,790, an increase of 42% since 1996.

Each State has its own individual police service which operates almost exclusively within its State boundaries. State police investigations include murder, robbery, street-level drug dealing, kidnapping, domestic violence and motor vehicle offences. State police activities are broadly known as community policing.

The role of the Australian Federal Police (AFP) is to enforce Commonwealth criminal law and protect Commonwealth and national interests from crime in Australia and overseas. Responsibilities include combating organized crime, transnational crime, money laundering, illicit drug trafficking, e-crime, the investigation of fraud against the Australian Government and handling special references from Government. The AFP also provides a protection service to dignitaries and crucial witnesses as well as community policing services to the people of the Australian Capital Territory, Jervis Bay and Australia's External Territories.

Total Australian Federal Police personnel (excluding ACT policing) as at 30 June 2003 was 3,496, of which 2,297 were sworn employees (police members) and 1,199 unsworn employees. There are approximately 48,000 police officers in Australia.

Education

The governments of the Australian States and Territories have the major responsibility for education, including the administration and substantial funding of primary, secondary, and technical and further education. In most States, a single education department is responsible for these three levels but in Queensland, Western Australia and the Northern Territory, separate departments deal with school-based and technical and further education issues.

School attendance is compulsory between the ages of six (five in Tasmania) and 17 years (with the exception of the Northern Territory where the leaving age is 15 years), at either a government school or a recognized non-government educational institution. Between the ages of 16 and 17 in some states students have the option of undertaking vocational training, apprenticeships or other government approved learning programmes. Many children attend pre-schools for a year before entering school (usually in sessions of two–three hours, for two–five days per week). Government schools are usually co-educational and comprehensive. Non-government schools have been traditionally single-sex, particularly in secondary schools, but there is a trend towards co-education. Tuition is free at government schools, but fees are normally charged at non-government schools.

In Aug. 2006 there were 6,902 government (and 2,710 non-government) primary and secondary schools with 2,248,229 (1,119,807) full-time pupils and 158,194 (81,445) full-time teachers.

Vocational education and training (VET) is essentially a partnership between the Commonwealth, the States and Territories and industry. In 2004 publicly-funded VET programmes were offered by some 68 TAFEs and other government institutions. A further 518 community education providers and over 1,300 other providers (mainly private providers) delivering VET were at least partly publicly funded. In 2004 there were over 1·6m. people enrolled in VET courses.

In 2004, 48 higher education institutions received Commonwealth Government funding including seven other education institutions with students on accredited higher education courses. There were 957,176 university students in 2005. Fields of university study with the largest number of award course students in 2005 were management and commerce (28·6%); society and culture (21·8%); health (11·3%); and education (10·0%).

International education is increasingly important, with 344,815 enrolments by full-fee overseas students at Australian educational institutions in 2005, an increase of 7·0% on the previous year. About 20% of university students are foreign, the highest proportion of any country.

Total operating expenses of Australian Government on education in 2005–06 were $A49,741m. Private expenditure on education in 2003–04 amounted to $A13,329m. The figures include government grants to the private sector which are also included in the operating expenses of Australian governments.

The adult literacy rate is at least 99%.

Health

In 2002–03 there were 729 public hospitals (including 19 psychiatric hospitals) and (in 2004–05) 532 private hospitals (including acute and psychiatric hospitals); there were an average 2·6 public hospital beds per 1,000 population (down from 3·0 in 1997–98). In 2002–03 there were 164,700 registered nurses, 36,700 general medical practitioners and 10,100 physiotherapists. The Royal Flying Doctor Service serves remote areas. Estimated total government expenditure on health goods and services (public and private sectors) in 2003–04 was $A78·6bn. ($A72·5bn. in the previous year), representing 9·7% of GDP. In 2004–05, 51% of Australians aged 15 years and over had private health insurance.

At 31 Dec. 2003 there were estimated to be 20,580 HIV cases, 9,380 AIDS diagnoses and 6,385 deaths following AIDS.

In 2005, 7·4m. people (54% of the adult population) aged 18 years and over were considered overweight or obese, compared to 45% in 1995.

Welfare

All Commonwealth government social security pensions, benefits and allowances are financed from the Commonwealth government's general revenue. In addition, assistance is provided for welfare services.

Age Pensions—age pensions are payable to men 65 years of age or more who have lived in Australia for a specified period and, unless permanently blind, also satisfy an income and assets test. The minimum age for women's eligibility was raised by six months to 62 years on 1 July 2001 and is being lifted in six-month increments every two years until 1 July 2013 when it will be 65 years. The qualifying age at 1 July 2006 was 63 years. In the year ending 30 June 2005, 1,915,036 age pensioners received a total of $A19,970·3m.

Disability Support Pension (DSP)—payable to persons aged 16 years or over with a physical, intellectual or psychiatric impairment of at least 20%, assessed as being unable to work for at least 15 hours a week. DSP for those of 21 years or over is paid at the same rate as Age Pensions and is subject to the same means test except for those who are permanently blind. In the year ending 30 June 2005, 706,782 disability support pensioners received a total of $A7,910·8m.

Carer Payment—payable to a person unable to support themselves owing to providing constant care and attention at home for a severely disabled person aged 16 or over, or a person who is frail aged, either permanently or for an extended period. Since 1 July 1998 Carer Payment has been extended to carers of children under 16 years of age with profound disabilities. Subject to income and assets tests, the rate of Carer Payment is the same as for other pensions. In the year ending 30 June 2005, 95,446 carers received a total of $A1,062·1m.

Carer Allowance—supplementary payment to a person providing constant care and attention at home for an adult or child with a disability or severe medical condition. The allowance is not income or assets tested. In the year ending 30 June 2005, 340,005 carers received a total of $A1,109·3m.

Sickness Allowance—paid to those over school-leaving age but below Age Pension age who are unable to work or continue full-time study temporarily owing to illness or injury. Eligibility rests on the person having a job or study course to which they can return. In the year ending 30 June 2005 a total of $A89·4m. was paid to 8,367 beneficiaries.

Family Tax Benefit (FTB)—replaced *Family Allowance* and *Family Tax Payment* on 1 July 2000. Family Tax Benefit Part A is paid to assist families with children under 21 years of age or dependent full-time students aged 21–24 years; Family Tax Benefit Part B provides additional assistance to families with only one income earner and children under 16 years of age or dependent full-time students aged 16–18 years. Both benefits are subject to an income and assets test. In the year ending 30 June 2005 FTB Part A and Part B payments were made to a total of 3·2m. families comprising 5·8m. children.

Parenting Payment (Single) and (Partnered)—is paid to assist those who care for children under 16, with income and assets under certain amounts, and have been an Australian resident for at least two years or a refugee or have become a lone parent while an Australian resident. Parenting Payment (Single) is paid to lone parents under pension rates and conditions; Parenting Payment (Partnered) is paid to one of the parents in the couple. [Since 1 July 2000 the basic component of Parenting Payment (Partnered) was incorporated into Family Tax Benefit with 375,233 beneficiaries transferring to Family Tax Benefit Part B.] In the year ending 30 June 2005, 448,566 Parenting Payment (Single) beneficiaries and 167,260 Parenting Payment (Partnered) beneficiaries received a total of $A6,157·0m.

Maternity Payment—was introduced as part of the 'More Help for Families' package in the 2004–05 budget. Recognizing the costs associated with a new baby, all families with a child born or adopted from 1 July 2004 are eligible for the payment with no income or assets test applying. This replaces the Maternity Allowance and Baby Bonus. The Maternity Immunization Allowance is not subject to an income test for children born on or after 1 Jan. 2003. In the year ended 30 June 2005 a total of $A770·1m. was paid (including Maternity Immunization Allowance).

Newstart Allowance (NSA)—payable to those who are unemployed and are over 21 years of age but less than Age Pension age. Eligibility is subject to income and assets tests and recipients must satisfy the 'activity test' whereby they are actively seeking and willing to undertake suitable paid work, including casual and part-time work. To be eligible for benefit a person must have resided in Australia for at least 12 months preceding his or her claim or intend to remain in Australia permanently; unemployment must not be as a result of industrial action by that person or by members of a union to which that person is a member. In the year ended 30 June 2005 a total of $A4,627·4m. was paid to 453,614 NSA beneficiaries.

Youth Allowance—replaced five former schemes for young people, including the Youth Training Allowance. In the year ending 30 June 2005 a total of $A2,218·5m. was paid to YA beneficiaries.

Mature Age Allowance (MAA)—paid to older long-term unemployed, over 60 years of age but less than Age Pension age. MAA is non-activity tested. In the year ended June 2005 a total of $A258·9m. was paid.

Service Pensions—are paid by the Department of Veterans' Affairs. Male veterans who have reached the age of 60 years or are permanently unemployable, and who served in a theatre of war, are eligible subject to an income and assets test. The minimum age for female veterans' eligibility is being lifted from 55 to 60 years in six-month increments every two years over the period 1995–2013. The qualifying age at 1 July 2006 was 57 years 6 months. Wives of service pensioners are also eligible, provided that they do not receive a pension from the Department of Social Security. Disability pension is a compensatory payment in respect of incapacity attributable to war service. It is paid at a rate commensurate with the degree of incapacity and is free of any income test. In the year ended 30 June 2005, $A2,816·4m. of service pensions and $A2,806·4m. of disability and war widows' dependants' pensions were paid out; at 30 June 2005 there were 299,774 eligible veterans.

Medicare—covers: automatic entitlement under a single public health fund to medical and optometrical benefits of 75% of the Medical Benefits Schedule fee, with a maximum patient payment for any service where the Schedule fee is charged; access without direct charge to public hospital accommodation and to inpatient and outpatient treatment by doctors appointed by the hospital; the restoration of funds for community health to approximately the same real level as 1975; a reduction in charges for private treatment in shared wards of public hospitals, and increases in the daily bed subsidy payable to private hospitals.

The Medicare programme is financed in part by a 1·5% levy on taxable incomes, with low income cut-off points, which were $A15,902 p.a. for a single person in 2004–05 and $A26,834 p.a. for a family with an extra allowance of $A2,464 for each child. A levy surcharge of 1% was introduced from 1 July 1997 for single individuals with taxable incomes in excess of $A50,000 p.a. and couples and families with combined taxable incomes in excess of $A100,000 who do not have private hospital cover through private health insurance.

Medicare benefits are available to all persons ordinarily resident in Australia. Visitors from the UK, New Zealand, Italy, Sweden, the Netherlands and Malta have immediate access to necessary medical treatment, as do all visitors staying more than six months.

RELIGION

Under the Constitution the Commonwealth cannot make any law to establish any religion, to impose any religious observance or to prohibit the free exercise of any religion. The following percentages refer to those religions with the largest number of adherents at the census of 2006. Answering the census question on religious adherence was not obligatory, however.

Christian, 63·9% of population: Catholic, 25·8%; Anglican, 18·7%; Uniting Church, 5·7%; Presbyterian and Reformed, 3·0%; Orthodox, 2·7%; Baptist, 1·6%; Lutheran, 1·3%; Pentecostal, 1·1%; Jehovah's Witnesses, 0·4%; Salvation Army, 0·3%; Churches of Christ, 0·3%; other Christian, 3·0%. Religions other than Christian, 6·2%: Buddhism, 2·1%; Islam, 1·7%; Hinduism, 0·7%; Judaism, 0·4%; other religions, 1·3%; no religion, 18·7%; no statement, 11·2%.

The Anglican Synod voted for the ordination of ten women in Nov. 1992. In Feb. 2010 the Roman Catholic church had three cardinals.

Thompson, R. C., *Religion in Australia, a History.* 1995

CULTURE

World Heritage Sites

There are 17 sites under Australian jurisdiction that appear on the UNESCO World Heritage List. They are (with year entered on list): Great Barrier Reef (1981), Kakadu National Park (1981, 1987 and 1992), Willandra Lakes Region (1981), Tasmanian Wilderness (1982 and 1989), Lord Howe Island Group (1982), Gondwana Rainforests of Australia (1986 and 1994), Uluru-Kata Tjuta National Park (1987 and 1994), Wet Tropics of Queensland (1988), Shark Bay (1991), Fraser Island (1992), Australian Fossil Mammal Sites (Riversleigh/Naracoorte) (1994), Heard and McDonald Islands (1997), Macquarie Island (1997), the Greater Blue Mountains Area (2000), Purnululu National Park (2003), Royal Exhibition Building and Carlton Gardens in Melbourne (2004) and Sydney Opera House (2007).

Broadcasting

Broadcasting is regulated by the Australian Communications and Media Authority (ACMA), established under the Broadcasting Services Act 1992. Foreign ownership of commercial radio and TV companies is limited by law. National and local public broadcasting is provided by the Australian Broadcasting Corporation (ABC), an independent statutory corporation, and the multilingual Special Broadcasting Service (SBS). ABC also runs Australia Network, an international television channel, and Radio Australia, an external service for the Asia-Pacific region. In addition there are national and local commercial radio and TV services, subscription TV services and community radio stations. As at 30 June 2004 the ACMA had licensed 53 commercial TV services, 274 commercial radio services and 341 community radio services. In 2006 there were 7·8m. television-equipped households. Colour is by PAL.

Press

There were 52 English daily metropolitan newspapers in 2007 (two national, 13 metropolitan, 36 regional and one suburban). There are also 11 metropolitan Sunday newspapers. The papers with the largest circulations are the *Sunday Telegraph* (New South Wales), with an average of 671,500 per issue in 2007; the *Sunday Herald Sun* (Victoria), with an average of 620,000 per issue; and the *Sunday Mail* (Queensland), with an average of 592,440 per issue. At least 24 magazines had an average circulation of over 100,000 copies per issue in 2004.

Tourism

In 2002–03 the total number of overseas visitors for the year stood at 4·7m. (a 2·0% decrease on 2001–02). The top source countries for visitors in 2002–03 were New Zealand (839,100); UK (627,800); Japan (627,700); USA (422,100); Singapore (253,400); and South Korea (207,300).

Festivals

In 2003 Australia hosted 176 performing arts festivals of more than two days' duration with a total estimated attendance of 7·5m. Among the largest events are the Sydney Festival (running for three weeks each Jan., with over 500 performers from across the arts), the National Multicultural Festival in Canberra (Feb.), the Perth International Arts Festival (Feb.), the Brisbane Festival (July) and the Melbourne International Arts Festival (Oct.). Adelaide and Darwin have their own large events too. Each June the Dreaming Festival in Woodford celebrates Indigenous culture.

Libraries

As at 30 June 2004 there were 540 public libraries and archive organizations operating through 1,733 locations. During 2003–04 there were 105m. visits to local government, national and state libraries. Total government funding for libraries in 2003–04 was $A781·2m.

Theatre and Opera

Opera Australia is the largest performing arts organization in the country with almost 250 performances staged annually. In 2005–06, 25·2% of the population aged 15 years and over (4·0m. people) attended at least one popular music concert; 17·0% (2·7m.), at least one theatre performance; 16·3% (2·6m.), at least one opera or musical.

Museums and Galleries

At 30 June 2004 there were 1,329 museums, including 673 social history museums, 160 art galleries and 381 historic properties, employing 28,067 people (including volunteers). In 2003–04 there were 31·2m. visitors to Australia's museums. Most admissions (66%) were free of charge. Government funding in 2003–04 represented 71% of the museums' total income of $A919·4m.

DIPLOMATIC REPRESENTATIVES

Of Australia in the United Kingdom (Australia House, Strand, London, WC2B 4LA)
High Commissioner: John Dauth.

Of the United Kingdom in Australia (Commonwealth Ave., Yarralumla, A.C.T. 2600)
High Commissioner: Rt Hon. Baroness Valerie Amos.

Of Australia in the USA (1601 Massachusetts Ave., NW, Washington, D.C., 20036)
Ambassador: Kim Beazley.

Of the USA in Australia (Moonah Pl., Yarralumla, A.C.T. 2600)
Ambassador: Jeffrey Bleich.

Of Australia to the United Nations
Ambassador: Gary Quinlan.

Of Australia to the European Union
Ambassador: Alan Thomas.

FURTHER READING

Australian Bureau of Statistics (ABS). *Year Book Australia*, since 1901.—*Australia at a Glance*, since 1994.—*Australian Economic Indicators* (absorbed *Monthly Summary of Statistics)* since 1994.—*Australian Social Trends*, since 1994. ABS also provide numerous online specialized statistical summaries.

Arthur, Bill and Morphy, Frances, *The Macquarie Atlas of Indigenous Australia.* 2006

Australian Encyclopædia. 12 vols. 1983

Blainey, G., *A Short History of Australia.* 1996
The Cambridge Encyclopedia of Australia. 1994
Clark, M., *Manning Clark's History of Australia*; abridged by M. Cathcart. 1994
Concise Oxford Dictionary of Australian History. 2nd ed. 1995
Davison, Graeme, *et al.*, (eds.) *The Oxford Companion to Australian History.* 2nd ed. 2002
Docherty, J. D., *Historical Dictionary of Australia.* 1993
Foster, S. G., Marsden, S. and Russell, R. (compilers) *Federation. A guide to records.* 2000
Gilbert, A. D. and Inglis, K. S. (eds.) *Australians: a Historical Library.* 5 vols. 1988
Hirst, John, *The Sentimental Nation: The Making of the Australian Commonwealth.* 2000.—*Australia's Democracy: A Short History.* 2002
Irving, H. (ed.) *The Centenary Companion to Australian Federation.* 2000
Knightley, Phillip, *Australia: A biography of a Nation.* 2000
Macintyre, S., *A Concise History of Australia.* 2000
Oxford History of Australia. vol 2: 1770–1860. 1992. vol 5: 1942–88. 1990
The Oxford Illustrated Dictionary of Australian History. 1993
Turnbull, M., *The Reluctant Republic.* 1994
Ward, Stuart, *Australia and the British Embrace: The Demise of the Imperial Ideal.* 2002

A more specialized title is listed under RELIGION, *above*

National library: The National Library, Canberra, ACT.
Website: http://www.nla.gov.au
National Statistical Office: Australian Bureau of Statistics (ABS), ABS House, 45 Benjamin Way, Belconnen, ACT 2617. The statistical services of the states are integrated with the Bureau.
ABS Website: http://www.abs.gov.au

AUSTRALIAN TERRITORIES AND STATES

Australian Capital Territory

KEY HISTORICAL EVENTS

The area that is now the Australian Capital Territory (ACT) was explored in 1820 by Charles Throsby who named it Limestone Plains. Settlement commenced in 1824. In 1901 the Commonwealth constitution stipulated that a land tract of at least 260 sq. km in area and not less than 160 km from Sydney be reserved as a capital district. The Canberra site was adopted by the Seat of Government Act 1908. The present site was surrendered by New South Wales and accepted by the Commonwealth in 1909. By subsequential proclamation the Territory became vested in the Commonwealth from 1 Jan. 1911. The Jervis Bay Territory was acquired by the Commonwealth of Australia from New South Wales in 1915 in order that the national seat of government at Canberra would have access to the sea. In 1911 an international competition for the city plan had been won by W. Burley Griffin of Chicago but construction was delayed by the First World War. It was not until 1927 that Canberra became the seat of government. Located on the Molonglo River surrounding an artificial lake, it was built as a compromise capital to stop squabbling between Melbourne and Sydney following the 1901 Federation of Australian States.

In Dec. 1988 self-government was proclaimed and in May 1989 the first ACT assembly was elected.

TERRITORY AND POPULATION

The total area is 2,349 sq. km, of which 60% is hilly or mountainous. Timbered mountains are located in the south and west, and plains and hill country in the north. The ACT lies within the upper Murrumbidgee River catchment, in the Murray-Darling Basin. The Murrumbidgee flows throughout the Territory from the south, and its tributary, the Molonglo, from the east. The Molonglo was dammed in 1964 to form Lake Burley Griffin. The Jervis Bay Territory (67 sq. km) is independent and administered by central government although the laws of the ACT apply. Population at the 2006 census was 324,034 (2001: 309,998).

SOCIAL STATISTICS

2007: births, 4,753; deaths, 1,597; marriages, 1,610; divorces, 1,333. Infant mortality rate (per 1,000 live births), 3·8. Expectation of life, 2007: males, 80·3 years; females, 84·0 years.

CLIMATE

ACT has a continental climate, characterized by a marked variation in temperature between seasons, with warm to hot summers and cold winters.

CONSTITUTION AND GOVERNMENT

The ACT became self-governing on 11 May 1989. It is represented by two members in the Commonwealth House of Representatives and two senators.

The parliament of the ACT, the *Legislative Assembly*, consists of 17 members elected for a three-year term. Its responsibilities are at State and Local government level. The Legislative Assembly elects a Chief Minister and a four-member cabinet.

Electors enrolled (30 June 2006) numbered 226,576.

RECENT ELECTIONS

At the elections of 18 Oct. 2008 the Labor Party won seven seats (37·4% of the vote) with the Liberal Party taking six seats (31·6%) and the Green Party four seats (15·6%).

CURRENT ADMINISTRATION

The ACT Australian Labor Party Ministry was as follows in Feb. 2010:

Chief Minister, Minister for Transport, Territory and Municipal Services, Business and Economic Development, Aboriginal and Torres Strait Islander Affairs, and the Arts and Heritage: Jon Stanhope.

Deputy Chief Minister, Treasurer, Minister for Health, and Industrial Relations: Katy Gallagher. *Attorney General, Minister for the Environment, Climate Change and Water, Energy, and Police and Emergency Services:* Simon Corbell. *Education and Training, Planning, Tourism, Sport and Recreation, and Gaming and Racing:* Andrew Barr. *Disability, Housing and Community Services, Children and Young People, Ageing, and Women:* Joy Burch.

Speaker: Shane Rattenbury.

ACT Government Website: http://www.act.gov.au

ECONOMY

Budget

The ACT fully participates in the federal-state model underpinning the Australian Federal System. As a city-State, the ACT Government reflects State and local (municipal) government responsibilities, which is unique within the federal system. However, the ACT is treated equitably with the other Australian jurisdictions regarding the distribution of federal funding.

In 2006 the Territory recorded total income of $A3,436m. (including the Territory's share of operating surplus from Joint Ventures accounted for using the Equity Method) and incurred expenditure of $A3,065m. achieving a surplus of $A372m. on accrual basis.

Banking and Finance

According to the Australian Prudential Regulation Authority, as at 30 June 2006 there were ten authorized banks with 66 branches; one building society with four branches and seven credit unions with 31 branches.

ENERGY AND NATURAL RESOURCES

Electricity

See NEW SOUTH WALES.

Water

ACTEW (Australian Capital Territory, Electricity & Water) provides more than 100m. litres of water each day to Canberra residents. There were 45 reservoirs in 2003 with a capacity of 215bn. litres.

Agriculture

Sheep and/or beef cattle farming is the main agricultural activity. In 2002–03 there were 91 farming establishments with a total area of 50,000 ha. Gross value of agricultural production in 2004–05: $A17·2m.

Forestry

There are about 10,000 ha. of plantation forest in the ACT (approximately 3·96% of the land area). Most of the area is managed for the production of softwood timber. The established pine forests, such as Kowen, Stromlo, Uriarra and Pierces Creek, are in the northern part of the Territory. After harvesting, 500–1,000 ha. of land are planted with new pine forest each year. No native forests or woodlands have been cleared for plantation since the mid-1970s.

INDUSTRY

Manufacturing industries in the year ended 30 June 2005 employed 5,100 persons and generated sales and service income of $A965m.

Labour

In June 2007 there were 187,900 employed persons and 6,000 unemployed persons, an unemployment rate of 3·1%.

In the year ending Feb. 2006, 25·7% of the ACT labour force was employed in public administration and defence; 14·9% in property and business services; 11·6% in retail trade. The average weekly wage in Nov. 2005 was $A1,191·20 (males $A1,275·60, females $A1,077·10).

Trade Unions

As at Aug. 2006 there were 31,000 people belonging to a trade union (17·7% of total employees).

INTERNATIONAL TRADE

Imports and Exports

In 2002–03 imports were valued at $A216·5m. ($A5·4m. in 2001–02); exports at $A4·3m. ($A10·6m. in 2001–02). Machinery and transport equipment accounted for 99% of total imports and 54% of total exports.

COMMUNICATIONS

Roads

At March 2004 there were 2,645 km of road. At 31 March 2006 there were 224,076 vehicles registered in the ACT. In 2004 there were ten road accident fatalities.

Civil Aviation

In 2004–05 Canberra International Airport handled an estimated 2,476,709 passengers.

Telecommunications

In 2005–06 there were 101,000 households with home computer access (82% of all households). In 2005–06, 89,000 households had home internet access (72%).

Postal Services

In the year ended 30 June 2006 there were 17 corporate outlets and 38 licensed post offices.

SOCIAL INSTITUTIONS

Justice

In 2004–05 there were 39,288 criminal incidents recorded by police. During the same year there were 606 full-time sworn police officers in the ACT and 196 unsworn police staff.

Education

In Feb. 2006 there were 221 schools comprising 82 pre-schools, 139 primary and secondary schools (including colleges) and five special schools. Of these 177 were government schools. There was a total of 60,142 full-time students. There were four higher education institutions in 2006: the Signadou Campus of the Australian Catholic University (ACU) had 596 students enrolled; the Australian National University, 14,476 students; the University of Canberra, 11,632; and the Australian Defence Force Academy, 2,136.

Health

The ACT is serviced by two public and nine private hospitals (six of the private hospitals are day surgery only). At 30 June 2005 there were 2,046 medical practitioners, 4,257 registered nurses, 250 dentists.

Welfare

At Dec. 2003 there were 17,643 age pensioners (5·4% of ACT population); 7,052 persons received disability support pension (2·2%).

RELIGION

At the 2006 census, 60·2% of the population were Christian. Of these, 46·5% were Roman Catholic and 27·8% Anglican. Non-Christian religions accounted for 6·2%, the largest groups being Buddhists, Muslims and Hindus.

CULTURE

Tourism

In 2003, 171,500 international visitors came to the ACT. Of these, the largest proportion (19%) was from the UK. At Dec. 2005 there were 58 hotels, guest houses and serviced apartments employing 2,379 persons.

FURTHER READING

Statistical Information: The State office of the Australian Bureau of Statistics (ABS) is at Level 5, QBE Insurance Building, 33–35 Ainslie Ave., Canberra City. Publications include: *Australian Capital Territory in Focus*. Annual (from 1994); *Australian Capital Territory at a Glance*, Annual (from 1995).

Sources: ACT in Focus 1307.8, Labour Force, Australia 6203.0 and Labour Force, New South Wales and Australian Capital Territory 6201.1.

Northern Territory

KEY HISTORICAL EVENTS

The Northern Territory, after forming part of New South Wales, was annexed on 6 July 1863 to South Australia. After the agreement of 7 Dec. 1907 for the transfer of the Northern Territory to the Commonwealth, it passed to the control of the Commonwealth government on 1 Jan. 1911. On 1 Feb. 1927 the Northern Territory was divided into two territories but in 1931 it was again administered as a single territory. The Legislative Council for the Northern Territory, constituted in 1947, was reconstituted in 1959. In that year, citizenship rights were granted to Aboriginal people of 'full descent'. On 1 July 1978 self-government was granted.

TERRITORY AND POPULATION

The Northern Territory's total area is 1,352,212 sq. km and includes adjacent islands. It has 5,100 km of mainland coastline and 2,100 km of coast around the islands. The greater part of the interior consists of a tableland with excellent pasturage. The southern part is generally sandy and has a small rainfall.

The 2006 census population was 192,898 (2001: 188,075). The capital, seat of government and principal port is Darwin, on the north coast; 2006 census population, 105,991. Other main centres (preliminary estimated 2006 totals) include Katherine (9,022); Alice Springs (27,018); Tennant Creek (3,068); Nhulunbuy (2004) (3,795); and Jabiru (2004) (1,168). There are also a number of large self-contained Aboriginal communities. People identifying themselves as indigenous numbered 53,662 at the 2006 census.

SOCIAL STATISTICS

2007 totals: births, 3,894; deaths, 1,001; marriages, 779; divorces, 417. Infant mortality rate per 1,000 live births, 8·5. Life expectancy, 2007: 72·4 years for males, 78·4 for females. The annual rates per 1,000 population in 2007 were: births, 18·1; deaths, 4·7; marriages, 3·6; divorces, 1·9.

CLIMATE

See AUSTRALIA: Climate.

The highest temperature ever recorded in the NT was 118·9°F (48·3°C) at Finke in 1960, while the lowest recorded temperature was 18·5°F (–7·5°C) at Alice Springs in 1976.

CONSTITUTION AND GOVERNMENT

The Northern Territory (Self-Government) Act 1978 established the Northern Territory as a body politic as from 1 July 1978, with Ministers having control over and responsibility for Territory finances and the administration of the functions of government as specified by the Federal government. Regulations have been made conferring executive authority for the bulk of administrative functions.

The Northern Territory has federal representation, electing one member to the House of Representatives and two members to the Senate.

The Legislative Assembly has 25 members, directly elected for a period of four years. The *Administrator* (Tom Pauling) appoints Ministers on the advice of the Leader of the majority party.

Electors enrolled (30 June 2006) numbered 111,254.

RECENT ELECTIONS

In parliamentary elections held on 9 Aug. 2008 the Australian Labor Party won 13 seats against 11 for the Country Liberal Party. One independent was elected.

CURRENT ADMINISTRATION

Administrator: Tom Pauling, AO, QC.

The NT Territory Labor Party Cabinet was as follows in Feb. 2010:

Chief Minister, Minister for Police, Fire and Emergency Services, Major Projects and Economic Development, Multicultural Affairs, and Defence Liaison: Paul Henderson.

Deputy Chief Minister, Treasurer, Minister for Justice and Attorney General, Racing, Gaming and Licensing, and Alcohol Policy: Delia Lawrie. *Education and Training, Public and Affordable Housing, and Public Employment:* Dr Chris Burns. *Health, Children and Families, Child Protection, Primary Industry, and Fisheries and Resources:* Konstantine Vatskalis. *Business and Employment, Trade, Asian Relations, Essential Services, Defence Support, Senior Territorians, and Young Territorians:* Rob Knight. *Local Government, Regional Government, Indigenous Development, Tourism, Women's Policy, and Statehood:* Malarndirri McCarthy. *Natural Resources, Environment and Heritage, Parks and Wildlife, Climate Change, Sport and Recreation, Information, Communications and Technology Policy, and Central Australia:* Karl Hampton. *Lands and Planning, Transport, Construction, Correctional Services, and Arts and Museums:* Gerald McCarthy.

NT Government Website: http://www.nt.gov.au

ECONOMY

Budget

Revenue and expenditure in $A1m.:

	2005–06	2006–07	2007–08[1]
Revenue	3,037	3,298	3,506
Expenditure	3,015	3,146	3,449

[1]Latest estimate from 2007–08 Mid-Year Report.

In 2007–08 total revenue was expected to be $A3,506m. of which $A2,770m. grants to the Northern Territory from the Commonwealth, $A386m. in state-like taxes and $A349m. Northern Territory Government own-source revenue.

Estimated expenditure in 2007–08 included $A772m. for health; $A741m. for education; $A432m. for public order and safety.

Banking and Finance

According to the Australian Prudential Regulation Authority, as at 30 June 2006 there were seven authorized banks with 39 branches; and six credit unions with 24 branches.

ENERGY AND NATURAL RESOURCES

Environment

There are 93 parks and reserves covering 43,709 sq. km. Twelve of the parks are classified as national parks, including the Kakadu and Uluru-Kata Tjuta National Park which are included on the World Heritage List.

Electricity

The Power and Water Corporation supplies power to 72 indigenous and remote communities as well as the major centres. In the year ended 30 June 2003 total electricity generated was 1,651 GWh; total consumption was 1,549m. kWh, including 1,055m. kWh by business customers.

Oil and Gas

The Timor Sea is a petroleum producing province with five fields and more than 22m. cu. ft of known gas reserves. Gas is currently supplied from the Palm Valley and Mereenie fields in the onshore Amadeus Basin to the Channel Island Power Station in Darwin via one of Australia's longest onshore gas pipelines. The total value of oil and gas production in 2004–05 was $A2,783m., an increase of $A821m. over 2003–04. The Northern Territory produced 2,640 megalitres of crude oil and 470m. cu. metres of natural gas in 2003–04.

Water

The Power and Water Corporation (PAWC) is responsible for providing water supply (also electric power and sewerage services) throughout the NT. PAWC's subsidiary, Indigenous Essential Services Pty Ltd, maintains water supply to the 72 remote communities and Aboriginal outstations.

Minerals

Mining is the major contributor to the Territory's economy. Compared to 2003–04 the overall value of production in the mining industry fell by 18·6% in 2004–05. Value of major mineral commodities production in 2003–04 (in $A1m.): bauxite/alumina, 591; gold, 342; manganese, 200; lead/zinc concentrate, 197; uranium, 184; diamonds (2002–03), 14.

Agriculture
In the year ending June 2005 there were 380 agricultural establishments with a total area under holding of 62·5m. ha. Gross value of agricultural production in 2004–05 rose by 4·2% to $A317m. Beef cattle production constitutes the largest farming industry. Total value of livestock slaughter and products in 2004–05 was $A249m., an increase of 23% on the previous year. 2004 fruit production (in tonnes): mangoes, 19,611; bananas, 2,898; table grapes, 1,508. There were six crocodile farms in 2005 producing a total of 13,513·5 kg of meat in the period Jan.–June 2005.

Forestry
In 2006 there were 27m. ha. of native forest, accounting for 20·2% of the Territory's total land area. As at June 2006 the total native forest cover consisted of 406,000 ha. closed forest, 7,139,000 ha. open forest and 25,290,000 ha. woodland. Total area of plantation forest was 26,000 ha., consisting mainly of softwoods. Hardwood plantations of fast-growing Acacia Mangium have been established on the Tiwi Islands for the production of woodchip for paper pulp. In addition, a number of operations for the production of sandalwood oil and neem products have been established near Batchelor.

Fisheries
Estimated total fisheries production in 2005–06 came to 8,257 tonnes with a gross value of $A98·0m. In the same year, aquaculture had a gross value of $A26·0m.

INDUSTRY
In the year ended 30 June 2005 the sales and service income generated by manufacturing industry was $A1,507m.; 4,200 persons were employed and salaries totalled $A209m. In Nov. 2006, 15,300 persons were employed in the wholesale and retail trade.

Labour
The labour force totalled 104,700 in Jan. 2007, of whom 102,100 were employed. The unemployment rate was 2·5%, down from 6·4% in Jan. 2006. The average weekly wage in Nov. 2006 was $A847·90 (males $A975·50, females $A724·80).

Trade Unions
As at Aug. 2006 there were 14,900 people belonging to a trade union (19·0% of total employees).[1]

[1]Mainly urban areas only, representing 77% of total population.

INTERNATIONAL TRADE
Imports and Exports
In 2005–06 the value of the Territory's imports totalled $A2,866·3m. Major sources of imports for 2005–06 (figures in $A1m.): France, 538·4; Singapore, 512·2; Thailand, 270·1; Kuwait, 149·8; Vietnam, 132·3; Japan, 117·9. 2005–06 exports totalled $A3,616·2m. Major export destinations (figures in $A1m.): Japan, 1,221·4; China, 741·4; Singapore, 439·8; Indonesia, 259·0; USA, 167·3; Canada, 120·6.

COMMUNICATIONS
Roads
At 30 June 2004 there were 22,097 km of roads. The number of registered motor vehicles (excluding tractors and trailers) at 31 March 2006 was 114,015, including 73,302 passenger vehicles, 28,872 light commercial vehicles, 4,725 trucks, 2,989 buses and 3,950 motorcycles. There were 45 road accident fatalities in 2006.

Rail
In 1980 Alice Springs was linked to the Trans-continental network by a standard (1,435 mm) gauge railway to Tarcoola in South Australia (830 km). A new 1,410 km standard gauge line operates between Darwin and Alice Springs. This $A1·3bn. AustralAsia Railway project links Darwin and Adelaide. The first train to complete the journey of 1,860 miles arrived in Darwin on 3 Feb. 2004.

Civil Aviation
Darwin and most regional centres in the Territory are serviced by daily flights to all State capitals and major cities. In 2003 there were direct international services connecting Darwin to Brunei, Hong Kong, Indonesia, Singapore and Timor-Leste. In 2003 Darwin airport handled 924,000 domestic and an estimated 77,700 international passengers, and Alice Springs (2003–04), 610,000 domestic passengers.

Shipping
In 2002–03, 704 commercial vessels called at Northern Territory ports. General cargo imported in 2002–03 was 117,794 mass tonnes and general cargo exported was 216,573 mass tonnes.

Telecommunications
In 2005–06 there were 41,000 households with home computer access (70% of all households). In 2005–06, 35,000 households had home internet access (60%).

Postal Services
In the year ended 30 June 2006 there were seven corporate outlets, 22 licensed post offices and 48 other agencies.

SOCIAL INSTITUTIONS
Justice
Voluntary euthanasia for the terminally ill was legalized in 1995 but the law was overturned by the Federal Senate on 24 March 1997. The first person to have recourse to legalized euthanasia died on 22 Sept. 1996.

Police personnel (sworn and unsworn) at 30 June 2007, 1,703 including 78 Aboriginal community police officers. In 2006–07 the Territory had two prisons with a daily average of 833 prisoners held.

Education
Education is compulsory from the age of six to 15 years. There were (Aug. 2006) 28,506 full-time students enrolled in 151 government schools and 9,074 enrolled in 35 non-government schools. Teaching staff in government and non-government schools totalled 3,205. The proportion of Indigenous students in the Territory is high, comprising 38·9% of all primary and secondary students at Aug. 2006. Bilingual programmes operate in some Aboriginal communities where traditional Aboriginal culture prevails.

The Northern Territory University (NTU), founded in 1989 by amalgamating the existing University College of the Northern Territory and the Darwin Institute of Technology, joined with the Alice Springs' Centralian College in 2004 to form the Charles Darwin University. At 31 March 2005, 2,519 students were enrolled in higher education courses of whom 7·5% were identified as Indigenous. The Batchelor Institute of Indigenous Tertiary Education, which provides higher and vocational education and training for Aboriginal and Torres Straits Islanders, had 593 students enrolled in higher education courses in 2005. In 2006 there were 29,817 enrolments in Vocational Education and Training activities.

Health
In 2005–06 there were five public hospitals with a total of 569 beds and two private hospitals. Community health services are provided from urban and rural Health Centres including mobile

units. Remote communities are served by resident nursing staff, aboriginal health workers and in larger communities, resident GPs. Emergency services are supported by the Aerial Medical Services throughout the Territory.

Welfare

Total social security and welfare expenditure for 2006–07 was $A175,331m. In the same year payments for welfare services for the aged totalled $A17,276m. and disability welfare services expenditure was $A50,811m.

RELIGION

Religious affiliation at the 2006 census: Roman Catholic, 21·1%; Anglican, 12·3%; Uniting Church, 7·0%; Lutheran, 3·9%; Baptist, 2·4%; other Christian, 8·0%; non-Christians, 5·1%; no religion, 23·1%; not stated, 17·1%.

CULTURE

Broadcasting

Darwin's radio services include four ABC stations, one SBS station, two commercial stations and a community station. Darwin has two commercial, one ABC and one SBS TV service. Most other Northern Territory centres have one commercial and one national radio service, with one each of ABC, SBS and commercial television.

Tourism

In 2003–04 a total of 1·5m. people visited the Northern Territory, a decrease of 10% over the previous year. In the same year tourist expenditure was $A1·2bn. Tourism is the second largest revenue earner after the mining industry.

FURTHER READING

Statistical Information: The State office of the Australian Bureau of Statistics (ABS) is at 7th Floor, AANT House, 81 Smith St., Darwin. Publications include: *Northern Territory at a Glance.* Annual (from 1994); *Regional Statistics, Northern Territory.* Annual (with exception of 1996) from 1995; and *National Regional Profile: Northern Territory* (from 2002).

The Northern Territory: Annual Report. Dept. of Territories, Canberra, from 1911. Dept. of the Interior, Canberra, from 1966–67. Dept. of Northern Territory, from 1972

Australian Territories, Dept. of Territories, Canberra, 1960 to 1973. Dept. of Special Minister of State, Canberra, 1973–75. Department of Administrative Services, 1976

Donovan, P. F., *A Land Full of Possibilities: A History of South Australia's Northern Territory 1863–1911.* 1981.—*At the Other End of Australia: The Commonwealth and the Northern Territory 1911–1978.* 1984

Heatley, A., *Almost Australians: the Politics of Northern Territory Self-Government.* 1990

Powell, A., *Far Country: A Short History of the Northern Territory.* 1996

State library: Northern Territory Library, Parliament House, State Sq., Darwin.

Website: http://www.ntl.nt.gov.au

New South Wales

KEY HISTORICAL EVENTS

The name New South Wales was applied to the entire east coast of Australia when Capt. James Cook claimed the land for the British Crown on 23 Aug. 1770. The separate colonies of Tasmania, South Australia, Victoria and Queensland were proclaimed in the 19th century. In 1911 and 1915 the Australian Capital Territory around Canberra and Jervis Bay was ceded to the Commonwealth. New South Wales was thus gradually reduced to its present area. The first settlement was made at Port Jackson in 1788 as a penal settlement. A partially elective council was established in 1843 and responsible government in 1856.

Gold discoveries from 1851 brought an influx of immigrants, and responsible government was at first unstable, with seven ministries holding office in the five years after 1856. Bitter conflict arose from land laws enacted in 1861. Lack of transport hampered agricultural expansion.

New South Wales federated with the other Australian states to form the Commonwealth of Australia in 1901.

TERRITORY AND POPULATION

New South Wales (NSW) is situated between the 29th and 38th parallels of S. lat. and 141st and 154th meridians of E. long., and comprises 801,352 sq. km, inclusive of Lord Howe Island, 17 sq. km, but exclusive of the Australian Capital Territory (2,349 sq. km) and 70 sq. km at Jervis Bay.

The population at the 2006 census was 6,549,177 (6,326,579 at 2001 census), of which 3,320,726 were female. In 2006 there were eight people per sq. km. Although NSW comprises only 10·4% of the total area of Australia, 33·0% of the Australian population live there. During the year ended June 2005, 44,700 permanent settlers arrived in New South Wales (40,600 June 2004).

The state is divided into 12 *Statistical Divisions.* The preliminary estimated population of these (in 1,000) at 30 June 2006 was: Sydney, 4,284·4; Hunter, 617·5; Illawarra, 414·5; Mid-North Coast, 297·0; Richmond-Tweed, 229·9; South Eastern, 207·2; Northern, 179·8; Central West, 178·5; Murrumbidgee, 154·2; North Western, 115·8; Murray, 115·6; Far West, 22·9. At June 2006 the preliminary estimated population of the Statistical Subdivisions Newcastle (within Hunter) and Wollongong (within Illawarra) was 517·5 and 278·1 respectively.

Lord Howe Island, 31° 33' 4" S., 159° 4' 26" E., which is part of New South Wales, is situated about 702 km northeast of Sydney; area, 1,654 ha., of which only about 120 ha. are arable; resident population (2006 census), 347 (175 females). The Island, which was discovered in 1788, is of volcanic origin. Mount Gower, the highest point, reaches a height of 866 metres.

The Lord Howe Island Board manages the affairs of the Island and supervises the Kentia palm-seed industry.

SOCIAL STATISTICS

Statistics for calendar years:

	Live births	*Deaths*	*Marriages*	*Divorces*
2004	85,894	46,440	37,431	15,007
2005	86,589	44,894	35,927	15,172
2006	87,336	46,034	38,071	14,482
2007	89,495	46,759	37,982	13,726

The annual rates per 1,000 of mean estimated resident population in 2007 were: births, 13·0; deaths, 6·8; marriages, 5·5; divorces, 2·0; infant mortality, 4·3 per 1,000 live births. Expectation of life in 2007: males, 79·1 years, females, 83·8.

CLIMATE

See AUSTRALIA: Climate.

CONSTITUTION AND GOVERNMENT

Within the State there are three levels of government: the Commonwealth government, with authority derived from a written constitution; the State government with residual powers; the local government authorities with powers based upon a State Act of Parliament, operating within incorporated areas extending over almost 90% of the State.

The Constitution of New South Wales is drawn from several diverse sources; certain Imperial statutes such as the Commonwealth of Australia Constitution Act (1900); the Australian States Constitution Act (1907); an element of inherited

English law; amendments to the Commonwealth of Australia Constitution Act; the (State) Constitution Act; the Australia Acts of 1986; the Constitution (Amendment) Act 1987 and certain other State Statutes; numerous legal decisions; and a large amount of English and local convention.

The Parliament of New South Wales may legislate for the peace, welfare and good government of the State in all matters not specifically reserved to the Commonwealth government. The State Legislature consists of the Sovereign, represented by the Governor, and two Houses of Parliament, the Legislative Council (upper house) and the Legislative Assembly (lower house). Australian citizens aged 18 and over, and other British subjects who were enrolled prior to 26 Jan. 1984, men and women aged 18 years and over, are entitled to the franchise. Enrolment and voting is compulsory. The optional preferential method of voting is used for both houses. The Legislative Council has 42 members elected for a term of office equivalent to two terms of the Legislative Assembly, with 21 members retiring at the same time as the Legislative Assembly elections. The whole State constitutes a single electoral district. The Legislative Assembly has 93 members elected in single-seat electoral districts for a maximum period of four years.

Electors enrolled (30 June 2006) numbered 4,299,510.

RECENT ELECTIONS

In elections held on 24 March 2007 the Australian Labor Party won 52 of 93 seats, the Liberal Party of Australia 22, the National Party 13 and ind. 6.

CURRENT ADMINISTRATION

In Feb. 2010 the Legislative Council consisted of the following parties: Australian Labor Party, 19; Liberal Party of Australia, 10; National Party, 5; Greens, 4; Shooters Party, 2; Christian Democratic Party (Fred Nile Group), 1; Family First Party, 1.

The Legislative Assembly, which was elected in 2007, consisted of the following parties in Feb. 2010: Australian Labor Party, 51 seats; Liberal Party of Australia, 23; National Party, 13; ind., 6.

Governor: Prof. Marie Bashir, AC.

The New South Wales ALP Ministry was as follows in Feb. 2010:

Premier, Minister for Redfern Waterloo: Kristina Keneally (b. 1968).

Deputy Premier, Minister for Health: Carmel Tebbutt. *Attorney General, Minister for Citizenship and Regulatory Reform:* John Hatzistergos. *Treasurer:* Eric Roozendaal. *Transport and Roads:* David Campbell. *Education and Training:* Verity Firth. *Planning, Infrastructure, and Lands:* Anthony Kelly. *Climate Change and the Environment:* Frank Sartor. *Community Services and State Plan:* Linda Burney. *Police and Finance:* Michael Daley. *Industrial Relations, Commerce, Energy and Public Sector Reform:* John Robertson. *State and Regional Development, Forest and Mineral Resources, and the Central Coast:* Ian Macdonald. *Ageing, Disability Services and Aboriginal Affairs:* Paul Lynch. *Emergency Services, Primary Industries and Rural Affairs:* Steven Whan. *Tourism, the Hunter, Women, and Science and Medical Research:* Jodi McKay. *Housing and Western Sydney:* David Borger. *Local Government:* Barbara Perry. *Water and Corrective Services:* Phillip Costa. *Gaming and Racing, Sport and Recreation:* Kevin Greene. *Fair Trading and the Arts:* Virginia Judge. *Juvenile Justice:* Graham West. *Ports and Waterways, and the Illawarra:* Paul McLeay. *Youth, Volunteering and Small Business:* Peter Primrose.

Speaker of the Legislative Assembly: Richard Torbay.

NSW Government Website: http://www.nsw.gov.au

ECONOMY

Budget

Government sector revenue and expenses ($A1m.):

	2005–06	2006–07	2007–08[1]
Revenue	41,220	42,196	44,068
Expenditure	40,576	42,892	43,690

[1]Forward estimate.

In 2006–07 State government revenue from taxes amounted to $A16,719m.; grants and subsidies totalled $A17,625m.

Performance

In 2002–03 the gross state product of New South Wales represented 34·95% of Australia's total GDP.

Banking and Finance

Lending activity of financial institutions in New South Wales in 2002–03 comprised (in $A1m.): commercial, 134,274; personal, 23,102; lease financing, 2,682. According to the Australian Prudential Regulation Authority, as at 30 June 2006 there were 27 authorized banks with 1,525 branches; seven building societies with 153 branches; and 87 credit unions with 397 branches.

ENERGY AND NATURAL RESOURCES

Electricity

In the year ended 30 June 2002 total consumption (including ACT total consumption) stood at 60,383m. kWh, of which 41,215m. kWh was by business customers. In 2001–02, 63,911m. kWh were produced, a fall of 1·4% on the previous year. Black coal is the main fuel source for electricity generation in the state, producing 89% of the total in the year ended 30 June 2007. Total installed capacity at 30 June 2002 was 12,147 MW.

Oil and Gas

No natural gas is produced in NSW. Almost all gas is imported from the Moomba field in South Australia plus, since 2001, a small amount from Bass Strait.

Water

Ground water represents the largest source with at least 130 communities relying on it for drinking water.

Minerals

New South Wales contains extensive mineral deposits. For the year ending 30 June 2005 there were 55 coal mines directly employing 11,290 people. The value of metallic minerals produced in 2004–05 was $A1·46bn.; construction materials, $A346m. Output of principal products, 2004–05 (in tonnes): coal, 156·3m.; zinc, 205,000; copper, 175,000; lead, 103,000; tin, 50; silver, 96; gold, 29.

Agriculture

NSW accounts for around 24% of the value of Australia's total agricultural production with a gross value of $A8·6bn. in 2004–05. In 2001–02 GDP at factor income for agriculture, forestry, hunting and fishing was $A5,808m. In the year ending 30 June 2005 there were 40,077 farming establishments with a total area under holding of 64·4m. ha. of which 7·67m. ha. were under crops.

Principal crops in 2004–05 with production in 1,000 tonnes: wheat for grain, 7,537; barley, 1,761; sorghum, 847; canola, 468. Value of crops, 2004–05, came to $A4·4bn. with wheat totalling $A1·4bn. and cotton $A526m. (Data relates to farms whose estimated value of agricultural operations was $A5,000 or more at the census.)

The total area under vines in 2005 was 39,278 ha. (including 3,501 ha. not yet bearing fruit); winegrape production totalled 508,286 tonnes.

In the year ending June 2005 there were an estimated 1,494 ha. of banana plantations, with production of 18,009 tonnes; 221,453 tonnes of oranges were produced (44·5% of the Australian total).

2004–05 gross value of livestock products was $A1·3bn., including wool produced, $A775m.; and milk, $A401m. In 2002–

03 production (in tonnes) of beef and veal, 488,000; mutton and lamb, 191,400; pig meat, 140,200.

Forestry

The area of forests managed by State Forests of NSW in 2002–03 totalled 2·9m. ha. of native forest; 212,000 ha. of softwood and 57,000 ha. of hardwood plantation with a total yield of 2·54m. cu. metres of sawlogs and veneer logs.

Fisheries

Estimated total fisheries production in 2005–06 came to 27,916 tonnes with a gross value of $A143·3m. In the same year aquaculture production was an estimated 5,212 tonnes with a gross value of $A45·03m.

INDUSTRY

A wide range of manufacturing is undertaken in the Sydney area, and there are large iron and steel works near the coalfields at Newcastle and Port Kembla. Around one-third of Australian manufacturing takes place in NSW.

Manufacturing establishments' operations in the year ended 30 June 2005:

Industry	*No. of persons employed (1,000)*	*Wages and salaries ($A1m.)*	*Sales and service income ($A1m.)*	*Industry value added ($A1m.)*
Food, beverages and tobacco	54·5	2,803	22,595	6,351
Textiles, clothing, footwear and leather	16·0	501	2,988	876
Wood and paper products	20·7	865	5,725	1,839
Printing, publishing and recorded media	41·6	2,196	10,185	4,080
Petroleum, coal, chemical and associated products	31·9	1,737	20,631	3,877
Non-metallic mineral products	14·1	752	4,513	1,600
Metal products	52·2	2,695	18,750	6,228
Machinery and equipment	63·9	3,157	15,783	5,441
Other manufacturing	22·1	717	4,181	1,273
Total manufacturing	317·0	15,425	105,352	31,564

Labour

In May 2003 the labour force was estimated to number 3,354,200 persons, of whom 3,152,100 were employed: 611,300 as professionals; 564,700 as intermediate clerical, sales and service workers; 390,500 as tradespersons and related workers; 275,900 as labourers and related workers; 262,900 as intermediate production and transport workers; 237,500 as managers and administrators; and 126,000 as advanced clerical and service workers. There were 169,900 unemployed (a rate of 4·8%) in June 2007. The average weekly wage in Nov. 2005 was $A1,089·00 (males $A1,157·40, females $A973·90).

Industrial tribunals are authorized to fix minimum rates of wages and other conditions of employment. Their awards may be enforced by law, as may be industrial agreements between employers and organizations of employees, when registered.

Trade Unions

Registration of trade unions is effected under the New South Wales Trade Union Act 1881, which follows substantially the Trade Union Acts of 1871 and 1876 of England. Registration confers a quasi-corporate existence with power to hold property, to sue and be sued, etc., and the various classes of employees covered by the union are required to be prescribed by the constitution of the union. For the purpose of bringing an industry under the review of the State industrial tribunals, or participating in proceedings relating to disputes before Commonwealth tribunals, employees and employers must be registered as industrial unions, under State or Commonwealth industrial legislation respectively. Trade union membership was held by 604,600 employees in Aug. 2006 (21·3% of employees).

INTERNATIONAL TRADE

Imports and Exports

External commerce, exclusive of interstate trade, is included in the statement of the commerce of Australia. Overseas commerce of New South Wales in $A1m. for years ending 30 June:

	Imports	*Exports*		*Imports*	*Exports*
2000–01	52,503	22,751	2003–04	53,763	19,091
2001–02	51,902	22,920	2004–05	60,107	23,003
2002–03	55,250	20,234	2005–06	64,885	26,840

The principal imports in 2005–06 (in $A1m.) were boilers, machinery, parts of mechanical appliances and nuclear reactors, 11,811; electrical machinery and equipment, sound recorders and reproducers, 9,692; vehicles other than railway or tramway rolling stock, 5,944; mineral fuels, mineral oils and products, 5,509. Major commodities exported were mineral fuels, mineral oils and products, 6,324; aluminium, 2,107; ores, slag and ash, 1,857; pharmaceutical products, 1,422.

Major sources of supply in 2005–06 (in $A1m.) were China, 11,479; USA, 9,625; Japan, 5,849; Germany, 3,291; UK, 3,010. Principal destinations of exports were Japan, 6,491; USA, 2,373; New Zealand, 2,228; China, 2,099; Republic of Korea, 1,815.

COMMUNICATIONS

Roads

At 30 June 2006 there were 183,120 km of public roads in total. The Roads and Traffic Authority of New South Wales is responsible for the administration and upkeep of major roads. In 2006 there were 20,699 km of roads under its control, comprising 4,250 km of national highways, 13,503 km of state roads and 2,946 km of regional and local roads.

The number of registered motor vehicles (excluding tractors and trailers) at 31 March 2006 was 4,268,631, including 3,395,905 passenger vehicles, 587,713 light commercial vehicles, 133,662 trucks, 20,733 buses and 122,211 motorcycles. There were 510 road accident fatalities in 2006.

Rail

Rail Corporation New South Wales (RailCorp) was formed in 2004 following a merger of the State Rail Authority and Rail Infrastructure Corporation. RailCorp owns, operates and maintains the rail tracks and related infrastructure, and provides metropolitan (CityRail) and long distance (CountryLink) passenger services and access to rail freight operators. In 2002–03, 273·5m. passengers were carried on CityRail and 2·1m. on Countrylink. In the year ended 31 March 2001, 112m. tonnes of freight were transported. Also open for traffic are 325 km of Victorian government railways which extend over the border, 68 km of private railways (mainly in mining districts) and 53 km of Commonwealth government-owned track.

A tramway opened in Sydney in 1996. There is also a small overhead railway in the city centre.

Civil Aviation

Sydney Airport (Kingsford Smith) is the major airport in New South Wales and Australia's principal international air terminal. In 2002 it was sold to Macquarie Airports. In 2002–03 it handled a total of 23,442,248 passengers (14,158,215 on domestic flights). It is also the leading airport for freight, handling 377,460 tonnes in 2002–03. At 13 Sept. 2003 registered aircraft totalled 3,593.

Shipping

The main ports are at Sydney, Newcastle, Port Kembla and Botany Bay. In 2002–03, 655 commercial vessels called at New South Wales ports. General cargo imported in 2002–03 was

25,992,725 mass tonnes and general cargo exported was 7,919,655 mass tonnes.

Telecommunications

At 30 June 2003 there were 14·3m. mobile telephone subscribers. In 2005–06 there were 1·82m. households with home computer access (69% of all households). In 2005–06, 1·57m. households had home internet access (60%).

Postal Services

In the year ended 30 June 2006 there were 267 corporate outlets, 881 licensed post offices and 100 other agencies.

SOCIAL INSTITUTIONS

Justice

Legal processes may be conducted in Local Courts presided over by magistrates or in higher courts (District Court or Supreme Court) presided over by judges. There is also an appellate jurisdiction. Persons charged with more serious crimes must be tried before a higher court.

Children's Courts remove children as far as possible from the atmosphere of a public court. There are also a number of tribunals exercising special jurisdiction, e.g. the Industrial Commission and the Compensation Court.

As at 30 June 2006 there was a daily average of 9,911 persons held in prison. Police personnel (sworn) at 30 June 2006, 14,634.

Education

The State government maintains a system of free primary and secondary education, and attendance at school is compulsory from the age of six years of age. Since Jan. 2010 it has been compulsory for young people aged 15–17 to remain in school or, by arrangement, take part in an approved education and training pathway such as an apprenticeship or traineeship. Non-government schools are subject to government inspection.

In Aug. 2006 there were 2,187 government schools with 740,415 pupils (434,366 primary, 306,049 secondary) and 51,385 teachers, and 912 non-government schools with 369,902 pupils (185,963 primary, 183,939 secondary) and 26,775 teachers. There were 297,200 students in higher education in 2005, with the largest numbers enrolled in management and commerce (29·1% of total enrolments) and society and culture (23·7%). Student enrolments in 2006: University of Sydney (founded 1850), 45,039; University of New England at Armidale (incorporated 1954), 17,854; University of New South Wales (founded 1949), 37,836; University of Newcastle (granted autonomy 1965), 22,997; University of Wollongong (founded 1951), 22,754; Macquarie University in Sydney (founded 1964), 31,660; University of Technology, Sydney, 32,708; University of Western Sydney, 35,061; Charles Sturt University, 34,261; Southern Cross University (founded 1994), 14,092. Colleges of advanced education were merged with universities in 1990. Post-school technical and further education is provided at State TAFE colleges. Enrolments in 2005 totalled 513,070.

Health

In 2005–06 there were 27,918 medical practitioners, 4,358 dentists and 82,740 registered nurses. In 2004–05 there were 232 public and 178 private hospitals.

Welfare

The number of income support payments in June 2003 included: age, 611,513; disability support, 219,820; single parent, 140,941; child care benefit, 224,820; carer payment, 26,910.

Direct State government social welfare services are limited, for the most part, to the assistance of persons not eligible for Commonwealth government pensions or benefits, and the provision of certain forms of assistance not available from the Commonwealth government. The State also subsidizes many approved services for needy persons.

RELIGION

At the 2006 census 28·2% of the population were Roman Catholic and 21·8% Anglican. These two religions combined had nearly 3·3m. followers.

CULTURE

Broadcasting

In addition to national broadcasting, at Sept. 2001 there were 22 commercial television services (including stations whose licence covers part of NSW as well as remote satellite services) and a total of 36 AM and 48 FM commercial radio services. The first cable-pay television service commenced in Sept. 1995, and satellite-delivered services in Nov. 1995.

Tourism

In 2003–04, 1·43m. overseas visitors arrived for short-term visits, a 7·4% increase on the previous year. At 30 June 2004 there were 1,350 hotels, motels, guest houses and serviced apartments providing 64,321 rooms.

FURTHER READING

Statistical Information: The NSW Government Statistician's Office was established in 1886, and in 1957 was integrated with the Commonwealth Bureau of Census and Statistics (now called the Australian Bureau of Statistics). The state office of: the Australian Bureau of Statistics is at 5th Floor, St Andrews House. Sydney Sq., Sydney). Publications include: *New South Wales in Focus.* Replaces *New South Wales Yearbook.* Annual, since 2005.—*Regional Statistics, New South Wales.*

State library: The State Library of NSW, Macquarie St., Sydney.
Website: http://www.sl.nsw.gov.au

Queensland

KEY HISTORICAL EVENTS

Queensland was discovered by Capt. Cook in 1770. From 1778 it was part of New South Wales and was made a separate colony, with the name of Queensland, by letters patent of 8 June 1859, when responsible government was conferred. Although by 1868 gold had been discovered, wool was the colony's principal product. The first railway line was opened in 1865. Queensland federated with the other Australian states to form the Commonwealth of Australia in 1901.

TERRITORY AND POPULATION

Queensland comprises the whole northeastern portion of the Australian continent, including the adjacent islands in the Pacific Ocean and in the Gulf of Carpentaria. Area, 1,734,190 sq. km.

At the 2006 census the population was 3,904,532 (3,522,044 at 2001 census), of which 1,969,151 were female. At the 2006 census there were 127,578 Aboriginals and Torres Strait Islanders. Statistics on birthplaces from the 2006 census are as follows: Australia, 75·2%; England, 4·1%; New Zealand, 3·8%; South Africa, 0·6%; Scotland, 0·6%.

Brisbane, the capital, had at the time of the 2006 census a resident population of 1,763,131 (Statistical Division). The resident populations of the other major centres (Statistical Districts) at 30 June 2005 were: Gold Coast-Tweed (Queensland component), 432,000; Sunshine Coast, 213,000; Townsville, 149,000; Cairns, 128,000; Mackay, 82,000; Rockhampton, 69,000; Bundaberg, 61,000; Gladstone, 43,000.

SOCIAL STATISTICS

Statistics (including Aboriginals) for calendar years:

	Births	*Deaths*	*Marriages*	*Divorces*
2004	49,593	24,657	24,312	13,279
2005	51,700	23,584	24,303	12,383
2006	52,665	24,473	25,043	12,175
2007	61,249	25,801	25,808	11,058

The annual rates per 1,000 population in 2007 were: births, 14·6; deaths, 6·2; marriages, 6·2; divorces, 2·6. The infant mortality rate in 2007 was 5·0 per 1,000 live births. Life expectancy, 2007: 78·9 years for males, 83·6 for females.

CLIMATE

A typical subtropical to tropical climate. High daytime temperatures during Oct. to March give a short spring and long summer. Centigrade temperatures in the hottest inland areas often exceed the high 30s before the official commencement of summer on 1 Dec. Daytime temperatures in winter are quite mild, in the low- to mid-20s. Average rainfall varies from about 150 mm in the desert in the extreme southwestern corner of the State to about 4,000 mm in parts of the sugar lands of the wet northeastern coast, the latter being the wettest part of Australia.

CONSTITUTION AND GOVERNMENT

Queensland, formerly a portion of New South Wales, was formed into a separate colony in 1859, and responsible government was conferred. The power of making laws and imposing taxes is vested in a parliament of one house—the *Legislative Assembly*—which comprises 89 members, returned from four electoral zones for three years, elected from single-member constituencies by compulsory ballot.

Queensland elects 26 members to the Commonwealth House of Representatives.

The Elections Act, 1983, provides franchise for all males and females, 18 years of age and over, qualified by six months' residence in Australia and three months in the electoral district. Electors enrolled (30 June 2006) numbered 2,458,457.

RECENT ELECTIONS

Legislative Assembly elections on 21 March 2009 gave the ruling Australian Labor Party (ALP) 51 seats and the newly-formed Liberal National Party (LNP) 34. Four independents were elected.

CURRENT ADMINISTRATION

Governor of Queensland: Penelope Wensley, AO (took office on 29 July 2008).

In Feb. 2010 the ALP administration was as follows:

Premier and Minister for the Arts: Anna Bligh (took office on 13 Sept. 2007).

Deputy Premier and Minister for Health: Paul Lucas. *Treasurer, and Minister for Employment and Economic Development:* Andrew Fraser. *Public Works, Information, and Communication Technology:* Rob Schwarten. *Natural Resources, Mines and Energy, and Trade:* Stephen Robertson. *Education and Training:* Geoff Wilson. *Police, Corrective Services, and Emergency Services:* Neil Roberts. *Main Roads:* Craig Wallace. *Primary Industries, Fisheries, and Rural and Regional Queensland:* Tim Mulherin. *Local Government, and Aboriginal and Torres Strait Islander Partnerships:* Desley Boyle. *Infrastructure and Planning:* Stirling Hinchliffe. *Transport:* Rachel Nolan. *Tourism and Fair Trading:* Peter Lawlor. *Child Safety and Sport:* Phil Reeves. *Community Services and Housing, and Women:* Karen Struthers. *Disability Services and Multicultural Affairs:* Annastacia Palaszczuk. *Climate Change and Sustainability:* Kate Jones. *Attorney General and Industrial Relations:* Cameron Dick.

Government Website: http://www.qld.gov.au

ECONOMY

Budget

In 2006–07 general government expenses by the state were expected to total $A28,825m.; revenue and grants received were expected to be $A29,070m.

Banking and Finance

According to the Australian Prudential Regulation Authority, as at 30 June 2006 there were 16 authorized banks with 1,151 branches; six building societies with 151 branches; and 24 credit unions with 148 branches.

ENERGY AND NATURAL RESOURCES

Electricity

The government-owned sector of the state's electricity industry has been restructured, and since Dec. 1998 it has operated as part of the wholesale national electricity market. Part of the restructuring was the formation of a single corporation, Ergon Energy, by the amalgamation of the six former regional distribution corporations. In the year ending 30 June 2002 total consumption stood at 39,544m. kWh by 1,684,488 customers, including 27,900m. kWh by business customers. Coal is the main fuel source for electricity generation in the state, producing 45,967m. kWh in the year ending 30 June 2002; installed generation capacity stood at 10,700 MW.

Water

In the western portion of the State water is comparatively easily found by sinking artesian bores. Monitoring of water quality in Queensland is carried out by the Department of the Environment (estuarine and coastal waters) and the Department of Natural Resources (fresh water).

Minerals

There are large reserves of coal, bauxite, gold, copper, silver, lead, zinc, nickel, phosphate rock and limestone. The state is the largest producer of black coal in Australia. Most of the coal produced comes from the Bowen Basin coalfields in central Queensland. Copper, lead, silver and zinc are mined in the northwest and the State's largest goldmines are in the north. The total value of metallic minerals in 2004–05 was $A4·62bn. In 2003–04 there were 45 coal mines in operation producing 160·06m. tonnes of saleable coal (an increase of 4·2% on the previous year); and at 30 June 2004, 13,192 persons were employed in mining.

Agriculture

Queensland is Australia's leading beef-producing state and its chief producer of fruit and vegetables. In the year ending 30 June 2005 there were 26,955 agricultural establishments farming 143·8m. ha. of which 2·7m. ha. were under crops. Livestock numbered (at 30 June 2005) 11,380,000 beef cattle; 4,949,000 sheep and lambs; and 666,000 pigs. Estimated total value of wool production, 2003–04: $A120m. The gross value of agricultural production in 2004–05 was $A8·3bn. which comprised crops, $A3·7bn.; livestock disposals, $4·2bn.; and livestock products, $A411m.

Forestry

Of a total of 56m. ha. of forests and woodlands in 2007, 9% was in national parks, World Heritage areas and other conservation reserves, while 5% was native forests in multiple use such as timber production. Queensland plantation forests comprise around 0·4% (225,000 ha.) of the state's total forest cover and supply around 10% of Australia's wood and paper products. The forestry industry is an important part of the state's economy, employing more than 19,000 people with an annual turnover of $A2·7bn.

Source: *Australia's Forests at a Glance 2007.* Australian Government Dept. of Agriculture, Fisheries and Forestry, Bureau of Rural Sciences publication, 2007.

Fisheries
Estimated total fisheries production in 2005–06 came to 34,417 tonnes with a gross value of $A322·6m. In the same year aquaculture production was an estimated 5,290 tonnes with a gross value of $A66·12m.

INDUSTRY
In the year ended 30 June 2005 manufacturing industry sales and service income was $A59,239m. with a total of 191,400 people employed. The largest manufacturing sector was food, beverages and tobacco (2004–05 sales and service income: $A14,995m.).

Labour
At Nov. 2006 the labour force numbered 2,163,900, of whom 2,082,900 (947,100 females) were employed. In June 2007 unemployment stood at 3·4%, down from 4·5% in June 2006. The average weekly wage in Nov. 2005 was $A959·60 (males $A1,014·00, females $A866·70).

Trade Unions
As at Aug. 2006 there were 363,600 people belonging to a trade union (20·7% of total employees).

INTERNATIONAL TRADE
Imports and Exports
Total value of direct overseas imports and exports f.o.b. port of shipment for both imports and exports in 2003–04: imports, $A18,052m.; exports, $A20,126m.

Chief sources of imports in 2003–04 (in $A1m.): USA, 3,052; Japan, 2,861; China, 1,614; Papua New Guinea, 920; Germany, 861. Exports went chiefly to (in $A1m.): Japan, 5,301; Republic of Korea, 2,194; USA, 1,421; China, 1,409; India, 1,041.

Principal overseas imports were (in $A1m.): passenger vehicles, 2,446; crude petroleum, 2,074; aircraft and parts, 1,199; motor vehicles for transporting goods, 815; non-monetary gold, 575; civil engineering equipment, 538. The chief exports overseas in 2003–04 (in $A1m.) were: coal, 5,929; bovine meat, 2,375; aluminium, 891; other ores, 807; copper, 490.

COMMUNICATIONS
Roads
At 30 June 2004 there were 181,305 km of roads open to the public. Of these, 70,608 km were surfaced with sealed pavement. The number of registered motor vehicles (excluding tractors and trailers) at 31 March 2006 was 2,897,867, including 2,138,364 passenger vehicles, 520,070 light commercial vehicles, 103,967 trucks, 16,516 buses and 110,501 motorcycles. There were 311 road accident fatalities in 2004.

Rail
Queensland Rail is a State government-owned corporation. Total length of line at 30 June 2006 was 8,360 km. In 2005–06, 54·1m. passengers and 183·5m. tonnes of freight were carried.

Civil Aviation
Queensland is well served with a network of air services, with overseas and interstate connections. Subsidiary companies provide planes for taxi and charter work, and the Flying Doctor Service operates throughout western Queensland. In 1997–98 all Federal airports were leased to private sector operators—Brisbane, Archerfield, Coolangatta, Mount Isa and Townsville Airports (the latter is operated jointly with the Department of Defence). In 2002–03 Brisbane handled 11,841,196 passengers (8,771,730 on domestic flights); Cairns, 2,900,472 passengers (1,899,991 on domestic flights). The number of aircraft registered at 31 Dec. 2005 was 2,715.

Shipping
Queensland has 14 modern trading ports, two community ports and a number of non-trading ports. In 2002–03 general cargo imported through Queensland ports was 1,588,964 mass tonnes and general cargo exported was 4,138,321 mass tonnes. There were 1,963 commercial ship calls during 2002–03.

Telecommunications
In 2005–06 there were 1·9m. households with home computer access (72% of all households). In 2005–06, 937,000 households had home internet access (61%).

Postal Services
In the year ended 30 June 2006 there were 173 corporate outlets, 463 licensed post offices and 186 other agencies.

SOCIAL INSTITUTIONS
Justice
Justice is administered by Higher Courts (Supreme and District), Magistrates' Courts and Children's Courts. The Supreme Court comprises the Chief Justice and 21 judges; the District Courts, 34 district court judges. Stipendiary magistrates preside over the Magistrates' and Children's Courts, except in the smaller centres, where justices of the peace officiate. A parole board may recommend prisoners for release.

Total police personnel (sworn and unsworn) at 30 June 2003 was 11,961. As at 30 June 2005 the average daily number of prisoners stood at 5,354.

Education
Education is compulsory between the ages of six and 16 years and is provided free in government schools. From 2008 students aged 15–17 must remain in school or, by arrangement, take part in an approved education and training pathway such as an apprenticeship or traineeship.

Primary and secondary education comprises 12 years of full-time formal schooling, and is provided by both the government and non-government sectors. In Aug. 2008 the State administered 1,250 schools with 308,771 primary students and 171,079 secondary students. In 2002 there were 35,071 teachers in government schools. There were 463 private schools in Aug. 2008 with 123,795 primary students and 102,817 secondary students. Educational programmes at private schools were provided by 13,803 teachers in 2002. In 2004 there were 278,800 subject enrolments in Vocational Education and Training activities. The one private and eight publicly-funded universities had approximately 190,000 full-time students in 2007.

Health
At 30 June 2003 there were 175 public acute hospitals and six public psychiatric hospitals. In 2005–06 there were 52 private free-standing day hospital facilities and 56 private acute and psychiatric hospitals. In 2003 Queensland had the highest rate of obesity in Australia (18·5% of the State's population).

Welfare
Welfare institutions providing shelter and social care for the aged, the handicapped and children are maintained or assisted by the State. A child health service is provided throughout the State. Age, invalid, widows', disability and war service pensions, family allowances, and unemployment and sickness benefits are paid by the Federal government. The number of age and disability pensions at 30 June 2003 was: age, 320,351; disability support, 129,406. There were 117,621 newstart allowance, 80,173 youth allowance and 97,730 single parent payments current at 30 June 2003.

RELIGION
Religious affiliation at the 2006 census: Roman Catholic, 24·0%; Anglican, 20·4%; Uniting Church, 7·2%; Presbyterian and Reformed, 3·7%; Lutheran, 2·0%; Baptist, 1·9%; other Christian, 7·2%; non-Christian, 3·3%; no religion, 18·6%; not stated, 11·7%.

CULTURE

Broadcasting

In addition to the national networks Queensland is served by 13 public radio stations (non-profit-making), 44 commercial radio stations and three commercial TV channels.

Tourism

Overseas visitors to Queensland in the year ending June 2004 totalled 1·96m., the main source being from Asia, with Japanese tourists totalling 454,157 (23% of the total). Visitors from New Zealand accounted for 17%; UK, 14%; and USA, 7%.

FURTHER READING

Statistical Information: The State office of the Australian Bureau of Statistics is at Level 3, 639 Wickham St., Brisbane. *A Queensland Official Year Book* was issued in 1901, the annual *ABC of Queensland Statistics* from 1905 to 1936 with exception of 1918 and 1922. Present publications include: *Queensland at a Glance*. Annual since 2000 with exception of 2001.—*Qld Stats*. Selected statistics available at *website:* http://www.abs.gov.au

Australian Sugar Year Book. From 1941
Johnston, W. R., *A Bibliography of Queensland History*. 1981.—*The Call of the Land: A History of Queensland to the Present Day*. 1982
Johnston, W. R. and Zerner, M., *Guide to the History of Queensland*. 1985

State library: The State Library of Queensland, Queensland Cultural Centre, PO Box 3488, South Bank, South Brisbane.
Website: http://www.slq.qld.gov.au
Local Statistical Office: Office of Economic and Statistical Research, PO Box 15037, City East, Qld 4002.
Website: http://www.oesr.qld.gov.au

South Australia

KEY HISTORICAL EVENTS

South Australia was surveyed by Tasman in 1644 and charted by Flinders in 1802. It was made into a British province by letters of patent of Feb. 1836, and a partially elective legislative council was established in 1851. From 6 July 1863 the Northern Territory was placed under the jurisdiction of South Australia until the establishment of the Commonwealth of Australia in 1911.

TERRITORY AND POPULATION

The total area of South Australia is 985,324 sq. km. The settled part is divided into counties and hundreds. There are 49 counties proclaimed, and 536 hundreds, covering 23m. ha., of which 19m. ha. are occupied. Outside this area there are extensive pastoral districts, covering 76m. ha., 49m. of which are under pastoral leases.

The 2006 census population was 1,514,337 (25,557 Aboriginal and Torres Strait Islanders). The 2001 census totalled 1,470,057.

At the 2006 census the Adelaide Statistical Division had a population of 1,105,839 persons (73·0% of South Australia's total population) in 25 councils and four municipalities and other districts. Urban centres outside this area (with estimated populations at 30 June 2007) are Mount Gambier (24,640), Whyalla (22,612), Port Pirie (17,869), Port Lincoln (14,298) and Port Augusta (14,215).

SOCIAL STATISTICS

Statistics for calendar years:

	Live Births	*Deaths*	*Marriages*	*Divorces*
2004	17,140	11,629	7,883	4,147
2005	17,800	11,984	7,630	3,669
2006	18,260	11,921	7,841	3,913
2007	19,662	12,345	8,095	3,534

The rates per 1,000 population in 2007 were: births, 12·4; deaths, 7·8; marriages, 5·1; divorces, 2·2. The infant mortality rate in 2007 was 4·5 per 1,000 live births. Life expectancy for 2007 was 78·8 years for men and 83·9 years for women.

CONSTITUTION AND GOVERNMENT

The present Constitution dates from 24 Oct. 1856. It vests the legislative power in an elected Parliament, consisting of a Legislative Council and a House of Assembly. The former is composed of 22 members. Eleven members are elected at alternate elections for a term of at least six years and are elected on the basis of preferential proportional representation with the State as one multi-member electorate. The House of Assembly consists of 47 members elected by a preferential system of voting for the term of a Parliament (four years). Election of members of both Houses takes place by secret ballot. Voting is compulsory for those on the Electoral Roll. The qualifications of an elector are to be an Australian citizen, or a British subject who was, at some time within the period of three months commencing on 26 Oct. 1983, enrolled under the Repealed Act as an Assembly elector or enrolled on an electoral roll maintained under the Commonwealth or a Commonwealth Territory, must be at least 18 years of age and have lived in the subdivision for which the person is enrolled for at least one month. By the Constitution Act Amendment Act, 1894, the franchise was extended to women, who voted for the first time at the general election of 25 April 1896. Certain persons are ineligible for election to either House.

The executive power is vested in a Governor appointed by the Crown and an Executive Council, consisting of the Governor and the Ministers of the Crown. The Governor has the power to dissolve the House of Assembly but not the Legislative Council, unless that Chamber has twice consecutively with an election intervening defeated the same or substantially the same Bill passed in the House of Assembly by an absolute majority.

Electors enrolled (30 June 2006) numbered 1,058,029.

RECENT ELECTIONS

The House of Assembly, elected on 20 March 2010, consisted of the following members: Australian Labor Party (ALP), 26; Liberal Party (LP), 18; Independent (ind.), 3.

CURRENT ADMINISTRATION

Governor: Kevin Scarce, AC, CSC.

In March 2010 the Labor Ministry was as follows:

Premier, Minister for Economic Development, Social Inclusion, the Arts, and Sustainability and Climate Change: Mike Rann.

Deputy Premier, Treasurer, Minister for Federal/State Relations and Defence Industries: Kevin Foley. *Mineral Resources Development, Urban Development and Planning, and Industrial Relations:* Paul Holloway. *Transport, Infrastructure and Energy:* Patrick Conlon. *Health, Mental Health and Substance Abuse, and the Southern Suburbs:* John Hill. *Police, Emergency Services, and Recreation, Sport and Racing:* Michael Wright. *Education and Early Childhood Development:* Jay Weatherill. *Families and Communities, Housing, Ageing, and Disability:* Jennifer Rankine. *Environment and Conservation, and River Murray, and Water:* Paul Caica. *State/Local Government Relations, Status of Women, Consumer Affairs, Government Enterprises, and Adelaide:* Gail Gago. *Industry and Trade, Small Business, Correctional Services, and Gambling:* Tom Koutsantonis. *Agriculture, Food and Fisheries, Forests, Regional Development, and the Northern Suburbs:* Michael O'Brien. *Employment, Training and Further Education, Science and Information Economy, Road Safety, and Veterans' Affairs:* Jack Snelling. *Attorney General, Justice, and Tourism:* John Rau. *Aboriginal Affairs and Reconciliation, Multicultural Affairs, Youth, and Volunteers:* Grace Portolesi.

Speaker: Jack Snelling (ALP).

President: Bob Sneath (ALP).

SA Government Website: http://www.sa.gov.au

ECONOMY

Budget

Estimated government sector revenue and expenses ($A1m.):

	2004–05	2005–06	2006–07
Revenue	10,592	11,088	11,264
Expenditure	10,368	10,942	11,173

In 2006–07 State government revenue from taxes amounted to $A3,086m.; grants and subsidies totalled $A5,792m.

Performance

South Australia's 2002–03 gross state product represented 6·63% of Australia's total GDP.

Banking and Finance

According to the Australian Prudential Regulation Authority, as at 30 June 2006 there were 14 authorized banks with 439 branches; one building society with one branch; and 14 credit unions with 75 branches.

ENERGY AND NATURAL RESOURCES

Electricity

In the year ending 30 June 2002 total consumption stood at 11,213m. kWh, including 6,813m. kWh by business customers. At June 2002 installed generation capacity stood at 3,479 MW.

Minerals

The principal metallic minerals produced are copper, iron ore, uranium oxide, gold and silver. The total value of metallic minerals produced in 2005–06 was $A2,077m. including copper, $A1,444m.; uranium oxide, $A288m.; iron ore, $A191m. Total value of opal production (2005–06), $A25·1m. In 2005–06 there were 4,141 persons employed in mining.

Agriculture

In the year ending 30 June 2005 there were 14,111 establishments mainly engaged in agriculture with a total area under holding of 54·1m. ha. of which 4·4m. ha. were under crops. The gross value of agricultural production in 2004–05 was $A3·9bn. Total value of wool production, $A267·0m. Value of chief crops in 2004–05: wheat, $A531m.; barley, $A304m.; potatoes, $A12m. Production of grapes (2005) was 861,518 tonnes with virtually all being used for winemaking (vineyards' total area, 71,413 ha., including 4,434 ha. not yet bearing). Fruit culture is extensive with citrus and orchard fruits. The most valuable vegetable crops are potatoes, onions and carrots.

Livestock, 30 June 2005: cattle, 1,223,000; sheep and lambs, 12,476,000; pigs, 335,000. Gross value of livestock slaughtered, 2004–05, $A839·9m.

Forestry

Total area of plantations at 31 Dec. 2006 totalled 172,000 ha. Production of sawn timber in 2005–06 was 493,900 cu. metres.

Fisheries

Estimated total fisheries production in 2005–06 came to 69,400 tonnes with a gross value of $A466·8m. In the same year aquaculture production was an estimated 16,935 tonnes with a gross value of $A214·5m.

INDUSTRY

Sales and service income for manufacturing industries for 2004–05 was $A27,182m.; wages and salaries totalled $A4,315m.

Industry sub-division	*No. of persons employed (1,000)*	*Wages and salaries ($A1m.)*	*Sales and service income ($A1m.)*	*Industry value added ($A1m.)*
Food, beverages and tobacco	19·2	845	5,993	1,987
Textile, clothing, footwear and leather manufacturing	2·7	78	475	118
Wood and paper products manufacturing	6·7	315	1,623	736
Printing, publishing and recorded media	7·8	296	1,332	608
Chemical, petroleum, coal and associated products	8·2	385	2,307	719
Non-metallic mineral products	3·2	162	1,299	422
Metal products manufacturing	12·7	569	3,616	1,024
Machinery and equipment	31·4	1,531	9,825	2,367
Other manufacturing	5·1	133	712	250
Total	97·1	4,315	27,182	8,140

Labour

In Nov. 2004 the labour force stood at 767,400. There were 38,100 unemployed in June 2007, a rate of 4·8%. The average weekly wage in Nov. 2005 was $A950·60 (males $A982·40, females $A891·00).

Trade Unions

As at Aug. 2006 there were 140,400 people belonging to a trade union (21·6% of total employees).

INTERNATIONAL TRADE

Imports and Exports

Overseas imports and exports in $A1m. (year ending 30 June):

	2001–02	2002–03	2003–04
Imports	5,347	5,724	5,163
Exports	9,103	8,365	7,604

Principal imports in 2003–04 were (with values in $A1m.): refined petroleum, 481; motor vehicles parts, 409; passenger motor vehicles, 384; internal combustion piston engines, 222; measuring and controlling instruments, 138. Principal exports in 2003–04 were (with values in $A1m.): alcoholic beverages, 1,411; passenger motor vehicles, 1,110; wheat, 693; copper, 398; fish 247; meat, excluding bovine, 217.

In 2003–04 the leading suppliers of imports were (with values in $A1m.): Japan, 891; USA, 652; Singapore, 547; China, 371; Canada, 311. Main export markets were the USA, 1,391; UK, 784; Japan, 695; New Zealand, 557; Saudi Arabia, 444.

COMMUNICATIONS

Roads

At 30 June 2004 there were 28,557 km of sealed and 68,017 km of unsealed roads. The number of registered motor vehicles (excluding tractors and trailers) at 31 March 2006 was 1,137,957, including 915,059 passenger vehicles, 145,643 light commercial vehicles, 34,994 trucks, 4,413 buses and 33,772 motorcycles. In 2004 there were 139 road accident fatalities.

Rail

In Aug. 1997 the passenger operations of Australian National Railways were sold to Great Southern Railway and the freight operations to Australian Southern Railroad. Australian National Railways operates 4,415 km of railway in country areas. TransAdelaide operates 120 km of railway in the metropolitan area of Adelaide. In the year ended 31 March 2001, 19m. tonnes of freight were carried.

There is a tramway in Adelaide that runs from the city centre to the coast. A joint South Australia and Northern Territory project, The AustralAsia Rail Project between Alice Springs and Darwin, carried its first passenger train in Feb. 2004.

Civil Aviation
The main airport is Adelaide International Airport, which handled 4,350,836 passengers (3,841,475 on domestic flights) in 2002–03.

Shipping
There are ten state and five private deep-sea ports. In 2002–03, 1,361 commercial vessels arrived in South Australia. General cargo imported in 2002–03 was 678,338 mass tonnes and general cargo exported was 1,610,919 mass tonnes.

Telecommunications
In 2004 residential telephone penetration was 93·1% (98% in 1998).[1] In 2005–06 there were 429,000 households with home computer access (67% of all households). In 2005–06, 356,000 households had home internet access (56%).

[1]Source: Roy Morgan Single Source January–March 2005

Postal Services
In the year ended 30 June 2006 there were 73 corporate outlets, 298 licensed post offices and 133 other agencies.

SOCIAL INSTITUTIONS

Justice
There is a Supreme Court, which incorporates admiralty, civil, criminal, land and valuation, and testamentary jurisdiction; district criminal courts, which have jurisdiction in many indictable offences; and magistrates courts, which include the Youth Court. Circuit courts are held at several places. At 30 June 2004 the police force numbered 3,910. The average daily number of prisoners at 30 June 2003 was 1,455.

Education
Education is compulsory for children between the ages of six and 16 years although most children are enrolled at age five or soon after. Since Jan. 2009 it has been compulsory for young people to remain in full-time education or training until they reach the age of 17. Primary and secondary education at government schools is secular and free. In March 2006 there were 805 schools operating, of which 602 were government and 203 non-government schools. In that year there were 107,611 children in government and 49,767 in non-government primary schools, and 63,576 children in government and 35,424 in non-government secondary schools. In 2004 there were 111,300 enrolments in Vocational Education and Training activities. There were 32,266 students enrolled at the University of South Australia in 2005; University of Adelaide, 19,224; and Flinders University, 15,110.

Health
In 2003–04 there were 80 public hospitals and 55 private hospitals. Beds available in public and private hospitals totalled 6,553.

Welfare
The number of age and disability pensions at 30 June 2003 was: age, 173,487; disability support, 64,414. There were 46,064 newstart allowance, 32,538 youth allowance and 35,686 single parent payments current at 30 June 2003.

RELIGION
Religious affiliation at the 2006 census: Catholic, 305,205; Anglican, 207,715; Uniting Church, 151,553; Lutheran, 71,251; Orthodox, 44,912; Baptist, 26,146; Presbyterian and Reformed, 21,030; other Christians, 78,252; non-Christians, 59,557; no religion, 367,161; not stated, 181,555.

CULTURE

Broadcasting
There are 131 radio stations (24 AM and 107 FM) and four commercial TV stations, one community service TV station and the national ABC service.

Tourism
In the year ended 30 June 2007 international visitors totalled 375,500 (around 48% from Europe), an increase of 8·5% on the previous year. At 30 June 2007 there were 253 hotels, motels, guest houses and serviced apartments with 11,547 rooms.

FURTHER READING
Statistical Information: The State office of the Australian Bureau of Statistics (ABS) is at 7th Floor East, Commonwealth Centre, 55 Currie St., Adelaide. Although the first printed statistical publication was the *Statistics of South Australia, 1854*, with the title altered to *Statistical Register* in 1859, there is a manuscript volume for each year back to 1838. These contain simple records of trade, demography, production, etc. and were prepared only for the information of the Colonial Office; one copy was retained in the State.

ABS publications include the *South Australian Year Book* (now discontinued)—*South Australia at a Glance*, annual since 2005.—*SA Stats*, a quarterly bulletin of economic, social and environment statistics.

Gibbs, R. M., *A History of South Australia: from Colonial Days to the Present.* 3rd ed. revised. 1995

Prest, Wilfred, Round, Kerrie and Fort, Carol, (eds.) *The Wakefield Companion to South Australian History.* 2002

Whitelock, D., *Adelaide from Colony to Jubilee: a Sense of Difference.* 1985

State library: The State Library of S.A., North Terrace, Adelaide.
Website: http://www.slsa.sa.gov.au/site/page.cfm

Tasmania

KEY HISTORICAL EVENTS
Abel Janszoon Tasman discovered Van Diemen's Land (Tasmania) on 24 Nov. 1642. The island became a British settlement in 1803 as a dependency of New South Wales. In 1825 its connection with New South Wales was terminated and in 1851 a partially elected Legislative Council was established. In 1856 a fully responsible government was inaugurated. On 1 Jan. 1901 Tasmania was federated with the other Australian states into the Commonwealth of Australia.

TERRITORY AND POPULATION
Tasmania is a group of islands separated from the mainland by Bass Strait with an area (including islands) of 67,914 sq. km, of which 63,447 sq. km form the area of the main island. The population at the 2006 census was 476,481 (460,672 at 2001 census), including 396,655 born in Australia, 18,918 in England and 4,158 in New Zealand.

The largest cities and towns (with populations at the 2006 census) are: Hobart (200,525), Launceston (103,325), Devonport (23,392) and Burnie (19,701).

SOCIAL STATISTICS
Statistics for calendar years:

	Births	*Deaths*	*Marriages*	*Divorces*
2004	5,809	3,892	2,648	1,404
2005	6,308	3,867	2,644	1,346
2006	6,475	3,934	2,664	1,233
2007	6,662	4,132	2,791	1,127

The annual rates per 1,000 of the mean resident population in 2007 were: births, 13·5; deaths, 8·4; marriages, 5·7; divorces, 2·3. Infant mortality rate, 2007, 4·2 per 1,000 live births. Expectation of life, 2007: males, 77·7 years; females, 82·4 years.

CLIMATE

Mostly a temperate maritime climate. The prevailing westerly airstream leads to a west coast and highlands that are cool, wet and cloudy, and an east coast and lowlands that are milder, drier and sunnier.

CONSTITUTION AND GOVERNMENT

Parliament consists of the Governor, the Legislative Council and the House of Assembly. The Council has 15 members, elected by adults with six months' residence. Members sit for six years, with either two or three retiring annually. There is no power to dissolve the Council. The House of Assembly has 25 members; the maximum term for the House of Assembly is four years. Women received the right to vote in 1903. Proportional representation was adopted in 1907, the method now being the single transferable vote in five member constituencies. Electors enrolled (30 June 2006) numbered 343,494.

A Minister must have a seat in one of the two Houses.

RECENT ELECTIONS

At the elections of 20 March 2010 the opposition Liberal Party won 10 seats in the House of Assembly, the ruling Australian Labor Party also 10 and the Tasmanian Greens 5.

CURRENT ADMINISTRATION

Governor: Peter Underwood, AO; b. 1937 (took office on 2 April 2008).

In April 2010 the Labor-Green government comprised:

Premier and Minister for Innovation, Science and Technology: David Bartlett (took office on 26 May 2008).

Deputy Premier, Attorney General and Minister for Justice, Economic Development and Infrastructure: Lara Giddings. *Treasurer and Minister for Industry:* Michael Aird. *Primary Industries and Water, Energy and Resources, Local Government, Planning, Racing and Veterans' Affairs:* Bryan Green. *Environment, Parks and Heritage, Workplace Relations, the Arts, Sport and Recreation, and Hospitality:* David O'Byrne. *Human Services, Corrections and Consumer Protection, Community Development, Climate Change, Sustainable Transport and Alternative Energy:* Nick McKim. *Health and Tourism:* Michelle O'Byrne. *Education and Skills, Children, and Police and Emergency Management:* Lin Thorp. *Leader of the Government in the Legislative Council:* Doug Parkinson.

Speaker of the House of Assembly: Michael Polley.

TAS Government Website: http://www.tas.gov.au

ECONOMY

Budget

Consolidated Revenue Fund receipts and expenditure, in $A1m., for financial years ending 30 June:

	2005–06	*2006–07*
Revenue	3,572	3,695
Expenditure	3,453	3,680

In 2007–08 estimated State government revenue from taxes amounted to $A752m.; grants and subsidies, $A2,391m.

Banking and Finance

According to the Australian Prudential Regulation Authority, as at 30 June 2006 there were seven authorized banks with 126 branches; one building society with nine branches; and three credit unions with 22 branches.

ENERGY AND NATURAL RESOURCES

Electricity

Installed capacity is 2,502 MW. In the year ended 30 June 2003 total consumption stood at 9,780m. kWh, including 1,820m. kWh by residential customers.

Minerals

Output of principal metallic minerals in 2004–05 was (in 1,000 tonnes): iron ore and concentrate, 2,174; zinc, 95; lead, 33; copper, 29; tin, 1·7.

Agriculture

There were 3,877 agricultural establishments at 30 June 2005 occupying a total area of 1·8m. ha. Principal crops in 2004–05 with estimated production in 1,000 tonnes: potatoes, 321; apples, 46; barley, 28; wheat, 30; oats, 9. Gross value of recorded production in 2004–05 was: crops, $A385m.; livestock products, $A259m.; total gross value of agricultural production, $A903m. Livestock, 2005–06: meat cattle, 501,000; sheep and lambs, 2,963,000; pigs, 17,000. Wool produced during 2001–02 was 14,268 tonnes.

Forestry

Indigenous forests, which cover a considerable part of the State, support sawmilling and woodchipping industries. Production of sawn timber in 2005–06 was 364,300 cu. metres. Newsprint and paper are produced from native hardwoods.

Fisheries

Estimated total fisheries production in 2005–06 came to 39,298 tonnes with a gross value of $A435·0m. In the same year aquaculture production was an estimated 22,756 tonnes with a gross value of $A247·2m.

INDUSTRY

The most important manufactures for export are refined metals, woodchips, newsprint and other paper manufactures, pigments, woollen goods, fruit pulp, confectionery, butter, cheese, preserved and dried vegetables, sawn timber and processed fish products. The electrolytic-zinc works at Risdon produce zinc, sulphuric acid, superphosphate, sulphate of ammonia, cadmium and other by-products. At George Town, large-scale plants produce refined aluminium and manganese alloys. In the year ending 30 June 2006 employment in manufacturing establishments was 21,400; wages and salaries totalled $A941m.

Labour

In 2006–07 the labour force stood at 238,000. In the same year there were 13,500 unemployed, a rate of 5·7%. The average weekly wage in Nov. 2005 was $A911·40 (males $A955·90, females $A827·60).

Trade Unions

As at Aug. 2006 there were 50,300 people belonging to a trade union (26·7% of total employees).

INTERNATIONAL TRADE

Imports and Exports

In 2003–04 direct imports into Tasmania totalled $A699m. In that year the principal suppliers of imports were (with values in $A1m.): Indonesia, 115; Germany, 100; USA, 71. In 2003–04 exports totalled $A2,312m. The principal countries of destination in 2003–04 (with values in $A1m.) for overseas exports were: Japan, 589; Hong Kong, 282; USA, 275; Republic of Korea, 207; China, 160. Commodities by value (in $A1m.) imported from overseas countries in 2003–04 included: ships, boats and floating structures, 172; pulp and waste paper, 68; rotating electric plant, 68. Commodities by value (in $A1m.) exported to overseas countries in 2003–04 included: zinc, 345; aluminium, 333; crustaceans, 90; bovine meat, 89.

COMMUNICATIONS

Roads

At 30 June 2004 there were 24,644 km of roads open to general traffic. The number of registered motor vehicles (excluding tractors and trailers) at 31 March 2006 was 374,846, including 271,365 passenger vehicles, 74,586 light commercial vehicles,

12,639 trucks, 2,219 buses and 10,488 motorcycles. In the year ended 31 Dec. 2004 there were 58 road accident fatalities.

Rail
Tasmania's rail network, incorporating 867 km of railways, is primarily a freight system with no regular passenger services. There are some small tourist railways, notably the newly rebuilt 34 km Abt Wilderness Railway on the west coast.

Civil Aviation
Regular passenger and freight services connect the south, north and northwest of the State with the mainland. The four main airports handled 2,559,656 passengers in 2004–05 and six leading airports handled 5,594 tonnes of freight in 2000–01.

Shipping
There are four major commercial ports: Burnie, Devonport, Launceston and Hobart. In 2002–03, 1,443 commercial vessels called at Tasmanian ports. General cargo imported in 2002–03 was 1,846,595 mass tonnes and general cargo exported was 2,852,972 mass tonnes. Passenger ferry services connect Tasmania with the mainland and offshore islands.

Telecommunications
In 2005–06 there were 121,000 households with home computer access (60% of all households). In 2006–07, 112,000 households had home internet access (56%).

Postal Services
In the year ended 30 June 2006 there were 28 corporate outlets, 146 licensed post offices and 27 other agencies.

SOCIAL INSTITUTIONS

Justice
The Supreme Court of Tasmania is a superior court of record, with both original and appellate jurisdiction, and consists of a Chief Justice and five puisne judges. There are also inferior civil courts with limited jurisdiction.

In 2002–03 there were 47,999 recorded offences, including 41,482 against property; 4,472 against the person; and 1,663 fraud and similar offences. Total police personnel (sworn and unsworn) at 30 June 2003 was 1,548. There are five prisons which in 2005–06 had a daily average of 504 prisoners held.

Education
Education is controlled by the State and is free, secular and compulsory between the ages of five and 16. Since Jan. 2008 it has been compulsory for students aged 16–17 to remain in school or, by arrangement, take part in an approved education and training pathway such as an apprenticeship or traineeship. In 2007, 212 government schools had a total enrolment of 58,926 pupils; 67 private schools had a total enrolment of 22,933 pupils.

In 2006 there were 41,800 students in Vocational Education and Training activities.

Tertiary education is offered at the University of Tasmania and the Australian Maritime College. In 2007 the University (established 1890) had 20,019 students and the Australian Maritime College 1,726 students.

Health
In 2002–03 there were 25 public hospitals with 1,136 beds and 11 private hospitals with 1,098 beds, a total of 4·7 beds per 1,000 population.

Welfare
The number of age and disability pensions at 30 June 2003 was: age, 51,015; disability support, 23,699. There were 19,350 newstart allowance, 13,007 youth allowance and 13,259 single parent payments current at 30 June 2003.

RELIGION
At the census of 2006 the following numbers of adherents of the principal religions were recorded:

Anglican Church	139,379	Not stated	58,135
Roman Catholic	87,784	No religion	102,577
Uniting Church	27,507	Non-Christian	9,696
Presbyterian and Reformed	12,125		
Baptist	8,664	Total	476,481
Other Christian	30,614		

CULTURE

Broadcasting
In 2002 there were four TV broadcasters and 21 radio stations.

Tourism
In 2007, 815,200 adult visitors arrived in Tasmania (748,500 in 2004).

FURTHER READING

Statistical Information: The State Government Statistical Office (200 Collins St., Hobart), established in 1877, became in 1924 the Tasmanian Office of the Australian Bureau of Statistics, but continues to serve State statistical needs as required.

Main publications: *Tasmanian Year Book.* Annual (from 1967; biennial from 1986), now discontinued.—*Tasmania at a Glance.* Annual (from 1994).—*Regional Statistics, Tasmania.* Annual (from 1999).—*Statistics–Tasmania.* Annual.

Email address: Sales and Inquiries: client.services@abs.gov.au

Website: http://www.abs.gov.au

Robson, L., *A History of Tasmania. Vol. 1: Van Diemen's Land from the Earliest Times to 1855.* 1983.—*A History of Tasmania. Vol. 2: Colony and State from 1856 to the 1980s.* 1990

State library: The State Library of Tasmania, 91 Murray St., Hobart, TAS 7000.

Website: http://www.statelibrary.tas.gov.au

Victoria

KEY HISTORICAL EVENTS
The first permanent settlement was formed at Portland Bay in 1834. A government was established in 1839. Victoria, formerly a portion of New South Wales, was proclaimed a separate colony in 1851 at much the same time as gold was discovered. A new constitution giving responsible government to the colony was proclaimed on 23 Nov. 1855. This event had far-reaching effects, as the population increased from 76,162 in 1850 to 589,160 in 1864. By this time the impetus for the search for gold had waned and new arrivals made a living from pastoral and agricultural holdings and from the development of manufacturing industries. Victoria federated with the other Australian states to form the Commonwealth of Australia in 1901.

TERRITORY AND POPULATION
The State has an area of 227,590 sq. km. The 2006 census population was 4,932,422 (4,660,991 at 2001 census). Victoria has the greatest proportion of people from non-English-speaking countries of any State or Territory, with (2006 census) 1·7% from Italy, 1·2% from Vietnam and 1·1% from China.

2006 census population, within 11 'Statistical Divisions': Melbourne, 3,592,590; Barwon, 259,015; Goulburn, 195,239; Loddon, 168,840; Gippsland, 159,485; Central Highlands, 142,210; Western District, 98,854; Ovens-Murray, 92,587; Mallee, 88,598; East Gippsland, 80,114; Wimmera, 48,441.

SOCIAL STATISTICS

Statistics for calendar years:

	Births	Deaths	Marriages	Divorces
2004	62,417	32,522	25,587	12,544
2005	63,287	32,605	25,266	12,512
2006	65,236	33,311	26,564	12,110
2007	70,313	33,930	26,967	11,833

The annual rates per 1,000 of the mean resident population in 2007 were: births, 13·5; deaths, 6·5; marriages, 5·2; divorces, 2·3. Infant mortality rate, 2007, 3·8 per 1,000 live births. Expectation of life, 2007: males, 79·3 years; females, 83·8 years.

CLIMATE

See AUSTRALIA: Climate.

CONSTITUTION AND GOVERNMENT

Victoria, formerly a portion of New South Wales, was, in 1851, proclaimed a separate colony, with a partially elective Legislative Council. In 1856 responsible government was conferred, the legislative power being vested in a parliament consisting of a Legislative Council (Upper House) and a Legislative Assembly (Lower House). At present the Council consists of 44 members who are elected for two terms of the Assembly, with half of the seats up for renewal at each election. The Assembly consists of 88 members, elected for four years from the date of its first meeting unless sooner dissolved by the Governor. Members and electors of both Houses must be aged 18 years and Australian citizens or those British subjects previously enrolled as electors, according to the Constitution Act 1975. Single voting (one elector one vote) and compulsory preferential voting apply to Council and Assembly elections. Enrolment for Council and Assembly electors is compulsory. The Council may not initiate or amend money bills, but may suggest amendments in such bills other than amendments which would increase any charge. A bill shall not become law unless passed by both Houses.

In the exercise of the executive power the Governor is advised by a Cabinet of responsible Ministers. Section 50 of the Constitution Act 1975 provides that the number of Ministers shall not at any one time exceed 22, of whom not more than six may sit in the Legislative Council and not more than 17 may sit in the Legislative Assembly.

Electors enrolled (30 June 2006) numbered 3,324,691.

RECENT ELECTIONS

In elections to the Legislative Assembly on 25 Nov. 2006 the Labor Party (ALP) won 55 seats with 43·1% of votes cast; the Liberal Party (LP), 23 (34·4%); the National Party (NP), 9 (5·2%). One independent was elected. The Greens took 10·0% of the vote but no seats and Family First 4·3% but no seats. Turnout was 92·7%.

In the simultaneous elections to the Legislative Council the ALP won 19 seats, the LP 15, the Greens 3, NP 2 and the Democratic Labor Party 1.

CURRENT ADMINISTRATION

Governor: Prof. David de Kretser, AC.

The Labor Cabinet was as follows in Feb. 2010:

Premier, Minister for Multicultural and Veterans' Affairs: John Brumby.

Deputy Premier, Attorney General and Minister for Racing: Rob Hulls. *Treasurer, Financial Services, and Information and Communication Technology:* John Lenders. *Industry and Trade, and Regional and Rural Development:* Jacinta Allan. *Health:* Daniel Andrews. *Arts, and Energy and Resources:* Peter Batchelor. *Police and Emergency Services, and Corrections:* Bob Cameron. *Community Development:* Lily D'Ambrosio. *Agriculture and Small Business:* Joe Helper. *Water, Finance, and Tourism and Major Events:* Tim Holding. *Environment and Climate Change, and Innovation:* Gavin Jennings. *Planning and the Respect Agenda:* Justin Madden. *Sport and Recreation, and Youth Affairs:* James Merlino. *Children and Early Childhood Development, and Women's Affairs:* Maxine Morand. *Mental Health, Community Services, and Senior Victorians:* Lisa Neville. *Industrial Relations and Public Transport:* Martin Pakula. *Roads and Ports, and Major Projects:* Tim Pallas. *Education, and Skills and Workforce Participation:* Bronwyn Pike. *Gaming and Consumer Affairs:* Tony Robinson. *Housing, Local Government and Aboriginal Affairs:* Richard Wynne.

Speaker of the Legislative Assembly: Jenny Lindell.

VIC Government Website: http://www.vic.gov.au

ECONOMY

Budget

In 2007–08 general government expenses by the state were estimated to total $A33,315·4m.; revenue and grants received were expected to increase by 2·9% to $A33,701·2m. ($A32,749·1m. in 2006–07).

Performance

In 2002–03 Victoria's gross state product represented 25·59% of Australia's total GDP.

Banking and Finance

The major trading banks in Victoria are the Commonwealth Bank of Australia, the Australia and New Zealand Banking Group, the Westpac Banking Corporation, the National Australia Bank, the St George Bank, the Bank of Queensland, Suncorp-Metway Bank, HSBC Bank Australia, Elders Rural Bank and the Bendigo Bank. According to the Australian Prudential Regulation Authority, as at 30 June 2006 there were 21 authorized banks with 1,282 branches; two building societies with five branches; and 45 credit unions with 139 branches.

ENERGY AND NATURAL RESOURCES

Electricity

In the year to 30 June 2002 total production was 49,438m. kWh; total consumption stood at 39,007m. kWh, including 28,156m. kWh by business customers.

In 1993 the State government began a major restructure of the government-owned electricity industry along competitive lines. The distribution sector was privatized in 1995, and four generator companies in 1997.

About 90% of power generated is supplied by four brown-coal fired generating stations. There are two other thermal stations and three hydro-electric stations in northeast Victoria. Victoria is also entitled to approximately 30% of the output of the Snowy Mountains hydro-electric scheme and half the output of the Hume hydro-electric station, both of which are in New South Wales.

Oil and Gas

Crude oil in commercially recoverable quantities was first discovered in 1967 in two large fields offshore, in East Gippsland in Bass Strait, between 65 and 80 km from land. These fields, with 20 other fields since discovered, have been assessed as containing initial recoverable oil reserves of 4,063m. bbls. Estimated remaining oil reserves as at May 2009 was 400·0m. bbls. Production of crude oil in the fiscal year 2002–03 was valued at about $A3·2bn. with output at 133,000 bbls per day (15% less than the previous year).

Natural gas was discovered offshore in East Gippsland in 1965. The initial recoverable gas reserves were 272·0m. cu. metres. Estimated remaining gas reserves (30 June 2005), 88·68m. cu. metres. Production of natural gas (2003–04), 7,973m. cu. metres.

Liquefied petroleum gas is produced after extraction of the propane and butane fractions from the untreated oil and gas.

Brown Coal

Major deposits of brown coal are located in the Latrobe Valley in the Central Gippsland region and comprise approximately 89% of the total resources in Victoria. In 2005 the resource was estimated to be 41,500 megatonnes, of which about 37,400 megatonnes were economically recoverable.

The primary use of these reserves is to fuel electricity generating stations. Production of brown coal in 2005–06 was 71·2m. tonnes.

Minerals

Production, 2003–04: limestone, 1,200,545 tonnes; kaolin, 251,392 tonnes. In 2002–03, 3,048 kg of gold were produced (around 32% of Australian gold production).

Agriculture

In the year ending 30 June 2004 there were an estimated 32,463 agricultural establishments (excluding those with an estimated value of agricultural operations less than $A5,000) with a total area of 13·6m. ha. of which around 3·5m. ha. were under crops. Gross value of agricultural production, 2004–05, $A8·4bn. Principal crops in 2004–05 with estimated production in 1,000 tonnes: wheat, 1,927; barley, 1,305; canola, 342; oats, 284.

Gross value of livestock production in 2004–05 totalled $A2·5bn., including wool production $A473m.

Grape growing, particularly for winemaking, is an important activity. In 2005, 551,214 tonnes of winegrapes were produced from 38,764 ha. of vineyards (including 3,715 ha. not yet bearing).

Forestry

Commercial timber production is an increasingly important source of income. As at Dec. 2006 there were 396,000 ha. of plantation. Of Victoria's 7·9m. ha. of native forest (Dec. 2005), 6·6m. ha. (83·4%) were publicly owned (3·1m. ha. in conservation reserves).

Fisheries

Estimated total fisheries production in 2005–06 came to 18,903 tonnes with a gross value of $A127·2m. In the same year aquaculture production was an estimated 3,034 tonnes with a gross value of $A21·6m.

INDUSTRY

Total sales and service income in manufacturing industry in the year ended 30 June 2005 was $A100,248m. In the same year there were 323,400 persons employed in the manufacturing sector with wages and salaries totalling $A15,359m.

Labour

At Aug. 2007 there were 2,706,600 persons in the labour force of whom 2,583,700 were employed: wholesale and retail trade, 503,600; finance, insurance, property and business services, 431,400; manufacturing, 330,600; health and community services, 264,000; construction, 211,900; education, 193,900; culture, recreation, personal and other services, 180,300; accommodation, cafes and restaurants, 118,100; transport and storage, 105,900; government administration and defence, 82,400; agriculture, forestry and fishing, 78,400; communication services, 50,100; electricity, gas and water supply, 20,400; mining, 12,600. There were 122,900 unemployed persons in Aug. 2007, a rate of 4·5%. The average weekly wage in Nov. 2005 was $A1,010·10 (males $A1,055·70, females $A915·00).

Trade Unions

As at Aug. 2006 there were 439,100 people belonging to a trade union (19·9% of total employees).

INTERNATIONAL TRADE

Imports and Exports

The total value of the overseas imports and exports of Victoria, including bullion and specie, was as follows (in $A1m.):

	2001–02	*2002–03*	*2003–04*
Imports	37,558	42,129	40,727
Exports[1]	22,237	18,904	18,102

[1]Includes re-exports.

The chief imports in 2003–04 (in $A1m.) were: passenger motor vehicles, 3,400; crude petroleum, 1,618; aircraft and parts, 1,571; medicaments (including veterinary), 1,012; telecommunications equipment, 945. Imports in 2003–04 (in $A1m.) came mainly from the USA, 6,530; China, 5,274; Japan, 4,963; Germany, 3,280; France, 1,926.

The chief exports in 2003–04 (in $A1m.) were: passenger motor vehicles, 1,467; aluminium, 1,081; milk and cream, 1,060; wool, 970; cheese and curd, 567. Exports in 2003–04 (in $A1m.) went mainly to New Zealand, 2,095; USA, 1,949; China, 1,889; Japan, 1,626; Saudi Arabia, 945.

COMMUNICATIONS

Roads

At 30 June 2004 there were 162,700 km of roads open to general traffic. The number of registered motor vehicles (excluding tractors and trailers) at 31 March 2006 was 3,740,726, including 2,997,856 passenger vehicles, 483,097 light commercial vehicles, 119,533 trucks, 16,508 buses and 114,438 motorcycles. There were 333 road accident fatalities in 2006.

Rail

The Victorian rail network is owned by the Victorian RailTrack Corporation (VicTrack), a Victorian Government corporation. Three interlinked rail networks operate in Victoria, comprising: 1,213 km of standard gauge interstate and intrastate non-urban track leased to the Australian Rail Track Corporation; 400 km of urban broad gauge track franchised to Metro Trains Melbourne, the metropolitan network access manager and passenger service operator; and 3,278 km of intrastate, non-urban rail network franchised to V/Line Passenger, the network access provider and regional passenger operator.

The regional instrastate rail network is leased to and managed by V/Line Passenger. Approximately 3m. tonnes of freight is transported on the instrastate rail network annually. There were more than 12m. passenger trips taken on regional train services in 2008–09.

Two new operators commenced operation from 30 Nov. 2009 following a competitive worldwide tender. The new train franchise agreement was awarded to Metro Trains Melbourne (Metro) and the new tram franchise to Keolis Downer EDI (KDR). The contracts operate for eight years with a possible extension of seven years based on good performance.

Melbourne's 249 km tramway and light rail network is operated by KDR (branded as Yarra Trams) across 28 main routes and had approximately 178·1m. passenger boardings in 2008–09. Melbourne's metropolitan passenger rail network, operated by Metro, comprises 15 lines and approximately 2,000 daily metropolitan rail services and had approximately 213·9m. passenger boardings in 2008–09.

Civil Aviation

There were 13,245,878 domestic and regional passenger movements and 3,136,420 international passenger movements in 2002–03 at Melbourne (Tullamarine) airport (Australia's second busiest airport after Sydney). Total freight handled in 2000 was 271,605 tonnes (international, 199,437; domestic, 72,168).

Shipping
The four major commercial ports are at Melbourne, Geelong, Portland and Hastings. In 2002–03, 3,687 commercial vessels called at Victorian ports. General cargo imported in 2002–03 was 9,573,802 mass tonnes and general cargo exported was 9,908,314 mass tonnes.

Telecommunications
In 2004, 94·2% of households had a fixed telephone connected[1]; 74·0% had mobile phones in 2002. In 2005–06 there were 1·36m. households with home computer access (69% of all households) and 1·16m. households with home internet access (59%).

[1]Source: Roy Morgan Single Source January–March 2005

Postal Services
In the year ended 30 June 2006 there were 203 corporate outlets, 828 licensed post offices and 37 other agencies.

SOCIAL INSTITUTIONS
Justice
There is a Supreme Court with a Chief Justice and 21 puisne judges. There are a county court, magistrates' courts, a court of licensing and a bankruptcy court.

In 1996–97 the State's prisons were upgraded with three new facilities developed, owned and operated by the private sector. In 2006–07 approximately 36% of Victoria's prison population was accommodated in the two private prisons still operating (one of the prisons having been returned to public ownership and operation in Nov. 2000). There are 12 public prisons remaining. At 30 June 2007 the number of prisoners held stood at 4,183. Police personnel (sworn and unsworn) at 30 June 2003, 12,924.

Education
In Feb. 2006 there were 1,606 government schools with 307,577 pupils in primary schools and 222,827 in secondary schools. In the same year there were 694 non-government schools with 140,683 pupils at primary schools; and 153,039 pupils at secondary schools.

All higher education institutions, excluding continuing education and technical and further education (TAFE), now fall under the Unified National System, and can no longer be split into universities and colleges of advanced education. In addition, a number of institutional amalgamations and name changes occurred in the 12 months prior to the commencement of the 1992 academic year. In 2004 there were 480,700 enrolments in Vocational Education and Training activities.

There are ten publicly funded higher education institutions including eight State universities, Marcus Oldham College and the Australian Catholic University (partly privately funded), and the Melbourne University Private, established in 1998. In 2005 there were 292,761 students in higher education.

Health
In 2002–03 there were 144 public hospitals with 11,938 beds, and 140 private hospitals with 6,628 beds. Total government outlay on health in 2002–03 was $A6,376m.

Welfare
Victoria was the first State of Australia to make a statutory provision for the payment of Age Pensions. The Act came into operation on 18 Jan. 1901, and continued until 1 July 1909, when the Australian Invalid and Old Age Pension Act came into force. The Social Services Consolidation Act, which came into operation on 1 July 1947, repealed the various legislative enactments relating to age and invalid pensions, maternity allowances, child endowment, unemployment and sickness benefits and, while following in general the Acts repealed, considerably liberalized many of their provisions.

The number of age and disability pensions at 30 June 2003 was: age, 472,068; disability support, 158,800. There were 128,395 newstart allowance, 102,612 youth allowance and 97,436 single parent payments current at 30 June 2003.

RELIGION
There is no State Church, and no State assistance has been given to religion since 1875. At the 2006 census the following were the enumerated numbers of the principal religions: Catholic, 1,355,904; Anglican, 671,774; Uniting Church, 274,056; Orthodox, 224,038; Presbyterian and Reformed, 143,146; other Christian, 316,887; Buddhist, 132,633; Muslim, 109,369; Hindu, 42,310; Jewish, 41,108; no religion, 1,007,415; not stated, 550,309.

CULTURE
Tourism
For the year ending June 2007 the number of short-term overseas visitors to Australia who specified Victoria as their main destination was 1·4m. (28·4% of total overseas visitors to Australia), with 1·02m. nominating 'holiday' or 'visiting friends/relatives' as purpose of their trip. The UK represented the major source of international visitors with 16·1%; followed by New Zealand (16·0%), China (9·9%), USA (8·6%), Singapore (4·5%) and Japan (4·2%).

Source: International Visitor Survey, year ending June 2007.

FURTHER READING
Statistical Information: The State office of the Australian Bureau of Statistics is at 5th Floor, Commercial Union Tower, 485 LaTrobe Street, Melbourne. Publications: *Victorian Year Book.* Annual.—*State and Regional Indicators.* Quarterly (from Sept. 2001).

State library: The State Library of Victoria, 328 Swanston St., Melbourne 3000.

Website: http://www.slv.vic.gov.au

Western Australia

KEY HISTORICAL EVENTS
In 1791 the British navigator George Vancouver took possession of the country around King George Sound. In 1826 the government of New South Wales sent 20 convicts and a detachment of soldiers to form a settlement then called Frederickstown. The following year, Capt. James Stirling surveyed the coast from King George Sound to the Swan River, and in May 1829 Capt. Charles Fremantle took possession of the territory. In June 1829 Capt. Stirling founded the Swan River Settlement (now the Commonwealth State of Western Australia) and the towns of Perth and Fremantle. He was appointed Lieut.-Governor.

Grants of land were made to the early settlers until, in 1850, with the colony languishing, they petitioned for the colony to be made a penal settlement. Between 1850 and 1868 (in which year transportation ceased), 9,668 convicts were sent out. In 1870 partially representative government was instituted. Western Australia federated with the other Australian states to form the Commonwealth of Australia in 1901.

In the 1914–18 war Western Australia provided more volunteers for overseas military service in proportion to population than any other State. The worldwide depression of 1929 brought unemployment (30% of trade union membership), and in 1933 over two-thirds voted to leave the Federation. While there were modest improvements in the standard of living through the 1930s, it was the 1939–45 war which brought full employment. Japanese aircraft attacked the Western Australia coast in 1942. Talk of a 'Brisbane line', which would abandon the West to invasion, only served to reinforce Western Australia's sense of isolation from the rest of the nation. The post-war years saw increasing demand for wheat and wool but the 1954–55 decline in farm incomes led to diversification. Work began in the early 1950s on steel production and oil processing. Oil was discovered in 1953 but it was not until 1966 that it was commercially exploited. The discovery of deposits of iron ore in the Pilbara, bauxite in the Darling scarp, nickel in Kambalda and ilmenite from mineral sands led to the State becoming a major world supplier of mineral exports by 1965.

TERRITORY AND POPULATION

Western Australia has an area of 2,532,422 sq. km and 12,500 km of coastline.

The population at the 2006 census was 1,959,088 (1,828,294 at 2001 census). Of the total, 1,279,224 (65·3%) were born in Australia and 982,966 were females. Perth, the capital, had a 2006 census population of 1,445,078.

Principal local government areas outside the metropolitan area, with estimated resident population at 30 June 2007: Mandurah, 60,560; Albany, 33,545; Bunbury, 31,638; Kalgoorlie-Boulder, 30,903; Busselton, 27,500; Geraldton, 20,333; Roebourne, 18,240; Port Hedland, 13,060.

SOCIAL STATISTICS

Statistics for calendar years[1]:

	Births	*Deaths*	*Marriages*	*Divorces*
2004	25,295	11,184	10,601	4,337
2005	26,253	11,297	11,124	5,265
2006	27,776	11,643	11,602	5,544
2007	29,164	12,283	12,290	4,932

[1]Figures are on state of usual residence basis.

The annual rates per 1,000 of the mean resident population in 2007 were: births, 13·8; deaths, 5·8; marriages, 5·8; divorces, 2·3. Infant mortality rate, 2007, 2·4 per 1,000 live births. Expectation of life, 2007: males, 79·2 years; females, 84·0 years.

CLIMATE

Western Australia is a region of several climate zones, ranging from the tropical north to the semi-arid interior and Mediterranean-style climate of the southwest. Most of the State is a plateau between 300 and 600 metres above sea level. Except in the far southwest coast, maximum temperatures in excess of 40°C have been recorded throughout the State. The normal average number of sunshine hours per day is 8·0.

CONSTITUTION AND GOVERNMENT

The *Legislative Council* consists of 36 members elected for a term of four years. There are six electoral regions for Legislative Council elections. Each electoral region returns six members. Each member represents the entire region.

There are 59 members of the *Legislative Assembly*, each member representing one of the 59 electoral districts of the State. Members are elected for a period of up to four years. A system of proportional representation is used to elect members.

Electors enrolled (30 June 2006) numbered 1,259,528.

RECENT ELECTIONS

In elections to the Legislative Assembly on 6 Sept. 2008 the Labor Party (ALP) won 28 seats with 35·9% of votes cast; the Liberal Party (LP), 24 (but 38·4% of the vote); the National Party (NP), 4 (4·9%); ind., 3 (4·6%). With the Liberals forming a coalition with the National Party, Western Australia became the first Australian state or territory in six years not to have a Labor government. The three independents also pledged their support for the minority government.

CURRENT ADMINISTRATION

Governor: Dr Ken Michael, AC.

Lieut.-Governor: David Kingsley Malcolm, AC.

In Feb. 2010 the Cabinet comprised:

Premier and Minister for State Development: Colin Barnett (Liberal Party).

Deputy Premier, Minister for Health and Indigenous Affairs: Kim Hames. *Mines and Petroleum, Fisheries, and Electoral Affairs:* Norman Moore. *Regional Development and Lands:* Brendon Grylls. *Education and Tourism:* Elizabeth Constable. *Transport and Disability Services:* Simon O'Brien. *Treasurer, Commerce, Science and Innovation, Housing and Works:* Troy Buswell. *Police, Emergency Services, and Road Safety:* Rob Johnson. *Sport and Recreation, Racing and Gaming:* Terry Waldron. *Planning, Culture and the Arts:* John Day. *Energy and Training:* Peter Collier. *Attorney General and Minister for Corrective Services:* Christian Porter. *Child Protection, Community Services, Seniors and Volunteering, and Women's Interests:* Robyn McSweeney. *Water and Mental Health:* Dr Graham Jacobs. *Local Government, Heritage, and Citizenship and Multicultural Interests:* John Castrilli. *Agriculture and Food, and Forestry:* Terry Redman. *Environment and Youth:* Donna Faragher.

Speaker of the Legislative Assembly: Grant Woodhams.

WA Government Website: http://wa.gov.au

ECONOMY

Budget

Revenue and expenditure (in $A1m.) in years ending 30 June:

	2005–06	*2006–07*	*2007–08*[1]
Revenue	16,123	16,510	17,593
Expenditure	14,141	15,234	16,141

[1]Projected.

A general government net operating surplus of $A1,853m. was projected for 2006–07, a decrease of $A812m. on the 2005–06 outcome.

Banking and Finance

According to the Australian Prudential Regulation Authority, as at 30 June 2006 there were 15 authorized banks with 519 branches; one building society with 19 branches; and 16 credit unions with 41 branches.

ENERGY AND NATURAL RESOURCES

Electricity

Deregulation of the energy industry was passed by the Office of Energy during 1996–97. Electricity users can obtain power from Western Power or private sector operators. In the year ended 30 June 2002 Western Power customer consumption stood at 12,081m. kWh, including 8,251m. kWh by business customers.

Oil and Gas

Petroleum continued to be the State's largest resource sector with sales increasing by 33% to $A22·3bn. in 2008. Owing to low oil prices in 2008–09 the value of crude oil sales decreased by 12% to $A7·7bn.; output was 81·4m. bbls. The State accounts for 66% of Australia's oil and condensate production.

Western Australia has significant natural gas resources and, with a $A2·4bn. expansion of the North West Shelf liquefied natural gas (LNG) project, exports are forecast to rise by around $A1bn. Total natural gas production, 2005–06: 25,887 gigalitres.

Source: Western Australian Department of Mineral and Petroleum Resources.

Minerals

Mining is a significant contributor to the Western Australia economy. The State is the world's third largest producer of iron ore and accounts for almost 88% of Australia's iron ore production.

Principal minerals produced in 2005–06 were: gold, 165 tonnes; iron ore and concentrate, 253·4m. tonnes; diamonds, 25·3m. carats. Most of the State's coal production (an estimated 6·2m. tonnes in 2004–05) is used by Western Power's electricity generation.

Agriculture

In the year ending 30 June 2005 there were 11,745 establishments mainly engaged in agriculture with a total area of 104·6m. ha. of which 8·33m. ha. were under crops. Gross value of agricultural production in 2004–05 totalled $A5·1bn., a reduction of 18% on the previous year.

Principal crops in 2004–05 with estimated production in 1,000 tonnes: wheat, 8,619; barley, 2,489; lupins for grain, 792; oats, 460; canola, 488.

Value of livestock products in 2004–05 totalled $A625m. Total value of wool produced in 2004–05 was $A490m.

Forestry

The area of State forests and timber reserves at 30 June 2003 was 1,169,300 ha. Jarrah and Karri hardwoods supply about 0·5m. cu. metres of sawn wood and pine plantations, 1m. cu. metres of logs for panel manufacture, sawmilling and export.

Fisheries

Estimated total fisheries production in 2005–06 came to 35,149 tonnes with a gross value of $A550·9m. In the same year aquaculture production was an estimated 848 tonnes with a gross value of $A127·91m. Pearling is the most valuable form of aquaculture in the State with the Pearl Oyster Fishery producing an estimated $A150m. worth of pearls from wild captured and hatchery produced oysters in 2003–04.

INDUSTRY

Heavy industry is concentrated in the southwest, and is largely tied to export-orientated mineral processing, especially alumina and nickel.

The following table shows manufacturing industry statistics for the year ended 30 June 2005:

Industry sub-division	*Persons employed 1,000*	*Wages and salaries $A1m.*	*Sales and service income $A1m.*
Food, beverages and tobacco	16·5	631	5,538
Textiles, clothing and leather products	3·8	107	539
Wood and paper products	4·6	170	966
Printing and publishing and recorded media	8·0	347	1,445
Petroleum, coal, chemical products	8·3	464	7,484
Non-metallic mineral products	6·0	276	1,799
Metal products	24·0	1,117	14,503
Machinery and equipment	18·3	749	4,171
Other manufacturing	8·8	225	1,263

Labour

The labour force comprised 1,054,800 employed and 44,500 unemployed persons in 2005 (an unemployment rate of 4·1%). The average weekly wage in Nov. 2005 was $A1,054·80 (males $A1,148·60, females $A863·40).

Trade Unions

As at Aug. 2006 there were 142,200 people belonging to a trade union (16·0% of total employees).

INTERNATIONAL TRADE

Imports and Exports

Value of foreign imports and exports (i.e. excluding inter-state trade) for years ending 30 June (in $A1m.):

	2002–03	*2003–04*	*2004–05*
Imports	11,755	11,690	14,157
Exports	32,439	32,220	38,835

The chief imports in 2003–04 (in $A1m.) were: non-monetary gold, 1,956; crude petroleum, 1,086; passenger motor vehicles, 954; refined petroleum, 572; motor vehicles for transporting goods, 420. Imports in 2003–04 (in $A1m.) came mainly from the USA, 1,340; Japan, 1,315; Indonesia, 1,246; Singapore, 870; China, 613.

The chief exports in 2003–04 (in $A1m.) were: non-monetary gold, 5,554; iron ore, 5,159; crude petroleum, 3,641; natural gas, 2,174; wheat, 1,785; nickel ores, 598. Exports in 2003–04 (in $A1m.) went mainly to Japan, 6,931; China, 4,400; Republic of Korea, 3,207; India, 2,809; UK, 1,916.

COMMUNICATIONS

The Public Transport Authority of Western Australian (PTA), which replaced the Western Australia Government Railways Commission in July 2003, is responsible for rail, bus and ferry services in the metropolitan area (Transperth); public transport services in regional centres; coach and rail passenger services in regional areas (Transwa); and school buses.

Roads

At 30 June 2004 there were 148,456 km of roads open to general traffic. The number of registered motor vehicles (excluding tractors and trailers) at 31 March 2006 was 1,600,566, including 1,205,266 passenger vehicles, 254,164 light commercial vehicles, 63,316 trucks, 11,051 buses and 59,675 motorcycles. In 2004 there were 178 road accident fatalities.

Rail

Transperth is responsible for metropolitan rail services and Transwa for rail passenger services to regional areas. In 1999–2000, 29·5m. passenger journeys were made on urban services. In the year ended 31 March 2001, 196m. tonnes of freight were carried.

Civil Aviation

An extensive system of regular air services operates for passengers, freight and mail. In 2002–03 Perth International Airport handled 5,189,365 passengers (3,402,600 on domestic flights).

Shipping

In 2002–03, 2,781 commercial vessels called at Western Australian ports (1,569 at Fremantle). General cargo imported in 2002–03 was 2,686,346 mass tonnes and general cargo exported was 3,033,257 mass tonnes.

Telecommunications

In 2005–06 there were 560,000 households with home computer access (71% of all households). In 2005–06, 484,000 households had home internet access (62%).

Postal Services

In the year ended 30 June 2006 there were 89 corporate outlets, 296 licensed post offices and 95 other agencies.

SOCIAL INSTITUTIONS

Justice

Justice is administered by a Supreme Court, consisting of a Chief Justice, 16 other judges and two masters; a District Court comprising a chief judge and 20 other judges; a Magistrates Court, a Chief Stipendiary Magistrate, 37 Stipendiary Magistrates and Justices of the Peace. All courts exercise both civil and criminal jurisdiction except Justices of the Peace who deal with summary criminal matters only. Juvenile offenders are dealt with by the

Children's Court. The Family Court also forms part of the justice system.

At 30 June 2005 there was a daily average of 3,482 prisoners held. At 30 June 2003 police personnel (sworn and unsworn) stood at 6,347.

Education

School attendance is compulsory from the age of six until the end of the year in which the child attains 16 years. Since Jan. 2008 young people aged 15–17 have been obliged to remain in school or, by arrangement, take part in an approved education and training pathway such as an apprenticeship or traineeship.

In Aug. 2006 there were 777 government primary and secondary schools (with 16,737 full-time equivalent teaching staff) providing free education to 131,294 primary and 83,064 secondary students; in the same year there were 303 non-government schools for 51,577 primary and 53,828 secondary students.

Higher education is available through four state universities and one private (Notre Dame). In 2004 there were 126,500 enrolments in Vocational Education and Training activities. In 2006 there were approximately 98,745 students in tertiary education at the University of Western Australia, Murdoch University, the University of Notre Dame Australia, Curtin University of Technology and the Edith Cowan University.

Health

In 2002–03 there were 93 acute public hospitals and one public psychiatric hospital. In 2005–06 there were 24 acute and psychiatric private hospitals and 13 private free-standing day hospitals.

Welfare

The Department for Community Development is responsible for the provision of welfare and community services throughout the State. The number of age and disability pensions at 30 June 2003 was: age, 156,550; disability support, 56,554. There were 52,988 newstart allowance, 37,972 youth allowance and 45,916 single parent payments current at 30 June 2003.

RELIGION

At the census of 2006 the principal denominations were: Catholic, 464,005; Anglican, 400,480; Uniting Church, 74,333; Presbyterian and Reformed, 43,807; Baptist, 32,730; other Christian, 147,171. There were 97,916 persons practising non-Christian religions and 448,435 persons had no religion.

CULTURE

Tourism

In 2002–03 there were 460,534 short-term overseas visitors. Of these, 24·3% were from the UK and Ireland, 18·5% from Singapore and 12·5% from Japan.

FURTHER READING

Statistical Information: The State Government Statistician's Office was established in 1897 and now functions as the Western Australian Office of the Australian Bureau of Statistics (Level 15, Exchange Plaza, Sherwood Court, Perth). Publications include: *Western Australia at a Glance*, Annual (from 1997). *Western Australia Statistical Indicators*, Quarterly (from Sept. 2000).

Broeze, F. J. A. (ed.) *Private Enterprise, Government and Society.* 1993
Crowley, F. K., *Australia's Western Third: A History of Western Australia from the First Settlements to Modern Times.* (Rev. ed.) 1970
Stannage, C. T. (ed.) *A New History of Western Australia.* 1980

State library: Alexander Library Building, Perth.
Website: http://www.slwa.wa.gov.au

AUSTRALIAN EXTERNAL TERRITORIES

Australian Antarctic Territory

An Imperial Order in Council of 7 Feb. 1933 placed under Australian authority all the islands and territories other than Adélie Land situated south of 60° S. lat. and lying between 160° E. long. and 45° E. long. The Order came into force with a Proclamation issued by the Governor-General on 24 Aug. 1936 after the passage of the Australian Antarctic Territory Acceptance Act 1933. The boundaries of Adélie Land were definitively fixed by a French Decree of 1 April 1938 as the islands and territories south of 60° S. lat. lying between 136° E. long. and 142° E. long. The Australian Antarctic Territory Act 1954 declared that the laws in force in the Australian Capital Territory are, so far as they are applicable and are not inconsistent with any ordinance made under the Act, in force in the Australian Antarctic Territory.

The area of the territory is estimated at 6,119,818 sq. km (2,362,875 sq. miles).

There is a research station on MacRobertson Land at lat. 67° 37' S. and long. 62° 52' E. (Mawson), one on the coast of Princess Elizabeth Land at lat. 68° 34' S. and long. 77° 58' E. (Davis), and one at lat. 66° 17' S. and long. 110° 32' E. (Casey). The Antarctic Division also operates a station on Macquarie Island.

Cocos (Keeling) Islands

GENERAL DETAILS

The Cocos (Keeling) Islands are two separate atolls comprising some 27 small coral islands with a total area of about 14·2 sq. km, and are situated in the Indian Ocean at 12° 05' S. lat. and 96° 53' E. long. They lie 2,950 km northwest of Perth. The islands are low-lying, flat and thickly covered by coconut palms, and surround a lagoon in which ships drawing up to seven metres may be anchored. There is an equable and pleasant climate, affected for much of the year by the southeast trade winds. Temperatures range over the year from 68° F (20° C) to 88° F (31° C) and rainfall averages 80" (2,000 mm) a year. Most of this rain falls between Nov. and May. Feb. and March are usually the wettest months.

The main islands are: West Island (the largest, about 14 km long), home to most of the European community; Home Island, occupied by the Cocos Malay community; Direction, South and Horsburgh Islands, and North Keeling Island, 24 km to the north of the group. The population of the Territory (2006 Census) was 571, distributed between Home Island (75%) and West Island (25%).

The islands were discovered in 1609 by Capt. William Keeling but remained uninhabited until 1826. In 1857 the islands were annexed to the Crown; the governments of Ceylon and Singapore held jurisdiction over the islands at different periods until they were placed under the authority of the Australian government as the Territory of Cocos (Keeling) Islands on 23 Nov. 1955. An *Administrator* (Brian Lacy; took office in Oct. 2009), appointed by the Governor-General, is the government's representative in the Territory and is responsible to the Minister for Territories and Local Government.

In 1978 and 1993 the Australian government purchased the various interests of the Clunies-Ross family, who had been granted the land in its entirety by Queen Victoria. A Cocos Malay co-operative was established to engage in local businesses.

CONSTITUTION AND GOVERNMENT

The Shire of Cocos (Keeling) Islands has seven members elected for terms of four years. Every two years half of the elected members' terms expire. The last Local Government elections were in Oct. 2009.

ECONOMY

Currency

The Australian dollar is legal tender.

ENERGY AND NATURAL RESOURCES

Electricity

Electricity consumption in 2005–06 was 5.3m. kWh.

COMMUNICATIONS

Roads

The Shire of Cocos (Keeling) Islands has responsibility for approximately 10 km of sealed roads and approximately 12 km of unsealed roads. As at Oct. 2006 there were 170 registered motor vehicles.

Civil Aviation

National Jet Systems operates two scheduled flights to and from Perth each week, a triangulated service with Christmas Island.

Shipping

There is approximately one general cargo ship every month and a tanker twice per year.

Postal Services

There is a post office on both West Island and Home Island, which are operated by Australia Post licensees.

SOCIAL INSTITUTIONS

Education

As at Oct. 2006 there were two school campuses catering for 128 students. The campus on Home Island caters for students up to secondary level and the campus on West Island for students from kindergarten to Year 10.

Health

There is a health centre on both West and Home Islands. As at Oct. 2006 there were one doctor, one nurse manager and nine staff across the two locations. The Christmas Island dentist visits the islands at regular intervals and a range of visiting medical specialists provides services to the island.

RELIGION

About 85% of the population are Muslim and 15% Christian.

CULTURE

Broadcasting

Television and radio operates from mainland Australia. Local radio 6CKI broadcasts English and Malay.

Christmas Island

GENERAL DETAILS

Christmas Island is an isolated peak in the Indian Ocean, lat. 10° 25' 22" S., long. 105° 39' 59" E. It lies 360 km S. 8° E. of Java Head, and 970 km N. 79° E. from Cocos (Keeling) Islands, 1,310 km from Singapore and 2,650 km from Perth. Area: 136·7 sq. km. The climate is tropical with temperatures varying little over the year at 27° C. The wet season lasts from Nov. to April with an average rainfall of 1,930 mm. The island was formally annexed by the UK on 6 June 1888, placed under the administration of the Governor of the Straits Settlements in 1889, and incorporated with the Settlement of Singapore in 1900. Sovereignty was transferred to the Australian government on 1 Oct. 1958. The population at the 2006 census was 1,347.

The legislative, judicial and administrative systems are regulated by the Christmas Island Act, 1958. The first Island Assembly was elected in Sept. 1985, and is now replaced by the elected members of the Shire of Christmas Island. The Territory underwent major changes to its legal system when the Federal Parliament passed the Territories Law Reform Bill of 1992; Commonwealth and State laws applying in the state of Western Australia now apply in the Territory as a result, although some Western Australia laws have been disallowed to take into account the unique status of the Territory.

Extraction and export of rock phosphate dust is the main industry. The government is also encouraging the private sector development of tourism.

CONSTITUTION AND GOVERNMENT

The Shire of Christmas Island has nine members elected for terms of four years. Every two years half of the positions are elected. The last elections were in Oct. 2007.

CURRENT ADMINISTRATION

Administrator: Brian Lacy (appointed 5 Oct. 2009).

ECONOMY

Currency

The Australian dollar is legal tender.

ENERGY AND NATURAL RESOURCES

Electricity

Electricity consumption in 2005–06 was 24·6m. kWh.

COMMUNICATIONS

Roads

The Shire of Christmas Island has responsibility for approximately 140 km of roads with the remaining 100 km of haul roads and tracks maintained by Christmas Island Phosphates and Park Australia North. As at Oct. 2006 there were 1,527 registered vehicles on the island.

Civil Aviation

National Jet Systems operates two scheduled flights weekly to and from Perth, a triangulated service with the Cocos (Keeling) Islands. Austasia Airlines have one scheduled return flight each week between Singapore and Christmas Island.

Shipping

There are up to eight phosphate ships a month, approximately 11 general cargo and seven fuel tankers visiting the island per year.

Postal Services

There is one post office, operated by Australia Post licensees.

SOCIAL INSTITUTIONS

Education

As at Oct. 2006 there were 335 students at the Christmas Island District High School, which caters for education under the

Western Australian curriculum for kindergarten through to Year 12.

Health
There is a nine-bed hospital staffed (as at Oct. 2006) by two doctors, one dentist, a Director of Nursing and 32 other on-island staff. A range of visiting medical specialists provides services to the island.

RELIGION
About 50% of the population are Buddhists or Taoists, 16% Muslims and 30% Christians.

CULTURE
Broadcasting
Television and radio operates from mainland Australia. Local Radio 6RCI broadcasts in English, Malay and Chinese.

Norfolk Island

KEY HISTORICAL EVENTS
The island was formerly part of the colony of New South Wales and then of Van Diemen's Land (now known as Tasmania). A penal colony between 1788–1814 and 1825–55, it was separated from the state of Tasmania in 1856 and placed under the jurisdiction of the Australian State of New South Wales. Following the Norfolk Island Act 1913 (Cth), the Island was accepted as a Territory of Australia with the Australian Federal Government having jurisdiction for the Island.

TERRITORY AND POPULATION
Situated 29° 02' S. lat. 167° 57' E. long.; area 3,455 ha.; permanent population (Aug. 2006 census), 1,576.

Descendants of the *Bounty* mutineer families constitute the 'original' settlers and are known locally as 'Islanders', while later settlers, mostly from Australia and New Zealand, are identified as 'mainlanders'. According to the Aug. 2006 census, 82% of the Island's permanent population are Australian citizens with 15% being New Zealand citizens. Descendants of the Pitcairn Islanders make up about 47·6% of the permanent resident population. Over the years the Islanders have preserved their own lifestyle and customs, and their language remains a mixture of West Country English, Gaelic and Tahitian.

SOCIAL STATISTICS
Births in 2004–05 totalled 25 and deaths 15.

CLIMATE
Sub-tropical. Summer temperatures (Dec.–March) average about 75°F (25°C), and 65°F (18°C) in winter (June–Sept.). Annual rainfall is approximately 50" (1,200 mm), most of which falls in winter.

CONSTITUTION AND GOVERNMENT
An *Administrator*, appointed by the Governor-General and responsible to the Minister for Territories and Local Government, is the senior government representative in the Territory. The seat of administration is Kingston.

The Norfolk Island Act 1979 gives Norfolk Island responsible legislative and executive government to enable it to run its own affairs. Wide powers are exercised by the Norfolk Island Legislative Assembly of nine members, elected for a period of three years, and by an Executive Council. The Norfolk Island Act also provides for consultation with the Federal Government in respect of certain types of laws proposed by Norfolk Island's Legislative Assembly.

RECENT ELECTIONS
At the last elections, on 17 March 2010, only non-partisans were elected.

CURRENT ADMINISTRATION
Administrator: Owen Walsh (since 7 Aug. 2007—acting until 2 Oct. 2008).

Chief Minister: Andre Neville Nobbs (since 28 March 2007).

ECONOMY
The office of the Administrator is financed from Commonwealth expenditure which in 2004–05 was $A1,195,000; local revenue for 2002–03 totalled $A23,251,000; expenditure, $A21,531,000.

Currency
Australian notes and coins are the legal currency.

Banking and Finance
There are two banks, Westpac and the Commonwealth Bank of Australia.

COMMUNICATIONS
Roads
There are 100 km of roads (53 km paved), some 2,800 passenger cars and 200 commercial vehicles.

Civil Aviation
In 2006 there were scheduled flights to Auckland (operated by Air New Zealand), Brisbane and Sydney (Norfolk Air).

Telecommunications
In 2006 there were 2,057 telephone lines in service.

Postal Services
There is one post office located in Burnt Pine.

SOCIAL INSTITUTIONS
Justice
The Island's Supreme Court sits as required and a Court of Petty Sessions exercises both civil and criminal jurisdiction. Appeals from decisions of the Norfolk Island Supreme Court are heard by the Federal Court of Australia and by the High Court of Australia.

Education
A school is run by the New South Wales Department of Education for children aged 5 to 12. It had 310 pupils in Aug. 2006. The Island also has a pre-school facility.

Health
In 2006 the Norfolk Island Hospital Enterprise had three doctors, one dentist, one physiotherapist, one radiographer, a pharmacist, a medical scientist, a generalist counsellor and registered nursing staff. The hospital had 24 beds. Visiting specialists attend the Island on a regular basis.

RELIGION
40% of the population are Anglicans.

CULTURE
Broadcasting
In 2006 there were 1,800 television receivers and 1,600 radio receivers.

Press
There is one weekly with a circulation of 1,200.

Tourism
In the year ended 30 June 2007, 34,318 tourists visited Norfolk Island.

Heard and McDonald Islands

These islands, about 2,500 miles southwest of Fremantle, were transferred from British to Australian control from 26 Dec. 1947. Heard Island is about 43 km long and 21 km wide; Shag Island is about 8 km north of Heard. The total area is 412 sq. km (159 sq. miles). The McDonald Islands are 42 km to the west of Heard. Heard is an active stratovolcano that has erupted eight times since 1910, most recently in 1993. A volcano on McDonald Island had been dormant for 75,000 years before it erupted in 1992. The most recent eruption was in 2005. In 1985–88 a major research programme was set up by the Australian National Antarctic Research Expeditions to investigate the wildlife as part of international studies of the Southern Ocean ecosystem. Subsequent expeditions followed from June 1990 through to 1992.

Territory of Ashmore and Cartier Islands

By Imperial Order in Council of 23 July 1931, Ashmore Islands (known as Middle, East and West Islands) and Cartier Island, situated in the Indian Ocean, some 320 km off the northwest coast of Australia (area, 5 sq. km), were placed under the authority of the Commonwealth. Under the Ashmore and Cartier Islands Acceptance Act, 1933, the islands were accepted by the Commonwealth as the Territory of Ashmore and Cartier Islands. It was the intention that the Territory should be administered by the State of Western Australia but owing to administrative difficulties the Territory was deemed to form part of the Northern Territory of Australia (by amendment to the Act in 1938). On 16 Aug. 1983 Ashmore Reef was declared a National Nature Reserve. The islands are uninhabited but Indonesian fishing boats fish within the Territory and land to collect water in accordance with an agreement between the governments of Australia and Indonesia. It is believed that the islands and their waters may house considerable oil reserves.

Territory of Coral Sea Islands

GENERAL DETAILS

The Coral Sea Islands, which became a Territory of the Commonwealth of Australia under the Coral Sea Islands Act 1969, comprises scattered reefs and islands over a sea area of about 1m. sq. km. The Territory is uninhabited apart from a meteorological station on Willis Island.

FURTHER READING

Australian Department of Arts, Sport, the Environment, Tourism and Territories. *Christmas Island: Annual Report.—Cocos (Keeling) Islands: Annual Report.—Norfolk Island: Annual Report.*

AUSTRIA

Republik Österreich
(Austrian Republic)

Capital: Vienna
Population estimate, 2010: 8·39m.
GDP per capita, 2007: (PPP$) 37,370
HDI/world rank: 0·955/14

KEY HISTORICAL EVENTS

The oldest historical site in Austria is at the Gudenus caves in the Kremstal valley, where hunters' stone implements and bones dating from the Paleolothic Age have been found. The Early Iron Age Hallstatt culture prevailed from around 750–400 BC, covering the area north of the Alps, large parts of Slovakia, the north Balkans and Hungary. This area became renowned for its ceramics, ornamental Hallstatt burial grounds and the development of salt mining.

In the 5th century BC Celtic tribes stormed the eastern Alps, their culture named after the site in Switzerland (La-Tène) where tools, weapons and other artefacts were found. La-Tène culture showed Greek and Etruscan influences. Around the middle of the second century BC some of these tribes united to found Noricum, the first recognizable state on Austrian territory. In 113 BC a treaty of friendship was signed between Rome and Noricum. Around 15 BC Noricum was incorporated into the Roman Empire. Present day Austria (with parts of Germany, Switzerland, Slovenia and Hungary) was eventually divided into the three Roman provinces of Raetia, Noricum and Pannonia.

Germanic tribes, in particular the Marcomanni and Quadi, later known as Bavarians, invaded in AD 166–80. Emperor Marcus Aurelius campaigned against them from Vindobona (Vienna), where he died in battle in AD 180. His successors fought unsuccessfully against the Alemanni and other invading tribes. Brigantium (Bregenz) became a border town of the Roman Empire after a peace agreement was signed with the Alemanni.

Charlemagne conquered the Bavarian duke Tassilo III and the Avars at the end of the 8th century and established a territory in the Danube Valley known as the Ostmark in 803. The church of Salzburg (Roman Juvavum) was founded at the end of the 8th century and consequently became the Bavarian-Frankish spiritual centre and archbishopric. Christianity spread throughout the region, led by the Slav apostles Cyril and Methodius.

The Magyar invasions culminated in the battle for Vienna in 881 and the loss of Lower Austrian territories. The Babenbergs took over the margravate of Bavaria in 976 under Leopold I. The name 'Ostarichi', originating from Old High German, first appeared in a document of Emperor Otto III in 996. In 1156 the margravate of Austria became a separate duchy.

From 1160–1200 Vienna, the most important trading town on the Danube, became the residence of the art-loving Babenberger dukes, receiving its town charter in 1198. In 1246 the last Babenberger, Friedrich II, fell in the battle of Leitha against King Bela IV of Hungary. Count Rudolf IV of Habsburg was elected German King Rudolf I in 1273 and set about conquering the former Babenberg lands, naming his son Duke Albert I the sole ruler in 1283. From the rule of Albert's son and successor Frederick I onwards, the territory of the Habsburgs was known as the *dominium Austriae*.

Holy Roman Empire

In 1452 Frederick III became Holy Roman Emperor. In one of the first of a series of dynastic marriages to expand the Habsburg realm, his son Maximilian I was married to Mary, the heiress of Burgundy. The marriage of their son, Philip the Handsome, to Juana, the heiress of the Spanish crowns, forged a massive and disparate Habsburg inheritance, encompassing Spain and its empire, Hungary, Bohemia, the Burgundian Netherlands and territory in Italy. Austria was harried by the Ottoman Turks, whose armies had advanced across southeast Europe as far as Hungary under Sultan Süleyman the Magnificent. A truce was agreed after the Ottoman defeat at Vienna in 1529.

The Reformation brought Protestantism to Austria but was resisted by Rudolf II. Brought up a strict Catholic, he embraced the Counter-Reformation in 1576. Tensions between Protestants and Catholics came to a head with the Defenestration of Prague in 1618, which led to the Thirty Years War. Peace was restored by the Treaty of Westphalia in 1648.

Philip, a grandson of Louis XIV of France, was designated heir to the last of the Spanish Habsburgs, Charles II. During the subsequent War of the Spanish Succession, Holland and England joined the coalition forces. Peace negotiations at Rastatt awarded Austria Spanish territory in Italy and the Netherlands. Austrian boundaries reached their furthest limit in 1720.

In 1740 Emperor Charles VI died without a male heir. By pragmatic sanction, his daughter Maria Theresa was allowed to succeed him as the first female Habsburg ruler, though she was denied the Imperial crown. Challenged by Prussia, the War of the Austrian Succession divided the two alliances of Bavaria, France, Spain and Prussia against Austria, Holland and Great Britain. Maria Theresa introduced a number of reforms aimed at strengthening the Habsburg monarchy. The army was almost doubled in size, a public education system was introduced and administrative and financial structures were overhauled, centralizing government and laying the foundations of a modern state. During the Seven Years' War (1756–63) Maria Theresa aimed to reconquer Silesia, lost in the War of the Austrian Succession. However, the Austrians, bereft of allies, were defeated at Burkersdorf in July 1762. Silesia was settled on Prussia by the Peace of Hubertusburg.

Enlightened Despotism

In 1772 Austria, Prussia and Russia carried out the first partition of Poland, with Austria gaining Galicia. Maria Theresa's youngest daughter of 16 children, Marie-Antoinette, married Louis XVI, thus achieving a closer political alliance with France. Maria Theresa was succeeded by Joseph, her eldest son. Also a reformist, and heavily influenced by the Enlightenment, Joseph II proclaimed the Edict of Toleration in 1781, giving more rights to faiths other than Catholicism. He also abolished serfdom and homogenized land tax laws. Not all of these changes were popular, such as the introduction of German as the official language in the Hungarian government. His heavy-handed reforms provoked resistance, leading to a revolt in the Austrian Netherlands opposing absolutist rule. In the face of widespread opposition to his reforms, Joseph revoked a number of them in 1790.

From 1792–1815 the Habsburgs were involved in almost continuous warfare. Austria and Prussia voiced their disapproval of the ideals of the French Revolution in the Declaration of Pillnitz. Ill-received by the French government, this led to a declaration of war followed by 23 years of hostilities and five separate wars. During the first, second and third coalition wars Vienna was occupied twice by French troops. Napoleon defeated Austria in the Battle of Austerlitz in 1805, forcing Francis to surrender his title of Holy Roman Emperor and to hand over one of his daughters, Archduchess Marie Louise, in marriage. After Napoleon was defeated and exiled to Elba in 1814, the Congress of Vienna met to re-establish Europe's internal borders. In charge of Austria's foreign policy, Prince von Metternich created the German confederation of 35 states and four free cities to succeed the Holy Roman Empire.

With the growth of the cities in the first half of the 19th century came an expansion of the markets for agricultural goods. The first Austrian railway, the Kaiser-Ferdinand Nordbahn, was built between Linz and Budweis and steam navigation started on the Danube. An uprising in Vienna in 1848 forced the Habsburgs to flee the city and Metternich to resign. Ferdinand I abdicated in Dec. and was succeeded by his 18-year-old nephew, Francis Joseph I. The pan-European wave of revolution spread to Hungary, where the fight for emancipation was led by Lajos Kossuth. The Habsburgs refused to accept Hungary's independence and enlisted Russian aid to quell the uprising. Italian and Slavic revolts followed. In 1859, during the Austro-Italian war, the Habsburgs were defeated and Italy was unified.

The German unification campaign was headed by Otto von Bismarck, who expanded Prussian influence by isolating Austria from her allies. This led to the Austro-Prussian war of 1866. Austria's defeat at the battle of Königgrätz stripped it of all presiding powers over Germany. The loss of Venetia in 1867 added a further blow to the shrinking Habsburg empire. Forced to compromise with Hungary, Emperor Francis Joseph I negotiated the 'Ausgleich' in 1867, giving Hungary its own constitution and quasi-independent status. Francis Joseph was henceforth recognized as the Apostolic king of Hungary and emperor of Austria within the Austro-Hungarian monarchy, also referred to as the Dual Monarchy. Foreign policy, the army and finances were administered jointly.

German Alliance

In 1879 Austria entered the Dual Alliance with the German Reich and the two states pledged mutual support in the eventuality of Russian aggression. Italy joined in 1882, making a Triple Alliance. Tensions between Austria and Russia heightened over territory in the Balkans, with an uprising in Macedonia in 1903. King Alexander of Serbia was assassinated while the Serbs were fighting for the unification of the Southern Slavs. The Habsburg empire responded with a livestock embargo, known as the Pig War. Austria-Hungary then annexed the two provinces of Bosnia and Herzegovina in 1908, prompting a Serb revolt and protests by the pan-Slav movement. Austria tried to gain control over Serbia during the Balkan wars of 1912–13. In June 1914 the heir to the Habsburg throne, Archduke Franz Ferdinand, and his wife were assassinated in Sarajevo by a Bosnian nationalist. The refusal of Serbia to accept the blame led to an Austrian declaration of war on Serbia in July. German backing for Austria encompassed a settling of its own scores with France and Russia. Austria was obliged to support Germany against France and Russia. Germany declared war on Russia and France in early Aug., beginning the First World War. The Austro-Hungarian army suffered major setbacks and the monarchy began to crumble after Francis Joseph I's death in 1916. His great-nephew, Charles I of Austria, succeeded him, trying but failing to achieve a secret truce with the Allies. A series of strikes, mutiny in the army and navy, and food shortages were among the factors that defeated Austro-Hungarian forces in the spring and summer of 1918. About 1·2m. soldiers from Austria-Hungary died during the war.

Emperor Charles I issued a manifesto on 17 Oct. 1918 guaranteeing the independence of the non-German speaking states. Each province established a national council which then developed into a government. The Poles declared themselves an independent unified state in Warsaw on 7 Oct. 1918; the Czechs founded an independent republic in Prague and the Southern Slavs merged with Serbia. An armistice was agreed on 3 Nov. and the Hungarian government announced its complete separation from Austria. Within days Austria and Hungary declared republics. The Habsburg monarchy was formally dissolved on 11 Nov. with the abdication of Charles I. The Treaty of Saint Germain in 1919 stipulated that the German–Austrian lands were not permitted to unite (*Anschluss*) with Germany without the consent of the League of Nations. Austria was declared a federal state on 1 Oct. 1920.

Nazism

The economic crises of the 1920s led to the rise of a nationalist movement much influenced by Germany's adoption of National Socialism. When Engelbert Dollfuss of the conservative Christian Socialists became chancellor in 1932 he faced Nazi and Marxist opposition. He dissolved parliament and governed by emergency decree, founding the conservative Fatherland Front in 1933. The anti-Marxist Heimwehr (home defence forces) supported him. When the Social Democrats fought back they were defeated by Dollfuss with the backing of the Heimwehr. All political parties except the Fatherland Front were subsequently banned. On 25 July 1934 a Nazi gang murdered Dollfuss but was forced to surrender and the coup leaders were executed. Dollfuss' successor, Kurt Schuschnigg, signed the Austrian–German agreement whereby Germany recognized Austria's sovereignty in return for Austria calling itself a German state. German Nazis pressurized Schuschnigg to allow them more influence, Hitler demanding that leading Nazis take on top positions in the Austrian cabinet. Schuschnigg planned a plebiscite to decide upon Anschluss but on 12 March 1938 German forces marched into Austria, establishing a Nazi government led by Arthur Seyss-Inquart. Renamed 'Ostmark', Austria was put under the central authority of the German Third Reich. After anti-Nazis were rounded up a plebiscite held on 10 April 1938 showed over 99% support for Hitler.

The Allied Moscow conference of 1943 agreed Austrian independence along the demarcation lines of 1937. The borders were finally set at the Yalta conference of Feb. 1945. On 13 April 1945 Vienna was liberated by Soviet troops. Two weeks later, Dr Karl Renner proclaimed a provisional government and Austria a republic, recognized officially by western powers at the Potsdam conference. The first elections were held in Nov., with former Nazis excluded from voting. Leopold Figl of the Austrian People's Party (Christian Socialists) became the first chancellor of the Second Republic, with Karl Renner as its first president. The Paris treaty of Sept. 1946 granted autonomy for South Tyrol within Italy, the Allies refusing to return it to Austria. Financial support from the United Nations and the Marshall Plan enabled Austria to begin rebuilding its economy.

The Soviet Union, Britain, France and the USA occupied Austria until 1955, when the country reaffirmed its neutrality. Full sovereignty was restored by the State Treaty in Vienna. Anschluss between Austria and Germany or restoration of the Habsburgs were expressly prohibited. The rights of ethnic minorities were guaranteed and former German assets confiscated by the Western allies were returned. The Soviet Union, however, demanded reparations including US$150m. for former German businesses.

Austria became a member of the United Nations in 1955 and subsequently joined EFTA in 1959 and the OECD in 1960.

The first all-socialist cabinet was formed in 1970 under Chancellor Bruno Kreisky, who established economic stability and prosperity throughout the 1970s. The late 1970s saw the emergence of the Green party, with the planned construction of a nuclear power station becoming a central political issue. Kreisky's achievements were followed by political scandals which led to his resignation in 1983.

Kurt Waldheim (elected as secretary general of the UN in 1971) became Austrian president in 1986 despite allegations of a Nazi past. Although this was never proved, his undisguised sympathies and political leanings caused him to be placed on the USA's list of undesirable aliens. In 1995 Austria became a member of the EU. In Jan. 2000 the Freedom Party, headed by the far-right leader Jörg Haider, joined the government. Although Haider, described as a 'dangerous extremist' by EU leaders, did not take a post in the government, he continued to exercise political influence and remained popular with the Austrian electorate. Sanctions against Austria were imposed by the European Union in Feb. 2000 but were lifted in Sept. 2000. In the parliamentary elections of Oct. 2002 the Freedom Party, with a new leader, saw its support fall by half. Nevertheless the Freedom Party was again invited to join a coalition government.

TERRITORY AND POPULATION

Austria is bounded in the north by Germany and the Czech Republic, east by Slovakia and Hungary, south by Slovenia and Italy, and west by Switzerland and Liechtenstein. It has an area of 83,858 sq. km (32,378 sq. miles). Population (2001 census) 8,032,926; density, 95·8 per sq. km. Previous population censuses: (1923) 6·53m., (1934) 6·76m., (1951) 6·93m., (1971) 7·49m., (1981) 7·56m., (1991) 7·96m. In 2005, 66·0% of the population lived in urban areas. The estimated population on 1 Jan. 2009 was 8,355,260.

In 2001, 91·1% of residents were of Austrian nationality and, in 2003, 92% were German-speaking. Principal minorities in 2003: former Yugoslavians, 175,000; Turks, 122,000; Hungarians, 34,000; Slovenes, 30,000; Czechs, 19,000. Since the mid-1980s the number of foreigners living in Austria has more than doubled, from just over 4% to nearly 9%.

The UN gives an estimated population for 2010 of 8·39m.

The areas, populations and capitals of the nine federal states:

Federal States	*Area (sq. km)*	*Population at censuses (1991)*	*(2001)*	*State capitals*
Vienna (Wien)	415	1,539,848	1,550,123	Vienna
Lower Austria (Niederösterreich)	19,174	1,473,813	1,545,804	St Pölten
Burgenland	3,965	270,880	277,569	Eisenstadt
Upper Austria (Oberösterreich)	11,980	1,333,480	1,376,797	Linz
Salzburg	7,154	482,365	515,327	Salzburg
Styria (Steiermark)	16,388	1,184,720	1,183,303	Graz
Carinthia (Kärnten)	9,533	547,798	559,404	Klagenfurt
Tyrol	12,648	631,410	673,504	Innsbruck
Vorarlberg	2,601	331,472	351,095	Bregenz

The populations of the principal towns at the census of 2001 (and 1991): Vienna, 1,550,123 (1,539,848); Graz, 226,244 (237,810); Linz, 183,504 (203,044); Salzburg, 142,662 (143,978); Innsbruck, 113,392 (118,112); Klagenfurt, 90,141 (89,415); Villach, 57,497 (54,640); Wels, 56,478 (52,594); St Pölten, 49,121 (50,026).

The official language is German. For orthographical changes agreed in 1996 *see* GERMANY: Territory and Population.

SOCIAL STATISTICS

Statistics, 2008: live births, 77,752 (rate of 9·3 per 1,000 population); deaths, 75,083 (rate of 9·0 per 1,000 population); infant deaths, 287; stillborn, 258; marriages, 35,223; divorces, 19,701. In 2007 there were 1,280 suicides (rate of 15·4 per 100,000 population), of which 965 males and 315 females. Average annual population growth rate, 2000–05, 0·5%. Life expectancy at birth, 2007, 82·5 years for women and 77·0 years for men. In 2003 the most popular age range for marrying was 30–34 for males and 25–29 for females. Infant mortality, 2005, was 4 per 1,000 live births; fertility rate, 2004, 1·4 children per woman. In 2000 some 370,700 Austrians resided permanently abroad: 186,000 lived in Germany, 28,000 in Switzerland, 17,000 in South Africa, and 16,000 in both Australia and the USA. In 2002 Austria received 37,074 asylum applications, equivalent to 4·6 per 1,000 inhabitants (the highest ratio in Europe).

CLIMATE

The climate is temperate and from west to east in transition from marine to more continental. Depending on the elevation, the climate is also predominated by alpine influence. Winters are cold with snowfall. In the eastern parts summers are warm and dry.

Vienna, Jan. 0·0°C, July 20·2°C. Annual rainfall 624 mm. Graz, Jan. –1·0°C, July 19·4°C. Annual rainfall 825 mm. Innsbruck, Jan. –1·7°C, July 18·1°C. Annual rainfall 885 mm. Salzburg, Jan. –0·9°C, July 18·6°C. Annual rainfall 1,174 mm.

CONSTITUTION AND GOVERNMENT

The constitution of 1 Oct. 1920 was revised in 1929 and restored on 1 May 1945. Austria is a democratic federal republic comprising nine states *(Länder)*, with a federal *President (Bundespräsident)* directly elected for not more than two successive six-year terms, and a bicameral National Assembly which comprises a National Council and a Federal Council.

The National Council *(Nationalrat)* comprises 183 members directly elected for a five-year term by proportional representation in a three-tier system by which seats are allocated at the level of 43 regional and nine state constituencies, and one federal constituency. Any party gaining 4% of votes cast nationally is represented in the National Council. In 2007 Austria's voting age was reduced to 16—the lowest for national elections in the EU.

The Federal Council *(Bundesrat)* has 62 members appointed by the nine states for the duration of the individual State Assemblies' terms; the number of deputies for each state is proportional to that state's population. In Jan. 2010 the ÖVP held 28 of the 62 seats, the SPÖ 24, the FPÖ 4 and non-attached 6.

The head of government is a *Federal Chancellor*, who is appointed by the President (usually the head of the party winning the most seats in National Council elections). The *Vice-Chancellor*, the *Federal Ministers* and the *State Secretaries* are appointed by the President at the Chancellor's recommendation.

National Anthem

'Land der Berge, Land am Strome' ('Land of mountains, land on the river'); words by Paula Preradovic; tune attributed to Mozart.

GOVERNMENT CHRONOLOGY

Presidents since 1945. (ÖVP = Austrian People's Party; SPÖ = Social Democratic Party)

1945–50	SPÖ	Karl Renner
1951–57	SPÖ	Theodor Körner
1957–65	SPÖ	Adolf Schärf
1965–74	SPÖ	Franz Joseph Jonas
1974–86	SPÖ	Rudolf Kirchschläger
1986–92	ÖVP	Kurt Josef Waldheim
1992–2004	ÖVP	Thomas Klestil
2004–	SPÖ	Heinz Fischer

Federal Chancellors since 1945.

1945	SPÖ	Karl Renner
1945–53	ÖVP	Leopold Figl
1953–61	ÖVP	Julius Raab
1961–64	ÖVP	Alfons Gorbach

1964–70	ÖVP	Josef Klaus
1970–83	SPÖ	Bruno Kreisky
1983–86	SPÖ	Alfred (Fred) Sinowatz
1986–97	SPÖ	Franz Vranitzky
1997–2000	SPÖ	Viktor Klima
2000–07	ÖVP	Wolfgang Schüssel
2007–08	SPÖ	Dr Alfred Gusenbauer
2008–	SPÖ	Werner Faymann

RECENT ELECTIONS

Elections were held on 28 Sept. 2008. The Social Democratic Party (SPÖ) won 57 seats with 29·3% of votes cast (68 with 35·3% in 2006); the Austrian People's Party (ÖVP), 51 with 26·0% (66 with 34·3%); the Freedom Party (FPÖ), 34 with 17·5% (21 with 11·0%); the Alliance for the Future of Austria (BZÖ), 21 with 10·7% (7 with 4·1%); the Greens, 20 with 10·4% (21 with 11·0%). Turnout was 78·8%.

In the presidential election held on 25 April 2010 incumbent Heinz Fischer (SPÖ) won 78·9% of the vote against 15·6% for Barbara Rosenkranz (FPÖ) and 5·4% for Rudolf Gehring (Christian Party of Austria). Turnout was 49·2%.

European Parliament

Austria has 17 (18 in 2004) representatives. At the June 2009 elections turnout was 46·0% (42·4% in 2004). The ÖVP won 6 with 30·0% of votes cast (political affiliation in European Parliament: European People's Party); the SPÖ 4 with 23·7% (Progressive Alliance of Socialists and Democrats); Liste Martin, 3 with 17·7% (non-attached); the FPÖ 2 with 12·7% (non-attached); the Greens, 2 with 9·9% (Greens/European Free Alliance).

CURRENT ADMINISTRATION

President: Dr Heinz Fischer; b. 1938 (SPÖ; took office on 8 July 2004 and re-elected 25 April 2010).

Following the elections of Sept. 2008 the SPÖ and the ÖVP agreed in Nov. 2008 to form a grand coalition, with Werner Faymann (SPÖ) as chancellor. In March 2010 the government comprised:

Chancellor: Werner Faymann; b. 1960 (SPÖ; sworn in 2 Dec. 2008).

Deputy-Chancellor and Minister for Finance: Josef Pröll (ÖVP).

Minister for European and International Affairs: Michael Spindelegger (ÖVP). *Defence and Sports:* Norbert Darabos (SPÖ). *Economy, Family and Youth:* Reinhold Mitterlehner (ÖVP). *Agriculture, Forestry, Environment and Water Management:* Nikolaus Berlakovich (ÖVP). *Health:* Alois Stöger (SPÖ). *Interior:* Maria Fekter (ÖVP). *Education, Art and Culture:* Claudia Schmied (SPÖ). *Science and Research:* Beatrix Karl (ÖVP). *Justice:* Claudia Bandion-Ortner (ÖVP). *Labour, Social Affairs and Consumer Protection:* Rudolf Hundstorfer (SPÖ). *Transport, Innovation and Technology:* Doris Bures (SPÖ). *Women and Public Administration:* Gabriele Heinisch-Hosek (SPÖ). *State Secretary in the Federal Chancellery:* Josef Ostermayer (SPÖ). *State Secretary in the Ministry for Economy, Family and Youth:* Christine Marek (ÖVP). *State Secretaries in the Ministry for Finance:* Reinhold Lopatka (ÖVP); Andreas Schieder (SPÖ).

Government Website: http://www.austria.gv.at

CURRENT LEADERS

Dr Heinz Fischer

Position

President

Introduction

Following his electoral victory on 25 April 2004 at the age of 65, Dr Heinz Fischer took office as Austria's first socialist federal president for 18 years on 8 July 2004. He is committed to maintaining the country's neutral foreign policy and the welfare state. Critics have labelled him a *Berufspolitiker* ('professional politician') who has tended to avoid controversy and conflict.

Early Life

Heinz Fischer was born into a political family in Graz on 9 Oct. 1938. His father was state secretary in the ministry of trade from 1954–56. Fischer attended the Humanistisches Gymnasium in Vienna and went on to study law and political science at the University of Vienna, attaining a PhD in 1961. He entered politics two years later, becoming secretary to the Social Democratic Party (SPÖ) in the Austrian parliament, a position he held until 1975. Despite being elected as a member of parliament in 1971, Fischer continued his academic career. He was appointed associate professor of political science at the University of Innsbruck in 1978 and was made a full professor in 1994.

Fischer served as federal minister of science and research from 1983–86, under a coalition government headed by Fred Sinowatz of the SPÖ. In 1986 the SPÖ joined the Austrian People's Party (ÖVP) in a 'grand coalition' that retained control of the government through the 1990s. Fischer was elected president of the National Council in Nov. 1990, holding the office for 12 years until Dec. 2002. He also served as a member of the national security council and the foreign affairs council.

He was elected federal president on 25 April 2004 as the SPÖ candidate, polling 52·4% of the vote to defeat Benita Ferrero-Waldner, foreign minister in the ruling ÖVP-led conservative coalition.

Career in Office

On 8 July 2004 Fischer was sworn in for a six-year term. Although a largely ceremonial post, the president is commander-in-chief of the military and has the constitutional power to reject nominations for cabinet ministers and to remove them from office. In his opening address, Fischer recalled how many Austrians had grown up 'sensitive to war and peace' and aware that 'peace and the politics to promote peace... must have a central role in our political efforts'. The consolidation of the basic values of democracy is another of his priorities: '...Consensus is very important to me. But consensus means to build bridges. Bridges between solid shores.'

Following the collapse of the governing coalition in July 2008, early parliamentary elections were held in Sept. Fischer subsequently asked SPÖ leader Werner Faymann, as head of the largest party, to form a new government. Faymann renewed the coalition with the ÖVP, excluding the resurgent far-right parties that had made gains in the elections, and his government took office in Dec. Fischer stressed that a stable and competent administration was in the national interest to deal with serious challenges confronting Austria, including the global financial crisis.

Fischer has written numerous books and publications on law and political science. He is also co-editor of the Austrian *Zeitschrift für Politikwissenschaft* (*Journal of Political Science*) and *Journal für Rechtspolitik* (*Journal of Law Policy*).

Fischer was elected for a further six-year term in the presidential election of April 2010.

Werner Faymann

Position

Chancellor

Introduction

A career politician, Werner Faymann became leader of the Social Democratic Party (SPÖ) in June 2008. He led the party to a narrow victory at the Sept. 2008 general election and heads a coalition government.

Early Life

Werner Faymann was born on 4 May 1960 in Vienna. He attended a grammar school in Vienna and studied law at the University of

Vienna before joining the youth branch of the Vienna SPÖ. There he led campaigns and protests, becoming the group's chairman in 1985. From 1985–88 he also worked as a consultant at the Zentralsparkasse (now Bank of Austria). In 1985 he was elected to the Vienna state parliament and from 1988–94 led the board for tenants' rights. He was appointed councillor for housing and urban development in Vienna in 1995, serving until 2007 when Chancellor Gusenbauer appointed him federal minister for transport, technology and development.

In June 2008, with the 'grand coalition' between the SPÖ and the Austrian People's Party (ÖVP) under strain, the SPÖ separated the role of chancellor from that of party leader. Faymann was chosen to head the party. Faymann and Gusenbauer then published an open letter that reversed earlier SPÖ policy by promising to put all amendments to EU treaties affecting the national interest to a referendum. The ÖVP consequently abandoned the coalition, triggering a general election.

Faymann fought the election on a platform of social investment and populist scepticism about the EU. On 28 Sept. 2008 the SPÖ won the most seats, although with a reduced share of the vote (just under 30%). Refusing to consider a coalition with the right-wing Alliance for the Future of Austria or the anti-immigration Freedom Party, he entered into an agreement in Nov. with the ÖVP under its new leader Josef Pröll. On 2 Dec. 2008 Faymann was sworn in as chancellor.

Career in Office

Faymann faced immediate challenges from the global economic crisis and in early 2009 introduced tax cuts to boost the economy. He advocates an EU aid package to support struggling European economies, in part to safeguard large loans Austria has made to eastern European countries.

DEFENCE

The Federal President is C.-in-C. of the armed forces. Conscription is for a six-month period, with liability for at least another 30 days' reservist refresher training spread over eight to ten years. Conscientious objectors can instead choose to undertake nine months' civilian service. Since 1992 the total 'on mobilization strength' of the forces has been reduced from approximately 200,000 to 110,000 troops. In 2002 approximately 1,000 personnel from so-called 'prepared units' were deployed in peace support operations in places such as Afghanistan, Bosnia, Cyprus, the Golan Heights and Syria.

Defence expenditure in 2006 totalled US$2,630m. (US$321 per capita), representing 0·8% of GDP.

Army

The Army is structured in five brigades and nine provincial military commands. Two brigades are mechanized, the rest infantry brigades. The mechanized brigades are equipped with Leopard 2/A4 main battle tanks. One of three infantry brigades is earmarked for airborne operations, the second is equipped with Pandur wheeled armoured personnel carriers and the third infantry brigade is specialized in mountain operations. The artillery units are brigade-directed. M-109 armoured self-propelled guns equip the artillery battalions. In addition to these standing units, some 20 infantry battalions under the direction of the provincial military commands are available on mobilization. Active personnel, 2002, 34,600 (to be 26,100) including 17,200 conscripts. Women started to serve in the armed forces on 1 April 1998.

Air Force

The Air Force Command comprises three aviation and three air-defence regiments with about 6,500 personnel, more than 150 aircraft and a number of fixed and mobile radar stations. Some 23 Draken interceptors equip a surveillance wing responsible for the defence of the Austrian air space and a fighter-bomber wing operates SAAB 105s. Helicopters including the S-70 Black Hawk equip six squadrons for transport/support, communication, observation, and search and rescue duties. Fixed-wing aircraft including PC-6s, PC-7s, Skyvans and C-130 Hercules are operated as trainers and for transport. The procurement of a fourth generation fighter is also planned for the near future.

INTERNATIONAL RELATIONS

Austria is a member of the UN, World Bank, IMF and several other UN specialized agencies, WTO, EU, Council of Europe, OSCE, CERN, CEI, Danube Commission, BIS, IOM, NATO Partnership for Peace, OECD, Inter-American Development Bank, Asian Development Bank and Antarctic Treaty. Austria is a signatory to the Schengen accord abolishing border controls between Austria, Belgium, Czech Republic, Denmark, Estonia, Finland, France, Germany, Greece, Hungary, Iceland, Italy, Latvia, Lithuania, Luxembourg, Malta, Netherlands, Norway, Poland, Portugal, Slovakia, Slovenia, Spain, Sweden and Switzerland.

ECONOMY

In 2007 agriculture accounted for 2% of GDP, industry 31% and services 67%.

According to the anti-corruption organization *Transparency International*, Austria ranked 16th in the world in a 2009 survey of the countries with the least corruption in business and government. It received 7·9 out of 10 in the annual index.

Overview

Austria has experienced one of the OECD's strongest productivity growth rates over the last decade while maintaining an unemployment rate below the OECD average. Market share in Central and Eastern European Countries (CEECs) has expanded significantly, while membership of the EU and the EMU has added momentum. EU membership has encouraged market liberalization and many companies have come under foreign (particularly German) ownership. Social partnership in the labour market has ensured wage moderation and low unemployment (5·0% in 2009). Tourism is important and benefits from Austria's central location and Alpine appeal. Austria is a net importer of research and development (R&D)-intensive products and the growth of R&D-intensive industries has been slow.

GDP growth accelerated in 2004 at its highest rate since 2000 and was higher still in the next three years, averaging 3·1% over four years until the global financial crisis and rising unemployment led to a fall in the growth rate in 2008 to 1·9%. Austria was particularly vulnerable because of its close economic ties with affected CEECs. Subsequent government stabilization measures are expected to increase the budget deficit.

Government spending accounts for about half of GDP, one of the highest levels in the OECD. The state controls many key industrial companies and utilities while local authorities control several savings banks. The government deficit, having met its target at the beginning of the 2000s, overshot in 2004. This was primarily for structural reasons, including increases in social and health care spending and reductions in corporate and personal income tax. It again met target levels each year through to 2008.

With one of the most expensive public pension systems in Europe, reforms were introduced in 2003 and 2005 to reduce the total cost to the benefit of long-term financial sustainability. The Austrian Medium-Term Budgetary Framework (MTBF), implemented in 2009 and aimed at balancing the budget, received cross-party political support.

Currency

On 1 Jan. 1999 the euro (EUR) became the legal currency in Austria at the irrevocable conversion rate of 13·7603 schillings to one euro. The euro, which consists of 100 cents, has been in circulation since 1 Jan. 2002. There are seven euro notes in different colours and sizes denominated in 500, 200, 100, 50, 20,

10 and 5 euros, and eight coins denominated in 2 and 1 euros, then 50, 20, 10, 5, 2 and 1 cents. On the introduction of the euro there was a 'dual circulation' period before the schilling ceased to be legal tender on 28 Feb. 2002.

Inflation rates (based on OECD statistics):

1999	2000	2001	2002	2003	2004	2005	2006	2007	2008
0·5%	2·0%	2·3%	1·7%	1·3%	2·0%	2·1%	1·7%	2·2%	3·2%

Foreign exchange reserves were US$5,269m. in Sept. 2009 and gold reserves 9·00m. troy oz. Total money supply was €96,422m. in Aug. 2009.

Budget
The federal budget for calendar years provided revenue and expenditure as follows (in €1m.):

	2003	2004	2005
Revenue	57,889	59,237	58,969
Expenditure	61,387	62,667	64,420

VAT is 20% (reduced rates, 12% and 10%).

Performance
Real GDP growth rates (based on OECD statistics):

1999	2000	2001	2002	2003	2004	2005	2006	2007	2008
3·7%	3·1%	0·8%	1·6%	0·8%	2·6%	2·9%	3·4%	3·4%	1·9%

Total GDP was US$416·4bn. in 2008.

Banking and Finance
The Oesterreichische Nationalbank, central bank of Austria, opened on 1 Jan. 1923 but was taken over by the German Reichsbank on 17 March 1938. It was re-established on 3 July 1945. Its *Governor* is Ewald Nowotny. At 31 Dec. 2002 it had total reserves of US$13·2bn.

In 2005 banking and insurance accounted for 4·8% of gross domestic product at current prices. In 2005 an average of 109,953 individuals were engaged in banking and insurance (76,730 in banking, 26,630 in insurance and 6,593 in banking and insurance), representing 3·4% of Austria's wage and salary earners.

In 2005 there were 880 bank and credit institution head offices and 4,317 branch offices. By June 2003, 40 credit institutions from countries outside the EU had established representative offices. The leading banks with total assets in 2005 (in €1bn.) were: Bank Austria Group of Companies, 158,879; Erste Bank, 152,660; Raiffeisen Zentralbank Österreich AG, 93,863; and Bank für Arbeit und Wirtschaft AG–PSK, 57,898.

There is a stock exchange in Vienna (VEX). It is one of the oldest in Europe and one of the smallest.

ENERGY AND NATURAL RESOURCES

Environment
Austria's carbon dioxide emissions from the consumption and flaring of fossil fuels were the equivalent of 8·6 tonnes per capita in 2008. An *Environmental Performance Index* compiled in 2008 ranked Austria sixth in the world, with 89·4%. The index examined various factors in six areas—air pollution, biodiversity and habitat, climate change, environmental health, productive natural resources and water resources.

Austria is one of the world leaders in recycling. In 2000, 50% of all municipal waste was recycled.

Electricity
The Austrian electricity market was fully liberalized on 1 Oct. 2001. Installed capacity was 21·0m. kW in 2004. Production in 2004 was 64·13bn. kWh. Consumption per capita, 2004: 8,256 kWh.

Oil and Gas
The commercial production of petroleum began in the early 1930s. Production of crude oil, 2006: 856,274 tonnes. Crude oil reserves, 2007, were 50m. bbls.

The Austrian gas market was fully liberalized on 1 Oct. 2002. Production of natural gas, 2008: 1,532m. cu. metres. Natural gas reserves in 2007 amounted to 16bn. cu. metres.

Minerals
The most important minerals are limestone and marble (2003 production, 24,476,840 tonnes), quartz and arenaceous quartz (2003 production, 7,305,244 tonnes), dolomite (2003 production, 5,468,300 tonnes), lignite (2003 production, 1,152,000 tonnes), basalt, clay and kaolin.

Agriculture
In 2005 the agricultural workforce numbered 520,984, with 243,715 persons employed in agriculture as their main occupation. There were 189,591 farms in 2005. There were 1·38m. ha. of arable land in 2007 and 68,000 ha. of permanent crops. In 2003 Austria set aside 297,000 ha. (11·6% of its agricultural land—the second highest proportion in the world after Liechtenstein) for the growth of organic crops. Agriculture accounted for 6·4% of exports and 6·3% of imports in 2004.

The chief products in 2003 (area in 1,000 ha.; yield in tonnes) were as follows: barley (212·3; 882,322); oats (34·4; 128,533); potatoes (21·1; 560,340); rye (40·0; 132,839); sugar beets (43·2; 2,485,386); wheat (272·0; 1,191,380). Other important agricultural products include apples (423,000 tonnes in 2003) and pears (175,000 tonnes in 2003). Wine production in 2007 totalled 2,628,021 hectolitres.

Livestock in 2006: cattle, 2,002,919; pigs, 3,139,438; sheep, 312,375; poultry (2003), 13,027,145.

Forestry
Forested area in 2005, 3·86m. ha. (46·7% of the land area), around three-quarters of which was coniferous. Felled timber, in 1,000 cu. metres: 2005, 16,470·7; 2006, 19,134·9; 2007, 21,317·3.

Fisheries
Total catch in 2005 came to 370 tonnes, exclusively from inland waters.

INDUSTRY
The leading companies by market capitalization in Austria in March 2009 were: Verbundgesellschaft, an electricity company (US$11·7bn.); OMV Group, an oil and gas company (US$10·0bn.); and Telekom Austria (US$7·0bn.).

Production (in 1,000 tonnes): pig iron (2002), 4,600; paper and paperboard (2003), 4,565; cement (2001), 3,863; distillate fuel oil (2004), 3,529; petrol (2004), 1,738; residual fuel oil (2004), 1,032; sawnwood (2003), 10·47m. cu. metres; soft drinks (2001), 1,524·3m. litres; beer (2001), 852·8m. litres.

Labour
Austria has one of the lowest unemployment rates in the European Union (5·4% in Dec. 2009).

In 2003 there were an average of 3,184,117 employed persons, with an average of 588,946 persons working in manufacturing; 493,288 in wholesale and retail trade, and repair of motor vehicles, motorcycles and personal and household goods; 471,062 in public administration and defence; 285,883 in real estate, renting and business activities; 237,677 in construction; and 215,243 in transport, storage and communication. In 2003 there were an average of 21,716 job vacancies.

The number of foreigners who may be employed in Austria is limited to 9% of the potential workforce. There were four strikes in 2002, with 6,305 participants (none in 2001). There were no strikes in 1996, 1998, 1999 or 2001. Between 1996 and 2005 strikes cost Austria an average of 41 days per 1,000 employees a year.

Austria has one of the lowest average retirement ages but reforms passed in 1997 now make it less attractive to retire before 60. Only 15% of men and 6% of women in the 60–65 age range work, although the legal retirement ages are 60 for women and 65 for men.

Trade Unions

The 13 unions in the Austrian Trade Union Confederation (Österreichischer Gewerkschaftsbund, ÖGB) had 1,385,000 members in Dec. 2003.

INTERNATIONAL TRADE

Imports and Exports

In 2006 imports were valued at US$133,661m. (US$113,806m. in 2005) and exports US$134,302m. (US$117,233m. in 2005).

Main import suppliers in 2003 (% of total imports): Germany, 41·0%; Italy, 7·0%; Switzerland, 4·1%; France, 3·9%; USA, 3·9%. Main export markets: Germany, 31·8%; Italy, 9·0%; Switzerland, 5·2%; USA, 5·2%; France, 4·4%. Other EU-member countries accounted for 65·9% of imports and 59·5% of exports.

In 2003 chemicals, manufactured goods classified chiefly by material and miscellaneous manufactured articles accounted for 43·0% of Austria's imports and 46·4% of exports; machinery and transport equipment 39·3% of imports and 41·9% of exports; food, live animals, beverages and tobacco 5·9% of imports and 5·8% of exports; mineral fuels, lubricants and related materials 8·0% of imports and 2·5% of exports; inedible crude materials, and animal and vegetable oil and fats 3·8% of imports and 3·4% of exports.

Trade Fairs

Vienna ranks as the fourth most popular convention city in the world (behind Singapore, Paris and Brussels) according to the Union des Associations Internationales (UAI), hosting 2·3% of all meetings held in 2008.

COMMUNICATIONS

Roads

In 2007 the road network totalled 107,262 km (Autobahn, 1,677 km; highways, 10,408 km; secondary roads, 23,657 km). In 2007 passenger cars in use numbered 4,245,600, lorries and vans 372,600, buses and coaches 9,300, and motorcycles and mopeds 642,800. There were 691 fatalities in road accidents in 2007.

Rail

The Austrian Federal Railways (ÖBB) has been restructured and was split up into ten new companies, which became operational on 1 Jan. 2005. Length of route in 2003, 5,656 km, of which 3,526 km were electrified. There are also a number of private railways with a total length of 589 km. In 2003, 183·73m. passengers and 87·0m. tonnes of freight were carried by Federal Railways. There is a metro and tramway in Vienna, and tramways in Gmunden, Graz, Innsbruck and Linz.

Civil Aviation

The national airline is Austrian Airlines, which was privatized after a takeover by Lufthansa in Sept. 2009. There are international airports at Vienna (Schwechat), Linz, Salzburg, Graz, Klagenfurt and Innsbruck. In 2003 services were provided by 62 other airlines. In 2003, 273,064 commercial aircraft and 16,344,253 passengers arrived and departed; 118,081 tonnes of freight and 11,554 tonnes of mail were handled. In 2003 Vienna handled 12,709,432 passengers and 115,686 tonnes of freight. Austrian Airlines carried 7,070,344 passengers in 2002.

Shipping

The Danube is an important waterway. Goods traffic (in 1,000 tonnes): 10,980 in 2000; 11,634 in 2001; 12,316 in 2002; 10,737 in 2003 (including the Rhine-Main-Danube Canal). The merchant shipping fleet totalled 30,000 GRT in 2002.

Telecommunications

Österreichische Industrie Holding AG, the Austrian investment and privatization agency, holds a 27·4% stake in Telekom Austria. In 2008 there were 3,285,000 main (fixed) telephone lines. In the same year mobile phone subscribers numbered 10,816,000 (1,297·3 per 1,000 persons). There were 5·0m. PCs in use in 2005 (611·2 per 1,000 persons) and 5·9m. internet users in 2008.

Postal Services

The Postal Savings Bank was privatized in 2000. In 2002 there were 1,669 post offices and 120 post-agencies, the so-called 'Post-Partner'. A total of 994m. domestic postal items were handled in 2005.

SOCIAL INSTITUTIONS

Justice

The Supreme Court of Justice *(Oberster Gerichtshof)* in Vienna is the highest court in civil and criminal cases. In addition, in 2003 there were four Courts of Appeal *(Oberlandesgerichte)*, 20 High Courts *(Landesgerichte)* and 148 District Courts *(Bezirksgerichte)*. There is also a Supreme Constitutional Court *(Verfassungsgerichtshof)* and a Supreme Administrative Court *(Verwaltungsgerichtshof)*, both seated in Vienna. In 2003 a total of 634,286 criminal offences were reported to the police and 41,749 people were convicted of offences. The population in penal institutions in Nov. 2003 was 8,114 (100 per 100,000 of national population).

Education

In 2006–07 there were 5,011 general compulsory schools (including special education) with 71,796 teachers and 639,433 pupils. Secondary schools totalled 1,676 in 2006–07, with 571,651 pupils. Secondary technical and vocational colleges numbered 317 in 2006–07, with 134,609 pupils.

The dominant institutions of higher education are the 16 public universities and six colleges of arts. Student fees were introduced in 2001, but in 2008 the government decided to eliminate fees for Austrian nationals who complete their studies within the minimum time.

In the winter term 2007–08 there were 224,597 students (46,102 foreign) enrolled at the public universities and 9,853 (5,934 foreign) at the colleges of arts. In 1994 Higher Technical Study Centres (*Fachhochschul-Studiengänge*, FHS) were established, which are private, but government-dependent, institutions. A federal law was passed in 1999 to allow the accreditation of private universities. In 2007 there were 11 accredited private universities.

In 2005 public expenditure on education came to 5·5% of GNI and 10·9% of total government spending. The adult literacy rate is at least 99%.

Health

In 2003 there were 37,447 doctors, 4,037 dentists, 40,113 nurses (2002) and 1,671 midwives. In 2002 there were 278 hospitals and 70,376 hospital beds. In 2007 Austria spent 10·1% of its GDP on health.

Welfare

Maternity/paternity leave is until the child's second birthday. A new parenting allowance was introduced on 1 Jan. 2002, replacing the maternity/paternity allowance. The latest formula is based on family benefit financed from the Family Fund. The basic allowance is €436 per month for a maximum of three years. In June 2003 a reform of the pensions system was approved involving the reduction of pension benefits by 10%, the raising of the retirement age to 65 by increasing the workers' contribution period from 40 to 45 years and the abolition of early retirement by 2017. These reforms provoked Austria's first general strike in over 50 years. There were 2,496,140 pensioners in Dec. 2003.

RELIGION

In 2001 there were 5,915,000 Roman Catholics (73·6%), 376,000 Evangelical Lutherans (4·7%), 339,000 Muslims (4·2%), 963,000 without religious allegiance (12·0%) and 439,000 others (5·5%). The Roman Catholic Church has two archbishoprics and seven bishoprics. In Feb. 2010 there was one cardinal.

CULTURE

World Heritage Sites

There are eight UNESCO sites in Austria. They are: the historic centre of the city of Salzburg (inscribed in 1996); the Palace and gardens of Schönbrunn (1996); Hallstatt-Dachstein Salzkammergut cultural landscape (1997); Semmering Railway (1998); the historic centre of the city of Graz (1999); the Wachau cultural landscape (2000); and the historic centre of the city of Vienna (2001).

Austria shares the Cultural Landscape of Fertö/Neusiedlersee site (2001) with Hungary.

Broadcasting

Legislation in 2001 established the Austrian Regulatory Authority for Broadcasting and Telecommunications. The public broadcaster Österreichischer Rundfunk (ORF) operates two national television channels, as well as national and regional radio stations and the external Ö1 International radio service. There has been growing competition from private broadcasters since the 1990s, with licences awarded to local commercial radio and television stations and (from 2000) to a national TV service, ATV. Cable and satellite services are widely available. There were 3·38m. TV-equipped households in 2006 (colour is by PAL) and 1,332,000 cable TV subscribers.

Press

There were 16 daily newspapers (seven of them in Vienna), 224 non-daily newspapers and 2,772 other periodicals in 2003. The most popular newspaper is the mass-market tabloid Neue Kronen-Zeitung, which is read on a daily basis by 42% of the population. In 2003 a total of 21,581 books were published, including 8,733 new titles.

Tourism

Tourism is an important industry. In 2003, 17,384 hotels and boarding houses had a total of 608,953 beds available. In 2005, 19,952,000 non-resident tourists stayed in holiday accommodation and tourist spending came to US$19·31bn. Of 117,966,984 overnight stays in tourist accommodation in 2003, 31,618,992 were by Austrians and 52,804,677 by Germans.

Festivals

The main festivals are Salzburger Festspiele, held every July–Aug. (219,944 visitors in 2003), and Bregenzer Festspiele, also held in July–Aug. (204,482 visitors in 2003). The Haydn Days in Eisenstadt, held every Sept., is also considered to be one of the leading annual festivals.

DIPLOMATIC REPRESENTATIVES

Of Austria in the United Kingdom (18 Belgrave Mews West, London, SW1X 8HU)
Ambassador: Gabriele Matzner-Holzer.

Of the United Kingdom in Austria (Jaurèsgasse 12, 1030 Vienna)
Ambassador: Simon Smith.

Of Austria in the USA (3524 International Court, NW, Washington, D.C., 20008)
Ambassador: Christian Prosl.

Of the USA in Austria (Boltzmanngasse 16, 1090 Vienna)
Ambassador: William C. Eacho.

Of Austria to the United Nations
Ambassador: Thomas Mayr-Harting.

Of Austria to the European Union
Permanent Representative: Hans-Dietmar Schweisgut.

FURTHER READING

Austrian Central Statistical Office. *Main publications: Statistisches Jahrbuch für die Republik Österreich.* New Series from 1950. Annual.—*Statistische Nachrichten.* Monthly.—*Beiträge zur österreichischen Statistik.*—*Statistik in Österreich 1918–1938.* [Bibliography] 1985.—*Veröffentlichungen des Österreichischen Statistischen Zentralamtes 1945–1985.* [Bibliography] 1990.—*Republik Österreich, 1945–1995.*

Bischof, Günter, Pelinka, Anton and Gehler, Michael, (eds.) *Austria in the European Union.* 2002.—*Austrian Foreign Policy in Historical Context.* 2005

Brook-Shepherd, G., *The Austrians: a Thousand-Year Odyssey.* 1997

Bruckmüller, Ernst, *Austrian Nation: Cultural Consciousness and Socio-Political Processes.* 2003

Pick, Hella, *Guilty Victim: Austria from the Holocaust to Haider.* 2000

Steininger, Rolf, *Austria in the Twentieth Century.* 2002

Wolfram, H. (ed.) *Österreichische Geschichte.* 10 vols. 1994

National library: Österreichische Nationalbibliothek, Josefsplatz, 1015 Vienna.

National Statistical Office: Austrian Central Statistical Office, Guglgasse 13, A-1110 Vienna.

Website: http://www.statistik.at

AZERBAIJAN

Azarbaijchan Respublikasy
(Republic of Azerbaijan)

Capital: Baku
Population estimate, 2010: 8·93m.
GDP per capita, 2007: (PPP$) 7,851
HDI/world rank: 0·787/86

KEY HISTORICAL EVENTS

Rock art at Gobustan, close to Azerbaijan's Caspian Sea coast, dates from as early as 20,000 BC. Part of southern Azerbaijan came under the influence of the Assyrian Empire around 800 BC and was later subsumed into the ancient kingdoms of Manue, Urartu and Medea. During the 6th century BC the Persian Akhemenid dynasty held sway in what was known as Caucasian Albania, fortified by the Zoroastrian religion. Persian influence continued in the form of the Parthian Empire from around 200 BC, followed by periods of Roman rule. The Arshakid dynasty, installed by the Romans to control much of the Caucasus, survived until the Persian Sassanid Empire asserted dominance in the 4th century AD.

Sassanid power reached its zenith under Khosrau II around AD 620, with a sphere of influence stretching from Egypt to the Caucasus, central Asia and northwest India. Arab tribes, newly united around Islam, made incursions into Azerbaijan from the mid-7th century and the territory came under the rule of Caliph Abu Abbas from 750, whose Abbasid dynasty was centred on Baghdad. Unpopular taxes and attacks on non-Muslims led to rebellions in Azerbaijan, including Babek's Khuramid Movement.

Arab control of Azerbaijan was waning by the late 10th century and the region dissolved into numerous fiefdoms, including Shirvan (centred on Shemakha) and Arran (based at Terter). The 11th century saw an influx of nomadic Oghuz Turks under the Seljuk dynasty from Central Asia. This began a process of Turkification that continued for the next three centuries, punctuated by Mongol incursions including the Golden Horde in 1319 and Timur in 1380.

At the end of the 15th century Azerbaijan became the power base of the Safavid dynasty, centred on Ardabil (now in northern Iran). Shah Ismail I forged a kingdom that controlled all Persia by 1520 and which promoted the Shia branch of Islam as the state religion. Conflict ensued with Ottoman Turkey, which followed Sunni Muslim traditions, and the Safavids shifted their focus eastwards from Azerbaijan, eventually establishing their capital in Esfahan.

The overthrow of Safavid control in Azerbaijan in 1722 preceded increasing Russian influence in the region, which led to the annexation of Georgia by Tsar Alexander I and the control of the khanates in Azerbaijan. By 1807 Nakhichevan remained the only independent khanate, although Russian forces had to fight off several Persian challenges for control. The territory of the present Azerbaijan was acquired by Russia from Persia through the treaties of Gulistan (1813) and Turkmenchai (1828). This period of Russian rule was marked by an influx of Armenians into western Azerbaijan, fleeing persecution from Ottoman Turkey and Persia.

Azerbaijan's oil industry, centred on Baku, began to develop in the 1870s. By the early 20th century half the world's production was supplied from Baku. Tensions between Azeris and Armenians rose against the backdrop of revolutions in Russia (1905–07) and Iran (1906–11), prompting the rise of Azeri nationalism. Following the Bolshevik revolution in 1917, Azerbaijan joined with Armenia and Georgia to form the short-lived Transcaucasian Federation. On 28 May 1918 the Azerbaijani Democratic Republic was declared, with Gandja as its capital. The fledgling nation was soon occupied, first by Ottoman troops and then by British forces until they withdrew in Aug. 1919. After the Red Army achieved victory in Russia's civil war in early 1920, it moved swiftly to secure control of oil-rich Azerbaijan, reaching Baku on 28 April 1920.

In 1922 Azerbaijan joined the Transcaucasian Soviet Federal Socialist Republic, whose administration was led by Nariman Narimanov. Stalin's administrative reorganization of 1936 led to Azerbaijan becoming a separate Soviet Republic, forced to retract links with other Turkic and Islamic states. Mass killings, deportations and imprisonments followed, reaching their height in the Stalinist purges of 1937. Baku's oilfields attracted Nazi forces in the Second World War but their defeat at Stalingrad meant that Azerbaijan remained under Soviet control.

Conflict with Armenia over the enclave of Nagorno-Karabakh escalated in 1988, leading to violent expulsions of Armenians in Azerbaijan and Azeris in Armenia. In 'Black January' 1990 Soviet tanks moved into Baku following rioting and over 100 civilians were killed. War broke out between the two countries in 1992 after the Armenian population of Nagorno-Karabakh declared independence from Azerbaijan. A ceasefire was agreed in 1994 but the dispute over territory remains unsettled, although negotiations in Florida in 2001 prompted hope of a peaceful solution.

On 18 Aug. 1991 the Supreme Soviet of Azerbaijan declared independence from the crumbling Soviet Union. Following an attempted coup in June 1993, Heidar Aliyev was appointed president by the national assembly and then confirmed in a general election in Oct. Parliament ratified association with the Commonwealth of Independent States on 20 Sept. 1993. A treaty of friendship and co-operation was signed with Russia on 3 July 1997 and Aliyev was re-elected in Oct. 1998, although the administration of the election was criticized by international observers. Following serious illness, Aliyev stood down from the presidency in Oct. 2003. He controversially appointed his son, Ilham, as the party's sole presidential candidate. Ilham Aliyev duly won the presidential election of 15 Oct. 2003 but international observers again criticized the contest as falling below expected standards. He was re-elected on 15 Oct. 2008 with 88·7% of the vote, although several major parties boycotted the election.

TERRITORY AND POPULATION

Azerbaijan is bounded in the west by Armenia, in the north by Georgia and the Russian Federation (Dagestan), in the east by the Caspian sea and in the south by Turkey and Iran. Its area is 86,600 sq. km (33,430 sq. miles), and it includes the Nakhichevan Autonomous Republic and the largely Armenian-inhabited Nagorno-Karabakh.

The population at the 1999 census was 7,953,000 (4,119,000 females); density, approximately 92 per sq. km. In 2005, 51·5% of the population lived in urban areas. The population breaks down into 82·7% Azerbaijanis, 5·6% Armenians, 5·6% Russians and 2·4% Lezgis (1999 census).

The UN gives an estimated population for 2010 of 8·93m.; density, 103 per sq. km.

Chief cities: Baku (at 1 Jan. 2004, 1,839,800), Gandja (303,100) and Sumgait (290,700). There are 66 districts and 13 cities.

The official language is Azeri. On 1 Aug. 2001 Azerbaijan abolished the use of the Cyrillic alphabet and switched to using Latin script.

SOCIAL STATISTICS

In 2003: births, 113,467; deaths, 49,001; marriages, 56,091; divorces, 6,671. Rates, 2003 (per 1,000 population): births, 14·0; deaths, 6·0; infant mortality (2005, per 1,000 live births), 74. Life expectancy in 2007: 72·3 years for females and 67·6 years for males. Annual population growth rate, 2000–05, 0·8%; fertility rate, 2004, 1·8 children per woman.

CLIMATE

The climate is almost tropical in summer and the winters slightly warmer than in regions north of the Caucasus. Cold spells do occur, however, both on the high mountains and in the enclosed valleys. There are nine climatic zones. Baku, Jan. –6°C, July 25°C. Annual rainfall 318 mm.

CONSTITUTION AND GOVERNMENT

Parliament is the 125-member *Melli-Majlis*, with all seats elected from single-member districts. A constitutional referendum and parliamentary elections were held on 12 Nov. 1995. Turnout for the referendum was 86%. The new Constitution was approved by 91·9% of votes cast. As a result of a referendum held on 24 Aug. 2002 a number of changes were made to the constitution, including the distribution of the *Melli-Majlis* seats—previously, 25 seats were distributed proportionally among political parties. The validity of the outcome of the referendum was questioned by international observers. In a referendum on 18 March 2009 a measure to abolish presidential term limits was approved, with 91·8% of votes cast in favour.

National Anthem

'Azerbaijan! Azerbaijan!'; words by A. Javad, tune by U. Hajibeyov.

RECENT ELECTIONS

At elections on 15 Oct. 2008 Ilham Aliyev of the New Azerbaijan Party (YAP) was re-elected president with 88·7% of votes cast. Igbal Aghazade of the Azerbaijan Hope Party (AUP) won 2·9%, Fazil Mustafayev of the Great Order Party (BQP) won 2·5%, Gudrat Hasanguliyev of the All-Azerbaijan Popular Front Party (BAKJP) won 2·3% and Gulamhuseyn Alibayli (ind.) won 2·2%. There were two other candidates who received less than 1% of the vote each. Turnout was 75·6%.

At the parliamentary elections held on 6 Nov. 2005 the YAP gained 56 seats; ind. 40 and the Azadlig (Freedom) opposition bloc 6 (the Musavat Party 5 and the Azerbaijan Popular Front Party 1). A number of smaller parties took either one or two seats. Turnout was 42·2%. International observers declared that the poll failed to meet international standards.

CURRENT ADMINISTRATION

President: Ilham Aliyev; b. 1961 (YAP; sworn in 31 Oct. 2003).

In March 2010 the government comprised:

Prime Minister: Artur Rasizade; b. 1935 (YAP; in office since 6 Aug. 2003, until 4 Nov. as acting prime minister, having previously been prime minister from 20 July 1996 to 4 Aug. 2003).

First Deputy Prime Minister: Yagub Eyyubov. *Deputy Prime Ministers:* Elchin Efendiyev; Ali Hasanov; Abid Sharifov.

Minister of Foreign Affairs: Elmar Mamedyarov. *Interior:* Ramil Usubov. *Culture and Tourism:* Abulfaz Garayev. *Education:* Misir Mardanov. *Emergency Situations:* Kamaladdin Heydarov. *National Security:* Eldar Mahmudov. *Defence:* Lieut.-Gen. Safar Abiyev. *Defence Industry:* Yavar Jamalov. *Communications and Information Technologies:* Ali Abbasov. *Agriculture and Food:* Ismat Abbasov. *Justice:* Fikret Mamedov. *Health:* Ogtay Shiraliyev. *Finance:* Samir Sharifov. *Labour and Social Protection:* Fizuli Alakbarov. *Youth and Sport:* Azad Rahimov. *Economic Development:* Shahin Mustafayev. *Ecology and Natural Resources:* Huseyngulu Bagirov. *Industry and Energy:* Natig Aliyev. *Taxation:* Fazil Mamedov. *Transport:* Ziya Mammadov.

Speaker of the National Assembly (Melli-Majlis): Ogtay Asadov.

Office of the President: http://www.president.az

CURRENT LEADERS

Ilham Aliyev

Position
President

Introduction
Ilham Aliyev succeeded his father, Heidar Aliyev, as president in Oct. 2003. The Moscow-educated politician has presided over a rapidly-growing economy but heightened political tension followed the parliamentary elections of 6 Nov. 2005. He was re-elected president in Oct. 2008, although most leading opposition candidates dismissed the poll as neither free nor fair.

Early Life
Ilham Heidar oglu Aliyev was born in Baku, capital of the Soviet Socialist Republic of Azerbaijan, on 24 Dec. 1961. His father was Heidar Aliyev, who became deputy prime minister of the Soviet Union under Mikhail Gorbachev and, in Oct. 1993, president of Azerbaijan. Ilham Aliyev graduated in history from the Moscow State Institute for International Relations in 1982. He subsequently gained a PhD in history and began teaching at the Institute. Plans to enter the diplomatic service were curtailed by the collapse of the Soviet Union in 1991 and he established 'business interests' in Moscow and İstanbul. Between 1991 and 1994 his flamboyant lifestyle attracted media attention and he was accused of accumulating large gambling debts.

In May 1994 Ilham Aliyev was appointed vice-president of Azerbaijan's state oil company. Four months later President Aliyev signed a 30-year deal valued at more than US$7bn. with eight foreign companies to develop the country's substantial oil reserves. In 1995 Ilham Aliyev was elected to parliament and was subsequently appointed president of the national Olympic committee and head of the Azerbaijan delegation to the Council of Europe. In Dec. 1999 he became a deputy of the ruling New Azerbaijan Party (YAP) and, in 2001, was appointed party vice president.

Following the surprise resignation of Prime Minister Artur Rasizade in Aug. 2003, Heidar Aliyev appointed his son as prime minister. The move was approved by a 101–1 vote in the National Assembly but opposition parties boycotted the election. Critics took the move as proof that the increasingly frail president planned to hand over power to his son (an amendment to the constitution in Aug. 2002 providing for the prime minister to become interim president in the event that the president dies in office or is incapacitated). A few weeks before the presidential elections of Oct. 2003 Heidar Aliyev pulled out of the running, leaving Ilham as the YAP's candidate.

Official results gave Aliyev victory with 76·8% of the vote but opposition parties staged mass protests over alleged intimidation and fraud, charges backed by international observers. Aliyev was sworn in as the president on 31 Oct. 2003. His father died on 12 Dec. 2003.

Career in Office

Aliyev has presided over a rapidly expanding economy, a consequence of the discovery of offshore gas fields, high international oil prices and the completion of pipelines crossing from the Caucasus to Turkey. Unemployment and poverty levels nonetheless remain high, especially in rural areas.

Aliyev released a number of opposition figures from prison in March 2005 following international pressure, particularly from the Council of Europe. However, his administration was criticized for intimidating opposition activists in the run-up to parliamentary elections in Nov. 2005. The YAP, led by Aliyev since March 2005, won 56 of 125 parliamentary seats but the OSCE's international election observer mission reported harassment and vote buying. The opposition Azadlig party refused to accept the election results and organized mass protests in Nov. and Dec. 2005. In Nov. 2006 an independent broadcaster was closed down and a newspaper evicted from offices in Baku. These measures were denounced by the opposition as a clampdown by the regime on freedom of speech. In Oct. 2008 Western observers judged that Aliyev's overwhelming re-election as president was an improvement on the conduct of previous polls but still fell short of fully-democratic standards. A constitutional amendment to abolish presidential term limits was approved in a referendum in March 2009 with nearly 92% of the vote, allowing Aliyev to stand for election a third time.

In Feb. 2006 Aliyev met Armenia's President Kocharian in Paris, France, but the two failed to agree on a 'declaration of principles' on the disputed territory of Nagorno-Karabakh. Azerbaijan has continued to reject any move towards independence for the Armenian enclave and in March 2008 fighting again broke out in the region, which left several soldiers dead on both sides. However, at a Russian-hosted meeting in Nov. 2008 Aliyev and new Armenian president Serzh Sargsyan agreed to intensify their efforts to find a political settlement over the territory.

Artur Rasizade

Position

Prime Minister

Introduction

Artur Rasizade, an oil engineer-turned-politician, has been prime minister since 1996. He was appointed by President Heidar Aliyev and has served under his son, Ilham Aliyev, since Oct. 2003.

Early Life

Artur Tahir oglu Rasizade was born on 26 Feb. 1935 in Gandja in the Transcaucasian Soviet Federated Socialist Republic. Educated at the Azerbaijan Institute of Industry in Baku, Azerbaijan Soviet Socialist Republic, Rasizade began work as an engineer at the Institute of Oil Machine Construction in 1957. He served as chief engineer at Trust Soyuzneftemash from 1973–77, before taking the post of deputy head of the Azerbaijan state planning committee.

In 1986, after five years as bureau chief of the central committee of the Communist Party of Azerbaijan, Rasizade became first deputy prime minister under Kamran Baghirov, who has been widely blamed for the Republic's economic stagnation and the escalating tension with Armenia over Nagorno-Karabakh.

Following the break-up of the Soviet Union and Azerbaijan's declaration of independence in Aug. 1991, Rasizade became an adviser to the foundation for economic reforms. He served as an assistant to President Heidar Aliyev in early 1996 and was then appointed first deputy prime minister. He was appointed prime minister when Fuad Kuliev resigned following accusations by Aliyev of economic mismanagement. The National Assembly endorsed Rasizade's appointment and he took office on 26 Dec. 1996.

Career in Office

Heidar Aliyev won the presidential election in Oct. 1998 and retained Rasizade (a fellow member of the New Azerbaijan Party) as prime minister until 4 Aug. 2003, when the premier unexpectedly resigned. Rasizade's departure, ostensibly for health reasons, paved the way for Ilham Aliyev to assume office. Ilham Aliyev contested the presidential election of 15 Oct. 2003 and emerged victorious, although the opposition staged mass protests, alleging intimidation and fraud. On 4 Nov. 2003 Rasizade was formally reinstated as prime minister. He was reappointed again in Oct. 2008 following Aliyev's re-election as president.

DEFENCE

Conscription is for 17 months. Defence expenditure in 2006 totalled US$658m. (US$82 per capita), representing 3·3% of GDP.

Army

Personnel, 2007, 56,840. In addition there is a reserve force of 300,000 Azerbaijanis who have received some kind of military service experience within the last 15 years. There is also a paramilitary Ministry of the Interior militia of more than 10,000 and a border guard of approximately 5,000.

Navy

The flotilla is based at Baku on the Caspian Sea. Equipment includes six patrol craft. Personnel numbered about 2,000 in 2007.

Air Force

How many ex-Soviet aircraft are usable is not known but there are 47 combat capable aircraft and 15 attack helicopters. Personnel, 7,900 in 2007.

INTERNATIONAL RELATIONS

Azerbaijan is a member of the UN, World Bank, IMF and several other UN specialized agencies, Council of Europe, OSCE, EBRD, BSEC, CIS, IOM, Islamic Development Bank, NATO Partnership for Peace, OIC and ECO. There is a dispute with Armenia over the status of the chiefly Armenian-populated Azerbaijani enclave of Nagorno-Karabakh. A ceasefire was negotiated from 1994 with 20% of Azerbaijan's land in Armenian hands and with 1m. Azeri refugees and displaced persons.

ECONOMY

In 2006 agriculture accounted for 7·4% of GDP, industry 70·1% and services 22·5%.

Overview

At 23% in 2007, Azerbaijan had one of the world's fastest growth rates. Lower oil prices have led to subsequent slower expansion but growth remained in double digits in 2008. Oil and gas make up 90% of exports and over 50% of GDP, although attempts are being made to diversify the economy.

After Azerbaijan gained independence in 1991, the economy suffered from corruption, distortion and weak social infrastructure. In 1994 the government signed a production-sharing agreement with a consortium of foreign companies, bringing together investments worth around US$7·5bn. to develop oil deposits in the Caspian Sea and transport oil from Azerbaijan to Turkey via Georgia through the Baku-Tbilisi-Ceyhan and Shah

Deniz pipelines. In 1999 the State Oil Fund was created to manage the oil boom by ensuring stabilization and enforcing savings. Its assets were valued at US$11·2bn. by the end of 2008.

Non-oil industries have also prospered, particularly the construction and service sectors, with growth at 12% in 2007 and 17% in 2008. However, around 20% of the population remains in poverty and corruption is endemic.

Currency
The *manat* (AZM) of 100 *gyapiks* replaced the rouble in Jan. 1994. It was in turn replaced in Jan. 2006 by the *new manat* (AZN), also of 100 *gyapiks*, at 1 new manat = 5,000 manats. Inflation, which had been 1·5% in 2001, rose to 16·6% in 2007 and 20·8% in 2008. Foreign exchange reserves were US$1,028m. in July 2005 and total money supply was 3,846·1bn. manats.

Budget
Government revenue and expenditure (in 1m. manats):

	2000	*2001*	*2002*	*2003*
Revenue	3,573,200	3,924,000	4,551,200	6,131,900
Expenditure	3,819,800	4,037,500	4,658,800	6,173,000

VAT (currently 18%) accounted for 2,048,600m. manats of the 2003 budget revenue and profits tax accounted for 891,500m. manats. Of the 2003 expenditure, education accounted for 1,170,000m. manats, social security and welfare 1,070,000m. manats, law enforcement 603,400m. manats, state administration bodies 289,500m. manats and health 276,600m. manats.

Performance
Total GDP was US$46·3bn. in 2008. Azerbaijan has one of the fastest-growing economies in the world. Real GDP growth was 24·3% in 2005, 30·5% in 2006 and 23·4% in 2007—the highest rates of any country in each of these years. This was largely thanks to foreign investment into the country and the oil boom. In 2008 growth slowed to 11·6%, although the rate was still one of the highest in the world.

Banking and Finance
The central bank and bank of issue is the National Bank (*Chairman*, Dr Elman Rustamov). In 2003 there were two state-owned banks (International Bank of Azerbaijan and the United Joint Stock Bank). In 2003 there were 46 privately-owned commercial banks of varying size.

ENERGY AND NATURAL RESOURCES

Environment
Azerbaijan's carbon dioxide emissions from the consumption and flaring of fossil fuels were the equivalent of 4·7 tonnes per capita in 2008.

Electricity
Output was 21·6bn. kWh in 2004; consumption per capita in 2004 was 2,770 kWh. Capacity in 2004 was an estimated 5·4m. kW.

Oil and Gas
The most important industry is crude oil extraction. Baku is at the centre of oil exploration in the Caspian. Partnerships with Turkish, western European and US companies have been forged.

In 2008 oil reserves totalled 7·0bn. bbls. A century ago Azerbaijan produced half of the world's oil, but output today is just 1% of the total (although production started to increase in the late 1990s, rising every year between 1997 and 2008). Oil production in 2008 was 44·7m. tonnes. In July 1999 BP Amoco announced a major natural gas discovery in the Shah Deniz offshore field, with reserves of at least 700bn. cu. metres and perhaps as much as 1,000bn. cu. metres. There were proven reserves of 1,200bn. cu. metres in 2008. Natural gas production in 2008 amounted to 14·7bn. cu. metres—an increase of 50% on 2007 and up from just 4·5bn. cu. metres in 2004.

Accords for the construction of an oil pipeline from Baku, the Azerbaijani capital, on the Caspian Sea through Georgia to Ceyhan in southern Turkey (the BTC pipeline) were signed in Nov. 1999. Work on the pipeline began in Sept. 2002 and it was officially opened in May 2005.

A gas pipeline from Baku through Georgia to Erzurum in Turkey (the South Caucasus pipeline) was commissioned in 2006, allowing Azerbaijan to become a net exporter of natural gas.

Minerals
The republic is rich in natural resources: iron, bauxite, manganese, aluminium, copper ores, lead, zinc, precious metals, sulphur pyrites, nepheline syenites, limestone and salt. Cobalt ore reserves have been discovered in Dashkasan, and Azerbaijan has the largest iodine-bromine ore reserves of the former Soviet Union (the Neftchala region has an iodine-bromine mill).

Agriculture
In 2003 the total area devoted to agriculture was 4·8m. ha., of which 1·8m. ha. was under crop and 223,774 ha. were orchards and vineyards. In 2007 there were 1·85m. ha. of arable land and 0·22m. ha. of permanent crops. 1·43m. ha. were irrigated in 2007. In 2003, 40% of the economically active population was engaged in agriculture. Principal crops include grain, cotton, rice, grapes, citrus fruit, vegetables, tobacco and silk.

Output of main agricultural products (in 1,000 tonnes) in 2003: wheat, 1,547; potatoes, 769; tomatoes, 421; melons and watermelons, 357; barley, 334; apples, 154.

Livestock (2003): cattle, 2·24m.; sheep, 6·68m.; goats, 604,000; chickens, 18m. Livestock products (2003, in 1,000 tonnes): beef and veal, 67; lamb and mutton, 39; cow's milk, 1,147; eggs, 38.

Forestry
In 2003 forests covered 1,037,000 ha., or 12·0% of the total land area. Timber production in 2007 was 7,000 cu. metres.

Fisheries
About ten tonnes of caviar from the Caspian sturgeon are produced annually. Total fish catch in 2005 came to 9,001 tonnes, exclusively from inland waters.

INDUSTRY

There are oil extraction and refining, oil-related machinery, iron and steel, aluminium, copper, chemical, cement, building materials, timber, synthetic rubber, salt, textiles, food and fishing industries. Production (2004) in 1,000 tonnes: residual fuel oil, 2,141; distillate fuel oil, 1,789; cement (2003), 1,012; petrol, 852; bread and bakery products (2003), 686; jet fuel, 647. Output of other products: footwear (2003), 455,900 pairs.

Labour
In 2003 the economically active workforce numbered 3,747,000. The main areas of activity were: agriculture, hunting and forestry, 1,497,000; wholesale and retail trade/repair of motor vehicles, motorcycles and personal and household goods, 618,300; education, 330,000; public administration and defence/compulsory social security, 265,000. The unemployment rate in 2003 was 10·9%. The average monthly salary in 2003 was 368,974 manats.

INTERNATIONAL TRADE

Total external debt was US$1,881m. in 2005.

Imports and Exports
In 2006 imports (f.o.b.) were valued at US$5,269·3m. and exports (f.o.b.) at US$13,014·6m.

Principal imports in 2003 were machinery, power, cereals, steel tubes, sugar and sweets. Petroleum and related products accounted for approximately 85% of exports. Cotton, chemicals, tobacco, beverages, air conditioners, wool and refrigerators are also important exports.

Leading import suppliers in 2003 were Russia (21·3%), UK (10·9%), Turkey (7·4%), Turkmenistan (7·2%), Germany (6·5%). The main export markets were Italy (51·7%), France (8·1%), Israel (5·3%), Russia (5·3%), Georgia (4·3%), Turkey (4·1%).

COMMUNICATIONS

Roads

There were 59,141 km of roads (6,928 km highways and main roads) in 2006. Passenger cars in use in 2006 totalled 548,979 (57 per 1,000 inhabitants in 2005). In addition, there were 9,916 lorries and vans, and 27,474 buses and coaches. There were 1,107 fatalities as a result of road accidents in 2007.

Rail

Total length in 2003 was 2,112 km of 1,520 mm gauge (1,270 km electrified). Passenger-km travelled in 2003 came to 654m. and freight tonne-km to 7·70bn.

There is a metro and tramway in Baku and a tramway in Sumgait.

Civil Aviation

There is an international airport at Baku. Azerbaijan Airlines had international flights in 2003 to Aktau, Aleppo, Ankara, Dubai, İstanbul, Kabul, Kyiv, London, Paris, Tbilisi, Tehran, Tel Aviv, Trabzon and Urumqi. There were direct flights in 2003 with other airlines to Almaty, Ashgabat, Bishkek, Donetsk, Ekaterinburg, Frankfurt, Kazan, Mineralnye Vody, Minsk, Moscow, Nizhnevartovsk, Novosibirsk, Omsk, St Petersburg, Samara, Surgut, Tashkent, Tyumen and Volgograd. The national airline is Azerbaijan Airlines. In 2005 scheduled airline traffic of Azerbaijan-based carriers flew 14·8m. km, carrying 494,800 passengers.

Shipping

In 2008 merchant shipping totalled 423,000 GRT (including oil tankers 229,000 GRT). In 2005 vessels totalling 1,627,000 NRT entered ports and vessels totalling 1,578,000 NRT cleared.

Telecommunications

Telephone subscribers numbered 3,333,400 in 2005 (396·3 per 1,000 inhabitants), including 2,242,000 mobile phone subscribers. Internet users numbered 678,800 in 2005.

Postal Services

There were 1,377 post offices in 2003.

SOCIAL INSTITUTIONS

Justice

The number of reported crimes in 2003 was 15,206, including 285 murders or attempted murders (449 in 1997). There were 187 crimes per 1,000 inhabitants and 94% of crimes were solved (80% in 1997).

The population in penal institutions in Jan. 2003 was 17,795 (217 per 100,000 of national population).

The death penalty was abolished in 1998.

Education

In 2003–04 there were 603,894 pupils and 40,876 teachers at 4,533 primary schools, and 1,070,636 pupils at secondary schools. There were 110,891 children enrolled at pre-school institutions. In 2003 there were 175,229 students at 42 institutes of higher education and 60 specialized secondary schools. There were 33 institutes of higher education in Baku, with 95,068 students in 2003–04 (including correspondence students). The Azerbaijan Academy of Sciences, founded in 1945, has 31 research institutes. Adult literacy is 98·8%.

In 2007 public expenditure on education came to 2·9% of GNI and represented 12·6% of total government expenditure.

Health

In 2003 there were 734 hospitals with 68,000 beds. There were 29,687 physicians, 2,275 dentists, 59,531 nurses, 1,842 pharmacists and 9,803 midwives in 2003.

Welfare

In Jan. 2004 there were 751,000 age pensioners and 576,000 other pensioners.

RELIGION

In 2003 the population was 92% Muslim (mostly Shia), the balance being mainly Russian Orthodox, Armenian Apostolic and Jewish.

CULTURE

World Heritage Sites

There are two UNESCO World Heritage sites in Azerbaijan: the Walled City of Baku with the Shirvanshah's Palace and Maiden Tower (2000), which was damaged by an earthquake in 2000, and the Gobustan rock art cultural landscape (2007).

Broadcasting

AzTV and Azerbaijan Radio are state-run broadcasting outlets, although legislation in 2004 provided for the establishment of the Public Television and Radio Broadcasting Company (ITV, launched in 2005), which is intended to be free from overt government control. There is an increasing number of private TV and radio stations. Russian and Turkish television services are also available. There were 2·85m. TV receivers in 2005.

Cinema

In 2008 there were 14 cinemas. Three feature films were produced in 2006.

Press

In 2002 Azerbaijan published 285 different newspapers, of which 25 were national daily newspapers with a combined circulation of 158,000. There is one daily, published by parliament, with a circulation of 5,000, and two independent thrice-weeklies with a combined circulation of 30,000. In 2002 a total of 478 book titles were published.

Tourism

In 2003 there were 1,066,000 foreign tourists; spending by tourists totalled US$58m. in 2003.

Libraries

There are 4,124 public libraries (2003).

Theatre and Opera

Azerbaijan had 27 professional theatres in 2003.

Museums and Galleries

There were 159 museums including a National Museum of History in 2003.

DIPLOMATIC REPRESENTATIVES

Of Azerbaijan in the United Kingdom (4 Kensington Court, London, W8 5DL)
Ambassador: Fakhraddin Gurbanov.

Of the United Kingdom in Azerbaijan (45 Khagani St., AZ-1010 Baku)
Ambassador: Dr Carolyn Browne.

Of Azerbaijan in the USA (2741 34th St., NW, Washington, D.C., 20008)
Ambassador: Yashar Aliyev.

Of the USA in Azerbaijan (83 Azadliq Prospect, AZ-1007 Baku)
Ambassador: Vacant.
Chargé d'Affaires a.i.: Donald Lu.

Of Azerbaijan to the United Nations
Ambassador: Agshin Mehdiyev.

Of Azerbaijan to the European Union
Ambassador: Emin Yaqub oglu Eyyubov.

FURTHER READING

Azerbaijan. A Country Study. 2004

Chorbajian, Levon, *The Making of Nagorno-Karabagh: From Secession to Republic.* 2001
De Waal, Thomas, *Black Garden: Armenia and Azerbaijan Through Peace and War.* 2003
Swietochowski, T., *Russia and a Divided Azerbaijan.* 1995
Van Der Leeuw, C., *Azerbaijan.* 1999

National Statistical Office: The State Statistical Committee of the Republic of Azerbaijan, Inshaatchilar Av., Baku AZ1136.

Nakhichevan

This territory, on the borders of Turkey and Iran, forms part of Azerbaijan although separated from it by the territory of Armenia. Its population in 1989 was 95·9% Azerbaijani. It was annexed by Russia in 1828. In June 1923 it was constituted as an Autonomous Region within Azerbaijan. On 9 Feb. 1924 it was elevated to the status of Autonomous Republic. The 1996 Azerbaijani Constitution defines it as an Autonomous State within Azerbaijan.

Area, 5,500 sq. km (2,120 sq. miles); population (Dec. 2003), 369,800. Capital, Nakhichevan (Jan. 2003, 64,400).

Chairman of the Supreme Council: Vasif Talybov.

Prime Minister: Alovsat Bakhshiyev.

There were 46,644 ha. of crops in 2003. Approximately 70% of the economically active population are engaged in agriculture of which the main branches are cotton and tobacco growing. Fruit and grapes are also produced.

In 2003–04 there were 232 primary and secondary schools with 72,179 pupils, and (1989–90) 2,200 students in higher educational institutions. There were 292 public libraries in Nakhichevan in 2003.

Nakhichevan had 52 hospitals and 3,540 hospital beds in 2003; there were 647 doctors and 2,765 paramedic staff.

Nagorno-Karabakh

Established on 7 July 1923 as an Autonomous Region within Azerbaijan, in 1989 the area was placed under a 'special form of administration' subordinate to the USSR government. In Sept. 1991 the regional Soviet and the Shaumyan district Soviet jointly declared a Nagorno-Karabakh republic, which declared itself independent with a 99·9% popular vote (only the Armenian community took part in this vote as the Azeri population had already been expelled from Nagorno-Karabakh) in Dec. 1991. The autonomous status of the region was meanwhile abolished by the Azerbaijan Supreme Soviet in Nov. 1991, and the capital renamed Khankendi. A presidential decree of Jan. 1992 placed the region under direct rule. Azeri-Armenian fighting for possession of the region culminated in its occupation by Armenia in 1993 (and the occupation of seven other Azerbaijani regions outside it), despite attempts at international mediation. Since May 1994 there has been a ceasefire. Negotiations on settlements are conducted within the OSCE Minsk Group. International pressure on Azerbaijan and Armenia to find a resolution to the conflict increased in 2005, following an OSCE fact-finding mission in the occupied provinces, but bilateral talks held in Aug. of that year proved to be inconclusive. In a referendum held on 10 Dec. 2006, 99% of votes cast were in favour of a constitution declaring a sovereign state with 1% against. Azerbaijan, the USA, the EU and the OSCE all refused to recognize the results.

Area, 4,400 sq. km (1,700 sq. miles); population (Jan. 2003 est.), 146,000. Capital, Khankendi (Jan. 2003 est., 54,600). It is populated by Armenians (76·9% at the 1989 census) and Azerbaijanis (21·5%).

In presidential elections held on 19 July 2007 Bako Sahakyan, backed by the ruling Democratic Artsakh Party, was elected with 85·1% of votes cast. The previous incumbent Arkady Gukasyan was constitutionally prevented from seeking a third term. Legislative elections were held on 19 June 2005. The Democratic Artsakh Party won 12 seats; the Free Motherland Party 10; ARF Dashnaktsutyun–Movement 88 Bloc 3; and ind. 8.

President: Bako Sahakyan.

Prime Minister: Araik Arutyunyan.

Main industries are silk, wine, dairying and building materials. Crop area is 67,200 ha.; cotton, grapes and winter wheat are grown. There are 33 collective and 38 state farms.

In 1989–90, 34,200 pupils were studying in primary and secondary schools, 2,400 in colleges and 2,100 in higher educational institutions.

BAHAMAS

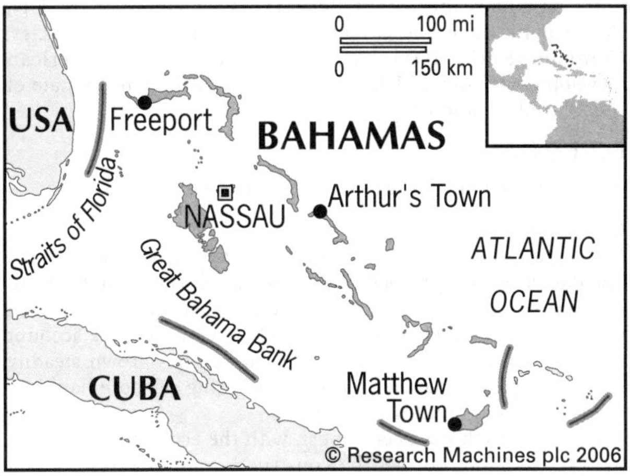

Commonwealth of The Bahamas

Capital: Nassau
Population estimate, 2010: 346,000
GDP per capita: not available
GNI per capita, 2007: US$21,109
HDI/world rank: 0·856/52

KEY HISTORICAL EVENTS

First inhabited in the 9th century by the Lucayans, a branch of the Arawaks, The Bahamas received their name 'Baja Mar' (low sea) from Christopher Columbus who landed on San Salvador in 1492. Colonized by English puritans from Bermuda during the 17th century, The Bahamas were later plagued by notorious pirates such as Blackbeard, until they were driven out by Governor Woodes Rogers in 1718. The Bahamas played an important part in the American Civil War—blockaded by the Union navy in 1861, the islanders traded Confederate cotton with Britain and supplied military equipment to the Confederacy. During Prohibition The Bahamas prospered as a rum-smuggling base but experienced a severe economic downturn when the Prohibition law was repealed in 1933. An important Atlantic base during WWII, the tourist industry benefited greatly from Cuba's closure to western visitors in the 1950s. Internal self-government with cabinet responsibility was introduced on 7 Jan. 1964 and full independence achieved on 10 July 1973.

TERRITORY AND POPULATION

The Commonwealth of The Bahamas consists of over 700 islands and inhabited cays off the southeast coast of Florida extending for about 260,000 sq. miles. Only 22 islands are inhabited. Land area, 5,382 sq. miles (13,939 sq. km).

The areas and populations of the 19 divisions used for the most recent census in 2000 were as follows:

	Area (in sq. km)	Population
New Providence	207	210,832
Grand Bahama	1,373	46,994
Abaco	1,681	13,170
Eleuthera	484	7,999
Andros	5,954	7,686
Exuma and Cays	290	3,571
Long Island	596	2,992
Biminis	23	1,717
Cat Island	388	1,647
Harbour Island	8	1,639
Spanish Wells	26	1,527
San Salvador	163	970
Inagua	1,551	969
Berry Islands	31	709
Acklins	497	428
Crooked Island	241	350
Mayaguana	285	259
Rum Cay	78	80
Ragged Island	36	72

Total census population for 2000 was 303,611 (155,833 females).

The UN gives an estimated population for 2010 of 346,000.

In 2005, 90·4% of the population were urban. The capital is Nassau on New Providence Island (210,832 in 2000); the other large town is Freeport (46,994 in 2000) on Grand Bahama.

English is the official language. Creole is spoken among Haitian immigrants.

SOCIAL STATISTICS

2003: births, 5,054; deaths, 1,649. Rates, 2003 (per 1,000 population): birth, 16·0; death, 5·2; infant mortality (per 1,000 live births), 2005, 13. Expectation of life was 70·4 years for males and 76·0 years for females in 2007. Annual population growth rate, 1992–2003, 1·9%; fertility rate, 2004, 2·3 children per woman.

CLIMATE

Winters are mild and summers pleasantly warm. Most rain falls in May, June, Sept. and Oct., and thunderstorms are frequent in summer. Rainfall amounts vary over the islands from 30" (750 mm) to 60" (1,500 mm). Nassau, Jan. 71°F (21·7°C), July 81°F (27·2°C). Annual rainfall 47" (1,179 mm).

CONSTITUTION AND GOVERNMENT

The Commonwealth of The Bahamas is a free and democratic sovereign state. Executive power rests with Her Majesty the Queen, who appoints a Governor-General to represent her, advised by a Cabinet whom he appoints. There is a bicameral legislature. The *Senate* comprises 16 members all appointed by the Governor-General for five-year terms, nine on the advice of the Prime Minister, four on the advice of the Leader of the Opposition, and three after consultation with both of them. The *House of Assembly* consists of 41 members elected from single-member constituencies for a maximum term of five years.

National Anthem

'Lift up your head to the rising sun, Bahamaland'; words and tune by T. Gibson.

RECENT ELECTIONS

In parliamentary elections held on 4 May 2007 the Free National Movement (FNM) won 49·9% of votes cast and 23 out of 41 seats (seven in 2002) against the ruling Progressive Liberal Party (PLP) with 47·0% and 18 seats (29 in 2002). Turnout was 91·2%.

CURRENT ADMINISTRATION

Governor-General: Arthur Dion Hanna; b. 1928 (sworn in 1 Feb. 2006).

In March 2010 the cabinet was composed as follows:

Prime Minister and Minister of Finance: Hubert Ingraham; b. 1947 (FNM; took office on 4 May 2007, having previously held office from Aug. 1992 to May 2002).

Deputy Prime Minister, Minister of Foreign Affairs, and Legal Affairs Minister and Attorney General (acting): Brent Symonette.

Minister of Agriculture and Marine Resources: Lawrence Cartwright. *Tourism and Aviation:* Vincent Vanderpool-Wallace. *Environment:* Earl Deveaux. *Health:* Hubert Minnis. *Labour and Social Development:* Dion Foulkes. *National Security:* Tommy Turnquest. *Education:* Carl Bethel. *Public Works and Transport:* Neko Grant. *Housing:* Kenneth Russell. *Youth, Sports and Culture:* Desmond Bannister.

Government Website: http://www.bahamas.gov.bs

CURRENT LEADERS

Hubert Ingraham

Position

Prime Minister

Introduction

Hubert Ingraham became prime minister for the second time on 4 May 2007, having secured a narrow victory for his Free National Movement (FNM) in the general election. The outgoing Progressive Liberal Party (PLP), led by Perry Christie, contested the result in several districts. Ingraham pledged to make government more accountable.

Early Life

Hubert Alexander Ingraham was born on 4 Aug. 1947 in Grand Bahama, then part of the British West Indies. He grew up in Cooper's Town on the island of Abaco and was educated in Nassau. After studying law, Ingraham was employed first by the Bahamas Telecommunications Corporation and then Chase Manhattan Bank. He was called to the Bahamas Bar in 1972 and worked in a private law practice.

Ingraham was elected to the national general council in the elections of 1977, representing the then ruling PLP. He served as a member of the standing committee on privilege and public accounts. Re-elected in 1982, he became minister of housing, national insurance and social service.

In 1984 Ingraham was dismissed from the Cabinet after an inquiry into drug-trafficking and alleged government corruption. He was expelled from the PLP in 1985, attributed in his official biography to his anti-corruption stance. Re-elected to parliament in 1987 as an independent, Ingraham joined the conservative FNM and became its leader in 1990. He led the party to an emphatic victory in the general election of Aug. 1992, ending Prime Minister Lynden Pindling's 25-year rule.

Career in Office

In 1993 Ingraham signed an agreement to establish an industrial park at Freeport for international high-tech companies. He led the FNM to victory in the March 1997 general election but was defeated by the PLP in May 2002. Ingraham nonetheless retained his North Abaco seat. During the party's Nov. 2005 convention, he was again elected FNM leader. In the run-up to the May 2007 parliamentary elections, he campaigned on issues of trust, criticizing the PLP for their involvement in a series of scandals. The FNM emerged victorious on 2 May 2007 with 23 of 41 available seats, although the PLP leader, Perry Christie, initially challenged the results. Ingraham pledged to improve the efficiency and transparency of government, to improve education and to tackle crime.

DEFENCE

The Royal Bahamian Defence Force is a primarily maritime force tasked with naval patrols and protection duties in the extensive waters of the archipelago. Personnel in 2007 numbered 860. The base is at Coral Harbour on New Providence Island.

In 2006 defence expenditure totalled US$40m. (US$132 per capita), representing 0·7% of GDP.

Navy

The Navy operates 14 patrol craft and four aircraft.

INTERNATIONAL RELATIONS

The Commonwealth of The Bahamas is a member of the UN, World Bank, IMF and several other UN specialized agencies, Commonwealth, IOM, ACS, CARICOM, Inter-American Development Bank, SELA, OAS and is an ACP member state of the ACP-EU relationship.

ECONOMY

Services contributed an estimated 92% of GDP in 2003.

Overview

Heavily dependent on its tourism and offshore banking sectors, The Bahamas has a prosperous developing economy with the third highest per capita income in the western hemisphere. Tourism together with related activities, notably in construction, account for approximately one-third of GDP, which has grown steadily in recent years. Financial services, including offshore banking, account for roughly 20% of GDP.

Recent growth has been robust, with the economy expanding by 3·4% in 2006, boosted by construction on new resorts and second-home projects, while inflation was at 1·8%. Short-term growth continues to rest heavily on the tourism sector, which in turn is dependent on the USA (responsible for 80% of visitors).

Currency

The unit of currency is the *Bahamian dollar* (BSD) of 100 *cents*. American currency is generally accepted. Inflation was 2·5% in 2007 and 4·5% in 2008. Foreign exchange reserves were US$731m. in July 2005 and total money supply was B$1,144m.

Budget

The fiscal year is 1 July–30 June.

Government revenue and expenditure (in B$1m.):

	2000	*2001*	*2002*	*2003*	*2004*
Revenue	958·0	857·0	902·0	944·0	1,052·0
Expenditure	933·0	1,000·3	1,047·0	1,075·0	1,185·0

The main sources of revenue are import duties, stamp duty from land sales, work permits and residence fees, and accommodation tax. There is no direct taxation.

Performance

The Bahamas experienced a recession during the period 1988–94; this was mainly owing to the recession in the USA leading to a fall in the number of American tourists. The economy has been growing since, and there are continuing efforts to diversify. Freeport's tax-free status was extended by 25 years in 1995, and import duties were reduced in the 1996–97 budget.

Real GDP growth was 0·7% in 2007 but the economy contracted by 1·7% in 2008. Total GDP in 2008 was US$6·9bn.

Banking and Finance

The Central Bank of The Bahamas was established in 1974. Its *Governor* is Wendy Craigg. The Bahamas is an important centre for offshore banking. Financial business produced 11·3% of GDP in 2004. In 2004, 259 banks and trust companies were licensed, about half being branches of foreign companies. Leading Bahamian-based banks include The Bank of Bahamas Ltd, The Commonwealth Bank Ltd and Private Investment Bank Ltd. There is also a Development Bank.

A stock exchange, the Bahamas International Securities Exchange (BISX) based in Nassau, was inaugurated in May 2000.

Weights and Measures

The Bahamas follows the USA in using linear, dry and liquid measures.

ENERGY AND NATURAL RESOURCES

Environment
The carbon dioxide emissions of The Bahamas from the consumption and flaring of fossil fuels were the equivalent of 17·5 tonnes per capita in 2008.

Electricity
In 2004 installed capacity was approximately 0·5m. kW, all thermal. Output in 2003 was 1·99bn. kWh; consumption per capita in 2003 was 6,700 kWh.

Oil and Gas
The Bahamas does not have reserves of either oil or gas, but oil is refined in The Bahamas. The Bahamas Oil Refining Company (BORCO), in Grand Bahama, operates as a terminal which trans-ships, stores and blends oil.

Minerals
Aragonite is extracted from the seabed.

Agriculture
In 2007 there were some 8,000 ha. of arable land and 4,000 ha. of permanent crops. Production (in 1,000 tonnes), 2003: sugarcane, 56; fruit, 28 (notably grapefruit, lemons and limes); vegetables, 24.

Livestock (2003): cattle, 1,000; sheep, 5,000; goats, 14,000; pigs, 6,000; chickens, 3m.

Forestry
In 2005 forests covered 515,000 ha. or 51·5% of the total land area. Timber production in 2007 was 50,000 cu. metres.

Fisheries
The estimated total catch in 2004 amounted to 5,128 tonnes, mainly lobsters, and exclusively from sea fishing. Total value in 2004 of fish landings was B$84·7m

INDUSTRY
Tourism and offshore banking are the main industries. Two industrial sites, one in New Providence and the other in Grand Bahama, have been developed as part of an industrialization programme. The main products are pharmaceutical chemicals, salt and rum.

Labour
A total of 176,330 persons were in employment in April 2004 (excluding armed forces). The main areas of activity were: wholesale and retail trade, restaurants and hotels, 32%; community, social and personal services, 30%; construction, 11%; financing, insurance, real estate and business services, 11%. Unemployment was 10·2% in 2004.

Trade Unions
In 2004 there were 34 unions, the largest being The Bahamas Hotel, Catering and Allied Workers' Union (6,000 members).

INTERNATIONAL TRADE
Public-sector foreign debt was US$289,837 in Dec. 2004. There is a free trade zone on Grand Bahama. Although a member of CARICOM, The Bahamas is not a signatory to its trade protocol.

Imports and Exports
Imports and exports for calendar years in US$1m.:

	2002	*2003*	*2004*	*2005*	*2006*
Imports f.o.b.	1,749	1,759	1,907	2,401	2,626
Exports f.o.b.	422	427	478	549	692

In 2004 the principal imports were (in US$1m.): machinery and transport equipment, 422; food and live animals, 310; and manufactured goods, 299. The principal exports were (in US$1m.): chemicals, 109; food and live animals, 90; and crude materials except fuels, 64. In 2004 the USA was the source of 86% of imports; the main export markets were the USA (76%) and France (9%).

COMMUNICATIONS

Roads
There were about 2,717 km of roads in 2002 (57·4% paved). In 2007 there were around 27,100 vehicles in use.

Civil Aviation
There are international airports at Nassau and Freeport (Grand Bahama Island). The national carrier is the state-owned Bahamasair, which in 2003 flew to Fort Lauderdale, Miami, Orlando and the Turks and Caicos Islands, as well as providing services between different parts of The Bahamas. There were direct flights in 2003 with other airlines to Atlanta, Baltimore, Boston, Charlotte, Cincinnati, Cleveland, Daytona Beach, Detroit, Hartford, Havana, Houston, Key West, Kingston, London, Manchester, Melbourne, Milwaukee, Montreal, New York, Philadelphia, Pittsburgh, Raleigh, Richmond, Rochester, Salt Lake City, San Diego, Tampa, Trinidad, Toronto, Washington, D.C. and West Palm Beach. In 2003 scheduled airline traffic of Bahamas-based carriers flew 6m. km, carrying 1,601,000 passengers (984,000 on international flights).

Shipping
The Bahamas' shipping registry consisted of a fleet of 35·6m. GRT in 2004, a figure exceeded only by the fleets of Panama and Liberia. There were 1,400 vessels in 2004, including 258 tankers.

Telecommunications
New Providence and most of the other major islands have automatic telephone systems in operation, interconnected by a radio network, while local distribution within the islands is by overhead and underground cables. In 2004 there were 325,900 telephone subscribers, or 1,022·5 per 1,000 inhabitants, including 186,000 mobile phone subscribers. International telecommunications service is provided by a submarine cable system to Florida, USA, and an INTELSAT Standard 'A' Earth Station and a Standard 'F2' Earth Station. International operator-assisted and direct dialling telephone services are available to all major countries. There is a packet switching system for data transmission, and land mobile and marine telephone services. There were 93,000 internet users in 2004.

Postal Services
In 2004 there were 158 post offices.

SOCIAL INSTITUTIONS

Justice
English Common Law is the basis of the Bahamian judicial system, although there is a large volume of Bahamian Statute Law. The highest tribunal in the country is the Court of Appeal. New Providence has 14 Magistrates' Courts, Grand Bahama has three and Abaco one.

The strength of the police force (2004) was 3,352 officers.

There were 44 murders in 2004 (a rate of 14·5 per 100,000 population). The death penalty is in force, the most recent execution being carried out in Jan. 2000. The population in penal institutions in Oct. 2004 was 1,515 (470 per 100,000 of national population).

Education
Education is compulsory between five and 16 years of age. The adult literacy rate in 2001 was 95·5% (94·6% among males and 96·3% among females). In 2004 there were 188 schools (30 independent). In 2004–05 there were 62,110 pupils with 1,365 teachers in primary schools and 26,185 pupils with 1,792 teachers in secondary education. Courses lead to The Bahamas General

Certificate of Secondary Education (BGCSE). Independent schools provide education at primary, secondary and high school levels.

The four institutions offering higher education are: the government-sponsored College of The Bahamas, established in 1974; the University of the West Indies (regional), affiliated with The Bahamas since 1960; The Bahamas Hotel Training College, sponsored by the Ministry of Education and the hotel industry; and The Bahamas Technical and Vocational Institute, established to provide basic skills. Several schools of continuing education offer secretarial and academic courses.

Health

In 2003 there was a government general hospital (423 beds) and a psychiatric/geriatric care centre (515 beds) in Nassau, and a hospital in Freeport (88 beds). The Family Islands, comprising 33 health districts, had 21 health centres and 66 main clinics in 2003. There were two private hospitals (495 beds) in New Providence in 2003. In 2004 there were 720 physicians, 76 dentists and 1,323 nurses.

Welfare

Social Services are provided by the Department of Social Services, a government agency which grants assistance to restore, reinforce and enhance the capacity of the individual to perform life tasks, and to provide for the protection of children in The Bahamas.

The Department's divisions include: community support services, child welfare, family services, senior citizens, disability affairs, Family Island and research planning, training and community relations.

RELIGION

In 2001, 44% of the population were Protestant, 16% Roman Catholic, 10% Anglican and the remainder other religions.

CULTURE

Broadcasting

The Broadcasting Corporation of The Bahamas is a government-owned company which operates a radio network and a television service (ZNS). Cable TV is widely available. In 2004, five independent radio stations were operating. There were 303,000 television receivers (colour by NTSC) in 2004.

Cinema

In 2004 there were four cinemas.

Press

There were three national dailies and one weekly in 2004.

Tourism

Tourism is the most important industry, accounting for about 70% of GDP. In 2003 there were 1,510,169 non-resident air arrivals and in 2004 there were 3,360,012 cruise ship visitors. Tourist expenditure was US$1,884m. in 2004.

Festivals

Junkanoo is the quintessential Bahamian celebration, a parade or 'rush-out' characterized by colourful costumes, goatskin drums, cowbells, horns and a brass section. It is staged in the early hours of 26 Dec. and the early hours of 1 Jan.

Libraries

There were 32 libraries in The Bahamas in 2004.

Theatre and Opera

The Bahamas had one National Theatre in 2004, the Dundas Centre for the Performing Arts.

Museums and Galleries

In 2004 there were four museums and 13 art galleries.

DIPLOMATIC REPRESENTATIVES

Of The Bahamas in the United Kingdom (10 Chesterfield St., London, W1J 5JL)
High Commissioner: Paul H. Farquharson.

Of the United Kingdom in The Bahamas
High Commissioner: Howard Drake, OBE (resides in Kingston, Jamaica).

Of The Bahamas in the USA (2220 Massachusetts Ave., NW, Washington, D.C., 20008)
Ambassador: Cornelius A. Smith.

Of the USA in The Bahamas (Mosmar Bldg, Queen St., Nassau)
Ambassador: Nicole A. Avant.

Of The Bahamas to the United Nations
Ambassador: Paulette Bethel.

Of The Bahamas to the European Union
Ambassador: Paul H. Farquharson.

FURTHER READING

Cash, P., *et al.*, *Making of Bahamian History.* 1991

Craton, M. and Saunders, G., *Islanders in the Stream: a History of the Bahamian People.* 2 vols. 1998

Storr, Virgil Henry, *Enterprising Slaves and Master Pirates: Understanding Economic Life in the Bahamas.* 2004

National Statistical Office: Department of Statistics, PO Box N-3904, Nassau.
Website: http://statistics.bahamas.gov.bs

BAHRAIN

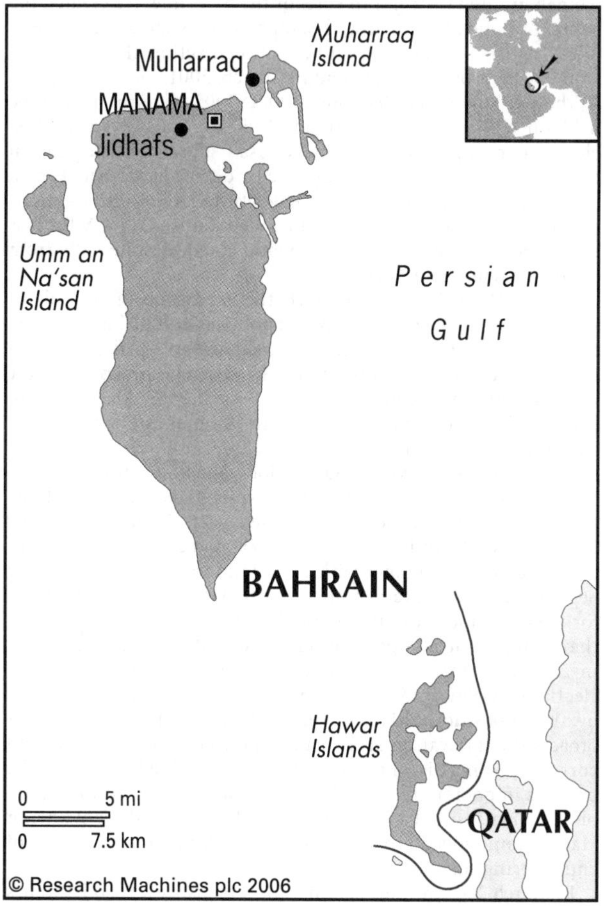

Al-Mamlaka Al-Bahrayn
(Kingdom of Bahrain)

Capital: Manama
Population estimate, 2010: 807,000
GDP per capita, 2005: (PPP$) 21,482
HDI/world rank: 0·895/39

KEY HISTORICAL EVENTS

Bahrain was controlled by the Portuguese from 1521 until 1602. The Khalifa family gained control in 1783 and has ruled since that date. British assistance was sought to retain independence and from 1861 until 1971 Bahrain was in all but name a British protectorate. Bahrain declared its independence in 1971. Sheikh Isa bin Salman Al-Khalifa became the Amir. A constitution was ratified in June 1973 providing for a National Assembly of 30 members, popularly elected for a four-year term, together with all members of the cabinet (appointed by the Amir). However, in 1975 the National Assembly was dissolved and the Amir began ruling by decree. In 1987 the main island was joined to the Saudi mainland by a causeway. In Feb. 2002 Bahrain became a kingdom, with the Amir proclaiming himself king.

TERRITORY AND POPULATION

The Kingdom of Bahrain forms an archipelago of 36 low-lying islands in the Persian Gulf, between the Qatar peninsula and the mainland of Saudi Arabia. The total area is 720 sq. km.

The island of Bahrain (578 sq. km) is connected by a 2·4 km causeway to the second largest island, Muharraq to the northeast, and by a causeway with the island of Sitra to the east. A causeway links Bahrain with Saudi Arabia. From Sitra, oil pipelines and a causeway carrying a road extend out to sea for 4·8 km to a deep-water anchorage.

Total census population in 2001 was 650,604. Population (2003 est.) 689,418 (males, 396,278; females, 293,140), of which 427,955 were Bahraini and 261,463 non-Bahraini. The population density was 957 per sq. km in 2003. In 2005, 96·5% of the population were urban.

The UN gives an estimated population for 2010 of 807,000.

There are five governorates: Capital, Central, Muharraq, Northern, Southern. Manama, the capital and commercial centre, had a 2001 census population of 143,035. Other towns (2001 census population) are Muharraq (91,307), Rifa'a (79,550), Hamad Town (52,718), Al-Ali (47,529) and Isa Town (36,833).

Arabic is the official language. English is widely used in business.

SOCIAL STATISTICS

Statistics, 2002: births, 13,576 (Bahraini, 10,539); deaths, 2,035 (Bahraini, 1,672). Rates (per 1,000 population) in 2002: birth, 20·2; death, 3·0. Infant mortality (per 1,000 live births), 9 (2005). Life expectancy at birth, 2007, was 74·2 years for men and 77·4 years for women. Annual population growth rate, 2000–05, 2·6%; fertility rate, 2004, 2·4 children per woman. In 2002 there were 4,909 marriages and 838 divorces.

CLIMATE

The climate is pleasantly warm between Dec. and March but from June to Sept. the conditions are very hot and humid. The period June to Nov. is virtually rainless. Bahrain, Jan. 66°F (19°C), July 97°F (36°C). Annual rainfall 5·2" (130 mm).

CONSTITUTION AND GOVERNMENT

The ruling family is the Al-Khalifa who have been in power since 1783.

The constitution changing Bahrain from an Emirate to a Kingdom dates from 14 Feb. 2002. The new constitutional hereditary monarchy has a bicameral legislature, inaugurated on 14 Dec. 2002. National elections for a legislative body took place on 24 and 31 Oct. 2002 (the first since the National Assembly was adjourned 27 years earlier). One chamber (*House of Deputies*) is a directly elected assembly while the second (upper) chamber, a *Shura* consultative council of experts, is appointed by the King. Both chambers have 40 members. All Bahraini citizens over the age of 21—men and women—are able to vote for the elected assembly. In the Oct. 2002 national elections women stood for office for the first time.

National Anthem

'Bahrain ona, baladolaman' ('Our Bahrain, secure as a country'); words by M. S. Ayyash, tune anonymous.

GOVERNMENT CHRONOLOGY

Heads of State since 1942.

Hakims

1942–61	Sheikh Salman bin Hamad Al-Khalifa
1961–71	Sheikh Isa bin Salman Al-Khalifa

Amirs

1971–99	Sheikh Isa bin Salman Al-Khalifa
1999–2002	Sheikh Hamad bin Isa Al-Khalifa

King
2002– Sheikh Hamad bin Isa Al-Khalifa

RECENT ELECTIONS

Parliamentary elections, held on 25 Nov. and 2 Dec. 2006, were dominated by Shia and Sunni Islamist candidates. The opposition Shia Al Wefaq party took 18 seats, while the Sunni Al Menbar and Al Asala groupings won 7 and 6 seats respectively. Independents won 9.

CURRENT ADMINISTRATION

The present king (formerly Amir), HH Sheikh Hamad bin Isa Al-Khalifa, KCMG (b. 1950), succeeded on 6 March 1999 and became king on 14 Feb. 2002.

In March 2010 the cabinet was composed as follows:

Prime Minister: Sheikh Khalifa bin Salman Al-Khalifa; b. 1936. He is currently the longest-serving prime minister of any sovereign country, having been Bahrain's prime minister since it became independent in Aug. 1971.

Deputy Prime Ministers: Jawad Al Arrayed; Sheikh Ali bin Khalifa Al-Khalifa; Sheikh Mohammed bin Mubarak Al-Khalifa.

Minister of Culture and Information: Shaikha Mai bin Mohammad Al-Khalifa. *Education:* Majid Ali Al-Nuaymi. *Electricity and Water:* Sheikh Abdulla bin Salman Al-Khalifa. *Finance:* Sheikh Ahmad bin Muhammad Al-Khalifa. *Foreign Affairs:* Sheikh Khalid bin Ahmed bin Mohammed Al-Khalifa. *Health:* Dr Faisal bin Yacoub Al-Hamar. *Industry and Commerce:* Dr Hassan bin Abdullah Fakhro. *Interior:* Gen. Rashed bin Abdullah bin Ahmed Al-Khalifa. *Justice and Islamic Affairs:* Sheikh Khalid bin Ali Al-Khalifa. *Labour:* Dr Majeed bin Mohsin Al-Alawi. *Municipalities and Agriculture:* Mansoor bin Rajab. *Oil and Gas Affairs:* Abdulhussain Mirza. *Prime Minister's Court:* Sheikh Khalid bin Abdulla Al-Khalifa. *Social Affairs:* Dr Fatima Ahmed Al-Beloushi. *Works and Housing:* Fahmi bin Ali Al-Jowdar.

Government Website: http://www.e.gov.bh

CURRENT LEADERS

HH Sheikh Hamad bin Isa Al-Khalifa

Position

King

Introduction

HH Sheikh Hamad bin Isa Al-Khalifa became Amir in March 1999. In Feb. 2001 his national action charter, encompassing a broad range of reforms, was approved by popular referendum. The state became a kingdom and Sheikh Hamad's title was changed to King. The king is the supreme authority in Bahrain, with members of the ruling family holding the majority of senior political and military positions.

Early Life

Sheikh Hamad bin Isa Al-Khalifa was born on 28 Jan. 1950 in Ar-Rifa', Bahrain. He was educated at Cambridge University in the UK before pursuing a military career. He attended Mons Officer Cadet School in Aldershot, UK, and continued his military training at the US Army Command and Staff College in Fort Leavenworth, Kansas. In 1968 Sheikh Hamad founded the Bahrain Defence Force (BDF) and served as the minister of defence from 1971–88. In Feb. 1979 he was awarded the British Knight of the Order of St Michael and St George.

Bahrain has been headed by the Al-Khalifa family since 1783 and Sheikh Hamad was crown prince from 1964 until he succeeded his father, Sheikh Isa bin Salman Al-Khalifa, as head of state in early 1999. As head of state he also became supreme commander of the BDF. Married to Sheikha Sabeeka Bint Ebrahim Al-Khalifa, he has four children. His interest in Arabian horses led him to establish the Amiri Stables in 1977.

Career in Office

On becoming Amir, Sheikh Hamad implemented changes to the running of the country. In June 1999 he released all political prisoners and in 2002 reintroduced parliamentary elections, with women granted the right to vote for the first time. He created the supreme judicial council and scrapped old state security laws. These reforms were based on his national action charter, which won 98% approval in a referendum in Feb. 2001.

The parliamentary elections of Oct. 2002 were the first to be held since Sheikh Isa bin Salman Al-Khalifa dissolved the first elected parliament in 1975. Sheikh Isa's subsequent suspension of the constitution and ensuing rule by decree led to widespread civil unrest amongst the Shia majority but the 2002 elections ensured the House of Deputies included a dozen Shia MPs. It is estimated that over 50% of the public voted, despite calls from Islamist parties for a boycott.

Sheikh Hamad has encouraged the expansion of the role of women within Bahraini society and politics. In 2000 he appointed four women to the consultative council and in April 2004 Nada Haffadh became the first woman to head a government ministry when she became health minister. In April 2005 Alees Samoan became the first woman, and the first non-Muslim, to chair a parliamentary session.

In a bid to ease inter-religious tensions, Sheikh Hamad pardoned Shia opposition leader Sheikh Abdel Amir Al-Jamin in July 1999, the day after he was sentenced to ten years imprisonment for inciting hostility. In Jan. 2000 Sheikh Hamad established ties with the Vatican when he met with Pope John Paul II. The following Sept. he appointed several non-Muslims to the consultative council for the first time. Despite support for his reforms, mainly among the Sunni minority population, thousands attended marches in 2005 to demand a fully elected government. Parliamentary elections in Nov. and Dec. 2006 resulted in a stronger showing by the opposition Shia Al Wefaq group, campaigning against broad social grievances such as unemployment, poor services and corruption. Shia discontent continued, provoking frequent public protests in poorer areas outside the predominantly Sunni capital of Manama in the early months of 2008. In April 2009 Sheikh Hamad announced a pardon for some 170 prisoners accused of endangering state security.

In March 2001 the international court of justice settled Bahrain's territorial dispute with Qatar over the Hawar Islands, declaring them the property of Bahrain. Sheikh Hamad subsequently invited international companies to drill for oil there. In Sept. 2004 Bahrain signed a free trade pact with the USA.

DEFENCE

The Crown Prince is C.-in-C. of the armed forces. An agreement with the USA in Oct. 1991 gave port facilities to the US Navy and provided for mutual manoeuvres.

Military expenditure totalled US$532m. in 2006 (US$761 per capita), representing 3·4% of GDP.

Army

The Army consists of one armoured brigade, one infantry brigade, one artillery brigade, one special forces battalion and one air defence battalion. Personnel, 2007, 6,000. In addition there is a National Guard of approximately 2,000 and a paramilitary police force of 9,000.

Navy

The Naval force based at Mina Sulman numbered 700 in 2007.

Air Force

Personnel (2007), 1,500. Equipment includes 33 combat capable aircraft and 24 attack helicopters.

INTERNATIONAL RELATIONS

Bahrain is a member of the UN, World Bank, IMF and several other UN specialized agencies, WTO, Islamic Development

Bank, OIC, Gulf Co-operation Council, League of Arab States and OAPEC (Organization of Arab Petroleum Exporting Countries).

In March 2001 the International Court of Justice ruled on a long-standing dispute between Bahrain and Qatar over the boundary between the two countries and ownership of certain islands. Both countries accepted the decision.

ECONOMY

Finance and real estate accounted for 30% of GDP in 2006, crude petroleum and natural gas 26%, and trade and restaurants 13%.

Overview

Although among the first countries in the Middle East to exploit its oil, the government has sought to diversify the economy to match the prosperity of neighbours with larger oil reserves. Leading sectors include aluminium production and oil-related services such as refining. Bahrain is also known for its financial services, which benefit from a sound regulatory system catering to both domestic and regional clients. In Aug. 2006 Bahrain became the first Gulf state to sign a free trade agreement with the USA.

The budgets for 2009 and 2010 showed an increasing deficit. The IMF predicted a decline in GDP growth from 6·1% in 2008 to 3·0% in 2009. With over 70% of state revenues derived from oil, the economy is vulnerable to price fluctuations. High unemployment, at around 15%, is an ongoing concern.

Currency

The unit of currency is the *Bahraini dinar* (BHD), divided into 1,000 *fils*. In Feb 2005 foreign exchange reserves were US$1,742m. Total money supply was BD948m. in April 2005 and gold reserves were 150,000 troy oz. Inflation was 3·5% in 2008.

In 2001 the six Gulf Arab states—Bahrain, along with Kuwait, Oman, Qatar, Saudi Arabia and the United Arab Emirates—signed an agreement to establish a single currency by 2010. In June 2009 it was agreed to postpone the implementation of the new currency, the *khaleeji*, until 2013. Both Oman and the United Arab Emirates have now withdrawn from the scheme, in 2007 and 2009 respectively.

Budget

Budgetary central government revenue and expenditure (in BD1m.):

	2004	*2005*	*2006*
Revenue	1,284·1	1,671·0	1,839·5
Expenditure	957·7	1,138·1	1,357·0

Performance

Total GDP in 2006 was US$15·8bn. Real GDP growth was 6·1% in 2008.

Banking and Finance

The Central Bank of Bahrain (*Chairman*, Qassim Mohammed Fakhro) has central banking powers. In 2001 Bahrain had 51 offshore banking units. Offshore banking units may not engage in local business; their assets totalled US$62,503m. in March 1996. In 2001 there were six locally incorporated commercial banks, ten foreign commercial banks and two specialized financial institutions. There were also several investment banks.

There is a stock exchange in Manama linked with those of Kuwait and Oman.

ENERGY AND NATURAL RESOURCES

Environment

Bahrain's carbon dioxide emissions from the consumption and flaring of fossil fuels in 2008 were the equivalent of 43·2 tonnes per capita, among the highest in the world.

Electricity

In 2003 installed capacity was 1·8m. kW; 8·45bn. kWh were produced in 2004. Electricity consumption per capita was 11,932 kWh in 2004.

Oil and Gas

In 1931 oil was discovered. Operations were at first conducted by the Bahrain Petroleum Co. (BAPCO) under concession. In 1975 the government assumed a 60% interest in the oilfield and related crude oil facilities of BAPCO. Oil reserves in 2005 were 125m. bbls. Production (2005) was 1·8m. tonnes. Refinery distillation output amounted to 12·6m. tonnes in 2004.

There were known natural gas reserves of 90bn. cu. metres in 2008. Production in 2008 was 13·4bn. cu. metres. Gas reserves are government-owned.

Water

Water is obtained from artesian wells and desalination plants and there is a piped supply to Manama, Muharraq, Isa Town, Rifa'a and most villages.

Minerals

Aluminium is Bahrain's oldest major industry after oil and gas; production in 2005 was 750,710 tonnes.

Agriculture

In 2007 there were some 2,000 ha. of arable land and 4,000 ha. of permanent crops. There are about 900 farms and smallholdings (average 2·5 ha.) operated by about 2,500 farmers who produce a wide variety of fruits (22,000 tonnes in 2003) including dates (17,000 tonnes). In 2003 an estimated 10,000 tonnes of vegetables were produced. The major crop is alfalfa for animal fodder.

Livestock (2003): cattle, 13,000; goats, 16,000; sheep, 18,000.

In 2003 an estimated 8,000 tonnes of lamb and mutton, 6,000 tonnes of poultry meat, 2,000 tonnes of eggs and 14,000 tonnes of fresh milk were produced.

Fisheries

The total catch in 2005 was 11,854 tonnes, exclusively from sea fishing.

INDUSTRY

Industry is being developed with foreign participation: aluminium smelting (and ancillary industries), shipbuilding and repair, petrochemicals, electronics assembly and light industry.

Traditional crafts include boatbuilding, weaving and pottery.

Labour

The workforce (estimate 2003) was 328,865 of which 136,215 were Bahraini. There were 16,965 unemployed persons in 2001.

Trade Unions

Trade unions have been permitted since 2002; all unions belong to the General Federation of Workers Trade Unions in Bahrain (GFWTUB).

INTERNATIONAL TRADE

Bahrain, along with Kuwait, Oman, Qatar, Saudi Arabia and the United Arab Emirates entered into a customs union in Jan. 2003.

Imports and Exports

In 2006 imports totalled US$8,565m. and exports US$11,703m. In 2003 petroleum products made up 38·3% of imports and 70·9% of exports. In 2001 the main import sources were Saudi Arabia, Australia and Japan; in 1999 the main export markets were Saudi Arabia, USA and India.

COMMUNICATIONS

Roads

A 25-km causeway links Bahrain with Saudi Arabia. In 2003 there were 3,498 km of roads (79·1% paved), including 440 km of main roads and 487 km of secondary roads. Bahrain has one of the densest road networks in the world. In 2008 there were 310,200 passenger cars in use (404 per 1,000 inhabitants in 2007). In 2007 there were 91 fatalities in road accidents.

Civil Aviation

The national carrier is Gulf Air, now fully owned by the government of Bahrain after the other three former partners, Qatar, Abu Dhabi and Oman, withdrew in 2002, 2006 and 2007 respectively. In 2001 Bahrain International Airport handled 3·44m. passengers (all on international flights) and 152,100 tonnes of freight. In 2003 scheduled airline traffic of Bahrain-based carriers flew 40m. km, carrying 1,850,000 passengers (all on international flights).

Shipping

In 2002 the merchant fleet totalled 288,000 GRT, including oil tankers 81,000 GRT. The port of Mina Sulman is a free transit and industrial area; about 800 vessels are handled annually.

Telecommunications

The telecommunications industry was fully liberalized on 1 July 2004. In 2005 there were 945,200 telephone subscribers (1,300·8 per 1,000 inhabitants), including 748,700 mobile phone subscribers. 121,000 PCs were in use in 2004 (169·0 for every 1,000 persons) and there were 152,700 internet users.

Postal Services

There were 13 post offices in 2003.

SOCIAL INSTITUTIONS

Justice

The new constitution which came into force in Feb. 2002 includes the creation of an independent judiciary. The State Security Law and the State Security Court were both abolished in the lead-up to the change to a constitutional monarchy.

The population in penal institutions in 2003 was 437 (62 per 100,000 of national population). The death penalty is still in force, though rarely used. There was one execution in 2008.

Education

Adult literacy was 87·7% in 2003 (male, 92·5%; female, 83·0%). Government schools provide free education from primary to technical college level. Schooling is in three stages: primary (six years), intermediate (three years) and secondary (three years). Secondary education may be general or specialized. In 2005–06 there were 67,528 primary school pupils, 32,359 intermediate school pupils and 29,223 secondary school pupils; there were a total of 203 schools and 10,836 teachers in 2005–06 including two religious institutes with 1,197 male students and 114 teachers.

In the private sector there were 56 schools with 34,378 pupils and 2,629 teachers in 2005–06.

There were 16 universities and similar institutions in 2005–06 with 29,678 students; and 2,392 persons attending adult education centres.

In 2006 expenditure on education came to 10·8% of total government spending.

Health

There is a free medical service for all residents. In 2003 there were 1,295 physicians, 186 dentists, 3,156 nurses and 158 pharmacists. In 2003 there were ten general hospitals (four government; six private), 21 health centres and five maternity hospitals.

Welfare

In 1976 a pensions, sickness benefits and unemployment, maternity and family allowances scheme was established. Employers contribute 7% of salaries and Bahraini employees 11%. In 1994, 36,612 persons received state benefit payments totalling BD3,715,158. A total of BD5,975,700 was paid out to pensioners, and BD306,600 to recipients of social insurance.

RELIGION

Islam is the state religion. In 2001, 87% of the population were Muslim (65% Shia and 22% Sunni). There are also Christian, Jewish, Bahai, Hindu and Parsee minorities.

CULTURE

World Heritage Sites

In 2005 Qal'at al-Bahrain archaeological site was added to the UNESCO World Heritage List (reinscribed in 2008). The site was an area of human occupation from about 2300 BC to the 16th century. It is now a site of major excavation.

Broadcasting

Broadcasting services are dominated by the state-controlled Bahrain Radio and Television Corporation. There were 306,000 TV receivers (colour by PAL) in 2006.

Cinema

There were 26 cinema screens in 2006.

Press

There were eight daily newspapers in 2006 with a combined average daily circulation of 150,000.

Tourism

In 2005 there were 3,914,000 non-resident tourists (up from 2,789,000 in 2001). Spending amounted to US$1,603m.; tourist expenditure by Bahrainis travelling abroad totalled US$574m.

Libraries

In 2003 there were ten public libraries; a total of 190,756 books were borrowed in that year.

DIPLOMATIC REPRESENTATIVES

Of Bahrain in the United Kingdom (30 Belgrave Square, London, SW1X 8QB)
Ambassador: Shaikh Khalifa bin Abdullah bin Mohammed Al Khalifa.

Of the United Kingdom in Bahrain (21 Government Ave., Manama 306, PO Box 114, Bahrain)
Ambassador: Jamie Bowden.

Of Bahrain in the USA (3502 International Dr., NW, Washington, D.C., 20008)
Ambassador: Houda Nonoo.

Of the USA in Bahrain (Building No. 979, Road No. 3119, Block 331, Zinj District, Manama)
Ambassador: Adam J. Ereli.

Of Bahrain to the United Nations
Ambassador: Tawfeeq Ahmed Khalil Almansoor.

Of Bahrain to the European Union
Ambassador: Muhammad Abdul Ghaffar.

FURTHER READING

Bahrain Monetary Authority. *Quarterly Statistical Bulletin.*
Central Statistics Organization. *Statistical Abstract.* Annual

Al-Khalifa, A. and Rice, M. (eds.) *Bahrain through the Ages.* 1993
Al-Khalifa, H. bin I., *First Light: Modern Bahrain and its Heritage.* 1995
Moore, Philip, *Bahrain: A New Era.* 2001

National Statistical Office: Central Statistics Organization, Council of Ministers, Manama.
Website: http://www.cio.gov.bh

BANGLADESH

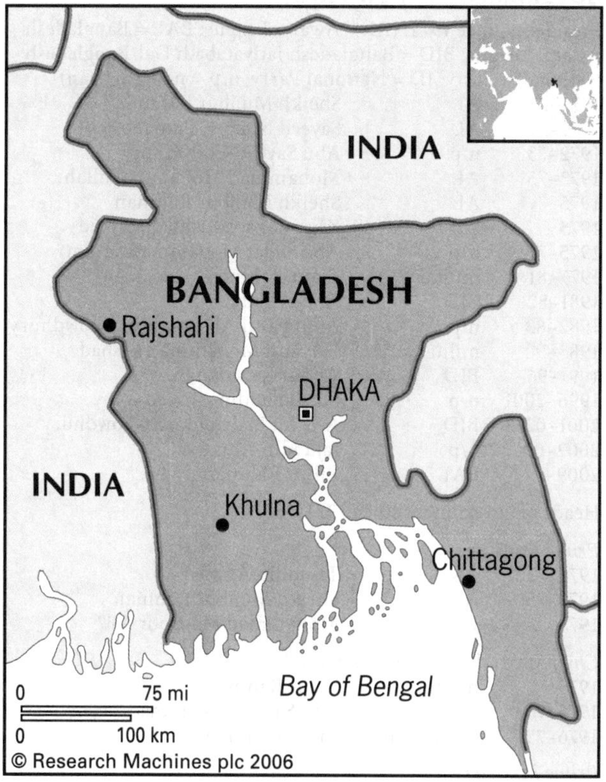

Gana Prajatantri Bangladesh
(People's Republic of Bangladesh)

Capital: Dhaka
Population estimate, 2010: 164·43m.
GDP per capita, 2007: (PPP$) 1,241
HDI/world rank: 0·543/146

KEY HISTORICAL EVENTS

India's Maurya Empire established Buddhism in Bengal (*Bangla*) in the 3rd century BC. The Buddhist Pala Dynasty ruled Bengal and Bihar independently from AD 750, exporting Buddhism to Tibet. Hinduism regained dominance under the Sena Dynasty in the 11th century until the Muslim invasions in 1203–04. Rule from Delhi was broken in the 14th century by local Bengali kings. The Afghan adventurer Sher Shah conquered Bengal in 1539 and defeated the Mughal Emperor Humayun, creating an extensive administrative empire in North India. However, Mughal power was re-established by Akbar in 1576.

The Portuguese arrived in the 15th century, drawn to the rich Bengali cotton trade. They were followed by the Dutch and the British, whose East India Company was centred at Calcutta. The Nawab of Bengal was defeated by Robert Clive's army at the Battle of Plassey in 1757. British rule was maintained through the mainly Hindu *zamindar* land-owners and the Company was replaced by the Crown in 1858.

The partition of Bengal in 1905 was an attempt to undermine the nationalist influence of the *bhadralok*, the Hindu middle-classes, by forming a Muslim-dominated eastern province. Religious violence increased and political interests were represented by newly formed parties, including the All-India Muslim League. The partition was reversed in 1912. Tensions between the Muslim and Hindu communities escalated in the 1930s. The League suffered electoral defeat in 1936 but calls for a Muslim state were strengthened by the Pakistan Resolution of 1940. An agreement between Hindu and Muslim leaders to create an independent, secular Bengal was resisted by Mahatma Gandhi. Further violence, such as the Great Calcutta Killing in 1946, put pressure on the administration and India was hastily partitioned—East Bengal was united with the northwestern Muslim provinces as Pakistan. East Pakistan (as East Bengal became under the 1956 constitution) received 0·7m. Muslims, mainly from Bihar and West Bengal, while over 2·5m. Hindus left for India.

Relations with West Pakistan were strained from the outset. Bengali demands for recognition of their language and resentment of preferential investment in their western partner led to the formation of the Awami League in 1949 to represent Bengali interests. Led by Sheikh Mujibur Rahman (Mujib), the Awami League triumphed as part of the 'United Front' in elections in 1954 but its government was dismissed by Governor-General Ghulam Mohammad after two months. A military government was installed from 1958–62 and in 1966 Mujib was arrested. Civilian government was again suspended in 1969 and in elections in 1970–71 the Awami League won all East Pakistani seats. While talks to form a government foundered, President Yahya Khan sent troops to the East and suspended the assembly, provoking a civil disobedience campaign. On 25 March 1971 the army began a crackdown. Members of the Awami League were arrested or fled to Calcutta, where they declared a provisional Bengali government. 10m. Bengalis fled to India to escape the bloody repression. India, with Soviet support, invaded on 3 Dec. 1971, forcing the surrender of the Pakistani army on 16 Dec. Mujib was released to become prime minister of independent Bangladesh.

Bangladesh suffered famine in 1974 and disorder led to Mujib assuming the presidency with dictatorial powers. Assassinated in Aug. 1975, a coup brought to power Maj.-Gen. Ziaur Rahman, who turned against the former ally, India. Rahman was assassinated in 1981. Hussain Mohammad Ershad became martial law administrator in 1982 and president in 1983. Ershad's National Party triumphed in parliamentary elections in May 1986 but presidential elections in Oct. were boycotted by opposition parties. A campaign of demonstrations and national strikes forced Ershad's resignation in 1990. Rahman's widow, Khaleda, became prime minister after her Bangladesh Nationalist Party won nearly half the seats. The Bangladesh Awami League's victory in 1996 brought Mujib's daughter, Sheikh Hasina Wajed, to the premiership but Khaleda Zia returned to power in 2001.

A state of emergency was declared in Jan. 2007 and elections were postponed following several weeks of violence that claimed more than 40 lives. The Bangladesh Awami League had previously announced that it would boycott the elections, maintaining that they were not free and fair. Sheikh Hasina Wajed became prime minister for a second time when the Bangladesh Awami League won elections held in Dec. 2008, at which time the state of emergency was lifted.

TERRITORY AND POPULATION

Bangladesh is bounded in the west and north by India, east by India and Myanmar and south by the Bay of Bengal. The area is 147,570 sq. km (56,977 sq. miles). In 1992 India granted a 999-year lease of the Tin Bigha corridor linking Bangladesh with its enclaves of Angarpota and Dahagram. At the 1991 census the population was 111,455,000 (54,141,000 females). The most recent census took place in Jan. 2001; population, 124,355,263 (64,091,508 males), giving a density of 843 persons per sq. km. The United Nations population estimate for 2001 was 143,289,000.

The UN gives an estimated population for 2010 of 164·43m.

In 2005, 74·9% of the population lived in rural areas. The country is administratively divided into six divisions, subdivided into 21 *anchal* and 64 *zila*. Area (in sq. km) and population (in 1,000) in 2001 of the six divisions:

	Area	*Population*
Barisal division	13,296	8,174
Chittagong division	33,771	24,290
Dhaka division	31,120	39,045
Khulna division	22,273	14,705
Rajshahi division	34,514	30,202
Sylhet division	12,596	7,939

The populations of the chief cities (2001 census) were as follows:

Dhaka[1]	7,673,032	Rajshahi	651,062
Chittagong	2,941,603	Mymensingh	332,721
Khulna	1,172,831	Sylhet	316,311
Narayanganj	1,133,191	Comilla	278,238
Gazipur	866,540	Rangpur	265,972

[1]Metropolitan area, 9,672,763.

The official language is Bengali. English is also in use for official, legal and commercial purposes.

SOCIAL STATISTICS

2002 births, 4,027,000; deaths, 1,150,000. In 2002 the birth rate was 28·0 per 1,000 population; death rate, 8·0; infant mortality, 2005, 54 per 1,000 live births. Life expectancy at birth, 2007, 66·7 years for females and 64·7 years for males. Annual population growth rate, 2000–05, 1·4%; fertility rate, 2004, 3·2 births per woman. Bangladesh has made some of the best progress in recent years in reducing child mortality. The number of deaths per 1,000 live births among children under five was reduced from nearly 150 in 1990 to 69 in 2003.

CLIMATE

A tropical monsoon climate with heat, extreme humidity and heavy rainfall in the monsoon season, from June to Oct. The short winter season (Nov.–Feb.) is mild and dry. Rainfall varies between 50" (1,250 mm) in the west to 100" (2,500 mm) in the southeast and up to 200" (5,000 mm) in the northeast. Dhaka, Jan. 66°F (19°C), July 84°F (28·9°C). Annual rainfall 81" (2,025 mm). Chittagong, Jan. 66°F (19°C), July 81°F (27·2°C). Annual rainfall 108" (2,831 mm).

CONSTITUTION AND GOVERNMENT

Bangladesh is a unitary republic. The Constitution came into force on 16 Dec. 1972 and provides for a parliamentary democracy. The head of state is the *President*, elected by parliament every five years, who appoints a *Vice-President*. A referendum of Sept. 1991 was in favour of abandoning the executive presidential system and opted for a parliamentary system. Turnout was low. An amendment to the constitution in 1996 allowed for a caretaker government, which the president may instal to supervise elections should the parliament be dissolved. There is a *Council of Ministers* to assist and advise the President. The President appoints the government ministers.

Following a constitutional amendment made in May 2004 parliament has one chamber of 345 members, 300 directly elected every five years by citizens over 18 and 45 reserved for women, elected by the 300 MPs based on proportional representation in parliament. Prior to the amendment the parliament had just contained 300 directly elected members.

National Anthem

'Amar Sonar Bangla, ami tomay bhalobashi' ('My Bengal of gold, I love you'); words and tune by Rabindranath Tagore.

GOVERNMENT CHRONOLOGY

Presidents since 1971. (AL = Awami League; BAL = Bangladesh Awami League; BJD = Bangladesh Jatiyatabadi Dal/Bangladesh Nationalist Party; JD = National Party; n/p = non-partisan)

1971–72	AL	Sheikh Mujibur Rahman
1971–72	AL	Sayeed Nazrul Islam (acting)
1972–73	n/p	Abu Sayeed Chowdhury
1973–75	AL	Mohammad Mohammadullah
1975	AL	Sheikh Mujibur Rahman
1975	AL	Khandakar Mushtaq Ahmed
1975–77	n/p	Abu Sadat Mohammad Sayem
1977–81	military/BJD	Ziaur Rahman
1981–82	BJD	Abdus Sattar
1982–83	n/p	Abul Fazal Ahsanuddin Chowdhury
1983–90	military/JD	Hossain Mohammad Ershad
1991–96	BJD	Abdur Rahman Biswas
1996–2001	n/p	Shahabuddin Ahmed
2001–02	BJD	A.Q.M. Badruddoza Chowdhury
2002–09	n/p	Iajuddin Ahmed
2009–	BAL	Zillur Rahman

Heads of government since 1971.

Prime Ministers

1971–72	AL	Tajuddin Ahmed
1972–75	AL	Sheikh Mujibur Rahman
1975		Mohammad Mansoor Ali

Chief Martial Law Administrators

1975	military	Ziaur Rahman
1975–76	n/p	Abu Sadat Mohammad Sayem
1976–79	military/BJD	Ziaur Rahman

Prime Ministers

1979–82	BJD	Shah Azizur Rahman
1984–86	JD	Ataur Rahman Khan
1986–88	JD	Mizanur Rahman Chowdhury
1988–89	JD	Moudud Ahmed
1989–90	JD	Kazi Zafar Ahmed
1991–96	BJD	Khaleda Zia
1996	n/p	Mohammad Habibur Rahman
1996–2001	BAL	Sheikh Hasina Wajed
2001	n/p	Latifur Rahman
2001–06	BJD	Khaleda Zia
2006–07	n/p	Iajuddin Ahmed
2007–09	n/p	Fakhruddin Ahmed
2009–	BAL	Sheikh Hasina Wajed

RECENT ELECTIONS

Zillur Rahman was declared president-elect on 11 Feb. 2009 after the opposition failed to put forward a rival candidate.

In parliamentary elections of 29 Dec. 2008 the Bangladesh Awami League (BAL) and its coalition partners gained 57·2% of votes cast. The BAL itself gained 230 seats, with allies the National Party (JD) gaining 27, Jatiyo Samajtantrik Dal (JSD) 3, the Workers Party of Bangladesh (WPB) 2 and the Liberal Democratic Party (LDP) 1. The Bangladesh Jatiyatabadi Dal/Bangladesh Nationalist Party (BJD) gained 30 seats (33·2%), the Jamaat-e-Islami Bangladesh (JIB) 2 and the Bangladesh Jatiya Party (BJP) 1 with remaining seats going to independents. Turnout was an estimated 87%.

CURRENT ADMINISTRATION

President: Zillur Rahman; b. 1929 (since 12 Feb. 2009).

In March 2010 the government comprised:

Prime Minister and Minister of Defence, Establishment, Housing and Public Works, Power, Energy and Mineral Resources, Religious

Affairs, and Women and Children's Affairs: Sheikh Hasina Wajed; b. 1947 (BAL; since 6 Jan. 2009, having previously held office from June 1996–July 2001).

Minister for Agriculture: Matia Chowdhury. *Civil Aviation and Tourism:* G. M. Qader. *Commerce:* Lieut.-Col. (retd) Faruq Khan. *Communications:* Syed Abul Hossain. *Education, and Primary and Mass Education:* Nurul Islam Naheed. *Finance:* Abul Maal Abdul Muhit. *Fisheries and Livestock:* Abdul Latif Biswas. *Food and Disaster Management:* Dr Abdur Razzak. *Foreign Affairs:* Dr Dipu Moni. *Health and Family Welfare:* Dr A. F. M. Ruhul Huq. *Home Affairs:* Sahara Khatun. *Industries:* Dilip Barua. *Information and Cultural Affairs:* Abul Kalam Azad. *Jute and Textiles:* Abdul Latif Siddiqui. *Labour and Employment, Overseas Employment and Expatriate Welfare:* Khandaker Mosharraf Hossain. *Land:* Rezaul Karim Hira. *Law, Justice and Parliamentary Affairs:* Shafiq Ahmed. *Local Government, Rural Development and Co-operatives:* Syed Ashraful Islam. *Planning:* A. K. Khandaker. *Post and Telecommunications:* Razi Uddin Ahmed Razu. *Shipping:* Dr Afsarul Amin. *Social Welfare:* Enamul Huq Mostafa Shaheed. *Water Resources:* Ramesh Chandra Sen.

Government Website: http://www.bangladesh.gov.bd

CURRENT LEADERS

Sheikh Hasina Wajed

Position
Prime Minister

Introduction
Sheikh Hasina, leader of the Bangladesh Awami League (BAL), was elected prime minister in Dec 2008 after two years of military government. It is her second term as premier, having previously served from 1996–2001.

Early Life
Sheikh Hasina was born on 28 Sept. 1947 in Tungipara, in the Gopalganj district of Bangladesh. She is the oldest of five children of Bangabandhu Sheikh Mujibar Rahman, former leader of the AL (which later became the BAL) and the nation's first head of state following the 1971 liberation war with Pakistan.

Politically active during her years at Eden College, Dhaka in the 1960s, Hasina was vice-president of the student union at the Government Intermediate College from 1966–67. She was a member of the AL's student Chhatra League while at Dhaka University, from where she graduated in 1973. In 1981 she was elected head of the BAL despite being in self-imposed exile, six years after the assassinations of her father, mother and three of her siblings.

Her chief political rival was Bangladesh Jatiyatabadi Dal/Bangladesh Nationalist Party (BJD) leader Khaleda Zia, widow of the assassinated military president Ziaur Rahman, who had taken power following the death of Hasina's father. Throughout the 1980s and early 1990s Hasina worked to remove the military government, including a BAL boycott of Zia's government in 1994. In 1996 a civilian caretaker government was established ahead of elections, which Hasina won with a landslide to become prime minister. As premier, she secured a 30-year Ganges Water Sharing Treaty with India and signed the Chittagong Hill Tract Peace Accords with rebel tribes in the southeast of the country. Nonetheless, Bangladesh descended into chaos and in 2001 Transparency International ranked it the most corrupt country in the world. In the same year the BJD won a landslide election victory.

Political violence involving supporters of the BJD and BAL escalated from 2004–07. In 2007 a military-backed caretaker government seized control after failed elections and implemented emergency rule. Hasina was arrested on charges of corruption, extortion and murder. She was briefly jailed before being released to seek medical care in the USA. Despite attempts to prevent Hasina from returning, she arrived in Bangladesh in time to lead the BAL to election victory on 29 Dec. 2008.

Career in Office
Hasina's primary challenge is to re-establish national stability. In Feb. 2009 a mutiny by border guards resulted in the deaths of an estimated 80 people, straining relations between the government and the Army. Also in Feb. 2009 the minister of finance acknowledged that global financial pressures were adversely affecting the economy. Relations with India were consolidated by the signing of two trade pacts and Hasina has begun talks on an anti-terrorism force with Pakistan and India.

DEFENCE

The supreme command of defence services is vested in the president. Defence expenditure in 2006 totalled US$938m. (US$6 per capita), representing 1·6% of GDP.

Army
Strength (2007) 120,000. There is also a 5,000-strong specialized police unit (the Armed Police), 20,000 security guards (Ansars) and the Bangladesh Rifles (border guard) numbering 38,000.

Navy
Naval bases are at Chittagong, Dhaka, Kaptai, Khulna and Mongla. The fleet comprises four frigates, nine missile craft, four torpedo craft and 25 patrol craft. Personnel in 2007 were estimated at 16,000.

Air Force
Personnel strength (2007) 14,000. There were 76 combat capable aircraft (mainly Chinese F-7s and A-5s) and 30 helicopters in 2007.

INTERNATIONAL RELATIONS

Bangladesh is a member of the UN, World Bank, IMF and several other UN specialized agencies, WTO, Commonwealth, IOM, Islamic Development Bank, Organization of the Islamic Conference, Asian Development Bank, Colombo Plan and SAARC.

ECONOMY

In 2006 agriculture accounted for 19·6% of GDP, industry 27·9% and services 52·5%.

Overview
Bangladesh has maintained macroeconomic stability in recent years, with growth rising to 6·4% in 2006 as a result of strong exports and private domestic investment. However, rising food and non-food prices have led to a pick-up in inflation. Foreign direct investment growth averaged 16% per year from 2002–07.

Despite political upheaval, international reserves have strengthened as a result of strong remittances and exports, both of which have annual growth rates of over 20%. Agriculture accounted for 19·6% of GDP in 2006. Although the service sector is the most dominant component of GDP, 48·4% of the population is employed in agriculture, hunting and fishing. With lower wages than China and other competitors, an increasing focus on textile production has boosted Bangladesh's export and employment prospects.

Continued reform efforts, buoyant exports and strong remittance flows are expected to maintain healthy growth rates but weak revenue collections, low skill levels and poor governance and infrastructure remain obstacles to sustained growth and poverty reduction.

Currency
The unit of currency is the *taka* (BDT) of 100 *poisha*, which was floated in 1976. Foreign exchange reserves in July 2005 were

US$2,780m., gold reserves were 113,000 troy oz and total money supply was Tk.384,290m. Inflation was 7·7% in 2008.

Budget

The fiscal year ends on 30 June. Budget, 2005–06: revenue, Tk.448·7bn.; expenditure, Tk.610·6bn.

VAT is 15%.

Performance

Real GDP growth was 6·3% in 2007 and 6·0% in 2008. Total GDP was US$79·0bn. in 2008.

Banking and Finance

Bangladesh Bank is the central bank (*Governor*, Dr Atiur Rahman). There are four nationalized commercial banks, 16 private commercial banks, nine foreign commercial banks and ten development finance organizations. In 1999 the Bangladesh Bank had Tk.9,118m. deposits. In 1999 Sonali Bank was the largest of the nationalized commercial banks with deposits of Tk.170,961m.

There are stock exchanges in Dhaka and Chittagong.

Weights and Measures

The metric system was introduced from July 1982, but some imperial and traditional measures are still in use. One *tola* = 11·66 g; one *maund* = 37·32 kg = 40 *seers*; one *seer* = 0·93 kg.

ENERGY AND NATURAL RESOURCES

Environment

Bangladesh's carbon dioxide emissions from the consumption and flaring of fossil fuels in 2008 were the equivalent of 0·3 tonnes per capita.

Electricity

Installed capacity was an estimated 3·1m. kW in 2004. Electricity generated, 2004, 21·47bn. kWh; consumption per capita in 2004 was 154 kWh.

Oil and Gas

In 2008 Bangladesh had proven natural gas reserves of 370bn. cu. metres in about 20 mainly onshore fields. Total natural gas production in 2008 amounted to 17·3bn. cu. metres.

Minerals

The principal minerals are lignite, limestone, china clay and glass sand. There are reserves of good-quality coal of 300m. tonnes. Production, 2001–02: limestone, 32,000 tonnes; kaolin, 8,100 tonnes.

Agriculture

In 2007 the agricultural population was approximately 76·11m., of whom 35·54m. were economically active. There were 7·96m. ha. of arable land in 2005 and some 0·5m. ha. of permanent crops. 5·60m. ha. were irrigated in 2005. Bangladesh is a major producer of jute: production, 2003, 801,000 tonnes. Rice is the most important food crop; production in 2003 (in 1m. metric tonnes), 38·06. Other major crops (1m. tonnes): sugarcane, 6·84; potatoes, 3·69; wheat, 1·55; bananas, 0·65. Livestock in 2003: goats, 34·50m.; cattle, 24·50m.; sheep, 1·24m.; buffalo, 850,000; chickens, 140m. Livestock products in 2003 (tonnes): beef and veal, 180,000; goat meat, 130,000; poultry meat, 115,000; goat's milk, 1·31m.; cow's milk, 797,000; sheep's milk, 25,000; buffalo's milk, 23,000; hen's eggs, 134,000. Bangladesh is the second largest producer of goat's milk, after India.

Forestry

In 2005 the area under forests was 871,000 ha., or 6·7% of the total land area. Timber production in 2007 was 27·79m. cu. metres.

Fisheries

Bangladesh is a major producer of fish and fish products. The total catch in 2005 amounted to 1,333,866 tonnes, of which 859,269 tonnes came from inland waters. Only China has a larger annual catch of freshwater fish.

INDUSTRY

Manufacturing contributes around 11% of GDP. The principal industries are jute and cotton textiles, tea, paper, newsprint, cement, chemical fertilizers and light engineering. Production, in 1,000 tonnes: cement (2000–01), 2,340; nitrogenous fertilizer (2001), 1,875; jute goods (2001–02), 536; sugar (2002), 229. Output of other products: cotton woven fabrics (2000–01), 63m. sq. metres; cigarettes (2000–01), 20·1bn. units; television sets (2001), 133,000 units; bicycles (2000–01), 13,000 units.

Labour

In 2000 the economically active workforce totalled 51,764,000 over the age of 15 years (32,369,000 males). The main areas of activity (in 1,000) were as follows: agriculture, hunting, forestry and fishing, 32,171; wholesale and retail trade, restaurants and hotels, 6,275; manufacturing, 3,783; community, social and personal services, 2,969; transport, storage and communication, 2,509; construction, 1,099. On average, wage rates (Tk.61 daily, 2003) are among the lowest of developing countries. In 1999–2000, 3·3% of the workforce aged 15 or over were unemployed.

INTERNATIONAL TRADE

Foreign debt was US$18,935m. in 2005.

Imports and Exports

In 2006 imports (f.o.b.) were valued at US$14,443·4m. (US$12,501·6m. in 2005) and exports (f.o.b.) at US$11,553·7m. (US$9,302·5m. in 2005). In 2003, 15·5% of imports came from India, 13·8% from China, 9·5% from Singapore and 6·7% from Japan. 24·6% of exports in 2003 went to the USA, 13·3% to Germany, 10·9% to the UK and 5·6% to France. The main imports are machinery, transport equipment, manufactured goods, minerals, fuels and lubricants, and the main exports are jute and jute goods, tea, hides and skins, newsprint, fish and garments. Since the early 1980s the garment industry has developed from virtually nothing to earn some 70% of the country's hard currency. Garment exports in 2003–04 earned US$5·7bn.

COMMUNICATIONS

Roads

In 2003 the total road network covered 239,226 km, including 22,378 km of national roads and 81,670 km of secondary roads. In 2007 there were 158,100 passenger cars, 168,600 vans and lorries, 31,600 buses and coaches, and 653,500 motorcycles and mopeds. There were 3,160 fatalities as a result of road accidents in 2006.

Rail

In 2005 there were 2,855 km of railways, comprising 660 km of 1,676 mm gauge, 1,830 km of metre gauge and 365 km of dual gauge. Passenger-km travelled in 2003 came to 402·4m. and freight tonne-km to 952m.

Civil Aviation

There are international airports at Dhaka (Zia) and Chittagong, and eight domestic airports. Biman Bangladesh Airlines is state-owned. In addition to domestic routes, in 2003 it operated international services to Abu Dhabi, Bahrain, Bangkok, Brussels, Dammam, Delhi, Doha, Dubai, Frankfurt, Hong Kong, Jeddah, Karachi, Kathmandu, Kolkata, Kuala Lumpur, Kuwait, London, Mumbai, Muscat, New York, Paris, Rangoon (Yangon), Riyadh, Rome, Singapore and Tokyo. There were direct flights in 2003 with other airlines to Madinah, Paro, Tashkent and Tehran. In 2001 Dhaka's Zia International Airport handled 2,863,575 passengers (2,322,743 on international flights) and 106,291 tonnes of freight. In 2003 scheduled airline traffic of Bangladesh-based carriers flew 29m. km, carrying 1,579,000 passengers (1,205,000 on international flights).

Shipping

There are sea ports at Chittagong and Mongla, and inland ports at Dhaka, Chandpur, Barisal, Khulna and five other towns. There are 8,000 km of navigable inland waterways. The Bangladesh Shipping Corporation owned 18 ships in 1994. Total tonnage registered, 2002, 432,000 GRT (including oil tankers 63,000 GRT). In 1993–94 the two sea ports handled 8·20m. tonnes of imports and 1·66m. tonnes of exports. In 1999–2000 vessels totalling 6,509,000 NRT entered ports and vessels totalling 2,949,000 NRT cleared. The Bangladesh Inland Water Transport Corporation had 288 vessels in 1994. 70·29m. passengers were carried in 1992–93.

Telecommunications

Telephone subscribers numbered 3,612,500 in 2004 (25·9 per 1,000 inhabitants), of which 2,781,600 were mobile phone subscribers. There were 1,650,000 PCs in use in 2004 (11·9 for every 1,000 persons) and 300,000 internet users.

Postal Services

There were 9,859 post offices in 2003.

SOCIAL INSTITUTIONS

Justice

The Supreme Court comprises an Appellate and a High Court Division, the latter having control over all subordinate courts. Judges are appointed by the President and retire at 65. There are benches at Comilla, Rangpur, Jessore, Barisal, Chittagong and Sylhet, and courts at District level.

The population in penal institutions in Sept. 2008 was 83,000 (51 per 100,000 of national population).

The death penalty is still in force. In 2009 there were three executions.

Education

In 2007 there were 16·3m. pupils and 364,494 teaching staff at primary schools; 10·4m. pupils and 413,746 teaching staff at secondary schools; 1·1m. students and 60,915 academic staff in tertiary education. In 2006 there were 78 universities of which 27 were public, 42 medical colleges (15 public), 171 polytechnic institutes (42 public) and 3,197 general colleges.

Adult literacy was 51·6% in 2004 (57·2% among males and 45·8% among females).

In 2007 public expenditure on education came to 2·4% of GNI and 15·8% of total government spending.

Health

In 1997 there were 976 hospitals, with the equivalent of four beds per 10,000 persons. There were 32,498 physicians, 938 dentists (1997), 18,135 nurses and 15,794 midwives in 2001.

RELIGION

Islam is the state religion. In 2001 the population was 87% Muslim and 12% Hindu.

CULTURE

World Heritage Sites

There are three UNESCO sites in Bangladesh: the Historic Mosque City of Bagerhat (inscribed in 1985); the Ruins of the Buddhist Vihara at Paharpur (1985); the Sundarbans (1997), 140,000 ha. of mangrove forest.

Broadcasting

Government-controlled Bangladesh Betar operates a dominant national radio network and an external service, while Bangladesh Television (BTV) transmits the sole terrestrial TV channel and a satellite service. A range of private satellite and cable channels is also available. There were 15·3m. TV receivers in 2006 (colour by PAL).

Press

In 2004 there were 388 daily newspapers (164 nationals and 224 regionals) with a combined circulation of 1·1m. In 1994, 1,258 book titles were published (122 in English).

Tourism

In 2005 there were 208,000 non-resident tourists, spending US$78m.

DIPLOMATIC REPRESENTATIVES

Of Bangladesh in the United Kingdom (28 Queen's Gate, London, SW7 5JA)
High Commissioner: Mohammad Sayeedur Rahman Khan.

Of the United Kingdom in Bangladesh (United Nations Rd, Baridhara, PO Box 6079, Dhaka 1212)
High Commissioner: Stephen Evans, CMG, OBE.

Of Bangladesh in the USA (3510 International Drive, NW, Washington, D.C., 20008)
Ambassador: Akramul Qader.

Of the USA in Bangladesh (Madani Ave., Baridhara, Dhaka 1212)
Ambassador: James F. Moriarty.

Of Bangladesh to the United Nations
Ambassador: Dr Abdul Momen.

Of Bangladesh to the European Union
Ambassador: A. H. M. Moniruzzaman.

FURTHER READING

Bangladesh Bureau of Statistics. *Statistical Yearbook of Bangladesh.—Statistical Pocket Book of Bangladesh.*

Bakshi, S. R., *Bangladesh: Government and Politics.* 2002
Baxter, Craig, *Historical Dictionary of Bangladesh.* 2003
Karlekar, Hiranmay, *Bangladesh: The Next Afghanistan?* 2006
Muhith, A. M. A., *Issues of Governance in Bangladesh.* 2000
Rashid, H. U., *Foreign Relations of Bangladesh.* 2001
Riaz, Ali, *God Willing: The Politics of Islamism in Bangladesh.* 2004.—*Unfolding State: The Transformation of Bangladesh.* 2005
Tajuddin, M., *Foreign Policy of Bangladesh: Liberation War to Sheikh Hasina.* 2001
Umar, Badruddin, *Emergence of Bangladesh.* 2004
Van Schendel, Willem, *A History of Bangladesh.* 2009

National Statistical Office: Bangladesh Bureau of Statistics, Ministry of Planning, E-27/A, Agargaon, Sher-e-banglanagar, Dhaka 1207.
Website: http://www.bbs.gov.bd

BARBADOS

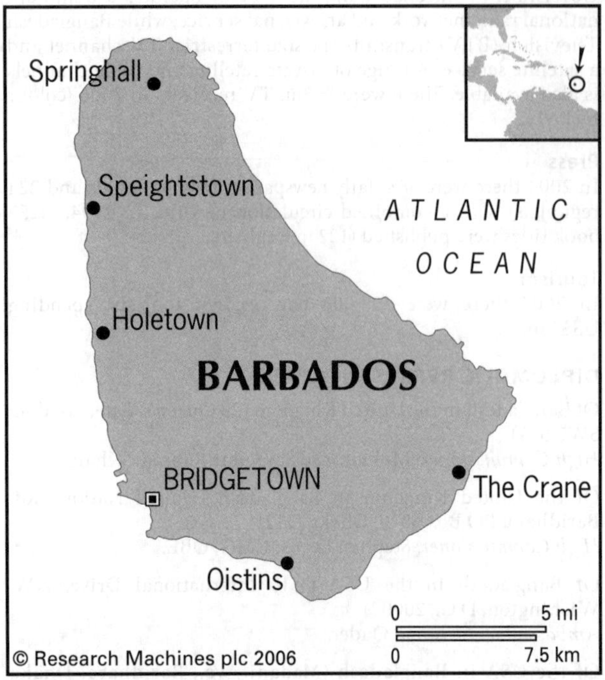

Capital: Bridgetown
Population estimate, 2010: 276,000
GDP per capita, 2006: (PPP$) 17,297
HDI/world rank: 0·903/37

KEY HISTORICAL EVENTS

Archaeological evidence suggests that Barbados was inhabited by Barrancoid Indians from at least 1000 BC, and by Arawak people for about 400 years from around AD 1000. Portuguese mariners who landed on the island in 1536 reported that it was uninhabited. An Englishman, William Courteen, established Jamestown in 1627. Sugar plantations were developed in the 1640s, using imported slave labour from Africa until the practice was abolished in 1834. In 1951 universal suffrage was introduced, followed in 1954 by cabinet government. Full internal self-government was attained in Oct. 1961. On 30 Nov. 1966 Barbados became an independent sovereign state within the British Commonwealth.

TERRITORY AND POPULATION

Barbados lies to the east of the Windward Islands. Area 430 sq. km (166 sq. miles). In 2000 the census population was 268,792; density 625·1 per sq. km.

The estimated population for 2010 is 276,000.

In 2005, 52·7% of the population were urban. Bridgetown is the principal city: population (including suburbs), 133,000 in 1999.

The official language is English.

SOCIAL STATISTICS

In 2003: births, 3,748; deaths, 2,274; birth rate, 13·0 per 1,000 population; death rate, 8·4; infant mortality (2005), 11 per 1,000 live births. Expectation of life, 2007, males 74·0 years and females 79·7. Population growth rate, 2005, 0·3%; fertility rate, 2004, 1·5 children per woman.

CLIMATE

An equable climate in winter, but the wet season, from June to Nov., is more humid. Rainfall varies from 50" (1,250 mm) on the coast to 75" (1,875 mm) in the higher interior. Bridgetown, Jan. 76°F (24·4°C), July 80°F (26·7°C). Annual rainfall 51" (1,275 mm).

CONSTITUTION AND GOVERNMENT

The head of state is the British sovereign, represented by an appointed Governor-General. The bicameral Parliament consists of a Senate and a House of Assembly. The *Senate* comprises 21 members appointed by the Governor-General, 12 being appointed on the advice of the Prime Minister, two on the advice of the Leader of the Opposition and seven at the Governor-General's discretion. The *House of Assembly* comprises 30 members elected every five years. In 1963 the voting age was reduced to 18.

The *Privy Council* is appointed by the Governor-General after consultation with the Prime Minister. It consists of 12 members and the Governor-General as chairman. It advises the Governor-General in the exercise of the royal prerogative of mercy and in the exercise of his disciplinary powers over members of the public and police services.

National Anthem

'In plenty and in time of need'; words by Irvine Burgie, tune by V. R. Edwards.

RECENT ELECTIONS

In the general election of 15 Jan. 2008 the opposition Democratic Labour Party (DLP) won 20 seats (53·2% of the total vote) and the Barbados Labour Party (BLP) 10 (46·5%). Two smaller parties and independents failed to win any seats.

CURRENT ADMINISTRATION

Governor-General: Sir Clifford Husbands, GCMG, KA; b. 1926.

In March 2010 the government comprised:

Prime Minister and Minister of Finance and Investment, the Civil Service and Energy: David Thompson; b. 1961 (DLP; appointed 16 Jan. 2008).

Deputy Prime Minister, Attorney General and Minister of Home Affairs: Freundel Stuart. *Minister of Agriculture:* Haynesley Benn. *Community Development and Culture:* Steve Blackett. *Economic Affairs and Empowerment, Innovation, and Trade, Industry and Commerce:* David Estwick. *Education and Human Resource Development:* Ronald Jones. *Environment, Water Resources and Drainage:* Dennis Lowe. *Family, Youth Affairs and Sport:* Stephen Lashley. *Foreign Affairs and Foreign Trade:* Maxine McClean. *Health:* Donville Inniss. *Housing and Lands:* Michael Lashley. *International Transport and International Business:* George Hutson. *Labour:* Dr Esther Byer-Suckoo. *Social Care, Constituency Empowerment, and Rural and Urban Development:* Christopher Sinckler. *Tourism:* Richard Sealy. *Transport and Works:* John Boyce.

Government of Barbados Information Network:
http://www.barbados.gov.bb

CURRENT LEADERS

David Thompson

Position
Prime Minister

Introduction
David Thompson, the leader of the Democratic Labour Party (DLP), became prime minister in Jan. 2008 after leading his party

to victory in a general election. Claiming 20 out of 30 available seats, the DLP returned to power after 14 years in opposition.

Early Life

David John Howard Thompson was born on 25 Dec. 1961 in London to Barbadian parents. He was educated at Combermere School before graduating in law from the University of the West Indies in 1984. While a student Thompson was active within the Young Democrats, the youth wing of the DLP, serving as its president from 1980–82. Thompson went on to the Hugh Wooding Law School at the University of the West Indies in Trinidad, obtaining his Legal Education Certificate. In 1986 he joined Trident Chambers, the chambers of Errol Barrow, Barbados' first prime minister. Between 1986 and 1988 Thompson was a part-time tutor at the University of the West Indies.

Following Barrow's death in 1987, Thompson won the by-election for Barrow's constituency of St John, which he has represented ever since. He was also selected as general secretary of the DLP, a position he retained until 1994. In 1991 he joined the cabinet of Prime Minister Lloyd Sandiford, in charge of the community development and culture portfolios. He moved to the ministry of finance in 1992 as minister of state. From 1993–94 he was minister of finance and oversaw the implementation of IMF structural reforms, and an overhaul of the sugar industry and offshore sector.

In 1994 Thompson became leader of the DLP after Sandiford lost a motion of no confidence. Thompson saw his party defeated in the general elections of 1994 and 1999 before he resigned as party head in Sept. 2001. He returned to his legal practice where he specialized in corporate, insurance, international business and property law. In Jan. 2006 he took up the DLP leadership again following the defection from the DLP of Clyde Mascoll, a former party leader. Thompson was widely lauded for his efforts to restore public confidence in the party. On 15 Jan. 2008 he was re-elected to his St John constituency with 84% of the vote and led his party to electoral victory.

Career in Office

In addition to the premiership, Thompson took over the portfolios of finance, economic affairs and development (since relinquished), labour, civil service and energy. He had campaigned on a platform of improving health care and transport infrastructure while fighting the rising cost of living. Although the collapse of a major Caribbean insurance conglomerate in early 2009 precipitated a financial crisis in Barbados, Thompson survived a consequent parliamentary motion of no confidence in March over his handling of the emergency.

DEFENCE

The Barbados Defence Force has a strength of about 610. In 2006 defence expenditure totalled US$25m. (US$89 per capita), representing 0·7% of GDP.

Army

Army strength was 500 with reserves numbering 430 in 2007.

Navy

A small maritime unit numbering 110 (2007) operates nine patrol vessels. The unit is based at St Ann's Fort Garrison, Bridgetown.

INTERNATIONAL RELATIONS

Barbados is a member of the UN, World Bank, IMF and several other UN specialized agencies, WTO, Commonwealth, ACS, CARICOM, Inter-American Development Bank, SELA, OAS and is an ACP member state of the ACP-EU relationship.

ECONOMY

In 2005 agriculture accounted for 4% of GDP, industry 18% and services 78%.

According to the anti-corruption organization *Transparency International*, Barbados ranked 20th in the world in a 2009 survey of the countries with the least corruption in business and government. It received 7·4 out of 10 in the annual index.

Overview

Since independence in 1966, Barbados has become an upper-middle-income economy with one of the highest per capita incomes in the region. Formerly dependent on sugar production, agriculture has played a diminishing role in the economy while tourism and financial services now account for around 75% of GDP.

Since 2004 economic performance has been positive, with real GDP growth averaging around 4% per year as a result of strong tourist receipts and construction activity, both contributing to record employment. Following two years of high inflation resulting from a temporary surcharge on consumer goods and higher oil prices, inflation fell in 2007 to 4·0%. The current account deficit is high despite easing in 2006 following an import slowdown, while official reserves have declined further relative to imports owing to lower capital inflows. The government began to liberalize the capital account in 2008 as a means of developing Barbados as a centre for tourism and financial services. Trade liberalization with CARICOM nations will extend to other countries.

Currency

The unit of currency is the *Barbados dollar* (BBD), usually written as BDS$, of 100 *cents*, which is pegged to the US dollar at BDS$2=US$1. Inflation was 4·0% in 2007 and 8·1% in 2008. Total money supply was BDS$1,691m. in June 2005. Foreign exchange reserves were US$575m. in July 2005.

Budget

The financial year runs from 1 April. Capital expenditure for 2003–04 was BDS$253·7m.; current expenditure for the same period was BDS$2,048·3m. The budget for 2003–04 put total revenue at an estimated BDS$1,850·5m. and recurrent expenditure at BDS$2,080·5m.

VAT at 15% was introduced in Jan. 1997.

Performance

Total GDP in 2007 was US$3·4bn. Real GDP growth was 3·4% in 2007 and 0·2% in 2008.

Banking and Finance

The central bank and bank of issue is the Central Bank of Barbados (*Governor*, Dr DeLisle Worrell), which had total assets of BDS$1,248·5m. in Dec. 2003. The provisional figures for the total assets of commercial banks in Dec. 2003 were BDS$6,812·6m. and savings banks' deposits BDS$5,493·8m. In 2003 there were 4,635 international business companies, 413 exempt insurance companies and 51 offshore banks. In addition, there were three commercial banks, one regional development bank, one National Bank (scheduled for privatization), three foreign banks and seven trust companies.

There is a stock exchange which participates in the regional Caribbean exchange.

Weights and Measures

Both Imperial and metric systems are in use.

ENERGY AND NATURAL RESOURCES

Environment

Carbon dioxide emissions from the consumption and flaring of fossil fuels in Barbados in 2008 were the equivalent of 5·0 tonnes per capita.

Electricity

Production in 2004, 895m. kWh. Capacity in 2004 was 0·2m. kW. Consumption per capita was 3,304 kWh in 2004.

Oil and Gas
Crude oil production in 2003 was 370,909 bbls and reserves in 2007 were 3·0m. bbls. Output of gas (2003) 22·4m. cu. metres, and reserves (2003) 130m. cu. metres. Production of Liquid Petroleum Gas (LPG) was 3,691 bbls in 2003.

Agriculture
The agricultural sector accounted for 4·4% of GDP in 2003 (24% in 1967). Of the total labour force in 2003, 4·6% were employed in agriculture. Of the total area of Barbados (42,995 ha.), about 16,000 ha. are arable land, which is intensively cultivated. In 2003, 7,515 ha. were under sugarcane cultivation. Production, 2003 (in tonnes): sugarcane, 48,500; sweet potatoes, 2,610; cucumbers, 2,018; okra, 1,446; tomatoes, 1,234; yams, 1,234; carrots, 1,012; cabbage, 640.

Meat and dairy products, 2003 (in tonnes): poultry, 11,458; cow's milk, 7,017; pork, 1,756; eggs, 1,620; beef, 346.

Livestock (2003): sheep, 27,000; pigs, 17,000; cattle, 14,000; chickens, 3m.

Forestry
Timber production in 2007 was 11,000 cu. metres.

Fisheries
In 2003 there were 954 fishing vessels employed during the flying-fish season. The catch in 2005 was 1,869 tonnes, exclusively from sea fishing.

INDUSTRY
Industry has traditionally been centred on sugar, but there is also light manufacturing and component assembly for export. In 2003, 36,300 tonnes of raw sugar were produced.

Labour
In 2003 the workforce was 145,500, of whom 129,500 were employed. Unemployment stood at 11·0%, down from 24·5% in 1993.

Trade Unions
About one-third of employees are unionized. The Barbados Workers' Union was founded in 1938 and has the majority of members. There are also a National Union of Public Workers and two teachers' unions.

INTERNATIONAL TRADE
External debt was BDS$2,224m. in 2004 (provisional).

Imports and Exports
In 2004 imports were valued at BDS$2,752m. and exports (excluding petroleum products) at BDS$498m. The main import suppliers in 2004 were the USA (37·0%), Trinidad and Tobago (18·9%), UK (6·0%) and Canada (3·9%). Principal export markets in 2004 were the USA (15·4%), Trinidad and Tobago (11·0%), UK (10·5%) and Jamaica (5·2%).

The main imports are foodstuffs, cars, chemicals, mineral fuels, and machinery and equipment. Main exports are electrical components, sugar, rum, cement, chemicals and petroleum (re-export) products.

COMMUNICATIONS
Roads
There were 1,600 km of roads in 2004. In 2007 there were 103,500 passenger cars, 15,200 lorries and vans, and 630 buses and coaches. There were 38 deaths as a result of road accidents in 2007.

Civil Aviation
The Grantley Adams International Airport is 16 km from Bridgetown. In 2001 it handled 1,763,500 passengers (all on international flights) and 14,094 tonnes of freight.

Shipping
There is a deep-water harbour at Bridgetown. 665,595 tonnes of cargo were handled in 1994. Shipping registered in 2002 totalled 328,000 GRT, including oil tankers 8,000 GRT. The number of merchant vessels entering in 2001 was 2,087 of 18·6m. net tonnes.

Telecommunications
In 2005 there were 341,100 telephone subscribers (1,267·9 per 1,000 inhabitants). There were 40,000 PCs in use in 2005 (148·7 per 1,000 inhabitants). Barbados had 206,200 mobile phone subscribers in 2005 and 160,000 internet users. There were 20·5 broadband subscribers per 100 inhabitants in June 2007.

Postal Services
There is a general post office in Bridgetown and 17 branches on the island.

SOCIAL INSTITUTIONS
Justice
Justice is administered by the Supreme Court and Justices' Appeal Court, and by magistrates' courts. All have both civil and criminal jurisdiction. There is a Chief Justice, three judges of appeal, five puisne judges of the Supreme Court and nine magistrates. The death penalty is authorized. Final appeal lies to the Privy Council in London. Barbados was one of ten countries to sign an agreement in Feb. 2001 establishing a Caribbean Court of Justice to replace the British Privy Council as the highest civil and criminal court. In the meantime the number of signatories has risen to twelve. The court was inaugurated at Port-of-Spain, Trinidad on 16 April 2005.

The population in penal institutions in Nov. 2003 was 992 (367 per 100,000 of national population).

Education
The adult literacy rate was 99·7% in 2003. There were 22,584 pupils at primary schools in 2007 with 1,553 teaching staff and 20,855 pupils at secondary schools in 2006 with 1,430 teaching staff. There were 23 public and eight private secondary schools in 2003. Education is free in all government-owned and government-maintained institutions from primary to university level.

In 2005 public expenditure on education came to 6·9% of GDP and 16·4% of total government spending.

In 2007 there were 11,405 students in higher education and 786 academic staff. One of the three main campuses of the University of the West Indies is in Barbados, at Cave Hill.

Health
In 2001 there was one general hospital, one psychiatric hospital, five district hospitals, eight health centres and two private hospitals with 35 beds. There were 2,049 hospital beds and 420 doctors in the same year.

Welfare
The National Insurance and Social Security Scheme provides contributory sickness, age, maternity, disability and survivors benefits. Sugar workers have their own scheme.

RELIGION
In 2001, 63% of the population were Protestants, 5% Roman Catholics and the remainder other religions.

CULTURE
Broadcasting
The Caribbean Broadcasting Corporation is the government-owned television and radio service. There are also various

commercial radio stations. In 2005 there were 90,000 television-equipped households (colour by NTSC).

Press

In 2003 there were two daily newspapers, the *Barbados Advocate* (est. 1895) and the *Daily Nation* (est. 1973), and a weekly business publication, the *Broad Street Journal*. The *Daily Nation* has an average daily circulation of 25,000; the *Barbados Advocate*, 15,000.

Tourism

There were 531,211 foreign tourists in 2003 (including 291,623 from elsewhere in the Americas and 233,791 from Europe), plus 559,119 cruise passenger arrivals, bringing revenue of BDS$1,493·8m. and contributing 11·8% of the country's GDP.

Festivals

The National Cultural Foundation organizes three annual national festivals: the nine-day Congaline Carnival which begins in the last week of April; Crop Over, a three-week festival held from mid-July until Aug.; the National Independence Festival of Creative Arts (NIFCA) which runs throughout Nov.

Libraries

The National Library Service operates seven branch libraries around the island and the Adult and Children's libraries in Bridgetown.

Museums and Galleries

There are four museums: the Barbados Museum at Bridgetown, which is housed in the former British military prison; Sunbury Plantation House; Hutson Sugar Museum; Tyrol Cot Heritage Village.

DIPLOMATIC REPRESENTATIVES

Of Barbados in the United Kingdom (1 Great Russell St., London, WC1B 3ND)
High Commissioner: Hugh Anthony Arthur.

Of the United Kingdom in Barbados (Lower Collymore Rock, PO Box 676, Bridgetown)
High Commissioner: Paul Brummell.

Of Barbados in the USA (2144 Wyoming Ave., NW, Washington, D.C. 20008)
Ambassador: John Beale.

Of the USA in Barbados (Wildey Business Park, Wildey, St Michael, BB 14006, Bridgetown)
Ambassador: Vacant.
Chargé d'Affaires a.i.: D. Brendt Hardt.

Of Barbados to the United Nations
Ambassador: Christopher Hackett.

Of Barbados to the European Union
Ambassador: Errol L. Humphrey.

FURTHER READING

Beckles, H., *A History of Barbados: from Amerindian Settlement to Nation-State.* 1990
Carmichael, Trevor A. (ed.) *Barbados: Thirty Years of Independence.* 1998
Carter, R. and Downes, A. S., *Analysis of Economic and Social Development in Barbados: A Model for Small Island Developing States.* 2000
Hoyos, F. A., *Tom Adams: a Biography.* 1988.—*Barbados: A History from the Amerindians to Independence.* 2nd ed. 1992

National Statistical Office: Barbados Statistical Service, Fairchild Street, Bridgetown.
Website: http://www.barstats.gov.bb

BELARUS

Respublika Belarus
(Republic of Belarus)

Capital: Minsk
Population estimate, 2010: 9·59m.
GDP per capita, 2007: (PPP$) 10,841
HDI/world rank: 0·826/68

KEY HISTORICAL EVENTS

Belarus was fully integrated with Russia until the Gorbachev reforms of the mid-1980s encouraged demands for greater freedom. On 25 Aug. 1991 Belarus declared its independence and in Dec. it became a founder member of the CIS. The Communists retained power in Belarus despite formidable opposition and it was not until a new constitution was adopted in March 1994 that the economic reformers began to influence events. Alyaksandr Lukashenka was elected president in July 1994. By 1996 only 11% of state enterprises had been privatized and the government remains pro-Russian, striving for eventual unification with Russia within the Russia–Belarus Union. A referendum held over 9–24 Nov. 1996 extended the President's term of office from three to five years and increased his powers to rule by decree. The last three parliamentary elections have been criticized by the OSCE for a lack of transparency.

TERRITORY AND POPULATION

Belarus is situated along the western Dvina and Dnieper. It is bounded in the west by Poland, north by Latvia and Lithuania, east by Russia and south by Ukraine. The area is 207,600 sq. km (80,155 sq. miles). The capital is Minsk. Other important towns are Homel, Vitebsk, Mahilyou, Bobruisk, Hrodno and Brest. On 2 Nov. 1939 western Belorussia was incorporated with an area of over 108,000 sq. km and a population of 4·8m. Census population, 1999, 10,045,237. Estimated population, Jan. 2009, 9,671,900; density, 46·6 per sq. km.

The UN gives an estimated population for 2010 of 9·59m.

In 2005, 72·2% of the population lived in urban areas. Major ethnic groups: 81·2% Belarusians, 11·4% Russians, 3·9% Poles, 2·4% Ukrainians, 1·1% others.

Belarus comprises six provinces. Areas and estimated populations:

Province	*Area sq. km*	*Population 2008*	*Capital*	*Population 2006*
Brest	32,300	1,435,100	Brest	301,400
Homel	40,400	1,468,600	Homel	481,500
Hrodno	25,000	1,106,600	Hrodno	318,600
Mahilyou	29,000	1,129,600	Mahilyou	367,700
Minsk	40,800	3,276,600	Minsk	1,741,000
Vitebsk	40,100	1,273,300	Vitebsk	343,600

Belarusian and Russian are both official languages.

SOCIAL STATISTICS

2007 births, 103,626 (rate of 10·7 per 1,000 population); deaths, 132,993 (rate of 13·7 per 1,000 population); marriages, 90,444; divorces, 36,146. Annual population growth rate, 2000–05, –0·5%. Life expectancy at birth, 2007, was 63·1 years for men and 75·2 years for women. Only Russia has a bigger difference between its male and female life expectancy. Infant mortality, 2007, 5·2 per 1,000 live births; fertility rate, 2004, 1·2 children per woman (one of the lowest rates in the world).

CLIMATE

Moderately continental and humid with temperatures averaging 20°F (–6°C) in Jan. and 64°F (18°C) in July. Annual precipitation is 22–28" (550–700 mm).

CONSTITUTION AND GOVERNMENT

A new constitution was adopted on 15 March 1994. It provides for a *President* who must be a citizen of at least 35 years of age, have resided for ten years in Belarus and whose candidacy must be supported by the signatures of 70 deputies or 100,000 electors. At a referendum held on 17 Oct. 2004, 86·2% of votes cast were in favour of the abolition of the two-term limit on the presidency. The vote was widely regarded as fraudulent.

There is an 11-member *Constitutional Court*. The chief justice and five other judges are appointed by the president.

Four referendums held on 14 May 1995 gave the president powers to dissolve parliament; work for closer economic integration with Russia; establish Russian as an official language of equal status with Belarusian; and introduce a new flag.

At a further referendum of 24 Nov. 1996 turnout was 84%. 79% of votes cast were in favour of the creation of an upper house of parliament nominated by provincial governors and 70% in favour of extending the presidential term of office by two years to five years. The Supreme Soviet was dissolved and a 110-member lower *House of Representatives* established, whose members are directly elected by universal adult suffrage every four years. The upper chamber is the *Council of the Republic* (64 seats; 56 members elected by regional councils and eight members appointed by the president, all for four-year terms). In practice, since 1996 the Belarusian parliament has only had a ceremonial function.

National Anthem

'My Bielarusy' ('We, the Belarusians'); words by M. Klimkovich and U. Karyzna, tune by Nester Sakalouski.

GOVERNMENT CHRONOLOGY

Heads of State since 1991.

Chairmen of the Supreme Council
1991–94 Stanislau Stanislavavich Shushkevich
1994 Myechyslau Ivanavich Hryb

President
1994– Alyaksandr Rygorovich Lukashenka

RECENT ELECTIONS

Parliamentary elections were held on 28 Sept. 2008. 110 deputies were elected, all supporters of the government. Of the 263 candidates, 82 represented political parties. Turnout was 76·7%. The results were widely disputed.

Presidential elections were held on 19 March 2006. Alyaksandr Lukashenka was re-elected with 87·5% of votes cast against 6·5% for Alyaksandr Milinkevich and 3·7% for Sergei Gaidukevich. The election took place amid accusations of vote rigging. No independent observers were allowed to watch the count. Turnout was 92·7%.

CURRENT ADMINISTRATION

President: Alyaksandr Lukashenka; b. 1954 (sworn in 20 July 1994 and re-elected in Sept. 2001 and March 2006).

Prime Minister: Sergei Sidorsky; b. 1954 (took office on 19 Dec. 2003).

In March 2010 the government comprised:

First Deputy Prime Minister: Vladimir Semashko. *Deputy Prime Ministers:* Ivan Bambiza; Viktor Burya; Andrei Kobyakov; Vladimir Potupchik.

Minister for Agriculture and Food: Semyon Shapiro. *Architecture and Construction:* Alexander Seleznyov. *Communications and Information Technology:* Nikolai Pantelei. *Culture:* Pavel Latushko. *Defence:* Yuri Zhadobin. *Economy:* Nikolai Snopkov. *Education:* Alexander Radkov. *Emergencies:* Enver Bariyev. *Energy:* Alexander Ozerets. *Finance:* Andrei Kharkovets. *Foreign Affairs:* Sergei Martynov. *Forestry:* Vacant. *Health:* Vasily Zharko. *Housing and Communal Services:* Vladimir Belokhvostov. *Industry:* Alexander Radevich. *Information:* Oleg Proleskovsky. *Internal Affairs:* Anatoly Kuleshov. *Justice:* Viktor Golovanov. *Labour and Social Protection:* Marianna Shchetkina. *Natural Resources and Environmental Protection:* Vladimir Tsalko. *Sports and Tourism:* Oleg Kachan. *Taxes and Duties:* Vladimir Poluyan. *Trade:* Valentin Chekanov. *Transport and Communications:* Ivan Shcherbo.

Government Website: http://www.government.by

CURRENT LEADERS

Alyaksandr Rygorovich Lukashenka

Position
President

Introduction
Alyaksandr Lukashenka has been president of Belarus since 1994. A member of the communist party from an early age, Lukashenka sought closer ties with Russia and rejected his predecessor's plans to implement free market policies. He has strengthened his powers within the constitution, but drawn international condemnation for his autocratic leadership and human rights abuses against opposition politicians and journalists.

Early Life
Lukashenka was born on 30 Aug. 1954 in Kepys. After studying history and agricultural economics, he taught at the Mahilyou Teaching Institute and the Belarusian SSR Agro-economics Academy. He was a member of Komsomol, a young communists' group, before working on collective farms while gaining political experience. After working in local politics, he became a deputy on the Belarusian Supreme Council in 1990. When Belarus gained independence the following year, he opposed the formation of the CIS, set up by Russia, Belarus and the Ukraine, as well as Stanislau Shushkevich's nationalist tendencies and his plans for privatization. By the time of the 1994 presidential elections, Shushkevich (the first post-independence leader) had been forced to stand down. Campaigning on a pro-Russian manifesto, Lukashenka stood against Shushkevich and took 45% of votes to 10%. In a second round run-off with former prime minister (1990–94) Vyachaslau Kebich, he received 80·1% of votes.

Career in Office
Following his election, Lukashenka set about increasing presidential powers and strengthening state control. Countering Shushkevich's efforts to promote Belarusian culture, he reinstated Russian as the official language and sought closer ties, not always successfully, with the Russian Federation. Trade agreements were made with Russia and several other former Soviet states. Establishing what he called a 'vertical' presidency, in 1996 he pressed through constitutional changes to give himself more power and to extend his term of office by two years to 2001. He reversed reforms made by his predecessor after the collapse of the Soviet Union and secured his control over the state-owned media and security services. This caused conflicts with the constitutional court as well as the Supreme Council. He also rejected Shushkevich's previous moves towards privatization.

Lukashenka used his presidential decree to impose restrictions on opponents, and journalists in particular were subject to harassment and censorship for criticizing his regime. He was condemned by the international community for human rights abuses and disregard for democracy.

In the 2000 parliamentary elections, Lukashenka's supporters won 81 of 110 seats. The following year Lukashenka won a second presidential term, taking 75·6% of the vote against 15·4% for Uladzimir Hancharyk. No independent observers were allowed to watch the count. However, experts estimated that the opposition actually gained between 30% and 40% of the vote. Both elections were criticized by international observers as undemocratic, with many opposition politicians either boycotting them or remaining in exile. International organizations continued to criticize Lukashenka's repressive regime during 2002 (when the authorities expelled an OSCE delegation) and 2003. The USA meanwhile passed legislation allowing the provision of financial support to the democratic opposition in Belarus.

Further parliamentary elections and a referendum were held on 17 Oct. 2004. No opposition candidates won a parliamentary seat in the poll, while Lukashenka claimed overwhelming support in the referendum for his intention to change the constitution and run for another presidential term. The results were dismissed as fraudulent by most international observers, raising fears among human rights activists and opposition politicians that his already authoritarian rule would progress to dictatorship.

Lukashenka was re-elected for a further term in March 2006, again amid accusations of vote rigging. Opponents staged a number of post-election demonstrations leading to many arrests, including that of rival presidential candidate Alyaksandr Kozulin who was jailed in July for five and a half years for inciting disorder. From April 2006 the European Union (EU) and the USA imposed travel bans and asset freezes on various Belarusian officials, including Lukashenka, deemed responsible for electoral fraud and civil repression.

In 2007 Belarus was in dispute with Russia over oil supplies, price rises and unpaid debts. Meanwhile, there were further violent demonstrations in Minsk in March by opposition supporters calling for an end to Lukashenka's rule, and in May Belarus' bid for a seat on the United Nations Human Rights Council was rejected.

In the spring of 2008 diplomatic relations with the USA deteriorated further, as Lukashenka's government expelled US diplomats for criticizing Belarus' human rights record. In Sept. 2008 candidates loyal to the president were again returned to every seat in parliamentary elections considered by European monitors to be only marginally less flawed than previous polls.

Following the lifting of the EU's travel ban in Oct. 2008, Lukashenka visited the Vatican in April 2009 for talks with Pope Benedict XVI in his first official visit to Western Europe since the mid-1990s.

DEFENCE

Conscription is for 18 months, or 12 in the case of university and college graduates. A treaty with Russia of April 1993 co-ordinates their military activities. All nuclear weapons had been transferred to Russia by Dec. 1996. Total active armed forces in 2007 numbered 72,940. In addition there are Ministry of Interior paramilitary troops numbering 110,000.

Defence expenditure in 2006 totalled US$279m. (US$29 per capita), representing 0·8% of GDP.

Army

In 2007 Army personnel numbered 29,600. In addition there were 289,500 reserves. Equipment in 2007 included 1,586 main battle tanks (T-55s, T-72s and T-80s).

Air Force

In 2007 the Air Force and Air Defence Forces operated 175 combat capable aircraft, including MiG-29s, Su-24s, Su-25s and Su-27s, and 50 attack helicopters. Personnel, 2007, 18,170.

INTERNATIONAL RELATIONS

A treaty of friendship with Russia was signed on 21 Feb. 1995. A further treaty signed by the respective presidents on 2 April 1997 provided for even closer integration.

Belarus is a member of the UN, World Bank, IMF and several other UN specialized agencies, OSCE, EBRD, CEI, CIS, IOM, NATO Partnership for Peace and Antarctic Treaty. In Jan. 2010 Belarus joined the newly established Customs Union, together with Kazakhstan and Russia. The three countries are now looking to enter the WTO as a single customs territory.

ECONOMY

In 2006 agriculture contributed 9·3% of GDP, industry 42·0% and services 48·7%. In 2006, 57·4% of economic output was being produced by the private sector.

Overview

Following the collapse of the Soviet Union, Belarus' economy significantly underperformed relative to other transition economies. From 1991 to 1995 the economy contracted at an average annual rate of 8·1% compared to the 0·6% contraction averaged by eastern European economies. In 1995 President Lukashenka reasserted state control with price controls, state intervention in private enterprise and the obstruction of foreign investment. In spite of this, the economy grew at an annual average rate of 6·9% in the decade 1996–2005.

A government programme was launched in 2007 to reduce the costs of doing business, with the aim of pushing Belarus into the top 30 countries by this measure. The economy grew at over 9% per year from 2003–07, in part because of much improved terms of trade. There has been a substantial decrease in poverty, from 30·5% of the population in 2002 to 7·7% in 2007, while income inequality remains low.

The economy is largely sustained by Russian oil subsidies and the processing and re-export of Russian oil at Belarus' two refining centres, Mozyr and Naftan. Russia's recent policy of increasing energy prices for Belarus to world market levels is likely to result in a slowdown in growth. The global financial crisis has also impacted, with demand for exports having fallen. In early 2009 the IMF approved a US$2·46bn. stand-by arrangement in support of the country's efforts to adjust to the crisis, and an additional US$1·1bn. was approved in June 2009.

Currency

The *rouble* was retained under an agreement of Sept. 1993 and a treaty with Russia on monetary union of April 1994. Foreign currencies ceased to be legal tender in Oct. 1994. Only banknotes are issued—there are no coins in circulation. In Jan. 2000 the Belarusian rouble was revalued at 1 new rouble (BYR) = 1,000 old roubles (BYB). In Nov. 2000 President Lukashenka and President Putin of Russia agreed the introduction of a single currency, but plans to introduce the Russian rouble to Belarus have since been postponed indefinitely. The inflation rate in 1994 was 2,434%. It has since fallen, to 7·0% in 2006, although it rose to 14·8% in 2008. Foreign exchange reserves in June 2005 were US$1,151m., total money supply was 4,025·7bn. roubles and gold reserves were 100,000 troy oz.

Budget

Central government revenue and expenditure (in 1bn. roubles):

	2004	2005	2006
Revenue	15,162	21,213	28,538
Expenditure	14,086	18,955	24,068

In 2006 tax revenue totalled 17,616bn. roubles (including domestic taxes on goods and services, 11,286bn. roubles). Main items of expenditure by economic type in 2006 were: social benefits, 9,619bn. roubles; grants, 4,286bn. roubles; compensation of employees, 2,987bn. roubles.

VAT is 20%.

Performance

Real GDP growth was 8·6% in 2007 and 10·0% in 2008. Total GDP in 2008 was US$60·3bn.

Banking and Finance

The central bank is the National Bank (*Chairman*, Petr P. Prokopovich). In 2003 there were 28 commercial banks. The largest banks are Belagroprombank, Belarusbank, Belinvestbank and BPS-Bank.

There is a stock exchange in Minsk.

ENERGY AND NATURAL RESOURCES

Environment

Carbon dioxide emissions from the consumption and flaring of fossil fuels in Belarus were the equivalent of 7·0 tonnes per capita in 2008.

Electricity

Installed capacity was an estimated 7·8m. kW in 2004. Production was 31·21bn. kWh in 2004. Consumption per capita in 2004 was 3,508 kWh.

Oil and Gas

In 2004 output of crude petroleum totalled 13m. bbls; reserves in 2007 were 198m. bbls. Natural gas production in 2004 was 255m. cu. metres; reserves were 2·8bn. cu. metres in 2007.

Minerals

Particular attention has been paid to the development of the peat industry with a view to making Belarus as far as possible self-supporting in fuel. There are over 6,500 peat deposits. There are rich deposits of rock salt and of iron ore.

Agriculture

Belarus is hilly, with a general slope towards the south. It contains large tracts of marshland, particularly to the southwest.

Agriculturally, it may be divided into three main sections—Northern: growing flax, fodder, grasses and breeding cattle for meat and dairy produce; Central: potato growing and pig breeding; Southern: good natural pasture land, hemp cultivation and cattle breeding for meat and dairy produce. In 2007 the agricultural population was around 972,000, of whom approximately 488,000 were economically active.

Output of main agricultural products (in 1m. tonnes) in 2007: potatoes, 8·74; sugar beets, 3·63; barley, 1·91; wheat, 1·40; rye, 1·31; oats, 0·58; cabbage, 0·56; milk, 5·91; eggs, 3,230m. units. In 2007 there were 3·99m. cattle; 3·64m. pigs; 156,200 horses; and 28·7m. poultry.

Since 1991 individuals may own land and pass it to their heirs, but not sell it. In 2006 there were 5·54m. ha. of arable land and 121,000 ha. of permanent crops. There were 4,723 farms in 2003. The private and commercial sectors accounted for 49% of the value of agricultural output in 2003, but only 20% of the total agricultural land. Agricultural output grew by 12·9% in 2004, the fifth successive year of growth. In 2004 state support for the agricultural sector accounted for 4% of GDP.

Forestry
Forests occupied 7·89m. ha., or 38·0% of the land area, in 2005. There are valuable reserves of oak, elm, maple and white beech. Timber production in 2007 was 8·76m. cu. metres.

Fisheries
Fish landings in 2004 amounted to 890 tonnes, exclusively from inland waters.

INDUSTRY

There are food-processing, chemical, textile, artificial silk, flax-spinning, motor vehicle, leather, machine-tool and agricultural machinery industries. Output in 1,000 tonnes (2004 unless otherwise indicated): distillate fuel oil, 5,845; residual fuel oil, 5,501; fertilizers, 5,403; petrol, 2,842; cement, 2,731; crude steel (2002), 1,607. Output of other products: 10,464m. cigarettes (2003); refrigerators (2003), 886,000; TV sets (2003), 690,000; tractors (2004), 34,000; lorries (2004), 21,500; beer (2003), 200m. litres; footwear (2002), 12·7m. pairs; cotton woven fabrics (2003), 57m. sq. metres; silk fabrics (2003), 40m. sq. metres; linen fabrics (2003), 30m. sq. metres. Machine-building equipment and chemical products are also important. Most industry is still state-controlled.

Labour
In 2007 the labour force totalled 4,525,200. In 2007, out of 4,476,600 economically active people, 1,183,400 were in industry; 638,700 in trade and public catering, material and technical supply and sale; 453,000 in education; and 441,900 in agriculture. In 2007 according to official statistics there were 48,600 unemployed persons, or 1·1% of the workforce, although some analysts maintain that unemployment is around 15%. The minimum unemployment benefit is the minimum wage and the maximum benefit is twice the minimum wage. The minimum wage in 2007 was 179,050 roubles a month.

Trade Unions
Trade unions are grouped in the Federation of Trade Unions of Belarus.

INTERNATIONAL TRADE

Foreign debt was US$4,734m. in 2005.

Imports and Exports
In 2006 imports were valued at US$22,237m. and exports at US$19,838m. The main import suppliers in 2006 were Russia (58·6%), Germany (7·5%), Ukraine (5·5%), Poland (3·4%) and China (2·5%). Principal export markets were Russia (34·7%), the Netherlands (17·7%), United Kingdom (7·5%), Ukraine (6·3%) and Poland (5·2%). Main import commodities are petroleum, natural gas, rolled metal and coal. Export commodities include machinery and transport equipment, diesel fuel, synthetic fibres and consumer goods.

COMMUNICATIONS

Roads
In 2005 there were 97,536 km of roads (88·0% paved), including 15,432 km of national roads. There were 2,329,200 passenger cars in use in 2007 (240 per 1,000 inhabitants). In 2007 public transport totalled 9,375m. passenger-km and freight 19,200m. tonne-km. There were 1,517 fatalities as a result of road accidents in 2007.

Rail
In 2005 there were 5,507 km of 1,520 mm gauge railways (874 km electrified). Passenger-km travelled in 2003 came to 13·3bn. and freight tonne-km to 38·4bn. There is a metro in Minsk.

Civil Aviation
The main airport is Minsk International 2, which handled 421,000 passengers (all international) and 2,700 tonnes of freight in 2001. The national carrier is Belavia. In 2003 Belavia flew on domestic routes and operated international services to Adler/Sochi, Baku, Berlin, Frankfurt, Hurghada, İstanbul, Kaliningrad, Kyiv, Larnaca, London, Moscow, Paris, Prague, Rome, Shannon, Stockholm, Tashkent, Tbilisi, Tel Aviv, Vienna, Warsaw and Yerevan. In 2003 scheduled airline traffic of Belarus-based carriers flew 7m. km, carrying 234,000 passengers (232,000 on international flights).

Shipping
In 2002 inland waterways carried 2m. passenger-km and 59m. tonne-km of freight.

Telecommunications
In 2005 there were 7,382,300 telephone subscribers in total (756·8 per 1,000 inhabitants). There were 4,098,000 mobile phone subscribers in 2005 and 3·4m. internet users.

Postal Services
In 2003 there were 3,752 post offices.

SOCIAL INSTITUTIONS

Justice
The death penalty is retained following the constitutional referendum of Nov. 1996; there were three executions in 2008 (although none in 2009).

There were 39,552 prisoners in 2007, at a rate of 408 prisoners per 100,000 population.

Education
Adult literacy rate in 2003 was 99·6%. In 2007 there were 365,298 children and 50,568 teachers at pre-school institutions, 362,282 pupils and 22,990 teachers at primary schools, 772,584 pupils and 99,011 teachers in secondary schools, and 576,679 students and 42,603 academic staff at institutions of tertiary education.

In 2007 there were 56 higher educational establishments (46 public and ten private) of which eight were general universities and 24 specialized universities (including four medical, three agricultural, three economics, three technical, two teacher training and two technological). There were also seven academies and 14 institutes. In 2007 there were 354,988 people enrolled at state higher education establishments.

Public expenditure on education in 2007 came to 5·3% of GNI.

Health
In 2007 there were 46,965 doctors (48·5 per 10,000 population), 1,964 dentists, 79,941 nurses, 4,921 midwives and 4,179 pharmacists. There were 112·4 hospital beds per 10,000 population in 2007.

Welfare
To qualify for an old-age pension men must be age 60 with 25 years of insurance coverage and women must be 55 with 20 years of insurance coverage. Minimum old-age pension is 25% of the average per capita subsistence budget. The maximum pension is 75% of wage base. Benefits are adjusted periodically according to changes in the minimum wage, which in 2009 was 229,000 roubles a month.

RELIGION

The Orthodox is the largest church. There is a Roman Catholic archdiocese of Minsk and Mahilyou, and five dioceses embracing 455 parishes. In 2001, 32% of the population were Belarusian Orthodox and 18% Roman Catholics. In Feb. 2010 there was one cardinal.

CULTURE

World Heritage Sites

There are four UNESCO sites in Belarus: the Mir Castle Complex, begun in the 15th century (inscribed on the list in 2000); the Radziwill Family complex at Nesvizh (2005); the Belovezhskaya Pushcha/Białowieża Forest site (1979 and 1992), shared with Poland; and the Struve Geodetic Arc (2005). The Arc is a chain of survey triangulations spanning from Norway to the Black Sea that helped establish the exact shape and size of the earth and is shared with nine other countries.

Broadcasting

Broadcasting is state-controlled. Belarus Television and Belarus Radio operate domestic TV and radio stations and an external radio service (transmitting in Belarusian, English, German and Russian). Nationwide TV is a state joint venture with a Russian television service. There were 3·08m. television-equipped households in 2005 (colour by SECAM H).

Press

There were two state-owned daily newspapers in Jan. 2006. The only independent daily newspaper, Narodnaya Volya, has been published in Russia since Oct. 2005. There is also a Belarusian edition of the Russian daily Komsomolskaya Pravda. The most widely read paper is Sovetskaya Belarussiya, with a daily circulation of 390,000 in 2006.

Tourism

In 2007 there were 105,400 foreign tourists on organized trips.

DIPLOMATIC REPRESENTATIVES

Of Belarus in the United Kingdom (6 Kensington Court, London, W8 5DL)
Ambassador: Aleksandr Mikhnevich.

Of the United Kingdom in Belarus (37 Karl Marx St., Minsk 220030)
Ambassador: Rosemary Thomas.

Of Belarus in the USA (1619 New Hampshire Ave., NW, Washington, D.C., 20009)
Ambassador: Vacant.
Chargé d'Affaires a.i.: Oleg Kravchenko.

Of the USA in Belarus (46 Starovilenskaya, Minsk 220002)
Ambassador: Vacant.
Chargé d'Affaires a.i.: Michael D. Scanlan.

Of Belarus to the United Nations
Ambassador: Andrei Dapkiunas.

Of Belarus to the European Union
Ambassador: Uladzimir L. Syanko.

FURTHER READING

Balmaceda, Margarita M., *Independent Belarus: Domestic Determinants, Regional Dynamics and Implications for the West.* 2003
Korosteleva, Elena, *Contemporary Belarus: Between Democracy and Dictatorship.* 2002
Marples, D. R., *Belarus: from Soviet Rule to Nuclear Catastrophe.* 1996
White, Stephen, *Postcommunist Belarus.* 2004
Zaprudnik, J., *Belarus at the Crossroads in History.* 1993

National Statistical Office: Ministry of Statistics and Analysis of the Republic of Belarus, 14 Partizansky Avenue, Minsk 220070.
Website: http://www.belstat.gov.by

BELGIUM

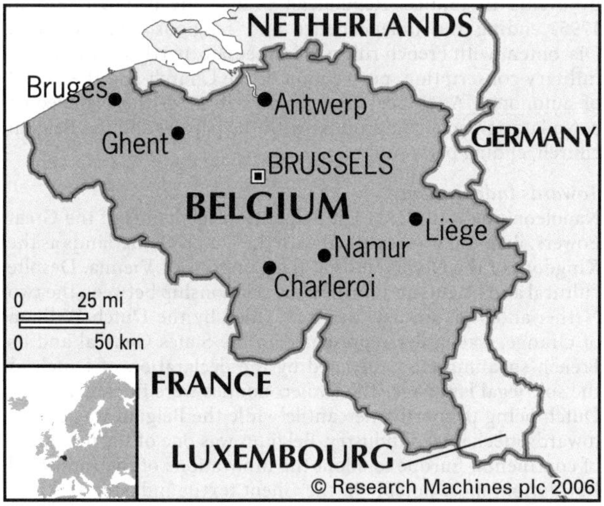

Royaume de Belgique — Koninkrijk België (Kingdom of Belgium)

Capital: Brussels
Population estimate, 2010: 10·70m.
GDP per capita, 2007: (PPP$) 34,935
HDI/world rank: 0·953/17

KEY HISTORICAL EVENTS

The Neanderthal Mousterian culture of the Ardennes region produced flint tools between 80–35,000 years ago. Omalien tribes of the early Neolithic period (5–4000 BC) developed settled agricultural practices, sophisticated tools and decorated black pottery. The Bronze Age Hilversum culture left evidence of contact overseas in Wessex, southern England. During the pre-Roman period Celtic and Germanic tribes moved across the region. Much of northern Gaul and southern Britain was settled by a Celtic group known as the Belgae, forming numerous tribes including the seafaring Morini and Menapii in what is now Flanders and the bellicose Nervii in Artois. In alliance with Germanic and other Belgic tribes, the Nervii led resistance to the invasion of Julius Caesar in 59 BC, succumbing five years later. Roman control was extended as far north as the Rhine and the area divided into the provinces of Gallia Belgica and Germania Inferior. Several tribes survived as Roman administrative *civitates*.

The network of Roman power, based around wealthy *villae* (country estates), declined from the mid-3rd century AD, despite the bolstering effect of the campaigns of Julian, who became emperor in AD 361. The massive influx of Germanic tribes (known commonly as the Barbarian invasions) over the Rhine in 406/7 effectively brought Roman rule in Belgium to an end. Chief among the German tribes were the Franks, who settled in Toxandria (modern Brabant). The Frankish Merovingian Empire, established by Childeric I, was based at Tournai and extended by Childeric's son, Clovis. The successors to the Merovingians, the Pippins (or Carolingians), ruled all but in name from Austrasia in the Ardennes. A partnership between the nobility and the church allowed the expansion of Frankish power north and east across the Rhine, bringing Christianity to the Low Countries by the 7th century, under the sees of Arras, Tournai, Cambrai and, from 720, Liège.

The death of Louis the Pious in 840 precipitated the fragmentation of Charlemagne's huge empire. Viking attacks on the Low Countries came at the end of the 8th century, intensifying in the period 841–75. Resistance began under Charlemagne; provincial princes capitalized on the fortification process and land reclamation to increase their own power. Baldwin 'Iron Arm', count of Flanders, fortified Ghent around 867, cementing his authority over the Flemish towns. His successors extended control into Artois (and to Hainault by personal union) in defiance of the French kings. Philippe IV of France was defeated in 1302 at the Battle of the Golden Spurs at Kortrijk, Flanders and formally recognized Flemish independence. Flanders' alliance with England during the Hundred Years War created an advantageous trading relationship, especially the importation of English wool for the textile industry. Brugge (Bruges), Ypres and Ghent flourished and in the 14th century had to be forcibly restrained from becoming city-states by Philip of Burgundy.

Other principalities emerged in the wake of the Carolingian empire, most notably the duchies of Brabant and Limburg and the prince-bishopric of Liège. Their union was forged under the dukes of Burgundy. The marriage of Philip the Bold, duke of Burgundy, to Margaret of Flanders in 1369 was the first step towards what became the Burgundian *Kreis* (lands) under Emperor Charles V. The addition of Hainault-Holland, Namur and Luxembourg encouraged Burgundian ambitions of centralization and even a unitary empire, vainly attempted by Duke Charles the Bold in the 1470s. The provinces and towns jealously guarded their imperial and local privileges and resisted the high taxation imposed by their Burgundian lord. Burgundian authority was reinforced by the 1477 marriage of Charles' daughter (and heir), Mary, to the Habsburg Maximilian of Austria, later Holy Roman Emperor, beginning over three centuries of Habsburg rule in the Low Countries.

Trade Centres

Brugge became the principal market of northwest Europe in the 14th century, ceding its role in the 1490s (on account of silting of its waterways) to Antwerp. The volume of Portuguese and English traders and Italian financiers testified to the importance of Antwerp as a mercantile and financial centre; the *Antwerpen beurs* (stock exchange) was established in 1531. Antwerp's population reached 100,000 in the mid-16th century. The artistic achievements of the 15th century were reliant on court patronage. Artists such as Rogier van der Weyden in Brussels and Jan van Eyck in Ghent formed part of a Flemish school that greatly influenced northern European art. The University of Louvain (Leuven), founded in 1425, was a centre of Dutch Humanism made famous by scholars such as Erasmus.

Dynastic pressures increased with the marriage of Archduke Philip the Handsome to the heiress of the Spanish crowns, Juana the Mad, leaving the Netherlands (the Burgundian Low Countries, including Belgium) under the supervision of governors-general in Brussels. Centralization continued under Philip's son, Charles of Ghent (Holy Roman Emperor Charles V), who regulated the succession to his Burgundian territories by pragmatic sanction. However, it was the imposition of a new ecclesiastical hierarchy by Charles' son, Philip II of Spain, that unified opposition in the Netherlands.

The Netherlands was highly receptive to religious reformist ideas, most notably those of Jean Calvin, whose influence had extended to Antwerp by 1545. Appealing to the urban middle classes and the lower nobility, Calvinism became the target of government repression, especially after the radical iconoclasm of 1566. The following year Philip sent the duke of Alba to stamp out the religious and political uprisings, sparking full revolt in Holland and other northern provinces. The execution of the counts of Hoorne and Egmond in Brussels in 1568 encouraged explicit rejection of 'Spanish rule'.

The secession of the northern Netherlands was partly the result of the inability of the Spanish armies to penetrate the marshes and dendritic waterways of Holland and Zeeland. Although Alba managed to reassert Philip's authority in the south, his armies never retook the provinces north of the Rhine after 1574. Separation was also caused by the extreme demands of the northern Calvinists, who alienated the more Catholic southern provinces. However, a measure of unity was achieved at the Pacification of Ghent after the atrocities of the 'Spanish Fury'—Spanish troops massacred 7,000 people in Antwerp in 1576.

In 1578 Philip appointed as governor-general Alessandro Farnese, duke of Parma, who ejected Protestants from the governments of the southern provinces and waged successful campaigns against the revolutionaries. The Union of Arras (1579), led by Flanders and Hainault, accepted the sovereignty of the Spanish king, supported Catholicism and ended the revolt of the southern provinces. In reaction the northern provinces drew up the Union of Utrecht, thus marking the birth of the 'Dutch Republic', though Philip was not rejected as sovereign in the north until 1581. Farnese took Antwerp in 1585, effectively creating the boundaries of the renegade Dutch state. Although fighting resumed after the Twelve Year Truce (1609–21), the Habsburg government accepted the independence of the Dutch Netherlands at the Peace of Westphalia in 1648.

The Spanish Netherlands was governed autonomously for much of the 17th century—Liège remained neutral in the revolt and separate until 1795. Antwerp was at first eclipsed as the principal trading centre of the region by Dutch Amsterdam, which attracted many of the south's skilled artisans and merchants. Economic recovery was helped by new industries such as linen production and diamond processing in Antwerp. Art was dominated by the Baroque style, patronized by the Catholic Church and adopted by Rubens, Van Dyck and Jordaens.

War of Succession

The death of Charles II of Spain without an heir in 1700 caused a constitutional crisis and the War of the Spanish Succession. Philip of Anjou, the heir-designate and a grandson of Louis XIV of France, was urged to hand over the Spanish Netherlands to France. The intervention of England and the Dutch was motivated by the fear of either Franco-Spanish union or the reuniting of the Austrian and Spanish Habsburgs. The Spanish Netherlands were finally settled on Emperor Charles VI after the Treaty of Utrecht in 1713, thus bringing the Netherlands under the sway of the Austrian Habsburgs.

Dynastic succession was again the cause of war after the death of Charles VI in 1740. By pragmatic sanction, his daughter, Archduchess Maria Theresa, succeeded to the Habsburg territories but was barred from the Imperial crown (it was secured for her husband, Francis Stephen of Lorraine). Supported by Great Britain, the Dutch and the Hungarian diet, Maria Theresa's armies repelled the French from the Austrian Netherlands, establishing her authority by the Treaty of Aix-la-Chapelle in 1748 (though she lost Silesia to Prussia). Her popular reign saw great economic gains in the Netherlands and the beginning of industrial capitalism thanks to good trading relations with Great Britain.

The Austrian regime lost popular support under Maria Theresa's successor, Emperor Joseph II, whose abolition of local privileges and his attempts to swap the Austrian Netherlands for Bavaria made him highly unpopular. Coupled with his attacks on the power of the Catholic Church, his 'Belgian' subjects—conservatives and progressives alike—revolted in 1789. The bulk of Joseph's forces being engaged on the Ottoman frontier, the Austrian army was easily routed at Turnhout. Conservative elements were victorious in the 'Brabant Revolution' and proclaimed the United States of Belgium in 1790.

Although Joseph's brother, Leopold II, reasserted Austrian authority, the seeds of revolution had been sown, encouraged by events in France. Republican France invaded Belgium in 1795, ending the independence and religious rule of Liège. Discontent with French rule was immediate, partly in reaction to military conscription, persecution of the Church and the denial of autonomy. After peasant uprisings in 1798 the Napoleonic consulate agreed a compromise with the papacy and the Belgian church, ending persecution.

Towards Independence

Napoleon's defeat in 1814 left Belgium in the hands of the Great Powers. Belgium was reunified with the Dutch Netherlands as the Kingdom of the Netherlands at the Congress of Vienna. Despite cultural and linguistic affinities, the relationship between the two Netherlands was uneasy. Belgium, ruled by the Dutch William of Orange, was under-represented in the States General and its French-speaking elite alienated by the declaration of Dutch as the sole legal language. The two economies were in contrast, the Dutch being primarily mercantile while the Belgian was geared towards mechanized industry. Belgium was one of the first areas of continental Europe to adopt the innovations of the Industrial Revolution, most notably in the Ghent textile industry and coal mining in Hainaut. The loss of the French market in 1814 and William's refusal to increase tariffs to protect Belgian industry impacted heavily on the Belgian economy.

Dissent paved the way for the Belgian Revolution of 1830. The secession of Belgium was secured by the intervention of France and Britain, which recognized Belgian independence in 1831. Repelled by the French, William accepted the loss of Belgium in 1838. Limburg and Luxembourg were partitioned and a liberal constitution implemented. The great powers insisted on a Belgian monarch and Prince Leopold of Saxe-Coburg was duly installed.

A Liberal government came to power in 1847 after three devastating harvests. The Liberal prime minister, Walthère Frère-Orban, championed the removal of church control of the schools. The Schools War dominated the political agenda and saw a conservative counter-offensive with the establishment of a network of independent Catholic schools. A conservative Catholic victory in 1884 brought Auguste Beernaert to the premiership. Closely associated with the Flemish revivalists, Beernaert managed the Flemish Equality Law, giving the Flemish language the same rights as French. Changes in the electoral system brought in full male suffrage (over 25 years of age) in 1893.

The Congo

Belgian foreign policy was bound by recognition (and imposition) of neutrality. King Leopold II, set on expanding his kingdom, looked to Africa. The Belgian Congo, acquired as his personal possession in 1885, was soon infamous for colonial abuse and exploitation. After widespread international condemnation, the 'Congo Free State' was formally annexed by Belgium in 1908, thus curbing Leopold's inhuman regime. In Europe, threats were perceived to the west and east. Attempts by Albert I (reigned 1909–34) to arm Belgium against French and German aggression were frustrated by the domestic pacifist movement led by Beernaert. Belgian neutrality was violated by Germany in 1914 after Albert's refusal to allow German free passage. Albert remained with his army on the Yser River throughout the First World War, supported by Allied troops. Neutrality, seen by many Belgians as a hindrance, was abolished under the Treaty of Versailles in 1919; Belgium was awarded the provinces of Eupen and Malmédy and jurisdiction over Ruanda-Urundi from the defeated Germany.

Belgium underwent massive change after the First World War. Its economy wrecked by German occupation—heavy industry in the south was particularly affected—the government followed an international economic policy. Economic union with Luxembourg was achieved in 1921 and the gold standard re-established to assist the export industry. The exploitative potential of the Belgian Congo was resolutely pursued once its wealth of minerals was discovered. Constitutional changes included equal suffrage of all men over 21 (women were denied the vote until 1948) and the formal linguistic separation of Flanders and Wallonia (excluding Brussels).

The 1930s was a time of rising unemployment—exports were seriously affected by the relinquishment of the British gold standard in 1931—and concern over German ambitions. Defences were built between Antwerp and Namur despite protestations of neutrality. Germany invaded Belgium on 10 May 1940. Capitulation after just 18 days made King Leopold III unpopular, despite his refusal to flee to France (and later to London) with the government. Collaboration with the German government of occupation was resisted and an underground army was active for much of the Second World War. Insurgents managed to protect the port of Antwerp, crucial for Allied support, during the liberation of Belgium in Sept. 1944.

The infrastructure of the economy was much less affected by the Second World War than the preceding occupation, allowing for a speedy recovery. Collaborators were treated harshly with many detentions. Political unity was disturbed by the royal question; a referendum on the return of the king from imprisonment in Austria caused violent protest in Wallonia and in 1951 Leopold was persuaded to abdicate in favour of his son, Baudouin.

European Union

Belgium embarked on international co-operation under the leadership of Prime Minister Paul-Henri Spaak. Economic union with Luxembourg was re-established and extended to include the Netherlands, forming the Benelux Economic Union. In 1949 Belgium joined the North Atlantic Treaty Organization (NATO) and in 1951 the European Coal and Steel Community (ECSC). Encouraged by the success of the ECSC, plans were laid for the establishment of two more communities. The European Economic Community (EEC) and the European Atomic Energy Community (Euratom) were subsequently created under separate treaties signed in Rome on 25 March 1957.

The administration of the Belgian Congo resisted political reform and demands for greater participation until the 1950s. After violent protest and agitation, moderate local government reform was passed in 1957 but was too late to quell the independence movement, led by Patrice Lumumba. In 1959 the Belgian government rushed through a decolonization programme, leaving the Congo abruptly in 1960. Rwanda and Burundi became independent in 1962.

A milestone in domestic politics was reached in 1958 with the School Pact, ending a century of conflict between secularists and conservative Catholics. Prime Minister Gaston Eyskens negotiated a guarantee of funding for state secondary schools and private religious schools. Relations between Walloon and Flemish society became difficult as a result of the decline of Walloon industry. Strikes and discontent with government subsidies set Belgium on the course of federalization. After the division of Brabant along linguistic lines Belgium officially became a federal state in 1993. King Baudouin, who died in 1993, was respected for his even-handed approach to Belgium's divided society and seen as an important symbol of unity. He was succeeded by his brother, Albert II.

Following elections in June 2007 won by the Christian Democratic and Flemish-New Flemish Alliance no new government was formed for 282 days. After a period of interim administration a coalition was eventually put together and took office in March 2008.

TERRITORY AND POPULATION

Belgium is bounded in the north by the Netherlands, northwest by the North Sea, west and south by France, and east by Germany and Luxembourg. Its area is 30,528 sq. km. Population (2001 census), 10,296,350. Population (at 1 Jan. 2008), 10,666,866 (5,442,557 females); density, 349·4 per sq. km. The Belgian exclave of Baarle-Hertog in the Netherlands has an area of seven sq. km and a population (2003) of 2,247. There were 971,448 resident foreign nationals as at 1 Jan. 2008. In 2005, 97·2% of the population lived in urban areas.

The UN gives an estimated population for 2010 of 10·70m.

Dutch (Flemish) is spoken by the Flemish section of the population in the north, French by the Walloon south. The linguistic frontier passes south of the capital, Brussels, which is bilingual. Some German is spoken in the east. Each language has official status in its own community. (Bracketed names below signify French/Dutch and where relevant English alternatives.)

Area, population and chief towns of the ten provinces on 1 Jan. 2007:

Province	*Area (sq. km)*	*Population*	*Chief Town*
Flemish Region			
Antwerp	2,867	1,700,570	Antwerp (Antwerpen/ Anvers)
East Flanders	2,982	1,398,253	Ghent (Gent/Gand)
West Flanders	3,144	1,145,878	Bruges (Brugge)
Flemish Brabant	2,106	1,052,467	Leuven (Louvain)
Limburg	2,422	820,272	Hasselt
Walloon Region			
Hainaut (Henegouwen)	3,786	1,294,844	Mons (Bergen)
Liège (Luik)	3,862	1,047,414	Liège (Luik)
Namur (Namen)	3,666	461,983	Namur (Namen)
Walloon Brabant	1,091	370,460	Wavre (Waver)
Luxembourg	4,440	261,178	Arlon (Aarlen)

Population of the regions on 1 Jan. 2007: Brussels-Capital Region, 1,031,215; Flemish Region, 6,117,440; Walloon Region, 3,435,879 (including the German-speaking Region, 73,675).

The most populous towns, with population on 1 Jan. 2007:

Brussels (Brussel/ Bruxelles)[1]	1,031,215	La Louvière	77,509
Antwerp (Antwerpen/ Anvers)	466,203	Kortrijk (Courtrai)	73,777
Ghent (Gent/Gand)	235,143	Hasselt	70,584
Charleroi	201,550	St Niklaas (St Nicolas)	70,016
Liège (Luik)	188,907	Ostend (Oostende/ Ostende)	69,115
Bruges (Brugge)	116,982	Tournai (Doornik)	67,844
Namur (Namen)	107,653	Genk	64,095
Leuven (Louvain)	91,942	Seraing	61,237
Mons (Bergen)	91,196	Roeselare (Roulers)	56,268
Mechelen (Malines)	78,900	Verviers	54,150
Aalst (Alost)	77,790	Mouscron (Moeskroen)	53,174

[1]19 communes.

SOCIAL STATISTICS

Statistics for calendar years:

	Births	*Deaths*	*Marriages*	*Divorces*	*Immigration*[1]	*Emigration*[1]
2001	114,172	103,447	42,110	29,314	524,626	489,263
2002	111,225	105,642	40,434	30,628	542,191	500,885
2003	112,149	107,039	41,777	31,355	552,608	512,592
2004	115,618	101,946	43,296	31,405	566,657	523,325
2005	118,002	103,278	43,141	30,840	581,702	535,057

[1]Including internal.

In 2004 Belgium received 15,357 asylum applications, equivalent to 1·5 per 1,000 inhabitants. Annual population growth rate, 2000–05, 0·4%. Life expectancy at birth, 2006, was 77·0 years for men and 82·7 years for women. 2005 birth rate (per 1,000 population): 11·3; death rate: 9·9. Infant mortality, 2005, four per 1,000 live births; fertility rate, 2004, 1·7 children per woman. In 2003 Belgium became the second country to legalize same-sex marriage.

CLIMATE

Cool temperate climate influenced by the sea, giving mild winters and cool summers. Brussels, Jan. 36°F (2·2°C), July 64°F (17·8°C). Annual rainfall 33" (825 mm). Ostend, Jan. 38°F (3·3°C), July 62°F (16·7°C). Annual rainfall 31" (775 mm).

CONSTITUTION AND GOVERNMENT

According to the constitution of 1831, Belgium is a constitutional, representative and hereditary monarchy. The legislative power is vested in the King, the federal parliament and the community and regional councils. The King convokes parliament after an election or the resignation of a government, and has the power to dissolve it in accordance with Article 46 of the Constitution.

The reigning King is **Albert II**, born 6 June 1934, who succeeded his brother, Baudouin, on 9 Aug. 1993. Married on 2 July 1959 to Paola Ruffo di Calabria, daughter of Don Fuleo and Donna Luisa Gazelli de Rossena. *Offspring*: Prince Philippe, Duke of Brabant, b. 15 April 1960; Princess Astrid, b. 5 June 1962; Prince Laurent, b. 19 Oct. 1963. Prince Philippe married Mathilde d'Udekem d'Acoz, 4 Dec. 1999. *Offspring*: Princess Elisabeth, b. 25 Oct. 2001; Prince Gabriel, b. 20 Aug. 2003; Prince Emmanuel, b. 4 Oct. 2005; Princess Eléonore, b. 16 April 2008. Princess Astrid married Archduke Lorenz of Austria, 22 Sept. 1984. *Offspring*: Prince Amedeo, b. 21 Feb. 1986; Princess Maria Laura, b. 26 Aug. 1988; Prince Joachim, b. 9 Dec. 1991; Princess Luisa Maria, b. 11 Oct. 1995; Princess Laetitia Maria, b. 23 April 2003. Prince Laurent married Claire Coombs, 12 April 2003. *Offspring*: Princess Louise, b. 6 Feb. 2004; Prince Nicolas, b. 13 Dec. 2005; Prince Aymeric, b. 13 Dec. 2005.

A constitutional amendment of June 1991 permits women to accede to the throne.

The King receives an allowance of €10,338,000 for 2010; Queen Fabiola receives €1,462,000; Prince Philippe, €935,000; Princess Astrid €324,000; and Prince Laurent, €311,000. For the first time in the history of the Belgian monarchy there was a reduction from the previous year's allowances.

Constitutional reforms begun in Dec. 1970 culminated in May 1993 in the transformation of Belgium from a unitary into a 'federal state, composed of communities and regions'. The communities are three in number and based on language: Flemish, French and German. The regions also number three, and are based territorially: Flemish, Walloon and the Brussels-Capital Region.

Since 1995 the federal parliament has consisted of a 150-member *Chamber of Representatives*, directly elected by obligatory universal suffrage from 20 constituencies on a proportional representation system for four-year terms; and a *Senate* of 71 members (excluding senators by right, i.e. certain members of the Royal Family). 25 senators are elected by a Dutch-speaking, and 15 by a French-speaking, electoral college; 21 are designated by community councils (ten Flemish, ten French and one German). These senators co-opt a further ten senators (six Dutch-speaking and four French-speaking).

The federal parliament's powers relate to constitutional reform, federal finance, foreign affairs, defence, justice, internal security, social security and some areas of public health. The Senate is essentially a revising chamber, though it may initiate certain legislation, and is equally competent with the Chamber of Representatives in matters concerning constitutional reform and the assent to international treaties.

The number of ministers in the federal government is limited to 15. The Council of Ministers, apart from the Prime Minister, must comprise an equal number of Dutch- and French-speakers. Members of parliament, if appointed ministers, are replaced in parliament by the runner-up on the electoral list for the minister's period of office. Community and regional councillors may not be members of the Chamber of Representatives or Senate.

National Anthem

'La Brabançonne'; words by A. Dechet, tune by F. van Campenhout. The Flemish version is 'O dierbaar België, O heilig land der vaad'ren' ('Noble Belgium, for ever a dear land').

GOVERNMENT CHRONOLOGY

Prime Ministers since 1939. (BSP/PSB = Belgian Socialist Party; Christian Democratic and Flemish = CD&V; CVP = Christian People's Party; CVP/PSC = Christian People's/Social Christian Party; VLD = Flemish Liberals and Democrats)

1939–45	CVP/PSC	Hubert Pierlot
1945–46	BSP/PSB	Achille Van Acker
1946	BSP/PSB	Paul-Henri Spaak
1946	BSP/PSB	Achille Van Acker
1946–47	BSP/PSB	Camille Huysmans
1947–49	BSP/PSB	Paul-Henri Spaak
1949–50	CVP/PSC	Gaston Eyskens
1950	CVP/PSC	Jean Pierre Duvieusart
1950–52	CVP/PSC	Louis Marie Joseph Pholien
1952–54	CVP/PSC	Jean Marie Van Houtte
1954–58	BSP/PSB	Achille Van Acker
1958–61	CVP/PSC	Gaston Eyskens
1961–65	CVP/PSC	Théodore Lefèvre
1965–66	CVP/PSC	Pierre Charles Harmel
1966–68	CVP/PSC	Paul Vanden Boeynants
1968–73	CVP	Gaston Eyskens
1973–74	BSP/PSB	Edmond Jules Leburton
1974–78	CVP	Léo Tindemans
1978–79	CVP	Paul Vanden Boeynants
1979–81	CVP	Wilfried Martens
1981	CVP	Mark Eyskens
1981–92	CVP	Wilfried Martens
1992–99	CVP	Jean-Luc Dehaene
1999–2008	VLD	Guy Verhofstadt
2008	CD&V	Yves Leterme
2008–09	CD&V	Herman Van Rompuy
2009–	CD&V	Yves Leterme

RECENT ELECTIONS

Elections to the 150-member Chamber of Representatives were held on 10 June 2007. The Christian Democratic and Flemish/New-Flemish Alliance (CD&V/N-VA) won 30 seats with 18·5% of votes cast; Reformist Movement (MR) won 23 seats (12·5%); Socialist Party (PS) won 20 seats (10·9%); Open Flemish Liberals and Democrats (Open Vld) won 18 seats (11·8%); Flemish Interest (VB) won 17 seats (12·0%); Socialist Party Alternative-Spirit (sp.a-spirit) won 14 seats (10·3%); the Humanist Democratic Centre (CDH) won 10 seats (6·1%); Ecolo won 8 seats (5·1%); List Dedecker won 5 seats (4·0%); Groen! won 4 seats (4·0%); and the National Front (FN) won 1 seat (2·0%). Turnout was 91·1%. A new government was eventually formed in March 2008.

Voting for the 40 electable seats in the Senate took place on the same day. CD&V/N-VA won 9 seats; MR won 6; Open Vld and VB, 5; PS and sp.a-spirit, 4; CDH and Ecolo, 2; and Groen!, List Dedecker and FN, 1. There are also 31 indirectly elected senators.

European Parliament

Belgium has 22 (24 in 2004) representatives. At the June 2009 elections turnout was 90·4% (90·8% in 2004). The CD&V won 3 seats with 14·4% of the vote (political affiliation in European Parliament: European People's Party); the Open Vld, 3 with 12·8% (Alliance of Liberals and Democrats for Europe); the PS, 3 with 10·9% (Progressive Alliance of Socialists and Democrats); the VB, 2 with 9·9% (non-attached); the MR, 2 with 9·7% (Alliance of Liberals and Democrats for Europe); Ecolo, 2 with 8·6% (Greens/European Free Alliance); sp.a, 2 with 8·2% (Progressive Alliance of Socialists and Democrats); the N-VA, 1 with 6·1% (Greens/European Free Alliance); the CDH, 1 with 5·0% (European People's Party); Groen!, 1 with 4·9% (Greens/European Free

Alliance); the LDD, 1 with 4·5% (European Conservatives and Reformists); the Christian-Social Party, 1 with 0·2% (European People's Party).

CURRENT ADMINISTRATION

In April 2010 the caretaker government comprised:

Prime Minister, in Charge of the Co-ordination of Immigration and Asylum Policy: Yves Leterme; b. 1960 (CD&V; sworn in 25 Nov. 2009, having previously been prime minister from March–Dec. 2008).

Deputy Prime Ministers: Didier Reynders (MR; also *Minister of Finance and Institutional Reform*); Laurette Onkelinx (PS; also *Minister of Social Affairs and Public Health and Minister in Charge of Social Integration*); Steven Vanackere (CD&V; also *Minister of Foreign Affairs and Institutional Reform*); Jöelle Milquet (CDH; also *Minister of Employment and Equal Opportunities and Minister in Charge of Immigration and Asylum Policy*); Guy Vanhengel (Open Vld; also *Minister of the Budget*).

Minister for Civil Service and Public Enterprises: Inge Vervotte (CD&V). *Climate and Energy:* Paul Magnette (PS). *Defence:* Pieter De Crem (CD&V). *Development Co-operation:* Charles Michel (MR). *Enterprise and Modernization of the Administration:* Vincent Van Quickenborne (Open Vld). *Interior:* Annemie Turtelboom (Open Vld). *Justice:* Stefaan De Clerck (CD&V). *Pensions and Urban Policy:* Michel Daerden (PS). *Small and Medium-Sized Enterprises, the Self-Employed, Agriculture and Scientific Policy:* Sabine Laruelle (MR).

Government Website: http://www.belgium.be

CURRENT LEADERS

Yves Leterme

Position
Prime Minister

Introduction
Yves Camille Désiré Leterme became prime minister of Belgium for the second time in Nov. 2009, replacing Herman Van Rompuy who had resigned to become the first president of the European Council. The Flemish Leterme is leader of the Christian Democratic and Flemish Party (CD&V) and a former minister-president of Flanders. He first served as prime minister from March to Dec. 2008.

Early Life
Yves Leterme was born in Wervik, West Flanders on 6 Oct. 1960. Brought up by his Dutch-speaking Flemish mother and French-speaking Walloon father, he is bilingual. He went to school in Ypres before graduating in law from the Catholic University of Leuven in 1981. After obtaining a BSc in political sciences from Ghent University, he earned an LLB in law and then a master's in public administration. In 1984 he also completed a postgraduate course at the International Centre for European Training.

After becoming involved in local youth politics, the Christian People's Party (CVP) invited Leterme to join them and in 1983 he became the chairman of the Youth-CVP Ypres group. He worked closely with the CVP for the next decade, supporting two CVP regional parliamentarians, acting as Ypres district CVP secretary (1985–87) and then serving as national vice-secretary (1989–91) and national secretary (1991–92). He worked at the Court of Audits for two years (1987–89) and in 1992 became a civil servant at the European Commission, where he stayed for five years. During this period he remained politically active, becoming a municipal councillor in 1995 and an MP in 1997. In 2001 he became head of the CD&V (ex-CVP) faction in the Chamber of Representatives and in 2003 he was elected party leader.

In 2004 Leterme was appointed minister-president of the Flemish government. There he made significant strides in eliminating the government's debt and introducing public-private partnerships as a means of boosting investment. Following the CD&V success in the June 2007 elections, King Albert invited Leterme to negotiate a coalition while Guy Verhofstadt remained as caretaker prime minister. Negotiations faltered over constitutional reforms aimed at devolving powers to the Dutch-, French- and German-speaking communities, with Leterme twice threatening to resign before talks finally failed. From Dec. 2007–March 2008 he served as minister of budget, transport, institutional reform and the North Sea (focusing on environmental issues).

Career in Office
Leterme finally assumed the premiership in March 2008, serving for nine months at the head of a five-party coalition. The central challenge he faced was pushing through reforms to allow greater independence for the separate language groups, most crucially in the Brussels-Halle-Vilvoorde region. His policy was widely rejected by the francophone community. Back in 2006 Leterme had angered parts of the Walloon community after a series of public relations blunders, including his comment that 'apparently the French speakers are intellectually not capable of learning Dutch'. He was subsequently caught out in an interview when he wrongly indentified the francophone Belgian national anthem. Nonetheless, his personal popularity remained high.

Leterme's failure to achieve a consensus on language reforms prompted him to offer his resignation in July 2008, which was refused by King Albert. In Sept. 2008, amid the worsening global economic climate, Belgium (together with the Netherlands and Luxembourg) agreed to inject funds into the ailing Fortis regional retail bank and (with France and Luxembourg) to rescue Dexia Bank, the world's biggest lender to local governments. The following month saw a nationwide strike over rising prices. On 19 Dec. 2008 Leterme again offered his resignation as a crisis grew over the sale of Fortis Bank to BNP Paribas, with shareholders taking the government to court over lack of consultation. His resignation, and that of the entire government, was accepted on 22 Dec. He remained in office until 30 Dec. 2008 when he was succeeded by Herman Van Rompuy, also of the CD&V.

In a cabinet reshuffle in July 2009 Leterme was named foreign minister. In this post he established bilateral relations with Vietnam, making it the only Asian country with preferential trade agreements with Belgium. Leterme became prime minister for a second time in Nov. 2009 after Van Rompuy was elected the first president of the European Council. Though he maintained his commitment to institutional reform, Leterme's main challenges were economic. In Jan. 2010 Opel revealed it was closing one of its factories and InBev announced a 10% workforce cut.

In April 2010 the Open Vld party withdrew from the ruling coalition causing the collapse of the government. Leterme remained in office as caretaker prime minister.

DEFENCE

Conscription was abolished in 1994 and the Armed Forces were restructured, with the aim of progressively reducing the size and making more use of civilian personnel. Since 1 Jan. 2002 they have been organized into one unified structure consisting of four main components: the Land Component (Army), Naval Component (Navy), Air Component (Air Force) and Medical Component.

In 2006 defence expenditure totalled US$4,428m. (US$427 per capita), representing 1·1% of GDP.

Army

The Land Component (formerly Army) has five 'capacities': the command capacity, the combat capacity, the support capacity, the services capacity and the training capacity. Total strength (2007) 12,571. In addition there are 2,040 reserves. All tracked vehicles are in the process of being phased out in favour of wheeled vehicles. The transition is scheduled to be completed by 2015.

Navy

The Naval Component (formerly Navy), based at Ostend and Zeebrugge, includes two frigates. Personnel (2007) totalled 1,605.

The naval air arm comprises three general utility helicopters.

Air Force

The Air Component (formerly Belgian Air Force) has a strength of (2007) 7,470 personnel. There are two tactical wings, based at Florennes and Kleine Brogel. Equipment in 2007 included 71 combat capable aircraft (Lockheed Martin F-16s), plus 44 helicopters.

INTERNATIONAL RELATIONS

Belgium is a member of the UN, World Bank, IMF and several other UN specialized agencies, WTO, EU, Council of Europe, WEU, OSCE, CERN, BIS, IOM, International Organization of the Francophonie, NATO, OECD, Inter-American Development Bank, Asian Development Bank and Antarctic Treaty. Belgium is a signatory to the Schengen accord abolishing border controls between Belgium, Austria, Czech Republic, Denmark, Estonia, Finland, France, Germany, Greece, Hungary, Iceland, Italy, Latvia, Lithuania, Luxembourg, Malta, Netherlands, Norway, Poland, Portugal, Slovakia, Slovenia, Spain, Sweden and Switzerland.

ECONOMY

Services contributed 75% of GDP in 2007, with industry accounting for 24% and agriculture 1%.

Overview

Belgium's open economy is closely linked with those of Germany, France and the Netherlands. These three countries account for 49% of Belgian exports. In recent years growth has outpaced key trading partners owing to strong household spending and residential investment, with the economy operating at near capacity. In 2007 the share of external trade in goods and services was 89% of GDP while trade in intermediate goods, distributed across neighbouring countries, accounted for 45% of trade. However, Belgium has lost export market share at approximately 1% per year over recent years as a result of the dominance of intermediate product exports such as chemicals and steel, which have lower structural growth than other products.

Inflexibilities in the labour market, including low labour mobility and wage inflexibility, have contributed to high unemployment. Labour utilization is low by OECD standards and, at 60·3% in 2006, the employment rate is the sixth lowest in the OECD. Employment is especially low for older workers (30·4% among people aged between 55 and 64), younger workers (26% among those aged between 15 and 24) and minorities. Employment for the rest of the prime-age population is close to international rates. Low employment rates among the young are predominantly found in the French community, reflecting poor education and high school drop-out rates. The unemployment rate of ethnic minorities is three times that of native Belgians, because of poorer education, language barriers and an inability to enforce anti-discrimination legislation. More than 60% of unemployed have been so for over two years and over 80% for at least one year. As a result of the economic downturn the unemployment rate is expected to increase from 7% in 2008 to 9% in the course of 2010.

In 2005 the government introduced the 'Generation Pact', a reform aimed at boosting employment. It limits the number of people taking early retirement in a bid to encourage employers to retain or hire older workers. In addition, cuts in social security contributions for the young and increased on-the-job training aim to increase employment opportunities for those entering the job market.

Economic activity slowed at the end of 2007 and in 2008, the result of low private consumption and investment as well as negative export growth stemming from the US sub-prime mortgage crisis. Bankruptcies increased by 12·5% year-on-year in Dec. 2008. The end of 2008 also saw a downturn in the manufacturing industry, although consumer confidence and activity in the trade and construction sectors was recovering slowly.

In Oct. 2008 the French bank BNP Paribas bailed out the Belgian part of Fortis, the Belgian-Dutch bank conglomerate, the Dutch part having been nationalized the same month. In Feb. 2009 Fortis shareholders voted against the sale of the bank to BNP Paribas and the Dutch government. A revised deal giving BNP Paribas a 75% stake in Fortis was approved by the Belgian government in March 2009.

After the severe downturn in 2008 and the early part of 2009, a slow recovery in GDP growth began in the third quarter of 2009 and is expected to continue through 2010, driven by a modest increase in private consumption and exports.

The OECD estimates that the old-age ratio will double by 2050, reducing economic growth and putting pressure on public finances. Since 2000 fiscal discipline has enabled a steady reduction in the public debt ratio. Public debt fell below 100% of GDP at the end of 2004 for the first time in 30 years and declined further to 84·2% in 2007. Loans and capital injections into financial institutions prompted debt to increase again in 2008, and it was predicted to reach 102% of GDP in 2010.

Currency

On 1 Jan. 1999 the euro (EUR) became the legal currency in Belgium at the irrevocable conversion rate of BEF40·3399 to EUR1. The euro, which consists of 100 cents, has been in circulation since 1 Jan. 2002. There are seven euro notes in different colours and sizes denominated in 500, 200, 100, 50, 20, 10 and 5 euros, and eight coins denominated in 2 and 1 euros, then 50, 20, 10, 5, 2 and 1 cents. On the introduction of the euro there was a 'dual circulation' period before the Belgian franc ceased to be legal tender on 28 Feb. 2002. Euro banknotes in circulation on 1 Jan. 2002 had a total value of €24·0bn.

Inflation rates (based on OECD statistics):

1999	*2000*	*2001*	*2002*	*2003*	*2004*	*2005*	*2006*	*2007*	*2008*
1·1%	2·7%	2·4%	1·6%	1·5%	1·9%	2·5%	2·3%	1·8%	4·5%

In Sept. 2009 gold reserves were 7·32m. troy oz and foreign exchange reserves US$8,060m. Total money supply was €97,656m. in Aug. 2009.

Budget

In 2005 central government revenue was €125,528m. (€120,136m. in 2004) and expenditure €126,142m. (€120,653m. in 2004). Principal sources of revenue in 2005: taxes on income, profits and capital gains, €46,518m.; social security contributions, €39,661m.; taxes on goods and services, €31,141m. Main items of expenditure by economic type in 2005: social benefits, €60,559m.; grants, €35,103m.; interest, €11,958m.

VAT is 21% (reduced rates, 12% and 6%).

Performance

Real GDP growth rates (based on OECD statistics):

1999	*2000*	*2001*	*2002*	*2003*	*2004*	*2005*	*2006*	*2007*	*2008*
3·5%	3·7%	0·8%	1·4%	0·8%	3·1%	2·0%	2·8%	2·8%	0·8%

Real GDP growth contracted by 3·0% in 2009 according to the National Bank of Belgium. Total GDP in 2008 was US$497·6bn.

Banking and Finance

The National Bank of Belgium was established in 1850. The *Governor*—Guy Quaden—was first appointed in 1999 for a five-year period; he was reappointed in 2004 and 2009. Its shares are listed on Euronext (Brussels).

The law of 22 Feb. 1998 has adapted the status of the National Bank of Belgium in view of the realization of the Economic and Monetary Union.

The National Bank of Belgium is within the ESCB-framework in charge of the issue of banknotes, the execution of exchange rate policy and monetary policy. Furthermore, it is the Bank of banks and the cashier of the federal state.

The law of 4 Dec. 1990 on financial transactions and financial markets defines the legal framework for collective investment institutions, the sole object of which is the collective investment of capital raised from the public. It transposes into Belgian legislation the European Directive of 20 Dec. 1985 on the co-ordination of laws, regulations and administrative provisions relating to undertakings for collective investment in transferable securities.

The law of 6 April 1995 relating to secondary markets, status and supervision of investment firms, intermediaries and investment consultants, provides the credit institutions with direct access to securities' stock exchanges. Stock exchange legislation was also subject to an important reform. The law fundamentally modifies the competitive environment and strengthens exercise conditions for securities' dealers.

On 30 June 2006, 103 credit institutions with a balance sheet totalling €1,150bn. were established in Belgium: 52 governed by Belgian law and 51 by foreign law. 372 collective investment institutions (152 Belgian and 220 foreign) were marketed in Belgium and supervised by the Banking, Finance and Insurance Commission; and 80 investment firms were operating in Belgium with the approval of the Banking, Finance and Insurance Commission.

There is a stock exchange (a component of Euronext) in Brussels. Euronext was created in Sept. 2000 through the merger of the Amsterdam, Brussels and Paris bourses.

ENERGY AND NATURAL RESOURCES

Environment

Belgium's carbon dioxide emissions from the consumption and flaring of fossil fuels were the equivalent of 14·9 tonnes per capita in 2008.

Electricity

The production of electricity amounted to 85·6bn. kWh in 2004; consumption per capita (2004) was 8,986 kWh. Installed capacity (2004) was 15·7m. kW. 55% of production in 2004 was nuclear-produced. Belgium had seven nuclear reactors in 2003.

Minerals

Belgium's mineral resources are very limited; the most abundantly occurring mineral is calcite.

Agriculture

There were, in 2006, 1,382,390 ha. under cultivation, of which 841,666 ha. were arable land. There were 49,850 farms in 2006.

	Area in ha.		*Produce in tonnes*	
Chief crops	*2005*	*2006*	*2005*	*2006*
Barley	39,965	49,008	301,647	367,348
Beet (fodder)	3,750	3,423	371,694	330,290
Beet (sugar)	85,527	82,912	5,983,173	5,666,621
Chicory	15,649	8,210	704,821	371,238
Maize (fodder)	163,825	161,178	7,745,553	6,600,738
Maize grain	54,256	56,500	634,088	575,898
Potatoes	64,952	67,267	2,780,865	2,592,820
Wheat	204,209	201,330	1,737,552	1,661,958

At the May 2006 agricultural census there were 6,294,904 pigs, 2,663,076 cattle, 153,976 sheep, 34,799 horses, 27,985 goats and 32,866,650 poultry.

Forestry

In 2005 forest covered 667,000 ha. (22·0% of the total land area). Timber production in 2007 was 4·95m. cu. metres.

Fisheries

In 2007 the fishing fleet had a total tonnage of 19,292 GRT. Total catch, 2005, 24,567 tonnes, almost entirely from marine waters.

INDUSTRY

The leading companies by market capitalization in March 2009 were: Anheuser-Busch InBev, a beverages company (US$44·1bn.); Groupe Bruxelles Lambert, a financial services company (US$11·0bn.); and Belgacom, a telecommunications company (US$10·6bn.).

Output, 2004 unless otherwise indicated, in 1,000 tonnes: distillate fuel oil, 12,327; crude steel (2006), 11,238; residual fuel oil, 8,380; cement (2006), 8,192; petrol, 5,789; sugar (2005), 3,394; beer (2006), 1,784·1m. litres; mineral water (2006), 1,066·8m. litres.

Labour

In 2002 (Labour Force Survey), 69,278 persons worked in the primary sector (agriculture, fishing and mining), 1,034,693 in the secondary sector (industry and construction) and 2,965,861 in the tertiary sector (services). The unemployment rate was 8·2% in Dec. 2009. In French-speaking Wallonia the rate is more than double that in Flemish-speaking Flanders. In 2006 the participation rate of the active population in the labour market was one of the lowest in the EU, at 60·3%.

Trade Unions

The main trade union organizations are the Confederation of Christian Trade Unions (CSC/ACV), the Belgian Socialist Confederation of Labour (FGTB/ABVV) and the Federation of Liberal Trade Unions of Belgium (CGSLB/ACLVB).

INTERNATIONAL TRADE

In 1922 the customs frontier between Belgium and Luxembourg was abolished; their foreign trade figures are amalgamated.

Imports and Exports

Imports and exports statistics (in €1m.):

	Imports	*Exports*
2002	168,392·1	178,760·6
2003	170,975·2	180,934·8
2004	188,874·8	197,062·5

Leading imports and exports (in €1m.):

	Imports		*Exports*	
	2003	*2004*	*2003*	*2004*
Machinery and appliances	29,893·4	31,372·5	25,906·4	27,395·3
Chemicals and pharmaceutical products	23,842·4	26,691·2	28,412·1	30,647·8
Transport equipment	22,554·4	25,435·8	26,913·9	29,047·0
Mineral products	19,515·0	24,042·2	12,555·1	14,731·2
Base metals	12,476·6	15,377·3	14,793·4	18,361·0
Plastics and rubber	10,114·4	11,100·5	15,408·6	17,270·1
Precious stones and precious metals	10,694·3	11,608·8	10,898·3	11,974·2
Food industry	7,328·6	7,466·9	9,150·5	9,562·5
Textile and textile articles	6,997·0	6,967·0	8,573·4	8,335·4
Paper and applications	4,911·3	4,882·1	4,852·9	5,009·3

Trade by selected countries (in €1m.):

	Imports from		*Exports to*	
	2003	*2004*	*2003*	*2004*
China	3,403·5	4,303·8	2,140·0	2,135·2
France	24,889·7	25,954·5	31,197·2	33,996·9
Germany	28,340·3	31,154·2	31,353·6	34,204·9
India	1,534·0	1,866·9	3,804·7	4,224·5

	Imports from		Exports to	
	2003	2004	2003	2004
Ireland	2,275·4	3,217·3	1,077·6	1,358·9
Israel	1,554·3	1,822·2	2,264·3	2,819·2
Italy	5,945·7	6,330·6	10,079·0	10,844·8
Japan	5,228·8	5,690·5	1,589·8	1,713·1
Luxembourg	1,304·9	1,628·5	3,980·3	4,555·0
Netherlands	33,096·0	37,380·5	23,232·2	25,549·9
Russia	2,093·6	2,912·1	1,217·3	1,514·5
Spain	3,848·1	4,146·4	7,454·5	8,017·9
Sweden	4,249·9	4,670·9	2,731·8	2,949·9
UK	14,883·5	14,973·3	16,232·2	17,125·0
USA	9,982·8	10,792·6	8,548·8	8,751·4

In 2004 other EU-member countries accounted for 77·2% of imports and 74·0% of exports.

Trade Fairs

Brussels ranks as the third most popular convention city behind Singapore and Paris according to the Union des Associations Internationales (UAI), hosting 2·7% of all international meetings held in 2008.

COMMUNICATIONS

Roads

Length of roads, 2006: motorways, 1,763 km; national roads, 12,585 km; secondary roads, 1,349 km; local roads, 136,559 km. Belgium has one of the densest road networks in the world. In 2007 there were 5,006,300 passenger cars in use, 29,000 buses and coaches, 696,700 lorries and vans, and 371,500 motorcycles and mopeds. Road accidents caused 1,089 fatalities in 2005 (1,486 in 2001).

Rail

The main Belgian lines were a State enterprise from their inception in 1834. In 1926 the Société Nationale des Chemins de Fer Belges (SNCB) was formed to take over the railways. In 2005 SNCB was divided into separate operating and infrastructure companies. The length of railway operated in 2005 was 3,696 km (electrified, 3,110 km). In 2003, 55·7m. tonnes of freight were carried; and, in 2005, 187m. passengers.

The regional transport undertakings Société Régionale Wallonne de Transport and Vlaamse Vervoermaatschappij operate tramways around Charleroi (20 km) and from De Panne to Knokke (55 km). There is also a metro and tramway in Brussels (175 km), and tramways in Antwerp (57 km) and Ghent (30 km).

Civil Aviation

The former national airline SABENA (*Société anonyme belge d'exploitation de la navigation aérienne*) was set up in 1923. However, in Nov. 2001 it filed for bankruptcy. Its successor, Delta Air Transport (DAT), a former SABENA subsidiary, was given a new identity in Feb. 2002 as SN Brussels Airlines. In Nov. 2006 SN Brussels Airlines merged with Virgin Express and since March 2007 has been trading under the name Brussels Airlines.

The busiest airport is Brussels National Airport (Zaventem), which handled 18,710,388 passengers in 2008 and 658,743 tonnes of freight. Charleroi is the second busiest airport in terms of passenger numbers and Liège the third busiest.

Shipping

In 2003 the merchant fleet comprised 17 vessels over 300 GRT. Total tonnage, 2002, 187,000 GRT. In 2004 vessels totalling 451,691,000 NRT entered ports and vessels totalling 444,956,000 NRT cleared. In 2002, 131,619,000 tonnes of cargo were handled at the port of Antwerp, with total container throughput 4,777,000 TEUs (twenty-foot equivalent units). Antwerp is Europe's second busiest port in terms of cargo handled after Rotterdam.

The length of navigable inland waterways was 1,516 km in 2004. 147·8m. tonnes of freight were carried on inland waterways in 2004.

Telecommunications

In 2008 there were 4,457,000 main (fixed) telephone lines. In the same year mobile phone subscribers numbered 11,822,000 (1,116·3 per 1,000 persons). There were 4·4m. PCs in use in 2006 and 7·3m. internet users in 2008. The broadband penetration rate in June 2008 was 26·4 subscribers per 100 inhabitants.

Postal Services

In 2007 there were 1,081 post offices and 286 post points. In 2001 a total of 3·7bn. items of mail were processed.

SOCIAL INSTITUTIONS

Justice

Judges are appointed for life. There is a court of cassation, five courts of appeal and assize courts for political and criminal cases. There are 27 judicial districts, each with a court of first instance. In each of the 222 cantons is a justice and judge of the peace. There are also various special tribunals. There is trial by jury in assize courts. The death penalty, which had been in abeyance for 45 years, was formally abolished in 1991.

The Gendarmerie ceased to be part of the Army in Jan. 1992.

The population in penal institutions in 2004 was 9,249 (89 per 100,000 of national population).

In Aug. 2003 a new act reformed war crimes legislation introduced in 1993 which allowed for charges to be brought against foreign nationals accused of abuses committed outside Belgian jurisdiction. The amendment requires that either accuser or defendant be a citizen of or resident in Belgium.

Education

Following the constitutional reform of 1988, education is the responsibility of the three Communities (the French Community, the Flemish Community and the German-speaking Community). Education is free and compulsory from the age of six to 18, although from 16 to 18 it may be part-time.

In 2007 there were 411,951 children and 29,550 teaching staff in pre-primary schools; 732,411 pupils and 65,378 teaching staff in primary schools; 825,293 pupils and (2006) 81,873 teaching staff in secondary schools; and 393,687 students and 26,298 academic staff in tertiary education. There were 16 universities and 73 non-university colleges and institutes in 2006–07. There are five royal academies of fine arts and six royal conservatoires at Brussels (one Flemish and one French), Liège, Ghent, Antwerp and Mons.

Public expenditure on education in 2005 amounted to 6·0% of GNI and represented 12·1% of total government expenditure.

The adult literacy rate is at least 99%.

Health

On 31 Dec. 2004 there were 41,730 physicians, 8,660 dentists and 11,620 pharmacists. There were 210 hospitals with 55,000 beds in 2007. Total health spending accounted for 10·3% of GDP in 2005. In Jan. 2000 the Belgian government agreed to decriminalize the use of cannabis. Euthanasia became legal on 24 Sept. 2002. The Belgian Chamber of Representatives had given its approval on 16 May 2002 to a measure adopted by the Senate on 26 Oct. 2001. Belgium was the second country to legalize euthanasia, after the Netherlands.

Welfare

Expenditure on social security, 2006: wage earners, €50,774·6m.; self employed, €3,858·9m. Expenditure on pensions, 2006: wage earners, €15,324·55m.; self employed, €2,192·28m.

The retirement age for men and women is 65. In 2005 the government announced plans to increase the early retirement age from 58 to 60 years of age. The move met with opposition from trade unions. A full pension is 60% of average lifetime earnings (75% for married couples). Based on size and sustainability of payments, a report by Aon Consulting in Nov. 2005 rated Belgium as the country with the worst pensions system of the 15 pre-expansion EU countries.

RELIGION

There is full religious liberty, and part of the income of the ministers of all denominations is paid by the State. In 2001 there were 8·31m. Roman Catholics. Numbers of clergy, 1996: Roman Catholic, 3,899; Protestant, 84; Anglican, 9; Jews, 26; Greek Orthodox, 39. There are eight Roman Catholic dioceses subdivided into 260 deaneries. In Feb. 2010 there was one cardinal. The Protestant (Evangelical) Church is under a synod. There is also a Central Jewish Consistory, a Central Committee of the Anglican Church and a Free Protestant Church.

CULTURE

World Heritage Sites

Belgium has ten sites which have been included on the UNESCO world heritage list. They are: the Flemish Beguinages (1998); the four lifts on the Canal du Centre and their environs (1998); La Grand Place in Brussels (1998); the historic centre of Bruges (2000); the major town houses of the architect Victor Horta in Brussels (2000); the Neolithic flint mines at Spiennes (2000); Notre Dame cathedral in Tournai (2000); the Plantin-Moretus Museum, a Renaissance printing and publishing house (2005); and Stoclet House in Brussels, a house designed by artists of the Vienna Secession movement (2009).

Belgium shares the belfries of Belgium and France (1999 and 2005) with France.

Broadcasting

Broadcasting is organized according to Belgium's language communities: VRT, RTBF and BRF provide public radio and television services in Dutch, French and German respectively. VRT has five radio networks and three TV stations; in July 2000 it started a new branch, e-VRT, responsible for the organization and development of a multimedia e-service platform and e-service network in Flanders. RTBF has five radio and three TV stations, and BRF transmits one TV and three radio services. Commercial TV networks include VTM (Dutch language), VT4 (Dutch) and RTL (French). Cable TV services are available to about 95% of the population. Number of TV receivers: 6·1m. (2006). TV colour is by PAL.

Cinema

In 2008 there were 491 cinemas, with an annual attendance of 21·9m.; gross box office receipts came to €128·0m.

Press

In 2002 there were 28 daily newspapers with a combined circulation of 1,479,000, at a rate of 143 per 1,000 inhabitants. Belgium's biggest-selling national daily is Het Laatste Nieuws, with an average daily circulation of 288,000 copies in 2006. The newspaper with the second highest circulation is the free Metro.

Tourism

In 2006, 29,372,011 tourist nights were spent in 3,485 establishments in accommodation for 367,866 persons. The number of overnight stays in 2006 accounted for by leisure, holiday and recreation was 22,611,797, with 3,622,212 for congresses and conferences, and 3,138,002 for other business purposes. Total number of tourists was 11,800,974 (8,372,294 leisure, 1,938,469 conference and 1,490,211 for other business purposes).

DIPLOMATIC REPRESENTATIVES

Of Belgium in the United Kingdom (17 Grosvenor Cres., London, SW1X 7EE)
Ambassador: Jean-Michel Veranneman de Watervliet.

Of the United Kingdom in Belgium (Av. d'Auderghem 10, Oudergemlaan, 1040 Brussels)
Ambassador: Dr Rachel Aron.

Of Belgium in the USA (3330 Garfield St., NW, Washington, D.C., 20008)
Ambassador: Jan Matthysen.

Of the USA in Belgium (Blvd du Régent 27, 1000 Brussels)
Ambassador: Howard. W. Gutman.

Of Belgium to the United Nations
Ambassador: Jan Grauls.

Of Belgium to the European Union
Permanent Representative: Jean De Ruyt.

FURTHER READING

The Institut National de Statistique. *Statistiques du commerce extérieur* (monthly). *Bulletin de Statistique.* Bi-monthly. *Annuaire Statistique de la Belgique* (from 1870).—*Annuaire statistique de poche* (from 1965).

Service Fédéral d'Information. *Guide de l'Administration Fédérale.* Occasional

Deprez, K., and Vos, L., *Nationalism in Belgium—Shifting Identities, 1780–1995.* 1998

Deschouwer, Kris, *The Politics of Belgium: Governing a Divided Society.* 2009

Fitzmaurice, J., *The Politics of Belgium: a Unique Federalism.* 1996

Hermans, T. J., *et al.*, (eds.) *The Flemish Movement: a Documentary History.* 1992

Witte, Els, *Political History of Belgium from 1830 Onwards.* 2000

National Statistical Office: Institut National de Statistique, Rue de Louvain 44, 1000 Brussels.
Service Fédérale d'Information: POB 3000, 1040 Brussels 4.
Website: http://statbel.fgov.be

BELIZE

Capital: Belmopan
Population estimate, 2010: 313,000
GDP per capita, 2007: (PPP$) 6,734
HDI/world rank: 0·772/93

KEY HISTORICAL EVENTS

Evidence of farming settlements at Cuello in northern Belize dates to around 2000 BC. Over the following centuries Mayan towns and villages encompassed Belize, Mexico's Yucatán peninsula and much of Guatemala. The city of Caracol, near Belize's border with Guatemala, is estimated to have spread over 140 sq. km, with some 180,000 residents at its height in the 7th century AD. However, the Mayan civilization declined rapidly after 900 AD for reasons that are still unclear (construction of the great pyramid temples ceased, literacy was abandoned and subsistence farming returned).

By 1525 the Spanish adventurer, Hernán Cortés, established a base in Honduras. Melchor and Alonso Pacheco took control of land around Tipu in southern Belize from 1543, which became nominally part of the Spanish Empire. However, Spanish control was limited and Tipu became a centre of Mayan resistance in the late 1630s. By the 1640s British buccaneers were staging attacks on Spanish ships from natural havens along Belize's coast. Some established settlements and traded logwood (then used in dyes). They were later joined by demobilized British soldiers and sailors, after the capture of Jamaica from Spain in 1655.

Spanish forces attempted to expel the British settlers during the 18th century until the defeat of the commander of Yucatán, Arturo O'Neill, at the Battle of St George's Caye in 1798. Belize was part of Britain's 'informal empire' during the 18th century. Logwood and mahogany were harvested by slaves, with British Honduras, as it was known, a focal point for Central American trade until the Panama railway was completed in 1855. In 1862 British Honduras was declared a British colony with a legislative assembly and a lieutenant-governor under the governor of Jamaica. The administrative connection with Jamaica was severed in 1884.

Belize's small economy was hit hard by the Great Depression in the 1930s and the capital, Belize City, was laid waste by a hurricane in Sept. 1931. Widespread protests over unemployment and poor living conditions in the mid-1930s were led by Antonio Soberanis Gómez. The establishment of the General Workers' Union became one of the foundations of Belize's nationalist movement after the Second World War. The People's United Party (PUP), formed in 1950, became the dominant political force under George Price. Universal suffrage was introduced in 1964 and thereafter the majority of the legislature were elected rather than appointed.

The road to independence from Britain was complicated by turbulent relations with Guatemala, which had long claimed Belize as its territory. Price rejected calls for an 'associated state' of Guatemala and full independence was achieved on 21 Sept. 1981, prompting Guatemala to threaten war. Price served as Belize's first prime minister but his party was defeated by the United Democratic Party (UDP) under Manuel Esquivel in Dec. 1984. Guatemala officially recognized Belize as an independent sovereign nation in Sept. 1991 but a border dispute rumbled on, remaining unresolved at the time of Dean Barrow's election as prime minister in Feb. 2008, following a landslide victory for the UDP.

TERRITORY AND POPULATION

Belize is bounded in the north by Mexico, west and south by Guatemala and east by the Caribbean. Fringing the coast there are three atolls and some 400 islets (cays) in the world's second longest barrier reef (140 miles), which was declared a world heritage site in 1996. Area, 22,964 sq. km.

There are six districts as follows, with area, population and chief city:

District	*Area (in sq. km)*	*Population 2007 (estimate)*	*Chief City*	*Population 2007 (estimate)*
Belize	4,204	93,200	Belize City	63,700
Cayo	5,338	73,300	San Ignacio/ Santa Elena	18,300
Corozal	1,860	36,400	Corozal	9,100
Orange Walk	4,737	47,100	Orange Walk	16,000
Stann Creek	2,176	32,200	Dangriga	11,600
Toledo	4,649	29,300	Punta Gorda	5,300

Population (2000 census), 240,204 (121,278 males); density, 10·5 per sq. km. 2007 official estimate: 311,500. The United Nations population estimate for 2007 was 295,000.

The UN gives an estimated population for 2010 of 313,000.

In 2007, 51·0% of the population were urban.

The capital is Belmopan (2007 estimated population, 16,400).

English is the official language. Spanish is widely spoken. In 2000 the main ethnic groups were Mestizo (Spanish-Maya), 48·7%; Creole (African descent), 24·9%; Mayans, 10·6%; and Garifuna (Caribs), 6·1%.

SOCIAL STATISTICS

2004 births (est.), 8,100; deaths (est.), 1,300. In 2004 (est.) the birth rate per 1,000 was 27·7 and the death rate 4·6; infant mortality in 2005 was 15 per 1,000 live births; there were 2,020 marriages in 2004. Life expectancy in 2007 was 74·2 years for males and 78·0 for females. Annual population growth rate, 2000–05, 3·1%; fertility rate, 2004, 3·1 children per woman.

CLIMATE

A tropical climate with high rainfall and small annual range of temperature. The driest months are Feb. and March. Belize City, Jan. 74°F (23·3°C), July 81°F (27·2°C). Annual rainfall 76" (1,890 mm).

CONSTITUTION AND GOVERNMENT

The head of state is the British sovereign, represented by an appointed Governor-General. The Constitution, which came into force on 21 Sept. 1981, provided for a National Assembly, with a five-year term, comprising a 31-member *House of Representatives* elected by universal suffrage, and a *Senate* consisting of 12 members, six appointed by the Governor-General on the advice of the Prime Minister, three on the advice of the Leader of the Opposition, one on the advice of the Belize Council of Churches and the Evangelical Association of Churches, one on the advice of the Belize Chamber of Commerce and Industry and the Belize Business Bureau and one on the advice of the National Trade Union Congress of Belize and the Civil Society Steering Committee.

National Anthem

'O, Land of the Free'; words by S. A. Haynes, tune by S. W. Young.

RECENT ELECTIONS

In elections to the House of Representatives held on 7 Feb. 2008 the opposition United Democratic Party won 25 of 31 seats with 56·6% of votes cast and the People's United Party 6 with 40·7%. Turnout was 74·5%.

CURRENT ADMINISTRATION

Governor-General: Sir Colville Young, GCMG; b. 1932 (sworn in 17 Nov. 1993).

In March 2010 the cabinet comprised as follows:

Prime Minister and Minister for Finance: Dean Barrow; b. 1951 (UDP; sworn in 8 Feb. 2008).

Deputy Prime Minister and Minister of Natural Resources and the Environment: Gaspar Vega. *Agriculture and Fisheries:* Rene Montero. *Attorney General and Minister of Foreign Affairs and Foreign Trade:* Wilfred Elrington. *Communications, Transport, Public Utilities and National Emergency Management:* Melvin Hulse. *Economic Development, Commerce, Industry and Consumer Protection:* Erwin Contreras. *Education:* Patrick Faber. *Health:* Pablo Marin. *Housing and Urban Development:* Michael Finnegan. *Human Development and Social Transformation:* Eden Martinez. *Labour, Local Government and Rural Development:* Gabriel Martinez. *National Security:* Carlos Perdomo. *Public Service, Governance Improvement, and Elections and Boundaries:* John Saldivar. *Tourism, Civil Aviation and Culture:* Manuel Heredia. *Works:* Anthony Martinez. *Youth, Sports, Information and Broadcasting:* Elvin Penner.

Government Website: http://www.belize.gov.bz

CURRENT LEADERS

Dean Barrow

Position
Prime Minister

Introduction
Dean Barrow, leader of the United Democratic Party (UDP), won a landslide victory in the Feb. 2008 general election to become Belize's first black prime minister. He took office promising to root out corruption, reduce crime and reform the faltering economy.

Early Life
Dean Barrow was born on 2 March 1951 in Belize City and was educated at St Michael's College. He studied law at the University of the West Indies, Barbados, and the Norman Manley Law School in Kingston, Jamaica. He entered the legal profession in 1975, joining his uncle Dean Lindo's Church Street Chambers in Belize City and becoming a partner in 1977. In the early 1980s he completed a Masters in international relations at the University of Miami.

In 1983 Barrow was elected to Belize City council. He successfully contested the Dec. 1984 general election for the UDP, winning the Queen's Square division. He was appointed attorney general and minister of foreign affairs, serving until 1989 when the UDP lost office. In 1989 Barrow set up with Rodwell Williams the law firm Barrow & Williams which has acted for influential clients including the Belize Bank and Belize Telecommunications Ltd (BTL). In 1990 Barrow became deputy leader of the UDP.

With the UDP victory at the 1993 general election, Barrow returned to his previous posts of attorney general and minister of foreign affairs but also took on responsibility for the national security, immigration and nationality, and media portfolios. This concentration of power attracted some criticism. In 1998, after the UDP lost all but three seats in the general election, Barrow became party head and oversaw the securing of seven seats in the 2003 election.

In opposition, Barrow argued for greater transparency in public finances and advocated building public infrastructure. In the Feb. 2008 general election the UDP upset predictions of a close result to win 25 out of 31 seats. Barrow took office as prime minister on 8 Feb. 2008 and on 11 Feb. announced his new cabinet with himself as minister of finance.

Career in Office
Barrow's early months in office were dominated by investigations into a financial scandal inherited from the previous administration, involving the alleged misuse of US$20m. of overseas grants. With politicians, the Belize Bank and a health care company all implicated, Barrow requested US assistance to set up an audit. Among Barrow's other major challenges are the revitalization of the economy, reducing high levels of crime and implementing a programme to build houses, roads and health centres.

DEFENCE

The Belize Defence Force numbers around 1,050 (2007) with 700 reservists. There is an Air Wing and a Maritime Wing.

In 2006 defence expenditure totalled US$18m. (US$63 per capita), representing 1·5% of GDP.

INTERNATIONAL RELATIONS

Belize is a member of the UN, World Bank, IMF and several other UN specialized agencies, WTO, Commonwealth, IOM, ACS, CARICOM, Inter-American Development Bank, SELA, OAS and is an ACP member state of the ACP-EU relationship.

ECONOMY

In 2006 agriculture accounted for 14·0% of GDP, industry 21·0% and services 65·0%.

Overview

Belize is classified as an upper middle-income country by the World Bank. In 2002, 33·5% of the population was living below the poverty line.

The largest industries by output are garment production, food processing, tourism, construction and oil. Since oil was discovered in 2005, crude petroleum has become a major export, contributing 40% of overall export earnings in 2008. Other exports include marine products, sugar, citrus fruits, bananas and papayas.

Agriculture accounts for 71% of total foreign exchange earnings. Efforts are being made to diversify the sector and to encourage industrial development. A Commercial Free Zone established in 1994 has seen FDI substantially increase since 2000. In Feb. 2007 the country restructured 98% of its external debt, worth around US$900m., but debt remains a concern.

Two tropical storms in 2008 caused damage to agriculture and infrastructure valued at 4·8% of GDP. The IMF approved US$6·9m. in early 2009 to aid economic recovery, to be repaid within 3¼–5 years.

Currency
The unit of currency is the *Belize dollar* (BZD) of 100 *cents*. Since 1976 \$B2 has been fixed at US\$1. Total money supply was \$B463m. in July 2005 and foreign exchange reserves were US\$101m. There was inflation of 4·2% in 2006, 2·3% in 2007 and 6·4% in 2008.

Budget
Revenues in 2006–07 were \$B598·0m. and expenditures \$B667·9m. Tax revenues accounted for 85·9% of total revenues; current expenditure accounted for 84·1% of total expenditures.

Performance
Real GDP growth was 4·7% in 2006, 1·2% in 2007 and 3·8% in 2008. Total GDP in 2008 was US\$1·4bn.

Banking and Finance
A Central Bank was established in 1981 (*Governor*, Glenford Ysaguirre) and in 2001 had deposits of \$B148m. There were (2001) one development bank and six other banks.

ENERGY AND NATURAL RESOURCES

Environment
Carbon dioxide emissions from the consumption and flaring of fossil fuels in Belize were the equivalent of 3·3 tonnes per capita in 2008.

Electricity
Installed capacity in 2004 was an estimated 48,000 kW. Production was approximately 169m. kWh in 2004 and consumption per capita about 707 kWh.

Oil and Gas
Oil was discovered in 2005 after several years of exploration, although additional testing will be required to determine the commercial viability of the site.

Agriculture
In 2005 there were 70,000 ha. of arable land and 32,000 ha. of permanent crops. Output, 2006 (in 1,000 tonnes): sugarcane, 1,192; oranges, 212; bananas, 87. Livestock (2001): cattle, 56,000; pigs, 28,000; horses, 5,000; mules, 4,000; chickens, 1m.

Forestry
In 2005, 1,653,000 ha. (72·5% of the total land area) were under forests. Timber production in 2007 was 711,000 cu. metres.

Fisheries
In 2007 there were five registered fishing co-operatives. The total catch in 2006 amounted to 7,790 tonnes, exclusively from sea fishing.

INDUSTRY
Manufacturing is mainly confined to processing agricultural products and timber. There is also a clothing industry. Sugar production in 2006 was 113,000 tonnes; molasses, 42,000 tonnes.

Labour
In 2004 the economically active labour force totalled 180,030; the unemployment rate in 2004 was 11·6%.

Trade Unions
There were ten accredited unions in 2006.

INTERNATIONAL TRADE
External debt was US\$1,057m. in 2007.

Imports and Exports
Imports (f.o.b.) in 2006 totalled US\$660·4m.; exports (f.o.b.) in 2006 amounted to US\$268·2m. Main imports in 2006 were: machinery and transport equipment (17%), mineral fuels and lubricants (16%), manufactured goods (12%) and food and live animals (9%); main exports were citrus concentrate (20%), sugar (19%), crude petroleum (17%) and marine products (16%). The USA is by far the leading trading partner, in 2003 accounting for 46·2% of imports and 56·4% of exports.

COMMUNICATIONS

Roads
In 2006 there were 575 km of main roads and 2,432 km of other roads. There were 40,000 passenger cars in use in 2006 and 14,800 trucks and vans. In 2004 there were 56 deaths as a result of road accidents.

Civil Aviation
There is an international airport (Philip S. W. Goldson) in Belize City. The national carrier is Maya Island Air, which in 2003 operated domestic services and international flights to Flores (Guatemala). There were direct flights in 2003 with other airlines to Boston, Charlotte, Dallas, Houston, Indianapolis, Las Vegas, McAllen, Miami, Montego Bay, New York, Raleigh, San Pedreo Sula, San Salvador and Washington, D.C. In 2001 Philip S. W. Goldson International handled 497,464 passengers (364,711 on international flights).

Shipping
The main port is Belize City, with a modern deep-water port able to handle containerized shipping. There are also ports at Commerce Bight and Big Creek. In 2002 the merchant marine totalled 1,473,000 GRT, including oil tankers 236,000 GRT. Nine cargo shipping lines serve Belize, and there are coastal passenger services to the offshore islands and Guatemala.

Telecommunications
Telephone subscribers numbered 126,400 in 2005, or 468·0 per 1,000 inhabitants, with 93,100 mobile telephone subscribers. There were 43,000 PCs in use in 2006 and 34,000 internet users in 2008.

Postal Services
In 2003 there were 136 post offices.

SOCIAL INSTITUTIONS

Justice
Each of the six judicial districts has summary jurisdiction courts (criminal) and district courts (civil), both of which are presided over by magistrates. There is a Supreme Court, a Court of Appeal and a Family Court. There is a Director of Public Prosecutions, a Chief Justice and two Puisne Judges. Belize was one of ten countries to sign an agreement in Feb. 2001 establishing a Caribbean Court of Justice to replace the British Privy Council as the highest civil and criminal court. In the meantime the number of signatories has risen to twelve. The court was inaugurated at Port-of-Spain, Trinidad on 16 April 2005.

The population in penal institutions in 2008 was 1,334 (455 per 100,000 of national population). Belize's prison population rate ranks in the top ten in the world.

Education
The adult literacy rate was 76·9% in 2003 (76·7% among males and 77·1% among females). Education is in English. State education is managed jointly by the government and the Roman Catholic and Anglican Churches. It is compulsory for children between five and 14 years and primary education is free, although there are plans to raise the leaving age to 16 by 2015. In 2003–04 there were 63,282 pupils at primary schools and 16,150 at secondary schools. There are two government-maintained special schools for disabled children. There is a teachers' training college. The University College of Belize opened in 1986. The University of the West Indies maintains an extramural department in Belize City.

In 2003 public expenditure on education came to 5·2% of GDP and 18·1% of total government spending.

Health

In 2006 there were 11 hospitals with 12 beds per 10,000 persons. There were 263 physicians, 12 dentists, 441 nurses and 46 pharmacists. Medical services in rural areas are provided by health care centres and mobile clinics.

RELIGION

In 2001, 58% of the population was Roman Catholic and 34% Protestant.

CULTURE

World Heritage Sites

The Belize Barrier Reef Reserve System was inscribed on the UNESCO World Heritage List in 1996.

Broadcasting

State-run radio broadcasting was privatized in 1998 heralding a range of commercial stations. There are also private television services (colour by NTSC), including cable TV in urban areas and satellite links. There were 120,000 TV sets in 2005.

Press

There are no daily newspapers although there were ten non-dailies in 2006, the largest of which were *The Amandala Press* and *The Reporter*.

Tourism

In 2008 there were 842,396 visitors of which 245,026 stayed overnight and 597,370 arrived on cruise ships. Tourism expenditure came to US$204m. in 2005 (excluding passenger transport). There were 561 hotels and 5,789 hotel rooms in 2006.

Festivals

The Belize Carnival is celebrated in the week before Lent begins, with particularly extravagant celebrations in San Pedro. There is also a series of Lobsterfests (at which lobsters prepared in many different ways are consumed) held at different venues throughout June and July. 10 Sept. is St George's Caye Day, held in memory of the defeat of Spanish forces in 1798 and including a battle re-enactment. National Independence Day follows on 21 Sept.

DIPLOMATIC REPRESENTATIVES

Of Belize in the United Kingdom (3rd Floor, 45 Crawford Place, London, W1H 4LP)
High Commissioner: Kamela Palma.

Of the United Kingdom in Belize (PO Box 91, Belmopan, Belize)
High Commissioner: Pat Ashworth.

Of Belize in the USA (2535 Massachusetts Ave., NW, Washington, D.C., 20008)
Ambassador: Nestor Mendez.

Of the USA in Belize (Floral Park Rd, Belmopan, Cayo)
Ambassador: Vinai Thummalapally.

Of Belize to the United Nations
Ambassador: Vacant.
Chargé d'Affaires a.i.: Janine Coye-Felson.

Of Belize to the European Union
Ambassador: Audrey Joy Grant.

FURTHER READING

Leslie, Robert, (ed.) *A History of Belize: Nation in the Making.* 2nd ed. 1995

Shoman, Assad, *Thirteen Chapters of a History of Belize.* 1994

Sutherland, Anne, *The Making of Belize: Globalization in the Margins.* 1998

Twigg, Alan, *Understanding Belize: A Historical Guide.* 2006

National Statistical Office: Central Statistical Office, Corner Culvert Rd and Mountain View Blvd, Belmopan.
Website: http://www.statisticsbelize.org.bz

BENIN

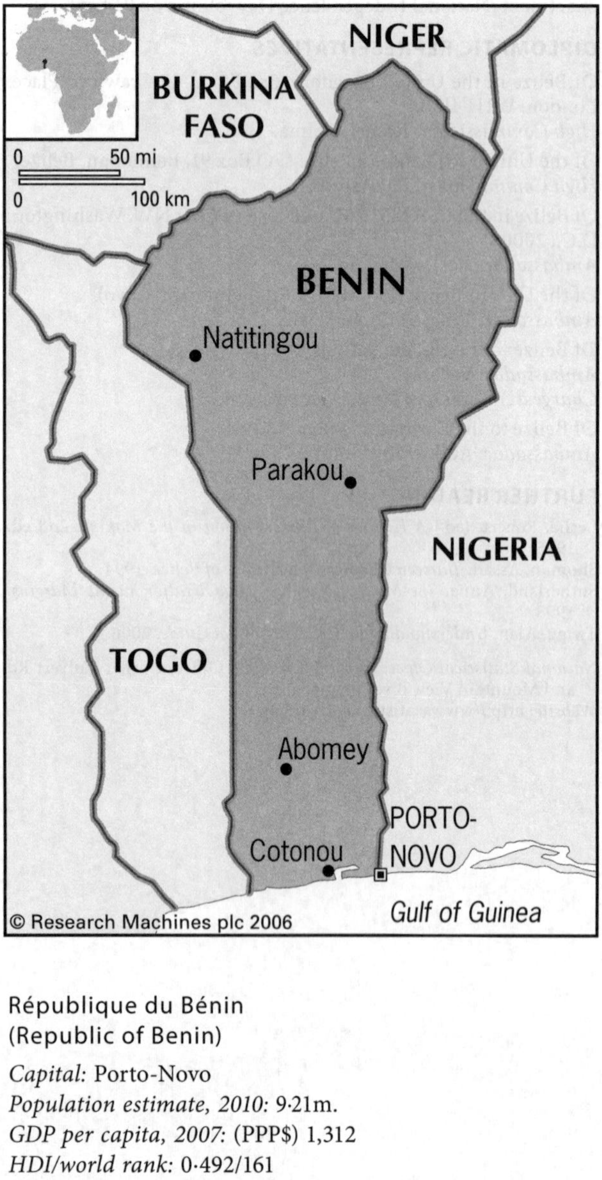

République du Bénin
(Republic of Benin)

Capital: Porto-Novo
Population estimate, 2010: 9·21m.
GDP per capita, 2007: (PPP$) 1,312
HDI/world rank: 0·492/161

KEY HISTORICAL EVENTS

The People's Republic of Benin is the former Republic of Dahomey. Dahomey was a powerful, well-organized state from the 17th century, trading extensively in slaves through the port of Whydah with the Portuguese, British and French. On the coast an educated African elite was established in the 19th century.

After the defeat of Dahomey, and the abolition of the monarchy, the French occupied territory inland up to the River Niger and created the colony of Dahomey as part of French West Africa. Protest against French rule grew after the Second World War.

After Dahomey became independent on 1 Aug. 1960 civilian government was interrupted by long periods of military rule. In Oct. 1972 Gen. Mathieu Kérékou seized power and installed a new left-wing regime committed to socialist policies. A constitution was adopted in 1977, based on a single Marxist-Leninist party, the *Parti de la Révolution Populaire du Bénin* (PRPB). Benin is beset with economic problems, factional fighting and frequent plots to overthrow the regime.

TERRITORY AND POPULATION

Benin is bounded in the east by Nigeria, north by Niger and Burkina Faso, west by Togo and south by the Gulf of Guinea. The area is 112,622 sq. km, and the population (census 2002) 6,769,914; density, 60·1 per sq. km. The United Nations population estimate for 2002 was 7,113,000.

The UN gives an estimated population for 2010 of 9·21m.

In 2005, 59·9% of the population were rural.

The areas and populations of the 12 departments are as follows:

Department	*Sq. km*	*Census 2002*	*Department*	*Sq. km*	*Census 2002*
Alibori	25,683	521,093	Donga	10,691	350,062
Atacora	20,459	549,417	Littoral	79	665,100
Atlantique	3,233	801,683	Mono	1,396	360,037
Borgou	25,310	724,171	Ouémé	2,835	730,772
Collines	13,561	535,923	Plateau	1,865	407,116
Couffo	2,404	524,586	Zou	5,106	599,954

Major towns, with 2002 census population: Cotonou, 665,100; Porto-Novo, 223,552; Parakou, 149,819; Bohicon, 65,974; Abomey, 59,672.

In 1992 the main ethnic groups numbered (in 1,000): Fon, 1,930; Yoruba, 590; Adja, 540; Aizo, 420; Bariba, 420; Somba, 320; Fulani, 270. The official language is French. Over half the people speak Fon.

SOCIAL STATISTICS

2006 (estimates) births, 303,000; deaths, 79,000. Rates, 2006 estimates (per 1,000 population): births, 38·7; deaths, 10·1. Infant mortality, 2005 (per 1,000 live births), 89. Expectation of life in 2007 was 59·8 years for males and 62·1 for females. Annual population growth rate, 1994–2004, 3·2%. Fertility rate, 2004, 5·7 children per woman.

CLIMATE

In coastal parts there is an equatorial climate, with a long rainy season from March to July and a short rainy season in Oct. and Nov. The dry season increases in length from the coast, with inland areas having rain only between May and Sept. Porto-Novo, Jan. 82°F (27·8°C), July 78°F (25·6°C). Annual rainfall 52" (1,300 mm). Cotonou, Jan. 81°F (27·2°C), July 77°F (25°C). Annual rainfall 53" (1,325 mm).

CONSTITUTION AND GOVERNMENT

The Benin Party of Popular Revolution (PRPB) held a monopoly of power from 1977 to 1989.

In Feb. 1990 a 'National Conference of the Active Forces of the Nation' proclaimed its sovereignty and appointed Nicéphore Soglo prime minister of a provisional government. At a referendum in Dec. 1990, 93·2% of votes cast were in favour of the new constitution, which introduced a presidential regime. The *President* is directly elected for renewable five-year terms. Parliament is the unicameral *National Assembly* of 83 members elected by proportional representation for four-year terms.

A 30-member advisory *Social and Economic Council* was set up in 1994. There is a *Constitutional Court.*

National Anthem

'L'Aube Nouvelle' ('The Dawn of a New Day'); words and tune by Gilbert Dagnon.

RECENT ELECTIONS

Presidential elections were held in two rounds on 5 and 19 March 2006. In the first round Yayi Boni (ind.) won 35·6% of the vote, former prime minister Adrien Houngbédji (Democratic Renewal Party) 24·1%, Bruno Amoussou (Social Democratic Party) 16·2% and Léhadi Vinagnon Soglo (Renaissance Party of Benin) 8·4%. There were a further 22 candidates. In the second round Boni won 74·5% of the vote against Houngbédji with 25·5%. Turnout in the first round was 76·9% and in the second round 69·5%.

Parliamentary elections were held on 31 March 2007. The Cauri Forces for an Emerging Benin, a coalition supporting President Yayi Boni, won 35 of 83 seats; the Alliance for Dynamism and Democracy, 20; the Democratic Renewal Party, 10; the Key Force, 4; the Union for Relief, 3; the Alliance for Revival, 2; the Coalition for an Emerging Benin, 2; Hope Force, 2; the National Union for Democracy and Progress, 2; the Alliance of the Forces of Progress, 1; the Party for Democracy and Social Progress, 1; and Restore the Hope, 1. Turnout was 58·7%.

CURRENT ADMINISTRATION

President: Yayi Boni; b. 1953 (ind.; sworn in 6 April 2006).

In March 2010 the government comprised:

Minister of State for Economic Forecasting, Development and Evaluation of Public Actions: Pascal Koupaki. *Minister of State for National Defence:* Issifou Kogui N'Douro.

Minister of Administrative and Institutional Reform: Joseph Ahanhanzo. *Agriculture, Husbandry and Fisheries:* Grégoire Akofodji. *Commerce:* Christine Ouinsavi. *Culture, Literacy and Promotion of National Languages:* Ganiou Soglo. *Decentralization, Local Government and Regional Planning:* Alassane Séïdou. *Economy and Finance:* Idrissou Daouda. *Energy and Water Resources:* Sacca Lafia. *Environment and Natural Protection:* Justin Adanmaï. *Family and Solidarity:* Mamatou Marie Joe Meba Bio Djossou. *Foreign Affairs, African Integration, Francophonie Affairs and Beninese Abroad:* Jean-Marie Ehouzou. *Handicrafts and Tourism:* Bako Mamata Djaouga. *Health:* Issifou Takpara. *Higher Education and Scientific Research:* François Abiola. *Industry:* Roger Dovonou. *Interior and Public Security:* Armand Zinzindohoué. *Justice, Legislation, Government Spokesperson, Human Rights and Keeper of the Seals:* Victor Topanou. *Labour and Civil Service:* Charles Kint Aguia. *Microfinance, and Youth and Women's Employment:* Rékya Madougou. *Petroleum and Mineral Research:* Barthélémy Kassa. *Pre-school and Primary Education:* Chabi Félicien Zachari. *Relations with Institutions:* Zakari Baba Body. *Secondary, Professional and Technical Education:* Bernard Lani Davo. *Small and Medium-Sized Enterprises and Promotion of the Private Sector:* Léandre Houage. *Urban Development, Housing, Land Reform and Coastal Erosion Prevention:* François Noudegbessi. *Youth, Sports and Leisure:* Étienne Kossi.

Government Website (French only): http://www.gouv.bj

CURRENT LEADERS

Yayi Boni

Position
President

Introduction
Yayi Boni, a former banker with little political experience and no party backing, won a run-off for the presidency by a landslide and was sworn in on 6 April 2006. He succeeded Gen. Mathieu Kérékou, who led the country for 30 of the 34 years following independence.

Early Life
Yayi Boni was born in 1952 in Tchaourou, northern Dahomey, then part of French West Africa. He attended schools in Tchaourou and Parakou, before studying economics at the National University of Benin and then banking and finance at the University of Dakar, Senegal. Boni later read politics and economics at the University of Orléans, France, and received a PhD in economics from Université Paris Dauphine in 1991.

Having worked at the Commercial Bank of Benin for two years, Boni joined the Central Bank of the States of West Africa in 1977. By the time he left in 1989, he was the organization's deputy director. Following a three-year spell as deputy director for professional development at the West African Centre for Banking Studies in Dakar, Boni returned to Benin as an adviser to President Nicéphore Soglo on banking and monetary policy.

Boni was appointed president of the Togo-based West African Development Bank in 1994 and oversaw a programme of modernization. Resigning in 2005 to contest Benin's presidential election, he campaigned on a platform of economic reforms aimed at reducing the country's dependence on cotton exports. Twenty-six candidates contested the first round of voting held on 5 March 2006, with Boni polling 36%. A run-off was held on 19 March between Boni and Adrien Houngbédji of the Democratic Renewal Party. Boni won with 74·5% of the vote and was sworn into office in Porto-Novo on 6 April 2006.

Career in Office
Boni promised sweeping reforms to tackle poverty and corruption and to strengthen the institutions of democracy. In March 2007 the pro-Boni Cauri Forces for an Emerging Benin won control of parliament in elections, and in April 2008 parties supporting the president won a majority of seats in polling for local councils.

DEFENCE

There is selective conscription for 18 months. Defence expenditure totalled US$47m. in 2006 (US$6 per capita), representing 1·0% of GDP.

Army
The Army strength (2007) was 4,300, with an additional 2,500-strong paramilitary gendarmerie.

Navy
Personnel in 2007 numbered about 100; the force is based at Cotonou.

Air Force
The Air Force has suffered a shortage of funds and operates no combat aircraft. Personnel, 2007, 350.

INTERNATIONAL RELATIONS

Benin is a member of the UN, World Bank, IMF and several other UN specialized agencies, WTO, IOM, International Organization of the Francophonie, Islamic Development Bank, OIC, African Development Bank, African Union, ECOWAS and is an ACP member state of the ACP-EU relationship.

ECONOMY

Agriculture accounted for 32% of GDP in 2005, industry 13% and services 54%.

Overview
Since the establishment of multiparty democracy in 1990, Benin has implemented market-oriented policies. Progress in recent years has centred on the agricultural and tertiary sectors. A debt reduction was announced by the G8 in July 2005 and GDP growth in 2008 was at its highest level since 2001. In light of the global economic downturn, growth for 2010 is forecast at around 3·0 %.

The rural development sector (incorporating agriculture, livestock, fisheries and water supply) is one of the leading sources of economic growth, employing 70% of the work force and accounting for over 80% of export earnings. Cotton represents approximately 80% of exports, with China a major partner. The country's geographical location enables it to function as a transit point to landlocked countries including Niger and Burkina Faso.

Improved growth rates are tied to strengthening public investment, rising cotton production and healthy activity in related transport and other services. In order to maintain growth and reduce susceptibility to external shocks, greater efforts are needed to fight corruption and to promote private sector development.

Currency

The unit of currency is the *franc CFA* (XOF) with a parity of 655·957 francs CFA to one euro. Total money supply was 394,434m. francs CFA in June 2005 and foreign exchange reserves were US$692m. Inflation was 1·3% in 2007, rising to 8·0% in 2008.

Budget

The fiscal year is the calendar year. In 2005 revenue was 422bn. francs CFA and expenditure 455bn. francs CFA.

VAT is 18%.

Performance

Real GDP growth was 4·6% in 2007 and 5·0% in 2008. Total GDP was US$6·7bn. in 2008.

Banking and Finance

The bank of issue and the central bank is the regional Central Bank of West African States (BCEAO). The *Governor* is Philippe-Henri Dacoury-Tabley. In Dec. 2001 it had total assets of 5,517,700m. francs CFA. There are five private commercial banks, one savings bank (total deposits 15,758m. francs CFA in 1997) and three credit institutions. The Caisse Autonome d'Amortissement du Bénin manages state funds.

ENERGY AND NATURAL RESOURCES

Environment

Benin's carbon dioxide emissions from the consumption and flaring of fossil fuels in 2008 were the equivalent of 0·4 tonnes per capita.

Electricity

Installed capacity in 2004 was 56,000 kW. In 2004 production was 81m. kWh; Benin also imported 578m. kWh. A solar energy programme was initiated in 1993. Consumption per capita in 2004 was 81 kWh.

Oil and Gas

The Semé oilfield, located 15 km offshore, was discovered in 1968. Production commenced in 1982 and was 100,000 bbls in 2004. Crude petroleum reserves in 2007 were 8m. bbls.

Agriculture

Benin's economy is underdeveloped, and is dependent on subsistence agriculture. In 2002, 3·69m. persons depended on agriculture, of whom 1·55m. were economically active. Small independent farms produce about 90% of output. In 2007 an estimated 2·7m. ha. were arable and 0·27m. ha. permanent crops; about 12,000 ha. were irrigated in 2002. There were 185 tractors in 2002. The chief agricultural products, 2002 (in 1,000 tonnes) were: cassava, 2,452; yams, 1,875; maize, 622; seed cotton, 486; cottonseed, 267; sorghum, 195; groundnuts, 146; tomatoes, 141.

Livestock, 2003 estimates: cattle, 1,600,000; goats, 1,300,000; sheep, 670,000; pigs, 550,000; chickens, 10m.

Livestock products, 2003 (estimates, in 1,000 tonnes): beef and veal, 19; pork, bacon and ham, 7; goat meat, 4; poultry meat, 12; eggs, 7; milk, 31.

Forestry

In 2005 there were 2·35m. ha. of forest (21·3% of the total land area), mainly in the north. Timber production in 2007 was 6·57m. cu. metres.

Fisheries

Total catch, 2005, 38,035 tonnes, of which freshwater fish approximately 74% and marine fish 26%.

INDUSTRY

Only about 2% of the workforce is employed in industry. The main activities include palm-oil processing, brewing and the manufacture of cement, sugar and textiles. Also important are cigarettes, food, construction materials and petroleum. Production (in 1,000 tonnes): cement (2000), 759; palm oil (2000), 15; wheat flour (1999), 9; beer (2002), 57m. litres.

Labour

The labour force numbered 2,490,000 in 1996 (52% males). Approximately half of the economically active population is engaged in agriculture, fishing and forestry.

Trade Unions

In 1973 all trade unions were amalgamated to form a single body, the Union Nationale des Syndicats des Travailleurs du Bénin. In 1990 some unions declared their independence from this Union, which itself broke its links with the PRPB. In 1992 there were three trade union federations.

INTERNATIONAL TRADE

Commercial and transport activities, which make up 36% of GDP, are extremely vulnerable to developments in neighbouring Nigeria, with which there is a significant amount of illegal trade. Foreign debt was US$1,855m. in 2005.

Imports and Exports

Imports (f.o.b.) in 2005 totalled US$865·7m.; exports (f.o.b.), US$578·3m.

Principal import suppliers, 2005: France, 18·4%; China, 8·8%; Ghana, 7·2%; Côte d'Ivoire, 6·9%; Thailand, 6·7%; UK, 5·7%. Principal export markets: China, 36·2%; India, 6·9%; Nigeria, 5·8%; Niger, 5·2%; Indonesia; 3·6%; Thailand, 3·6%.

Main imports in 2005 were: petroleum and petroleum products (13·8%); machinery and transport equipment (12·2%); rice (11·2%); chemicals and related products (6·7%). The main exports were: cotton (58·0%); cashew nuts (6·9%); cigarettes (6·7%); cement (4·1%).

COMMUNICATIONS

Roads

There were 19,000 km of roads in 2004, of which 9·5% were paved. Passenger cars in use in 2007 totalled 149,300, buses and coaches 1,100, and lorries and vans 35,700.

Rail

In 2005 there were 438 km of metre-gauge railway. In 2003, 0·7m. passengers were carried and 0·6m. tonnes of freight.

Civil Aviation

The international airport is at Cotonou (Cadjehoun), which in 2001 handled 227,000 passengers (all on international flights) and 3,200 tonnes of freight. In 2001 scheduled airline traffic of Benin-based carriers flew 1m. km, carrying 46,000 passengers (all on international flights). In 2003 Trans African Airlines flew to Abidjan, Bamako, Brazzaville, Dakar, Lomé and Pointe-Noire; Trans Air Benin operated services to Abidjan, Brazzaville and Lomé; and Aero Benin flew to Bamako, Brazzaville, Johannesburg, Libreville and Ouagadougou.

Shipping

There is a port at Cotonou. In 2002 the merchant fleet totalled 1,000 GRT. In 2003 vessels totalling 1,539,000 NRT entered ports and vessels totalling 8,450,000 NRT cleared.

Telecommunications

In 2008 there were 103,200 main (fixed) telephone lines; mobile phone subscribers numbered 3,625,400 in 2008 (41·9 per 100 persons). There were 50,000 PCs in use in 2006 and 160,000 internet users in 2008.

Postal Services
In 2003 there were 174 post offices.

SOCIAL INSTITUTIONS

Justice
The Supreme Court is at Cotonou. There are Magistrates Courts and a *tribunal de conciliation* in each district. The legal system is based on French civil law and customary law.

The population in penal institutions in May 2006 was 5,834 (75 per 100,000 of national population).

Education
Adult literacy rate was 33·6% in 2003 (46·4% among males and 22·6% among females). In 2006 there were 1,356,818 pupils in primary schools with 31,103 teaching staff; and, in 2004, 344,890 pupils in secondary schools with 14,410 teaching staff. There were 42,603 students in higher education in 2006. The leading institution in the tertiary sector is the National University of Benin (Université Nationale du Bénin), located in Cotonou.

In 2006 public expenditure on education came to 3·9% of GNI and 18·0% of total government spending.

Health
In 2006 there were 1,088 physicians, 3,563 nurses and 999 midwives. There were three hospital beds per 10,000 inhabitants in 2006.

RELIGION

Some 51% of the population follow traditional animist beliefs. Voodoo became an official religion in 1996. In 2001 there were 1·37m. Roman Catholics and 1·32m. Muslims.

CULTURE

World Heritage Sites
The Royal Palaces of Abomey joined the World Heritage List in 1985 (reinscribed in 2007). They preserve the remains of the palaces of 12 kings who ruled the former kingdom of Abomey between 1625 and 1900.

Broadcasting
The Office de Radiodiffusion et Télévision du Bénin operates the state television (colour by SECAM V) and radio services. There are a few commercial TV channels, but numerous radio stations. In 2006 there were 395,000 TV receivers.

Press
In 2005 there were 20 daily newspapers with a circulation of 38,000. The main newspapers are Le Matinal, Les Echos du Jour and the government-controlled La Nation.

Tourism
In 2005 there were an estimated 176,000 non-resident tourists. Tourist spending totalled US$122m. in 2004.

DIPLOMATIC REPRESENTATIVES

Of Benin in the United Kingdom
Ambassador: Albert Agossou (resides in Paris).
Honorary Consul: Lawrence Landau (Millennium House, Humber Rd, London, NW2 6DW).

Of the United Kingdom in Benin
Ambassador: Robert Dewar, CMG (resides in Abuja, Nigeria).

Of Benin in the USA (2124 Kalorama Rd, NW, Washington, D.C., 20008)
Ambassador: Segbe Cyrille Oguin.

Of the USA in Benin (Rue Caporal Bernard Anani, Cotonou)
Ambassador: James Alcorn Knight.

Of Benin to the United Nations
Ambassador: Jean-Francis Régis Zinsou.

Of Benin to the European Union
Ambassador: Charles Borromée Todjinou.

FURTHER READING

Bay, E., *Wives of the Leopard: Gender, Politics, and Culture in the Kingdom of Dahomey.* 1998

National Statistical Office: Institut National de la Statistique et de l'Analyse Économique, 01 BP 323, Cotonou.
Website (French only): http://www.insae-bj.org

BHUTAN

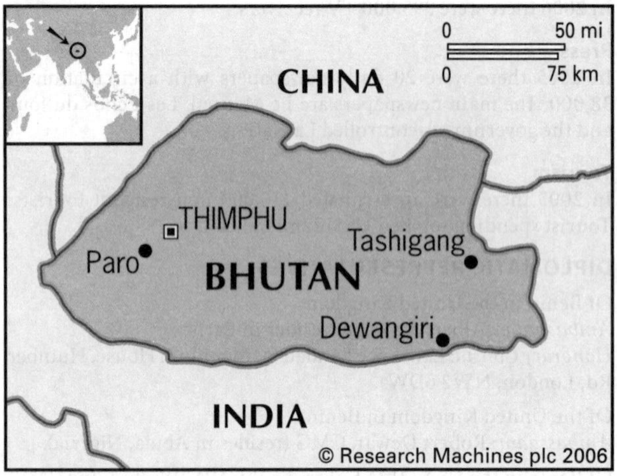

Druk-yul
(Kingdom of Bhutan)

Capital: Thimphu
Population estimate, 2010: 708,000
GDP per capita, 2007: (PPP$) 4,837
HDI/world rank: 0·619/132

KEY HISTORICAL EVENTS

Indigenous Monpa clans established settlements in the eastern Himalayas by around 2000 BC. Buddhism was brought to Bhutan in the 7th century AD when Tibetan lamas (monks) founded monasteries at Bumthang and Kyichi, although animist beliefs persisted among the scattered villages. It was the arrival in 1616 of a monk, Zhabdrung Nawang Namgyal, fleeing persecution in Tibet, which led to the foundation of the kingdom of Bhutan. Over a period of 35 years Zhabdrung and his followers built fortresses and monasteries and established the Drukpa sect of Buddhism as well as a dual system of governance known as the Chhoesid. Power was split between the Deb Raja, the head of secular affairs (responsible for four regional governors) and the Dharma Raja, the spiritual head who was charged with enacting laws. In 1720 the Ch'ing dynasty took control of Tibet, claiming suzerainty of it and neighbouring Bhutan.

Tensions between Bhutan and Bengal to the south culminated in a Bhutanese invasion of Cooch Behar in 1772. This prompted the governor of the province to seek military assistance from the British who had defeated the Nawab of Bengal in 1757. Skirmishes continued for two years until peace was brokered by Tashi Lama, then Regent of Tibet. British attempts to develop trade with Bhutan in the 1780s were unsuccessful and new tensions emerged when British India took control of neighbouring Assam in 1826. In 1864 British India claimed ownership of a strip of southern Bhutan known as the Duars. It was formally ceded to India the following year, although the Treaty of Sinchula provided for an annual subsidy to Bhutan as compensation.

In 1907 the office of Dharma Raja came to an end. The governor of Tongsa, Ugyen Wangchuck, was then chosen as Maharajah of Bhutan, the first of a hereditary line (the title is now King of Bhutan). He concluded a treaty with British India in 1910 which allowed for internal autonomy with British control of foreign policy in return for a doubling of Britain's annual subsidy to the kingdom. After Indian independence, a treaty of 1949 returned the Duars to Bhutan. The kingdom continued to manage its internal affairs while India inherited control of Bhutan's defence and foreign affairs.

When Communist Chinese forces invaded Tibet in 1950, Bhutan was claimed as part of 'Greater Tibet'. In response, India closed the Bhutan–Tibet border and upgraded roads linking Bengal with Bhutan. Amid mounting Indo-Sino tensions in the early 1960s, Bhutan established a small army, trained and equipped by India. The reign of the third king, Jigme Dorji Wangchuk (1952–72), was marked by gradual economic development and an opening up to the outside world. The 151-seat National Assembly was established in 1952 and Bhutan became a member of the United Nations in 1971, since when relations with China have slowly thawed.

In the early 1990s, tens of thousands of 'illegal immigrants', mostly Nepali-speaking Hindus, were forcibly expelled from southern and western Bhutan. More than 15 years on, there are still more than 85,000 people claiming to be Bhutanese refugees in camps set up by the UNHCR in eastern Nepal, although around 23,000 have been resettled in the USA and Europe since March 2008. Bhutan was ruled from 1972–2006 by King Jigme Singye Wangchuck. He abdicated in Dec. 2006 in favour of his son, Jigme Kesar Namgyel Wangchuck. In Dec. 2007 and March 2008 Bhutan held its first democratic parliamentary elections, in which two parties stood. The leader of the Druk Phuensum Tshogpa (Bhutan Peace and Prosperity Party), Jigme Thinley, took office as the first elected prime minister of Bhutan on 9 April 2008.

TERRITORY AND POPULATION

Bhutan is situated in the eastern Himalayas, bounded in the north by Tibet and on all other sides by India. In 1949 India retroceded 83 sq. km of Dewangiri, annexed in 1865. Area 46,650 sq. km (18,012 sq. miles); 2005 census population, 672,425 (364,482 males), giving a density of 14 per sq. km.

The UN gives an estimated population for 2010 of 708,000.

In 2005, 88·9% of the population lived in rural areas. A Nepalese minority makes up 30–35% of the population, mainly in the south. The capital is Thimphu (2005 population, 79,185). The country is divided into 20 districts (*dzongkhag*).

The official language is Dzongkha.

SOCIAL STATISTICS

2002 (estimates) births, 77,000 (rate of 34·9 per 1,000 population); deaths, 19,000 (rate of 8·7 per 1,000 population). Life expectancy at birth, 2007, was 64·0 years for men and 67·6 years for women. Infant mortality, 2005, 65 per 1,000 live births. Annual population growth rate, 1992–2002, 2·8%; fertility rate, 2004, 4·2 children per woman.

CLIMATE

The climate is largely controlled by altitude. The mountainous north is cold, with perpetual snow on the summits, but the centre has a more moderate climate, though winters are cold, with rainfall under 40" (1,000 mm). In the south, the climate is humid sub-tropical and rainfall approaches 200" (5,000 mm).

CONSTITUTION AND GOVERNMENT

There is as yet no formal constitution, although a draft constitution was unveiled in March 2005 that transforms Bhutan into a two-party democratic system. There is a bicameral parliament. The lower house is the 47-member *National Assembly* (all elected) and the upper house the 25-member *National Council* (with 20 members elected and five appointed by the king). All Bhutanese over 30 years may be candidates.

The reigning King is Jigme Kesar Namgyel Wangchuck (b. 1980), who succeeded his father King Jigme Singye Wangchuck (abdicated 14 Dec. 2006). He was crowned on 6 Nov. 2008. With the introduction of democratic elections in 2007–08, the King's role became more ceremonial. Nonetheless, all leading political parties have affirmed their loyalty to the monarchy, which remains central to political life.

In 1907 the Tongsa Penlop (the governor of the province of Tongsa in central Bhutan), Sir Ugyen Wangchuck, GCIE, KCSI, was elected as the first hereditary Maharaja of Bhutan. The Bhutanese title is Druk Gyalpo, and his successors are addressed as King of Bhutan. The stated goal is to increase Gross National Happiness.

12 monastic representatives are elected by the central and regional ecclesiastical bodies, while the remaining members are nominated by the King, and include members of the Council of Ministers (the Cabinet) and the Royal Advisory Council.

National Anthem

'Druk tsendhen koipi gyelknap na' ('In the Thunder Dragon Kingdom'); words by Gyaldun Dasho Thinley Dorji, tune by A. Tongmi.

RECENT ELECTIONS

Bhutan's first ever elections were held on 31 Dec. 2007 when 15 members (all independents) were elected to the National Council (the non-partisan upper house of Bhutan's bicameral parliament). A further five members were elected on 29 Jan. 2008, after voting in these districts was postponed because there were not at least two candidates (as required by the Electoral Commission of Bhutan) at the time of the original deadline for nominations.

On 22 March 2008 elections were held for Bhutan's National Assembly. The 47 seats were contested by two parties—the Druk Phuensum Tshogpa (DPT; Bhutan Peace and Prosperity Party), led by former prime minister Jigme Thinley, and the People's Democratic Party (PDP), led by another former prime minister, Sangay Ngedup. The DPT won 45 of the 47 seats with 67·0% of the vote. The PDP gained only two seats, with 33·0% of the vote.

CURRENT ADMINISTRATION

In March 2010 the government comprised:

Prime Minister: Jigme Thinley; b. 1952 (took office for the third time on 9 April 2008, having previously been prime minister from July 1998–July 1999 and Aug. 2003–Aug. 2004).

Minister for Economy: Khandu Wangchuk. *Information and Communication:* Nandalal Rai. *Education:* Thakur Singh Powdyel. *Finance:* Wangdi Norbu. *Health:* Zangley Dukpa. *Labour and Human Resources:* Dorji Wangdi. *Home and Cultural Affairs:* Minjur Dorji. *Agriculture:* Pema Gyamtsho. *Foreign Affairs:* Ugyen Tshering. *Works and Human Settlement:* Yeshey Zimba. *Chief Justice:* Sonam Tobgye.

Speaker: Jigme Tshultim.

CURRENT LEADERS

Jigme Thinley

Position
Prime Minister

Introduction
Jigme Thinley, a civil servant and former government minister, became Bhutan's first ever democratically elected prime minister on 24 March 2008.

Early Life
Jigme Yoser Thinley was born in 1952 in Bumthang, northern Bhutan and educated at Dr Graham's Homes in Kalimpong, northeastern India. He graduated from St Stephen's College at the University of Delhi and subsequently earned a masters degree in public administration from Penn State University in the USA. He later studied manpower planning and management at Manchester University in the UK.

Having joined Bhutan's civil service in 1974 as a trainee officer in the ministry of home affairs, Thinley went on to hold a range of posts including, in 1990, administrator of Bhutan's six eastern districts. He became a secretary in the ministry of home affairs in 1992 and was promoted to deputy minister in 1994. In the same year he was appointed as Bhutan's permanent representative to the UN and other international organizations.

Career in Office
From July 1998 to July 1999 and again from Aug. 2003 to Aug. 2004, Thinley was the royal appointee as prime minister. He also served as minister of foreign affairs between 1998–2003. In March 2008, in the run-up to Bhutan's first multi-party elections, Thinley stood as leader of the new DPT. The party won 45 of the 47 seats in the National Assembly, making Thinley the country's first democratically elected premier. He took office on 9 April 2008, promising to make democracy a success and to provide a transparent and corruption-free government.

DEFENCE

In 2003 defence spending totalled US$22m. (US$25 per capita), representing 3·3% of GDP.

Army

In 2007 the Royal Bhutan Army had a strength of 9,021. It is lightly armed, mainly with weapons supplied by India. There is also an Air Wing of around 80 personnel.

INTERNATIONAL RELATIONS

Bhutan is a member of the UN, World Bank, IMF and several other UN specialized agencies, Asian Development Bank, Colombo Plan and SAARC.

ECONOMY

Agriculture accounted for 22·3% of GDP in 2006, with industry accounting for 37·9% and services 39·8%.

Overview

One of the smallest economies in the world, 26% of the population lived on less than US$1·25 per day in 2005. Over 90% of the poor reside in rural areas and 63% of the labour force is employed in agriculture, although agriculture's share of GDP has steadily declined in recent years. Public expenditure, guided by the government ideology of Gross National Happiness, has increasingly focused on health and education.

The economy is closely tied to that of India. The currency, the ngultrum, is pegged to the Indian rupee and the Indian government finances a large part of Bhutan's budget expenditures. India is by far the country's largest trading partner, followed by Indonesia and Singapore. Exports to India increased from Nu5·9bn. in 2003 to Nu22·7bn. in 2007. Sales of electricity, the chief export to India, more than doubled between 2006 and 2007.

Annual GDP growth has been impressive in recent years, notably with an increase of 21·4% in 2007. Development is focused on roads and telecommunications, although progress is slowed by the mountainous terrain and a shortage of skilled labour.

Currency

The unit of currency is the *ngultrum* (BTN) of 100 *chetrum*, at parity with the Indian rupee. Indian currency is also legal tender. Foreign exchange reserves were US$425m. in May 2005 and total money supply was Nu8,088m. Inflation was 5·3% in 2005, 5·0% in 2006, 5·2% in 2007 and 8·4% in 2008.

Budget
Revenues for 2004–05 were Nu11,352m. and expenditures Nu13,622m.

Performance
Real GDP growth was 6·5% in 2005, 6·3% in 2006, 21·4% in 2007 (one of the highest rates for the year in the world) and 7·6% in 2008. Total GDP in 2008 was US$1·4bn.

Banking and Finance
The Royal Monetary Authority (founded 1982; *Managing Director*, Daw Tenzin) acts as the central bank. Deposits (Dec. 1995) Nu2,816·3m. Foreign exchange reserves in 1997: US$120m. The Bank of Bhutan, a commercial bank, was established in 1968. The headquarters are at Phuentsholing with 26 branches throughout the country. It is 80%-owned by the government of Bhutan and 20%-owned by the Indian government. There is another commercial bank (the Bhutan National Bank), a development bank (the Bhutan Development Finance Corporation) and a stock exchange in Thimphu.

ENERGY AND NATURAL RESOURCES

Environment
Bhutan's carbon dioxide emissions from the consumption and flaring of fossil fuels in 2008 were the equivalent of 0·5 tonnes per capita.

Electricity
Installed capacity in 2007 was 486,000 kW (all hydro-electric). Production (2007) was 4·5bn. kWh. Consumption per capita in 2004 was about 229 kWh. Bhutan exports electricity to India.

In March 2007 the Tala hydro-electric plant was commissioned. A joint project between Bhutan and India, it is designed to generate 4·9bn. kWh annually.

Minerals
Large deposits of limestone, marble, dolomite, slate, graphite, lead, copper, coal, talc, gypsum, beryl, mica, pyrites and tufa have been found. Most mining activity (principally limestone, coal, slate and dolomite) is on a small-scale. Output, 2004 estimates: limestone, 288,000 tonnes; dolomite, 275,000 tonnes; coal, 67,000 tonnes.

Agriculture
The area under cultivation in 1996 was 0·36m. ha. In 2007 there were an estimated 128,000 ha. of arable land and 27,000 ha. of permanent crops. The chief products (2000 production in 1,000 tonnes) are maize (70), oranges (58), rice (50), potatoes (34), wheat (20) and sugarcane (13).

Livestock (2000): cattle, 435,000; pigs, 75,000; sheep, 59,000; goats, 42,000; horses, 30,000.

Forestry
In 2005, 3·20m. ha. (68·0% of the land area) were forested. Timber production in 2007 was 4·80m. cu. metres.

Fisheries
The total catch in 2005 amounted to an estimated 300 tonnes, exclusively from inland waters.

INDUSTRY

Industries in Bhutan include cement, wood products, processed fruits, alcoholic beverages and calcium carbide. 2001 production: cement, 160,000 tonnes; veneer sheets, 16,000 cu. metres; particle board, 12,000 cu. metres; plywood, 4,000 cu. metres. In 2001 there were 12,878 licensed industrial establishments, of which 8,536 were construction, 3,773 service and 569 manufacturing industries. The latter included 317 forest-based companies, 116 agriculture-based and 46 mineral-based.

Labour
In 2005 the economically active population was 256,895. Of those in employment, 63·5% were males. Unemployment in 2005 was 3·1%.

INTERNATIONAL TRADE

External debt in 2007 amounted to US$775m.

Financial support is received from India, the UN and other international aid organizations.

Imports and Exports
Trade with India dominates but oranges and apples, timber, cardamom and liquor are also exported to the Middle East, Singapore and Europe. Imports in 2005 amounted to Nu17,035m. and exports to Nu11,386m. In 2005 India accounted for 75·1% of imports and 87·6% of exports.

COMMUNICATIONS

Roads
In 2006 there were about 4,153 km of roads, of which 1,577 km were highways. In 2007 there were 19,600 passenger cars, 180 buses and coaches, 5,400 lorries and vans, and 7,500 motorcycles and mopeds. A number of sets of traffic lights were installed during the late 1990s but all have subsequently been removed as they were considered to be eyesores. There had previously been just one set. There were 111 fatalities in road accidents in 2007.

Civil Aviation
In 2003 Druk-Air flew from Paro to Bangkok, Delhi, Dhaka, Kathmandu, Calcutta and Rangoon (Yangon). In 2003 Druk-Air flew 2m. km, carrying 36,000 passengers (all on international flights).

Telecommunications
In 2004 there were 49,400 telephone subscribers (63·4 per 1,000 inhabitants), including 19,100 mobile phone subscribers. There were 13,000 PCs in use in 2005 and 25,000 internet users. The country's first internet cafe was opened in March 2000 in the capital Thimphu.

Postal Services
In 2003 there were 110 post offices. Prior to the opening of the country to tourism in 1974 the main source of foreign exchange was the sale of commemorative postage stamps.

SOCIAL INSTITUTIONS

Justice
The High Court consists of eight judges appointed by the King. There is a Magistrate's Court in each district, under a *Thrimpon*, from which appeal is to the High Court at Thimphu. The death penalty, which had not been used for 40 years, was abolished in 2004.

Education
In 2004 there were 24,533 pupils and 707 teachers in community primary schools, 26,508 pupils and 752 teachers in primary schools and 79,729 pupils with 2,630 teachers in secondary schools. In 2006 there were 4,141 students in tertiary education and 375 academic staff. Adult literacy was 47·0% in 2004.

In 2005 public expenditure on education came to 7·1% of GNI and 17·2% of total government spending.

Health
In 2000 there were 29 hospitals, 160 basic health units, 447 outreach clinics and 18 indigenous hospital units. There were 140

doctors, 493 nurses and 144 health assistants in 2003. Free health facilities are available to 90% of the population.

RELIGION

The state religion of Bhutan is the Drukpa Kagyupa, a branch of Mahayana Buddhism. There are also Hindu and Muslim minorities.

CULTURE

Broadcasting

Radio broadcasting began in 1973, but television was not introduced until 1999. The state-owned Bhutan Broadcasting Service is the national radio and television provider. Although there are no private broadcasters, cable TV is available. There were 25,000 TV receivers in 2004.

Cinema

There are two cinemas in Thimphu and four others.

Press

Until 2006 there was only one newspaper, the government-controlled Kuensel (circulation of 15,000 in 2005), which is published in English, Dzongkha and Nepali. Two private weeklies were launched in 2006.

Tourism

Bhutan was not formally opened to foreign tourists until 1974, but tourism is now the largest source of foreign exchange. In 2003, 6,000 tourists visited Bhutan; revenue totalled US$8m.

Festivals

Bhutan's most famous festival is Tshechu, a religious celebration of Guru Padsambhava held throughout the country at the end of the harvest. The Thimphu Tshechu takes place around mid-Sept. and includes spectacular masked dances performed by monks. Other important festivals include Dromche (to honour the protective deities of the Bhutanese people) and Jambay Lhakhan Drup (including a fire dance to promote fertility).

DIPLOMATIC REPRESENTATIVES

Of Bhutan to the United Nations
Ambassador: Lhato Wangchuk.

Of Bhutan to the European Union
Ambassador: Sonam Tobden Rabgye.

FURTHER READING

Crossette, B., *So Close to Heaven: The Vanishing Buddhist Kingdoms of the Himalayas.* 1995
Das, B. N., *Mission to Bhutan: a Nation in Transition.* 1995
Hutt, M., *Bhutan: Perspectives on Conflict and Dissent.* 1994
Parmanand, Parashar, *The Politics of Bhutan: Retrospect and Prospect.* 2002
Savada, A. M. (ed.) *Nepal and Bhutan: Country Studies.* 1993
Sinha, A. C., *Bhutan: Ethnic Identity and National Dilemma.* 1998

National Statistical Office: Central Statistical Organization, Thimphu.
Website: http://www.nsb.gov.bt

BOLIVIA

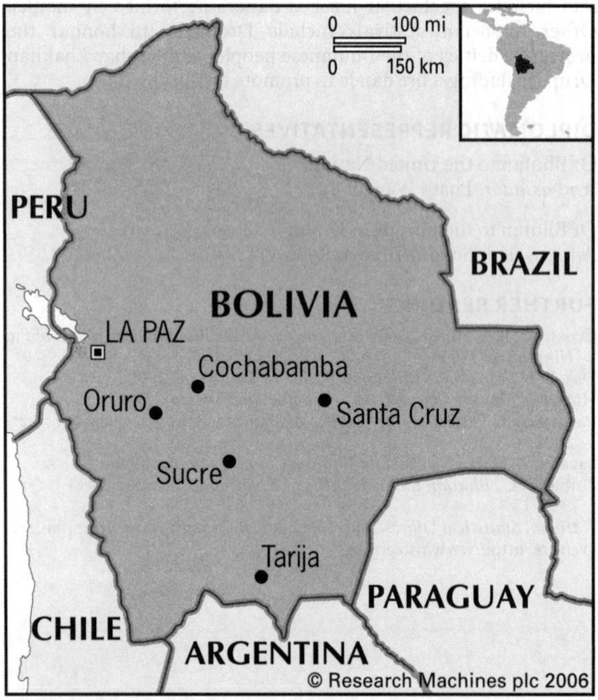

Estado Plurinacional de Bolivia
(Plurinational State of Bolivia)

Capital: Sucre
Seat of government: La Paz
Population estimate, 2010: 10·03m.
GDP per capita, 2007: (PPP$) 4,206
HDI/world rank: 0·729/113

KEY HISTORICAL EVENTS

Bolivia was part of the Inca Empire until conquered by the Spanish in the 16th century. Independence was won and the Republic of Bolivia was proclaimed on 6 Aug. 1825. During the first 154 years of its independence, Bolivia had 189 governments, many of them installed by coups. In the 1960s the Argentinian revolutionary and former minister of the Cuban government, Ernesto 'Che' Guevara, was killed in Bolivia while fighting with a left-wing guerrilla group. In 1971 Bolivian instability reached a peak with the brief establishment of a revolutionary Popular Assembly during the regime of Gen. Torres. Later repression under Gen. Hugo Banzer took a heavy toll on the left-wing parties. Banzer was followed by a succession of military-led governments until civilian rule was restored in Oct. 1982 when Dr Siles Zuazo became president. He introduced a period of economic reform embracing free markets and open trade, which succeeded in restoring stability but also widened the gap between rich and poor. Amid growing discontent, in Dec. 2005 Evo Morales Ayma was elected as the country's first indigenous president.

TERRITORY AND POPULATION

Bolivia is a landlocked state bounded in the north and east by Brazil, south by Paraguay and Argentina, and west by Chile and Peru, with an area of some 1,098,581 sq. km (424,165 sq. miles). A coastal strip of land on the Pacific passed to Chile after a war in 1884. In 1953 Chile declared Arica a free port and Bolivia has certain privileges there.

Population (2001 census): 8,274,325; density, 7·5 per sq. km. In 2005, 64·2% of the population lived in urban areas.

The UN gives an estimated population for 2010 of 10·03m.

Area and population of the departments (capitals in brackets) at the 1992 and 2001 censuses:

Departments	*Area (sq. km)*	*Census 1992*	*Census 2001*
Beni (Trinidad)	213,564	276,174	362,521
Chuquisaca (Sucre)	51,524	453,756	531,522
Cochabamba (Cochabamba)	55,631	1,110,205	1,455,711
La Paz (La Paz)	133,985	1,900,786	2,350,466
Oruro (Oruro)	53,588	340,114	391,870
Pando (Cobija)	63,827	38,072	52,525
Potosí (Potosí)	118,218	645,889	709,013
Santa Cruz (Santa Cruz de la Sierra)	370,621	1,364,389	2,029,471
Tarija (Tarija)	37,623	291,407	391,226
Total	1,098,581	6,420,792	8,274,325

Population (2001, in 1,000) of the principal towns: Santa Cruz de la Sierra, 1,114; La Paz, 790; El Alto, 647; Cochabamba, 517; Oruro, 201; Sucre, 194; Tarija, 136; Potosí, 133.

Spanish along with the Amerindian languages Quechua and Aymará are all official languages; Tupi Guaraní is also spoken. Indigenous peoples account for 50% of the population.

SOCIAL STATISTICS

In 2000 births totalled an estimated 265,000 (birth rate of 32·4 per 1,000 population); deaths totalled an estimated 72,000 (rate, 8·8 per 1,000); infant mortality (2005), 52 per 1,000 live births, the highest in South America. Expectation of life (2007) was 63·3 years for men and 67·5 years for women. Annual population growth rate, 2000–05, 2·2%. Fertility rate, 2004, 3·8 children per woman (along with Paraguay the highest in South America).

CLIMATE

The varied geography produces different climates. The low-lying areas in the Amazon Basin are warm and damp throughout the year, with heavy rainfall from Nov. to March; the Altiplano is generally dry between May and Nov. with sunshine but cold nights in June and July, while the months from Dec. to March are the wettest. La Paz, Jan. 55·9°F (13·3°C), July 50·5°F (10·3°C). Annual rainfall 20·8" (529 mm). Sucre, Jan. 58·5°F (14·7°C), July 52·7°F (11·5°C). Annual rainfall 20·1" (510 mm).

CONSTITUTION AND GOVERNMENT

Bolivia's first constitution was adopted on 19 Nov. 1826. The present constitution, the fifteenth, came into effect following its acceptance in a referendum on 25 Jan. 2009 and defined Bolivia as 'a United Social State of Plurinational Communitarian Law'. Under its terms, running to 411 articles, the majority indigenous population has been granted increased rights (including recognition of indigenous systems of justice), state control is extended over the exploitation of natural resources and regional autonomy is enhanced. The separation of church and state is recognized and land reforms in favour of indigenous populations enshrined. A new 'plurinational legislative assembly', consisting of a 130-member *Chamber of Deputies* and a 36-member *Senate*, took office following elections in Dec. 2009. The constitution also allows for the president to serve a maximum of two consecutive terms.

National Anthem

'Bolivianos, el hado propicio' ('Bolivians, a favourable destiny'); words by José Ignacio Sanjinés, tune by Benedetto Vincenti.

GOVERNMENT CHRONOLOGY

Heads of State since 1943. (ADN = Nationalist Democratic Action; FRB = Front of the Bolivian Revolution; MAS = Movement Towards Socialism; MIR = Movement of Revolutionary Left; MNR = Nationalist Revolutionary Movement; MNRI = Nationalist Revolutionary Movement of the Left; PSD = Social Democratic Party; PURS = Party of the Republican Socialist Union; n/p = non-partisan)

President of the Republic		
1943–	military	Gualberto Villarroel López
Presidents of the Provisional Junta of Government		
1946	n/p	Néstor Guillén Olmos
1946–47	n/p	Tomás Monje Gutiérrez
Presidents of the Republic		
1947–49	PURS	José Enrique Hertzog Garaizábal
1949–51	PURS	Mamerto Urriolagoitia Harriague
President of the Military Junta of Government		
1951–52	military	Hugo Ballivián Rojas
Presidents of the Republic		
1952	MNR	Hernán Siles Zuazo
1952–56	MNR	Ángel Víctor Paz Estenssoro
1956–60	MNR	Hernán Siles Zuazo
1960–64	MNR	Ángel Víctor Paz Estenssoro
Presidents of the Military Junta of Government		
1964	military	Alfredo Ovando Candía
1964–65	military	René Barrientos Ortuño
1965–66	military	René Barrientos Ortuño + Alfredo Ovando Candía
1966	military	Alfredo Ovando Candía
Presidents of the Republic		
1966–69	FRB	René Barrientos Ortuño
1969	PSD-FRB	Luis Adolfo Siles Salinas
1969–70	military	Alfredo Ovando Candía
1970–71	military	Juan José Torres González
1971–78	military	Hugo Banzer Suárez
1978	military	Juan Pereda Asbún
President of the Military Junta of Government		
1978–79	military	David Padilla Arancibia
Presidents of the Republic		
1979	military	Alberto Natusch Busch
1980–81	military	Luis García Meza Tejada
1981–82	military	Celso Torrelio Villa
1982	military	Guido Vildoso Calderón
1982–85	MNRI	Hernán Siles Zuazo
1985–89	MNR	Ángel Víctor Paz Estenssoro
1989–93	MIR	Jaime Paz Zamora
1993–97	MNR	Gonzalo Sánchez de Lozada
1997–2001	ADN	Hugo Banzer Suárez
2001–02	ADN	Jorge Fernando Quiroga Ramírez
2002–03	MNR	Gonzalo Sánchez de Lozada
2003–05	MNR	Carlos Diego Mesa Gisbert
2005–06	n/p	Eduardo Rodríguez Veltzé
2006–	MAS	Evo Morales Ayma

RECENT ELECTIONS

Presidential elections were held on 6 Dec. 2009. Evo Morales Ayma (Movement Towards Socialism) won 64·1% of votes cast against 26·6% for Manfred Reyes Villa (Progress Plan for Bolivia), 5·7% for Samuel Doria Medina (National Unity Front) and 2·3% for René Joaquino (Social Alliance). There were four other candidates.

In elections to the Chamber of Deputies, also held on 6 Dec. 2009, the Movement Towards Socialism won 88 seats with 64·2% of the vote, Progress Plan for Bolivia 37 with 26·5%, the National Unity Front 3 with 5·7% and the Social Alliance 2 with 2·3%. In Senate elections of the same day Movement Towards Socialism won 26 seats and Progress Plan for Bolivia 10.

CURRENT ADMINISTRATION

President: Evo Morales Ayma; b. 1959 (Movement Towards Socialism; sworn in 22 Jan. 2006 and re-elected 6 Dec. 2009).

Vice-President: Álvaro García Linera.

In March 2010 the cabinet was composed as follows:

Minister of Autonomy: Carlos Romero. *Culture:* Zulma Yugar Párraga. *Economy and Public Finance:* Luis Alberto Arce Catacora. *Education:* Roberto Aguilar. *Environment and Water:* María Esther Udaeta Velásquez. *Foreign Relations and Worship:* David Choquehuanca Céspedes. *Health:* Sonia Polo Andrade. *Hydrocarbons and Energy:* Fernando Vincenti Vargas. *Institutional Transparency and the Fight Against Corruption:* Nardy Suxo. *Interior:* Sacha Sergio Llorenti. *Justice:* Nilda Copa Condori. *Labour, Employment and Social Security:* Carmen Trujillo Cárdenas. *Legal Defence of the State:* Elizabeth Arismendi Chumacero. *Mining and Metals:* José Antonio Pimentel Castillo. *National Defence:* Rubén Saavedra Soto. *Planning and Development:* Elba Viviana Caro Hinojosa. *Presidency:* Oscar Coca Antezana. *Presidential Spokesperson:* Iván Canelas Alurralde. *Productive Development:* Antonia Rodríguez Medrano. *Public Works, Services and Housing:* Wálter Delgadillo. *Rural Affairs and Lands:* Nemecia Achacollo Tola.

Office of the President (Spanish only):
http://www.presidencia.gov.bo

CURRENT LEADERS

Juan Evo Morales Ayma

Position
President

Introduction
Evo Morales Ayma became Bolivia's first indigenous president in Jan. 2006, having promised to transform the fortunes of South America's poorest country. The former coca farmer and left-wing activist has sought to revise the constitution to embed a state-led socialist economy and strengthen presidential powers, and has been a leading critic of US intervention in Bolivia. He was re-elected in Dec. 2009.

Early Life
Evo Morales Ayma was born in the mining town of Orinoca, Oruro on 26 Oct. 1959. When the mines began to close in the early 1980s, his family moved to the southeastern lowland to become farmers. Settling in Chapare as a coca farmer, Morales became a leader of the *cocaleros* and during the 1990s came into conflict with successive governments, particularly that of the former right-wing military dictator, Hugo Banzer Suárez. Banzer joined the US 'war on drugs' and introduced a five-year 'Dignity Plan' which aimed to eradicate coca cultivation and pressurize the *cocaleros* into growing alternative crops. In 1997 Morales, by then a member of the Movement Towards Socialism (MAS), was elected to Congress where he continued to fight the government's coca eradication policy, arguing that coca leaf and tea consumption was an accepted part of daily life for workers and that the West had a responsibility to suppress cocaine demand.

In Jan. 2002 he was removed from his seat in Congress on a terrorism charge related to riots in Sacaba over coca eradication, though many claimed his dismissal followed pressure from the US embassy. Morales nevertheless declared his candidacy for the congressional and presidential elections, held in June 2002, on a platform of nationalizing strategic industries, providing basic services for all, land reform and tackling corruption. The MAS came second with 20·9% of the vote, with Morales crediting much of his success to inflammatory comments made against him by the then US ambassador to Bolivia, Manuel Rocha. Refusing to join a coalition with the Nationalist Revolutionary Movement (MNR), led by President Gonzalo Sánchez de Lozada, the MAS became the leading opposition party.

Following a general strike, Morales was involved in an uprising that led to the ousting of de Lozada in Oct. 2003. He was also a key figure in the mass protests that gripped La Paz in April 2005, when demonstrators called for an end to poverty and a greater share of profits from the country's gas reserves. A blockade led to food and fuel shortages in La Paz and when clashes erupted between the police and protesters, Carlos Mesa, the new president, fled the city under armed escort. In fresh elections in Dec. 2005, Morales defeated the conservative former president, Jorge Quiroga, with 53·7% of the vote. He was sworn in as president on 22 Jan. 2006.

Career in Office

In his inaugural address Morales promised to deliver 'equality and justice' for the poor and marginalized. He pledged to secure a new constitution providing greater legal representation and more rights for indigenous people. His choice of inexperienced left-wing activists to fill most of the cabinet led to comparisons with Venezuela's president, Hugo Chávez. Morales swiftly signed a co-operation accord with Chávez under which Venezuela's state-owned oil company would help Bolivia develop its energy reserves. Close links have also been forged with communist Cuba, but relations with the USA have remained strained (leading to the expulsion of the US ambassador, Philip Goldberg, and the suspension of operations of the US drug enforcement agency in Bolivia in Oct.–Nov. 2008).

On 1 May 2006 Morales announced the nationalization of Bolivia's oil and gas industry. The decree required foreign energy companies already operating in the market, including Brazil's Petrobras, to accept harsh new contracts within six months. However, a temporary suspension of the nationalization programme was announced in Aug. owing to shortage of finance, and the terms accepted by foreign companies by the end of Oct. were less draconian than in the May decree.

In July 2006 Morales and the MAS claimed victory in elections for a new Constituent Assembly to revise Bolivia's constitution, taking 137 of the 255 seats. The result, however, fell well short of the two-thirds majority needed to rewrite the constitution at will. This led MAS delegates to introduce a controversial measure in Sept. allowing the Assembly to approve individual clauses by simple majority vote. Opponents of the move, including many of the country's elected departmental governors, feared the loss of regional autonomy and the greater centralization of political power in the president's hands. There was also resistance from senators representing large landowners to Morales' land redistribution reform in favour of the indigenous majority, which passed into law in Nov. 2006. Although Morales retained majority support among the electorate, he remained locked in a power struggle over the proposed constitution with the wealthier eastern departments, four of which declared autonomy in protest. In response, Morales staged a recall referendum on his leadership in Aug. 2008, which he won convincingly. In Oct. Congress approved the text of the new constitution, which was accepted in a referendum on 25 Jan. 2009.

In April 2009 Morales claimed that a plot to assassinate him had been foiled in a raid against a group of alleged foreign mercenaries by government troops in Santa Cruz. Presidential and parliamentary elections in Dec. saw Morales returned to office in a landslide victory with about 64% of the vote, while his MAS won solid majorities in both the Chamber of Deputies and Senate.

DEFENCE

In 2006 defence expenditure totalled US$156m. (US$17 per capita), representing 1·4% of GDP.

Army

There are six military regions. Strength (2007): 34,800 (25,000 conscripts), including a Presidential Guard infantry regiment under direct headquarters command.

Navy

A small force exists for river and lake patrol duties. Personnel in 2007 totalled 4,800, including 1,700 marines. There were six Naval Districts in 2007. The Navy had 73 vessels in 2007, including 54 patrol craft.

Air Force

The Air Force, established in 1923, had 33 combat capable aircraft and 15 armed helicopters in 2007. Personnel strength (2007): 6,500.

INTERNATIONAL RELATIONS

Bolivia is a member of the UN, World Bank, IMF and several other UN specialized agencies, WTO, IOM, the Andean Community, Inter-American Development Bank, SELA, LAIA, OAS, UNASUR and is an associate member of MERCOSUR.

ECONOMY

In 2007 agriculture accounted for 12·9% of GDP, industry 36·4% and services 50·7%.

Overview

Bolivia is the poorest country in Latin America, with an estimated 60% of the population living below the poverty line. There are severe inequalities in wealth distribution and most industries are capital intensive with restricted employment opportunities. Yet the country is resource rich. Home to the largest natural gas reserves in Latin America, it exports an abundance of minerals and agricultural goods. It is also among the world's largest producers of coca (the raw material for cocaine); government efforts to eradicate production in 1999–2000 exacerbated poverty among small farmers. While agriculture employs about 40% of the population, it accounted for only 11·3% of GDP in 2008.

Growth has been volatile over the decades. The 1960s and 1970s were boom years owing to a flourishing mining sector and capital inflows, while the 1980s were marked by hyperinflation, high debt and political crises. In the 1990s consumption-driven expansion led to an average annual investment growth rate of 4–5%. The state privatized some utilities but by the end of the decade growth was slowed by the knock-on effect of the economic crises in Brazil and Argentina, both major trading partners.

Between 2004–07 growth rates improved to around 4% per year as a result of rising prices for hydrocarbons and mining products. Remittances also substantially increased during the decade. Inflation accelerated in 2007 and was 14·0% in 2008, its highest rate since the early 1990s. External debt was significantly reduced through the Multilateral Debt Relief Initiative.

Currency

The unit of currency is the *boliviano* (BOB) of 100 *centavos*, which replaced the *peso* on 1 Jan. 1987 at a rate of one boliviano = 1m. pesos. Inflation was 8·7% in 2007, rising to 14·0% in 2008. In July 2005 foreign exchange reserves were US$922m., total money supply was 7,481m. bolivianos and gold reserves totalled 911,000 troy oz.

Budget

Budgetary central government revenue was 23,485m. bolivianos in 2005 (18,390m. bolivianos in 2004) and expenditure 22,027m. bolivianos (19,110m. bolivianos in 2004).

Performance
Real GDP growth was 4·6% in 2007 and 6·1% in 2008. Total GDP was US$16·7bn. in 2008.

Banking and Finance
The Central Bank (*President*, Gabriel Loza Tellería) is the bank of issue. In 2000 there were eight commercial banks and five foreign banks.

There is a stock exchange in La Paz.

ENERGY AND NATURAL RESOURCES

Environment
In 2008 Bolivia's carbon dioxide emissions from the consumption and flaring of fossil fuels were the equivalent of 1·4 tonnes per capita.

Electricity
Installed capacity was 1·6m. kW in 2004. Production from all sources (2004), 4·54bn. kWh; consumption per capita was 493 kWh in 2004.

Oil and Gas
There are petroleum and natural gas deposits in the Tarija, Santa Cruz and Cochabamba areas. Production of oil in 2005 was 15,416,919 bbls. Reserves in 2005 were 465m. bbls. The US$2·2bn. Bolivia-Brazil pipeline was completed in 2000 and is the longest natural gas pipeline in South America. The 3,150 km pipeline connects Bolivia's gas sources with the southeast regions of Brazil. Natural gas output in 2008 was 13·9bn. cu. metres, with proven reserves of 710bn. cu. metres. In May 2006 Bolivia nationalized the oil and natural gas industries and six months later, in Nov., Bolivia signed up 40 new contracts with oil and natural gas enterprises.

Minerals
Mining accounted for 4% of GDP in 2005. Tin-mining had been the mainstay of the economy until the collapse of the international tin market in 1985. Estimated production in 2005 (preliminary, in tonnes): zinc, 157,019; tin, 18,694; lead, 11,093; antimony, 5,225; wolfram, 658; silver, 420; gold, 8,906 fine kg.

Agriculture
The agricultural population was 3·17m. in 2002, of whom 1·56m. were economically active. There were 2·35m. ha. of arable land in 2004–05. Output in 1,000 tonnes in 2004–05 was: sugarcane, 5,328; soybeans, 1,689; maize, 817; potatoes, 762; rice, 479; bananas, 443; cassava, 370; sorghum, 246; alfalfa, 167. In 2004, 49,000 tonnes of coca (the source of cocaine) were grown. Since 1987 Bolivia has received international (mainly US) aid to reduce the amount of coca grown, with compensation for farmers who co-operate.

Livestock, 2005: cattle, 7,314,000; sheep, 8,816,000; pigs, 2,390,000; goats, 1,896,000; llamas, 2,130,000; asses (2003), 635,000; horses (2003), 323,000; alpacas, 255,000; chickens (2003), 75m.

Forestry
Forests covered 58·74m. ha. (54·2% of the land area) in 2005. Tropical forests with woods ranging from the 'iron tree' to the light balsa are exploited. Timber production in 2007 was 3·10m. cu. metres.

Fisheries
In 2005 the total catch was 6,660 tonnes, exclusively from inland waters.

INDUSTRY
In 2007 industry accounted for 36·4% of GDP, with manufacturing contributing 14·7%. The principal manufactures are mining, petroleum, smelting, foodstuffs, tobacco and textiles.

Labour
Out of 3,884,251 people (54·8% male) in employment in 2001, 44·1% were in agriculture, ranching and hunting, 14·0% in retail and repair, 9·2% in industrial manufacturing and 4·9% in construction. The unemployment rate in 2004 was 8·7%. In 2006 the minimum wage was 500 bolivianos a month.

Trade Unions
Unions are grouped in the Central Obrera Boliviana (COB).

INTERNATIONAL TRADE
An agreement of Jan. 1992 with Peru gives Bolivia duty-free transit for imports and exports through a corridor leading to the Peruvian Pacific port of Ilo from the Bolivian frontier town of Desaguadero, in return for Peruvian access to the Atlantic via Bolivia's roads and railways. Foreign debt was US$6,390m. in 2005.

Imports and Exports
In 2005 imports (f.o.b.) amounted to US$2,191·8m.; exports (f.o.b.) US$2,810·4m. Main import commodities are road vehicles and parts, machinery for specific industries, cereals and cereal preparations, general industrial machinery, chemicals, petroleum, food, and iron and steel. Main exports in 2005 (provisional, in US$1m.): natural gas, 984·0; soybeans and products, 340·1; fuels, 314·8; zinc, 200·1; metallic tin, 102·0; silver ore, 88·3; metallic gold, 78·6; nuts, 74·4; wood and wood products, 67·4.

Main import suppliers in 2005 (provisional, in US$1m.): Brazil, 486·0; Argentina, 370·2; USA, 294·2; Chile, 154·3; Peru, 145·6; Japan, 135·9. Main export markets in 2005 (provisional, in US$1m.): Brazil, 1,011·6; USA, 385·3; Argentina, 260·5; Colombia, 180·5; Venezuela, 154·3; Japan, 134·3.

COMMUNICATIONS

Roads
The total length of the road system was 62,479 km in 2004, of which 14,336 km were national roads. Total passenger cars in use in 2007 numbered 174,900, lorries and vans 468,800, and buses and coaches 7,000. There were 1,073 road accident fatalities in 2007.

Rail
In 2002 the railway network totalled 3,815 km of metre gauge track. Passenger-km travelled in 2002 came to 356m. and freight tonne-km to 1,044m. In July 2007 President Morales announced plans to nationalize the railways.

Civil Aviation
The three international airports are La Paz (El Alto), Santa Cruz de la Sierra (Viru Viru) and Cochabamba (Jorge Wisterman). The main airline is Aerosur, which in 2007 ran scheduled services to Asunción, Buenos Aires, Lima, Salta and São Paulo, as well as internal services. The operations of Lloyd Aéreo Boliviano, for many years the national airline, were suspended in April 2007 owing to financial problems but charter flights were resumed in Dec. In Oct. 2007 the government announced the creation of a new airline, Boliviana de Aviación, as a successor flag carrier. It began commercial flights in March 2009, initially on domestic routes only although it is expected to serve international routes too in due course. In 2005 scheduled airline traffic of Bolivian-based carriers flew 17·1m. km, carrying 1,396,400 passengers.

Shipping
Lake Titicaca and about 19,000 km of rivers are open to navigation. In 2002 the merchant marine totalled 358,000 GRT, including oil tankers 242,000 GRT.

Telecommunications
In June 2006 there were 3,186,900 telephone subscribers (331·0 per 1,000 persons), including 2,534,000 mobile phone subscribers

(263·2 per 1,000 persons). Internet users numbered 480,000 in 2005.

Postal Services
In 2001 there were 142 post offices, or one for every 59,500 persons.

SOCIAL INSTITUTIONS

Justice
Justice is administered by the Supreme Court, superior department courts (of five or seven judges) and courts of local justice. The Supreme Court, with headquarters at Sucre, is divided into two sections, civil and criminal, of five justices each, with the Chief Justice presiding over both. Members of the Supreme Court are chosen on a two-thirds vote of Congress. The death penalty was abolished for ordinary crimes in 1997.

The population in penal institutions in Dec. 2003 was 6,768 (76 per 100,000 of national population).

Education
Adult literacy was 86·9% in 2004 (male, 94·1%; female, 80·4%). Primary instruction is free and obligatory between the ages of six and 14 years. In 2004 there were 14,504 schooling facilities, with 1,743,643 pupils and 78,747 teachers in primary schools, 523,835 pupils and 22,043 teachers in secondary schools, and 205,774 students and 4,525 academic staff in tertiary education. The national rate of school attendance (4–17 year-olds) reached 79·5% in 2004.

In 2005 there were ten universities, two technical universities, one Roman Catholic university, one musical conservatory, and colleges in the following fields: business, six; teacher training, four; industry, one; nursing, one; technical teacher training, one; fine arts, one; rural education, one; physical education, one. In 2004 state universities had 256,140 students and 4,614 teaching staff. There were 35 private universities with 61,414 students and 5,395 teaching staff in 2003.

In 2003 public expenditure on education came to 6·6% of GNI and 18·1% of total government expenditure.

Health
In 2001 there were 1,999 doctors and 4,025 nurses. There were 241 hospitals with 9,886 hospital beds (one per 954 persons) in 2005.

Welfare
The pensions and social security systems in Bolivia were reformed in 1996. Instead of a defined-benefit publicly managed pension system, a defined-contribution system based on privately managed individual capitalization accounts was introduced. There are now two funds: the Collective Capitalization Fund, made up of 50% of the shares of capitalized companies formerly owned by the state, and the Individual Capitalization Fund, made up of contributions of those associated to the new system with a monthly income of above US$50. A solidarity bonus, BONOSOL—worth approximately US$225 a year—is paid to all Bolivians over the age of 65.

RELIGION
The Roman Catholic church was disestablished in 1961. It is under a cardinal (in Sucre), an archbishop (in La Paz), six bishops and vicars apostolic. It had 7·54m. adherents in 2001. In 2001, 78% of the population were Roman Catholics and 16% Protestants. In Feb. 2010 there was one cardinal.

CULTURE

World Heritage Sites
There are six UNESCO sites in Bolivia: the City of Potosí (inscribed in 1987), the largest industrial mining complex of the 16th century; the Jesuit Missions of the Chiquitos (1990), six settlements for converted Indians built between 1696 and 1760; the Historic City of Sucre (1991), containing 16th century colonial architecture; El Fuerte de Samaipata (1998), a pre-Hispanic sculptured rock and political and religious centre; Noel Kempff Mercado National Park (2000), a 1,523,000 ha. park in the Amazon Basin; and Tiwanaku: Spiritual and Political Centre of the Tiwanaku Culture (2000), monumental remains from AD 500 to 900.

Broadcasting
The broadcasting authority is the Superintendencia de Telecomunicaciones (SITTEL). There is a government-operated TV service (Televisión Boliviana) and state-run radio networks (Radio Illimani and Radio Patria Nueva), as well as numerous private TV outlets and hundreds of independent radio stations. In 2006 televisions totalled 1,450,000 (colour by NTSC).

Cinema
In 2005 there were 48 cinema screens, with a total attendance for the year of 1·5m.

Press
There were 29 daily newspapers in 1998 with a combined circulation of 788,000, at a rate of 99 per 1,000 inhabitants.

Tourism
In 2005 there were 504,000 foreign tourists; total revenue from tourism was US$346m. in 2005.

DIPLOMATIC REPRESENTATIVES
Of Bolivia in the United Kingdom (106 Eaton Sq., London, SW1W 9AD)
Ambassador: María Beatriz Souvirón Crespo.

Of the United Kingdom in Bolivia (Avenida Arce 2732, Casilla 694, La Paz)
Ambassador: Nigel Baker.

Of Bolivia in the USA (3014 Massachusetts Ave., NW, Washington, D.C., 20008)
Ambassador: Vacant.
Chargé d'Affaires a.i.: Erika Duenas.

Of the USA in Bolivia (Avenida Arce 2780, Casilla 425, La Paz)
Ambassador: Vacant.
Chargé d'Affaires a.i.: John S. Creamer.

Of Bolivia to the United Nations
Ambassador: Vacant.
Chargé d'Affaires a.i.: Pablo Solón-Romero.

Of Bolivia to the European Union
Ambassador: Vacant.

FURTHER READING
Jemio, Luis Carlos, *Debt, Crisis and Reform in Bolivia: Biting the Bullet.* 2001
Klein, Herbert S., *A Concise History of Bolivia.* 2003
Morales, Waltraud Q., *Bolivia.* 2004
Muñoz-Pogossian, Betilde, *Electoral Rules and the Transformation of Bolivian Politics: The Rise of Evo Morales.* 2008

National Statistical Office: Instituto Nacional de Estadistica, Av. José Carrasco 1391, CP 6129, La Paz.
Website (Spanish only): http://www.ine.gov.bo

BOSNIA AND HERZEGOVINA

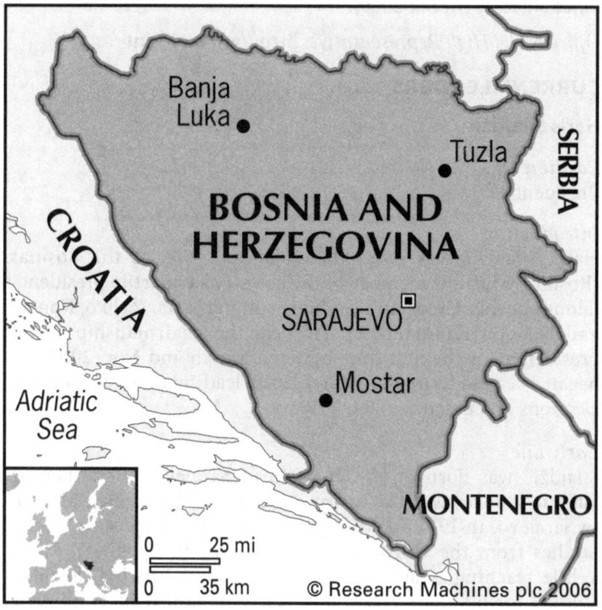

Republika Bosna i Hercegovina
(Republic of Bosnia and Herzegovina)

Capital: Sarajevo
Population estimate, 2010: 3·76m.
GDP per capita, 2007: (PPP$) 7,764
HDI/world rank: 0·812/76

KEY HISTORICAL EVENTS

Settled by Slavs in the 7th century, Bosnia was conquered by the Turks in 1463 when much of the population was gradually converted to Islam. At the Congress of Berlin (1878) the territory was assigned to Austro-Hungarian administration under nominal Turkish suzerainty. Austria-Hungary's outright annexation in 1908 generated international tensions which contributed to the outbreak of the First World War. After 1918 Bosnia and Herzegovina became part of a new Kingdom of Serbs, Croats and Slovenes under the Serbian monarchy. Its name was changed to Yugoslavia in 1929. (See SERBIA and MONTENEGRO for developments up to and beyond the Second World War.)

On 15 Oct. 1991 the National Assembly adopted a 'Memorandum on Sovereignty', the Serbian deputies abstaining. This envisaged Bosnian autonomy within a Yugoslav federation. Though boycotted by Serbs, a referendum in March 1992 supported independence. In March 1992 an agreement was reached by Muslims, Serbs and Croats to set up three autonomous ethnic communities under a central Bosnian authority.

Bosnia and Herzegovina declared independence on 5 April 1992. Fighting broke out between the Serb, Croat and Muslim communities, with particularly heavy casualties and destruction in Sarajevo, leading to extensive Muslim territorial losses and an exodus of refugees. UN-sponsored ceasefires were repeatedly violated.

On 13 Aug. 1992 the UN Security Council voted to authorize the use of force to ensure the delivery of humanitarian aid to besieged civilians. Internationally sponsored peace talks were held in Geneva in 1993, but Serb-Muslim-Croat fighting continued. In April 1993 the UN established havens for Muslim civilians in Sarajevo, Srebrenica and Goražde.

In Dec. 1994 Bosnian Serbs and Muslims signed a countrywide interim ceasefire. Bosnian Croats also signed in Jan. 1995. However, Croatian Serbs and the Muslim secessionist forces under Fikret Abdić did not sign the agreement, and fighting continued. On 16 June 1995 Bosnian government forces launched an attack to break the Bosnian Serb siege of Sarajevo. On 11 July Bosnian Serb forces began to occupy UN security zones despite retaliatory NATO air strikes, and on 28 Aug. shelled Sarajevo. In July Srebrenica was the scene of the worst massacre of the war, when Bosnian Serb troops killed over 7,000 Muslim boys and men after Dutch peacekeeping forces were withdrawn from the city.

To stop the shelling of UN safe areas, more than 60 NATO aircraft attacked Bosnian Serb military installations on 30–31 Aug. On 26 Sept. in Washington the foreign ministers of Bosnia, Croatia and Yugoslavia (the latter negotiating for the Bosnian Serbs) agreed a draft Bosnian constitution under which a central government would handle foreign affairs and commerce and a Serb Zone, and a Muslim-Croat Federation would run their internal affairs. A ceasefire came into force on 12 Oct. 1995.

In Dayton (Ohio) on 21 Nov. 1995 the prime ministers of Bosnia, Croatia and Yugoslavia initialled a US-brokered agreement to end hostilities. The Bosnian state was divided into a Croat-Muslim Federation containing 51% of Bosnian territory and a Serb Republic containing 49%. A central government authority representing all ethnic groups with responsibility for foreign and monetary policy and citizenship issues was established and free elections held. On 20 Dec. 1995 a NATO contingent (IFOR) took over from UN peacekeeping forces to enforce the Paris peace agreements and set up a 4 km separation zone between the Serb and Muslim-Croat territories. After a year IFOR was replaced by SFOR, a 'Stabilization Force'. On 2 Dec. 2004 a 7,000-strong European Union force 'EUFOR' took over from SFOR.

TERRITORY AND POPULATION

The republic is bounded in the north and west by Croatia, in the east by Serbia and in the southeast by Montenegro. It has a coastline of only 20 km with no harbours. Its area is 51,129 sq. km. The capital is Sarajevo (estimated population, 2005: 380,000).

Population at the 1991 census: 4,377,033, of which the predominating ethnic groups were Muslims (1,905,829), Serbs (1,369,258) and Croats (755,892). Population of the principal cities in 1991: Sarajevo, 415,631 (est. 1999, 522,000); Banja Luka, 142,644; Zenica, 96,238. By 1996, following the civil war, 1,319,250 Bosnians had taken refuge abroad, including 0·45m. in Serbia and Montenegro, 0·32m. in Germany, 0·17m. in Croatia and 0·12m. in Sweden.

The UN gives an estimated population for 2010 of 3·76m.; density, 74 per sq. km.

In 2005, 54·3% of the population lived in rural areas.

The official languages are Bosnian, Croatian and Serbian.

SOCIAL STATISTICS

2004 births, 35,151; deaths, 32,616. Rates per 1,000, 2004: birth, 9·1; death, 8·5. Annual population growth rate, 2000–05, 0·3%. Life expectancy at birth, 2007, was 72·4 years for men and 77·7 years for women. Infant mortality, 2005, 13 per 1,000 live births; fertility rate, 2004, 1·2 children per woman.

CLIMATE

The climate is generally continental with steady rainfall throughout the year, although in areas nearer the coast it is more Mediterranean.

CONSTITUTION AND GOVERNMENT

On 18 March 1994, in Washington, Bosnian Muslims and Croats reached an agreement for the creation of a federation of cantons with a central government responsible for foreign affairs, defence and commerce. It was envisaged that there would be a president elected by a two-house legislature alternating annually between the nationalities.

On 31 May 1994 the National Assembly approved the creation of the Muslim Croat federation. Alija Izetbegović remained the unitary states' President. An interim government with Hasan Muratović as Prime Minister was formed on 30 Jan. 1996.

The Dayton Agreement including the new constitution was signed and came into force on 14 Dec. 1995. The government structure was established in 1996 as follows:

Heading the state is a three-member *Presidency* (one Croat, one Muslim, one Serb) with a rotating president. The Presidency is elected by direct universal suffrage, and is responsible for foreign affairs and the nomination of the prime minister. There is a two-chamber parliament: the *House of Representatives* (which meets in Sarajevo) comprises 42 directly elected deputies, two-thirds Croat and Muslim and one-third Serb; and the *House of Peoples* (which meets in Lukavica) comprises five Croat, five Muslim and five Serb delegates.

Below the national level the country is divided into two self-governing entities along ethnic lines.

The Bosniak-Croat Federation of Bosnia and Herzegovina (Federacija Bosna i Hercegovina) is headed by a President and Vice-President, alternately Croat and Muslim, a 98-member Chamber of Representatives and a 58-member Chamber of Peoples. The Serb Republic (Republika Srpska) is also headed by an elected President and Vice-President, and there is a National Assembly of 83 members, elected by proportional representation.

Central government is conducted by a *Council of Ministers*, which comprises Muslim and Serb Co-Prime Ministers and a Croat Deputy Prime Minister. The Co-Prime Ministers alternate in office every week.

In Nov. 2005 leaders of the three main ethnic groups agreed on a series of constitutional reforms aimed at enhancing the authority of the central government, reducing the powers of the Federation of Bosnia and Herzegovina and the Serb Republic, and streamlining the parliament and the office of the presidency.

National Anthem

'Intermezzo'; tune by Dusan Sestić; no words.

RECENT ELECTIONS

Elections were held on 1 Oct. 2006 for the Presidium and the federal parliament. Elected to the Presidency were: Haris Silajdžić (Muslim; Party for Bosnia and Herzegovina—SBiH); Željko Komšić (Croat; Social Democratic Party—SDP); and Nebojša Radmanović (Serb; Alliance of Independent Social Democrats—SNSD). In the parliamentary elections the Party for Democratic Action won 9 seats with 238,474 votes, the SBiH 8 with 219,477 votes, the SNSD 7 with 269,468 votes, the SDP 5, the Croatian Democratic Community 3 and the Serb Democratic Party 3.

CURRENT ADMINISTRATION

Presidency Chairman: Haris Silajdžić (Muslim; SBiH, took rotating presidency on 6 March 2010). *Presidency Members:* Nebojša Radmanović (Serb, SNSD); Željko Komšić (Croat, SDP).

In March 2010 the cabinet comprised:

Prime Minister: Nikola Špirić (Muslim; SNSD); b. 1956 (in office since 11 Jan. 2007).

Deputy Prime Minister and Minister of Finance and Treasury: Dragan Vrankić. *Deputy Prime Minister and Minister of Security:* Sadik Ahmetović.

Minister of Civil Affairs: Sredoje Nović. *Defence:* Selmo Cikotić. *Foreign Affairs:* Sven Alkalaj. *Foreign Trade and Economic Relations:* Mladen Zirojević. *Human Rights and Refugees:* Safet Halilović. *Justice:* Bariša Čolak. *Transportation and Communications:* Rudo Vidović.

UN High Representative: Valentin Inzko (Austria); b. 1949 (in office since 26 March 2009).

Office of the High Representative: http://www.ohr.int

CURRENT LEADERS

Haris Silajdžić

Position

President

Introduction

Haris Silajdžić was sworn in on 6 Oct. 2006 as the Bosniak (Bosnian Muslim) member of the country's tripartite presidency (alongside his Croat and Serbian counterparts, Željko Komšić and Nebojša Radmanović). He held the chairmanship of the presidency for the first time between March and Nov. 2008 and began a second term on 6 March 2010, leading up to presidential elections scheduled for Oct. 2010.

Early Life

Silajdžić was born on 1 Oct. 1945 in Sarajevo. His father, an Islamic scholar, was the imam of the Gazi Husrev-Beg Mosque in Sarajevo. In 1971 Silajdžić graduated with a degree in Islamic Studies from the University of Garyounis in Benghazi, Libya. While teaching Arabic at the University of Priština, Silajdžić studied for his master's degree which he gained in 1979. After finishing a doctorate on American-Albanian relations, he took up a professorship at the University of Sarajevo. He was also invited to guest lecture at Harvard University and Chatham House.

In May 1990 Silajdžić helped establish the Party for Democratic Action (SDA), eventually becoming its vice-president. Following the triumph of the SDA at the Nov. 1990 general elections, Silajdžić was appointed chairman of the Bosnia-Herzegovina Republican Committee for International Cooperation, which was to become the foreign ministry. Between 1993 and 1996 he was prime minister and made powerful appeals for financial and military assistance for Bosnian self-defence. In 1995 he joined the Bosnian delegation to negotiate in the US-brokered Dayton Accords.

Silajdžić left the SDA and resigned as prime minister in 1996, after a power struggle within the SDA-controlled government and Silajdžić's concern at the party's brush with Islamic fundamentalism. He founded his own party, the Party for Bosnia and Herzegovina, which he still heads. He stood for the Bosniak presidential seat in the Oct. 2002 general election but lost to the SDA leader, Sulejman Tihić. Contesting the seat again in Oct. 2006, on a platform of uniting the country under a strong central government, he received over 60% of the Bosniak vote. In 2007 he expressed disappointment at the International Court of Justice's judgment that Serbia was not directly involved in the Bosnian genocide of the 1990s.

Career in Office

Silajdžić supports constitutional reform and the abolition of the country's two composite entities, the Federation of Bosnia and Herzegovina and the Serb Republic. His second term began against the backdrop of a dispute over the arrest of former president Ejup Ganić at London's Heathrow airport on war crimes charges. Silajdžić flew to London to oppose Ganić's extradition to Serbia. His Serbian counterpart in the tripartite presidency, Nebojša Radmanović, accused Silajdžić of seeking to create a 'private Bosnian state'.

DEFENCE

Defence expenditure in 2006 totalled US$142m. (US$32 per capita), representing 1·2% of GDP.

An EU-led peacekeeping contingent 'EUFOR' took over military operations from the NATO-led 'SFOR' on 2 Dec. 2004. Its mission is to focus on the apprehension of indicted war criminals and counter-terrorism, and provide advice on defence reform. Initially numbering 7,000 personnel, by the end of 2007 the strength had been reduced to 2,200.

Army

Reform of the defence forces began in 2003 and resulted, in 2006, in the establishment of a single state army (in place of the previously separate armed forces of the Federation of Bosnia and Herzegovina and the Serb Republic). Its personnel—including that of the Air Force and Anti-Air Defence Brigade—totalled 9,007 in 2007. The Army had 325 main battle tanks in 2007 plus 193 armoured personnel carriers and 132 armoured infantry fighting vehicles.

Air Force

The Air Force and Anti-Aircraft Defence was established in 2006. It had 17 combat capable aircraft and 21 helicopters in 2007.

INTERNATIONAL RELATIONS

Bosnia and Herzegovina is a member of the UN, World Bank, IMF and several other UN specialized agencies, OSCE, BIS, Central European Initiative, IOM and NATO Partnership for Peace.

The Serb Republic and the then Yugoslavia signed an agreement on 28 Feb. 1997 establishing 'special parallel relations' between them. The agreement envisages co-operation in cultural, commercial, security and foreign policy matters, allows visa-free transit of borders and includes a non-aggression pact. A customs agreement followed on 31 March.

ECONOMY

In 2004 agriculture accounted for 11·9% of GDP, industry 27·5% and services 60·6%.

Overview

Infrastructure and output were damaged by war in the early 1990s but growth has been continuous since the Dayton Accords ended fighting in 1995, although the economy is yet to reach pre-war levels. Policy has focused on restoring social stability and securing international aid. It is estimated that donor commitment from international assistance programmes totals US$5·4bn.

Unemployment has remained high with the global financial slowdown. Remittances and exports have grown rapidly in recent years. In the post-war decade GDP tripled and exports expanded ten-fold. Exports, however, dropped 22% during the first two months of 2009 as a result of the global financial crisis. Around 66% of the economy is generated by services. The financial sector plays an important role, with the banking sector dominated by foreign banks. The country became a full member of the Central European Free Trade Agreement in Sept. 2007.

Currency

A new currency, the *konvertibilna marka* (BAM) consisting of 100 *pfennig*, was introduced in June 1998. Initially trading at a strict 1-to-1 against the Deutsche Mark, it is now pegged to the euro at a rate of 1·95583 convertible marks to the euro. Inflation was 7·4% in 2008. Total money supply was 4,193m. convertible marks in July 2005.

Budget

Revenue in 2004 was 3,725m. convertible marks; expenditure was 3,489m. convertible marks. VAT of 17% was introduced on 1 Jan. 2006.

Performance

Real GDP grew by 6·8% in 2007 and 5·5% in 2008. Total GDP was US$18·5bn. in 2008.

Banking and Finance

There is a Central Bank (*Governor*, Kemal Kozarić). In 2005 there were 28 commercial banks (19 in the Federation and 9 in the Serb Republic). There are stock exchanges in Banja Luka and Sarajevo.

ENERGY AND NATURAL RESOURCES

Environment

Bosnia and Herzegovina's carbon dioxide emissions from the consumption and flaring of fossil fuels in 2008 were the equivalent of 4·1 tonnes per capita.

Electricity

Bosnia and Herzegovina is rich in hydro-electric potential and is a net exporter of electricity. Installed capacity was estimated at 2·7m. kW in 2004. Production in 2004 was 12·60bn. kWh. In 2004 consumption per capita was 2,690 kWh.

Minerals

Output in 2006: lignite, 10·0m. tonnes; iron ore, 3·4m. tonnes; bauxite, 817,000 tonnes; aluminium, 136,000 tonnes.

Agriculture

In 2007 there were 1·02m. ha. of arable land and 95,000 ha. of permanent crops. 2003 production (in 1,000 tonnes): maize, 545; potatoes, 302; wheat, 160; plums, 88; cabbage, 71; oats, 50; apples, 41; barley, 40. Livestock in 2003: sheep, 670,000; cattle, 440,000; pigs, 300,000; poultry, 5m.

Forestry

In 2005 forests covered 2·19m. ha., or 43·1% of the total land area. Timber production in 2007 was 3·75m. cu. metres.

Fisheries

Estimated total fish catch in 2005: 2,000 tonnes (exclusively freshwater).

INDUSTRY

Output (in 1,000 tonnes): cement (2000), 300; crude steel (2001), 80. Other products (1990): cars, 38,000 units; tractors, 34,000 units; lorries, 16,000 units; televisions, 21,000 sets.

Labour

The labour force totalled 1,719,000 in 1996 (62% males). Unemployment in 2004 was nearly 40%.

INTERNATIONAL TRADE

External debt was US$5,564m. in 2005.

Imports and Exports

2007 external trade (in US$1m.): imports (c.i.f.), 9,720·1; exports (f.o.b.), 4,152·0. Principal import sources in 2007 were Croatia, 17·6%; Germany, 12·5%; Serbia, 10·2%, Italy, 9·0%; Slovenia, 6·4%; main export markets were Croatia, 18·4%; Serbia, 13·7%; Italy, 13·1%; Germany, 12·8%; Slovenia, 10·9%.

COMMUNICATIONS

Roads

In 2005 there were an estimated 22,419 km of roads (4,104 km main roads). There were 96,182 passenger cars in use in 1996 (23 per 1,000 inhabitants) and 9,783 vans and trucks. There were 428 road accident fatalities in 2007.

Rail

There were 1,028 km of railways in 2005 (777 km electrified). It is estimated that up to 80% of the rail network was destroyed in the civil war, and it was not until July 2001 that the first international services were resumed. There are two state-owned rail companies—the Bosnia & Herzegovina Railways Public Corporation (BHŽJK) and the Railway of the Serb Republic (ŽRS). BHŽJK carried 6·7m. tonnes of freight and 346,000 passengers in 2005; ŽRS carried 1·2m. passengers and 1·1m. tonnes of freight in 2003.

Civil Aviation

There are airports at Sarajevo (Butmir), Tuzla, Banja Luka and Mostar. In 2005 there were direct flights to Belgrade, Cologne/Bonn, Düsseldorf, Frankfurt, İstanbul, İzmir, Ljubljana, Milan, Prague, Stockholm, Stuttgart, Vienna, Zagreb and Zürich. In 2001 Sarajevo handled 313,000 passengers (all international) and 1,300 tonnes of freight.

Telecommunications

Telephone subscribers numbered 2,563,200 in 2005, equivalent to 656·1 per 1,000 inhabitants. There were 1,594,400 mobile phone subscribers in 2005 and 806,400 internet users. Three state-owned companies run the telephone networks in different parts of the country, the largest of which is the Sarajevo-based PTT Bih.

Postal Services

In 2003 there were 243 post offices.

SOCIAL INSTITUTIONS

Justice

The population in penal institutions in April 2003 was 2,283.

Police

The European Union Police Mission (EUPM) in Bosnia and Herzegovina, the EU's first civilian crisis management operation, took over from the UN's International Police Task Force on 1 Jan. 2003. It aims to help the authorities develop their police forces to the highest European and international standards.

Education

The adult literacy rate was 94·6% in 2003 (male, 98·4%; female, 91·1%). In 2003–04 there were 375,213 pupils in 1,993 primary schools (21,763 teachers), 168,592 in 303 secondary schools (10,892 teachers) and 76,979 students in seven universities.

Health

In 2001 there were 5,443 physicians, 679 dentists, 16,708 nurses and 350 pharmacists. In 1996 there were 48 hospital beds per 10,000 inhabitants.

Welfare

There were 380,000 pensions in 1990 (including 140,000 old age).

RELIGION

In 2001 there were estimated to be 1,690,000 Sunni Muslims, 1,180,000 Serbian Orthodox, 710,000 Roman Catholics and 350,000 followers of other religions. In Feb. 2010 the Roman Catholic church had one cardinal.

CULTURE

World Heritage Sites

There are two UNESCO World Heritage sites in Bosnia and Herzegovina: the Old Bridge area of the Old City of Mostar (inscribed on the list in 2005), an important Ottoman frontier town, and the Mehmed Paša Sokolović Bridge in Višegrad (2007), constructed in the 16th century.

Broadcasting

The main public broadcasters are: the Public Broadcasting Service of Bosnia and Herzegovina, which operates the national BHTV1 and BH Radio 1 networks; Serb Republic Radio-TV (RTRS), which runs services in the Serb self-governing entity; and Federation TV (FTV) and Radio FBiH in the Bosniak-Croat Federation. There is also a large number of commercial radio and TV stations. The Communications Regulatory Agency was established in 2001 with jurisdiction over broadcasting and telecommunications. In 2005 there were 1·1m. TV receivers.

Press

There were seven daily newspapers in 2006 with a combined circulation of 100,000. Less than 17% of the population regularly reads a daily newspaper.

Tourism

In 2005, 217,000 non-resident tourists stayed in holiday accommodation; spending by tourists totalled US$604m.

DIPLOMATIC REPRESENTATIVES

Of Bosnia and Herzegovina in the United Kingdom (5–7 Lexham Gdns, London, W8 5JJ)
Ambassador: Jadranka Negodić.

Of the United Kingdom in Bosnia and Herzegovina (8 Tina Ujevića, Sarajevo)
Ambassador: Michael Tatham.

Of Bosnia and Herzegovina in the USA (2109 E St., NW, Washington, D.C., 20037)
Ambassador: Mitar Kujundžić.

Of the USA in Bosnia and Herzegovina (Alipasina 43, 71000, Sarajevo)
Ambassador: Charles English.

Of Bosnia and Herzegovina to the United Nations
Ambassador: Ivan Barbalić.

Of Bosnia and Herzegovina to the European Union
Ambassador: Osman Topčagić.

FURTHER READING

Bieber, Florian, *Post-War Bosnia: Ethnicity, Inequality and Public Sector Governance.* 2005

Burg, Steven L. and Shoup, Paul S., *The War in Bosnia-Herzegovina.* 1999

Cigar, N., *Genocide in Bosnia: the Policy of Ethnic Cleansing.* 1995

Fine, J. V. A. and Donia, R. J., *Bosnia-Hercegovina: a Tradition Betrayed.* 1994

Friedman, F., *The Bosnian Muslims: Denial of a Nation.* 1996

Hoare, Marko Attila, *The History of Bosnia: From the Middle Ages to the Present Day.* 2006

Holbrooke, R., *To End a War.* 1998

Malcolm, N., *Bosnia: a Short History.* 2nd ed. 1996

O'Ballance, E., *Civil War in Bosnia, 1992–94.* 1995

Rieff, D., *Slaughterhouse: Bosnia and the Failure of the West.* 1997

Sells, M. A., *The Bridge Betrayed: Religion and Genocide in Bosnia.* 1996

National Statistical Office: Agency for Statistics of Bosnia and Herzegovina, Zelenih beretki 26, 71000 Sarajevo. *Director:* Zdenko Milinović.
Website: http://www.bhas.ba

BOTSWANA

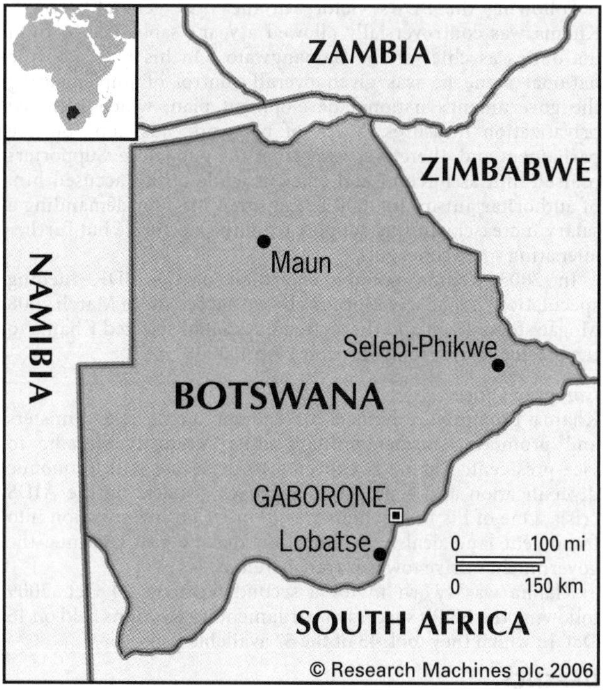

Lefatshe la Botswana
(Republic of Botswana)

Capital: Gaborone
Population estimate, 2010: 1·98m.
GDP per capita, 2007: (PPP$) 13,604
HDI/world rank: 0·694/125

KEY HISTORICAL EVENTS

The Tswana or Batswana people are the principal inhabitants of the country formerly known as Bechuanaland. The territory was declared a British protectorate in 1895. Britain ruled through her High Commissioner in South Africa until the post was abolished in 1964. Frequent suggestions for the addition of Bechuanaland and the other two High Commission Territories to South Africa were rejected, the Africans being strongly against the idea. Economically, however, the country was very closely tied to that of South Africa and has remained so. In Dec. 1960 Bechuanaland received its first constitution. Further constitutional change brought full self-government in 1965 and full independence on 30 Sept. 1966. For years Botswana had great difficulties with the neighbouring settler regime in Rhodesia, until that country became Zimbabwe in 1980. Relations with South Africa were also strained until the ending of apartheid. Today the country enjoys stability and a fast-growing economy.

'The sole country in Africa with a record of consistently strong political and economic progress is Botswana' (*The Economist*, 11 Oct. 2008).

TERRITORY AND POPULATION

Botswana is bounded in the west and north by Namibia, northeast by Zambia and Zimbabwe, and east and south by South Africa. The area is 581,730 sq. km. Population (2001 census), 1,680,863; density, 2·9 per sq. km. In 2001, 49·4% of the population was urban.

The UN gives an estimated population for 2010 of 1·98m.

In 2005, 57·4% of the population were urban.

The country is divided into nine districts (Central, Ghanzi, Kgalagadi, Kgatleng, Kweneng, Ngwaketse, North East, North West and South East).

The main towns (with population, 2001) are Gaborone (186,007), Francistown (83,023), Molepolole (54,561), Selebi-Phikwe (49,849), Maun (43,776), Serowe (42,444), Kanye (40,628), Mahalapye (39,719), Mochudi (36,962), Mogoditshane (32,843) and Lobatse (29,689).

The official languages are Setswana and English. Setswana is spoken by over 90% of the population and English by approximately 40%. More than ten other languages, including Herero, Hottentot, Kalanga, Mbukushu, San and Sekgalagadi are spoken in various tribal areas. The main ethnic groups are the Tswana (67%), Kalanga (15%) and Ndebele (2%).

SOCIAL STATISTICS

2001 (estimates) births, 49,000; deaths, 21,000. Rates, 2001 estimates (per 1,000 population): births, 28·9; deaths, 12·4. Infant mortality, 2005 (per 1,000 live births), 86. Expectation of life in 2007 was 53·2 years for males and 53·3 for females. In 2007, 23·9% of all adults between 15 and 49 were infected with HIV. Annual population growth rate, 1992–2002, 2·1%. Fertility rate, 2004, 3·1 children per woman.

CLIMATE

In winter, days are warm and nights cold, with occasional frosts. Summer heat is tempered by prevailing northeast winds. Rainfall comes mainly in summer, from Oct. to April, while the rest of the year is almost completely dry with very high sunshine amounts. Gaborone, Jan. 79°F (26·1°C), July 55°F (12·8°C). Annual rainfall varies from 650 mm in the north to 250 mm in the southeast. The country is prone to droughts.

CONSTITUTION AND GOVERNMENT

The Constitution was adopted in March 1965 and became effective on 30 Sept. 1966. It provides for a republican form of government headed by the President with three main organs: the Legislature, the Executive and the Judiciary. The executive rests with the President who is responsible to the National Assembly. The President is elected for five-year terms by the National Assembly.

The *National Assembly* consists of 63 members, of which 57 are elected by universal suffrage, four are specially elected members and two, the President and the Speaker, are *ex officio*.

Elections are held every five years. Voting is on the first-past-the-post system.

There is also a *House of Chiefs* to advise the government. It consists of the Chiefs of the eight tribes who were autonomous during the days of the British protectorate, plus four members elected by and from among the sub-chiefs in four districts; these 12 members elect a further three politically independent members.

National Anthem

'Fatshe leno la rona' ('Blessed be this noble land'); words and tune by K. T. Motsete.

GOVERNMENT CHRONOLOGY

Presidents since 1966. (BDP = Botswana Democratic Party)

1966–80	BDP	Seretse Khama
1980–98	BDP	Quett Ketumile Joni Masire
1998–2008	BDP	Festus Gontebanye Mogae
2008–	BDP	Lieut.-Gen. Seretse Khama Ian Khama

RECENT ELECTIONS

In National Assembly elections held on 16 Oct. 2009 the Botswana Democratic Party (BDP) gained 45 seats with 53·3% of the vote, the Botswana National Front 6 with 21·9%, the Botswana Congress Party 4 with 19·2%, the Botswana Alliance Movement 1 with 2·3% and ind. 1 with 1·9%. Turnout was 76·7%.

CURRENT ADMINISTRATION

President: Lieut.-Gen. Seretse Khama Ian Khama; b. 1953 (BDP; sworn in 1 April 2008).

Vice-President: Lieut.-Gen. Mompati Merafhe.

In March 2010 the cabinet was as follows:

Minister of Presidential Affairs and Public Administration: Lesego Motsumi. *Defence, Justice and Security:* Dikgakgamatso Seretse. *Foreign Affairs and International Co-operation:* Phandu Skelemani. *Finance and Development Planning:* Kenneth Matambo. *Infrastructure, Science and Technology:* Johnnie Swartz. *Lands and Housing:* Nonofo Molefhi. *Labour and Home Affairs:* Peter Siele. *Youth, Sports and Culture:* Shaw Kgathi. *Trade and Industry:* Baledzi Gaolathe. *Local Government:* Lebonamang Mokalake. *Agriculture:* Christian de Graaf. *Transport and Communications:* Frank Ramsden. *Minerals, Energy and Water Resources:* Ponatshego Kedikilwe. *Education and Skills Development:* Pelonomi Venson-Moitoi. *Environment, Wildlife and Tourism:* Kitso Mokaila. *Health:* John Seakgosing.

Government Website: http://www.gov.bw

CURRENT LEADERS

Lieut.-Gen. Seretse Khama Ian Khama

Position

President

Introduction

Lieut.-Gen. (retd) Seretse Khama Ian Khama succeeded Festus Mogae as president in 2008. Formerly head of the army and a paramount chief of the Bamangwato people, Khama retains a reputation as a military man rather than a career politician. Since entering politics in 1998 he has been closely associated with the government's programme to diversify the economy and promote transparency.

Early Life

Seretse Khama Ian Khama was born in the UK on 27 Feb. 1953, the son of Seretse Khama (who later became Botswana's first president) and his English wife. Following the family's return to Botswana in 1956, Khama grew up in his father's home village of Serowe and attended the local school. He pursued further studies in Zimbabwe (then Rhodesia), Swaziland and Switzerland, before enrolling at Sandhurst Military Academy in the UK. After graduating from Sandhurst, he joined the Botswana Defence Force (BDF) and rose rapidly through the ranks. In 1977 he was promoted to brigadier and became deputy commander of the BDF under Lieut.-Gen. Mompati Merafhe.

In 1979 he was made paramount chief of the Bamangwato people, Botswana's largest tribal group. However, Khama continued to devote his time to the army and in 1989, when Merafhe retired to enter politics, became its commander. Under Khama the BDF developed into a professional force, participating in international peacekeeping, disaster relief and anti-poaching missions.

On 1 April 1998 Khama, newly retired from the army, was named vice-president by the incoming president Festus Mogae. The appointment was widely seen as an attempt to inject new blood into the ruling Botswana Democratic Party (BDP) and to tap into Khama's reputation and influence. Initially unable to take up his post because he did not hold a seat in the National Assembly, Khama was sworn in on 13 July 1998 after winning a by-election in Serowe North. He was put in charge of presidential administration and public affairs and became an arbiter of complaints against government ministers, which made him some political enemies.

Following the BDF's victory in the 1999 general election, Khama was controversially allowed a year's sabbatical to fulfil his duties as chief of the Bamangwato. On his return to the national scene he was given overall control of implementing the government's national development plan, which included privatization measures. Much of his work was done outside parliament and, therefore, away from the public eye. Supporters praised him as forceful and efficient while critics accused him of authoritarianism. In 2000 he censured MPs for demanding a salary increase, winning support from the electorate but further alienating some colleagues.

In 2003 Khama became chairman of the BDP, fuelling speculation that he was Mogae's chosen successor. In March 2008 Mogae stood down and the National Assembly elected Khama to the presidency. He took office on 1 April 2008.

Career in Office

Khama promptly reshuffled his cabinet, firing five ministers and promoting former military chief Mompati Merafhe to vice-president. Khama is expected to persevere with economic diversification and a proactive approach to tackling the AIDS crisis. One of his first actions was to order an investigation into fraudulent land deals, an indication that he will continue the government's drive towards transparency.

Khama was sworn in for a second term on 20 Oct. 2009 following the BDP's success in parliamentary elections held on 16 Oct. in which they took 45 of the 57 available seats.

DEFENCE

In 2006 defence expenditure totalled US$289m. (US$176 per capita), representing 3·0% of GDP.

Army

The Army personnel (2007) numbered 8,500. There is also a 1,500-strong paramilitary force.

Air Force

The Air Wing operated 31 combat capable aircraft in 2007 and numbered 500.

INTERNATIONAL RELATIONS

Botswana is a member of the UN, World Bank, IMF and several other UN specialized agencies, WTO, Commonwealth, African Development Bank, African Union, SADC and is an ACP member state of the ACP-EU relationship.

ECONOMY

Industry accounted for 55·2% of GDP in 2006, services 42·9% and agriculture 1·9%.

Overview

Until recently Botswana's economic performance was seen as an example to other developing countries. From the 1980s until the early 2000s Botswana recorded 8% annual growth, fuelled by the diamond industry. From one of the world's poorest countries in the 1960s, it achieved middle income status and today holds the highest sovereign credit rating in Africa. This impressive development resulted from healthy management of resources and prudent government expenditure. However, 25% of the population is in poverty and inequality is high. The HIV/AIDS rate is the second highest in the world. Alongside a slowdown in diamond production, the global economic crisis of 2007–08 saw the growth rate dwindle to 2·9% in 2008.

When Botswana gained independence in 1966 mining accounted for only 1% of GDP but today accounts for 36%. Nickel and copper exports are also important. Manufacturing, construction and agriculture each comprise 2–6% of the economy. Agricultural development is limited by the naturally dry landscape. The government is attempting to diversify the economy by developing the financial services sector and safari tourism. In 1994 Botswana was the first country to be removed from the UN's list of Least Developed Countries (LDCs).

Currency

The unit of currency is the *pula* (BWP) of 100 *thebe*. The pula was devalued by 7·5% in Feb. 2004 and 12·5% in May 2005. Inflation was 7·1% in 2007 and 12·6% in 2008. Foreign exchange reserves were US$5,770m. in June 2005 and total money supply was P3,878m.

Budget

The fiscal year begins in April. Government finance for recent years (in P1m.):

	2001–02	*2002–03*	*2003–04*
Revenue	7,907·5	8,829·1	9,746·7
Expenditure	8,143·3	9,469·9	10,082·2

2003–04 revenue (in P1m.) comprised: mineral taxes, 4,930·0; customs pool, 1,394·1; other revenue, 3,422·6. Expenditure included: recurrent, 7,327·6; development, 2,462·6.

VAT is 10%.

Performance

Real GDP grew by 4·4% in 2007 and 2·9% in 2008. Total GDP in 2008 was US$13·0bn.

Banking and Finance

There were five commercial banks in 2004. Total assets were P24,718·2m. at July 2004. The Bank of Botswana (*Governor*, Linah Mohohlo), established in 1976, is the central bank. The National Development Bank, founded in 1964, has six regional offices, and agricultural, industrial and commercial development divisions. The Botswana Co-operative Bank is banker to co-operatives and to thrift and loan societies. The government-owned Post Office Savings Bank (Botswana Post) operates throughout the country.

There is a stock exchange in Gaborone.

ENERGY AND NATURAL RESOURCES

Environment

Botswana's carbon dioxide emissions from the consumption and flaring of fossil fuels in 2008 were the equivalent of 2·4 tonnes per capita.

Electricity

Installed capacity was 132,000 kW in 2003. Production in 2005 was 867m. kWh. The coal-fired power station at Morupule supplies cities and major towns.

Minerals

Botswana is the world's biggest diamond producer in terms of value; in 2003 the total value was estimated to be US$2·5bn. Diamonds were first discovered in Botswana in 1967. Debswana, a partnership between the government and De Beers, runs three mines producing around 30m. carats a year, with plans to double the capacity of the largest mine from 6m. to 12m. carats a year. Coal reserves are estimated at 17bn. tonnes. There is also copper, salt and soda ash. Estimated diamond production in 2005, 31·9m. carats (the third largest quantity after Australia and Russia). Other mineral production, 2003: coal, 823,000 tonnes; salt, 30,000 tonnes; copper, 8,000 tonnes; gold, 8 kg.

Agriculture

70% of the total land area is desert. 80% of the population is rural, 71% of all land is 'tribal', protected and allocated to prevent overgrazing, maintain small farmers and foster commercial ranching. Agriculture provides a livelihood for over 70% of the population, but accounts for only 2·4% of GDP (2003). In 2003, 360,000 ha. were arable and 3,000 ha. permanent crops. There were 7,000 tractors in 2004 and 102 harvester-threshers. Cattle-rearing is the chief industry after diamond-mining, and the country is more a pastoral than an agricultural one, crops depending entirely upon the rainfall. In 2007 an estimated 295,000 persons were economically active in agriculture. In 2004 there were: cattle, 2·2m.; goats, 1·6m.; asses, 330,000 (estimate); sheep, 244,000; chickens, 4·5m. (estimate). A serious outbreak of cattle lung disease in 1995–96 led to the slaughter of around 300,000 animals.

Production in 2004 (in 1,000 tonnes) included: sorghum, 12; maize, 8; millet, 3; beans and pulses, 2.

17% of the land is set aside for wildlife conservation and 20% for wildlife management areas, with four national parks and game reserves.

Forestry

Forests covered 139,000 sq. km, or 25·2% of the total land area, in 2003. There are forest nurseries and plantations. Concessions have been granted to harvest 7,500 cu. metres in Kasane and Chobe Forestry Reserves, and up to 2,500 cu. metres in the Masame area. In 2007, 774,000 cu. metres of roundwood were cut.

Fisheries

In 2005 the total catch was 132 tonnes, exclusively from inland waters.

INDUSTRY

The most important sector is the diamond industry. A diamond-processing plant opened in Gaborone in March 2008. Meat is processed, and beer, soft drinks, textiles and foodstuffs manufactured. Rural technology is being developed and traditional crafts encouraged. In June 2003 there were 16,773 enterprises operating in Botswana, of which a third were in the wholesale and retail trade.

Labour

In 2005–06, 787,962 persons were economically active, of which 539,150 persons were in employment; 29·9% worked in agriculture, 14·4% in wholesale and retail trade, 8·0% in education and 6·9% in public administration. In March 2005 there were an estimated 288,800 paid employees (including 86,700 in central government and 24,700 in local government). Botswana's biggest individual employer is the Debswana Diamond Company, with a workforce of 4,000. In 2005–06 the unemployment rate was 17·5%.

INTERNATIONAL TRADE

Botswana is a member of the Southern African Customs Union (SACU) with Lesotho, Namibia, South Africa and Swaziland. There are no foreign exchange restrictions. External debt in 2005 totalled US$473m.

Imports and Exports

In 2006 imports (f.o.b.) totalled US$2,616·5m. More than three-quarters of all imports are from the SACU countries, the main commodities being machinery and electrical equipment, foodstuffs, vehicles and transport equipment, textiles, and petroleum products.

In 2006 exports (f.o.b.) totalled US$4,520·8m., including diamonds, vehicles, copper, nickel and beef.

Principal import sources in 2003 were Southern African Customs Union (SACU), 86·6%; UK, 2·5%; Zimbabwe, 1·5%; USA, 0·7%. Main export markets were the UK, 77·6%; SACU, 8·8%; Zimbabwe, 2·9%; USA, 0·4%.

COMMUNICATIONS

Roads

In 2004 the total road network was estimated to be 21,133 km (8,916 km national roads). In Nov. 2004 there were 220,663 motor vehicles registered. In 2007 there were 497 deaths in road accidents.

Rail

The main line from Mafeking in South Africa to Bulawayo in Zimbabwe traverses Botswana. The total length of the rail system was 888 km in 2005, including two branch lines. In 2006, 426,894 passengers and 1,712,607 tonnes of freight were carried.

Civil Aviation

There are international airports at Gaborone (Sir Seretse Khama) and at Maun and six domestic airports. The national carrier is the state-owned Air Botswana. In 2003 direct flights were operated to Harare and Johannesburg. In 2003 scheduled airline traffic of Botswana-based carriers flew 3m. km, carrying 189,000 passengers (131,000 on international flights). In Oct. 1999 an Air Botswana pilot who had been suspended two months earlier crashed an empty passenger plane into the airline's two serviceable aeroplanes at Gaborone Airport, killing himself and destroying the airline's complete fleet in the process. In 2006 Gaborone handled 289,550 passengers.

Telecommunications

Botswana had 955,100 telephone subscribers in 2005 (541·1 per 1,000 inhabitants), including 823,100 mobile phone subscribers. There were 80,000 PCs in use in 2004 (45·2 per 1,000 inhabitants) and 60,000 internet users.

Postal Services

There were 113 post offices and 70 postal agencies in Nov. 2004. The Botswana Post offers many services including Western Union Money Transfers.

SOCIAL INSTITUTIONS

Justice

Law is based on the Roman-Dutch law of the former Cape Colony, but judges and magistrates are also qualified in English common law. The Court of Appeal has jurisdiction in respect of criminal and civil appeals emanating from the High Court, and in all criminal and civil cases and proceedings. Magistrates' courts and traditional courts are in each administrative district. As well as a national police force there are local customary law enforcement officers. The death penalty is still in force. There was one execution in 2009. The population in penal institutions in Nov. 2003 was 5,890 (327 per 100,000 of national population).

Education

Adult literacy rate in 2003 was 81·2%. Basic free education, introduced in 1986, consists of seven years of primary and three years of junior secondary schooling. In 2005 enrolment in primary schools was 326,500 with 13,472 teaching staff, and 168,720 pupils at secondary level with 12,371 teaching staff. There were 10,950 students is higher education in 2005 with 529 academic staff. 'Brigades' (community-managed private bodies) provide lower-level vocational training. The Department of Non-Formal Education offers secondary-level correspondence courses and is the executing agency for the National Literacy Programme.

In 2003–04 expenditure on education came to US$797·4m.

Health

In 2004 there were 16 primary hospitals, one mental hospital, three referral hospitals, 15 health centres, 257 clinics and 366 health posts. There were also 761 stops for mobile health teams. In 2004 there were 89 doctors and 2,129 nurses in government health facilities. There are other private health facilities with more personnel.

RELIGION

Freedom of worship is guaranteed under the Constitution. About 43% of the population is Christian. Non-Christian religions include Bahais, Muslims and Hindus.

CULTURE

World Heritage Sites

Tsodilo was created a UNESCO World Heritage Site in 2001. It is the site of over 4,500 prehistoric rock paintings in the Kalahari Desert.

Broadcasting

Radio Botswana and Botswana Television (BTV) are state-run. There is an independent TV service run by the Gaborone Broadcasting Company (colour by PAL). Yarona FM and Gabz FM are private radio stations. 9·5% of households were equipped with televisions in 2005.

Press

The government-owned Daily News is distributed free (circulation, 2006: 65,000). There is one other daily, the independent Mmegi (The Reporter), and 11 non-dailies.

Tourism

There were 1·1m. foreign visitors in 2003 with tourism receipts totalling US$356m.

DIPLOMATIC REPRESENTATIVES

Of Botswana in the United Kingdom (6 Stratford Pl., London, W1C 1AY)
High Commissioner: Roy Warren Blackbeard.

Of the United Kingdom in Botswana (Private Bag 0023, Gaborone)
High Commissioner: Jennifer Anderson.

Of Botswana in the USA (1531–1533 New Hampshire Ave., NW, Washington, D.C., 20036)
Ambassador: Lapologang Caesar Lekoa.

Of the USA in Botswana (PO Box 90, Gaborone)
Ambassador: Stephen Nolan.

Of Botswana to the United Nations
Ambassador: Charles Thembani Ntwaagae.

Of Botswana to the European Union
Ambassador: Claurinah Tshenolo Modise.

FURTHER READING

Central Statistics Office. *Statistical Bulletin* (Quarterly).

Ministry of Information and Broadcasting. *Botswana Handbook.—Kutlwano* (Monthly).

Molomo, M. G. and Mokopakgosi, B. (eds.) *Multi-Party Democracy in Botswana.* 1991

Perrings, C., *Sustainable Development and Poverty Alleviation in Sub-Saharan Africa: the Case of Botswana.* 1995

National Statistical Office: Central Statistics Office, Private Bag 0024, Gaborone.
Website: http://www.cso.gov.bw

BRAZIL

República Federativa do Brasil
(Federative Republic of Brazil)

Capital: Brasília (Federal District)
Population estimate, 2010: 195·42m.
GDP per capita, 2007: (PPP$) 9,567
HDI/world rank: 0·813/75

KEY HISTORICAL EVENTS

There is evidence of human habitation in Brazil dating back to 9000 BC. Before the Portuguese discovery and occupation of Brazil there was a large indigenous population. This population was fragmented into a number of smaller tribes, the largest of which was the Tupi-Guarani, who survived the sub-tropical environment by clearing just enough land for their crops.

The first Europeans to come into contact with the indigenous peoples were exiled criminals, or degredados, who learned their language and skills in farming and hunting. Jesuit missionaries later attempted to convert the native people with limited success.

The first Portuguese contact with Brazil was Pedro Alvares Cabral who left Lisbon in 1500 with orders to travel along the Cape of Good Hope route discovered by the Portuguese navigator Vasco da Gama in 1497–98. In an attempt to avoid storms he set a course more westerly than da Gama's and was carried still farther westward by currents, landing in a place he named *Terra da Vera Cruz* (Land of the True Cross) and later renamed *Terra do Brasil* (Land of Brazil).

Although the official motive for Portuguese exploration was religious—the conversion of the natives to the Catholic faith—the greater incentive was to find a direct all-water trade route with Asia and thereby break Italy's commercial domination. Early Portuguese economic activity in Brazil revolved around the exploitation of the huge timber (Brazilwood) resources. This was soon superseded by sugarcane and, to a lesser extent, tobacco, harvested on plantations that sprang up in the interior in the 16th and 17th centuries. As these industries came to dominate the economy, the need for large-scale labour became more pressing. Where the indigenous people proved unsuitable or unavailable, largely owing to ill health from newly introduced European diseases, millions of Africans were enslaved and shipped to the region.

The first attempt to establish a working government came in 1533 when the Portuguese divided the land into 15 captaincies, subdivided into leagues and ruled by selected governors (*donatários*). In 1549 John III sought to establish a more centralized power structure and appointed Tomé de Sousa as governor general, ruling from the newly founded capital, Salvador (Bahia). In 1567 Governor-General Mem da Sá founded Rio de Janeiro to protect its harbour from French incursions. During the Union of Portugal and Spain (1580–1640), Brazil became subject to attacks from Spanish enemies, notably the Netherlands, whose forces were not expelled until 1654.

The Portuguese settlers had set about conquering the vast Brazilian interior by the late 17th century. Early excursions were made by *bandeirantes*, men pursuing private enterprise and dreams of vast personal wealth. It was these men who, in forging waterways and paths into the interior, discovered the first gold in the region at Minas Gerais in 1695. This opened up a whole new resource for exploitation by the Portuguese crown. Rio de Janeiro benefited greatly from mining wealth and in 1763 became the colonial capital in place of Salvador. Recife and Ouro Preto were the only other major colonial urban centres.

The third quarter of the 18th century saw Spain accept many of Portugal's claims in the region. Portuguese Prime Minister Sebastião José de Carvalho e Mello ended the rule of the *donatários*, expelled the Jesuits, gave new freedoms to the native population and established two companies to regulate Brazilian trade. As Brazilian government became increasingly centralized a burgeoning nationalism emerged, most famously in the failed rebellion against the Portuguese led by Joaquim José da Silva Xavier (Tiradentes) in 1789.

In 1807 an invasion of Portugal by the French forces of Napoleon Bonaparte forced the royal family to flee Portugal and take refuge in Rio, declaring it the temporary capital of the Portuguese Empire. In 1816 King João VI ascended to the Portuguese throne but refused to return to Lisbon until revolts demanded his presence there five years later. While in Brazil he initiated reforms which ended Portugal's commercial monopoly and in 1815 granted Brazil equal status with Portugal when he established the United Kingdom of Portugal, Brazil and the Algarves. On his return to Portugal João's son, Pedro, became Brazil's regent.

Independence

Pedro's regency ran into trouble when he battled the demands of the Cortes (the Portuguese parliamentary body) for him to return to Portugal. The Cortes repealed many of João's reforms for the former colony and sought to reduce it to its earlier colonial status. When in Sept. 1822 the Cortes decided to reduce Pedro's powers he called for Brazilian independence. On 1 Dec. 1822 he was crowned Constitutional Emperor and Perpetual Defender of Brazil. The United States recognized Brazil's independence in May 1824 followed by Portugal itself in 1825.

Pedro was forced to abdicate in 1831 following a disastrous war with Argentina and a money crisis deepened by his promise to free the slaves. He left his five-year old son Pedro II as the ruler in waiting. In 1840 Pedro II ascended the throne after nine years of weak rule and civil strife. Pedro proceeded to establish himself as leader, free of all political influences, by 1847. He ruled for nearly 50 years and despite a series of uprisings Brazil remained relatively stable and its economy strong.

Pedro was instrumental in the overthrow of Juan Manuel de Rosas in Argentina in the 1850s and became involved in Uruguay's civil war in the 1860s. In the 1870s the three nations united to repel the advances of the Paraguayan forces of Francisco Solano López. Pedro initiated the gradual abolition of slavery by outlawing the slave trade in 1854. Emancipation was achieved in 1888 when three quarters of a million slaves were freed without compensation to their owners. In 1889 Gen. Manuel Deodoro da Fonseca led a military revolt which forced Pedro's abdication. A republic was proclaimed, headed by Fonseca, which instigated the separation of church and state. In Feb. 1891 Brazil officially became a Federal Republic with Fonseca elected as its first president. Forced to resign when he attempted to bypass congress, he was succeeded by Floriano Peixoto who used the military to restore order. In 1894 he was replaced by Brazil's first civilian head of state, Prudente de Morais, the first of a succession of leaders who enjoyed relative peace as Brazil grew rich on coffee exports.

Brazil underwent significant territorial expansion in the early years of the 20th century during the Baron of Rio Branco's tenure as foreign minister. As well as winning 900,000 sq. km of land from other South American nations, he pursued close relations with the USA and UK, which led to a declaration of war against Germany in 1917. However, by the 1920s there was growing internal resentment at the wealth of the coffee barons and in 1922 a failed military coup initiated eight years of civil strife. Amid economic crisis in 1930 Getúlio Vargas lost the presidential election but was swept to power by a military junta which dismissed the legitimately elected government.

The constitution of 1934 provided for universal suffrage and three years later a new constitution, drafted in the aftermath of a failed coup, gave Vargas greatly extended power. During his period of rule some areas, including São Paulo, saw considerable industrial development, helping Brazil to create a modern economy. In the 1940s the first steel plant was built in the state of Rio de Janeiro at Volta Redonda with US financing. In 1942 Brazil followed the lead of the USA and declared war against the Axis powers. In Oct. 1945 the military staged a coup and Vargas was forced to step down.

Economic Problems

The subsequent election was won by Eurico Gaspar Dutra, a favourite of Vargas, whose government promulgated a constitution which set presidential terms at five years and reduced the power of central government. Vargas was returned to power in 1950 but failed to dominate as he had previously. Brazil's economic problems spiralled and in 1954 Vargas was implicated in the attempted murder of a journalist critical of him. When the High Command demanded his resignation Vargas committed suicide by shooting himself.

Juscelino Kubitschek, popularly known as JK, was elected president in 1956. He instigated massive public expenditure including road and hydroelectric schemes and the creation of a new capital, Brasília. It was hoped these programmes would be the catalyst for the development of Brazil's huge interior but instead brought uncontrollable inflation. Jânio Quadros became president in 1961 on a wave of euphoria but his decoration of Che Guevara in a public ceremony antagonized the right wing military and he resigned after six months in office. Vice-president João Goulart took over but his leftist policies led to his overthrow by the military in 1964.

There followed 20 years of single party rule and censored press. Humberto Castelo Branco was installed as president in April 1964. Chosen by the military to enforce fundamental political and economic reforms, Branco instead sought to introduce change through democratic channels. He narrowly survived a coup in 1965 but was forced by the military powerbrokers to take a radical line. Laws passed in Oct. 1965 suspended political parties and gave the president emergency powers. An ostensibly two-party state was created, consisting of the government-backed National Renewal Alliance (ARENA) and the Brazilian Democratic Movement (MDB). The MDB declined to field a candidate at the presidential elections of 1966 and ARENA's Costa e Silva took the presidency.

Brazil's military regime was not as brutal as those of Chile or Argentina, but at its height, around 1968 and 1969 when Costa e Silva awarded himself emergency powers, the use of torture was widespread. Costa e Silva had a stroke in Aug. 1970 and was replaced by Gen. Emílio Garrastazú Médici in Oct. He was succeeded in early 1974 by Gen. Ernesto Geisel. Geisel promoted measures to reduce censorship and increase political freedom but reverted to political oppression when electoral victory seemed doubtful. In April 1977 he dismissed congress when it failed to pass judicial reforms and governed using emergency powers. He resigned in 1979 to be replaced by his favoured successor, Gen. João Baptista de Oliveira Figueiredo. The generals benefited from the Brazilian economic miracle in the late 1960s and '70s, when the economy was growing by more than 10% per year. However, uncoordinated growth led to rampant bureaucracy, corruption and inflation.

Return to Democracy

Confronted with hyperinflation, Figueiredo introduced reforms but conditions for the majority failed to improve. In 1979 the government authorized the restitution of political rights which had been eroded since Quadros came to power. In 1980 a militant working-class movement sprang up under the charismatic leadership of a worker, Luiz Inácio Lula da Silva (better known as Lula). Popular opposition, together with economic problems, forced Figueiredo to adopt the *abertura* (opening)—a slow process of returning to democratic government.

Tancredo Neves, leader of the Partido do Movimento Democratico Brasiliero (PMDB), the main opposition party, surprised his military opponents by winning the 1985 elections, but died shortly before assuming power. José Sarney, his vice-president, took over and successfully guided the country through the difficult transition from military to civilian rule as well as overseeing the drafting and implementation of a new democratic constitution. Despite this political success the country drifted into the economic chaos which afflicted the whole continent, with finance ministers changing frequently and foreign debt reaching CR$115,000m. Price and wage freezes set out in Sarney's Cruzado Plan succeeded briefly in bringing down inflation but ultimately failed. In the presidential run-off of Dec. 1989 voters backed two of Sarney's most vociferous critics, with Fernando Collor de Mello narrowly defeating Labour Party candidate, Lula.

Collor, of the National Reconstruction party, promised reductions in inflation and corruption. In March 1990 he confiscated 80% of every bank account worth more than US$1,200, promising to release them 18 months later with interest. He also announced the privatization of state-owned companies and the opening of Brazilian markets to foreign competition and capital. By 1992 Collor's government had failed to reach many of its targets and was embroiled in scandals and corruption, some of which were linked directly to his family. Parliament, under public pressure, forced an impeachment and Itamar Franco, Collor's vice-president, took office until elections were held in Oct. 1994. Under Franco inflation leapt towards 3,000% but his fourth finance minister, Fernando Henrique Cardoso, was responsible for the introduction of successful economic reforms.

In 1994 Cardoso was elected president for the Partido da Social Democracia Brasiliera, formed in 1990 by PMDB dissidents. He oversaw an economic revolution that included a radical privatization programme, the lowering of trade barriers and the introduction of a new currency, the *real*. A constitutional amendment in 1997 provided for consecutive presidential terms and the following year Cardoso won re-election although Brazil had already begun to feel the effects of the economic turbulence in the Far East and was reliant on IMF loans. In Jan. 1999 the *real* was devalued, losing 35% of its value against the dollar in two months. In Cardoso's second term the public debt reached US$260bn. and the government was forced to reduce spending on health and welfare while increasing taxes. His government failed to address the problems of social inequality and official corruption and at the 2002 presidential elections Cardoso's successor, José Serra, was defeated by the left-wing leader, Luiz Inácio Lula da Silva.

Lula, the country's first elected socialist president, pledged to combat Brazil's widespread poverty while co-operating with the business sector and international community. In May 2003 he invited the Democratic Movement into government to ensure the passage of key economic reforms.

TERRITORY AND POPULATION

Brazil is bounded in the east by the Atlantic and on its northern, western and southern borders by all the South American countries except Chile and Ecuador. The total area (including inland water) is 8,514,877 sq. km. Population as at the census of 2000 and population count of 2007:

Federal Unit and Capital	*Area (sq. km)*	*Census 2000*	*Population Count 2007*
North	3,853,327		
Rondônia (Porto Velho)	237,576	1,379,787	1,453,756
Acre (Rio Branco)	164,165	557,526	655,385
Amazonas (Manaus)	1,559,161	2,812,557	3,221,939
Roraima (Boa Vista)	224,299	324,397	395,725
Pará (Belém)	1,247,690	6,192,307	7,065,573
Amapá (Macapá)	142,815	477,032	587,311
Tocantins (Palmas)	277,621	1,157,098	1,243,627
North-East	1,554,257[1]		
Maranhão (São Luís)	331,983	5,651,475	6,118,995
Piauí (Teresina)	251,529	2,843,278	3,032,421
Ceará (Fortaleza)	148,826	7,430,661	8,185,286
Rio Grande do Norte (Natal)	52,797	2,776,782	3,013,740
Paraíba (João Pessoa)	56,440	3,443,825	3,641,395
Pernambuco (Recife)	98,312	7,918,344	8,485,386
Alagoas (Maceió)	27,768	2,822,621	3,037,103
Sergipe (Aracaju)	21,910	1,784,475	1,939,426
Bahia (Salvador)	564,693	13,070,250	14,080,654
South-East	924,511		
Minas Gerais (Belo Horizonte)	586,528	17,891,494	19,273,506
Espírito Santo (Vitória)	46,078	3,097,232	3,351,669
Rio de Janeiro (Rio de Janeiro)	43,696	14,391,282	15,420,375
São Paulo (São Paulo)	248,209	37,032,403	39,827,570
South	576,410		
Paraná (Curitiba)	199,315	9,563,458	10,284,503
Santa Catarina (Florianópolis)	95,346	5,356,360	5,866,252
Rio Grande do Sul (Porto Alegre)	281,749	10,187,798	10,582,840
Central West	1,606,372		
Mato Grosso (Cuiabá)	903,358	2,504,353	2,854,642
Mato Grosso do Sul (Campo Grande)	357,125	2,078,001	2,265,274
Goiás (Goiânia)	340,087	5,003,228	5,647,035
Distrito Federal (Brasília)	5,802	2,051,146	2,455,903
Total	8,514,877	169,799,170	183,987,291

[1]Including disputed areas between states of Piauí and Ceará.

Population density, 2007, 21·6 per sq. km. The 2000 census showed 83,576,015 males and 86,233,155 females. The United Nations population estimate for 2000 was 174·17m. The urban population comprised 84·2% of the population in 2005.

The UN gives an estimated population for 2010 of 195·42m.

The official language is Portuguese.

Population of principal cities (2007 population count):

São Paulo	10,990,249	Guarulhos	1,279,202
Rio de Janeiro	6,161,047	Goiânia	1,265,394
Salvador	2,948,733	Campinas	1,056,644
Brasília	2,557,158	São Luís	986,826
Fortaleza	2,473,614	São Gonçalo	982,832
Belo Horizonte	2,434,642	Maceió	924,143
Curitiba	1,828,092	Duque de Caxias	864,392
Manaus	1,709,010	Nova Iguaçu	855,500
Recife	1,549,980	São Bernardo do Campo	801,580
Porto Alegre	1,430,220		
Belém	1,424,124	Natal	798,065

Teresina	793,915	Londrina	505,184
Campo Grande	747,189	Belford Roxo	495,694
Osasco	713,066	Ananindeua	495,480
João Pessoa	693,082	Aparecida de Goiânia	494,919
Jaboatão dos Guararapes	678,346	Joinville	492,101
		Niterói	477,912
Santo André	671,696	São João de Meriti	468,309
Uberlândia	622,441	Campos dos Goytacazes	431,839
Contagem	617,749		
São José dos Campos	609,229	Betim	429,507
Feira de Santana	584,497	Santos	417,518
Sorocaba	576,312	São José do Rio Preto	414,272
Ribeirão Preto	558,136	Mauá	412,753
Cuiabá	544,737	Vila Velha	407,579
Aracaju	536,785	Caxias do Sul	405,858
Juiz de Fora	520,612	Florianópolis	402,346

The principal metropolitan areas (census, 2000) were São Paulo (17,834,664), Rio de Janeiro (10,872,768), Belo Horizonte (4,811,760), Porto Alegre (3,655,834), Recife (3,335,704), Salvador (3,018,285), Fortaleza (2,975,703), Curitiba (2,725,629) and Belém (1,794,981).

Approximately 54% of the population of Brazil is White, 40% mixed White and Black, and 5% Black. There are some 260,000 native Indians.

SOCIAL STATISTICS

The total number of registered live births in 2006 was 2,799,128 (rate of 15·4 per 1,000 population); deaths, 1,020,211 (5·6); marriages, 889,828 (4·9); divorces 162,244 (0·9). The average age at first marriage in 2006 was 28·3 years for men and 25·4 for women. Life expectancy in 2006 was 68·5 years for males and 76·1 for females. Annual population growth rate, 2000–05, 1·5%; infant mortality, 2006, 25 per 1,000 live births; fertility rate, 2006, 2·0 children per woman. Brazil's recent economic advances enabled 6m. people to move out of poverty in 2006.

CLIMATE

Because of its latitude, the climate is predominantly tropical, but factors such as altitude, prevailing winds and distance from the sea cause certain variations, though temperatures are not notably extreme. In tropical parts, winters are dry and summers wet, while in Amazonia conditions are constantly warm and humid. The northeast *sertão* is hot and arid, with frequent droughts. In the south and east, spring and autumn are sunny and warm, summers are hot, but winters can be cold when polar air-masses impinge. Brasília, Jan. 72°F (22·3°C), July 68°F (19·8°C). Annual rainfall 60" (1,512 mm). Belém, Jan. 78°F (25·8°C), July 80°F (26·4°C). Annual rainfall 105" (2,664 mm). Manaus, Jan. 79°F (26·1°C), July 80°F (26·7°C). Annual rainfall 92" (2,329 mm). Recife, Jan. 80°F (26·6°C), July 77°F (24·8°C). Annual rainfall 75" (1,907 mm). Rio de Janeiro, Jan. 83°F (28·5°C), July 67°F (19·6°C). Annual rainfall 67" (1,758 mm). São Paulo, Jan. 75°F (24°C), July 57°F (13·7°C). Annual rainfall 62" (1,584 mm). Salvador, Jan. 80°F (26·5°C), July 74°F (23·5°C). Annual rainfall 105" (2,669 mm). Porto Alegre, Jan. 75°F (23·9°C), July 62°F (16·7°C). Annual rainfall 59" (1,502 mm).

CONSTITUTION AND GOVERNMENT

The present Constitution came into force on 5 Oct. 1988, the eighth since independence. The *President* and *Vice-President* are elected for a four-year term. To be elected candidates must secure 50% plus one vote of all the valid votes, otherwise a second round of voting is held to elect the President between the two most voted candidates. Voting is compulsory for men and women between the ages of 18 and 70 apart from illiterates (for whom it is optional); it is also optional for persons from 16 to 18 years old and persons over 70. A referendum on constitutional change was held on 21 April 1993. Turnout was 80%. 66·1% of votes cast were in favour of retaining a republican form of government, and 10·2% for re-establishing a monarchy. 56·4% favoured an executive presidency, 24·7% parliamentary supremacy.

A constitutional amendment of June 1997 authorizes the re-election of the President for one extra term of four years.

Congress consists of an 81-member *Senate* (three Senators per federal unit plus three from the Federal District of Brasília) and a 513-member *Chamber of Deputies*. The Senate is directly elected (half of it elected for eight years in rotation). The Chamber of Deputies is elected by universal franchise for four years. There is a *Council of the Republic* which is convened only in national emergencies.

Baaklini, A. I., *The Brazilian Legislature and Political System*. 1992
Martinez-Lara, J., *Building Democracy in Brazil: the Politics of Constitutional Change*. 1996

National Anthem

'Ouviram do Ipiranga às margens plácidas de um povo heróico o brado retumbante' ('The peaceful banks of the Ipiranga heard the resounding cry of an heroic people'); words by J. O. Duque Estrada, tune by F. M. da Silva.

GOVERNMENT CHRONOLOGY

Presidents since 1930. (ARENA = National Renewal Alliance; PMDB = Brazilian Democratic Movement Party; PRN = Party for National Reconstruction; PSD = Social Democratic Party; PSDB = Brazilian Social Democracy Party; PT = Workers' Party; PTB = Brazilian Labour Party; n/p = non-partisan)

1930–45	n/p	Getúlio Dornelles Vargas
1945–46	n/p	José Linhares
1946–51	military/PSD	Eurico Gaspar Dutra
1951–54	PTB	Getúlio Dornelles Vargas
1954–56	PTB	João Fernandes de Campos Café (Filho)
1956–61	PSD	Juscelino Kubitschek de Oliveira
1961	n/p	Jânio da Silva Quadros
1961–64	PTB	João Belchior Marques Goulart
1964–67	military	Humberto de Alencar Castelo Branco
1967–69	military	Artur da Costa e Silva
1969	Triumvirate (military)	Augusto Hamann Rademaker Grünewald, Aurélio de Lyra Tavares, Márcio de Souza e Mello
1969–74	military/ARENA	Emílio Garrastazú Médici
1974–79	military/ARENA	Ernesto (Beckmann) Geisel
1979–85	military/ARENA/ PDS	João Baptista de Oliveira Figueiredo
1985–90	PMDB	José Sarney Costa
1990–92	PRN	Fernando Affonso Collor de Mello
1992–95	n/p	Itamar Augusto Cautiero Franco
1995–2003	PSDB	Fernando Henrique Silva Cardoso
2003–	PT	Luiz Inácio Lula da Silva

RECENT ELECTIONS

In the first round of presidential elections held on 1 Oct. 2006, incumbent Luiz Inácio Lula da Silva (Workers' Party) won 48·6% of votes cast, Geraldo Alckmin of the Brazilian Social Democracy Party (PSDB) 41·6%, Heloísa Helena of the Socialism and Freedom Party (PSOL) 6·9% and Cristovam Buarque of the Democratic Labour Party (PDT) 2·6%. There were three other candidates. In the run-off held on 29 Oct. 2006 Luiz Inácio Lula da Silva won 60·8% against 39·2% for Geraldo Alckmin.

Parliamentary elections were also held on 1 Oct. 2006 for both the Chamber of Deputies and the Senate.

In the elections to the 513-seat Chamber of Deputies, the Brazilian Democratic Movement Party (PMDB) won 89 seats; Workers' Party (PT), 83; Brazilian Social Democracy Party (PSDB), 65; Liberal Front Party (PFL), 65; Progressive Party (PP), 42; Brazilian Socialist Party (PSB), 27; Democratic Labour Party (PDT), 24; Liberal Party (PL), 23; Brazilian Labour Party (PTB), 22; Socialist People's Party (PPS), 21; Green Party (PV), 13; Communist Party of Brazil (PCdoB), 13; Christian Social Party (PSC), 9. Other parties won four seats or fewer.

Following the Senate elections of 1 Oct. 2006 the Liberal Front Party had 18 seats; Brazilian Social Democracy Party, 15; Brazilian Democratic Movement Party, 15; Workers' Party, 11; Democratic Labour Party, 5; Brazilian Labour Party, 4; Brazilian Socialist Party, 3; Liberal Party, 3; Brazilian Republican Party, 2; Communist Party of Brazil, 2; Brazilian Labour Renewal Party, 1; Progressive Party, 1; Socialist People's Party, 1.

Presidential and parliamentary elections are scheduled to take place on 3 Oct. 2010.

CURRENT ADMINISTRATION

President: Luiz Inácio Lula da Silva 'Lula'; b. 1945 (Workers' Party; sworn in 1 Jan. 2003 and re-elected 29 Oct. 2006).

Vice-President: José Alencar.

In March 2010 the coalition government was composed as follows:

Minister of Agrarian Development: Guilherme Cassel. *Agriculture, Livestock and Supply:* Reinhold Stephanes. *Communications:* Hélio Costa. *Culture:* Juca Ferreira. *Defence:* Nelson Jobim. *Development, Industry and Foreign Trade:* Miguel Jorge. *Education:* Fernando Haddad. *Environment:* Carlos Minc. *Finance:* Guido Mantega. *Foreign Relations:* Celso Amorim. *Health:* José Gomes Temporão. *Institutional Relations:* Alexandre Rocha Santos Padilha. *Justice:* Luiz Paulo Barreto. *Labour:* Carlos Lupi. *Mines and Energy:* Edison Lobão. *National Integration:* Geddel Vieira Lima. *Planning, Budget and Administration:* Paulo Bernardo Silva. *Science and Technology:* Sérgio Rezende. *Social Development and Hunger Alleviation:* Patrus Ananias. *Social Security:* José Pimentel. *Sport:* Orlando Silva de Jesus Júnior. *Strategic Affairs:* Samuel Pinheiro Guimarães Neto. *Tourism:* Luiz Eduardo Pereira Barretto Filho. *Transport:* Alfredo Nascimento. *Urban Affairs:* Márcio Fortes.

Government Website: http://www.brasil.gov.br

CURRENT LEADERS

Luiz Inácio Lula da Silva

Position
President

Introduction
A former factory worker and trade union activist, Luiz Inácio Lula da Silva, better known as Lula, was elected president of Brazil in 2002 at his fourth attempt, representing the Workers' Party (PT; Partido dos Trabalhadores). The country's first elected socialist leader, he pledged to combat Brazil's widespread poverty while co-operating with the business sector and international community. He was re-elected in Oct. 2006.

Early Life
Lula was born on 27 Oct. 1945 in Garanhans in the northeastern state of Pernambuco, the seventh of eight surviving siblings. In 1952 his family moved to São Paulo state where his father worked as a docker. Living in Guarujá and Santos, Lula initially worked as a street vendor and shoe-shine boy and had little formal education. When his parents separated in 1956, he moved with his mother to the state capital. Following two years of odd jobs in the city's factories, he was employed from the age of 14 as a lathe operator in a São Paulo metalworks. He continued to work in the industry for the next 20 years.

In the late 1960s, when Brazil was under military rule, Lula became politically active in the metalworkers' trade union. Progressing through the union hierarchy, he was elected leader in 1975 with 92% support. He was re-elected just as emphatically three years later. In 1980 he founded the radical PT as a combination of trade unionists, left-wing groups and church activists. Contesting its first elections in 1982, the PT took only six seats, but increased its representation to 19 four years later.

Lula first stood for the presidency in 1989 coming second to the National Reconstruction candidate Fernando Collor. Through the 1990s the party's rhetoric softened, although it continued its commitment to aiding the poor. Nonetheless, in the 1994 and 1998 presidential elections, Lula came second to the Social Democrat candidate Fernando Cardoso.

At the time of the Oct. 2002 elections, Brazil was suffering from the economic fall-out of a growing trade deficit, tax increases and reduced government spending. In the first round, Lula came first with 46·4% of votes. In the second round run-off with the Social Democrat candidate, José Serra, he took 61·3%. The PT also won the most seats in the Chamber of Deputies.

Career in Office
Lula took office in Jan. 2003, having pledged to reduce poverty and hunger by redistributing wealth, improving education and health, and implementing agrarian reform, with the creation of a new 'social emergency' ministry. Brazil's financial markets were nervous, and the *real* faltered at the prospect of a socialist revolution. However, Lula also promised to co-operate with the business and banking communities, to adhere to IMF guidelines, to repay foreign debt and to continue his predecessor's attempts to control inflation. His government has since pursued sound macroeconomic policies, taking credit for low inflation, significant job creation and strong annual growth in GDP.

From May 2005 the PT was undermined politically by financial corruption scandals, leading to the resignations of several senior party officials and Lula allies, which tarnished the government's claim to probity and threatened to jeopardize the president's hopes of re-election. However, in Oct. 2006 Lula secured a second term of office after two rounds of voting in the presidential elections. The PT lost ground marginally in the parliamentary poll to become the second largest party in the Chamber of Deputies. In 2007 corruption allegations continued to haunt Lula's administration as the Supreme Court indicted 40 people in Aug., including the president's former chief of staff and other senior PT politicians. Nevertheless, the president maintained his personal popularity, achieving a 78% approval rating in a poll in late 2008. He also drew political credit for the resilience of Brazil's economy which, although not immune to the global financial crisis that unfolded in the latter half of 2008, was quick to rebound through 2009, reflecting the sound financial system, robust domestic demand and diverse trading partnerships.

In foreign affairs, Lula has sought increasing engagement with other emerging powers on the world stage, particularly India and China, and expanded Brazil's diplomatic representation in Africa. He has also championed the country's candidacy for a permanent seat on the United Nations Security Council. Lula was closely involved in Rio de Janeiro's successful lobbying for selection to host the 2016 summer Olympic Games, which was confirmed in Oct. 2009.

DEFENCE

Conscription is for 12 months.

In 2008 defence expenditure totalled US$23,302m. (US$120 per capita), a 5% real-term year-on-year increase. In 2007 defence spending represented 1·5% of GDP. Brazil is responsible for 48% of South America's military spending.

As at Oct. 2009, 1,347 personnel (1,288 troops, 47 military observers and 12 police) were deployed in UN peacekeeping operations.

Army

There are seven military commands and 12 military regions. Strength, 2007, 238,200 (including 89,000 conscripts). Equipment in 2007 included 224 main battle tanks.

Navy

The principal ship of the Navy and Brazil's only aircraft carrier is the 32,700-tonne *São Paulo* (formerly the French *Foch*), commissioned in 1963 and purchased in 2000. There are also five diesel submarines and ten frigates including three bought from the UK in 1995 and 1996.

Naval bases are at Rio de Janeiro, Salvador, Natal, Belém, Rio Grande and São Paulo, with river bases at Brasília, Ladário and Manaus.

Active personnel, 2007, totalled 62,261 (more than 11,000 conscripts), including 14,500 Marines and 1,300 in Naval Aviation.

Air Force

The Air Force has four commands: COMGAR (operations), COMDABRA (aerospace defence), COMGAP (logistics) and COMGEP (personnel). There are seven air regions. Personnel strength, 2007, 67,440. There were 309 combat aircraft in 2007, including Mirage F-2000s and F-5Es.

INTERNATIONAL RELATIONS

Brazil is a member of the UN, World Bank, IMF and several other UN specialized agencies, WTO, BIS, IOM, Inter-American Development Bank, SELA, LAIA, OAS, MERCOSUR, UNASUR and Antarctic Treaty.

In Dec. 2005 the government repaid the country's entire US$15·5bn. debt to the IMF two years ahead of schedule.

ECONOMY

Agriculture accounted for 5·1% of GDP in 2006, industry 30·9% and services 64·0%.

Overview

Rich in natural resources, Brazil is South America's largest economy. Following the Second World War it developed a diversified industrial sector protected by tariff barriers. By the 1980s, import substituting industrialization (ISI) was no longer sustaining high growth. From 1981–90 annual growth averaged only 1·7%, compared to an average of 8·5% from 1971–80. The 1990s saw market reforms and outward-looking development. Average annual growth improved to 2·7% for 1991–2000. A period of hyperinflation was broken in the mid-1990s and since 1999 inflation-targeting monetary policy has held levels under 10%, except for 2003. The overvaluation of the pegged currency in the 1990s kept exports from making a significant contribution to GDP.

In 1999 the crawling-peg exchange rate was replaced by a managed-float, when unsustainable debt maintenance and failing investor confidence (stemming from the Russian bond default and the East Asian crisis) forced the central bank to devalue the currency.

In the last decade exports have gained importance, with Brazil enjoying a competitive advantage in agriculture. However, the economy remains relatively closed to imports, particularly those from outside the Southern Common Market (MERCOSUR), to which Brazil belongs. Major exports include transport equipment, iron ore, soybeans, footwear and coffee.

In 2002–03, against a backdrop of poor global economic conditions, Brazil's currency came under pressure. Under the threat of debt default, the government, in collaboration with the IMF, avoided serious trouble by sound macroeconomic management. Tight fiscal and monetary policies protected the economy but stymied growth in 2003. In 2004 the economy rebounded, growing at its highest rate for over a decade. Public debt was reduced from 60% of GDP in 2003 to 36·5% in 2008. Brazil is no longer an IMF borrower and outstanding IMF debt was paid off two years ahead of schedule.

Growth averaged 4·7% between 2004 and 2008 which, combined with well implemented social policies, reduced the poverty rate from 32·9% in 2003 to 25·6% in 2006, as measured by the minimum wage. Capital inflows, including FDI, have helped to more than double international reserves. In mid-2008 Brazil achieved an investment grade rating by Standard & Poor's and Fitch as a result of its strong growth prospects and continued sound macroeconomic policies. In 2007 the government launched the Growth Acceleration Plan to stimulate public and private investment and to provide tax incentives for faster growth, spurring 5·1% growth in 2008.

The global financial crisis saw a curtailment in external credit, as well as a decline in commodity prices and export demand. GDP shrank by 4·5% in the last quarter of 2008 and the first quarter of 2009, when the government adopted countercyclical measures. Private consumption and a healthy financial system helped ensure a recovery beginning in the second quarter of 2009. The limited impact of the global financial turmoil highlighted the economy's ability to withstand changes in the external environment.

A BRIC summit in 2008 provided further evidence of the strengthening alliance with the similarly fast-growing nations of Russia, India and China. However, poverty and inequality remain high, while barriers and regulations hinder the country's ability to reach its growth potential.

Currency

The unit of currency is the *real* (BRL) of 100 *centavos*, which was introduced on 1 July 1994 to replace the former *cruzeiro real* at a rate of 1 real (R$1) = 2,750 cruzeiros reais (CR$2,750). The *real* was devalued in Sept. 1994, March 1995, June 1995 and Jan. 1999, when it was allowed to float. Inflation rates (based on IMF statistics):

1999	*2000*	*2001*	*2002*	*2003*	*2004*	*2005*	*2006*	*2007*	*2008*
4·9%	7·1%	6·8%	8·4%	14·8%	6·6%	6·9%	4·2%	3·6%	5·7%

In 1990 inflation had been 2,948%.

In Sept. 2009 foreign exchange reserves were US$215,978m. (US$32,434m. in 2000); gold reserves totalled 1·08m. troy oz. Total money supply in Aug. 2009 was R$201,761m.

Budget

2004 (in R$1m.): revenue was 422,450 and expenditure 372,730. Tax revenues accounted for 76·4% of revenues in 2004; social security and welfare accounted for 33·8% of expenditures.

Performance

Real GDP growth rates (based on IMF statistics):

1999	*2000*	*2001*	*2002*	*2003*	*2004*	*2005*	*2006*	*2007*	*2008*
0·3%	4·3%	1·3%	2·7%	1·1%	5·7%	3·2%	4·0%	5·7%	5·1%

In March 1999 an IMF agreement introduced a tight monetary policy with an emphasis on reducing the ratio of debt to GDP. Total GDP in 2008 was US$1,612·5bn., making Brazil the world's eighth largest economy.

Banking and Finance

On 31 Dec. 1964 the Banco Central do Brasil (*President*, Henrique Meirelles) was founded as the national bank of issue and at Dec. 2002 had total reserves of US$37·84bn.

The Banco do Brasil/Bank of Brazil (founded in 1853 and reorganized in 1906) is a state-owned commercial bank; it had 4,048 branches in 2007 throughout the country. In Nov. 2008

Banco Itaú and Unibanco agreed to merge in a move that would create South America's biggest bank, with assets of approximately R$608bn. (US$338bn.). However, operations are not expected to be fully integrated until 2011. In March 2007 total deposits in banks were R$386·8bn.

In Nov. 1998 the IMF announced a US$41·5bn. financing package to help shore up the Brazilian economy. In Aug. 2001 it gave approval for a new US$15bn. stand-by credit, and in Aug. 2002 granted an additional US$30bn. loan to try to prevent a financial meltdown that was threatening to devastate the region. In Dec. 2005 Brazil repaid all its IMF debts.

Brazil received a record US$45·1bn. worth of foreign direct investment in 2008, up from US$34·6bn. in 2007 and US$18·8bn. in 2006.

There is a stock exchange in São Paulo.

ENERGY AND NATURAL RESOURCES

Environment

Brazil's carbon dioxide emissions from the consumption and flaring of fossil fuels in 2008 were the equivalent of 2·2 tonnes per capita. An *Environmental Performance Index* compiled in 2008 ranked Brazil 35th in the world, with 82·7%. The index examined various factors in six areas—air pollution, biodiversity and habitat, climate change, environmental health, productive natural resources and water resources.

Brazil has the world's biggest river system and about a quarter of the world's primary rainforest. Current environmental issues are deforestation in the Amazon Basin, air and water pollution in Rio de Janeiro and São Paulo (the world's fourth largest city), and land degradation and water pollution caused by improper mining activities. Contaminated drinking water causes 70% of child deaths.

Electricity

Hydro-electric power accounts for over 80% of Brazil's total electricity output. Although Brazil was only the tenth largest electricity producer overall in the world in 2004, it was the third largest producer of hydro-electric power. Installed electric capacity (2004) was 90·7m. kW, of which 69·0m. kW hydro-electric. There were two nuclear power plants in 2004, supplying some 2·9% of total output. Production (2004) 387,451 GWh. Consumption per capita in 2004 was 2,340 kWh.

Oil and Gas

There are 13 oil refineries, of which 11 are state-owned. Oil production in 2008 was a record 93·9m. tonnes. Production rose every year between 2004 and 2008. Proven oil reserves were 12·6bn. bbls in 2008. Brazil began to open its markets in 1999 by inviting foreign companies to drill for oil, and in 2000 the monopoly of the state-owned Petrobras on importing oil products was removed. In Nov. 2007 the discovery of a huge offshore oilfield was announced off Brazil's southeastern Atlantic coast that could increase the country's oil reserves by as much as 40%. The Tupi field, which contains reserves estimated at between 5bn. and 8bn. bbls of oil, is the largest new oilfield discovered since Kazakhstan's Kashagan field in 2000.

Natural gas production in 2008 was 13·9bn. cu. metres (up from 11·3bn. cu. metres in 2007) with reserves of 330bn. cu. metres. One of the most significant developments has been the construction of the 3,150-km Bolivia–Brazil gas pipeline, one of Latin America's biggest infrastructure projects, costing around US$2bn. (£1·2bn.). The pipeline runs from the Bolivian interior across the Brazilian border at Puerto Suárez-Corumbá to the far southern port city of Porto Alegre. Gas from Bolivia began to be pumped to São Paulo in 1999.

Ethanol

Brazil is the second largest producer of ethanol (after the USA) and by far the largest exporter. Production, almost exclusively from sugarcane, totalled 17·0bn. litres in 2006. Ethanol accounts for half of all the transport fuel used in Brazil.

Minerals

The chief minerals are bauxite, gold, iron ore, manganese, nickel, phosphates, platinum, tin and uranium. Output figures, 2004 (in 1,000 tonnes): phosphate rock, 35,000; bauxite (2003), 17,363; salt, 6,648; hard coal, 5,077; asbestos (crude ore), 3,950; manganese ore, 3,143; aluminium (2003), 1,381; magnesite, 1,339; graphite, 650; chrome (crude ore, 2003), 404; zinc, 159; barytes, 64; nickel ore, 52; zirconium, 35; copper (2003), 26; lead (lead content in concentrate), 15; tin (tin content), 12. Deposits of coal exist in Rio Grande do Sul, Santa Catarina and Paraná. Total reserves were estimated at 9,920m. tonnes in 2005.

Iron is found chiefly in Minas Gerais, notably the Cauê Peak at Itabira. Proven reserves of iron ore amounted to around 15,800m. tonnes in 2005. Total output of iron ore, 2004 was 261·7m. tonnes. Brazil is the second largest producer of iron ore after China.

Gold is chiefly from Pará, Mato Grosso and Minas Gerais; total production (2004), 47·6 tonnes. Silver output (2004), 35·5 tonnes. Diamond output in 2005 was an estimated 900,000 carats, mainly from Minas Gerais and Mato Grosso.

Agriculture

In 2007 the agricultural population was an estimated 23·06m. There were 5·2m. farms in 2006. There were some 59·5m. ha. of arable land in 2007 and 7·0m. ha. of permanent crops. 2·92m. ha. were irrigated in 2002.

Production (in tonnes):

	2004	*2005*
Apples	980,203	850,535
Bananas	6,583,564	6,703,400
Beans	2,967,007	3,021,641
Cassava	23,926,553	25,872,015
Coconut (1,000 fruits)	2,078,226	2,079,291
Coffee	2,465,710	2,140,169
Cotton	3,801,382	3,668,283
Grapes	1,291,382	1,232,564
Maize	41,787,558	35,113,312
Onions	1,157,562	1,137,684
Oranges	18,313,717	17,853,443
Pineapples (1,000 fruits)	1,477,299	1,528,313
Potatoes	3,047,083	3,130,174
Rice	13,277,008	13,192,863
Soya	49,549,941	51,182,074
Sugarcane	415,205,835	422,956,646
Tomatoes	3,515,567	3,452,973
Wheat	5,818,846	4,658,790

Brazil is the world's leading producer of sugarcane, oranges and coffee (and the second largest consumer of coffee after the USA). Harvested coffee area, 2005, 2,325,920 ha., principally in the states of Minas Gerais, Espírito Santo, São Paulo and Paraná. Harvested cocoa area, 2005, 625,384 ha. Bahia furnished 65% of the output in 2005. Two crops a year are grown. Brazil accounts for more than a quarter of annual coffee production worldwide. Harvested castor-bean area, 2005, 230,911 ha. Tobacco is grown chiefly in Rio Grande do Sul and Santa Catarina. Rubber is produced chiefly in the states of São Paulo, Mato Grosso, Bahia, Espírito Santo and Minas Gerais. Output, 2005, 172,847 tonnes.

Livestock, 2005: cattle, 207·2m.; pigs, 34·1m.; sheep, 15·6m.; goats, 10·3m.; horses, 5·8m.; mules, 1·4m.; asses, 1·2m.; chickens and other poultry, 999·0m.

Livestock products, 2005 (in 1,000 tonnes): beef and veal, 6,346; pork, bacon and ham, 2,157; poultry meat, 7,866; milk, 24·6bn. litres; hen's eggs, 2·8bn. dozen; wool, 11; honey, 34.

Forestry

With forest lands covering 477,698,000 ha. in 2005, only Russia had a larger area of forests. In 2005, 57·2% of the total land area of Brazil was under forests. The annual loss of 3,103,000 ha. of forests between 2000 and 2005 was the biggest in any country in the world over the same period.

In 1996 the government ruled that Amazonian landowners could log only 20% of their holdings, instead of 50%, as had previously been permitted. Timber production in 2007 totalled 244·96m. cu. metres, a figure exceeded only in the USA, India and China. By Dec. 2003 the government had seized illegally-cut mahogany to the value of US$60m. Between Aug. 2004 and Aug. 2006 the government's environmental agency, Ibama, issued fines worth R$4·97bn. for illegal logging, but only 2·5% of these were actually collected. The government has pledged to end net deforestation by 2015, although Amazon deforestation increased in 2007–08 for the first time since 2003–04.

Fisheries

In 2005 the fishing industry had a catch of 750,283 tonnes (68% sea fishing and 32% inland).

INDUSTRY

The leading companies by market capitalization in Brazil in March 2009 were: Petrobras (US$123·9bn.); Companhia Vale do Rio Doce, the world's largest iron ore producer (US$68·3bn.); and Itaú Unibanco (US$42·6bn.).

The main industries are textiles, shoes, chemicals, cement, lumber, iron ore, tin, steel, aircraft, motor vehicles and parts, and other machinery and equipment. The National Iron and Steel Co. at Volta Redonda, State of Rio de Janeiro, furnishes a substantial part of Brazil's steel. Production (in 1,000 tonnes): distillate fuel oil (2004), 34,079; cement (2003), 34,010; pig iron (2003), 32,036; crude steel (2003), 31,150; cast iron (2000), 27,854; sugar (2002), 23,567; rolled steel (2000), 18,201; residual fuel oil (2004), 16,074; petrol (2004), 13,738; paper and paperboard (2003), 7,811. Output of other products in 2001: 5·46m. TV sets; 3·37m. refrigerators; 34·4m. rubber tyres for motor vehicles; 1·72m. motor vehicles (2002); beer, 6,790·5m. litres; soft drinks, 6,226·1m. litres.

Labour

In 2004 a total of 84,596,000 persons were in employment (49,242,000 males), including: 17,330,000 engaged in agriculture, hunting and forestry; 14,653,000 in wholesale and retail trade; 11,724,000 in manufacturing; 6,472,000 in private households with employed persons; 5,354,000 in construction. A constitutional amendment of Oct. 1996 prohibits the employment of children under 14 years. However, in 2000 more than 14% of children between 10 and 14 were working. At March 2008 there was a minimum monthly wage of R$415. In Jan. 2008, 8·0% of the workforce was unemployed (9·3% in Jan. 2007).

Trade Unions

The main union is the United Workers' Centre (CUT).

INTERNATIONAL TRADE

In 1990 Brazil repealed most of its protectionist legislation. Import tariffs on some 13,000 items were reduced in 1995. In 1991 the government permitted an annual US$100m. of foreign debt to be converted into funds for environmental protection. Total foreign debt in 2005 was US$187,994m., a figure exceeded only by China and Russia.

Imports and Exports

Imports and exports for calendar years (in US$1m.):

	2003	2004	2005	2006
Imports	48,290	62,809	73,551	91,355
Exports	73,084	96,475	118,308	137,470

Principal imports in 2004 were: machinery and transport equipment, 34·8%; chemicals and related products, 22·1%; mineral fuels, lubricants and related materials, 18·8%; manufactured goods, 9·9%; and miscellaneous manufactured articles, 5·7%.

Principal exports in 2004 were: machinery and transport equipment, 25·5%; manufactured goods, 19·6%; food and live animals, 19·4% (including coffee, 2·2%); crude materials (excluding fuels), 16·4%; chemicals and related products, 6·0%. Brazil is the world's largest exporter of a number of commodities including coffee, sugar and orange juice.

The leading import suppliers in 2004 were: USA, 18·3%; Argentina, 9·0%; Germany, 7·5%; China, 6·2%; Nigeria, 5·5%; Japan, 4·6%. The principal export destinations in 2004 were: USA, 21·4%; Argentina, 7·8%; Netherlands, 6·2%; China, 5·7%; Germany, 4·2%; Mexico, 4·2%. China has in the meantime become Brazil's largest export market.

COMMUNICATIONS

Roads

In 2004 there were 1,751,868 km of roads, of which 93,071 km were highways, national and main roads. In 2004 there were 31,231,000 vehicles in use, including 24,937,000 passenger cars. There were 112,457 road accidents in 2004 resulting in 6,119 deaths.

Rail

The Brazilian railways have largely been privatized: all six branches of the large RFFSA network are now under private management. The largest areas of the network are now run by América Latina Logística (7,228 km of metre gauge in 2005) and Ferrovia Centro-Atlântica (7,080 km of metre-gauge). The Rio de Janeiro suburban network is run by SuperVia (114m. passengers in 2003) and the São Paulo network by Cia Paulista de Trens Metropolitanos (390m. passengers in 2005).

Several other freight routes operate independently and are mainly used by the mining industry. There are metros in Belo Horizonte (30 km), Brasília (40 km), Porto Alegre (31 km), Recife (39 km), Rio de Janeiro (46 km) and São Paulo (57 km).

Civil Aviation

There are major international airports at Rio de Janeiro-Galeão (Antonio Carlos Jobim International) and São Paulo (Guarulhos) and some international flights from Brasília, Porto Alegre, Recife and Salvador. The main airlines are TAM (with 38% of the market in 2005) and Gol (a low-cost airline launched in 2001). In 2005 TAM carried 17,109,193 passengers and Varig 13,268,869 passengers. Varig was previously Brazil's biggest airline but was surpassed by TAM and was bought by Gol in April 2007.

Brazil's busiest airport is Guarulhos (São Paulo), which handled 18,795,596 passengers in 2007, followed by Congonhas (São Paulo) with 15,244,401 passengers (all on domestic flights) and Brasília International with 11,119,872 passengers.

Shipping

Inland waterways, mostly rivers, are open to navigation over some 43,000 km. Tubarão and Itaqui are the leading ports. In 2007 Santos, the leading container port, handled 2·45m. TEUs (twenty-foot equivalent units). Vessels totalling 88,562,000 NRT entered Brazilian ports in 2001 and vessels totalling 258,962,000 NRT cleared. In Jan. 2003 the merchant fleet comprised 179 vessels over 300 GRT (52 oil tankers). In 2004 total tonnage registered was 2·63m. GRT, including oil tankers 1·12m. GRT. In 2007 the cargo moved through Brazilian ports and terminals totalled 754·7m. tonnes of which 35·44% was iron ore.

Telecommunications

The state-owned telephone system was privatized in 1998. There were 41,141,000 main (fixed) telephone lines in 2008. Mobile phone services were opened to the private sector in 1996. In 2008 there were 150,641,000 mobile phone subscribers. There were 72·0m. internet users in 2008 and PCs numbered 30·0m. in 2005.

Postal Services

In 2005 there were 12,531 post offices. A total of 8,271m. pieces of mail were handled in 2005.

SOCIAL INSTITUTIONS

Justice

There is a Supreme Federal Court of Justice at Brasília composed of 11 judges, and a Supreme Court of Justice; all judges are appointed by the President with the approval of the Senate. There are also Regional Federal Courts, Labour Courts, Electoral Courts and Military Courts. Each state organizes its own courts and judicial system in accordance with the federal Constitution.

In Dec. 1999 President Cardoso created the country's first intelligence agency (the Brazilian Intelligence Agency) under civilian rule. It replaced informal networks which were a legacy of the military dictatorship, and helps authorities crack down on organized drug gangs.

The prison population was 285,000 in June 2003 (160 per 100,000 of national population). Brazil's annual murder rate fell slightly between 2001 and 2004 but remains in excess of 25 per 100,000 population, around five times that of the USA.

Education

Elementary education is compulsory from seven to 14. Adult literacy in 2004 was 88·6% (male, 88·4%; female, 88·8%). In 2006 there were 107,375 pre-primary schools, with 5,588,153 pupils and 310,241 teachers; 159,016 elementary schools, with 33,282,663 pupils and 1,665,341 teachers; 24,131 secondary schools, with 8,906,820 pupils and 519,935 teachers. In 2003 there were 1,637 higher education institutions, with 3,479,913 students and 227,844 teachers. In 2006, 97·6% of children between the ages of seven and 14 were enrolled at schools.

There were 1,859 universities in Brazil in 2003, of which 207 were public and 1,652 were private. Of the 207 public universities, 83 were federal, 65 were state and 59 were municipal institutions.

In 2004 total expenditure on education came to 4·0% of GDP and 12·3% of total government spending.

Health

In 2005 there were 62,483 hospitals, clinics and health centres (18,496 private). There were a total of 443,210 beds at hospitals, clinics and health centres in 2005 (294,244 private). In 2001 there were 357,888 doctors, 165,599 dentists, 89,710 nurses and 66,727 pharmacists. In 2006 there were 115 physicians per 100,000 population.

Brazil has been one of the most successful countries in the developing world in the campaign against AIDS. In Rio de Janeiro there was a 47·5% reduction in AIDS-related deaths between 1995 and 2003.

Welfare

Old-age pensions begin at 65 years (men) or 60 years (women) for employees and the urban self-employed, and ages 60 (men) or 55 (women) for the rural self-employed. To qualify there must be at least 35 years contributions for men or 30 years contributions for women. The maximum monthly pension was R$1,869·34 in June 2003.

Unemployment benefits vary depending on insurance but, as a general rule, cover 50% of average earnings in the last three months of employment, up to three times the minimum wage. The minimum benefit is 100% of the minimum monthly wage (R$415 in March 2008).

Family allowances are granted to low-income families with one or more children under the age of 14 or with disabled children attending school. In 2003, R$13·48 a month was provided for each child.

RELIGION

In 2000 there were 124,980,000 Roman Catholics (including syncretic Afro-Catholic cults having spiritualist beliefs and rituals) and 26,185,000 Evangelical Protestants, with 5,274,000 followers of other religions. Roman Catholic estimates in 1991 suggest that 90% were baptized Roman Catholic but only 35% were regular attenders. In 1991 there were 338 bishops and some 14,000 priests. In Feb. 2010 there were eight cardinals. There are numerous sects, some evangelical, some African-derived (e.g. *Candomble*).

CULTURE

World Heritage Sites

The sites under Brazilian jurisdiction entered on the UNESCO World Heritage List (with year entered) are: the Historic Town of Ouro Preto (1980), the centre of the gold rush founded at the end of the 17th century; the Historic Centre of Olinda (1982), founded by the Portuguese in the 16th century and largely rebuilt in the 18th century; the centre of Salvador de Bahia, Brazil's first capital (1549–1763), with its early mix of European, African and Amerindian cultures and many colonial buildings; and the Sanctuary of Bom Jesus do Congonhas, an ornate church dating to the late 18th century (both 1985); the Iguaçu National Park (1986), with its 2,700 metre waterfall and an impressive range of flora and fauna, shared with the Iguazu National Park in Argentina; Brasília (1987), Brazil's purpose built capital city; Serra da Capivara National Park (1991) including cave paintings over 25,000 years old; the Historic Centre of São Luís (1997), which has examples of late 17th-century architecture; the Historic Centre of Diamantina, a colonial village inhabited by diamond prospectors in the 18th century; the Discovery Coast Atlantic Forest Reserves, incorporating eight separate areas protecting 100,000 ha. of Atlantic forest; and Atlantic Forest Southeast Reserves, covering 470,000 ha. over 25 protected areas (all 1999); the Pantanal Conservation Area (2000), incorporating four protected areas covering 188,000 ha. and offering access to a major freshwater wetland ecosystem; the Central Amazon Conservation Complex, covering over 6m. ha. of Amazon basin (2000 and 2003); the Cerrado Protected Areas, comprising Chapada dos Veadeiros and Emas National Parks, home to a diverse tropical ecosystem; Brazilian Atlantic Islands, comprising Fernando de Noronha and Atol das Rocas Reserves, protecting important marine flora and fauna such as dolphins and turtles and a large concentration of tropical seabirds; and the Historic Centre of Goiás, established by colonizing powers in the 18th and 19th centuries (all 2001).

Brazil shares the Jesuit Missions of the Guaranis (1983 and 1984), the ruins of five Jesuit missions in the tropical rainforest dating from the 17th and 18th centuries, with Argentina.

Broadcasting

There are thousands of radio services and hundreds of TV outlets under concentrated commercial ownership, particularly the Globo conglomerate. Radiobras is the state-run broadcaster. The regulatory authority is Agencia Nacional de Telecomunicações (ANATEL).

There were 50·8m. television-equipped households in 2006 (colour by PAL M).

Cinema

In 2005 there were 2,045 cinema screens. Total admissions were 89·7m. in 2005; 47 Brazilian films were released in 2005.

Press

In 2002 there were 523 daily newspapers with a combined circulation of 6,972,000, at a rate of 40 per 1,000 inhabitants. In 2002 a total of 43,028 book titles were published.

Tourism

In 2004, 4,794,000 tourists visited Brazil (4,133,000 in 2003). Argentina is the country of origin of the largest number of visitors, ahead of the USA, Uruguay and Paraguay. Receipts in 2004 totalled US$3·34bn. (US$2·67bn. in 2003).

Festivals

New Year's Eve in Rio de Janeiro is always marked with special celebrations, with a major fireworks display at Copacabana

Beach. Immediately afterwards, preparations start for Carnival, which in 2011 will be held from 4–8 March. Other notable cultural festivals include the Parintins Folk Festival, held at the end of June and attracting over 40,000 people, and the Bahia Carnival, held in Salvador in Feb. to celebrate African influences in the region.

Libraries

In 2008 Brazil's National Library housed 9m. items. In 2007 there were around 6,545 public libraries.

DIPLOMATIC REPRESENTATIVES

Of Brazil in the United Kingdom (32 Green St., London, W1K 7AT)
Ambassador: Carlos Augusto Rego Santos-Neves.

Of the United Kingdom in Brazil (Setor de Embaixadas Sul, Quadra 801, Lote 8, CEP 70408-900, Brasília, DF)
Ambassador: Alan Charlton.

Of Brazil in the USA (3006 Massachusetts Ave., NW, Washington, D.C. 20008)
Ambassador: Mauro Luiz Iecker Vieira.

Of the USA in Brazil (Av. das Nações, Quadra 801, Lote 03, CEP: 70403-900, Brasília, D.F.)
Ambassador: Thomas A. Shannon, Jr.

Of Brazil to the United Nations
Ambassador: Maria Luiza Ribeiro Viotti.

Of Brazil to the European Union
Ambassador: Ricardo Neiva Tavares.

FURTHER READING

Instituto Brasileiro de Geografia e Estatística. *Anuário Estatístico do Brasil.—Censo Demográfico de 1991.—Indicadores IBGE.* Monthly

Boletim do Banco Central do Brasil. Banco Central do Brasil. Brasília. Monthly

Baer, W., *The Brazilian Economy: Growth and Development.* 5th ed. 2001

Eakin, Marshall C., *Brazil: The Once and Future Country.* 1997

Falk, P. S. and Fleischer, D. V., *Brazil's Economic and Political Future.* 1988

Fausto, Boris, *A Concise History of Brazil.* 1999

Font, M. A., *Coffee, Contention and Change in the Making of Modern Brazil.* 1990

Guimarães, R. P., *Politics and Environment in Brazil: Ecopolitics of Development in the Third World.* 1991

Klein, Herbert, *Brazil Since 1980.* 2006

Levine, Robert M., *History of Brazil.* 2003

Love, Jospeh L. and Baer, Werner (eds.) *Brazil Under Lula: Economy, Politics, and Society Under the Worker-President.* 2009

Montero, Alfred, *Brazilian Politics: Reforming a Democratic State in a Changing World.* 2006

Stepan, A. (ed.) *Democratizing Brazil: Problems of Transition and Consolidation.* 1993

For other more specialized titles see under CONSTITUTION AND GOVERNMENT *above.*

National library: Biblioteca Nacional, Avenida Rio Branco 219, 22040-008 Rio de Janeiro, RJ.

National Statistical Office: Instituto Brasileiro de Geografia e Estatística (IBGE), Avenida Franklin Roosevelt 166, 20021-120 Rio de Janeiro, RJ.

Website: http://www.ibge.gov.br

BRUNEI

Negara Brunei Darussalam
(State of Brunei Darussalam)

Capital: Bandar Seri Begawan
Population estimate, 2010: 407,000
GDP per capita, 2007: (PPP$) 50,200
HDI/world rank: 0·920/30

KEY HISTORICAL EVENTS

Brunei became an independent Sultanate in the 15th century, controlling most of Borneo, its neighbouring islands and the Suhi Archipelago. By the end of the 16th century, however, the power of Brunei was on the wane. By the middle of the 19th century the State had been reduced to its present limits. Brunei became a British protectorate in 1888. The discovery of major oilfields in the western end of the State in the 1920s brought economic stability and created a new lifestyle for the population. Brunei was occupied by the Japanese in 1941 and liberated by the Australians in 1945. Self-government was introduced in 1959 but Britain retained responsibility for foreign affairs. In 1965 constitutional changes were made which led to direct elections for a new Legislative Council. Full independence and sovereignty were gained in Jan. 1984.

TERRITORY AND POPULATION

Brunei, on the coast of Borneo, is bounded in the northwest by the South China Sea and on all other sides by Sarawak (Malaysia), which splits it into two parts, the smaller portion forming the Temburong district. Area, 5,765 sq. km (2,226 sq. miles). Population (2001 census) 332,844 (168,925 males), giving a density of 57·8 per sq. km.

The UN gives an estimated population for 2010 of 407,000.

In 2005, 73·5% of the population lived in urban areas. The four districts are Brunei/Muara (2005: 255,600), Belait (61,800), Tutong (43,200) and Temburong (9,500). The capital is Bandar Seri Begawan (estimate 2001: 27,285); other large towns are Kuala Belait (2001: 27,975) and Seria (2001: 15,819). Ethnic groups include Malays 67% and Chinese 11%.

The official language is Malay but English is in use.

SOCIAL STATISTICS

2005 births, 6,933; deaths, 1,072. Rates, 2005: birth per 1,000 population, 18·7; death, 2·9. There were 2,018 marriages in 2005. Life expectancy in 2007: males, 74·9 years; females, 79·6. Annual population growth rate, 1995–2005, 2·5%. Infant mortality, 2005, 7·4 per 1,000 live births; fertility rate, 2005, 2·1 children per woman.

CLIMATE

The climate is tropical marine, hot and moist, but nights are cool. Humidity is high and rainfall heavy, varying from 100" (2,500 mm) on the coast to 200" (5,000 mm) inland. There is no dry season. Bandar Seri Begawan, Jan. 80°F (26·7°C), July 82°F (27·8°C). Annual rainfall 131" (3,275 mm).

CONSTITUTION AND GOVERNMENT

The Sultan and Yang Di Pertuan of Brunei Darussalam is HM Paduka Seri Baginda Sultan Haji Hassanal Bolkiah Mu'izzadin Waddaulah. He succeeded on 5 Oct. 1967 at his father's abdication and was crowned on 1 Aug. 1968. On 10 Aug. 1998 his son, Oxford-graduate Prince Al-Muhtadee Billah, was inaugurated as Crown Prince and heir apparent.

On 29 Sept. 1959 the Sultan promulgated a constitution, but parts of it have been in abeyance since Dec. 1962 under emergency powers assumed by the Sultan. Since 1984 the Legislative Council (*Majlis Masyuarat Megeri*) has been effectively replaced by a Council of Cabinet Ministers appointed and presided over by the Sultan. The constitution was amended in Sept. 2004, allowing for the Legislative Council to be reconvened, but with no independent executive powers and its 21 members chosen by the Sultan. The amendment allowed for the first elections since 1962, with a third of the members of a new 45-member parliament to be directly elected. However, no date has been set for elections and in Sept. 2005 a 29-member Legislative Council including five indirectly-elected members was appointed. The Sultan is both the head of state and head of government.

National Anthem

'Ya Allah, lanjutkan lah usia' ('God bless His Majesty'); words by P. Rahim, tune by I. Sagap.

CURRENT ADMINISTRATION

In March 2010 the Council of Ministers was composed as follows:

Prime Minister, Minister of Defence and of Finance: The Sultan.

Minister of Communications: Pehin Dato Seri Haji Awang Abu Bakar bin Haji Apong. *Culture, Youth and Sports:* Pehin Dato Seri Setia Dr Haji Ahmad Haji Jumat. *Development:* Pehin Dato Paduka Awang Haji Abdullah. *Education:* Pehin Dato Haji Awang Abdul Rahman. *Energy:* Pehin Dato Seri Pahlawan Haji Mohammad Haji Daud. *Finance (No. 2):* Pehin Dato Haji Abdul Rahman bin Haji Ibrahim. *Foreign Affairs and Trade:* Prince Haji Mohammad Bolkiah. *Foreign Affairs and Trade (No. 2):* Pehin Dato Seri Paduka Lim Jock Seng. *Health:* Pehin Dato Paduka Haji Suyoi bin Haji Osman. *Home Affairs:* Pehin Dato Paduka Haji Adanan. *Industry and Primary Resources:* Pehin Dato Seri Setia Haji Yahya Begawan Mudim Dato Paduka Haji Bakar. *Religious Affairs:* Pehin Dato Dr Haji Mohammad Zain bin Serudin.

Government Website: http://www.brunei.gov.bn

CURRENT LEADERS

Sultan Sir Hassanal Bolkiah (Sultan of Brunei)

Position
Head of State

Introduction
The Sultan was crowned Brunei's 29th head of state on 1 Aug. 1968 following the abdication of his father. He is among the world's richest men.

Early Life
The Sultan was born on the 15 July 1946 in Bandar Seri Begawan. He was educated in Darussalam, Brunei and Malaysia. He became the Crown Prince of Brunei in 1961 and in 1966–67 he enlisted as an officer cadet at the Royal Military Academy in Sandhurst in the UK.

In 1978 he led the mission to London which paved the way for Brunei to become a sovereign state. On 1 Jan. 1984 a treaty of friendship ended British control over Brunei's foreign affairs and defence.

Career in Office
The Sultan is head of government as well as head of state. He is prime minister, minister of defence and minister of finance. Under the 1959 constitution and the Malay Muslim Monarchy tradition, he is assisted by a council of cabinet ministers, a privy council, council of succession and a religious council. A legislative council (a third of whose 45 members will, following a constitutional amendment in Sept. 2004, be directly elected) is to be revived, although elections have yet to be scheduled.

Brunei's wealth originates from the country's large oil and gas reserves, although earnings from overseas investments have exceeded those from exports. The people of Brunei enjoy high subsidies and pay no taxes.

DEFENCE

In 2006 military expenditure totalled US$328m. (US$864 per capita), representing 2·8% of GDP.

Army
The armed forces are known as the Task Force and contain the naval and air elements. Only Malays are eligible for service. Strength (2007): 4,900.

There is a Gurkha reserve unit of 400–500.

Navy
The Royal Brunei Armed Forces Flotilla includes three fast missile-armed attack craft. Personnel in 2007 numbered 1,000.

Air Force
The Royal Brunei Air Force (formerly known as the Air Wing) was formed in 1965. Personnel (2007), 1,100. There are no combat aircraft.

INTERNATIONAL RELATIONS

Brunei is a member of the UN, World Bank, IMF and several other UN specialized agencies, WTO, Commonwealth, Islamic Development Bank, OIC, Asian Development Bank, APEC, ASEAN and Mekong Group.

ECONOMY

In 2005 agriculture, forestry and fisheries accounted for 0·9% of GDP, industry 71·6% and services 27·5%. The fall in oil prices in 1997–98 led to the setting up of an Economic Council to advise the Sultan on reforms. An investigation was mounted into the affairs of the Amedeo Corporation, Brunei's largest private company run by Prince Jefri, the Sultan's brother.

Overview
Since independence in 1984, Brunei has boasted one of the highest standards of living in the world, largely thanks to the substantial income derived from its oil and gas resources. GDP per capita is estimated at around US$25,754, far greater than for most other developing countries. Crude oil and natural gas account for approximately half of real GDP and over 90% of total export earnings and government revenues. However, performance was disappointing for several years up to 2005 with GDP growth averaging roughly 2% over a five-year period, reflecting declines in the oil and gas sectors arising from disruption caused by repairs and upgrades to production facilities. 2006 saw higher growth, mainly thanks to high world oil prices and strong demand from neighbouring Asian economies. Growth in the short to medium term is expected to strengthen as more production facilities become available, the macroeconomic environment remains stable and revenues from energy-related ventures stay high. Inflation has remained at around 1%, partly as a result of the exchange rate being set on a par with the Singapore dollar. The state is actively promoting tourism to boost that sector's contribution to GDP.

Currency
The unit of currency is the *Brunei dollar* (BND) of 100 cents, which is at parity with the Singapore dollar (also legal tender). Inflation was 1·1% in 2005, 0·2% in 2006, 0·3% in 2007 and 2·7% in 2008.

Budget
The fiscal year ends on 31 March. Revenues in 2005–06 were B$8,441m.; expenditures were B$5,086m. Tax revenues accounted for 62·2% of revenues in 2005–06; current expenditure accounted for 80·1% of total expenditures.

Performance
Real GDP growth was 0·4% in 2005, 4·4% in 2006 and 0·6% in 2007 although the economy then shrank by 1·5% in 2008. Total GDP in 2006 was US$11·5bn.

Banking and Finance
The Brunei Currency Board is the note-issuing monetary authority. In 2002 there were three commercial banks, six foreign banks and one off-shore bank. Total bank assets in 2005 were B$16,971m.

The International Brunei Exchange Ltd (IBX) established an international securities exchange in May 2002.

ENERGY AND NATURAL RESOURCES

Environment
Brunei's carbon dioxide emissions from the consumption and flaring of fossil fuels were the equivalent of 27·3 tonnes per capita in 2008.

Electricity
Installed capacity was 0·8m. kW in 2005. Production in 2005 was 2·91bn. kWh and consumption per capita 7,280 kWh.

Oil and Gas
The Seria oilfield, discovered in 1929, has passed its peak production. The high level of crude oil production is maintained through the increase of offshore oilfields production. Output was 8·5m. tonnes in 2008. The crude oil is exported directly, and only a small amount is refined at Seria for domestic uses. There were proven oil reserves of 1·1bn. bbls in 2008.

Natural gas is produced (12·1bn. cu. metres in 2008) at one of the largest liquefied natural gas plants in the world and is exported to Japan. There were proven reserves of 350bn. cu. metres in 2008.

Agriculture

In 2007 there were about 3,000 ha. of arable land and 5,000 ha. of permanent crops. The main crops produced in 2005 were (estimates, in 1,000 tonnes): vegetables, 11; fruit, 5 (notably bananas and pineapples); rice, 1.

Livestock in 2005: cattle, 1,079; buffaloes, 4,790; goats, 2,578; pigs (2003), 1,000; chickens (2003), 11m.

Livestock products (2003 estimates, in 1,000 tonnes): beef and veal, 3; poultry meat, 24; eggs, 6.

Forestry

Forests covered 449,700 ha., or 78·0% of the total land area, in 2005. Most of the interior is under forest, containing large potential supplies of serviceable timber. Timber production in 2007 was 124,000 cu. metres.

Fisheries

The 2004 catch totalled 2,428 tonnes.

INDUSTRY

Although Brunei has long been dependent on its oil and gas industry, the government has begun a programme of diversification, recognizing oil and gas as non-renewable resources. Greater emphasis is now placed on other sectors such as manufacturing, services, tourism and high technology, but oil still accounted for nearly two-thirds of total GDP in 2004.

Labour

The labour force totalled 169,200 in 2005 (60·4% males). Unemployment in 2005 was 4·3%.

INTERNATIONAL TRADE

Imports and Exports

Imports totalled B$2,481m. in 2005 and exports B$10,397m.

In 2005 basic manufactures constituted 35·4% of imports, with machinery and transport equipment accounting for 32·0%; crude petroleum and partly refined petroleum made up 62·9% of exports in 2005 and natural gas 31·3%.

Malaysia and Singapore both supplied 19% of imports in 2005 with the USA providing 10%. Japan took 37% of all exports, Indonesia 19% and South Korea 13%.

COMMUNICATIONS

Roads

There were an estimated 3,560 km of roads in 2005. The main road connects Bandar Seri Begawan with Kuala Belait and Seria. In 2007 there were 252,700 passenger cars in use (649 per 1,000 inhabitants—one of the highest rates in the world), 16,700 vans and lorries, 1,500 buses and coaches, and 12,200 motorcycles and mopeds. There were 38 fatalities in road accidents in 2005.

Civil Aviation

Brunei International Airport (Bandar Seri Begawan) handled 1,262,343 passengers (all international) in 2005. The national carrier is the state-owned Royal Brunei Airlines (RBA). In 2006 RBA operated services to Auckland, Bangkok, Brisbane, Darwin, Denpasar Bali, Dubai, Frankfurt, Ho Chi Minh City, Hong Kong, Jakarta, Jeddah, Kota Kinabalu, Kuala Lumpur, London, Manila, Perth, Shanghai, Sharjah, Singapore, Surabaya and Sydney. In 2003 RBA flew 28m. km, carrying 956,000 passengers (all on international flights).

Shipping

Regular shipping services operate from Singapore, Hong Kong, Sarawak and Sabah to Bandar Seri Begawan, and there is a daily passenger ferry between Bandar Seri Begawan and Labuan. In 2005 merchant shipping totalled 2·4m. GRT. In 2005 vessels totalling 1,066,381 NRT entered ports and vessels totalling 1,061,339 NRT cleared.

Telecommunications

There is a telephone network linking the main centres. Brunei had 381,600 telephone subscribers in 2006 (or 999·2 per 1,000 inhabitants), including 301,400 mobile phone subscribers. There were 31,000 PCs in 2004 (84·7 for every 1,000 persons) and 56,000 internet users.

Postal Services

There were 22 post offices in 2005.

SOCIAL INSTITUTIONS

Justice

The Supreme Court comprises a High Court and a Court of Appeal and the Magistrates' Courts. The High Court receives appeals from subordinate courts in the districts and is itself a court of first instance for criminal and civil cases. The Judicial Committee of the Privy Council in London is the final court of appeal. Sharia Courts deal with Islamic law. 4,552 crimes were reported in 2005.

The population in penal institutions in Aug. 2007 was 486 (124 per 100,000 of national population).

Education

The government provides free education to all citizens from pre-school up to the highest level at local and overseas universities and institutions. In 2005 there were 12,999 children and 701 teachers in pre-primary education; 46,012 pupils and 4,548 teachers in primary education; 41,107 pupils and 3,907 teachers in secondary education; 4,154 students and 658 academic staff in tertiary education. The University of Brunei Darussalam was founded in 1985; in 2006 there were also eight technical and vocational colleges, one teacher training college and an institute of advanced education.

Adult literacy rate, 2003, 92·7% (male, 95·2%; female, 90·2%). Total expenditure on education in 2000–01 came to 4·8% of GDP and approximately 9% of total government spending.

Health

Medical and health services are free to citizens and those in government service and their dependants. Citizens are sent overseas, at government expense, for medical care not available in Brunei. Flying medical services are provided to remote areas. In 2005 there were four government hospitals and the Jerudong Park private hospital with a total of 1,154 beds; there were 390 physicians, 73 dentists, 1,789 nurses, 748 midwives and 41 pharmacists.

RELIGION

The official religion is Islam. In 2001, 75% of the population were Muslim (mostly Malays). There are Buddhist and Christian minorities.

CULTURE

Broadcasting

All broadcasting media is state-controlled through Radio Television Brunei. Foreign television is available through cable services. Number of receivers (2006): radio, 381,150; television, 225,750 (colour by PAL).

Press

In 2006 there were three daily newspapers with an average circulation of 35,000. The Borneo Bulletin and the Brunei Times are English-language papers, while Media Permata is a Malay paper.

Tourism

In 2005 there were 815,000 foreign tourists (including 791,000 from other Asian countries and Oceania and 14,000 from Europe).

DIPLOMATIC REPRESENTATIVES

Of Brunei in the United Kingdom (19/20 Belgrave Sq., London, SW1X 8PG)
High Commissioner: Pengiran Dato Maidin Hashim.

Of the United Kingdom in Brunei (2.01, 2nd Floor, Block D, Kompleks Yayasan Sultan Haji Hassanal Bolkiah, Bandar Seri Begawan, BS 8711)
High Commissioner: Rob Fenn.

Of Brunei in the USA (3520 International Court, NW, Washington, D.C., 20008)
Ambassador: Dato Yusoff Abd Hamid.

Of the USA in Brunei (3rd Floor, Teck Guan Plaza, Jalan Sultan, Bandar Seri Begawan 2085)
Ambassador: William Todd.

Of Brunei to the United Nations
Ambassador: Latif bin Tuah.

Of Brunei to the European Union
Ambassador: Pengiran Alihashim.

FURTHER READING

Department of Economic Planning and Development, Prime Minister's Office. *Brunei Darussalam Statistical Yearbook.*

Cleary, M. and Wong, S. Y., *Oil, Economic Development and Diversification in Brunei.* 1994

Horton, A. V. M., *A Critical Guide to Source Material Relating to Brunei with Special Reference to the British Residential Era, 1906–1959.* 1995

Saunders, G., *History of Brunei.* 1996

National Statistical Office: Department of Statistics, Department of Economic Planning and Development, Prime Minister's Office, Block 2A, Jalan Ong Sum Ping, Bandar Seri Begawan, BA 1311.

BULGARIA

Republika Bulgaria
(Republic of Bulgaria)

Capital: Sofia
Population estimate, 2010: 7·50m.
GDP per capita, 2007: (PPP$) 11,222
HDI/world rank: 0·840/61

KEY HISTORICAL EVENTS

The Bulgarians take their name from an invading Asiatic horde (Bulgars) and their language from the Slav population, with whom they merged after 680. The Bulgarians carved out empires against a background of conflict with Byzantium and Serbia but after the Serb-Bulgarian defeat at Kosovo in 1389 Bulgaria finally succumbed to Ottoman encroachment. The Ottoman empire's decline, however, engendered rebellion which met with brutal repression, provoking great power intervention. By the Treaty of Berlin (1878), Macedonia and Thrace reverted to Turkey, Eastern Rumelia became semi-autonomous and Bulgaria proper became a principality under Turkish suzerainty.

After Austria annexed Bosnia in 1908, Bulgaria declared itself independent. To block Austrian expansion into the Balkans, Russia encouraged Greece, Serbia, Montenegro and Bulgaria to attack Turkey (First Balkan War, 1912), but in the dispute which followed over the territorial spoils Bulgaria failed to secure her claims against her formal allies by force (Second Balkan War, 1913). Territorial aspirations led Bulgaria to join the First World War on the German side.

Economic decline caused by the war produced social unrest. Tsar Ferdinand I, who succeeded Prince Alexander of Battenberg in 1887, was forced to abdicate in favour of his son, Boris III, in Oct. 1918. Bedevilled by Macedonian terrorism and the effects of the world economic depression, parliamentary government was ended by a military coup in May 1934. In 1935 Boris established a royal dictatorship under which political parties were banned. Boris died in 1943 and was succeeded by a regency.

Increasingly drawn into the German economic orbit, Bulgaria joined the Nazis against Britain in March 1941. In Sept. 1944 the Soviet Union declared war and sent its troops across the frontiers. The Communist-dominated Fatherland Front formed a government and a referendum in 1946 abolished the monarchy. Demonstrations in Sofia in Nov. 1989, occasioned by the Helsinki Agreement ecological conference, broadened into demands for political reform. In Dec. the National Assembly approved 21 measures of constitutional reform, including the abolition of the Communist Party's sole right to govern. But attempts at economic reform led to strikes and unrest. In 1996 Petar Stoyanov was elected as an anti-Communist pro-reform President. In the election the following April the anti-Communist Union of Democratic Forces coalition, led by Ivan Kostov and Alexander Bozhkov, swept back to power.

Bulgaria was one of seven countries to join NATO in 2004. It became a member of the European Union on 1 Jan. 2007.

TERRITORY AND POPULATION

The area of Bulgaria is 110,994 sq. km (42,855 sq. miles). It is bounded in the north by Romania, east by the Black Sea, south by Turkey and Greece, and west by Serbia and the Republic of Macedonia. The country is divided into 28 districts.

Area and population in 2001 (census):

District	*Area (sq. km)*	*Population*	*District*	*Area (sq. km)*	*Population*
Blagoevgrad	6,452	341,245	Shumen	3,380	204,395
Bourgas	7,753	423,608	Silistra	2,844	142,003
Dobrich	4,711	215,232	Sliven	3,544	218,474
Gabrovo	2,046	144,150	Smolyan	3,194	140,067
Haskovo	5,543	277,483	Sofia (city)	1,311	1,173,988
Kardzhali	3,410	164,019	Sofia (district)	7,020	273,252
Kyustendil	3,048	162,622	Stara Zagora	5,147	370,665
Lovech	4,132	169,951	Targovishte	2,732	137,689
Montana	3,618	182,267	Varna	3,820	462,218
Pazardzhik	4,458	310,741	Veliko		
Pernik	2,027	149,856	Turnovo	4,666	293,294
Pleven	4,656	312,018	Vidin	3,022	130,094
Plovdiv	5,928	715,904	Vratsa	4,006	243,039
Razgrad	2,415	152,417	Yambol	3,336	156,080
Rousse	2,775	266,213	*Total*	*110,994*	*7,932,984*

The capital, Sofia, has district status.

The population of Bulgaria at the census of 2001 was 7,932,984 (females, 4,066,436); population density 71·5 per sq. km. Bulgaria's population has been declining since the mid-1980s. It has been falling at such a rate that by 2010 it was the same as it had been in the late 1950s. In 2005, 70·0% of the population were urban.

The UN gives an estimated population for 2010 of 7·50m.

Population of principal towns (2001 census): Sofia, 1,173,988; Plovdiv, 338,302; Varna, 320,668; Bourgas, 209,479; Rousse, 178,435; Stara Zagora, 167,708; Pleven, 149,174; Sliven, 136,148; Pazardzhik, 127,918.

Ethnic groups at the 2001 census: Bulgarians, 6,655,210; Turks, 746,664; Roma (Gypsies), 370,908.

Bulgarian is the official language.

SOCIAL STATISTICS

2008: live births, 77,712; deaths, 110,523; marriages, 27,722; divorces, 14,104. Rates per 1,000 population, 2008: birth, 10·2; death, 14·5; marriage, 3·6; divorce, 1·9; infant mortality, 12 per 1,000 live births (2005). There were 37,272 reported abortions in 2006. In 2005 the most popular age range for marrying was 25–29 for males and 20–24 for females. Expectation of life in 2007 was 69·6 years among males and 76·7 years among females. The annual population growth rate for the period 2000–05 was –1·1%, giving Bulgaria one of the fastest declining populations of any country. Fertility rate, 2004, 1·2 children per woman (one of the lowest rates in the world).

CLIMATE

The southern parts have a Mediterranean climate, with winters mild and moist and summers hot and dry, but further north the conditions become more Continental, with a larger range of temperature and greater amounts of rainfall in summer and early autumn. Sofia, Jan. 28°F (–2·2°C), July 69°F (20·6°C). Annual rainfall 25·4" (635 mm).

CONSTITUTION AND GOVERNMENT

A new constitution was adopted at Turnovo on 12 July 1991. The *President* is directly elected for not more than two five-year terms. Candidates for the presidency must be at least 40 years old and have lived for the last five years in Bulgaria. American-style primary elections were introduced in 1996; voting is open to all the electorate.

The 240-member *National Assembly* is directly elected by proportional representation. The *President* nominates a candidate from the largest parliamentary party as *Prime Minister*.

National Anthem

'Gorda stara planina' ('Proud and ancient mountains'); words and tune by T. Radoslavov.

GOVERNMENT CHRONOLOGY

(BKP = Bulgarian Communist Party; BSP = Bulgarian Socialist Party; GERB = Citizens for the European Development of Bulgaria; NMS = National Movement Simeon II; SDS = Union of Democratic Forces; Zveno = People's League Zveno; n/p = non-party)

Heads of State since 1943.

King

1943–46	Simeon II (Simeon Sakskoburggotski)	

Chairman of Provisional Presidency

1946–47	BKP	Vasil Petrov Kolarov

Chairmen of the Presidium of the National Assembly

1947–50	BKP	Mincho Kolev Neychev
1950–58	BKP	Georgi Parvanov Damyanov
1958–64	BKP	Dimitar Ganev Varbanov
1964–71	BKP	Georgi Traykov Girovski

Chairmen of the Council of State

1971–89	BKP	Todor Khristov Zhivkov
1989–90	BKP	Petar Toshev Mladenov

Presidents of the Republic

1990	n/p	Petar Toshev Mladenov
1990–97	SDS	Zhelyu Mitev Zhelev
1997–2002	SDS	Petar Stefanov Stoyanov
2002–	BSP	Georgi Sedefchov Parvanov

Prime Ministers since 1944.

1944–46	Zveno	Kimon Gheorgiev Stoyanov
1946–49	BKP	Georgi Mihaylov Dimitrov
1949–50	BKP	Vasil Petrov Kolarov
1950–56	BKP	Vûlko Velov Chervenkov
1956–62	BKP	Anton Tanev Yugov
1962–71	BKP	Todor Khristov Zhivkov
1971–81	BKP	Stanko Todorov Georgiev
1981–86	BKP	Grisha Stanchev Filipov
1986–90	BKP	Georgi Ivanov Atanasov
1990	BSP	Andrey Karlov Lukanov
1990–91	n/p	Dimitar Popov
1991–92	SDS	Filip Dimitrov Dimitrov
1992–94	n/p	Lyuben Borisov Berov
1995–97	BSP	Zhan Vasilev Videnov
1997–01	SDS	Ivan Yordanov Kostov
2001–05	NMS	Simeon Borisov Sakskoburggotski
2005–09	BSP	Sergey Dimitrievich Stanishev
2009–	GERB	Boyko Metodiev Borisov

RECENT ELECTIONS

Presidential elections were held in two rounds on 22 and 29 Oct. 2006. Incumbent Georgi Parvanov won the first round with 64·0% of votes cast, ahead of Volen Siderov with 21·5%, Nedelcho Beronov with 9·8% and Georgy Markov with 2·7%. A further three candidates received less than 1% of the votes each. Turnout at 44·3% was below the 50% required to make the election valid. Parvanov also won the run-off round, with 75·9% of votes cast, against 24·1% for Volen Siderov; turnout in the second round (for which the 50% minimum does not apply) was 42·5%.

At the elections of 5 July 2009 Citizens for the European Development of Bulgaria won 116 of 240 seats with 39·7% of the vote; the Coalition for Bulgaria (headed by the Bulgarian Socialist Party) won 40 seats with 17·7% of the vote; the Movement for Rights and Freedoms won 38 seats with 14·5%; the Attack coalition 21 with 9·4%; the Blue Coalition 15 with 6·8%; and Order, Law and Justice 10 with 4·1%. Turnout was 60·2%.

European Parliament

Bulgaria has 17 (18 in 2007) representatives. At the June 2009 elections turnout was 39·0% (29·2% in 2007). Citizens for the European Development of Bulgaria won 5 seats with 24·4% of the vote (political affiliation in European Parliament: European People's Party); the Coalition for Bulgaria, 4 with 18·5% (Progressive Alliance of Socialists and Democrats); the Movement for Rights and Freedoms, 3 with 14·1% (Alliance of Liberals and Democrats for Europe); the Attack coalition, 2 with 12·0% (non-attached); the National Movement for Stability and Progress, 2 with 8·0% (Alliance of Liberals and Democrats for Europe); the Blue Coalition, 1 with 8·0% (European People's Party).

CURRENT ADMINISTRATION

President: Georgi Parvanov; b. 1957 (Bulgarian Socialist Party; in office since 22 Jan. 2002 and re-elected in Oct. 2006).

Vice-President: Angel Marin.

In April 2010 the government comprised:

Chairman of the Council of Ministers (Prime Minister): Boyko Borisov; b. 1959 (Citizens for the European Development of Bulgaria; sworn in 27 July 2009).

Deputy Prime Ministers: Simeon Dyankov (also *Minister of Finance*); Tsvetan Tsvetanov (also *Minister of the Interior*); Tomislav Dontchev (also *Minister of European Union Funds*).

Minister of Agriculture and Food Industry: Miroslav Naidenov. *Culture:* Vezhdi Rashidov. *Defence:* Anyu Angelov. *Economy, Energy and Tourism:* Traicho Traikov. *Education, Youth and Science:* Sergey Ignatov. *Environment and Water:* Nona Karadjova. *Foreign Affairs:* Nikolai Mladenov. *Healthcare:* Dr Anna-Maria Borisova. *Justice:* Margarita Popova. *Labour and Social Policy:* Totyu Mladenov. *Regional Development:* Rossen Plevneliev. *Sport:* Svilen Neikov. *Transport, Communications and Information Technology:* Alexander Tsvetkov. *Minister without Portfolio:* Bozhidar Dimitrov.

Government Website: http://www.government.bg

CURRENT LEADERS

Georgi Parvanov

Position

President

Introduction

Georgi Parvanov, leader of the Socialist party, was elected president of Bulgaria in Nov. 2001, defeating his predecessor, Petar Stoyanov. He was sworn into office in Jan. 2002. Re-elected in Oct. 2006, he became the first Bulgarian president to retain office through a democratic mandate, albeit in a very low turnout. The role of the presidency is largely ceremonial, as legislative power is exercised by the prime minister and National Assembly.

Early Life

Georgi Sedefchov Parvanov was born in Sirishtchnik, Bulgaria on 28 June 1957. He graduated from Mathematics High School in Pernik in 1975 then studied for an MA and a PhD in history at Sofia University St Kliment Ohridski.

Parvanov joined the Bulgarian Communist Party (BCP) in 1981 as a researcher in its institute of history. By 1989 he held the post of senior research associate. In 1990 the BCP changed its name to the Bulgarian Socialist Party (BSP), a year after dethroning their chairman Todor Zhivkov, and in 1991 Parvanov was elected to a party post for the first time. He began a steady climb up the party ladder, becoming deputy chairman in 1994 and in 1996 replacing Zhan Videnov as the elected chairman of the BSP supreme council. He won the post again in 2000.

As an MP from 1994–2001, Parvanov held several posts, including chairman of the parliamentary group for friendship with Greece (1994–97), chairman of the parliamentary group of the Democratic Left (1997–2001) and chairman of the parliamentary group of the Coalition for Bulgaria (1997–2001). In 1999, during NATO's air bombing campaign of Yugoslavia, Parvanov led his parliamentary group in a vote against granting NATO access to Bulgarian air space. However, a year later he announced his party's support for Bulgaria's admission to NATO and the European Union.

Career in Office

Georgi Parvanov became the first former communist to win a presidential election in post-communist Bulgaria. His priorities have included stabilizing the country's economy, modernizing the Bulgarian army and fighting crime and corruption. He has sought a stronger role for the state in national life and supports closer ties with former allies such as Russia and Ukraine. In Dec. 2001 parliament agreed to the destruction of Soviet-made missiles.

In Nov. 2002 Bulgaria was invited to join NATO and in March 2004 was granted admission. In April 2005 it signed the EU accession treaty and became a full member on 1 Jan. 2007. Parvanov was re-elected as president over two rounds of voting in Oct. 2006. Following parliamentary elections in July 2009, Parvanov asked Boyko Borisov, the leader of the populist centre-right Citizens for the European Development of Bulgaria which emerged as the largest party, to form a new government in place of the outgoing Socialist Party administration.

Boyko Borisov

Position

Prime Minister

Introduction

Boyko Metodiev Borisov was sworn in as prime minister on 27 July 2009, following electoral victory for his GERB (Citizens for the European Development of Bulgaria) party. An outspoken former bodyguard who rose to high rank in the Sofia police department and at the interior ministry, Borisov was mayor of Sofia from 2005–09.

Early Life

Borisov was born in Bankya, western Bulgaria, in June 1959. Like his father, he worked in the interior ministry, graduating from its academy in 1982 with an engineering degree. In the same year he started work at the Sofia fire directorate, commanding first a platoon and later a company. Between 1985 and 1990 he was a professor at the interior ministry's police academy, where he was awarded a PhD in 'Psychological and Physical Training of Operatives'. He resigned in 1990 to found one of Bulgaria's largest security firms, IPON, in which role he worked as a personal bodyguard to former communist leader, Todor Zhivkov, and to the then-exiled King Simeon II during the king's private visits to Bulgaria. Since this period Borisov has been dogged by associations with senior figures in Bulgaria's criminal underworld. He claims to have met them when, using the same sports facilities to hone his karate expertise, he was coach for the national karate squad.

In 2001 Borisov was named chief secretary of the interior ministry and in 2004 he was appointed lieutenant-general. The following year he surrendered his parliamentary seat and gave up his interior ministry post to run for mayor of Sofia. He won the election with a landslide following the mid-term resignation of his predecessor Stefan Sofiyanski. He took office in Nov. 2005.

Borisov ran as a candidate for his own party, GERB, at the 2007 local elections and again won comfortably. Unable to take on the role of party leader by a law which prohibits a mayor from heading a political party, GERB was headed by Tsvetan Tsvetanov, a close associate of Borisov. The centre-right party won the largest share of votes in Bulgaria's first European parliamentary elections in June 2007 and became a member of the European People's Party in early 2008.

In Feb. 2009 Borisov courted controversy by making disparaging remarks about his country's Roma and ethnic Turkish populations. He dedicated his victory in parliamentary elections in July 2009 to the memory of his grandfather, who was executed by the communist regime in the wake of the Bulgarian coup d'état in 1944.

Career in Office

Borisov ran for office on a platform of fiscal responsibility and put a balanced budget among his top priorities. He has pledged to restore EU trust in Bulgaria and to reduce the nation's dependence on Russia for its energy supplies. In Oct. 2009 he berated Czech President Vaclav Klaus for refusing to sign the Lisbon Treaty.

In Jan. 2010 Borisov was unanimously elected by his party to be chairman of GERB, replacing Tsvetanov at the helm. In the same month he received domestic and foreign criticism for his nomination of Rumiana Jeleva, Bulgaria's foreign minister and a senior member of GERB, as EU Aid Commissioner. Amid questions about her personal financial interests, Jeleva resigned her posts a little over a week later, signalling an early blow to Borisov's tenure.

Borisov has a reputation as a strongman on issues of law and order, having gained a name for tackling fraud and embezzlement during his time as mayor of Sofia. He has promised to widen the fight against corruption.

DEFENCE

Since 1 Jan. 2008 Bulgaria has had an all-volunteer professional army. Following restructuring the total strength of the armed forces has been reduced from more than 68,000 in 2002 to less than 41,000 in 2007.

Defence expenditure in 2006 totalled US$703m. (US$95 per capita), representing 2·3% of GDP. In 1985 the total had been US$1,424m.

Army

In 2007 the Army had a strength of 18,773. In addition there are reserves of 250,500, 12,000 border guards and 18,000 railway and construction troops.

Navy

The Navy, mostly ex-Soviet or Soviet-built, includes one old diesel submarine and two small frigates. The Naval Aviation Wing operates six armed helicopters. The naval headquarters are at Varna (Northern Command) and Bourgas (Southern Command), and there are further bases at Atiya, Vidin, Balchik and Sozopol. Personnel in 2007 totalled 4,100, with 7,500 reservists.

Air Force

The Air Force had (2007) 9,344 personnel, with 45,000 reservists. There were 80 combat capable aircraft in 2007, including MiG-21s, MiG-29s and Su-25s, and 18 attack helicopters.

INTERNATIONAL RELATIONS

Bulgaria is a member of the UN, World Bank, IMF and several other UN specialized agencies, WTO, EU, Council of Europe, OSCE, CEI, BSEC, Danube Commission, BIS, IOM, the International Organization of the Francophonie, NATO, Antarctic Treaty and is an associate partner of the WEU. At the European Union's Helsinki Summit in Dec. 1999 Bulgaria, along with five other countries, was invited to begin full negotiations for membership in Feb. 2000. Bulgaria joined the EU on 1 Jan. 2007. It became a member of NATO on 29 March 2004.

ECONOMY

Agriculture accounted for 8·5% of GDP in 2006, industry 31·2% and services 60·3%.

Overview

After communism, Bulgaria was slow to adapt to the market economy. In early 1997 the collapse of the banking system led to a currency crisis and a sharp decline in GDP. Government reforms later that year privatized state-owned enterprises and liberalized prices. The creation of a privatized financial sector inspired high growth rates in the private sector. Prime Minister Simeon Sakskoburggotski (formerly King Simeon II), who served from 2001–05, adopted further market reforms designed by international authorities to meet EU regulations. Unemployment dropped and inflation rates slowed.

Bulgaria joined the EU in Jan. 2007 after preparing its economy for entry following an accession treaty in 2005. This led to increased capital inflows and a credit boom, generating GDP growth of over 6% per annum. However, strong growth in domestic demand resulted in overheating and a sharp widening of the current account deficit, while rising food and oil prices have caused a surge of inflation. The global financial crisis is expected to erode capital inflows and slow economic growth but the banking sector remains well capitalized and highly profitable.

Currency

The unit of currency is the *lev* (BGN) of 100 *stotinki*. In May 1996 the lev was devalued by 68%. A new *lev* was introduced on 5 July 1999, at 1 new *lev* = 1,000 old *leva*. Runaway inflation (123·0% in 1996 rising to 1,061% in 1997) forced the closure of 14 banks in 1996. However, by 1999 the rate had slowed to 2·6%, and has remained relatively stable ever since. Inflation was 7·6% in 2007 and 12·0% in 2008. In June 1997 the new government introduced a currency board financial system which stabilized the lev and renewed economic growth. Under it, the lev is pegged to the euro at one euro = 1·95583 new leva. Foreign exchange reserves were US$7,792m. in July 2005, gold reserves were 1·28m. troy oz and total money supply was 11,494m. leva.

Budget

The fiscal year is the calendar year.

Central government revenue and expenditure (in 1m. new leva):

	2004	*2005*	*2006*
Revenue	14,950	16,877	18,683
Expenditure	13,426	14,396	15,637

VAT is 20%.

Performance

Total GDP in 2008 was US$49·9bn. Real GDP growth was 6·2% in 2007 and 6·0% in 2008.

Banking and Finance

The National Bank (*Governor*, Ivan Iskrov) is the central bank and bank of issue. There is also a Currency Board, established in 1997. The DSK Bank became the last state bank to be privatized in 2003. There were 34 commercial banks in 2003. Foreign direct investment totalled US$1,419m. in 2003 (26% from privatization revenues).

There is a stock exchange in Sofia.

ENERGY AND NATURAL RESOURCES

Environment

Bulgaria's carbon dioxide emissions from the consumption and flaring of fossil fuels were the equivalent of 7·3 tonnes per capita in 2008.

Electricity

In 2007 there were two nuclear reactors in use, at the country's sole nuclear power plant in Kozloduy (dating from the 1970s). The two oldest of the plant's six reactors closed in Dec. 2002. A further two closed in Dec. 2006, as a condition of Bulgaria's accession to the EU. To compensate, the government has approved plans to complete a nuclear plant in Belene, started in the 1980s but suspended in 1990 because of lack of funds and environmental protests. Installed electrical capacity was 12·0m. kW in 2004. Output, 2004, 41·62bn. kWh (52% thermal, 40% nuclear and 8% hydro-electric). Consumption per capita: 4,582 kWh (2004).

Oil and Gas

Oil is extracted in the Balchik district on the Black Sea coast, in an area 100 km north of Varna, and at Dolni Dubnik near Pleven. There are refineries at Bourgas (annual capacity 5m. tonnes) and Dolni Dubnik (7m. tonnes). Crude oil production (2007) was 26,000 tonnes; natural gas (2004), 353m. cu. metres.

Minerals

Output in 2004 (in tonnes): lignite, 26·45m.; iron ore, 83,000; coal, 33,000. There are also deposits of gold, silver and copper.

Agriculture

In 2002 the total area of land in agricultural use was 5,796,208 ha. (52·2% of the overall territory of the country); there were 3,080,829 ha. under crops (including 2,217,560 ha. for cereals), 2,502,723 ha. of permanent grassland (including meadows and orchards), and 212,656 ha. of perennial plantations. There were 32,000 tractors in use in 2002 and 9,000 harvester-threshers.

Legislation of 1991 and 1992 provided for the redistribution of collectivized land to its former owners up to 30 ha. In 2002 there were 37,836 registered agricultural producers, including 33,633 individual farmers. The agricultural workforce was 222,000 in 2004.

Production in 2002 (in 1,000 tonnes): wheat, 4,123; maize, 1,288; sunflower seeds, 645; potatoes, 627; barley, 569; grapes, 409; tomatoes, 390; watermelons, 200; chillies and green peppers, 167; cucumbers and gherkins, 125; cabbage, 109. Bulgaria is a leading producer of attar of roses (rose oil). Bulgaria produced 205,000 tonnes of wine in 2002. Other products (in 1,000 tonnes) in 2002: meat, 488; cow's milk, 1,306; goat's milk, 105; sheep's milk, 93; eggs, 91.

Livestock (2002), in 1,000: cattle, 635; sheep, 1,571; pigs, 1,014; goats, 899; chickens, 18,000.

Forestry

In 2005 forests covered 3·63m. ha., or 32·8% of the total land area (3·37m. ha. in 2000). Timber production in 2007 totalled 5·70m. cu. metres.

Fisheries

In 2005 total catch was 5,434 tonnes, mainly from sea fishing. As recently as 1988 the catch amounted to 106,000 tonnes.

INDUSTRY

In 2005 the total output of industrial enterprises was 35,260m. new leva, of which 31,459m. new leva (89·2%) came from the private and 3,801m. new leva (10·8·%) from the public sector.

Output in 1,000 tonnes (2004 unless otherwise indicated): cement (2005), 3,618; crude steel, 2,106; distillate fuel oil, 1,912; rolled steel (2005), 1,817; petrol, 1,401; pig iron (2002), 1,100; residual fuel oil, 958; sulphuric acid (2001), 620; nitrogenous fertilizers (2002), 193; paper (2002), 171. Production of other products: cotton fabrics (2005), 67·7m. sq. metres; silk fabrics (2005), 18·3m. sq. metres; woollen fabrics (2005), 9·9m. sq. metres; 26·7bn. cigarettes (2001); 145,000 refrigerators (2001).

Labour

There is a 40-hour five-day working week. The average annual salary in 2006 was 4,225 new leva. In 2001 the labour force numbered 3,412,600. A total of 2,940,300 persons were in employment in 2001 (excluding the armed forces), with the leading areas of activity as follows: agriculture, fishing, forestry and hunting, 774,100; manufacturing, 591,800; wholesale and retail trade/ repair of motor vehicles, motorcycles and personal and household goods, 355,200; transport, storage and communications, 214,200; and health and social work, 138,300. Unemployment was 11·7% in Sept. 2004, the lowest rate in five years.

Trade Unions

The former official Central Council of Trade Unions reconstituted itself in 1990 as the Confederation of Independent Trade Unions; in 2003 it had 390,000 members. An independent white-collar trade union movement, Podkrepa, was formed in 1989; there were an estimated 109,000 members in 2003.

INTERNATIONAL TRADE

Legislation in force as of Feb. 1992 abolished restrictions imposed in 1990 on the repatriation of profits and allows foreign nationals to own and set up companies in Bulgaria. Western share participation in joint ventures may exceed 50%. Total foreign debt was US$16,786m. in 2005.

Imports and Exports

Imports (c.i.f.) and exports (f.o.b.) for calendar years in US$1m.:

	2001	*2002*	*2003*	*2004*	*2005*
Imports	7,260·8	7,903·4	10,753·6	14,380·4	18,312·3
Exports	5,112·9	5,692·1	7,444·8	9,877·0	11,835·2

Leading import commodities are mineral products, machinery and apparatus, electrical equipment and parts, textile materials and articles, and transportation facilities. Leading export commodities are non-precious metals and articles, textile materials and articles, mineral products and chemical industry produce.

Leading import suppliers in 2005: Russia, 15·6%; Germany, 13·6%; Italy, 9·0%; Turkey, 6·1%; Greece, 5·0%; France, 4·7%. Main export markets in 2005: Italy, 12·0%; Turkey, 10·5%; Germany, 9·8%; Greece, 9·4%; Belgium, 6·0%; France, 4·6%. Trade with the European Union grew steadily in the years prior to Bulgaria becoming a member in Jan. 2007, with imports from the EU rising from 35% of the total in 1996 to 50% in 2005 and exports to the EU increasing from 39% of all exports in 1996 to 56% in 2005.

COMMUNICATIONS

Roads

In 2005 Bulgaria had 40,231 km of roads, including 331 km of motorways and 2,961 km of main roads. In 2007 there were 1,971,500 passenger cars (257 per 1,000 inhabitants), 262,900 lorries and vans, 26,300 buses and coaches, and 78,900 motorcycles and mopeds. In 2005 public transport totalled 13·7bn. passenger-km. There were 6,905 road accidents in 2004 with 943 fatalities.

Rail

In 2005 there were 5,040 km of 1,435 mm gauge railway (3,900 km electrified) and 245 km of 760 mm gauge. Passenger-km travelled in 2004 came to 2·60bn. and freight tonne-km to 4·63bn.

There is a tramway and a metro in Sofia.

Civil Aviation

There is an international airport at Sofia (Vrazhdebna), which handled 1,101,734 passengers (1,049,738 on international flights) and 7,395 tonnes of freight in 2001. The bankrupt former state-owned Balkan Bulgarian Airlines was replaced by Balkan Air Tour in 2002 as the new national flag carrier. In 2003 Balkan Air Tour operated direct services to Berlin, Brussels, Budapest, Copenhagen, Frankfurt, Lisbon, London, Madrid, Moscow, Paris, Prague, Rome, Stockholm, Tel Aviv, Vienna, Warsaw and Zürich. Balkan Air Tour has in the meantime been renamed Bulgaria Air. The independent Hemus Air operated services in 2003 to Athens, Beirut, Bucharest, Damascus, Dubai, Larnaca, Tirana and Tripoli. In 2003 scheduled airline traffic of Bulgarian-based carriers flew 7m. km, carrying 311,000 passengers (270,000 on international flights).

Shipping

In 2002 the merchant fleet totalled 889,000 GRT, including oil tankers 114,000 GRT. Bourgas is a fishing and oil-port. Varna is the other important port. There is a rail ferry between Varna and Ilitchovsk (Ukraine). In 2002, 15·5m. tonnes of cargo were carried on international and coastal sea traffic; 60,000 passengers and 1·6m. tonnes of freight were carried on inland waterways.

Telecommunications

The Bulgarian Telecommunications Company was privatized in Jan. 2004. About 26% of main lines had been digitalized by 2003. There were 8,728,200 telephone subscribers in 2005 (1,129·7 per 1,000 inhabitants), of which 6,244,700 were mobile phone subscribers. There were 461,000 PCs in use in 2004 (59·4 per 1,000 persons) and 1,591,700 internet users in 2005.

Postal Services

In 2002 there were 3,021 post offices.

SOCIAL INSTITUTIONS

Justice

A law of Nov. 1982 provides for the election (and recall) of all judges by the National Assembly. There are a Supreme Court, 28 provincial courts (including Sofia) and regional courts. Jurors are elected at the local government elections. The Prosecutor General and judges are elected by the Supreme Judicial Council established in 1992.

The population in penal institutions in Sept. 2003 was 10,500 (134 per 100,000 of national population). The maximum term of imprisonment is 20 years. The death penalty was abolished for all crimes in 1998.

Education

Adult literacy rate in 2003 was 98·2% (male, 98·7%; female, 97·7%). Education is free, and compulsory for children between the ages of 7 and 16.

In 2003–04 there were 6,648 educational establishments: 3,278 kindergartens, 2,823 general and special schools, 496 vocational schools and 51 higher education institutions. There were 122,986 teaching staff (22,532 in higher education) and 1,451,284 pupils and students (228,468 in higher education); 114 schools (with 8,721 pupils) and 14 higher institutions (with 32,802 students) were private. There are eight state universities, four private universities and several specialized higher education institutions, some of which have university status. The Academy of Sciences was founded in 1869.

In 2006 public expenditure on education came to 4·3% of GNI and 11·6% of total government spending.

Health

All medical services are free. Private medical services were authorized in Jan. 1991. In 2003 there were 249 hospitals with 58 beds per 10,000 inhabitants. There were 28,128 physicians, 6,475 dentists, 29,650 nurses, 381 pharmacists and 3,456 midwives in 2003. In 2004 health spending represented 8·0% of GDP.

Welfare

In 2000 Bulgaria's official retirement age remained unchanged since the Soviet era at 60 years (men) and 55 years (women). However, as part of EU accession reform, the age level increased gradually until 2009 when retirement ages were 63 (men) and 60 (women). The minimum old-age pension is 113 leva a month and the social pension is 84 leva a month.

The family allowance is 30 leva a month for each child below age 16 (or age 18 if the child attends secondary school).

Unemployment benefits are calculated as 60% of average earnings for the previous nine months.

RELIGION

'The traditional church of the Bulgarian people' (as it is officially described) is that of the Eastern Orthodox Church. It was disestablished under the 1947 constitution. In 1953 the Bulgarian Patriarchate was revived. The Patriarch is Maksim (enthroned 1971). The seat of the Patriarch is at Sofia. There are 11 dioceses (each under a Metropolitan), ten bishops, 2,600 parishes, 1,500 priests, 120 monasteries (with about 400 monks and nuns), 3,700 churches and chapels, one seminary and one theological college.

In 2002 there were some 80,000 Roman Catholics with 51 priests and 54 parishes in three bishoprics. At the 2001 census, 6,638,870 Christians were recorded and 966,978 Muslims (Pomaks). There is a Chief Mufti elected by regional muftis.

CULTURE

World Heritage Sites

There are nine Bulgarian sites that appear on the UNESCO World Heritage List. They are (with year entered on list): Boyana Church (1979); Madara Rider (1979), an 8th century sculpture carved into a rockface; Rock-hewn Churches of Ivanovo (1979); Thracian Tomb of Kazanlak (1979); Ancient City of Nessebar (1983); Srebarna Nature Reserve (1983); Pirin National Park (1983); Rila Monastery (1983 and 2008); Thracian tomb of Sveshtari (1985).

Broadcasting

Bulgarian National Radio and Bulgarian National Television are the public broadcasters. The first national commercial TV service, BTV, was launched in 2000, and Nova TV was awarded the second national licence in 2003. There are several commercial regional TV channels and numerous licensed radio stations provide national and local coverage. In total there were 98 TV channels (colour by SECAM V) and 89 radio stations in 2003. There were 2·7m. television-equipped households in 2006. The Council for Electronic Media is the regulatory authority for broadcasting.

Cinema

There were 149 cinemas with 52,865 seats in 2003 (attendance, 3·53m.). In 2005, three full-length films of Bulgarian initiative were produced.

Press

In 2002 there were 48 daily newspapers with a combined daily circulation of 1·40m., giving a rate of 173 per 1,000 persons. The two biggest circulation dailies are Trud, the only title from the socialist era that survived after 1989, and 24 Chasa, Bulgaria's first private newspaper. A total of 6,432 book titles were published in 2004, including 2,047 in sociology and politics and 1,756 literary texts for adults.

Tourism

There were 3,531,567 foreign tourists in 2003. Most arrived from Serbia and Montenegro, Macedonia, Greece and Germany. In 2003, 903,133 Bulgarians made visits abroad as tourists. Earnings from tourism were US$1,623m. in 2003.

Libraries

In 2005 there were 4,552 public libraries. They held a combined 68,531,000 volumes for 1,336,000 registered users.

DIPLOMATIC REPRESENTATIVES

Of Bulgaria in the United Kingdom (186–188 Queen's Gate, London, SW7 5HL)
Ambassador: Lyubomir Kyuchukov.

Of the United Kingdom in Bulgaria (9 Moskovska St., Sofia 1000)
Ambassador: Steve Williams.

Of Bulgaria in the USA (1621 22nd St., NW, Washington, D.C., 20008)
Ambassador: Vacant.
Chargé d'Affaires a.i.: Tihomir Anguelov Stoytchev.

Of the USA in Bulgaria (16 Kozyak St., 1407 Sofia)
Ambassador: James B. Warlick, Jr.

Of Bulgaria to the United Nations
Ambassador: Rayko Raytchev.

Of Bulgaria to the European Union
Permanent Representative: Boyko Kotzev.

FURTHER READING

Central Statistical Office. *Statisticheski Godishnik.—Statisticheski Spravochnik* (annual).—*Statistical Reference Book of Republic of Bulgaria* (annual).

Crampton, Richard J., *A Concise History of Bulgaria.* 2nd ed. 2005
Melone, A., *Creating Parliamentary Government: The Transition to Democracy in Bulgaria.* 1998

National Statistical Office: Natsionalen Statisticheski Institut, Sofia. *President:* Mariana Kotzeva.
Website: http://www.nsi.bg

BURKINA FASO

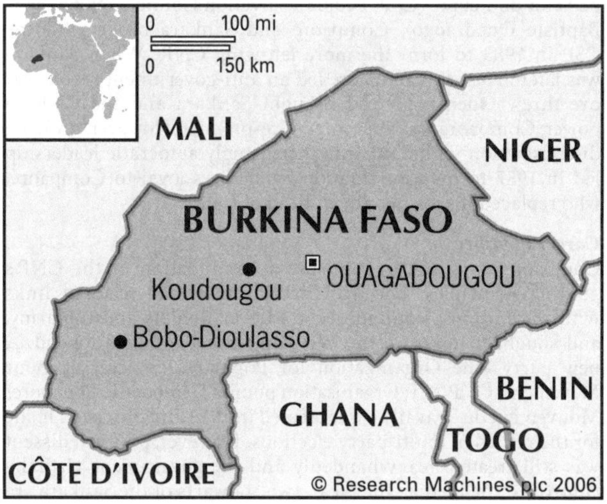

République Démocratique du Burkina Faso
(Democratic Republic of Burkina Faso)

Capital: Ouagadougou
Population estimate, 2010: 16·29m.
GDP per capita, 2007: (PPP$) 1,124
HDI/world rank: 0·389/177

KEY HISTORICAL EVENTS

Formerly known as Upper Volta, the country's name was changed in 1984 to Burkina Faso, meaning 'the land of honest men'. The area it covers was settled by farming communities until their invasion by the Mossi people in the 11th century. The Mossi successfully resisted Islamic crusades and attacks by neighbouring empires for seven centuries until conquered by the French between 1895 and 1903.

France made Upper Volta a separate colony in 1919, only to abolish it as such in 1932, dividing its territory between the Ivory Coast (now Côte d'Ivoire), French Sudan (now Mali) and Niger. In 1947 the territory of Upper Volta was reconstituted as a territory within French West Africa. In 1958 it was granted the status of autonomous republic within the French Community before winning full independence two years later.

Upper Volta remained a desperately poor country often hit by drought, particularly in 1972–74 and again in 1982–84. The military has held power for most of the period after independence. In Aug. 1983 a coup brought to power Capt. Thomas Sankara, a leading radical, who headed a left-wing regime. Sankara was overthrown and killed in a coup on 15 Oct. 1987, the fifth since 1960, led by his former friend Capt. Blaise Compaoré.

TERRITORY AND POPULATION

Burkina Faso is bounded in the north and west by Mali, east by Niger and south by Benin, Togo, Ghana and Côte d'Ivoire. Area: 270,764 sq. km; 2006 census population, 14,017,262, giving a density of 51·8 per sq. km. The United Nations population estimate for 2006 was 14·26m. In 2005 the population was 81·7% rural.

The UN gives an estimated population for 2010 of 16·29m.

The largest cities in 2006 were Ouagadougou, the capital (1,475,223), Bobo-Dioulasso (489,967), Koudougou (88,184), Banfora (75,917), Ouahigouya (73,153) and Pouytenga (60,618).

Areas and populations of the 45 provinces:

Province	*Sq. km*	*Population 2006*	*Province*	*Sq. km*	*Population 2006*
Balé	4,596	213,423	Mouhoun	6,659	297,350
Bam	4,084	275,191	Nahouri	3,748	157,071
Banwa	5,888	269,375	Namentenga	6,466	328,820
Bazéga	3,964	238,425	Nayala	3,923	163,433
Bougouriba	2,815	101,479	Noumbiel	2,736	70,036
Boulgou	6,687	543,570	Oubritenga	2,778	238,775
Boulkiemdé	4,268	505,206	Oudalan	9,832	195,964
Comoé	15,302	407,528	Passoré	3,866	323,222
Ganzourgou	4,179	319,380	Poni	7,351	256,931
Gnagna	8,470	408,669	Sanguié	5,183	297,036
Gourma	11,145	305,936	Sanmatenga	9,290	598,014
Houet	11,571	955,451	Séno	6,866	264,991
Ioba	3,251	192,321	Sissili	7,147	208,409
Kadiogo	2,805	1,727,390	Soum	12,205	347,335
Kénédougou	8,139	285,695	Sourou	5,768	220,622
Komondjari	5,043	79,507	Tapoa	14,572	342,305
Kompienga	6,998	75,867	Tuy	5,633	228,458
Kossi	7,328	278,546	Yagha	6,457	160,152
Koulpélogo	5,348	258,667	Yatenga	6,987	553,164
Kouritenga	2,621	329,779	Ziro	5,128	175,915
Kourwéogo	1,588	138,217	Zondoma	1,759	166,557
Léraba	3,132	124,280	Zoundwéogo	3,601	245,947
Loroum	3,587	142,853			

The principal ethnic groups are the Mossi (48%), Fulani (10%), Bobo (7%), Lobi (7%), Mandé (7%), Grosi (5%), Gurma (5%), Sénoufo (5%) and Tuareg (3%).

French is the official language.

SOCIAL STATISTICS

2000 births (estimates), 557,000; deaths, 189,000. Estimated birth rate in 2000 was 46·8 per 1,000 population; estimated death rate, 15·9. Annual population growth rate, 2000–05, 2·4%. Expectation of life at birth, 2007, 54·0 years for females and 51·4 for males. Infant mortality, 2005 (per 1,000 live births), 96. Fertility rate, 2004, 6·6 children per woman.

CLIMATE

A tropical climate with a wet season from May to Nov. and a dry season from Dec. to April. Rainfall decreases from south to north. Ouagadougou, Jan. 76°F (24·4°C), July 83°F (28·3°C). Annual rainfall 36" (894 mm).

CONSTITUTION AND GOVERNMENT

At a referendum in June 1991 a new constitution was approved; there is an executive presidency and a multi-party system. Parliament consists of the 111-member *National Assembly*, elected by universal suffrage. The *Chamber of Representatives*, a consultative body representing social, religious, professional and political organizations, was abolished in 2002. There is also an *Economic and Social Council*. In April 2000 parliament passed a law reducing presidential terms from seven to five years, with a maximum of two terms. The new law did not affect President Blaise Compaoré's seven-year term which was to expire in Nov. 2005, and he has now been elected for a further term.

National Anthem

'Contre la férule humiliante' ('Against the shameful fetters'); words by T. Sankara, tune anonymous.

RECENT ELECTIONS

At the presidential elections of 13 Nov. 2005 Blaise Compaoré was re-elected by 80·3% of votes cast against 12 other candidates. Turnout was 57·7%.

Parliamentary elections were held on 6 May 2007. The Congress for Democracy and Progress (CDP) won 73 out of 111 seats; the Alliance for Democracy and Federation–African Democratic Rally (ADF–RDA), 14; the Union for the Republic (UPR), 5; the Union for Rebirth/Sankarist Movement, 4; the Convention of the Democratic Forces of Burkina, 3; the Party for Democracy and Progress/Socialist Party, 2; the Party for Democracy and Socialism, 2; the Rally for the Development of Burkina, 2; the Union of Sankarist Parties, 2; the African Independence Party, 1; Citizen's Popular Rally, 1; the National Rebirth Party, 1; and the Union for Democracy and Social Progress, 1. Turnout was 56·4%.

Presidential elections are scheduled to take place on 21 Nov. 2010.

CURRENT ADMINISTRATION

President: Capt. Blaise Compaoré; b. 1951 (CDP; in office since 1987, most recently re-elected 13 Nov. 2005).

In March 2010 the government comprised:

Prime Minister: Tertius Zongo; b. 1957 (ind.; sworn in 4 June 2007).

Minister of State and Minister for Foreign Affairs and Regional Co-operation: Alain Bédouma Yoda.

Minister of Agriculture, Water and Water Resources: Laurent Sédogo. *Animal Resources:* Sékou Bâ. *Basic Education and Mass Literacy:* Odile Bonkoungou. *Civil Service and State Reform:* Soungalo Ouattara. *Culture, Tourism, Communication and Government Spokesperson:* Filippe Savadogo. *Defence:* Yéro Boli. *Economy and Finance:* Lucien Marie Noël Bembamba. *Environment and Quality of Life:* Salifou Sawadogo. *Health:* Seydou Bouda. *Housing and Town Planning:* Vincent Dabilougou. *Human Rights Promotion:* Salamata Sawadogo-Tapsoba. *Infrastructure and Rural Public Works Development:* Seydou Kaboré. *Justice and Keeper of the Seals:* Zakalia Koté. *Labour and Social Security:* Amadou Adrien Koné. *Mines and Energy:* Abdoulaye Abdoulkader Cissé. *Post, Information Technologies and Communications:* Noël Kabouré. *Promotion of Women:* Céline Yoda-Konkobo. *Relations with Parliament:* Cécile Béloum Ouédraogo. *Secondary and Higher Education and Scientific Research:* Joseph Paré. *Security:* Emile Ouédraogo. *Social Affairs and National Solidarity:* Pascaline Tamini. *Sports and Leisure:* Mori Ardjouma Jean Pierre Palm. *Territorial Administration and Decentralization:* Clément Sawadogo. *Trade, Promotion of Enterprise and Handicrafts:* Léonce Koné. *Transport:* Gilbert Noël Ouédraogo. *Youth and Employment:* Justin Koutaba.

Office of the Prime Minister (French only): http://www.primature.gov.bf

CURRENT LEADERS

Blaise Compaoré

Position

President

Introduction

Blaise Compaoré came to power in 1987 after the assassination of Thomas Sankara, the president of the Conseil National de la Révolution (CNR; National Revolutionary Council). Compaoré has attempted to deregulate the economy and improve relations with the West. He has said that he wants to make the country democratic, but his tenure has been marked by strikes, unrest and political murders. His human rights record has also attracted international condemnation.

Early Life

Born on 3 Feb. 1951 in Ouagadougou, Compaoré received his early education in Burkina Faso and became a secondary school teacher. In 1971 he joined the army and in 1975 went to Cameroon and France for military training. His friendship with Sankara began in Morocco in 1978 while he was serving as a parachute instructor. By 1981 Compaoré had achieved the rank of captain.

Although involved in the establishment in 1982 of the Conseil de Salut du Peuple (CSP; People's Salvation Council, led by Jean-Baptiste Ouedraogo), Compaoré and Sankara broke with the CSP in 1983 to form the more left-wing CNR. When Sankara was later arrested, Compaoré led an anti-government revolt that overthrew Ouedraogo and brought Sankara and the CNR to power. Compaoré was appointed vice-premier. However, growing dissatisfaction with Sankara's increasingly autocratic leadership led in 1987 to his assassination by soldiers loyal to Compaoré, who replaced his former ally as head of state.

Career in Office

Compaoré took office promising a continuation of the CNR's guiding principles, but with 'rectification'. He restored links with the business community, traditional chiefs and the army, and sought to reassure the West on whom he relied for aid. A new party—the Organization for Popular Democracy/Labour Movement (ODP/MT; Organisation pour la Démocratie Populaire/Mouvement du Travail)—was created in 1989 and provision made for the return of multi-party elections. However, political dissent was still treated heavy-handedly and the government virtually controlled the media. That year, two stalwarts of the Sankara era still holding senior office (Boukari Lingani and Henri Zongo) were accused of plotting a coup and executed. In 1991 an amnesty was called on all those guilty of 'political crimes' since 1960 and exiles were offered safe return.

Despite Compaoré's ostensible democratization of the election process and more moderate regime, the 1991 elections were boycotted by opposition groups. Compaoré, the sole candidate, won 90·4% of votes but less than 25% of the population participated. He was sworn in as president on 24 Dec. 1991. Amid high political tension, the assassination of opposition leader Clement Oumarou Ouedraogo and the postponement of legislative elections, Compaoré called a development forum of diverse political and social leaders. In the same year he agreed to a World Bank structural adjustment programme, although the resultant austerity measures led to strikes and protests by students.

The 1991 constitution was amended in 1997, allowing the president to stand for re-election more than once, and also restructuring parliament and provincial government. In addition the national anthem and the flag were modified to break with the revolutionary past. Compaoré was re-elected president in Nov. 1998 with more than 87% of votes (in a 56·1% turnout), although doubt was cast on the legitimacy of the electoral process. On 13 Dec. 1998 a journalist critical of Compaoré, Norbert Zongo, and three of his colleagues were murdered. There followed public protests and the arrest of opposition leaders.

A report of May 1999 suggested that the presidential bodyguard was behind the murders of Zongo and his colleagues. The conclusions led to student protests in the capital. Compaoré's human rights record fell under further scrutiny as more opposition leaders and independent journalists were arrested. Despite the offer of compensation to the victims' families and the release of several political prisoners, tensions remained high, and strikes and other protests persisted.

In parliamentary elections in May 2002, despite a stronger opposition performance, the pro-Compaoré Congress for Democracy and Progress (CDP) won 57 of the 111 National Assembly seats, and it took 73 of the 111 seats in the May 2007 elections. Meanwhile, although deemed unconstitutional by opposition politicians, Compaoré was re-elected for a further presidential term in Nov. 2005, winning over 80% of the vote. In April 2009 the parliament adopted legislation requiring at least 30% of political party candidates in future elections to be women.

In foreign policy, Compaoré has forged close links with both Libya and France. However, his regime has been accused more recently of destabilizing interference in civil wars in Liberia and Sierra Leone.

DEFENCE

There are three military regions. Defence expenditure totalled US$85m. in 2006 (US$6 per capita), representing 1·4% of GDP.

Army

Strength (2007), 6,400 with a paramilitary Gendarmerie of 4,200. In addition there is a People's Militia of 45,000.

Air Force

Personnel total (2007), 200 with five combat capable aircraft.

INTERNATIONAL RELATIONS

Burkina Faso is a member of the UN, World Bank, IMF and several other UN specialized agencies, WTO, IOM, International Organization of the Francophonie, Islamic Development Bank, OIC, African Development Bank, African Union, ECOWAS and is an ACP member state of the ACP-EU relationship.

ECONOMY

In 2006 agriculture accounted for 33·3% of GDP, industry 22·4% and services 44·4%.

Overview

Burkina Faso is ranked among the world's poorest nations, with per capita income of US$400 in 2005 (compared to a US$590 average for low income countries) and is listed at 177 out of 182 in the Human Development Index. Although there are large deposits of gold in the country, the economy is dependent on cotton exports that are susceptible to droughts and changes in world prices.

Macroeconomic performance has been sound since the late 1990s, with real GDP growth averaging around 5·5% per year. Tourism has benefited from the country's popularity as a venue for international conferences. Since 1991 the IMF and World Bank have helped implement economic and social reforms aimed at liberalizing the economy and developing the private sector. However, the economy remains heavily dependent on agriculture. Spending on poverty reduction rose from 4·7% of GDP in 2003 to 5·5% in 2005.

Currency

The unit of currency is the *franc CFA* (XOF) with a parity of 655·957 francs CFA to one euro. Foreign exchange reserves were US$520m. in June 2005 and total money supply was 375,711m. francs CFA. There was inflation of 10·7% in 2008, following deflation of 0·2% in 2007.

Budget

Total revenues in 2006 were 793·0bn. francs CFA and expenditures 892·1bn. francs CFA.

VAT is 18%.

Performance

Real GDP growth was 3·6% in 2007 and 5·0% in 2008. Total GDP was US$7·9bn. in 2008.

Banking and Finance

The bank of issue which functions as the central bank is the regional Central Bank of West African States (BCEAO; *Governor*, Philippe-Henri Dacoury-Tabley). There are seven other banks and three credit institutions. There is a stock exchange in Ouagadougou.

ENERGY AND NATURAL RESOURCES

Environment

Burkina Faso's carbon dioxide emissions from the consumption and flaring of fossil fuels in 2008 were the equivalent of 0·1 tonnes per capita. An *Environmental Performance Index* compiled in 2008 ranked Burkina Faso 144th in the world out of 149 countries analysed, with 44·3%. The index examined various factors in six areas—air pollution, biodiversity and habitat, climate change, environmental health, productive natural resources and water resources.

Electricity

Production of electricity (2004) was 400m. kWh. Thermal capacity in 2004 was approximately 48,000 kW; hydro-electric capacity in 2004 was around 30,000 kW. Total installed capacity was an estimated 78,000 kW in 2004. Consumption per capita was 31 kWh in 2004.

Minerals

There are deposits of manganese, zinc, limestone, phosphate and diamonds. Gold production was 770 kg in 2003.

Agriculture

In 2007 there were about 5·2m. ha. of arable land and 60,000 ha. of permanent crops. 25,000 ha. were irrigated in 2001. There were four tractors per 10,000 ha. of arable land in 2006. The agricultural population in 2007 totalled approximately 13·56m., of whom 6·12m. were economically active. Production (2003, in 1,000 tonnes): sorghum, 1,519; millet, 1,214; maize, 738; seed cotton, 500; sugarcane, 420; groundnuts, 301; cottonseed, 250.

Livestock (2003 estimates): goats, 8·8m.; sheep, 6·8m.; cattle, 5·0m.; pigs, 640,000; asses, 531,000; chickens, 24m. Livestock products, 2003 estimates (in 1,000 tonnes): beef and veal, 62; goat meat, 24; poultry meat, 28; cow's milk, 180; goat's milk, 54; eggs, 18.

Forestry

In 2005 forests covered 6,794,000 ha., or 29·0% of the total land area. Timber production in 2007 was 13·41m. cu. metres.

Fisheries

In 2005 total catch was 9,000 tonnes, exclusively from inland waters. There is some fish farming.

INDUSTRY

In 2002 manufacturing contributed 14·5% of GDP, primarily food-processing and textiles. Industry is underdeveloped and employs only 1% of the workforce. The country's manufactures are mainly restricted to basic consumer goods and processed foods. Output of major products, in 1,000 tonnes: vegetable oil (2000), 31; sugar (2002), 35; flour (2002), 10; soap (2002), 10; beer (2003), 55·0m. litres; printed fabric (2000), 275,000 sq. metres.

Labour

In 2003 the labour force was 5,918,880 (54% males). Over 90% of the economically active population are engaged in agriculture, fishing and forestry.

Trade Unions

There were six trade union federations in 2009: Confédération Générale du Travail du Burkina (CGT-B), Confédération Nationale des Travailleurs Burkinabé (CNTB), Confédération Syndicale Burkinabé (CSB), Force Ouvrière/Union Nationale des Syndicats Libres (FO/UNSL), Organisation Nationale des Syndicats Libres (ONSL) and Union Syndicale des Travailleurs du Burkina (USTB).

INTERNATIONAL TRADE

Foreign debt was US$2,045m. in 2005.

Imports and Exports

In 2004 imports totalled US$1,267·2m. and exports US$396·5m. Principal import suppliers, 2003: Togo, 29·1%; France, 17·1%; Benin, 10·3%. Principal export markets, 2003: Togo, 45·8%; Ghana,

25·8%; France, 5·6%. Cotton is the main export, accounting for 71·5% of the country's export income in 2004.

COMMUNICATIONS

Roads

The road system comprised 92,495 km in 2004 (including 15,271 km of main roads). There were 97,100 passenger cars (seven per 1,000 inhabitants), 55,700 lorries and vans, and 356,400 motorcycles and mopeds in use in 2007.

Rail

The railway from Abidjan in Côte d'Ivoire to Kaya (600 km of metre gauge within Burkina Faso) is operated by the mixed public-private company Sitarail, a concessionaire to both governments. Across both countries Sitarail carried 156,569 passengers in 2004 and 759,957 tonnes of freight in 2005.

Civil Aviation

The international airports are Ouagadougou (which handled 337,000 passengers in 2007) and Bobo-Dioulasso. The national carrier is Air Burkina, which in 2003 flew to Abidjan, Bamako, Cotonou, Dakar, Lomé and Niamey in addition to operating on domestic routes. In 2003 scheduled airline traffic of Burkina Faso-based carriers flew 1m. km, carrying 54,000 passengers (36,000 on international flights).

Telecommunications

There were 669,600 telephone subscribers in 2005, equivalent to 50·6 per 1,000 inhabitants, of which mobile phone subscribers numbered 572,200. In 2005, 31,000 PCs were in use (2·4 per 1,000 persons) and there were 64,600 internet users.

Postal Services

There were 73 post offices in 2003.

SOCIAL INSTITUTIONS

Justice

Civilian courts replaced revolutionary tribunals in 1993. A law passed in April 2000 split the supreme court into four separate entities—a constitutional court, an appeal court, a council of state and a government audit office.

The population in penal institutions in Dec. 2006 was 3,108 (22 per 100,000 of national population).

Education

In 2005 adult literacy was 23·6%, among the lowest in the world. The 1994–96 development programme established an adult literacy campaign, and centres for the education of 10–15-year-old non-school attenders. In 2007 there were 1,561,258 pupils at primary schools with 32,760 teaching staff. During the period 1990–95 only 24% of females of primary school age were enrolled in school but by 2006 this had increased to 42%. In 2007 there were 352,376 pupils and 12,498 teaching staff in secondary schools, and 33,459 students in higher education with 1,886 academic staff.

In 2006 public expenditure on education came to 4·5% of GNI and 15·4% of total government expenditure.

Health

In 2007 there were three national hospitals, nine regional hospitals and 75 medical centres. There were 441 physicians, 38 dentists, 4,262 nurses, 604 midwives and 58 pharmacists in the public sector in 2007.

RELIGION

In 2001 there were 5·96m. Muslims and 2·04m. Christians (mainly Roman Catholic). Many of the remaining population follow traditional animist religions.

CULTURE

World Heritage Sites

The Ruins of Loropéni were inscribed on the UNESCO World Heritage List in 2009. At least 1,000 years old, Loropéni is the best preserved of ten similar fortresses in the Lobi area and is part of a larger group of around 100 stone-built enclosures with ties to the trans-Saharan gold trade.

Broadcasting

State-controlled Télévision Nationale du Burkina (colour by NTSC) and Radio Burkina operate national (and regional radio) broadcasting networks. Canal 3 is a commercial TV channel and there are numerous private and community radio stations. There were 260,000 television receivers in 2006.

Press

There were five dailies (two government-owned) with a combined circulation of 33,000 in 2006.

Tourism

In 2005, 245,000 non-resident tourists stayed in hotels or similar accommodation.

DIPLOMATIC REPRESENTATIVES

Of Burkina Faso in the United Kingdom
Ambassador: Kadré Désiré Ouedraogo (resides in Brussels).
Honorary Consul: Colin Seelig (The Lilacs, Stane St., Ockley, Surrey, RH5 5LU).

Of the United Kingdom in Burkina Faso
Ambassador: Dr Nicholas Westcott, CMG (resides in Accra, Ghana).

Of Burkina Faso in the USA (2340 Massachusetts Ave., NW, Washington, D.C., 20008)
Ambassador: Parmanga Ernest Yonli.

Of the USA in Burkina Faso (602 avenue Raoul Follereau, 01 BP 35, Ouagadougou 01)
Ambassador: Vacant.
Chargé d'Affaires a.i.: Samuel C. Laeuchli.

Of Burkina Faso to the United Nations
Ambassador: Michel Kafando.

Of Burkina Faso to the European Union
Ambassador: Kadré Désiré Ouedraogo.

FURTHER READING

Nnaji, B. O., *Blaise Compaoré: Architect of the Burkina Faso Revolution.* 1991

National Statistical Office: Institut National de la Statistique et de la Démographie (INSD), 555 Boulevard de l'Indépendance, 01 BP 374, Ouagadougou.
Website (French only): http://www.insd.bf

BURUNDI

Republika y'Uburundi
(Republic of Burundi)

Capital: Bujumbura
Population estimate, 2010: 8·52m.
GDP per capita, 2007: (PPP$) 341
HDI/world rank: 0·394/174

KEY HISTORICAL EVENTS

From 1890 Burundi was part of German East Africa and from 1919 part of Ruanda-Urundi, administered by Belgium as a League of Nations mandate. Internal self-government was granted on 1 Jan. 1962, followed by independence on 1 July 1962. In April 1972 fighting broke out between rebels from both Burundi and neighbouring countries and the ruling Tutsi, apparently with the intention of destroying the Tutsi hegemony. Up to 120,000 died. On 1 Nov. 1976 President Micombero was deposed by the Army, as was President Bagaza on 3 Sept. 1987. Maj. Pierre Buyoya assumed the presidency on 1 Oct. 1987.

On 1 June 1993 President Buyoya was defeated in elections by Melchior Ndadaye, who thus became the country's first elected president and the first Hutu president, but on 21 Oct. 1993 President Ndadaye and six ministers were killed in an attempted military coup. A wave of Tutsi-Hutu massacres broke out, costing thousands of lives. On 6 April 1994 the new president, Cyprien Ntaryamira, was also killed, possibly assassinated, together with the president of Rwanda.

On 25 July 1996 the army seized power, installing Maj. Pierre Buyoya, a Tutsi, as president for the second time. In June 1998 Buyoya drew up a settlement for a power-sharing transitional government and the replacement of the prime minister by two vice-presidents, one Hutu and one Tutsi. Extremists on both sides denounced the agreement. An attempted coup in April 2001 failed. In July 2001 it was agreed that a three-year transitional government should be installed with Buyoya as president and Domitien Ndayizeye, a Hutu, as vice-president for the first 18 months, after which the roles would be reversed. A further attempted coup shortly after the announcement of the agreement also failed, although fighting continued. A ceasefire accord was eventually signed in Dec. 2002 by the government and the Forces for the Defense of Democracy (FDD), the country's principal rebel movement. In Oct. 2003 the FDD and the government sealed a peace deal to end the civil war and put into practice the ceasefire agreed in 2002. More than 200,000 people have been killed in civil conflict since 1993. However, developments in recent years, including the holding of a referendum on the post-transition constitution, suggest a more peaceful future.

TERRITORY AND POPULATION

Burundi is bounded in the north by Rwanda, east and south by Tanzania and west by the Democratic Republic of the Congo, and has an area (including inland water) of 27,834 sq. km (10,759 sq. miles). The population at the 1990 census was 5,292,793. In 2005, 90·0% of the population lived in rural areas (the largest proportion of any country in the world).

The UN gives an estimated population for 2010 of 8·52m.; density, 306 per sq. km.

There are 17 regions, all named after their chief towns. Area and population:

Region	*Area (in sq. km.)*	*Population (1999)*
Bubanza	1,089	289,060
Bujumbura Mairie	87	319,098
Bujumbura Rural	1,089	436,896
Bururi	2,465	437,931
Cankuzo	1,965	172,477
Cibitoke	1,636	385,438
Gitega	1,979	628,872
Karusi	1,457	384,187
Kayanza	1,233	458,815
Kirundo	1,703	502,171
Makamba	1,960	357,492
Muramvya	696	252,833
Muyinga	1,836	485,347
Mwaro	840	229,013
Ngozi	1,474	601,382
Rutana	1,959	244,939
Ruyigi	2,339	304,567

The capital, Bujumbura, had an estimated population of 319,098 in 1999. The second largest town, Gitega, had a population in 1990 of 102,000.

There are four ethnic groups—Hutu (Bantu, forming 81% of the total); Tutsi (Nilotic, 16%); Lingala (2%); Twa (pygmoids, 1%). The local language, Kirundi, and French are both official languages. Kiswahili is spoken in the commercial centres.

SOCIAL STATISTICS

2000 estimates: births, 288,000; deaths, 130,000. Rates, 2000 estimates (per 1,000 population): birth, 43·5; death, 20·8. Life expectancy at birth, 2007, was 48·6 years for men and 51·4 years for women. Infant mortality, 2005, 114 per 1,000 live births. Annual population growth rate, 1992–2002, 1·3%; fertility rate, 2004, 6·8 children per woman.

CLIMATE

An equatorial climate, modified by altitude. The eastern plateau is generally cool, the easternmost savanna several degrees hotter. The wet seasons are from March to May and Sept. to Dec. Bujumbura, Jan. 73°F (22·8°C), July 73°F (22·8°C). Annual rainfall 33" (825 mm).

CONSTITUTION AND GOVERNMENT

The constitution of 1981 provided for a one-party state. In Jan. 1991 the government of President Maj. Pierre Buyoya, leader of the sole party, the Union for National Progress (UPRONA), proposed a new constitution which was approved by a referendum in March 1992 (with 89% of votes cast in favour), legalizing parties not based on ethnic group, region or religion and providing for presidential elections by direct universal suffrage. On 28 Feb. 2005 citizens voted overwhelmingly to adopt a new constitution laying the foundations for the end of a 12-year civil war, with 92% of votes cast in favour of the constitution. The constitution gives Tutsis (who have traditionally held power in Burundi but only make up 15% of the population) 40% of seats in the National Assembly, while the Hutus, who constitute 83% of the population, are given 60% of the seats.

Burundi has a bicameral legislature, consisting of the *National Assembly* of 118 members, with 100 members elected to serve five-year terms and 18 appointed to ensure that ethnic and gender quotas are met, and the *Senate* of 49 members (34 elected and 15 appointed, including four former presidents).

In July 2001 agreement was reached on President Buyoya's presidency for the first 18 months of a three-year transition period of multi-ethnic broad-based government. In accordance with the terms of the Arusha peace accord, initially he was being assisted by Hutu Vice-President Domitien Ndayizeye, after which the roles were to be reversed for the second 18 months. The transitional government was established on 1 Nov. 2001. On 30 April 2003 Ndayizeye became president but Alphonse Marie Kadege, like Buyoya a Tutsi from the Party of Unity and National Progress, became the vice-president. In Oct. 2004 the transitional government was extended for a further six months, with elections scheduled for 22 April 2005. In April 2005 the transitional period was extended for a further four months and a new deadline of 19 Aug. 2005 set for elections. The success of the referendum in Feb. 2005 held under 1993 electoral laws was seen as proof that presidential elections need not be postponed further. Parliamentary elections that were generally deemed free and fair were held in July 2005, with presidential elections following in Aug.

National Anthem

'Burundi Bwacu' ('Dear Burundi'); words by a committee, tune by M. Barengayabo.

RECENT ELECTIONS

Burundi's parliament elected Pierre Nkurunziza, the only candidate, president on 19 Aug. 2005 by 151 votes to nine with one abstention and one null vote. A former Hutu rebel, he thus became the country's first president chosen through democratic means since the assassination of President Melchior Ndadaye in 1993.

At the parliamentary elections of 4 July 2005 the National Council for the Defense of Democracy–Forces for the Defense of Democracy (CNDD–FDD) won 64 of 118 seats with 58·6% of the vote, President Domitien Ndayizeye's ruling Front for Democracy in Burundi (FRODEBU) 30 with 21·7%, the Union for National Progress (UPRONA) 15 with 7·2%, National Council for the Defense of Democracy (CNDD) 4 with 4·1% and Movement for the Rehabilitation of Citizens–Rurenzangemero (MRC–Rurenzangemero) 2 with 2·1%. In addition, three ethnic Twa members were appointed to the National Assembly. In indirect Senate elections held on 29 July 2005 the National Council for the Defense of Democracy–Forces for the Defense of Democracy won 32 of 49 seats, the Front for Democracy in Burundi 7, the Union for National Progress 3, the National Council for the Defense of Democracy 3, ethnic Twa members 3 and the Party for National Recovery (PARENA) 1.

Presidential elections were scheduled to take place on 28 June 2010 and parliamentary elections on 23 July 2010.

CURRENT ADMINISTRATION

President: Pierre Nkurunziza; b. 1963 (CNDD–FDD; sworn in 26 Aug. 2005).

In March 2010 the government comprised:

Minister of Agriculture and Livestock: Ferdinand Nderagakura. *Civil Service, Labour and Social Security:* Anonciate Sendazirasa. *Decentralization and Communal Development:* Mupira Pierre. *East African Community Affairs:* Hafsa Mossi. *Energy and Mining:* Moïse Bucumi. *External Relations and International Co-operation:* Augustin Nsanze. *Fight Against Aids:* Spéciose Baransata. *Finance:* Clotilde Nizigama. *Higher Education and Scientific Research:* Saïdi Kebeya. *Human Rights and Gender:* Christine Ndayishimiye. *Information, Communication and Parliamentary Relations:* Vénérand Bakevyumusaya. *Interior:* Edouard Nduwimana. *Justice and Keeper of the Seals:* Jean-Bosco Ndikumana. *National Defence and War Veterans:* Maj.-Gen. Germain Niyoyankana. *National Solidarity, Repatriation of Refugees, National Reconstruction and Social Integration:* Immaculée Nahayo. *Planning and Reconstruction:* Tabu Abdallah Manirakiza. *Primary and Secondary Education:* Ernest Mberamiheto. *Public Health:* Dr Emmanuel Gikoro. *Public Security:* Alain Guillaume Bunyoni. *Public Works and Equipment:* Anatole Kanyenkiko. *Technical Education, Professional Training and Literacy:* Rose Gahiru. *Trade, Industry and Tourism:* Euphrasie Bigirimana. *Transport, Posts and Telecommunications:* Philippe Njoni. *Water, Environment, Territorial Development and Public Works:* Déogratias Nduwimana. *Youth, Sports and Culture:* Jean-Jacques Nyenimigabo.

Government Website (French only): http://www.burundi-gov.bi

CURRENT LEADERS

Pierre Nkurunziza

Position
President

Introduction
Pierre Nkurunziza became president in Aug. 2005 in the country's first democratic elections since the start of the civil war in 1993. The key challenges facing the former leader of Burundi's largest ethnic Hutu rebel group have been the rebuilding of the economy, overseeing the repatriation of tens of thousands of refugees and maintaining relations with the Tutsi minority.

Early Life
Pierre Nkurunziza was born in Burundi's capital, Bujumbura, on 18 Dec. 1963, the son of Eustache Ngabisha, who was the governor of Ngozi and Kayansi provinces and a member of parliament from 1965. He attended primary school in the northern town of Ngozi and was there in 1972 when his father was killed in a wave of ethnic violence that claimed over 100,000 lives. The family moved to Gitega, where Nkurunziza attended secondary school. He studied physical education at the University of Burundi in Bujumbura and became closely involved with the New Sporting football club as both player and coach. Having graduated in 1990, he combined teaching at Muramvya High School with further studies in psychology and pedagogy. A year later he began lecturing in physical education both at the country's leading military academy and at the University of Burundi.

Civil war was ignited in Oct. 1993 by the assassination of Burundi's first ethnic Hutu president, Melchior Ndadaye, and spilled on to the University of Burundi campus in 1995 when 200 Hutu students were killed by Tutsi militia. Nkurunziza was reportedly shot at but managed to escape and left the capital to join the National Council for the Defense of Democracy–Forces for the Defense of Democracy (CNDD–FDD) as a soldier. The group was one of several rebel Hutu groups that fought the Tutsi-dominated army, a conflict which killed thousands and had created an estimated 700,000 refugees by the late 1990s. In 1998 Nkurunziza was promoted to deputy secretary-general and co-ordinated the activities of the armed and political wings of the CNDD–FDD. In the same year he was sentenced to death by a Burundian court for alleged involvement in a series of ambushes but was granted immunity during peace talks that culminated in the Arusha Peace Accord of Aug. 2000.

Elected chairman of the CNDD–FDD at its first congress in 2001, Nkurunziza began negotiations with Burundi's transitional government. In Nov. 2003 he signed a ceasefire accord, winning official recognition of the CNDD–FDD as a political party. Nkurunziza became state minister of good governance in the transitional government led by Domitien Ndayizeye. As such, he was a key figure in forging a power-sharing agreement and setting a timetable for democratic elections, ratified by heads of state from the Great Lakes region in Aug. 2004.

Following a series of CNDD–FDD victories in elections held in June and July 2005, Nkurunziza was nominated as the party's presidential candidate. He won an overwhelming victory in a vote by members of parliament (acting as an electoral college) on 19 Aug. and was sworn in as president on 26 Aug. 2005.

Career in Office

President Nkurunziza called for the Palipehutu–FNL opposition to lay down arms and rejoin negotiations. He appointed a cabinet of 20 ministers comprising 11 Hutus and nine Tutsis in accordance with the fixed quotas stipulated in the constitution. He announced that free primary education would be available to all children with immediate effect. He also promised to facilitate the return of Burundian refugees from Tanzania and Rwanda. In Aug. 2006 Nkurunziza's government claimed to have foiled a coup attempt, which prompted a crackdown on opposition and the arrest of several prominent political and military figures. The following month the government signed a ceasefire agreement with the Palipehutu–FNL rebel group which finally entered the peace process. In 2007, despite some residual violence attributed to the FNL, the United Nations completed its peacekeeping mandate in Burundi. In April 2008 a renewal of fighting between government forces and the FNL left around 100 people dead before another ceasefire was negotiated the following month. Then, in April 2009, the FNL officially disarmed and transformed into a legal political party.

DEFENCE

A new National Defence Force combining government forces and rebels from the FDD was created following the Oct. 2003 peace settlement.

Defence expenditure totalled US$49m. in 2006 (US$6 per capita), representing 5·1% of GDP.

Army

The Army had a strength (2007) of 35,000 including an air wing.

Air Force

There were 200 air wing personnel in 2007 with two combat capable aircraft and two attack helicopters.

INTERNATIONAL RELATIONS

Burundi is a member of the UN, World Bank, IMF and several other UN specialized agencies, WTO, IOM, International Organization of the Francophonie, African Development Bank, African Union, COMESA, EAC, CEEAC and is an ACP member state of the ACP-EU relationship.

ECONOMY

Agriculture accounted for 35% of GDP in 2005, industry 20% and services 45%.

Overview

Being landlocked and among the poorest countries in the world, Burundi is dependent on foreign aid. 90% of the population relies on agriculture for subsistence living. The economy is driven primarily by coffee exports and, to a lesser extent, tea, sugar, cotton and hides. Ethnic tensions from the civil war that ended in 2005 still persist, particularly in light of the Tutsi minority effectively controlling the coffee trade.

In 2007 GDP reached US$1bn. Over the decade to 2007 GDP increased slowly with slight fluctuations. There was real GDP growth of more than 4% in 2002, 2004, 2006 and 2008 but the economy shrank in 2000 and 2003. Although the economy is showing signs of activity, endemic poverty and the weak legal system will render it dependent on foreign aid for the foreseeable future.

Currency

The unit of currency is the *Burundi franc* (BIF) of 100 *centimes*. Inflation was 8·3% in 2007, rising to 24·4% in 2008. In July 2005 gold reserves were 1,000 troy oz and foreign exchange reserves US$88m. Total money supply was 139,353m. Burundi francs in Sept. 2004.

Budget

Total revenues in 2004 were 218,892·5m. Burundi francs and expenditures 292,854·9m. Burundi francs. Tax revenue accounted for 53·6% of revenues in 2004; current expenditure accounted for 64·4% of expenditures.

VAT of 18% was introduced in July 2009, replacing the 17% transaction tax.

Performance

Real GDP growth was 4·5% in 2008 (3·6% in 2007). Total GDP in 2008 was US$1·2bn.

Banking and Finance

The Bank of the Republic of Burundi is the central bank and bank of issue. Its *Governor* is Gaspard Sindayigaya. In 1999 it had deposits of 11·23bn. Burundi francs. There are seven commercial banks, a development bank and a co-operative bank.

ENERGY AND NATURAL RESOURCES

Environment

Burundi's carbon dioxide emissions from the consumption and flaring of fossil fuels in 2008 were the equivalent of less than 0·1 tonnes per capita.

Electricity

Installed capacity was approximately 33,000 kW in 2004. Production was an estimated 135m. kWh in 2004. Consumption per capita in 2004 was about 22 kWh.

Minerals

Gold is mined on a small scale. Deposits of nickel (280m. tonnes) and vanadium remain to be exploited. There are proven reserves of phosphates of 17·6m. tonnes.

Agriculture

The main economic activity is agriculture, which contributed 35% of GDP in 2005. In 2007, 0·96m. ha. were arable and 0·35m. ha. permanent crops. 74,000 ha. were irrigated in 2001. There were 170 tractors in 2001. Beans, cassava, maize, sweet potatoes, groundnuts, peas, sorghum and bananas are grown according to the climate and the region.

The main cash crop is coffee, of which about 95% is arabica. It accounts for 90% of exports, and taxes and levies on coffee constitute a major source of revenue. Production (2003) 36,000 tonnes. The main agricultural crops (2002 production, in 1,000 tonnes) are bananas (1,603), sweet potatoes (833), cassava (750), dry beans (245), sugarcane (176) and maize (127).

Livestock (2002): 750,000 goats, 324,000 cattle, 230,000 sheep, 70,000 pigs and 4m. chickens.

Forestry
Forests covered 152,000 ha., or 5·9% of the total land area, in 2005. Timber production in 2007 was 9·16m. cu. metres, the majority of it for fuel.

Fisheries
In 2004 the total catch was 13,855 tonnes, exclusively from inland waters.

INDUSTRY
In 2003 production of sugar totalled 20,000 tonnes. Other major products are beer (87·5m. litres in 2003), soft drinks (12·1m. litres in 2003), cigarettes (354m. units in 2003) and blankets (123,000 units in 2003).

Labour
In 2004 there were 3,335,000 employed persons.

INTERNATIONAL TRADE
With Rwanda and the Democratic Republic of the Congo, Burundi forms part of the Economic Community of the Great Lakes. Foreign debt was US$1,322m. in 2005.

Imports and Exports
Imports and exports for calendar years in US$1m.:

	2002	*2003*	*2004*	*2005*	*2006*
Imports f.o.b.	104·8	130·0	157·7	210·6	249·5
Exports f.o.b.	31·0	37·5	47·9	56·9	58·7

Main exports are coffee, manufactures and tea. Main import suppliers, 2003: Belgium-Luxembourg, 14·8%; Kenya, 14·4%; Tanzania, 11·7%; Uganda, 5·9%; Zambia, 5·2%. Main export markets, 2003: Switzerland, 32·0%; UK, 16·4%; Rwanda, 5·7%; Belgium-Luxembourg, 5·7%; Netherlands, 4·5%.

COMMUNICATIONS
Roads
In 2004 there were 12,322 km of roads of which 10·4% were paved. There were 15,500 passenger cars (two per 1,000 inhabitants) and 32,700 lorries and vans in use in 2007.

Civil Aviation
There were direct flights to Addis Ababa, Douala, Entebbe/Kampala, Kigali and Nairobi in 2003. In 1998 scheduled airline traffic of Burundi-based carriers flew 800,000 km, carrying 12,000 passengers (all on international flights). Bujumbura International airport handled 86,353 passengers and 2,240 tonnes of freight in 2003.

Shipping
There are lake services from Bujumbura to Kigoma (Tanzania) and Kalémie (Democratic Republic of the Congo). The main route for exports and imports is via Kigoma, and thence by rail to Dar es Salaam.

Telecommunications
In 2004 there were 128,300 telephone subscribers (18·2 per 1,000 inhabitants), including 100,600 mobile phone subscribers. 34,000 PCs were in use in 2004 (4·8 per 1,000 persons) and the number of internet users was 25,000.

Postal Services
In 2003 there were 29 post offices, equivalent to one for every 235,000 persons.

SOCIAL INSTITUTIONS
Justice
There is a Supreme Court, an appeal court and a court of first instance at Bujumbura, and provincial courts in each provincial capital.

The death penalty was abolished in April 2009. The population in penal institutions in May 2008 was 9,114 (104 per 100,000 of national population).

Education
Adult literacy rate was 58·9% in 2003 (66·8% among males and 51·9% among females). In 2007 there were 1,490,844 pupils in primary schools with 28,671 teachers and 209,945 pupils in secondary schools with 7,501 teachers. There were 15,623 students in higher education in 2007 and 1,007 academic staff. The leading institution in the tertiary sector is the Université du Burundi, located in Bujumbura.

In 2005 public expenditure on education came to 5·2% of GNI.

Health
In 2000 there were 323 doctors and 1,783 nurses. In 1996 there was less than one hospital bed per 10,000 inhabitants.

RELIGION
In 2001 there were 4·05m. Roman Catholics with an archbishop and three bishops. About 3% of the population are Pentecostal, 1% Anglican and 1% Muslim, while the balance follow traditional tribal beliefs.

CULTURE
Broadcasting
The national services are provided by the state controlled Radiodiffusion et Télévision Nationale du Burundi (RTNB), broadcasting in Swahili, Kirundi, French and English. A few private radio stations operate with mainly international funding. There were 280,000 TV receivers in 2006 (colour by SECAM V).

Press
There was one state-controlled daily newspaper (Le Renouveau) in 2006 with a circulation of 20,000.

Tourism
There were 148,000 foreign tourists in 2005. Receipts totalled US$2m.

DIPLOMATIC REPRESENTATIVES
Of Burundi in the United Kingdom (26 Armitage Rd, London, NW11 8RD)
Ambassador: Laurent Kavakure (resides at Brussels).

Of the United Kingdom in Burundi
Ambassador: Nicholas Cannon, OBE (resides in Kigali, Rwanda).

Of Burundi in the USA (2233 Wisconsin Ave., NW, Suite 212, Washington, D.C., 20007)
Ambassador: Angele Niyuhire.

Of the USA in Burundi (PO Box 1720, Ave. des Etats-Unis, Bujumbura)
Ambassador: Pamela J. H. Slutz.

Of Burundi to the United Nations
Ambassador: Zacharie Gahutu.

Of Burundi to the European Union
Ambassador: Laurent Kavakure.

FURTHER READING
Lemarchand, R., *Burundi: Ethnic Conflict and Genocide.* 1996
Melson, Robert, *Genocide and Crisis in Central Africa: Conflict Roots, Mass Violence and Regional War.* 2001

National Statistical Office: Service des Études et Statistiques, Ministère du Plan, Bujumbura.
Website (French only): http://burundistats.org

CAMBODIA

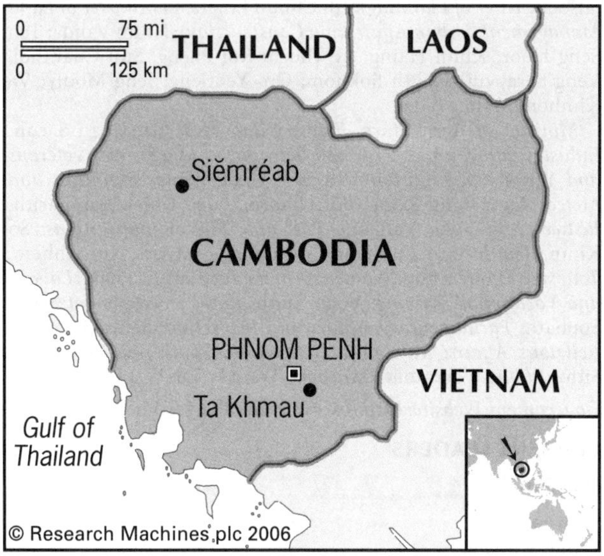

Preah Reach Ana Pak Kampuchea
(Kingdom of Cambodia)

Capital: Phnom Penh
Population estimate, 2010: 15·05m.
GDP per capita, 2007: (PPP$) 1,802
HDI/world rank: 0·593/137

KEY HISTORICAL EVENTS

Neolithic communities, probably linked to migration from southeast China, were established by 1000 BC in the Kompong Cham province of eastern Cambodia. From around 300 BC the Indianized Funan kingdom held sway across much of present-day Cambodia, with trading links to China, India, the Middle East and Rome. The state of Chenla broke away from Funan control during the 6th century and over the next 300 years its influence spread to include western Cambodia, central Laos and northern Thailand. Cambodia's southern coast came under Javanese control in the eighth century, forcing Khmer-speaking groups inland. The crowning of Jayavarman II as a deva-raja (or god king) in 802 heralded a long period of regional Khmer domination centred around Angkor.

The Indian-influenced civilization prospered through the development of agriculture and trade, notably under King Yasovarman I around 900 AD and during the reign of Suryavarman II (1113–50), when the temple complex at Angkor Wat was constructed. The empire was attacked by the Islamic Kingdom of Champa (now in central Vietnam) in the 12th and 13th centuries and was subsequently vulnerable to Thai incursions from Ayudhya. Thai forces sacked Angkor in 1432, ushering in a period of dominance by the kings of Siam on Cambodia's western frontier and pressure from Annam to the east. Cambodian nobility established a capital at Phnom Penh in the 16th century, although its influence was limited and the city was sacked by Rama I of Siam in 1772. In 1811–12 Siamese and Vietnamese forces fought for control of Cambodia, with the kingdom coming under Vietnam's control in 1835–40. King Ang Doung wrested back control in 1848 and appealed for military assistance from France, a major naval force in the region with bases in southern Vietnam. Under King Norodom I, a French protectorate was established in 1863, although resentment grew as French control extended beyond foreign affairs and defence. Rebellions were suppressed in the 1870s and 1880s and Cambodia became part of the Union of Indochina in 1887.

Anti-French feeling strengthened in 1940–41 when the Vichy French submitted to Japanese demands for bases in Cambodia. Son Ngoc Thanh was one of the leaders of a nascent nationalist movement after French control was reasserted in 1945. Having returned to Cambodia in 1951, he joined the Khmer Issarak guerrillas to fight the French. Independence was achieved on 9 Nov. 1953, the result of deft diplomacy by King Norodom Sihanouk and France's increasingly weak position in a war against Vietnam's communist revolutionaries. Sihanouk abdicated in 1955 to form the popular Socialist Party, which dominated the general election of that year. He served as the country's leader until 1970, when he was deposed by the US-backed Lon Nol amid growing communist incursions from North Vietnam, a rapidly deteriorating economy and political corruption.

The country's name was changed to the Khmer Republic in Oct. 1970. US forces attacked Cambodia's communist strongholds, which led to the rise of the Khmer Rouge. In 1973 direct US involvement came to an end, precipitating a civil war between the Khmer Republic and the United National Cambodian Front (including the Khmer Rouge), supported by North Vietnam and China. After unsuccessful attempts to capture Phnom Penh in 1973 and 1974, the Khmer Rouge, led by Pol Pot, overthrew Lon Nol's government in April 1975.

Renaming the country Democratic Kampuchea, Pol Pot instituted a harsh and highly centralized regime. All cities and towns were forcibly evacuated and citizens set to work in the fields. Intellectuals, members of the professional classes and people identified as enemies of the Khmer Rouge were murdered in their hundreds of thousands and many more died as a result of disease, malnutrition and overwork, resulting in the loss of an estimated 2m. Cambodian lives from 1975–79. In response to repeated border attacks, Vietnam invaded Cambodia in 1978. On 7 Jan. 1979 Phnom Penh was captured by the Vietnamese and Pol Pot fled. During the 1980s the country was destabilized by warring factions fighting both the Vietnamese and the Khmer Rouge. On 23 Oct. 1991 an agreement was signed in Paris by the warring factions and 19 countries, instituting a UN-monitored ceasefire.

A new constitution was promulgated in 1993 restoring parliamentary monarchy. The Khmer Rouge continued hostilities, refusing to take part in the 1993 elections, and by 1996 had split into two factions. The leader of one faction, Ieng Sary, had been sentenced to death *in absentia* for genocide but was pardoned in Sept. 1996. In Nov. 1996 Ieng Sary and 4,000 of his troops joined with government forces. Prince Norodom Ranariddh, styled as First Prime Minister of the Royal Government, was exiled in July 1997 and coup-leader Hun Sen appointed himself prime minister. In March 1998 Ranariddh returned with a Japanese-brokered plan to ensure 'fair and free' elections, which took place in July 1998. Against a background of violence Hun Sen's Cambodian People's Party (KPK) declared victory.

King Norodom Sihanouk abdicated in Oct. 2004 for health reasons and was succeeded by his son, Norodom Sihamoni. In July 2007 UN-backed tribunals investigated allegations of genocide by the Khmer Rouge. The KPK claimed victory in the parliamentary elections of July 2008 and announced that it would remain in coalition with the depleted Royalist FUNCINPEC (National United Front for an Independent, Neutral, Peaceful and Co-operative Cambodia).

TERRITORY AND POPULATION

Cambodia is bounded in the north by Laos and Thailand, west by Thailand, east by Vietnam and south by the Gulf of Thailand. It has an area of about 181,035 sq. km (69,898 sq. miles).

Population, 13,388,910 (2008 census, provisional), of whom 6,893,398 were females; density, 74·0 per sq. km. The United Nations population estimate for 2008 was 14·56m. In 2005, 80·3% of the population lived in rural areas.

The UN gives an estimated population for 2010 of 15·05m.

The capital, Phnom Penh, had an estimated population of 1,157,000 in 2003. Other cities are Kompong Cham and Battambang. Ethnic composition, 2000: Khmer, 85%; Chinese, 6%; Vietnamese, 3%; Cham, 2%; Lao-Thai, 1%.

Khmer is the official language.

SOCIAL STATISTICS

2002 estimated births, 467,000; deaths, 138,000. Rates, 2002 estimates (per 1,000 population): births, 33·8; deaths, 10·0. Infant mortality, 2005 (per 1,000 live births), 98. Expectation of life in 2007 was 58·6 years for males and 62·3 for females. Annual population growth rate, 2000–05, 1·5%. Fertility rate, 2004, 4·0 children per woman.

CLIMATE

A tropical climate, with high temperatures all the year. Phnom Penh, Jan. 78°F (25·6°C), July 84°F (28·9°C). Annual rainfall 52" (1,308 mm).

CONSTITUTION AND GOVERNMENT

A parliamentary monarchy was re-established by the 1993 constitution. King Norodom Sihamoni (b. 14 May 1953; appointed 14 Oct. 2004 and sworn in on 29 Oct. 2004) was chosen in the first ever meeting of the nine-member Throne Council following the abdication of his father King Norodom Sihanouk (b. 31 Oct. 1922) on health grounds. As the Cambodian constitution allowed for a succession only in the event of the monarch's death, a new law had to be approved after King Norodom Sihanouk announced his abdication.

Cambodia has a bicameral legislature. There is a 123-member *National Assembly*, which on 14 June 1993 elected Prince Sihanouk head of state. On 21 Sept. it adopted a constitution (promulgated on 24 Sept.) by 113 votes to five with two abstentions making him monarch of a parliamentary democracy. Its members are elected by popular vote to serve five-year terms. There is also a 61-member *Senate*, established in 1999.

National Anthem

'Nokoreach' ('Royal kingdom'); words by Chuon Nat, tune adapted from a Cambodian folk song.

RECENT ELECTIONS

Parliamentary elections were held on 27 July 2008; turnout was 75·2%. The Cambodian People's Party (KPK) won 90 seats with 58·1% of the vote, the party of government critic Sam Rainsy won 26 seats with 21·9%, the Human Rights Party won three seats with 6·6%, the party of Prince Norodom Ranariddh two seats with 5·6% and the royalist FUNCINPEC party two seats with 5·1%.

CURRENT ADMINISTRATION

In March 2010 the government comprised:

Prime Minister: Hun Sen; b. 1951 (KPK; sworn in 30 Nov. 1998 and reappointed 14 July 2004 and 25 Sept. 2008 having first become prime minister in 1985).

Deputy Prime Ministers: Men Sam An; Sar Kheng (also *Minister of Internal Affairs*); Sok An (also *Minister in Charge of the Office of the Council of Ministers*); Gen. Tea Banh (also *Minister of Defence*); Hor Nam Hong (also *Minister of Foreign Affairs and International Co-operation*); Keat Chhon (also *Minister of Economy and Finance*); Bin Chhin; Nhek Bunchhay; Yim Chhai Ly.

Senior Ministers: Cham Prasidh (also *Minister of Commerce*); Dr Mok Mareth (also *Minister of Environment*); Chhay Than (also *Minister of Planning*); Im Chhun Lim (also *Minister of Land Management, Urban Affairs and Construction*); Nhim Vanda; Tao Seng Huor; Khun Haing; Ly Thuch; Kol Pheng; Sun Chanthol; Veng Sereyvuth; Nuth Sokhom; Om Yentieng; Ieng Mouly; Va Kimhong; Yim Nol La.

Minister of Agriculture, Forestry and Fisheries: Chan Sarun. *Industry, Mines and Energy:* Suy Sem. *Social Affairs, War Veterans and Youth Rehabilitation:* Ith Sam Heng. *Water Resources and Meteorology:* Lim Kean Hor. *Information:* Khieu Kanharith. *Justice:* Ang Vong Vathana. *Post and Telecommunications:* So Khun. *Health:* Mam Bunheng. *Culture and Fine Arts:* Him Chhem. *Tourism:* Thong Khon. *Women's Affairs:* Ing Kantha Phavi. *Labour and Vocational Training:* Vong Sauth. *Rural Development:* Chea Sophara. *Parliamentary Affairs and Inspection:* Sam Kim Suor. *Religious Affairs:* Min Khin. *Education, Youth and Sports:* Im Sithy. *Public Works and Transport:* Tram Iv Tek.

Government Website: http://www.cambodia.gov.kh

CURRENT LEADERS

Hun Sen

Position

Prime Minister

Introduction

Hun Sen has been the dominant figure in Cambodian politics since becoming prime minister in 1985. His tenure has coincided with national recovery from the rule of the Khmer Rouge in the 1970s and the subsequent occupation by Vietnamese forces. He has been criticized for the tactics he has used to retain power. The economy has suffered from endemic corruption and a failure to attract foreign investment. However, Hun Sen has moved the economy away from state socialism towards one based on free market principles. A tribunal to investigate charges of genocide against prominent Khmer Rouge figures may conclude that turbulent period in the nation's history.

Early Life

Hun Sen was born into a peasant family in Kompang in 1952 and was educated in Phnom Penh by Buddhist monks. In 1970 he joined the Khmer Rouge, losing an eye in battle in 1975, but in 1977 he joined anti-Khmer Rouge forces operating out of Vietnam. After Vietnamese troops invaded Kampuchea in 1979, Hun Sen was appointed foreign minister in the newly-established People's Republic of Kampuchea. He became prime minister in 1985.

Career in Office

On assuming office, Hun Sen was confronted with a country in turmoil as pro- and anti-Vietnamese forces waged guerrilla war. In 1989 Vietnamese forces withdrew from the country, which was renamed the State of Cambodia. Buddhism was re-established as the state religion and Hun Sen announced the end of state socialism. In 1991 the UN brokered a peace treaty and a transitional government was installed, with Prince Sihanouk as head of state.

FUNCINPEC, the royalist party of Prince Norodom Ranariddh, was victorious at the 1993 elections but Hun Sen refused to relinquish power. A compromise government was formed with Ranariddh as first prime minister and Hun Sen as his deputy. In 1997 Hun Sen received international condemnation and saw Cambodia expelled from ASEAN for deposing Ranariddh while he was absent from the country. The Cambodian People's Party (KPK) won the 1998 elections but did not gain enough seats to form a government. Hun Sen agreed to head a coalition that included FUNCINPEC. Ranariddh was found guilty in absentia of arms smuggling but received a royal pardon and was named president of the National Assembly. Pol Pot died that year, having been sentenced to life imprisonment for his crimes the previous year.

In 2001 Prince Norodom Sirivudh became leader of the opposition FUNCINPEC party, having received a royal pardon in 1999 for a ten-year prison sentence he received in absentia for his alleged involvement in an assassination plot against Hun Sen. In the same year the east and west of the country were connected for the first time by a bridge across the Mekong River.

In 2002 Thailand agreed to extradite Sok Yoeun, a leading figure in the Cambodian Sam Rainsy Party, for alleged involvement in an assassination plot against Hun Sen. Sok Yoeun declared that the charges were part of a political attack and Amnesty International classified him as a prisoner of conscience.

In 2002 the KPK was the dominant party at the country's first multi-party local elections, although opposition groups claimed ballots were rigged. At the general elections of 2003 the KPK emerged as the single biggest party but fell short of the two thirds majority required to form the government. Coalition talks were frosty and relations were not improved when Hun Sen removed 17 FUNCINPEC politicians from senior posts, claiming neglect of duty. The opposition FUNCINPEC and Sam Rainsy parties agreed to join a ruling coalition but not under Hun Sen. The king finally confirmed Hun Sen as head of government in July 2004, after almost a year without a properly functioning administration.

After winning senate approval, Cambodia began talks with the UN on a tribunal to try former Khmer Rouge leaders for genocide. Negotiations were protracted and in 2003 the UN concluded that the tribunal was unlikely to function alongside Cambodia's existing judicial system, which claimed precedence over international law. The issue was further complicated by Khmer Rouge leaders transferring allegiance to the government in the years following Pol Pot's fall from power. Hun Sen himself was a soldier in the Khmer Rouge, though he denied claims that he ever held a senior position. Nevertheless, the UN-backed tribunal, run by Cambodian and international judges, finally held its first public hearing in Nov. 2007.

In 2003 a Thai celebrity suggested that the religious complex of Angkor Wat had been stolen by Cambodia from Thailand. The comments caused outrage in Cambodia and led to a siege of the Thai embassy in Phnom Penh. Observers accused Hun Sen of aggravating the situation. In 2004 Hun Sen threatened to boycott a joint Asian-European summit if, as the EU was requesting, Myanmar was banned from attending. In the same year, with economic growth and foreign investment falling, Hun Sen outlined proposals to cut business costs, reduce red tape and counter corruption. He also promised to increase civil service salaries. However, he did not offer a timeframe for these developments. Entry into the WTO was ratified in Aug. 2004 after long delays.

Other significant problems confronting Hun Sen's government have included deforestation and the spread of AIDS. In Aug.–Sept. 2006 he pushed two controversial measures through the National Assembly. The first curtailed the right of parliamentarians to speak openly without fear of prosecution and the second imposed a ban on adultery.

Following public criticism by Hun Sen, Prince Ranariddh resigned as president of the National Assembly and in March 2007 was sentenced in absentia to 18 months imprisonment for breach of trust over the sale of the FUNCINPEC headquarters.

On 26 Sept. 2008 Hun Sen was reappointed prime minister after the KPK had secured over two-thirds of the seats in the National Assembly in elections in July that were criticized by European Union monitors as falling short of international standards.

In Oct. 2008 tensions between Cambodia and Thailand worsened as border skirmishes resulted in the deaths of two Cambodian soldiers in a disputed area around Preah Vihear, an ancient temple and (since July 2008) a UNESCO World Heritage site. Further exchanges of gunfire on the border were reported in spring 2009.

DEFENCE

The King is C.-in-C. of the Royal Cambodian Armed Forces (RCAF). Conscription has not been implemented since 1993 although it is authorized. Defence expenditure in 2006 totalled US$123m. (US$9 per capita), representing 1·7% of GDP.

Army

Strength in 2007 was an estimated 75,000. There are also provincial forces numbering some 45,000 and paramilitary local forces organized at village level.

Navy

Naval personnel in 2007 totalled about 2,800 including a naval infantry of 1,500. In 2007 there were two coastal fast patrol craft, two riverine patrol craft and six patrol boats.

Air Force

Aviation operations were resumed in 1988, initially under the aegis of the Army and since 1993 as part of the RCAF. Personnel (2007), 1,500. There are 24 combat capable aircraft but serviceability is in doubt.

INTERNATIONAL RELATIONS

Cambodia is a member of the UN, World Bank, IMF and several other UN specialized agencies, WTO, IOM, International Organization of the Francophonie, Asian Development Bank, ASEAN and Mekong Group.

ECONOMY

Agriculture accounted for 30·1% of GDP in 2006, industry 26·2% and services 43·7%.

Overview

Cambodia is among the poorest countries in the world, with per capita income at US$290 in 2004. Efforts to reduce poverty have been frustrated by low agricultural productivity, inadequate infrastructure and a stifling regulatory environment.

The economy was devastated by the Khmer Rouge regime of 1975–79 when trade collapsed to an agrarian barter system, the industrial base was destroyed and the banking system and domestic currency abolished. Economic progress remained slow until the Paris Peace Accord of 1991 brought about a ceasefire in the civil war. At the time of signing Cambodia faced rapid inflation, significant exchange rate depreciation, monetary instability, negative real interest rates and high fiscal deficits. Since the Accord, and with the aid of the World Bank and the IMF, the government has tried to restore monetary stability and improve fiscal performance. Privatization of state-owned enterprises was completed by 1996 and the trade regime was liberalized as Cambodia joined ASEAN and prepared for WTO accession.

Growth has averaged over 9% since 2000 and reached a record of 13·3% in 2005, thanks to continued growth in agriculture, buoyant exports and a healthy urban economy underpinned by construction, services and the financial sector. The overall poverty rate declined from 47% in 1993 to 35% in 2004 but inequality has increased, largely because rural poverty remains high. Government instability and endemic corruption continue to hamper private sector development, limiting foreign direct investment and eroding the tax base.

Currency

The unit of currency is the *riel* (KHR) of 100 *sen*. In July 2005 total money supply was 1,222·4bn. riels, foreign exchange reserves were US$937m. and gold reserves 400,000 troy oz. Inflation was 6·1% in 2006, rising to 7·7% in 2007 and further still to 25·0% in 2008.

Budget
In 2005 revenues were 3,280bn. riels and expenditures 3,295bn. riels. Tax revenue accounted for 58·3% of revenues in 2005; current expenditure accounted for 59·7% of expenditures.

VAT is 10%.

Performance
Real GDP growth was 10·8% in 2006, 10·2% in 2007 and 6·7% in 2008. Total GDP in 2008 was US$9·6bn.

Banking and Finance
The National Bank of Cambodia (*Governor*, Chea Chanto) is the bank of issue. In 2001 there were operating: one state-owned bank; three specialized banks; 12 locally-incorporated private banks; and five foreign banks. In 2001, 11 banks were closed for failing to comply with new banking legislation.

ENERGY AND NATURAL RESOURCES

Environment
Carbon dioxide emissions from the consumption and flaring of fossil fuels were the equivalent of less than 0·3 tonnes per capita in 2008.

Electricity
Installed capacity was an estimated 35,000 kW in 2004. Production (2004) was around 130m. kWh. Consumption per capita was an estimated 10 kWh—the lowest in the world—in 2004. A long-term plan for hydro-electricity has been issued by the government.

Oil and Gas
Oil was discovered in 2005 off the coast of Cambodia. The reserves are estimated to total at least 400m. bbls. It is hoped that production will start by 2013.

Minerals
There are phosphates and high-grade iron-ore deposits. Some small-scale gold panning and gem (mainly zircon) mining is carried out.

Agriculture
The majority of the population is engaged in agriculture, fishing or forestry. Before the spread of war in the 1970s the high productivity provided for a low but well-fed standard of living for the peasant farmers, the majority of whom owned the land they worked before agriculture was collectivized. A relatively small proportion of the food production entered the cash economy. The war and unwise pricing policies led to a disastrous reduction in production, so much so that the country became a net importer of rice. Private ownership of land was restored by the 1989 constitution. In 2007 there were around 3·80m. ha. of arable land and 155,000 ha. of permanent crops.

A crop of 3·82m. tonnes of rice was produced in 2002. Production of other crops, 2002 (in 1,000 tonnes): sugarcane, 209; maize, 149; bananas, 146; cassava, 122; coconuts, 70; oranges, 63.

Livestock (2002): cattle, 2·92m.; pigs, 2·11m.; buffaloes, 626,000; poultry, 17m.

Livestock products, 2003 (in 1,000 tonnes): pork, bacon and ham, 105; beef and veal, 54; poultry meat, 28; buffalo meat, 13; eggs, 17; milk, 20.

Forestry
Some 10·45m. ha., or 59·2% of the land area, were covered by forests in 2005. Nearly half of the forested area in 1995 was reserved by the government to be awarded to concessionaires. Such areas are not at present worked to any extent. The remainder is available for exploitation by the local residents, and as a result some areas are over-exploited and conservation is not practised. Timber exports have been banned since Dec. 1996. There are substantial reserves of pitch pine. Rubber plantations are a valuable asset with production at around 40,000 tonnes per year. There are plans to expand the area under rubber cultivation from 50,000 ha. to 800,000 ha. Timber production in 2007 was 9·00m. cu. metres.

Fisheries
2005 catch was 384,000 tonnes (84% from inland waters).

INDUSTRY
Some development of industry had taken place before the spread of open warfare in 1970, but little was in operation by the 1990s except for rubber processing, sea-food processing, jute sack making and cigarette manufacture. Garment manufacture, rice milling, wood and wood products, rubber, cement and textiles production are the main industries. In the private sector small family concerns produce a wide range of goods. Light industry is generally better developed than heavy industry.

Labour
In 2004 the labour force was 7,496,000. Females constituted 51·8% of the labour force in 2001—among the highest proportions of women in the workforce in the world. More than 66% of employed persons are engaged in agriculture, fishing and forestry.

INTERNATIONAL TRADE
Foreign investment has been encouraged since 1989. Legislation of 1994 exempts profits from taxation for eight years, removes duties from various raw and semi-finished materials and offers tax incentives to investors in tourism, energy, the infrastructure and labour-intensive industries. External debt was US$3,515m. in 2005.

Imports and Exports
Imports and exports for calendar years in US$1m.:

	2000	*2001*	*2002*	*2003*	*2004*
Imports f.o.b.	2,792·0	3,430·8	2,318·0	2,559·9	3,193·3
Exports f.o.b.	1,961·2	2,490·1	1,753·8	2,027·2	2,475·5

The main imports include cigarettes, construction materials, petroleum products, machinery and motor vehicles. Main exports are timber, rubber, soybeans and sesame.

Major import sources, 2003: Thailand (27·0%), Hong Kong (14·7%) and Singapore (12·1%). Principal export destinations, 2003: USA (59·8%), Germany (10·4%) and the UK (7·4%).

COMMUNICATIONS

Roads
There were 8,257 km of roads in 2004, of which 6·3% were paved. In 2005 there were 195,300 passenger cars in use plus 3,200 buses and coaches, 32,100 lorries and vans and 566,300 motorcycles and mopeds. There were 1,545 fatalities in road accidents in 2007.

Rail
Main lines link Phnom Penh with Sisophon near the Thai border and the port of Kompong Som (total 601 km, metre gauge). After a long period of disruption owing to political unrest, limited services were restored on both lines in 1992. Passenger-km travelled in 2000 came to 15m. and freight tonne-km to 91m.

Civil Aviation
Pochentong airport is 8 km from Phnom Penh and handled 895,000 passengers (670,000 on international flights) in 2001. There are regular domestic services; airlines with international flights are Angkor Airways, PMTair, President Airlines, Royal Khmer Airlines, Royal Phnom Penh Airways and Siem Riep Airways International.

Shipping
There is an ocean port at Kompong Som; the port of Phnom Penh can be reached by the Mekong (through Vietnam) by ships of between 3,000 and 4,000 tonnes. In 2002 merchant shipping totalled 2,426,000 GRT, including oil tankers 141,000 GRT.

Telecommunications
In 2008 Cambodia had just 43,100 main (fixed) telephone lines, but there were 4,237,000 mobile phone subscribers (291·0 for every 1,000 persons). Cambodia has among the highest ratios of mobile phone subscriptions to fixed telephone lines. There were 38,000 PCs in use in 2004 and 74,000 internet users in 2008 (5·1 for every 1,000 persons).

Postal Services
In 2003 there were 79 post offices, or one for every 179,000 persons.

SOCIAL INSTITUTIONS

Justice
The population in penal institutions in 2007 was 10,337 (71 per 100,000 of national population). In March 2003 the government announced plans to establish a special court in partnership with the UN to try leaders of the former Khmer Rouge regime. The death penalty was abolished in 1989.

Education
In 2004–05 there were 6,990 schools of which 6,180 were primary, 578 junior high and 232 senior high. There were 111,090 pupils in pre-primary schools and 4,415 teaching staff in 2007; 2,479,644 pupils and 48,736 teaching staff in primary schools; and in general secondary education 30,258 teaching staff for 875,120 pupils. There were 92,340 students in tertiary education in 2007 and (2006) 3,261 academic staff. Adult literacy in 2003 was 73·6% (male, 84·7%; female, 64·1%).

In 2007 public expenditure on education came to 1·7% of GNI and 12·4% of total government spending.

Health
In 2000 there were 2,047 physicians, 209 dentists, 8,085 nurses and 3,040 midwives. Only 30% of the population had access to safe drinking water in 2000.

RELIGION
The constitution of 1989 reinstated Buddhism as the state religion; it had 10·8m. adherents in 2001. About 2,800 monasteries were active in 1994. There are small Roman Catholic and Muslim minorities.

CULTURE

World Heritage Sites
There are two UNESCO world heritage sites in Cambodia: Angkor (inscribed in 1992), an archaeological park that was the site of various capitals of the Khmer Empire from the 9th to the 15th centuries containing the Temple of Angkor Wat and the Bayon Temple at Angkor Thom; and the Temple of Preah Vihear (2008), an outstanding example of Khmer architecture that dates back to the first half of the 11th century and is composed of a series of sanctuaries linked by a system of pavements and staircases.

Broadcasting
National Television of Cambodia and National Radio of Cambodia are the state broadcasters. There are also commercial radio services, and a number of independent TV stations (including TV5, CTN, Bayon TV and CTV9) which often depend on political patronage. Foreign radio broadcasts and TV services from regional satellite networks are also available. There were 1·1m. television-equipped households (colour by PAL) in 2005.

Press
There were 20 daily newspapers in 2006 with a combined circulation of 55,000, including the English-language *Cambodia Daily*.

Tourism
In 2005 there were 1,422,000 foreign visitors (including 794,000 from elsewhere in Asia and Oceania and 310,000 from Europe), up from 605,000 in 2001. Receipts in 2005 totalled US$927m., compared to US$429m. in 2001.

DIPLOMATIC REPRESENTATIVES
Of Cambodia in the United Kingdom (64 Brondesbury Park, London, NW6 7AT)
Ambassador: Hor Nambora.

Of the United Kingdom in Cambodia (27–29 St. 75, Phnom Penh)
Ambassador: Andrew Mace.

Of Cambodia in the USA (4530 16th St., NW, Washington, D.C., 20011)
Ambassador: Hem Heng.

Of the USA in Cambodia (1 St. 96, Phnom Penh)
Ambassador: Carol A. Rodley.

Of Cambodia to the United Nations
Ambassador: Sea Kosal.

Of Cambodia to the European Union
Ambassador: Hem Saem.

FURTHER READING

Chandler, D. P., *A History of Cambodia.* 2nd ed. 1996
Etcheson, Craig, *After the Killing Fields: Lessons from the Cambodian Genocide.* 2005
Gottesman, Evan R., *Cambodia After the Khmer Rouge: Inside the Politics of Nation Building.* 2004
Martin, M. A, *Cambodia: A Shattered Society.* 1994
Peschoux, C., *Le Cambodge dans la Tourmente: le Troisième Conflit Indochinois, 1978–1991.* 1992.—*Les 'Nouveaux' Khmers Rouges.* 1992
Short, Philip, *Pol Pot: The History of a Nightmare.* 2004

National Statistical Office: National Institute of Statistics, Ministry of Planning, Preah Monivong Blvd, Sankat Boeung Keng Kang 1, Phnom Penh.
Website: http://www.nis.gov.kh

CAMEROON

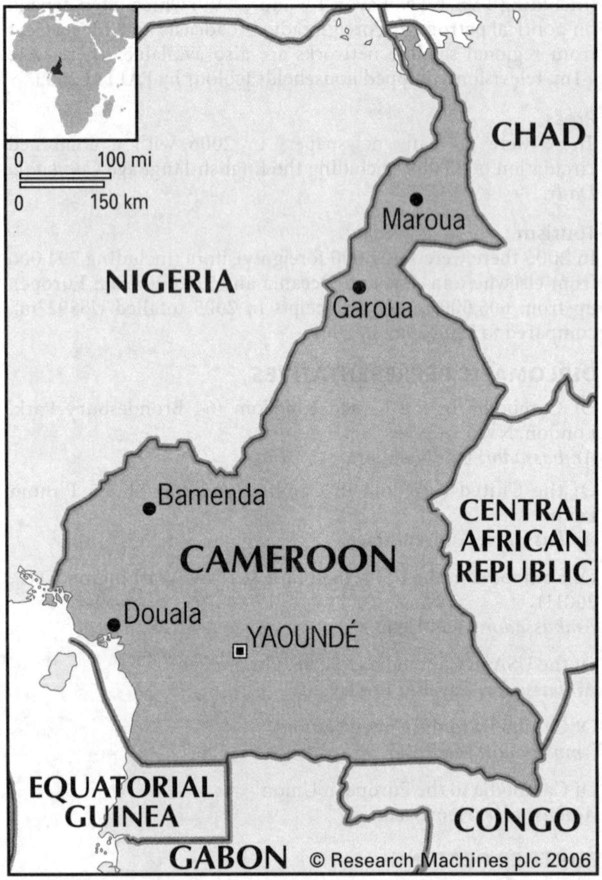

République du Cameroun
(Republic of Cameroon)

Capital: Yaoundé
Population estimate, 2010: 19·96m.
GDP per capita, 2007: (PPP$) 2,128
HDI/world rank: 0·523/153

KEY HISTORICAL EVENTS

The name Cameroon derives from *camarães* (prawns), introduced by Portuguese navigators. Called Kamerun in German and Cameroun in French, the estuary was later called the Cameroons River by British navigators. The Duala people living there were traders, selling slaves and later palm oil to Europeans. On 12 July 1884 they signed a treaty establishing German rule over Kamerun. Originally covering the Duala's territory on the Wouri, this German colony later expanded to cover a large area inland, home to a number of African peoples. In the First World War Allied forces occupied the territory which was partitioned between France and Britain. British Cameroons consisted of British Southern Cameroons and British Northern Cameroons, adjoining Nigeria. France's mandated territory of Cameroun occupied most of the former German colony.

In 1946 the French and British territories became Trust Territories of the UN. In French Cameroun the *Union des Populations du Cameroun* (UPC), founded in 1948, became the major nationalist party, calling for independence and 'reunification' with British Cameroons. In Dec. 1956, when elections were held prior to self-government, the UPC began a guerrilla war against the French and the new Cameroonian government. On 1 Jan. 1960 French Cameroun gained independence. The UPC guerrillas were largely defeated by 1963. On 11 Feb. 1961 British Southern Cameroons voted in a referendum to join ex-French Cameroun, while British Northern Cameroons chose to join Nigeria. The country's name was changed to the Republic of Cameroon in 1984.

TERRITORY AND POPULATION

Cameroon is bounded in the west by the Gulf of Guinea, northwest by Nigeria, east by Chad and the Central African Republic, and south by the Republic of the Congo, Gabon and Equatorial Guinea. The total area (including inland water) is 475,440 sq. km. On 29 March 1994 Cameroon asked the International Court of Justice to confirm its sovereignty over the oil-rich Bakassi Peninsula, occupied by Nigerian troops. The dispute continued for eight years, with Equatorial Guinea also subsequently becoming involved. In Oct. 2002 the International Court of Justice rejected Nigeria's claims and awarded the peninsula to Cameroon. All parties agreed to accept the Court's judgment. At 1987 census, the population was 10,494,000. A census was held in 2005 although the results have yet to be released.

The UN gives an estimated population for 2010 of 19·96m.; density, 42 per sq. km.

In 2005, 54·6% of the population were urban.

The areas, estimated populations and chief towns of the ten provinces are:

Province	*Sq. km*	*Estimate 2007*	*Chief town*	*Estimate 2001*
Adamaoua	63,691	859,000	Ngaoundéré	189,800
Centre	68,926	2,969,300	Yaoundé	1,248,200
Est	109,011	896,400	Bertoua	173,000
Extrême-Nord	34,246	3,230,700	Maroua	271,700
Littoral	20,239	2,614,400	Douala	1,494,700
Nord (Bénoué)	65,576	1,456,600	Garoua	356,900
Nord-Ouest	17,810	2,184,900	Bamenda	316,100
Ouest	13,872	2,353,000	Bafoussam	242,000
Sud	47,110	634,900	Ebolowa	79,500
Sud-Ouest	24,471	1,475,300	Buéa	47,300

The population is composed of Sudanic-speaking people in the north (Fulani, Sao and others) and Bantu-speaking groups, mainly Bamileke, Beti, Bulu, Tikar, Bassa and Duala, in the rest of the country. The official languages are French and English.

SOCIAL STATISTICS

2000 estimates: births, 549,000; deaths, 221,000. Rates, 2000 estimates (per 1,000 population): birth, 36·3; death, 14·6. Annual population growth rate, 1992–2002, 2·4%. Infant mortality, 2005, 87 per 1,000 live births. Life expectancy in 2007: males, 50·3 years; females, 51·4. Fertility rate, 2004, 4·5 children per woman.

CLIMATE

An equatorial climate, with high temperatures and plentiful rain, especially from March to June and Sept. to Nov. Further inland, rain occurs at all seasons. Yaoundé, Jan. 76°F (24·4°C), July 73°F (22·8°C). Annual rainfall 62" (1,555 mm). Douala, Jan. 79°F (26·1°C), July 75°F (23·9°C). Annual rainfall 160" (4,026 mm).

CONSTITUTION AND GOVERNMENT

The constitution was approved by referendum on 20 May 1972 and became effective on 2 June; it was amended in Jan. 1996. It provides for a *President* as head of state and government. The President is directly elected for a seven-year term, and there is a *Council of Ministers* whose members must not be members of parliament. A constitutional bill removing a two-term presidential limit was adopted in April 2008.

The *National Assembly*, elected by universal adult suffrage for five years, consists of 180 representatives. After 1966 the sole legal party was the Cameroon People's Democratic Movement (RDPC), but in Dec. 1990 the National Assembly legalized opposition parties.

National Anthem

'O Cameroon, Thou Cradle of our Fathers'/'O Cameroun, Berceau de nos Ancêtres'; words by R. Afame, tune by R. Afame, S. Bamba and M. Nko'o.

GOVERNMENT CHRONOLOGY

Presidents since 1960. (UC = Cameroonian Union; UNC = Cameroonian National Union; RDPC = Cameroonian People's Democratic Rally)

1960–82	UC, UNC	Ahmadou Babatoura Ahidjo
1982–	UNC, RDPC	Paul Biya

RECENT ELECTIONS

Presidential elections were held on 11 Oct. 2004. Incumbent Paul Biya was re-elected with 70·9% of the votes ahead of John Fru Ndi with 17·4%, Adamou Ndam Njoya with 4·5% and Garga Haman Adji with 3·7%. The opposition denounced the election as fraudulent. Turnout was 82·8%.

The most recent National Assembly elections were held on 22 July and 30 Sept. 2007. The ruling Cameroon People's Democratic Movement (Rassemblement Démocratique du Peuple Camerounais; RDPC) won 153 seats, Social-Democratic Front (Front Social-Démocratique; SDF) 16, National Union for Democracy and Progress (Union Nationale pour la Démocratie et le Progrès; UNDP) 6, Democratic Union of Cameroon (Union Démocratique du Cameroun; UDC) 4 and Progressive Movement (Mouvement Progressiste; MP) 1.

CURRENT ADMINISTRATION

President: Paul Biya; b. 1933 (RDPC; assumed office 6 Nov. 1982, elected 14 Jan. 1984, re-elected 24 April 1988, also 10 Oct. 1992, 12 Oct. 1997 and once again re-elected 11 Oct. 2004).

In March 2010 the cabinet comprised:

Prime Minister: Philémon Yang; b. 1947 (RDPC; in office since 30 June 2009).

Deputy Prime Minister for Justice and Guardian of the Seals: Amadou Ali. *Deputy Prime Minister for Agriculture and Rural Development:* Jean Nkuété.

Minister of State for Territorial Administration and Decentralization: Marafa Hamidou Yaya. *Transport:* Bello Bouba Maïgari. *Secretary General at the Presidency:* Laurent Esso.

Minister for Basic Education: Alim Youssouf. *Commerce:* Luc Magoire Mbarga Atangana. *Communication:* Issa Tchiroma Bakari. *Culture:* Ama Tutu Muna. *Economy, Planning and Regional Development:* Louis Paul Motaze. *Employment and Professional Training:* Zacharie Perevet. *Energy and Water Resources:* Tomdjo Michael Ngako. *Environment and Nature Protection:* Pierre Hélé. *External Relations:* Henri Eyebe Ayissi. *Finance:* Lazare Essimi Menye. *Forests and Wildlife:* Elvis Ngolle Ngolle. *Health:* Andre Mama Fouda. *Higher Education:* Jacques Fame Ndongo. *Industry, Mines and Technological Development:* Badel Ndanga Ndinga. *Labour and Social Insurance:* Robert Nkili. *Lands and Land Titles:* Jean-Baptiste Béleoken. *Livestock, Fisheries and Animal Industries:* Aboubakari Sarki. *Posts and Telecommunications:* Jean-Pierre Biyiti Bi Essam. *Promotion of Women and Family Affairs:* Marie-Thérèse Abena Ondoa. *Public Service and Administrative Reforms:* Emmanuel Bondé. *Public Works:* Bernard Messengue Avom. *Scientific Research and Innovation:* Madeleine Tchuenté. *Secondary Education:* Louis Bapes Bapes. *Small and Medium-Sized Enterprises, Social Economy and Handicrafts:* Laurent Etoundi Ngoa. *Social Affairs:* Cathérine Bakang Mbock. *Sports and Physical Education:* Michel Zoah. *Tourism:* Baba Hamadou. *Urban Development and Housing:* Clobaire Tchatat. *Youth:* Adoum Garoua. *Minister Delegate at the Presidency in Charge of Defence:* Edgard Alain Mebe Ngo'o.

Office of the President: http://www.prc.cm

CURRENT LEADERS

Paul Biya

Position
President

Introduction
President since 1982, Biya has kept tight control over Cameroon, despite some concessions to democracy. His international profile has been low, although he has fostered close relations with France. Cameroon's place on the UN Security Council during the 2003 Iraq crisis brought increased international attention. Biya's relationship with the then French President Jacques Chirac ensured that Cameroon did not support the pro-war stance of the USA and UK.

Early Life
Born on 13 Feb. 1933 in Mvomeka'a, Sud Province, Biya attended a Catholic mission school and, in the early 1950s, a seminary. He specialized in philosophy at the Lycée Général Leclerc in Yaoundé before studying law at the Université de la Sorbonne, Paris. His postgraduate studies included a diploma in public law from the Institut des Hautes Etudes d'Outre-Mer.

Biya's political career began in 1962 as chargé de mission at the Presidency of the Republic. He became secretary-general of the ministry of national education in 1965. In 1970 he was made a minister of state, serving as secretary-general to the Presidency. On 30 June 1975 Biya was appointed prime minister by President Ahmadou Ahidjo. An amendment to the constitution in 1979, designating the prime minister as successor to the president in case of vacancy, allowed Biya to assume the presidency on 6 Nov. 1982 following Ahidjo's resignation.

Career in Office
The succession, although constitutional, was not peaceful. In Aug. 1983 Biya forced Ahidjo into exile, and then consolidated his position by replacing Ahidjo's northern supporters with fellow southerners. Direct presidential elections by universal suffrage were instituted in Jan. 1984, which Biya won. Despite his initial democratic and modernizing aspirations, freedom of speech and the press were soon curtailed, largely as a result of problems with the old regime. The Republican Guard revolt of April 1984 provoked Biya to reform the sole political party, the Cameroon National Union (UNC), which was seen as Ahidjo's personal support base. Transformed into the Cameroon People's Democratic Movement (RDPC; Rassemblement Démocratique du Peuple Camerounais), it elected Biya as party president in March 1985.

In the early 1980s Cameroon's economy suffered from a downturn in the commodity export trade. Biya only admitted the severity of the economic crisis in 1987, submitting the national economy to scrutiny and assistance from the World Bank. Despite popular dissatisfaction, he was re-elected in April 1988.

Opposition political parties were legalized in Dec. 1990, although the delay in organizing multi-party elections and a ban on opposition party meetings caused rioting and a general strike in 1991. Biya relented in Oct. promising elections, which took place in March 1992. The RDPC was forced into coalition with the Movement for the Defence of the Republic (MDR; Mouvement pour la Défense de la République) to attain a majority in the National Assembly. Biya himself was re-elected in Oct. by a narrow majority.

Conflict over the Bakassi Peninsula, on the Nigerian border, and its oil and fishing rights began when the Nigerian leader Gen. Abacha sent troops to claim the area. Biya responded with military force and appealed to the International Court of Justice, which ruled in Cameroon's favour in 2002 (with Cameroon eventually taking control of the territory in Aug. 2008).

The presidential elections of Oct. 1997 were boycotted by the three main opposition parties after a year of popular unrest. The removal of elected mayors after the 1996 municipal elections and the Supreme Court's controversial rulings concerning the May 1997 National Assembly elections were two of the more prominent causes of the boycott. Biya was re-elected with a large majority of the vote.

By that time, Biya's presidency was marked by anglophone separatist unrest and allegations of corruption and human rights abuses. The secessionist Southern Cameroon National Council (SCNC), claiming to represent the country's 5m. English speakers, was targeted by the government and its leaders charged with treason. In 1998 Transparency International, the Berlin-based anti-corruption organization, classed Cameroon as the most corrupt country of the 85 covered by their survey. Amnesty International meanwhile claimed that extrajudicial executions and politically-motivated detentions were continuing despite international pressure.

In parliamentary elections in 2002 the RDPC won 149 of the 180 seats in National Assembly. On 11 Oct. 2004 Biya was re-elected for a further presidential term with over 70% of the vote, although opposition parties alleged widespread fraud and international observers said the poll lacked credibility in key areas. By 2006 new measures against corruption were in place, including a law requiring the declaration of assets by public officials and the establishment of an anti-corruption commission. In the 2007 legislative elections the RDPC retained its overwhelming majority and in April 2008 parliament approved a controversial constitutional amendment enabling Biya to run for a third term of office in 2011.

DEFENCE

The President of the Republic is C.-in-C. of the armed forces. Defence expenditure totalled US$257m. in 2006 (US$15 per capita), representing 1·4% of GDP.

Army

Total strength (2007) is 12,500 and includes a Presidential Guard; there is a Gendarmerie 9,000 strong.

Navy

Personnel in 2007 numbered about 1,300. There are bases at Douala (HQ), Limbe and Kribi.

Air Force

Aircraft availability is low because of funding problems. Personnel (2007), 300. There are 15 combat capable aircraft.

INTERNATIONAL RELATIONS

Cameroon is a member of the UN, World Bank, IMF and several other UN specialized agencies, WTO, Commonwealth, IOM, International Organization of the Francophonie, Islamic Development Bank, OIC, African Development Bank, African Union, CEEAC, Lake Chad Basin Commission and is an ACP member state of the ACP-EU relationship.

ECONOMY

In 2006 agriculture accounted for 19·9% of GDP, industry 31·4% and services 48·7%.

Overview

Regarded as an African success story in the early 1980s, Cameroon's economic downfall was triggered in 1985 by a sharp price fall in primary products such as cocoa and oil.

Underlying the external trade shock were weak economic and political structures, a fiscal crisis and an overvalued exchange rate. In 1994 the national currency was devalued and annual inflation fell from 32·5% to just 0·3% by 2004. Though devaluation reduced external debt, it remained high and stood at 80% of GDP in 2001.

A programme of privatization began in 1995, taking in the major export, infrastructure, banking and insurance sectors. Cameroon's main industries include crude oil and petroleum products, timber, cocoa, aluminium, coffee and cotton. Oil accounts for 60% of exports, making the economy vulnerable to global economic developments.

In 1996, supported by the IMF and World Bank, the government adopted structural reforms and macroeconomic policies encompassing forestry, banking, transportation and privatization of public utilities. Despite these reforms, corruption and poor resource management remain problems. There are large income inequalities and around 40% of the population lives in poverty. In April 2006 Cameroon graduated from the Enhanced Heavily Indebted Poor Countries (HIPC) Initiative and became eligible for further debt relief.

Currency

The unit of currency is the *franc CFA* (XAF) with a parity of 655·957 francs CFA to one euro. In June 2005 foreign exchange reserves were US$759m. (negligible in 1997), total money supply was 757,006m. francs CFA and gold reserves were 30,000 troy oz. Inflation was 1·1% in 2007 and 5·3% in 2008.

Budget

The financial year used to end on 30 June but since 2003 has been the calendar year. In 2005 revenues totalled 1,590bn. francs CFA and expenditures 1,278bn. francs CFA.

VAT is 19·25%.

Performance

Real GDP growth was 3·3% in 2007 and 2·9% in 2008. Total GDP in 2008 was US$23·4bn.

Banking and Finance

The Banque des États de l'Afrique Centrale (*Governor*, Philibert Andzembe) is the sole bank of issue. There are in addition nine commercial banks, three development banks and five other financial institutions.

The Douala Stock Exchange was opened in April 2003.

ENERGY AND NATURAL RESOURCES

Environment

Cameroon's carbon dioxide emissions from the consumption and flaring of fossil fuels in 2008 were the equivalent of 0·4 tonnes per capita.

Electricity

Installed capacity in 2003 was 0·9m. kW. Total production in 2004 was 4·11bn. kWh (95% hydro-electric), with consumption per capita (2004) 256 kWh.

Oil and Gas

Oil production (2008), mainly from Kole oilfield, was 4·3m. tonnes. In 2007 there were proven reserves of 400m. bbls. In June 2000 the World Bank approved funding for a 1,000-km US$4bn. pipeline to run from 300 new oil wells in Chad through Cameroon to the Atlantic Ocean. Oil started pumping in July 2003. Revenues are projected to reach US$20m. per annum.

Minerals
Tin ore and limestone are extracted. There are deposits of aluminium, bauxite, uranium, nickel, gold, cassiterite and kyanite. Aluminium production in 2004 was 85,900 tonnes.

Agriculture
In 2002, 57·1% of the economically active population were engaged in agriculture. In 2001 there were 5·96m. ha. of arable land and 1·20m. ha. of permanent crops. 33,000 ha. were irrigated in 2001. There were 500 tractors in 2001. Main agricultural crops (with 2003 production in 1,000 tonnes): cassava, 2,619; sugarcane, 1,350; plantains, 1,200; maize, 1,040; bananas, 689; tomatoes, 419; sorghum, 331; yams, 311; groundnuts, 295; seed cotton, 244; sweet potatoes, 234; millet, 196; dry beans, 182; potatoes, 162; palm oil, 144; cocoa beans, 125; pumpkins and squash, 122; cucumbers and gherkins, 115.

Livestock (2003): 5·9m. cattle; 4·4m. goats; 3·8m. sheep; 1·3m. pigs; 24m. chickens.

Livestock products (in 1,000 tonnes), 2003: beef and veal, 95; lamb and mutton, 16; pork, bacon and ham, 16; goat meat, 15; poultry meat, 29; cow's milk, 125; goat's milk, 42; sheep's milk, 17; eggs, 13.

Forestry
Forests covered 21·25m. ha. in 2005 (45·6% of the total land area), ranging from tropical rain forests in the south (producing hardwoods such as mahogany, ebony and sapele) to semi-deciduous forests in the centre and wooded savannah in the north. Timber production in 2007 was 11·45m. cu. metres.

Fisheries
In 2005 the total catch was 142,345 tonnes, of which freshwater fish approximately 53% and marine fish 47%.

INDUSTRY
Manufacturing is largely small-scale, with only some 30 firms employing more than ten workers. Output in 1,000 tonnes (2004 unless otherwise indicated): cement (2003), 949; distillate fuel oil, 607; petrol, 402; residual fuel oil, 388; kerosene, 258; sugar (2002), 104. In 2001, 374m. litres of beer and 2·8bn. cigarettes were produced. There are also factories producing shoes, soap, oil and food products.

Labour
In 2001 there were 5,465,000 employed persons, of whom 58·5% were occupied in agriculture.

Trade Unions
The principal trade union federation is the Organisation des syndicats des travailleurs camerounais (OSTC), established on 7 Dec. 1985 to replace the former body, the UNTC.

INTERNATIONAL TRADE
Foreign debt was US$7,151m. in 2005.

Imports and Exports
In 2004 total imports amounted to 1,294·6bn. francs CFA and exports to 1,425·4bn. francs CFA. Principal exports, 2003: crude petroleum, 49·9%; aluminium, 7·3%; cocoa beans, 7·0%; cotton, 6·6%; sawn wood, 6·5%.

Main import suppliers, 2003: France, 30·5%; Nigeria, 13·5%; Belgium, 5·9%. Main export markets, 2003: Spain, 20·3%; Italy, 15·0%; Netherlands, 11·9%.

COMMUNICATIONS
Roads
There were about 51,300 km of roads in 2004, of which 8·4% were paved. In 2005 there were 174,900 passenger cars, 56,200 lorries and vans, 15,600 buses and coaches, and 65,600 motorcycles and mopeds.

Rail
Cameroon Railways (Camrail), 987 km in 2005, link Douala with Nkongsamba and Ngaoundéré, with branches from M'Banga to Kumba and Makak to M'Balmayo. In 2003 railways carried 1·1m. passengers and 1·8m. tonnes of freight.

Civil Aviation
There are 45 airports including three international airports at Douala, Garoua and Yaoundé (Nsimalen). In 2001 Douala handled 485,000 passengers (386,000 on international flights). In 2003 Cameroon Airlines (Camair), the national carrier, operated on domestic routes and provided international services to Abidjan, Bamako, Bangui, Brazzaville, Bujumbura, Cotonou, Dakar, Johannesburg, Kigali, Kinshasa, Lagos, Libreville, Malabo, N'Djaména, Paris and Pointe-Noire. In 2003 scheduled airline traffic of Cameroon-based carriers flew 9m. km, carrying 315,000 passengers (225,000 on international flights).

Shipping
In 2002 the merchant marine totalled 17,000 GRT. In 2002 vessels totalling 1,278,000 NRT entered ports. The main port is Douala; other ports are Bota, Campo, Garoua (only navigable in the rainy season), Kribi and Limbo-Tiko.

Telecommunications
In 2004 there were 1,636,000 telephone subscribers, or 100·4 per 1,000 inhabitants, including 1,536,600 mobile phone subscribers. There were 160,000 PCs in use (9·8 per 1,000 persons) in 2004 and 167,000 internet users.

Postal Services
There were 259 post offices in 2003.

SOCIAL INSTITUTIONS
Justice
The Supreme Court sits at Yaoundé, as does the High Court of Justice (consisting of nine titular judges and six surrogates all appointed by the National Assembly). There are magistrates' courts situated in the provinces.

The average population in penal institutions in 2004–05 was 22,734 (139 per 100,000 of national population).

Education
In 2007 there were 217,284 children and 12,349 teaching staff at pre-primary schools. There were 3,120,357 pupils in primary schools in 2007 with 70,230 teaching staff and 750,777 secondary level pupils with (2006) 43,193 teaching staff.

In 2007, 132,134 students were in tertiary education with 3,040 academic staff. There were six public universities and five private universities in 2007. The adult literacy rate in 2003 was 67·9% (77·0% among males and 59·8% among females).

In 2007 public expenditure on education came to 3·9% of GNI and 17·0% of total government spending.

Health
In 2004 there were 3,124 physicians, 147 dentists, 26,042 nurses and 700 pharmacists. There were 15 hospital beds per 10,000 population in 2006.

RELIGION
In 2001 there were 4·18m. Roman Catholics, 3·35m. Muslims and 3·27m. Protestants. Some of the population follow traditional animist religions. In Feb. 2010 there was one cardinal.

CULTURE
World Heritage Sites
The Dja Faunal Reserve was inscribed on the UNESCO World Heritage List in 1987. Surrounded by the Dja River, it is one of Africa's largest rainforests.

Broadcasting

The state-controlled Cameroon Radio Television (CRTC) provides public, national and provincial radio programmes and a national TV service (colour by PAL). Broadcasting was liberalized in 2000, heralding the establishment of private TV and radio stations. There were 850,000 TV receivers in 2006.

Press

In 2006 there was one national government-owned daily newspaper with a circulation of 25,000, three privately-owned dailies and about 500 other periodicals.

Tourism

In 2005, 176,000 non-resident tourists stayed in hotels or similar accommodation (including 89,000 from other African countries and 68,000 from Europe). Receipts from tourism totalled US$162m. in 2003.

DIPLOMATIC REPRESENTATIVES

Of Cameroon in the United Kingdom (84 Holland Park, London, W11 3SB)
High Commissioner: Nkwelle Ekaney.

Of the United Kingdom in Cameroon (Ave. Winston Churchill, BP 547, Yaoundé)
High Commissioner: Bharat Joshi.

Of Cameroon in the USA (2349 Massachusetts Ave., NW, Washington, D.C., 20008)
Ambassador: Joseph Foe-Atangana.

Of the USA in Cameroon (Ave. Rosa Parks, BP 817, Yaoundé)
Ambassador: Janet E. Garvey.

Of Cameroon to the United Nations
Ambassador: Michel Tommo Monthe.

Of Cameroon to the European Union
Ambassador: Daniel Evina Abe'e.

FURTHER READING

Ardener, E., *Kingdom on Mount Cameroon: Studies in the History of the Cameroon Coast 1500–1970.* 1996

DeLancey, M. W., *Cameroon: Dependence and Independence.* 1989

Gros, Jean-Germain, *Cameroon: Politics and Society in Critical Perspective.* 2003

National Statistical Office: Direction de la Statistique et de la Comptabilité Nationale, Ministère du Plan et de l'Aménagement du Territoire, Yaoundé.

Website (French only): http://www.statistics-cameroon.org

CANADA

Capital: Ottawa
Population estimate, 2010: 33·89m.
GDP per capita, 2007: (PPP$) 35,812
HDI/world rank: 0·966/4

KEY HISTORICAL EVENTS

The first habitation in Canada dates from the last stages of the Pleistocene Ice Age up to 30,000 years ago. Mongoloid tribes from Asia crossed the Bering Strait by a land bridge in search of mammoth, bison and elk. These hunter-gatherers were the forefathers of some of Canada's native people referred to today as the First Nations. There are currently two other Aboriginal groups; the Inuit (Arctic people, formerly known as Eskimos) and the Métis. The Inuit were one of the last groups to arrive, around 1000 BC, whereas the Métis evolved from the union of natives and Europeans (mostly French).

The numerous tribes that made up the First Nations consisted of 12 major language groups with a number of sub groups with diverse spiritual beliefs, laws and customs. Around 6000 BC, during the Boreal Archaic age, the glaciers of the Canadian Shield melted and lakes were formed. The Iroquois speaking tribes, including the Mohawks and the Huron, settled along the St Lawrence River and the Great Lakes. Excellent farmers, they lived in large communities. Trade flourished but tribal wars were common. By 1000 BC the Early Woodland Culture had developed in the east. Among the eight tribes were the Algonquin, one of the largest language groups, who spread west to the Plains to hunt buffalo along with the Blackfoot, Sioux and Cree. The tribes of the Pacific Coast, such as the Tlingit and Salish, made a living from whaling and salmon fishing and enjoyed a more elaborate social structure. The peoples in the north around Yukon and Mackenzie River basins and the Inuit around the Arctic were nomadic hunters foraging for limited food in small family groups. However, one factor common to all was that they were self-governing and politically independent.

In 1963 remains of a Viking settlement were found at L'Anse aux Meadows in Newfoundland dating from AD 1000. Trade had been established between the Norse men and the Inuit but settlements were abandoned when the Norse withdrew from Greenland. John Cabot, an Italian navigator, commissioned by King Henry VII of England in 1497, charted the coasts around Labrador and Newfoundland and found large resources of fish. The Frenchman, Jacques Cartier, discovered the Gulf of St

Lawrence in 1534 and claimed it for the French crown. In the following years fisheries were set up by the English and French with Indians bringing valuable furs, mostly beaver, to trade for iron and other goods. Realising the potential, the French sent Samuel de Champlain in 1604 to establish a fur trade and organize a settlement. This he achieved in 1605 in an area called Acadia (now New Brunswick, Nova Scotia and Prince Edward Island). The French traded with the Algonquin and Huron and supported them during fierce raids by the Iroquois. In retaliation the Iroquois later became the fur trading allies of the Dutch and then the English. Champlain, having founded Quebec City, went on to explore Huron territory, now central Ontario, and is considered by many to be the father of New France.

English–French Rivalry

In opposition to French expansion, England sent explorers such as Martin Frobisher, William Baffin and Henry Hudson to claim new territory. Colonies sprang up along the English coast and the Hudson Bay Company was formed in 1670 to gain a fur-trading monopoly over the area. Rivalry between the English and French for trade at Hudson Bay persisted throughout the 17th century. In 1713 the Treaty of Utrecht, signed by Queen Anne of England and Louis XIV, gave England complete control of the Hudson Bay territory, Acadia and Newfoundland. France, however, retained Cape Breton Island, the St Lawrence Islands and fishing rights in Newfoundland. Led by Gen. Wolfe, Britain's victory over France at the Battle of the Plains of Abraham in 1759 gained Quebec, and in 1760 Montreal too was taken. This brought an end to the Seven Years' War (1756–63) confirmed in 1763 by the Treaty of Paris in which all French Canadian territory was ceded to the British.

Relations with Indian tribes formerly allied to the French were strained and there was much resentment at the invasion of their lands by white settlers. The Royal Proclamation of 1763, administered by the Indian Department, ruled that aboriginal peoples could only sell land to crown representatives. Numerous treaties were signed over the following decades, redistributing thousands of acres of land. To soothe the British rule of a French speaking colony, the British government passed the Quebec Act in 1774 allowing French Canadians religious and linguistic freedom, the right to collect tithes and recognition of French civil law.

The attack on Montreal in 1775, during the American War of Independence, failed and Americans, loyal to Britain, sought refuge in Canada. Around 50,000 emigrated to Nova Scotia, from which New Brunswick was created in 1784. In an attempt to keep the peace the Constitutional Act of 1791 divided Quebec into Lower Canada (mostly French) and Upper Canada (mostly British from America).

Exploration continued on the Pacific Coast and into the Plains and the Northwest. Capt. James Cook charted the Pacific Coast from Vancouver to Alaska in 1778. From trading posts set up by the Hudson Bay Company (HBC) expeditions were made by traders including Samuel Hearne who, in 1771, was the first man to reach the Arctic Ocean by land. A rival company, the North West Company (NWC), was set up in Montreal in 1783. In 1793 Alexander Mackenzie, from the NWC, crossed the Rocky Mountains and reached the coast making him the first man to cross the continent. Competition between the two companies erupted into violence between new settlers and established traders including the Métis who were hired, mainly by NWC, to transport furs and supply food. To resolve the conflict the British government pressed for the merger of the two companies. This was achieved in 1821.

After the American war against Britain in Canada in 1812 (which ended in stalemate), large numbers of English, Scottish and Irish settlers swelled the English-speaking population. By 1837 radical reformers were seeking accountable government with a broader electorate. Rebellions led by William Lyon Mackenzie in Upper Canada and by Louis-Joseph Papineau in Lower Canada were quashed by government troops. Following a report by Lord Durham, who was sent from England as governor-general to conduct an enquiry, the two colonies were united under one central government in 1841 with both enjoying equal representation. Vancouver Island was acknowledged to be British by the Oregon Boundary Treaty of 1846. The 1850s saw a significant period of growth. Railways were built and industry and commerce thrived, enhanced by the Reciprocity Treaty of 1854 with the USA.

Dominion Status

However, by the 1860s ethnic clashes had made Canada almost ungovernable. The American Civil War also posed a threat. Three political leaders, George Étienne Cartier (Conservative–Canada East), George Brown (Reform Movement–Canada West) and John A. Macdonald (Conservative–Canada West) formed a coalition government in 1864. Nova Scotia, New Brunswick and the Canadas (now Ontario and Quebec) were united in 1867 as the Dominion of Canada. What became known as the Constitution Act, confirmed the language and legal rights of the French and provided for the division of power between the federal government and the provinces. John Macdonald was elected prime minister.

One of the first actions of the new federal government was to purchase the Northwest Territories from the HBC, a move that led to rebellion by white settlers and the Métis, under Louis Riel. The result was the creation of Manitoba in 1870 with political power divided between the French and English. British Columbia joined the federation in 1871 and Prince Edward Island in 1873. The former agreed to join on the promise of a federally financed railway. To make way for new settlers from 1868–77, treaties were negotiated with Indians from Ontario to the Rocky Mountains. In return for moving to reserves the Indians were to receive financial support and other concessions. They were also to be assimilated into Christian society. In the years following the government failed in its obligations and many Plains Indians suffered poverty, starvation and disease. Later legislation even outlawed traditional practices such as the Sun Dance and the potlatch (exchange of gifts). Many Métis had moved out of Manitoba and settled further west but were not awarded the same rights as those of the Aboriginal Indians. Resistance grew, and Riel, who had emigrated to Montana, was urged to lead a revolt. In response, troops were rushed in by rail and the rebellion was crushed. The importance of the railway became evident and money was found for its completion across the Rockies. The new railway was opened in 1885, the same year in which Riel was executed.

Prosperity and Reform

Following the death of Macdonald in 1891, the Liberal leader Wilfrid Laurier came to power in 1896 and there followed a period of growth and stability. Mineral resources were found in British Columbia and Ontario as well as gold which precipitated the Klondike gold rush of 1897. The Yukon territory was established in 1898 to ensure Canadian jurisdiction over the exploitation of gold. The provinces of Saskatchewan and Alberta were created in 1905, each with its own premier and elected assembly. By 1911 the population in the provinces had doubled and there was a powerful business sector. When reformers called for action to alleviate conditions in overcrowded cities, health and welfare programmes were introduced. A new women's movement campaigned for equal rights and women's suffrage. Anti-monopoly legislation was passed in 1910. However, much industrial investment was backed by American money and many French Canadians began to agitate for autonomy. In 1910 Laurier founded the Canadian Navy with the provision that in time of war it would be placed under British command. This further angered the French Canadians. Laurier's decision to negotiate a new trade agreement with the USA, coupled with the navy issue, lost him the 1911 election to the Conservatives. Robert Laird Borden became prime minister.

When the First World War broke out in 1914 thousands of British-born Canadians volunteered to fight. At first troops were under British command, but by the time conscription had been introduced in 1917 they were under Canadian leadership. Around 60,000 men lost their lives in the battles of Ypres, Vimy Ridge and Passchendaele, and another 173,000 were wounded. Having won recognition for its contribution to the war effort, Canada participated as an independent state at the Paris Peace Conference and joined the League of Nations. At home the French Canadians had been bitterly opposed to Borden's implementation of conscription and to counteract this he formed a joint government of Liberals and Conservatives. This was split into the English speaking Unionists and the French speaking Liberals. At the election in 1917 the Unionists won every province but Quebec.

Women's suffrage was granted in 1918. 1921 saw the Liberals back in power under William Lyon Mackenzie King who strove to unify the nation and gain autonomy. This was achieved in 1931 by the Statute of Westminster in which Canada was granted complete independence. In the same year Norway formally recognized the Canadian title to the Sverdrup group of Arctic islands. Canada thus holds sovereignty in the whole Arctic sector north of the Canadian mainland.

Following the Wall Street Crash of 1929, the country chose the Conservatives under the leadership of Richard Bedford Bennett in the election of 1930. Despite measures to alleviate the effects of the depression and the severe drought in the prairies, Bennett was unsuccessful and in 1935 King was re-elected. King introduced a new Reciprocity Treaty (1936) with the USA, nationalized the Bank of Canada, created the Canadian Broadcasting Corporation and made available federal money to provide social services.

Post-War Politics

Canada's contribution in the Second World War was even more extensive than that in the First World War although casualties were lower. A post-war plan introduced unemployment insurance, family allowances, veterans' benefits, subsidized housing, health plans and improved pensions. Industrial controls were lifted and trade was encouraged. Canada became a founder member of the United Nations in 1945 and has been active in a peacekeeping role ever since. King retired in 1948 to be succeeded by Louis St Laurent, a Quebec lawyer, who won an overwhelming victory in 1949. In the same year, Newfoundland—including Labrador—became a Canadian province thus completing the Confederation. Also in that year, Canada joined NATO.

An amendment to the Indian Act in 1959 increased opportunities for Indians to influence decisions affecting them, and in 1960 the federal government granted the franchise to all Indians, with several provinces following suit.

For 20 years after 1950 Canada enjoyed growth, prosperity and a 'baby boom'. The face of industrial Canada changed with the discovery of radium, petroleum and natural gas. Canada took a more active part in foreign affairs, especially in the Suez Canal crisis for which Lester B. Pearson, external affairs minister, won the Nobel Peace Prize. The North American Air Defense Command (NORAD) was formed with the USA in 1957. In the same year, after 22 years of Liberal rule, the Conservatives won the election with John Diefenbaker as leader. However, internal struggles and an economic recession saw the return of the Liberals in 1963 under Pearson. During his five years as prime minister Canada gained a national flag, a social security system and medical care for all its citizens. Expo '67 was held in Montreal as part of the celebrations of the Centennial of Canadian Confederation and the Order of Canada was instituted to award outstanding merit and service.

Having chosen Pierre Trudeau to succeed Pearson, the Liberals won the 1968 election. At the same time there was a revival of French nationalism, especially in Quebec, with the formation of the Parti Québécois (PQ) led by René Levasque. Keen to preserve national unity, Trudeau passed the Official Languages Act in 1969 which affirmed the equality of French and English in all governmental activities. However, in 1970 he had to send troops into Quebec following the murder of the Labour minister, Pierre Laporte, by the separatist Front de Libération du Québec. In 1976 the Olympic Games were hosted in Montreal. Also in that year a pledge on separatism won the PQ the provincial election and French became the official language of Quebec. Despite these milestones, a referendum to make the province an independent country was rejected by Quebec voters in 1980.

Indian Rights

In the sixties and seventies Indians sought special rights and settlement of their outstanding treaty claims. The National Indian Brotherhood was formed in 1968 to represent the interest of Indians at federal level. By 1973 the Department of Indian Affairs and Northern Development was instructed to resolve these claims. In 1982, with the exception of Quebec, the country agreed to a new constitution giving Canada, as opposed to the British Parliament, prerogative over all future constitutional changes. At the same time a charter of Rights and Freedoms was introduced recognizing the nation's multi-cultural heritage, affirming the existing rights of native peoples and the principle of equality of benefits to the provinces.

Retiring in 1984, Trudeau was succeeded by John Turner who was ousted the same year by the Conservative leader Brian Mulroney. In 1987 at a meeting in Meech Lake, a series of constitutional amendments were drawn up to win Quebec's acceptance of the new constitution. English Canadians objected to the Meech Lake Accord and it was rejected by Newfoundland and Manitoba. This failure sparked another separatist revival in Quebec leading to the drafting of the Charlottetown Accord incorporating extensive amendments, including recognition of Quebec as a 'distinct society', offering better representation in parliament, and self-government for indigenous peoples. This was defeated in a national referendum in 1992.

Mulroney negotiated a free trade agreement with the United States which went into effect in 1989. This was followed in 1994 by North American Free Trade Agreement (NAFTA) with the USA and Mexico. Voter opposition coupled with a recession in the early nineties forced Mulroney to resign in 1993. He was replaced by Kim Campbell, Canada's first female prime minister. In the Oct. election of that year, Campbell and the Conservatives suffered a major defeat retaining only two of their 154 seats. Led by Jean Chrétien, the Liberals won 177 seats and the Reform Party 52 seats. The PQ became the major opposition party with 54 seats.

Another referendum on Quebec's independence from Canada failed narrowly in 1995. Again in 1997 leaders of all provinces and territories (apart from Quebec) met in Calgary and signed a declaration recognizing the 'unique character' of Quebec's society. The following year the Supreme Court ruled that Quebec was prohibited from declaring itself independent without first negotiating an agreement with the federal government and other provinces.

In the 1990s further protests were made by native peoples anxious to claim their territory. In 1997 the Supreme Court ruled that two aboriginal groups had title to 22,000 square miles of ancestral lands in British Columbia. The following year a formal apology was issued by the government for the treatment Indian and Inuit peoples had received since the arrival of the Europeans. After decades of complex negotiations, the Inuit were granted their own territory of Nunavut in 1999, an area once part of the Northwest Territories. In the same year the government agreed that Indians and the Inuit should have the right of self-government.

Following a period of economic growth Chrétien's government made major tax cuts in 2000. In an attempt to form a more effective opposition, the Reform Party accepted the 'united alternative' proposed by party leader Preston Manning which resulted in the Canadian Alliance (Canadian Reform Conservative Alliance), a broad-based conservative party with Stockwell Day as its first leader. However, with the Progressive Conservative Party declining to join forces, Chrétien was returned for a third term in Nov. 2000 with an increased majority.

Chrétien stood down from the premiership in late 2003 and was replaced by his Liberal colleague, Paul Martin. Martin and his party soon became embroiled in a financial scandal over misuse of government money for advertising. In the Jan. 2006 general election the Conservative Party, led by Stephen Harper, defeated the Liberals, taking power for the first time in 12 years.

TERRITORY AND POPULATION

Canada is bounded in the northwest by the Beaufort Sea, north by the Arctic Ocean, northeast by Baffin Bay, east by the Davis Strait, Labrador Sea and Atlantic Ocean, south by the USA and west by the Pacific Ocean and USA (Alaska). The area is 9,984,670 sq. km, of which 891,163 sq. km are fresh water. 2006 census population, 31,612,897 (51·0% female), giving a density of 3·2 per sq. km. Population estimate, 1 Oct. 2009, was 33,873,400. In 2005, 80·1% of the population were urban.

The UN gives an estimated population for 2010 of 33·89m.

Population at previous censuses:

1861	3,229,633	1921	8,787,949	1976[1]	22,992,604
1871	3,689,257	1931	10,376,786	1981	24,343,181
1881	4,324,810	1941	11,506,655	1986[1]	25,309,331
1891	4,833,239	1951	14,009,429	1991	27,296,859[2]
1901	5,371,315	1961	18,238,247	1996[1]	28,848,761[2]
1911	7,206,643	1971	21,568,311	2001	30,007,094

[1]It became a statutory requirement to conduct a census every five years in 1971. [2]Excludes data from incompletely enumerated Indian reserves and Indian settlements.

Figures for the 2006 census population according to ethnic origin (leading categories), were[1]:

Canadian	10,066,290	Chinese	1,346,510
English	6,570,015	North American Indian	1,253,260
French	4,941,210	Ukrainian	1,209,090
Scottish	4,719,850	Dutch	1,035,965
Irish	4,354,155	Polish	984,565
German	3,179,425	East Indian	962,670
Italian	1,445,330	Russian	500,500

[1]Census respondents who reported multiple ethnic origins are counted for each origin they reported.

The aboriginal population (those persons identifying with at least one aboriginal group, and including North American Indian, Métis or Inuit) numbered 1,172,785 in 2006. In 2006, 57·2% of the population gave their mother tongue as English and 21·8% as French (English and French are both official languages); Chinese was reported as the third most common language, accounting for 3·2% of the total population. In 2006, 1·2m. residents were immigrants who had arrived between 2001 and 2006, accounting for 3·8% of the total population; 40·8% of all immigrants in 2006 were from Asia (including the Middle East), 36·8% from Europe, 11·3% from the Caribbean, Central and South America, 6·1% from Africa, 4·0% from the USA and 1·0% from Oceania and other countries.

Of the total population in 2006, 80·4% were Canadian-born. The percentage of the population in each of the provinces and territories in 2006 born outside Canada was as follows: Ontario, 27·9%; British Columbia, 27·2%; Alberta, 16·0%; Manitoba, 13·2%; Quebec, 11·3%; Yukon, 9·9%; Northwest Territories, 6·8%; Saskatchewan, 5·0%; Nova Scotia, 4·9%; New Brunswick, 3·6%; Prince Edward Island, 3·5%; Newfoundland, 1·7%; Nunavut, 1·5%.

Alberta had the biggest population increase between 2001 and 2006 with 10·6%, whilst Newfoundland had the biggest population reduction with –1·5%.

Populations of Census Metropolitan Areas (CMA) and Cities (proper), 2006 census:

	CMA	*City proper*		*CMA*	*City proper*
Toronto	5,113,149	2,503,281	Halifax	372,858	372,679
Montreal	3,635,571	1,620,693	Oshawa	330,594	141,590
Vancouver	2,116,581	578,041	Victoria	330,088	78,057
Ottawa-Gatineau	1,130,761	—	Windsor	323,342	216,473
Ottawa	—	812,129	Saskatoon	233,923	202,340
Gatineau	—	242,124	Regina	194,971	179,246
Calgary	1,079,310	988,193	Sherbrooke	186,952	147,427
Edmonton	1,034,945	730,372	St John's	181,113	100,646
Quebec	715,515	491,142	Barrie	177,061	128,430
Winnipeg	694,668	633,451	Kelowna	162,276	106,707
Hamilton	692,911	504,559	Abbotsford	159,020	123,864
London	457,720	352,395	Greater Sudbury	158,258	157,857
Kitchener	451,235	204,668	Kingston	152,358	117,207
St Catharines-Niagara	390,317	—	Saguenay	151,643	143,692
St Catharines	—	131,989	Trois-Rivières	141,529	126,323
Niagara Falls	—	82,184	Guelph	127,009	114,943

SOCIAL STATISTICS

Statistics for period from July–June:

	Live births	*Deaths*
2004–05	339,270	229,906
2005–06	346,082	225,489
2006–07	360,916	233,172
2007–08	370,859	238,330

Average annual population growth rate, 2000–05, 1·0%. Birth rate, 2007–08 (per 1,000 population), 11·2; death rate, 7·2. Marriages, 2006, numbered 147,084; divorces, 2005, 71,269. In 2003 the average age for first-time opposite-sex marriage (excluding Ontario) was 30·6 for males and 28·5 for females. Suicides, 2005, 3,743 (11·6 per 100,000 population). Life expectancy at birth, 2007, was 78·2 years for men and 82·9 years for women. Infant mortality, 2005, 5 per 1,000 live births; fertility rate, 2004, 1·5 children per woman. Canada legalized same-sex marriage in 2005.

CLIMATE

The climate ranges from polar conditions in the north to cool temperate in the south, but with considerable differences between east coast, west coast and the interior, affecting temperatures, rainfall amounts and seasonal distribution. Winters are very severe over much of the country, but summers can be very hot inland. *See* individual provinces for climatic details.

CONSTITUTION AND GOVERNMENT

In Nov. 1981 the Canadian government agreed on the provisions of an amended constitution, to the end that it should replace the British North America Act and that its future amendment should be the prerogative of Canada. These proposals were adopted by the Parliament of Canada and were enacted by the UK Parliament as the Canada Act of 1982. This was the final act of the UK Parliament in Canadian constitutional development. The Act gave to Canada the power to amend the Constitution according to procedures determined by the Constitutional Act 1982. The latter added to the Canadian Constitution a charter of Rights and Freedoms, and provisions which recognize the nation's multi-cultural heritage, affirm the existing rights of native peoples, confirm the principle of equalization of benefits among the provinces, and strengthen provincial ownership of natural resources.

Under the Constitution legislative power is vested in Parliament, consisting of the Queen, represented by a Governor-General, a Senate and a House of Commons. The members of the *Senate* are appointed until age 75 by summons of the Governor-General under the Great Seal of Canada. Members appointed before 2 June 1965 may remain in office for life. The Senate consists of 105 senators: 24 from Ontario, 24 from Quebec, 10 from Nova Scotia, 10 from New Brunswick, 6 from Manitoba, 6 from British Columbia, 6 from Alberta, 6 from Saskatchewan, 6 from Newfoundland, 4 from Prince Edward Island, 1 from Yukon, 1 from the Northwest Territories, and 1 from Nunavut. Each senator must be at least 30 years of age and reside in the province for which he or she is appointed. The *House of Commons*, currently of 308 members, is elected by universal secret suffrage, by a first-past-the-post system. Legislation that came into force in May 2007 stipulates that elections will be held on the third Monday of Oct. in the fourth calendar year following the previous general election, except when a government loses a vote of confidence. Representation is based on the population of all the provinces taken as a whole with readjustments made after each census. State of the parties in the Senate (March 2010): Conservatives, 51; Liberals, 49; Progressive Conservatives, 2; ind., 2; non-aligned, 1.

The First Nations have representation in the *Assembly of First Nations* (National Chief: Shawn A-in-chut Atleo, elected July 2009).

The office and appointment of the Governor-General are regulated by letters patent of 1947. In 1977 the Queen approved the transfer to the Governor-General of functions discharged by the Sovereign. The Governor-General is assisted by a *Privy Council* composed of Cabinet Ministers.

Canadian Parliamentary Guide. Annual.
Bejermi, J., *Canadian Parliamentary Handbook*. 2008
Cairns, A. C., *Charter versus Federalism: the Dilemmas of Constitutional Reform*. 1992
Canada: The State of the Federation. Queen's Univ., annual
Forsey, E. A., *How Canadians Govern Themselves*. 1991
Fox, P. W. and White, G., *Politics Canada*. 8th ed. 1995
Hogg, P. W., *Constitutional Law of Canada*. 2001
Kaplan, W. (ed.) *Belonging: the Meaning and Future of Canadian Citizenship*. 1993
Kernaghan, K., *Public Administration in Canada: a Text*. 1991
Mahler, G., *Contemporary Canadian Politics, 1970–1994: an Annotated Bibliography*. 2 vols. 1995
Osbaldston, G. F., *Organizing to Govern*. 1992
Reesor, B., *The Canadian Constitution in Historical Perspective*. 1992
Tardi, G., *The Legal Framework of Government: a Canadian Guide*. 1992

National Anthem

'O Canada, our home and native land'/'O Canada, terre de nos aïeux'; words by A. Routhier, tune by C. Lavallée.

GOVERNMENT CHRONOLOGY

Prime Ministers since 1935. (CPC = Conservative Party of Canada; LP = Liberal Party; PC = Progressive Conservative Party)

1935–48	LP	William Lyon Mackenzie King
1948–57	LP	Louis Stephen Saint Laurent
1957–63	PC	John George Diefenbaker
1963–68	LP	Lester Bowles Pearson
1968–79	LP	Pierre Elliott Trudeau
1979–80	PC	Charles Joseph (Joe) Clark
1980–84	LP	Pierre Elliott Trudeau
1984	LP	John Napier Turner
1984–93	PC	Martin Brian Mulroney
1993	PC	Avril Phaedra (Kim) Campbell
1993–2003	LP	Joseph Jacques Jean Chrétien
2003–06	LP	Paul Joseph Martin (Jr)
2006–	CPC	Stephen Joseph Harper

RECENT ELECTIONS

At the elections of 14 Oct. 2008 the incumbent Conservative Party won 143 seats (124 in 2006) with 37·6% (36·3% in 2006) of votes cast; the Liberal Party 76 with 26·2% (103 in 2006 with 30·2%); the Bloc Québécois 50 with 10·0% (51 in 2006 with 10·5%) and the New Democratic Party 37 with 18·2% (29 in 2006 with 17·5%). The Green Party polled 6·8% and took no seats. Two independents were elected. Turnout was 59·1% (64·9% in 2006).

CURRENT ADMINISTRATION

Governor-General: Michaëlle Jean (b. 1957; sworn in 27 Sept. 2005).

In March 2010 the Conservative cabinet comprised:

Prime Minister: Stephen Harper; b. 1959 (Conservative Party; took office on 6 Feb. 2006).

Minister of Agriculture and Agri-Food, and the Canadian Wheat Board: Gerry Ritz. *Canadian Heritage and Official Languages:* James Moore. *Citizenship, Immigration and Multiculturalism:* Jason Kenney. *Environment:* Jim Prentice. *Finance:* James Flaherty. *Fisheries and Oceans:* Gail Shea. *Foreign Affairs:* Lawrence Cannon. *Health:* Leona Aglukkaq. *Human Resources and Skills Development:* Diane Finley. *Indian Affairs and Northern Development, Federal Interlocutor for Métis and Non-Status Indians, and Minister of the Canadian Northern Economic Development Agency:* Chuck Strahl. *Industry:* Tony Clement. *International Co-operation:* Beverley Oda. *International Trade:* Peter Van Loan. *Justice and Attorney General:* Robert Nicholson. *Labour:* Lisa Raitt. *National Defence:* Peter MacKay. *National Revenue, Atlantic Canada Opportunities Agency and the Atlantic Gateway:* Keith Ashfield. *Natural Resources:* Christian Paradis. *Public Safety:* Vic Toews. *Public Works and Government Services, and Status of Women:* Rona Ambrose. *Transport, Infrastructure and Communities:* John Baird. *Veterans' Affairs:* Jean-Pierre Blackburn. *Leader of the Government in the House of Commons:* Jay Hill. *Leader of the Government in the Senate:* Marjory LeBreton. *President of the Queen's Privy Council for Canada, Minister of Intergovernmental Affairs and Francophonie:* Josée Verner. *President of the Treasury Board, Minister for the Asia-Pacific Gateway:* Stockwell Day.

The *Leader of the Opposition* is Michael Ignatieff.

Office of the Prime Minister: http://www.pm.gc.ca

CURRENT LEADERS

Stephen Harper

Position

Prime Minister

Introduction

Stephen Harper's victory in federal elections in Jan. 2006 represented a shift to the right after 12 years of Liberal government overshadowed by allegations of corruption. The free-market economist and leader of the Conservative Party cast himself as a moderate, progressive, centre-right politician and promised to tackle corruption, reduce taxes and lead a more efficient government. He retained power after the Conservatives won the Oct. 2008 election.

Early Life

Stephen Harper was born on 30 April 1959 in Toronto, Canada. He graduated from Richview Collegiate Institute in 1978 and moved to Edmonton, Alberta, where he worked as a computer programmer in the oil and gas industry. While studying economics at the University of Calgary in the early 1980s, Harper was influenced by the right-wing monetarist ideas espoused by Ronald Reagan in the USA and Margaret Thatcher in the UK. He graduated with a BA in economics in 1985 and began working for a Conservative member of parliament, Jim Hawkes.

Disillusioned with the Progressive Conservatives (PC) and the government of Brian Mulroney, Harper joined the newly established Reform Party of Canada in 1987, led by the economist Preston Manning. As chief policy officer, Harper helped draft the party's manifesto for the elections of 1988. He became legislative assistant to the Reform Party MP, Deborah Gray, after she won a by-election to represent Beaver River, Alberta in March 1989.

At the elections of Oct. 1993 Harper beat Jim Hawkes to win Calgary West for the Reform Party and became the party's spokesman on finance and national unity. In a run-up to a referendum in Oct. 1995 on the status of Quebec, Harper argued to maintain but decentralize the federation. Disagreements with Manning led to Harper's decision in late 1996 not to stand in the next election. He resigned his seat in Jan. 1997 and was appointed vice president of the conservative lobby group, the National Citizens Coalition. He also worked as a regular political commentator for the Canadian Broadcasting Corporation.

Harper rejected invitations to run for the PC leadership but returned to politics in March 2002 when he was elected to succeed Stockwell Day as leader of the Canadian Alliance party. He successfully contested a by-election for Calgary Southwest two months later and returned to the House of Commons as leader of the opposition. Following protracted negotiations, Harper reached agreement with the PC leader, Peter MacKay, on a merger between the two parties to form the Conservative Party of Canada in Dec. 2003.

Harper won the new party's leadership election in March 2004 and fought the Liberal prime minister, Paul Martin, in the 2004 election. After taking an early lead in the polls, the Conservatives lost ground. Harper was criticized for his support of the US-led war on Iraq in March 2003. The election, on 28 June 2004, saw a victory for the Liberals, who took 135 seats against 99 for the Conservatives.

When the Liberals became mired in a corruption scandal in April 2005, Harper argued that the government had 'lost the moral authority to govern'. He introduced a motion of no confidence in Paul Martin's administration on 24 Nov. 2005, which was passed by 171–133. Parliament was dissolved and elections were scheduled for 23 Jan. 2006. Harper's campaign presented him as head of a modernizing centre-right party that would stimulate economic growth by lowering taxes. Having held a comfortable lead in the opinion polls, the Conservatives won the elections with 36% of the vote, though short of a parliamentary majority. Harper was sworn in as prime minister on 6 Feb. 2006.

Career in Office

Harper promised a smaller 'more focused and effective' government and his first cabinet had 27 posts, 12 fewer than Paul Martin's. Eager to pursue closer relations with the USA, he announced a settlement in April of Canada's long-running dispute over softwood timber exports to its neighbour. He also promised more respect for provincial autonomy, particularly in relation to French-speaking Quebec. In Nov. 2006 his proposal to recognize Quebec 'as a nation within a united Canada' was approved by the House of Commons. In foreign policy, he maintained the previous administration's position on Afghanistan and extended Canada's military deployment there until 2011. In June 2006 police arrested 17 Islamic extremists allegedly intending to kill the prime minister during a planned wave of bomb attacks.

In Oct. 2007 Harper set out a new government programme focusing on the environment, tax cuts, the fiscal imbalance between the provinces and the federal government, and reform of political institutions (to include an elected Senate rather than an appointed body). He also promised a parliamentary vote on any extension of the Canadian military mission in Afghanistan.

Despite the shadow of global financial turmoil and opposition accusations of economic complacency, Harper sought a more secure mandate for his administration by calling early an early general election for Oct. 2008 (although he had earlier pushed through legislation fixing the normal life of a parliament at four years). The Conservatives improved their representation in the House of Commons but again failed to achieve a parliamentary majority. In Dec. the opposition parties sought to bring down the minority government over its response to the economic situation, but Harper asked the Governor-General to suspend parliament until Jan. 2009 thereby postponing a no-confidence vote. When parliament resumed in late Jan. the opposition alliance backed down and in Feb. the government secured approval of its 2009 budget, including a two-year stimulus package for the economy, with conditional Liberal Party support which ensured Harper's political survival. However, in Oct. 2009 the Liberals tabled a no-confidence motion accusing the government of having lost control of the public finances. The motion was defeated by 144 votes to 117 with the help of the New Democratic Party and Bloc Québécois, and in Nov. the Conservatives gained two seats in four parliamentary by-elections, suggesting some improvement in the government's standing with the electorate.

DEFENCE

The armed forces are unified as the Canadian Armed Forces and organized in functional commands: Land Forces (army), Air Command (air forces) and Maritime Command (naval and naval air forces). In 2007 the armed forces numbered 64,000; reserves, 65,800.

Military expenditure totalled US$19,290m. in 2008 (US$581 per capita). In 2007 defence spending represented 1·2% of GDP.

Army

The Land Forces numbered 33,300 in 2007; reserves include a Militia of 24,700.

Navy

The naval combatant force, which forms part of the Maritime Command of the unified armed forces, is headquartered at Halifax (Nova Scotia), and includes four diesel submarines, three destroyers and 12 helicopter-carrying frigates. Naval personnel in 2007 numbered about 11,100, with 4,200 reserves. The main bases are Halifax, where about two-thirds of the fleet is based, and Esquimalt (British Columbia).

Air Force

The air forces numbered 19,600 in 2007 with 107 combat capable aircraft (mainly CF-18s).

INTERNATIONAL RELATIONS

Canada is a member of the UN, World Bank, IMF and several other UN specialized agencies, WTO, OSCE, BIS, Commonwealth, IOM, International Organization of the Francophonie, NATO, OECD, Inter-American Development Bank, OAS, Asian Development Bank, APEC, Antarctic Treaty and the North American Free Trade Agreement.

ECONOMY

Services accounted for 69% of GDP in 2005, industry 29% and agriculture, forestry, fisheries and hunting 2%.

According to the anti-corruption organization *Transparency International*, Canada ranked equal eighth in the world in a 2009 survey of the countries with the least corruption in business and government. It received 8·7 out of 10 in the annual index.

Overview

While Canada's development record is impressive, its GDP per capita has not kept up with that of the USA over the last three decades. However, it has a greater degree of income equality than its neighbour and a higher index rating in the UN Human Development Report.

Canada has vast natural resources, a skilled labour force, modern technological capabilities and a diversified economy. The services sector accounted for just under 70% of GDP in 2005 and employs approximately three-quarters of the population. Industry contributes slightly over a quarter of GDP. The primary sector accounts for roughly 2% of GDP but contributes a quarter of total export earnings and is the leading source of income for several provinces.

Structural reforms in the 1980s helped pave the way for productivity gains in the 1990s. Fiscal consolidation and a credible monetary policy improved the macroeconomic framework, lowering sustainable real interest rates and increasing the effectiveness of counter-cyclical monetary policy. Between 1992–2000 Canada achieved strong labour productivity and total factor productivity growth. Labour productivity continued to grow at an annual average of 1·6% between 1997 and 2005. Advantage Canada, the government's structural policy blueprint published in late 2006, prioritized productivity. The 1989 US–Canada Free Trade Agreement and the 1994 North American Free Trade Agreement (which includes Mexico) touched off a dramatic increase in trade and economic integration. By 1994 the USA accounted for 80% of Canada's exports. The figure increased to 87% in 2000, although the share of exports going to the USA has since fallen to 79% in 2007.

Following a decade of strong economic performance, the global slowdown has resulted in a decline in growth, driven by a deterioration in domestic demand, the tightening of financial conditions and the sharp downturn in the USA. Policy response has been strong, with tax relief and fiscal stimulus measures, a 425 basis point reduction in interest rates to a historic low of 0·25%, and a flexible exchange rate. No Canadian bank has required public capital injections or guarantees, a benefit of strong long-term supervision and regulation. According to the OECD, external demand and domestic investment rebounded during the second half of 2009, with growth set to reach 2% in 2010.

Annual inflation was brought down from double-digit growth in the early 1980s to less than 2% in 1992 and has remained stable ever since. The budget was in surplus from 1997–2008, helping Canada to achieve the lowest debt-to-GDP ratio among G7 countries. However, fiscal stimulus packages and the downturn have ended this string of annual fiscal surpluses. Once the outlook becomes clearer, new debt reduction plans will be needed to maintain fiscal credibility and to provide fiscal space for costs related to population aging and health care.

Currency

The unit of currency is the *Canadian dollar* (CAD) of 100 *cents*. In Sept. 2009 gold reserves were 0·11m. troy oz and foreign exchange reserves totalled US$46,327m. Total money supply was $434,519m. CDN in Dec. 2008.

Inflation rates (based on OECD statistics):

1999	*2000*	*2001*	*2002*	*2003*	*2004*	*2005*	*2006*	*2007*	*2008*
1·7%	2·7%	2·5%	2·3%	2·8%	1·9%	2·2%	2·0%	2·1%	2·4%

Budget

Consolidated federal, provincial, territorial and local government revenue and expenditure for fiscal years ending 31 March (in $1m. CDN):

	2002–03	*2003–04*	*2004–05*	*2005–06*
Revenue	447,861	468,040	500,411	532,183
Expenditure	455,442	476,284	496,111	515,019

In 2005–06 revenue included (in $1m. CDN): income taxes, 224,189; consumption taxes, 107,510; property and related taxes, 48,784; investment income, 44,954; sales of goods and services, 42,592. Expenditure included: social services, 131,146; health, 102,286; education, 82,762; debt charges, 48,068.

On 1 Jan. 1991 a 7% Goods and Services Tax (GST) was introduced, superseding a 13·5% Manufacturers' Sales Tax. This was reduced to 5% from 1 Jan. 2008. A Harmonized Sales Tax (HST) of 14% applies in New Brunswick, Newfoundland and Labrador and Nova Scotia.

Performance

Real GDP growth rates (based on OECD statistics):

1999	*2000*	*2001*	*2002*	*2003*	*2004*	*2005*	*2006*	*2007*	*2008*
5·5%	5·2%	1·8%	2·9%	1·9%	3·1%	3·0%	2·9%	2·5%	0·4%

Real GDP growth contracted by 2·6% in 2009 according to Statistics Canada. Total GDP was US$1,400·1bn. in 2008.

Banking and Finance

The Bank of Canada (established 1935) is the central bank and bank of issue. The *Governor* (Mark J. Carney) is appointed by the Bank's directors for seven-year terms. The Minister of Finance owns the capital stock of the Bank on behalf of Canada. Banks in Canada are chartered under the terms of the Bank Act, which imposes strict conditions on capital reserves, returns to the federal government, types of lending operations, ownership and other matters. As of June 2008 there were 20 domestic banks, 24 foreign bank subsidiaries, 22 full service foreign bank branches and seven foreign bank lending branches operating in Canada; these manage over $2·7trn. CDN in assets between them. Chartered banks accounted collectively for over 70% of the total assets of the Canadian financial services sector, with the six largest domestic banks (Canadian Imperial Bank of Commerce, Bank of Nova Scotia, Bank of Montreal, National Bank of Canada, TD Canada Trust and Royal Bank of Canada) accounting for over 90% of the total assets held by the banking industry. In 2006 Canada had the highest number of automated bank machines per capita in the world (at 1,735 per 1m. inhabitants). The First Nations Bank was founded in Dec. 1996 to provide finance to Inuit and Indian entrepreneurs.

The activities of banks are monitored by the federal Office of the Superintendent of Financial Institutions (OSFI), which reports to the Minister of Finance. Canada's federal financial institutions legislation is reviewed at least every five years. Significant legislative changes were made in 1992, updating the regulatory framework and removing barriers separating the activities of various types of financial institutions. In 1999 legislation was passed allowing foreign banks to establish operations in Canada without having to set up Canadian-incorporated subsidiaries. In 2001 Bill C-8, establishing the Financial Consumer Agency of Canada (the FCAC), was implemented. It aimed to foster competition in the financial sector and provide a holding company option allowing additional organizational flexibility to banks and insurance companies. The FCAC is responsible for enforcing consumer-related provisions of laws governing federal financial institutions.

There are stock exchanges at Calgary (Alberta Stock Exchange), Montreal, Toronto, Vancouver and Winnipeg.

ENERGY AND NATURAL RESOURCES

Environment

Canada's carbon dioxide emissions from the consumption and flaring of fossil fuels in 2008 were the equivalent of 17·3 tonnes per capita.

An *Environmental Performance Index* compiled in 2008 ranked Canada 12th in the world, with 86·6%. The index examined various factors in six areas—air pollution, biodiversity and habitat, climate change, environmental health, productive natural resources and water resources.

Electricity

Generating capacity, 2004, 118·6m. kW. Production, 2004, 598·51bn. kWh (341·06bn. kWh hydro-electric, 165·63bn. kWh thermal and 90·39bn. kWh nuclear); consumption per capita was 18,408 kWh in 2004. In 2003 there were 17 nuclear reactors in use. Canada is one of the world's leading exporters of electricity, with 33·2bn. kWh in 2004.

Oil and Gas

Oil reserves in 2006 were 178·6bn. bbls (5·4bn. bbls of conventional crude oil and condensate reserves and 173·2bn. bbls of oil sands reserves in Alberta). Natural gas reserves in 2008 were 1,630bn. cu. metres. Production of oil, 2008, 156·7m. tonnes; natural gas, 175·2bn. cu. metres.

Canada is the third largest producer of natural gas, after Russia and the USA. Canada's first off-shore field, 250 km off Nova Scotia, began producing in June 1992.

Water

Annual average water usage in Canada is 1,600 cu. metres per person—less than in the USA but nearly twice the average for an industrialized nation.

Minerals

Mineral production in 1,000 tonnes (in 2004 unless otherwise indicated): sand and gravel, 248,159; lignite, 36,736; coal, 29,261; iron ore, 28,596; salt, 13,903; gypsum and anhydrite, 9,339; aluminium, 2,642; lime, 2,410; peat, 1,180; zinc, 791; copper, 563; asbestos, 201; nickel, 187; lead, 77; uranium (2005), 9·9 (the highest of any country in the world); cobalt, 5·1; silver, 1·34; gold, 129 tonnes; diamonds (2005), 12·3m. carats.

Agriculture

Grain growing, dairy farming, fruit farming, ranching and fur farming are all practised. In 2006 over 346,000 people were engaged in agriculture (2% of the labour force).

According to the 2006 census the total land area was 9,220,770 sq. km, of which 675,867 sq. km were on farms. There were 229,373 farms in 2006 (246,923 in 2001); average size, 294·6 ha. Total farm cash receipts (2006), $36,949,543,000 CDN. There were 733,182 tractors in 2006 and 102,924 combine harvesters.

The following table shows the value of receipts for selected agricultural commodities in 2003 (in $1m. CDN):

Crops	13,055	*Livestock and products*	16,213
Barley	387	Beef	5,194
Canola	1,755	Dairy	4,496
Corn for grain	784	Hogs	3,390
Soybeans	715	Poultry	1,785
Wheat	2,441		
Other crops	6,966		

Output (in 1,000 tonnes) and harvested area (in 1,000 ha.) of crops:

	Output		*Harvested Area*	
	2002	*2003*	*2002*	*2003*
Wheat	16,198	23,552	8,836	10,467
Barley	7,489	12,328	3,348	4,446
Maize	8,999	9,587	1,283	1,226
Rapeseeds	4,178	6,669	3,262	4,689
Potatoes	4,697	5,324	171	180
Oats	2,911	3,691	1,379	1,575
Soybeans	2,336	2,268	1,024	1,047
Peas	1,366	2,124	1,050	1,271
Linseeds	679	754	633	728
Tomatoes	792	712	9	9
Sugar beets	345	680	10	12
Lentils	354	520	387	536
Beans	407	346	215	162
Rye	134	327	77	147
Carrots	286	298	8	9
Cabbage	159	179	9	9
Cucumbers and gherkins	170	177	5	5
Onions	168	170	5	6
Sunflower seeds	157	150	95	114

Canada is the world's second largest producer of barley, rapeseeds and oats.

Livestock

In parts of Saskatchewan and Alberta, stockraising is still carried on as a primary industry, but the livestock industry of the country at large is mainly a subsidiary of mixed farming. The following table shows the numbers of livestock (in 1,000) by provinces in July 2009:

Provinces	*Total cattle and calves (including milch cows)*	*Milch cows*	*Sheep and lambs*	*Pigs*
Newfoundland and Labrador	11·80	6·2	4·0	1·8
Prince Edward Island	68·5	13·0	4·1	48·8
Nova Scotia	88·8	22·2	26·2	16·4
New Brunswick	82·1	18·9	8·1	81·2
Quebec	1,385·0	366·0	285·0	3,870·0
Ontario	1,828·8	321·0	315·0	3,064·8
Manitoba	1,430·0	45·5	71·0	2,530·0
Saskatchewan	3,370·0	29·5	114·0	810·0
Alberta	5,870·0	88·5	177·0	1,530·0
British Columbia	705·0	72·0	58·0	112·0
Total	14,840·0	982·8	1,062·4	12,065·0

Other livestock totals (2007 estimates): chickens, 165m.; turkeys, 5·6m.

Livestock products

Slaughterings in 2003: pigs, 23·22m.; cattle, 3·45m.; sheep, 0·72m. Production, 2003 (in 1,000 tonnes): pork, bacon and ham, 1,952; beef and veal, 1,171; poultry meat, 1,091; horse meat, 18; lamb and mutton, 15; cow's milk, 7,880; hens' eggs, 394; cheese, 363; honey, 34; hides, 86.

Fruit production in 2007, in 1,000 tonnes: apples, 446; blueberries, 78; grapes, 76; cranberries, 71; peaches, 34; strawberries, 24; raspberries, 12; pears, 12.

Forestry

Forests make up nearly half of Canada's landmass and 10% of the world's forest cover. Forestry is of great economic importance, and forestry products (pulp, newsprint, building timber) constitute Canada's most valuable exports. In 2007 Canada had 310·1m. ha. of forest land and 92·0m. ha. of other wooded land. 1·7m. ha. were burned by forest fires in 2007. 195·91m. cu. metres of roundwood was produced in 2007.

Fur Trade

In 2006, 1,047,400 wildlife pelts (valued at $25,777,200 CDN) and 1,652,200 ranch-raised pelts (valued at $90,176,000 CDN) were produced.

Fisheries

In 2007 landings of commercial fisheries totalled 1,019,224 tonnes with a value of $1,951m. CDN. More than 96% of the total catch in 2007 was from sea fishing; Atlantic landings totalled 815,903 tonnes and Pacific landings 171,019 tonnes, with freshwater fish totalling 32,303 tonnes. Value of sea fish landed in 2007 was $1,888m. CDN and of freshwater fish $64m. CDN.

INDUSTRY

The leading companies by market capitalization in Canada in March 2009 were: Royal Bank of Canada (US$41·1bn.); Imperial Oil (US$31·3bn.); and EnCana, a gas company (US$30·8bn.).

Value of manufacturing shipments for all industries in 2008 was $598,217·1m. CDN. Principal manufactures in 1,000 tonnes: petrol (2004), 33,024; distillate fuel oil (2004), 31,590; wood pulp (2007), 22,381; paper and paperboard (2007), 18,113; crude steel (2003), 17,000; cement (producers' shipments, 2003), 14,190; pig iron (2003), 8,800; residual fuel oil (2004), 8,724; newsprint (2007), 6,640; jet fuel (2004), 4,597; sulphuric acid (2001), 3,846; kerosene (2004), 1,519; synthetic rubber (2002), 150; sugar (2002), 64. Output of other products: 2·6m. motor vehicles (2003); 44·4bn. cigarettes (2001); sawn lumber (2008), 57·25m. cu. metres; chipboard (2001), 10·73m. cu. metres; plywood (2007), 2·07m. cu. metres.

According to the World Bank's *Doing Business 2010* Canada is the second easiest country in which to start a business, after New Zealand, and the eighth easiest country in which to do business.

Labour

In 2008 there were (in 1,000), 17,125·8 (8,104·5 females) in employment, with principal areas of activity as follows: trade, 2,678·8; manufacturing, 1,970·3; health care and social assistance, 1,903·4; construction, 1,232·2; educational services, 1,192·8; finance, insurance, real estate and leasing, 1,075·4; accommodation and food services, 1,073·5; public administration, 925·7; transport and warehousing, 857·7. In Jan. 2010 the unemployment rate was 8·3%.

In 2006, 813,000 working days were lost in industrial disputes, a sharp decline from 4·1m. in 2005. Between 1996 and 2005 strikes cost Canada an average of 208 days per 1,000 employees a year. Canada's figure was one of the highest in the industrialized world.

Trade Unions

Union membership in 2007 was 4,480,020, of whom 70·8% belonged to the Canadian Labour Congress. Individual unions with the largest memberships in 2007 were the Canadian Union of Public Employees (548,880), National Union of Public and General Employees (340,000), United Steel, Paper and Forestry, Rubber, Manufacturing, Energy, Allied Industrial and Services Workers International Union (280,000), National Automobile, Aerospace, Transportation and General Workers Union of Canada (265,000) and United Food and Commercial Workers Canada (245,330).

A trade union to which the majority of employees in a unit suitable for collective bargaining belong generally has certain rights and duties. An employer is required to negotiate with that union to determine wage rates and other working conditions of employees. The employer, trade union and employees affected are bound by the resulting agreement. Generally, work stoppages do not take place until an established conciliation or mediation procedure has been carried out, and are prohibited while an agreement is in effect.

INTERNATIONAL TRADE

A North American Free Trade Agreement (NAFTA) between Canada, Mexico and the USA was signed on 7 Oct. 1992 and came into force on 1 Jan. 1994.

Imports and Exports

Trade in $1m. CDN:

	2004	2005	2006	2007	2008
Imports	363,158	387,838	404,346	415,229	442,988
Exports	429,006	450,210	453,951	463,127	489,857

Canada is heavily dependent on foreign trade. In 2006 imports of goods and services were equivalent to 34% of GDP and exports equivalent to 36%.

Leading import suppliers, 2007: USA, 54·2%; China, 9·4%; Mexico, 4·2%; Japan, 3·8%; Germany, 2·8%; UK, 2·8%. Leading export markets, 2007: USA, 79·0%; UK, 2·8%; China, 2·1%; Japan, 2·0%; Mexico, 1·1%; Germany, 0·9%.

Main categories of imports, 2008 (in $1m. CDN): machinery and equipment, 122,628·3 (industrial and agricultural machinery, 34,251·8; aircraft and other transportation equipment, 17,544·2); industrial goods and materials, 91,573·8 (metals and metal ores, 32,573·2; chemicals and plastics, 31,561·7); automotive products, 71,959·0 (motor vehicle parts, 30,847·2). Exports, 2008 (in $1m. CDN): energy products, 125,792·2 (crude petroleum, 60,969·7; natural gas, 33,046·0); industrial goods and materials, 111,511·5 (metals and alloys, 39,976·7; chemicals, plastics and fertilizers, 35,910·1); machinery and equipment, 92,994·4 (industrial and agricultural machinery, 23,442·6; aircraft and other transport equipment, 20,339·6); automotive products, 61,082·6 (passenger cars and chassis, 34,069·2; motor vehicle parts, 19,749·5); forestry products, 25,659·2 (newsprint and other paper and paperboard products, 10,092·0; lumber and sawmill products, 9,169·0).

COMMUNICATIONS

Roads

In 2007 there were 1,409,000 km of public roads, including 17,000 km of motorways, 86,000 km of main roads and 115,000 km of secondary roads. The National Highway System, spanning almost 25,000 km, includes the Trans-Canada Highway and other major east–west and north–south highways. While representing only 3% of total road infrastructure, the system carries about 30% of all vehicle travel in Canada.

Registered road motor vehicles totalled 18,868,756 in 2003; they comprised 17,755,082 passenger cars and light vehicles, 660,437 trucks and truck tractors (weighing at least 4,500 kg), 79,875 buses and 373,362 motorcycles and mopeds.

In 2003 freight transport totalled 184,774m. tonne-km.

There were 2,891 fatalities (a rate of 8·8 deaths per 100,000 population) in road accidents in 2006.

Rail

Canada has two great trans-continental systems: the Canadian National Railway system (CN), a body privatized in 1995 which operated 25,185 km of routes in 2005, and the Canadian Pacific Railway (CP), operating 22,370 km. A government-funded organization, VIA Rail, operates passenger services in all regions of Canada; 3·8m. passengers were carried in 2003. There are several provincial and private railways operating 12,705 km (2005).

There are metros in Montreal and Toronto, and tram/light rail systems in Calgary, Edmonton, Ottawa, Toronto and Vancouver.

Civil Aviation

Civil aviation is under the jurisdiction of the federal government. The technical and administrative aspects are supervised by Transport Canada, while the economic functions are assigned to the Canadian Transportation Agency.

The busiest Canadian airport is Toronto Pearson International, which in 2008 handled 32,335,000 passengers (18,439,000 on international flights), ahead of Vancouver International, with 17,852,000 passengers (9,345,000 on domestic flights) and Montreal (Pierre Elliot Trudeau International), with 12,813,000 passengers (5,278,000 on domestic flights). Toronto is also the busiest airport for freight, handling 483,975 tonnes in 2008.

Air Canada (privatized in July 1989) took over its main competitor, Canadian Airlines, in April 2000. In 2005 Air Canada carried 23·5m. passengers (11·9m. on international flights); passenger-km totalled 71·0bn. Other major Canadian airlines are Air Transat and WestJet.

Shipping

In 2000 the merchant marine comprised 861 vessels over 100 GRT including 25 oil tankers. Total tonnage, 2002, 2·80m. GRT, including oil tankers 0·40m. GRT. In 2004 vessels totalling 90,984,000 NRT entered ports and vessels totalling 124,221,000 NRT cleared.

In 2004 the total tonnage handled by Canadian ports was 452·3m. tonnes (265·0m. loaded and 187·3m. unloaded). Canada's leading port in terms of cargo handled is Vancouver. Other major ports are Saint John, Fraser River, Montreal and Quebec.

The major canals are those of the St Lawrence Seaway. Main commodities moved along the seaway are grain, iron ore, coal, other bulk and steel. The St Lawrence Seaway Management Corporation was established in 1998 as a non-profit making corporation to operate the Canadian assets of the seaway for the federal government under a long-term agreement with Transport Canada.

In 2003 total traffic on the Montreal-Lake Ontario (MLO) section of the seaway was 28,900,440 tonnes; on the Welland Canal section it was 31,870,466 tonnes. There were 3,886 vessel transits in 2003, generating $62,257,197 CDN in toll revenue.

Telecommunications

In 2008 there were 18,250,000 main (fixed) telephone lines. In the same year mobile phone subscribers numbered 22,093,000 (664·2 per 1,000 persons). Canada had 25·1m. internet users in 2008 and 30·8m. PCs were in use in 2006. The broadband penetration rate in June 2008 was 27·9 subscribers per 100 inhabitants.

Postal Services

The Canada Post Corporation processed 10·7bn. pieces of mail in 2003. Revenue from operations reached $6·3bn. CDN, an increase of $190m. CDN over 2002. Consolidated net income for 2003 was $253m. CDN, an increase of $182m. CDN over 2002. The Corporation had 23,765 retail points of access at the end of 2003.

SOCIAL INSTITUTIONS

Justice

The courts in Canada are organized in a four-tier structure. The Supreme Court of Canada, based in Ottawa, is the highest court, having general appellate jurisdiction in civil and criminal cases throughout the country. It is comprised of a Chief Justice and eight puisne judges appointed by the Governor-in-Council, with a minimum of three judges coming from Quebec. The second tier consists of the Federal Court of Appeal and the various provincial courts of appeal. The third tier consists of the Federal Court (which replaced the Exchequer Court in 1971), the Tax Court of Canada and the provincial and territorial superior courts (which include both a court of general trial jurisdiction and a provincial court of appeal). The majority of cases are heard by the provincial courts, the fourth tier in the hierarchy. They are generally divided within each province into various divisions defined by the subject matter of their respective jurisdictions (for example a Traffic Division, a Small Claims Division, a Family Division and a Criminal Division).

There were 2,504,559 Criminal Code Offences (excluding traffic) reported in 2005. There were 963 violent crimes per 100,000 population in 2003. In 2003 there were 548 homicides in Canada, giving a rate of 1·7 homicides per 100,000 population (the lowest rate since 1967). In 2007–08 the average daily population in penal institutions (including pre-trial detainees) was 38,348 (116 per 100,000 of national population). The death penalty was abolished for all crimes in 1998.

Police

Total police officers in Canada in 2008 numbered 65,283. There were 12,207 female police officers, up from 3,573 in June 1990. Policing costs in 2007 totalled $10·54bn. CDN.

Royal Canadian Mounted Police (RCMP)

The RCMP is Canada's national police force maintained by the federal government. Established in 1873 as the North-West Mounted Police, it became the Royal Northwest Mounted Police in 1904. Its sphere of operations was expanded in 1918 to include all of Canada west of Thunder Bay, Ontario. In 1920 the force absorbed the Dominion Police and its headquarters was transferred from Regina, Saskatchewan to Ottawa, Ontario. Its title also changed to Royal Canadian Mounted Police. The RCMP is responsible to the Minister of Public Safety and Emergency Preparedness Canada and is controlled by a Commissioner who is empowered to appoint peace officers in all the provinces and territories of Canada.

The responsibilities of the RCMP are national in scope. The administration of justice within the provinces, including the enforcement of the Criminal Code of Canada, is the responsibility of provincial governments, but all the provinces except Ontario and Quebec have entered into contracts with the RCMP to enforce criminal and provincial laws under the direction of the respective Attorneys-General. In these eight provinces the RCMP is under agreement to provide police services to municipalities as well. The RCMP is also responsible for all police work in the three territories—Yukon, Northwest Territories and Nunavut—enforcing federal law and territorial ordinances. The 16 Divisions, alphabetically designated, make up the strength of the RCMP across Canada; they comprise 740 detachments containing varying numbers of police officers. Headquarters Division, as well as the Office of the Commissioner, is located in Ottawa.

Supporting Canada's law enforcement agencies, the RCMP's National Police Services includes seven diverse service lines providing a broad range of programmes and services throughout Canada. It comprises Information and Identification Services, Forensic Laboratory Services, Canadian Police College, Criminal Intelligence Service Canada, Technical Operations, National Child Exploitation Coordination Centre and Chief Information Officer.

In 2005 the Force had a total strength of over 22,000 including regular members, special constables, civilian members and public service employees. It maintained 10,385 motor vehicles, 112 police dog teams across Canada and 195 horses.

The Force has 16 divisions actively engaged in law enforcement, one Headquarters Division and one training division. Marine services are divisional responsibilities and the Force currently has 308 boats at various points across Canada. The Air Services Branch has offices throughout the country and maintains a fleet of 34 operational aircraft.

Education

Under the Constitution the provincial legislatures have powers over education. These are subject to certain qualifications respecting the rights of denominational and minority language schools. School board revenues derive from local taxation on real property, and government grants from general provincial revenue.

In 2006–07 there were 5,162,363 pupils enrolled in elementary and secondary public schools and 376,294 educators (including teaching support staff and administrators).

Enrolment for Indian and Inuit children in elementary/secondary schools for 2003–04: federal schools, 1,686; First Nation managed schools, 72,469; provincial/private schools, 46,266; giving a total of 120,421 students funded by Indian and Northern Affairs Canada (INAC). However, this total represents only a portion of Indian and Inuit students attending elementary/secondary schools.

The Association of Universities and Colleges of Canada represents 94 public and private not-for-profit universities and degree-level colleges. In 2005–06 there were 781,440 full-time and 266,070 part-time students enrolled in universities and 461,589 full-time and 151,911 part-time students enrolled in colleges. Full-time faculty staff in universities numbered 40,800 (13,400 women) in 2006. According to 2006 census data, 3,985,745 adults aged between 25 and 64 had a university degree (up 24% from 3,207,440 in 2001). Six out of every ten adults between 25 and 64 (10,541,900 people according to the census) had completed some form of post-secondary education in 2006, with a university degree, college diploma or post-secondary certificate.

The adult literacy rate is at least 99%.

In 2006–07 public education expenditure represented 3·3% of GDP.

Health

Constitutional responsibility for health care services rests with the provinces and territories. Accordingly, Canada's national health insurance system consists of an interlocking set of provincial and territorial hospital and medical insurance plans conforming to certain national standards rather than a single national programme. The Canada Health Act (which took effect from April 1984 and consolidated the original federal health insurance legislation) sets out the national standards that provinces and territories are required to meet in order to qualify for full federal health contributions, including: provision of a comprehensive range of hospital and medical benefits; universal population coverage; access to necessary services on uniform terms and conditions; portability of benefits; and public administration of provincial and territorial insurance plans. From 1996–97 the federal government's contribution to provincial health and social programmes was consolidated into a single block transfer—the Canada Health and Social Transfer (CHST). However, following reforms introduced by the 2003 Accord on Health Care Renewal to improve health spending accountability it was split into the Canada Health Transfer (CHT) for health and the Canada Social Transfer (CST) for post-secondary education, social service and social assistance in April 2004. The CHT is the federal government's largest transfer and funding is provided to provinces as a combination of cash contributions and tax transfers. In 2009–10 the provinces and territories were to receive a CHT cash transfer of $24·0bn. CDN and CHT tax transfers of $13·9bn. CDN. Over and above these health transfers, the federal government also provides financial support for such provincial and territorial extended health care service programmes as nursing-home care, certain home care services, ambulatory health care services and adult residential care services.

The approach taken by Canada is one of state-sponsored health insurance. The advent of insurance programmes produced little change in the ownership of hospitals, almost all of which are owned by non-government non-profit corporations, or in the rights and privileges of private medical practice. Patients are free to choose their own general practitioner. Except for a small percentage of the population whose care is provided for under other legislation (such as serving members of the Canadian Armed Forces and inmates of federal penitentiaries), all residents are eligible, regardless of whether they are in the workforce. Benefits are available without upper limit so long as they are medically necessary, provided any registration obligations are met.

In addition to the benefits qualifying for federal contributions, provinces and territories provide additional benefits at their own discretion. Most fund their portion of health costs out of general provincial and territorial revenues. Most have charges for long-term chronic hospital care geared, approximately, to the room and board portion of the OAS–GIS payment mentioned under Welfare *below*. Health spending accounted for 10·1% of GDP in 2007.

In 2006 there were: 62,307 physicians, giving a rate of 19 per 10,000 population; 38,310 dentists (12 per 10,000 population); and 327,224 nursing and midwifery personnel (101 per 10,000 population).

Welfare

The social security system provides financial benefits and social services to individuals and their families through programmes administered by federal, provincial and municipal governments and voluntary organizations. Federally, Human Resources and Skills Development is responsible for research into the areas of social issues, provision of grants and contributions for various social services and the administration of income security programmes, including the Old Age Security (OAS) programme, the Guaranteed Income Supplement, the Spouse's Allowance and the Canada Pension Plan (CPP).

The Old Age Security pension is payable to persons 65 years of age and over who satisfy the residence requirements stipulated in the Old Age Security Act. The amount payable, whether full or partial, is also governed by stipulated conditions, as is the payment of an OAS pension to a recipient who absents himself from Canada. OAS pensioners with little or no income apart from OAS may, upon application, receive a full or partial supplement known as the Guaranteed Income Supplement (GIS). Entitlement is normally based on the pensioner's income in the preceding year, calculated in accordance with the Income Tax Act. The spouse of an OAS pensioner, aged 60 to 64, meeting the same residence requirements as those stipulated for OAS, may be eligible for a full or partial Spouse's Allowance (SPA). SPA is payable, on application, depending on the annual combined income of the couple (not including the pensioner spouse's basic OAS pension or GIS). In 1979 the SPA programme was expanded to include a spouse, who is eligible for SPA in the month the pensioner spouse dies, until the age of 65 or until remarriage (Extended Spouse's Allowance). Since Sept. 1985 SPA has also been available to low income widow(er)s aged 60–64 regardless of the age of their spouse at death.

As of 1 July 2004 the basic OAS pension was $466·63 CDN monthly; the maximum Guaranteed Income Supplement was $554·59 CDN monthly for a single pensioner or a married pensioner whose spouse was not receiving a pension or a Spouse's Allowance, and $361·24 CDN monthly for each spouse of a married couple where both were pensioners.

The Canada Pension Plan is designed to provide workers with a basic level of income protection in the event of retirement, disability or death. Benefits may be payable to a contributor, a surviving spouse or an eligible child. Actuarially adjusted retirement benefits may begin as early as age 60 or as late as age 70. Benefits are determined by the contributor's earnings and contributions made to the Plan. Contribution is compulsory for most employed and self-employed Canadians aged 18 to 65. The CPP does not operate in Quebec, which has exercised its constitutional prerogative to establish a similar plan. In 2004 the maximum retirement pension payable under CPP was $814·17 CDN; the maximum disability pension was $992·80 CDN; and the maximum surviving spouse's pension was $488·50 CDN (for survivors 65 years of age and over) or 60% of the retirement pension which the deceased contributor would have received at age 65. The survivor pension payable to a surviving spouse under 65 (maximum of $454·42 CDN in 2004) is composed of two parts: a flat-rate component and an earnings-related portion.

As projections indicated that the CPP was lacking sufficient assets to meet long-term obligations, contribution rates were increased from 6% in 1997 to 9·9% of maximum pensionable earnings by 2003. The Canada Pension Plan Investment Board, an independent investment organization separate from the CPP, was established to invest excess CPP funds in a diversified portfolio of securities, beginning operations in April 1998. In 2004 the range of yearly pensionable earnings was from $3,500 CDN to $40,500 CDN. A total of 4·5m. Canadians received Canada Pension Plan benefits amounting to $23·8bn. CDN in fiscal year 2004–05. Social security agreements co-ordinate the operation of the Old Age Security and the CPP with the comparable social security programmes of certain other countries.

Canada Child Tax Benefit (CCTB) is a tax-free monthly payment made to eligible families to help them with the cost of raising children under 18. Included with the CCTB is the National Child Benefit Supplement (NCBS), a monthly benefit for low-income families with children.

RELIGION

Membership of religious denominations (according to census analysis):

	1991	*2001*	*% change 1991–2001*
Anglican Church of Canada	2,188,110	2,035,500	–7·0
Canadian Baptist Ministries	663,360	729,470	10·0
Christian Orthodox	387,395	479,620	23·8
Lutheran Church	636,205	606,590	–4·7
Pentecostal Assemblies of Canada	436,435	369,475	–15·3
Presbyterian Church	636,295	409,830	–35·6
Roman Catholic Church	12,203,625	12,793,125	4·8
United Church of Canada	3,093,120	2,839,125	–8·2

Membership of other denominations in 2001 (census figures): Jehovah's Witnesses, 154,745; Jews, 329,995; Latter-day Saints

(Mormons), 104,750; Mennonites, 191,465; Muslims, 579,640; Salvation Army, 87,785. In Feb. 2010 the Roman Catholic church had three cardinals.

CULTURE

World Heritage Sites

Sites under Canadian jurisdiction which appear on UNESCO's world heritage list are (with year entered on list): L'Anse aux Meadows National Historic Site (1978), the remains of an 11th-century Viking settlement in Newfoundland; Nahanni National Park (1978), containing canyons, waterfalls and a limestone cave system—fauna includes wolves, grizzly bears, caribou, Dall's sheep and mountain goats; Dinosaur Provincial Park (1979), in Alberta, a major area for fossil discoveries, including 35 species of dinosaur; SGaang Gwaii (Anthony Island) (1981), illustrating the Haida people's art and way of life; Head-Smashed-In Buffalo Jump (1981), in southwest Alberta, incorporating an aboriginal camp—the name relates to the aboriginal custom of killing buffalo by chasing them over a precipice; Wood Buffalo National Park (1983), in north-central Canada, home to America's largest population of wild bison as well as important fauna; Canadian Rocky Mountain Parks (1984 and 1990), incorporating the neighbouring parks of Banff, Jasper, Kootenay and Yoho, as well as the Mount Robson, Mount Assiniboine and Hamber provincial parks, and the Burgess Shale fossil site; Historic District of Québec (1985), retaining aspects of its French colonial past; Gros Morne National Park (1987), in Newfoundland; Old Town Lunenburg (1995), a well-preserved British colonial settlement established in 1753; Miguasha Park (1999), among the world's most important fossil sites for fish species of the Devonian age, forerunners of the first four-legged, air-breathing terrestrial vertebrates (tetrapods); Rideau Canal (2007), a 19th century monumental canal running from Ottawa to Kingston Harbour; and Joggins Fossil Cliffs (2008), a 689 ha. palaeontological site along the coast of Nova Scotia.

Two UNESCO World Heritage Sites fall under joint Canadian and US jurisdiction: Kluane/Wrangell-St Elias/Glacier Bay/Tatshenshini-Alsek (1979, 1992 and 1994), parks in Yukon, British Columbia and Alaska, include the world's largest non-polar icefield, glaciers and high peaks, and important fauna; Waterton Glacier International Peace Park (1995), in Alberta and Montana, with collections of plant and mammal species as well as prairie, forest, and alpine and glacial features.

Broadcasting

The independent Canadian Radio-Television and Telecommunications Commission (CRTC) regulates broadcasting and telecommunications. The Canadian Broadcasting Corporation (CBC) is the public broadcaster. Transmitting in English and French, CBC operates two national TV channels and four radio networks. Radio Canada International is the external service. There are also major commercial television networks (including CTV broadcasting in English and TVA in French) and around 2,000 licensed radio stations.

In 2006 there were 12·4m. TV-equipped households (colour by NTSC) and 7,782,000 subscribers to cable television. The number of digital cable TV subscriptions has grown steadily; as at Aug. 2007 there were 3·3m., representing four out of ten cable TV subscribers. Cable operators earned $1·6bn. CDN in 2007.

Cinema

In 2004–05 there were 2,933 cinema screens (including 91 drive-ins); total admissions were 120·3m. In 2006, 74 feature films were produced in Canada.

Press

In 2003 there were 101 daily papers with a total average circulation of 4·93m.; *The Toronto Star* had the largest circulation at 460,000, then *The Globe and Mail* with 315,000. There were 1,071 non-daily papers in 2003, with a circulation of 21,235,000. In 2004 a total of 16,776 book titles were published.

Tourism

In 2008 foreign visitors made 16·97m. overnight trips to Canada (provisional) of which 73·6% were made by Americans. The next biggest tourist markets are the UK, France, Germany and Japan. Tourism expenditure amounted to US$15·83bn. in 2005. In 2008, 662,900 were employed in tourism.

Festivals

The Quebec Winter Festival is held each Feb. The Montreal Jazz Festival is in June while the Calgary Stampede (the world's largest rodeo, incorporating a series of concerts and a carnival) is in July. Also in July are the Ottawa International Jazz Festival, the Québec Festival d'Été/Summer Festival (featuring music and art performances) and the Montréal Juste Pour Rire/Just for Laughs comedy festival. The Toronto international film festival takes place in Sept. and the Vancouver international film festival is the following month. Canada Day, held each July, is marked nationwide with firework displays, parades and parties.

Libraries

In 2002 the National Library and the National Archives of Canada amalgamated to create the Library and Archives of Canada. Collections comprise some 20m. books, periodicals, newspapers, microfilms, literary texts and government publications.

Museums and Galleries

In 2002–03 there were 2,517 heritage institutions (excluding nature parks) attracting 58·8m. visits and generating operating revenues of $1·3bn. CDN.

DIPLOMATIC REPRESENTATIVES

Of Canada in the United Kingdom (Macdonald House, 1 Grosvenor Sq., London, W1K 4AB)
High Commissioner: James R. Wright.

Of the United Kingdom in Canada (80 Elgin St., Ottawa, K1P 5K7)
High Commissioner: Anthony Cary, CMG.

Of Canada in the USA (501 Pennsylvania Ave., NW, Washington, D.C., 20001)
Ambassador: Gary Doer.

Of the USA in Canada (490 Sussex Drive, Ottawa, K1N 1G8)
Ambassador: David Jacobson.

Of Canada to the United Nations
Ambassador: John McNee.

Of Canada to the European Union
Ambassador: Ross Hornby.

FURTHER READING

Canadian Annual Review of Politics and Public Affairs. From 1960
Canadian Encyclopedia. 2000
Brown, R. C., *An Illustrated History of Canada.* 1991
Cook, C., *Canada after the Referendum of 1992.* 1994
Dawson, R. M. and Dawson, W. F., *Democratic Government in Canada.* 5th ed. 1989
Fierlbeck, Katherine, *The Development of Political Thought in Canada: An Anthology.* 2005
Jackson, R. J. and Jackson, D., *Politics in Canada: Culture, Institutions, Behaviour and Public Policy.* 6th ed. 2006
Longille, P., *Changing the Guard: Canada's Defence in a World in Transition.* 1991
O'Reilly, Marc, *Handbook of Canadian Foreign Policy.* 2006
Silver, A. I. (ed.) *Introduction to Canadian History.* 1994

Other more specialized titles are listed under CONSTITUTION AND GOVERNMENT *above.*

Library and Archives Canada: 395 Wellington Street, Ottawa, K1A ON4.
Librarian and Archivist of Canada: Daniel J. Caron.
National Statistical Office: Statistics Canada, Ottawa, K1A 0T6.
Website: http://www.statcan.gc.ca

CANADIAN PROVINCES

GENERAL DETAILS

The ten provinces each have a separate parliament and administration, with a Lieut.-Governor, appointed by the Governor-General in Council at the head of the executive. They have full powers to regulate their own local affairs and dispose of their revenues, provided that they do not interfere with the action and policy of the central administration. Among the subjects assigned exclusively to the provincial legislatures are: the amendment of the provincial constitution, except as regards the office of the Lieut.-Governor; property and civil rights; direct taxation for revenue purposes; borrowing; management and sale of Crown lands; provincial hospitals, reformatories, etc.; shop, saloon, tavern, auctioneer and other licences for local or provincial purposes; local works and undertakings, except lines of ships, railways, canals, telegraphs, etc., extending beyond the province or connecting with other provinces, and excepting also such works as the Canadian Parliament declares are for the general good; marriages, administration of justice within the province; education. On 18 July 1994 the federal and provincial governments signed an agreement easing inter-provincial barriers on government procurement, labour mobility, transport licences and product standards. Federal legislation of Dec. 1995 grants provinces a right of constitutional veto.

For the administration of the three territories *see* Northwest Territories, Nunavut and Yukon *below*.

Areas of the ten provinces and three territories (Northwest Territories, Nunavut and Yukon) (in sq. km) and population at recent censuses:

Province	*Land area*	*Total land and fresh water area*	*Population, 1996*	*Population, 2001*	*Population, 2006*
Newfoundland (Nfld.)	373,872	405,212	551,792	512,930	505,469
Prince Edward Island (PEI)	5,660	5,660	134,557	135,294	135,851
Nova Scotia (NS)	53,338	55,284	909,282	908,007	913,462
New Brunswick (NB)	71,450	72,908	738,133	729,498	729,997
Quebec (Que.)[1]	1,365,128	1,542,056	7,138,795	7,237,479	7,546,131
Ontario (Ont.)[1]	917,741	1,076,395	10,753,573	11,410,046	12,160,282
Manitoba (Man.)	553,556	647,797	1,113,898	1,119,583	1,148,401
Saskatchewan (Sask.)[1]	591,670	651,036	990,237	978,933	968,157
Alberta (Alta.)[1]	642,317	661,848	2,696,826	2,974,807	3,290,350
British Columbia (BC)[1]	925,186	944,735	3,724,500	3,907,738	4,113,487
Nunavut (Nvt.)	1,936,113	2,093,190		26,745[2]	29,474
Northwest Territories (NWT)	1,183,085	1,346,106	64,402	37,360[3]	41,464
Yukon (YT)	474,391	482,443	30,766	28,674	30,372

[1]Excludes population data from incompletely enumerated Indian reserves and Indian settlements.
[2]Nunavut only came into existence in 1999.
[3]The population of the Northwest Territories declined so steeply between 1996 and 2001 because of the formation of Nunavut, previously part of the Northwest Territories, in 1999.

Local Government

Under the terms of the British North America Act the provinces are given full powers over local government. All local government institutions are, therefore, supervised by the provinces, and are incorporated and function under provincial acts.

The acts under which municipalities operate vary from province to province. A municipal corporation is usually administered by an elected council headed by a mayor or reeve, whose powers to administer affairs and to raise funds by taxation and other methods are set forth in provincial laws, as is the scope of its obligations to, and on behalf of, the citizens. Similarly, the types of municipal corporations, their official designations and the requirements for their incorporation vary between provinces. The following table sets out the classifications as at the 2006 census:

	Federal electoral districts	*Economic regions*	*Census divisions*
Nfld.	7	4	11
PEI	4	1	3[1]
NS	11	5	18[1]
NB	10	5	15[1]
Que.	75	17	98[2]
Ont.	106	11	49[3]
Man.	14	8	23
Sask.	14	6	18
Alta.	28	8	19
BC	36	8	28[4]
Nvt.	1	1	3[5]
NWT	1	1	2[5]
YT	1	1	1[6]

[1]Counties. [2]81 municipalités régionales de comté, 12 territoires équivalents, 5 census divisions.
[3]19 counties, 10 districts, 9 census divisions, 6 regional municipalities, 3 united counties, 1 district municipality, 1 management board. [4]27 regional districts, 1 region.
[5]Regions. [6]Territory.

SOCIAL INSTITUTIONS

Justice

The administration of justice within the provinces, including the enforcement of the Criminal Code of Canada, is the responsibility of provincial governments, but all the provinces except Ontario and Quebec have entered into contracts with the Royal Canadian Mounted Police (RCMP) to enforce criminal and provincial law. In addition, in these eight provinces the RCMP is under agreement to provide police services to municipalities.

Alberta

KEY HISTORICAL EVENTS

The southern half of Alberta was administered from 1670 as part of Rupert's land by the Hudson's Bay Company. Trading posts were set up after 1783 when the North West Company took a share in the fur trade. In 1869 Rupert's land was transferred from the Hudson's Bay Company (which had absorbed its rival in 1821) to the new Dominion and in the following year this land was combined with the former Crown land of the North Western Territories to form the Northwest Territories. In 1882 'Alberta' first appeared as a provisional 'district', consisting of the southern half of the present province. In 1905 the Athabasca district to the north was added when provincial status was granted to Alberta.

TERRITORY AND POPULATION

The area of the province is 661,848 sq. km, 642,317 sq. km being land area and 16,531 sq. km water area. The population at the 2006 census was 3,290,350; Oct. 2009 estimate, 3,704,000. Alberta had the fastest-growing population of any Canadian province between 1996 and 2006, with a 25·2% increase over the ten-year period. The urban population (2006), centres of 1,000 or over, was 82·1% and the rural 17·9%. Population (2006 census) of the 16 cities, as well as the two largest specialized municipalities: Calgary, 988,193; Edmonton, 730,372; Red Deer, 82,772; Lethbridge, 74,637; St Albert, 57,719; Medicine Hat, 56,997; Grande Prairie, 47,076; Airdrie, 28,927; Spruce Grove, 19,496; Leduc, 16,967; Lloydminster (Alberta portion), 15,910; Camrose, 15,620; Fort Saskatchewan, 14,957; Brooks, 12,498; Cold Lake, 11,991; Wetaskiwin, 11,673; Specialized Municipality of Strathcona County (Sherwood Park), 82,551; Specialized Municipality of Wood Buffalo (Fort McMurray), 51,496.

SOCIAL STATISTICS

Births in 2007–08 numbered 49,568 (a rate of 13·9 per 1,000 population) and deaths 20,699 (rate of 5·8 per 1,000 population). There were 18,632 marriages in 2006 and 8,075 divorces in 2005.

CLIMATE

Alberta has a continental climate of warm summers and cold winters—extremes of temperature. For the capital city, Edmonton, the hottest month is usually July (mean 17·5°C), while the coldest are Dec. and Jan. (–12°C). Rainfall amounts are greatest between May and Sept. In a year, the average precipitation is 461 mm (19·6") with about 129·6 cm of snowfall.

CONSTITUTION AND GOVERNMENT

The constitution of Alberta is contained in the British North America Act of 1867, and amending Acts; also in the Alberta Act of 1905, passed by the Parliament of the Dominion of Canada, which created the province out of the then Northwest Territories. The province is represented by five members in the Senate and 26 in the House of Commons of Canada.

The executive is vested nominally in the Lieut.-Governor, who is appointed by the federal government, but actually in the Executive Council or the Cabinet of the legislature. Legislative power is vested in the Assembly in the name of the Queen.

Members of the 83-member Legislative Assembly are elected by the universal vote of adults, 18 years of age and older.

RECENT ELECTIONS

In elections on 3 March 2008 the Progressive Conservative Party won 52·7% of the vote (taking 72 of 83 seats), the Liberal Party 26·4% (9), the New Democrats 8·5% (2), the Wildrose Alliance Party 6·8% (0) and the Green Party 4·6% (0). Turnout was 40·7%.

CURRENT ADMINISTRATION

Lieut.-Governor: Normie Kwong (sworn in 20 Jan. 2005).

As of Feb. 2010 the members of the Executive Council were as follows:

Premier, President of Executive Council: Ed Stelmach; b. 1951 (Progressive Conservative; sworn in 14 Dec. 2006).

Deputy Premier and Minister of Advanced Education and Technology: Doug Horner. *Finance and Enterprise:* Ted Morton. *Education:* David Hancock. *President of the Treasury Board:* Lloyd Snelgrove. *International and Intergovernmental Relations:* Iris Evans. *Energy:* Ron Liepert. *Transportation:* Luke Ouellette. *Sustainable Resource Development:* Mel Knight. *Attorney General and Minister of Justice:* Alison Redford. *Environment:* Rob Renner. *Health and Wellness:* Gene Zwozdesky. *Children and Youth Services:* Yvonne Fritz. *Agriculture and Rural Development:* Jack Hayden. *Infrastructure:* Ray Danyluk. *Seniors and Community Support:* Mary Anne Jablonski. *Culture and Community Spirit:* Lindsay Blackett. *Service Alberta:* Heather Klimchuk. *Tourism, Parks and Recreation:* Cindy Ady. *Municipal Affairs:* Hector Goudreau. *Solicitor General and Minister of Public Security:* Franke Oberle. *Aboriginal Relations:* Len Webber. *Housing and Urban Affairs:* Jonathan Denis. *Employment and Immigration:* Thomas Lukaszuk.

Office of the Premier: http://premier.alberta.ca

ECONOMY

GDP per person in 2004 was $58,537 CDN.

Budget

The budgetary revenue and expenditure (in $1m. CDN) for years ending 31 March were as follows:

	2000–01	*2001–02*	*2002–03*	*2003–04*	*2004–05*
Revenue	25,527	21,926	22,662	25,887	29,328
Expenditure	18,956	20,845	20,529	21,751	24,153

Performance

Real GDP growth was 6·6% in 2006 (5·3% in 2005 and 5·2% in 2004). Alberta had the highest GDP growth rate of all the Canadian provinces and territories in 2004, 2005 and 2006.

Banking and Finance

Personal income per capita (2004), $34,713 CDN.

ENERGY AND NATURAL RESOURCES

Environment

There are five national parks in Alberta totalling 63,045 sq. km, the largest area of any province in Canada. There are also 519 parks and protected areas in Alberta covering 2,755,634 ha.

Oil and Gas

Oil sands underlie some 60,000 sq. km of Alberta, the four major deposits being: the Athabasca, Cold Lake, Peace River and Buffalo Head Hills deposits. Some 7% (3,250 sq. km) of the Athabasca deposit can be recovered by open-pit mining techniques. The rest of the Athabasca, and all the deposits in the other areas, are deeper reserves which must be developed through *in situ* techniques. These reserves reach depths of 760 metres. In 2004 Alberta produced 773,300 bbls per day of crude oil and 962,300 bbls per day of synthetic crude oil and bitumen. The 2004 value of Albertan producers' sales of crude oil, condensate and pentanes was $40·94bn. CDN. Sales of oilsands were worth $14·94bn. CDN. Alberta produced 67% of Canada's crude petroleum output in 2004.

Natural gas is found in abundance in numerous localities. In 2004, 4,923bn. cu. ft valued at $31·1bn. CDN were produced in Alberta.

Minerals

Coal production in 2004 was 27·2m. tonnes with 1·7m. tonnes of coal being exported.

The preliminary value of mineral production in 2004 (excluding oil and gas) was $1,200·0m. CDN.

Agriculture

There were 49,431 farms in Alberta in 2006 with a total area of 21,095,393 ha.; 9,621,606 ha. were land in crop in 2006. The majority of farms are made up of cattle, followed by grains and oilseed, and wheat. For particulars of livestock *see* CANADA: Agriculture.

Farm cash receipts in 2004 totalled $8,043·4m. CDN of which crops contributed $2,616·8m. CDN, livestock and products $3,993·3m. CDN and direct payments $1,433·3m. CDN.

Forestry

Forest and other wooded land in 2001 covered some 36,388,000 ha. In 2003–04 Alberta had a regulated harvest of 24,819,100 cu. metres of net merchantable forest.

Fisheries

The largest catch in commercial fishing is whitefish. Perch, tullibee, walleye, pike and lake trout are also caught in smaller quantities. Commercial fish production in 2003–04 was 2,127 tonnes, value $3·46m. CDN.

INDUSTRY

The leading manufacturing industries are food and beverages, petroleum refining, metal fabricating, wood industries, primary metal, chemical and chemical products and non-metallic mineral products.

Manufacturing shipments had a total value of $52,965·8m. CDN in 2004. Greatest among these shipments were (in $1m. CDN): refined petroleum and coal products, 10,018; chemicals and chemical products, 9,645; food, 9,087; fabricated metal products, 4,135; machinery, 4,062; wood products, 3,753; primary metal, 2,137; paper and allied products, 1,784; non-metal mineral products, 1,695; and computer and electronic products, 1,471.

Total retail sales in 2004 were $43,703m. CDN, as compared to 2003 with $38,925m. CDN in sales. Main sales in 2004 were (in $1m. CDN): automobiles, 10,007·8; food, 7,650·9; general merchandise, 5,032·2; fuel 4,072·8; and pharmacies and personal care, 2,111·8.

Labour

In 2004 the labour force was 1,843,400 (837,200 females), of whom approximately 1,757,900 (797,700) were employed. In 2004 a total of 40,000 new jobs were created. Alberta's unemployment rate dropped to 4·6% in 2004, compared to the national average of 7·2%.

INTERNATIONAL TRADE

Imports and Exports

Alberta's exports were valued at a record $80·6bn. CDN in 2007, an increase of 3·7% on 2006. The largest export markets were the USA, China, Japan, Mexico and the Netherlands, which together accounted for 93% of Alberta's international exports. Energy accounted for 68% of exports in 2007.

COMMUNICATIONS

Roads

In 2005 there were 30,800 km of provincial highways and 153,500 km of local roads.

On 31 March 2005 there were 2,459,926 motor vehicles registered.

Rail

In 2003 the length of main railway lines was 7,136 km. There are light rail networks in Edmonton (12·3 km) and Calgary (35·7 km).

Civil Aviation

Calgary International is a major international airport. It handled 10,149,000 passengers (7,377,000 on domestic flights) in 2005.

Telecommunications

The primary telephone system is owned and operated by the Telus Corporation. Telus Corporation had 1,998,366 telephone subscriber lines (including residential and business lines) in service in 2002; in all, 98·2% of Alberta's households had fixed telephone lines. In 2002, 60·9% of households had mobile phones. Alberta also had the second highest percentage of households with computers in Canada at 70·6%.

SOCIAL INSTITUTIONS

Justice

The Supreme Judicial authority of the province is the Court of Appeal. Judges of the Court of Appeal and Court of Queen's Bench are appointed by the Federal government and hold office until retirement at the age of 75. There are courts of lesser jurisdiction in both civil and criminal matters. The Court of Queen's Bench has full jurisdiction over civil proceedings. A Provincial Court which has jurisdiction in civil matters up to $2,000 CDN is presided over by provincially appointed judges. Youth Courts have power to try boys and girls 12–17 years old inclusive for offences against the Young Offenders Act.

The jurisdiction of all criminal courts in Alberta is enacted in the provisions of the Criminal Code. The system of procedure in civil and criminal cases conforms as nearly as possible to the English system. In 2003, 325,894 Criminal Code offences were reported, including 63 homicides.

Education

Schools of all grades are included under the term of public school (including those in the separate school system, which are publicly supported). The same board of trustees controls the schools from kindergarten to university entrance. In 2001–02 there were approximately 546,961 pupils enrolled in grades 1–12, including private schools and special education programmes. The University of Alberta (in Edmonton), founded in 1907, had, in 2004–05, 35,666 students; the University of Calgary had 28,306 students; Athabasca University had 29,542 students; the University of Lethbridge had 7,086 students. Alberta has 34 post-secondary institutions including four universities and two technical colleges.

CULTURE

Tourism

Alberta attracted more than 4,661,000 visitors from outside the province in 2003. It is known for its mountains, museums, parks and festivals. Total tourism receipts in 2003 were $4·3bn. CDN.

FURTHER READING

Savage, H., Kroetsch, R., Wiebe, R., *Alberta*. 1993

Statistical office: Alberta Finance, Statistics, Room 259, Terrace Bldg, 9515–107 St., Edmonton, AB T5K 2C3.
Websites: http://www.albertacanada.com; http://www.discoveralberta.com

---

British Columbia

KEY HISTORICAL EVENTS

British Columbia, formerly known as New Caledonia, was first administered by the Hudson's Bay Company. In 1849 Vancouver Island was given crown colony status and in 1853 the Queen Charlotte Islands became a dependency. The discovery of gold on the Fraser river and the following influx of population resulted in the creation in 1858 of the mainland crown colony of British Columbia, to which the Strikine Territory (established 1862) was later added. In 1866 the two colonies were united.

TERRITORY AND POPULATION

British Columbia has an area of 944,735 sq. km of which land area is 925,186 sq. km. The capital is Victoria. The province is bordered westerly by the Pacific Ocean and Alaska Panhandle, northerly by the Yukon and Northwest Territories, easterly by the Province of Alberta and southerly by the USA along the 49th parallel. A chain of islands, the largest of which are Vancouver Island and the Queen Charlotte Islands, affords protection to the mainland coast.

The population at the 2006 census was 4,113,487; Oct. 2009 estimate, 4,479,900.

The principal metropolitan areas and cities and their population census for 2006 are as follows: Metropolitan Vancouver, 2,116,581; Metropolitan Victoria, 330,088; Abbotsford (amalgamated with Matsqui), 123,864; Kelowna, 106,707; Kamloops, 80,376; Nanaimo, 78,692; Prince George, 70,981; Chilliwack, 69,217; Vernon, 35,944; Penticton, 31,909; Campbell River, 29,572;

Courtenay, 21,940; Cranbrook, 18,267; Port Alberni, 17,548; Fort St John, 17,402; Salmon Arm, 16,012.

SOCIAL STATISTICS

Births in 2007–08 numbered 44,087 (a rate of 10·1 per 1,000 population) and deaths 31,789 (rate of 7·3 per 1,000 population). There were 20,665 marriages in 2006 and 9,954 divorces in 2005. Life expectancy, at 81·4 years in 2006, is the highest in Canada.

CLIMATE

The climate is cool temperate, but mountain influences affect temperatures and rainfall considerably. Driest months occur in summer. Vancouver, Jan. 36°F (2·2°C), July 64°F (17·8°C). Annual rainfall 58" (1,458 mm).

CONSTITUTION AND GOVERNMENT

The British North America Act of 1867 provided for eventual admission into Canadian Confederation, and on 20 July 1871 British Columbia became the sixth province of the Dominion.

British Columbia has a unicameral legislature of 85 elected members. Government policy is determined by the Executive Council responsible to the Legislature. The Lieut.-Governor is appointed by the Governor-General of Canada, usually for a term of five years, and is the head of the executive government of the province.

The Legislative Assembly is elected for a maximum term of five years. There are 85 electoral districts. Every Canadian citizen 18 years and over, having resided a minimum of six months in the province, duly registered, is entitled to vote. The province is represented in the Federal Parliament by 36 members in the House of Commons and six Senators.

RECENT ELECTIONS

At the Legislative Assembly elections of 12 May 2009 the Liberal Party won 46·0% of the vote and 49 of the 85 available seats, the New Democratic Party won 42·1% and 35 seats, and the Green Party 8·1%; an independent took one seat. Turnout was 51%.

CURRENT ADMINISTRATION

Lieut.-Governor: Steven Point (sworn in 1 Oct. 2007).

The Liberal Executive Council comprised in Feb. 2010:

Premier, President of the Executive Council: Gordon Campbell.

Deputy Premier and Minister for Finance: Colin Hansen. *Aboriginal Relations and Reconciliation:* George Abbott. *Advanced Education and Labour Market Development:* Moira Stilwell. *Agriculture and Lands:* Steve Thomson. *Children and Family Development and Minister Responsible for Child Care:* Mary Polak. *Citizens' Services:* Ben Stewart. *Community and Rural Development:* Bill Bennett. *Education and Minister Responsible for Early Learning and Literacy:* Dr Margaret MacDiarmid. *Energy, Mines and Petroleum Resources:* Blair Lekstrom. *Environment:* Barry Penner. *Forests and Range and Minister Responsible for the Integrated Land Management Bureau:* Pat Bell. *Health Services:* Kevin Falcon. *Healthy Living and Sport:* Ida Chong. *Housing and Social Development:* Rich Coleman. *Labour:* Murray Coell. *Public Safety and Solicitor General:* Kash Heed. *Small Business, Technology and Economic Development:* Iain Black. *Tourism, Culture and the Arts:* Kevin Krueger. *Transportation and Infrastructure:* Shirley Bond. *Minister of State for Climate Action:* John Yap. *Minister of State for Intergovernmental Relations:* Naomi Yamamoto. *Minister of State for Mining:* Randy Hawes. *Minister Responsible for the Olympics and ActNow BC:* Mary McNeil. *Attorney General:* Mike de Jong.

Office of the Premier: http://www.gov.bc.ca/prem

ECONOMY

GDP per person in 2004 was $37,289 CDN.

Budget

Total revenue in 2005–06 was $34,070m. CDN (own source revenue, $28,333m. CDN; general purpose transfers, $2,086m. CDN; special purpose transfers, $3,651m. CDN). Total expenditures in 2005–06 came to $32,910m. CDN (including: health, $12,468m. CDN; education, $6,562m. CDN; social services, $4,923m. CDN; debt charges, $2,602m. CDN; transport and communication, $1,671m. CDN; resource conservation and industrial development, $1,452m. CDN).

ENERGY AND NATURAL RESOURCES

Electricity

Generation in 2007 totalled 71,820 GWh (64,337 GWh from hydro-electric sources), of which 10,984 GWh were delivered outside the province. Available within the province were 68,863 GWh (with imports of 8,027 GWh).

Oil and Gas

In 2004 natural gas production, from the northeastern part of the province, was valued at $5·83bn. CDN.

Water

Canada accounts for a quarter of the world's fresh water supply, a third of which is located in British Columbia. An extensive hydro-electric generation system has been developed in the province.

Minerals

Coal, copper, gold, zinc, silver and molybdenum are the most important minerals produced but natural gas amounts to approximately half of the value of mineral and fuel extraction. The value of mineral production in 2006 was estimated at $5·99bn. CDN. Coal production (from the northeastern and southeastern regions) was valued at $2·11bn. CDN. Copper was the most valuable metal with production totalling $2·19bn. CDN; gold production amounted to $344m. CDN.

Agriculture

Only 3% of the total land area is arable or potentially arable. Farm holdings (19,844 in 2006) cover 2·8m. ha. with an average size of 143 ha. Farm cash receipts in 2007 were $2·4bn. CDN, led by dairy products valued at $424m. CDN, floriculture and nursery products valued at $404m. CDN and poultry and eggs valued at $382m. CDN. For particulars of livestock *see* CANADA: Agriculture.

Forestry

Around 49·9m. ha. are considered productive forest land of which 48·0m. ha. are provincial crown lands managed by the Ministry of Forests. Approximately 96% of the forested land is coniferous. The total timber harvest in 2007 was 72·9m. cu. metres. Output of forest-based products, 2007: lumber, 3·7m. cu. metres; plywood (2006), 1·6m. cu. metres; pulp, 4·7m. tonnes; newsprint, paper and paperboard, 2·5m. tonnes.

Fisheries

In 2006 the total landed value of the catch was $786m. CDN; wholesale value $1·3bn. CDN. Salmon (wild and farmed) generated 53% of the wholesale value of seafood products, followed by groundfish and shellfish. In 2006, 7,800 people worked in the commercial fishery, aquaculture and fish processing industries.

INDUSTRY

The value of shipments from all manufacturing industries reached $42·2bn. CDN in 2004, including wood ($13·0bn. CDN), paper ($5·9bn. CDN), food ($5·0bn. CDN) and primary metals ($2·4bn. CDN).

Labour

In 2007 the labour force averaged 2,366,000 persons with 2,266,000 employed (47% female) and 100,000 unemployed

(4·2%). Of the employed workforce 1·77m. were in service industries and 496,000 in goods production. There were 365,000 employed in trade, 240,000 in healthcare and social assistance, 205,000 in manufacturing, 197,000 in construction and 173,000 in accommodation and food industries.

Trade Unions

In 2007, 32% of the province's paid workers were unionized. The largest unions are: Canadian Union of Public Employees (110,000 members in 2006); B.C. Government and Service Employees' Union and affiliates (60,000 in 2006); and B.C. Teachers' Federation (45,000 in 2006).

INTERNATIONAL TRADE

Imports and Exports

Imports in 2007 totalled $38,687m. CDN in value, while exports amounted to $31,459m. CDN. The USA is the largest market for products exported through British Columbia customs ports ($19,009m. CDN in 2007), followed by Japan ($4,102m. CDN) and People's Republic of China, excluding Hong Kong ($1,744m. CDN).

Wood products accounted for 22·7% of exports in 2007, energy products 19·6%, pulp and paper products 16·2%, machinery and equipment 11·0% and metallic mineral products 10·9%.

COMMUNICATIONS

Roads

In 2001 there were 42,440 km of provincial highway, of which 23,710 km were paved. In 2007, 1,995,000 passenger cars and 664,000 commercial vehicles were registered.

Rail

The province is served by two transcontinental railways, the Canadian Pacific Railway and the Canadian National Railway. Passenger service is provided by VIA Rail, a Crown Corporation, and the publicly owned British Columbia Railway. In 1995 the American company Amtrak began operating a service between Seattle and Vancouver after a 14-year hiatus. British Columbia is also served by the freight trains of the B.C. Hydro and Power Authority, the Northern Alberta Railways Company and the Burlington Northern and Southern Railways Inc. The combined route-mileage of mainline track operated by the CPR, CNR and BCR totals 6,800 km. The system also includes CPR and CNR wagon ferry connections to Vancouver Island, between Prince Rupert and Alaska, and interchanges with American railways at southern border points. There is a light rail system in Vancouver, opened in 1985 (50 km). A commuter rail service linking Vancouver and the Fraser Valley was established in 1995 (69 km).

Civil Aviation

International airports are located at Vancouver and Victoria. Total passenger arrivals and departures on scheduled services made by 85 foreign and domestic airlines were 17·5m. in 2007 at Vancouver and 1·5m. at Victoria. Daily interprovincial and intraprovincial flights serve all main population centres. Small public and private airstrips are located throughout the province.

Shipping

The major ports are Vancouver (the largest dry cargo port on the North American Pacific coast), Prince Rupert and ports on the Fraser River. Other deep-sea ports include Nanaimo, Port Alberni, Campbell River, Powell River, Kitimat, Stewart and Squamish. Total cargo shipped through the port of Vancouver in 2007 was 82·7m. tonnes. 961,000 cruise passengers visited Vancouver in 2007.

British Columbia Ferries—one of the largest ferry systems in the world—connect Vancouver Island with the mainland and also provide service to other coastal points; in 2006–07, over 21m. passengers and more than 8·5m. vehicles were carried. Service by other ferry systems is also provided between Vancouver Island and the USA. The Alaska State Ferries connect Prince Rupert with centres in Alaska.

Telecommunications

In Dec. 2006, 91·5% of households had a landline telephone and 69·3% of households at least one cellular phone.

SOCIAL INSTITUTIONS

Justice

The judicial system is composed of the Court of Appeal, the Supreme Court, County Courts and various Provincial Courts, including Magistrates' Courts and Small Claims Courts. The federal courts include the Supreme Court of Canada and the Federal Court of Canada.

In 2002, 478,635 Criminal Code offences were reported, including 126 homicides.

Education

Education, free up to Grade XII level, is financed jointly from municipal and provincial government revenues. Attendance is compulsory from the age of five to 16. There were 582,691 pupils enrolled in 1,634 public schools from kindergarten to Grade 12 in Sept. 2007.

The universities had a full-time enrolment of 114,536 for 2006–07. Enrolment at the six universities (2006–07): the University of British Columbia, 48,293; Simon Fraser University, 24,842; University of Victoria, 19,372; Thompson Rivers University, 14,711; University of Northern British Columbia, 3,672; Royal Roads University, 3,646. There were three university-colleges in 2006: Kwantlen University College, Surrey; Malaspina University-College, Nanaimo; University College of the Fraser Valley, Abbotsford. British Columbia also had 12 colleges and five institutes in 2006: Camosun College, Victoria; Capilano College, North Vancouver; College of New Caledonia, Prince George; College of the Rockies, Cranbrook; Douglas College, New Westminster; Langara College, Vancouver; North Island College, Courtenay; Northern Lights College, Dawson Creek; Northwest Community College, Terrace; Okanagan College, Kelowna; Selkirk College, Castlegar; Vancouver Community College, Vancouver; British Columbia Institute of Technology, Burnaby; Emily Carr Institute of Art and Design, Vancouver; Institute of Indigenous Government, Burnaby; Justice Institute of British Columbia, New Westminster; Nicola Valley Institute of Technology, Merritt.

Televised distance education and special programmes through KNOW, the Knowledge Network of the West, are also provided.

Health

The government operates a hospital insurance scheme giving universal coverage after a qualifying period of three months' residence in the province. The province has come under a national medicare scheme which is partially subsidized by the provincial government and partially by the federal government. In March 2003 there were approximately 8,400 acute care and rehabilitation hospital beds. The provincial government spent an estimated $12·1bn. CDN on health programmes in 2006–07. 38% of the government's total expenditure was for health care in 2005–06.

CULTURE

Tourism

British Columbia's greatest attractions are Vancouver, and the provincial parks and ecological reserves that make up the Protected Areas System. There were more than 11,000 campsites and over 6,000 km of hiking trails in 2007. In 2003, 21·87m. tourists spent $8·95n. CDN in the province.

FURTHER READING

Barman, J., *The West beyond the West: a History of British Columbia.* 1991

Statistical office: BC STATS, Ministry of Finance and Corporate Relations, P.O. Box 9410, Stn. Prov. Govt., Victoria V8W 9V1.
Website: http://www.bcstats.gov.bc.ca

Manitoba

KEY HISTORICAL EVENTS

Manitoba was known as the Red River Settlement before it entered the dominion in 1870. During the 18th century its only inhabitants were fur-trappers, but a more settled colonization began in the 19th century. The area was administered by the Hudson's Bay Company until 1869 when it was purchased by the new dominion. In 1870 it was given provincial status. It was enlarged in 1881 and again in 1912 by the addition of part of the Northwest Territories.

TERRITORY AND POPULATION

The area of the province is 647,797 sq. km (250,114 sq. miles), of which 553,556 sq. km are land and 94,241 sq. km water. From north to south it is 1,225 km, and at the widest point it is 793 km.

The population at the 2006 census was 1,148,401; Oct. 2009 estimate, 1,226,200. The 2006 census showed the following figures for areas of population of over 10,000 people: Winnipeg, the province's capital and largest city, 694,668; Brandon, 41,511; Thompson, 13,446; Portage la Prairie, 12,773; Steinbach, 11,066.

SOCIAL STATISTICS

Births in 2007–08 numbered 15,417 (a rate of 12·8 per 1,000 population) and deaths 10,137 (rate of 8·4 per 1,000 population). There were 5,722 marriages in 2006 and 2,429 divorces in 2005.

CLIMATE

The climate is cold continental, with very severe winters but pleasantly warm summers. Rainfall amounts are greatest in the months May to Sept. Winnipeg, Jan. –3°F (–19·3°C), July 67°F (19·6°C). Annual rainfall 21" (539 mm).

CONSTITUTION AND GOVERNMENT

The provincial government is administered by a *Lieut.-Governor* assisted by an *Executive Council* (Cabinet), which is appointed from and responsible to a *Legislative Assembly* of 57 members elected for five years. Women were enfranchised in 1916. The Electoral Division Act, 1955, created 57 single-member constituencies and abolished the transferable vote. There are 26 rural electoral divisions and 31 urban electoral divisions. The province is represented by six members in the Senate and 14 in the House of Commons of Canada.

RECENT ELECTIONS

In elections to the Legislative Assembly held on 22 May 2007 the New Democratic Party won 36 out of 57 seats (47·7% of the vote), the Progressive Conservative Party 19 seats (38·2%) and the Liberal Party 2 seats (12·4%).

CURRENT ADMINISTRATION

Lieut.-Governor: Philip S. Lee; b. 1944 (took office on 4 Aug. 2009).

The members of the New Democratic Party Ministry in Feb. 2010 were:

Premier, President of the Executive Council, Minister of Federal-Provincial Relations: Greg Selinger; b. 1951.

Minister of Aboriginal and Northern Affairs: Eric Robinson. *Advanced Education and Literacy:* Diane McGifford. *Agriculture, Food and Rural Initiatives:* Stan Struthers. *Conservation:* Bill Blaikie. *Culture, Heritage and Tourism:* Flor Marcelino. *Education:* Nancy Allan. *Entrepreneurship, Training and Trade:* Peter Bjornson. *Family Services and Consumer Affairs:* Gord Mackintosh. *Finance:* Rosann Wowchuk. *Health:* Theresa Oswald. *Healthy Living, Youth and Seniors:* Jim Rondeau. *Housing and Community Development:* Kerri Irvin-Ross. *Infrastructure and Transportation:* Steve Ashton. *Innovation, Energy and Mines:* Dave Chomiak. *Justice and Attorney General:* Andrew Swan. *Labour and Immigration:* Jennifer Howard. *Local Government:* Ron Lemieux. *Water Stewardship:* Christine Melnick.

Manitoba Government Website: http://www.gov.mb.ca

ECONOMY

GDP per capita was $34,407 CDN in 2004.

Budget

Total revenue in 2008–09 was $11,791m. CDN (own source revenue, $8,004m. CDN; general purpose transfers, $2,458m. CDN; special purpose transfers, $1,328m. CDN). Total expenditures in 2008–09 amounted to $11,713m. CDN (including: health, $3,979m. CDN; education, $1,983m. CDN; social services, $1,859m. CDN).

Performance

Real GDP growth was 3·2% in 2006 (2·7% in 2005).

ENERGY AND NATURAL RESOURCES

Electricity

The province's electrical utility, Manitoba Hydro, has a total net generating capacity of 5,466,000 kW. In the year ending 31 March 2003 the provincial Crown corporation produced 29,178m. kWh of electricity. In 2002–03 scheduled power purchases from elsewhere in Canada and the USA totalled 3,043m. kWh. Manitoba provided 18,953m. kWh to its domestic customers. Energy sold outside Manitoba was 9,735m. kWh. This represented a decline in extraprovincial sales for the first time in six years. Revenue declined to $463m. CDN, $125m. CDN less than revenues reported in 2001–02. Of total extraprovincial revenue, $379m. CDN or 82% was derived from the US market while $84m. CDN or 18% was from sales to other Canadian provinces.

Oil and Gas

The value of oil production in 2002 was $152·6m. CDN, up 10·5% from 2001.

Minerals

Principal minerals mined are nickel, zinc, copper, gold and small quantities of silver. The value of mineral production declined 4% in 2002 to $982m. CDN. At $398m. CDN, nickel is Manitoba's most important mineral product, accounting for 40·5% of the province's total value of mineral production. Zinc accounted for 11% of the value of mineral production in 2002. Copper, which accounts for 9% of Manitoba's mineral production, saw moderate declines in both price and volume of production in 2002.

Agriculture

Rich farmland is the main primary resource, although the area in farms is only about 14% of the total land area. In 2002 total farm cash receipts increased by 2·9% to $3·76bn. CDN. Crop receipts surged 24·4% to $1·85bn. CDN while livestock receipts fell 5·2% to $1·7bn. CDN. Crop receipts accounted for 52% of total market receipts while livestock accounted for 48%. The growth of a number of non-traditional crops, such as dry beans and potatoes, underscores the continuing diversification of Manitoba's agricultural base. Manitoba's share of Canada's dry bean production has increased from 7% in 1993 to 57% in 2002. For particulars of livestock *see* CANADA: Agriculture.

Fisheries
From about 57,000 sq. km of rivers and lakes, the value of fisheries production to fishers was about $32·2m. CDN in 2001–02 representing about 14,800 tonnes of fish. Whitefish, sauger, pickerel and pike are the principal varieties of fish caught.

INDUSTRY
Manitoba's diverse manufacturing sector is the province's largest industry, accounting for approximately 12·5% of total GDP. The value of manufacturing shipments grew 0·6% in 2002 to $11·5bn. CDN.

Labour
Manitoba's total employment rose by 9,100 in 2002 (3,500 full-time and 5,600 part-time jobs), a 1·6% increase, bringing employment to a record-high level of 567,000. Manitoba had the lowest unemployment rate among the Canadian provinces at 5·2%. It also had the lowest youth unemployment rate in the country at 10·2%.

INTERNATIONAL TRADE
Products grown and manufactured in Manitoba find ready markets in other parts of Canada, in the USA, particularly the upper Midwest region, and in other countries.

Imports and Exports
In 2002 Manitoba merchandise exports to the US rose 1% to $7·6bn. CDN. Manitoba is the only province in Canada to record higher exports to the USA in 2001 and 2002. Merchandise exports to the USA comprise 82% of Manitoba's total foreign merchandise exports. In 2002 merchandise exports to Japan (Manitoba's second-most important foreign market) increased 3·2% while exports declined to Mexico, Hong Kong, Belgium and China. Manufacturing industries' exports, which account for about two-thirds of Manitoba's total foreign exports, increased by 1%. Gains were posted by four of the five largest manufacturing industry categories. Leading growth export industries include machinery, printing and wood products.

COMMUNICATIONS

Roads
Highways and provincial roads total 18,500 km, with 2,800 bridges and other structures. In 2003 there were 498,880 passenger vehicles (including taxis), 118,823 trucks, 51,122 farm trucks, 27,978 off-road vehicles and 9,138 motorcycles registered in the province.

Rail
The province has about 5,650 km of commercial track, not including industrial track, yards and sidings. Most of the track belongs to the country's two national railways. Canadian Pacific owns about 1,950 km and Canadian National about 2,400 km. The Hudson Bay Railway, operated by Denver-based Omnitrax, has about 1,300 km of track. Fort Worth-based Burlington Northern's railcars are moved in Manitoba on CN and CP tracks and trains.

Civil Aviation
In 2003 there were 61 domestic commercial aviation operators flying from bases in Manitoba. Three were designated private. Fifty-four air taxi companies were licensed to carry fewer than ten passengers; and six commuter operations were licensed to carry up to 19 passengers. Twelve national airlines were licensed to carry more than 19 passengers. Five foreign airlines were landing in the province (cargo and passenger). In addition, 36 aerial services were licensed (largely for agricultural chemical spraying).

Telecommunications
In 2002 Manitoba Telecom Services provided over 700,000 access services on its wireline network, more than 230,000 cellular subscribers and more than 115,000 internet access customers.

SOCIAL INSTITUTIONS

Justice
In 2002, 129,935 Criminal Code offences (excluding traffic offences) were reported in Manitoba (a ratio of 11,290 per 100,000 people), including 36 homicides (a ratio of three per 100,000 people).

Education
Education is controlled through locally elected school divisions. There were 179,287 students enrolled in the province's public schools in the 2003–04 school year. Student teacher ratios (including all instructors but excluding school-based administrators) averaged one teacher for every 18·1 students.

Manitoba has four universities with a total full- and part-time undergraduate and graduate enrolment for the 2003–04 academic year of 39,500. They are the University of Manitoba, founded in 1877; the University of Winnipeg; Brandon University; and the Collège universitaire de Saint Boniface.

Community colleges in Brandon, The Pas and Winnipeg offer two-year diploma courses in a number of fields, as well as specialized training in many trades. They also give a large number and variety of shorter courses, both at their campuses and in many communities throughout the province. Provincial government expenditure on education and training for the 2003–04 fiscal year is budgeted at $1·59bn. CDN.

CULTURE

Tourism
Between 2000 and 2002 Manitoba's tourism sector grew 28% and now brings in $1·3bn. CDN a year. Tourism and related industries have created 60,000 jobs in the province, employing one in ten people. For the period ending 30 Nov. 2002 the total number of overseas tourists entering Manitoba for one or more nights increased by 1·4%. Manitoba was the only Canadian jurisdiction to record positive growth of overseas tourists in the period in question.

FURTHER READING
General Information: Inquiries may be addressed to Manitoba Government Inquiry. *Email:* mgi@gov.mb.ca

---

New Brunswick

KEY HISTORICAL EVENTS
Visited by Jacques Cartier in 1534, New Brunswick was first explored by Samuel de Champlain in 1604. With Nova Scotia, it originally formed one French colony called Acadia. It was ceded by the French in the Treaty of Utrecht in 1713 and became a permanent British possession in 1759. It was first settled by British colonists in 1764 but was separated from Nova Scotia, and became a province in June 1784 as a result of the great influx of United Empire Loyalists. Responsible government from 1848 consisted of an executive council, a legislative council (later abolished) and a House of Assembly. In 1867 New Brunswick entered the Confederation.

TERRITORY AND POPULATION
The area of the province is 72,908 sq. km (28,150 sq. miles), of which 71,450 sq. km (27,587 sq. miles) is land area. The 2006 census counted 729,997 people in New Brunswick; Oct. 2009 estimate, 750,500. At the time of the 2006 census, the most frequently reported ethnic origin, whether reported alone or in combination with other origins, was Canadian (53%). French was the second most frequently reported ancestry (27%), followed by English (25%), Irish (21%) and Scottish (20%). A total of 36,015

persons in New Brunswick identified themselves as Aboriginal (that is, as a North American Indian, Métis or Inuit) in 2006.

The seven urban centres of the province and their respective populations based on 2006 census figures are: Moncton, 126,424; Saint John, 122,389; Fredericton (capital), 85,688; Bathurst, 31,424; Miramichi, 24,737; Edmundston, 21,442; Campbellton (part only), 14,826. The official languages are English and French.

SOCIAL STATISTICS

Births in 2007–08 numbered 7,120 (a rate of 9·5 per 1,000 population) and deaths 6,277 (rate of 8·4 per 1,000 population). There were 3,497 marriages in 2006 and 1,444 divorces in 2005.

CLIMATE

A cool temperate climate, with rain in all seasons but temperatures modified by the influence of the Gulf Stream. Annual average total precipitation in Fredericton: 1,131 mm. Warmest month, July (average high) 25·6°C.

CONSTITUTION AND GOVERNMENT

The government is vested in a Lieut.-Governor, appointed by the Queen's representative in New Brunswick, and a Legislative Assembly of 55 members, each of whom is individually elected to represent the voters in one constituency or riding. The political party with the largest number of elected representatives, after a Provincial election, forms the government.

The province has ten appointed members in the Canadian Senate and elects ten members in the House of Commons.

RECENT ELECTIONS

Elections to the provincial assembly were held on 18 Sept. 2006. The opposition Liberal Party won 29 seats (with 47·1% of the vote), the Progressive Conservative Party 26 seats (with 47·5%) and the New Democratic Party no seats (5·1%).

CURRENT ADMINISTRATION

Lieut.-Governor: Graydon Nicholas; b. 1946 (took office on 30 Sept. 2009).

The members of the Liberal government were as follows in Feb. 2010:

Premier, President of Executive Council Office, and Minister of Intergovernmental Affairs: Shawn Graham; b. 1968.

Attorney General, Minister of Social Development: Kelly Lamrock. *Solicitor General and Minister of Public Safety:* John Foran. *Finance:* Greg Byrne. *Supply and Services:* Edward Doherty. *Transportation:* Denis Landry. *Natural Resources:* Wally Stiles. *Energy:* Jack Keir. *Agriculture and Aquaculture:* Ronald Ouellette. *Fisheries:* Rick Doucet. *Health:* Mary Schryer. *Wellness, Culture and Sport, and Tourism and Parks (acting):* Hédard Albert. *Office of Human Resources:* Rick Brewer. *Post-Secondary Education, Training and Labour:* Donald Arseneault. *Education:* Roland Haché. *Environment:* Rick Miles. *Local Government:* Chris Collins. *Business New Brunswick:* Victor Boudreau.

Government of New Brunswick Website: http://www.gnb.ca

ECONOMY

GDP per capita in 2004 was $31,101 CDN; personal income per person was $25,699 CDN.

Budget

The ordinary budget (in $1m. CDN) is shown as follows (financial years ended 31 March):

	2001–02	2002–03	2003–04	2004–05	2005–06
Gross revenue	5,251·4	5,261·1	5,479·8	5,994·1	6,325·5
Gross expenditure	5,072·9	5,370·5	5,571·0	5,848·7	6,202·9

Funded debt and capital loans outstanding (exclusive of Treasury Bills) as of 31 March 2006 was $6,685·1m. CDN.

ENERGY AND NATURAL RESOURCES

Electricity

Hydro-electric, thermal and nuclear generating stations of NB Power had an installed capacity of 3,769 MW at 31 March 2002, consisting of 15 generating stations. The sale of out-of-province power accounted for 17·8% of revenue in 2002–03. Total revenue amounted to $1,273m. CDN.

Oil and Gas

In 2002 Enbridge Gas New Brunswick continued developing the natural gas distribution system in the province, which is now available in Fredericton, Moncton, St John, St George and Oromocto.

Minerals

The total value of minerals produced in 2006 was $1,538·6m. CDN. The top four contributors to mineral production are zinc, lead, silver and peat, accounting for 79·7% of total value in 2006. In 2007 New Brunswick ranked first in Canada for the production of zinc, bismuth and lead, second for silver and sixth for copper.

Agriculture

The total area under crops was 151,996 ha. in 2006. Farms numbered 2,776 and averaged 142 ha. (census 2006). Potatoes account for 33% of total farm cash receipts and dairy products 11%. New Brunswick is self-sufficient in fluid milk and supplies a processing industry. For particulars of livestock *see* CANADA: Agriculture. Net farm income in 2005 was $25·4m. CDN.

Forestry

New Brunswick contains some 6m. ha. of productive forest lands. The value of manufacturing shipments for the wood-related industries in 2002 was just over $3·8bn. CDN. The paper and allied industry group is the largest component of the industry, contributing 55·2% of forestry output. In 2002 nearly 15,750 people were employed in all aspects of the forest industry.

Fisheries

Commercial fishing is one of the most important primary industries of the province, employing 6,959 in 2002. Landings in 2005 (117,295 tonnes) amounted to $197m. CDN. In 2005 molluscs and crustaceans ranked first with a value of $178m. CDN, 90% of the total landed value. Exports in 2005, totalling $653·4m. CDN, went mainly to the USA and Japan.

INDUSTRY

Important industries include food and beverages, paper and allied industries, and timber products.

Labour

New Brunswick's labour force increased by 2·4% in 2002 to 385,700 while employment increased to 345,000. Goods producing industries employed 79,700 and the service-producing industries employed 253,700. Nearly 20% of the industrial labour force work in Saint John. In 2002 unemployment was 10·4%.

INTERNATIONAL TRADE

Imports and Exports

New Brunswick's location, with deepwater harbours open throughout the year and container facilities at Saint John, makes it ideal for exporting. The main exports include lumber, wood pulp, newsprint, refined petroleum products and electricity. In 2002 the major trading partners of the province were the USA with 89·2% of total exports, followed by Japan with 2·4% and the UK with 1·4% of total exports. Imports totalled $5,720m. CDN while exports reached $8,160·8m. CDN in 2002.

COMMUNICATIONS

Roads

There are 21,423 km of roads in the Provincial Highway system, of which 8,333 km consists of arterial, collector and local roads that provide access to most areas. The main highway system, including approximately 964 km of the Trans-Canada Highway, links the province with the principal roads in Quebec, Nova Scotia and Prince Edward Island, as well as the Interstate Highway System in the eastern seaboard states of the USA. At 31 March 2002 total road motor vehicle registrations numbered 549,061 of which 370,990 were passenger automobiles, 147,149 were truck and truck tractors, 13,406 motorcycles and mopeds, and 4,387 other vehicles.

Rail

New Brunswick is served by the Canadian National Railways, Springfield Terminal Railway, New Brunswick Southern Railway, New Brunswick East Coast Railway, Le Chemin de fer de la Matapédia et du Golfe and VIA Rail. The Salem-Hillsborough rail is popular with tourists.

Civil Aviation

There are three major airports at Fredericton, Moncton and Saint John. There are also a number of small regional airports.

Shipping

New Brunswick has five major ports. The Port of Saint John handles approximately 20m. tonnes of cargo each year including forest products, steel, potash and petroleum. The Port of Belledune is a deep-water port and open all year round. Other ports are Dalhousie, Bayside/St Andrews and Miramichi.

Telecommunications

In 2003, 282,000 households (96·8%) had telephones.

SOCIAL INSTITUTIONS

Justice

In 2002, 56,856 Criminal Code offences were reported, including nine homicides.

Education

Public education is free and non-sectarian.

There were, in Sept. 2002, 120,600 students (including kindergarten) and 7,469 full-time equivalent/professional educational staff in the province's 342 schools.

There are four universities. The University of New Brunswick at Fredericton (founded 13 Dec. 1785 by the Loyalists, elevated to university status in 1823, and reorganized as the University of New Brunswick in 1859) had 9,007 full-time students at the Fredericton campus and 3,017 full-time students at the Saint John campus (2002–03); the Université de Moncton at Moncton, 5,089 full-time students; St Thomas University at Fredericton, 2,897 full-time students; Mount Allison University at Sackville had 2,199 full-time students.

CULTURE

Broadcasting

The province is served by 57 radio stations and a number of television stations, the majority of which broadcast exclusively in English; the remainder broadcast in French (some radio stations are bilingual).

Press

In 2002 New Brunswick had five daily newspapers (one in French), and 23 weekly newspapers, five in French and two bilingual.

Tourism

New Brunswick has a number of historic buildings as well as libraries, museums and other cultural sites. Tourism is one of the leading contributors to the economy. In 2002 tourism revenues reached $1·2bn. CDN.

FURTHER READING

Industrial Information: Dept. of Business New Brunswick, Fredericton. *Economic Information:* Dept. of Finance, New Brunswick Statistics Agency, Fredericton. *General Information:* Communications New Brunswick, Fredericton.

Newfoundland and Labrador

KEY HISTORICAL EVENTS

Archaeological finds at L'Anse aux Meadows in northern Newfoundland show that the Vikings established a colony here in about AD 1000. This site is the only known Viking colony in North America. Newfoundland was discovered by John Cabot on 24 June 1497, and was soon frequented in the summer months by the Portuguese, Spanish and French for its fisheries. It was formally occupied in Aug. 1583 by Sir Humphrey Gilbert on behalf of the English Crown but various attempts to colonize the island remained unsuccessful. Although British sovereignty was recognized in 1713 by the Treaty of Utrecht, disputes over fishing rights with the French were not finally settled until 1904. By the Anglo-French Convention of 1904, France renounced her exclusive fishing rights along part of the coast, granted under the Treaty of Utrecht, but retained sovereignty of the offshore islands of St Pierre and Miquelon. Self-governing from 1855, the colony remained outside of the Canadian confederation in 1867 and continued to govern itself until 1934, when a commission of government appointed by the British Crown assumed responsibility for governing the colony and Labrador. This body controlled the country until union with Canada in 1949.

TERRITORY AND POPULATION

Area, 405,212 sq. km (156,452 sq. miles), of which freshwater, 31,340 sq. km (12,100 sq. miles). In March 1927 the Privy Council decided the boundary between Canada and Newfoundland in Labrador. This area, now part of the Province of Newfoundland and Labrador, is 294,330 sq. km (113,641 sq. miles) of land area.

Newfoundland island's coastline is punctuated with numerous bays, fjords and inlets, providing many good deep water harbours. Approximately one-third of the area is covered by water. Grand Lake, the largest body of water, has an area of about 530 sq. km. Good agricultural land is generally found in the valleys of the Terra Nova River, the Gander River, the Exploits River and the Humber River, which are also heavily timbered. The Strait of Belle Isle separates the island from Labrador to the north. Bordering on the Canadian province of Quebec, Labrador is a vast, pristine wilderness and extremely sparsely populated (approximately 10 sq. km per person). Labrador's Lake Melville is 2,934 sq. km and its highest peak, Mount Caubvick, is 1,700 metres.

The population at the 2006 census was 505,469; population estimate, 1 Oct. 2009, was 510,300.

The capital of the province is the City of St John's (2006 census population, 100,646). The other cities are Mt Pearl (24,671 in 2006) and Corner Brook (20,083); important towns are Conception Bay South (21,966), Grand Falls-Windsor (13,558), Paradise (12,584), Gander (9,951), Happy Valley-Goose Bay (7,572), Labrador City (7,240), Stephenville (6,588), Portugal Cove-St Philip's (6,575), Torbay (6,281), Marystown (5,436), Bay Roberts (5,414) and Clarenville (5,274).

SOCIAL STATISTICS

Births in 2007–08 numbered 4,521 (a rate of 8·9 per 1,000 population) and deaths 4,656 (rate of 9·2 per 1,000 population).

Newfoundland and Labrador was the only province in which deaths exceeded births in 2007–08. There were 2,722 marriages in 2006 and 789 divorces in 2005.

CLIMATE

The cool temperate climate is marked by heavy precipitation, distributed evenly over the year, a cool summer and frequent fogs in spring. St. John's, Jan. –4°C, July 15·8°C. Annual rainfall 1,240 mm.

CONSTITUTION AND GOVERNMENT

Until 1832 Newfoundland was ruled by a British Governor. In that year a Legislature was brought into existence, but the Governor and his Executive Council were not responsible to it. Under the constitution of 1855, the government was administered by the Governor appointed by the Crown with an Executive Council responsible to the House of Assembly.

Parliamentary government was suspended in 1933 on financial grounds and Government by Commission was inaugurated on 16 Feb. 1934. Confederation with Canada was approved by a referendum in July 1948. In the Canadian Senate on 18 Feb. 1949 Royal Assent was given to the terms of union of Newfoundland and Labrador with Canada, and on 23 March 1949, in the House of Lords, London, Royal Assent was given to an amendment to the British North America Act, made necessary by the inclusion of Newfoundland and Labrador as the tenth Province of Canada.

The province is represented by six members in the Senate and by seven members in the House of Commons of Canada.

RECENT ELECTIONS

Elections were held on 9 Oct. 2007. The ruling Progressive Conservative Party (PC) won 43 of the 48 seats in the House of Assembly with 69·7% of the vote; the Liberal Party (Lib.), 3 (22·0%); and the New Democratic Party (NDP), 1 (8·2%). Turnout was 61·7%.

CURRENT ADMINISTRATION

Lieut.-Governor: John Crosbie; b. 1931 (assumed office 4 Feb. 2008).

In Feb. 2010 the Progressive Conservative Cabinet was composed as follows:

Premier: Danny Williams; b. 1950 (sworn in 6 Nov. 2003).

Deputy Premier, Minister of Natural Resources, and Minister Responsible for the Forestry and Agrifoods Agency and for the Status of Women: Kathy Dunderdale. *Aboriginal Affairs:* Patty Pottle. *Business:* Ross Wiseman. *Child, Youth and Family Services:* Joan Burke. *Education:* Darin King. *Environment and Conservation:* Charlene Johnson. *Finance, President of the Treasury Board, and Minister Responsible for the Public Service Secretariat and for the Office of the Chief Information Officer:* Thomas Marshall, QC. *Fisheries and Aquaculture:* Clyde Jackman. *Government Services and Minister Responsible for the Government Purchasing Agency:* Kevin O'Brien. *Health and Community Services:* Jerome Kennedy, QC. *Human Resources, Labour and Employment, and Minister Responsible for the Status of Persons with Disabilities, the Labour Relations Agency, Francophone Affairs and Youth Engagement:* Susan Sullivan. *Innovation, Trade and Rural Development and Minister Responsible for the Rural Secretariat:* Shawn Skinner. *Intergovernmental Affairs and Minister Responsible for the Volunteer and Non-Profit Sector:* Dave Denine. *Justice and Attorney General:* Felix Collins. *Labrador Affairs:* John Hickey. *Municipal Affairs, Minister Responsible for Emergency Preparedness and Registrar General:* Dianne Whalen. *Tourism, Culture and Recreation:* Terry French. *Transportation and Works, and Minister Responsible for the Newfoundland and Labrador Housing Corporation:* Thomas Hedderson.

Speaker of the House of Assembly: Roger Fitzgerald.

Office of the Premier: http://www.premier.gov.nl.ca/premier

ECONOMY

GDP per capita was $37,837 CDN in 2004. Inflation for 2003 was estimated to be 2·2%. Real GDP growth for 2006 was forecast to be 3·0%.

Budget

Government budget in $1,000 CDN in fiscal years ending 31 March:

	2004–05	*2005–06*	*2006–07*[1]
Gross Revenue	4,153,356	4,928,642	4,909,628
Gross Expenditure	4,009,775	4,229,153	4,599,079

[1]Estimate.

ENERGY AND NATURAL RESOURCES

Electricity

Newfoundland and Labrador is served by two physically independent electrical systems with a total of 7,427 MW of operational electrical generating capacity. In 2004 total provincial electricity generation equalled 41·4bn. kWh, of which about 96% was from hydro-electric sources. Approximately 72% of total electricity generation was exported outside the province. Electricity service for a total of 259,000 retail customers is provided by two utilities and regulated by the Board of Commissioners of Public Utilities.

Oil and Gas

Since 1965, 140 wells have been drilled on the Continental Margin of the Province. Only the Hibernia discovery has had commercial capability with production starting in the early 1990s. In 2005 oil production from Hibernia reached 72·6m. bbls. 2006 production was expected to fall to around 66m. bbls. The Terra Nova development started producing oil in Jan. 2002 and is permitted to produce almost 59m. bbls annually, although production declined in 2005 to 36·2m. bbls.

Minerals

The mineral resources are vast but only partially documented. Large deposits of iron ore, with an ore reserve of over 5,000m. tonnes at Labrador City, Wabush City and in the Knob Lake area, are supplying approximately half of Canada's production. Other large deposits of iron ore are known to exist in the Julienne Lake area. The Central Mineral Belt, which extends from the Smallwood Reservoir to the Atlantic coast near Makkovik, holds uranium, copper, beryllium and molybdenite potential.

The percentage share of mineral shipment value in 2005 stood at 84% for iron ore. Other major mineral products were gold, silver, pyrophyllite, limestone and gypsum. The value of mineral shipments in 2005 totalled $1·5bn. CDN, representing a 120% increase over 2004.

Agriculture

The value of farm production in 2005 was $91·0m. CDN, an increase of 2·9% on 2004. In 2002 dairy products accounted for 34% of total receipts, hens and chickens 20%, eggs 13% and floriculture and nursery 13%. For particulars of livestock *see* CANADA: Agriculture.

Forestry

The forestry economy in the province is mainly dependent on the operation of three newsprint mills—Corner Brook Pulp and Paper and Abitibi-Consolidated (which operates two mills). In 2005 the value of newsprint exported totalled $563m. CDN, an increase of 7·5% over 2004. Lumber mills and saw-log operations produced 125m. flat bd ft in 2005.

Fisheries

Closure of the northern cod and other groundfish fisheries has switched attention to secondary seafood production and aquaculture. The total catch in 2004 fell by 2·5% to 326,300 tonnes valued at $461m. CDN (a reduction in value of 23·9%). Shellfish accounted for 53·8% of total landings and 75·9% of landed value. 16,200 people were employed in the fishing industry in 2002.

INDUSTRY

The total value of manufacturing shipments in 2005 was $2·98bn. CDN, a 2·8% reduction on 2004. This consisted largely of fish products, refined petroleum and newsprint.

Labour

In 2005 those in employment numbered 214,100 with 16,800 workers employed in manufacturing. The unemployment rate was 15·2% in 2005 (15·7% in 2004).

Trade Unions

In 2005 union membership was 37% of the employed workforce. The Newfoundland and Labrador Federation of Labour (NLFL) has approximately 70,000 members; the Newfoundland and Labrador Association of Public and Private Employees (NAPE) has more than 19,000.

COMMUNICATIONS

Roads

In 2007 there were 19,250 km of roads, of which 10,595 km were paved. In 2005 there were 266,716 motor vehicles registered.

Rail

The Quebec North Shore and Labrador Railway operated both freight and passenger services on its 588 km main line from Sept-Iles, Quebec, to Shefferville, Quebec and its 58 km spur line from Ross Bay Junction to Labrador City, Newfoundland. In 2006 iron ore freight totalled 20·0m. tonnes.

Civil Aviation

The province is linked to the rest of Canada by regular air services provided by Air Canada and a number of smaller air carriers.

Shipping

At Jan. 2006 there were 1,851 ships on register in Newfoundland. Marine Atlantic, a federal crown corporation, provides a freight and passenger service all year round from Channel-Port aux Basques to North Sydney, Nova Scotia; and seasonal ferries connect Argentia with North Sydney, and Lewisporte with Goose Bay, Labrador.

Telecommunications

In 2004, 195,000 households (98·7%) had telephones.

Postal Services

There were 442 full service post office outlets in 2005.

SOCIAL INSTITUTIONS

Justice

In 2005, 31,416 Criminal Code offences (excluding traffic offences) were reported, including nine homicides.

Education

In 2005–06 total enrolment for elementary and secondary education was 76,763; full time teachers numbered 5,485; total number of schools was 294. Memorial University, offering courses in arts, science, engineering, education, nursing and medicine, had 15,000 full-time students in 2004–05.

CULTURE

Tourism

In 2005, 469,600 non-resident tourists (449,300 in 2004) spent approximately $336·4m. CDN in the province.

FURTHER READING

Statistical office: Newfoundland Labrador Statistics Agency, POB 8700, St John's, NL A1B 4J6.
Website: http://www.stats.gov.nl.ca

Nova Scotia

KEY HISTORICAL EVENTS

Nova Scotia was visited by John and Sebastian Cabot in 1497–98. In 1605 a number of French colonists settled at Port Royal. The old name of the colony, Acadia, was changed in 1621 to Nova Scotia. The French were granted possession of the colony by the Treaty of St-Germain-en-Laye (1632). In 1654 Oliver Cromwell sent a force to occupy the settlement. Charles II, by the Treaty of Breda (1667), restored Nova Scotia to the French. It was finally ceded to the British by the Treaty of Utrecht in 1713. In the Treaty of Paris (1763) France resigned all claims and in 1820 Cape Breton Island united with Nova Scotia. Representative government was granted as early as 1758 and a fully responsible legislative assembly was established in 1848. In 1867 the province entered the dominion of Canada.

TERRITORY AND POPULATION

The area of the province is 55,284 sq. km (21,345 sq. miles), of which 53,338 sq. km are land area and 1,946 sq. km water area. The population at the 2006 census was 913,462; Oct. 2009 estimate, 940,400.

Population of the major urban areas (2006 census): Halifax Regional Municipality, 372,679; Cape Breton Regional Municipality, 102,250. Principal towns (2006 census): Truro, 11,765; Amherst, 9,505; New Glasgow, 9,455; Bridgewater, 7,944; Yarmouth, 7,162; Kentville, 5,815.

SOCIAL STATISTICS

Births in 2007–08 numbered 8,848 (a rate of 9·5 per 1,000 population) and deaths 8,401 (rate of 9·0 per 1,000 population). There were 4,513 marriages in 2006 and 1,961 divorces in 2005.

CLIMATE

A cool temperate climate, with rainfall occurring evenly over the year. The Gulf Stream moderates the temperatures in winter so that ports remain ice-free. Halifax, Jan. 23·7°F (–4·6°C), July 63·5°F (17·5°C). Annual rainfall 54" (1,371 mm).

CONSTITUTION AND GOVERNMENT

Under the British North America Act of 1867 the legislature of Nova Scotia may exclusively make laws in relation to local matters, including direct taxation within the province, education and the administration of justice. The legislature of Nova Scotia consists of a Lieut.-Governor, appointed and paid by the federal government, and holding office for five years, and a House of Assembly of 52 members, chosen by popular vote at least every five years. The province is represented in the Canadian Senate by ten members, and in the House of Commons by 11.

RECENT ELECTIONS

At the provincial elections of 9 June 2009 the New Democratic Party won 31 seats (45·3% of the vote), the Liberals 11 (27·2%) and the Progressive Conservatives 10 (24·5% of the vote). Turnout was 58%.

CURRENT ADMINISTRATION

Lieut.-Governor: Mayann Francis.

The members of Nova Scotia's first ever New Democratic cabinet in Feb. 2010 were:

Premier, President of the Executive Council and Minister of Policy and Priorities, Intergovernmental Affairs and Aboriginal Affairs: Darrell Dexter.

Deputy Premier, Deputy President of the Executive Council, Minister of the Public Service Commission, Communications Nova Scotia and Information Management: Frank Corbett. *Health, Health Promotion and Protection, and Gaelic Affairs:* Maureen MacDonald. *Agriculture, and Natural Resources:* John MacDonell. *Transportation and Infrastructure Renewal, and Energy:* Bill Estabrooks. *Finance, and Acadian Affairs:* Graham Steele. *Education, Labour and Workforce Development:* Marilyn More. *Fisheries and Aquaculture, and Environment:* Sterling Belliveau. *Economic and Rural Development, Tourism, Culture and Heritage, and African Nova Scotian Affairs:* Percy Paris. *Community Services, and Seniors:* Denise Peterson-Rafuse. *Service Nova Scotia and Municipal Relations, Emergency Management, and Immigration:* Ramona Jennex. *Attorney General and Minister of Justice:* Ross Landry.

Speaker of the House of Assembly: Charlie Parker.

Government of Nova Scotia Website: http://www.gov.ns.ca

ECONOMY

Budget

Summary of operations and net funding requirements for the consolidated entity (in $1m. CDN) for fiscal years ending 31 March:

	2004[1]	2005[2]	2006[3]
Revenues	5,857·7	6,267·7	6,587·3
Net Programme Expenditures/Expenses	5,192·7	5,588·4	5,987·2
Net Debt Servicing Costs	890·3	872·1	884·6
Pension Valuation Adjustment	6·3	38·3	33·2
Total Net Expenditures/Expenses	6,089·4	6,498·7	6,905·0
Consolidation Adjustment	47·5	35·5	54·5
Net Income from Government Business Enterprises	349·5	346·6	335·1
Surplus (Deficit)	166·3	151·0	71·9

[1]Actual. [2]Forecast. [3]Estimate.

Performance

GDP (market prices) was $31,344m. CDN in 2005, an increase of 5·0% on 2004. GDP per person in 2005 was $33,487 CDN.

Banking and Finance

Revenue is derived from provincial sources, payments from the federal government under the equalization agreements and the Canada Health and Social Transfer (CHST).

In the fourth quarter of 2005 deposits with chartered banks totalled $8,641m. CDN.

ENERGY AND NATURAL RESOURCES

Electricity

In 2005 production was 12,371,688 kWh, of which 98% came from thermal sources and the rest from hydro-electric, wind and tidal sources.

Oil and Gas

Significant finds of offshore natural gas are currently under development. Gas is flowing to markets in Canada and the USA (the pipeline was completed in 1999). Total marketable gas receipts for 2005 was 3·9bn. cu. metres.

Minerals

Principal minerals in 2005 were: gypsum, 6·8m. tonnes, valued at $81·1m. CDN; stone, 10·8m. tonnes, valued at $73·0m. CDN. Total value of mineral production in 2005 was $286·1m. CDN.

Agriculture

In 2006 there were 3,795 farms in the province with 116,609 ha. of land under crops. Dairying, poultry and egg production, livestock and fruit growing are the most important branches. Farm cash receipts for 2005 were $453·4m. CDN. Cash receipts from sale of dairy products were $107·0m. CDN, with total milk and cream sales of 166·7m. litres. The production of poultry meat in 2005 was 37,030 tonnes, of which 33,508 tonnes were chicken and 3,522 tonnes were turkey. Egg production in 2005 was 17·9m. dozen. For particulars of livestock *see* CANADA: Agriculture.

The main fruit crops in 2005 were apples, 39,372 tonnes; blueberries, 16,239 tonnes; strawberries, 1,769 tonnes.

Forestry

The estimated forest area of Nova Scotia is 15,830 sq. miles (40,990 sq. km), of which about 28% is owned by the province. Softwood species represented 89·4% of the 6,254,716 cu. metres of the forest round products produced in 2005. Employment in the forest sector was 4,100 persons in 2005.

Fisheries

The fisheries of the province in 2005 had a landed value of $647m. CDN of sea fish; including lobster fishery, $339m. CDN; and crab fishery, $73m. CDN. Aquaculture production in 2005 was 8,917 tonnes with a value of $40·4m. CDN; finfish accounted for 64% of total value while shellfish made up the remainder.

INDUSTRY

The number of employees in manufacturing establishments was 38,055 in 2004; wages and salaries totalled $1,444m. CDN. The value of shipments in 2005 was $10,596m. CDN, and the leading industries were food, paper production, and plastic and rubber products.

Labour

In 2005 the labour force was 483,900 (232,100 females), of whom 443,100 (214,500) were employed. The provincial unemployment rate stood at 8·4% while the participation rate was 63·6%.

Trade Unions

Total union membership in 2005 was 112,300 or 29·4% of employees. The largest union membership was in the service sector, followed by public administration and defence.

INTERNATIONAL TRADE

Imports and Exports

Total of imports and exports to and from Nova Scotia (in $1m. CDN):

	2002	2003	2004	2005
Imports	5,140	5,816	6,590	6,989
Exports	5,345	5,477	5,859	5,815

The main exports in 2005 included fish and fish products, natural gas and paper. Major trading partners were the USA with 80·1% of total exports, followed by Japan and the United Kingdom.

COMMUNICATIONS

Roads

In 2005 there were 26,000 km of highways, of which 13,600 km were paved. The Trans Canada and 100 series highways are limited access, all-weather, rapid transit routes. The province's first toll road opened in Dec. 1997. In 2005 total road vehicle registrations numbered 561,325 and over 600,000 persons had road motor vehicle operators licences.

Rail

The province has an 805-km network of mainline track operated predominantly by Canadian National Railways. The Cape Breton and Central Nova Scotia Railway operates between Truro and Cape Breton Island. The Windsor and Hantsport Railway operates in the Annapolis Valley region. VIA Rail operates the Ocean for six days a week, a transcontinental service between Halifax and Montreal.

Civil Aviation

There are direct air services to all major Canadian points, and international scheduled services in 2006 to Bermuda, Boston, Frankfurt, London and New York. Halifax International Airport is the largest airport, and there are also major airports at Yarmouth and Sydney.

Shipping

Ferry services connect Nova Scotia to the provinces of Newfoundland, Prince Edward Island and New Brunswick as well as to the USA. The deep-water, ice-free Port of Halifax handles about 14m. tonnes of cargo annually.

Telecommunications

In 2004, 357,000 households (96·1%) had telephones. Household internet use was 59·0% in 2005.

Postal Services

The postal service is provided by the Federal Crown Corporation Canada Post.

SOCIAL INSTITUTIONS

Justice

The Supreme Court (Trial Division and Appeal Division) is the superior court of Nova Scotia and has original and appellate jurisdiction in all civil and criminal matters unless they have been specifically assigned to another court by Statute. An appeal from the Supreme Court, Appeal Division, is to the Supreme Court of Canada.

For the year ending 31 March 2005 there were 1,660 admissions to provincial sentenced custody. In 2003, 86,150 Criminal Code offences were reported, including five homicides.

Education

Public education in Nova Scotia is free, compulsory and undenominational through elementary and high school. Attendance is compulsory to the age of 16. In 2004–05 there were 438 elementary-secondary public schools, with 9,581 full-time teachers and 145,396 pupils. The province has eleven degree-granting institutions. The Nova Scotia Agricultural College is located at Truro. The Technical University of Nova Scotia, which grants degrees in engineering and architecture, amalgamated with Dalhousie University and is now known as DalTech.

The Nova Scotia government offers financial support and organizational assistance to local school boards for provision of weekend and evening courses in academic and vocational subjects, and citizenship for new Canadians.

Health

A provincial retail sales tax of 8% provides funds for free hospital in-patient care up to ward level and free medically required services of physicians. The Queen Elizabeth II Hospital in Halifax is the overall referral hospital for the province and, in many instances, for the Atlantic region. The Izaak Walton Killam Hospital provides similar regional specialization for children.

Welfare

General and specialized welfare services in the province are under the jurisdiction of the Department of Community Services. The provincial government funds all of the costs.

RELIGION

The population is predominantly Christian. In 2001, 36·6% were Roman Catholic, 15·9% were United Church, 13·4% Anglicans, 10·6% Baptist and 2·5% Presbyterian.

CULTURE

Broadcasting

Nova Scotia has 22 radio stations and nine television stations. In 2005 there were six operating cable television systems.

Press

Nova Scotia has approximately 50 newspapers, including eight dailies. Daily newspapers with the largest circulations are *The Chronicle Herald* and *Mail Star* of Halifax, *The Daily News* of Dartmouth and *The Cape Breton Post* of Sydney.

Tourism

Tourism revenues were $1·3bn. CDN in 2005. Total number of visitors in 2005 was 2,114,000.

FURTHER READING

Nova Scotia Statistical Review. 2007
Nova Scotia at a Glance. 2006

Statistical office: Statistics Division, Department of Finance, POB 187, Halifax, Nova Scotia B3J 2N3.
Website: http://www.gov.ns.ca/finance/statistics/agency/index.asp

---

Ontario

KEY HISTORICAL EVENTS

The French explorer Samuel de Champlain explored the Ottawa River from 1613. The area was governed by the French, first under a joint stock company and then as a royal province, from 1627 and was ceded to Great Britain in 1763. A constitutional act of 1791 created there the province of Upper Canada, largely to accommodate loyalists of English descent who had immigrated after the United States war of independence. Upper Canada entered the Confederation as Ontario in 1867.

TERRITORY AND POPULATION

The area is 1,076,395 sq. km (415,596 sq. miles), of which some 917,741 sq. km (354,340 sq. miles) are land area and some 158,654 sq. km (61,256 sq. miles) are lakes and fresh water rivers. The province extends 1,690 km (1,050 miles) from east to west and 1,730 km (1,075 miles) from north to south. It is bounded in the north by the Hudson and James Bays, in the east by Quebec, in the west by Manitoba, and in the south by the USA, the Great Lakes and the St Lawrence Seaway.

The census population in 2006 was 12,160,282. Population estimate, 1 Oct. 2009, was 13,119,300. Population of the principal cities (2006 census):

Toronto[1]	2,503,281	Windsor	216,473	Oshawa	141,590
Ottawa	812,129	Kitchener	204,668	St Catharines	131,989
Mississauga	668,549	Oakville	165,613	Barrie	128,430
Hamilton	504,559	Burlington	164,415	Cambridge	120,371
Brampton	433,806	Richmond Hill	162,704	Kingston	117,207
London	352,395	Greater Sudbury	157,857	Guelph	114,943
Markham	261,573			Whitby	111,184
Vaughan	238,866			Thunder Bay	109,140

[1]The new City of Toronto was created on 1 Jan. 1998 through the amalgamation of seven municipalities: Metropolitan Toronto and six local area municipalities of Toronto, North York, Scarborough, Etobicoke, East York and York.

There are over 1m. French-speaking people and 0·25m. native Indians. An agreement with the Ontario government of Aug. 1991 recognized Indians' right to self-government.

SOCIAL STATISTICS

Births in 2007–08 numbered 138,985 (a rate of 10·8 per 1,000 population) and deaths 89,141 (a rate of 6·9 per 1,000 population). There were 63,151 marriages in 2006 and 28,805 divorces in 2005.

CLIMATE

A temperate continental climate, but conditions can be quite severe in winter, though proximity to the Great Lakes has a moderating influence on temperatures. Ottawa, average temperature, Jan. –10·8°C, July 20·8°C. Annual rainfall (including snow) 911 mm. Toronto, average temperature, Jan. –4·5°C, July 22·1°C. Annual rainfall (including snow) 818 mm.

CONSTITUTION AND GOVERNMENT

The provincial government is administered by a *Lieut.-Governor*, a cabinet and a single-chamber 107-member *Legislative Assembly* elected by a general franchise for a period of no longer than five years. The minimum voting age is 18 years.

RECENT ELECTIONS

At the elections on 10 Oct. 2007 to the Legislative Assembly the governing Liberal Party won 71 of a possible 107 seats (with 42·2% of the vote), the Progressive Conservative Party 26 seats (31·6%) and the New Democratic Party 10 seats (16·8%). The Greens took 8·0% of the vote but did not win any seats.

CURRENT ADMINISTRATION

Lieut.-Governor: David Onley, O.Ont.; b. 1950 (in office since 5 Sept. 2007).

In Feb. 2010 the Executive Council comprised:

Premier: Dalton McGuinty; b. 1955 (sworn in 23 Oct. 2003).

Deputy Premier: Vacant. *Agriculture, Food and Rural Affairs:* Carol Mitchell. *Attorney General and Minister of Aboriginal Affairs:* Chris Bentley. *Children and Youth Services, and Minister Responsible for Women's Issues:* Laurel Broten. *Citizenship and Immigration:* Dr Eric Hoskins. *Community and Social Services, and Minister Responsible for Francophone Affairs:* Madeleine Meilleur. *Community Safety and Correctional Services:* Rick Bartolucci. *Consumer Services:* Sophia Aggelonitis. *Economic Development and Trade:* Sandra Pupatello. *Education:* Leona Dombrowsky. *Energy and Infrastructure:* Brad Duguid. *Environment:* John Gerretsen. *Finance:* Dwight Duncan. *Government Services:* Harinder Takhar. *Health and Long-Term Care:* Deb Matthews. *Health Promotion:* Margarett Best. *Intergovernmental Affairs:* Monique Smith. *Labour:* Peter Fonseca. *Municipal Affairs and Housing:* Jim Bradley. *Natural Resources:* Linda Jeffrey. *Northern Development, Mines and Forestry:* Michael Gravelle. *Revenue:* John Wilkinson. *Tourism and Culture:* Michael Chan. *Training, Colleges and Universities, and Research and Innovation:* John Milloy. *Transportation:* Kathleen Wynne. *Minister Responsible for Seniors:* Gerry Phillips.

Office of the Premier: http://www.premier.gov.on.ca

ECONOMY

GDP per person in 2004 was $41,768 CDN.

Budget

Provincial revenue and expenditure (in $1m. CDN) for years ending 31 March:

	2001–02	2002–03	2003–04	2004–05	2005–06
Gross revenue	71,013	71,585	72,432	80,247	86,811
Gross expenditure	68,626	72,106	77,807	83,747	89,061

Performance

In 2006 real GDP grew at a rate of 2·1% (2·9% in 2005).

ENERGY AND NATURAL RESOURCES

Electricity

In 2006 Ontario Power Generation, which is responsible for 70% of the province's electric production, had an installed capacity of 22,100 MW and generated 105·2bn. kWh of electricity. In 2006 throughout Ontario there were 180 hydro-electric, 60 gas-fired, four coal-fired and five nuclear generating stations in operation. There were also four major wind farms. Nuclear energy accounted for 54% of electricity generation in 2006. Following restructuring in 2002, the industry is evolving into a hybrid system with both administered and competitive markets, serving about 4·5m. customers through 90 distribution utilities.

Oil and Gas

Ontario is Canada's leading petroleum refining region. The province's five refineries have an annual capacity of 170m. bbls (27m. cu. metres).

Minerals

The total value of mineral production in 2002 was $5·7bn. CDN. In 2003 the most valuable commodities (production in $1m. CDN) were: gold, 1,253; nickel, 1,192; cement, 614; stone, 506; sand and gravel, 410; copper, 393. Total direct employment in the mining industry was 14,000 (9,000, metals) in 2002.

Agriculture

In 2006, 57,211 census farms operated on 5,386,453 ha.; total gross farm receipts in 2005 (excluding forest products sold) were $10·3bn. CDN. Net farm income in 2005 totalled $341·8m. CDN. For particulars of livestock *see* CANADA: Agriculture.

Forestry

The forested area totals 69·1m. ha., approximately 65% of Ontario's total area. Composition of Ontario forests: conifer, 56%; mixed, 26%; deciduous, 18%. The total growing stock (62% conifer, 38% hardwood) equals 5·3bn. cu. metres with an annual harvest level of 23m. cu. metres.

INDUSTRY

Ontario is Canada's most industrialized province, with GDP in 2007 of $532,842m. CDN, or 40·5% of the Canadian total. In 2006 manufacturing accounted for 19·1% of Ontario's GDP.

Leading manufacturing industries include: motor vehicles and parts; office and industrial electrical equipment; food processing; chemicals; and steel.

In 2006 Ontario was responsible for about 43% ($177·4bn. CDN) of Canada's merchandise exports, and for 96% ($69·2bn. CDN) of exports of motor vehicles and motor vehicle parts.

Labour

In 2006 the labour force was 6,928,000, of whom 6,493,000 were employed (4,388,000 in the private sector, 1,170,000 in the public sector and 935,000 self-employed). The major employers (2006 in thousands) were: trade, 1,016; manufacturing, 1,007; health care and social assistance, 638; finance, insurance, real estate and leasing, 477; professional, scientific and technical services, 454; educational services, 445; construction, 405. The unemployment rate in 2006 was 6·3%.

INTERNATIONAL TRADE

Imports and Exports

Ontario's imports were $209·9bn. CDN in 2003, down from $224·7bn. CDN in 2003. Exports were $189·1bn. CDN in 2003, down from $206·5bn. CDN.

COMMUNICATIONS

Roads
Almost 40% of the population of North America is within one day's drive of Ontario. There were, in 1998, 159,456 km of roads (municipal, 143,000). Motor licences (on the road) numbered (2004) 10,360,891, of which 6,218,458 were passenger cars, 1,267,244 commercial vehicles, 31,038 buses, 2,100,511 trailers, 158,103 motorcycles and 306,479 snow vehicles.

Rail
In 2007 there were 17 short lines (eight provincially-licensed freight railways, four provincially-licensed tourist railways and five federally-licensed railways), plus the provincially-owned Ontario Northland Railway. The Canadian National and Canadian Pacific Railways operate in Ontario. Total track length, approximately 11,800 km. There is a metro and tramway network in Toronto.

Civil Aviation
Toronto's Lester B. Pearson International Airport is Canada's busiest, serving approximately 28m. passengers annually.

Shipping
The Great Lakes/St Lawrence Seaway, a 3,747 km system of locks, canal and natural water connecting Ontario to the Atlantic Ocean, has 95,000 sq. miles of navigable waters and serves the water-borne cargo needs of four Canadian provinces and 17 American States.

Telecommunications
In 2003, 4,431,000 households (97·2%) had telephones.

SOCIAL INSTITUTIONS

Justice
In 2003 there were 6,097 criminal code offences per 100,000 population, compared to a national average of 8,132 per 100,000 population.

Education
There is a provincial system of publicly financed elementary and secondary schools as well as private schools. Publicly financed elementary and secondary schools had a total enrolment of 2,118,544 pupils in 2005–06 (1,411,011 elementary and 707,533 secondary) and 114,191 teachers in 2004–05. In 2001–02, of the $64,270m. CDN total expenditure, 18·5% was on education.

There are 18 publicly funded universities (Brock, Carleton, Dominican, Guelph, Lakehead, Laurentian, McMaster, Nipissing, Ottawa, Queen's, Ryerson, Toronto, Trent, Waterloo, Western Ontario, Wilfred Laurier, Windsor and York), the Royal Military College of Canada and the University of Ontario Institute of Technology as well as one institute of equivalent status (Ontario College of Art and Design) with full-time enrolment for 2004–05 of 333,219. All receive operating grants from the Ontario government. There are also 24 publicly financed Colleges of Applied Arts and Technology, with a full-time enrolment of 150,000 in 2005–06.

Government funding for education in Ontario in 2005–06 was $17·2bn. CDN.

Health
Ontario Health Insurance Plan health care services are available to eligible Ontario residents at no cost. The Ontario Health Insurance Plan (OHIP) is funded, in part, by an Employer Health Tax.

FURTHER READING

Statistical Information: Annual publications of the Ontario Ministry of Finance include: *Ontario Statistics; Ontario Budget; Public Accounts; Financial Report.*

Prince Edward Island

KEY HISTORICAL EVENTS

The first recorded European visit was by Jacques Cartier in 1534, who named it Isle St-Jean. In 1719 it was settled by the French, but was taken from them by the English in 1758, annexed to Nova Scotia in 1763, and constituted a separate colony in 1769. Named Prince Edward Island in honour of Prince Edward, Duke of Kent, in 1799, it joined the Canadian Confederation on 1 July 1873.

TERRITORY AND POPULATION

The province lies in the Gulf of St Lawrence, and is separated from the mainland of New Brunswick and Nova Scotia by Northumberland Strait. The area of the island is 5,660 sq. km (2,185 sq. miles). The population at the 2006 census was 135,851; Oct. 2009 estimate, 141,400. Population of the principal cities (2006): Charlottetown (capital), 32,174; Summerside, 14,500.

SOCIAL STATISTICS

Births in 2007–08 numbered 1,388 (a rate of 10·0 per 1,000 population) and deaths 1,217 (rate of 8·8 per 1,000 population). There were 844 marriages in 2006 and 283 divorces in 2005.

CLIMATE

The cool temperate climate is affected in winter by the freezing of the St Lawrence, which reduces winter temperatures. Charlottetown, Jan. –3°C to –11°C, July 14°C to 23°C. Annual rainfall 853·5 mm.

CONSTITUTION AND GOVERNMENT

The provincial government is administered by a Lieut.-Governor-in-Council (Cabinet) and a Legislative Assembly of 27 members who are elected for up to five years.

RECENT ELECTIONS

At provincial elections on 28 May 2007 the opposition Liberal Party won 23 of the available 27 seats (with 52·9% of the vote) and the Progressive Conservatives took four seats (41·3%). The Greens and the New Democratic Party won no seats (3·0% and 2·0% respectively). Turnout was 83·8%.

CURRENT ADMINISTRATION

Lieut.-Governor: Barbara Hagerman, O.PEI; b. 1943 (sworn in 31 July 2006).

The Liberal Party Executive Council was composed as follows in Feb. 2010:

Premier, President of the Executive Council and Minister Responsible for Intergovernmental Affairs: Robert Ghiz; b. 1974.

Deputy Premier and Minister of Agriculture: George Webster. *Community Services, Seniors and Labour:* Janice Sherry. *Education and Early Childhood Development, and Attorney General:* Doug Currie. *Environment, Energy and Forestry:* Richard Brown. *Finance and Municipal Affairs:* Wesley Sheridan. *Fisheries, Aquaculture and Rural Development:* Neil LeClair. *Health and Wellness (including Aboriginal Affairs):* Carolyn Bertram. *Innovation and Advanced Learning:* Allan Campbell. *Tourism and Culture:* Robert Vessey. *Transportation and Infrastructure Renewal:* Ron MacKinley.

Office of the Premier: http://www.gov.pe.ca/premier

ECONOMY

GDP per person was $29,014 CDN in 2004.

Budget
Total revenue in 2005–06 was $1,196m. CDN (own source revenue, $746m. CDN; general purpose transfers, $319m. CDN; special purpose transfers, $132m. CDN). Total expenditures in 2005–06

amounted to $1,213m. CDN (including: health, $365m. CDN; education, $232m. CDN; debt charges, $124m. CDN; resource conservation and industrial development, $112m. CDN; social services, $107m. CDN).

ENERGY AND NATURAL RESOURCES

Electricity

Prince Edward Island's electricity supply in 2003 was 1,138,554 MWh, an increase of 5·7% over the preceding year. All but 4% was accessed from other provinces, via an underwater cable which spans the Northumberland Strait. Wind generated power accounted for 11% of the total capacity within the province in 2003.

Oil and Gas

In 2006 Prince Edward Island had more than 400,000 ha. under permit for oil and natural gas exploration.

Agriculture

Total area of farmland occupies approximately half of the total land area of 566,177 ha. Farm cash receipts in 2003 were $353m. CDN, with cash receipts from potatoes accounting for about 50% of the total. Cash receipts from dairy products, hogs and cattle followed in importance. For particulars of livestock, *see* CANADA: Agriculture.

Forestry

Total forested area is 280,000 ha. Of this 87% is owned by 12,000 woodlot owners. Most of the harvest takes place on private woodlots. The forest cover is 23% softwood, 29% hardwood and 48% mixed wood. In 2003 the volume of wood harvested reached 677,031 cu. metres, an increase of 5·2% on the previous year. The total value of wood industry shipments was $50·6m. CDN in 2003.

Fisheries

The total catch of 147m. lb in 2003 had a landed value of $169·6m. CDN. Lobsters accounted for $108·3m. CDN, around two-thirds of the total value; other shellfish, $47·1m. CDN; pelagic and estuarial, $10·7m. CDN; groundfish, $0·6m. CDN; seaplants, $2·7m. CDN.

INDUSTRY

Value of manufacturing shipments for all industries in 2003 was $1,356·1m. CDN. In 2003 (provisional) provincial GDP in constant prices for manufacturing was $394·9m. CDN; construction, $160·7m. CDN. In 2003 the total value of retail trade was $1,318·0m. CDN.

Labour

The average weekly wage (industrial aggregate) rose from $540·77 CDN in 2002 to $547·04 CDN in 2003. The labour force averaged 78,500 in 2004, with employment averaging 69,600. The unemployment rate was 11·1% in 2003.

COMMUNICATIONS

Roads

In 2006 there were 3,700 km of paved highway and 1,900 km of unpaved road as well as 1,200 bridge structures. The Confederation Bridge, a 12·9-km two-lane bridge that joins Borden-Carleton with Cape Jourimain in New Brunswick, was opened in June 1997. A bus service operates twice daily to the mainland.

Civil Aviation

In 2003 Air Canada provided daily services from Charlottetown to Halifax and Toronto. Canadian Airlines International operated daily services to Boston and Halifax, and there were also services to Moncton, Montreal and St John.

Shipping

Car ferries link the Island to New Brunswick year-round, with ice-breaking ferries during the winter months. Ferry services are operated to Nova Scotia from late April to mid-Dec. A service to the Magdalen Islands (Quebec) operates from 1 April to 31 Jan. The main ports are Summerside and Charlottetown, with additional capacity provided at Souris and Georgetown.

Telecommunications

In 2003, 53,000 households (98·7%) had telephones.

SOCIAL INSTITUTIONS

Justice

In 2003 there were 8,619 Criminal Code offences per 100,000 population, including one homicide.

Education

In 2003–04 there were 10,731 elementary students and 12,352 secondary students in both private and public schools. There is one undergraduate university (3,294 full-time and 599 part-time students), a veterinary college (237 students), and a Master of Science programme (33 students), all in Charlottetown. Holland College provides training for employment in business, applied arts and technology, with approximately 2,500 full-time students in post-secondary and vocational career programmes. The college offers extensive academic and career preparation programmes for adults.

Estimated government expenditure on education, 2000–01, $183·4m. CDN.

CULTURE

Tourism

The value of the tourist industry was estimated at $350m. CDN in 2003, with 1·1m. visitors in that year.

FURTHER READING

Baldwin, D. O., *Abegweit: Land of the Red Soil.* 1985

Quebec—Québec

KEY HISTORICAL EVENTS

Quebec was known as New France from 1534 to 1763; as the province of Quebec from 1763 to 1790; as Lower Canada from 1791 to 1846; as Canada East from 1846 to 1867, and when, by the union of the four original provinces, the Confederation of the Dominion of Canada was formed, it again became known as the province of Quebec (Québec).

The Quebec Act, passed by the British Parliament in 1774, guaranteed to the people of the newly conquered French territory in North America security in their religion and language, their customs and tenures, under their own civil laws. In a referendum on 20 May 1980, 59·5% voted against 'separatism'. At a further referendum on 30 Oct. 1995, 50·6% of votes cast were against Quebec becoming 'sovereign in a new economic and political partnership' with Canada. The electorate was 5m.; turnout was 93%. On 20 Aug. 1998 Canada's supreme court ruled that Quebec was prohibited by both the constitution and international law from seceding unilaterally from the rest of the country but that a clear majority in a referendum would impose a duty on the Canadian government to negotiate. Both sides claimed victory. On 27 Nov. 2006 Canada's parliament passed a motion recognizing that 'the Québécois form a nation within a united Canada'.

TERRITORY AND POPULATION

The area of Quebec (as amended by the Labrador Boundary Award) is 1,542,056 sq. km (595,388 sq. miles), of which 1,365,128 sq. km is land area (including the Territory of Ungava, annexed in 1912 under the Quebec Boundaries Extension Act). The population at the 2006 census was 7,546,131. Population estimate, 1 Oct. 2009, was 7,856,900.

Principal cities (2006 census populations): Montreal, 1,620,693; Quebec (capital), 491,142; Laval, 368,709; Gatineau, 242,124; Longueuil, 229,330; Sherbrooke, 147,427; Saguenay, 143,692; Lévis, 130,006; Trois-Rivières, 126,323; Terrebonne, 94,703; Saint-Jean-sur-Richelieu, 87,492; Repentigny, 76,237; Brossard, 71,154; Drummondville, 67,392; Saint-Jérôme, 63,729; Shawnigan, 51,904; Sainte-Hyacinthe, 51,616.

SOCIAL STATISTICS

Births in 2007–08 numbered 85,608 (a rate of 11·1 per 1,000 population) and deaths 56,200 (rate of 7·3 per 1,000 population). There were 21,956 marriages in 2006 and 15,423 divorces in 2005.

CLIMATE

Cool temperate in the south, but conditions are more extreme towards the north. Winters are severe and snowfall considerable, but summer temperatures are quite warm. Quebec, Jan. –12·5°C, July 19·1°C. Annual rainfall 1,123 mm. Montreal, Jan. –10·7°C, July 20·2°C. Annual rainfall 936 mm.

CONSTITUTION AND GOVERNMENT

There is a Legislative Assembly consisting of 125 members, elected in 125 electoral districts for four years.

RECENT ELECTIONS

At the elections of 8 Dec. 2008 the Quebec Liberal Party won 66 seats with 42·1% of votes cast, the Parti Québécois won 51 seats with 35·2%, the Action Démocratique won 7 seats with 16·4% and Québec Solidaire won 1 seat with 3·8%.

CURRENT ADMINISTRATION

Lieut.-Governor: Pierre Duchesne (took office on 7 June 2007).

Members of the Quebec Liberal Party Cabinet in Feb. 2010:

Premier: Jean Charest; b. 1958.

Deputy Premier and Minister of Natural Resources and Wildlife: Nathalie Normandeau. *Chair of the Conseil du trésor:* Monique Gagnon-Tremblay. *Public Security and Government House Leader:* Jacques Dupuis. *Sustainable Development, Environment and Parks:* Line Beauchamp. *Education, Recreation and Sports:* Michelle Courchesne. *Agriculture, Fisheries and Food:* Claude Béchard. *Finance:* Raymond Bachand. *Health and Social Services:* Yves Bolduc. *Transport:* Julie Boulet. *Municipal Affairs, Regions and Land Occupancy:* Laurent Lessard. *Employment and Social Solidarity:* Sam Hamad. *Economic Development, Innovation and Export Trade:* Clément Gignac. *Immigration and Cultural Communities:* Yolande James. *Culture, Communications and the Status of Women:* Christine St-Pierre. *Revenue:* Robert Dutil. *International Relations:* Pierre Arcand. *Justice:* Kathleen Weil. *Tourism:* Nicole Ménard. *Families:* Tony Tomassi. *Government Services:* Dominique Vien.

In addition to the above, the Cabinet also includes 'Ministers for' (full ministers who assist senior ministers).

Government of Quebec Website: http://www.gouv.qc.ca

ECONOMY

GDP per person in 2004 was $35,402 CDN.

Budget

Revenue and expenditure (in $1,000 CDN) for fiscal years ending 31 March:

	2002–03	*2003–04*	*2004–05*	*2005–06*
Revenue	58,186,000	60,808,000	64,439,000	69,311,000
Expenditure	60,469,000	63,135,000	66,833,000	69,832,000

The total net debt at 31 March 2004 was $97,647m. CDN.

ENERGY AND NATURAL RESOURCES

Electricity

Water power is one of the most important natural resources of Quebec. At the end of 2005 the installed generating capacity was 44,308 MW. Production, 2004, was 206,970 MWh. Quebec produced 6·9% of the world's total hydroelectric power in 2004.

Water

There are 4,500 rivers and 500,000 lakes in Quebec, which possesses 3% of the world's freshwater resources.

Minerals

For 2006 the value of mineral production was $4,826m. CDN. Chief minerals: iron ore (confidential); nickel, $628·1m. CDN; gold, $508·3m. CDN; zinc, $319·0m. CDN; copper, $144·6m. CDN. Non-metallic minerals produced include: asbestos, titanium-dioxide, peat and quartz (silica). Among the building materials produced were: stone, $367·8m. CDN; cement, $329·0m. CDN; sand and gravel, $90·0m. CDN.

Agriculture

In 2005 the agricultural area was 3,386,800 ha. The yield of the principal crops was (2005 in 1,000 tonnes):

Crops	*Yield*	*Crops*	*Yield*
Corn for grain	3,450	Barley	340
Tame hay	3,435	Oats	265
Fodder corn	1,800	Wheat	162
Soya	505	Mixed grains	65

There were 29,876 farms operating in 2005. Cash receipts, 2005, $6,191m. CDN (livestock, 32·3%; by-products including milk and eggs, 32·3%; crops, 22·7%). Quebec is a net exporter of food and agricultural produce. For particulars of livestock *see* CANADA: Agriculture.

Forestry

Forests cover an area of 591,549 sq. km. 424,114 sq. km are classified as productive forests, of which 355,004 sq. km are provincial forest land and 66,198 sq. km are privately owned. Quebec leads the Canadian provinces in paper production, having nearly half of the Canadian estimated total.

In 2006 production of pulp, paper and cardboard was 9,832,000 tonnes.

Fisheries

The principal fish and seafood are brown bullhead, eel, smelt, herring, snow crab and shrimp. The landed value in 2005 of fish, seafood and shellfish was $158m. CDN.

INDUSTRY

In 2001 there were 15,191 industrial establishments in the province; employees, 567,999; salaries and wages, $20,691m. CDN; value of shipments, $141,537m. CDN. Among the leading industries are petroleum refining, pulp and paper mills, smelting and refining, dairy products, slaughtering and meat processing, motor vehicle manufacturing, women's clothing, sawmills and planing mills, iron and steel mills, and commercial printing.

Labour

In 2003 there were 3,650,000 persons (1,689,400 female) in employment.

INTERNATIONAL TRADE

Imports and Exports

In 2003 the value of Canadian imports through Quebec custom ports was $64,228m. CDN; value of exports, $63,635m. CDN.

COMMUNICATIONS

Roads

In 2007 there were 30,086 km of roads and (2006) 5,402,353 registered motor vehicles.

Rail

There were (2003) 8,977 km of railway. There is a metro system in Montreal (65 km).

Civil Aviation

There are two international airports, Dorval (Montreal) and Mirabel (Laurentides).

Telecommunications

In 2003, 2,994,000 households (96·1%) had telephones.

SOCIAL INSTITUTIONS

Justice

In 2002, 476,543 Criminal Code offences were reported; there were 121 homicides.

Education

Education is compulsory for children aged 6–16. Pre-school education and elementary and secondary training are free in some 2,520 public schools. In July 1998 the number of school boards was reduced to 72. These were organized along linguistic lines, 60 French, nine English and three special school boards that served native students in the Côte-Nord and Nord-du-Québec regions. Around 12% of the student population attends private schools: in 2004–05, 348 establishments were authorized to provide pre-school, elementary and secondary education. After six years of elementary and five years of secondary school education, students attend Cegep, a post-secondary educational institution. In 2004–05 college, pre-university and technical training for young and adult students was provided by 52 Cegeps, 11 government schools and 60 private establishments.

In 2005–06 in pre-kindergartens there were 14,808 pupils; in kindergartens, 74,123; in primary schools, 510,340; in secondary schools, 489,054; in general education for adults, 257,443; in colleges (post-secondary, non-university), 188,549; and in universities, 264,240.

The operating expenditures of education institutions totalled $14,663·0m. CDN in 2004–05. This included $4,163·2m. CDN for universities, $8,000·3m. CDN for public primary and secondary schools, $873·6m. CDN for private primary and secondary schools and $1,625·9m. CDN for colleges.

In 2004–05 the province had 19 universities and affiliated schools of which seven were major universities: four French-language universities—Université Laval (Quebec, founded 1852), Université de Montréal (opened 1876 as a branch of Laval, independent 1920), Université de Sherbrooke (founded 1954), Université du Québec (founded 1968); and three English-language universities—McGill University (Montreal, founded 1821), Bishop's University (Lennoxville, founded 1843) and Concordia University (Montreal, granted a charter 1975). Université de Montréal has two affiliated schools: HEC Montréal (École des Hautes Études Commerciales), a business school founded in 1907; and École Polytechnique de Montréal, an engineering school founded in 1873. In 2004–05 there were 164,644 full-time university students and 97,045 part-time.

Health

Quebec's socio-health network consisted of 478 public and private establishments in 2001, of which 348 were public.

CULTURE

Broadcasting

In 2004 there were 58 television and 148 radio stations.

Press

In 2007 there were five major French-language newspapers (La Presse, Le Devoir, Le Journal de Québec, Le Journal de Montréal and Le Soleil) and one major English-language newspaper (The Gazette).

FURTHER READING

Dickinson, J. A. and Young, B., *A Short History of Quebec*. 4th ed. 2008
Young, R. A., *The Secession of Quebec and the Future of Canada*. 1995

Statistical office: Institut de la statistique du Québec, 200 chemin Sainte-Foy, Québec, G1R 5T4.
Website: http://www.stat.gouv.qc.ca

Saskatchewan

KEY HISTORICAL EVENTS

Saskatchewan derives its name from its major river system, which the Cree Indians called 'Kis-is-ska-tche-wan', meaning 'swift flowing'. It officially became a province when it joined the Confederation on 1 Sept. 1905.

In 1670 King Charles II granted to Prince Rupert and his friends a charter covering exclusive trading rights in 'all the land drained by streams finding their outlet in the Hudson Bay'. This included what is now Saskatchewan. The trading company was first known as The Governor and Company of Adventurers of England; later as the Hudson's Bay Company. In 1869 the Northwest Territories was formed, and this included Saskatchewan. The North-West Mounted Police Force was inaugurated four years later. In 1882 the District of Saskatchewan was formed and in 1885 the Canadian Pacific Railway's transcontinental line was completed, bringing a stream of immigrants to southern Saskatchewan. The Hudson's Bay Company surrendered its claim to territory in return for cash and land around the existing trading posts.

TERRITORY AND POPULATION

Saskatchewan is bounded in the west by Alberta, in the east by Manitoba, in the north by the Northwest Territories and in the south by the USA. The area of the province is 651,036 sq. km (251,365 sq. miles), of which 591,670 sq. km is land area and 59,366 sq. km is water. The population at the 2006 census was 968,157. Population estimate, 1 Oct. 2009, was 1,035,000. Population of cities, 2006 census: Saskatoon, 202,340; Regina (capital), 179,246; Prince Albert, 34,138; Moose Jaw, 32,132; Yorkton, 15,038; Swift Current, 14,946; North Battleford, 13,190; Estevan, 10,084; Weyburn, 9,433; Lloydminster, 8,118; Melfort, 5,192; Humboldt, 4,998; Melville, 4,149.

SOCIAL STATISTICS

Births in 2007–08 numbered 13,438 (a rate of 13·3 per 1,000 population) and deaths 9,295 (rate of 9·2 per 1,000 population). There were 5,030 marriages in 2006 and 1,922 divorces in 2005.

CLIMATE

A cold continental climate, with severe winters and warm summers. Rainfall amounts are greatest from May to Aug. Regina, Jan. 0°F (–17·8°C), July 65°F (18·3°C). Annual rainfall 15" (373 mm).

CONSTITUTION AND GOVERNMENT

The provincial government is vested in a Lieut.-Governor, an Executive Council and a Legislative Assembly, elected for five years. Women were given the franchise in 1916.

RECENT ELECTIONS

In elections on 7 Nov. 2007 the opposition Saskatchewan Party (SP) won 38 of 58 seats (50·9% of the vote); the New Democrats (NDP), 20 (37·2%). The Liberal Party received 9·4% of the vote but did not win any seats.

CURRENT ADMINISTRATION

Lieut.-Governor: Gordon Barnhart (took office 1 Aug. 2006).

The Saskatchewan Party ministry comprised as follows in Feb. 2010:

Premier, President of the Executive Council: Brad Wall.

Deputy Premier and Minister of Education: Ken Krawetz. *Energy and Resources:* Bill Boyd. *Finance and Government House Leader:* Rod Gantefoer. *First Nations and Métis Relations:* Bill Hutchinson. *Health:* Don McMorris. *Highways and Infrastructure:* Jim Reiter. *Justice and Attorney General:* Don Morgan, QC. *Government Services:* Christine Tell. *Agriculture:* Bob Bjornerud. *Enterprise:* Ken Cheveldayoff. *Social Services:* Donna Harpauer. *Environment:* Nancy Heppner. *Tourism, Parks, Culture and Sport:* Dustin Duncan. *Advanced Education, Employment and Labour:* Rob Norris. *Municipal Affairs:* Jeremy Harrison. *Corrections, Public Safety and Policing:* Yogi Huyghebaert. *Minister Responsible for Crown Investments Corporation:* June Draude.

Office of the Premier: http://www.gov.sk.ca/premier

ECONOMY

GDP per capita in 2004 was $40,643 CDN.

Budget

Budget and net assets (years ending 31 March) in $1,000 CDN:

	2002–03	*2003–04*	*2004–05*	*2005–06*
Budgetary revenue	6,094,300	6,228,000	6,590,500	7,006,800
Budgetary expenditure	6,319,255	6,561,383	6,761,533	7,151,731

ENERGY AND NATURAL RESOURCES

Agriculture used to dominate the history and economics of Saskatchewan, but the 'prairie province' is now a rapidly developing mining and manufacturing area. It is a major supplier of oil, has the world's largest deposits of potash and the net value of its non-agricultural production accounted for (2005 estimate) 93·0% of the provincial economy.

Electricity

The Saskatchewan Power Corporation generated 18,803m. kWh in 2005.

Minerals

In 2005 mineral sales were valued at $13,050m. CDN, including (in $1m. CDN): petroleum, 6,671·5; potash, 2,697·8; natural gas, 2,095·9; coal and others, 889·9; salt, 24·6. Other major minerals included copper, zinc, potassium sulphate, ammonium sulphate, bentonite, uranium, gold and base metals.

Agriculture

Saskatchewan normally produces about two-thirds of Canada's wheat. Wheat production in 2005 (in 1,000 tonnes) was 13,742 (12,261 in 2004) from 14·0m. acres; barley, 5,345 from 4·8m. acres; canola, 4,633 from 6·6m. acres; oats, 1,672 from 2·0m. acres; flax, 881 from 1·6m. acres; rye, 184 from 195,000 acres. Livestock (1 July 2005): cattle and calves, 3·7m.; swine, 1·4m.; sheep and lambs, 145,000. Poultry in 2005: chickens, 22·0m.; turkeys, 674,000. Cash income from the sale of farm products in 2005 was $6,355m. CDN. At the 2006 census there were 44,329 farms in the province covering an area of 26,002,605 ha. (with 14,960,103 ha. of land under crops).

The South Saskatchewan River irrigation project, the main feature of which is the Gardiner Dam, was completed in 1967. It will ultimately provide for an area of 0·2m. to 0·5m. acres of irrigated cultivation in Central Saskatchewan. As of 2006, 247,158 acres were intensively irrigated. Total irrigated land in the province, 339,583 acres.

Forestry

Half of Saskatchewan's area is forested, but only 115,000 sq. km are of commercial value at present. Forest products valued at $612m. CDN were produced in 2003–04.

Fur Production

In 2003–04 wild fur production was estimated at $1,687,708 CDN. Ranch-raised fur production amounted to $8,290 CDN in 2004 and $18,170 CDN in 2005.

Fisheries

The lakeside value of the 2002–03 commercial fish catch of 3·5m. kg was $4·6m. CDN.

INDUSTRY

In 2005 there were 1,008 manufacturing establishments, employing 20,293 persons. In 2005 manufacturing contributed $2,336·1m. CDN and construction $1,776·0m. CDN to total GDP at basic prices of $31,575·0m. CDN.

Labour

In 2005 the labour force was 509,400 (234,700 females), of whom 483,500 (224,000) were employed.

COMMUNICATIONS

Roads

In 2005 there were 26,168 km of provincial highways and 198,375 km of municipal roads (including prairie trails). Motor vehicles registered totalled 750,640 (2005). Bus services are provided by two major lines.

Rail

In 2005 there were approximately 9,513 km of railway track.

Civil Aviation

There were two major airports and 148 airports and landing strips in 2005.

Telecommunications

There were 604,279 telephone network access services to the Saskatchewan Telecommunications system in 2005.

Postal Services

In 2005 there were 475 post offices (excluding sub-post offices).

SOCIAL INSTITUTIONS

Justice

In 2005, 142,354 Criminal Code offences were reported, including 43 homicides.

Education

The Saskatchewan education system in 2005–06 consisted of 28 school divisions, of which nine are Roman Catholic, serving 107,331 elementary pupils, 59,801 high-school students and 1,577 students enrolled in special classes. In addition, the Saskatchewan Institute of Applied Science and Technology (SIAST) had approximately 13,200 full-time and 29,000 part-time and extension course registration students in 2005–06. There are also eight regional colleges with an enrolment of approximately 19,700 students in 2004–05.

The University of Saskatchewan was established at Saskatoon in 1907. In 2005–06 it had 15,300 full-time students, 4,000 part-time students and 961 full-time academic staff. The University of Regina, established in 1974, had 9,678 full-time and 2,977 part-time students and 425 full-time academic staff in 2005–06.

CULTURE

Broadcasting

In 2005 there were 58 TV and rebroadcasting stations, and 54 AM and FM radio stations.

Tourism

An estimated 1·8m. out-of-province tourists spent $513·3m. CDN in 2004.

FURTHER READING

Archer, J. H., *Saskatchewan: A History.* 1980
Arora, V., *The Saskatchewan Bibliography.* 1980

Statistical office: Bureau of Statistics, 9th Floor, 2350 Albert St., Regina, SK, S4P 4A6.
Website: http://www.stats.gov.sk.ca

The Northwest Territories

KEY HISTORICAL EVENTS

The Territory was developed by the Hudson's Bay Company and the North West Company (of Montreal) from the 17th century. The Canadian government bought out the Hudson's Bay Company in 1869 and the Territory was annexed to Canada in 1870. The Arctic Islands lying north of the Canadian mainland were annexed to Canada in 1880.

A plebiscite held in March 1992 approved the division of the Northwest Territories into two separate territories. (For the new territory of Nunavut *see* CONSTITUTION AND GOVERNMENT *below*, and NUNAVUT on page 291).

TERRITORY AND POPULATION

The Northwest Territories comprises all that portion of Canada lying north of the 60th parallel of N. lat. except those portions within Nunavut, Yukon and the provinces of Quebec and Newfoundland. The total area of the Territories was 3,426,320 sq. km, but since the formation of Nunavut is now 1,346,106 km. Of its five former administrative regions—Fort Smith, Inuvik, Kitikmeot, Keewatin and Baffin—only Fort Smith and Inuvik remain in the Northwest Territories.

The population at the 2006 census was 41,464, 54% of whom were aboriginal. Population estimate, 1 Oct. 2009, was 43,200. The capital is Yellowknife, population (2006); 18,700. Other main centres (with population in 2006): Hay River (3,648), Inuvik (3,484), Fort Smith (2,364), Behchokò (1,894). Iqaluit and Rankin Inlet, formerly in the Northwest Territories, are now in Nunavut. In Aug. 2003 an agreement was reached for the Tlicho First Nation to assume control over 39,000 sq. km of land in the Northwest Territories (including Canada's two diamond mines), creating the largest single block of First Nation-owned land in Canada.

SOCIAL STATISTICS

Births in 2007–08 numbered 727 (a rate of 16·7 per 1,000 population) and deaths 193 (rate of 4·4 per 1,000 population). There were 129 marriages in 2006 and 65 divorces in 2005.

CLIMATE

Conditions range from cold continental to polar, with long hard winters and short cool summers. Precipitation is low. Yellowknife, Jan. mean high –24·7°C, low –33°C; July mean high 20·7°C, low 11·8°C. Annual rainfall 26·7 cm.

CONSTITUTION AND GOVERNMENT

The Northwest Territories is governed by a Premier, with a cabinet (the Executive Council) of eight members including the Speaker, and a Legislative Assembly, who choose the premier and ministers by consensus. There are no political parties. The Assembly is composed of 19 members elected for a four-year term of office. A Commissioner of the Northwest Territories is the federal government's senior representative in the Territorial government. The seat of government was transferred from Ottawa to Yellowknife when it was named Territorial Capital on 18 Jan. 1967. On 10 Nov. 1997 the governments of Canada and the Northwest Territories signed an agreement so that the territorial government could assume full responsibility to manage its elections.

Legislative powers are exercised by the Executive Council on such matters as taxation within the Territories in order to raise revenue, maintenance of justice, licences, solemnization of marriages, education, public health, property, civil rights and generally all matters of a local nature.

The Territorial government has assumed most of the responsibility for the administration of the Northwest Territories but political control of Crown lands. In a Territory-wide plebiscite in April 1982, a majority of residents voted in favour of dividing the Northwest Territories into two jurisdictions, east and west. Constitutions for an eastern and western government have been under discussion since 1992. A referendum was held in Nov. 1992 among the Inuit on the formation of a third territory, **Nunavut** ('Our Land'), in the eastern Arctic. Nunavut became Canada's third territory on 1 April 1999.

RECENT ELECTIONS

On 1 Oct. 2007, 16 members (MLAs) were returned to the 16th Legislative Assembly. There were 55 candidates, three of whom had been previously returned unopposed. All members are independent.

CURRENT ADMINISTRATION

Commissioner: Tony Whitford, b. 1941 (took office in April 2005).

Members of the Executive Council of Ministers in Feb. 2010:

Premier, Minister of Aboriginal Affairs and Intergovernmental Relations: Floyd Roland; b. 1961.

Deputy Premier, Minister of Finance, and Environment and Natural Resources: Michael Miltenberger. *Justice, and Education, Culture and Employment:* Jackson Lafferty. *Municipal and Community Affairs:* Robert McLeod. *Health and Social Services:* Sandy Lee. *Public Works and Services, and Transportation:* Michael McLeod. *Human Resources, and Industry, Tourism and Investment:* Bob McLeod.

Speaker: Paul Delorey.

Government of the Northwest Territories Website:
http://www.gov.nt.ca

ECONOMY

GDP per person in 2003 was $85,983 CDN, the highest of any Canadian province or territory.

Budget

Total revenue in 2005–06 was $1,259m. CDN (own source revenue, $268m. CDN; general purpose transfers, $801m. CDN; special purpose transfers, $190m. CDN). Total expenditures in 2005–06 amounted to $1,333m. CDN (including: health, $264m. CDN; education, $251m. CDN; social services, $137m. CDN).

Performance

In 2006 real GDP growth was –0·4%.

ENERGY AND NATURAL RESOURCES

Oil and Gas

Crude petroleum production was 1,373,000 cu. metres in 2003; natural gas production was 780m. cu. metres in 2003.

Minerals

Mineral production in 2006: diamonds, 12,976,000 carats ($1,567,019,000 CDN); sand and gravel (including Nunavut), 362,000 tonnes ($2,157,000 CDN); stone, 461,000 tonnes ($4,500,000 CDN); tungsten, 2,500 tonnes ($64,497,000 CDN). Total mineral production in 2006 was valued at $1·64bn. CDN.

Forestry

Forest land area in the Northwest Territories consists of 61·4m. ha., about 18% of the total land area. The principal trees are white and black spruce, jack-pine, tamarack, balsam poplar, aspen and birch. In 2000, 22,000 cu. metres of timber were produced.

Trapping and Game

Wildlife harvesting is the largest economic activity undertaken by aboriginal residents in the Northwest Territories. The value of the subsistence food harvest is estimated at $28m. CDN annually in terms of imports replaced. Fur-trapping (the most valuable pelts being white fox, wolverine, beaver, mink, lynx, and red fox) was once a major industry, but has been hit by anti-fur campaigns. In 1999–2000, 37,124 pelts worth $842,049 CDN were sold.

Fisheries

Fish marketed through the Freshwater Fish Marketing Corporation in 2005–06 totalled 734,000 kg at a value of $705,000 CDN, principally whitefish, northern pike and trout.

INDUSTRY

Co-operatives

There are 37 active co-operatives, including two housing co-operatives and two central organizations to service local co-operatives, in the Northwest Territories. They are active in handicrafts, furs, fisheries, retail stores, hotels, cable TV, post offices, petroleum delivery and print shops. Total revenue in 2000 was about $97m. CDN.

COMMUNICATIONS

Roads

The Mackenzie Route connects Grimshaw, Alberta, with Hay River, Pine Point, Fort Smith, Fort Providence, Rae-Edzo and Yellowknife. The Mackenzie Highway extension to Fort Simpson and a road between Pine Point and Fort Resolution have both been opened.

Highway service to Inuvik in the Mackenzie Delta was opened in spring 1980, extending north from Dawson, Yukon as the Dempster Highway. The Liard Highway connecting the communities of the Liard River valley to British Columbia opened in 1984.

In 2005 there were a total of 28,212 vehicle registrations, including 23,184 road motor vehicles and 3,864 trailers.

Rail

There is one small railway system in the north which runs from Hay River, on the south shore of Great Slave Lake, 435 miles south to Grimshaw, Alberta, where it connects with the Canadian National Railways, but it is not in use.

Civil Aviation

In 2003 there were 130,310 take-offs and landings in the Northwest Territories.

Shipping

A direct inland-water transportation route for about 1,700 miles is provided by the Mackenzie River and its tributaries, the Athabasca and Slave rivers. Subsidiary routes on Lake Athabasca, Great Slave Lake and Great Bear Lake total more than 800 miles. Communities in the eastern Arctic are resupplied by ship each summer via the Atlantic and Arctic Oceans or Hudson Bay.

Telecommunications

In 2003, 13,000 households (95·5%) had telephones. Those few communities without a telephone service have high frequency or very high frequency radios for emergency use.

Postal Services

There is a postal service in all communities.

SOCIAL INSTITUTIONS

Education

The Education System in the Northwest Territories is comprised of eight regional bodies (boards) that have responsibilities for the K-12 education programme. Three of these jurisdictions are located in Yellowknife; a public school authority, a catholic school authority and a Commission scolaire francophone that oversees a school operating in Yellowknife, and one in Hay River.

For the 2000–01 school year there were 49 public plus two (small) private schools operating in the NWT. Within this system there were 667 teachers, including Aboriginal Language Specialists, for 9,855 students. 98% of students have access to high school programmes in their home communities. There is a full range of courses available in the school system, including academic, French immersion, Aboriginal language, cultural programmes, technical and occupational programmes.

A range of post secondary programmes are available through the Northwest Territories' Aurora College. The majority of these programmes are offered at the three main campus locations: Inuvik, Yellowknife and Fort Smith.

Health

In 2004 there were eight separate regional boards. Expenditure on health totalled $159·4m. CDN in 1999–2000.

Welfare

Welfare services are provided by professional social workers. Facilities included (2006): family violence services in seven communities, eight helplines, seven group homes or shelters and one residential treatment centre.

FURTHER READING

Northwest Territories—2008: By the Numbers. 2009
Zaslow, M., *The Opening of the Canadian North 1870–1914.* 1971

Statistical office: Bureau of Statistics, Government of the Northwest Territories, PO Box 1320, Yellowknife, NWT X1A 2L9.
Website: http://www.stats.gov.nt.ca

Nunavut

KEY HISTORICAL EVENTS

Inuit communities started entering and moving around what is now the Canadian Arctic between 4500 BC and AD 1000. By the 19th century these communities were under the jurisdiction of the Northwest Territories. In 1963 the Canadian government first introduced legislation to divide the territory, a proposal that failed at the order paper stage. In 1973 the Comprehensive Land Claims Policy was established which sought to define the rights and benefits of the Aboriginal population in a land claim settlement agreement. The Northwest Territories Legislative Assembly voted in favour of dividing the territory in 1980, and in a public referendum of 1982, 56% of votes cast were also for the division. In 1992 the proposed boundary was ratified in a public vote and the Inuit population approved their land claim settlement. A year later, the Nunavut Act (creating the territory) and the Nunavut Land Claim Agreement Act were passed by parliament. Iqaluit was selected as the capital in 1995.

On 15 Feb. 1999 Nunavut held elections for its Legislative Assembly and on 1 April 1999 the territory was officially designated and the government inaugurated.

TERRITORY AND POPULATION

The total area of the region is 2,093,190 sq. km or about 21% of Canada's total mass, making Nunavut Canada's largest territory. It contains seven of Canada's 12 largest islands and two-thirds of the country's coastline. The territory is divided into three regions: Qikiqtaaluk (Baffin), Kivalliq (Keewatin) and Kitikmeot. The total population at the 2006 census was 29,474 (51·2% males) or 141 persons per 10,000 sq. km. 85% of the population are Inuit. Population estimate, 1 Oct. 2009, was 32,400. The population is divided up into 25 communities of which the largest is in the capital Iqaluit, numbering 6,184.

The native Inuit language is Inuktitut.

SOCIAL STATISTICS

Births in 2007–08 numbered 797 (a rate of 25·3 per 1,000 population) and deaths 136 (rate of 4·3 per 1,000 population). Nunavut's birth rate is the highest in Canada and is more than twice the national average of 11·2 per 1,000 births. It also has the lowest death rate. Life expectancy, at 70·4 years in 2004, is the lowest in Canada.

CLIMATE

Conditions range from cold continental to polar, with long hard winters and short cool summers. In Iqaluit there can be as little as four hours sunshine per day in winter and up to 21 hours per day at the summer solstice. Iqaluit, Jan. mean high –22°C; July mean high, 15°C.

CONSTITUTION AND GOVERNMENT

Government is by a Legislative Assembly of 19 elected members, who then choose a leader and ministers by consensus. There are no political parties. Government is highly decentralized, consisting of ten departments spread over 11 different communities. By 2020 Inuktitut is intended to be the working language of government but government agencies will also offer services in English and French. Although the Inuits are the dominant force in public government, non-Inuit citizens have the same voting rights.

RECENT ELECTIONS

Legislative Assembly elections were held on 27 Oct. 2008 (3 Nov. 2008 in one district). There were 50 non-partisan candidates; 18 were elected (one woman) with the election in one district cancelled.

CURRENT ADMINISTRATION

Commissioner: Ann Meekitjuk Hanson (took office in April 2005).

In Feb. 2010 the cabinet was as follows:

Premier and Minister of Executive and Intergovernmental Affairs, and Minister Responsible for the Status of Women and Immigration: Eva Aariak (took office on 19 Nov. 2008).

Deputy Premier, Minister of Economic Development and Transportation, and Minister Responsible for the Nunavut Business Credit Corporation, the Nunavut Development Corporation, and Mines: Peter Taptuna. *Community and Government Services, and Energy:* Lorne Kusugak. *Finance and Justice:* Keith Peterson. *Human Resources, Environment and Minister Responsible for Nunavut Arctic College:* Daniel Shewchuk. *Health and Social Services, and Minister Responsible for the Utility Rates Review Council and the Workers' Safety and Compensation Commission:* Tagak Curley. *Government House Leader, Minister of Culture, Language, Elders and Youth, Education, Languages and Aboriginal Affairs:* Louis Tapardjuk. *Minister Responsible for the Qullig Energy Corporation, Nunavut Housing Corporation, and Homelessness:* Hunter Tootoo.

Speaker: James Arreak.

Government of Nunavut Website: http://www.gov.nu.ca

ECONOMY

While the cost of living in Nunavut is around 160–200% that of southern Canadians, the average household income is $31,471 CDN compared to $45,251 CDN for Canada as a whole. With unemployment running high, transport costs expensive and education limited, self-sufficiency is unlikely to be achieved soon.

Currency

The Canadian dollar is the standard currency.

Budget

Total revenue in 2005–06 was $1,181m. CDN (own source revenue, $111m. CDN; general purpose transfers, $877m. CDN; special purpose transfers, $192m.). Total expenditures in 2005–06 amounted to $1,119m. CDN (including: health, $256m. CDN; education, $192m. CDN; housing, $145m. CDN).

Performance

Real GDP growth was 3·4% in 2006, the second highest among Canada's provinces and territories after Alberta.

Banking and Finance

Few banks have branches in the province. Iqaluit has two automated cash machines and stores are increasingly installing debit card facilities.

ENERGY AND NATURAL RESOURCES

Minerals

There are two lead and zinc mines operating in the High Arctic region. There are also known deposits of copper, gold, silver and diamonds.

Hunting and Trapping

Most communities still rely on traditional foodstuffs such as caribou and seal. The Canadian government now provides meat inspections so that caribou and musk ox meat can be sold across the country.

Fisheries

Fishing is still very important in Inuit life. The principal catches are shrimp, scallop and arctic char.

INDUSTRY

The main industries are mining, tourism, fishing, hunting and trapping and arts and crafts production.

Labour

The unemployment rate was 15·6% in May 2006.

COMMUNICATIONS

Roads

There is one 21-km government-maintained road between Arctic Bay and Nanisivik. There are a few paved roads in Iqaluit and Rankin Inlet, but most are unpaved. Some communities have local roads and tracks but Kivalliq has no direct land connections with southern Canada.

Civil Aviation

There are air connections between communities and a daily air connection between Iqaluit and Montreal/Ottawa.

Shipping
There is an annual summer sea-lift by ship and barge for transport of construction materials, dry goods, non-perishable food, trucks and cars.

Telecommunications
In 2003, 6,000 households (84·9%) had telephones. Because of the wide distances between communities, there is a very high rate of internet use in Nunavut. However, line speeds are slow and there is a problem with satellite bounce.

Postal Services
There is no door-to-door delivery service, so correspondence has to be retrieved from post offices.

SOCIAL INSTITUTIONS

Justice
A territorial court has been put in place. Policing is by the Royal Canadian Mounted Police (RCMP).

Education
Approximately one quarter of Nunavut's population aged over 15 have less than Grade 9 schooling. Training and development is seen as central to securing a firm economic foundation for the province.

Courses in computer science, business management and public administration may be undertaken at Arctic College. In 1997–98 there were 39 schools with 7,770 students.

Health
There is one hospital in Iqaluit. 26 health centres provide nursing care for communities. For more specialized treatment, patients of Qikiqtaaluk may be flown to Montreal, patients in Kivalliq to Churchill or Winnipeg and patients in Kitikmeot to Yellowknife's Stanton Regional Hospital.

CULTURE

Broadcasting
The Canadian Broadcasting Corporation (CBC) North transmits television to Iqaluit and other communities. The Inuit Broadcasting Corporation (IBC) transmits in Inuktitut and Television Northern Canada (TVNC) is devoted to programming by and for northerners and native citizens. There are 5½ hours of Inuktitut television programming per week. Cable satellite television is also widely available. CBC is the only local radio station accessible in all Nunavut communities.

Tourism
Auyuittuq National Park is one of the principal tourist attractions, along with the opportunity of seeing Inuit life first-hand. Under the terms of the land claim settlement, three more national parks are planned. It is also hoped that the publicity surrounding the new territory will encourage visitors.

FURTHER READING
The Nunavut Handbook. 2004

Yukon

KEY HISTORICAL EVENTS
The territory owes its fame to the discovery of gold in the Klondike at the end of the 19th century. Formerly part of the Northwest Territories, the Yukon was joined to the Dominion as a separate territory on 13 June 1898.

Yukon First Nations People lived a semi-nomadic subsistence lifestyle in the region long before it was established as a territory. The earliest evidence of human activity was found in caves containing stone tools and animal bones estimated to be 20,000 years old. The Athapaskan cultural linguistic tradition to which most Yukon First Nations belong is more than 1,000 years old. The territory's name comes from the native 'Yu-kun-ah' for the great river that drains most of this area.

The Yukon was created as a district of the Northwest Territories in 1895. The Klondike Gold Rush in the late 1890s saw thousands of stampeders pouring into the gold fields of the Canadian northwest. Population at the peak of the rush reached 40,000. This event spurred the federal government to set up basic administrative structures in the Yukon. The territory was given the status of a separate geographical and political entity with an appointed legislative council in 1898. In 1953 the capital was moved south from Dawson City to Whitehorse, where most of the economic activity was centred. The federal government granted the Yukon responsible government in 1979.

The *Yukon Act* of 1 April 2003 gave the territory more control over its own governance and changed its name from the Yukon Territory to Yukon.

TERRITORY AND POPULATION
The territory consists of one city, three towns, four villages, two hamlets, 13 unincorporated communities and eight rural communities. It is situated in the northwestern region of Canada and comprises 482,443 sq. km of which 8,052 sq. km is fresh water.

The population at the 2006 census was 30,372; Oct. 2009 estimate, 34,000.

Principal centres in 2006 were Whitehorse, the capital, 20,461; Dawson City, 1,327; Watson Lake, 846; Haines Junction, 589; Carmacks, 425.

Yukon represents 4·8% of Canada's total land area.

SOCIAL STATISTICS
Births in 2007–08 numbered 355 (a rate of 10·8 per 1,000 population) and deaths 189 (rate of 5·7 per 1,000 population). There were 152 marriages in 2006 and 109 divorces in 2005.

CLIMATE
Temperatures in Yukon are usually more extreme than those experienced in the southern provinces of Canada. A cold climate in winter with moderate temperatures in summer provide a considerable annual range of temperature and moderate rainfall.

Whitehorse, Jan. –18·7°C (–2·0°F), July 14°C (57·2°F). Annual precipitation 268·8 mm. Dawson City, Jan. –30·7°C (–23·3°F), July 15·6°C (60·1°F). Annual precipitation 182·7 mm.

CONSTITUTION AND GOVERNMENT
Yukon was constituted a separate territory on 13 June 1898. The Yukon Legislative Assembly consists of 18 elected members and functions in much the same way as a provincial legislature. The seat of government is at Whitehorse. It consists of an executive council with parliamentary powers similar to those of a provincial cabinet. The Yukon government consists of 12 departments, as well as a Women's Directorate and four Crown corporations.

RECENT ELECTIONS
At elections held on 10 Oct. 2006 the Yukon Party took 10 of the available 18 seats; the Liberal Party 5; and the New Democratic Party 3.

CURRENT ADMINISTRATION
Commissioner: Geraldine Van Bibber (took office on 1 Dec. 2005).

In Feb. 2010 the Yukon Party Ministry comprised:

Premier, Minister Responsible for Executive Council Office, Yukon Development Corporation and Yukon Energy Corporation, and Minister of Finance: Dennis Fentie.

Deputy Premier, Minister of Tourism and Culture: Elaine Taylor. *Justice:* Marian Horne. *Highways and Public Works, and Community Services:* Archie Lang. *Health and Social Services:* Glenn Hart. *Economic Development:* Jim Kenyon. *Education, and Energy, Mines and Resources:* Patrick Rouble. *Environment:* John Edzerza.

Speaker: Ted Staffen.

Government of Yukon Website: http://www.gov.yk.ca

ECONOMY

The key sectors of the economy are government, tourism, finance, insurance and real estate.

Budget

Total revenue in 2005–06 was $776m. CDN (own source revenue, $136m. CDN; general purpose transfers, $545m. CDN; special purpose transfers, $95m. CDN). Total expenditures in 2005–06 amounted to $784m. CDN (including: education, $129m. CDN; health, $125m. CDN; transport and communication, $124m. CDN).

Performance

GDP at basic prices in 2005 for all industries was $1,176m. CDN (at market prices, GDP was $1,521m. CDN). Mining, oil and gas production was estimated at $55·5m. CDN in 2005 and shipments in the manufacturing sector were valued at $24·6m. CDN. Revenue from agriculture, forestry, hunting and fishing was estimated at $3·5m. CDN. GDP per person in 2005 was $49,065 CDN.

ENERGY AND NATURAL RESOURCES

Environment

Yukon is recognized as a critical habitat for many species of rare and endangered flowers, big game animals, birds of prey and migratory birds. There are 278 species of birds and 38 species of fish. The vegetation is classified as sub-arctic and alpine.

Three national parks (total area 36,572 sq. km), five territorial parks (7,861 sq. km), two ecological reserves (181 sq. km), eight wildlife management areas (10,651 sq. km) and one wildlife sanctuary (6,450 sq. km) have been established to protect fragile and significant areas for the future.

Electricity

Yukon currently depends on imported refined petroleum products for 6·6% of the energy it uses. At the same time, 93·4% (2006 figure) of the territory's electrical supply comes from four utility-owned hydro-electrical facilities. Hydro-generated power is supplemented with diesel power plants which are located in most communities. Total generation for 2006 was 359 GWh.

Oil and Gas

In 1997 the Yukon Oil and Gas Act was passed, replacing the federal legislation. This Act provides for the transfer of responsibility for oil and gas resources to Yukon jurisdiction. Five unexplored oil and gas basins with rich potential exist. Current net production is about 1·7m. cu. metres of natural gas per day.

Minerals

Gold and silver are the chief minerals. There are also deposits of lead, zinc, copper, tungsten and iron ore. Gold deposits, both hard rock and placer, are being mined.

Estimates for 2006 mineral production: gold, $37·5m. CDN; and silver, $0·2m. CDN. Total: $37·7m. CDN.

Agriculture

Many areas have suitable soils and climate for the production of forages, vegetables, domestic livestock and game farming. The greenhouse industry is Yukon's largest horticulture sector.

In 2006 there were 148 farms operating full- and part-time. The total area of farms was 10,125 ha. of which 2,658 ha. were in crops.

Gross farm receipts in 2005 were estimated at $4·1m. CDN. Total farm capital at market value in 2006 was $66·1m. CDN.

Forestry

The forests, covering 281,000 sq. km of the territory, are part of the great Boreal forest region of Canada, which covers 58% of Yukon.

Fur Trade

The fur-trapping industry is considered vital to rural and remote residents and especially First Nations people wishing to maintain a traditional lifestyle. Preliminary fur production in 2006 (mostly marten, lynx, wolverine, wolf, beaver and muskrat) was valued at $428,810 CDN.

Fisheries

Commercial fishing concentrates on chinook salmon, chum salmon, lake trout and whitefish.

INDUSTRY

The key sectors of the economy are tourism and government.

Labour

The 2006 labour force average was 16,200, of whom 15,500 were employed.

INTERNATIONAL TRADE

Imports and Exports

In 2003 exports made up 15·6% of Yukon goods and services produced. In 2003 exports were valued at $353m. CDN.

COMMUNICATIONS

Roads

The Alaska Highway and branch highway systems connect Yukon's main communities with Alaska, the Northwest Territories, southern Canada and the United States. The 733-km Dempster Highway north of Dawson City connects with Inuvik, in the Northwest Territories. In 2006 there were 4,902·5 km of roads maintained by the government of Yukon: 3,780·8 km is primary (including the 998·1 km Alaska Highway); 1,121·7 km is secondary. Vehicles registered in 2006 totalled 29,003 (excluding buses, motorcycles and trailers), including 26,621 passenger vehicles.

Rail

The 176-km White Pass and Yukon Railway connected Whitehorse with year-round ocean shipping at Skagway, Alaska, but was closed in 1982. A modified passenger service was restarted in 1988 to take cruise ship tourists from Skagway to Carcross, Yukon, over the White Pass summit.

Civil Aviation

Whitehorse has an international airport with direct daily flights from Vancouver, Alaska and the Northwest Territories. In the summer there are regular scheduled flights from Europe. There are ten airports throughout the territory, with many smaller airstrips and aerodromes in remote areas. Commercial airlines offering charter services are located throughout the territory.

Shipping

The majority of goods are shipped into the territory by truck over the Alaska and Stewart-Cassiar Highways. Some goods are shipped through the ports of Skagway and Haines, Alaska, and then trucked to Whitehorse for distribution throughout the territory.

Telecommunications

All telephone and telecommunications, including internet access in most communities, are provided by Northwestel, a subsidiary of Bell Canada Enterprises. In 2003, 10,000 households (93·4%) had telephones.

SOCIAL INSTITUTIONS

Education

The Yukon Department of Education operates (with the assistance of elected school boards) the territory's 29 schools, both public and private, from kindergarten to grade 12. In May 2006 there were 5,148 pupils. There is also one French First Language school and three Roman Catholic schools. The total enrolment figure for Yukon College in 2005–06 was 5,057. The Whitehorse campus is the administrative and programme centre for 13 other campuses located throughout the territory. In 2005–06 a total of 600 full-time and 4,457 part-time students enrolled in programmes and courses.

Health

In 2006 there were two hospitals with 71 staffed beds, 14 health centres, 74 resident doctors and 16 resident dentists.

CULTURE

Broadcasting

There are three radio stations in Whitehorse and 15 low-power relay radio transmitters operated by CBC, and six operated by the Yukon government. CHON-FM, operated by Northern Native Broadcasting, is broadcast to virtually all Yukon communities by satellite. There are also 27 basic and 36 extended pay-cable TV channels in Whitehorse, and private cable operations in some communities. Live CBC national television and TVNC is provided by satellite and relayed to all communities.

Press

In 2006 there was one daily and one semi-weekly newspaper printed in Whitehorse, and a semi-weekly (summer only) and a monthly newspaper in Dawson City. In total, the territory publishes five newspapers which range in publication from daily to annual.

Tourism

In 2006, 396,377 visitors came to Yukon. Tourism is the largest private sector employer. In 2005 approximately 80% of employees in Yukon worked for businesses that reported some level of tourism revenue. In 2005, 15% of businesses generated more than a third of gross revenues from tourism.

FURTHER READING

Annual Report of the Government of Yukon.
Yukon Executive Council, *Annual Statistical Review.*

Berton, P., *Klondike.* (Rev. ed.) 1987
Coates, K. and Morrison, W., *Land of the Midnight Sun: A History of the Yukon.* 1988

Statistical office: Bureau of Statistics, Executive Council Office, Box 2703, Whitehorse, Yukon Y1A 2C6. There is also a Yukon Archive at Yukon College, Whitehorse.
Website: http://www.eco.gov.yk.ca/stats

CAPE VERDE

República de Cabo Verde
(Republic of Cape Verde)

Capital: Praia
Population estimate, 2010: 513,000
GDP per capita, 2007: (PPP$) 3,041
HDI/world rank: 0·708/121

KEY HISTORICAL EVENTS

During centuries of Portuguese rule the islands were gradually peopled with Portuguese, slaves from Africa and people of mixed African-European descent who became the majority. While retaining some African culture, the Cape Verdians spoke Portuguese or the Portuguese-derived Crioulo (Creole) language and became Catholics. In 1956 nationalists from Cape Verde and Portuguese Guinea formed the *Partido Africano da Independência da Guiné e Cabo Verde* (PAIGC). In the 1960s the PAIGC waged a successful guerrilla war. On 5 July 1975 Cape Verde became independent, ruled by the PAIGC, which was already the ruling party in the former Portuguese colony of Guinea-Bissau. But resentment at Cape Verdians' privileged position in Guinea-Bissau led to the end of the ties between the two countries' ruling parties. Although the PAIGC retained its name in Guinea-Bissau, in Jan. 1981 it was renamed the *Partido Africano da Independência do Cabo Verde* (PAICV) in Cape Verde. The constitution of 1981 made the PAICV the sole legal party but in Sept. 1990 the National Assembly abolished its monopoly and free elections were permitted.

TERRITORY AND POPULATION

Cape Verde is situated in the Atlantic Ocean 620 km off west Africa and consists of ten islands (Boa Vista, Brava, Fogo, Maio, Sal, Santa Luzia, Santo Antão, São Nicolau, São Tiago and São Vicente) and five islets. The islands are divided into two groups, named Barlavento (windward) and Sotavento (leeward). The total area is 4,033 sq. km (1,557 sq. miles). The 2000 census population was 436,823, giving a density of 108·3 per sq. km. In 2005, 57·3% of the population lived in urban areas.

The UN gives an estimated population for 2010 of 513,000.

Over 600,000 Cape Verdeans live abroad (more than still live in the country), mainly in the USA.

Areas and populations of the islands:

Island	*Area (sq. km)*	*Population Census 1990*	*Population Census 2000*
Santo Antão	779	43,845	47,389
São Vicente[1]	227	51,277	67,511
São Nicolau	388	13,665	13,735
Sal	216	7,715	14,892
Boa Vista	620	3,452	4,225
Barlavento	*2,230*	*119,954*	*147,752*
Maio	269	4,969	6,788
São Tiago	991	175,691	237,828
Fogo	476	33,902	37,617
Brava	67	6,975	6,838
Sotavento	*1,803*	*221,537*	*289,071*

[1]Including Santa Luzia island, which is uninhabited.

The main towns are Praia, the capital, on São Tiago (94,361, 2000 census) and Mindelo on São Vicente (63,315, 2000 census). Ethnic groups in 2000 included: Mixed, 70%; Fulani, 12%; Balanta, 10%; Mandyako, 5%. The official language is Portuguese; a creole (Crioulo) is in ordinary use.

SOCIAL STATISTICS

2000 estimates: births, 12,600; deaths, 2,400. Rates, 2000 estimates (per 1,000 population): birth, 29·1; death, 5·6. Annual population growth rate, 1992–2002, 2·2%. Annual emigration varies between 2,000 and 10,000. Life expectancy at birth, 2007, was 68·2 years for men and 73·5 years for women. Infant mortality, 2005, 26 per 1,000 live births; fertility rate, 2004, 3·6 children per woman.

CLIMATE

The climate is arid, with a cool dry season from Dec. to June and warm dry conditions for the rest of the year. Rainfall is sparse, rarely exceeding 5" (127 mm) in the northern islands or 12" (304 mm) in the southern ones. There are periodic severe droughts. Praia, Jan. 72°F (22·2°C), July 77°F (25°C). Annual rainfall 10" (250 mm).

CONSTITUTION AND GOVERNMENT

The Constitution was adopted in Sept. 1992 and was revised in 1995 and 1999.

A constitutional referendum was held on 28 Dec. 1994; turnout was 45%. 82·06% of votes cast favoured a reform extending the powers of the presidency and strengthening the autonomy of local authorities. The *President* is elected for five-year terms by universal suffrage.

The 72-member *National Assembly* (*Assembleia Nacional*) is elected for five-year terms.

National Anthem

'Cântico da Liberdade' ('Song of Freedom'); words by A. S. Lopes, tune by A. H. T. Silva.

RECENT ELECTIONS

Elections for the National Assembly of 72 members were held on 22 Jan. 2006. Turnout was 52·2%. The PAICV won 41 seats with 52·2% of votes cast, the Movement for Democracy (MPD) won 29 seats with 44·0% and the Christian, Independent and

Democratic Union won 2 with 2·6%. Two smaller parties failed to win any seats.

Presidential elections took place on 12 Feb. 2006. Incumbent Pedro Pires was re-elected with 51·0% of the vote against Carlos Veiga with 49·0%. Turnout was 53·1%.

CURRENT ADMINISTRATION

President: Pedro Pires; b. 1934 (PAICV; sworn in 22 March 2001 and re-elected in Feb. 2006).

In March 2010 the government comprised:

Prime Minister: José Maria Neves; b. 1959 (PAICV; sworn in 1 Feb. 2001).

Secretary of State in the Prime Minister's Office in Charge of Economy, Growth and Competitiveness: Humberto Brito.

Senior Minister for Health: Dr Basílio Mosso Ramos. *Senior Minister for Infrastructure and Transport, and Telecommunications:* Manuel Inocêncio Sousa. *Minister for Decentralization, Housing and Regional Development:* Sara Lopes. *Defence and State Reform:* Maria Cristina Fontes Lima. *Education and Sports:* Octávio Ramos Tavares. *Environment, and Rural and Marine Resource Development:* José Maria Veiga. *Finance:* Cristina Duarte. *Foreign Affairs:* José Brito. *Higher Education, Science and Culture:* Fernanda Marques. *Immigrant Communities:* Sidónio Monteiro. *Industry, Tourism and Energy:* Fátima Maria Carvalho Fialho. *Internal Administration:* Lívio Fernandes Lopes. *Justice:* Marisa Helena Morais. *Labour, Family and Solidarity:* Madalena Neves. *Youth, Parliamentary Affairs and Government Spokesperson:* Janira Hopffer Almada.

Government Website: http://www.governo.cv

CURRENT LEADERS

Pedro Pires

Position
President

Introduction
A veteran politician, Pedro Pires was sworn in as the third president of Cape Verde in March 2001, having previously served three terms as prime minister. As a founder member of the African Party for the Independence of Cape Verde (PAICV), he played a prominent role in Cape Verde's independence movement, taking part in the negotiations with the colonial power, Portugal. He won a further term as president in Feb. 2006.

Early Life
Pedro Verona Rodrigues Pires was born on 29 April 1934 on Fogo Island, where he attended comprehensive school in São Filipe before going on to high school in the capital, Praia. He studied at the Science Faculty of the University of Lisbon in the 1950s and stayed in Portugal to carry out his compulsory military service in the Portuguese Air Force. Contact with nationalists from other Portuguese colonies led to his involvement with Amilcar Cabral's African Party for the Independence of Guinea and Cape Verde (PAIGC). Following the death of the Portuguese dictator, Salazar, in 1975 Portugal relinquished its sovereignty over Cape Verde.

Career in Office
Pires was the first prime minister of the independent Cape Verde, taking office in July 1975. The first multi-party elections were held peacefully in 1991. Pires' PAICV lost to the Movement for Democracy (MPD), the first instance of a West African country seeing a single-party government accept defeat at the polls. The 1992 constitution reduced the powers of the president and increased those of parliament.

The perceived sluggishness of economic reform and factionalism within the MPD allowed the return of the PAICV to power after the parliamentary elections of Jan. 2001. José Maria Neves took office as prime minister. After the presidential elections of Feb. 2001, the MPD candidate Carlos Veiga refused to accept a narrow win for Pires by 17 votes, appealing to the Supreme Court on the basis of electoral irregularities. However, Pires' win was confirmed and he took office on 22 March.

After reversing his decision not to stand in the presidential election of Feb. 2006, Pires again defeated Veiga, winning 51% of the vote, to claim a new five-year term.

DEFENCE

The President of the Republic is C.-in-C. of the armed forces. Defence expenditure totalled US$7m. in 2006 (US$17 per capita), representing 0·6% of GDP.

Army
The Army is composed of two battalions and had a strength of 1,000 in 2007.

Navy
There is a coast guard of about 100 (2007) with two patrol craft.

Air Force
The Air Force had under 100 personnel and no combat aircraft in 2007.

INTERNATIONAL RELATIONS

Cape Verde is a member of the UN, World Bank, IMF and several other UN specialized agencies, WTO, IOM, International Organization of the Francophonie, African Development Bank, African Union, ECOWAS and is an ACP member state of the ACP-EU relationship. It became the 153rd member of the WTO in July 2008.

ECONOMY

Agriculture accounted for 8·8% of GDP in 2006, industry 16·3% and services 74·9%.

Overview
Despite poor natural resources and its small island status, Cape Verde has achieved remarkable growth in recent years. Real per capita GDP has expanded on average by 7% per year, a figure greater than other small island economies and countries within sub-Saharan Africa. Real GDP growth peaked in 2006, with strong performance in the tourism, telecommunications and construction sectors. Inflation in 2006 was 5·4% but is expected to stabilize at around 2–3%, consistent with the currency peg to the euro. A target of domestic debt at 20% of GDP was reached two years ahead of schedule in 2007 owing to higher tax revenues, improved tax administration and spending restraint. Poverty fell from 37% to 29% between 2001–06, while unemployment declined by more than 10% during the same period.

The economy's success derives from a government programme, notably tax reforms to reduce domestic debt, the attraction of significant tourism-related foreign direct investment (enhancing credibility of the exchange rate peg) and enhanced private sector involvement in the economy. Strong performance led to Cape Verde's acceptance as a special partner of the EU, an invitation to join the WTO in 2007 and exit from the UN's least-developed country (LDC) status in 2008.

Currency
The unit of currency is the *Cape Verde escudo* (CVE) of 100 *centavos*, which is pegged at 110·6521 to the euro. Foreign exchange reserves were US$164m. in June 2005 and total money supply was 25,156m. escudos. There was inflation of 4·4% in 2007 and 6·8% in 2008.

Budget
Revenues in 2006 were 34,603m. escudos (tax revenue, 68·1%) and expenditures 36,309m. escudos (current expenditure, 59·7%).

VAT is 15%.

Performance
Real GDP growth was 7·8% in 2007 and 5·9% in 2008. Total GDP in 2008 was US$1·7bn.

Banking and Finance
The Banco de Cabo Verde is the central bank (*Governor*, Carlos Burgo) and bank of issue, and was also previously a commercial bank. Its latter functions have been taken over by the Banco Comercial do Atlântico, mainly financed by public funds. The Caixa Econômica de Cabo Verde (CECV) has been upgraded into a commercial and development bank. Two foreign banks have also been established there. In addition, the Fundo de Solidariedade Nacional acts as the country's leading savings institution while the Fundo de Desenvoluimento Nacional administers public investment resources and the Instituto Caboverdiano channels international aid.

ENERGY AND NATURAL RESOURCES

Environment
Cape Verde's carbon dioxide emissions from the consumption and flaring of fossil fuels in 2008 were the equivalent of 0·7 tonnes per capita.

Electricity
Installed capacity was 80,000 kW in 2004. Production was 220m. kWh in 2004. Consumption per capita in 2004 was 529 kWh.

Minerals
Salt is obtained on the islands of Sal, Boa Vista and Maio. Volcanic rock (pozzolana) is mined for export. There are also deposits of kaolin, clay, gypsum and basalt.

Agriculture
In 2002, 21·7% of the economically active population were engaged in agriculture. Some 10–15% of the land area is suitable for farming. In 2003, 46,000 ha. were arable and 3,000 ha. permanent crops, mainly confined to inland valleys. 3,000 ha. were irrigated in 2003. The chief crops (production, 2002, in 1,000 tonnes) are: sugarcane, 14; bananas, 6; coconuts, 6; maize, 5; cabbage, 4; mangoes, 4; sweet potatoes, 4; tomatoes, 4.

Livestock (2003): 200,000 pigs, 112,000 goats, 22,000 cattle, 14,000 asses.

Forestry
In 2005 the woodland area was 84,000 ha., or 20·7% of the total land area.

Fisheries
In 2005 the total catch was 7,742 tonnes (mainly tuna), exclusively from marine waters. About 200 tonnes of lobsters are caught annually.

INDUSTRY
The main industries are the manufacture of paint, beer, soft drinks, rum, flour, cigarettes, canned tuna and shoes.

Labour
In 1996 the workforce was 157,000 (62% males).

INTERNATIONAL TRADE
Foreign debt was US$599m. in 2007.

Imports and Exports
Imports and exports (f.o.b.) for calendar years in US$1m.:

	2001	*2002*	*2003*	*2004*
Imports	233·8	313·7	355·0	421·5
Exports (including re-exports)	32·1	40·9	49·9	53·2

In 2004 machinery and transport equipment constituted 30·8% of imports, with food and live animals accounting for 22·3% and manufactured goods 16·4%; clothing made up 57·4% of exports, footwear 31·2% and seafood 8·2%.

Main import suppliers, 2004: Portugal, 42·5%; Netherlands, 13·7%; USA, 13·2%. Leading export markets, 2004: Portugal, 78·3%; USA, 19·4%; Guinea-Bissau, 0·6%.

COMMUNICATIONS

Roads
In 2002 there were an estimated 1,100 km of roads (78% paved); in 2005 there were 2,244 registered vehicles.

Civil Aviation
Amilcar Cabral International Airport, at Espargos on Sal, is a major refuelling point on flights to Africa and Latin America. A new international airport, Praia International Airport, has been built at Praia on São Tiago, and was opened in 2005. Transportes Aéreos de Cabo Verde (TACV), the national carrier, provided services to most of the other islands in 2003, and internationally to Abidjan, Amsterdam, Bamako, Bissau, Conakry, Dakar, Fortaleza, Las Palmas, Lisbon, Madrid, Milan, Munich, Paris and Zürich. In 2006 Amilcar Cabral International Airport handled 562,972 passengers and 1,415 tonnes of freight. In 2003 scheduled airline traffic of Cape Verde-based carriers flew 5m. km, carrying 253,000 passengers (86,000 on international flights).

Shipping
The main ports are Mindelo and Praia. In 2002 the merchant marine totalled 16,000 GRT. There is a state-owned ferry service between the islands.

Telecommunications
There were 153,100 telephone subscribers in 2005 (302·0 per 1,000 persons), including 81,700 mobile phone subscribers. 48,000 PCs were in use in 2004 (102·7 per 1,000 persons) and there were 25,000 internet users.

Postal Services
In 2003 there were 53 post offices.

SOCIAL INSTITUTIONS

Justice
There is a network of People's Tribunals, with a Supreme Court in Praia. The Supreme Court is composed of a minimum of five Judges, of whom one is appointed by the President, one elected by the National Assembly and the other by the Supreme Council of Magistrates.

The population in penal institutions in Dec. 1999 was 755 (178 per 100,000 of national population). The death penalty was abolished in 1981.

Education
Adult literacy in 2004 was 81·2%. Primary schooling is followed by lower (13–15 years) and upper (16–18 years) secondary education options. In 2005–06 there were 3,196 primary school teachers for 81,162 pupils; and 2,363 teachers for 52,969 pupils at secondary schools. There are two universities: the Jean Piaget University of Cape Verde and the University of Cape Verde.

In 2007 public expenditure on education came to 5·9% of GNI.

Health
In 1996 there were two central and three regional hospitals, 15 health centres, 22 dispensaries and 60 community health clinics. There were 217 physicians and 471 nurses in 2006.

RELIGION
In 2001, 83% of the population were Roman Catholic and 8% were followers of other religions.

CULTURE

World Heritage Sites

Cidade Velha, the historic centre of Ribeira Grande, was inscribed on the UNESCO World Heritage List in 2009. It was the first European colonial town to be built in the tropics.

Broadcasting

Televisão Nacional de Cabo Verde (TNCV) and Radio Nacional de Cabo Verde (RNCV) are the state-run national broadcasting services. Private radio broadcasting is expanding, and Portuguese and French international radio and TV services can also be received. There were 65,000 television receivers in 2005. 61% of households had a television in 2005.

Press

In 2006 there were four national newspapers, none of which were published daily, a state-owned bi-weekly (circulation 5,000) and three independent newspapers..

Tourism

Tourism has experienced huge growth in the past few years. There were 242,000 foreign tourists in 2006 (of which 208,000 were from Europe), compared to just 126,000 in 2002. In 2006 tourist spending totalled US$286m.

DIPLOMATIC REPRESENTATIVES

Of Cape Verde in the United Kingdom
Ambassador: Fernando Jorge Wahnon Ferreira (resides in Brussels).
Honorary Consul: João Roberto (20 Stanley St., Liverpool, L1 6AF)

Of the United Kingdom in Cape Verde
Ambassador: Christopher Trott (resides in Dakar, Senegal).

Of Cape Verde in the USA (3415 Massachusetts Ave., NW, Washington, D.C., 20007)
Ambassador: Maria de Fatima Lima da Veiga.

Of the USA in Cape Verde (Rua Abilio Macedo 6, Praia)
Ambassador: Marianne M. Myles.

Of Cape Verde to the United Nations
Ambassador: António Pedro Monteiro Lima.

Of Cape Verde to the European Union
Ambassador: Fernando Jorge Wahnon Ferreira.

FURTHER READING

National Statistical Office: Instituto Nacional de Estatística, Praia.
Website (Portuguese only): http://www.ine.cv

CENTRAL AFRICAN REPUBLIC

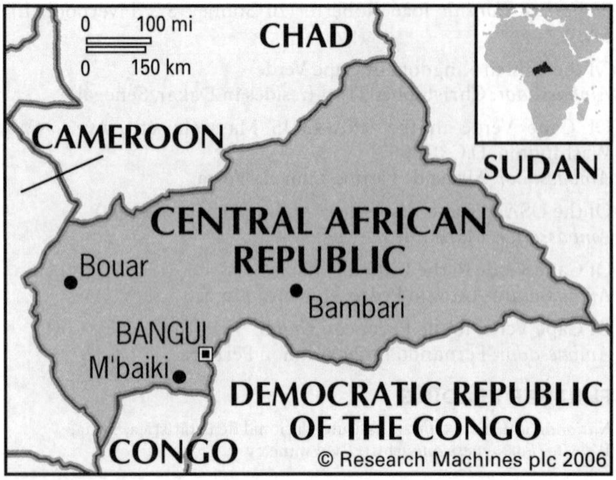

République Centrafricaine

Capital: Bangui
Population estimate, 2010: 4·51m.
GDP per capita, 2007: (PPP$) 713
HDI/world rank: 0·369/179

KEY HISTORICAL EVENTS

Central African Republic became independent on 13 Aug. 1960, after having been one of the four territories of French Equatorial Africa. A constitution of 1976 provided for a parliamentary democracy to be known as the Central African Empire. President Bokassa became Emperor Bokassa I. He was overthrown in 1979. In 1981 Gen. André Kolingba took power, initiating a gradual return to constitutional rule.

On 5 June 1996, following an army mutiny, President Patassé accepted an agreement brokered by France which led to the formation of a government of national unity. But mutineers demanded the replacement of President Patassé. France chaired a mediation committee of various neighbouring French-speaking states. An agreement to end the mutiny was signed in 1997 and a peacekeeping force from neighbouring states, MISAB, was set up. Conflicts between the mutineers and MISAB continued until a ceasefire was concluded on 2 July 1997. There was an attempted coup on 28 May 2001, allegedly led by Gen. Kolingba, who had been the country's military ruler from 1981 to 1993. However, it failed following several days of fighting in and around the capital, Bangui. Fighting erupted once more in Oct. 2002 after another coup attempt. In March 2003 a further coup saw Gen. François Bozizé, a former army chief, seize power.

TERRITORY AND POPULATION

The republic is bounded in the north by Chad, east by Sudan, south by the Democratic Republic of the Congo and the Republic of the Congo, and west by Cameroon. The area (including inland water) covers 622,984 sq. km (240,534 sq. miles). The population at the 2003 census was 3,895,139, giving a density of 6 per sq. km. In 2005, 62·0% of the population were rural. The United Nations population estimate for 2003 was 3,959,000.

The UN gives an estimated population for 2010 of 4·51m.

The areas, populations and capitals of the prefectures are as follows:

Prefecture	*Sq. km*	*2003 census*	*Capital*
Bamingui-Bangoran	58,200	43,229	Ndele
Bangui[1]	67	622,771	Bangui
Basse-Kotto	17,604	249,150	Mobaye
Haute-Kotto	86,650	90,316	Bria
Haut-M'bomou	55,530	57,602	Obo
Kemo	17,204	118,420	Sibut
Lobaye	19,235	246,875	M'baiki
Mambere Kadéi	30,203	364,795	Berbérati
M'bomou	61,150	164,009	Bangassou
Nana Grebizi	19,996	117,816	Kaga-Bandoro
Nana-Mambere	26,600	233,666	Bouar
Ombella-M'poko	31,835	356,725	Bimbo
Ouaka	49,900	276,710	Bambari
Ouham	50,250	369,220	Bossangoa
Ouham-Pendé	32,100	430,506	Bozoum
Sangha M'baéré	19,412	101,074	Nola
Vakaga	46,500	52,255	Birao

[1]Autonomous commune.

The capital, Bangui, had a census population in 2003 of 622,771. Other main towns, with 2003 census populations, are Bimbo (124,176), Bebérati (76,918), Carnot (45,421), Bambari (41,356) and Bouar (40,353).

There are a number of ethnic groups, the largest being Gbaya (34%), Banda (27%) and Mandja (21%).

Sango and French are the official languages.

SOCIAL STATISTICS

2000 births (estimates), 139,000; deaths, 69,000. Estimated birth rate in 2000 was 37·5 per 1,000 population; estimated death rate, 18·6. Infant mortality, 2005 (per 1,000 live births), 115. Expectation of life in 2007 was 45·1 years for males and 48·2 for females. Annual population growth rate, 1992–2002, 2·1%. Fertility rate, 2004, 4·9 children per woman.

CLIMATE

A tropical climate with little variation in temperature. The wet months are May, June, Oct. and Nov. Bangui, Jan. 31·9°C, July 20·7°C. Annual rainfall 1,289·3 mm. Ndele, Jan. 36·3°C, July 30·5°C. Annual rainfall 203·6 mm.

CONSTITUTION AND GOVERNMENT

Under the Constitution adopted by a referendum on 21 Nov. 1986, the sole legal political party was the *Rassemblement Démocratique Centrafricain*. In Aug. 1992 the Constitution was revised to permit multi-party democracy. Further constitutional reforms followed a referendum in Dec. 1994, including the establishment of a *Constitutional Court*. Following the coup of March 2003 Gen. François Bozizé suspended the constitution and dissolved parliament. However, at a referendum on 5 Dec. 2004, 90·4% of voters approved the adoption of a new constitution; voter participation was 77·4%. The new constitution resembles the previous one but permits the *President* to serve not more than two terms of five years. The President appoints the *Prime Minister* and leads the *Council of Ministers*. There is a 105-member *National Assembly*, with members elected in single-member constituencies for a five-year term.

National Anthem

'La Renaissance' ('Rebirth'); words by B. Boganda, tune by H. Pepper.

RECENT ELECTIONS

At the presidential elections held on 13 March 2005 there were 11 presidential candidates. Incumbent president Gen. François Bozizé received 42·9% of the vote, ahead of former prime minister

Martin Ziguélé (Liberation Movement of the Central African People) with 23·5% and former president André Kolingba (Central African Democratic Rally) 16·4%. In the second round on 8 May 2005 Gen. François Bozizé won 64·7% of the vote against Martin Ziguélé who won 35·3%. Turnout was 64·6%.

In National Assembly elections on 13 March and 8 May 2005 the National Convergence coalition gained 42 seats (including the National Unity Party with 3 seats and the Movement for Democracy and Development with 2), the Liberation Movement of the Central African People 11, the Central African Democratic Rally 8, Social Democratic Party 4, Patriotic Front for Progress 2, Alliance for Democracy and Progress 2, the Londo Association 1 and ind. 34.

CURRENT ADMINISTRATION

Former army chief Gen. François Bozizé seized power on 15 March 2003 in a coup and the following day declared himself president, saying that he had dissolved the National Assembly and government. A transitional government was formed comprising representatives of civil society and all political parties. Gen. Bozizé said that a transition period would last between one and three years, after which elections would be held to decide on a new government. Bozizé reshuffled the transitional government in Dec. 2003 and in Sept. 2004. The period of transitional government ended with the 2005 elections, following which Gen. François Bozizé again reshuffled the government. In March 2010 it comprised the following:

President and Minister of Defence, Veterans, War Victims, Disarmament and Army Restructuring: Gen. François Bozizé; b. 1946 (since 16 March 2003).

Prime Minister: Faustin-Archange Touadéra; b. 1957 (took office on 22 Jan. 2008).

Minister of State for Economy, Planning and International Co-operation: Sylvain Maliko. *Mines, Energy and Water Resources:* Sylvain Ndoutingaï. *Transport and Civil Aviation:* Parfait-Anicet M'bay. *Communication, Social Cohesion, Dialogue and National Reconciliation:* Cyriaque Gonda.

Minister of Agriculture and Rural Development: Fidèle Ngouandjika. *Civil Service, Labour, Social Security and Youth Employment Promotion:* Gaston Mackouzangba. *Commerce and Industry:* Emilie Béatrice Epaye. *Environment and Ecology:* François Naoyama. *Equipment and Rural Public Works Development:* Cyriaque Samba Panza. *Family, Social Affairs and National Solidarity:* Bernadette Sayo. *Finance and Budget:* Albert Bessé. *Foreign Affairs, Regional Integration and Francophonie:* Gen. Antoine Gambi. *Housing:* Djomo Didou. *Justice and Keeper of the Seals:* Laurent Gon Baba. *National Education, Higher Education and Research:* Ambroise Zawa. *National Security and Public Order:* Gen. Jules Bernard Ouandé. *Post, Telecommunications and New Technologies:* Thierry Malhéyombo. *Public Health, Population and the Fight against AIDS:* André Nalke-Dorogo. *Reconstruction of Public Buildings and Town Planning:* Faustin Ntenombi. *Small and Medium-Sized Enterprises:* Moïse Kotayé. *Territorial Administration and Decentralization:* Élie Wefio. *Tourism Development and Handicrafts:* Solange Pagonéndji Ndackala. *Water, Forests, Hunting, Fishing and the Environment:* Emmanuel Bizot. *Youth, Sport, Art and Culture:* Aurélien Simplice Zingas. *Secretary General of the Government, in Charge of Relations with Parliament:* Guy Désiré Kolingba.

CURRENT LEADERS

François Bozizé

Position
President

Introduction
Gen. François Bozizé declared himself president of the Central African Republic following a military coup in March 2003, having been a prominent figure on the CAR's political scene during the regimes of Andre Kolingba and Ange-Félix Patassé. He was suspected of involvement in coup attempts in 1983, 2001 and 2002 before seizing control.

Early Life
Bozizé was born in 1946. He came to political prominence as a leading critic of Kolingba's military rule which began in 1981. Having led an unsuccessful coup in 1983, he was arrested and tortured by government forces before going into exile in Togo. There he met Patassé with whom he established strong ties. The two stood against each other at the free elections of 1993 and Bozizé lost. Nonetheless, he remained a Patassé ally, defending him against several uprisings during 1996 and 1997.

However, the relationship became increasingly strained. Bozizé accused Patassé's regime of mismanagement as popular discontent grew at government corruption and failure to pay salaries. In May 2001 Patassé used Libyan forces to put down a coup headed by former president Kolingba, who had been assisted by Bozizé. Bozizé was sacked as head of the army. In Nov. 2001 government troops attempted to arrest Bozizé, but fighting broke out with forces loyal to him. Bozizé held the north of Bangui for a period before taking around 300 troops into exile in Chad. In Oct. 2002 pro-Bozizé factions attempted to depose Patassé, but were defeated amid allegations that Bozizé had instigated the coup with support from Chad.

Career in Office
While Patassé was away in Niger in March 2003 Bozizé led around 1,000 troops into Bangui. They faced little opposition and secured vital strategic locations within a day. Patassé attempted to fly back into the city but was diverted to Cameroon. The Congolese rebels, on whose support Patassé had relied, meanwhile fled over the country.

Having seized power, Bozizé imposed a curfew, dissolved parliament, suspended the constitution and was named president amid promises of free elections. He announced plans to negotiate aid from the IMF and World Bank and promised to address government inefficiency and corruption, disunity in the armed forces and the growing AIDS threat.

Reaction to the coup was mixed. Opposition groups within the CAR welcomed the removal of Patassé, as did many central African nations. However, France, the former colonial power, described the coup as 'unacceptable' and the African Union threatened the CAR's expulsion. There was widespread looting and rioting in Bangui in the days following Bozizé's assumption of power and he appealed to the Economic Community of Central African States to restore order. He was also accused of using backing from Chad in the coup, a charge which provoked widespread unease throughout the country. There followed a period of transitional government until the 2005 presidential and parliamentary elections, in which Bozizé retained power with 43% of the vote.

The poverty-stricken country has, however, remained unstable owing to continuing violence spilling over from the conflict in Darfur in neighbouring Sudan and internal rebel violence in the northeast of the country. In Jan. 2008 civil servants and teachers began a series of strikes in protest at unpaid salaries over several months. At the same time, the prime minister, Élie Doté, resigned and was replaced by Faustin-Archange Touadéra, an academic with no previous political experience.

Following the adoption of an amnesty law, the government reached a peace accord with rebel forces in Dec. 2008 envisaging the formation of a unity government and fresh elections in March 2010—although they were subsequently postponed initially until April 2010 and then until May, when they were delayed yet again. In Jan. 2009 Bozizé dissolved the government and reappointed Touadéra as prime minister of a reshuffled cabinet including representatives of rebel groups. However, sporadic clashes between government and rebel forces have since continued.

DEFENCE

Selective national service for a two-year period is in force.

Defence expenditure totalled US$16m. in 2006 (US$4 per capita), representing 1·0% of GDP.

Army

The Army consisted (2007) of about 2,000 personnel. There is a territorial defence regiment, a combined arms regiment and a support/HQ regiment. In addition there are some 1,000 personnel in the paramilitary Gendarmerie.

Navy

The Army includes a small naval wing operating a handful of patrol craft.

Air Force

Personnel strength (2007) was 150. There are no combat aircraft.

INTERNATIONAL RELATIONS

The Central African Republic is a member of the UN, World Bank, IMF and several other UN specialized agencies, WTO, International Organization of the Francophonie, African Development Bank, African Union, CEEAC, Lake Chad Basin Commission and is an ACP member state of the ACP-EU relationship.

ECONOMY

Agriculture accounted for 55·8% of GDP in 2006, industry 15·5% and services 28·7%.

Overview

Despite being rich in natural resources including diamonds, gold, timber and uranium, and having favourable agricultural conditions, the CAR remains one of the world's poorest countries. Political turmoil and armed conflict have hampered growth over a number of decades, along with droughts, the nation's landlocked position and its poor transport system, together with misdirected government initiatives.

A coup d'état in 2003 preceded two years of transition culminating in legislative and presidential elections in May 2005. The return to representative government prompted the strongest economic growth for a decade. GDP growth was around 4% in 2006 owing to increased private consumption following the resumption of regular salary payments to civil servants, a pick-up in investment, a recovery in diamond and timber exports, and an upturn in agriculture (the economy's largest sector). Inflation moderated to 1% in 2007 as a result of the recovery in agriculture, while the fiscal position has improved as a result of better management.

The economy receives significant international aid, including from the IMF-backed Poverty Reduction and Growth Facility (approved in Dec. 2006) and from the Heavily Indebted Poor Countries initiative (approved in Sept. 2007). However, domestic debt is at 23% of GDP, 60% of which is arrears, with some civil servants owed years of salary.

Currency

The unit of currency is the *franc CFA* (XAF) with a parity of 655·957 francs CFA to one euro. Total money supply in June 2005 was 98,664m. francs CFA, with foreign exchange reserves US$132m. and gold reserves 11,000 troy oz. Inflation was 0·9% in 2007, rising to 9·3% in 2008.

Budget

In 2005 revenue totalled 88,000m. francs CFA and expenditure 120,400m. francs CFA.

VAT is 19%.

Performance

Total GDP in 2008 was US$2·0bn. Real GDP growth was 2·2% in 2008 (3·7% in 2007).

Banking and Finance

The Banque des États de l'Afrique Centrale (BEAC) acts as the central bank and bank of issue. The *Governor* is Philibert Andzembe. There are three commercial banks, a development bank and an investment bank.

ENERGY AND NATURAL RESOURCES

Environment

The Central African Republic's carbon dioxide emissions from the consumption and flaring of fossil fuels in 2008 were the equivalent of 0·1 tonnes per capita.

Electricity

Installed capacity was an estimated 43,000 kW in 2004. Production in 2004 totalled approximately 110m. kWh (around 76% hydro-electric). Consumption per capita in 2004 was about 26 kWh.

Minerals

In 2005 an estimated 265,000 carats of gem diamonds and 88,000 carats of industrial diamonds were mined; and, in 2002, 16 kg of gold. There are also oil, uranium and other mineral deposits which are for the most part unexploited.

Agriculture

In 2002 the agricultural population numbered 2·21m. persons, of whom 1·27m. were economically active. In 2002 about 1·93m. ha. were arable and 94,000 ha. permanent crops. The main crops (production 2002, in 1,000 tonnes) are cassava, 563; yams, 350; groundnuts, 128; bananas, 115; maize, 113; taro, 100; sugarcane, 90; plantains, 82; sorghum, 48.

Livestock, 2002: cattle, 3·27m.; goats, 2·92m.; pigs, 738,000; sheep, 246,000; chickens, 5m.

Forestry

There were 22·76m. ha. of forest in 2005, or 36·5% of the total land area. The extensive hardwood forests, particularly in the southwest, provide mahogany, obeche and limba. Timber production in 2007 was 2·83m. cu. metres.

Fisheries

The catch in 2005 was approximately 15,000 tonnes, exclusively from inland waters.

INDUSTRY

The small industrial sector includes factories producing wood products, cotton fabrics, footwear, beer and radios. Output: sugar (2001), 13,000 tonnes; oils and fats (2000), 7,000 tonnes; beer (2003), 12·2m. litres; cotton fabrics (1992), 5·32m. metres; sawnwood (2001), 150,000 cu. metres.

Labour

In 2003 there were 1,162,000 employed persons (53% males).

INTERNATIONAL TRADE

External debt was US$1,016m. in 2005.

Imports and Exports

Imports in 2000 totalled US$247m. (US$253m. in 1999); exports in 2000 totalled US$181m. (US$178m. in 1999).

Main import suppliers, 1999: France, 33·8%; Cameroon, 12·2%; Belgium-Luxembourg, 7·4%; UK, 4·1%. Main export markets, 2000: Belgium-Luxembourg, 64·7%; Spain, 6·3%; France, 3·2%; Taiwan, 3·2%. Main imports include food, textiles, petroleum products, machinery, electrical equipment and motor vehicles. Main exports are diamonds, coffee, timber and cotton.

COMMUNICATIONS

Roads

There were 23,417 km of roads in 2002, including 5,200 km of highways or main roads. In 2007 there were 1,200 passenger cars,

58 lorries and vans, and 4,500 motorcycles and mopeds. There were 77 road accident deaths in 2000.

Civil Aviation

There is an international airport at M'Poko, near Bangui, which handled 44,000 passengers (41,000 on international flights) in 2001. In 2003 there were direct services operating to Douala, Khartoum, Nyala, Paris and Yaoundé. In 2001 scheduled airline traffic of Central African Republic-based carriers flew 1m. km, carrying 46,000 passengers (all on international flights).

Shipping

Timber and barges are taken to Brazzaville (Republic of the Congo).

Telecommunications

There were 70,000 telephone subscribers in 2004 (equivalent to 17·9 per 1,000 persons), including 60,000 mobile phone subscribers. There were 11,000 PCs in use (2·8 per 1,000 persons) in 2004 and 9,000 internet users.

Postal Services

In 2003 there were 32 post offices.

SOCIAL INSTITUTIONS

Justice

The Criminal Court and Supreme Court are situated in Bangui. There are 16 high courts throughout the country. The population in penal institutions in 2001 was 4,168 (110 per 100,000 of national population).

Education

Adult literacy rate was 48·6% in 2003 (64·8% among males and 33·5% among females).

In 2002–03 there were 284,869 pupils at the *fondamental 1* (lower primary) level; 49,922 pupils at *fondamental 2*; and 9,945 pupils at secondary schools. The University of Bangui, founded in 1969, is the leading institution in the tertiary sector. In 2006 there were 4,462 students in total in higher education.

Public expenditure on education came to 1·3% of GNI in 2006.

Health

In 1990 there were 255 hospitals and health centres with 4,120 beds (4,126 beds in 2000). In 2000 there were 114 doctors, 179 midwives and 217 state qualified nurses. The government's health care budget for 2000 was 5·4m. francs CFA and foreign aid amounted to 5·3m. francs CFA.

RELIGION

In 2001 there were 660,000 Roman Catholics, 560,000 Muslims and 520,000 Protestants. Traditional animist beliefs are still widespread.

CULTURE

World Heritage Sites

The Manovo-Gounda St Floris National Park was inscribed on the UNESCO World Heritage List in 1988. Poaching and violence closed the park to tourism in 1997.

Broadcasting

Broadcasting is state-controlled through the Radiodiffusion-Télévision Centrafricaine, although the United Nations-sponsored Radio Ndeke Luka station in Bangui rebroadcasts international news programmes. There were 42,000 TV sets in 2005 (colour by SECAM V).

Press

In 2006 there were six daily newspapers with a circulation of 5,000, although none of these were distributed outside the Bangui area.

Tourism

In 2005, 12,000 non-resident tourists arrived by air; spending by tourists totalled US$4m. in 2004.

DIPLOMATIC REPRESENTATIVES

Of Central African Republic in the United Kingdom
Ambassador: Jean Willybiro Sako (resides in Paris).

Of the United Kingdom in Central African Republic
Ambassador: Bharat Joshi (resides in Yaoundé, Cameroon).

Of Central African Republic in the USA (1618 22nd St., NW, Washington, D.C., 20008)
Ambassador: Stanislas Moussa-Kembe.

Of the USA in Central African Republic (Ave. David Dacko, Bangui)
Ambassador: Frederick B. Cook.

Of Central African Republic to the United Nations
Ambassador: Fernand Poukré-Kono.

Of Central African Republic to the European Union
Ambassador: Armand-Guy Zounguere-Sokambi.

FURTHER READING

Kalck, Pierre, *Historical Dictionary of the Central African Republic.* 3rd ed. 2004
Titley, B., *Dark Age: The Political Odyssey of Emperor Bokassa.* 1997

National Statistical Office: Division des Statistiques, des Études Économiques et Sociales, BP 696, Bangui.
Website (French only): http://www.stat-centrafrique.com

CHAD

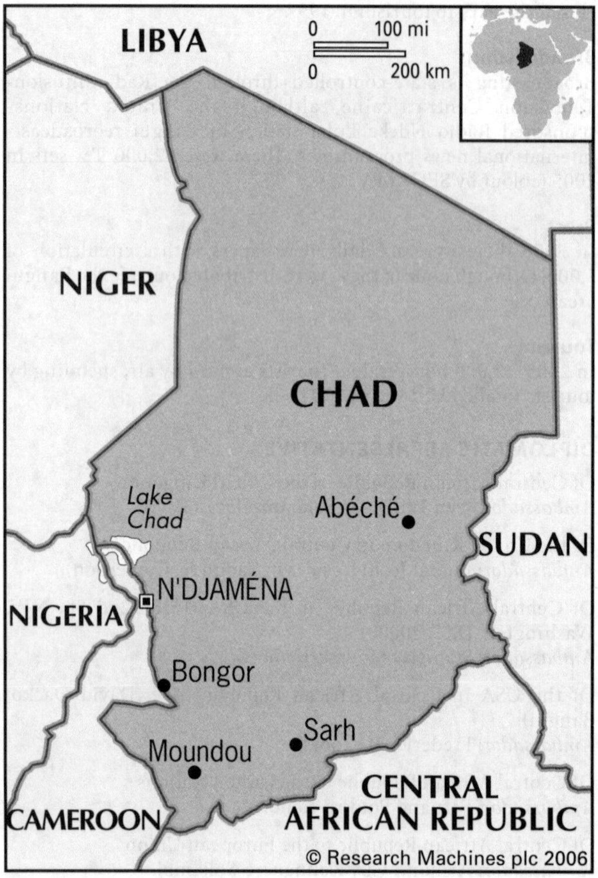

République du Tchad
(Republic of Chad)

Capital: N'Djaména
Population estimate, 2010: 11·51m.
GDP per capita, 2007: (PPP$) 1,477
HDI/world rank: 0·392/175

KEY HISTORICAL EVENTS

France proclaimed a protectorate over Chad in 1900 and in July 1908 the territory was incorporated into French Equatorial Africa. It became a separate colony in 1920, and in 1946 one of the four constituent territories of French Equatorial Africa. It achieved full independence on 11 Aug. 1960. Conflicts between the government and secessionist groups, particularly in the Muslim north and centre, began in 1965 and developed into civil war. In 1982 forces led by Hissène Habré gained control of the country. In June 1983 Libyan-backed forces reoccupied some territory but a ceasefire took effect in Sept. 1987. Rebel forces of the Popular Salvation Movement led by Idriss Déby entered Chad from Sudan in Nov. 1990. On 4 Dec. 1990 Déby declared himself President. In Feb. 2000 Hissène Habré was charged with torture and barbarity and put under house arrest in Senegal, where he had lived since being toppled in 1990.

TERRITORY AND POPULATION

Chad is bounded in the west by Cameroon, Nigeria and Niger, north by Libya, east by Sudan and south by the Central African Republic. In Feb. 1994 the International Court of Justice ruled that the Aozou Strip along the Libyan border, occupied by Libya since 1973, was part of Chad. Area, 1,284,000 sq. km. At the 2009 census the provisional population was 11,175,915. In 1993, 94% of the population were settled (of whom 22% were urban and 6% nomadic).

The UN gives an estimated population for 2010 of 11·51m.; density, 9 per sq. km.

In 2005, 74·7% of the population were rural. The capital is N'Djaména with 993,492 inhabitants (2009 census, provisional), other large towns being (2009 provisional census figures) Moundou (132,411) and Sarh (99,099).

Following administrative reforms of 2002 and 2008, Chad's 14 prefectures were divided into 22 regions, including the City of N'Djaména (which is a commune governed by a special statute). The 22 regions are (with 2009 provisional census population and capital): Barh el Ghazel, population 260,865 (Moussoro); Batha, 527,031 (Ati); Bourkou, 97,251 (Faya); Chari-Baguirmi, 621,785 (Massénya); Ennedi, 173,606 (Fada); Guéra, 553,795 (Mongo); Hadjer-Lamis, 562,957 (Massakory); Kanem, 354,603 (Mao); Lac, 451,369 (Bol); Logone Occidental, 683,293 (Moundou); Logone Oriental, 796,453 (Doba); Mandoul, 637,086 (Koumra); Mayo-Kebbi Est, 769,178 (Bongor); Mayo-Kebbi Ouest, 565,087 (Pala); Moyen-Chari, 598,284 (Sarh); N'Djaména, 993,492 (N'Djaména); Ouaddaï, 731,679 (Abéché); Salamat, 308,605 (Am-Timan); Sila, 289,776 (Goz Beïda); Tandjilé, 682,817 (Laï); Tibesti, 21,970 (Bardaï); Wadi Fira, 494,933 (Biltine).

The official languages are French and Arabic, but more than 100 different languages and dialects are spoken. The largest ethnic group is the Sara of southern Chad (27·7% of the total population), followed by the Sudanic Arabs (11·5%).

SOCIAL STATISTICS

2001 estimates: births, 398,000; deaths, 138,000. Rates, 2001 estimates (per 1,000 population): births, 49·1; deaths, 17·0. Annual rate of growth, 1992–2002, 3·1%. Expectation of life in 2007 was 47·3 years among males and 49·9 among females. Infant mortality, 2005 (per 1,000 live births), 124. Fertility rate, 2004, 6·7 children per woman.

CLIMATE

A tropical climate, with adequate rainfall in the south, though Nov. to April are virtually rainless months. Further north, desert conditions prevail. N'Djaména, Jan. 75°F (23·9°C), July 82°F (27·8°C). Annual rainfall 30" (744 mm).

CONSTITUTION AND GOVERNMENT

After overthrowing the regime of Hissène Habré, Idriss Déby proclaimed himself *President* and was sworn in on 4 March 1991.

A law of Oct. 1991 permits the formation of political parties provided they are not based on regionalism, tribalism or intolerance. There were 59 parties in 1996.

At a referendum on 31 March 1996 a new constitution was approved by 63·5% of votes cast. It defines Chad as a unitary state. The head of state is the *President*, elected by universal suffrage. On 26 May 2004 the *National Assembly* passed an amendment scrapping the two-term limit on the presidency, replacing it with an age limit of 70. The amendment was approved by referendum in June 2005.

The National Assembly has 155 members, elected for a four-year term. A *Senate* was stipulated in the 1996 constitution, but has yet to be created.

National Anthem

'Peuple tchadien, debout et à l'ouvrage' ('People of Chad, arise and take up the task'); words by L. Gidrol, tune by P. Villard.

RECENT ELECTIONS

Presidential elections were held on 3 May 2006. Turnout was 53·1%. Incumbent Idriss Déby won re-election, with 64·7% of the vote, against 15·1% for Delwa Kassiré Koumakoye, 7·8% for Albert Pahimi Padacké, 7·1% for Mahamat Abdoulaye and 5·3% for Brahim Koulamallah.

In parliamentary elections held on 21 April 2002 the Patriotic Salvation Movement (MPS) of President Idriss Déby won 102 seats, the Rally for Democracy and Progress (RDP) 12, the Federation Action for the Republic 11, the VIVA-National Rally for Development and Progress 5, the National Union for Democracy and Renewal 5 and the Union for Renewal and Democracy 3. Turnout was 52·8%.

Parliamentary elections are scheduled to take place on 28 Nov. 2010.

CURRENT ADMINISTRATION

President: Lieut.-Gen. Idriss Déby; b. 1954 (MPS; in office since Dec. 1990 and re-elected 3 July 1996, 20 May 2001 and 3 May 2006).

In March 2010 the government comprised:

Prime Minister: Emmanuel Nadingar; b. 1951 (in office since 5 March 2010).

Minister of Agriculture and Irrigation: Albert Pahimi Padacké. *Civil Service and Labour:* Abdoulaye Abakar. *Commerce and Industry:* Youssouf Abassallah. *Communications and Government Spokesman:* Kedallah Younous. *Culture, Youth and Sport:* Djibert Younous. *Defence:* Gen. Wadal Abdelkader Kamougué. *Economy and Planning:* Mahamat Ali Hassan. *Environment and Fisheries:* Hassan Terap. *Finance and Budget:* Gata Ngoulou. *Foreign Affairs, African Integration and International Co-operation:* Moussa Faki Mahamat. *Higher Education, Scientific Research and Professional Training:* Ahmad Taboye. *Infrastructure and Transport:* Adoum Younousmi. *Interior and Public Security:* Ahamat Mahamat Bachir. *Justice and Keeper of the Seals:* Mbailaou Naembave Lossimian. *Land Management, Town Planning and Housing:* Djimrangar Dadnadji. *Livestock and Animal Resources:* Ahmat Rakhis Mannany. *Mines and Geology:* Hassan Saline. *National Education:* Abderahim Yunous Ali. *Oil Resources and Energy:* Eugène Tabé. *Posts, New Technology and Communications:* Jean Bawoyeu Alingué. *Public Health:* Dr Toupta Boguena. *Public Sanitation and Good Governance:* Ahmadaye Al Hassan. *Social Action, National Solidarity and Family Affairs:* Ngarmbatina Carmel Sou IV. *Tourism Development and Handicrafts:* Mahamat Allaou Taher. *Water:* Ahmat Mahamat Karambale. *Minister in Charge of Human Rights and the Promotion of Liberty:* Abderamane Djasnabaille. *Minister in Charge of Microfinance and the Fight Against Poverty:* Fatime Tchombi.

Government Website (French only):
http://www.primature-tchad.org

CURRENT LEADERS

Idriss Déby

Position
President

Introduction
Lieut.-Gen. Idriss Déby became president in Feb. 1991 after participating in a coup to overthrow Hissène Habré. He oversaw multi-party elections, but opponents cited electoral irregularities after Déby's victories at the 1996 and 2001 polls and largely boycotted the 2006 presidential contest. His tenure has been marked by civil war and an overspill of fighting from Darfur in neighbouring Sudan, hindering attempts at reducing Chad's extreme poverty. The country's recently acquired status as an oil exporter may boost the economy.

Early Life
Déby was born in 1952 into the Bidyate clan of the Zaghawa peoples. While serving in the army he helped Hissène Habré take power in 1982, overthrowing Goukouki Queddei in a coup. His relationship with Habré declined and in 1989 Déby was accused of involvement in an alleged coup and went into exile in Sudan. In Dec. 1990, as head of the Patriotic Salvation Movement (MPS) and with the support of Libya, he removed Habré from power. Déby was proclaimed president in Feb. 1991 and in 1993 was appointed interim head of a transitional government charged with preparing democratic elections to be held within a year.

Career in Office
Déby went on to establish a multi-party constitution and triumphed at presidential elections held in 1996. The MPS won elections to the legislative assembly the following year.

Déby has had to cope with tensions between the largely Arab-Muslim north and the mainly Christian and animist south. In 1998 there was a surge in rebel activity in the north, spearheaded by the Movement for Democracy and Justice in Chad (MDJT), led by Déby's former defence minister Youssouf Togoimi. In early 2002 Libyan leader Col. Qadhafi, formerly a supporter of Chadian rebel movements, brokered a peace agreement which included provision for an amnesty for MDJT members. It soon failed but in Jan. 2003 the government reached a peace agreement with the rebel National Resistance Army in the east and in Dec. that year a new accord was signed with the MDJT.

Déby was re-elected in 2001 although the electoral commission discounted results from 25% of polling stations for electoral irregularities. Six of Déby's defeated rivals were subsequently arrested for 'inciting violence and civil disobedience' but later released as human rights organizations and trades unions pressed for a general strike. Déby was sworn in to office in Aug. 2001. In 2001 the Senegalese judicial system concluded that it lacked the authority to try Habré, the deposed former president in exile in Senegal, on charges of authorizing torture. A constitutional amendment in June 2005 permitted Déby to stand for a third term of office, which he did successfully in May 2006 as the main opposition parties boycotted the poll.

Since 2003 fighting has spilled over the border from Darfur in neighbouring Sudan. There has been a large influx of refugees from Darfur into the Chadian interior, many under the supervision of the UNHCR. From 2005 Chad accused Sudan of supporting Chadian rebels, who made unsuccessful assaults on the capital, N'Djaména, in April 2006 and Feb. 2008. The government meanwhile declared a state of emergency in eastern provinces in Nov. 2006 and again in Oct. 2007. In March 2008 Déby and Sudan's president signed an accord aimed at stopping hostilities between their two countries. However, alleged Chadian involvement in a rebel attack on Omdurman, close to the Sudanese capital of Khartoum, in May prompted Sudan to sever diplomatic relations and Déby to close Chad's borders and cut economic links in retaliation. In Jan. 2009 several rebel groups united to form a new alliance named the Union of Resistance Forces (UFR), which in May launched a major offensive in eastern Chad from bases in Sudan. The offensive was repelled, but the action further exacerbated tensions between the Chadian and Sudanese governments.

Déby's political survival has been attributed in large part to the presence of French forces in the country, although his tenure has seen a steady worsening in relations with the former colonial power.

DEFENCE

There are seven military regions. Total armed forces personnel numbered 25,350 in 2007, including republican guards. Defence expenditure totalled US$59m. in 2006 (US$6 per capita), representing 0·9% of GDP.

Army

In 2007 the strength was about 17,000 although it is being reorganized. In addition there was a paramilitary Gendarmerie of 4,500 and a Republican Guard of 5,000.

Air Force

Personnel (2007), 350 including four combat capable aircraft and two attack helicopters.

INTERNATIONAL RELATIONS

Chad is a member of the UN, World Bank, IMF and several other UN specialized agencies, WTO, International Organization of the Francophonie, Islamic Development Bank, OIC, African Development Bank, African Union, CEEAC, Lake Chad Basin Commission and is an ACP member state of the ACP-EU relationship.

ECONOMY

Agriculture accounted for 20·5% of GDP in 2006, industry 54·8% and services 24·7%.

Chad featured among the ten most corrupt countries in the world in a 2009 survey of 180 countries carried out by the anti-corruption organization *Transparency International*.

Overview

After 30 years of civil war, Chad is dependent on external aid (chiefly from the IMF, the World Bank and the EU) while the agrarian sector supports 80% of the population despite accounting for less than 40% of GDP. Per capita income is less than US$250 per annum, with economic development hindered by political instability, droughts and primitive infrastructure.

However, there has been substantial recent economic growth resulting from oil-related investments and the completion of the Chad–Cameroon oil pipeline in July 2003. The majority of Chad's oil revenues have been earmarked for priority sectors such as education, health care, infrastructure and rural development. Since the mid-1990s real GDP growth has averaged 5·2%, with growth of 10% since 2001 and peaking at over 30% in 2004. Growth in the non-oil sector is more volatile, reflecting the vulnerability of the cotton sector to declines in world prices, bad weather and disease-based shocks. Growth has slowed since 2005, owing to technical problems with oil production and difficulties in the cotton sector. Domestic debt continues to rise, reflecting weak public finance management.

Chad became a member of CAEMU (the Central African Economic and Monetary Union) in 2004. The currency is pegged to the euro and managed by the Banque des États de l'Afrique Centrale.

Currency

The unit of currency is the *franc CFA* (XAF) with a parity of 655·957 francs CFA to one euro. There was deflation of 7·4% in 2007, but then inflation of 8·3% in 2008. Foreign exchange reserves were US$214m. in June 2005, total money supply was 213,920m. francs CFA and gold reserves were 11,000 troy oz.

Budget

Revenues in 2004 were 239·0bn. francs CFA (tax revenue, 52·3%) and expenditures 296·0bn. francs CFA (current expenditure, 55·3%).

VAT is 18%.

Performance

In 2008 Chad suffered negative growth, with economy shrinking by 0·2%. As recently as 2004 there had been growth of 33·6%, thanks mainly to the construction of an oil pipeline from landlocked Chad to Cameroon. Chad became the world's newest oil producer in 2003, and as a result in 2004 recorded the highest economic growth of any country. In 2008 total GDP was US$8·4bn.

Banking and Finance

The Banque des États de l'Afrique Centrale (*Governor*, Philibert Andzembe) is the bank of issue. Other leading banks include: Banque Agricole du Soudan au Tchad; Banque Commerciale du Chari; Banque Internationale de l'Afrique au Tchad; Commercial Bank Tchad; Financial Bank Tchad; and Société Générale Tchadienne de Banque.

ENERGY AND NATURAL RESOURCES

Environment

Carbon dioxide emissions from the consumption and flaring of fossil fuels were the equivalent of less than 0·1 tonnes per capita in 2008. An *Environmental Performance Index* compiled in 2008 ranked Chad 143rd in the world out of 149 countries analysed, with 45·9%. The index examined various factors in six areas—air pollution, biodiversity and habitat, climate change, environmental health, productive natural resources and water resources.

Electricity

Installed capacity was estimated at 29,000 kW in 2004. Production in 2004 amounted to about 99m. kWh. Consumption per capita was an estimated 11 kWh in 2004.

Oil and Gas

The oilfield in Kanem prefecture has been linked by pipeline to a new refinery at N'Djaména but production has remained minimal. There is a larger oilfield in the Doba Basin. In June 2000 the World Bank approved funding for a 1,070-km US$4bn. pipeline to run from 300 new oil wells in Chad through Cameroon to the Atlantic Ocean. Oil started pumping in July 2003. Oil production in 2008 was 6·7m. tonnes. Proven reserves totalled 0·9bn. bbls in 2008. Revenues are expected to reach US$80m. per annum.

Minerals

Salt (about 4,000 tonnes per annum) is mined around Lake Chad, and there are deposits of uranium, gold, iron ore and bauxite. There are small-scale workings for gold and iron.

Agriculture

Some 80% of the workforce is involved in subsistence agriculture and fisheries. In 2001, 3·60m. ha. were arable and 30,000 ha. permanent crops. There were 175 tractors in 2001. Cotton growing (in the south) and animal husbandry (in the central zone) are the most important branches. Production, 2002 (in 1,000 tonnes): sorghum, 481; groundnuts (2001), 477; millet, 357; sugarcane, 355; cassava (2001), 306; yams, 230; seed cotton, 170; rice, 135; cottonseed, 100; maize, 84; dry beans, 78.

Livestock, 2001: cattle, 5,992,000; goats, 5,304,000; sheep, 2,431,000; camels, 725,000; chickens, 5m.

Forestry

In 2005 the area under forests was 11·92m. ha., or 9·5% of the total land area. Timber production in 2007 was 7·47m. cu. metres.

Fisheries

Total catches, from Lake Chad and the Chari and Logone rivers, were approximately 70,000 tonnes in 2005.

INDUSTRY

Output: cotton fibre (1998), 86,260 tonnes; sugar (2002), 32,000 tonnes; soap (1996), 2,958 tonnes; edible oil (1996), 12·55m. litres; beer (2003), 21·6m. litres; cigarettes (2000), 30m. packets; bicycles (1996), 3,444 units.

Labour

In 2003 the labour force was 4,171,710 (55% males). In 2003 approximately 72% of the economically active population were engaged in agriculture.

INTERNATIONAL TRADE

External debt was US$1,633m. in 2005.

Imports and Exports

Imports in 2000 totalled US$450m. (US$474m. in 1999); exports in 2000 totalled US$233m. (US$242m. in 1999).

Main import suppliers in 1997 were France, 41·3%; Nigeria, 10·1%; Cameroon, 7·2%; India, 5·8%; Belgium-Luxembourg, 5·1%; Italy, 4·3%. Main export markets were Portugal, 29·9%; Germany, 14·2%; Thailand, 7·5%; Costa Rica, 6·0%; Hong Kong, 4·8%; Taiwan, 4·8%. The principal imports are machinery and transportation equipment, industrial goods, petroleum products and foodstuffs. Cotton exports in 1994, 28,857m. francs CFA; cattle, 15,401 francs CFA. Apart from cotton and cattle, other important exports are textiles and fish.

COMMUNICATIONS

Roads

In 2006 there were around 40,000 km of roads. 18,900 passenger cars were in use in 2006, plus 3,300 buses and coaches, 35,400 lorries and vans, and 63,000 motorcycles and mopeds.

Civil Aviation

There is an international airport at N'Djaména, from which there were direct flights in 2003 to Addis Ababa, Bamako, Bangui, Douala, Garoua, Kano, Paris, Tripoli and Yaoundé. In 2001 scheduled airline traffic of Chad-based carriers flew 1m. km, carrying 46,000 passengers (all on international flights). In 2000 N'Djaména handled 17,000 passengers and 2,300 tonnes of freight.

Telecommunications

In 2004 telephone subscribers numbered 136,000 (15·4 per 1,000 persons), of which 123,000 were mobile phone subscribers. There were 15,000 PCs in use (1·7 per 1,000 persons) in 2004 and 35,000 internet users.

Postal Services

In 2003 there were 42 post offices, or one for every 204,700 persons.

SOCIAL INSTITUTIONS

Justice

There are criminal courts and magistrates courts in N'Djaména, Moundou, Sarh and Abéché, with a Court of Appeal situated in N'Djaména.

The population in penal institutions in Aug. 2005 was 3,416 (35 per 100,000 of national population).

The death penalty is still in force. In 2003 there were nine executions (the first since 1991).

Education

In 2007 there were 1,324,298 pupils in primary schools with 21,933 teaching staff and 314,470 pupils in secondary schools with 9,555 teaching staff. In 2005 there were 10,468 students with 1,100 academic staff at institutes of tertiary education. Adult literacy rate was 25·5% in 2003 (male, 40·6%; female, 12·7%).

In 2005 public expenditure on education came to 2·3% of GNI and 10·1% of total government spending.

Health

In 2001 there were 4,105 hospital beds. There were 205 doctors, 1,220 nurses, 161 midwives and 38 pharmacists in 2001.

Chad has made significant progress in the reduction of undernourishment in the past 15 years. Between the period 1990–92 and 2001–03 the proportion of undernourished people declined from 58% of the population to 33%.

RELIGION

The northern and central parts of the country are predominantly Muslim. In 2001 there were estimated to be 4,690,000 Muslims, 1,770,000 Roman Catholics and 1,250,000 Protestants. Traditional beliefs are still widespread.

CULTURE

Broadcasting

Radiodiffusion Nationale Tchadienne (RNT), which broadcasts national and regional radio services, and Télé-Tchad, the only television station (colour by SECAM V), are state-controlled. There are a few private radio services. There were 90,000 TV receivers in 2006.

Press

There are no daily newspapers; there were five non-dailies in 2006, including the government-owned Info-Tchad. Combined circulation was 4,000.

Tourism

In 2005, 29,000 non-resident tourists stayed in hotels or similar accommodation.

DIPLOMATIC REPRESENTATIVES

Of Chad in the United Kingdom
Ambassador: Ahmat Abderaman Haggar (resides in Brussels).

Of the United Kingdom in Chad
Ambassador: Bharat Joshi (resides in Yaoundé, Cameroon).

Of Chad in the USA (2002 R. St., NW, Washington, D.C., 20009)
Ambassador: Mahamoud Adam Bechir.

Of the USA in Chad (Ave. Felix Eboue, N'Djaména)
Ambassador: Louis Nigro.

Of Chad to the United Nations
Ambassador: Ahmad Alaam-mi.

Of Chad to the European Union
Ambassador: Maïtine Djoumbe.

FURTHER READING

National Statistical Office: Direction de la Statistique des Études Économiques et Démographiques, Ministère du Plan et de la Coopération, 453 N'Djaména.
Website (French only): http://www.inseed-tchad.org

CHILE

República de Chile
(Republic of Chile)

Capitals: Santiago (Administrative), Valparaíso (Legislative)
Population estimate, 2010: 17·14m.
GDP per capita, 2007: (PPP$) 13,880
HDI/world rank: 0·878/44

KEY HISTORICAL EVENTS

Archaeological evidence suggests the earliest settlements in Chile date from around 10,500 BC. A discovery at Monte Verde, near Puerto Montt in southern Chile, indicates that its inhabitants were hunter-gatherers in a temperate rainforest. They were probably the descendents of Paleo-Indians who crossed from Siberia by way of the Bering Strait (at various times a land bridge). Prior to the arrival of Europeans, the indigenous peoples included the Atacameno (living in small settlements in the northern deserts and influenced by the cultures of the central Andes, such as the Inca empires of Chincha and Quechua), the Araucanians (farmers in the more temperate valleys of central Chile) and the Chono (Alacaluf and Yahgan nomads from the mountainous southern areas).

Ferdinand Magellan was the first European to glimpse what is now Chile in 1520, when he sailed through the bleak archipelago at the tip of South America en route for the Pacific Ocean. Fifteen years later a Spanish expeditionary force, led by Diego de Almagro, set off from the newly-captured Inca city of Cusco to explore land to the south. Almagro travelled as far as the Itata river but came under repeated attacks from hostile Araucanians and was unable to establish a foothold. He returned to Peru in 1536, with news only of 'a cursed land without gold, inhabited by savages of the worst kind.' Five years passed before the next Spanish expedition to Chile left Cusco, headed by Pedro de Valdivia. After months of hardship, battles with Araucanians and internal divisions, Valdivia's forces established the settlement of Santiago in early 1541. In the next ten years the Spanish built fortified towns at Concepción, La Serena, Valdivia and Villarrica. North of Concepción, they began to convert the Araucanians to Christianity and established mines run on forced labour. Subjugating the indigenous people south of Concepción, however, proved difficult. In that region, Araucanians known as Mapuche fought hard and quickly adapted their weapons and tactics to become effective guerrilla fighters. 50 years after Valdivia's forces arrived in Chile, the colony remained a frontier, dependent on the Viceroyalty of Peru and governed by military officers based in dispersed fort towns. Gold was discovered but the wealth it generated was minimal compared with the riches that poured out of Mexico and Peru.

Opposition to Spain

Following further military defeats at the hands of the Mapuche and the destruction of Concepción in an earthquake in 1570, King Felipe II of Spain named a veteran conquistador, Rodrigo de Quiroga, as governor of Chile. After 1575 Quiroga attempted to quell rebellion with a brutal campaign against the Araucanians, capturing them for forced labour and mutilating their feet to prevent escape. A subsequent governor, Garcia Onez de Loyola, attempted to moderate these abuses, but was eventually killed at the battle of Curalaba in 1598. Subsequently, all major Spanish settlements south of the Bíobío river were destroyed or abandoned. In 1600 the king of Spain granted a permanent military subsidy to fund the war in Chile and in 1608 he signed a royal decree legalizing the enslavement of 'rebellious' Indians. At around this time, coastal settlements such as Valparaíso came under attack from English and Dutch adventurers and pirates, in search of wealth and as part of a prolonged effort to force Spain to allow other nations to trade with its colonies. The relative lack of mineral wealth in Chile led the 5,000 or so Spanish settlers to develop a pastoral and agricultural society; they grew a wide range of cereals and raised livestock. North of the Bíobío river, there was considerable intermarriage and the rapid growth of a mestizo (mixed Amerindian and European) group. The social status of mestizos was determined by the extent to which they were Hispanicized and by their kinship ties with the landed class.

In 1664 the governorship of Chile passed to Francisco de Meneses, an opportunist who took advantage of the warfare economy, taxing ships unless they carried his merchandise. He demanded bribes and accumulated vast wealth from the slave trade. An earthquake that shook Lima in 1687 severely disrupted the supply of food to the Peruvian city for some years. Chilean merchants cashed in by shipping wheat from the country's central belt and there was a rapid expansion in wheat production. The wheat 'boom' continued until 1700 and the trade was controlled by a clique of merchants who colluded with corrupt officials. Attempts by successive governors to make peace with the Mapuche (the Pact of Quillin) ended in failure, and sporadic fighting continued throughout the 17th and 18th centuries. Many thousands of Mapuche migrated eastwards across the Andes to Argentina.

Bourbon Rule

The Habsburg dynasty's rule over Spain ended in 1700. They were succeeded by the Bourbons who tried to improve the empire's productivity and defence. The Bourbon rulers gave the *audiencia* of Chile (based in Santiago) greater independence from the Viceroyalty of Peru. One of the most charismatic governors of the Bourbon era was the Irish-born Ambrosio O'Higgins, who presided over increased economic production and strengthened the military. In 1791 he also outlawed forced labour. Economic links with Argentina increased after it became the Viceroyalty of the Río de la Plata in 1776 and by the end of the 18th century Chile was engaging in direct trade with Europe. Freer trade brought with it knowledge of politics abroad, particularly the spread of liberalism in Europe and American independence. The Royal University of San Felipe was established at Santiago in 1758 but most educated Chileans followed the traditional ideology of the Spanish crown and the Roman Catholic Church, while the majority of mestizos and Araucanians remained illiterate and subordinate.

The French Revolution and Napoleon Bonaparte's subsequent invasion of Spain in 1807 sent shockwaves through the Spanish colonies, eventually leading to greater autonomy and independence. On 18 Sept. 1810 the Santiago elite, employing the town council as a junta, announced their intention to govern the colony until Fernando VII was reinstated. They remained loyal to the ousted Spanish king but insisted they had the right to rule and immediately relaxed trade restrictions. Chile's first government was led by José Miguel Carrera Verdugo. Carrera and his brothers, as well as Bernardo O'Higgins (son of former governor Ambrosio O'Higgins) soon saw the opportunity to replace temporary self-rule with permanent independence, although others remained loyal to Spain and civil conflict ensued. 1814 saw the start of the Reconquest (*La Reconquista*), and the Spanish authorities managed to reassert control of Chile by winning the Battle of Rancagua. O'Higgins and many of the Chilean rebels escaped to Argentina, from where they plotted to liberate their country. O'Higgins won the support of the revolutionary government in Buenos Aires under José de San Martín, and their joint forces freed Chile in 1817, defeating the Spaniards and their supporters at the Battle of Chacabuco.

Independence

From 1817–23 Bernardo O'Higgins ruled Chile as supreme director, formally proclaiming independence on 12 Feb. 1818 at Talca. He founded schools and expelled the remaining Spaniards but his authoritarian style and attempted reforms of the land tenure system aroused resistance. The combination of unrest among the powerful landowners and a succession of poor harvests forced him to abdicate in 1823. Civil conflict continued throughout the 1820s, owing largely to a split between the Chilean oligarchs and the army. The civil struggle's harmful effects on the economy, particularly exports, prompted conservatives to seize control in 1830. Diego Portales reached a compromise between the oligarchs and promulgated a constitution in 1833, beginning a prolonged period of political stability and economic revival. A free port was created at Valparaíso to encourage trade with foreign, especially British, merchants. Chilean landowners and merchants profited from new export markets in California and Australia in the 1850s. Economic improvement was underpinned by discoveries of silver and copper in northern Chile and significant coal deposits around Concepción. The period after 1860, known as the 'Liberal Republic', saw the emergence of many rival political groups, most of which were influenced by new economic, scientific and literary ideas brought from Europe. Great Britain became the main trading partner and British entrepreneurs invested in the railways and the modernization of the ports.

A weakening currency and the threat of economic decline attracted Chile to valuable saltpetre (nitrate) deposits in the far north, bordering Peru and Bolivia. Arguments over the ill-defined borders led to the War of the Pacific (1879–83), in which the Chilean army and navy prevailed. During the presidency of José Manuel de Balmaceda (1886–91) the government attempted to use revenue from mineral extraction to strengthen its administration, a policy that was opposed by the oligarchs and led to a brief civil war, forcing Balmaceda's abdication. Thereafter Chile's presidential republic was transformed into a parliamentary republic; the following 20 years saw the emergence of new political parties that tried to represent the emerging working and middle classes. The Democratic Party was formed in 1887 to represent artisans and urban workers, while the Radical Party was backed by the middle class. Marxist ideology spread among workers in the late 1890s and the Socialist Party was established in 1901. By the start of the 20th century Chile was becoming increasingly urbanized; workers poured into the cities from rural areas. Society was polarized, with parts of Santiago and Valparaíso mirroring prosperous and elegant European cities, while the masses remained largely poverty stricken and illiterate.

The outbreak of the First World War brought disaster to the Chilean economy, as Britain and Germany were leading trading partners. Demand for saltpetre fell away and thousands of workers lost their jobs. Dissatisfied Chileans elected the reformist president Arturo Alessandri Palma in 1920 but his initiatives were blocked by the legislature and he resigned. The army intervened and returned Alessandri to power in 1925, after which the constitution was amended to strengthen the executive at the expense of the legislature. It established a presidential republic, separated church and state, and enshrined new labour and welfare legislation. Various economic reforms attempted to reduce the power of the oligarchs, but failed. Alessandri resigned for a second time and was replaced by Carlos Ibáñez del Campo in 1927. His military dictatorship led to improvements in education and public services but also failed to address the economic power of the oligarchs. The world depression of the 1930s was hard on Chile as demand for mineral exports plummeted. A democratic-leftist coalition, the Popular Front, took power following the elections of 1938. Chile remained neutral in the Second World War until 1942, when President Juan Antonio Ríos declared war on Germany, Italy and Japan.

Conflict with the USA

The Radical Party joined with the Communists to field a left-wing Radical, Gabriel González Videla, for president in the 1946 election. Once in office, González Videla (president, 1946–52) turned against his Communist allies, expelling them from his cabinet and banning them completely in 1948. He also severed relations with the Soviet Union, prompting accusations of a Cold War agreement with the United States. The early 1950s were characterized by slow economic growth, spiralling inflation and increasing social demands, and the political arena became increasingly crowded and heated. By 1952 Chileans were alienated by multi-party politics and reacted by turning to two symbols of the past, firstly the 1920s dictator Ibáñez and, following the 1958 elections, the son of former president Alessandri. The Christian Democrat party, under the leadership of Eduardo Frei Montalva, undertook a 'Chileanization programme', wresting back control from the US-owned copper mines and making progress in land reform (by establishing peasant co-operatives). There were also advances in education and housing. The agrarian reforms led to an increased politicization of the working classes, who tended to join the various Socialist and Communist parties. In 1969 they formed the Popular Unity coalition, headed by the Marxist Salvador Allende Gossens, who was elected president in 1970. Allende nationalized many private companies, attempted to improve conditions for the working classes and established ties with other socialist states. The first year was heralded a success, but in 1971–72 Chile was afflicted by a series of economic woes including rapid inflation and shortages of foods and consumer goods. The United States, which had become by far the largest foreign investor in the decades that followed the Second World War, withdrew much of its backing.

In Sept. 1973, with covert American support, the armed forces staged a coup and Allende died during an assault on the presidential palace in Santiago. Gen. Augusto Pinochet Ugarte was installed as president and he argued that a dictatorship was a necessary transitory stage to restore the economy. The military closed Congress, censored the media, purged the universities and banned Marxist parties and union activities. It is estimated that over 3,000 of Allende's supporters lost their lives, over 30,000 were forced into exile and more than 130,000 were arrested over a three-year period. The return to market capitalism led to steady economic improvement from 1976 but falling copper prices and mounting foreign debt led to spiralling inflation and growing unemployment in the early 1980s. In 1981 a new constitution was approved, guaranteeing an eight-year extension to Pinochet's rule but also allowing a transition to civilian government by the end of the decade. The first free elections since the 1973 coup took place in Dec. 1989 and Patricio Aylwin Azócar emerged victorious, heading a coalition of left and centrist parties. The 1990s saw a rapid strengthening of the economy, underpinned by large inflows of foreign investment.

Pinochet remained head of the military until 1998, after which he claimed his constitutional right to become a senator for life (and hence immune from prosecution). While visiting Britain for medical treatment in 1998, Pinochet was arrested and held on human rights charges instigated by Spain. In early 2000 he returned to Chile after the British government ruled he was too ill to be extradited to Spain to face charges. Despite being stripped of his immunity from prosecution, he died in Dec. 2006 having never faced trial. On his election in Jan. 2000, Ricardo Lagos Escobar, leader of the Coalition of Parties for Democracy (CPD) pledged to reform the labour code, increase the minimum wage, introduce unemployment insurance and provide better health care, education and housing. In March 2003 Lagos' government faced allegations of financial corruption, which damaged investor confidence.

In Jan. 2006 Michelle Bachelet, of the centre-left Concertación coalition, became Chile's first female president.

TERRITORY AND POPULATION

Chile is bounded in the north by Peru, east by Bolivia and Argentina, and south and west by the Pacific Ocean. The area is 756,096 sq. km (291,928 sq. miles) excluding the claimed Antarctic territory. Many islands to the west and south belong to Chile: the Islas Juan Fernández (147 sq. km with 633 inhabitants in 2002) lie about 600 km west of Valparaíso, and the volcanic Isla de Pascua (Easter Island or Rapa Nui, 164 sq. km with 3,791 inhabitants in 2002), lies about 3,000 km west-northwest of Valparaíso. Small uninhabited dependencies include Sala y Goméz (400 km east of Easter Is.), San Félix and San Ambrosio (1,000 km northwest of Valparaíso, and 20 km apart) and Islas Diego Ramírez (100 km southwest of Cape Horn).

In 1940 Chile declared, and in each subsequent year has reaffirmed, its ownership of the sector of the Antarctic lying between 53° and 90° W. long., and asserted that the British claim to the sector between the meridians 20° and 80° W. long. overlapped the Chilean by 27°. Seven Chilean bases exist in Antarctica. A law of 1955 put the governor of Magallanes in charge of the 'Chilean Antarctic Territory' which has an area of 1,250,000 sq. km and a population (2002) of 2,392.

The population at the census of April 2002 was 15,116,435 (7,668,740 females and 7,447,695 males); density, 20·0 per sq. km. The United Nations population estimate for 2002 was 15·78m. 87·6% of the population lived in urban areas in 2005.

The UN gives an estimated population for 2010 of 17·14m.

Area, population and capitals of the 15 regions:

Region	*Sq. km*	*Population (2002 census)*	*Capital*	*Population (2002 census)*
Aisén del Gral. Carlos Ibáñez del Campo	108,494	91,492	Coihaique	50,041
De Antofagasta	126,049	493,984	Antofagasta	296,905
De La Araucanía	31,842	869,535	Temuco	245,347
De Arica-Parinacota[1]	16,873	189,644	Arica	185,268
De Atacama	75,176	254,336	Copiapó	129,091
Del Bíobío	37,063	1,861,562	Concepción	216,061
De Coquimbo	40,580	603,210	La Serena	160,148
Del Libertador Gral. B. O'Higgins	16,387	780,627	Rancagua	214,344
De Los Lagos	48,584	716,739	Puerto Montt	175,938
De Los Ríos[2]	18,430	356,396	Valdivia	140,559
De Magallanes y de la Antártica Chilena	132,297	150,826	Punta Arenas	119,496
Del Maule	30,296	908,097	Talca	201,797
Metropolitana de Santiago	15,403	6,061,185	Santiago	4,668,473
De Tarapacá	42,226	238,950	Iquique	216,419
De Valparaíso	16,396	1,539,852	Valparaíso	275,982

[1]Created in June 2007—formerly part of Región de Tarapacá.
[2]Created in June 2007—formerly part of Región de Los Lagos.

Other large towns (June 2002 populations) are: Puente Alto (458,906), Viña del Mar (350,221), Talcahuano (288,666), San Bernardo (262,623), Arica (189,743), Chillán (176,863), Coquimbo (141,796), Calama (135,526) and Osorno (135,204). 69·7% of the population is mixed or mestizo, 20% are of European descent and 10·3% declared themselves to be indigenous Amerindians of the Mapuche, Aymara, Atacameño and Quechua groups. Language and culture remain of European origin, with 604,349 Mapudungun-speaking (mainly Mapuche) Indians the only sizeable minority.

The official language is Spanish.

SOCIAL STATISTICS

2007 births, 240,569; deaths, 93,000; marriages, 57,792. Rates, 2007 (per 1,000 population): birth, 14·6; death, 5·6; marriage, 3·5. Divorce was only made legal in 2004; abortion remains illegal. Annual population growth rate, 2000–05, 1·1%. Infant mortality, 2005 (per 1,000 live births), 8. In 2003 the most popular age range for marrying was 25–29 for males and 20–24 for females. Expectation of life at birth (2007): males 75·5 years, females 81·6 years. Chile has the highest life expectancy in South America. Fertility rate, 2004, 2·0 children per woman.

CLIMATE

With its enormous range of latitude and the influence of the Andean Cordillera, the climate of Chile is very complex, ranging from extreme aridity in the north, through a Mediterranean climate in Central Chile, where winters are wet and summers dry, to a cool temperate zone in the south, with rain at all seasons. In the extreme south, conditions are very wet and stormy. Santiago, Jan. 67°F (19·5°C), July 46°F (8°C). Annual rainfall 15" (375 mm). Antofagasta, Jan. 69°F (20·6°C), July 57°F (14°C). Annual rainfall 0·5" (12·7 mm). Valparaíso, Jan. 64°F (17·8°C), July 53°F (11·7°C). Annual rainfall 20" (505 mm).

CONSTITUTION AND GOVERNMENT

A new Constitution was approved by 67·5% of the voters on 11 Sept. 1980 and came into force on 11 March 1981. It provided for a return to democracy after a minimum period of eight years. Gen. Pinochet would remain in office during this period after which the government would nominate a single candidate for President. At a plebiscite on 5 Oct. 1988 President Pinochet was rejected as a presidential candidate by 54·6% of votes cast. The Constitution has been amended on a number of occasions since then.

The *President* is directly elected for a non-renewable four-year term. Parliament consists of a 120-member *Chamber of Deputies* and a *Senate* of 38 members. In March 2006 the Senate became fully elected, by abolishing non-elected senators and eliminating life seats for former presidents. Senators are elected for an eight-year term.

Santiago is the administrative capital of Chile, but since 11 March 1990 Valparaíso has been the legislative capital.

National Anthem

'Dulce patria, recibe los votos' ('Sweet Fatherland, receive the vows'); words by E. Lillo, tune by Ramón Carnicer.

GOVERNMENT CHRONOLOGY

Heads of State since 1942. (APL = Popular Liberating Alliance; FP = Popular Front; PC = Conservative Party; PDC = Christian Democratic Party; PS = Socialist Party; RN = National Renewal)

Presidents of the Republic

1942–46	FP	Juan Antonio Ríos Morales
1946–52	FP	Gabriel González Videla
1952–58	APL	Carlos Ibáñez del Campo
1958–64	PC	Jorge Alessandri Rodríguez
1964–70	PDC	Eduardo Nicanor Frei Montalva
1970–73	PS	Salvador Allende Gossens

Military Junta

1973–74		Gen. Augusto J. R. Pinochet (chair); Gen. César Raúl Benavides Escobar; Admr. José Toribio Merino Castro; Gen. Gustavo Leigh Guzmán; Gen. Fernando Matthei Aubel; Gen. César Mendoza Durán; Gen. Rodolfo Stange Oelckers

Presidents of the Republic

1974–90	military	Augusto J. R. Pinochet
1990–94	PDC	Patricio Aylwin
1994–2000	PDC	Eduardo Frei Ruiz-Tagle
2000–06	PS	Ricardo Froilán Lagos
2006–10	PS	Michelle Bachelet
2010–	RN	Sebastián Piñera Echenique

RECENT ELECTIONS

In the presidential run-off held on 17 Jan. 2010 the centre-right candidate Sebastián Piñera Echenique (National Renewal) polled 51·6%, defeating the ruling leftist 'Concertación' candidate Eduardo Frei Ruiz-Tagle (Christian Democratic Party), with 48·4%. Two other candidates had participated in the first round of voting on 13 Dec. 2009.

In elections to the Chamber of Deputies on 13 Dec. 2009 the Coalition for Change won 58 seats with 43·4% of the vote (Independent Democratic Union, 37 and 23·0%; National Renewal, 18 and 17·8%; ind. 3 and 2·3%) against 57 seats (44·4%) for the Coalition of Parties for Democracy/Concertación (Christian Democratic Party, 19 and 14·2%; Party for Democracy, 18 and 12·7%; Socialist Party, 11 and 9·9%; Radical Social Democratic Party, 5 and 3·8%; Communist Party, 3 and 2·0%; ind., 1 and 1·8%) and 3 for Clean Chile Vote Happy (5·4%). The remaining two seats went to independent candidates. After partial elections to the Senate on the same day the composition in the Senate was: Coalition of Parties for Democracy, 19 seats; Coalition for Change, 16; Clean Chile Vote Happy, 1; and ind., 2.

CURRENT ADMINISTRATION

President: Sebastián Piñera; b. 1949 (National Renewal; sworn in 11 March 2010).

In March 2010 the government comprised:

Minister of Agriculture: José Antonio Galilea. *Culture and the Arts:* Luciano Cruz-Coke. *Economy and Reconstruction:* Juan Andrés Fontaine. *Education:* Joaquín Lavín. *Energy:* Ricardo Rainieri. *Environment:* María Ignacia Benitez. *Finance:* Felipe Larraín. *Foreign Affairs:* Alfredo Moreno. *Health:* Jaime Mañalich. *Housing and Urban Development:* Magdalena Matte. *Interior:* Rodrigo Hinzpeter. *Justice:* Felipe Bulnes. *Labour and Social Security:* Camila Merino. *Mining:* Laurence Golborne. *National Defence:* Jaime Ravinet. *National Property:* Catalina Parot. *National Women's Service:* Carolina Schmidt. *Planning and Co-operation:* Felipe Kast. *Public Works:* Hernán Solminihac. *Transport and Telecommunications:* Felipe Morandé Lavín. *General Secretary of the Government:* Ena von Baer. *General Secretary of the Presidency:* Cristián Larroulet.

Government Website (Spanish only):
http://www.gobiernodechile.cl

CURRENT LEADERS

Sebastián Piñera Echenique

Position
President

Introduction
Sebastián Piñera became president in March 2010 in the aftermath of a severe earthquake. A billionaire and right-of-centre politician, his victory ended 22 years of centre-left rule. He is expected to focus on strengthening the economy and increasing employment, while promising to maintain many existing social policies.

Early Life
Miguel Juan Sebastián Piñera Echenique was born on 1 Dec. 1949 in Santiago, the son of a diplomat. He grew up in Belgium, New York and Chile, where he attended the College of the Divine Word until 1967. He graduated in economics from the Pontifical Catholic University of Chile in 1971, then worked as a university tutor for two years. He undertook postgraduate studies at Harvard University from 1973–76, gaining a doctorate in economics. Returning to Chile, he continued to teach economics while amassing personal wealth by establishing a credit card business and, from 1977–80, serving as general manager of the Bank of Talca.

In 1982 allegations of fraud relating to the bank led to the issue of an arrest warrant but the case against him was dropped. In 1989, following President Pinochet's relinquishing of power, Piñera entered politics to lead the presidential campaign of Hernán Büchi, a former finance minister. From 1990–98 Piñera was senator for East Santiago, representing the centre-right party, National Renewal. During this period he served on the senate financial committee and in 1992 made an unsuccessful attempt to win the party's presidential candidacy. In 1993 he created the Future Foundation, later renamed the Foundation for Culture and Society, to develop policies on social justice, human rights and the environment.

From 2001–04 he was party president and in 2005 contested the presidential election, coming second behind Michelle Bachelet of the governing centre-left coalition. He made another run for the presidency in 2009, promising to increase economic growth to 6% and create a million new jobs. He pledged to privatize 20% of state-owned Codelco, the world's largest copper-producing company, while continuing many existing social policies. With a lead from the first round of voting on 13 Dec. 2009, he won the run-off with 52% of the vote on 17 Jan. 2010.

Career in Office

Piñera took office on 11 March 2010 as Chile struggled to cope with the impact of the previous month's earthquake when hundreds of people died and approximately half a million homes were destroyed. Restoring the social fabric is likely to be his main challenge, together with rebuilding the economy. Internationally, he has signalled his intention to distance Chile from Venezuela and Cuba and to strengthen bonds with Colombia and other right-of-centre neighbours.

DEFENCE

Military service is voluntary and is currently for one year in the Army and 22 months in the Air Force and Navy.

In 2006 defence expenditure totalled US$4,677m. (US$290 per capita), representing 3·2% of GDP. In 1985 defence spending had accounted for 10·0% of GDP.

Army

Strength (2005): 41,000 (18,366 conscripts) with 50,000 reserves. There is a 36,800-strong force of Carabineros.

Navy

The principal ships of the Navy are three ex-British destroyers, three diesel submarines and three frigates. There is a Naval Air Service numbering 600 personnel with 13 combat aircraft.

Naval personnel in 2005 totalled 20,092 (1,030 conscripts) including 3,800 marines and 1,300 Coast Guard. There are HQs at Iquique, Valparaíso, Talcahuano and Punta Arenas.

Air Force

Strength (2005) was 9,971 personnel (950 conscripts). There are 76 combat aircraft made up largely of Mirage jets.

INTERNATIONAL RELATIONS

Chile is a member of the UN, World Bank, IMF and several other UN specialized agencies, WTO, IOM, Inter-American Development Bank, SELA, LAIA, OAS, UNASUR, APEC, Antarctic Treaty and has a free trade agreement with MERCOSUR.

ECONOMY

Agriculture accounted for 8·9% of GDP in 2004, industry 34·5% and services 56·6%.

Overview

Chile's economy was liberalized under the Pinochet regime (1973–90) ahead of the rest of Latin America and economic reform continued under the democratic government of the 1990s. The country had the highest foreign direct investment to GDP ratio in Latin America and strong growth for most of the decade. In 1998 growth was curtailed by monetary tightening aimed at reversing current account deficits caused by low export earnings in a period of global financial crisis. In 1999 the economy shrank by 0·4%. Growth resumed at an average rate of 4% from 2000–04. Since 2005 Chile has experienced a broad-based resurgence, the result of buoyant domestic demand and a strong external climate, aided by supportive macroeconomic policies. Inflation in 2006 was above target at 3·4% owing to high world energy and food prices but medium-term expectations remain around the government target of 3%.

Strong in mining, Chile is the world's leading copper and iodine producer and, increasingly, a source of gold and non-metallic minerals. Manufacturing's share of GDP has gradually declined while sectors including wood products, fruit, salmon, wines and methanol production have grown. Increasingly diversified export production has been a key engine of growth. In 1999–2000 a floating exchange rate regime was introduced and a counter-cyclical fiscal policy was implemented. The country has signed many foreign trade agreements, notably with the USA, the EU and China. Poverty has declined by roughly two-thirds since 1990 but, despite the implementation of well-directed social programmes, income inequality remains high and extreme poverty is endemic.

Currency

The unit of currency is the *Chilean peso* (CLP) of 100 *centavos.* The peso was revalued 3·5% against the US dollar in Nov. 1994. In Sept. 1999 the managed exchange-rate system was abandoned and the peso allowed to float. Inflation rates (based on IMF statistics):

1999	*2000*	*2001*	*2002*	*2003*	*2004*	*2005*	*2006*	*2007*	*2008*
3·3%	3·8%	3·6%	2·5%	2·8%	1·1%	3·1%	3·4%	4·4%	8·7%

In Aug. 2009 gold reserves were 8,000 troy oz and foreign exchange reserves US$23,711m. Total money supply was 9,687·2bn. pesos in May 2009.

Budget

The fiscal year is the calendar year.

Budgetary central government revenue and expenditure (in 1bn. pesos):

	2005	*2006*	*2007*
Revenue	15,304·0	19,382·0	22,784·1
Expenditure	11,481·0	12,701·0	14,175·9

VAT is 19%.

Performance

Real GDP growth rates (based on IMF statistics):

1999	*2000*	*2001*	*2002*	*2003*	*2004*	*2005*	*2006*	*2007*	*2008*
–0·4%	4·5%	3·5%	2·2%	4·0%	6·0%	5·6%	4·6%	4·7%	3·2%

Total GDP in 2008 was US$169·5bn.

Banking and Finance

The Superintendencia de Bancos e Instituciones Financieras, affiliated to the finance ministry, is the banking supervisory authority. There is a Central Bank and a State Bank. The Central Bank was made independent of government control in March 1990. The *President* is José de Gregorio. There were 21 domestic and six foreign banks in 2005. In Jan. 2005 deposits in domestic banks totalled 25,779,053m. pesos; in foreign banks, 2,163,183m. pesos, and in other finance companies, 4,829,090m. pesos.

There are stock exchanges in Santiago and Valparaíso.

ENERGY AND NATURAL RESOURCES

Environment

Chile's carbon dioxide emissions from the consumption and flaring of fossil fuels in 2008 were the equivalent of 3·9 tonnes per capita.

Electricity

Installed capacity was 12·3m. kW in 2004. Production of electricity was 51·98bn. kWh in 2004, of which 41% was hydro-electric. Consumption per capita in 2004 was 3,347 kWh.

Oil and Gas

Production of crude oil, 2004, was 1·3m. bbls. Gas production, 2003, was 85 petajoules. Chile imports nearly all of its oil and around 75% of the natural gas that it consumes.

Minerals

The wealth of the country consists chiefly in its minerals. Chile is the world's largest copper producer; copper is the most important source of foreign exchange and government revenues. Production, 2004, 5,418,800 fine tonnes. Coal is low-grade and mining is difficult, made possible by state subsidies. Production, 2004, 238,307 tonnes.

Output of other minerals, 2004 (in tonnes): iron ore, 8,003,491; limestone, 6,653,343; salt, 4,938,928; molybdenum, 41,883; zinc,

27,635; manganese, 7,188; silver, 1,360. Gold (39,986 kg in 2004), lithium, nitrate, iodine and sodium sulphate are also produced.

Agriculture

In 2007, 1·29m. ha. were arable land and 0·46m. ha. permanent crops. 0·96m. ha. were irrigated in 2007. There were 400 tractors and 66 harvester-threshers per 10,000 ha. of arable land in 2006.

Principal crops were as follows:

Crop	Area harvested, 1,000 ha 2004	Production, 1,000 tonnes 2004	Crop	Area harvested, 1,000 ha 2004	Production, 1,000 tonnes 2004
Sugarbeets	31	2,598	Tomatoes	7	470
Wheat	420	1,852	Oats	77	357
Maize	134	1,508	Onions	6	290[1]
Potatoes	56	1,116	Rice	25	117

[1]2003.

Fruit production, 2004 (in 1,000 tonnes): apples, 1,300; grapes, 1,150; peaches and nectarines, 311; plums, 250; pears, 210; lemons and limes, 165; oranges, 140. Wine production in 2005 totalled 7,886,000 hectolitres.

Livestock, 2003: sheep, 4·1m.; cattle, 3·9m.; pigs, 3·2m.; goats, 1·0m.; horses, 700,000; poultry, 98m. Livestock products, 2003 (in 1,000 tonnes): pork, bacon and ham, 386; beef and veal, 190; poultry meat, 457; milk, 2,180; eggs, 116.

Since 1985 agricultural trade has been consistently in surplus. Wine exports rose from US$52m. in 1990 to US$844m. in 2004.

Forestry

In 2004, 15·64m. ha., or 20·7% of the total land area, was under forests. There were 13·4m. ha. of natural forest and woodland (larch, araucaria, lenga, coihue and oak are important species), representing 85·9% of the total forested area, and 2·1m. ha. of planted forest. Timber production in 2007 was 52·91m. cu. metres.

Fisheries

Chile has 4,200 km of coastline and exclusive fishing rights to 1·6m. sq. km. There are 220 species of edible fish. The catch in 2005 was 4,330,325 tonnes, entirely from sea fishing. Exports of fishery commodities in 2004 were valued at US$2·58bn., against imports of US$38·9m. Fish farms produced 486,850 tonnes of salmon in 2003.

INDUSTRY

The leading companies by market capitalization in Chile in Feb. 2009 were: SQM (Sociedad Química y Minera de Chile), a chemicals manufacturer (US$8·0bn.); Falabella, a retail company (US$7·3bn.); and Antarchile, an investment company (US$4·9bn.).

Output of major products in 2003 unless otherwise indicated (in 1,000 tonnes): distillate fuel oil (2004), 3,693; cement, 2,870; sulphuric acid, 2,866; petrol (2004), 2,383; residual fuel oil (2004), 2,294; cellulose, 1,430; fishmeal, 580; iron or steel plates, 403; sugar (2004), 401; newsprint, 177; paper and cardboard, 113. Output of other products: soft drinks, 796m. litres; beer, 192m. litres; 20,136 motor vehicles (2001); 4·74m. motor tyres.

Labour

In 2005 there were 5,779,660 people in employment (1,997,690 women). In Sept. 2005, 1,678,880 persons were employed in social or personal services, 1,117,900 in trade, 765,580 in manufacturing, 683,100 in agriculture, forestry and fisheries, and 470,110 in transport and communications. In 2005 there was a monthly minimum wage of 127,500 pesos. In the fourth quarter of 2009, 8·6% of the workforce was unemployed, down from 9·1% in the third quarter but up from 7·5% in the fourth quarter of 2008.

Trade Unions

Trade unions were established in the mid-1880s.

INTERNATIONAL TRADE

Foreign debt was US$45,154m. in 2005.

Imports and Exports

Trade in US$1m.:

	2000	2001	2002	2003	2004
Imports f.o.b.	17,091	16,411	15,827	18,001	23,006
Exports f.o.b.	19,210	18,466	18,340	21,524	32,025

In 2004 the principal exports were (in US$1m.): minerals, 16,633·6 (of which copper, 14,358·4, equivalent to 87·2% of all exports); manufactures, 11,928·7; and agricultural products, 2,339·3. Principal imports in 2004 were (in US$1m.): manufactures, 17,928·7; minerals, 3,919·6; and agricultural products, 416·9. Major import suppliers (as % of total), 2004: Argentina, 18·5; USA, 15·1; Brazil, 12·4; China, 8·3; Germany 3·7. Major export markets, 2004: USA, 14·8; Japan, 12·0; China, 10·4; South Korea, 5·8; Netherlands, 5·4.

COMMUNICATIONS

Roads

In 2004 there were 80,505 km of roads, but only 20·8% were hard-surfaced. There were 2,414 km of motorways and 16,785 km of main roads. In 2004 there were 1,303,554 private cars, 633,853 trucks and vans, 61,152 buses and coaches and 22,870 motorcycles and mopeds. In 2006 there were 2,280 road accident fatalities.

Rail

The total length of railway lines was (2004) 5,775 km, including 1,051 km electrified, of broad- and metre-gauge. The state railway (EFE) is now mainly a passenger carrier, and transported 13·3m. passengers in 2004. Freight operations are in the hands of the semi-private companies Ferronor, Pacifico and the Antofagasta (Chili) and Bolivia Railway (973 km, metre-gauge) which links the port of Antofagasta with Bolivia and Argentina. Freight carried totalled 25·3m. tonnes in 2004. Passenger-km travelled in 2004 came to 820m. and freight tonne-km to 3,897m.

There are metro systems in Santiago (46·2 km) and Valparaíso (42·5 km).

Civil Aviation

There are 389 airports, with nine international airports at Antofagasta, Arica, Coihaique, Concepción, Easter Island (Isla de Pascua), Iquique, Puerto Montt, Punta Arenas and Santiago (Comodoro Arturo Merino Benítez). The largest airline is LAN Airlines, formerly Línea Aérea Nacional Chile (LAN-Chile); in 2001 LAN-Chile flew 70·3m. km and carried 5,046,600 passengers. In 2004 Santiago handled 6,057,279 passengers (3,603,267 on international flights) and 269,660 tonnes of freight.

Shipping

The mercantile marine in 2001 totalled 647,820 GRT, including oil tankers 160,179 GRT. The five major ports, Valparaíso, San Antonio, Antofagasta, Arica and Iquique, are state-owned; there are 11 smaller private ports. Valparaíso, the largest port, handled 4,469,302 tonnes of freight in 2001.

Telecommunications

In 2008 there were 3,252,000 main (fixed) telephone lines. In the same year mobile phone subscribers numbered 14,797,000 (880·5 per 1,000 persons). There were 2·3m. PCs in use (147·5 for every 1,000 persons) in 2005 and 5·7m. internet users in 2006.

Postal Services

In 2002 there were 752 post offices.

SOCIAL INSTITUTIONS

Justice

There is a High Court of Justice in the capital, 16 courts of appeal distributed over the republic, courts of first instance in the departmental capitals and second-class judges in the sub-delegations. There were 642 public prosecutors, 782 judges and 417 defence lawyers in 2002.

The population in penal institutions in Dec. 2004 was 65,262 (417 per 100,000 of national population).

The death penalty for ordinary crimes was abolished in 2001.

Education

In 2004 there were 287,454 children at pre-primary schools, 2·27m. primary school pupils and 989,039 pupils at secondary level. Adult literacy rate in 2003 was 95·7% (male, 95·8%; female, 95·6%).

In 2004 there were 567,114 students in higher education. There were 162 universities with 403,370 students, 140 professional institutes with 101,674 students and 211 technical education centres with 62,070 students. The number of students at higher education institutions has doubled since 1990.

In 2007 public expenditure on education came to 3·8% of GNI and represented 18·2% of total government expenditure.

Health

There were 846 hospitals in 2002. In 2003 there were 15,006 doctors, 2,846 dentists and 6,900 university nurses in the public sector. In 2004 there were 20,776 junior doctors.

Welfare

In 1981 Chile abolished its state-sponsored pension plan and became the first country to establish private mandatory retirement savings. The system is managed by competitive private companies called AFPs (Pension Fund Administrators). Employees are required to save 13% of their pay. In April 2005 it had 7,132,983 members and assets of 35,051,470m. pesos. In 2005 about 65% of the population over the age of 14 had private health insurance.

RELIGION

At the 2002 census Chile had 7,853,428 Roman Catholics. In Jan. 2002 there were five archbishops, 25 bishops and two vicars apostolic. There were two cardinals in Feb. 2010. In 2002 there were 1,699,725 Evangelical Christians, 119,455 Jehovah's Witnesses, 103,735 Latter-day Saints, 14,976 Jews, 6,959 Orthodox Christians and 2,894 Muslims.

CULTURE

World Heritage Sites

Chile's five UNESCO protected sites are the Rapa Nui National Park, the Churches of Chiloé, the Historic Quarter of the Seaport of Valparaíso, the Humberstone and Santa Laura Saltpeter Works, and the Sewell Mining Town. Entered on the list in 1995, the Rapa Nui National Park encompasses much of the coastline of Easter Island and protects the shrines and statues (*Moai*) carved between the 10th–16th centuries. On the island of Chiloé off the Región de Los Lagos coastline, wooden churches were built by Jesuit missionaries at the turn of the 17th century. The churches were entered on the list in 2000. The Valparaíso site was inscribed on the list in 2003 as a model of urban and architectural development in 19th-century Latin America. The Humberstone and Santa Laura Saltpeter Works were inscribed in 2005 and are where workers from Peru, Chile and Bolivia formed a distinctive communal pampinos culture. The Sewell Mining Town, inscribed in 2006, is an example of the company towns that existed in the early 20th century in many remote parts of the world.

Broadcasting

In 2004 there were 1,128 (mostly commercial) radio broadcasting stations. Televisión Nacional de Chile is state-owned and broadcasts nationally. There are also private national and local terrestrial television services, as well as cable TV networks carrying overseas stations. There were 4·1m. TV-equipped households in 2005.

Cinema

In 2004 there were 271 cinema screens; total admissions in 2005 were 9·6m.

Press

In 2005 there were 93 national daily newspapers; Chile's daily newspapers had total annual sales of 354m. copies. In 2004 a total of 3,151 book titles were published.

Tourism

There were 1,785,024 foreign visitors in 2004. Tourist receipts were US$1,396m. in 2004.

DIPLOMATIC REPRESENTATIVES

Of Chile in the United Kingdom (37–41 Old Queen St., London, SW1H 9JA)
Ambassador: Rafael Moreno.

Of the United Kingdom in Chile (Av. El Bosque Norte 0125, Piso 2, Las Condes, Santiago)
Ambassador: Jon Benjamin.

Of Chile in the USA (1732 Massachusetts Ave., NW, Washington, D.C., 20036)
Ambassador: José Goñi Carrasco.

Of the USA in Chile (Av. Andrés Bello 2800, Las Condes, Santiago)
Ambassador: Paul Simons.

Of Chile to the United Nations
Ambassador: Heraldo Muñoz Valenzuela.

Of Chile to the European Union
Ambassador: Juan Arturo Salazar Sparks.

FURTHER READING

Banco Central de Chile. *Boletín Mensual.*
Bethell, L. (ed.) *Chile since Independence.* 1993
Bizzarro, Salvatore, *Historical Dictionary of Chile.* 2005
Collier, S. and Sater, W. F., *A History of Chile, 1808–1994.* 1996
Hickman, J., *News From the End of the Earth: A Portrait of Chile.* 1998
Hojman, D. E., *Chile: the Political Economy of Development and Democracy in the 1990s.* 1993.—(ed.) *Change in the Chilean Countryside: from Pinochet to Aylwin and Beyond.* 1993
Oppenheim, L. H., *Politics in Chile: Democracy, Authoritarianism and the Search for Development.* 1993
Rector, John L., *The History of Chile.* 2006

National Statistical Office: Instituto Nacional de Estadísticas (INE), Paseo Bulnes 418, Santiago.
Website: http://www.ine.cl

CHINA

Zhonghua Renmin Gonghe Guo
(People's Republic of China)

Capital: Beijing (Peking)
Population estimate, 2010: 1,354·15m.
GDP per capita, 2007: (PPP$) 5,383
HDI/world rank: 0·772/92

KEY HISTORICAL EVENTS

An embryonic Chinese state emerged in the fertile Huang He (Yellow River) basin before 4000 BC. Chinese culture reached the Chang Jiang (Yangtze) basin by 2500 BC and within 500 years the far south was also within the Chinese orbit. Four thousand years ago the Xia dynasty ruled in the Huang He basin. About 1500 BC it was supplanted by the Shang dynasty, under which writing developed using recognizable Chinese characters. The remains of the Shang period show that their state was the cultural ancestor of modern China.

Shang civilization spread out from the Huang He region. In the west, the Shang state came into conflict with the Zhou state, whose rulers replaced the Shang dynasty around 1000 BC. Under the Zhou, a centralized administration developed. In about 500 BC one court official, Kongfuzi (Confucius), outlined his vision of society. Confucianism, which introduced a system of civil service recruitment through examination, remained the principal Chinese belief system until the mid-20th century.

The Zhou expanded the Chinese state south beyond the Chang Jiang. There, dependent territories emerged which, by the 5th century, had become independent Warring States. These insubordinate kingdoms periodically rebelled against the central authority and fought one another. In 221 BC the ruler of the Warring State of Qin became the first emperor of China. He built an empire extending from the South China Sea to the edge of Central Asia, where work was begun on the Great Wall of China, a massive fortification to keep threatening nomads at bay. The Qin dynasty standardized laws, money and administration throughout the empire but it was short-lived. By 206 BC the state had divided into three.

Reunification came gradually under the Han dynasty (202 BC–AD 200). Han emperors ruled through an efficient, centralized bureaucracy. They established a state whose boundaries were similar to those of modern China. Some of the peripheral possessions proved too distant to hold and the Han empire collapsed through rebellion and invasion. It was followed by the Jin (265–316) and Sui (589–612) dynasties, interspersed by a period of inter-state war and anarchy. Reunification was achieved by the Tang dynasty, whose efficient reforming rule brought new prosperity to China from 618–917. Eventually the Tang empire too collapsed as separatism grew.

Under the next dynasty, the Song (960–1127), the balance of power within China shifted south. Song China expanded trade with the rest of Asia. In 1126 nomads from Manchuria invaded the north. The Song state lost control of the area north of the Chang Jiang. A declining Song empire persisted in the south until 1279.

Genghis Khan

The northern invaders were overthrown by the Mongols, led by Genghis Khan (c. 1162–1227), who went on to claim the rest of China. In 1280 their ruler Kublai Khan (1251–94), who had founded the Yuan dynasty in 1271, swept into southern China. The Mongol Yuan dynasty adopted Chinese ways but was overthrown by a nationalist uprising in 1368, led by Hongwu (1328–98), a former beggar who established the Ming dynasty. Hongwu, and several later Ming emperors, made important reforms, resulting in increased levels of prosperity and extended borders.

The Ming empire collapsed in a peasants' revolt in 1644. The capital, Beijing (Peking), was only 64 km from the Great Wall and vulnerable to attack from nomads to the north. Within months the peasants' leader was swept aside by the invasion of the Manchus, whose Qing dynasty ruled China until 1911. Preoccupied with threats from the north, China neglected its southern coastal frontier where European traders were attempting to open up the country. The Portuguese, who landed on the Chinese coast in 1516, were followed by the Dutch in 1622 and the English in 1637.

Qing emperors initially ruled fairly and adopted Chinese ways and customs. The empire expanded into Mongolia, Tibet, Vietnam and Kazakhstan. By the 19th century imperial China was suffering from corruption. Under pressure from rural revolts, ignited by crippling taxation and poverty, the Qing empire started to collapse. Through the two Opium Wars (1838–42; 1856–58), Britain forced China to allow the import of opium from India into China, while Britain, France, Germany and other European states gained concessions in 'treaty ports' that virtually came under foreign rule.

The Taiping Rebellion (1851–64) set up a revolutionary egalitarian state in southern China. The European powers intervened to crush the rebellion, but in 1860 British and French forces invaded Beijing and burnt the imperial palace. The Europeans extracted further trading concessions from China. A weakened China was defeated by Japan in 1895 and lost both Taiwan and Korea.

The xenophobic Boxer Rebellion, led by members of a secret society called the Fists of Righteous Harmony, broke out in 1900. The Guangxu emperor (1875–1908) attempted modernization in the Hundred Days Reform, but was taken captive by the conservative dowager empress who harnessed the Boxer Rebellion to her own ends. The rebellion was put down by European troops in 1901. China was then divided into zones of influence between the major European states and Japan.

With imperial authority so weakened, much of the country was ungovernable and ripe for rebellion. The turning point came in 1911 when a revolution led by the Kuomintang (Guomintang or Nationalist movement) of Sun Yet-sen (Sun Zhong Shan; 1866–1925) overthrew the emperor and the imperial system. The revolution was followed by a period of anarchy, which included an attempted imperial restoration. The authoritarian Yuan Shih-kai ruled as president from 1913 to 1916. Following the overthrow of Yuan, China disintegrated at the hands of local warlords.

In 1916 Sun founded a republic in southern China. The north remained beyond his control. Sun reorganized the Nationalist party on Soviet lines. At this stage the Nationalists co-operated with the Communists to re-establish national unity, but rivalry between the two parties increased, particularly after the death of Sun in 1925.

Nationalism and Communism

After Sun's death the nationalist movement was taken over by his ally Chiang Kai-shek (Jiang Jie Shi; 1887–1976). As commander in chief of the Nationalist army from 1925, Chiang's power grew. In April 1927 he tried to suppress the Chinese Communist Party in a bloody campaign in which thousands of Communists were slaughtered. The remains of the party fled to the far western province of Jiangxi, beyond the reach of the Nationalists. In 1928 Chiang's army entered Beijing. With the greater part of the country reunited under Chiang's rule, he formed a government in Nanjing, which became the capital of China.

In 1934 the Communists were forced to retreat from Jiangxi province. Led by Mao Zedong (Mao Tse-tung; 1893–1976) they trekked for more than a year on the 5,600-mile Long March. Harried during their journey, they were besieged by the Nationalists when they eventually took refuge in Shaanxi province.

In 1931, against this backdrop of civil unrest, the Japanese had invaded Manchuria and set up the last emperor of China as puppet emperor of Manchukuo. By 1937 the Japanese had seized Beijing and most of coastal China. The Nationalists and Communists finally co-operated against the invader, although the Chinese were unable to achieve much against the superior Japanese forces.

During the Second World War (1939–45), a Nationalist government provided largely ineffectual rule of unoccupied China from a temporary capital in Chongqing. At the end of the war, Nationalist-Communist co-operation was short-lived. The Soviet Union sponsored the Communist Party, which marched into Manchuria in 1946. This action began the civil war which lasted until 1949. Although the Nationalist forces of Chiang Kai-shek received support from some western countries, particularly the United States, the Communists were victorious. On 1 Oct. 1949 Mao declared the People's Republic of China in Beijing.

Chiang fled with the remains of his Nationalist forces to the island of Taiwan, where he established a government that claimed to be a continuation of the Republic of China. At first, that administration was recognized as the government of China by most Western countries and Taiwan kept China's Security Council seat at the United Nations until 1971. Chiang's authoritarian regime was periodically challenged by Red China, which bombed Taiwan's small offshore islands near the mainland. But, supported by the United States, Taiwan endured. In the 1960s and 1970s, Taiwan gradually lost recognition as the legitimate government of China and in 1978 the USA recognized the People's Republic of China.

Expansionism

In 1950 China invaded Tibet, which had been independent in practice since 1916. Repressive Chinese rule quickly alienated the Tibetans, who rose in rebellion in 1959. The Tibetan religious leader, the Dalai Lama, was forced to flee to India. Since then, the settlement of large numbers of ethnic Chinese in the main cities of Tibet has threatened to swamp Tibetan culture.

During the 1950s and 1960s China was involved in a number of border disputes and wars in neighbouring states. The Communists posted 'volunteers' to fight alongside Communist North Korea during the Korean War (1950–53). There were clashes on the Soviet border in the 1950s and the Indian border in the 1960s, when China occupied some Indian territory.

From the establishment of the Peoples' Republic of China, Communist China and the Soviet Union were allies. Communist China initially depended upon Soviet assistance for economic development. A Soviet-style five-year plan was put into action in 1953, but the relationship with Moscow was already showing signs of strain. The two Communist powers fell out regarding their different interpretations of Marxist orthodoxy. By the end of the 1950s the Soviet Union and China were rivals, spurring the Chinese arms race. Chinese research into atomic weapons culminated in the testing of the first Chinese atomic bomb in 1964.

Mao introduced rapid collectivization of farms in 1955. The countryside was to take the lead in implementing Communist economics. Mao's idea was not met with universal approval in the Communist Party but its implementation demonstrated his complete authority over the fortunes of the nation. In 1956 he launched the doctrine of letting a 'hundred flowers bloom', encouraging intellectual debate. However, the new freedoms took a turn Mao did not expect and led to the questioning of the role of the party. Strict controls were reimposed and free-thinkers were sent to work in the countryside to be 're-educated'.

In May 1958 Mao launched another ill-fated policy, the Great Leap Forward. To promote rapid industrialization and socialism, the collectives were reorganized into larger units. Neither the resources nor trained personnel were available for this huge task. Backyard blast furnaces were set up to increase production of iron and steel. The Great Leap Forward was a disaster. It is believed that 30m. died from famine. Soviet advice against the project was ignored and a complete rift in relations with Moscow came in 1963, when Soviet assistance was withdrawn. As relations between the former friends cooled, a rapprochement with the United States was achieved in the early 1970s.

Cultural Revolution

Having published his 'Thoughts' in the 'Little Red Book' in 1964, Mao set the Cultural Revolution in motion. Militant students were organized into groups of Red Guards to attack the party hierarchy. Anyone perceived to lack enthusiasm for Mao Zedong Thought was denounced. Thousands died as the students lost control and the army was eventually called in to restore order.

After Mao's death in 1976 the Gang of Four, led by Mao's widow Jiang Qing, attempted to seize power. These hard-liners were denounced and arrested. China effectively came under the control of Deng Xiaoping, despite the fact that he held none of the great offices of state. Deng placed an emphasis on economic reform. The country was opened to Western investment. Special Economic Zones and 'open cities' were designated and private enterprise gradually returned, on a small scale at first.

Greatly improved standards of living and a thriving economy increased expectations for civil liberties. The demand for political change climaxed in demonstrations by workers and students in April 1989, following the funeral of Communist Party leader Hu Yaobang. Protests were held in several major cities. In Beijing where demonstrators peacefully occupied Tiananmen Square, they were evicted by the military who opened fire, killing more than 1,500. Hard-liners took control of the government, and martial law was imposed from May 1989 to Jan. 1990.

Since 1989 the leadership has concentrated on economic development. Hong Kong was returned to China from British rule in 1997 and Macao from Portuguese rule in 1999. The late 1990s saw a cautious extension of civil liberties, but the leadership still denies Chinese citizens most basic political rights.

Beijing was chosen for the 2008 Olympic Games. China's treatment of Tibet came under the international spotlight in the build-up to the games, following violent protests in Tibet's capital city, Lhasa.

For the background to the handover of Hong Kong in 1997, *see* page 328.

TERRITORY AND POPULATION

China is bounded in the north by Russia and Mongolia; east by North Korea, the Yellow Sea and the East China Sea, with Hong Kong and Macao as enclaves on the southeast coast; south by Vietnam, Laos, Myanmar, India, Bhutan and Nepal; west by India, Pakistan, Afghanistan, Tajikistan, Kyrgyzstan and Kazakhstan. The total area (including Taiwan, Hong Kong and Macao) is estimated at 9,572,900 sq. km (3,696,100 sq. miles). A law of Feb. 1992 claimed the Spratly, Paracel and Diaoyutasi Islands. An agreement of 7 Sept. 1993 at prime ministerial level settled Sino-Indian border disputes which had first emerged in the war of 1962.

China's fifth national census was held on 1 Nov. 2000. The total population of the 31 provinces, autonomous regions and municipalities on the mainland was 1,242,612,226 (602,336,257 females, representing 48·47%); density, 130 per sq. km. The population rose by 111,789,233 (or 9·89%) since the census in 1990. There were 458,770,983 urban residents, accounting for 36·9% of the population. The proportion of the population living in urban areas has more than doubled since 1975. An estimated 300m. people have migrated from the countryside to cities since the economy was opened up in the late 1970s, and a further 300m. are expected to move to towns and cities by 2020. China has a fast-growing ageing population. Whereas in 1980 only 4·7% of the population was aged 65 or over and by 2005 this had increased to 7·6%, by 2030 it is expected to rise to 16·3%. Long-term projections suggest that in 2050 as much as 23·6% of the population will be 65 or older. The estimated population in 2006 was 1,314·48m. (nearly a fifth of the world's total population), with 577,060,000 urban residents (43·9% of the population).

The UN gives an estimated population for 2010 of 1,354·15m.

China is set to lose its status as the world's most populous country to India in about 2030, and according to UN projections its population will begin to decline around the same time.

1979 regulations restricting married couples to a single child, a policy enforced by compulsory abortions and economic sanctions, have been widely ignored, and it was admitted in 1988 that the population target of 1,200m. by 2000 would have to be revised to 1,270m. Since 1988 peasant couples have been permitted a second child after four years if the first born is a girl, a measure to combat infanticide. In 1999 China started to implement a more widespread gradual relaxation of the one-child policy.

An estimated 55m. persons of Chinese origin lived abroad in 2005.

A number of widely divergent varieties of Chinese are spoken. The official 'Modern Standard Chinese' is based on the dialect of North China. Mandarin in one form or another is spoken by 885m. people in China, or around 70% of the population of mainland China. The Wu language and its dialects has some 77m. native speakers and Cantonese 66m. The ideographic writing system of 'characters' is uniform throughout the country, and has undergone systematic simplification. In 1958 a phonetic alphabet (*Pinyin*) was devised to transcribe the characters, and in 1979 this was officially adopted for use in all texts in the Roman alphabet. The previous transcription scheme (Wade) is still used in Taiwan and Hong Kong.

Mainland China is administratively divided into 22 provinces, five autonomous regions (originally entirely or largely inhabited by ethnic minorities, though in some regions now outnumbered by Han immigrants) and four government-controlled municipalities. These are in turn divided into 332 prefectures, 658 cities (of which 265 are at prefecture level and 393 at county level), 2,053 counties and 808 urban districts.

Government-controlled municipalities	*Area (in 1,000 sq. km)*	*Population (2000 census, in 1,000)*	*Density per sq. km (in 2000)*	*Capital*
Beijing	16·8	13,569	808	—
Chongqing	82·0	30,512	372	—
Shanghai	6·2	16,407	2,646	—
Tianjin	11·3	9,849	872	—
Provinces				
Anhui	139·9	59,000	422	Hefei
Fujian	123·1	34,098	277	Fuzhou
Gansu[1]	366·5	25,124	69	Lanzhou
Guangdong[1]	197·1	85,225	432	Guangzhou
Guizhou[1]	174·0	35,248	203	Guiyang
Hainan[1]	34·3	7,559	220	Haikou
Hebei[1]	202·7	66,684	329	Shijiazhuang

Provinces	Area (in 1,000 sq. km)	Population (2000 census, in 1,000)	Density per sq. km (in 2000)	Capital
Heilongjiang[1]	463·6	36,238	78	Haerbin
Henan	167·0	91,237	546	Zhengzhou
Hubei[1]	187·5	59,509	317	Wuhan
Hunan[1]	210·5	63,274	301	Changsha
Jiangsu	102·6	73,044	712	Nanjing
Jiangxi	164·8	40,398	245	Nanchang
Jilin[1]	187·0	26,802	143	Changchun
Liaoning[1]	151·0	41,824	277	Shenyang
Qinghai[1]	721·0	4,823	7	Xining
Shaanxi	195·8	35,365	181	Xian
Shandong	153·3	89,972	587	Jinan
Shanxi	157·1	32,471	207	Taiyuan
Sichuan[1]	487·0	82,348	169	Chengdu
Yunnan[1]	436·2	42,360	97	Kunming
Zhejiang[1]	101·8	45,931	451	Hangzhou
Autonomous regions				
Guangxi Zhuang	220·4	43,855	199	Nanning
Inner Mongolia	1,177·5	23,323	20	Hohhot
Ningxia Hui	66·4	5,486	83	Yinchuan
Tibet[2]	1,221·6	2,616	2	Lhasa
Xinjiang Uighur	1,646·9	18,460	11	Urumqi

[1]Also designated minority nationality autonomous area.
[2]See also Tibet below.

Population of largest cities in 2000: Shanghai, 14·23m.; Beijing (Peking), 10·30m.; Guangzhou (Canton), 7·55m.; Tianjin, 6·84m.; Wuhan, 6·79m.; Shenzhen, 6·48m.; Chongqing, 5·09m.; Shenyang, 4·60m.; Chengdu, 4·27m.; Foshan, 4·01m.; Xian, 3·87m.; Dongguan, 3·87m.; Nanjing, 3·78m.; Haerbin, 3·63m.; Hangzhou, 3·24m.; Shantou, 3·07m.; Dalian, 2·87m.; Jinan, 2·80m.; Changchun, 2·75m.; Qingdao, 2·72m.; Kunming, 2·55m.; Taiyuan, 2·54m.; Zhengzhou, 2·50m.; Changsha, 2·12m.; Fuzhou, 2·03m.; Shijiazhuang, 1·94m.; Zibo, 1·93m.; Lanzhou, 1·91m.; Guiyang, 1·89m.; Wuxi, 1·87m.; Suzhou, 1·75m.; Urumqi (Wulumuqi), 1·73m.; Ningbo, 1·70m.; Nanchang, 1·68m.; Nanning, 1·67m.; Tangshan, 1·66m.; Wenzhou, 1·58m.; Hefei, 1·55m.; Changzhou, 1·51m.

China has 56 ethnic groups. According to the 2000 census 1,159,400,000 people (91·6%) were of Han nationality and 106,430,000 (8·4%) were from national minorities (including Zhuang, Manchu, Hui, Miao, Uighur, Yi, Tujia, Mongolian and Tibetan). Compared with the 1990 census, the Han population increased by almost 116,920,000 (11·2%), while the ethnic minorities increased by 15,230,000 (16·7%). Non-Han populations predominate in the autonomous regions, most notably in Tibet where national minorities accounted for 96·8% of the population in 2006.

Li Chengrui, *The Population of China.* 1992

Tibet

After the 1959 revolt was suppressed, the Preparatory Committee for the Autonomous Region of Tibet (set up in 1955) took over the functions of local government, led by its Vice-Chairman, the Panchen Lama, in the absence of its Chairman, the Dalai Lama, who had fled to India in 1959. In Dec. 1964 both the Dalai and Panchen Lamas were removed from their posts and on 9 Sept. 1965 Tibet became an Autonomous Region. 301 delegates were elected to the first People's Congress, of whom 226 were Tibetans. The senior spiritual leader, the Dalai Lama, is in exile. He was awarded the Nobel Peace Prize in 1989. Following the death of the 10th Panchen Lama (Tibet's second most important spiritual leader) in Jan. 1989, the Dalai Lama announced Gendun Choekyi Nyima (b. 1989) as the 11th Panchen Lama in May 1995. Beijing rejected the choice and appointed Gyaltsen Norbu (b. 1989) in his place. Gendu Choekyi Nyima has been missing since 1995. The borders were opened for trade with neighbouring countries in 1980. In July 1988 Tibetan was reinstated as a 'major official language', competence in which is required of all administrative officials. Monasteries and shrines have been renovated and reopened. There were some 46,000 monks and nuns in 2004. In 1984 a Buddhist seminary in Lhasa opened with 200 students. A further softening of Beijing's attitude towards Tibet was shown during President Bill Clinton's visit to China in June 1998. Jiang Zemin, China's president, said he was prepared to meet the Dalai Lama provided he acknowledged Chinese sovereignty over Tibet and Taiwan. In Sept. 2002 direct contact between the exiled government and China was re-established after a nine-year gap.

In March 2008 anti-Chinese protests in Lhasa, the regional capital, ended in violence, with dozens reportedly killed by the Chinese authorities. The episode focused international attention on China's human rights record ahead of the 2008 Olympic Games in Beijing.

At the 2000 census Tibet had a population of 2·62m., of which 2·42m. were Tibetans and the remainder from other ethnic groups. The average population density was 2·02 persons per sq. km, although the majority of residents live in the southern and eastern parts of the region. The estimated population in 2006 was 2·69m. Birth rate (per 1,000), 2006, 17·4; death rate, 5·7. Population of the Lhasa (capital) region in 2000 was 403,700.

About 80% of the population is engaged in the dominant industries of farming and animal husbandry. In 2006 the total sown area was 233,000 ha. (including 171,700 ha. of grain crops). Output in 2006: total grain crops, 923,700 tonnes; vegetables, 450,000 tonnes. In 2005 there were 10·7m. sheep, 6·3m. cattle and buffaloes, 6·3m. goats and 0·4m. horses.

Tibet has over 2,000 mineral ore fields. Minerals output, 2006: copper, 1,260,000 tonnes; vanadium, 415,000 tonnes; chrome, 121,800 tonnes. Cement production, 2006: 1·66m. tonnes. Timber output, 2007: 356,800 cu. metres.

In 2006 there were 44,813 km of roads (21,842 km in 1990). There are airports at Lhasa, Bangda and (since 2006) Nyingchi providing external links. In 2006, 154,800 foreign tourists visited Tibet. In July 2006 a 1,142-km railway linking Lhasa with the town of Golmud opened. It is the highest railway in the world. Direct services have subsequently been introduced between Lhasa and a number of major Chinese cities, including Beijing and Shanghai.

In Dec. 2006 Tibet had 890 elementary schools and 1,568 teaching centres (with 329,500 pupils), 93 junior middle schools (127,900 pupils), 13 senior middle schools (37,700 pupils) and ten secondary vocational schools (14,775 pupils). There were also six higher education institutes (including Tibet University, Tibet Nationalities Institute, Tibet Agriculture and Animal Husbandry College, and Institute of Tibetan Medicines) with 23,327 enrolled students. The illiteracy rate of young and middle-aged people fell from 39% in 2000 to below 10% in 2006.

In 2006 there were 10,746 medical personnel (including 4,310 doctors and 2,000 registered nurses) and 1,349 medical institutions, with a total of 7,496 beds.

Barnett, R. and Akiner, S. (eds.) *Resistance and Reform in Tibet.* 1994
Margolis, Eric, *War at the Top of the World: The Struggle for Afghanistan, Kashmir and Tibet.* 2001
Pinfold, John, *Tibet* [Bibliography]. 1991
Schwartz, R. D., *Circle of Protest: Political Ritual in the Tibetan Uprising.* 1994
Smith, W. W., *A History of Tibet: Nationalism and Self-Determination.* 1996

SOCIAL STATISTICS

Births, 2005, 16,210,000; deaths, 8,510,000. 2005 birth rate (per 1,000 population), 12·40; death rate, 6·51. In 2005 the birth rate rose for the first time since 1987. There were 9,450,000 marriages and 1,893,000 divorces in 2006. In April 2001 parliament passed revisions to the marriage law prohibiting bigamy and cohabitation outside marriage. The World Health Organization estimated in 2005 that the suicide rate in China was about 17·4 per 100,000 population. China is the only major country in which the suicide rate is higher among females—over half the world's female suicides occur in China. Life expectancy at birth, 2007, was 71·3 years for men and 74·7 years for women. Infant mortality, 2005, 23 per 1,000 live births. Fertility rate, 2004, 1·7 births per woman. Annual population growth rate, 2000–05, 0·6%. According to the World Bank, the number of people living in poverty (less than US$1·25 a day) at purchasing power parity declined from 835m. in 1981 to 207m. in 2005.

CLIMATE

Most of China has a temperate climate but, with such a large country, extending far inland and embracing a wide range of latitude as well as containing large areas at high altitude, many parts experience extremes of climate, especially in winter. Most rain falls during the summer, from May to Sept., though amounts decrease inland. Monthly average temperatures and annual rainfall (2006): Beijing (Peking), Jan. 28·6°F (–1·9°C), July 78·6°F (25·9°C). Annual rainfall 12·5" (318 mm). Chongqing, Jan. 46·0°F (7·8°C), July 87·8°F (31·0°C). Annual rainfall 33·1" (840 mm). Shanghai, Jan. 42·3°F (5·7°C), July 84·9°F (29·4°C). Annual rainfall 45·3" (1,150 mm). Tianjin, Jan. 27·1°F (–2·7°C), July 78·6°F (25·9°C). Annual rainfall 16·3" (415 mm).

CONSTITUTION AND GOVERNMENT

On 21 Sept. 1949 the *Chinese People's Political Consultative Conference* met in Beijing, convened by the Chinese Communist Party. The Conference adopted a 'Common Programme' of 60 articles and the 'Organic Law of the Central People's Government' (31 articles). Both became the basis of the Constitution adopted on 20 Sept. 1954 by the 1st National People's Congress, the supreme legislative body. The Consultative Conference continued to exist after 1954 as an advisory body. Three further constitutions have been promulgated under Communist rule—in 1975, 1978 and 1982 (currently in force). The latter was partially amended in 1988, 1993 and 1999, endorsing the principles of a socialist market economy and of private ownership.

The unicameral *National People's Congress* is the highest organ of state power. Usually meeting for one session a year, it can amend the constitution and nominally elects and has power to remove from office the highest officers of state. There are 2,987 members of the Congress, who are elected to serve five-year terms by municipal, regional and provincial people's congresses. The Congress elects a *Standing Committee* (which supervises the *State Council*) and the *President* and *Vice-President* for a five-year term. When not in session, Congress business is carried on by the *Standing Committee*.

The *State Council* is the supreme executive organ and comprises the Prime Minister, Deputy Prime Ministers and State Councillors.

The *Central Military Commission* is the highest state military organ.

National Anthem

'March of the Volunteers'; words by Tien Han, tune by Nie Er.

GOVERNMENT CHRONOLOGY

Leaders of the Communist Party of China since 1935.

Chairmen

1935–76	Mao Zedong
1976–81	Hua Guofeng
1981–82	Hu Yaobang

General Secretaries

1956–57	Deng Xiaoping
1980–87	Hu Yaobang
1987–89	Zhao Ziyang
1989–2002	Jiang Zemin
2002–	Hu Jintao

De facto ruler

1978–97	Deng Xiaoping

Heads of State since 1949.

Chairman of the Central People's Government

1949–54	Mao Zedong

Chairmen (Presidents)

1954–59	Mao Zedong
1959–68	Liu Shaoqi
1968–75	Dong Biwu

Chairmen of the Standing Committee of the National People's Congress

1975–76	Zhu De
1978–83	Ye Jianying

Presidents of the Republic

1983–88	Li Xiannian
1988–93	Yang Shangkun
1993–2003	Jiang Zemin
2003–	Hu Jintao

Prime Ministers since 1949.

1949–76	Zhou Enlai
1976–80	Hua Guofeng
1980–87	Zhao Ziyang
1987–1998	Li Peng
1998–2003	Zhu Rongji
2003–	Wen Jiabao

RECENT ELECTIONS

Elections of delegates to the 11th National People's Congress were held between Oct. 2007 and Feb. 2008 by municipal, regional and provincial people's congresses. At its annual session in March 2008 the Congress re-elected Hu Jintao as President and elected Xi Jinping as Vice-President.

CURRENT ADMINISTRATION

President and Chairman of Central Military Commission: Hu Jintao; b. 1942 (Chinese Communist Party; elected 15 March 2003 and re-elected 15 March 2008).

Deputy President: Xi Jinping.

In March 2010 the government comprised:

Prime Minister: Wen Jiabao; b. 1942 (Chinese Communist Party; appointed 16 March 2003).

Deputy Prime Ministers: Li Keqiang; Zhang Dejiang; Wang Qishan; Hui Liangyu.

Minister of Agriculture: Han Changfu. *Civil Administration:* Li Xueju. *Commerce:* Chen Deming. *Culture:* Cai Wu. *Education:* Zhou Ji. *Environmental Protection:* Zhou Shengxian. *Finance:* Xie Xuren. *Foreign Affairs:* Yang Jiechi. *Health:* Chen Zhu. *Housing and Construction:* Jiang Weixin. *Human Resources and Social Security:* Yin Weimin. *Industry and Information:* Li Yizhong. *Justice:* Wu Aiying. *Land and Resources:* Xu Shaoshi. *National Defence:* Liang Guanglie. *Public Security:* Meng Jianzhu. *Railways:* Liu Zhijun. *Science and Technology:* Wan Gang. *State Security:* Geng Huichang. *Supervision:* Ma Wen. *Transport:* Li Shenglin. *Water Resources:* Chen Lei.

Ministers heading State Commissions: *Ethnic Affairs*, Yang Jing. *National Development and Reform*, Zhang Ping. *National Population and Family Planning*, Li Bin.

De facto power is in the hands of the Communist Party of China, which had 66m. members in 2002. There are eight other parties, all members of the Chinese People's Political Consultative Conference.

The members of the Standing Committee of the Politburo in March 2010 were: Hu Jintao (*General Secretary*); Wu Bangguo; Wen Jiabao; Jia Qinglin; Li Changchun; Xi Jinping; Li Keqiang; He Guoqiang; Zhou Yongkang.

Government Website: http://www.gov.cn

CURRENT LEADERS

Hu Jintao

Position
President

Introduction
Hu Jintao was nominated general secretary of the Chinese Communist Party (CCP) in Nov. 2002, formally succeeding Jiang Zemin as head of state in March 2003 and as chairman of the Central Military Commission in Sept. 2004. Although widely perceived as a conservative—having supported the Tiananmen Square massacres in the late 1980s and cracked down on separatism in Tibet—he has continued Jiang's cautious reformist policies. He has maintained the drive for rapid industrial growth and also further developed China's international contacts, undertaking visits as state president to Latin America, Australia, Canada, Central Asia, the UK, USA and, in particular, Africa.

Early Life
Much of Hu's early history is disputed. He is believed to have been born in Dec. 1942 in Jixi, Anhui Province. His mother died when he was six and he was subsequently raised by an aunt. In 1959 he began engineering studies at Qinghua University and graduated in 1964, the same year in which he joined the CCP. He then held a variety of posts at the University and the ministry of water conservancy.

He is reported to have distanced himself from Mao's Cultural Revolution of the mid-1960s and was sentenced to two months of 'reform through labour'. Later, he worked on large-scale engineering projects in Gansu province. By the late 1970s Hu was a favourite of Deng Xiaoping, who became China's effective leader. He settled in Beijing in 1980, and within two years he was the youngest member of the party's central committee. Having risen through the ranks of the Communist Youth League, in 1985 he was appointed provincial party secretary for Guizhou. In 1988 he became party secretary in charge of Tibet and authorized the killing of several independence protesters in March 1989. Shortly afterwards he declared martial law and oversaw the introduction of 100,000 troops into the region. Later in the year he was among the first of the provincial party secretaries to express his support for those who took part in the Tiananmen Square massacres.

In 1992 Hu was responsible for organizing Jiang's first party congress as leader, and soon after was designated a member of the Politburo Standing Committee. In 1998 he was named vice-president, from which point on he was Jiang's acknowledged successor. The following year he was prominent in protests at the US and British embassies in Beijing over the accidental bombing of the Chinese embassy in Belgrade during NATO military action against Serbia. He was also named deputy chairman of the Central Military Commission at that time.

Career in Office
At the CCP congress of Nov. 2002, Hu replaced Jiang as party general secretary and then succeeded him as state president in March 2003. Hu expressed his commitment to Jiang's *Theory of Three Representations* (treatise on Chinese political thought), suggesting a continuity of government style.

Hu has nevertheless pursued an active foreign policy, breaking from the Deng model which proscribed taking the lead in diplomatic negotiations. He has sought to resolve the issue of North Korea's nuclear ambitions through the ongoing six-nations talks between North and South Korea, China, Japan, Russia and the USA. He has also developed relations with neighbouring India and Pakistan, establishing military links with both countries in Nov. 2003. Earlier, in June 2003, Hu received the visiting Indian prime minister who conceded recognition of Tibet as an autonomous region of the People's Republic of China. As president, Hu has travelled widely, visiting Australia, Africa, Latin America, Canada and Central Asia in pursuit of closer economic and commercial links to supply the resources for China's industrial machine. In Nov. 2006 he hosted a Sino-African summit in Beijing attended by more than 40 African heads of state and government, and in 2007 undertook a tour of eight African countries to boost trade and investment. In July 2008 China and Russia finalized a treaty formally ending a 40-year-old border dispute that had provoked armed clashes during the Cold War.

Human rights, Taiwan and Tibet remain difficult issues in Sino-US relations. Perennial US accusations of 'backsliding' in human rights have been vigorously denied, and Hu's government has pointed to US foreign policy as aggressive and harmful to the rights of civilians. Former President George W. Bush's less conciliatory attitude towards China over Taiwan led to a more turbulent relationship between the two countries, although Hu made a seemingly successful first presidential visit to the USA in April 2006. In Nov. 2009 US President Obama made his first visit to China, heralding declarations of bilateral co-operation on trade, climate change and other issues. At the CCP congress in Oct. 2007, Hu offered a peace agreement with Taiwan as long as the territory did not explicitly renounce its links with mainland China, and in June 2008 the first formal bilateral talks since 1999 took place. In July 2009 Hu exchanged direct messages with the president of Taiwan, the first such exchange between the national leaders in more than 60 years.

In March 2008 the worst ethnic violence in two decades in Tibet against continuing Chinese rule prompted a security crackdown against separatist protesters and widespread international criticism of Hu's government ahead of the summer Olympic Games staged in Beijing in Aug. Further ethnic violence erupted in July 2009 in Urumqi, the capital of China's northwestern Xinjiang province, between indigenous Muslim Uighurs and Han Chinese settlers, which left around 200 people dead and 1,700 injured.

Hu's domestic agenda has focused on continuing China's rapid economic development and alleviating the poverty of the peasant population, while an anti-corruption drive has included the sacking and even execution of high-ranking state officials. His government has also pledged increases in agricultural subsidies and the eventual termination of agricultural taxes—a programme interpreted as an attempt to create a larger middle class, committed to the CCP hegemony.

Hu was re-elected for a further term in March 2008. In Oct. 2009 he oversaw the mass celebrations to mark the 60th anniversary of the Communist Party's assumption of power.

Wen Jiabao

Position
Prime Minister

Introduction
Wen Jiabao was confirmed as China's prime minister in March 2003. Although relatively low-profile, he has established a reputation for reliability and durability. A leading figure in the liberalization of China's economic and environmental policies in the 1990s, he has promoted the development of the traditionally poorer and less urban west of the country.

Early Life
Wen Jiabao was born in Tianjin in the east of China in Sept. 1942. In 1965 he obtained a degree from the Beijing Institute of Geology and joined the Chinese Communist Party (CCP). In 1968 he received his master's degree and began working with the geomechanics survey team at the Gansu provincial geological bureau (until 1982).

Wen then moved to Beijing to work at the ministry of geology and mineral resources. After heading the policy and research section he was appointed vice-minister. In 1985 he was made deputy director of the general office of the CCP central committee, working closely with the party chairman, Hu Yaobang. Wen emerged unscathed after Hu's 1987 purge and took over as director of the general office as well as becoming an alternate member of the Politburo of the CCP central committee and secretary of the central committee's work committee of departments.

In 1989 Wen was in attendance when General Secretary Zhao Ziyang visited Tiananmen Square during the student protests. Zhao was subsequently purged, but again Wen's position remained secure. In 1992 he took on additional roles within the CCP central committee. Having led the team responsible for drafting the national five-year plan in 1995, Wen won full membership of the Politburo of the central committee two years later.

Throughout the 1990s Wen was a prominent figure in the formation of the party's economic policy. He was involved in banking reform and the restructuring of the finance ministry. By the late 1990s he was increasingly involved in environmental and rural affairs. In March 2003 Wen was confirmed as Zhu Rhongji's successor to the premiership with 99·3% support from the National People's Congress.

Career in Office

Although perceived as less charismatic than Zhu, Wen has won respect within the Chinese political establishment for his longevity and experience. His management style has traditionally been based on seeking consensus.

When he was in Gansu, Wen became one of the few leading Chinese politicians to work for an extended period in the economically less prosperous west of the country. He has stated that his aim is to narrow the prosperity gap between the east and west of China. In addition, many observers hope that he can confront the problems of China's economically weak agricultural sector. Under Jiang, Wen did much to promote the land rights of the rural peasant population. In addition, he has pushed for a reduction in the tax burden on rural communities and promoted freedom for farmers to sell their holdings.

Despite his contribution to banking reform in the 1990s, Wen was not expected to champion radical reforms to counter the crippling problem of bad debts. In 2002 he called for a 'gradual approach' to further deregulation and in 2003 he stated that China would not be pressured by the international community into a revaluation of the yuan (renminbi). Nevertheless, in July 2005 China did revalue the currency, abandoning its 11-year peg to the US dollar and linking it to a basket of currencies.

Wen's programme for assisting the rural poor took shape at the opening of the National People's Congress in March 2004. Stressing the importance of social development in poorer regions, he highlighted the damaging disparity in wealth between the rich, industrial coastal provinces and the poorer rural provinces of the interior. He promised investment in agriculture, emphasizing the need to increase overall grain production capability. His programme also included the recognition of private property, requiring an amendment to the constitution, designed to prevent the unlawful requisition of property by officials.

However, the government's slow reaction to SARS, originating in Guangdong in 2002 and 2003, was criticized by the international community as nearly 350 people died from the virus, despite quarantines and travel bans. Then the government was criticized for its attitude towards HIV/AIDS, prompting the health minister in 2004 to announce plans to combat the epidemic. Furthermore, in Sept. 2008 a scandal over tainted milk supplies, which caused around 50,000 children to fall ill, prompted a public apology by Wen.

In April 2007 Wen visited Japan and became the first Chinese premier to make a formal address to the Japanese legislature, in which he urged friendship and reconciliation after their countries' difficult shared history.

Wen was re-elected for a further term in March 2008. In Nov. he disclosed that the effects of the global financial crisis on China were worse than had been expected, prompting the government to announce a US$586bn. spending stimulus to boost the economy. In March 2009 China's central bank called for a new global reserve currency run by the International Monetary Fund to replace the US dollar and Wen, while voicing his confidence in the Chinese economy, expressed concern over China's significant holdings of US government bonds.

DEFENCE

The Chinese president is chairman of the State and Party's Military Commissions. China is divided into seven military regions. The military commander also commands the air, naval and civilian militia forces assigned to each region.

China's armed forces, totalling more than 2·2m. in 2006, are the largest of any country.

Conscription is compulsory, but for organizational reasons, is selective: only some 10% of potential recruits are called up. Service is for two years. A military academy to train senior officers in modern warfare was established in 1985.

Defence expenditure in 2008 was estimated at 590bn. yuan (US$84,900m., equivalent to US$63 per capita). Defence spending in 2007 represented an estimated 2·0% of GDP. Only the USA spent more on defence in 2008, but China's defence expenditure totalled around a seventh of that of the USA. In the period 2004–08 China's expenditure on major conventional weapons was the highest in the world at US$13·0bn. In March 2007 it was announced that defence budget for the year would rise by 17·8%. Military spending rose by an estimated 194% in real terms between 1999 and 2008.

Nuclear Weapons

Having carried out its first test in 1964, there have been 45 tests in all at Lop Nur, in Xinjiang (the last in 1996). The nuclear arsenal consisted of approximately 186 warheads in Jan. 2009 according to the Stockholm International Peace Research Institute. China has been helping Pakistan with its nuclear efforts. Despite China's official position, *Deadly Arsenals*, published by the Carnegie Endowment for International Peace, alleges that the Chinese government is secretly pursuing chemical and biological weapons programmes.

Army

The Army (PLA: 'People's Liberation Army') is divided into main and local forces. Main forces, administered by the seven military regions in which they are stationed, but commanded by the Ministry of Defence, are available for operation anywhere and are better equipped. Local forces concentrate on the defence of their own regions. There are 18 Integrated Group Armies comprising 42 infantry divisions, nine armoured divisions, 12 armoured brigades, one mechanized infantry, 22 motorized infantry brigades, seven artillery divisions, 14 artillery brigades, one anti-tank brigade, nine surface-to-air missile brigades and 12 anti-aircraft artillery brigades. Total strength in 2006 was 1·60m. including some 800,000 conscripts. Reserve forces are undergoing major reorganization on a provincial basis but are estimated to number some 800,000.

In Sept. 2003 it was announced that the strength of the PLA was to be reduced by 200,000 as part of a move to modernize the military.

There is a paramilitary People's Armed Police force estimated at 1·5m. under PLA command.

Navy

The naval arm of the PLA comprises one nuclear-powered ballistic missile armed submarine, four nuclear-propelled fleet submarines, one diesel-powered cruise missile submarine and some 51 patrol submarines. Surface combatant forces include 27 missile-armed destroyers, 44 frigates and some 52 missile craft.

There is a land-based naval air force of about 792 combat aircraft, primarily for defensive and anti-submarine service. The force includes H-5 torpedo bombers, Q-5 fighter/ground attack aircraft, J-6 (MiG-19) and J-7 (MiG-21) fighters.

The naval arm is split into a North Sea Fleet, an East Sea Fleet and a South Sea Fleet.

In 2006 naval personnel were estimated at 255,000, including 26,000 in the naval air force and 40,000 conscripts.

Air Force

There are 32 air divisions. Up to four squadrons make up an air regiment and three air regiments form an air division. The Air Force has an estimated 2,600 combat aircraft.

Equipment includes J-7 (MiG-21) interceptors and fighter-bombers, H-5 (Il-28) jet bombers, H-6 Chinese-built copies of Tu-16 strategic bombers, Q-5 fighter-bombers (evolved from the MiG-19) and Su-27 fighters supplied by Russia. About 165 of a locally-developed fighter designated J-8 (known in the West as 'Finback') are in service.

Total strength (2006) was 400,000 (150,000 conscripts), including 210,000 in air defence organization. The Air Force headquarters are in Beijing.

INTERNATIONAL RELATIONS

The People's Republic of China is a member of the UN (and a permanent member of its Security Council), World Bank, IMF and several other UN specialized agencies, WTO, BIS, Inter-American Development Bank, Asian Development Bank, APEC, Mekong Group and Antarctic Treaty.

In 2005 China made the transition from receiver of foreign aid to donor as a consequence of several years of rapid economic growth.

ECONOMY

In 2006 agriculture accounted for 11·7% of GDP, industry 48·1% and services 40·2%.

Overview

China's economic performance has been marked by high rates of growth for over 25 years. GDP growth in the early 2000s consistently exceeded 10% until suffering a slump following the global financial crisis. China holds the world's largest foreign reserves, is among the top recipients of foreign direct investment and is the world's largest producer and consumer of coal. It is also a key player in Africa's development, having signed business deals worth US$2bn. by 2006.

The first steps towards a more market-oriented economy were taken by Deng Xiaoping in the late 1970s. He opened the economy to foreign trade and investment, decentralized industrial management and allowed the private sector to flourish. In 2001 China became a member of the WTO, establishing trade relations with many countries. Much of China's recent dynamism has come from 'collective' enterprises, particularly those at township and village level run by managers under the auspices of local government. Local governments have an incentive to see enterprises run efficiently as officials are allowed to keep surplus revenues. Much of the productivity-enhancing competition that China has experienced is therefore competition between local or regional governments with direct interests in productive enterprise.

Private entrepreneurs and foreign investors have played an important role in manufacturing output. Even before 1978 the economy was heavily skewed towards manufacturing but thereafter output increased and there was a structural shift away from large state-owned enterprises (SOEs), although SOEs remain a significant part of the economy. Many new enterprises are labour-intensive industries as distinct from the capital-intensive SOEs. Estimates of the private sector's share of total economic activity differ significantly, with the Chinese government and some foreign banks putting it as low as a quarter while the OECD estimate is two-thirds. Growth has been fuelled by low added value, labour-intensive exports but the country has moved up the added value curve and Chinese firms are predicted to become increasingly competitive with higher added value producers, such as South Korea.

There are several threats to continued growth. Inefficient production and outmoded equipment have led to a deterioration of the environment, especially in the north. Air pollution, soil erosion and a declining water table are particular problems, although under China's 11th Five Year Plan (2006–10) the government aims to reduce major pollutants by 10%.

The global economic crisis of 2008 reduced the rate of growth and the inflow of FDI but China's recovery was among the earliest and most spectacular. GDP growth was 7·9% in the second quarter of 2009, up from a two-decade low of 6·1% in the first quarter of that year. Recent growth has been rooted in a government stimulus package of 4trn. yuan (US$586bn. or 13% of 2008 GDP), including fiscal spending and interest rate cuts, as well as expansionary monetary policy. The government committed 1·18trn. yuan with the rest of the package coming from local government, banks and SOEs. The Asian Development Bank forecasts GDP growth of 8·9% for 2010. The fiscal position remains strong with total government debt totalling 15·9% of GDP in 2008. Although exports declined by around 17% in 2009, other countries fared worse and China's share of world exports increased to nearly 10% (up from 3% in 1999), making it the world's largest exporter.

Efforts to restructure the economy away from investment and export-led growth towards more private consumption have been interrupted by the global crisis. Nonetheless, structural reforms to redirect the export-oriented economy include increased worker mobility and improved public sector efficiency. The economy's dynamism is handicapped by the heavy capitalization required for start-ups, bias against small private companies by state-controlled banks and a deficient stock market that makes family and friends a key source of financing. SOEs continue to dominate 'strategic' industries and remain burdened by excess labour. China also faces the growing burden of an ageing population.

The World Bank estimates that the number of people living on a dollar a day declined by 391m. between 1990 and 2005. However, the 204m. who still have consumption levels below one dollar a day are located mainly in remote and resource-poor regions, particularly in the west and the interior.

Currency

The currency is called Renminbi (i.e. People's Currency). The unit of currency is the *yuan* (CNY) which is divided into ten *jiao*, the *jiao* being divided into ten *fen*. The yuan was floated to reflect market forces on 1 Jan. 1994 while remaining state-controlled. For 11 years the People's Bank of China maintained the yuan at about 8·28 to the US dollar, allowing it to fluctuate but only by a fraction of 1% in closely supervised trading. However, on 21 July 2005 it was revalued and is now pegged against a 'market basket' of currencies the central parities of which are determined every night. The exchange rate was changed from 8·28 yuan to the dollar to 8·11 yuan to the dollar. Since July 2005 the yuan has been allowed to appreciate slowly, and the dollar to yuan exchange rate has gone from 8·11 to 6·83. In Aug. 2009 total money supply was 20,039·5bn. yuan, gold reserves were 33·89m. troy oz and foreign exchange reserves US$2,210·8bn. (US$75·4bn. in 1995). China's reserves are the highest of any country, having overtaken those of Japan in Feb. 2006.

Inflation rates (based on IMF statistics):

1999	*2000*	*2001*	*2002*	*2003*	*2004*	*2005*	*2006*	*2007*	*2008*
–1·4%	0·4%	0·7%	–0·8%	1·2%	3·9%	1·8%	1·5%	4·8%	5·9%

China's economy overheated in the early 1990s, leading to inflation rates of 14·7% in 1993, 24·1% in 1994 and 17·1% in 1995. The 2008 rate was the highest since 1996.

Budget

Total revenue and expenditure (in 1bn. yuan):

	2002	2003	2004	2005	2006
Revenue	1,890·4	2,171·5	2,639·6	3,164·9	3,876·0
Expenditure	2,205·3	2,465·0	2,848·7	3,393·0	4,042·3

Total revenue in the central budget for 2006 was 2,123·2bn. yuan, comprising 2,045·0bn. yuan in revenue collected by central government and 78·3bn. yuan transferred to central government from local authorities. Total expenditure in the central budget amounted to 2,348·2bn. yuan, of which 999·2bn. yuan of expenditure for the central government and 1,349·1bn. yuan in the form of subsidies for local authorities. Local government revenue in 2006 came to 3,177·2bn. yuan (1,828·1bn. yuan in revenue collected by local authorities and 1,349·1bn. yuan in central government subsidies) and expenditure amounted to 3,100·4bn. yuan (3,022·2bn. yuan of expenditure in local budgets and 78·3bn. yuan transferred to central government). The deficit in the central budget in 2006 was 275·0bn. yuan.

Performance

GDP totalled US$4,326·2bn. in 2008, the third highest behind the USA and Japan. It is forecast that by 2050 China will have overtaken the USA to become the world's largest economy. Real GDP growth rates (based on IMF statistics):

1999	2000	2001	2002	2003	2004	2005	2006	2007	2008
7·6%	8·4%	8·3%	9·1%	10·0%	10·1%	10·4%	11·6%	13·0%	9·0%

GDP growth in 2009 was 8·7% according to the National Bureau of Statistics. In spite of high growth in recent years, China's GDP per capita at purchasing power parity was $5,383 in 2007 compared to the very high human development average of $37,272.

Banking and Finance

The People's Bank of China is the central bank and bank of issue (*Governor*, Zhou Xiaochuan). There are three state policy banks—the State Development Bank, Export and Import Bank of China and Agricultural Development Bank of China—and four national specialized banks (the Bank of China, Industrial and Commercial Bank of China, Agricultural Bank of China and China Construction Bank). The Bank of China, Industrial and Commercial Bank of China and China Construction Bank have all sold minority stakes to foreign investors. The Bank of China is responsible for foreign banking operations. In April 2003 the China Banking Regulatory Commission was launched, taking over the role of regulating and supervising the country's banks and other deposit-taking financial institutions from the central bank. Legislation of 1995 permitted the establishment of commercial banks; credit co-operatives may be transformed into banks, mainly to provide credit to small businesses. In Oct. 2005 there were 30,438 rural credit co-operatives and 626 urban credit co-operatives. In mid-2002 deposits in rural co-operatives amounted to 1,870bn. yuan and loans reached 1,360bn. yuan. Insurance is handled by the People's Insurance Company.

Savings deposits in various forms in all banking institutions totalled 30,020·9bn. yuan at the end of 2005; loans amounted to 20,683·8bn. yuan.

There are stock exchanges in the Shenzhen Special Economic Zone and in Shanghai. A securities trading system linking six cities (Securities Automated Quotations System) was inaugurated in 1990 for trading in government bonds.

China received US$83·5bn. worth of foreign direct investment in 2007 and a record US$108·3bn. in 2008.

Weights and Measures

The metric system is in general use alongside traditional units of measurement.

ENERGY AND NATURAL RESOURCES

Environment

China's carbon dioxide emissions from the consumption and flaring of fossil fuels in 2008 accounted for 21·5% of the world total (the biggest emissions producer having overtaken the USA in 2007) and were equivalent to 4·9 tonnes per capita. An *Environmental Performance Index* compiled in 2008 ranked China 105th in the world out of 149 countries analysed, with 65·1%. The index examined various factors in six areas—air pollution, biodiversity and habitat, climate change, environmental health, productive natural resources and water resources. Pollution is estimated to cost China about 10% of GDP annually.

Electricity

Installed generating capacity in 2005 was 510m. kW, compared with 254m. kW in 1997. In 2005 electricity output was 2,474,700 GWh, a 12·8% increase over 2004. Consumption per capita was 1,684 kWh in 2004. Rapidly increasing demand has meant that more than half of China's provinces have had to ration power. Sources of electricity in 2005 as percentage of total production: coal, 81·5%; hydro-electric power, 16·0%; nuclear, 2·1%; others, 0·4%. In 2003 there were eight nuclear reactors in use with a further three under construction. Generating electricity is not centralized; local units range between 30 and 60 MW of output. In Dec. 2002 China formally broke up its state power monopoly, creating instead five generating and two transmission firms. The Three Gorges dam project on the Yangtze river was launched in 1993 and is intended to produce abundant hydro-electricity (as well as helping flood control). The first three 700,000-kW generators in service at the project's hydro-power station began commercial operation in July 2003. The original specification was completed in Oct. 2008, although six more generators are to be added (bringing the total to 32) that are not scheduled for completion until 2011. When the project is completed, it will have an overall capacity of 18·9 GW.

Oil and Gas

On-shore oil reserves are found mainly in the northeast (particularly the Daqing and Liaohe fields) and northwest. There are off-shore fields in the continental shelves of east China. Oil production was 189·7m. tonnes in 2008. China is the second largest consumer of oil after the USA. Ever-growing demand has meant that increasing amounts of oil are having to be imported. Domestic production now accounts for only 55% of consumption, compared to nearly 85% in 1998. Proven reserves in 2008 were 15·5bn. bbls, but they are expected to be exhausted by 2019.

The largest natural gas reserves are located in the western and north-central regions. Production was 76·1bn. cu. metres in 2008, with proven reserves of 2,460bn. cu. metres.

Minerals

In 2006 there were 158 varieties of proven mineral deposits in China, making it the third richest in the world in total reserves. Recoverable deposits of coal totalled 3,334·8bn. tonnes, mainly distributed in north China (particularly Shanxi province and the Inner Mongolia Autonomous Region). Coal production was 2,320m. tonnes in 2006. Annual coal production has increased every year since 2000. Growing domestic demand meant that China became a net importer of coal in 2007.

The iron ore reserve base was 46bn. tonnes in 2005. Deposits are abundant in the anthracite field of Shanxi, in Hebei and in Shandong, and are found in conjunction with coal and worked in the northeast. Production in 2006 was 601m. tonnes, making China the world's leading iron ore producer.

Tin ore is plentiful in Yunnan, where the tin-mining industry has long existed. Tin production was 126,000 tonnes in 2006.

China is a major producer of wolfram (tungsten ore). There is mining of wolfram in Hunan, Guangdong and Yunnan.

Salt production was 56·6m. tonnes in 2006; gold production was 245 tonnes. Output of other minerals (in 1,000 tonnes) in

2006: bauxite, 21,000; aluminium, 13,700; zinc, 2,840; lead, 1,330; copper, 873. Estimated diamond production in 2005, 1,060,000 carats. Other minerals produced: nickel, barite, bismuth, graphite, gypsum, mercury, molybdenum, silver. Reserves (in tonnes) of salt, 402,400m.; phosphate ore, 15,766m.; sylvite, 458m. China's gold production rose to 276 tonnes in 2007, in the process surpassing South Africa as the world's leading gold producer.

Agriculture

Agriculture accounted for approximately 15·4% of GDP in 2002, compared to over 50% in 1949 at the time of the birth of the People's Republic of China and over 30% in 1980. In 2003 areas harvested for major crops were (in 1m. ha.): rice, 27·40; maize, 23·52; wheat, 22·04; soybeans, 9·50; rapeseed, 7·20; sweet potatoes, 5·31. Intensive agriculture and horticulture have been practised for millennia. Present-day policy aims to avert the traditional threats from floods and droughts by soil conservancy, afforestation, irrigation and drainage projects, and to increase the 'high stable yields' areas by introducing fertilizers, pesticides and improved crops. In Aug. 1998 more than 21m. ha., notably in the Yangtze valley, were under water as China experienced its worst flooding since the 1950s. The 1998 flood season claimed over 4,100 lives.

'Township and village enterprises' in agriculture comprise enterprises previously run by the communes of the Maoist era, co-operatives run by rural labourers and individual firms of a certain size. Such enterprises employed 146·8m. people in 2006. There were 1,896 state farms in 2006 with 3·29m. employees. In 2005 there were 252·22m. rural households. The rural workforce in 2005 was 503·87m., of whom 299·76m. were employed in agriculture, fishing or land management. Net per capita annual peasant income, 2006: 3,587 yuan. Around 40% of the total workforce is engaged in agriculture, down from 68% in 1980. In 2006 rural residents accounted for 56·1% of the population (1996, 69·5%).

In 2002 there were 142,621,000 ha. of arable land and 11,335,000 ha. of permanent cropland; 54·9m. ha. were irrigated. There were 926,031 tractors in 2002 and 197,000 harvester-threshers.

Agricultural production of main crops (in 1m. tonnes), 2003: rice, 166·42; maize, 114·18; sweet potatoes, 100·19; sugarcane, 92·37; wheat, 86·10; melons and watermelons, 80·19; potatoes, 66·82; cabbage, 30·68; tomatoes, 28·85; cucumbers and gherkins, 25·07; onions, 17·55; soybeans, 16·50; aubergines, 16·03; seed cotton, 15·60; groundnuts, 13·45; chillies and green peppers, 11·54; rapeseeds, 11·41; cottonseed, 10·40; garlic, 10·08; pears, 9·42; tangerines and mandarins, 9·00. Tea production in 2003 was just 800,000 tonnes. China is the world's leading producer of a number of agricultural crops, including rice, sweet potatoes, wheat, potatoes, watermelons, groundnuts and honey. The gross value of agricultural output in 2006 was 4,242,400m. yuan.

Livestock, 2003: pigs, 469,804,000; goats, 172,921,000; sheep, 143,793,000; cattle, 103,470,000; buffaloes, 22,733,000; horses, 8,090,000; chickens, 3·98bn.; ducks, 660m. China has more sheep, goats, pigs, horses and chickens than any other country. China also has nearly two-thirds of the world's ducks. Meat production in 2003 was 71·04m. tonnes; milk, 14·34m. tonnes; eggs, 22·33m. tonnes; honey, 273,000 tonnes. China is the world's leading producer of meat and eggs.

Powell, S. G., *Agricultural Reform in China: from Communes to Commodity Economy, 1978–1990.* 1992

Forestry

In 2005 the area under forests was 197·29m. ha., or 21·2% of the total land area. The average annual increase in forest cover of 4,058,000 ha. between 2000 and 2005 was the highest of any country in the world. Total roundwood production in 2007 was 294·40m. cu. metres, making China the world's third largest timber producer (8·2% of the world total in 2007). It is the world's leading importer of roundwood, accounting for 28·2% of world timber imports in 2007.

Fisheries

Total catch, 2005: 17,053,191 tonnes, of which 14,502,515 tonnes were from marine waters. China's annual catch is the largest in the world, and currently accounts for approximately 18% of the world total. In 1989 the annual catch had been just 5·3m. tonnes.

INDUSTRY

The leading companies by market capitalization in China in April 2009 were PetroChina (US$270·6bn.); China Mobile (Hong Kong), a telecommunications company (US$175·9bn.); and Industrial and the Commercial Bank of China (US$170·8bn.). In Nov. 2007 PetroChina was briefly the world's largest company after its flotation on the Shanghai stock market, with a market capitalization in excess of US$1trn.; in April 2009 it ranked second after the USA's Exxon Mobil.

Industry accounted for 52·9% of GDP in 2004, up from 21% in 1949 when the People's Republic of China came into existence. Cottage industries persist into the 21st century. Industrial output grew by 11·1% in 2004. Modern industrial development began with the manufacture of cotton textiles and the establishment of silk filatures, steel plants, flour mills and match factories. In 2006 there were 287,406 non-state-owned industrial enterprises with an annual revenue of more than 5m. yuan, and a combined gross industrial output value of 28,586·1bn. yuan. Of these enterprises, 226,534 were domestically funded, 31,691 were foreign funded and 29,181 were dependent on funds from Hong Kong, Macao and Taiwan. There were 14,555 state-owned industrial enterprises in total, with a gross output value of 3,072·8bn. yuan.

Output of major products, 2004 (in tonnes): cement, 970·0m. (nearly half of the world total); rolled steel, 297·2m.; crude steel, 272·8m.; pig iron, 251·9m.; distillate fuel oil, 98·4m.; petrol, 52·2m.; chemical fertilizers (2002), 37·9m.; paper and paperboard (2003), 37·9m.; sulphuric acid (2002), 30·5m.; residual fuel oil, 20·3m.; sugar (2002), 9·26m.; cotton yarn (2002), 8·50m. Also produced in 2002: cloth, 3,220m. metres; woollen fabrics, 326·9m. metres; beer (2003), 25,404·8m. litres; 181m. watches (2003); 303·5m. mobile telephones (2005); 81·99m. cameras (2005); 69m. bicycles (2005); 51·55m. TV sets; 31·55m. air conditioners; 30·36m. washing machines (2005); 15·99m. refrigerators; 14·64m. micro-computers; 14·61m. motorcycles and scooters (2003); 5·71m. motor vehicles (2005); 2,207 ships. China is the world's leading cement, steel and pig iron manufacturer (producing 47% of the world's cement, 36% of crude steel and 47% of pig iron); output of cement has doubled and of rolled steel, crude steel and pig iron trebled since 2000.

Labour

The employed population at the 1990 census was 647·2m. (291·1m. female). By 2005 it had risen to 758·3m. (6·3m. more than in 2004), of whom 484·9m. worked in rural areas (2·3m. fewer than in 2004) and 273·3m. in urban areas (8·6m. more than in 2004). By 2015 China's working age population will begin to decline as a consequence of the country's one-child policy. In Sept. 2005 China's registered urban jobless was 4·2%, with 8·35m. registered unemployed in the country's cities. Between 1995 and 2002, 15m. jobs were lost owing to the closure of state-owned factories. The number of state-controlled companies has halved since 1995. In 2005 there were 312·06m. people working in agriculture, forestry and fisheries; 80·80m. in manufacturing; 49·66m. in wholesale and retail trade, restaurants and hotels; 45·22m. in community, social and personal services; and 40·77m. in construction.

In 2006 China had 149,736 private industrial enterprises employing almost 20m. people. It was not until the late 1970s that the private sector even came into existence in China.

The average non-agricultural annual wage in 2005 was 18,364 yuan: 11,283 yuan, urban collectives; 19,313 yuan, state-owned enterprises; 18,244 yuan, other enterprises. There is a 6-day 48-hour working week. Minimum working age was fixed at 16 in 1991. There were 260,000 labour disputes in 2004, up from 8,000 in 1989.

Trade Unions

The All-China Federation of Trade Unions, founded in 1925, is headed by Wang Zhaoguo. In 2003 there were 134m. members. It consists of 31 federations of trade unions. Its National Congress convenes every five years.

INTERNATIONAL TRADE

Foreign debt was US$281,612m. in 2005.

There are five Special Economic Zones at Shenzhen, Xiamen, Zhuhai, Shantou and Hainan in which concessions are made to foreign businessmen. The Pudong New Area in Shanghai is also designated a special development area. Since 1979 joint ventures with foreign firms have been permitted. A law of April 1991 reduced taxation on joint ventures to 33%. There is no maximum limit on the foreign share of the holdings; the minimum limit is 25%.

In May 2000 the USA granted normal trade relations to China, a progression after a number of years when China was accorded 'most favoured nation' status. China subsequently joined the World Trade Organization on 11 Dec. 2001.

Pearson, M. M., *Joint Ventures in the People's Republic of China: the Control of Foreign Direct Investment under Socialism.* 1991

Imports and Exports

Trade in US$1m.:

	2001	*2002*	*2003*	*2004*	*2005*	*2006*
Imports	243,553	295,170	412,760	561,229	659,953	791,461
Exports	266,098	325,596	438,228	593,326	761,953	968,936

China is the third largest trading nation in the world after the USA and Germany, in 2008 accounting for 6·9% of global imports by value and 8·9% of global exports. Provisional figures indicate that it overtook Germany as the largest exporter in 2009.

Main imports in 2004 (in US$1bn.): electrical machinery and parts, 110·7; petroleum and petroleum products, 44·5; industrial machinery, 26·3; organic chemicals, 23·7; iron and steel, 23·4; plastics, 22·0. Major exports in 2004 (in US$1bn.): office machinery and computers, 87·1; telecommunications equipment, 68·5; clothing, 61·9; electrical machinery and appliances, 59·5; textile yarn and fabrics, 33·4; industrial machinery, 25·5. Chinese exports trebled between 2001 and 2006, largely thanks to foreign investment.

Main import suppliers, 2004: Japan, 16·8%; South Korea, 11·1%; USA, 8·0%; Germany, 5·4%. Main export markets in 2004: USA, 21·1%; Hong Kong, 17·0%; Japan, 12·4%; South Korea, 4·7%. Customs duties with Taiwan were abolished in 1980. Trade with the European Union is fast expanding, having more than trebled since 2000.

COMMUNICATIONS

Roads

The total road length in 2005 was 1,931,000 km, including 41,000 km of motorways (there had not been any motorways as recently as the mid-1980s). 14,663m. tonnes of freight and 18,605m. persons were transported by road in 2006. The number of civil motor vehicles was 31·60m. in 2005, including 21·32m. buses and cars and 9·56m. trucks. China is the world's fastest-growing car market. There were 378,871 traffic accidents in 2006, with 89,455 fatalities.

Rail

In 2006 there were 77,100 km of railway including 23,400 km electrified. Gauge is standard except for some 600 mm track in Yunnan. Passenger-km travelled in 2006 came to 662·2bn. and freight tonne-km to 2,195·4bn. China's railways are the busiest in the world, carrying 24% of global rail traffic. There are metro systems in Beijing, Dalian, Guangzhou, Nanjing, Shanghai, Shenzhen, Tianjin and Wuhan.

Civil Aviation

There are major international airports at Beijing (Capital), Guangzhou (Baiyun), Hong Kong (Chek Lap Kok) and Shanghai (Hongqiao and Pudong). In 2006 there were 142 civil airports for regular flights. The national and major airlines are state-owned, except Shanghai Airlines (75% municipality-owned, 25% private) and Shenzhen Airlines (private). The leading Chinese airlines operating scheduled services in 2006 were China Southern Airlines (49·2m. passengers), China Eastern Airlines (35·0m.) and Air China (34·0m.). Other Chinese airlines include Changan Airlines, Hainan Airlines, Shandong Airlines, Shanghai Airlines, Shanxi Airlines, Shenzhen Airlines, Sichuan Airlines and Xiamen Airlines.

In 2007 the busiest airport was Beijing (Capital), with 53,611,747 passengers; followed by Hong Kong International (Chek Lap Kok), with 47,042,419 passengers; Guangzhou (Baiyun), with 30,958,467 passengers; and Shanghai (Pudong), with 28,920,432 passengers. Shanghai (Pudong) is the busiest airport for freight, with 2,559,246 tonnes of cargo handled in 2007. In 2006 China had a total of 1,336 scheduled flight routes, of which 1,068 were domestic air routes and 268 were international air routes. Total passenger traffic in 2006 reached 159·68m.; freight traffic totalled 3·49m. tonnes.

Regular direct flights between mainland China and Taiwan resumed in July 2008 for the first time since 1949.

Shipping

In Jan. 2003 the merchant fleet consisted of 2,136 vessels of 300 GRT and over (including 410 oil tankers), totalling 16·09m. GRT (oil tankers, 2·53m. GRT).

In 2003, 2,011m. tonnes of freight were handled in major coastal ports, including: Shanghai, 316·2m. tonnes; Ningbo, 185·4m.; Guangzhou (Canton), 171·9m.; Tianjin, 161·8m.; Qingdao, 140·9m.; Dalian, 126·0m.; Qinhuangdao, 125·6m. Cargo traffic at Tianjin grew at an average annual rate of 17·3% between 1998 and 2002, the highest rate of growth of any port in the world over the same period. In 2005 Shanghai replaced Singapore as the largest cargo port in the world as its turnover reached 443m. tonnes; in 2006 it handled 21·7m. 20-ft equivalent units (TEUs), making it the world's third busiest container port in terms of number of containers handled. Construction began in 2002 on the 14·31bn. yuan Yangshan deep-water port to the south of Shanghai that should make Shanghai the world's third busiest port. On completion in 2020 it is estimated that it will have a capacity of 13m. TEUs.

In Jan. 2001 the first legal direct shipping links between the Chinese mainland and Taiwanese islands in more than 50 years were inaugurated.

Inland waterways totalled 123,400 km in 2006; 2,487·0m. tonnes of freight and 220·47m. passengers were carried. In June 2003 the Three Gorges Reservoir on the Chang Jiang River, the largest water control project in the world, reached sufficient depth to support the resumption of passenger and cargo shipping.

Telecommunications

In 2008 there were 340,810,000 main (fixed) telephone lines. In the same year mobile phone subscribers numbered 641,230,000 (479·5 per 1,000 persons), making China the biggest market for mobile phones in the world. The two main mobile operators are China Mobile and China Unicom. The main landline operators are China Telecom and China Netcom. In 1998 there were around 500,000 internet users, but by 2008 this had risen to 298·0m. China has by far the most internet users of any country. In 2006, 74·1m. PCs were in use.

Postal Services

There were 63,555 post offices in 2003. The use of *Pinyin* transcription of place names has been requested for mail to addresses in China (e.g. 'Beijing' not 'Peking').

SOCIAL INSTITUTIONS

Justice

Six new codes of law (including criminal and electoral) came into force in 1980, to regularize the legal unorthodoxy of previous years. There is no provision for *habeas corpus*. The death penalty has been extended from treason and murder to include rape, embezzlement, smuggling, fraud, theft, drug-dealing, bribery and robbery with violence. China does not divulge figures on its use of the death penalty; however, Amnesty International reported that there were at least 1,718 executions in 2008, representing more than 70% of the world's total. 'People's courts' are divided into some 30 higher, 200 intermediate and 2,000 basic-level courts, and headed by the Supreme People's Court. The latter, the highest state judicial organ, tries cases, hears appeals and supervises the people's courts. It is responsible to the National People's Congress and its Standing Committee. People's courts are composed of a president, vice-presidents, judges and 'people's assessors' who are the equivalent of jurors. 'People's conciliation committees' are charged with settling minor disputes. There are also special military courts. Procuratorial powers and functions are exercised by the Supreme People's Procuracy and local procuracies.

The number of sentenced prisoners in Dec. 2005 was 1,565,771 (119 per 100,000 of national population).

Education

An educational reform of 1985 brought in compulsory nine-year education consisting of six years of primary schooling and three years of secondary schooling, to replace a previous five-year system.

In mainland China the 2000 population census revealed the following levels of educational attainment: 45·71m. people had finished university education; 141·09m. had received senior secondary education; 429·89m. had received junior secondary education; and 451·91m. had had primary education. 85·07m. people over 15 years of age or 6·72% of the population were illiterate, although this compared favourably with a 15·88% rate of illiteracy recorded in the 1990 census. In 2006 there were 130,495 kindergartens with 22·64m. children and 776,500 teachers; 396,567 primary schools with 109·77m. pupils and 5·63m. teachers; 94,116 secondary schools (of which: 16,992 senior secondary; 62,431 junior secondary; 6,048 specialized; 5,765 vocational; and 2,880 technical) with 103·50m. pupils and 5·67m. teachers. There were also 363,000 children at 1,605 special education schools. Institutes of higher education, including universities, numbered 1,867 in 2006, with 17·39m. undergraduates and 1·10m. postgraduate level students, and 1·08m. teaching staff. In 2003, 17% of school-leavers went to university, compared to fewer than 3% in the 1980s. A national system of student loans was established in 1999. The number of Chinese students studying abroad has exceeded 100,000 annually since 2002 (making the country the largest exporter of students in the world); in 2006 the figure was 134,000.

There are more than 1,300 non-governmental private higher education institutions (including 12 private universities) with 1·5m. students, or 39% of the total college and university students nationwide.

There is an Academy of Sciences with provincial branches. An Academy of Social Sciences was established in 1977.

In 2005 total expenditure on education came to 841,884m. yuan; government appropriation was 516,108m. yuan.

Health

Medical treatment is free only for certain groups of employees, but where costs are incurred they are partly borne by the patient's employing organization.

In 2006 there were 308,969 health institutions throughout China, comprising 60,037 hospitals and health centres, 264 sanatoriums, 212,243 clinics, 1,402 specialized prevention and treatment centres, 3,548 centres for disease control and prevention, 3,003 maternity and child care centres, 248 medical research institutions and 28,224 other institutions; the number of beds totalled 3·51m.

China's first AIDS case was reported in 1985. Approximately 700,000 Chinese were HIV-infected in 2007.

In the first half of 2003 China was struck by an epidemic of a pneumonia-type virus identified as SARS (severe acute respiratory syndrome). The virus was first detected in southern China and was subsequently reported in over 30 other countries. According to the Ministry of Health, by the time the outbreak had been contained a total of 5,327 cases had been reported on the Chinese mainland; 4,959 patients were cured and discharged from hospital, and 349 died.

In 2002 some 61% of males smoked, but fewer than 4% of females; 30% of the world's smokers are in China.

In the period 2001–03, 12% of the population were undernourished compared to 22% in 1979.

Welfare

In 2006 there were 30,199 social welfare enterprises with 1,512,000 inmates. Numbers (in 1,000) of beneficiaries of relief funds: persons receiving minimum living allowance and traditional relief in rural areas, 29,878; persons receiving minimum living allowance in urban areas, 22,401; persons receiving temporary relief in poor rural households, 9,638; persons receiving temporary relief in poor urban households, 1,230; persons in rural households entitled to 'the five guarantees' (food, clothing, medical care, housing, education for children or funeral expenses), 5,033.

RELIGION

Non-religious persons account for 52% of the population. The government accords legality to five religions only: Buddhism, Islam, Protestantism, Roman Catholicism and Taoism. Confucianism, Buddhism and Taoism have long been practised. Confucianism has no ecclesiastical organization and appears rather as a philosophy of ethics and government. Taoism—of Chinese origin—copied Buddhist ceremonial soon after the arrival of Buddhism two millennia ago. Buddhism in return adopted many Taoist beliefs and practices. A more tolerant attitude towards religion had emerged by 1979, and the government's Bureau of Religious Affairs was reactivated.

Ceremonies of reverence to ancestors have been observed by the whole population regardless of philosophical or religious beliefs.

A new quasi-religious movement, Falun Gong, was founded in 1992, but has since been banned by the authorities. The movement claims it has some 100m. adherents, although the Chinese government has maintained the real number is closer to 2m.

Muslims are found in every province of China, being most numerous in the Ningxia-Hui Autonomous Region, Yunnan, Shaanxi, Gansu, Hebei, Henan, Shandong, Sichuan, Xinjiang and Shanxi. They totalled 18·4m. in 2001.

Roman Catholicism has had a footing in China for more than three centuries. In 2002 there were an estimated 4m. Catholic believers, 4,000 clergy and 4,600 churches and meeting places. Catholics are members of the Patriotic Catholic Association, which declared its independence from Rome in 1958. Protestants are members of the All-China Conference of Protestant Churches. In 2002 they numbered 10m. There were an estimated 76·5m. Christians in total in 2001.

In 2001 there were also estimated to be 256·3m. Chinese folk-religionists, 153·0m. atheists, 108·1m. Buddhists and 1·3m. advocates of traditional beliefs.

Legislation of 1994 prohibits foreign nationals from setting up religious organizations.

CULTURE

World Heritage Sites

There are 38 sites in the People's Republic of China that appear on the UNESCO World Heritage List. They are (with year entered on list): the Great Wall of China (1987), Zhoukoudian, the Peking

Man site (1987), Imperial Palaces of the Ming and Qing Dynasties in Beijing and Shenyang (1987 and 2004), mausoleum of first Qing dynasty emperor, Beijing (1987), Taishan mountain (1987), Mogao Caves (1987), Mount Huangshan (1990), Huanglong Scenic Reserve (1992), Jiuzhaigou National Reserve (1992), Wulingyuan Scenic Reserve (1992), Chengde mountain resort and temples (1994), Potala palace, Lhasa (1994, 2000 and 2001), ancient building complex in the Wudang Mountains (1994), Qufu temple, cemetery and mansion of Confucius (1994), Mount Emei Scenic Reserve, including the Leshan Buddha (1996), Lushan National Park (1996), Lijiang old town (1997), Ping Yao old town (1997), Suzhou classical gardens (1997 and 2000), Summer Palace, Beijing (1998), Temple of Heaven, Beijing (1998), Mount Wuyi (1999), Dazu rock carvings (1999), Mount Qincheng and Dujiangyan irrigation system (2000), Xidi and Hongcun ancient villages, Anhui (2000), Longmen grottoes (2000), Ming and Qing dynasty tombs (2000, 2003 and 2004), the Yungang Grottoes (2001), the Three Parallel Rivers of Yunnan Protected Areas (2003), the Capital Cities and Tombs of the Ancient Koguryo Kingdom (2004), the historic centre of Macao (2005), the Sichuan Giant Panda sanctuaries (2006), Yin Xu (2006), Kaiping Diaolou and villages (2007), South China Karst (2007), Fuijan Tulou (2008), Mount Sanqingshan National Park (2008) and Mount Wutai (2009).

Broadcasting

Broadcasting is tightly controlled by the Communist authorities through the State Administration for Radio, Film and Television. The availability of foreign services is limited. By 2003 there were 494m. television receivers in China, the greatest number in any country in the world and an increase of 485m. since 1980. In 2006 there were 296 local and regional TV stations, offering programmes to 96·2% of the total population. China Central Television is the largest national station. Cable TV subscribers numbered 139·9m. by the end of 2006 (compared to 50m. in 1997). China National Radio operates the national radio network, with six nationwide services (including services to Taiwan). China Radio International is the external broadcaster, with programmes in more than 40 languages. There were 267 local and regional radio broadcasting stations and 800 medium- and short-wave transmitting and relaying stations throughout China in 2006, reaching 95·0% of the population.

Cinema

There were 39,425 cinema screens in 2005. A total of 330 feature films and 62 scientific, documentary and cartoon films were produced in 2006.

Press

China has two news agencies: Xinhua (New China) News Agency (the nation's official agency) and China News Service. In 2006 there were 1,938 newspapers and 9,468 magazines; 42,500m. copies of newspapers and 2,850m. copies of magazines were published. In 1980 there were fewer than 400 newspapers. The Communist Party newspaper is Renmin Ribao (People's Daily), which had a daily circulation of 2·8m. in 2006. The most widely read newspaper is Cankao Xiaoxi, with a daily circulation of 3·2m. in 2006. China has the highest circulation of daily newspapers in the world, with an average daily total of 99·04m. in 2005. In July 2003 the State Administration of Press and Publication abolished compulsory subscription to state newspapers and magazines and funding for subscription-dependent publications, which amount to 40% of the press. By Nov. 2003, 673 newspapers had ceased publication.

In 2006, 6,410m. volumes of books were produced.

Tourism

In 2005 tourist numbers totalled 46·8m. The World Tourism Organization predicts that China will overtake France as the world's most visited destination by 2020. It is currently the fourth most visited destination after France, Spain and the USA. More than 31m. Chinese travelled outside mainland China in 2005, up from under 5m. in 1995. Income from tourists in 2005 was US$29·3bn., ranking it fifth behind the USA, Spain, France and Italy.

Festivals

The lunar New Year, also known as the 'Spring Festival', is a time of great excitement for the Chinese people. The festivities get under way 22 days prior to the New Year date and continue for 15 days afterwards. Dates of the lunar New Year: Year of the Tiger, 14 Feb. 2010; Year of the Rabbit, 3 Feb. 2011. Lantern Festival, or Yuanxiao Jie, is an important, traditional Chinese festival, which is on the 15th of the first month of the Chinese New Year. Guanyin's Birthday is on the 19th day of the second month of the Chinese lunar calendar. Guanyin is the Chinese goddess of mercy. Tomb Sweeping Day, as the name implies, is a day for visiting and cleaning the ancestral tomb and usually falls on 5 April. Dragon Boat Festival is called Duan Wu Jie in Chinese. The festival is celebrated on the 5th of the 5th month of the Chinese lunar calendar. The Moon Festival is on the 15th of the 8th lunar month. It is sometimes called Mid-Autumn Festival. The Moon Festival is an occasion for family reunion.

Libraries

In 2006 there were 2,778 public libraries. The National Library of China, with 23·7m. items, is the largest library in Asia and fifth largest in the world. Shanghai library is China's biggest provincial-level library.

Museums and Galleries

There were 1,617 museums in 2006, of which 33 were in Beijing.

DIPLOMATIC REPRESENTATIVES

Of China in the United Kingdom (49–51 Portland Pl., London, W1B 1JL)
Ambassador: Fu Ying.

Of the United Kingdom in China (11 Guang Hua Lu, Jian Guo Men Wai, Beijing 100600)
Ambassador: Sebastian Wood, CMG.

Of China in the USA (2300 Connecticut Ave., NW, Washington, D.C. 20008)
Ambassador: Zhou Wenzhong.

Of the USA in China (55 An Jia Lou Lu, 100600 Beijing)
Ambassador: Jon M. Huntsman, Jr.

Of China to the United Nations
Ambassador: Li Baodong.

Of China to the European Union
Ambassador: Song Zhe.

FURTHER READING

State Statistical Bureau. *China Statistical Yearbook*
China Directory [in Pinyin and Chinese]. Annual

Adshead, S. A. M., *China in World History.* 1999
Baum, R., *Burying Mao: Chinese Politics in the Age of Deng Xiaoping.* 1994
Becker, Jasper, *The Chinese.* 2000
Breslin, Shaun, *China and the Global Political Economy.* 2007
Brown, Raj, *Overseas Chinese Merchants.* 1999
The Cambridge Encyclopaedia of China. 2nd ed. 1991
The Cambridge History of China. 14 vols. 1978 ff.
Chang, David Wen-Wei and Chuang, Richard Y., *The Politics of Hong Kong's Reversion to China.* 1999
Chang, Jung and Halliday, Jon, *Mao: The Unknown Story.* 2005
Cook, Sarah, Yao, Shujie and Zhuang, Juzhong, (eds.) *The Chinese Economy Under Transition.* 1999
De Crespigny, R., *China This Century.* 2nd ed. 1993
Dillon, Michael, *China: A Modern History.* 2006
Dittmer, Lowell, *China's Deep Reform: Domestic Politics in Transition.* 2006

Dixin, Xu and Chengming, Wu, (eds.) *Chinese Capitalism, 1522–1840.* 1999
Dreyer, J. T., *China's Political System: Modernization and Tradition.* 2nd ed. 1996
Evans, R., *Deng Xiaoping and the Making of Modern China.* 1993
Fairbank, J. K., *The Great Chinese Revolution 1800–1985.* 1987.—*China: a New History.* 1992
Glassman, R. M., *China in Transition: Communism, Capitalism and Democracy.* 1991
Goldman, M., *Sowing the Seeds of Democracy in China: Political Reform in the Deng Xiaoping Era.* 1994
Guo, Jian, *Historical Dictionary of the Chinese Cultural Revolution.* 2006
Ho, Samuel P. S. and Kueh, Y. Y. (eds.) *Sustainable Economic Development in South China.* 1999
Hsü, Immanuel C. Y., *The Rise of Modern China.* 6th ed. 2000
Huang, R., *China: a Macro History.* 2nd ed. 1997
Hunter, A. and Sexton, J., *Contemporary China.* 1999
Kruger, Rayne, *All Under Heaven: A Complete History of China.* 2004
Lam, Willy Wo-Lap, *Chinese Politics in the Hu Jintao Era: New Leaders, New Challenges.* 2006
Lieberthal, K. G., *From Revolution through Reform.* 1995.
Lieberthal, K. G. and Lampton, D. M. (eds.) *Bureaucracy, Politics and Decision-Making in Post-Mao China.* 1992
Lynch, Michael, *Modern China.* 2006
Ma, Jun, *Chinese Economy in the 1990s.* 1999
MacFarquhar, R. (ed.) *The Politics of China: the Eras of Mao and Deng.* 2nd ed. 1997.—*The Origins of the Cultural Revolution.* 3 vols. 1998
Mok, Ka-Ho, *Social and Political Development in Post-Reform China.* 1999
Nolan, Peter, *China and the Global Economy.* 2001
Phillips, R. T., *China Since 1911.* 1996
Roberts, J. A. G., *A History of China.* 2nd ed. 2006
Saich, Tony, *Governance and Politics of China.* 2nd ed. 2004
Schram, S. (ed.) *Mao's Road to Power: Revolutionary Writings 1912–1949.* 4 vols. 1998
Shen, Xiobai, *The Chinese Road to High Technology.* 1999
Sheng Hua, *et al.*, *China: from Revolution to Reform.* 1992
Shenkar, Oded, *The Chinese Century: The Rising Chinese Economy and Its Impact on the Global Economy, the Balance of Power, and Your Job.* 2004
Short, Philip, *Mao: A Life.* 2000
Spence, Jonathan, D., *The Chan's Great Continent: China in Western Minds.* 1998.—*Mao Zedong.* 2000
Suyin, H., *Eldest Son, Zhou Enlai and The Making of Modern China.* 1995
Tseng, Wanda and Cowen, David, *India's and China's Recent Experience with Reform and Growth.* 2007
Tubilewicz, Czeslaw, *Critical Issues in Contemporary China.* 2006
Yan, Yanni, *International Joint Ventures in China.* 1999
Yeung, Henry Wai-Cheung and Olds, Kristopher, (eds.) *The Globalisation of Chinese Business Firms.* 1999
Zhang, Xiao-Guang, *China's Trade Patterns and International Comparative Advantage.* 1999

Other more specialized titles are listed under TERRITORY AND POPULATION; TIBET; AGRICULTURE; INTERNATIONAL TRADE.

National Statistical Office: National Bureau of Statistics, 57 Yuetan Nanjie, Beijing 100826.
Website: http://www.stats.gov.cn

Hong Kong

Xianggang

Population estimate, 2010: 7·07m.
GDP per capita, 2007: (PPP$) 43,306
HDI/world rank: 0·944/24

KEY HISTORICAL EVENTS

Hong Kong island and the southern tip of the Kowloon peninsula were ceded in perpetuity to the British Crown in 1841 and 1860 respectively. The area lying immediately to the north of Kowloon known as the New Territories was leased to Britain for 99 years in 1898. Talks began in Sept. 1982 between Britain and China over the future of Hong Kong after the lease expiry in 1997. On 19 Dec. 1984 the two countries signed a Joint Declaration by which Hong Kong became, with effect from 1 July 1997, a Special Administrative Region of the People's Republic of China, enjoying a high degree of autonomy and vested with executive, legislative and independent judicial power, including that of final adjudication. The existing social and economic systems were to remain unchanged for another 50 years. This 'one country, two systems' principle, embodied in the Basic Law, became the constitution for the Hong Kong Special Administrative Region of the People's Republic of China.

TERRITORY AND POPULATION

Hong Kong ('Xianggang' in Mandarin *Pinyin*) island is situated off the southern coast of the Chinese mainland 32 km east of the mouth of the Pearl River. The area of the island is 80 sq. km. It is separated from the mainland by a fine natural harbour. On the opposite side is the peninsula of Kowloon (47 sq. km). The 'New Territories' include the mainland area lying to the north of Kowloon together with over 200 offshore islands (974 sq. km). Total area of the Territory is 1,101 sq. km, a large part of it being steep and unproductive hillside. Country parks and special areas cover over 40% of the land area. Since 1945 the government has reclaimed over 5,400 ha. from the sea, principally from the seafronts of Hong Kong and Kowloon, facing the harbour.

Based on the results of the 2006 population census Hong Kong's resident population in March 2006 was 6,864,346 and the population density 6,235 per sq. km. 60·3% of the population was born in Hong Kong, 33·5% in other parts of China and 6·2% in the rest of the world.

In 2005, 100% of the population lived in urban areas. Some 9,800 persons emigrated in 2005. The British Nationality Scheme enables persons to acquire citizenship without leaving Hong Kong. There were 38,100 legal entrants (one-way permit holders) from the mainland of China in 2003–04.

The UN gives an estimated population for 2010 of 7·07m.

The official languages are Chinese and English.

SOCIAL STATISTICS

Annual population growth rate, 2000–05, 0·4%. Vital statistics, 2001: known births, 48,200; known deaths, 33,400; registered marriages, 32,800. Rates (per 1,000): birth, 7·2; death, 5·0; marriage, 4·8; infant mortality, 2001, 2·6 per 1,000 live births (one of the lowest rates in the world). Expectation of life at birth, 2007: males, 79·3 years; females, 85·1. The median age for marrying in 2001 was 31·3 years for males and 28·1 for females. Total fertility rate, 2001, 0·9 child per woman.

CLIMATE

The climate is sub-tropical, tending towards temperate for nearly half the year, the winter being cool and dry and the summer hot and humid, May to Sept. being the wettest months. Normal temperatures are Jan. 60°F (15·8°C), July 84°F (28·8°C). Annual rainfall 87" (2,214·3 mm).

THE BRITISH ADMINISTRATION

Hong Kong used to be administered by the Hong Kong government. The Governor was the head of government and presided over the *Executive Council*, which advised the Governor on all important matters. The last British Governor was Chris Patten. In Oct. 1996 the Executive Council consisted of three *ex officio* members and ten appointed members, of whom one was an official member. The chief functions of the *Legislative Council* were to enact laws, control public expenditure and put questions to the administration on matters of public interest. The Legislative Council elected in Sept. 1995 was, for the first time, constituted solely by election. It comprised 60 members, of whom 20 were elected from geographical constituencies, 30 from functional constituencies encompassing all eligible persons in a workforce of 2·9m., and ten from an election committee formed by members of 18 district boards. A president was elected from and by the members.

At the elections on 17 Sept. 1995 turnout for the geographical seats was 35·79%, and for the functional seats (21 of which were contested), 40·42%. The Democratic Party and its allies gained 29 seats, the Liberal Party 10 and the pro-Beijing Democratic Alliance 6. The remaining seats went to independents.

CONSTITUTION AND GOVERNMENT

In Dec. 1995 the Standing Committee of China's National People's Congress set up a Preparatory Committee of 150 members (including 94 from Hong Kong) to oversee the retrocession of Hong Kong to China on 1 July 1997. In Nov. 1996 the Preparatory Committee nominated a 400-member Selection Committee to select the *Chief Executive of Hong Kong* and a provisional legislature to replace the Legislative Council. The Selection Committee was composed of Hong Kong residents, with 60 seats reserved for delegates to the National People's Congress and appointees of the People's Political Consultative Conference. On 11 Dec. 1996 Tung Chee Hwa was elected Chief Executive by 80% of the Selection Committee's votes.

On 21 Dec. 1996 the Selection Committee selected a provisional legislature which began its activities in Jan. 1997 while the Legislative Council was still functioning. In Jan. 1997 the provisional legislature started its work by enacting legislation which would be applicable to the Hong Kong Special Administrative Region and compatible with the Basic Law.

Constitutionally Hong Kong is a Special Administrative Region of the People's Republic of China. The Basic Law enables Hong Kong to retain a high degree of autonomy. It provides that the legislative, judicial and administrative systems which were previously in operation are to remain in place. The Special Administrative Region Government is also empowered to decide on Hong Kong's monetary and economic policies independent of China.

In July 1997 the first-past-the-post system of returning members from geographical constituencies to the Legislative Council was replaced by proportional representation. There were 20 directly elected seats out of 60 for the first elections to the Legislative Council following Hong Kong's return to Chinese sovereignty, increasing in accordance with the Basic Law to 24 for the 2000 election with 36 indirectly elected. In the Sept. 2004 Legislative Council election (and that of Sept. 2008) 30 of the 60 seats were directly elected. The Chief Executive is chosen by a Beijing-backed 796-member election committee, although it has been stated that universal suffrage is the ultimate aim—potentially in 2017 for the Chief Executive and 2020 for all Legislative Council seats.

In July 2002 a new accountability or 'ministerial' system was introduced, under which the Chief Executive nominates for appointment 14 policy secretaries, who report directly to the Chief Executive. The Chief Executive is aided by the *Executive Council*, consisting of the three senior Secretaries of Department (the Chief Secretary, the Financial Secretary and the Secretary for Justice) and eleven other secretaries plus five non-officials.

RECENT ELECTIONS

In the Legislative Council election held on 7 Sept. 2008 turnout was 45%, down from 56% at the 2004 vote. 30 of the 60 seats were directly elected, the other 30 being returned by committees and professional associations. Pro-Beijing parties won 35 of the 60 seats (34 in 2004) including 11 of the 30 that were directly elected; pro-democracy parties won 23 (25 in 2004), including 19 of the 30 that were directly elected. Independents won the remaining two seats (an independent took one seat in 2004).

CURRENT ADMINISTRATION

In March 2010 the government of the Hong Kong Special Administrative Region comprised:

Chief Executive: Donald Tsang, OBE; b. 1944 (since 24 June 2005, having previously been acting Chief Executive from 12 March 2005–1 June 2005; re-elected on 25 March 2007).

Chief Secretary for Administration: Henry Tang Ying-yen. *Financial Secretary:* John Tsang Chun-wah. *Secretary for Justice:* Wong Yan Lung. *Education:* Michael Suen Ming-yeung. *Commerce and Economic Development:* Rita Lau Ng Wai-lan. *Constitutional and Mainland Affairs:* Stephen Lam Sui-lung. *Security:* Ambrose Lee Siu-kwong. *Food and Health:* Dr York Chow. *Civil Service:* Denise Yue Chung-yee. *Home Affairs:* Tsang Tak-sing. *Labour and Welfare:* Matthew Cheung Kin-chung. *Financial Services and the Treasury:* Prof. K. C. Chan. *Development:* Carrie Lam Cheng Yuet-ngor. *Environment:* Edward Yau Tang-wah. *Transport and Housing:* Eva Cheng.

Government Website: http://www.gov.hk

ECONOMY

Trade accounted for 27·8% of GDP in 2005; finance, insurance and real estate 22·2%; public administration, defence and services 16·6%; and transport and communications 10·4%.

According to the anti-corruption organization *Transparency International*, Hong Kong ranked equal 12th in the world in a 2009 survey of the countries and regions with the least corruption in business and government. It received 8·2 out of 10 in the annual index.

Hong Kong adopted a flat tax rate in 1948. Income tax is a flat 16% and only 25% of the population pay any tax at all. 6% of the population pays 80% of the total income tax bill. Hong Kong represents 20% of China's total worth.

Overview

Hong Kong has a per capita GDP that compares favourably with other OECD countries. Its economic rise was founded on its position as an international trade emporium. After developing as a successful low-cost, labour-intensive manufacturing centre, the structure of the economy has now shifted towards services. The island is dependant on trade for food and other resources. In 1998 and the first quarter of 1999 Hong Kong sank into recession as a result of the Asian financial crisis. Later in 1999 the economy bounced back and in 2000 grew by 10·2%, the highest rate since 1987. In the second quarter of 2001 the economy sank back into recession for three consecutive quarters as a result of the slowdown in the US and global economy. After briefly rebounding, the economy shrank again for one quarter in 2003 following the SARS outbreak. However, the economy again proved resilient and in 2004 and 2005 grew strongly on the back of a rise in Chinese tourism, strong global demand for its exports and growing domestic consumer confidence. Growth moderated in 2006 and 2007 but remains strong, whilst job creation continues to rise at all levels, with unemployment in 2007 at 4·0%.

Hong Kong's main engine of growth is its re-export business to and from China. Despite the overwhelming importance of China to Hong Kong's economy, the USA plays an important role as the second most important export destination. Near-term risks include a downturn in global demand (particularly from the USA) and an increase in protectionist sentiments against China. Continued financial integration with Mainland China is key to strong growth in the medium-term.

Currency

The unit of currency is the *Hong Kong dollar* (HKD) of 100 *cents*. It is pegged at a rate of HK$7·8 to the US dollar. Banknotes are issued by the Hongkong and Shanghai Banking Corporation and the Standard Chartered Bank, and, from May 1994, the Bank of China. Total money supply was HK$529,161m. in July 2009. In

Aug. 2009 gold reserves were 67,000 troy oz and foreign exchange reserves were US$223,211m.

Inflation rates (based on IMF statistics):

1999	2000	2001	2002	2003	2004	2005	2006	2007	2008
−3·9%	−3·7%	−1·6%	−3·0%	−2·6%	−0·4%	0·9%	2·0%	2·0%	4·3%

Budget

In 2005–06 revenue totalled HK$247·0bn. and expenditure HK$245·0bn. Earnings and profits taxes accounted for 45·6% of revenues in 2005–06 and indirect taxes 20·4%; education accounted for 22·0% of expenditures and social welfare 13·6%.

Performance

Total GDP was US$215·4bn. in 2008. Real GDP growth rates (based on IMF statistics):

1999	2000	2001	2002	2003	2004	2005	2006	2007	2008
2·6%	8·0%	0·5%	1·8%	3·0%	8·5%	7·1%	7·0%	6·4%	2·4%

The economy contracted by 6·0% in 1998, representing Hong Kong's most severe recession since the 1970s. In the 2009 *World Competitiveness Yearbook*, compiled by the International Institute for Management Development, Hong Kong came second in the world ranking.

Banking and Finance

The Hong Kong Monetary Authority acts as a central bank. The *Chief Executive* is Norman Chan. As at Dec. 2003 there were 133 banks licensed under the Banking Ordinance, of which 26 were locally incorporated, 46 restricted licence banks, 45 deposit-taking companies and 94 representative offices of foreign banks. Licensed bank deposits were HK$5,193,003m. in July 2007; restricted licence bank deposits were HK$22,065m. There are three banks of issue: Bank of China (Hong Kong); The Hong Kong and Shanghai Banking Corporation; and Standard Chartered Bank.

In March 2000 the stock exchange, the futures exchange and the clearing settlement merged into Hong Kong Exchanges and Clearing (HKEx).

Weights and Measures

The metric system is standard but British Imperial and traditional Chinese measurements are still in use.

ENERGY AND NATURAL RESOURCES

Environment

Hong Kong's carbon dioxide emissions from the consumption and flaring of fossil fuels in 2008 were the equivalent of 12·0 tonnes per capita.

Electricity

Installed capacity was 11·7m. kW in 2004. Production in 2004 was 37·13bn. kWh. Hong Kong is a net importer of electricity. Consumption in 2004 was 43·88bn. kWh.

Agriculture

The local agricultural industry is directed towards the production of high quality fresh food through intensive land use and modern farming techniques. Out of the territory's total land area of 1,103 sq. km, only 60 sq. km is currently farmed. In 2006 local production accounted for 55% of live poultry consumed, 23% of live pigs and 4% of fresh vegetables. The gross value of local agricultural production totalled HK$1,184m. in 2006, with pig production valued at HK$585m., poultry production (including eggs) at HK$340m., and vegetable and flower production at HK$254m.

Fisheries

In 2006 the capture and mariculture fisheries supplied about 21% of seafood consumed in Hong Kong and pond fish farms produced about 5% of the freshwater fish consumed. The capture fishing fleet comprises some 3,900 fishing vessels, almost all mechanized. In 2006 the industry produced 155,000 tonnes of fisheries produce, valued at HK$1·6bn. There are 26 fish culture zones occupying a total sea area of 209 ha. with some 1,080 licensed operators. The estimated production in 2006 was 1,488 tonnes. The inland fish ponds, covering a total of 1,024 ha., produced 1,943 tonnes of freshwater fish in 2006.

INDUSTRY

The leading companies by market capitalization in Hong Kong in March 2009 were: China Mobile (Hong Kong), a mobile telecommunications company (US$174·7bn.); CNOOC, an oil and natural gas company (US$44·3bn.); and China Unicom (Hong Kong), a mobile telecommunications company (US$25·4bn.).

Industry is mainly export-oriented. In Sept. 2001 there were 19,801 manufacturing establishments employing 209,329 persons. Other establishment statistics by product type (and persons engaged) were: printing, publishing and allied industries, 4,778 (42,963); textiles and clothing, 3,696 (58,821); plastics, 973 (5,938); electronics, 748 (20,939); watches and clocks, 347 (2,945); shipbuilding, 325 (3,173); electrical appliances, 49 (390).

Labour

In 2001 the size of the labour force (synonymous with the economically active population) was 3,427,100 (1,461,900 females). The persons engaged in Sept. 2001 included 1,027,000 people in wholesale, retail and import/export trades, restaurants and hotels, 437,000 in finance, insurance, real estate and business services, 209,000 in manufacturing, 177,000 in the civil service and 77,000 in construction sites (manual workers only).

Unemployment stood at 4·0% in 2007.

EXTERNAL ECONOMIC RELATIONS

Imports and Exports

In 2006 the total value of imports (f.o.b.) was US$331,634m. and total exports (f.o.b.) US$317,600m. The main suppliers of imports in 2003 were mainland China (43·5%), Japan (11·9%), Taiwan (6·9%), USA (5·5%) and Singapore (5·0%). In 2003, 42·6% of total exports went to mainland China, 18·6% to the USA, 5·2% to Japan, 3·3% to the United Kingdom and 3·2% to Germany.

The chief import items in 2004 were: electrical machinery, apparatus and appliances, etc. (21·6%); telecommunications, sound recording and reproducing equipment (12·4%); office machines and automatic data processing machines (9·8%); articles of apparel and clothing accessories (6·3%). The main exports in 2004 were: electrical machinery, apparatus and appliances, etc. (19·2%); telecommunications, sound recording and reproducing equipment (13·9%); office machines and automatic data processing machines (10·7%); articles of apparel and clothing accessories (9·5%).

Hong Kong has a free exchange market. Foreign merchants may remit profits or repatriate capital. Import and export controls are kept to the minimum, consistent with strategic requirements.

COMMUNICATIONS

Roads

In 2005 there were 1,955 km of roads, around 50% of which were in the New Territories. There are 12 road tunnels, including three under Victoria Harbour. In 2005 there were 351,000 private cars, 111,000 goods vehicles, 19,000 buses and coaches, and 34,000 motorcycles and mopeds. There were 15,062 road accidents in 2005, 135 fatal. A total of 18·3m. tonnes of cargo were transported by road in 2005.

Hong Kong was ranked third for its road infrastructure in the World Economic Forum's *Global Competitiveness Report 2009–2010*.

Rail

The railway network covers around 229 km. The electrified Kowloon-Canton Railway, East Rail, runs for 53·9 km from the terminus at East Tsim Sha Tsui in Kowloon to border points at Lo Wu and Lok Ma Chau. Ma On Shan Rail branches off the main East Rail at Tai Wai and runs to Wu Kai Sha. East Rail and Ma On Shan Rail together carried 337m. passenger in 2006; cargo transported in 2006 totalled 184,000 tonnes. Another passenger rail service, West Rail, runs for 30·5 km from Tuen Mun in the New Territories to Nam Cheong in West Kowloon. It carried 72m. passengers in 2006. A light rail system (36 km and 58 stops) is operated by the Kowloon-Canton Railway Corporation in Tuen Mun, Yuen Long and Tin Shui Wai; it carried 136m. passengers in 2006.

The electric tramway on the northern shore of Hong Kong Island commenced operating in 1904 and has a total track length of 16 km. The Peak Tram, a funicular railway connecting the Peak district with the lower levels in Victoria, has a track length of 1·4 km and two tramcars (each with a capacity of 120 passengers per trip).

A metro, the Mass Transit Railway system, comprises 91 km with 53 stations and carried 867m. passengers in 2006.

The Airport Express Line (35 km) opened in 1998 and carried a total of 9·6m. passengers in 2006.

In 2006 a total of 4·1bn. passenger journeys were made on public transport (including local railways, buses, etc.).

In the World Economic Forum's *Global Competitiveness Report 2009–2010* Hong Kong ranked third for quality of rail infrastructure.

Civil Aviation

The new Hong Kong International Airport (generally known as Chek Lap Kok), built on reclaimed land off Lantau Island to the west of Hong Kong, was opened on 6 July 1998 to replace the old Hong Kong International Airport at Kai Tak, which was situated on the north shore of Kowloon Bay. More than 85 airlines now operate scheduled services to and from Hong Kong. In 2006 Cathay Pacific Airways, the largest Hong Kong-based airline, operated approximately 1,250 passenger and cargo services weekly to 96 destinations in Europe, the Far and Middle East, South Africa, Australasia and North America. Cathay Pacific carried 15,438,243 passengers and 1·12m. tonnes of cargo in 2005. Dragonair, a Cathay Pacific subsidiary, provided scheduled services to 21 cities in Mainland China and ten other destinations in Asia in 2006, plus about 70 cargo services per week to Anchorage, New York, Osaka, Shanghai, Taipei and Xiamen. In 2006 Air Hong Kong, an all-cargo operator, provided scheduled services to and from Bangkok, Osaka, Penang, Seoul, Shanghai, Singapore, Taipei and Tokyo. Hong Kong International Airport handled more international freight in 2001 than any other airport. In 2006, 280,490 aircraft arrived and departed and 44·5m. passengers and 3·58m. tonnes of freight were carried on aircraft.

Hong Kong was second, behind only Singapore, in the rankings for air transport infrastructure in the World Economic Forum's *Global Competitiveness Report 2009–2010*.

Shipping

The port of Hong Kong handled 23·5m. 20-ft equivalent units (TEUs) in 2006, making it the world's second busiest container port after Singapore. The Kwai Chung Container Port has 24 berths with 7,694 metres of quay backed by 275 ha. of cargo handling area. Merchant shipping in 2004 totalled 25,562,000 GRT, including oil tankers 5,416,000 GRT. In 2004, 35,900 ocean-going vessels, 117,540 river cargo vessels and 71,980 river passenger vessels called at Hong Kong. In 2004, 221m. tonnes of freight were handled. In 2004 vessels totalling 399,031,000 NRT entered ports and vessels totalling 399,025,000 NRT cleared.

Only Singapore ranked ahead of Hong Kong for quality of port facilities in the World Economic Forum's *Global Competitiveness Report 2009–2010*.

Telecommunications

In 2008 there were 4,099,900 main (fixed) telephone lines. The local fixed telecommunications network services (FTNS) market in Hong Kong was liberalized in 1995. In Oct. 2007 there were five mobile network operators in Hong Kong. There were ten wireline-based local FTNS operators in Oct. 2007 and one wireless-based FTNS operator. There were only 687,600 mobile phone subscribers in 1995, since when the sector has expanded substantially. In 2008 there were 11,580,100 mobile phone subscribers (1,658·5 per 1,000 population). The internet market has also seen considerable growth. In 2008 there were 4·7m. internet users, up from 1·9m. in 2000. There were 26·1 broadband subscribers per 100 inhabitants in June 2007. In 2006 there were 4·5m. PCs in use.

The external telecommunications services market has been fully liberalized since 1 Jan. 1999.

Postal Services

In Dec. 2002 there were 131 post offices. In 2006 Hongkong Post handled 1,322m. letters and 929,000 parcels.

SOCIAL INSTITUTIONS

Justice

The Hong Kong Act of 1985 provided for Hong Kong ordinances to replace English laws in specified fields.

The courts of justice comprise the Court of Final Appeal (inaugurated 1 July 1997) which hears appeals on civil and criminal matters from the High Court; the High Court (consisting of the Court of Appeal and the Court of First Instance); the Lands Tribunal which determines on statutory claims for compensation over land and certain landlord and tenant matters; the District Court (which includes the Family Court); the Magistracies (including the Juvenile Court); the Coroner's Court; the Labour Tribunal, which provides a quick and inexpensive method of settling disputes between employers and employees; the Small Claims Tribunal, which deals with monetary claims involving amounts not exceeding HK$50,000; and the Obscene Articles Tribunal.

While the High Court has unlimited jurisdiction in both civil and criminal matters, the District Court has limited jurisdiction. The maximum term of imprisonment it may impose is seven years. Magistracies exercise criminal jurisdiction over a wide range of offences, and the powers of punishment are generally restricted to a maximum of two years' imprisonment or a fine of HK$100,000.

After being in abeyance for 25 years, the death penalty was abolished in 1992.

77,437 crimes were reported in 2005, of which 13,890 were violent crimes. 40,804 people were arrested in 2005, of whom 9,339 were for violent crimes. The prison population was 11,580 in Oct. 2006 (168 per 100,000 of national population).

Education

Adult literacy was 93·5% in 2001 (96·9% among males and 89·6% among females). Universal basic education is available to all children aged from six to 15 years. In around three-quarters of the ordinary secondary day schools teaching has been in Cantonese since 1998–99, with about a quarter of ordinary secondary day schools still using English. In 2005 there were 149,141 pupils in 1,062 kindergartens, 425,864 full-time students in 720 ordinary primary day schools (26,958 in private schools) and 478,440 in 37 government, 375 aided and 89 private ordinary secondary day schools.

The Hong Kong Technical Institutes and the Hong Kong Technical Colleges were renamed the Hong Kong Institutes of Vocational Education in 1999. In the academic year 2005–06 there were 55,531 students enrolled in Hong Kong Institutes of Vocational Education.

The University of Hong Kong (founded 1911) had 11,377 full-time and 1,114 part-time students in 2005–06; the Chinese

University of Hong Kong (founded 1963), 11,605 full-time and 931 part-time students; the Hong Kong University of Science and Technology (founded 1991), 6,598 full-time and 211 part-time students; the Hong Kong Polytechnic University (founded 1972 as the Hong Kong Polytechnic), 12,282 full-time and 3,241 part-time students; the City University of Hong Kong (founded 1984 as the City Polytechnic of Hong Kong), 11,334 full-time and 1,418 part-time students; the Hong Kong Baptist University (founded 1956 as the Hong Kong Baptist College), 4,894 full-time and 637 part-time students; the Lingnan University (founded 1967 as the Lingnan College), 2,288 full-time and ten part-time students; and the Hong Kong Institute of Education (founded 1994), 2,666 full-time and 4,153 part-time students.

Estimated total government expenditure on education in 2005–06 was HK$55·6bn. (24·0% of total government spending; 3·9% of GDP). In 2004–05: 22·9% of total government spending; 4·1% of GDP.

According to the OECD's 2006 PISA (Programme for International Student Assessment) study, 15-year-olds in Hong Kong rank second in science and third in mathematics and reading. The three-yearly study compares educational achievement of pupils in the major industrialized countries.

Health

The Department of Health (DH) is the Government's health adviser and regulatory authority. The Hospital Authority (HA) is an independent body responsible for the management of all public hospitals. In 2002 there were 9,021 doctors on the local list, equivalent to 1·5 doctors per 1,000 population. In 2001 there were 1,900 dentists, 42,000 nurses and 136 midwives. In 2002 the total number of hospital beds was 35,100, including 29,432 beds in 41 public hospitals under the HA and 2,928 beds in 12 private hospitals. The bed-population ratio was 5·2 beds per thousand population.

The Chinese Medicine Ordinance was passed by the Legislative Council in July 1999 to establish a statutory framework to control the practice, use, manufacture and trading of Chinese medicine.

Recurrent spending on health amounts to US$4·15bn. (HK$324bn.), an increase of 4% in real terms over the latest estimated spending for 2001–02.

Welfare

Social welfare programmes include social security, family services, child care, services for the elderly, medical social services, youth and community work, probation, and corrections and rehabilitation. 181 non-governmental organizations are subsidized by public funds.

The government gives non-contributory cash assistance to needy families, unemployed able-bodied adults, the severely disabled and the elderly. Caseload as at 31 Dec. 2004 totalled 295,694. Victims of natural disasters, crimes of violence and traffic accidents are financially assisted. Estimated total government expenditure on social welfare for 2004–05 was HK$33·7bn.

RELIGION

In 2001 there were 4,970,000 Buddhists and Taoists, 290,000 Protestants and 280,000 Roman Catholics. The remainder of the population are followers of other religions. Joseph Zen Ze-kiun became Hong Kong's first cardinal in 2006.

CULTURE

Broadcasting

Broadcasting is regulated by the Broadcasting Authority, a statutory body comprising three government officers and nine non-official members.

There is a public broadcasting station, Radio Television Hong Kong (colour by PAL), which broadcasts seven channels (three Chinese, one English, one bilingual and one Putonhua service, and one for the relay of the BBC World Service), six of which provide a 24-hour service. Hong Kong Commercial Broadcasting Co. Ltd and Metro Broadcast Co. Ltd transmit commercial sound programmes on six channels. Television Broadcasts Ltd and Asia Television Ltd transmit domestic free television programme services in English and Chinese on four channels. Hong Kong Cable Television Ltd offers over 30 TV channels on a subscription basis.

In 2006 TV receivers numbered 3·47m.

Press

In 2006 there were 48 newspapers of which 21 were Chinese-language dailies, 14 English dailies, eight bilingual dailies and five Japanese dailies. The newspapers with the highest circulation figures are all Chinese-language papers—*Oriental Daily News*, *Apple Daily* and *The Sun*. Circulation of dailies (including free papers) in 2006 was 3·2m. (2·0m. paid-for and 1·2m. free). Daily newspapers reached 75% of the population in 2005. A number of news agency bulletins are registered as newspapers.

Tourism

There were a record 21,811,000 visitor arrivals in 2004. Tourism receipts totalled HK$91,850·0m. in 2004.

FURTHER READING

Statistical Information: The Census and Statistics Department is responsible for the preparation and collation of government statistics. These statistics are published mainly in the *Hong Kong Monthly Digest of Statistics*. The Department also publishes monthly trade statistics, economic indicators and an annual review of overseas trade, etc. *Website:* http://www.info.gov.hk/censtatd

Hong Kong [various years] Hong Kong Government Press
Brown, J. M. (ed.) *Hong Kong's Transitions, 1842–1997.* 1997
Buckley, R., *Hong Kong: the Road to 1997.* 1997
Cottrell, R., *The End of Hong Kong: the Secret Diplomacy of Imperial Retreat.* 1993
Courtauld, C. and Holdsworth, M., *The Hong Kong Story.* 1997
Flowerdew, J., *The Final Years of British Hong Kong: the Discourse of Colonial Withdrawal.* 1997
Keay, J., *Last Post: the End of Empire in the Far East.* 1997
Lo, C. P., *Hong Kong.* 1992
Lo, S.-H., *The Politics of Democratization in Hong Kong.* 1997
Lok, Sang Ho and Ash, Robert, *China, Hong Kong and the World Economy.* 2006
Morris, J., *Hong Kong: Epilogue to an Empire.* 2nd ed. [of *Hong Kong: Xianggang*]. 1993
Roberti, M., *The Fall of Hong Kong: China's Triumph and Britain's Betrayal.* 2nd ed. 1997
Roberts, E. V., *et al.*, *Historical Dictionary of Hong Kong and Macau.* 1993
Shipp, S., *Hong Kong, China: a Political History of the British Crown Colony's Transfer to Chinese Rule.* 1995
Tsang, S. Y., *Hong Kong: an Appointment with China.* 1997
Wang, G. and Wong, S. L. (eds.) *Hong Kong's Transition: a Decade after the Deal.* 1996
Welsh, F., *A History of Hong Kong.* 3rd ed. 1997
Yahuda, M., *Hong Kong: China's Challenge.* 1996

Macao

Região Administrativa Especial de Macau (Macao Special Administrative Region)

Population estimate, 2010: 548,000
GDP per capita: not available
GNI per capita, 2007: US$39,336

KEY HISTORICAL EVENTS

Macao was visited by Portuguese traders from 1513 and became a Portuguese colony in 1557. Initially sovereignty remained vested in China, with the Portuguese paying an annual rent. In 1848–

49 the Portuguese declared Macao a free port and established jurisdiction over the territory. On 6 Jan. 1987 Portugal agreed to return Macao to China on 20 Dec. 1999 under a plan in which it would become a special administrative zone of China, with considerable autonomy.

TERRITORY AND POPULATION

The Macao Special Administrative Region, which lies at the mouth of the Pearl River, comprises a peninsula (8·8 sq. km) connected by a narrow isthmus to the People's Republic of China, on which is built the city of Santa Nome de Deus de Macao, the islands of Taipa (6·4 sq. km), linked to Macao by a 2-km bridge, and Colôane (7·6 sq. km) linked to Taipa by a 2-km causeway, and Cotai, a strip of reclaimed land between Colôane and Taipa (4·7 km). The total area of Macao is 27·5 sq. km. Additional land continues to be reclaimed from the sea. The population (2001 census) was 435,235 (266,370 females). Population on 31 Dec. 2006, 513,427 (260,952 females); density, 18,670 people per sq. km. The population increased by 6·0% in 2006. An estimated 99·5% of the population lived in urban areas in 2004. The official languages are Chinese and Portuguese, with the majority speaking the Cantonese dialect. Only about 2,000 people speak Portuguese as their first language.

The UN gives an estimated population for 2010 of 548,000.

In Dec. 2003, 32,167 foreigners were legally registered for residency in Macao. There were 2,451 legal immigrants from mainland China.

SOCIAL STATISTICS

2003: births, 3,212 (7·2 per 1,000 population); deaths, 1,474 (3·3); marriages, 1,309 (2·9); divorces, 440 (1·0). Infant mortality, 2001, 4·3 per 1,000 live births. Life expectancy at birth (1998–2001), 78·9 years.

CLIMATE

Sub-tropical tending towards temperate, with an average temperature of 23·0°C. The number of rainy days is around a third of the year. Average annual rainfall varies from 47–87" (1,200–2,200 mm). It is very humid from May to Sept.

CONSTITUTION AND GOVERNMENT

Macao's constitution is the 'Basic Law', promulgated by China's National People's Congress on 31 March 1993 and in effect since 20 Dec. 1999. It is a Special Administrative Region (SAR) of the People's Republic of China, and is directly under the Central People's Government while enjoying a high degree of autonomy.

RECENT ELECTIONS

At the elections held on 20 Sept. 2009 the Union for Development won two of 12 elected seats with 14·9% of votes cast, the Association of United Citizens of Macau two with 12·0% and the Democratic Prosperous Macau Association two with 11·6%. Six other parties won a single seat each. Turnout was 59·9%.

Fernando Chui Sai-on was elected chief executive on 26 July 2009, receiving 282 out of 296 votes in the Election Committee.

CURRENT ADMINISTRATION

Chief Executive: Fernando Chui Sai-on; b. 1957 (sworn in 20 Dec. 2009).

Government Website: http://www.gov.mo

ECONOMY

Gaming is of major importance to the economy of Macao, accounting for around one third of total GDP (2002) and providing billions of dollars in taxes. In 2003, 7·5% of the workforce was directly employed by the casinos. In 2006 Macao overtook Las Vegas as the world's largest gaming market.

Overview

Since its transfer of sovereignty to the People's Republic of China in 1999, Macao has achieved high growth as a result of expansion in the tourism and gaming sectors. China's relaxation of travel restrictions since 1999 has resulted in a large increase in mainland visitors, with the total number of visitors reaching nearly 27m. in 2007 (up from 7m. in 1999) according to the public administration of Macao. The cessation of Stanley Ho's monopoly of the local gaming industry in 2001 and its opening up to foreign competition has led to an influx of foreign investment that saw Macao become the world's biggest gaming centre in 2006.

The economy grew an average 13·1% per year from 2001–06, with gaming, tourism and hospitality contributing an estimated 50% of GDP. Dependence on one service industry leaves the economy susceptible to shock, as does the slow decline of traditional manufacturing industries and the transfer of much of the textile industry to the Chinese mainland following the 2005 termination of the Multi-Fibre Agreement that provided a near-guarantee of export markets.

Currency

The unit of currency is the *pataca* (MOP) of 100 *avos* which is tied to the Hong Kong dollar at parity. Inflation was –2·6% in 2002 and –1·6% in 2003. Foreign exchange reserves were US$4,343m. in 2003. Total money supply was 8,790m. patacas in 2003.

Budget

Final budget figures for 2003 were: revenue, 15,578·0m. patacas; expenditure, 15,578·0m. patacas. Actual figures were: revenue, 18,370·6m. patacas; expenditure, 15,713·0m. patacas.

Performance

Real GDP growth was 6·9% in 2005, rising to 16·6% in 2006. Total GDP in 2006 was US$14·2bn.

Banking and Finance

There are two note-issuing banks in Macao—the Macao branch of the Bank of China and the Macao branch of the Banco Nacional Ultramarino. The Monetary Authority of Macao functions as a central bank (*Director,* Teng Lin Seng). Commercial business is handled (2003) by 23 banks, ten of which are local and 13 foreign. Total deposits, 2003 (including non-resident deposits), 124,977·4m. patacas. There are no foreign-exchange controls within Macao.

ENERGY AND NATURAL RESOURCES

Environment

Macao's carbon dioxide emissions from the consumption and flaring of fossil fuels in 2008 were the equivalent of 4·4 tonnes per capita.

Electricity

Installed capacity was 0·49m. kW in 2004; production, 1·97bn. kWh. Macao imported 151m. kWh of electricity in 2004.

Oil and Gas

311,324,000 litres of fuel oil were imported in 2003.

Fisheries

The catch in 2005 was approximately 1,500 tonnes.

INDUSTRY

Although the economy is based on gaming and tourism there is a light industrial base of textiles and garments. In 2002 the number of manufacturing establishments was 1,162 (textiles and clothing, 500; metal products, 138; foods, 119; publishing and printing, 117).

Labour

In 2003 a total of 202,588 people were in employment, including 37,077 (18·3%) in manufacturing; 32,824 (16·2%), wholesale and retail trade, repair of motor vehicles, motorcycles and personal and household goods; 23,469 (11·6%), community, social and other personal services; 22,114 (10·9%), hotels, restaurants and similar activities; 17,812 (8·8%), public administration, defence and compulsory social security; 16,283 (8·0%), construction. Employment in 2003 was 60·9% of the labour force (62·3% in 2002); unemployment rate stood at 6·0% (6·3% in 2002).

INTERNATIONAL TRADE

Imports and Exports

In 2006 imports were valued at US$5,271m., of which the main products were textile yarn, fabrics and finished articles; clothing and apparel; telecommunications, sound recording and reproducing equipment; and petroleum and petroleum products. Main import suppliers in 2004: mainland China, 44·4%; Hong Kong, 10·6%; Japan, 9·6%.

2006 exports were valued at US$2,478m., of which the leading products were clothing and apparel; textile yarn, fabrics and finished articles; footwear; and petroleum and related products. Main export markets in 2004: USA, 48·7%; mainland China, 13·9%; Germany, 8·3%.

COMMUNICATIONS

Roads

In 2007 there were 401 km of roads. In 2007 there were 68,800 passenger cars in use (143 cars per 1,000 inhabitants), 2,100 buses and coaches, 4,600 lorries and vans, and 85,400 motorcycles and mopeds. There were 17 fatalities in road accidents in 2007.

Civil Aviation

An international airport opened in Dec. 1995. In 2003 Macau International Airport handled 2,904,118 passengers and 141,223 tonnes of freight (including transit cargo). In 2003 Air Macau flew to Bangkok, Beijing, Chengdu, Guilin, Haikou, Kaohsiung, Kota Kinabalu, Kuala Lumpur, Kunming, Manila, Nanjing, Ningbo, Shanghai, Singapore, Taipei and Xiamen. In 2003 scheduled airline traffic of Macao-based carriers flew a total of 15m. km, carrying 1,212,000 passengers.

Shipping

Regular services connect Macao with Hong Kong, 65 km to the northeast. In 2002 merchant shipping totalled 4,000 GRT. In 2003 cargo vessel departures by flag totalled 2,451,106 NRT.

Telecommunications

In 2005 there were 707,100 telephone subscribers (1,537·3 per 1,000 inhabitants), including 532,800 mobile phone subscribers. There were 35,000 PCs in use (290·1 for every 1,000 persons) in 2004 and 170,000 internet users in 2005. In June 2007 there were 23·0 broadband subscribers per 100 inhabitants.

Postal Services

21,076,438 letters and parcels were posted in 2003.

SOCIAL INSTITUTIONS

Justice

There is a judicial district court, a criminal court and an administrative court with 24 magistrates in all.

In 2003 there were 9,920 crimes, of which 5,445 were against property. There were 928 persons in prison in 2003.

Education

There are three types of schools: public, church-run and private. In 2002–03 there were 142 schools and colleges with 110,266 students and 5,324 teachers. Numbers of schools and colleges by category (number of students at the end of the 2002–03 academic year): pre-primary, 62 (12,737); primary, 83 (41,535); secondary, 56 (41,551); technical/professional secondary, 4 (2,448); higher, 12 (11,995). In 2002–03 there were 132 adult education institutions with a total of 86,578 students enrolled.

In 2003 total expenditure on education came to 2·9% of GNP and 15·2% of total government spending.

Health

In 2003 there were 986 doctors, 91 dentists and 1,010 nurses. In 2003 there were 444 inhabitants per doctor and 447 per hospital bed.

RELIGION

Non-religious persons account for 62% of the population. About 17% are Buddhists and 7% Roman Catholics.

CULTURE

Broadcasting

One government and one private commercial radio station are in operation on medium wave broadcasting in Portuguese and Chinese. Macao receives television broadcasts from Hong Kong and in 1984 a public bilingual TV station began operating. There were, in 2006, 130,000 TV-equipped households (colour by PAL).

Press

In 2003 there were 11 daily newspapers (three in Portuguese and eight in Chinese) and six weekly newspapers (one in Portuguese and five in Chinese), plus four Chinese periodicals.

Tourism

Tourism is one of the mainstays of the economy. In 2006 there were 22·0m. tourists (of which 12·0m. were from mainland China, 6·9m. from Hong Kong and 1·4m. from Taiwan), up 17% on the 2005 total and more than double the 2001 total. Receipts in 2003 totalled US$4,836m.

FURTHER READING

Direcção dos Serviços de Estatística e Censos. *Anuário Estatístico/Yearbook of Statistics Macau in Figures.* Annual

Porter, J., *Macau, the Imaginary City: Culture and Society, 1557 to the Present.* 1996

Roberts, E. V., *Historical Dictionary of Hong Kong and Macau.* 1993

Statistics and Census Service Website: http://www.dsec.gov.mo

---

Taiwan[1]

Zhonghua Minguo
('Republic of China')

Capital: Taipei
Population, 2007: 23·0m.
GDP per capita: not available

KEY HISTORICAL EVENTS

Taiwan, christened Ilha Formosa ('beautiful island') by the Portuguese, was ceded to Japan by China by the Treaty of Shimonoseki in 1895. After the Second World War the island was surrendered to Gen. Chiang Kai-shek who made it the headquarters for his crumbling Nationalist Government. Until 1970 the USA supported Taiwan's claims to represent all of China. Only in 1971 did the government of the People's Republic of China manage to replace that of Chiang Kai-shek at the UN. In Jan. 1979 the UN established formal diplomatic relations with the People's Republic of China, breaking off all formal ties with Taiwan. Taiwan itself has continued to reject all attempts at reunification, and although there have been frequent threats from mainland China to precipitate direct action (including military manoeuvres

[1]See note on transcription of names in CHINA: Territory and Population.

off the Taiwanese coast) the prospect of confrontation with the USA supports the status quo.

In July 1999 President Lee Teng-hui repudiated Taiwan's 50-year-old One China policy—the pretence of a common goal of unification—arguing that Taiwan and China should maintain equal 'state to state' relations. This was a rejection of Beijing's view that Taiwan is no more than a renegade Chinese province which must be reunited with the mainland, by force if necessary. In the presidential election of 18 March 2000 Chen Shui-bian, leader of the Democratic Progressive Party, was elected, together with Annette Lu Hsiu-lien as his Vice President. Both support independence although Chen Shui-bian has made friendly gestures towards China and has distanced himself from colleagues who want an immediate declaration of independence. Following his wife's indictment on embezzlement charges in Nov. 2006, President Chen survived three parliamentary attempts to impeach him.

TERRITORY AND POPULATION

Taiwan lies between the East and South China Seas about 160 km from the coast of Fujian. The territories currently under the control of the Republic of China include Taiwan, Penghu (the Pescadores), Kinmen (Quemoy) and Lienchiang (the Matsu Islands), as well as the archipelagos in the South China Sea. Off the Pacific coast of Taiwan are Green Island and Orchid Island. To the northeast of Taiwan are the Tiaoyutai Islets. The total area of Taiwan Island, the Penghu Archipelago and the Kinmen area (including the fortified offshore islands of Quemoy and Matsu) is 36,188 sq. km (13,973 sq. miles). Population (2008), 23,037,031. The ethnic composition is 84% native Taiwanese (including 15% of Hakka), 14% of Mainland Chinese, and 2% aborigine of Malayo-Polynesian origin. There were also 494,107 aboriginals of Malay origin in Dec. 2008. Population density: 637 per sq. km.

Taiwan's administrative units comprise (with 2008 populations): two special municipalities: Taipei, the capital (2,622,923) and Kaohsiung (1,525,642); five cities outside the county structure: Chiayi (273,793), Hsinchu (405,371), Keelung (388,979), Taichung (1,066,128), Tainan (768,453); 16 counties (*hsien*) in Taiwan Province: Changhwa (1,312,935), Chiayi (548,731), Hsinchu (503,273), Hualien (341,433), Ilan (460,902), Kaohsiung (1,243,412), Miaoli (560,397), Nantou (531,753), Penghu (93,308), Pingtung (884,838), Taichung (1,557,944), Tainan (1,104,552), Taipei (3,833,730), Taitung (231,849), Taoyuan (1,958,686), Yunlin (723,674); two counties in Fujian Province: Kinmen (84,570), Lienchiang (9,755).

SOCIAL STATISTICS

In 2006 the birth rate was 9·0 per 1,000 population; death rate, 6·0 per 1,000. Population growth rate, 2006, 0·5%. Life expectancy, 2006: males, 74·1 years; females, 80·2 years. Infant mortality, 2006, 5·8 per 1,000 live births.

CLIMATE

The climate is subtropical in the north and tropical in the south. The typhoon season extends from July to Sept. The average monthly temperatures of Jan. and July in Taipei are 59·5°F (15·3°C) and 83·3°F (28·5°C) respectively, and average annual rainfall is 84·99" (2,158·8 mm). Kaohsiung's average monthly temperatures of Jan. and July are 65·66°F (18·9°C) and 83·3°F (28·5°C) respectively, and average annual rainfall is 69·65" (1,769·2 mm).

CONSTITUTION AND GOVERNMENT

The ROC Constitution is based on the Principles of Nationalism, Democracy and Social Wellbeing formulated by Dr Sun Yat-sen, the founding father of the Republic of China. The ROC government is divided into three main levels: central, provincial/municipal and county/city, each of which has well-defined powers.

The central government consists of the Office of the President, the National Assembly, which is specially elected only for constitutional amendment, and five governing branches called '*yuan*', namely the Executive Yuan, the Legislative Yuan, the Judicial Yuan, the Examination Yuan and the Control Yuan. Beginning with the elections to the seventh Legislative Yuan held on 12 Jan. 2008 the Legislative Yuan has 113 members (formerly 225).

From 5 May to 23 July 1997 the *Additional Articles of the Constitution of the Republic of China* underwent yet another amendment. As a result a resolution on the impeachment of the President or Vice President is no longer to be instituted by the Control Yuan but rather by the Legislative Yuan. The Legislative Yuan has the power to pass a no-confidence vote against the premier of the Executive Yuan, while the president of the Republic has the power to dissolve the Legislative Yuan. The premier of the Executive Yuan is now directly appointed by the president of the Republic. Hence the consent of the Legislative Yuan is no longer needed.

In Dec. 2003 a law came into effect allowing for referendums to be held.

National Anthem

'San Min Chu I'; words by Dr Sun Yat-sen, tune by Cheng Mao-yun.

RECENT ELECTIONS

Presidential elections took place on 22 March 2008. Ma Ying-jeou (Nationalist Party/Kuomintang) won 58·4% of the vote and Frank Hsieh (Democratic Progressive Party) 41·6%.

Elections to the Legislative Yuan were held on 13 Jan. 2008. The Nationalist Party won 81 seats with 71·7% of votes cast; the Democratic Progressive Party, 27 seats (23·9%); the Non-Partisan Solidarity Union, 3 seats (2·7%); the People First Party, 1 seat (0·9%); ind., 1 seat (0·9%).

Elections for an *ad hoc* National Assembly charged with amending the constitution were held on 14 May 2005. The Democratic Progressive Party took 127 of 300 seats (with 42·5% of the vote), the Nationalist Party 117 (38·9%), the Taiwan Solidarity Union 21 (7·1%), the People First Party 18 (6·1%) and the Jhang Ya Jhong Union 5 (1·7%). Turnout was 23·4%.

CURRENT ADMINISTRATION

President: Ma Ying-jeou; b. 1950 (Nationalist Party/Kuomintang; sworn in 20 May 2008).

Vice President: Vincent Siew.

Prime Minister and *President of the Executive Yuan:* Wu Den-yih; b. 1948 (Nationalist Party/Kuomintang; sworn in 10 Sept. 2009). There are eight ministries under the Executive Yuan: Interior; Foreign Affairs; National Defence; Finance; Education; Justice; Economic Affairs; Transport and Communications.

Vice President of the Executive Yuan (Deputy Premier) and Minister for the Consumer Protection Commission: Eric Liluan Chu. *President, Control Yuan:* Wang Chien-shien. *President, Examination Yuan:* Kuan John Chung. *President, Judicial Yuan:* Lai In-jaw. *President, Legislative Yuan:* Wang Jin-ping. *Secretary General, Executive Yuan:* Lin Join-sane. *Minister of Interior:* Jiang Yi-huah. *Foreign Affairs:* Timothy Yang. *National Defence:* Kao Hua-chu. *Finance:* Li Sush-der. *Education:* Wu Ching-chi. *Justice:* Wang Ching-feng. *Economic Affairs:* Shih Yen-shiang. *Transport and Communications:* Mao Chi-kuo. *Ministers without Portfolio:* Tsai Hsung-hsiung (also Chair of the *Council for Economic Planning and Development*); Chang Jin-fu; Fan Liang-shiow; James Cherng-Tay Hsueh; Ovid Tzeng; Yiin Chii-ming; Liang Chi-yuan.

A number of commissions and subordinate organizations have been formed with the resolution of the Executive Yuan Council and the Legislature to meet new demands and handle new affairs. Examples include the Mongolian and Tibetan Affairs

Commission; the Mainland Affairs Council; the Fair Trade Commission; the Public Construction Commission; and the Financial Supervisory Commission. These commissions, councils and agencies are headed by:

Council of Agriculture: Chen Wu-hsiung. *Atomic Energy Council:* Tsai Chuen-horng. *Aviation Safety Council:* Wu Jing-shown. *Directorate General of Budget, Accounting and Statistics:* Shih Su-mei. *Central Election Commission:* Lai Hau-min. *Central Personnel Administration:* Wu Tai-cheng. *Coast Guard Administration:* Wang Ginn-wang. *Council for Cultural Affairs:* Emile Chih-jen Sheng. *Environmental Protection Administration:* Stephen Shu-hung Shen. *Fair Trade Commission (acting):* Wu Shiow-ming. *Financial Supervisory Commission:* Sean Chen. *Government Information Office:* Su Jun-pin. *Council for Hakka Affairs:* Huang Yu-cheng. *Department of Health:* Yaung Chih-liang. *Council of Indigenous Peoples:* Sun Ta-chuan. *Council of Labour Affairs:* Wang Ju-hsuan. *Mainland Affairs Council:* Lai Shin-yuan. *Mongolian and Tibetan Affairs Commission:* Kao Su-po. *National Communications Commission:* Bonnie Peng. *National Science Council:* Lee Lou-chuang. *National Youth Commission:* Wang Yu-ting. *Overseas Compatriot Affairs Commission:* Wu Ying-yih. *Public Construction Commission:* Fan Liang-shiow. *Research, Development and Evaluation Commission:* Chu Chin-peng. *Sports Affairs Council:* Tai Hsia-ling. *Veterans' Affairs Commission:* Tseng Jing-ling.

Government Website: http://www.gio.gov.tw

DEFENCE

Conscription was reduced from 16 months to 14 months in July 2007. Defence expenditure in 2006 totalled US$7,738m. (US$336 per capita), representing 2·2% of GDP.

Army

The Army was estimated to number about 190,000 in 2000, including military police. Army reserves numbered 2·7m. In addition the Ministry of Justice, Ministry of Interior and the Ministry of Defence each command paramilitary forces totalling 25,000 personnel in all. The Army consists of Army Corps, Defence Commands, Airborne Cavalry Brigades, Armoured Brigades, Motorized Rifle Brigades, Infantry Brigades, Special Warfare Brigades and Missile Command.

Navy

Active personnel in the Navy in 2000 totalled 50,000. There are 425,000 naval reservists. The operational and land-based forces consist of four submarines, 16 destroyers and 21 frigates. There is a naval air wing operating 31 combat aircraft and 21 armed helicopters.

Air Force

Units in the operational system are equipped with aircraft that include locally developed IDF, F-16, Mirage 2000-5 and F-5E fighter-interceptors. There were 50,000 Air Force personnel in 2000 and 334,000 reservists.

INTERNATIONAL RELATIONS

By a treaty of 2 Dec. 1954 the USA pledged to defend Taiwan, but this treaty lapsed one year after the USA established diplomatic relations with the People's Republic of China on 1 Jan. 1979. In April 1979 the Taiwan Relations Act was passed by the US Congress to maintain commercial, cultural and other relations between USA and Taiwan through the American Institute in Taiwan and its Taiwan counterpart, the Co-ordination Council for North American Affairs in the USA, which were accorded quasi-diplomatic status in 1980. The People's Republic took over the China seat in the UN from Taiwan on 25 Oct. 1971. In May 1991 Taiwan ended its formal state of war with the People's Republic. Taiwan became a member of the World Trade Organization on 1 Jan. 2002.

In Jan. 2008 Taiwan had formal diplomatic ties with 23 countries after Malaŵi agreed to recognize the People's Republic of China instead. In Aug. 2007, 15 of the diplomatic allies sponsored an unsuccessful proposal for Taiwan to join the UN.

ECONOMY

Overview

Taiwan has made a successful transition from an agricultural economy to one based on high-tech electronics. The agricultural, industrial and service sectors account for approximately 2%, 20% and 68% of GDP respectively. Taiwan has experienced average economic growth of 8% during the last three decades, driven primarily by high value added manufacturing and exports, especially in electronics and computers.

In 1989 the government began to privatize government-owned enterprises, including banks, telecommunication firms and industrial firms. Though largely escaping the effects of the 1997 Asian financial crisis, the economy has suffered recent setbacks, partly owing to policy co-ordination problems and bad debts in the banking system. The economy went into recession in 2001 when the first year of negative growth ever was recorded and unemployment reached record highs. Strong export performance has subsequently stimulated a recovery, with annual GDP growth above 3% since 2004, unemployment falling below 4% in 2007 and inflation consistently low. Taiwan has successfully diversified its trade, with China overtaking the USA as the prime export market. It ranks among the world's most export-dependent economies. China is also the main destination for Taiwan's foreign direct investment.

Currency

The unit of currency is the *New Taiwan dollar* (TWD) of 100 *cents*. Gold reserves were 13·61m. oz in Sept. 2005. There was inflation of 1·8% in 2007 and 3·5% in 2008. Foreign exchange reserves were US$241·7bn. in Dec. 2004.

Budget

As a result of the constitutional amendment to abolish the provincial government, the central government budget has been enlarged to include the former provincial government since the fiscal year 2000. The central government's general budget for the fiscal year 2002 (beginning on 1 Jan.) was NT$1,518,724m. Expenditure planned: 18·1% on education, science and culture; 17·6% on economic development; 17·5% on social security; 15% on defence.

Performance

Taiwan sustained rapid economic growth at an annual rate of 9·2% from 1960 up to 1990. The rate slipped to 6·4% in the 1990s and 5·9% in 2000; Taiwan suffered from the Asian financial crisis, though less than its neighbours. Consumer prices showed increasing stability, rising at an average annual rate of 6·3% from 1960 to 1989, 2·9% in the 1990s and 1·3% in 2000. In 2001 global economic sluggishness and the events of 11 Sept. in the USA severely affected Taiwan's economy, which contracted by 2·2%. Per capita GNP stood at US$12,876, while consumer prices remained almost unchanged. Subsequent economic recovery led to growth of 4·8% in 2006 and 5·7% in 2007, although growth was just 0·1% in 2008.

Banking and Finance

The Central Bank of The Republic of China (Taiwan), reactivated in 1961, regulates the money supply, manages foreign exchange and issues currency. The *Governor* is Perng Fai-nan. The Bank of Taiwan is the largest commercial bank and the fiscal agent of the government. There are seven domestic banks, 38 commercial banks and 36 foreign banks.

There are two stock exchanges in Taipei.

ENERGY AND NATURAL RESOURCES

Environment

Taiwan's carbon dioxide emissions from the consumption and flaring of fossil fuels in 2008 were the equivalent of 13·3 tonnes per capita.

Electricity

Output of electricity in 2001 was 188·5m. MWh; total installed capacity was 35,568 MW, of which 77·1% is held by the Taiwan Power Company. There were six units in three nuclear power stations in 2003. Consumption per capita stood at 4,257 litres of oil equivalent in 2001.

Oil and Gas

Crude oil production in 2004 was 2·8m. bbls; natural gas, 850m. cu. metres.

Minerals

Coal production ceased by 2001 because of competitive imports and increasing local production costs.

Agriculture

In 2001 the cultivated area was 848,743 ha., of which 438,974 ha. were paddy fields. Rice production totalled 1,396,274 tonnes. Livestock production was valued at more than NT$101,205m., accounting for 28·67% of Taiwan's total agricultural production value.

Forestry

Forest area, 2001: 2,101,719 ha. Forest reserves: trees, 357,492,423 cu. metres; bamboo, 1,109m. poles. Timber production, 26,401 cu. metres.

Fisheries

The catch in 2005 was 1,017,243 tonnes, almost exclusively from sea fishing.

INDUSTRY

The largest companies in Taiwan by market capitalization in March 2009 were: Taiwan Semicon. Mnfg (US$38·8bn.), Formosa Petrochemical (US$18·3bn.) and Chunghwa Telecom (US$17·7bn.).

Output (in tonnes) in 2005: cement, 19·9m.; crude steel, 18·6m.; sugar (2002), 0·2m.; cotton fabrics (1999), 1,061m. sq. metres; portable computers (1999), 9·95m. units; desktop computers (1999), 3·01m. units. Taiwan is the third largest information technology producer after the USA and Japan. The IT sector has replaced traditional industries as the engine for growth.

Labour

In Sept. 2002 the total labour force was 9·97m., of whom 9·44m. were employed. Of the employed population, 55·09% worked in the service sector (including 22·70% in trade and 16·11% in accommodation and eating and drinking establishments); 37·28% in industry (including 27·05% in manufacturing and 7·64% in construction); and 7·63% in agriculture, forestry and fisheries. The unemployment rate was 5·32%.

INTERNATIONAL TRADE

Restrictions on the repatriation of investment earnings by foreign nationals were removed in 1994.

Imports and Exports

Imports in 2007 totalled US$219,252m. and exports US$246,677m.

In 2001 the main import suppliers were Japan (24·1%), USA (17·0%), South Korea (6·3%) and Germany (4·0%). The main export markets were the USA (22·5%), Hong Kong (21·9%), Japan (10·4%) and Germany (3·6%).

Principal imports (2001), in US$1bn.: machinery and electrical equipment, 47·55; minerals, 12·76; chemicals, 10·23; basic metals and articles, 7·78; precision instruments, clocks and watches, and musical instruments, 6·21; vehicles and transport equipment, 4·24; textile products, 2·36.

Principal exports (2001), in US$1bn.: machinery and electrical equipment, 66·85; textiles, 12·63; basic metals and articles, 11·33; plastic and rubber products, 7·99; vehicles and transport equipment, 4·44; toys, games and sports equipment, 1·79; footwear, headwear and umbrellas, 0·79. By 2001 high-tech products were responsible for more than 54% of exports.

COMMUNICATIONS

Roads

In 2006 there were 39,286 km of roads. In 2007, 5·7m. passenger cars, 117,100 buses and coaches, 1·0m. lorries and vans, and 13·9m. motorcycles and mopeds were in use. 1,007m. passengers and 594m. tonnes of freight were transported in 2006. There were 3,140 fatalities in road accidents in 2006.

Rail

In 2005 freight traffic amounted to 13m. tonnes and passenger traffic to 169m. Total route length was 1,450 km. There are metro systems in Taipei (opened in 1996) and in Kaohsiung (opened in 2008).

Civil Aviation

There are currently two international airports: Chiang Kai-shek International at Taoyuan near Taipei, and Kaohsiung International in the south. In addition there are 14 domestic airports: Taipei, Hualien, Taitung, Taichung, Tainan, Chiayi, Pingtung, Makung, Chimei, Orchid Island, Green Island, Wangan, Kinmen and Matsu (Peikan). A second passenger terminal at Chiang Kai-shek International Airport opened in July 2000 as part of a US$800m. expansion project, which included aircraft bays, airport connection roads, a rapid transit link with Taipei, car parks and the expansion of air freight facilities, begun in 1989. The planned facilities are designed to allow the airport to handle an additional 14m. passengers annually by the year 2010.

In June 2002, 38 airlines including code-share airlines provided flights to destinations in Taiwan, of which 32 foreign and six Taiwanese carriers—China Airlines (CAL), EVA Airways, Mandarin Airlines (MDA; CAL's subsidiary), Trans Asia Airways (TNA), UNI Airways and the now defunct Far Eastern Air Transport Corp.—operated international services. In 2001, 44·1m. passengers and 1·3m. tonnes of freight were flown.

Regular direct flights between Taiwan and mainland China resumed in July 2008 for the first time since 1949.

Shipping

Maritime transportation is vital to the trade-oriented economy of Taiwan. At the end of 2001 Taiwan's shipping fleet totalled 249 national-flagged ships (over 100 GRT), amounting to 4·7m. GRT and 7·4m. DWT. There are six international ports: Kaohsiung, Keelung, Hualien, Taichung, Anping and Suao. The first two are container centres, Kaohsiung handling 7·54m. 20-ft equivalent units in 2001, making it the world's fourth busiest container port in terms of number of containers handled. Suao port is an auxiliary port to Keelung. In Jan. 2001 the first legal direct shipping links between Taiwanese islands and the Chinese mainland in more than 50 years were inaugurated.

Telecommunications

In Sept. 2006 there were 36,491,200 telephone subscribers (1,597·8 per 1,000 inhabitants) and PCs numbered 13·1m. (575·2 per 1,000 inhabitants). Taiwan's biggest telecommunications firm, the state-owned Chunghwa Telecom, lost its fixed-line monopoly in Aug. 2001. In Sept. 2006 there were 22,978,100 mobile phone subscribers, equivalent to 1,006·1 per 1,000 persons. There were approximately 13·21m. internet users in 2005. There were 20·9 broadband subscribers per 100 inhabitants in June 2007.

SOCIAL INSTITUTIONS

Justice

The Judicial Yuan is the supreme judicial organ of state. Comprising 15 grand justices, since 2003 these have been nominated and, with the consent of the Legislative Yuan, appointed by the President of the Republic. The grand justices hold meetings to interpret the Constitution and unify the interpretation of laws and orders. There are three levels of judiciary: district courts and their branches deal with civil and criminal cases in the first instance; high courts and their branches deal with appeals against judgments of district courts; the Supreme Court reviews judgments by the lower courts. There is also the Supreme Administrative Court, high administrative courts and a Commission on the Disciplinary Sanctions of Public Functionaries. Criminal cases relating to rebellion, treason and offences against friendly relations with foreign states are handled by high courts as the courts of first instance.

The death penalty is still in force. There were three confirmed executions in 2005, but none since. The population in penal institutions in Oct. 2008 was 63,370 (276 per 100,000 of national population).

Education

Since 1968 there has been compulsory education for six to 15-year-olds with free tuition. The illiteracy rate dropped from 7·1% in 1989 to 2·5% by 2006. There were 2,654 primary schools, 1,061 secondary schools and 156 vocational schools in 2008; and 102 universities, 45 colleges and 15 junior colleges. In 2005–06 there were 1,831,913 pupils with 101,682 teaching staff at elementary schools; 951,236 pupils and 48,816 teaching staff at junior high schools; 420,608 pupils and 34,112 teaching staff at senior high schools; and 331,604 students and 15,590 teaching staff at senior vocational schools. There were 1,259,490 students in universities and colleges in 2005–06 with 48,047 academic staff.

According to the OECD's 2006 PISA (Programme for International Student Assessment) study, 15-year-olds in Taiwan rank first in mathematics and fourth in science. The three-yearly study compares educational achievement of pupils in the major industrialized countries.

Health

In 2001 there was one physician serving every 733 persons, one doctor of Chinese medicine per 5,631 persons and one dentist per 2,505 persons. Some 114,179 beds were provided by the 92 public and 501 private hospitals, averaging nearly 57 beds per 10,000 persons. In addition to the 492 public and 17,136 private clinics, there were 369 health stations and 503 health rooms serving residents in the sparsely populated areas. In 2001 acute infectious diseases were no longer the number one killer. Malignant neoplasms, cerebrovascular diseases, heart diseases and accidents and adverse effects were the first four leading causes of death.

Welfare

A universal health insurance scheme came into force in March 1995 as an extension to 13 social insurance plans which cover only 59% of Taiwan's population. Premium shares among the government, employer and insured are varied according to the insured statuses. By the end of 2001 about 21·65m. people or 96% of the population were covered by the National Health Insurance programme.

RELIGION

According to the registered statistics of Municipality, County and City Government there were 827,135 Taoists in 2001 (and 7,714 temples), 382,437 Protestants (and 2,387 churches), 216,495 Buddhists (and 1,966 temples) and 182,814 Catholics (and 728 churches). In Feb. 2010 there was one cardinal.

CULTURE

Broadcasting

At Oct. 2002 there were 174 radio stations, one public and four commercial terrestrial TV services and 65 cable systems. The Public Television Service (PTS) is the public broadcaster. The commercial networks tend to be politically partisan. Cable TV services reach about 85% of the population. In 2006 there were 9·8m. TV receivers. The Broadcasting Corporation of China operates national and regional radio networks; CBS-Radio Taiwan is also a national broadcaster. There are around 170 local radio stations. TV colour is by NTSC.

Press

There were 267 domestic news agencies, 454 newspapers and 7,236 periodicals in 2001.

Tourism

In 2006, 3,520,000 international tourists visited Taiwan. Receipts totalled US$5,136m.

FURTHER READING

Statistical Yearbook of the Republic of China. Annual. *The Republic of China Yearbook*. Annual. *Taiwan Statistical Data Book*. Annual. *Annual Review of Government Administration, Republic of China*. Annual.

Arrigo, L. G., *et al.*, *The Other Taiwan: 1945 to the Present Day*. 1994
Cooper, J. F., *Historical Dictionary of Taiwan*. 1993
Hughes, C., *Taiwan and Chinese Nationalism: National Identity and Status in International Society*. 1997
Lary, Diana, *China's Republic*. 2006
Long, S., *Taiwan: China's Last Frontier*. 1991
Moody, P. R., *Political Change in Taiwan: a Study of Ruling Party Adaptability*. 1992
Smith, H., *Industry Policy in Taiwan and Korea in the 1980s*. 2000
Tsang, S. (ed.) *In the Shadow of China: Political Developments in Taiwan since 1949*. 1994

National library: National Central Library, Taipei (established 1986).
National Statistics Website: http://www.stat.gov.tw

COLOMBIA

República de Colombia
(Republic of Colombia)

Capital: Bogotá
Population estimate, 2010: 46·30m.
GDP per capita, 2007: (PPP$) 8,587
HDI/world rank: 0·807/77

KEY HISTORICAL EVENTS

In 1564 the Spanish Crown appointed a President of New Granada, which included the territories of Colombia, Panama and Venezuela. In 1718 a viceroyalty of New Granada was created. This viceroyalty gained its independence from Spain in 1819, and together with the present territories of Panama, Venezuela and Ecuador was officially constituted as the state of 'Greater Colombia'. This new state lasted only until 1830 when it split up into Venezuela, Ecuador and the republic of New Granada, later renamed *Estados Unidos de Colombia*. The constitution of 5 Aug. 1886, forming the Republic of Colombia, abolished the sovereignty of the states, converting them into departments with governors appointed by the President of the Republic. The department of Panama, however, became an independent country in 1903. Conservatives and Liberals fought a civil war from 1948 to 1957 (*La Violencia)* during which some 300,000 people were killed. Subsequently, powerful drugs lords have made violence endemic. Two Marxist guerrilla forces are active, the Colombian Revolutionary Armed Forces (FARC), and the smaller National Liberation Army (ELN). They are opposed by a well-armed paramilitary organization which emerged after the setting up of rural self-defence groups. Killings and other abuses by paramilitary squads, guerrillas and the military in 1996 made it the most infamous year in the nation's history for human rights violations. On average, ten Colombians were killed every day for political or ideological reasons, while one person disappeared every two days.

There were hopes of a fresh start in 1998 when Andrés Pastrana was elected president. Offers to talk peace were taken up by the rebels and by their paramilitary enemies. But political differences are wide, with FARC demanding sweeping agrarian reform and a redistribution of wealth. FARC controls around 40% of the country including areas which produce the bulk of illegal drugs. Approximately 80% of the cocaine and 60% of the heroin sold in the USA originates in Colombia. In Feb. 2002, following the kidnapping of a prominent senator, President Pastrana broke off three years of peace talks. In May 2002 Álvaro Uribe Vélez became president, but within days of his inauguration, amidst mounting violence, he called a state of emergency.

TERRITORY AND POPULATION

Colombia is bounded in the north by the Caribbean Sea, northwest by Panama, west by the Pacific Ocean, southwest by Ecuador and Peru, northeast by Venezuela and southeast by Brazil. The estimated area is 1,141,748 sq. km (440,829 sq. miles). Population census (2005), 42,888,592; density, 37·6 per sq. km.

The UN gives an estimated population for 2010 of 46·30m.

In 2005, 72·7% lived in urban areas. Bogotá, the capital (census 2005): 6,824,510.

The following table gives census populations for departments and their capitals for 2005:

Departments	*Area (sq. km)*	*Population*	*Capital*	*Population*
Amazonas	109,665	67,726	Leticia	23,811
Antioquia	63,612	5,682,276	Medellín	2,175,681
Arauca	23,818	232,118	Arauca	62,634
Atlántico	3,388	2,166,156	Barranquilla	1,142,312
Bogotá[1]	1,587	6,840,116	—	—
Bolívar	25,978	1,878,993	Cartagena	842,228
Boyacá	23,189	1,255,311	Tunja	146,621
Caldas	7,888	968,740	Manizales	353,312
Caquetá	88,965	420,337	Florencia	121,898
Casanare	44,640	295,353	Yopal	90,218
Cauca	29,308	1,268,937	Popayán	226,978
Cesar	22,905	903,279	Valledupar	299,065
Chocó	46,530	454,030	Quibdó	101,134
Córdoba	25,020	1,467,929	Montería	286,575
Cundinamarca	22,623	2,280,037	Bogotá	—
Guainía	72,238	35,230	Puerto Inírida	10,793
Guaviare	42,327	95,551	San José del Guaviare	34,863
Huila	19,890	1,011,418	Neiva	295,961
La Guajira	20,848	681,575	Riohacha	136,183
Magdalena	23,188	1,149,917	Santa Marta	385,122
Meta	85,635	783,168	Villavicencio	356,464
Nariño	33,268	1,541,956	Pasto	312,377
Norte de Santander	21,658	1,243,975	Cúcuta	567,664
Putumayo	24,885	310,132	Mocoa	25,751
Quindío	1,845	534,552	Armenia	273,114
Risaralda	4,140	897,509	Pereira	371,239
San Andrés y Providencia	44	70,554	San Andrés	48,421
Santander	30,537	1,957,789	Bucaramanga	509,216
Sucre	10,917	772,010	Sincelejo	219,639
Tolima	23,562	1,365,342	Ibagué	468,647
Valle del Cauca	22,140	4,161,425	Cali	2,083,171
Vaupés	65,268	39,279	Mitú	13,066
Vichada	100,242	55,872	Puerto Carreño	10,032

[1]Capital District.

Ethnic divisions (2000): Mestizo 47%, Mulatto 23%, White 20%, Black 6%, Indian 3%, mixed Black-Indian 1%.

The official language is Spanish.

SOCIAL STATISTICS

2000 estimates: births, 734,000; deaths, 184,000. Rates, 2000 estimates (per 1,000 population): births, 17·4; deaths, 4·4. Annual population growth rate, 2000–05, 1·7%. Life expectancy at birth, 2007, was 69·1 years for men and 76·5 years for women. Infant mortality, 2005, 17 per 1,000 live births; fertility rate, 2004, 2·6 children per woman. Abortion is illegal.

CLIMATE

The climate includes equatorial and tropical conditions, according to situation and altitude. In tropical areas, the wettest months are March to May and Oct. to Nov. Bogotá, Jan. 58°F (14·4°C), July 57°F (13·9°C). Annual rainfall 42" (1,052 mm). Barranquilla, Jan. 80°F (26·7°C), July 82°F (27·8°C). Annual rainfall 32" (799 mm). Cali, Jan. 75°F (23·9°C), July 75°F (23·9°C). Annual rainfall 37" (915 mm). Medellín, Jan. 71°F (21·7°C), July 72°F (22·2°C). Annual rainfall 64" (1,606 mm).

CONSTITUTION AND GOVERNMENT

Simultaneously with the presidential elections of May 1990, a referendum was held in which 7m. votes were cast for the establishment of a special assembly to draft a new constitution. Elections were held on 9 Dec. 1990 for this 74-member 'Constitutional Assembly' which operated from Feb. to July 1991. The electorate was 14·2m.; turnout was 3·7m. The Liberals gained 24 seats, M19 (a former guerrilla organization), 19. The Assembly produced a new constitution which came into force on 5 July 1991. It stresses the state's obligation to protect human rights, and establishes constitutional rights to health care, social security and leisure. Indians are allotted two Senate seats. Congress may dismiss ministers, and representatives may be recalled by their electors.

The *President* is elected by direct vote. In Oct. 2005 the constitution was amended to allow a president to be re-elected for a second term. A vice-presidency was instituted in July 1991.

The legislative power rests with a *Congress* of two houses, the *Senate*, of 102 members (including two elected from a special list set aside for American Indian communities), and the *House of Representatives*, of 166 members, both elected for four years by proportional representation. Congress meets annually at Bogotá on 20 July.

National Anthem

'O! Gloria inmarcesible' ('Oh unfading Glory!'); words by R. Núñez, tune by O. Síndici.

GOVERNMENT CHRONOLOGY

Heads of State since 1945. (PLC = Liberal Party; PSC = Colombian Conservative Party/Colombian Social Conservative Party; n/p = non-partisan)

Presidents

1945–46	PLC	Alberto Lleras Camargo
1946–50	PSC	Luis Mariano Ospina Pérez
1950–51	PSC	Laureano Eleuterio Gómez Castro
1951–53	PSC	Roberto Urdaneta Arbeláez
1953	PSC	Laureano Eleuterio Gómez Castro
1953–57	military	Gustavo Rojas Pinilla

Military Junta

1957–58	Gabriel Paris Gordillo (chair); Rubén Piedrahíta Arango; Deogracias Fonseca Espinosa; Luis Ernesto Ordóñez Castillo; Rafael Navas Pardo

Presidents

1958–62	PLC	Alberto Lleras Camargo
1962–66	PSC	Guillermo León Valencia Muñoz
1966–70	PLC	Carlos Lleras Restrepo
1970–74	PSC	Misael Eduardo Pastrana Borrero
1974–78	PLC	Alfonso López Michelsen
1978–82	PLC	Julio César Turbay Ayala
1982–86	PSC	Belisario Betancur Cuartas
1986–90	PLC	Virgilio Barco Vargas
1990–94	PLC	César Augusto Gaviria Trujillo
1994–98	PLC	Ernesto Samper Pizano
1998–2002	PSC	Andrés Pastrana Arango
2002–	n/p	Álvaro Uribe Vélez

RECENT ELECTIONS

Presidential elections were held on 28 May 2006, in which incumbent Álvaro Uribe Vélez (ind.) won with 62·3% of votes cast, against 22·0% for Carlos Gaviria Díaz (Democratic Alternative Pole Party), 11·8% for Horacio Serpa (Colombian Liberal Party) and 1·2% for Antanas Mockus Sivickas (Indigenous Social Alliance Movement). Three other candidates received less than 1% of the vote each. Turnout was 45·1%.

Congressional elections were held on 12 March 2006. In elections to the House of Representatives the Colombian Liberal Party won 38 seats, the Social National Unity Party 30, the Colombian Conservative Party 29, the Radical Change Party 20, the Democratic Alternative Pole Party 9, the Citizens' Convergence Party 8 and the Wings Colombia Team 7, with the remaining seats going to smaller parties. In the elections to the Senate the Social National Unity Party won 20 seats, the Colombian Conservative Party 18, the Colombian Liberal Party 17, the Radical Change Party 15 and the Democratic Alternative Pole Party 11, with smaller parties accounting for the remainder.

Presidential elections were scheduled to take place on 30 May 2010.

CURRENT ADMINISTRATION

President: Álvaro Uribe Vélez; b. 1952 (ind.; sworn in 7 Aug. 2002 and re-elected in May 2006).

Vice President: Francisco Santos Calderón.

In March 2010 the government comprised:

Minister of Agriculture and Rural Development: Andrés Fernández Acosta. *Communications:* María del Rosario Guerra de la Espriella. *Culture:* Paula Marcela Moreno Zapata. *Defence:* Gabriel Silva Luján. *Environment, Housing and Territorial Development:* Carlos Costa Posada. *Finance:* Óscar Iván Zuluaga. *Foreign Relations:* Jaime Bermúdez Merizalde. *Interior and Justice:* Fabio Valencia Cossio. *Mines and Energy:* Hernán Martínez Torres. *National Education:* Cecilia María Vélez White. *Social Welfare:* Diego Palacio Betancourt. *Trade, Industry and Tourism:* Luis Guillermo Plata. *Transport:* Andrés Uriel Gallego Henao.

Office of the President (limited English):
http://www.presidencia.gov.co

CURRENT LEADERS

Álvaro Uribe Vélez

Position

President

Introduction

Álvaro Uribe Vélez was elected president of Colombia in May 2002 in an outright first-round victory. An independent candidate, his hardline mandate of combating left-wing guerrillas and right-wing paramilitaries found popularity with the electorate after attempts at peace talks by his predecessor Andrés Pastrana had failed. He was re-elected in May 2006.

Early Life

Uribe was born on 4 July 1952 in Medellín. After completing a law degree at the Universidad de Antioquia, he studied management at Harvard University in the USA and worked as an associate professor at Oxford University in England.

At the age of 24 he began working for Medellín's public works, following which he was secretary general of the labour ministry (1977–78), worked for the civil aeronautics department (1980–82) and was then mayor of Medellín. His career in his native region continued between 1995–97 when he served as governor of the Antioquia region. As such he streamlined the local government department and increased spending on education, health and road infrastructure. He set up the 'Convivirs' security networks which diminished the presence of the left-wing guerrilla Fuerzas Armadas Revolucionarias de Colombia (FARC; Colombian Revolutionary Armed Forces) in Antioquia. But he was criticized for allowing the right-wing paramilitary Autodefensas Unidas de Colombia (AUC; United Self-Defence Forces of Colombia) to take advantage of the reduced FARC profile.

Uribe's hardline view on guerrilla activity in part stems from his father's assassination in 1983 by FARC members during a bungled kidnapping attempt. Combating terrorism was made the central issue of his 2002 presidential campaign. Peace talks between incumbent president Pastrana and FARC leaders had failed to stem violence and kidnappings, and Uribe's pledge to forcefully oppose terrorist activity was well received among voters. Violence increased in the lead-up to the polls, including numerous assassination attempts on Uribe and the kidnapping of the independent candidate Ingrid Betancourt. The election itself passed relatively peacefully and, with a turnout of 47%, Uribe beat the Colombian Liberal Party candidate Horacio Serpa by 53% of votes to 32%. Despite a military presence of 20,000, Uribe's inauguration in Aug. 2002 was marred by explosions around Bogotá which killed 20 people and injured 60.

Career in Office

On election Uribe planned to double the size of the army and create a 1m.-strong civil militia. He also sought to amend the constitution to allow for martial law and states of siege. His plans received a positive response from the USA, with the possibility of increased military aid, although FARC promised to resist the government forces. Unlike his predecessor, Uribe demanded a full FARC ceasefire and halt in kidnappings before any peace talks could be brokered. FARC demanded control of two southern provinces, Caquetá and Putumayo, in return. Although Uribe also targeted terrorism by the smaller left-wing Ejército de Liberación Nacional (ELN; National Liberation Army) and the AUC, the latter responded positively to the president's election and formal peace talks began in mid-2003, leading to an AUC commitment to demobilize in exchange for amnesty.

In July 2005 the 'justice and peace' law won congressional approval, making generous concessions to illegal fighters in return for laying down their arms. Human rights groups have been critical of the law, however, viewing it as a charter of impunity for war criminals. The government announced in April 2006 that the demobilization of the AUC had been completed.

In 2007 Uribe offered to free guerrilla prisoners and start peace talks with FARC in exchange for the release of hostages, and invited President Hugo Chávez of Venezuela to try and broker a deal. However, Uribe ended Chávez's involvement in Nov. after a series of apparent diplomatic breaches. In 2008 the release of several high-profile FARC hostages was secured and there were signs of reconciliation between Uribe and Chávez, but links with Ecuador were seriously undermined by a cross-border Colombian strike against a FARC target in Ecuadorian territory. Relations with Venezuela were again strained in 2009 by Uribe's agreement to allow US armed forces to use Colombian military bases for joint operations against drug trafficking and guerrillas and by Venezuela's alleged supply of arms to FARC.

In Oct. 2005 the Constitutional Court had upheld an amendment to the constitution allowing presidential re-election and the following month set out conditions under which an incumbent could stand, so allowing Uribe to campaign for a second term in elections which he won in May 2006. He was formally inaugurated in Aug. that year. Then, in Sept. 2009, the House of Representatives approved the final text of a law to call a referendum on changing the constitution to allow Uribe to run for an unprecedented third consecutive term in presidential elections scheduled for May 2010. However, the Constitutional Court blocked the plans after ruling that they were unconstitutional.

Uribe's other aims during his presidency have included tackling corruption, targeting crime and drug trafficking and, on his Antioquia model, reducing expenditure on public administration. The drug trade has been closely linked to guerrilla and paramilitary activities, and in May 2008 the government extradited 14 paramilitary leaders to the USA to stand trial on trafficking charges.

DEFENCE

Selective conscription at 18 years is for two years' service. In 2006 defence expenditure totalled US$5,377m. (US$123 per capita), representing 4·0% of GDP. In 1985 expenditure had been US$823m. Colombia is the second largest military spender in South America, after Brazil.

Army

Personnel (2007) 217,000 (conscripts, 173,000); reserves number 54,700. The national police numbered (2007) 136,100.

Navy

The Navy has two diesel powered submarines, two midget submarines and four small frigates. Naval personnel in 2007 totalled 27,600. There are also two brigades of marines numbering 14,000. An air arm operates light reconnaissance aircraft.

The Navy's main ocean base is Cartagena with Pacific bases at Buenaventura and Málaga. There are in addition numerous river bases.

Air Force

The Air Force has been independent of the Army and Navy since 1943, when its reorganization began with US assistance. It has 115 combat capable aircraft and 31 attack helicopters. There are six combat air commands plus a command responsible for air operations in a specific geographical area. Total strength (2006), 8,600 personnel, including 1,900 conscripts.

INTERNATIONAL RELATIONS

Colombia is a member of the UN, World Bank, IMF and several other UN specialized agencies, WTO, IOM, Andean Community, ACS, Inter-American Development Bank, SELA, LAIA, OAS, UNASUR and Antarctic Treaty.

It was announced in Aug. 2000 that Colombia would receive US$1·3bn. in anti drug-trafficking aid (mostly of a military nature) from the USA as part of 'Plan Colombia', a five-year long series of projects intended to serve as a foundation for stability and peace of which the focal point is the fight against drugs. By May 2005 the USA had given aid amounting to US$4·5bn.

In March 2008 Colombian forces killed a high-level member of the rebel FARC movement during an unsanctioned raid over the Ecuadorian border. A week-long diplomatic incident ensued, in which both Ecuador and Venezuela massed military personnel on their respective borders with Colombia.

ECONOMY

In 2006 agriculture accounted for 12·0% of GDP, industry 35·7% and services 52·3%.

Overview
Colombia's economic progress has been blighted by guerrilla insurgencies, drug cartels, human rights violations and an unsustainable fiscal deficit. The country produces 80% of the world's cocaine and a third of the world's marijuana. It is estimated that trade in illegal drugs accounts for 3% of GDP.

Colombia has a diversified economic base. The second largest exporter of coffee in the world, it is endowed with substantial oil reserves and is a major producer of gold, silver, emeralds, platinum and coal. Until 1996 Colombia enjoyed relatively high and stable rates of growth but in 1998–99 the economy suffered its worst economic crisis since the 1930s as poverty and unemployment escalated.

Since the 1970s violence and crime have significantly diminished the economy. The World Bank estimates that ongoing conflict in the last 20 years has reduced growth by 2% per year, reducing GDP per capita by two-thirds. After 20 years of sustained poverty reduction, the situation reversed in the late 1990s with over 65% of the population below the poverty line by mid-2000.

More recently growth has been strong, reaching 7·7% in 2007, its highest rate since the late 1970s. Unemployment and poverty remain high but are falling, while inflation is above the official government target of 3·5–4·5% owing to high demand and rising food prices. The external current account deficit is among the highest in the region at 4% of GDP. The IMF has advised that tighter fiscal policy could alleviate overheating and reduce the external deficit.

Currency
The unit of currency is the *Colombian peso* (COP) of 100 *centavos*. Inflation rates (based on IMF statistics):

1999	*2000*	*2001*	*2002*	*2003*	*2004*	*2005*	*2006*	*2007*	*2008*
10·9%	9·2%	8·0%	6·3%	7·1%	5·9%	5·0%	4·3%	5·5%	7·0%

In Sept. 2009 gold reserves were 221,000 troy oz and foreign exchange reserves US$22,926m. Total money supply was 41,403bn. pesos in Aug. 2009.

Budget
In 2003 budgetary central government revenue was 42,446bn. pesos (34,476bn. pesos in 2002) and expenditure 51,849bn. pesos (43,315bn. pesos in 2002).

VAT is 16%.

Performance
Real GDP growth rates (based on IMF statistics):

1999	*2000*	*2001*	*2002*	*2003*	*2004*	*2005*	*2006*	*2007*	*2008*
–4·2%	2·9%	2·2%	2·5%	4·6%	4·7%	5·7%	6·9%	7·5%	2·5%

GDP shrank by 4·2% in 1999 when Colombia experienced its worst recession since the 1930s. Total GDP in 2008 was US$242·3bn.

Banking and Finance
In 1923 the Bank of the Republic (*General Manager*, José Darío Uribe Escobar) was inaugurated as a semi-official central bank, with the exclusive privilege of issuing banknotes. Its note issues must be covered by a reserve in gold of foreign exchange of 25% of their value. Interest rates of 40% plus are imposed.

There are 24 commercial banks, of which 18 are private or mixed, and six official. There is also an Agricultural, Industrial and Mining Credit Institute, a Central Mortgage Bank and a Social Savings Bank. Demand deposits totalled 11,256bn. pesos in Dec. 2002. The Superintendencia Bancaria acts as a supervising body.

There are stock exchanges in Bogotá, Medellín and Cali.

Weights and Measures
The metric system is standard but traditional Spanish weights and measures are still used, e.g. *botella* (750 grammes), *galón* (5 *botellas*), *vara* (70 cm) and *fanegada* (1,000 square varas).

ENERGY AND NATURAL RESOURCES

Environment
In 2008 Colombia's carbon dioxide emissions from the consumption and flaring of fossil fuels were the equivalent of 1·5 tonnes per capita. An *Environmental Performance Index* compiled in 2008 ranked Colombia ninth in the world, with 88·3%. The index examined various factors in six areas—air pollution, biodiversity and habitat, climate change, environmental health, productive natural resources and water resources.

Electricity
Installed capacity of electric power (2004) was 13·8m. kW. In 2003 production was 47·68bn. kWh and consumption per capita 1,045 kWh. Colombia exported 1·68bn. kWh of electricity in 2004.

Oil and Gas
Oil production (2008) 30·5m. tonnes. Natural gas production in 2008 totalled 9·1bn. cu. metres. In 2008 there were proven oil reserves of 1·4bn. bbls and proven natural gas reserves of 110bn. cu. metres.

Minerals
Production (2005): gold, 35,785 kg; silver, 7,142 kg; platinum, 1,082 kg. Other important minerals include: copper, lead, mercury, manganese, nickel and emeralds (of which Colombia accounts for about half of world production).

Coal production (2004): 53·69m. tonnes; iron ore (2005): 498,623 tonnes; salt production (2005): 473,996 tonnes.

Agriculture
There is a wide range of climate and, consequently, crops. In 2002 there were 2·29m. ha. of arable land and 1·56m. ha. of permanent crops.

In 2002, 19·3% of the economically active population were engaged in agriculture. Production, 2002 (in 1,000 tonnes): sugarcane, 35,800; plantains, 2,921; potatoes, 2,841; rice, 2,347; cassava, 1,768; bananas, 1,424; maize, 1,189; coffee, 691. Coca was cultivated in 2005 on approximately 144,000 ha., up from 34,000 ha. in 1988. Estimated coca leaf production in 2005 totalled 170,730 tonnes, making Colombia the world's largest producer of coca leaves, the raw material for cocaine. Production of cocaine was estimated at 640 tonnes.

Livestock (2002): 24·76m. cattle; 2·65m. horses; 2·26m. sheep; 2·23m. pigs; 1·10m. goats; 723,000 asses; 115m. chickens.

Livestock products, 2002: beef and veal, 6·76m. tonnes; poultry meat, 629,000 tonnes; pork, bacon and ham, 110,000 tonnes; milk, 6,021,000 tonnes; eggs, 314,000 tonnes.

Forestry
In 2005 the area under forests was 60·73m. ha., or 58·5% of the total land area. Timber production in 2007 was 10·44m. cu. metres.

Fisheries
Total catch (2004) was 111,860 tonnes, of which 75% was from marine waters.

INDUSTRY
Production, 2004 unless otherwise indicated (in tonnes): cement (2001), 6,776,000; petrol, 4,963,000; distillate fuel oil, 3,689,000; residual fuel oil, 3,330,000; sugar (2002), 2,522,637; steel ingots (1998), 264,466; soft drinks (2001), 1,832·5m. litres; beer (2001), 1,421·3m. litres; passenger cars (1998), 49,807 units; industrial vehicles (1998), 14,162 units.

Labour

The economically active workforce in 2001 was 18·65m., of which 16·62m. were employed. The main areas of activity in 2001 were: wholesale and retail trade, restaurants and hotels (employing 4·19m. persons); community, social and personal services (3·74m.); and agriculture, hunting, forestry and fishing (3·49m.). The unemployment rate in 2002 was 15·7%.

INTERNATIONAL TRADE

Foreign companies are liable for basic income tax of 30% and surtax of 7·5%. Since 1993 tax on profit remittance has started at 12%, reducing (except for oil companies) to 7% after three years. Foreign debt was US$37,656m. in 2005.

The Group of Three (G-3) free trade pact with Mexico and Venezuela came into effect on 1 Jan. 1995. In Nov. 2006 Colombia and the USA signed a free trade agreement that eliminates tariffs on each other's goods, but it has yet to be ratified and faces opposition in the USA from the Democrats.

Imports and Exports

In US$1m.:

	2003	*2004*	*2005*	*2006*	*2007*
Imports c.i.f.	13,881	17,100	21,204	26,162	32,897
Exports f.o.b.	13,092	16,730	21,190	24,391	29,991

Major import suppliers, 2006: USA (26·6%), Mexico (8·8%), China (8·5%), Brazil (7·2%). Major export markets, 2006: USA (40·8%), Venezuela (11·1%), Ecuador (5·1%), Spain (3·0%).

Main imports in 2006 were (in US$1m.): machinery and transport equipment (10,508·9), chemicals and related products (5,230·2), food and live animals (1,890·2), iron and steel (1,257·5), textile yarn and fabrics (863·5). Main exports in 2006 were (in US$1m.): petroleum and petroleum products (6,309·8), coal (2,807·2), chemicals and related products (2,024·4), coffee and coffee substitutes (1,633·7), machinery and transport equipment (1,519·8).

COMMUNICATIONS

Roads

Total length of roads was 164,278 km in 2006 (including 14,143 km of main roads). In 2005 there were 2,686,000 vehicles in use, including 1,607,000 passenger cars. There were 5,486 road accident fatalities in 2006.

Rail

The National Railways (2,532 km of route, 914 mm gauge) went into liquidation in 1990 prior to takeover of services and obligations by three new public companies in 1992. Freight tonne-km came to 374m. in 2002. Total rail track, 3,304 km. A metro system operates in Medellín.

Civil Aviation

There are international airports at Barranquilla, Bogotá (Eldorado), Cali, Cartagena, Medellín and San Andrés. The main Colombian airline is Avianca. In 2005 scheduled traffic of Colombian-based carriers flew 132·5m. km and carried 9,933,100 passengers. The busiest airport is Bogotá, which in 2000 handled 7,154,312 passengers (5,234,807 on domestic flights) and 372,957 tonnes of freight.

Shipping

Vessels entering Colombian ports in 1995 unloaded 13,806,000 tonnes of imports and loaded 26,284,000 tonnes of exports. In 2000 vessels totalling 52,442,000 NRT entered ports and vessels totalling 50,787,000 NRT cleared. The merchant marine totalled 68,000 GRT in 2002, including oil tankers 6,000 GRT.

The Magdalena River is subject to drought, and navigation is always impeded during the dry season, but it is an important artery of passenger and goods traffic. The river is navigable for 1,400 km; steamers ascend to La Dorada, 953 km from Barranquilla.

Telecommunications

In 2008 there were 8,054,000 main (fixed) telephone lines. In the same year mobile phone subscribers numbered 41,365,000 (919·0 per 1,000 persons). There were 2,488,000 PCs in use in 2006 and 17,330,000 internet users in 2008.

Postal Services

In 2003 there were 2,174 post offices.

SOCIAL INSTITUTIONS

Justice

The July 1991 constitution introduced the offices of public prosecutor and public defence. The Supreme Court, at Bogotá, of 20 members, is divided into three chambers—civil cassation (six), criminal cassation (eight), labour cassation (six). Each of the 61 judicial districts has a superior court with various sub-dependent tribunals of lower juridical grade. In Dec. 1997 the constitution was amended to allow the extradition of Colombian nationals.

In 2006 there were 17,479 murders, continuing a downward trend since the high of 28,837 in 2002. Colombia's murder rate, at 39 per 100,000 persons, although declining is still among the highest in the world. In 2008 the reported number of kidnappings totalled 437, down from 3,572 in 2000.

Colombia abolished the death penalty in 1997. The population in penal institutions in May 2001 was 54,034 (126 per 100,000 of national population).

Education

Education between the ages of five and 15 became compulsory in 1991. Schools are both state and privately controlled. In 2007 there were 49,538 teaching staff for 1,081,343 children in pre-primary schools; 187,821 teaching staff for 5,298,567 pupils in primary schools; and 4,657,360 pupils with 164,484 teaching staff in secondary schools. In 2008 there were 44,757 pre-primary schools, 57,711 primary schools and 18,412 secondary schools.

There were 32 public universities in 2007. The National University of Colombia (Universidad Nacional de Colombia), founded in 1867, is the leading institution in the tertiary sector. Colombia also has many private universities and colleges of art and music. In 2007 there were 1,372,674 students in total in higher education and 88,337 academic staff.

Adult literacy in 2003 was 94·2% (93·7% among males and 94·6% among females).

In 2007 public expenditure on education came to 5·1% of GNI and represented 12·6% of total government expenditure.

Health

In 2003 there were 1,165 hospitals with 49,000 beds. Medical personnel (2002) was as follows: doctors, 58,761; dentists, 33,951; nurses and midwives, 103,158.

Welfare

The retirement age is 60 (men), or 55 (women); to be eligible for a state pension 1,000 weeks of contributions are required. The minimum social insurance pension is equal to the minimum wage. If a private pension is less than the minimum pension set by law, the government makes up the difference.

Unemployment benefit is a month's wage for every year of employment.

RELIGION

The religion is Roman Catholic (39·59m. adherents in 2001), with the Cardinal Archbishop of Bogotá as Primate of Colombia and nine other archbishoprics. There are also 44 bishops, 8 apostolic vicars, 5 apostolic prefects and 2 prelates. In Feb. 2010 there were two cardinals. Other forms of religion are permitted so long as their exercise is 'not contrary to Christian morals or the law'. In 2001 there were 3·48m. followers of other religions.

CULTURE

World Heritage Sites

Colombia's heritage sites as classified by UNESCO (with year entered on list) are: the Port, Fortresses and Group of Monuments, Cartagena (1984)—on the Caribbean coast, Cartagena was one of the first cities to be founded in South America and has the most extensive fortifications in the continent; Los Katíos National Park (1994) covers 72,000 ha. in northwest Colombia; founded 200 km inland on the River Magdalena in the 1530s, the Historic Centre of Santa Cruz de Mompox (1995), or Mompós, was a focal point for colonization and a vital trade post between the Caribbean coast and the interior—its colonial aspect has been preserved; the National Archaeological Park of Tierradentro (1995) in the southwest contains statues and elaborately decorated underground tombs dating from the 6th–10th centuries; the San Agustín Archaeological Park (1995) protects religious monuments and sculptures from the 1st–8th centuries; the Malpelo Fauna and Flora sanctuary (2006) provides a critical habitat for internationally threatened marine species.

Broadcasting

Señal Colombia and Radio Nacional de Colombia are state-run TV and radio networks. There are also a number of commercial TV services, and hundreds of private radio stations registered with the Ministry of Communications. In 2006 there were 13·07m. TV sets (colour by NTSC).

Cinema

In 2004 there were 406 cinema screens; total admissions in 2004 were 16·2m.

Press

There were 23 daily newspapers in 2002, with daily circulation totalling 1·1m.

Tourism

In 2004 there were 791,000 foreign tourists (including 618,000 from elsewhere in the Americas and 156,000 from Europe), bringing revenue of US$1,340m.

DIPLOMATIC REPRESENTATIVES

Of Colombia in the United Kingdom (Flat 3a, 3 Hans Cres., London, SW1X 0LN)
Ambassador: Dr José Mauricio Rodríguez Múnera.

Of the United Kingdom in Colombia (Edificio Ing. Barings, Carrera 9 No 76–49, Piso 8, Bogotá)
Ambassador: John Dew.

Of Colombia in the USA (2118 Leroy Pl., NW, Washington, D.C., 20008)
Ambassador: María Carolina Barco Isakson.

Of the USA in Colombia (Carrera 45 # 22D-45, Bogotá)
Ambassador: William Brownfield.

Of Colombia to the United Nations
Ambassador: Claudia Blum.

Of Colombia to the European Union
Ambassador: Carlos Holmes Trujillo García.

FURTHER READING

Departamento Administrativo Nacional de Estadística. *Boletín de Estadística.* Monthly.

Dudley, Steven, *Walking Ghosts: Murder and Guerrilla Politics in Colombia.* 2004

Hylton, Forrest, *Evil Hour in Colombia.* 2006

Palacios, Marco, *Between Legitimacy and Violence: A History of Colombia, 1875–2002.* 2006

Thorp, R., *Economic Management and Economic Development in Peru and Colombia.* 1991

National Statistical Office: Departamento Administrativo Nacional de Estadística (DANE), AA 80043, Zona Postal 611, Bogotá.
Website (limited English): http://www.dane.gov.co

COMOROS

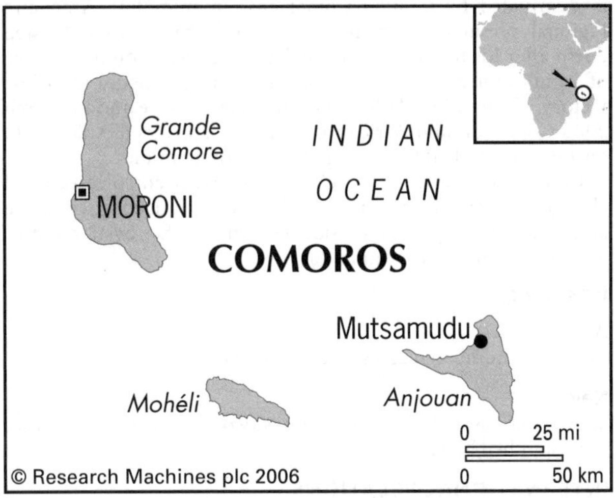

Union des Îles Comores
(Union of Comoros Islands)

Capital: Moroni
Population estimate, 2010: 691,000
GDP per capita, 2007: (PPP$) 1,143
HDI/world rank: 0·576/139

KEY HISTORICAL EVENTS

The three islands forming the present state became French protectorates at the end of the 19th century and were proclaimed colonies in 1912. With neighbouring Mayotte they were administratively attached to Madagascar from 1914 until 1947 when the four islands became a French Overseas Territory, achieving internal self-government in Dec. 1961. In referendums held on each island on 22 Dec. 1974, the three western islands voted overwhelmingly for independence, while Mayotte voted to remain French. There have been more than 20 coups or attempted takeovers since independence, with recent years marked by political disruption. In 1997 the islands of Anjouan and Mohéli attempted to secede from the federation.

In April 1999 an agreement was brokered on a federal structure for the three main islands—Grand Comore, Anjouan and Mohéli—to be known as the Union of Comoros Islands. However, the delegates from Anjouan did not sign the agreement. Violence broke out in the capital, Moroni, against Anjouans living there. A military coup followed on 30 April 1999, led by Col. Azaly Assoumani. He subsequently dissolved the government and the constitution, declaring a transitional government.

TERRITORY AND POPULATION

The Comoros consist of three islands in the Indian Ocean between the African mainland and Madagascar with a total area of 1,862 sq. km (719 sq. miles). The population at the 2003 census was 575,660 (285,590 males), giving a density of 309 per sq. km.

The UN gives an estimated population for 2010 of 691,000.

In 2005, 63·0% of the population were rural.

The areas, populations and chief towns of the islands are:

	Area (sq. km)	*Population (2003 census)*	*Chief town*
Njazídja (Grande Comore)	1,148	296,177	Moroni
Nzwani (Anjouan)	424	243,732	Mutsamudu
Mwali (Mohéli)	290	35,751	Fomboni

Estimated population of the chief towns (2002): Moroni, 40,275; Mutsamudu, 21,558; Domoni, 13,254; Fomboni, 13,053.

The indigenous population are a mixture of Malagasy, African, Malay and Arab peoples; the vast majority speak Comorian, an Arabized dialect of Swahili and one of the three official languages, but a small proportion speak one of the other official languages, French and Arabic, or Makua (a Bantu language).

SOCIAL STATISTICS

2000 births (estimates), 26,600; deaths, 6,000. Estimated birth rate in 2000 was 37·7 per 1,000 population; estimated death rate, 8·5. Annual population growth rate, 1992–2002, 3·0%. Infant mortality, 53 per 1,000 live births (2005). Expectation of life in 2007 was 62·8 years among men and 67·2 among females. Fertility rate, 2004, 4·7 children per woman.

CLIMATE

There is a tropical climate, affected by Indian monsoon winds from the north, which gives a wet season from Nov. to April. Moroni, Jan. 81°F (27·2°C), July 75°F (23·9°C). Annual rainfall, 113" (2,825 mm).

CONSTITUTION AND GOVERNMENT

At a referendum on 23 Dec. 2001, 77% of voters approved a new constitution that keeps the three islands as one country while granting each one greater autonomy.

The *President of the Union* is Head of State.

There used to be a *Federal Assembly* comprised of 42 democratically elected officials and a 15-member *Senate* chosen by an electoral college, but these were dissolved after the 1999 coup. A new 33-member *Federal Parliament* was established following the elections of April 2004. In 2004 there were 15 deputies selected by the individual islands' parliaments and 18 by universal suffrage but this was changed to nine selected by the individual islands' parliaments and 24 by universal suffrage for the 2009 elections.

National Anthem

'Udzima wa ya Masiwa' ('The union of the islands'); words by S. H. Abderamane, tune by K. Abdallah and S. H. Abderamane.

RECENT ELECTIONS

In the first round of presidential elections held on 16 April 2006 on Anjouan, Ahmed Abdallah Mohamed Sambi won 23·7% of the votes, Mohamed Djaanfari 13·1%, Ibrahim Halidi 10·4% and Caabi El-Yachroutu 9·6%. Turnout was 54·9%. The top three candidates qualified for the run-off election on 14 May, in which Ahmed Abdallah Mohamed Sambi gained 58·0% of votes cast, against 28·3% for Ibrahim Halidi and 13·7% for Mohamed Djaanfari. Turnout in the run-off was 57·3%.

Parliamentary elections were held on 6 and 20 Dec. 2009. The pro-presidential party and its allies won 20 of 33 seats while the opposition won four. The remaining nine were allocated to regional assembly representatives.

CURRENT ADMINISTRATION

President of the Union: Ahmed Abdallah Mohamed Sambi; b. 1958 (sworn in 26 May 2006).

In March 2010 the government comprised:

Vice President for Agriculture, Fisheries and Environment, Energy, Industry and Handicrafts: Idi Nadhoim. *Vice President for Finance and Budget, and the Professional Status of Women:* Ikililou Dhoinine.

Chief of the Cabinet, in Charge of Defence: Mohamed Bacar Dossar.

Minister of Foreign Affairs and Co-operation, in Charge of Comorians Abroad, Francophonie and Relations with the Arab World: Ahmed Ben Saïd Djaffar. *Economy, Labour, Employment and International Trade, in Charge of Parliamentary Relations:* Hassane Ahmed el Barwane. *Justice, Prison Administration, Islamic Affairs and Keeper of the Seals:* Abdouroihmane Ibrahim. *Interior and Information:* Bourhane Hamidou. *National Education, Research, Culture, Arts and Government Spokesman:* Kamalidine Afraitane. *Health, Solidarity and Gender:* Hodhoaer Inzouddine. *Transport, Tourism and Investments:* Mikidar Houmadi. *Land Management, Infrastructure, Town Planning and Housing:* Mohamed Larif Oukacha. *Civil Service, Administrative and Institutional Reform, and Human Rights:* Fouad Ben Mohadji. *Post and Telecommunications, and in Charge of Communication and the Promotion of New Technology:* Djae Ahamada.

Office of the President (French only): http://www.beit-salam.km

CURRENT LEADERS

Ahmed Abdallah Mohamed Sambi

Position
President

Introduction
Known as the 'Ayatollah' after studying in Iran, Ahmed Abdallah Sambi was elected president in May 2006, marking the country's first peaceful handover of power. A moderate Islamist, Sambi defeated two other candidates from the island of Anjouan, in accordance with the federal power-rotation agreement between the three islands.

Early Life
Ahmed Abdallah Mohamed Sambi was born on the 5 June 1958 at Mutsamadu on the Comorian island of Anjouan (Nzwani), where he attended primary and secondary school. He later studied in Saudi Arabia, Sudan and Iran. In 1980 he launched the first Comorian periodical, *Retour à la Source*. His preaching took him to Madagascar in 1982 and Mauritius in 1984 before he returned to the Comoros in 1986. On Anjouan he founded a girls' school and organized evening lectures which were banned by the police and led to his arrest. In 1987 he lectured on Grande Comore (Njazídja) and met Comorian scholars in Cairo.

In 1990 Sambi entered politics, helping to form the Front National pour la Justice, which supported Mohamed Taki Abdoulkarim (who later became president). In 1993 he was active in raising money for Bosnian Muslims and the following year opposed the establishment of diplomatic relations with Israel. He was elected to the then Federal Assembly in Dec. 1996 and was appointed president of the Law Commission. Sambi opposed the central government's crackdown on Anjouan in Aug. 1997 and was forced to resign his seat in the Assembly. Despite urging Anjouan's separatists to negotiate, he fled to Madagascar in Jan. 1999 amid accusations of separatist sympathies. He went into manufacturing in 2000, producing mattresses and perfume. In May 2005 he announced his candidacy for the presidency and came first in the April 2006 primary, held only on Anjouan.

Career in Office
Supervised by South African peacekeepers, Sambi defeated two secular candidates, Deputy Speaker Mohamed Djaanfari and the veteran politician Ibrahim Halidi, in a national vote in May 2006, although his rivals alleged fraud. Sambi has voiced support for the reinstitution of an Islamic state in the Comoros, sparking fears of Islamic radicalization and restrictions on women's freedoms. Doubts have been raised concerning the authority of an Anjouanais over the central government bureaucracy, which is dominated by Grande Comorians. In mid-2007 Anjouan's regional president Mohamed Bacar, who had refused to step down after his five-year term, held an illegal election in defiance of Sambi and the federal government and claimed a landslide victory. Negotiations failed to resolve the impasse and in March 2008 Comorian and African Union troops invaded Anjouan to oust Bacar who fled to the French island of Réunion.

In May 2009 voters in a referendum approved constitutional changes to streamline the complex decentralized governance system and to extend the president's term of office by 12 months, allowing Sambi to serve until 2011.

DEFENCE

Army
The Army numbered an estimated 1,060 in 2008.

Navy
There is no navy. The Army operates two small patrol boats that were supplied by Japan in 1982.

INTERNATIONAL RELATIONS

The Comoros is a member of the UN, World Bank, IMF and several other UN specialized agencies, International Organization of the Francophonie, Islamic Development Bank, OIC, African Development Bank, COMESA, League of Arab States and is an ACP member state of the ACP-EU relationship.

ECONOMY

Agriculture accounted for 45·2% of GDP in 2006 and industry 11·8%.

Currency
The unit of currency is the *Comorian franc* (KMF) of 100 *centimes*. It is pegged to the euro at 491·96775 *Comorian francs* to the euro. Foreign exchange reserves were US$92m. in July 2005, total money supply was 24,096m. Comorian francs and gold reserves were 1,000 troy oz. There was inflation of 4·5% in 2007 and 4·8% in 2008.

Budget
Revenues in 2005 were 30·5bn. Comorian francs and expenditures 30·4bn. Comorian francs.

VAT is 10%.

Performance
Real GDP growth was 0·5% in 2007 and 1·0% in 2008. In 2008 total GDP was US$0·5bn.

Banking and Finance
The Central Bank is the bank of issue. Chief commercial banks include the Banque Internationale des Comores, the Banque de Développement des Comores and the Banque pour l'Industrie et le Commerce-Comores.

ENERGY AND NATURAL RESOURCES

Environment
Carbon dioxide emissions from the consumption and flaring of fossil fuels were the equivalent of 0·2 tonnes per capita in 2008.

Electricity
In 2004 estimated installed capacity was 4,000 kW. Production was approximately 20m. kWh in 2004; consumption per capita was an estimated 31 kWh in 2004.

Agriculture
80% of the economically active population depends upon agriculture, which (including fishing, hunting and forestry)

contributed 41% to GDP in 2002. There were about 80,000 ha. of arable land in 2002 and 52,000 ha. of permanent crops. The chief product was formerly sugarcane, but now vanilla, copra, maize and other food crops, cloves and essential oils (citronella, ylang-ylang, lemongrass) are the most important products. Production (2002 in 1,000 tonnes): coconuts, 77; bananas, 61; cassava, 55; rice, 17; taro, 9; copra, 8; sweet potatoes, 5.

Livestock (2003): goats, 115,000; cattle, 52,000; sheep, 21,000; asses, 5,000.

Forestry
In 2005 the area under forest was 5,000 ha., or 2·9% of the total land area. The forested area has been severely reduced because of the shortage of cultivable land and ylang-ylang production. In 2007, 9,000 cu. metres of timber were cut.

Fisheries
Fishing is on an individual basis, without modern equipment. The catch totalled 15,070 tonnes in 2005.

INDUSTRY
Branches include perfume distillation, textiles, furniture, jewellery, soft drinks and the processing of vanilla and copra.

Labour
The workforce in 1996 was 286,000 (58% males).

INTERNATIONAL TRADE
Total foreign debt was US$291m. in 2007.

Imports and Exports
In 2006 imports amounted to US$101·4m. (up from US$65·0m. in 2004) and exports to US$2·6m. (down from US$7·9m. in 2004).

Main import suppliers, 2006: United Arab Emirates, 30·7%; France, 21·3%; South Africa, 9·5%. Main export markets, 2006: France, 53·8%; India, 15·4%; Germany, 11·5%. The principal imports are machinery and transport equipment (35·0% of total imports in 2006), food and live animals (25·1% in 2006), cement (6·6% in 2006), petroleum and petroleum products, chemicals and related products, and iron and steel. Main exports are vanilla (53·8% in 2006) and cloves (30·8% in 2006).

COMMUNICATIONS

Roads
In 2002 there were 880 km of roads, of which 76·5% were paved.

Civil Aviation
There is an international airport at Moroni (International Prince Said Ibrahim). In 2001 it handled 108,000 passengers (78,000 on international flights).

Shipping
In 2002 the merchant marine totalled 407,000 GRT.

Telecommunications
There were 33,000 telephone subscribers in 2005 (41·4 per 1,000 persons), including 16,100 mobile subscribers. There were 5,000 PCs in use (6·3 per 1,000 persons) in 2004 and internet users numbered 20,000 in 2005.

Postal Services
In 2001 there were 29 post offices.

SOCIAL INSTITUTIONS

Justice
French and Muslim law is in a new consolidated code. The Supreme Court comprises seven members, two each appointed by the President and the Federal Assembly, and one by each island's Legislative Council. The death penalty is authorized for murder. The last execution was in 1996.

Education
After two pre-primary years at Koran school, which 50% of children attend, there are six years of primary schooling for seven- to 13-year-olds followed by a four-year secondary stage attended by 25% of children. Some 5% of 17- to 20-year-olds conclude schooling at *lycées*. There were 106,700 pupils with 3,050 teaching staff in primary schools in 2005 and 43,349 pupils at secondary schools with 3,138 teaching staff. At the tertiary level there were 1,779 students in 2004 and 130 academic staff.

The adult literacy rate in 2002 was 56·2% (63·5% among males and 49·1% among females).

In 2002 public expenditure on education came to 3·8% of GDP.

Health
In 1997 there were 64 physicians, 180 nurses and 74 midwives. In 1995 there were 29 hospital beds per 10,000 inhabitants.

RELIGION
Islam is the official religion: 98% of the population are Muslims; there is a small Christian minority. Following the coup of April 1999 the federal government discouraged the practice of religions other than Islam, with Christians especially facing restrictions on worship.

CULTURE

Broadcasting
The state-owned national broadcasting services, Télévision Nationale Comorienne and Radio Comoros, are run by the Office de la Radio et de la Télévision des Comoros. There are also regional government radio and TV outlets and some private stations. Radio France Internationale is relayed in the capital, Moroni. There were 13,000 television receivers in 2002.

Press
There was one daily newspaper in 2005. There were also five non-dailies.

Tourism
In 2004 there were 18,000 foreign tourists, bringing revenue of US$10m.

DIPLOMATIC REPRESENTATIVES
Of the Comoros in the United Kingdom
Honorary Consul: Khaled Chehabi (Flat 6, 24–26 Avenue Rd, London, NW8 6BU).

Of the United Kingdom in the Comoros
Ambassador: Dr John Murton (resides in Port Louis, Mauritius).

Of the Comoros in the USA (Temporary: c/o the Permanent Mission of the Union of the Comoros to the United Nations, 420 E 50th St., N.Y. 10022)
Ambassador: Mohamed Toihiri.

Of the USA in the Comoros
Ambassador: R. Niels Marquardt (resides in Antananarivo, Madagascar).

Of the Comoros to the United Nations
Ambassador: Mohamed Toihiri.

Of the Comoros to the European Union
Ambassador: Vacant.

FURTHER READING
Ottenheimer, M. and Ottenheimer, H. J., *Historical Dictionary of the Comoro Islands.* 1994

CONGO, DEMOCRATIC REPUBLIC OF THE

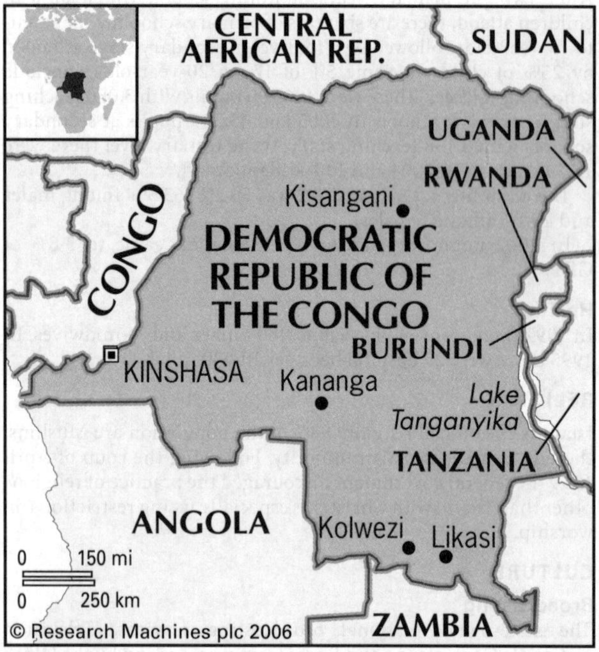

République Démocratique du Congo

Capital: Kinshasa
Population estimate, 2010: 67·83m.
GDP per capita, 2007: (PPP$) 298
HDI/world rank: 0·389/176

KEY HISTORICAL EVENTS

Bantu tribes migrated to the Congo basin from the northwest in the first millennium AD, forming several kingdoms and many smaller forest communities. Congo emerged as a kingdom on the Atlantic coast in the 14th century. King Nzinga Mbemba entered into diplomatic relations with Portugal after 1492. The Luba kingdom was centred on the marshy Upemba depression in the southeast. Expansion began in the late 18th century under Ilungu Sungu. In central Congo the Kuba kingdom was established in the 17th century as a federation of Bantu groups. Agriculture became the mainstay of the Kuba economy, strengthened by the introduction of American crops by Europeans. Trade made the Kuba elite, especially the Bushoong group, wealthy and encouraged the development of art and decorated cloth. Kuba thrived until the incursions of the Nsapo in the late 19th century.

King Leopold II of the Belgians claimed the Congo Basin as a personal possession in 1885. Exploitation of the native population provoked international condemnation. The Belgian government responded by annexing the Congo in 1908. Political representation was denied the Congolese until 1957, when the colonial administration introduced the *statut des villes* in response to the revolutionary demands of the *Alliance des BaKongo* (Abako). Political violence increased, instigated by the *Mouvement National Congolais* (MNC), led by Patrice Lumumba. Local elections were held in Dec. 1959 and in Jan. 1960 the Belgian government announced a rapid independence programme. After general elections in May, the Republic of the Congo became independent on 1 June 1960, with Lumumba as prime minister and Joseph Kasavubu, the Abako leader, as president.

Independence and Anarchy

The country descended into anarchy, with the mineral-rich Katanga region declaring independence. Lumumba was ousted and in 1961 was assassinated. Only in 2002 did Belgium admit to participating in his murder. Lieut.-Gen. Joseph-Désiré Mobutu (later Sese Seko) seized power in 1965. At first he was seen as a strongman who could hold together a huge, unstable country comprising hundreds of tribes and language groups. He changed the country's name to Zaïre in 1971. In the 1970s he was feted by the USA, which used Zaïre as a springboard for operations into neighbouring Angola where western-backed Unita rebels were locked in civil war with a Cuban and Soviet-backed government. Because Mobutu was useful in the fight against Communism the brutality and repressiveness of his regime was ignored.

After armed insurrection by Tutsi rebels in the province of Kivu, the government alleged pro-Tutsi intervention by the armies of Burundi and Rwanda and on 25 Oct. 1996 declared a state of emergency. By Dec. the secessionist forces of Laurent-Désiré Kabila, the *Alliance des Forces Démocratiques pour la Libération du Congo-Zaïre* (AFDL), had begun to drive the regular Zaïrean army out of Kivu and an attempt was made to establish a rebel administration, called 'Democratic Congo'. In the face of continuing rebel military successes and the disaffection of the army, the Government accepted a UN resolution demanding the immediate cessation of hostilities. The Security Council asked the rebels to make a public declaration of their acceptance. However, they continued in their victorious advance westwards, capturing Kisangani on 15 March 1997, then Kasai and Shaba, giving Kabila control of eastern Zaïre, and crucially the country's mineral wealth. After a futile attempt to deploy Serbian mercenaries, Mobutu succumbed to pressure from the USA and South Africa to meet Kabila, an occasion that had all the trappings of a symbolic surrender. Mobutu fled on the night of 15–16 May 1997. One of the most destructive tyrants of the African independence era, he died of cancer four months later.

On coming to power Kabila changed the name of the country to the Democratic Republic of the Congo. Hopes for democratic and economic renewal were soon disappointed. The Kabila regime relied too closely on its military backup, mainly Rwandans and eastern Congolese from the Tutsi minority who seemed more interested in eliminating tribal enemies in eastern border areas than in establishing democracy. As a result, Rwanda and Uganda switched support to rebel forces. When Zimbabwe and Angola sent in troops to help President Kabila, full-scale civil war threatened. A ceasefire was negotiated at a Franco-African summit in Nov. 1998 but the military build-up continued into the new year and violence intensified.

A ceasefire was signed by leaders from more than a dozen African countries in July 1999. Rival factions of the *Rassemblement Congolais pour la Démocratie* (RCD), the main rebel group opposed to the president, also signed the accord, but not until Sept.

Violence and Collapse

On 16 Jan. 2001 President Kabila was assassinated, allegedly by one of his own bodyguards. He was succeeded by his son, Joseph. Prospects for peace improved dramatically in Feb. 2001 when the UN Security Council approved the deployment of 3,000 UN-supported peacekeepers. In early 2002 talks between the government and rebels on how to end the conflict ended without agreement. However, in July 2002 the presidents of the Democratic

Republic of the Congo and neighbouring Rwanda signed a peace deal that was expected to be the first stage towards ending a war that has claimed more than 3m. lives. In Oct. 2002 Rwanda completed the withdrawal of its forces. The Democratic Republic of the Congo and Uganda also signed a peace agreement.

The conflict, described as Africa's first continental war, had drawn in Zimbabwe, Angola and Namibia (and, for a time, Sudan and Chad) on the side of the government, which controls the west of the country, while Rwanda and Uganda backed other rival factions. The RCD, which controls areas in the east, was backed by Rwanda, while Uganda supported the *Mouvement de Libération du Congo* (MLC), based in the north and northeast of the country. Burundi also had troops in the country, allied to the Rwandans, although they stayed close to the border with Burundi. In addition to the huge death toll, large numbers of people were displaced and sought asylum in Tanzania and Zambia. In Dec. 2002 the government and leading rebel forces reached an agreement on power-sharing. Its terms allowed for Joseph Kabila to remain as president until elections which, after several postponements, were held in July 2006. Kabila was elected president in a second round run-off in Oct. 2006 that signalled the end of the period of transitional government. The war is now more or less over, with the government having made peace with most of the principal rebel groups.

In April 2007 the Democratic Republic of the Congo resurrected the Economic Community of the Great Lakes alongside Rwanda and Burundi. Political instability within the country continued, particularly in eastern areas. In Jan. 2008 the government signed a peace deal with militia groups, including that of the renegade Gen. Laurent Nkunda. However, fighting between the army and Rwandan Hutu militias had resumed by April. In Oct. the government accused Rwanda of secretly backing Nkunda. Fighting intensified and Goma, the provincial capital of Nord-Kivu, was paralysed as rebel forces encroached and some 200,000 people were displaced. In Jan. 2009 Rwandan forces arrested Nkunda, signalling a new diplomatic direction.

TERRITORY AND POPULATION

The Democratic Republic of the Congo, sometimes referred to as Congo (Kinshasa), is bounded in the north by the Central African Republic, northeast by Sudan, east by Uganda, Rwanda, Burundi and Lake Tanganyika, south by Zambia, southwest by Angola and northwest by the Republic of the Congo. There is a 37-km stretch of coastline which gives access to the Atlantic Ocean, with the Angolan exclave of Cabinda to the immediate north, and Angola itself to the south. Area, 2,344,798 sq. km (905,327 sq. miles). At the last census, in 1988, the population was 34·7m. 67·9% of the population was rural in 2005.

The UN gives an estimated population for 2010 of 67·83m.; density, 29 per sq. km.

More than 200,000 refugees who escaped the fighting between Hutus and Tutsis in Rwanda and Burundi in 1994 are still in the Democratic Republic of the Congo (out of 1m. who came originally), and there are also 100,000 Angolan and 100,000 Sudanese refugees in the country.

Area and populations (1998 estimate) of the provinces (plus Kinshasa City), with their chief towns (2004 population estimates):

Region	*Area (sq. km)*	*Population (in 1,000)*	*Chief town*	*Population*
Bandundu	295,658	5,201	Bandundu	117,197
Bas-Congo	53,920	2,835	Matadi	245,862
Equateur	403,292	4,820	Mbandaka	262,814
Kasai Occidental	154,742	3,337	Kananga	720,362
Kasai Oriental	170,302	3,830	Mbuji-Mayi	1,213,726
Katanga	496,877	4,125	Lubumbashi	1,283,380
Maniema	132,250	1,247	Kindu	135,534
Nord-Kivu	59,483	3,564	Goma	249,862
Orientale	503,239	5,566	Kisangani	682,599
Sud-Kivu	65,070	2,838	Bukavu	471,789
Kinshasa City[1]	9,965	4,787	Kinshasa	7,273,947

[1]Neutral city.

Other large cities (with estimated 2004 population): Kolwezi (456,446), Likasi (367,219), Tshikapa (366,503), Kikwit (294,210).

The population is Bantu, with minorities of Sudanese (in the north), Nilotes (northeast), Pygmies and Hamites (in the east). French is the official language, but of more than 200 languages spoken, four are recognized as national languages: Kiswahili, Tshiluba, Kikongo and Lingala. Lingala has become the *lingua franca* after French.

SOCIAL STATISTICS

2000 estimates: births, 2,293,000; deaths, 661,000. Rates (2000 estimates, per 1,000 population); birth, 47·2; death, 13·6. Annual population growth rate, 1992–2002, 2·4%. Infant mortality in 2005 was 129 per 1,000 live births. Expectation of life in 2007 was 46·1 years for men and 49·2 for females. Fertility rate, 2004, 6·7 children per woman.

CLIMATE

The climate is varied, the central region having an equatorial climate, with year-long high temperatures and rain at all seasons. Elsewhere, depending on position north or south of the Equator, there are well-marked wet and dry seasons. The mountains of the east and south have a temperate mountain climate, with the highest summits having considerable snowfall. Kinshasa, Jan. 79°F (26·1°C), July 73°F (22·8°C). Annual rainfall 45" (1,125 mm). Kananga, Jan. 76°F (24·4°C), July 74°F (23·3°C). Annual rainfall 62" (1,584 mm). Kisangani, Jan. 78°F (25·6°C), July 75°F (23·9°C). Annual rainfall 68" (1,704 mm). Lubumbashi, Jan. 72°F (22·2°C), July 61°F (16·1°C). Annual rainfall 50" (1,237 mm).

CONSTITUTION AND GOVERNMENT

A new constitution was adopted by the transitional parliament on 16 May 2005. It limits the powers of the president, who may now serve a maximum of two five-year terms and lowers the minimum age for presidential candidates from 35 to 30. It allows a greater degree of federalism and recognises as citizens all ethnic groups at the time of independence in 1960. It also called for presidential elections by June 2006. In a referendum held on 18–19 Dec. 2005, 83% of voters approved the constitution in the country's first free vote in 40 years. The constitution was promulgated on 18 Feb. 2006.

The 240-member *Constituent and Legislative Assembly* was appointed in Aug. 2000 by former President Laurent Désiré Kabila. In Aug. 2003 a new bicameral parliament of 500 members and 120 senators met in Kinshasa. The representatives were chosen from the groups that comprised the newly-formed transitional government. In accordance with the constitution of the time, for the 2006 presidential election the *President* was elected by direct popular vote to serve a five-year term. In the *National Assembly*, 60 members were elected by majority vote in single-member constituencies and 440 members by open list proportional representation in multi-member constituencies to serve five-year terms. The 108 members of the *Senate* were elected by indirect vote, by provincial deputies, to serve five-year terms.

National Anthem

'Debout Congolais' ('Stand up, Congolese'); words and tune by J. Lutumba and S. Boka di Mpasi Londi.

RECENT ELECTIONS

Presidential and parliamentary elections, the first since the Democratic Republic of the Congo's became independent in 1960, were held on 30 July 2006. In the presidential election incumbent

Joseph Kabila received 44·8% of votes cast, Jean-Pierre Bemba 20·0%, Antoine Gizenga 13·1%, Nzanga Mobutu 4·8% and Oscar Kashala 3·5%. There were 28 other candidates who received 2% of the votes or less. Turnout was 70·5%. In a run-off poll held on 29 Oct. 2006, Kabila took 58·1% of the vote to Bemba's 41·9%. The result was disputed by Bemba but ratified by the Supreme Court in Nov. 2006.

In the parliamentary elections of 30 July 2006 the People's Party for Reconstruction and Democracy won 111 of 500 seats, the Movement for the Liberation of Congo 64, the Unified Lumumbist Party 34, the Social Movement for Renewal 27, the Forces of Renewal 26, the Congolese Rally for Democracy 15, the Coalition of Congolese Democrats 10 and the Convention of Christian Democrats 10, the remaining seats going to minor parties and independents.

The July elections were conducted relatively peacefully, but the subsequent counting of the results proved chaotic, leading to armed clashes that resulted in several deaths. Further violence followed the run-off presidential election in Oct. 2006.

CURRENT ADMINISTRATION

President: Joseph Kabila; b. 1971 (in office since 17 Jan. 2001 and elected on 29 Oct. 2006).

In March 2010 the coalition government comprised:

Prime Minister: Adolphe Muzito; b. 1947 (Unified Lumumbist Party; in office since 10 Oct. 2008).

Deputy Prime Ministers: François Joseph Mobutu Nzanga (also *Minister of Employment, Labour and Social Welfare*); Adolphe Mulenda Bwana Sefu (also *Minister of the Interior and Security*); Simon Bulupi Galati (also *Minister of Post, Telephones and Telecommunications*).

Minister of Agriculture, Fisheries and Livestock: Norbert Basengezi Katitima. *Budget:* Jean-Baptiste Ntawa Derwa. *Civil Service:* Dieudonné Upira Sunguma. *Communications and Media:* Lambert Mende Omalanga. *Culture and Arts:* Jeannette Kavira Mapera. *Decentralization and Land Management:* Antipas Mbusa Nyamwisi. *Energy:* Gilbert Tshiongo Tshibinkubula wa Ntumba. *Environment, Conservation and Tourism:* José Endundo Bononge. *Finance:* Matata Mponyo Mapon. *Foreign Affairs:* Alexis Thambwe Mwamba. *Gender, Family and Children's Affairs:* Marie-Ange Lukiana Mufwankol. *Higher Education:* Léonard Mashako Mamba. *Hydrocarbons:* Célestin Mbuyu Kabangu. *Industry:* Anicet Kuzunda Mutangisha. *Infrastructure, Public Works and Reconstruction:* Fridolin Kaswesi Kusoka. *International and Regional Co-operation:* Raymond Tshibanda Ntunga Mulongo. *Justice:* Luzolo Bambi Lessa. *Land:* Kisimba Ngoy Maj. *Mines:* Martin Kabwelulu Labilo. *National Defence and Veterans Affairs:* Charles Mwando Nsimba. *National Economy:* Jean-Marie Bulambo Kiloso. *Parastatals:* Jeannine Mabunda Lioko. *Planning:* Olivier Kamitatu Etsu. *Primary and Secondary Education:* Macaire Mwangu Famba. *Public Health:* Victor Makwenge Kaputu. *Relations with Parliament:* Richard Muyez Mangez. *Rural Development:* Philippe Undji Yangia. *Scientific Research:* Jean-Pierre Bokole Ompaka. *Small and Medium Businesses:* Claude Basibuhe Nyamulabu. *Social and Humanitarian Affairs and National Solidarity:* Ferdinand Kambere Kalubi. *Town Planning and Housing:* César Lubamba Ngimbi. *Transportation and Networks:* Laure Marie-Louise Kabwanda Kayende. *Youth and Sports:* Claude Bazibure Nyabugabu.

CURRENT LEADERS

Joseph Kabila

Position
President

Introduction
Joseph Kabila is the son of the former president Laurent Kabila who was assassinated on 16 Jan. 2001. Despite being little known outside his own group, Joseph Kabila was appointed president. He inherited a country divided by civil war which had spanned his father's tenure. Although promising unification in Congo, many need to be persuaded that Kabila has the necessary authority to restore peace to a country split along tribal lines and, despite its rich natural resources, suffering from poverty and economic instability. He was elected president following two rounds of voting held in July and Oct. 2006.

Early Life
Joseph Kabila was born on 4 Dec. 1971 at Laurent Kabila's anti-Mobutu guerrilla movement's headquarters (Hewa Bora) in the Fizi territory of Sud-Kivu. He was educated at a French-language school in Tanzania and then studied at the Makerere University in Uganda. He also did military training in China.

Career in Office
Following his father's death, Kabila replaced him as president. In his inaugural speech in 2001, he promised a ceasefire with rebel forces, an end to corruption and an improvement in living standards. He pledged to lead the country into multi-party democracy, and in May 2001 he lifted restrictions on political parties. Subsequently, over 200 parties were registered.

Peace negotiations brokered by South Africa in 2002 between the Kabila government and rebel factions led to agreement in Dec. on a power-sharing accord. Kabila was to remain as president pending future democratic elections, while his supporters, the civilian political opposition and two main rebel groups would each appoint a vice-president and seven ministers to serve under him on an interim basis. On 30 June 2003 Kabila announced the composition of the new transitional government. Although this was a major breakthrough, members of the new government feared for their safety in Kinshasa amid the mistrust between the various factions. The new government was inaugurated in Kinshasa in July 2003, but subsequent political progress was very slow and lawlessness and human rights abuses continued, particularly in the east and northeast of the country. Following a referendum on a new constitution in Dec. 2005, elections were scheduled for mid-2006. In the first round of the presidential poll in July, Kabila won 45% of the vote while his main rival, vice-president and former rebel Jean-Pierre Bemba, took 20%. In the Oct. 2006 run-off, Kabila claimed victory with 58%. The result was ratified by the Supreme Court the following month. Although Bemba denounced the outcome as rigged and his supporters reacted violently, he ultimately conceded defeat and in Dec. 2006 Kabila was sworn in as the country's first freely-elected president in more than 40 years.

Nevertheless, violence has persisted between government troops, rebel groups and militias, which have displaced and abused many thousands of civilians, particularly in the east of the country where swathes of Congolese territory remain lawless despite the presence of the world's largest UN peacekeeping mission.

DEFENCE

Following the overthrow of the Mobutu regime in May 1997, the former Zaïrean armed forces were in disarray. In June 2003 command of ground forces and naval forces were handed over to the RCD-Goma and MLC factions respectively as part of the power-sharing transitional government. Supreme command of the armed forces will remain in the hands of the former government faction.

A UN mission, MONUC, has been in the Democratic Republic of the Congo since 1999. With 20,509 uniformed personnel in Dec. 2009 it is the largest UN peacekeeping force in the world.

Defence expenditure totalled US$163m. in 2006 (US$3 per capita), representing 1·9% of GDP.

Army

The total strength of the Army was estimated at 125,000 (2007), including some 14,000 republican guards. There is an additional paramilitary National Police Force of unknown size. There are thought to be 14 infantry brigades, one mechanized infantry brigade and two commando regiments.

Navy

Naval strength (2007), 6,700.

Air Force

Personnel (2007), 2,500.

INTERNATIONAL RELATIONS

The Democratic Republic of the Congo is a member of the UN, World Bank, IMF and several other UN specialized agencies, WTO, IOM, International Organization of the Francophonie, African Development Bank, African Union, COMESA, CEEAC and is an ACP member state of the ACP-EU relationship.

ECONOMY

Agriculture accounted for 45·7% of GDP in 2006 (one of the highest percentages of any country), industry 27·7% and services 26·6%.

Overview

The Democratic Republic of the Congo has suffered severe economic difficulties since the mid-1980s owing to socio-political unrest. Per capita income has dropped steadily since independence, from US$250 in 1960 to US$139 in 2006.

Ceasefire agreements in 1999 and 2001 led to economic and social reforms. Stabilization measures launched in May 2001 brought inflation down from 630% in 2000 to 4·4% in 2003. After a decade of contraction, growth increased after 2002 to over 6% in 2005. Growth slowed to 5·1% in 2006 owing to weak manufacturing production and falling diamond exports while inflation increased to 13·2%, the result of government overspending on security and electioneering. The oil sector accounts for over 25% of GDP and 75% of export earnings. The economy is heavily indebted, with external debt representing 225% of GDP and 1,280% of exports. Mineral smuggling, particularly of gold, costs the country millions of dollars every month.

Currency

The unit of currency is the *Congolese franc* (CDF) which replaced the former *zaïre* in July 1998. The value of the new currency fell by two-thirds in the six months following its launch. Total money supply was 120,605m. Congolese francs in July 2005. Inflation, which reached 23,760% in 1994, had declined to 4·0% by 2004 before rising to 18·0% in 2008. In May 2001 the franc was floated in an effort to overcome the economic chaos caused by three years of state control and inter-regional war.

Budget

In 2005 revenues totalled 564·9bn. Congolese francs and expenditures 655·5bn. Congolese francs.

Performance

Real GDP growth was 6·3% in 2007 and 6·2% in 2008. In Feb. 1998 GDP was reported to be 65% lower than it was in 1960, when the country gained independence. Total GDP in 2008 was US$11·6bn.

Banking and Finance

The central bank, the Banque Centrale du Congo (*Governor*, Jean-Claude Masangu), achieved independence in May 2002. There are 14 commercial banks. In 2003 the largest was the Banque Commerciale Congolaise, in which the Société Générale of Belgium had a 25% stake through its subsidiary, Belgolaise. Other banks included Citibank and Stanbic. A 40% state-owned investment bank, Société Financière de Développement (Sofide), lent mainly to agriculture and manufacturing.

ENERGY AND NATURAL RESOURCES

Environment

Carbon dioxide emissions from the consumption and flaring of fossil fuels were the equivalent of less than 0·1 tonnes per capita in 2008. An *Environmental Performance Index* compiled in 2008 ranked Democratic Republic of the Congo 142nd in the world out of 149 countries analysed, with 47·3%. The index examined various factors in six areas—air pollution, biodiversity and habitat, climate change, environmental health, productive natural resources and water resources.

Electricity

Production (2004), 6·9bn. kWh. Installed capacity was an estimated 2·6m. kW in 2004. Consumption per capita was 92 kWh in 2004.

Oil and Gas

Offshore oil production began in Nov. 1975; crude production (2004) was 7·5m. bbls. Reserves in 2007 were 180m. bbls. There is an oil refinery at Kinlao-Muanda.

Minerals

Production, 2004 (in 1,000 tonnes): coal, 108; copper, 70; cobalt (estimate), 20; gold (estimate), 10,500 kg. Diamond production, 2004: 29·5m. carats. Only Australia, Russia and Botswana produce more diamonds. The country holds an estimated 80% of the world's coltan (columbite-tantalite) reserves. Coal, tin and silver are also found. The most important mining area is in the province of Katanga.

Agriculture

There were, in 2001, 6·70m. ha. of arable land and 1·18m. ha. of permanent crops. 11,000 ha. were irrigated in 2001. There were 2,430 tractors in 2001. The main agricultural crops (2002 production in 1,000 tonnes) are: cassava, 14,929; sugarcane, 1,650; plantains (2001), 1,216; maize, 1,154; groundnuts, 355; yams, 320; rice, 315; bananas, 313; sweet potatoes, 220; papayas, 210. Livestock (2002): goats, 4,004,000; pigs, 953,000; sheep, 897,000; cattle, 761,000; poultry, 20m.

Forestry

Forests covered 133·61m. ha. in 2005, or 58·9% of the land area. Timber production in 2007 was 77·66m. cu. metres.

Fisheries

The catch for 2005 was approximately 220,000 tonnes, almost entirely from inland waters.

INDUSTRY

The main manufactures are foodstuffs, beverages, tobacco, textiles, rubber, leather, wood products, cement and building materials, metallurgy and metal extraction, metal items, transport vehicles, electrical equipment and bicycles. Main products in 1,000 tonnes: cement (2001), 192; steel (2001), 80; sugar (2002), 65; soap (1995), 47; tyres (1995), 50,000 units; printed fabrics (1995), 15·73m. sq. metres; shoes (1995), 1·6m. pairs; beer (2003), 149·6m. litres.

Labour

In 1996 the workforce was 19·62m. (56% males). Agriculture employs around 65% of the total economically active population.

INTERNATIONAL TRADE

External debt was US$10,600m. in 2005.

Imports and Exports

Imports in 2004 were US$2,056m.; exports were US$1,813m. Main commodities for import are consumer goods, foodstuffs, mining and other machinery, transport equipment and fuels; and for export: diamonds, copper, coffee, cobalt and crude oil. Principal import suppliers in 2004 were South Africa, 18·5%; Belgium, 15·6%; France, 10·9%; USA, 6·2%. Principal export markets (2004) were Belgium, 42·5%; Finland, 17·8%; Zimbabwe, 12·2%; USA, 9·2%.

COMMUNICATIONS

Roads

In 2004 there were 153,497 km of roads (1·8% paved). There were an estimated 26,200 passenger cars in use in 2000 plus 20,400 trucks and vans.

Rail

Total route length was 4,499 km on three gauges in 2004, of which 858 km was electrified. However, the length of track actually in use has been severely reduced by the civil conflict and only amounted to 3,641 km. In 2001 the state-owned railway company carried 900,000 passengers and 1m. tonnes of freight.

Civil Aviation

There is an international airport at Kinshasa (Ndjili). Other major airports are at Lubumbashi (Luano), Bukavu, Goma and Kisangani. The national carrier is Congo Airlines. In 2001 Kinshasa handled 278,000 passengers (142,000 on international flights) and 41,500 tonnes of freight.

Shipping

The River Congo and its tributaries are navigable to 300-tonne vessels for about 14,500 km. Regular traffic has been established between Kinshasa and Kisangani as well as Ilebo, on the Lualaba (i.e. the river above Kisangani), on some tributaries and on the lakes. The Democratic Republic of the Congo has only 37 km of sea coast. In 2002 merchant shipping totalled 13,000 GRT. Matadi, Kinshasa and Kalemie are the main seaports.

Telecommunications

Telephone subscribers numbered 2,756,600 in 2005, or 47·9 per 1,000 inhabitants, including 2,746,000 mobile phone subscribers. With 99·6% of all telephone subscribers being mobile users, no other country has such a high ratio of mobile subscribers to landline subscribers. In 2005 there were 140,600 internet users.

Postal Services

In 2003 there were 280 post offices.

SOCIAL INSTITUTIONS

Justice

There is a Supreme Court at Kinshasa, 11 courts of appeal, 36 courts of first instance and 24 'peace tribunals'. The death penalty is in force.

The population in penal institutions in Jan. 2004 was approximately 30,000 (57 per 100,000 of national population).

Education

In 2007 there were 230,834 teaching staff in primary schools for 8·8m. pupils, and 2·8m. pupils in secondary schools with 179,635 teaching staff. In 2007 there were 237,836 students in higher education and 16,913 academic staff. The largest public universities are the University of Kinshasa, the University of Kisangani and the University of Lubumbashi.

Adult literacy rate was 65·3% in 2003 (male, 79·8%; female, 51·9%).

Health

In 1996 there were 3,224 physicians, 514 dentists and 20,652 nurses.

The Democratic Republic of the Congo has been one of the least successful countries in the battle against undernourishment in the past 15 years. The proportion of the population classified as undernourished increased from 31% in 1990–92 to 72% by 2001–03.

RELIGION

In 2001 there were 21·99m. Roman Catholics, 16·95m. Protestants, 7·17m. Kimbanguistes (African Christians) and 0·75m. Muslims. Animist beliefs persist.

CULTURE

World Heritage Sites

(With year entered on list). Virunga National Park (1979); Kahuzi-Biega National Park (1980); Garamba National Park (1980); Salonga National Park (1984); and Okapi Wildlife Reserve (1996).

Broadcasting

Radio-Télévision Nationale Congolaise is the state-run national broadcasting authority. There are also a number of private TV and radio outlets. Radio Okapi is a United Nations-sponsored independent service. There 146,000 TV receivers in 2003 (colour by SECAM V).

Press

In 2006 there were 11 daily newspapers with a combined circulation of 50,000.

Tourism

In 2004 there were 30,000 foreign tourists; spending by tourists totalled US$1m.

DIPLOMATIC REPRESENTATIVES

Of the Democratic Republic of the Congo in the United Kingdom (281 Gray's Inn Rd, London, WC1X 8QF)
Ambassador: Dr Barnabe Kikaya Bin Karubi.

Of the United Kingdom in the Democratic Republic of the Congo (83 Ave. du Roi Baudouin, Kinshasa)
Ambassador: Nick Kay, CMG.

Of the Democratic Republic of the Congo in the USA (1726 M St., Suite 601, NW, Washington, D.C., 20009)
Ambassador: Faida Mitifu.

Of the USA in the Democratic Republic of the Congo (310 Ave. des Aviateurs, Kinshasa)
Ambassador: William. J. Garvelink.

Of the Democratic Republic of the Congo to the United Nations
Ambassador: Atoki Ileka.

Of the Democratic Republic of the Congo to the European Union
Ambassador: Corneille Yambu-A-Ngoyi.

FURTHER READING

Gondola, Didier, *The History of Congo.* 2003
Hochschild, Adam, *King Leopold's Ghost: A Study of Greed, Terror and Heroism in Colonial Africa.* 1999
Melson, Robert, *Genocide and Crisis in Central Africa: Conflict Roots, Mass Violence and Regional War.* 2001
Renton, David, *The Congo: Plunder and Resistance.* 2006
Wrong, Michaela, *In the Footsteps of Mr Kurtz: Living on the Brink of Disaster in the Congo.* 2000

CONGO, REPUBLIC OF THE

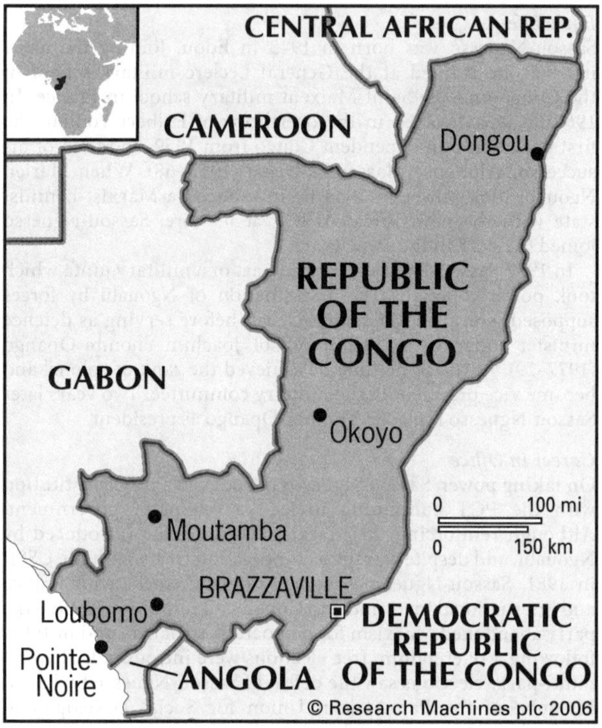

République du Congo

Capital: Brazzaville
Population estimate, 2010: 3·76m.
GDP per capita, 2007: (PPP$) 3,511
HDI/world rank: 0·601/136

KEY HISTORICAL EVENTS

First occupied by France in 1882, the Congo became a territory of French Equatorial Africa from 1910–58, and then a member state of the French Community. Between 1940 and 1944, thanks to Equatorial Africa's allegiance to Gen. de Gaulle, he named Brazzaville the capital of the Empire and Liberated France. Independence was granted in 1960. A Marxist-Leninist state was introduced in 1970. Free elections were restored in 1992 but violence erupted when, in June 1997, President Lissouba tried to disarm opposition militia ahead of a fresh election. There followed four months of civil war with fighting concentrated on Brazzaville which became a ghost town. In Oct. Gen. Sassou-Nguesso proclaimed victory, having relied upon military support from Angola. President Lissouba went into hiding in Burkina Faso. A peace agreement signed in Nov. 1999 between President Sassou-Nguesso and the 'Cocoye' and 'Ninja' militias brought a period of relative stability.

TERRITORY AND POPULATION

The Republic of the Congo, sometimes referred to as Congo (Brazzaville), is bounded by Cameroon and the Central African Republic in the north, the Democratic Republic of the Congo to the east and south, Angola and the Atlantic Ocean to the southwest and Gabon to the west, and covers 341,821 sq. km. At the census of 1996 the population was 2,591,271.

The UN gives an estimated population for 2010 of 3·76m.; density, 11 per sq. km.

In 2005, 60·2% of the population were urban. Census population of major cities in 1996: Brazzaville, the capital, 856,410; Pointe-Noire, 455,131; Loubomo (Dolisie), 79,852; N'Kayi, 46,727; Ouesso, 17,784; Mossendjo, 16,458.

Area, census population and county towns of the regions in 1996 were:

Region	*Sq. km*	*Population*	*County town*
Bouenza	12,258	236,566	Madingou
Capital District	100	856,410	Brazzaville
Cuvette	74,850	112,946	Owando
Cuvette Ouest		49,422	Ewo
Kouilou	13,650	532,179	Pointe-Noire
Lékoumou	20,950	75,734	Sibiti
Likouala	66,044	66,252	Impfondo
Niari	25,918	199,988	Loubomo (Dolisie)
Plateaux	38,400	139,371	Djambala
Pool	33,955	265,180	Kinkala
Sangha	55,795	57,223	Ouesso

Main ethnic groups are: Kongo (48%), Sangha (20%), Teke (17%) and M'Bochi (12%).

French is the official language. Kongo languages are widely spoken. Monokutuba and Lingala serve as *lingua francas*.

SOCIAL STATISTICS

2000 estimates: births, 152,000; deaths, 48,000. Rates, 2000 estimates (per 1,000 population): births, 44·2; deaths, 14·0. Infant mortality, 2005 (per 1,000 live births), 79. Expectation of life in 2007 was 52·5 years for males and 54·4 for females. Annual population growth rate, 1992–2002, 3·2%. Fertility rate, 2001, 6·3 children per woman.

CLIMATE

An equatorial climate, with moderate rainfall and a small range of temperature. There is a long dry season from May to Oct. in the southwest plateaux, but the Congo Basin in the northeast is more humid, with rainfall approaching 100" (2,500 mm). Brazzaville, Jan. 78°F (25·6°C), July 73°F (22·8°C). Annual rainfall 59" (1,473 mm).

CONSTITUTION AND GOVERNMENT

A new constitution was approved in a referendum held in Jan. 2002. Under the new constitution the president's term of office is increased from five to seven years. The constitution provides for a new two-chamber assembly consisting of a house of representatives and a senate. The president may also appoint and dismiss ministers. 84·3% of voters were in favour of the draft constitution and 11·3% against. Turnout was 78%, despite calls from opposition parties for a boycott. The new constitution came into force in Aug. 2002.

There is a 137-seat *National Assembly*, with members elected for a five-year term in single-seat constituencies, and a 66-seat *Senate*, with members elected for a six-year term (one third of members every two years).

National Anthem

'La Congolaise'; words by Levent Kimbangui, tune by Français Jacques Tondra.

RECENT ELECTIONS

Presidential elections were held on 12 July 2009. Incumbent Denis Sassou-Nguesso won with 78·6% of votes cast, against 7·5% for Joseph Kignoumbi Kia Mboungou and 7·0% for Nicéphore

Antoine Fylla de Saint-Eudes. The turnout was 66·4%. There were ten other candidates. Six opposition candidates boycotted the elections, claiming that the electoral lists were flawed.

Parliamentary elections were held on 24 June and 5 Aug. 2007. President Denis Sassou-Nguesso's Congolese Labour Party won 46 out of 137 seats; Congolese Movement for Democracy and Integral Development, 11; Pan-African Union for Social Democracy, 11; Action Movement for Renewal, 5; Movement for Solidarity and Development, 5; Club 2002, 3; Take Action for Congo, 3. A total of 11 other parties won either one or two seats. The Congolese Labour Party and its allies won 124 seats in total, with only 11 going to the opposition (Pan-African Union for Social Democracy). There were also two vacant seats. A number of opposition parties boycotted the elections, claiming that they were not free and fair.

CURRENT ADMINISTRATION

President: Denis Sassou-Nguesso; b. 1943 (Congolese Labour Party; sworn in 25 Oct. 1997 for a second time and re-elected in March 2002 and July 2009, having previously held office 1979–92).

In March 2010 the government comprised:

Minister at the Presidency in Charge of Defence: Charles Zacharie Bowao. *Minister at the Presidency in Charge of Special Economic Zones:* Alain Akouala Atipault.

State Minister of Economy, Planning, Land Management and Integration: Pierre Moussa. *Justice, Guardian of the Seals and Human Rights:* Aimé Emmanuel Yoka. *Transport, Civil Aviation and the Merchant Marine:* Isidore Mvouba. *Work and Social Security:* Florent Tsiba. *Industrial Development and Promotion of the Private Sector:* Rodolphe Adada.

Minister of Agriculture and Livestock: Rigobert Maboundou. *Civic Education and Youth:* Zacharie Kimpomi. *Civil Service and State Reform:* Guy Brice Parfait Kolélas. *Commerce and Supplies:* Claudine Munari. *Communications and Relations with Parliament:* Bienvenu Okiemy. *Construction, Town Planning and Housing:* Claude Alphonse Nsilou. *Culture and the Arts:* Jean-Claude Gakosso. *Energy and Water Resources:* Bruno Jean-Richard Itoua. *Equipment and Public Works:* Émile Ouosso. *Finance and Budget:* Gilbert Ondongo. *Fishing and Aquaculture:* Hellot Mampouy Matson. *Foreign Affairs and Co-operation:* Basile Ikouébé. *Health and Population:* Georges Moyen. *Higher Education:* Ange Antoine Abena. *Hydrocarbons:* André Raphaël Loemba. *Land Affairs and Public Territory:* Pierre Mabiala. *Mines, Mining Industry and Geology:* Pierre Oba. *Posts, Telecommunications and New Technologies:* Thierry Moungala. *Primary and Secondary Education and Literacy:* Rosalie Kama-Niamayoua. *Promotion of Women and the Involvement of Women in Development:* Jeanne Françoise Leckomba Loumeto-Pombo. *Scientific Research:* Henri Ossebi. *Small and Medium-Sized Businesses, and Handicrafts:* Adélaïde Moundélé-Ngollo. *Social Affairs, Humanitarian Affairs and Solidarity:* Émilienne Raoul. *Sports and Physical* Education: Jacques Yvon Ndolou. *Sustainable Development, Forest Economy and the Environment:* Henri Djombo. *Technical and Vocational Training, and Employment:* André Okombi Salissa. *Territorial Administration and Decentralization:* Raymond Mboulou. *Tourist Industry and Leisure:* Mathieu Martial Kani.

CURRENT LEADERS

Denis Sassou-Nguesso

Position
President

Introduction
A military leader from the 1960s, Denis Sassou-Nguesso ruled the Republic of the Congo between 1979–92, regaining power in 1997 in a coup. He maintained Congo's one-party Marxist-Leninist state—through the Congolese Labour Party (PCT; Parti Congolais du Travail)—until 1992, when he introduced free elections in which he was defeated. His latest tenure since 1997 has been marred by civil war and economic crises.

Early Life
Sassou-Nguesso was born in 1943 in Edou. Joining the army in 1960, he trained at the General Leclerc military school in the Congo and the Saint-Maixent military school in France. In 1963 he was involved in the overthrow of Fulbert Youlou, the first president of independent Congo from 1959, and then of his successor Alphonse Massemba-Débat (1963–68). When Marien Ngouabi took power in 1969 he introduced a Marxist-Leninist state with the newly-created PCT at its core. Sassou-Nguesso joined the PCT in the same year.

In 1977 Sassou-Nguesso formed part of a military junta which took power following the assassination of Ngouabi by forces supposedly loyal to Massemba-Débat, before serving as defence minister under the leadership of Col. Joachim Yhombi-Opango (1977–79). At the same time he achieved the rank of colonel and became vice president of the military committee. Two years later Sassou-Nguesso replaced Yhombi-Opango as president.

Career in Office
On taking power, Sassou-Nguesso introduced a new constitution with the PCT continuing to lead a one-party government. Although reinforcing the Marxist-Leninist state introduced by Ngouabi, and despite signing a co-operation treaty with the USSR in 1981, Sassou-Nguesso sought a rapprochement with France and international investment in Congo's oil resources. In 1990 the party abandoned Marxism for democratic socialism and in 1992, following a referendum, free elections were introduced. The first multi-party elections saw the defeat of Sassou-Nguesso by Pascal Lissouba of the Pan-African Union for Social Development. Sassou-Nguesso came third with 16·9% of votes.

Thereafter, tension between the governing and opposition parties led to recurring violence between their respective militias, including the 'Cobra' militia loyal to Sassou-Nguesso. Violence increased ahead of elections scheduled for 1997, accelerating from June 1997 into four months of civil war. Sassou-Nguesso, with the aid of Angolan soldiers, finally ousted Lissouba. The latter went into hiding in Burkina Faso and Sassou-Nguesso was sworn in as president again in Oct. 1997. Between 10,000–15,000 people were killed in the conflict and the capital's infrastructure was destroyed.

Fighting erupted again in Jan. 1999 as 'Cocoye' rebels loyal to Lissouba attacked Brazzaville. In April there was an attack on Pointe-Noire by the 'Ninja' rebels loyal to former prime minister Bernard Kolélas. The conflict caused many to flee to the Democratic Republic of the Congo. In Aug. 1999 peace talks were held by Sassou-Nguesso, Lissouba and Kolélas at which a ceasefire was agreed. Congo's economy, still affected by the civil war of 1997, suffered further.

In Jan. 2001 Sassou-Nguesso passed a new constitution which increased the president's term from five to seven years and strengthened presidential powers. In presidential elections held in March 2002, Sassou-Nguesso won 89·4% of votes. The new constitution deemed Lissouba and Kolélas ineligible to stand, while another opposition candidate, Andre Milongo, refused to participate claiming 'irregularities'. The elections were marred by violence between the 'Ninja' rebels and government forces in the Pool area of the country, which caused the displacement of around 66,000 people. Legislative elections which followed in May and June 2002 resulted in a large parliamentary majority for the PCT and its allies, although the results were criticized by international observers and provoked further widespread militia violence. A peace agreement reached in March 2003 has remained fragile. Following the most recent parliamentary elections in mid-2007 the PCT remained the largest party in the National Assembly. In

July 2009 Sassou-Nguesso was re-elected for a further seven-year presidential term, claiming 78·6% of the vote. The conduct of the poll was criticized by a European Commission delegation and the results were disputed, provoking street protests in Brazzaville that were dispersed by riot police.

In a cabinet reshuffle in Sept. 2009, Sassou-Nguesso abolished the post of prime minister and took over those duties himself under the mantle of the presidency.

DEFENCE

In 2006 military expenditure totalled US$84m. (US$23 per capita), representing 1·2% of GDP.

Army

Total personnel (2007) 8,000. There is a Gendarmerie of 2,000.

Navy

Personnel in 2007 totalled about 800. The Navy is based at Pointe Noire.

Air Force

The Air Force had (2007) about 1,200 personnel and 24 aircraft although none are combat capable and their serviceability is questionable.

INTERNATIONAL RELATIONS

The Republic of the Congo is a member of the UN, World Bank, IMF and several other UN specialized agencies, WTO, IOM, International Organization of the Francophonie, African Development Bank, African Union, CEEAC and is an ACP member state of the ACP-EU relationship.

ECONOMY

Agriculture produced 4·0% of GDP in 2006, industry 70·2% and services 25·8%.

Overview

Oil accounts for just over half of GDP and over 85% of exports, making the economy vulnerable to external price shocks. A third of the population is employed in agriculture which accounts for roughly 5% of GDP. The Republic of the Congo is eligible for debt relief under the World Bank's Enhanced Heavily Indebted Poor Countries (HIPC) initiative. This creates conditions for sustainable growth in partnership with increased oil exports and fiscal revenues.

Inflation has accelerated with the expansionary fiscal policy and transportation disruptions. Non-oil fiscal deficits are amongst the highest in Africa and are not sustainable in the long-term given that oil production is expected to peak during 2010. Under the HIPC Initiative there are plans to reduce poverty, improve the public management finance system and strengthen governance. Civil war and poor governance during the 1990s damaged the health and education systems as well as the transport infrastructure.

Currency

The unit of currency is the *franc CFA* (XAF) with a parity of 655·957 francs CFA to one euro. Total money supply in June 2005 was 322,269m. francs CFA and foreign exchange reserves were US$226m. Gold reserves were 11,000 troy oz in July 2005. There was inflation of 2·6% in 2007 and 6·0% in 2008.

Budget

Budgetary central government revenue totalled 1,302·2bn. francs CFA in 2005 (866·8bn. francs CFA in 2004) and expenditure 461·8bn. francs CFA (451·7bn. francs CFA in 2004).

VAT is 18%.

Performance

Total GDP in 2008 was US$10·7bn. Real GDP growth was –1·6% in 2007 and 5·6% in 2008.

Banking and Finance

The Banque des États de l'Afrique Centrale (*Governor*, Philibert Andzembe) is the bank of issue. There are four commercial banks and a development bank, in all of which the government has majority stakes. There is also a co-operative banking organization (Mutuelle Congolaise de l'Épargne et de Crédit).

ENERGY AND NATURAL RESOURCES

Environment

Carbon dioxide emissions from the consumption and flaring of fossil fuels in 2008 were the equivalent of 1·4 tonnes per capita.

Electricity

Installed capacity was an estimated 93,000 kW in 2004. Total production in 2004 was 399m. kWh and consumption per capita 229 kWh.

Oil and Gas

Oil was discovered in the mid-1960s when Elf Aquitaine was given exclusive rights to production. Elf still has the lion's share but Agip Congo is also involved in oil exploitation. In 2008 production was 12·9m. tonnes. Proven reserves in 2008 were 1·9bn. bbls, including major off-shore deposits. Oil provides about 90% of government revenue and exports. There is a refinery at Pointe-Noire, the second largest city. There were proven natural gas reserves of 91bn. cu. metres in 2007.

Minerals

A government mine produces several metals; gold and diamonds are extracted by individuals. There are reserves of potash (4·5m. tonnes), iron ore (1,000m. tonnes), and also clay, bituminous sand, phosphates, zinc and lead.

Agriculture

In 2001 there were 175,000 ha. of arable land and 45,000 ha. of permanent crops. There were some 700 tractors and 85 thresher-harvesters in use in 2001. Production (2002, in thousand tonnes): cassava, 862; sugarcane, 459; bananas, 84; plantains, 71; mangoes, 25; groundnuts, 24; palm oil, 17; yams, 11; maize, 7.

Livestock (2002): goats, 294,000; sheep, 98,000; cattle, 93,000; pigs, 46,000; poultry, 2m.

Forestry

In 2005 equatorial forests covered 22·47m. ha. (65·8% of the total land area). In 2007, 3·71m. cu. metres of timber were produced, mainly okoumé from the south and sapele from the north. Timber companies are required to replant, and to process at least 60% of their production locally. Before the development of the oil industry, forestry was the mainstay of the economy.

Fisheries

The catch for 2005 was 58,368 tonnes, of which 56% was from inland waters and 44% from marine waters.

INDUSTRY

There is a growing manufacturing sector, located mainly in the four major towns, producing processed foods, textiles, cement, metal goods and chemicals. Industry produced 65·2% of GDP in 2001, including 4·1% from manufacturing. Production (2004): residual fuel oil, 295,000 tonnes; distillate fuel oil, 120,000 tonnes; petrol, 49,000 tonnes; kerosene, 19,000 tonnes; cigarettes (1994), 655m. cartons; beer (2003), 66·0m. litres; veneer sheets (2001), 12,000 cu. metres; cotton textiles (1993), 1·8m. metres.

Labour

In 1996 the labour force was 1,105,000 (57% males). More than 50% of the economically active population were engaged in agriculture.

Trade Unions

In 1964 the existing unions merged into one national body, the Confédération Syndicale Congolaise. The 40,000-strong

Confédération Syndicale des Travailleurs Congolais split off from the latter in 1993.

INTERNATIONAL TRADE

Foreign debt was US$5,936m. in 2005.

Imports and Exports

Imports and exports for calendar years in US$1m.:

	2001	*2002*	*2003*	*2004*	*2005*
Imports f.o.b	681	691	831	969	1,356
Exports f.o.b	2,055	2,289	2,637	3,433	4,730

Principal imported commodities are intermediate manufactures, capital equipment, construction materials, foodstuffs and petroleum products. Apart from crude oil, other significant commodities for export are lumber, plywood, sugar, cocoa, coffee and diamonds. In 2003 the main import suppliers were the Netherlands, France, USA, Italy and Germany. The main export markets were China, South Korea, USA, North Korea and France.

COMMUNICATIONS

Roads

In 2004 there were 17,289 km of roads (5·0% paved). Passenger cars in use in 2007 numbered 56,000 (15 per 1,000 inhabitants). There were 126 deaths in road accidents in 2004.

Rail

A railway connects Brazzaville with Pointe-Noire via Loubomo and Bilinga, and a branch links Mont-Belo with Mbinda on the Gabon border. Total length in 2005 was 797 km (1,067 mm gauge). In 2003 passenger-km totalled 76m. and freight tonne-km 307m.

Civil Aviation

The principal airports are at Brazzaville (Maya Maya) and Pointe-Noire. In 2003 Trans Air Congo operated services to Abidjan, Cotonou and Lomé, as well as domestic services. Trans African Airlines flew to Abidjan, Bamako, Cotonou, Dakar and Lomé. In 2001 Brazzaville handled 433,000 passengers (341,000 on domestic flights) and 27,000 tonnes of freight.

Shipping

The only seaport is Pointe-Noire. The merchant marine totalled 3,000 GRT in 2002. There are some 5,000 km of navigable rivers, and river transport is an important service for timber and other freight as well as passengers. There are hydrofoil connections from Brazzaville to Kinshasa.

Telecommunications

There were 397,500 telephone subscribers in 2004 (104·1 per 1,000 persons), including 383,700 mobile phone subscribers. In 2004, 96·5% of all telephone subscribers were mobile phone subscribers—among the highest ratios of mobile to fixed-line subscribers in the world. There were 17,000 PCs in use (4·5 per 1,000 persons) in 2004 and 36,000 internet users.

Postal Services

There were 37 post offices in 2003.

SOCIAL INSTITUTIONS

Justice

The Supreme Court, Court of Appeal and a criminal court are situated in Brazzaville, with a network of *tribunaux de grande instance* and *tribunaux d'instance* in the regions.

Education

In 2007 there were 10,631 teaching staff for 621,702 pupils at primary schools and (2004) 6,965 secondary school teaching staff for 232,026 pupils. There were 12,456 students at tertiary level in 2003 with 894 academic staff. Adult literacy rate in 2004 was 84·7%.

In 2005 public expenditure on education came to 1·8% of GDP and 8·1% of total government spending.

Health

In 2001 there were 103 hospitals with 5,195 beds. In 2000 there were 540 physicians, 75 pharmacists, 1,439 nurses and 579 midwives.

RELIGION

In 2001 there were 1·43m. Roman Catholics, 0·49m. Protestants and 0·36m. Kimbanguistes (African Christians). Traditional animist beliefs are still widespread.

CULTURE

Broadcasting

Nearly all broadcasting is under government control through the Radiodiffusion-Télévision Congolaise, which operates Congo TV, Radio Congo and Radio Brazzaville. There were 40,000 TV receivers in 2002.

Press

In 2006 there were four daily newspapers with a combined circulation of 8,000.

Tourism

There were 22,000 foreign tourists in 2002; spending by tourists in 2003 totalled US$20m.

DIPLOMATIC REPRESENTATIVES

Of the Republic of the Congo in the United Kingdom
Ambassador: Henri Marie Joseph Lopes (resides in Paris).
Honorary Consul: Louis Muzzu (The Arena, 24 Southwark Bridge Rd, London, SE1 9HF).

Of the United Kingdom in the Republic of the Congo
Ambassador: Nick Kay, CMG (resides in Kinshasa, Democratic Republic of the Congo).

Of the Republic of the Congo in the USA (4891 Colorado Ave., NW, Washington, D.C., 20011)
Ambassador: Serge Mombouli.

Of the USA in the Republic of the Congo (BDEAC Building 4th Floor, Boulevard de la Révolution, Brazzaville)
Ambassador: Alan W. Eastham.

Of the Republic of the Congo to the United Nations
Ambassador: Raymond Serge Balé.

Of the Republic of the Congo to the European Union
Ambassador: Jacques Obia.

FURTHER READING

Thompson, V. and Adloff, R., *Historical Dictionary of the People's Republic of the Congo*. 2nd ed. 1984

National Statistical Office: Centre National de la Statistique et des Études Économiques, BP 2031, Brazzaville.
Website (French only): http://www.cnsee.org

COSTA RICA

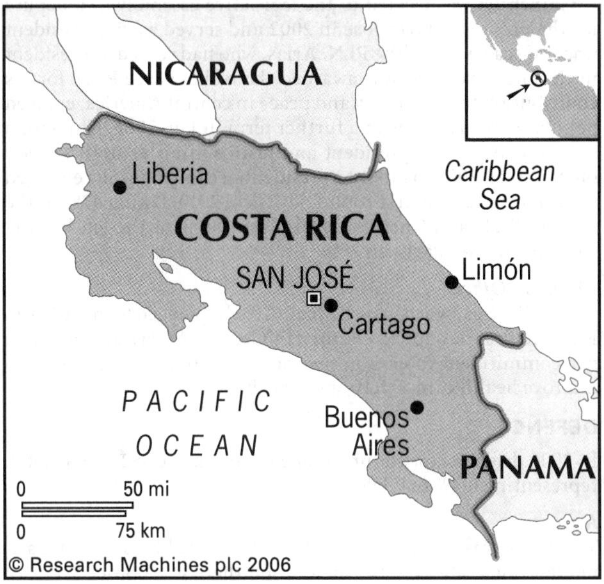

República de Costa Rica
(Republic of Costa Rica)

Capital: San José
Population estimate, 2010: 4·64m.
GDP per capita, 2007: (PPP$) 10,842
HDI/world rank: 0·854/54

KEY HISTORICAL EVENTS

Discovered by Columbus in 1502 on his last voyage, Costa Rica (Rich Coast) was part of the Spanish viceroyalty of New Spain from 1540 to 1821, then of the Central American Federation until 1838 when it achieved full independence. Coffee was introduced in 1808 and became a mainstay of the economy, helping to create a peasant land-owning class. In 1948 accusations of election fraud led to a six-week civil war, at the conclusion of which José Figueres Ferrer won power at the head of a revolutionary junta. A new constitution abolished the Army. In 1986 Oscar Arias Sánchez was elected president. He promised to prevent Nicaraguan anti-Sandinista (*contra*) forces using Costa Rica as a base. In 1987 he received the Nobel Peace Prize as recognition of his Central American peace plan, agreed to by the other Central American states. Costa Rica was beset with economic problems in the early 1990s when several politicians, including President Calderón, were accused of profiting from drug trafficking.

TERRITORY AND POPULATION

Costa Rica is bounded in the north by Nicaragua, east by the Caribbean, southeast by Panama, and south and west by the Pacific. The area is estimated at 51,100 sq. km (19,730 sq. miles). The population at the census of July 2000 was 3,810,179; density, 71·4 per sq. km. In 2005, 61·7% of the population were urban.

The UN gives an estimated population for 2010 of 4·64m.

There are seven provinces (with 2000 population): Alajuela (716,286); Cartago (432,395); Guanacaste (264,238); Heredia (354,732); Limón (339,295); Puntarenas (357,483); San José (1,345,750). The largest cities, with estimated 2000 populations, are San José (346,600); Limón (62,000); and Alajuela (53,900).

Ethnic divisions (2000): White 77%, Mestizo 17%, Mulatto 3%, East Asian (predominantly Chinese) 2%, Amerindian 1%.

Spanish is the official language.

SOCIAL STATISTICS

Statistics for calendar years:

	Marriages	*Births*	*Deaths*
2002	23,926	71,144	15,004
2003	24,448	72,938	15,800
2004	25,370	72,247	15,949
2005	25,631	71,548	16,139

2005 rates per 1,000 population: births, 16·6; deaths, 3·7. Annual population growth rate, 2000–05, 2·3%. Life expectancy at birth, 2007, was 76·4 years for men and 81·3 years for women. Infant mortality, 2005, 9·8 per 1,000 live births; fertility rate, 2004, 2·2 children per woman.

CLIMATE

The climate is tropical, with a small range of temperature and abundant rain. The dry season is from Dec. to April. San José, Jan. 66°F (18·9°C), July 69°F (20·6°C). Annual rainfall 72" (1,793 mm).

CONSTITUTION AND GOVERNMENT

The Constitution was promulgated on 7 Nov. 1949. The legislative power is vested in a single-chamber *Legislative Assembly* of 57 deputies elected for four years. The *President* and two *Vice-Presidents* are elected for four years; the candidate receiving the largest vote, provided it is over 40% of the total, is declared elected, but a second ballot is required if no candidate gets 40% of the total. Since 2003 former presidents have been permitted to stand again. Elections are normally held on the first Sunday in Feb.

The President may appoint and remove members of the cabinet.

National Anthem

'Noble patria, tu hermosa bandera' ('Noble fatherland, thy beautiful banner'); words by J. M. Zeledón Brenes, tune by M. M. Gutiérrez.

GOVERNMENT CHRONOLOGY

Presidents since 1944. (PLN = National Liberation Party; PRD = Party of the Democratic Renewal; PRN = National Republican Party; PUN = National Union Party; PUSC = Social Christian Unity Party)

1944–48	PRN	Teodoro Picado Michalski
1948–49	military	José María Figueres Ferrer
1949–53	PUN	Luis Otilio Ulate Blanco
1953–58	PLN	José María Figueres Ferrer
1958–62	PUN	Mario José Echandi Jiménez
1962–66	PLN	Francisco José Orlich Bolmarcich
1966–70	PUN	José Joaquín Trejos Fernández
1970–74	PLN	José María Figueres Ferrer
1974–78	PLN	Daniel Oduber Quirós
1978–82	PRD	Rodrigo José Carazo Odio
1982–86	PLN	Luis Alberto Monge Álvarez
1986–90	PLN	Óscar Rafael Arias Sánchez
1990–94	PUSC	Rafael Ángel Calderón Fournier
1994–98	PLN	José María Figueres Olsen
1998–2002	PUSC	Miguel Ángel Rodríguez Echeverría
2002–06	PUSC	Abel Pacheco de la Espriella

2006–10 PLN Óscar Rafael Arias Sánchez
2010– PLN Laura Chinchilla Miranda

RECENT ELECTIONS

In presidential elections held on 7 Feb. 2010 vice-president Laura Chinchilla of the National Liberation Party (PLN) won 46·8% of the vote, Ottón Solís of the Citizens' Action Party (PAC) 25·2%, Otto Guevara of the Libertarian Movement (ML) 20·8% and Luis Fishman of the Social Christian Unity Party (PUSC) 3·9%. There were five other candidates. Turnout was 69·1%. In parliamentary elections held on the same day the PLN won 24 of 57 seats with 37·3% of votes cast, the PAC 11 (17·6%), the ML 9 (14·5%), the PUSC 6 (8·2%), the PASE (Accessibility Without Exclusion Party) 4 (9·0%), with three parties each winning one seat.

CURRENT ADMINISTRATION

President: Laura Chinchilla Miranda; b. 1959 (PLN; sworn in 8 May 2010).

In March 2010 the government comprised:

Minister of Agriculture and Livestock: Javier Flores Galarza. *Communications:* Mayi Antillón Guerrero. *Competitiveness:* Jorge Woodbridge González. *Culture and Youth:* María Elena Carballo Castegnaro. *Economy, Industry and Commerce:* José Eduardo Sibaja Arias. *Environment, Energy and Telecommunications:* Jorge Rodríguez Quirós. *Finance:* Jenny Phillips Aguilar. *Foreign Relations and Religion:* Bruno Stagno Ugarte. *Foreign Trade:* Marco Vinicio Ruiz Gutiérrez. *Housing:* Clara Zomer Rezler. *Institutional Co-ordination, and Public Works and Transportation:* Marco Antonio Vargas Díaz. *Interior, Police and Public Security:* Janina del Vecchio Ugalde. *Justice:* Hernando París Rodríguez. *Labour and Social Security:* Álvaro González Alfaro. *Planning and Economic Policy:* Roberto Gallardo Núñez. *Public Education:* Leonardo Garnier Rimolo. *Public Health:* María Luisa Ávila Agüero. *Science and Technology:* Eugenia Flores Vindas. *Tourism:* Carlos Ricardo Benavides. *Minister of the Presidency:* Rodrigo Arias Sánchez.

Government Website (Spanish only): http://www.casapres.go.cr

CURRENT LEADERS

Laura Chinchilla

Position
President

Introduction
Laura Chinchilla was elected Costa Rica's first female president in Feb. 2010, continuing the centre-right National Liberation Party's (PLN) hold on government. A former justice minister, she has won praise for her attempts to tackle drug networks and improve public security.

Early Life
Laura Chinchilla Miranda was born on 28 March 1959 in Desamparados, a suburb of the capital, San José. She graduated in political science from the University of Costa Rica in 1981 and went on to earn a master's in public administration from Georgetown University in the USA. Returning to Costa Rica, she worked as a consultant to various international organizations including the US Agency for International Development, the UN Development Program and the Inter-American Development Bank, on issues such as public safety, border security, human rights and judicial reform.

Consultancy for the ministry of national planning and economic policy in the early 1990s led to Chinchilla being offered a senior role in government. In May 1994 she was appointed deputy minister of public security in the administration of José María Figueres Olsen, whose PLN had won the general election three months earlier. Chinchilla also led the national council of migration and foreign affairs and was a member of the board of the national drug council. She was promoted to minister for public security in 1996 and gained a reputation for her tough stance on criminal drugs activities.

Chinchilla was elected to the legislative assembly as a deputy for the province of San José in 2002 and served as vice-president under Oscar Arias of the PLN. Arias, who had served as president in the late 1980s and was awarded the Nobel Peace Prize for his contribution to democracy and peace in central America, enjoyed popular support and won a further term in Jan. 2006. Chinchilla served as both vice-president and justice minister until she left office in Oct. 2008 to mount a presidential campaign. She emerged victorious after the first round on 7 Feb. 2010, taking 47% of the vote, well ahead of nearest rival Ottón Solís of the left-leaning Citizens' Action Party on 25%.

Career in Office
Chinchilla was sworn in on 8 May 2010. She pledged to make Costa Rica the first developed country in Central America, confirmed her commitment to carbon neutrality by 2021 and promised to improve health care, safety and security.

DEFENCE

In 2006 defence expenditure totalled US$99m. (US$24 per capita), representing 0·4% of GDP.

Army
The Army was abolished in 1948 and replaced by a Civil Guard numbering 4,500 in 2007. In addition there is a Border Security Police of 2,500 and a Rural Guard, 2,000-strong.

Navy
The paramilitary Coast Guard Unit numbered (2007) 400.

Air Wing
There is a 400-strong Air Surveillance Unit attached to the ministry of public security, equipped with ten light planes and two helicopters.

INTERNATIONAL RELATIONS

Costa Rica is a member of the UN, World Bank, IMF and several other UN specialized agencies, WTO, IOM, ACS, CACM, Inter-American Development Bank, SELA and OAS.

ECONOMY

Agriculture accounted for 8·8% of GDP in 2006, industry 29·4% and services 61·8%.

Overview
Growth rates dipped in the mid-1990s and early in the 2000s but otherwise the economy has grown at a healthy pace. Following the economic crisis of the 1980s, which was in part brought on by a fall in the prices of key exports (bananas, pineapples and coffee), the country diversified into manufacturing. Tax-free trade zones were established to attract foreign companies. Foreign direct investment (FDI) was initially for assembly plants producing clothing for the US market. Later, investment in skilled labour attracted electronics and telecommunications equipment manufacturers shifting production from the USA to lower-cost locations. The most significant foreign investment was the opening of an Intel computer chip assembly and testing plant in 1998. Since then other US manufacturing companies have chosen the country as an FDI destination because of its proximity, relative political stability and well-educated, English-speaking, population. On 1 Jan. 2009 the US–Central American Free Trade Agreement came into force.

Preliminary figures suggest economic growth slowed in 2009 owing to reduced demand for exports and a reduction in investment. Central government expenditure has increased in response and the World Bank approved a US$500m. credit line in April 2009.

Currency
The unit of currency is the *Costa Rican colón* (CRC) of 100 *céntimos*. The official rate is used for all imports on an essential list and by the government and autonomous institutions, and a free rate is used for all other transactions. In July 2005 total money supply was 1,101·6bn. colones, foreign exchange reserves were US$2,215m. and gold reserves were 2,000 troy oz. Inflation was 9·4% in 2007 and 13·4% in 2008.

Budget
In 2006 central government revenues were 2,750·0bn. colones (2,189·2bn. colones in 2005) and expenditures 2,508·6bn. colones (2,168·8bn. colones in 2005).

There is a sales tax of 13%.

Performance
Costa Rica, considered to be amongst the most stable countries in Central America, experienced real GDP growth of 7·8% in 2007 and 2·6% in 2008. Total GDP in 2008 was US$29·8bn.

Banking and Finance
The bank of issue is the Central Bank (founded 1950) which supervises the national monetary system, foreign exchange dealings and banking operations. The bank has a board of seven directors appointed by the government, including *ex officio* the Minister of Finance and the Planning Office Director. The *Governor* is Francisco de Paula Gutiérrez Gutiérrez.

There are three state-owned banks (Banco de Costa Rica, Banco Nacional de Costa Rica and Banco Popular y de Desarrollo Comunal), 17 private banks and one credit co-operative.

There is a stock exchange in San José.

Weights and Measures
The metric system is obligatory but Imperial Spanish measurements are still used.

ENERGY AND NATURAL RESOURCES

Environment
Costa Rica's carbon dioxide emissions from the consumption and flaring of fossil fuels in 2008 were the equivalent of 1·7 tonnes per capita. An *Environmental Performance Index* compiled in 2008 ranked Costa Rica fifth in the world, with 90·5%. The index examined various factors in six areas—air pollution, biodiversity and habitat, climate change, environmental health, productive natural resources and water resources.

Electricity
Installed capacity was an estimated 2·0m. kW in 2004. Production was 8·21bn. kWh in 2004; consumption per capita in 2004 was 1,876 kWh.

Minerals
In 2005 gold output was 424 kg and salt production was an estimated 37,000 tonnes.

Agriculture
Agriculture is a key sector, with an estimated 327,000 people being economically active in 2007. There were about 0·2m. ha. of arable land in 2007 and 0·3m. ha. of permanent crops. The principal agricultural products are coffee, bananas and sugar. Cattle are also of great importance. Production figures for 2003 (in 1,000 tonnes): sugarcane, 3,924; bananas, 1,863; pineapples, 725; oranges, 367; melons and watermelons, 292; rice, 180; coffee, 132; palm oil, 131; cassava, 94; potatoes, 82; plantains, 70.

Livestock (2003): cattle, 1·15m.; pigs, 500,000; horses, 115,000; chickens, 18m.

Forestry
In 2005 forests covered 2·39m. ha., or 46·8% of the land area. Timber production in 2007 was 4·61m. cu. metres.

Fisheries
Total catch in 2005 amounted to 22,340 tonnes, mostly from sea fishing.

INDUSTRY
The main manufactured goods are foodstuffs, palm oil, textiles, fertilizers, pharmaceuticals, furniture, cement, tyres, canning, clothing, plastic goods, plywood and electrical equipment.

Labour
In July 2001 there were 1,552,920 people in employment. In July 2001 there were 100,397 unemployed persons, or 6·1% of the workforce. The main area of employment is transport, storage and communications (303,000 people in 2002), followed by agriculture, hunting, forestry and fisheries (243,000 in 2002).

Trade Unions
There are two main trade unions, Rerum Novarum (anti-Communist) and Confederación General de Trabajadores Costarricenses (Communist).

INTERNATIONAL TRADE
A free trade agreement was signed with Mexico in March 1994. Some 2,300 products were freed from tariffs, with others to follow over ten years. In 2007 a national referendum approved the adoption of the Central America-Dominican Republic-United States Free Trade Agreement (CAFTA-DR), which establishes a free trade zone with the Dominican Republic, El Salvador, Guatemala, Honduras, Nicaragua and the USA. It was approved by the Legislative Assembly in Nov. 2008 and subsequently entered into force on 1 Jan. 2009. External debt was US$6,223m. in 2005.

Imports and Exports
The value of imports and exports in US$1m. was:

	2002	*2003*	*2004*	*2005*	*2006*
Imports f.o.b.	6,547·7	7,252·3	7,791·0	9,242·0	10,810·8
Exports f.o.b.	5,269·9	6,163·0	6,369·7	7,099·6	8,067·5

Principal imports: machinery and apparatus, chemicals and chemical products, mineral fuels, food. Chief exports: manufactured goods and other products, coffee, bananas, sugar, cocoa. Main import suppliers, 2006: USA, 39·6%; Japan, 5·3%; Venezuela, 5·3%; Mexico, 5·2%. Major export markets, 2006: USA, 42·5%; China, 7·7%; Hong Kong, 7·2%; Netherlands, 6·9%.

COMMUNICATIONS

Roads
In 2007 there were 36,654 km of roads, including 7,640 km of main roads. On the Costa Rica section of the Inter-American Highway it is possible to drive to Panama during the dry season. The Pan-American Highway into Nicaragua is metalled for most of the way and a new highway between San José and Caldera opened in Jan. 2010. Passenger cars in use in 2007 numbered 525,400, buses and coaches 12,300, vans and lorries 139,600 and motorcycles and mopeds 100,100. There were 339 fatalities as a result of road accidents in 2007.

Rail
The nationalized railway system (Incofer) was closed in 1995 following an earthquake in 1991. Freight services and some commuter services have now been resumed. In 2003 the railways carried 5,000 passengers and 14,000 tonnes of freight.

Civil Aviation
There are international airports at San José (Juan Santamaria) and Liberia (Daniel Oduber Quirós). The national carrier is Líneas Aéreas Costarriquenses (LACSA). In 2003 scheduled airline traffic of Costa Rican-based carriers flew 20m. km, carrying 750,000 passengers (584,000 on international flights). In 2001 San

José handled 2,108,713 passengers (1,972,606 on international flights) and 67,858 tonnes of freight.

Shipping

The chief ports are Limón on the Atlantic and Caldera on the Pacific. The merchant marine totalled 4,000 GRT in 2002. In 2005 vessels totalling 2,012,000 NRT entered ports and vessels totalling 2,012,000 NRT cleared.

Telecommunications

Costa Rica had 2,489,500 telephone subscribers in 2005 (575·3 per 1,000 inhabitants), including 1,101,000 mobile phone subscribers. There were 930,000 PCs in use (218·9 for every 1,000 persons) in 2004 and 1m. internet users.

Postal Services

In 2003 there were 121 post offices.

SOCIAL INSTITUTIONS

Justice

Justice is administered by the Supreme Court and five appeal courts divided into five chambers—the Court of Cassation, the Higher and Lower Criminal Courts, and the Higher and Lower Civil Courts. There are also subordinate courts in the separate provinces and local justices throughout the republic. There is no capital punishment.

The population in penal institutions in Nov. 2004 was 7,619 (177 per 100,000 of national population).

Education

The adult literacy rate in 2005 was 97·4% (96·0% among males and 96·2% among females). Primary instruction is compulsory and free from six to 14 years; secondary education (since 1949) is also free. Primary schools are provided and maintained by local school councils, while the national government pays the teachers, besides making subventions in aid of local funds. In 2006 there were 4,026 public and private primary schools with 35,413 teachers and administrative staff and 521,505 enrolled pupils, and 752 public and private secondary schools with 24,445 teachers and 338,508 pupils. In 2004 there were 166,417 university students. The largest of the four public universities is the University of Costa Rica (Universidad de Costa Rica). There are also a number of private universities.

In 2006 public expenditure on education came to 4·9% of GNI, representing 20·6% of total government expenditure.

Health

In 2006 there were 6,987 doctors, 2,800 dentists, 6,943 nurses, 3,058 pharmacists and 29 hospitals. There were 14 beds per 10,000 inhabitants in 2006.

RELIGION

Roman Catholicism is the state religion; it had 3·38m. adherents in 2001. There is entire religious liberty under the constitution. The Archbishop of Costa Rica has six bishops at Alajuela, Ciudad Quesada, Limón, Puntarenas, San Isidro el General and Tilarán. There were 360,000 Protestants in 2001. The remainder of the population are followers of other religions.

CULTURE

World Heritage Sites

Costa Rica has three sites on the UNESCO World Heritage List: Cocos Island National Park (1997 and 2002); and the Area de Conservación Guanacaste (1999 and 2004), an important dry forest habitat.

Costa Rica shares a UNESCO site with Panama: the Talamanca Range-La Amistad Reserves (1983 and 1990), an important cross-breeding site for North and South American flora and fauna.

Broadcasting

There are various private and public television and radio services; cable TV is widely available. In 2006 there were 1·1m. television receivers (colour by NTSC).

Press

There were six daily newspapers in 2006 with a combined circulation of 199,000, and 34 non-dailies. The most widely read dailies are La Nación, Diario Extra and Al Día.

Tourism

In 2005 there were 1,679,000 non-resident tourists, spending US$1,804m.

Theatre and Opera

There are eight national theatres.

Museums and Galleries

Costa Rica has three museums.

DIPLOMATIC REPRESENTATIVES

Of Costa Rica in the United Kingdom (Flat 1, 14 Lancaster Gate, London, W2 3LH)
Ambassador: Pilar Saborío Rocafort.

Of the United Kingdom in Costa Rica (Edificio Centro Colón, 11th Floor, Apartado 815, San José 1007)
Ambassador: Tom Kennedy.

Of Costa Rica in the USA (2114 S St., NW, Washington, D.C., 20008)
Ambassador: Luis Diego Escalante.

Of the USA in Costa Rica (Calle 120 Avenida 0, Pavas, San José)
Ambassador: Anne Slaughter Andrew.

Of Costa Rica to the United Nations
Ambassador: Jorge Urbina.

Of Costa Rica to the European Union
Ambassador: Roberto Echandi.

FURTHER READING

Biesanz, R., *et al.*, *The Costa Ricans.* 1982
Bird, L., *Costa Rica: Unarmed Democracy.* 1984
Creedman, T. S., *Historical Dictionary of Costa Rica.* 2nd ed. 1991
Cruz, Consuelo, *Political Culture and Institutional Development in Costa Rica and Nicaragua: World Making in the Tropics.* 2005

National Statistical Office: Instituto Nacional de Estadística y Censos, San José.
Website (Spanish only): http://www.inec.go.cr

CÔTE D'IVOIRE

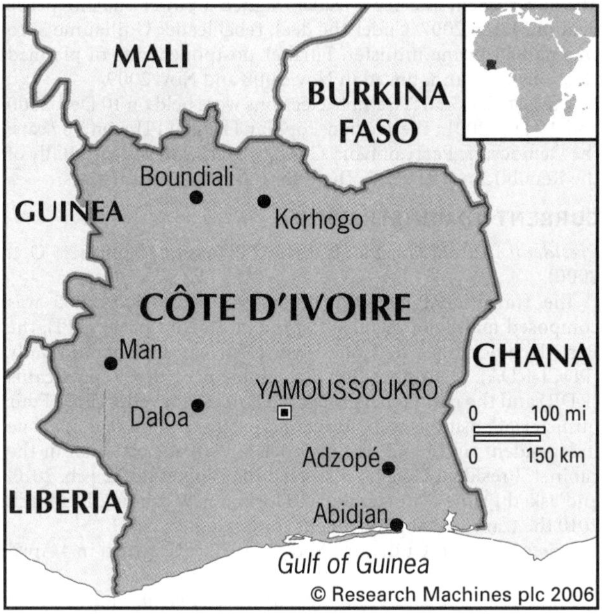

République de la Côte d'Ivoire
(Republic of Côte d'Ivoire)

Capital: Yamoussoukro
Seat of government: Abidjan
Population estimate, 2010: 21·57m.
GDP per capita, 2007: (PPP$) 1,690
HDI/world rank: 0·484/163

KEY HISTORICAL EVENTS

France obtained rights on the coast in 1842 but did not occupy the territory until 1882. In the early 1870s a French offer to exchange Côte d'Ivoire with the British for the Gambia, which bisected the French colony of Senegal, was refused. Rumours of gold later rekindled French interest and in 1889 Côte d'Ivoire was declared a French protectorate. Governors appointed from France administered the colony using a system of centralized rule that allowed little room for local participation. In 1946 Côte d'Ivoire's first political party, the Democratic Party of Côte d'Ivoire, was created under the leadership of Félix Houphouët-Boigny who eventually adopted a policy of co-operation with the French authorities. By the mid-1950s the country was the wealthiest in French West Africa and in 1958 Côte d'Ivoire became an autonomous republic within the French Community. Côte d'Ivoire achieved full independence on 7 Aug. 1960, with Félix Houphouët-Boigny as its first president.

On 23 Dec. 1999 President Henri Konan Bédié was ousted in a military coup led by Gen. Robert Guéï, the country's military chief from 1990 to 1995. On 6 Oct. 2000 a state of emergency was declared ahead of a Supreme Court announcement on the candidates allowed to stand for the presidential election on 22 Oct. 2000. After Robert Guéï declared himself the winner in the election, a violent uprising in which over 2,000 people were killed resulted in Gen. Guéï fleeing to Benin. The veteran opposition candidate Laurent Gbagbo was then declared the rightful winner. In Sept. 2002 there was a failed coup by mutinous soldiers that claimed more than 20 lives, including those of both Gen. Guéï and the interior minister. Côte d'Ivoire then descended further into civil war, with the country divided between the rebel-held north and the government-held south. A peace agreement was reached in Jan. 2003 but was not implemented in full. In April 2005 government, rebel and opposition leaders signed a deal to end the civil war and pledged to hold elections in Oct., but these were subsequently postponed owing to the ongoing crisis. Under a power-sharing peace deal agreed in March 2007 between the government and the New Forces rebels, the New Forces leader, Guillaume Soro, became prime minister. A joint military command was planned.

TERRITORY AND POPULATION

Côte d'Ivoire is bounded in the west by Liberia and Guinea, north by Mali and Burkina Faso, east by Ghana, and south by the Gulf of Guinea. It has an area (including inland water) of 322,460 sq. km. The population at the 1998 census was 15,366,672; density, 47·7 per sq. km. The population was 55·0% rural in 2005.

The UN gives an estimated population for 2010 of 21·57m.

Since 2000 the country has been divided into 19 regions comprising 58 departments.

Areas, populations (1998 census) and capitals of the regions are:

Region	*Area (in sq. km)*	*Population*	*Capital*
Agnéby	9,080	525,211	Agboville
Bafing	8,720	139,251	Touba
Bas-Sassandra	25,800	1,395,251	San-Pédro
Denguélé	20,600	222,446	Odienné
Dix-Huit Montagnes	16,600	936,510	Man
Fromager	6,900	542,992	Gagnoa
Haut-Sassandra	15,200	1,071,977	Daloa
Lacs	8,920	476,235	Yamoussoukro
Lagunes	14,200	3,733,413	Abidjan
Marahoué	8,500	554,807	Bouaflé
Moyen-Cavally	14,150	508,733	Guiglo
Moyen-Comoé	6,900	394,761	Abengourou
N'zi-Comoé	19,560	633,927	Dimbokro
Savanes	40,323	929,673	Korhogo
Sud-Bandama	10,650	682,021	Divo
Sud-Comoé	6,250	459,487	Aboisso
Vallée du Bandama	28,530	1,080,509	Bouaké
Worodougou	21,900	378,463	Séguéla
Zanzan	38,000	701,005	Bondoukou

In 2000 the population of Abidjan stood at 3,790,000. Other major towns (with 1998 census population): Bouaké, 461,618; Yamoussoukro, 299,243; Daloa, 173,107; Korhogo, 142,093.

There are about 60 ethnic groups, the principal ones being the Baoulé (23%), the Bété (18%) and the Sénoufo (15%). A referendum held in July 2000 on the adoption of a new constitution set eligibility conditions for presidential candidates (the candidate and both his parents had to be Ivorian). This excluded a northern Muslim leader and in effect made foreigners out of millions of Ivorians. The north of the country is predominantly Muslim and the south predominantly Christian and animist.

Approximately 30% of the population are immigrants, in particular from Burkina Faso, Mali, Guinea and Senegal.

French is the official language.

SOCIAL STATISTICS

2000 estimates: births, 559,000; deaths, 242,000. Rates (2000 estimates, per 1,000 population); birth, 35·3; death, 15·3. Expectation of life in 2007 was 55·7 years for males and 58·3 for females. Annual population growth rate, 2000–05, 3·0%. Infant mortality, 2005, 118 per 1,000 live births; fertility rate, 2004, 4·9 births per woman. 29% of the population are migrants.

CLIMATE

A tropical climate, affected by distance from the sea. In coastal areas, there are wet seasons from May to July and in Oct. and Nov., but in central areas the periods are March to May and July to Nov. In the north, there is one wet season from June to Oct. Abidjan, Jan. 81°F (27·2°C), July 75°F (23·9°C). Annual rainfall 84" (2,100 mm). Bouaké, Jan. 81°F (27·2°C), July 77°F (25°C). Annual rainfall 48" (1,200 mm).

CONSTITUTION AND GOVERNMENT

The 1960 constitution was amended in 1971, 1975, 1980, 1985, 1986, 1990, 1998 and 2000. The sole legal party was the Democratic Party of Côte d'Ivoire, but opposition parties were legalized in 1990. There is a 225-member *National Assembly* elected by universal suffrage for a five-year term. The *President* is also directly elected for a five-year term (renewable). He appoints and leads a Council of Ministers.

In Nov. 1990 the National Assembly voted that its Speaker should become President in the event of the latter's incapacity, and created the post of Prime Minister to be appointed by the President. Following the death of President Houphouët-Boigny on 7 Dec. 1993, the speaker, Henri Konan Bédié, proclaimed himself head of state till the end of the presidential term in Sept. 1995.

Following the coup of Dec. 1999 a referendum was held on 23 July 2000 on the adoption of a new constitution, which set eligibility conditions for presidential candidates (the candidate and both his parents must be Ivorian), reduced the voting age from 21 to 18, and abolished the death penalty. It also offered an amnesty to soldiers who staged the coup and the junta, but committed the junta to hand over power to an elected civilian head of state and parliament within six months of the proclamation of the text. Approximately 87% of votes cast were in favour of the new constitution. This was subsequently adopted on 4 Aug. 2000.

National Anthem

'L'Abidjanaise' ('Song of Abidjan'); words by M. Ekra, J. Bony and P. M. Coty, tune by P. M. Pango.

GOVERNMENT CHRONOLOGY

Presidents since 1960. (PDCI-RDA = Democratic Party of Ivory Coast-African Democratic Rally; FPI = Ivorian Popular Front)

1960–93	PDCI-RDA	Félix Houphouët-Boigny
1993–99	PDCI-RDA	Aimé Henri Konan Bédié
1999–2000	military	Robert Guéï
2000–	FPI	Laurent Gbagbo

RECENT ELECTIONS

Presidential elections were last held on 22 Oct. 2000, but were boycotted by the former ruling Parti Démocratique de Côte d'Ivoire/Democratic Party of Ivory Coast and the Rassemblement des Républicains/Rally of the Republicans. Laurent Gbagbo (Front Populaire Ivorienne/Ivorian Popular Front) obtained 59·4% of votes cast against 32·7% for Robert Guéï, who had seized power in a coup in Dec. 1999. Initially Robert Guéï claimed victory but following a violent uprising accepted defeat (the first time in Africa that a popular rising had succeeded in toppling a military regime). There were three other candidates.

Presidential and parliamentary elections scheduled for 30 Oct. 2005 were postponed in view of the continuing instability. In order to avert a constitutional crisis, the UN Security Council recommended that the president remain in office for a further year and that an interim prime minister be appointed. On 4 Dec. 2005 international mediators chose Charles Konan Banny, governor of the Central Bank of West African States, as prime minister for a ten-month period that was set to end in Oct. 2006. However, elections that were scheduled to take place in Oct. 2006 were again postponed owing to the delay in preparations. In Nov. the Security Council voted to extend the mandates of President Gbagbo and Prime Minister Banny for another year. The government and rebel leaders signed a power-sharing peace deal in March 2007. Under the deal, rebel leader Guillaume Soro was named prime minister. Further postponements of planned elections were announced in Nov. 2008 and Nov. 2009.

The last National Assembly elections were held on 10 Dec. 2000 and 14 Jan. 2001. The Ivorian Popular Front (FPI) won 96 seats; the Democratic Party of Ivory Coast (PDCI) won 94 seats; Rally of the Republicans (RDR), 5. There were also two vacant seats.

CURRENT ADMINISTRATION

President: Laurent Gbagbo; b. 1945 (FPI; assumed office 26 Oct. 2000).

The transitional government appointed in Dec. 2005 was composed mainly of members of the president's party (FPI), the Parti Démocratique de Côte d'Ivoire-African Democratic Rally (PDCI-RDA), the opposition Rassemblement des Républicains (RDR) and the main rebel group, the Forces Nouvelles (FN). Four ministerial positions went to smaller parties and there is also one independent (ind.) and one member of civil society (c.s.) in the cabinet. President Gbagbo dissolved the cabinet on 12 Feb. 2010, and asked Prime Minister Soro to form a new cabinet. In March 2010 the transitional government comprised:

Prime Minister: Guillaume Soro; b. 1972 (FN; sworn in 4 April 2007).

Minister of State for Planning and Development: Paul Antoine Bohoun Bouabré (FPI). *Minister of State for Justice, Human Rights and Keeper of the Seals:* Mamadou Koné (FN). *Minister of Agriculture:* Mamadou Sangafowa Coulibaly (RDR). *Animal Production and Fishery Resources:* Alphonse Douaty (FPI). *Civil Service, Employment and Administrative Reform:* Émile Guiriehoulou (FPI). *Commerce:* Calice Yapo Yapo (PDCI-RDA). *Communication:* Ibrahim Sy Savané (FN). *Construction, Housing and Town Planning:* Tiémoko Koné (FN). *Culture and Francophonie:* Moutaye Azoumana (Movement of Future Forces). *Defence:* Michel Amani N'Guessan (FPI). *Economic Infrastructure:* Dagobert Banzio (PDCI-RDA). *Economy and Finance:* Charles Diby Koffi (c.s.). *Environment, Water and Forests:* Karim Fadiga (Ivorian Workers' Party). *Family, Women and Social Affairs:* Vacant. *Fight Against AIDS:* Christine Adjobi (FPI). *Foreign Affairs and African Integration:* Jean-Marie Kacou Gervais (PDCI-RDA). *Health and Public Hygiene:* Eugène Aouélé Aka (PDCI-RDA). *Higher Education and Scientific Research:* Vacant. *Industry and Promotion of the Private Sector:* Moussa Dosso (FN). *Interior:* Désiré Tagro (FPI). *Mines and Energy:* Augustin Komoé Kouadio (FPI). *National Education:* Gilbert Bleu Lainé (ind.). *New Information Technologies and Telecommunications:* Jacques Gohorey Houga Bi (RDR). *Technical Education and Professional Training:* Benjamin Yapo Atsé (FPI). *Tourism and Handicrafts:* Sidiki Konaté (FN). *Transport:* Albert Flindé (Union for Democracy and Peace in Côte d'Ivoire). *Youth, Civic Education and Sports:* Théodore Mel Eg (Union Démocratique Citoyenne).

Office of the President (French only): http://www.cotedivoirepr.ci

CURRENT LEADERS

Laurent Gbagbo

Position
President

Introduction
Laurent Gbagbo took over the presidency in Oct. 2000, succeeding Robert Guéï who had been forced into exile after claiming victory in a disputed presidential election. Gbagbo subsequently oversaw a long period of political and economic instability and fighting

between the rebel, largely Muslim, north of the country and the government-controlled and mainly Christian south before a more enduring power-sharing agreement was concluded in March 2007.

Early Life

Gbagbo was born on 31 May 1945 in Gagnoa in the mid-west of the country. He graduated in history and was jailed in the early 1970s for subversive teaching. Increasingly involved in trade union politics, he was a critic of the regime of Félix Houphouët-Boigny who had been in power since 1960.

In the 1980s Gbagbo went into exile in France, from where he established the Ivorian Popular Front (FPI) and developed a nationalist agenda. Gbagbo returned to the country in 1988 and two years later Houphouët-Boigny agreed to multi-party elections. In 1993 Houphouët-Boigny was succeeded by Henri Konan Bédié, who remained in power until 1999, when he was deposed by Gen. Robert Guéï in a military coup.

Guéï announced new presidential elections in which he excluded anyone unable to prove 'pure' Ivorian heritage from running. This removed 15 candidates, including a major opposition leader, Alassane Ouattara of the Rally of the Republicans (RDR), which had widespread support in the Muslim north. Guéï claimed victory although Gbagbo was widely believed to have polled most votes. Popular protests forced Guéï to resign and Gbagbo assumed the presidency on 26 Oct. 2000.

Career in Office

Ouattara immediately urged Gbagbo to call new elections, but Gbagbo refused. Fighting broke out between Ouattara's Muslim supporters in the north and Gbagbo's Christian supporters in the south. In parliamentary elections held at the end of 2000, the FPI emerged as the largest party, although only one third of those eligible voted. In Jan. 2001 Gbagbo survived an attempted coup.

As well as increasing ethnic friction, he was confronted by an economy suffering from a decline in the global cocoa market (Côte d'Ivoire being the world's largest producer of cocoa). Also, his broad nationalist position led him to announce a ban on foreign ownership of property, causing unease among the country's immigrants making up around 30% of the population.

Gbagbo's human rights record has received widespread criticism. Leading opposition politicians have been arrested on disputed charges, and from 2001 the US embassy and Amnesty International voiced concerns over arbitrary detention and mistreatment. Alleged use of child slave labour further tarnished Gbagbo's regime. Côte d'Ivoire consequently suffered cuts in international aid, with the UN refusing to resume assistance until a domestic reconciliation process was in place.

In Sept. 2002 fighting erupted in Abidjan when 700 troops, believed to be loyal to Guéï, mutinied. Guéï was killed by government forces. There was further violence in Bouaké and several other towns which had been seized by rebels. ECOWAS agreed to broker negotiations between the government and the rebel factions and a short-lived ceasefire was signed in Oct. In Jan. 2003 the French authorities brokered another ceasefire and a power-sharing agreement to end the civil war (despite violent anti-French protests in Abidjan by pro-government supporters). Under the agreement Gbagbo would remain president, with a prime minister approved by consensus serving alongside. Seydou Diarra was chosen to serve as prime minister until elections scheduled for 2005. However, little progress was made in disarming militia forces or implementing political reform before a serious resurgence of conflict in Nov. 2004. Following an attack by government forces across the ceasefire line against the rebels and on French peacekeeping troops, the French military retaliated by destroying the Ivorian air force, provoking more rioting by pro-government supporters in Abidjan. Further attempts at reconciliation, brokered by South Africa, resulted in a new agreement in April 2005 to revitalize power sharing, but it remained fragile and elections scheduled firstly for late 2005 and then for Oct. 2006 were postponed. In Nov. 2006 the UN Security Council extended Gbagbo's presidential mandate. Earlier, in Sept., Gbagbo accepted Prime Minister Banny's resignation over an environmental scandal in which toxic waste contaminated residential areas of Abidjan, the largest city, but subsequently asked him to form a new administration.

In March 2007 Gbagbo agreed a further power-sharing deal in an attempt to unify the country, under which the FN rebel leader, Guillaume Soro, became prime minister in a new administration. Nevertheless, the threat of further violence has remained (Soro survived a rocket attack on his plane in June 2007) and presidential elections have been postponed several times (most recently in Nov. 2009), mainly owing to security concerns and to problems over who is qualified to vote and the validity of identity cards. In Oct. 2008 the UN extended its arms embargo and sanctions on Côte d'Ivoire's diamond trade for a further year, but agreed to review the embargo once presidential elections had been held. In May 2009 former rebel forces relinquished territory in ten northern zones of the country to state control under civilian administrators appointed by Gbagbo.

DEFENCE

Defence expenditure totalled US$266m. in 2006 (US$15 per capita), representing 1·5% of GDP.

About 7,200 UN troops, aided by 900 French soldiers, are in the country to maintain a ceasefire.

Army

Total strength (2007), 6,500. In addition there is a Presidential Guard of 1,350, a Gendarmerie of 7,600 and a Militia of 1,500.

Navy

Personnel in 2007 totalled about 900 with the force based at Locodjo (Abidjan).

Air Force

There are six combat capable aircraft, although their serviceability is in doubt. Personnel (2007) 700.

INTERNATIONAL RELATIONS

Côte d'Ivoire is a member of the UN, World Bank, IMF and several other UN specialized agencies, WTO, IOM, International Organization of the Francophonie, Islamic Development Bank, OIC, African Development Bank, African Union, ECOWAS, UEMOA and is an ACP member state of the ACP-EU relationship.

ECONOMY

Agriculture accounted for 23·1% of GDP in 2006, industry 26·8% and services 50·2%.

Overview

After a burst of economic expansion following independence from France in the 1960s, Côte d'Ivoire has seen little growth. The civil war that began in 2002 held growth rates at around 1% per year for most of the 2000s. The economy began to recover in 2008, spurred by the Ouagadougou Political Accord of 2007 which reunified the country. With a steadily improving security situation, the World Bank expects growth to increase gradually over the next few years.

Export industries include cocoa beans, crude oil and manufactures. Côte d'Ivoire is the world's largest producer of cocoa but, since 2006, oil and gas production have become more important for the economy. Unemployment is estimated to be as high as 50%.

The economy constitutes 40% of the GDP of the West African Economic and Monetary Union (UEMOA), largely as a result of the dependence of several neighbouring countries (including

Burkina Faso, Mali and Guinea) on Côte d'Ivoire for transport and remittances from migrant nationals.

Currency
The unit of currency is the *franc CFA* (XOF) with a parity of 655·957 francs CFA to one euro. Foreign exchange reserves were US$1,379m. in June 2005 and total money supply was 1,225·0bn. francs CFA. Inflation was 1·9% in 2007 and 6·3% in 2008.

Budget
Revenues in 2005 were 1,566bn. francs CFA (tax revenue, 79·9%) and expenditures 1,537bn. francs CFA (current expenditure, 78·4%).

VAT is 18%.

Performance
Real GDP growth was 1·6% in 2007 and 2·3% in 2008. Total GDP in 2008 was US$23·4bn.

Banking and Finance
The regional Banque Centrale des États de l'Afrique de l'Ouest is the central bank and bank of issue. The *Governor* is Philippe-Henri Dacoury-Tabley. In 2002 there were 13 commercial banks and six credit institutions. The African Development Bank is based in Abidjan.

ENERGY AND NATURAL RESOURCES

Environment
Carbon dioxide emissions from the consumption and flaring of fossil fuels in 2008 were the equivalent of 0·3 tonnes per capita.

Electricity
The electricity industry was privatized in 1990. Installed capacity was an estimated 1·4m. kW in 2004. Production in 2004 amounted to 5·41bn. kWh, with consumption per capita 224 kWh.

Oil and Gas
Petroleum has been produced (offshore) since Oct. 1977. Production (2004), 9·5m. bbls. Oil reserves, 2007, 100m. bbls. Natural gas reserves, 2007, 28bn. cu. metres; production (2004), 1,016m. cu. metres.

Minerals
Côte d'Ivoire has large deposits of iron ores, bauxite, tantalite, diamonds, gold, nickel and manganese, most of which are untapped. Gold production totalled 3·6 tonnes in 2002. Estimated diamond production, 2005: 300,000 carats.

Agriculture
In 2002 the agricultural population was 9·09m., of whom 3·13m. were economically active. In 2002 agriculture accounted for 58% of exports. There were 3·10m. ha. of arable land in 2001 and 4·40m. ha. of permanent crops. 73,000 ha. were irrigated in 2001. There were 3,800 tractors in 2001 and 70 harvester-threshers. Côte d'Ivoire is the world's largest producer and exporter of cocoa beans, with an output of 1·23m. tonnes in 2003 (more than 37% of the world total). It is also a leading coffee producer, although production dropped from 365,000 tonnes in 2000 to 160,000 tonnes in 2003. The cocoa and coffee industries have for years relied on foreign workers, but tens of thousands have left the country since the 1999 coup resulting in labour shortages. Other main crops, with 2001 production figures in 1,000 tonnes, are: yams (2,938), cassava (1,688), plantains (1,410), rice (1,212), sugarcane (1,155), maize (573), taro (369), seed cotton (287), bananas (270), coconuts (240), pineapples (235), palm oil (205), tomatoes (170), cottonseed (162), groundnuts (145), natural rubber (128) and cotton lint (124). Côte d'Ivoire is the biggest producer of rubber outside of Asia.

Livestock, 2002: 1·52m. sheep, 1·48m. cattle, 1·19m. goats, 356,000 pigs and 33m. chickens.

Forestry
In 2005 the rainforest covered 10·41m. ha., or 32·7% of the total land area. Products include teak, mahogany and ebony. In 2007, 10·25m. cu. metres of roundwood were produced.

Fisheries
The catch in 2004 amounted to 54,398 tonnes, of which marine fish approximately 91% and freshwater fish 9%.

INDUSTRY
Industrialization has developed rapidly since independence, particularly food processing, textiles and sawmills. Output in 2004 (in 1,000 tonnes): distillate fuel oil, 1,313; kerosene, 940; cement (2001), 650; petrol, 589; residual fuel oil, 209; sugar (2002), 177; sawnwood (2001), 630,000 cu. metres; veneer sheets (2001), 296,000 cu. metres.

Labour
In 2003 the workforce was 7·3m. (60% males).

Trade Unions
The main trade union is the Union Générale des Travailleurs de Côte d'Ivoire, with over 100,000 members.

INTERNATIONAL TRADE
External debt was US$10,735m. in 2005.

Imports and Exports
Imports and exports for calendar years in US$1m.:

	2003	2004	2005	2006	2007
Imports c.i.f.	3,536·3	4,714·7	5,865·0	5,820·4	6,683·1
Exports f.o.b.	5,493·4	6,578·9	7,247·9	8,147·7	8,067·7

Main imports, 2007: petroleum and petroleum products, 30·0%; machinery and transport equipment, 19·7%; food and live animals, 15·3%; chemicals and related products, 11·0%; arms and ammunition, 3·9%. Principal exports, 2007: petroleum and petroleum products, 32·6%; cocoa, 26·4%; machinery and transport equipment, 4·9%; natural rubber, 4·4%; arms and ammunition, 4·0%. Main import suppliers, 2007: Nigeria, 24·1%; France, 21·7%; China, 6·6%; Venezuela, 3·2%; Thailand, 2·8%. Main export markets, 2007: France, 20·5%; Netherlands, 9·1%; Nigeria, 8·0%; USA, 6·8%; Burkina Faso, 4·2%.

COMMUNICATIONS

Roads
In 2004 roads totalled about 80,000 km. There were about 114,000 passenger cars in 2002 (6·4 per 1,000 inhabitants).

Rail
From Abidjan a metre-gauge railway runs to Léraba on the border with Burkina Faso (660 km), and thence through Burkina Faso to Ouagadougou and Kaya. Operation of the railway in both countries is franchised to the mixed public-private company Sitarail. Across both countries Sitarail carried 156,569 passengers in 2004 and 759,957 tonnes of freight in 2005.

Civil Aviation
There is an international airport at Abidjan (Félix Houphouët-Boigny Airport), which in 2001 handled 912,000 passengers (all on international flights) and 19,100 tonnes of freight. The national carrier is the state-owned Air Ivoire. It provides domestic services and in 2003 operated international flights to Accra, Bamako, Conakry, Cotonou, Dakar, Douala, Libreville, Lomé, Niamey and Ouagadougou. There were direct flights in 2003 with other airlines to Addis Ababa, Banjul, Beirut, Bobo Dioulasso, Brazzaville, Brussels, Cairo, Casablanca, Freetown, Johannesburg, Lagos, Monrovia, Nairobi, Nouakchott, Paris, Pointe-Noire and Tripoli. In 2001 scheduled airline traffic of Côte d'Ivoire-based carriers

flew 1m. km, carrying 46,000 passengers (all on international flights).

Shipping

The main ports are Abidjan and San-Pédro. Abidjan handled 15m. tonnes of cargo for the first time in 1998 and is the busiest port in West Africa. Some US$200m. have been earmarked for continued expansion of the port. In 2002 the merchant marine totalled 9,000 GRT, including oil tankers 1,000 GRT.

Telecommunications

In 2003 there were 1,518,700 telephone subscribers, or 91·3 per 1,000 inhabitants, of which 1,280,700 were mobile phone subscribers. There were 262,000 PCs in use (15·5 per 1,000 persons) in 2004 and 160,000 internet users.

Postal Services

In 2003 there were 194 post offices.

SOCIAL INSTITUTIONS

Justice

There are 28 courts of first instance and three assize courts in Abidjan, Bouaké and Daloa, two courts of appeal in Abidjan and Bouaké, and a supreme court in Abidjan. Côte d'Ivoire abolished the death penalty in 2000.

The population in penal institutions under government control was 10,621 (55 per 100,000 of national population) in Dec. 2007.

Education

The adult literacy rate in 2003 was 48·1% (60·1% among males and 38·2% among females). There were, in 2007, 2,179,801 pupils with 53,161 teaching staff in primary schools and (2000–01) 663,636 pupils with 23,184 teachers at secondary schools. In 2007 there were 156,772 students in higher education. In 1995–96 there was one university with 21,000 students and 730 academic staff, and three university centres. There were six other institutions of higher education.

In 2000–01 expenditure on education came to 4·9% of GNP and 21·5% of total government spending.

Health

In 1993 there were five hospital beds per 10,000 inhabitants. In 1996 there were 1,318 physicians, 4,568 nurses and 2,196 midwives.

RELIGION

In 2001 there were 6·3m. Muslims (mainly in the north) and 4·3m. Christians (chiefly Roman Catholics in the south). Although Christians are in the majority among Ivorians, when Côte d'Ivoire's large immigrant population is taken into account Muslims are in the majority. Traditional animist beliefs are also practised. In Feb. 2010 the Roman Catholic church had one cardinal.

CULTURE

World Heritage Sites

UNESCO world heritage sites in Côte d'Ivoire are: Taï National Park (inscribed on the list in 1982); the Comoé National Park (1983); and the Mount Nimba Strict Nature Reserve (1981 and 1982), shared with Guinea.

Broadcasting

The government-controlled Radiodiffusion Télévision Ivoirienne operates two television services (La Première and TV2) and two radio stations. There is no private terrestrial TV, but some pay-TV services are available. Independent radio services include Christian community radio stations and Onuci FM (launched by United Nations peacekeeping forces). There were 800,000 television sets (colour by SECAM V) in 2005.

Press

In 2005 there were 21 daily newspapers with a combined circulation of 190,000.

Tourism

There were 479,000 foreign tourists in 2002; spending by tourists totalled US$74m.

DIPLOMATIC REPRESENTATIVES

Of Côte d'Ivoire in the United Kingdom (2 Upper Belgrave St., London, SW1X 8BJ)
Ambassador: Philippe D. Djangoné-Bi.

Of the United Kingdom in Côte d'Ivoire (staff withdrawn from embassy in Abidjan)
Ambassador: Dr Nicholas Westcott, CMG (resides in Accra, Ghana).

Of Côte d'Ivoire in the USA (temporary address: 3421 Massachusetts Ave., NW, Washington, D.C., 20008)
Ambassador: Yao Charles Koffi.

Of the USA in Côte d'Ivoire (Riviera Golf, 01 B.P. 1712, Abidjan)
Ambassador: Wanda Nesbitt.

Of Côte d'Ivoire to the United Nations
Ambassador: Ilahiri A. Djédjé.

Of Côte d'Ivoire to the European Union
Ambassador: Marie Gosset.

FURTHER READING

Direction de la Statistique. *Bulletin Mensuel de Statistique.*
McGovern, Mike, *Making War in Côte d'Ivoire.* 2006
Mundt, Robert J., *Historical Dictionary of Côte d'Ivoire.* 1995

National Statistical Office: Institut National de la Statistique, BP V 55, Abidjan 01.
Website (French only): http://www.ins.ci

CROATIA

Republika Hrvatska
(Republic of Croatia)

Capital: Zagreb
Population estimate, 2010: 4·43m.
GDP per capita, 2007: (PPP$) 16,027
HDI/world rank: 0·871/45

KEY HISTORICAL EVENTS

Croatia was united with Hungary in 1091 and remained under Hungarian administration until the end of the First World War. On 1 Dec. 1918 Croatia became a part of the new Kingdom of Serbs, Croats and Slovenes, which was renamed Yugoslavia in 1929. During the Second World War an independent fascist (Ustaša) state was set up under the aegis of the German occupiers. During the Communist period Croatia became one of the six 'Socialist Republics' constituting the Yugoslav federation led by Marshal Tito. With the collapse of Communism, an independence movement gained momentum.

In a referendum on 19 May 1991, 94·17% of votes cast were in favour of Croatia becoming an independent sovereign state with the option of joining a future Yugoslav confederation as opposed to remaining in the existing Yugoslav federation. The Krajina and other predominantly Serbian areas of Croatia wanted union with Serbia and seized power. Croatian forces and Serb insurgents backed by federal forces became embroiled in a conflict throughout 1991 until the arrival of a UN peacekeeping mission at the beginning of 1992 and the establishment of four UN peacekeeping zones ('pink zones'). In early May 1995 Croatian forces retook Western Slavonia from the Serbs and opened the Zagreb-Belgrade highway. In a 60-hour operation mounted on 4 Aug. 1995 the former self-declared Serb Republic of Krajina was occupied, provoking an exodus of 180,000 Serb refugees. Croats who had left the area in 1991 began to return. On 12 Nov. 1995 the Croatian government and Bosnian Serbs reached an agreement to place Eastern Slavonia, the last Croatian territory still under Bosnian Serb control, under UN administration.

TERRITORY AND POPULATION

Croatia is bounded in the north by Slovenia and Hungary, in the east by Serbia and Bosnia and Herzegovina and in the southeast by Montenegro. It includes the areas of Dalmatia, Istria and Slavonia which no longer have administrative status. Its area is 56,542 sq. km. Population at the 2001 census was 4,437,460 (4,784,265 in 1991), of whom the predominating ethnic groups were Croats (90%) and Serbs (5%); population density, 78·5 per sq. km.

The estimated population for 2010 is 4·43m.

In 2005, 56·5% of the population lived in urban areas.

The area, population and capital (2001 census) of the 20 counties and one city:

County	*Area (in sq. km)*	*Population*	*Capital*
Bjelovarska-Bilogorska	2,638	133,084	Bjelovar
Brodsko-Posavska	2,027	176,765	Slavonski Brod
Dubrovačko-Neretvanska	1,782	122,870	Dubrovnik
Istarska	2,813	206,344	Pazin
Karlovačka	3,622	141,787	Karlovac
Koprivničko-Križevačka	1,734	124,467	Koprivnica
Krapinsko-Zagorska	1,230	142,432	Krapina
Ličko-Senjska	5,350	53,677	Gospić
Međimurska	730	118,426	Čakovec
Osječko-Baranjska	4,149	330,506	Osijek
Požeško-Slavonska	1,821	85,831	Požega
Primorsko-Goranska	3,590	305,505	Rijeka
Šibensko-Kninska	2,994	112,891	Šibenik
Sisačko-Moslavačka	4,448	185,387	Sisak
Splitsko-Dalmatinska	4,524	463,676	Split
Varaždinska	1,260	184,769	Varaždin
Virovitičko-Podravska	2,021	93,389	Virovitica
Vukovarsko-Srijemska	2,448	204,768	Vukovar
Zadarska	3,643	162,045	Zadar
Zagrebačka	3,078	309,696	Zagreb
Zagreb (city)	640	779,145	Zagreb

Zagreb, the capital, had a 2001 population of 691,724. Other major towns (with 2001 census population): Split (188,694), Rijeka (143,800) and Osijek (90,411).

At the beginning of 1991 there were some 0·6m. resident Serbs. A law of Dec. 1991 guaranteed the autonomy of Serbs in areas where they are in a majority after the establishment of a permanent peace.

The official language is Croatian.

SOCIAL STATISTICS

2007: births, 41,910 (9·4 per 1,000 population); deaths, 52,367 (11·8); marriages, 23,140 (5·2); divorces, 4,785 (1·1); suicides, 776 (17·5 per 100,000). Infant mortality, 2005, 6 per 1,000 live births. Annual population growth rate, 2004–07, 0·0%. In 2004 the most popular age range for marrying was 25–29 for males and 20–24 for females. Life expectancy at birth, 2007, was 72·6 years for males and 79·4 years for females. Fertility rate, 2004, 1·3 children per woman.

CLIMATE

Inland Croatia has a central European type of climate, with cold winters and hot summers, but the Adriatic coastal region experiences a Mediterranean climate with mild, moist winters and hot, brilliantly sunny summers with less than average rainfall. Average annual temperature and rainfall: Dubrovnik, 16·6°C and 1,051 mm. Zadar, 15·6°C and 963 mm. Rijeka, 14·3°C and 1,809 mm. Zagreb, 12·4°C and 1,000 mm. Osijek, 11·3°C and 683 mm.

CONSTITUTION AND GOVERNMENT

A new constitution was adopted on 22 Dec. 1990 and was revised in both 2000 and 2001. The *President* is elected for renewable five-year terms. There is a unicameral Parliament (*Hrvatski Sabor*), consisting of 153 deputies; 140 members are elected from multi-seat constituencies for a four-year term, eight seats are reserved for national minorities and five members representing Croatians abroad are chosen by proportional representation. The upper house, the *Chamber of Counties*, was abolished in 2001.

National Anthem

'Lijepa nasva domovino' ('Beautiful our homeland'); words by A. Mihanović, tune by J. Runjanin.

GOVERNMENT CHRONOLOGY

(HDZ = Croatian Democratic Union; SDP = Social Democratic Party of Croatia; n/p = non-partisan)

Presidents since 1990.

1990–99	HDZ	Franjo Tuđman
2000–10	n/p	Stjepan (Stipe) Mesić
2010–	SDP	Ivo Josipović

Prime Ministers since 1990.

1990	HDZ	Stjepan (Stipe) Mesić
1990–91	HDZ	Josip Manolić
1991–92	HDZ	Franjo Gregurić
1992–93	HDZ	Hrvoje Šarinić
1993–95	HDZ	Nikica Valentić
1995–2000	HDZ	Zlatko Mateša
2000–03	SDP	Ivica Račan
2003–09	HDZ	Ivo Sanader
2009–	HDZ	Jadranka Kosor

RECENT ELECTIONS

Presidential elections were held on 27 Dec. 2009. Ivo Josipović (Social Democratic Party of Croatia/SDP) received 32·4% of the vote, Milan Bandić (ind.) 14·8%, Andrija Hebrang (Croatian Democratic Union/HDZ) 12·0% and Nadan Vidošević (ind.) 11·3%. There were eight other candidates. Turnout was 44·0%. As a result a second round was required. In the run-off on 10 Jan. 2010 Ivo Josipović received 60·3% of votes cast, against 39·7% for Milan Bandić.

Elections to the Sabor were held on 25 Nov. 2007. The HDZ won 66 seats (43·1% of the vote), the SDP 56 (36·6%), the coalition of the Croatian Peasant Party and the Croatian Social Liberal Party 8 (5·2%), the Croatian People's Party–Liberal Democrats 7 (4·6%), the Croatian Democratic Alliance of Slavonija and Baranja 3 (2·0%) and the Istrian Democratic Assembly also 3 (2·0%). Other parties and national minority representatives took ten seats. Turnout was 63·5%.

CURRENT ADMINISTRATION

President: Ivo Josipović; b. 1957 (SDP; sworn in 18 Feb. 2010).

Following the election of 25 Nov. 2007, a coalition government was formed between the Croatian Democratic Union, the Croatian Social Liberal Party, the Croatian Peasant Party and the Independent Democratic Serbian Party.

In March 2010 the government comprised:

Prime Minister: Jadranka Kosor; b. 1953 (Croatian Democratic Union; sworn in 6 July 2009).

Deputy Prime Ministers: Ivan Šuker (also *Minister of Finance*); Darko Milinović (also *Health and Social Welfare*); Slobodan Uzelac (also *Social Issues and Human Rights*); Božidar Pankretić (also *Regional Development, Forestry and Water Management*); Đurđa Adlešič.

Minister of Agriculture, Fisheries and Rural Development: Petar Čobanković. *Culture:* Božo Biškupić. *Defence:* Branko Vukelić. *Economy, Labour and Entrepreneurship:* Đuro Popijač. *Environmental Protection, Physical Planning and Construction:* Marina Matulović Dropulić. *Family, Veterans' Affairs and Intergenerational Solidarity:* Tomislav Ivić. *Foreign Affairs and European Integration:* Gordan Jandroković. *Interior:* Tomislav Karamarko. *Justice:* Ivan Šimonović. *Public Administration:* Davorin Mlakar. *Science, Education and Sports:* Radovan Fuchs. *Sea, Transport and Infrastructure:* Božidar Kalmeta. *Tourism:* Damir Bajs. *Minister without Portfolio:* Bianca Matković.

Government Website: http://www.vlada.hr

CURRENT LEADERS

Ivo Josipović

Position
President

Introduction
Ivo Josipović was sworn in as president on 18 Feb. 2010 after winning the second round of elections on 10 Jan. 2010 on an anti-corruption platform. His five-year term will be largely ceremonial and he is expected to preside over Croatia's entry into the EU, while seeking improved relations with the country's ex-Yugoslav neighbours.

Early Life
Josipović was born on 28 Aug.1957 in Zagreb. He studied law at the University of Zagreb, qualifying for the bar in 1980. He returned as a lecturer in 1984, specializing in criminal procedure and international crime. In 1985 he gained an MA in criminal law and in 1994 received his PhD in criminal sciences. Josipović also pursued musical interests, graduating from the composition department of the Zagreb Music Academy in 1983. From 1987–2004 he taught at the Academy and has written over 50 compositions and won several awards for his work.

He began his political career in 1980 when he joined the League of Communists of Croatia (SKH). The party rebranded its image in the early 1990s, with Josipović helping to write the first statutes of the new Social Democratic Party of Croatia (SDP). In 1994 he retired from politics to work as an international law specialist in cooperation with the International Criminal Tribunal for the former Yugoslavia in The Hague. He was a key author of Croatia's genocide case against Serbia before the International Court of Justice.

In 2003 Josipović returned to politics. Elected into parliament as an independent MP, he was selected as vice-president of the SDP Representatives' Group in parliament. In 2005 he became a representative in the City of Zagreb assembly and was re-elected to parliament in 2007, formally rejoining the SDP a year later. On 12 July 2009 he was selected as the SDP presidential candidate and on 27 Dec. 2009 won the first round of voting with 32% of the vote. He received 60% in the second round to secure the presidency.

Career in Office
Josipović's top priority is to fight corruption, a pre-requisite to Croatia's anticipated membership of the EU in 2012. He also faces the challenge of mending ties with ex-Yugoslav neighbours, most notably Serbia which on 4 Jan. 2010 filed a counter-genocide complaint against Croatia.

Jadranka Kosor

Position
Prime Minister

Introduction
Jadranka Kosor became Croatia's first female prime minister on 1 July 2009 following Ivo Sanader's resignation. Amid opposition calls for early elections, Kosor's premiership was endorsed with 83 votes from the 153-seat parliament on 6 July 2009. Her priority is to deal with the country's economic crisis.

Early Life

Kosor was born on 1 July 1953 in Pakrac. Having graduated in law from Zagreb University, in 1972 she became a print and radio journalist. From 1991–95, during Croatia's war of independence, she hosted a radio show for refugees on Croatian Radio.

Elected as an MP in 1995, Kosor became vice-president of the House of Representatives after Franjo Tuđman invited her to join the Croatian Democratic Union (HDZ), of which she was also vice-president from 1995–97 (and again from 2002–09). From 1998–2000 she headed the conservative HDZ Women's Association, named after Katarina Zrinski. Under her leadership the number of female candidates standing for the HDZ in the 2000 elections doubled from the previous election. In 2003 Kosor was appointed to Sanader's government as deputy prime minister and minister of family, veterans' affairs and intergenerational solidarity. She ran for the presidency in 2005 but was defeated in the run-off by the incumbent, Stjepan Mesić.

Recommended as a possible successor to the premiership by Sanader on his resignation in July 2009, Kosor was endorsed by parliament on 6 July 2009. On 4 July 2009 she was also named president of the HDZ.

Career in Office

Kosor has pledged to continue the policies of her predecessor. Proposed budget cuts were an early test of her government's strength, with the prospect of an IMF bailout looming if they were rejected. Party in-fighting grew after the HDZ's poor showing at the first round of the presidential elections in Dec. 2009. On 4 Jan. 2010 Kosor took the decision to expel Sanader from the HDZ after alleged interference with her leadership.

Among her key challenges is to restart talks on EU accession. In Nov. 2009 Kosor met with her Slovenian counterpart in Stockholm to sign an agreement to bring their border dispute (over the bay of Piran on the Adriatic coast) to international arbitration. On 1 Jan. 2010 Serbia announced it was filing a genocide counter-complaint to the International Court of Justice against Croatia for events that took place in the 1990s.

DEFENCE

Conscription was abolished on 1 Jan. 2008. Defence expenditure in 2006 totalled US$693m. (US$154 per capita), representing 1·6% of GDP.

Army

Personnel, 2007, 12,300 (around 1,300 conscripts). Paramilitary forces include an armed police of 3,000. There are 95,000 reserves.

Navy

In 2007 the fleet included two tactical submarines and two missile-armed corvettes. Total personnel in 2007 numbered 1,700 (250 conscripts), including two companies of marines.

Air Force

Personnel, 2007, 1,800 (including Air Defence and 200 conscripts). There were 12 combat capable aircraft (MiG-21s) in 2007.

INTERNATIONAL RELATIONS

Croatia is a member of the UN, World Bank, IMF and several other UN specialized agencies, WTO, Council of Europe, OSCE, Central European Initiative, Danube Commission, BIS, IOM, NATO and Inter-American Development Bank. Croatia applied for European Union membership in 2003 and was accepted as an official candidate country in 2004. It is expected to become a member in 2012.

ECONOMY

Agriculture contributed 7·4% of GDP in 2006, industry 31·6% and services 60·9%.

Overview

In the 1990s the economy was rocked by war and international isolation. Increased political stability from 2000 onwards spurred a recovery that saw the economy expanding at an average of 4·8% per annum between 2001–06. Structural reforms included a privatization programme and modernization of the bankruptcy, company and labour laws. There was also strong investment in fixed capital which had been neglected in the previous decade.

Tourism potential has attracted investment. Household consumption has expanded at rates slightly below economic growth but has acted as an anchor for domestic demand. The banking sector is almost entirely owned by foreign banks that have benefited from borrowing at low external interest rates and lending at higher rates in Croatia, fuelling a domestic credit boom. This credit boom is in large part responsible for the recent deterioration of Croatia's external financial position. In 2006 the current-account deficit was 7·4% of GDP while the external debt position reached 89% of GDP by the end of the year.

Industry is expected to benefit from integration with other European economies but, dependent on imported raw materials, it is fuelling import demand and widening the current account deficit. The National Bank has taken measures to restrict the growth of domestic credit and though foreign banks often find ways to circumvent restrictions, inflation has been modest relative to other Central and Eastern European economies. In 2006 consumer price growth stood at 3·2%. The aim now is to hold back inflation and current account deterioration while pursuing privatization beyond telecommunications and banking and reforming the labour market and legal system.

Currency

On 30 May 1994 the *kuna* (HRK; a name used in 1941–45) of 100 *lipa* replaced the Croatian dinar at one kuna = 1,000 dinars. Foreign exchange reserves were US$8,529m. in July 2005 and total money supply was 38,305m. kuna. Inflation was 2·9% in 2007 and 6·1% in 2008.

Budget

Budgetary central government revenue and expenditure (1m. kuna):

	2004	*2005*	*2006*
Revenue	80,464	85,653	95,236
Expenditure	83,131	87,858	95,950

Principal sources of revenue in 2006 were: taxes on goods and services, 47,546m. kuna; social security contributions, 33,877m. kuna. Main items of expenditure by economic type in 2006: social benefits, 43,445m. kuna; compensation of employees, 24,314m. kuna.

VAT is 23%.

Performance

Real GDP growth was 5·5% in 2007 and 2·4% in 2008. Total GDP was US$69·3bn. in 2008.

Banking and Finance

The National Bank of Croatia (*Governor*, Željko Rohatinski) is the bank of issue. In 2001 there were 43 registered banks. The largest banks are Zagrebačka Banka, with assets in Dec. 2006 of US$12·6bn., and Privredna Banka Zagreb. There are stock exchanges in Zagreb and Varaždin.

Total foreign direct investment in 2008 was US$4,383m., down from US$4,982m. in 2007.

ENERGY AND NATURAL RESOURCES

Environment

Croatia's carbon dioxide emissions from the consumption and flaring of fossil fuels in 2008 were the equivalent of 5·4 tonnes per capita.

Electricity
Installed capacity in 2003 was 3·9m. kW. Output was 13·30bn. kWh in 2004, with consumption per capita 3,818 kWh in 2004.

Oil and Gas
In 2004, 6·5m. bbls of crude oil were produced. Natural gas output totalled 2·4bn. cu. metres in 2004; reserves were 34bn. cu. metres in 2005.

Minerals
Production (in 1,000 tonnes): salt (2006), 30.

Agriculture
Agriculture and fishing generate approximately 9% of GDP. The agricultural workforce was 154,000 in 2002. Agricultural land totals 3·15m. ha. (63·4% is cultivated). There were 1·46m. ha. of arable land in 2002 and 126,000 ha. of permanent crops. Production (in 1,000 tonnes, 2003): maize, 1,569; sugar beets, 678; wheat, 609; potatoes, 375; grapes, 333; wine, 200; barley, 134.

Livestock, 2003: cattle, 444,000; sheep, 587,000; pigs, 1,347,000; chickens, 12m. Livestock products, 2002: milk, 705,000 tonnes; meat, 192,000 tonnes; eggs, 46,000 tonnes; cheese, 24,000 tonnes.

Forestry
Forests covered 1·96m. ha. in 2002, of which 80% are state owned. In 2007, 4·21m. cu. metres of roundwood were produced.

Fisheries
Total catch in 2005 was 34,669 tonnes, almost exclusively from sea fishing.

INDUSTRY

The largest company in Croatia in March 2009 was T-HT (T-Hrvatski Telekom), with a market capitalization of US$3,168m.

In 2001 industrial production growth totalled 6% in comparison with 2000. Output: cement (2004), 3,811,000 tonnes; distillate fuel oil (2004), 1,741,000 tonnes; petrol (2004), 1,226,000 tonnes; residual fuel oil (2004), 1,012,000 tonnes; paper and paperboard (2002), 467,000 tonnes; passenger cars (2002), 1,244,300 units; cigarettes (2001), 14,738m. units; cotton woven fabrics (2002), 35m. sq. metres; beer (2001), 379·9m. litres.

Labour
In 2001 the number of employees was 1,469,500 and unemployment was 24·7%. Among 15 to 30-year-olds unemployment is around 40%. The main areas of activity in 2001 were manufacturing (employing 305,600 persons), agriculture, hunting and forestry (224,500), wholesale and retail trade/repair of motor vehicles, motorcycles and personal and household goods (211,300) and public administration and defence/compulsory social security (105,500).

INTERNATIONAL TRADE

Total foreign debt was US$30,169m. in 2005.

Imports and Exports
Imports for 2004 came to US$16,589m. Exports in 2004 were valued at US$8,024m.

Principal imports in 2004 were: machinery and transport equipment, 34·9%; manufactured goods, 19·6%; mineral fuels, 12·0%; miscellaneous manufactured articles, 11·9%; chemicals, 11·2%; food and live animals, 7·2%. Main exports in 2004 were: machinery and transport equipment, 32·3%; miscellaneous manufactured articles, 17·8%; manufactured goods, 14·8%; mineral fuels, 11·3%; chemicals, 9·4%; food and live animals, 6·3%.

In 2004 the main import suppliers were (in US$1m.): Italy (2,819); Germany (2,569); Russia (1,206); Slovenia (1,179); Austria (1,131). Main export markets (in US$1m.): Italy (1,834); Bosnia and Herzegovina (1,154); Germany (895); Austria (757); Slovenia (601).

COMMUNICATIONS

Roads
There were 28,472 km of roads in 2005 (including 731 km of motorways and 6,822 km of highways, national and main roads). In 2004 there were 1,337,538 passenger cars, 4,869 buses and coaches, and 154,790 vans and trucks. 65m. passengers and 55·3m. tonnes of freight were carried by road transport in 2004. There were 608 deaths in road accidents in 2004.

Rail
There were 2,726 km of 1,435 mm gauge rail in 2004 (984 km electrified). In 2004 railways carried 36·7m. passengers and 12·2m. tonnes of freight.

Civil Aviation
The biggest international airports are Zagreb (Pleso), Split and Dubrovnik. The national carrier is Croatia Airlines. In 2004 scheduled airline traffic of Croatian-based carriers flew 12m. km, carrying 1,336,411 passengers (886,215 on international flights). In 2004 Zagreb handled 1,389,537 passengers (926,011 on international flights) and 7,692 tonnes of freight, Dubrovnik 860,672 passengers (704,331 on international flights) and Split 768,706 passengers (575,019 on international flights).

Shipping
The main port is Rijeka, which handled 2·1m. tonnes of freight in 2004. Figures for 2004 show that 22·6m. passengers and 25·2m. tonnes of cargo were transported. In 2002 merchant shipping totalled 835,000 GRT, including oil tankers 8,000 GRT. In 2004 vessels totalling 212,282,000 GRT entered ports and vessels totalling 214,231,000 GRT cleared.

Telecommunications
The telephone density (the number of lines per 1,000 population) rose from 17·2% in 1990 to 42% in 2004.

In 2004 there were 1,676,482 fixed telephone subscribers and 2,842,377 mobile subscribers (pre-paid included). Internet subscribers numbered 834,468 in 2004 (excluding 87,152 subscribers using the services of the non-profit Croatian Academic and Research Network).

Postal Services
In 2004 there were 1,158 post offices.

SOCIAL INSTITUTIONS

Justice
The population in penal institutions in Oct. 2005 was 3,594 (81 per 100,000 of national population).

Education
In 2004–05 there were 1,190 pre-school institutions with 104,987 children and 8,476 childcare workers; 2,141 primary schools with 391,744 pupils and 29,485 teachers; 665 secondary schools with 192,076 pupils and 20,701 teachers. In 2004–05 there were 103 institutes of higher education with 134,583 students and 8,764 academic staff. In 2004–05 there were six universities (Zagreb, Osijek, Rijeka, Split, Dubrovnik and Zadar). Adult literacy rate in 2003 was 98·1% (male, 99·3%; female, 97·1%).

In 2003 public expenditure on education came to 4·5% of GDP and represented 10·0% of total government expenditure.

Health
In 2003 there were 73 hospitals with 25,000 beds. In 2001 there were 10,552 physicians, 3,021 dentists, 22,185 nurses, 2,235 pharmacists and 1,491 midwives.

Welfare

The official retirement age is 65 years (men) and 60 years (women). It was gradually increased in six-month increments over four years from the 2004 levels of 63 (men) and 58 (women). The old-age pension is dependent on wages earned in relation to the average wage of all employed persons. The minimum old-age pension is defined for every year of the qualifying period as 0·825% of the average gross salary of all employees in 1998. This amount (39·86 kuna from Jan. 2002) is adjusted for inflation. The minimum unemployment benefit was 725 kuna a month in 2002 and the maximum benefit was 900 kuna a month.

RELIGION

In 2001 there were 3,890,000 Roman Catholics, 250,000 Serbian Orthodox and 100,000 Sunni Muslims. The remainder of the population were followers of other religions. In Feb. 2010 there was one cardinal.

CULTURE

World Heritage Sites

Croatia has seven UNESCO protected sites: the Old City of Dubrovnik (entered on the List in 1979 and 1994), known as the 'Pearl of the Adriatic'; the Historic Complex of Split with the Palace of Diocletian (1979), including Roman Emperor Diocletian's mausoleum, now the cathedral; Plitvice Lakes National Park (1979 and 2000), a series of lakes and waterfalls and a habitat for bears and wolves; the Episcopal Complex of the Euphrasian Basilica in the Historical Centre of Poreč (1997); the Historic City of Trogir (1997), a Venetian city based on a Hellenistic plan; the Cathedral of St James in Šibenik (2000), built in the Gothic and Renaissance styles between 1431–1535; and Stari Grad Plain (2008), agricultural land on the island of Hvar that was first cultivated by the Greeks in the 4th century BC.

Broadcasting

Croatian Radio-Television is the state-owned public broadcaster, operating several national television and radio networks. There are also national commercial TV services (RTL Televizja and Nova TV) and many private local stations. In 2004 there were 129 radio and 16 TV stations, 1·19m. radio subscribers and 1·11m. television subscribers. Colour is by PAL.

Cinema

In 2004 there were 141 cinemas (of which two were multiplexes, one with 13 screens and one with five screens) with a total attendance of 3·0m. Four feature films were made in 2004.

Press

In 2003 there were 12 daily newspapers; in 2002 the dailies had a circulation of 597,000, at a rate of 135 per 1,000 inhabitants. In 2003 a total of 6,447 book titles and brochures were published.

Tourism

In 2005, 8,467,000 tourists visited Croatia (7,912,000 in 2004). Receipts in 2005 totalled US$7·5bn., up from US$6·8bn. in 2004.

Festivals

Croatia has a number of cultural and traditional festivals, including the Zagreb Summer Festival (July–Aug.); the International Folk Dance Festival in Zagreb (July); Dubrovnik Summer Festival (July–Aug.); Split Summer (July–Aug.); Alka Festival (traditional medieval tilting), Sinj (Aug.).

DIPLOMATIC REPRESENTATIVES

Of Croatia in the United Kingdom (21 Conway St., London, W1T 6BN)
Ambassador: Dr Ivica Tomić.

Of the United Kingdom in Croatia (Ivana Lučića 4, 10000 Zagreb)
Ambassador: David Blunt.

Of Croatia in the USA (2343 Massachusetts Ave., NW, Washington, D.C., 20008)
Ambassador: Kolinda Grabar-Kitarović.

Of the USA in Croatia (Thomasa Jeffersona 2, 10010 Zagreb)
Ambassador: James Brendan Foley.

Of Croatia to the United Nations
Ambassador: Ranko Vilović.

Of Croatia to the European Union
Ambassador: Branco Baričević.

FURTHER READING

Central Bureau of Statistics. *Statistical Yearbook, Monthly Statistical Report, Statistical Information, Statistical Reports.*
Fisher, Sharon, *Political Change in Post-Communist Slovakia and Croatia: From Nationalist to Europeanist.* 2006
Jovanovic, Nikolina, *Croatia: A History.* Translated from Croatian. 2000
Stallaerts, Robert, *Historical Dictionary of the Republic of Croatia.* 2nd ed. 2003
Tanner, M. C., *A Nation Forged in War.* 1997
Uzelac, Gordana, *The Development of the Croatian Nation: An Historical and Sociological Analysis.* 2006

National Statistical Office: Central Bureau of Statistics, 3 Ilica, 10000 Zagreb. *Director:* Ivan Kovač.
Website: http://www.dzs.hr

CUBA

República de Cuba
(Republic of Cuba)

Capital: Havana
Population estimate, 2010: 11·20m.
GDP per capita: not available
GNI per capita, 2007: US$5,145
HDI/world rank: 0·863/51

KEY HISTORICAL EVENTS

Cuba's first inhabitants were the Taíno, Ciboney and Guanahatabey tribes. Christopher Columbus landed in 1492 and a permanent settlement was established by Diego Velázquez in 1511. Oppression and European diseases virtually exterminated the indigenous population within 50 years and African slaves were imported as replacements. In 1607 Havana was declared the capital.

Resistance to Spanish rule grew after the removal of Cuban delegates from the Spanish *Cortes* in 1837. Repeated offers by the USA to buy Cuba were rejected. Slavery was suppressed from the 1850s though not abolished until 1886. The first rebellion, the Ten-Year War, broke out in 1868 and was led by Gen. Máximo Gómez. An assembly was granted in 1869. However, José Martí y Pérez created the Cuban Revolutionary Party from New York and launched an invasion of Cuba in 1895 with Gómez and Antonio Maceo. The USA intervened in 1898, winning control of Cuba from Spain at the Treaty of Paris. Municipal elections in 1900 rejected annexationist policies and Cuba achieved independence in 1902. The Platt Amendment allowed for US intervention to preserve independence and stability and awarded the USA control of Guantánamo Bay. At the request of President Estrada Palma, US forces were installed on the island between 1906 and 1909. In 1912 and 1917 there were further interventions by American forces.

Gerardo Machado's dictatorial presidency began in 1925 and was ended by a coup in 1933. The Revolt of the Sergeants brought Fulgencio Batista y Zaldívar to power. The Platt Amendment was revoked and in 1940 a socially progressive constitution was inaugurated. Batista was returned at disputed elections in 1940 but was voted out of office four years later. He ran for re-election in 1952 but, with little chance of victory, led a bloodless coup before elections could be held, suspending the constitution and instigating a repressive and corrupt regime.

Fidel Castro, imprisoned in 1953 after a failed revolt, arrived from Mexico with 80 men in 1956. Castro and Che Guevara led a guerrilla war from the Sierra Maestra mountains and, despite US financial support, Batista fled after revolutionaries seized Havana in Jan. 1959. The USA recognized the new regime but relations soon deteriorated. Castro, as prime minister, launched a nationalization programme, seizing American assets and outlawing foreign land ownership. In Oct. 1960 the USA's trade embargo began and diplomatic relations were broken in Jan. 1961. Close relations between Cuba and the USSR provoked covert US support for the doomed Bay of Pigs invasion in April 1961, in which an offensive by a group of exiled Cubans was defeated by Castro's troops. Castro declared Cuba to be a socialist state. In 1962 the USA and USSR neared nuclear conflict during the Cuban Missile Crisis, with the US Navy imposing a blockade on Cuba from 22 Oct. until 22 Nov. to force the USSR to withdraw Soviet missile bases. In return, the USA guaranteed not to invade Cuba. Between 1965 and 1973, 250,000 Cubans left for America on Freedom Flights agreed between the two nations. In 1976 a new constitution consolidated Castro's power as head of state, government and the armed forces.

Cuba continued to receive financial aid and technical advice from the USSR until the early 1990s when subsidies were suspended. This led to a 40% drop in GDP between 1989 and 1993. The USA has maintained an economic embargo against the island and relations between Cuba and the USA have remained embittered, although contact between the two countries has been growing in recent years. From Jan. 2002 suspected al-Qaeda and Taliban prisoners were brought from Afghanistan to the military prison at the American naval base at Guantánamo Bay.

In July 2006 Castro was hospitalized and temporarily handed power to his brother, Raúl. When Fidel failed to appear at a series of high-profile presidential appointments, there was speculation that the power transfer would become permanent. In Feb. 2008 Fidel announced his resignation and was immediately replaced by Raúl.

TERRITORY AND POPULATION

The island of Cuba forms the largest and most westerly of the Greater Antilles group and lies 215 km (135 miles) south of the tip of Florida, USA. The area is 110,861 sq. km, and comprises the island of Cuba (104,748 sq. km); the Isle of Youth (Isla de la Juventud, formerly the Isle of Pines; 2,398 sq. km); and some 1,600 small isles ('cays'; 3,715 sq. km). Population, census (2002), 11,177,743, giving a density of 100·8 per sq. km. In 2005, 75·5% of the population were urban.

The UN gives an estimated population for 2010 of 11·20m.

The area and population of the 14 provinces and the special Municipality of the Isle of Youth (Isla de la Juventud) were as follows (2002):

	Area (sq. km)	*Population*
Ciudad de La Habana	727	2,201,610
Santiago de Cuba	6,170	1,036,281
Holguín	9,301	1,021,321
Villa Clara	8,662	817,395
Granma	8,372	822,452
Camagüey	15,990	784,178
Pinar del Río	10,925	726,574
La Habana	5,731	711,066
Matanzas	11,978	670,427
Las Tunas	6,589	525,485
Guantánamo	6,186	507,118
Sancti Spíritus	6,744	460,328
Ciego de Avila	6,910	411,766
Cienfuegos	4,178	395,183
Isla de la Juventud	2,398	86,559

The capital city, Havana, had a population in 2002 of 2,201,610. Other major cities (2002 census populations in 1,000): Santiago de Cuba (423), Camagüey (302), Holguín (270), Santa Clara (210),

Guantánamo (208), Bayamo (145), Las Tunas (144), Cienfuegos (141), Pinar del Río (139) and Matanzas (127).

The official language is Spanish.

SOCIAL STATISTICS

2008 births, 122,569; deaths, 86,357; marriages, 61,852; divorces, 35,882; suicides, 1,357. Rates, 2008 (per 1,000 population): birth, 10·9; death, 7·7; marriage, 5·5; divorce, 3·2; suicide, 12·1 per 100,000 population. Infant mortality rate, 2008, 4·7 per 1,000 live births. Annual population growth rate, 2000–05, 0·2%. Life expectancy, 2005–07: 76·0 years for males and 80·0 for females. The fertility rate in 2008 was 1·6 births per woman.

CLIMATE

Situated in the sub-tropical zone, Cuba has a generally rainy climate, affected by the Gulf Stream and the N.E. Trades, although winters are comparatively dry after the heaviest rains in Sept. and Oct. Hurricanes are liable to occur between June and Nov. Havana, Jan. 72°F (22·2°C), July 82°F (27·8°C). Annual rainfall 48" (1,224 mm).

CONSTITUTION AND GOVERNMENT

A Communist Constitution came into force on 24 Feb. 1976. It was amended in July 1992 to permit direct parliamentary elections and in June 2002 to make the country's socialist system 'irrevocable'.

Legislative power is vested in the *National Assembly of People's Power*, which meets twice a year and consists of 614 deputies elected for a five-year term by universal suffrage. Citizens are entitled to vote at the age of 16. Lists of candidates are drawn up by mass organizations (trade unions, etc.). The National Assembly elects a 31-member *Council of State* as its permanent organ. The Council of State's President, who is head of state and of government, nominates and leads a Council of Ministers approved by the National Assembly.

National Anthem

'Al combate corred bayameses' ('Run, Bayamans, to the combat'); words and tune by P. Figueredo.

RECENT ELECTIONS

Elections to the National Assembly were held on 20 Jan. 2008. 50% of candidates must come from municipal assemblies, with the other 50% being candidates of national or provincial importance. All 614 candidates received the requisite 50% of votes for election.

CURRENT ADMINISTRATION

President: Gen. Raúl Castro Ruz (b. 1931) became *President* of the Council of State and of the Council of Ministers on 24 Feb. 2008.

In March 2010 the government comprised:

First Vice-President of the Council of State and of the Council of Ministers: José Ramón Machado.

Vice-Presidents of the Council of Ministers: José Ramón Fernández Alvarez, Ramiro Valdés Menendéz (also *Minister of Information Science and Communications*), Ulises Rosales del Toro (also *Minister of Agriculture*), Jorge Luis Sierra Cruz (also *Minister of Transport*), Ricardo Cabrisas Ruiz, Marino Murillo Jorge (also *Minister of Economy and Planning*). *Secretary of the Council of Ministers:* Brig. Gen. José Amado Ricardo Guerra.

Minister of Basic Industries: Yadira García Vera. *Construction:* Fidel Figueroa de la Paz. *Culture:* Abel Prieto Jiménez. *Defence:* Julio Casas Regueiro. *Domestic Trade:* Jacinto Angulo Pardo. *Education:* Ena Elsa Velázquez Cobiella. *Finance and Prices:* Lina Pedraza Rodríguez. *Food Industry:* María del Carmen Concepción González. *Foreign Relations:* Bruno Rodríguez Parrilla. *Foreign Trade and Investment:* Rodrigo Malmierca Díaz. *Higher Education:* Miguel Díaz-Canel Bermúdez. *Interior:* Gen. Abelardo Colomé Ibarra. *Iron, Steel and Engineering Industries:* Brig. Gen. Salvador Pardo Cruz. *Justice:* María Esther Reus. *Labour and Social Security:* Margarita Marlene González Fernández. *Light Industry:* José Hernández Bernárdez. *Public Health:* José Ramón Balaguer Cabrera. *Science, Technology and Environment:* José Miyar Barruecos. *Sugar Industry:* Luís Manuel Avila González. *Tourism:* Manual Marrero Cruz.

The Congress of the Cuban Communist Party (PCC) elects a Central Committee of 150 members, which in turn appoints a Political Bureau comprising 25 members.

Government Website (Spanish only): http://www.cubagob.cu

CURRENT LEADERS

Raúl Modesto Castro Ruz

Position
President

Introduction
Raúl Castro was elected president by the National Assembly of People's Power on 24 Feb. 2008. His five-year term began when he replaced his brother, Fidel, who had held office for 49 years. While less charismatic than his brother, he is committed to preserving the essence of Cuba's specific brand of socialism.

Early Life
Raúl Castro was born on 3 June 1931 in Birán, in the Oriente province (now Santiago de Cuba) in eastern Cuba. His father was a sugar plantation owner of Spanish origin and his mother a housemaid. After expulsion from his first school Raúl attended the Jesuit-run Colegio Dolores in Santiago and the Belén School in Havana, before graduating as a sergeant from military college. He attended the University of Havana until 1953, when his involvement in politics cut short his studies.

Raúl was a member of the Socialist Youth group, affiliated to the Moscow-orientated Popular Socialist Party. Although the party supported President Fulgencio Batista, Raúl's travels to the Soviet bloc in 1953 prompted him to turn against Batista which culminated that year in the failed 26 July attack on the Moncada barracks alongside brother Fidel. Both were sentenced to 13 years imprisonment but were freed and exiled to Mexico 22 months later, where Raúl reputedly introduced Che Guevara into his brother's circle. Raúl subsequently helped organize the 26 July Revolutionary Movement and the failed coup attempt of 1956.

Raúl found refuge in the Sierra Maestra mountains before taking charge of the military campaign in the east of the country, where he gained notoriety for his ruthlessness. Military victory was achieved in 1959 and Batista went into exile. Raúl secured his place as Fidel's right hand man, politically and militarily, and oversaw the summary execution of large numbers of Batista troops. In 1959 he married Vilma Espín Guillois, a fellow revolutionary veteran. He was appointed minister for the Revolutionary Armed Forces (FAR) and played a key role during the Bay of Pigs invasion of 1961 and in the Cuban missile crisis the following year.

In 1965 he was promoted to the eight-seat Cuban Communist Party (PCC) Politburo and made second secretary of the central committee behind Fidel. In 1972 he became first vice premier and four years later the new National Assembly of People's Power elected him vice president. The Castro hierarchy was endorsed with total support at each of the congressional party sessions from 1975–97 and at the National Assembly sessions from 1981–2003.

As vice president he was pivotal in the close relationship with the Eastern European communist bloc until the 1990s when he engineered the economic shift away from former Soviet dependency and introduced some freedom in the agricultural sector. From 2000–02 his public profile grew as he stood in for Fidel on diplomatic tours of China and South East Asia.

When Fidel underwent abdominal surgery in July 2006, Raúl became acting president. On 19 Feb. 2008 Fidel announced his formal resignation and Raúl was elected his successor by the National Assembly nine days later.

Career in Office
Raúl's key challenges are economic and he has promised to reduce red tape and to revise the dual-currency system. Early signs of greater market freedom included allowing Cubans to stay in tourist hotels and rent cars and the lifting of bans on ownership of consumer products such as mobile phones, computers and DVD players (although such products remain unaffordable to average citizens).

In mid-2008 the government relaxed restrictions on the amount of idle state-owned land available to private farmers and announced plans to abandon salary equality in a radical departure from Marxist principles. In the wake of two hurricanes in 2008 that devastated homes and crops in Cuba, a US offer of emergency aid was rejected by Raúl, who instead demanded a lifting of the longstanding US trade embargo.

In March 2009 the Obama administration eased the US embargo, lifting restrictions on remittances and visits to Cuba by Cuban-Americans and holding talks on restarting postal services. However, despite this slight thaw in bilateral relations and Cuba's acute economic problems, Raúl has continued to crack down on political dissent and has insisted on the maintenance of the country's communist system.

In June 2009 the Organization of American States voted to end Cuba's diplomatic suspension dating back to 1962.

DEFENCE

The National Defence Council is headed by the president of the republic. Conscription is for two years.

In 2006 defence expenditure totalled US$1,660m. (US$146 per capita), representing 4·0% of GDP.

Army
The strength was estimated at 38,000 in 2006, with 39,000 reservists. Border Guard and State Security forces total 26,500. The Territorial Militia is estimated at 1m. (reservists), all armed. In addition there is a Youth Labour Army of 70,000 and a Civil Defence Force of 50,000.

Navy
Personnel in 2006 totalled about 3,000 including some 550 marines. The Navy has five patrol and coastal combatants, five mine warfare vessels and one support vessel. Main bases are at Cabañas and Holguín. The USA still occupies the Guantánamo naval base.

Air Force
In 2006 the Air Force had a strength of some 8,000 and about 130 combat aircraft of which only around 25 are thought to be operational. They include MiG-29, MiG-23 and MiG-21 jet fighters.

INTERNATIONAL RELATIONS

Cuba is a member of the UN, ILO, WTO, ACS, SELA (Latin American Economic System), LAIA, OAS and Antarctic Treaty.

ECONOMY

Services account for about 68% of GDP, industry 27% and agriculture 5%.

Overview
Cuba is classified as a middle income country with a GDP per capita of US$2,500. Since the withdrawal of subsidies worth US$4–6bn. from the USSR in 1990, the economy has had to cope with falling tourism, low export prices and hurricane damage. Cuba fell into deep recession in the early 1990s from which it is only now emerging. The US trade embargo on Cuba, imposed in 1963, blocks access to funds from the IMF and the World Bank but the UN is able to continue operating in Cuba. The black market is bigger than the legal economy and basic economic activities (such as the sale of milk and bread) take place in the informal sector.

Following the collapse of the Soviet Union, the government helped stimulate growth through legalization of US tender in shops and other businesses. However, commercial transactions in dollars were banned in Nov. 2004 in response to tighter US sanctions. Growth has also been helped by significant aid from Venezuela.

In Jan. 2009 near-term growth was predicted to be around 4·3%, significantly lower than earlier predictions, as a result of rising international food prices, the damage caused by Hurricanes Gustav and Ike and a fall in the price of nickel, Cuba's principal export. The subsidized food ration system allows the higher cost of food to be absorbed by the state budget, reducing the impact on consumer spending. In 2007–08 tourism experienced an upsurge following a two-year downturn.

Currency
There are two currencies in Cuba. The official currency (‘*moneda nacional*’) is the *Cuban peso* (CUP) of 100 *centavos*. The *Convertible peso* (CUC), introduced in 1994 (pegged since April 2005 at 1 Convertible peso = US$1·08), is the ‘tourist’ currency. The US dollar ceased to be legal tender in 2004. 9,710m. pesos were in circulation in 1998. Inflation is low, averaging 1·8% between 1995–2002.

Budget
The 2006 revenue totalled 30,012m. pesos and expenditure 31,742m. pesos. Hard-currency earners and the self-employed became liable to a 10–50% income tax in Nov. 1995.

Performance
Cuba's economic growth was officially put as 4·3% in 2008, down from 7·5% in 2007 and 12·5% in 2006.

Banking and Finance
The Central Bank of Cuba (*Governor*, Ernesto Medina Villaveirán) replaced the National Bank of Cuba as the central bank in June 1997. On 14 Oct. 1960 all banks were nationalized. Changes to the banking structure beginning in 1996 divested the National Bank of its commercial functions, and created new commercial and investment institutions. The Grupa Nueva Banca has majority holdings in each institution of the new structure. There were eight commercial banks in March 2002 and 18 local non-banking financial institutions. In addition, there were 13 representative offices of foreign banks and four representative offices of non-banking financial institutions. All insurance business was nationalized in Jan. 1964. A National Savings Bank was established in 1983.

Weights and Measures
The metric system is legally compulsory, but the American and old Spanish systems are much used. The sugar industry uses the Spanish long ton (1·03 tonnes) and short ton (0·92 tonne). Cuba sugar sack = 329·59 lb or 149·49 kg. Land is measured in *caballerías* (of 13·4 ha. or 33 acres).

ENERGY AND NATURAL RESOURCES

Environment
Cuba's carbon dioxide emissions from the consumption and flaring of fossil fuels were the equivalent of 2·3 tonnes per capita in 2008.

Electricity
Installed capacity was 4·0m. kW in 2004. Production was 15·7bn. kWh in 2004; consumption per capita in 2004 was 1,380 kWh.

Oil and Gas
Crude oil production (2004), 21m. bbls. There were known natural gas reserves of 71bn. cu. metres in 2005. Natural gas production (2004), 704m. cu. metres.

Minerals

Iron ore abounds, with deposits estimated at 3,500m. tonnes; output (2006), 7·8m. tonnes. The output of salt was 180,000 tonnes in 2006; nickel, 74,000 tonnes (2005); chromite, 34,000 tonnes (2005); lime, 34,000 tonnes (2005). Other minerals are cobalt and silica. Nickel is Cuba's second largest foreign exchange earner, after tourism. Gold is also worked.

Agriculture

In 1959 all land over 30 *caballerías* was nationalized and eventually turned into state farms. In 2007 there were 3·0m. ha. of arable land and 1·8m. ha. of permanent crops. Under legislation of 1993, state farms were reorganized as 'units of basic co-operative production'. Unit workers select their own managers and are paid an advance on earnings. In 1963 private holdings were reduced to a maximum of five *caballerías*. In 1994 farmers were permitted to trade on free market principles after state delivery quotas had been met. In 2008 private farmers were granted access to underused government land in the form of ten-year leases in an effort to boost food production and curb dependence on imported produce.

During the 1980s average annual sugar production totalled 7·5m. tonnes making it one of the country's most important crops. However, the negative economic impact of the collapse of the Soviet Union in 1991 followed by a series of weather disasters in subsequent years resulted in production shrinking to 3·2m. tonnes in 1998, the smallest crop for 50 years. In 2002 the government closed over half of the 156 sugar mills and by 2007–08 production had fallen to 1·4m. tonnes with the country relying on imports to meet domestic demand. Production of other crops in 2008 was (in 1,000 tonnes): bananas, 758; tomatoes, 576; rice, 436; sweet potatoes, 375; cassava, 340; maize, 326; oranges, 200; potatoes, 196; pomelos, 166.

In 2008 livestock included 3·8m. cattle; 1·9m. pigs; 1·1m. goats; 565,000 horses; 277,500 sheep; 29m. chickens.

Forestry

Cuba had 2·71m. ha. of forests in 2005, representing 24·7% of the land area. These forests contain valuable cabinet woods, such as mahogany and cedar, besides dye-woods, fibres, gums, resins and oils. Cedar is used locally for cigar boxes, and mahogany is exported. In 2007, 2·35m. cu. metres of roundwood were produced.

Fisheries

Fishing ranks among the most important export industries. The total catch was 29,710 tonnes in 2005, of which 28,149 tonnes were from marine waters.

INDUSTRY

The gross value of the manufacturing industry in 1998 was 4,290·7m. pesos. All industrial enterprises had been state-controlled, but in 1995 the economy was officially stated to comprise state property, commercial property based on activity by state enterprises, joint co-operative and private property. Production (in 1,000 tonnes): sugar (2002), 3,522; cement (2000), 1,633; residual fuel oil (2004), 858; distillate fuel oil (2004), 385; sulphuric acid (1989), 381; petrol (2004), 331; steel (1998), 278; complete fertilizers (1998), 157; tobacco (1998), 40. Also in 1998: 160m. cigars; textiles, 54m. sq. metres. The sugar industry, once the backbone of the country's economy, is being restructured. Plans emerged in April 2010 to replace the sugar ministry with a state-run corporation and to introduce foreign investors.

Labour

In 2005 the labour force was 6,679,900, with 4,722,500 in employment. Self-employment was legalized in 1993. Under legislation of Sept. 1994 employees made redundant must be assigned to other jobs or to strategic social or economic tasks; failing this, they are paid 60% of former salary.

Trade Unions

The Workers' Central Union of Cuba groups 23 unions.

INTERNATIONAL TRADE

Foreign debt to non-communist countries was US$12·3bn. in 2000. Since July 1992 foreign investment has been permitted in selected state enterprises, and Cuban companies have been able to import and export without seeking government permission. Foreign ownership is recognized in joint ventures. A free-trade zone opened at Havana in 1993. In 1994 the productive, real estate and service sectors were opened to foreign investment. Legislation of 1995 opened all sectors of the economy to foreign investment except defence, education and health services. 100% foreign-owned investments and investments in property are now permitted.

The Helms-Burton Law of March 1996 gives US nationals the right to sue foreign companies investing in Cuban estate expropriated by the Cuban government.

Imports and Exports

In 2004 imports totalled US$5,610m. and exports US$2,332m. The principal exports are nickel, sugar, tobacco, medical products and shellfish. Sugar used to account for more than half of Cuba's export revenues, but revenues have been gradually declining and constituted less than 1% of the total in 2006.

In 2004 the chief import sources (in US$1m.) were: Venezuela (1,143); Spain (644); China (590); USA (449); Canada (298). The chief export markets (in US$1m.) were: Netherlands (647); Canada (487); Venezuela (367); Spain (174); Russia (121).

COMMUNICATIONS

Roads

In 2002 there were estimated to be 60,856 km of roads (including 638 km of motorways), of which 29,819 km were paved. Vehicles in use in 1997 included 172,500 passenger cars (15·6 per 1,000 inhabitants) and 156,600 trucks and vans. There were 1,309 fatalities as a result of road accidents in 1997.

Rail

There were 4,066 km of public railway (1,435 mm gauge) in 2005, of which 140 km was electrified. Passenger-km travelled in 2003 came to 1,736m. and freight tonne-km to 783m. In addition, the large sugar estates have 7,162 km of lines in total on 1,435 mm, 914 mm and 760 mm gauges.

Civil Aviation

There is an international airport at Havana (Jose Martí). The state airline Cubana operates all services internally, and in 2003 had international flights from Havana to Bogotá, Buenos Aires, Cancún, Caracas, Curaçao, Fort de France, Guatemala City, Guayaquil, Kingston, Las Palmas, London, Madrid, Mexico City, Montego Bay, Montreal, Moscow, Panama City, Paris, Pointe-à-Pitre, Quito, Rome, San José (Costa Rica), Santiago, Santo Domingo, São Paulo and Toronto. In 2003 scheduled airline traffic of Cuban-based carriers flew 19m. km, carrying 664,000 passengers (429,000 on international flights). In 2001 Havana Jose Martí International handled 2,472,300 passengers (2,056,500 on international flights) and 19,302 tonnes of freight.

Shipping

There are 11 ports, the largest being Havana, Cienfuegos and Mariel. The merchant marine in 2002 totalled 103,000 GRT, including oil tankers 5,000 GRT.

Telecommunications

There were 984,400 telephone subscribers in 2005 (87·4 for every 1,000 persons), including 134,500 mobile phone subscribers. There were 377,000 PCs in use (33·5 for every 1,000 persons) in 2005 and internet users numbered 190,000.

Postal Services
In 2001 there were 1,044 post offices, or one for every 10,800 persons.

SOCIAL INSTITUTIONS

Justice
There is a Supreme Court in Havana and seven regional courts of appeal. The provinces are divided into judicial districts, with courts for civil and criminal actions, and municipal courts for minor offences. The civil code guarantees aliens the same property and personal rights as those enjoyed by nationals.

The 1959 Agrarian Reform Law and the Urban Reform Law passed on 14 Oct. 1960 have placed certain restrictions on both. Revolutionary Summary Tribunals have wide powers.

The death penalty is still in force. There were three executions in 2003, but none since then.

The population in penal institutions in 2003 was approximately 55,000 (487 per 100,000 of national population).

Education
Education is compulsory (between the ages of six and 14), free and universal. In 2007 there were 883,132 pupils in primary school and 91,530 teaching staff; and 898,833 secondary school pupils with 93,311 teaching staff. There were 864,846 students and 135,800 academic staff in higher education in 2007.

There are four universities, and ten teacher training, two agricultural, four medical and ten other higher educational institutions.

The adult literacy rate was 99·8% in 2002.

In 2007 public expenditure on education came to 13·6% of GNI and 20·6% of total government spending.

Health
In 2002 there were 67,079 physicians, 9,955 dentists and 83,880 nurses. There were 266 hospitals in 2002 with 63 beds per 10,000 population.

Free medical services are provided by the state polyclinics, though a few doctors still have private practices.

Welfare
The official retirement age is 60 (men) or 55 (women). However, the qualifying age falls to 55 (men) or 50 (women) if the last 12 years of employment or 75% of employment was in dangerous or arduous work. The minimum pension in 2003 was 59 pesos a month, or 79 pesos a month, or 80% of wages, depending on average earnings and the number of years of employment. The maximum pension is 90% of average earnings.

Cuba has a sickness and maternity support programme.

RELIGION
Religious liberty was constitutionally guaranteed in July 1992. 40% of the population was estimated to be Roman Catholic in 2001. In 1994 Cardinal Jaime Ortega (b. 1936) was nominated Primate by Pope John Paul II. In Feb. 2010 there was one cardinal. In 2002 there were 180 Roman Catholic priests, approximately half of them foreign nationals. There is a seminary in Havana which had 61 students in 1996. There is a bishop of the American Episcopal Church in Havana; there are congregations of Methodists in Havana and in the provinces as well as Baptists and other denominations. Cults of African origin (mainly Santería) still persist.

CULTURE

World Heritage Sites
There are nine UNESCO sites in Cuba: Old Havana and its fortifications (inscribed in 1982), Trinidad and the Valley de los Ingenios (19th century sugar mills; 1988), San Pedro de la Roca Castle in Santiago de Cuba (1997), Desembarco del Granma National Park (marine terraces; 1999), Viñales Valley (1999), the 19th-century coffee plantations at Sierra Maestra (2000), Alejandro de Humboldt National Park (2001), the urban historic centre of Cienfuegos (2005) and the historic centre of Camagüey (2008).

Broadcasting
All broadcasting is state-controlled through the Instituto Cubano de Radio y Televisión. Cubavisión and Tele-Rebelde are TV channels (colour by NTSC), and there are national, provincial and local radio stations. Radio Habana is the external service. There were 2·4m. TV sets in 2005.

Press
There were (2006) four national daily newspapers and 14 regional and local dailies with a combined circulation of 1·8m. The most widely read newspaper is the Communist Party's Granma.

Tourism
Tourism is Cuba's largest foreign exchange earner, and for some years was growing by nearly 20% per year. There were 1,847,000 foreign tourists in 2003 (1,656,000 in 2002). Total receipts from tourism in 2003 amounted to US$1,846m.

DIPLOMATIC REPRESENTATIVES
Of Cuba in the United Kingdom (167 High Holborn, London, WC1 6PA)
Ambassador: René Juan Mujica Cantelar.

Of the United Kingdom in Cuba (Calle 34, No. 702/4, entre 7 ma Avenida y 17 Miramar, Havana)
Ambassador: Dianna Melrose.

Of Cuba to the United Nations
Ambassador: Pedro Núñez Mosquera.

Of Cuba to the European Union
Ambassador: Elio Rodríguez Perdomo.

The USA broke off diplomatic relations with Cuba on 3 Jan. 1961 but Cuba has an Interests Section in the Swiss Embassy in Washington, D.C., and the USA has an Interests Section in the Swiss Embassy in Havana.

FURTHER READING

Bethell, L. (ed.) *Cuba: a Short History.* 1993

Bunck, J. M., *Fidel Castro and the Quest for a Revolutionary Culture in Cuba.* 1994

Cabrera Infantye, G., *Mea Cuba*; translated into English from Spanish. 1994

Cardoso, E. and Helwege, A., *Cuba after Communism.* 1992

Dosal, Paul J., *Cuba Libre: A Brief History of Cuba.* 2006

Eckstein, S. E., *Back from the Future: Cuba under Castro.* 1994

Fursenko, A. and Naftali, T., *'One Hell of a Gamble': Khrushchev, Castro and Kennedy, 1958–1964.* 1997

Gott, Richard, *Cuba: A New History.* 2004

Levine, Robert, *Secret Missions to Cuba: Fidel Castro, Bernardo Benes, and Cuban Miami.* 2002

May, E. R. and Zelikow, P. D., *The Kennedy Tapes: Inside the White House during the Cuban Missile Crisis.* 1997

Mesa-Lago, C. (ed.) *Cuba: After the Cold War.* 1993

Sweig, Julia, *Inside the Cuban Revolution.* 2002

Thomas, Hugh, *Cuba, or the Pursuit of Freedom.* 1971; 2nd ed. 1998

National Statistical Office: Oficina Nacional de Estadísticas, Paseo No. 60e/3ra y 5ta, Vedado, Plaza de la Revolución, Havana, CP 10400.
Website (Spanish only): http://www.one.cu

CYPRUS

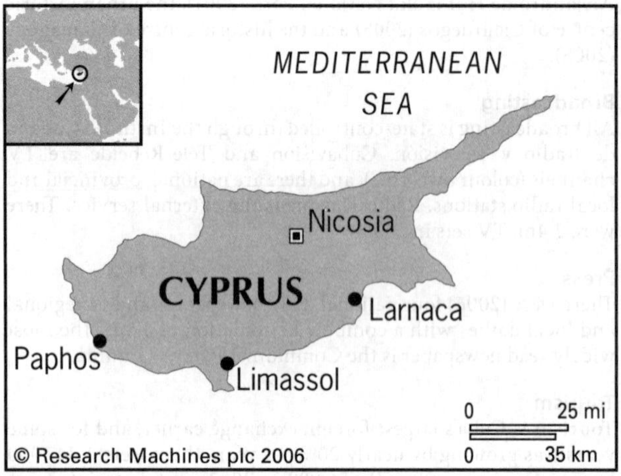

Kypriaki Dimokratia—Kibris Çumhuriyeti (Republic of Cyprus)

Capital: Nicosia
Population estimate, 2010: 880,000
GDP per capita, 2007: (PPP$) 24,789
HDI/world rank: 0·914/32

KEY HISTORICAL EVENTS

Cyprus has been settled since the early Neolithic period in the 9th millennium BC. During the 2nd millennium BC cities were built and extensive trading developed: Greek colonies were established and Greek culture predominated. Cyprus then came under Assyrian and Egyptian rule, subsequently becoming part of the Persian Empire. In the 2nd and 1st centuries BC the island was Hellenized. It became a Roman province in 58 BC and remained within the Roman Empire for most of the next three centuries, during which time it was Christianized.

The island became part of the Byzantine Empire in AD 364. In 488 the Church of Cyprus was confirmed as independent. Successive Arab invasions in the 7th century led to joint rule by Arabs and Byzantines until 965, when Byzantium regained sole rule. From 1191 Cyprus came under attack from Crusaders and in 1193 it became a Frankish kingdom under Guy de Lusignan. The Venetians ruled it as a dependency from 1489–1571, when it was taken by the Ottoman Turks. Under the Ottomans, the population was divided between Muslim Turks and Christian Greeks. After Greece achieved independence in 1829, some Greek Cypriots called for a union between Cyprus and Greece. On 4 June 1878 Great Britain and the Ottomans signed the Cyprus Convention, which gave Cyprus to Britain as a protectorate, in return for Britain supporting Turkey against Russia. In 1914, in response to Turkey's alliance with Germany, Britain annexed Cyprus. On 1 May 1925 it became a Crown Colony.

In the 1930s Greek Cypriots began campaigning for union with Greece (*enosis*). In 1955 the EOKA (National Organization of Cypriot Fighters), an anti-British guerrilla movement, was formed, led by Archbishop Makarios, head of the Greek Orthodox Church in Cyprus. In 1959 Greek and Turkish Cypriots agreed a constitution for an independent Cyprus and Makarios was elected president. On 16 June 1960 Cyprus became an independent state.

In Dec. 1963 conflict over proposed changes to the power-sharing mechanisms led to the Turkish Cypriots withdrawing from government. Fighting broke out and a UN peacekeeping force was deployed in 1964. Further fighting occurred in 1967–68, after which the Turkish Cypriots formed a provisional administration to run their community's affairs. Some Turkish Cypriots began to call for *taksim*, division of the island. On 15 July 1974 the Greek Cypriot National Guard staged a coup, with backing from Athens, and deposed President Makarios. On 20 July 1974 Turkey invaded the island. Turkish forces rapidly occupied the northern third of the island and, as the coup collapsed, enforced partition between north and south. During the fighting, and later as part of a UN-supervised population transfer, 200,000 Greek Cypriots moved south, while an estimated 65,000 Turkish Cypriots moved north.

In Dec. 1974 Makarios returned as president. In 1975 a Turkish Cypriot Federated State was proclaimed in the north, with Rauf Denktaş its president. In 1983 the Turkish state unilaterally proclaimed itself the 'Turkish Republic of Northern Cyprus' ('TRNC'). UN-sponsored peace talks continued without success throughout the 1980s. In 1991 the UN rejected Rauf Denktaş' demands for recognition of the 'TRNC', including the right to secession. In 1998 the Greek and Cypriot governments rejected Denktaş' proposal that the Greek and Turkish communities should join in a federation recognizing 'the equal and sovereign status of Cyprus' Greek and Turkish parts'.

In 2002 Cyprus was one of ten countries to be granted EU membership starting in 2004; the 'TRNC' would be included only if UN-brokered talks to reunify the country succeeded. In Nov. 2002 the UN presented a peace plan to the Greek Cypriot and Turkish Cypriot leaders for a 'common' state with two 'component' states and a rotating presidency. In March 2003 UN-brokered talks to pave the way for this reunification collapsed. However, as a goodwill measure the 'TRNC' opened the 'Green Line' separating the island's two sectors in April 2003. In a referendum held in the Greek-speaking and the Turkish-speaking areas on 24 April 2004, Turkish Cypriots voted in favour of a UN plan to reunite the island but Greek Cypriots voted overwhelmingly against. This result meant that after EU accession, EU benefits and laws would apply only to Greek Cypriots. On 1 May 2004, under these conditions, Cyprus became a member of the EU.

In Dec. 2004 Turkey extended its EU customs union agreement to Cyprus but declared that this did not amount to a recognition of Cyprus. In 2006 at UN-sponsored talks, a series of confidence building measures were agreed by Greek and Turkish Cypriots. However, in Nov. 2006 EU-Turkish talks on Cyprus broke down. Hopes of finding a solution were boosted with the election in March 2008 of President Dimitris Christofias who vowed to resurrect negotiations with Turkey. A month later the Ledra Street crossing that had symbolized the island's division since its closure 44 years earlier was reopened.

TERRITORY AND POPULATION

The island lies in the Mediterranean, about 60 km off the south coast of Turkey and 90 km off the coast of Syria. Area, 9,251 sq. km (3,572 sq. miles). The Turkish-occupied area is 3,335 sq. km. Population of Cyprus by ethnic group:

Ethnic group	*1960 census*	*1973 census*	*1992*	*2002*
Greek Cypriot	452,291	498,511	599,200	642,600
Turkish Cypriot	104,942	116,000	94,500[1]	87,400[1]
Others	16,333	17,267	20,000	72,500[2]
Total	573,566	631,778	713,700[1]	802,500[1]

[1]Excluding Turkish settlers and troops.
[2]Including foreign workers and residents.

The 2001 census population (government-controlled area only) was 703,529; estimate, 2007, 789,300. The United Nations population estimate for 2001 was 797,000.

The UN gives an estimated population for 2010 of 880,000; density, 95 per sq. km.

69·3% of the population lived in urban areas in 2005. Principal towns with populations (2007 estimate): Nicosia (the capital), 310,900; Limassol, 226,700; Larnaca, 131,900; Paphos, 76,100.

As a result of the Turkish occupation of the northern part of Cyprus, 0·2m. Greek Cypriots were displaced and forced to find refuge in the south. The urban centres of Famagusta, Kyrenia and Morphou were completely evacuated. *See below* for details on the 'Turkish Republic of Northern Cyprus'. (The 'TRNC' was unilaterally declared as a 'state' in 1983 in the area of the Republic of Cyprus, which has been under Turkish occupation since 1974, when Turkish forces invaded the island. The establishment of the 'TRNC' was declared illegal by UN Security Resolutions 541/83 and 550/84. The 'TRNC' is not recognized by any country in the world except Turkey). Nicosia is a divided city, with the UN-patrolled Green Line passing through it.

Greek and Turkish are official languages. English is widely spoken.

SOCIAL STATISTICS

2005 births, 8,243; deaths, 5,425; marriages, 5,881; divorces, 1,514. Rates, 2005 (per 1,000 population): birth, 10·9; death, 7·2; marriage, 7·8; divorce, 2·0. Life expectancy at birth, 2007, was 77·3 years for males and 81·9 years for females. Annual population growth rate, 2000–05, 1·8%; infant mortality, 2005, 4·6 per 1,000 live births; fertility rate, 2004, 1·6 children per woman. In 2005 the average age of first marriage was 29·1 years for men and 26·7 years for women.

CLIMATE

The climate is Mediterranean, with very hot, dry summers and variable winters. Maximum temperatures may reach 112°F (44·5°C) in July and Aug., but minimum figures may fall to 22°F (-5·5°C) in the mountains in winter, when snow is experienced. Rainfall is generally between 10" and 27" (250 and 675 mm) and occurs mainly in the winter months, but it may reach 48" (1,200 mm) in the Troodos mountains. Nicosia, Jan. 50°F (10·0°C), July 83°F (28·3°C). Annual rainfall 19·6" (500 mm).

CONSTITUTION AND GOVERNMENT

Under the 1960 constitution executive power is vested in a *President* elected for a five-year term by universal suffrage, and exercised through a Council of Ministers appointed by him or her. The *House of Representatives* exercises legislative power. It is elected by universal suffrage for five-year terms, and consists of 80 members, of whom 56 are elected by the Greek Cypriot and 24 by the Turkish Cypriot community. As from Dec. 1963 the Turkish Cypriot members have ceased to attend, and the 24 seats allocated to the Turkish Cypriot community are no longer contested. Voting is compulsory, and is by preferential vote in a proportional representation system with reallocation of votes at national level.

National Anthem

'Imnos eis tin Eleftherian' ('Hymn to Freedom'); words by Dionysios Solomos, tune by N. Mantzaros.

(Same as Greece.)

GOVERNMENT CHRONOLOGY

Presidents since 1960. AKEL = Progressive Party of the Working People; DIKO = Democratic Party; DISI = Democratic Rally; EOKA = National Organization of Cypriot Fighters; n/p = non-partisan)

1960–74	n/p	Makarios III
1974	EOKA	Nikolaos (Nikos) Sampson
1974–77	n/p	Makarios III
1977–88	DIKO	Spyros Achilleos Kyprianou
1988–93	n/p	Georgios Vasou Vasiliou
1993–2003	DISI	Glafcos Ioannou Clerides
2003–08	DIKO	Tassos Nikolaou Papadopoulos
2008–	AKEL	Dimitris Christofias

RECENT ELECTIONS

Parliamentary elections were held on 21 May 2006. The Progressive Party of the Working People (AKEL) won 18 of 56 available seats with 31·2% of votes cast, followed by the Democratic Rally (DISI) with 18 and 30·3%, the Democratic Party (DIKO) 11 and 17·9%, the Socialist Party (EDEK) 5 and 8·9%, the European Party (Evroko) 3 and 5·7% and the Ecological and Environmental Movement (KOP) 1 and 2·0%. The electorate was 501,024 and turnout was 89·0%.

Presidential elections were held in Feb. 2008. Incumbent Tassos Papadopoulos (DIKO) was eliminated in the first round, held on 17 Feb., after gaining 31·8% of the vote, behind Ioannis Kasoulidis (DISI) with 33·5% and Dimitris Christofias (AKEL) with 33·3%. A run-off, held on 24 Feb., was won by Christofias with 53·4% of the vote, against 46·6% for Kasoulidis. Turnout was 89·6% in the first round and 90·8% in the second.

European Parliament

Cyprus has six representatives. At the June 2009 elections turnout was 59·4% (72·5% in 2004). The DISI won 2 seats with 35·7% of votes cast (political affiliation in European Parliament: European People's Party), AKEL 2 seats with 34·9% (European United Left/Nordic Green Left), DIKO 1 seat with 12·3% (Progressive Alliance of Socialists and Democrats) and EDEK 1 seat with 9·9% (Progressive Alliance of Socialists and Democrats).

CURRENT ADMINISTRATION

President: Dimitris Christofias; b. 1946 (Progressive Party of the Working People; sworn in 28 Feb. 2008).

In March 2010 the Council of Ministers consisted of:

Minister of Foreign Affairs: Markos Kyprianou. *Interior:* Neoklis Sylikiotis. *Defence:* Costas Papacostas. *Agriculture, Natural Resources and Environment:* Michalis Polynikis. *Commerce, Industry and Tourism:* Antonis Paschalides. *Health:* Christos Patsallides. *Communications and Works:* Nicos Nicolaides. *Finance:* Charilaos Stavrakis. *Education and Culture:* Andreas Demetriou. *Labour and Social Insurance:* Sotiroulla Charalambous. *Justice and Public Order:* Kypros Chrysostomides.

Government Website: http://www.cyprus.gov.cy

CURRENT LEADERS

Dimitris Christofias

Position

President

Introduction

Dimitris Christofias became the European Union's only communist head of state when he was sworn in as president in Feb. 2008. Christofias, the leader of the far-left Progressive Party of the Working People (AKEL), was elected after two rounds of presidential elections. He vowed to pursue talks with the 'Turkish Republic of Northern Cyprus'/'TRNC' to find a solution to the division of the island.

Early Life

Christofias was born on 29 Aug. 1946 in Kato Dikomo, Kyrenia province, which is now under Turkish control. His father was a member of the Pancyprian Federation of Labour (PEO), an umbrella organization of trade unions in Cyprus with close ties to the AKEL. Christofias attended the Nicosia Commercial Lyceum where he joined the Pancyprian United Student Organization (PEOM) at the age of 14. In 1969 he became a member of AKEL, PEO and the United Democratic Youth Organization (EDON; AKEL's youth wing). At the fifth congress of EDON held the same year, Christofias was elected to the central council. From 1969–74 Christofias studied at the Institute of Social Sciences and the Academy of Social Sciences in Moscow, where he graduated with a doctorate in history.

On his return to Cyprus in 1974, Christofias was elected to the post of central organizing secretary of EDON. In 1976 he was elected member of the Nicosia-Kyrenia district committee of AKEL and the following year became general secretary of EDON. He was appointed to the AKEL central committee in 1982 and was elected a member of the political bureau of the central committee in 1986. In 1987 he resigned as general secretary of EDON to take on his new post on the secretariat of the AKEL central committee. Following the death of Ezekias Papaioannou in April 1988, Christofias was made general secretary of the central committee of AKEL, a post he still holds.

In the 1991 parliamentary elections Christofias was voted into the House of Representatives, winning re-election in 1996 and 2001. On 7 June 2001 he became president of the House and retained the post in 2006. In his capacity as general secretary of AKEL and president of the House of Representatives, Christofias was a member of the national council, the advisory body to the president on the 'Cyprus problem'.

Ahead of the 2008 presidential election Christofias campaigned on finding a solution to reunite the divided island—despite backing the 2004 rejection of a UN reunification plan. In the first round of voting on 17 Feb. he came second with 33·3% of the vote, displacing the incumbent Tassos Papadopoulos of DIKO (Democratic Party). In the second round he received the support of DIKO and defeated right-winger Ioannis Kasoulidis, obtaining 53·4% of the vote.

Career in Office

Despite widespread reservations about his communist background, Christofias promised to preserve the country's market economy. He also quickly kick-started talks with Northern Cyprus, meeting Turkish Cypriot leader Mehmet Ali Talat in March 2008. Agreement was reached on reopening a key crossing in the divided capital, Nicosia, and they declared their intention to relaunch formal reunification talks. Meeting again in May, they acknowledged their differences but reaffirmed their commitment to 'a bi-zonal, bi-communal federation with political equality'. Following a further review in July, Christofias and Talat met again in Nicosia in Sept. to begin direct intensive negotiations.

Substantive progress has nevertheless been slow, reflecting the underlying fragility of the peace process and the complexity of the issues of contention, such as governance and power-sharing, territorial adjustment, property ownership and security guarantees. Furthermore, parliamentary elections in the 'TRNC' in April 2009 were won by the right-wing nationalist National Unity Party, weakening the negotiating position of Mehmet Ali Talat and casting doubts on the prospects for a reunification settlement.

DEFENCE

Conscription is for 25 months. Defence expenditure in 2006 totalled US$240m. (US$306 per capita), representing 1·3% of GDP. In 1998 the president cancelled a US$450m. contract with Russia for the deployment of S-300 anti-aircraft missiles on the island and negotiated to place them on Crete instead. The defence policy was revised in 2004 to include the threats identified in the European Security Strategy.

National Guard

Total strength (2007) 10,000 (8,700 conscripts). There is also a paramilitary force of some 500 armed police.

There are two British bases (Army and Royal Air Force) and some 3,250 personnel. Greek (1,150) and UN peacekeeping (909 uniformed personnel; UNFICYP) forces are also stationed on the island.

There are approximately 36,000 Turkish troops stationed in the occupied area of Cyprus. The Turkish Cypriot Security Force amounts to around 5,000 troops, with 26,000 reservists and a paramilitary armed police of approximately 150.

Navy

The Maritime Wing of the National Guard operates six vessels. In the Turkish-occupied area of Cyprus the Coast Guard operates six patrol craft.

Air Force

The Air Wing of the National Guard operates a handful of aircraft and 16 attack helicopters, including 12 Mi-35s.

INTERNATIONAL RELATIONS

Cyprus is a member of the UN, World Bank, IMF and several other UN specialized agencies, WTO, EU, Council of Europe, OSCE, Commonwealth and IOM. It became a member of the EU on 1 May 2004.

ECONOMY

Overview

The leading economic sectors are tourism, financial services and real estate. There is an active insurance market and a developing securities market. Following an invitation in 2002 to join the EU, Cyprus has adopted stringent policies to meet EU requirements. The southern part of Cyprus became an EU member in 2004 and adopted the euro as the national currency in Jan. 2008. Major changes in regulatory and institutional structures have been implemented since 2004, including low tax incentives targeted to attract international corporations to the island.

The economy expanded at around 4% per annum for several years before the global downturn but in 2009 it is estimated to have contracted by 1·7%. The tourism and construction sectors have experienced the brunt of this decline.

Though there have been attempts to develop the northern part of Cyprus, where the informal market comprises 30–40% of the economy, little progress has been made in bringing the economies together. The 'Turkish Republic of Northern Cyprus' lacks an independent monetary policy, suffers from high inflation and relies on Turkey for fiscal transfers and trade. Turkey provides US$400m. annually in aid.

Currency

On 1 Jan. 2008 the euro (EUR) replaced the Cyprus pound (CYP) as the legal currency of Cyprus at the irrevocable conversion rate of £C0·585274 to one euro. Inflation was 2·0% in 2005, 2·2% in both 2006 and 2007, and 4·4% in 2008.

In July 2005 gold reserves were 465,000 troy oz, foreign exchange reserves were US$3,655m. and total money supply was £C1,504m.

Budget

Revenue in 2003 (2002) was £C2·4bn. (£C2·1bn.) and expenditure £C2·8bn. (£C2·4bn.). Main sources of revenue in 2003 (in £C1m.) were: tax revenue, 1,700; non-tax revenue, 377.

Main divisions of expenditure in 2003 (in £C1m.): wages and salaries, 727; social security payments, 387; other goods and services, 242.

Capital expenditure for 2003 totalled £C305m., of which £C219m. was investment expenditure.

The outstanding domestic debt at 31 Dec. 2003 was £C3,681·7m. and the foreign debt was £C1,063·0m.

VAT is 15·0% (reduced rates, 8·0% and 5·0%).

Performance
Real GDP growth was 3·9% in 2005, 4·1% in 2006, 4·4% in 2007 and 3·6% in 2008. Cyprus went into recession in the second quarter of 2009, with the economy shrinking by an estimated 1·7% in the year as a whole. Total GDP in 2007 was US$21·3bn.

Banking and Finance
The Central Bank of Cyprus, established in 1963, is the bank of issue. It regulates money supply, credit and foreign exchange and supervises the banking system. The *Governor* is Athanasios Orphanides.

In 2004 there were 14 domestic banks, 29 International Banking Units and one representative office of a foreign bank. The leading banks are Bank of Cyprus, Marfin Popular Bank and Hellenic Bank.

At 30 Sept. 2004 banks' total deposits and lending amounted to £C13,054m. and £C9,003m. respectively.

There is a stock exchange in Nicosia.

ENERGY AND NATURAL RESOURCES

Environment
Carbon dioxide emissions from the consumption and flaring of fossil fuels in Cyprus were the equivalent of 9·5 tonnes per capita in 2008.

Electricity
Installed capacity was 1·0m. kW in 2004. Production in 2004 was 4·18bn. kWh and consumption 5,718m. kWh.

Water
In 2004, £C16·3m. was spent on water dams, water supplies, hydrological research and geophysical surveys. A further £C16·7m. was spent on the production of desalinated sea water. Existing dams had (2004) a capacity of 327m. cu. metres.

Minerals
The principal minerals extracted in 2004 were (in tonnes): gypsum, 234,000; bentonite, 170,000; umber, 5,205; copper, 1,240.

Agriculture
28% of the government-controlled area is cultivated. There were 138,500 ha. of arable land in 2006 and 41,100 ha. of permanent crops. 32,600 ha. were irrigated in 2006. About 6·9% (2002) of the economically active population were engaged in agriculture.

Chief agricultural products in 2002 (1,000 tonnes): milk, 200·6; potatoes, 148·5; cereals (wheat and barley), 141·3; citrus fruit, 137·8; meat, 104·1; grapes, 62·4; fresh fruit, 38·3; olives, 27·5; eggs, 12·3; carobs, 7·2; almonds, 2·0; carrots, 1·9; other vegetables, 141·2.

Livestock in 2002: cattle, 58,300; sheep, 294,000; goats, 459,500; pigs, 491,400; poultry, 3·59m.

Forestry
Total forest area in 2004 was 172,000 ha. (18·6% of the land area). In 2007, 20,000 cu. metres of timber were produced.

Fisheries
Catches in 2005 totalled 1,916 tonnes; aquaculture production in 2004 amounted to 1,820 tonnes.

INDUSTRY
The most important industries in 2003 were: food, beverages and tobacco, metal products, machinery and equipment, other non-metallic mineral products, refined petroleum products, chemicals, chemical products and plastic, wood and wood products, textiles and leather products. The manufacturing industry in 2003 contributed about 9·0% of the GDP.

Labour
Out of an average of 377,948 people in employment in 2007, 67,979 were in wholesale and retail trade/repair of motor vehicles, motorcycles and personal and household goods; 44,669 in construction; and 37,180 in manufacturing. The unemployment rate was 3·1% in Sept. 2003.

Trade Unions
About 80% of the workforce is organized and the majority of workers belong either to the Pancyprian Federation of Labour or the Cyprus Workers Confederation.

INTERNATIONAL TRADE

Imports and Exports
Trade figures for calendar years were (in £C1,000):

	2000	*2001*	*2002*	*2003*
Imports	2,401,826	2,528,720	2,486,612	2,314,248
Exports	591,864	628,029	511,277	476,799

Chief imports, 2003 (in £C1,000):

Machinery, electrical equipment, sound and television recorders	384,280
Vehicles, aircraft, vessels and equipment	288,300
Mineral products	233,282
Products of chemical or allied industries	208,729
Prepared foodstuffs, beverages and tobacco	168,799
Textiles and textile articles	163,621
Base metal and articles of base metal	161,095
Plastics and rubber and articles thereof	88,161
Pulp, waste paper and paperboard and articles thereof	82,046
Vegetable products	71,507
Articles of stone, plaster, cement, etc., ceramic and glass products	65,414
Optical, photographic, medical, musical and other instruments, clocks and watches	48,568
Wood and articles, charcoal, cork, etc.	43,077
Footwear, headgear, umbrellas, prepared leathers, etc.	32,640
Live animals and animal products	32,640
Pearls, precious stones and metals, semi-precious stones and articles	22,310

Chief domestic exports, 2003 (in £C1,000):

Medicinal and pharmaceutical products	38,742	Cement	9,110
Citrus fruit	19,018	Cigarettes	6,839
Potatoes	15,051	Wine	6,127
Cheese	11,656	Fruit, preserved and juices	4,869
Clothing	9,810	Footwear	1,374

Main import suppliers, 2003: Greece, 11·9%; Italy, 9·8%; UK, 8·3%; Germany, 7·5%. Main export markets, 2003: UK, 32·0%; Greece, 9·2%; Germany, 3·9%; Lebanon, 3·4%.

COMMUNICATIONS

Roads
In 2007 the total length of roads in the government-controlled area was 12,246 km, of which 64·0% were paved. In 2004 there were 321,634 passenger cars, 117,819 trucks and vans, 3,199 buses and coaches and 41,396 motorcycles and mopeds. There were 117 deaths as a result of road accidents in 2004.

The area controlled by the government of the Republic and that controlled by the 'TRNC' are now served by separate transport systems, and there are no services linking the two areas.

Civil Aviation
Nicosia airport has been closed since the Turkish invasion in 1974. It is situated in the UN controlled buffer zone. There are international airports at Larnaca (the main airport) and Paphos. In 2003, 6,483,037 passengers, 58,358 aircraft and 31,725 tonnes of commercial freight went through these airports. Both are set to

be expanded with a view to increasing annual capacity by 3m. In 2003 Larnaca handled 4,804,471 passengers (all on international flights) and (2000) 32,077 tonnes of freight. In 2003 Paphos handled 1,679,566 passengers (all on international flights) and (2000) 1,396 tonnes of freight. The national carrier is Cyprus Airways, which is 69·62% state-owned. In 2003 scheduled airline traffic of Cyprus-based carriers flew 30m. km, carrying 1,883,000 passengers (all on international flights).

Shipping

The two main ports are Limassol and Larnaca. In 2007, 4,279 ships of 22,296,482 net registered tons entered Cyprus ports carrying 9,038,002 tonnes of cargo from, to and via Cyprus. In 2002 the merchant marine totalled 23·0m. GRT, including oil tankers 3·6m. GRT. In 2004 the fleet consisted of 1,400 vessels (150 tankers). In 2004 vessels totalling 18,465,000 NRT entered ports. The port in Famagusta has been closed to international traffic since the Turkish invasion in 1974.

Telecommunications

Telephone subscribers numbered 1,138,900 in 2005 (1,363·9 for every 1,000 inhabitants), with 718,800 mobile phone subscribers. There were 249,000 PCs in use (308·6 per 1,000 persons) in 2004 and 298,000 internet users. The Cyprus Telecommunications Authority provides telephone and data transmission services nationally, and to 253 countries automatically. The liberalization of the telecommunications market began in Aug. 2003 when the Electricity Authority of Cyprus was awarded a licence to provide landline telephone services.

Postal Services

In 2003 there were 52 post offices and 912 postal agencies.

SOCIAL INSTITUTIONS

Justice

There is a Supreme Court, Assize Courts and District Courts. The Supreme Court is composed of 13 judges, one of whom is the President of the Court. The Assize Courts have unlimited criminal jurisdiction, and may order the payment of compensation up to £C3,000. The District Courts exercise civil and criminal jurisdiction, the extent of which varies with the composition of the Bench.

A Supreme Council of Judicature, consisting of the President and Judges of the Supreme Court, is entrusted with the appointment, promotion, transfers, termination of appointment and disciplinary control over all judicial officers, other than the Judges of the Supreme Court. The Attorney-General (Petros Clerides) is head of the independent Law Office and legal adviser to the President and his Ministers.

The population in penal institutions in the government-controlled area in Aug. 2008 was 671 (83 per 100,000 of national population).

The death penalty was abolished for all crimes in 2002.

Education

Greek-Cypriot Education. Elementary education is compulsory and is provided free in six grades to children between 5 years 8 months and 11 years 8 months. There are also schools for the deaf and blind, and nine schools for handicapped children. In 2004 the Ministry of Education and Culture ran 238 kindergartens for children in the age group 3–5 years 8 months; there were also 70 communal and 89 private kindergartens. There were 348 primary schools in 2004 with 58,373 pupils and 4,409 teachers.

Secondary education is also free and attendance for the first cycle is compulsory. The secondary school is six years—three years at the gymnasium followed by three years at the *lykeion* (lyceum) or three years at one of the technical schools which provide technical and vocational education for industry. In 2004 there were 120 secondary schools with 6,200 teachers and 56,634 pupils.

Post-secondary education is provided at seven public institutions: the University of Cyprus, which admitted its first students in Sept. 1992 and had 4,603 students in 2004; the Higher Technical Institute, which provides courses lasting three to four years for technicians in civil, electrical, mechanical and marine engineering; the Cyprus Forestry College (administered by the Ministry of Agriculture, Natural Resources and Environment); the Higher Hotel Institute (Ministry of Labour and Social Insurance); the Mediterranean Institute of Management (Ministry of Labour and Social Insurance); the School of Nursing (Ministry of Health) which runs courses lasting two to three years; the Cyprus Police Academy which provides a three-year training programme.

There are also various public and private institutions which provide courses at various levels. These include the Apprenticeship Training Scheme and Evening Technical Classes, and other vocational and technical courses organized by the Human Resources Development Authority.

In 2003 the adult literacy rate was 96·8% (98·6% among males, 95·1% among females). The percentage of the population aged 20 years and over that has attended school was 88·0% in 2003.

In 2006 public expenditure on education came to 7·3% of GNI and 9·5% of total government spending.

Health

In 2004 there were 1,952 doctors, 714 dentists, 3,613 nurses and 800 pharmacists. There were 84 registered private hospitals/clinics, five government hospitals, three rural hospitals, 25 rural health centres and one government psychiatric hospital.

Welfare

Cyprus has a compulsory earnings-related Social Insurance Scheme financed by tripartite contributions, which covers all the gainfully employed population. Employees in the broader public sector are covered by supplementary mandatory pension schemes or provident funds. A large proportion of the private sector's employees have supplementary coverage under non-statutory provident funds established by collective agreements.

RELIGION

The Greek Cypriots are predominantly Greek Orthodox Christians, and almost all Turkish Cypriots are Muslims (mostly Sunnis of the Hanafi sect). There are also small groups of the Armenian Apostolic Church, Roman Catholics (Maronites and Latin Rite) and Protestants (mainly Anglicans). *See also* CYPRUS: Territory and Population.

CULTURE

World Heritage Sites

There are three sites under Cypriot jurisdiction in the World Heritage List: Paphos (entered on the list in 1980); the churches of the Troodos region (1985, 2001); and Choirokoitia (1998). Paphos was a site of worship of the goddess Aphrodite. The Troodos region has one of the largest groups of Byzantine churches and monasteries. The Neolithic settlement of Choirokoitia dates from the 7th to the 4th millennium BC.

Broadcasting

Cyprus Broadcasting Corporation is the public broadcaster, providing four radio networks (mainly in Greek, but also in Turkish, English and Armenian) and two television channels (colour by SECAM H). Commercial broadcasting was legalized in 1990. By 2004 there were five independent radio stations broadcasting nationwide, numerous local radio stations, four private TV stations and two private pay-TV services. Relays of Greek and Turkish stations are also available. There were 302,000 TV sets in 2006; nearly all households possessed at least one television in 2007.

Cinema
In the government-controlled area there were 11 cinemas and 33 screens in 2004. Admissions in 2004 totalled 960,000.

Press
In 2004 there were six daily newspapers with a circulation of 120,000; and 60 other newspapers with a circulation of 250,000.

Tourism
There were 2,470,000 non-resident tourist arrivals in 2005. Visitors from the UK account for some 50% of all tourist arrivals. Tourist spending in 2005 totalled US$2,644m.

Libraries
In 2004 there were 162 public libraries and one national library, holding a combined 580,000 volumes for 60,000 registered users.

Museums and Galleries
In 2003 there were 27 museums which received 1,227,519 visitors.

DIPLOMATIC REPRESENTATIVES
Of Cyprus in the United Kingdom (13 St James' Sq., London, SW1Y 4LB)
High Commissioner: Alexandros N. Zenon.

Of the United Kingdom in Cyprus (Alexander Pallis St., Nicosia)
High Commissioner: Peter Millett.

Of Cyprus in the USA (2211 R St., NW, Washington, D.C., 20008)
Ambassador: Andreas S. Kakouris.

Of the USA in Cyprus (Metochiou and Ploutarchou Streets, Engomi, Nicosia)
Ambassador: Frank C. Urbancic, Jr.

Of Cyprus to the United Nations
Ambassador: Minas Hadjimichael.

Of Cyprus to the European Union
Permanent Representative: Andreas Mavroyiannis.

FURTHER READING
Calotychos, V., *Cyprus and Its People: Nation, Identity and Experience in an Unimaginable Community 1955–1997.* 1999
Christodolou, D., *Inside the Cyprus Miracle: the Labours of an Embattled Mini-Economy.* 1992
Mallinson, William, *Cyprus: A Modern History.* 2005
Pace, Roderick, *The European Union's Mediterranean Enlargement: Cyprus and Malta.* 2006
Papadakis, Yiannis, *Divided Cyprus: Modernity, History and an Island in Conflict.* 2006
Salem N. (ed.) *Cyprus: a Regional Conflict and its Resolution.* 1992

Statistical Information: Statistical Service of the Republic of Cyprus, Michalakis Karaolis Street, 1444 Nicosia.
Website: http://www.mof.gov.cy/mof/cystat/statistics.nsf

'Turkish Republic of Northern Cyprus (TRNC)'

Kuzey Kıbrıs Türk Cumhuriyeti

KEY HISTORICAL EVENTS
See CYPRUS: Key Historical Events.

TERRITORY AND POPULATION
The Turkish Republic of Northern Cyprus occupies 3,355 sq. km (about 33% of the island of Cyprus) and its census population in 2006 was 256,644 (Turkish Cypriots, plus Turkish settlers and troops). Distribution of population by districts (2006): Lefkoşa (Nicosia), 84,231; Mağusa (Famagusta), 63,091; Girne (Kyrenia), 58,438; Güzelyurt (Morphou), 29,481; İskele (Trikomo), 21,403.

CONSTITUTION AND GOVERNMENT
The Turkish Republic of Northern Cyprus was proclaimed on 15 Nov. 1983. The 50 members of the *Legislative Assembly* are elected under a proportional representation system.

RECENT ELECTIONS
Presidential elections were held on 18 April 2010. Prime Minister Derviş Eroğlu (National Unity Party/UBP) won 50·4% against incumbent president, Mehmet Ali Talat (ind.), who claimed 42·9%. Turnout was 76·4%.

In parliamentary elections on 19 April 2009 the opposition National Unity Party won 44·1% of the vote (26 of 50 seats), the ruling Republican Turkish Party-United Forces 29·2% (15), the Democrat Party 10·7% (5), the Communal Democracy Party 6·9% (2) and the Freedom and Reform Party 6·2% (2). Turnout was 81·4%.

CURRENT ADMINISTRATION
President: Derviş Eroğlu; b. 1938 (sworn in 23 April 2010).

In April 2010 the interim government consisted of:

Acting Prime Minister and Minister for Foreign Affairs: Hüseyin Özgürgün; b. 1965 (UBP; since 23 April 2010).

Minister for Agriculture and Natural Resources: Nazim Çavuşoğlu. *Economy and Energy:* Sunat Atun. *Education, Youth and Sport:* Kemal Dürüst. *Finance:* Erşin Tatar. *Foreign Minister:* Hüseyin Özgürgün. *Health:* Ahmet Kaşif. *Interior and Local Administration:* İlkay Kamil. *Labour and Social Security:* Türkay Toker. *Public Works and Communications:* Hasan Taçoy. *Tourism, Environment and Culture:* Hamza Ersan Saner.

Speaker of the Assembly: Hasan Bozer.

DEFENCE
In 2007 around 36,000 members of Turkey's armed forces were stationed in the TRNC with eight main battle tanks (plus 441 tanks for training purposes). TRNC forces comprise seven infantry battalions with an estimated total personnel strength of 5,000. Conscription is for 15 months.

INTERNATIONAL RELATIONS
In April 2004 the European Union pledged to release almost US$310m. as a reward for approval of a UN plan to reunify the island, although it will not be coming into force as it was rejected by the Greek Cypriot south.

ECONOMY

Currency
The Turkish lira is used.

Budget
Revenue in 2003 (in US$1m.) was 696·1 (of which local revenues 404·3 and foreign aid and loans 291·8); expenditure, 691·4.

Performance
The economy grew by 13·5% in 2005.

Banking and Finance
46 banks, including 21 offshore banks, were operating in 2004. Control is exercised by the Central Bank of the TRNC.

ENERGY AND NATURAL RESOURCES

Agriculture
Agriculture accounted for 10·6% of GDP in 2003 (provisional figure).

INTERNATIONAL TRADE

Exports earned US$68·1m. in 2005. Imports cost US$1,255·5m. Customs tariffs with Turkey were reduced in July 1990. There is a free port at Famagusta.

COMMUNICATIONS

Civil Aviation

There is an international airport at Ercan. In 2004 there were flights to Adana, Ankara, Antalya, Dalaman, İstanbul and İzmir with Turkish Airlines and Cyprus Turkish Airlines.

SOCIAL INSTITUTIONS

Education

In 2003 there were 15,482 pupils and 1,156 teachers in primary schools; 15,910 pupils and 1,504 teachers in secondary and general high schools; 1,985 students and 435 teachers in technical and vocational schools; and 29,054 students in higher education. There are four private colleges and five universities.

Health

In 2002 there were 338 doctors, 115 dentists, 167 pharmacists and 1,121 beds in state hospitals and private clinics.

CULTURE

Broadcasting

The Bayrak Radio and Television Corporation is the TRNC's quasi-official broadcasting service, operating two TV channels (BRT 1 and BRT 2) and five radio stations. Colour is by PAL.

Press

In 2006 there were 11 daily and five weekly newspapers. The most widely read paper is the Turkish-language Kibris.

Tourism

There were 715,749 tourists in 2006, of which 572,633 were from Turkey and 143,116 from other countries.

FURTHER READING

North Cyprus Almanack. 1987

Dodd, C. H. (ed.) *The Political, Social and Economic Development of Northern Cyprus.* 1993

Hanworth, R., *The Heritage of Northern Cyprus.* 1993

Ioannides, C. P., *In Turkey's Image: the Transformation of Occupied Cyprus into a Turkish Province.* 1991

CZECH REPUBLIC

Česká Republika

Capital: Prague
Population estimate, 2010: 10·41m.
GDP per capita, 2007: (PPP$) 24,144
HDI/world rank: 0·903/36

KEY HISTORICAL EVENTS

The area that is today the Czech Republic was originally inhabited by Celts around the 4th century BC. The Celtic Boii tribe gave the country its Latin name—Boiohaemum (Bohemia)—but was driven out by Germanic tribes. Slav tribes migrated to central Europe during the period known as the Migration of Peoples and were well established by the 6th century. The first half of the 7th century saw allied Slavonic tribes defending their territory from the Avar Empire in the Hungarian lowlands and from Frank attackers to the West.

Mojmír established The Great Moravian Empire in 830, comprising Bohemia, Moravia and Slovakia. The Empire reached its height under Moravian ruler Svatopluk, but was engulfed and destroyed by the Magyars around 903–07. In 1041, after the defeat of Prince Břetislav the Restorer by the German Emperor Henry III, Bohemia became a fief of the Holy Roman Empire. Dynastic squabbles, exacerbated by German interference, weakened the power of the dukes, but in 1212 Otakar I (1197–1230) was granted a hereditary kingship from the Holy Roman Emperor who also declared the indivisibility of Bohemia which became a key independent state within the realm.

A period of prosperity followed, aided by the immigration of German miners and merchants. Bohemia expanded under the last Přemysl kings: Wenceslas I (1230–53) seized Austria in 1251, though it passed to the Habsburgs when Otakar II was killed at the battle of Marchfeld in 1278. His son Wenceslas II was elected king of Poland in 1300. Wenceslas III was assassinated in 1306, thus ending the Přemysl line. After four years of struggle John of Luxemburg succeeded the throne in 1310.

John's son Charles (1346–78) became Holy Roman Emperor as Charles IV (Charles I of Bohemia) in 1355. He declared Prague the capital of the German Empire and decreed the realm the Crownlands of Bohemia which included parts of modern Germany and Poland. The Golden Bull of Nürnberg in 1356 granted the king of Bohemia first place among the empire's electors.

In what became known as the Golden Age, Charles fostered the commercial and cultural development of Bohemia. In 1348 he founded Prague University, the first university in Central Europe. Work started on the building of St Vitus cathedral, Charles Bridge and the Czech castle of the Grail in Karlstejn during his reign.

Hussite Revolution

Dissatisfaction with the Catholic church in the 14th and 15th centuries climaxed with the Hussite Revolution, the clerical reform movement associated with Jan Hus. The movement had undertones of anti-German Czech nationalism and found support amongst the urban middle classes and lesser rural gentry as well as the urban poor and peasantry. Hus was condemned as a heretic and burnt at the stake in Constance in 1415. Anti-Hussite rulings by Wenceslas IV led to the first 'Defenestration of Prague' in 1419, when Catholic councillors were thrown from the Town Hall windows. In the ensuing Hussite wars Sigismund, the Hungarian Holy Roman Emperor, failed to recover the Bohemian crown. Five crusades were launched against the Hussites in the years 1420–31, all of which were defeated.

The Hussites were eventually weakened by divisions between moderates, the Utraquists, and radicals, the Taborites (originating from the town of Tabor in South Bohemia). The latter's militant leader, Jan Žižka, was defeated in the battle of Lipany in 1434 by the Prague faction supported by Sigismund. This victory allowed for a temporary agreement between Hussite Bohemia and Catholic Europe, known as the Compacts of Basle, which reunited the Utraquist faction with Rome in 1436. A degree of post-war recovery followed under the moderate Hussite king, George of Poděbrady (1457–71), who crushed the radical Taborite dissidents.

In 1471 Vladislav Jagellonský, son of King Casimir IV of Poland, was elected King of Bohemia. His son Louis inherited the throne but was killed at Mohás fighting the Turks in 1526. From 1490, Hungary and Bohemia were both ruled by the Jagiellon Dynasty. Under their rule, the provincial diet of three estates (nobility, gentry and burgesses) acted to enhance the power of the nobility and diminish that of the burgesses. Religious struggles between the Hussite church and the minority Catholic Church continued.

In 1526, after the extinction of the Jagiellon line, Czech nobles elected Archduke Ferdinand. The advent of the Habsburgs saw Roman Catholicism reintroduced and the Crownlands of Bohemia remained in the Habsburg empire until 1918. When Rudolf II (1576–1611) left Vienna to make Prague the capital of the German Empire and the seat of a papal nuncio, the city became a centre of European culture. However, religious divisions with the beginnings of the Counter-Reformation led to the second Defenestration of Prague. Two Catholic governors and their secretary were thrown from a window of Prague Castle, an action which sparked off the Thirty Years' War (1618–48). This brought political disorder and economic devastation to the country with the Habsburg forces wiping out a third of the Bohemian population. The estates deposed Emperor Ferdinand II in favour of the Calvinist Frederick V but the latter's forces were defeated at the battle of White Mountain in 1620. A period of Habsburg hegemony ensued.

After the suppression of the Taborites, the only remaining Protestant Church in Bohemia was the Unity of Czech Brethren, to which Catholics, Utraquists and Lutherans were opposed. The Czech nobility was replaced by German-speaking adventurers, the burgesses lost their rights, the peasantry suffered severe hardships and citizens were forced to embrace the Catholic faith or emigrate. The throne of Bohemia was made hereditary in the

Habsburg Dynasty and the most important offices transferred to Vienna. Risings were savagely repressed. The next two centuries became known as the Dark Ages.

Enlightened Despotism

In the Enlightenment of the late 18th century, Empress Maria Theresa and her son Joseph II granted freedom of worship and movement to the peasantry in 1781, a precondition for the industrial revolution of the next century which made Bohemia the most developed economy within the Empire. Bohemia and Moravia each became independent parts of the Habsburg Monarchy, although conversely the reforms led to greater Germanization and centralization of power, threatening the Slavic identities of the Empire's subjects.

The revival of the Czech nation, which began as a cultural movement, soon progressed into a struggle for political emancipation. Calls for the promotion of the Czech language encouraged Czech nationalists to campaign for the formation of a new Czechoslovakia. It was a concept fostered by Tomáš Garrigue Masaryk, a philosophy professor at the University of Prague and Professor for Slavonic Studies at King's College, London, who was to become the first president of the Czechoslovak Republic.

Male suffrage was granted in 1906 but the chamber of deputies was constantly bypassed by the emperor. The First World War brought estrangement between the Czechs and the Germans, the latter supporting the war effort, the former seeing it as a clash of monarchy versus democracy. Masaryk went into exile in London, where he committed himself to enlisting the support of Britain, France, Russia and the United States in founding a post-war independent Czechoslovak state. He worked with other exiled Czechs and Slovaks, including Dr Edvard Beneš, who later also became president of Czechoslovakia. In 1916 a Czechoslovak National Council was set up in Paris under Masaryk's chairmanship.

In 1918 Masaryk secured the support of US president Woodrow Wilson for Czech and Slovak unity and in May the Pittsburgh agreement was signed in the USA by exiles of both lands. On 18 Oct. 1918 the National Council transformed itself into a provisional government, and was recognized by the Allies.

Creation of the State

Austria accepted President Wilson's terms on 27 Oct. 1918, and the next day a republic was proclaimed with Masaryk, almost 70, as president, and Beneš as foreign minister. In drawing up the frontiers of the new state the principles of Wilsonian self-determination were defeated by the ethnic mix; other criteria employed were the partial restoration of the historic provinces and the need to establish an economically viable and defensible state. Among the minorities were 3·25m. Sudeten Germans. Borders were confirmed in the Treaty of Versailles in June 1919 (although Hungary subsequently called for these to be reformed) along with the official recognition of the state of Czechoslovakia by the international community.

The constitution of 1920 provided for a two-chamber parliament with adult suffrage. The French Constitution and the American Declaration of Rights were both used as models. The electoral system worked so that all governments were coalitions. Slovakia was granted an assembly in 1927, but the state was basically centralist, and the Slovaks maintained their own parties. Between the wars Czechoslovakia became one of the ten most developed and stable countries of the world, although it suffered severe economic depression in the 1930s.

In Nov. 1935 Masaryk was succeeded by Beneš. Meanwhile in Germany, Hitler's designs on expanding the Third Reich stirred up nationalist agitation among the Sudeten Germans. The 1930 census showed 22·3% of the Czechoslovak population were ethnic Germans. In 1933 the German National Socialist Worker's Party in Czechoslovakia, directly affiliated to the Nazi party in Germany, was banned. The Sudeten German Party, led by Konrad Henlein, was formed in its place and won 67% of the German vote in the parliamentary elections of 1935. Czechoslovakia had relied on its 1925 pact with France to defend it against the threat of German aggression, but in the Munich Conference of 29 Sept. 1938 France sided with Britain and Italy in stipulating that all districts with a German population of more than 50% should be ceded to Germany. This legitimized the annexing of the Czech Sudetenland to Germany.

On 5 Oct. 1938 Beneš resigned and went into exile in Britain, and on 15 March 1939 Hitler's troops invaded Prague, contravening the Munich agreement. Slovakia declared itself independent under the fascist leadership of Jozef Tiso, though it was allied to the Germans, and the Czech lands became the German Protectorate of Bohemia-Moravia.

Czechoslovakia suffered further territorial losses to Poland and Hungary under the Vienna Arbitration of 2 Nov. 1938. Altogether it had lost 30% of its territory and almost 34% of its population. Over 1m. Czechs, Slovaks and Ukrainians came under German, Polish and Hungarian rule. Hitler's declared aim was to drive the Czechs out of Central Europe. The Protectorate became a centre for arms production.

Nazi Occupation

Initial attempts at resistance were brutally crushed. On 17 Nov. 1939 German occupiers closed down all Czech universities, executed nine of the leaders of the student movement and transported scores of other students to concentration camps. In 1940 the Gestapo transformed the town of Terezín (Theresienstadt) near Prague into a concentration camp, evacuating the pre-war population to accommodate 140,000 Jews from all parts of the Reich, the majority from the Protectorate of Bohemia-Moravia. 85,000 were then transported to death camps in the East, chiefly to Auschwitz, and over 30,000 prisoners were held in the fortress. Many Communists and Czech resistance fighters also met their deaths there.

Mass expulsions were a regular feature of the Protectorate. In 1942, 30,000 people were forced to leave their homes in order to make way for the military. In another case around 5,000 families were expelled from around 30 villages in Moravia in an attempt to create an ethnic German enclave. Growing resistance led to the appointment of SS General Reinhard Heydrich, head of the Reich's Security Office, who launched a savage offensive against underground organizations, and executed general Alois Elias, head of the Protectorate's government, for his connections with the Beneš government in Britain. The latter, along with the Allies, were in turn behind the assassination of Heydrich, carried out on 27 May 1942 by two paratroopers. The Nazis responded with a frenzy of terror known as the 'Heydrichiade'. Revenge murders of the entire populations of Lidice (on 10 June 1942) and Lezáky (24 June 1942) were carried out.

The Beneš government in exile in London, with Jan Šrámek as prime minister, was officially recognized by Britain and the USSR on 18 June 1941. A 20-year treaty of alliance with the USSR was signed on 12 Dec. 1943 and, in March 1945, Beneš went to Moscow to prepare for post-war government in the wake of the Soviet Army advance. Liberation by the Soviet Army and US forces was completed in 1945 following an insurrection on 5 May. Territories taken by Germans, Poles and Hungarians were restored to Czechoslovakia. Subcarparthian Ruthenia (now in Ukraine) was transferred to the USSR, creating a common border with the Soviet state.

The Sudeten Germans suffered brutal expulsions, during which up to 250,000 died, 6,000 of whom were murdered. The 'resettlement' of ethnic Germans was officially approved at the Potsdam Conference on 1 Aug. 1945, when the USA and Britain insisted on humane transfer, subsequently supervised by the Allies and the Red Cross. German or Hungarian Czechs had their citizenship taken away unless they were naturalized Czechs or Slovaks. In order to stay, German or Hungarian Czechs had to prove that they had remained faithful to the Czechoslovak Republic, had fought in the resistance, or had personally suffered at the hands of fascists. Further decrees expropriated property and agricultural land. A total of 2,700,000 Germans were expelled, and in the Czech census of March 1991 only 47,000 claimed German as their nationality. A Czech–German Declaration of 21 Jan. 1997 saw both sides admit to and apologize for their atrocities during the period.

Soviet Domination

Beneš once again became president of Czechoslovakia but, under pressure from the USSR, measures were taken to confiscate and redistribute property and to take key industries into public ownership. Before 1939 the Communist party of Czechoslovakia (CPCz) had never gained more than 13% of the vote, but its patriotic stance in the late 1930s as well as its clear affiliation with the country's main liberator the USSR, led to a sharp increase in popularity. In the elections of 26 May 1946 the Communists won almost 40% of the vote in Czech areas and 30% in Slovakia. This made the party the largest group in the new Constituent National Assembly, with 114 of the 300 seats and Klement Gottwald as premier. Its leaders pledged commitment to democratic traditions while pursuing a 'specific Czechoslovak road to socialism'.

The party's independence was first put into question when Czechoslovakia was pressurized by Stalin into withdrawing from the American Marshall plan for economic rejuvenation, seen from Moscow as a threat to its own influence. Stalin's encouragement of the CPCz grew in the autumn of 1947 when a people's militia was formed and non-communist parties in the governing coalition found their influence eroded. In protest, 12 non-communist ministers handed in their resignations. The CPCz adroitly handled this situation to its own advantage, forcing President Beneš to appoint a predominantly communist government on 25 Feb. 1948.

A new constitution, declaring Czechoslovakia a 'people's democracy' was approved on 9 May 1948, and elections were held on 30 May with a single list of candidates, resulting in an 89% majority for the government. Beneš resigned on 2 June after refusing to ratify the Communist Constitution. 12 days later Gottwald succeeded him as President. Civil rights were severely restricted; from 1950 monasteries and convents were nationalized, with 219 monasteries being taken over by the People's Militia on the night of 13 April alone; monastic orders were abolished.

The secret service became one of the most systematic and omnipresent in the Soviet bloc. Unsubstantiated charges of treason and resistance to the communist cause led to a series of show trials and executions, with many victims from the CPCz itself. It is estimated that between 200,000 and 280,000 suffered death or persecution during the Stalin era. Stalin died on 5 March 1953, and Gottwald just a week later, but the communists maintained their grip. Workers' demonstrations in Plzeň and other Czech towns against price rises and currency reform, which devalued savings, were brutally suppressed by the military in June that year. Political trials of 'Slovak nationalists' in 1954 had many Slovak Communists imprisoned, including Gustáv Husák, who later went on to become secretary-general of the CPCz and president of Czechoslovakia.

The Soviet five-year economic plans emphasized engineering, arms production and heavy industry. A third of Czechoslovak output came from the arms industry. The service and consumer goods industries were virtually abolished and all farms collectivized. The founding of COMECON on 1 Jan. 1949 and the signing of the Warsaw Pact in 1955 limited Czechoslovakia's trading partners to the Eastern bloc.

A new constitution, introduced in 1960, reinforced the power of the Communist Party and changed the country's name to the Socialist Republic of Czechoslovakia (ČSSR).

Prague Spring

The failure of the third five-year plan to meet its targets gave a push to economic reform. A mixed economy was introduced, which led to a period of cultural liberalization. Support for political reform grew within party ranks. Antonín Novotný was persuaded to resign as CPCz leader on 5 Jan. 1968. He was replaced by Alexander Dubček, leader of the Communist Party of Slovakia. On 22 March, Novotný resigned as president in favour of Gen. Ludvík Svoboda, who was elected by the National Assembly. Precipitating what became known as the Prague Spring, Dubček introduced many reforms in his pursuit of 'socialism with a human face'. New political bodies were formed, breaking up the monopoly of the Communist Party. Press censorship was abolished and restraints on freedom of expression relaxed.

The reforms caused unrest in Moscow. Brezhnev unsuccessfully put pressure on Czechoslovakia between May and Aug. He then ordered the invasion of Czechoslovakia by troops of the Warsaw Pact countries (with the exception of Romania), whose tanks rolled in on 20–21 Aug. The Soviet intention of replacing Dubček and his government with more hard-line Communists failed when President Svoboda turned down Soviet nominees. Dubček and other party leaders were then abducted to Moscow and forced to sign an agreement to keep Soviet troops stationed in Czechoslovakia. The Prague Spring all but withered. The only surviving measure of reform was the introduction of the federal system on 1 Jan. 1969. Separate Czech and Slovak states came into force within a Czechoslovak federation, a move that satisfied the Slovaks who had been seeking autonomy for some time. Each state was awarded its own administration and a national council, and the National Assembly divided into two chambers. All other reforms of the Dubček administration were stamped out or reversed and the Soviet policy of 'normalization' took hold.

In protest at the Soviet repression, student Jan Palach set fire to himself in Wenceslas Square on 16 Jan. 1969. On 28 March when the Czechoslovak national ice hockey team beat the Soviets, celebrations turned into anti-Soviet demonstrations and led to many arrests. On 17 April Dubček was forced from office and replaced with the hard-liner, Gustáv Husák. Repression led to mass emigrations. So-called 'enemies of the state' were put under constant surveillance, blacklisted for jobs and their children denied university places. Freedom to travel abroad was no longer granted to ordinary citizens. Protest resurfaced again in 1977, with the signing of Charter 77 and founding of the Committee for the Defence of the Rights of the Unjustly Persecuted (VONS). These two organizations, led by artists and intellectuals, alerted the public to civil rights abuses and campaigned for civil and political rights.

Velvet Revolution

The advent of Mikhail Gorbachev's *glasnost* and *perestroika* in the mid-1980s initially changed little. Husák was replaced as leader of the CPCz by Miloš Jakeš, who had been responsible for Party purges in 1970. But there were renewed demonstrations in Aug. 1988 on the 20th anniversary of the Soviet invasion, in Oct. on the 70th anniversary of the founding of Czechoslovakia and in Jan. 1989 on the 20th anniversary of Jan Palach's suicide when the crowd was brutally dispersed and leading dissidents, including Václav Havel, arrested and imprisoned. Protests, petitions and further demonstrations followed in May, Aug. and Oct. of 1989. The fall of the Berlin Wall on 9 Nov. 1989 galvanized the pro-democracy movement. Another major demonstration by students on 17 Nov. led to further protests until the entire CPCz leadership resigned on 24 Nov. Civic Forum (OF) in the Czech Republic and the Public Against Violence (VPN) in Slovakia were formed to co-ordinate all pro-democratic forces, and an interim broad coalition 'Government of National Understanding' with a minority of Communists took over. These non-violent events became known as the Velvet Revolution. Václav Havel was unanimously elected president of Czechoslovakia by the Federal Assembly on 29 Dec. 1989.

The first free elections since the Second World War were held in June 1990, with a turnout of 96·4%. The Communists were roundly defeated, and Civic Forum won 52% of the votes. Second parliamentary elections were fixed for mid-1992, by which time neither Civic Forum (OF) nor VPN any longer existed, having been replaced by fully-fledged parties across the political spectrum. In the Czech lands, the right wing emerged as the strongest element, with the Civic Democratic party (ODS) the largest coalition party. Its leader, Václav Klaus, who was also finance minister, became prime minister and stayed in the post until Nov. 1997.

By contrast, in Slovakia, Vladimír Mečiar's Democratic Slovakia party and other post-communists were successful in the elections. A continuing Slovak desire for independence from Prague, along with differences in opinion on economic policy and the role of the state, strained relations between the two federal partners. An agreement to a 'velvet divorce' was reached and from 1 Jan. 1993 the two devolved into separate sovereign states. Economic property was divided in accordance with a federal law of 13 Nov. 1992 and real estate became the property of the republic in which it was located. Other property was divided by specially-constituted commissions in the proportion of 2 (Czech Republic) to 1 (Slovakia) on the basis of population. Military material was also divided on the 2:1 principle, and regular military personnel were invited to choose in which army they would serve.

The Czech Republic showed greater eagerness than its former partner to become westernized. Although many feared a precipitous move towards a market economy, Klaus argued that danger lay in delaying reform, and that the creation of a market economy would lead the 'return to Europe' and the opening up of new markets.

Klaus immediately embarked on a series of radical reforms, impressing Western investors with his Thatcherite rhetoric, policies and publications. A programme of mass privatization was implemented, at first successfully, and the early to mid-nineties were a time of economic boom, with the Czech Republic a leading contender for Western trade and investment. However, many of the tough policies were not fully implemented and an increasing number of financial scandals were associated with the Klaus administration. 1997 also saw a currency crisis, where the crown devalued 12% against the dollar. Klaus was forced to resign as prime minister on 18 Nov. 1997.

Josef Tošovský formed a caretaker government until 1998 when Miloš Zeman formed a minority Social Democratic government, the country's first left-wing government since the fall of socialism. The Czech Republic joined NATO in 1999 and in 2001 Vladimír Špidla succeeded Zeman as party leader and prime minister. The Czech Republic became a member of the EU on 1 May 2004.

Following an inconclusive election in June 2006 there were seven months of political deadlock during which the country was without a government. A new centre-right coalition was formed under Mirek Topolánek in Jan. 2007.

TERRITORY AND POPULATION

The Czech Republic is bounded in the west by Germany, north by Poland, east by Slovakia and south by Austria. Minor exchanges of territory to straighten their mutual border were agreed between the Czech Republic and Slovakia on 4 Jan. 1996, but the Czech parliament refused to ratify them on 24 April 1996. Its area is 78,866 sq. km (30,450 sq. miles). At the 2001 census the population was 10,230,060 (51·3% female); density, 129·7 per sq. km. The estimated population at 1 Jan. 2009 was 10,467,542. The United Nations population estimate for 2009 was 10·37m. In 2005, 73·5% of the population lived in urban areas.

The UN gives an estimated population for 2010 of 10·41m.

There are 14 administrative regions *(Kraj)*, one of which is the capital, Prague (Praha).

Region	*Chief city*	*Area in sq. km*	*Population 2001 census*
Jihočeský	České Budějovice	10,056	625,267
Jihomoravský	Brno	7,067	1,127,718
Karlovarský	Karlovy Vary	3,315	304,343
Královéhradecký	Hradec Králové	4,757	550,724
Liberecký	Liberec	3,163	428,184
Moravskoslezský	Ostrava	5,555	1,269,467
Olomoucký	Olomouc	5,139	639,369
Pardubický	Pardubice	4,519	508,281
Plzeňský	Pilsen (Plzeň)	7,560	550,688
Prague (Praha)	—	496	1,169,106
Středočeský	Prague (Praha)	11,014	1,122,473
Ústecký	Ústí nad Labem	5,335	820,219
Vysočina	Jihlava	6,925	519,211
Zlínský	Zlín	3,965	595,010

The estimated population of the principal towns in 2006 (in 1,000):

Prague (Praha)	1,182	Liberec	98	Havířrov	84
Brno	367	České Budějovice	95	Zlín	78
Ostrava	310	Hradec Králové	94	Kladno	69
Pilsen (Plzeň)	163	Ústí nad Labem	94	Most	68
Olomouc	100	Pardubice	88	Karviná	63

At the 2001 census 90·4% of the population was Czech, 3·7% Moravian and 1·9% Slovak. There were also (in 1,000): Poles, 52; Germans, 39; Roma (Gypsies), 12; Silesians, 11.

The official language is Czech.

SOCIAL STATISTICS

2005 births, 102,211; deaths, 107,938; marriages, 51,829; divorces, 31,288. Rates (per 1,000 population), 2005: birth, 10·0; death, 10·5; marriage, 5·1; divorce, 3·1. Life expectancy at birth, 2007, 73·2 years for males and 79·4 years for females. In 2005 the most popular age range for marrying was 25–29 for both males and females. Annual population growth rate, 2000–05, –0·1%. Infant mortality, 2005, 3·4 per 1,000 live births; fertility rate, 2004, 1·2 children per woman (one of the lowest rates in the world).

CLIMATE

A humid continental climate, with warm summers and cold winters. Precipitation is generally greater in summer, with thunderstorms. Autumn, with dry clear weather, and spring, which is damp, are each of short duration. Prague, Jan. 29·5°F (–1·5°C), July 67°F (19·4°C). Annual rainfall 19·3" (483 mm). Brno, Jan. 31°F (–0·6°C), July 67°F (19·4°C). Annual rainfall 21" (525 mm).

CONSTITUTION AND GOVERNMENT

The constitution of 1 Jan. 1993 provides for a parliament comprising a 200-member *Chamber of Deputies*, elected for four-year terms by proportional representation, and an 81-member *Senate* elected for six-year terms in single-member districts, 27 senators being elected every two years. The main function of the Senate is to scrutinize proposed legislation. Senators must be at least 40 years of age, and are elected on a first-past-the-post basis, with a run-off in constituencies where no candidate wins more than half the votes cast. For the House of Representatives there is a 5% threshold; votes for parties failing to surmount this are redistributed on the basis of results in each of the eight electoral districts.

There is a *Constitutional Court* at Brno, whose 15 members are nominated by the President and approved by the Senate for ten-year terms.

The *President* of the Republic is elected for a five-year term. He or she must be at least 40 years of age and must win the votes in both chambers of parliament to be declared the winner. If after two rounds of voting the houses cannot unite in their support for one candidate then the election proceeds to a ballot incorporating both chambers, in which a winner must gain the vote of over half the lawmakers present. If this does not give a conclusive result the whole process is repeated. The President names the Prime Minister at the suggestion of the Speaker.

National Anthem

'Kde domov můj?' ('Where is my homeland?'); words by J. K. Tyl, tune by F. J. Škroup.

GOVERNMENT CHRONOLOGY

(ČSSD = Czech Social Democratic Party; ODS = Civic Democratic Party; n/p = non-partisan)

Presidents since 1993.

1993–2003	n/p	Václav Havel
2003–	ODS	Václav Klaus

Prime Ministers since 1993.

1993–97	ODS	Václav Klaus
1997–98	n/p	Josef Tošovský
1998–2002	ČSSD	Miloš Zeman
2002–04	ČSSD	Vladimír Špidla
2004–05	ČSSD	Stanislav Gross
2005–06	ČSSD	Jiří Paroubek
2006–09	ODS	Mirek Topolánek
2009–	n/p	Jan Fischer

RECENT ELECTIONS

Incumbent president and former prime minister Václav Klaus (Civic Democratic Party/ODS) was re-elected by parliament for a second term on 15 Feb. 2008. In the first round of voting, held on 8 Feb., he won the Senate 47–32, but his opponent Jan Švejnar (ind.) won the lower house 106–92. A second vote, held the following day, was also inconclusive. In the third round on 15 Feb., in which votes from both chambers were counted together, Klaus won a majority with 141 votes against 111 for Švejnar.

Elections to the National Assembly were held on 2 and 3 June 2006; turnout was 64·5%. The Civic Democratic Party (ODS) gained 81 seats with 35·4% of votes cast; the Czech Social Democratic Party (ČSSD) gained 74 with 32·3%; the Communist Party of Bohemia and Moravia (KSČM), 26 with 12·8%; the coalition of the Christian and Democratic Union (KDU) and the Czechoslovak People's Party (ČSL) 13 with 7·2% and the Green Party (SZ) 6 with 6·3%. The Civic Democratic Party's result was the best achieved by any party since the Czech Republic came into existence in 1993. After seven months of political deadlock a three-party coalition government was formed in Jan. 2007 between ODS, KDU–ČSL and SZ.

Elections for a third of the seats in the Senate were held on 17, 18, 24 and 25 Oct. 2008. As a result ODS had 35 seats in the Senate; ČSSD 29; the coalition of KDU and ČSL 7; KSČM 3; the SNK European Democrats 2; with ind. and a number of other parties holding one seat.

Parliamentary elections were scheduled to take place on 28 and 29 May 2010.

European Parliament

The Czech Republic has 22 (24 in 2004) representatives. At the June 2009 elections turnout was 28·2% (28·3% in 2004). The ODS won 9 seats with 31·5% of votes cast (political affiliation in European Parliament: European Conservatives and Reformists); ČSSD, 7 with 22·4% (Progressive Alliance of Socialists and Democrats); KSČM, 4 with 14·2% (European United Left/Nordic Green Left); KDU–ČSL, 2 with 7·6% (European People's Party).

CURRENT ADMINISTRATION

President: Václav Klaus; b. 1941 (ODS; sworn in 7 March 2003 and re-elected 15 Feb. 2008).

Prime Minister and Minister for Human Rights: Jan Fischer; b. 1951 (ind.; sworn in 8 May 2009).

In April 2010 the government comprised:

Deputy Prime Minister and Minister for Foreign Affairs: Jan Kohout. *Deputy Prime Minister and Minister for Defence:* Martin Barták.

Minister of Agriculture: Jakub Šebesta. *Culture:* Václav Riedlbauch. *Education:* Miroslava Kopicová. *Environment:* Rut Bízková. *European Affairs:* Juraj Chmiel. *Finance:* Eduard Janota. *Health:* Dana Jurásková. *Industry and Trade:* Vladimír Tošovský. *Interior:* Martin Pecina. *Justice and Head of Government Legislative Council:* Daniela Kovářová. *Labour and Social Affairs:* Petr Šimerka. *Regional Development:* Rostislav Vondruška. *Transport:* Gustáv Slamečka.

Government Website: http://www.vlada.cz

CURRENT LEADERS

Václav Klaus

Position

President

Introduction

Dr Václav Klaus, a member of the Civic Forum movement and later the centre-right Civic Democratic Party (ODS; Obcanská Demokratická Strana), was Czechoslovakia's first minister of finance following the Velvet Revolution of 1989. He was elected prime minister in 1992 and oversaw the Czech Republic's transition from a state-planned economy to a free market system. His reforms led initially to economic growth unparalleled among any of the other post-communist nations in the region. However, by the late 1990s the economy was suffering and Klaus resigned in 1997 following a party financing scandal. He succeeded Václav Havel as president in March 2003 and was re-elected in Feb. 2008. A noted eurosceptic, Klaus was the last head of state to sign the European Union's Lisbon Treaty on institutional and administrative reform in Nov. 2009.

Early Life

Born on 19 April 1941 in Prague, Klaus graduated from the Prague School of Economics in 1963, continuing his education in Naples, Italy and at Cornell University in New York. He was then employed as a researcher at the Institute of Economics of the Czechoslovak Academy of Sciences until 1970, when he was removed as an anti-socialist element. During that time he came into contact with Václav Havel, the dissident writer and future Czech president, when both were on the editorial board of a magazine.

From 1971 until 1987, Klaus held a succession of posts at the Czechoslovak State Bank before joining the Academy of Sciences' Economic Forecasting Institute. On 17 Nov. 1989, while the Velvet Revolution was in its infancy, Klaus returned from lecturing in Vienna to find that his son had only just escaped a serious beating from police in Prague's Wenceslas Square. Two days later he became a founder member of the Civic Forum, the movement that would be instrumental in the overthrow of the Communist regime in the coming days. He was appointed finance minister in the first post-revolution government in Dec. 1989, implementing a range of reformist policies influenced by free market economics.

The Civic Forum, which had been a loose alliance of anti-communists, began to splinter and Klaus became a prominent member of the centre-right ODS, which had an ambitious agenda to restructure, deregulate and liberalize the market. In April 1991 he became party chairman, in Oct. 1991 he was appointed deputy premier and in June 1992 he became prime minister, following the ODS electoral victory.

Career in Office

Following the split with Slovakia, the Czech Republic underwent a programme of rapid reform and privatization that saw the economy eclipse those of its former communist neighbours.

Klaus was acclaimed internationally as the architect of an economic miracle and praised for his publications (such as *Ten Commandments of Systematic Reform* and *Rebirth of a Nation*).

However, the ODS faired less well than expected at the elections of July 1996 and the governing coalition lost their majority in the House of Representatives. For the first time, Klaus' authority within the ODS had been challenged and was further weakened during that year when his foreign minister, Josef Zieleniec, made public a feud between them. The economy was also beginning to suffer, and there followed a series of crisis budgets, austerity measures and ultimately devaluation in 1997. A number of further problems for Klaus included the resignation of Zieleniec, popular protests against the government and, most damagingly, the re-emergence of corruption allegations concerning ODS party funding. The charges concerned improper donations in return for preferential treatment in relation to privatization, but Klaus vigorously denied all knowledge. Zieleniec publicly declared that Klaus had been aware of a number of certain key donations, and President Havel called for the government to step down. Klaus resigned on 29 Nov. 1997, still denying any wrongdoing.

Although corruption allegations were the catalyst for Klaus' fall from power, his government had been under pressure as the Czech Republic failed to sustain its economic lead over its former communist rivals. However, he retained significant influence as speaker of the Chamber of Deputies for four years from 1998. In Jan. 2003 he twice stood for election to the presidency in succession to Havel but, despite winning most votes on both occasions, failed to secure the requisite 50%. Havel resigned on 3 Feb. 2003 and Klaus was chosen to succeed him at the third attempt.

In June 2003 membership of the EU, scheduled for 2004, won 77% approval in a national referendum. Klaus, however, had described entry into the EU as a 'marriage of convenience rather than love' and refused to reveal which way he had voted. Parliamentary elections in June 2006 resulted in a political stalemate and a failure to negotiate any workable government until Sept., when a centre-right minority administration took office under Mirek Topolánek of the ODS. However, this government collapsed the following month after losing a vote of confidence. In Nov. President Klaus again designated Topolánek as prime minister and a new coalition government took office in Jan. 2007. Klaus was re-elected for a second term in Feb. 2008.

Topolánek resigned in March 2009 after his government lost a parliamentary vote of confidence and Klaus appointed Jan Fischer, an economist, as interim prime minister. Meanwhile, with the Czech Republic having assumed the six-month presidency of the EU in Jan. 2009, Klaus made plain his distrust of the Union's Lisbon Treaty for national sovereignty reasons. However, having unsuccessfully sought a national opt-out from aspects of the treaty, Klaus eventually signed it in Nov. 2009 following a ruling by the Czech Constitutional Court on its legitimacy.

Jan Fischer

Position

Prime Minister

Introduction

Jan Fischer took over as prime minister on 8 May 2009. His appointment followed the collapse of Mirek Topolánek's government in March 2009. Fischer, the head of the Czech Statistical Office (ČSÚ), was approved for the role by the three centre-right governing coalition parties and the senior opposition, the Social Democrats.

Early Life

Fischer was born in Prague in Jan. 1951 into a family of professional mathematicians. Following his parents into statistical analysis, Fischer specialized in statistics and econometrics during his undergraduate study at Prague's University of Economics. He completed postgraduate studies in economic statistics at the same university in 1985. Fischer was a member of the Communist Party of Czechoslovakia from 1980–89. He has said that he became a member of the party only to ensure that he would not be obstructed in his career.

Having begun work at Czechoslovakia's central statistical office upon graduation, Fischer was appointed vice-president of the institution in 1990, a post he retained when the ČSÚ was created following the dissolution of Czechoslovakia in 1993. He was made head of the ČSÚ in April 2003 and was often required to attend cabinet meetings. As rival parliamentary parties sought a politically neutral figure with a good understanding of the political agenda to succeed Topolánek, Fischer was chosen as interim prime minister.

Career in Office

On assuming office Fischer said that he had no political ambitions. He aimed to focus on completing the Czech Republic's EU Presidency, leading the government until elections in May 2010, and then returning to his post at the statistical office.

DEFENCE

Conscription ended in Dec. 2004 when the armed forces became all-volunteer. Defence expenditure in 2006 totalled US$2,464m. (US$241 per capita), representing 1·7% of GDP.

Army

Strength (2007) 16,960. There are also paramilitary Border Guards (3,000-strong) and Internal Security Forces (100).

Air Force

The Air Force has a strength of 6,130 including Air Defence Forces. There were 50 combat capable aircraft in 2007 (L-159s and JAS 39s) and 38 attack helicopters.

INTERNATIONAL RELATIONS

In 1974 the Federal Republic of Germany and Czechoslovakia annulled the Munich agreement of 1938. On 14 Feb. 1997 the Czech parliament ratified a declaration of German–Czech reconciliation, with particular reference to the Sudeten German problems.

The Czech Republic is a member of the UN, World Bank, IMF and several other UN specialized agencies, WTO, EU, Council of Europe, OSCE, CERN, CEI, BIS, IOM, NATO, OECD and Antarctic Treaty, and is an associate member of WEU. The Czech Republic became a member of the EU on 1 May 2004. A referendum held on 13–14 June 2003 approved accession, with 77·3% of votes cast for membership and 22·7% against. In 2000 a visa requirement for Russians entering the country was introduced as one of the conditions for EU membership.

In Dec. 2007 the Czech Republic acceded to the Schengen accord, which abolishes border controls between the Czech Republic, Austria, Belgium, Denmark, Estonia, Finland, France, Germany, Greece, Hungary, Iceland, Italy, Latvia, Lithuania, Luxembourg, Malta, Netherlands, Norway, Poland, Portugal, Slovakia, Slovenia, Spain, Sweden and Switzerland.

The Czech Republic's Senate approved the European Union's Treaty of Lisbon on 6 May 2009, after the Chamber of Deputies had done so on 18 Feb. 2009. However, President Klaus stated that he would not sign it until Ireland had ratified it (which happened after a second referendum held on 2 Oct. 2009). Klaus subsequently gave his presidential assent on 3 Nov. 2009, making the Czech Republic the last country to ratify it.

ECONOMY

Agriculture accounted for 2% of GDP in 2008, industry 38% and services 60%.

Overview

Until 1996 the Czech Republic was viewed as the most successful European transition economy. Industrial production and employment declined significantly during the transition from communism but job losses were contained by rising service sector employment and soft loans given to loss-making enterprises by state-banks. After four years of 3% average annual growth, the economy fell into recession in 1997–98. In May 1997 large current account deficits fuelled a speculative attack on the *koruna*, forcing the country to adopt a tight monetary policy and fiscal austerity. With a financial sector no longer able to subsidize loss-making industrial enterprises, industry was forced to make costly financial and enterprise reforms. Foreign direct investment began flowing from the West in 1999 and solid growth resumed in the 2000s without high inflation.

With strength in engineering, low labour costs, good infrastructure and a favourable geographical position, the Czech Republic's diversified industrial export sector has been a key engine of growth. A strengthening *koruna* has kept inflation down and moderated the current account deficit. A favourable trend in public finances was reversed in 2006 as the government deficit increased, reflecting pre-election tax cuts and an expansion of social transfers for pensions and health care. An increase in mandatory social spending in the 2007 budget was expected to worsen the fiscal position. Faced with an ageing population, strong fiscal consolidation and improved labour market flexibility are required to sustain growth and allow for the successful adoption of the euro.

Currency

The unit of currency is the *koruna* (CZK) or crown of 100 *haler*, introduced on 8 Feb. 1993 at parity with the former Czechoslovakian koruna. Gold reserves were 415,000 troy oz in Sept. 2009 and foreign exchange reserves were US$39,101m. Total money supply was Kč. 1,736·0bn in Aug. 2009.

Inflation rates (based on OECD statistics):

1999	*2000*	*2001*	*2002*	*2003*	*2004*	*2005*	*2006*	*2007*	*2008*
2·1%	3·9%	4·7%	1·8%	0·1%	2·8%	1·9%	2·6%	3·0%	6·3%

The koruna became convertible on 1 Oct. 1995. In May 1997 the koruna was devalued 10% and allowed to float.

Budget

Budgetary central government revenue in 2005 totalled Kč. 813·69bn. (Kč. 762·12bn. in 2004) and expenditure Kč. 856·91bn. (Kč. 806·62bn. in 2004).

Principal sources of revenue in 2003 were: social security contributions, Kč. 273·11bn.; taxes on goods and services, Kč. 203·10bn.; taxes on income, profits and capital gains, Kč. 172·91bn. Main items of expenditure by economic type in 2003: social benefits, Kč. 305·03bn.; grants, Kč. 170·74bn.; compensation of employees, Kč. 79·26bn.

VAT is 20% (reduced rate, 10%).

Performance

Real GDP growth rates (based on OECD statistics):

1999	*2000*	*2001*	*2002*	*2003*	*2004*	*2005*	*2006*	*2007*	*2008*
1·2%	3·9%	2·4%	1·8%	3·6%	4·3%	6·4%	7·0%	6·1%	2·6%

GDP growth in 2009 was –4·2% according to the Czech Statistical Office. Total GDP was US$216·5bn. in 2008.

Banking and Finance

The central bank and bank of issue is the Czech National Bank (*Governor*, Zdeněk Tůma), which also acts as banking supervisor and regulator. Decentralization of the banking system began in 1991, and private banks began to operate. The Czech banking sector accounted for 78·3% of total financial sector assets at the end of 2002, representing Kč. 2,504bn. or 110% of GDP in 2002. The only legal form of domestically operating banks are joint stock companies (27 at 30 June 2003) and branches of foreign banks (nine at 30 June 2003). The Commercial Bank and Investment Bank are privatized nationwide networks with a significant government holding. Specialized banks include the Czech Savings Bank and the Czech Commercial Bank (for foreign trade payments). Private banks tend to be on a regional basis, many of them agricultural banks. In Nov. 1997 the cabinet agreed to sell off large stakes in three of the largest state-held banks to individual foreign investors through tenders, in preparation for European Union entry. In June 2000 the country's fourth largest bank, Československá obchodní banka (ČSOB), acquired the operations of the third largest bank, IPB (Investiční a Poštovní banka). The newly-formed institution (which retained the name ČSOB) is the largest bank in central and eastern Europe, with assets of US$51·3bn. in Dec. 2007. Other major banks are Česká Spořitelna (assets of US$51·6bn. in Sept. 2008) and Komerční banka (assets of US$37·2bn. in Dec. 2008). Foreign shareholders controlled 94·5% of the total assets of the banking sector at June 2003, most of them from EU countries. Other capital market participants are subject to the supervision of the Czech Securities Commission. Savings deposits were Kč. 1,467,270m. in 2002.

Foreign direct investment was US$10·7bn. in 2008 (US$10·4bn. in 2007).

A stock exchange was founded in Prague in 1992.

ENERGY AND NATURAL RESOURCES

Environment

The Czech Republic's carbon dioxide emissions from the consumption and flaring of fossil fuels in 2008 were the equivalent of 9·9 tonnes per capita.

Electricity

Installed capacity was 17·4m. kW in 2004. Production in 2004 was 84·33bn. kWh. 66% of electricity was produced by thermal power stations (mainly using brown coal) and 31% was nuclear. In 2003 there were six nuclear reactors in operation. Consumption per capita in 2004 was 6,720 kWh.

Oil and Gas

Natural gas reserves in 2005 totalled 4·0bn. cu. metres. Production in 2004 was 229m. cu. metres. In 2005 crude petroleum reserves were 15m. bbls; production was 2·1m. bbls in 2004.

Minerals

There are hard coal and lignite reserves (chief fields: Most, Chomutov, Kladno, Ostrava and Sokolov). Lignite production in 2004 was 48·5m. tonnes; coal production in 2004 was 15·6m. tonnes.

Agriculture

In 2002 there were 4,273,000 ha. of agricultural land. In 2002 there were 3·07m. ha. of arable land and 0·97m. ha. of permanent crops. Approximately 19,900 ha. were irrigated in 2007. Agriculture employs just 4·9% of the workforce—the smallest proportion of any of the ex-Communist countries in eastern Europe. A law of May 1991 returned land seized by the Communist regime to its original owners, to a maximum of 150 ha. of arable to a single owner. Main agricultural production figures, 2002 (1,000 tonnes): wheat, 3,867; sugar beets, 3,833; barley, 1,793; potatoes, 901; rapeseed, 710; apples, 339; maize, 304; rye, 119. Livestock, 2003: cattle, 1·47m.; pigs, 3·36m.; sheep, 103,000; poultry, 27m. In 2002 production of meat was 787,000 tonnes; cheese, 146,000 tonnes; milk, 2,728m. litres; 1,829m. eggs.

Forestry

In 2002 forests covered 2,643,000 ha. (34% of the total land area). Timber production in 2007 was 18·51m. cu. metres.

Fisheries

Ponds created for fish-farming number 21,800 and cover about 41,000 ha., the largest of them being two lakes in southern

Bohemia. Fish landings in 2005 amounted to 4,242 tonnes, entirely from inland waters.

INDUSTRY

The leading company in the Czech Republic in March 2009 was ČEZ (České Energetické Závody a.s.), with a market capitalization of US$19·1bn.

In 2008 there were 1,747,020 small private businesses (of which 17,448 were incorporated), 311,309 companies and partnerships (of which 22,700 were joint-stock companies), 15,338 co-operatives and 526 state enterprises. Output (2008 unless otherwise indicated) includes: crude steel, 6·4m. tonnes; cement (2007), 4·9m. tonnes; pig iron, 4·7m. tonnes; 940,300 cars; soft drinks, 2,935·4m. litres; beer, 1,904·4m. litres.

Labour

In 2002 the economically active population numbered 5,139,000. The major areas of activity were 1·32m. persons employed in mining and manufacturing; 619,800 in trade; 425,200 in construction; 367,600 in transport, storage and communications; and 325,700 in public administration and defence. In Dec. 2009 the unemployment rate was 8·0% (up from 4·4% in 2008 as a whole). The average monthly wage was Kč. 18,133 in 2002. Pay increases are regulated in firms where wages grow faster than production. Fines are levied if wages rise by more than 15% over four years. There were 36,000 industrial disputes in 2003 (20,000 in 2002).

INTERNATIONAL TRADE

Imports and Exports

Trading with EU and EFTA countries has increased significantly while trading with all post-communist states has fallen.

Trade, 2005, in US$1m. (2004 in brackets): imports f.o.b., 76,342 (66,962); exports f.o.b., 78,135 (66,161). Main import suppliers, 2005: Germany, 30·0%; Russia, 5·6%; Slovakia, 5·4%; China, 5·1%; Poland, 4·9%; Italy, 4·7%. Main export markets, 2005: Germany, 33·3%; Slovakia, 8·7%; Austria, 5·5%; Poland, 5·5%; France, 5·3%; United Kingdom, 4·6%. In 2005 other EU countries accounted for 70·8% of the Czech Republic's imports and 84·3% of exports.

In 2005 machinery and transport equipment accounted for 51·0% of the Czech Republic's imports and 40·2% of exports; chemicals, manufactured goods classified chiefly by material and miscellaneous manufactured articles 39·6% of imports and 42·4% of exports; food, live animals, beverages and tobacco 3·8% of imports and 5·1% of exports; mineral fuels, lubricants and related materials 3·1% of imports and 9·2% of exports; inedible crude materials, and animal and vegetable oil and fats 2·6% of imports and 3·0% of exports.

COMMUNICATIONS

Roads

In 2007 there were 657 km of motorways, 6,191 km of highways and main roads, 48,736 km of secondary roads and 72,927 km of other roads, forming a total network of 128,511 km. Passenger cars in use in 2007 numbered 4,280,100 (414 per 1,000 inhabitants), and there were also 555,200 lorries and vans and 20,400 buses and coaches. Motorcycles and mopeds numbered 860,100. There were 1,382 deaths as a result of road accidents in 2004.

Rail

In 2002 Czech State Railways had a route length of 9,600 km (1,435 mm gauge), of which 2,926 km were electrified. Passenger-km travelled in 2002 came to 6·60bn. and freight tonne-km to 15·81bn. There is a metro (44 km) and tram/light rail system (496 km) in Prague, and also tram/light rail networks in Brno, Liberec, Most, Olomouc, Ostrava and Plzeň.

Civil Aviation

There are international airports at Prague (Ruzyně), Ostrava (Mošnov) and Brno (Turany). The national carrier is Czech Airlines, 91·51% of which is owned by the state. In 2007 it flew 82·9m. km and carried 5,492,200 passengers (5,379,500 on international flights). In 2007 Prague handled 12,436,254 passengers; there were a total of 174,662 take-offs and landings.

Shipping

1·3m. tonnes of freight were carried by inland waterways in 2004.

Telecommunications

In 2008 there were 2,264,000 main (fixed) telephone lines. In the same year mobile phone subscribers numbered 13,780,000 (1,335·4 per 1,000 persons). Český Telecom was sold to the Spanish telecommunications firm Telefónica in April 2005. It has since become Telefónica O2 Czech Republic. There were 2·8m. PCs in 2005 and 6·0m. internet users in 2008.

Postal Services

In 2002 there were 3,407 post offices.

SOCIAL INSTITUTIONS

Justice

The post-Communist judicial system was established in July 1991. This provides for a unified system of civil, criminal, commercial and administrative courts. Commercial courts arbitrate in disputes arising from business activities. Administrative courts examine the legality of the decisions of state institutions when appealed by citizens. In addition, there are military courts which operate under the jurisdiction of the Ministry of Defence. There is a Supreme Court, and a hierarchy of courts under the Ministry of Justice at republic, region and district level. District courts are courts of first instance. Cases are usually decided by senates comprising a judge and two associate judges, though occasionally by a single judge. (Associate judges are citizens in good standing over the age of 25 who are elected for four-year terms). Regional courts are courts of first instance in more serious cases and also courts of appeal for district courts. Cases are usually decided by a senate of two judges and three associate judges, although occasionally by a single judge. There is also a Supreme Administrative Court. The Supreme Court interprets law as a guide to other courts and functions also as a court of appeal. Decisions are made by senates of three judges. Judges are appointed for life by the National Council.

There is no death penalty. In 2002, 372,341 crimes were reported, of which 40·7% were solved. The population in penal institutions in Oct. 2003 was 17,360.

Education

Elementary education up to age 15 is compulsory. 52% of children continue their education in vocational schools and 48% move on to secondary schools. In 2007 there were 462,820 children in primary schools with 24,713 teaching staff and 937,026 secondary school pupils with (2006) 91,622 teaching staff.

In 2003–04 there were nine universities, four technical universities, one university for economics, one for agriculture, one for agriculture and forestry, one for veterinary sciences, one for pharmaceutical sciences, one for chemical technology, four academies for performing arts, music and dramatic arts, fine arts and arts, architecture and industrial design, and a higher school of teacher training. There were 363,277 students in higher education in 2007 and (2006) 22,549 academic staff.

In 2006 public expenditure on education came to 4·8% of GNI and 10·5% of total government spending.

The adult literacy rate is at least 99%.

Health

In 2002 there were 201 hospitals with a provision of 65 beds per 10,000 inhabitants. There were 34,437 physicians, 6,595 dentists, 77,956 nurses, 5,583 pharmacists and 3,842 midwives in 2007. In 2007 the Czech Republic spent 6·8% of its GDP on health.

Welfare

Since 1 Jan. 1996 the retirement age has been gradually increasing by two months per year for men and by four months per year for women. The retirement age, as of Sept. 2006, was 61 years 6 months (men) and 55 to 59 (women), according to the number of children. The target age will be 63 by the end of 2015 for men and by the end of 2028 for childless women, and between 59 and 62 for women depending on the number of children.

The old-age pension is calculated as a flat-rate basic amount of Kč. 1,310 plus an earnings-related percentage calculated on personal assessment and the number of years of insurance. In 2002 the minimum monthly pension was Kč. 2,080. Early pensions are available up to three years before the standard date of retirement, with the claimant required to have at least 25 years of contributions.

To qualify for unemployment benefit the applicant must have been in employment for at least 12 months in the previous three years. The maximum unemployment benefit in 2006 was Kč. 11,050 per month.

RELIGION

In 2009 there were 25 registered churches and religious societies. In 2001 church membership was estimated to be: Roman Catholic, 2,740,800; Evangelical Church of the Czech Brethren, 117,200; Hussites, 99,100; Eastern Orthodox, 23,000; Silesian Evangelicals, 14,000. 6,040,000 persons were classified as atheist or non-religious, and there were 331,000 adherents of other religions.

Dominik Duka (b. 1943) was installed as Archbishop of Prague and Primate of Bohemia in April 2010. The national Czech church, created in 1918, took the name 'Hussite' in 1972. In 1991 it had a patriarch, five bishops and 300 pastors (40% women). In 1991 there were also around a dozen other Protestant churches, the largest being the Evangelical which unites Calvinists and Lutherans, and numbered about 200,000. In Nov. 2009 the Roman Catholic church had two cardinals.

CULTURE

World Heritage Sites

Sites under Czech jurisdiction which appear on UNESCO's World Heritage List are (with year entered on list): Historic Centre of Prague (1992); Historic Centre of Český Krumlov (1992); Historic Centre of Telč (1992); Pilgrimage Church of St John of Nipomuk at Zelená Hora in Ždár nad Sázavou (1994); Kutná Hora—the Historical Town Centre with the Church of Saint Barbara and the Cathedral of our Lady at Sedlec (1995); Lednice-Valtice Cultural Landscape (1996); Holašovice Historical Village Reservation (1998); Gardens and Castle at Kroměříž (1998); Litomyšl Castle (1999); Holy Trinity Column in Olomouc (2000); Tugendhat Villa in Brno (2001); and the Jewish Quarter and St Procopius' Basilica in Třebíč (2003).

Broadcasting

Broadcasting is the responsibility of the independent Board for Radio and Television. Czech Television (ČTV, colour by SECAM H) and Czech Radio are public corporations. ČTV operates two national terrestrial networks and a news channel; Czech Radio transmits national and regional services and the external Radio Prague. TV Nova and Prima are national commercial television channels, and there are a number of private radio stations. There were 4·66m. TV receivers in 2006.

Press

There were 93 daily newspapers in 2002 with a total readership of 2,620,000 (256 per 1,000 inhabitants). There were also 3,636 non-dailies with total readership of 4,200,000 (410 per 1,000 inhabitants).

Tourism

In 2005, 6,336,000 non-resident tourists stayed in holiday accommodation; receipts from tourism in 2005 were US$5,580m.

DIPLOMATIC REPRESENTATIVES

Of the Czech Republic in the United Kingdom (26 Kensington Palace Gdns, London, W8 4QY)
Ambassador: Michael Žantovský.

Of the United Kingdom in the Czech Republic (Thunovská 14, 118 00 Prague 1)
Ambassador: Sian MacLeod, OBE.

Of the Czech Republic in the USA (3900 Spring of Freedom St., NW, Washington, D.C., 20008)
Ambassador: Petr Kolář.

Of the USA in the Czech Republic (Tržiste 15, 118 01 Prague 1)
Ambassador: Vacant.
Chargé d'Affaires a.i.: Mary Thompson-Jones.

Of the Czech Republic to the United Nations
Ambassador: Martin Palouš.

Of the Czech Republic to the European Union
Permanent Representative: Milena Vicenová.

FURTHER READING

Czech Statistical Office. *Statistical Yearbook of the Czech Republic.*

Havel, V., *Disturbing the Peace.* 1990.—*Living in Truth: Twenty-Two Essays.* 1990.—*Summer Meditations.* 1992

Kalvoda, J., *The Genesis of Czechoslovakia.* 1986

Krejcí, Jaroslav and Machonin, Pavel, *Czechoslovakia 1918–1992: A Laboratory for Social Change.* 1996

Leff, C. S., *National Conflict in Czechoslovakia: The Making and Remaking of a State, 1918–1987.* 1988

Simmons, M., *The Reluctant President: a Political Life of Vaclav Havel.* 1992

National Statistical Office: Czech Statistical Office, Na Padesátém 81, 100 82 Prague 10.
Website: http://www.czso.cz

DENMARK

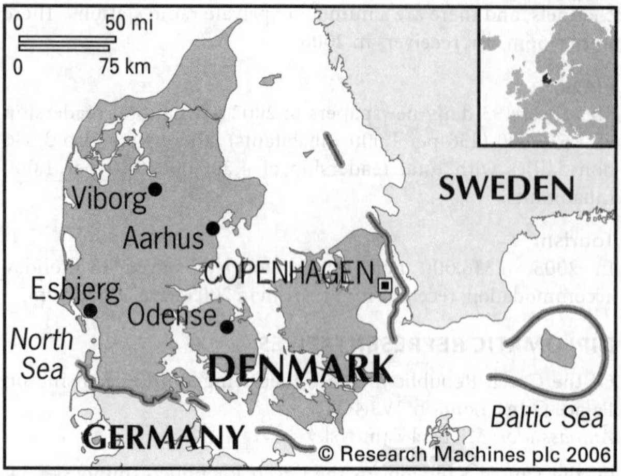

Kongeriget Danmark
(Kingdom of Denmark)

Capital: Copenhagen
Population estimate, 2010: 5·48m.
GDP per capita, 2007: (PPP$) 36,130
HDI/world rank: 0·955/16

KEY HISTORICAL EVENTS

Evidence of habitation exists from the Bølling period (12500–12000 BC). By 7700 BC reindeer hunters were settled on the Jutland Peninsula and around 3900 BC agriculture developed. Metal tools and weapons were imported in the Dagger Period (c. 2000 BC) but trading stations on the coast did not appear until around AD 300. The first towns developed in the Germanic Iron Age (AD 400–750). The first trading market was held in the 8th century in Hedeby. Denmark was converted to Christianity in 860 when Ansgar built churches in Hedeby and Ribe.

Danish Vikings first attacked England's northeast coast in 793. In about 900 Harold Bluetooth became the first king of Denmark and Skåne. His grandson, Canute the Great, fought successfully to incorporate England into his North Sea Empire and from 1018–35, Denmark, England and Norway were one nation. However, civil war broke out and in 1146 the kingdom was divided between Magnus the Strong and Knud Lavard. In 1157 Knud's son Valdemar was recognized as the ruler of Denmark. By 1200 Skåne, Halland and Blekinge in the South of Sweden were part of the Danish kingdom. The southern border of Denmark extended to the Eider in what is today northern Germany. In 1219 Valdemar conquered Estonia. He also established a code of law and a land register (Jordebog). The first written constitution was a coronation charter signed by Erik V in 1282.

In the 13th century, agriculture was supplemented by the expansion of fishing to supply inland Europe. Other industries also benefited and this brought with it a passion for building, particularly cathedrals and churches. Economic growth strengthened German influence. The Hanseatic League of German entrepreneurs was granted trade concessions for herring, salt and grain and also played a leading role in the country's political affairs. Valdemar IV Atterdag was crowned king in 1340. He challenged the privileges of the Hanseatic League, and was brought into conflict with Sweden over the southern provinces of Skåne, Halland and Blekinge. In 1361 Valdemar Atterdag took Gotland in one of the bloodiest of Nordic battles. When the king died in 1375, his daughter Margaret (married to King Håkon of Norway) claimed the throne on behalf of her five-year-old son Olav. After Håkon's death in 1388 she also became regent of Norway. While resisting the Hanseatic League, she succeeded in defeating her opponent Albrecht of Mecklenburg, king of Sweden, thus clearing the way to a Nordic union. In 1397, after Olav's death, Margaret's nephew Erik of Pomerania became king of Denmark, Norway and Sweden. In 1412 Erik was opposed by the Swedish nobles, who resented being taxed to finance Danish wars in northern Germany. When Erik abdicated, Christian I was elected king of Denmark and Norway in 1448.

By the 16th century Scandinavia was divided between Denmark–Norway (including Iceland and Greenland) and Sweden–Finland. In 1520 a power struggle in Sweden made the country vulnerable to a Danish invasion. Christian II was crowned king of Sweden but was soon challenged by Gustav Vasa, who replaced Christian II in 1521 as king of Sweden. In 1523 Christian was succeeded by Frederick I, who ended the union with Sweden. Following the Lutheran Reformation, the monarchy enhanced its power by confiscating the property of the Roman Catholic Church.

Imperial Rise and Fall

Christian IV (1577–1648) is regarded as one of Denmark's greatest rulers. Around this time overseas colonies were established, including Tranquebar (India), Danish Gold Coast (Ghana) and the Danish West Indies (the US Virgin Islands). However, in 1626 Denmark was defeated in the Thirty Years' War. Denmark lost Gotland and the Norwegian territories of Jämtland and Härjedalen to Sweden. In 1660 Sweden gained Skåne, Halland and Blekinge. A new constitution proclaimed the Danish king absolute sovereign. In 1661 the Supreme Court was established and in 1683 the law was codified.

In the Great Northern War, Denmark allied itself with Russia, the Netherlands and France, a policy which lasted for the rest of the 18th century. In the Napoleonic Wars, Denmark, smarting under the British bombardment of Copenhagen, allied itself to Napoleon. The price Denmark had to pay was signing away its rights to Norway, which it did by the treaty of Kiel in 1814. Danish possessions were now reduced to Iceland, Greenland, the Faroes and Schleswig-Holstein. Holstein was lost to Germany in 1863 and Schleswig a year later. The surrender of so much rich agricultural land, with nearly 1m. inhabitants, brought Denmark to the edge of bankruptcy. But within a few years the country managed to pull itself back from one of the lowest points in its history. The economy benefited from a land-reclamation programme in Jutland. Socially, Bishop Grundtvig (founder of the folk high-schools), who reconciled patriotism with a reduced status for Denmark in European affairs, had a great influence. There were demands for a liberal constitution. In 1846 Anton Frederik Tscherning founded the Society of the Friends of the Peasant (Bondevennernes Selskab), which later became the Liberal Party (Venstre).

Social Reform

In 1901 the Left Reform Party (Venstrereformparti) came to power to introduce free-trade, popular education and changes in the revenue system to make income rather than land the criterion for taxation. The First World War gave neutral Denmark an improved export market but there was a shortage of raw materials. In 1929 a Social Democrat government, with Thorvald Stauning as prime minister, combined rural and urban interests in one of the most ambitious programmes of social reforms ever mounted. The 1930s Great Depression led to unemployment made worse when Britain favoured Commonwealth food imports over those from Denmark. In the late 1930s trade improved and industry expanded.

In 1939 when the Second World War broke out, Denmark again declared neutrality. On 9 April 1940 German troops entered and occupied the country. The Germans permitted Danish self-government until growing resistance led to a state of emergency. After the liberation a Liberal government was elected with Knud Kristensen as prime minister. Kristensen's campaign for the return of southern Schleswig from Germany brought down his government in 1947. Denmark joined NATO in 1949.

With its share of the Marshall Plan, Denmark entered on a new industrial revolution. By the mid-1950s the value of manufacturing equalled that of agriculture. However, there was a high rate of inflation. In 1953 the Social Democrats came back to power where they remained until the mid-1960s. By then the rate of inflation was higher than in any comparable country. In 1968 a centre-right coalition was elected, led by Hilmar Baunsgaard. But the change of government did not signify a change in strategy. Taxes were kept high and the budget expanded to increase social welfare. After the 1971 election, the Social Democrat leader Jens Otto Krag negotiated entry into the European Union, making Copenhagen the bridge between the Nordic capitals and Brussels. In 1982 a Conservative-led minority government was formed, led by Poul Schlüter, the first Conservative prime minister since 1901. He remained in power until 1993 when a Social Democratic coalition led by Poul Nyrup Rasmussen took office. Following the 2001 election, a right-wing government came to power. The new prime minister, Anders Fogh Rasmussen, advocated joining EMU (European Monetary Union) but this was rejected in a referendum in 2000.

TERRITORY AND POPULATION

Denmark is bounded in the west by the North Sea, northwest and north by the Skagerrak and Kattegat straits (separating it from Norway and Sweden), and south by Germany. A 16-km long fixed link with Sweden was opened in July 2000 when the Øresund motorway and railway bridge between Copenhagen and Malmö was completed.

Regions	*Area (sq. km)*	*Population 1 Jan. 2008*	*Population per sq. km 2008*
Capital Region (Hovedstaden)	2,561	1,645,825	642·6
Central Jutland (Midtjylland)	13,053	1,237,041	94·3
North Jutland (Nordjylland)	8,020	578,839	73·0
Zealand (Sjælland)	7,273	819,427	112·7
South Denmark (Syddanmark)	12,191	1,194,659	97·9
Total	43,094	5,475,791	127·1

The UN gives an estimated population for 2010 of 5·48m.

In 2008 an estimated 86·3% of the population lived in urban areas. In 2008, 92·0% of the inhabitants were born in Denmark, including the Faroe Islands and Greenland.

On 1 Jan. 2008 the population of the capital, Copenhagen (comprising Copenhagen, Frederiksberg and Gentofte municipalities), was 672,218; Aarhus, 298,538; Aalborg, 193,145; Odense, 186,932; Esbjerg, 114,244; Vejle, 104,933; Randers, 93,644; Viborg, 92,084; Kolding, 87,781; Silkeborg, 87,371.

The official language is Danish.

SOCIAL STATISTICS

Statistics for calendar years:

	Live births	*Marriages*	*Divorces*	*Deaths*	*Emigration*	*Immigration*
2003	64,599	35,041	15,763	57,574	43,466	49,754
2004	64,609	37,711	15,774	55,806	45,017	49,860
2005	64,282	36,148	15,300	54,962	45,869	52,458
2006	64,984	36,452	14,343	55,477	46,786	56,750
2007	64,082	36,576	14,066	55,604	41,566	64,656

2007 rates per 1,000 population: birth, 11·7; death, 10·2. Births outside marriage: 2004, 45·4%; 2005, 45·7%; 2006, 46·4%; 2007, 46·1%. Annual population growth rate, 1995–2005, 0·3%. Suicide rate, 2005 (per 100,000 population) was 11·6 (men, 17·0; women, 6·3). Life expectancy at birth, 2007, was 76·0 years for males and 80·5 years for females. In 2007 the most popular age range for marrying was 30–34 for males and 25–29 for females. Denmark was the first country to legalize same-sex unions, in 1989. Infant mortality, 2007, 4·0 per 1,000 live births. Fertility rate, 2007, 1·8 births per woman. In 2007 Denmark received 2,246 asylum applications, equivalent to 0·4 per 1,000 inhabitants. In July 2002 a controversial new immigration law was introduced in an attempt to deter potential asylum seekers.

A UNICEF report published in 2005 showed that 2·4% of children in Denmark live in poverty (in households with income below 50% of the national median), the lowest percentage of any country.

CLIMATE

The climate is much modified by marine influences and the effect of the Gulf Stream, to give winters that may be both cold or mild and often cloudy. Summers may be warm and sunny or chilly and rainy. Generally the east is drier than the west. Long periods of calm weather are exceptional and windy conditions are common. Copenhagen, Jan. 33°F (0·5°C), July 63°F (17°C). Annual rainfall 650 mm. Esbjerg, Jan. 33°F (0·5°C), July 61°F (16°C). Annual rainfall 800 mm. In general 10% of precipitation is snow.

CONSTITUTION AND GOVERNMENT

The present constitution is founded upon the Basic Law of 5 June 1953. The legislative power lies with the Queen and the *Folketing* (parliament) jointly. The executive power is vested in the monarch, who exercises authority through the ministers.

The reigning Queen is **Margrethe II**, b. 16 April 1940; married 10 June 1967 to Prince Henrik, b. Count de Monpezat. She succeeded to the throne on the death of her father, King Frederik IX, on 14 Jan. 1972. *Offspring:* Crown Prince Frederik, b. 26 May 1968, married 14 May 2004 Mary Elizabeth Donaldson, b. 5 Feb. 1972 (*offspring:* Prince Christian Valdemar Henri John, b. 15 Oct 2005; Princess Isabella Henrietta Ingrid Margrethe, b. 21 April 2007); Prince Joachim, b. 7 June 1969, married 18 Nov. 1995 Alexandra Manley, b. 30 June 1964, divorced 8 April 2005 (*offspring:* Prince Nikolai William Alexander Frederik, b. 28 Aug. 1999; Prince Felix Henrik Valdemar Christian, b. 22 July 2002), married 24 May 2008 Marie Cavallier, b. 6 Feb. 1976.

Sisters of the Queen. Princess Benedikte, b. 29 April 1944; married 3 Feb. 1968 to Prince Richard of Sayn-Wittgenstein-Berleburg; Princess Anne-Marie, b. 30 Aug. 1946; married 18 Sept. 1964 to King Constantine of Greece.

The crown was elective from the earliest times but became hereditary by right in 1660. The direct male line of the house of Oldenburg became extinct with King Frederik VII on 15 Nov. 1863. In view of the death of the king, without direct heirs, the Great Powers signed a treaty at London on 8 May 1852, by the terms of which the succession to the crown was made over to Prince Christian of Schleswig-Holstein-Sonderburg-Glücksburg, and to the direct male descendants of his union with the Princess Louise of Hesse-Cassel. This became law on 31 July 1853. Linked to the constitution of 5 June 1953, a new law of succession, dated 27 March 1953, has come into force, which restricts the right of succession to the descendants of King Christian X and Queen Alexandrine, and admits the sovereign's daughters to the line of succession, ranking after the sovereign's sons.

The Queen receives a tax-free annual sum of 65·9m. kroner from the state (2008).

The judicial power is with the courts. The monarch must be a member of the Evangelical-Lutheran Church, the official Church of the State, and may not assume major international obligations without the consent of the Folketing. The Folketing consists of one chamber. All men and women of Danish nationality of more than 18 years of age and permanently resident in Denmark possess the franchise, and are eligible for election to the Folketing, which is at present composed of 179 members; 135 members are elected by the method of proportional representation in 17 constituencies. In order to attain an equal representation of the different parties, 40 additional seats are divided among such parties which have not obtained sufficient returns at the constituency elections. Two members are elected for the Faroe Islands and two for Greenland. The term of the legislature is four years, but a general election may be called at any time. The Folketing convenes every year on the first Tuesday in Oct. Besides its legislative functions, every six years it appoints judges who, together with the ordinary members of the Supreme Court, form the *Rigsret*, a tribunal which can alone try parliamentary impeachments.

National Anthem

'Kong Kristian stod ved højen mast' ('King Christian stood by the lofty mast'); words by J. Ewald, tune by D. L. Rogert.

GOVERNMENT CHRONOLOGY

Prime Ministers since 1945. (KF = Conservative Party; RV = Radical Liberal Party; SD = Social Democratic Party; V = Liberal Party)

1945	SD	Vilhelm Buhl
1945–47	V	Knud Kristensen
1947–50	SD	Hans Hedtoft
1950–53	V	Erik Eriksen
1953–55	SD	Hans Hedtoft
1955–60	SD	Hans Christian Hansen
1960–62	SD	Viggo Kampmann
1962–68	SD	Jens Otto Krag
1968–71	RV	Hilmar Baunsgaard
1971–72	SD	Jens Otto Krag
1972–73	SD	Anker Jørgensen
1973–75	V	Poul Hartling
1975–82	SD	Anker Jørgensen
1982–93	KF	Poul Holmskov Schlüter
1993–2001	SD	Poul Nyrup Rasmussen
2001–09	V	Anders Fogh Rasmussen
2009–	V	Lars Løkke Rasmussen

RECENT ELECTIONS

Parliamentary elections were held on 13 Nov. 2007; turnout was 86·6%. The Liberal Party (V) won 46 seats, with 26·3% of votes cast (52 seats with 29·1% in 2005); the Social Democratic Party (SD) 45 with 25·5% (47 with 25·9%); the Danish People's Party (DF) 25 with 13·8% (24 with 13·2%); the Socialist People's Party (SF) 23 with 13·0% (11 with 6·0%); the Conservative Party (KF) 18 with 10·4% (18 with 10·3%); the Radical Liberal Party (RV) 9 with 5·1% (17 with 9·2%); the New Alliance 5 with 2·8%; the Unity List—the Red Greens (E) 4 with 2·2% (6 with 3·4%). Four remaining seats go to representative parties from the Faroe Islands and Greenland.

European Parliament

Denmark has 13 (14 in 2004) representatives. At the June 2009 elections turnout was 59·5% (47·9% in 2004). The SD won 4 seats with 20·9% of votes cast (political affiliation in European Parliament: Progressive Alliance of Socialists and Democrats); V, 3 with 19·6% (Alliance of Liberals and Democrats for Europe); the SF, 2 with 15·4% (Greens/European Free Alliance); DF, 2 with 14·8% (Europe of Freedom and Democracy); KF, 1 with 12·3% (European People's Party); the People's Movement Against the EU, 1 with 7·0% (European United Left/Nordic Green Left).

CURRENT ADMINISTRATION

Following the appointment of Prime Minister Anders Fogh Rasmussen as NATO Secretary General in April 2009, Finance Minister Lars Løkke Rasmussen was appointed prime minister. The coalition government of the Liberal Party (V) and Conservatives (KF) came to power in 2001 and was re-elected in Feb. 2005 and Nov. 2007 but relies on the support of the far-right, anti-immigrant Danish People's Party, although it is not represented in the cabinet. In March 2010 the government comprised:

Prime Minister: Lars Løkke Rasmussen; b. 1964 (V; sworn in 5 April 2009).

Minister for Climate and Energy, and Gender Equality: Lykke Friis (V). *Culture:* Dr Per Stig Møller (KF). *Defence:* Gitte Lillelund Bech (V). *Development Co-operation:* Søren Pind (V). *Economic and Business Affairs:* Brian Mikkelsen (KF). *Education:* Tina Nedergaard (V). *Employment:* Inger Støjberg (V). *Environment and Nordic Co-operation:* Karen Ellemann (V). *Finance:* Claus Hjort Frederiksen (V). *Food, Agriculture and Fisheries:* Henrik Høegh (V). *Foreign Affairs:* Lene Espersen (KF). *Interior and Health:* Bertel Haarder (V). *Justice:* Lars Barfoed (KF). *Refugee, Immigration and Integration Affairs, and Ecclesiastical Affairs:* Birthe Rønn Hornbech (V). *Science, Technology and Innovation:* Charlotte Sahl-Madsen (KF). *Social Welfare:* Benedikte Kiær (KF). *Taxation:* Troels Lund Poulsen (V). *Transport:* Hans Christian Schmidt (V).

Office of the Prime Minister: http://www.statsministeriet.dk

CURRENT LEADERS

Lars Løkke Rasmussen

Position

Prime Minister

Introduction

On 5 April 2009 Lars Løkke Rasmussen was appointed prime minister and acting leader of the Liberal Party (V), succeeding Anders Fogh Rasmussen (no relation), who resigned to become NATO Secretary General. Løkke Rasmussen heads a coalition consisting of V, the KF and the DF. His prime ministerial tenure runs until a general election scheduled for 2011.

Early Life

Løkke Rasmussen was born on 15 May 1964 in Vejle, in Denmark's Syddanmark Region. He attended Graested School until 1980 and Helsinge Upper Secondary School until 1983, from where he matriculated in social studies and mathematics. After leaving Helsinge, Løkke Rasmussen studied law at Copenhagen University. During this period he became politically active, volunteering for V, working in the Graested-Gilleleje municipal council in Frederiksborg County (1986–97) and serving as national chairman of the Young Liberals (1986–89). He graduated from Copenhagen University in 1992.

In 1994 Løkke Rasmussen was elected first deputy mayor of Graested-Gilleleje, a post he held for three years, and also entered parliament. In 1998 he became mayor of Frederiksborg County and was named deputy chairman of the V party under Fogh Rasmussen, who served as prime minister from 2001–09. Between 2001–07 Løkke Rasmussen served as the minister for the interior and for health. He oversaw the passage of municipal reforms that came into practice in Jan. 2007, replacing 14 administrative counties and 271 municipalities with five regions and 98 municipalities. He also championed policies aimed at cutting hospital waiting lists.

In 2007 he was appointed finance minister, representing the government in negotiations to share tax revenues between richer and poorer municipalities. In response to the global financial slowdown in 2008, Løkke Rasmussen was responsible for providing funds to troubled banks and for creating a national economic stimulus package. In Feb. 2009 he cut the rate of income tax and increased taxes on pollution, fulfilling party campaign promises. These reforms received a mixed reception from both the public and opposition parties.

On 4 April Fogh Rasmussen resigned the premiership to take up the post of NATO secretary general, leaving Løkke Rasmussen to take over as prime minister and party leader the following day.

Career in Office

On 7 April 2009 Løkke Rasmussen reappointed the majority of Fogh Rasmussen's cabinet, the most notable change being the conversion of the social welfare ministry into two separate portfolios. Other changes included the appointment of two female V MPs to head the ministry of employment and gender equality and the newly created interior and social affairs ministry. With almost half the cabinet made up of women, Denmark has one of the world's highest levels of female representation in government.

In foreign policy, Løkke Rasmussen is expected to push for a resolution to the fighting in Afghanistan where Denmark had 700 troops stationed in April 2009. In Dec. 2009 he chaired a major international climate change conference hosted by Denmark in Copenhagen.

Løkke Rasmussen is expected to continue broadly the economic policies of his predecessor, with a referendum on adoption of the euro likely in late 2010 (having previously been rejected in a referendum in 2000).

DEFENCE

Pursuant to the Defence Agreement covering 2005–09 the Danish defence system is being completely restructured. A new security mechanism is being built from scratch to make it relevant in today's security environment. The entire transformation process centres on increasing Denmark's deployable capabilities. The composition of armed forces personnel has changed to 60:40 in favour of operational elements. Change has been accomplished by establishing so-called functional services in a number of areas formerly run by each individual service, and by reducing the staff- and support structure.

Denmark will be able simultaneously to deploy 2,000 soldiers on international missions and offer considerable High Readiness forces to NATO or coalition partners. The Armed Forces as a whole have been professionalized. Formal conscription still exists, but no specific combat training takes place. New conscripts train for four months in basic Homeland Defence, for example fire fighting, relief work during *force majeure* and basic weapons handling. The 20% of conscripts expected to sign up for additional time undergo military training focusing on participation in international operations for eight months and then deploy on an international assignment for six months.

The overall organization of the Danish Armed Forces includes the Ministry of Defence (MoD), the Danish Defence Command, the Army, the Navy, the Air Force, Functional Services and Schools and several joint service institutions and authorities; to this should be added the Home Guard, which is an integral part of Danish military defence. The Chief of Defence (CHOD), answering to the Minister of Defence, is in full command of the Army, the Navy and the Air Force.

Denmark has a compulsory military service with mobilization based on the constitution of 1849. This states that it is the duty of every fit man to contribute to the national defence. In 2007 defence expenditure totalled US$3,788m. (US$692 per capita), representing 1·3% of GDP.

Army

The Danish Army is comprised of field army formations and local defence forces. The strength of the Danish Army is approximately 10,600. The Danish Army is organized in two brigades, the first made up of professional soldiers and the second functioning as a training structure for conscripts.

Navy

The strength of the Royal Danish Navy is approximately 3,500. The two main naval bases are located at Frederikshavn and Korsør.

Air Force

The strength of the Royal Danish Air Force is approximately 3,500. The Royal Danish Air Force consists of Tactical Air Command Denmark and the Danish Air Materiel Command.

Home Guard (Hjemmeværnet)

The overall Home Guard organization comprises the Home Guard Command, the Army Home Guard, the Naval Home Guard, the Air Force Home Guard and supporting institutions. The personnel are recruited on a voluntary basis. The personnel establishment of the Home Guard is approximately 50,000 soldiers.

INTERNATIONAL RELATIONS

In a referendum in June 1992 the electorate voted against ratifying the Maastricht Treaty for closer political union within the EU. Turnout was 82%. 50·7% of votes were against ratification, 49·3% in favour. However, a second referendum on 18 May 1993 reversed this result, with 56·8% of votes cast in favour of ratification and 43·2% against. Turnout was 86·2%. In a referendum held on 28 Sept. 2000 Danish voters rejected their country's entry into the common European currency, 53·2% opposing membership of the euro against 46·8% voting in favour. Turnout was 87·6%.

Denmark is a member of the UN, World Bank, IMF and several other UN specialized agencies, WTO, EU, Council of Europe, OSCE, CERN, Nordic Council, Council of the Baltic Sea States, BIS, IOM, NATO, OECD, Inter-American Development Bank, Asian Development Bank and Antarctic Treaty. On 19 Dec. 1996 Denmark acceded to the Schengen accord of June 1990 which abolishes border controls between Denmark, Austria, Belgium, Czech Republic, Estonia, Finland, France, Germany, Greece, Hungary, Iceland, Italy, Latvia, Lithuania, Luxembourg, Malta, Netherlands, Norway, Poland, Portugal, Slovakia, Slovenia, Spain, Sweden and Switzerland.

Denmark gave US$2·6bn. in international aid in 2007, equivalent to 0·81% of GNI (making Denmark one of only five countries to exceed the UN target of 0·7%).

ECONOMY

In 2007 agriculture accounted for 1% of GDP, industry 26% and services 73%.

According to the Berlin-based organization *Transparency International*, Denmark ranked second in the world in a 2009 survey of countries with the least corruption in business and government. It received 9·3 out of 10 in the corruption perceptions index.

Overview

After weak growth during the Scandinavian banking crisis of 1991–93 the economy grew robustly from 1994–2007. In the period 2001–03 Denmark avoided recession in the face of a global economic slowdown but averaged annual growth of less than 1%. The growth of both foreign and domestic demand was instrumental in the economic revival from 2004. Income tax cuts passed in 2004 and a thriving real estate market boosted consumer demand in 2005. Investment growth and a strong export performance also helped economic expansion. Denmark has enjoyed a comfortable balance of payments surplus in recent years and is a net exporter of both food and energy. In early 2007 the housing boom ended and the economy began to slow, exacerbated by the global financial crisis. The economy shrank by 5% in 2009, although a gradual recovery is expected to begin during 2010.

Until the 1960s the economy was heavily based on its competitive agricultural sector. 57% of the labour force was employed in agriculture, fisheries, manufacturing and industry in 1960. By 2007 the percentage of the labour force employed in these sectors had declined to 26%. Almost three-quarters of the workforce are employed in services. The segment of the economy with the greatest proportional gain in employment in the last half-century is public services, accounting for 29% of total employment in 2007 compared to only 10% in 1960.

The research and development (R&D) expenditure-to-GDP ratio has increased substantially since the early 1990s. In the period 1993–2003 total R&D expenditure nearly doubled, with expenditure in the private sector accounting for over two-thirds of total R&D spending. Since 2002 R&D expenditure as a share of GDP has been around 2·5% annually, well above both the EU and OECD averages. R&D is particularly high in manufacturing, knowledge services and, increasingly, in financial services.

Denmark is ranked first in the world in terms of the Gini coefficient, a measure of income equality, and fifth in the World Economic Forum's *Global Competitiveness Report 2009–2010*. An absence of corruption has ensured that government revenues have helped to build world-class educational establishments and a social safety net that does not create a disincentive to work. In the latter half of the 1990s unemployment fell from double-digits and stood at 6·0% in 2009.

Currency

The monetary unit is the *Danish krone* (DKK) of 100 *øre*. Inflation rates (based on OECD statistics):

1999	*2000*	*2001*	*2002*	*2003*	*2004*	*2005*	*2006*	*2007*	*2008*
2·5%	2·9%	2·3%	2·4%	2·1%	1·2%	1·8%	1·9%	1·7%	3·4%

In Aug. 2009 foreign exchange reserves were US$67,774m., gold reserves were 2·14m. troy oz and total money supply was 832·2bn. kroner.

While not participating directly in EMU, the Danish krone is pegged to the euro in ERM-2, the successor to the exchange rate mechanism.

Budget

The following shows the actual revenue and expenditure in central government accounts for the calendar years 2006 and 2007, the approved budget figures for 2008 and the budget for 2009 (in 1,000 kroner):

	2006	*2007*	*2008*	*2009*
Revenue[1]	562,987,500	649,559,500	647,946,900	669,496,400
Expenditure[1]	459,623,500	535,301,500	556,050,500	597,606,700

[1]Receipts and expenditures of special government funds and expenditures on public works are included.

The 2009 budget envisaged revenue of 335,266·7m. kroner from income and property taxes and 279,872·0m. kroner from consumer taxes. The central government debt on 31 Dec. 2007 amounted to 255,074m. kroner.

In 2007 tax revenues were 48·9% of GDP (the highest percentage of any developed country).

VAT is 25%.

Performance

Real GDP growth rates (based on OECD statistics):

1999	*2000*	*2001*	*2002*	*2003*	*2004*	*2005*	*2006*	*2007*	*2008*
2·6%	3·5%	0·7%	0·5%	0·4%	2·3%	2·4%	3·3%	1·6%	–1·2%

The real GDP growth rate in 2009 according to Danmarks National Bank was –5·1%. Total GDP was US$342·7bn. in 2008.

Banking and Finance

In 2007 the accounts of the National Bank (*Governor*, Nils Bernstein) balanced at 424,540m. kroner. The assets included official net foreign reserves of 169,600m. kroner. The liabilities included notes and coins totalling 61,553m. kroner. On 31 Dec. 2006 there were 152 commercial banks and savings banks, with deposits of 1,287,502m. kroner.

The two largest commercial banks are Danske Bank and Nordea Bank Danmark. The supervisory boards of all banks must include public representation.

There is a stock exchange in Copenhagen.

ENERGY AND NATURAL RESOURCES

Environment

Denmark's carbon dioxide emissions from the consumption and flaring of fossil fuels in 2008 were the equivalent of 9·9 tonnes per capita.

Electricity

Installed capacity was 13·0m. kW in 2007. Production (2007), 39,157m. kWh. Consumption per capita in 2007 was 6,505 kWh. In 2007 some 5,212 wind turbines produced 19·7% of output.

Oil and Gas

Oil production was (2008) 14·0m. tonnes with 800m. bbls of proven reserves. Production of natural gas was (2008) 10·1bn. cu. metres with 60bn. cu. metres of proven reserves.

Wind

Denmark is one of the world's largest wind-power producers, with an installed capacity of 3,124 MW at the end of 2007. Denmark generates 19·7% of its electricity from wind, the highest proportion of any country.

Agriculture

Agriculture accounted for 8·9% of exports and 2·1% of imports in 2005. Land ownership is widely distributed. In June 2007 there were 44,618 holdings with at least 5 ha. of agricultural area (or at least a production equivalent to that from 5 ha. of barley). There were 10,460 small holdings (with less than 10 ha.), 18,887 medium-sized holdings (10–50 ha.) and 15,270 holdings with more than 50 ha. Approximately 5·0% of all agricultural land is used for organic farming. There were 24,675 agricultural workers in 2007. In 2007 Denmark had 2·30m. ha. of arable land and 8,000 ha. of permanent cultures.

In 2007 the cultivated area was (in 1,000 ha.): grain, 1,445; green fodder and grass, 668; set aside, 184; root crops, 84; other crops, 276; pulses, 6; total cultivated area, 2,663.

	Area (1,000 ha.)				*Production (in 1,000 tonnes)*			
Chief crops	*2004*	*2005*	*2006*	*2007*	*2004*	*2005*	*2006*	*2007*
Wheat	666	676	692	692	4,759	4,887	4,802	4,519
Barley	697	705	688	626	3,589	3,797	3,265	3,104
Potatoes	41	40	38	41	1,629	1,576	1,361	1,626
Oats	62	69	60	56	310	315	274	312
Rye	32	27	30	30	146	132	130	135
Other root crops	55	52	46	43	3,268	3,095	2,584	3,518

Livestock, 2007 (in 1,000): pigs, 13,723; cattle, 1,566; sheep, 157; horses, 53; poultry, 16,385.

Production (in 1,000 tonnes) in 2007: pork and bacon, 2,046; beef, 141; milk, 4,515; cheese, 346; eggs, 78; butter, 36.

In 2005 tractors numbered 106,500 and harvester-threshers 19,400.

Forestry

The area under forests in 2005 was 500,000 ha., or 11·8% of the total land area. Timber production in 2007 was 2·57m. cu. metres.

Fisheries

The total value of the fish caught was (in 1m. kroner): 1950, 156; 1960, 376; 1970, 854; 1980, 2,888; 1985, 3,542; 1990, 3,485; 1995, 3,020; 2000, 3,141; 2005, 2,781.

In 2005 the total catch was 839,441 tonnes, almost exclusively from sea fishing. Denmark is one of the leading fishing nations in the EU.

INDUSTRY

The leading companies by market capitalization in Denmark in March 2009 were: Novo Nordisk A/S, a health care company (US$25·2bn.); A. P. Møller-Mærsk, a shipping company (US$19·2bn.); and Vestas Windsystems, an alternative energy company (US$8·1bn.).

The following table is of gross value added by kind of activity (in 1m. kroner; 2000 constant prices):

	2005	2006	2007
Total	1,161,529	1,196,403	1,216,864
Agriculture, fishing and quarrying	62,712	57,099	51,219
Manufacturing	173,524	180,718	187,263
Electricity, gas and water supply	22,516	21,632	18,174
Construction	60,125	70,281	73,052
Wholesale and retail trade	160,475	166,392	169,638
Transport, post and telecommunication	98,965	104,117	109,910
Financial and business activities	284,136	293,989	303,262
Public and personal services	299,010	302,092	306,488

In the following table 'number of jobs' refers to 18,779 local activity units including single-proprietor units (Nov. 2006):

Branch of industry	*Number of jobs*
Food, beverages and tobacco	72,508
Textiles, wearing apparel, leather	8,963
Wood and wood products	15,537
Paper products	44,541
Refined petroleum products	1,008
Chemicals and man-made fibres	27,940
Rubber and plastic products	21,157
Non-metallic mineral products	16,585
Basic metals	52,902
Machinery and equipment	62,976
Electrical and optical equipment	47,873
Transport equipment	15,040
Furniture, other manufactures	26,510
Total manufacturing	413,540

Labour

In 2007 the labour force was 2,901,911. 36·8% of the working population in 2007 were in public and personal services; 19·3% in wholesale and retail trade, hotels and restaurants; 15·6% in financial intermediation, commerce, etc.; 14·6% in manufacturing; 7·1% in construction; 6·4% in transport, storage and telecommunications; 3·3% in agriculture, fisheries and quarrying; and 0·5% in electricity, gas and water supply. In 2007, 396,257 persons were employed in manufacturing. Retirement age is 65. In Dec. 2009 the unemployment rate was 7·4% (up from 3·4% in 2008 as a whole). In 2007 Denmark lost 32 working days to strikes per 1,000 employees.

INTERNATIONAL TRADE

Imports and Exports

In 2007 imports totalled 531,793m. kroner and exports 551,296m. kroner.

Imports and exports (in 1m. kroner) for calendar years:

	2006		2007	
Leading commodities	*Imports*	*Exports*	*Imports*	*Exports*
Live animals, meat and meat preparations	5,255	32,026	7,418	31,452
Dairy products and eggs	3,633	11,978	3,998	12,335
Fish, crustaceans, etc. and preparations	10,654	17,124	10,329	16,693
Cereals and cereal preparations	3,810	4,921	4,570	5,552
Fodder for animals	5,684	5,386	6,619	5,188
Wood and cork	5,799	811	6,055	1,055
Textile fibres, yarns, fabrics, etc.	8,429	7,716	8,540	7,594
Mineral fuels, lubricants, etc.	31,307	59,331	24,684	45,775
Chemicals and plastics, etc.	29,430	21,752	31,145	23,773
Medicine and pharmaceutical products	15,410	38,657	16,286	39,881
Metals, manufacture of metals	46,373	27,920	52,101	30,741
Machinery, electrical, equipment, etc.	128,094	122,634	131,586	129,331
Transport equipment	54,140	22,799	56,032	20,376
Furniture, etc.	8,164	15,953	9,161	15,895
Clothing and clothing accessories	22,786	19,341	24,124	19,959

Distribution of foreign trade (in 1m. kroner) according to countries of origin and destination for 2007:

Countries	*Imports*	*Exports*
Austria	5,947·2	4,394·6
Belgium	18,918·0	8,292·7
Canada	3,062·6	5,178·4
China	29,974·2	9,672·9
Finland	12,057·7	15,894·7
France and Monaco	21,736·6	24,875·0
Germany	115,838·8	91,900·8
Greece	1,079·7	4,072·8
Greenland	2,217·7	2,776·4
Hong Kong	2,159·3	4,325·1
Ireland	6,138·3	8,581·3
Italy	21,975·8	18,217·1
Japan	3,928·1	10,334·1
Netherlands	36,121·0	25,092·9
Norway	22,445·0	33,026·1
Poland	13,384·8	12,697·7
Russia	7,928·2	10,532·2
South Korea	3,064·9	3,798·3
Spain	9,834·2	15,774·4
Sweden	76,494·0	80,892·4
Switzerland	4,623·5	4,753·3
Turkey	5,590·1	3,189·4
United Kingdom	27,236·4	43,905·5
United States of America	18,500·4	34,935·3

In 2006 other European Union member countries accounted for 72·6% of imports and 69·1% of exports.

COMMUNICATIONS

Roads

Denmark proper had (1 Jan. 2008) 1,111 km of motorways, 2,755 km of other state roads, and 69,331 km of other commercial roads. Motor vehicles registered at 1 Jan. 2008 comprised 2,068,493 passenger cars, 35,442 trucks, 485,786 vans, 25,578 taxi cabs (including 19,978 for private hire), 14,482 buses and 133,914 motorcycles. There were 7,062 casualties in road accidents in 2008, resulting in 406 fatalities.

Rail

In 2007 there were 2,132 km of State railways of 1,435 mm gauge (619 km electrified), which carried 164m. passengers and 6·85m. tonnes of freight. There were also 514 km of private railways. A metro system was opened in Copenhagen in 2002.

Civil Aviation

The main international airport is at Copenhagen (Kastrup), and there are also international flights from Aalborg, Aarhus, Billund and Esbjerg. The Scandinavian Airlines System (SAS) resulted from the 1950 merger of the three former Scandinavian airlines. SAS Denmark A/S is the Danish partner (SAS Norge ASA and SAS Sverige AB being the other two). Denmark and Norway each hold 14·3% of the capital of SAS and Sweden 21·4%. The remaining 50% of SAS shares are listed on the stock exchanges of Copenhagen, Oslo and Stockholm.

On 1 Jan. 2008 Denmark had 1,077 aircraft with a capacity of 19,949 seats. In 2007 there were 272,000 take-offs and landings to and from abroad, and 215,000 to and from Danish airports. Copenhagen (Kastrup) handled 10,748,000 departing passengers in 2007, Billund 1,134,000, Aalborg 499,000 and Aarhus 288,000.

Shipping

On 1 Jan. 2008 the merchant fleet consisted of 610 vessels (above 20 GRT) totalling 9·2m. GRT. In 2007, 47m. tonnes of cargo were unloaded and 35m. tonnes were loaded in Danish ports; traffic by passenger ships and ferries is not included.

Telecommunications

In 2008 there were 2,491,000 main (fixed) telephone lines. In the same year mobile phone subscribers numbered 6,862,000 (1,257·2 per 1,000 persons). In 2008, 85% of the population had access to the internet at home and 88% had access to a computer at home. Denmark has the second highest broadband penetration rate (after Bermuda), at 36·7 subscribers per 100 inhabitants in June 2008.

According to the World Economic Forum's *Global Information Technology Report 2008–2009* Denmark is the world's leading country in exploiting global information technology developments.

Postal Services

In 2007 there were 768 post offices.

SOCIAL INSTITUTIONS

Justice

The lowest courts of justice are organized in 24 tribunals *(byretter)*, where minor cases are dealt with by a single judge. The tribunal at Copenhagen has one president and 42 other judges; and Aarhus one president and 13 other judges; the other tribunals have one to 11 judges. Cases of greater consequence are dealt with by the two High Courts *(Landsretterne)*; these courts are also courts of appeal for minor cases. The Eastern High Court in Copenhagen has one president and 60 other judges; and the Western in Viborg one president and 39 other judges. From these an appeal lies to the Supreme Court in Copenhagen, composed of a president and 19 other judges. Judges under 65 years of age can be removed only by judicial sentence.

In 2007 there were 11,386 convictions for males and 1,961 for females for violations of the criminal code, fines not included. In 2007 the daily average population in penal institutions was 3,646 (66·9 per 100,000 of national population).

Education

Education has been compulsory since 1814. The first stage of the Danish education system is the basic school (education at first level). This starts with a pre-school year (education preceding the first level), which has been compulsory since the beginning of the 2009–10 school year, and continues up to and including the optional 10th year in the *folkeskole* (municipal primary and lower secondary school). In 2006, 649,000 pupils attended education at first level and second level, first stage. The number of pupils beginning their education at pre-school was 67,600.

Of all students leaving basic school in 2006, 77% had commenced further education within three months. Almost two-thirds of the students had elected to attend general upper-secondary education (general programmes of education at secondary level, second stage), while one-third opted for a vocational education at secondary level, second stage.

Education that qualifies students for tertiary level education is called general upper-secondary education and comprises general upper-secondary education (general programmes of education at secondary level, second stage), such as *gymnasium* (upper-secondary school), higher preparatory examination and adult upper-secondary level courses as well as general/vocational upper-secondary education at the vocational education institutions. In 2006, 138,000 students attended general upper-secondary education and 126,000 students attended upper-secondary vocational education.

Higher education is divided into three levels: short-cycle higher education involves two years of training, sometimes practical, after completion of upper-secondary education (29,000 students in 2006); medium-cycle higher education involves two–four years of mainly theoretical training (80,000 students in 2006); long-cycle higher education requires more than four years of education, mainly theoretical, divided between a bachelor's degree, candidate programme and PhD programme (bachelor's students in 2006: 60,000; master's: 58,000; PhD: 5,200).

Universities have been reorganized as a result of several mergers in Jan. 2007. The universities ranked by student population are: the University of Copenhagen (founded 1479), 36,600 students; the University of Aarhus (1928), 30,100; the University of Southern Denmark (1964), 14,300; the Copenhagen Business School, 13,900; the University of Aalborg (1974), 11,300; Roskilde University (1972), 8,100; the Technical University of Denmark, 6,200; the IT University of Copenhagen, 1,300.

Other types of post-secondary education have also been reorganized through mergers of institutions. Eight university colleges have been formed with student numbers ranging from 3,000 to 13,000. The university colleges encompass: schools of nursing; schools of midwifery education; colleges of physiotherapy; social education colleges; teacher training colleges; engineering colleges. There are also post-secondary educational institutions in the cultural sector in areas such as music, architecture, media and the visual arts.

In 2005 public expenditure on education was 15·5% of total government spending.

The adult literacy rate in 2003 was at least 99%.

Health

In 2005 there were 17,350 doctors (321 per 100,000 persons), 4,634 dentists, 52,843 nurses, 27,072 auxiliary nurses and 1,304 midwives. There were 59 hospitals in 2005 (20,058 beds). In 2007 Denmark spent 9·8% of its GDP on health. In 2006 an estimated 26% of men and 23% of women smoked.

Welfare

The main body of Danish social welfare legislation is consolidated in seven acts concerning: (1) public health security, (2) sick-day benefits, (3) social pensions (for early retirement and old age), (4) employment injuries insurance, (5) employment services, unemployment insurance and activation measures, (6) social assistance including assistance to handicapped, rehabilitation, child and juvenile guidance, daycare institutions, care of the aged and sick, and (7) family allowances.

Public health security, covering the entire population, provides free medical care, substantial subsidies for certain essential medicines together with some dental care, and a funeral allowance. Hospitals are primarily municipal and treatment is normally free. All employed workers are granted daily sickness allowances; others can have limited daily sickness allowances. Daily cash benefits are granted in the case of temporary incapacity because of illness, injury or childbirth to all persons in paid employment. The benefit is paid up to the rate of 100% of the average weekly earnings. There is, however, a maximum rate of 3,415 kroner a week.

Social pensions cover the entire population. Entitlement to the old-age pension at the full rate is subject to the condition that the beneficiary has been ordinarily resident in Denmark for 40 years. For a shorter period of residence, the benefits are reduced proportionally. The basic amount of the old-age pension in Jan. 2007 was 174,720 kroner a year to married couples and 119,244 to single persons. Various supplementary allowances, depending on age and income, may be payable with the basic amount. The retirement age is 65, or 67 for those born before 1 July 1939. Depending on health and income, persons aged 60–64 (60–66 for those born before 1 July 1939) may apply for an early retirement pension. Persons over 65 (or 67) years of age are entitled to the basic amount. The pensions to a married couple are calculated and paid to the husband and the wife separately. Early retirement pension to a disabled person is payable at ages 18–64 (or 66) years, at a rate of 177,636 kroner to a single person. Early retirement pensions may be subject to income regulation. The same applies to the old-age pension.

Employment injuries insurance provides for disability or survivors' pensions and compensations. The scheme covers practically all employees.

Employment services are provided by regional public employment agencies. Insurance against unemployment provides daily allowances and covers about 85% of the unemployed. The unemployment insurance system is based on state subsidized insurance funds linked to the trade unions. The unemployment insurance funds had a membership of 2,091,368 in Dec. 2007.

The *Social Assistance Act* comprises three acts (the act on active social policy, the act on social service and the act on integration of foreigners). From these acts individual benefits are applied, in contrast to the other fields of social legislation which apply to fixed benefits. Total social expenditure, including hospital and health services, statutory pensions, etc. amounted in the financial year 2006 to 464,768·0m. kroner.

RELIGION

There is complete religious liberty. The state church is the Evangelical-Lutheran to which 82·1% of the population belonged in Jan. 2008. There are ten dioceses, each with a Bishop. The Bishop together with the Chief Administrative Officer of the county make up the diocesan-governing body, responsible for all matters of ecclesiastical local finance and general administration. Bishops are appointed by the Crown after an election by the clergy and parish council members. Each diocese is divided into a number of deaneries (107 in the whole country), each with its own Dean and Deanery Committee, who have certain financial powers. 81% of church finance derives from a voluntary tax paid by members, at a rate between 0·4–1·5% of income depending upon location. A further 12% comes from state subsidiaries and 7% from other sources, such as church lands.

CULTURE

World Heritage Sites

Denmark has four sites on the UNESCO World Heritage List: the burial mounds, runic stones and church at Jelling (inscribed on the list in 1994); Roskilde Cathedral (1995); Kronborg Castle (2000); and Ilulissat Icefjord (2004), the sea mouth of Sermeq Kujalleq in Greenland.

Broadcasting

Public broadcaster DR (Danmarks Radio) operates two television networks and four radio stations nationally, as well as regional radio services. There are also private terrestrial, satellite cable TV services and around 250 local commercial and community radio stations. Number of licences (2004): TV, 2·24m., including 2·23m. colour sets. Denmark had 2·18m. cable TV subscribers in 2006. There were 2·41m. television equipped households in 2006 (95·9% of all households). Colour is by PAL.

Press

In 2007 there were 36 daily newspapers with a combined circulation of 1·73m. The newspaper with the largest average circulation in the period July–Dec. 2007 was Urban (a free paper; 246,000 on weekdays), followed by Metro (also a free paper; 244,000 on weekdays) and Jyllands-Posten (140,000 on weekdays and 189,000 on Sundays).

Tourism

In 2004, 3,663,000 foreign tourists visited Denmark. In 2007 foreign tourists spent some 37,159m. kroner. Foreigners spent 5,825,000 nights in hotels and 3,007,000 nights at camping sites in 2007.

Festivals

Roskilde, one of Europe's largest music festivals, is held annually in July. Other festivals include the Carnival in Aalborg, held every May, the Copenhagen Jazz Festival in July, the Aarhus Festival (performing arts) in Aug./Sept. and the Copenhagen International Film Festival in Sept./Oct.

DIPLOMATIC REPRESENTATIVES

Of Denmark in the United Kingdom (55 Sloane St., London, SW1X 9SR)
Ambassador: Birger Riis Jørgensen.

Of the United Kingdom in Denmark (Kastelsvej 36–40, DK-2100, Copenhagen Ø)
Ambassador: Nick Archer.

Of Denmark in the USA (3200 Whitehaven St., NW, Washington, D.C., 20008)
Ambassador: Arne Friis Petersen.

Of the USA in Denmark (Dag Hammarskjölds Allé 24, DK-2100, Copenhagen Ø)
Ambassador: Laurie S. Fulton.

Of Denmark to the United Nations
Ambassador: Carsten Staur.

Of Denmark to the European Union
Permanent Representative: Poul Skytte Christoffersen.

FURTHER READING

Statistical Information: Danmarks Statistik was founded in 1849 and reorganized in 1966 as an independent institution; it is administratively placed under the Minister of Economic Affairs. Its main publications are: *Statistisk Årbog* (Statistical Yearbook). From 1896: *Statistiske Efterretninger* (Statistical News). *Konjunkturstatistik* (Main indicators); *Statistisk Tiårsoversigt* (Statistical Ten-Year Review).

Dania polyglotta. Annual Bibliography of Books . . . in Foreign Languages. Annual
Kongelig Dansk Hof og Statskalender. Annual
Jespersen, Knud J. V., *History of Denmark.* 2004
Larsen, Henrik, *Analysing Small State Foreign Policy in the EU: The Case of Denmark.* 2005
Petersson, O., *The Government and Politics of the Nordic Countries.* 1994

National library: Det kongelige Bibliotek, POB 2149, DK-1016 Copenhagen K. *Director:* Erland Kolding Nielsen.
National Statistical Office: Statistics Denmark, Sejrøgade 11, DK-2100 Copenhagen Ø. *Director General:* Jan Plovsing.
Website: http://www.dst.dk

The Faroe Islands

Føroyar/Færøerne

KEY HISTORICAL EVENTS

A Norwegian province until the peace treaty of 14 Jan. 1814, the islands have been represented by two members in the Danish parliament since 1851. In 1852 they were granted an elected parliament which in 1948 secured a degree of home-rule. The islands are not part of the EU. Recently, negotiations for independence were given a push by the prospect of exploiting offshore oil and gas.

TERRITORY AND POPULATION

The archipelago is situated due north of Scotland, 300 km from the Shetland Islands, 675 km from Norway and 450 km from Iceland, with a total land area of 1,399 sq. km (540 sq. miles). There are 17 inhabited islands (the main ones being Streymoy, Eysturoy, Vágoy, Suðuroy, Sandoy and Borðoy) and numerous islets, all mountainous and of volcanic origin. Population in Jan. 2008 was 48,430; density, 34·6 per sq. km. In 2003 an estimated 61·4% of the population lived in rural areas. The capital is Tórshavn (12,340 residents in Jan. 2008) on Streymoy.

The official languages are Faroese and Danish.

SOCIAL STATISTICS

Birth rate per 1,000 inhabitants (2005), 14·8; death rate, 8·7. Life expectancy at birth (2001–05): 77·8 years.

CONSTITUTION AND GOVERNMENT

The parliament comprises 33 members elected by proportional representation by universal suffrage at age 18. Parliament elects a government of at least three members which administers home rule. Denmark is represented in parliament by the high commissioner. A referendum was to be held on 26 May 2001 on the government's plan to move towards full sovereignty, but it was called off after the Danish prime minister at the time Poul Nyrup Rasmussen stated that subsidies would cease after four years if the islanders voted for independence.

RECENT ELECTIONS

Parliamentary elections were held on 19 Jan. 2008: the Republican Party (TF) won 8 seats with 23·3% of the vote; the Union Party (SF) 7 seats (21·0%); the People's Party (FF) 7 (20·1%); the Social Democratic Party (JF) 6 (19·4%); the Centre Party (MF) 3 (8·4%); and the Self-Government Party (SSF) 2 (7·2%).

CURRENT ADMINISTRATION

High Commissioner: Dan M. Knudsen (b. 1962; took office on 1 Jan. 2008).

Prime Minister: Kaj Leo Johannesen; b. 1964 (SF; took office on 26 Sept. 2008).

Office of the Prime Minister: http://www.tinganes.fo

ECONOMY

Currency

Since 1940 the currency has been the Faroese *króna* (kr.) which remains freely interchangeable with the Danish krone.

Budget

In 2003 revenues totalled 5,737m. kr. and expenditures 5,329m. kr.

Banking and Finance

The largest bank is the state-owned Føroya Banki. There are four other banks.

ENERGY AND NATURAL RESOURCES

Environment

Carbon dioxide emissions from the consumption and flaring of fossil fuels in 2008 were the equivalent of 16·8 tonnes per capita.

Electricity

Installed capacity was 87,000 kW in 2004. Total production in 2004 was 290m. kWh, of which 31% was hydro-electric. There are five hydro-electric stations at Vestmanna on Streymoy and one at Eiði on Eysturoy. Consumption per capita was an estimated 6,215 kWh in 2004.

Agriculture

Only 2% of the surface is cultivated; it is chiefly used for sheep and cattle grazing. Potatoes are grown for home consumption. Livestock (2002): sheep, 68,000; cattle, 2,000.

Fisheries

Deep-sea fishing now forms the most important sector (90%) of the economy, primarily in the 200-mile exclusive zone, but also off Greenland, Iceland, Svalbard and Newfoundland and in the Barents Sea. Total catch (2005) 565,260 tonnes, primarily cod, coalfish, redfish, mackerel, blue whiting, capelin, prawns and herring.

INTERNATIONAL TRADE

Imports and Exports

Trade, 2006, in US$1m. (2005 in brackets): imports c.i.f., 783·2 (746·6); exports f.o.b., 631·0 (601·8). In 2006 machinery and transport equipment accounted for 28·3% of imports, mineral fuels 18·8% and manufactured goods 14·1%. Chilled and frozen fish constituted 61·1% of exports in 2006, salted and smoked fish 15·2% and feeding stuff for animals 11·4%. Denmark supplied 30·1% of imports in 2006, Norway 20·3% and Germany 7·6%; the United Kingdom took 27·2% of exports in 2006, Denmark 12·2% and Norway 10·3%.

COMMUNICATIONS

Roads

In 2005 there were 463 km of highways. At 1 Jan. 2006 there were 18,041 private cars and 4,017 lorries and vans.

Civil Aviation

The airport is on Vágoy, from which there are regular services to Aberdeen, Billund, Copenhagen and Reykjavík.

Shipping

The chief port is Tórshavn, with smaller ports at Klaksvik, Vestmanna, Skálafjørður, Tvøroyri, Vágur and Fuglafjørður. In 2002 merchant shipping totalled 200,000 GRT, including oil tankers 80,000 GRT.

Telecommunications

There were 66,400 telephone subscribers in 2005, including 42,500 mobile phone subscribers. In 2005 internet users numbered 33,000.

SOCIAL INSTITUTIONS

Education

In 2008–09 there were 5,113 primary and 1,899 secondary school pupils (total of 649 teachers).

Health

In 2003 there were 83 physicians, 38 dentists and 360 nurses. In 2003 there were three hospitals with 290 beds.

RELIGION

About 80% are Evangelical Lutherans and 20% are Plymouth Brethren, or belong to small communities of Roman Catholics, Pentecostalists, Adventists, Jehovah's Witnesses and Bahais.

CULTURE

Broadcasting

Radio and TV broadcasting (colour by PAL) are provided by Utvarp Føroya and Sjónvarp Føroya respectively. In 2004 there were 25,000 TV receivers.

Press

In 2004 there were 13 newspapers per week, with a combined circulation of 22,100.

FURTHER READING

Árbók fyri Føroyar. Annual.
Rutherford, G. K. (ed.) *The Physical Environment of the Færoe Islands.* 1982
Wylie, J., *The Faroe Islands: Interpretations of History.* 1987

National Statistical Office: Hagstova Føroya, Glyvursvegur 1, PO Box 2068, FO-165 Argir.
Website: http://www.hagstova.fo

Greenland

Grønland/Kalaallit Nunaat

KEY HISTORICAL EVENTS

A Danish possession since 1380, Greenland became an integral part of the Danish kingdom on 5 June 1953. Following a referendum in Jan. 1979, home rule was introduced from 1 May 1979. In June 2009 laws providing for an extension of Greenland's autonomy came into force, providing Greenland with increased control over its energy resources and the adoption of Greenlandic as the sole official language.

TERRITORY AND POPULATION

Area, 2,166,086 sq. km (840,000 sq. miles), made up of 1,755,437 sq. km of ice cap and 410,449 sq. km of ice-free land. The population at 1 Jan. 2007 was 56,648, of whom 50,366 were born in Greenland and 6,282 were born outside Greenland; density 0·03 per sq. km. In Jan. 2007 the population of West Greenland was 52,004; East Greenland, 3,598; North Greenland (Thule/Qaanaaq), 846; and 200 not belonging to any specific municipality. The capital is Nuuk (Godthåb), with a population in Jan. 2007 of 14,719. In Jan. 2007, 47,000 persons were urban (83%).

The predominant language is Kalaallisut (Greenlandic), which since June 2009 has been the sole official language. Most of the population also speak Danish, which was also had official status until June 2009.

SOCIAL STATISTICS

Live births (2005), 887; deaths (2005), 466. Number of abortions (2005): 899. Birth rate per 1,000 population (2005), 15·7; death rate per 1,000 population (2005), 8·2. There were 49 suicides in 2005. Population growth rate (2005), –0·1%.

CONSTITUTION AND GOVERNMENT

There is a 31-member Home Rule Parliament, which is elected for four-year terms and meets two to three times a year. The seven-member cabinet is elected by parliament. Ministers need not be members of parliament. In accordance with the Home Rule Act, the Greenland Home Rule government is constituted by an elected parliament, *Landstinget* (The Greenland Parliament), and an administration headed by a local government, *Landsstyret* (The Cabinet).

Greenland elects two representatives to the Danish parliament (Folketing). Denmark is represented by an appointed High Commissioner. Following a referendum in Nov. 2008 approved by 75·5% of voters and ratification by the parliaments of Greenland and Denmark, a series of autonomous reforms came into operation on 21 June 2009. These include extending Greenland's authority over its police force, courts and coastguard as well as revenues derived from its natural resources. Greenlandic is the sole official language. Denmark, meanwhile, has cut its annual subsidies to the island. The moves are considered a major staging post to independence.

RECENT ELECTIONS

At parliamentary elections held on 2 June 2009 the opposition Inuit Ataqatigiit (leftist) won 14 of 31 seats and 43·7% of votes cast, the ruling Siumut (Social Democratic) 9 and 26·5%, the Democrats 4 and 12·7%, Atássut (Liberal) 3 and 10·9%, and the Association of Candidates 1 with 3·8%. As a result Siumut lost power after 30 years as the ruling party. Turnout was 71·3%.

CURRENT ADMINISTRATION

A coalition government of Inuit Ataqatigiit, the Democrats and the Association of Candidates was formed in June 2009.

Prime Minister: Kuupik Kleist; b. 1958 (Inuit Ataqatigiit, in office since 12 June 2009).

High Commissioner: Søren Hald Møller (appointed 2005).

Greenland Home Rule Website: http://www.nanoq.gl

ECONOMY

Currency

The Danish krone is the legal currency.

Budget

The budget (*finanslovsforslag*) for the following year must be approved by the Home Rule Parliament (*Landstinget*) no later than 31 Oct.

The following table shows the actual revenue and expenditure as shown in Home Rule government accounts for the calendar years 2003–05 and the approved budget figures for 2006 and 2007. Figures are in 1m. kroner.

	2003	*2004*	*2005*	*2006*	*2007*
Revenue	5,315	5,395	5,648	5,834	5,808
Expenditure	5,184	5,294	5,341	5,473	5,670

Performance

Since 2004 the rate of economic growth has quickened, primarily as a result of high growth rates in private consumption expenditure and investment in new buildings. In 2005 GDP at market prices was 10,210m. kroner and gross national disposable income was 13,630m. kroner. In 2005 the real GDP growth rate was 2·0% (in 1981 prices).

Banking and Finance

There are two private banks, Grønlandsbanken and Sparbank Vest.

ENERGY AND NATURAL RESOURCES

Environment

Greenland's carbon dioxide emissions from the consumption and flaring of fossil fuels in 2008 were the equivalent of 11·2 tonnes per capita.

Electricity

In 2005 the production of electricity in the cities totalled 331m. kWh.

Oil and Gas

Imports of fuel and fuel oil (2005), 275·5m. litres, with a value of 741·6m. kroner.

Agriculture

Livestock, 2003: sheep, 19,259; reindeer, 3,100. There are about 57 sheep-breeding farms in southwest Greenland.

Fisheries

Fishing and product-processing are the principal industry. The total catch in 2004 was 262,172 tonnes. In 2006, 84% of Greenland's total exports were derived from fish products, particularly prawns and halibut. In 2006, 192 large whales and

2,787 smaller cetacean mammals such as porpoise were caught (subject to the International Whaling Commission's regulations); plus 130,927 seals.

INDUSTRY

Six shipyards repair and maintain ships and produce industrial tanks, containers and steel constructions for building.

Labour

At 1 Jan. 2007 the potential labour force was 38,652.

INTERNATIONAL TRADE

Imports and Exports

In 2006 imports totalled 3,454m. kroner and exports 2,418m. kroner.

Principal import commodities in 2006 were machinery and vehicles (22%); mineral fuels (22%); and food, beverages and tobacco products (19%). Main export commodities were fish and fish products (84%), notably shrimp and halibut.

Principal import sources, 2006: Denmark, 59·7%; Sweden, 22·5%; Germany, 3·8%; Norway, 1·8%. Main export markets, 2006: Denmark, 86·6%; Spain, 7·0%; UK, 1·9%; Iceland, 1·6%.

COMMUNICATIONS

Roads

There are no roads between towns. Registered vehicles (2003): passenger cars, 2,974; commercial vehicles and trucks, 1,389; total (including others), 4,842.

Civil Aviation

Number of passengers to/from Greenland (2003): 98,118. Domestic flights—number of passengers (2003): aeroplanes, 177,554; helicopters, 39,457. Air Greenland operates domestic services and international flights to Denmark and Baltimore in the USA. There are international airports at Kangerlussuaq (Søndre Strømfjord), Narsarsuaq and Kulusuk and 18 local airports/heliports with scheduled services. There are cargo services to Denmark, Iceland and Canada.

Shipping

There are no overseas passenger services. In 2006, 43,448 passengers were carried on coastal services. There are cargo services to Denmark, Iceland and St John's (Canada).

Telecommunications

In 2008 there were 22,800 main (fixed) telephone lines; mobile phone subscribers numbered 55,800 in 2008 (97·4 per 100 persons). In 2004 there were 38,000 internet users.

SOCIAL INSTITUTIONS

Justice

Cases in the High Court in Nuuk are led by one professional judge and two lay magistrates, while there are 18 district courts under lay assessors.

The population in penal institutions in Oct. 2005 was 112 (199 per 100,000 of national population).

Education

Education is compulsory from six to 15 years. A further three years of schooling are optional. Primary schools (2006–07) had 10,688 pupils and 1,216 teachers; secondary schools, 780 pupils.

Health

The medical service is free to all citizens. There is a central hospital in Nuuk and 15 smaller district hospitals. In 2006 there were 95 doctors.

Non-natural death occurred in approximately one-fifth of all deaths in 2005. Suicide is the most dominant non-natural cause of death.

Welfare

Pensions are granted to persons who are 63 or above. The right to maternity leave has been extended to two weeks before the expected birth and up to 20 weeks after birth against a total of 21 weeks in earlier regulations. The father's right to one week's paternity leave in connection with the birth was extended to three weeks from 1 Jan. 2000. Wage earners who are members of SIK (The National Workers' Union) receive financial assistance (unemployment benefit) according to fixed rates, in case of unemployment or illness.

RELIGION

About 80% of the population are Evangelical Lutherans. In 2006 there were 17 parishes with 92 churches and chapels, and 27 ministers.

CULTURE

Broadcasting

The public TV and radio station Kalaallit Nunaata Radioa (KNR) provides broadcasting services, and there are also local services. Several towns have local television stations. In 2006 locally produced broadcasts accounted for 6% of KNR's television output and 29% of its radio output.

Press

In 2006 there were two national newspapers with a combined circulation of 8,500.

Tourism

In 2006 visitors stayed 245,432 nights in hotels (including 104,012 Greenlandic visitors).

FURTHER READING

Statistics Greenland. *Greenland 2001–2002* in English. *Greenland in Figures 2009* in English

Gad, F., *A History of Greenland*. 2 vols. 1970–73

Greenland National Library, P.O. Box 1011, DK-3900 Nuuk
National Statistical Office: Statistics Greenland, PO Box 1025, DK-3900 Nuuk.
Website: http://www.stat.gl

DJIBOUTI

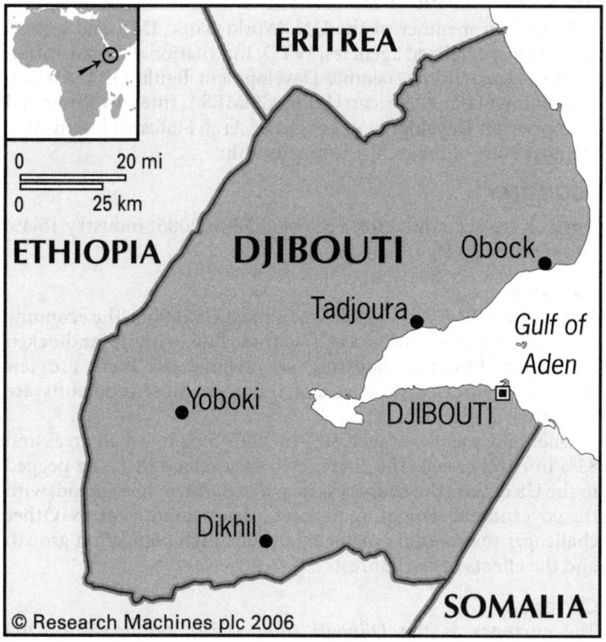

Jumhouriyya Djibouti
(Republic of Djibouti)

Capital: Djibouti
Population estimate, 2010: 879,000
GDP per capita, 2007: (PPP$) 2,061
HDI/world rank: 0·520/155

KEY HISTORICAL EVENTS

At a referendum held on 19 March 1967, 60% of the electorate voted for continued association with France rather than independence. France affirmed that the Territory of the Afars and the Issas was destined for independence but no date was fixed. Independence as the Republic of Djibouti was achieved on 27 June 1977. Afar rebels in the north, belonging to the Front for the Restoration of Unity and Democracy (FRUD), signed a 'Peace and National Reconciliation Agreement' with the government on 26 Dec. 1994, envisaging the formation of a national coalition government, the redrafting of the electoral roll and the integration of FRUD militants into the armed forces and civil service.

TERRITORY AND POPULATION

Djibouti is in effect a city-state surrounded by a semi-desert hinterland. It is bounded in the northwest by Eritrea, northeast by the Gulf of Aden, southeast by Somalia and southwest by Ethiopia. The area is 23,200 sq. km (8,958 sq. miles). The population was estimated in 2005 at 804,000 (86·1% urban), of whom about half were Somali (Issa, Gadaboursi and Issaq), 35% Afar, and some Europeans (mainly French) and Arabs.

The UN gives an estimated population for 2010 of 879,000; density, 38 per sq. km.

There are five administrative regions, plus the city of Djibouti (areas in sq. km): Ali-Sabieh (2,200); Arta (1,800); Dikhil (7,200); Djibouti (200); Obock (4,700); Tadjoura (7,100). The capital is Djibouti (2003 population, 502,000).

French and Arabic are official languages; Somali and Afar are also spoken.

SOCIAL STATISTICS

1999 estimates: births, 24,000; deaths, 10,000. Rates (1999 estimates, per 1,000 population); birth, 37; death, 15. Annual population growth rate, 1992–2002, 2·3%. Infant mortality, 2005, 88 per 1,000 live births. Expectation of life, 2007: 53·7 years for men, 56·5 for women. Fertility rate, 2004, 4·9 children per woman

CLIMATE

Conditions are hot throughout the year, with very little rain. Djibouti, Jan. 78°F (25·6°C), July 96°F (35·6°C). Annual rainfall 5" (130 mm).

CONSTITUTION AND GOVERNMENT

After a referendum at which turnout was 70%, a new constitution was approved on 4 Sept. 1992 by 96·63% of votes cast, which permits the existence of up to four political parties. Parties are required to maintain an ethnic balance in their membership. The *President* is directly elected for a renewable six-year term. Parliament is a 65-member *Chamber of Deputies* elected for five-year terms.

National Anthem

'Hinjinne u sara kaca' ('Arise with strength'); words by A. Elmi, tune by A. Robleh.

RECENT ELECTIONS

In the presidential election on 8 April 2005 Ismail Omar Guelleh was re-elected with 100% of the votes cast. There were no other candidates. Turnout was 78·9%.

At the parliamentary elections of 8 Feb. 2008 the Union for a Presidential Majority—a coalition of RPP (People's Rally for Progress), FRUD (Front for the Restoration of Unity and Democracy), PND (National Democratic Party) and PPSD (Social Democratic People's Party)—won all 65 seats with 94·1% of votes cast. The opposition boycotted the election. Turnout was 72·6%.

CURRENT ADMINISTRATION

President: Ismail Omar Guelleh; b. 1947 (RPP; sworn in 8 May 1999 and re-elected in April 2005).

In March 2010 the Council of Ministers comprised:

Prime Minister: Dilleita Mohamed Dilleita; b. 1958 (RPP; sworn in 7 March 2001).

Minister of Agriculture, Fisheries and Livestock: Abdoulkader Kamil Mohamed. *Commerce and Industry:* Rifki Abdoulkader Bamakhrama. *Communications, Culture, Post and Telecommunications, and Government Spokesperson:* Ali Abdi Farah. *Defence:* Ougoureh Kifleh Ahmed. *Economy, Finance and Privatization:* Ali Farah Assoweh. *Employment and National Solidarity:* Houmed Mohamed Dini. *Energy and Natural Resources:* Mohamed Ali Mohamed. *Equipment and Transport:* Ismael Ibrahim Houmed. *Foreign Affairs and International Co-operation:* Mahamoud Ali Youssouf. *Health:* Abdallah Abdillahi Miguil. *Housing, Town Planning, Environment and Parliamentary Relations:* Elmi Obsieh Waiss. *Interior and Decentralization:* Yacin Elmi Bouh. *Justice, Penal and Muslim Affairs, and Human Rights:* Mohamed Barkat Abdillahi. *National and Higher Education:* Abdi Ibrahim Absieh. *Presidential Affairs and Investment Promotion:* Osman Ahmed Moussa. *Youth, Sports, Leisure and Tourism:* Hassan Farah Miguil.

Government Website (French only): http://www.presidence.dj

CURRENT LEADERS

Ismail Omar Guelleh

Position
President

Introduction
Ismail Omar Guelleh was elected unopposed for a second six-year term as president in April 2005. He succeeded his uncle in 1999, becoming the country's second president since independence in 1977. He has proved an able diplomat, brokering peace between Djibouti's two main ethnic groups.

Early Life
Ismail Omar Guelleh was born on 27 Nov. 1947 in Dire Dawa, Ethiopia. He is the grandson of Guelleh Batal, one of the chiefs of the Issa clan who signed the 1917 agreement placing the Issa territories under French administration. From 1974 Guelleh became increasingly involved in the fight for independence as a member of the African Popular League for Independence (LPAI). Following Djibouti's declaration of independence on 27 June 1977, Guelleh was appointed principal private secretary to the president, his uncle, Hassan Gouled Aptidon.

Guelleh became head of the security services and joined the People's Rally for Progress (RPP) when it was established in March 1979. He became head of the party's cultural commission in 1981, the year in which Gouled made the Issa-dominated RPP the country's only legal political party, causing resentment among the Afar community. Civil war followed in 1991. When Gouled announced that he would not contest the April 1999 presidential elections, Guelleh stood as the RPP candidate. He was sworn in as president on 8 May 1999.

Career in Office
In Feb. 2000 Guelleh signed a peace agreement with the radical faction of the Afar party, the Front for the Restoration of Unity and Democracy (FRUD), ending nine years of civil war. During the multi-party elections of Jan. 2003 the coalition supporting him—the Union for a Presidential Majority—won all 65 seats, prompting opposition accusations of vote-rigging. In the run-up to the April 2005 presidential election, Guelleh pledged to reduce poverty and the country's dependence on food imports while boosting women's rights and institutional accountability. The election was boycotted by the opposition and he was sworn in for a second six-year term with 100% of votes cast. In Feb. 2008 the Union for a Presidential Majority again won all 65 seats in parliamentary elections boycotted by the main opposition parties.

In Sept. 2002, in support of the US-led war on terror, Guelleh allowed 900 US troops to be based in Djibouti. Although his government has denied interference in neighbouring Somalia's affairs, US air strikes in Jan. 2007 on the retreating Islamist militias which in the second half of 2006 had taken control of the Somali capital, Mogadishu, and much of the south of the country, were launched from the US base in Djibouti. In June 2008 border clashes between troops from Djibouti and Eritrea led Guelleh to announce a declaration of war with the neighbouring state.

DEFENCE

France maintains a naval base and forces numbering 2,850 under an agreement renewed in Feb. 1991. Defence expenditure totalled US$17m. in 2006 (US$36 per capita), representing 2·3% of GDP.

Army

There are three Army commands: North, Central and South. The strength of the Army in 2007 was approximately 8,000. There is also a paramilitary Gendarmerie of 1,400, and an Interior Ministry National Security Force of some 2,500.

Navy

A coastal patrol is maintained. Personnel (2007 estimate), 200.

Air Force

There is a small Air Force with no combat capable aircraft. Personnel (2007), 250.

INTERNATIONAL RELATIONS

Djibouti is a member of the UN, World Bank, IMF and several other UN specialized agencies, WTO, International Organization of the Francophonie, Islamic Development Bank, OIC, African Development Bank, African Union, COMESA, Intergovernmental Authority on Development, League of Arab States and is an ACP member state of the ACP-EU relationship.

ECONOMY

Agriculture accounted for 3·5% of GDP in 2006, industry 16·4% and services 80·1%.

Overview

Djibouti's GDP (PPP) in 2008 was almost US$1·9bn. The economy relies on Djibouti's status as a free trade hub, with its landlocked neighbour, Ethiopia, boosting sea commerce. There are few natural resources and a lack of industry. Most foodstuffs are imported.

Unemployment averaged 60% in 2007 (59% in urban areas and 83% in rural areas). The currency is overvalued by being pegged to the US dollar. The country is heavily reliant on foreign aid, with the government struggling to meet foreign donors' terms. Other challenges to economic wellbeing include high population growth and the effects of civil unrest.

Currency

The currency is the *Djibouti franc* (DJF), notionally of 100 *centimes*. Foreign exchange reserves were US$90m. in July 2005 and total money supply was 49,822m. Djibouti francs. Inflation was 5·0% in 2007, rising to 12·0% in 2008.

Budget

Revenues in 2004 were 42·1bn. Djibouti francs and expenditures 44·6bn. Djibouti francs.

Performance

Real GDP growth was 5·1% in 2007 and 5·8% in 2008. Total GDP in 2008 was US$0·9bn.

Banking and Finance

The Banque Nationale de Djibouti is the bank of issue (*Governor*, Djama Mahamoud Haid). There are three commercial banks and a development bank.

ENERGY AND NATURAL RESOURCES

Environment

Djibouti's carbon dioxide emissions from the consumption and flaring of fossil fuels in 2008 were the equivalent of 2·6 tonnes per capita.

Electricity

Installed capacity in 2004 was an estimated 88,000 kW. Production in 2004 was 200m. kWh; consumption per capita was 260 kWh in 2004.

Agriculture

There were around 1,000 ha. of arable land in 2002. Production is dependent on irrigation which in 2002 covered 1,000 ha. Vegetable production (2003) 24,000 tonnes. The most common crops are tomatoes, mangoes, papayas and melons. Livestock (2003 estimates): goats, 512,000; sheep, 466,000; cattle, 297,000; camels, 69,000. Livestock products, 2003 estimates: meat, 11,000 tonnes; milk, 8,000 tonnes.

Forestry

In 2005 the area under forests was 6,000 ha., or 0·2% of the total land area.

Fisheries
In 2005 the catch was approximately 260 tonnes, entirely from sea fishing.

INDUSTRY

Labour
In 1991 the estimated labour force totalled 282,000, with 75% employed in agriculture, 14% in services and 11% in industry. Unemployment in 2007 was estimated at 60%.

INTERNATIONAL TRADE
Foreign debt totalled US$472m. in 2007.

Imports and Exports
The main economic activity is the operation of the port; in 1990 only 36% of imports were destined for Djibouti. Exports are largely re-exports. In 2006 imports totalled US$335·7m. and exports US$55·2m. The chief imports are cotton goods, sugar, cement, flour, fuel oil and vehicles; the chief exports are hides, cattle and coffee (transit from Ethiopia).

Main import suppliers, 1998 (% of total trade): France, 12·5%; Ethiopia, 12·0%; Italy, 9·2%. Main export markets, 1998: Somalia, 53·0%; Yemen, 22·5%; Ethiopia, 5·0%.

COMMUNICATIONS

Roads
In 2002 there were estimated to be 2,890 km of roads, of which 12·6% were hard-surfaced. An estimated 15,700 passenger cars were in use in 2002 (23·5 per 1,000 inhabitants), plus 3,200 vans and trucks.

Rail
For the line from Djibouti to Addis Ababa, of which 97 km lie within Djibouti, *see* ETHIOPIA: Communications. Traffic carried is mainly in transit to and from Ethiopia.

Civil Aviation
There is an international airport at Djibouti (Ambouli), 5 km south of Djibouti. Djibouti-based carriers are Daallo Airlines and Djibouti Airlines. They operated flights in 2003 to Addis Ababa, Asmara, Borama, Bossaso, Burao, Dire Dawa, Dubai, Galcaio, Hargeisa, Jeddah, London, Mogadishu, Paris and Ta'iz.

Shipping
Djibouti is a free port and container terminal. 1,138 ships berthed in 1999 (including 117 warships), totalling 5·93m. NRT. 7,238 passengers embarked or disembarked, and 3·88m. tonnes of cargo were handled. In 2002 the merchant marine totalled 3,000 GRT.

Telecommunications
Djibouti had 45,600 telephone subscribers in 2004 (67·0 for every 1,000 inhabitants), of which 34,500 were mobile phone subscribers. There were 21,000 PCs in use in 2004 and 9,000 internet users.

Postal Services
There were ten post offices in 2003.

SOCIAL INSTITUTIONS

Justice
There is a Court of First Instance and a Court of Appeal in the capital. The judicial system is based on Islamic law. The death penalty was abolished for all crimes in 1994.

The population in penal institutions in 2005 was 1,479 (184 per 100,000 of national population).

Education
Adult literacy in 2001 was 65·5% (76·1% of men; 55·5% of women). In 2007 there were 56,667 pupils and 1,597 teaching staff in primary schools, and 34,667 pupils and 1,021 teachers in secondary schools. In 2007 there were 2,192 students at tertiary education institutions and 121 academic staff.

In 2007 public expenditure on education came to 7·8% of GNI.

Health
In 2007 there were a total of 1,220 hospital beds. There were 85 physicians, nine dentists, 196 nurses, 90 midwives and eight pharmacists in 2007.

RELIGION
In 2001, 96% of the population were Muslim; there were small Roman Catholic, Protestant and Orthodox minorities.

CULTURE

Broadcasting
The state-run Radiodiffusion-Télévision de Djibouti broadcasts through Radio Djibouti in French, Somali, Afar and Arabic, and operates the national television service. There is no private broadcasting. US-sponsored Arabic-language programming is transmitted from Djibouti to the Gulf states and East Africa. In 2005 there were 53,000 television receivers (colour by SECAM V).

Press
There are no daily newspapers; in 2006 the government-owned La Nation was published three times a week.

Tourism
There were 26,000 foreign tourists in 2004; tourist spending totalled US$7m.

DIPLOMATIC REPRESENTATIVES
Of Djibouti in the United Kingdom
Ambassador: Rachad Farah (resides in Paris).

Of the United Kingdom in Djibouti
Ambassador: Norman Ling (resides in Addis Ababa, Ethiopia).

Of Djibouti in the USA and to the United Nations (1156 15th St., NW, Suite 515, Washington, D.C., 20005)
Ambassador: Roble Olhaye.

Of the USA in Djibouti (Plateau du Serpent, Blvd Marechal Joffre, Djibouti)
Ambassador: James Swan.

Of Djibouti to the European Union
Ambassador: Mohamed Moussa Chehem.

FURTHER READING
Direction Nationale de la Statistique. *Annuaire Statistique de Djibouti*
Alwan, Daoud A., *Historical Dictionary of Djibouti.* 2000

National Statistical Office: Direction Nationale de la Statistique, Ministère de l'Économie, des Finances et de la Planification chargé de la Privatisation, BP 13, Djibouti.

DOMINICA

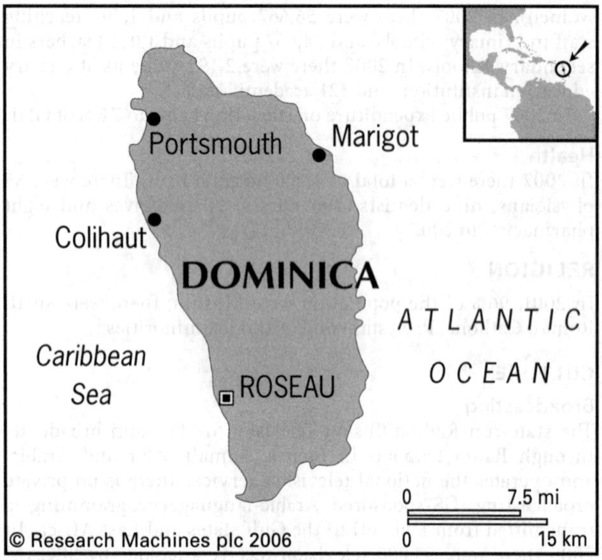

Commonwealth of Dominica

Capital: Roseau
Population, 2001: 71,000
GDP per capita, 2007: (PPP$) 7,893
HDI/world rank: 0·814/73

KEY HISTORICAL EVENTS

When Christopher Columbus sighted Dominica on 3 Nov. 1493 it was occupied by Carib Indians, who are thought to have overrun the previous inhabitants, the Arawak, from around 1300. Dominica remained a 'Carib Isle' until the 1630s, when French farmers and missionaries established sugar plantations. Control was contested between the British and French until it was awarded to the British by the Treaty of Versailles in 1783. In March 1967 Dominica became a self-governing state within the West Indies Associated States, with Britain retaining control of external relations and defence. The island became an independent republic, the Commonwealth of Dominica, on 3 Nov. 1978.

TERRITORY AND POPULATION

Dominica is an island in the Windward group of the West Indies situated between Martinique and Guadeloupe. It has an area of 750 sq. km (290 sq. miles) and a population at the 2001 census of 71,474. The population density in 2001 was 95·0 per sq. km.

In 2005, 72·9% of the population were urban. The chief town, Roseau, had 14,847 inhabitants in 2001.

The population is mainly of African and mixed origins, with small white and Asian minorities. There is a Carib settlement of about 500, almost entirely of mixed blood.

The official language is English, although 90% of the population also speak a French Creole.

SOCIAL STATISTICS

Births, 2000, 1,199 (rate of 16·8 per 1,000 population); deaths, 503 (rate of 7·0); marriages (1999), 339 (rate of 4·7); divorces (1999), 61 (rate of 0·9). Life expectancy, 2003: male, 71·0 years; female, 76·0 years. Annual population growth rate, 1992–2002, 0·0%. Infant mortality rate, 2005, 13 per 1,000 live births. Fertility rate, 2004, 2·0 births per woman.

CLIMATE

A tropical climate, with pleasant conditions between Dec. and March, but there is a rainy season from June to Oct., when hurricanes may occur. Rainfall is heavy, with coastal areas having 70" (1,750 mm) but the mountains may have up to 225" (6,250 mm). Roseau, Jan. 76°F (24·2°C), July 81°F (27·2°C). Annual rainfall 78" (1,956 mm).

CONSTITUTION AND GOVERNMENT

The head of state is the *President*, nominated by the Prime Minister and the Leader of the Opposition, and elected for a five-year term (renewable once) by the House of Assembly. The *House of Assembly* has 30 members, of whom 21 members are elected and nine nominated by the President.

National Anthem

'Isle of beauty, isle of splendour'; words by W. Pond, tune by L. M. Christian.

RECENT ELECTIONS

Elections were held on 18 Dec. 2009. The ruling Dominica Labour Party (DLP) won 18 of 21 elected seats (12 in 2005), the United Workers Party (UWP) won 3 seats (8 in 2005). The Dominica Freedom Party (DFP) did not win any seats.

CURRENT ADMINISTRATION

President: Dr Nicholas Liverpool; b. 1934 (took office on 2 Oct. 2003 and sworn in for a second term on 2 Oct. 2008).

Prime Minister, Minister of Finance, Foreign Affairs and Information Technology: Roosevelt Skerrit; b. 1972 (DLP; sworn in 8 Jan. 2004 and again on 21 Dec. 2009).

In March 2010 the cabinet comprised:

Minister of Agriculture and Forestry: Matthew Walter. *Carib Affairs:* Ashton Graneau. *Culture, Youth and Sports:* Justina Charles. *Education and Human Resource Development:* Petter Saint-Jean. *Employment, Trade, Industry and Diaspora Affairs:* Colin McIntyre. *Environment, Natural Resources, Physical Planning and Fisheries:* Kenneth Darroux. *Health:* Julius Timothy. *Information, Telecommunications and Constituency Empowerment:* Ambrose George. *Lands, Housing, Settlements and Water Resource Management:* Reginald Austrie. *National Security, Labour and Immigration:* Charles Savarin. *Public Works, Energy and Ports:* Rayburn Blackmore. *Social Services, Community Development and Gender Affairs:* Gloria Shillingford. *Tourism and Legal Affairs:* Ian Douglas. *Attorney General:* Francine Baron-Royer.

Government Website: http://www.dominica.gov.dm

CURRENT LEADERS

Dr Nicholas Liverpool

Position
President

Introduction
Dr Nicholas Liverpool became Dominica's eighth president in Oct. 2003, calling for national unity and emphasizing the importance of focusing on the needs of the nation's youth. In Oct. 2008 he began a second term in office.

Early Life
Nicholas Joseph Orville Liverpool was born in Grand Bay, Dominica in 1934. After studying law, he was called to the Bar in London in 1961 and completed a doctorate at Sheffield University

in 1965. He then spent 18 years as a law lecturer at the University of the West Indies in Barbados and in 1992 became dean of its law school. He served as a regional judge and then an appeal court judge in several Caribbean countries including Belize and Grenada. He also served as a high court judge in Antigua and Montserrat and on a number of tribunals and commissions for legal reform. In 2002 he was chairman of the constitutional review commission for Grenada.

In 1998 Liverpool became Dominica's ambassador to the USA, serving under the United Workers Party administration and the succeeding Dominica Labour Party–Dominica Freedom Party (DLP–DFP) coalition. In Oct. 2003 all three main political parties backed his appointment as president.

Career in Office

Liverpool took office on 2 Oct. 2003. After becoming president he was awarded the Dominican award of honour for his contribution to law and jurisprudence in the Caribbean.

When Prime Minister Pierre Charles died suddenly in Jan. 2004 it fell to Liverpool to appoint his successor. He selected Roosevelt Skerrit on the recommendation of the ruling DLP–DFP coalition.

In 2005 Liverpool suggested changes to the constitution and the structure and role of parliament, proposing the merger of the presidential and prime ministerial roles into a single directly elected executive presidency. Following the joint nomination of the prime minister and leader of the opposition, he took office for a second presidential term in Oct. 2008.

Roosevelt Skerrit

Position

Prime Minister

Introduction

Roosevelt Skerrit became Dominica's youngest ever prime minister in Jan. 2004 when he took office following the death of his predecessor, Pierre Charles. Appointed by parliamentary recommendation to lead the coalition government, he was returned as prime minister in the May 2005 general election when the Dominica Labour Party (DLP) won an outright majority, and again in Dec. 2009.

Early Life

Roosevelt Skerrit was born in 1972 and grew up in Vieille Case in northeast Dominica. From 1994–97 he studied psychology and English at the University of Mississippi and New Mexico State University. On his return to Dominica he worked as a teacher, first in a high school then at the Dominica Community College. In 1999 he entered politics and in 2000 was elected as a DLP representative to the House of Assembly.

In the coalition government of the DLP and the Dominica Freedom Party (DFP), Skerrit served as minister for sports and youth affairs and later also for education. When Pierre Charles died of a heart attack in Jan. 2004, President Liverpool appointed Skerrit as his replacement.

Career in Office

Skerrit inherited a small working majority and sought to maintain unity in the coalition government. Against a background of economic troubles, the government introduced unpopular austerity measures, with a combination of spending cuts and higher taxes prompting strikes. During his first year in office he pursued a CARICOM initiative to raise US$50m. of aid and has subsequently been involved in developing a regional stabilization fund under the auspices of the Caribbean Development Bank.

In March 2004 Skerrit reversed Dominica's traditional policy of pursuing diplomatic ties with Taiwan in preference to relations with China, obtaining a six-year aid package from China worth US$117m. In an attempt to reduce Dominica's dependence on agriculture, the government has invested in tourism and major infrastructure projects.

In the election of 5 May 2005 Skerrit led the DLP to victory with 12 of 21 elected seats. In Sept. 2005 Dominica was one of several CARICOM countries to enter into an oil-purchasing deal with Venezuela and in Oct. 2005 he secured around US$2m. of direct US aid for public and private sector investment. The International Monetary Fund commended his government in Dec. 2006 for its successful economic programme, including significant progress in debt restructuring. In Feb. 2009 Skerrit announced that his government had secured US$49m. in grants from Venezuela within the framework of the ALBA (Alianza Bolivariana para los Pueblos de Nuestra América) trade group of leftist Latin American states. In the Dec. 2009 election Skerrit again led the DLP to victory, this time with 18 of the 21 elected seats.

INTERNATIONAL RELATIONS

Dominica is a member of the UN, World Bank, IMF and several other UN specialized agencies, WTO, Commonwealth, International Organization of the Francophonie, ACS, CARICOM, OECS, OAS and is an ACP member state of the ACP-EU relationship.

ECONOMY

Agriculture accounted for 18% of GDP in 2005, industry 24% and services 58%.

Currency

The *East Caribbean dollar* (XCD) and the US dollar are legal tender. Foreign exchange reserves were US$50m. in July 2005 and total money supply was EC$149m. Inflation was 6·3% in 2008.

Budget

The fiscal year begins on 1 July. Revenues for the fiscal year 2005–06 were EC$325·0m. and expenditures EC$315·3m.

Performance

Dominica has recovered from a recession, during which the economy shrank by 4·2% in 2001 and 5·1% in 2002, to record real GDP growth of 1·8% in 2007 and 3·2% in 2008. In 2008 total GDP was US$0·4bn.

Banking and Finance

The East Caribbean Central Bank based in St Kitts and Nevis functions as a central bank. The *Governor* is Sir Dwight Venner. In 2001 there were five commercial banks (four foreign, one domestic), a development bank and a credit union. Dominica is affiliated to the Eastern Caribbean Securities Exchange in Basseterre, St Kitts and Nevis.

ENERGY AND NATURAL RESOURCES

Environment

Carbon dioxide emissions from the consumption and flaring of fossil fuels in 2008 were the equivalent of 1·7 tonnes per capita.

Electricity

Installed capacity was 22,000 kW in 2004. Production in 2004 was 79m. kWh. Consumption per capita in 2004 was 1,129 kWh. There is a hydro-electric power station.

Agriculture

Agriculture employs 26% of the labour force. In 2007 there were around 5,000 ha. of arable land and 16,000 ha. of permanent crops. Estimated production, 2003, in 1,000 tonnes): bananas, 29; grapefruit and pomelos, 17; coconuts, 12; taro, 11; yams, 8; oranges, 7; plantains, 6. Livestock (2003 estimates): cattle, 13,000; goats, 10,000; sheep, 8,000; pigs, 5,000.

Forestry

In 2005 forests covered 46,000 ha., or 61·3% of the total land area.

Fisheries
In 2005 fish landings were 579 tonnes, exclusively from sea fishing.

INDUSTRY
Manufactures include soap (10,500 tonnes in 2001), coconut oil, copra, cement blocks, furniture and footwear.

Labour
Around 25% of the economically active population are engaged in agriculture, fishing and forestry. In 2006 the minimum wage was US$0·75 an hour. The unemployment rate in 2003 was 15·7%.

INTERNATIONAL TRADE
Total foreign debt was US$290m. in 2007.

Imports and Exports
In 2005 imports (c.i.f.) totalled US$165·3m. and exports (f.o.b.) US$41·8m. Main imports in 2004 (in US$1m.): machinery and transport equipment, 36·6; manufactured goods, 24·7; food, 24·0; chemicals, 16·2; petroleum and petroleum products, 14·6. Main exports (2004, in US$1m.): soap, 12·7; bananas, 8·8. Fruit, perfumes and sand are also exported. Main import suppliers, 2004: USA, 36·7%; Trinidad and Tobago, 18·1%; UK, 6·5%; France, 5·0%. Main export markets, 2004: Jamaica, 20·1%; UK, 17·9%; Antigua and Barbuda, 9·9%; France, 9·4%.

COMMUNICATIONS

Roads
In 2002 there were an estimated 788 km of roads, of which 50·4% were paved. Approximately 10,300 passenger cars and 3,500 commercial vehicles were in use in 2002.

Civil Aviation
There are international airports at Melville Hall and Cane Field. In 2003 there were direct flights to Anguilla, Antigua, Barbados, British Virgin Islands, Grenada, Guadeloupe, Martinique, Puerto Rico, St Kitts, St Lucia, St Maarten, St Vincent, Trinidad and the US Virgin Islands.

Shipping
There are deep-water harbours at Roseau and Woodbridge Bay. Roseau has a cruise ship berth. In 2002 merchant shipping totalled 4,000 GRT. In 2005 vessels totalling 1,302,000 NRT entered ports and vessels totalling 1,302,000 NRT cleared.

Telecommunications
In 2004 there were 62,800 telephone subscribers, equivalent to 880·8 per 1,000 inhabitants, with 41,800 mobile phone subscribers. There were 13,000 PCs in use (182·3 for every 1,000 persons) in 2004 and 20,500 internet users.

Postal Services
In 2001 there were 72 post offices, or one for every 1,090 persons.

SOCIAL INSTITUTIONS

Justice
There is a supreme court and 14 magistrates courts. Law is based on UK common law as exercised by the Eastern Caribbean Supreme Court on St Lucia. Final appeal lies to the UK Privy Council. Dominica was one of twelve countries to sign an agreement establishing a Caribbean Court of Justice to replace the British Privy Council as the highest civil and criminal court. The court was inaugurated at Port-of-Spain, Trinidad on 16 April 2005.

The police force has a residual responsibility for defence. The population in penal institutions in Dec. 2003 was 243 (equivalent to 337 per 100,000 of national population).

Education
In 1998 adult literacy was 94%. Education is free and compulsory between the ages of five and 16 years. In 2007 there were 499 teaching staff and 8,643 pupils in primary schools, and 469 teaching staff and 7,481 pupils in general secondary level education. The leading higher education institution is Ross University School of Medicine, established in 1978. In 2007 public expenditure on education came to 5·5% of GNI.

Health
In 1994 there were 53 hospitals and health centres with 25 beds per 10,000 inhabitants. There were 38 physicians, ten dentists and 361 nurses in 1998. Large numbers of professional nurses take up employment abroad, especially in the USA, causing a shortage of health care workers in Dominica.

RELIGION
70% of the population was Roman Catholic in 2001.

CULTURE

World Heritage Sites
Dominica has one site on the UNESCO World Heritage List: Morne Trois Pitons National Park (1997), a tropical forest centred on the Morne Trois Pitons volcano.

Broadcasting
Radio services are provided by the Dominica Broadcasting Corporation and by private stations. There is a commercial cable TV network (colour by NTSC). There were 15,700 TV sets in 2000.

Press
In 2006 there were three newspapers—*The Chronicle*, *The Sun* and *The Tropical Star*.

Tourism
In 2003 there were 72,948 stop-over and 177,044 cruise ship visitors. Tourism receipts in 2002 totalled US$36m.

DIPLOMATIC REPRESENTATIVES
Of Dominica in the United Kingdom (1 Collingham Gdns, South Kensington, London, SW5 0HW)
Acting High Commissioner: Agnes Adonis.

Of the United Kingdom in Dominica
High Commissioner: Paul Brummell (resides in Bridgetown, Barbados).

Of Dominica in the USA (3216 New Mexico Ave., NW, Washington, D.C., 20016)
Ambassador: Vacant.
Chargé d'Affaires a.i.: Judith Ann Rolle.

Of the USA in Dominica
Ambassador: Vacant (resides in Bridgetown, Barbados).
Chargé d'Affaires a.i.: D. Brendt Hardt.

Of Dominica to the United Nations
Ambassador: Crispin Gregoire.

Of Dominica to the European Union
Ambassador: Shirley Skerritt-Andrew.

FURTHER READING
Baker, P. L., *Centring the Periphery: Chaos, Order and the Ethnohistory of Dominica.* 1994
Honychurch, L., *The Dominica Story: a History of the Island.* 2nd ed. 1995

National Statistical Office: Central Statistical Office, Kennedy Avenue, Roseau.

DOMINICAN REPUBLIC

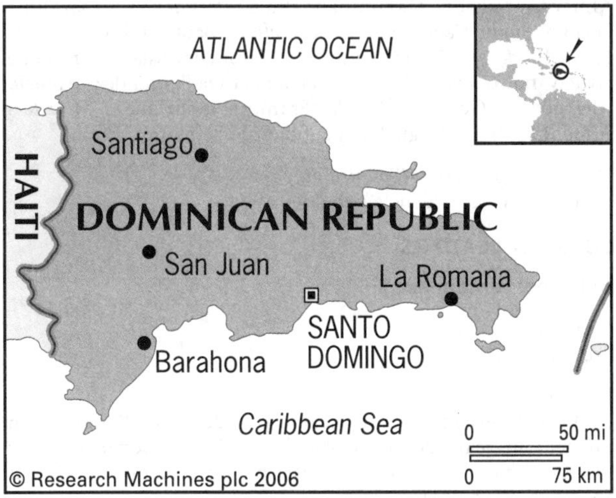

República Dominicana

Capital: Santo Domingo
Population estimate, 2010: 10·23m.
GDP per capita, 2007: (PPP$) 6,706
HDI/world rank: 0·777/90

KEY HISTORICAL EVENTS

In 1492 Columbus discovered the island of Hispaniola, which he called La Isla Española, and which for a time was also known as Santo Domingo. The city of Santo Domingo, founded by his brother, Bartholomew, in 1496, is the oldest city in the Americas. The western third of the island—now the Republic of Haiti—was later occupied and colonized by the French, to whom the Spanish colony of Santo Domingo was also ceded in 1795. In 1808 the Dominican population routed the French at the battle of Palo Hincado. Eventually, with the aid of a British naval squadron, the French were forced to return the colony to Spanish rule, from which it declared its independence in 1821. It was invaded and held by the Haitians from 1822 to 1844, when the Dominican Republic was founded and a constitution adopted.

Thereafter the rule was dictatorship interspersed with brief democratic interludes. Between 1916 and 1924 the country was under US military occupation. From 1930 until his assassination in 1961, Rafael Trujillo was one of Latin America's legendary dictators. The conservative pro-American Joaquin Balaguer was president from 1966 to 1978. In 1986 Balaguer returned to power at the head of the Socialist Christian Reform Party, leading the way to economic reforms. But there was violent opposition to spending cuts and general austerity. The 1996 elections brought in a reforming government pledged to act against corruption.

TERRITORY AND POPULATION

The Dominican Republic occupies the eastern portion (about two-thirds) of the island of Hispaniola, the western division forming the Republic of Haiti. The area is 48,137 sq. km (18,586 sq. miles). The area and 2002 census populations of the provinces and National District (Santo Domingo area) were:

	Area (in sq. km)	*Population*
La Altagracia	2,474	182,020
Azua	2,532	208,857
Bahoruco	1,282	91,480
Barahona	1,739	179,239
Dajabón	1,021	62,046
Distrito Nacional (Santo Domingo area)	1,401	2,731,294
Duarte	1,605	283,805
Elías Piña	1,426	63,879
Espaillat	839	225,091
Hato Mayor	1,329	87,631
Independencia	2,006	50,833
María Trinidad Sánchez	1,272	135,727
Monseñor Nouel	992	167,618
Monte Cristi	1,924	111,014
Monte Plata	2,632	180,376
Pedernales	2,075	21,207
Peravia	998	232,233
Puerto Plata	1,857	312,706
La Romana	654	219,812
Salcedo[1]	440	96,356
Samaná	854	91,875
Sánchez Ramírez	1,196	151,179
San Cristóbal	1,266	532,880
San José de Ocoa[2]	650	—
San Juan	3,569	241,105
San Pedro de Macorís	1,255	301,744
Santiago	2,839	908,250
Santiago Rodríguez	1,111	59,629
Santo Domingo[3]	1,296	—
El Seíbo	1,787	89,261
Valverde	823	158,293
La Vega	2,287	385,101

[1]Renamed Hermanas Mirabel in 2007.
[2]Created in 2002; formerly part of Peravia.
[3]Created in 2001; formerly part of Distrito Nacional.

Census population (2002), 8,562,541 (4,297,326 females). In 2005 the population was 66·8% urban.

The UN gives an estimated population for 2010 of 10·23m.

Population of the main towns (2002 census, in 1,000): Santo Domingo, the capital, 1,888; Santiago de los Caballeros, 507; San Pedro de Macorís, 194; La Romana, 191; Los Alcarrizos, 167.

The population is mainly composed of a mixed race of European (Spanish) and African blood. The official language is Spanish; about 0·18m. persons speak a Haitian-French Creole.

SOCIAL STATISTICS

2004 estimates: births, 210,000; deaths, 61,000. Rates, 2004 estimates (per 1,000 population): birth, 24; death, 7. Annual population growth rate, 2000–05, 1·1%. Life expectancy, 2007: male, 69·8 years; female, 75·2 years. Infant mortality, 2005, 26 per 1,000 live births. Fertility rate, 2004, 2·7 children per woman.

CLIMATE

A tropical maritime climate with most rain falling in the summer months. The rainy season extends from May to Nov. and amounts are greatest in the north and east. Hurricanes may occur from June to Nov. Santo Domingo, Jan. 75°F (23·9°C), July 81°F (27·2°C). Annual rainfall 56" (1,400 mm).

CONSTITUTION AND GOVERNMENT

The constitution dates from 28 Nov. 1966 and was amended on 25 July 2002. The *President* is elected for four years, by direct vote, and has executive power. A constitutional amendment of Aug. 1994 prohibits the president from serving consecutive terms. In 1994 the constitution was amended to allow for a second round of voting in a presidential election, when no candidate secures an absolute majority in the first ballot. There is a bicameral legislature, the *Congress*, comprising a 32-member Senate (one member for each province and one for the National District of Santo Domingo) and a 178-member *Chamber of Deputies*, both elected for four-year terms. Citizens are entitled to vote at the age of 18, or less when married.

National Anthem

'Quisqueyanos valientes, alcemos' ('Valiant Quisqueyans, Let us raise our voices'); words by E. Prud'homme, tune by J. Reyes.

GOVERNMENT CHRONOLOGY

Heads of State since 1942. (PD = Dominican Party; PLD = Dominican Liberation Party; PR = Reformist Party; PRD = Dominican Revolutionary Party; PRSC = Social Christian Reformist Party; REP = Republican Party; UCN = National Civic Union; n/p = non-partisan)

Presidents		
1942–52	PD/military	Rafael Leonidas Trujillo Molina
1952–60	PD	Héctor Bienvenido Trujillo Molina
1960–62	PD	Joaquín Antonio Balaguer Ricardo
1962–63	REP	Rafael Filiberto Bonelly Fondeur
1963	PRD	Juan Emilio Bosch Gaviño
Chairmen of the Triumvirate		
1963	n/p	Emilio de los Santos
1963–65	UCN	Donald Joseph Reid Cabral
Chairman of Military Junta of Government		
1965	military	Pedro Bartolomé Benoit Vanderhorst
President of the Government of National Reconstruction		
1965	military	Antonio Cosme Imbert Barrera
Presidents		
1965	military	Francisco Alberto Caamaño Deñó
1965–66	PR	Héctor Federico García-Godoy Cáceres
1966–78	PR	Joaquín Antonio Balaguer Ricardo
1978–82	PRD	Silvestre Antonio Guzmán Fernández
1982	PRD	Jacobo Majluta Azar
1982–86	PRD	Salvador Jorge Blanco
1986–96	PRSC	Joaquín Antonio Balaguer Ricardo
1996–2000	PLD	Leonel Antonio Fernández Reyna
2000–04	PRD	Rafael Hipólito Mejía Domínguez
2004–	PLD	Leonel Antonio Fernández Reyna

RECENT ELECTIONS

Presidential elections were held on 16 May 2008. Incumbent Leonel Antonio Fernández Reyna of the Dominican Liberation Party (PLD) won 53·8% of the votes, Miguel Vargas Maldonado of the Dominican Revolutionary Party (PRD) 40·5% and Amable Aristy Castro of the Social Christian Reformist Party (PRSC) 4·6%. Turnout was 70·7%.

Parliamentary elections were held on 16 May 2006. In the election to the Chamber of the Deputies the PLD and its allies won 96 seats with 52·4% of the vote, the PRD and its allies 60 (21·9%) and the PRSC and its allies 22 (23·3%). In the Senate elections of the same day, the PLD and its allies won 22 seats, the PRD and its allies 6 and the PRSC 4 and its allies. Turnout was 56·5%.

Parliamentary elections were scheduled to take place on 16 May 2010.

CURRENT ADMINISTRATION

President: Leonel Antonio Fernández; b. 1953 (PLD; sworn in 16 Aug. 2004 and re-elected 16 May 2008, having previously been president from 1996–2000).

Vice-President: Rafael Alburquerque.

In March 2010 the government comprised:

Secretary of State for Agriculture: Salvador Jiménez. *Armed Forces:* Gen. Pedro Rafael Peña Antonio. *Culture:* José Rafael Lantigua. *Economy, Planning and Development:* Juan Temístocles Montas. *Education:* Melanio Paredes. *Environment and Natural Resources:* Jaime David Fernández Mirabal. *Finance:* Vicente Bengoa. *Foreign Relations:* Carlos Morales Troncoso. *Higher Education, Science and Technology:* Ligia Amada Melo. *Industry and Commerce:* José Ramón Fadul. *Interior and Police:* Franklin Almeyda. *Labour:* Maximiliano Puig. *Presidency:* César Pina Toribio. *Public Health and Social Welfare:* Bautista Rojas Gómez. *Public Works and Communications:* Víctor Díaz Rua. *Sport:* Felipe Jay Payano. *Tourism:* Francisco Javier García Fernández. *Women:* Alejandrina Germán. *Youth:* Franklin Rodríguez. *Ministers without Portfolio:* Miguel Mejía; Eduardo Selman.

Office of the President (Spanish only):
http://www.presidencia.gob.do

CURRENT LEADERS

Dr Leonel Fernández

Position
President

Introduction
Dr Leonel Fernández first became president in 1996 and won further four-year terms in 2004 and 2008. He has won plaudits for easing the country's economic crisis, but poverty, unemployment and corruption persist.

Early Life
Leonel Antonio Fernández Reyna was born on 26 Dec. 1953 in Santo Domingo, the capital city. In 1962 his family moved to New York, where he attended school before returning to Santo Domingo in 1971. He enrolled at the Independent University of Santo Domingo (UASD) to study law. In 1973 Fernández joined the leftist Dominican Liberation Party (PLD), the movement founded by his professor and mentor, the former president, Juan Bosch. Following his graduation with a doctorate in 1978, Fernández worked as a political journalist. He subsequently lectured at the UASD and the Latin American Faculty of Social Science in Santo Domingo. Elected to the PLD's central committee in 1985, he rose through the party's administrative ranks and stood as Bosch's running mate at the 1994 presidential election (won by Joaquín Balaguer). Balaguer was barred from running in the May 1996 elections and Fernández defeated José Francisco Peña Gómez in a run-off a month later.

Career in Office
Sworn in as president on 16 Aug. 1996, Fernández brought in sweeping economic and judicial reforms. However, despite increased foreign investment, economic growth and infrastructural improvements, he was displaced as president by Hipólito Mejía of the Dominican Revolutionary Party (PRD) in Aug. 2000 amid discontent over power cuts in the previously privatized electricity industry. Mejía presided over a deepening economic crisis and spiralling crime and unemployment. Fernández was re-elected president on 16 May 2004 and introduced austerity measures and succeeded in stabilizing inflation and the currency. However, attempts to tackle poverty and corruption and to resolve the energy crisis were less successful. A free trade agreement with the USA and the countries of Central America was ratified by the government in 2005. In parliamentary elections in May 2006 the PLD and its allies secured a majority of congressional seats and in May 2008 Fernández was again re-elected to the presidency.

DEFENCE

In 2006 defence expenditure totalled US$256m. (US$28 per capita), representing 0·7% of GDP.

Army

There are five defence zones. The Army has a strength (2007) of 15,000 and includes a special forces unit and a Presidential Guard. There is a paramilitary National Police 15,000-strong.

Navy
The Navy is equipped with former US vessels. Personnel in 2007 totalled 4,000, based at Santo Domingo and Las Calderas.

Air Force
The Air Force, with HQ at San Isidoro, has 11 aircraft. Personnel strength (2007), 5,500.

INTERNATIONAL RELATIONS

The Dominican Republic is a member of the UN, World Bank, IMF and several other UN specialized agencies, WTO, IOM, ACS, Inter-American Development Bank, SELA, OAS and is an ACP member state of the ACP-EU relationship.

ECONOMY

In 2006 agriculture accounted for 11·9% of GDP, industry 25·9% and services 62·1%.

Overview
The Dominican Republic is noted for its plantation crop exports of sugar, cocoa, coffee and tobacco. Although these products remain important, their combined share of total exports has declined to one-tenth. The pillars of the economy are now tourism, worker remittances from the USA and the free trade zones where in-bond factories (known as *maquillas*) produce clothing for big name brands.

Economic growth was interrupted in 2003 when a banking crisis, triggered by corruption, sent the sovereign debt to the brink of default while the *peso* depreciated dramatically and inflation soared. Tight fiscal and monetary policy measures, as well as renewed strength in the US economy (on which exports are heavily dependent), helped lift the country out of crisis. Real growth has averaged near double digits since the crisis, peaking at 10·7% in 2006. Strong fiscal consolidation has helped reduce public debt ratios.

In March 2007 the Dominican Republic–Central America–United States Free Trade Agreement (DR–CAFTA) came into effect, providing free access to the US market. A spate of natural disasters in late 2007 and the onset of the global economic slowdown threatened near-term growth. However, domestic banks' limited exposure to foreign credit lines and their strong liquidity position stand them in good stead to weather further shocks.

Currency
The unit of currency is the *peso* (DOP), written as RD$, of 100 *centavos*. Gold reserves were 18,000 troy oz in July 2005, foreign exchange reserves US$1,537m. and total money supply was RD$78,490m. Inflation spiralled to 51·5% in 2004, second in the world only to Zimbabwe, but has since slowed with rates of 6·1% in 2007 and 10·6% in 2008.

Budget
Budgetary central government revenue totalled RD$192,577m. and expenditure RD$183,795m. in 2006. Tax revenues in 2006 were RD$176,581m. Main items of expenditure by economic type in 2006 were: compensation of employees (RD$44,270m.) and grants (RD$31,240m.).

Performance
Real GDP growth was 8·5% in 2007 and 5·3% in 2008. Total GDP in 2008 was US$45·8bn.

Banking and Finance
In 1947 the Central Bank was established (*Governor*, Héctor Valdez Albizu). Its total assets were RD$34,958·7m. in 1993. In 2002 there were 12 commercial banks, two foreign banks and nine development banks.

The Santo Domingo Securities Exchange is a member of the Association of Central American Stock Exchanges (Bolcen).

Weights and Measures
The metric system is in force but US units are in common use. Rural land is measured with the *tarea* (624 sq. metres).

ENERGY AND NATURAL RESOURCES

Environment
Carbon dioxide emissions from the consumption and flaring of fossil fuels in 2008 were the equivalent of 2·0 tonnes per capita.

Electricity
Installed capacity was 5·4m. kW in 2004. Production was 13·76bn. kWh in 2004; consumption per capita was 1,536 kWh. Power failures are frequent.

Minerals
Bauxite output in 1988 was 167,800 tonnes, but had declined to nil by 1992. Output: nickel (2002), 38,859 tonnes; gold (1999), 651 kg. Gold production had been declining over the previous few years and has since been suspended.

Agriculture
Agriculture and processing are the chief sources of income, sugar cultivation being the principal industry. In 2001 there were 1·1m. ha. of arable land and 500,000 ha. of permanent cropland. 275,000 ha. were irrigated in 2001.

Production, 2003 (in 1,000 tonnes): sugarcane, 5,036; rice, 609; bananas, 481; plantains, 192; mangoes, 186; coconuts, 178; tomatoes, 155; avocados, 150; cassava, 124; pineapples, 110; oranges, 88.

Livestock in 2003: 2·16m. cattle; 578,000 pigs; 342,000 horses; 188,000 goats; 46m. chickens. Livestock products, 2003 (in 1,000 tonnes): poultry meat, 186; beef and veal, 72; pork, bacon and ham, 65; eggs, 83; milk, 520.

Forestry
Forests and woodlands covered 1·38m. ha. in 2005, representing 28·4% of the total land area. In 2007, 903,000 cu. metres of timber were cut.

Fisheries
The total catch in 2005 was 11,106 tonnes, mainly from sea fishing.

INDUSTRY

Production, 2004 unless otherwise indicated (in 1,000 tonnes): cement (2001), 2,758; residual fuel oil, 843; sugar (2002), 516; petrol, 445; distillate fuel oil, 430; kerosene (2003), 190; rum (1995–96), 395·6m. litres; beer (2003), 337·0m. litres; cigarettes (1999), 4·0bn. units.

Labour
In 2005 the economically active population was 4,026,000. The unemployment rate in 2005 was 19·3%.

INTERNATIONAL TRADE

On 1 March 2007 the Central America-Dominican Republic-United States Free Trade Agreement (CAFTA-DR) entered into force between the Dominican Republic and El Salvador, Guatemala, Honduras, Nicaragua and the USA. Costa Rica implemented the agreement on 1 Jan. 2009. Foreign debt was US$7,398m. in 2005.

Imports and Exports
Trade, 2006, in US$1m.: imports (f.o.b.), 11,190·2; exports (f.o.b.), 6,440·0. Main imports, 1995: oil and products, 21·7%; agricultural products, 17·2%. Main exports: ferronickel, 31·6%; raw sugar, 13·3%; coffee, 10·6%; cocoa, 7·1%; gold, 5·4%. Main import suppliers, 1997: USA, 56%; Venezuela, 23%; Mexico, 9%. Main export markets: USA, 54%; Belgium, 12%; Puerto Rico, 7%.

COMMUNICATIONS

Roads

In 2002 the road network covered an estimated 19,705 km, of which 51·2% were paved. In 2007 there were 602,700 passenger cars (62 per 1,000 inhabitants), 525,400 lorries and vans, and 64,200 buses and coaches. Motorcycles and mopeds numbered 1·04m. In 1998 there were 1,494 road accidents resulting in 1,683 deaths.

Rail

The railway system has been closed down with the exception of 142 km line from Guayubin to the port of Pepillo, used primarily for the banana trade.

There is a metro in Santo Domingo.

Civil Aviation

There are international airports at Santo Domingo (Las Americas), Puerto Plata and Punta Cana. In 2000 Santo Domingo was the busiest airport, handling 4,652,000 passengers, followed by Puerto Plata (estimated at 2,023,000 passengers) and Punta Cana (1,745,000).

Shipping

The main ports are Santo Domingo, Puerto Plata, La Romana and Haina. In 2002 the merchant marine totalled 9,000 GRT. In 2004 vessels totalling 12,730,000 NRT entered and vessels totalling 2,144,000 NRT cleared.

Telecommunications

In 2005 there were 4,517,800 telephone subscribers (507·2 for every 1,000 inhabitants), of which 3,623,300 were mobile phone subscribers. There were 938,300 internet users in 2005.

Postal Services

In 2003 there were 278 post offices.

SOCIAL INSTITUTIONS

Justice

The judicial power resides in the Supreme Court of Justice, the courts of appeal, the courts of first instance, the communal courts and other tribunals created by special laws, such as the land courts. The Supreme Court, consisting of a president and eight judges chosen by the Senate, and the procurator-general, appointed by the executive, supervises the lower courts. Each province forms a judicial district, as does the National District, and each has its own procurator fiscal and court of first instance; these districts are subdivided, in all, into 97 municipalities, each with one or more local justices. The death penalty was abolished in 1924.

The population in penal institutions in June 2003 was 16,789 (193 per 100,000 of national population).

Education

Primary instruction is free and compulsory for children between five and 14 years of age; there are also secondary, normal, vocational and special schools, all of which are either wholly maintained by the State or state-aided. In 2007 there were 1,355,085 primary school pupils with 56,744 teaching staff and 920,494 pupils at secondary level with 31,710 teaching staff. The Universidad Autónoma de Santo Domingo, founded in 1914, is the leading public university; there were 141,929 students enrolled in 2004. The leading private university is the Universidad Tecnológica de Santiago, created in 1976. There were 293,565 students and 11,367 academic staff in tertiary education in 2004. Adult literacy was 87·7% in 2003 (88·0% among males and 87·3% among females).

In 2007 public expenditure on education came to 2·6% of GNI and 11·0% of total government spending.

Health

In 2000 there were 15,670 physicians, 7,000 dentists, 15,352 nurses and 3,330 pharmacists. There were 723 government hospitals in 1992.

RELIGION

The religion of the state is Roman Catholic; there were 7·11m. adherents in 2001. Protestants numbered 560,000 in 2001. In Feb. 2010 there was one cardinal.

CULTURE

World Heritage Sites

The Dominican Republic has one site on the UNESCO World Heritage List: the Colonial City of Santo Domingo (1990)—founded in 1492, it is the site of the first cathedral and university in the Americas.

Broadcasting

The government-owned Corporación Estatal de Radio y Televisión operates public radio and television networks (colour by NTSC). There are also private terrestrial and cable TV services, and more than 200 radio stations. In 2006 there were 2·1m. television receivers.

Press

In 2006 there were 11 dailies with a combined circulation of 605,000.

Tourism

In 2006 there were 3,965,055 non-resident air arrivals and 303,489 cruise ship visitors. Tourism receipts in 2006 totalled US$3,917m. In 2005 there were 59,870 hotel rooms.

DIPLOMATIC REPRESENTATIVES

Of the Dominican Republic in the United Kingdom (139 Inverness Terrace, London, W2 6JF)
Ambassador: Aníbal de Castro.

Of the United Kingdom in the Dominican Republic (Edificio Corominas Pepin, Ave. 27 de Febrero 233, Santo Domingo)
Ambassador: Stephen Fisher.

Of the Dominican Republic in the USA (1715 22nd St., NW, Washington, D.C., 20008)
Ambassador: Roberto B. Saladin.

Of the USA in the Dominican Republic (Calle Cesar Nicolas Penson, Santo Domingo)
Ambassador: Vacant.
Chargé d'Affaires a.i.: Christopher Lambert.

Of the Dominican Republic to the United Nations
Ambassador: Federico Alberto Cuello Camilo.

Of the Dominican Republic to the European Union
Ambassador: Alejandro González Pons.

FURTHER READING

Black, J. K., *The Dominican Republic: Politics and Development in an Unsovereign State.* 1986

Gregory, Steven, *The Devil Behind the Mirror: Globalization and Politics in the Dominican Republic.* 2006

Hartlyn, Jonathan, *The Struggle for Democratic Politics in the Dominican Republic.* 1998

Peguero, Valentina, *The Militarization of Culture in the Dominican Republic, from the Captains General to General Trujillo.* 2004

Wucker, Michele, *Why the Cocks Fight: Dominicans, Haitians, and the Struggle for Hispaniola.* 2000

National Statistical Office: Oficina Nacional de Estadística, Av. México esq. Leopoldo Navarro, Edificio Oficinas Gubernamentales 'Juan Pablo Duarte' Pisos 8 y 9 Gazcue, Santo Domingo.
Website (Spanish only): http://www.one.gov.do

ECUADOR

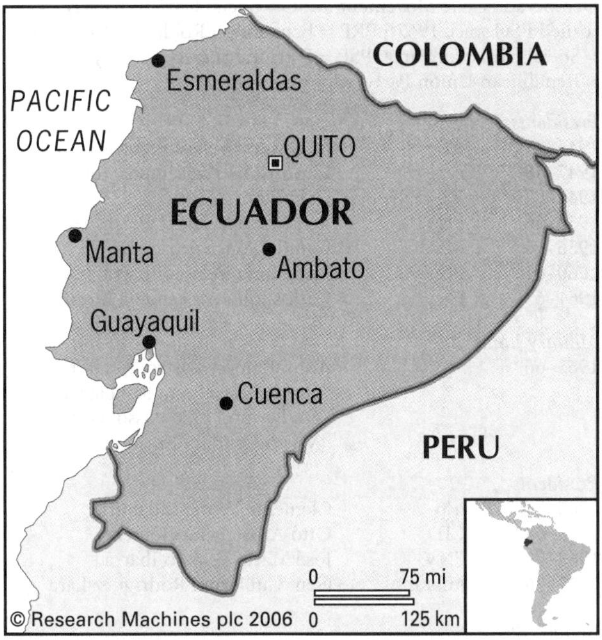

República del Ecuador
(Republic of Ecuador)

Capital: Quito
Population estimate, 2010: 13·78m.
GDP per capita, 2007: (PPP$) 7,449
HDI/world rank: 0·806/80

KEY HISTORICAL EVENTS

In 1532 the Spaniards founded a colony in Ecuador, then called Quito. In 1821 a revolt led to the defeat of the Spaniards at Pichincha and thus independence from Spain. On 13 March 1830, Quito became the Republic of Ecuador. Political instability was endemic. From the mid-1930s, President José Maria Velasco Ibarra was deposed by military coups from four of his five presidencies.

From 1963 to 1966 and from 1976 to 1979 military juntas ruled the country. The second of these juntas produced a new constitution which came into force on 10 Aug. 1979. Presidencies were more stable but civil unrest continued in the wake of economic reforms and attempts to combat political corruption.

In Jan. 2000 President Mahaud declared a state of emergency when protesters demanded his resignation over his handling of an economic crisis. There was a coup on 21 Jan. but, after five hours in control, the military junta handed power to the former vice-president, Gustavo Noboa.

In April 2005 President Lucio Gutiérrez was ousted by Ecuador's congress after public protest at his attempts to implement IMF-backed economic policies and his substitution of 27 out of 31 Supreme Court judges with his allies. The replacement judges promptly dropped corruption charges against two former presidents, increasing public outcry. Four days after being dismissed, Gutiérrez fled to Brazil. He was replaced by Alfredo Palacio, who immediately issued a warrant for Gutiérrez's arrest. Gutiérrez was arrested in Oct. 2005 and charged with endangering national security but was freed in March 2006 when a judge dismissed the claims. Palacio was defeated in the elections of Nov. 2006, with Rafael Correa taking over as president.

TERRITORY AND POPULATION

Ecuador is bounded in the north by Colombia, in the east and south by Peru and in the west by the Pacific ocean. The frontier with Peru has long been a source of dispute. It was delimited in the Treaty of Rio, 29 Jan. 1942, when, after being invaded by Peru, Ecuador lost over half her Amazonian territories. Ecuador unilaterally denounced this treaty in Sept. 1961. Fighting between Peru and Ecuador began again in Jan. 1981 over this border issue but a ceasefire was agreed in early Feb. Following a confrontation of soldiers in Aug. 1991 the foreign ministers of both countries signed a pact creating a security zone, and took their cases to the UN in Oct. 1991. On 26 Jan. 1995 further armed clashes broke out with Peruvian forces in the undemarcated mutual border area (*Cordillera del Cóndor*). On 2 Feb. talks were held under the auspices of the guarantor nations of the 1942 Protocol of Rio de Janeiro (Argentina, Brazil, Chile and the USA) but fighting continued. A ceasefire was agreed on 17 Feb., which was broken, and again on 28 Feb. On 25 July 1995 an agreement between Ecuador and Peru established a demilitarized zone along their joint frontier. The frontier was reopened on 4 Sept. 1995. Since 23 Feb. 1996 Ecuador and Peru have signed three further agreements to regulate the dispute. The dispute was settled in Oct. 1998. Confirming the Peruvian claim that the border lies along the high peaks of the Cóndor, Ecuador gained navigation rights on the Amazon within Peru.

No definite figure of the area of the country can yet be given. One estimate of the area of Ecuador is 272,045 sq. km, excluding the litigation zone between Peru and Ecuador, which is 190,807 sq. km, but including the **Galápagos** Archipelago (8,010 sq. km), situated in the Pacific ocean about 960 km west of Ecuador, and comprising 13 islands and 19 islets. These were discovered in 1535 by Fray Tomás de Berlanga and had a population of 10,207 in 1996. They constitute a national park, and had about 80,000 visitors in 1995.

The population is an amalgam of European, Amerindian and African origins. Some 41% of the population is Amerindian: Quechua, Shiwiar, Achuar and Zaparo. In May 1992 they were granted title to the 1m. ha. of land they occupy in Pastaza.

The official language is Spanish. Quechua and other languages are also spoken.

Census population in 2001, 12,156,608; density, 45 per sq. km. In 2005, 62·8% lived in urban areas.

The UN gives an estimated population for 2010 of 13·78m.

The population was distributed by provinces as follows in 2001 (census figures):

Province	*Sq. km*	*Population*	*Capital*	*Population*
Azuay	8,124·7	599,546	Cuenca	277,374
Bolívar	3,939·9	169,370	Guaranda	20,742
Cañar	3,122·1	206,981	Azogues	27,866
Carchi	3,605·1	152,939	Tulcán	47,359
Chimborazo	6,569·3	403,632	Riobamba	124,807
Cotopaxi	6,071·9	349,540	Latacunga	51,689
El Oro	5,850·1	525,763	Machala	204,578
Esmeraldas	15,239·1	385,223	Esmeraldas	95,124
Guayas	20,502·5	3,309,034	Guayaquil	1,985,379
Imbabura	4,559·3	344,044	Ibarra	108,535
Loja	11,026·5	404,835	Loja	118,532
Los Ríos	7,175·0	650,178	Babahoyo	76,869
Manabi	18,878·8	1,186,025	Portoviejo	171,847

Province	Sq. km	Population	Capital	Population
Morona-Santiago	25,690·0	115,412	Macas	13,602
Napo	11,430·9	79,139	Tena	16,669
Orellana	22,500·0	86,493	Francisco de Orellana	18,298
Pastaza	29,773·7	61,779	Puyo	24,432
Pichincha	12,914·7	2,388,817	Quito	1,399,378
Sucumbíos	18,327·5	128,995	Nueva Loja	34,106
Tungurahua	3,334·8	441,034	Ambato	154,095
Zamora-Chinchipe	23,110·8	76,601	Zamora	10,355
Galápagos	8,010·0	18,640	Puerto Baquerizo Moreno	4,908
Non-delimited zones	2,288·8	72,588		

Following an administrative reorganization in 2007, two new provinces were created (with capitals): Santa Elena (Santa Elena) and Santo Domingo de los Tsáchilas (Santo Domingo de los Colorados).

SOCIAL STATISTICS

2001 estimates: births, 328,000; deaths, 68,000. Rates, 2001 estimates (per 1,000 population): birth, 26·0; death, 5·4. Life expectancy at birth, 2007, was 72·1 years for males and 78·0 years for females. Annual population growth rate, 2000–05, 1·4%. Infant mortality, 2005, 22 per 1,000 live births; fertility rate, 2004, 2·7 children per woman. In 2003 the most popular age for marrying was 20–24 for both men and women.

CLIMATE

The climate varies from equatorial, through warm temperate to mountain conditions, according to altitude, which affects temperatures and rainfall. In coastal areas, the dry season is from May to Dec., but only from June to Sept. in mountainous parts, where temperatures may be 20°F colder than on the coast. Quito, Jan. 59°F (15°C), July 58°F (14·4°C). Annual rainfall 44" (1,115 mm). Guayaquil, Jan. 79°F (26·1°C), July 75°F (23·9°C). Annual rainfall 39" (986 mm).

CONSTITUTION AND GOVERNMENT

An executive president and a vice-president are directly elected by universal suffrage. The president appoints and leads a *Council of Ministers*, and determines the number and functions of the ministries that comprise the executive branch. Legislative power is vested in a *National Assembly* of 124 members, popularly elected by province. One seat is reserved for overseas voters. Voting is obligatory for all literate citizens of 18–65 years.

A new constitution came into force on 20 Oct. 2008. It was drafted by a Constituent Assembly set up by President Correa in Nov. 2007 and was approved with 63·9% of the vote in a referendum on 28 Sept. 2008. It superseded the previous constitution that had been in place for ten years. The 2008 constitution, which includes 444 articles, allows a president to run for two consecutive four-year terms, dissolve parliament and call early elections, and set monetary policy. The *National Congress* was abolished and replaced by a new *National Assembly*. The constitution also allows for tighter control of key industries, the expropriation and redistribution of idle farm land, free health care for the elderly and the legalization of same-sex civil marriages. The government can also declare some foreign loans illegitimate.

National Anthem

'Salve, Oh Patria, mil veces, Oh Patria' ('Hail, Oh Fatherland, a thousand times, Oh Fatherland'); words by J. L. Mera, tune by A. Neumane.

GOVERNMENT CHRONOLOGY

Heads of State since 1944. (AD = Democratic Alliance; Alianza PAIS = Proud and Sovereign Fatherland Alliance; CFP = Concentration of Popular Forces; CID = Democratic Institutional Coalition; DP–UDC = People's Democracy–Christian Democratic Union; FNV = National Velasquista Federation; FRA = Alfarista Radical Front; ID = Democratic Left; MCDN = Nacional Democratic Civic Movement; MSC = Social Christian Party [called PSC since 1967]; PRE = Ecuadorian Roldosist Party; PSC = Social Christian Party; PSP = Patriotic Society January 21; PUR = Republican Union Party; n/p = non-party)

Presidents		
1944–47	AD	José María Velasco Ibarra
1947–48	n/p	Carlos Julio Arosemena Tola
1948–52	MCDN	Galo Plaza Lasso
1952–56	FNV	José María Velasco Ibarra
1956–60	MSC	Camilo Ponce Enríquez
1960–61	FNV	José María Velasco Ibarra
1961–63	FNV	Carlos Julio Arosemena Monroy
Military Junta		
1963–66		Adm. Ramón Castro Jijón (chair); Gen. Luis Cabrera Sevilla; Col. Guillermo Freile Posso; Gen. Mario Gándara Enríquez
Presidents		
1966	n/p	Clemente Yerovi Indaburu
1966–68	CID	Otto Arosemena Gómez
1968–72	FNV	José María Velasco Ibarra
1972–76	military	Gen. Guillermo Rodríguez Lara
Military Junta		
1976–79		Admr. Alfredo Ernesto Poveda Burbano (chair); Gen. Luis Leoro Franco; Gen. Luis G. Durán Arcentales
Presidents		
1979–81	CFP	Jaime Roldós Aguilera
1981–84	DP–UDC	Osvaldo Hurtado Larrea
1984–88	PSC	León Esteban Febres Cordero
1988–92	ID	Rodrigo Borja Cevallos
1992–96	PUR	Sixto Alfonso Durán-Ballén
1996–97	PRE	Abdalá Jaime Bucaram Ortiz
1997–98	FRA	Fabián Ernesto Alarcón Rivera
1998–2000	DP–UDC	Jorge Jamil Mahuad Witt
2000–03	DP–UDC	Gustavo Noboa Bejarano
2003–05	PSP	Lucio Edwin Gutiérrez Borbúa
2005–07	n/p	Luis Alfredo Palacio González
2007–	Alianza PAIS	Rafael Vicente Correa Delgado

RECENT ELECTIONS

In the presidential elections held on 26 April 2009 Rafael Vicente Correa Delgado won 51·9% of the vote, against 27·9% for Lucio Edwin Gutiérrez Borbúa, 11·7% for Álvaro Fernando Noboa Pontón, 4·4% for Martha Roldós Bucaram, 1·6% for Carlos Sagñay de la Bastida and 1·3% for Melba Yolanda Jácome Marín. There were two other candidates who each received less than 1% of the vote. Correa was the first incumbent president to seek re-election, following constitutional changes made in Oct. 2008.

In National Congress elections on 26 April 2009 the Proud and Sovereign Fatherland Alliance (PAIS) won 59 seats with 45·8% of votes cast, Patriotic Society January 21 (PSP) 19 with 14·9%, Social Christian Party (PSC) 11 with 13·6%, the National Action Institutional Renewal Party (PRIAN) 7 with 5·8%, Popular Democratic Movement (MPD) 5 with 4·1%, Municipalist Movement for National Integrity 5 with 1·8%, Plurinational Pachakutik Unity-New Country (MUPP-NP) 4 with 1·4%, Ecuadorian Roldosist Party (PRE) 3 with 4·1% and Democratic Left (ID) 3 with 1·4%. Eight other parties won one seat each.

CURRENT ADMINISTRATION

President: Rafael Correa; b. 1963 (Alianza PAIS; sworn in 15 Jan. 2007 and re-elected 26 April 2009).

Vice-President: Lenín Moreno.

In March 2010 the cabinet comprised:

Minister of Agriculture, Livestock, Aquaculture and Fisheries: Ramón Espinel. *Coast:* Nicolás Issa Wagner. *Communication and Information Society:* Jorge Glas Espinel. *Culture:* Ramiro Noriega. *Defence:* Javier Ponce. *Economic and Social Inclusion:* María de los Ángeles Duarte. *Education:* Raúl Vallejo Corral. *Electricity and Renewable Energy:* Miguel Calahorrano. *Environment:* Marcela Aguiñaga. *Finance:* María Elsa Viteri Acaiturri. *Foreign Relations, Trade and Integration:* Ricardo Patiño. *Government, Religion, Police and Municipalities:* Gustavo Jalkh. *Industry and Competitiveness:* Xavier Abad Vicuña. *Justice and Human Rights:* Néstor Arbito Chica. *Labour and Employment:* Richard Espinoza. *Mines and Petroleum:* Germánico Pinto. *Public Health:* Caroline Chang. *Sport:* Sandra Vela. *Tourism:* Verónica Sión. *Transport and Public Works:* David Ortiz. *Urban Development and Housing:* Walter Solís.

Office of the President (Spanish only):
http://www.presidencia.gov.ec

CURRENT LEADERS

Rafael Correa

Position
President

Introduction
Correa started his four year presidential term in Jan. 2007. An economist educated in Europe and the USA, he has enjoyed strong popular support and was re-elected at the presidential election of April 2009.

Early Life
Correa was born in April 1963 in Ecuador's principal port and second city, Guayaquil. He graduated in economics from the Catholic University of Guayaquil and worked for a year in an indigenous community in the Cotopaxi region. He went on to postgraduate studies at the Catholic University of Leuven (Belgium) and the University of Illinois at Urbana-Champaign (USA).

Correa embarked on an academic career, rising to become dean of economics at the private University San Francisco de Quito. An economic analyst known for his anti-neoliberal and nationalist stance, he worked as a consultant for the UN development programme and the Japanese Development Bank among others. He was a notable opponent of Ecuadorian dollarization in 2000.

When popular revolts forced Lucio Gutiérrez to resign as president in April 2005, his successor Alfredo Palacio appointed Correa as finance minister. Correa held the position for four months, during which time he was critical of the World Bank and IMF and advocated poverty reduction and economic sovereignty schemes. When the World Bank withheld a loan in protest at various economic policies, Correa resigned his office amid a groundswell of popular support. In 2006 he founded the Alianza PAIS movement which allied itself with the Socialist Party in the run-up to general elections.

Career in Office
Correa campaigned on a platform of sustainable socio-economic revolution and Latin American integration. On taking office, he pledged a referendum on the establishment of a constitutional assembly to draft a new constitution, announced his intention to maintain good relations with the USA (although his rejection of a free trade agreement and Ecuador's refusal to extend Washington's use of the Manta military base in the Pacific have strained ties) and promised that dollarization would remain in place during his tenure. He also guaranteed Ecuador's non-involvement in Colombia's internal conflict but promised that any FARC members straying into Ecuadorian territory would be arrested. Other policies included engagement with Colombia and Brazil in trade negotiations and talks with Argentina to renegotiate the terms of Ecuador's multi-billion dollar debt. In addition, Correa announced that he would renegotiate 'entrapping' oil contracts with transnational companies, consider Ecuador's re-entry into OPEC (which happened in Nov. 2007) and limit debt repayment in favour of social spending (although quick repayment of IMF debts would remain on the agenda).

In April 2007 he overwhelmingly won referendum approval to set up a constituent assembly to rewrite the constitution. Elections to the assembly in Sept. resulted in a majority victory for Correa's allies and supporters over opposition parties dominating the Congress since the Oct. 2006 polls. In Nov. 2007 the assembly voted to dissolve the Congress and proceeded to act as a legislature. A new draft constitution increasing presidential powers and tenure, banning foreign military bases and enhancing state influence over the economy was approved by the assembly in July 2008 and endorsed in a national referendum on 28 Sept.

In March 2008 Ecuador's relations with Colombia were seriously undermined by a cross-border Colombian strike against a FARC guerrilla target in Ecuadorian territory, prompting Correa to cut diplomatic ties and send troops to the border. Relations worsened in July 2009 as a FARC military commander claimed that his organization had contributed funding to Correa's 2006 election campaign.

Correa won a landslide victory in the April 2009 presidential elections, receiving 52% of the vote and in the process avoiding the need for a second round run-off. His party also won a legislative majority at the same time.

DEFENCE

Military service is selective, with a one-year period of conscription. The country is divided into four military zones, with headquarters at Quito, Guayaquil, Cuenca and Pastaza.

In 2006 defence expenditure totalled US$653m. (US$48 per capita), representing 1·9% of GDP.

Army

Strength (2007) 47,000.

Navy

Navy combatant forces include two diesel submarines (although their serviceability is in doubt) and two ex-UK frigates. The Naval Aviation has 12 aircraft but no combat capable aircraft. Naval personnel in 2007 totalled 6,100 including 1,500 marines.

Air Force

The Air Force had a 2007 strength of 4,000 personnel and some 57 combat capable aircraft, and includes Cessna A-37s, Mirage F-1s and Kfirs.

INTERNATIONAL RELATIONS

Ecuador is a member of the UN, World Bank, IMF and several other UN specialized agencies, WTO, IOM, Andean Community, Inter-American Development Bank, SELA, LAIA, OAS, UNASUR, OPEC and Antarctic Treaty.

In March 2008 Ecuador responded to a Colombian incursion into its territory, during which a senior figure in the rebel FARC movement was killed, by sending troops to the border with Colombia. Venezuela made a similar gesture in sympathy before a diplomatic solution to the stand-off came into effect a week later.

ECONOMY

Agriculture accounted for 6·7% of GDP in 2006, industry 34·6% and services 58·7%.

Overview
In the 1980s and 1990s Ecuador's per capita income stagnated at a level above the Latin American average but below the world average. Heavily dependent on oil exports, the fall in oil prices in the late 1990s combined with natural disasters to trigger a momentary but sharp collapse in GDP and income levels. Since the early 2000s high oil prices have reinvigorated growth. However, the recent fall in business confidence and private investment have led to a sharp deceleration in growth.

The public debt to GDP ratio has declined significantly as a result of robust growth and sustained primary surpluses. The government is implementing major political and economic reforms to tackle poverty, promote equity-enhancing growth and create an efficient financial system. Nonetheless, poverty continues to afflict much of the population, particularly in rural areas where levels are over double those in urban areas. Violent protests are a threat to the maintenance of oil output levels and corruption remains endemic.

Currency
The monetary unit is the US dollar. Inflation was 8·4% in 2008. In March 2000 the government passed a law to phase out the former national currency, the *sucre*, to be replaced by the US dollar, and in April bank cash machines began dispensing dollars instead of sucres. On 11 Sept. 2000 the dollar became the only legal currency. Foreign exchange reserves were US$1,398m. in July 2005 with gold reserves of 845,000 troy oz.

Budget
Revenues in 2006 totalled US$6,895m. and expenditures US$7,011m.

VAT is 12% and corporate tax 25%.

Performance
Real GDP growth was 6·5% in 2008. Total GDP in 2008 was US$52·6bn.

Banking and Finance
The Central Bank of Ecuador (*President of the Directorate*, Diego Borja), the bank of issue, with a capital and reserves of US$1,557m. at 31 Dec. 1995, is modelled after the Federal Reserve Banks of the USA; through branches opened in 16 towns, it now deals in mortgage bonds. There are five other state banks, 16 commercial banks, four foreign banks and a *Multibanco.* All commercial banks must be affiliated to the Central Bank. The national monetary board is based in Quito.

There are stock exchanges in Quito and Guayaquil.

Weights and Measures
The metric system is standard but some US measures are used.

ENERGY AND NATURAL RESOURCES

Environment
Ecuador's carbon dioxide emissions from the consumption and flaring of fossil fuels were the equivalent of 2·0 tonnes per capita in 2008.

Electricity
Installed capacity was 3·20m. kW in 2004. Production was 11·70bn. kWh in 2004; consumption per capita was 1,024 kWh.

Oil and Gas
Production of oil in 2008 was 26·2m. tonnes. Estimated reserves, 2008, 3·8bn. bbls. In 2004 natural gas production was 352m. cu. metres. Proven reserves (2007), 90bn. cu. metres.

Minerals
Main products are silver, gold, copper and zinc. The country also has some iron, uranium, lead, coal, cobalt, manganese and titanium.

Agriculture
There were 1·20m. ha. of arable land in 2007 and 1·22m. ha. of permanent crops. In 2007 the agricultural population was an estimated 2·86m., of which about 1·19m. were economically active.

Main crops, in 1,000 tonnes, in 2003: sugarcane, 5,691; bananas, 5,609; rice, 1,236; plantains, 860; maize, 677; potatoes, 427; palm oil, 244; oranges, 189; soybeans, 111.

Livestock, 2003: cattle, 4·98m.; pigs, 3·01m.; sheep, 2·65m.; horses, 530,000; asses, 280,000; goats, 279,000; chickens, 142m.

Forestry
Excepting the agricultural zones and a few arid spots on the Pacific coast, Ecuador is a vast forest. 10·85m. ha., or 39·2% of the land area, was forested in 2005, but much of the forest is not commercially accessible. In 2007, 6·08m. cu. metres of roundwood were produced.

Fisheries
Fish landings in 2005 were 407,723 tonnes (almost entirely from sea fishing). Exports of fishery commodities were valued at US$761m. in 2004.

INDUSTRY
Industry produced 34·6% of GDP in 2006, including 9·0% from manufacturing. Manufacturing showed an annual increase of 8·5% in 2006. Main products include (2004, in 1,000 tonnes): residual fuel oil, 3,657; cement (2002), 2,947; distillate fuel oil, 1,621; petrol, 895.

Labour
Out of 3,673,200 people in urban employment in 2001, 1,026,700 were in wholesale and retail trade/repair of motor vehicles, motorcycles and personal and household goods; 610,600 in manufacturing; 244,600 in transport, storage and communications; and 239,800 in agriculture, hunting and forestry. In June 2001, 10·4% of the workforce was unemployed, down from 14·1% in June 2000.

Trade Unions
The main trade union federation is the United Workers' Front.

INTERNATIONAL TRADE
Most restrictions on foreign investment were removed in 1992 and the repatriation of profits was permitted. Foreign debt was US$17,129m. in 2005.

Imports and Exports
In 2004 imports totalled US$7,861m. (US$6,534m. in 2003); exports, US$7,606m. (US$6,039m. in 2003).

Main imports in 2004 were (in US$1m.): road vehicles, 835·2; telecommunications, sound recording and reproducing equipment, 615·3; iron and steel, 477·7; petroleum and petroleum products, 378·8; medicinal and pharmaceutical products, 377·1. Ecuador is the world's leading exporter of bananas (US$1,022·9m. in 2004), with approximately a third of world banana exports. Other major exports (2004, in US$1m.): petroleum and petroleum products, 4,233·8; fish and seafood, 734·6; cut flowers and foliage, 342·2; cocoa, 145·7. Main import suppliers, 2004: USA, 20·7%; Colombia, 14·6%; Venezuela, 6·8%; Brazil, 6·1%.

Main export markets in 2004: USA, 42·9%; Peru, 7·9%; Italy, 4·6%; Colombia, 3·9%.

COMMUNICATIONS

Roads
In 2007 there were 43,670 km of roads. There were 507,500 passenger cars in 2007 (38 per 1,000 inhabitants) and 323,500 lorries and vans. There were 1,848 fatalities in road accidents in 2007.

In 1998 storms and floods on the coast, caused by El Niño, resulted in 2,000 km of roads being damaged or destroyed.

Rail
The railway network, once 971 km long, now has a total length of just 204 km. In 2002 passenger-km travelled came to 33m.

Civil Aviation
There are international airports at Quito (Mariscal Sucre) and Guayaquil (Simón Bolívar). The main Ecuadorian carriers are Tame Línea Aérea del Ecuador and Icaro. In 2001 Quito handled 2,213,000 passengers (1,140,000 on domestic flights) and 105,400 tonnes of freight, and Guayaquil handled 1,416,000 passengers (749,000 on domestic flights) and 40,500 tonnes of freight.

Shipping
Ecuador has three major seaports, of which Guayaquil is the most important, and six minor ones. In 2002 the merchant navy totalled 313,000 GRT of ocean-going vessels, including oil tankers 219,000 GRT. In 2001 vessels totalling 3,064,000 NRT entered ports and vessels totalling 18,761,000 NRT cleared.

Telecommunications
Ecuador had 7,947,800 telephone subscribers in 2005, equivalent to 600·8 for every 1,000 persons, with 6,246,300 mobile phone subscribers. In 2005, 514,000 PCs were in use (38·9 for every 1,000 persons) and internet users numbered 616,000.

Postal Services
In 2003 there were 254 post offices.

SOCIAL INSTITUTIONS

Justice
The Supreme Court in Quito, consisting of a President and 30 Justices, comprises ten chambers each of three Justices. It is also a Court of Appeal. There is a Superior Court in each province, comprising chambers (as appointed by the Supreme Court) of three magistrates each. The Superior Courts are at the apex of a hierarchy of various tribunals. There is no death penalty.

The population in penal institutions in Aug. 2008 was 17,065 (126 per 100,000 of national population).

Education
In 2000–01 there were 199,588 pre-primary pupils with 13,755 teachers. Primary education is free and compulsory. Private schools, both primary and secondary, are under some state supervision. In 2007 there were 2·04m. pupils and 90,366 teaching staff in primary schools; and 1·14m. pupils with 77,904 teaching staff in secondary schools. In the public sector in 2000–01 there were: 9 universities, 8 technical universities, 2 institutes of technology, 1 polytechnical university, 1 military polytechnic and 1 agricultural university; and in the private sector: 9 universities, 3 Roman Catholic universities, 4 institutes of technology, 2 polytechnic institutes and 1 technical university. There were 443,509 students in tertiary education in 2007 with 22,714 academic staff. Adult literacy was 91·0% in 2003 (male, 92·3%; female, 89·7%).

In 2000–01 total expenditure on education came to 1·7% of GNP and 8·0% of total government spending.

Health
In 2002 there were 3,496 hospitals and clinics with 14 beds per 10,000 inhabitants. There were 18,335 physicians, 2,062 dentists, 19,549 nurses and 1,037 midwives in 2000.

Welfare
Those who qualify for a pension must be aged 55 and have 360 months of contributions if born before 30 Nov. 1946, or be aged 65 with 180 months of contributions. A scheme to change the age of retirement to 60 with 360 months of contributions is being phased in gradually. In 2003 the minimum monthly pension was US$25, and the maximum pension was US$125.

Social insurance providing lump-sum benefits for unemployment is gradually being phased out in favour of a system linking payments to income and length of employment.

RELIGION
The state recognizes no religion and grants freedom of worship to all. In 2001 there were 11·91m. Roman Catholics. There were also small numbers of Protestants and followers of other faiths.

CULTURE

World Heritage Sites
Ecuador has four sites on the UNESCO World Heritage List: the Galápagos Islands (inscribed on the list in 1978 and 2001); the City of Quito (1978); Sangay National Park (1983); and the Historic Centre of Santa Ana de los Ríos de Cuenca (1999).

Broadcasting
Radio and television services are dominated by private operators. Radio is the more widely available medium, and there are hundreds of independent stations. There were 3·5m. TV receivers in 2006 (colour by NTSC).

Press
There were 19 daily newspapers in 2006, with a circulation of 670,000.

Tourism
Foreign visitors numbered 861,000 in 2005, spending US$488m.

DIPLOMATIC REPRESENTATIVES
Of Ecuador in the United Kingdom (Flat 3b, 3 Hans Cres., London, SW1X 0LS)
Ambassador: Eduardo Cabezas Molina.

Of the United Kingdom in Ecuador (Citiplaza Bldg, Naciones Unidas Ave., & República de El Salvador, 14th Floor, Quito)
Ambassador: Linda Cross.

Of Ecuador in the USA (2535 15th St., NW, Washington, D.C., 20009)
Ambassador: Luis Gallegos Chiriboga.

Of the USA in Ecuador (Avenida Avigiras E12–170 y Avenida Eloy Alfaro, Quito)
Ambassador: Heather M. Hodges.

Of Ecuador to the United Nations
Ambassador: Francisco Carrión Mena.

Of Ecuador to the European Union
Ambassador: Fernando Yépez Lasso.

FURTHER READING

Pineo, R. F., *Social and Economic Reform in Ecuador.* 1996

Roos, W. and van Renterghem, O., *Ecuador in Focus: A Guide to the People, Politics and Culture.* 1997

Sawyer, Suzana, *Crude Chronicles: Indigenous Politics, Multinational Oil, and Neoliberalism in Ecuador.* 2004

Selverston-Scher, M., *Ethnopolitics in Ecuador: Indigenous Rights and the Strengthening of Democracy.* 2001

National Statistical Office: Instituto Nacional de Estadística y Censos (INEC), Juan Larrea 534 y Riofrío, Quito.
Website (Spanish only): http://www.inec.gov.ec

EGYPT

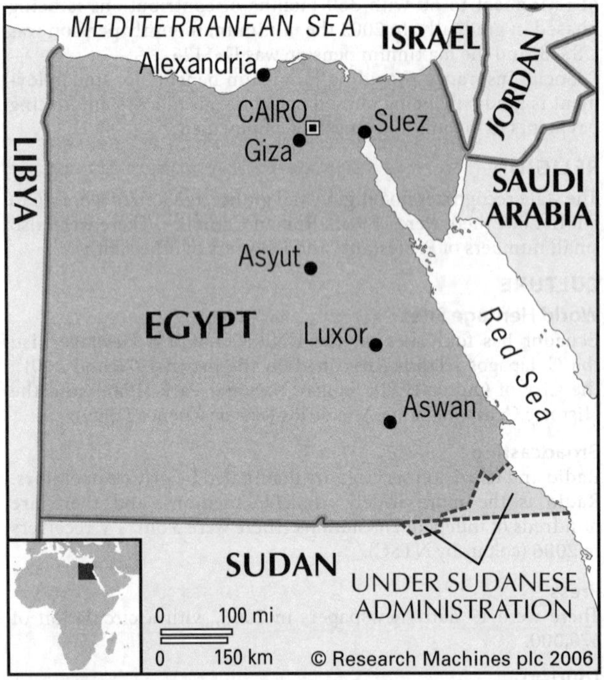

Jumhuriyat Misr al-Arabiya
(Arab Republic of Egypt)

Capital: Cairo
Population estimate, 2010: 84·47m.
GDP per capita, 2007: (PPP$) 5,349
HDI/world rank: 0·703/123

KEY HISTORICAL EVENTS

There is evidence of pastoralism and the cultivation of cereals in southwest Egypt from as early as 7000 BC. Settlements grew along the Nile valley, though Upper and Lower Egypt only united around 3100 BC under Pharoah Menes. The subsequent Early Dynastic period was marked by flourishing trade with Sinai, the Levant and as far north as the Black Sea. The astonishing artistic and intellectual developments of the Old Kingdom began during the IVth dynasty (2575–2465 BC), when sun-worship took hold and temples and pyramids, including those at Giza, were constructed. Egypt was governed from the city of Memphis, south of modern Cairo, reaching its height during the VIth dynasty before losing power to local rulers from around 2200 BC.

Centralized power was restored at Thebes from 2134 BC. The Middle Kingdom (XIIth dynasty) saw Egypt expand south into Nubia under Amenemhat I. A cultural flowering included the invention of a writing system. The XIIth dynasty ended in 1786 BC when the region was invaded by the Hyksos, a nomadic Asiatic tribe. The New Kingdom came into being with the expulsion of the Hyksos around 1550 BC and lasted until 1050 BC. It was now that Egypt achieved its greatest territorial dominance, with Syria, Palestine and northern Iraq all under Egyptian jurisdiction. The conquests brought great prosperity and bold architecture, which reached its zenith under the XVIIIth dynasty pharaohs, Tuthmosis III and Tutankhamun.

Ancient Egyptian civilization began to fragment amid conflict with Hittite invaders during the XIXth dynasty (around 1250 BC). The subsequent rise of Assyria to the northeast and Nubian conquests from the south hastened the decline. The last pharaoh was ousted by Persian invading forces led by Cambyses in 525 BC. The Persians remained in power until overrun by Alexander the Great in 332 BC. He founded the port of Alexandria, including its great lighthouse, and made the city the commercial and cultural centre of the Greek world. On his death in 305 BC, Ptolemy of Macedonia seized power, establishing a dynasty which lasted until 30 BC and the suicide of Cleopatra.

Egypt then became a province of the Roman Empire until Arabian forces invaded in AD 642, absorbing the Nile valley into the Ummayad Caliphate, centred on Damascus. The Arabic language became the official language of government in 706. The Abbasid defeat of the Ummayad dynasty in 750 brought a shift of Arab power to the new city of Baghdad. Abdullah bin Tahir sent a deputy to rule Egypt. The Fatimid caliphs, whose origins were in Tunisia, entered Egypt in 960 and founded Cairo as their capital, later establishing the Muslim university. Over the next 200 years they built an empire that stretched from Tunisia to Syria and Yemen, with extensive trade routes across the Mediterranean and into the Indian Ocean.

Weakened by the Christian Crusades, the Fatimid caliphate fell to the Ayyubid dynasty in 1169, led by Tikrit-born Saladin (Salahuddin al-Ayyubi). Operating from Damascus, he fought the Crusader States and by the end of the 12th century controlled much of the Eastern Mediterranean. Egypt was largely governed by his deputy, Karaksh. In 1250 Egypt was seized by Saif ad Din Qutuz, a Turkic former slave who founded the Mamluk Sultanate. There were frequent revolts and changes of leaders (*beys*, or princes), but the Sultanate survived until 1517 when Egypt was absorbed into the Ottoman empire.

Napoleonic forces seized the country between 1798 and 1801 but were forced out by a combined Anglo-Ottoman force. Muhammad Ali, appointed Egyptian pasha by the Ottoman emperor in 1805, swiftly destroyed the remnants of Mamluk power. He introduced sweeping political and social reforms and modernized agriculture. Like many of his predecessors he took control of Syria, Nubia and part of the Arabian peninsula. The opening of the Suez Canal during the reign of Muhammad Said Pasha in 1867 heralded an era of foreign intervention and domination, with Said selling his shares in the Suez Canal to the British in 1875. British forces occupied Alexandria and then Cairo in 1882, ruling the country through the consul general, Lord Cromer. During the First World War, Britain declared Egypt a British Protectorate, ousting the khedive, Abbas I, for supporting Germany. Calls for independence grew louder after the war ended and Fuad I ruled a partially independent Egypt from 1923.

Although Egypt was officially neutral until the last days of the Second World War, Britain was the dominant power. From 1940 it was the arena for the Desert War that saw Allied forces ultimately repel Axis attempts to occupy Egypt, take control of the Suez Canal and open up access to the oil fields of the Middle East. The decisive victory came when Gen. Montgomery's Eighth Army overpowered the German and Italian forces under Gen. Rommel at the Second Battle of El Alamein in July 1942.

Following a revolution in July 1952 led by Gen. Neguib, King Farouk abdicated in favour of his son but in 1953 the monarchy was abolished. Neguib became president but encountered opposition from the military when he attempted to move towards a parliamentary republic. Col. Gamal Abdel Nasser became head of state on 14 June 1954 (president from 1956). In 1956 Egypt nationalized the Suez Canal, a move which led Britain, France and Israel to mount military attacks against Egypt until UN and US pressure forced a withdrawal.

The 1960s and 1970s were years of conflict with Israel, notably the Six-Day War in June 1967, when Egypt (together with Syria and Jordan) declared war on Israel but were defeated despite having more troops and armaments. After the war Egypt received economic and military aid from the Soviet Union. Following Nasser's death in Sept. 1970 Muhammad Anwar Sadat took over as president. Having launched a peace initiative during a visit to Jerusalem in 1977, Sadat secured a peace treaty with Israel in March 1979. Sadat was assassinated on 6 Oct. 1981 and was succeeded by his vice-president, Lieut.-Gen. Muhammad Hosni Mubarak of the National Democratic Party (NDP). He gained a fifth consecutive term after emerging victorious in presidential elections in Sept. 2005 (the first multi-candidate presidential poll) to become the country's longest-serving leader since Muhammad Ali.

TERRITORY AND POPULATION

Egypt is bounded in the east by Israel and Palestine, the Gulf of Aqaba and the Red Sea, south by Sudan, west by Libya and north by the Mediterranean. The total area (including inland waters) is 1,009,450 sq. km, but the cultivated and settled area, that is the Nile Valley, Delta and oases, covers only 35,000 sq. km. A number of new desert cities are being developed to entice people away from the overcrowded Nile valley, where 99% of the population lives. The 2006 census population was 72,798,031; density 72·1 per sq. km. The United Nations population estimate for 2006 was 78,602,000. In 2005, 57·2% of the population were rural.

The UN gives an estimated population for 2010 of 84·47m.

3·9m. Egyptians were living abroad in 2006.

Area, population and capitals of the governorates (1996 and 2006 censuses):

Governorate	Area (in sq. km)	Population (1996 census)	Population (2006 census)	Capital
Alexandria	2,300	3,339,076	4,123,869	Alexandria
Aswan	62,726	960,510	1,186,482	Aswan
Asyut	25,926	2,802,334	3,444,967	Asyut
Behera	9,826	3,994,297	4,747,283	Damanhur
Beni Suef	10,954	1,859,213	2,291,618	Beni Suef
Cairo	3,085	6,800,991	6,758,581	Cairo
Dakahlia	3,716	4,223,338	4,989,997	Mansura
Damietta	910	913,555	1,097,339	Damietta
Fayum	6,068	1,989,772	2,511,027	Fayum
Gharbia	1,948	3,404,339	4,011,320	Tanta
Giza	13,184	4,784,095	3,143,486	Giza
Helwan[1]	—	—	1,713,278	Helwan
Ismailia	5,067	714,828	953,006	Ismailia
Kafr El Shaikh	3,748	2,223,383	2,620,208	Kafr El Shaikh
Kalyubia	1,124	3,281,135	4,251,672	Benha
Luxor	2,410	361,138	457,286	Luxor
Matruh	166,563	212,001	323,381	Matruh
Menia	32,279	3,310,129	4,166,299	Menia
Menufia	2,499	2,760,429	3,270,431	Shibin Al Kom
New Valley	440,098	141,774	187,263	Al Kharija
Port Said	1,351	472,331	570,603	Port Said
Qena	10,798	2,442,016	3,001,681	Qena
Red Sea	119,099	157,314	288,661	El Gurdakah
Sharkia	4,911	4,281,068	5,354,041	Zagazig
North Sinai	27,564	252,160	343,681	Al Arish
6th October[2]	—	—	2,581,059	6th October City
South Sinai	31,272	54,806	150,088	At Tur
Suez	9,002	417,526	512,135	Suez
Suhag	11,022	3,123,114	3,747,289	Suhag

[1]Helwan, formerly part of Cairo, was created in 2008.
[2]6th October, formerly part of Giza, was created in 2008.

The capital, Cairo, had a census population in 2006 of 6,758,581. Other major cities, with populations at the 2006 census (in 1,000): Alexandria, 4,085; Giza, 2,891; Shubra Al Khayma, 1,026; Helwan, 650; Port Said, 571; Suez (2005 estimate), 489.

Smaller cities, with 2006 populations (in 1,000): Mahalla Al Kubra, 443; Mansura, 439; Tanta, 423; Asyut, 389; Fayum, 316; Zagazig, 303; Ismailia, 293; Al Khusus, 291; Aswan, 266; Damanhur, 244; Menia, 236; Damietta, 207; Luxor (Uqsur), 202; Qena, 201.

The official language is Arabic, although French and English are widely spoken.

SOCIAL STATISTICS

Births, 2003, 1,776,000 (26·1 per 1,000 population); deaths, 440,000 (6·5); marriages, 537,000 (rate per 1,000 population, 7·9); divorces, 70,000 (1·0). Annual population growth rate, 2000–05, 2·3%. In 2004, 78% of the population was under 40 years old. Life expectancy at birth, 2007, was 68·2 years for males and 71·7 years for females. Fertility rate, 2004, 3·2 births per woman; infant mortality, 2005, 28 per 1,000 live births. Egypt has made some of the best progress in recent years in reducing child mortality. The number of deaths per 1,000 live births among children under five was reduced from more than 100 in 1990 to 26 in 2005.

CLIMATE

The climate is mainly dry, but there are winter rains along the Mediterranean coast. Elsewhere, rainfall is very low and erratic in its distribution. Winter temperatures are comfortable everywhere, but summer temperatures are very high, especially in the south. Cairo, Jan. 56°F (13·3°C), July 83°F (28·3°C). Annual rainfall 1·2" (28 mm). Alexandria, Jan. 58°F (14·4°C), July 79°F (26·1°C). Annual rainfall 7" (178 mm). Aswan, Jan. 62°F (16·7°C), July 92°F (33·3°C). Annual rainfall (trace). Giza, Jan. 55°F (12·8°C), July 78°F (25·6°C). Annual rainfall 16" (389 mm). Ismailia, Jan. 56°F (13·3°C), July 84°F (28·9°C). Annual rainfall 1·5" (37 mm). Luxor, Jan. 59°F (15°C), July 86°F (30°C). Annual rainfall (trace). Port Said, Jan. 58°F (14·4°C), July 78°F (27·2°C). Annual rainfall 3" (76 mm).

CONSTITUTION AND GOVERNMENT

The Constitution was approved by referendum on 11 Sept. 1971 and was amended on 22 May 1980. It defines Egypt as 'an Arab Republic with a democratic, socialist system' and the Egyptian people as 'part of the Arab nation'. The *President* was to be nominated by the People's Assembly and confirmed by plebiscite for a six-year term. However, in March 2005 parliament approved a proposal by President Mubarak to amend the constitution to allow for multi-candidate presidential elections. This was approved in a referendum on 25 May 2005. Further amendments to the constitution, on matters regarding the conduct of elections and anti-terror legislation, were approved in a referendum on 26 March 2007. Turnout was low. The President may appoint one or more *Vice-Presidents.*

The *People's Assembly* consists of 454 members, 444 directly elected and ten appointed by the president. An upper house, the *Shura Council*, was established in 1980 but it has a consultative role only. It has 264 members, 176 elected by popular vote and 88 appointed by the president for six-year terms. One half of the Shura Council is renewed every three years. There is a *Constitutional Court.*

The President appoints the Prime Minister and a Council of Ministers. It is traditional for two ministers to be Coptic Christians.

National Anthem

'Biladi' ('My homeland'); words and tune by S. Darwish.

GOVERNMENT CHRONOLOGY

Heads of State since 1953. (ASU = Arab Socialist Union; LR = Liberation Rally; NDP = National Democratic Party; NU = National Union)

President		
1953–54	military, LR	Muhammad Neguib
Chairman of the Revolutionary Command Council		
1954	military, LR	Gamal Abdel Nasser
President		
1954	military, LR	Muhammad Neguib
Chairman of the Revolutionary Command Council		
1954–56	military, LR	Gamal Abdel Nasser
Presidents		
1956–70	NU, ASU	Gamal Abdel Nasser
1970–81	ASU, NDP	Muhammad Anwar Sadat
1981–	NDP	Muhammad Hosni Mubarak

RECENT ELECTIONS

Elections for the People's Assembly were held in six rounds between 9 Nov. 2005 and 7 Dec. 2005. Turnout was 26·2%. The National Democratic Party (NDP) gained 388 seats; ind., 112 (of which 88 with the Muslim Brotherhood); New Wafd Party, 6; Al-Tagamu, 2; Al-Ghad 1.

In Shura Council elections held on 11 and 18 June 2007 the National Democratic Party took 84 of the 88 seats and the National Progressive Unionist Party 1. Three independents were elected.

The first multi-party election in Egypt's history took place on 7 Sept. 2005 when Hosni Mubarak was re-elected president with 88·6% of the votes against 7·3% for Ayman Nour and 2·8% for Noaman Gomaa. There were some allegations of ballot stuffing, vote buying and voter intimidation. Turnout was 23%.

CURRENT ADMINISTRATION

President: Hosni Mubarak; b. 1928 (NDP; first sworn in 14 Oct. 1981 and most recently re-elected in Sept. 2005).

In March 2010 the cabinet comprised:

Prime Minister: Ahmad Mahmoud Nazif; b. 1952 (NDP; sworn in 14 July 2004).

Minister of Agriculture and Land Reclamation: Amin Abaza. *Civil Aviation:* Ahmed Mohammed Shafique. *Communications and Information Technology:* Tarek Mohamed Kamel Mahmoud. *Culture:* Farouk Abdel Aziz Hosni. *Defence and Military Production:* Field Marshal Mohamed Hussein Tantawi. *Education:* Ahmed Badr. *Electricity and Energy:* Hassan Ahmed Younis. *Finance:* Yousef Boutrous Ghali. *Foreign Affairs:* Ahmed Ali Ahmed Abou Elgheit. *Health:* Hatem el-Gabali. *Higher Education and Scientific Research:* Hani Helal. *Housing:* Ahmed el-Maghrabi. *Information:* Anas el-Fiqqi. *Interior:* Habib Ibrahim Al-Adly. *International Co-operation:* Fayza Abu el-Naga. *Investment:* Mahmoud Safwat Mohyee El-Din. *Irrigation and Water Resources:* Mohamed Nasr Eldin Allam. *Justice:* Mamdouh Marei. *Manpower and Immigration:* Aicha Abdel Hadi. *Petroleum:* Amin Sameh Fahmy. *Religious Affairs (Awqaf):* Mahmoud Hamdi Zakzouk. *Social Solidarity:* Ali Al-Sayed Al-Moselhi. *Tourism:* Zuheir Garana. *Trade and Industry:* Rasheed Mohamed Rasheed Hussein. *Transport:* Alaa Eldin Fahmi.

Egyptian Parliament: http://www.parliament.gov.eg

CURRENT LEADERS

Muhammad Hosni Mubarak

Position

President

Introduction

Following a career in the Air Force, Hosni Mubarak was appointed vice-president of Egypt in April 1975 and then became president in Oct. 1981 shortly after the assassination of Anwar Sadat by militant Islamic fundamentalists. He has since been re-elected as president on four occasions—in 1987, 1993, 1999 and 2005—and remains chairman of the dominant National Democratic Party (NDP). Mubarak kept faith with most of his predecessor's policies, in particular reconciliation with the Western powers (after Gamal Abdel Nasser's pro-Soviet stance) and Egypt's controversial peace accord with Israel. However, he also sought to re-establish links with Arab states. He has taken a hard line with Muslim extremists and has been the target of several assassination plots.

Early Life

Born in Kafr al Musailha on 4 May 1928, Mubarak attended high school and graduated from the military academy in Cairo before joining the Egyptian Air Force in 1950. He was promoted successively to squadron leader, base commander, director of the Air Force Academy (1967–69) and chief of staff (1969–72), before his appointment as commander of the Air Force and deputy minister for military affairs in 1972. In the 1973 war with Israel he was acclaimed for his command of Egyptian air operations. Two years later, in April 1975, Sadat made Mubarak his vice-president.

Career in Office

Following Sadat's assassination, Mubarak was inaugurated as president and prime minister on 14 Oct. 1981 (although he relinquished the latter post in Jan. 1982). Under his presidency, Egypt's isolation in the Arab world in the wake of Sadat's peace treaty with Israel came to an end. By the end of the 1980s the country had resumed a leading role in regional politics. Mubarak supported UN sanctions against Iraq after its occupation of Kuwait in 1990, and Egypt participated in the Gulf War of 1991 in support of the Western-led coalition against the Iraqi president Saddam Hussein. Thereafter, Egypt's foreign policy focused on a comprehensive settlement between Israel and other neighbouring Arab states, with particular emphasis on resolving Palestinian grievances. This policy, however, was undermined by the outbreak from Sept. 2000 of the Palestinian intifada in opposition to Israeli occupation.

Since the 11 Sept. 2001 attacks on the USA, Mubarak has been a key supporter of the US campaign against terrorism, and Egypt itself has been the target of several terrorist attacks directed mainly against the tourism industry, a major source of revenue. Mubarak hosted summits on the Middle East peace process in 2000–03, and worked with Israel and the Palestinian Authority during 2004–05 to facilitate stability following Israel's withdrawal from Gaza.

Domestically Mubarak has maintained the political status quo, albeit with a measure of liberalization. However, his economic reforms have struggled to keep pace with inflation and rapid population growth, and he has alienated poorer sections of society. There was a resurgence of violent Islamic fundamentalism in the 1990s, targeted in particular at foreign tourists. Mubarak narrowly survived an assassination attempt by Egyptian militants in Addis Ababa, Ethiopia, in June 1995. His NDP government responded with a security crackdown on activists.

In early 2005 political reformers and opposition activists mounted a series of anti-government demonstrations. In Feb. Mubarak proposed amending the constitution to allow for the country's first multi-candidate presidential elections. That amendment was approved in a referendum in May, albeit with restrictions including a five-year registration for parties wanting to nominate candidates. As expected, Mubarak was re-elected for a fifth consecutive term in Sept. with 88·6% of the vote. However, only 23% of the eligible electorate turned out and there were allegations of vote buying and intimidation. In Dec. 2005 parliamentary elections ended with clashes between police and opposition supporters. Although the NDP retained its parliamentary majority, the Muslim Brotherhood won a record number of seats.

Following three bomb explosions in the resort town of Dahab on the Red Sea coast in April 2006, killing over 20 people, Mubarak extended controversial emergency legislation giving the security forces broad powers of arrest and detention. He had earlier promised to abolish the emergency regime during his campaign for re-election in 2005, but then claimed that it was necessary to combat Islamist terrorism. Despite opposition scepticism, he promised during an address to parliament in Nov. 2006 that he would introduce democratic and constitutional reform. A referendum was subsequently held in March 2007, in which amendments to the constitution, including controversial judicial and security provisions and a formal ban on religious parties, were approved by 76% of voters. Opponents of Mubarak's government, however, rejected the measures as a 'constitutional coup'. Elections to the Shura Council (upper house of parliament) in June 2007 were dominated by the NDP as most Muslim Brotherhood candidates were barred from running and none won a seat. In April 2008, in the run-up to elections for local councils, the government imposed a further crackdown on the Brotherhood, sentencing 25 members to stiff prison terms and arresting about 800 others. In response, the Brotherhood boycotted the polls.

In April 2009 the Egyptian authorities accused Hizbollah—Lebanon's radical Shia militia aligned with Syria, Iran and the Palestinian Hamas Islamist movement in an anti-Israeli front—of espionage activities aimed against Mubarak's regime. Around 50 people were arrested in connection with the charges.

Speculation about Mubarak's prospective successors has escalated as rumours of the ageing president's ill-health have spread.

DEFENCE

Conscription is selective, and for 12–36 months, depending on the level of education. Military expenditure totalled US$4,337m. in 2006 (US$55 per capita), representing 4·0% of GDP. According to *Deadly Arsenals*, published by the Carnegie Endowment for International Peace, Egypt has a chemical and biological weapons programme.

Army

Estimated strength (2007) 310,000 (around 205,000 conscripts). In addition there were 375,000 reservists, a Central Security Force of 325,000, a National Guard of 60,000 and 12,000 Border Guards.

Navy

Major surface combatants include one destroyer and ten frigates. A small shore-based naval aviation branch operates 20 helicopters. There are naval bases at Al Ghardaqah, Alexandria, Hurghada, Mersa Matruh, Port Said, Port Tewfik, Safaqa and Suez. Naval personnel in 2007 totalled an estimated 18,500 (including 10,000 conscripts and 2,000 coast guards).

Air Force

Until 1979 the Air Force was equipped largely with aircraft of USSR design, but subsequent re-equipment involves aircraft bought in the West, as well as some supplied by China. Strength (2007) is about 30,000 personnel (10,000 conscripts), 115 attack helicopters and 489 combat capable aircraft including F-7s, F-16s and *Mirages*.

INTERNATIONAL RELATIONS

Egypt is a member of the UN, World Bank, IMF and several other UN specialized agencies, WTO, IOM, International Organization of the Francophonie, Islamic Development Bank, OIC, African Development Bank, African Union, COMESA, League of Arab States and OAPEC (Organization of Arab Petroleum Exporting Countries).

ECONOMY

In 2006 agriculture accounted for 14·1% of GDP, industry 38·4% and services 47·5%.

Overview

The 1980s was a decade of macroeconomic disorder in Egypt. In the 1990s the government implemented an IMF-backed reform programme and the economy achieved stability. Reform started with a privatization push in the early 1990s and by the end of 2000 around 50% of state-owned enterprises were fully privatized. However, the late 1990s saw an economic downturn and privatization efforts stalled in the early 2000s. In 2004 an economically liberal cabinet was appointed and the reform agenda was revived, with President Mubarak investing political capital in structural reforms to generate jobs and promote foreign investment. Cuts have been made in customs duties and income taxes and the government has tackled problems in the banking system which accumulated large non-performing loans during the economic slowdown of the late 1990s.

In 2007 the economy recorded its strongest real GDP growth since 1998 at over 7%. The broad-based nature of the growth, in particular within the labour-intensive agriculture, manufacturing, construction and services sectors, helped reduce unemployment from 11·8% in 2004 to roughly 9% by March 2007. The economy enjoyed record levels of foreign direct investment in 2007 and structural reforms have helped promote a private sector-driven economy. However, high imported food prices and domestic demand continue to create inflationary pressures. The budget deficit remains high but is declining, with the government committed to reducing the fiscal deficit to 3% of GDP by 2011.

Currency

The monetary unit is the *Egyptian pound* (EGP) of 100 *piastres*. Inflation rates (based on IMF statistics) for fiscal years:

1999	*2000*	*2001*	*2002*	*2003*	*2004*	*2005*	*2006*	*2007*	*2008*
3·7%	2·8%	2·4%	2·4%	3·2%	8·1%	8·8%	4·2%	11·0%	11·7%

Faced with slowing economic activity, the country devalued the Egyptian pound four times in 2001. In Jan. 2003 the Egyptian pound was allowed to float against the dollar after years of a government-controlled foreign exchange regime. In June 2009 foreign exchange reserves were US$29,278m., gold reserves totalled 2·43m. troy oz and total money supply was £E182,991m.

Budget

The financial year runs from 1 July. Revenues in 2003–04 were £E116,490m. and expenditures £E159,600m. Main sources of revenue were income and profits taxes, 28·3%; sales taxes, 19·4%; customs duties, 13·0%; Suez Canal fees, 4·4%. Current expenditure accounted for 76·6% of total expenditures and capital expenditure 23·4%.

Performance

Real GDP growth rates (based on IMF statistics):

1999	*2000*	*2001*	*2002*	*2003*	*2004*	*2005*	*2006*	*2007*	*2008*
6·1%	5·4%	3·5%	3·2%	3·2%	4·1%	4·5%	6·8%	7·1%	7·2%

Total GDP in 2008 was US$162·8bn.

Banking and Finance

The Central Bank of Egypt (founded 1960) is the central bank and bank of issue. The *Governor* is Farouk el-Okdah.

In 2003, four major public-sector commercial banks accounted for some 77% of all banking assets: the National Bank of Egypt (the largest bank, with assets of nearly £E74bn. in 1999), the Banque Misr, the Bank of Alexandria and the Banque du Caïre. There were 40 banks in total in 2008. Foreign banks have only been allowed to operate since 1996.

Foreign direct investment inflows, which were just US$237m. in 2003, rose to US$11·6bn. in 2007 although they fell to US$9·5bn. in 2008.

There are stock exchanges in Cairo and Alexandria.

Weights and Measures

The metric system is official with the exception of the *feddan* (= 0·42 ha.) to measure land. However, other traditional measures are still in use: *Kadah* = 1·91 litres; *Rob* = 4 kadahs; *Keila* = 8 kadahs; *Ardeb* = 96 kadahs; *Dirhem* = 3·12 grams; *Rotl* = 144 dirhems (0·449 kg); *Oke* = 400 dirhems; *Qantar* = 100 rotls or 36 okes.

ENERGY AND NATURAL RESOURCES

Environment

Egypt's carbon dioxide emissions from the consumption and flaring of fossil fuels in 2008 were the equivalent of 2·1 tonnes per capita.

Electricity

Installed capacity was 16·9m. kW in 2003. Electricity generated in 2003–04 was 95·18bn. kWh. Consumption per capita was an estimated 1,465 kWh in 2004. The use of solar energy is expanding. There are plans to build a nuclear power station to help meet the growing demand for electricity.

Oil and Gas

Oil was discovered in 1909. Oil policy is controlled by the state-owned Egyptian General Petroleum Corporation, whole or part-owner of the production and refining companies. Oil production in 2008 was 34·6m. tonnes with 4·3bn. bbls of proven reserves.

As a result of a series of new discoveries in 1999 and 2000 gas reserves have been steadily increasing. Egypt began exporting natural gas in 2003 and is now a major exporter. 2008 total production amounted to 58·9bn. cu. metres. There were proven natural gas reserves of 2,170bn. cu. metres in 2008.

Water

The Aswan High Dam, completed in 1970, allows for a perennial irrigation system.

The Mubarak Pumping Station, the world's largest, has been operational since Jan. 2003. Located behind the Aswan High Dam at Lake Nasser, since its inauguration it has been pumping 14·5m. cu. metres of water per day into a 67 km canal to irrigate approximately 540,000 feddans of desert land in Toshka.

Minerals

Production (2003–04, in tonnes): phosphate, 2·08m.; iron ore, 1·98m.; salt, 1·55m.; kaolin, 221,000; aluminium (2002 estimate), 190,000; quartz, 19,000; asbestos (2002 estimate), 2,000.

Agriculture

There were 2·86m. ha. of arable land in 2001 and 0·48m. ha. of permanent crops. In 1996, of the total cultivated area 18·4% was reclaimed desert. Irrigation is vital to agriculture and is being developed by government programmes; it now reaches most cultivated areas and in 2001 covered 3·34m. ha. The Nile provides 85% of the water used in irrigation, some 55,000m. cu. metres annually. There were 102,584 tractors in 2007 and 2,451 harvester-threshers.

In 1994 there were 5,214 agricultural co-operatives. 0·71m. feddan of land had been distributed by 1991 to 0·35m. families under an agrarian reform programme. In 2001, 5·07m. persons were engaged in agriculture. Cotton, sugarcane and rice are subject to government price controls and procurement quotas.

Output (in 1,000 tonnes), 2007: sugarcane, 17,014; tomatoes, 8,695; wheat, 7,379; maize, 6,930; rice, 6,877; sugar beets, 5,458; potatoes, 2,760; melons and watermelons, 2,121; oranges, 2,055; dry onions, 1,756; grapes, 1,485; dates, 1,314; aubergines, 1,160; bananas, 945; sorghum, 844; mandarins, 748; pumpkins and squash, 727; green peppers, 652; seed cotton, 621; cabbage, 618; apples, 558; peaches, 425; garlic, 309; dry broad beans, 305. Egypt is Africa's largest producer of a number of crops, including wheat, rice, tomatoes, potatoes and oranges.

Livestock, 2000: sheep, 4·45m.; goats, 3·30m.; buffaloes, 3·20m.; cattle, 3·18m.; asses, 3·05m.; camels, 120,000; chickens, 88m. Livestock products in 2000 (in 1,000 tonnes): buffalo's milk, 2,079; cow's milk, 1,645; meat, 1,391; eggs, 170. 464,000 tonnes of cheese were produced in 2000, making Egypt the largest cheese producer in Africa.

Forestry

In 2005 forests covered 67,000 ha., representing 0·1% of the total land area. In 2007, 17·44m. cu. metres of roundwood were produced.

Fisheries

The catch in 2005 was 349,553 tonnes, of which 242,100 tonnes were freshwater fish.

INDUSTRY

The largest companies by market capitalization in Egypt in Feb. 2009 were: Telecom Egypt (US$4·5bn.); Orascom Construction Industries (US$4·2bn.); and Orascom Telecom (US$3·2bn.).

Almost all large-scale enterprises are in the public sector, and these account for about two-thirds of total output. The private sector, dominated by food processing and textiles, consists of about 150,000 small and medium businesses, most employing fewer than 50 workers. Industrial production in 2001 showed a growth rate of 0·7% compared to 2000, although manufacturing grew by 4·5%.

Production, in 1,000 tonnes: cement (2001), 26,811; residual fuel oil, 11,273 (2004); distillate fuel oil (2004), 7,922; crude steel (2002), 4,300; petrol (2005), 2,972; sugar (2001–02), 1,555; fertilizers (2002), 1,269; tobacco (1997–98), 595; paper and paperboard (2001), 460; cotton yarn (2000), 164. Motor vehicles (2002), 46,479 units; washing machines (1999), 252,000 units; cigarettes (2000), 53·0bn. units.

Labour

In 2002–03 the labour force was 19·9m. In 2003, 29·0% of employed persons were engaged in agriculture, hunting and forestry; 11·9% in wholesale and retail trade/repair of motor vehicles, motorcycles and personal and household goods; 11·2% in public administration, defence and compulsory social security; and 10·9% in manufacturing. Unemployment was 9·9% in 2003. The high birth rate of the 1980s has meant that there are now some 800,000 new entrants into the job market annually.

INTERNATIONAL TRADE

Foreign debt totalled US$34,114m. in 2005.

Imports and Exports

Imports and exports for calendar years in US$1m.:

	2002	*2003*	*2004*	*2005*	*2006*
Imports (f.o.b.)	12,879	13,189	18,895	23,818	28,984
Exports (f.o.b.)	7,118	8,987	12,320	16,073	20,546

Imports of principal commodities in 2004: machinery and apparatus, 15·9%; vegetable products, 11·4%; metal products, 10·0%; chemicals and chemical products, 9·1%. Exports, 2004: petroleum, 40·0%; finished goods, 27·2%; semi-manufactured goods, 14·1%; raw cotton, 6·3%. Egypt exports less than 20% of its manufactured goods. Much higher exports are deemed necessary to accelerate growth and job creation.

Main import suppliers in 2004: Free zones, 11·8%; USA, 10·3%; Germany, 6·6%; China, 5·1%; Italy, 4·9%. Main export markets, 2004: Italy, 12·5%; Bunkers and ship's stores, 9·8%; USA, 7·5%; Free zones, 5·7%; Spain, 5·5%.

COMMUNICATIONS

Roads

In 2006 there were 99,672 km of roads, of which 81·0% were paved. The road link between Sinai and the mainland across the Suez Canal was opened in 1996. Vehicles in use in 2006 (in 1,000): passenger cars, 2,372 (29 per 1,000 inhabitants in 2005); lorries and vans, 1,463; motorcycles and mopeds, 751; buses and coaches, 79. There were 12,295 fatalities as a result of road accidents in 2007.

Rail

In 2005 there were 5,063 km of state railways (1,435 mm gauge), of which 42 km were electrified. Passenger-km travelled in 2004 came to 40·8bn. and freight tonne-km to 4·2bn.

There are tramway networks in Cairo, Heliopolis and Alexandria, and a metro (63 km) opened in Cairo in 1987.

Civil Aviation

There are international airports at Cairo, Luxor, Alexandria, Hurghada and Sharm El-Sheikh. The national carrier is Egyptair. In 2003 scheduled airline traffic of Egyptian-based carriers flew 63m. km, carrying 4,181,000 passengers (2,916,000 on international flights). In 2003 Cairo handled 8,337,000 passengers and 187,280 tonnes of freight. Sharm El-Sheikh was the second busiest in 2003, with 3,423,000 passengers.

Shipping

In 2004 the merchant marine totalled 1,143,000 GRT, including oil tankers 225,000 GRT. In 2004 vessels totalling 50,931,000 NRT entered ports and vessels totalling 32,077,000 NRT cleared. The leading ports are Adabeya, Alexandria, Damietta, Dekheila, Port Said and Sokhna.

Suez Canal

The Suez Canal was opened for navigation on 17 Nov. 1869 and nationalized in June 1956. By the convention of Constantinople of 29 Oct. 1888, the canal is open to vessels of all nations and is free from blockade, except in time of war. It is 190 km long, connecting the Mediterranean with the Red Sea. It has a maximum depth of 22·5 metres and a maximum width of 365 metres. Vessels of up to 210,000 DWT fully laden are able to pass through the canal.

In 2004, 16,850 vessels (net tonnage, 621m.) went through the canal. In 2004, 521m. tonnes of cargo were transported. Toll revenue in 2004 was US$3,085m. Tolls for tankers were increased by 3% from Feb. 2005.

Telecommunications

In 2008 there were 11,936,000 main (fixed) telephone lines. In the same year mobile phone subscribers numbered 41,273,000 (506·2 per 1,000 persons). In Dec. 2005 the Egyptian government sold 20% of its holding in Telecom Egypt. There were 13,573,000 internet users in 2008 and 3,160,000 PCs were in use in 2006.

Postal Services

There were 5,530 post offices in 2003, or one for every 13,000 persons.

SOCIAL INSTITUTIONS

Justice

The court system comprises: a Court of Cassation with a bench of five judges which constitutes the highest court of appeal in both criminal and civil cases; five Courts of Appeal with three judges; Assize Courts with three judges which deal with all cases of serious crime; Central Tribunals with three judges which deal with ordinary civil and commercial cases; Summary Tribunals presided over by a single judge which hear minor civil disputes and criminal offences. Contempt for religion and what is judged to be a false interpretation of the Koran may result in prison sentences.

The population in penal institutions in Dec. 2006 was 64,378 (87 per 100,000 of national population). The death penalty is in force; Amnesty International reported that there were at least five executions in 2009.

Education

The adult literacy rate in 2005 was 71·4%. Free compulsory education is provided in primary schools (eight years). Secondary and technical education is also free. In 2002–03, 53·9% of girls and 46·1% of boys were enrolled in the primary school system. In 2004–05 there were 5,845 pre-primary schools with 494,334 pupils. In 2004–05 there were 16,369 primary schools with 8,634,115 pupils, 8,757 preparatory schools with 2,889,212 pupils and 2,170 general secondary schools with 1,299,233 pupils. In 2004–05 there were 788,017 students in 841 commercial secondary schools, 1,050,970 in 855 industrial secondary schools and 251,021 in 172 agricultural secondary schools.

Al Azhar institutes educate students who intend enrolling at Al Azhar University, one of the world's oldest universities and Sunni Islam's foremost seat of learning. In 2003–04 there were 6,690 institutes in the Al Azhar system with 1,449,048 pupils.

In 2002–03 there were 12 state universities, the Al Azhar university and five private universities including a French and a German university. There were 2·0m. students enrolled in university and higher education.

Public education expenditure in 2007 was 3·7% of GNI and 12·6% of total government spending.

Health

At 1 Jan. 2002 there were 1,112 hospitals with 80,519 beds. There were 157,000 physicians and 188,000 nurses in 2005. In 2004–05 health expenditure represented 3·4% of GDP.

Welfare

In 2003–04 there were 18·7m. welfare beneficiaries including, in 2002–03, 7·4m. recipients of pensions.

RELIGION

Islam is constitutionally the state religion. In 2001 there were 58·1m. Sunni Muslims (84% of the population); some 9% of the population are Coptic Christians, the remainder being Roman Catholics, Protestants or Greek Orthodox, with a small number of Jews. A Patriarch heads the Coptic Church, and there are 25 metropolitans and bishops in Egypt; four metropolitans for Ethiopia, Jerusalem, Khartoum and Omdurman, and 12 bishops in Ethiopia. The Copts use the Diocletian (or Martyrs') calendar, which begins in AD 284.

CULTURE

World Heritage Sites

There are seven sites under Egyptian jurisdiction that appear on the UNESCO World Heritage List. The first five were entered on the list in 1979. They are: Memphis and its Necropolis (the Pyramid Fields from Giza to Dahshur); Ancient Thebes with its Necropolis; Nubian Monuments from Abu Simbel to Philae; Historic Cairo; and Abu Mena. Memphis was considered one of the Seven Wonders of the World. Ancient Thebes was the capital of Egypt during the period of the middle (c. 2000 BC) and new (c. 1600 BC) kingdoms. The Nubian monuments include the temples of Ramses II in Abu Simbel and the Sanctuary of Isis in Philae. Historic Cairo, founded in the 10th century, became the centre of the Islamic world. Abu Mena was an early Christian holy city.

The Saint Catherine Area was added to the list in 2002. It included Saint Catherine's Monastery, an outstanding example of an Orthodox Christian monastic settlement, dating from the 6th century AD. The area is centred on Mount Sinai (Jebel Musa or Mount Horeb). In 2005 Wadi Al-Hitan (Whale Valley) was inscribed on the list. The site is an area rich in fossil remains in Egypt's western desert.

Broadcasting

The Ministry of Information operates public television and radio services through the Egyptian Radio and Television Union (ERTU). ERTU runs two national terrestrial TV channels and six regional channels. It also operates eight national radio networks and the external services Radio Cairo and Voice of the Arabs. The state monopoly on radio broadcasting ended in 2003 when private music stations were licensed. Egypt has been a leader in regional satellite TV development; in 1998 it became the first Arab nation to launch its own satellite, Nilesat 101, devoted to state-owned TV channel and multimedia transmission. Two private satellite networks, Dream TV and al-Mihwar, have also been broadcasting since 2001. Number of TV receivers (2005), 18·0m. Colour is by SECAM V.

Cinema

There were 146 cinemas in 2003. Attendances totalled 15,602,000.

Press

In 2003 there were 16 dailies with a total average circulation of 1·28m. To set up a newspaper requires permission from the prime minister. In 2002 a total of 976 book titles were published.

Tourism

There were 8·24m. non-resident tourists in 2005; tourist spending in 2005 reached a record US$7·2bn. Tourism is the leading source of foreign revenue and contributes 7% of GDP.

Libraries

In 2003 there were 357 public libraries and 36 national libraries. They held a combined 2,558,000 volumes.

DIPLOMATIC REPRESENTATIVES

Of Egypt in the United Kingdom (26 South Sq, London, W1K 1DWA)
Ambassador: Hatem Seif El-Nasr.

Of the United Kingdom in Egypt (7 Ahmed Ragheb St., Garden City, Cairo)
Ambassador: Dominic Asquith, CMG.

Of Egypt in the USA (3521 International Court, NW, Washington, D.C., 20008)
Ambassador: Sameh Shoukry.

Of the USA in Egypt (8 Kamal el-Din Salah St., Garden City, Cairo)
Ambassador: Margaret M. Scobey.

Of Egypt to the United Nations
Ambassador: Maged Abdelfattah Abdelaziz.

Of Egypt to the European Union
Ambassador: Fatma Elzahraa Etman.

FURTHER READING

CAPMAS, *Statistical Year Book, Arab Republic of Egypt*

Abdel-Khalek, G., *Stabilization and Adjustment in Egypt*. 2001
Baker, Raymond William, *Islam without Fear: Egypt and the New Islamists*. 2006
Daly, M. W. (ed.) *The Cambridge History of Egypt*. 2 vols. 2000
El-Mikawy, Noha and Handoussa, Heba, (eds.) *Institutional Reform and Economic Development in Egypt*. 2004
Hopwood, D., *Egypt: Politics and Society 1945–1990*. 3rd ed. 1992
Ibrahim, Fouad N. and Ibrahim, Barbara, *Egypt: An Economic Geography*. 2001
King, J. W., *Historical Dictionary of Egypt*. 2nd ed. Revised by A. Goldschmidt. 1995
Malek, J. (ed.) *Egypt*. 1993
Raymond, André, *Cairo*. 2001
Rodenbeck, M., *Cairo—the City Victorious*. 1998
Rubin, Barry, *Islamic Fundamentalism in Egyptian Politics*. 2002
Vatikiotis, P. J., *History of Modern Egypt: from Muhammad Ali to Mubarak*. 1991

National Statistical Office: Central Agency for Public Mobilization and Statistics (CAPMAS), Nasr City, Cairo.
Website: http://www.capmas.gov.eg

EL SALVADOR

República de El Salvador
(Republic of El Salvador)

Capital: San Salvador
Population estimate, 2010: 6·19m.
GDP per capita, 2007: (PPP$) 5,804
HDI/world rank: 0·747/106

KEY HISTORICAL EVENTS

Conquered by Spain in 1526, El Salvador remained under Spanish rule until 1821. Thereafter, El Salvador was a member of the Central American Federation comprising the states of El Salvador, Guatemala, Honduras, Nicaragua and Costa Rica until this federation was dissolved in 1839. In 1841 El Salvador declared itself an independent republic.

The country's history has been marked by political violence. The repressive dictatorship of President Maximiliano Hernandez Martínez lasted from 1931 to 1944 when he was deposed as were his successors in 1948 and 1960. The military junta that followed gave way to more secure presidential succession although left-wing guerrilla groups were fighting government troops in the late 1970s. As the guerrillas grew stronger and gained control over a part of the country, the USA sent economic aid and assisted in the training of Salvadorean troops. A new constitution was enacted in Dec. 1983 but the presidential election was boycotted by the main left-wing organization, the Favabundo Marti National Liberation Front (FMLN). Talks between the government and the FMLN in April 1991 led to constitutional reforms in May, envisaging the establishment of civilian control over the armed forces and a reduction in their size. On 16 Jan. 1992 the government and the FMLN signed a peace agreement.

TERRITORY AND POPULATION

El Salvador is bounded in the northwest by Guatemala, northeast and east by Honduras and south by the Pacific Ocean. The area (including 247 sq. km of inland lakes) is 21,040 sq. km. Population (2007 census), 5,744,113 (female 53%), giving a population density of 273 per sq. km. The United Nations population estimate for 2007 was 6,107,000.

The UN gives an estimated population for 2010 of 6·19m.

In 2007, 62·7% of the population were urban. Some 2·5m. Salvadoreans live abroad, mainly in the USA.

The republic is divided into 14 departments. Areas (in sq. km) and 2007 populations:

Department	*Area*	*Population*	*Chief town*	*Population*
Ahuachapán	1,240	319,503	Ahuachapán	63,981
Cabañas	1,104	149,326	Sensuntepeque	15,395
Chalatenango	2,017	192,788	Chalatenango	16,976
Cuscatlán	756	231,480	Cojutepeque	41,072
La Libertad	1,653	660,652	Santa Tecla	108,840
La Paz	1,224	308,087	Zacatecoluca	42,127
La Unión	2,074	238,217	La Unión	18,046
Morazán	1,447	174,406	San Francisco	15,307
San Miguel	2,077	434,003	San Miguel	158,136
San Salvador	886	1,567,156	San Salvador	316,090[1]
San Vicente	1,184	161,645	San Vicente	36,700
Santa Ana	2,023	523,655	Santa Ana	204,340
Sonsonate	1,225	438,960	Sonsonate	49,129
Usulatán	2,130	344,235	Usulután	51,496

[1]Greater San Salvador conurbation (2007), 1,566,629.

The official language is Spanish.

SOCIAL STATISTICS

2004 births, 119,710; deaths, 30,058. Rates (2004, per 1,000 population): births, 17·7; deaths, 4·4. Life expectancy at birth in 2007 was 66·4 years for males and 75·9 years for females. Annual population growth rate, 2000–05, 1·8%. Infant mortality, 2005, 23 per 1,000 live births; fertility rate, 2004, 2·8 births per woman. Abortion is illegal.

CLIMATE

Despite its proximity to the equator, the climate is warm rather than hot, and nights are cool inland. Light rains occur in the dry season from Nov. to April, while the rest of the year has heavy rains, especially on the coastal plain. San Salvador, Jan. 71°F (21·7°C), July 75°F (23·9°C). Annual rainfall 71" (1,775 mm). San Miguel, Jan. 77°F (25°C), July 83°F (28·3°C). Annual rainfall 68" (1,700 mm).

CONSTITUTION AND GOVERNMENT

A new constitution was enacted in Dec. 1983. Executive power is vested in a *President* and *Vice-President* elected for a non-renewable term of five years. There is a *Legislative Assembly* of 84 members elected by universal suffrage and proportional representation: 64 locally and 20 nationally, for a term of three years.

National Anthem

'Saludemos la patria orgullosos' ('We proudly salute the Fatherland'); words by J. J. Cañas, tune by J. Aberle.

GOVERNMENT CHRONOLOGY

Heads of State since 1944. (ARENA = Nationalist Republican Alliance; FMLN = Farabundo Martí National Liberation Front; PCN = National Conciliation Party; PDC = Christian Democratic Party; PRUD = Revolutionary Party of Democratic Unification; n/p = non-party)

Presidents

1944–45	military	Osmín Aguirre y Salinas
1945–48	military	Salvador Castaneda Castro

Military Junta

1948–50		Manuel de Jesús Córdova; Óscar Osorio Hernández; Reinaldo Galindo Pohl; Óscar A.Bolaños; Humberto Costa

Presidents

1950–56	military, PRUD	Óscar Osorio Hernández
1956–60	military, PRUD	José María Lemus López

Junta

1960–61		Miguel Ángel Castillo; César Yanes Urías; Rubén Alonso Rosales; Ricardo Falla Cáceres; Fabio Castillo Figueroa; Rene Fortín Magaña

Civic-Military Directory

1961–62		José Antonio Rodríguez Porth; José Francisco Valiente; Feliciano Avelar; Aníbal Portillo; Julio Adalberto Rivera Carballo; Mariano Castro Morán

Presidents

1962	n/p	Eusebio Rodolfo Cordón Cea
1962–67	military, PCN	Julio Adalberto Rivera Carballo
1967–72	military, PCN	Fidel Sánchez Hernández
1972–77	military, PCN	Arturo Armando Molina Barraza
1977–79	military, PCN	Carlos Humberto Romero Mena

Revolutionary Junta of Government (I)

1979–80		Adolfo Arnaldo Majano Ramos; Jaime Abdul Gutiérrez Avendaño; Román Mayorga Quirós; Guillermo Manuel Ungo Revelo; Mario Antonio Andino

Revolutionary Junta of Government (II)

1980		Adolfo Arnaldo Majano Ramos (military); Jaime Abdul Gutiérrez Avendaño (military); José Antonio Morales Ehrlich (PDC); Héctor Miguel Dada Hirezi (PDC); José Napoleón Duarte Fuentes (PDC); José Ramón Ávalos Navarrete (n/p)

Chairman of the Revolutionary Junta of Government

1980–82	PDC	José Napoleón Duarte Fuentes

Presidents

1982–84	n/p	Álvaro Alfredo Magaña Borja
1984–89	PDC	José Napoleón Duarte Fuentes
1989–94	ARENA	Alfredo Félix Cristiani Burkard
1994–99	ARENA	Armando Calderón Sol
1999–2004	ARENA	Francisco Guillermo Flores Pérez
2004–09	ARENA	Elías Antonio Saca González
2009–	FMLN	Carlos Mauricio Funes Cartagena

RECENT ELECTIONS

Presidential elections were held on 15 March 2009. Mauricio Funes (Farabundo Martí National Liberation Front; FMLN) received 51·3% of votes cast against Rodrigo Ávila (Nationalist Republican Alliance; ARENA) with 48·7%.

In parliamentary elections on 18 Jan. 2009 the FMLN gained 35 of a possible 84 seats in the Legislative Assembly, ahead of the ARENA with 32, the National Conciliation Party (PCN) 11, the Christian Democratic Party (PDC) 5 and the United Democratic Centre (CDU) 1. Turnout was 52·8%.

CURRENT ADMINISTRATION

President: Mauricio Funes; b. 1959 (FMLN; sworn in 1 June 2009).

In March 2010 the cabinet comprised:

Vice-President and Minister of Education: Prof. Salvador Sánchez Cerén.

Minister of Agriculture and Livestock: Manuel Ramón Sevilla Avilés. *Defence:* Col. David Victoriano Munguía Payés. *Economy:* Héctor Miguel Antonio Dada Hirezi. *Environment and Natural Resources:* Hermán Humberto Rosa Chávez. *Finance:* Juan Ramón Carlos Enrique Cáceres Chávez. *Foreign Affairs:* Hugo Roger Martínez Bonilla. *Governance:* Humberto Centeno Najarro. *Health:* Dr María Isabel Rodríguez. *Justice and Public Security:* José Manuel Melgar Henriquez. *Labour and Social Welfare:* Victoria de Avilés. *Public Works:* Manuel Orlando Quinteros Aguilar. *Tourism:* José Napoleón Duarte Durán.

Office of the President (Spanish only):
http://www.presidencia.gob.sv

CURRENT LEADERS

Carlos Mauricio Funes Cartagena

Position
President

Introduction
Mauricio Funes took office in June 2009 at the head of the left-wing Farabundo Martí National Liberation Front (FMLN) administration, ending 20 years of Nationalist Republican Alliance (ARENA) government.

Early Life
Funes was born on 18 Oct. 1959 in San Salvador. Schooled at the Colegio Centroamérica and then the private Colegio Externado San José, in 1975 he went to study literature at the city's José Simón Cañas University.

In 1980 civil war broke out between the authoritarian government and armed leftist organizations, from which the FMLN was created. Roberto Funes, Mauricio's older brother, was killed by police during a student demonstration. Mauricio left his studies and taught literature in San Salvador until becoming a reporter for state television news in 1986. In 1997 he became head of news at Canal 12. However, after several run-ins—notably over criticism of the government after a 2001 earthquake—he left the station in 2005.

His public popularity paved the way for a move into politics, where he established a relationship with the FMLN. In Sept. 2007 the party chose him as its presidential candidate, a month before Funes' son was murdered during a fight in Paris. Funes is the first FMLN leader not to have fought as a guerrilla. At the presidential elections in March 2009 Funes defeated Rodrigo Ávila of the Nationalist Republican Alliance, winning over 50% of the vote.

Career in Office
Amid claims that an FMLN victory would jeopardize US relations and turn the country into a satellite of Venezuela, Funes declared he would maintain a good relationship with Washington and that El Salvador would remain part of the Central American Free Trade Agreement, signed by ARENA in 2006. Meanwhile, he re-established ties with Cuba, cut off since 1961.

He offered ministerial portfolios to supporters from a range of political backgrounds. His primary challenge is to address the troubled economy and reduce the large deficit (aided by loans from the IMF and development banks). He must do so in co-operation with a congress where the opposition hold a small majority.

DEFENCE

There is selective conscription for 18 months. In 2006 defence expenditure totalled US$106m. (US$16 per capita), representing 0·6% of GDP.

Army

Strength (2007): 13,850 (4,000 conscripts). The National Civilian Police numbers about 12,000.

Navy
There is a small coastguard force with 860 (2007) personnel including one company of Naval Infantry numbering 160 and one company of Commandos numbering 90.

Air Force
Estimated strength (2007): 950 personnel (200 conscripts). There are some 15 combat capable aircraft and 33 helicopters.

INTERNATIONAL RELATIONS
El Salvador is a member of the UN, World Bank, IMF and several other UN specialized agencies, WTO, IOM, ACS, CACM, Inter-American Development Bank and OAS.

ECONOMY
Agriculture accounted for 10·9% of GDP in 2006, industry 29·4% and services 59·7%.

Overview
Economic performance in the early- to mid-2000s was the result of wide-ranging reforms initiated in the early 1990s, which called for more open trade, and changes to pension and fiscal policies. In 2001 the US dollar replaced the *colón* as the official currency. In March 2006 El Salvador was the first country to enter into the Central America–Dominican Republic–United States Free Trade Agreement (CAFTA–DR) with the USA, followed by Honduras, Nicaragua, Guatemala, the Dominican Republic and Costa Rica.

Key industries include coffee and textiles, making the economy vulnerable to external factors including the weather and variations in the international market. Remittances contributed 18% of GDP in 2007. 47% of exports go to the USA and remittance inflows from the USA are the largest in the region.

After achieving its highest growth rates in a decade in 2007, El Salvador was hit hard by the global financial crisis. Remittances decreased by nearly 10% while GDP contracted by 2·5% in 2009. A US$250m. assistance package to tackle the effects of the financial crisis was announced by the World Bank in July 2009.

Currency
The *dollar* (USD) replaced the *colón* as the legal currency of El Salvador in 2003. Inflation was 4·6% in 2007 and 7·3% in 2008. Foreign exchange reserves were US$1,741m. and gold reserves 326,000 troy oz in May 2005.

Budget
Budgetary central government revenue totalled US$2,711·9m. in 2006 and expenditure US$3,010·7m.

VAT is 13%.

Performance
Real GDP growth was 4·7% in 2007 and 2·5% in 2008. Total GDP in 2008 was US$22·1bn.

Banking and Finance
The bank of issue is the Central Reserve Bank (*President*, Carlos Acevedo), formed in 1934 and nationalized in 1961. There are 15 commercial banks (two foreign). Individual private holdings may not exceed 5% of the total equity.

There is a stock exchange in San Salvador, founded in 1992.

Weights and Measures
The metric system is standard with US gallons.

ENERGY AND NATURAL RESOURCES

Environment
El Salvador's carbon dioxide emissions from the consumption and flaring of fossil fuels were the equivalent of 0·9 tonnes per capita in 2008.

Electricity
Installed capacity in 2004 was 1,187,000 kW, of which 442,000 kW hydro-electric. Production in 2004 was 4·56bn. kWh; consumption per capita was 732 kWh in 2004.

Minerals
El Salvador has few mineral resources. In 2002 an estimated 3·2m. tonnes of limestone were produced. Annual marine salt production averages 30,000 tonnes.

Agriculture
27% of the land surface is given over to arable farming. There were about 682,000 ha. of arable land in 2007 and 237,000 ha. of permanent crops. In 2007 the agricultural population was an estimated 1,696,000, of which about 608,000 were economically active. Large landholdings have been progressively expropriated and redistributed in accordance with legislation initiated in 1980. Since the mid-19th century El Salvador's economy has been dominated by coffee. Output, in 1,000 tonnes (2003): sugarcane, 4,532; maize, 618; sorghum, 144; coffee, 92; melons and watermelons, 90; dry beans, 78; bananas, 65. Livestock (2003): 1·0m. cattle, 153,000 pigs, 96,000 horses, 8m. chickens.

Forestry
Forest area was 298,000 ha. (14·4% of the land area) in 2005. Balsam trees abound: El Salvador is the world's principal source of this medicinal gum. In 2007, 4·89m. cu. metres of roundwood were cut.

Fisheries
The catch in 2005 was 41,114 tonnes (95% from marine waters).

INDUSTRY
Production in 1,000 tonnes (2004 unless otherwise indicated): cement (2001), 1,174; residual fuel oil, 543; sugar (2002), 476; distillate fuel oil, 199; petrol, 143; paper and paperboard (2001), 56. Traditional industries include food processing and textiles.

Labour
Out of 2,412,800 people in employment in 2002, 688,500 were in wholesale and retail trade/repair of motor vehicles, motorcycles and personal and household goods/hotels and restaurants; 458,400 in agriculture, forestry and hunting; 434,100 in manufacturing; and 155,400 in health and social work, and other community, social and personal service activities. There were 160,200 unemployed persons, or 6·2% of the workforce, in 2002.

INTERNATIONAL TRADE
In 2004 El Salvador signed the Central America-Dominican Republic-United States Free Trade Agreement (CAFTA-DR), along with Costa Rica, the Dominican Republic, Guatemala, Honduras, Nicaragua and the USA. The agreement entered into force for El Salvador on March 1 2006. External debt was US$7,088m. in 2005.

Imports and Exports
Imports and exports in calendar years (in US$1m.):

	2000	*2001*	*2002*	*2003*	*2004*
Imports f.o.b.	4,702·8	4,824·1	4,884·7	5,428·0	5,948·8
Exports f.o.b.	2,963·2	2,891·6	3,019·7	3,152·6	3,329·6

Principal import suppliers, 2004: USA, 46·3%; Guatemala, 8·1%; Costa Rica, 2·8%; Honduras, 2·5%. Principal export markets, 2004: USA, 65·4%; Guatemala, 11·7%; Honduras, 6·3%; Nicaragua, 3·9%. Main import commodities are chemicals and chemical products, transport equipment, and food and beverages; main export commodities are coffee, paper and paper products, and clothing.

COMMUNICATIONS

Roads

In 2002 there were an estimated 10,029 km of roads, including 327 km of motorways. Vehicles in use in 2002: passenger cars, 112,700; trucks and vans, 234,500. There were 656 fatalities in road accidents in 1997.

Rail

There are 555 km of 914 mm gauge railway. The railway was closed from 2002–06 but a limited service resumed in 2007 and continues to operate.

Civil Aviation

The international airport is El Salvador International in San Salvador. The national carrier is Taca International Airlines. In 2003 scheduled airline traffic of El Salvador-based carriers flew 34m. km, carrying 2,271,000 passengers (2,182,000 on international flights). It flies to various destinations in the USA, Mexico and all Central American countries. In 2001 El Salvador International handled 1,294,864 passengers on international flights and 26,276 tonnes of international freight.

Shipping

The main ports are Acajutla and Cutuco. Merchant shipping totalled 6,000 GRT in 2002. In 2003 vessels totalling 6,983,000 NRT entered ports and vessels totalling 694,000 NRT cleared.

Telecommunications

The telephone system has been privatized and is owned by two international telephone companies. In 2005 there were 3,383,200 telephone subscribers (491·7 per 1,000 inhabitants), including 2,411,800 mobile phone subscribers. There were 350,000 PCs in use in 2005 and 637,100 internet users.

Postal Services

In 2003 there were 313 post offices.

SOCIAL INSTITUTIONS

Justice

Justice is administered by the Supreme Court (six members appointed for three-year terms by the Legislative Assembly and six by bar associations), courts of first and second instance, and minor tribunals. Following the disbanding of security forces in Jan. 1992 a new National Civilian Police Force was created which numbered 12,000 by 2002. The population in penal institutions in July 2002 was 10,278 (158 per 100,000 of national population).

El Salvador has among the highest annual murder rates in the world, at 55 per 100,000 people (3,812 homicides in total in 2005).

Education

The adult literacy rate in 2004 was 80·6%. Education, run by the state, is free and compulsory. In 2007 there were 229,539 children in nursery schools, 1,075,041 in primary schools and 536,017 in secondary schools. The University of El Salvador (Universidad de El Salvador), founded in 1841, is the country's oldest and largest public university. There are also several private universities. In 2007 there were 132,246 students and 8,370 academic staff in tertiary education.

In 2007 public expenditure on education came to 3·1% of GNI and 13·1% of total government spending.

Health

In 2003 there were 30 hospitals with nine beds per 10,000 inhabitants. There were 8,171 physicians, 3,573 dentists and 11,777 nurses in 2002.

Welfare

There are old age, disability and survivors' pensions and sickness, maternity and work injury benefits. The official retirement age is 55 years (women) and 60 years (men). The minimum monthly old age pension is US$143·64. Maternity benefit is equal to 75% of average monthly earnings for up to 12 weeks.

RELIGION

In 2001 there were 4,880,000 Roman Catholics. Under the 1962 constitution, churches are exempted from the property tax; the Catholic Church is recognized as a legal person, and other churches are entitled to secure similar recognition. There is an archbishop in San Salvador and bishops at Santa Ana, San Miguel, San Vicente, Santiago de María, Usulután, Sonsonate and Zacatecoluca. There were about 1,070,000 Protestants in 2001 and 290,000 followers of other religions.

CULTURE

World Heritage Sites

El Salvador has one site on the UNESCO World Heritage List: the Joya de Cerén Archaeological Site (1993), a pre-Hispanic farming community preserved under volcanic ash.

Broadcasting

Radio and television networks are predominantly under commercial operation. Cable television is widely available and carries international channels. There were 1·56m. television sets in 2005 (colour by NTSC).

Press

In 2005 there were five daily newspapers with a combined circulation of 250,000.

Tourism

There were 1,154,000 foreign tourists in 2005, spending US$838m.

DIPLOMATIC REPRESENTATIVES

Of El Salvador in the United Kingdom (8 Dorset Sq., London, NW1 6PU)
Ambassador: Dr Roberto Ricardo Ávila Avilez.

Of the United Kingdom in El Salvador (embassy in San Salvador closed in July 2003)
Ambassador: Julie Chappell, OBE (resides in Guatemala City).

Of El Salvador in the USA (1400 16th St., NW, Suite 100, Washington, D.C., 20036)
Ambassador: Vacant.
Chargé d'Affaires a.i.: Francisco Altschul.

Of the USA in El Salvador (Urbanización Santa Elena, Antiguo Cuscatlán, San Salvador)
Ambassador: Vacant.
Chargé d'Affaires a.i.: Robert Blau.

Of El Salvador to the United Nations
Ambassador: Carmen María Gallardo Hernández.

Of El Salvador to the European Union
Ambassador: Héctor Gonzalez Urrutia.

FURTHER READING

Lauria-Santiago, Aldo and Binford, Leigh, (eds.) *Landscapes of Struggle: Politics, Society and Community in El Salvador.* 2004
Ladutke, Lawrence Michael, *Freedom of Expression in El Salvador: The Struggle for Human Rights and Democracy.* 2004
Tilley, Virginia Q., *Seeing Indians: A Study of Race, Nation, and Power in El Salvador.* 2005

National Statistical Office: Dirección General de Estadística y Censos, Av. Juan Bertis No. 79, Ciudad Delgado, San Salvador.
Website (Spanish only): http://www.digestyc.gob.sv

EQUATORIAL GUINEA

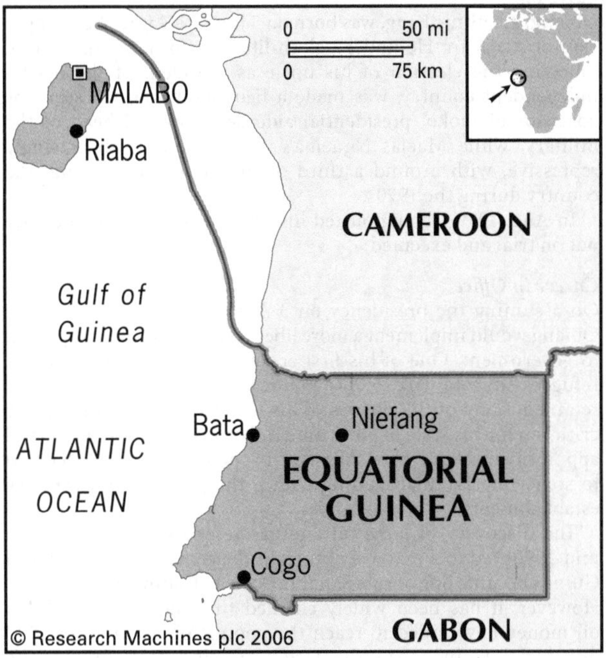

República de Guinea Ecuatorial
(Republic of Equatorial Guinea)

Capital: Malabo
Population estimate, 2010: 693,000
GDP per capita, 2007: (PPP$) 30,627
HDI/world rank: 0·719/118

KEY HISTORICAL EVENTS

Equatorial Guinea consists of the island of Bioko, for centuries called Fernando Pó; other smaller islands and the mainland territory of Rio Muni. Fernando Pó was named after the Portuguese navigator Fernão do Pó. The island was then ruled for three centuries by Portugal until 1778 when it was ceded to Spain. For some decades after taking possession of Fernando Pó, Spain did not have a strong presence. Britain was permitted to establish a naval base at Clarence (later Santa Isabel), which was central to the suppression of slave trading over a wide area. Spain asserted its rule from the 1840s. On Fernando Pó the Spanish grew cocoa on European-owned plantations using imported African labour. This traffic led to an international scandal in 1930 when Liberians were found to be held in virtual slavery. Later many Nigerians were employed, often in poor conditions.

African nationalist movements began in the 1950s. Internal self-government was granted in 1963. In 1969 Spain suspended the constitution but then, in 1969, agreed to a referendum, which supported independence. The two parts of Equatorial Guinea were united under Macías Nguema who established single-party rule. Up to a third of the population was killed or else left the country. Macías was declared President-for-Life in July 1972 but was overthrown by a military coup on 3 Aug. 1979.

A constitution approved by a referendum on 3 Aug. 1982 restored some institutions but a Supreme Military Council remained the sole political body until constitutional rule was resumed on 12 Oct. 1982.

TERRITORY AND POPULATION

The mainland part of Equatorial Guinea is bounded in the north by Cameroon, east and south by Gabon, and west by the Gulf of Guinea, in which lie the islands of Bioko (formerly Macías Nguema, formerly Fernando Pó) and Annobón (called Pagalu from 1973 to 1979). The total area is 28,051 sq. km (10,831 sq. miles) and the population at the 1994 census was 406,151. Another 110,000 are estimated to remain in exile abroad.

The UN gives an estimated population for 2010 of 693,000; density, 25 per sq. km.

In 2005, 61·1% of the population were rural.

The seven provinces are grouped into two regions—Continental (C), chief town Bata; and Insular (I), chief town Malabo—with areas and populations as follows:

	Sq. km	*Census 1994 (estimate)*	*Chief town*
Annobón (I)	17	2,800	San Antonio de Palea
Bioko Norte (I)	776	75,100	Malabo
Bioko Sur (I)	1,241	12,600	Luba
Centro Sur (C)	9,931	60,300	Evinayong
Kié-Ntem (C)	3,943	92,800	Ebebiyin
Litoral (C)	6,665[1]	100,000	Bata
Wele-Nzas (C)	5,478	62,500	Mongomo

[1]Including the adjacent islets of Corisco, Elobey Grande and Elobey Chico (17 sq. km).

In 2003 the capital, Malabo, had an estimated population of 92,900.

The main ethnic group on the mainland is the Fang, which comprises 85% of the total population; there are several minority groups along the coast and adjacent islets. On Bioko the indigenous inhabitants (Bubis) constitute 60% of the population there, the balance being mainly Fang and coast people. On Annobón the indigenous inhabitants are the descendants of Portuguese slaves and still speak a Portuguese patois. The official languages are French, Portuguese and Spanish.

SOCIAL STATISTICS

2000 estimates: births, 19,700; deaths, 6,900. Rates (2000 estimates, per 1,000 population); birth, 43·2; death, 15·1. Life expectancy (2007): male, 48·7 years; female, 51·1. Annual population growth rate, 1992–2002, 2·6%. Infant mortality, 2005, 123 per 1,000 live births; fertility rate, 2004, 5·9 births per woman.

CLIMATE

The climate is equatorial, with alternate wet and dry seasons. In Rio Muni, the wet season lasts from Dec. to Feb.

CONSTITUTION AND GOVERNMENT

A Constitution was approved in a plebiscite in Aug. 1982 by 95% of the votes cast and was amended in Jan. 1995. It provided for an 11-member Council of State, and for a 41-member House of Representatives of the People. The President presides over a Council of Ministers.

On 12 Oct. 1987 a single new political party was formed as the *Partido Democrático de Guinea Ecuatorial.*

A referendum on 17 Nov. 1991 approved the institution of multi-party democracy, and a law to this effect was passed in Jan. 1992. The electorate is restricted to citizens who have resided in Equatorial Guinea for at least ten years. A parliament created as a result, the *Cámara de Representantes del Pueblo* (*House of People's Representatives*), has 100 seats, with members elected for a five-year term by proportional representation in multi-member constituencies.

National Anthem

'Caminemos pisando las sendas' ('Let us journey treading the pathways'); words by A. N. Miyongo, tune anonymous.

RECENT ELECTIONS

At parliamentary elections on 4 May 2008, boycotted by most opposition parties, the ruling Democratic Party of Equatorial Guinea (PDGE) won 89 of the 100 seats and its allies (the so-called 'democratic opposition') won 10. The Convergence for Social Democracy (CPDS) won the remaining seat.

Presidential elections were held on 29 Nov. 2009. President Nguema Mbasogo was re-elected with 95·4% of votes cast. His main rival, opposition candidate Plácido Micó Abogo of the CPDS, received 3·6% but refused to accept the result, citing fraud. Turnout was 93·5%.

CURRENT ADMINISTRATION

President of the Supreme Military Council: Brig.-Gen. Teodoro Obiang Nguema Mbasogo; b. 1943 (PDGE; in office since 1979, most recently re-elected in 2009).

In March 2010 the government comprised:

Prime Minister: Ignacio Milam Tang; b. 1940 (ind.; sworn in 8 July 2008).

First Deputy Prime Minister, in Charge of Social and Human Rights: Salomon Nguema Owono. *Second Deputy Prime Minister, in Charge of Economic and Financial Affairs:* Aniceto Ebiaca Moete. *Third Deputy Prime Minister, in Charge of Political and Democracy Affairs:* Demetrio Elo Ndong Nsefumu.

Minister of National Defence: Gen. Antonio Mba Nguema. *National Security:* Nicolas Obama Nchama. *Foreign Affairs and International Co-operation:* Micha Ondo Bilé. *Agriculture and Forestry:* Teodoro Nguema Obiang Mangue. *Interior and Local Corporations:* Clemente Engonga Nguema Onguene. *Mines, Industry and Energy:* Marcelino Owono Edu. *Transport, Technology, Posts and Communications:* Vicente Ehate Tomi. *Infrastructure and Urban Planning:* Vacant. *Minister in Charge of Relations with Parliament:* Angel Masie Mibuy. *Minister in Charge of Administrative Co-ordination:* Mauricio Bokung Asumu. *Regional Integration:* Baltasar Engonga Edjo. *Justice, Religion and Penitentiary Institutions:* Salvador Ondo Nkumu. *Economy and Commerce:* Pedro Ondo Nguema. *Planning, Economic Development and Public Investment:* Jose Ela Oyana. *Finance and Budget:* Melchor Esono Edjo. *Education, Science and Sports:* Filiberto Ntutunu Nguema. *Health and Social Welfare:* Francisco Obama. *Labour and Social Security:* Estanislao Don Malavo. *Social Affairs and Women's Development:* Eulalia Envo Bela. *Environment and Fisheries:* Anastasio Asumu Mum Muñoz. *Information, Culture, Tourism and Government Spokesperson:* Jeronimo Osa Osa Ecoro. *Public Administration and Administrative Planning:* Tomas Esono Ava. *Minister at the Presidency in Charge of Missions:* Alejandro Evuna Owono Asangono. *Minister at the Presidency in Charge of the Civilian Cabinet:* Braulio Ncogo Abegue.

Government Website: http://guinea-equatorial.com

CURRENT LEADERS

Brig.-Gen. Teodoro Obiang Nguema Mbasogo

Position

President

Introduction

Brig.-Gen. Teodoro Obiang Nguema Mbasogo became president of Equatorial Guinea in Aug. 1979, having led a coup d'état against the dictatorial regime of his uncle, Macías Nguema. After introducing some liberalizing reforms, Obiang himself adopted an authoritarian form of government, leading to widespread allegations of civil rights abuses and electoral fraud. The discovery of major fossil fuel reserves in the mid-1990s has created an economic boom, although Obiang has been criticized for the government's lack of transparency in administering this new wealth.

Early Life

Obiang, an ethnic Fang, was born on 5 June 1942 into the Esangui clan of Acoacán. He undertook military training in Spain and, following the election of his uncle as president of the newly-independent country, was made a lieutenant. He had stints as governor of Bioko, presidential aide-de-camp and head of the military, while Macías Nguema's regime became increasingly repressive, with around a third of the population leaving the country during the 1970s.

In Aug. 1979 Obiang ousted his uncle, who was subsequently put on trial and executed.

Career in Office

On assuming the presidency on 3 Aug. 1979 it was hoped that Obiang would implement a more liberal and democratic approach to government. One of his first acts was to call an amnesty on refugees and to free 5,000 political prisoners. However, he retained many of the powers of his uncle and soon came under criticism for his style of government. Local and national political appointments have been blighted by nepotism, which has led to some interfamilial feuding within the political and military establishments.

The discovery of large oil and gas reserves off Bioko in the mid-1990s led to a massive upturn in the economy as Equatorial Guinea became one of sub-Saharan Africa's leading oil exporters. However, it has been widely claimed that the benefits of this oil money have failed to reach the population at large. In 1997 Equatorial Guinea had the fastest-growing economy on the continent (although the rate of growth subsequently dropped). The IMF and the World Bank demanded increased transparency concerning government oil revenues, which Obiang claimed were a state secret, and warned against an over-reliance on the oil reserves (although they are not expected to start running out until 2012 at the earliest). It was also reported that the US senate was investigating several hundred million dollars worth of deposits in US accounts belonging to members of Obiang's family.

The country's first multi-party elections in 1993 were won by Obiang's Democratic Party of Equatorial Guinea (PDGE), but boycotted by most of the opposition parties. Then, in the presidential election in Feb. 1996, he was returned with a reported 99% of the vote. At the presidential election of Dec. 2002 he again claimed over 97% of the vote and opposition parties accused the government of vote rigging. A government-in-exile formed by Obiang's opponents was established in Spain. Obiang's treatment of opposition politicians has received condemnation from, among others, the EU and Amnesty International and the president has been accused of using torture on political prisoners. There have also been high-profile public trials such as that in 2002 which resulted in the one-year imprisonment of opposition leader Fabian Nseu Guema for insulting Obiang on a website. In Nov. 2009 Obiang was again re-elected overwhelmingly as president in polling that was denounced by opposition figures as fraudulent and manipulated.

In foreign policy, Obiang has been in dispute with Gabon over the latter's long-term occupation of Mbagne, an island in the Bay of Corisco thought to contain further significant oil supplies. In 2000 he called on the people of Equatorial Guinea to be permanently vigilant against unspecified neighbouring countries accused of attempting to destabilize the nation. In 2002 he signed an agreement with Nigeria for the development of the Zafiro-Ekanga oil field along their joint maritime border.

In 2004 a plane flying from Zimbabwe was intercepted after Obiang announced it was carrying mercenaries preparing a coup against him. Those accused of involvement included Mark Thatcher (son of former British prime minister Margaret

Thatcher), who was arrested in South Africa and later fined and given a suspended prison term, and British mercenary Simon Mann, arrested in Zimbabwe. Obiang claimed that the arrests were evidence of a plot by the secret services of the USA, UK and Spain to overthrow him. In Feb. 2008 Mann was extradited from Zimbabwe to stand trial for his alleged role in the coup and in July was sentenced to 34 years' imprisonment. However, he was granted a presidential pardon in Nov. 2009 on humanitarian grounds.

The PDGE retained its dominance in parliamentary elections in April 2004, but most opposition parties boycotted the poll and foreign observers claimed that there were serious irregularities. In Aug. 2006 Obiang accepted the resignation of Abia Biteo's government, having accused it of corruption and poor leadership. Ricardo Mangue Obama Nfubea was appointed as the new prime minister, but he also submitted the resignation of his government in July 2008 after further accusations by Obiang of corruption and mismanagement and was replaced as prime minister by Ignacio Milam Tang.

DEFENCE

In 2006 defence expenditure totalled US$8m. (US$14 per capita), representing 0·1% of GDP.

Army

The Army consists of three infantry battalions with (2007) 1,100 personnel. There is also a paramilitary Guardia Civil.

Navy

A small force, numbering an estimated 120 in 2007 and based at Malabo and Bata, operates five patrol and coastal combatants.

Air Force

There are no combat capable aircraft or armed helicopters. Personnel (2007), 100.

INTERNATIONAL RELATIONS

Equatorial Guinea is a member of the UN, World Bank, IMF and several other UN specialized agencies, International Organization of the Francophonie, African Development Bank, African Union, and is an ACP member state of the ACP-EU relationship.

ECONOMY

Agriculture accounted for 2% of GDP in 2008, industry 96% (the highest percentage of any country) and services 2%.

Overview

Equatorial Guinea has been one of the world's fastest growing economies since the discovery of oil reserves in the 1990s. Oil revenues grew from US$3m. in 1993 to US$3·3bn. in 2006, making it the third largest oil producer in Sub-Saharan Africa (behind Nigeria and Angola). GDP growth performance has been exceptional since the late 1990s, although a recent slowdown in hydrocarbon production, which accounted for over 80% of GDP in 2005, has resulted in reduced GDP growth. In 2005 GDP growth was 6·9%, down from a high of 71·2% in 1997. Non-oil GDP growth has remained positive, with large public infrastructure investment and private housing construction the main drivers of growth. The oil boom has generated inflationary pressures, averaging 6% since the early 2000s, but public investment in infrastructure projects has helped offset these pressures.

Despite per capita income rising to that of middle-income countries, living standards remain poor. Poverty remains widespread, life expectancy low and access to safe water among the worst in the world. The economy is equipped to make socio-economic progress but a stronger institutional capacity to direct resources to priority areas is needed.

Currency

On 2 Jan. 1985 the country joined the Franc Zone and the *ekpwele* was replaced by the *franc CFA* (XAF) which now has a parity value of 655·957 francs CFA to one euro. Foreign exchange reserves were US$1,416m. in June 2005 and total money supply was 209,768m. francs CFA. Inflation was 2·8% in 2007 and 5·9% in 2008.

Budget

In 2005 revenue was 1,529bn. francs CFA and expenditure 698bn. francs CFA. Oil revenue accounted for 94·3% of revenues in 2005; capital expenditure accounted for 63·9% of total expenditures in 2005.

Performance

Equatorial Guinea has been one of the world's fastest-growing economies in recent years thanks to the rapid expansion of its oil sector. The economy grew by a record 71·2% in 1997. More recently this strong performance has continued with growth in both 2007 and 2008 among the highest in the world, at 21·4% and 11·3% respectively.

Banking and Finance

The Banque des États de l'Afrique Centrale (*Governor*, Philibert Andzembe) became the bank of issue in Jan. 1985. There are two commercial banks (Caisse Commune d'Épargne et d'Investissement Guinée Equatoriale; Société Générale des Banques GE) and two development banks.

ENERGY AND NATURAL RESOURCES

Environment

Carbon dioxide emissions from the consumption and flaring of fossil fuels in 2008 were the equivalent of 7·4 tonnes per capita.

Electricity

There are two hydro-electric plants. Installed capacity was an estimated 13,000 kW in 2004. Production was around 27m. kWh in 2004; consumption per capita in 2004 was approximately 52 kWh.

Oil and Gas

Oil production started in 1992 and in 2005 totalled 17·6m. tonnes, up from 5·8m. tonnes in 2000. There were proven reserves of 1·8bn. bbls in 2005. Mobil is the biggest operator in the country but other US-based oil companies are investing heavily. Since oil in commercial quantities was discovered in 1995 Equatorial Guinea has attracted more than US$12bn. in foreign direct investment.

Natural gas reserves were 37bn. cu. metres in 2007.

Minerals

There is some small-scale alluvial gold production.

Agriculture

There were an estimated 130,000 ha. of arable land in 2007 and 90,000 ha. of permanent crops. Subsistence farming predominates. In 2007 the agricultural population was approximately 425,000 of which about 164,000 were economically active. The major crops (estimated production, 2003, in 1,000 tonnes) are: cassava, 45; sweet potatoes, 36; plantains, 31; bananas, 20; coconuts, 6; cocoa beans, 4; coffee, 4; palm oil, 4. Plantations in the hinterland have been abandoned by their Spanish former owners and, except for cocoa and coffee, commercial agriculture is in serious difficulties. Livestock, 2003 estimates: cattle, 5,000; goats, 9,000; pigs, 6,000; sheep, 38,000.

Forestry

In 2005 forests covered 1·63m. ha., or 58·2% of the total land area. Timber production in 2007 totalled 606,000 cu. metres.

Fisheries

The total catch in 2005 was estimated to be 3,500 tonnes (71% from sea fishing). Tuna and shellfish are caught.

INDUSTRY

The once-flourishing light industry collapsed under the Macías regime. Oil production is now the major activity. Production of veneer sheets, 2001, 15,000 cu. metres. Food processing is also being developed.

Labour

In 1996 the labour force was 171,000 (65% males). The wage-earning non-agricultural workforce is small.

INTERNATIONAL TRADE

Foreign debt was US$260m. in 2002.

Imports and Exports

In 2004 imports were 1,442·9bn. francs CFA and exports 2,479·3bn. francs CFA.

Main import suppliers, 2003: USA, 30·6%; UK, 16·0%; France, 15·0%; Côte d'Ivoire, 11·9%; Spain, 8·2%. Main export markets, 2003: USA, 33·2%; Spain, 25·4%; China, 14·2%; Canada, 12·7%; Italy, 6·3%. Principal import commodities are machinery and transport equipment, and petroleum and petroleum products; principal export commodities are petroleum, cocoa and timber.

COMMUNICATIONS

Roads

In 2002 the road network covered 2,880 km. Most roads are in a state of disrepair. There were 4,700 passenger cars (9·6 per 1,000 inhabitants) and 3,600 vans and trucks in 2002.

Civil Aviation

There is an international airport at Malabo. There were international flights in 2003 to Cotonou, Douala, Libreville, Madrid, Yaoundé and Zürich. In 1998 Malabo handled 54,000 passengers.

Shipping

Bata is the main port, handling mainly timber. The other ports are Luba, formerly San Carlos, in Bioko, and Malabo, Evinayong and Mbini on the mainland. Ocean-going shipping totalled 29,000 GRT in 2002.

Telecommunications

In 2005 there were 106,900 telephone subscribers (212·5 for every 1,000 persons), with 96,900 mobile phone subscribers. The number of PCs in use was 7,000 (13·8 per 1,000 persons) in 2004 and there were 5,000 internet users.

SOCIAL INSTITUTIONS

Justice

The Constitution guarantees an independent judiciary. The Supreme Tribunal, the highest court of appeal, is located at Malabo. There are Courts of First Instance and Courts of Appeal at Malabo and Bata. The death penalty is in force; there were three reported executions in 2007 but none in 2008.

Education

In 2000–01 there were 596 teachers for 16,654 children in pre-primary schools; 1,754 teachers for 72,791 pupils in primary schools; and (1999–2000) 20,679 secondary pupils with 836 teachers. In 1993 there were 2 teacher training colleges, 2 post-secondary vocational schools and 1 agricultural institute. Adult literacy was 84·2% in 2003 (male, 92·1%; female, 76·4%). The rate for males is second only to Zimbabwe among African countries. In 2003 public expenditure on education came to 1·3% of GNP.

Health

In 1990 there were 29 hospital beds per 10,000 inhabitants. There were 105 physicians, four dentists, 169 nurses and nine midwives in 1996.

RELIGION

Christianity was proscribed under President Macías but reinstated in 1979. In 2001 there were 390,000 Roman Catholics with the remainder of the population followers of other religions.

CULTURE

Broadcasting

The state-controlled Radio Nacional de Guinea Ecuatorial and Televisión Nacional are the main broadcasters. Radio France Internationale (RFI) is available in the capital. There are some commercial radio stations. In 2002 there were 55,000 TV receivers (colour by SECAM).

Press

There are no daily newspapers, although there are a number of periodicals that are published at varying degrees of regularity. There are no printing presses in the country, and international newspapers and magazines may not be distributed without government permission.

Tourism

Foreign tourists brought in revenue of US$14m. in 2001.

DIPLOMATIC REPRESENTATIVES

Of Equatorial Guinea in the United Kingdom (13 Park Place, London, SW1A 1LP)
Ambassador: Agustin Nze Nfumu.

Of the United Kingdom in Equatorial Guinea
Ambassador: Robert Dewar, CMG (resides in Abuja, Nigeria).

Of Equatorial Guinea in the USA (2020 16th St., NW, Washington, D.C., 20009)
Ambassador: Purificación Angue Ondo.

Of the USA in Equatorial Guinea (Carretera de Aeropuerto, K-3 El Paraiso, Apt 95, Malabo)
Ambassador: Alberto M. Fernandez.

Of Equatorial Guinea to the United Nations
Ambassador: Anatolio Ndong Mba.

Of Equatorial Guinea to the European Union
Ambassador: Victorino Nka Obiang Maye.

FURTHER READING

Fegley, Randall, *Equatorial Guinea, an African Tragedy.* 1989
Liniger-Goumaz, M., *Guinea Ecuatorial: Bibliografía General.* 1974–91.—*Small is Not Always Beautiful: The Story of Equatorial Guinea.* 1988.—*Historical Dictionary of Equatorial Guinea.* 2000
Molino, A. M. del, *La Ciudad de Clarence.* 1994

National Statistical Office: Dirección General de Estadísticas y Cuentas Nacionales.
Website (Spanish only): http://www.dgecnstat-ge.org

ERITREA

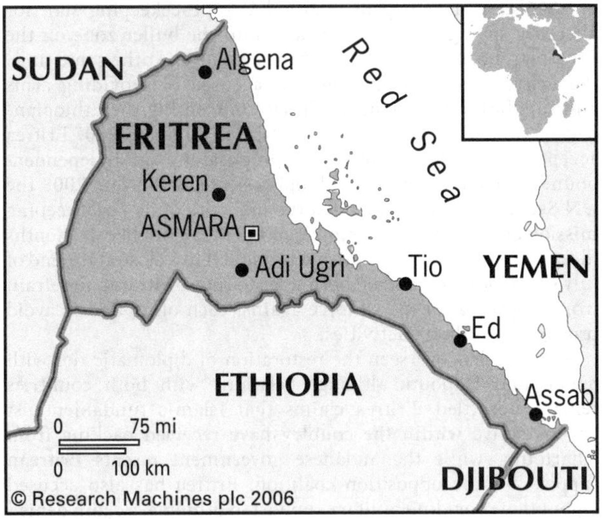

Hagere Ertra
(State of Eritrea)

Capital: Asmara
Population estimate, 2010: 5·22m.
GDP per capita, 2007: (PPP$) 626
HDI/world rank: 0·472/165

KEY HISTORICAL EVENTS

Italy was the colonial ruler from 1890 until 1941 when Eritrea fell to British forces. A British protectorate ended in 1952 when the UN sanctioned federation with Ethiopia. In 1962 Ethiopia became a unitary state and Eritrea was incorporated as a province. Eritreans began an armed struggle for independence under the leadership of the Eritrean People's Liberation Front (EPLF) which culminated successfully in the capture of Asmara on 24 May 1991. Thereafter the EPLF maintained a *de facto* independent administration recognized by the Ethiopian government. Sovereignty was proclaimed on 24 May 1993. In 1999 fighting broke out along the border with Ethiopia, following a series of skirmishes the previous year. After the failure of international mediation, the 13-month long-truce between Eritrea and Ethiopia ended in May 2000. Ethiopia launched a major offensive in the ongoing war over territorial disputes and claimed victory. In June both sides agreed to an Organization of African Unity peace deal to end the two-year border war. Dec. 2000 saw the establishment of commissions to oversee border demarcation, refugee issues and prisoner exchanges.

In 2003 the border commission's award of the disputed town of Badame to Eritrea was rejected by Ethiopia, leading to a standoff between the two nations. Eritrea's relations with the UN deteriorated until UN helicopters were banned from Eritrean airspace in Nov. 2005. The following month Eritrea expelled all North American and European UN representatives, with the UN threatening sanctions against both countries unless they adhered to the 2000 peace plan. Meanwhile, the international commission in The Hague judged that Eritrea's 1998 attacks on Ethiopia breached international law.

Eritrean relations with the UN deteriorated further throughout 2006, with five UN staff expelled on charges of spying in Sept. In Oct. 2006 Kofi Annan, the then UN secretary general, exhorted Eritrea to withdraw its troops from a buffer zone on the Ethiopian border.

TERRITORY AND POPULATION

Eritrea is bounded in the northeast by the Red Sea, southeast by Djibouti, south by Ethiopia and west by Sudan. Some 300 islands form the Dahlak Archipelago, most of them uninhabited. For the dispute with Yemen over the islands of Greater and Lesser Hanish *see* YEMEN: Territory and Population. Its area is 121,100 sq. km (46,800 sq. miles). There has not been a census since Eritrea became independent in 1993. 80·6% of the population was rural in 2005.

The UN gives an estimated population for 2010 of 5·22m.; density, 43 per sq. km

In 1995, 1m. Eritreans lived abroad, 0·5m. as refugees in Sudan. A UN Programme for Refugee Reintegration and Rehabilitation of Resettlement Areas in Eritrea (PROFERI) is in operation.

There are six regions: Anseba, Debub, Debubawi Keyih Bahri, Gash Barka, Maekel and Semenawi Keyih Bahri. The capital is Asmara (2002 estimated population, 500,600). Other large towns (with 2002 populations) are Keren (74,800) and Adi Ugri (25,700). An agreement of July 1993 gives Ethiopia rights to use the ports of Assab and Massawa.

49% of the population speak Tigrinya and 32% Tigré, and there are seven other indigenous languages. Arabic is spoken on the coast and along the Sudanese border, and English is used in secondary schools. Arabic and Tigrinya are the official languages.

SOCIAL STATISTICS

2000 births (estimates), 143,000; deaths, 49,000. Estimated birth rate in 2000 was 38·5 per 1,000 population; estimated death rate, 13·3. Annual population growth rate, 1992–2002, 2·4%. Life expectancy at birth, 2007, was 56·8 years for males and 61·4 years for females. Infant mortality, 2005, 50 per 1,000 live births; fertility rate, 2004, 5·4 births per woman.

CLIMATE

Massawa, Jan. 78°F (25·6°C), July 94°F (34·4°C). Annual rainfall 8" (193 mm).

CONSTITUTION AND GOVERNMENT

A referendum to approve independence was held on 23–25 April 1993. The electorate was 1,173,506. 99·8% of votes cast were in favour.

The transitional government consists of the *President* and a 150-member *National Assembly*. It elects the President, who in turn appoints the *State Council* made up of 14 ministers and the governors of the ten provinces. The President chairs both the State Council and the National Assembly.

National Anthem

'Ertra, Ertra, Ertra' ('Eritrea, Eritrea, Eritrea'); words by S. Beraki, tune by I. Meharezghi and A. Tesfatsion.

RECENT ELECTIONS

In the presidential and legislative elections in May 1997, President Afewerki was re-elected to office. National Assembly elections, postponed in 1998, were set to take place before the end of 2003 but have been put back indefinitely. In the meantime several dissident politicians have been jailed.

CURRENT ADMINISTRATION

President: Issaias Afewerki; b. 1945 (People's Front for Democracy and Justice, formerly the Eritrean People's Liberation Front; elected 22 May 1993 and re-elected in May 1997).

In March 2010 the ministers in the State Council were:

Minister of Agriculture: Arefaine Berhe. *Construction:* Abraha Asfaha. *Defence:* Sebhat Ephrem. *Education:* Semere Russom. *Energy and Mining:* Tesfai Ghebreselassie. *Finance:* Berhane Abrehe. *Fisheries and Maritime Resources:* Ahmed Haj Ali. *Foreign Affairs:* Osman Saleh. *Health:* Saleh Meki. *Information:* Ali Abdu. *Justice:* Fozia Hashim. *Labour and Human Welfare:* Askalu Menkerios. *Land, Water and Environment:* Woldemichael Ghebremariam. *National Development:* Wolday Futur. *Tourism:* Amna Nur Husayn. *Trade and Industry:* Giorgis Teklemikael. *Transport and Communications:* Woldemikael Abraha.

CURRENT LEADERS

Issaias Afewerki

Position
President

Introduction
Issaias Afewerki has been president of Eritrea since it achieved independence from Ethiopia in 1993, having been a leading campaigner for secession since the mid-1960s. However, his tenure has been marked by civil rights abuses. In foreign policy he has overseen a bloody war with Ethiopia in 1999–2000, which has since threatened to reignite over an unresolved border dispute.

Early Life
Issaias Afewerki was born in 1945 in Asmara, Eritrea's capital, which was then under British administration. Eritrea became part of Ethiopia in 1962 and in 1966 Afewerki joined the secessionist Eritrean Liberation Front (ELF). Having received military training in China, he became a deputy divisional commander. In 1970 he helped found the Eritrean People's Liberation Front (EPLF), becoming its general secretary in 1987.

Following the collapse of the Mengistu military regime in Ethiopia in 1991, the new government agreed to a referendum on Eritrean independence. The referendum was held in 1993 and Eritrea declared independence in May of that year. Eritrea's National Assembly selected Afewerki as the country's first president.

Career in Office
The EPLF initially suggested a multi-party political system and in the early stages of his tenure Afewerki advocated close economic relations with Ethiopia. However, in Feb. 2002 the National Assembly, composed of EPLF representatives, refused to ratify a bill on the establishment of new political parties. Multi-party elections, previously scheduled for the end of 2001, were shelved.

In 2001 Afewerki authorized the arrest of critical journalists and political opponents. The move was condemned internationally and the Italian ambassador, who had voiced concerns over human rights violations, was expelled. International aid was consequently cut. In 2002 Afewerki set out his plans for the creation of a 'responsible' press, soon after an opposition party—the Eritrean People's Liberation Front Democratic Party—had emerged to challenge him. The party was believed to have been co-founded by Mesfin Hagos, Afewerki's former defence minister.

In 1999 border disputes escalated into full-scale war between Ethiopian and Eritrean forces which resulted in 70,000 deaths. A ceasefire was agreed in June 2000, with Ethiopia withdrawing its forces under UN supervision. A formal peace treaty was signed in Dec. 2000. Tensions remained, particularly concerning the ownership of the small border settlement of Badame, and in May 2001 the countries agreed to abide by the decision of an international boundary commission. The commission awarded Badame to Eritrea, but Ethiopia refused to accept the decision. Fears of a renewed conflict mounted in late 2005 after Eritrea expelled UN observers policing the militarized border region.

Relations with the UN deteriorated further during the autumn of 2006 as Eritrea expelled several UN peacekeeping staff for allegedly spying and moved troops into the buffer zone on the Ethiopian border in violation of the ceasefire. At the same time, the Eritrean government was also accused of providing arms and supplies to the Islamist militias confronting the Ethiopian-backed transitional government in Somalia. In Nov. 2007 Eritrea accepted a border demarcation proposal by an independent boundary commission but Ethiopia rejected it. In Jan. 2008 the UN Security Council extended the mandate of its peacekeeping mission on the Eritrean-Ethiopian border for a further six months (despite Eritrean opposition), but brought it to a close at the end of July. The Council called on both sides to show restraint, to refrain from any threat or use of force against each other and to avoid provocative military activities.

Afewerki has overseen the restoration of diplomatic ties with Sudan and Djibouti, although relations with both countries remain unsettled. Eritrea claims that Islamic fundamentalist groups active within the country have received backing from Khartoum, while the Sudanese government resents Eritrean support for the opposition coalition. Eritrea has also accused Djibouti of providing military support to Ethiopia, a claim denied by Djibouti. In June 2008 there were border clashes between troops from Djibouti and Eritrea following several weeks of rising tensions.

In mid-2009 the African Union (AU) rebuked Afewerki's regime for continuing to aid Islamist insurgents in Somalia, so endangering civilians and AU peacekeeping forces, and called on the United Nations to impose punitive sanctions.

DEFENCE

Conscription for 18 months was introduced in 1994 for all Eritreans between the ages of 18 and 40, with some exceptions. It has since been reduced to 16 months. The total strength of all forces was estimated at 201,750 in 2007.

Defence expenditure totalled US$65m. in 2005 (US$14 per capita and 6·3% of GDP).

Army

The Army had a strength of around 200,000 in 2007. There were also approximately 120,000 reservists available.

Navy

Most of the former Ethiopian Navy is now in Eritrean hands. The main bases and training establishments are at Massawa, Assab and Dahlak. Personnel numbered 1,400 in 2007.

Air Force

Personnel numbers were estimated at 350 in 2007. There were 18 combat capable aircraft including MiG-29s, MiG-23s and MiG-21s.

INTERNATIONAL RELATIONS

A border dispute between Eritrea and Ethiopia broke out in May 1998. Eritrean troops took over the border town of Badame after a skirmish between Ethiopian police units and armed men from Eritrea. Ethiopia maintained that Badame and Sheraro, a nearby town, had always been part of Ethiopia and called Eritrea's action an invasion. An agreement ending hostilities was signed in June 2000, followed by a peace accord in Dec. A buffer zone has been created to separate the armies, but tensions do still arise from time to time, notably in late 2005 following a further dispute between the two countries over Badame.

Eritrea is a member of the UN, World Bank, IMF and several other UN specialized agencies, African Development Bank,

African Union, COMESA and is an ACP member state of the ACP-EU relationship.

ECONOMY

In 2007 agriculture accounted for 24·3% of GDP, industry 19·2% and services 56·5%.

Eritrea's resources are meagre, the population small and poorly-educated; communications are difficult and there is a shortage of energy.

Overview

In the half decade following Eritrea's declaration of independence in 1993 and after 30 years of war with Ethiopia, the average annual growth rate was 10·9%. However, renewed conflict with Ethiopia between 1998–2000 damaged much of the economic and social infrastructure and displaced a large part of the population. Eritrea now stands as one of the world's poorest countries, with the government focussed on continued tensions with Ethiopia rather than on righting imbalances in the economy.

Subsistence agriculture is the main economic activity. Economic growth averaged 1% between 2005–07, hindered by vulnerability to droughts and severe food shortages. Inflation is high, reaching 15·1% in 2006, but is reported to be on a downward trend. A third of the population is in extreme poverty according to the IMF. Sustained real economic growth of above 7% is required in order to significantly reduce the number of people living in long-term extreme poverty.

Currency

The *nakfa* (ERN) replaced the Ethiopian currency, the *birr*, in 1997. However, its introduction led to tensions with Ethiopia, adversely affecting cross-border trade. Inflation was 9·3% in 2007 and 12·6% in 2008. Total money supply was 8,063m. nafka in May 2005.

Budget

Revenues in 2002 were 3,410m. nafka and expenditures 6,138m. nafka.

Performance

Total GDP in 2008 was US$1·7bn. The economy expanded by 8·8% in 2001 following the end of the conflict with neighbouring Ethiopia but both 2003 and 2006 saw negative growth. More recently the real GDP growth rate was 1·3% in 2007 and 1·0% in 2008.

Banking and Finance

The central bank is the National Bank of Eritrea (*Governor*, Tekie Beyene). All banks and financial institutions are state-run. There is a Commercial Bank of Eritrea with 15 branches, an Eritrean Investment and Development Bank with 13 branches, a Housing and Commercial Bank of Eritrea with seven branches and an Insurance Corporation.

ENERGY AND NATURAL RESOURCES

Environment

Carbon dioxide emissions from the consumption and flaring of fossil fuels were the equivalent of 0·1 tonnes per capita in 2008.

Electricity

Installed capacity was an estimated 0·2m. kW in 2004. Electricity is provided to only some 10% of the population. Total production was 283m. kWh in 2004.

Minerals

There are deposits of gold, silver, copper, zinc, sulphur, nickel, chrome and potash. Basalt, limestone, marble, sand and silicates are extracted. Oil exploration is taking place in the Red Sea. Salt production totals 200,000 tonnes annually.

Agriculture

Agriculture engaged approximately 77% of the economically active population in 2002. Several systems of land ownership (state, colonial, traditional) co-exist. In 1994 the PFDJ proclaimed the sole right of the state to own land. There were 500,000 ha. of arable land in 2001 and 3,000 ha. of permanent crops. 21,000 ha. were irrigated in 2001. There were 463 tractors in 2001 and 125 harvester-threshers.

Main agricultural products, 2003 (in 1,000 tonnes): sorghum, 64; potatoes, 33; millet, 17; barley, 9; wheat, 5; maize, 4.

Livestock, 2003: sheep, 2·1m.; cattle, 1·9m.; goats, 1·7m.; camels, 75,000; chickens, 1m.

Livestock products, 2003 (in 1,000 tonnes): beef and veal, 14; goat meat, 6; lamb and mutton, 6; poultry meat, 2; milk, 51.

Forestry

In 2005 forests covered 1·55m. ha., or 15·4% of the total land area. Timber production in 2007 was 2·53m. cu. metres.

Fisheries

The total catch in 2005 was 4,027 tonnes, exclusively from marine waters, but a joint French–Eritrean project to assess fish stocks in the Red Sea has suggested a sustainable yield of up to 70,000 tonnes a year.

INDUSTRY

Light industry was well developed in the colonial period but capability has declined. Processed food, textiles, leatherwear, building materials, glassware and oil products are produced. Industrial production accounted for 19·2% of GDP in 2007, with the manufacturing sector providing 5·5%.

Labour

In 1996 the labour force was 1,649,000 (53% males).

INTERNATIONAL TRADE

Eritrea is dependent on foreign aid for most of its capital expenditure. Total external debt in 2005 was US$736m.

Imports and Exports

In 2003 imports (c.i.f.) were valued at US$432·8m. and exports (f.o.b.) at US$6·6m. The leading imports are machinery and transport equipment, basic manufactures, and food and live animals. The main exports are drinks, leather and products, textiles and oil products. Principal import suppliers, 2003: USA, 15·9%; UAE, 12·2%; Italy, 11·6%; Saudi Arabia, 10·5%; India, 6·3%. Principal export markets, 2003: Sudan, 19·7%; Italy, 12·1%; Singapore, 12·1%; Netherlands, 10·6%; India, 7·6%.

COMMUNICATIONS

Roads

There were some 4,010 km of roads in 2000, of which 21·8% were paved. A tarmac road links the capital Asmara with one of the main ports, Massawa. In 1996 passenger cars in use numbered 5,940 (1·5 per 1,000 inhabitants). About 500 buses operate regular services.

Rail

In 2000 the reconstruction of the 117 km Massawa–Asmara line reached Embatkala, thus opening up an 80 km stretch from Massawa on the coast. In 2003 the line was rebuilt right through to Asmara.

Civil Aviation

There is an international airport at Asmara (Yohannes IV Airport). In 2003 there were scheduled flights to Cairo, Djibouti, Dubai, Frankfurt, Jeddah, Milan, Nairobi and Sana'a. In 2001 Asmara handled 140,000 passengers (129,000 on international flights) and 3,200 tonnes of freight.

Shipping
Massawa is the main port; Assab used to be the main port for imports to Ethiopia. Both were free ports for Ethiopia until the onset of hostilities. Merchant shipping totalled 21,000 GRT in 2002.

Telecommunications
International telephone links were restored in 1992. There were 78,200 telephone subscribers in 2005 (17·8 for every 1,000 inhabitants), including 40,400 mobile phone subscribers. Eritrea had 70,000 internet users in 2005 and 35,000 PCs were in use (8·0 per 1,000 inhabitants).

Postal Services
In 2003 there were 64 post offices, equivalent to one for every 64,700 persons.

SOCIAL INSTITUTIONS

Justice
The legal system derives from a decree of May 1993.

Education
Adult literacy was about 56·7% in 2001 (68·2% among males and 34·6% among females). In 2007 there were 331,855 pupils and 6,933 teaching staff in primary schools, and 218,369 pupils at secondary schools with 4,425 teaching staff. There were 4,612 students and 429 academic staff in tertiary education in 2004. In 2006 public expenditure on education came to 2·4% of GNI.

Health
In 1993 there were 10 small regional hospitals, 32 health centres and 65 medical posts. In 1996 there were 108 physicians, 4 dentists, 574 nurses and 79 midwives.

Eritrea has one of the highest rates of undernourishment of any country. The proportion of the population classified as undernourished was 73% in the period 2001–03, up from 68% in 1995–97.

RELIGION
Half the population are Sunni Muslims (along the coast and in the north), and half Coptic Christians (in the south).

CULTURE

Broadcasting
All television and radio broadcasting is controlled through Eri TV, Radio Zara and the Voice of the Broad Masses of Eritrea radio networks. In 2006 TV receivers numbered 305,000.

Press
In 2006 there were three government newspapers, one published three times a week and the others once a week. In Sept. 2001 the government closed down the country's eight independent newspapers. A number of journalists have been jailed.

Tourism
There were 82,000 non-resident visitors in 2005; tourist spending totalled US$66m.

DIPLOMATIC REPRESENTATIVES
Of Eritrea in the United Kingdom (96 White Lion St., London, N1 9PF)
Ambassador: Tesfamicael Gerahtu Ogbaghiorghis.

Of the United Kingdom in Eritrea (66–68 Mariam Ghimbi St., PO Box 5584, Asmara)
Ambassador: Andrea Reidy, OBE.

Of Eritrea in the USA (1708 New Hampshire Ave., NW, Washington, D.C., 20009)
Ambassador: Ghirmai Ghebremariam.

Of the USA in Eritrea (179 Alaa St., POB 211, Asmara)
Ambassador: Ronald K. McMullen.

Of Eritrea to the United Nations
Ambassador: Araya Desta.

Of Eritrea to the European Union
Ambassador: Girma Asmerom Tesfay.

FURTHER READING
Connel, D., *Against All Odds: a Chronicle of the Eritrean Revolution*. 1993
Henze, Paul, *Eritrea's War: Confrontation, International Response, Outcome, Prospects*. 2001
Lewis, R., *Eritrea: Africa's Newest Country*. 1993
Mengisteab, Kidane, *Anatomy of an African Tragedy: Political, Economic and Foreign Policy Crisis in Post-Independence Eritrea*. 2005
Negash, Tekeste and Tronvoll, Kjetil, *Brothers at War: Making Sense of the Eritrean–Ethiopian War*. 2001
Wrong, Michaela, *I Didn't Do It For You: How the World Betrayed a Small African Nation*. 2005

ESTONIA

Eesti Vabariik
(Republic of Estonia)

Capital: Tallinn
Population estimate, 2010: 1·34m.
GDP per capita, 2007: (PPP$) 20,361
HDI/world rank: 0·883/40

KEY HISTORICAL EVENTS

There is evidence of human habitation from around 8000 BC. Remnants of a 'comb' pottery culture show the arrival around 5000 BC of the ancestors of the Eestii, one of the first known peoples to inhabit the Baltic's eastern shores and the forerunners of modern Estonians. Before the arrival of Christianity the cult of Tharapita (or Taara), a god of war, was popular in northern Estonia and the island of Saaremaa.

The failed Danish invasion of Saaremaa in 1206 under the bishop of Lund marked the first attempt at the Christianization of Estonia. German invasions began in 1208 with the capture of Otepää in the southeast. The Sword Brothers, a military order that became the Livonian Order, took Livonia (including southern Estonia) in 1217. Valdemar II of Denmark invaded the north in 1219, establishing Tanin Lidna (later Tallinn) at Reval on the Gulf of Finland. Danish forces prevailed in 1227, taking Saaremaa (Ösel). In 1238 Wilhelm of Modena, the papal legate, negotiated the re-establishment of Danish power in the north after its seizure by the Sword Brothers, who shared the rest of the land with the prince-bishops of Ösel-Wiek and Dorpat (Tartu). The eastward expansion of the Sword Brothers was checked in 1242 at Lake Peipus by Alexander Nevsky, prince of Novgorod.

A large immigrant population of 'Coastal Swedes' arrived from the mid-13th century and a significant German merchant class emerged in the towns. The St George's Night Uprising on 23 April 1343 saw Estonians revolt against Danish rule. The peasant army appealed to Swedish Finland for help but were defeated by the Danish vice-regents, who called on the Livonian Order. Indigenous peasants were increasingly subjugated to the benefit of landlords and immigrant vassals. In 1346 Denmark's Valdemar IV sold his share of Estonia to the Teutonic Knights who gave control to the Livonian Order.

The Reformation reached Estonia's semi-autonomous cities in the 1520s but met rural resistance from the Livonian Order. In 1558 Tsar Ivan IV demanded extortionate taxes from the bishopric of Dorpat (Tartu) as a pretext to invading the Livonian Confederation and gaining access to the Baltic Sea. The weakened Livonian Order disbanded in 1561 and Estland was given to Sweden while Ösel was sold to Denmark. By 1600 Sweden, repelling the incursions of Muscovy, had strengthened its hold over Estland. Sweden's Gustavus Adolphus attempted to build a Reformist Baltic empire, winning all of Estonia in 1629 and reducing the power of German landowners while defending the country from Polish and Russian attacks. In 1645 the Danes ceded Ösel to the Swedes. Estonian territories were badly affected by the Great Famine of 1695–97, when over 70,000 people (around 20% of the population) died.

Russian ambitions to establish a Baltic coast presence and Danish resentment of Swedish hegemony led to the Great Northern War (1700–21). Swedish forces won a string of victories under Charles XII, routing Peter the Great's army at Narva in 1700. However, Charles' over-ambitious attack on Poland led to a Swedish collapse. Peter seized Ingria (where he built St Petersburg) and ravaged Livonia. The Swedish defeat at Poltava in 1709 led to Estonia passing to Russia by the 1721 Treaty of Nystad.

Estonia remained dominated by German aristocrats after the reversal of Swedish land seizures and the reinforcement of serfdom. Estonian nationalism and 'Estophilia' emerged in the mid-19th century but anti-(Baltic) German policies of Russification were introduced in the 1880s to prevent the Empire's fragmentation. After nationalist success in the municipal elections of 1904, many Estonians joined the all-Russia workers' strikes of 1905, which were brutally suppressed. In the ensuing anti-landlord violence, about a fifth of German-owned manors were destroyed by ethnic Estonians.

Russia's provisional government amalgamated Estonia and Estonian-speaking northern Livonia in April 1917 and workers' and soldiers' Soviets came to prominence. Germany invaded in early 1918 and took Estonia by the Treaty of Brest-Litovsk but withdrew later that year to be replaced by Russian Bolsheviks. However, they were ejected in May 1919 (with British naval support) and the Estonians proclaimed a democratic republic.

Estonian incursions into Russia won slices of Estonian-speaking territories beyond the River Narva and in Pskov province. In March 1934 this regime was, in turn, overthrown by a fascist coup. The secret protocol of the Soviet-German agreement of Aug. 1939 assigned Estonia to the Soviet sphere of interest. An ultimatum in June 1940 saw the formation of the Estonian Soviet Socialist Republic but a German occupation lasted from June 1941–Sept. 1944. The return to the Soviet sphere saw the loss of 2,200 sq. km of Estonian territory to Pskov Oblast. There followed a severe Sovietization programme that lasted until the mid-1980s. The Estonian Supreme Soviet declared a sovereign republic in Nov. 1988.

In a 1991 popular referendum 77·8% voted in favour of independence and the USSR recognized the new state on 6 Sept. 1991. Estonia was admitted to the Council of Europe in 1993 and all Russian troops were withdrawn by Aug. 1994, though a sizeable Russian/East Slavic population remains (around a third of the total). Estonia became a member of NATO in March 2004 and the European Union in May 2004.

TERRITORY AND POPULATION

Estonia is bounded in the west and north by the Baltic Sea, east by Russia and south by Latvia. There are 1,521 offshore islands, of which the largest are Saaremaa and Hiiumaa, but only 12 are permanently inhabited. Area, 45,227 sq. km (17,462 sq. miles). The census population in 2000 was 1,370,052; Jan. 2008 estimate, 1,340,935, giving a density of 29·6 per sq.

The UN gives an estimated population for 2010 of 1·34m.

In 2005, 69·1% of the population lived in urban areas. Of the whole population, Estonians accounted for 67·9%, Russians 25·6%, Ukrainians 2·1%, Belarusians 1·3% and Finns 0·9%. The capital is Tallinn (population, 397,200 or 29·3%). Other large towns are Tartu (101,200), Narva (67,800), Kohtla-Järve (46,800) and Pärnu (44,800). There are 15 counties, 47 towns and 202 rural municipalities.

The official language is Estonian.

SOCIAL STATISTICS

2003 registered births, 13,198; deaths, 18,231. Rates (per 1,000 population): birth, 9·7; death, 13·4. There were 9,394 reported abortions in 2006. Expectation of life in 2007 was 67·3 years for males and 78·3 for females. The annual population growth rate in the period 2000–05 was –0·3%. The suicide rate was 20·3 per 100,000 population in 2005 (rate among males, 35·5). The rate has nearly halved in ten years, having been 40·1 per 100,000 in 1995. Infant mortality in 2005 was six per 1,000 births. In 2004 total fertility rate was 1·4 births per woman.

CLIMATE

Because of its maritime location Estonia has a moderate climate, with cool summers and mild winters. Average daily temperatures in 2008: Jan. –1·5°C; July 17·0°C. Rainfall is heavy, 600–800 mm per year, and evaporation low.

CONSTITUTION AND GOVERNMENT

A draft constitution drawn up by a constitutional assembly was approved by 91·1% of votes cast at a referendum on 28 June 1992. Turnout was 66·6%. The constitution came into effect on 3 July 1992. It defines Estonia as a 'democratic state guided by the rule of law, where universally recognized norms of international law are an inseparable part of the legal system.' It provides for a 101-member national assembly (*Riigikogu*) elected for four-year terms. There are 12 electoral districts with eight to 12 mandates each. Candidates may be elected: a) by gaining more than 'quota', i.e. the number of votes cast in a district divided by the number of its mandates; b) by standing for a party which attracts for all of its candidates more than the quota, in order of listing; c) by being listed nationally for parties which clear a 5% threshold and eligible for the seats remaining according to position on the lists. The head of state is the *President*, elected by the Riigikogu for five-year terms. Presidential candidates must gain the nominations of at least 20% of parliamentary deputies. If no candidate wins a two-thirds majority in any of three rounds, the Speaker convenes an electoral college, composed of parliamentary deputies and local councillors. At this stage any 21 electors may nominate an additional candidate. The electoral college elects the President by a simple majority.

Citizenship requirements are two years residence and competence in Estonian for existing residents. For residents immigrating after 1 April 1995, five years qualifying residence is required.

National Anthem

'Mu isamaa, mu õnn ja rõõm' ('My native land, my pride and joy'); words by J. V. Jannsen, tune by F. Pacius (same as Finland).

GOVERNMENT CHRONOLOGY

Heads of State since independence.

Chairman of the Supreme Council

1991–92	Arnold Rüütel

Presidents

1992–2001	Lennart Georg Meri
2001–06	Arnold Rüütel
2006–	Toomas Hendrik Ilves

Prime Ministers since independence. (IERSP (Isamaaliit) = Pro Patria Union; KMÜ-K = Estonian Coalition Party; n/p = non-party; Rahvarinne = Popular Front of Estonia; RE (Reformierakond) = Estonian Reform Party; ResP = Union for the Republic-Res Publica; RK Isamaa = National Coalition Party Pro Patria)

1990–92	Rahvarinne	Edgar Savisaar
1992	n/p	Tiit Vähi
1992–94	RK Isamaa	Mart Laar
1994–95	n/p	Andres Tarand
1995–97	KMÜ-K	Tiit Vähi
1997–99	KMÜ-K	Mart Siimann
1999–2002	IERSP	Mart Laar
2002–03	RE	Siim Kallas
2003–05	ResP	Juhan Parts
2005–	RE	Andrus Ansip

RECENT ELECTIONS

Parliamentary elections were held on 4 March 2007; turnout was 61·9%. The Estonian Reform Party (Reform) won 31 of 101 seats (with 27·8% of the total votes); Estonian Centre Party (Kesk), 29 seats (26·1%); Union of Pro Patria and Res Publica (IRPL), 19 seats (17·9%); Social Democratic Party (SDE), 10 seats (10·6%); Greens, 6 seats (7·1%); Estonian People's Union (Rahvaliit), 6 seats (7·1%). Six other parties failed to win seats.

An electoral college elected the president on 23 Sept. 2006 after parliament had failed to do so in three rounds on 28–29 Aug. 2006. Toomas Ilves was elected with 174 votes in the 345-member electoral college, against 162 votes for incumbent Arnold Rüütel.

European Parliament

Estonia has six representatives. At the June 2009 elections turnout was 43·9% (26·8% in 2004). Kesk won 2 seats with 26·1% of the vote (political affiliation in European Parliament: Alliance of Liberals and Democrats for Europe); Reform, 1 with 15·3% (Alliance of Liberals and Democrats for Europe); IRPL, 1 with 12·2% (European People's Party); SDE, 1 with 8·7% (Progressive Alliance of Socialists and Democrats). One independent was elected, with 25·8% (Greens/European Free Alliance).

CURRENT ADMINISTRATION

President: Toomas Ilves; b. 1953 (sworn in 9 Oct. 2006).

In March 2010 the coalition government comprised:

Prime Minister: Andrus Ansip; b. 1956 (Reform; in office since 13 April 2005).

Minister of Agriculture: Helir-Valdor Seeder (IRPL). *Culture:* Laine Jänes (Reform). *Defence:* Jaak Aaviksoo (IRPL). *Economic Affairs and Communications:* Juhan Parts (IRPL). *Education and Research:* Tõnis Lukas (IRPL). *Environment:* Jaanus Tamkivi (Reform). *Finance:* Jürgen Ligi (Reform). *Foreign Affairs:* Urmas Paet (Reform). *Internal Affairs:* Marko Pomerants (IRPL). *Justice:* Rein Lang (Reform). *Regional Affairs:* Siim-Valmar Kiisler (IRPL). *Social Affairs:* Hanno Pevkur (Reform).

Government Website: http://www.riik.ee

CURRENT LEADERS

Toomas Hendrik Ilves

Position

President

Introduction

Toomas Ilves began his five-year term as president on 9 Oct. 2006, replacing Arnold Rüütel. The office is largely ceremonial.

Early Life

Toomas Hendrik Ilves was born on 26 Dec. 1953 in Sweden, his parents having fled Estonia during the Soviet occupation in the 1940s. Ilves studied psychology in the USA, first at Columbia

University before completing his MA at Pennsylvania University. He then lectured in Vancouver on Estonian literature and linguistics before working as an analyst and researcher for Radio Free Europe.

He returned to Estonia in 1993, two years after the country regained independence. In the late 1990s he served as ambassador to the USA, Canada and Mexico. He also had two spells as minister for foreign affairs and was chairman of the North American Institute. From 2004–06 he was a member of the European parliament, representing the Social Democratic Party.

Career in Office

Ilves' principal duty as president is to represent the country abroad. In Nov. 2006 George W. Bush became the first US president to visit Estonia. Ilves has justified the participation of Estonian forces in Afghanistan as a necessary duty of NATO membership, and an increase in the Estonian deployment was approved by parliament in June 2009.

Ilves wants greater integration of Estonia's large Russian-speaking minority. Relations between Estonia and Russia were tense during the early months of Ilves' tenure, particularly over the relocation by the Estonian government of a prominent Soviet war memorial out of the centre of Tallinn.

Andrus Ansip

Position

Prime Minister

Introduction

When Andrus Ansip was sworn in as prime minister of Estonia on 13 April 2005, he took charge of the country's 12th government since its independence in 1991. A right-leaning former investment banker who was mayor of the second largest city, Tartu, for six years, Ansip pledged to implement policies that would attract investment and strengthen Estonia's position as a dynamic, post-industrial economy. His coalition government retained power in parliamentary elections in March 2007.

Early Life

Ansip was born in Tartu in the Soviet Republic of Estonia (ESSR) on 1 Oct. 1956. He attended local schools and graduated from the University of Tartu with a diploma in chemistry in 1979. He remained at the historic university to undertake further academic study, and later joined the municipal Committee of the Estonian Communist Party (ECP), which had been led, since 1978, by Karl Vaino, a Russian-born Estonian. The ESSR experienced increased Russification and 'Sovietization' in the early 1980s, in accordance with the policy of the Soviet leader, Leonid Brezhnev. By 1988 however, there was growing opposition to the communist leadership and, against a backdrop of gradual economic liberalization, Ansip joined Estkompexim, a 'joint-venture' specializing in the import and export of foodstuffs. He was head of Estkompexim's Tartu office during 1991, when, following the collapse of the USSR, Estonia was internationally recognized as an independent nation. The following year Ansip attended a business management course at the University of York in Toronto, Canada.

On his return to Estonia in 1993, Ansip entered the rapidly evolving banking and investment sector, serving as a member of the board of directors of Rahvapank (the People's Bank) until 1995 and then chairman of the board of Livonia Privatization. In 1997 he was chief executive officer of the investment fund, Fondiinvesteeringu Maakler AS, as well as chairman of the board of Radio Tartu. The following year he was elected Mayor of Tartu as a candidate of the centre-right Estonian Reform Party (Reform), established in 1994 by Siim Kallas, a former governor of Estonia's central bank. A popular mayor, Ansip was credited with attracting investment to the country's second city and overseeing developments such as the Baltic Defence College and a new biomedical research institute which capitalized on Tartu's long-standing reputation as an academic centre.

On 13 Sept. 2004, shortly after Estonia joined the EU and NATO, Ansip was nominated to replace Meelis Atonen as the minister of economic affairs and communications. Two months later, he became chairman of Reform, which had formed part of the Res Publica-led coalition government under Juhan Parts since March 2003. His appointment followed the departure of Reform's leader (and former prime minister), Siim Kallas, to Brussels to become an EU commissioner. When, in March 2005, the *Riigikogu* (parliament) passed a vote of no confidence in the country's justice minister over proposed anti-corruption measures, Parts resigned as prime minister. On 31 March 2005 the president, Arnold Rüütel, asked Ansip to form a new government. He succeeded in forging a coalition with the Estonian Centre Party (Kesk) and the Estonian Peoples' Union (Rahvaliit). Ansip was backed by 53 out of 101 members of the *Riigikogu*, and was inaugurated as prime minister on 13 April 2005.

Career in Office

Ansip confirmed Estonia's aspiration to adopt the single European currency. However, he acknowledged that it would be tough to fulfil the criterion of holding inflation to no more than 1·5 percentage points above that of the three lowest-inflation EU countries, given that Estonia's economy was growing at that time at around 7% a year and its exports had risen by 20% in its first 12 months in the EU. He pledged to maintain the previous government's tax-cutting agenda, as well as increasing social welfare measures to bridge the gap between the relatively wealthy, young urban population and poorer rural citizens whose skills date from the Soviet period. He retained the premiership following legislative elections in March 2007, forming a new Reform coalition with Union of Pro Patria and Res Publica (IRPL) and the Social Democratic Party.

Despite a sharp economic contraction in the wake of the global financial crisis that unfolded in the latter half of 2008, Estonia fared better than its Baltic neighbours in the ensuing downturn. The government acted quickly to implement spending cuts and adjustments to stem the rise in the budget deficit, while earlier prudent management of the public finances provided a buffer of fiscal reserves, with no requirement for support from the International Monetary Fund. The country was also expected to remain on track to meet the criteria for joining the eurozone in 2011.

In May 2009 the government lost its parliamentary majority as Ansip dismissed the three Social Democratic ministers from the coalition cabinet in a dispute over economic policy, replacing them in June with IRPL members and continuing on a minority basis.

In foreign affairs, Ansip's government formally signed a border treaty agreement with Russia in May 2005. However, Russia subsequently withdrew from the agreement because Estonia had attached an unacceptable preamble to the text referring to the Soviet occupation. Relations with Russia soured further in early 2007 when the Estonian parliament passed legislation banning monuments glorifying Soviet rule and the government approved the removal of a Soviet war memorial in Tallinn.

DEFENCE

The President is the head of national defence. Conscription is eight to 11 months for men and voluntary for women. Conscientious objectors may opt for 16 months civilian service instead.

Defence expenditure in 2006 totalled US$238m. (US$179 per capita), representing 1·4% of GDP.

The Estonian Defence Forces (EDF) regular component is divided into the Army, the Air Force and the Navy.

Army

The Army consists of seven battalions (three infantry, one reconnaissance, one artillery, one guard and one peacekeeping).

The total number of personnel in the Army in 2007 was 3,600 (1,200 conscripts). There is a Border Guard numbering 2,600.

Navy

The Navy consists of the Naval Staff (Naval HQ), the Naval Base, and the Mine Countermeasures (MCM) Squadron. The total number of personnel in the Navy in 2007 was 300 including a platoon-sized conscript unit. Estonia, Latvia and Lithuania have established a joint naval unit 'BALTRON' (Baltic Naval Squadron), with bases at Tallinn in Estonia, Liepāja, Riga and Ventspils in Latvia, and Klaipėda in Lithuania.

Air Force

The Air Force consists of an Air Force Staff, Air Force Base and Air Surveillance Wing. The total number of personnel in the Air Force in 2007 was 200.

INTERNATIONAL RELATIONS

Estonia is a member of the UN, World Bank, IMF and several other UN specialized agencies, WTO, EU, Council of Europe, OSCE, Council of the Baltic Sea States, BIS, IOM, NATO and is an associate partner of WEU. Estonia became a member of NATO on 29 March 2004 and of the EU on 1 May 2004. Estonia held a referendum on EU membership on 14 Sept. 2003, in which 66·9% of votes cast were in favour of accession, with 33·1% against.

In Dec. 2007 Estonia acceded to the Schengen accord, which abolishes border controls between Estonia, Austria, Belgium, Czech Republic, Denmark, Finland, France, Germany, Greece, Hungary, Iceland, Italy, Latvia, Lithuania, Luxembourg, Malta, Netherlands, Norway, Poland, Portugal, Slovakia, Slovenia, Spain, Sweden and Switzerland.

ECONOMY

Agriculture contributed 3% of GDP in 2007, industry 30% and services 67%.

Overview

Estonia is a gateway for trade with the Nordic countries, especially Finland, the destination for 18·3% of Estonian exports in 2008. When Estonia gained independence in 1991 it was among the most competitive of the former Soviet Union countries, boasting the highest per capital income, strong infrastructure and high education levels compared to its neighbours.

The cornerstones of economic reform were the introduction of a new currency, tight budgetary control, privatization programmes and trade liberalization. In 1999 a number of tariff and non-tariff barriers were abolished in line with WTO rules.

Since independence, Estonia has been among the fastest growing of the EU accession countries (it joined the EU in 2004), with per capita GDP almost doubling between 1993–2003 to reach about 45% of the EU average in purchasing power parity terms. Performance has been in large part driven by low unemployment, strong domestic demand and buoyant exports, with GDP growth averaging 8% per year between 2003–07. Unemployment dropped from 11% in 2003 to 4·7% in 2007.

However, the economy began to slow in 2007 and fell into recession as the global financial crisis hit. Growth contracted by 14·1% in 2009, with the worst three-month period being the second quarter when the economy shrank by 16·1%. Unemployment soared and was predicted to exceed 16% at the end of 2009. Nonetheless, the IMF argues that adoption of the euro in 2011 remains within reach. Growth is expected to resume in mid-2010.

Currency

The unit of currency is the *kroon* (EEK) of 100 *sents*. The kroon is pegged to the euro at a rate of 15·6466 *krooni* to one euro. Foreign exchange reserves were US$1,768m. in July 2005, gold reserves 8,000 troy oz and total money supply was 42,396m. krooni. Inflation was 6·6% in 2007 and 10·4% in 2008. In June 2004 the kroon was included in the Exchange Rate Mechanism II (ERM II); the fixed exchange rate with the euro remains unchanged. Estonia hopes to be the next country to adopt the euro, possibly in 2011. There are no restrictions on the free movement of capital between Estonia and foreign countries.

Budget

Budgetary central government revenue and expenditure in 1m. krooni for calendar years:

	2005	*2006*	*2007*[1]
Revenue	46,639	57,735	69,028
Expenditure	41,634	49,296	57,919

[1]Provisional.

Tax revenue provided 33,862m. krooni in 2006; social benefits (16,263m. krooni) were the main item of expenditure. There is a flat tax rate of 21% that is set to be reduced to 20% in the course of 2010; VAT is 20% (reduced rate, 9%).

Performance

Estonia's economy expanded by 10·0% in 2006 and 7·2% in 2007 but Estonia then suffered particularly badly in the global downturn with the economy shrinking by 3·6% in 2008 and 14·1% in 2009. Total GDP in 2008 was US$23·1bn.

Banking and Finance

A central bank, the Bank of Estonia, was re-established in 1990 (*Governor*, Andres Lipstok). The Estonian Investment Bank was established in 1992 to provide financing for privatized and private companies. Since 1 Jan. 1996 banks have been required to have an equity of at least 50m. krooni. As of Dec. 2004 there were six Estonian authorized commercial banks, three foreign banks' branches and five foreign banks' representative offices. As a result of a wave of mergers the two largest groups, Hansabank and the Union Bank of Estonia, control 80% of the market. Total assets and liabilities of commercial banks at Nov. 2004 were 128,211m. krooni. The Estonian Banking Association was founded in 1992.

In 2008 Estonia received US$2·0bn. worth of foreign direct investment.

A stock exchange opened in Tallinn in 1996.

ENERGY AND NATURAL RESOURCES

Environment

Estonia's carbon dioxide emissions from the consumption and flaring of fossil fuels in 2008 were the equivalent of 15·8 tonnes per capita.

Electricity

Estonia is a net electricity exporter. In 2005 installed capacity was 2·7m. kW, with production of 9·1bn. kWh. Consumption per capita was 6,733 kWh in 2005. 91% of electricity was produced by burning oil shale. Production of hydro and wind energy accounted for about 0·7% of total electricity production. About 20% of net production was exported, mainly to Latvia.

Oil and Gas

Oil shale deposits were estimated at 4,898m. tonnes in 2006. A factory for the production of gas from shale and a 208 km-pipeline from Kohtla-Järve supplies shale gas to Tallinn, and exports to St Petersburg. Natural gas is imported from Russia.

Minerals

Oil shale is the most valuable mineral resource. Production volume has decreased (from 21m. tonnes in 1990 to 12m. tonnes in 2006) because of falls in exports and domestic electricity consumption, and an increase in the use of natural gas. Peatlands occupy about 22% of Estonia's territory; there are extensive deposits, totalling an estimated 1·64bn. tonnes in 2004. Phosphorites and super-phosphates are found and refined, and lignite (13·99m. tonnes in 2004), limestone, dolomite, clay, sand and gravel are mined.

Agriculture
Farming employed 6·1% of the population in 2003. In 2005 there were 27,747 holdings (55,748 in 2001). In 2007 there were 598,000 ha. of arable land and 9,000 ha. of permanent crops. Total agricultural output in 2003 was valued at 7,044m. krooni, including: animal production 3,388m. krooni; crop production, 2,616m. krooni; agricultural services and other non-agricultural production, 1,040m. krooni.

Output of main agricultural products (in 1,000 tonnes) in 2003: barley, 254; potatoes, 244; wheat, 145; rapeseed, 64; oats, 63; rye, 23.

In 2003 there were 340,800 pigs, 253,900 cattle, 29,900 sheep and 2,096,000 chickens.

Livestock products (in 1,000 tonnes), 2003: meat, 105; milk, 611; eggs, 15.

Forestry
In 2005, 2·28m. ha. were covered by forests (53·9% of the total land area), which provide material for sawmills, furniture, and the match and pulp industries, as well as wood fuel. Private, municipal and state ownership of forests is allowed. In 2007 the annual timber cut was 5·90m. cu. metres.

Fisheries
In 2004 the Estonian fishing fleet numbered 1,044 vessels of 24,954 gross tonnes. The total catch in 2005 was 98,772 tonnes.

INDUSTRY
Important industries are engineering, metalworking, food products, wood products, furniture and textiles. In 2005 manufacturing accounted for 18·5% of GDP.

Labour
The workforce in 2003 totalled 660,500, of whom 594,300 were employed. The monthly average gross wage in 2003 was 6,723 krooni. The unemployment rate in the fourth quarter of 2009 was 15·5% (7·6% in the fourth quarter of 2008).

Retirement age was 63 years for both men and women in 2004.

Trade Unions
The main trade union organization in Estonia is the Estonian Association of Trade Unions, which represents the interests of industrial, service, trade, public and agricultural employees.

INTERNATIONAL TRADE
External debt was US$11,255m. in 2005.

Imports and Exports
Imports in 2006 (and 2005) were valued at US$12,373·6m. (US$9,627·8m.); exports, US$9,635·1m. (US$7,783·0m.).

Main import suppliers in 2003: Finland, 15·9%; Germany, 11·3%; Sweden, 8·8%; Russia, 8·6%; China, 4·5%. Main export markets, 2003: Finland, 25·9%; Sweden, 15·3%; Germany, 9·9%; Latvia, 7·0%; UK, 4·2%.

Around 80% of Estonian trade is with EU member countries, and 41% with Finland and Sweden alone.

COMMUNICATIONS
Roads
As of 1 Jan. 2004 there were 16,452 km of national roads (29·4% of the total Estonian road and street network of 55,592 km), of which 52·3% were paved. In 2007 there were 523,800 registered passenger cars in use, plus 80,300 lorries and vans, 4,300 buses and coaches, and 12,200 motorcycles and mopeds. There were 2,446 road accidents and 196 fatalities in 2007.

Rail
Length of railways in 2002 was 968 km (1,520 mm gauge), of which 132 km was electrified. In 2003, 5·06m. passengers and 65·6m. tonnes of freight were carried.

Civil Aviation
In 2002 there were 38 airports in Estonia. There is an international airport at Tallinn (Ulemiste), which handled 570,919 passengers (566,551 on international flights) and 2,181 tonnes of freight in 2001. The national carrier is Estonian Air, 34% state-owned. In 2003 Estonian Air operated services to Copenhagen, Frankfurt, Hamburg, Kyiv, London, Moscow, Paris, Riga, Stockholm and Vilnius. In 2003 scheduled airline traffic of Estonian-based carriers flew 7m. km, carrying 395,000 passengers (389,000 on international flights).

Shipping
There are six major shipping companies, all of which are privatized. There are ice-free, deep-water ports at Tallinn and Muuga (state-owned). Tallinn handled 85% of the total turnover of goods in Estonia in 2000. The port of Tallinn makes most of its money by shipping out Russian oil and importing goods destined for Russia. In 2002 the merchant shipping fleet comprised 33 vessels of 1,000 GRT or over.

Telecommunications
Estonia had 1,887,300 telephone subscribers in 2005 (1,420·1 per 1,000 persons), with 1,445,300 mobile phone subscribers. There were 650,000 PCs (489·1 per 1,000 persons) in use in 2005 and 690,000 internet users. In Feb. 2000 the Estonian parliament voted to guarantee internet access to its citizens.

Postal Services
As of 1 Jan. 2004, the state-owned Eesti Post had 12 main post offices, 395 other post offices and 154 postal agencies, employing 4,237 persons.

SOCIAL INSTITUTIONS
Justice
A post-Soviet criminal code was introduced in 1992. There is a three-tier court system with the State Court at its apex, and there are both city and district courts. The latter act as courts of appeal. The State Court is the final court of appeal, and also functions as a constitutional court. There are also administrative courts for petty offences. Judges are appointed for life. City and district judges are appointed by the President; State Court judges are elected by Parliament.

In 2003, 53,595 crimes were recorded; there were 38 murders and attempted murders (down from 200 in 1999). There are nine prisons; in May 2003, 4,874 persons were in custody (361 per 100,000 of national population—one of the highest rates in Europe).

The death penalty was abolished for all crimes in 1998.

Education
Adult literacy rate in 2003 was 99·8% (99·8% for both males and females). There are nine years of comprehensive school starting at age six, followed by three years secondary school. In 2002–03 there were 636 general education schools: 65 nursery/primary, 52 primary, 279 basic and 240 secondary/upper secondary. Of these, 525 were Estonian-language, 89 Russian-language and 22 mixed-language. There were 45 schools for children with special needs. The total number of pupils at basic school level in general education in 2002–03 was 165,486 (115,204 at urban schools and 50,282 at rural schools). At the start of the 2003–04 academic year there were 65,659 higher education students studying at six public universities, six private universities, seven state higher schools and 17 private higher schools; 11 vocational educational institutions also provide higher education.

In 2006 central government expenditure on education came to 4,510·5m. krooni. In 2006 total education expenditure came to 6·1% of GDP.

Health
Estonia had 51 hospitals (14 private) in 2002, down from 78 hospitals (28 private) in 1999. There were 8,248 hospital beds

in 2002. In 2003 there were 4,293 doctors (1,245 in private medicine).

Welfare
In 2005 there were 0·38m. pensioners. The average monthly pension was 2,315 krooni in 2005. An official poverty line was introduced in 1993 (then 280 krooni per month). Persons receiving less than the subsistence level (750 krooni per month in 2005) are entitled to state benefit. Unemployment benefit was 400 krooni a month in 2005.

RELIGION
There is freedom of religion in Estonia and no state church, although most of the population is Lutheran. The Estonian Orthodox Church owed allegiance to Constantinople until it was forcibly brought under Moscow's control in 1940; a synod of the free Estonian Orthodox Church was established in Stockholm. Returning from exile, it registered itself in 1993 as the Estonian Apostolic Orthodox Church. By an agreement in 1996 between the Moscow and Constantinople Orthodox Patriarchates, there are now two Orthodox jurisdictions in Estonia. In 2000 there were 152,000 Lutherans and 144,000 Orthodox. Other Christian denominations, including Methodist, Baptist and Roman Catholic, are also represented.

CULTURE
Tallinn will be one of two European Capitals of Culture for 2011. The title attracts large European Union grants.

World Heritage Sites
Estonia has two sites on the UNESCO World Heritage List: the Historic Centre (Old Town) of Tallinn (1997 and 2008) and the Struve Geodetic Arc (2005). The Arc is a chain of survey triangulations spanning from Norway to the Black Sea that helped establish the exact shape and size of the earth and is shared with nine other countries.

Broadcasting
The two former public broadcasting organizations, Eesti Televisioon (ETV) and Eesti Raadio (ER), were merged in June 2007 to form Eesti Rahvusringhääling (Estonian Public Broadcasting or ERR). ERR is regulated by the Estonian Broadcasting Council. There are four public radio networks and numerous private radio stations. TV3 and Kanal 2 are major commercial TV stations. Cable television is widely available. There were 685,000 TV receivers (colour by PAL) in 2003; in 2007, 96% of households were equipped with colour TV.

Cinema
In 2003 there were 69 cinemas (81 screens); attendances totalled 1·27m. Three full-length films were released in 2003.

Press
In 2006 there were 13 daily newspapers (combined circulation of 334,000) and 29 non-dailies (250,000). *The Baltic Times* is an English-language weekly covering news from Estonia, Latvia and Lithuania.

Tourism
There were 1·9m. non-resident tourists in 2005 who spent US$1,207m.

Festivals
Festivals include: International Folklore Festival, BALTICA, which is staged every three years; Festival of Baroque Music; Jazz festival, JAZZKAAR; Pärnu International Documentary and Anthropology Film Festival and the Viljandi Folk Music Festival. Estonia's Song Festival, which was first held in 1869, is held every five years and is next scheduled to take place in 2014.

Baltoscandal, an international theatre festival which takes place every two years, celebrated its 10th staging in July 2008.

Libraries
The Eesti Rahvusraamatukogu (National Library of Estonia) was founded in 1918 and opened in its new building in 1993. Other libraries include the Tartu University Library (1802); Technical University Library (1919); and the Estonian Academic Library (1946). In 2005 there were 562 public libraries and 70 scientific and specialized libraries (including the National Library and 23 Higher Education libraries). They held a combined 21,441,000 volumes for 605,240 registered users.

Theatre and Opera
Most performances are in the Estonian language with the exception of a few theatre performances in Russian and operas, which are usually performed in their original language. There were nine state and three municipal theatres in 2007; 18 private theatres received state funding in 2007.

DIPLOMATIC REPRESENTATIVES
Of Estonia in the United Kingdom (16 Hyde Park Gate, London, SW7 5DG)
Ambassador: Dr Margus Laidre.

Of the United Kingdom in Estonia (Wismari 6, 10136 Tallinn)
Ambassador: Peter Carter.

Of Estonia in the USA (2131 Massachusetts Ave., NW, Washington, D.C., 20036)
Ambassador: Vaïno Reinart.

Of the USA in Estonia (Kentmanni 20, 15099 Tallinn)
Ambassador: Michael C. Polt.

Of Estonia to the United Nations
Ambassador: Tiina Intelmann.

Of Estonia to the European Union
Permanent Representative: Raul Mälk.

FURTHER READING
Statistical Office of Estonia. *Statistical Yearbook.*
Ministry of the Economy. *Estonian Economy.* Annual

Hood, N., *et al.*, (eds.) *Transition in the Baltic States.* 1997
Kolsto, Pal, *National Integration and Violent Conflict in Post-Soviet Societies: The Cases of Estonia and Moldova.* 2002
Lieven, A., *The Baltic Revolution: Estonia, Latvia, Lithuania and the Path to Independence.* 2nd ed. 1994
Misiunas, R.-J. and Taagepera, R., *The Baltic States: Years of Dependence 1940–1991.* 2nd ed. 1993
O'Connor, Kevin, *The History of the Baltic States.* 2003
Smith, David J., Purs, Aldis, Pabriks, Artis and Lane, Thomas, (eds.) *The Baltic States: Estonia, Latvia and Lithuania.* 2002
Taagepera, R., *Estonia: Return to Independence.* 1993

National Statistical Office: Statistical Office of Estonia, Endla 15, 15174 Tallinn.
Website: http://www.stat.ee

ETHIOPIA

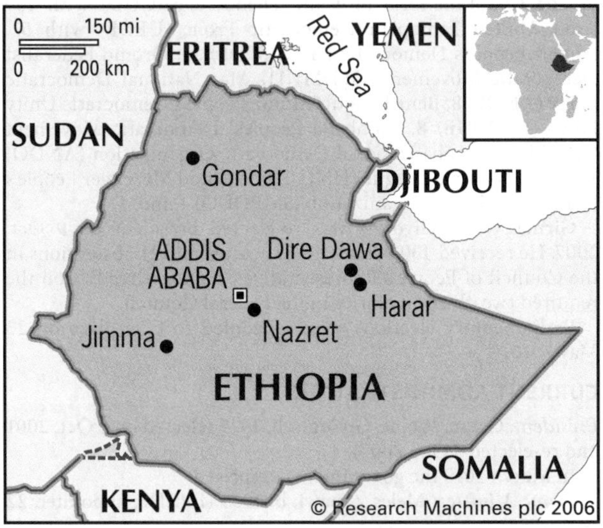

Ye-Ityoppya Federalawi Dimokrasiyawi Ripeblik
(Federal Democratic Republic of Ethiopia)

Capital: Addis Ababa
Population estimate, 2010: 84·98m.
GDP per capita, 2007: (PPP$) 779
HDI/world rank: 0·414/171

KEY HISTORICAL EVENTS

From as early as 3000 BC Egyptian Pharaohs referred to northern Ethiopia as the Land of Punt, rich in precious resources including gold, myrrh and ivory. Its inhabitants are thought to have been predominantly Cushitic speakers. The region was in contact with southern Arabia by around 2000 BC, with settlers bringing Semitic languages and stone-building techniques. Early in the 1st century AD a prosperous and advanced civilization arose in the northern highlands, centred on Aksum. Christianity reached Aksum in the 4th century AD when King Ezana was converted by Frumentius of Tyre. At its height in the 6th century AD the Aksumite empire controlled much of the Red Sea coast and traded with the Mediterranean powers, as well as Persia and India.

Between the 8th–10th centuries the declining Aksumite realm shifted southwards, while northern Ethiopia increasingly came under Arabian influence. Christianity held sway in the highlands and was central to the culture of the post-Aksumite Zagwe kingdom, founded in 1137. The first of the rock-hewn churches at Lalibela were constructed at this time. The Zagwe were ousted around 1270 by Yekuno Amlak, an Amharic warrior who restored the Solomonic dynasty which claimed descent from Aksum, King Solomon and the Queen of Sheba. The kingdom expanded to the south, particularly under Zara Jakob (ruled 1434–68).

Portuguese mariners reached the Red Sea in the early 1500s and a diplomatic mission arrived in Ethiopia in 1508. Faced with raids from neighbouring Islamic states, Emperor Lebna Dengel sought an alliance with the Portuguese who, in 1543, assisted in defeating Ahmad ibn Ibrahim al Ghazi, the conqueror of much of southern and eastern Ethiopia. The Solomonic monarchy was reinstated in 1632 by Emperor Fasidas, who established a new capital at Gondar. The coastal provinces came largely under Ottoman rule. By 1700 Gondar was a leading centre of education and the arts.

Tigray and Amhara experienced sporadic civil wars until the emergence of Lij Kasa in the 19th century. Crowned Emperor Tewodros II in 1855, he set about unifying the country although his efforts to end the slave trade led to tensions with local rulers. Following disagreements with Britain, Tewodros arrested several British officials including the consul. Britain responded by sending 12,000 troops to Ethiopia under Robert Napier. When Napier overwhelmed the fortress at Magdala, Tewodros committed suicide, igniting civil war.

The opening of the Suez Canal in 1869 intensified the regional scramble for influence among the European powers. At the same time Ethiopia faced armed incursions from Egypt and the Madhists in Sudan. Menelik II, ruler of Shoa in central Ethiopia, increased his power base with Italian support and seized control of Ethiopia in 1889. He renounced Italian claims to Ethiopia and defeated the Italian army at Adwa in 1896 before founding a new capital at Addis Ababa. Menelik II centralized authority and developed the country's infrastructure. He was succeeded in 1913 by his grandson, Lij Iyasu, who was deposed three years later in favour of Empress Zawaditu, with Ras Tafari Makonnen as regent and heir apparent. Following Empress Zawaditu's death in 1930 Ras Tafari became emperor as Haile Selassie I, claiming direct descent from King Solomon and the Queen of Sheba.

Although Ethiopia was recognized as independent in 1923, the League of Nations was unable to prevent Benito Mussolini from launching a second Italian invasion from Eritrea on 3 Oct. 1935. When Addis Ababa was captured in May 1936 Haile Selassie fled to Britain, only returning when Allied forces defeated the Italians in 1941. He brought in social and political reforms and established a national assembly. In 1950 Eritrea, an Italian colony under British military administration since 1941, was handed over to Ethiopia. A secessionist movement, the Eritrean Peoples' Liberation Front (EPLF), began a guerrilla war for independence. Following famine and economic decline, a military government (the Dirgue) assumed power on 12 Sept. 1974 under Lieut. Col. Mengistu Haile Mariam. It deposed Haile Selassie (who was murdered in prison in 1975), abolished the monarchy and mounted an agricultural collectivization programme.

In 1977 Somalia invaded Ethiopia and took control of the Ogaden region. After a counter offensive, with Soviet and Cuban support, the area was recaptured. Droughts in the late 1970s and early 1980s led to a devastating famine, which received international attention in 1984 when the death toll had already reached 200,000. War-torn Tigray and Eritrea were again at conflict in 1989. In 1991 the Ethiopian People's Revolutionary Democratic Front (EPRDF), led by Meles Zenawi, defeated the Ethiopian army, forcing Mengistu to flee to Zimbabwe. In July 1991 a conference of 24 political groups, called to appoint a transitional government, agreed a democratic charter. Eritrea seceded and became independent on 24 May 1993.

In 1994 a new constitution established a bicameral legislature and a judicial system. Meles Zenawi was elected prime minister in May 1995 with Negasso Gidada as president. The ongoing conflict with Eritrea flared up in 1999 and many thousands were killed before a peace deal was brokered in June 2000. Economic progress, including market-led reforms, raised hopes of higher living standards until three successive years of drought left food resources seriously depleted. Widespread malnutrition was alleviated by international aid. Zenawi's EPRDF won contested elections in May 2005, paving the way for his third five-year stint as prime minister. Opposition supporters took to the streets and around 35 were killed in subsequent clashes.

TERRITORY AND POPULATION

Ethiopia is bounded in the northeast by Eritrea, east by Djibouti and Somalia, south by Kenya and west by Sudan. It has a total area of 1,127,127 sq. km. The secession of Eritrea in 1993 left Ethiopia without a coastline. An Eritrean–Ethiopian agreement of July 1993 gives Ethiopia rights to use the Eritrean ports of Assab and Massawa.

The first census was carried out in 1984: population, 42,616,876 (including Eritrea). 1994 census population: 53,477,265. 2007 census population (provisional): 73,918,505, of which 36,621,848 were female; density, 65·6 per sq. km. The United Nations population estimate for 2007 was 78·65m. In 2005, 84·0% of the population lived in rural areas.

The UN gives an estimated population for 2010 of 84·98m.

Ethiopia has eleven administrative divisions—eight states (Afar, Amhara, Benshangul/Gumaz, Gambella, Oromia, the Peoples of the South, Somalia and Tigre) and three cities (Addis Ababa, Dire Dawa and Harar).

The population of the capital, Addis Ababa, was 2,738,248 in 2007 (provisional). Other large towns: Dire Dawa, 232,854; Nazret, 222,035; Mekele, 215,546; Gonder, 206,987; Bahir Dar, 180,094.

There are six major ethnic groups (in % of total population in 1996): Oromo, 31%; Amhara, 30%; Tigrinya, 7%; Gurage, 5%; Somali, 4%; Sidamo, 3%. There are also some 60 minor ethnic groups and 286 languages are spoken. The *de facto* official language is Amharic (which uses its own alphabet), though Oromo-speakers form the largest group.

SOCIAL STATISTICS

Births, 1999, 2,186,000; deaths, 1,062,000. Rates per 1,000 population, 1999: births, 34·2; deaths, 16·6. Expectation of life at birth in 2007 was 53·3 years for males and 56·2 years for females. Annual population growth rate, 1992–2002, 2·8%; infant mortality, 2005, 109 per 1,000 live births; fertility rate, 2004, 5·7 births per woman.

CLIMATE

The wide range of latitude produces many climatic variations between the high, temperate plateaus and the hot, humid lowlands. The main rainy season lasts from June to Aug., with light rains from Feb. to April, but the country is very vulnerable to drought. Addis Ababa, Jan. 59°F (15°C), July 59°F (15°C). Annual rainfall 50" (1,237 mm). Harar, Jan. 65°F (18·3°C), July 64°F (17·8°C). Annual rainfall 35" (897 mm). Massawa, Jan. 78°F (25·6°C), July 94°F (34·4°C). Annual rainfall 8" (193 mm).

CONSTITUTION AND GOVERNMENT

A 548-member constituent assembly was elected on 5 June 1994; turnout was 55%. The EPRDF gained 484 seats. On 8 Dec. 1994 it unanimously adopted a new federal constitution which became effective on 22 Aug. 1995. It provided for the creation of a federation of nine regions based (except the capital and the southern region) on a predominant ethnic group. These regions have the right of secession after a referendum. The *President*, a largely ceremonial post, is elected for a six-year term by both chambers of parliament. The lower house is the 547-member *Council of People's Representatives*; the upper house the 112-member *Federal Council*.

National Anthem

'Yazegennat keber ba-Ityop yachchen santo' ('In our Ethiopia our civic pride is strong'); words by D. M. Mengesha, tune by S. Lulu Mitiku.

RECENT ELECTIONS

Parliamentary elections were held on 15 May 2005 with repeat elections on 21 Aug. where irregularities had been reported or results were challenged. The bitterly contested elections resulted in more than 30 deaths and hundreds of arrests. Official results eventually released on 5 Sept. 2005 gave the Ethiopian People's Revolutionary Democratic Front (EPRDF) 327 seats, followed by the Coalition for Unity and Democracy (CUD) with 109 seats, United Ethiopian Democratic Front (UEDF) with 52, Somali People's Democratic Party (SPDP) 23, Oromo Federalist Democratic Movement (OFDM) 11, Afar National Democratic Party (ANDP) 8, Benishangul Gumuz People's Democratic Unity Front (BGPDUF) 8, Gambella Peoples' Democratic Movement (GPDM) 3, Argoba National Democratic Organization (ANDO) 1, Hareri National League (HNL) 1, Sheko and Mezenger People's Democratic Unity Organization (SMPDUO) 1, ind. 1.

Girma Wolde-Giyorgis was re-elected president on 9 Oct. 2007. He received 430 votes with 88 against and 11 abstentions in the Council of People's Representatives, having already won the required two-thirds majority in the Federal Council.

Parliamentary elections were scheduled to take place on 23 May 2010.

CURRENT ADMINISTRATION

President: Girma Wolde-Giyorgis; b. 1925 (elected on 8 Oct. 2001 and re-elected 9 Oct. 2007).

In March 2010 the government comprised:

Prime Minister: Meles Zenawi; b. 1955 (EPRDF; appointed 22 Aug. 1995).

Deputy Prime Minister: Adisu Legesse.

Minister of Agriculture and Rural Development: Tefera Deribew. *Capacity Building:* Tefera Walwa. *Communication Affairs:* Bereket Simon. *Culture and Tourism:* Mahmud Dirir. *Defence:* Siraj Fegeta. *Education:* Demeke Mekonnen. *Federal Affairs:* Dr Shiferaw Tekle-Mariam. *Finance and Economic Development:* Sufyan Ahmad. *Foreign Affairs:* Seyoum Mesfin. *Health:* Dr Tewodros Adhanom. *Justice:* Berhan Hailu. *Labour and Social Affairs:* Hassan Abdella. *Mines and Energy:* Alemayehu Tegenu. *Revenue:* Melaku Fenta. *Science and Technology:* Junedi Sado. *Trade and Industry:* Girma Birru. *Transport and Communications:* Diriba Kuma. *Water Resources:* Asefaw Dingam. *Women's Affairs:* Muferiat Kamil. *Works and Urban Development:* Kasu Ilala. *Youth and Sports:* Aster Mamo.

Ethiopian Parliament: http://www.ethiopar.net

CURRENT LEADERS

Meles Zenawi

Position

Prime Minister

Introduction

Meles Zenawi headed Ethiopia's transitional government from 1991–95. He was then appointed prime minister, the most important executive position in the country. He has had to cope with one of the world's weakest economies threatened by famine. His tenure has witnessed a border war with Eritrea, which officially ended in 2000 but remains a source of contention. Relations with Sudan have improved under Meles' guidance, but he remains troubled by separatist fighters in western Ethiopia. In late 2006 he launched a military offensive by Ethiopian forces to oust hostile Islamist militias that had taken control of much of neighbouring Somalia. Continuing insecurity prevented an early military withdrawal until late 2008 when, amid rising casualties and financial costs, Meles' government announced its decision to leave Somalia.

Early Life

Meles Zenawi Asres was born in Adwa, in Ethiopia's Tigre region in 1955. He attended school in Adwa and Addis Ababa. In 1972 he began studying medicine at Addis Ababa University but left two years later to join the Tigre People's Liberation Front (TPLF) to fight against the Dirgue military government of Lieut. Col. Mengistu Haile Mariam. He served on the organization's central committee between 1979 and 1983 and sat on the executive council from 1983 until 1989. In 1989 he was elected chairman of the TPLF and of the Ethiopian People's Revolutionary Democratic Front (EPRDF), an alliance formed that year between the TPLF and the Ethiopian People's Democratic Movement.

Career in Office

Alongside his role as EPRDF chair, Meles was president of Ethiopia's transitional government, established after the overthrow of the Mengistu regime, from 1991 until 1995. During this period he oversaw the secession of Eritrea and the drafting of a new constitution which divided Ethiopia into ethnic regions. In 1995 the EPRDF-dominated elections were boycotted by the major opposition groups. In Aug. 1995 Meles was elected prime minister of the newly established Federal Democratic Republic of Ethiopia, while Negasso Gidada took the largely ceremonial role of president. Meles was also voted chairman of the Organization of African Unity (now the African Union) for 1995–96.

In 2000 the EPRDF again dominated parliamentary elections and Meles was confirmed in office as prime minister. Despite the liberalization of the media and a move away from the human rights abuses of the Mengistu years, there remained opposition to Meles' government, and in 2001 there were mass protests in the capital against police brutality and political and academic oppression. In May 2005 Meles won a third term of office in further elections that were bitterly contested. Following allegations of fraud, there were violent protests and elections were rerun in some constituencies in Aug. In Sept. the Election Board confirmed the final results giving the EPRDF and its affiliates a solid parliamentary majority. Meanwhile, however, opposition parties and demonstrators continued to contest the outcome, clashing in June with security forces in Addis Ababa where 36 people were killed. In Nov. at least 46 more protesters died during renewed violence between security forces and opposition supporters. In May 2006 anti-Meles political parties and armed groups formed an opposition Alliance for Freedom and Democracy at a meeting in the Netherlands. In July 2007 Meles pardoned 38 opposition figures who had earlier been sentenced to life imprisonment on charges relating to the protests that followed the 2005 elections. In Jan. 2009 legislation was passed banning foreign agencies from work related to human rights or conflict resolution in Ethiopia in an apparent move to deter outside interference.

On the economic front, Meles—formerly an advocate of Marxist-Leninism—has adopted free market reforms that have generated considerable growth, although the country remains among the world's poorest. In 2002 an Economic Commission for Africa report highlighted excessive bureaucracy and the HIV/AIDS pandemic as major obstacles to sustained development.

In 1999 border fighting between Ethiopian and Eritrean forces escalated into a full-scale war, which cost 70,000 lives. A ceasefire was agreed in June 2000, with Ethiopia withdrawing its forces under UN supervision. A formal peace treaty was signed in Dec. 2000. Tensions remained, particularly concerning the control of the small border settlement of Badame. In May 2001 the countries agreed to abide by the decision of an international boundary commission. The commission awarded Badame to Eritrea, but Meles refused to accept the decision. Fears of a renewed conflict mounted in late 2005, after Eritrea expelled UN observers policing the militarized border region, and again in the autumn of 2006 as Eritrea moved troops into the buffer zone on the Ethiopian border in violation of the ceasefire. In Nov. 2007 Eritrea accepted a border demarcation proposal by an independent boundary commission but Ethiopia rejected it. In Jan. 2008 the UN Security Council extended the mandate of its peacekeeping mission on the border for a further six months (despite Eritrean opposition), but brought it to a close at the end of July. The Council called on both sides to show restraint, to refrain from any threat or use of force against each other and to avoid provocative military activities.

Tensions with neighbouring Somalia took a new turn in Dec. 2006. Ethiopian troops launched an offensive in support of the weak, but internationally-recognized, transitional Somali administration (established in 2004) against Islamist militias that had seized control of the capital, Mogadishu, and much of the south of the country from clan warlords earlier in the year. Meles was determined not to allow an enemy Islamic state on Ethiopia's borders. The Islamist forces were initially defeated and dispersed by Jan. 2007, and nominal authority was restored to the transitional government. However, insecurity continued and in Nov. 2008, embroiled in a stalemate situation, the Ethiopian government announced that its troops would leave Somalia at the end of the year, raising the spectre of a renewed takeover of the country by Islamist groups. The troop withdrawal was completed in Jan. 2009, although the government disclosed in the middle of the year that it was maintaining reconnaissance operations in Somalia.

In May 2008 the exiled former dictator Mengistu Haile Mariam was sentenced in absentia to death by Ethiopia's Supreme Court.

DEFENCE

In 2006 defence expenditure totalled US$345m. (US$5 per capita), representing 2·6% of GDP.

Army

Following the overthrow of President Mengistu's government Ethiopian armed forces were constituted from former members of the Tigray People's Liberation Front. The strength of the Army was 135,000 in 2007.

Air Force

Owing to its role in the war with Eritrea aircraft operability has improved. There were 48 combat capable aircraft in 2007, including MiG-21s and MiG-23s, and 25 attack helicopters. Personnel numbered 3,000 in 2007.

INTERNATIONAL RELATIONS

A border dispute between Ethiopia and Eritrea broke out in May 1998. Eritrean troops took over the border town of Badame after a skirmish between Ethiopian police units and armed men from Eritrea. Ethiopia maintained that Badame and Sheraro, a nearby town, had always been part of Ethiopia and called Eritrea's action an invasion. An agreement ending hostilities was signed in June 2000, followed by a peace accord in Dec. A buffer zone has been created to separate the armies but tensions do still arise from time to time, notably in late 2005 following a further dispute between the two countries over Badame.

Ethiopia is a member of the UN, World Bank, IMF and several other UN specialized agencies, African Development Bank, African Union, COMESA, Intergovernmental Authority on Development and is an ACP member state of the ACP-EU relationship.

ECONOMY

Agriculture accounted for 46·3% of GDP in 2007, industry 13·3% and services 40·4%.

Overview

Ethiopia is among the poorest countries in the world. Ongoing conflict with Eritrea since the late 1990s, as well as frequent droughts, has stalled economic development.

In 2000 Ethiopia embarked on a poverty reduction programme sponsored by the IMF, aimed at restoring macroeconomic stability. Donor assistance increased significantly in 2004 under the IMF-World Bank Indebted Poor Country Initiative and the country qualified for debt relief under the Multilateral Debt Relief Initiative of Dec. 2005.

Despite many obstacles, economic growth averaged around 11% between 2005–08. The percentage of the population living below the poverty line fell from 56% in 1999–2000 to 39% in 2006–07. The IMF, however, estimates growth will drop to around 7% over the period 2009–14.

Currency

The *birr* (ETB), of 100 *cents*, is the unit of currency. The birr was devalued in Oct. 1992. In April 2005 total money supply was 24,297m. birr. Foreign exchange reserves were US$1,444m. in May 2005. There was inflation of 15·8% in 2007, rising to 25·3% in 2008.

Budget

The fiscal year ends on 7 July. Revenue, 2004–05, 20,032m. birrs; expenditure, 24,551m. birrs.

VAT of 15% was introduced in 2003.

Performance

After the economy contracted by 3·5% in 2003 there was a recovery with growth of 13·1% in 2004. Real GDP growth was 11·5% in 2007 and 11·6% in 2008. Total GDP was US$26·5bn. in 2008.

Banking and Finance

The central bank and bank of issue is the National Bank of Ethiopia (founded 1964; *Governor*, Teklewold Atnafu). The country's largest bank is the state-owned Commercial Bank of Ethiopia. The complete monopoly held by the bank ended with deregulation in 1994, but it still commands about 90% of the market share. There are eight other banks. On 1 Jan. 1975 the government nationalized all banks, mortgage and insurance companies.

Weights and Measures

The metric system is official. Traditional units include the *feresula* (= approximately 17 kg), and the *gasha* (based on family land-ownership), which is officially 40 ha. but can be up to 120 ha.

ENERGY AND NATURAL RESOURCES

Environment

Carbon dioxide emissions from the consumption and flaring of fossil fuels were the equivalent of 0·1 tonnes per capita in 2008.

Electricity

Installed capacity in 2004 was an estimated 0·5m. kW. Production in 2004 was 2·55bn. kWh. Hydro-electricity accounts for 99% of generation. Consumption per capita was 36 kWh in 2004. Supply: 220 volts; 50 Hz. In 2008 only 15% of the population had access to electricity, although the stated aim is for electricity to be available to the entire country by 2018.

Oil and Gas

The Calub gas field in the southeast of Ethiopia had proven reserves of 25bn. cu. metres in 2007.

Minerals

Gold and salt are produced. Lege Dembi, an open-pit gold mine in the south of the country, has proven reserves of over 62 tonnes and produces more than five tonnes a year.

Agriculture

Small-scale farmers make up about 85% of Ethiopia's population. There were 10·7m. ha. of arable land in 2001 and 750,000 ha. of permanent crops. 190,000 ha. were irrigated in 2001. There were 3,000 tractors in 2001 and 100 harvester-threshers. Land remains the property of the state, but individuals are granted rights of usage which can be passed to their children, and produce may be sold on the open market instead of compulsorily to the state at low fixed prices.

Coffee is by far the most important source of rural income. Main agricultural products (2002, in 1,000 tonnes): maize, 2,968; sugarcane, 2,232; sorghum, 1,566; wheat, 1,478; barley, 1,093; broad beans, 447; potatoes, 385; millet, 308; yams, 300; papayas, 226; coffee, 220. Teff (*Eragrastis abyssinica*) and durra are also major products.

Livestock, 2002: cattle, 35·5m.; sheep, 11·4m.; goats, 9·6m.; asses, 3·4m.; horses, 1·3m.; camels, 326,000; chickens, 38m.

Forestry

In 2005 forests covered 13·0m. ha., representing 11·9% of the land area. Ethiopia is Africa's leading roundwood producer, with removals totalling 100·06m. cu. metres in 2007.

Fisheries

The catch in 2005 was 9,450 tonnes, entirely from inland waters.

INDUSTRY

Most public industrial enterprises are controlled by the state. Industrial activity is centred around Addis Ababa. Processed food, cement, textiles and drinks are the main commodities produced. Industrial production accounted for 13·3% of GDP in 2007, including 5·0% from manufacturing.

Labour

The labour force in 1996 was 25,392,000 (59% males); it was estimated by the UN that 30% were unemployed. Coffee provided a livelihood to a quarter of the population.

INTERNATIONAL TRADE

Foreign debt was US$6,259m. in 2005.

Imports and Exports

Imports and exports for calendar years in US$1m.:

	2002	2003	2004	2005	2006
Imports f.o.b.	1,455·0	1,895·0	2,768·5	3,700·9	4,105·6
Exports f.o.b.	480·2	496·4	678·3	917·3	1,024·7

Principal imports (2006): machinery and transport equipment (35·6%); petroleum and petroleum products (19·8%); manufactured goods (16·1%); chemicals and chemical products (11·0%). Principal exports (2006): coffee and coffee substitutes (40·8%); sesame seeds (15·4%); crude vegetable materials (12·4%); gold (6·2%). Other important exports include leather, chick-peas, hides and skins, and cattle.

Major import suppliers, 2006: Saudi Arabia, 17·9%; China, 12·3%; Italy, 7·7%. Main export markets, 2006: Germany, 12·6%; China, 9·7%; Japan, 8·4%.

COMMUNICATIONS

Roads

There were 36,469 km of roads in 2004, 19·1% of which were paved. Passenger cars in use in 2007 numbered 70,900 (one per 1,000 inhabitants) and there were also 149,000 lorries and vans, and 17,100 buses and coaches. In 2007 there were 2,517 deaths in road accidents.

Rail

The Ethiopian-Djibouti Railway has a length of 781 km (metre-gauge), but much of the route is in need of renovation. Passenger-km travelled in 2005 came to 145m. and freight tonne-km to 118m.

Civil Aviation

There are international airports at Addis Ababa (Bole) and Dire Dawa. The national carrier is the state-owned Ethiopian Airlines. In 2003 it served 43 international and 25 domestic destinations. In 2003 scheduled airline traffic of Ethiopian-based carriers flew 35m. km, carrying 1,147,000 passengers (881,000 on international flights). In 2001 Addis Ababa (Bole) handled 1,096,500 passengers and 26,490 tonnes of freight.

Shipping
Merchant shipping totalled 82,000 GRT in 2002, including oil tankers 2,000 GRT.

Telecommunications
All the main centres are connected with Addis Ababa by telephone or radio telegraph. In 2003 there were 532,800 telephone subscribers (7·7 per 1,000 persons), including 97,800 mobile phone subscribers. There were 225,000 PCs in use in 2004 (3·1 per 1,000 persons) and 113,000 internet users.

Postal Services
In 2003 there were 611 post offices, or one for every 116,000 persons.

SOCIAL INSTITUTIONS

Justice
The legal system is based on the Justinian Code. A new penal code came into force in 1958 and Special Penal Law in 1974. Codes of criminal procedure, civil, commercial and maritime codes have since been promulgated. Provincial and district courts have been established, and High Court judges visit the provincial courts on circuit. The Supreme Court at Addis Ababa is presided over by the Chief Justice. The death penalty is in force; there was one execution in 2007 but none in 2008.

The population in penal institutions in 2003 was approximately 65,000 (92 per 100,000 of national population).

Education
The adult literacy rate in 2004 was 35·9%. Primary education commences at seven years and continues with optional secondary education at 13 years. Up to the age of 12, education is in the local language of the federal region. In 2007 there were 12·17m. pupils at primary schools and 3·43m. pupils at secondary schools. During the period 1990–95 only 19% of females of primary school age were enrolled in school but this had increased to 62% by 2006. There were 21 public universities in 2007, with many having just opened in the previous few years. There were 210,456 students in tertiary education in 2007 and 8,355 academic staff.

In 2007 public expenditure on education came to 5·5% of GNI and 23·3% of total government spending.

Health
In 2002 there were 1,971 physicians, 61 dentists, 13,018 nurses, 1,142 midwives and 125 pharmacists. In 2000 only 24% of the population had access to safe drinking water.

RELIGION
About 59% of the population are Christian, mainly belonging to the Ethiopian Orthodox Church, and 32% Sunni Muslims. Amhara, Tigreans and some Oromos are Christian. Somalis, Afars and some Oromos are Muslims. About 5% of the population follow traditional animist beliefs.

CULTURE

World Heritage Sites
There are eight sites in Ethiopia that appear on the UNESCO World Heritage List. They are (with the year entered on list): the Rock-hewn Churches at Laibela (1978), 11 monolithic 13th century churches; Simien National Park (1978); Fasil Ghebbi, Gondar Region (1979), a 16th century fortress city; Aksum (1980), the capital of the ancient Kingdom of Aksum, containing tombs and castles dating from the first millennium AD; the Lower Valley of the Awash (1980), an important palaeontological site; the Lower Valley of the Omo (1980), where *Homo gracilis* was discovered; Tiya (1980), a group of archaeological sites south of Addis Ababa; and Harar Jugol (2006), a fortified historic town.

Broadcasting
Ethiopian Television (ETV) and most radio stations are government-controlled. Radio Ethiopia operates a national service, an external service and regional stations. Private radio stations have been permitted since 2004. In 2006 there were 700,000 TV-equipped households (colour by PAL).

Press
In 2006 there were three daily newspapers with a combined circulation of 92,000 and 53 non-dailies.

Tourism
In 2005 there were 227,000 foreign visitors. Revenue from tourists totalled US$533m.

Calendar
The Ethiopian calendar is based on the ancient Coptic calendar; the year has 13 months (12 months with 30 days and one month with five or six, depending on the leap-year). It begins on 11 or 12 Sept. (Gregorian) and is seven or eight years behind the Gregorian calendar.

DIPLOMATIC REPRESENTATIVES
Of Ethiopia in the United Kingdom (17 Prince's Gate, London, SW7 1PZ)
Ambassador: Ato Berhanu Kebede.

Of the United Kingdom in Ethiopia (Comoros St., Addis Ababa)
Ambassador: Norman Ling.

Of Ethiopia in the USA (3506 International Drive, NW, Washington, D.C., 20008)
Ambassador: Vacant.
Chargé d'Affaires a.i.: Wondimu Asamnew Chefchife.

Of the USA in Ethiopia (Entoto St., Addis Ababa)
Ambassador: Vacant.
Chargé d'Affaires a.i.: John M. Yates.

Of Ethiopia to the United Nations
Ambassador: Dawit Yohannes.

Of Ethiopia to the European Union
Ambassador: Ato Berhane Gebre-Christos.

FURTHER READING

Araia, G., *Ethiopia: the Political Economy of Transition.* 1995

Bigsten, Arne, Shimeles, Adebe and Kebede, Bereket, (eds.) *Poverty, Income Distribution and Labour Markets in Ethiopia.* 2005

Crummey, Donald, *Land and Society in the Christian Kingdom of Ethiopia: From the Thirteenth to the Twentieth Century.* 2000

Dejene, Alemneh, *Environment, Famine and Politics in Ethiopia: a View from the Village.* 1991

Henze, Paul B., *Layers of Time: A History of Ethiopia.* 2000

Marcus, H. G., *A History of Ethiopia.* 1994

Negash, Tekeste and Tronvoll, Kjetil, *Brothers at War: Making Sense of the Eritrean–Ethiopian War.* 2001

Pankhurst, Richard, *The Ethiopians.* 1999

Woodward, Peter, *The Horn of Africa: Politics and International Relations.* 2002

National Statistical Office: Central Statistical Office, Addis Ababa.

FIJI ISLANDS

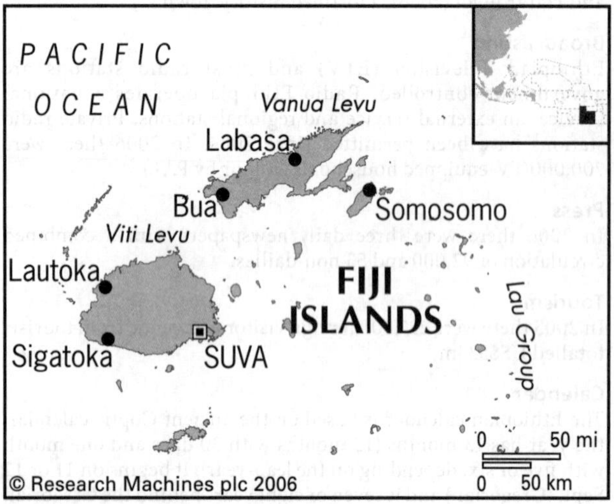

Kai Vakarairai ni Fiji
(Republic of the Fiji Islands)

Capital: Suva

Population estimate, 2010: 854,000

GDP per capita, 2007: (PPP$) 4,304

HDI/world rank: 0·741/108

KEY HISTORICAL EVENTS

The Fiji Islands were first recorded in detail by Capt. Bligh after the mutiny of the *Bounty* (1789). In the 19th century the demand for sandalwood attracted merchant ships. Deserters and shipwrecked men stayed. Tribal wars were bloody and widespread until Fiji was ceded to Britain on 10 Oct. 1874. Fiji gained independence on 10 Oct. 1970. It remained an independent state within the Commonwealth with a Governor-General appointed by the Queen until 1987. In the general election of 12 April 1987 a left-wing coalition came to power with the support of the Indian population who outnumbered the indigenous Fijians by 50% to 44%. However, it was overthrown in a military coup. A month later, Fiji declared itself a Republic and Fiji's Commonwealth membership lapsed.

In 1990 a new coalition restored civilian rule but made it impossible for Fijian Indians to hold power. A rapprochement with Indian leaders led to an agreement to restore multi-racial government in 1998. Fiji rejoined the Commonwealth in 1997. On 27 July 1998 a new constitution changed the country's name from Fiji to Fiji Islands.

A coup was staged in May 2000 under the leadership of George Speight, a failed businessman. His main aim was to exclude Indians from the government. An interim government, excluding Speight supporters, was appointed on 3 July 2000 to rule for 18 months. On 26 July George Speight and 400 of his supporters were arrested. On 18 Feb. 2002 Speight was sentenced to death although this was subsequently commuted to life imprisonment.

On 5 Dec. 2006 the Fiji Islands suffered their fourth coup in less than 20 years when Commodore Frank Bainimarama ousted Prime Minister Laisenia Qarase, placing him under house arrest. Bainimarama assumed the powers of president and prime minister, although he subsequently restored his predecessor, Ratu Josefa Iloilo, to the presidency.

TERRITORY AND POPULATION

The Fiji Islands comprise 332 islands and islets (about one-third are inhabited) lying between 15° and 22° S. lat. and 174° E. and 178° W. long. The largest is Viti Levu, area 10,429 sq. km (4,027 sq. miles); followed by Vanua Levu, 5,556 sq. km (2,145 sq. miles). The island of Rotuma (47 sq. km, 18 sq. miles), about 12° 30′ S. lat., 178° E. long., was added to the colony in 1881. Total area, 18,333 sq. km (7,078 sq. miles). Total population (2007 census), 837,271 (females, 410,095); ethnic groups: Fijian, 475,739; Indian, 313,798; other Pacific islanders, 15,311; part-European/European, 13,724; Rotuman, 10,335; Chinese, 4,704; other, 3,660. Population density (2007), 45·7 per sq. km; 50·7% of the population lived in urban areas in 2007.

The UN gives an estimated population for 2010 of 854,000.

The population of the capital, Suva (including Nasinu), was 173,137 at the 2007 census. Other large towns are Lautoka (52,220), Nausori (47,604) and Nadi (42,284).

English, Fijian and Hindustani are all official languages.

SOCIAL STATISTICS

Births, 2003, 17,701; deaths, 5,068; marriages, 7,440. 2003 birth rate per 1,000 population, 21·2; death rate per 1,000 population, 6·1. Annual population growth rate, 2000–05, 0·8%. Life expectancy at birth in 2007 was 66·5 years for males and 71·0 years for females. Infant mortality, 2005, 16 per 1,000 live births; fertility rate, 2004, 2·9 births per woman.

CLIMATE

A tropical climate, but oceanic influences prevent undue extremes of heat or humidity. The S. E. Trades blow from May to Nov., during which time nights are cool and rainfall amounts least. Suva, Jan. 80°F (26·7°C), July 73°F (22·8°C). Annual rainfall 117″ (2,974 mm).

CONSTITUTION AND GOVERNMENT

The executive authority of the State is vested in the *President*, who is appointed by the Bose Levu Vakaturaga (Great Council of Chiefs). The *Prime Minister* is appointed by the President. The Prime Minister must establish a multi-party cabinet. The President's term of office is five years.

A new Constitution unanimously passed by Parliament and assented to by H.E. the President came into force on 27 July 1998. The country's name was changed from Fiji to Fiji Islands and the people were to be known as Fiji Islanders instead of Fijians. The new Constitution stated that it was no longer a condition to have an indigenous Prime Minister and established a 71-seat *House of Representatives* (Lower House), with 46 elected on a communal role and 25 from an open electoral roll. Of the 46, 23 are elected from a roll of voters registered as Fijians, 19 from a roll of voters registered as Indians, one from a roll of voters registered as Rotumans and three from a roll of voters registered who are none of these. The Upper House or *Senate* has 32 members, 14 appointed by the Great Council of Chiefs, nine appointed on the advice of the prime minister, eight on the advice of the leader of the opposition and one appointed by the Council of Rotuma.

Parliament was reopened in Oct. 2001, having been suspended following a coup in May 2000. In 2006 another coup brought Commodore Frank Bainimarama to power but on 9 April 2009 the court of appeal declared his government illegal and he stood down. The next day the president repealed the constitution and assumed all governing power. The court was disbanded and Bainimarama's government restored on 12 April for the next five years. Elections were delayed indefinitely resulting in suspension from the Pacific Islands Forum.

National Anthem

'Meda Dau Doka' ('God Bless Fiji'); words and tune by M. Prescott.

RECENT ELECTIONS

Mahendra Chaudhry, the Fiji Labour Party leader, became the country's first Indian prime minister in 1999, but was ousted in the coup of May 2000 after just over a year in office. In parliamentary elections held between 6–13 May 2006, incumbent Prime Minister Laisenia Qarase's Fiji United Party won 36 of 71 available seats with 44·6% of votes cast, followed by the Fiji Labour Party with 31 (39·2%), the United People's Party 2 (0·8%) and ind. 2 (4·9%). Turnout was 87·7%.

CURRENT ADMINISTRATION

President: Ratu Epeli Nailatikau; b. 1941 (sworn in 5 Nov. 2009, having been acting president since 30 July 2009).

In March 2010 the interim government comprised:

Prime Minister, Minister for Public Service, People's Charter for Change, and Information, Acting Minister for Finance and National Planning, International Co-operation, Civil Aviation, Provincial Development, Indigenous Affairs and Multi-Ethnic Affairs: Commodore Frank Bainimarama; b. 1954 (sworn in 5 Jan. 2007, then briefly ousted from 9–12 April 2009).

Minister of Defence, National Security and Immigration: Ratu Epeli Galinau. *Education, National Heritage, Culture and the Arts, Youth and Sports, and Acting Minister for Labour, Industrial Relations, Employment, Local Government, Urban Development, Housing and the Environment:* Filipe Bole. *Foreign Affairs:* Ratu Inoke Kubuabola. *Primary Industries:* Joketani Cokanasiga. *Health:* Dr Neil Sharma. *Women, Social Welfare and Poverty Alleviation:* Dr Jiko Luveni. *Justice and Attorney General, Electoral Reform, Public Enterprise, Anti Corruption, and Acting Minister for Industry, Tourism, and Trade and Communication:* Aiyaz Sayed-Khaiyum. *Lands and Mineral Resources:* Netani Sukanaivalu. *Public Utilities, Works and Transport:* Timoci Lesi Natuva.

Fiji Islands Government Online: http://www.fiji.gov.fj

CURRENT LEADERS

Ratu Epeli Nailatikau

Position
President

Introduction
Ratu Epeli Nailatikau was sworn into office on 5 Nov 2009. He had been acting president for the previous three months following the resignation of Ratu Josefa Iloilo on 30 July 2009.

Early Life
Nailatikau was born on 5 July 1941 to a family of politically powerful chieftains. After completing his education in Fiji, he joined the armed forces and was sent for training in New Zealand. In 1966 he was posted with the 1st Battalion, Royal New Zealand Infantry Regiment to Sarawak, Malaysia during the Indonesia–Malaysia confrontation. On his return to Fiji, he joined the Fiji Infantry Regiment, rising steadily through the ranks. By 1987 he was a Brigadier-General and Commander of the Royal Fiji Military Forces but was ousted in a military coup headed by Sitiveni Rabuka.

Pursuing a new career in the diplomatic service, Nailatikau completed the foreign service programme at the University of Oxford and was appointed High Commissioner to the United Kingdom, a portfolio that also included Denmark, Egypt, Germany, Israel and the Holy See. He went on to become Roving Ambassador and High Commissioner to the member states of the South Pacific Forum and, in 1999, was appointed permanent secretary for foreign affairs and external trade.

Following a coup in 2000, which he had strongly opposed, Nailatikau was nominated as prime minister in the subsequent interim military government of Commodore Frank Bainimarama. However, within 24 hours Nailatikau had withdrawn in favour of Laisenia Qarase, instead taking the posts of deputy prime minister and minister for Fijian affairs. At the 2001 general election he put himself forward as speaker of the House of Representatives, a post he held until 2006. On 14 June 2005, Nailatikau was appointed the UNAIDS (The United Nations Joint Programme on HIV/AIDS) Special Representative for the Pacific. Outspoken in his campaign to tackle the AIDS crisis, he attracted controversy when he called for a public endorsement of safe sex.

In Jan. 2007 Nailatikau joined Bainimarama's interim government, formed in the wake of another coup d'état in Dec. 2006. He served as minister of foreign affairs, international co-operation and civil aviation. On 10 April 2007 he was nominated as vice-president by the newly reinstalled President Iloilo but his appointment was rejected by the Grand Council of Chiefs. Nailatikau took over the portfolio for provincial development and multi-ethnic affairs from Prime Minister Bainimarama in Oct. 2008, with his previous duties reassigned to the premier.

Nailatikau became vice-president on 17 April 2009 following a constitutional crisis in which the appeal court ruled that the military regime formed in 2006 was illegal, prompting Iloilo to repeal the constitution and sack the appeal court judges. With Bainimarama restored to the premiership, Nailatikau took over the presidency on 30 July 2009 in an acting capacity, until 5 Nov. 2009 when he was sworn in as Iloilo's successor.

Career in Office
Nailatikau's appointment, made behind closed doors, signalled that the military would continue to play a pivotal in Fijian politics. On 29 Jan. 2010 Nailatikau signed an extension of the public emergency regulation, in place since April 2009 to give power to the authorities to stop events they deem to be a threat to national security.

Josaia Voreqe Bainimarama

Position
Prime Minister

Introduction
Voreqe Bainimarama, military commander of the Fiji Islands, became prime minister after leading a coup in Dec. 2006 against the incumbent, Laisenia Qarase. Previously a Qarase ally, Bainimarama was a key figure in defeating a coup attempt by George Speight in 2000 and installing Qarase to the premiership. Bainimarama's relationship with Qarase deteriorated in 2006 and Bainimarama deposed him. He appointed himself as president before relinquishing that position to become prime minister. He is popularly known in the Fiji Islands as 'Frank' Bainimarama.

Early Life
An ethnic Fijian, Bainimarama was born on 27 April 1954 on Bau Island and educated at the Marist Brothers High School. He enlisted in the navy in July 1975 and received his first command post in the early 1980s. He was promoted to lieutenant commander in Feb. 1986 and then served with the Multinational Force and Observers peacekeeping force in the Sinai Peninsula until returning to Fiji in Sept. 1987. He was appointed commander of the navy in Oct. 1988.

During his term as commander Bainimarama undertook extensive training, including in maritime surveillance, in disaster management and in exclusive economic zone management. He became acting chief of staff in Nov. 1997, and was promoted to the rank of commodore and appointed commander of the armed forces in March 1999.

In May 2000 George Speight led a coup with the declared aim of promoting Fijian nationalism and excluding ethnic Indians from government. Prime Minister Chaudhry was deposed and when President Mara fled, Bainimarama declared martial law. On 30 May he appointed an interim military government and appointed Laisenia Qarase as prime minister on 4 July. On 6 July the interim government responded to a military mutiny by signing an accord with Speight granting him immunity from prosecution. On 13 July it installed Iloilo as president, together with a pro-Speight vice-president, Jope Seniloli.

On 27 July the interim government revoked Speight's immunity, with Bainimarama claiming that the accord had been signed under duress. Speight and 369 others were arrested. On 2 Nov. pro-Speight soldiers mutinied in Suva, forcing Bainimarama to flee. The mutiny was quelled and Bainimarama accused a former prime minister, Sitiveni Rabuka, of involvement. He persisted in attempts to prove the involvement of Rabuka and other alleged conspirators and vehemently opposed Prime Minister Qarase's proposals in 2006 to offer amnesty to the rebels.

In Oct. 2006 Qarase attempted unsuccessfully to replace Bainimarama as commander of the armed forces while he was out of the country. Bainimarama then staged a coup on 5 Dec. 2006, with the support of senior military figures. Claiming he wanted to end corruption and stop racial divisions threatening national unity, he dismissed Qarase's government and appointed himself acting president. He placed government ministries under the control of their chief executive officers and appointed Jona Senilagakali as acting prime minister. International pressure forced Bainimarama to return the presidency to Iloilo on 4 Jan. 2007 and on 5 Jan. he replaced Senilagakali as interim prime minister.

Career in Office

Bainimarama's political legitimacy has since come under intense scrutiny domestically and internationally. Australia and New Zealand called for him to relinquish power and refused visas to members of his government. At home political opponents and leading institutions, including the influential Methodist Church, condemned the coup alleging human rights abuses although talks in Feb. 2007 led to the Methodist Church declaring its support for the interim government. Internationally, particularly within the Pacific islands region, pressure continued to mount. In Feb. 2007 Bainimarama promised to work towards democratic elections, but initially would not commit to a time-frame. Then, in Oct. 2007 at the Pacific Islands Forum annual summit in Tonga, he agreed to hold a general election by March 2009. However, in July 2008 he reneged on this commitment on the grounds that electoral reforms could not be completed in time.

Having briefly reimposed a state of emergency from Sept.–Oct. 2007 he claimed the following month to have foiled a plot to assassinate him. On 9 April 2009 Bainimarama stood down following a court of appeal judgment that his government was illegal. However, President Iloilo reinstated the cabinet on 12 April for another five years after having dismissed the judiciary and annulled the constitution.

In Sept. 2009 the Commonwealth suspended the Fiji Islands' membership and cut off all aid because of the country's lack of progress in re-establishing democracy. Bainimarama incurred further diplomatic reproach in Nov. when he accused Australia and New Zealand of interfering in the Fiji Islands' internal affairs and expelled their high commissioners.

DEFENCE

In 2006 defence expenditure totalled US$43m. (US$47 per capita), representing 1·5% of GDP.

As at Oct. 2009, 277 personnel (including 221 troops and 49 police) were deployed in UN peacekeeping operations although a ban preventing the Fiji Islands from joining any new UN peacekeeping forces was enacted in June 2009.

Army

Personnel in 2007 numbered 3,200 including 300 recalled reserves. There is an additional reserve force of around 6,000.

Navy

A small naval division of the armed forces numbered 300 in 2007.

INTERNATIONAL RELATIONS

The Fiji Islands are a member of the UN, World Bank, IMF and several other UN specialized agencies, WTO, Asian Development Bank, Colombo Plan, SPC and is an ACP member state of the ACP-EU relationship.

ECONOMY

Agriculture accounted for 15·0% of GDP in 2006, industry 25·8% and services 59·2%.

Overview

Following a military coup in 2000 the Fiji Islands experienced high levels of growth. Political turmoil led to a contraction of the economy by 2·8% that year and growth of only 1% in 2001. However, according to the IMF, real GDP growth averaged 4·5% between 2002–04, above the average 1990s growth rate of 3·2%. It was driven primarily by high domestic demand, increased construction and tourism.

The growing tourism sector, sugar exports and remittances from citizens working abroad have been the main sources of foreign exchange for Fiji in recent years. GDP growth in 2005 was moderate at 0·7%, partly reflecting the loss of preferential trade agreements with the USA and the EU in the garment and sugar industries. After another coup in Dec. 2006, tourist arrivals fell by 6% in 2007 and the business climate was plagued by uncertainty. Low investment, uncertain property rights and inefficient budget management remain long-term problems.

Currency

The unit of currency is the *Fiji dollar* (FJD) of 100 *cents*. In June 2005 total money supply was $F1,082m., foreign exchange reserves were US$397m. and gold reserves 1,000 troy oz. Inflation in 2008 was 7·8%. The Fiji dollar was devalued by 20% in Jan. 1998 and again in April 2009.

Budget

Revenues in 2005 totalled $F1,218·3m. and expenditures $F1,231·6m.

VAT of 10% was introduced in 1992 (increased to 12·5% in 2003).

Performance

The economy contracted by 6·6% in 2007, although there was a slight recovery in 2008 when the economy grew by 0·2%. Total GDP in 2008 was US$3·5bn.

Banking and Finance

The financial system in the Fiji Islands comprises the central bank, banking, insurance and superannuation industries, non-bank financial institutions (NBFIs), restricted foreign exchange dealers and money changers, and the South Pacific Stock Exchange.

The central bank and bank of issue is the Reserve Bank of Fiji (*Governor*, Sada Reddy). Total assets at 31 Dec. 2007 were $F1,170m.

Total assets of commercial banks were $F3,957m. at the end of 2007. Total assets for the Fiji National Provident Fund (the sole player in the superannuation industry) at 31 Dec. 2007 were $F3,437m. Non-regulated financial institutions include the Fiji Development Bank, Housing Authority and Unit Trust of Fiji. Their assets totalled $F738m. in Dec. 2007.

The South Pacific Stock Exchange is based in Suva.

ENERGY AND NATURAL RESOURCES

Environment

Carbon dioxide emissions from the consumption and flaring of fossil fuels in 2008 were the equivalent of 2·9 tonnes per capita.

Electricity

The Fiji Electricity Authority is responsible for the generation, transmission and distribution of electricity in most of the country. It operates 13 power stations, three of which are operated on hydro power, and one 10 MW wind farm. The largest energy project is one of hydro-electricity that is capable of generating 70% of the main island's electric needs. Two rural hydro schemes have been completed, one private generating 100 kW and the other—operated by the Authority—producing 800 kW.

Installed capacity in 2004 was about 140,000 kW. Production in 2004 was around 540m. kWh with consumption per capita an estimated 613 kWh.

Minerals

The main gold-mine normally accounts for about a twelfth of the country's exports. Gold has for many years been one of the Fiji Islands' main exports. However, after an extended closure in 2006–07 gold production in 2007 was only 77 kg, valued at $F2·55m.

Agriculture

With a total land area of 1·8m. ha., only 16% is suitable for farming. In 2007 there were an estimated 170,000 ha. of arable land and 83,000 ha. of permanent crops. Arable land: 24% sugarcane, 23% coconut and 53% other crops. Production figures for 2003 (in 1,000 tonnes): sugarcane, 3,300; coconut, 170; taro, 38; cassava, 33; rice, 16; copra, 14; bananas, 6; sweet potatoes, 6. Ginger is becoming increasingly important.

Livestock (2003): cattle, 320,000; goats, 248,000; pigs, 139,000; chickens, 4m. Products, 2003 (in 1,000 tonnes): beef and veal, 9; poultry meat, 9; pork, bacon and ham, 4; eggs, 3. Total production of milk was 58,000 tonnes in 2003.

Forestry

Forests covered 1·0m. ha.—54·7% of the land area—in 2005. Forestry contributed about 0·5% of GDP in 2007. It is the sixth most important export commodity, valued at $F48m. in 2007, of which $F27m. was in the form of wood chips. Hardwood plantations covered over 67,000 ha. in 2007. About 42,000 ha. of softwood plantations were held by Fiji Pine Ltd in 2007. There was no export of unprocessed timber. Roundwood production in 2007 was 509,000 cu. metres.

Fisheries

The catch in 2004 was 46,635 tonnes, of which 43,642 tonnes came from sea fishing. In 2007 fisheries accounted for around 2% of GDP, valued at $F101·3m. Mainstay of export fisheries are the skipjack and albacore tuna for canning. There was an increase in export of fresh and chilled tuna from 53 tonnes in 1989 to over 3,000 tonnes in 1995.

INDUSTRY

The main industries are tourism, sugar, fish, mineral water, garments and gold which in 2007 accounted for 12·6%, 3·4%, 1·9%, 1·9%, 1·8% and 0·5% of GDP respectively.

Output, 2007 (in tonnes): sugar, 240,000; cement, 144,000; flour, 52,677; animal feed, 37,820; coconut oil, 9,657; soap, 5,556; soft drinks, 213·4m. litres; beer, 19·0m. litres; cigarettes, 401m. units.

Labour

The labour force was estimated at 371,400 in 2003. In 2002 there were 23,000 people out of work and seeking employment—the number of unemployed people doubled between 1996 and 2002.

INTERNATIONAL TRADE

The Tax Free Factory/Tax Free Zone Scheme was introduced in 1987 to stimulate investment and encourage export-oriented businesses.

Foreign debt was US$387m. in 2007.

Imports and Exports

Imports totalled US$1,640·1m. in 2006; exports US$712·9m.

Chief exports are clothing and apparel, sugar, gold, prepared and preserved fish, beverages, and cereal and cereal preparations. Principal import suppliers, 2004: Australia, 34·0%; New Zealand, 20·4%; Singapore, 12·5%. Main export markets, 2004: Australia, 29·6%; USA, 27·2%; UK, 16·0%.

COMMUNICATIONS

Roads

Total road length in 2002 was an estimated 3,440 km, of which almost half were surfaced. There were a total of 94,400 passenger cars and 48,000 lorries and vans in 2007. In 2006, 89 fatalities were caused by road accidents.

Rail

Fiji Sugar Cane Corporation runs 600 mm gauge railways at four of its mills on Viti Levu and Vanua Levu, totalling 597 km in 2005.

Civil Aviation

There are international airports at Nadi and Suva. The national carrier is Air Pacific (51% government-owned). In 2003 it provided services to Australia, Japan, New Zealand, USA and a number of Pacific island nations. Air Fiji only operates on domestic routes. In 2001 Nadi handled 911,000 passengers (808,000 on international flights).

Shipping

The three main ports are Suva, Lautoka and Levuka. The gross registered tonnage of ocean-going shipping entering the ports in 2007 totalled 8,361,785 GRT including liquid bulk carriers of 2,530,718 GRT. A total of 694 foreign vessels called into Suva port in 2007, 348 into Lautoka and 93 into Levuka. The inter-island shipping fleet is made up of private and government vessels.

Telecommunications

In 2008 there were 129,100 main (fixed) telephone lines; mobile phone subscribers numbered 530,000 in 2008 (63·2 per 100 persons). In 2004 there were 44,000 PCs in use (51·9 per 1,000 persons) and 61,000 internet users.

Postal Services

There were 142 post offices in 2003, or one for every 5,910 persons. A total of 37m. pieces of mail were processed in 2003.

SOCIAL INSTITUTIONS

Justice

An independent Judiciary is guaranteed under the constitution. A High Court has unlimited original jurisdiction to hear and determine any civil or criminal proceedings under any law. The High Court also has jurisdiction to hear and determine constitutional and electoral questions including the membership of the House of Representatives. The Chief Justice of the Fiji Islands is appointed by the President after consultation with the Prime Minister. The substantive Chief Justice was removed from office following the Dec. 2006 military coup and was replaced by an Acting Chief Justice in Jan. 2007.

The Fiji Islands' Court of Appeal, of which the Chief Justice is *ex officio* President, is formed by three specially appointed Justices of Appeal, appointed by the President after consultation with the Judicial and Legal Services Commission. Generally, any person convicted of an offence has a right of appeal from the High Court of Appeal. The final appellant court is the Supreme Court.

Most matters coming before the Superior Courts originate in Magistrates' Courts.

The population in penal institutions in 2007 was 841 (100 per 100,000 of national population).

Police

In 2008 the Royal Fiji Police Force had a total strength of 2,655 established officers, 60 support staff and 1,600 Special Constables.

Education

Adult literacy rate was 93·2% in 2001 (95·2% among males and 91·2% among females). Total enrolment: pre-primary schools (2004), 8,628; primary schools (2005), 141,089 (with 5,006 teachers); secondary schools (2005), 68,521 (with 4,141 teachers); special schools (2005), 1,007 (with 103 teachers); teacher training (2005), 713 (with 87 teachers); technical/vocational education (2005), 2,115 (1,048 teachers in 2004). There were 531 pre-primary schools, 719 primary schools, 162 secondary schools, 17 special schools, 4 teacher training schools and 63 technical/vocational schools in 2005.

The University of the South Pacific, which is located in Suva, serves 12 countries in the South Pacific region. The Fiji Islands also has a college of agriculture, school of medicine and nursing, an institute of technology, a primary school teacher training college and an advanced college of education.

In 2005 public expenditure on education came to 6·2% of GDP.

Health

In 2007 there were 25 public hospitals with 1,727 beds, two private hospitals, 76 health centres and 101 nursing stations. There were 318 doctors, 196 dental staff and 1,820 nurses.

Through its national health service system, the government continues to provide the bulk of health services both in the curative and public health programmes.

RELIGION

In 2001 the population consisted of 53% Christians, 38% Hindus, 8% Muslims and 1% others.

CULTURE

Broadcasting

The state-owned Fiji Broadcasting Corporation runs two public and several commercial radio services (broadcasting in Fijian, Hindustani and English). Communications Fiji Ltd, the South Pacific's largest broadcast organization, operates four radio networks in the Fiji Islands. Fiji Television is a commercial network that has one free-to-air and one pay-TV channel (colour by NTSC). In 2005 TV receivers numbered 99,000.

Press

In 2006 there were three national dailies with a combined circulation of 40,000. However, the *Fiji Times* and *The Daily Post* were closed down following the coup in Dec. 2006.

Tourism

Visitor arrivals in 2003 totalled 431,000; earnings from tourism in 2003 amounted to US$340m.

DIPLOMATIC REPRESENTATIVES

Of the Fiji Islands in the United Kingdom (34 Hyde Park Gate, London, SW7 5DN)
High Commissioner: Pio Bosco Tikoisuva.

Of the United Kingdom in the Fiji Islands (Victoria House, 47 Gladstone Rd, Suva)
High Commissioner: Mac McLachlan, MBE.

Of the Fiji Islands in the USA (2233 Wisconsin Ave., NW, Washington, D.C., 20007)
Ambassador: Winston Thompson.

Of the USA in the Fiji Islands (31 Loftus St., Suva)
Ambassador: C. Steven McGann.

Of the Fiji Islands to the United Nations
Ambassador: Peter Thomson.

Of the Fiji Islands to the European Union
Ambassador: Ratu Seremaia Tuinosori Cavuilati.

FURTHER READING

Bureau of Statistics. *Annual Report; Current Economic Statistics.* Quarterly

Reserve Bank of Fiji. *Quarterly Review*

Belshaw, Cyril S., *Under the Ivi Tree: Society and Economic Growth in Rural Fiji.* 2004

Kelly, John D. and Kaplan, Martha, *Represented Communities: Fiji and World Decolonization.* 2001

Lal, B. J., *Broken Waves: a History of the Fiji Islands in the Twentieth Century.* 1992

Robertson, Robert and Sutherland, William, *Government by the Gun: Fiji and the 2000 Coup.* 2002

Sutherland, W., *Beyond the Politics of Race: an Alternative History of Fiji to 1992.* 1992

National Statistical Office: Bureau of Statistics, POB 2221, Government Buildings, Suva.

Website: http://www.statsfiji.gov.fj

FINLAND

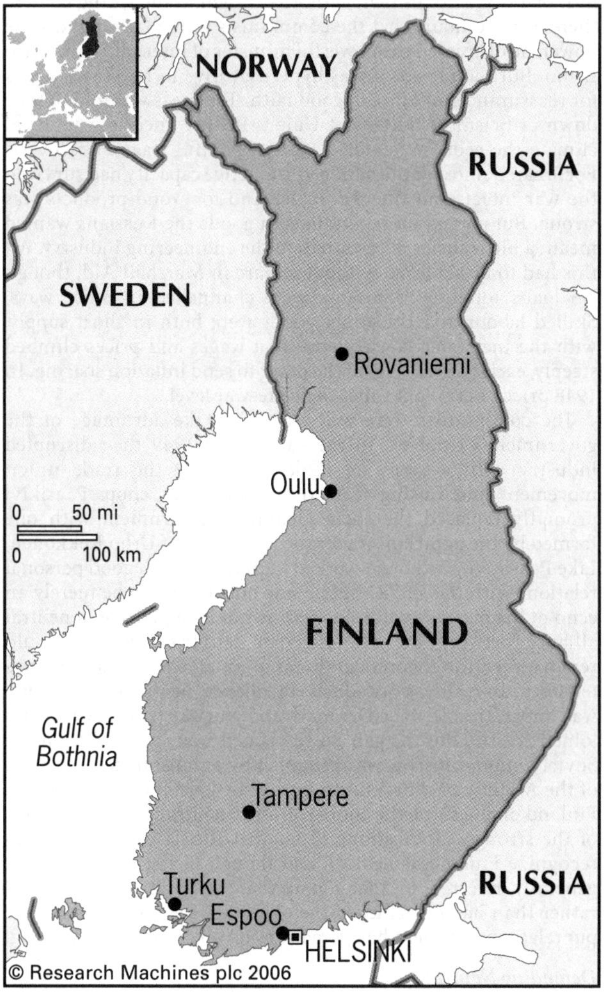

Suomen Tasavalta—Republiken Finland (Republic of Finland)

Capital: Helsinki
Population estimate, 2010: 5·35m.
GDP per capita, 2007: (PPP$) 34,526
HDI/world rank: 0·959/12

KEY HISTORICAL EVENTS

Finland's first inhabitants moved northwards at the end of the Ice Age. Further waves of settlement came in 4000 BC and 1000 BC and although the population was spread out, distinct social groups began to develop. During the Viking era Finland's location on the trade route between Russia and Sweden brought prosperity and conflict in equal measure, with attacks frequently made on Finnish trading posts by the Swedes and the Danes.

In the 12th century economic and religious rivalry between Sweden and Russia was centred on Finland. Sweden, supported by the Papacy in Rome, began a succession of crusades to draw Finland into its sphere of control. The defeat of Birger Jarl in 1240 marked the end of the Swedish incursions into Finland but efforts at strengthening the Swedish presence in areas it already held were intensified. By 1323 Russia was forced to recognize a boundary marking off those parts of Finland which were under Swedish control including all of western and southern Finland. Finland remained a duchy of Sweden until 1581 when it was made a grand duchy.

In the 18th century Russian forces conquered the southeast territory. The rest of the country was ceded to Russia by the treaty of Hamina in 1809 when Finland became an autonomous grand duchy, retaining its laws and institutions but owing allegiance to the tsar of Russia.

Throughout the 19th century Finland remained in Russia's shadow. Under Alexander II Finland built on her status as a grand duchy, so that by the 1880s she had control over her own army. This proved too much for the Russian military, who feared that moves towards Finnish separatism would make more difficult their task of defending the long western border. With the appointment of Gen. Bobrikov as governor general in 1898 a start was made on bringing Finland back into the imperial fold. The army was put under Russian command, the Russian language was made compulsory for the civil service and for schools and decision-making reverted to the tsar's appointees.

Resistance first took the form of non-cooperation but as the Russian revolutionary movement gathered pace, their allies in Finland became bolder. In June 1904 Bobrikov was assassinated and in 1916 the Marxists won an absolute majority in parliamentary elections. It was a short-lived victory but the far left held its popular appeal.

Civil War

Following the revolution, on 6 Dec. 1917 Finland declared independence. This was recognized by the Russian Bolsheviks on 31 Dec. By this time, however, a breach between the left and right parties in Finland had become irreconcilable. In Jan. 1918 the Whites (the government forces) took the western, Russian-controlled province of Ostrobothnia while the Reds (the left-wing forces, supported by the Bolsheviks) seized power in the south. At the end of Jan. the Reds staged a coup and the Whites were forced to abandon Helsinki, relocating to Vaasa. Civil war ensued which the government forces won, led by Gen. Gustaf Mannerheim and aided by German troops.

Parliament approved a new constitution in which a German prince, Friedrich Karl, would become regent. However, such plans were halted with the collapse of Germany at the end of the First World War. In the summer of 1919 Finland became a republic with K. J. Ståhlberg elected as its first president.

Throughout the 1920s and early 1930s the class antagonism inherited from the civil war remained the dominant political issue. As a conciliatory measure the Social Democrats were brought into government and the party formed a minority government in 1926–27. In the early 1930s fascism entered domestic politics with the emergence of the Lapua Movement. After an unsuccessful coup attempt in 1932 the movement was banned. In common with its Scandinavian neighbours, Finland was hit by the Great Depression but cushioned by the dominant role of agriculture in the Finnish economy, industrialization and urbanization both continued throughout the inter-war years.

Winter War

As Europe was anticipating German aggression, the Finns were taking up arms to resist Moscow's territorial demands. Outnumbered and outmatched in arms and equipment, their hopes were pinned on foreign involvement. When this failed to materialize, there was no option but to give the Russians all they wanted, including the Karelian Isthmus. The 1940 treaty, which ended the Winter War, required the resettlement of 12% of the Finnish population. Fearing worse to come from the Soviet Union, Helsinki opened up contacts with the Germans, allowing transit for military traffic in return for food and armaments.

There followed the German invasion of Russia, a campaign which Mannerheim, in justifying the active participation of his army, described as a 'holy war' to restore Finnish borders. Having achieved this objective with remarkable ease, the Finns wanted out, a desire which became all the more determined as the German advance ground to a halt at Stalingrad. But there was no basis for a settlement and the Finns could only wait for the inevitable Russian counter-attack. When it came, retreating Germans took revenge by devastating everything in their path.

Having fought first against Russia then against Germany, the country emerged from the Second World War defeated, demoralized and in political disarray. The peace treaty with the Soviet Union was still to be agreed, but the terms of the 1944 armistice—the surrender of one-twelfth of Finnish territory and reparations to be paid in goods valued at US$300m. at 1938 prices—suggested that Russia had no inhibitions about leaning heavily on her weaker neighbour.

If the public looked anywhere for a leader it was to the presidency, and to Field-Marshal Mannerheim. Revered as a national hero by the right, Mannerheim extended his reputation by bringing his country through the Winter War and by his initial success in the renewed hostilities with Russia in 1941. Though he was not much loved by the Soviets they acknowledged Mannerheim's unique personal authority. Carl Enckell, a close and trusted associate of Mannerheim for many years, took charge of foreign affairs while Juho Paasikivi was appointed premier. The 1945 election confirmed Paasikivi and Enckell in their jobs and a cabinet was formed giving roughly equal representation to the social democrats, communists and the farmers' party. When Mannerheim, who had turned 78 and was ailing fast, was persuaded to stand down in mid-term of his presidency, Paasikivi was the obvious successor.

The peace treaty with Russia was signed in Feb. 1947. Though severe, the terms confirmed what had already been provisionally agreed by the 1944 armistice. Finland lost 12% of her border territory to the Soviet Union, including the country's second largest city, Viipuri, and the port and province of Petsamo on the Arctic coast. With a large part of the province of Karelia taken over by the Russians the frontier was moved back from a distance of only 31 km from Leningrad to a new line 180 km from the former Russian capital. 400,000 people had to be resettled. The Åland Islands were to remain demilitarized and limitations were imposed on the size of the Finnish armed forces and its weaponry.

Pacifying Russia

The Russians then raised the stakes with an 'invitation' to negotiate a mutual assistance agreement. It seemed as if nothing less than an administration directly answerable to Moscow would satisfy the Russians. Paasikivi opened negotiations by arguing that the interests of the Soviet Union on her northwestern border (the only part of Finland that really mattered to the Russian military) could best be served by a sovereign Finland whose sympathetic relations with her eastern neighbour precluded her territory being used as a platform for attack. Skilfully, Paasikivi shifted the emphasis away from Russian ambitions for making Finland an ally towards the far more attractive prospect of the two countries' entering into a joint security arrangement which would allow Finland to stand aside from big power politics. In the end it was a matter of interpretation. Finland promised to defend herself against an attack from Germany or an allied state, to confer with Russia in case of war or threat of war and, if necessary, to accept Russian aid. Great play was made of Finland's ambition 'to remain outside the conflicting interests of the great powers'.

The popular view in Europe was that Finland had tied herself to the Soviet Union and was as much under the control of Moscow as any of the communist satellites. Paasikivi did his best to counteract this impression and reacted decisively if there was any hint of a threat to his own authority. When in the spring of 1948 there were rumours that the communists were planning to seize power, he dismissed the powerful minister of internal affairs, Yrjö Leino. But the president was hyper-sensitive to Moscow's needs for reassurances of Finnish good faith. The press was told to tone down criticism of the Soviet Union. In this uncertain political climate the economy entered its first painful stage of recovery. Fortunately, most of the nation's productive capacity had survived the war intact, and the export demand for wood products was strong. But paying off reparations in goods the Russians wanted meant a big transfer of resources to the engineering industry. All this had to be achieved without a share in Marshall Aid, though US loans totalling US$150m. were channelled in other ways. Skilled labour and consumer goods were both in short supply, with the inevitable consequence that wages and prices climbed steeply, each one feeding off the other to send inflation soaring. In 1948 prices were eight times their pre-war level.

The communists were well placed to take advantage of the government's troubles. In the summer of 1949 they disrupted industry with a series of strikes, splitting the trade union movement and raising fears of an imminent coup. Paasikivi promptly replaced the social democrat government with one formed by the agrarians under the leadership of Urho Kekkonen. Like Paasikivi, Kekkonen worked hard to establish good personal relations with the USSR. But he was not content to be merely an echo of his master's voice. In 1952 he put up a plan for 'a neutral alliance between the Scandinavian countries', which 'would remove even the theoretical threat of an attack … via Finland's territory'. In reality, a Scandinavian alliance, neutral or otherwise, was impracticable since Denmark and Norway had only recently joined NATO. But the gain to Kekkonen was approval from the Soviet Union. Moscow was delighted by an unsolicited rejection of the Atlantic pact by a north European state and congratulated Finland on pursuing the course of 'strict neutrality'. This was one of the strongest indications so far that Russia was prepared to recognize Finland as neutral, and though Soviet commentators generally referred to that country as 'striving for neutrality' rather than having achieved the objective, Kekkonen's initiative put relations between the two nations on an entirely new footing.

Defending Neutrality

In 1955, two years after the death of Stalin had brought the first signs of an easing in the cold war, Finland negotiated the return of the Porkkala base near Helsinki, which had been leased to the Soviet Union for 50 years. This meant the departure of the last Soviet troops on Finnish territory—the most powerful boost to national morale of the early post-war years. That same year Finland joined the United Nations but stayed out of the latest formation of Soviet defence, the Warsaw Pact. In 1956 Kekkonen succeeded Paasikivi as president. A succession of weak governments consolidated presidential power and confirmed Kekkonen as the only leader capable of handling the Russians. Enjoying his enhanced prestige he was soon back on course with his policy of trying to establish Finland as an independent neutral.

His first move was to assert his country's freedom of action, by suggesting that Finland might come to a deal with the European Community. In response, the Soviet Union activated article 2 of the 1948 Treaty by demanding consultation on measures to ensure the defence of their frontiers. It was the most serious challenge yet to Finnish neutrality. It had been said that article 2 could be acted upon only when both parties agreed that a threat existed; it came as a shock to realize that a unilateral declaration of interest by the stronger partner was sufficient to start the process of military consultation. If the Soviet claim went uncontested Finnish independence would be seen as a sham.

Western observers expected the worst; nothing less than military bases on Finnish soil would satisfy Moscow. But Kekkonen remained placid. His compromise strategy called for a postponement of military talks in favour of discussions aimed at reassuring the Kremlin that Finland would remain true to her foreign policy. This was accompanied by a warning that if military consultations went ahead there would be a war scare in Scandinavia, possibly leading to counter-measures by the West. When the Soviet Union backed down Kekkonen was feted as the country's saviour. He was elected for a second six-year term by an overwhelming majority on the first round of voting.

In 1981 the ailing Kekkonen was replaced by Mauno Koivisto. At first he adopted the foreign policy of his predecessor but with the collapse of the Soviet Union at the end of the 1980s he was able to move Finland towards closer ties with Western Europe. Koivisto played a major role in dismantling the 1948 Treaty and in the early 1990s fostered close relations with the EU. A referendum held in 1995 paved the way for Finland to join the EU.

TERRITORY AND POPULATION

Finland, a country of lakes and forests, is bounded in the northwest and north by Norway, east by Russia, south by the Baltic Sea and west by the Gulf of Bothnia and Sweden. The most recent ten-yearly census took place on 31 Dec. 2000. The areas, populations and population densities of Finland and its provinces and regions on 31 Dec. 2007 (Swedish names in brackets) were as follows:

Provinces (in italics) and Regions	*Area (sq. km)*[1]	*Population*	*Population per sq. km*
Etelä-Suomi (Södra Finland)	*30,183*	*2,173,509*	*70·0*
Uusimaa (Nyland)	6,371	1,388,964	218·0
Itä-Uusimaa (Östra Nyland)	2,761	94,755	34·3
Kanta-Häme (Egentliga Tavastland)	5,199	171,449	33·0
Päijät-Häme (Päijänne-Tavastland)	5,127	200,061	39·0
Kymenlaakso (Kymmenedalen)	5,112	183,564	35·9
Etelä-Karjala (Södra Karelen)	5,613	134,716	24·0
Itä-Suomi (Östra Finland)	*48,523*	*573,478*	*11·8*
Etelä-Savo (Södra Savolax)	13,989	157,862	11·3
Pohjois-Savo (Norra Savolax)	16,771	248,872	14·8
Pohjois-Karjala (Norra Karelen)	17,763	166,744	9·4
Länsi-Suomi (Västra Finland)	*74,240*	*1,874,573*	*25·3*
Varsinais-Suomi (Egentliga Finland)	10,664	459,235	43·1
Satakunta	7,956	228,431	28·7
Pirkanmaa (Birkaland)	12,447	476,631	38·3
Keski-Suomi (Mellersta Finland)	16,708	270,701	16·2
Etelä-Pohjanmaa (Södra Österbotten)	13,444	193,815	14·4
Pohjanmaa (Österbotten)	7,749	174,987	22·6
Keski-Pohjanmaa (Mellersta Österbotten)	5,273	70,964	13·5
Lappi (Lappland)	*92,666*	*184,390*	*2·0*
Oulu (Uleåborg)	*56,736*	*467,190*	*8·2*
Pohjois-Pohjanmaa (Norra Österbotten)	35,230	383,411	10·9
Kainuu (Kajanaland)	21,506	83,779	3·9
Ahvenanmaa (Åland)	*1,553*	*27,153*	*17·5*
Total	303,901	5,300,484	17·4

[1]Excluding inland water area which totals 34,519 sq. km.

The semi-autonomous province of the **Åland Islands** (Ahvenanmaa) occupies a special position as a demilitarized area and is 91% Swedish-speaking. **Åland** elects a 30-member parliament (*Lagting*), which in turn elects the provincial government (*Landskapsstyrelse*). It has a population of 27,000. The capital is Mariehamn (Maarianhamina).

The growth of Finland's population, which was 421,500 in 1750, has been:

End of year	*Urban*[1]	*Semi-urban*[2]	*Rural*	*Total*	*Percentage urban*
1800	46,600	—	786,100	832,700	5·6
1900	333,300	—	2,322,600	2,655,900	12·5
1950	1,302,400	—	2,727,400	4,029,800	32·3
1970	2,340,300	—	2,258,000	4,598,300	50·9
1980	2,865,100	—	1,922,700	4,787,800	59·8
1990	2,846,220	803,224	1,349,034	4,998,500	56·9
2000	3,167,668	898,860	1,114,587	5,181,115	61·1
2005	3,294,777	896,181	1,064,622	5,255,580	62·7
2006	3,327,207	913,614	1,036,134	5,276,955	63·1
2007	3,444,620	852,225	1,003,639	5,300,484	65·0

The classification urban/rural has been revised as follows: [1]Urban—at least 90% of the population lives in urban settlements, or in which the population of the largest settlement is at least 15,000. [2]Semi-urban—at least 60% but less than 90% live in urban settlements, or the population of the largest settlement is more than 4,000 but less than 15,000.

The population on 31 Dec. 2007 by language spoken: Finnish, 4,836,183; Swedish, 289,596; Lappish, 1,777; other languages, 172,928.

The UN estimated population for 2010 is 5·35m.

The principal towns with resident population, 31 Dec. 2007, are (Swedish names in brackets):

Helsinki (Helsingfors)—capital	568,531	Järvenpää	37,989
Espoo (Esbo)	238,047	Lohja (Lojo)	37,352
Tampere (Tammerfors)	207,866	Seinäjoki	37,336
Vantaa (Vanda)	192,522	Kokkola (Karleby)	36,966
Turku (Åbo)	175,286	Rauma (Raumo)	36,783
Oulu (Uleåborg)	131,585	Jyväskylän maalaiskunta	36,100
Lahti	99,308		
Kuopio	91,320	Tuusula (Tusby)	35,968
Jyväskylä	85,402	Kirkkonummi (Kyrkslätt)	35,141
Pori (Björneborg)	76,255		
Lappeenranta (Villmanstrand)	59,286	Kerava (Kervo)	33,181
Rovaniemi	58,825	Kouvola	30,701
Vaasa (Vasa)	57,998	Nokia	30,485
Joensuu	57,677	Imatra	29,155
Kotka	54,679	Riihimäki	28,023
Mikkeli (St Michel)	48,720	Kangasala	27,733
Hämeenlinna (Tavastehus)	48,414	Vihti (Vichtis)	27,040
Porvoo (Borgå)	47,832	Savonlinna (Nyslott)	26,775
Hyvinkää (Hyvinge)	44,652	Ylöjärvi	26,384
Nurmijärvi	38,633	Salo	25,802
Kajaani (Kajana)	38,089		

In 2007, 65·0% of the population lived in urban areas. Nearly one-fifth of the total population lives in the Helsinki metropolitan region.

Finnish and Swedish are the official languages. Sami is spoken in Lapland.

SOCIAL STATISTICS

Statistics in calendar years:

	Living births	*Of which outside marriage*	*Still-born*	*Marriages*	*Deaths (exclusive of still-born)*	*Emigration*
2003	56,630	22,649	178	25,815	48,996	12,083
2004	57,758	23,554	187	29,342	47,600	13,656
2005	57,745	23,319	182	29,283	47,928	12,369
2006	58,840	23,858	193	28,236	48,065	12,107
2007	58,729	23,824	204	29,497	49,077	12,443

In 2007 the rate per 1,000 population was: births, 11; deaths, 9; marriages, 6; infant deaths (per 1,000 live births), 2·7. Annual population growth rate, 1997–2007, 0·3%. In 2006 the suicide rate per 100,000 population was 30·0 among men and 8·9 among women, giving Finland one of the highest suicide rates in Europe. Life expectancy at birth, 2007, 75·8 years for males and 82·9 years for females. In 2007 the most popular age range for marrying was 25–29 for both males and females. Fertility rate, 2007, 1·8 births per woman. In 2007 Finland received 1,505 asylum applications, equivalent to 0·3 per 1,000 inhabitants.

A UNICEF report published in 2005 showed that 2·8% of children in Finland live in poverty (in households with income below 50% of the national median), the second lowest percentage of any country behind Denmark.

CLIMATE

A quarter of Finland lies north of the Arctic Circle. The climate is severe in winter, which lasts about six months, but mean temperatures in the south and southwest are less harsh, 21°F (–6°C). In the north, mean temperatures may fall to 8·5°F (–13°C). Snow covers the ground for three months in the south and for over six months in the far north. Summers are short but quite warm, with occasional very hot days. Precipitation is light throughout the country, with one third falling as snow, the remainder mainly as rain in summer and autumn. Helsinki (Helsingfors), Jan. 30·2°F (–1·0°C), July 68·4°F (20·2°C). Annual rainfall 27·9" (708·7 mm).

CONSTITUTION AND GOVERNMENT

Finland is a republic governed by the constitution of 1 March 2000 (which replaced the previous constitution dating from 1919). Although the president used to choose who formed the government, under the new constitution it is the responsibility of parliament to select the prime minister. The government is in charge of domestic and EU affairs with the president responsible for foreign policy 'in co-operation with the government'.

Parliament consists of one chamber (*Eduskunta*) of 200 members chosen by direct and proportional election by all citizens of 18 or over. The country is divided into 15 electoral districts, with a representation proportional to their population. Every citizen over the age of 18 is eligible for parliament, which is elected for four years, but can be dissolved sooner by the president.

The *president* is elected for six years by direct popular vote. In the event of no candidate winning an absolute majority, a second round is held between the two most successful candidates.

National Anthem

'Maamme'/'Vårt land' ('Our land'); words by J. L. Runeberg, tune by F. Pacius (same as Estonia).

GOVERNMENT CHRONOLOGY

(KESK = Centre Party; KOK = National Coalition Party; ML = Agrarian League; SDP = Social Democratic Party; SFP = Swedish People's Party; SKDL = Finnish People's Democratic League; VL = Liberal League; n/p = non-partisan)

Presidents of the Republic

1944–46	military	Carl Gustaf Emil Mannerheim
1946–56	KOK	Juho Kusti Paasikivi
1956–82	ML/KESK	Urho Kaleva Kekkonen
1982–94	SDP	Mauno Henrik Koivisto
1994–2000	SDP	Martti Oiva Kalevi Ahtisaari
2000–	SDP	Tarja Kaarina Halonen

Prime Ministers

1944–46	KOK	Juho Kusti Paasikivi
1946–48	SKDL	Mauno Pekkala
1948–50	SDP	Karl-August Fagerholm
1950–53	ML	Urho Kaleva Kekkonen
1953–54	VL	Sakari Severi Tuomioja
1954	SFP	Ralf Johan Gustaf Törngren
1954–56	ML	Urho Kaleva Kekkonen
1956–57	SDP	Karl-August Fagerholm
1957	ML	Väinö Johannes Sukselainen
1957–58	n/p	Berndt Rainer von Fieandt
1958	n/p	Reino Iisakki Kuuskoski
1958–59	SDP	Karl-August Fagerholm
1959–61	ML	Väinö Johannes Sukselainen
1961–62	ML	Martti Juhani Miettunen
1962–63	ML	Ahti Kalle Samuli Karjalainen
1963–64	n/p	Reino Ragnar Lehto
1964–66	ML/KESK	Johannes Virolainen
1966–68	SDP	Kustaa Rafael Paasio
1968–1970	SDP	Mauno Henrik Koivisto
1970	n/p	Teuvo Ensio Aura
1970–71	KESK	Ahti Kalle Samuli Karjalainen
1971–72	n/p	Teuvo Ensio Aura
1972	SDP	Kustaa Rafael Paasio
1972–75	SDP	Taisto Kalevi Sorsa
1975	n/p	Keijo Antero Liinamaa
1975–77	KESK	Martti Juhani Miettunen
1977–79	SDP	Taisto Kalevi Sorsa
1979–81	SDP	Mauno Henrik Koivisto
1982–87	SDP	Taisto Kalevi Sorsa
1987–91	KOK	Harri Hermanni Holkeri
1991–95	KESK	Esko Tapani Aho
1995–2003	SDP	Paavo Tapio Lipponen
2003	KESK	Anneli Tuulikki Jäätteenmäki
2003–	KESK	Matti Taneli Vanhanen

RECENT ELECTIONS

Presidential elections were held on 15 Jan. 2006 with a second round on 29 Jan. In the first round incumbent president and Social Democratic Party candidate Tarja Halonen came first with 46·3% of the vote, followed by Sauli Niinistö (National Coalition Party) with 24·1%, Prime Minister Matti Vanhanen (Centre Party) 18·6% and Heidi Hautala (Green League) 3·5%. There were five other candidates. In the run-off Halonen won with 51·8% against 48·2% for Niinistö. Turnout was 73·9% in the first round and 77·2% in the run-off.

At the elections for the 200-member parliament on 18 March 2007, turnout was 67·8%. The Centre Party (KESK) won 51 seats with 23·1% of votes cast (55 seats in 2003), the National Coalition Party (KOK) 50 with 22·3% (40 seats in 2003), the Social Democratic Party (SDP) 45 with 21·4% (53 seats in 2003), the Left Alliance 17 with 8·8% (19), the Green League 15 with 8·5% (14), the Swedish People's Party (SFP) 9 with 4·6% (8), the Christian Democrats 7 with 4·9% (7) and True Finns 5 with 4·1% (3). One representative from the province of Åland was also elected. Following the March 2007 election 42·0% of the seats in parliament were held by women.

European Parliament

Finland has 13 (14 in 2004) representatives. At the June 2009 elections turnout was 40·3% (39·4% in 2004). KOK won 3 seats with 23·2% of votes cast (political affiliation in European Parliament: European People's Party); KESK, 3 with 19·0% (Alliance of Liberals and Democrats for Europe); SDP, 2 with 17·5% (Progressive Alliance of Socialists and Democrats); Christian Democrats-True Finns, 2 with 14·0% (one with European People's Party and one with Europe of Freedom and Democracy); Green League, 2 with 12·4% (Greens/European Free Alliance); the Swedish People's Party, 1 with 6·1% (Alliance of Liberals and Democrats for Europe).

CURRENT ADMINISTRATION

President: Tarja Halonen; b. 1943 (Social Democrat; sworn in 1 March 2000 and re-elected in Jan. 2006).

The Council of State (Cabinet) is composed of a coalition of the Centre Party (KESK), the National Coalition Party (KOK), the Green League and the Swedish People's Party (SFP). The 20-member cabinet, consisting of eight men and 12 women (the highest proportion of women in any country's cabinet), comprised in March 2010:

Prime Minister: Matti Vanhanen; b. 1955 (KESK; sworn in 24 June 2003 and re-elected by parliament in April 2007).

Deputy Prime Minister and Minister of Finance: Jyrki Katainen (KOK). *Foreign Affairs:* Alexander Stubb (KOK). *Justice:* Tuija Brax (Green League). *Education:* Henna Virkkunen (KOK). *Culture and Sport:* Stefan Wallin (SFP). *Interior:* Anne Holmlund (KOK). *Economic Affairs:* Mauri Pekkarinen (KESK). *Transport:* Anu Vehviläinen (KESK). *Social Affairs and Health:* Liisa Hyssälä (KESK). *Health and Social Services:* Paula Risikko (KOK). *Labour:* Anni Sinnemäki (Green League). *Defence:* Jyri Häkämies (KOK). *Environment:* Paula Lehtomäki (KESK). *Foreign Trade and Development:* Paavo Väyrynen (KESK). *Agriculture and Forestry:* Sirkka-Liisa Anttila (KESK). *Migration and European Affairs:* Astrid Thors (SFP). *Public Administration and Local Government:* Mari Kiviniemi (KESK). *Housing:* Jan Vapaavuori (KOK). *Communications:* Suvi Lindén (KOK).

The *Speaker* is Sauli Niinistö.

Government Website: http://www.valtioneuvosto.fi

CURRENT LEADERS

Tarja Halonen

Position
President

Introduction
The first woman president in Finnish history, Tarja Kaarina Halonen began her term in office on 1 March 2000. She won a second term in Jan. 2006. A member of parliament from 1979 until her election to the presidency, she also served as a minister in three governments from 1987. From 1995–2000 she was the country's foreign minister.

Early Life
Tarja Halonen was born on 24 Dec. 1943. She was educated at the University of Helsinki where she received a degree in law. She was actively involved in student politics and served as the general secretary for the National Union of Finnish Students. From 1970–74 she was a lawyer with the central organization of Finnish Trade Unions. In 1974 she became the parliamentary secretary to prime minister Kalevi Sorsa, holding this position until Sorsa's term ended in 1975. Halonen was then elected to the Helsinki City council in 1977 (remaining a councillor until 1996) and two years later was elected a member of the Finnish parliament. She was chairman of the parliamentary social affairs committee (from 1984–87) before being appointed minister of social affairs and health. She went on to hold two further ministerial positions, serving as minister for Nordic co-operation (1989–91) and minister of justice (1990–91), before becoming the minister of foreign affairs in April 1995. In this role she oversaw Finland's assimilation into the European Union. In Jan. 2000 Halonen stood for election as the Social Democratic Party candidate for the presidency, campaigning on a liberal and feminist manifesto. She received 51·6% of the total votes cast in the second round of the presidential elections on 6 Feb. 2000, narrowly defeating the Centre Party's Esko Aho.

Career in Office
On the day of her inauguration, a new national constitution came into effect which reduced presidential powers and expanded and emphasized parliament as the most important body in the Finnish political system. The president was still granted a significant role in foreign policy, a fact which suited Halonen's diplomatic and linguistic skills. She has continued her country's pro-European Union policies, although her position on NATO has been less certain.

In Nov. 2005 the SDP nominated Halonen for re-election as its presidential candidate. Having failed to secure a majority in the first round of voting, she narrowly defeated the Conservative candidate, Sauli Niinistö, in a run-off in Jan. 2006.

Matti Vanhanen

Position
Prime Minister

Introduction
Matti Vanhanen took over as Finland's prime minister in June 2003 when the three-month tenure of Anneli Jäätteenmäki ended amid political scandal. A member of the Centre Party like his predecessor, Vanhanen is widely regarded as a cautious and reliable politician. He retained the premiership following parliamentary elections in March 2007.

Early Life
Matti Taneli Vanhanen was born 4 Nov. 1955 in Jyväskylä, Finland. From 1980–83 he was chairman of the Centre Party's youth organization, and in 1989 completed a university degree in political science. His early career as a journalist, working as editor-in-chief of Kehäsanomat from 1988–91, won him a reputation as an expert on the European Union. In 1991 he was elected to the Finnish parliament, where he became vice-president of the party and, later, defence minister.

On 18 June 2003 Jäätteenmäki resigned from both her role as prime minister and as leader of the Centre Party, following allegations over her use of information concerning her predecessor, Paavo Lipponen, in the build-up to the elections of March 2003. Jäätteenmäki was in office for just 63 days.

Career in Office
Observers viewed the appointment of Vanhanen as an attempt to restore calm to Finnish national politics and one of his principal tasks was to win back public trust. He initially headed a coalition comprising the Centre Party, the Social Democrats and the Swedish People's Party, and was expected to pursue a similar economic programme to that of Jäätteenmäki. He spoke out against plans for a proposed EU common defence policy, was a leading advocate of ecological and environmental issues, and voiced his opposition to plans to build a fifth nuclear reactor in Finland.

In 2005 a seven-week industrial dispute in the paper mill industry over pay and conditions caused nationwide strikes before being settled by mediation. Losses in export earnings were expected to reach €5bn. and Vanhanen's government faced considerable losses in tax revenue.

In Oct. 2005 Vanhanen was nominated as the presidential candidate of the Centre Party for the Jan. 2006 election but came third with just under 19% of the vote. During Finland's six-month presidency of the EU from July–Dec. 2006, he sought to build a wider consensus among Europe's leaders on reviving the stalled EU constitution and on conditions for future membership expansion, particularly in relation to Turkey.

He was re-elected as prime minister by parliament in April 2007, following the Centre's Party's narrow victory in parliamentary polls in March, and formed a new centre-right coalition government with the Swedish People's Party, the National Rally Party and the Green League.

In Sept. 2008 he called for stricter firearms controls after a gunman killed nine students and a teacher at a college in the town of Kauhajoki before taking his own life.

Alleged election financing irregularities by the Centre Party led to the tabling of a parliamentary no-confidence motion in Vanhanen's coalition by opposition left-wing parties in Oct. 2009, but this was defeated by 117–27 votes with 56 abstentions.

DEFENCE

Conscript service is 6–12 months. Total strength of trained and equipped reserves is about 490,000 (to be 350,000).

In 2007 defence expenditure totalled €2,203m. (€416 per capita), representing 1·2% of GDP.

Army

The Army consists of one armoured training brigade, three readiness brigades, three infantry training brigades, three jaeger regiments, one artillery brigade, three brigade artillery regiments, two air defence regiments, one engineer regiment (including ABC school), three brigade engineer battalions, one signals regiment, four brigade signals battalions and a reserve officer school. Total strength of 37,700 (26,000 conscripts).

Frontier Guard

This comes under the purview of the Ministry of the Interior, but is militarily organized to participate in the defence of the country. It is in charge of border surveillance and border controls. It is also responsible for conducting maritime search and rescue operations. If necessary in the interests of defence capability, the frontier troops or parts thereof may be attached to the Defence Forces. Personnel, 2004, 3,200 (professional) with a potential mobilizational force of 22,000 (to be 8,500).

Navy

The organization of the Navy was changed on 1 July 1998. The Coastal Defence, comprising the coast artillery and naval infantry, was merged into the Navy.

About 50% of the combatant units are kept manned, with the others on short-notice reserve and reactivated on a regular basis. Naval bases exist at Upinniemi (near Helsinki), Turku and Kotka. Naval Infantry mobile troops are trained at Tammisaari. Total personnel strength (2006) was 6,600, of whom 4,300 were conscripts.

Air Force

Personnel (2006), 4,600 (1,500 conscripts). Equipment included 62 F-18 Hornets.

INTERNATIONAL RELATIONS

Finland is a member of the UN, World Bank, IMF and several other UN specialized agencies, WTO, EU, Council of Europe, OSCE, CERN, Nordic Council, Council of the Baltic Sea States, BIS, IOM, NATO Partnership for Peace, OECD, Inter-American Development Bank, Asian Development Bank and Antarctic Treaty. Finland has acceded to the Schengen accord, which abolishes border controls between Finland, Austria, Belgium, Czech Republic, Denmark, Estonia, France, Germany, Greece, Hungary, Iceland, Italy, Latvia, Lithuania, Luxembourg, Malta, Netherlands, Norway, Poland, Portugal, Slovakia, Slovenia, Spain, Sweden and Switzerland.

ECONOMY

Agriculture accounted for 3% of GDP in 2007, industry 33% and services 64%.

According to the Berlin-based organization *Transparency International*, Finland ranked equal sixth in a 2009 survey of countries with the least corruption in business and government. It received 8·9 out of 10 in the corruption perceptions index.

Overview

The economy, once based on basic metals and forestry, has evolved to become a leading force in knowledge-based, high-tech production. Finland is one of the world's leading information and communications technology (ICT) producers. The emergence of venture capital financing in the 1990s created opportunities for high-risk technology start-ups and the rapid increase in research and development (R&D) also pushed the economic transformation. Expenditure on R&D has risen significantly since the 1980s. Its share of GDP was 3·5% in 2004, one of the highest levels in the world. The economy's structural transition began to produce significant economic results after the Scandinavian banking crisis and four years of negative annual growth in the period 1990–93. Strong global demand in the ICT sector in the late 1990s helped boost the economy. From 1994–2000 real GDP growth averaged a robust 3·9% annually. By 2000 almost one third of Finnish exports were from the ICT sector.

The downturn in the demand for ICT goods beginning in 2001 slowed real GDP growth from 2001–03. In 2004 an investment-led recovery once again pushed annual growth above 3%. Key sectors in the 2004 rebound were electronics, paper, forestry and metals. Strong growth of approaching 5% in 2006 reflected a rebound in the paper sector following a labour dispute in 2005, together with buoyant exports to local trading partners and sound private consumption growth.

In 2005 Finland was ranked first in the *World Economic Forum*'s global competitiveness report. However, Finland's own ministry of finance estimates that in the medium-term the pace of economic growth will be less than 2%. Three factors impeding growth are an ageing population, the relocation of production overseas and the slow rate of production capacity increases. The combination of a decrease in labour supply owing to an increase in the number of pensioners and high structural unemployment will limit economic growth on the demand side. On the supply side there are fears that companies will increasingly look to outsource production to areas either closer to large markets or with lower labour costs. The key to Finland's growth performance will be the pace of productivity gains. Yet productivity growth is not expected to be strong as the economy is increasingly service-based where productivity gains are harder to achieve, while the contracting supply of skilled labour threatens to raise labour costs.

Exports are relatively narrow and concentrated in two sectors, telecommunications and paper products, which pose risks to future growth prospects. Fiscal surpluses, which the government has been running since 1998, are necessary to finance the growing number of pensioners. The IMF suggests that a uniform improvement in the primary surplus of around 2% of GDP beyond 2011, together with a reduction in public spending growth, will be needed to prepare for expenditures relating to population ageing.

Currency

On 1 Jan. 1999 the euro (EUR) became the legal currency in Finland at the irrevocable conversion rate of 5·94573 marks to one euro. The euro, which consists of 100 cents, has been in circulation since 1 Jan. 2002. There are seven euro notes in different colours and sizes denominated in 500, 200, 100, 50, 20, 10 and 5 euros, and eight coins denominated in 2 and 1 euros, then 50, 20, 10, 5, 2 and 1 cents. On the introduction of the euro there was a 'dual circulation' period before the mark ceased to be legal tender on 28 Feb. 2002. Euro banknotes in circulation on 31 Dec. 2007 had a total value of €11·1bn.

Inflation rates (based on OECD statistics):

1999	*2000*	*2001*	*2002*	*2003*	*2004*	*2005*	*2006*	*2007*	*2008*
1·3%	2·9%	2·7%	2·0%	1·3%	0·1%	0·8%	1·3%	1·6%	3·9%

Foreign exchange reserves were US$7,002m. in Sept. 2009 and gold reserves were 1·58m. troy oz. Total money supply was €62,585m. in Aug. 2009.

Budget

Revenue and expenditure for the calendar years 2003–07 in €1m:

	2003	*2004*	*2005*	*2006*	*2007*
Revenue	36,413	38,525	39,023	40,979	43,212
Expenditure	36,897	36,320	41,247	40,871	43,252

Of the total revenue in 2007, 35% derived from income and property tax, 31% from value added tax, 11% from excise duties, 7% from other taxes and similar revenue and 16% from miscellaneous sources. Of the total expenditure, 2007, 30% went to health and social security, 15% to education, 6% to agriculture and forestry, 5% to defence, 4% to transport and 40% to other expenditure.

VAT was 22% in 2009 (reduced rates, 17% and 8%).

At the end of Dec. 2007 the central government debt totalled €56,068m. Foreign debt amounted to €45m. at the end of 2006.

Performance

Real GDP growth rates (based on OECD statistics):

1999	*2000*	*2001*	*2002*	*2003*	*2004*	*2005*	*2006*	*2007*	*2008*
4·0%	5·0%	2·5%	1·5%	2·0%	3·7%	3·0%	4·9%	4·1%	0·8%

The real GDP growth rate (provisional) in 2009 according to Statistics Finland was –7·8%. Total GDP was US$271·3bn. in 2008.

Banking and Finance

The central bank is the Bank of Finland (founded in 1811), operating under the guarantee and supervision of parliament. The Bank is a member of the European System of Central Banks. As a member of the euro area, the Bank issues euro banknotes and coins in Finland by permission of the European Central Bank. The *Governor* is Erkki Liikanen.

The most important groups of banking institutions in 2007 were:

	Number of institutions	*Number of branches*	*Deposits (€1m.)*	*Loans (€1m.)*
Commercial banks	14	491	47,865	72,177
Savings banks	39	277	7,690	7,418
Co-operative banks	271	735	28,150	32,529
Foreign banks	15	67	—	—

The three largest banks are Nordea Bank Finland (formed in 1997 as MeritaNordbanken when Nordbanken of Sweden merged with Merita of Finland), Sampo Bank (formerly Leonia) and Pohjola Bank (previously OKO). In March 2000 MeritaNordbanken acquired Denmark's Unidanmark, thereby becoming the Nordic region's biggest bank in terms of assets. It has also become Europe's leading Internet bank, by July 2000 having 1·4m. Internet banking clients. By early 2001 approximately 40% of the Finnish population were using e-banking, the highest percentage in any country.

In 2007 Finland received US$11·4bn. worth of foreign direct investment.

There is a stock exchange in Helsinki.

ENERGY AND NATURAL RESOURCES

Environment

Finland's carbon dioxide emissions in 2008 were the equivalent of 10·4 tonnes per capita. An *Environmental Performance Index* compiled in 2008 ranked Finland fourth in the world, with 91·4%. The index examined various factors in six areas—air pollution, biodiversity and habitat, climate change, environmental health, productive natural resources and water resources.

Electricity

Installed capacity was 16·9m. kW at the beginning of 2007. Production was 78,623m. kWh. in 2006 (14% hydro-electric). Consumption per capita in 2006 was an estimated 17,060 kWh. In 2006 there were four nuclear reactors, which contributed 28% of production. In May 2002 parliament approved the construction of a fifth reactor, on the island of Olkiluoto, which is scheduled for completion in 2012.

Water

Finland has abundant surface water and groundwater resources relative to its population and level of consumption. The total groundwater yield is estimated to be 10–30m. cu. metres a day, of which some 6m. is suitable for water supplies. Approximately 15% of this latter figure is made use of at the present time.

Minerals

Notable of the mines are Pyhäsalmi (zinc–copper), Pahtavaara (gold ore), Hitura (nickel) and Keminmaa (chromium). In 2006 the metal content (in tonnes) of the output of zinc ore was 35,700; of copper ore, 13,000; of nickel ore, 2,800; of chromium, 264,500.

Agriculture

The cultivated area covers only 7% of the land, and of the economically active population 4% were employed in agriculture and forestry in 2007. In 2007 there were 2·26m. ha. of arable land. This arable area was divided into 66,938 farms (including 442 farms with under one hectare of arable land). The distribution of this area by the size of the farms was: less than 5 ha. cultivated, 5,366 farms; 5–20 ha., 23,357 farms; 20–50 ha., 24,171 farms; 50–100 ha., 10,909 farms; over 100 ha., 3,135 farms.

Agriculture accounted for 0·8% of exports and 3·1% of imports in 2007.

The principal crops (area in 1,000 ha., yield in 1,000 tonnes) were in 2007:

Crop	*Area*	*Yield*
Barley	550·1	1,984·4
Oats	361·5	1,222·0
Wheat	203·9	796·8
Potatoes	27·6	701·6
Hay	103·1	382·6

The total area under cultivation in 2006 was 2,278,417 ha. Approximately 6·5% of all agricultural land is used for organic farming. Production of dairy butter in 2007 was 48,283 tonnes; and of cheese, 94,156 tonnes.

Livestock (2007): pigs, 1,448,000; cattle, 926,700; reindeer, 193,000; horses, 68,000 (including trotting and riding horses, and ponies); poultry, 3,898,300.

Forestry

Forests covered 26·3m. ha. in 2007, or 86·4% of the total land area. The productive forest land covers 20·2m. ha. Timber production in 2007 was 57·7m. cu. metres. Finland is one of the largest producers of roundwood in Europe. Finland's per capita consumption of roundwood is the highest in the world, at 11·2 cu. metres per person in 2007.

Fisheries

The catch in 2007 was 122,355 tonnes, of which 117,857 tonnes came from sea fishing. In 2007 there were 201 food fish production farms in operation, of which 61 were freshwater farms. Their total production amounted to 13,031 tonnes. In addition there were 108 fry-farms and 235 natural food rearers, most of these in freshwater.

INDUSTRY

The leading companies by market capitalization in Finland in March 2009 were: Nokia, the world's leading mobile phone producer (US$44·2bn.); Fortum, an energy company (US$16·9bn.); and Sampo, an insurance company (US$8·3bn.).

Forests are still Finland's most crucial raw material resource, although the metal and engineering industry has long been Finland's leading branch of manufacturing, both in terms of value added and as an employer. In 2006 there were 28,628 establishments in industry (of which 26,129 were manufacturing concerns) with 416,018 personnel (of whom 396,266 were in manufacturing). Gross value of industrial production in 2006 was €126,152m., of which manufacturing accounted for €118,265m.

Labour

In 2007 the labour force was 2,675,000 (52% males). Of this total, 69·6% of the economically active population worked in services (including 15·9% in trade and restaurants) and 18·7% in manufacturing. In Dec. 2009 unemployment was 8·8%.

Trade Unions

There are three labour organizations: the Confederation of Unions for Academic Professionals—Akateemisten Toimihenkilöiden Keskusjarjesto (AKAVA); the Finnish Confederation of Salaried Employees—Toimihenkilokeskusjarjesto (STTK); and the Central Organization of Finnish Trade Unions (SAK). According to an incomes policy agreement reached by the central labour market organizations in Sept. 2007, which is in force until Jan. 2010, wages and salaries were to increase by about 11% over the period covered by the agreement.

INTERNATIONAL TRADE

At the start of the 1990s a collapse in trade with Russia led to the worst recession in the country's recent history. Today, exports to Russia are about 10% of the total.

Imports and Exports

In 1960 the wood and paper industry dominated exports with 69% of the total, but today the metal and engineering industry is the largest export sector.

Imports and exports for calendar years, in €1m.:

	2004	*2005*	*2006*	*2007*
Imports	40,730	47,027	55,253	59,616
Exports	48,917	52,453	61,489	65,688

Use of Goods	*Imports 2007*
Raw materials, production necessities	39%
Investment goods	24%
Energy	14%
Durable consumer goods	10%
Other	13%

Industry	*Exports 2007*
Metal, engineering, electronics	59%
Forest industry	20%
Chemical industry	7%
Other	14%

Region	*Imports 2007*	*Exports 2007*
European Union	56%	57%
Other Europe	21%	21%
(EFTA	3%	4%)
Developing countries	17%	16%
Other countries	6%	6%

Trade with principal partners in 2007 was as follows (in €1m.):

	Imports	*Exports*		*Imports*	*Exports*
Australia	953	481	Netherlands	2,726	3,650
Belgium	1,285	1,596	Norway	1,296	2,045
China	4,458	2,161	Poland	797	1,549
Denmark	1,515	1,296	Russia	8,411	6,724
Estonia	1,253	1,750	South Korea	1,085	582
France	2,134	2,331	Spain	990	1,799
Germany	8,416	7,162	Sweden	5,900	7,035
Italy	2,068	1,842	UK	2,903	3,824
Japan	1,606	1,174	USA	2,010	4,194

COMMUNICATIONS

Roads

At 1 Jan. 2008 there were 78,161 km of public roads, of which 50,836 km were paved. At the end of 2007 there were 2,570,356 registered cars, 77,817 lorries, 297,531 vans and pick-ups, 11,543 buses and coaches and 13,264 special automobiles. Road accidents caused 380 fatalities in 2007.

Rail

In 2007 the total length of the line operated was 5,899 km (3,047 km electrified), all of it owned by the State. The gauge is 1,524 mm. In 2007, 66·7m. passengers and 40·3m. tonnes of freight were carried. There is a metro (21 km) and tram/light rail network (85 km) in Helsinki.

Civil Aviation

The main international airport is at Helsinki (Vantaa), and there are also international airports at Turku, Tampere, Rovaniemi and Oulu. The national carrier is Finnair. Scheduled traffic of Finnish airlines covered 178m. km in 2007. The number of passengers was 11·0m. and the number of passenger-km 22,704m.; the air transport of freight and mail amounted to 508·6m. tonne-km. Helsinki-Vantaa handled 13,141,622 passengers in 2007 (10,266,326 on international flights) and 145,482 tonnes of freight and mail. Oulu is the second busiest airport, handling 840,158 passengers in 2007, and Tampere-Pirkkala the third busiest, with 687,690 in 2007.

Shipping

The total registered mercantile marine in 2007 was 635 vessels of 1,555,000 GRT. In 2007 the total number of vessels arriving in Finland from abroad was 38,741 and the goods discharged amounted to 57·9m. tonnes. The goods loaded for export from Finnish ports amounted to 44·7m. tonnes.

The lakes, rivers and canals are navigable for about 9,541 km. Timber floating has some importance, and there are about 9,149 km of floatable inland waterways. In 2005 bundle floating was about 0·5m. tonnes.

Finland was ranked fourth in the World Economic Forum's *Global Competitiveness Report 2009–2010* for the quality of its port facilities.

Telecommunications

In 2008 there were 1,650,000 main (fixed) telephone lines. In the same year mobile phone subscribers numbered 6,830,000 (1,287·6 per 1,000 persons). In Nov. 2008 around 98% of Finnish households owned at least one mobile phone. The rate among 18- and 19-year-olds is almost 100%. In Nov. 2008 approximately 69% of Finnish households only had a mobile phone and did not have a fixed-line phone at all. The Finnish company Nokia is the world's biggest manufacturer of mobile phones, having a 38% share of the world mobile phone market. It is by far the biggest company in Finland, accounting for 21·7% of the country's GDP in 2005 and more than 30% of the value of its stock exchange. Finland has the lowest rates in Europe for both fixed and mobile phone calls.

There were 2·6m. PCs in use in 2005 (499·5 per 1,000 persons) and 4·4m. internet users in 2008. There were 30·7 broadband subscribers per 100 inhabitants in June 2008.

Postal Services

In 2007 there were 208 primary post offices and 1,014 agents providing postal services in Finland.

SOCIAL INSTITUTIONS

Justice

The lowest court of justice is the District Court. In most civil cases a District Court has a quorum of three legally qualified members. In criminal cases as well as in some cases related to family law the District Court has a quorum with a chair and three lay judges. In the preliminary preparation of a civil case and in a criminal case concerning a minor offence, a District Court is composed of the chair only. From the District Court an appeal lies to the courts of appeal in Turku, Vaasa, Kuopio, Helsinki, Kouvola and Rovaniemi. The Supreme Court sits in Helsinki. Appeals from the decisions of administrative authorities are in the final instance decided by the Supreme Administrative Court, also in Helsinki. Judges can be removed only by judicial sentence. Two functionaries, the Chancellor of Justice and the Ombudsman or Solicitor-General, exercise control over the administration of justice. The former acts also as counsel and public prosecutor for the government; the latter is appointed by Parliament.

At the end of 2007 the daily average number of prisoners was 3,551 of which 244 were women. The number of convictions in 2006 was 295,008, of which 26,496 carried a penalty of imprisonment. 10,956 of the prison sentences were unconditional.

Education

Number of institutions, teachers and students (2007):

Primary and Secondary Education

	Number of institutions	Teachers[1]	Students
First-level Education (Lower sections of the comprehensive schools, grades I–VI)	3,669	54,191	370,328[2]
Second-level Education General education (Upper sections of the comprehensive schools, grades VII–IX, and upper secondary general schools)			315,614
Vocational Education	233[3]	16,751[4]	266,419

[1]Data for teachers refers to 2006.
[2]Including pre-primary education (12,925 pupils) in comprehensive schools.
[3]Numbers of institutions for vocational education refer to secondary and tertiary education.
[4]Number of teachers for vocational education refer to secondary and tertiary education.

Tertiary Education

Vocational education at tertiary education level was provided for 60 students in 2007. In 2007 polytechnic education was provided at 30 polytechnics with 133,284 students and 5,431 teachers (2006). In 2007, 26·3% of the population aged 15 years or over had been through tertiary education.

University Education

Universities with the number of teachers and students in 2007:

	Founded[1]	Teachers	Students Total	Students Women
Universities				
Helsinki	1640	1,600	38,365	24,781
Turku (Swedish)	1918	326	6,662	4,033
Turku (Finnish)	1922	784	16,204	10,285
Tampere	1925	591	15,725	10,344
Jyväskylä	1934	732	13,748	8,689
Oulu	1958	823	15,793	7,745
Vaasa	1968	167	5,055	2,693
Joensuu	1969	412	8,328	5,206
Kuopio	1972	345	6,229	4,109
Lapland	1979	200	4,742	3,352
Universities of Technology				
Helsinki	1849	482	14,535	3,179
Tampere	1965	343	11,850	2,493
Lappeenranta	1969	194	5,784	1,695
Schools of Economics and Business Administration				
Helsinki (Swedish)	1909	102	2,465	1,090
Helsinki (Finnish)	1911	162	4,274	1,931
Turku (Finnish)	1950	118	2,473	1,213
Universities of Art				
Academy of Fine Arts	1848	35	272	143
University of Art and Design	1871	165	1,900	1,199
Sibelius Academy	1882	228	1,475	854
Theatre Academy	1943	52	425	247
Total		7,861	176,304	95,281

[1]Year when the institution was founded regardless of status at the time.

Adult Education

Adult education provided by educational institutions in 2007:

Type of institution	*Participants*[1]
General education institutions[2]	1,684,500
Vocational education institutions	412,900
Permanent polytechnics	76,600
Universities[3]	159,900
Summer universities	95,300
	2,429,200

[1]Participants are persons who have attended adult education courses run by educational institutions in the course of the calendar year. The same person may have attended a number of different courses and has been recorded as a participant in each one of them. [2]Including study centres. [3]Adult education at continuing education centres of universities.

In 2005 public expenditure on education came to 6·3% of GNP and 12·5% of total government spending.

The adult literacy rate in 2007 was almost 100%.

According to the OECD's 2006 PISA (Programme for International Student Assessment) study, 15-year-olds in Finland rank first in science and second in mathematics and reading. The three-yearly study compares educational achievement of pupils in the major industrialized countries. Although education is only compulsory until 16, 80% of pupils stay on at school to 18.

Health

In 2007 there were 18,843 physicians, 4,540 dentists and 35,024 hospital beds. The average Finnish adult smokes 3·5 cigarettes a day and drinks 10·1 litres of alcohol a year.

In 2007 Finland spent 8·2% of its GDP on health.

Welfare

The Social Insurance Institution administers old-age pensions (to all persons over 65 years of age and disabled younger persons) and health insurance. There is also a system of special assistance for resident immigrants over 65. The universal old-age pension paid between €11·38 and €510·80 per month in 2006. An additional system of compulsory old-age pensions paid for by employers is in force and works through the Central Pension Security Institute. Reforms of 2005 provided for pensions to be linked to life expectancy, early retirement to be phased out and the pension age to rise to 63. Incentives to encourage workers to carry on after retirement age are a bid to counter the problems posed by an ageing population and a shortage of younger workers. Pensioners are predicted to account for 25% of the population by 2020. Systems for other public aid are administered by the communes and supervised by the National Social Board and the Ministry of Social Affairs and Health.

The total cost of social security amounted to €43,802m. in 2006. Of this €19,900m. (45%) was spent on old age and disability, €11,139m. (25%) on health, €6,355m. (15%) on family allowances and child welfare, €3,622m. (8%) on unemployment and €2,786m. (6%) on general welfare purposes and administration. Out of the total expenditure, 38·3% was financed by employers, 25·1% by the State, 18·8% by local authorities, 11·8% by the insured and 6·0% by property income.

RELIGION

Liberty of conscience is guaranteed to members of all religions. National churches are the Lutheran National Church and the Greek Orthodox Church of Finland. The Lutheran Church is divided into eight bishoprics (Turku being the archiepiscopal see), 80 provostships and 567 parishes. The Greek Orthodox Church is divided into three bishoprics (Kuopio being the archiepiscopal see) and 27 parishes, in addition to which there are a monastery and a convent. Percentage of the total population at the end of 2007: Lutherans, 81·8; Greek Orthodox, 1·1; others, 1·2; not members of any religion, 15·9.

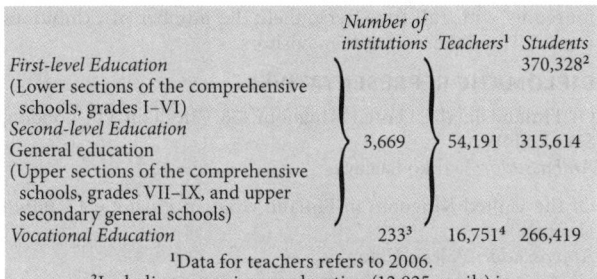

CULTURE

Turku will be one of two European Capitals of Culture for 2011. The title attracts large European Union grants.

World Heritage Sites

There are seven UNESCO sites in Finland: Old Rauma harbour (inscribed in 1991); the sea fortress of Suomenlinna (1991); the old church of Petäjävesi (1994); Verla groundwood and board mill (1996); the Bronze Age burial site of Sammallahdenmäki (1999); the Kvarken Archipelago and High Coast (2000 and 2006), shared with Sweden; and the Struve Geodetic Arc (2005). The Arc is a chain of survey triangulations spanning from Norway to the Black Sea that helped establish the exact shape and size of the earth and is shared with nine other countries.

Broadcasting

The Finnish Broadcasting Company, YLE, is the public national television service provider, operating several channels in Finnish and Swedish. The largest private television broadcaster is MTV3. The private TV channel Nelonen (Channel Four) started in 1997. There are numerous pay-TV and local television stations. There were 2·09m. TV-equipped households in 2006 (86·8% of all households). On 31 Dec. 2007 the number of television licences was 1,947,044. The only radio broadcaster with full national coverage is YLE, which transmits channels in Finnish, Swedish and Sami (Lappish) and has an external service. At the end of 2006 there were 76 local radio stations. Two of them, the news and music stations Nova and Classic, cover almost 60% of the population.

Cinema

In 2007 there were 316 cinema halls; total attendance was 6·5m. and gross box office receipts came to €50·8m.

Press

Finland has 53 newspapers that are published four to seven times a week, nine of which are in Swedish, and 151 with one to three issues per week. The total circulation of all newspapers is 3·2m. There are 4,801 registered periodicals with a total circulation of over 15m. The bestselling newspapers in 2007 were Helsingin Sanomat (average daily circulation, 419,791 copies), Ilta-Sanomat (176,351) and Aamulehti (139,165). In 2007 a total of 14,154 book titles were published.

Tourism

There were 2,472,449 foreign tourists in 2007; the income from tourism was €2,070m. and the expenses were €2,908m.

Major international tourist attractions include Uspensky Cathedral, Helsinki Cathedral and Suomenlinna (all in Helsinki). Helsinki's churches and Santa Park in Rovaniemi are particularly popular among foreigners, who account for the majority of their visitors.

Festivals

Major festivals are the Helsinki Festival Week, the Maritime Festival in Kotka, the Lakeside Blues Festival in Järvenpää, Pori Jazz Festival, Kaustinen Folk Music Festival, Tampere Theatre Festival and Seinäjoki's Tango Festival.

Libraries

The Helsinki University Library doubles as a national library. The public library network is comprehensive with 895 libraries altogether. In 2007 there were over 2·2m. registered borrowers.

Theatre and Opera

A new opera house and a new 14,000-seat Arena Show Hall opened in 1999 in Helsinki. The city hosts both the National Theatre and the National Opera. All major cities have theatres and show halls. In 2007 there were 12,956 performances in total with over 2·6m. tickets sold.

Museums and Galleries

The National Museum as well as the National Gallery (the Atheneum) are located in Helsinki. In 2006 there were 163 museums with full-time personnel. The number of exhibitions was 1,279 and there were 4·5m. visitors.

DIPLOMATIC REPRESENTATIVES

Of Finland in the United Kingdom (38 Chesham Pl., London, SW1X 8HW)
Ambassador: Jaakko Laajava.

Of the United Kingdom in Finland (Itäinen Puistotie 17, 00140 Helsinki)
Ambassador: Valerie Caton.

Of Finland in the USA (3301 Massachusetts Ave., NW, Washington, D.C., 20008)
Ambassador: Pekka Lintu.

Of the USA in Finland (Itäinen Puistotie 14, Helsinki 00140)
Ambassador: Bruce Oreck.

Of Finland to the United Nations
Ambassador: Jarmo Viinanen.

Of Finland to the European Union
Permanent Representative: Jan Store.

FURTHER READING

Statistics Finland. *Statistical Yearbook of Finland* (from 1879).—*Bulletin of Statistics* (quarterly, from 1971).

Constitution Act and Parliament Act of Finland. 1999

Suomen valtiokalenteri—Finlands statskalender (State Calendar of Finland). Annual

Facts About Finland. Annual

Finland in Figures. Annual

Jussila, Osmo, Hentila, Seppo and Nevakivi, Jukka, *From Grand Duchy to a Modern State: A Political History of Finland since 1809.* 2000

Kirby, D. G., *A Concise History of Finland.* 2006

Klinge, M., *A Brief History of Finland.* 1987

Lewis, Richard D., *Finland, Cultural Lone Wolf.* 2004

Pesonen, Pertti and Riihinen, Olavi, *Dynamic Finland: The Political System and the Welfare State.* 2004

Raunio, Tapio and Tiilikainen, Teija, *Finland in the European Union.* 2003

Singleton, F., *A Short History of Finland.* 2nd ed. 1998

National Statistical Office: Statistics Finland, FIN-00022.
Website: http://www.stat.fi

FRANCE

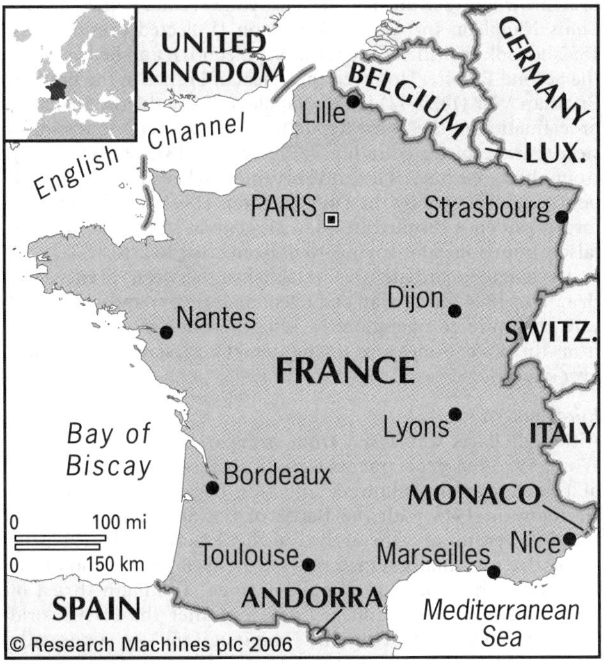

République Française
(French Republic)

Capital: Paris
Population estimate, 2010: 62·64m.
GDP per capita, 2007: (PPP$) 33,674
HDI/world rank: 0·961/8

KEY HISTORICAL EVENTS

The Dordogne has evidence of Mousterian industry from 40,000 BC and of Cro-Magnon man of the Upper Paleolithic period. With the end of the Ice Age, agricultural settlement appeared around 7000 BC. By the beginning of the 8th century BC, Celtic tribes from Central Europe were inhabiting the Rhône valley of Gaul (now France) while the Greeks were building cities such as Massalia (Marseille) along the southern coast. The Romans crossed the Alps into southern France in 121 BC and Gaul was conquered by Julius Caesar in 52 BC. The country benefited from protected trade routes and from Roman infrastructure, speech and government. Roman rule was consolidated by the reign of Augustus at the end of the 1st century AD. But the Empire was threatened by Germanic ('barbarian') incursions from the north and east. Many of these tribes were assimilated as *foederati* (treaty nations) into the Gallo-Roman Empire but they assumed authority in their domains as Roman government receded in the 4th and 5th centuries. After the repulse of Attila and his Huns in 451, the Salian Franks emerged as the strongest of the Germanic tribes—their leader, Merovius, was the progenitor of the Merovingian dynasty that ruled France until the beginning of the 8th century.

On the death of Merovius' grandson, Clovis, the kingdom was divided between his three sons. The Merovingians remained in power for two centuries but their rule, weakened by internecine warfare, gave way to the Carolingian dynasty in 751. Having extended his empire over Germany and Italy, Charlemagne was crowned emperor of the West by the pope in 800. He moved his seat of government to Aix-la-Chapelle (Aachen) where he presided over a revival of learning and education.

Charlemagne died in 814 and his empire was fought over by his grandsons before the 843 Treaty of Verdun officially split the territories. Charles le Chauve (823–77) inherited the western territories, an area roughly corresponding to modern day France. But by 912 Vikings had settled in Rouen, having laid siege to Paris. Further threats came from Muslim Saracens in the south and Hungarian Magyars in the east. The Carolingians struggled to keep their power for another century but they were weakened by unrest and disunity. In 987 Hugh Capet, the duke of the Franks, ousted the legitimate claimant to the throne, Charles of Lorraine, and appointed himself king. To control a diverse country, power was centralized on Paris.

Between 1150 and 1300 France underwent a period of economic expansion, though the 12th century also saw the Holy Land crusades and the expulsion of the Jews, followed by the bloody Albigensian Crusade against the heretical Cathars of Languedoc in 1209. The last Capetian king, Charles IV, died in 1328 (leaving only daughters) and the Capetian dynasty gave way to the House of Valois. However, King Edward III of England disputed Philippe de Valois' claim to the French throne, prompting the start of the Hundred Years War (1337–1453). With his son the Black Prince, Edward III's successful invasion led to the Treaty of Brétigny in 1360, which ceded Aquitaine to England. Edward renounced all claims to the French throne but the warfare continued until Charles V (ruled 1364–80) won back most of their territories.

In 1415 Henry V of England, with the backing of the Burgundians, defeated the French at Agincourt. He married the daughter of Charles IV and obtained the right of succession to the French throne. The war continued between his son Henry VI and the dauphin Charles (VI) who enlisted the help of Joan of Arc (Jeanne d'Arc). After leading a series of successful campaigns against the English, she was captured, tried as a heretic by a court of Burgundian ecclesiastics and burnt at the stake in Rouen in 1431. Nevertheless, French successes continued and eventually the English were driven from all their French possessions except Calais.

Rising Power

The reign of Louis XI (1461–83) saw a change from a medieval social system to a more modern state. Provincial governments were set up in major cities and nobles wielding independent power were crushed. In 1494 Charles VIII, encouraged to pursue his claim to the crown of Naples by Ludovico Sforza, duke of Milan, invaded Italy. The speed of his advance shocked the Italian cities into an alliance to expel his army. The appearance of Spanish power in Naples began the Habsburg-Valois wars that used Italy as a battlefield until the Peace of Cateau-Cambrésis in 1559. François I is considered the first Renaissance French king. He patronized some of Italy's greatest artists, commissioning palaces such as the Château de Chambord and rebuilding the Louvre and Château de Fontainebleau. To finance his cultural interests and his military failures in Italy—he was captured by Spanish forces at the Battle of Pavia in 1525—François imposed huge tax rises, severely straining the French economy.

Between 1562–98 the Wars of Religion raged in France between the Protestant Huguenots and the Spanish-supported Catholic League. The civil war reached its peak with the 1572 St Bartholomew's Day massacre, in which 20,000 Huguenots were killed, before ending with Henry of Navarre's conversion to Catholicism. He did not abandon his Huguenot roots, however, and the 1598 Edict of Nantes guaranteed Protestants political and religious rights.

After Henry's assassination in 1610 the young Louis XIII took the throne with his mother, Marie de Médicis, acting as regent. Between 1624–42 Cardinal Richelieu held the reins of government and set about establishing absolute royal power in France, with the suppression of Protestant influences. This policy was continued for the next twenty years by his successor Cardinal Mazarin. On Mazarin's death Louis XIV (1643–1715) was able to govern alone. Louis, the 'Sun King', attempted to impose a centralized absolutism, gathering the aristocracy around him and thus denying it traditional regional power. The king formally revoked the Edict of Nantes, Protestant churches were destroyed and religious minorities persecuted. His successor, Louis XV, married Maria, the daughter of the deposed king of Poland, who drew France into the War of the Polish Succession. Further costly military disasters followed including the Seven Years' War, in which France lost her colonies in India, North America and the West Indies.

When Louis XVI succeeded to the throne in 1774, financial crises caused by prolonged military failure coupled with a succession of bad harvests led to grain riots in 1787–88 in Paris, Lyon, Nantes and Grenoble. The subsequent reforms were rejected by the aristocracy (*les privilégiés*), the upper ranks of the clergy (the First Estate) and the majority of the nobility (the Second Estate), who feared a reduction in their tax-levying privileges. Meanwhile, Louis XVI supported the American colonies in their struggle for independence from Britain, a policy that was financially disastrous and also did much to disseminate revolutionary and democratic ideals in France.

Revolution

The French Revolution erupted in 1789 when the Third Estate (the non-privilégiés) assumed power in the National Assembly and overthrew the government. Riots broke out across France, culminating in the storming of the Bastille in Paris on 14 July 1789. A new legislative assembly was formed and although the moderate Girondins held power at the start, the more extreme followers of Danton, Robespierre and Marat—the Jacobins—seized power and in 1792 declared a republic.

On 21 Jan. 1793 Louis XVI was guillotined in the Place de la Révolution. After his death a reign of terror led by Maximilien Robespierre followed in which thousands of people were guillotined. Despite the efforts of the royalists to re-establish a monarchy, in 1795 the 'Directory of Five' was appointed to run the country. As one of these five, Paul Barras had been responsible for the promotion of a young Corsican, Napoleon Bonaparte, to the rank of general. Over four years, Napoleon commanded the French troops in a series of successful campaigns against the Austrians and the British. On his return to Paris, he found the Directory in disarray and in 1799 overthrew the government and declared himself first consul. Napoleon immediately faced a hostile coalition of England, Austria and Russia. In 1805 he defeated Austria and Russia at the Battle of Austerlitz but the British naval victory at the Battle of Trafalgar earlier the same year gave Britain maritime supremacy. Napoleon's best troops were bogged down supporting his brother Joseph in the Peninsula War in Spain and his success at Borodino, Russia in 1812 was followed by the army's forced retreat from Moscow during the harsh winter months. The Prussian army retaliated at Leipzig, entered France and forced the surrender of Paris in March 1814. Napoleon abdicated at Fontainebleau on 20 April 1814 and retired to Elba. But when Louis XVIII returned from exile in England later that year, Napoleon left Elba to attempt to recover his empire. He marched north towards Paris, gathering support on the way. But his defeat in 1815 at Waterloo by the Allies led by the duke of Wellington ended his 'Hundred Days' reign. He was exiled to the island of St Helena where he died in 1821.

Second Empire

The monarchy was restored with the Bourbon family. A revolution in 1830 brought Louis Philippe, son of the duke of Orléans, to the throne as a constitutional monarch. This 'July Monarchy' was overthrown in 1848 and superseded by the Second Republic, with Louis Napoleon (nephew of Napoleon I) elected president. In 1852 he took the title of Emperor Napoleon III, and hence began the Second Empire. However, the defeat of France in the Franco-Prussian War (1870–71) led to Napoleon being deposed and the proclamation of the Third Republic in 1870. After a four-month siege, Paris capitulated in Jan. 1871. By Sept. 1873 the occupying troops had gone but Alsace and Lorraine had been lost and French politics, embittered by the Dreyfus Affair (1894–1906), in which forged evidence resulted in a Jewish general staff captain being falsely imprisoned for spying, went from crisis to crisis.

An entente cordiale was established between France and Britain in 1904, putting an end to colonial rivalry and paving the way for future co-operation. In 1905 the Church was separated from the State, a measure to counteract ecclesiastical influence over education.

European War

Although Paris was saved from occupation during the First World War, ten departments were overrun and four long years of trench warfare followed. The tide began to turn against Germany in 1916 with the Battle of the Somme, the French stand at Verdun and the arrival of the Americans in 1917; the Armistice was finally signed on 11 Nov. 1918. By the end of the war France had lost a total of 1·3m. men. The main thrust of France's efforts to rebuild her defences after the First World War was concentrated on the 'Maginot Line'—a supposedly impregnable barrier running along the German frontier, but which was sidestepped by the advancing German forces in 1939. Demoralized French troops, unable to resist the German advance, were forced to retreat towards Dunkerque (Dunkirk). The French government capitulated and a pro-German government presided over by Marshal Pétain (a hero of the Battle of Verdun) was established at Vichy. A truce was signed with Germany agreeing German occupation in the northern third of the country and collaborationist government control in the south. Gen. Charles de Gaulle established the Forces Françaises Libres (Free French Forces) and declared the Comité National Français to be the true French government-in-exile with its headquarters first in London and then in Algiers. With help from the Resistance in France, in Aug. 1944 de Gaulle returned at the head of the allied armies and liberated Paris. An armistice with Germany was signed in March 1945.

In Oct. 1946 the Fourth Republic, institutionally similar to the Third Republic, was established but during prolonged wrangling over the form of the new constitution Gen. de Gaulle retired. Despite frequent changes of government and defeat in Indo-China, France achieved economic recovery. In 1957 a European common market was established of which France, West Germany, Italy and the Benelux countries were founder members.

Fifth Republic

Between 1954–62 France was embroiled in a war of independence with Algeria that split public and political opinion. In 1958 de Gaulle prepared a new constitution and was persuaded to return first as prime minister and then, by popular election, as the first president of the newly declared Fifth Republic. The new constitution greatly enhanced the power of the president. The politics of the early Fifth Republic was dominated by the centre-right, with a succession of parties (including the Union of Democrats for the Republic, Union of Democrats for the V Republic, Union for the New Republic, Union for the French Republic-Democratic Union of Labour) working to a Gaullist agenda. There was an emphasis on national independence, government involvement in the economy and broadly conservative social policies.

In 1962 Algeria gained independence. De Gaulle continued to preside over a period of relative stability and economic growth but serious student riots in Paris in 1968 precipitated reforms to the authoritarian system of education. The students were joined by workers wanting better pay and conditions. The National Assembly was dissolved and, although the Gaullists were returned to power in the new election, de Gaulle's referendum proposing decentralization was defeated and in 1969 he resigned. Georges Pompidou, who had been de Gaulle's prime minister, succeeded him. Pompidou attempted to consolidate de Gaulle's legacy by concentrating on economic reform. When he died in office in 1974 he was succeeded by Valéry Giscard d'Estaing who continued right-wing policies, eventually precipitating a swing to the left. In 1981 the Socialist leader François Mitterrand was elected president. He immediately implemented widespread social reforms but a deep recession in 1983 forced him to take a series of unpopular deflationary measures.

When the ailing Mitterrand's term of office expired in 1995, Jacques Chirac was elected president with Alain Juppé as prime minister. After the Socialists won an assembly majority in 1997, Juppé resigned making way for the Socialist leader Lionel Jospin to take over as prime minister. The right and leftwing *cohabitation* lasted five years until Jospin retired after a disastrous result in the first round presidential elections. Chirac's second electoral success was consolidated by the moderate right taking an assembly majority in the 2002 legislative elections.

In Oct. 2005 the death of two youths of African origin led to several days of rioting in immigrant ghettoes, prompting the government to declare a state of emergency, which was lifted in Jan. 2006. In May 2007 Nicolas Sarkozy was elected president. In 2009 he led France back into NATO's integrated military command after a 43-year absence.

TERRITORY AND POPULATION

France is bounded in the north by the English Channel *(La Manche)*, northeast by Belgium and Luxembourg, east by Germany, Switzerland and Italy, south by the Mediterranean (with Monaco as a coastal enclave), southwest by Spain and Andorra, and west by the Atlantic Ocean. The total area of metropolitan France is 543,965 sq. km. Paris is the most populous agglomeration in Europe, with a population of over 10·1m. More than 14% of the population of Paris are foreign and 19% are foreign born.

The population was 58,518,395 at the census of 1999 and 61,795,550 on 1 Jan. 2007 (density, 113·6 persons per sq. km).

The UN gives an estimated population for 2010 of 62·64m.

In 2005, 76·7% of the population lived in urban areas.

The growth of the population has been as follows:

Census	*Population*	*Census*	*Population*	*Census*	*Population*
1801	27,349,003	1946	40,506,639	1982	54,334,871
1861	37,386,313	1954	42,777,174	1990	56,615,155
1901	38,961,945	1962	46,519,997	1999	58,518,395
1921	39,209,518	1968	49,778,540	2006[1]	61,399,733
1931	41,834,923	1975	52,655,802	2007[2]	61,795,550

[1]First recorded figure using the new 'rolling census' method of calculating the population that came into effect in Jan. 2004.
[2]Calculated using the 'rolling census' method.

According to the 1999 census, there were 3·26m. people of foreign extraction in France (5·6% of the population). The largest groups of foreigners with residence permits in 1999 were: Portuguese (573,000), Algerians (545,000) and Moroccans (445,000). France's Muslim population, at 5m., is the highest in Europe.

Controls on illegal immigration were tightened in July 1991. Automatic right to citizenship for those born on French soil was restored in 1997 by the new left-wing coalition government. New immigration legislation, which came into force in 1998, brought in harsher penalties for organized traffic in illegal immigrants and extended asylum laws to include people whose lives are at risk from non-state as well as state groups. It also extended nationality at the age of 18 to those born in France of non-French parents, provided they have lived a minimum of five years in France since the age of 11.

The areas, recorded populations and chief towns of the 22 metropolitan regions in 2006 were as follows:

Regions	*Area (sq. km)*	*Population*	*Chief town*
Alsace	8,280	1,815,493	Strasbourg
Aquitaine	41,309	3,119,778	Bordeaux
Auvergne	26,013	1,335,938	Clermont-Ferrand
Basse-Normandie	17,589	1,456,793	Caen
Bourgogne (Burgundy)	31,582	1,628,837	Dijon
Bretagne (Brittany)	27,209	3,094,534	Rennes
Centre	39,151	2,519,567	Orléans
Champagne-Ardenne	25,606	1,338,850	Reims
Corse (Corsica)	8,680	294,118	Ajaccio
Franche-Comté	16,202	1,150,624	Besançon
Haute-Normandie	12,318	1,811,055	Rouen
Île-de-France	12,011	11,532,398	Paris
Languedoc-Roussillon	27,376	2,534,144	Montpellier
Limousin	16,942	730,920	Limoges
Lorraine	23,542	2,335,749	Nancy
Midi-Pyrénées	45,348	2,776,822	Toulouse
Nord-Pas-de-Calais	12,414	4,018,644	Lille
Pays de la Loire	32,082	3,450,413	Nantes
Picardie	19,399	1,894,355	Amiens
Poitou-Charentes	25,809	1,724,123	Poitiers
Provence-Alpes-Côte d'Azur	31,400	4,815,232	Marseille
Rhône-Alpes	43,698	6,021,346	Lyon

The 22 regions are divided into 96 metropolitan *départements*, which in 2007 consisted of 36,569 communes.

Populations of the principal conurbations (in descending order of size) and towns in 2006:

	Conurbation	*Town*
Paris	10,142,977[1]	2,181,371
Marseille–Aix-en-Provence	1,418,481[2]	839,043
Lyon	1,417,463[3]	472,305
Lille	1,016,205[4]	226,014
Nice	940,017	347,060
Toulouse	850,873	437,715
Bordeaux	803,117	232,260
Nantes	568,743	282,853
Toulon	543,065	167,816
Douai–Lens	512,462	...[5]
Strasbourg	440,265	272,975
Grenoble	427,658	156,107
Rouen	388,798	107,904
Valenciennes	355,660	42,426
Nancy	331,279	105,468
Metz	322,946	124,435
Montpellier	318,225	251,634
Tours	306,974	136,942
Saint-Étienne	286,400	177,480
Rennes	282,550	209,613
Avignon	273,359	92,454
Orléans	269,283	113,130
Clermont-Ferrand	260,657	138,992
Béthune	259,293	26,472
Le Havre	238,776	182,580
Mulhouse	238,638	110,514
Dijon	238,088	151,504
Angers	227,771	152,337
Reims	212,021	183,837
Brest	206,394	144,548
Caen	196,323	110,399
Pau	193,991	83,903
Le Mans	192,910	144,016
Bayonne	189,836	44,406
Dunkerque	182,973	69,274
Perpignan	178,501	115,326
Limoges	177,439	136,539

	Conurbation	Town
Nîmes	161,565	144,092
Amiens	161,311	136,105
Annecy	144,682	51,023
Saint-Nazaire	143,106	68,838
Besançon	134,951	117,080
Troyes	131,039	61,344
Thionville	130,437	41,127
Poitiers	126,652	88,776
Valence	120,922	65,263
La Rochelle	119,702	77,196
Chambéry	119,266	57,543
Genève–Annemasse	118,554	...[6]
Lorient	116,764	58,547
Montbéliard	109,118	26,535
Angoulême	105,021	42,096
Calais	103,277	74,888
Creil	101,100	33,479

[1]Including Boulogne-Billancourt (110,251), Argenteuil (102,683), Montreuil (101,587), Versailles (87,549), Saint-Denis (97,875), Nanterre (88,316), Créteil (88,939), Aulnay-sous-Bois (81,600), Vitry-sur-Seine (82,902). [2]Including Aix-en-Provence (142,534). [3]Including Villeurbanne (136,473), Vénissieux (57,179). [4]Including Roubaix (97,952), Tourcoing (92,357). [5]Including Douai (42,766), Lens (35,583). [6]Including Annemasse (28,572).

France (including its overseas territories) has nine national parks, 45 regional nature parks and 164 national nature reserves.

Languages

The official language is French. Breton and Basque are spoken in their regions. The *Toubon* legislation of 1994 seeks to restrict the use of foreign words in official communications, broadcasting and advertisements (a previous such decree dated from 1975). The Constitutional Court has since ruled that imposing such restrictions on private citizens would infringe their freedom of expression.

SOCIAL STATISTICS

Statistics for calendar years:

	Births	Deaths	Marriages	Divorces
2002	761,630	535,144	279,087	115,861
2003	761,464	552,339	275,963	125,175
2004	767,816	509,429	271,598	131,335
2005	774,355	527,533	276,303	152,050
2006	796,896	516,416	267,260	135,910
2007	785,985	521,016	267,194	131,316

Live birth rate (2006) was 13·0 per 1,000 population; death rate, 8·4; marriage rate, 4·4; divorce rate, 2·2. 50·5% of births in 2006 were outside marriage. In 2006 the average age at first marriage was 31·3 years for males and 29·3 years for females. Abortions were legalized in 1975; there were an estimated 209,700 in 2006. Life expectancy at birth, 2006, 77·2 years for males and 84·2 years for females. Annual population growth rate, 2000–05, 0·6%. In 2005 the suicide rate per 100,000 population was 17·6 (males, 26·4; females, 9·2). Infant mortality, 2006, 3·6 per 1,000 live births; fertility rate, 2004, 1·9 births per woman. In 2005 France received 49,733 asylum applications (58,545 in 2004 and 59,768 in 2003).

CLIMATE

The northwest has a moderate maritime climate, with small temperature range and abundant rainfall; inland, rainfall becomes more seasonal, with a summer maximum, and the annual range of temperature increases. Southern France has a Mediterranean climate, with mild moist winters and hot dry summers. Eastern France has a continental climate and a rainfall maximum in summer, with thunderstorms prevalent. Paris, Jan. 37°F (3°C), July 64°F (18°C). Annual rainfall 22·9" (573 mm). Bordeaux, Jan. 41°F (5°C), July 68°F (20°C). Annual rainfall 31·4" (786 mm). Lyon, Jan. 37°F (3°C), July 68°F (20°C). Annual rainfall 31·8" (794 mm).

CONSTITUTION AND GOVERNMENT

The Constitution of the Fifth Republic, superseding that of 1946, came into force on 4 Oct. 1958. It consists of a preamble, dealing with the Rights of Man, and 89 articles.

France is a decentralized republic, indivisible, secular, democratic and social; all citizens are equal before the law (Art. 1). National sovereignty resides with the people, who exercise it through their representatives and by referendums (Art. 3). Constitutional reforms of July 1995 widened the range of issues on which referendums may be called. Political parties carry out their activities freely, but must respect the principles of national sovereignty and democracy (Art. 4).

A constitutional amendment of 4 Aug. 1995 deleted all references to the 'community' (*communauté*) between France and her overseas possessions, representing an important step towards the constitutional dismantling of the former French colonial empire.

The head of state is the *President*, who sees that the Constitution is respected; ensures the regular functioning of the public authorities, as well as the continuity of the state; is the protector of national independence and territorial integrity (Art. 5). As a result of a referendum held on 24 Sept. 2000 the President is elected for five years by direct universal suffrage (Art. 6). Previously the term of office had been seven years. The President appoints (and dismisses) a Prime Minister and, on the latter's advice, appoints and dismisses the other members of the government (*Council of Ministers*) (Art. 8); presides over the Council of Ministers (Art. 9); may dissolve the National Assembly, after consultation with the Prime Minister and the Presidents of the two Houses (Art. 12); appoints to the civil and military offices of the state (Art. 13). In times of crisis, the President may take such emergency powers as the circumstances demand; the National Assembly cannot be dissolved during such a period (Art. 16).

Parliament consists of the National Assembly and the Senate. The *National Assembly* is elected by direct suffrage by the second ballot system (by which candidates winning 50% or more of the vote in their constituencies are elected, candidates winning less than 12·5% are eliminated and other candidates go on to a second round of voting); the Senate is elected by indirect suffrage (Art. 24). Since 1996 the National Assembly has convened for an annual nine-month session. It comprises 577 deputies, elected by a two-ballot system for a five-year term from single-member constituencies (555 in Metropolitan France, 22 in the overseas departments and dependencies), and may be dissolved by the President.

The *Senate* comprises 343 senators (rising to 348 in 2011) elected for six-year terms (one-half every three years) by an electoral college in each Department or overseas dependency, made up of all members of the Departmental Council or its equivalent in overseas dependencies, together with all members of Municipal Councils within that area. The *President* of the Senate deputizes for the President of the Republic in the event of the latter's incapacity. Senate elections were last held on 21 Sept. 2008.

The *Constitutional Council* is composed of nine members whose term of office is nine years (non-renewable), one-third every three years; three are appointed by the President of the Republic, three by the President of the National Assembly, three by the President of the Senate; in addition, former Presidents of the Republic are, by right, life members of the Constitutional Council (Art. 56). It oversees the fairness of the elections of the President (Art. 58) and Parliament (Art. 59), and of referendums (Art. 60), and acts as a guardian of the Constitution (Art. 61). Its *President* is Jean-Louis Debré (appointed 5 March 2007).

The *Economic and Social Council* advises on Government and Private Members' Bills (Art. 69). It comprises representatives of employers', workers' and farmers' organizations in each Department and Overseas Territory.

Constitutional amendments of 25 March 2003 and 1 March 2005 added provisions for European Union arrest warrants and allowed for a referendum on the European Union constitution.

The annual salary of the president is €253,600.

Ameller, M., *L'Assemblée Nationale.* 1994
Duhamel, O. and Mény, Y., *Dictionnaire Constitutionnel.* 1992
Elgie, R. (ed.) *Electing the French President: the 1995 Presidential Election.* 1996

Local Government

The traditional system of centralized government was overhauled in 1982 to provide local government with greater power. There are three basic layers of local government: *régions* (of which there are 22), *départements* (of which there are 96) and *communes* (which number about 36,000). Paris, Lyon and Marseille each have special status.

Régions—Mainland France comprises 22 *régions*, which are principally responsible for economic development, town and country planning and education. Government is through regional councils, with members elected every six years. The council works with an economic and social committee, which includes representatives from business and commerce, trade unions, voluntary bodies and other organizations. The council elects a president every three years.

Départements—Government at the department level is principally concerned with health and social welfare, rural capital works, highways and the administration of colleges. A prefect, appointed by the government, oversees the work of the department administration. Decision-making rests with a general council, with members elected every six years. Each department is divided into *cantons* (of which there are around 4,000 in France) to serve as electoral constituencies. The council elects a chairman who holds executive power.

Communes—These municipalities can vary greatly in size. Around 80% of communes have fewer than 1,000 citizens. As a result, smaller communes will often group themselves together, either as urban communities (*communautés urbaines*) or as associations called *syndicats intercommunaux*. Municipal government consists of a decision-making municipal council and a mayor, elected by the council, who wields executive power and also acts as the state's representative. The size of a municipal council is dependent on the size of the commune and members are elected every six years. The council oversees management in areas such as schools and the environment. In addition, the mayor has jurisdiction in security, public health and crime, as well as responsibility for registering births, deaths and marriages.

National Anthem

'La Marseillaise'; words and tune by C. Rouget de Lisle.

GOVERNMENT CHRONOLOGY

(CD = Democratic Centre; CNIP = National Centre of Independents and Peasants; DL = Liberal Democracy; FNRI = National Federation of Independent Republicans; MRP = People's Republican Movement; PR = Republican Party; PS = Socialist Party; Rad. = Radical Party; RPR = Rally for the Republic; SFIO = French Section of the Workers International; UDF = Union for the French Democracy; UDR = Union of Democrats for the Republic; UDSR = Democratic and Social Union of the Resistance; UDT = Democratic Union of Labour; UDVe = Union of Democrats for the V Republic; UMP = Union for a Popular Movement; UNR = Union for the New Republic; UNR-UDT = Union for the French Republic-Democratic Union of Labour; n/p = non-partisan)

Presidents of the French Republic since the Second World War.

1947–54	SFIO	Vincent Auriol
1954–59	CNIP	René Coty

With the advent of the Fifth Republic the power of the president gained at the expense of the prime minister.

1959–69	UNR, UNR-UDT, UDVe, UDR	Charles de Gaulle
1969	CD	Alain Poher
1969–74	UDR	Georges Pompidou
1974	CD	Alain Poher
1974–81	FNRI, PR-UDF	Valéry Giscard d'Estaing
1981–95	PS	François Mitterrand
1995–2007	RPR, UMP	Jacques Chirac
2007–	UMP	Nicolas Sarkozy

Heads of Government since 1944.

Chairmen of the Provisional Government of the French Republic

1944–46	n/p	Charles de Gaulle
1946	SFIO	Félix Gouin
1946	MRP	Georges Bidault
1946–47	SFIO	Léon Blum

Chairmen of the Council of Ministers

1947	SFIO	Paul Ramadier
1947–48	MRP	Robert Schuman
1948	Rad.	André Marie
1948	MRP	Robert Schuman
1948–49	Rad.	Antoine Henri Queuille
1949–50	MRP	Georges Bidault
1950	Rad.	Antoine Henri Queuille
1950–51	UDSR	René Pleven
1951	Rad.	Antoine Henri Queuille
1951–52	UDSR	René Pleven
1952	Rad.	Edgar Faure
1952–53	CNIP	Antoine Pinay
1953	Rad.	René Mayer
1953–54	CNIP	Joseph Laniel
1954–55	Rad.	Pierre Mendès France
1955–56	Rad.	Edgar Faure
1956–57	SFIO	Guy Mollet
1957	Rad.	Maurice Bourgès-Maunoury
1957–58	Rad.	Félix Gaillard
1958	MRP	Pierre Pflimlin
1958–59	UNR	Charles de Gaulle

Prime Ministers

1959–62	UNR	Michel Debré
1962–68	UNR, UNR-UDT, UDVe	Georges Pompidou
1968–69	UDVe, UDR	Maurice Couve de Murville
1969–72	UDR	Jacques Chaban-Delmas
1972–74	UDR	Pierre Messmer
1974–76	UDR	Jacques Chirac
1976–81	n/p, UDF	Raymond Barre
1981–84	PS	Pierre Mauroy
1984–86	PS	Laurent Fabius
1986–88	RPR	Jacques Chirac
1988–91	PS	Michel Rocard
1991–92	PS	Édith Cresson
1992–93	PS	Pierre Bérégovoy
1993–95	RPR	Édouard Balladur
1995–97	RPR	Alain Juppé
1997–2002	PS	Lionel Jospin
2002–05	DL, UMP	Jean-Pierre Raffarin
2005–07	UMP	Dominique de Villepin
2007–	UMP	François Fillon

RECENT ELECTIONS

At the first round of presidential elections on 22 April 2007 Nicolas Sarkozy, the Union for a Popular Movement candidate, gained the largest number of votes (31·18% of those cast) against 11 opponents. His nearest rivals were the Socialist Party candidate Ségolène Royal, who came second with 25·87% of votes cast, and the Union for French Democracy candidate François Bayrou, with 18·57%. National Front leader Jean-Marie Le Pen, who reached the second round in 2002 against a backdrop of widespread protest, won only 10·44% of votes cast. In the second round of voting, held on 6 May 2007, Sarkozy was elected president with 53·06% of votes cast against 46·94% for Royal. Turnout was 84·0% in the second round (83·9% in the first round).

Elections to the National Assembly were held on 10 and 17 June 2007. The Union for a Popular Movement (UMP) won a slightly reduced majority, gaining 314 of the 577 available seats; the Socialist Party (PS), 185; the New Centre (NC), 22; the French Communist Party (PCF), 15; the Left Radical Party (PRG), 7; the Greens, 4; the Democratic Movement (MoDem), 3; the Movement for France (MPF), 2; and others, 22. A centrist 'Presidential Majority' grouping including the UMP, the New Centre and the Movement for France was formed following the election, giving Sarkozy the parliamentary support of 345 deputies. Only 107 of the 577 deputies elected in June 2007 were women.

Following the indirect election held on 21 Sept. 2008, the Senate was composed of (by group, including affiliates): Union for a Popular Movement, 151; the Socialist Group, 116; the Centrist Group, 29; Républicain, Communiste et Citoyen (RCC), 23; Democratic and Social European Rally, 17; Unattached, 7. The number of senators rose from 331 elected in 2004 to 343, and is scheduled to increase to 348 in 2011. In Oct. 2008 Gérard Larcher (UMP) was elected *President* of the Senate for a three-year term.

European Parliament

France has 72 (78 in 2004) representatives. At the June 2009 elections turnout was 40·6% (42·8% in 2004). The UMP won 29 seats with 27·8% of votes cast (political affiliation in European Parliament: European People's Party); PS 14 with 16·5% (Progressive Alliance of Socialists and Democrats); Europe Ecologie 14 with 16·3% (Greens/European Free Alliance); MoDem, 6 with 8·4% (Alliance of Liberals and Democrats for Europe); Front de Gauche, 4 with 6·0% (European United Left/Nordic Green Left); Front National, 3 with 6·3% (non-attached); Libertas, 1 with 4·6% (Europe of Freedom and Democracy); Alliance des Outre-mers, 1 with 0·4% (European United Left/Nordic Green Left).

CURRENT ADMINISTRATION

President: Nicolas Sarkozy; b. 1955 (Union for a Popular Movement; sworn in 16 May 2007).

In March 2010 the cabinet comprised:

Prime Minister: François Fillon; b. 1954 (Union for a Popular Movement; sworn in 17 May 2007).

Minister of State, Minister for Ecology, Energy, Sustainable Development and the Sea, Green Technologies and Climate Change Negotiations: Jean-Louis Borloo. *Minister of State, Keeper of the Seals and Minister for Justice and Liberty:* Michèle Alliot-Marie.

Minister of Foreign and European Affairs: Bernard Kouchner. *Economy, Industry and Employment:* Christine Lagarde. *Interior, Overseas France and Territorial Communities:* Brice Hortefeux. *Labour, Solidarity and the Civil Service:* Éric Woerth. *National Education and Government Spokesperson:* Luc Chatel. *Higher Education and Research:* Valérie Pécresse. *Defence:* Hervé Morin. *Health and Sports:* Roselyne Bachelot-Narquin. *Budget, Public Spending and State Reform:* François Baroin. *Food, Agriculture and Fisheries:* Bruno Le Maire. *Culture and Communication:* Frédéric Mitterrand. *Immigration, Integration, National Identity and Mutually-Supportive Development:* Éric Besson. *Rural Territories and Planning:* Michel Mercier. *Youth and Active Solidarity:* Marc-Philippe Daubresse.

President of the National Assembly: Bernard Accoyer.

Office of the Prime Minister:
http://www.premier-ministre.gouv.fr

CURRENT LEADERS

Nicolas Sarkozy

Position

President

Introduction

Nicolas Sarkozy became president in May 2007, succeeding Jacques Chirac. Having been minister of the interior and the economy, he defeated the Socialist Ségolène Royal and ten other candidates for the presidency. Despite his electoral mandate to introduce modernizing reforms and his commitment to reinvigorating the economy and reducing unemployment, he encountered widespread labour opposition in his first months in office and has since been confronted by the impact of the global credit crisis and ensuing downturn in the French economy. He has nevertheless pursued an active and influential role on the world diplomatic stage, particularly during France's six-month presidency of the European Union from July–Dec. 2008.

Early Life

Nicolas Sarkozy de Nagy-Bosca was born in Paris on 28 Jan. 1955, the son of a Hungarian aristocrat and a French-Jewish mother. Educated at a private Catholic school, he graduated in political science and law and undertook further studies at the Institut d'études politiques de Paris, although he did not graduate. He entered the legal profession as a barrister specializing in business law and began his political life in 1977 as a councillor for Neuilly-sur-Seine. He became a national youth delegate for the newly founded neo-Gaullist Rally for the Republic (RPR) a year later. In 1979 Sarkozy was elected president of the RPR's youth wing under the party's leader Jacques Chirac, who subsequently lost the 1981 presidential campaign to the Socialist, François Mitterrand.

In 1983 Sarkozy was elected mayor of Neuilly-sur-Seine. A member of the Île-de-France Regional Council from 1983–88, he was elected as a parliamentary deputy for the département of Hauts-de-Seine in June 1988 following Mitterrand's re-election as president. Sarkozy was re-elected to the National Assembly at the 1993 elections, in which the RPR made significant progress and the Socialists were reduced to their weakest position since 1958. Sarkozy was appointed minister for the budget before becoming spokesman for the executive in the cabinet of Prime Minister Édouard Balladur.

His decision to back Balladur rather than his mentor, Chirac, in the presidential election of 1995 led to a prolonged rift. Sarkozy retreated into the RPR's internal politics, becoming the party's secretary general in 1998 and its interim president a year later. He also sat as an MEP in 1999.

When Chirac won a landslide victory in the 2002 presidential election he appointed Jean-Pierre Raffarin as prime minister and made Sarkozy minister of the interior. Sarkozy's 'tough on crime' policies divided opinion with his critics claiming that his measures infringed civil rights.

As minister for the economy, finance and industry from 2002–04 Sarkozy introduced market-led reforms, including the reduction of the government's stake in France Télécom. However, he also backed a partial renationalization of the troubled manufacturing company, Alstom. In Nov. 2004 Sarkozy was elected to succeed Alain Juppé as leader of the Union for a Popular Movement (UMP, which grew out of a merger of the RPR and Liberal Democracy in 2002). Reappointed minister of the interior in the government of Dominique de Villepin in June 2005, Sarkozy responded to rioting in some suburbs of Paris by promising to toughen justice measures for delinquents and to counter illegal immigration.

Having been endorsed by the UMP as its candidate in the 2007 presidential election, Sarkozy pledged his support for reducing bureaucracy to help create jobs and to nurture an entrepreneurial culture.

Career in Office

Having defeated Ségolène Royal in a second round of voting held on 6 May 2007, Sarkozy outlined plans for a more dynamic economy with France playing a more prominent global role. He announced his cabinet on 18 May 2007, including François Fillon as prime minister. In June 2007 the UMP won the parliamentary elections, but with a reduced majority. Also in June, Sarkozy enjoyed a successful diplomatic debut at the European Union summit of heads of government, where a new draft treaty on the Union's institutional structure and decision-making process was agreed (and which eventually came into force in Dec. 2009). Later in 2007 his plans for public sector pension benefits provoked paralysing strike action in Nov. by civil servants and workers in the transport and energy sectors. Also in Nov. he was confronted with a renewed, although brief, eruption of rioting in poor immigrant suburbs in Paris and Toulouse.

Public attention in early 2008 focused largely on Sarkozy's private life and remarriage before his UMP party fared badly against the Socialists in municipal elections in March. However, after France assumed the rotating EU presidency in July, he took a prominent role in calling for reform of the world's financial system in response to the global credit crisis and, acting in the name of the EU, helped to secure a ceasefire in the violent conflict that erupted in Aug. between Russia and Georgia. Also in July, a new Union for the Mediterranean was launched at a summit of regional heads of state and government hosted by Sarkozy in Paris.

In early 2009 the government faced strikes and protests in response to the economic downturn. However, France unexpectedly pulled out of recession with a return to growth in the second quarter of the year and Sarkozy's UMP party topped the polls in French elections to the European Parliament in June.

In March 2009, in a significant foreign policy move, Sarkozy confirmed that France would rejoin NATO's integrated military command, reversing its withdrawal of 43 years earlier. Then in May he opened France's first military base in the Persian Gulf area with the stationing of forces in the United Arab Emirates.

In June 2009 the president courted religious controversy by declaring that the burqa, a woman's Islamic garment, was 'not welcome on French territory'.

François Fillon

Position

Prime Minister

Introduction

François Fillon was appointed prime minister on 17 May 2007 by the recently-elected centre-right president, Nicolas Sarkozy. Fillon is a career politician from the left of the conservative Union for Popular Movement (UMP). A former ally of Jacques Chirac, Fillon backed Sarkozy as the UMP presidential candidate and was a leading architect of his election campaign.

Early Life

François Fillon was born on 4 March 1954 in Le Mans, Sarthe. He took an MA in public law at the Université du Maine in Le Mans in 1976, before further study at the Université de Paris V: René Descartes. He subsequently received a DEA in political science from the Fondation Nationale des Sciences Politiques in Paris. From 1977 he was a parliamentary assistant to Joel le Theule, the deputy for Sarthe, continuing when Theule became minister of transport in 1978, then minister of defence in 1980.

Fillon's parliamentary career began in June 1981 when he was elected deputy of the 4th district of Sarthe, representing the conservative-Gaullist Rally for the Republic (RPR). He was also elected to serve on the council of Sable-sur-Sarthe, becoming town mayor in 1983, a position he would hold for 18 years. Fillon was appointed minister of higher education and research in 1993, serving under the RPR prime minister Édouard Balladur until 1995. Fillon then became minister for information technology and the post office. He regained his National Assembly seat at the 1997 elections, although Chirac's ruling centre-right grouping lost its parliamentary majority to a coalition of Socialists, Communists and Greens against a backdrop of rising unemployment and public discontent. That year Fillon was elected national secretary of the RPR and in 1998 he became president of the regional council of Pays de la Loire.

In the aftermath of Chirac's landslide re-election as president in April 2002, Fillon co-founded the UMP to fight in the forthcoming legislative elections. Formed from the merger of the RPR, Liberal Democracy (DL) and the Union for French Democracy (UDF), it won control of the government in the elections of June 2002. Fillon was named minister of social affairs in the administration of Jean-Pierre Raffarin, introducing controversial reforms to the 35-hour working week and to the pensions system.

As minister for education and research from 2004–05, Fillon's proposals for sweeping reforms to the national curriculum met with mass student protests. Nevertheless, the 'Fillon law' was adopted in April 2005. He was not given a ministerial position in Prime Minister Dominique de Villepin's administration, formed in May 2005, and pledged his loyalty to Nicolas Sarkozy in the subsequent presidential election. Later in 2005 he was elected senator for the Sarthe *département*.

Fillon won plaudits for his management of Sarkozy's slick election campaign, which saw Sarkozy consistently polling ahead of rival Socialist candidate Ségolène Royal. Sarkozy emerged as president in the run-off on 6 May 2007 and on 17 May 2007 he appointed Fillon as prime minister.

Career in office

Fillon took control of a slimmed-down government of 15 ministers, half its previous number. At the legislative elections of June 2007 the UMP won a majority, claiming 314 of 577 seats, down from 359. Fillon was expected to play a leading role in President Sarkozy's programme of employment and welfare reform, although these plans attracted a hostile response from public sector workers during the government's first months in office. In late 2008 Fillon threatened to nationalize banks unless they responded positively to the global credit crisis and lent more to French companies. Fillon won a parliamentary vote of confidence in March 2009, sparked by a debate over plans to rejoin NATO's military command, and retained the premiership in a cabinet reshuffle in June. He survived a further reshuffle in March 2010 following poor results for the UMP in regional elections.

DEFENCE

The President of the Republic is the supreme head of defence policy and exercises command over the Armed Forces. He is the only person empowered to give the order to use nuclear weapons. He is assisted by the Council of Ministers, which studies defence problems, and by the Defence Council and the Restricted Defence Committee, which formulate directives.

Legislation of 1996 inaugurated a wide-ranging reform of the defence system over 1997–2002, with regard to the professionalization of the armed forces (brought about by the ending of military conscription and consequent switch to an all-volunteer defence force), the modification and modernization of equipment and the restructuring of the defence industry. In 2008 defence expenditure totalled US$65,675m. (equivalent to US$1,061 per capita), ensuring France overtook the UK as the country with the world's third highest defence expenditure.

Defence spending as a proportion of GDP has fallen from 3·9% in 1985 to 2·3% in 2008.

France rejoined NATO as a full member in April 2009, having withdrawn from its integrated military structure in 1966. In 2006 French military personnel were stationed in a number of countries outside France, including Afghanistan, Bosnia and Herzegovina, the Democratic Republic of the Congo, Côte d'Ivoire, Lebanon and Macedonia.

Conscription was for ten months, but France officially ended its military draft on 27 June 2001 with a reprieve granted to all conscripts (barring those serving in civil positions) on 30 Nov. 2001.

Nuclear Weapons

Having carried out its first test in 1960, there have been 210 tests in all. The last French test was in 1996 (this compares with the last UK test in 1991 and the last US test in 1993). The nuclear arsenal consisted of approximately 300 warheads in Jan. 2009 according to the Stockholm International Peace Research Institute. In 2008 France announced a 33% reduction in the airborne component of its nuclear forces.

Army

The Army comprises the Logistic Force (CFLT), based in Montlhéry with two logistic brigades, and the Land Force Command (CFAT), based in Lille. Apart from the Franco-German brigade, there are 13 brigades, each made up of between four and seven battalions, including one airmobile brigade.

Personnel numbered (2006) 133,500 including 14,700 marines and a Foreign Legion of 7,700. There were 11,350 army reservists in 2006. The 1997–2002 Programming Act provided for the following force at the end of the transitional period: 16,000 officers, 50,000 NCOs, 66,500 army enlistees, 5,500 volunteers, 34,000 civilians and 30,000 reservists. Equipment levels in 2006 included 926 main battle tanks and 393 helicopters.

Gendarmerie

The paramilitary police force exists to ensure public security and maintain law and order, as well as participate in the operational defence of French territory as part of the armed forces. On 1 Jan. 2009 budgetary responsibility for the Gendarmerie was transferred from the ministry of defence to the ministry of the interior. It consisted in 2006 of 102,322 personnel including 1,953 civilians. It comprises a territorial force of 66,537 personnel throughout the country, a mobile force of 16,859 personnel and specialized formations including the Republican Guard, the Air Force and Naval Gendarmeries, and an anti-terrorist unit.

Navy

The missions of the Navy are to provide the prime element of the French independent nuclear deterrent through its force of strategic submarines; to assure the security of the French offshore zones; to contribute to NATO's missions; and to provide on-station and deployment forces overseas in support of French territorial interests and UN commitments. French territorial seas and economic zones are organized into two maritime districts (with headquarters in Brest and Toulon).

The strategic deterrent force comprises four nuclear-powered strategic-missile submarines, including three new-generation vessels of a much larger class (*Le Triomphant*, *Le Téméraire* and *Le Vigilant*, which entered service in 1997, 1999 and 2004 respectively).

Until it was withdrawn from service in 2000, the *Foch*, of 33,000 tonnes, was the principal surface ship. The 40,000-tonne nuclear-powered replacement *Charles de Gaulle*, which was launched at Brest in 1994, commissioned in Oct. 2000. There is one cruiser, the *Jeanne d'Arc*, completed in 1964 and used in peacetime as a training vessel. Other surface combatants include 13 destroyers and 20 frigates.

The naval air arm, *Aviation Navale*, numbers some 6,400 personnel. Operational aircraft include Super-Étendard nuclear-capable strike aircraft, Étendard reconnaissance aircraft and maritime Rafale combat aircraft. A small Marine force of 1,550 *Fusiliers Marins* provides assault groups.

Personnel in 2006 numbered 43,995, including 10,265 civilians. There were 6,000 reserves in 2006.

Air Force

Created in 1934, the Air Force was reorganized in June 1994. The Conventional Forces in Europe (CFE) Agreement imposes a ceiling of 800 combat aircraft. In 2006 there were 304 combat aircraft, 157 transport aircraft and 342 aircraft for training purposes.

Personnel (2006) 63,600. Air Force reserves in 2006 numbered 4,300.

INTERNATIONAL RELATIONS

France is a member of the UN (and a permanent member of its Security Council), World Bank, IMF and several other UN specialized agencies, EU, Council of Europe, WEU, OSCE, CERN, BIS, IOM, International Organization of the Francophonie, NATO, OECD, Inter-American Development Bank, Asian Development Bank, SPC and Antarctic Treaty. France is a signatory to the Schengen accord, which abolishes border controls between France, Austria, Belgium, Czech Republic, Denmark, Estonia, Finland, Germany, Greece, Hungary, Iceland, Italy, Latvia, Lithuania, Luxembourg, Malta, Netherlands, Norway, Poland, Portugal, Slovakia, Slovenia, Spain, Sweden and Switzerland.

At a referendum in Sept. 1992 to approve the ratification of the Maastricht treaty on European union of 7 Feb. 1992, 12,967,498 votes (50·8%) were cast for and 12,550,651 (49·2%) against. On 29 May 2005 France became the first European Union member to reject the proposed EU constitution, with 54·67% of votes cast in a referendum against the constitution and only 45·33% in favour.

France is the focus of the *Communauté Francophone* (French-speaking Community) which formally links France with many of its former colonies in Africa. A wide range of agreements, both with members of the Community and with other French-speaking countries, extend to economic and technical matters, and in particular to the disbursement of overseas aid.

ECONOMY

Agriculture accounted for 2% of GDP in 2007, industry 21% and services 77%.

Overview

France enjoys high per capita income but GDP growth has lagged behind other major European economies. Growth averaged 2% from 2003–07, driven by private consumption resulting from a steady increase in real disposable income, although the failure of domestic supply to keep up with demand resulted in a net external drag on growth of roughly 0·5% of GDP per year over the period. Since 2002 France has fallen from 12th to 23rd position in per capita GDP rankings according to IMF data.

Business sector productivity is high and from 1996–2005 labour productivity grew at an average annual rate of 1·23%, higher than Germany's average of 1·05% (reported by the Economist Intelligence Unit). By 2000, labour productivity had surpassed that of the USA. However, per capita income in France has remained below that of the USA primarily because the French, like other Europeans, work shorter hours. Total factor productivity grew at only 0·47% on average over the decade, compared to Germany's average of 0·64%.

The agricultural sector is large compared with other developed countries. While agriculture accounts for an average 1·3% of GDP among G7 countries, it accounts for nearly twice as much in France and employs more than 3% of the workforce. France secured the common agricultural policy (CAP), which subsidizes European agriculture, as a condition for establishing the EU. It is the largest beneficiary of CAP, receiving around 25% of all EU farm subsidies valued at €40bn. a year (or 40% of the total EU budget). In 2003 CAP reform saw most subsidies converted from price supports to direct income payments. While this creates less trade distortion, farm support remains a major point of contention in EU budget and WTO trade negotiations.

The tax burden in France is among the highest in Europe, equating to almost 50% of GDP in 2005. Labour force participation is particularly low with structural unemployment high. The re-emergence of government-aided jobs and labour market reforms have aided employment growth but continued rises in the minimum wage and pension reform allowing early retirement have held back job creation. Having reached a low of 7·6% in March 2008, unemployment rose steeply from late 2008 owing to the economic downturn. By Nov. 2009 the rate had reached 10%. The IMF suggests efforts to foster job creation, especially for young, low-skilled and senior workers, would aid efforts to boost growth and competitiveness, safeguard fiscal sustainability and boost welfare.

The global financial crisis forced the economy into recession in 2008. Following four successive quarters of contraction, France exited from recession in the second quarter of 2009 but GDP declined by 2·2% for the year as a whole. Policy response has included a fiscal stimulus package comprising temporary investment expenditures and tax breaks, and measures to recapitalize banks to support liquidity.

In 2002 France breached the 3% GDP budget deficit limit set by the euro zone's growth and stability pact, causing public debt to exceed 60% of GDP in 2003. It reduced its deficit to less than 3% of GDP in 2005, while healthcare spending was on target for the first time in recent history and real government spending remained constant for four years running. Given the recession, authorities have aimed to manage short-term stimulus without derailing medium-term fiscal consolidation plans. Steps to consolidate have so far included adoption of a multi-year budgeting framework, zero-growth expenditure at central government level, and ongoing reductions in public sector employment. Efforts to tackle population ageing remain an obstacle to future growth until public debt is tackled and structural reforms are implemented.

The IMF suggests introducing further product market reforms to boost consumer welfare. It reports that consumers would benefit from increased competition, demonstrated by the competition authority's action over collusion in the telecommunications industry. According to the IMF and OECD further consumer benefits would come from simpler administrative procedures for new businesses and prompt implementation of the EU services directive.

The IMF reports that service sector liberalization is likely to raise economic efficiency, though proposed reforms were a primary reason for the rejection of the EU constitution in a 2005 referendum. The government has taken an increasingly conservative stance on EU issues and in late 2005 announced that it would protect 11 sectors of the economy from foreign acquisitions.

Currency

On 1 Jan. 1999 the euro (EUR) became the legal currency in France at the irrevocable conversion rate of 6·55957 francs to one euro. The euro, which consists of 100 cents, has been in circulation since 1 Jan. 2002. There are seven euro notes in different colours and sizes denominated in 500, 200, 100, 50, 20, 10 and 5 euros, and eight coins denominated in 2 and 1 euros, then 50, 20, 10, 5, 2 and 1 cents. On the introduction of the euro there was a 'dual circulation' period before the franc ceased to be legal tender on 17 Feb. 2002. Euro banknotes in circulation on 1 Jan. 2002 had a total value of €84·2bn.

Foreign exchange reserves were US$26,170m. in Sept. 2009 and gold reserves 78·30m. troy oz. Total money supply was €431,879m. in Aug. 2009. Inflation rates (based on OECD statistics):

1999	*2000*	*2001*	*2002*	*2003*	*2004*	*2005*	*2006*	*2007*	*2008*
0·6%	1·8%	1·8%	1·9%	2·2%	2·3%	1·9%	1·9%	1·6%	3·2%

Franc Zone

13 former French colonies (Benin, Burkina Faso, Cameroon, Central African Republic, Chad, Comoros, the Republic of the Congo, Côte d'Ivoire, Gabon, Mali, Niger, Senegal and Togo), the former Spanish colony of Equatorial Guinea and the former Portuguese colony of Guinea-Bissau are members of a Franc Zone, the CFA (*Communauté Financière Africaine*). Comoros uses the Comorian franc. The *franc CFA* is pegged to the euro at a rate of 655·957 francs CFA to one euro. The franc CFP *(Comptoirs Français du Pacifique)* is the common currency of French Polynesia, New Caledonia and Wallis and Futuna. It is pegged to the euro at 119·3317422 francs CFP to the euro.

Budget

Central government revenue and expenditure in €1m.:

	2005	*2006*	*2007*[1]
Revenue	744,640	775,020	798,780
Expenditure	789,750	814,350	841,170

[1]Provisional

Principal sources of revenue in 2006 were: social security contributions, €327·60bn.; taxes on income, profits and capital gains, €194·06bn.; taxes on goods and services, €184·19bn. Main items of expenditure by economic type in 2006: social benefits, €403·58bn.; compensation of employees, €178·70bn.; use of goods and services, €51·59bn.

The standard rate of VAT is 19·6% (reduced rates, 5·5% and 2·1%). In 2009 the top rate of income tax was 40·0% and corporate tax was 33·3%.

Performance

Real GDP growth rates (based on OECD statistics):

1999	*2000*	*2001*	*2002*	*2003*	*2004*	*2005*	*2006*	*2007*	*2008*
3·2%	4·1%	1·8%	1·1%	1·1%	2·3%	1·9%	2·4%	2·3%	0·3%

The real GDP growth rate in 2009 according to INSEE, the French National Institute for Statistics and Economic Studies, was –2·2%. Total GDP in 2008 was US$2,853·1bn.

Banking and Finance

The central bank and bank of issue is the Banque de France (*Governor*, Christian Noyer, appointed 2003), founded in 1800, and nationalized on 2 Dec. 1945. The Governor is appointed for a six-year term (renewable once) and heads the nine-member Council of Monetary Policy.

The National Credit Council, formed in 1945 to regulate banking activity and consulted in all political decisions on monetary policy, comprises 51 members nominated by the government; its president is the minister for the economy; its vice-president is the governor of the Banque de France.

In 2003 there were 1,518 banks and other credit institutions, including 304 banks and 593 investment firms. Four principal deposit banks were nationalized in 1945, the remainder in 1982; the latter were privatized in 1987. The banking and insurance sectors underwent a flurry of mergers, privatizations, foreign investment, corporate restructuring and consolidation in 1997, in both the national and international fields. The largest banks in April 2009 by assets were BNP Paribas (US$2,888·73bn.) and Crédit Agricole (US$2,064·17bn.). In April 2010 the largest banks by market capitalization were BNP Paribas (US$68·44bn.) and Société Générale (US$34·25bn.).

The former state banks, the Caisses d'Épargne, became co-operative savings banks in 1999 although the group remains partly state-owned. There is a state-owned postal bank, La Banque Postale. Deposited funds are centralized by a non-banking body, the Caisse des Dépôts et Consignations, which finances a large number of local authorities and state-aided housing projects, and carries an important portfolio of transferable securities.

France attracted US$117·5bn. worth of foreign direct investment in 2008, down from the record level of US$157·8bn. in 2007.

There is a stock exchange (*Bourse*) in Paris; it is a component of Euronext, which was created in Sept. 2000 through the merger of the Paris, Brussels and Amsterdam bourses.

ENERGY AND NATURAL RESOURCES

Environment

France's carbon dioxide emissions from the consumption and flaring of fossil fuels in 2008 were the equivalent of 6·5 tonnes per capita. An *Environmental Performance Index* compiled in 2008 ranked France tenth in the world, with 87·8%. The index examined various factors in six areas—air pollution, biodiversity and habitat, climate change, environmental health, productive natural resources and water resources.

Electricity

EDF is responsible for power generation and supply. It was privatized in Nov. 2005 when the government sold a 15·5% stake in the company. Installed capacity was 120·4m. kW in 2004. Electricity production in 2004: 572·24bn. kWh, of which 78·3% was nuclear. Hydro-electric power contributes about 11·3% of total electricity output. Consumption per capita in 2004 was 8,231 kWh. In 2004 France was the world's biggest exporter of electricity, with 68·6bn. kWh. EDF is Europe's leading electricity producer, generating 610·6bn. kWh in 2007.

France, not rich in natural energy resources, is at the centre of Europe's nuclear energy industry. In 2004 there were 59 nuclear reactors in operation—more than in any other country in the world apart from the USA—with a generating capacity of 63,363 MW. France has the highest percentage of its electricity generated through nuclear power of any country.

Oil and Gas

In 2004, 8·3m. bbls of crude oil were produced. The greater part came from the Parentis oilfield in the Landes. Reserves in 2007 totalled 122m. bbls. The importation and distribution of natural gas is the responsibility of GDF Suez, a company formed in July 2008 following a merger between Gaz de France and fellow utility group Suez. The French government has a 35·6% stake in the combined company. Production of natural gas (2004, including Monaco) was 1·4bn. cu. metres. Natural gas reserves were 9·7bn. cu. metres in 2007.

Minerals

France is a significant producer of nickel, uranium, iron ore, bauxite, potash, pig iron, aluminium and coal. Société Le Nickel extracts in New Caledonia and is the world's third largest nickel producer.

Coal production in 2004 was 0·9m. tonnes. France's last coal mine closed in April 2004. Production of other principal minerals and metals, in 1,000 tonnes: salt (2006), 9,371; aluminium (2006), 442; gold (2003), 1,470 kg.

Agriculture

France has the highest agricultural production in Europe. In 2004 the agricultural sector employed about 929,000 people, down from 1,869,000 in 1980. Agriculture accounts for 14·5% of exports and 11·4% of imports.

In 2003 there were 590,000 holdings (average size 45 ha.), down from over 1m. in 1988. Co-operatives account for between 30–50% of output. There were 1,264,000 tractors and 200,000 harvester-threshers in 2002. Although the total number of tractors has been declining steadily in recent years, increasingly more powerful ones are being used. In 2000, 427,000 tractors in use were of 80 hp or higher, compared to 96,000 in 1979.

Of the total area of France (54·9m. ha.), the utilized agricultural area comprised 29·68m. ha. in 2003. 18·30m. ha. were arable, 10·12m. ha. were under pasture and 1·12m. ha. were under permanent crops including vines (0·88m. ha.).

Area under cultivation and yield for principal crops:

	Area (1,000 ha.)			*Production (1,000 tonnes)*		
	2001	*2002*	*2003*	*2001*	*2002*	*2003*
Wheat	4,767	5,230	4,905	31,540	38,934	30,582
Sugar beets	429	438	402	26,841	33,450	29,238
Maize	1,916	1,831	1,667	16,408	16,440	11,898
Barley	1,705	1,643	1,750	9,799	10,988	9,818
Potatoes	162	162	156	6,078	6,877	6,235
Rapeseeds	1,083	1,036	1,080	2,878	3,317	3,341
Peas	417	339	367	2,134	2,085	2,013
Sunflower seeds	708	616	689	1,584	1,497	1,494

Production of principal fruit crops (in 1,000 tonnes) as follows:

	2001	*2002*	*2003*
Apples	2,397	2,478	2,402
Melons	318	282	297
Plums	272	253	247
Pears	260	268	210
Peaches	263	264	192

Total fruit and vegetable production in 2003 was 18,371,000 tonnes. Other important vegetables include tomatoes (834,000 tonnes in 2003), carrots (682,000 tonnes), onions (393,000 tonnes) and cauliflowers (390,000 tonnes). France is the world's leading producer of sugar beets. Total area under cultivation and yield of grapes from the vine (2003): 851,000 ha.; 6·31m. tonnes. Wine production (2006): 57,127,000 hectolitres. France was the largest wine producer in the world in 2006 (18·4% of the world total), having overtaken Italy in 1999. Consumption in France has declined dramatically in recent times, from nearly 120 litres per person in 1966 to 55 litres per person in 2004.

In 2005 France set aside 560,838 ha. (1·9% of its agricultural land) for the growth of organic crops, compared to the EU average of 3·6%.

Livestock (2003, in 1,000): cattle, 19,517; pigs, 15,058; sheep, 9,204; goats, 1,214; horses, 345; chickens, 220,000; turkeys, 42,000; ducks, 25,000. Livestock products (2002, in 1,000 tonnes): pork, bacon and ham, 2,346; beef and veal, 1,640; lamb and mutton, 128; horse, 10; poultry, 2,105; eggs, 989. Milk production, 2002 (in 1,000 tonnes): cow, 25,197; goat, 536; sheep, 257. Cheese production, 1,783,000 tonnes. France is the second largest cheese producer in the world after the USA.

Source: SCEES/Agreste

Forestry

Forestry is France's richest natural resource and employs 550,000 people. In 2005 forest covered 15·55m. ha. (28·3% of the land area). In 1990 the area under forests had been 14·23m. ha., or 25·9% of the land area. 65% of forest is privately owned. 51,000 ha. of land in France is reforested annually. Timber production in 2007 was 62·76m. cu. metres.

Fisheries

In 2008 there were 7,389 fishing vessels (of which 4,979 were in mainland France), and (in 2006) 17,088 fishermen. Catch in 2005 was 574,358 tonnes, of which 572,248 tonnes were from marine waters.

INDUSTRY

The leading companies by market capitalization in France in March 2009 were: Total, an integrated oil company (US$117·9bn.); GDF Suez, an energy company (US$75·3bn.); and Sanofi-Aventis, a pharmaceuticals company (US$74·0bn.).

The industrial sector employs about 19% of the workforce. Chief industries: steel, chemicals, textiles, aircraft, machinery, electronic equipment, tourism, wine and perfume.

Industrial production, 2004 (in 1,000 tonnes): distillate fuel oil, 34,421; crude steel (2003), 19,803; cement (2003), 19,660; petrol, 16,878; pig iron (2003), 12,756; residual fuel oil, 11,887; jet fuel, 5,616; sulphuric acid (2001), 2,051; caustic soda (2002), 1,829. France is one of the biggest producers of mineral water, with 6,283m. litres in 2001; soft drinks production in 2003, 2,510m. litres; beer production in 2001, 1,572m. litres; cigarette production in 2001, 41·8bn. units.

Engineering production (in 1,000 units): passenger cars (2005), 3,112; car tyres (2001), 63,790; television sets (2002), 5,375; radio sets (2002), 3,357.

Labour

Of 25,628,000 people in employment in 2008, 46·9% were women. By sector, 74·5% worked in services (58·1% in 1980), 22·0% in industry and construction (33·1% in 1980) and 3·4% in agriculture (8·8% in 1980). Some 3·1m. people work in the public sector at national and local level.

A new definition of 'unemployed' was adopted in Aug. 1995, omitting persons who had worked at least 78 hours in the previous month. The unemployment rate was 10·0% in Dec. 2009. The rate among the under 25s is more than double the overall national rate.

Conciliation boards (*conseils de prud'hommes*) mediate in labour disputes. They are elected for five-year terms by two colleges of employers and employees. There were a total of 1,415,000 working days lost to strike action in 2006. Between 1996 and 2005 strikes cost France an average of 53 days per 1,000 employees a year. In Jan. 2010 the minimum wage (SMIC) was raised to €8·86 an hour (€1,343·77 a month for a 35-hour week); it affected about 3·4m. wage-earners in July 2008. The average annual salary in the private and semi-public sectors was €31,932 in 2007. Retirement age is 60, although the average actual age for retirement is 57. A five-week annual holiday is statutory.

In March 2005 the National Assembly voted by 350 to 135 to amend the working hours law restricting the legal working week to 35 hours, introduced by the former Socialist government between 1998–2000. Under the new proposals employees can, in agreement with their employer, work up to 48 hours per week. There is no change in the legal working week: any increased hours are on a voluntary basis. The proposal also allows for the increase of overtime hours from 180 to 220 per year, payable at 125% of the normal hourly rate. To encourage the working of longer hours, payment of overtime work is now exempt from individual income tax, social contributions and social taxes (since 1 Oct. 2007).

Trade Unions

The main trade union confederations are as follows: the Communist-led CGT (Confédération Générale du Travail), founded 1895; the CGT-FO (Confédération Générale du Travail–Force Ouvrière) which broke away from the CGT in 1948; the CFTC (Confédération Française des Travailleurs Chrétiens), founded in 1919 and divided in 1964, with a breakaway group retaining the old name and the main body continuing under the new name of CFDT (Confédération Française Démocratique du Travail); and the CGC-CFE (Confédération Générale des Cadres-Confédération Française de l'Encadrement) formed in 1946, which represents managerial and supervisory staff. The main haulage confederation is the FNTR; the leading employers' association is MEDEF (Mouvement des Entreprises de France), formerly known as the CNPF. Unions are not required to publish membership figures, but in 2008 the two largest federations, the CFDT and the CGT, had an estimated 0·81m. and (in 2006) 0·71m. members respectively.

Although France has the lowest rate of trade union membership in Europe (8% in 2007, compared to 20% in Germany, 26% in the UK and more than 70% in Finland and Sweden), its trade unionists have considerable clout: they run France's welfare system; staff the country's dispute-settling industrial tribunals (*conseils de prud'hommes*); and fix national agreements on wages and working conditions. A union call to strike is invariably answered by more than a union's membership.

INTERNATIONAL TRADE

Imports and Exports

In 2008 imports (c.i.f.) totalled US$696·65bn. (US$619·27bn. in 2007); exports (f.o.b.), US$596·10bn. (US$542·64bn. in 2007). Principal imports include: oil, machinery and equipment, chemicals, iron and steel, and foodstuffs. Major exports: metals, chemicals, industrial equipment, consumer goods and agricultural products.

In 2007 chemicals and manufactured goods accounted for 41·4% of France's imports and 42·6% of exports; machinery and transport equipment 35·0% of imports and 40·1% of exports; food, live animals, beverages and tobacco 7·3% of imports and 10·7% of exports; mineral fuels, lubricants and related materials 13·5% of imports and 3·9% of exports; inedible crude materials, and animal and vegetable oil and fats 2·7% of imports and 2·6% of exports.

In 2007 the chief import sources (as % of total imports) were as follows: Germany, 16·6%; Italy, 8·5%; Belgium, 8·3%; Spain, 7·0%; China, 6·3%. The chief export markets (as % of total) were: Germany, 14·4%; Spain, 9·6%; Italy, 9·2%; UK, 8·4%; Belgium, 7·5%. Imports from fellow European Union members accounted for 62·0% of all imports, and exports to other European Union members constituted 65·5% of the total.

Trade Fairs

Paris ranks as the second most popular convention city behind Singapore according to the Union des Associations Internationales (UAI), hosting 3·8% of all international meetings held in 2008.

COMMUNICATIONS

Roads

In 2007 there were 951,125 km of road, including 11,010 km of motorway and 9,115 km of highways and main roads. France has the longest road network in the EU. Around 90% of all freight is transported by road. In 2007 there were 30·70m. passenger cars (498 per 1,000 inhabitants), 6·27m. lorries and vans, and 83,000 buses and coaches. Road passenger traffic in 2007 totalled 775bn. passenger-km. In 2007 there were 4,620 road deaths, down from 8,445 in 1997.

Only Singapore ranked ahead of France for quality of road infrastructure in the World Economic Forum's *Global Competitiveness Report 2009–2010.*

Rail

In 1938 all the independent railway companies were merged with the existing state railway system in a Société Nationale des Chemins de Fer Français (SNCF), which became a public industrial and commercial establishment in 1983. Legislation came into effect in 1997 which vested ownership of the railway infrastructure (track and signalling) in a newly established public corporation, the Réseau Ferré de France (RFF/French Rail Network). The RFF is funded by payments for usage from the SNCF, government and local subventions and authority capital made available by the state derived from the proceeds of privatization. The SNCF remains responsible for maintenance and management of the rail network. The legislation also envisages the establishment of regional railway services which receive funds previously given to the SNCF as well as a state subvention. These regional bodies negotiate with SNCF for the provision of suitable services for their area. SNCF is the most heavily indebted and subsidized company in France.

In 2001 the RFF-managed network totalled 31,385 km of track (14,464 km electrified). High-speed TGV lines link Paris to the south and west of France, and Paris and Lille to the Channel Tunnel (Eurostar). The high-speed TGV line appeared in 1983; it had 2,110 km of track in 2001, and another 4,000 km planned by 2015. Services from London through the Channel Tunnel began operating in 1994. Rail passenger traffic in 2001 totalled 71·6bn. passenger km and freight tonne-km came to 50·4bn.

The Paris transport network consisted in 2005 of 212 km of metro (297 stations), 115 km of regional express railways and 31 km of tramway. There are metros in Lille (67 km), Lyon (29 km), Marseille (19 km), Rennes (9 km) and Toulouse (12 km), and tram/light railway networks in Bordeaux (25 km), Clermont-Ferrand (14 km), Grenoble (28 km), Le Mans (15 km), Lille (22 km), Lyon (18 km), Marseille (12 km), Montpellier (12 km), Mulhouse (12 km), Nantes (40 km), Nice (9 km), Orléans (18 km), Rouen (15 km), St Étienne (9 km), Strasbourg (25 km) and Valenciennes (9 km).

France was ranked fourth for rail infrastructure in the World Economic Forum's *Global Competitiveness Report 2009–2010*.

Civil Aviation

The main international airports are at Paris (Charles de Gaulle), Paris (Orly), Bordeaux (Mérignac), Lyon (Satolas), Marseille-Provence, Nice-Côte d'Azur, Strasbourg (Entzheim), Toulouse (Blagnac), Clermont-Ferrand (Aulunat) and Nantes (Atlantique). The following had international flights to only a few destinations in 2003: Brest, Caen, Carcassonne, Le Havre, Le Touquet, Lille, Pau, Rennes, Rouen and Saint-Étienne. The national airline, Air France, was 54·4% state-owned but merged in Oct. 2003 with the Dutch carrier KLM to form Air France-KLM. In the process the share owned by the French state fell to 44·2%. In Dec. 2004 the government sold off a further 18·4% to reduce its stake to 25·8%, and in the meantime the government's share has come down still further to 15·7%. In 2005 Air France carried 42·9m. passengers (25·9m. on international flights); passenger-km totalled 115·1bn. The main other French airline is Corsairfly. In 2008 Charles de Gaulle airport handled 60,874,681 passengers (55,825,413 on international flights) and 2,039,460 tonnes of freight. Only Heathrow handled more international passengers in 2008. Orly was the second busiest airport, handling 26,209,703 passengers (11,825,460 on domestic flights) and 95,770 tonnes of freight. Nice was the third busiest for passengers, with 10,382,566 (6,061,002 on international flights).

In April 2003 Air France announced that Concorde, the world's first supersonic jet which began commercial service in 1976, would be permanently grounded from Oct. 2003.

Shipping

In Jan. 2003 the merchant fleet comprised 221 vessels of 300 gross tons or over totalling 6·49m. DWT, including 52 tankers (4·33m. DWT). In 2002 vessels totalling 2,439m. NRT entered ports. In 2003, 248m. tonnes of cargo were unloaded, including 137m. tonnes of crude and refined petroleum products, and 110m. tonnes were loaded; total passenger traffic was 28·6m. Chief ports: Marseille, Le Havre, Dunkerque, Saint-Nazaire and Calais.

France has extensive inland waterways. Canals are administered by the public authority France Navigable Waterways (VNF). In 2003 there were 8,501 km of navigable rivers, waterways and canals (of which 1,621 km were accessible to vessels over 3,000 tons), with a total traffic of 54·7m. tonnes.

Telecommunications

France Télécom became a limited company on 1 Jan. 1997. In 2007 there were 34·8m. main (fixed) telephone lines. In the same year mobile phone subscribers numbered 55·4m. (897·0 per 1,000 persons). The largest operators are Orange France, with a 43% share of the market, and SFR, with a 33% share. There were 40·0m. PCs in use in 2006 and 42·3m. internet users in 2008. The broadband penetration rate in June 2008 was 26·4 subscribers per 100 inhabitants.

Postal Services

There were 16,992 post offices in 2003. A total of 17,201m. pieces of mail were processed in 2003, or 286 items per person. La Poste is a public enterprise under autonomous management responsible for mail delivery and financial services.

SOCIAL INSTITUTIONS

Justice

The system of justice is divided into two jurisdictions: the judicial and the administrative. Within the judicial jurisdiction are common law courts including 473 lower courts (*tribunaux d'instance*, 11 in overseas departments), 181 higher courts (*tribunaux de grande instance*, 5 *tribunaux de première instance* in the overseas territories) and 454 police courts (*tribunaux de police*, 11 in overseas departments).

The *tribunaux d'instance* are presided over by a single judge. The *tribunaux de grande instance* usually have a collegiate composition, but may be presided over by a single judge in some civil cases. The *tribunaux de police*, presided over by a judge on duty in the *tribunal d'instance*, deal with petty offences (*contraventions*); correctional chambers (*chambres correctionelles*, of which there is at least one in each *tribunal de grande instance*) deal with graver offences (*délits*), including cases involving imprisonment up to five years. Correctional chambers normally consist of three judges of a *tribunal de grande instance* (a single judge in some cases). Sometimes in cases of *délit*, and in all cases of more serious *crimes*, a preliminary inquiry is made in secrecy by one of 569 examining magistrates (*juges d'instruction*), who either dismisses the case or sends it for trial before a public prosecutor.

Within the judicial jurisdiction are various specialized courts, including 191 commercial courts (*tribunaux de commerce*), composed of tradesmen and manufacturers elected for two years initially, and then for four years; 271 conciliation boards (*conseils de prud'hommes*), composed of an equal number of employers and employees elected for five years to deal with labour disputes; 437 courts for settling rural landholding disputes (*tribunaux paritaires des baux ruraux*, 11 in overseas departments); and 116 social security courts (*tribunaux des affaires de sécurité sociale*).

When the decisions of any of these courts are susceptible of appeal, the case goes to one of the 35 courts of appeal (*cours d'appel*), composed each of a president and a variable number of members. There are 104 courts of assize (*cours d'assises*), each composed of a president who is a member of the court of appeal, and two other magistrates, and assisted by a lay jury of nine members. These try crimes involving imprisonment of over five years. The decisions of the courts of appeal and the courts of assize are final. However, the Court of Cassation (*cour de cassation*) has discretion to verify if the law has been correctly interpreted and if the rules of procedure have been followed exactly. The Court of Cassation may annul any judgment, following which the cases must be retried by a court of appeal or a court of assizes.

The administrative jurisdiction exists to resolve conflicts arising between citizens and central and local government authorities. It consists of 36 administrative courts (*tribunaux administratifs*, of which eight are in overseas departments and territories) and 15 administrative courts of appeal (*cours administratives d'appel*, of which eight are in overseas departments and territories). The Council of State is the final court of appeal in administrative cases, though it may also act as a court of first instance.

Cases of doubt as to whether the judicial or administrative jurisdiction is competent in any case are resolved by a *Tribunal de conflits* composed in equal measure of members of the Court of Cassation and the Council of State. In 1997 the government restricted its ability to intervene in individual cases of justice.

Penal code

A revised penal code came into force on 1 March 1994, replacing the *Code Napoléon* of 1810. Penal institutions consist of: (1) *maisons d'arrêt*, where persons awaiting trial as well as those condemned to short periods of imprisonment are kept; (2) punishment institutions – (a) central prisons (*maisons centrales*) for those sentenced to long imprisonment, (b) detention centres for offenders showing promise of rehabilitation, and (c) penitentiary centres, establishments combining (a) and (b); (3) hospitals for the sick. Special attention is being paid to classified treatment and the rehabilitation and vocational re-education of prisoners including work in open-air and semi-free establishments. Juvenile delinquents go before special judges in 139 (11 in overseas departments and territories) juvenile courts (*tribunaux pour enfants*); they are sent to public or private institutions of supervision and re-education.

The first Ombudsman (*Médiateur*) was appointed for a six-year period in Jan. 1973. The present incumbent is Jean-Paul Delevoye (appointed 2004).

Capital punishment was abolished in Aug. 1981. In metropolitan France the detention rate in 2006 was 98·4 prisoners per 100,000 population, up from 50 per 100,000 in 1975. The average period of detention in 2004 was 8·4 months. The principal offences committed were: theft, 21·1%; drink driving, 20·6%; assault (including rape), 16·8%; drug-related offences, 5·8%. The population of the 194 penal establishments (six for minors) in 2008 was 64,003, including 2,379 women.

Weston, M., *English Reader's Guide to the French Legal System*. 1991

Education

The primary, secondary and higher state schools constitute the 'Université de France'. Its Supreme Council of 84 members has deliberative, administrative and judiciary functions, and as a consultative committee advises respecting the working of the school system; the inspectors-general are in direct communication with the Minister. For local education administration France is divided into 25 academic areas, each of which has an Academic Council whose members include a certain number elected by the professors or teachers. The Academic Council deals with all grades of education. Each is under a Rector, and each is provided with academy inspectors, one for each department.

Compulsory education is provided for children of 6–16. The educational stages are as follows:

1. Non-compulsory pre-school instruction for children aged 2–5, to be given in infant schools or infant classes attached to primary schools.

2. Compulsory elementary instruction for children aged 6–11, to be given in primary schools and certain classes of the *lycées*. It consists of three courses: preparatory (one year), elementary (two years) and intermediary (two years). Children with special needs are cared for in special institutions or special classes of primary schools.

3. Lower secondary education (*Enseignement du premier cycle du Second Degré*) for pupils aged 11–15, consists of four years of study in the *lycées* (grammar schools), *Collèges d'Enseignement Technique* (CES) or *Collèges d'Enseignement Général* (CEG).

4. Upper secondary education (*Enseignement du second cycle du Second Degré*) for pupils aged 15–18: (1) *Long, général* or *professionel* provided by the *lycées* and leading to the *baccalauréat* or to the *baccalauréat de technicien* after three years; and (2) *Court*, professional courses of three, two and one year are taught in the *lycées d'enseignement professionel*, or the specialized sections of the *lycées*, CES or CEG.

The following table shows the number of schools in 2006–07 and the numbers of teaching staff and pupils in 2007:

	Number of schools	*Teaching staff*	*Pupils*
Nursery	17,410	141,476	2,594,074
Primary	38,257	216,654	4,105,628
Secondary	11,410	490,955	5,940,366

Higher education is provided by the state free of charge in universities and in special schools, and by private individuals in the free faculties and schools. Legislation of 1968 redefined the activities and workings of universities. Bringing several disciplines together, 780 units for teaching and research (*UER—Unités d'Enseignement et de Recherche*) were formed which decided their own teaching activities, research programmes and procedures for checking the level of knowledge gained. In 1984 they were reclassified as units for training and research (*UFR—Unités de Formation et de Recherche*). They and the other parts of each university must respect the rules designed to maintain the national standard of qualifications. The UFRs form the basic units of the 78 state universities in mainland France and three national polytechnic institutes (with university status), which are grouped into 25 administrative Académies. Private universities include seven Catholic universities, in Angers, Lille, Lyon, Paris, Rennes, Toulouse and La Roche-sur-Yon in the Vendée region. There were 2,179,505 students in higher education in 2007.

Outside the university system, higher education (academic, professional and technical) is provided by over 400 schools and institutes, including the 177 *Grandes Écoles*, which are highly selective public or private institutions offering mainly technological or commercial curricula. These have an annual output of about 20,000 graduates, and in 2004–05 there were also 73,147 students in preparatory classes leading to the *Grandes Écoles;* 230,275 students were registered in the Sections de Techniciens Supérieurs and 100,899 in the Écoles d'Ingénieurs.

The adult literacy rate is at least 99%.

In 2006 public expenditure on education came to 5·6% of GNI and represented 10·6% of total government expenditure.

Health

Ordinances of 1996 created a new regional regime of hospital administration and introduced a system of patients' records to prevent abuses of public health benefits. In 2007 there were 972 public and 1,800 private health care establishments with 316,551 and 174,925 beds respectively. There were 208,191 physicians, 41,444 dentists, 483,380 nurses, 70,498 pharmacists and 17,483 midwives in 2007.

In 2007 France spent 11·0% of its GDP on health (the highest percentage in the EU), with public spending amounting to 79·0% of the total.

In 2005 an estimated 19·2% of the population were regular smokers. The average French adult drinks 13·0 litres of alcohol a year.

Welfare

An order of 4 Oct. 1945 laid down the framework of a comprehensive plan of Social Security and created a single organization which superseded the various laws relating to social insurance, workmen's compensation, health insurance, family allowances, etc. All previous matters relating to Social Security are dealt with in the Social Security Code, 1956; this has been revised several times. The Chamber of Deputies and Senate, meeting as Congress on 19 Feb. 1996, adopted an important revision of the Constitution giving parliament powers to review annually the funding of social security (previously managed by the trade unions and employers' associations), and to fix targets for expenditure in the light of anticipated receipts.

In 2002 the welfare system accounted for €381bn., representing 35% of GDP. The Social Security budget had a deficit of some €11·9bn. in 2004.

Contributions. The general social security contribution (CSG) introduced in 1991 was raised by 4% to 7·5% in 1997 by the Jospin administration in an attempt to dramatically reduce the deficit on social security spending, effectively almost doubling the CSG. All wage-earning workers or those of equivalent status are insured regardless of the amount or the nature of the salary or earnings. The funds for the general scheme are raised mainly from professional contributions, these being fixed within the limits of a ceiling and calculated as a percentage of the salaries. The calculation of contributions payable for family allowances, old age and industrial injuries relates only to this amount; on the other hand, the amount payable for sickness, maternity expenses, disability and death is calculated partly within the limit of the 'ceiling' and partly on the whole salary. These contributions are the responsibility of both employer and employee, except in the case of family allowances or industrial injuries, where they are the sole responsibility of the employer.

Self-employed Workers. From 17 Jan. 1948 allowances and old-age pensions were paid to self-employed workers by independent insurance funds set up within their own profession, trade or business. Schemes of compulsory insurance for sickness were instituted in 1961 for farmers, and in 1966, with modifications in 1970, for other non-wage-earning workers.

Social Insurance. The orders laid down in Aug. 1967 ensure that the whole population can benefit from the Social Security Scheme; at present all elderly persons who have been engaged in the professions, as well as the surviving spouse, are entitled to claim an old-age benefit.

Sickness Insurance refunds the costs of treatment required by the insured and the needs of dependants.

Maternity Insurance covers the costs of medical treatment relating to the pregnancy, confinement and lying-in period; the beneficiaries being the insured person or the spouse.

Insurance for Invalids is divided into three categories: (1) those who are capable of working; (2) those who cannot work; (3) those who, in addition, are in need of the help of another person. According to the category, the pension rate varies from 30 to 50% of the average salary for the last ten years, with additional allowance for home help for the third category.

Old-Age Pensions for workers were introduced in 1910. Over the period 2003–08 the duration a private sector wage-earner or standard civil servant had to work in order to qualify for a pension was raised from 37½ years to 40 years. As a result, standard public sector workers were required to contribute for the same period as private sector workers. The contribution period is set to rise to 41 years by 2012 and to 42 years subsequently. Pensions are payable at 60 to anyone with at least 25% insurance coverage. A pension worth 50% of the adjusted average salary is provided to those who have paid a full 40 years (160 quarters) worth of insurance. The pension is proportionately reduced for coverage less than 160 quarters (or less than 150 quarters for those claiming their pension before 2004). The exception is the special retirement plan for which employees of several state-owned companies (notably the SNCF) and organizations including the military and the police are eligible, allowing them to claim a full pension after 37½ years' contribution.

There is also an allowance payable to low-income pensioners, who also receive an old-age supplement at 65. A child's supplement, worth 10% of the pension, is awarded to those who have three or more children. Citizens who do not qualify for a pension may be allowed to claim an old-age special allowance.

Family Allowances. A controversial programme of means-testing for Family Allowance was introduced in 1997 by the new administration. The Family Allowance benefit system comprises: (a) Family allowances proper, equivalent to 25·5% of the basic monthly salary for two dependent children, 46% for the third child, 41% for the fourth child, and 39% for the fifth and each subsequent child; a supplement equivalent to 9% of the basic monthly salary for the second and each subsequent dependent child more than ten years old, and 16% for each dependent child over 15 years. (b) Family supplement for persons with at least three children or one child aged less than three years. (c) Ante-natal grants. (d) Maternity grant is equal to 260% of basic salary. Increase for multiple births or adoptions, 198%; increase for birth or adoption of third or subsequent child, 457%. (e) Allowance for specialized education of handicapped children. (f) Allowance for orphans. (g) Single parent allowance. (h) Allowance for opening of school term. (i) Allowance for accommodation, under certain circumstances. (j) Minimum family income for those with at least three children. Allowances (b), (g), (h) and (j) only apply to those whose annual income falls below a specified level.

Workmen's Compensation. The law passed by the National Assembly on 30 Oct. 1946 forms part of the Social Security Code and is administered by the Social Security Organization. Employers are invited to take preventive measures. The application of these measures is supervised by consulting engineers (assessors) of the local funds dealing with sickness insurance, who may compel employers who do not respect these measures to make additional contributions; they may, in like manner, grant rebates to employers who have in operation suitable preventive measures. The injured person receives free treatment, the insurance fund reimburses the practitioners, hospitals and suppliers chosen freely by the injured. In cases of temporary disablement, the daily payments are equal to half the total daily wage received by the injured. In case of permanent disablement, the injured person receives a pension, the amount of which varies according to the degree of disablement and the salary received during the past 12 months.

Unemployment Benefits vary according to circumstances (full or partial unemployment) which are means-tested.

Ambler, J. S. (ed.) *The French Welfare State: Surviving Social and Ideological Change.* 1992

RELIGION

A law of 1905 separated church and state. In 2005 there were 96 Roman Catholic dioceses in metropolitan France and 106 bishops. In Feb. 2010 there were nine cardinals. In 2001 there were 38·69m. Roman Catholics (over 65% of the population), 4·18m. Muslims, 0·72m. Protestants and 0·59m. Jews. France has both the highest number of Muslims and of Jews of any EU member country. An estimated 9·23m. people were non-religious in 2001 and there were 2·38m. atheists.

CULTURE

World Heritage Sites

There are 33 sites under French jurisdiction that appear on the UNESCO World Heritage List. They are (with year entered on list): Mont-Saint-Michel and its Bay, the Versailles Palace and Park, the church and hill at Vézelay, Burgundy (all 1979 and 2007); the prehistoric sites and decorated grottoes of the Vézère Valley (Dordogne) and Chartres Cathedral (both 1979); Fontainebleau Palace and Park, Amiens Cathedral, and the Roman and Romanesque monuments of Arles (all 1981); Fontenay's Cistercian Abbey and Orange's Roman theatre and Arc de Triomphe (both 1981 and 2007); from the Great Saltworks of Salins-les-Bains to the Royal Saltworks of Arc-et-Senans, Franche-Comté (1982 and 2009); the Place Stanislas, Place de la Carrière and Place d'Alliance in Nancy and the Gulf of Porto (the Gulf of Girolata, Scandola Nature Reserve and the Calanche of Piana) in Corsica (both 1983); the Church of Saint-Savin-sur-Gartempe in Poitou-Charentes (1983 and 2007); the Pont du Gard Roman aqueduct, Languedoc (1985 and 2007); Grande-Île, Strasbourg (1988); the Banks of the Seine and Reims' Notre Dame Cathedral, Abbey of Saint-Remi and Tau Palace (both 1991); Bourges Cathedral (1992); Avignon's historic centre (1995); the Canal du Midi, Languedoc (1996); the Historic Fortified City of Carcassonne (1997); Lyon's historic sites and the route of Santiago de Compostela (both 1998); Saint-Émilion Jurisdiction (1999); the Loire Valley between Sully-sur-Loire and Chalonnes-sur-Loire (2000); Provins, the

Town of Medieval Fairs (2001); the city of Le Havre (2005); the historic centre of Bordeaux (2007); fortifications of Vauban and the lagoons of New Caledonia: reef diversity and associated ecosystems (both 2008).

France shares the Pyrénées–Mount Perdu site (1997 and 1999) with Spain and the Belfries of Belgium and France (1999 and 2005) with Belgium.

Broadcasting

The broadcasting authority (an independent regulatory commission) is the Conseil Supérieur de l'Audiovisuel (CSA). Public radio is provided by Radio France broadcasting nationally, Réseau France Outre-mer (RFO, which broadcasts in the French Overseas Departments and Territories) and an external service, Radio France Internationale (RFI, founded in 1931). There are several thousand private local radio stations. Europe 1, RTL and NRJ are major commercial stations. There are three public national TV channels that together form the France Télévisions group—France 2, France 3 and France 5. The main terrestrial channels broadcasting nationwide are: TF1, a former state channel privatized in 1987; M6, established in 1987; Arte, a joint Franco-German cultural channel; and Canal+, a subscription channel. Colour is by SECAM H. French TV broadcasts (terrestrial and satellite) must contain at least 60% EU-generated programmes and 50% of these must be French. A government-funded round-the-clock news channel, France 24, was launched in Dec. 2006; it broadcasts in French, English and Arabic. In April 2008 President Sarkozy created a new holding company, Audiovisuel Extérieur de la France ('AEF', formerly known as France Monde), which incorporates France 24, TV5 Monde and Radio France International (including its subsidiary, Monte Carlo Doualiya). The restructuring is intended to co-ordinate and modernize France's public service broadcasting activities. The expansion of satellite and cable broadcasting has led to a proliferation of channels. The two largest satellite TV operators are Canal Satellite and TPS. Digital television began in 1996. By 2002 there were about 850 TV channels, and there were 8·8m. satellite and cable TV subscribers. There were 24·5m. television-equipped households in 2006 (97·0% of all households).

Cinema

There were 5,366 cinema screens in 2005. Attendances totalled 175·4m. in 2005 (130·2m. in 1995); gross box office receipts came to €1,023·1m. in 2005. A record 187 full-length films of French initiative were produced in 2005. In 2007 French films took 36·5% of the national market.

Press

There were 87 daily papers (18 nationals, 69 provincials) in 2008. The leading dailies are: Ouest-France (average circulation, 792,000), Le Figaro (average circulation, 333,000), Le Monde (average circulation, 332,000), Le Parisien, L'Équipe, Sud Ouest, Voix du Nord and Le Dauphiné Libéré. The Journal du Dimanche is the only national Sunday paper. In 2006 total average daily press circulation was 9·3m. copies. In 2004 a total of 65,268 book titles were published.

Tourism

There were 78,900,000 foreign tourists in 2006; tourism receipts were US$46·3bn. France is the most popular tourist destination in the world, and receipts from tourism in 2006 were exceeded only in the USA and Spain. The most visited tourist attractions in 2007 were Disneyland Paris (14·5m.), the Louvre (8·2m.) and the Eiffel Tower (6·8m.). Around 17m. foreigners a year visit Paris. In 2004, 90·1% of visitors to France were from elsewhere in Europe and 5·6% from the Americas. Most visitors come from the UK, Germany, Belgium/Luxembourg, the Netherlands, Italy and Switzerland. There were 614,532 classified hotel rooms in 17,721 hotels in 2008.

Festivals

Religious Festivals

Ascension Day (40 days after Easter Sunday), Assumption of the Blessed Virgin Mary (15 Aug.) and All Saints Day (1 Nov.) are all public holidays.

Cultural Festivals

The Grande Parade de Montmartre, Paris (1 Jan.); the Carnival of Nice (Feb.–March); the Fête de la Victoire (8 May), celebrates victory in World War Two; the May Feasts take place in Nice regularly throughout May; the prestigious Cannes Film Festival, which has been running since 1946, lasts two weeks in mid-May; the Avignon Festival is a celebration of theatre that attracts average attendances of 140,000 each year and runs for most of July; Bastille Day (14 July) sees celebrations, parties and fireworks across the country. The Festival International d'Art Lyrique, focusing on classical music, opera and ballet, takes place in Aix-en-Provence every July. There are also annual festivals of opera at Orange (July–Aug.) and baroque music at Ambronay (Sept.–Oct.).

Libraries

In 2001 there were 3,884 public libraries, one national library and 396 higher education Libraries. Public and higher education libraries held 152,185,000 volumes.

Museums and Galleries

In 2007, 25m. people visited France's 34 national museums: the Musée du Louvre received 8·22m. visitors; the Château de Versailles, 5·33m.; the Musée d'Orsay, 3·17m.

DIPLOMATIC REPRESENTATIVES

Of France in the United Kingdom (58 Knightsbridge, London, SW1X 7JT)
Ambassador: Maurice Gourdault-Montagne.

Of the United Kingdom in France (35 rue du Faubourg St Honoré, 75363 Paris Cedex 08)
Ambassador: Sir Peter Westmacott, KCMG, LVO.

Of France in the USA (4101 Reservoir Rd, NW, Washington, D.C., 20007)
Ambassador: Pierre Vimont.

Of the USA in France (2 Ave. Gabriel, 75382 Paris Cedex 08)
Ambassador: Charles H. Rivkin.

Of France to the United Nations
Ambassador: Gérard Araud.

Of France to the European Union
Permanent Representative: Philippe Étienne.

FURTHER READING

Institut National de la Statistique et des Études Économiques: *Annuaire statistique de la France* (from 1878); *Bulletin mensuel de statistique* (monthly); *Documentation économique* (bi-monthly); *Économie et Statistique* (monthly); *Tableaux de l'Économie Française* (biennially, from 1956); *Tendances de la Conjoncture* (monthly).

Agulhon, Maurice, *De Gaulle: Histoire, Symbole, Mythe.* 2000
Agulhon, M., and Nevill, A., *The French Republic, 1879–1992.* 1993
Ardagh, John, *France in the New Century: Portrait of a Changing Society.* 1999
Ardant, P., *Les Institutions de la Ve République.* 1992
Bell, David, *Presidential Power in Fifth Republic France.* 2000.—*Parties and Democracy in France: Parties under Presidentialism.* 2000
Brouard, Sylvain, Appelton, Andrew M. and Mazur, Amy G. (eds.) *The French Fifth Republic at Fifty: Beyond Stereotypes.* 2008
Chafer, Tony and Sackur, Amanda, (eds.) *French Colonial Empire and the Popular Front.* 1999
Cole, Alistair, Le Galès, Patrick and Levy, Jonah, (eds.) *Developments in French Politics 4.* 2008
Cubertafond, A., *Le Pouvoir, la Politique et l'État en France.* 1993
Culpepper, Pepper D., Hall, Peter A. and Palier, Bruno, (eds.) *Changing France: The Politics that Markets Make.* 2008

L'État de la France. Annual
Friend, Julius W., *The Long Presidency: France in the Mitterrand Years, 1981–95.* 1999
Gildea, R., *France since 1945.* 1996
Guyard, Marius-François, (ed.) *Charles de Gaulle: Mémoires.* 2000
Hollifield, J. F. and Ross, G., *Searching for the New France.* 1991
Hudson, G. L., *Corsica.* [World Bibliographic Series, vol. 202] 1997
Jack, A., *The French Exception.* 1999
Jones, C., *The Cambridge Illustrated History of France.* 1994
Kedward, Rod, *France and the French: A Modern History.* 2007
Knapp, Andrew, *Parties and the Party System in France: A Disconnected Democracy?* 2004
Lacoutre, Jean, *Mitterrand: Une histoire de Français.* 2 vols. 1999
Lewis-Beck, Michael S., *The French Voter: Before and After the 2002 Elections.*2004
MacLean, Mairi, *The Mitterrand Years: Legacy and Evaluation.* 1999
McMillan, J. F., *Twentieth-Century France: Politics and Society in France, 1898–1991.* 2nd ed. [of *Dreyfus to De Gaulle*] 1992
Menon, Anand, *France, NATO and the Limits of Independence, 1918–97.* 1999
Milner, Susan and Parsons, Nick, (eds.) *Reinventing France: State and Society in the 21st Century.* 2004
Noin, D. and White, P., *Paris.* 1998
Peyrefitte, Alain, *C'était de Gaulle.* 2000
Popkin, J. D., *A History of Modern France.* 1994
Price, Roger, *A Concise History of France.* 1993
Raymond, Gino G. (ed.) *Structures of Power in Modern France.* 1999
Stevens, Anne, *Government and Politics of France.* 2003
Tiersky, Ronald, *Mitterrand in Light and Shadow.* 1999.—*François Mitterrand: The Last French President.* 2000
Tippett-Spiritou, Sandy, *French Catholicism.* 1999
Zeldin, T., *The French.* 1997
(Also see specialized titles listed under relevant sections, above.)

National Statistical Office: Institut National de la Statistique et des Études Économiques (INSEE), 75582 Paris Cedex 12.
Website: http://www.insee.fr

DEPARTMENTS AND COLLECTIVITIES OVERSEAS

Départements (DOM) et collectivités d'outre-mer (COM)

GENERAL DETAILS

These fall into two main categories: *Overseas Departments and Regions* (French Guiana, Guadeloupe, Martinique, Réunion) and *Overseas Collectivities* (French Polynesia, Mayotte, St Barthélemy, St Martin, St Pierre and Miquelon, Wallis and Futuna). In addition there are two *Sui Generis Collectivities* (New Caledonia, Southern and Antarctic Territories) and one *Minor Territory* (Clipperton Island).

FURTHER READING

Aldrich, R. and Connell, J., *France's Overseas Frontier: Départements et Territoires d'Outre-Mer.* 1992

OVERSEAS DEPARTMENTS AND REGIONS

Départements et régions d'outre-mer

French Guiana

Guyane Française

KEY HISTORICAL EVENTS

A French settlement on the island of Cayenne was established in 1604 and the territory between the Maroni and Oyapock rivers finally became a French possession in 1817. Convict settlements were established from 1852, that on Devil's Island being the most notorious; all were closed by 1945. On 19 March 1946 the status of French Guiana was changed to that of an Overseas Department.

TERRITORY AND POPULATION

French Guiana is situated on the northeast coast of Latin America, and is bounded in the northeast by the Atlantic Ocean, west by Suriname, and south and east by Brazil. It includes the offshore Devil's Island, Royal Island and St Joseph, and has an area of 85,534 sq. km. Recorded population in 2007: 213,031; density: 2·5 per sq. km. The UN gives an estimated population for 2010 of 231,000. In 2005 an estimated 75·6% lived in urban areas. The chief towns are (with 2007 recorded populations): the capital, Cayenne (58,008 inhabitants), Saint-Laurent-du-Maroni (34,149) and Kourou (25,688). About 58% of inhabitants are of African descent.

The official language is French.

SOCIAL STATISTICS

2007 births, 6,386; deaths, 690. 40% of the population are migrants. Average annual population growth rate, 2000–05, 4·0%.

CLIMATE

Equatorial type climate with most of the country having a main rainy season between April and July and a fairly dry period between Aug. and Dec. Both temperatures and humidity are high the whole year round. Cayenne, Jan. 26°C, July 29°C. Annual rainfall 3,202 mm.

CONSTITUTION AND GOVERNMENT

French Guiana is administered by a General Council of 19 members directly elected for five-year terms, and by a Regional Council of 31 members. It is represented in the National Assembly by two deputies; in the Senate by one senator. The French government is represented by a Prefect. There are two *arrondissements* (Cayenne and Saint Laurent-du-Maroni) sub-divided into 22 communes and 19 cantons.

70·2% of voters rejected proposals for greater autonomy from France in a referendum on 10 Jan. 2010. However, a second referendum on 24 Jan. proposing a change in status from department to unique collectivity was passed with 57·5% of the vote and is scheduled to take effect in 2012. The General Council and the Regional Council will be combined as a sole entity.

CURRENT ADMINISTRATION

Prefect: Daniel Ferey.

President of the General Council: Alain Tien-Long (Divers Gauche).

President of the Regional Council: Rodolphe Alexandre (Divers Gauche).

Government Website (French only):
http://www.guyane.pref.gouv.fr

ECONOMY

Currency

Since 1 Jan. 2002 the euro has been the official currency as in metropolitan France.

Performance

In 2003 GDP was €2,207m.; GDP per capita was €13,139 in 2005. Real GDP growth was –2·1% in 2003.

Banking and Finance

The Caisse Centrale de Coopération Économique is the bank of issue. In 2001 commercial banks included the Banque Nationale de Paris-Guyane, Crédit Populaire Guyanais and Banque Française Commerciale.

ENERGY AND NATURAL RESOURCES

Electricity

Installed capacity was 0·1m. kW in 2004. Production in 2004 was about 430m. kWh.

Minerals

Placer gold mining is the most important industry in French Guiana. In 2005, 1,955 kg of gold were produced.

Agriculture

There were 13,280 ha. of arable land in 2006. Principal crops (2006, in 1,000 tonnes): cassava, 30; rice, 15; passion fruit, 8; sugarcane, 7.

Livestock (2003): 9,702 cattle; 6,928 pigs; 1,604 goats; 1,547 sheep; 98,774 poultry.

Forestry

The country has immense forests which are rich in many kinds of timber. In 2005 forests covered 8·06m. ha., or 91·8% of the total land area. Roundwood production (2007) 177,000 cu. metres. The trees also yield oils, essences and gum products.

Fisheries

The catch in 2005 was an estimated 5,265 tonnes. Shrimp account for nearly 55% of the total catch.

INDUSTRY

Important products include rum, rosewood essence and beer. The island has sawmills and one sugar factory.

Labour

In 2006 there were 47,500 people in paid work and 6,100 in unpaid work. In Jan. 2010 the minimum wage (SMIC) was raised to €8·86 an hour (€1,343·77 a month for a 35-hour week). There were 11,697 jobseekers in 2007.

INTERNATIONAL TRADE

Imports and Exports

Imports (2006), €2,504m.; exports (2006), €489m. Main import suppliers are France, Trinidad and Tobago and Germany. Leading export markets are France, Switzerland and Italy.

COMMUNICATIONS

Roads

There were (1996) 356 km of national and 366 km of departmental roads. In 2002 there were 30,000 passenger cars and 11,200 commercial vehicles.

Civil Aviation

In 2007 Rochambeau International Airport (Cayenne) handled 383,168 passengers. There are smaller airports at Maripasoula and Saul for internal flights. The base of the European Space Agency (ESA) is located near Kourou and has been operational since 1979.

Shipping

359 vessels arrived and departed in 1993; 249,160 tonnes of petroleum products and 230,179 tonnes of other products were discharged, and 69,185 tonnes of freight loaded. Chief ports: Cayenne, St-Laurent-du-Maroni and Kourou. There are also inland waterways navigable by small craft.

Telecommunications

In 2008 there were 51,000 main (fixed) telephone lines. Mobile phone subscribers numbered 98,000 in 2004. There were 33,000 PCs in use (180·3 for every 1,000 persons) in 2004 and 38,000 internet users.

SOCIAL INSTITUTIONS

Justice

At Cayenne there is a tribunal d'instance and a tribunal de grande instance, from which appeal is to the regional cour d'appel in Martinique.

The population in penal institutions in April 2003 was 5,900 (324 per 100,000 population).

Education

Primary education is free and compulsory. In 2008–09 there were 40,890 pupils at pre-elementary and primary schools, and 28,758 at secondary level. In 2004–05 there were 1,775 students at the French Guiana campuses of the University of Antilles-Guyana.

Health

In 2007 there were 804 hospital beds. There were (2003) 319 doctors, 38 dentists, 70 pharmacists, 47 midwives and 371 nursing personnel.

RELIGION

In 2001 approximately 55% of the population was Roman Catholic.

CULTURE

Broadcasting

Radiodiffusion Française d'Outre-Mer-Guyane broadcasts for 133 hours each week on medium and short wave, and FM in French. Television is broadcast for 60 hours each week on two channels. There were 37,000 TV receivers in 1998; colour is by SECAM.

Press

There were two daily newspapers in 2006 with a combined circulation of 15,000.

Tourism

Total number of non-resident tourists (2005), 95,000; receipts totalled US$45m.

FURTHER READING

Redfield, Peter, *Space in the Tropics: From Convicts to Rockets in French Guiana.* 2000

Guadeloupe

KEY HISTORICAL EVENTS

The islands were discovered by Columbus in 1493. The Carib inhabitants resisted Spanish attempts to colonize. A French colony was established on 28 June 1635, and apart from short periods of occupancy by British forces, Guadeloupe has since remained a French possession. On 19 March 1946 Guadeloupe became an Overseas Department.

TERRITORY AND POPULATION

Guadeloupe consists of a group of islands in the Lesser Antilles with a total area of 1,630 sq. km. The two main islands, Basse-Terre (to the west) and Grande-Terre (to the east), are joined by a bridge over a narrow channel. Adjacent to these are the islands of Marie-Galante (to the southeast), La Désirade (to the east), and the Îles des Saintes (to the south). The islands of St Martin (2007 population of 35,925) and St Barthélemy (2007 population of 8,450) seceded from Guadeloupe in Feb. 2007.

Island	*Area (sq. km)*	*2007 populations*	*Chief town*
Grande-Terre	590	197,600	Pointe-à-Pitre
Basse-Terre	848	186,600	Basse-Terre
Marie-Galante	158	11,939	Grand-Bourg
Îles des Saintes	13	2,854	Terre-de-Bas
La Désirade	20	1,591	Grande Anse

Recorded population in 2007, 400,584 excluding St Martin and St Barthélemy (422,496 at 1999 census with St Martin and St Barthélemy; 386,566 without). An estimated 99·8% of the population were urban in 2005. Basse-Terre (2007 population, 12,451) is the seat of government, while larger Pointe-à-Pitre (2007 population, 17,408) is the department's main economic centre and port; Les Abymes (2007 population, 59,404) is a 'suburb' of Pointe-à-Pitre.

French is the official language, but Creole is spoken by the vast majority.

SOCIAL STATISTICS

2004: live births, 7,273; deaths, 2,676; marriages, 1,751. 2004 rates (per 1,000 population): birth, 16·4; death, 6·0. Annual population growth rate, 2000–05, 0·8%. Life expectancy at birth, 2005, 75·3 years for males and 81·6 years for females.

CLIMATE

Warm and humid. Pointe-à-Pitre, Jan. 74°F (23·4°C), July 80°F (26·7°C). Annual rainfall 71" (1,814 mm).

CONSTITUTION AND GOVERNMENT

Guadeloupe is administered by a General Council of 42 members directly elected for six-year terms (assisted by an Economic and Social Committee of 40 members) and by a Regional Council of 41 members. It is represented in the National Assembly by four deputies; in the Senate by two senators; and on the Economic and Social Council by one councillor. There are four *arrondissements*, sub-divided into 42 cantons and 34 communes, each administered by an elected municipal council. The French government is represented by an appointed Prefect.

CURRENT ADMINISTRATION

Prefect: Jean-Luc Fabre.

President of the General Council: Jacques Gillot.

President of the Regional Council: Victorin Lurel.

Government Website (French only):
http://www.guadeloupe.pref.gouv.fr

ECONOMY

Currency

Since 1 Jan. 2002 the euro has been the official currency as in metropolitan France.

Performance

In 2005 GDP was €7,388m.; GDP per capita was €16,584. Real GDP growth was 6·1% in 2005.

Banking and Finance

The Caisse Française de Développement is the official bank of the department. The main commercial banks in 1995 (with number of branches) were: Banque des Antilles Françaises (six), Banque Régionale d'Escompte et de Depôts (five), Banque Nationale de Paris (eight), Crédit Agricole (18), Banque Française Commerciale (eight), Société Générale de Banque aux Antilles (five), Le Crédit Lyonnais (six), Crédit Martiniquais (three), Banque Inschauspé et Cie (one).

ENERGY AND NATURAL RESOURCES

Electricity

Total production (2003): 1·17bn. kWh. Installed capacity was 0·4m. kW in 2004.

Agriculture

Chief products (2007, in 1,000 tonnes): sugarcane, 789; bananas, 45; melons, 9; pineapples, 7; cucumbers, 6. Other fruits and vegetables are also grown for both export and domestic consumption.

Livestock (2003): cattle, 54,940; goats, 34,216; pigs, 24,675.

Forestry

In 2005 forests covered 80,000 ha., or 47·2% of the total land area. Timber production in 2007 was 32,000 cu. metres.

Fisheries

Total catch in 2005 amounted to an estimated 10,100 tonnes, exclusively from sea fishing.

INDUSTRY

The main industries are sugar refining, food processing and rum distilling, carried out by small and medium-sized businesses. Other important industries are cement production and tourism.

Labour

The economically active population in 2005 was 160,000. In Jan. 2010 the minimum wage (SMIC) was raised to €8·86 an hour (€1,343·77 a month for a 35-hour week). The unemployment rate was 23·9% in 2005.

INTERNATIONAL TRADE

Imports and Exports

Total imports (2006): €2,310m.; total exports (2006): €164m. Main export commodities are bananas, sugar and rum. Main import sources in 2006 were France, 60·8%; Italy, 3·5%; Germany, 3·4%; Trinidad and Tobago, 3·0%. Main export markets in 2006 were France, 54·9%; Martinique, 30·7%; French Guiana, 2·9%; Venezuela, 2·6%.

COMMUNICATIONS

Roads

In 1996 there were 3,200 km of roads. In 1993 there were 101,600 passenger cars and 37,500 commercial vehicles. There were 76 road-related fatalities in 2004.

Civil Aviation

Air France and six other airlines call at Guadeloupe airport. In 2007 there were 1,707,781 passengers on domestic flights and 155,582 passengers on international flights at Le Raizet (Pointe-à-Pitre) airport. There is a smaller airport at Marie-Galante only for internal flights. Most domestic services are operated by Air Caraibes.

Shipping

In 2008, 3,582,054 tonnes of freight passed through the Port autonome de la Guadeloupe (2,841,539 tonnes inbound and 740,515 tonnes outbound).

Telecommunications

In 2008 there were 246,000 main (fixed) telephone lines. Mobile phone subscribers numbered 314,700 in 2004. There were 90,000

PCs (203·2 per 1,000 inhabitants) in use in 2004 and 79,000 internet users.

SOCIAL INSTITUTIONS

Justice

There are four tribunaux d'instance and two tribunaux de grande instance at Basse-Terre and Pointe-à-Pitre; there is also a court of appeal and a court of assizes.

The population in penal institutions in April 2003 was 695 (159 per 100,000 population).

Education

Education is free and compulsory from six to 16 years. In 2008–09 there were 60,741 pupils at pre-elementary and primary schools, and 52,547 at secondary level. In 2004–05 there were 5,965 students at the Guadeloupe campuses of the University of Antilles-Guyana.

Health

In 2004 there were 3,556 beds in health care establishments. In 2003 there were 924 physicians, 151 dentists, 1,957 nurses, 265 pharmacists and 148 midwives.

RELIGION

The majority of the population are Roman Catholic.

CULTURE

Broadcasting

Radiodiffusion Française d'Outre-Mer broadcasts for 17 hours a day in French. There is a local region radio station, and several private stations. There are two television channels (one regional; one satellite) broadcasting for six hours a day (colour by SECAM V). There were 118,000 TV receivers in 1999.

Press

There was (1996) one daily newspaper with a circulation of 30,000.

Tourism

Tourism is the chief economic activity. In 2004, 455,981 non-resident tourists stayed in hotels and similar accommodation (excluding the north islands of St Martin and St Barthélemy, which at the time were under Guadeloupe's jurisdiction).

Martinique

KEY HISTORICAL EVENTS

Discovered by Columbus in 1502, Martinique became a French colony in 1635 and apart from brief periods of British occupation the island has since remained under French control. On 19 March 1946 its status was altered to that of an Overseas Department.

TERRITORY AND POPULATION

The island, situated in the Lesser Antilles between Dominica and St Lucia, occupies an area of 1,128 sq. km. Recorded population in 2007, 397,730; density, 353 per sq. km. The UN gives an estimated population for 2010 of 406,000. An estimated 97·9% of the population were urban in 2005. Recorded population of principal towns in 2007: the capital and main port Fort-de-France, 89,794; Le Lamentin, 39,442; Le Robert, 24,068; Schoelcher, 21,510; Le François, 19,333; Sainte-Marie, 19,249.

French is the official language but the majority of people speak Creole.

SOCIAL STATISTICS

2002: live births, 5,446; deaths, 2,681. 2002 estimates per 1,000 population: birth rate, 14·0; death rate, 6·9. Average annual population growth rate, 2000–05, 0·7%. Life expectancy at birth, 2002, 75·4 years for males and 82·2 years for females.

CLIMATE

The dry season is from Dec. to May, and the humid season from June to Nov. Fort-de-France, Jan. 74°F (23·5°C), July 78°F (25·6°C). Annual rainfall 72" (1,840 mm).

CONSTITUTION AND GOVERNMENT

The island is administered by a General Council of 45 members directly elected for six-year terms and by a Regional Council of 42 members. The French government is represented by an appointed Prefect. There are four *arrondissements*, sub-divided into 45 cantons and 34 communes, each administered by an elected municipal council. Martinique is represented in the National Assembly by four deputies, in the Senate by two senators and on the Economic and Social Council by one councillor.

79·3% of voters rejected proposals for greater autonomy from France in a referendum on 10 Jan. 2010. However, a second referendum on 24 Jan. proposing a change in status from department to unique collectivity was passed with 68·3% of the vote and is scheduled to take effect in 2012. The General Council and the Regional Council will be combined as a sole entity.

CURRENT ADMINISTRATION

Prefect: Ange Mancini; b. 1944 (took office on 2 Aug. 2007).

President of the General Council: Claude Lise.

President of the Regional Council: Serge Letchimy.

Government Website: http://www.martinique.pref.gouv.fr

ECONOMY

Main sectors of activity: tradeable services, distribution, industry, building and public works, transport and telecommunications, agriculture and tourism.

Currency

Since 1 Jan. 2002 the euro has been the official currency as in metropolitan France.

Performance

In 2003 GDP was €6,442m.; GDP per capita in 2005 was €18,207. Real GDP growth was 5·5% in 2003.

Banking and Finance

The Agence Française de Développement is the government's vehicle for the promotion of economic development in the region. There were five commercial banks, four co-operative banks, one savings bank, five investment companies and two specialized financial institutions in 1999.

ENERGY AND NATURAL RESOURCES

Electricity

A network of 4,262 km of cables covers 98% of Martinique and supplies more than 142,000 customers. Electricity is produced by two fuel-powered electricity stations. Total production (2002): 1·18bn. kWh. Installed capacity (2004 estimate): 0·4m. kW.

Agriculture

Crops in 2003 by area: bananas, 10,000 ha.; sugarcane, 3,740 ha.; pineapples, 416 ha. Production (2007, in 1,000 tonnes): sugarcane, 226; bananas, 144; cucumbers, 7; tomatoes, 3.

Livestock (2003): 23,183 cattle; 19,035 pigs; 13,074 sheep; 12,678 goats; 331,926 poultry.

Forestry

In 2005 there were 46,000 ha. of forest, or 43·9% of the total land area. Timber production in 2007 was 26,000 cu. metres.

Fisheries

The catch in 2005 was 5,500 tonnes, exclusively from sea fishing.

INDUSTRY

Some food processing and chemical engineering is carried out by small and medium-size businesses. There were 33,063 businesses in 2006. There is an important cement industry; there are also 11 rum distilleries and an oil refinery, with an annual treatment capacity of 0·75m. tonnes. Martinique has five industrial zones.

Labour

In 2006, 4·6% of the employed population worked in agriculture, 12·0% in commerce, 6·2% in construction, 7·6% in industry and 69·6% in services. There were 120,900 people in paid work in 2006 and 11,100 in unpaid work. In Jan. 2010 the minimum wage (SMIC) was raised to €8·86 an hour (€1,343·77 a month for a 35-hour week). There were 34,463 jobseekers in 2007.

INTERNATIONAL TRADE

Imports and Exports

Martinique has a structural trade deficit owing to the nature of goods traded. It imports high-value-added goods (foodstuffs, capital goods, consumer goods and motor vehicles) and exports agricultural produce (bananas) and refined oil.

In 2006 imports were valued at €2,504m.; exports at €489m. Main trading partners: France, the UK, Guadeloupe, the USA and Italy. Trade with France accounted for 55·6% of imports and 21·8% of exports in 2006.

COMMUNICATIONS

Roads

Martinique has 2,176 km of roads. In 1993 there were 108,300 passenger cars and 32,200 commercial vehicles.

Civil Aviation

There is an international airport at Fort-de-France (Lamentin), which handled 1,482,465 passengers on internal flights and 119,919 on international flights in 2007.

Shipping

The island is visited regularly by French, American and other lines. The main sea links to and from Martinique are ensured by CGM Sud. It links Martinique to Europe and some African and American companies. Since 1995 new scheduled links have been introduced between Martinique, French Guiana, Haiti and Panama. These new links facilitate exchanges between Martinique, Latin America and the Caribbean, especially Cuba. In 1993, 2,856 vessels called at Martinique and discharged 80,605 passengers and 1,612,000 tonnes of freight, and embarked 82,119 passengers and 789,000 tonnes of freight.

Telecommunications

In 2008 there were 172,000 main (fixed) telephone lines. Mobile phone subscribers numbered 295,400 in 2004. The main operator is France Télécom. There were 82,000 PCs in use (equivalent to 207·6 for every 1,000 persons) in 2004 and 107,000 internet users.

SOCIAL INSTITUTIONS

Justice

Justice is administered by two lower courts (tribunaux d'instance), a higher court (tribunal de grande instance), a regional court of appeal, a commercial court and an administrative court.

The population in penal institutions in April 2003 was 643 (164 per 100,000 population).

Education

Education is compulsory between the ages of six and 16 years. In 2002–03 there were 51,926 pupils in nursery and primary schools, and 47,770 pupils in secondary schools. There were 29 institutes of higher education in 1994. In 2004–05 there were 5,417 students at the Martinique campus of the University of Antilles-Guyana.

Health

In 1995 there were eight hospitals, three private clinics and seven nursing homes. Total number of beds, 2,100. There were 909 physicians, 148 dentists, 2,229 nurses, 271 pharmacists and 149 midwives in 2003.

RELIGION

In 2001, 87% of the population was Roman Catholic.

CULTURE

Broadcasting

Radiodiffusion Française d'Outre-Mer broadcasts on FM wave, and operates two channels (one satellite). There are also two commercial TV stations. There were 66,000 TV receivers in 1999 (colour by SECAM V).

Press

In 2006 there was one daily newspaper with a circulation of 65,000.

Tourism

In 2006 there were 503,475 staying visitors and 96,089 cruise passenger arrivals. Tourism receipts totalled US$291m. in 2004. In 2006 there were 99 classified hotels, with 4,747 rooms.

Réunion

KEY HISTORICAL EVENTS

Réunion (formerly Île Bourbon) became a French possession in 1638 and remained so until 19 March 1946, when its status was altered to that of an Overseas Department.

TERRITORY AND POPULATION

The island of Réunion lies in the Indian Ocean, about 880 km east of Madagascar and 210 km southwest of Mauritius. It has an area of 2,507 sq. km. Recorded population in 2007: 794,107, giving a density of 317 per sq. km. An estimated 92·4% of the population were urban in 2005. The capital is Saint-Denis (population, 2007: 140,733); other large towns are Saint-Paul (101,023), Saint-Pierre (75,265) and le Tampon (70,539).

The UN gives an estimated population for 2010 of 837,000.

French is the official language, but Creole is also spoken.

SOCIAL STATISTICS

2005: births, 14,610; deaths, 4,255; marriages, 3,115; divorces, 1,499. Rates per 1,000 population (2005): birth, 18·7; death, 5·5. Average annual population growth rate, 2000–05, 1·5%. Life expectancy at birth, 2005, 72·4 years for males and 80·0 years for females. Infant mortality, 2005, 7·9 per 1,000 live births; fertility rate, 2005, 2·4 births per woman.

CLIMATE

There is a sub-tropical maritime climate, free from extremes of weather, although the island lies in the cyclone belt of the Indian Ocean. Conditions are generally humid and there is no well-defined dry season. Saint-Denis, Jan. 80°F (26·7°C), July 70°F (21·1°C). Annual rainfall 56" (1,400 mm).

CONSTITUTION AND GOVERNMENT

Réunion is administered by a General Council of 47 members directly elected for six-year terms, and by a Regional Council of 45 members. Réunion is represented in the National Assembly in Paris by five deputies; in the Senate by three senators; and in the Economic and Social Council by one councillor. There are four *arrondissements* sub-divided into 47 cantons and 24 communes, each administered by an elected municipal council. The French government is represented by an appointed Prefect.

CURRENT ADMINISTRATION

Prefect: Pierre-Henry Maccioni.

President of the General Council: Nassimah Dindar-Mangrolia.

President of the Regional Council: Didier Robert.

Government Website (French only): http://www.reunion.pref.gouv.fr

ECONOMY

Currency

Since 1 Jan. 2002 the euro has been the official currency as in metropolitan France. Owing to its geographical location, Réunion was, by two hours, the first territory to introduce the euro.

Performance

GDP was €12,061m. in 2005; real GDP growth was 7·4% in 2004. GDP per capita in 2005 was €15,475.

Banking and Finance

The Institut d'Émission des Départements d'Outre-mer has the right to issue bank-notes. Banks operating in Réunion are the Banque de la Réunion (Caisse d'Épargne), the Banque Nationale de Paris Intercontinentale, the Crédit Agricole de la Réunion, the Banque Française Commerciale (BFC) CCP, Trésorerie Générale and the Banque de la Réunion pour l'Économie et le Développement (BRED).

ENERGY AND NATURAL RESOURCES

Electricity

Production in 2004 was about 1,620m. kWh. Estimated consumption per capita (2004), 2,114 kWh. Installed capacity (2004 estimate): 0·4m. kW.

Agriculture

There were 47,425 ha. of land used for agriculture in 2006 of which 25,569 ha. were planted with sugarcane. Main agricultural products (2006 in 1,000 tonnes): sugarcane, 1,864; pineapples, 16; bananas, 10; citrus fruits, 8; tomatoes, 8.

Livestock (2006): 73,000 pigs, 36,000 cattle, 36,000 goats, 14·9m. poultry (estimate). Meat production (2004, in tonnes): pork, 12,394; beef and veal, 1,723; poultry, 8,319. Milk production (2004), 238,470 hectolitres.

Forestry

There were 84,000 ha. of forest in 2005, or 33·6% of the total land area. Timber production in 2007 was 36,000 cu. metres.

Fisheries

In 2005 the catch was 4,596 tonnes, almost entirely from marine waters.

INDUSTRY

The major industries are electricity and sugar. Food processing, chemical engineering, printing and the production of perfume, textiles, leathers, tobacco, wood and construction materials are carried out by small and medium-sized businesses. In 2004 there were 9,018 craft businesses employing about 27,000 persons. Production of sugar was 220,470 tonnes in 2004; rum, 86,130 hectolitres.

Labour

In 2006 there were 197,800 people in paid work and 24,100 in unpaid work. In Jan. 2010 the minimum wage (SMIC) was raised to €8·86 an hour (€1,343·77 a month for a 35-hour week). In 2007 the unemployment rate was 24·2%. Among the under 25s the unemployment rate is nearly 50%.

INTERNATIONAL TRADE

Imports and Exports

In 2006 imports totalled €3,912m. and exports €238m. The chief export is sugar, accounting for 41·0% of total exports in 2006. France provided 42·2% of imports in 2006 and took 59·6% of exports.

COMMUNICATIONS

Roads

There were, in 2001, 2,914 km of roads and 258,400 registered vehicles. There were 67 road-related fatalities in 2004.

Civil Aviation

In 2007 Roland Garros Saint-Denis airport handled 1,049,791 passengers on domestic flights and 470,171 passengers on international flights.

Shipping

753 vessels visited the island in 2000, unloading 2,783,700 tonnes of freight and loading 482,300 tonnes at Port-Réunion.

Telecommunications

In 2008 there were 440,000 main (fixed) telephone lines. Mobile phone subscribers numbered 579,200 in 2004. There were 278,000 PCs in use (363·1 per 1,000 persons) in 2004 and internet users numbered 200,000.

SOCIAL INSTITUTIONS

Justice

There are three lower courts (tribunaux d'instance), two higher courts (tribunaux de grande instance), one appeal, one administrative court and one conciliation board.

The population in penal institutions in April 2003 was 1,071 (143 per 100,000 population).

Education

In 2008–09 there were 122,298 pupils in primary schools and 101,262 in secondary schools. The *Université Française de l'Océan Indien* (founded 1971) had 12,267 students in 2007–08.

Health

In 2007 there were 1,359 hospital beds and 2,130 doctors. There were 105 general doctors per 100,000 inhabitants in 2007.

RELIGION

In 2001, 82% of the population was Roman Catholic.

CULTURE

Broadcasting

Radiodiffusion Française d'Outre-Mer broadcasts in French on medium and short wave for more than 18 hours a day. There are two national television channels (RFD1 and Tempo) and three independent channels (Antenne Réunion, Canal Réunion/Canal+ and Parabole Réunion). Colour transmission is by SECAM V. There were 138,000 TV receivers in 2002.

Press

There were three daily newspapers (Quotidien, Journal de l'Île and Témoignages) in 2006 with a combined circulation of 73,000.

Tourism

Tourism is a major resource industry. There were 409,000 visitors in 2005 (430,000 in 2004). Receipts in 2004 totalled US$448m. In 2008 there were 49 classified hotels with 2,127 rooms.

FURTHER READING

Institut National de la Statistique et des Études Économiques: *Tableau Économique de la Réunion.* Annual

Bertile, W., *Atlas Thématique et Régional.* 1990

OVERSEAS COLLECTIVITIES

Collectivités d'outre-mer

French Polynesia

Territoire de la Polynésie Française

KEY HISTORICAL EVENTS

French protectorates since 1843, these islands were annexed to France 1880–82 to form 'French Settlements in Oceania', which opted in Nov. 1958 for the status of an overseas territory within the French Community. In March 2003 French Polynesia became an Overseas Collectivity.

TERRITORY AND POPULATION

The total land area of these five archipelagoes, comprising 121 volcanic islands and coral atolls (76 inhabited) scattered over a wide area in the eastern Pacific, is 3,521 sq. km. The population (2007 census) was 259,596; density, 74 per sq. km. In 2007 French forces stationed in Polynesia numbered 1,500 (based mostly on Tahiti). In 2005 an estimated 51·7% of the population lived in urban areas.

The UN gives an estimated population for 2010 of 272,000.

The official languages are French and Tahitian.

The islands are administratively divided into five *subdivisions administratives* as follows:

Windward Islands (Îles du Vent) (194,623 inhabitants, 2007) comprise Tahiti with an area of 1,042 sq. km and 178,132 inhabitants in 2007; Mooréa with an area of 132 sq. km and 16,191 inhabitants in 2007; Maiao (Tubuai Manu) with an area of 9 sq. km and 299 inhabitants in 2007; and the smaller Mehetia (uninhabited) and Tetiaroa (population of one). The capital is Papeete, Tahiti (26,017 inhabitants in 2007, excluding suburbs; urban area, 131,693).

Leeward Islands (Îles sous le Vent) comprise the five volcanic islands of Raiatéa, Tahaa, Huahine, Bora-Bora and Maupiti, together with four small atolls (Tupai, Mopelia, Scilly, Bellinghausen), the group having a total land area of 404 sq. km and 33,184 inhabitants in 2007. The chief town is Uturoa on Raiatéa. The Windward and Leeward Islands together are called the Society Archipelago (Archipel de la Société). Tahitian, a Polynesian language, is spoken throughout the archipelago and used as a *lingua franca* in the rest of the territory.

Marquesas Islands 12 islands lying north of the Tuamotu Archipelago, with a total area of 1,049 sq. km and 8,632 inhabitants in 2007. There are six inhabited islands: Nuku Hiva, Ua Pou, Ua Uka, Hiva Oa, Tahuata, Fatu Hiva; and six smaller (uninhabited) ones; the chief centre is Taiohae on Nuku Hiva.

Austral or Tubuai Islands lying south of the Society Archipelago, comprise a 1,300 km chain of volcanic islands and reefs. There are five inhabited islands (Rimatara, Rurutu, Tubuai, Raivavae and, 500 km to the south, Rapa), with a combined area of 148 sq. km (6,310 inhabitants in 2007); the chief centre is Mataura on Tubuai.

Tuamotu and Gambier Islands comprise the Tuamotu Islands, two parallel ranges of 76 atolls (53 inhabited) lying north and east of the Society Archipelago with a total area of 690 sq. km and 15,510 inhabitants in 2007; and the Gambier Islands to the southeast of the Tuamotu Islands with a total area of 36 sq. km and 1,337 inhabitants in 2007. The most populous atolls are Rangiroa (3,210 inhabitants in 2007), Manihi (1,379 in 2007) and Hao (1,342 in 2007).

The Mururoa and Fangataufa atolls in the southeast of the group were ceded to France in 1964 by the Territorial Assembly, and were used by France for nuclear tests from 1966–96. The Pacific Testing Centre (CEP) was dismantled in 1998. A small military presence remains to ensure permanent radiological control.

SOCIAL STATISTICS

2005: births, 4,467; deaths, 1,239. Average annual population growth rate, 2000–05, 1·6%. Life expectancy at birth, 2005, 71·4 years for males and 76·4 years for females. Infant mortality, 2005, 6·3 per 1,000 live births; fertility rate, 2·2 births per woman.

CLIMATE

Papeete, Jan. 81°F (27·1°C), July 75°F (24°C). Annual rainfall 83" (2,106 mm).

CONSTITUTION AND GOVERNMENT

Under the 1984 constitution, the Territory is administered by a Council of Ministers, whose President is elected by the Territorial Assembly from among its own members; the President appoints a Vice-President and 14 other ministers. French Polynesia is represented in the French Assembly by two deputies and in the Senate by one senator. The French government is represented by a High Commissioner. The Territorial Assembly comprises 57 members elected every five years from five constituencies by universal suffrage, using the same proportional representation system as in metropolitan French regional elections. To be elected a party must gain at least 5% of votes cast.

In Dec. 2003 French Polynesia's status was changed to that of an Overseas Country within the French Republic. However, the designation has no legal consequences and the 2004 status of French Polynesia acknowledged that it belongs to the category of Overseas Collectivity.

RECENT ELECTIONS

Elections were held on 27 Jan. and 10 Feb. 2008. The anti-independence Our Home alliance (To Tatou Ai'a) of former president Gaston Tong Sang won 27 seats (with 45·1% of the vote), the Union for Democracy alliance (UPD) 20 seats with 37·2% and the Popular Rally (Tahoera'a Huiraatira) 10 with 17·2%. An indirect presidential election was held on 11 Feb. 2009 in the Territorial Assembly. In the first round Oscar Temaru (Tavini Huiraatira/People's Servant Party) received 24 votes against 20 for outgoing president Gaston Tong Sang (To Tatou Ai'a), 12 for Edouard Fritch (Tahoera'a Huiraatira) and 1 for Sandra Levy-Agami (ind.). Temaru defeated Tong Sang in the second round by 37 votes to 20.

CURRENT ADMINISTRATION

High Commissioner: Adolphe Colrat; b. 1955 (took office on 11 June 2008).

President: Gaston Tong Sang; b. 1949 (To Tatou Ai'a/Our Home alliance; took office for a third time on 24 Nov. 2009).

Government Website (French only):
http://www.polynesie-francaise.pref.gouv.fr

ECONOMY

Currency

The unit of currency is the franc CFP (XPF). Up to 31 Dec. 1998, its parity was to the French franc: 1 franc CFP = 0·055 French francs; from 1 Jan. 1999 parity was linked to the euro: 119·3317422 francs CPF = one euro.

Budget

Revenues totalled 100·3bn. francs CPF in 2005 and expenditures 148·6bn. francs CPF.

Performance
Total GDP was US$6,172m. in 2007; GDP per capita was US$23,488. Real GDP growth was 3·0% in 2007.

Banking and Finance
There are four commercial banks: Banque de Tahiti, Banque de Polynésie, Société de Crédit et de Développement de l'Océanie and the Banque Westpac.

ENERGY AND NATURAL RESOURCES
French Polynesia is heavily dependent on external sources for its energy.

Environment
Carbon dioxide emissions from the consumption and flaring of fossil fuels in 2008 were the equivalent of 3·8 tonnes per capita.

Electricity
Production (2003) was 479m. kWh, of which approximately 19% was hydro-electric. Consumption per capita in 2003 was 1,963 kWh.

Agriculture
Agriculture used to be the primary economic sector but now accounts for only 2% of GDP. Important products are copra (coconut trees cover the coastal plains of the mountainous islands and the greater part of the low-lying islands) and the nono fruit, which has medicinal value. Production in tonnes (2007): copra, 9,508; fruit, 8,920; vegetables, 5,675; nono, 2,089; vanilla, 37. Tropical fruits, such as bananas, pineapples and oranges, are grown for local consumption.

Livestock (2006 estimates): cattle 12,000; goats 17,000; pigs 27,000; poultry 232,000.

Forestry
There were 105,000 ha. of forest in 2005, or 28·7% of the total land area.

Fisheries
Polynesia has an exclusive zone of 5·2m. sq. km, one of the largest in the world. The industry employs some 2,000 people, including 700 traditional fishermen. Catch (2005): 12,152 tonnes, almost exclusively from sea fishing.

INDUSTRY
Some 2,218 industrial enterprises employ 5,800 people. Principal industries include food and drink products, cosmetics, clothing and jewellery, furniture-making, metalwork and shipbuilding.

INTERNATIONAL TRADE

Imports and Exports
French Polynesia imports a great deal and exports very little. Trade, 2004, in US$1m. (2003 in brackets): imports f.o.b., 1,440 (1,530); exports f.o.b., 179 (149).

The chief exports are pearls, aircraft and associated equipment, fruit and vegetables, precious jewellery and fish. Polynesia is among the world's largest producers of pearls. While pearl production remains the second largest industry in Polynesia after tourism, the number of pearl farms has shrunk in recent years from over 2,500 in 2001 to just 516 in 2006 as a result of over-production and declining pearl quality.

The major trading partner overall is France, although Japan (41% of pearl exports) is the leading export market. There is also a significant amount of trade with the USA and Australia. France accounted for 34% of imports and 14% of exports in 2004.

COMMUNICATIONS

Roads
There were estimated to be 2,590 km of roads in 1999, 67% paved.

Civil Aviation
The main airport is at Papeete (Tahiti-Faa'a). Air France and nine other international airlines (including Air New Zealand, Qantas and LAN Airlines) connect Tahiti International Airport with Paris, Auckland, Honolulu, Los Angeles, Osaka, Santiago, Tokyo and many Pacific islands. In 2007, 1,788 flights landed at Papeete and 1,786 took off. 332,444 passengers arrived in 2007, 332,894 departed and 17,342 were in transit.

Shipping
Ten shipping companies connect France, San Francisco, New Zealand, Japan, Australia, southeast Asia and most Pacific locations with Papeete. In 2005 vessels totalling 19,749,378 GRT passed through Papeete's main port. Around 1·4m. people pass through the port each year.

Telecommunications
There were 125,800 telephone subscribers in 2004 (507·3 per 1,000 inhabitants), including 72,500 mobile phone subscribers. In 2005 there were 28,000 PCs in use (109·4 per 1,000 inhabitants) and 55,000 internet users.

SOCIAL INSTITUTIONS

Justice
There is a tribunal de première instance and a cour d'appel at Papeete. The population in penal institutions in April 2003 was 291 (120 per 100,000 population).

Education
In 2006–07 there were 165 primary schools and 99 secondary schools. 15,249 children attended pre-primary schools in 2006–07, 24,961 pupils primary schools and 33,845 pupils secondary schools. The University of French Polynesia (Université de la Polynésie Française) was formed from the Tahitian campus of the now-defunct French University of the Pacific (UFP) in 1999. In 2008–09 student enrolments numbered 2,664.

Health
In 2007 there were a total of 613 beds in public sector establishments and 260 in the private sector. Medical personnel in 2007 numbered 609 doctors, 1,123 nurses, 149 pharmacists, 128 midwives and 113 dentists.

RELIGION
In 2001 there were approximately 119,000 protestants (about 49% of the population) and 94,000 Roman Catholics (39%).

CULTURE

Broadcasting
There are three TV broadcasters (one public, two independent): Radio Télévision Française d'Outre-mer (RFO) which broadcasts on two channels in French, Tahitian and English; Canal+ Polynésie; and Telefenua which broadcasts across 16 channels. There are also 11 private radio stations. Number of TV receivers (2005): 56,000 (colour by SECAM H).

Press
In 2006 there were two daily newspapers with a combined circulation of 22,000.

Tourism
Tourism is the main industry. There were 218,241 tourist arrivals in 2007.

FURTHER READING
Local Statistical Office: Institut Statistique de Polynésie Française, Immeuble Uupa, 1st Floor, Rue Edouard Ahnne, Papeete.
Website (French only): http://www.ispf.pf

Mayotte

KEY HISTORICAL EVENTS

Mayotte was a French colony from 1843 until 1914 when it was attached, with the other Comoro islands, to the government-general of Madagascar. The Comoro group was granted administrative autonomy within the French Republic and became an Overseas Territory. When the other three islands voted to become independent (as the Comoro state) in 1974, Mayotte voted against and remained a French dependency. In Dec. 1976, following a further referendum, it became a Territorial Collectivity. On 11 July 2001 Mayotte became a Departmental Collectivity—a constitutional innovation—as a result of a referendum. This was denounced by the Comorian authorities, who claim Mayotte as part of the Union of Comoros Islands. On 28 March 2003 it became an Overseas Collectivity. As a result of a further referendum held on 29 March 2009 the island is scheduled to become an Overseas Department in 2011.

TERRITORY AND POPULATION

Mayotte, east of the Comoros, had a total population at the 2007 census of 186,452 (population density of 499 persons per sq. km). The whole territory covers 374 sq. km (144 sq. miles). It consists of a main island (363 sq. km) with (2007 census) 162,036 inhabitants, containing the chief town, Mamoudzou (53,022 inhabitants in 2007); and the smaller island of Pamanzi (11 sq. km) lying 2 km to the east (24,416 in 2007) containing the old capital of Dzaoudzi (15,339 in 2007).

The UN gives an estimated population for 2010 of 199,000.

The spoken language is Shimaoré (akin to Comorian, an Arabized dialect of Swahili), but French remains the official, commercial and administrative language.

SOCIAL STATISTICS

There were 7,643 births and 572 deaths in 2004.

CLIMATE

The dry and sunniest season is from May to Oct. The hot but rainy season is from Nov. to April. Average temperatures are 27°C from Dec. to March and 24°C from May to Sept.

CONSTITUTION AND GOVERNMENT

The island is administered by a General Council of 19 members, directly elected for a six-year term. The French government is represented by an appointed Prefect. In accordance with the legislation of 11 July 2001 executive powers were transferred from the prefect to the president of the General Council in March 2004. Mayotte is represented by one deputy in the National Assembly and by one member in the Senate. There are 17 communes, including two on Pamanzi.

RECENT ELECTIONS

At the General Council elections on 21 and 28 March 2004 the Union pour un Mouvement Populaire (UMP) won nine seats (with 22·8% of the vote), the Mouvement Départementaliste Mahorais (MDM) won six (23·3%) and the Mouvement Républicain et Citoyen (MRC) won two (8·9%). The Mouvement Populaire Mahorais (MPM) and Divers Gauche (DVG) took one seat each. The Parti Socialiste (PS) took 10·2% of the vote but no seats.

CURRENT ADMINISTRATION

Prefect: Hubert Derache.

President of the General Council: Ahmed Attoumani Douchina (UMP).

Government Website (French only):
http://www.mayotte.pref.gouv.fr

ECONOMY

Currency

Since 1 Jan. 2002 the euro has been the official currency as in metropolitan France.

Banking and Finance

The Institut d'Émission d'Outre-mer and the Banque Française Commerciale both have branches in Dzaoudzi and Mamoudzou.

ENERGY AND NATURAL RESOURCES

Agriculture

Agricultural land in Mayotte totalled 20,250 ha. in 2003. Mayotte is the world's second largest producer of ylang-ylang essence. Important cash crops include cinnamon, ylang-ylang, vanilla and coconut. The main food crops (2004) were bananas (11,500 tonnes) and cassava (9,000 tonnes). Livestock (2004): cattle, 17,235; goats, 22,811; sheep, 1,430.

Forestry

There are some 19,750 ha. of forest, of which 1,150 ha. are primary, 15,000 ha. secondary and 3,600 ha. badlands (uncultivable or eroded).

Fisheries

A lobster and shrimp industry has been created. Fish landings in 2005 totalled 2,214 tonnes.

INDUSTRY

Labour

In 2007, 19% of the active population was engaged in education, health and social care; 17% in public administration; 13% in transport, real estate and services; and 12% in commerce. Unemployment rate, 2007, 26·4%.

INTERNATIONAL TRADE

Imports and Exports

In 2004 imports totalled €212·9m. and exports €3·7m. Main export commodities are fish, ylang-ylang, vanilla, cinnamon and coconut. Main imports sources in 2003: France, 55·1%; South Africa, 4·8%. Main export destinations, 2003: France, 61·4%; Comoros, 25·0%.

COMMUNICATIONS

Roads

In 2002 there were 224 km of main roads, all of which are paved, and 1,528 motor vehicles.

Civil Aviation

There is an airport at Pamandzi, with scheduled services in 2002 provided to the Comoros, Kenya, Madagascar, Mozambique, Réunion, Seychelles and South Africa.

Shipping

There are services provided by Tratringa and Ville de Sima to Anjouan (Comoros) and Moroni (Comoros).

Telecommunications

In 2008 there were 10,000 main (fixed) telephone lines. There were 48,100 mobile phone subscribers in 2004.

SOCIAL INSTITUTIONS

Justice

There is a tribunal de première instance and a tribunal supérieur d'appel.

Education

In 2004 there were 39,807 pupils in nursery and primary schools, and 17,316 pupils at 16 collèges and 4 lycées at secondary level.

There were also 3,011 pupils enrolled in pre-professional classes and professional lycées. There is a teacher training college.

Health

There were two hospitals with 242 beds in 2004. In 2001 there were 112 doctors, 11 dentists, 19 pharmacists, 91 midwives and 284 nursing personnel.

RELIGION

The population is 97% Sunni Muslim, with a small Christian (mainly Roman Catholic) minority.

CULTURE

Broadcasting

Broadcasting is conducted by Radio Télévision Française d'Outre-Mer (RFO-Mayotte) with one hour a day in Shimaoré. Télé Mayotte RFO on Petite Terre transmits from 6 a.m. to around midnight every day. There are two private radio stations. In 2000 there were an estimated 5,000 TV receivers; colour is by SECAM. Since 1999, two satellite TV programmes have been available.

Press

In 2006 there was one newspaper, Kwezi, which was published weekly and also distributed in the Comoros.

Tourism

In 2001 there were 23,000 visitors. In 2005, 58% of visitors came from Réunion, 29% from mainland France and 13% from other countries. The average length of stay was 16 days.

St Barthélemy

Saint-Barthélemy

KEY HISTORICAL EVENTS

There is evidence of habitation dating to 1000 BC. Columbus visited in 1493 but it was the French who settled St Barthélemy in 1648. The island came under Swedish rule in 1784, after which it prospered as a free port. The British briefly held sway in 1801–02 but the French regained control in 1878 and the island was administered by Guadeloupe until seceding on 22 Feb. 2007 to become a French overseas collectivity.

TERRITORY AND POPULATION

The island has an area of 21 sq. km and is situated 200 km northwest of Guadeloupe. 2007 recorded population, 8,450. The capital is Gustavia.

CONSTITUTION AND GOVERNMENT

The laws of France are enforceable. Government on the island is by a 19-seat Territorial Council, elected by popular vote every five years. The council elects a President and the French government appoints a Prefect.

RECENT ELECTIONS

Elections to the Territorial Council were held in July 2007. Saint Barth First!/UMP won 16 seats and three other parties won one seat each.

CURRENT ADMINISTRATION

Prefect: Jacques Simonnet.

President of the Territorial Council: Bruno Magras.

St Martin

Saint-Martin

KEY HISTORICAL EVENTS

Sighted by Columbus in 1493, St Martin was settled by the Dutch in 1631. The Spanish claimed dominion in 1633 but by 1648 the island was divided between Dutch and French interests. The French part of the island was administered by Guadeloupe until it seceded on 22 Feb. 2007 to become a French overseas collectivity (encompassing several neighbouring islets including Île Tintamarre).

TERRITORY AND POPULATION

St Martin is situated 300 km southeast of Puerto Rico. The French-run part of the island covers roughly the northern two-thirds while the southern third (Sint Maarten) is part of the Netherlands Antilles. The French area is 53 sq. km; the recorded population in 2007 was 35,925. Marigot is the capital.

CONSTITUTION AND GOVERNMENT

The laws of France are enforceable. Government on the island is by a 23-seat Territorial Council, elected by popular vote every five years. The council elects a President and the French government appoints a Prefect.

RECENT ELECTIONS

Elections to the Territorial Council were held in July 2007. Union for Progress/UMP won 16 seats; Rally Responsibility Success, 6; and Succeed Saint Martin, 1.

CURRENT ADMINISTRATION

Prefect: Jacques Simonnet.

President of the Territorial Council: Frantz Gumbs.

St Pierre and Miquelon

Saint-Pierre et Miquelon

KEY HISTORICAL EVENTS

The only remaining fragment of the once-extensive French possessions in North America, the archipelago was settled from France in the 17th century. It was a French colony from 1816 until 1976, an overseas department until 1985, and is now an Overseas Collectivity.

TERRITORY AND POPULATION

The archipelago consists of two islands off the south coast of Newfoundland, with a total area of 242 sq. km, comprising the Saint-Pierre group (26 sq. km) and the Miquelon-Langlade group (216 sq. km). The recorded population at 2007 was 6,099 (6,316 at the 1999 census). Approximately 90% of the population lives on Saint-Pierre. The chief town is St Pierre.

The official language is French.

SOCIAL STATISTICS

2000: births, 51; deaths, 35; marriages, 24; divorces, 7.

CONSTITUTION AND GOVERNMENT

The Overseas Collectivity is administered by a Territorial Council of 19 members directly elected for a six-year term. It is represented in the National Assembly in Paris by one deputy, in the Senate by one senator and in the Economic and Social Council by one councillor. The French government is represented by a Prefect.

RECENT ELECTIONS

At the Territorial Council elections on 19 March 2006, 16 seats went to Archipel Demain, 2 to Cap sur l'Avenir and 1 to SPM Ensemble.

CURRENT ADMINISTRATION

Prefect: Jean-Régis Borius.

President of the Territorial Council: Stéphane Artano.

Government Website (French only): http://www.saint-pierre-et-miquelon.pref.gouv.fr

ECONOMY

Currency

Since 1 Jan. 2002 the euro has been the official currency as in metropolitan France.

Budget

The budget for 2000 balanced at 270m. French francs.

Banking and Finance

Banks include the Banque des Îles Saint-Pierre et Miquelon, the Crédit Saint-Pierrais and the Caisse d'Épargne.

A Development Agency was created in 1996 to help with investment projects.

ENERGY AND NATURAL RESOURCES

Environment

Carbon dioxide emissions from the consumption and flaring of fossil fuels in 2008 were the equivalent of 12·9 tonnes per capita.

Electricity

Production (2004 estimate): 52m. kWh. Installed capacity (2004 estimate): 27,000 kW.

Agriculture

The islands, being mostly barren rock, are unsuited for agriculture, but some vegetables are grown and livestock is kept for local consumption.

Fisheries

In June 1992 an international tribunal awarded France a 24-mile fishery and economic zone around the islands and a 10·5-mile-wide corridor extending for 200 miles to the high seas. The 2005 catch amounted to 3,084 tonnes, chiefly snow crab, cod, lumpfish, shark and scallops. A Franco-Canadian agreement regulating fishing in the area was signed in Dec. 1994. The total annual catch has declined dramatically in the past 15 years.

INDUSTRY

In 1994 there were 351 businesses (including 144 services, 69 public works, 45 food trade, 8 manufacturing and 2 agriculture). The main industry, fish processing, resumed in 1994 after a temporary cessation owing to lack of supplies in 1992. Diversification activities are in progress (aquaculture, sea products processing, scallops plant).

Labour

The economically active population in 2000 was 3,261. In Jan. 2010 the minimum wage (SMIC) was raised to €8·86 an hour (€1,343·77 a month for a 35-hour week). In 1996, 11% of the labour force was registered as unemployed.

INTERNATIONAL TRADE

Imports and Exports

Trade in 1m. French francs (2000): imports, 371 (51% from Canada); exports, 50.

COMMUNICATIONS

Roads

In 2000 there were 117 km of roads, of which 80 km were surfaced. There were 2,508 passenger cars and 1,254 commercial vehicles in use.

Civil Aviation

Air Saint-Pierre connects St Pierre with Halifax, Montreal, Sydney (Nova Scotia) and St John's (Newfoundland). In addition, a new airport capable of receiving medium-haul aeroplanes was opened in 1999.

Shipping

St Pierre has regular services to Fortune and Halifax in Canada. In 1999, 893 vessels called at St Pierre; 17,067 tonnes of freight were unloaded and 3,020 tonnes were loaded.

Telecommunications

There were 4,800 main (fixed) telephone lines in 2008.

SOCIAL INSTITUTIONS

Justice

There is a court of first instance and a higher court of appeal at St Pierre.

Education

Primary instruction is free. In 2000 there were three nursery and five primary schools with 799 pupils; three secondary schools with 564 pupils; and two technical schools with 199 pupils.

Health

In 2000 there was one hospital with 45 beds, one convalescent home with 20 beds, one retirement home with 40 beds; 15 doctors and one dentist.

RELIGION

The population is chiefly Roman Catholic.

CULTURE

Broadcasting

Radio Télévision Française d'Outre Mer (RFO) broadcasts in French on medium wave and on two television channels (one satellite). In 2000 there were 35 cable television channels from Canada and USA. In 2000 there were also approximately 4,500 television sets in use.

Tourism

In 2000 there were 10,090 visitors.

Wallis and Futuna

Wallis et Futuna

KEY HISTORICAL EVENTS

French dependencies since 1842, the inhabitants of these islands voted on 22 Dec. 1959 by 4,307 votes out of 4,576 in favour of exchanging their status to that of an overseas territory, which took effect from 29 July 1961. In March 2003 Wallis and Futuna became an Overseas Collectivity.

TERRITORY AND POPULATION

The territory comprises two groups of islands in the central Pacific (total area, 274 sq. km; census population, 13,445 in 2008). The Îles de Hoorn lie 255 km northeast of the Fiji Islands and consist of two main islands: Futuna (64 sq. km, 4,238 inhabitants) and uninhabited Alofi (51 sq. km). The Wallis Archipelago lies another 160 km further northeast, and has an area of 159 sq. km (9,207 inhabitants). It comprises the main island of Uvéa (60 sq. km) and neighbouring uninhabited islands, with a surrounding coral reef. The capital is Mata-Utu (2008 census population of 1,126) on Uvéa. Wallisian and Futunian are distinct Polynesian languages.

SOCIAL STATISTICS

Estimates per 1,000 population, 2003: birth rate, 19·4; death rate, 5·9.

CONSTITUTION AND GOVERNMENT

A Prefect represents the French government and carries out the duties of head of the territory, assisted by a 20-member Territorial Assembly directly elected for a five-year term, and a six-member Territorial Council, comprising the three traditional chiefs and three nominees of the Prefect agreed by the Territorial Assembly. The territory is represented by one deputy in the French National Assembly, by one senator in the Senate, and by one member on the Economic and Social Council. There are three districts: Singave and Alo (both on Futuna), and Wallis; in each, tribal kings exercise customary powers assisted by ministers and district and village chiefs.

RECENT ELECTIONS

Territorial Assembly elections were held on 1 April 2007. Union pour un Mouvement Populaire–Divers Droite won 12 of the 20 seats, with 8 going to Parti Socialiste–Divers Gauche.

CURRENT ADMINISTRATION

Prefect: Philippe Paolantoni.

President of the Territorial Assembly: Victor Brial.

ECONOMY

Currency

The unit of currency is the franc CFP (XPF), with a parity of 119·3317422 francs CPF to the euro.

Budget

The budget for 2005 balanced at 2,623m. francs CFP.

Banking and Finance

There is a branch of Banque Indosuez at Mata-Utu.

ENERGY AND NATURAL RESOURCES

Electricity

There is a thermal power station at Mata-Utu.

Agriculture

The chief products are bananas, coconuts, copra, cassava, yams and taro.

Livestock (2002): 25,000 pigs; 7,000 goats.

Fisheries

The catch in 2005 was approximately 300 tonnes.

COMMUNICATIONS

Roads

There are about 100 km of roads on Uvéa.

Civil Aviation

There is an airport on Wallis, at Hihifo, and another near Alo on Futuna. Eight flights a week link Wallis and Futuna. Air Calédonie International operates two flights a week to Nouméa (three in the summer) and two flights a week to Nadi.

Shipping

A regular cargo service links Mata-Utu (Wallis) and Singave (Futuna) with Nouméa (New Caledonia). In 2002 merchant shipping totalled 158,000 GRT.

Telecommunications

There were 2,143 main telephone lines in 2006.

SOCIAL INSTITUTIONS

Justice

There is a court of first instance, from which appeals can be made to the Court of Appeal in New Caledonia.

Education

In 2005 there were 2,573 pupils in nursery and primary schools and 2,355 in secondary schools. The South Pacific University Institute for Teacher Training, founded in 1992 (part of the French University of the Pacific, UFP) has three colleges: in Wallis and Futuna, French Polynesia and Nouméa (New Caledonia), where it is headquartered.

Health

In 2005 there were two hospitals with 72 beds, and three dispensaries.

RELIGION

The majority of the population is Roman Catholic.

CULTURE

Broadcasting

Since Aug. 2000 Réseau Français d'Outre-Mer (RFO) Wallis et Futuna radio has broadcast 24 hours a day. Télé Wallis et Futuna is the only television station.

SUI GENERIS COLLECTIVITIES

Collectivités sui generis

New Caledonia

Nouvelle-Calédonie

KEY HISTORICAL EVENTS

From the 11th century Melanesians settled in the islands that now form New Caledonia and dependencies. Capt. James Cook was the first European to arrive on Grande Terre on 4 Sept. 1774. The first European settlers (English Protestants and French Catholics) came in 1840. In 1853 New Caledonia was annexed by France and was used as a penal colony, taking in 21,000 convicts by 1897. Nickel was discovered in 1863, the mining of which provoked revolt among the Kanak tribes. During the Second World War, New Caledonia was used as a military base by the USA. Having fought for France during the war, the Kanaks were awarded citizenship in 1946. Together with most of its former dependencies, New Caledonia was made an Overseas Territory in 1958. It became a Territorial Collectivity under the Nouméa Accord of May 1998, which agreed on a gradual handover of responsibilities and the creation of New Caledonian citizenship. New Caledonia became a *Sui Generis* Collectivity (one that does not conform to the normal administrative structure) in March 2003. A referendum on independence is set to be held between 2014 and 2018.

TERRITORY AND POPULATION

The territory comprises Grande Terre (New Caledonia mainland) and various outlying islands, all situated in the southwest Pacific (Melanesia) with a total land area of 18,575 sq. km (7,172 sq. miles). New Caledonia has the second biggest coral reef in the world. The population (2009 census, provisional) was 245,580; density, 13·2 per sq. km. The main ethnic groups are the native Melanesians (Kanaks) and the Europeans (mostly French). There are also Wallisians and Futunians, Tahitians and Vietnamese and smaller minorities. In 2004 an estimated 63% of the population lived in urban areas. The UN gives an estimated population for 2010 of 254,000. The capital, Nouméa, had 91,386 inhabitants in 2004.

There are four main islands (or groups of):

Grande Terre An area of 16,372 sq. km (about 400 km long, 50 km wide) with a population (2004 census) of 205,939. A central mountain range separates a humid east coast and a drier temperate west coast. The east coast is predominantly Melanesian; the Nouméa region predominantly European; and the rest of the west coast is of mixed population.

Loyalty Islands 100 km (60 miles) east of New Caledonia, consisting of four large islands: Maré, Lifou, Uvéa and Tiga. It has a total area of 1,981 sq. km and a population (2004) of 22,080.

Isle of Pines A tourist and fishing centre 50 km (30 miles) to the southeast of Nouméa, with an area of 152 sq. km and a population (2004) of 1,840.

Bélep Archipelago About 50 km northwest of New Caledonia, with an area of 70 sq. km and a population (2004) of 930.

The remaining islands are very small and have no permanent inhabitants.

At the 1996 census there were 341 tribes (which have legal status under a high chief) living in 160 reserves, covering a surface area of 392,550 ha. (21% of total land), and representing about 28·7% of the population. 80,443 Melanesians belong to a tribe.

New Caledonia has a remarkable diversity of Melanesian languages (29 vernacular), divided into four main groups (Northern, Central, Southern and Loyalty Islands). There were 62,648 speakers in 2004. In 2006, eight Melanesian languages were taught in schools.

SOCIAL STATISTICS

2003: live births, 4,102; deaths, 1,121; marriages, 873; divorces, 246. Annual population growth rate, 1·3%. Life expectancy at birth, 2005, 75·2 years. Infant mortality, 2003, 5·9 per 1,000 live births; fertility rate, 2·3 births per woman.

CLIMATE

2006: Nouméa, Jan. 25·5°C, July 20·5°C (average temperature, 23·2°C; max. 33·8°C, min. 14·6°C). Annual rainfall 739 mm.

CONSTITUTION AND GOVERNMENT

Subsequent to the referendum law of 9 Nov. 1988, the organic and ordinary laws of 19 March 1999 define New Caledonia's new statute. In March 2003 New Caledonia became a *Sui Generis* Collectivity with specific status endowed with wide autonomy. New Caledonia's institutions comprise the congress, government, economic and social council (CES), the customary senate and customary councils. The congress is made up of 54 members called 'Councillors of New Caledonia' from the provincial assemblies. The 11-member government is elected by congress on a proportional ballot from party lists. The president is elected by majority vote of all members. Each member is allocated to lead and control a given sector in the administration. The government's mandate ends when the mandate of the Congress that elected it comes to an end. New Caledonia is represented by two deputies and one senator in the French parliament.

RECENT ELECTIONS

On 8 Nov. 1998 there was a referendum for the agreement of the Nouméa accords. Nearly 72% of those who voted approved. Turnout was 74·2%. Voting was restricted to those people resident in New Caledonia before 1998.

In elections to the Territorial Congress on 10 May 2009 the conservative Rassemblement-UMP won 13 of 54 seats, Calédonie Ensemble 10, Union Calédonienne 8, Union Nationale pour l'Indépendance–Front de Libération Nationale Kanak et Socialiste (UNI–FLNKS) 8, Avenir Ensemble–Le Mouvement de la Diversité 6, FLNKS 3, Parti Travailliste 3, Rassemblement pour la Calédonie 2 and Libération Kanak Socialiste 1. Turnout was 72·3%.

CURRENT ADMINISTRATION

High Commissioner: Yves Dassonville; b. 1948 (took office on 9 Nov. 2007).

President: Philippe Gomès; b. 1958 (Calédonie Ensemble; took office on 5 June 2009).

Vice-President: Pierre Ngaiohni (FLNKS).

President of the Congress: Harold Martin (Avenir Ensemble).

Government Website (French only):
http://www.nouvelle-caledonie.gouv.fr

ECONOMY

Currency

The unit of currency is the *franc CFP* (XPF), with a parity of 1,000 francs CPF = 8·38 euros. 344,036m. francs CFP were in circulation in Dec. 2006.

Budget

New Caledonia's expenditures in 2005 totalled 107,665m. francs CFP and receipts 117,765m. francs CFP.

Performance

Total GDP was 518·5bn. francs CFP in 2003.

Banking and Finance

In 2006 the banks were: Banque Calédonienne d'Investissement (BCI), Banque de Nouvelle-Calédonie (BNC), Banque Nationale de Paris/Nouvelle-Calédonie (BNP/NC), Société Générale Calédonienne de Banque (SGCB) and Caisse d'Épargne.

ENERGY AND NATURAL RESOURCES

Environment

Carbon dioxide emissions from the consumption and flaring of fossil fuels in 2008 were the equivalent of 12·8 tonnes per capita.

Electricity

Production (2004): 1,678m. kWh. Installed capacity was 0·4m. kW in 2004.

Minerals

A wide range of minerals has been found in New Caledonia including: nickel, copper and lead, gold, chrome, gypsum and platinum metals. The nickel deposits are of special value, being without arsenic, and constitute between 20–40% of the world's known nickel resources located on land.

Production of nickel ore (2006): 102,986 tonnes, of which saprolitic ore (80,794 tonnes) and lateritic ore (22,192).

Agriculture

In 2002, 6,441 persons worked in the agricultural sector. In 2001 there were an estimated 7,000 ha. of arable land and 6,000 ha. of permanent crops. In 2002 livestock numbered: pigs, 25,447; goats, 8,130; deer, 14,361; horses, 7,512; poultry, 382,800; cattle, 111,308. The chief products are beef, pork, poultry, coffee, copra, maize, fruit and vegetables. Production (2002 estimates, in 1,000 tonnes): coconuts, 16; yams, 11; cassava, 3; sweet potatoes, 3.

Forestry
There were 717,000 ha. of forest in 2005, or 39·2% of the total land area. Timber production (2007), 5,000 cu. metres.

Fisheries
Total catch in 2005 was 3,315 tonnes. In 2005 there were 216 fishing boats. Aquaculture (consisting mainly of saltwater prawns) provides New Caledonia's second highest source of export income after nickel.

INDUSTRY
Up until the end of the 1970s the New Caledonia economy was almost totally dependent on the nickel industry. Subsequently transformation or processing industries gained in importance to reach levels similar to those in metallurgic industries.

Labour
The employed population (2005) was 70,291. In Feb. 2009 the guaranteed monthly minimum wage was 125,464 francs CFP. In 2004 the unemployment rate stood at 16·3%.

INTERNATIONAL TRADE

Imports and Exports
Trade, 2004, in US$1m.: imports f.o.b., 1,473; exports f.o.b., 1,009. In 2003, 50·0% of imports came from France, 10·4% from Singapore and 10·2% from Australia. In 2003, 26·0% of exports went to France, 21·4% to Japan and 16·6% to Taiwan. In 2004 machinery and apparatus accounted for 20·9% of imports, transportation equipment 17·6% and food 13·9%. Ferro-nickel accounted for 60·6% of exports, nickel ore 16·1% and nickel matte 14·3%.

COMMUNICATIONS

Roads
In 2006 there were 5,622 km of roads and 110,000 vehicles. In 2006 road accidents injured 878 and killed 56 persons.

Civil Aviation
New Caledonia is connected by air routes with Australia, Japan, Vanuatu, Wallis and Futuna, Fiji Islands, New Zealand and French Polynesia. Regular domestic air services are provided by Air Calédonie from Magenta aerodrome in Nouméa. In 2006 there were 297,257 passengers recorded at Magenta Aerodrome. Internal services with Air Calédonie link Nouméa to a number of domestic airfields.

In 2006, 414,990 passengers and 5,440 tonnes of freight were carried via La Tontouta International Airport, near Nouméa.

Shipping
In 2005, 235 vessels unloaded 1,566,000 tonnes of freight in New Caledonia; 341 vessels loaded 3,643,000 tonnes of cargo.

Telecommunications
In 2005 there were 189,600 telephone subscribers (799·9 per 1,000 inhabitants), of which 134,300 were mobile phone subscribers. In 2005 there were 76,000 internet users.

Postal Services
In 2003 there were 54 post offices.

SOCIAL INSTITUTIONS

Justice
There are courts at Nouméa, Koné and Wé (on Lifou Island), a court of appeal, a labour court and a joint commerce tribunal. There were 3,916 cases judged in the magistrates courts in 2005; 226 went before the court of appeal, 16 were sentenced in the court of assizes.

The population in penal institutions in 2005 was 285 (123 per 100,000 population).

Education
In 2005 there were 37,245 pupils and 1,883 teachers in 287 primary schools; 31,987 pupils and 2,727 teachers in 93 secondary schools; and 2,926 students at university with 111 teaching staff. By decree of 1999 the New Caledonia campus of the French University of the Pacific (UFP), established in 1987, was separated from the campus, to become University of New Caledonia (UNC).

Health
In 2003 there were 481 doctors, 132 dentists, 116 pharmacists, 1,228 nursing personnel and 96 midwives. There were 26 socio-medical districts, with four hospitals and three private clinics; beds totalled 840.

Welfare
There are two main forms of social security cover: Free Medical Aid provides total sickness cover for non-waged persons and low-income earners; the Family Benefit, Workplace Injury and Contingency Fund for Workers in New Caledonia (CAFAT). There are also numerous mutual benefit societies. In 2006 Free Medical Aid had 57,873 beneficiaries; CAFAT had 214,638 beneficiaries.

RELIGION
There were about 130,000 Roman Catholics in 2001.

CULTURE

Broadcasting
Television broadcasting was, for a long time, limited to one or two state-owned stations (today Télé Nouvelle-Calédonie and Tempo). A private channel (Canal+) began broadcasting in 1994, and in late 1999 a digital service (Canal'Sat) was launched that in 2007 had 45 paying channels. By the end of 2005 Canal Calédonie had 26,000 Canal'Sat subscribers and/or Canal+ subscribers.

There were 68,000 TV sets in use in 2005.

Press
In 2001 there was one daily newspaper, Les Nouvelles Calédoniennes.

Tourism
In 2005 New Caledonia welcomed 101,000 tourists. In 2004 there were 91 hotels providing 2,295 beds.

FURTHER READING
Institut de la Statistique et des Études Économiques: *Tableaux de l'Économie Calédonienne/New Caledonia: Facts & Figures (TEC 2006)* (every three years); *Informations Statistiques Rapides de Nouvelle-Calédonie* (monthly).

Imprimerie Administrative, Nouméa: *Journal Officiel de la Nouvelle Calédonie.*

Local Statistical Office: Institut Territorial de la Statistique et des Études Économiques, BP 823, 98845 Nouméa.

Website: http://www.isee.nc

Southern and Antarctic Territories

Terres Australes et Antarctiques Françaises (TAAF)

GENERAL DETAILS
The Territory of the TAAF was created on 6 Aug. 1955. It comprises the Kerguelen and Crozet archipelagoes, the islands of Saint-Paul and Amsterdam (formerly Nouvelle Amsterdam) and the Scattered Islands group, all in the southern Indian Ocean, plus Terre Adélie. It has been classified as a *Sui Generis* Collectivity (one that does not conform to the normal administrative structure) since 2007. The Scattered Islands were incorporated into the TAAF in Feb. 2007.

Since 2 April 1997 the administration has had its seat in Saint-Pierre, Réunion; before that it was in Paris. The Administrator is assisted by a seven-member consultative council which meets twice yearly in Paris; its members are nominated by the government for five years. The 15-member Polar Environment Committee, which in 1993 replaced the former Consultative Committee on the Environment (est. 1982), meets at least once a year to discuss all problems relating to the preservation of the environment

The French Institute for Polar Research and Technology was set up to organize scientific research and expeditions in Jan. 1992. The staff of the permanent scientific stations of the TAAF (approximately 200 in 2005) is renewed every 6 or 12 months and forms the only population.

Administrateur Supérieur: Rollon Mouchel-Blaisot.

Amsterdam and **Saint-Paul Islands** Situated 38–39° S. lat., 77° E. long. Amsterdam, with an area of 54 sq. km (21 sq. miles) was discovered in 1522 by Magellan's companions; Saint-Paul, lying about 100 km to the south, with an area of 7 sq. km (2·7 sq. miles), was probably discovered in 1559 by Portuguese sailors. Both were first visited in 1633 by the Dutch explorer, Van Diemen, and were annexed by France in 1843. They are both extinct volcanoes. The only inhabitants are at Base Martin de Vivies (est. 1949 on Amsterdam Island), including several scientific research stations, a hospital, communication and other facilities (ranging from 25–45 persons). Crayfish are caught commercially on Amsterdam.

Crozet Islands Situated 46° S. lat., 50–52° E. long.; consists of five larger and 15 tiny islands, with a total area of 505 sq. km (195 sq. miles). The western group includes Apostles, Pigs and Penguins islands; the eastern group, Possession and Eastern islands. The archipelago was discovered in 1772 by Marion Dufresne, whose first mate, Crozet, annexed it for Louis XV. A meteorological and scientific station (ranging from 25–45 persons) at Base Alfred-Faure on Possession Island was built in 1964.

Kerguelen Islands Situated 48–50° S. lat., 68–70° E. long.; consists of one large and 85 smaller islands, and over 200 islets and rocks, with a total area of 7,215 sq. km (2,786 sq. miles) of which Grande Terre occupies 6,675 sq. km (2,577 sq. miles). It was discovered in 1772 by Yves de Kerguelen, but was effectively occupied by France only in 1949. Port-aux-Français has several scientific research stations (ranging from 70–110 persons). Reindeer, trout and sheep have been acclimatized.

Scattered Islands Situated in the Indian Ocean around Madagascar between 11–22° S. lat., 39–54° E. long., comprising Bassas da India, Europa Island, the Glorieuses Islands, Juan de Nova Island and Tromelin Island. Formerly French minor territories, the islands—which have a total area of 39 sq. km (15 sq. miles)—were incorporated into the TAAF in Feb. 2007. Sovereignty of individual islands is disputed, with the Comoros, Madagascar, Mauritius and the Seychelles all making claims. The population numbers around 50. The islands are designated as nature reserves and support a range of meteorological stations, military garrisons and radio stations. About 12,000 tonnes of guano are mined annually on Juan de Nova Island.

Terre Adélie Comprises that section of the Antarctic continent between 136° and 142° E. long., south of 60° S. lat. The ice-covered plateau has an area of about 432,000 sq. km (166,800 sq. miles), and was discovered in 1840 by Dumont d'Urville. A research station (ranging from 30–110 persons) is situated at Base Dumont d'Urville, which is maintained by the French Institute for Polar Research and Technology.

MINOR TERRITORIES

Dépendances

Clipperton Island

Île Clipperton

In the 18th century the island was the hideout of a pirate, John Clipperton, for whom it was named. In 1855 it was claimed by France, and in 1897 by Mexico. It was awarded to France by international arbitration in 1935. Clipperton Island is a Pacific atoll, 3 km long, some 1,120 km southwest of the coast of Mexico. It covers an area of 7 sq. km and is uninhabited. The island is administered by the Minister of Overseas France. The island is occasionally visited by tuna fishermen.

GABON

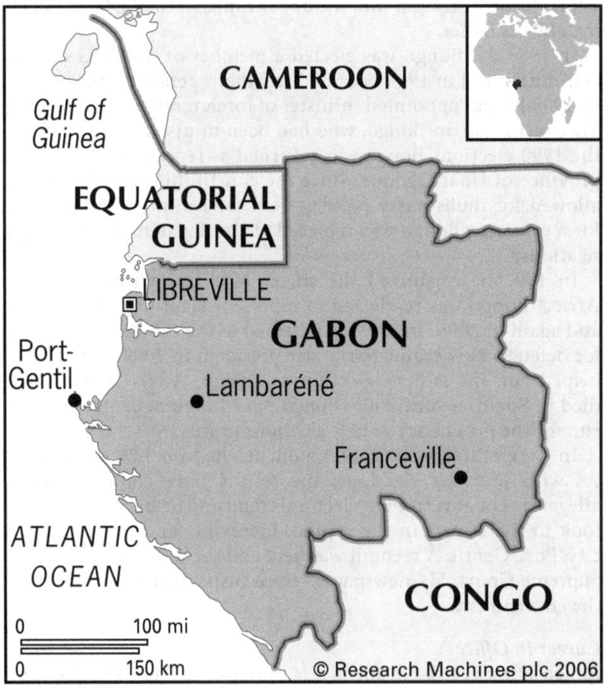

République Gabonaise
(Gabonese Republic)

Capital: Libreville
Population estimate, 2010: 1·50m.
GDP per capita, 2007: (PPP$) 15,167
HDI/world rank: 0·755/103

KEY HISTORICAL EVENTS

Between the 16th and 18th centuries, the Fang and other peoples in the region of present-day Gabon were part of a federation of chiefdoms. The country's capital, Libreville, grew from a settlement of slaves who were rescued from captivity by the French in 1849. Colonized by France around this period, the territory was annexed to French Congo in 1888. There was resistance by the indigenous people between 1905 and 1911 to the depredations of colonial rule, but the country became a separate colony in 1910 as one of the four territories of French Equatorial Africa. Gabon became an autonomous republic within the French Community on 28 Nov. 1958 and achieved independence on 17 Aug. 1960.

TERRITORY AND POPULATION

Gabon is bounded in the west by the Atlantic Ocean, north by Equatorial Guinea and Cameroon and east and south by the Republic of the Congo. The area covers 267,667 sq. km. Its population at the 1993 census was 1,014,976; density, 3·8 per sq. km. In 2005, 83·6% of the population were urban.

The UN gives an estimated population for 2010 of 1·50m.; density, 6 per sq. km.

The capital is Libreville (611,000 inhabitants, 2003 estimate), other large towns (1993 census) being Port-Gentil (79,225), Franceville (31,183), Oyem (22,404) and Moanda (21,882).

Provincial areas, populations and capitals:

Province	*Area in sq. km*	*Population 1993 census*	*Capital*
Estuaire	20,740	463,187	Libreville
Haut-Ogooué	36,547	104,301	Franceville (Masuku)
Moyen-Ogooué	18,535	42,316	Lambaréné
Ngounié	37,750	77,781	Mouila
Nyanga	21,285	39,430	Tchibanga
Ogooué-Ivindo	46,075	48,862	Makokou
Ogooué-Lolo	25,380	43,915	Koulamoutou
Ogooué-Maritime	22,890	97,913	Port-Gentil
Woleu-Ntem	38,465	97,271	Oyem

The largest ethnic groups are the Fangs (25%) in the north and the Bapounou (24%) in the south. There are some 40 smaller groups. French is the official language.

SOCIAL STATISTICS

2003 estimates: births, 41,000; deaths, 16,000. Estimated rates, 2003 (per 1,000 population): births, 31; deaths, 12. Annual population growth rate, 1992–2002, 2·6%. Expectation of life at birth, 2007, 58·7 years for males and 61·5 years for females. Infant mortality, 2005, 59 per 1,000 live births; fertility rate, 2004, 3·9 births per woman.

CLIMATE

The climate is equatorial, with high temperatures and considerable rainfall. Mid-May to mid-Sept. is the long dry season, followed by a short rainy season, then a dry season again from mid-Dec. to mid-Feb., and finally a long rainy season once more. Libreville, Jan. 80°F (26·7°C), July 75°F (23·9°C). Annual rainfall 99" (2,510 mm).

CONSTITUTION AND GOVERNMENT

On 21 March 1997 the government presented to the Parliament legislation aimed at reforming the constitution in a number of key areas: notably, the bill mandated the creation of a Vice-President of the Republic, the extension of the presidential term of office from five to seven years, and the transformation of the Senate into an Upper Chamber of Parliament. Gabon has a bicameral legislature, consisting of a 120-member *National Assembly* (with members elected by direct, popular vote to serve five-year terms) and a 102-member *Senate* (elected for six-year terms in single-seat constituencies by local and departmental councillors). At a referendum on electoral reform on 23 July 1995, 96·48% of votes cast were in favour; turnout was 63·45%. The 1991 constitution provides for an Executive *President* directly elected for a five-year term (renewable once only). In July 2003 Gabon's parliament approved an amendment to the constitution that allows the president to seek re-election indefinitely. The head of government is the *Prime Minister*, who appoints a Council of Ministers.

National Anthem

'La concorde' ('The Concord'); words and tune by G. Damas Aleka.

RECENT ELECTIONS

Presidential elections were held on 30 Aug. 2009. The late president's son, Ali Bongo Ondimba, was elected with 41·7% of votes cast against 25·9% for Andre Mba Obame and 25·2% for Pierre Mamboundou. There were 15 other candidates. Bongo's victory was marred by accusations of vote-rigging and post-election violence.

Elections for the National Assembly were held in two rounds on 17 and 24 Dec. 2006. The Gabonese Democratic Party (PDG) won 82 seats; allied parties 17 (including National Woodcutter's Party/Rally for Gabon 8, Democratic and Republican Alliance 3, Circle of Reformist Liberals 2, Social Democratic Party 1); opposition parties 17 (including Gabonese People's Union 8 and Gabonese Union for Democracy and Development 4); ind. 4.

Senate elections were held on 18 Jan. 2009. The PDG won 75 of 102 seats; Rally for Gabon, 6; Gabonese Union for Democracy and Development, 3. Independents claimed nine seats and the remaining nine went to minor parties.

CURRENT ADMINISTRATION

President: Ali Bongo Ondimba; b. 1959 (PDG; sworn in 16 Oct. 2009).

Vice President: Didjob Divungi Di Ndinge.

In March 2010 the Council of Ministers comprised:

Prime Minister: Paul Biyoghé Mba; b. 1953 (sworn in 17 July 2009).

Minister for Agriculture, Livestock and Rural Development: Raymond Ndong Sima. *Budget, Public Finance and Civil Service, and Minister in Charge of State Reform:* Blaise Louembé. *Communications, Posts and Information Technology:* Laure Olga Gondjoult. *Culture, and Youth, Sports and Leisure:* René Ndemozo'o Obiang. *Defence:* Angélique Ngoma. *Economy, Commerce, Industry and Tourism:* Magloire Ngambia. *Energy and Hydraulics:* Régis Imongault. *Equipment, Infrastructure and Land Management:* Gen. Flavien Nziengui Nzoundou. *Foreign Affairs, International Co-operation and Francophonie Affairs:* Paul Toungui. *Health, Social Affairs, National Solidarity and Family:* Alphonsine Mvié Na. *Housing and Urban Affairs:* Rufin Pacome Ondzouga. *Interior, Public Security, Immigration and Decentralization:* Jean François Ndongou. *Justice and Keeper of the Seals:* Anicette Nanga Origa. *Mining, Petrol and Hydrocarbons:* Julien Nkogue Békalé. *National Education, Higher Education, Scientific Research and Innovation and Government Spokesperson:* Séraphin Moundounga. *Parliamentary Relations and Constitutional Affairs, Regional Integration and Minister in Charge of Human Rights:* Émile Doumba. *Small and Medium-sized Enterprise and Handicrafts:* Jean-Félix Mouloungui. *Technical Education and Professional Training:* Léon Zouba. *Transport:* Rémy Ossélé Ndong. *Water and Forests, Environment and Sustainable Development:* Martin Mabala. *Work, Employment and Social Security:* Maxime Ngohou Ifoundou.

Gabonese Parliament (French only): http://www.assemblee.ga

CURRENT LEADERS

Ali-Ben Bongo Ondimba

Position

President

Introduction

Ali-Ben Bongo Ondimba was elected president in Aug. 2009 following the death of his father, Omar Bongo Ondimba (president from 1967–2009). Ali Bongo served as minister of foreign affairs under his father, as well as deputy of the national assembly, minister of defence and vice-president of the Gabonese Democratic Party (PDG).

Early Life

Ali-Ben Bongo Ondimba is the oldest son of Omar Bongo, the country's longest-serving president. He was born Alain-Bernard Bongo in Feb. 1959 in Brazzaville, Republic of the Congo. His mother, Gabonese singer Josephine Kama (later Patience Dabany), was 15 at the time of his birth.

The family moved to Gabon in 1960, just after its independence from France. Alain-Bernard spent most of his youth in France, studying at a protestant primary school in Cévennes and then the Catholic College Notre-Dame de Sainte-Croix, on the outskirts of Paris. In 1973 Albert-Bernard Bongo and Alain-Bernard Bongo changed their names to Omar and Ali-Ben, taking the second name Ondimba as part of their conversion to Islam. Ali graduated in law from the Sorbonne before returning to Gabon in 1981. He went straight into the upper ranks of the PDG, presided over by his father.

In 1983 Ali Bongo was elected a member of the PDG central committee and in 1984 became his father's personal spokesman. In 1989 he was appointed minister of foreign relations, replacing his cousin Martin Bongo, who had been minister since 1976. At the 1990 elections Bongo was returned as representative for the province of Haut-Ogooué. Since the constitution of 1991, which allowed for multi-party politics, also set a minimum age of 35 for a minister, Bongo was replaced at the department of foreign relations.

In 1992 he organized the singer Michael Jackson's tour of Africa. Bongo was re-elected to represent Haut-Ogooué in 1996 and again in 2006. In 1999 he returned to the cabinet as minister for defence. He became party vice president in 2003 and in 2005 helped run his father's election campaign. After Omar Bongo died in Spain in June 2009, Bongo put himself at centre stage to run for the presidency in new elections in Aug.

In competition against 17 opponents, he won 42% of the vote. As with previous elections, the results were contested amid allegations of government electoral fraud and bribery. Thousands took to the streets in the capital, Libreville, and in the second city, Port-Gentil. A recount was held and the result upheld by the Supreme Court. Six newspapers were suspended for criticism of the government.

Career in Office

Bongo's first act as president was to reinstate Paul Biyoghé Mba as head of the cabinet and to cut down the number of ministers, having pledged to slash government expenditure. Ministers have undergone curbs on privileges and been subject to pay cuts. In Nov. 2009 Bongo travelled to Paris to meet French president Nicolas Sarkozy and in Dec. 2009 he made a state visit to the Pope.

Bongo has pledged to fight corruption. Nonetheless, Transparency International and other NGOs have pushed for investigations into the Bongo family's finances.

Paul Biyoghé Mba

Position

Prime Minister

Introduction

Paul Biyoghé Mba is a career civil servant who served as a minister under Gabon's autocratic president, Omar Bongo. In Oct. 2009 he was appointed prime minister by the late president's controversial successor, Ali Bongo.

Early Life

Biyoghé Mba was born on 18 April 1953 in Donguila, Estuaire province, in western Gabon. In the early 1970s he studied business administration at the University of Rennes, France, before returning to Gabon to work at the Banque Gabonaise de Développement. Biyoghé Mba served as the bank's deputy director from 1977–80, before joining the civil service, initially as an adviser to Omar Bongo on commercial, industrial and investment affairs (1980–83). This was when high international oil prices brought prosperity to Gabon and to the president personally.

Biyoghé Mba was deputy director to the presidential cabinet from 1984–89, when he helped secure US investment in a period of economic downturn. Disillusionment with Bongo's repressive policies brought demands for multi-party democracy. In 1990 Gabon held its first multi-party legislative elections for 22 years.

Biyoghé Mba was elected for the Gabonese Democratic Party (PDG), which gained a majority in the National Assembly. He served as a deputy for two years until he was appointed minister of state control, parastatal reform and privatization.

Biyoghé Mba supported Bongo's re-election as president in 1993 but resigned from the government and the PDG the following year in protest at Bongo's authoritarian response to riots in Libreville and Port-Gentil. Returning to the National Assembly, he created a new party, the Communal Movement for Development (MCD), which eventually merged with the PDG in 2002. Elected to the newly established Senate in 1997, he was the minister responsible for small and medium-sized enterprises from 1999–2003. As Gabon's minister of trade and industrial development (2003–08) he was responsible for the New Partnership for Africa's Development. In Oct. 2008 he became minister for agriculture in Jean Eyeghe Ndong's government.

Career in Office

In the political upheaval that followed Bongo's death on 8 June 2009 (ending his 41-year rule), his son, Ali Bongo (then minister of defence) became the PDG's presidential candidate. Ndong resigned as prime minister to fight the election as an independent.

On 17 July 2009 the interim president, Rose Francine Rogombé, named Biyoghé Mba as interim prime minister. Ali-Ben Bongo Ondimba was sworn in as the new president on 16 Oct. 2009, nearly two months after his disputed election victory had triggered widespread civil unrest. On the same day, Bongo appointed Biyoghé Mba as prime minister, praising his managerial skills and experience. Biyoghé Mba named a government of 30 ministers (slimmed down from 44), which included 12 members from his previous cabinet.

DEFENCE

In 2006 military expenditure totalled US$21m. (US$15 per capita), representing 0·2% of GDP.

Army

The Army totalled (2007) 3,200. A referendum of 23 July 1995 favoured the transformation of the Presidential Guard into a republican guard. There is also a paramilitary Gendarmerie of 2,000. France maintains 700 Army personnel in Gabon.

Navy

There is a small naval flotilla, about 500 strong in 2007. France maintains 1,560 Naval personnel in Gabon.

Air Force

Personnel (2007) 1,000. There are around 16 combat capable aircraft (including nine Mirage 5s) and five attack helicopters.

INTERNATIONAL RELATIONS

Gabon is a member of the UN, World Bank, IMF and several other UN specialized agencies, WTO, IOM, International Organization of the Francophonie, Islamic Development Bank, Organization of the Islamic Conference, African Development Bank, African Union, Economic Community of the Central African States (CEEAC) and is an ACP member state of the ACP-EU relationship.

ECONOMY

Agriculture accounted for 4·9% of GDP in 2006, industry 61·2% and services 33·9%.

Overview

Income per capita is over five times greater than the sub-Saharan Africa average. Although extreme poverty has been cut drastically over the years, a large section of the population continues to live in sub-standard conditions.

Principal exports were timber and manganese until the early 1970s when offshore oil deposits were discovered. Because of the heavy role of the oil industry in the economy, the agricultural sector accounts for a small percentage of total output relative to other low-income countries. Since the oil rush there has been volatile growth marked by fiscal mismanagement which in 1994 led to the devaluation of the currency by 50%. In the years since there has been an inflationary spike and significant French, American and IMF financial support agreements. Among oil-exporting African nations, Gabon stands out as a growth laggard in recent years, averaging only 1·1% annual growth from 1996–2005 compared to a 9·1% average among the continent's top seven oil exporters. Performance is particularly disappointing given that World Bank studies suggest that since 1995 growth rates in Africa have been highly correlated with the demand for minerals, with oil exporters performing markedly better than other countries. Unlike other regional exporters, Gabon has seen significant drops in oil production in recent years, with few additional deposits expected to be found.

Some progress has been made in diversifying the economy and development indicators have shown improvement. A major challenge is posed by HIV, with 8·1% of the population infected.

Currency

The unit of currency is the *franc CFA* (XAF) with a parity of 655·957 francs CFA to one euro. Foreign exchange reserves were US$466m. in June 2005 and total money supply was 416,653m. francs CFA. Gold reserves were 13,000 troy oz in July 2005. Inflation was 5·0% in 2007 and 5·3% in 2008.

Budget

In 2004 revenue totalled 1,113·6bn. francs CFA and expenditure 827·1bn. francs CFA. Oil revenues account for more than half of all revenues.

The standard rate of VAT is 18% (reduced rate, 10%).

Performance

Real GDP growth was 5·6% in 2007, followed by 2·3% in 2008. Total GDP in 2008 was US$14·4bn.

Banking and Finance

The Banque des États de l'Afrique Centrale (*Governor*, Philibert Andzembe) is the bank of issue. There are five commercial banks. The largest are Banque Internationale pour le Commerce et l'Industrie du Gabon, BGFIBANK and Union Gabonaise de Banque, which between them had 80% of the market share in 2003.

ENERGY AND NATURAL RESOURCES

Environment

Gabon's carbon dioxide emissions from the consumption and flaring of fossil fuels in 2008 were the equivalent of 3·1 tonnes per capita.

Electricity

Installed capacity was an estimated 0·4m. kW in 2004. Production totalled 1·54bn. kWh in 2004 (approximately 58% hydro-electric and 42% thermal). Consumption per capita was an estimated 1,128 kWh in 2004.

Oil and Gas

Proven oil reserves (2008), 3·2bn. bbls. Production, 2008, 11·8m. tonnes. There were proven natural gas reserves of 28bn. cu. metres in 2007. Natural gas production (2004) was 126m. cu. metres.

Minerals

There are an estimated 200m. tonnes of manganese ore and 850m. tonnes of iron ore deposits. Gold, zinc and phosphates also occur. Output, 2006: manganese ore, 2·98m. tonnes.

Agriculture
In 2007 the agricultural population was approximately 415,000, of whom 192,000 were economically active. There were 325,000 ha. of arable land in 2001 and 170,000 ha. of permanent crops. 15,000 ha. were irrigated in 2001.

The major crops (estimated production, 2003, in 1,000 tonnes) are: plantains, 270; sugarcane, 235; cassava, 230; yams, 155; taro, 59; maize, 31; groundnuts, 20; bananas, 12; rubber, 11. Other important products include palm oil, sweet potatoes and soybeans.

Livestock (2002 estimates): 212,000 pigs; 195,000 sheep; 90,000 goats; 35,000 cattle; 3m. chickens.

In 2002 an estimated 32,000 tonnes of meat, 2,000 tonnes of eggs and 2,000 tonnes of fresh milk were produced.

Forestry
Equatorial forests covered 21·78m. ha. in 2005, or 84·5% of the total land area. Timber production in 2007 was 3·93m. cu. metres.

Since 2002 a tenth of the country has been transformed into 13 national parks covering nearly 30,000 sq. km.

Fisheries
The catch in 2005 was 43,863 tonnes, of which 34,163 tonnes were from marine waters. Industrial fleets account for about 25% of the catch.

INDUSTRY
Most manufacturing is based on the processing of food (particularly sugar), timber and mineral resources, cement and chemical production and oil refining.

Production figures in 1,000 tonnes: residual fuel oil (2004), 324; cement (2006), 260; distillate fuel oil (2004), 228; petrol (2004), 68; beer (2003), 75·4m. litres; soft drinks (2005), 60·7m. litres.

Labour
The economically active workforce in 2005 numbered 664,000 (59% males). The unemployment rate was 14·8% in 2005. In 2007 the legal minimum monthly wage was 80,000 francs CFA. There is a 40-hour working week.

INTERNATIONAL TRADE
Foreign debt was US$3,902m. in 2005. The government retains the right to participate in foreign investment in oil and mineral extraction.

Imports and Exports
In 2006 imports (c.i.f.) totalled US$1,724·9m. and exports (f.o.b.) US$6,015·2m.

Machinery and transport equipment accounted for 42·8% of imports in 2006, food and live animals 13·0%, chemicals and related products 9·2% and iron and steel 7·4%. Petroleum and petroleum products constituted 85·6% of exports in 2006, and cork and wood 6·3%.

Main import suppliers, 2006: France, 39·9%; Belgium, 14·2%; USA, 7·3%. Main export markets, 2006: USA, 58·4%; China, 10·6%; France, 7·1%.

COMMUNICATIONS
Roads
In 2004 there were an estimated 9,170 km of roads (10·2% paved); and in 2002 some 25,600 passenger cars plus 17,000 trucks and vans. There were 293 deaths in road accidents in 2000.

Rail
The 657 km standard gauge Transgabonais railway runs from the port of Owendo to Franceville. Total length of railways, 2005, 649 km. In 2003 passenger-km travelled came to 86m. and freight tonne-km to 2,998m.

Civil Aviation
There are international airports at Libreville (Léon M'Ba Airport), Port-Gentil and Franceville (Masuku); scheduled internal services link these to a number of domestic airfields. Libreville, the main airport, handled 757,000 passengers and 17,700 tonnes of freight in 2001. In 2003 scheduled airline traffic of Gabonese-based carriers flew 8m. km, carrying 386,000 passengers (170,000 on international flights). Gabon Airlines was established in July 2006 as a successor to the bankrupt national carrier Air Gabon.

Shipping
In 2002 the merchant marine totalled 13,000 GRT, including oil tankers 1,000 GRT. Owendo (near Libreville), Mayumba and Port-Gentil are the main ports. In 2000, 18m. tonnes of cargo were handled at the ports. Rivers are an important means of inland transport.

Telecommunications
In 2005 Gabon had 688,900 telephone subscribers (497·8 per 1,000 inhabitants), including 649,800 mobile phone subscribers. 45,000 PCs were in use (32·5 per 1,000 inhabitants) in 2005 and internet users numbered 67,000.

Postal Services
There were 59 post offices in 2003.

SOCIAL INSTITUTIONS
Justice
There are Tribunaux de grande instance at Libreville, Port-Gentil, Lambaréné, Mouila, Oyem, Franceville (Masuku) and Koulamoutou, from which cases move progressively to a central Criminal Court, Court of Appeal and Supreme Court, all three located in Libreville. Civil police number about 900.

Education
The adult literacy rate in 2004 was 84·0%. Education is compulsory between 6–16 years. In 2000–01 there were 265,714 pupils and 5,399 teachers in primary schools, and 101,681 pupils with 2,727 (1996–97) teachers at secondary schools; in 1996–97 there were 6,703 students in 11 technical and professional schools and 76 students in two teacher-training establishments.

In 1996–97 there was one university at Libreville (the Omar Bongo University) and one university of science and technology at Franceville (Masuku), with a total of 6,800 students and 506 academic staff. In 2004 a university of health sciences (previously part of the Omar Bongo University) was created in Libreville.

In 2000–01 total expenditure on education came to 4·6% of GNP.

Health
In 2004 there were 395 physicians, 66 dentistry personnel, 63 pharmaceutical personnel and 6,778 nursing and midwifery personnel. In 2006 there were 20 hospital beds per 10,000 inhabitants.

RELIGION
In 2001 there were 0·69m. Roman Catholics, 0·22m. Protestants and 0·17m. followers of African Christian sects. The majority of the remaining population follow animist beliefs. There are about 12,000 Muslims.

CULTURE
World Heritage Sites
Gabon has one site on the UNESCO World Heritage List: the ecosystem and relict cultural landscape of Lopé-Okanda (inscribed on the list in 2007), an area of rainforest and savannah containing the remains of Neolithic and Iron Age settlements.

Broadcasting
Broadcasting is the responsibility of the state-controlled Radiodiffusion Télévision Gabonaise (RTG), which operates

two television stations and a radio network, as well as provincial services. There are a few private broadcasters. There were 227,000 TV sets in 2006 (colour by SECAM).

Press

In 2006 there was one government-controlled daily newspaper (L'Union) with a circulation of 20,000.

Tourism

222,000 non-resident tourists arrived at Libreville airport in 2003 (169,000 in 2001). In 2004 tourist spending amounted to US$74m.

DIPLOMATIC REPRESENTATIVES

Of Gabon in the United Kingdom (27 Elvaston Place, London, SW7 5NL)
Ambassador: Omer Piankali.

Of the United Kingdom in Gabon
Ambassador: Bharat Joshi (resides in Yaoundé, Cameroon).

Of Gabon in the USA (2034 20th St., NW, Suite 200, Washington, D.C., 20009)
Ambassador: Carlos Boungou.

Of the USA in Gabon (Blvd du Bord de Mer, Libreville)
Ambassador: Eunice Reddick.

Of Gabon to the United Nations
Ambassador: Emanuel Issoze-Ngondet.

Of Gabon to the European Union
Ambassador: René Makongo.

FURTHER READING

Barnes, J. F. G., *Gabon: Beyond the Colonial Legacy.* 1992
Gardinier, David E., *Historical Dictionary of Gabon.* 3rd ed. 2006
Saint Paul, M. A., *Gabon: the Development of a Nation.* 1989

National Statistical Office: Direction Générale de la Statistique et des Études Économiques, Ministère de la Planification et de la Programmation du Développement, BP 2119, Libreville.
Website (French only): http://www.stat-gabon.ga

THE GAMBIA

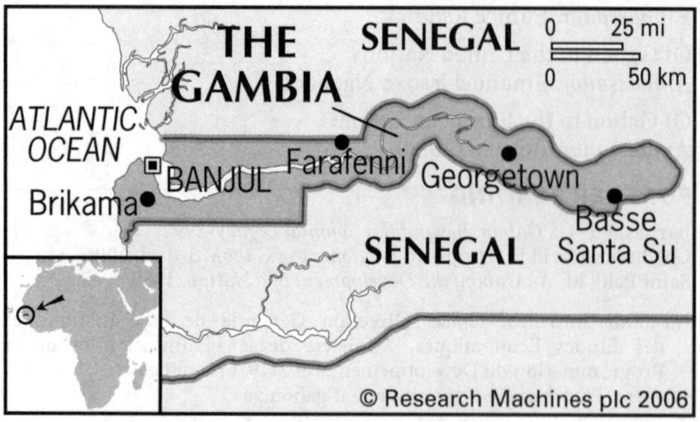

Republic of The Gambia

Capital: Banjul
Population estimate, 2010: 1·75m.
GDP per capita, 2007: (PPP$) 1,225
HDI/world rank: 0·456/168

KEY HISTORICAL EVENTS

Stone circles thought to have been constructed by ancestors of the Jola people are estimated to date from AD 600. Kingdoms of Mandinka-speaking people were established near the Gambia River from around 1100. State-building by the Jolof and Serer groups gathered pace from around 1400. Portuguese mariners entered the Gambia River in 1455 but the first permanent European settlement was founded by traders from the Baltic Duchy of Courland (Latvia) in 1651. English and French merchants subsequently vied for control of the region (Senegambia). The British Captain, Alexander Grant, established Bathurst (Banjul) as a garrison in 1816 and it was controlled from the Freetown Colony (Sierra Leone). The Gambia became an independent member of the British Commonwealth on 18 Feb. 1965 and an independent republic on 24 April 1970.

TERRITORY AND POPULATION

The Gambia takes its name from the River Gambia, and consists of a strip of territory never wider than 10 km on both banks. It is bounded in the west by the Atlantic Ocean and on all other sides by Senegal. The area is 10,690 sq. km, including 2,077 sq. km of inland water. Population (census, 2003), 1,360,681; density, 127 per sq. km. The United Nations population estimate for 2003 was 1,436,000. In 2005, 53·9% of the population were urban.

The UN gives an estimated population for 2010 of 1·75m.

The largest ethnic group is the Mandingo, followed by the Wolofs, Fulas, Jolas and Sarahuley. The country is administratively divided into eight local government areas (LGAs).

The eight LGAs, with their areas, populations and chief towns are:

Division	*Area in sq. km*	*Population 2003 census*	*Chief town*
Banjul	12	35,061	Banjul
Basse	2,070	182,586	Basse Santa Su
Brikama	1,764	389,594	Brikama
Janjangbureh	1,428	107,212	Janjangbureh
Kanifeng	76	322,735	Kanifeng
Kerewan	2,255	172,835	Kerewan
Kuntaur	1,467	78,491	Kuntaur
Mansakonko	1,618	72,167	Mansakonko

The official language is English.

SOCIAL STATISTICS

2000 estimates: births, 49,000; deaths, 22,000. Estimated birth rate in 2000 was 37·2 per 1,000 population; estimated death rate, 17·0. Annual population growth rate, 1992–2002, 3·3%. Expectation of life, 2007, was 54·1 years for males and 57·3 for females. Fertility rate, 2004, 4·6 births per woman; infant mortality, 2005, 97 per 1,000 live births. The Gambia has made some of the best progress in recent years in reducing child mortality. The number of deaths per 1,000 live births among children under five was reduced from around 130 in 1990 to approximately 80 in 1999.

CLIMATE

The climate is characterized by two very different seasons. The dry season lasts from Nov. to May, when precipitation is very light and humidity moderate. Days are warm but nights quite cool. The SW monsoon is likely to set in with spectacular storms and produces considerable rainfall from July to Oct., with increased humidity. Banjul, Jan. 73°F (22·8°C), July 80°F (26·7°C). Annual rainfall 52" (1,295 mm).

CONSTITUTION AND GOVERNMENT

The 1970 constitution provided for an executive *President* elected directly for renewable five-year terms. The President appoints a *Vice-President* who is the government's chief minister. The single-chamber *National Assembly* has 53 members (48 elected by universal adult suffrage for a five-year term and five appointed by the President).

A referendum of 8 Aug. 1996 approved a new constitution by 70·4% of votes cast. It took effect in Jan. 1997 and thereby created the Second Republic. Under this, the ban on political parties imposed in July 1994 was lifted. Members of the ruling Military Council resigned from their military positions before joining the Alliance for Patriotic Reorientation and Construction (APRC).

National Anthem

'For the Gambia, our homeland'; words by V. J. Howe, tune traditional.

RECENT ELECTIONS

Presidential elections were held on 22 Sept. 2006. President Jammeh (Alliance for Patriotic Reorientation and Construction) was re-elected with 67·3% of the vote, against 26·7% for Ousainou Darboe (United Democratic Party) and 6·0% for Halifa Sallah (National Alliance for Democracy and Development). Turnout was 58·6%.

Parliamentary elections were held on 25 Jan. 2007. The Alliance for Patriotic Reorientation and Construction (APRC) won 42 seats, the United Democratic Party 4, the National Alliance for Democracy and Development 1, and ind. 1. Turn-out was 41·7%.

CURRENT ADMINISTRATION

President, and C.-in.-C. of the Armed Forces, Responsible for Agriculture, Mineral Resources, Oil, Religious Affairs, and Public Works and Infrastructure: Col. (retd) Yahya Jammeh; b. 1965 (APRC; seized power 22 July 1994; elected 26 Sept. 1996 and re-elected in 2001 and 2006).

In March 2010 the government comprised:

Vice-President and Secretary of State for Women's Affairs: Isatou Njie Saidy.

Secretary of State for Basic and Secondary Education: Fatou Faye. *Economic Planning and Industrial Development:* Yusupha Kah. *Energy:* Sirra Wally Ndow-Njie. *Finance and Economic Affairs:* Abdou Kolley. *Fisheries, Natural Resources and National Assembly Affairs:* Lamin Kaba Bajo. *Foreign Affairs and Gambians*

Abroad: Ousman Jammeh. *Forestry and Environment:* Jato Sillah. *Health and Social Welfare:* Dr Abubacarr Gaye. *Higher Education, Research, Science and Technology:* Dr Mamadou Tangara. *Information and Communication Infrastructure:* Alhaji Cham. *Interior:* Ousman Sonko. *Justice and Attorney General:* Marie Saine Firdaus. *Local Government and Lands:* Pierre Tamba. *Tourism and Culture:* Fatou Mass Jobe-Njie. *Trade and Employment:* Babucarr Jallow. *Youth and Sports:* Sheriff Gomez.

Office of the President: http://www.statehouse.gm

CURRENT LEADERS

Retd Col. Yahya Jammeh

Position
President

Introduction
Former army colonel Yahya Jammeh came to power in a military coup in July 1994. Leading the APRC, he was elected to office in 1996 and re-elected in 2001 and 2006.

Early Life
Yahya A. J. J. Jammeh was born in the Foni Kansala district of The Gambia on 25 May 1965, the year in which the country gained independence from the United Kingdom. He joined the army in 1984, rising to captain by 1992, and on 22 July 1994 led a successful coup against Sir Dawda Jawara, the president since 1970.

Career in Office
In 1996 a new constitution was approved by national referendum. Jammeh was confirmed as president in Sept. that year and his Alliance for Patriotic Reorientation and Construction (APRC) secured a majority of seats in parliamentary elections in Jan. 1997. He was re-elected president in Oct. 2001. The 2002 parliamentary elections, in which the APRC won nearly all the seats, were boycotted by the main opposition party.

Legislation passed in 2004 set jail terms for journalists guilty of libel while broadcast news has remained tightly controlled. In April 2006 the regime was threatened by a coup attempt, leading to numerous arrests and the disappearance of the former army chief of staff. Jammeh was re-elected again in Sept. 2006, defeating two opposition party candidates. The poll was considered free and fair on the day by observers, but the Commonwealth Secretariat noted 'abuses of incumbency' before the vote.

Acknowledged in The Gambia as a herbalist, Jammeh has claimed to have found a cure for HIV/AIDS, although his assertion has been dismissed by most medical opinion around the world.

In Dec. 2008 two British missionaries were sentenced to one year in prison for sedition after allegedly writing letters spreading disaffection against Jammeh and the Gambian government. Seven journalists were similarly charged with sedition in June 2009 after criticizing the president, in an apparent move to eradicate opposition.

DEFENCE

The Gambian National Army, 800 strong, has two infantry battalions, one engineer squadron and one company of presidential guards.

The marine unit of the Army consisted in 2007 of approximately 70 personnel operating four inshore patrol craft, based at Banjul.

Defence expenditure totalled US$2m. in 2006 (US$1 per capita), representing 0·3% of GDP.

INTERNATIONAL RELATIONS

The Gambia is a member of the UN, World Bank, IMF and several other UN specialized agencies, WTO, Commonwealth, IOM, Islamic Development Bank, OIC, African Development Bank, African Union, ECOWAS and is an ACP member state of the ACP-EU relationship.

ECONOMY

Agriculture accounted for 29% of GDP in 2007, industry 15% and services 56%.

Currency

The unit of currency is the *dalasi* (GMD), of 100 *butut*. Inflation was 5·4% in 2007 and 4·5% in 2008. Foreign exchange reserves were US$90m. in July 2005. Total money supply in June 2005 was 3,256m. dalasis.

Budget

In 2003 revenues were 1,776·3m. dalasis and expenditures 2,327·9m. dalasis. Tax revenue accounted for 77·2% of revenues in 2003; current expenditure accounted for 72·2% of expenditures.

Performance

Real GDP growth was 6·3% in 2007 and 6·1% in 2008. Total GDP was US$0·8bn. in 2008.

Banking and Finance

The Central Bank of The Gambia (founded 1971; *Governor*, Momodou Bamba Saho) is the bank of issue. There are six other banks: Standard Chartered, Trust Bank, Arab Gambian Islamic Bank, Continent Bank, First International and the International Bank for Commerce and Industry.

ENERGY AND NATURAL RESOURCES

Environment

Carbon dioxide emissions from the consumption and flaring of fossil fuels in 2008 were the equivalent of 0·2 tonnes per capita.

Electricity

Installed capacity was an estimated 29,000 kW in 2004. Production was approximately 151m. kWh in 2004; consumption per capita in 2004 was about 98 kWh.

Oil and Gas

President Jammeh announced in Feb. 2004 that large quantities of oil had been discovered in waters off The Gambia's coast.

Minerals

Heavy minerals, including ilmenite, zircon and rutile, have been discovered in Sanyang, Batokunku and Kartong areas.

Agriculture

About 68% of the population depend upon agriculture. There were 0·25m. ha. of arable land in 2001 and 5,000 ha. of permanent crops. Almost all commercial activity centres upon the marketing of groundnuts, which is the only export crop of financial significance. Cotton is also exported on a limited scale. Rice is of increasing importance for local consumption. Major products (2002, in 1,000 tonnes), are: millet, 85; groundnuts, 72; rice, 20; maize, 19; sorghum, 15; cassava, 8.

Livestock (2002): 327,000 cattle, 262,000 goats, 146,000 sheep and 1m. poultry.

Forestry

In 2005 forests covered 471,000 ha., or 41·7% of the land area. Timber production in 2007 was 778,000 cu. metres.

Fisheries

The total catch in 2004 was estimated at 31,423 tonnes, of which marine fish approximately 92% and freshwater fish 8%.

INDUSTRY

Labour

The labour force in 1996 totalled 579,000 (55% males). Around 78% of the economically active population are engaged in agriculture.

INTERNATIONAL TRADE

Foreign debt was US$672m. in 2005.

Imports and Exports

In 2006 imports (f.o.b.) were valued at US$221·8m. and exports (f.o.b.) at US$108·7m. Re-exports account for more than 70% of total exports. Chief imports in 2006 were: machinery and transport equipment, 25·2%; food and live animals, 22·8%; petroleum and petroleum products, 17·2%. In 2006 groundnuts accounted for 47·8% of domestic exports, fruit and vegetables 28·7% and machinery and transport equipment 9·6%. Main import sources, 2006: Denmark, 16·5%; USA, 12·0%; China, 9·3%; Côte d'Ivoire, 8·6%. Leading markets for domestic exports, 2006: UK, 48·7%; Senegal, 30·4%; France, 4·3%; Germany, 4·3%.

COMMUNICATIONS

Roads

There were some 3,742 km of roads in 2004, of which 19·3% were paved. Number of vehicles (2007): 8,800 passenger cars; 2,600 lorries and vans.

Civil Aviation

There is an international airport at Banjul (Yundum). The national carrier is Gambia International Airlines. Banjul handled 300,000 passengers in 2001 (all on international flights) and 2,700 tonnes of freight.

Shipping

The chief port is Banjul. Ocean-going vessels can travel up the Gambia River as far as Kuntaur. The merchant marine totalled 2,000 GRT in 2002.

Telecommunications

The Gambia had 291,500 telephone subscribers in 2005, or 192·1 per 1,000 population, of which 247,500 were mobile phone subscribers. There were 23,000 PCs in use in 2004 and 49,000 internet users.

Postal Services

There were 14 post offices in 2003; postal facilities are also afforded to all towns.

SOCIAL INSTITUTIONS

Justice

Justice is administered by a Supreme Court consisting of a chief justice and puisne judges. The High Court has unlimited original jurisdiction in civil and criminal matters. The Supreme Court is the highest court of appeal and succeeds the judicial committee of the Privy Council in London. There are Magistrates Courts in each of the divisions plus one in Banjul and two in nearby Kombo St Mary's Division—eight in all. There are resident magistrates in provincial areas. There are also Muslim courts, district tribunals dealing with cases concerned with customary law, and two juvenile courts.

The death penalty, last used in 1981, was abolished in 1993 but restored by decree in 1995. The population in penal institutions in Sept. 2002 was 450 (32 per 100,000 of national population).

Education

The adult literacy rate in 2001 was 37·8% (45·0% among males and 30·9% among females). In 2007 there were 218,341 pupils with 5,341 teaching staff at primary schools and 101,670 pupils with 4,475 teachers at secondary schools. Higher education institutes include The Gambia College, a technical training institute, a management development institute, a multi-media training institute and a hotel training school. In 2004 there were 1,530 students and 134 academic staff in tertiary education.

In 2004 public expenditure on education came to 2·1% of GNI.

Health

In 1994 there were two hospitals, one clinic, ten health centres and some 60 dispensaries. There were 43 physicians, 155 nurses, six pharmacists and 102 midwives in 1997.

RELIGION

More than 90% of the population is Muslim. Banjul is the seat of an Anglican and a Roman Catholic bishop. There is a Methodist mission. A few sections of the population retain their original animist beliefs.

CULTURE

World Heritage Sites

The Gambia has two sites on the UNESCO World Heritage List: James Island and Related Sites (inscribed on the list in 2003), containing important evidence of early Afro-European encounters and the slave trade.

The Gambia shares a UNESCO site with Senegal: the Stone Circles of Senegambia (added in 2006) is a collection of 93 stone circles, tumuli and burial mounds from between the 3rd century BC and the 16th century AD.

Broadcasting

Gambia Radio and Television Services (GRTS) is the government broadcasting agency. Gambia Television (colour by PAL) and Gambia Radio operate the state-run national services. Premium TV Network is an independent satellite TV channel and there are private radio stations. There were 20,400 television-equipped households in 2005.

Press

In 2006 there were two daily newspapers—the *Daily Observer* and the government-owned *Gambia Daily*.

Tourism

Tourism is The Gambia's biggest foreign exchange earner. In 2004 there were 90,095 non-resident charter tourists; spending by tourists totalled US$57m. in 2005.

DIPLOMATIC REPRESENTATIVES

Of The Gambia in the United Kingdom (57 Kensington Ct., London, W8 5DG)
High Commissioner: Elizabeth Ya Eli Harding.

Of the United Kingdom in The Gambia (48 Atlantic Rd, Fajara, Banjul)
High Commissioner: Phil Sinkinson.

Of The Gambia in USA (Suite 600, 1424 K St., NW, Washington, D.C., 20005)
Ambassador: Vacant.
Chargé d'Affaires a.i.: Musa Mboob.

Of the USA in The Gambia (Fajara (East), Kairaba Ave., Banjul)
Ambassador: Barry L. Wells.

Of The Gambia to the United Nations
Ambassador: Susan Waffa-Ogoo.

Of The Gambia to the European Union
Ambassador: Mamour A. Jagne.

FURTHER READING

Gailey, Harry A., *Historical Dictionary of the Gambia*. 1999
Hughes, A. and Perfect, D., *A Political History of The Gambia, 1816–1994*. 2006

National Statistical Office: The Gambia Bureau of Statistics, Kanifing Institutional Layout, Serekunda, P.O. Box 3504, Serekunda.
Website: http://www.gbos.gm

GEORGIA

Sakartvelos Respublika
(Republic of Georgia)

Capital: Tbilisi
Population estimate, 2010: 4·22m.
GDP per capita, 2007: (PPP$) 4,662
HDI/world rank: 0·778/89

KEY HISTORICAL EVENTS

By the 1st millennium BC the Diakhi (Taokhi) and the Qolha (Colchis) tribal groups had coalesced and developed bronze casting techniques. A two-state confederation emerged as early as the 6th century BC, with Colchis (Egrisi) in the west and Kartli (Iberia) in the east. The Greeks established Black Sea colonies from the 6th century BC, including Phasis (present-day Poti), Gyenos (Ochamchire) and Dioscuras (Sukhumi). Parnavaz I ruled a united Kartli (or Georgia) from his citadel of Armaztsikhe from *c.* 302–237 BC.

The Romans under Pompey attacked Kartli in 65 BC, defeating King Artag and establishing a client state. In the first half of the 2nd century AD Kartli grew under Parsman II. Rome, realizing its value as an ally against Parthia (Iran), recognized Kartli's extended borders. In 298 the Sassanid Iranians acknowledged Roman jurisdiction over Kartli-Iberia and recognized King Mirian III (284–361), who adopted Christianity as the state religion. Christianity brought close ties with Rome's successor, Byzantium, though Persia controlled Kartli for much of the 4th–6th centuries.

Tbilisi fell to an Arab army in 645 but Kartli retained considerable autonomy under local Arab rulers. In 813 the Armenian prince Ashot I of the Bagrationi family took control of Georgia, beginning nearly a millennium of Bagratid rule. Bagrat V (1027–72) united west and east and David IV ('the Builder', 1099–1125) presided over a golden age, repulsing the Seljuk Turks and disseminating Georgian influence in the Caucasus.

The Mongols invaded in 1236 and the Turkic conqueror Timur destroyed Tbilisi in 1386. Turkish dominance was sealed when the Byzantine Empire collapsed. By the 18th century the Bagratids had regained autonomy under nominal Persian rule. In 1762 Herekle II took control of the eastern regions of Kartli and Kakhetia, reducing the powers of the Georgian nobility. Herekle opened channels with Russia to gain protection from the Turks, though Russo-Turkish rivalry soon afflicted Georgia. After the Persians sacked Tbilisi in 1795 Herekle again sought Russian protection, leading to annexation.

In 1801 Tsar Alexander I abolished the kingdom of Kartli-Kakhetia (Eastern Georgia). Western Georgia (Imeretia) was annexed in 1804 and the Georgian Orthodox Church lost its autocephalous status in 1811. Russification intensified in the second half of the 19th century but a national liberation movement emerged in the 20th century, with Russia declaring martial law in 1905 following peasant revolts and general strikes. Revolutionaries split between the gradualist Mensheviks and the radical Bolsheviks (led by Ioseb Jugashvili, later Joseph Stalin).

The Caucasus became a major battleground in 1915 when Russia invaded Turkey. In May 1918 Georgia declared independence under the protection of Germany (to prevent invasion by the Turks). Lenin gave recognition in May 1920 and the Menshevik-dominated government redistributed swathes of aristocratic landholdings. In 1921 the Bolshevik Red Army invaded Georgia. From 1922–36 Georgia was part of the Transcaucasian Soviet Federated Socialist Republic within the USSR. In 1936 the republic was divided into Armenia, Azerbaijan and Georgia.

Over 500,000 Georgians served in the Red Army in the Second World War and the autonomy of the Georgian Orthodox Church was restored in 1943. Stalin oversaw forced urbanization and industrialization and although he and Lavrenti Beria (chief of secret police) were Georgians, Georgia suffered greatly under his regime. Nonetheless, criticism of Stalin in Georgia only gained momentum under Gorbachev's *glasnost* policy of the late 1980s. In 1972 Eduard Shevardnadze took control of the Georgian Communist Party. His purges of officials prompted dissident nationalists (led by the academic, Zviad Gamsakhurdia) to stress the threat of Russification. In 1978 leaders of the Abkhazian Autonomous Republic threatened to secede from Georgia. Shevardnadze took steps to diffuse the crisis, including an affirmative action programme for ethnic Abkhaz. When Shevardnadze became Soviet foreign minister in 1985, his successor Jumber Patiashvili removed some of the Shevardnadze appointees, forcing reformist leaders underground.

In April 1989 Soviet troops broke up peaceful demonstrations in Tbilisi and 20 Georgians, mostly women and children, were killed. Following the 'April Tragedy' Shevardnadze was sent to restore calm. Multiparty elections in Oct. 1990 saw Gamsakhurdia's Round Table/Free Georgia coalition win a solid majority. Supported by a referendum, parliament declared independence and declined to participate in the Commonwealth of Independent States.

In May 1991 Gamsakhurdia was elected president but the National Guard joined the opposition. When fighting in central Tbilisi in late Dec. forced Gamsakhurdia to flee to Chechnya, a military council took control and invited Shevardnadze to return in March 1992. Post-Soviet Georgia was dogged by separatism, especially in South Ossetia and Abkhazia. Relations with Russia were strained by its support for these insurgencies. In 1990 Gamsakhurdia had removed South Ossetia's autonomous status. When the South Ossetian regional legislature attempted to unite with Russian North Ossetia, Georgian forces invaded. Thousands died and tens of thousands were displaced before Yeltsin mediated a ceasefire in July 1992.

In Abkhazia the ethnic Abkhaz population feared cultural annihilation while the Georgian majority resented disproportionate allocation of political and administrative positions to the Abkhaz. In July 1992 the Abkhazian Supreme Soviet voted to separate from Georgia. In Aug. 1992 the National Guard seized the Abkhazian capital, Sukhumi. Hundreds died and refugees fled to Russia and other parts of Georgia. The Abkhazian government requested Russian intervention, retaking Sukhumi and forcing the Georgian army out in 1993. A ceasefire began in early 1994. When Gamsakhurdia invaded Mingrelia (his home region where he had retained support) Shevardnadze asked for Russian military assistance. Defeated, Gamsakhurdia committed suicide in Jan. 1994.

Opposition to Shevardnadze's increasingly corrupt rule grew in the late 1990s, despite advantageous relations with the West and a US$3bn. Baku-Tbilisi-Ceyhan oil pipeline deal. In Nov. 2003 Shevardnadze resigned after opposition forces stormed parliament amid allegations of electoral fraud. Following the 'Rose Revolution' Mikheil Saakashvili became president in Jan. 2004. Saakashvili's presidency has been dominated by diplomatic sparring with Russia over Russian interference in Abkhazia and South Ossetia. Relations reached a new low in the months following Saakashvili's re-election in Jan. 2008. In March Abkhazia's separatist government requested that the UN recognize the region's independence and in April 2008 Moscow announced closer ties with both regions. In Aug. Saakashvili sent troops into South Ossetia to attack separatist forces. Russia claimed its citizens were under attack and responded by sending in several thousand troops. A week of fierce fighting was brought to an end by a French-brokered peace deal, with Russia recognizing independence for both South Ossetia and Abkhazia. Moscow was subsequently accused of delaying its troop withdrawal. Adjara, another autonomous region, was brought under Tbilisi's control with the ejection of its populist leader, Aslan Abashidze, in 2004.

TERRITORY AND POPULATION

Georgia is bounded in the west by the Black Sea and south by Turkey, Armenia and Azerbaijan. Area, 69,700 sq. km (26,900 sq. miles). Its census population in 2002 was 4,371,535 (excluding Abkhazia and South Ossetia); density (excluding Abkhazia and South Ossetia), 76 per sq. km.

The UN gives an estimated population for 2010 of 4·22m.

In 2005, 52·5% of the population lived in urban areas. The capital is Tbilisi (2005 population estimate, 1·10m.). Other principal towns (with 2005 populations in brackets): Kutaisi (190,100), Batumi (122,100), Rustavi (118,200). After Russian-backed Abkhaz forces and their allies took Sukhumi in 1993, non-Abkhaz residents were ejected from the region. Sukhumi's population fell from 121,000 in 1991 to an estimated 45,000 in 2002.

Georgians accounted for 83·8% of the 2002 census population; others included 6·5% Azerbaijanis, 5·7% Armenians and 1·5% Russians. Georgia includes the Autonomous Republics of Abkhazia and Adjara and the former Autonomous Region of South Ossetia.

Georgian is the official language. Armenian, Russian and Azeri are also spoken.

SOCIAL STATISTICS

Births, 2005, 46,512; deaths, 42,984. Rates, 2005: birth, 10·7 per 1,000 population; death, 9·9 per 1,000. Annual population growth rate, 2000–05, –0·3%. Life expectancy, 2007, 68·1 years for males and 75·0 years for females. Infant mortality, 2005, 41 per 1,000 live births; fertility rate, 2004, 1·4 births per woman.

CLIMATE

The Georgian climate is extremely varied. The relatively small territory covers different climatic zones, ranging from humid sub-tropical zones to permanent snow and glaciers. In Tbilisi summer is hot: 25–35°C. Nov. sees the beginning of the Georgian winter and the temperature in Tbilisi can drop to –8°C; however, average temperature ranges from 2–6°C.

CONSTITUTION AND GOVERNMENT

A new constitution of 24 Aug. 1995 defines Georgia as a presidential republic with federal elements. The head of state is the *President*, elected by universal suffrage for not more than two five-year terms. The 150-member *Supreme Council* is elected for four-year terms, with 75 members elected in single-seat constituencies and 75 by proportional representation. There is a 5% threshold.

National Anthem

'Tavisupleba' ('Freedom'); words by Dawit Magradse, tune by Zakaria Paliashvili.

RECENT ELECTIONS

At the presidential election held on 5 Jan. 2008 Mikheil Saakashvili of the United National Movement was re-elected president with 53·5% of the vote. Levan Gachechiladze took 25·7% and Badri Patarkatsishvili 7·1%. Turnout was 56·2%.

At the parliamentary elections of 21 May 2008 the United National Movement won 119 of the 150 seats (with 59·2% of the vote). The Joint Opposition (a coalition of the National Council and New Rights) won 17 seats (17·7%), the Christian Democrats 6 (8·7%), the Labour Party 6 (7·4%) and the Party of Republicans 2 (3·8%). Turnout was 53·9%.

CURRENT ADMINISTRATION

President: Mikheil Saakashvili; b. 1967 (United National Movement; since 20 Jan. 2008, having previously been president from Jan. 2004 to Nov. 2007).

In March 2010 the government comprised:

Prime Minister: Nika Gilauri; b. 1975 (ind.; sworn in 6 Feb. 2009).

Vice Prime Minister and Minister of State for European and Euro-Atlantic Integration: Giorgi Baramidze.

Minister of State for Diaspora Issues: Iulon Gagoshidze. *Reintegration:* Temur Iakobashvili.

Minister of Agriculture: Bakur Kvezereli. *Corrections and Legal Assistance:* Khatuna Kalmakhelidze. *Culture and Sport:* Nikoloz Rurua. *Defence:* Bacho Akhalaia. *Economic Development:* Zurab Pololikashvili. *Education and Science:* Dimitri Shashkin. *Energy:* Alexander Khetaguri. *Environment and Natural Resources:* Giorgi Khachidze. *Finance:* Kakha Baindurashvili. *Foreign Affairs:* Grigol Vashadze. *Health, Labour and Social Affairs:* Sandro Kvitashvili. *Interior:* Vano Merabishvili. *Justice:* Zurab Adeishvili. *Refugees and Resettlement:* Koba Subeliani. *Regional Development and Infrastructure:* Davit Tkeshelashvili.

The *Speaker* is David Bakradze.

Georgian Parliament: http://www.parliament.ge

CURRENT LEADERS

Mikheil Saakashvili

Position

President

Introduction

Mikheil Saakashvili was first elected president on 4 Jan. 2004. A former protégé of President Eduard Shevardnadze, he led opposition to the rigged parliamentary elections of Nov. 2003 and forced the president to resign. Saakashvili's peaceful management of the 'rose revolution' earned him respect at home and abroad and even the support of the ousted Shevardnadze. However, more recently he has been undermined by increasing domestic opposition, in response to which he imposed a state of emergency in Nov. 2007. He nevertheless secured re-election as president in Jan. 2008 but with a much reduced majority. Relations with Russia, already fragile, were shattered in Aug. 2008 when Georgian military action against the separatist enclave of South Ossetia provoked a retaliatory invasion by Russian forces. Saakashvili is fluent in Georgian, Russian, English, French and Ukrainian.

Early Life

Mikheil (Mikhail in Russian) Saakashvili was born on 21 Dec. 1967 in Tbilisi. He received law degrees from Kyiv University, Ukraine in 1992 and Columbia University, New York in 1994 and completed a doctorate in juridical science at George Washington University, Washington, D.C. He pursued further studies in Florence and Strasbourg.

While working for a New York law firm, Saakashvili was approached by Zurab Zhvania, speaker of the Georgian parliament. The Georgian leader, Eduard Shevardnadze, was seeking potential parliamentary candidates, unconnected to the Soviet system. Saakashvili returned home and was elected to parliament in Dec. 1995. As a member of Shevardnadze's Citizens' Union and a trained jurist, his political career developed rapidly. He served as chairman of the parliamentary committee on electoral reform and contributed to the drafting of the 1995 constitution. He led the Citizens' Union in parliament from 1998–99 and was appointed vice-president of the Council of Europe's parliamentary assembly in Jan. 2000.

Appointed justice minister in Oct. 2000, Saakashvili attempted an overhaul of the judicial system, condemned by international observers as highly corrupt. He also tried to reform the prison system and proposed a bill on illegal property confiscation, which was blocked by Shevardnadze. His programme was cut short when he openly accused the ministers for economics and state security and Tbilisi's head of police of corruption and profiteering. Shevardnadze, then president, refused to act on these charges, forcing Saakashvili to resign in Sept. 2001.

Having left the government, he continued his anti-corruption programme by forming a party, the United National Movement, to represent Georgia's reformist elements. Coalition partners included the small ideological Republican Party and the Union of National Forces. Support was widened by alliances with Zurab Zhvania's United Democrats and the Burjanadze-Democrats, led by Nino Burjanadze, Zhvania's replacement as speaker. Saakashvili was elected chairman of the Tbilisi Assembly in June 2002.

Saakashvili campaigned for the Nov. 2003 parliamentary elections on an anti-Shevardnadze platform, drawing large crowds with his energetic rhetoric, especially in Adjara, in the southwest, and Kvemo Kartli, a province in the southeast with a large Azeri minority. Despite OSCE sponsorship, the elections on 2 Nov. were chaotic and heavily rigged by the ruling Citizens' Union. The delayed announcement of provisional results provoked accusations of electoral fraud. Burjanadze and Zhvania agreed to form a coalition with Saakashvili—the United Opposition Front—and massive demonstrations were organized night after night in Tbilisi. After the results were announced, putting Saakashvili's United National Movement in third place, a boycott of parliament was declared by the coalition. Shevardnadze refused to compromise and opened parliament on 22 Nov. Saakashvili responded by summoning his national supporters to Tbilisi and demanded the president's resignation. During Shevardnadze's opening address Saakashvili burst into the assembly, brandishing a rose, the symbol of the peaceful demonstrations. His supporters occupied the chancellery, causing the president to declare a state of emergency.

Bereft of support from abroad and in his own government, Shevardnadze finally resigned on 23 Nov. His avoidance of a military solution was praised internationally and by the opposition leaders. In the wake of his resignation, Saakashvili, Burjanadze and Zhvania agreed to present a united front in immediate presidential elections, the former gaining the support from the other two in exchange for senior government positions. On 4 Jan. 2004 Saakashvili won the presidential election with just over 96% of the votes. His electoral promises were broad and ambitious: the abolition of taxes on small businesses, doubling of pensions and public sector salaries and swift punishment for the worst abuses of the previous regime. His campaign was strengthened by the co-operation of Shevardnadze, who voted for his successor.

Career in Office

Saakashvili declared his priorities in office as maintaining the territorial integrity of Georgia and his anti-corruption programme. He consolidated his political position in March 2004 when the National Movement–Democrats bloc won the parliamentary elections with a substantial majority of seats. Tension increased with Adjara's president, Aslan Abashidze, who declared a state of emergency in his jurisdiction and rejected the new central government's authority. Saakashvili reasserted direct control over Adjara in May 2004 after popular demonstrations in Batumi forced Abashidze to step down. Elsewhere, Saakashvili proposed giving greater autonomy—but not full independence—to the separatist regions of South Ossetia and Abkhazia.

Despite friction with Russia over its links with these regions, its military bases in Georgia and the conflict in Chechnya (where Russia has accused Georgia of aiding Chechen fighters), Saakashvili initially sought to improve relations between the two countries. Nevertheless, bilateral tensions resurfaced in 2006 as energy supplies from Russia were disrupted in Jan., Russia suspended imports of Georgian wine and mineral water on health grounds in March–May, and Georgia briefly detained and then expelled four Russian army officers on spying charges in Sept.–Oct. (in retaliation for which Russia imposed a transport blockade and adopted punitive measures against ethnic Georgians living in Russia). In Dec. 2006 the Georgian government accepted a doubling of the price of Russian natural gas supplies, but accused its powerful neighbour of political blackmail.

Tension continued through 2007, as Georgia accused Russia of violations of its airspace in Aug. and of orchestrating mass opposition demonstrations in Tbilisi against Saakashvili's government which in Nov. led to a police crackdown and temporary state of emergency. The protests were sparked particularly by allegations of corruption and murder against Saakashvili made by a former defence minister in Sept. Despite his apparent unpopularity and opposition claims of fraud and vote rigging, Saakashvili was re-elected as president in polling in Jan. 2008, and in May the ruling United National Movement won a landslide victory in parliamentary elections.

Meanwhile, suspicious of Georgia's aspirations to join NATO, Russia stated in April 2008 that it would strengthen its links with South Ossetia and Abkhazia. This prompted the Georgian government to accuse Russia of planning military intervention and annexation of the regions. In Aug. continuing tensions escalated into outright military conflict between Georgia and Russia after Georgian troops had mounted an attack of separatist forces in South Ossetia. Russian forces occupied the enclaves and advanced deep into Georgian territory, destroying strategic targets, before agreeing a French-brokered ceasefire following diplomatic intervention by the European Union. Later in the month, Russia unilaterally recognized the independence of Abkhazia and South Ossetia, a move rejected by Saakashvili and the Western nations. In Sept. Russia announced that it would keep troops in Abkhazia and South Ossetia but completed the withdrawal from the rest of Georgia in Oct.

Also in Oct., Saakashvili's former ally, Nino Burjanadze, announced the creation of a new opposition group, claiming that the government was not capable of protecting the country and should face fresh elections. At the same time, Saakashvili dismissed Prime Minister Vladimir Gurgenidze and nominated Grigol Mgaloblishvili to succeed him, an appointment confirmed by parliament the following month. However, Mgaloblishvili stepped down in 2009 owing to ill health and was replaced by Nika Gilauri in Feb. Opposition agitation against the president and his powers has since continued and in May the authorities quelled a military mutiny.

DEFENCE

The total strength of the Armed Forces consisted of 21,150 personnel in 2007. The UN peacekeeping mission (United Nations Observer Mission in Georgia, or UNOMIG, which was established in Aug. 1993) ended in June 2009 owing to a lack of consensus among Security Council members on mandate extension. Following the collapse of the USSR in 1991 Russia maintained two bases in Georgia with some 4,000 personnel. The last Russian troops left Georgia in Nov. 2007. However, several thousand soldiers returned in Aug. 2008 when Moscow responded to Georgia's military attack on separatist forces in South Ossetia. Despite a subsequent withdrawal, some forces remain as part of a 'buffer zone' around South Ossetia and Abkhazia.

Defence expenditure in 2006 totalled US$339m. (US$73 per capita), representing 4·4% of GDP.

Army

The Army totalled 17,767 (3,767 conscripts) in 2007. In addition there were 1,578 active reservists in the National Guard and 6,300 Ministry of the Interior troops. A paramilitary border guard exists, estimated at 5,400.

Navy

Former Soviet facilities at Poti have been taken over. The headquarters are at Tbilisi. Personnel, 2007, 495.

Air Force

Personnel, 2007, 1,310 (290 conscripts). There were nine combat capable aircraft in 2007 (mainly Su-25 fighter-bombers) and nine attack helicopters.

INTERNATIONAL RELATIONS

Georgia is a member of the UN, World Bank, IMF and several other UN specialized agencies, WTO, Council of Europe, OSCE, BSEC, IOM, NATO Partnership for Peace and Asian Development Bank. Georgia hopes to become a member of NATO.

ECONOMY

Agriculture accounted for 12·8% of GDP in 2006, industry 24·9% and services 62·3%.

Overview

Georgia is a small lower-income transition economy. After independence in 1991, civil war and the loss of markets in the former Soviet Union led to economic collapse. Georgia suffered the worst declines experienced by any of the transition economies, with exports declining by 90% and output falling by 70%. Political tensions, declining living standards and low tax revenues undermined the funding of basic state functions. Progress towards macroeconomic stabilization was made in the late 1990s but was disrupted by internal fragmentation, drought and the 1998 financial crisis in Russia. IMF-supported programmes between 2001–04 aided growth recovery and price stability.

More recently, prudent macroeconomic policies and structural reforms, notably a privatization programme, have helped achieve strong growth and single-digit inflation. Anti-corruption initiatives and government efforts to create a more business-friendly environment saw the World Bank label the economy as the world's number one reformer in a 2006 'Doing Business' survey. Sanctions imposed by Russia, its major export market, have been offset by reform-led growth momentum but uncertainty remains over their future effects and Georgia's ability to generate greater foreign inflows.

Military conflict with Russia in Aug. 2008 damaged the economy. Real GDP fell sharply around the second quarter and inflation slowed post-conflict. Imports decreased by less than exports in Oct. 2008, resulting in a negative year-on-year trade balance, and the current account deficit hit an all-time high of US$900m. in mid-2008.

Currency

The unit of currency is the *lari* (GEL) of 100 *tetri*, which replaced coupons at 1 lari = 1m. coupons on 25 Sept. 1995. Inflation was 10·0% in 2008, having been 163% in 1995 and 15,606% in 1994. Gold reserves are negligible. Total money supply was 882m. laris in July 2005.

Budget

Revenues in 2005 totalled 3,257m. laris and expenditures 3,281m. laris. Tax revenue accounted for 74·0% of total revenues; social security and welfare accounted for 19·1% of total expenditures and defence 12·1%.

VAT is 18%.

Performance

Real GDP growth was 9·4% in 2006, 12·3 in 2007 and 2·1% in 2008. Georgia's economy continues to recover from the suffering it endured in the wake of the political and economic reforms that took place across central and eastern Europe in 1989. In both 1996 and 1997 growth had exceeded 10%, but prior to that the economy had suffered a sharp downturn, contracting by 45% in 1992, 29% in 1993 and 10% in 1994.

Total GDP was US$12·8bn. in 2008.

Banking and Finance

The *President* of the Central Bank is Giorgi Kadagidze. In 2005 there were 19 commercial banks. Two foreign banks had representative offices.

ENERGY AND NATURAL RESOURCES

Environment

Carbon dioxide emissions from the consumption and flaring of fossil fuels in Georgia were the equivalent of 1·2 tonnes per capita in 2008.

Electricity

The many fast-flowing rivers provide an important hydro-electric resource. Installed capacity was around 4·4m. kW in 2004. Production in 2004 was 6·92bn. kWh; consumption per capita in 2004 was 1,577 kWh.

Oil and Gas

Output (2004) of crude petroleum, 700,000 bbls. A 930 km long oil pipeline from an offshore Azerbaijani oilfield in the Caspian Sea across Azerbaijan and Georgia to a new oil terminal at Supsa, near Poti, on the Black Sea Coast started pumping oil in early 1999; the US$600m. pipeline allowed Georgia to create 25,000 new jobs. However, Georgia is still heavily dependent on Russia for natural gas. Accords for the construction of a second oil pipeline through Georgia were signed in Nov. 1999, to take oil from Azerbaijan to Turkey via Georgia. Work on the pipeline began in Sept. 2002 and it was officially opened in May 2005. Natural gas production was 12m. cu. metres in 2004.

A gas pipeline from Baku through Georgia to Erzurum in Turkey was commissioned in June 2006.

Minerals

Manganese deposits are calculated at 250m. tonnes. Other important minerals are barytes, clays, gold, diatomite shale, agate, marble, alabaster, iron and other ores, building stone, arsenic, molybdenum, tungsten and mercury.

Agriculture

Agriculture plays an important part in Georgia's economy, contributing 12·8% of GDP in 2006. In 2001 there were 795,000 ha. of arable land and 268,000 ha. of permanent crops. 469,000 ha. were irrigated in 2001.

Output of main agricultural products (in 1,000 tonnes) in 2003: maize, 450; potatoes, 425; wheat, 225; grapes, 200; tomatoes, 185; cabbage, 148; onions, 98; apples, 86; wine, 80; watermelons (including melons, pumpkins and squash), 60. Livestock, 2003:

cattle, 1,216,000; sheep, 611,000; pigs, 446,000; chickens, 10m. Livestock products, 2003 (in 1,000 tonnes): meat, 109; milk, 762; eggs, 24.

Forestry
There were 2·76m. ha. of forest in 2005, or 39·7% of the total land area. Timber production in 2007 was 616,000 cu. metres.

Fisheries
The catch in 2004 was 2,951 tonnes, down from 147,688 tonnes in 1989.

INDUSTRY

Industry accounted for 24·3% of GDP in 2002. There is a metallurgical plant and a motor works. There are factories for processing tea, creameries and breweries. There are also textile and silk industries.

Production (in 1,000 tonnes): cement (2003), 345; nitrogenous fertilizer (2003), 260; flour (2002), 78; ferroalloys (2003 estimate), 64; footwear (2001), 45,000 pairs; beer (2002), 27·0m. litres; spirits (2002), 2·1m. litres; cigarettes (2001), 1,615m. units.

Labour
The economically active workforce numbered 1,877,600 in 2001 (966,600 males), including: 989,600 in agriculture, hunting and forestry; 181,500 in wholesale and retail trade/repair of motor vehicles, motorcycles and personal and household goods; 138,700 in education; 105,600 in public administration and defence/compulsory social security; and 102,400 in manufacturing. The unemployment rate was 11·5% in 2003. Approximately 500,000 Georgians, or a tenth of the population, work in Russia, but in Dec. 2000 Russia began requiring Georgians to have a visa to visit the country.

INTERNATIONAL TRADE

Total foreign debt was US$1,911m. in 2005. The debt was mainly as a result of the importing of natural gas from Turkmenistan.

Imports and Exports
Imports and exports for calendar years in US$1m.:

	2000	*2001*	*2002*	*2003*	*2004*
Imports c.i.f.	650·7	678·7	793·3	1,140·9	1,847·0
Exports f.o.b.	329·9	320·0	346·3	465·3	648·8

Major commodities imported are machinery and transport equipment, food products and mineral fuels. Major commodities for export are iron and steel products, food and beverages, and machinery.

The leading import suppliers in 2004 were: Russia, 14·0%; Turkey, 10·9%; UK, 9·3%; Azerbaijan, 8·5%. Principal export markets in 2004 were: Turkey, 18·3%; Turkmenistan, 17·7%; Russia, 16·1%; Armenia, 8·4%.

COMMUNICATIONS

Roads
There were 20,329 km of roads in 2007 (94·1% hard-surfaced). Passenger cars in use in 2007 numbered 416,300, and there were also 51,500 lorries and vans and 42,800 buses and coaches. In 2007 there were 737 road deaths.

Rail
Total length in 2005 was 1,522 km of 1,520 mm gauge (1,481 km electrified). In 2005 railways carried 19m. tonnes of freight and 3·6m. passengers. There is a metro system in Tbilisi.

Civil Aviation
The main airport is at Tbilisi (Novo-Alexeyevka). The main Georgian carrier is Georgian Airways. In 2007 it had flights to Amsterdam, Athens, Dubai, Frankfurt, Kyiv, Minsk, Moscow, Paris, Tel Aviv and Vienna. In 2001 Tbilisi airport handled 250,000 passengers (all on international flights) and 4,300 tonnes of freight.

Shipping
In 2002 sea-going shipping totalled 569,000 GRT, of which oil tankers accounted for 41,000 GRT.

Telecommunications
There were 544,000 main line telephone subscribers in 2005, or 124·6 per 1,000 persons; mobile phone subscribers numbered 1,544,800. There were 192,000 PCs (42·5 per 1,000 inhabitants) in 2004 and 193,000 internet users in 2005.

Postal Services
There were 1,025 post offices in 2003.

SOCIAL INSTITUTIONS

Justice
The population in penal institutions in Jan. 2008 was 18,170 (415 per 100,000 of national population). The death penalty was abolished in 1997.

Education
In 2005 there were 1,214 public pre-primary schools with 6,883 teachers for 76,416 pupils. In 2005–06 there were 2,744 public and private schools with 74,300 teachers and 634,700 pupils (326,600 at primary level and 308,100 at secondary). In 2005–06 there were 171 higher education institutions with 144,300 students and 11,280 academic staff; the largest is Tbilisi State University with 35,000 students in 2005–06. Adult literacy rate in 2002 was over 99%.

Public spending on education in 2007 came to 2·6% of GNI and 7·8% of total government expenditure.

Health
Georgia had 18,200 hospital beds in 2003. In 2002 there were 20,225 physicians, 1,532 dentists, 19,298 nurses, 364 pharmacists and 1,500 midwives.

Welfare
In 2005 there were 549,900 age and 352,200 other pensioners.

RELIGION

The Georgian Orthodox Church has its own organization under Catholicos (patriarch) Ilia II who is resident in Tbilisi. In 2001 there were 1·8m. Georgian Orthodox, 550,000 Sunni Muslims, 280,000 Armenian Apostolic (Orthodox) and 130,000 Russian Orthodox.

CULTURE

World Heritage Sites
Georgia has three sites on the UNESCO World Heritage List: City-Museum Reserve of Mtskheta (inscribed on the list in 1994), churches of the former Georgian capital; Bagrati Cathedral and Gelati Monastery (1994); and Upper Svaneti (1996), a mountainous area of medieval villages.

Broadcasting
Georgian Public Broadcasting is the national public broadcaster, operating two television channels and two radio networks. Rustavi-2, Imedi TV and Mze TV are major independent television services; there are also a number of cable TV operators and private radio stations. Colour is by SECAM V. There were 2·04m. TV receivers in 2004.

Press
In 2006 there were ten dailies with a combined circulation of 24,000, as well as 81 non-dailies.

Tourism
Investment in tourism has increased substantially in recent years, and large numbers of hotels have been built. In 2005 there were 560,000 non-resident tourists, spending US$288m.

DIPLOMATIC REPRESENTATIVES

Of Georgia in the United Kingdom (4 Russell Gdns, London, W14 8EZ)
Ambassador: Giorgi Badridze.

Of the United Kingdom in Georgia (GMT Plaza, 4 Freedom Sq., 0105 Tbilisi)
Ambassador: Denis Keefe.

Of Georgia in the USA (2209 Massachusetts Ave., Washington, D.C., 20008)
Ambassador: Batu Kutelia.

Of the USA in Georgia (11 George Balanchine St., 0131 Tbilisi)
Ambassador: John Bass.

Of Georgia to the United Nations
Ambassador: Alexander Lomaia.

Of Georgia to the European Union
Ambassador: Salome Samadashvili.

FURTHER READING

Areshidze, Irakly, *Democracy and Autocracy in Eurasia: Georgia in Transition.* 2007
Brook, S., *Claws of the Crab: Georgia and Armenia in Crisis.* 1992
Coppieters, Bruno and Legvold, Robert, (eds.) *Statehood and Security: Georgia after the Rose Revolution.* 2005
Gachechiladze, R., *The New Georgia: Space, Society, Politics.* 1995
Mikaberidze, Alexander, *Historical Dictionary of Georgia.* 2007
Nasmyth, P., *Georgia: a Rebel in the Caucasus.* 1992
Nodia, Ghia and Scholtbach, Alvaro Pinto, *The Political Landscape of Georgia: Political Parties, Achievements, Challenges, and Prospects.* 2007
Pelkmans, Mathijs, *Defending the Border: Identity, Religion, and Modernity in the Republic of Georgia.* 2006
Suny, R. G., *The Making of the Georgian Nation.* 2nd ed. 1994
Wheatley, Jonathan, *Georgia from National Awakening to Rose Revolution: Delayed Transition in the Former Soviet Union.* 2005

State Department for Statistics Website: http://www.statistics.ge

Abkhazia

GENERAL DETAILS

Area, 8,600 sq. km (3,320 sq. miles); population (Jan. 2004 est.), 178,600. Capital, Sukhumi (2002 population, 45,000). This area, the ancient Colchis, saw the establishment of a West Georgian kingdom in the 4th century and a Russian protectorate in 1810. In March 1921 a congress of local Soviets proclaimed it a Soviet Republic, and its status as an Autonomous Republic, within Georgia, was confirmed on 17 April 1930 and again by the Georgian Constitution of 1995.

Around 300,000 ethnic Georgians were displaced as a result of the 1992–94 war and ethnic Abkhazians are now thought to constitute the majority population followed by Armenians and Russians with Georgians in the minority.

In July 1992 the Abkhazian parliament declared sovereignty under the presidency of Vladislav Ardzinba and the restoration of its 1925 constitution. Fighting broke out as Georgian forces moved into Abkhazia. On 3 Sept. and on 19 Nov. ceasefires were agreed, but fighting continued into 1993 and by Sept. Georgian forces were driven out. On 15 May 1994 Georgian and Abkhazian delegates under Russian auspices signed an agreement on a ceasefire and deployment of 2,500 Russian troops as a peacekeeping force. On 26 Nov. 1994 parliament adopted a new constitution proclaiming Abkhazian sovereignty. CIS economic sanctions were imposed in Jan. 1996. Parliamentary elections were held on 23 Nov. 1996. Neither the constitution nor the elections were recognized by the Georgian government or the international community. Fighting flared up between rival militia forces again in May 1998 after Abkhazian forces ejected thousands of ethnic Mingrelian and Georgian refugees who had returned to the southern Abkhazian region of Gali. After the fighting in 1998, the worst in five years, both sides declared a ceasefire. Up to 20,000 Georgians lost their homes. Abkhazia has expressed a desire to join the Russian Federation. In March 2008 Abkhazia appealed to the UN to have its independence recognized. Following fighting between Russian and Georgian forces in Aug. 2008, after Tbilisi sent troops into South Ossetia, Russia confirmed its recognition of Abkhazia as an independent state (as have Nicaragua and Venezuela in the meantime).

President: Sergei Bagapsh (elected on 3 Oct. 2004). In elections held on 12 Dec. 2009 incumbent Sergei Bagapsh was re-elected with 61·2% of the vote, against 15·3% for Raul Khadjimba. There were three other candidates. Turnout was 73·5%. The USA, the European Union and Georgia refused to recognize the election.

Prime Minister: Sergey Shamba (appointed on 13 Feb. 2010).

The unit of currency is the Russian *rouble* (RUB), of 100 *kopeks.* Imports, 2006: 3,270·2m. roubles; exports, 2006: 627·2m. roubles. Since 1997 the EU has provided over €20m. in funding for humanitarian projects. The European Commission provided €9·4m. for the restoration of the Inguri hydro power station, which was inaugurated in Oct. 2006 having fallen into severe disrepair in the early 1990s.

The republic has coal, electric power, building materials and light industries. Tourism is an important growth industry. In the first nine months of 2009, 88,865 tourists stayed in Abkhazian hotels and resorts (up from 68,905 for 2008 as a whole).

All agricultural land is owned by the state and private ownership is forbidden under still prevailing Soviet-era regulations. 90% of all households keep cattle. During the Soviet era Abkhazia provided 15–20% of tea for the USSR but since its collapse the industry has declined by around 80%. Tobacco production has also virtually ceased. Peak annual production levels were 120,000 tonnes of citrus fruits, 110,000 tonnes of tea and 14,000 of tonnes of tobacco. Current cash crops are citrus fruits and hazelnuts.

There is a university at Sukhumi.

FURTHER READING

Coppieters, Bruno, Darchiashvili, David and Akaba, Natella, *Federal Practice: Exploring Alternatives for Georgia and Abkhazia.* 2001

Adjara

Area, 2,900 sq. km (1,160 sq. miles); census population (2002): 376,016. Density, 129 per sq. km. Capital, Batumi (2002 population, 121,806, mostly Sunni Muslim). Adjara fell under Turkish rule in the 17th century, and was annexed to Russia (rejoining Georgia) after the Berlin Treaty of 1878. On 16 July 1921 the territory was constituted as an Autonomous Republic within the Georgian SSR, a status confirmed by the Georgian Constitution of 1995. In Jan. 2004 Adjaran leader Aslan Abashidze refused to acknowledge the central government of Mikheil Saakashvili and declared a state of emergency. Fearing a Georgian invasion, Abashidze destroyed road and rail links to the rest of Georgia but was forced to step down on 6 May after popular demonstrations in Batumi. Saakashvili imposed direct rule over Adjara. Elections were held on 20 June 2004. Saakashvili's Victorious Adjara group took 72·1% of the vote and 28 of the 30 seats in the *Supreme Council*, Adjara's parliament. Two seats went to the Republican

Party (13·5% of the vote). The last Russian troops left the military base in Batumi in Nov. 2007.

Ethnic groups at the 2002 census: Georgians, 93·4%; Russians, 2·4%; Armenians, 2·3%.

Chairman of the Supreme Council: Mikheil Makharadze.

Prime Minister: Levan Varshalomidze.

Adjara specializes in sub-tropical agricultural products. These include tea, citruses, bamboo, eucalyptus and tobacco. Livestock (Dec. 2003): 128,400 cattle, 1,900 pigs, 16,100 sheep and goats.

There is a port and a shipyard at Batumi, oil-refining, food-processing and canning factories, clothing, building materials and pharmaceutical factories. The reconstructed Batumi airport opened in May 2007 with flights to Turkey and Ukraine.

Approximately 166,300 persons were in paid employment in 2003; the unemployment rate was 12·1%.

South Ossetia

Area, 3,900 sq. km (1,505 sq. miles); population (Jan. 2004 est.), 49,200. Ethnic groups include Ossetians, Georgians, Russians and Armenians. The capital, Tskhinvali, had a population of approximately 30,000 before the 2008 conflict with Georgia. The UN High Commission for Refugees reported that some 30,000 people were displaced within South Ossetia as a result of the 2008 conflict.

This area was populated by Ossetians from across the Caucasus (North Ossetia), driven out by the Mongols in the 13th century. The region was set up within the Georgian SSR on 20 April 1922. Formerly an Autonomous Region, its administrative autonomy was abolished by the Georgian Supreme Soviet on 11 Dec. 1990, and it has been named the Tskhinvali Region.

Fighting broke out in 1990 between insurgents wishing to unite with North Ossetia and Georgian forces. By a Russo-Georgian agreement of July 1992 Russian peacekeeping forces moved into a seven-km buffer zone between South Ossetia and Georgia pending negotiations. An OSCE peacekeeping force has been deployed since 1992.

At elections not recognized by the Georgian government on 10 Nov. 1996, Lyudvig Chibirov was elected president. Though maintaining a commitment to independence, President Chibirov came to a political agreement with the Georgian government in 1996 that neither force nor sanctions should be applied. In July 2003 his successor, President Eduard Kokoyty, asked Vladimir Putin to let South Ossetia become a member of the Russian Federation. Georgian President Mikheil Saakashvili, who took office in Jan. 2004, has made clear his wish to revive the authority of the Georgian government in the regions. In Aug. 2008 he sent in troops against the region's separatist forces. Moscow responded by mobilizing troops, leading to a week of fierce fighting. Russia subsequently recognized South Ossetian independence, as have Nicaragua and Venezuela in the meantime.

President: Eduard Kokoyty (elected on 6 Dec. 2001).

Prime Minister: Vadim Brovtsev (in office since 5 Aug. 2009).

Parliamentary elections were held on 31 May 2009. The ruling Unity Party won 17 of 34 seats, the People's Party of South Ossetia 9 and the Communist Party of South Ossetia 8. Both NATO and the EU refused to recognize the elections, which were illegal under Georgian law.

Main industries are mining, timber, electrical engineering and building materials.

GERMANY

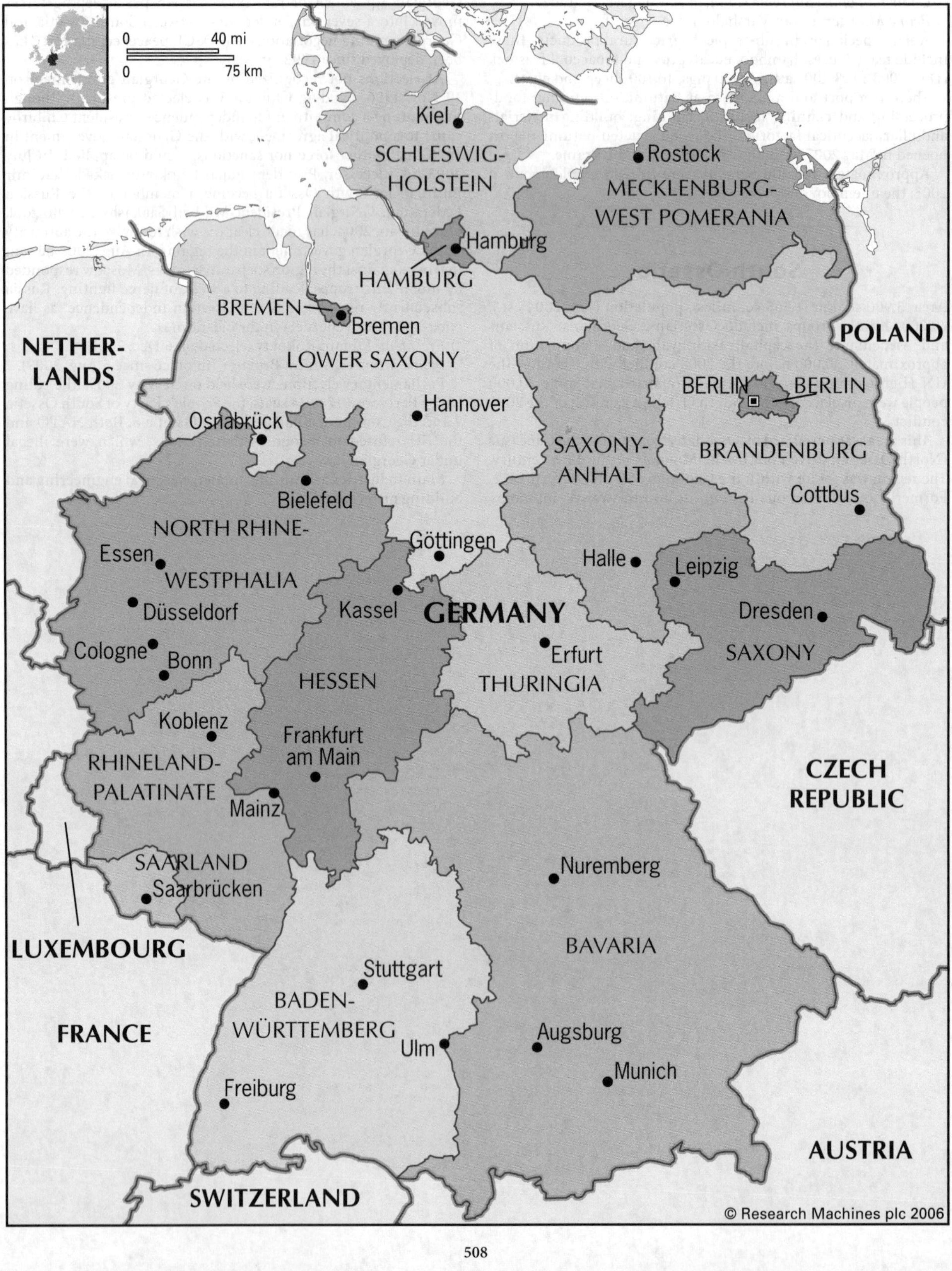

0
40 mi
0
75 km
Kiel
SCHLESWIG-
HOLSTEIN
Rostock
MECKLENBURG-
WEST POMERANIA
Hamburg
HAMBURG
BREMEN
Bremen
LOWER SAXONY
POLAND
NETHER-
LANDS
BERLIN
BERLIN
Hannover
Osnabrück
SAXONY-
ANHALT
BRANDENBURG
Bielefeld
Cottbus
NORTH RHINE-
WESTPHALIA
Essen
Göttingen
Halle
Leipzig
Düsseldorf
Kassel
GERMANY
Dresden
Cologne
Bonn
Erfurt
SAXONY
HESSEN
THURINGIA
Koblenz
Frankfurt
am Main
RHINELAND-
PALATINATE
Mainz
CZECH
REPUBLIC
SAARLAND
Saarbrücken
Nuremberg
LUXEMBOURG
BAVARIA
Stuttgart
BADEN-
WÜRTTEMBERG
FRANCE
Ulm
Augsburg
Munich
Freiburg
AUSTRIA
SWITZERLAND
© Research Machines plc 2006

Bundesrepublik Deutschland (Federal Republic of Germany)

Capital: Berlin
Seat of Government: Berlin/Bonn
Population estimate, 2010: 82·06m.
GDP per capita, 2007: (PPP$) 34,401
HDI/world rank: 0·947/22

KEY HISTORICAL EVENTS

From the 8th century BC the Celtic peoples inhabited a vast proportion of present-day Germany but by about 500 BC warlike Germanic tribes had pushed their way north and settled in the Celtic lands. The expanding Roman Empire established its boundaries along the Rhine and the Danube rivers but attempts to move further east had to be abandoned after the Roman provincial Governor Varius was defeated in AD 9 by the Germanic forces under Arminius. For the next thousand years the towns of Trier, Regensburg, Augsburg, Mainz and Cologne, founded by the Romans, formed the main centres of urban settlement. Christianity was introduced under Emperor Constantine and the first bishopric north of the Alps was established in Trier in AD 314.

At the start of the 5th century the Huns forced the indigenous Saxons north, towards Britain. However, the Franks, who came from the lowlands and were to become the founders of a civilized German state, gradually asserted themselves over all the other Germanic people. Towards the end of the 5th century a powerful Rhenish state was founded under King Clovis, a descendant of Merovech (Merovius), a Salian Frankish king. The powerful Merovingian dynasty eventually gave way to the Carolingians, whose authority was strengthened by papal support.

Charlemagne succeeded to the throne in 768, founding what was later known as the First Reich (Empire). The Franks continued to thrive until their influence stretched from Rome to the North Sea and from the Pyrenees to the River Elbe. The Pope crowned Charlemagne emperor on Christmas Day 800, creating what was to become known as the Holy Roman Empire. But the empire was too unwieldy to survive Charlemagne. On his death in 814 it began to break up. The Treaty of Verdun in 843 divided the French and German people for the first time, creating a Germanic Central Europe and a Latin Western Europe. The first king of the newly formed eastern kingdom was Ludwig the German and under him a specific German race and culture began to take shape. The last of Charlemagne's descendants died in 911 and with it the Carolingian dynasty. Power shifted, via Conrad I, duke of Franconia, to Henry I, duke of Saxony. Henry's son Otto the Great crushed the increasing power of the hereditary duchies and by making grants of land to the Church he strengthened ties with Rome. His coronation as emperor of the Romans in 962 was the first to associate German kingship with the office of the Holy Roman Emperor.

Over two centuries, powerful dynasties emerged to threaten the position of the emperor. After an intense feud the Hohenstaufens (of Swabia) gained supremacy over the Guelfs (the counts of Bavaria; later denoting anti-imperial loyalties and the papal faction) and managed to keep the upper hand for well over a century. Frederick Barbarossa, descended from both dynasties, led several expeditions to subjugate Italy and died on the Third Crusade. The Knights of the Teutonic Order set about converting Eastern Europe to Christianity and by the 14th century they had conquered much of the Baltic. By controlling the lucrative grain trade Germany grew rich.

Habsburg Rule

The Golden Bull of 1356 established the method for electing an emperor by setting up an Electoral College composed of seven princes or *electors*. Three of these were drawn from the church (the archbishops of Cologne, Mainz and Trier), and four from the nobility (the king of Bohemia, the duke of Saxony, the margrave of Brandenburg and the count palatine of the Rhine), all of whom had the right to build castles, mint their own coinage, impose taxes and act as judges. The title of Holy Roman Emperor nearly always went to an outsider and increasingly to members of the Austrian Habsburg dynasty. In 1273 Count Rudolph IV was the first Habsburg to be crowned king of the Germans. The Great Schism of 1378–1417, which resulted in rival popes holding court in Rome and Avignon, effectively ended the church's residual power over German affairs.

The Hundred Years War between France and England benefited the growing number of Free Imperial Cities along the German trading routes. Merchants and craftsmen organized themselves into guilds, wresting control of civic life away from the nobility and laying the foundations for a capitalist economy. Founded as a defence and trading league at Lübeck, the Hanseatic League combated piracy and established Germanic economic and political domination of the Baltic and North Sea. German communities were founded in Scandinavia and along the opposite coast as far as Estonia.

In the 14th century the bubonic plague wiped out a quarter of the German population. Rather than put the onus on their own tradesmen returning from Asia, it was the Jews, living in tightly-knit segregated communities, who were blamed. Excluded from guilds and trades they took to money lending, an occupation forbidden to Christians, and one which engendered envy and suspicion.

In 1273 Count Rudolph IV was the first Habsburg to be crowned king of the Germans. Over two centuries the Habsburg dynasty became increasingly powerful, retaining the title of Holy Roman Emperor from 1432 until its abolition nearly four centuries later. Succeeding to the title in 1493 Maximilian I gained the Netherlands by his marriage to Mary of Burgundy and control of Hungary and Bohemia by other marital alliances. Spain was added to the Habsburg dominions by the marriage of Maximilian's son, Philip, to Juana the Mad.

Reformation

In the early part of the 15th century the unpopularity of the church was linked to corruption coupled with a growing trade in the sale of indulgences. Huge land taxes were levied to pay for St Peter's Church and other sacred buildings in Rome. In 1517 an Augustinian monk named Martin Luther, professor of theology at the University of Wittenberg, made his famous protest with 95 Theses or arguments against indulgences nailed to the door of the Schlosskirche in Wittenberg. This was seen as an open attack on the Church of Rome and marked the beginning of the Reformation. Luther challenged the power of the pope, the privileged position of the priests and the doctrine of transubstantiation that had always been at the heart of Catholic dogma. But for the death of Maximilian I in 1519 and the subsequent power struggle for the title of Holy Roman Emperor, Luther might well have been executed as a heretic.

Following Maximilian's death, Francis I of France staked a claim to the succession in an attempt to avoid the concentration of power that would result in the election of the Habsburg candidate, Charles I of Spain. To placate the electors of Germany, the pope named Luther's patron, Frederick the Wise of Saxony, as a compromise candidate. This gained Luther only a temporary reprieve as, after much intrigue, the king of Spain was elected. Although Luther was excommunicated in 1520, he had the right to a hearing before an Imperial Diet (court). This was convened at Worms and although he was branded an outlaw and his books were ordered to be burned, he was given safe haven in Wartburg Castle where he translated the Bible into German, with the help of Philipp Melanchthon. Thanks to the revolutionary system of printing invented by Johannes Gutenberg, Luther's ideas spread quickly throughout Germany. His doctrine of 'justification by faith alone', with its apparent invitation to resist the authority of the church, was one of the main causes of the Peasants' War of 1524–25 that led to wholesale destruction of monasteries and castles. To the surprise of the rebels, Luther aligned himself with the authorities and so the uprising was brutally crushed. The Reformation thus gained political authority. By 1555 so many of the small independent German states had joined what was now known as the Protestant cause that Charles V admitted defeat and abdicated, retiring to a monastery in Spain. His brother Ferdinand succeeded him and signed the Peace of Augsburg. This agreement gave the secular rulers of each state the right to decide on their own religious practices (*cuius regio, eius religio*), so dividing Germany between Catholics and Lutherans.

Thirty Years War

Martin Luther died in 1546. The Catholics then launched a Counter-Reformation following the church reforms agreed at the Council of Trent. Bavaria's annexation of the mostly Protestant free city of Donauwörth in 1608 led to the formation of the Protestant Union, an armed alliance under the leadership of the Palatinate. The Catholic League, set up by the Bavarians the following year, created a sharp division in Germany. Rudolf II, who reigned as emperor for 36 years, chose Prague as his power base, thus weakening his authority over his more distant territories. After he was deposed in 1611 a series of dynastic and religious conflicts set in train what came to be known as the Thirty Years' War. Germany was devastated; the countryside was laid waste, towns were pillaged and mass slaughter reduced the population by as much as a third. Although the Catholics were the early victors, Denmark and Sweden as well as Catholic France (who preferred the Protestants to the Habsburgs) backed the Protestants while Spain supported the Catholics. After repeated attempts to end the war, the Peace of Westphalia (signed in 1648) brought peace but deprived the emperor of much of his authority. Power was divided between 300 principalities, and over 1,000 other territories.

During the 17th and 18th centuries the German princes consolidated their power, building vast palaces to bolster their claim to divine right. The Hanoverian branch of the Welf family inherited the British Crown in 1714; a royal union that was to last until 1837.

Meanwhile, the Habsburgs were struggling to hold on to the title of Holy Roman Emperor. The Turks reached Vienna in 1683 but after they were repulsed, the Austrians pushed eastwards and began to build up an empire in the Balkans. This left their western borders vulnerable where the French, who had long regarded the Rhine as the natural limit of their territory to their east, annexed Alsace and Strasbourg in 1688 and 1697. To the north, the presence of Brandenburg-Prussia under the Hohenzollern family was beginning to be felt. Throughout the 18th century Prussia was built up into a powerful independent state with its capital in Berlin. Strong militarism and a strict class-dominated society helped Prussia to become a major European power. When Frederick the Great came to the throne in 1740, he softened his country's military image by introducing reforms and by creating a cultured life at his court. His main preoccupation, however, continued to be expansion by force. His annexation of Silesia (under an old Brandenburg claim) provoked the Habsburgs to retaliate and, backed by Russia and France, they launched the Seven Years' War. Frederick had only the tacit support of Hanover and Britain to fall back on and, within three years, the Prussian armies were seriously overextended. But Frederick engineered a dramatic change in his fortunes by swelling the ranks of his armies with fresh recruits and in 1772, helped by the collapse of the alliance between Austria and Russia, he annexed most of Poland, achieving his goal of establishing his version of Austria in north Germany.

Unification

Revolutionary France had expanded east and when the left bank of the Rhine fell under French control during the War of the First Coalition of 1792–97 the way was paved for the unification of Germany. After Napoleon Bonaparte defeated Austria in 1802 he redrew the map of Germany. All but a few of the free German cities and all the ecclesiastical territories were stripped of their independence. In their place he created a series of buffer states. Bavaria, Württemberg and Saxony were raised to the status of kingdoms, with Baden and Hesse-Darmstadt as duchies. In 1806 the Holy Roman Empire was officially abolished. The Habsburgs promoted themselves from archdukes to emperors of Austria and set about consolidating their position in the Balkans. After the defeat of Prussia and the occupation of Berlin by Napoleon, the country was forced to sign away half its territory. In the aftermath, Prussia abolished serfdom and allowed the cities to develop their own municipal governments. Prussia played a critical role in the defeat of Napoleon at Waterloo in 1815. The Congress of Vienna, which met to determine the structure of post-Napoleon Europe, established Prussian dominance in German affairs. Westphalia and the Rhineland were added to its territories and although there were still 39 independent states, much of Napoleon's original vision for the reorganization of the Holy Roman Empire was ratified. A German Confederation was established, each state was represented in the Frankfurt-based Diet and Austria held the permanent right to the presidency with Prussia holding the vice-presidency.

The dominant political forces in Germany after the Congress of Vienna were still extremely conservative, but the rapid advance of the industrial revolution brought about the emergence of a new social order, with wage-earning workers and a growing bourgeoisie. The workers were quick to agitate for better working conditions and the middle classes for political representation. Adding to the social unrest was the peasant class, whose poor living standards were made worse by the failed harvests of the late 1840s. By 1848 violence had erupted all over Europe, forcing the Prussian king to allow elections to the National Assembly in Frankfurt. Although this presented an opportunity for the electorate to introduce widespread liberal social reforms, the middle class members of the Assembly blocked all radical measures. When armed rebellions broke out in 1849, the National Assembly was disbanded and the Prussian army, backed by other German kingdoms and principalities, seized power. From the 1850s, Prussia was in an unassailable position. Realizing the importance of industrial might, Prussia became the driving force for creating a single German market.

Bismarck

In 1862 Wilhelm I appointed Otto von Bismarck as chancellor. Although a leading member of the Junker class, he set about introducing widespread reforms. In order to unite the liberal and conservative wings, he backed the demands for universal male suffrage and, in return for the Chancellor's support for a united Germany, the liberals supported his plans for modernizing the army. Bismarck persuaded Austria to back him in a war against Denmark, which resulted in the recapture of Schleswig and Holstein, and in a subsequent row with Austria over the spoils (the Seven Years' War) Austria was crushed by the superior strength of Prussian arms and military organization. Austria was forced out of German affairs and the previously neutral Hanover and Hesse-Kassel joined the other small German states under Prussia to form a North German Confederation. Bismarck still needed to bring the southern German states into the fold and, in 1870, he rallied all the German states to provoke a war with France. The outcome of the Franco-Prussian War of 1870–71 was the defeat of France and the creation of a united Germany (including the long disputed provinces of Alsace and Lorraine). Wilhelm I of Prussia was named kaiser and the empire was dubbed the Second Reich, commemorating the revival of German imperial tradition after a hiatus of 65 years.

At home, Bismarck continued with his liberal reforms. Uniform systems of law, currency, banking and administration were introduced nationwide, restrictions on trade and labour movements were lifted and the cities were given civic autonomy. These measures were designed to contain the liberals while he set about trying to undermine the influence of the Catholic Church. Although he forced the Catholics to support his agricultural policies designed to protect the interests of the Junker landowners, he had to back down on other issues. Despite the introduction of welfare benefits, opposition to Bismarck grew with the formation of the Social Democratic Party (SPD) in 1870.

Meanwhile, Bismarck was competing with Britain and France in the acquisition of colonies in Africa and the Pacific. In Germany he managed a political balancing act, on one hand creating an alliance of the three great imperial powers of Germany, Russia and Austria and on the other a Mediterranean alliance with Britain to prevent Russia from expanding into the Balkans. When Wilhelm I died in 1888, he was succeeded by his son, Friedrich III, who died after only a few months, and then by his grandson Kaiser Wilhelm II, a firm believer in the divine right of kings. After dismissing Bismarck from office in 1890, he appointed a series of 'yes men' to run his government, thereby seriously undermining the strength and stability that had been built up under Bismarck in the previous decade. Britain had long been an ally of Germany, bound by the ties of dynasty and common distrust of France but after the Kaiser came out in open support of the South African Boers, with whom Britain was in conflict, relations between the two countries plummeted, and the European arms race accelerated. Bismarck's juggling of alliances collapsed and Europe was divided into two hostile camps. On one side, Germany was allied once more with Austria (who needed help in propping up her collapsing Eastern Empire) and with Italy. On the other, France and Russia, united in common mistrust of the German-speaking nations, drew Britain closer to them. The European war that was brewing was set in motion in 1914 when a Bosnian nationalist assassinated the Austrian Archduke Franz Ferdinand at Sarajevo. Austria sent a threatening memo falsely accusing Serbia of causing the assassination. This led Russia to mobilize in defence of her Slavic neighbours. Seeing this as an excuse to strike first, Germany attacked France. Belgium's neutrality (which had been guaranteed by Britain) was violated when the German armies marched through on their way to France and Britain declared war on Germany in 1914.

First World War

The German generals miscalculated the strength of the resistance from France and Russia. They had counted on a capitulation within a short time and when this did not happen, they found they were fighting a war on two fronts. A new form of warfare emerged with the digging of trenches all along Northern France and Belgium. The injury and loss of life suffered by both sides during the next four years was to damage an entire generation of young men all over Europe. In 1917 the United States entered the war and although the Bolshevik revolution in Russia that same year gained Germany a reprieve, allowing the transfer of vast numbers of troops from the eastern to western fronts, the respite was short-lived. Troops returning from Russia agitated against the war. At the same time, the German lines were weakened by over-extension. On 8 Aug. 1918 the German defences were finally broken and the armies routed. In 1916 the Kaiser had handed over military and political power to Generals Paul von Hindenburg and Erich Ludendorff. As the threat of defeat came closer and in an attempt to minimize the potential damage of a harsh peace treaty, Ludendorff decided to leave the peace negotiations to a parliamentary delegation. He felt they would be more likely to gain lenient terms and this might serve to nip a possible Bolshevik-style revolution in the bud. Two months of frenzied political activity followed which resulted in the abdication of the Kaiser and the announcement of a new German republic. The First World War ended on 11 Nov. 1918.

The Elections that followed confirmed the Social Democratic Party as the new political force in Germany. Friedrich Ebert, leader of the SPD, was made president, with Philip Scheidmann as chancellor. In 1919 a new constitution was drawn up at Weimar and a republican government under Chancellor Ebert attempted to restore political and economic stability. But the Treaty of Versailles had exacted painful losses. The rich industrial regions of Saarland and Alsace-Lorraine were ceded to France and Upper Silesia was given to a resurrected Poland. A Polish corridor to the sea effectively cut off East Prussia from the rest of the country and all Germany's overseas colonies were confiscated. The Rhineland was declared a demilitarized zone and the size of the armed forces was severely limited. The German economy was burdened with a heavy reparation bill.

Feeling betrayed by what they saw as a harsh settlement, the German military fostered the 'stab in the back' excuse for failure, which was readily accepted by a disillusioned public. Scheidmann was forced to resign and in the elections of 1920 the SPD withdrew altogether, leaving power in the hands of minorities drawn from the liberal and moderate conservative parties. The reparation payments were having such an effect on the economy that payments were withheld, giving France the excuse to occupy the industrial region of the Ruhr in 1923. Passive resistance by the German workers meant that production ground to a halt and galloping inflation quickly ruined the middle class as the currency became worthless. Although the Weimar Republic seemed bound to fail, a new chancellor, Gustav Stresemann, realised the danger of economic collapse and ended the passive resistance to the allies in the Ruhr. He also negotiated enormous loans from the United States to help rebuild Germany's economy.

Rise of Hitler

By Oct. 1924 the currency was re-established at more or less its former value and (very nearly) full employment and general prosperity followed. Scheidmann went on to serve as foreign secretary when he re-established Germany as a world power. Reparation payments were scaled down and more US aid was negotiated. Even though in 1925 the ailing and aged Hindenburg was elected president, the German Republic seemed secure.

The National Socialist German Workers' Party was founded in 1918. Its first leader, a locksmith named Anton Drexler, was soon ousted by Adolf Hitler, a former soldier from Austria whose fanaticism had been fed by defeat in 1918. The party attracted political extremists and misfits, whose views mixed the extremes of right and left wing opinion. The party's constitution was based on a combination of Communism and Italian fascism.

After forming its own army, the Brown Shirts or Storm Troopers (SA), Hitler led a failed *Putsch* in Bavaria in 1923. He was arrested and convicted of high treason. He served only nine months of his sentence and emerged having used his time in prison to write his political manifesto, *Mein Kampf*. Initially, sales of *Mein Kampf* were negligible and Hitler's views were treated as something of a joke. Only the power of his personality, and Joseph Goebbels' propaganda skills, sustained the National Socialists on the German political scene.

The recession of the late 1920s proved fertile ground for Hitler's ideas, which began to appeal to wounded national pride and seemed to offer an attractive solution to the growing economic crisis. Elections were held in 1930 and the Nazi party gained an astonishing 6·4m. votes, becoming the country's second largest party.

The young, the unemployed and the impoverished middle classes were Hitler's main supporters but it was the decision of the right wing traditionalists to back Hitler in order to gain control over his supporters that gave him respectability. Financial support from leading industrialists and giant corporations followed, enabling the Nazi party to fight a strong campaign in the 1932 presidential elections. Hindenburg, backed by the SPD and other democratic parties, scraped a victory. Appointed chancellor, Heinrich

Brüning introduced a series of economic reforms, negotiated the end of reparation payments and regained Germany's right to arms equality. But his attempt to introduce land reform lost him the support of the landowners, who undermined his efforts to make the Republic work. Two short-term chancellors followed—Franz von Papen and Gen. Kurt von Schleicher. In 1932 one inconclusive election followed another. Hitler, greatly helped by a campaign of terror by his storm troopers, won increased support. Von Papen, who plotted to persuade Hindenburg to declare Hitler chancellor, mistakenly believed that his party's majority in the Reichstag would enable him to retain control. Hitler was sworn in as chancellor on 30 Jan. 1933.

No sooner had Hitler assumed power than he set about destroying all opposition, stepping up the campaign of terror, which was now backed by the apparatus of the state. He was greatly helped by Hermann Göring who, as Prussian minister of the interior, had control of the police. A month later, the Reichstag was burned down and Hindenburg was obliged to declare a state of emergency, giving Hitler the excuse to silence his opponents legally. Hitler was now the country's dictator, declaring himself president of the Third Reich in 1934.

Race to War

Hitler's policies embraced a theory of Aryan racial supremacy by which, during the following decade, millions of Jews, gypsies, and other non-Aryan 'undesirables' were persecuted, used as slave labour, shipped off to concentration camps, murdered and their assets confiscated. Hitler's expansionism led to his annexation of Austria (the *Anschluss*) and German-speaking Czechoslovakia (the Sudetenland) in 1938. The following year he declared all of Bohemia-Moravia a German protectorate and invaded Poland, attempting to restore the authority exercised there by Prussia before 1918. After the invasion of Czechoslovakia, Britain and France signed an agreement with Germany sacrificing Czech national integrity in return for what they believed would be world peace. Interpreting this as a sign of weakness, Hitler ordered the invasion of Poland, signed a non-aggression pact with Russia and expected a similar collapse of resistance on the part of other western powers. However, by now Britain and France had realized that the Munich agreement was a humiliating sham and that Hitler's invasion of Poland on 1 Sept. 1939 meant that he would pursue his policy of *Lebensraum* ('living space'). Two days after German tanks rolled into Poland, Britain and France declared war on Germany and the Second World War began.

Germany was well prepared for conflict and to begin with the war went well for Hitler. The fall of Poland was quickly followed by the defeat of the Low Countries and in 1940 France was forced to sign an armistice with Germany and to set up a puppet government in Vichy. Hitler bombarded Britain from the air but held back from invasion. Instead, he turned to the east, subduing the Balkans and, in 1941, planned an invasion of the Soviet Union. In Dec. 1941, after Hitler's Japanese allies attacked the United States naval base at Pearl Harbor, America declared war on the Axis powers. By this time, Germany was hopelessly overextended. Defeat in North Africa, in May 1943, was followed by the halt of the German advance on Russia. The Allies invaded France in June 1944, liberating Paris in Aug. while Russian troops advanced from the east. Hitler was faced with certain defeat but refused to surrender, ordering the German people to defend every square inch of German territory to the death. On 30 April 1945, as Soviet forces marched into Berlin, Hitler committed suicide in his bunker. Germany surrendered unconditionally on 7 May 1945, bringing the Third Reich to an end.

Post-War Period

The Allied forces occupied Germany—the UK, the USA and France holding the west and the USSR the east. By the Berlin Declaration of 5 June 1945 each was allocated a zone of occupation. The zone commanders-in-chief together made up the Allied Control Council in Berlin. The area of Greater Berlin was also divided into four sectors.

At the Potsdam Conference of 1945 northern East Prussia was transferred to the USSR. It was also agreed that, pending a final peace settlement, Poland should administer the areas east of the rivers Oder and Neisse, with the frontier fixed on the Oder and Western Neisse down to the Czechoslovak frontier.

By 1948 it had become clear that there would be no agreement between the occupying powers as to the future of Germany. Accordingly, the western allies united their zones into one unit in March 1948. In protest, the USSR withdrew from the Allied Control Council, blockaded Berlin until May 1949, and consolidated control of eastern Germany, establishing the German Democratic Republic (GDR).

A People's Council appointed in 1948 drew up a constitution for the GDR that came into force in Oct. 1949, providing for a communist state of five Länder with a centrally planned economy. In 1952 the government marked the division between its own territory and that of the Federal Republic (West Germany), with a three-mile cordon fenced along the frontier. Berlin was closed as a migration route by the construction of a concrete boundary wall in 1961. In 1953 there were popular revolts against food shortages and the pressure to collectivize. In 1954 the government eased economic restraints, the USSR ceased to collect reparation payments, and sovereignty was granted. The GDR signed the Warsaw Pact in 1955. Socialist policies were stepped up in 1958, leading to flight to the West of skilled workers.

Meanwhile, a constituent assembly met in Bonn in Sept. 1948 and drafted a Basic Law, which came into force in May 1949. In Sept. 1949 the occupation forces limited their own powers and the Federal Republic of Germany came into existence. The occupation forces retained some powers, however, and the Republic did not become a sovereign state until 1955 when the Occupation Statute was revoked.

The Republic consisted of the states of Schleswig-Holstein, Hamburg, Lower Saxony, Bremen, North Rhine-Westphalia, Hessen, Rhineland-Palatinate, Baden-Württemberg, Bavaria and Saarland, together with West Berlin.

The first chancellor, Konrad Adenauer (1949–63), was committed to the ultimate reunification of Germany and refused to acknowledge the German Democratic Republic. It was not until 1972 that the two German states signed an agreement of mutual recognition and intent to co-operate, forged by West German Chancellor Willy Brandt.

The most marked feature of post-war West Germany was rapid population and economic growth. Immigration from the German Democratic Republic, about 3m. since 1945, stopped when the Berlin Wall was built in 1961; however, there was a strong movement of German-speaking people from German settlements in countries of the Soviet bloc. Industrial growth also attracted labour from Turkey, Yugoslavia, Italy and Spain.

Reunification

The Paris Treaty, which came into force in 1955, ensured the Republic's contribution to NATO and NATO forces were stationed along the Rhine in large numbers, with consequent dispute about the deployment of nuclear missiles on German soil. Even before sovereignty, the Republic had begun negotiations for a measure of European unity, and joined in creating the European Coal and Steel Community in 1951 and the European Economic Community in 1957. In Jan. 1957 the Saarland was returned to full German control. In 1973 the Federal Republic entered the UN.

In the autumn of 1989 movements for political liberalization in the GDR and reunification with Federal Germany gathered strength. Erich Honecker and other long-serving Communist leaders were dismissed in Oct.–Nov. The Berlin Wall was breached on 9 Nov. Following the reforms in the GDR in Nov. 1989 the Federal Chancellor Helmut Kohl issued a plan for German confederation. The ambassadors of the four wartime allies met in Berlin in Dec. After talks with Chancellor Kohl on 11 Feb. 1990, President Gorbachev said the USSR would raise no objection to German reunification. The Allies agreed a formula for reunification talks to begin after the GDR elections on 18 March. On 18 May Federal Germany and the GDR signed a treaty extending Federal Germany's currency, together with its economic, monetary and social legislation, to the GDR as of 1 July. On 23 Aug. the *Volkskammer* (the parliament of the GDR) by 294 votes to 62 'declared its accession to the jurisdiction of the Federal Republic as from 3 Oct. according to article 23 of the Basic Law', which provided for the Länder of pre-war Germany to accede to the Federal Republic. On 12 Sept. the Treaty on the Final Settlement with Respect to Germany was signed by the Federal Republic of Germany, the GDR and the four wartime allies: France, the USSR, the UK and the USA.

The single most important event in German post-war history took place on 3 Oct. 1990 with the reunification of the Federal Republic and the former GDR. That it happened at all was remarkable enough but that it was achieved without major social and political disruption was a huge tribute to the strength of a still young democracy. That is not to say that reunification has been trouble free. Notwithstanding the injection of billions of deutschemarks of public subsidy which transformed the infrastructure and restored urban areas, the easterners found the transition from communism to capitalism more painful than they had anticipated. Part of the problem was the adoption of the Deutsche Mark which, by virtue of its strength as an international currency, inspired confidence but at the same time made it harder for export markets in central and eastern Europe to afford to buy German. The collapse of much traditional industry in the east was hastened by wage equalization deals, pushing up labour costs. As a result, unemployment rose before being brought under relative control in the late 2000s.

The Federal Assembly (*Bundestag*) moved from Bonn to the renovated *Reichstag* in Berlin in 1999. As a psychological factor, the government move to Berlin was calculated to do much to bring eastern Germany back into the centre of national life as an equal part of the country. Gerhard Schröder served as chancellor from 1998 until 2005, when he was replaced by Angela Merkel of the Christian Democratic Union. She headed a 'grand coalition' of the Christian Democratic Union and the Social Democratic Party until securing a further term in 2009 with the Free Democratic Party as coalition partners.

TERRITORY AND POPULATION

Germany is bounded in the north by Denmark and the North and Baltic Seas, east by Poland, east and southeast by the Czech Republic, southeast and south by Austria, south by Switzerland and west by France, Luxembourg, Belgium and the Netherlands. Area: 357,104 sq. km. Population estimate, 31 Dec. 2008: 82,002,000 (41,818,000 females); density 230 per sq. km. Of the total population of 82,002,000 in Dec. 2008, 65,541,000 lived in the former Federal Republic of Germany (excluding West Berlin), 13,029,000 in the five new states of the former German Democratic Republic and 3,432,000 in Berlin. In 2005, 75·2% of the population lived in urban areas. There were 40·08m. households in 2008 of which 15·79m. were single-person. Germany has an ageing population. The proportion of the population over 60 has been steadily rising, and that of the under 20s steadily declining. By the mid-1990s the number of over 60s had surpassed the number of under 20s and now stands at 25% of the total population.

The UN gives an estimated population for 2010 of 82·06m.

On 14 Nov. 1990 Germany and Poland signed a treaty confirming Poland's existing western frontier and renouncing German claims to territory lost as a result of the Second World War.

The capital is Berlin; the Federal German government moved from Bonn to Berlin in 1999.

The Federation comprises 16 *Bundesländer* (states). Area and population:

Bundesländer	*Area in sq. km*	*Population (in 1,000) 1987 census*	*Population (in 1,000) 2008 estimate*	*Density per sq. km (2008)*
Baden-Württemberg (BW)	35,751	9,286	10,747[1]	301[1]
Bavaria (BY)	70,552	10,903	12,520	177
Berlin (BE)[2]	892	—	3,432	3,849
Brandenburg (BB)[3]	29,481	—	2,522	86
Bremen (HB)	404	660	662	1,638
Hamburg (HH)	755	1,593	1,772	2,346
Hessen (HE)	21,115	5,508	6,065	287
Lower Saxony (NI)	47,627	7,162	7,947	167
Mecklenburg-West Pomerania (MV)[3]	23,186	—	1,664	72
North Rhine-Westphalia (NW)	34,086	16,712	17,933	526
Rhineland-Palatinate (RP)	19,854	3,631	4,028	203
Saarland (SL)	2,570	1,056	1,030	401
Saxony (SN)[3]	18,419	—	4,193	228
Saxony-Anhalt (ST)[3]	20,448	—	2,382	116
Schleswig-Holstein (SH)	15,799	2,554	2,834	179
Thuringia (TH)[3]	16,172	—	2,268	140

[1]March 2009. [2]1987 census population of West Berlin: 2,013,000. [3]Reconstituted in 1990 in the Federal Republic.

On 31 Dec. 2008 there were 6,727,600 resident foreigners, including 1,688,400 Turks, 523,200 Italians, 393,800 Poles and 287,200 Greeks. More than 1·6m. of these were born in Germany. In 2008 Germany received 22,085 asylum applications, compared to 438,200 in 1992. The main countries of origin in 2008 were Iraq (6,836), Turkey (1,408) and Vietnam (1,042). Tighter controls on entry from abroad were applied as from 1993. 113,030 persons were naturalized in 2007, of whom 28,861 were from Turkey. In 2007 there were 636,900 emigrants and 680,800 immigrants. New citizenship laws were introduced on 1 Jan. 2000, whereby a child of non-Germans will have German citizenship automatically if the birth is in Germany, if at the time of the birth one parent has made Germany his or her customary legal place of abode for at least eight years, and if this parent has had an unlimited residence permit for at least three years. Previously at least one parent had to hold German citizenship for the child to become a German national.

Populations of the 81 towns of over 100,000 inhabitants in Dec. 2007 (in 1,000):

Town (and Bundesland)	*Population in 1,000)*	*Ranking by population*	*Town (and Bundesland)*	*Population in 1,000)*	*Ranking by population*
Aachen (NW)	259·0	27	Essen (NW)	583·1	8
Augsburg (BY)	263·0	25	Frankfurt am Main (HE)	659·0	5
Bergisch Gladbach (NW)	105·8	73	Freiburg im Breisgau (BW)	219·4	34
Berlin (BE)	3,416·3	1	Fürth (BY)	114·1	68
Bielefeld (NW)	324·9	18	Gelsenkirchen (NW)	264·8	24
Bochum (NW)	381·5	16	Gera (TH)	101·6	81
Bonn (NW)	316·4	19	Göttingen (NI)	121·5	60
Bottrop (NW)	118·6	65	Hagen (NW)	193·7	41
Braunschweig (NI)	245·8	28	Halle (ST)	234·3	32
Bremen (HB)	547·8	10	Hamburg (HH)	1,770·6	2
Bremerhaven (HB)	115·3	67	Hamm (NW)	183·1	42
Chemnitz (SN)	245·0	29	Hanover (NI)	518·1	11
Cologne/Köln (NW)	995·4	4	Heidelberg (BW)	145·3	53
Cottbus (BB)	102·8	79=	Heilbronn (BW)	121·6	59
Darmstadt (HE)	142·2	55	Herne (NW)	168·5	45
Dortmund (NW)	586·9	7	Hildesheim (NI)	103·6	78
Dresden (SN)	507·5	13	Ingolstadt (BY)	123·1	58
Duisburg (NW)	496·7	15	Jena (TH)	102·8	79=
Düsseldorf (NW)	581·1	9	Karlsruhe (BW)	288·9	21
Erfurt (TH)	202·9	37	Kassel (HE)	193·8	40
Erlangen (BY)	104·7	76	Kiel (SH)	236·9	30
			Koblenz (RP)	106·1	72

Town (and Bundesland)	*Population in 1,000)*	*Ranking by population*
Krefeld (NW)	236·5	31
Leipzig (SN)	510·5	12
Leverkusen (NW)	161·3	49
Lübeck (SH)	211·5	36
Ludwigshafen am Rhein (RP)	163·8	46
Magdeburg (ST)	230·1	33
Mainz (RP)	198·1	39
Mannheim (BW)	309·8	20
Moers (NW)	107·1	71
Mönchengladbach (NW)	260·0	26
Mülheim a. d. Ruhr (NW)	168·9	44
Munich/München (BY)	1,311·6	3
Münster (NW)	273·0	23
Neuss (NW)	151·4	51
Nuremberg/Nürnberg (BY)	503·1	14
Oberhausen (NW)	217·1	35
Offenbach am Main (HE)	118·2	66
Oldenburg (NI)	159·6	50
Osnabrück (NI)	162·9	47
Paderborn (NW)	144·2	54
Pforzheim (BW)	119·4	64
Potsdam (BB)	150·8	52
Recklinghausen (NW)	120·5	62
Regensburg (BY)	132·5	57
Remscheid (NW)	113·9	69
Reutlingen (BW)	112·5	70
Rostock (MV)	200·4	38
Saarbrücken (SL)	176·5	43
Salzgitter (NI)	105·3	74
Siegen (NW)	105·0	75
Solingen (NW)	162·6	48
Stuttgart (BW)	597·2	6
Trier (RP)	103·9	77
Ulm (BW)	121·4	61
Wiesbaden (HE)	275·8	22
Wolfsburg (NI)	120·0	63
Wuppertal (NW)	356·4	17
Würzburg (BY)	135·2	56

The official language is German. Minor orthographical amendments were agreed in 1995. An agreement between German-speaking countries on 1 July 1996 in Vienna provided for minor orthographical changes and established a Commission for German Orthography in Mannheim. There have been objections within Germany, particularly in the North, and many *Bundesländer* are to decide their own language programmes for schools. Generally, both old and new spellings are acceptable.

SOCIAL STATISTICS

Calendar years:

	Marriages	*Live births*	*Of these to single parents*	*Deaths*	*Divorces*
2003	382,911	706,721	190,641	853,946	213,975
2004	395,992	705,622	197,129	818,271	213,691
2005	388,451	685,795	200,122	830,227	201,693
2006	373,681	672,724	201,519	821,627	190,928
2007	368,922	684,862	211,053	827,155	187,072

The annual number of births declined every year between 1997 and 2006, when the number of births reached a post-war low, before rising in 2007. Of the 368,922 marriages in 2007, 25,907 involved a foreign male and 32,232 involved a foreign female. The average age of bridegrooms in 2007 was 36·7 years, and of brides 33·5. The average first-time marrying age for men was 32·7 and for women 29·8.

Rates (per 1,000 population), 2007: birth, 8·3; death, 10·1; marriage, 4·5; infant mortality, 3·9 per 1,000 births; stillborn rate, 3·5 per 1,000 births. Life expectancy, 2007: men, 77·0 years; women, 82·3. Suicide rates, 2007, per 100,000 population, 11·4 (men, 17·4; women, 5·7). Annual population growth rate, 2000–05, 0·1%; fertility rate, 2004, 1·3 births per woman.

Legislation of 1995 categorizes abortions as illegal, but stipulates that prosecutions will not be brought if they are performed in the first three months of pregnancy after consultation with a doctor.

Since 1 Aug. 2001 same-sex couples have been permitted to exchange vows at registry offices. The law also gives them the same rights as heterosexual couples in inheritance and insurance law.

A UNICEF report published in 2005 showed that 10·2% of children in Germany live in poverty (in households with income below 50% of the national median).

CLIMATE

Oceanic influences are only found in the northwest where winters are quite mild but stormy. Elsewhere a continental climate is general. To the east and south, winter temperatures are lower, with bright frosty weather and considerable snowfall. Summer temperatures are fairly uniform throughout. Berlin, Jan. 31°F (–0·5°C), July 66°F (19°C). Annual rainfall 22·5" (563 mm). Cologne, Jan. 36°F (2·2°C), July 66°F (18·9°C). Annual rainfall 27" (676 mm). Dresden, Jan. 30°F (–0·1°C), July 65°F (18·5°C). Annual rainfall 27·2" (680 mm). Frankfurt, Jan. 33°F (0·6°C), July 66°F (18·9°C). Annual rainfall 24" (601 mm). Hamburg, Jan. 31°F (–0·6°C), July 63°F (17·2°C). Annual rainfall 29" (726 mm). Hanover, Jan. 33°F (0·6°C), July 64°F (17·8°C). Annual rainfall 24" (604 mm). Munich, Jan. 28°F (–2·2°C), July 63°F (17·2°C). Annual rainfall 34" (855 mm). Stuttgart, Jan. 33°F (0·6°C), July 66°F (18·9°C). Annual rainfall 27" (677 mm).

CONSTITUTION AND GOVERNMENT

The Basic Law (*Grundgesetz*) was approved by the parliaments of the participating *Bundesländer* and came into force on 23 May 1949. It is to remain in force until 'a constitution adopted by a free decision of the German people comes into being'. The Federal Republic is a democratic and social constitutional state on a parliamentary basis. The federation is constituted by the 16 *Bundesländer* (states). The Basic Law decrees that the general rules of international law form part of the federal law. The constitutions of the *Bundesländer* must conform to the principles of a republican, democratic and social state based on the rule of law. Executive power is vested in the *Bundesländer*, unless the Basic Law prescribes or permits otherwise. Federal law takes precedence over state law.

Legislative power is vested in the *Bundestag* (Federal Assembly) and the *Bundesrat* (Federal Council). The Bundestag is currently composed of 622 members and is elected in universal, free, equal and secret elections for a term of four years. A party must gain 5% of total votes cast in order to gain representation in the Bundestag, although if a party has three candidates elected directly, they may take their seats even if the party obtains less than 5% of the national vote. The electoral system combines relative-majority and proportional voting; each voter has two votes, the first for the direct constituency representative, the second for the competing party lists in the *Bundesländer*. All directly elected constituency representatives enter parliament, but if a party receives more 'indirect' than 'direct' votes, the first name in order on the party list not to have a seat becomes a member—the number of seats is increased by the difference ('overhang votes'). Thus the number of seats in the Bundestag varies, but is 598 regular members (for the 2009 election, the same as in 2005 and 2002, but down from 656 for the previous elections since reunification) plus the 'overhang votes' (24 at the 2009 election, giving a total of 622 members). The Bundesrat consists of 69 members appointed by the governments of the *Bundesländer* in proportions determined by the number of inhabitants. Each *Bundesland* has at least three votes.

The Head of State is the Federal *President*, who is elected for a five-year term by a *Federal Convention* specially convened for this purpose. This Convention consists of all the members of the Bundestag and an equal number of members elected by the *Bundesländer* parliaments in accordance with party strengths, but who need not themselves be members of the parliaments. No president may serve more than two terms. Executive power is vested in the Federal government, which consists of the Federal *Chancellor*, elected by the Bundestag on the proposal of the Federal President, and the Federal Ministers, who are appointed and dismissed by the Federal President upon the proposal of the Federal Chancellor.

The Federal Republic has exclusive legislation on: (1) foreign affairs; (2) federal citizenship; (3) freedom of movement, passports, immigration and emigration, and extradition; (4)

currency, money and coinage, weights and measures, and regulation of time and calendar; (5) customs, commercial and navigation agreements, traffic in goods and payments with foreign countries, including customs and frontier protection; (6) federal railways and air traffic; (7) post and telecommunications; (8) the legal status of persons in the employment of the Federation and of public law corporations under direct supervision of the Federal government; (9) trade marks, copyright and publishing rights; (10) co-operation of the Federal Republic and the *Bundesländer* in the criminal police and in matters concerning the protection of the constitution, the establishment of a Federal Office of Criminal Police, as well as the combating of international crime; (11) federal statistics.

In the field of finance the Federal Republic has exclusive legislation on customs and financial monopolies and concurrent legislation on: (1) excise taxes and taxes on transactions, in particular, taxes on real-estate acquisition, incremented value and on fire protection; (2) taxes on income, property, inheritance and donations; (3) real estate, industrial and trade taxes, with the exception of the determining of the tax rates.

Federal laws are passed by the Bundestag and after their adoption submitted to the Bundesrat, which has a limited veto. The Basic Law may be amended only upon the approval of two-thirds of the members of the Bundestag and two-thirds of the votes of the Bundesrat.

Die Bundesrepublik Deutschland: Staatshandbuch. Annual

National Anthem

'Einigkeit und Recht und Freiheit' ('Unity and right and freedom'); words by H. Hoffmann, tune by J. Haydn.

GOVERNMENT CHRONOLOGY

Federal Republic of Germany (prior to reunification).
Chancellors since 1949 (CDU = Christian Democratic Union; FDP = Free Democratic Party; SPD = Social Democratic Party)

1949–63	CDU	Konrad Adenauer
1963–66	CDU	Ludwig Erhard
1966–69	CDU	Kurt Georg Kiesinger
1969–74	SPD	Willy Brandt
1974	FDP	Walter Scheel
1974–82	SPD	Helmut Schmidt
1982–90	CDU	Helmut Kohl

German Democratic Republic = Presidents of the Republic (1949–60) then Leaders of the Council of State. (LDPD = Liberal Democratic Party of Germany; SED = Socialist Unity Party of Germany)

1949	LDPD	Johannes Dieckmann
1949–60	SED	Willhelm Pieck
1960	LDPD	Johannes Dieckmann
1960–73	SED	Walter Ulbricht
1973	SED	Friedrich Ebert
1973–76	SED	Willi Stoph
1976–89	SED	Erich Honecker
1989	SED	Egon Krenz
1989–90	LDPD	Manfred Gerlach

Federal Republic of Germany.
Chancellors since reunification.

1990–98	CDU	Helmut Kohl
1998–2005	SPD	Gerhard Schröder
2005–	CDU	Angela Merkel

Presidents since 1949.

1949–59	FDP	Theodor Heuss
1959–69	CDU	Karl Heinrich Lübke
1969–74	SPD	Gustav Heinemann
1974–79	FDP	Walter Scheel
1979–84	CDU	Karl Carstens
1984–94	CDU	Richard von Weizsäcker
1994–99	CDU	Roman Herzog
1999–2004	SPD	Johannes Rau
2004–	CDU	Horst Köhler

RECENT ELECTIONS

On 23 May 2009 incumbent Horst Köhler was re-elected Federal President by the Federal Convention, defeating Gesine Schwan and Peter Sodann in the first round.

Bundestag elections were held on 27 Sept. 2009. The Christian Democratic Union/Christian Social Union of Chancellor Angela Merkel (CDU/CSU; the CSU is a Bavarian party where the CDU does not stand) won 239 seats with 33·8% of votes cast (226 with 35·2% in 2005); the Social Democratic Party (SPD) won 146 with 23·0% (222 seats with 34·2%); the Free Democratic Party (FDP), 93 with 14·6% (61 with 9·8%); the Left Party (former Party for Democratic Socialism), 76 with 11·9% (54 with 8·7%); the Greens, 68 with 10·7% (51 with 8·1%). Turnout was 70·8% (77·7% in 2005). The CDU formed a coalition with the FDP to create Germany's first centre-right government since 1998.

European Parliament

Germany has 99 representatives. At the June 2009 elections turnout was 43·3% (43·0% in 2004). The CDU/CSU won 42 seats—CDU 34 and CSU 8—with 37·9% of votes cast (political affiliation in European Parliament: European People's Party); the SPD, 23 with 20·8% (Progressive Alliance of Socialists and Democrats); the Greens, 14 with 12·1% (Greens/European Free Alliance); the FDP, 12 with 11·0% (Alliance of Liberals and Democrats for Europe); the Left Party, 8 with 7·5% (European Left/Nordic Green Left).

CURRENT ADMINISTRATION

Federal President: Horst Köhler; b. 1943 (CDU; sworn in 1 July 2004 and re-elected in May 2009).

Chancellor: Angela Merkel; b. 1954 (CDU; sworn in 22 Nov. 2005 and re-elected in Oct. 2009). In March 2010 the cabinet comprised:

Vice Chancellor and Minister for Foreign Affairs: Guido Westerwelle (FDP). *Interior:* Thomas de Maizière (CDU). *Justice:* Sabine Leutheusser-Schnarrenberger (FDP). *Finance:* Wolfgang Schäuble (CDU). *Economics and Technology:* Rainer Brüderle (FDP). *Labour and Social Affairs:* Ursula von der Leyen (CDU). *Food, Agriculture and Consumer Protection:* Ilse Aigner (CSU). *Defence:* Karl-Theodor Freiherr zu Guttenberg (CSU). *Family Affairs, Senior Citizens, Women and Youth:* Kristina Schröder (CDU). *Health:* Philipp Rösler (FDP). *Transport, Building and Urban Development:* Peter Ramsauer (CSU). *Environment, Nature Conservation and Nuclear Safety:* Norbert Röttgen (CDU). *Education and Research:* Annette Schavan (CDU). *Economic Co-operation and Development:* Dirk Niebel (FDP). *Head of the Federal Chancellery and Minister for Special Tasks:* Ronald Pofalla (CDU).

President of the Bundestag: Norbert Lammert (CDU; elected Oct. 2005).

Government Website: http://www.bundesregierung.de

CURRENT LEADERS

Horst Köhler

Position

President

Introduction

Horst Köhler took office as federal president of Germany on 1 July 2004, having previously served as the first German managing director of the International Monetary Fund (IMF) from 2000–04. Prior to the IMF, he was involved in German financial politics, particularly in regard to German reunification and the European Union Maastricht Treaty negotiations in 1991.

Early Life

Köhler was born on 22 Feb. 1943 in Skierbieszów, Poland. Following the Soviet invasion in the Second World War, his family fled to East Germany. In 1953 they moved into West Germany. He earned a doctorate in economics and politics from the University of Tübingen, where he was a scientific research assistant at the Institute for Applied Economic Research during 1969–76. Between 1976–89 he held various posts in Germany's ministries of economics and finance. He played an important role in the economic planning for Germany's reunification and assisted in providing aid to Russia after the collapse of the USSR. In 1991 Köhler was Germany's lead official in the negotiations that led to the Maastricht Treaty. From 1990–93 he served as Germany's deputy finance minister and from 1993–98 he was president of the German Savings Bank Association. In 1998 Köhler was appointed president of the European Bank for Reconstruction and Development (EBRD). He took part in focusing the EBRD's priorities on small businesses rather than large infrastructure projects. During his presidency the EBRD improved its finances, from having lost US$2,528m. in 1998 to making a profit of US$41m. in 1999. In addition he was deputy governor for Germany at the World Bank and was the personal representative of the federal chancellor in the preparation of the Group of Seven (G7) economic summits from 1990–93.

On 23 March 2000 Köhler was elected managing director and chairman of the Executive Board of the IMF, the first German to hold the post. His appointment came after the then chancellor, Gerhard Schröder, had campaigned to persuade European nations to back him. In 2002 his plan to allow indebted countries to file for bankruptcy caused protests from international financial markets.

Career in Office

Relinquishing his position at the IMF, Köhler was elected federal president of Germany on 23 May 2004. In his inaugural speech he encouraged the government to persevere with its economic reform programme, despite the short-term hardships that it would present. Following inconclusive parliamentary elections in Sept. 2005, he formally appointed Angela Merkel of the CDU as the first female federal chancellor at the head of a new coalition government in Nov. 2005. In May 2008 Köhler announced his candidacy for a second term as president in elections scheduled for May 2009. He went on to win re-election, defeating two opponents.

Angela Merkel

Position

Chancellor

Introduction

Angela Merkel became Germany's first female chancellor in Nov. 2005. Her appointment came after three weeks of negotiations following elections that failed to give a parliamentary majority to either her party, the Christian Democrats (CDU), or the Social Democrats (SPD) of incumbent Gerhard Schröder. Despite her initial success in re-energizing Germany's economy, global turmoil in financial markets led to recession in 2008, which highlighted considerable differences in her uneasy CDU–SPD coalition over the appropriate policy response. She has nevertheless maintained her personal popularity among voters, with over half claiming that they would vote for her if the chancellor was elected directly. She was re-elected Chancellor in the elections of Sept. 2009.

Early Life

Angela Dorothea Kasner was born on 17 July 1954 in Hamburg, West Germany, the daughter of a Lutheran pastor and a teacher. Later in 1954 her father received a pastorship in East Germany (GDR) and the family moved to Templin, 50 km north of Berlin. Merkel was educated in Templin before studying physics at the University of Leipzig from 1973–78. Having married Ulrich Merkel in 1977, she continued her studies at the Academy of Sciences in East Berlin, receiving a doctorate in 1986, and subsequently combined research in quantum chemistry with lecturing. While a student, she was secretary for propaganda in the FDJ, an East German youth organization loyal to the ruling Socialist Unity Party of Germany. Following the fall of the Berlin Wall in Nov. 1989 she joined the new Democratic Awakening party.

Following democratic elections in the GDR on 18 March 1990, Merkel became a member of the East German Christian Democratic Union (CDU) and deputy spokesperson of the new government under Lothar de Maizière. She was elected to the *Bundestag* in the first post-unification general elections in Dec. 1990, representing the united CDU in a Baltic coast constituency encompassing Rügen and the city of Stralsund. She was also appointed to Chancellor Helmut Kohl's cabinet as minister for women and youth, a position she held until being promoted to minister for the environment in 1994.

Merkel lost ministerial office in 1998 when the CDU were defeated in federal elections but later that year was appointed secretary-general of the CDU. She oversaw a string of CDU provincial election victories in 1999, although it was a party funding scandal implicating the CDU's chairman, Wolfgang Schäuble, and Kohl himself, which thrust Merkel into the limelight. She criticized Kohl (who was later stripped of his title of the CDU's honorary chairman), called for a fresh start for the party and was duly elected president of the CDU on 10 April 2000.

Unable to garner sufficient support to challenge Chancellor Schröder in the 2002 federal elections, Merkel ceded that role to Edmund Stoiber, leader of the CDU's sister party, the Bavarian Christian Social Union (CSU). Following Stoiber's narrow defeat, Merkel became leader of the conservative opposition in the *Bundestag*. She advocated institutional reform through simplifying the tax code and lowering taxes, simplifying health care and radically overhauling pensions. She also argued for a loosening of German labour law and, in 2003, controversially backed the US-led invasion of Iraq.

On 30 May 2005 Merkel won the CDU/CSU nomination as challenger to Schröder in the 2005 elections. The CDU began with a 21% lead in opinion polls but Merkel trailed Schröder in terms of personal popularity. In the elections on 18 Sept. the CDU/CSU won 35·2% of the vote to the SPD's 34·2%. Both Merkel and Schröder claimed victory and weeks of wrangling ensued. A deal for a grand coalition was eventually reached whereby Merkel would become chancellor and the SPD would hold eight of the fourteen cabinet posts. Merkel was elected chancellor by a majority of delegates in the *Bundestag* on 22 Nov. 2005.

Career in Office

Merkel won plaudits for brokering an EU budget deal between France's Jacques Chirac and Britain's Tony Blair within weeks of becoming chancellor. Although early opinion polls were favourable, countering high unemployment and the sluggish German economy, and delivering health care and tax reforms, were likely to prove difficult. Nevertheless, by Aug. 2006 she claimed that the country had 'turned the corner', with a reduction in the budget deficit and lower unemployment. The economy was forecast to grow by 2·5% in 2007 and in the first half of the year the public sector recorded a surplus for the first time since unification in 1990. Meanwhile, in Jan. 2007 Germany took over the six-month rotating presidency of the EU and Merkel was instrumental in facilitating agreement among the heads of government on a new draft treaty streamlining the Union's institutional structure and decision-making process (which, officially concluded as the Treaty of Lisbon in Dec. 2007, eventually entered into force in Dec. 2009).

In March 2008 Merkel made an historic address to the Israeli parliament, the first by a German head of government, during a visit marking the 60th anniversary of the founding of Israel.

As the global financial crisis began to bite through 2008, Germany's economy slipped into recession. In the autumn the government stepped in to prevent the collapse of one of the country's largest banks, Hypo Real Estate, and made €500bn. available in loan guarantees and capital to bolster the banking system. Merkel remained unconvinced, however, about the wisdom of the huge economic stimulus packages unveiled by many of her EU partners and said that Germany would not engage in a 'pointless race to spend billions'. This apparent inaction in the face of a worsening recession generated external and internal opposition, and Merkel subsequently endorsed a co-ordinated economic recovery package (and joint action on global warming) agreed at a summit of EU leaders in mid-Dec. 2008. Also in Dec., Merkel was re-elected overwhelmingly as the leader of her Christian Democratic Union.

Merkel's CDU emerged as the largest party in the German elections to the European Parliament in June 2009 and increased its majority in the Federal Assembly in general elections in Sept. In Oct. Merkel was sworn in as chancellor for a second term at the head of a new centre-right coalition with the Free Democratic Party (FDP).

DEFENCE

Conscription was reduced from ten months to nine months from Jan. 2002. In July 1994 the Constitutional Court ruled that German armed forces might be sent on peacekeeping missions abroad. Germany has increased the number of professionals available for military missions abroad and sent troops to Afghanistan as part of the international alliance against terrorism in the aftermath of 11 Sept. 2001. The first time that German armed forces were deployed in this way since the Second World War, the move provoked controversy in Germany. In 2006 there were over 8,000 German troops abroad. In addition to those in Afghanistan (nearly half of all German troops deployed abroad) there were German peacekeepers in various parts of the world including Kosovo, Lebanon, Bosnia and Sudan. Since Jan. 2001 women have been allowed to serve in all branches of the military on the same basis as men.

In 2008 defence expenditure totalled US$46,759m. (US$568 per capita). In 2007 defence spending represented 1·3% of GDP. Military spending fell by 11·0% in real terms between 1999 and 2008.

Army

The Army is organized in the Army Forces Command. The equipment of the former East German army is in store. Total strength was (2006) 191,350 (conscripts 73,450). There are Army reserves of 297,300.

The Territorial Army is organized into five Military Districts, under three Territorial Commands. Its main task is to defend rear areas and remains under national control even in wartime.

Navy

The Fleet Commander operates from a modern Maritime Headquarters at Glücksburg, close to the Danish border.

The fleet includes 14 diesel coastal submarines and 14 frigates. The main naval bases are at Wilhelmshaven, Olpenitz, Kiel, Eckernförde and Warnemünde.

The Naval Air Arm, 3,700 strong, is organized into two wings and includes 16 combat aircraft (Atlantics) and 29 armed helicopters.

Personnel in 2006 numbered 20,700, including 4,950 conscripts.

Air Force

Since 1970 the *Luftwaffe* has comprised the following commands: German Air Force Tactical Command, German Air Force Support Command (including two German Air Force Regional Support Commands—North and South) and General Air Force Office. Personnel in 2006 was 51,400 (16,100 conscripts). There were 426 combat aircraft, including *Tornados*, F-4Fs, T-37Bs and T-38As.

INTERNATIONAL RELATIONS

A treaty of friendship with Poland signed on 17 June 1991 recognized the Oder-Neisse border and guaranteed minorities' rights in both countries.

Germany is a member of the UN, World Bank, IMF and several other UN specialized agencies, WTO, EU, Council of Europe, WEU, OSCE, CERN, Council of the Baltic Sea States, Danube Commission, BIS, IOM, NATO, OECD, Inter-American Development Bank, Asian Development Bank and Antarctic Treaty. Germany is a signatory to the Schengen accord which abolishes border controls between Germany, Austria, Belgium, Czech Republic, Denmark, Estonia, Finland, France, Greece, Hungary, Iceland, Italy, Latvia, Lithuania, Luxembourg, Malta, Netherlands, Norway, Poland, Portugal, Slovakia, Slovenia, Spain, Sweden and Switzerland.

ECONOMY

Services accounted for 69% of GDP in 2007, industry 30% and agriculture 1%.

According to the anti-corruption organization *Transparency International*, Germany ranked equal 14th in the world in a 2009 survey of the countries with the least corruption in business and government. It received 8·0 out of 10 in the annual index.

Overview

Measured on an international exchange rate basis, Germany is the third largest economy in the world after the USA and Japan. However, the reunification of the two Germanies in 1989 proved costly for the more prosperous West Germans. GDP growth averaged 4·5% per annum in the 1960s but slowed to under 1% in the first half of the 2000s, the lowest in the eurozone alongside Italy. In 2006 the economy recorded its highest growth since 2000, spurred by an increase in exports and a burst of domestic demand prior to a 3% VAT increase implemented in Jan. 2007.

The principal manufacturing is in the auto and chemical industries, with telecommunications an increasingly important sector. Manufacturing (especially of automobiles) and related services rank higher in the economy than in other developed countries. This leaves the country vulnerable to slowdowns or recessions in its principal export markets.

The post-Second World War economic miracle (*Wirtschaftswunder*) was marked by prudent fiscal and monetary policy, the growth of a globally competitive manufacturing sector and good industrial relations. The economy is described as a 'social market' in that it embraces enlightened company management and social welfare. Companies are managed on the 'stakeholder' concept, which means they are responsible not only to their shareholders but also to employees, customers, suppliers and local communities. However, the system is changing in response to the internationalization of ownership, corporate mergers, the revitalization of the stock exchange and the ending of large cross-shareholdings by companies and banks. This has led to a weakening of previously interlocking structures in commerce and finance.

Low growth in recent years has been attributed to weaknesses in the labour market and the high cost of restructuring the economy of the former GDR. Employment flexibility has diminished owing to high labour costs, generous unemployment benefits and early retirement policies. Unemployment has been persistently high, at almost twice the OECD average. The GDP per capita gap relative to the upper half of OECD countries has widened since the mid-1990s, reflecting weak labour utilization. Unemployment benefits and social security have been merged for long-term claimants (known as the Hartz IV reforms).

Since 2007 the global economic slowdown, high commodity prices and financial tensions have damaged the economy. In Oct. 2008 the finance ministry agreed a €50bn. plan to rescue Hypo Real Estate, one of the country's biggest banks. In Jan. 2009 Commerzbank became the first German bank to be partly nationalized via a government bail-out fund. The government also announced a €50bn. stimulus package of public investment and tax cuts aimed at halting a descent into severe recession, alongside a €100bn. fund to underwrite fresh credit to companies starved of new loans. In June 2009 the German cabinet approved a 'bad bank' scheme aimed at removing toxic assets from the balance sheets of troubled regional banks. In the period April–June 2009 the economy emerged from recession, growing by 0·4% on the back of increasing exports, government fiscal stimulus, stronger private consumption and construction investment. Having contracted by 4·9% in 2009, growth is expected in 2010 and 2011, although lower demand for exports and cautious domestic consumer spending will restrain its extent.

Having achieved a balanced budget in 2008, the government deficit is expected to increase to 5·5% of GDP in 2010, nearly double the 3% target set by the EU's Stability and Growth Pact (SGP). The government has committed to bringing it down to its target by 2013, leading to the implementation of fiscal consolidation measures as soon as the recovery has firmed up. The goal of a close-to-balanced federal, structural budget by 2016 aims to allow Germany to regain the fiscal space lost to the crisis and prepare for the rising costs of its ageing population.

Currency

On 1 Jan. 1999 the euro (EUR) became the legal currency in Germany at the irrevocable conversion rate of 1·95583 DM (deutschemark) to one euro. The euro, which consists of 100 cents, has been in circulation since 1 Jan. 2002. There are seven euro notes in different colours and sizes denominated in 500, 200, 100, 50, 20, 10 and 5 euros, and eight coins denominated in 2 and 1 euros, then 50, 20, 10, 5, 2 and 1 cents. It was still possible to make cash transactions in German marks until 28 Feb. 2002, although formally the mark had ceased to be legal tender on 31 Dec. 2001. Euro banknotes in circulation on 1 Jan. 2002 had a total value of €254·2bn.

Foreign exchange reserves were US$37,492m. in Sept. 2009 and gold reserves were 109·56m. troy oz. Only the USA, with 261·50m. troy oz, had more in Sept. 2009. Total money supply was €934,352m. in Aug. 2009.

Inflation rates (based on OECD statistics):

1999	*2000*	*2001*	*2002*	*2003*	*2004*	*2005*	*2006*	*2007*	*2008*
0·6%	1·4%	1·9%	1·4%	1·0%	1·8%	1·9%	1·8%	2·3%	2·8%

The inflation rate in 2009 according to Destatis, the Federal Statistical Office, was at 0·4% the lowest year-on-year rate of price increase since reunification.

Budget

In July 2000 the then Chancellor Schröder pushed through a tax-cutting package which included from 2001 a reduction in corporation tax from 40%/30% to 25%. The top rate of income tax was to be reduced gradually from 51% to 42% by 2005. In March 2003 Schröder announced 'Agenda 2010', to include cuts in unemployment benefits, an easing of job protection rules and trimmed state pensions. The health system, among the world's most expensive, was also a core target. 'Agenda 2010' encountered criticism from trade unionists and left-wingers within the SPD. In July 2003 the German government announced that it would bring forward the tax cuts scheduled for 2005 and combine them with those planned for 2004, bringing the total tax cut for 2004 to €15·5bn.

VAT is (since 1 Jan. 2007) 19% (reduced rate, 7%). In 2006 the federal government and the *Bundesländer* each received 42·5% of income tax and the local authorities 15%. Corporation tax was equally split between the federal government and the *Bundesländer*. In 2007 the federal government received approximately 55% of VAT, the *Bundesländer* around 43% and the local authorities about 2%.

Budget for 2008 (in €1m.):

	All public authorities	*Federal portion*
Revenue	*Current*	
Taxes	944,570	260,945
Economic activities	19,417	5,400
Interest	6,733	1,443
Current allocations and subsidies	288,994	26,107
Other receipts	36,251	6,607
minus equalising payments	267,277	11,817
	1,028,689	288,685
Revenue	*Capital*	
Sale of assets	12,817	7,068
Allocations for investment	20,601	244
Repayment of loans	5,253	2,909
Public sector borrowing	640	174
minus equalising payments	17,311	185
	22,000	10,209
Total revenues	1,050,689	298,895
Expenditure	*Current*	
Staff	201,417	40,205
Materials	253,149	19,842
Interest	67,863	40,856
Allocations and subsidies	717,250	192,074
Other current expenditures	262	—
minus equalising payments	267,277	11,817
	972,664	281,162
Expenditure	*Capital*	
Construction	26,189	5,778
Acquisition of property	9,314	1,425
Allocations and subsidies	42,473	17,074
Loans	4,798	2,425
Acquisition of shares	13,826	8,904
Repayments in the public sector	779	—
Other expenditures	459	—
minus equalising payments	17,311	185
	80,524	35,419
Total expenditures	1,053,188	316,581

Performance

Real GDP growth rates (based on OECD statistics):

1999	*2000*	*2001*	*2002*	*2003*	*2004*	*2005*	*2006*	*2007*	*2008*
1·9%	3·5%	1·4%	0·0%	–0·2%	0·7%	0·9%	3·4%	2·6%	1·0%

In 2002 real GDP growth was 0·0%, the lowest since 1993, and in 2003 the economy contracted by 0·2%, although Germany came out of recession in the second half of the year. Germany had four quarters of negative growth from the second quarter of 2008 but emerged from recession in the second quarter of 2009. The real GDP growth rate in 2009 according to Destatis, the Federal Statistical Office, was –4·9%. Total GDP in 2008 was US$3,652·8bn., the fourth highest in the world.

Banking and Finance

The Deutsche Bundesbank (German Federal Bank) is the central bank and bank of issue. Its duty is to protect the stability of the currency. It is independent of the government but obliged to support the government's general policy. Its Governor is appointed by the government for eight years. The *President* is Axel Weber. Its assets were €373,535m. in Dec. 2006. The largest private banks are the Deutsche Bank, Commerzbank, Dresdner Bank and DZ Bank. In April 2001 Dresdner Bank accepted a takeover offer from Allianz, the country's largest insurance company. Commerzbank in turn agreed to buy Dresdner Bank from Allianz in Aug. 2008.

In June 2005 Italy's UniCredit finalized an agreement to acquire HypoVereinsbank in Europe's biggest cross-border banking takeover.

In 2008 there were 2,169 credit institutes, including 283 banks, 438 savings banks, 25 mortgage lenders and 1,199 credit societies. They are represented in the wholesale market by the ten public sector *Bundesländer* banks. Total assets, 2008, €7,956,390m. Savings deposits were €544,121m. in 2008. In 2007 approximately 39% of the German population were using e-banking.

A single stock exchange, the Deutsche Börse, was created in 1992, based on the former Frankfurt stock exchange in a union with the smaller exchanges in Berlin, Bremen, Düsseldorf, Hamburg, Hanover, Munich and Stuttgart. Frankfurt processes 90% of equities trading in the country.

Germany attracted US$50·92bn. worth of foreign direct investment in 2007, compared to a record US$198·28bn. in 2000.

Gull, L., *et al.*, *The Deutsche Bank, 1870–1995*. 1996

ENERGY AND NATURAL RESOURCES

Environment

Germany's carbon dioxide emissions from the consumption and flaring of fossil fuels were the equivalent of 10·1 tonnes per capita in 2008. An *Environmental Performance Index* compiled in 2008 ranked Germany 13th in the world, with 86·3%. The index examined various factors in six areas—air pollution, biodiversity and habitat, climate change, environmental health, productive natural resources and water resources.

Germany is one of the world leaders in recycling. In 2004, 56% of all household waste was recycled.

Electricity

Installed capacity in 2007 was 115·32m. kW. In 2009 there were 17 nuclear reactors in operation, but in Dec. 2001 the German parliament decided to decommission the country's nuclear reactors over the next two decades. Production of electricity was 576·02bn. kWh in 2007, of which about 24% was nuclear. There is a moratorium on further nuclear plant construction, and the SPD-Green coalition government agreed in 2000 to begin phasing out nuclear power, with the final plant closure scheduled for 2022. Consumption per capita was 7,442 kWh in 2004. In April 1998 the electricity market was liberalized, leading to huge cuts in bills for both industrial and residential customers. In June 2000 Veba and Viag merged to form E.ON, which became the world's largest private energy service provider. Germany is the second largest exporter of electricity (after France), with 50·8bn. kWh in 2004.

New European targets proposed by the European Commission in Jan. 2007, since approved by the German Energy Council, aim for renewable sources to account for 20% of the total by 2020. The share of electricity consumption from renewables reached 14·2% in 2007, up from 6·3% in 2000.

Oil and Gas

The chief oilfields are in Emsland (Lower Saxony). In 2008, 2·59m. tonnes of crude oil were produced. Natural gas production was 13·0bn. cu. metres in 2008. Natural gas reserves were 120bn. cu. metres in 2008; crude petroleum reserves were 367m. bbls in 2007.

Wind

Germany is the world's leading producer of wind-power. By the end of 2007 there were 19,460 wind turbines with a total rated power of 22,247 MW (23·7% of the world total). Production of wind-generated electricity in 2007 totalled 39·5bn. kWh.

Minerals

The main production areas are: North Rhine-Westphalia (for coal, iron and metal smelting-works), Central Germany (for lignite) and Lower Saxony (Salzgitter for iron ore; the Harz for metal ore).

Production (in 1,000 tonnes), 2006: lignite, 176,290; coal, 20,882; salt, 17,480. In 2005 recoverable coal reserves were estimated at 6·7bn. tonnes. Germany is the world's largest lignite producer and the third largest salt producer after China and the USA.

Agriculture

In 2008 there were 11·93m. ha. of arable land. Sown areas in 2008 (in 1,000 ha.) included: wheat, 3,213·5; fodder, 2,203·5; barley, 1,961·7; rape, 1,370·7; rye, 736·9; maize, 520·5; sugar beets, 369·3; potatoes (2007), 275·0; oats, 179·5. Crop production, 2008 (in 1,000 tonnes): fodder, 75,876; wheat, 26,001; sugar beets, 23,004; barley, 11,972; potatoes (2007), 11,646; maize, 5,158; rapeseed, 5,154; rye, 3,743; oats, 793. Germany is the world's largest producer of hops (39,700 tonnes in 2008) and the second largest producer of rye.

In 2008, 5·4% of agricultural land was farmed organically in Germany. Organic food sales for Germany in 2008 were valued at €5·8bn. (the second highest in the world behind the USA).

In 2007 there were 374,514 farms, of which 60,405 were between two and five ha. and 31,879 over 100 ha. In 2007 there were 346,300 farmers assisted by 382,200 household members and 522,900 hired labourers (336,300 of them seasonal).

In 2008 wine production was 999·1m. litres.

Livestock, 2008 (in 1,000): beef cattle, 12,987·5; milch cows, 4,229·1; sheep, 2,437·0; pigs, 26,718·6; horses (2007), 541·9; poultry (2007), 111,522·6. Livestock products, 2008 (in 1,000 tonnes): milk, 28,656; meat, 6,304; cheese (except soft cheese and cottage cheese), 1,487; eggs, 9,617m. units.

Forestry

Forest area in 2007 was 8,824,500 ha., of which about half was owned by the State. Timber production was 76·73m. cu metres in 2007. In recent years depredation has occurred through pollution with acid rain.

Fisheries

The total catch in 2005 was 285,668 tonnes (264,268 tonnes from marine waters). Germany's total catch increased every year between 2001 and 2005. In 2005 the fishing fleet consisted of 2,121 vessels totalling 64,075 GT. About 3,700 people were engaged in fisheries in 2005.

INDUSTRY

The leading companies by market capitalization in Germany in March 2009 were: Volkswagen (US$96·6bn.); E.ON, an energy service provider (US$55·6bn.); and Deutsche Telekom (US$54·1bn.).

In 2008 a total of 833,281 firms were registered (728,978 in 2001).

Output of major industrial products, 2008 unless otherwise indicated (in 1,000 tonnes): distillate fuel oil (2004), 49,551; crude steel (2007), 48,550; rolled steel products (2007), 41,999; cement, 33,983; pig iron (2004), 30,018; unleaded petrol, 23,692; plastics, 17,274; residual fuel oil (2004), 14,013; paper, 12,882; flour, 5,044; jet fuel (2004), 4,424; sulphuric acid, 2,125; nitrogenous fertilizers, 1,329; synthetic fibre (2006), 406; passenger cars, 6,100,000 units; household dishwashing machines, 3,178,000 units; refrigerators, 2,957,000 units; glass bottles, 9,323m. units; TV sets, 2,180,000; beer, 9,112m. litres; soft drinks (excluding milk-based beverages), 22,308m. litres (2007).

Labour

Retirement age is normally 65 years. In 2008 the workforce was 43·39m., of whom 40·33m. were working and 3·27m. (1·60m. females) were registered as unemployed. In 2008 there were 35·87m. employees and 4·47m. self-employed (including those helping family members). 3·13m. foreign workers were employed in 2008, making up 7% of the workforce. Of the total workforce in 2007 the year average for the number of employees in each industry was as follows: 9,343,000 in the mining, processing and manufacturing industries; 5,182,000 in the vehicle trade and maintenance; 4,785,000 in real estate and corporate services; 3,710,000 in health, veterinary and social services; 2,652,000 in the civil service and armed forces; 2,226,000 in education; 2,049,000 in transport and communications; 1,751,000 in the construction industry; 1,481,000 in the hotel and catering industries; 1,055,000 in banking and insurance; and 445,000 in agriculture, forestry and fisheries. In 2008 there were 568,513 job vacancies. By 2000 there was a shortfall of 75,000 people in the information technology industry. In Aug. 2000 Germany launched a 'Green Card' project, aimed at attracting 20,000 telecommunication and information technology specialists from non-European Union countries in a bid to make up for the shortfall in qualified personnel. The card authorized the holder to unrestricted employment in Germany for five years. By July 2003 more than 14,000 recruits had found work. The scheme was halted at the end of 2004 and a new Immigration Act came into effect from 1 Jan. 2005 which provides a legislative framework for controlling and restricting immigration. The standardized unemployment rate was 7·5% in Dec. 2009 (down from 8·0% in Dec. 2007 but up from 7·1% in Dec. 2008); the rate in the former GDR is more than double that in the states of the former Federal Republic of Germany. In Jan. 2005 the number of people out of work reached 5m., the highest total since the 1930s. The gross annual earnings of full-time employees in the industry and services sector amounted to an average of €41,509 per person in 2008. There is no national minimum wage in Germany.

Trade Unions

Germany's largest trade union is Vereinigte Dienstleistungsgewerkschaft, or ver.di, created in March 2001 as a result of the merger of five smaller unions. Representing 3m. workers in the service industry, it is the largest trade union outside of China.

The majority of trade unions belong to the Deutscher Gewerkschaftsbund (DGB, German Trade Union Federation), which had 6·4m. (2·0m. women) members in Dec. 2008. It functions as an umbrella organization for its eight member unions. DGB unions are organized in industrial branches such that only one union operates within each enterprise. The official GDR trade union organization (FDGB) was merged in the Deutscher Gewerkschaftsbund. Strikes are not legal unless called by a union with the backing of 75% of members. Certain public service employees are contractually not permitted to strike. 131,679 days were lost through strikes in 2008, up substantially from 2005 (18,633 days lost). Between 1996 and 2005 strikes cost Germany an average of three days per 1,000 employees a year, one of the lowest rates in the EU.

INTERNATIONAL TRADE

In 2007 Germany had its highest ever annual trade surplus, at €195·3bn. for the year compared to €159·0bn. a year earlier.

Imports and Exports

Trade in €1m.:

	2005	*2006*	*2007*	*2008*[1]
Imports	628,087	733,994	769,887	818,621
Exports	786,266	893,042	965,236	994,870

[1]Provisional.

Most important trading partners in 2008 (provisional trade figures in €1m.). Imports: Netherlands, 72,083; France, 66,710; China, 59,378; USA, 46,060; Italy, 45,962; UK, 44,261; Belgium, 39,775; Russia, 35,909; Austria, 33,148. Exports: France, 96,859; USA, 71,467; UK, 66,788; Netherlands, 65,644; Italy, 64,003; Austria, 53,841; Belgium, 51,635; Spain, 43,704; Poland, 40,149.

Distribution of imports and exports by commodities in 2008 (provisional, in €1m.) includes: finished goods, 524,325 and 829,172; semi-finished goods, 71,972 and 57,219; foodstuffs, 49,476 and 40,606; raw materials, 98,118 and 9,310; alcohol and tobacco, 8,036 and 8,321; live animals, 1,088 and 718.

Germany is the second largest trading nation in the world after the USA, but in 2003 took over from the USA as the world's leading exporter and in 2008 accounted for 8·1% of global exports. However, provisional figures indicate that China took over as the largest exporter in 2009.

Trade Fairs

Germany has a number of major annual trade fairs, among the most important of which are Internationale Grüne Woche Berlin (International Green Week Berlin—Exhibition for the Food Industry, Agriculture and Horticulture), held in Berlin in Jan.; Ambiente (for high quality consumer goods and new products), held in Frankfurt in Feb.; ITB Berlin (International Tourism Exchange), held in Berlin in March; CeBit (World Business Fair for Office Automation, Information Technology and Telecommunications), held in Hanover in March; Hannover Messe (the World's Leading Fair for Industry, Automation and Innovation), held in Hanover, in April; Internationale Funkausstellung Berlin (Your World of Consumer Electronics), held in Berlin in late Aug./early Sept.; and Frankfurter Buchmesse (Frankfurt Book Fair) held in Frankfurt in Oct. Hanover's trade fair site is the largest in Europe and Frankfurt's the second largest.

COMMUNICATIONS

Roads

In 2008 the total length of the road network was 231,181 km, including 12,594 km of motorway *(Autobahn)*, 40,416 km of federal highways and 86,607 km of secondary roads. The motorway network is the largest in Europe. On 1 Jan. 2009 there were 49,602,600 motor vehicles, including: passenger cars, 41,321,200 (approximately one car for every two persons); lorries, 2,346,700; buses, 75,300; motorcycles, 3,658,600. In 2007, 9,052m. passengers were transported by scheduled road transport services. In 2008, 320,614 motorists were arrested at the scene of an accident (resulting in injury) for driving offences, of which 18,383 were alcohol related and 55,710 for exceeding speed limits. Road casualties in 2008 totalled 413,524, with 409,047 injured and 4,477 killed. In 2008 there were 5·5 fatalities per 100,000 population.

Germany was ranked fifth for its road infrastructure in the World Economic Forum's *Global Competitiveness Report 2009–2010*.

Rail

Legislation of 1993 provides for the eventual privatization of the railways, but the state-owned Deutsche Bahn still dominates the market. On 1 Jan. 1994 West German Bundesbahn and the former GDR Reichsbahn were amalgamated as the Deutsche Bahn, a joint-stock company in which track, long-distance passenger traffic, regional passenger traffic, goods traffic and railway stations/services are run as five separate administrative entities. These were intended after 3–5 years to become companies themselves, at first under a holding company, and ultimately independent. In 2008 the total length of railway track of all kinds was 40,953 km (nearly all 1,435 mm gauge track). In 2005, 22,064 km was electrified. 2,330m. passengers and 371·3m. tonnes of freight were carried in 2008.

There are metros in Berlin (152 km), Hamburg (101 km), Munich (101 km) and Nuremberg (35 km), and tram/light rail networks in over 50 cities.

In the World Economic Forum's *Global Competitiveness Report 2009–2010* Germany ranked fifth for quality of rail infrastructure.

Civil Aviation

Lufthansa, the largest carrier, was set up in 1953 and was originally 75% state-owned. The government sold its final shares in 1997. Other airlines include Air Berlin, Condor, Eurowings,

Germanwings and TUIfly. In 2005 Lufthansa carried 49·0m. passengers (35·7m. on international flights); passenger-km totalled 112·8bn. Lufthansa carries more passengers on international flights than any other airline. In 2008 civil aviation had 775 aircraft over 20 tonnes (751 jets).

In 2008 there were 95·11m. passenger arrivals and 95·26m. departures. Main international airports: Bremen, Cologne-Bonn, Düsseldorf, Frankfurt am Main, Hamburg (Fuhlsbüttel), Hanover, Leipzig, Munich, Nuremberg, Stuttgart and two at Berlin (Tegel and Schönefeld). Airports at Dortmund, Dresden, Frankfurt (Hahn), Lübeck, Paderborn, Rostock and Saarbrücken are used for only a few scheduled international flights in addition to domestic flights.

In 2008 Frankfurt am Main handled 53·4m. passengers and 2,037,000 tonnes of freight. It is the busiest airport in Europe in terms of freight handled. Munich was the second busiest German airport in terms of passenger traffic in 2008 (34·5m.) but fourth for freight. Cologne-Bonn was the second busiest in 2008 for freight, with 584,000 tonnes, but only sixth for passenger traffic.

Shipping

At 31 Dec. 2008 the mercantile marine comprised 1,170 ocean-going vessels of 16,280,000 GRT. Sea-going ships in 2008 carried 321m. tonnes of cargo. Navigable rivers and canals have a total length of 7,476 km. The inland-waterways fleet on 31 Dec. 2008 included 921 motor freight vessels totalling 1·15m. tonnes and 398 tankers of 683,924 tonnes. 246m. tonnes of freight were transported in 2008. In 2005 vessels totalling 918,038,000 GRT entered ports and vessels totalling 880,784,000 GRT cleared. The busiest port, Hamburg, handled 118·9m. tonnes of cargo in 2008, ranking it third in Europe behind Rotterdam and Antwerp. Hamburg is Europe's second busiest container port after Rotterdam.

Germany was ranked fifth in the World Economic Forum's *Global Competitiveness Report 2009–2010* for the quality of its port facilities.

Telecommunications

Telecommunications were deregulated in 1989. On 1 Jan. 1995, three state-owned joint-stock companies were set up: Deutsche Telekom, Postdienst and Postbank. The partial privatization of Deutsche Telekom began in Nov. 1996; in 2007 the German government held only 14·8% of shares directly, and a further 16·9% indirectly through the government bank KfW.

In 2008 there were 51·4m. main (fixed) telephone lines. In 2004, 98·8% of all households had a private telephone. Mobile phone subscribers numbered 105·5m. in 2008 (1,282·7 per 1,000 persons). T-Mobile and D2 Vodafone are the largest networks, with 36% and 32% of the market share respectively. There were 54·0m. PCs in use in 2006. Germany has the highest number of internet users in Europe, with 62·0m. in 2008. The broadband penetration rate in June 2008 was 26·2 subscribers per 100 inhabitants.

Postal Services

In 2007 there were 12,617 post offices and 5,440 affiliated agents. A total of 17,585m. pieces of mail were processed in 2007.

SOCIAL INSTITUTIONS

Justice

Justice is administered by the federal courts and by the courts of the *Bundesländer*. In criminal procedures, civil cases and procedures of non-contentious jurisdiction the courts on the state level are the local courts *(Amtsgerichte)*, the regional courts *(Landgerichte)* and the courts of appeal *(Oberlandesgerichte)*. Constitutional federal disputes are dealt with by the Federal Constitutional Court *(Bundesverfassungsgericht)* elected by the Bundestag and Bundesrat. The *Bundesländer* also have constitutional courts. In labour law disputes the courts of the first and second instance are the labour courts and the *Bundesland* labour courts, and in the third instance the Federal Labour Court *(Bundesarbeitsgericht)*. Disputes about public law in matters of social security, unemployment insurance, maintenance of war victims and similar cases are dealt with in the first and second instances by the social courts and the *Bundesland* social courts and in the third instance by the Federal Social Court *(Bundessozialgericht)*. In most tax matters the finance courts of the *Bundesländer* are competent, and in the second instance the Federal Finance Court *(Bundesfinanzhof)*. Other controversies of public law in non-constitutional matters are decided in the first and second instance by the administrative and the higher administrative courts *(Oberverwaltungsgerichte)* of the *Bundesländer*, and in the third instance by the Federal Administrative Court *(Bundesverwaltungsgericht)*.

For inquiries into maritime accidents the admiralty courts *(Seeämter)* are competent on the state level and in the second instance the Federal Admiralty Court *(Bundesoberseeamt)* in Hamburg.

The death sentence was abolished in the Federal Republic of Germany in 1949 and in the German Democratic Republic in 1987.

The population in penal institutions at 31 March 2008 was 61,900. 1,985 prisoners were serving life sentences.

Education

Education is compulsory for children aged 6 to 15, although between the ages of 15 and 18 young people are obliged to pursue at least part-time vocational secondary education. After the first four (or six) years at primary school *(Grundschulen)* children attend post-primary *(Hauptschulen)*, secondary modern *(Realschulen)*, grammar *(Gymnasien)*, or comprehensive schools *(Integrierte Gesamtschulen)*. Secondary modern school lasts six years and grammar school nine. Entry to higher education is by the final Grammar School Certificate (*Abitur*—Higher School Certificate). There are also schools for physically disabled children and those with other special needs *(Sonderschulen)*.

In 2007–08 there were 1,598 kindergartens with 28,136 pupils and 2,549 teachers; 16,649 primary schools with 3,082,499 pupils and 189,389 teachers; 3,360 special schools with 400,399 pupils and 71,724 teachers; 8,415 secondary modern schools with 2,268,788 pupils and 151,016 teachers; 3,078 grammar schools with 2,466,041 pupils and 169,790 teachers; 869 comprehensive schools with 578,624 pupils and 44,523 teachers.

In 2007–08 there were 665,118 working teachers, of whom 459,326 were female.

The adult literacy rate is at least 99%.

In 2006 total expenditure on education came to €142·9bn. In 2006 public expenditure on education came to 4·4% of GNI and represented 9·7% of total government expenditure.

Vocational education is provided in part-time, full-time and advanced vocational schools (*Berufs-, Berufsaufbau-, Berufsfach-* and *Fachschulen*, including *Fachschulen für Technik* and *Schulen des Gesundheitswesens)*. Occupation-related, part-time vocational training of six to 12 hours per week is compulsory for all (including unemployed) up to the age of 18 years or until the completion of the practical vocational training. Full-time vocational schools comprise courses of at least one year. They prepare for commercial and domestic occupations as well as specialized occupations in the field of handicrafts. Advanced full-time vocational schools are attended by pupils over 18. Courses vary from six months to three or more years.

In 2007–08 there were 8,981 full- and part-time vocational schools with 2,802,776 students and 123,620 teachers.

Higher Education. In the winter term of the 2008–09 academic year there were 394 institutes of higher education *(Hochschulen)* with 1,996,062 students, including 104 universities (1,341,352 students), six teacher training colleges (20,033), 14 theological seminaries (2,611), 51 schools of art (31,977), 189 technical colleges (572,751) and 30 management schools (27,338). Only 335,554 students (16·8%) were in their first year.

Health

In 2007 there were 314,912 doctors, 65,929 dentists and 56,719 pharmacists. In 2007 there were 2,087 hospitals with 506,954 beds (61·7 for every 10,000 people). In 2007 Germany spent 10·4% of its GDP on health, with public spending amounting to 76·9% of the total. In 2007 total expenditure on health came to €252·8bn.

Welfare

Social Health Insurance (introduced in 1883). Wage-earners and apprentices, salaried employees with an income below a certain limit and social insurance pensioners are compulsorily insured within the state system. Voluntary insurance is also possible.

Benefits: medical treatment, medicines, hospital and nursing care, maternity benefits, death benefits for the insured and their families, sickness payments and out-patients' allowances. Economy measures of Dec. 1992 introduced prescription charges related to recipients' income.

As part of a series of measures to tackle a funding shortfall in the health service, a patient charge of €10 was introduced from Jan. 2004, payable for the first visit only per quarter to a doctor.

50·97m. persons were insured in 2008 (29·64m. compulsorily). Number of cases of incapacity for work (2007) totalled 30·34m., and the number of working days lost were 197·33m. (men) and 179·81m. (women). Total disbursements in 2007 were €153,876m.

Accident Insurance (introduced in 1884). Those insured are all persons in employment or service, apprentices and the majority of the self-employed and the unpaid family workers.

Benefits in the case of industrial injuries and occupational diseases: medical treatment and nursing care, sickness payments, pensions and other payments in cash and in kind, surviving dependants' pensions.

Number of insured in 2007, 59·93m.; number of current pensions, 1,046,345; total disbursements, €9,757m.

Workers' and Employees' Old-Age Insurance Scheme (introduced in 1889). All wage-earners and salaried employees, the members of certain liberal professions and—subject to certain conditions—self-employed craftsmen are compulsorily insured. The insured may voluntarily continue to insure when no longer liable to do so or increase the insurance.

Benefits: measures designed to maintain, improve and restore the earning capacity; pensions paid to persons incapable of work, old age and surviving dependants' pensions.

Number of current pensions in July 2008, 24·69m. (including old age pensions, 17·32m.; pensions to widows and widowers, 5·40m.). Total disbursements in 2007, €249,497m.

There are also special retirement and unemployment pension schemes for miners and farmers, assistance for war victims and compensation payments to members of German minorities in East European countries expelled after the Second World War and persons who suffered damage because of the war or in connection with the currency reform.

Family Allowances. €28·89bn. were dispensed to 8·95m. recipients (1·08m. foreigners) in 2008 on behalf of 14·77m. children. Paid child care leave is available for three years to mothers or fathers.

Unemployment Allowances. In 2008, 0·92m. persons (0·42m. women) were receiving unemployment benefit and 1·90m. (0·92m. women) earnings-related benefit. Total expenditure on these and similar benefits (e.g. short-working supplement, job creation schemes) was €39·41bn. in 2008. Unemployment assistance was abolished in Jan. 2005 and replaced with a new so-called 'Unemployment benefit II'. The new benefit is no longer tied to the former income of the recipient but is around the same flat-rate level as the social assistance benefit.

Public Welfare. In 2007, €21·13bn. were distributed to 312,000 recipients (156,000 women).

Public Youth Welfare. For supervision of foster children, official guardianship, assistance with adoptions and affiliations, social assistance in juvenile courts, educational assistance and correctional education under a court order. A total of €22·20bn. was spent on recipients in 2007.

Pension Reform. A major reform of the German pension system became law on 11 May 2001. The changes entail a cut in the value of the average state pension from 70% to approximately 67% of average final earnings by 2030. There will be incentives in the form of tax concessions and direct payments to encourage individuals to build up supplementary provision by contributing up to 4% of their earnings into private-sector personal pensions. In the long term these could supply up to 40% of overall pension income, with 60% coming from the state as opposed to 85% prior to the changes.

A survey by Aon Consulting in 2005 which ranked the pension systems of the 15 pre-expansion EU countries (based on size and sustainability of payments) placed Germany's system at 13th. The OECD notes that Germany has one of the smallest active workforces aged between 55 and 65 (with a participation rate of 40%). Future reforms are expected to increase employee contributions. Workers and employers currently contribute around 20% of salary, with the state contributing a further 10%.

The retirement age is to be increased gradually from 65 to 67 starting in 2012. By 2029 Germans will only be eligible for a state pension at the age of 67.

RELIGION

In 2007 there were 25,461,000 Roman Catholics in 12,265 parishes, 24,832,000 Protestants in 15,603 parishes; and in 2008, 106,435 Jews with 46 rabbis and 92 synagogues. The Federal Ministry of the Interior estimated in 2007 that there were between 3·1m and 3·4m. Muslims resident in Germany, a number exceeded in the EU only in France.

There are seven Roman Catholic archbishoprics (Bamberg, Berlin, Cologne, Freiburg, Hamburg, Munich and Freising, Paderborn) and 20 bishoprics. Chairman of the German Bishops' Conference is Robert Zollitsch, Archbishop of Freiburg im Breisgau. A concordat between Germany and the Holy See dates from 10 Sept. 1933. In April 2005 Cardinal Joseph Ratzinger, former archbishop of Munich and Freising, was elected Pope as Benedict XVI. In Feb. 2010 there were seven cardinals.

The Evangelical (Protestant) Church (EKD) consists of 22 member-churches comprising nine Lutheran Churches, 11 United-Lutheran-Reformed Churches and two Reformed Churches. Its organs are the Synod, the Church Conference and the Council under the chairmanship of Margot Kässmann. The Free Evangelical Church (BFeG) has some 420 communities.

CULTURE

Essen is one of three European Capitals of Culture for 2010. The title attracts large European Union grants.

World Heritage Sites

Germany has 33 sites on the UNESCO World Heritage List (date of inscription on the list in brackets): Aachen Cathedral (1978), begun in the 8th century under Charlemagne; Speyer Cathedral (1981), founded in 1030 and constructed in the Romanesque style; Würzburg Residence, with the Court Gardens and Residence Square (1981), an 18th century Baroque palace; Pilgrimage Church of Wies (1983), an 18th century Baroque-Rococo church; Castles of Augustusburg and Falkenlust at Brühl (1984), early examples of 18th century Rococo architecture; St Mary's Cathedral and St

Michael's Church at Hildesheim (1985 and 2008), Romanesque constructions from the 11th century; Roman Monuments in Trier (1986), a Roman colony from the 1st century, and the Cathedral of St Peter and Church of Our Lady; Hanseatic City of Lübeck (1987), founded in the 12th century; Palaces and Parks of Potsdam and Berlin (1990, 1992 and 1999), an eclectic mix of 150 buildings covering 500 hectares built between 1730 and 1916; Abbey and Altenmünster of Lorsch (1991), an example of Carolignian architecture; Mines of Rammelsberg and Historic Town of Goslar (1992 and 2008), with a well-preserved historic centre; Town of Bamberg (1993), the country's biggest intact historical city core; Maulbronn Monastery Complex (1993), a former Cistercian abbey over 850 years old; Collegiate Church, Castle, and Old Town of Quedlinburg (1994), capital of the East Franconian German Empire; Völklingen Ironworks (1994), a preserved 19th/20th centuries ironworks; Messel Pit Fossil site (1995), containing important fossils from 57m.–36m. BC; Cologne Cathedral (1996 and 2008), a Gothic masterpiece begun in 1248; Bauhaus and its sites in Weimar and Dessau (1996), buildings of the influential early-20th century architectural movement; Luther Memorials in Eisleben and Wittenberg (1996), including his birthplace, baptism church and religious sites; Classical Weimar (1998), a cultural epicentre during the 18th and early 19th centuries; Museumsinsel (Museum Island), Berlin (1999), including Altes Museum, Bodemuseum, Neues Museum and Pergamonmuseum; Wartburg Castle (1999), dating from the feudal period and rebuilt in the 19th century—Luther translated the New Testament here; Garden Kingdom of Dessau-Wörlitz (2000), an 18th century landscaped garden in the Enlightenment style; Monastic Island of Reichenau (2000), on Lake Constance, incorporating medieval churches and the remains of an 8th century Benedictine monastery; Zollverein Coal Mine Industrial Complex in Essen (2001), a 20th century mining complex with modernist buildings; Upper Middle Rhine Valley (2002), a 65 km-stretch of one of Europe's most important historical transport conduits; Historic Centres of Stralsund and Wismar (2002), Hanseatic towns; Town Hall and Roland on the Marketplace of Bremen (2004); Old Town of Regensburg with Stadtamhof (2006); and the Berlin Modernism Housing Estates (2008).

Germany and Poland are jointly responsible for Muskauer Park/ Park Muzakowski (2004), a landscaped park astride the Neisse river. Germany and the United Kingdom share the Frontiers of the Roman Empire sites (1987, 2005 and 2008), which contain the border line of the Roman Empire at its greatest extent in the 2nd century AD. The Wadden Sea, the largest unbroken system of intertidal sand and mud flats in the world (2009), is located in Germany and the Netherlands.

Broadcasting

ARD (Arbeitsgemeinschaft der öffentlich-rechtlichen Rundfunkanstalten der Bundesrepublik Deutschland) and ZDF (Zweites Deutsches Fernsehen) are national public broadcasting organizations, although each of the country's 16 states regulates its own public and private broadcasting. There is a great variety of free-to-view public and commercial television channels and most households have access to cable and satellite services. Digital broadcasting is expanding; the government aims to end analogue transmissions by 2012. National public service radio is provided by DeutschlandRadio through its Deutschlandfunk and Deutschlandradio Kultur networks. Private radio stations also broadcast in the regions. Deutsche Welle (DW-radio) broadcasts overseas. In 2008 there were 36·87m. TV licences and 43·06m. radio licences.

Cinema

There were 4,639 cinemas in 2008 with a total seating capacity of 852,529. In 2008, 125 feature films were made. A total of 129m. visits to the cinema were made in 2008; gross box office receipts came to €794·7m. in 2008. In 2008 German films took 27% of the national market, up from 16% in 2001.

Press

The daily press is mainly regional. The dailies with the highest circulation are (average figures for July–Sept. 2008): the tabloid Bild (3·36m. copies per day); Süddeutsche Zeitung (Munich, 0·44m.); Frankfurter Allgemeine Zeitung (0·37m.); and die Welt (which in 2007 made the first profit in its 60-year history, 0·27m.). Other important opinion leaders are the weeklies Die Zeit, Die Woche and Rheinischer Merkur. Bild has the highest circulation of any paper in Europe. In the period April–June 2009 the total circulation figures for some 350 German daily newspapers came to 25·3m. The entire range of popular magazines includes some 2,300 publications and has a total circulation of more than 120m. The total circulation of daily newspapers in Germany is the highest in Europe. 78% of the population over the age of 14 regularly read a daily newspaper. There were also 267 online daily newspapers in 2008. Among magazines the most widely read are Der Spiegel (1·04m. weekly) and Stern (1·02m. weekly). In 2006 a total of 87,510 book titles were published.

Tourism

In 2008 there were 52,143 places of accommodation with 2,585,761 beds (including 13,281 hotels with 1,023,804 beds). 24,884,017 foreign visitors and 108,074,890 tourists resident in Germany spent a total of 369,579,835 nights in holiday accommodation. The most visited city is Berlin with 7,905,145 visitors in 2008; Bavaria is the most visited *Bundesland* with 26,664,538 (4,830,393 visited Munich). In 2008 the Netherlands was the country of origin of the largest number of visitors (3,584,865), ahead of the USA (1,973,686) and the UK (1,968,477). In 2007 tourism brought in €26,296m.

Festivals

The Munich Opera Festival takes place annually in June–July, and the Wagner Festspiele (the Wagner Festival) in Bayreuth is held from late July to the end of Aug. The Oberammergau Passion Play, which takes place every ten years, was last held in 2000. Karneval (Fasching in some areas), in Jan./Feb./March, is a major event in the annual calendar in cities such as Cologne, Munich, Düsseldorf and Mainz. The annual Berlin Film Festival (Berlinale) takes place over a two-week period in Feb. The Love Parade, which takes place in mid-July, is Europe's second largest street party. Oktoberfest, Munich's famous beer festival which first began in 1810, takes place each year in late Sept. and early Oct. and regularly attracts 7m. visitors.

Libraries

In 2008 there were 8,393 public libraries, five national libraries and 204 higher education libraries; they and other libraries held a combined 369,307,000 volumes. There were 10,702,000 active users in 2008, with 451,011,000 loans.

Theatre and Opera

In 2006–07 there were 143 theatre companies, performing on 826 stages. Audiences totalled 18·78m.

Museums and Galleries

In 2007 there were 4,712 museums which attracted 107,304,000 visitors.

DIPLOMATIC REPRESENTATIVES

Of Germany in the United Kingdom (23 Belgrave Sq., London, SW1X 8PZ)
Ambassador: Georg Boomgaarden.

Of the United Kingdom in Germany (Wilhelmstrasse 70, 10117 Berlin)
Ambassador: Sir Michael Arthur, KCMG.

Of Germany in the USA (4645 Reservoir Rd, NW, Washington, D.C., 20007)
Ambassador: Klaus Scharioth.

Of the USA in Germany (Pariser Platz 2, 10117 Berlin)
Ambassador: Philip D. Murphy.

Of Germany to the United Nations
Ambassador: Peter Wittig.

Of Germany to the European Union
Permanent Representative: Edmund Duckwitz.

FURTHER READING

Statistisches Bundesamt. *Statistisches Jahrbuch für die Bundesrepublik Deutschland; Wirtschaft und Statistik* (monthly, from 1949); *Das Arbeitsgebiet der Bundesstatistik* (latest issue 1997; Abridged English version: *Survey of German Federal Statistics*).

Ardagh, J., *Germany and the Germans.* 3rd ed. 1996
Balfour, M., *Germany: the Tides of Power.* 1992
Bark, D. L. and Gress, D. R., *A History of West Germany, 1945–1991.* 2nd ed. 1993
Betz, H. G., *Postmodern Politics in Germany.* 1991
Blackbourn, D., *Fontana History of Germany, 1780–1918: The Long Nineteenth Century.* 1997
Blackbourn, D. and Eley, G., *The Peculiarities of German History.* 1985
Carr, W., *A History of Germany, 1815–1990.* 4th ed. 1995
Childs, D., *Germany in the 20th Century.* 1991.—*The Stasi: The East German Intelligence and Security Service.* 1999
Dennis, M., *The German Democratic Republic: Politics, Economics and Society.* 1987
Fulbrook, Mary, *A Concise History of Germany.* 1991.—*The Divided Nation: A History of Germany, 1918–1990.* 1992.—*German National Identity After the Holocaust.* 1999.—*Interpretation of the Two Germanies, 1945–1997.* 1999
Glees, A., *Reinventing Germany: German Political Development since 1945.* 1996
Heneghan, Tom, *Unchained Eagle: Germany After the Wall.* 2000
Huelshoff, M. G., *et al.*, (eds.) *From Bundesrepublik to Deutschland: German Politics after Reunification.* 1993
Kielinger, T., *Crossroads and Roundabouts, Junctions in German-British Relations.* 1997
Langewiesche, Dieter, *Liberalism in Germany.* 1999
Lees, Charles, *Party Politics in Germany.* 2005
Loth, W., *Stalin's Unwanted Child—The Soviet Union, the German Question and the Founding of the GDR.* 1998
Maier, C. S., *Dissolution: The Crisis of Communism and the End of East Germany.* 1997
Marsh, D., *The New Germany: At the Crossroads.* 1990
Marshall, B., *The Origins of Post-War West German Politics.* 1988
Maull, Hanns W., *German Foreign Policy Since Reunification.* 2005
Merkl, Peter H. (ed.) *The Federal Republic of Germany at Fifty: The End of a Century of Turmoil.* 1999
Miskimmon, Alister, *Germany and the Common Foreign and Security Policy of the European Union: Between Europeanization and National Adaptation.* 2007
Miskimmon, Alister, Paterson, William E. and Sloam, James, (eds.) *Germany's Gathering Crisis: The 2005 Federal Election and the Grand Coalition.* 2008
Müller, Jan-Werner, *Another Country: German Intellectuals, Unification and National Identity.* 2000
Neville, P., *Appeasing Hitler: The Diplomacy of Sir Neville Henderson.* 1999
Nicholls, A. J., *The Bonn Republic: West German Democracy, 1945–1990.* 1998
Olsen, Jonathan, *Nature and Nationalism: Right-wing Ecology and the Politics of Identity in Contemporary Germany.* 2000
Orlow, D., *A History of Modern Germany, 1871 to the Present.* 4th ed. 1994
Padgett, Stephen, Paterson, William E. and Smith, Gordon, (eds.) *Developments in German Politics 3.* 2003
Parkes, K. S., *Understanding Contemporary Germany.* 1996
Pulzer, P., *German Politics, 1945–1995.* 1995
Schwartz, H-P., translator, Willmot, L., *Konrad Adenauer Vol 1: From the German Empire to the Federal Republic, 1876–1952.* 1995.—*Konrad Adenauer Vol 2: The Statesman: 1952–1967.* 1997
Schweitzer, C.-C., Karsten, D., Spencer, R., Cole, R. T., Kommers, D. P. and Nicholls, A. J. (eds.) *Politics and Government in Germany, 1944–1994: Basic Documents.* 2nd ed. 1995
Sereny, Gitta, *The German Trauma: Experiences and Reflections, 1938–99.* 2000
Sinn, G. and Sinn, H.-W., *Jumpstart: the Economic Reunification of Germany.* 1993
Smyser, W. R., *The Economy of United Germany: Colossus at the Crossroads.* 1992.—*From Yalta to Berlin: The Cold War Struggle over Germany.* 1999
Speirs, Ronald and Breuilly, John, (eds.) *Germany's Two Unifications: Anticipations, Experiences, Responses.* 2005
Taylor, R., *Berlin and its Culture.* 1997
Thompson, W. C., *et al.*, *Historical Dictionary of Germany.* 1995
Turner, H. A., *Germany from Partition to Reunification.* 2nd ed. [of *Two Germanies since 1945*]. 1993
Tusa, A., *The Last Division – A History of Berlin, 1945–1989.* 1997
Watson, A., *The Germans: Who Are They Now?* 2nd ed. 1994
Wende, Peter, *History of Germany.* 2004
Williams, C., *Adenauer: The Father of the New Germany.* 2000

Other more specialized titles are listed under CONSTITUTION AND GOVERNMENT *and* BANKING AND FINANCE, *above.*

National libraries: Deutsche Bibliothek, Adickesallee 1, 60322 Frankfurt am Main. *Director General:* Elisabeth Niggemann; (Berliner) Staatsbibliothek Preussischer Kulturbesitz, Potsdamer Str. 33, Postfach 1407, 10785 Berlin. *Director:* Barbara Schneider-Kempf.

National Statistical Office: Statistisches Bundesamt, 65189 Wiesbaden, Gustav Stresemann Ring 11. *President:* Roderich Egeler.

Website: http://www.destatis.de

THE BUNDESLÄNDER

Baden-Württemberg

KEY HISTORICAL EVENTS

The *Bundesland* is a combination of former states. Baden (the western part of the present *Bundesland*) became a united margravate in 1771, after being divided as Baden-Baden and Baden-Durlach since 1535; Baden-Baden was predominantly Catholic, and Baden-Durlach predominantly Protestant. The margrave became an ally of Napoleon, ceding land west of the Rhine and receiving northern and southern territory as compensation. In 1805 Baden became a grand duchy and in 1806 a member state of the Confederation of the Rhine, extending from the Main to Lake Constance. In 1815 it was a founder-state of the German Confederation. A constitution was granted by the grand duke in 1818, but later rulers were less liberal and there was revolution in 1848, put down with Prussian help. The grand Duchy was abolished and replaced by a *Bundesland* in 1919.

In 1949 Baden was combined with Württemberg to form three states; the three joined as one in 1952.

Württemberg, having been a duchy since 1495, became a kingdom in 1805 and joined the Confederations as did Baden. A constitution was granted in 1819 and the state remained liberal. In 1866 the king allied himself with Austria against Prussia, but in 1870 joined Prussia in war against France. The liberal monarchy came to an end with the abdication of William II in 1918, and Württemberg became a state of the German Republic. In 1945 the state was divided between Allied occupation authorities but the divisions ended in 1952.

TERRITORY AND POPULATION

Baden-Württemberg comprises 35,751 sq. km, with a population (at 31 March 2009) of 10,744,383 (5,459,572 females, 5,284,811 males).

The *Bundesland* is divided into four administrative regions, nine urban and 35 rural districts, and numbers 1,102 communes. The capital is Stuttgart.

SOCIAL STATISTICS

Statistics for calendar years:

	Live births	*Marriages*	*Divorces*	*Deaths*
2005	94,279	50,272	23,854	94,074
2006	91,955	48,780	22,686	92,662
2007	92,823	47,233	22,145	94,079
2008	91,909	48,612	22,792	96,431

CONSTITUTION AND GOVERNMENT

Baden-Württemberg is a merger of Baden, Württemberg-Baden and Württemberg-Hohenzollern, which were formed after 1945. The merger was approved by a plebiscite held on 9 Dec. 1951, when 70% of the population voted in its favour. It has six votes in the Bundesrat.

RECENT ELECTIONS

At the elections to the 139-member Diet of 26 March 2006, turnout was 53·4%. The Christian Democrats won 69 seats with 44·2% of the vote, the Social Democrats 38 with 25·2%, the Greens 17 with 11·7% and the Free Democrats 15 with 10·7%. The Election Alternative Labour and Social Justice only received 3·1% of the vote, and therefore won no seats.

CURRENT ADMINISTRATION

Stefan Mappus (CDU) is *Prime Minister.*

Government Website: http://www.baden-wuerttemberg.de

ECONOMY

Performance

GDP in 2008 was €364,304m., which amounted to 14·6% of Germany's total GDP. Industries (*Produzierendes Gewerbe*) provide around 39·3% of GDP (44·6% in 1991). Real GDP growth in 2008 was 1·9%. Service enterprises account for 60·0% of GDP.

Banking and Finance

There is a stock exchange in Stuttgart. Turnover of shares and bonds in 2008 was €154·3bn.

ENERGY AND NATURAL RESOURCES

Electricity

Hydro-electric power is a significant source of electricity in the *Bundesland.*

Agriculture

Area and yield of the most important crops:

	Area (in 1,000 ha.)			*Yield (in 1,000 tonnes)*		
	2006	*2007*	*2008*	*2006*	*2007*	*2008*
Wheat	227·0	224·6	236·0	1,659·1	1,614·3	1,750·4
Sugar beet	17·7	18·4	17·3	1,179·4	1,187·6	1,156·0
Barley	183·4	187·6	192·6	1,045·8	997·0	1,079·6
Potatoes	6·5	5·9	5·5	209·4	208·1	197·5
Oats	30·9	30·1	28·6	160·7	134·5	158·9
Rye	7·7	9·4	10·0	42·4	49·9	58·8

Livestock in May 2009 (in thousands): cattle, 1,044·6 (including 358·1 milch cows); pigs, 2,103·6; sheep, 282·6; poultry (2007), 4,728·0.

Forestry

Total area covered by forests is 13,675 sq. km or 38·3% of the total area.

INDUSTRY

Baden-Württemberg is one of Germany's most industrialized states. In 2008, 8,491 establishments (with 20 or more employees) employed 1,254,198 persons; of these, 292,526 were employed in machine construction; 245,931 in car manufacture; 196,381 in electrical and optical equipment; 14,404 in the textile industry.

Labour

Economically active persons totalled 5,372,200 at the 1%-EU-sample survey of May 2008: 4·79m. were employees and 586,100 were self-employed (including family workers); 2,010,600 were engaged in power supply, mining, manufacturing and building; 1,082,400 in commerce and transport; 102,800 in agriculture and forestry; 2,176,400 in other industries and services. There were 229,129 unemployed in 2008, a rate of 4·1%.

INTERNATIONAL TRADE

Imports and Exports

Total imports (2008): €130,294m. Total exports: €151,229m., of which €89,009m. went to the EU. Automotive exports totalled €34,667m. and machinery exports €35,816m.

COMMUNICATIONS

Roads

On 1 Jan. 2009 there were 27,426 km of 'classified' roads, comprising 1,039 km of Autobahn, 4,371 km of federal roads, 9,938 km of first-class and 12,078 km of second-class highways. Motor vehicles, at 1 Jan. 2009, numbered 6,867,506, including 5,663,963 passenger cars, 8,458 buses, 278,813 lorries, 339,583 tractors and 546,877 motorcycles.

Civil Aviation

The largest airport in Baden-Württemberg is at Stuttgart, which in 2008 handled 9,877,000 passengers and 28,890 tonnes of freight. There are two further airports, Karlsruhe/Baden-Baden and Friedrichshafen.

Shipping

The harbour in Mannheim is the largest in Baden-Württemberg. In 2008 it handled 7·9m. tonnes of freight, compared to 7·1m. tonnes in Karlsruhe.

SOCIAL INSTITUTIONS

Justice

There are a constitutional court *(Staatsgerichtshof)*, two courts of appeal, 17 regional courts, 108 local courts, a *Bundesland* labour court, nine labour courts, a *Bundesland* social court, eight social courts, a finance court, a higher administrative court *(Verwaltungsgerichtshof)* and four administrative courts.

Education

In 2008–09 there were 2,720 primary schools (*Grund- und Hauptschulen*) with 35,049 teachers and 582,595 pupils; 577 special schools with 11,580 teachers and 53,927 pupils; 478 intermediate schools with 13,282 teachers and 246,656 pupils; 444 high schools with 22,496 teachers and 343,421 pupils; 55 *Freie Waldorf* schools with 1,625 teachers and 23,069 pupils. Other general schools had 655 teachers and 10,592 pupils in total; there were also 775 vocational schools with 434,595 pupils. There were 41 *Fachhochschulen* (colleges of engineering and others) with 98,880 students in winter term 2008–09.

In the winter term 2008–09 there were nine universities (Freiburg, 19,682 students; Heidelberg, 24,918; Hohenheim, 6,676; Karlsruhe, 18,113; Konstanz, 8,820; Mannheim, 9,840; Stuttgart, 18,491; Tübingen, 21,461; Ulm 6,998); six teacher-training colleges with 19,690 students; five colleges of music and three colleges of fine arts with a total of 4,274 students.

Health

In 2008 the 297 hospitals in Baden-Württemberg had 59,224 beds and treated 1,976,987 patients. The average occupancy rate was 74·5%.

Welfare

At 31 Dec. 2006 there were approximately 177,500 persons receiving benefits of all kinds. 2007 expenditure on social welfare was €2,100m.

RELIGION

In 2006, 37·5% of the population were Roman Catholics and 33·6% were Protestants.

CULTURE

Tourism

In 2008, 16,487,947 visitors spent a total of 43,616,862 nights in Baden-Württemberg. Only Bavaria of the German *Bundesländer* recorded more overnight stays.

FURTHER READING

Statistical Information: Statistisches Landesamt Baden-Württemberg (P.O.B. 10 60 33, 70049 Stuttgart) (*President:* Dr Carmina Brenner), publishes: *Statistisches Monatsheft* (monthly); *Trends und Fakten* (latest issue 2007); *Statistisches Taschenbuch* (latest issue 2009).

State libraries: Württembergische Landesbibliothek, Konrad-Adenauer-Str. 8, 70173 Stuttgart. Badische Landesbibliothek Karlsruhe, Erbprinzenstr. 15, 76133 Karlsruhe.

Bavaria

Bayern

KEY HISTORICAL EVENTS

Bavaria was ruled by the Wittelsbach family from 1180. The duchy remained Catholic after the Reformation, which made it a natural ally of Austria and the Habsburg Emperors.

The present boundaries were reached during the Napoleonic wars, and Bavaria became a kingdom in 1806. Despite the granting of a constitution and parliament, radical feeling forced the abdication of King Ludwig I in 1848. Maximilian II was followed by Ludwig II who allied himself with Austria against Prussia in 1866, but was reconciled with Prussia and entered the German Empire in 1871. In 1918 the King Ludwig III abdicated. The first years of republican government were filled with unrest, attempts at the overthrow of the state by both communist and right-wing groups culminating in an unsuccessful coup by Adolf Hitler in 1923.

The state of Bavaria included the Palatinate from 1214 until 1945, when it was taken from Bavaria and added to the Rhineland. The present *Bundesland* of Bavaria was formed in 1946. Munich became capital of Bavaria in the reign of Albert IV (1467–1508) and remains capital of the *Bundesland.*

TERRITORY AND POPULATION

Bavaria has an area of 70,552 sq. km. The capital is Munich. There are seven administrative regions, 25 urban districts, 71 rural districts, 203 unincorporated areas and 2,056 communes, 987 of which are members of 313 administrative associations (as of 31 Dec. 2008). The population (31 Dec. 2008) numbered 12,519,728 (6,138,101 males, 6,381,627 females).

SOCIAL STATISTICS

Statistics for calendar years:

	Live births	*Marriages*	*Divorces*	*Deaths*
2005	107,308	59,617	28,417	119,326
2006	104,822	57,387	27,326	118,733
2007	106,870	57,220	27,154	118,432
2008	106,298	58,300	27,566	121,109

CONSTITUTION AND GOVERNMENT

The Constituent Assembly, elected on 30 June 1946, passed a constitution on the lines of the democratic constitution of 1919, but with greater emphasis on state rights; this was agreed upon by the Christian Social Union (CSU) and the Social Democrats (SPD). Bavaria has six seats in the Bundesrat. The CSU replaces the Christian Democratic Party in Bavaria.

RECENT ELECTIONS

At the Diet elections on 28 Sept. 2008 the CSU won 92 seats with 43·4% of votes cast (down from 60·7% in 2003), the SPD 39 with 18·6%, the Free Voters 21 with 10·2%, the Alliance '90/Greens 19 with 9·4% and the Free Democratic Party 16 with 8·0%. The Left took 4·3% but won no seats. As a result the CSU lost its absolute majority for the first time since 1962. Turnout was 57·9%.

CURRENT ADMINISTRATION

The *Prime Minister* is Horst Seehofer (CSU).

Government Website: http://www.bayern.de

ECONOMY

Performance

Real GDP growth in 2008 was 1·5%, down from 3·0% in 2007.

ENERGY AND NATURAL RESOURCES

Agriculture

Area and yield of the most important products:

	Area (in 1,000 ha.)			*Yield (in 1,000 tonnes)*		
	2006	*2007*	*2008*	*2006*	*2007*	*2008*
Sugar beet	60·8	66·0	62·8	3,999·0	4,856·6	4,328·4
Wheat	492·0	481·2	524·2	3,358·7	3,572·3	3,857·6
Barley	441·6	436·6	433·5	2,224·4	2,303·4	2,308·3
Potatoes	48·9	48·0	45·8	1,895·2	2,092·5	1,934·0
Rye	32·0	40·5	45·5	156·4	213·3	249·9
Oats	39·9	37·8	33·1	173·5	160·5	149·7

Livestock, 2007: 3,444,600 cattle (including 1,229,400 milch cows); 98,200 horses; 3,760,000 pigs; 441,600 sheep; 10,502,000 poultry.

INDUSTRY

On 30 Sept. 2008, 7,547 establishments (with 20 or more employees) employed 1,227,753 persons; of these, 220,001 were employed in the manufacture of machinery and equipment, 184,909 in the manufacture of motor vehicles and 26,610 in the manufacture of textiles and textile products.

Labour

The economically active persons totalled 6,301,000 at the 1% sample survey of the microcensus of 2008. Of the total, 5,452,000 were employees, 754,000 were self-employed, 95,000 were unpaid family workers; 2,039,000 worked in power supply, mining, manufacturing and building; 1,386,000 in commerce, hotels and restaurants, and transport; 192,000 in agriculture and forestry; 2,683,000 in other services.

COMMUNICATIONS

Roads

There were, on 1 Jan. 2009, 41,882 km of 'classified' roads, comprising 2,491 km of Autobahn, 6,583 km of federal roads, 14,022 km of first-class and 18,786 km of second-class highways. Number of motor vehicles on 1 Jan. 2009 was 8,499,456, including 6,772,212 passenger cars, 346,851 lorries, 12,849 buses and 728,882 motorcycles.

Civil Aviation

Munich airport handled 34,402,131 passengers (24,560,299 on international flights) and 247,238 tonnes of freight in 2008.

Nuremberg handled 4,229,582 (2,688,178 on international flights) and 10,276 tonnes of freight in 2008.

SOCIAL INSTITUTIONS

Justice

There are a constitutional court *(Verfassungsgerichtshof)*, three courts of appeal, 22 regional courts, 72 local courts, two *Bundesland* labour courts, 11 labour courts, a *Bundesland* social court, seven social courts, two finance courts, a higher administrative court *(Verwaltungsgerichtshof)* and six administrative courts. The supreme *Bundesland* court *(Oberstes Landesgericht)* was abolished in June 2006. Since 1 Jan. 2005 new cases have been transferred to the courts of appeal.

Education

In 2008–09 there were 2,858 primary schools with 45,577 teachers and 720,445 pupils; 359 special schools with 8,156 teachers and 58,467 pupils; 352 intermediate schools with 13,265 teachers and 235,538 pupils; 408 high schools with 25,110 teachers and 377,356 pupils; 228 part-time vocational schools with 8,021 teachers and 301,949 pupils, including 48 special part-time vocational schools with 1,105 teachers and 15,600 pupils; 832 full-time vocational schools with 5,435 teachers and 75,631 pupils including 436 schools for public health occupations with 1,806 teachers and 25,476 pupils; 272 advanced full-time vocational schools with 1,640 teachers and 21,211 pupils; 145 vocational high schools *(Berufsoberschulen, Fachoberschulen)* with 2,828 teachers and 50,114 pupils.

In 2008–09 there were 12 universities with 174,065 students (Augsburg, 13,692; Bamberg, 8,098; Bayreuth, 8,704; Eichstätt, 4,306; Erlangen-Nuremberg, 25,036; Munich, 41,776; Passau, 8,287; Regensburg, 16,633; Würzburg, 19,861; the Technical University of Munich, 23,186; University of the Federal Armed Forces, Munich *(Universität der Bundeswehr)*, 3,961; the college of politics, Munich, 525; plus the college of philosophy, Munich, 323), and two philosophical-theological colleges with 285 students in total (Benediktbeuern, 109; Neuendettelsau, 176). There were also five colleges of music, two colleges of fine arts and one college of television and film, with 3,303 students in total; 26 vocational colleges *(Fachhochschulen)* with 80,863 students including one for the civil service *(Bayerische Beamtenfachhochschule)* with 3,128 students.

Welfare

In Dec. 2008 there were 44,218 persons receiving benefits of all kinds.

RELIGION

In 2006, 57·2% of the population were Roman Catholics and 21·2% were Protestants.

CULTURE

Tourism

In June 2008 there were 13,807 places of accommodation (with nine beds or more) providing beds for 554,422 people. In 2008 they received 26,664,538 guests of whom 5,999,338 were foreigners. They stayed an average of 2·9 nights each, totalling 76,910,271 nights (12,830,381 nights stayed by foreign visitors).

Festivals

Oktoberfest, Munich's famous beer festival, takes place each year from the penultimate Saturday in Sept. through to the first Sunday in Oct. (extended to 3 Oct. if the last Sunday of the festival falls on 1 or 2 Oct.). There were 5·7m. visitors at the 176th Oktoberfest in 2009.

FURTHER READING

Statistical Information: Bayerisches Landesamt für Statistik und Datenverarbeitung, Neuhauser Str. 8, 80331 Munich. *President:* Karlheinz Anding. It publishes: *Statistisches Jahrbuch für Bayern.* 1894 ff.—*Bayern in Zahlen.* Monthly (from Jan. 1947).—*Zeitschrift des Bayerischen Statistischen Landesamts.* July 1869–1943; 1948 ff.—*Beiträge zur Statistik Bayerns.* 1850 ff.—*Statistische Berichte.* 1951 ff.—*Kreisdaten.* 1972–2001 (from 2003 incorporated in *Statistisches Jahrbuch für Bayern*).—*Gemeindedaten.* 1973 ff.

State library: Bayerische Staatsbibliothek, Ludwigstr. 16, 80539 Munich. *Director General:* Dr Rolf Griebel.

Berlin

KEY HISTORICAL EVENTS

After the end of World War II, Berlin was divided into four occupied sectors, each with a military governor from one of the victorious Allied Powers (the USA, the Soviet Union, Britain and France). In March 1948 the USSR withdrew from the Allied Control Council and in June blockaded West Berlin until May 1949. In response, the allies flew food and other supplies into the city in what became known as the Berlin Airlift. On 30 Nov. 1948 a separate municipal government was set up in the Soviet sector which led to the political division of the city. In contravention of the special Allied status agreed for the city, East Berlin became 'Capital of the GDR' in 1949 and thus increasingly integrated into the GDR as a whole. In West Berlin, the formal authority of the western allies lasted until 1990.

On 17 June 1953 the protest by workers in East Berlin against political oppression and economic hardship was suppressed by Soviet military forces. To stop refugees, the east German government erected the Berlin Wall to seal off West Berlin's borders on 13 Aug. 1961.

The Berlin Wall was breached on 9 Nov. 1989 as the regime in the GDR bowed to the internal pressure which had been building for months. East and West Berlin were amalgamated on the reunification of Germany in Oct. 1990. In April 1994 the *Bundesland* governments of Berlin and Brandenburg agreed to merge the two *Bundesländer* in 1999 or 2002, subject to the approval of their respective parliaments, and of their electorates in referendums held in May 1996. In Berlin 53·4% of votes were cast in favour, but in Brandenburg 62·8% were against. A further referendum on the proposed merger is likely to take place in the next few years.

With the move of the national government, the parliament (Bundestag), and the federal organ of the *Bundesländer* (Bundesrat) in 1999, Berlin is once again a capital city.

TERRITORY AND POPULATION

The area is 891·5 sq. km. Population, 31 Dec. 2008, 3,431,675 (1,751,173 females), including 480,403 foreign nationals; density, 3,849·3 per sq. km.

SOCIAL STATISTICS

Statistics for calendar years:

	Live births	*Marriages*	*Divorces*	*Deaths*
2005	28,976	12,058	9,785	31,985
2006	29,627	11,634	8,317	31,523
2007	31,174	11,511	7,760	30,980
2008	31,936	11,762	7,716	31,911

CONSTITUTION AND GOVERNMENT

According to the constitutions of Sept. 1950 and Oct. 1995, Berlin is simultaneously a *Bundesland* of the Federal Republic and a city. It is governed by a House of Representatives (of at least 130 members); executive power is vested in a Senate, consisting of the Governing Mayor, two Mayors and not more than eight senators. Since 1992 adherence to the constitution has been watched over by a Constitutional Court.

After a proposed merger was rejected by Brandenburg in the 1996 referendum, a Joint Berlin-Brandenburg Co-operation Council was set up.

Berlin has four seats in the Bundesrat.

RECENT ELECTIONS

At the elections of 17 Sept. 2006 turnout was 58·0%. The Social Democratic Party (SPD) won 53 seats with 30·8% of votes cast; the Christian Democratic Union (CDU) 37, with 21·3%; the Left Party 23, with 13·4%; the Greens 23, with 13·1%; and the Free Democratic Party 13, with 7·6%.

CURRENT ADMINISTRATION

The *Governing Mayor* is Klaus Wowereit (SPD).

Government Website: http://www.berlin.de

ECONOMY

Berlin's real GDP growth in 2008 was 1·6%.

INDUSTRY

In Sept. 2008 there were 787 industrial concerns employing 99,817 people. The main industries in terms of percentage of the labour force employed were: electronics, 28·9%; paper, printing and publishing, 14·0%; chemicals, 11·7%; food and tobacco, 11·7%; machine-building, 10·8%; vehicle production, 8·8%; metallurgy, 8·0%.

Labour

In 2008 the workforce was 1,638,000. There were 233,737 persons registered unemployed in 2008 and 1,285 on short time. An average of 33,222 jobs were available at any one time in 2008. The unemployment rate in 2008 was 13·9%.

COMMUNICATIONS

Roads

On 1 Jan. 2009 there were 5,375·8 km of roads (248·9 km of 'classified' roads, made up of 76·7 km of Autobahn and 172·2 km of federal roads). In Jan. 2009, 1,266,879 motor vehicles were registered, including 1,088,221 passenger cars, 73,929 lorries, 2,078 buses and 90,292 motorcycles. There were 123,592 road accidents in 2008 of which 16,102 involved badly damaged vehicles or injured persons, of whom there were 17,685.

Civil Aviation

234,650 flights were made from Berlin's three airports—Tegel, Tempelhof and Schönefeld—in 2008, carrying a total of 21,347,776 passengers. Tempelhof closed in Oct. 2008.

SOCIAL INSTITUTIONS

Justice

There are a court of appeal *(Kammergericht)*, a regional court, nine local courts, a *Bundesland* Labour court, a labour court, a *Bundesland* social court, a social court, a higher administrative court, an administrative court and a finance court.

Education

In the autumn of 2008 there were 323,220 pupils attending schools. There were 436 primary schools with 157,057 pupils, 52 schools for practical education with 11,587 pupils, 92 special schools with 12,297 pupils, 73 secondary modern schools with 19,998 pupils, 108 grammar schools with 78,000 pupils, 53 comprehensive schools with 40,978 pupils and nine *Freie Waldorf* schools with 3,303 pupils. In 2008–09 there were two universities and two technical universities, four arts colleges and 23 technical colleges. There were a total of 135,327 students in higher education.

Health

In 2008 there were 74 hospitals with 19,407 beds, 6,079 doctors, 3,112 dentists and 892 pharmacies.

RELIGION

In Dec. 2008 membership and number of places of worship for major religions was as follows:

Religion	*Members*	*Places of Worship*
Protestant	675,779	460[1]
Roman Catholic	318,438	108
Jewish	11,696	8
Muslim	248,200	128

[1]2007.

CULTURE

Tourism

In 2008 Berlin had 648 places of accommodation providing 97,205 beds for 7,905,145 visitors.

FURTHER READING

Statistical Information: The Amt für Statistik Berlin-Brandenburg (Dortustrasse 46, 14467 Potsdam) was created in Jan. 2007 through the merger of the Statistisches Landesamt Berlin and the Landesbetrieb für Datenverarbeitung und Statistik Land Brandenburg. *President:* Prof. Dr Ulrike Rockmann. It publishes: *Statistisches Jahrbuch* (from 1867): *Zeitschrift für amtliche Statistik Berlin-Brandenburg* (six a year from 2007).—*100 Jahre Berliner Statistik* (1962). *Website (German only):* http://www.statistik-berlin-brandenburg.de

Large, David Clay, *Berlin.* 2000
Read, A., and Fisher, D., *Berlin, Biography of a City.* 1994
Richie, Alexandra, *Faust's Metropolis: A History of Berlin.* 1999
Taylor, R., *Berlin and its Culture.* 1997
Till, Karen, E., *The New Berlin: Memory, Politics, Place.* 2005

State library: Zentral- und Landesbibliothek, Blücherplatz 1, 10961 Berlin. *Director General:* Claudia Lux.

Brandenburg

KEY HISTORICAL EVENTS

For the proposed merger with Berlin *see* BERLIN: Key Historical Events.

Brandenburg surrounds the capital city of Germany, Berlin, but the people of the state voted against the recommendations of the Berlin House of Representatives and the Brandenburg State Parliament that the two states should merge around the year 2000. The state capital, Potsdam, is the ancient city of the Emperor Frederic II 'The Great' who transformed the garrison town of his father Frederic I 'The Soldier' into an elegant city.

TERRITORY AND POPULATION

The area is 29,481 sq. km. Population on 31 Dec. 2008 was 2,522,493 (1,273,181 females). Foreigners accounted for 2·6% of the total population. There are four urban districts, 14 rural districts and 420 communes (31 Dec. 2008). The capital is Potsdam, with a population (31 Dec. 2008) of 152,966.

SOCIAL STATISTICS

Statistics for calendar years:

	Live births	*Marriages*	*Divorces*	*Deaths*
2005	17,910	11,504	5,792	26,069
2006	17,883	11,316	5,525	26,348
2007	18,589	11,430	5,127	26,666
2008	18,808	11,757	5,060	26,807

CONSTITUTION AND GOVERNMENT

The *Bundesland* was reconstituted on former GDR territory on 14 Oct. 1990. Brandenburg has four seats in the Bundesrat and following the 2005 election 21 in the Bundestag.

After a proposed merger was rejected by Brandenburg in the 1996 referendum, a Joint Berlin-Brandenburg Co-operation Council was set up.

At a referendum on 14 June 1992, 93·5% of votes cast were in favour of a new constitution guaranteeing direct democracy and the right to work and housing.

RECENT ELECTIONS

At the Diet elections on 27 Sept. 2009 the Social Democrats (SPD) won 31 seats with 33·0% of the vote; the Left 26, with 27·2%; the Christian Democrats (CDU) 19, with 19·8%; the Free Democratic Party (FDP) 7, with 7·2%; the Greens 5, with 5·6%. Turnout was 67·0%.

CURRENT ADMINISTRATION

The *Prime Minister* is Matthias Platzeck (SPD).

Government Website: http://www.brandenburg.de

ECONOMY

Performance

GDP in 2008 was €54,900m.

ENERGY AND NATURAL RESOURCES

Electricity

Power stations in Brandenburg produced 37,242m. kWh in 2007. A minimal amount was produced from hydro-electric power.

Agriculture

Area and yield of the most important crops:

	Area (in 1,000 ha.)			*Yield (in 1,000 tonnes)*		
	2007	*2008*	*2009*	*2007*	*2008*	*2009*
Rye	208·6	227·0	226·2	688·5	933·4	1,101·1
Wheat	133·6	143·5	143·4	741·8	943·5	987·2
Rape	133·1	121·6	131·2	401·1	431·0	538·5
Barley	84·0	84·4	89·7	409·3	455·9	522·3
Sugar beet	9·0	7·1	7·2	509·8	321·3	448·6
Potatoes	10·4	9·5	9·6	337·0	298·1	340·6

Livestock on 3 May 2009: cattle, 587,000 (including 166,000 milch cows); pigs, 772,000; sheep, 124,000; horses (2007), 20,200; poultry (2007), 8,480,500.

INDUSTRY

In 2008, 1,116 establishments (20 or more employees) in the mining and manufacturing industries employed 94,675 persons, the main areas being: the food industry; vehicle construction; manufacture of chemical products; metal production and treatment; and the wood industry. There were 4,703 establishments in the building industry in 2009, employing 33,021 persons.

Labour

In 2008 at the 1%-sample of the microcensus, 1,229,000 persons were economically active, of which 712,000 non-manual workers and civil servants, 381,200 manual workers, and 132,300 self-employed and family assistants. In 2008 there were on average 175,459 unemployed persons (14·5%).

INTERNATIONAL TRADE

Imports and Exports

Total imports (2008): €14,099m. Total exports: €11,877m.

COMMUNICATIONS

Roads

On 1 Jan. 2009 there were 1,546,337 registered vehicles including 1,295,571 passenger cars.

SOCIAL INSTITUTIONS

Education

In 2008–09 there were 869 schools providing general education (including special schools) with 221,778 pupils and 72 vocational schools with 68,777 pupils.

In the winter term 2008–09 there were three universities and 11 colleges with 46,865 students.

RELIGION

In 2006 there were 461,155 Protestants and 79,351 Roman Catholics.

CULTURE

Tourism

In 2008 there were 1,420 places of accommodation (with nine or more beds), including 458 hotels—providing a total of 78,152 beds—and 172 campsites. 3,727,756 visitors (347,995 foreign) spent a total of 10,171,976 nights (including camping) in Brandenburg in 2008.

FURTHER READING

Statistical office: The Amt für Statistik Berlin-Brandenburg (Dortustrasse 46, 14467 Potsdam) was created in Jan. 2007 through the merger of the Landesbetrieb für Datenverarbeitung und Statistik Land Brandenburg and the Statistisches Landesamt Berlin. *Director:* Prof. Dr Ulrike Rockmann. It publishes *Statistisches Jahrbuch Land Brandenburg* (since 1991).

Website (German only): http://www.statistik-berlin-brandenburg.de

---

Bremen

Freie Hansestadt Bremen

KEY HISTORICAL EVENTS

The state is dominated by the Free City of Bremen and its port, Bremerhaven. In 1815, when it joined the German Confederation, Bremen was an autonomous city and Hanse port with important Baltic trade. In 1827 the expansion of trade inspired the founding of Bremerhaven on land ceded by Hanover at the confluence of the Geest and Weser rivers. Further expansion followed the founding of the Nord-deutscher Lloyd Shipping Company in 1857. Merchant shipping, associated trade and fishing were dominant until 1940 but there was diversification in the post-war years. In 1939 Bremerhaven was absorbed by the Hanoverian town of Wesermünde. The combined port was returned to the jurisdiction of Bremen in 1947.

TERRITORY AND POPULATION

The area of the *Bundesland*, consisting of the two urban districts and ports of Bremen and Bremerhaven, is 404 sq. km. Population, 31 Dec. 2008, 661,866 (321,814 males, 340,052 females).

SOCIAL STATISTICS

Statistics for calendar years:

	Live births	*Marriages*	*Divorces*	*Deaths*
2005	5,489	2,960	1,777	7,419
2006	5,506	2,850	1,647	7,211
2007	5,591	2,762	1,599	7,300
2008	5,569	2,804	1,647	7,353

CONSTITUTION AND GOVERNMENT

Political power is vested in the 83-member House of Burgesses (*Bürgerschaft*) which appoints the executive, called the Senate. Bremen has three seats in the Bundesrat.

RECENT ELECTIONS

At the elections of 13 May 2007 the Social Democratic Party won 33 seats with 36·7% of votes cast; the Christian Democratic Union 23 with 25·7%; Alliance '90/Greens 14 with 16·5%; the Left Party 7 with 8·4%; the Free Democratic Party 5 with 6·0%; and the German People's Union 1 with 2·7%. Turnout was 57·6%.

CURRENT ADMINISTRATION

The *Burgomaster* is Jens Böhrnsen (Social Democrat).

Government Website: http://www.bremen.de

ENERGY AND NATURAL RESOURCES

Agriculture

Agricultural area comprised (2007) 11,450 ha. Livestock in May 2007: 10,976 cattle (including 3,226 milch cows); 894 horses; 608 pigs; 438 sheep.

INDUSTRY

In 2008, 149 establishments (50 or more employees) employed 49,678 persons; of these, 20,782 were employed in the production of cars and car parts and other vehicles; 6,473 were employed in machine construction; 3,121 in electrical engineering; 2,175 in fish processing; 1,495 in shipbuilding (except naval engineering); 1,132 in coffee and tea processing.

Labour

The economically active persons totalled 287,900 at the microcensus of 2008. Of the total, 259,400 were employees, 27,700 self-employed; 79,300 in commerce, trade and communications, 70,300 in production industries, 135,900 in other industries and services.

COMMUNICATIONS

Roads

On 1 Jan. 2008 there were 113 km of 'classified' roads, of which 71 km were Autobahn and 42 km federal roads. Registered motor vehicles on 1 Jan. 2009 numbered 299,283, including 259,335 passenger cars, 15,806 lorries, 502 buses, 3,318 tractors and 18,813 motorcycles.

Civil Aviation

Bremen airport handled 2,486,337 passengers in 2008.

Shipping

Vessels entered in 2008, 9,646 of 200,408,000 GRT; cleared, 9,536 of 197,131,000 GRT. Sea traffic, 2008, incoming 38,810,000 tonnes; outgoing, 35,715,000 tonnes.

SOCIAL INSTITUTIONS

Justice

There are a constitutional court *(Staatsgerichtshof)*, a court of appeal, a regional court, three local courts, a *Bundesland* labour court, two labour courts, a *Bundesland* social court, a finance court, a higher administrative court and an administrative court.

Education

In 2007 there were 294 schools of general education with 5,295 teachers and 67,458 pupils; 40 vocational schools (part-time and full-time) with 19,381 pupils; 24 advanced vocational schools (including institutions for the training of technicians) with 2,993 pupils; six schools for public health occupations with 811 pupils. In 2007 there were 26 special schools with 617 teachers and 2,727 pupils.

In the winter term 2008–09, 17,326 students were enrolled at the University of Bremen and 1,189 at the Jacobs University Bremen. In addition to the universities there were five other colleges in 2008–09 with 11,999 students.

RELIGION

In 2006, 41·4% of the population were Protestants and 13·4% Roman Catholics.

CULTURE

Tourism

In 2008 there were 96 places of accommodation (with nine beds or more) providing 9,700 beds. Of the 934,300 visitors 20% were from abroad.

FURTHER READING

Statistical Information: Statistisches Landesamt Bremen (An der Weide 14–16, D-28195 Bremen), founded in 1850. *Director:* Jürgen Wayand. Its current publications include: *Statistisches Jahrbuch Bremen* (from 1992).—*Statistische Mitteilungen* (from 1948).—*Statistische Monatsberichte* (1954–2004).—*Statistische Hefte* (from 2005).—*Statistische Berichte* (from 1956).—*Statistisches Handbuch Bremen (1950–60,* 1961; *1960–64,* 1967; *1965–69,* 1971; *1970–74,* 1975; *1975–80,* 1982; *1981–85,* 1987).—*Bremen im statistischen Zeitvergleich 1950–1976.* 1977.—*Bremen in Zahlen* (from 1975). *Website (German only):* http://www.statistik.bremen.de

State and University Library: Bibliotheksstraße, 28359 Bremen. *Director:* Maria Elisabeth Müller.

Hamburg

Freie und Hansestadt Hamburg

KEY HISTORICAL EVENTS

Hamburg was a free Hanse town owing nominal allegiance to the Holy Roman Emperor until 1806. In 1815 it became part of the German Confederation, sharing a seat in the Federal Diet with Lübeck, Bremen and Frankfurt. During the Empire it retained its autonomy. By 1938 it had become the third largest port in the world and its territory was extended by the cession of land (three urban and 27 rural districts) from Prussia. After World War II, Hamburg became a *Bundesland* of the Federal Republic with its 1938 boundaries.

TERRITORY AND POPULATION

Total area, 755·3 sq. km (2008), including the islands Neuwerk and Scharhörn (7·6 sq. km). Population (31 Dec. 2008), 1,772,100 (865,900 males; 906,200 females). The *Bundesland* forms a single urban district *(Stadtstaat)* with seven administrative subdivisions.

SOCIAL STATISTICS

Statistics for calendar years:

	Live births	*Marriages*	*Divorces*	*Deaths*
2005	16,179	6,976	4,994	17,374
2006	16,089	6,921	4,583	17,101
2007	16,727	6,661	4,385	17,036
2008	16,751	6,615	4,476	17,091

CONSTITUTION AND GOVERNMENT

The constitution of 6 June 1952 vests the supreme power in the House of Burgesses *(Bürgerschaft)* of 121 members. The executive is in the hands of the Senate, whose members are elected by the Bürgerschaft. Hamburg has three seats in the Bundesrat.

RECENT ELECTIONS

The elections of 24 Feb. 2008 had the following results: Christian Democrats, 56 seats with 42·6% of votes cast; Social Democrats, 45 with 34·1%; the Greens, 12 with 9·6%; the Left, 8 (6·4%); Free Democrats, no seats (4·8%). There were nine other parties. Turnout was 63·4%.

CURRENT ADMINISTRATION

The mayor is Ole von Beust (Christian Democrat).

Government Website: http://www.hamburg.de

ENERGY AND NATURAL RESOURCES

Agriculture

The agricultural area comprised 14,015 ha. in 2007.

Livestock (2007): cattle, 6,559 (including 966 milch cows); horses, 3,107; pigs, 432; sheep, 1,957; poultry, 3,485.

INDUSTRY

In Sept. 2008, 514 establishments (with 20 or more employees) employed 91,512 persons; of these, 26,516 were employed in manufacturing transport equipment (including motor vehicles, aircraft and ships), 13,860 in manufacturing machinery, 12,703 in manufacturing electrical and optical equipment, 4,446 in the mineral oil industry and 4,372 in manufacturing chemical products.

Labour

Economically active persons totalled 861,000 at the 1%-sample survey of the microcensus of 2008. Of the total, 735,000 were employees and 126,000 were self-employed or unpaid family workers; 254,000 were engaged in commerce and transport, 154,000 in power supply, mining, manufacturing and building, 8,000 in agriculture and forestry, 446,000 in other industries and services.

COMMUNICATIONS

Roads

In 2008 there were 3,956 km of roads, including 82 km of Autobahn and 120 km of federal roads. Number of motor vehicles (1 Jan. 2009), 818,189, of which 711,450 were passenger cars, 47,626 lorries, 1,462 buses, 46,651 motorcycles and 11,000 other motor vehicles.

Civil Aviation

Hamburg airport handled 12,782,352 passengers and 34,734 tonnes of freight in 2008.

Shipping

Hamburg is the largest sea port in Germany.

Vessels		*2006*	*2007*	*2008*
Entered:	Number	12,373	12,217	11,899
	Tonnage (gross)	210,291,766	217,159,591	228,584,052
Cleared:	Number	12,400	12,238	11,922
	Tonnage (gross)	210,735,192	216,758,850	228,779,297

SOCIAL INSTITUTIONS

Justice

There is a constitutional court *(Verfassungsgericht)*, a court of appeal *(Oberlandesgericht)*, a regional court *(Landgericht)*, eight local courts *(Amtsgerichte)*, a *Bundesland* labour court, a labour court, a *Bundesland* social court, a social court, a finance court, a higher administrative court and an administrative court.

Education

In 2008 there were 400 schools of general education (not including the *Internationale Schule*) with 183,213 pupils; 45 special schools with 7,091 pupils; 44 part-time vocational schools with 39,604 pupils; 41 schools with 3,990 pupils in manual instruction classes; 45 full-time vocational schools with 9,913 pupils; nine economic secondary schools with 2,298 pupils; two technical *Gymnasien* with 435 pupils; one pedagogical *Gymnasium* with 111 pupils; 18 advanced vocational schools with 4,301 pupils; 34 schools for public health occupations with 3,210 pupils; and 17 technical superior schools with 1,311 pupils.

In the winter term 2008–09 there was one university with 36,108 students; one technical university with 4,950 students; one college of music and one college of fine arts with 1,498 students in total; one university of the *Bundeswehr* (Helmut Schmidt University) with 3,240 students; eight professional colleges with a total of 23,219 students.

Health

In 2008 there were 46 hospitals with 11,426 beds, 10,198 doctors and 1,800 dentists.

RELIGION

In 2006, 31·2% of the population went to the Evangelical Church and Free Churches, whilst 10·3% were Roman Catholic.

CULTURE

Tourism

At Dec. 2008 there were 292 places of accommodation with 39,528 beds. Of the 4,116,335 visitors in 2008, 18·6% were foreigners.

FURTHER READING

Statistical Information: Statistisches Amt für Hamburg und Schleswig-Holstein (Standort Hamburg, Steckelhörn 12, 20457 Hamburg). *Director:* Dr Wolfgang Bick. Publications: *Statistische Berichte, Statistisches Jahrbuch, NORD.regional, Statistik informiert spezial.*

Hamburger Sparkasse, *Hamburg: von Altona bis Zollspieker.* 2002
Hamburgische Gesellschaft für Wirtschaftsförderung mbH, *Hamburg.* 1993
Klessmann, E., *Geschichte der Stadt Hamburg.* 7th ed. 1994
Kopitzsch, F. and Brietzke, D., *Hamburgische Biografie, Personenlexikon.* Vol. 1. 2001
Kopitzsch, F. and Tilgner, D., *Hamburg Lexikon.* 1998
Möller, I., *Hamburg.* 2nd ed. 1999
Schubert, D. and Harms, H., *Wohnen am Hafen.* 1993
Schütt, E. C., *Die Chronik Hamburgs.* 1991

State library: Staats- und Universitätsbibliothek, Carl von Ossietzky, Von-Melle-Park 3, 20146 Hamburg. *Director:* Prof. Dr Gabriele Beger.

Hessen

KEY HISTORICAL EVENTS

The *Bundesland* consists of the former states of Hesse-Darmstadt and Hesse-Kassel, and Nassau. Hesse-Darmstadt was ruled by the Landgrave Louis X from 1790. He became grand duke in 1806 with absolute power, having dismissed the parliament in 1803. However, he granted a constitution and bicameral parliament in 1820. Hesse-Darmstadt lost land to Prussia in the Seven Weeks' War of 1866, but retained its independence, both then and as a state of the German Empire after 1871. In 1918 the grand duke abdicated and the territory became a state of the German Republic. In 1945 areas west of the Rhine were incorporated into the new *Bundesland* of Rhineland-Palatinate, areas east of the Rhine became part of the *Bundesland* of Greater Hesse.

Hesse-Kassel was ruled by the Landgrave William IX from 1785 until he became Elector in 1805. In 1807 the Electorate was absorbed into the Kingdom of Westphalia (a Napoleonic creation), becoming independent again in 1815 as a state of the German Confederation. In 1831 a constitution and parliament were granted but the Electors remained strongly conservative.

In 1866 the Diet approved alliance with Prussia against Austria; the Elector nevertheless supported Austria. He was defeated by the Prussians and exiled and Hesse-Kassel was annexed to Prussia. In 1867 it was combined with Frankfurt and some areas taken from Nassau and Hesse-Darmstadt to form a Prussian province (Hesse-Nassau). In 1801 Nassau west of the Rhine passed to France; Napoleon also took the northern state in 1806. The remnant of the southern states allied in 1803 and three years later they became a duchy. In 1866 the duke supported Austria against Prussia and the duchy was annexed by Prussia as a result. In 1944 the Prussian province of Hesse-Nassau was split in two: Nassau and Electoral Hesse, also called Kurhessen. The following year these were combined with Hesse-Darmstadt as the *Bundesland* of Greater Hesse which became known as Hessen.

TERRITORY AND POPULATION

Area, 21,115 sq. km. The capital is Wiesbaden. There are three administrative regions with five urban and 21 rural districts and 426 communes. Population, 31 Dec. 2008, was 6,064,953 (2,970,447 males, 3,094,506 females).

SOCIAL STATISTICS

Statistics for calendar years:

	Live births	*Marriages*	*Divorces*	*Deaths*
2005	53,369	28,669	15,552	58,548
2006	51,404	27,644	15,405	57,840
2007	52,616	26,928	15,469	59,137
2008	51,752	26,685	15,437	60,083

CONSTITUTION AND GOVERNMENT

The constitution was put into force by popular referendum on 1 Dec. 1946. Hessen has five seats in the Bundesrat.

RECENT ELECTIONS

At the Diet elections on 18 Jan. 2009 the Christian Democratic Union (CDU) won 46 of 118 seats with 37·2% of votes cast (up from 36·8% in 2008), the Social Democratic Party (SPD) 29 with 23·7% (down from 36·7% in 2008), the Free Democratic Party (FDP) 20 with 16·2%, the Greens 17 with 13·7% and the Left 6 with 5·4%.

CURRENT ADMINISTRATION

The cabinet is headed by *Prime Minister* Roland Koch (Christian Democrats; CDU).

Government Website (German only): http://www.hessen.de

ECONOMY

Performance

In 2008 the price-adjusted growth of the gross domestic product at market prices (GDP) was 2·6% in comparison with the previous year. The total amount at current prices was €220·8bn. in 2008. The GDP (at current prices) per person engaged in labour productivity was €70,597 in 2008 (€69,678 in 2007).

ENERGY AND NATURAL RESOURCES

Electricity

Electricity production in 2008 was 31,139m. kWh (gross) and 29,168m. kWh (net). Total electricity consumption in 2008 was 36,149m. kWh.

Oil and Gas

Gas consumption in 2008 was 65,594m. kWh. All gas was imported from other parts of Germany.

Agriculture

Area and yield of the most important crops:

	Area (in 1,000 ha.)			*Yield (in 1,000 tonnes)*		
	2006	*2007*	*2008*	*2006*	*2007*	*2008*
Wheat	156·6	153·3	160·9	1,181·4	1,102·4	1,359·8
Sugar beet	15·5	16·8	15·0	942·5	1,033·7	957·3
Barley	102·4	101·3	101·8	637·0	565·7	618·5
Rape	63·1	65·9	61·2	242·2	233·7	219·5
Potatoes	4·8	4·9	4·5	154·1	175·6	162·5
Rye	13·8	15·4	16·4	85·3	83·6	98·7
Oats	14·4	13·2	12·9	68·6	60·7	65·2

Livestock, May 2009: cattle, 485,159 (including 151,303 milch cows); pigs, 718,486; sheep, 148,191; horses (2007), 37,593; poultry (2007), 1·68m.

INDUSTRY

In Sept. 2009, 1,395 establishments (with 50 or more employees) employed 345,333 persons; of these, 56,566 were employed in the chemical industry; 47,028 in car building; 37,596 in machine construction; 30,435 in production of metal products.

Labour

The economically active persons totalled 2,872,000 at the 1% sample survey of the microcensus in 2008. Of the total, 2,540,000 were employees; 309,000 self-employed, 24,000 unpaid family workers; 759,000 were engaged in power supply, mining, manufacturing and building, 690,000 in commerce, transport, hotels and restaurants, 47,000 in agriculture and forestry and 1,376,000 in other services.

COMMUNICATIONS

Roads

On 1 Jan. 2009 there were 16,640 km of 'classified' roads, comprising 972 km of Autobahn, 3,463 km of federal highways, 7,229 km of first-class highways and 4,976 km of second-class highways. Motor vehicles licensed on 1 Jan. 2009 totalled 3,860,815, including 3,243,845 passenger cars, 5,772 buses, 167,525 lorries, 134,494 tractors and 289,033 motorcycles.

Civil Aviation

Frankfurt/Main airport is one of the most important freight airports in the world. In 2008, 485,783 aeroplanes took off and landed, carrying 53,472,915 passengers, 2,042,956 tonnes of air freight and 90,346 tonnes of air mail.

Shipping

Frankfurt/Main harbour and Hanau harbour are the two most important harbours. In 2008, 8·5m. tonnes of goods were imported into the *Bundesland* and 2·3m. tonnes were exported.

SOCIAL INSTITUTIONS

Justice

There are a constitutional court *(Staatsgerichtshof)*, a court of appeal, nine regional courts, 46 local courts, a *Bundesland* labour court, 12 labour courts, a *Bundesland* social court, seven social courts, a finance court, a higher administrative court *(Verwaltungsgerichtshof)* and five administrative courts.

Education

In 2008 there were 1,258 primary schools with 248,505 pupils (including *Förderstufen*); 162 intermediate schools with 51,068 pupils; 19,222 teachers in the primary and intermediate schools; 237 special schools with 5,059 teachers and 25,450 pupils; 172 high schools with 10,870 teachers and 160,595 pupils; 215 *Gesamtschulen* (comprehensive schools) with 12,784 teachers and 184,240 pupils; 117 part-time vocational schools with 126,646 pupils; 263 full-time vocational schools with 56,363 pupils; 111 advanced vocational schools with 11,862 pupils; 9,076 teachers in the vocational schools.

In the winter term 2008–09 there were four universities (Frankfurt/Main, 32,961 students; Giessen, 22,508; Marburg/Lahn, 19,142; Kassel, 17,868); one technical university in Darmstadt (18,175); two private *Wissenschaftliche Hochschulen* (2,353); 17 *Fachhochschulen* (56,429); two Roman Catholic theological colleges and one Protestant theological college with a total of 357 students; one college of music and two colleges of fine arts with 1,456 students in total.

RELIGION

In 2007 the churches in Hessen reported 2,504,000 (41·2%) Protestants and 1,532,000 (25·2%) Roman Catholics.

CULTURE

Press

In 2008 there were 76 newspapers published in Hessen with a combined circulation of 1·7m.

Tourism

In 2008, 11·5m. visitors stayed 27·3m. nights in Hessen.

FURTHER READING

Statistical Information: The Hessisches Statistisches Landesamt (Rheinstr. 35–37, 65175 Wiesbaden). *President:* Eckart Hohmann. Main publications: *Statistisches Jahrbuch für das Land Hessen* (biannual).—*Staat und Wirtschaft in Hessen* (monthly).—*Statistische Berichte.*—*Hessische Gemeindestatistik* (annual, 1980 ff.). *Website (German only):* http://www.statistik-hessen.de

State library: Hessische Landesbibliothek Wiesbaden, Rheinstr. 55–57, 65185 Wiesbaden. *Director:* Vacant.

Website (German only): http://www.hlb-wiesbaden.de

Lower Saxony

Niedersachsen

KEY HISTORICAL EVENTS

The *Bundesland* consists of the former states of Hanover, Oldenburg, Schaumburg-Lippe and Brunswick. It does not include the cities of Bremen or Bremerhaven. Oldenburg, Danish from 1667, passed to the bishopric of Lübeck in 1773; the Holy Roman Emperor made it a duchy in 1777. As a small state of the Confederation after 1815 it supported Prussia, becoming a member of the Prussian Zollverein (1853) and North German Confederation (1867). The grand duke abdicated in 1918 and was replaced by an elected government.

Schaumburg-Lippe was a small sovereign principality. As such it became a member of the Confederation of the Rhine in 1807 and of the German Confederation in 1815. Surrounded by Prussian territory, it also joined the Prussian-led North German Confederation in 1867. Part of the Empire until 1918, it then became a state of the new republic.

Brunswick, a small duchy, was taken into the Kingdom of Westphalia by Napoleon in 1806 but restored to independence in 1814. In 1830 the duke, Charles II, was forced into exile and replaced in 1831 by his more liberal brother, William. The succession passed to a Hanoverian claimant in 1913 but the duchy ended with the Empire in 1918.

As a state of the republican Germany, Brunswick was greatly reduced under the Third Reich. Its boundaries were restored by the British occupation forces in 1945.

Hanover was an autonomous Electorate of the Holy Roman Empire whose rulers were also kings of Great Britain from 1714 to 1837. From 1762 they ruled almost entirely from England. After Napoleonic invasions Hanover was restored in 1815. A constitution of 1819 made no radical change and had to be followed by more liberal versions in 1833 and 1848. Prussia annexed Hanover in 1866; it remained a Prussian province until 1946. On 1 Nov. 1946 all four states were combined by the British military administration to form the *Bundesland* of Lower Saxony.

TERRITORY AND POPULATION

Lower Saxony has an area of 47,627 sq. km, and is divided into eight urban districts, 38 rural districts and 1,022 communes; capital, Hanover. Population, on 31 Dec. 2008, was 7,947,244 (3,901,052 males; 4,046,192 females).

SOCIAL STATISTICS

Statistics for calendar years:

	Live births	*Marriages*	*Divorces*	*Deaths*
2005	66,993	40,687	20,177	82,976
2006	65,327	39,091	19,058	82,121
2007	65,326	38,036	19,682	82,277
2008	64,887	39,234	20,368	84,874

CONSTITUTION AND GOVERNMENT

The *Bundesland* Niedersachsen was formed on 1 Nov. 1946 by merging the former Prussian province of Hanover with Brunswick, Oldenburg and Schaumburg-Lippe. Lower Saxony has seven seats in the Bundesrat.

RECENT ELECTIONS

At the Diet elections on 27 Jan. 2008 the Christian Democratic Union won 68 of 152 seats, receiving 42·5% of votes cast (down from 48·3% in 2003), the Social Democratic Party 48 with 30·3% (down from 33·4% in 2003), the Free Democrats 13 with 8·2%, the Greens 12 with 8·0% and the Left 11 with 7·1%.

CURRENT ADMINISTRATION

The *Prime Minister* is Christian Wulff (CDU).

Government Website: http://www.niedersachsen.de

ECONOMY

Banking and Finance

193 credit institutions were operating in 2008. Deposits totalled €47,635m.

ENERGY AND NATURAL RESOURCES

Electricity

Electricity production in 2008 was 52,280m. kWh.

Agriculture

Area and yield of the most important crops:

	Area (in 1,000 ha.)			*Yield (in 1,000 tonnes)*		
	2006	*2007*	*2008*	*2006*	*2007*	*2008*
Sugar beet	87	101	98	4,780	6,381	6,319
Potatoes	119	120	114	4,417	5,225	5,257
Wheat	427	400	434	3,401	2,883	3,867
Barley	272	243	247	1,704	1,210	1,527
Rye	120	142	142	695	596	858
Oats	16	17	18	72	66	77

Livestock, 3 May 2007: cattle, 2,497,000 (including 704,700 milch cows); horses, 84,900; pigs, 8,202,700; sheep, 248,900; poultry, 52,523,900.

INDUSTRY

In Sept. 2008, 3,863 establishments employed 521,206 persons; of these 61,125 were employed in machine construction; 50,899 in electrical engineering.

Labour

The economically active persons totalled 3,603,000 in 2008. Of the total, 3,205,500 were employees, 358,200 self-employed, 39,400 unpaid family workers; 1,019,900 were engaged in power supply, mining, manufacturing and building, 875,700 in commerce and transport, 107,900 in agriculture and forestry, and 1,599,500 in other industries and services.

COMMUNICATIONS

Roads

At 1 Jan. 2009 there were 28,076 km of 'classified' roads, comprising 1,341 km of Autobahn, 4,715 km of federal roads, 8,213 km of first-class and 13,653 km of second-class highways. Number of motor vehicles, 1 Jan. 2009, was 4,895,553 including 4,058,368 passenger cars, 218,887 lorries, 7,402 buses, 223,244 tractors and 360,579 motorcycles.

Rail
In 2008, 41·5m. tonnes of freight came into the *Bundesland* by rail and 36·1m. tonnes left by rail.

Civil Aviation
72,340 planes landed at Hanover airport in 2008, which saw 2,788,094 passenger arrivals and 2,781,887 departures. 3,408 tonnes of freight left by air and 2,858 tonnes came in.

SOCIAL INSTITUTIONS
Justice
There are a constitutional court *(Staatsgerichtshof)*, three courts of appeal, 11 regional courts, 79 local courts, a *Bundesland* labour court, 15 labour courts, a *Bundesland* social court, eight social courts, a finance court, a higher administrative court and seven administrative courts.

Education
In 2008–09 there were 1,833 primary schools with 314,897 pupils; 480 post-primary schools with 86,154 pupils; 338 special schools with 36,912 pupils; 466 secondary modern schools with 176,164 pupils; 259 grammar schools with 256,199 pupils; 33 co-operative comprehensive schools with 40,296 pupils; and 32 integrated comprehensive schools with 31,726 pupils.

In the winter term 2008–09 there were seven universities (Göttingen, 23,129 students; Hanover, 19,943; Hildesheim, 4,570; Lüneburg, 8,020; Oldenburg, 8,311; Osnabrück, 9,736; Vechta, 3,418); two technical universities (Braunschweig, 12,683; Clausthal, 3,124); the medical college of Hanover (2,844); the veterinary college in Hanover (2,319).

Health
In 2008 there were 27,227 doctors and 196 hospitals with 5·3 beds per 1,000 population.

RELIGION
In 2007 there were 50·8% Protestants and 17·8% Roman Catholics.

CULTURE
Broadcasting
Norddeutscher Rundfunk is the public broadcasting service for Lower Saxony.

Tourism
In 2008, 10,592,827 guests spent 33,714,415 nights in Lower Saxony.

FURTHER READING
Statistical Information: Niedersächsischer Landesbetrieb für Statistik und Kommunikationstechnologie, Postfach 910764, 30427 Hanover. *Chairman:* Dr Christoph Lahmann. Main publications are: *Statistische Monatshefte Niedersachsen* (from 1947).—*Statistische Berichte Niedersachsen.*—*Statistisches Taschenbuch Niedersachsen 2008* (biennial).

State libraries: Niedersächsische Staats- und Universitätsbibliothek, Platz der Göttinger Sieben 1, 37073 Göttingen. *Director:* Prof. Dr Elmar Mittler; Gottfried Wilhelm Leibniz Bibliothek—Niedersächsische Landesbibliothek, Waterloostr. 8, 30169 Hanover. *Director:* Dr Georg Ruppelt.

Mecklenburg-West Pomerania

Mecklenburg-Vorpommern

KEY HISTORICAL EVENTS
Pomerania was at one time under Swedish control while Mecklenburg was an independent part of the German Empire. The two states were not united until after the Second World War, and after a short period when it was subdivided into three districts under the GDR, it became a state of the Federal Republic of Germany in 1990. The people of the region speak a dialect known as Plattdeutsch (Low German). The four main cities of this state are Hanseatic towns from the period when the area dominated trade with Scandinavia. Rostock on the North Sea coast became the home of the GDR's biggest shipyards.

TERRITORY AND POPULATION
The area is 23,186 sq. km. It is divided into six urban districts, 12 rural districts and 848 communes. Population on 31 Dec. 2008 was 1,664,356 (839,232 females). It is the most sparsely populated of the German *Bundesländer*, with a population density of 72 per sq. km in 2008. The capital is Schwerin.

SOCIAL STATISTICS
Statistics for calendar years:

	Live births	*Marriages*	*Divorces*	*Deaths*
2005	12,357	9,743	3,858	17,384
2006	12,638	9,440	3,213	17,285
2007	12,786	9,747	3,000	17,595
2008	13,098	10,464	3,195	17,818

CONSTITUTION AND GOVERNMENT
The *Bundesland* was reconstituted on former GDR territory in 1990. It has three seats in the Bundesrat.

RECENT ELECTIONS
At the Diet elections of 17 Sept. 2006 the Social Democrats (SPD) won 23 seats with 30·2% of the vote; the Christian Democrats (CDU), 22 with 28·8%; the Left Party, 13 with 16·8%; the Free Democrats, 7 with 9·6%; the far-right National Democratic Party, 6 with 7·3%; the Greens, no seats with 3·4%. Turnout was 59·1%.

CURRENT ADMINISTRATION
The *Prime Minister* is Erwin Sellering (SPD).

Government Website: http://www.mecklenburg-vorpommern.eu

ENERGY AND NATURAL RESOURCES
Agriculture
Area and yield of the most important crops:

	Area (in 1,000 ha.)			*Yield (in 1,000 tonnes)*		
	2006	*2007*	*2008*	*2006*	*2007*	*2008*
Wheat	330·0	312·2	337·2	2,653·4	2,156·7	2,698·8
Sugar beet	21·0	24·5	22·6	1,062·6	1,342·5	1,043·6
Barley	155·7	140·8	139·3	999·8	818·1	965·1
Rape	244·3	259·0	223·7	936·0	878·6	887·1
Potatoes	16·6	15·9	14·6	512·4	612·3	502·9
Rye	50·0	64·5	87·2	226·9	246·2	431·3

Livestock in 2008: cattle, 565,297 (including 174,882 milch cows); pigs, 746,600; sheep, 104,300; horses (2007), 15,420; poultry (2007), 7,425,550.

Fisheries
Sea catch, 2008: 29,072 tonnes (5,535 tonnes frozen, 23,537 tonnes fresh). Freshwater catch, 2008: 585 tonnes (mainly carp, pike, perch and eels). Fish farming, 2008: 518 tonnes.

INDUSTRY
In 2008 there were 746 enterprises (with 20 or more employees) employing 59,969 persons.

Labour
776,200 persons (358,100 females) were employed at the 1%-sample survey of the microcensus (2008 average at the place of residence), including 400,500 white-collar workers, 263,000 manual workers and 76,500 self-employed and family assistants. 32,700 persons were employed as officials. Employment by sector (2008 average at the place of work): public and private services, 273,800; trade, guest business, transport and communications, 190,100; financing, leasing and services for enterprises, 102,900; manufacturing, 78,400; construction, 51,190; agriculture, forestry and fisheries, 28,800; mining, energy and water resources, 6,200; total, 732,100.

COMMUNICATIONS

Roads
In 2008 there were 9,985 km of 'classified' roads, comprising 538 km of Autobahn, 2,004 km of federal roads, 3,298 km of first-class and 4,145 km of second-class highways. Number of motor vehicles at 1 Jan. 2009 was 951,827, including 801,800 passenger cars, 63,967 lorries, 1,604 buses and 50,373 motorcycles.

Shipping
There is a lake district of some 554 lakes greater than 0·1 sq. km. The ports of Rostock, Stralsund and Wismar are important for shipbuilding and repairs. In 2008 the cargo fleet consisted of 120 vessels (including 11 tankers) of 2,422,000 GT. Sea traffic, 2008, incoming 15,394,912 tonnes; outgoing 12,751,739 tonnes.

SOCIAL INSTITUTIONS

Justice
There is a court of appeal (*Oberlandesgericht*), four regional courts (*Landgerichte*), 21 local courts (*Amtsgerichte*), four labour courts, four social courts, a finance court and two administrative courts.

Education
In 2008 there were 592 schools with 128,295 pupils, including 48,173 pupils in primary schools, 55,040 in secondary schools and 14,590 candidates for the school-leaving examination; and 10,399 pupils in special needs schools.

There are universities at Rostock and Greifswald with (in 2008–09) 26,370 students and 5,491 academic staff, and six institutions of equivalent status with 10,633 students and 1,247 academic staff.

RELIGION
In 2007 the Evangelical Lutheran Church of Mecklenburg had 204,800 adherents, 244 pastors and 296 parishes. The Pomeranian Evangelical Church had 100,400 adherents, 108 pastors and 228 parishes in 2007. Roman Catholics numbered 55,700, with 47 priests and 40 parishes.

CULTURE

Tourism
In July 2008 there were 2,740 places of accommodation (with nine or more beds) providing a total of 174,874 beds. 5,772,984 guests stayed an average of 4·1 nights each in 2008.

FURTHER READING
Statistical office: Statistisches Amt Mecklenburg-Vorpommern, Postfach 120135, 19018 Schwerin.

Main publications are: *Statistische Hefte* (formerly *Statistische Monatshefte*) *Mecklenburg-Vorpommern* (since 1991); *Gemeindedaten Mecklenburg-Vorpommern* (since 1999; electronic); *Statistische Berichte* (since 1991; various); *Statistisches Jahrbuch Mecklenburg-Vorpommern* (since 1991); *Statistische Sonderhefte* (since 1992; various). *Website (German only):* http://www.statistik-mv.de

North Rhine-Westphalia

Nordrhein-Westfalen

KEY HISTORICAL EVENTS
Historical Westphalia consisted of many small political units, most of them absorbed by Prussia and Hanover before 1800. In 1807 Napoleon created a Kingdom of Westphalia for his brother Joseph. This included Hesse-Kassel, but was formed mainly from the Prussian and Hanoverian lands between the rivers Elbe and Weser.

In 1815 the kingdom ended with Napoleon's defeat. Most of the area was given to Prussia, with the small principalities of Lippe and Waldeck surviving as independent states. Both joined the North German Confederation in 1867. Lippe remained autonomous after the end of the Empire in 1918; Waldeck was absorbed into Prussia in 1929.

In 1946 the occupying forces combined Lippe with most of the Prussian province of Westphalia to form the *Bundesland* of North Rhine-Westphalia. On 1 March 1947 the allied Control Council formally abolished Prussia.

TERRITORY AND POPULATION
The *Bundesland* comprises 34,086 sq. km. It is divided into five administrative regions, 23 urban districts, 31 rural districts and 396 communes. Capital: Düsseldorf. Population, 31 Dec. 2008, 17,933,064 (9,186,645 females, 8,746,419 males).

SOCIAL STATISTICS
Statistics for calendar years:

	Live births	*Marriages*	*Divorces*	*Deaths*
2005	153,372	85,528	47,480	186,427
2006	149,925	81,502	45,665	183,741
2007	151,168	80,091	43,104	184,954
2008	150,007	81,515	46,098	189,586

CONSTITUTION AND GOVERNMENT
Since Oct. 1990 North Rhine-Westphalia has had six seats in the Bundesrat.

RECENT ELECTIONS
The Diet elected on 22 May 2005 consisted of 89 Christian Democrats (44·8% of votes cast), 74 Social Democrats (37·1%—their worst showing in North Rhine-Westphalia in 50 years), 12 Free Democrats (6·2%) and 12 Greens (6·2%). Turnout was 63·0%.

CURRENT ADMINISTRATION
North Rhine-Westphalia is governed by the Christian Democrats (CDU) and the Free Democrats (FDP).

Prime Minister: Dr Jürgen Rüttgers (CDU).

Government Website (German only): http://www.nrw.de

ECONOMY
North Rhine-Westphalia has the highest GDP of any German *Bundesland* (€529·4bn. in 2007). Foreign direct investment is also higher than in any other *Bundesland*.

Budget
The predicted total revenue for 2009 was €52,704·2m. and the predicted total expenditure was also €52,704·1m.

ENERGY AND NATURAL RESOURCES

Agriculture
Area and yield of the most important crops:

	Area (in 1,000 ha.)			Yield (in 1,000 tonnes)		
	2006	2007	2008	2006	2007	2008
Sugar beet	56·7	62·0	53·6	3,400·0	4,119·8	3,572·8
Wheat	278·7	269·5	292·8	2,176·5	1,961·5	2,607·8
Potatoes	30·5	31·7	30·0	1,308·8	1,430·6	1,611·0
Barley	203·8	189·3	188·1	1,373·6	1,062·3	1,314·4
Rye	19·2	20·2	18·5	126·6	93·7	123·7
Oats	18·4	17·0	17·4	88·4	73·1	88·9

Livestock, 3 May 2008: cattle, 1,421,326 (including 396,400 milch cows); pigs, 6,366,355; sheep, 173,830; poultry (2007), 10,133,143.

INDUSTRY

In Sept. 2008, 10,322 establishments (with 20 or more employees) employed 1,297,140 persons: 297,504 were employed in metal production and manufacture of metal goods; 230,130 in machine construction; 140,982 in manufacture of office machines, computers, electrical and precision engineering and optics; 105,690 in the chemical industry; 97,347 in production of food and tobacco; and 96,453 in motor vehicle manufacture. 69% of the workforce is now employed in the services industry. Of the total population, 9·8% were engaged in industry.

Labour

The economically active persons totalled 8,093,000 at the 1%-sample survey of the microcensus of 2008. Of the total, 7,225,000 were employees, 803,500 self-employed and 64,000 unpaid family workers; 2,398,000 were engaged in power supply, mining, manufacturing, water supply and building, 1,881,000 in commerce, hotel trade and transport, 121,000 in agriculture, forestry and fishing, and 3,694,000 in other industries and services.

COMMUNICATIONS

Roads

There were (1 Jan. 2009) 29,605 km of 'classified' roads, comprising 2,186 km of Autobahn, 4,875 km of federal roads, 12,773 km of first-class and 9,772 km of second-class highways. Number of motor vehicles (1 Jan. 2009): 10,318,681, including 8,820,040 passenger cars, 465,188 lorries, 16,003 buses and 754,622 motorcycles.

Civil Aviation

In 2008, 111,792 aircraft landed at Düsseldorf, bringing 9,065,373 incoming passengers; and 64,403 aircraft landed at Cologne-Bonn, bringing 5,133,037 incoming passengers.

SOCIAL INSTITUTIONS

Justice

There are a constitutional court *(Verfassungsgerichtshof)*, three courts of appeal, 19 regional courts, 130 local courts, three *Bundesland* labour courts, 30 labour courts, one *Bundesland* social court, eight social courts, three finance courts, a higher administrative court and seven administrative courts.

Education

In 2008 there were 3,971 primary schools with 58,233 teachers and 912,495 pupils; 708 special schools with 17,939 teachers and 101,480 pupils; 557 intermediate schools with 17,995 teachers and 320,895 pupils; 268 *Gesamtschulen* (comprehensive schools) with 18,876 teachers and 251,069 pupils; 629 high schools with 36,950 teachers and 593,080 pupils; there were 289 part-time vocational schools with 387,674 pupils; 215 vocational preparatory year schools with 24,121 pupils; 313 full-time vocational schools with 114,613 pupils; 193 vocational high schools with 27,425 pupils; 195 full-time vocational schools leading up to vocational colleges with 24,623 pupils; 260 advanced full-time vocational schools with 41,988 pupils; 444 schools for public health occupations with 13,112 teachers and 41,588 pupils.

In the winter term 2008–09 there were 15 universities (Bielefeld, 17,629 students; Bochum, 30,763; Bonn, 26,343; Cologne, 40,458; Dortmund, 21,654; Düsseldorf, 16,415; Duisburg-Essen, 30,953; Münster, 35,922; Paderborn, 13,023; Siegen, 12,198; Witten/Herdecke, 1,072; Wuppertal, 13,414; the Technical University of Aachen, 31,422; Fernuniversität at Hagen, 42,035; German Police University/DHPol, 100); the College for physical education in Cologne, 4,543; three Roman Catholic and two Protestant theological colleges with a total of 539 students. There were also four colleges of music, four colleges of fine arts with 5,442 students in total; 28 *Fachhochschulen* (vocational colleges) with 127,376 students.

Health

In 2008 there were 418 hospitals in North Rhine-Westphalia with 122,803 beds, which had an average occupancy rate of 75·7%.

RELIGION

In 2006 there were 42·5% Roman Catholics and 28·2% Protestants.

CULTURE

Tourism

In Dec. 2008 there were 5,530 places of accommodation (nine beds or more) providing 295,267 beds altogether. In 2008, 17,683,902 visitors (3,569,313 foreigners) spent 41,521,488 nights in North Rhine-Westphalia.

FURTHER READING

Statistical Information: Information und Technik Nordrhein-Westfalen (IT NRW) (Mauerstr. 51, 40476 Düsseldorf) was founded in 1946 as the Landesamt für Datenverabeitung und Statistik Nordrhein-Westfalen by amalgamating the provincial statistical offices of Rhineland and Westphalia. It was renamed on 1 Jan. 2009. *President:* Hans-Josef Fischer. IT NRW publishes (from 1949): *Statistisches Jahrbuch Nordrhein-Westfalen.* More than 550 other publications yearly. *Website (German only):* http://www.it.nrw.de

Bundesland Library: Universitätsbibliothek, Universitätsstr. 1, 40225 Düsseldorf. *Director:* Dr Irmgard Siebert.

Rhineland-Palatinate

Rheinland-Pfalz

KEY HISTORICAL EVENTS

The *Bundesland* was formed from the Rhenisch Palatinate and the Rhine valley areas of Prussia, Hesse-Darmstadt, Hesse-Kassel and Bavaria.

From 1214 the Palatinate was ruled by the Bavarian house of Wittelsbach, with its capital as Heidelberg. In 1797 the land west of the Rhine was taken into France, and Napoleon divided the eastern land between Baden and Hesse. In 1815 the territory taken by France was restored to Germany and allotted to Bavaria. The area and its neighbours formed the strategically important Bavarian Circle of the Rhine. The rule of the Wittelsbachs ended in 1918 but the Palatinate remained part of Bavaria until the American occupying forces detached it in 1946. The new *Bundesland*, incorporating the Palatinate and other territory, received its constitution in April 1947.

TERRITORY AND POPULATION

Rhineland-Palatinate has an area of 19,854 sq. km. It comprises 12 urban districts, 24 rural districts and 2,306 other communes. The capital is Mainz. Population (at 31 Dec. 2008), 4,028,351 (2,051,320 females).

SOCIAL STATISTICS

Statistics for calendar years:

	Live births	*Marriages*	*Divorces*	*Deaths*
2005	32,592	20,265	10,653	42,784
2006	31,755	20,003	10,078	41,973
2007	32,536	19,542	10,324	42,165
2008	32,223	20,059	10,273	42,932

CONSTITUTION AND GOVERNMENT

The constitution of the *Bundesland* Rheinland-Pfalz was approved by the Consultative Assembly on 25 April 1947 and by referendum on 18 May 1947, when 579,002 voted for and 514,338 against its acceptance. It has four seats in the Bundesrat.

RECENT ELECTIONS

At the elections of 26 March 2006 the Social Democratic Party won 53 seats of the 101 in the state parliament with 45·6% of votes cast; the Christian Democrats 38 with 32·8% (their worst result ever in Rheinland-Pfalz); the Free Democrats 10 with 8·0%. The Greens only received 4·6% of the vote and the Election Alternative Labour and Social Justice 2·6%; therefore neither party won any seats. Turnout was 58·2%.

CURRENT ADMINISTRATION

The cabinet is headed by *Prime Minister* Kurt Beck (b. 1949; Social Democrat).

Government Website: http://www.rlp.de

ENERGY AND NATURAL RESOURCES

Agriculture

Area and yield of the most important products:

	Area (in 1,000 ha.)			*Yield (in 1,000 tonnes)*		
	2006	*2007*	*2008*	*2006*	*2007*	*2008*
Sugar beet	18·8	19·8	18·9	1,227·5	1,316·7	1,156·9
Wheat	101·6	102·8	111·5	709·7	650·1	825·7
Barley	89·8	91·6	96·9	505·7	414·2	548·5
Potatoes	8·4	8·5	8·5	293·6	311·3	282·2
Rye	9·1	9·8	12·0	50·6	49·4	75·9
Oats	8·2	7·0	7·1	35·3	25·0	31·9
Wine	61·8	62·1	62·3	5,907·8[1]	6,796·6[1]	6,612·5[1]

[1]1,000 hectolitres.

Livestock (2008, in 1,000): cattle, 391·6 (including milch cows, 119·3); pigs, 285·7; sheep, 108·0; horses (2007), 25·2; poultry (2007), 1,674·8.

Forestry

Total area covered by forests in Dec. 2008 was 8,321·0 sq. km or 41·9% of the total area.

INDUSTRY

In 2008, 2,119 establishments (with 20 or more employees) employed 291,066 persons; of these 55,023 were employed in the chemical industry; 40,827 in metal production and manufacture of metal goods; 38,844 in machine construction; 31,793 in motor vehicle manufacture; 27,076 in production of food and tobacco.

Labour

The economically active persons totalled 1,922,600 in 2008. Of the total, 1,698,700 were employees, 202,900 were self-employed, 21,100 were unpaid family workers; 572,300 were engaged in power supply, mining, manufacturing and building, 449,000 in commerce, transport, hotels and restaurants, 48,000 in agriculture and forestry, 853,400 in other industries and services.

COMMUNICATIONS

Roads

In 2009 there were 18,450 km of 'classified' roads, comprising 872 km of Autobahn, 2,948 km of federal roads, 7,221 km of first-class and 7,409 km of second-class highways. Number of motor vehicles, 1 Jan. 2009, was 2,671,389, including 2,195,226 passenger cars, 111,889 lorries, 4,699 buses, 134,116 tractors and 211,508 motorcycles.

SOCIAL INSTITUTIONS

Justice

There are a constitutional court *(Verfassungsgerichtshof)*, two courts of appeal, eight regional courts, 47 local courts, a *Bundesland* labour court, five labour courts, a *Bundesland* social court, four social courts, a finance court, a higher administrative court and four administrative courts.

Education

In 2008 there were 996 primary schools with 10,519 teachers and 157,042 pupils; 566 secondary schools with 21,240 teachers and 295,271 pupils; 141 special schools with 2,843 teachers and 15,868 pupils; 103 vocational and advanced vocational schools with 5,724 teachers and 132,833 pupils.

In higher education, in the winter term 2009–10 (provisional figures) there were the University of Mainz (34,277 students), the University of Trier (14,320 students), the University of Koblenz-Landau (12,991 students), the University of Kaiserslautern (12,008 students), the *Deutsche Hochschule für Verwaltungswissenschaften* in Speyer (332 students), the *Wissenschaftliche Hochschule für Unternehmensführung* (Otto Beisheim Graduate School) in Vallendar (622 students), the Roman Catholic Theological College in Trier (404 students) and the Roman Catholic Theological College in Vallendar (179 students). There were also nine *Fachhochschulen* with 32,753 students and three *Verwaltungsfachhochschulen* with 2,194 students.

RELIGION

In 2007 there were 45·8% Roman Catholics and 31·3% Protestants.

CULTURE

Tourism

In 2008, 3,581 places of accommodation provided 153,458 beds for 6,926,215 visitors.

FURTHER READING

Statistical Information: Statistisches Landesamt Rheinland-Pfalz (Mainzer Str., 14–16, 56130 Bad Ems). *President:* Jörg Berres. Its publications include: *Statistisches Jahrbuch Rheinland-Pfalz* (since 1948); *Statistische Monatshefte Rheinland-Pfalz* (since 1958); *Rheinland-Pfalz heute* (since 1973); *Statistik von Rheinland-Pfalz* (from 1946 to 2004), then renamed *Statistische Bände* (since 2004) 397 vols. to date; *Kreisfreie Städte und Landkreise* (since 2004); *Rheinland-Pfalz ein Ländervergleich* (since 2005); *Die Wirtschaft in Rheinland-Pfalz* (since 2007).

Saarland

KEY HISTORICAL EVENTS

Long disputed between Germany and France, the area was occupied by France in 1792. Most of it was allotted to Prussia at the close of the Napoleonic wars in 1815. In 1870 Prussia defeated France and when, in 1871, the German Empire was founded under Prussian leadership, it was able to incorporate Lorraine. This part of France was the Saar territory's western neighbour so the Saar was no longer a vulnerable boundary state. It began to develop industrially, exploiting Lorraine coal and iron.

In 1919 the League of Nations took control of the Saar until a plebiscite of 1935 favoured return to Germany. In 1945 there was a French occupation, and in 1947 the Saar was made an international area, but in economic union with France. In 1954

France and Germany agreed that the Saar should be a separate and autonomous state, under an independent commissioner. This was rejected by referendum and France agreed to return Saarland to Germany; it became a *Bundesland* of the Federal Republic on 1 Jan. 1957.

TERRITORY AND POPULATION

Saarland has an area of 2,570 sq. km (including a mutual area with Luxembourg). It comprises six rural districts and 52 communes. The capital is Saarbrücken. Population, 31 Dec. 2008, 1,030,324 (501,185 males, 529,139 females).

SOCIAL STATISTICS

Statistics for calendar years:

	Live births	*Marriages*	*Divorces*	*Deaths*
2005	7,484	5,069	2,924	12,312
2006	7,222	4,670	2,497	12,296
2007	7,274	4,774	2,802	12,327
2008	7,158	4,936	2,734	12,547

CONSTITUTION AND GOVERNMENT

Saarland has three seats in the Bundesrat.

RECENT ELECTIONS

At the elections to the Saar Diet of 30 Aug. 2009 the Christian Democrats (CDU) won 19 of 51 seats with 34·5% of votes cast, the Social Democrats (SPD) 13, with 24·5%; the Left 11, with 21·3%; the Free Democrats (FDP) 5, with 9·2%; and the Greens 3, with 5·9%. Turnout was 67·6%.

CURRENT ADMINISTRATION

In Oct. 2009 the rightist CDU, the right-of-centre FDP and the Greens agreed to form Germany's first ever so-called 'Jamaica coalition' (the traditional colours of the three parties—black, yellow and green—being the same as those of the Jamaican flag). The *Prime Minister* is Peter Müller (Christian Democrat).

Government Website: http://www.saarland.de

ENERGY AND NATURAL RESOURCES

Electricity

In 2008 electricity production was 9,179m. kWh. End-user consumption totalled 8,907m. kWh in 2007.

Oil and Gas

9,107m. kWh of gas was used in 2007.

Agriculture

The cultivated area (2008) occupied 112,341 ha. or 43·7% of the total area.

Area and yield of the most important crops:

	Area (in 1,000 ha.)			*Yield (in 1,000 tonnes)*		
	2007	*2008*	*2009*	*2007*	*2008*	*2009*
Wheat	8·7	9·7	9·5	51·2	67·0	66·5
Barley	5·8	6·1	5·1	26·4	31·0	28·0
Rye	3·6	4·4	4·1	16·5	25·1	24·4
Oats	2·7	2·4	2·1	9·6	10·0	9·2
Potatoes	0·2	0·1	0·2	5·6	3·8	5·9

Livestock, May 2009: cattle, 52,795 (including 14,084 milch cows); pigs, 11,681; sheep, 14,448; horses (2007), 5,930; poultry (2007), 166,180.

Forestry

The forest area (86,148 ha.) comprises 34·0% of the total (256,969 ha.).

INDUSTRY

In June 2009, 253 establishments (with 50 or more employees) employed 84,799 persons; of these 22,899 were engaged in manufacturing of motor vehicles, parts and accessories, 10,871 in iron and steel production, 10,012 in machine construction, 4,403 in coalmining and quarrying of stone, sand and clay, 2,818 in steel construction and 2,074 in electrical engineering. In 2008 the coalmines produced 1·0m. tonnes of coal. Two blast furnaces and seven steel furnaces produced 4·4m. tonnes of pig iron and 5·7m. tonnes of crude steel in 2008.

Labour

The economically active persons totalled 454,700 at the 1%-sample survey of the microcensus of 2008. Of the total, 416,300 were employees and 38,400 self-employed; 126,000 were engaged in power supply, mining, manufacturing and building, 106,600 in commerce and transport, fewer than 5,000 in agriculture and forestry, and 218,000 in other industries and services.

COMMUNICATIONS

Roads

At 1 Jan. 2009 there were 2,042 km of classified roads, comprising 240 km of Autobahn, 331 km of federal roads, 845 km of first-class and 626 km of second-class highways. Number of registered motor vehicles, 1 Jan. 2009, 678,332, including 575,317 passenger cars, 28,753 lorries, 1,294 buses, 15,606 tractors and 54,314 motorcycles.

Shipping

In 2008, 1,902 ships docked in Saarland ports, bringing 2·5m. tonnes of freight. In the same year 1,903 ships left the ports, carrying 1·5m. tonnes of freight.

SOCIAL INSTITUTIONS

Justice

There are a constitutional court *(Verfassungsgerichtshof)*, a regional court of appeal, a regional court, ten local courts, a *Bundesland* labour court, three labour courts, a *Bundesland* social court, a social court, a finance court, a higher administrative court and an administrative court.

Education

In 2008–09 there were 160 primary schools with 33,675 pupils; 41 special schools with 3,858 pupils; 54 *Realschulen* and *Erweiterte Realschulen* with 21,609 pupils; 35 high schools with 30,462 pupils; 18 comprehensive high schools with 12,059 pupils; four *Freie Waldorfschulen* with 1,401 pupils; two evening intermediate schools with 304 pupils; one evening high school with 185 pupils; one Saarland College with 68 pupils; 38 part-time vocational schools with 21,908 pupils; year of commercial basic training: 53 institutions with 2,475 pupils; 13 advanced full-time vocational schools and schools for technicians with 1,899 pupils; 41 full-time vocational schools with 4,335 pupils; 34 *Fachoberschulen* (full-time vocational schools leading up to vocational colleges) with 7,451 pupils; seven business and technical grammar schools with 1,082 pupils; 33 schools for public health occupations with 2,478 pupils. The number of pupils attending the vocational schools amounts to 41,474.

In the winter term 2008–09 there was the University of the Saarland with 14,883 students; one academy of fine art with 285 students; one academy of music with 361 students; one vocational college (economics and technics) with 4,021 students; one vocational college for social affairs with 13 students; one vocational college for public administration with 334 students; and one university of applied science (health care and prevention) with 1,721 students.

Health

In 2008 the 25 hospitals in the Saarland contained 6,671 beds and treated 255,747 patients. The average occupancy rate was 85·1%. There were also 19 out-patient and rehabilitation centres which treated 28,855 patients in 2008. On average they were using 76·6% of their capacity.

RELIGION

In 2006, 64·9% of the population were Roman Catholics and 19·7% were Protestants.

CULTURE

Tourism

In 2008, 18,921 beds were available in 285 places of accommodation (of nine or more beds). 768,463 guests spent 2,264,108 nights in the Saarland, staying an average of 2·9 days each.

FURTHER READING

Statistical Information: Landesamt für Zentrale Dienste, Statistisches Amt Saarland (Virchowstrasse 7, 66119 Saarbrücken). *Director:* Michael Sossong. The most important publications are: *Statistisches Jahrbuch Saarland* (annual).—*Saarland in Zahlen* (special issues).—*Einzelschriften zur Statistik des Saarlandes* (special issues).—*Statistik-Journal* (quarterly magazine).

Website (German only): http://www.saarland.de/statistik.htm

Saxony

Freistaat Sachsen

KEY HISTORICAL EVENTS

The former kingdom of Saxony was a member state of the German Empire from 1871 until 1918, when it became the state of Saxony and joined the Weimar Republic. After the Second World War it was one of the five states in the German Democratic Republic until German reunification in 1990. It has been home to much of Germany's cultural history. In the 18th century, the capital of Saxony, Dresden, became the cultural capital of northern Europe earning the title 'Florence of the North', and the other great eastern German city, Leipzig, was a lively commercial city with strong artistic trends. The three cities of Dresden, Chemnitz and Leipzig formed the industrial heartland of Germany which, after World War II, was the manufacturing centre of the GDR.

TERRITORY AND POPULATION

The area is 18,419 sq. km. It is divided into three administrative regions, three urban districts, ten rural districts and 493 communes. Population on 31 Dec. 2008 was 4,192,801 (2,143,628 females, 2,049,173 males); density, 228 per sq. km. The capital is Dresden.

SOCIAL STATISTICS

Statistics for calendar years:

	Live births	*Marriages*	*Divorces*	*Deaths*
2005	32,581	17,156	8,429	48,908
2006	32,556	16,754	7,759	48,228
2007	33,858	16,965	7,749	49,069
2008	34,411	17,397	7,715	48,997

CONSTITUTION AND GOVERNMENT

The *Bundesland* was reconstituted as the Free State of Saxony on former GDR territory in 1990. It has four seats in the Bundesrat.

RECENT ELECTIONS

At the Diet elections of 30 Aug. 2009 the Christian Democratic Union won 58 of 132 seats, with 40·2% of the vote; the Left, 29, with 20·6%; the Social Democratic Party, 14, with 10·4%; the Free Democrats, 14, with 10·0%; the Greens, 9, with 6·4% and the extreme right-wing National Democratic Party, 8, with 5·6%. Turnout was 52·2%.

CURRENT ADMINISTRATION

The *Prime Minister* is Stanislaw Tillich (b. 1959; Christian Democrat).

Government Website: http://www.sachsen.de

ENERGY AND NATURAL RESOURCES

Agriculture

Area and yield of the most important crops:

	Area (in 1,000 ha.)			*Yield (in 1,000 tonnes)*		
	2007	*2008*	*2009*	*2007*	*2008*	*2009*
Maize	76·2	83·3	81·6	2,891·0	2,933·0	3,019·4
Fodder	208·3	210·7	204·4	1,683·9	1,638·3	1,668·5
Wheat	175·8	185·9	190·7	1,206·7	1,420·6	1,367·5
Barley	135·1	145·2	139·0	800·7	883·9	891·6
Potatoes	8·0	7·2	7·1	343·4	286·7	305·5
Rye	39·4	39·4	44·0	174·0	210·2	230·7

Livestock in May 2008 (in 1,000): cattle, 504 (including milch cows, 192); pigs, 616; sheep, 125.

INDUSTRY

In Sept. 2009, 1,277 establishments (with 50 or more employees) employed 190,529 persons.

Labour

The unemployment rate was 13·0% in Oct. 2009.

COMMUNICATIONS

Roads

On 1 Jan. 2009 there were 529·5 km of autobahn and 2,519·9 km of main roads. There were 2,405,706 registered motor vehicles, including 2,049,158 passenger cars, 208,315 lorries and tractors, 3,695 buses and 130,270 motorcycles.

Civil Aviation

Leipzig/Halle airport handled 2,457,077 passengers in 2008.

SOCIAL INSTITUTIONS

Education

In 2009–10 there were 839 primary schools (*Grundschulen*) with 120,763 pupils and 8,746 teachers; 333 secondary schools (*Mittelschulen*) with 81,276 pupils and 9,416 teachers; 145 grammar schools (*Gymnasien*) with 79,078 pupils and 8,296 teachers; and 158 high schools (*Förderschulen*) with 18,821 pupils and 3,223 teachers. There were three *Freie Waldorfschulen* (private) with 1,314 pupils and 109 teachers; 298 professional training schools with 137,196 students and 6,721 teachers; and ten adult education colleges with 2,775 students and 213 teachers. In 2008–09 there were seven universities with 75,429 students, 11 polytechnics with 28,191 students, six art schools with 2,749 students and two management colleges with 985 students; in 2008–09 there were a total of 107,355 students in higher education institutions.

Health

In 2008 there were 80 hospitals with 26,316 beds. There were 14,564 doctors and 3,824 dentists.

RELIGION

In 2007, 20·9% of the population belonged to the Evangelical Church and 3·6% were Roman Catholic.

CULTURE

Tourism

In 2008 there were 115,309 beds in 2,121 places of accommodation. There were 5,911,979 visitors during the year.

FURTHER READING

Statistical office: Statistisches Landesamt des Freistaates Sachsen, Postfach 1105, 01911 Kamenz. It publishes *Statistisches Jahrbuch des Freistaates Sachsen* (since 1990).

Saxony-Anhalt

Sachsen-Anhalt

KEY HISTORICAL EVENTS

Saxony-Anhalt has a short history as a state in its own right. Made up of a patchwork of older regions ruled by other states, Saxony-Anhalt existed between 1947 and 1952 and then, after reunification in 1990, it was re-established. Geographically, it lies at the very heart of Germany and despite the brevity of its federal status, the region has some of the oldest heartlands of German culture.

TERRITORY AND POPULATION

The area is 20,448 sq. km. It is divided into three county-free cities, 11 rural districts and 1,012 communes. Population on 31 Dec. 2008 was 2,381,872. The capital is Magdeburg.

SOCIAL STATISTICS

Statistics for calendar years:

	Live births	*Marriages*	*Divorces*	*Deaths*
2005	17,166	10,980	5,227	29,277
2006	16,927	10,114	5,097	29,151
2007	17,387	10,117	4,924	29,392
2008	17,697	10,515	4,994	29,905

CONSTITUTION AND GOVERNMENT

The *Bundesland* was reconstituted on former GDR territory in 1990. It has four seats in the Bundesrat.

RECENT ELECTIONS

At the Diet election on 26 March 2006 the CDU received 36·2% of votes cast giving them 40 of 97 seats, the Left Party (former Party for Democratic Socialism) 24·1% (26 seats), the SPD 21·4% (24 seats) and the Free Democratic Party 6·7% (7). The Green Party only received 3·6% of the vote, and therefore won no seats. Turnout was 44·4%.

CURRENT ADMINISTRATION

The *Prime Minister* is Wolfgang Böhmer (CDU).

Government Website: http://www.sachsen-anhalt.de

ENERGY AND NATURAL RESOURCES

Agriculture

Area and yield of the most important crops:

	Area (in 1,000 ha.)			*Yield (in 1,000 tonnes)*		
	2006	*2007*	*2008*	*2006*	*2007*	*2008*
Cereals	580·7	557·4	598·9	3,729·7	3,389·2	4,450·1
Sugar beet	39·7	48·3	45·6	1,877·8	2,949·9	2,643·5
Potatoes	13·0	12·8	12·6	450·9	584·1	560·0
Maize	18·3	14·5	22·1	119·3	135·3	186·9

Livestock in 2008 (in 1,000): cattle, 354·2 (including milch cows, 128·1); pigs, 1,053·5; sheep, 111·4 (2007).

INDUSTRY

In 2008, 1,489 establishments (with 20 or more employees) employed 129,294 persons; of these, 59,286 were employed in basic industry, 38,404 in the capital goods industry and 21,588 in the food industry. Major sectors are extraction of metal, metal working, metal articles, the nutrition industry, mechanical engineering and the chemical industry.

Labour

The economically active persons totalled 1,089,400 in 2008. Of the total, 999,500 were employees, 87,900 self-employed, 2,000 unpaid family workers; 315,700 were engaged in power supply, mining, manufacturing and building, 254,400 in commerce and transport, 33,600 in agriculture and forestry, 485,700 in other industries and services.

COMMUNICATIONS

Roads

In 2009 there were 549 km of motorways, 2,305 km of main and 3,858 km of local roads. At 1 Jan. 2008 there were 1,384,383 registered motor vehicles, including 1,184,174 passenger cars, 84,233 lorries, 2,170 buses and 71,183 motorcycles.

SOCIAL INSTITUTIONS

Education

In 2008–09 there were 952 schools with 175,575 pupils. There were 11 universities and institutes of equivalent status with 52,034 students in 2006.

RELIGION

In 2006, 15·3% of the population were Protestants and 3·8% were Roman Catholics.

CULTURE

Tourism

1,045 places of accommodation provided 52,698 beds in Dec. 2008. There were 2,641,801 visitors during the year.

FURTHER READING

Statistical office: Statistisches Landesamt Sachsen-Anhalt, Postfach 20 11 56, 06012 Halle. It publishes *Statistisches Jahrbuch des Landes Sachsen-Anhalt* (since 1991).

Schleswig-Holstein

KEY HISTORICAL EVENTS

The *Bundesland* is formed from two states formerly contested between Germany and Denmark. Schleswig was a Danish dependency ruled since 1474 by the King of Denmark as Duke of Schleswig. He also ruled Holstein, its southern neighbour, as Duke of Holstein, but he did so recognizing that it was a fief of the Holy Roman Empire. As such, Holstein joined the German Confederation which replaced the Empire in 1815.

Disputes between Denmark and the powerful German states were accompanied by rising national feeling in the duchies, where the population was part-Danish and part-German. There was war in 1848–50 and in 1864, when Denmark surrendered its claims to Prussia and Austria. Following her defeat of Austria in 1866 Prussia annexed both duchies.

North Schleswig (predominantly Danish) was awarded to Denmark in 1920. Prussian Holstein and south Schleswig became the present *Bundesland* in 1946.

TERRITORY AND POPULATION

The area of Schleswig-Holstein is 15,799 sq. km. It is divided into four urban and 11 rural districts and 1,127 communes. The capital is Kiel. The population (estimate, 31 Dec. 2008) numbered 2,834,260 (1,387,798 males, 1,446,462 females).

SOCIAL STATISTICS

Statistics for calendar years:

	Live births	*Marriages*	*Divorces*	*Deaths*
2005	23,027	17,131	7,940	29,699
2006	22,686	16,263	7,524	29,815
2007	22,961	16,451	7,434	29,934
2008	22,678	16,590	7,459	30,719

CONSTITUTION AND GOVERNMENT

The *Bundesland* has four seats in the Bundesrat.

RECENT ELECTIONS

At the elections of 27 Sept. 2009 the Christian Democrats won 34 of the 95 available seats with 31·5% of votes cast, the Social Democrats 25 with 25·4%, the Free Democrats 15 with 14·9%, the Greens 12 with 12·4%, the Left 5 with 6·0% and the (Danish) South Schleswig Voters Association 4 with 4·3%. Turnout was 73·6%.

CURRENT ADMINISTRATION

The *Prime Minister* is Peter Harry Carstensen (b. 1947; CDU).

Government Website: http://www.schleswig-holstein.de

ENERGY AND NATURAL RESOURCES

Agriculture

Area and yield of the most important crops:

	Area (in 1,000 ha.)			*Yield (in 1,000 tonnes)*		
	2006	*2007*	*2008*	*2006*	*2007*	*2008*
Wheat	195	192	217	1,699	1,453	2,064
Barley	84	71	80	616	460	603
Sugar beet	10	11	7	581	657	421
Potatoes	5	6	5	181	207	191
Rye	19	23	29	101	107	168
Oats	8	8	9	43	43	45

Livestock, May 2007: 1,149,373 cattle (including 334,205 milch cows); 51,659 horses; 1,519,690 pigs; 367,350 sheep; 2,738,258 poultry.

Fisheries

In 2008 the yield of small-scale deep-sea and inshore fisheries was 44,463 tonnes. The catch was valued at €59·8m. in 2008.

INDUSTRY

In Sept. 2008, 1,313 mining, quarrying and manufacturing establishments (with 20 or more employees) employed 129,644 persons; of these, 24,070 were employed in machine construction; 20,725 in food and related industries; 8,467 in electrical engineering; 5,143 in shipbuilding (except naval engineering).

Labour

The economically active persons totalled 1,334,000 in 2008. Of the total, 1,149,000 were employees, 164,000 were self-employed or unpaid family workers; 345,000 were engaged in commerce and transport, 298,000 in power supply, mining, manufacturing and building, 44,000 in agriculture and forestry, and 647,000 in other industries and services.

COMMUNICATIONS

Roads

There were (1 Jan. 2009) 9,884 km of 'classified' roads, comprising 511 km of Autobahn, 1,580 km of federal roads, 3,678 km of first-class and 4,115 km of second-class highways. In Jan. 2009 the number of motor vehicles was 1,730,033, including 1,432,290 passenger cars, 87,784 lorries, 2,541 buses, 61,311 tractors and 127,441 motorcycles.

Shipping

The Kiel Canal (*Nord-Ostsee-Kanal*) is 98·7 km long; in 2007, 43,378 vessels of 82m. NRT passed through it.

SOCIAL INSTITUTIONS

Justice

There are a court of appeal, four regional courts, 25 local courts, a *Bundesland* labour court, five labour courts, a *Bundesland* social court, four social courts, a finance court, an upper administrative court and an administrative court.

Education

In 2008–09 there were 632 primary schools with 7,815 teachers and 113,516 pupils; 229 elementary schools with 2,192 teachers and 28,718 pupils; 169 intermediate schools with 3,878 teachers and 57,045 pupils; 106 grammar schools (*Gymnasien*) with 5,975 teachers and 86,381 pupils; 129 comprehensive schools with 2,265 teachers and 27,918 pupils; 195 other schools (including special schools) with 2,369 teachers and 16,721 pupils; 306 vocational schools with 4,648 teachers and 101,584 pupils.

In the winter term of the academic year 2008–09 there were 28,643 students at the three universities (Kiel, Flensburg and Lübeck) and 19,723 students at 11 further education colleges.

RELIGION

In 2006, 55·1% of the population were Protestants and 6·1% Roman Catholics.

CULTURE

Tourism

4,317 places of accommodation provided 176,138 beds in 2008 for 5,028,049 visitors.

FURTHER READING

Statistical Information: Statistisches Amt für Hamburg und Schleswig-Holstein (Fröbel Str. 15–17, 24113 Kiel). *Director:* Dr Wolfgang Bick. Publications: *Statistisches Taschenbuch Schleswig-Holstein,* since 1954.—*Statistisches Jahrbuch Schleswig-Holstein,* since 1951.—*Statistische Monatshefte Schleswig-Holstein,* since 1949.—*Statistische Berichte,* since 1947.—*Beitrage zur historischen Statistik Schleswig-Holstein,* from 1967.—*Lange Reihen,* from 1977. *Website (German only):* http://www.statistik-nord.de

Handbuch für Schleswig-Holstein. 34th ed. 2008

Ibs, Jürgen, (ed.) *Historischer Atlas Schleswig-Holstein: Vom Mittelalter bis 1867.* 2004

Lange, Ulrich, (ed.) *Historischer Atlas Schleswig-Holstein: seit 1945.* 1999

Momsen, Ingwer, (ed.) *Historischer Atlas Schleswig-Holstein: 1867 bis 1945.* 2001

State library: Schleswig-Holsteinische Landesbibliothek, Kiel, Schloss. *Director:* Dr Jens Ahlers.

Thuringia

Thüringen

KEY HISTORICAL EVENTS

Thuringia with its capital Erfurt is criss-crossed by the rivers Saale, Werra and Weisse Elster and dominated in the south by the mountains of the Thuringian Forest. Martin Luther spent his exile in Eisenach where he translated the New Testament into German while he lived in protective custody in the castle. Weimar became the centre of German intellectual life in the 18th century. In 1919 Weimar was the seat of a briefly liberal Republic. Only ten miles from Weimar lies Buchenwald, the site of a war-time Nazi concentration camp, which is now a national monument to the victims of fascism.

TERRITORY AND POPULATION

The area is 16,172 sq. km. Population on 31 Dec. 2008 was 2,267,763 (1,118,827 females); density, 140 per sq. km. It is divided into six urban districts, 17 rural districts and 959 communes. The capital is Erfurt.

SOCIAL STATISTICS

Statistics for calendar years:

	Live births	Marriages	Divorces	Deaths
2005	16,713	9,836	4,834	25,695
2006	16,402	9,312	4,617	25,599
2007	17,176	9,454	4,418	25,812
2008	17,332	9,810	4,417	26,276

CONSTITUTION AND GOVERNMENT

The *Bundesland* was reconstituted on former GDR territory in 1990. It has four seats in the Bundesrat.

RECENT ELECTIONS

At the Diet elections of 30 Aug. 2009 the Christian Democrats (CDU) won 30 of 88 seats, with 31·2% of the vote; the Left 27, with 27·4%; the Social Democrats (SPD) 18, with 18·5%; the Free Democrats (FDP) 7, with 7·6%; and the Greens 6, with 6·2%. Turnout was 56·2%.

CURRENT ADMINISTRATION

The *Prime Minister* is Christine Lieberknecht (CDU).

Government Website: http://www.thueringen.de

ENERGY AND NATURAL RESOURCES

Agriculture

Area and yield of the most important crops:

	Area (in 1,000 ha.)			Yield (in 1,000 tonnes)		
	2006	2007	2008	2006	2007	2008
Wheat	222·1	216·8	223·2	1,487·2	1,461·3	1,709·2
Barley	117·0	111·9	121·2	694·6	668·2	736·9
Sugar beet	9·0	10·6	8·7	487·4	637·5	487·4
Potatoes	2·4	2·5	2·3	84·1	111·2	81·3
Rye	8·4	11·6	11·9	52·1	71·4	78·1
Oats	5·7	5·5	6·1	27·6	22·8	26·1

Livestock, 2008: 351,114 cattle (including 116,226 milch cows); 714,315 pigs; 201,360 sheep; 9,464 horses (2007); 3,837,086 poultry (2007).

INDUSTRY

In 2008, 1,838 establishments (with 20 or more employees) employed 162,942 persons; of these, 77,485 were employed by producers of materials and supplies, 49,800 by producers of investment goods, 8,309 by producers of durables and 27,348 by producers of non-durables.

Labour

The economically active persons totalled 1,088,000 in 2008, including 534,000 professional workers, 390,000 manual workers and 117,000 self-employed. 367,000 were engaged in production industries, 235,000 in commerce, transport and communications, 31,000 persons in agriculture and forestry, and 456,000 in other sectors. The unemployment rate in 2008 was 11·3%.

COMMUNICATIONS

Roads

At 1 Jan. 2009 there were 481 km of motorways, 1,700 km of federal roads, 4,737 km of first- and second-class highways and 2,948 km of district highways. Number of registered motor vehicles, Jan. 2009, 1,368,347, including 1,146,044 private cars, 87,096 lorries, 2,274 buses, 44,235 tractors and 79,757 motorcycles.

SOCIAL INSTITUTIONS

Education

In 2008–09 there were 470 primary schools with 64,790 pupils, 245 core curriculum schools with 43,353 pupils, 97 grammar schools with 48,019 pupils and 90 special schools with 11,435 pupils; there were 75,295 pupils in technical and professional education, and 3,741 in professional training for the disabled; there were 13 universities and colleges with 50,724 students enrolled.

Health

In 2008 there were 43 hospitals with 15,954 beds. There were 8,038 doctors (one doctor per 282 population).

Welfare

2008 expenditure on social welfare was €438m.

RELIGION

In 2006, 589,749 persons were Protestant and 183,308 persons were Roman Catholic. In 2007, 750 were Jewish.

CULTURE

Tourism

In July 2008 there were 1,371 places of accommodation (with nine or more beds). There were 3,326,300 visitors who stayed 9,247,500 nights in 2008.

FURTHER READING

Statistical information: Thüringer Landesamt für Statistik (Postfach 900163, 99104 Erfurt; Europaplatz 3, 99091 Erfurt). *President:* Günter Krombholz. Publications: *Statistisches Jahrbuch Thüringen*, since 1993. *Kreiszahlen für Thüringen*, since 1995. *Gemeindezahlen für Thüringen*, since 1998. *Thüringen-Atlas*, since 1999. *Statistische Monatshefte Thüringen*, since 1994. *Statistische Berichte*, since 1991. *Faltblätter*, since 1991.

Website (German only): http://www.statistik.thueringen.de

State library: Thüringer Universitäts- und Landesbibliothek, Jena. *Director:* Dr Sabine Wefers.

GHANA

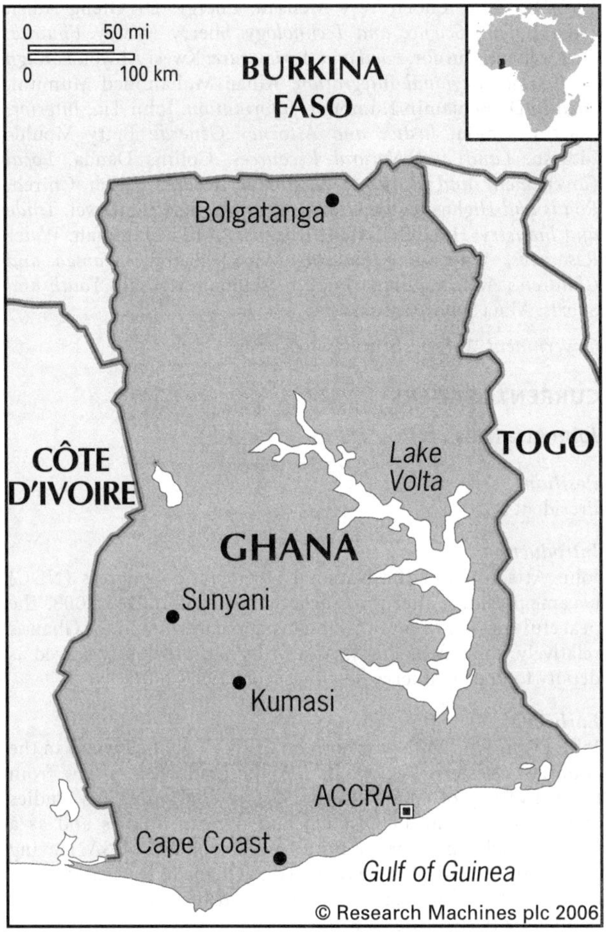

Republic of Ghana

Capital: Accra
Population estimate, 2010: 24·33m.
GDP per capita, 2007: (PPP$) 1,334
HDI/world rank: 0·526/152

KEY HISTORICAL EVENTS

By the 17th century, strong chiefdoms and warrior states, notably the Ashanti, dominated the territory. The Ashanti state was strengthened by its collaboration with the slave trade but by 1874 it had been conquered by Britain and made a colony. The hinterland became a protectorate in 1901. British rule was challenged after the Second World War by Kwame Nkrumah and the Convention People's Party (CPP), formed in 1949. The state of Ghana came into existence on 6 March 1957 when the former Colony of the Gold Coast with the Trusteeship Territory of Togoland attained Dominion status. The country was declared a Republic within the Commonwealth on 1 July 1960 with Dr Kwame Nkrumah as the first President.

In 1966 the Nkrumah regime was overthrown by the military who ruled until 1969 when they handed over to a civilian regime under a new constitution. On 13 Jan. 1972 the armed forces regained power. In 1979 the Supreme Military Council (SMC) was toppled in a coup led by Flight-Lieut. J. J. Rawlings. The new government permitted elections already scheduled and these resulted in a victory for Dr Hilla Limann and his People's National Party. However, on 31 Dec. 1981 another coup led by Rawlings dismissed the government and Parliament, suspended the constitution and established a Provisional National Defence Council to exercise all government powers. A new pluralist democratic constitution was approved by referendum in April 1992. The Fourth Republic was proclaimed on 7 Jan. 1993.

TERRITORY AND POPULATION

Ghana is bounded west by Côte d'Ivoire, north by Burkina Faso, east by Togo and south by the Gulf of Guinea. The area is 238,533 sq. km; the 2000 census population was 18,912,079, giving a density of 79·3 persons per sq. km.

The UN gives an estimated population for 2010 of 24·33m.

In 2005, 52·2% of the population was rural. 1m. Ghanaians lived abroad in 1995.

Ghana is divided into ten regions:

Regions	*Area (sq. km)*	*Population, census 2000*	*Capital*
Ashanti	24,389	3,612,950	Kumasi
Brong-Ahafo	39,557	1,815,408	Sunyani
Central	9,826	1,593,823	Cape Coast
Eastern	19,323	2,106,696	Koforidua
Greater Accra	3,245	2,095,726	Accra
Northern	70,384	1,820,806	Tamale
Upper East	8,842	920,089	Bolgatanga
Upper West	18,476	576,583	Wa
Volta	20,570	1,635,421	Ho
Western	23,921	1,924,577	Sekondi-Takoradi

In 2000 the capital, Accra, had a population of 1,658,937. Other major cities are Kumasi, Tamale, Sekondi-Takoradi and Ashiaman.

About 42% of the population are Akan. Other tribal groups include Moshi (23%), Ewe (10%) and Ga-Adangme (7%). About 75 languages are spoken; the official language is English.

SOCIAL STATISTICS

2000 estimates: births, 639,000; deaths, 204,000. Rates, 2000 estimates (per 1,000 population): births, 32·6; deaths, 10·4. 2007 life expectancy, 55·6 years for men and 57·4 for women. Infant mortality, 68 per 1,000 live births (2005). Annual population growth rate, 1992–2002, 2·4%; fertility rate, 2004, 4·2 births per woman.

CLIMATE

The climate ranges from the equatorial type on the coast to savannah in the north and is typified by the existence of well-marked dry and wet seasons. Temperatures are relatively high throughout the year. The amount, duration and seasonal distribution of rain is very marked, from the south, with over 80" (2,000 mm), to the north, with under 50" (1,250 mm). In the extreme north, the wet season is from March to Aug., but further south it lasts until Oct. Near Kumasi, two wet seasons occur, in May and June and again in Oct., and this is repeated, with greater amounts, along the coast of Ghana. Accra, Jan. 80°F (26·7°C), July 77°F (25°C). Annual rainfall 29" (724 mm). Kumasi, Jan. 77°F (25°C), July 76°F (24·4°C). Annual rainfall 58" (1,402 mm). Sekondi-Takoradi, Jan. 77°F (25°C), July 76°F (24·4°C). Annual rainfall 47" (1,181 mm). Tamale, Jan. 82°F (27·8°C), July 78°F (25·6°C). Annual rainfall 41" (1,026 mm).

CONSTITUTION AND GOVERNMENT

After the coup of 31 Dec. 1981, supreme power was vested in the Provisional National Defence Council (PNDC), chaired by Flight-Lieut. Jerry John Rawlings.

A new constitution was approved by 92·6% of votes cast at a referendum on 28 April 1992. The electorate was 8,255,690; turnout was 43·8%. The constitution sets up a presidential system on the US model, with a multi-party parliament and an independent judiciary. The *President* is elected by universal suffrage for a four-year term renewable once.

The unicameral *Parliament* has 230 members, elected for a four-year term in single-seat constituencies.

National Anthem

'God bless our Homeland, Ghana'; words by the government, tune by P. Gbeho.

GOVERNMENT CHRONOLOGY

Heads of State since 1960. (CPP = Convention People's Party; PNP = People's National Party; NDC = National Democratic Congress; NPP = New Patriotic Party; n/p = non-partisan)

President of the Republic

1960–66 CPP Kofi Kwame Nkrumah

Chairmen of the National Liberation Council

1966–69 military Joseph Arthur Ankrah
1969 military Akwasi Amankwaa Afrifa

Presidential Commission

1969–1970 Akwasi Amankwaa Afrifa (chairman), John Willie Kofi Harlley, Albert Kwesi Ocran

Presidents of the Republic

1970–72 n/p Edward Akufo-Addo

Chairman of the National Redemption Council

1972–75 military Ignatius Kutu Acheampong

Chairmen of the Supreme Military Council

1975–78 military Ignatius Kutu Acheampong
1978–79 military Frederick Kwasi Akuffo

Chairman of the Armed Forces Revolutionary Council

1979 military Jerry John Rawlings

President of the Republic

1979–81 PNP Hilla Limann

Chairman of the Provisional National Defence Council

1981–93 military Jerry John Rawlings

Presidents of the Republic

1993–2001 NDC Jerry John Rawlings
2001–09 NPP John Agyekum Kufuor
2009– NDC John Atta Mills

RECENT ELECTIONS

Presidential elections were held on 7 and 28 Dec. 2008. In the first round Nana Addo Dankwa Akufo-Addo of the New Patriotic Party (NPP) won 49·1% of the vote and John Atta Mills of the National Democratic Congress (NDC) 47·9%. There were six other candidates. In the run-off on 28 Dec. Atta Mills was elected with 50·2% of the vote, against Akufo-Addo with 49·8%. Turnout was 69·5% in the first round and 72·9% in the second round. In parliamentary elections held on 7 Dec. 2008, the NDC won 114 of 230 seats, the NPP 107, ind. 4, the People's National Convention 2 and the Convention People's Party 1. There were also two vacant seats.

CURRENT ADMINISTRATION

President: John Atta Mills; b. 1944 (NDC; sworn in 7 Jan. 2009).

Vice-President: John Dramani Mahama.

In March 2010 the government comprised the following:

Minister of Chieftancy and Culture: Alexander Asuom Ahinsa. *Communications:* Haruna Iddrisu. *Defence:* Retd Lieut.-Gen. J. H. Smith. *Education:* Alex Tetteh-Enyo. *Employment and Social Welfare:* Enoch Teye Mensah. *Energy:* Dr Oteng Adjei. *Environment, Science and Technology:* Sherry Ayittey. *Finance:* Dr Kwabena Dufuor. *Food and Agriculture:* Kwesi Ahwoi. *Foreign Affairs and Regional Integration:* Alhaji Muhammed Mumuni. *Health:* Dr Benjamin Kumbuor. *Information:* John Tia. *Interior:* Martin Amidu. *Justice and Attorney General:* Betty Mould-Iddrisu. *Land and Natural Resources:* Collins Dauda. *Local Government and Rural Development:* Joseph Yieleh Chireh. *Roads and Highways:* Joe Gidisu. *Tourism:* Zita Okaikwei. *Trade and Industry:* Hannah Tetteh. *Transport:* Mike Hammah. *Water Resources, Works and Housing:* Alban Bagbin. *Women and Children's Affairs:* Juliana Jocelyn Azumah-Mensah. *Youth and Sports:* Akua Sena Dansua.

Government Website: http://www.ghana.gov.gh

CURRENT LEADERS

John Atta Mills

Position

President

Introduction

John Atta Mills of the National Democratic Congress (NDC) became president after winning a tight run-off in Dec. 2008. The peaceful transfer of power was considered a triumph for Ghana's relatively stable democracy. Atta Mills had previously served as deputy to President Jerry Rawlings from 1997–2001.

Early Life

John Evans Atta Mills was born on 21 July 1944 in Tarkwa in the country's Western Region. In 1967 he graduated in Law from the University of Ghana, Legon, before continuing his studies at London's School of Oriental and African Studies and as a Fulbright scholar at the Stanford Law School in the USA. Having gained his PhD in 1971, he returned to Ghana to teach at the Law faculty of his alma mater. He continued to work in academia, publishing twelve scholarly titles.

In 1988 President Rawlings, leader of the NDC, appointed Atta Mills as commissioner of the internal revenue service. Nine years later Rawlings invited him to be his vice-president. In 2000 Rawlings, who had served the maximum two terms of office, nominated Atta Mills as the NDC candidate in the election of that year. Atta Mills lost the presidential race, and again in 2004, to John Kufuor of the New Patriotic Party (NPP).

Nonetheless, his party re-selected him, ahead of three rivals, to fight a third election in Dec. 2008. With Kufuor constitutionally banned from seeking another term, the NPP's Nana Akufo-Addo emerged from the first round of elections in the lead, though just short of the overall majority required to claim victory. The second round was dogged by claims of electoral malpractice on both sides but, after a re-run of voting in one rural constituency, Atta Mills received 50·2% of the vote, beating his opponent by less than 0·5%.

Career in Office

Atta Mills has presented himself as a social democrat and has vowed to work towards national unity. He has attempted to distance himself from earlier pronouncements that as president he would consult with Rawlings, a highly divisive figure in Ghanaian politics. In July 2009 Ghana secured a US$600m. three-year loan from the International Monetary Fund, and a further economic boost is expected in late 2010 when Ghana hopes to start producing oil.

DEFENCE

Defence expenditure totalled US$83m. in 2006 (US$4 per capita), representing 0·7% of GDP.

Army

Total strength (2007), 10,000.

Navy

The Navy, based at Sekondi and Tema, numbered 2,000 in 2007.

Air Force

The main air base is at Accra. Personnel strength (2007), 1,500. There were nine combat capable aircraft although their serviceability was in doubt.

INTERNATIONAL RELATIONS

Ghana is a member of the UN, World Bank, ILO, WTO, Commonwealth, African Development Bank, African Union, ECOWAS and is an ACP member state of the ACP-EU relationship.

ECONOMY

Agriculture accounted for 38·0% of GDP in 2006, industry 25·8% and services 36·3%.

Overview

Ghana, one of Africa's biggest borrowers, is committed to the reform programmes of the IMF and World Bank. In 2005 aid amounted to 11% of GNI, or three times the value of Ghana's exports. Ghana's completion of the Heavily Indebted Poor Countries (HIPC) scheme in 2004 paved the way for debt cancellation by major bilateral donors, helping to bring down national debt. Nonetheless, the country's infrastructure (particularly power, water and roads) is in urgent need of improvement and stands as an obstacle to economic growth and a disincentive to foreign investment.

Steady growth averaging 3–6% since the mid 1980s has resulted from careful macroeconomic management and an increase in exports. More recently growth has been driven by increases in both private and public investment in road-building and agricultural upgrading. A privatization programme was mounted in 1988, with 132 state-owned enterprises sold off to become 232 privately-owned companies by April 2000. Privatization deals raised over US$800m. between 1990 and 1996, including the Ashanti Goldfields sell-off worth more than US$400m. Only South Africa among sub-Saharan African nations has raised more from privatization.

The economy relies on mining and agricultural products such as cocoa, timber and pineapples. The country is the second largest gold exporter after South Africa and the second largest cocoa producer after Côte d'Ivoire. Cocoa, gold and timber comprise 75% of Ghana's exports. Building, tourism, technology and financial services account for up to 50% of national income. Tourism is increasingly important and is now the third largest revenue earner after gold and cocoa.

Currency

The monetary unit is the *cedi* (GHS) of 100 *pesewas*. It was introduced in July 2007 and is equal to 10,000 old cedi (GHC). Inflation was 10·7% in 2007 and 16·5% in 2008. Foreign exchange reserves were US$1,343m. in June 2005 and gold reserves 281,000 troy oz in July 2005. Total money supply in April 2005 was ₵13,257·7bn.

Budget

In 2004 revenues totalled ₵23,938bn. and expenditures ₵26,229bn.

Performance

Real GDP growth was 5·7% in 2007 and 7·3% in 2008. Total GDP was US$16·1bn. in 2008.

Banking and Finance

The Bank of Ghana (*Governor*, Kwesi Bekoe Amissah-Arthur) was established in 1957 as the central bank and bank of issue. At Dec. 1995 its total assets were ₵3,272,946·6m. There were in 1998 nine commercial banks, four merchant banks and 130 rural banks. There are two discount houses. Banks are required to have a capital base of at least 6% of net assets. At Dec. 1995 assets of commercial banks totalled ₵1,900,327·1m.

Foreign investment is actively encouraged with the Ghana Free Zone Scheme offering particular incentives such as full exemption of duties and levies on all imports for production and exports from the zones, full exemption on tax on profits for ten years, and no more than 8% after ten years. It is a condition of the scheme that at least 70% of goods made within the zones must be exported. Within 18 months of the scheme being set up in 1995, 50 projects had been registered.

There is a stock exchange in Accra.

ENERGY AND NATURAL RESOURCES

Ghana is facing an energy crisis, with power cuts of up to 12 hours a day because drought has caused the level of Lake Volta to drop to below the danger level.

Environment

Ghana's carbon dioxide emissions from the consumption and flaring of fossil fuels in 2008 were the equivalent of 0·3 tonnes per capita.

Electricity

Installed capacity was 1·5m. kW in 2004. Production (2004) 6·04bn. kWh, mainly from two hydro-electric stations operated by the Volta River Authority, Akosombo (six units) and Kpong (four units). Consumption per capita was 289 kWh in 2004. Since 1998 droughts have caused power cuts owing to the reliance on hydro-electricity. However, production is becoming more dependent on gas—the 678-km West Africa Gas Pipeline bringing gas flows from Nigeria resumed operations in March 2010 following a year-long suspension.

Oil and Gas

Ghana is pursuing the development of its own gas fields and plans to harness gas at the North and South Tano fields located off the western coast. Natural gas reserves, 2005, totalled 24bn. cu. metres. Oil reserves in 2005 were 17m. bbls, although the discovery of an offshore field containing in excess of 300m. bbls of oil was announced in June 2007. Two months later a second offshore field was discovered, potentially with even larger oil resources. Ghana hopes to become an oil producer before the end of 2010.

Minerals

Gold is one of the mainstays of the economy; Ghana ranks second only to South Africa among African gold producers. Production in 2005 was 63,100 kg. In 2005 estimated diamond production was 1·0m. carats; manganese (2002), 1·14m. tonnes; bauxite (2002), 684,000 tonnes; aluminium (2002), 117,000 tonnes.

Agriculture

The rural poor earn little and many small farmers have reverted to subsistence farming. The agricultural population in 2002 was 12·97m., of whom 5·74m. were economically active. There were 7·15m. ha. of land under cultivation in 2007 and 11,000 ha. were irrigated. There were 154 registered combine harvesters in 2007. In southern and central Ghana the main food crops are maize, rice, cassava, plantains, groundnuts, yam and taro; and in northern Ghana groundnuts, rice, maize, sorghum, millet and yams. Agriculture presently operates at only 20% of its potential and is an area that is to be a major focus of investment.

Production of main food crops (2007 unless otherwise indicated, in 1,000 tonnes): cassava, 10,218; yams, 4,376; plantains,

3,234; cocoyams, 1,690; maize 1,220; cocoa beans (2006–07), 615; coconuts (2002), 315; oranges (2002), 300; chillies and green peppers (2002), 270; rice (milled), 185; sorghum, 155; millet, 133. Cocoa is the main cash crop. The government estimates that more than 40% of the population relies either directly or indirectly on cocoa as a source of income. It contributes approximately 13% of GDP. Ghana is the second largest cocoa bean producer in the world after Côte d'Ivoire, and the second largest producer of both yams and cocoyams, after Nigeria.

Livestock, 2002: goats, 3·23m.; sheep, 2·92m.; cattle, 1·33m.; pigs, 310,000; chickens, 24m.

Forestry

There were 5·52m. ha. of forest in 2005, or 24·2% of the total land area. Reserves account for some 30% of the total forest lands. Timber production in 2007 was 35·49m. cu. metres.

Fisheries

In 2005 total catch was 392,274 tonnes, of which 317,274 tonnes came from sea fishing.

INDUSTRY

Ghana's industries include mining, lumbering, light manufacturing and food processing.

Labour

In 2000 the number of economically active persons totalled 8,292,100. Females constituted 50% of the workforce in 2000. Ghana has among the highest proportions of women in the workforce in the world.

The unemployment rate was 8·2% in 2000.

INTERNATIONAL TRADE

Foreign debt was US$6,739m. in 2005.

Imports and Exports

In 2007 imports (c.i.f.) were valued at US$7,206·7m.; exports (f.o.b.) totalled US$4,186·7m. Principal imported commodities, 2007: machinery and transport equipment, 46·4%; manufactured goods, 17·9%; food and live animals, 12·9%; chemicals and related products, 12·4%. Principal exports, 2007: gold, 34·8%; cocoa, 25·1%; fruit and vegetables, 7·9%; animal and vegetable oils and fats, 7·0%. Main import suppliers in 2007: Germany, 14·6%; China, 11·2%; USA, 7·7%. Main export markets in 2007: South Africa, 31·3%; Netherlands, 16·9%; USA, 10·8%.

COMMUNICATIONS

Roads

In 2005 there were 57,614 km of roads, including 11,177 km of highways, main and national roads. About 14·9% of all roads are paved. A Road Sector Strategy and Programme to develop the road network ran from 1995 to 2000. There were 493,800 passenger cars in use in 2007, 158,400 lorries and vans, and 121,100 buses and coaches. Motorcycles and mopeds numbered 149,100.

Rail

Total length of railways in 2005 was 953 km of 1,067 mm gauge. In 2005 railways carried 1·8m. tonnes of freight and 2·3m. passengers.

Civil Aviation

There is an international airport at Accra (Kotoka). In 2003 scheduled airline traffic of Ghana-based carriers flew 12m. km, carrying 241,000 passengers (all on international flights). Accra handled 623,000 passengers (all on international flights) in 2001.

Shipping

The chief ports are Tema and Takoradi. In 2002, 6·8m. tonnes of cargo were handled at Tema and 3·4m. tonnes at Takoradi. There is inland water transport on Lake Volta. In 2002 the merchant marine totalled 126,000 GRT, including oil tankers 8,000 GRT. The Volta, Ankobra and Tano rivers provide 168 km of navigable waterways for launches and lighters.

Telecommunications

Ghana Telecom was privatized in 1996. In 2004 Ghana had 2,008,300 telephone subscribers, or 93·9 for every 1,000 inhabitants, with 1,695,000 mobile phone subscribers. There were 112,000 PCs in use (5·2 per 1,000 persons) in 2004 and 368,000 internet users.

Postal Services

In 2003 there were 730 post offices.

SOCIAL INSTITUTIONS

Justice

The Courts are constituted as follows:

Supreme Court. The Supreme Court consists of the Chief Justice who is also the President, and not less than four other Justices of the Supreme Court. The Supreme Court is the final court of appeal in Ghana. The final interpretation of the constitution is entrusted to the Supreme Court.

Court of Appeal. The Court of Appeal consists of the Chief Justice with not less than five other Justices of the Appeal court and such other Justices of Superior Courts as the Chief Justice may nominate. The Court of Appeal is duly constituted by three Justices. The Court of Appeal is bound by its own previous decisions and all courts inferior to the Court of Appeal are bound to follow the decisions of the Court of Appeal on questions of law. Divisions of the appeal court may be created, subject to the discretion of the Chief Justice.

High Court of Justice. The Court has jurisdiction in civil and criminal matters as well as those relating to industrial and labour disputes including administrative complaints. The High Court of Justice has supervisory jurisdiction over all inferior Courts and any adjudicating authority and in exercise of its supervisory jurisdiction has power to issue such directions, orders or writs including writs or orders in the nature of habeas corpus, certiorari, mandamus, prohibition and quo warranto. The High Court of Justice has no jurisdiction in cases of treason. The High Court consists of the Chief Justice and not less than 12 other judges and such other Justices of the Superior Court as the Chief Justice may appoint.

Under the Provisional National Defence Council which ruled from 1981 to 2001 public tribunals were established in addition to the traditional courts of justice.

The population in penal institutions in Sept. 2006 was 12,736 (55 per 100,000 of national population).

Education

Schooling is free and compulsory, and consists of six years of primary, three years of junior secondary and three years of senior secondary education. In 2006–07 there were 3·37m. pupils in primary schools with 105,257 teachers; and 1·13m. pupils with 67,005 teachers in junior secondary schools. University education is free. In 2007 there were 140,017 students in tertiary education and 4,011 academic staff. Adult literacy in 2003 was 54·1% (62·9% among men and 45·7% among women). In 1970 adult literacy was just 31%.

In 2005 public expenditure on education came to 5·5% of GNI.

Health

In 2002 there were 1,842 physicians, 13,102 nurses, 4,094 midwives and 1,433 pharmacists. In 2003 there were an estimated 350,000 people living with HIV, mainly women.

Ghana has been one of the most successful countries in reducing undernourishment in the past 15 years. Between 1990–92 and 2001–03 the proportion of undernourished people declined from 37% of the population to just 12%.

RELIGION

An estimated 30% of the population are Muslim and 24% Christian, with 38% adherents to indigenous beliefs and 8% other religions. In Feb. 2010 the Roman Catholic church had one cardinal.

CULTURE

World Heritage Sites

Ghana has two sites on the UNESCO World Heritage List: Forts and Castles, Volta, Greater Accra, Central and Western Regions (inscribed on the list in 1979), Portuguese trading posts built between 1482 and 1786 along the coast; Asante Traditional Buildings (1980), the remains of the Asante civilization that peaked in the 18th century.

Broadcasting

The state-run Ghana Broadcasting Corporation operates the national GTV service, the Radio One and Radio Two networks and also regional radio services. Metro TV is under joint government-private ownership. TV3 and MultiChoice (pay TV) are independent services. There are a number of commercial radio stations. There were 1·35m. television-equipped households (colour by PAL) in 2006.

Press

There were 11 daily newspapers in 2006 with a combined circulation of 215,000.

Tourism

There were 587,000 foreign tourists in 2007, spending US$1,172m.

DIPLOMATIC REPRESENTATIVES

Of Ghana in the United Kingdom (13 Belgrave Sq., London, SW1X 8PN)
High Commissioner: Prof. Kwaku Danso-Boafo.

Of the United Kingdom in Ghana (Osu Link, off Gamel Abdul Nasser Ave., Accra)
High Commissioner: Dr Nicholas Westcott, CMG.

Of Ghana in the USA (3512 International Dr., NW, Washington, D.C., 20008)
Ambassador: Daniel Ohene Agyekum.

Of the USA in Ghana (24, 4th Circular Rd, Cantonments, Accra)
Ambassador: Donald G. Teitelbaum.

Of Ghana to the United Nations
Ambassador: Leslie Kojo Christian.

Of Ghana to the European Union
Ambassador: Nana Bema Kumi.

FURTHER READING

Boafo-Arthur, Kwame, (ed.) *Ghana: One Decade of the Liberal State.* 2007
Carmichael, J., *Profile of Ghana.* 1992.—*African Eldorado: Ghana from Gold Coast to Independence.* 1993
Herbst, J., *The Politics of Reform in Ghana, 1982–1991.* 1993
Ninsin, Kwame A. (ed.) *Ghana: Transition to Democracy.* 2002
Odotei, Irene K. and Awedoba, Albert K. (eds.) *Chieftaincy in Ghana: Culture, Governance and Development.* 2006
Petchenkine, Y., *Ghana in Search of Stability, 1957–1992.* 1992
Ray, D. I., *Ghana: Politics, Economics and Society.* 1986
Rimmer, D., *Staying Poor: Ghana's Political Economy, 1950–1990.* 1993
Rothchild., D. (ed.) *Ghana: the Political Economy of Recovery.* 1991
Tettey, Wisdom, Puplampu, Korbia P. and Berman, Bruce J., (eds.) *Critical Perspectives in Politics and Socio-Economic Development in Ghana.* 2003

National Statistical Office: Ghana Statistical Service, P. O. Box GP 1098, Ministry of Finance and Economic Planning (MoFEP) Head Office Building, Accra.
Website: http://www.statsghana.gov.gh

GREECE

Elliniki Dimokratia
(Hellenic Republic)

Capital: Athens
Population estimate, 2010: 11·18m.
GDP per capita, 2007: (PPP$) 28,517
HDI/world rank: 0·942/25

KEY HISTORICAL EVENTS

The land that is now Greece was first inhabited between 2000–1700 BC by tribes from the North. This period was followed by the Mycenaean Civilization which was overthrown by the Dorians at the end of the 12th century BC. Its dominant citadels were at Tiryns and Mycenae. What little is known about this period is from stories such as those by Homer written in the 9th or 8th century BC.

The following period, known as the Greek Dark Ages, ended by the 6th century BC when the *polis*, or city state, was formed. Built mainly on coastal plains, the two principal cities were Sparta and Athens. With government based on consensus of a ruling class, and rich in theatre, art and philosophy, the *polis* was the pinnacle of the Greek Classical Age. It was the era of Euripides, Theusidades and Socrates. With strong trade links, Greece also had territories in Southern Italy, Sicily, Southern France and Asia Minor.

Two Persian invasions in the 5th century were checked at Marathon (490 BC) and Thermopylae (480 BC) where Spartans held off a great force of Persian soldiers. In 431 BC rivalry between the dominant city states erupted into the Peloponnesian War. In 404 BC Sparta defeated Athens, but in the next century Sparta itself fell to Thebes (371 BC).

Led by Philip II of Macedon, the Macedonians defeated the city states in 338 BC. The *poleis* were forced to unify under his rule. With Plato and Aristotle active at this time, the latter serving as a tutor to Philip's son Alexander, this was a period of cultural enrichment. When Philip was assassinated in 336 BC, Alexander, then aged of 20, succeeded him. He spent the next thirteen years on a relentless campaign to expand the Macedonian territories. The Greek Empire stretched to the edge of India and encompassed most of the known civilized world.

Following Alexander's death in 323 BC, the empire gradually disintegrated. By the end of the 2nd century AD, the Romans had defeated the Macedonians and Greece was incorporated into the Roman Empire. It remained in Roman hands until it became part of the Byzantine Empire in the 4th century AD. A population of Greek-speaking Christians had its power base in Constantinople.

Over the next six centuries Greece was invaded by Franks, Normans and Arabs but remained part of the Byzantine Empire. Following the Empire's decline in the 11th century, Greece was incorporated into the Ottoman Empire in 1460. Apart from a period under Venetian control between 1686–1715, Greece was part of Turkey until the Greek War of Independence.

Greece broke away from the Ottoman Empire in the 1820s and was declared a kingdom under the protection of Great Britain, France and Russia. Many Greeks were left outside the new state but Greece's area increased by 70%, the population growing from 2·8m. to 4·8m., after the Treaty of Bucharest (1913) recognized Greek sovereignty over Crete.

King Constantine opted for neutrality in the First World War, while Prime Minister Venezelos favoured the Entente powers. This National Schism led to British and French intervention which deposed Constantine on 11 June 1917. When his son Alexander died on 25 Oct. 1920, he returned and reigned until 1922. He was forced to abdicate by a coup after defeat by Turkey and the loss of Smyrna. The Treaty of Lausanne (1923) recognized Smyrna as Turkish with Eastern Thrace and the islands of Imvros and Tenedos, all of which had been ceded to Greece by the 1920 Treaty of Sevres. An exchange of Christian and Muslim populations followed. Resistance to Italian demands brought Greece into the Second World War when Germany had to come to the aid of the hard-pressed Italians. Athens was occupied on 27 April 1941. The occupation lasted until 15 Oct. 1944.

Shortly before the German withdrawal the leading communist resistance movement established a provisional government to supplant the monarchy and the existing government-in-exile. British attempts to oversee a coalition government between the communists and royalist groups collapsed in Dec. 1944. Two months of fierce fighting saw the communists claim most of the country bar Athens and Salonika, before the uprising was suppressed by the British. The communists boycotted the general election of March 1946, which returned a royalist government. When the king was restored to the throne in Sept. 1946 the communists responded with a guerrilla war. The Greek army, heavily backed by the USA, defeated the insurgents and the civil war came to an end in Oct. 1949, with 50,000 dead and around half a million people displaced.

The late 1950s saw the emergence of the Left, capitalizing on the movement for union with Cyprus and unease over NATO membership (1952). A military coup in 1967 led to the authoritarian rule of the 'Colonels' headed by George Papadopoulos. A republic was declared on 29 July 1973.

Papadopoulos was ousted by Brigadier-General Demetrios Ioannidis, head of the military police, who returned some civil powers but kept much power for himself. In 1974 an Athens-supported coup attempt against Cyprus's President Makarios led to a Turkish invasion of the island and the establishment of the 'Turkish Republic of Northern Cyprus'. Ioannidis' government fell and Konstantinos Karamanlis returned from 13 years in exile to head a civilian government of national unity. The monarchy was abolished by a referendum on 8 Dec. 1974 and a new constitution the following year established a parliamentary republic with an executive president. The 1981 election brought Andreas Papandreou to power at the head of a socialist government. Earlier that year Greece had become the tenth member of the EU. Re-elected in 1985, Papandreou imposed economic austerity to combat inflation and soaring budgets but industrial unrest and evidence of widespread corruption led to his fall and a succession of weak governments. Papandreou returned to power in Oct. 1993 but ill-health forced his resignation two years later. His successor Constantinos Simitis took a more pro-European stance, instituting economic reforms to prepare the way for entry into European Monetary Union (EMU).

Kostas Karamanlis led the Conservative New Democracy party to power in 2004, ending over a decade of rule by Pasok. In the same year Athens hosted the Olympic Games. Karamanlis won a second term in Sept. 2007. In March 2008 his government blocked Macedonia's accession to NATO because of a long-running dispute about Macedonia's name. Greece already has a constituent province called Macedonia.

TERRITORY AND POPULATION

Greece is bounded in the north by Albania, the Former Yugoslav Republic of Macedonia (FYROM) and Bulgaria, east by Turkey and the Aegean Sea, south by the Mediterranean and west by the Ionian Sea. The total area is 131,957 sq. km (50,949 sq. miles), of which the islands account for 25,026 sq. km (9,663 sq. miles).

The population was 10,964,020 (5,536,338 females) according to the census of March 2001; density, 83·1 per sq. km.

The UN gives an estimated population for 2010 of 11·18m.

In 2005, 59·0% of the population lived in urban areas. There were 761,813 resident foreign nationals in 2001. A further 5m. Greeks are estimated to live abroad.

In 1987 the territory of Greece was administratively reorganized into 13 *regions* comprising in all 51 *departments*. Areas and populations according to the 2001 census:

Geographic Region/ Department	*Area in sq. km*	*Population*[1]	*Chief town*
Aegean Islands	*9,122*	*508,807*	
Chios	904	53,408	Chios
Cyclades	2,572	112,615	Hermoupolis
Dodecanese	2,714	190,071	Rhodes
Lesbos	2,154	109,118	Mytilene
Samos	778	43,595	Samos
Attica[2]	*3,808*	*3,761,810*	*Athens (Athinai)*
Central Greece and Euboea	*21,010*	*829,758*	
Aetolia and Acarnania	5,461	224,429	Messolonghi
Boeotia	2,952	131,085	Levadeia
Euboea	4,167	215,136	Chalcis
Evrytania	1,869	32,053	Karpenissi
Phocis	2,120	48,284	Amphissa
Phthiotis	4,441	178,771	Lamia
Crete	*8,336*	*601,131*	
Canea	2,376	150,387	Canea
Heraklion	2,641	292,489	Heraklion
Lassithi	1,823	76,319	Aghios Nikolaos
Rethymnon	1,496	81,936	Rethymnon
Epirus	*9,203*	*353,820*	
Arta	1,662	78,134	Arta
Ioannina	4,990	170,239	Ioannina
Preveza	1,036	59,356	Preveza
Thesprotia	1,515	46,091	Hegoumenitsa
Ionian Islands	*2,307*	*212,984*	
Cephalonia	904	39,488	Argostoli
Corfu	641	111,975	Corfu
Leucas	356	22,506	Leucas
Zante	406	39,015	Zante
Macedonia	*34,177*	*2,424,765*	
Cavalla	2,111	145,054	Cavalla
Chalcidice	2,918	104,894	Polygyros
Drama	3,468	103,975	Drama
Florina	1,924	54,768	Florina
Grevena	2,291	37,947	Grevena
Imathia	1,701	143,618	Veroia
Kastoria	1,720	53,483	Kastoria
Kilkis	2,519	89,056	Kilkis
Kozani	3,516	155,324	Kozani
Mount Athos[3]	336	2,262	Karyai
Pella	2,506	145,797	Edessa
Pieria	1,516	129,846	Katerini
Serres	3,968	200,916	Serres
Thessaloniki (Salonika)	3,683	1,057,825	Thessaloniki
Peloponnese	*21,379*	*1,155,019*	
Achaia	3,271	322,789	Patras
Arcadia	4,419	102,035	Tripolis
Argolis	2,154	105,770	Nauplion
Corinth	2,290	154,624	Corinthos
Elia	2,618	193,288	Pyrgos
Laconia	3,636	99,637	Sparti
Messenia	2,991	176,876	Calamata
Thessaly	*14,037*	*753,888*	
Karditsa	2,636	129,541	Karditsa
Larissa	5,381	279,305	Larissa
Magnesia	2,636	206,995	Volos
Trikala	3,384	138,047	Trikala
Thrace	*8,578*	*362,038*	
Evros	4,242	149,354	Alexandroupolis
Rhodope	2,543	110,828	Comotini
Xanthi	1,793	101,856	Xanthi

[1]*De facto* population. [2]Attica is both region and department. [3]Autonomous region.

The largest cities (2001 census populations) are Athens (the capital), 745,514; Thessaloniki, 363,987; Piraeus, 175,697; Patras, 160,400; Peristerion, 137,918; Heraklion, 130,914; Larissa, 124,394; Kallithea, 109,609; Volos, 82,439. The department of Attica, composed of Athens, the port of Piraeus and a number of suburbs, contains about one third of the Greek population. It also contains about 50% of the country's industry and is the principal commercial, financial and diplomatic centre. Efforts have, however, been made to decentralize the economy. The second city, Thessaloniki, with its major port, has grown rapidly in population and industrial development.

The Monastic Republic of **Mount Athos** (or Agion Oros, i.e. 'Holy Mountain'), the easternmost of the three prongs of the peninsula of Chalcidice, is a self-governing community composed of 20 monasteries. The peninsula is administered by a Council of four members and an Assembly of 20 members, one deputy from each monastery. The constitution of 1927 gives legal sanction to the Charter of Mount Athos, drawn up by representatives of the 20 monasteries on 20 May 1924, and its status is confirmed by the 1952 and 1975 constitutions. Women are not permitted to enter. Population, 2001, 2,262.

The modern Greek language had two contesting literary standard forms, the archaizing *Katharevousa* ('purist'), and a version based on the spoken vernacular, 'Demotic'. In 1976 Standard Modern Greek was adopted as the official language, with Demotic as its core.

SOCIAL STATISTICS

2005: 107,545 live births; 105,091 deaths; 61,043 marriages; 13,494 divorces; 421 still births; 5,485 births to unmarried mothers. 2005 rates: birth (per 1,000 population), 9·7; death, 9·5; marriage, 5·5; divorce, 1·2. Population growth rate, 2005, 0·4%. In 2004 the suicide rate per 100,000 population was 3·2 (men, 5·2; women, 1·2). Expectation of life at birth, 2007, 76·9 years for males and 81·3 years for females. In 2005 the most popular age range for marrying was 25–29 for females and 30–34 for males. Infant mortality, 2005, 3·8 per 1,000 live births; fertility rate, 2005, 1·2 births per woman (one of the lowest rates in the world). In 2004 Greece received 4,469 asylum applications, equivalent to 0·4 per 1,000 inhabitants.

CLIMATE

Coastal regions and the islands have typical Mediterranean conditions, with mild, rainy winters and hot, dry, sunny summers. Rainfall comes almost entirely in the winter months, though amounts vary widely according to position and relief. Continental conditions affect the northern mountainous areas, with severe winters, deep snow cover and heavy precipitation, but summers are hot. Athens, Jan. 48°F (8·6°C), July 82·5°F (28·2°C). Annual rainfall 16·6" (414·3 mm).

CONSTITUTION AND GOVERNMENT

Greece is a presidential parliamentary democracy. A new constitution was introduced in June 1975 and was amended in March 1986 and April 2001. The 300-member *Chamber of Deputies* is elected for four-year terms by proportional representation. There is a 3% threshold. Extra seats are awarded to the party which leads in an election. The Chamber of Deputies elects the head of state, the *President*, for a five-year term.

National Anthem

'Imnos eis tin Eleftherian' ('Hymn to Freedom'); words by Dionysios Solomos, tune by N. Mantzaros.
(Same as Cyprus.)

GOVERNMENT CHRONOLOGY

(EEK = National Unionist Party; EK = Center Union; EPEK = National Progressive Center Union; ERE = National Radical Union; ES = Hellenic Union; FDK = Liberal Democratic Center; KF = Liberal Party; LK = People's Party; ND = New Democracy; Pasok = Panhellenic Socialist Movement; n/p = non-partisan)

Presidents since 1973.

1973	n/p	Georgios C. (George) Papadopoulos
1973–74	military	Phaidon D. Gizikis
1974–75	n/p	Michail D. Stasinopoulos
1975–80	ND	Konstantinos D. Tsatsos
1980–85	ND	Konstantinos G. Karamanlis
1985–90	n/p	Christos A. Sartzetakis
1990–95	ND	Konstantinos G. Karamanlis
1995–2005	n/p	Konstantinos (Kostis) Stephanopoulos
2005–	Pasok	Karolos G. Papoulias

Prime Ministers since 1945.

1945	military	Nikolaos Plastiras
1945	military	Petros Voulgaris
1945	EEK	Panagiotis Kanellopoulos
1945–46	KF	Themistoklis P. Sophoulis
1946	n/p	Panagiotis Poulitsas
1946–47	LK	Konstantinos S. Tsaldaris
1947	n/p	Dimitrios E. Maximos
1947	LK	Konstantinos S. Tsaldaris
1947–49	KF	Themistoklis P. Sophoulis
1949–50	n/p	Alexandros N. Diomidis
1950	LK	Ioannis G. Theotokis
1950	KF	Sophoklis E. Venizelos
1950	EPEK	Nikolaos Plastiras
1950–51	KF	Sophoklis E. Venizelos
1951–52	EPEK	Nikolaos Plastiras
1952	n/p	Dimitrios Kiousopoulos
1952–55	ES	Alexandros L. Papagos
1955–58	ES, ERE	Konstantinos G. Karamanlis
1958–61	ERE	Konstantinos G. Karamanlis
1961–63	ERE	Konstantinos G. Karamanlis
1963	ERE	Panagiotis Pipinelis
1963	n/p	Stilianos Mavromichalis
1963	EK	Georgios A. Papandreou, Sr
1963–64	n/p	Ioannis Paraskevopoulos
1964–65	EK	Georgios A. Papandreou, Sr
1965	EK	Georgios T. Athanasiadis-Novas
1965	n/p	Elias I. Tsirimokos
1965–66	FDK	Stephanos C. Stephanopoulos
1966–67	n/p	Ioannis Paraskevopoulos
1967	ERE	Panagiotis Kanellopoulos
1967	n/p	Konstantinos V. Kollias
1967–73	military	Georgios C. (George) Papadopoulos
1973	n/p	Spiros V. Markezinis
1973–74	n/p	Adamantios Androutsopoulos
1974–80	ND	Konstantinos G. Karamanlis
1980–81	ND	Georgios I. Rallis
1981–89	Pasok	Andreas G. Papandreou
1989	ND	Tzannis P. Tzannetakis
1989–90	n/p	Xenophon E. Zolotas
1990–93	ND	Konstantinos K. Mitsotakis
1993–96	Pasok	Andreas G. Papandreou
1996–2004	Pasok	Costantinos G. (Kostas) Simitis
2004–09	ND	Konstantinos A. (Kostas) Karamanlis
2009–	Pasok	Georgios Papandreou

RECENT ELECTIONS

Karolos Papoulias was re-elected president by the 300-member parliament on 3 Feb. 2010, receiving 266 votes. No other candidates stood.

Parliamentary elections were held on 4 Oct. 2009. Turnout was 70·9%. Seats gained (and % of vote): the opposition Pasok (Panhellenic Socialist Movement), 160 (43·9%); the ruling New Democracy (ND), 91 (33·5%); Communist Party, 21 (7·5%); Popular Orthodox Rally (LAOS), 15 (5·6%); Coalition of the Radical Left (SIN), 13 (4·6%).

European Parliament

Greece has 22 (24 in 2004) representatives. At the June 2009 elections turnout was 52·6% (63·2% in 2004). Pasok won 8 seats with 36·7% of votes cast (political affiliation in European Parliament: Progressive Alliance of Socialists and Democrats); ND, 8 with 32·3% (European People's Party); the Communist Party, 2 with 8·4% (European United Left/Nordic Green Left); the LAOS, 2 with 7·2% (Europe of Freedom and Democracy); the SIN, 1 with 4·7% (European United Left/Nordic Green Left); the Ecologist Greens, 1 with 3·5% (Greens/European Free Alliance).

CURRENT ADMINISTRATION

President: Karolos Papoulias; b. 1929 (Pasok; sworn in 12 March 2005 and re-elected 3 Feb. 2010).

In March 2010 the government comprised:

Prime Minister and Minister of Foreign Affairs: Georgios Papandreou; b. 1952 (Pasok; sworn in 6 Oct. 2009).

Vice Prime Minister, Responsible for Co-ordination of the Foreign Policy and Defence Committee and Economic and Social Policy Committee: Theodoros Pangalos.

Minister of Interior, Decentralization and E-Governance: Yiannis Ragoussis. *Finance:* Georgios Papaconstantinou. *National Defence:* Evengelos Venizelos. *Economy, Competitiveness and Shipping:* Louka Katseli. *Environment, Energy and Climate Change:* Tina Birbili. *Education, Lifelong Learning and Religious Affairs:* Anna Diamantopoulou. *Infrastructure, Transport and Networks:* Dimitris Reppas. *Labour and Social Security:* Andreas Loverdos. *Health and Social Solidarity:* Mariliza Xenoyiannakopoulou. *Agricultural Development and Food:* Katerina Batzeli. *Justice, Transparency and Human Rights:* Haris Kastanidis. *Citizens' Protection:* Mihalis Chrysohoidis. *Culture and Tourism:* Pavlos Geroulanos.

Office of the Prime Minister: http://www.primeminister.gr

CURRENT LEADERS

Karolos Papoulias

Position
President

Introduction
Karolos Papoulias was sworn in as president of Greece on 12 March 2005, having been elected by an unprecedented parliamentary majority of 279 out of the 300 available votes. A founding member of the Panhellenic Socialist Movement (Pasok) and foreign minister throughout the 1980s and 1990s, Papoulias succeeded Kostis Stephanopoulos in this largely ceremonial role.

Early Life
Papoulias was born on 4 June 1929 in the northwestern city of Ioannina and went on to study law at the University of Athens and at the University of Milan in Italy, followed by a doctorate in private international law at the University of Cologne in Germany.

In 1967, following a coup that saw the right-wing Greek government replaced by a military dictatorship under Georgios Papadopoulos, Papoulias left Greece for Cologne. There he founded the resistance organization, the Overseas Socialist Democratic Union, which mobilized exiled Greeks against the military regime. From 1967–74 Papoulias broadcast regularly on Deutsche Welle Radio's Greek programme, denouncing the military government. With the fall of the Papadopoulos dictatorship and the establishment of the democratic Third Hellenic Republic in 1974, Papoulias returned to Greece, where, with fellow returned exile Andreas Papandreou, he helped to found Pasok. With its principles of 'National Independence, Popular Sovereignty, Social Emancipation and Democratic Process', Pasok was to dominate Greek political life throughout the 1980s and 1990s.

At the Nov. 1974 elections Pasok won 13·5% of the vote, coming third in the electoral battle behind the Liberal Party and the conservative New Democracy Party. By Nov. 1977, however, Pasok had doubled its percentage of the votes and become the official opposition. In the elections of Oct. 1981 Pasok won a resounding 48% of the vote and, with Papoulias' long-time associate Andreas Papandreou as prime minister, formed the first socialist government in the history of Greece. Papoulias served as secretary of Pasok's International Relations Committee from 1975–85, and from 1976–80 he was also a member of the party's Co-ordinating Council. In 1977 Papoulias entered parliament for the first time, representing Ioannina as a Pasok member. He was to be re-elected eight times, serving a total of 27 years continuously until 2004. In Oct. 1981 Papoulias gave up his law practice to take up a full-time post as deputy foreign minister in the Pasok government. He held his post until 1984, becoming foreign minister from 1985–90, and again from 1993–96.

Under the leadership of Papoulias, Pasok foreign policy in the Balkan states contributed significantly to the stability of at least some parts of this historically volatile area. In 1976 the Greek government initiated an inter-Balkan conference on economic and technical co-operation, attended by representatives of Yugoslavia, Romania, Bulgaria and Turkey. Similar conferences followed in 1979 and 1982, leading in 1984 to talks on the denuclearization of the Balkan region. Despite the two counties having been officially at war since 1940, Greco-Albanian relations improved dramatically during the mid-1980s and, in 1985, the Greco-Albanian border was reopened for the first time in 45 years, with full normalization of relations in 1987.

Following the death of Andreas Papandreou in June 1996, and the general election of Sept. of that year, Papoulias left the cabinet to become the Greek representative at the Organization for Security and Co-operation in Europe (OSCE).

On 12 Dec. 2004 Prime Minister Karamanlis (New Democracy) and leader of the opposition George Papandreou (Pasok) named Papoulias as the only presidential candidate in the Feb. 2005 election. Gaining 279 out of 300 votes Papoulias was elected by a huge majority of MPs representing all the parliamentary parties.

Career in Office
The appointment of Papoulias to the role of president of the Third Hellenic Republic ended months of speculation that Pasok MPs might withhold the votes required for the endorsement of a new president, forcing early elections just one year after the centre-right New Democracy Party came to power. Papoulias, who has enjoyed popularity across the political spectrum, has spoken of his desire to see a united Cyprus and expressed hope that Turkey's EU membership talks would be a trigger for progress on the issue. Following defeat in a snap general election in Oct. 2009, Prime Minister Karamanlis resigned and Papoulias asked Georgios Papandreou, the leader of Pasok, to form a new government. Papoulias was re-elected for a second term unopposed in Feb. 2010.

Georgios Papandreou

Position
Prime Minister

Introduction
Georgios Papandreou assumed office as prime minister on 6 Oct. 2009 after leading his party, the Panhellenic Socialist Movement (Pasok), to victory over the conservative New Democracy party in snap legislative elections. Having previously served as foreign minister from 1999–2004, Papandreou is also president of Socialist International, a worldwide collective of socialist parties. He is the third generation of his family to serve as prime minister of Greece, following his grandfather (also Georgios) and father (Andreas).

Early Life
Papandreou was born in St Paul, Minnesota, USA, where his father held a teaching post, in June 1952. He read sociology at the University of Massachusetts Amherst and gained a master's in the same subject from the London School of Economics. He also studied in Stockholm and in 1992 he was made a fellow at Harvard's Centre for International Affairs.

Papandreou returned to Greece after the fall of the military junta in 1974, when his father established the centre-left Pasok. In 1981, the year that his father became prime minister, he was elected MP for Achaia. He served as minister of education and religious affairs and deputy foreign minister before becoming foreign minister in Feb. 1999. During his five years in the post Papandreou sought closer relations with Greece's neighbours, particularly Albania and Bulgaria. He was praised for achieving a partial rapprochement with Turkey, resulting in the accession of the Republic of Cyprus to the EU.

He replaced the former prime minister, Kostas Simitis, as leader of Pasok in 2004, before losing a general election in the same year. He held on to the party leadership and in 2009 secured an absolute majority against an incumbent government made unpopular by allegations of corruption.

Career in Office
Papandreou has pledged to restore the struggling economy with a €3bn. (US$4·4bn.) stimulus package. However, the prospects for a speedy recovery were undermined by the acknowledgment that the financial situation was considerably worse than had been reported by the preceding administration. In order to slash the budget deficit of 12·7%, four times higher than the limit allowed to eurozone members, Papandreou imposed wide-ranging austerity measures, likening the crisis to a 'wartime situation'. While parliament passed swingeing cuts to public sector pay and a freeze on pensions, a wave of public unrest grew as the crisis threatened to sour Greece's relations with EU partners, notably Germany. In March 2010 Papandreou caused controversy by refusing to rule

out an application to the IMF if the EU refused sufficient financial support.

DEFENCE

Prior to 2001 conscription was generally: (Army) 18 months, (Navy) 21 months, (Air Force) 20 months. However, following a gradual shortening of military service, in 2009 conscription was 12 months for all three branches of the armed forces.

In 2006 defence expenditure totalled US$7,286m. (US$682 per capita), representing 2·4% of GDP (the highest percentage in the EU).

Army

The Field Army is currently being reorganized. There are three military regions, with one Army, five corps and five divisional headquarters. Total Army strength (2007) 93,500 (around 38% conscripts). There is also a National Guard of 34,500 whose role is internal security.

Navy

The current strength of the Hellenic Navy includes eight diesel submarines, 14 frigates and three corvettes. Main bases are at Salamis, Patras and Soudha Bay (Crete). Personnel in 2007 totalled 20,000 (including 4,000 conscripts).

Air Force

The Hellenic Air Force (HAF) had a strength (2007) of 31,500 (including 11,000 conscripts). There were 357 combat capable aircraft including A-7s, F-4s, F-16s and Mirage 2000s. The HAF is organized into Tactical, Air Defence, Air Support and Air Training Commands.

INTERNATIONAL RELATIONS

Greece is a member of the UN, World Bank, IMF and several other UN specialized agencies, WTO, EU, Council of Europe, WEU, OSCE, CERN, BSEC, BIS, IOM, NATO, OECD, International Organization of the Francophonie and Antarctic Treaty. Greece is a signatory to the Schengen accord which abolishes border controls between Greece, Austria, Belgium, Czech Republic, Denmark, Estonia, Finland, France, Germany, Hungary, Iceland, Italy, Latvia, Lithuania, Luxembourg, Malta, Netherlands, Norway, Poland, Portugal, Slovakia, Slovenia, Spain, Sweden and Switzerland.

In 2006 Greece gave US$384m. in international aid. In terms of a percentage of GNI, however, Greece was one of the least generous major industrialized countries, giving just 0·16%.

ECONOMY

Agriculture accounted for 4% of GDP in 2007, industry 23% and services 73%.

Overview

Greece's economy is the smallest of the old EU-15 and its income per capita is the lowest among the group. As a reflection of its relative backwardness, agriculture's share of GDP is roughly twice the OECD average. The industrial base is also small compared to other developed countries. Until the early 1990s the state was responsible for up to 70% of all industrial assets but in 1998 the government began a programme of privatization to meet EU membership criteria. The mining and extractive metallurgy sectors are central to the economy. Government attempts to decentralize industry have not reached the country's northern regions or its islands, owing to poor infrastructure. However, financial aid from the EU has brought improvements in road, rail, harbour and airport links.

Greece ranks among the top 20 tourism destinations in the world according to the UNWTO and in 2005 attracted over 14m. foreign tourists, mainly from Western Europe. The economy grew strongly in the 2000s, outstripping both EU and OECD average growth rates. Real GDP grew by nearly 4% per year on average in the period 1995–2007. It has benefited substantially from EU aid, equal to 3·3% of annual GDP, and growth was boosted by spending on the 2004 Olympic Games. The combination of low interest rates inherited when joining the euro and financial market reform also helped boost investment spending.

However, much of this development was reversed with the global financial crisis. Real GDP contracted by 2% in 2009 but was expected to gain momentum by 2011 as the external climate improved. The government deficit was 12·7% of GDP in 2009 while public debt was 112·6%, among the highest in the euro area. In addition, interest on loans increased following the downgrading of its credit rating in Dec. 2009. In early 2009 the government announced a civil servant wage freeze and a surcharge on higher income earners. In Dec. 2009 Prime Minister Papandreou outlined proposals to further reduce public spending and counter rampant tax evasion. Under EU pressure, he set out plans to overhaul pensions by the end of 2010, reduce the budget deficit to 3% of GDP by 2013 and bring debt beneath 4% of GDP by the same time.

In early 2010 the government pledged to reduce the budget deficit to 8·7% by the end of the year and to under 3·0% by 2012. A US$11·2bn. austerity plan was passed in March 2010, including US$6·5bn. in savings through rises in sales tax, lower holiday bonuses to civil servants and a pension freeze. Public anger over the measures resulted in a succession of general strikes and concerns over Greek finances contributed to a plunge in the value of the euro in early 2010.

In March 2010 the 16 eurozone members reached an agreement, in conjunction with the IMF, to provide loans worth up to €22bn. in the event that Greece was unable to secure market loans. In late April 2010 Prime Minister Papandreou requested a bail-out, arguing that high interest rates for Greece prohibited further market borrowing. On 2 May 2010 the EU and the IMF agreed to provide up to €110bn. over three years (€80bn. from the EU and €30bn. from the IMF). In return, Greece agreed to implement still deeper spending cuts and improve revenue raising, prompting popular protests.

The OECD has long argued that Greece's tax system is one of the most complex and inequitable among developed countries. In 2005 the ministry of economy and finance began simplifying tax regulations, speeding up bureaucratic procedures and reducing the corporate tax rate from 35% to 25%, a process completed at the beginning of 2007. The OECD has also warned that rigidities in the labour market must be tackled if unemployment is to fall significantly below 10%.

Currency

In June 2000 EU leaders approved a recommendation for Greece to join the European single currency, the euro, and on 1 Jan. 2001 the euro (EUR) became the legal currency at the irrevocable conversion rate of 340·750 drachmas to 1 euro. The euro, which consists of 100 cents, has been in circulation since 1 Jan. 2002. There are seven euro notes in different colours and sizes denominated in 500, 200, 100, 50, 20, 10 and 5 euros, and eight coins denominated in 2 and 1 euros, then 50, 20, 10, 5, 2 and 1 cents. On the introduction of the euro there was a 'dual circulation' period before the drachma ceased to be legal tender on 28 Feb. 2002. Euro banknotes in circulation on 1 Jan. 2002 had a total value of €13·4bn.

Inflation rates (based on OECD statistics):

1999	*2000*	*2001*	*2002*	*2003*	*2004*	*2005*	*2006*	*2007*	*2008*
2·1%	2·9%	3·7%	3·9%	3·4%	3·0%	3·5%	3·3%	3·0%	4·2%

Foreign exchange reserves were US$116m. in Sept. 2009 (US$17,726m. in 1999) and gold reserves 3·61m. troy oz. Total money supply in Aug. 2009 was €97,507m.

Budget
Revenues in 2006 totalled €48,600m. (92·2% tax revenues) and expenditures €50,413m. (38·8% pensions and salaries, and 18·9% interest payments).

VAT is 19% (reduced rates, 9% and 4·5%).

Performance
Real GDP growth rates (based on OECD statistics):

1999	*2000*	*2001*	*2002*	*2003*	*2004*	*2005*	*2006*	*2007*	*2008*
3·4%	4·5%	4·2%	3·4%	5·9%	4·6%	2·2%	4·5%	4·5%	2·0%

According to the Bank of Greece, real GDP growth was –2% in 2009. Up until 2008 Greece had recorded economic growth above the EU average every year since 1996. Total GDP in 2008 was US$356·8bn.

Banking and Finance
The central bank and bank of issue is the Bank of Greece. Its *Governor* is George Provopoulos. There were 39 commercial banks in 2002 (17 Greek and 22 foreign). Total assets of all banks were 41,819bn. drachmas (€127,295m.) in 1999. The six leading banks in 2000 accounted for nearly 80% of assets of all Greek banks. Ranked by size of assets the largest banks were National Bank of Greece, Alpha Bank, Agricultural Bank, Emporiki Bank, EFG Eurobank and Piraeus Bank. Foreign direct investment was US$5,093m. in 2008.

There is a stock exchange in Athens.

ENERGY AND NATURAL RESOURCES

Environment
Carbon dioxide emissions from the consumption and flaring of fossil fuels in Greece were the equivalent of 10·0 tonnes per capita in 2008.

Electricity
Installed capacity in 2004 was 12·7m. kW. A national grid supplies the mainland, and islands near its coast. Power is produced in remoter islands by local generators. Total production in 2004 was 59·34bn. kWh; consumption per capita in 2004 was 5,630 kWh. 89% of electricity was produced in 2004 by thermal power stations (mainly using lignite) and the rest was from hydro-electric and geothermal generation. Electricity supply is: domestic, 220v, 50 cycles AC; industrial, 280v, AC 3 phase.

Oil and Gas
Output of crude petroleum, 2004, 0·8m. bbls; proven reserves, 2007, 5m. bbls. The oil sector plays a critical role in the Greek economy, accounting for more than 70% of total energy demand. Supply is mostly imported but oil prospecting is intensifying. Natural gas was introduced in Greece in 1997 through a pipeline from Russia, and an additional source of supply is liquefied natural gas from Algeria. Demand for natural gas is in its infancy; however, in 2004 production ran to 34m. cu. metres. The public monopoly in natural gas, DEPA, has developed only a few sales contracts to some large industrial groups, outside a large contract with DEH.

Minerals
Greece produces a variety of ores and minerals, including in 2004 (with production, in tonnes): bauxite (2,444,000); pumice (893,000 in 2003); gypsum and anhydrite (731,785 in 2003); magnesite (549,049 in 2003); white and coloured marble (276,200 in 2003); aluminium (167,300); caustic magnesia (98,357 in 2003); zinc (30,400 in 2003); nickel ore (21,700); silver (79 in 2003). There is little coal, and the lignite is of indifferent quality (70·04m. tonnes in 2004). Salt production (2003) 205,162 tonnes.

Agriculture
In 2002 there were 2·72m. ha. of arable land and 1·13m. ha. of permanent crops.

The Greek economy was traditionally based on agriculture, with small-scale farming predominating, except in a few areas in the north. There were 824,000 farms in 2003. However, there has been a steady shift towards industry and although agriculture still employs nearly 17% of the population, it accounted for only 7% of GDP in 2002. Nevertheless, prior to the accession of the ten new member countries in May 2004 Greece had a higher percentage of its population working in agriculture than any other European Union member country. Agriculture accounts for 33·1% of exports and 17·9% of imports.

Production (2002, in 1,000 tonnes):

Olives	2,863	Oranges	1,193
Sugarbeets	2,834	Potatoes	901
Maize	2,219	Grapes	747
Wheat	2,038	Watermelons	696
Tomatoes	1,753	Peaches	687
Cotton	1,306	Olive oil	382
Alfalfa	1,230	Must	368

Livestock (2003, in 1,000): 9,426 sheep, 5,287 goats, 1,082 pigs, 733 cattle, 56 asses, 28 horses, 28 mules, 38,500 poultry. Livestock products, 2002 (in 1,000 tonnes): milk, 2,069; meat, 472; cheese, 170.

Forestry
Area covered by forests in 2005 was 3·75m. ha., or 29·1% of the total land area. Timber production in 2007 was 1·74m. cu. metres.

Fisheries
Total catch in 2005 was 90,445 tonnes, mainly from sea fishing. In 2005, 13,926 fishermen were active. 3,000 kg of sponges were produced in 2005.

INDUSTRY
The leading companies by market capitalization in Greece in March 2009 were: OPAP (Greek Organization of Football Prognostics), a betting company (US$8·4bn.); the National Bank of Greece (NBG), US$7·5bn.; and Coca-Cola Hellenic Bottling Company (US$5·2bn.).

The main products are canned vegetables and fruit, fruit juice, beer, wine, other alcoholic beverages, cigarettes, textiles, yarn, leather, shoes, synthetic timber, paper, plastics, rubber products, chemical acids, pigments, pharmaceutical products, cosmetics, soap, disinfectants, fertilizers, glassware, porcelain sanitary items, wire and power coils and household instruments.

Production in 1,000 tonnes (2002): cement, 14,981; residual fuel oil (2004), 7,095; distillate fuel oil (2004), 5,369; petrol (2004), 3,629; crude steel, 1,840; jet fuel (2004), 1,720; iron (concrete-reinforcing bars), 1,454; fertilizers, 1,374; alumina, 750; sulphuric acid, 468; packing materials, 318; soap, washing powder and detergents, 239; textile yarns, 130; soft drinks, 573·6m. litres; beer, 465·1m. litres; wine, 167·2m. litres; cigarettes, 30·5bn. units; glass (2001), 382,343 sq. metres.

Although manufacturing accounts for more than 21% of GDP, Greece's performance is hampered by the proliferation of small, traditional, low-tech firms, often run as family businesses. Food, drink and tobacco processing are the most important sectors, but there are also some steel mills and several shipyards. Shipping is of prime importance to the economy. In addition, there are major programmes under way in the fields of power, irrigation and land reclamation.

Labour
Of the total workforce of 4,822,800 in the period April–June 2004, 4,329,700 persons were employed. 748,200 were engaged in wholesale and retail trade; 569,700 in manufacturing; 533,100 in agriculture, animal breeding, hunting and forestry; and 350,000 in construction. Workers in Greece put in among the longest hours of any country in the world. In 2005 the average worker put

in 2,053 hours. Automatic index-linking of wages was abolished at the end of 1990. Since 1989 a statutory minimum of wage-bills must be spent on training (0·45%). Retirement age is 65 years for men and 60 for women, although most men retire before the age of 60. Unemployment was 9·7% in Sept. 2009 (up from 7·7% in 2008 as a whole); unemployment among under 25s stood at 20·6% in 2008.

Trade Unions

The status of trade unions is regulated by the Associations Act 1914. Trade union liberties are guaranteed under the Constitution, and a law of June 1982 altered the unions' right to strike.

The national body of trade unions is the Greek General Confederation of Labour.

INTERNATIONAL TRADE

Following the normalization of their relations, Greece lifted its trade embargo (imposed in Feb. 1994) on Macedonia on 13 Oct. 1995. There are quarrels with Turkey over Cyprus, oil rights under the Aegean and ownership of uninhabited islands close to the Turkish coast.

Imports and Exports

In 2004 imports (c.i.f.) were valued at US$52,809m. and exports (f.o.b.) at US$15,224m. In 2003 principal imports were: machinery and transport equipment, 35·2%; manufactured goods classified chiefly by material, 13·5%; minerals, fuels and lubricants, 13·5%; chemicals, 12·8%; miscellaneous manufactured articles, 10·9%. Principal exports in 2003 were: manufactured goods classified chiefly by material, 20·1%; miscellaneous manufactured articles, 18·1%; food and live animals, 14·8%; machinery and transport equipment, 12·9%; chemicals, 12·3%.

In 2004 Germany was the principal supplier of imports (13·4% of the total), ahead of Italy (12·9%), France (6·4%), the Netherlands (5·6%) and Russia (5·4%). Germany was the leading export market (13·2% of the total), followed by Italy (10·1%), UK (7·6%), Bulgaria (6·3%) and USA (5·3%). Fellow EU member countries accounted for 57·1% of imports in 2004 and 52·5% of all exports.

COMMUNICATIONS

Roads

There were 116,631 km of roads in 2005, including 868 km of motorway, 9,299 km of national roads and 30,864 km of secondary roads. Number of motor vehicles in 2005: 4,303,129 passenger cars (388 per 1,000 inhabitants), 1,186,483 trucks and vans, 1,124,172 motorcycles and 26,829 buses. There were 1,612 road deaths in 2007. With 14·4 deaths per 100,000 population in 2007, Greece has among the highest death rates in road accidents of any industrialized country. Road projects include improved links to Turkey and Bulgaria.

Rail

In 2005 the state network, Hellenic Railways (OSE), totalled 2,576 km, of which 1,743 km were of standard 1,435 mm gauge and 833 km were of narrow gauge (1,000 mm, 750 mm and 600 mm). Railways carried 3·0m. tonnes of freight and 10·0m. passengers in 2005. The Greek Railways Organization is investing US$23bn. in the link from Athens to the northern Bulgarian border. A 52-km long metro opened in Athens in Jan. 2000.

Civil Aviation

There are international airports at Athens (Spata 'Eleftherios Venizelos') and Thessaloniki-Makedonia. The airport at Spata opened in March 2001. The old airport at Hellenikon has now closed down. The national carrier is Olympic Airlines, serving some 30 towns and islands. Several failed attempts to privatize its predecessor, Olympic Airways, by selling a 51% stake led to the establishment of Olympic Airlines in Dec. 2003. Apart from the international airports there are a further 25 provincial airports. 5·70m. passengers were carried in 2005, of whom 2·90m. were on domestic and 2·80m. on international flights. Olympic Airlines operates routes from Athens to all important cities of the country, Europe, the Middle East and USA. In 2006 Athens airport (Spata) handled 15,079,708 passengers (9,611,095 on international flights).

Shipping

In 2005 the merchant navy totalled 33,020,000 GRT, of which oil tankers 17,234,000 GRT. Greek-owned ships under foreign flags numbered 80 of 2,413,000 GRT in 2005. In 2002 vessels totalling 50,856,000 NRT entered ports and vessels totalling 21,808,000 NRT cleared.

There is a canal (opened 9 Nov. 1893) across the Isthmus of Corinth (about 7 km). The principal seaports are Piraeus, Thessaloniki, Patras, Volos, Igoumenitsa and Heraklion. Greece has 123 seaports with cargo and passenger handling facilities. Container terminals at the port of Piraeus are to be expanded to 1m. TEUs (twenty-foot equivalent units).

Telecommunications

In 2008 there were 5,975,000 main (fixed) telephone lines. In the same year active mobile phone subscribers numbered 13,799,000 (1,239·0 per 1,000 persons). There were 4,845,000 internet users in 2008 and 1,045,000 PCs in use in 2006. There were 11·2 broadband subscribers per 100 inhabitants in June 2008.

Postal Services

In 2003 there were 2,218 post offices, or one for every 4,950 persons. A total of 622m. pieces of mail were processed, or 57 items per person.

SOCIAL INSTITUTIONS

Justice

Judges are appointed for life by the President after consultation with the judicial council. Judges enjoy personal and functional independence. There are three divisions of the courts—administrative, civil and criminal—and they must not give decisions which are contrary to the Constitution. Final jurisdiction lies with a Special Supreme Tribunal.

The Office of Ombudsman (*Synigoros*), currently Giorgos Kaminis, was instituted in 1998.

The population in penal institutions in Nov. 2008 was 12,300 (109 per 100,000 of national population). The death penalty was abolished for all crimes in 2004.

Education

Public education is provided in nursery, primary and secondary schools, starting at 5½–6½ years of age and free at all levels. Adult literacy rate, 2003, 91·0% (male 94·0%; female 88·3%).

In 2005–06 there were 5,715 nursery schools with 11,461 teachers and 143,401 pupils; 5,753 primary schools with 58,376 teachers and 639,685 pupils; 3,308 high schools (lycea) with 62,149 teachers and 569,887 pupils; 660 secondary technical, vocational and ecclesiastic schools with 16,066 teachers and 123,436 students. In 2002–03 there were 68 technical, vocational and ecclesiastic schools in third level education with 11,357 teachers and 146,270 students; and 19 universities with 11,079 academic staff and 175,597 students.

In 2005 public expenditure on education came to 3·5% of GNI and 9·2% of total government spending.

Health

Doctor and hospital treatment within the Greek national health system is free, but patients have to pay 25% of prescription charges. Those living in remote areas can reclaim a proportion of private medical expenses. In 2002 there were 326 hospitals with a total of 51,781 beds, plus 188 health centres. In 2002 there were 50,374 doctors and 13,107 dentists. In 2007 Greece spent 9·6% of its GDP on health. In 2008, 46·3% of Greek adult males and 33·5%

of females smoked on a daily basis. Greece has among the highest smoking rates of any country.

Welfare

The majority of employees are covered by the Social Insurance Institute, financed by employer and employee contributions. Benefits include pensions, medical expenses and long-term disability payments. Social insurance expenditure in 2004 totalled 36,038bn. euros.

The basic pension is available to men (aged 65) and women (aged 60), who have at least 4,500 days of contributions. Men aged 62 and women aged 57 qualify if they have 10,000 days of contributions, and men and women aged 58 can claim if they have 10,500 days. The basic pension is calculated on the length of the insurance period and on pensionable earnings in the last five years. A reduced early pension is available to men aged 60 and women aged 55 with 4,500 days of contributions. The minimum pension for a single person is €392 per month and the maximum is €2,966.

RELIGION

The Christian Eastern (Greek) Orthodox Church is the established religion to which 91% of the population belong. It is under an archbishop and 67 metropolitans, one archbishop and seven metropolitans in Crete, and four metropolitans in the Dodecanese. The head of the Greek Orthodox Church is Archbishop Ieronymos II of Athens and All Greece (b. 1938). Roman Catholics have three archbishops (in Naxos and Corfu and, not recognized by the State, in Athens) and one bishop (for Syra and Santorin). The Exarchs of the Greek Catholics and the Armenians are not recognized by the State. There are 360,000 Muslims.

Complete religious freedom is recognized by the constitution of 1974, but proselytizing from, and interference with, the Greek Orthodox Church is forbidden.

CULTURE

World Heritage Sites

Greece has 17 sites on the UNESCO World Heritage List: the Temple of Apollo Epicurius at Bassae (1986); the archaeological site of Delphi (1987); The Acropolis, Athens (1987); Mount Athos (1988); Meteora (1988); the Paleochristian and Byzantine monuments of Thessaloniki (1988); the Archaeological Site of Epidaurus (1988); the Medieval City of Rhodes (1988); the archaeological site of Olympia (1989); Mystras (1989); Delos (1990); the monasteries of Daphni, Hossios Luckas and Nea Moni of Chios (1990); the Pythagoreion and Heraion of Samos (1992); the archaeological site of Vergina (1996); the archaeological sites of Mycenae and Tiryns (1999); the historical sites on the Island of Patmos (1999); and the old town of Corfu (2007).

Broadcasting

Elliniki Radiofonia Tileorasi (ERT—Hellenic Radio and Television) is the state-owned public radio and television broadcasting corporation. ERT operates four national radio networks, regional services and an external service, Voice of Greece. The ERT national terrestrial network comprises three channels—ET1, NET and ET3. Major commercial television stations include Mega TV, ANT1 and Alpha TV. The number of private radio stations has spiralled since the late 1980s, many of them unlicensed. Number of television-equipped households (2006): 3·65m. TV colour is by SECAM H.

Press

There were 32 daily newspapers published in 2002 with a combined daily circulation of 628,000. A total of 6,826 book titles were published.

Tourism

Tourism is Greece's biggest industry with tourist spending amounting to US$13·70bn. in 2005; in 2004 tourism contributed approximately 14% of GDP. Tourists in 2008 numbered 18·8m. There were 700,933 hotel beds in 2007 (285,956 in 1981). A total of 56,385,986 nights were spent in hotels in 2007, 41,002,800 by foreigners and 15,383,186 by nationals.

Libraries

In 2006 there were 477 public libraries, one national library and 113 higher education libraries; they held a combined 14,782,000 volumes. There were 3,912,000 visits to the libraries in 2006.

Theatre and Opera

There are two national theatres and one opera house.

Museums and Galleries

Amongst Greece's most important museums are the Acropolis Museum, the Museum of the City of Athens, the National Archaeological Museum and the National Historical Museum. In 2005 there were 107 museums with 2,692,128 visitors.

DIPLOMATIC REPRESENTATIVES

Of Greece in the United Kingdom (1A Holland Park, London, W11 3TP)
Ambassador: Vassilis-Achilleas Pispinis.

Of the United Kingdom in Greece (1 Ploutarchou St., 106 75 Athens)
Ambassador: Dr David Landsman, OBE.

Of Greece in the USA (2221 Massachusetts Ave., NW, Washington, D.C., 20008)
Ambassador: Vassilis Kaskarelis.

Of the USA in Greece (91 Vasilissis Sophias Blvd, 101 60 Athens)
Ambassador: Daniel Speckhard.

Of Greece to the United Nations
Ambassador: Anastasios Mitsialis.

Of Greece to the European Union
Permanent Representative: Theodoros Sotiropoulos.

FURTHER READING

Clogg, Richard, *A Concise History of Greece.* 2nd ed. 2002
Couloumbis, Theodore A., Kariotis, Theodore and Bellou, Fotini, (eds.) *Greece in the Twentieth Century.* 2003
Dimitrakopoulos, Dionyssis G. and Passas, Argyris G. (eds.) *Greece in the European Union.* 2004
Jougnatos, G. A., *Development of the Greek Economy, 1950–91: an Historical, Empirical and Econometric Analysis.* 1992
Legg, K. R. and Roberts, J. M., *Modern Greece: A Civilization on the Periphery.* 1997
Pettifer, J., *The Greeks: the Land and the People since the War.* 1994
Sarafis, M. and Eve, M. (eds.) *Background to Contemporary Greece.* 1990
Tsakalotos, E., *Alternative Economic Strategies: the Case of Greece.* 1991
Veremis, T., *The Military in Greek Politics: From Independence to Democracy.* 1997
Woodhouse, C. M., *Modern Greece: a Short History.* Rev. ed. 1991

National Statistical Office: National Statistical Service; 14–16 Lycourgou St., Athens.
Website: http://www.statistics.gr

GRENADA

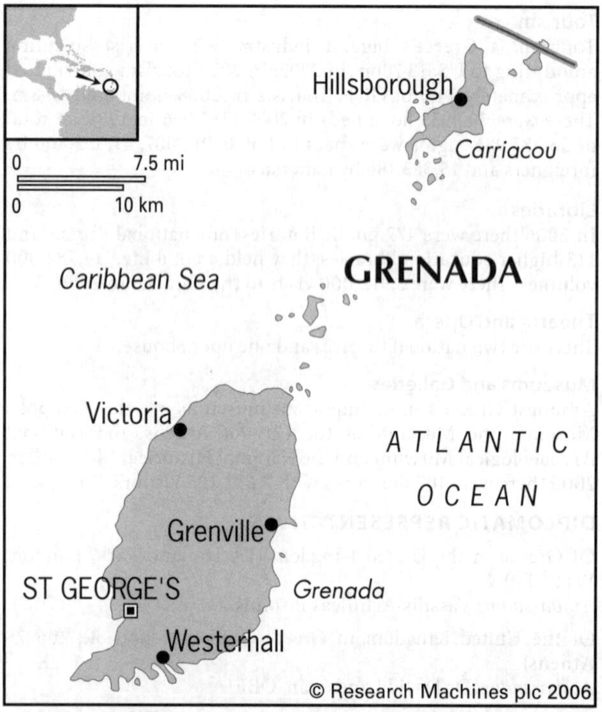

Capital: St George's
Population estimate, 2010: 104,000
GDP per capita, 2007: (PPP$) 7,344
HDI/world rank: 0·813/74

KEY HISTORICAL EVENTS

Carib Indians inhabited Grenada when it was sighted by Christopher Columbus in 1498. The Caribs prevented European settlement until French forces landed in 1654. The British took control of Grenada in 1783 and established sugar plantations using African slave labour. Eric Gairy led a violent uprising of impoverished plantation workers in 1951 and became the island's dominant political figure in the lead-up to independence on 7 Feb. 1974. He was ousted by a leftist coup on 13 March 1979. The army took control on 19 Oct. 1983 after a power struggle led to the killing of the prime minister, Maurice Bishop. At the request of a group of Caribbean countries, Grenada was invaded by US-led forces on 25–28 Oct. On 1 Nov. a state of emergency was imposed which ended later in the year with the restoration of the 1973 constitution.

TERRITORY AND POPULATION

Grenada is the most southerly island of the Windward Islands with an area of 344 sq. km (133 sq. miles); the state also includes the Southern Grenadine Islands to the north, chiefly Carriacou (58·3 sq. km) and Petit Martinique. The total population at the 2001 census was 102,632; density, 298 per sq. km.

The UN gives an estimated population for 2010 of 104,000.

In 2005, 69·4% of the population were rural. The Borough of St George's, the capital, had 35,559 inhabitants in 2001. 52% of the population is Black, 40% of mixed origins, 4% Indian and 1% White.

The official language is English. A French-African patois is also spoken.

SOCIAL STATISTICS

Births, 2001, 1,899; deaths, 727. Rates per 1,000 population, 2001: birth, 18·8; death, 7·2. Life expectancy, 2007: 73·7 years for males, 76·7 years for females. Infant mortality, 2005, 17 per 1,000 live births. Annual population growth rate, 1995–2001, 0·4%; fertility rate, 2004, 2·4 births per woman.

CLIMATE

The tropical climate is very agreeable in the dry season, from Jan. to May, when days are warm and nights quite cool, but in the wet season there is very little difference between day and night temperatures. On the coast, annual rainfall is about 60" (1,500 mm) but it is as high as 150–200" (3,750–5,000 mm) in the mountains. Average temperature, 27°C.

CONSTITUTION AND GOVERNMENT

The head of state is the British sovereign, represented by an appointed Governor-General. There is a bicameral legislature, consisting of a 13-member *Senate*, appointed by the Governor-General, and a 15-member *House of Representatives*, elected by universal suffrage.

National Anthem

'Hail Grenada, land of ours'; words by I. M. Baptiste, tune by L. A. Masanto.

RECENT ELECTIONS

At the elections of 8 July 2008 for the House of Representatives the opposition National Democratic Congress won 11 seats, with 51·0% of the votes cast, against 4 and 47·8% for the New National Party. Turnout was 80·3%.

CURRENT ADMINISTRATION

Governor-General: Sir Carlyle Glean.

In March 2010 the government comprised:

Prime Minister, Minister of Culture, Information, Information Technology, National Security and Public Administration: Tillman Thomas; b. 1945 (NDC; in office since 9 July 2008).

Minister of Agriculture, Forestry and Fisheries: Michael Lett. *Carriacou and Petite Martinique Affairs:* George Prime. *Education and Human Resources:* Franca Bernadine. *Environment, Foreign Trade and Export Development:* Michael Church. *Finance, Planning, Economy, Energy and Co-operatives:* Nazim Burke. *Foreign Affairs:* Peter David. *Health:* Anne Peters. *Housing, Lands and Community Development:* Alleyne Walker. *Labour, Social Security and Ecclesiastical Affairs:* Karl Hood. *Social Development:* Sylvester Quarless. *Tourism and Civil Aviation:* Glynis Roberts. *Works, Physical Development and Public Utilities:* Joseph Gilbert. *Youth Empowerment and Sports:* Patrick Simmons. *Attorney-General (acting):* Rohan Phillip.

Government Website: http://www.gov.gd

CURRENT LEADERS

Tillman Thomas

Position
Prime Minister

Introduction
Tillman Thomas was appointed prime minister on 9 July 2008, ending 13 years of rule by Keith Mitchell and his New National Party. As leader of the National Democratic Congress (NDC), Thomas gained advantage from the reaction against Mitchell's increasingly autocratic rule. A veteran legislator and one-time

political prisoner, Thomas promised to fashion a more open and inclusive government.

Early Life

Thomas was born in 1945 in Hermitage in St Patrick, Grenada's northernmost parish. A graduate of the University of West Indies and Trinidad's Hugh Wooding Law School, he began his career as an attorney. He was imprisoned on political grounds in 1981 during the Marxist and Cuba-aligned regime of Maurice Bishop, who had come to power following a coup. Thomas was released in 1983 following a military invasion by US and Caribbean troops.

In 1984 Thomas was elected to the House of Representatives as the New National Party member for St Patrick East. In 1987 he was one of the founding members of the NDC, serving for six years as its assistant general secretary. Despite losing his seat at the 1990 general election, Thomas was appointed minister of works, communications and public utilities in 1991. He subsequently served as minister of finance and as minister of tourism, culture, civil aviation and sports.

Following the NDC's failure to gain a single seat in the 1999 general election, Thomas was appointed party leader. The NDC came close to gaining power in 2003, winning seven of the 15 available seats, with Thomas reclaiming St Patrick East. As leader of the opposition, he accused Mitchell of mismanagement and played upon voter frustration with rising prices and a tourist-based economy struggling to recover from the devastation wreaked by Hurricane Ivan in 2004.

Career in Office

The NDC won a resounding victory at the 2008 general election, taking 11 of the 15 seats. One of Thomas' first actions was to repeal the national reconstruction levy, a tax of 3% on income over EC$1,000 per month imposed in the aftermath of Hurricane Ivan. Thomas has also promised free school books for all primary and secondary schools. He has vowed to create a more participatory government focusing on improving the economy and lowering the cost of living for Grenada's poorest families.

DEFENCE

Royal Grenada Police Force

Modelled on the British system, the 730-strong police force includes an 80-member paramilitary unit and a 30-member coastguard.

INTERNATIONAL RELATIONS

Grenada is a member of the UN, World Bank, IMF and several other UN specialized agencies, WTO, Commonwealth, IOM, ACS, CARICOM, SELA, OECS, OAS and is an ACP member state of the ACP-EU relationship.

ECONOMY

Agriculture accounted for 6·7% of GDP in 2006, industry 29·0% and services 64·3%.

Overview

Massive damage caused by hurricanes in 2004 and 2005 led the government to launch a medium-term economic reform package to tackle the large public debt, ensure sustainable growth and alleviate poverty. This was supported by the IMF's Poverty Reduction and Growth Facility arrangement, with the first review completed in 2008.

Following near-zero levels in 2006, growth rebounded to over 4% in 2007 owing to strong tourism, the Cricket World Cup and the expansion of an offshore university. Strong growth helped reduce the GDP-to-debt ratio from 117% at the end of 2006 to 112% a year later. However, while the outlook is positive, challenges remain. Annual inflation has risen sharply as a result of increasing world food and fuel prices and the depreciating US dollar, while fiscal performance deteriorated further in 2007, reflecting high capital expenditure and shortfalls in grants (from, among others, the EU). Economic growth is expected to slow down in the short term as a result of the global downturn.

Currency

The unit of currency is the *East Caribbean dollar* (XCD). Foreign exchange reserves were US$100m. in July 2005 and total money supply was EC$380m. Inflation was 3·9% in 2007 and 8·0% in 2008.

Budget

In 2006 revenue was EC$490·8m. and expenditure EC$588·8m. Income tax has been abolished. VAT of 15% (reduced rate, 10%) was introduced on 1 Feb. 2010.

Performance

Real GDP growth was 4·9% in 2007 and 2·2% in 2008. Total GDP in 2008 was US$0·6bn.

Banking and Finance

Grenada is a member of the Eastern Caribbean Central Bank. The *Governor* is Sir Dwight Venner. In 2002 there were three commercial banks and four foreign banks. The Grenada Agricultural Bank was established in 1965 to encourage agricultural development; in 1975 it became the Grenada Agricultural and Industrial Development Corporation. In 1995 bank deposits were EC$666·8m. (US$249·7m.). Total foreign currency deposits in 1995 amounted to US$11·8m.

Grenada is affiliated to the Eastern Caribbean Securities Exchange in Basseterre, St Kitts and Nevis.

ENERGY AND NATURAL RESOURCES

Environment

Grenada's carbon dioxide emissions from the consumption and flaring of fossil fuels in 2008 were the equivalent of 3·7 tonnes per capita.

Electricity

Installed capacity in 2004 was an estimated 27,000 kW. Production in 2004 was 157m. kWh, with consumption per capita 1,963 kWh.

Agriculture

There were about 2,000 ha. of arable land in 2007 and 10,000 ha. of permanent crops. Principal crop production (2003, in 1,000 tonnes): sugarcane, 7; coconuts, 6; bananas, 4; avocados, 2; grapefruit and pomelos, 2; mangoes, 2. Nutmeg, corn, pigeon peas, citrus, root-crops and vegetables are also grown, in addition to small scattered cultivations of cotton, cloves, cinnamon, pimento, coffee and fruit trees. Grenada is the second largest producer of nutmeg in the world, after Indonesia.

Livestock (2003): sheep, 13,000; goats, 7,000; pigs, 5,000; cattle, 4,000.

Forestry

In 2005 the area under forests was 4,000 ha., or 12·2% of the total land area.

Fisheries

The catch in 2004 was 2,039 tonnes, entirely from marine waters.

INDUSTRY

Main products are wheat flour, soft drinks, beer, animal feed, rum and cigarettes.

Labour

In 1993 the labour force was estimated at 27,820. Unemployment was 11% in Dec. 2000.

INTERNATIONAL TRADE

Total external debt amounted to US$525m. in 2007.

Imports and Exports

In 2005 imports totalled US$287·7m. and exports US$32·8m. Major import commodities in 2005 were: machinery and transport equipment, 23·4%; food and live animals, 14·2%; manufactures of metals, 6·9%. The principal exports were: nutmeg, mace and cardamom, 29·7%; machinery and transport equipment, 15·2%; fish and shellfish, 12·7%.

In 2005 the main import suppliers were the USA (37·5%), Trinidad and Tobago (21·0%), UK (5·8%), Japan (4·0%) and China (3·2%). Main export destinations were the USA (21·4%), Netherlands (14·1%), Trinidad and Tobago (10·1%), St Lucia (9·4%) and Barbados (6·2%).

COMMUNICATIONS

Roads

In 2000 there were 1,127 km of roads, of which 61·0% were hard-surfaced.

Civil Aviation

The main airport is Point Salines International. Union Island and Carriacou have smaller airports. There were direct flights from Point Salines in 2003 to Anguilla, Antigua, Barbados, the British Virgin Islands, Dominica, Frankfurt, London, Montego Bay, New York, Philadelphia, Puerto Rico, St Kitts, St Lucia, St Maarten, St Vincent, Tobago and Trinidad. In 2001 Point Salines handled 344,064 passengers (342,124 on international flights) and 2,747 tonnes of freight.

Shipping

The main port is at St George's; there are eight minor ports. Total number of containers handled in 1991 was 5,161; cargo landed, 187,039 tonnes; cargo loaded, 24,786 tonnes. Sea-going shipping totalled 1,000 GRT in 2002.

Telecommunications

Telephone subscribers numbered 76,000 in 2004 (743·4 per 1,000 persons), of which 43,300 were mobile phone subscribers. There were 16,000 PCs in use (156·5 for every 1,000 persons) in 2004 and 19,000 internet users in 2003.

Postal Services

In 2003 there were 52 post offices.

SOCIAL INSTITUTIONS

Justice

The Grenada Supreme Court, situated in St George's, comprises a High Court of Justice, a Court of Magisterial Appeal (which hears appeals from the lower Magistrates' Courts exercising summary jurisdiction) and an Itinerant Court of Appeal (to hear appeals from the High Court). Grenada was one of ten countries to sign an agreement in Feb. 2001 establishing a Caribbean Court of Justice to replace the British Privy Council as the highest civil and criminal court. In the meantime the number of signatories has risen to twelve. The court was inaugurated at Port-of-Spain, Trinidad on 16 April 2005. For police *see* DEFENCE, *above*.

The population in penal institutions in 2007 was 367 (equivalent to 408 per 100,000 of national population).

Education

Adult literacy was 96·0% in 2004. In 2007 there were 13,733 pupils in primary schools (871 teaching staff) and 13,060 pupils (886 teaching staff in 2005) in secondary schools. The Grenada National College was established in 1988. There is also a branch of the University of the West Indies. In 2003 public expenditure on education amounted to 5·9% of GNI and 12·9% of total government spending.

Health

In 1996 there were three general hospitals with a provision of 35 beds per 10,000 inhabitants. There were 96 physicians, 14 dentists, 232 nurses and 47 pharmacists in 1996. 16·2% of the 2001 budget was allocated to health.

RELIGION

At the 2001 census 53% of the population were Roman Catholic, 14% Anglican and the remainder other religions.

CULTURE

Broadcasting

The Grenada Broadcasting Network, which is jointly owned by the government and the Caribbean Communications Network, operates the main television station (GBN TV—colour by NTSC) and two radio services. MTV is a private television station, and there are several independent radio stations, based largely in St George's. There were 38,000 television receivers in 2001.

Press

In 2006 there were five weekly newspapers and several others that were published irregularly.

Tourism

In 2005 there were 98,548 non-resident tourists and 275,080 cruise passenger arrivals. Tourism receipts (excluding passenger transport) totalled US$71m. in 2005.

DIPLOMATIC REPRESENTATIVES

Of Grenada in the United Kingdom (The Chapel, Archel Rd, London, W14 9QH)
High Commissioner: Ruth Elizabeth Rouse.

Of the United Kingdom in Grenada
High Commissioner: Paul Brummell (resides in Bridgetown, Barbados).

Of Grenada in the USA (1701 New Hampshire Ave., NW, Washington, D.C., 20009)
Ambassador: Gillian M. S. Bristol.

Of the USA in Grenada
Ambassador: Vacant (resides in Bridgetown, Barbados).
Chargé d'Affaires a.i.: D. Brendt Hardt.

Of Grenada to the United Nations
Ambassador: Dessima Williams.

Of Grenada to the European Union
Ambassador: Stephen Fletcher.

FURTHER READING

Ferguson, J., *Grenada: Revolution in Reverse.* 1991
Heine, J. (ed.) *A Revolution Aborted: the Lessons of Grenada.* 1990
Steele, Beverley A., *Grenada: A History of its People.* 2003

GUATEMALA

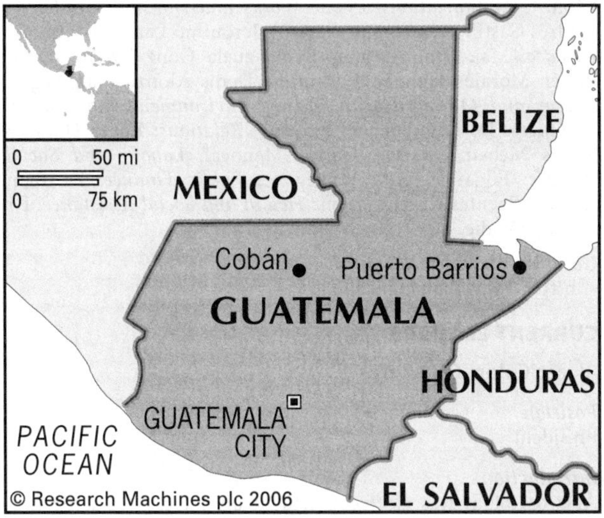

República de Guatemala
(Republic of Guatemala)

Capital: Guatemala City
Population estimate, 2010: 14·38m.
GDP per capita, 2007: (PPP$) 4,562
HDI/world rank: 0·704/122

KEY HISTORICAL EVENTS

From 1524 Guatemala was part of a Spanish captaincy-general, comprising the whole of Central America. It became independent in 1821 and formed part of the Confederation of Central America from 1823 to 1839. The overthrow of the right-wing dictator Jorge Ubico in 1944 opened a decade of left-wing activity which alarmed the USA. In 1954 the leftist regime of Jacobo Arbenz Guzmán was overthrown by a CIA-supported coup. A series of right-wing governments failed to produce stability while the toll on human life and the violation of human rights was such as to cause thousands of refugees to flee to Mexico. Elections to a National Constituent Assembly were held on 1 July 1984, and a new constitution was promulgated in May 1985. Amidst violence and assassinations, the presidential election was won by Marco Vinicio Cerezo Arévalo. On 14 Jan. 1986 Cerezo's civilian government was installed—the first for 16 years and only the second since 1954. Violence continued, however, and there were frequent reports of torture and killings by right-wing 'death squads'. The presidential and legislative elections of Nov. 1995 saw the return of open politics for the first time in over 40 years. Meanwhile the Guatemalan Revolutionary Unit (URNG) declared a ceasefire. On 6 May and 19 Sept. 1996 the government agreed reforms to military, internal security, judicial and agrarian institutions. A ceasefire was concluded in Oslo on 4 Dec. 1996 and a final peace treaty was signed on 29 Dec. 1996. In Nov. 1999 the country's first presidential elections took place since the end of the 36-year-long civil war, which had claimed over 200,000 lives.

TERRITORY AND POPULATION

Guatemala is bounded on the north and west by Mexico, south by the Pacific ocean and east by El Salvador, Honduras and Belize, and the area is 108,889 sq. km (42,042 sq. miles). In March 1936 Guatemala, El Salvador and Honduras agreed to accept the peak of Mount Montecristo as the common boundary point.

The population was 11,237,196 at the census of Nov. 2002; density, 103 per sq. km. The estimated population in 2006 was 12,988,000.

The UN gives an estimated population for 2010 of 14·38m.

In 2005, 52·8% of the population were rural. In 2000, 33% were Amerindian, of 21 different groups descended from the Maya; 64% Mestizo (mixed Amerindian and Spanish). 51% speak Spanish, the official language of Guatemala, with the remainder speaking one or a combination of the 23 Indian dialects.

Guatemala is administratively divided into 22 departments, each with a governor appointed by the president. Area and population, 2002:

Departments	*Area (sq. km)*	*Population*	*Departments*	*Area (sq. km)*	*Population*
Alta Verapaz	8,686	776,246	Petén	35,854	366,735
Baja Verapaz	3,124	215,915	Quezaltenango	1,951	624,716
Chimaltenango	1,979	446,133	Quiché	8,378	655,510
Chiquimula	2,376	302,485	Retalhuleu	1,858	241,411
El Progreso	1,922	139,490	Sacatepéquez	465	248,019
Escuintla	4,384	538,746	San Marcos	3,791	794,951
Guatemala City	2,126	2,541,581	Santa Rosa	2,955	301,370
Huehuetenango	7,403	846,544	Sololá	1,061	307,661
Izabal	9,038	314,306	Suchitepéquez	2,510	403,945
Jalapa	2,063	242,926	Totonicapán	1,061	339,254
Jutiapa	3,219	389,085	Zacapa	2,690	200,167

In 2002 Guatemala City, the capital, had a population of 942,348. Populations of other major towns, 2002 (in 1,000): Mixco, 384; Villa Nueva, 302; Quezaltenango, 120; Petapa, 94; Escuintla, 87.

SOCIAL STATISTICS

Births, 2006, 368,399; deaths, 69,756. 2006 rates per 1,000 population: birth, 28·4; death, 5·4. Life expectancy, 2007: male 66·7 years, female 73·7. Annual population growth rate, 2000–05, 2·2%. Infant mortality, 2005, 32 per 1,000 live births; fertility rate, 2004, 4·5 births per woman.

CLIMATE

A tropical climate, with little variation in temperature and a well marked wet season from May to Oct. Guatemala City, Jan. 63°F (17·2°C), July 69°F (20·6°C). Annual rainfall 53" (1,316 mm).

CONSTITUTION AND GOVERNMENT

A new Constitution, drawn up by the Constituent Assembly elected on 1 July 1984, was promulgated in June 1985 and came into force on 14 Jan. 1986. In 1993, 43 amendments were adopted, reducing *inter alia* the President's term of office from five to four years. The President and Vice-President are elected by direct election (with a second round of voting if no candidate secures 50% of the first-round votes) for a non-renewable four-year term. The unicameral *Congreso de la República* comprises 158 members, elected partly from constituencies and partly by proportional representation to serve four-year terms.

National Anthem

'¡Guatemala Feliz!' ('Happy Guatemala'); words by J. J. Palma, tune by R. Alvárez.

GOVERNMENT CHRONOLOGY

Heads of State since 1944. (CAO = Organized Aranista Central; DCG = Guatemalan Christian Democracy; FRG = Guatemalan Republican Front; GANA = Grand National Alliance; MAS

= Solidarity Action Movement; MLN = National Liberation Movement; PAN = National Advancement Party; PAR = Revolutionary Action Party; PID = Democratic Institutional Party; PR = Revolutionary Party; PRDN = National Democratic Reconciliation/Redemption Party; UNE = National Union of Hope; n/p = non-partisan)

Military Junta		
1944–45		Maj. Francisco Javier Arana; Capt. Jacobo Arbenz Guzmán; Jorge Toriello Garrido
Presidents		
1945–51	PAR	Juan José Arévalo Bermejo
1951–54	PAR	Jacobo Arbenz Guzmán
1954	military	Carlos Enrique Díaz de León
Military Juntas		
1954		Col. Elfego Hernán Monzón Aguirre; Col. José Ángel Sánchez; Col. José Luis Cruz Salazar; Col. Carlos Enrique Díaz de León; Col. Mauricio Dubois
1954		Col. Carlos Castillo Armas; Col. Mauricio Dubois; Maj. Enrique Trinidad Oliva; Col. Elfego Hernán Monzón Aguirre; Col. José Luis Cruz Salazar
Presidents		
1954–57	military	Carlos Castillo Armas
1957–58	military	Guillermo Flores Avendaño
1958–63	PRDN	José Ramón Ydígoras Fuentes
1963–66	military	Alfredo Enrique Peralta Azurdia
1966–70	PR	Julio César Méndez Montenegro
1970–74	military, MLN	Carlos Manuel Arana Osorio
1974–78	military, MLN/PID	Kjell Eugenio Laugerud García
1978–82	military, PID/PR/CAO	Fernando Romeo Lucas García
1982–83	military	José Efraín Ríos Montt
1983–86	military	Óscar Humberto Mejía Víctores
1986–91	DCG	Marco Vinicio Cerezo Arévalo
1991–93	MAS	Jorge Antonio Serrano Elías
1993–96	n/p	Ramiro de León Carpio
1996–2000	PAN	Álvaro Enrique Arzú Yrigoyen
2000–04	FRG	Alfonso Antonio Portillo Cabrera
2004–08	GANA	Óscar Rafael Berger Perdomo
2008–	UNE	Álvaro Colom Caballeros

RECENT ELECTIONS

In a run-off for the presidency on 4 Nov. 2007 Álvaro Colom Caballeros of the Unidad Nacional de la Esperanza (UNE, National Union of Hope) won with 52·8% of the vote against Otto Pérez Molina of the Partido Patriota (PP, Patriotic Party) with 47·2%. In the first round of voting on 9 Sept. 2007 there had been 12 other candidates. Turnout was 60·5% in the first round and 48·3% in the second.

Congressional elections were held on 9 Sept. 2007. UNE won 48 seats with 22·8% of the vote, the Gran Alianza Nacional/Grand National Alliance (comprising the Reformist Movement and the National Solidarity Party) 37 with 16·5%; Partido Patriota (Patriotic Party) 30 with 15·9%; Frente Republicano Guatemalteco (Guatemalan Republican Front) 15 with 9·8%; Partido Unionista (Unionist Party) 8 with 6·1%; and Centro de Acción Social (Social Action Centre) 5 with 4·9%. Five other parties won four seats or fewer. Turnout was 60·5%.

CURRENT ADMINISTRATION

President: Álvaro Colom Caballeros; b. 1951 (UNE; sworn in 14 Jan. 2008).

Vice-President: Dr Rafael Espada; b. 1944 (UNE; took office on 14 Jan. 2008).

In March 2010 the government comprised:

Minister of Agriculture, Livestock and Food: Juan Alfonzo de Léon. *Communications, Public Works and Housing:* Guillermo Andrés Castillo. *Culture and Sports:* Jerónimo Lancevio Chingo. *Defence:* Maj.-Gen. Abraham Valenzuela González. *Economy:* Rubén Morales Monroy. *Education:* Denis Alonzo Mazariegos. *Energy and Mining:* Carlos Meany. *Environment and Natural Resources:* Dr Luis Ferraté. *External Relations:* Roger Haraldo Rodas Melgar. *Interior:* Carlos Menocal. *Labour and Social Welfare:* Edgar Alfredo Rodríguez. *Public Finance:* Dr Juan Alberto Fuentes Knight. *Public Health and Social Assistance:* Dr Ludwig Ovalle.

Government Website (Spanish only): http://www.guatemala.gob.gt

CURRENT LEADERS

Álvaro Colom Caballeros

Position
President

Introduction
Álvaro Colom was elected president on 4 Nov. 2007, the first social democrat to hold the office since 1954. Colom replaced Oscar Berger of the Gran Alianza Nacional.

Early Life
Colom was born into a politically active family in June 1951 in Guatemala City. He studied at the Liceo Guatemala, a private Catholic school, and then the state University of San Carlos (USAC). After graduating in 1974 as an industrial engineer, he entered the textile industry, becoming a leading representative in the 1980s.

In 1990 President Jorge Serrano Elias—a fellow alumnus of both Liceo Guatemala and USAC—appointed Colom vice minister for the economy and director of the Fund for Peace (FONAPAZ). After the 1997 peace accords ended decades of civil war, Colom worked in land conflict resolution and the promotion of reconciliation.

In 1999 he unsuccessfully ran for president for the centre-left ANN party. In 2003 he ran again, this time for the social democratic UNE, but was defeated by Oscar Berger in the second round. Nonetheless, it was the best left-wing showing in an election for almost 50 years though critics accused him of illegal campaign financing.

Career in Office
Colom's 2007 campaign centred on his 'Plan de la Esperanza', extending to 2032. As well as pledging to fight poverty and improve health, education and public security, he promised to create 700,000 new jobs, build 200,000 new homes and increase GDP growth to 6%. In May 2009 the government denied any complicity in the murder of a prominent lawyer who had claimed that Colom was seeking to kill him.

DEFENCE

In 2006 defence expenditure totalled US$146m. (US$12 per capita), representing 0·4% of GDP.

Army

The Army numbered (2007) 13,400 and is organized in 15 military zones. It includes a special forces unit. There is a paramilitary national police of 19,000 including 2,500 treasury police.

Navy

The Navy was (2007) 990-strong of whom 650 were marines. Main bases are Santo Tomás de Castilla (on the Atlantic Coast) and Puerto Quetzal (Pacific).

Air Force
There is an Air Force with ten combat capable aircraft (PC-7s and A-37s). Strength was (2007) 1,070.

INTERNATIONAL RELATIONS
Guatemala is a member of the UN, World Bank, IMF and several other UN specialized agencies, WTO, IOM, ACS, CACM, Inter-American Development Bank, SELA and OAS.

ECONOMY
In 2007 agriculture accounted for 11% of GDP, industry 28% and services 62%.

Overview
Guatemala's income per capita is high relative to other Central American countries. However, income inequality is particularly high and around half the population lives in poverty. Social indicators fall below the average of low-income countries. The agricultural sector accounts for about 25% of the economy, almost half of all employment, and a large part of exports. Remittances, though, are the primary source of foreign income, exceeding the combined value of all exports. Guatemala spent most of the first half of the decade in recession but since 2004 the economy has expanded, albeit at an unimpressive rate given its low starting point. Consumer price inflation fell from 36·9% in 1986 to 6·6% in 2006. While exports have risen slowly over the years, import growth has accelerated—imports now total more than twice the value of exports. Rising energy costs in particular contributed to the import surge. Food imports grew from US$627m. to US$1,493m. between 1996–2000. Since the end of the civil war in 1996 the economy has drawn more foreign capital investment, which has also contributed to the growth of imports. Nonetheless, the country has had a persistently negative but stable current account balance, averaging about –4% of GDP since 2003.

Currency
The unit of currency is the *quetzal* (GTQ) of 100 *centavos*, established on 7 May 1925. In July 2005 foreign exchange reserves were US$3,685m., total money supply was Q.30,083m. and gold reserves were 221,000 troy oz. Inflation was 11·4% in 2008.

Budget
Budgetary central government revenue in 2003 totalled Q.21,694·4m. (Q.20,715·6m. in 2002) and expenditure was Q.24,968·6m. (Q.20,758·7m. in 2002).

VAT is 12%.

Performance
Real GDP growth was 4·0% in 2008. Total GDP in 2008 was US$39·0bn.

Banking and Finance
The Banco de Guatemala is the central bank and bank of issue (*President*, María Antonieta de Bonilla). In 2002 there were 27 national banks (four state-owned and 23 private). The international banks and the foreign banks are authorized to operate as commercial banks.

There are two stock exchanges.

Weights and Measures
The metric system is official but the imperial is still used locally.

ENERGY AND NATURAL RESOURCES

Environment
Carbon dioxide emissions from the consumption and flaring of fossil fuels in 2008 were the equivalent of 0·9 tonnes per capita.

Electricity
Installed capacity in 2004 was an estimated 1·8m. kW. Production, 2004, 7·01bn. kWh. Consumption per capita in 2004 was 532 kWh.

Oil and Gas
There were proven natural gas reserves in 2007 of 3·1bn. cu. metres. Production (2002), 11m. cu. metres. In 2007 crude petroleum reserves were 83m. bbls; output in 2004 was 7·3m. bbls.

Minerals
There are deposits of gold, silver and nickel.

Agriculture
There were 1·36m. ha. of arable land in 2001 and 0·55m. ha. of permanent crops. 130,000 ha. were irrigated in 2001. Output, 2003 estimates (in 1,000 tonnes): sugarcane, 17,500; maize, 1,054; bananas, 1,000; melons and watermelons, 314; plantains, 268; potatoes, 248; coffee, 210. Guatemala is one of the largest producers of essential oils (citronella and lemongrass). Livestock (2003 estimates): cattle, 2·54m.; pigs, 780,000; sheep, 260,000; horses, 124,000; goats, 112,000; chickens, 27m.

Forestry
In 2005 the area under forests was 3·94m. ha., or 36·3% of the total land area. Timber production in 2007 was 17·41m. cu. metres.

Fisheries
In 2005 the total catch was 12,248 tonnes, of which freshwater fish 60% and marine fish 40%.

INDUSTRY
Manufacturing contributed 12·9% of GDP in 2001. The principal industries are food and beverages, tobacco, chemicals, hides and skins, textiles, garments and non-metallic minerals. Cement production in 2004 was an estimated 1,800,000 tonnes; raw sugar production was 1,661,000 tonnes in 2001.

Labour
In 2002 there were 3,463,000 employed persons. The main areas of activity were: agriculture, hunting, forestry and fishing, 1,457,000; wholesale and retail trade and restaurants and hotels, 571,700; manufacturing, 466,000; services, 266,000; construction, 207,900. There is a working week of a maximum of 44 hours.

Trade Unions
There are three federations for private sector workers.

INTERNATIONAL TRADE
In 2004 Guatemala signed the Central America-Dominican Republic-United States Free Trade Agreement (CAFTA-DR), along with Costa Rica, the Dominican Republic, El Salvador, Honduras, Nicaragua and the USA. The agreement entered into force for Guatemala on 1 July 2006. External debt was US$5,349m. in 2005.

Imports and Exports
Values in US$1m. were:

	2003	*2004*	*2005*	*2006*	*2007*
Imports c.i.f.	6,718·7	7,812·1	10,499·5	9,539·7	12,731·4
Exports f.o.b.	2,634·7	2,931·8	5,380·8	3,198·1	6,900·4

In 2007 the main imports were: machinery and transport equipment, 25·1%; petroleum and petroleum products, 16·1%; chemicals and related products, 14·8%; food and live animals, 9·8%. Principal exports in 2007 were: apparel and clothing accessories, 20·1%; chemicals and related products, 10·8%; coffee and coffee substitutes, 8·5%; cane sugar, 5·2%; bananas, 4·7%. Main import suppliers, 2007: USA, 34·1%; Mexico, 8·8%; China, 5·7%; El Salvador, 4·8%; South Korea, 3·4%. Main export markets, 2007: USA, 42·6%; El Salvador, 12·2%; Honduras, 8·6%; Mexico, 6·7%; Nicaragua, 3·9%.

COMMUNICATIONS

Roads
In 2002 there were 14,891 km of roads, of which 74 km were motorways. 37·6% of all roads were paved in 2002. There is a

highway from coast to coast via Guatemala City. There are two highways from the Mexican to the Salvadorean frontier: the Pacific Highway serving the fertile coastal plain and the Pan-American Highway running through the highlands and Guatemala City. Vehicles in use in 2007 numbered 1,558,100.

Rail

The state-owned Ferrocarriles de Guatemala operated 788 km of railway in 2005, linking east and west coast seaports to Guatemala City, with branch lines to the north and south borders. Passenger-km travelled in 1994 came to 991m. and freight tonne-km in 2000 to 2·2bn.

Civil Aviation

There are international airports at Guatemala City (La Aurora) and Flores. In 2000 La Aurora handled 1,258,919 passengers and 58,118 tonnes of freight. In 1999 scheduled airline traffic of Guatemalan-based carriers flew 5·3m. km, carrying 506,000 passengers (472,000 on international flights).

Shipping

The chief ports on the Atlantic coast are Puerto Barrios and Santo Tomás de Castilla: on the Pacific coast, Puerto Quetzal and Champerico. Merchant shipping totalled 9,000 GRT in 2002. In 2004 vessels totalling 9,534,000 NRT entered ports and vessels totalling 5,211,000 NRT cleared.

Telecommunications

The government own and operate the telecommunications services. In 2004 there were 4,300,400 telephone subscribers, or 339·7 for every 1,000 persons, including 3,168,300 mobile phone subscribers. 231,000 PCs were in use (18·2 for every 1,000 persons) in 2004 and there were 756,000 internet users.

Postal Services

There were 434 post offices in 2003.

SOCIAL INSTITUTIONS

Justice

Justice is administered in a Constitution Court, a Supreme Court, six appeal courts and 28 courts of first instance. Supreme Court and appeal court judges are elected by Congress. Judges of first instance are appointed by the Supreme Court.

The death penalty is authorized for murder and kidnapping. There were 5,885 homicides in 2006. At 46 per 100,000 persons, Guatemala has among the highest murder rates in the world. There were two executions in 2000, but none since.

A new National Civil Police force under the authority of the Minister of the Interior was created in 1996. It was 19,000-strong in 2007.

The population in penal institutions in Dec. 2006 was 7,477 (57 per 100,000 of national population).

Education

In 2007 there were 2,448,976 pupils at primary schools and 864,154 pupils at secondary level. The adult literacy rate in 2003 was 69·1% (male, 75·4%; female, 63·3%). There is one state university—the University of San Carlos of Guatemala (Universidad de San Carlos de Guatemala), founded in 1676—as well as several private universities. In 2006 there were 112,215 students and 3,843 academic staff in tertiary education.

In 2007 public expenditure on education came to 3·1% of GNI.

Health

Guatemala had 9,965 physicians and 2,046 dentists in 1999. There were 49 hospitals, 257 country health centres and 1,288 community health clinics in 2000.

Welfare

A comprehensive system of social security was outlined in a law of 30 Oct. 1946.

RELIGION

Roman Catholicism is the prevailing faith (8·9m. adherents in 2001) and there is a Roman Catholic archbishopric. In Feb. 2010 there was one cardinal. The remainder of the population are followers of other religions (mainly Evangelical Protestantism).

CULTURE

World Heritage Sites

There are three UNESCO sites in Guatemala: Tikal National Park (inscribed on the list in 1979); Antigua Guatemala (1979); and the Archaeological Park and Ruins of Quiriguá (1981).

Broadcasting

Broadcasting is dominated by commercial operators. The main private television services are Radio-TV Guatemala, Teleonce, Televisiete and Trecevision: two state TV channels are also licensed to broadcast. La Voz de Guatemala is a government-owned radio station. There were 2·1m. TV receivers (colour by NTSC) in 2006.

Press

In 2006 there were ten daily newspapers, the main ones being Nuestro Diario and Prensa Libre.

Tourism

Tourism is an important source of foreign exchange (receipts totalled US$883m. in 2005). There were 1,316,000 non-resident tourists in 2005.

DIPLOMATIC REPRESENTATIVES

Of Guatemala in the United Kingdom (13A Fawcett St., London, SW10 9HN)
Ambassador: Alfonso Matta Fahsen.

Of the United Kingdom in Guatemala (Avenida La Reforma 16-00, Zona 10, Edificio Torre Internacional, Nivel 11, Guatemala City)
Ambassador: Julie Chappell, OBE.

Of Guatemala in the USA (2220 R. St., NW, Washington, D.C., 20008)
Ambassador: Francisco Villagrán de León.

Of the USA in Guatemala (7–01 Avenida de la Reforma, Zone 10, Guatemala City)
Ambassador: Stephen G. McFarland.

Of Guatemala to the United Nations
Ambassador: Gert Rosenthal.

Of Guatemala to the European Union
Ambassador: Antonio Fernando Arenales Forno.

FURTHER READING

Benson, Peter and Fischer, Edward F., *Broccoli and Desire: Global Connections and Maya Struggles in Post-War Guatemala.* 2006

Jonas, Susanne, *Of Centaurs and Doves: Guatemala's Peace Process.* 2001

Reeves, René, *Ladinos with Ladinos, Indians with Indians: Land, Labor, and Regional Ethnic Conflict in the Making of Guatemala.* 2006

Sanford, Victoria, *Buried Secrets: Truth and Human Rights in Guatemala.* 2003

National library: Biblioteca Nacional, 5a Avenida y 8a Calle, Zona 1, Guatemala City.

National Institute of Statistics Website (Spanish only): http://www.ine.gob.gt

GUINEA

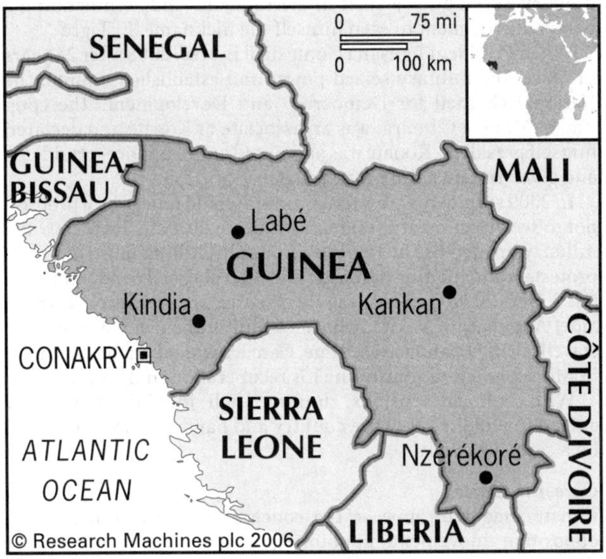

République de Guinée
(Republic of Guinea)

Capital: Conakry
Population estimate, 2010: 10·32m.
GDP per capita, 2007: (PPP$) 1,140
HDI/world rank: 0·435/170

KEY HISTORICAL EVENTS

In 1888 Guinea became a French protectorate, in 1893 a colony, and in 1904 a constituent territory of French West Africa. Forced labour and other colonial depredations ensued, although a form of representation was introduced in 1946. The independent Republic of Guinea was proclaimed on 2 Oct. 1958, after the territory of French Guinea had decided to leave the French community. Guinea became a single-party state. In 1980 the armed forces staged a coup and dissolved the National Assembly. Following popular disturbances a multi-party system was introduced in April 1992.

In 2000 fierce fighting broke out between Guinean government troops and rebels, believed to be a mix of Guinean dissidents and mercenaries from Liberia and Sierra Leone. More than 250,000 refugees were caught up in what the United Nations High Commissioner for Refugees described as the world's worst refugee crisis. In 2003 the governments of Guinea, Liberia and Sierra Leone reached a deal on measures to secure mutual borders and to fight insurgency.

In 2008 President Lansana Conté died after 24 years of authoritarian rule. Power fell to the military, who appointed Capt. Moussa Dadis Camara as president. Camara promised presidential elections in Jan. 2010 and parliamentary elections in March 2010. In Sept. 2009 the army opened fire on an opposition rally, killing at least 150 people. The European Union, African Union and USA imposed sanctions the following month, the UN set up an enquiry into the incident and in Feb. 2010 the International Criminal Court condemned the massacre as a crime against humanity. After surviving an attempted assassination in Dec. 2009, Camara agreed to recuperate abroad while rule fell to his deputy, Gen. Sekouba Konaté. Konaté appointed Jean-Marie Doré as interim prime minister to oversee a return to civilian rule.

TERRITORY AND POPULATION

Guinea is bounded in the northwest by Guinea-Bissau and Senegal, northeast by Mali, southeast by Côte d'Ivoire, south by Liberia and Sierra Leone, and west by the Atlantic Ocean.

The area is 245,857 sq. km (94,926 sq. miles). In 1996 the census population was 7,156,406 (density 29·1 per sq. km).

The UN gives an estimated population for 2010 of 10·32m.; density, 42 per sq. km.

The capital is Conakry. In 2005, 67·0% of the population were rural.

Guinea is divided into seven provinces and a special zone (national capital). These are in turn divided into 34 administrative regions. The major divisions (with their areas in sq. km) are: Boké, 34,231; Conakry (special zone—national capital), 308; Faranah, 38,272; Kankan, 71,085; Kindia, 26,749; Labé, 21,150; Mamou, 13,560; Nzérékoré, 40,502.

The main towns are Conakry (population estimate, 2003, 1,366,000), Kindia, Nzérékoré, Kankan, Guéckédougou and Kissidougou.

The ethnic composition is Fulani (38·6%, predominant in Moyenne-Guinée), Malinké (or Mandingo, 23·2%, prominent in Haute-Guinée), Susu (11·0%, prominent in Guinée-Maritime), Kissi (6·0%) and Kpelle (4·6%) in Guinée-Forestière, and Dialonka, Loma and others (16·6%).

The official language is French.

SOCIAL STATISTICS

2000 estimates: births, 352,000; deaths, 136,000. Rates, 2000 estimates (per 1,000 population): births, 43·4; deaths, 16·8. infant mortality, 2005, 98 per 1,000 live births. Life expectancy, 2007, 55·3 years for males and 59·3 for females. Annual population growth rate, 1992–2002, 2·4%; fertility rate, 2004, 5·8 births per woman.

CLIMATE

A tropical climate, with high rainfall near the coast and constant heat, but conditions are a little cooler on the plateau. The wet season on the coast lasts from May to Nov., but only to Oct. inland. Conakry, Jan. 80°F (26·7°C), July 77°F (25°C). Annual rainfall 172" (4,293 mm).

CONSTITUTION AND GOVERNMENT

There is a 114-member *National Assembly* (currently suspended), 38 of whose members are elected on a first-past-the-post system, and the remainder from national lists by proportional representation. It was dissolved following the military coup of Dec. 2008.

On 11 Nov. 2001 a referendum was held in which 98·4% of votes cast were in favour of President Conté remaining in office for a third term, requiring an amendment to the constitution (previously allowing a maximum two presidential terms). The referendum, which also increased the presidential mandate from five to seven years, was boycotted by opposition parties.

National Anthem

'Peuple d'Afrique, le passé historique' ('People of Africa, the historic past'); words anonymous, tune by Fodeba Keita.

RECENT ELECTIONS

Presidential elections were held on 21 Dec. 2003. President Lansana Conté of the Party of Unity and Progress (PUP) was re-elected with 95·6% of the vote against 4·4% won by Mamadou Bhoye Barry of the Union for National Progress (UPN). Opposition parties boycotted the elections. Turnout was reported to be 82·8%.

Parliamentary elections took place on 30 June 2002. The PUP gained 85 out of 114 seats with 61·6% of votes cast, Union for Progress and Renewal (UPR) 20 seats with 26·6%, Union for the Progress of Guinea (UPG) 3 with 4·1%, Democratic Party of Guinea (PDG) 3 with 3·4%, National Alliance for Progress (ANP) 2 with 2·0% and Party of the Union for Development (PUD) 1 with 0·7%. Turnout was 71·6%. The Rally of the Guinean People, the main opposition party, boycotted the election.

Presidential elections were scheduled to take place on 27 June 2010.

CURRENT ADMINISTRATION

President (acting): Sékouba Konaté; b. 1966 (National Council for Democracy and Development/CNDD; since 5 Dec. 2009).

In March 2010 the cabinet comprised:

Prime Minister: Jean-Marie Doré; b. 1938 (Union for the Progress of Guinea/UPG; since 26 Jan. 2010).

Minister of State for Foreign Affairs, African Integration and Francophonie: Bakary Fofana. *Minister of State for Public Service, Administrative Reform, Labour and Employment:* Penda Diallo. *Minister of State for Security and Civil Protection:* Gen. Mamadouba Toto Camara.

Minister of Agriculture: Lieut.-Col. Kélétigui Faro. *Arts and Culture:* Fodéba Isto Kéira. *Commerce, Industry, and Promotion of the Private Sector:* Mamadou Niaré. *Communication:* Aboubacar Sylla. *Construction, Urban Affairs and Housing:* Mansour Kaba. *Decentralization and Local Civic Development:* Aly Gilbert Ifono. *Economic Control and Auditing:* Kerfala Camara. *Economy and Finance:* Kerfala Yansané. *Energy and Hydraulics:* Capt. Mamadou Sandé. *Environment, Water and Forests, and Sustainable Development:* Georges Niakoye Délamou. *Fisheries and Aquaculture:* Col. Mamadou Korka Diallo. *Guineans Abroad:* Lucien Bendou Guilao. *Health and Public Sanitation:* Dr Ibrahima Sow. *Higher Education and Scientific Research:* Georges Ghandi Tounkara. *Justice and Keeper of the Seals:* Cdr Siba Loalamou. *Literacy and Promotion of National Languages:* Bamba Camara. *Livestock:* Mouctar Diallo. *Microfinance, Informal Sector, and Female and Youth Employment:* Dr Mariame Béavogui. *Mines and Energy:* Mamoudou Thiam. *National Solidarity, and Promotion of Women and Children:* Nanfadima Magassouba. *Planning and International Co-operation:* Zénab Saïfon Diallo. *Pre-university Education and Civic Education:* Amadou Lélouma Diallo. *Public Works:* Yamodou Touré. *Technical and Professional Training:* Dr Mamadou Saliou Bella Diallo. *Telecommunications and Information Technology:* Talibé Diallo. *Territorial Administration and Political Affairs:* Nawa Damey. *Tourism, Hotels and Handicrafts:* Sy Mariame Diallo. *Transport:* Col. Mathurin Bangoura. *Youth and Sports:* Thierno Aliou Diaouné. *Secretary General for Religious Affairs:* Moustapha Koutoubou Sanoh. *Secretary General to the Government:* Sékou Kissi Camara.

Government Website (French only): http://www.guinee.gov.gn

CURRENT LEADERS

Sékouba Konaté

Position

Acting President

Introduction

Brigadier General Sékouba Konaté took over duties as head of state in Dec. 2009 after President Lansana Conté, who had seized power in a military takeover in 2008, was shot by an aide. It is hoped that Konaté will oversee the reimplementation of civilian rule.

Early Life

Sékouba Konaté was born in 1964 in the capital, Conakry, to Mandinka parents. He graduated in 1990 from the Académie Militaire Royale in Meknès, Morocco and then joined the Guinean military, serving for a spell in Sierra Leone and commanding a parachute regiment to earn himself the nickname 'El Tigre'.

When President Lansana Conté died in Dec. 2008 after 24 years in office, the military seized power and established a junta, the National Council for Democracy and Development. The coup leader, Moussa Camara, was an associate of Konaté and declared himself president. Konaté was appointed one of his vice-presidents and given responsibility for the defence portfolio.

In 2009 suspicions grew that Camara would renege on a promise not to seek election at presidential polls in 2010. In Sept. 2009 the military opened fire at an opposition rally, killing more than 150 protesters and inciting domestic and international condemnation. On 3 Dec. 2009 Camara was involved in an altercation with an aide, Aboubacar Diakité, who shot him in the head. Konaté was travelling in Lebanon at the time. Camara was taken for treatment in Morocco before continuing his recuperation in Burkina Faso.

With political tensions running high in Guinea, Camara agreed to remain out of the country and handed power to Konaté on a caretaker basis.

Career in Office

Konaté sought to appease the concerns of the pro-democracy opposition movement, appointing civilian leader Jean-Marie Doré as prime minister. Konaté heads a coalition government with a remit to restore civilian rule. On the international stage the White House expressed its preference for Konaté over Camara, urging the former to remain in power until elections can be held. In Feb. 2010 the International Criminal Court condemned the opposition massacre carried out under Camara as a crime against humanity. Konaté has removed from office dozens of officials linked to the attack.

DEFENCE

Conscription is for two years. Defence expenditure totalled US$36m. in 2006 (US$4 per capita), representing 1·2% of GDP.

Army

The Army strength (2007) was 8,500. There are also three paramilitary forces: People's Militia (7,000), Gendarmerie (1,000) and Republican Guard (1,600) although only 2,600 are active.

Navy

A small force of around 400 (2007) operates from bases at Conakry and Kakanda.

Air Force

Personnel (2007) 800. There were seven combat capable aircraft including MiG-17s and MiG-21s, although their serviceability was in doubt.

INTERNATIONAL RELATIONS

Guinea is a member of the UN, World Bank, IMF and several other UN specialized agencies, WTO, IOM, International Organization of the Francophonie, Islamic Development Bank, OIC, African Development Bank, ECOWAS and is an ACP member state of the ACP-EU relationship.

ECONOMY

Agriculture produced 13·4% of GDP in 2006, industry 38·9% and services 47·7%.

Overview

Having achieved relatively strong growth in the 1990s, economic performance since 2000 has deteriorated. Rich in natural resources, with around a third of the world's bauxite reserves as well as large amounts of gold and diamond deposits, Guinea achieved its 1990s growth on the back of tight financial policies and favourable commodity prices. Inflation was also kept low. Subsequent poor performance stems from a weaker policy framework, the knock-on effect of conflicts in neighbouring countries and a fall in commodity export prices (including bauxite, which accounts for 50% of exports). GDP growth has slowed to an average 2·5% per year since 2000 while inflation has accelerated.

This decade's disappointing performance has been reflected in declining levels of foreign assistance. Aid from the Heavily Indebted Poor Countries (HIPC) initiative fell from 3·7% of GDP in the late 1990s to 0·6% in 2004. In 2003 the IMF and the African Development Bank suspended interim HIPC assistance following Guinea's weak performance under an IMF Poverty Reduction and Growth Facility (PGRF) programme.

Currency

The monetary unit is the *Guinean franc* (GNF). Inflation was 22·9% in 2007 and 18·4% in 2008. Foreign exchange reserves were US$95m. in Dec. 2005 and total money supply was 1,394·2bn. Guinean francs.

Budget

Revenue for 2006 was 2,397,800m. Guinean francs and expenditure 2,871,400m. Guinean francs.

Of total government revenue in 2006, mining sector revenue accounted for 28·2%, taxes on domestic production and trade 25·9% and taxes on international trade 18·2%. Current expenditure accounted for 76·2% of total expenditure and capital expenditure 23·4%.

VAT is 18%.

Performance

Real GDP growth in 2008 was 4·9% (1·8% in 2007). Total GDP in 2008 was US$4·3bn.

Banking and Finance

In 1986 the Central Bank (*Governor*, Alhassane Barry) and commercial banking were restructured, and commercial banks returned to the private sector. There were seven commercial banks in 2002. There is an Islamic bank.

ENERGY AND NATURAL RESOURCES

Environment

Guinea's carbon dioxide emissions from the consumption and flaring of fossil fuels in 2008 were the equivalent of 0·1 tonnes per capita.

Electricity

In 2004 installed capacity was estimated at 0·2m. kW. Production was approximately 801m. kWh in 2004; consumption per capita was an estimated 87 kWh.

Minerals

Mining accounted for 23% of state revenue in 2007. Guinea has the world's largest bauxite reserves, possessing nearly a third of global total, and is the fifth largest producer. Output: bauxite (2008), 17,682,300 tonnes; alumina (2008), 593,900 tonnes; gold (2006), 16,922 kg. Diamond production in 2008, 445,400 carats. There are also deposits of granite, iron ore, chrome, copper, lead, manganese, molybdenum, nickel, platinum, uranium and zinc.

Agriculture

Subsistence agriculture supports about 70% of the population. There were around 2·2m. ha. of arable land in 2007 and 670,000 ha. of permanent crops. The chief crops (production, 2008, in 1,000 tonnes) are: rice, 1,534; cassava, 1,122; maize, 952; plantains, 436 (2007 estimate); millet, 323 (2007 estimate); groundnuts, 316; sugarcane, 283 (2007 estimate); sweet potatoes, 200 (2007); mangoes and guavas, 165 (2007 estimate); bananas, 160 (2007 estimate); cocoyams and taro, 105; pineapples, 102.

Livestock (2008): cattle, 4·15m.; goats, 1·53m.; sheep, 1·28m.; pigs, 82,000; chickens, 18m. (2007 estimate).

Forestry

The area under forests in 2005 was 6·72m. ha., or 27·4% of the total land area. In 2007, 12·44m. cu. metres of roundwood were cut.

Fisheries

In 2004 the total catch was 93,947 tonnes, almost entirely from sea fishing.

INDUSTRY

Manufacturing accounted for 3·8% of GDP in 2006. Cement, corrugated and sheet iron, beer, soft drinks and cigarettes are produced.

Labour

In 1996 the labour force was 3,565,000 (53% males). The agricultural sector employs 80% of the workforce.

INTERNATIONAL TRADE

Foreign debt was US$3,247m. in 2005.

Imports and Exports

Imports and exports for calendar years in US$1m.:

	2000	*2001*	*2002*	*2003*	*2004*
Imports f.o.b.	587·1	561·9	668·5	644·3	688·4
Exports f.o.b.	666·3	731·1	708·6	609·3	725·6

Main imports by value, 2004: machinery and apparatus, 28·0%; food, 20·6%; refined petroleum, 18·9%. Principal import suppliers, 2004: France, 14·6%; China, 9·6%; Netherlands, 6·8%; Belgium, 6·0%; USA, 5·9%. Main exports by value, 2004: bauxite, 39·0%; alumina, 20·3%; gold, 18·9%. Principal export markets, 2004: South Korea, 15·6%; Russia, 13·1%; Spain, 12·3%; Ireland, 9·1%; USA, 7·5%. Guinea is the world's largest exporter of bauxite.

COMMUNICATIONS

Roads

In 2008 there were 6,758 km of roads, 35·4% of which were asphalted. In 2003 there were an estimated 47,500 passenger cars, 11,500 trucks and vans and 20,900 buses.

Rail

A railway connects Conakry with Kankan (662 km). A line 134 km long linking bauxite deposits at Sangaredi with Port Kamsar was opened in 1973 (carried 17m. tonnes in 2004) and a third line links Conakry and Fria (144 km; carried 1·2m. tonnes in 2004). The Kindia Bauxite Railway (102 km), linking Débéle with Conakry, carried 2·5m. tonnes in 2004. A further railway used by the bauxite industry runs from Tougué to Dabola (130 km).

Civil Aviation

There is an international airport at Conakry (Gbessia). In 2003 there were scheduled flights to Abidjan, Accra, Bamako, Banjul, Bissau, Brussels, Casablanca, Dakar, Freetown, Lagos and Paris. In 2006 there were 103,200 air arrivals and 153,800 departures plus 9,600 passengers in transit. A total of 8·53m. tonnes of air freight were handled in 2006.

Shipping

There are ports at Conakry and for bauxite exports at Kamsar (opened 1973). Merchant shipping totalled 12,000 GRT in 2002.

Telecommunications

The Société des Télécommunications de Guinée, which was privatized in 1995, became 100% state-owned again in 2008 after Telekom Malaysia sold its 60% stake in the company. In 2003 there were 137,700 telephone subscribers, equivalent to 17·8 per 1,000 population; mobile phone subscribers numbered 189,000 in

2005. In 2004 Guinea had 46,000 internet users and 44,000 PCs were in use (5·6 per 1,000 persons).

Postal Services

In 2003 there were 61 post offices, or one for every 139,000 persons.

SOCIAL INSTITUTIONS

Justice

There are *tribunaux du premier degré* at Conakry and Kankan, and a *juge de paix* at Nzérékoré. The High Court, Court of Appeal and Superior Tribunal of Cassation are at Conakry. The death penalty is in force, and was used in 2001 for the first time in 17 years.

The population in penal institutions in 2002 was 3,070 (37 per 100,000 of national population).

Education

In 2004 adult literacy was 29·5%. In 2007 there were 1,317,791 pupils with 29,049 teaching staff in primary schools; and 530,590 pupils with 13,907 teaching staff in secondary schools. In 2006 there were 42,711 students and 1,439 academic staff in tertiary education.

Besides French, there are eight official languages taught in schools: Fulani, Malinké, Susu, Kissi, Kpelle, Loma, Basari and Koniagi.

In 2005 public expenditure on education came to 1·7% of GNI.

Health

In 2006 there were 35 hospitals. There were (2006) 689 doctors, 109 pharmacists, 279 midwives and (2004) 4,061 nursing personnel.

RELIGION

79% of the population are Muslim, 9% Christian. Traditional animist beliefs are still found.

CULTURE

World Heritage Sites

Guinea shares one site with Côte d'Ivoire on the UNESCO World Heritage List: Mount Nimba Strict Nature Reserve (inscribed on the list in 1981 and 1982). The dense forested slopes are home to viviparous toads and chimpanzees among other fauna.

Broadcasting

Broadcasting is state controlled though the Radiodiffusion Télévision Guineénne. Although the government licensed independent radio broadcasting in 2006, it reimposed controls (including the closure of several private stations) in early 2007 in response to civil unrest. There were 140,000 TV receivers (colour by SECAM H) in 2004.

Press

In 2006 there were two daily newspapers (circulation 25,000).

Tourism

In 2005, 45,000 non-resident tourists arrived at Conakry airport. Receipts (excluding passenger transport) came to US$30m. in 2004.

DIPLOMATIC REPRESENTATIVES

Of Guinea in the United Kingdom (258 Belsize Rd, London, NW6 4BT)
Ambassador: Lansana Keïta.

Of the United Kingdom in Guinea (BP 6729, Conakry)
Ambassador: Ian Felton.

Of Guinea in the USA (2112 Leroy Pl., NW, Washington, D.C., 20008)
Ambassador: Mory Karamoko Kaba.

Of the USA in Guinea (Transversale 2, Ratoma, Conakry)
Ambassador: Patricia Newton Moller.

Of Guinea to the United Nations
Ambassador: Alpha Ibrahima Sow.

Of Guinea to the European Union
Ambassador: Ahmed Tidiane Sakho.

FURTHER READING

Bulletin Statistique et Économique de la Guinée. Monthly.

National Statistical Office: Direction Nationale de la Statistique, BP 221, Conakry.
Website (French only): http://www.stat-guinee.org

GUINEA-BISSAU

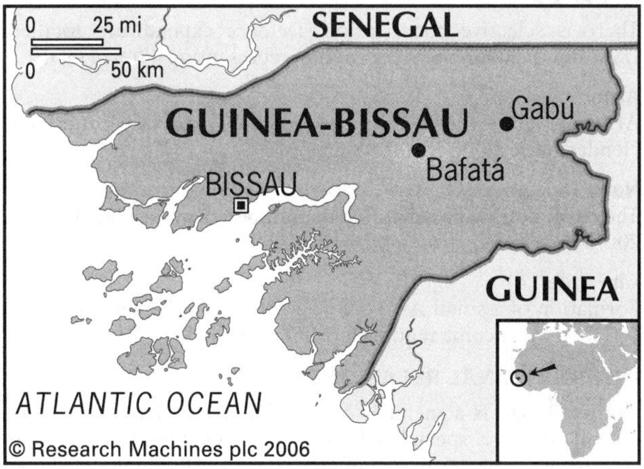

Republica da Guiné-Bissau
(Republic of Guinea-Bissau)

Capital: Bissau
Population estimate, 2010: 1·65m.
GDP per capita, 2007: (PPP$) 477
HDI/world rank: 0·396/173

KEY HISTORICAL EVENTS

Portugal was the major power in the area throughout the colonial period. In 1974, after the Portuguese revolution, Portugal abandoned the struggle to keep Guinea-Bissau and independence was formally recognized on 10 Sept. 1974. In 1975 Cape Verde also became independent but the two countries remained separate sovereign states. On 14 Nov. 1980 a coup d'état was in part inspired by resentment in Guinea-Bissau over the privileges enjoyed by Cape Verdians. Guineans obtained a more prominent role under the new government. On 16 May 1984 a new constitution was approved based on Marxist principles but after 1986 there was a return to private enterprise in an attempt to solve critical economic problems and to lift the country out of poverty. A year-long civil war broke out in 1998 between army rebels and the country's long-time ruler. Neighbouring Senegal and Guinea sent troops in to aid the government. On 7 May 1999 President João Bernardo Vieira was ousted in a military coup led by former chief of staff Gen. Ansumane Mané, whom the president had dismissed in 1998. Following the coup Mané briefly headed a military junta before National Assembly speaker Malam Bacai Sanhá took power as acting president. After presidential elections in Nov. 1999 and Jan. 2000 Kumba Ialá gained the presidency in a landslide victory. Marking a change towards a democratic future in Guinea-Bissau's politics, Ialá rejected a demand made by the outgoing junta for special consultative status following the elections. Kumba Ialá was overthrown in a coup in Sept. 2003 led by army chief of staff Gen. Veríssimo Correia Seabra. Vieira returned from exile to win the 2005 presidential election but was murdered in March 2009 by a group of soldiers following the assassination of his rival Batista Tagme Na Waie, the Army Chief of Staff.

TERRITORY AND POPULATION

Guinea-Bissau is bounded by Senegal in the north, the Atlantic Ocean in the west and by Guinea in the east and south. It includes the adjacent archipelago of Bijagós. Area, 36,125 sq. km (13,948 sq. miles). 2009 census population (provisional), 1,548,159; density, 42·9 per sq. km. The United Nations population estimate for 2009 was 1·61m. In 2005, 70·4% of the population were rural.

The UN gives an estimated population for 2010 of 1·65m.

The area, population, and chief town of the capital and the eight regions:

Region	*Area in sq. km*	*Population (2009 census, provisional)*	*Chief town*
Bissau City	78	384,960	—
Bafatá	5,981	225,516	Bafatá
Biombo	838	94,869	Quinhámel
Bolama	2,624	33,929	Bolama
Cacheu	5,175	199,674	Cacheu
Gabú	9,150	214,520	Gabú
Oio	5,403	226,263	Farim
Quinara	3,138	65,946	Fulacunda
Tombali	3,736	102,482	Catió

The main ethnic groups were (1998) the Balante (30%), Fulani (20%), Manjaco (14%), Mandingo (13%) and Papeis (7%). Portuguese remains the official language, but Crioulo is spoken throughout the country.

SOCIAL STATISTICS

2000 births (estimates), 61,000; deaths, 26,000. Estimated rates per 1,000 population, 2000: births, 44·6; deaths, 19·3. Annual population growth rate, 1992–2002, 3·0%. Life expectancy, 2007: male, 46·0 years; female, 49·1. Infant mortality, 2005, 124 per 1,000 live births; fertility rate, 2004, 7·1 births per woman.

CLIMATE

The tropical climate has a wet season from June to Nov., when rains are abundant, but the hot, dry Harmattan wind blows from Dec. to May. Bissau, Jan. 76°F (24·4°C), July 80°F (26·7°C). Annual rainfall 78" (1,950 mm).

CONSTITUTION AND GOVERNMENT

A new constitution was promulgated on 16 May 1984 and has been amended five times since, most recently in 1996. The Revolutionary Council, established following the 1980 coup, was replaced by a 15-member Council of State, while in April 1984 a new National People's Assembly was elected comprising 150 representatives elected by and from the directly-elected regional councils for five-year terms. The sole political movement was the *Partido Africano da Independência da Guiné e Cabo Verde* (PAIGC), but in Dec. 1990 a policy of 'integral multi-partyism' was announced, and in May 1991 the National Assembly voted unanimously to abolish the law making the PAIGC the sole party. The *President* is Head of State and Government and is elected for a five-year term. The *National Assembly* now has 100 members.

National Anthem

'Sol, suor, o verde e mar' ('Sun, sweat, the green and the sea'); words and tune by A. Lopes Cabral.

RECENT ELECTIONS

Presidential elections were held in two rounds on 28 June and 26 July 2009. In the first round former acting president Malam Bacaï Sanhá (African Party for the Independence of Guinea and Cape Verde/PAIGC) took 39·6% of votes cast, ahead of former president Mohamed Ialá Embaló (formerly known as Kumba Ialá) (Party for Social Renewal/PRS) with 29·4%, former interim president Henrique Rosa (ind.) with 24·2% and Iaya Djalo (New

Democracy Party) with 3·1%. Turnout was 60%. In the second round turnout was 61%. Malam Bacaï Sanhá won with 63·3% of the vote, against 36·7% for Mohamed Ialá Embaló.

At the parliamentary elections on 16 Nov. 2008 turnout was 82%. The PAIGC won 49·8% of the vote (67 of 100 seats), the PRS 25·3% (28 seats) and the Republican Party for Independence and Development (PRID) 7·5% (3 seats). Two parties took one seat each.

CURRENT ADMINISTRATION

President: Malam Bacaï Sanhá; b. 1947 (PAIGC; sworn in 8 Sept. 2009, having previously been acting president from May 1999–Feb. 2000).

In March 2010 the government comprised:

Prime Minister: Carlos Gomes Júnior; b. 1949 (PAIGC; since 2 Jan. 2009, having previously been in office from May 2004–Nov. 2005).

Minister of Agriculture and Rural Development: Bacar Banjai Barros. *Civil Service, Labour and State Modernization:* Fernando Gomes. *Commerce, Industry, Tourism and Handicrafts:* Botché Candé. *Culture, Education, Science, Youth and Sport:* Artur Silva. *Defence:* Aristides Ocante da Silva. *Economy, Planning and Regional Integration:* Helena Nosolini Embaló. *Energy and Natural Resources:* Higino Cardoso. *Finance:* José Mário Vaz. *Foreign Affairs, International Co-operation and Communities:* Adelino Mano Quetá. *Health:* Camilo Simões Pereira. *Infrastructure:* José António da Cruz Almeida. *Interior:* Adja Satú Camará Pinto. *Justice:* Mama Saliu Djaló Pires. *Territorial Administration:* Luís Oliveira Sanca. *Women's Affairs, Family, Social Solidarity and the Fight Against Poverty:* Lurdes Vaz. *Minister of the Presidency of the Council of Ministers and Social Communication and Parliamentary Affairs:* Maria Adiatú Djaló Nandingna.

Government Website: http://www.gov.gw

CURRENT LEADERS

Malam Bacaï Sanha

Position
President

Introduction
Malam Bacaï Sanha was sworn in as president in Sept. 2009 after elections praised by the international community for their orderly running. He is a member of the African Party for the Independence of Guinea and Cape Verde (PAIGC).

Early Life
Sanha was born on 5 May 1947 in Dar Salam in the Quinara region. He worked as an aide to Amilcar Cabral, the founder of the PAIGC, and served as governor of the Gabú and Biombo regions. From 1994–99 he was president of the National People's Assembly and from 14 May 1999 to 17 Feb 2000 he was acting head of state, having been appointed by the military following the ousting of João Bernardo Vieira in the 1998–99 civil war.

Sanha, a vociferous critic of Vieira, finished second to Kumba Ialá in the presidential elections that straddled 1999 and 2000 and again in 2005 (a result Sanha challenged). In 2008 he unsuccessfully challenged Carlos Gomes Júnior for the PAIGC leadership.

In March 2009 President Vieira was assassinated and presidential elections were scheduled for June. Sanha led the polls after the first round of voting and defeated Mohamed Ialá Embaló in a second round in July. He was sworn into office on 8 Sept.

Career in Office
In his inaugural speech Sanha promised to investigate the March 2009 killings of Vieira and Army Chief of Staff Batista Tagme Na Waie. He has also prioritized the fight against crime, particularly drug trafficking and corruption. In Sept. 2009 China pledged US$1·5m. to help feed the Guinea-Bissau army and in Dec. 2009 the EU promised US$37m. to help pay Guinea-Bissau's domestic debt and the salaries of government workers.

DEFENCE

There is selective conscription. Defence expenditure totalled US$13m. in 2006 (US$9 per capita), representing 4·0% of GDP.

Army
Army personnel in 2007 numbered 6,800. There is a paramilitary Gendarmerie 2,000 strong.

Navy
The naval flotilla, based at Bissau, numbered an estimated 350 in 2007.

Air Force
Formation of a small Air Force began in 1978. Personnel (2007) 100 with three combat aircraft (MiG-17s).

INTERNATIONAL RELATIONS

Guinea-Bissau is a member of the UN, World Bank, IMF and several other UN specialized agencies, WTO, IOM, International Organization of the Francophonie, Islamic Development Bank, OIC, African Development Bank, African Union, ECOWAS and is an ACP member state of the ACP-EU relationship.

ECONOMY

In 2006 agriculture accounted for 61·8% of GDP (the highest percentage of any country), industry 11·5% and services 26·8%.

Currency
On 2 May 1997 Guinea-Bissau joined the French Franc Zone, and the *peso* was replaced by the franc CFA at 65 pesos = one franc CFA. The *franc CFA* (XOF) has a parity rate of 655·957 francs CFA to one euro. Foreign exchange reserves were US$96m. in June 2005 and total money supply was 58,030m. francs CFA. Inflation was 4·6% in 2007 and 10·4% in 2008.

Budget
Revenue in 2005 was 41,378m. francs CFA; expenditure totalled 60,524m. francs CFA.

Performance
Real GDP growth in 2008 was 3·3% (2·7% in 2007). Total GDP in 2008 was US$0·4bn. Guinea-Bissau is more reliant than any other country on remittances from abroad, which accounted for 48·7% of total GDP in 2006.

Banking and Finance
The bank of issue and the central bank is the regional Central Bank of West African States (BCEAO). The *Governor* is Philippe-Henri Dacoury-Tabley. There are four other banks (Banco da Africa Occidental; Banco Internacional de Guiné-Bissau; Caixa de Crédito de Guiné; Caixa Económica Postal).

The stock exchange of the Economic and Monetary Union of West Africa is in Abidjan.

ENERGY AND NATURAL RESOURCES

Environment
Carbon dioxide emissions from the consumption and flaring of fossil fuels in 2008 were the equivalent of 0·3 tonnes per capita. An *Environmental Performance Index* compiled in 2008 ranked Guinea-Bissau 140th in the world out of 149 countries analysed, with 49·7%. The index examined various factors in six areas—air pollution, biodiversity and habitat, climate change, environmental health, productive natural resources and water resources.

Electricity
Installed capacity in 2004 was estimated at 21,000 kW. Production was about 61m. kWh in 2004; consumption per capita was an estimated 44 kWh.

Minerals
Mineral resources are not exploited. There are estimated to be 200m. tonnes of bauxite and 112m. tonnes of phosphate.

Agriculture
Agriculture employs 80% of the labour force. There were an estimated 300,000 ha. of arable land in 2007 and 250,000 ha. of permanent crops. Chief crops (production, 2003 estimates, in 1,000 tonnes) are: rice, 97; cashew nuts, 80; coconuts, 46; plantains, 38; cassava, 34; millet, 22; maize, 20. Livestock (2003 estimates): cattle, 520,000; pigs, 360,000; goats, 300,000; sheep, 290,000; chickens, 2m.

Forestry
The area covered by forests in 2005 was 2·07m. ha., or 73·7% of the total land area. In 2007, 592,000 cu. metres of roundwood were cut.

Fisheries
Total catch in 2005 came to approximately 6,200 tonnes, of which 98% was from sea fishing. Revenue from fishing licences may be worth as much as 45% of government revenue.

INDUSTRY
Manufacturing accounted for 10·1% of GDP in 2001. Output of main products: vegetable oils (3·4m. litres in 2000), sawnwood (16,000 tonnes in 2001), soap (2,500 tonnes in 2000) and animal hides and skins (1,400 tonnes in 2001).

Labour
The labour force in 1996 was 514,000 (60% males).

INTERNATIONAL TRADE
Foreign debt totalled US$693m. in 2005.

Imports and Exports
Imports in 2004 were US$82·9m. and exports US$75·8m. Main imports in 2001 were: foodstuffs, 18·7%; transport equipment, 13·2%; equipment and machinery, 7·7%. Exports: cashew nuts, 95·6%; cotton, 2·3%; logs, 1·5%. Guinea-Bissau supplies more than 10% of the world market of cashew nuts. Main import suppliers, 2001: Portugal, 30·9%; Senegal, 28·3%; China, 11·3%; Netherlands, 6·8%. Main export markets, 2001: India, 85·6%; Portugal, 3·8%; Senegal, 2·5%; France, 1·7%.

COMMUNICATIONS

Roads
In 2002 there were about 4,400 km of roads, of which 2,400 km were national roads. In 2008 there were 42,200 passenger cars in use (27 per 1,000 inhabitants in 2007) and 9,300 lorries and vans.

Civil Aviation
The national carrier is Transportes Aéreos de Guiné-Bissau. There is an international airport serving Bissau (Osvaldo Vieira). In 2003 there were scheduled flights to Banjul, Conakry, Dakar, Lisbon, Nouakchott, Praia and Sal.

Shipping
The main port is Bissau; minor ports are Bolama, Cacheu and Catió. In 2002 the merchant marine totalled 6,000 GRT.

Telecommunications
Guinea-Bissau had 11,800 telephone subscribers in 2003 (9·2 per 1,000 persons); mobile phone subscribers numbered 67,000 in 2005. There were 26,000 internet users in 2004.

Postal Services
In 2003 there were 20 post offices.

SOCIAL INSTITUTIONS

Justice
The death penalty was abolished for all crimes in 1993.

Education
Adult literacy was 39·6% in 2001 (male, 55·2%; female, 24·7%). In 1999–2000 there were 150,041 pupils at primary schools (3,405 teachers), 25,736 at secondary schools (1,226 teachers) and 463 students in tertiary education. In 1999–2000 total expenditure on education came to 2·3% of GNP.

Health
In 1999 there were two national, seven regional hospitals and 26 prefectorial hospitals. In 2003 there were 893 physicians and dentists, 1,092 nurses and 193 pharmacists.

RELIGION
In 2001 about 38% of the population were Muslim and about 12% Christian (mainly Roman Catholic). The remainder held traditional animist beliefs.

CULTURE

Broadcasting
Rádio Televisão da Guiné-Bissau is the state-run broadcaster. There were 44,000 TV receivers in 2001. Colour is by SECAM V.

Press
There are no daily newspapers. In 2006 the Gazeta de Notícias and the Correio de Bissau were published weekly.

Tourism
In 2005, 5,000 non-resident tourists arrived by air.

DIPLOMATIC REPRESENTATIVES
Of Guinea-Bissau in the United Kingdom
Ambassador: Vacant (resides in Paris).
Chargé d'Affaires a.i.: Fali Embalo.

Of the United Kingdom in Guinea-Bissau
Ambassador: Christopher Trott (resides in Dakar, Senegal).

Of Guinea-Bissau in the USA (P.O. Box 33813, Washington, D.C., 20033)
Ambassador: Vacant.

Of the USA in Guinea-Bissau
Ambassador: Marcia S. Bernicat (resides in Dakar, Senegal).

Of Guinea-Bissau to the United Nations
Ambassador: Alfredo Lopes Cabral.

Of Guinea-Bissau to the European Union
Ambassador: Henrique Adriano da Silva.

FURTHER READING
Barry, Boubacar-Sid, Creppy, Edward G. E., Gacitua-Mario, Estanislao and Wodon, Quentin, *Conflict, Livelihoods, and Poverty in Guinea-Bissau.* 2007

Forrest, J. B., *Lineages of State Fragility: Rural Civil Society in Guinea-Bissau.* 2003

National Statistical Office: Instituto Nacional de Estadística e Censos (INEC), CP 06 Bissau.
Website (Portuguese only): http://www.stat-guinebissau.com

GUYANA

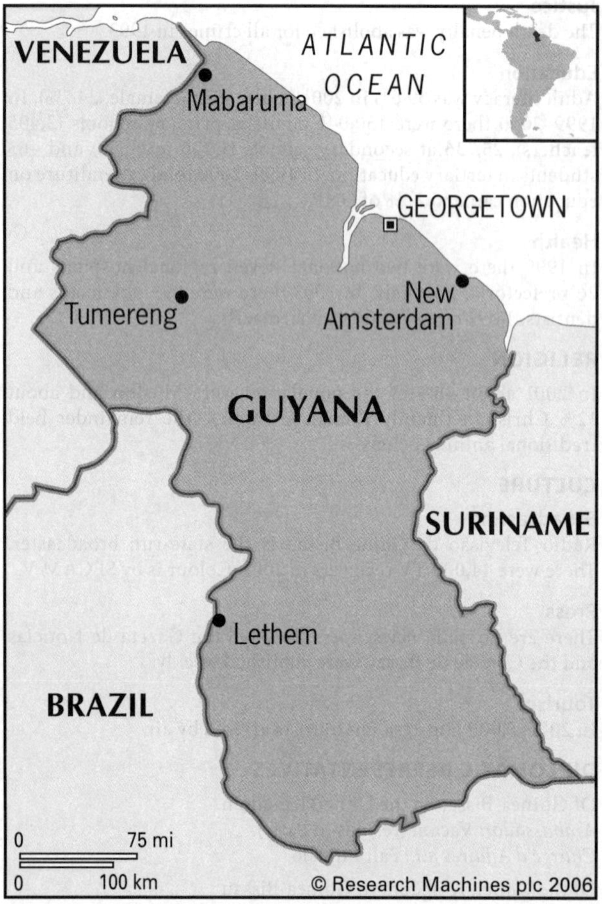

Co-operative Republic of Guyana

Capital: Georgetown
Population estimate, 2010: 761,000
GDP per capita, 2007: (PPP$) 2,782
HDI/world rank: 0·729/114

KEY HISTORICAL EVENTS

First settled by the Dutch West Indian Company about 1620, the territory was captured by Britain to which it was ceded in 1814 and named British Guiana. African slaves were transported to Guyana in the 18th century to work the sugar plantations, with East Indian and Chinese indentured labourers following in the 19th century. From 1950 the anti-colonial struggle was spearheaded by the People's Progressive Party (PPP) led by Cheddi Jagan and Forbes Burnham. By the time internal autonomy was granted in 1961 Burnham had split with Jagan to form the more moderate People's National Congress (PNC). Guyana became an independent member of the Commonwealth in 1966 with Burnham as the first prime minister, later president. By the 1980s, desperate economic straits had forced Guyana to seek outside help which came on condition of restoring free elections. Dr Jagan returned to power in 1992. Following his death in March 1997 his wife, Janet Jagan, was sworn in as president.

TERRITORY AND POPULATION

Guyana is situated on the northeast coast of Latin America on the Atlantic Ocean, with Suriname on the east, Venezuela on the west and Brazil on the south and west. Area, 214,999 sq. km (83,013 sq. miles). In 2002 the census population was 751,223; density 3·5 per sq. km.

The UN gives an estimated population for 2010 of 761,000.

Guyana has the highest proportion of rural population in South America, with only 28·2% living in urban areas in 2005. Ethnic groups by origin: 49% Indian, 36% African, 7% mixed race, 7% Amerindian and 1% others. The capital is Georgetown (2002 census population, 33,366; urban agglomeration, 134,497); other towns are Linden, New Amsterdam, Anna Regina and Corriverton.

Venezuela demanded the return of the Essequibo region in 1963 (nearly 75% of the area of Guyana). It was finally agreed in March 1983 that the UN Secretary-General should mediate, but the dispute is ongoing. There is also an ongoing unresolved claim by Suriname for the return of a triangle of uninhabited rainforest between the New River and the Courantyne River, near the Brazilian border. In Sept. 2007 the UN settled a long-standing maritime boundary dispute between Guyana and Suriname. The coastal area off both countries is believed to hold significant oil and gas deposits.

The official language is English.

SOCIAL STATISTICS

2004 estimates: births, 16,000; deaths, 7,000. Rates, 2004 estimates (per 1,000 population): birth, 21; death, 9. Life expectancy at birth in 2007: male 63·7 years and female 69·6 years. Annual population growth rate, 2000–05, 0·4%. Infant mortality, 2005, 47 per 1,000 live births; fertility rate, 2004, 2·2 births per woman.

CLIMATE

A tropical climate, with rainy seasons from April to July and Nov. to Jan. Humidity is high all the year but temperatures are moderated by sea-breezes. Rainfall increases from 90" (2,280 mm) on the coast to 140" (3,560 mm) in the forest zone. Georgetown, Jan. 79°F (26·1°C), July 81°F (27·2°C). Annual rainfall 87" (2,175 mm).

CONSTITUTION AND GOVERNMENT

A new Constitution was promulgated in Oct. 1980. There is an *Executive Presidency* and a *National Assembly*. The president is elected by simple majority vote as the designated candidate of a party list in parliamentary elections; there are no term limits. The National Assembly has 65 elected members who serve five-year terms, plus not more than four non-voting members and two non-voting parliamentary secretaries appointed by the president. Of the 65 elected members, 25 are elected in multi-seat constituencies and 40 through a party-list proportional representation system.

National Anthem

'Dear land of Guyana'; words by A. L. Luker, tune by R. Potter.

RECENT ELECTIONS

Bharrat Jagdeo and the People's Progressive Party (PPP) won the presidential and parliamentary elections of 28 Aug. 2006. In the presidential election incumbent Bharrat Jagdeo received 183,887 votes (54·7% of the vote), with Robert Corbin of the People's National Congress (PNC) receiving 114,608 (34·1%). The PPP won 36 seats in the parliamentary election, followed by the PNC with

22, Alliance for Change with 5, Guyana Action Party with 1 and the United Force also with 1.

CURRENT ADMINISTRATION

President: Bharrat Jagdeo; b. 1964 (PPP; sworn in 11 Aug. 1999 and re-elected in March 2001 and Aug. 2006).

In March 2010 the government comprised:

Prime Minister and Minister of Public Works and Communications: Samuel Hinds; b. 1943 (PPP; first sworn in 9 Oct. 1992 and now in office for the third time).

Head of the Presidential Secretariat: Roger Luncheon. *Attorney General and Minister of Legal Affairs:* Charles Ramson. *Minister of Finance:* Ashni Kumar Singh. *Foreign Affairs:* Carolyn Rodrigues-Birkett. *Foreign Trade and International Co-operation:* Vacant. *Health:* Dr Leslie Ramsammy. *Education:* Shaik Baksh. *Home Affairs:* Clement Rohee. *Culture, Youth and Sports:* Frank Anthony. *Tourism, Industry and Commerce:* Manniram Prashad. *Amerindian Affairs:* Pauline Sukhai. *Housing and Water:* Irfaan Ali. *Labour:* Mansoor Nadir. *Local Government and Regional Development:* Kellawan Lall. *Human Services and Social Security:* Priya Manickchand. *Public Service:* Jennifer Westford. *Agriculture:* Robert Persaud. *Transport and Hydraulics:* Robeson Benn.

Government Information Agency Website:
http://www.gina.gov.gy

CURRENT LEADERS

Bharrat Jagdeo

Position
President

Introduction
Bharrat Jagdeo, representing the People's Progressive Party (PPP), took over from President Janet Jagan in 1999, when the latter retired on health grounds, and was re-elected in 2001 and 2006. Jagdeo's main challenges have been placating civil unrest caused by rivalry between supporters of the PPP and the opposition People's National Congress (PNC) and negotiating settlements of border disputes with Suriname and Venezuela.

Early Life
Jagdeo was born on 23 Jan. 1964. He studied economics before taking a masters degree at the Friendship University in Moscow, Russia. He had joined the PPP's youth group, the Progress Youth Organization, in 1977, becoming a full PPP member three years later. In 1990 he worked as an economist in the state planning secretariat. When the PPP came to power in 1992 he was appointed special adviser to the finance ministry from which he progressed to the post of junior finance minister the following year. He also served on various PPP committees. In 1995 he became finance minister (occasionally acting as prime minister), a position he kept when Janet Jagan came to power in 1997. In April 1999 Jagdeo negotiated with workers from the Guyana Public Service Union who went on strike for a 40% wage increase. The strike eventually ended after eight weeks of suspended public services.

Career in Office
Favoured by Jagan as her successor, Jagdeo took over the presidency following her resignation in 1999. However, he inherited ongoing political and civil disputes between politicians and followers of the PPP and those of the PNC, despite both being socialist parties. The PNC claimed that the 1997 elections had been fixed and had never accepted Jagan, subsequently refusing to recognize the Jagdeo presidency. During negotiations in 1998 directed by CARICOM, the PPP agreed to shorten the presidential term by two years.

In 2001 the two parties and their followers were caught up in more widespread racial tensions that traditionally erupted around elections (the PPP representing the Indo-Guyanese population and the PNC the Afro-Guyanese community). For this reason the elections that year were closely monitored by international observers and a special commission. They passed off without too much trouble, and Jagdeo was elected with 53·1% of the vote against 41·7% for Desmond Hoyte of the PNC. Hoyte accused the PPP of fraud, claiming many voters had disappeared from the electoral role. Jagdeo admitted this, but said that both parties had been affected by the discrepancies. In Aug. 2006 he was again re-elected for a further five-year term. Polling passed off peacefully despite the earlier murder in April of the agriculture minister.

On the international level, there have been border disputes with Venezuela and Suriname. In June 2000 a Surinamese naval ship expelled a Canadian-owned oil rig which had been granted a licence for oil exploration by Guyana but was said to be in waters claimed by Suriname. Talks between Jagdeo and the then Surinamese president under the mediation of then Jamaican prime minister P. J. Patterson failed. At the same time, Jagdeo agreed the construction of a rocket launch site by a US company 40 km from the Venezuelan border. Claiming a large portion of Guyanese land up to the Essequibo River, Venezuela argued that the project could be used for military purposes. The PNC also voiced its opposition to the proposed site. In June 2004 the United Nations set up a tribunal to resolve Guyana's maritime border issues with Suriname, which was settled in Sept. 2007.

In Oct. 2008 Jagdeo signed up to a trade agreement between the European Union and a number of Caribbean countries, having earlier accused the EU of economic bullying in negotiations.

DEFENCE

In 2003 defence expenditure totalled US$5m. (US$7 per capita), representing 0·7% of GDP. The army, navy and air force are combined in a 1,100-strong Guyana Defence Force.

Army
The Guyana Army had (2007) a strength of 1,400 including 500 reserves. There is a paramilitary Guyana People's Militia approximately 1,500 strong.

Navy
The Coast Guard is an integral part of the Guyana Defence Force. In 2007 it had 100 personnel and five patrol and coastal combatants. It is based at Georgetown and New Providence, Bahamas.

Air Force
The Air Command has no combat capable aircraft. It was equipped in 2007 with one light aircraft and two helicopters. Personnel (2007) 100.

INTERNATIONAL RELATIONS

Guyana is a member of the UN, World Bank, IMF and several other UN specialized agencies, WTO, Commonwealth, ACS, CARICOM, Inter-American Development Bank, SELA, OAS, UNASUR, OIC and is an ACP member state of the ACP-EU relationship.

ECONOMY

Agriculture accounted for 31% of GDP in 2005, industry 25% and services 44%.

Overview
Nominal GDP remained constant below US$1bn. throughout the 1990s and until 2007. Since then it has gradually increased, reaching its peak in 2008 when nominal GDP at current prices rose to US$1·13bn. This growth is largely attributable to development in the mining and agricultural sectors that has helped stabilize the exchange rate, keep inflation low and precipitate closer co-operation with international organizations.

Agriculture remains an important sector although its contribution to GDP fell from 30·8% in 2002 to 25% in 2008. An acute shortage of skilled labour is a problem, along with a sub-standard infrastructure. Main exports include bauxite, gold, molasses, rice, rum, shrimp, sugar and timber. Sugar accounts for 28% of export revenues. Increasingly, the country benefits from high FDI inflows, especially in the mining sector. Guyana has been a member of CARICOM since 1973.

Currency
The unit of currency is the *Guyana dollar* (GYD) of 100 *cents*. Inflation was 12·2% in 2007 and 8·1% in 2008. Foreign exchange reserves were US$223m. in July 2005 and total money supply was G$35·3bn.

Budget
Revenues in 2005 totalled G$69,415m. (tax revenue, 76·2%) and expenditures G$88,861m. (current expenditure, 60·5%).

VAT of 16% was introduced in 2007.

Performance
Real GDP growth was 5·4% in 2007 and 3·0% in 2008. Total GDP was US$1·2bn. in 2008.

Banking and Finance
The bank of issue is the Bank of Guyana (*Governor*, Lawrence Williams), established 1965. There are five commercial banks and three foreign-owned. At Dec. 2006 the total assets of commercial banks were G$180,208·3m. Savings deposits were G$88,599·5m.

ENERGY AND NATURAL RESOURCES

Environment
Guyana's carbon dioxide emissions from the consumption and flaring of fossil fuels were the equivalent of 2·2 tonnes per capita in 2008.

Electricity
Capacity in 2004 was 0·3m. kW. In 2004 production was 835m. kWh and consumption per capita 1,090 kWh.

Minerals
Placer gold mining commenced in 1884, and was followed by diamond mining in 1887. In 2007 output of bauxite was 2,242,928 tonnes, and (in 2005) of gold 11,102 kg. Other minerals include copper, tungsten, iron, nickel, quartz and molybdenum.

Agriculture
In 2003 Guyana had 480,000 ha. of arable land and 30,000 ha. of permanent crops. 150,000 ha. were irrigated in 2003. Agricultural production, 2006 (in 1,000 tonnes): rice, 307; sugarcane, 260; coconuts (2003 estimate), 45; cassava, 23; mangoes (2003 estimate), 12; pumpkins and squash (2003 estimate), 10; bananas, 7; plantains, 4.

Livestock (2003 estimate): sheep, 130,000; cattle, 110,000; goats, 79,000; pigs, 20,000; chickens, 21m. Livestock products, 2003 estimates (in 1,000 tonnes): meat, 27; milk, 30; eggs, 2.

Forestry
In 2005 the area under forests totalled 15·10m. ha. (76·7% of the land area). Timber production in 2007 was 426,000 cu. metres.

Fisheries
Fish landings in 2005 came to 53,372 tonnes, of which 99% was from sea fishing.

INDUSTRY
The main industries are agro-processing (particularly sugar and rice) and mining (notably gold and bauxite). Production (2006): sugar, 259,588 tonnes; rum, 11·9m. litres; beer, 8·6m. litres; soft drinks, 4,050,000 cases; clothes, 1,685,000 items; footwear, 9,435 pairs; margarine, 2,264,626 kg; edible oil (2005), 928,500 litres; paint, 2,403,534 litres.

Labour
In 2002 the labour force was 271,728 (69% males).

INTERNATIONAL TRADE
Guyana's external debt in 2007 was US$734m.

Imports and Exports
In 2006 imports were valued at US$817m. and exports at US$563m. Main commodities imported, 2004: petroleum, petroleum products and related materials, 27·4%; machinery and transport equipment, 23·0%; manufactured goods, 16·3%; food and live animals, 10·9%. Principal commodities exported, 2004: sugar, 20·5%; gold, 18·4%; diamonds, 16·4%; fish, crustaceans and molluscs, 11·4%. Rice, timber and bauxite are also exported. Major import suppliers, 2004: USA, 30%; Trinidad and Tobago, 27%; Netherlands Antilles, 9%; Japan, 6%; UK, 5%. Main export markets in 2004: Canada, 19%; USA, 16%; Belgium, 14%; UK, 12%; Trinidad and Tobago, 7%.

COMMUNICATIONS

Roads
In 2002 there were an estimated 7,970 km of roads, of which 590 km were paved. In 2008 there were 44,700 passenger cars in use, plus 28,100 lorries and vans, and 37,100 motorcycles and mopeds.

Rail
There is a government-owned railway in the North West District, while the Guyana Mining Enterprise operates a standard gauge railway of 133 km from Linden on the Demerara River to Ituni and Coomacka.

Civil Aviation
There is an international airport at Georgetown (Timehri), which handled 465,962 passengers in 2007. In 2003 there were direct flights to Anguilla, Antigua, Barbados, Dominica, Miami, New York, Paramaribo, Port of Spain, St Kitts and the British Virgin Islands.

Shipping
The major port is Georgetown; there are two other ports. In 2002 merchant shipping totalled 15,000 GRT. There are 217 nautical miles of river navigation. There are ferry services across the mouths of the Demerara, Berbice and Essequibo rivers.

Telecommunications
The inland public telegraph and radio communication services are operated by the Guyana Telephone and Telegraph Company Ltd. In 2005 there were 360,100 telephone subscribers, equivalent to 479·4 per 1,000 population, of which 281,400 were mobile phone subscribers. There were 29,000 PCs (or 38·6 for every 1,000 persons) in use in 2005 and 160,000 internet users.

Postal Services
In 2003 there were 89 post offices.

SOCIAL INSTITUTIONS

Justice
The law, both civil and criminal, is based on the common and statute law of England, save that the principles of the Roman-Dutch law have been retained for the registration, conveyance and mortgaging of land.

The Supreme Court of Judicature consists of a Court of Appeal, a High Court and a number of courts of summary jurisdiction. Guyana was one of ten countries to sign an agreement in Feb. 2001 establishing a Caribbean Court of Justice to replace the British Privy Council as the highest civil and criminal court. In the meantime the number of signatories has risen to twelve. The court was inaugurated at Port-of-Spain, Trinidad on 16 April 2005.

In 2006 there were 2,756 reported serious crimes, including 173 homicides. The population in penal institutions in Dec. 2005 was 1,525 (199 per 100,000 of national population).

Education

In 2004–05 there were 428 pre-primary schools with 1,958 teachers for 31,730 pupils; 440 primary schools with 4,013 teachers for 113,971 pupils; and 349 secondary schools with 3,392 teachers for 65,638 pupils. In 2004–05 there were 7,689 students at university level.

Adult literacy in 2001 was 98·6% (male, 99·0%; female, 98·2%). The literacy rates are the highest in South America. An OECD report published in 2005 showed that Guyana loses a greater proportion of its graduates (83%) to OECD member countries than any other non-OECD member.

In 2004–05 total expenditure on education came to 7·4% of GNP and 12·4% of total government spending.

Health

In 2004 there were 43 hospitals (seven private), 116 health centres and 194 health posts. There were 1,887 hospital beds in 2004. There were 5·1 physicians per 10,000 inhabitants in 2007 and 9·9 nurses per 10,000 inhabitants.

RELIGION

In 2002, 28·8% of the population were Hindus, 17·0% Pentecostalists, 8·1% Roman Catholics, 7·3% Muslims and 7·0% Anglicans. There were also significant numbers of other Christians.

CULTURE

Broadcasting

In 2004 the Guyana Broadcasting Corporation merged with the Guyana Television Broadcasting Company to form the state-owned National Communications Network (NCN). NCN operates radio services (Voice of Guyana, Radio Roraima, Hot FM) and a television channel. There are also private radio stations. There were 125,000 TV receivers (colour by PAL) in 2003.

Press

In 2006 there were three daily newspapers (the state-owned *Guyana Chronicle* and the privately-owned *Kaieteur News* and *Stabroek News*) with a combined circulation of 32,000.

Tourism

117,000 non-resident tourists arrived at Timehri airport in 2005; receipts totalled US$37m.

Festivals

There are a number of Christian, Hindu and Muslim festivals throughout the year.

Libraries

There is a national library in Georgetown.

Museums and Galleries

The Guyana National Museum contains a broad selection of animal life and Guyanese heritage. Castellani House, the National Gallery, is home to the finest art collection in Guyana.

DIPLOMATIC REPRESENTATIVES

Of Guyana in the United Kingdom (3 Palace Ct, London, W2 4LP)
High Commissioner: Laleshwar K. N. Singh.

Of the United Kingdom in Guyana (44 Main St., Georgetown)
High Commissioner: Fraser Wheeler.

Of Guyana in the USA (2490 Tracy Pl., NW, Washington, D.C., 20008)
Ambassador: Bayney R. Karran.

Of the USA in Guyana (99–100 Young and Duke Streets, Kingston, Georgetown)
Ambassador: Vacant.
Chargé d'Affaires a.i.: Karen L. Williams.

Of Guyana to the United Nations
Ambassador: Vacant.
Chargé d'Affaires a.i.: George Talbot.

Of Guyana to the European Union
Ambassador: Patrick Ignatius Gomes.

FURTHER READING

Braveboy-Wagner, J. A., *The Venezuela-Guyana Border Dispute: Britain's Colonial Legacy in Latin America.* 1984
Daly, V. T., *A Short History of the Guyanese People.* 3rd. ed. 1992
Gafar, John, *Guyana: From State Control to Free Markets.* 2003
Seecoomar, Judaman, *Democratic Advance and Conflict Resolution in Post-Colonial Guyana.* 2006
Williams, B. F., *Stains on My Name, War in My Veins: Guyana and the Politics of Cultural Struggle.* 1992

National Statistical Office: Bureau of Statistics, Avenue of the Republic and Brickdam, Georgetown.
Website: http://www.statisticsguyana.gov.gy

HAITI

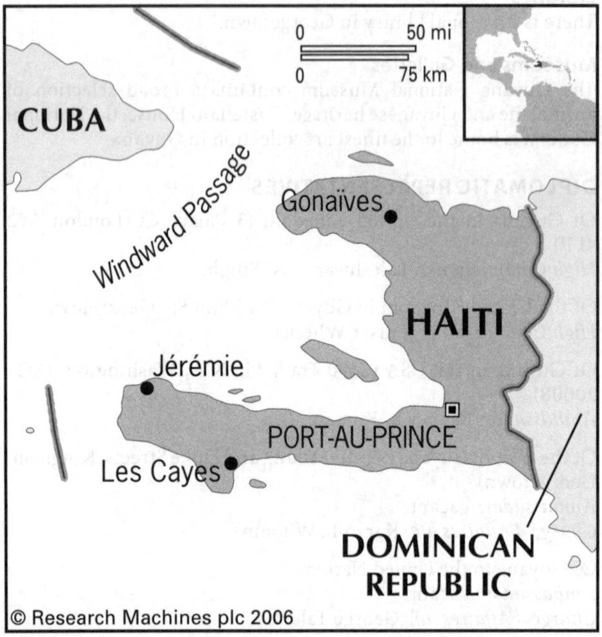

République d'Haïti
(Republic of Haiti)

Capital: Port-au-Prince
Population estimate, 2010: 10·19m.
GDP per capita, 2007: (PPP$) 1,155
HDI/world rank: 0·532/149

KEY HISTORICAL EVENTS

In the 16th century, Spain imported large numbers of African slaves whose descendants now populate the country. The colony subsequently fell under French rule. In 1791 a slave uprising led to the 13-year-long Haitian Revolution. In 1801 Toussaint Louverture, one of the leaders of the revolution, succeeded in eradicating slavery. He proclaimed himself governor-general for life over the whole island. He was captured and sent to France, but Jean-Jacques Dessalines, one of his generals, led the final battle that defeated Napoleon's forces. The newly-named Haiti declared its independence on 1 Jan. 1804, becoming the first independent black republic in the world. Ruled by a succession of self-appointed monarchs, Haiti became a republic in the mid-19th century. From 1915 to 1934 Haiti was under United States occupation.

A corrupt regime was dominated by François Duvalier from 1957 to 1964 when he was succeeded by his son, Jean-Claude Duvalier. He fled the country on 7 Feb. 1986. After a period of military rule, Father Jean-Bertrand Aristide was elected president in Dec. 1990.

On 30 Sept. 1991 President Aristide was deposed by a military junta and went into exile. Under international pressure, parliament again recognized Aristide as president in June 1993. However, despite a UN led naval blockade, the junta showed no sign of stepping down. 20,000 US troops moved into Haiti on 19 Sept. in an uncontested occupation. President Aristide returned to office on 15 Oct. 1994 and on 1 April 1995 a UN peacekeeping force (MANUH) took over from the US military mission. Aristide was succeeded by René Préval who was generally assumed to be a stand-in for his predecessor. Jean-Bertrand Aristide subsequently won the presidential elections held in Nov. 2000. In Dec. 2001 there was an unsuccessful coup led by former police and army officers. After armed rebels took control of the north of the country President Aristide stood down in Feb. 2004 and fled into exile.

After a period of interim government, René Préval was elected president for a second time in 2006. In July 2009 the World Bank and IMF cancelled US$1·2bn. (80%) of the national debt. In Jan. 2010 an earthquake of magnitude 7·0 hit the capital, Port-au-Prince, and its surrounding region, killing at least 217,000 people, displacing over 1m. and seriously undermining Haiti's economic prospects.

TERRITORY AND POPULATION

Haiti is bounded in the east by the Dominican Republic, to the north by the Atlantic and elsewhere by the Caribbean Sea. The area is 27,700 sq. km (10,695 sq. miles). The Île de la Gonâve, some 40 miles long, lies in the gulf of the same name. Among other islands is La Tortue, off the north peninsula. Census population, 2003, 8,373,750; density, 302 per sq. km. The United Nations population estimate for 2003 was 9,105,000. In 2005, 61·2% of the population were rural.

The UN gives an estimated population for 2010 of 10·19m.

Areas, populations and chief towns of the ten departments:

Department	*Area (in sq. km)*	*2003 census population (provisional)*	*Chief town*
Artibonite	4,984	1,299,398	Gonaïves
Centre	3,675	581,505	Hinche
Grande Anse	3,310	626,928	Jérémie
Nippes[1]	—	—	Miragoâne
Nord	2,106	823,043	Cap Haïtien
Nord-Est	1,805	308,385	Fort-Liberté
Nord-Ouest	2,176	531,198	Port-de-Paix
Ouest	4,827	3,096,967	Port-au-Prince
Sud	2,794	621,651	Les Cayes
Sud-Est	2,023	484,675	Jacmel

[1]Created since 2003 census—formerly part of Grande Anse.

The capital is Port-au-Prince (2003 census provisional population, 703,023; urban agglomeration, 1,977,036); other towns are Cap Haïtien (111,094 in 2003), Gonaïves (104,825 in 2003) and Les Cayes (48,095 in 2003). Most of the population is of African or mixed origin.

The official languages are French and Créole. Créole is spoken by all Haitians; French by only a small minority.

SOCIAL STATISTICS

2004 estimates: births, 247,000; deaths, 107,000. Rates, 2004 estimates (per 1,000 population): birth, 30; death, 13. Annual population growth rate, 1992–2002, 1·4%. Expectation of life at birth, 2007, 59·1 years for males and 62·9 years for females. Infant mortality, 2005, 83 per 1,000 live births; fertility rate, 2004, 3·9 births per woman.

CLIMATE

A tropical climate, but the central mountains can cause semi-arid conditions in their lee. There are rainy seasons from April to June and Aug. to Nov. Hurricanes and severe thunderstorms can occur. The annual temperature range is small. Port-au-Prince, Jan. 77°F (25°C), July 84°F (28·9°C). Annual rainfall 53" (1,321 mm).

CONSTITUTION AND GOVERNMENT

The 1987 constitution, ratified by a referendum, provides for a bicameral legislature (a 99-member *Chamber of Deputies* and a

30-member *Senate*), and an executive *President*, directly elected for a five-year term. The President can stand for a second term but only after a five-year interval. The constitution was suspended in 1988 but the country returned to constitutional rule in Oct. 1994.

National Anthem

'La Dessalinienne' ('The Dessalines Song'); words by J. Lhérisson, tune by N. Geffrard.

RECENT ELECTIONS

After several postponements, presidential elections were held on 7 Feb. 2006. Former president René Préval won 51·2% of the vote, former president Leslie Manigat 12·4% and Charles Henry Baker 8·2%. There were 32 other candidates. Initial results gave Préval less than the 50% needed to avoid a second round run-off, but following several days of protests amid claims of irregularities the provisional results were amended and Préval was declared the winner.

Delayed parliamentary elections were held on 7 Feb. and 21 April 2006, with 11 seats decided in a run-off on 3 Dec. after violence or other problems delayed the April vote. In the vote for the Chamber of Deputies, Lespwa won 22 seats, Fusion Social and Democratic Party 16, Democratic Alliance Party 11, Struggling People's Organization 10, Lavalas Family Party 6 and Union 6. The remaining seats went to 13 smaller parties with the result for one seat still to be confirmed. Elections for ten seats in the Senate were held on 19 April and 21 June 2009 alongside by-elections to two other vacant seats. Lespwa took 6 of the 12 available seats, Fusion Social and Democratic Party 1, L'Artibonite in Action 1, Co-operative Action to Build Haiti 1, Struggling People's Organization 1 and independents also 1. There was one vacant seat.

CURRENT ADMINISTRATION

President: René Préval; b. 1943 (Lespwa; sworn in 14 May 2006 having previously been president from Feb. 1996 to Feb. 2001).

In March 2010 the government comprised:

Prime Minister and Minister for Planning and International Co-operation: Jean-Max Bellerive; b. 1958 (Lespwa; sworn in 11 Nov. 2009).

Minister of Interior and Territorial Collectivities: Paul Antoine Bien-Aimé. *Economy and Finance:* Ronald Baudin. *Public Health:* Alex Larsen. *Foreign Affairs and Cults:* Marie-Michèle Rey. *Environment:* Jean Marie Claude Germain. *Education:* Joël Desrosiers Jean-Pierre. *Public Works:* Jacques Gabriel. *Youth and Sports:* Evans Lescouflair. *Culture and Communication:* Marie-Laurence Lassègue. *Women's Affairs:* Marjorie Michel. *Agriculture:* Joanas Gué. *Tourism:* Patrick Delatour. *Haitians Living Abroad:* Edwin Paraison. *Justice and Public Security:* Paul Denis. *Social Affairs and Labour:* Yves Cristallin. *Commerce and Industry:* Josseline Colimon-Féthière. *Minister Delegate in the Office of the Prime Minister in Charge of Relations with Parliament:* Joseph Jasmin.

CURRENT LEADERS

René Préval

Position
President

Introduction
René Préval won a controversial election in Feb. 2006 to become president of Haiti for the second time, with the difficult task of restoring stability and hope to the poorest nation in the western hemisphere.

Early Life
René Garcia Préval was born on 17 Jan. 1943 in Port-au-Prince. The son of a politician, his family were forced into exile in 1963 by the dictator, François 'Papa Doc' Duvalier. He studied agronomy at the College of Gembloux, Belgium, before moving to New York, USA in 1970, where he lived for five years. Having returned to Haiti, he became active in politics and charity work following the fall of Jean-Claude 'Baby Doc' Duvalier in Feb. 1986. He grew close to the radical slum preacher, Jean-Bertrand Aristide, who in Dec. 1990 was elected president. Préval was appointed prime minister in Feb. 1991 but was forced to flee the country shortly after a military coup led by Gen. Raoul Cedras in Sept. 1991.

Joining the exiled constitutional government in Washington, D.C., USA in 1992, Préval held the prime minister's portfolio. Aristide was reinstated as president in Oct. 1994 but was constitutionally barred from running in the Dec. 1995 election. Préval emerged victorious with 88% of the vote and took office on 7 Feb. 1996, inheriting a country with a devastated economy. In Jan 1999, following a series of disagreements with legislators, Préval began to rule by decree. Following Aristide's return to power after a controversial presidential election in Nov. 2000, Préval, whose relationship with Aristide had deteriorated from the mid-1990s, retreated from politics.

Poverty and massive unemployment, together with Aristide's increasingly authoritarian rule, led to violent protests which forced the president into exile in Feb. 2004. His successor, former chief justice Boniface Alexandre, worked with a US-led international force to stabilize the country and prepare for fresh elections. Préval unexpectedly returned to the fray, running as the candidate for Lespwa and distancing himself from his time as an ally of Aristide and his Lavalas movement. Following repeated delays, the presidential election was held on 7 Feb. 2006 and Préval was subsequently declared the outright winner, with 51·2% of the vote. He was sworn in as president on 14 May 2006.

Career in Office
Préval pledged to create 'cohesion' in Haiti's fractured society and restore peace in an effort to revive the ailing economy and provide employment. However, political in-fighting, economic vulnerability, organized crime and natural disasters have continued to undermine the stability of the country. In April 2008 violent protests against rising staple food prices led to the dismissal of the prime minister, Jacques-Edouard Alexis. In May Préval sought increased help from Brazilian peacekeeping forces to combat a wave of kidnappings. Then, in Aug. and Sept. 2008, tropical storms caused extensive flooding across the country and claimed 800 lives.

Further political uncertainty surfaced in late 2009 as the Senate voted in Oct. to dismiss Prime Minister Michèle Pierre-Louis after little more than a year in office and despite her reputation among Haiti's aid donors for integrity and administrative capability. Préval named the planning minister, Jean-Max Bellerive, as the new premier and his appointment was endorsed by the Senate in early Nov. In Jan. 2010 Port-au-Prince and the surrounding region were hit by an earthquake that left over 200,000 dead and severely threatened the country's chances of mid- to long-term economic growth.

DEFENCE

After the restoration of civilian rule in 1994 the armed forces and police were disbanded and an Interim Public Security Force formed, although this was later also dissolved. In 1995 a new police force—Police Nationale d'Haiti (PNH)—was recruited from former military personnel and others not implicated in human rights violations. The PNH currently has about 2,000 members. A UN peacekeeping force, MINUSTAH, has been in Haiti since 2004. Following the earthquake of Jan. 2010 the UN Security Council passed a resolution recommending an increase in overall force levels to support the immediate recovery, reconstruction and stability efforts in the country. As of Feb. 2010 MINUSTAH consisted of 9,087 uniformed personnel.

In 2003 defence expenditure totalled US$22m. (US$3 per capita), representing 0·8% of GDP.

Army

The Army was disbanded in 1995.

Navy

There is a small Coast Guard, which was created in 1996 and is a specialized unit of the PNH.

Air Force

The Air Force was disbanded in 1995.

INTERNATIONAL RELATIONS

Haiti is a member of the UN, World Bank, IMF and several other UN specialized agencies, WTO, IOM, International Organization of the Francophonie, ACS, CARICOM, Inter-American Development Bank, SELA, OAS and is an ACP member state of the ACP-EU relationship.

ECONOMY

Trade and restaurants accounted for 26·8% of GDP in 2006–07, agriculture and forestry 25·3%, and finance and real estate 12·1%.

Overview

Haiti is the poorest economy in the western hemisphere following decades of economic decline and instability. Real per capita GDP has declined on average by 0·7% per year over the past 40 years. The economy has been characterized by macroeconomic instability, rampant inflation and susceptibility to external shocks. Social and environmental indicators are both poor.

Nonetheless, performance in recent years suggested some progress was being made, with inflation falling and GDP recording some modest growth. However, on 12 Jan. 2010 an earthquake hit Haiti, killing around 217 000, as well as destroying several government ministries and 25,000 commercial buildings. Over US$2bn. of relief funding was pledged within two weeks of the disaster but officials estimated that recovery will likely take a decade and cost, according to the Inter-American Development Bank, between US$8–14bn.

Currency

The unit of currency is the *gourde* (HTG) of 100 *centimes*. Inflation was 14·4% in 2008. In July 2005 foreign exchange reserves were US$74m. and total money supply was 19,263m. gourdes.

Budget

The fiscal year begins on 1 Oct. In 2003–04 revenues were 12,474m. gourdes and expenditures 17,165m. gourdes.

Performance

There was negative growth in 2004, with the economy contracting by 3·5%. Since then the economy has recovered slightly, growing by 3·4% in 2007 and 1·2% in 2008. Total GDP in 2008 was US$7·0bn.

Banking and Finance

The Banque Nationale de la République d'Haïti is the central bank and bank of issue (*Governor*, Charles Castel). In 1999 there were 12 commercial banks (three foreign-owned) and a development bank.

Weights and Measures

The metric system and British imperial and US measures are in use.

ENERGY AND NATURAL RESOURCES

Environment

Carbon dioxide emissions from the consumption and flaring of fossil fuels in 2008 were the equivalent of 0·2 tonnes per capita.

Electricity

Most of the country is only provided with around four hours of electricity a day, supplied by the state-owned Électricité d'Haiti. Installed capacity was 0·2m. kW in 2004. Production in 2004 was an estimated 547m. kWh, with consumption per capita around 61 kWh.

Minerals

Until the supply was exhausted in the 1970s, a small quantity of bauxite was mined.

Agriculture

There were 780,000 ha. of arable land in 2001 and 320,000 ha. of permanent crops. 65% of the workforce, mainly smallholders, make a living by agriculture carried on in seven large plains, from 0·2m. to 25,000 acres, and in 15 smaller plains down to 2,000 acres. Irrigation is used in some areas and in 2001 covered 75,000 ha. The main crops are (2003 production estimates, in 1,000 tonnes): sugarcane, 1,050; cassava, 340; bananas, 300; plantains, 283; mangoes, 261; yams, 199; maize, 198; sweet potatoes, 175; rice, 105; sorghum, 95. Livestock (2003 estimates): goats, 1·9m.; cattle, 1·5m.; pigs, 1·0m.; horses, 500,000; chickens, 6m.

Forestry

The area under forests in 2005 was 105,000 ha., or 3·8% of the total land area. In 2007, 2·26m. cu. metres of roundwood were cut.

Fisheries

The total catch in 2004 was 8,300 tonnes, of which 96% was from marine waters.

INDUSTRY

Manufacturing is largely based on the assembly of imported components: toys, sports equipment, clothing, electronic and electrical equipment. Textiles, steel, soap, chemicals, paint and shoes are also produced. Many jobs were lost to other Central American and Caribbean countries during the 1991–94 trade embargo, after President Aristide was deposed.

Labour

In 1996 the labour force was 3,209,000 (57% males). The unemployment rate in July 1998 was around 60%.

Trade Unions

Whilst at least six unions exist, their influence is very limited.

INTERNATIONAL TRADE

Foreign debt was US$1,323m. in 2005.

Imports and Exports

In 2006 imports totalled US$1,548·2m. and exports US$494·4m. The leading imports are petroleum products, foodstuffs, textiles, machinery, animal and vegetable oils, chemicals, pharmaceuticals, raw materials for transformation industries and vehicles. The USA is by far the leading trading partner. Main import suppliers in 1999 were the USA, 60%; Dominican Republic, 4%; France, 3%; Japan, 3%. The USA accounted for 90% of exports in 1999.

COMMUNICATIONS

Roads

Total length of roads was estimated at 4,160 km in 2002, of which 1,010 km were surfaced. There were 58,100 passenger cars in 2002 (7·1 per 1,000 inhabitants), plus 39,100 trucks and vans.

Civil Aviation

There is an international airport at Port-au-Prince. Cap Haïtien also has scheduled flights to the Turks and Caicos Islands. In 2003 there were international flights to Aruba, Boston, Cayenne, Curaçao, Fort de France, Kingston, Miami, Montego Bay, Montreal, New York, Panama City, Paramaribo, Pointe-à-Pitre, Raleigh/Durham, Sint Maarten, Santiago (Cuba), Santiago

(Dominican Republic), Santo Domingo and Washington, D.C. In 2001 Port-au-Prince handled 913,022 passengers (771,656 on international flights) and 13,455 tonnes of freight.

Shipping

Port-au-Prince and Cap Haïtien are the principal ports, and there are 12 minor ports. In 2002 the merchant marine totalled 1,000 GRT. In 1997 vessels totalling 1,304,000 NRT entered ports.

Telecommunications

The state telecommunications agency is Teleco. Telephone subscribers in 2004 numbered 540,000 (65·8 for every 1,000 inhabitants), including 400,000 mobile phone subscribers. In 2004 there were 500,000 internet users.

Postal Services

There were 24 post offices in 2003, equivalent to one for every 347,000 persons (the lowest ratio of any country). The postal service is fairly reliable in the capital and major towns. Many businesses, however, prefer to use express courier services (DHL and Federal Express).

SOCIAL INSTITUTIONS

Justice

The Court of Cassation is the highest court in the judicial system. There are four Courts of Appeal and four Civil Courts. Judges are appointed by the President. The legal system is basically French.

The population in penal institutions in 2003 was 3,519 (42 per 100,000 of national population).

Education

The adult literacy rate in 2002 was 51·9% (53·8% among males and 50·0% among females). Education is divided into nine years 'education fondamentale', followed by four years to 'Baccalaureate' and university/higher education. The school system is based on the French system and instruction is in French and Créole. About 20% of education is provided by state schools; the remaining 80% by private schools, including Church and Mission schools.

In 1994–95 there were 360 primary schools (221 state, 139 religious), 21 public *lycées*, 123 private secondary schools, 18 vocational training centres and 42 domestic science centres.

There is a state university, several private universities and an Institute of Administration and Management.

In 2000–01 total expenditure on education came to 1·1% of GNP and 10·9% of total government spending.

Health

In 1996 there were 773 physicians and 2,630 nurses. There were 49 hospitals with a provision of ten beds per 10,000 population in 1994.

RELIGION

Since the Concordat of 1860 Roman Catholicism has been given special recognition, under an archbishop with nine bishops. The Episcopal Church has one bishop. 60% of the population are nominally Roman Catholic, while other Christian churches number perhaps 20%. Probably two-thirds of the population to some extent adhere to Voodoo, recognized as an official religion in 2003.

CULTURE

World Heritage Sites

Haiti has one site on the UNESCO World Heritage List: National History Park—Citadel, Sans-Souci, Ramiers (inscribed on the list in 1982), 19th century monuments to independence.

Broadcasting

Radio is the principal media, with more than 250 private radio stations on the air. Télévision Nationale is a government-owned service (colour by SECAM V). There were 60,000 TV sets in 2003.

Press

There were two daily newspapers in 2006 with a combined circulation of 8,000.

Tourism

In 2005 there were 112,267 tourists, spending US$110m. (excluding passenger transport). Cruise passenger arrivals in 2005 numbered 368,021. There are only about 1,000 hotel rooms in the whole country.

DIPLOMATIC REPRESENTATIVES

The Haitian Embassy in London closed on 30 March 1987.

Of the United Kingdom in Haiti
Ambassador: Stephen Fisher (resides in Santo Domingo, Dominican Republic).

Of Haiti in the USA (2311 Massachusetts Ave., NW, Washington, D.C., 20008)
Ambassador: Raymond Alcide Joseph.

Of the USA in Haiti (Tabarre 41, Blvd 15 Octobre, Port-au-Prince)
Ambassador: Kenneth H. Merten.

Of Haiti to the United Nations
Ambassador: Leo Merores.

Of Haiti to the European Union
Ambassador: Raymond Lafontant.

FURTHER READING

Girard, Philippe, *Paradise Lost: Haiti's Tumultuous Journey from Pearl of the Caribbean to Third World Hotspot.* 2005

Heinl, Robert & Nancy, revised by Michael Heinl, *Written in Blood.* 1996

Nicholls, D., *From Dessalines to Duvalier: Race, Colour and National Independence in Haiti.* 2nd ed. 1992

Pierre, Hyppolite, *Haiti, Rising Flames from Burning Ashes: Haiti the Phoenix.* 2006

Shamsie, Yasmine and Thompson, Andrew S., (eds.) *Haiti: Hope for a Fragile State.* 2006

Thomson, I., *Bonjour Blanc: a Journey through Haiti.* 1992

Weinstein, B. and Segal, A., *Haiti: the Failure of Politics.* 1992

Wucker, Michele, *Why the Cocks Fight: Dominicans, Haitians, and the Struggle for Hispaniola.* 2000

National library: Bibliothèque Nationale, 193 Rue du Centre, Port-au-Prince.

National Statistical Office: Institut Haïtien de Statistique et d'Informatique (IHSI), 1 Angle rue Joseph Janvier et Blvd Harry Truman, HT6110 Port-au-Prince.

Website (French only): http://www.ihsi.ht

HONDURAS

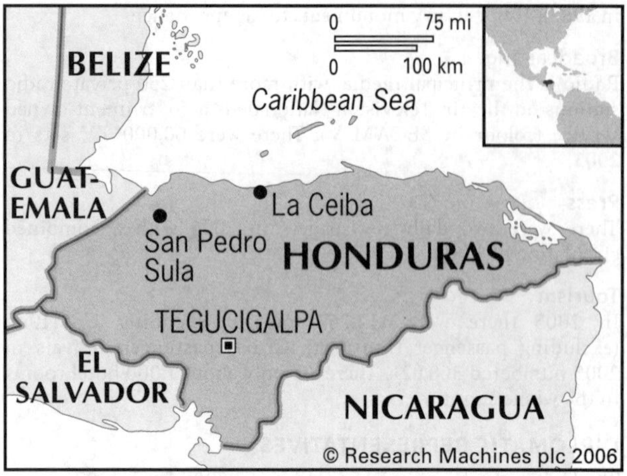

República de Honduras
(Republic of Honduras)

Capital: Tegucigalpa
Population estimate, 2010: 7·62m.
GDP per capita, 2007: (PPP$) 3,796
HDI/world rank: 0·732/112

KEY HISTORICAL EVENTS

Discovered by Columbus in 1502, Honduras was ruled by Spain until independence in 1821. Political instability was endemic throughout the 19th and most of the 20th century. The end of military rule seemed to come in 1981 when a general election gave victory to the more liberal and non-military party, PLH (Partido Liberal de Honduras). However, power remained with the armed forces. Internal unrest continued into the 1990s with politicians and military leaders at loggerheads, particularly over attempts to investigate violations of human rights. In Oct. 1998 Honduras was devastated by Hurricane Mitch, the worst natural disaster to hit the area in modern times. In June 2009 President Manuel Zelaya was deposed in a military coup, leading to international condemnation and the suspension of aid. A presidential poll was held in Nov. 2009, with Porfirio Lobo Sosa of the National Party emerging victorious after Zelaya's refusal to recognize the election. The following month Congress rejected proposals to return Zelaya to power and in Jan. 2010 Porfirio Lobo was sworn in as Zelaya went into exile.

TERRITORY AND POPULATION

Honduras is bounded in the north by the Caribbean, east and southeast by Nicaragua, west by Guatemala, southwest by El Salvador and south by the Pacific Ocean. The area is 112,492 sq. km (43,433 sq. miles). In 2001 the census population was 6,535,344 (3,304,386 females), giving a density of 58·1 per sq. km. In 2005, 53·5% of the population lived in rural areas.

The UN gives an estimated population for 2010 of 7·62m.

The chief cities and towns are (2001 census populations): Tegucigalpa, the capital (819,867), San Pedro Sula (483,384), La Ceiba (126,721), Choloma (126,042), El Progreso (94,797), Choluteca (76,135), Comayagua (60,078), Danlí (47,310), Catacamas (35,995), Juticalpa (33,698).

Areas and 2001 populations of the 18 departments:

Department	*Area (in sq. km)*	*Population*
Atlántida	4,372	344,099
Choluteca	3,923	390,085
Colón	4,360	246,708
Comayagua	8,249	352,881
Copán	5,124	288,766
Cortés	3,242	1,202,510
El Paraíso	7,489	350,054
Francisco Morazán	8,619	1,180,676
Gracias a Dios	16,997	67,384
Intibucá	3,123	179,862
Islas de la Bahía	236	38,073
La Paz	2,525	156,560
Lempira	4,228	250,067
Ocotepeque	1,630	108,029
Olancho	23,905	419,561
Santa Bárbara	5,024	342,054
Valle	1,665	151,841
Yoro	7,781	465,414

The official language is Spanish. The Spanish-speaking population is of mixed Spanish and Amerindian descent (87%), with 6% Amerindians.

SOCIAL STATISTICS

2004 estimates: births, 204,000; deaths, 42,000. Rates, 2004 estimates (per 1,000 population): birth, 29; death, 6. 2007 life expectancy, 69·6 years for men and 74·4 for women. Annual population growth rate, 1992–2002, 2·8%. Infant mortality, 2005, 31 per 1,000 live births; fertility rate, 2004, 3·6 births per woman. Abortion is illegal.

CLIMATE

The climate is tropical, with a small annual range of temperature but with high rainfall. Upland areas have two wet seasons, from May to July and in Sept. and Oct. The Caribbean Coast has most rain in Dec. and Jan. and temperatures are generally higher than inland. Tegucigalpa, Jan. 66°F (19°C), July 74°F (23·3°C). Annual rainfall 64" (1,621 mm).

CONSTITUTION AND GOVERNMENT

The present Constitution came into force in 1982 and was amended in 1995. The *President* is elected for a single four-year term. Members of the *National Congress* (total 128 seats) and municipal mayors are elected simultaneously on a proportional basis, according to combined votes cast for the Presidential candidate of their party.

In March 2009 the incumbent president, Manuel Zelaya, proposed a referendum to approve an assembly to revise the constitution. His opponents feared that he was seeking revisions to allow him to stand for re-election. A constitutional crisis culminated in a military coup and Zelaya's exile to Costa Rica.

National Anthem

'Tu bandera' ('Thy Banner'); words by A. C. Coello, tune by C. Hartling.

RECENT ELECTIONS

Presidential and parliamentary elections took place on 29 Nov. 2009. In the presidential elections Porfirio Lobo Sosa (National Party, PNH) won 56·5% of votes cast against 38·1% for his chief rival, Elvin Santos (Liberal Party, PLH). There were three other candidates. Turnout was 50·0%. In the elections to the National Congress held on the same day the National Party won 71 of 128 seats, the Liberal Party 45, the Christian Democratic Party 5,

Democratic Unification Party 4 and the Innovation and Unity Party 3.

CURRENT ADMINISTRATION

On 28 June 2009 the government was ousted in a military coup. In March 2010 the new government consisted of:

President: Porfirio Lobo Sosa; b. 1947 (PNH; sworn in 27 Jan. 2010).

Vice-presidents: María Antonieta de Bográn *(also Minister of the Presidency)*; Marlón Tábora.

Minister of Agriculture: Jacobo Regalado. *Communications:* Miguel Ángel Bonilla. *Culture, Art and Sport:* Bernard Martínez. *Defence:* Marlon Pascua. *Education:* Alejandro Ventura. *Family:* María Elena Zepeda. *Finance:* William Chong Wong. *Foreign Relations:* Mario Canahuati. *Health:* Arturo Bendaña. *Industry and Commerce:* Oscar Escalante. *Interior:* Áfrico Madrid. *Labour:* Felicito Ávila. *National Institute of Women:* María Antonieta Botto. *Natural Resources and Environment:* Rigoberto Cuéllar. *Public Works, Transport and Housing:* Miguel Pastor. *Security:* Oscar Álvarez. *Tourism:* Nelly Jérez.

Office of the President (Spanish only):
http://www.presidencia.gob.hn

CURRENT LEADERS

Porfirio Lobo Sosa

Position
President

Introduction
Porfirio Lobo Sosa was elected president on 29 Nov. 2009, ending months of political turmoil that followed the ousting of President Zelaya in a coup. The right-wing former agronomist will need to draw on his long political experience to unite the country and re-establish regional alliances.

Early Life
Porfirio Lobo Sosa was born on 22 Dec. 1947 in Trujillo, Colón district, the son of a wealthy politician who served in Honduras' National Congress in the 1950s. Lobo grew up on a ranch near Juticalpa, Olancho, attending a local Catholic school and then the San Francisco Institute of Tegucigalpa from 1961–65. He went to the University of Miami in 1966 to study business administration before returning to Honduras in 1970 to work in his family's agricultural business and to teach politics and economics at a college in Juticalpa. In the 1970s Lobo travelled to the Soviet Union and enrolled at Patrice Lumumba University in Moscow. He is reputed to have joined the Communist Party of Honduras on his return before making a political U-turn to join the right-wing National Party (PNH), becoming president of the party's Olancho branch in 1986.

In the general election of Nov. 1989 Lobo secured a seat in the National Congress for the PNH. He worked in the department for agriculture and economics under the new president, Rafael Leonardo Callejas, and headed the corporation for forestry development until 1994. Lobo was elected president of the PNH's central committee in June 1999 and served as president of congress from 2002–06. Selected as the PNH candidate to contest the presidential election of 27 Nov. 2005, he took a hard line on crime, promising the death penalty for convicted gang members. This contrasted with the approach of his rival, José Manuel Zelaya, of the centre-right Liberal Party (PLH) who pledged to introduce re-education programmes for criminals. Lobo was defeated with 46% of the vote to Zelaya's 50%.

Lobo took over as leader of the opposition PNH in Jan. 2006. He criticized Zelaya's lurch to the political left in 2007 and the president's alliance with the Venezuelan leader, Hugo Chávez, who persuaded Honduras to join the leftist alliances, Petrocaribe and the Bolivarian Alternative for Latin America and the Caribbean (ALBA). Zelaya's popularity was dented by his attempts in 2008 to hold a referendum to change the constitution that barred him from standing for re-election—a path taken by Chávez in Venezuela and President Morales in Bolivia. Zelaya pushed ahead with the referendum, despite opposition from the PNH, national legal bodies and much of the military.

On 28 June 2009, after the Supreme Court had ruled that the bid to change the constitution was illegal, the army launched a coup and forced Zelaya into exile in Costa Rica. A wave of international criticism ushered in five months of sometimes violent turmoil between Zelaya's supporters and backers of the interim president, Roberto Micheletti. In the presidential election of 29 Nov. 2009 (scheduled prior to the coup), Lobo secured 56% of the vote and was sworn in on 27 Jan. 2010.

Career in Office
Lobo promptly granted amnesty to those who were involved in the political crisis and paved the way for Zelaya to leave for exile in the Dominican Republic. The move was one of the conditions of the Tegucigalpa–San José Accord, signed in Oct. 2009 after efforts by the Organization of American States to broker a solution to the political crisis. Lobo promised to 're-establish channels of friendship with all nations' and to seek foreign investment to revive the economy and create jobs. In early Feb. 2010 President Chávez urged the region not to recognize Lobo's government.

DEFENCE

Conscription was abolished in 1995. In 2006 defence expenditure totalled US$55m. (US$8 per capita), representing 0·6% of GDP.

Army

The Army numbered (2007) 8,300. There is also a paramilitary Public Security Force of 8,000.

Navy

Personnel (2007), 1,400 including 830 marines. Bases are at Puerto Cortés, Puerto Castilla and Amapala.

Air Force

There were 16 combat capable aircraft in 2007 (A-37B Dragonfly and F-5E/F Tiger II fighters). Total strength was (2007) 2,300 personnel.

INTERNATIONAL RELATIONS

Honduras is a member of the UN, World Bank, IMF and several other UN specialized agencies, WTO, IOM, ACS, CACM, Inter-American Development Bank and SELA.

ECONOMY

Agriculture accounted for 13·5% of GDP in 2006, industry 28·3% and services 58·2%.

Overview

Honduras is a lower middle income country with a diversified economy based on international trading of manufactures and agricultural commodities. One of the poorest countries in Latin America with social indicators among the weakest in the region, the economy is highly susceptible to external shocks and natural disasters.

GDP fell by 0·5% a year for three years after Hurricane Mitch (1998) ruined many small-scale farmers with knock-on damage to banking. Debt relief from the Enhanced Heavily Indebted Poor Countries Initiative, Paris Club creditors, Multilateral Debt Relief Initiative and Inter-American Development Bank helped reduce external debt from 78% of GDP in 1999 to 16% in 2007. In the five years to 2008 growth had been above the Latin American average although living standards for the majority barely improved.

Growth is largely attributed to increased remittances and strong export performance, particularly by the *maquila* sector (re-export business), and private investment arising from the Central American Free Trade Agreement (CAFTA). The US recession has resulted in a decline in remittances, FDI and exports from *maquilas*, and GDP growth fell by 2·1% in 2009 according to the Banco Central de Honduras.

In Jan. 2010 Porfirio Lobo Sosa became president following a military-backed coup against President Zelaya in June 2009. Political uncertainty is likely to hinder sustained economic progress.

Currency

The unit of currency is the *lempira* (HNL) of 100 *centavos*. In July 2005 foreign exchange reserves were US$2,164m., total money supply was 19,865m. lempiras and gold reserves were 21,000 troy oz. Inflation was 6·9% in 2007 and 11·4% in 2008.

Budget

In 2005 revenues were 32,305m. lempiras and expenditures 37,018m. lempiras. Tax revenue accounted for 82·7% of revenues in 2005; current expenditure accounted for 78·6% of expenditures.

There is a sales tax of 12%.

Performance

Real GDP growth was 6·3% in 2007 and 4·0% in 2008. Total GDP in 2008 was US$14·1bn.

Banking and Finance

The central bank of issue is the Banco Central de Honduras (*President*, María Elena Mondragón). It had total reserves at Dec. 2002 of US$1,531m. There is an agricultural development bank, Banadesa, for small grain producers, a state land bank and a network of rural credit agencies managed by peasant organizations. The Central American Bank for Economic Integration (CABEI) has its head office in Tegucigalpa. In 1999 there were 40 private banks, including four foreign.

There are stock exchanges in Tegucigalpa and San Pedro Sula.

Weights and Measures

The metric system is official but some local measures are used, such as the *manzana* (= 0·7 ha.) and the *vara* (= 88 mm).

ENERGY AND NATURAL RESOURCES

Environment

Carbon dioxide emissions from the consumption and flaring of fossil fuels in 2008 were the equivalent of 1·1 tonnes per capita.

Electricity

Installed capacity was around 1·0m. kW in 2004 (0·5m. kW hydro-electric). Production in 2004 was 4·88m. kWh (48% hydro-electric); consumption per capita (2004) was 730 kWh.

Minerals

Output in 2006: zinc, 37,646 tonnes; lead, 11,775 tonnes; silver, 55,036 kg. Small quantities of gold are mined, and there are also deposits of tin, iron, copper, coal, antimony and pitchblende.

Agriculture

There were around 1·07m. ha. of arable land in 2007 and 0·36m. ha. of permanent crops. Legislation of 1975 provided for the compulsory redistribution of land, but in 1992 the grounds for this were much reduced, and a 5-ha. minimum area for land titles was abolished. Members of the 2,800 co-operatives set up in 1975 received individual shareholdings which can be broken up into personal units. Since 1992 women may have tenure in their own right. The state monopoly of the foreign grain trade was abolished in 1992. In 1996 the Agricultural Incentive Program was created (Ley de Incentivo Agrícola, LIA) which involves the redistribution of land for agricultural development.

Estimated crop production in 2003 (in 1,000 tonnes): sugarcane, 4,200; bananas, 965; maize, 502; plantains, 260; oranges, 167; coffee, 150; melons and watermelons, 145; palm oil, 112; dry beans, 69; pineapples, 62; sorghum, 52.

Livestock (2003 estimates): cattle, 2·40m.; pigs, 478,000; horses, 181,000; mules, 70,000; chickens, 19m.

Forestry

In 2005 forests covered 4·65m. ha., or 41·5% of the total land area. In 2007, 9·46m. cu. metres of roundwood were cut.

Fisheries

Shrimp and lobster are important catches. The total catch in 2005 was approximately 19,200 tonnes, almost entirely from sea fishing.

INDUSTRY

Industry is small-scale and local. 2001 output (in 1,000 tonnes): cement, 1,100; raw sugar, 316; wheat flour, 113; fabrics (1995), 11,641 metres; beer (2003), 96·1m. litres; rum (1995), 2·37m. litres.

Labour

The workforce was 2,438,000 in Sept. 2001. Of 2,334,600 persons in employment in Sept. 2001, 766,800 were in agriculture, hunting, forestry and fishing, 559,200 in wholesale and retail trade and restaurants and hotels, 380,300 in community, social and personal services and 356,000 in manufacturing. Unemployment rate, Sept. 2001: 4·2%.

Trade Unions

About 346,000 workers were unionized in 1994.

INTERNATIONAL TRADE

In 2004 Honduras signed the Central America-Dominican Republic-United States Free Trade Agreement (CAFTA-DR), along with Costa Rica, the Dominican Republic, El Salvador, Guatemala, Nicaragua and the USA. The agreement entered into force for Honduras on 1 April 2006. Foreign debt was US$5,242m. in 2005.

Imports and Exports

Imports in 2004 were valued at US$3,921·8m. and exports at US$1,533·9m.

Main imports are machinery and electrical equipment, industrial chemicals, and mineral products and lubricants. Main exports are coffee, bananas, shrimp and lobster, gold, lead and zinc, timber and refrigerated meats. Principal import suppliers, 2004: USA, 34·6%; Guatemala, 7·7%; El Salvador, 5·0%; Costa Rica, 4·9%. Principal export markets, 2004: USA, 41·5%; El Salvador, 10·9%; Guatemala, 7·3%; Germany, 5·9%.

COMMUNICATIONS

Roads

Honduras is connected with Guatemala, El Salvador and Nicaragua by the Pan-American Highway. Out of a total of 13,603 km of roads in 2002, 20·4% were paved. In 2007 there were 487,700 passenger cars in use, 31,500 buses and coaches, 165,200 lorries and vans, and 94,400 motorcycles and mopeds.

Rail

The small government-run railway was built to serve the banana industry and is confined to the northern coastal region and does not reach Tegucigalpa. In 2005 there were 595 km of track in three gauges, which in 1994 carried 1m. passengers and 1·2m. tonnes of freight.

Civil Aviation

There are four international airports: San Pedro Sula (Ramon Villeda) and Tegucigalpa (Toncontín) are the main ones, plus Roatún and La Ceiba, with over 80 smaller airstrips in various parts of the country. In addition to domestic flights and services to other parts of central America and the Caribbean, there were flights in 2003 to Barcelona, Dallas/Fort Worth, Houston, Las Vegas, Los Angeles, Madrid, Miami, New Orleans, New York, Oklahoma City, Orange County, Phoenix and San Jose. In 2001 San Pedro Sula handled 496,000 passengers (386,000 on international flights) and 7,500 tonnes of freight, and Tegucigalpa handled 451,000 passengers (327,000 on international flights) and 3,800 tonnes of freight.

Shipping

The largest port is Puerto Cortés on the Atlantic coast. There are also ports at Henecán (on the Pacific) and Puerto Castilla and Tela (northern coast). In 2002 the merchant marine totalled 933,000 GRT, including oil tankers 214,000 GRT. Honduras is a flag of convenience registry.

Telecommunications

In 2005 there were 1,775,800 telephone subscribers, or 246·5 for every 1,000 persons, with 1,281,500 mobile phone subscribers. There were 110,000 PCs in use (15·7 for every 1,000 persons) in 2004 and 222,300 internet users.

Postal Services

There were 290 post offices in 2003.

SOCIAL INSTITUTIONS

Justice

Judicial power is vested in the Supreme Court, with nine judges elected by the National Congress for four years; it appoints the judges of the courts of appeal, and justices of the peace.

There were 2,772 homicides in 2005. At 39 per 100,000 persons, Honduras has among the highest murder rates in the world.

The population in penal institutions in Dec. 2005 was 11,589 (161 per 100,000 of national population).

Education

Adult literacy in 2003 was 80·0% (male, 79·8%; female, 80·2%). Education is free, compulsory (from 6 to 15 years) and secular. There is a high drop-out rate after the first years in primary education. In 2007 there were 214,051 children in pre-primary schools (8,178 teaching staff in 2006); 1,308,119 children in primary schools (46,308 teaching staff in 2006); 554,297 pupils in secondary schools (16,667 teaching staff in 2004). There were 122,874 students in tertiary education in 2004 and 7,170 academic staff. The leading institution of higher learning is the National Autonomous University of Honduras (Universidad Nacional Autónoma de Honduras), founded in 1847, in Tegucigalpa.

In 1998–99 expenditure on education came to 4·2% of GNP.

Health

In 1997 there were 4,896 physicians, 989 dentists and 6,152 nurses. In 1994 there were 29 public hospitals and 32 private, with 4,737 beds, and 849 health centres.

RELIGION

Roman Catholicism is the prevailing religion (5,740,000 followers in 2001), but the constitution guarantees freedom to all creeds, and the State does not contribute to the support of any. In 2001 there were 690,000 Evangelical Protestants with the remainder of the population followers of other faiths. In Feb. 2010 there was one cardinal.

CULTURE

World Heritage Sites

Honduras has two sites on the UNESCO World Heritage List: Maya Site of Copán (inscribed on the list in 1980), a centre of the Mayan civilization abandoned in the early 10th century; and Río Plátano Biosphere Reserve (1982), one of the few remains of the Central American rain forest.

Broadcasting

Televicentro operates the main television services. Other commercial channels include CBC Canal 6, Vica TV and SOTEL Canal 11. Radio America and Radio HRN are private national stations. There were 1·1m. TV sets in 2006 (colour by NTSC).

Press

Honduras had five national daily papers in 2006, with a combined circulation of 160,000.

Tourism

In 2005 there were 673,000 non-resident tourists, spending US$476m.

Festivals

There are a number of festivals and religious celebrations held throughout the year in Honduras. The Fiesta de San Isidro is a week-long carnival held in May every year to honour the city's patron saint.

DIPLOMATIC REPRESENTATIVES

Of Honduras in the United Kingdom (115 Gloucester Pl., London, W1U 6JT)
Ambassador: Iván Romero-Martínez.

Of the United Kingdom in Honduras (embassy in Tegucigalpa closed in Dec. 2003)
Ambassador: Julie Chappell, OBE (resides in Guatemala City).

Of Honduras in the USA (3007 Tilden St., NW, Washington, D.C., 20008)
Ambassador: Vacant.
Chargé d'Affaires a.i.: Eduardo Enrique Reina.

Of the USA in Honduras (Av. La Paz, Tegucigalpa)
Ambassador: Hugo Llorens.

Of Honduras to the United Nations
Ambassador: Jorge Arturo Reina Idiaquez.

Of Honduras to the European Union
Ambassador: Ramón Custodio Espinoza.

FURTHER READING

Banco Central de Honduras. *Honduras en Cifras 2006–08.* Online only
Euraque, Darío A., *Reinterpreting the Banana Republic: Region and State in Honduras, 1870–1972.* 1997
Loker, William M., *Changing Places: Environment, Development and Social Change in Rural Honduras.* 2004
Meyer, H. K. and Meyer, J. H., *Historical Dictionary of Honduras.* 2nd ed. 1994

National Statistical Office: Instituto Nacional de Estadísticas, Tegucigalpa.
Website (Spanish only): http://www.ine-hn.org

HUNGARY

Magyar Köztársaság
(Hungarian Republic)

Capital: Budapest
Population estimate, 2010: 9·97m.
GDP per capita, 2007: (PPP$) 18,755
HDI/world rank: 0·879/43

KEY HISTORICAL EVENTS

Records date back to 9 BC, when the Romans subdued the Celts to establish Pannonia. From the 5th century both Romans and Celts retreated before attacks from the Huns who were followed by the Avars in the 7th century and the Magyars in the 9th. It was then that the name *On ogur* ('ten arrows') was adopted for the country that was to become Hungary. The founding date of Hungary is put at 896 after which Árpád, leader of one of the Magyar tribes, forged a dynasty which ruled Hungary until 1301. Forays into Italy, Germany, the Balkans and Spain ended after the Magyars were defeated by Holy Roman Emperor Otto I at the battle of Lechfeld in 955, and the Ostmark (Austria) was returned to Germanic control.

In seeking a truce with Otto I, the Árpád leader Géza invited him to send Catholic missionaries into Hungary. He had his son István (Stephen) crowned as King of Hungary and replaced the tribal structure with a system of counties (*megye*), administered by royal officials. A disputed succession led to intervention by the Holy Roman Emperor who established temporary suzerainty over Hungary. By the end of the 11th century, Slovakia, Carpathian Ruthenia and Transylvania were all under the crown of St Stephen. In a struggle for control of the ports on the Adriatic, Venice and Hungary went to war on 21 occasions between 1115–1420.

Andrew III, the last Árpád monarch, could do little to hold the country together against the opposition of feuding nobles. His death in 1301 led to a seven-year interregnum, after which, with two exceptions, Hungary was ruled by foreign kings. Linked to the Árpáds through marriage, Charles Robert of Anjou was elected to the throne. His primary task was to restore royal authority over the nobles. An economic boom coincided with Hungary becoming the leading gold producer in Europe and trade links with European neighbours were fostered.

Ottoman Threat

His successors had to contend with the growing power of the Ottoman Empire. Assaults on Hungary increased after the fall of Constantinople in 1453, but in 1456 János Hunyadi, acting as military regent, broke the siege of Belgrade to keep the Turks at bay for another 70 years.

Rival magnates reacted to Hunyadi's death from the plague in 1456 by trying to wipe out the omnipotent Hunyadi clan, but in 1457 the Diet appointed his 15-year-old son Matthias Corvinus as king. Matthias was an enlightened despot. He built up one of Europe's finest libraries—destroyed a century later by the Ottomans—and encouraged writers and artists, many of whom were Italian, to come and work in Hungary. The heirless Matthias was succeeded in 1490 by Bohemia's ruler Vladislav, or King Ulászló II (1490–1516), known as 'Rex Bene', because 'dobre', or 'good' was his reply to almost everything. He managed to repel a Habsburg invasion of Hungary but indulged the nobles with disproportionate powers and relied heavily on foreign financing. Vladislav II was succeeded in 1516 by his son Louis II, who held both the Hungarian and Bohemian thrones. A ten-year-old, he could do little to discourage the onslaught of the Turks, to whom Belgrade was lost in 1521. The Hungarians were defeated by the Turks under Suleiman II at the battle of Mohács on 29 Aug. 1526. Louis was killed in battle and Hungary lost its independence, not to be regained until 1918.

Hungary was partitioned, the largest section going to the Turks, royal Hungary to the Habsburgs and Transylvania, though theoretically autonomous, becoming a vassal state of the Ottomans. The Transylvanians were at constant war with the Habsburgs, who in turn fought the Ottomans. The economy along with the Magyar language declined and much agricultural land, mainly the Hungarian Plain, went to waste.

The Treaty of Vienna of 1606 was meant to set peaceful boundaries, but was soon violated. A series of costly territorial struggles culminated in the Ottoman siege of Vienna in 1683. Repelled by the Habsburgs, it marked a turning point for the Turks who, by 1699, had ceded most of their Hungarian territory. The Habsburgs became hereditary rulers pursuing a policy of divide and rule which led to anti-Habsburg risings. The second, under Ferenc Rákóczi, the last independent prince of Transylvania, united both nobles and peasants, and lasted from 1703–11. It was concluded by the signing of the Peace of Szatmár, in which the Habsburgs guaranteed political freedom for the three 'nations'—the ethnic Magyar, Saxon and Székelys groups. State education, introduced by Maria Theresa and Joseph II, led to greater Germanization.

Challenge to Habsburg Rule

Power was concentrated on the Magyar nobility, descendents of the Árpád royal line, who owned vast estates and were exempt from land tax. In March 1848 the Hungarian Diet renounced Viennese rule and legislated for a sovereign Magyar state, which was approved by Emperor Ferdinand. However, what began peacefully soon deteriorated as national minorities such as the Croats, the Romanians, Serbs and Slovaks demanded the same rights. In the War of Independence, heavy fighting broke out between the Hungarians and the Austrians, the Hungarians being led by Lajos Kossuth (1802–94).

When Emperor Franz Joseph I took the throne in 1848, the Hungarians refused to recognize him. This provoked an Austrian invasion, which was repelled, and in Feb. 1849 the diet in Debrecen declared Hungary an independent republic under Kossuth's leadership. Franz Joseph reacted by accepting the assistance of Tsar Nicholas I of Russia in suppressing the revolution. The Magyars chose to surrender to the Russians rather than the Austrians but the aftermath of the war witnessed mass executions and imprisonment of rebel factions. Kossuth escaped into exile. Direct rule was imposed from Vienna.

Dual Monarchy

Having lost territory to Sardinia in 1859 and to Prussia in 1866, Austria recognized the need for a compromise with Hungary. What became known as the 'Ausgleich' created a dual monarchy to preside over the Austro-Hungarian Empire. Hungary gained internal autonomy but while the Ausgleich profited Magyars and Austro-Germans it did little to benefit national minorities.

Bosnia and Herzegovina were annexed in 1908, which outraged Serbia, but Austria tried a number of tricks to prevent retaliation including the Zagreb Treason Trial of 1909, when evidence was produced of a Serb-Croat conspiracy to bring down the Habsburgs. It was the Czech professor and future president Tomáš Masaryk who proved the evidence to be fake.

On 28 June 1914 the heir to the Habsburg throne, Archduke Franz Ferdinand, and his wife were shot in Sarajevo by a Bosnian Serb. Austria-Hungary declared war on Serbia a month later, precipitating the First World War. The Entente of France, Britain and Russia united against the Central Powers of Germany and Austria-Hungary, with other nations soon joining in one or other alliance. By the Treaty of Versailles, the territories of Hungary and Austria were reduced drastically. Hungary became a republic in Nov. 1918, with Mihály Károlyi as president. Transylvania was handed over to Romania. New countries including Czechoslovakia and Yugoslavia were created, all of which gained former Hungarian territory.

On 21 March 1919, Károlyi was replaced by the Bolshevik leader, Béla Kun, who was in power for 133 days. His downfall was brought about by a non-communist revolutionary movement fighting to regain Slovakia and Romania. The Allies persuaded Romania to retreat, and Hungary's borders were finalized by the Treaty of Trianon on 4 June 1920. Two-thirds of Hungary's territory and over half of the population were assigned to neighbouring countries.

In 1919 the Hungarian Kingdom was restored under Count Miklós Horthy, who ruled as regent and appointed a chiefly aristocratic government. Despite Horthy's efforts to amend the Trianon treaty, Hungary's boundaries remained unchanged until the Second World War. Germany and Italy backed the 'Vienna awards' of Nov. 1938 which restored to Hungary southern Slovakia and southern Subcarparthian Ruth, and in Aug. 1940, Transylvanian and Romanian territory. Hitler's support, including favourable trading terms, drew Hungary into fighting with Germany against the Soviet army in 1941, a tactical error which led to enormous losses.

In March 1944 the Germans occupied Hungary. Horthy was forced to abdicate and Hitler appointed a government of Ferenc Szálasi and his fascist Arrow Cross movement. Large-scale deportation of Jews and political dissidents began. Around 400,000 Jews are estimated to have been murdered. With civilian and military losses, almost a million Hungarians died in the war.

Soviet Rule

With the Soviets as the occupying power, post-war Communist rule was established in 1948–49 after a three-year multi-party democracy which the Communists conspired to undermine. Mátyás Rákosi and his Hungarian Workers' Party headed a dictatorship which went unchallenged until 1953, the year of Stalin's death. In July of that year Rákosi was ousted by reformers led by Imre Nagy. Appointed prime minister, Nagy began what he called 'the new stage in building socialism', which entailed industrial and economic reforms and the restoration of human rights. But disagreements within the Soviet leadership gave an advantage to Rákosi who was still general secretary of the Workers' Party. Nagy was forced out of office in April 1955.

On 23 Oct. 1956 a student-led demonstration demanded democratic reforms and Nagy's reinstatement as prime minister. Soviet troops fired into crowds trying to occupy the radio station. The next day Imre Nagy was reappointed prime minister but was unable to quell the riots. Revolutionary committees were set up and there was a general strike to promote the three aims of the revolution: national independence, a democratic political structure and the protection of social benefits. All of this, along with armed rebels in the capital, put pressure on the hardliners in the party to accept reform.

A ceasefire, called by Nagy on 28 Oct., was honoured and Soviet troops retreated from Budapest. A multi-party democracy was announced, and the State Security Authority abolished. Even so, there were continuing demands for a clean sweep of all Stalinist-Rákosist ministers and total Soviet withdrawal. Nagy believed that such a transition should occur gradually and peacefully, but when he voiced the nation's support for neutrality and a withdrawal from the Warsaw pact, it was a step too far for Moscow. János Kádár was encouraged to form a counter-government with Soviet military backing. The Soviet Army marched into Budapest on 4 Nov., crushing all resistance.

Soviet hopes that Nagy would resign after this resounding defeat and support Kádár were disappointed. Kádár returned from Moscow on 7 Nov. after the heaviest fighting was over, to be confronted by a less than compromising nation. The renamed Hungarian Socialist Workers' Party declared all Oct. events as a counter-revolution, and began a series of revenge attacks. Nagy was hanged on 16 June 1958 along with several of his reformist associates. Many opponents of the regime were deported to labour camps in the Soviet Union and over 200,000 people fled the country.

Gradual Reform

János Kádár was party leader from 1956–89, and prime minister in the years 1956–58 and 1961–65. In the early '60s Kádár made a gradual shift towards liberalization. After the wave of executions, a distinction was made between political crime and mere error, and people were no longer required to be active in the party in order to succeed professionally. Trade unions were allowed to play a more active role, as was the press, so long as the government was not openly criticized.

The now-recognized need to loosen state control of the economy gave rise to the New Economic Mechanism (NEM) in 1968, which relaxed price controls, acknowledged the profit motive, improved manufacturing quality and shifted the emphasis from heavy to light industry. Subsidies were reduced and enterprise encouraged. Growing demands for a more open market economy coincided with the first signs of a weakening of the Soviet system. A group of Hungarian dissidents were sufficiently encouraged by the liberal trend in Moscow to form the Hungarian Democratic Forum. Led by their secretary general, Imre Pozsgay, they produced a manifesto 'Turn and Reform' which argued for a total overhaul of the economy.

The subsequent debate reopened divisions between hardliners and reformists, and throughout the country there were demonstrations and strikes. The conservative old school of the Hungarian Socialist Workers' Party was gradually phased out by the reformists. A committee was set up to investigate the events of 1956, which concluded that it had been a popular uprising and not a counter-revolution. This called for the ceremonial reburial of Imre Nagy's remains on 16 June 1989, an event attended by a quarter of a million people who gathered in Heroes' Square, Budapest.

Post Communism

When prime minister Miklós Németh opened the borders with Austria, the flood of refugees from East Germany precipitated the fall of the Berlin wall. Multi-party democracy was enshrined in law in Sept. 1989 and Hungary ceased to be a People's Republic on 23 Oct. A unicameral National Assembly was formed and the first free elections took place on 25 March 1990. Of the 386 members elected to the National Assembly, only 21 had ever served in parliament before, and of the six successful parties, three were entirely new. The Hungarian Democratic Forum (MDF) and Alliance of Free Democrats advocated democracy, political pluralism, a market economy and a 'return' to Europe. The MDF came out ahead but having failed to secure a majority, formed a coalition with the Independent Smallholders' Party and the Christian Democratic People's Party.

A largely inexperienced government set about economic reform while trying to contain trade and budget deficits and high inflation. Social unrest prompted the government to slow down its privatization programme which proved popular with the electorate until they realized that the economy was stalling. In 1993 Iván Szabó became finance minister and adopted much stricter policies, cutting social budgets and devaluing the forint. This again led to domestic hardship. Unemployment, a hitherto unknown phenomenon, grew to over 12%. A nostalgia for a Communist past where jobs, housing and benefits were secure was perceptible in voting patterns at the 1994 elections.

Although the MDF's 'shock tactic' policies were praised by the West, and attracted foreign investment, the electorate opted for an updated version of the Hungarian Socialist Party (MSzP). Former Communist and leader Gyula Horn touted the party as one free of ideological limitations, playing down the traditional left and promising a higher standard of living along with continued economic reform under the guidance of László Bekesy, finance minister of the former Communist government. Horn became prime minister of a coalition led by the Alliance of Free Democrats (SzDSz) and the MSzP. Economic reforms were put back on the agenda but the government moved cautiously in an effort to carry public opinion.

The 1998 elections produced another coalition led by Viktor Orbán of the Federation of Young Democrats (later called Fidesz). He was succeeded in May 2002 by Péter Medgyessy, the Socialists' candidate, who formed a coalition with the SzDSz. In June 2002 revelations that Medgyessy had worked as a counter-intelligence agent for the communist regime highlighted the transitional problems for former Eastern Bloc nations. Hungary became a member of NATO in 1999 and of the EU on 1 May 2004.

TERRITORY AND POPULATION

Hungary is bounded in the north by Slovakia, northeast by Ukraine, east by Romania, south by Croatia and Serbia, southwest by Slovenia and west by Austria. The peace treaty of 10 Feb. 1947 restored the frontiers as of 1 Jan. 1938. The area of Hungary is 93,030 sq. km (35,919 sq. miles).

At the census of 1 Feb. 2001 the population was 10,198,315 (5,347,665 females); Jan. 2009 official estimate, 10,030,975.

The UN gives an estimated population for 2010 of 9·97m.

67·7% of the population was urban in Jan. 2008; population density, Jan. 2009, 107·8 per sq. km. Hungary's population has been falling at such a steady rate since 1980 that its 2009 population was the same as that in the early 1960s.

Ethnic minorities, 2001: Roma (Gypsies), 5·3%; Ruthenians, 2·9%; Germans, 2·4%; Romanians, 1·0%; Slovaks, 0·9%. A law of 1993 permits ethnic minorities to set up self-governing councils. There is a worldwide Hungarian diaspora of about 4·7m. (including 1·5m. in the USA and Canada; 1·4m. in Romania; 0·5m. in Slovakia; 0·3m. in Serbia, mainly in Vojvodina; 0·2m. in Israel; 0·2m. in Ukraine; 0·1m. in Brazil; 0·1m. in Germany). In total, 2·5m. Hungarians live in neighbouring countries.

Hungary is divided into 19 counties (*megyék*) and the capital, Budapest, which has county status.

Area (in sq. km) and population (in 1,000) of counties and chief towns:

Counties	*Area*	*2009 population*	*Chief town*	*2009 population*
Bács-Kiskun	8,445	530	Kecskemét	111
Baranya	4,430	395	Pécs	157
Békés	5,631	371	Békéscsaba	65
Borsod-Abaúj-Zemplén	7,247	701	Miskolc	170
Csongrád	4,263	424	Szeged	169
Fejér	4,359	428	Székesfehérvár	102
Győr-Moson-Sopron	4,089	447	Győr	130
Hajdú-Bihar	6,211	542	Debrecen	206
Heves	3,637	314	Eger	56
Jász-Nagykún-Szolnok	5,582	395	Szolnok	75
Komárom-Esztergom	2,265	314	Tatabánya	70
Nógrád	2,544	208	Salgótarján	38
Pest	6,393[1]	1,213[2]	Budapest	1,712
Somogy	6,036	322	Kaposvár	68
Szabolcs-Szatmár-Bereg	5,936	565	Nyíregyháza	118
Tolna	3,703	236	Szekszárd	34
Vas	3,336	261	Szombathely	80
Veszprém	4,613	360	Veszprém	63
Zala	3,784	290	Zalaegerszeg	62
Budapest	525	1,712	(has county status)	

[1]Excluding area of Budapest. [2]Excluding population of Budapest.

The official language is Hungarian. 98·5% of the population have Hungarian as their mother tongue. Ethnic minorities have the right to education in their own language.

SOCIAL STATISTICS

2007: births, 97,613; deaths, 132,938; marriages, 40,842; divorces, 25,160. In 2000 the number of births rose for the first time in a decade. There were 2,450 suicides in 2007. Rates (per 1,000 population), 2007: birth, 9·7; death, 13·2; marriage, 4·1; divorce, 2·5. Population growth rate, 2005, –0·2%. The suicide rate, at 26·0 per 100,000 population in 2005, is one of the highest in the world. Among males it was nearly four times as high as among females. Expectation of life at birth, 2007, 69·2 years for males and 77·3 years for females. Infant mortality, 2007, 5·9 per 1,000 live births. Fertility rate, 2007, 1·3 births per woman.

CLIMATE

A humid continental climate, with warm summers and cold winters. Precipitation is generally greater in summer, with thunderstorms. Dry, clear weather is likely in autumn, but spring is damp and both seasons are of short duration. Budapest, Jan. 32°F (0°C), July 71°F (21·5°C). Annual rainfall 25" (625 mm). Pécs, Jan. 30°F (–0·7°C), July 71°F (21·5°C). Annual rainfall 26·4" (661 mm).

CONSTITUTION AND GOVERNMENT

On 18 Oct. 1989 the National Assembly approved by an 88% majority a constitution which abolished the People's Republic, and established Hungary as an independent, democratic, law-based state. The constitution was amended in 1997.

The head of state is the *President*, who is elected for five-year terms by the National Assembly.

The single-chamber *National Assembly* has 386 members, made up of 176 individual constituency winners, 152 allotted by proportional representation from county party lists and 58 from a national list. It is elected for four-year terms. A *Constitutional Court* was established in Jan. 1990 to review laws under consideration.

National Anthem

'Isten áldd meg a magyart' ('God bless the Hungarians'); words by Ferenc Kölcsey, tune by Ferenc Erkel.

GOVERNMENT CHRONOLOGY

(Fidesz-MPP = Fidesz-Hungarian Civic Party; FKgP = Independent Party of Smallholders, Agrarian Workers and Citizens; MDF = Hungarian Democratic Forum; MDP = Hungarian Workers' Party; MKP = Hungarian Communist Party; MSzMP = Hungarian Socialist Workers' Party; MSzP = Hungarian Socialist Party; SzDSz = Alliance of Free Democrats; n/p = non-partisan)

Presidents since 1946.

1946–48	FKgP	Zoltán Tildy
1948–50	MDP	Árpád Szakasits
1950–52	MDP	Sándor Rónai
1952–67	MSzMP	István Dobi
1967–87	MSzMP	Pál Losonczi
1987–88	MSzMP	Károly Németh
1988–89	MSzMP	Bruno Ferenc Straub
1989–90	MSzP	Mátyás Szűrös
1990–2000	SzDSz	Árpád Göncz
2000–05	n/p	Ferenc Mádl
2005–	n/p	László Sólyom

Prime Ministers since 1946.

1946–47	FKgP	Ferenc Nagy
1947–48	FKgP	Lajos Dinnyés
1948–52	MDP	István Dobi
1952–53	MDP	Mátyás Rákosi
1953–55	MDP	Imre Nagy
1955–56	MDP	András Hegedüs
1956	MDP	Imre Nagy
1956–58	MSzMP	János Kádár
1958–61	MSzMP	Ferenc Münnich
1961–65	MSzMP	János Kádár
1965–67	MSzMP	Gyula Kállai
1967–75	MSzMP	Jenő Fock
1975–87	MSzMP	György Lázár
1987–88	MSzMP	Károly Grósz
1988–90	MSzP	Miklós Németh
1990–93	MDF	József Antall
1993–94	MDF	Péter Boross
1994–98	MSzP	Gyula Horn
1998–2002	Fidesz-MPP	Viktor Orbán
2002–04	n/p (MSzP)	Péter Medgyessy
2004–09	MSzP	Ferenc Gyurcsány
2009–	n/p	Gordon Bajnai

Leaders of the Communist Party, 1945–89.

General Secretary of MKP/MDP

1945–	Mátyás Rákosi

First Secretaries of MDP/MSzMP

1953–56	Mátyás Rákosi
1956	Ernő Gerő
1956–88	János Kádár
1988–89	Károly Grósz

Collective Chairmanship of MSzMP

1989	Rezső Nyers; Miklós Németh; Károly Grósz; Imre Pozsgay

RECENT ELECTIONS

László Sólyom was elected president by the National Assembly on 7 June 2005 by 185 votes to 182. In two previous rounds he had failed to achieve the required two-thirds majority.

In the Hungarian parliamentary elections on 11 and 25 April 2010 the Fidesz-Hungarian Civic Union (Fidesz-MPP) won 263 seats in the 386-seat National Assembly (164 in 2006); the Socialist Party (MSzP) 59 (186 in 2006); Movement for a Better Hungary (Jobbik) 47 (none in 2006); Politics Can Be Different (LMP) 16 (none in 2006). One seat went to an independent candidate. Turnout in the first round was 64·4% and in the second round 44·2%.

European Parliament
Hungary has 22 (24 in 2004) representatives. At the June 2009 elections turnout was 36·3% (38·5% in 2004). Fidesz-Christian Democratic People's Party (Fidesz-KDNP) won 14 seats with 56·4% of votes cast (political affiliation in European Parliament: European People's Party); the MSzP, 4 with 17·4% (Progressive Alliance of Socialists and Democrats); Jobbik, 3 with 14·8% (non-attached); the MDF, 1 with 5·3% (European Conservatives and Reformists).

CURRENT ADMINISTRATION

President: László Sólyom; b. 1968 (in office since 5 Aug. 2005).

After Prime Minister Ferenc Gyurcsány announced his resignation in March 2009, Gordon Bajnai was the only candidate to receive cross-party support. He took office after a constructive vote of no-confidence in April 2009. Following the elections of April 2006 a coalition government was formed between the MSzP and the SzDSz. However, the SzDSz left the coalition in April 2008 resulting in a minority government consisting in March 2010 of:

Prime Minister: Gordon Bajnai; b. 1942 (ind.; sworn in 14 April 2009).

Head of Prime Minister's Office: Csaba Molnár. *Minister of Agriculture and Regional Development:* József Gráf. *Defence:* Imre Szekeres. *Education and Culture:* István Hiller. *Environment and Water:* Imre Szabó. *Finance:* Péter Oszkó. *Foreign Affairs:* Péter Balázs. *Health:* Dr Tamás Székely. *Justice and Law Enforcement:* Imre Forgács. *Local Government:* Zoltán Varga. *National Development and Economy:* István Varga. *Social Affairs and Labour:* László Herczog. *Transport, Telecommunication and Energy:* Péter Hónig. *Minister without Portfolio in Charge of Social Policy:* Péter Kiss. *Minister without Portfolio in Charge of Civilian Secret Services:* Gábor Juhász.

Office of the Prime Minister: http://www.meh.hu

CURRENT LEADERS

László Sólyom

Position
President

Introduction
As a professor of law and an environmental activist, László Sólyom was closely involved in the negotiations between opposition civic groups and the Communist regime that led to the fall of the Iron Curtain. For most of the 1990s Sólyom was chief justice in Hungary's newly-established constitutional court, overseeing sweeping reforms to the country's legal system. He became president on 5 Aug. 2005.

Early Life
László Sólyom was born in the southern Hungarian city of Pécs on 3 Jan. 1942. In 1965 he graduated in law from the University of Pécs. Later that year he qualified as a librarian at the National Széchenyi Library in Budapest. Between 1966 and 1969 he studied for a doctorate and worked as assistant lecturer at the institute of civil law at the Friedrich Schiller University in Jena in East Germany, an institution known as a dissident stronghold. Returning to Budapest in 1969, Sólyom became a fellow of the institute of political and legal sciences at the Hungarian Academy of Sciences (MTA). He also worked as a librarian at the library of parliament. In 1978 Sólyom joined the Eötvös Loránd University in Budapest as an assistant professor in the department of civil law. Five years later he became a professor at the university. He specialized in the field of the right to privacy, and was largely responsible for the introduction of data protection legislation in

Hungary. Sólyom also worked as a legal adviser to some of the country's new and radical civil and environmental organizations during the 1980s, and helped to prevent the construction of the controversial Nagymaros dam on the river Danube.

Sólyom was one of a group of dissident intellectuals that met at the town of Lakitelek in Sept. 1987 and formed the Hungarian Democratic Forum (MDF), which became a fully-fledged political party six months later. As a member of the MDF's executive committee, Sólyom participated in roundtable negotiations that precipitated the end of Hungary's Communist regime and the dismantling of the Iron Curtain between Hungary and Austria in May 1989. Sólyom was elected onto the newly-established constitutional court of Hungary on 24 Nov. 1989, and was made the court's chief justice shortly afterwards. He remained in this post for nine years, playing a key role in strengthening democracy in Hungary. Highly activist, with the power to review and invalidate parliamentary acts, the court did much to promote freedom of opinion and the removal of capital punishment.

When his mandate expired in 1998 Sólyom continued his academic career, lecturing at universities throughout Hungary and internationally, including the University of Cologne (Köln), Germany, where he was visiting professor in 1999 and 2000. He joined numerous boards and committees, including the Council of Europe's Commission for Democracy through Law, the Hungarian Accreditation Commission and the Geneva-based International Commission of Jurists. He became a member of the Védegylet (an environmental and civil-society organization) when it was founded in early 2000 and it was this group which nominated him to replace Ferenc Mádl as the country's president in 2005. Backed by the right-leaning opposition MDF and Fidesz, Sólyom went head-to-head with Katalin Szili, the parliamentary speaker and candidate of the Socialist-led coalition government. In a third-round run-off on 7 June 2005, Sólyom emerged victorious with 185 votes to Szili's 182.

Career in Office

Sólyom was inaugurated as president on 5 Aug. 2005. He has been critical of some politicians, accusing them of spending their time attacking each other instead of dealing with the key issues at hand. Although the position of president is largely a ceremonial role in Hungary, Sólyom can exercise his right to forward legislation to the constitutional court for review.

Gordon Bajnai

Position

Prime Minister

Introduction

Gordon Bajnai took office as prime minister in April 2009, following the resignation of Prime Minister Ferenc Gyurcsány. A career banker, Bajnai had previously served in the ministry of economics and pledged to introduce a raft of economic reforms. He did not stand for re-election in April 2010 and was scheduled to leave office on 14 May.

Early Life

Born on 5 March 1968 in the southern Hungarian town of Szeged, György Gordon Bajnai was raised in Baja. He studied international relations at the Budapest University of Economic Sciences (now Corvinus University) before entering the banking sector, working from 1991–93 at Creditum Financial Consulting Ltd. Following a 1993 internship at the European Bank for Reconstruction and Development in London, he joined Eurocorp International Finance Ltd (then under the directorship of Ferenc Gyurcsány).

From 1995–2000 Bajnai was managing director and then deputy chief executive officer of brokerage firm CA-IB Securities, where he oversaw the listing of several major companies on the stock exchange. From 2000–05 he was chief executive officer of Wallis ZRT, a trade and investment group with extensive holdings. During this period he served as a member of the board of directors of Graboplast, a flooring firm in which Wallis ZRT acquired a majority shareholding, and oversaw the liquidation of poultry-producing company Hajdu-Bet.

Bajnai became president of Budapest Airport Inc. in 2005, when he was also appointed to the supervisory committee of Zwack Inc. and became a member of the economic council of Corvinus University. On 1 July 2006 Prime Minister Gyurcsány appointed him head of the National Development Agency as part of a drive to prepare Hungary for eurozone membership. Bajnai became local government minister in 2007. In Oct. 2008, after the Alliance of Free Democrats (SzDSz) left the coalition government in protest at the slowing of economic reforms, Bajnai's department was renamed the ministry for national development and economy.

In March 2009, against a background of political deadlock, Gyurcsány announced that he would stand down and pass the premiership to the candidate with the greatest parliamentary support. On 30 March 2009 Bajnai won the backing of both the ruling Socialist Party (MSzP) and the SzDSz for his manifesto of economic reforms that combined cuts in welfare benefits with a stimulus package for business. Presenting himself as politically independent, Bajnai promised not to stand for re-election in polling scheduled for April 2010. On 14 April 2009 Gyurcsány initiated a constructive vote of no confidence and resigned in favour of Bajnai.

Career in Office

Bajnai was sworn in as prime minister on 14 April 2009 with 204 votes in favour and none against. He emphasized the severity of Hungary's economic crisis, predicting that the economy could shrink by up to 6% over the following year and advocating stringent austerity measures to reverse the decline. He identified his primary task as crisis management and announced that his new cabinet was selected on the basis of expertise rather than party allegiance. His early moves to cut state benefits, restructure taxes and invest in industry were well received by international markets. However, he faced severe challenges in winning public acceptance of his welfare reforms, especially changes to pension and benefit entitlement. He did not contest the general election of April 2010, having previously announced that he would not hold office for more than a year. He was scheduled to hand over power to Viktor Orbán of Fidesz-MPP on 14 May 2010.

DEFENCE

The President of the Republic is C.-in-C. of the armed forces.

Conscription was abolished in 2004.

In 2006 defence expenditure totalled US$1,323m. (US$133 per capita), representing 1·2% of GDP. In 1985 defence expenditure had represented 6·8% of GDP.

Army

The strength of the Army was (2005) 15,814. There is an additional force of 12,000 border guards.

Air Force

The Air Force had a strength (2005) of 6,545. There were 77 combat aircraft in 2005, including MiG-21s, MiG-23s, MiG-29s and Su-22s, plus 55 in store, and 45 attack helicopters.

INTERNATIONAL RELATIONS

Hungary is a member of the UN, World Bank, IMF and several other UN specialized agencies, WTO, EU, Council of Europe, OSCE, CERN, CEI, Danube Commission, BIS, IOM, NATO, OECD, Antarctic Treaty and is an associate member of the WEU. Hungary held a referendum on EU membership on 12 April 2003, in which 83·8% of votes cast were in favour of accession, with 16·2% against, although turnout was only 45·6%. It became a member of the EU on 1 May 2004. In 2000 Hungary introduced a visa requirement for Russians entering the country as one of the conditions for EU membership.

In Dec. 2007 Hungary acceded to the Schengen accord, which abolishes border controls between Hungary, Austria, Belgium, Czech Republic, Denmark, Estonia, Finland, France, Germany, Greece, Iceland, Italy, Latvia, Lithuania, Luxembourg, Malta, Netherlands, Norway, Poland, Portugal, Slovakia, Slovenia, Spain, Sweden and Switzerland.

Hungary has had a long-standing dispute with Slovakia over the Gabčíkovo-Nagymaros Project, involving the building of dam structures in both countries for the production of electric power, flood control and improvement of navigation on the Danube as agreed in a treaty signed in 1977 between Hungary and Czechoslovakia. In late 1998 Slovakia and Hungary signed a protocol easing tensions between the two nations and settling differences over the dam.

ECONOMY

Agriculture accounted for 4% of GDP in 2008, industry 29% and services 66%.

Overview

Aided by market-oriented policies in the last two decades of communist rule and structural and stabilization measures implemented in the 1990s, Hungary's transition from communism was among the smoothest of the former Eastern Bloc nations. Since the collapse of communism, services have accounted for an increasing share of GDP. However, manufacturing, concentrated in low-cost industrial assembly and processing, has been the main engine of growth.

Hungary has attracted the highest level of foreign direct investment in the region after the Czech Republic. This has helped to modernize production and to redirect trade from east to west. Since the mid-1990s the majority of state assets have been privatized and the private sector now accounts for over 80% of GDP. However, growth has slowed since 2005 and was further weakened by a fiscal consolidation package in mid-2006. Unemployment levels are high and rising, reaching 10·1% in 2009 (compared to 7·8% in 2008). The labour force participation rate (the proportion of economically active working-age persons in an economy) is among the lowest in the OECD.

In the second half of 2008 the Hungarian forint lost nearly 20% of its value against the euro and the dollar. High levels of foreign debt increased strain. In Oct. 2008 a US$25bn. rescue package was agreed jointly with the IMF, EU and the World Bank to alleviate the effects of the global financial crisis. A series of measures were implemented to restore economic health, with investor trust increasing during 2009. The government raised a further €1bn. in July 2009 by selling bonds on international capital markets. Eurozone recovery has prompted rising demand for Hungarian exports, which account for 80% of GDP.

Currency

A decree of 26 July 1946 instituted a new monetary unit, the *forint* (HUF) of 100 *fillér*. The forint was made fully convertible in Jan. 1991 and moves in a 15% band against the euro either side of a central rate of €1=282·4 forints. Inflation rates (based on OECD statistics):

1999	*2000*	*2001*	*2002*	*2003*	*2004*	*2005*	*2006*	*2007*	*2008*
10·0%	9·8%	9·1%	5·3%	4·7%	6·7%	3·6%	3·9%	8·0%	6·0%

The inflation rate of 3·6% in 2005 was the lowest in more than 25 years. Foreign exchange reserves were US$42,988m. in Sept. 2009 and gold reserves 99,000 troy oz. Total money supply in Aug. 2009 was 5,930·4bn. forints.

Budget

Budgetary central government revenues totalled 6,109·6bn. forints in 2006 (5,584·5bn. forints in 2005); expenditures totalled 8,321·0bn. forints in 2006 (6,988·9bn. forints in 2005). Principal sources of revenue in 2006: taxes on goods and services, 2,940·1bn. forints; taxes on income, profits and capital gains, 1,693·8bn. forints; grants, 335·4bn. forints. Main items of expenditure by economic type in 2006: grants, 2,664·8bn. forints; compensation of employees, 1,370·9bn. forints; social benefits, 1,169·5bn. forints.

VAT is 25% (reduced rates, 18% and 5%).

Performance

Real GDP growth rates (based on OECD statistics):

1999	*2000*	*2001*	*2002*	*2003*	*2004*	*2005*	*2006*	*2007*	2008
4·2%	4·9%	4·1%	4·4%	4·3%	4·9%	3·5%	4·0%	1·0%	0·6%

Real GDP growth was –6·3% in 2009 according to the Hungarian Central Statistical Office. Total GDP was US$154·7bn. in 2008.

Banking and Finance

In 1987 a two-tier system was established. The National Bank (*Director,* András Simor) remained the central state financial institution. It is responsible for the operation of monetary policy and the foreign exchange system. In Sept. 2004 the Hungarian financial system comprised 32 banks, 5 specialized credit institutions, 178 co-operatives, 199 financial enterprises, 18 investment enterprises, 24 investment funds, 65 insurance companies and 168 pension/health related funds. They are all supervised by the Hungarian Financial Supervisory Authority (HFSA).

The largest bank is OTP Bank Rt. (the National Savings and Commercial Bank of Hungary), with assets in 2002 of 2,393bn. forints. Other leading banks are K+H (Hungarian Commercial and Credit Bank) and MKB (Hungarian Foreign Trade Bank). A law of June 1991 sets capital and reserve requirements, and provides for foreign investment in Hungarian banks. Permission is needed for investments of more than 10%. Privatization of the banking system is well under way.

At the end of 2008 foreign direct investment stocks totalled US$63·7bn.

The Hungarian International Trade Bank opened in London in 1973. In 1980 the Central European International Bank was set up in Budapest with seven western banks holding 66% of the shares.

A stock exchange was opened in Budapest in Jan. 1989.

ENERGY AND NATURAL RESOURCES

Environment

Hungary's carbon dioxide emissions from the consumption and flaring of fossil fuels in 2008 were the equivalent of 5·7 tonnes per capita.

Electricity

Installed capacity in 2004 was 8·6m. kW, about a fifth of which is nuclear. There is an 880 MW nuclear power station at Paks with four reactors. It produced 35% of total output in 2004. In 2004 Hungary produced 33·7bn. kWh of electricity and 10·5bn. kWh were imported. Total consumption in 2004 (including domestic consumption, power station consumption, network losses and exports) was 41·2bn. kWh. Consumption per capita in 2004 was 4,070 kWh.

Oil and Gas

Oil and natural gas are found in the Szeged basin and Zala county. Oil production in 2004 was 7m. bbls. Natural gas production in 2007 was 2·7bn. cu. metres, with proven reserves of 8bn. cu. metres in the same year. Hungary relies on Russia for almost all of its oil and much of its gas.

Minerals
Production in 1,000 tonnes (2004): lignite, 8,470; bauxite, 647; hard coal, 259.

Agriculture
Agricultural land was collectivized in 1950. It was announced in 1990 that land would be restored to its pre-collectivization owners if they wished to cultivate it. A law of April 1994 restricts the area of land that may be bought by individuals to 300 ha., and prohibits the sale of arable land and land in conservation zones to companies and foreign nationals. Today, although 90% of all cultivated land is in private hands, most farms are little more than smallholdings. In 2003 the agricultural area was 5·87m. ha. (equivalent to 63% of the total land area); arable land constituted 4·52m. ha.

Agricultural production dropped drastically from 1989 to 2003, but made a recovery in 2004. Production figures (2004, in 1,000 tonnes): maize, 8,317 (6,747 in 1989); wheat, 6,020 (6,509 in 1989); sugar beets, 3,130 (5,277 in 1989); barley, 1,423; sunflower seeds, 1,198; grapes, 772; potatoes, 767; apples, 666.

Livestock has also drastically decreased since 1989 from 7·7m. pigs to 4·1m. by 2004, from 1·6m. cattle to 723,000, and from 2·1m. sheep to 1·4m. Thus the pig stock, cattle stock and sheep stock have all declined to levels not seen in fifty years.

The north shore of Lake Balaton, Villány and the Tokaj area are important wine-producing districts. Wine production in 2003 was 388m. litres.

Forestry
The forest area in 2003 was 1·77m. ha., or 19·1% of the land area. Timber production in 2007 was 5·64m. cu. metres.

Fisheries
There are fisheries in the rivers Danube and Tisza and Lake Balaton. In 2003 there were 33,100 ha. of commercial fishponds. In 2005 total catch was 7,609 tonnes, exclusively from inland fishing.

INDUSTRY
The leading companies by market capitalization in Hungary in March 2009 were MOL Magyar Olaj-és Gázipari Rt (Hungarian Oil and Gas Plc), US$4·7bn.; Magyar Telekom, US$2·4bn.; and OTP Bank Rt., US$2·3bn.

Manufacturing output grew by an average of 8·5% annually between 1992 and 2002.

Production, 2007, in 1,000 tonnes: rolled steel products, 103,347; distillate fuel oil, 3,720; cement, 3,552; crude steel, 2,232; plastics, 1,672; petrol (2004), 1,465; fertilizers, 359; residual fuel oil (2004), 313; alumina (2006), 270; refrigerators, 2,909,786 units; radio sets, 2,367,763 units; beer, 749·7m. litres.

Labour
In 2005 out of an economically active population of 4,205,400 there were 3,901,500 employed persons, of which 3,367,300 were employees. Among the employed persons in 2001, 59·6% worked in services, 34·2% in industry and construction, and 6·2% in agriculture. Average gross monthly wages of full-time employees in 2007: 185,004 forints. Minimum monthly wage, 2006, 62,500 forints (more than twice the 2000 level). In Dec. 2009 Hungary had an unemployment rate of 10·7%. The normal retirement age is 62 but it is set to be increased gradually to 65 for both men and women by 2017.

Trade Unions
The former official Communist organization (National Council of Trade Unions), renamed the National Confederation of Hungarian Trade Unions (MSZOSZ), groups 70 organizations and claimed 240,000 members in 2003. A law of 1991 abolished its obligatory levy on pay packets. Other major workers' organizations are (with 2003 membership): the Association of Autonomous Trade Unions (ASZSZ, 150,000); Co-operation Forum of Trade Unions (SZEF, 270,000); Confederation of Unions of Professionals (ESZT, 85,000); Democratic League of Independent Trade Unions (Liga, 100,000); National Federation of Workers' Councils (MOSZ, 56,000).

INTERNATIONAL TRADE
Foreign debt was US$66,119m. in 2005. An import surcharge imposed in March 1995 was abolished in July 1997.

Imports and Exports
In 2007 the value of imports was US$93,147m. and that of exports US$92,986m. (up from US$46,753m. and US$43,475m. respectively in 2003). Hungary's foreign trade has been expanding at a very fast rate, with the value of both its imports and its exports trebling between 1996 and 2004.

Machinery and transport equipment accounted for 52·5% of imports and 62·4% of exports in 2007, and manufactured goods 32·1% of imports and 26·5% of exports. 79·1% of exports in 2007 went to European Union member countries, the highest share of any of the central and eastern European countries that joined the EU in May 2004. In 2007, 26·8% of imports came from Germany and 28·4% of exports went to Germany. Russia was the second biggest supplier of imports in 2007 (6·9% of the total) and Italy the second biggest market for exports (5·6%). In 2007, 3·1% of exports went to Russia, down from 13·1% in 1992.

COMMUNICATIONS
Roads
In 2007 there were 195,719 km of roads, including 1,157 km of motorways, 6,745 km of main roads and 23,280 of secondary roads. Passenger cars numbered (2007) 3,012,200; lorries and vans, 829,800; motorcycles and mopeds, 135,900; and buses and coaches, 17,900. In 2007 there were 20,635 road accidents with 1,232 fatalities.

Rail
In 2003 the rail network was 7,685 km in length; 49·9m. tonnes of freight and 159·8m. passengers were carried. There is a metro in Budapest (30·1 km), and tram/light rail networks in Budapest (332·0 km), Debrecen, Miskolc and Szeged.

Civil Aviation
Budapest airport (Ferihegy) handled 4,482,000 passengers in 2002 (all on international flights) and 42,380 tonnes of freight. The national carrier, Malév, was privatized in Feb. 2007. It carried 2,354,080 passengers in 2003.

Shipping
There are 1,622 km of navigable waterways. In 2002, along the Hungarian section of the Danube River, 4,801 vessels entered the country on their way to a Hungarian destination, 4,916 vessels left Hungary for other countries and 3,331 vessels were in transit. In 2003, 2·06m. tonnes of cargo and 1·42m. passengers were carried. Merchant shipping totalled 4,000 GRT in 2002. The Hungarian Shipping Company (MAHART) has agencies at Amsterdam, Alexandria, Algiers, Beirut, Rijeka and Trieste. It has 23 ships and runs scheduled services between Budapest and Esztergom.

Telecommunications
In 2008 there were 3,094,000 main (fixed) telephone lines. In the same year mobile phone subscribers numbered 12,224,000 (1,220·9 per 1,000 persons). Matav, the privatized former national telephone company, still has more than 80% of the fixed line market. There were 3,201,000 PCs in use in 2006 and internet users numbered 5,873,000 in 2008. There were 15·7 broadband subscribers per 100 inhabitants in June 2008.

Postal Services
In 2007 there were 2,744 post offices.

SOCIAL INSTITUTIONS

Justice

The administration of justice is the responsibility of the Procurator-General, elected by Parliament for six years. There are 111 local courts, 20 labour law courts, 20 county courts, six district courts and a Supreme Court. Criminal proceedings are dealt with by the regional courts through three-member councils and by the county courts and the Supreme Court in five-member councils. A new Civil Code was adopted in 1978 and a new Criminal Code in 1979.

Regional courts act as courts of first instance; county courts as either courts of first instance or of appeal. The Supreme Court acts normally as an appeal court, but may act as a court of first instance in cases submitted to it by the Public Prosecutor. All courts, when acting as courts of first instance, consist of one professional judge and two lay assessors, and, as courts of appeal, of three professional judges. Local government Executive Committees may try petty offences.

Regional and county judges and assessors are elected by the appropriate local councils; members of the Supreme Court by Parliament.

The Office of Ombudsman was instituted in 1993. He or she is elected by parliament for a six-year term, renewable once.

There are also military courts of the first instance. Military cases of the second instance go before the Supreme Court.

The death penalty was abolished in Oct. 1990.

The population in penal institutions in Nov. 2003 was 16,700 (165 per 100,000 of national population). There were 87,476 convictions of adults and 6,726 of juvenile offenders in 2003; 34% of convictions resulted in custodial sentences (most of them suspended). 18,000 crimes against the person were detected in 2003, including 227 homicides.

Education

Adult literacy rate in 2003 was 99·3% (male, 99·4%; female, 99·3%). Education is free and compulsory from five to 16. Primary schooling ends at 14; thereafter education is continued at secondary, secondary technical or secondary vocational schools, which offer diplomas entitling students to apply for higher education, or at vocational training schools which offer tradesmen's diplomas. Students at the latter may also take the secondary school diploma examinations after two years of evening or correspondence study. Optional religious education was introduced in schools in 1990.

In 2003–04 there were: 4,610 kindergartens with 31,383 teachers and 327,500 pupils; 3,748 primary schools with 89,784 teachers and 913,600 pupils; and 1,622 secondary schools (including vocational schools) with 38,479 teachers and 531,400 pupils (of which 438,100 were full-time). 409,075 students were enrolled in tertiary education at 68 institutions in 2003–04: of these, 366,947 were at university and college level (204,910 full-time and 162,037 part-time). In 1990 only 11% of 18- to 23-year-olds were enrolled in higher education. By 2000 the proportion had risen to 35%; 53% of 18- to 22-year olds were enrolled in full-time courses in 2007–08, exceeding the target of 50% set for 2010.

In 2007–08 total expenditure on education came to 5·2% of GNI and 14·4% of total government spending.

Health

In 2003 there were 32,877 doctors, 5,347 dentists, 5,125 pharmacists, 4,949 midwives and 87,381 nurses. While there is an excess supply of doctors, there are too few nurses and wages for both groups are exceptionally low. In 2003 there were 178 hospitals with 79,368 beds. Spending on health accounted for 7·4% of GDP in 2007.

Welfare

In 1998 the Hungarian parliament decided to place the financial funds of health and pension insurance under government supervision. The self-governing bodies which had previously been responsible for this were dissolved. Medical treatment is free. Patients bear 15% of the cost of medicines. Sickness benefit is 75% of wages, old age pensions 60–70%. In 2003, 1·9trn. forints was spent on pensions and pension-like benefits for 3·05m. recipients (old age 53%, disability or reduced working ability 34%, and widows and other pensions 13%); the average monthly amount of benefit per capita was 50,428 forints. Family benefits totalled about 2·1% of GDP in 2006. On a monthly basis as of Jan. 2004, 1·3m. families were receiving family allowance on behalf of 2·1m. children and child care allowance was being paid for 164,000 children.

RELIGION

Church-state affairs are regulated by a law of Feb. 1990 which guarantees freedom of conscience and religion and separates church and state by prohibiting state interference in church affairs. Religious matters are the concern of the Department for Church Relations, under the auspices of the Prime Minister's Office.

According to the 2001 census, 51·9% of the population was Roman Catholic (5·3m. people), 15·9% Calvinist (1·6m.), 3·0% Lutheran (0·3m.) and 2·6% Greek Catholic (0·27m.). Adherents to smaller Christian faiths, including Baptists, other Protestant groups, Adventists and a range of Orthodox denominations, numbered around 98,000. About 0·1% of the population was Jewish in 2001.

The Primate of Hungary is Péter Erdő, Archbishop of Esztergom-Budapest, installed in Jan. 2003. There are 11 dioceses, all with bishops or archbishops. There is one Uniate bishopric. In Feb. 2010 the Roman Catholic church had two cardinals.

CULTURE

Pécs is one of three European Capitals of Culture for 2010. The title attracts large European Union grants.

World Heritage Sites

Sites under Hungarian jurisdiction which appear on UNESCO's World Heritage List are (with year entered on list): Budapest, and specifically the Banks of the Danube and the Buda Castle Quarter (1987 and 2002); Hollókő (1987), a preserved settlement developed during the 17th and 18th centuries; Millenary Benedictine Monastery of Pannonhalma and its Natural Environment (1996), first settled by Benedictine monks in 996; Hortobágy National Park (1999), a large area of plains and wetlands in eastern Hungary; Pécs (Sopianae) Early Christian Cemetery (2000), a series of decorated tombs dating from the 4th century; Tokaj Wine Region Historic Cultural Landscape (2002), a thousand-year-old wine-producing area.

Hungary also shares two UNESCO sites: the Caves of Aggtelek and Slovak Karst (1995, 2000 and 2008), a complex of 712 temperate-zone karstic caves, is shared with Slovakia; the Cultural Landscape of Fertö/Neusiedlersee (2001), an area that has acted as a meeting place for different cultures for 8,000 years, is shared with Austria.

Broadcasting

Magyar Rádió operates three public networks and an external service, Rádió Budapest. There are numerous commercial and local radio stations. State-owned Magyar Televízió operates two TV channels (colour by PAL). Duna Televízió broadcasts by satellite to Hungarians abroad. TV2 and RTL-KLUB are national private terrestrial channels. There were 5·76m. TV sets in use in 2006.

Cinema

There were 400 cinema screens in 2007; attendances in 2007 totalled 10·9m. In 2006, 46 full-length feature films were made.

Press
In 2006 there were 31 daily newspapers with a combined circulation of 1,775,000, at a rate of 176 per 1,000 inhabitants. The most widely read newspapers are the free tabloid Metro and the broadsheets Blikk and Észak-Keleti Napló. In 2004 there were 244 non-dailies (211 paid-for and 33 free). A total of 13,239 book titles were published in 2007 in 42·63m. copies.

Tourism
In 2005 there were 38·56m. foreign tourists. 18·62m. Hungarians travelled abroad in 2005. Tourist receipts in 2005 amounted to US$4·58bn. 5% of GDP is produced by tourism.

Festivals
The Budapest Spring Festival, comprising music, theatre, dance etc., takes place in March. The Balaton Festival is in May and the Szeged Open-Air Theatre Festival is in July–Aug.

Libraries
In 2007 there were 2,965 public libraries and 15 national and special libraries. They held a combined 56,075,000 volumes for 1,488,000 registered users.

Theatre and Opera
Hungary had 54 theatres in 2003.

Museums and Galleries
There were 794 museums in 2003. 10·3m. people visited museums in the same year.

DIPLOMATIC REPRESENTATIVES
Of Hungary in the United Kingdom (35 Eaton Pl., London, SW1X 8BY)
Ambassador: Borbála Czakó.

Of the United Kingdom in Hungary (Harmincad Utca 6, Budapest 1051)
Ambassador: Greg Dorey.

Of Hungary in the USA (3910 Shoemaker St., NW, Washington, D.C., 20008)
Ambassador: Béla Szombati.

Of the USA in Hungary (Szabadság Tér 12, Budapest 1054)
Ambassador: Eleni Tsakopoulos Kounalakis.

Of Hungary to the United Nations
Ambassador: Márta Horváth Fekszi.

Of Hungary to the European Union
Permanent Representative: Gábor Iván.

FURTHER READING

Central Statistical Office. *Statisztikai Évkönyv.* Annual since 1871.—*Magyar Statisztikai Zsebkönyv.* Annual.—*Statistical Yearbook.*—*Statistical Handbook of Hungary.*—*Monthly Bulletin of Statistics.*

Bozóki, A., *et al.*, (eds.) *Post-Communist Transition: Emerging Pluralism in Hungary.* 1992

Burawoy, M. and Lukács, J., *The Radiant Past: Ideology and Reality in Hungary's Road to Capitalism.* 1992

Cox, T. and Furlong, A. (eds.) *Hungary: the Politics of Transition.* 1995

Geró, A., *Modern Hungarian Society in the Making: the Unfinished Experience*; translated from Hungarian. 1995

Kontler, László, *A History of Hungary.* 2002

Mitchell, K. D. (ed.) *Political Pluralism in Hungary and Poland: Perspectives on the Reforms.* 1992

Molnár, Miklós, *A Concise History of Hungary.* 2001

Rose-Ackerman, Susan, *From Elections to Democracy: Building Accountable Government in Hungary and Poland.* 2007

Schiemann, John W., *The Politics of Pact-Making: Hungary's Negotiated Transition to Democracy in Comparative Perspective.* 2005

Szekely, I. P., *Hungary: an Economy in Transition.* 1993

National library: Széchényi Library, Budavári Palota F épület, 1827 Budapest. *Director General:* István Monok.

National Statistical Office: Központi Statisztikai Hivatal/Central Statistical Office, Keleti Károly u. 5/7, H-1024 Budapest. *Director:* Dr Pál Belyó.

Website: http://portal.ksh.hu

ICELAND

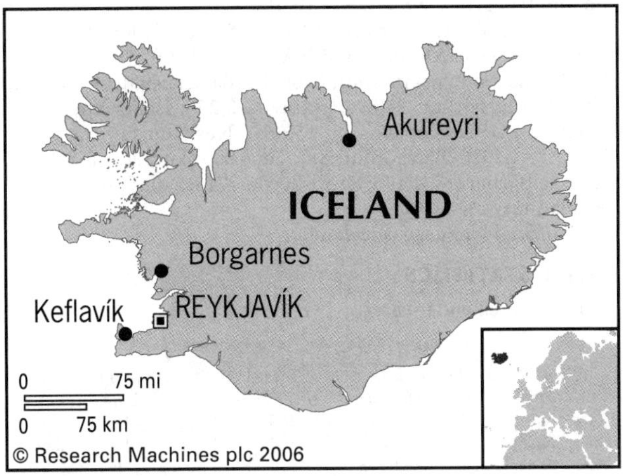

Lyðveldið Ísland
(Republic of Iceland)

Capital: Reykjavík
Population estimate, 2010: 329,000
GDP per capita, 2007: (PPP$) 35,742
HDI/world rank: 0·969/3

KEY HISTORICAL EVENTS

Scandinavia's North Atlantic outpost was first settled in 874. According to the *Landnámabók* or 'book of settlements', the first to land was Ingólfr Arnarson, who came from Norway to live on the site of present-day Reykjavík. He was followed by some 400 migrants, mainly from Norway but also from other Nordic countries and from Norse settlements in the British Isles.

A ruling class was soon formed by chieftains, known as the *godar*. In 930 they established the first ever democratic national assembly, the *Alþingi* (Althing). Primarily an adjudicating body, it also served as a legislature and as a fair, a marriage mart and as a national celebration in which a large proportion of the Icelandic population participated for two weeks each June. The first notable event in its history occurred in 1000 when, by majority decision, Christianity was adopted as Iceland's official religion. Despite the change, the *godar* remained politically important and some of them were ordained. Bishoprics were established at Skálholt in 1056 and at Hólar in 1106. It was not until the 1800s, after the bishoprics were united, that Reykjavík became the new episcopal see, making it the leading community.

Trade flourished with homespun woollen cloth as the chief export, although certain materials such as grain and timber had to be imported. Iceland's only indigenous wood, birchwood, which grew in abundance yet proved unsuitable for building, later became valuable in making charcoal.

In the mid-13th century there were power struggles between the *godar*. With the 'Old Treaty' of 1262, the *godar* were persuaded to swear allegiance to the king of Norway, bringing Iceland under Norwegian rule but leaving it with internal autonomy. When Norway was joined with Denmark in 1380, Iceland still retained the Althing as well as its own code of law.

In the 14th century, the expansion of fishing to satisfy European demand stimulated agriculture and other basic industries. Iceland's newfound prosperity encouraged trade between the Icelandic fisherman and traders in Bergen, Norway. English traders in Bergen were keen to bypass Norwegian importers and instead began trading directly with Iceland. The Danish were largely unsuccessful in preventing this and it was not until the 16th century, when the English turned to the North American fishing grounds, that hostilities ceased.

Iceland's economic progress was checked when birchwood became depleted. Coupled with over-grazing, this led to soil erosion and put an end to crop growth. Further troubles came in the 15th century when Iceland fell victim to the Black Death, on two occasions losing around half of the population.

With the advent of Lutheranism in the first half of the 16th century, Iceland resisted Denmark's efforts to impose the Reformation on their North Atlantic possession. The bishoprics of Skálholt and Hólar were eventually overcome in 1550, marking the consolidation of Danish power over Iceland. In 1602 a royal decree gave all foreign trading rights in Iceland exclusively to Danish merchants. This restriction, which lasted until 1787, virtually ended Iceland's contacts with England and Germany, their one-time trading partners. Absolutism in Denmark and Norway under King Frederick III was recognized by Iceland in 1662, further strengthening external rule, and after economic hardship in the 18th century (in the 1780s famine killed one-fifth of the population) Iceland's receding status was confirmed. When Norway split from Denmark in 1814 there were no similar calls for secession from Iceland.

Home Rule

In the 1830s a Danish consultative assembly was formed in which Iceland was given two seats. Denmark's transition to a system of representative democratic government after Frederick VII relinquished absolute power in 1848 did not extend to Iceland. After failures to reach agreement over the country's status, the Althing decided that 1874, the year that marked a thousand years of settlement, should be chosen as the year when it gained a new constitution. This was to provide the Althing with legislative if not executive control. During this period Iceland's economy continued to fare badly. With soil erosion still a problem, the strains of population growth forced mass emigration to North America. Around 15,000 emigrants left Iceland between 1870 and 1914. In 1904, after several decades of pressure for autonomy and, from 1901 onwards, support from the governing Danish Liberal party, Iceland finally achieved home rule.

Economic progress was led by the motorization of the fishing industry and an expanded labour force. In 1916 a national trade unions organization was established and a process of urbanization began as the population moved towards the coastal fishing villages. Educational reform brought the introduction of compulsory education and in 1911, the establishment of the University of Iceland at Reykjavík.

In 1918 Iceland became a separate state under the Danish crown, with only foreign affairs remaining under Danish jurisdiction. The following decades were overshadowed by the influence of the 1930s' depression and the Spanish Civil War in 1936, the latter bringing an end to the lucrative fish trade with Spain.

In 1944 Iceland declared independence since Denmark was then occupied by Nazi Germany. The termination of the union was little more than a formality, the German invasion of Denmark in 1940 having effectively ended that country's responsibility for Iceland's foreign relations.

Iceland was occupied peacefully by Britain in 1940 but US troops took over a year later. They improved roads and docks, built an airport and paid high wages. An American request for a long-term lease on three military bases was reviewed sympathetically. But the continuing presence of American forces somehow gave the lie to the independence so recently celebrated. The answer was for Iceland to join NATO. Objections to the American-run Keflavík airbase were gradually withdrawn and in 1951 a defence agreement with the United States allowed for an increase in the number of troops brought in 'to defend Iceland and ... to ensure the security of the seas around the country'. Greater integration with Europe came with joining the European Free Trade Association in 1970.

Fish remained central to the economy, accounting for 90% of the export trade. But there were worries about over-dependence on a single product and concern that other nations were taking too large a share of the Icelandic catch. In 1948 the demarcation of new fishing zones was made subject to Icelandic jurisdiction. Two years later one mile was added to the three-mile offshore zone which Iceland had administered since 1901. This was just acceptable to other fishing nations but when, in 1958, the limit was extended to 12 miles, Britain sent naval vessels to protect trawlers from harassment and arrest. This was the first Cod War, a cat-and-mouse game between the British navy and coastguard patrols which continued to 1961. At that point Britain and West Germany, the other fishing nation involved in the dispute, accepted the 12-mile zone on condition that if Iceland intended to widen her jurisdiction still further she had to give six months' notice of her intention and, if challenged, refer her claims to the International Court of Justice at The Hague.

In 1971, however, the government fulfilled its promise to do something about over-fishing by unilaterally extending the offshore zone to 50 miles. Despite a clear contravention of treaty commitment, Iceland gained sympathy as the tiny nation fighting the giants. Also in Iceland's favour was the move by Britain and members of the European Community to extend their jurisdiction over the continental shelf. A law officially expanding the Icelandic fishery limits to 50 miles came into force on 1 Sept. 1972. However, a second Cod War began shortly after as British and German trawlers continued to fish within the new zone. Hostility quickly intensified, with the Icelandic Coast Guard deploying net cutters to prevent the ships securing their catch. An agreement was signed on 8 Nov. 1973 confining British trawlers to specific areas within the 50 mile catch zone, and limiting their annual catch to 130,000 tonnes.

This agreement expired in Nov. 1975, after which Iceland declared the ocean up to 200 miles from its coast to be under Icelandic authority, and a third Cod War began. Britain protested at the 200-mile limit but when the talks reached stalemate in Dec. 1976, British vessels were nevertheless banned from Icelandic waters.

TERRITORY AND POPULATION

Iceland is an island in the North Atlantic, close to the Arctic Circle. Area, 102,819 sq. km (39,698 sq. miles).

There are eight regions:

Region	*Inhabited land (sq. km)*	*Mountain pasture (sq. km)*	*Waste-land (sq. km)*	*Total area (sq. km)*	*Population (1 Jan. 2008)*
Capital area	1,266	716	—	1,982	196,564
Southern Peninsula					20,446
West	5,011	3,415	275	8,701	15,462
Western Fjords	4,130	3,698	1,652	9,470	7,299
Northland West	4,867	5,278	2,948	13,093	7,360
Northland East	9,890	6,727	5,751	22,368	28,821
East	16,921	17,929	12,555	21,991	13,919
South				25,214	23,505
Iceland	42,085	37,553	23,181	102,819	313,376

Of the population of 313,376 in 2008, 21,406 were domiciled in rural districts and 291,970 (93·2%) in towns and villages (of over 200 inhabitants). Population density (2008), 3·0 per sq. km.

The UN gives an estimated population for 2010 of 329,000.

The population is predominantly Icelandic. On 1 Jan. 2008 foreigners numbered 21,434 (8,488 Polish, 1,332 Lithuanian, 984 German, 966 Danish, 890 Portuguese, 743 Filipinos, 651 Serbs and Montenegrins, 598 US, 545 Thai).

The capital, Reykjavík, had on 1 Jan. 2008 a population of 116,992; other towns were: Akranes, 6,359; Akureyri, 17,097; Bolungarvík, 905; Dalvík, 1,410; Eskifjörður, 1,100; Garðabær, 9,931; Grindavík, 2,762; Hafnarfjörður, 24,895; Húsavík, 2,256; Ísafjörður, 2,690; Keflavík, 8,192; Kópavogur, 28,665; Neskaupstaður, 1,436; Njarðvík, 4,402; Ólafsfjörður, 881; Sauðárkrókur, 2,554; Selfoss, 6,275; Seltjarnarnes, 4,446; Seyðisfjörður, 713; Siglufjörður, 1,307; Vestmannaeyjar, 4,036.

The official language is Icelandic.

SOCIAL STATISTICS

Statistics for calendar years:

	Live births	*Still-born*	*Marriages*	*Divorces*	*Deaths*	*Infant deaths*	*Net immi-gration*
2004	4,234	15	1,515	560	1,824	12	530
2005	4,280	8	1,607	564	1,838	10	3,860
2006	4,415	13	1,753	516	1,903	6	5,255
2007	4,560	7	1,708	515	1,943	9	3,097

2007 rates per 1,000 population: births, 14·6; deaths, 6·2. 63·8% of births are to unmarried mothers, the highest percentage in Europe. Population growth rate, 2007, 1·9%. In 2007 the most popular age range for marrying was 30–34 for both males and females. Life expectancy, 2007: males, 79·4 years; females, 82·9. Iceland has the highest male life expectancy of any country. Infant mortality, 2007, 2·0 per 1,000 live births (one of the lowest rates in the world); fertility rate, 2007, 2·1 births per woman.

CLIMATE

The climate is cool temperate oceanic and rather changeable, but mild for its latitude because of the Gulf Stream and prevailing S.W. winds. Precipitation is high in upland areas, mainly in the form of snow. Reykjavík, Jan. 30·9°F (–0·6°C), July 55·0°F (12·8°C). Annual rainfall, 2007: 44·3" (1,125 mm).

CONSTITUTION AND GOVERNMENT

The present constitution came into force on 17 June 1944 and has been amended four times since, most recently on 24 June 1999. The President is elected by direct, popular vote for a period of four years.

The *Alþingi* (parliament) is elected in accordance with the electoral law of 1999, which provides for an *Alþingi* of 63 members. The country is divided into a minimum of six and a maximum of seven constituencies. There are currently six constituencies: Northwest (10 seats); Northeast (10 seats); South (10); Southwest (11); Reykjavík north (11); and Reykjavík south (11).

National Anthem

'Ó Guð vors lands' ('Oh God of Our Country'); words by M. Jochumsson, tune by S. Sveinbjörnsson.

GOVERNMENT CHRONOLOGY

Presidents since 1944.

1944–52	Sveinn Björnsson
1952–68	Ásgeir Ásgeirsson
1968–80	Kristján Thórarinsson Eldjárn
1980–96	Vigdís Finnbogadóttir
1996–	Ólafur Ragnar Grímsson

Prime Ministers since 1944. (AF = People's Party; FSF = Progressive Party; SF = Social Democratic Alliance; SSF = Independence Party)

1944–47	SSF	Ólafur Thors
1947–49	AF	Stefán Jóhann Stefánsson

1949–50	SSF	Ólafur Thors
1950–53	FSF	Steingrímur Steinthórsson
1953–56	SSF	Ólafur Thors
1956–58	FSF	Hermann Jónasson
1958–59	AF	Emil Jónsson
1959–63	SSF	Ólafur Thors
1963–70	SSF	Bjarni Benediktsson
1970–71	SSF	Jóhann Hafstein
1971–74	FSF	Ólafur Jóhannesson
1974–78	SSF	Geir Hallgrímsson
1978–79	FSF	Ólafur Jóhannesson
1979–80	AF	Benedikt Gröndal
1980–83	SSF	Gunnar Thoroddsen
1983–87	FSF	Steingrímur Hermannsson
1987–88	SSF	Thorsteinn Pálsson
1988–91	FSF	Steingrímur Hermannsson
1991–2004	SSF	Davíð Oddsson
2004–06	FSF	Halldór Ásgrímsson
2006–09	SSF	Geir Haarde
2009–	SF	Jóhanna Sigurðardóttir

RECENT ELECTIONS

President Ólafur Ragnar Grímsson was reappointed for a second term on 1 Aug. 2000, no opposing candidates having come forward. On 26 June 2004 he stood for popular election and gained 85·6% of the vote. Baldur Ágústsson won 12·5% and Ástþór Magnússon won 1·9%. Turnout was 63·0%. He was reappointed for a fourth term on 1 Aug. 2008, again no opposing candidates having come forward.

In the parliamentary election held on 25 April 2009, the Social Democratic Alliance (SF)—consisting of the People's Alliance, the People's Party and the Alliance of the Women's List—won 20 of the 63 seats with 29·8% of the votes cast, the conservative Independence Party (SSF) 16 with 23·7%, the Left-Green Movement (VG) 14 with 21·7%, the Progressive Party (FSF) 9 with 14·8% and the Citizens' Movement 4 with 7·2%. Turnout was 85·1%. Following the election the Social Democratic Alliance continued its coalition with the Left-Green Movement.

CURRENT ADMINISTRATION

President: Ólafur Ragnar Grímsson; b. 1943 (People's Alliance; sworn in 1 Aug. 1996, reappointed 1 Aug. 2000 and re-elected 26 June 2004, and sworn in for another term on 1 Aug. 2008).

The interim government appointed following the resignation of the government on 26 Jan. 2009 won the 25 April elections and maintained its coalition with the Left-Green Movement. In March 2010 it comprised:

Prime Minister: Jóhanna Sigurðardóttir; b. 1942 (SF; sworn in 1 Feb. 2009).

Minister of Finance: Steingrímur J. Sigfússon (VG). *Foreign Affairs:* Össur Skarphéðinsson (SF). *Health:* Álfheiður Ingadóttir (VG). *Communications:* Kristján L. Möller (SF). *Education, Science and Culture:* Katrín Jakobsdóttir (VG). *Justice and Ecclesiastical Affairs:* Ragna Árnadóttir (ind.). *Business Affairs:* Gylfi Magnússon (ind.). *Industry, Energy, and Tourism:* Katrín Júlíusdóttir (SF). *Fisheries and Agriculture:* Jón Bjarnason (VG). *Social Affairs and Social Security:* Árni Páll Árnason (SF). *Environment:* Svandís Svavarsdóttir (VG).

Government Offices of Iceland Website:
http://www.government.is

CURRENT LEADERS

Ólafur Ragnar Grímsson

Position
President

Introduction
Ólafur Ragnar Grímsson was leader of the People's Alliance until becoming president in 1996. Observers feared his background would politicize the presidency, which is traditionally a non-partisan, ceremonial post, but he has enjoyed broad popular support and retained the office in 2000, 2004 and 2008.

Early Life
Grímsson was born on 14 May 1943 in Ísafjörður. He studied economics and political science at Manchester University in the UK, graduating with a doctorate in 1970. He took up a lecturing post at the University of Iceland and was appointed professor in 1973. From 1966 until 1973 he was on the board of the youth wing of the Progressive Party and between 1971 and 1973 he sat on the party's executive board.

He moved to the People's Alliance and was elected to the *Alþingi* (Parliament) in 1978 as a member for Reykjavík. From 1980 until 1983, when he failed to win re-election to parliament, Grímsson led the People's Alliance in the *Alþingi.* During 1987–96 he was party chairman and between 1988–91 served as the minister of finance. Between 1984–90 he held senior posts with Parliamentarians for Global Action, an international organization with a membership of 1,800 throughout the world. Grímsson also held positions in the Council of Europe during the 1980s and 1990s.

In 1995 he led the People's Alliance to a poor showing at the polls, in which they secured less than 15% of the vote. Shortly afterwards Grímsson announced his candidacy for the presidency at the following year's elections. In June 1996 he was elected with 41% of the vote, defeating three other candidates.

Career in Office
The presidency is a largely ceremonial office and Grímsson's election prompted some observers to fear he would politicize the position. His relationship with the then prime minister, Davíð Oddsson, had been poor ever since the two had clashed as leaders of rival parties. Nevertheless, Grímsson was reappointed as president for a second term (without an election as there were no opposing candidates) and then re-elected by popular vote on 26 June 2004 with nearly 86% of the poll. During his presidency Grímsson has used his international profile to vigorously promote Iceland and its industrial potential, particularly in emerging sectors such as information technology. His reappointment in Aug. 2008 was unopposed.

Jóhanna Sigurðardóttir

Position
Prime Minister

Introduction
Jóhanna Sigurðardóttir became prime minister in Jan. 2009 following economic crisis and the collapse of Geir Haarde's administration. Heading a coalition including her centre-left Social Democratic Alliance (SF) along with the Left-Green Movement (VG), she is the country's first female leader.

Early Life
Sigurðardóttir was born on 4 Oct. 1942 in Reykjavík. After studying business at Iceland's Commercial College, she undertook a varied career that included flight attendant, trade union organizer and office administrator. In 1978 she entered *Alþingi* (Parliament) as the Social Democratic Party representative for the Reykjavík constituency. Subsequent boundary changes saw her become the MP for Reykjavík South and then for the North. In 1979 and from 1983–84 she was the speaker of the *Alþingi* and from 1987–94 she was minister of social affairs but resigned and made an unsuccessful run for her party's leadership.

She subsequently left the Social Democrats to form a new party, the National Movement, which won four seats at the 1995 general election. It merged five years later with her old party and two others to form the SF in a bid to end the dominance of the Independence Party (SSF). In 2007 the Alliance joined the Independence Party in a coalition headed by Haarde. Sigurðardóttir was reappointed to the social affairs portfolio. Working on behalf of the elderly, disabled and disadvantaged, she retained high personal approval ratings even in the depths of the national financial crisis in 2008.

When the country's independent banking system collapsed in late 2008, Haarde and his cabinet came under pressure to resign. On 23 Jan. 2009 Haarde called elections for early May but within three days the coalition had fallen apart. Talks between the SF and the SSF to form a new coalition failed and Alliance turned instead to the Left-Green Movement. With SF leader Ingibjorg Gisladóttir suffering ill health, Sigurðardóttir was proposed for prime minister. By the end of the month VG had agreed to form a coalition ahead of a general election scheduled for 25 April.

Career in Office

Sigurðardóttir's appointment received international media coverage as she became not only the first woman premier of Iceland but also the world's first openly gay head of government. She led her party to victory at the general election held on 25 April, receiving 29·8% of the vote.

Her major challenge has been to restore economic stability. In Feb. 2009 she engineered the removal of the head of the central bank, former prime minister Davíð Oddsson, who was widely blamed for the banking collapse, and in July her government formally applied for membership of the European Union after the *Alþingi* had voted in favour of accession.

DEFENCE

Iceland possesses no armed forces. Under the North Atlantic Treaty, US forces were stationed for many years in Iceland as the Iceland Defence Force. In Sept. 2006 an agreement was signed between USA and Iceland, withdrawing all US forces from the island.

Navy

There is a paramilitary coastguard of 120.

INTERNATIONAL RELATIONS

Iceland is a member of the UN, World Bank, IMF and several other UN specialized agencies, WTO, Council of Europe, OSCE, EFTA, Nordic Council, Council of the Baltic Sea States, BIS, NATO, OECD and is an associate member of WEU. Iceland has acceded to the Schengen accord, which abolishes border controls between Iceland, Austria, Belgium, Czech Republic, Denmark, Estonia, Finland, France, Germany, Greece, Hungary, Italy, Latvia, Lithuania, Luxembourg, Malta, Netherlands, Norway, Poland, Portugal, Slovakia, Slovenia, Spain, Sweden and Switzerland. Iceland applied to join the European Union in July 2009 and hopes to become a member by 2012.

ECONOMY

Agriculture and fishing contributed 6·0% of GDP in 2007, industry 25·7% and services 68·3%.

According to the anti-corruption organization *Transparency International*, Iceland ranked equal eighth in a 2009 survey of countries with the least corruption in business and government. It received 8·7 out of 10 in the annual index.

Overview

The economy experienced strong growth in the mid-1990s as a result of privatization and deregulation, per capita income doubling in the two decades to 2007. The strong housing market, in combination with a tight job market, fuelled domestic demand. Favourable household spending conditions further contributed to the growth of GDP, which expanded by more than 20% between 2003–08.

However, this rapid expansion left the economy with large macroeconomic imbalances and high dependency on foreign financing. Financial sector assets amounted to over 1,000% of GDP and gross external indebtedness roughly 550% of GDP by the end of 2007. The global credit squeeze had a significant impact on domestic financial markets. In Oct. 2008 all three of the country's major banks were nationalized in order to stabilize the financial system. The IMF approved a US$2·1bn. loan in Nov. 2008, supplemented by US$3bn. in loans from Iceland's neighbours, to support the króna. The key interest rate reached a record high of 18% and in Jan. 2009 the government collapsed following political turmoil prompted by the crisis.

A new government was elected in April 2009 and has worked in consultation with the IMF on measures to rebuild the economy. Among the most divisive questions has been how to repay the Dutch and British governments for bailing out their depositors in Icesave, owned by the failed Icelandic bank Landsbanki. A law outlining a repayment programme was narrowly passed by parliament in Dec. 2009 but a presidential refusal to ratify the draft law led to a referendum on 6 March 2010 in which 93·2% of voters rejected the legislation. Ahead of the result the government had entered into negotiations on a new deal with the Dutch and British.

Unemployment exceeded 7% in 2009, up from 1% in 2007, but an IMF mission in late 2009 pronounced the recession to be less severe than predicted. Preliminary figures prompted the IMF to anticipate the resumption of GDP growth in 2010.

Currency

The unit of currency is the *króna* (ISK) of 100 *aurar* (singular: *eyrir*). Foreign exchange markets were deregulated on 1 Jan. 1992. The króna was devalued 7·5% in June 1993. Inflation rates (based on OECD statistics):

1999	*2000*	*2001*	*2002*	*2003*	*2004*	*2005*	*2006*	*2007*	*2008*
3·2%	5·1%	6·4%	5·2%	2·1%	3·2%	4·0%	6·7%	5·1%	12·7%

Foreign exchange reserves were US$3,263m. and gold reserves 64,000 troy oz in Sept. 2009. Total money supply in April 2008 was 420,423m. kr. Note and coin circulation on 31 Dec. 2007 was 15,735m. kr.

Budget

Total central government revenue and expenditure for calendar years (in 1m. kr.):

	2002	*2003*	*2004*	*2005*	*2006*	*2007*
Revenue	252,775	268,032	306,851	363,568	412,839	454,588
Expenditure	263,109	283,278	297,591	317,986	350,866	403,199

Central government debt was 252,990m. kr. on 31 Dec. 2004. Foreign debt amounted to 154,352m. kr. in 2007. VAT is 25·5% (reduced rate, 7%). Iceland has the highest standard VAT rate of any country

Performance

Real GDP growth rates (based on OECD statistics):

1999	*2000*	*2001*	*2002*	*2003*	*2004*	*2005*	*2006*	*2007*	*2008*
4·1%	4·3%	3·9%	0·1%	2·4%	7·7%	7·5%	4·3%	5·6%	1·3%

GDP in 2008 totalled US$16·7bn. In 2007 GDP per capita was US$64,871.

Banking and Finance

The Central Bank of Iceland (founded 1961; *Governor*, Már Guðmundsson) is responsible for note issue and carries out the central banking functions. There were 16 savings banks in 2008. On 31 Dec. 2007 the accounts of the Central Bank balanced at 476,859m. kr.; commercial bank deposits were 2,562,438m. kr. in 2007.

There is a stock exchange in Reykjavík.

ENERGY AND NATURAL RESOURCES

Iceland is aiming to become the world's first 'hydrogen economy'; its buses started to convert to fuel cell-powered vehicles in late 2003. Ultimately it aims to run all its transport and even its fishing fleet on hydrogen produced in Iceland.

Environment

Iceland's carbon dioxide emissions from the consumption and flaring of fossil fuels in 2008 were the equivalent of 11·1 tonnes per capita. An *Environmental Performance Index* compiled in 2008 ranked Iceland 11th in the world, with 87·6%. The index examined various factors in six areas—air pollution, biodiversity and habitat, climate change, environmental health, productive natural resources and water resources.

Electricity

The installed capacity of public electrical power plants at the end of 2007 totalled 2,363,700 kWh; installed capacity of hydro-electric plants was 1,758,300 kWh. Electricity production in public-owned plants totalled 11,976m. kWh in 2007. Virtually all of Iceland's electricity is produced from hydro power and geothermal energy. Consumption per capita was estimated in 2007 to be 38,566 kWh (the highest in the world).

Agriculture

Of the total area, about six-sevenths is unproductive, but only about 1·3% is under cultivation, which is largely confined to hay and potatoes. Arable land totalled 15,500 ha. in 2007. In 2007 the total hay crop was 1,993,773 cu. metres; the crop of potatoes, 13,000 tonnes; of tomatoes, 1,603 tonnes; and of cucumbers, 1,343 tonnes. Livestock (2007): sheep, 454,812; horses, 76,982; cattle, 70,660 (milch cows, 26,048); pigs, 4,147; poultry, 41,296. Livestock products (2007): lamb and mutton, 8,644 tonnes; poultry, 7,597 tonnes; pork, 6,088 tonnes; beef, 3,557 tonnes. Consumption of dairy products (2007): milk, 124,817 tonnes; cheese, 4,903 tonnes; butter and dairy margarines, 1,753 tonnes.

Forestry

In 2005 forests covered 46,000 ha., or approximately 0·5% of the total land area.

Fisheries

Fishing is of vital importance to the economy. Fishing vessels in 2007 numbered 1,642 with a gross tonnage of 169,279. Total catch in 2004: 1,727,785; 2005: 1,668,927; 2006: 1,322,914; 2007: 1,395,716. Virtually all the fish caught is from marine waters. Iceland has received international praise for its management system which aims to avoid the over-fishing that has decimated stocks in other parts of the world. Commercial whaling was prohibited in 1989, but recommenced in 2006. In 2007 fisheries accounted for 6·6% of GDP, down from 16·8% in 1996. The per capita consumption of fish and fishery products is the second highest in the world, after that of the Maldives.

INDUSTRY

Production, 2007, in 1,000 tonnes: aluminium, 446·3; ferro-silicon, 114·9. 132,438 tonnes of cement were sold in 2007.

Labour

In 2007 the economically active population was 181,500. The standardized unemployment rate in 2009 was 7·2% (up from 3·0% in 2008). In the period 1996–2005 Iceland averaged 401 working days lost to strikes per 1,000 employees—the highest number in any western European country. In 2007 agriculture and fishing employed 5·9% of the economically active population, industry 20·6% and services 73·1% (including: health services and social work, 14·7%; wholesale, retail trade and repairs, 14·3%).

Trade Unions

In 2004 trade union membership was 94·3% of the workforce.

INTERNATIONAL TRADE

The economy is heavily trade-dependent.

Imports and Exports

Total value of imports (c.i.f.) and exports (f.o.b.) in 1m. kr.:

	2003	*2004*	*2005*	*2006*	*2007*
Imports	216,525	260,431	313,855	432,106	427,383
Exports	182,580	202,373	194,355	242,740	305,096

Main imports, 2007 (in 1m. kr.): industrial supplies, 114,314 (of which primary, 5,858; processed, 108,456); transport equipment, 87,625 (of which passenger motor cars, 29,571); fuels and lubricants, 37,186; food and beverages, 28,913. Main exports, 2007 (in 1m. kr.): marine products, 127,619; manufactured goods, 90,291 (of which aluminium, 80,324); transport equipment 49,696; animal feeds, 10,572.

Value of trade with principal countries for three years (in 1,000 kr.):

	2005		*2006*		*2007*	
	Imports (c.i.f.)	*Exports* (f.o.b.)	*Imports* (c.i.f.)	*Exports* (f.o.b.)	*Imports* (c.i.f.)	*Exports* (f.o.b.)
Belgium	4,951,700	4,094,500	6,656,200	4,734,700	6,725,400	4,997,700
Canada	4,744,300	1,922,500	12,302,500	1,395,000	7,583,100	1,463,800
China	16,055,300	1,694,400	22,700,400	2,753,200	21,601,800	2,375,900
Denmark	22,321,400	8,083,000	26,276,400	8,501,700	31,660,900	10,080,300
France	10,662,900	7,235,600	16,950,500	8,224,500	12,201,000	7,827,300
Germany	43,446,100	30,800,900	53,046,100	36,345,500	51,582,500	40,815,000
Ireland	7,886,600	2,173,300	8,479,300	1,208,200	5,106,700	23,077,400
Italy	11,349,500	1,886,500	14,089,500	1,829,300	14,550,000	1,991,200
Japan	16,525,200	6,262,100	17,931,100	5,019,200	20,161,600	12,775,600
Netherlands	15,080,400	24,296,700	20,956,500	40,317,700	24,012,800	64,885,800
Norway	21,904,400	5,202,000	30,395,800	9,633,100	19,682,300	11,565,000
Poland	4,799,500	3,983,900	4,718,700	1,900,700	7,305,500	1,909,400
Portugal	1,195,300	5,152,200	1,774,800	5,458,300	1,012,200	7,560,000
Russia	1,501,100	2,770,400	1,507,400	4,653,400	4,895,400	4,185,600
Spain	4,121,600	14,442,400	5,805,100	15,452,200	5,694,200	14,158,800
Sweden	26,458,700	2,093,600	30,067,000	2,201,500	42,848,300	2,214,400
Switzerland	5,229,900	2,438,200	9,667,900	5,879,000	8,555,200	3,856,600
UK	18,062,800	34,614,500	22,744,900	37,939,300	22,875,100	40,333,800
USA	29,281,400	16,299,200	55,465,400	26,131,300	57,558,600	16,049,700

COMMUNICATIONS

Roads

On 31 Dec. 2007 the length of the public roads (including roads in towns) was 13,048 km. Of these 8,223 km were main and secondary roads and 4,822 km were provincial roads. Total length of surfaced roads was 4,492 km. A ring road of 1,400 km runs just inland from much of the coast; about 80% of it is smooth-surfaced. Motor vehicles registered at the end of 2007 numbered 240,551, of which 209,456 were passenger cars (668 per 1,000 inhabitants—the highest rate of any country) and 31,095 lorries; there were also 8,074 motorcycles. There were 15 fatal road accidents in 2007 with 15 persons killed.

Civil Aviation

Icelandair is the national carrier. In 2007 it served 18 destinations in western Europe and six in north America. In 2004 it carried 1·3m. passengers. The main international airport is at Keflavík (Leifsstöd), with Reykjavík for flights to the Faroe Islands, Greenland and domestic services. Keflavík handled 2,182,232 passengers in 2007 (of which 298,547 transit passengers) and 59,742 tonnes of freight.

Shipping

On 1 Jan. 2008 the merchant fleet consisted of 52 vessels totalling 8,515 GT, including 49 passenger ships and ferries of 7,669 GT.

Telecommunications

The number of telephone main lines was 186,688 in 2007; mobile phone subscribers, 311,785 (approximately 99% of the population). In 2008, 90·6% of the population (the highest percentage in the world) were internet users. The broadband penetration rate in June 2008 was 32·3 subscribers per 100 inhabitants.

Postal Services

There were 83 post offices in 2007.

SOCIAL INSTITUTIONS

Justice

In 1992 jurisdiction in civil and criminal cases was transferred from the provincial magistrates to eight new district courts, separating the judiciary from the prosecution. From the district courts there is an appeal to the Supreme Court in Reykjavík, which has eight judges. The population in penal institutions in Sept. 2005 was 119 (40 per 100,000 of national population).

Education

Primary education is compulsory and free from 6–16 years of age. Optional secondary education from 16 to 19 is also free. In 2007 there were 43,841 pupils in primary schools, 26,186 in secondary schools (21,401 on day courses) and 16,630 tertiary-level students (14,394 on day courses). Some 14·1% of tertiary-level students study abroad.

There are seven universities and five specialized colleges at tertiary level in Iceland. A total of 17,449 students were enrolled in universities in 2007. Universities (with total students, 2007): University of Iceland (founded 1911), Reykjavík, 9,586; Reykjavík University, 2,907; Iceland University of Education, 2,241; University of Akureyri, 1,305; Bifröst University, 744; Iceland Academy of Arts, 380; Agricultural University of Iceland, 286.

In 2007 public sector spending on education was 7·5% of GDP.

The adult literacy rate is at least 99%.

Health

In 2002 there were 23 hospitals with 2,228 beds, equivalent to 78 per 10,000 population. In 2007 there were 1,157 doctors, 2,729 nurses, 327 pharmacists and 294 dentists. There were 3·7 doctors per 1,000 inhabitants in 2007. Iceland has one of the lowest alcohol consumption rates in Europe, at 7·53 litres of alcohol per adult per year (2007). Iceland spent 9·3% of its GDP on health in 2007.

Welfare

The main body of social welfare legislation is consolidated in six acts:

(i) *The social security legislation (a)* health insurance, including sickness benefits; *(b)* social security pensions, mainly consisting of old age pension, disablement pension and widows' pension, and also children's pension; *(c)* employment injuries insurance.

(ii) *The unemployment insurance legislation,* where daily allowances are paid to those who have met certain conditions.

(iii) *The subsistence legislation.* This is controlled by municipal government.

(iv) *The tax legislation.* Prior to 1988 children's support was included in the tax legislation. Since 1988 family allowances are paid directly to all children age 0–15 years. The amount is increased with the second child in the family, and children under the age of seven get additional benefits. Single parents receive additional allowances.

(v) *The rehabilitation legislation*

(vi) *Child and juvenile guidance*

Health insurance covers the entire population. Citizenship is not demanded and there is a six-month waiting period. Most hospitals are both municipally and state run, a few solely state run and all offer free medical help. Medical treatment out of hospitals is partly paid by the patient; the same applies to medicines, except medicines of lifelong necessary use, which are paid in full by the health insurance. Dental care is partly paid by the state for children under 17 years old and also for old age and disabled pensioners. Sickness benefits are paid to those who lose income because of periodical illness.

The pension system is composed of the public social security system and some 90 private pension funds. The social security system pays basic old age and disablement pensions of a fixed amount regardless of past or present income, as well as supplementary pensions to individuals with low present income. The pensions are index-linked, i.e. are changed in line with changes in wage and salary rates in the labour market. In the public social security system, entitlement to old age and disablement pensions at the full rates is subject to the condition that the beneficiary has been resident in Iceland for 40 years at the age period of 16–67. For shorter periods of residence, the benefits are reduced proportionally. Entitled to old age pension are all those who are 67 years old, and have been residents in Iceland for three years of the age period of 16–67. Old age and disablement pension are of equally high amount; in the year 2007 the total sum was 297,972 kr. for an individual. Married pensioners receive double the basic pension. Pensioners with little or no other income are entitled to an income supplement; in 2007 the maximum annual income supplement was 981,775 kr.

The employment injuries insurance covers medical care, daily allowances, disablement pension and survivors' pension and is applicable to practically all employees.

RELIGION

The national church, the Evangelical Lutheran, is endowed by the state. There is complete religious liberty. The affairs of the national church are under the superintendence of a bishop. In 2008, 252,624 persons (80·6% of the population) were members of it (93·2% in 1980). 15,305 persons (4·9%) belonged to Lutheran free churches. 36,665 persons (11·7%) belonged to other religious organizations and 8,782 persons (2·8%) did not belong to any religious community.

CULTURE

World Heritage Sites

There are two UNESCO sites in Iceland: Þingvellir National Park (2004), located on an active volcanic site; and Surtsey (2008), an island formed by volcanic eruptions in 1963–67.

Broadcasting

The state owned Icelandic State Broadcasting Service operates two national radio networks and four regional stations, and one national public TV network. 15 privately-owned radio stations and nine private TV stations were in operation in 2007. 97% of households had TV sets in 2007. Licensed TVs at 31 Dec. 2007: colour, 107,535; black and white, 375.

Cinema

There were 21 cinemas with 44 screens in 2007 of which the capital had seven cinemas and 26 screens. Total admissions numbered 1,487,663 in 2007, with the Reykjavík area accounting for 1,262,303. In 2006 gross box office receipts came to 1,069·8m. kr.

Press

In 2006 there were four daily newspapers (two paid-for and two free) and 24 non-daily newspapers. Combined circulation was 338,000 (of which dailies accounted for 251,000 and non-dailies 87,000). Iceland has among the highest circulation rates of daily newspapers in the world, at 1,087 per 1,000 adult inhabitants in 2005.

Iceland publishes more books per person than any other country in the world. In 2006, 1,419 volumes of books and booklets were published.

Tourism

There were 458,889 visitors in 2007 (up 15·1% on 2006); revenue totalled 56,215m. kr. Overnight stays in hotels and guest houses in 2007 numbered 1,916,579 (of which foreign travellers, 1,480,025; Icelanders, 436,554). Tourism accounts for 12·7% of foreign currency earnings.

Festivals

The Reykjavík Arts Festival, an annual programme of international artists and performers, is held every May–June.

Libraries

The National and University Library of Iceland is in Reykjavík and contains 980,350 volumes. The seven university libraries contain 208,287 volumes. There were 57 public libraries with 2,235,658 volumes in 2001.

Theatre and Opera

In 2007 there were six professional theatres operated on a yearly basis (of which five were in the capital region). There were 259,030 admissions to performances of the professional theatres in 2007, 70,781 admissions to the National Theatre and 121,807 admissions to the City Theatre. Total audience of the Icelandic Opera was 9,585.

There is one symphonic orchestra operated on a regular basis, the Icelandic Symphony Orchestra. In 2007 the orchestra performed 64 times, with audiences totalling 52,154.

Museums and Galleries

In 2006 there were 124 museums, botanical gardens, aquariums and zoos in operation, with a total of 1·4m. visitors. The National Museum reopened in Sept. 2004 after extensive renovation, and received 88,195 visitors in 2006. The National Gallery received 51,818 visitors and 155,200 attended the Reykjavík Municipal Art Museum.

DIPLOMATIC REPRESENTATIVES

Of Iceland in the United Kingdom (2A Hans St., London, SW1X 0JE)
Ambassador: Benedikt Jónsson.

Of the United Kingdom in Iceland (Laufásvegur 31, 101 Reykjavík)
Ambassador: Ian Whitting.

Of Iceland in the USA (2900 K St. NW, Suites 508/509, Washington, D.C., 20007)
Ambassador: Hjálmar W. Hannesson.

Of the USA in Iceland (Laufásvegur 21, 101 Reykjavík)
Ambassador: Carol van Voorst.

Of Iceland to the United Nations
Ambassador: Gunnar Pálsson.

Of Iceland to the European Union
Ambassador: Stéfan Hankur Jóhannesson.

FURTHER READING

Statistics Iceland, *Landshagir* (Statistical Yearbook of Iceland).—*Hagtíðindi* (Statistical Series)
Central Bank of Iceland. *Monetary Bulletin.—The Economy of Iceland.* (Latest issue 2010)

Boyes, Roger, *Meltdown Iceland.* 2009
Byock, Jesse, *Viking Age Iceland.* 2001
Karlsson, G., *The History of Iceland.* 2000
Smiley, Jane, (ed.) *The Sagas of Icelanders: A Selection.* 2002
Thorhallsson, Baldur, (ed.) *Iceland and European Integration: On the Edge.* 2004

National library: Landsbókasafn Islands—Háskólabókasafn, Arngrímsgata 3, 107 Reykjavík. *Librarian:* Ingibjörg Steinunn Sverrisdóttir.
National Statistical Office: Statistics Iceland, Bogartúni 21a, IS-150 Reykjavík.
Website: http://www.hagstofa.is
Central Bank of Iceland: Kalkofnsvegi 1, 150 Reykjavik
Website: http://www.sedlabanki.is

INDIA

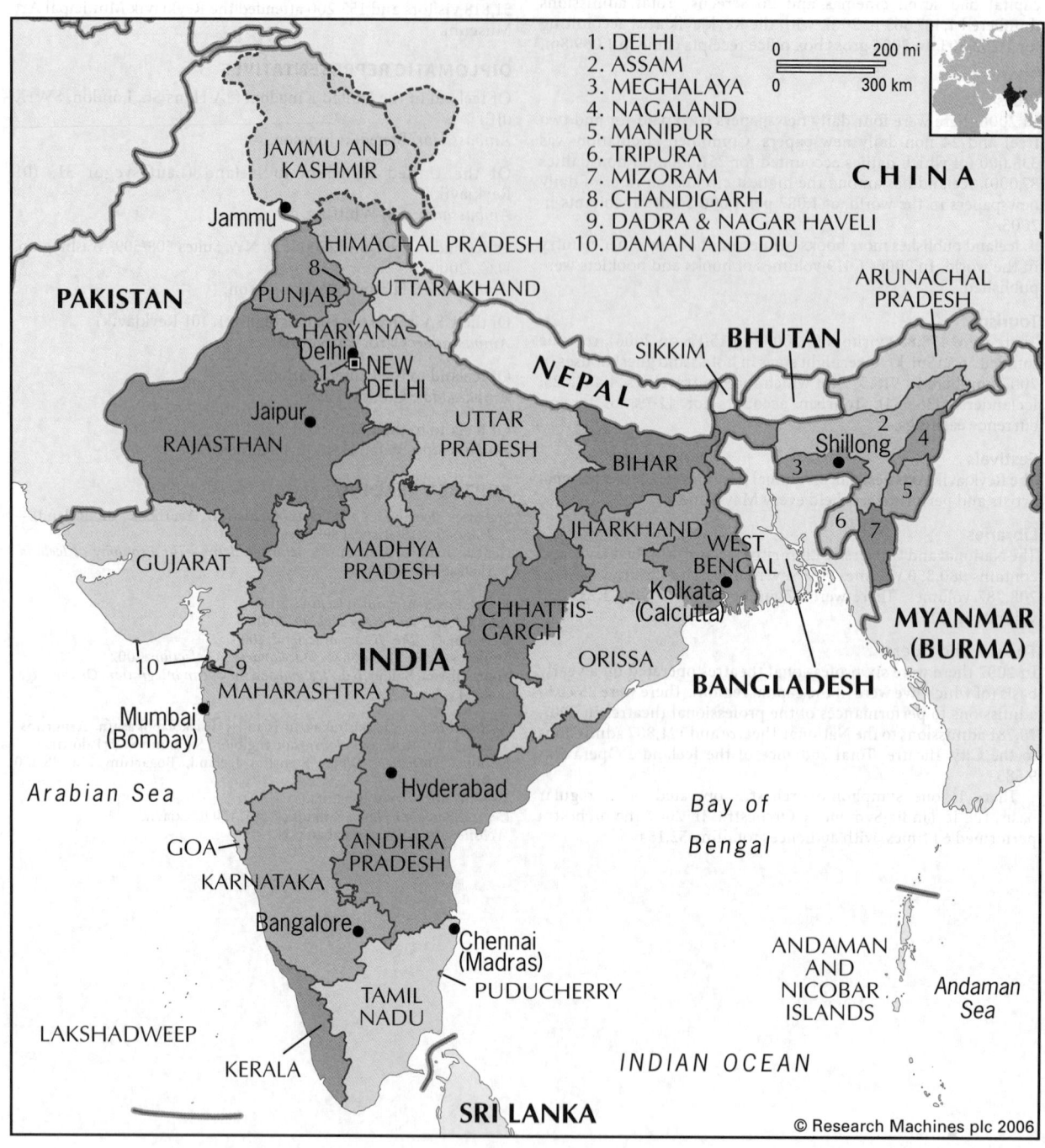

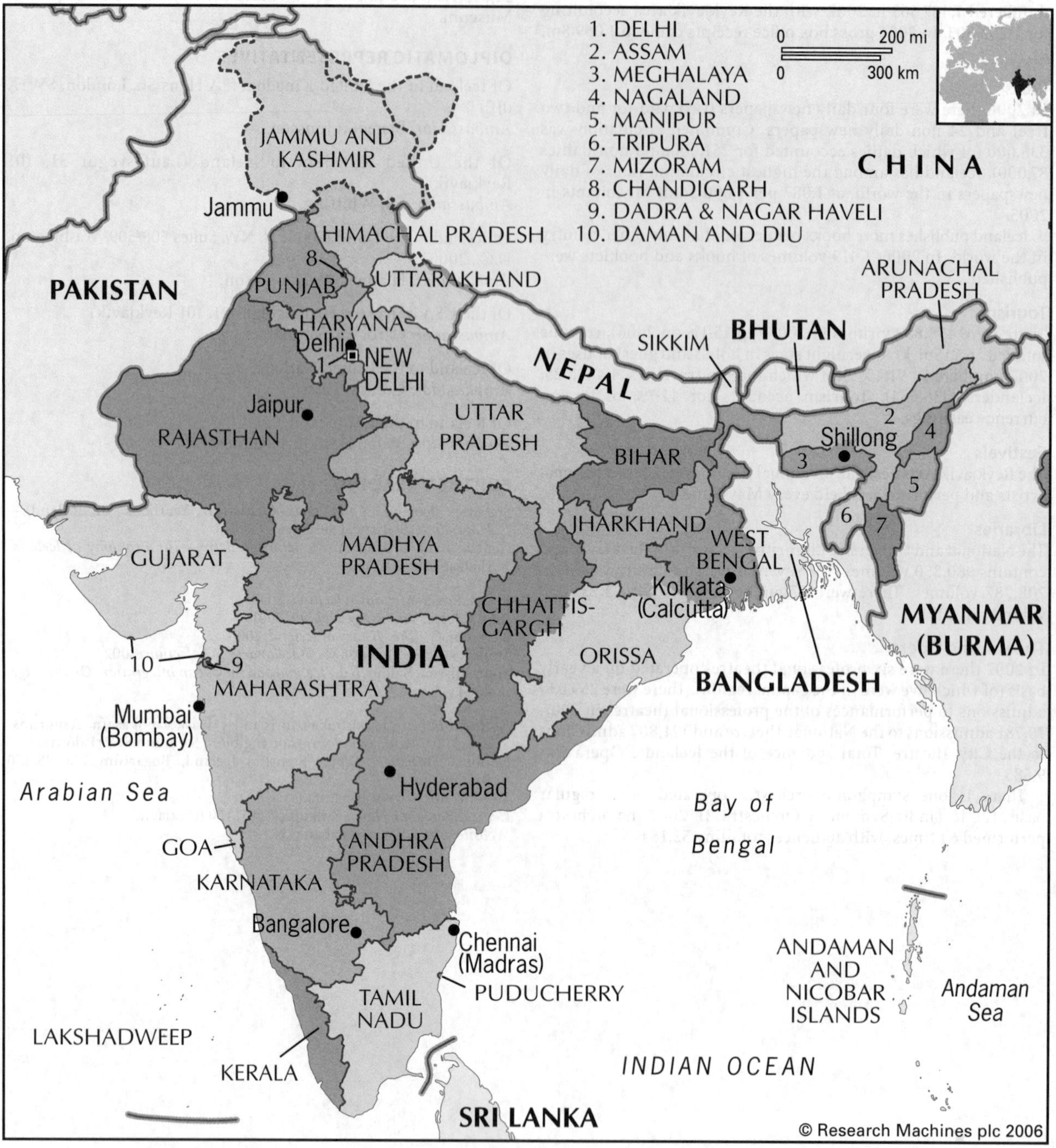

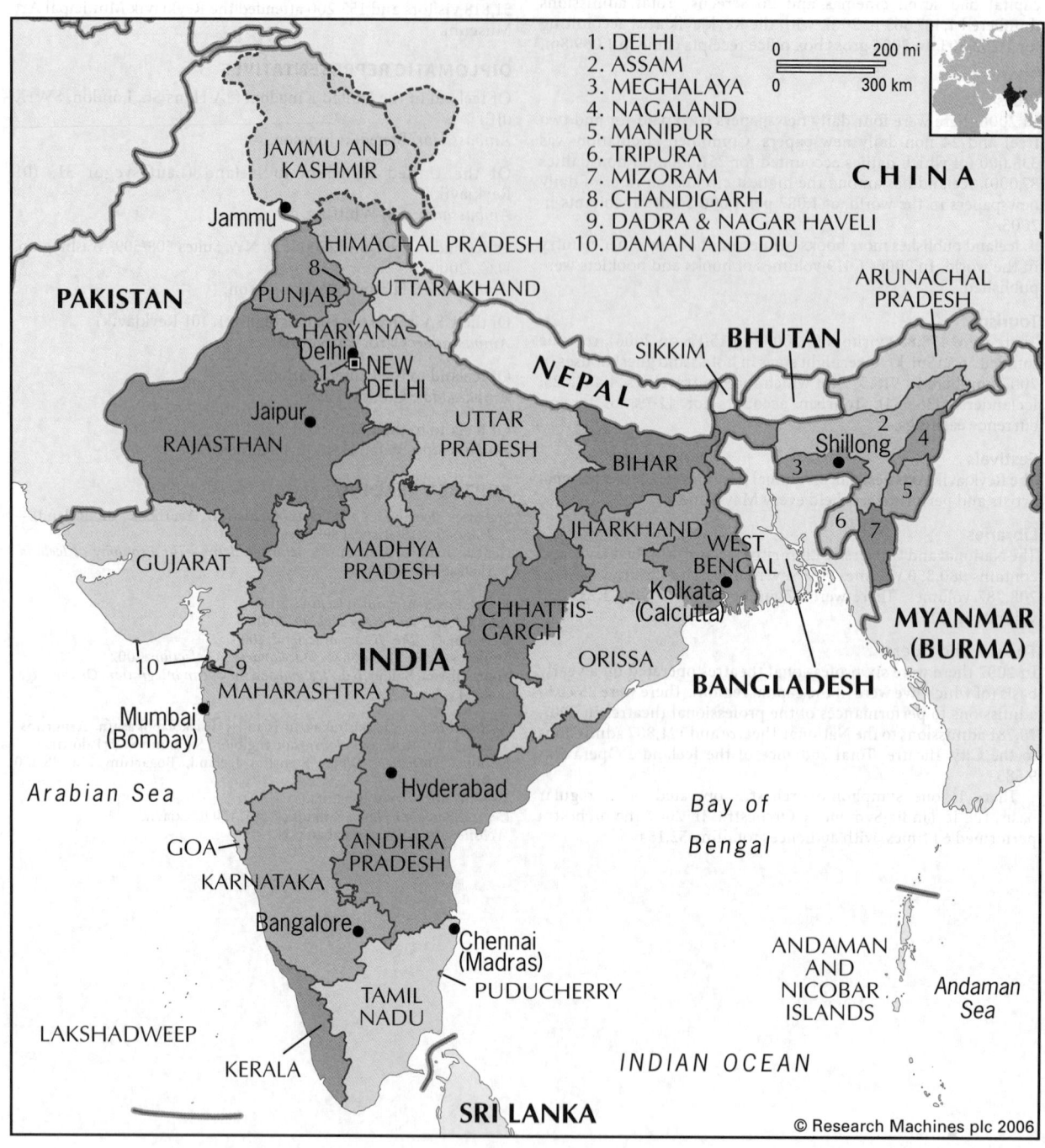

Map. Based upon Survey of India Map with the permission of the Surveyor General of India. The responsibility for the correctness of internal details rests with the publisher. The territorial waters of India extend into the sea to a distance of 12 nautical miles measured from the appropriate base line. The external boundaries and coatlines of India agree with the Record/Master Copy certified by the Survey of India.

Bharat
(Republic of India)

Capital: New Delhi
Population estimate, 2010: 1,214·46m.
GDP per capita, 2007: (PPP$) 2,753
HDI/world rank 0·612/134

KEY HISTORICAL EVENTS

The valley of the Indus and its tributaries is divided today between India and Pakistan. Some 7,000 years ago the valley was one of the cradles of civilization. From the Indus Valley, Dravidian peoples spread agriculture and fixed settlements gradually across India, arriving in the far south by about 4,000 years ago. The Indus Valley Harappan civilization, a Bronze Age culture, flourished from around 2300 to 1500 BC and had links with western Asian civilizations in Iran. The two great cities of the Harappan civilization—Mohenjo-Daro and Harappa—were in what is now Pakistan, but Harappan culture also thrived in modern-day northwestern India. Writing, fine jewellery and textile production, town planning, metalworking and pottery were the hallmarks of an advanced urban society, which collapsed for reasons that are still not fully understood.

At the same time, another Bronze Age civilization existed in the Ganges Valley. This civilization, whose links were with southeastern Asia, was based on a rice-growing rural economy, which supported a number of city-states. Around 1500 BC a pastoral people, the Aryans, invaded the Indus Valley from Iran and Central Asia. Their arrival completed the destruction of the Harappan civilization and shifted the balance of power in the subcontinent to the Ganges Valley.

The Aryans took over northern and central India, merging their culture with that of the Dravidians. The caste system, still a feature of Indian society, dates back to the Dravidians, but the languages of northern and central India, and the polytheistic religion that is now followed by the majority of the inhabitants of the subcontinent, are both Aryan in origin. From these two cultures, a Hindu civilization emerged.

By 800 BC a series of Hindu kingdoms had developed in the Ganges Valley. This region gave birth to one of the world's great religions: Buddhism. Prince Gautama, the Buddha (*c.* 563–483 BC), renounced a life of wealth to seek enlightenment. His creed of non-violence was spread throughout India and, later, southeastern Asia. However, Buddhism was partly instrumental in destroying the most powerful of ancient states of the Ganges Valley: Magdalha.

Magdalha was ruled by the Nanda dynasty in the 4th century BC. In 321 BC the Nandas were replaced by the Mauryans under Chandragupta Maurya (reigned 321–297 BC). Chandragupta conquered most of northern India before his ascetic death from self-imposed starvation. His grandson, Ashoka, ruled an empire that stretched from the Deccan to Afghanistan from *c.* 272–*c.* 231, but he is mainly remembered for his enthusiasm for Buddhist pacifism. Attacked by enemies who did not share this creed, the Mauryan empire collapsed soon after Ashoka's death.

To the west, the Indus Valley had passed to the Persian Empire by the 5th century BC and then fell to Alexander the Great. After Alexander's death in 323 BC, Greek influences continued to be felt in the northwest of the subcontinent where an Indo-Greek civilization flourished for at least 200 years. This was brought to an end by nomadic invasions from Central Asia between the 1st and 5th centuries AD. By then, India had been divided into many small warring states, most of which were short-lived.

Empire Building

However, two strong states emerged briefly to reunite much of India: the Gupta empire and the Harsa empire. The Gupta empire was founded in the Ganges Valley by Chandragupta I (reigned *c.* 320–30). His warrior son, Samudragupta (reigned *c.* 330–80), won most of north India, but the empire was destroyed by succession disputes and a Hun invasion in the middle of the 5th century. The Harsa empire was the personal creation of a Buddhist convert, Harsa (reigned 606–47), who briefly ruled most of the north of the subcontinent. With his death, his empire fell apart and India was once more divided into many rival kingdoms.

Although no Hindu state managed to unite India, the Hindu religion and culture proved powerful influences throughout the region. The agents of Hinduism were not kings or soldiers but merchants. By about 500 BC Sri Lanka was within the Hindu sphere of influence. Over the next 800 years Hindu kingdoms were established in Burma, Cambodia, Sumatra, Thailand and Java. From the 4th century BC, Indian merchants also spread Buddhism through southeastern Asia. The great Hindu kingdoms flourished far beyond the subcontinent. The most splendid were the Khmer kingdom based on Angkor Wat in Cambodia and the maritime kingdom of Sriwijaya, based in Sumatra.

While Indian religion and culture spread south and east, an invasion from the west threatened to change the subcontinent. In 713 a Muslim army conquered Sind. For the next 300 years, Islamic rulers were largely confined to what is now Pakistan, but in 1000 a raid by the ruler of Ghazni (now in Afghanistan) overran the Punjab. During the 11th and 12th centuries the Hindu states of the Ganges Valley were toppled by Muslim invaders.

The principal Islamic state of India, following the Muslim conquest of northern India, was the sultanate of Delhi. This powerful state was founded by Qutb-ud-Din Aybak (reigned *c.* 1208–10), a former slave, who united the Indus and Ganges valleys and founded the Mu'izzi dynasty. Under the short-lived Khaljis dynasty, the sultanate became the leading power in India, largely owing to the military prowess of Sultan 'Ala-ud-Din Khalji (reigned 1296–1316). But by 1388, following the inept rule of the three sultans of the Tughluq dynasty, the sultanate had ceased to be important.

The Delhi sultanate was eventually replaced in the north by the Mughal Empire, which was founded by Babur (reigned 1526–30), a descendant of Timur and Genghis Khan. Akbar the Great (reigned 1556–1605) extended the Mughal Empire, conquering Baluchistan, Gujarat, Bengal, Orissa, Rajasthan, Afghanistan and Bihar. In his campaign against Gujarat, Akbar marched his army 800 km (500 miles) in only 11 days. His grandson, Shah Jahan (reigned 1628–58), a pleasure-seeking ruler, is remembered for constructing the Taj Mahal as a memorial to his favourite wife.

The decline of the Mughal Empire began under Shah Jahan's son, Aurangzeb I (reigned 1658–1707). Aurangzeb persecuted Hindus with a vengeance. Inter-community violence and wars against Hindu states weakened the empire. Throughout the 18th century, disputed successions and fears of assassination diverted the Mughal emperors. By the close of the 18th century the last emperor was nominal ruler of the environs of Delhi.

The main Hindu state of the subcontinent from the 14th century to the 17th century was the kingdom of Vijayanagar, which occupied most of southern India. Harihara I (reigned 1336–54), who had been governor of part of central India for the Mughal emperor, rebelled and established his own kingdom. Under Devaraya II (reigned 1425–47), Vijayanagar included virtually all of southern India and much of Sri Lanka. This kingdom reached its zenith under Krsnadevaraya (reigned 1509–29). He encouraged good relations with the Portuguese who had founded trading posts on his shores. Vijayanagar collapsed in civil wars (1614–46).

The Bahmani sultanate of the Deccan was an Islamic state, which dominated central India from the mid-14th century until the 16th century. This state was founded by 'Ala-ud-Din Hasan Bahmani Shah (reigned 1347–58), the local governor for the sultan of Delhi who rebelled against Delhi and established his own dynasty. For a time the Bahmani sultanate was the most powerful state in central India, but defeats at the hands of the kingdom of Vijayanagar in the 15th century weakened the Bahmani sultans. On the death of the last Bahmani sultan in 1518 the kingdom was divided by the provincial governors into small states.

European Influence

By the 16th century European traders were established along India's coasts. The first to arrive were the Portuguese in 1498. In 1510 the Portuguese took Goa, which was to remain the centre of the fragmented possessions of Portuguese India until 1962. The creation of the (English) East India Company in 1600 heralded the beginning of what was to become the British Indian Empire. Forts were established on the coast in 1619 and in 1661 England took possession of Bombay.

Initially, the Europeans were only interested in trade but they soon became involved in local politics, in particular, the disputed successions that bedevilled Indian states. Portugal and England were not alone in attempting to establish outposts in India. The Dutch were active in the 17th century but were effectively eliminated from the competition before 1759, when Britain took Chinsura, the headquarters of Dutch administration in India. Two small Danish colonies lasted from 1618 until 1858. However, the main threat to British rule in India was France. Although the East India Company controlled parts of Bengal and the Ganges Valley, France was supreme in the Deccan where French forces, and Indian rulers allied to France, held sway over an area twice the size of France itself.

In the 1750s Britain and France fought out their European wars overseas. The defeat of French forces, and France's Indian allies, at the battle of Plassey (1757), by British forces led by Robert Clive (1725–74), confirmed British rule in Bengal and Bihar and ejected France from the Deccan. Henceforth, France was restricted to five small coastal possessions.

The Maratha state was the major power in central and southern India in the 17th and 18th centuries. This empire was founded by Sivaji (1627–80), who built the state between 1653 and 1660. The Hindu Sivaji came into conflict with the fanatical Muslim Mughal emperor Aurangzeb, who imprisoned Sivaji. After his famous escape from captivity, concealed in a fruit basket, Sivaji made himself emperor of his Maratha state in 1674. This pious monarch ruled competently, establishing an efficient administration, but by the time of his grandson, Shahu (reigned 1707–27), the power of the Maratha emperors had been eclipsed by that of their hereditary chief minister, the Peshwa. In 1727 the Peshwa Baji Rao I (reigned 1720–40) effectively replaced the emperor and established his own dynasty. Baji Rao made the Maratha state the strongest in India. His descendant, Baji Rao II (reigned 1795–1817), raised a weakened state against the British and was crushed. He was the last important Indian monarch outside British influence.

East India Company

In the first half of the 19th century, wars against Sind (1843) and the Sikhs in Punjab (1849) extended the borders of British India. By the middle of the 19th century about 60% of the subcontinent was controlled by the East India Company. The remaining 40% was divided between about 620 Indian states, which were, in theory, still sovereign and ruled by their own maharajas, sultans, nawabs and other monarchs, each advised by a British resident. The Indian states ranged from large entities the size of European countries (such as Hyderabad, Baroda, Mysore and Indore) to tiny states no bigger than an English parish.

British rule brought land reform in the areas controlled by the East India Company. The traditional patterns of land holdings was broken up and private land ownership was introduced. This had the unintended result of concentrating ownership in the hands of a small number of powerful landlords. As a result, landless peasants and dispossessed princes united in their opposition to British rule. In 1857 a mutiny by soldiers of the East India Company quickly spread into full-scale rebellion. Throughout India those who resented the speed and nature of the changes brought about by British rule made one final attempt to eject the occupiers. The Indian Mutiny took 14 months to put down.

After the Mutiny the British government replaced the East India Company as the ruler of an Indian colonial empire (1858), and the modernization of India began apace. Emphasis was placed on building up an Indian infrastructure, particularly roads and railways. The participation of Indians within the civil administration, the construction of a vast national railway system and the imposition of the English language did much to forge a national identity overriding the divisions of local state and caste. But in deference to British manufacturers industry in India remained backward. In 1877 the Indian Empire was proclaimed and Queen Victoria became Empress of India (Kaiser-i-Hind).

Growing Nationalism

The (Hindu-dominated) Indian National Congress, the forerunner of the Congress Party, first met in 1885, and in 1906 the rival Muslim League was founded. Demands for Home Rule grew in the early years of the 20th century, and nationalist feeling was fuelled when British troops fired on a nationalist protest meeting—the Amritsar Massacre (1919).

Realizing that change was inevitable, the British government reformed the administration in 1919 and 1935. The creation of an Indian federation removed many of the differences between the Crown territories and the Indian states and granted an Indian government limited autonomy. The pace of reform was, however, too slow for popular opinion.

In 1920 the Congress party began a campaign of non-violence and non-cooperation with the British colonial authorities. Congress was led in its struggle by the charismatic figure of Mahatma Gandhi (1869–1948). The British authorities were forced to concede Gandhi's moral influence but he himself was opposed by the traditional rulers of the Indian states, whose own positions were at risk.

By the start of the Second World War (1939–45), relations between the Hindu and Muslim communities in India had broken down, with the Muslims demanding a separate independent Islamic state, later, Pakistan. During the war, Assam and other northeastern areas were faced with the threat of a Japanese invasion. Although many Indians served in the Allied forces during the war, a minority supported Japan as a possible liberator.

In 1945 Britain had neither the will nor the resources to maintain the Indian Empire. But while Britain accepted independence, religious tension made partition inevitable. In 1947 the sub-continent was divided between India, a predominantly Hindu state led by Jawaharlal (Pandit) Nehru (1889–1964) of the Congress Party, and Pakistan, a Muslim state led by Mohammad Ali Jinnah (1876–1948) of the Muslim League. The rulers of the Indian states were entitled to choose their allegiance while British Crown territories were assigned to either India or Pakistan.

Partitions

Partition brought enormous upheaval. More than 70m. Hindus and Muslims became refugees as they trekked across the new boundaries. Many thousands were killed in intercommunal violence. The Muslim ruler of the large, mainly Hindu, southern Indian state of Hyderabad, declared independence and the adherence of his state to India was only achieved through Indian military intervention. The Hindu ruler of mainly Muslim Kashmir opted to join India, against the wishes of his people. Elsewhere the border remained disputed in many places. Tension increased when Gandhi was assassinated by a Hindu fundamentalist (1948). In 1950 India became a republic.

Tension between India and Pakistan erupted into war in 1947–49 when the two countries fought over Kashmir. The region was divided along a ceasefire line, although neither side recognized this as an international border. India and Pakistan went to war again over Kashmir in 1965 and again in 1971 when Bangladesh (formerly East Pakistan) gained its independence as a result of Indian military intervention. Indian forces saw action in 1961 when Indian troops invaded and annexed Portuguese India and in 1962 in a border war with China. France had already ceded its small enclaves to India in 1950 and 1955. In 1975 India annexed the small Himalayan kingdom of Sikkim.

Despite its involvement in several wars, India assumed joint leadership of the non-aligned world. Pandit Nehru, premier from 1947 to 1964, was briefly succeeded by Lal Bahadur Shastri. In 1966 Nehru's daughter Indira Gandhi (1917–84) became premier. Under Mrs Gandhi, India continued to assert itself as a regional power and the rival of Pakistan. Although non-aligned, India developed close relations with the Soviet Union.

In 1971 Mrs Gandhi's government abolished the titles, pensions and privileges guaranteed to the Indian princes at independence as compensation for merging their states into India. India was wracked by local separatism and communal unrest. From 1975 to 1977 Mrs Gandhi imposed a state of emergency. Her actions split the Congress Party, allowing Morarji Desai (1896–1995) of the Janata Party to form India's first non-Congress administration. However, his coalition soon shattered and a wing of Congress, led by Mrs Gandhi, was returned to power in 1980.

Violence in Sikh areas, fanned by demands by militant Sikhs for an independent homeland (called Khalistan) increased tensions. In 1984 Mrs Gandhi ordered that the Golden Temple in Amritsar be stormed after it had been turned into a storehouse for weapons by Sikh extremists. Soon afterwards, Mrs Gandhi was assassinated by her Sikh bodyguards.

Mrs Gandhi was succeeded as premier by her son, Rajiv (1944–91), during whose period of office India became involved in Sri Lanka, supporting the central government against the separatist Tamil Tigers movement. Rajiv Gandhi was assassinated by a Tamil Tiger suicide bomber during the 1991 election campaign.

Recent Politics

By 1989 personality clashes and separatists tendencies had shattered the unity of the once all-powerful Congress Party. Regional parties and Hindu nationalist parties came to the fore and, since 1989, when Rajiv Gandhi left office, coalitions have held office. Seven prime ministers have led India since 1989: the longest periods in office were enjoyed by P. V. Narasimha Rao (born 1921), who led a coalition from 1991 to 1996, and Atal Bihari Vajpayee (born 1924), who was premier in 1996 and held office again from 1998–2004. The right-wing Hindu nationalist Bharatiya Janata Party (BJP) has joined most of these coalitions. Support for the BJP increased following violence between Hindus and Muslims over a campaign, begun in 1990, to build a Hindu temple on the site of a mosque in the holy city of Ayodhya.

Since the fall of the Soviet Union (1991), India has retreated from state ownership and protectionism. Privatization has been accompanied by an economic revolution that has seen the development of high tech industries. At the same time, India has become a nuclear power. Although India exploded its first nuclear device in 1974, tests in 1998 confirmed the nation's capability to deliver these weapons.

There have been 35,000 deaths since the outbreak of the Kashmir insurgency in 1988. Negotiations with Pakistan over the future of the disputed territory began in July 1999. Hopes of avoiding further violence were set back in Dec. 2001, in an attack on the Indian parliament by suicide bombers. 13 people died. Although no group claimed responsibility, Kashmiri separatists were blamed. However, Pakistani President Pervez Musharraf's subsequent crackdown on militants helped to bring the two countries back from the brink of war. Tension between India and Pakistan increased following an attack on an Indian army base in Indian-occupied Kashmir on 14 May 2002. The attack, which killed 31 people, was linked to Islamic terrorists infiltrating the Kashmir valley from Pakistan. It drew widespread criticism of President Musharraf for failing to combat terrorism in the disputed region. In Feb. 2002, 58 Hindu pilgrims returning from Ayodhya were killed when their train was set on fire following a confrontation with a Muslim crowd at Godhra in Gujarat. The incident led to three months of intermittent communal rioting, during which at least 800 Muslims died in attacks by Hindus. Relations between India and Pakistan cooled again in Aug. 2003 when 50 people were killed by terrorist bombings in Mumbai (Bombay). The two countries then embarked on a new phase of peace negotiations. In May 2004 India elected Manmohan Singh as its first Sikh prime minister. The peace process was set back when unidentified terrorists killed over 200 people and injured 700 more in a series of co-ordinated train bombings in Mumbai on 11 July 2006. In Dec. 2008 talks were temporarily suspended, a month after nearly 200 people died when gunmen launched a series of attacks on buildings in Mumbai's tourism and financial district. India claimed that Pakistani-based militants were responsible.

TERRITORY AND POPULATION

India is bounded in the northwest by Pakistan, north by China (Tibet), Nepal and Bhutan, east by Myanmar, and southeast, south and southwest by the Indian Ocean. The far eastern states and territories are almost separated from the rest by Bangladesh. The area is 3,166,285 sq. km. A Sino-Indian agreement of 7 Sept. 1993 settled frontier disputes dating from the war of 1962. Population, 2001 census population: 1,028,610,328 (496,453,556 females), giving a density of 325 persons per sq. km. There are also 20m. Indians and ethnic Indians living abroad, notably in Malaysia, the USA, Saudi Arabia, the UK and South Africa. 71·3% of the population was rural in 2005. Goa is the most urban state, at 49·8% in 2001; and Himachal Pradesh the most rural, at 90·2% in 2001. More than 45% of Indians are under 20.

The UN gives an estimated population for 2010 of 1,214·46m.

By 2050 India is expected to have a population of 1·66bn. It is projected to overtake China as the world's most populous country around 2025.

Area and population of states and union territories:

States	*Area in sq. km*	*Population 2001 census*	*Density per sq. km (2001)*
Andhra Pradesh (And P)	275,069	76,210,007	277
Arunachal Pradesh (Arun P)	83,743	1,097,968	13
Assam (Ass)	78,438	26,655,528	340
Bihar (Bih)	94,163	82,998,509	881
Chhattisgarh (Chh)	135,191	20,833,803	154
Goa	3,702	1,347,668	364
Gujarat (Guj)	196,024	50,671,017	258
Haryana (Har)	44,212	21,144,564	478
Himachal Pradesh (Him P)	55,673	6,077,900	109
Jammu and Kashmir (J and K)	101,387	10,143,700	100
Jharkhand (Jha)	79,714	26,945,829	338
Karnataka (Kar)	191,791	52,850,562	276
Kerala (Ker)	38,863	31,841,374	819
Madhya Pradesh (MP)	308,245	60,348,023	196
Maharashtra (Mah)	307,577	96,878,627	315
Manipur (Man)	22,327	2,166,788	97
Meghalaya (Meg)	22,429	2,318,822	103
Mizoram (Miz)	21,087	888,573	42
Nagaland (Nag)	16,579	1,990,036	120
Orissa (Or)	155,707	36,804,660	236
Punjab (Pun)	50,362	24,358,999	484
Rajasthan (Raj)	342,239	56,507,188	165
Sikkim (Sik)	7,096	540,851	76
Tamil Nadu (TN)	130,058	62,405,679	480
Tripura (Tri)	10,486	3,199,203	305
Uttar Pradesh (UP)	240,928	166,197,921	690
Uttarakhand (formerly Uttaranchal) (Uan)	53,483	8,489,349	159
West Bengal (WB)	88,752	80,176,197	903

Union Territories	Area in sq. km	Population 2001 census	Density per sq. km (2001)
Andaman and Nicobar Islands (ANI)	8,248	356,152	43
Chandigarh (Chan)	114	900,635	7,900
Dadra and Nagar Haveli (DNH)	491	220,490	449
Daman and Diu (D and D)	112	158,204	1,413
Delhi (Del)	1,483	13,850,507	9,340
Lakshadweep (Lak)	32	60,650	1,895
Puducherry (formerly Pondicherry) (Pdy)	480	974,345	2,030

Urban agglomerations with populations over 2m., together with their core cities at the 2001 census:

	State/ Union Territory	Urban agglomeration	Core city
Mumbai (Bombay)	Maharashtra	16,434,386	11,978,450
Kolkata (Calcutta)	West Bengal	13,211,853	4,572,876
Delhi	Delhi	12,877,470	9,879,172
Chennai (Madras)	Tamil Nadu	6,560,242	4,343,645
Hyderabad	Andhra Pradesh	5,742,036	3,637,483
Bangalore	Karnataka	5,701,456	4,301,326
Ahmedabad	Gujarat	4,518,240	3,520,085
Pune (Poona)	Maharashtra	3,760,636	2,538,473
Surat	Gujarat	2,811,614	2,433,835
Kanpur	Uttar Pradesh	2,715,555	2,551,337
Jaipur	Rajasthan	2,322,575	2,322,575
Lucknow	Uttar Pradesh	2,245,509	2,185,927
Nagpur	Maharashtra	2,129,500	2,052,066

Smaller urban agglomerations and cities with populations over 250,000 (with 2001 census populations, in 1,000):

Agra (UP)	1,331	Firozabad (UP)	433
Ahmadnagar (Mah)	348	Gaya (Bih)	395
Ajmer (Raj)	491	Ghaziabad (UP)	968
Akola (Mah)	401	Gorakhpur (UP)	623
Alappuzha (Ker)	283	Gulbarga (Kar)	430
Aligarh (UP)	669	Guntur (And P)	514
Allahabad (UP)	1,042	Guwahati (Ass)	819
Alwar (Raj)	266	Gwalior (MP)	866
Amravati (Mah)	550	Hisar (Har)	263
Amritsar (Pun)	1,004	Hubli-Dharwad (Kar)	786
Asansol (WB)	1,067	Ichalkaranji (Mah)	286
Aurangabad (Mah)	892	Imphal (Man)	250
Barddhaman (WB)	286	Indore (MP)	1,506
Bareilly (UP)	748	Jabalpur (MP)	1,098
Belgaum (Kar)	506	Jalandhar (Pun)	714
Bellary (Kar)	317	Jalgaon (Mah)	369
Bhagalpur (Bih)	350	Jammu (J and K)	612
Bhavnagar (Guj)	518	Jamnagar (Guj)	557
Bhilai (Chh)	928	Jamshedpur (Jha)	1,105
Bhilwara (Raj)	280	Jhansi (UP)	460
Bhiwandi (Mah)	621	Jodhpur (Raj)	861
Bhopal (MP)	1,458	Junagadh (Guj)	252
Bhubaneswar (Or)	658	Kakinada (And P)	296
Bijapur (Kar)	254	Kharagpur (WB)	273
Bikaner (Raj)	530	Kochi (Ker)	1,356
Bilaspur (Chh)	335	Kolhapur (Mah)	506
Bokaro Steel City (Jha)	498	Kollam (Ker)	380
Brahmapur (OR)	308	Korba (Chh)	316
Chandigarh (Chan)	809	Kota (Raj)	703
Chandrapur (Mah)	289	Kozhikode (Ker)	880
Coimbatore (TN)	1,461	Kurnool (And P)	343
Cuddapah (And P)	263	Latur (Mah)	300
Cuttack (Or)	587	Ludhiana (Pun)	1,398
Darbhanga (Bih)	267	Madurai (TN)	1,203
Davangere (Kar)	365	Malegaon (Mah)	409
Dehra Dun (Uan)	530	Mangalore (Kar)	539
Dhanbad (Jha)	1,065	Mathura (UP)	323
Dhule (Mah)	342	Meerut (UP)	1,162
Durgapur (WB)	493	Moradabad (UP)	642
Erode (TN)	390	Muzaffarnagar (UP)	332
Faridabad Complex (Har)	1,056	Muzaffarpur (Bih)	306
Mysore (Kar)	799	Shahjahanpur (UP)	322
Nanded (Mah)	431	Shiliguri (WB)	285
Nashik (Mah)	1,152	Shillong (Meg)	268
Nellore (And P)	405	Shimoga (Kar)	274
Nizamabad (And P)	289	Sholapur (Mah)	872
Noida (UP)	305	Srinagar (J and K)	988
Panipat (Har)	354	Thalassery (Ker)	498
Parbhani (Mah)	259	Thiruvananthapuram (Ker)	890
Patiala (Pun)	324	Thrissur (Ker)	330
Patna (Bih)	1,698	Tiruchirapalli (TN)	866
Puducherry (Pdy)	506	Tirunelveli (TN)	433
Raipur (Chh)	700	Tirupati (And P)	304
Rajahmundry (And P)	414	Tiruppur (TN)	551
Rajkot (Guj)	1,003	Udaipur (Raj)	389
Rampur (UP)	281	Ujjain (MP)	431
Ranchi (Jha)	863	Vadodara (Guj)	1,491
Rohtak (Har)	295	Varanasi (UP)	1,204
Rourkela (OR)	485	Vellore (TN)	387
Sagar (MP)	309	Vijayawada (And P)	1,040
Saharanpur (UP)	456	Visakhapatnam (And P)	1,346
Salem (TN)	751	Warangal (And P)	579
Sangli-Miraj (Mah)	448	Yamunanagar (Har)	307

SOCIAL STATISTICS

Many births and deaths go unregistered. The Registrar General's data suggests a birth rate for 2003 of 23·3 per 1,000 population and a death rate of 8·5, which would indicate in a year approximately 24,860,000 births and 9,070,000 deaths. The growth rate is, however, slowing, and by 2003 had dropped below 1·5%, having been over 2% in 1991. Expectation of life at birth, 2007, 62·0 years for males and 64·9 years for females. In 2005, 52% of the population was aged under 25.

Marriages and divorces are not registered. The minimum age for a civil marriage is 18 for women and 21 for men; for a sacramental marriage, 14 for females and 18 for males. Population growth rate, 1991–2001, 21·54% (the lowest since 1961–71). Infant mortality, 2005, 56 per 1,000 live births; fertility rate, 2004, 3·0 births per woman. Child deaths (under the age of five) fell from 123 per 1,000 in 1990 to 74 per 1,000 in 2005.

CLIMATE

India has a variety of climatic sub-divisions. In general, there are four seasons. The cool one lasts from Dec. to March, the hot season is in April and May, the rainy season is June to Sept., followed by a further dry season until Nov. Rainfall, however, varies considerably, from 4" (100 mm) in the N.W. desert to over 400" (10,000 mm) in parts of Assam.

Range of temperature and rainfall: New Delhi, Jan. 57°F (13·9°C), July 88°F (31·1°C). Annual rainfall 26" (640 mm). Chennai, Jan. 76°F (24·4°C), July 87°F (30·6°C). Annual rainfall 51" (1,270 mm). Cherrapunji, Jan. 53°F (11·7°C), July 68°F (20°C). Annual rainfall 432" (10,798 mm). Darjeeling, Jan. 41°F (5°C), July 62°F (16·7°C). Annual rainfall 121" (3,035 mm). Hyderabad, Jan. 72°F (22·2°C), July 80°F (26·7°C). Annual rainfall 30" (752 mm). Kochi, Jan. 80°F (26·7°C), July 79°F (26·1°C). Annual rainfall 117" (2,929 mm). Kolkata, Jan. 67°F (19·4°C), July 84°F (28·9°C). Annual rainfall 64" (1,600 mm). Mumbai, Jan. 75°F (23·9°C), July 81°F (27·2°C). Annual rainfall 72" (1,809 mm). Patna, Jan. 63°F (17·2°C), July 90°F (32·2°C). Annual rainfall 46" (1,150 mm).

On 26 Dec. 2004 an undersea earthquake centred off the Indonesian island of Sumatra caused a huge tsunami that flooded coastal areas in southern India resulting in 16,000 deaths. In total there were more than 225,000 deaths in 14 countries.

CONSTITUTION AND GOVERNMENT

The Constitution was passed by the Constituent Assembly on 26 Nov. 1949 and came into force on 26 Jan. 1950. It has since been amended 93 times.

India is a republic and comprises a Union of 28 States and seven Union Territories. Each State is administered by a Governor appointed by the President for a term of five years while each Union Territory is administered by the President through a Lieut.-Governor or an administrator appointed by him. The head of the Union (head of state) is the *President* in whom all executive power is vested, to be exercised on the advice of ministers responsible to Parliament. The President, who must be an Indian citizen at least 35 years old and eligible for election to the House of the People, is elected by an electoral college of all the elected members of Parliament and of the state legislative assemblies, holds office for five years and is eligible for re-election. There is also a *Vice-President* who is *ex officio* chairman of the Council of States.

There is a *Council of Ministers* to aid and advise the President; this comprises Ministers who are members of the Cabinet and Ministers of State and deputy ministers who are not. A Minister who for any period of six consecutive months is not a member of either House of Parliament ceases to be a Minister at the expiration of that period. The *Prime Minister* is appointed by the President; other Ministers are appointed by the President on the Prime Minister's advice. The salary of each Minister is Rs 16,000 per month.

Parliament consists of the President, the *Council of States* (*Rajya Sabha*) and the *House of the People* (*Lok Sabha*). The Council of States, or the Upper House, consists of not more than 250 members; in July 2005 there were 233 elected members and 11 members nominated by the President. The election to this house is indirect; the representatives of each State are elected by the elected members of the Legislative Assembly of that State. The Council of States is a permanent body not liable to dissolution, but one-third of the members retire every second year. The House of the People, or the Lower House, normally consists of 545 members, 543 directly elected on the basis of adult suffrage from territorial constituencies in the States, and the Union territories; in July 2005 there were 540 elected members, two nominated members and three vacancies. The House of the People unless sooner dissolved continues for a period of five years from the date appointed for its first meeting; in emergency, Parliament can extend the term by one year.

State Legislatures

For every State there is a legislature which consists of the Governor, and (a) two Houses, a Legislative Assembly and a Legislative Council, in the States of Bihar, Jammu and Kashmir, Karnataka, Madhya Pradesh (where it is provided for but not in operation), Maharashtra and Uttar Pradesh, and (b) one House, a Legislative Assembly, in the other States. Every Legislative Assembly, unless sooner dissolved, continues for five years from the date appointed for its first meeting. In emergency the term can be extended by one year. Every State Legislative Council is a permanent body and is not subject to dissolution, but one-third of the members retire every second year. Parliament can, however, abolish an existing Legislative Council or create a new one, if the proposal is supported by a resolution of the Legislative Assembly concerned.

Legislation

The various subjects of legislation are enumerated in three lists in the seventh schedule to the constitution. List I, the Union List, consists of 97 subjects (including defence, foreign affairs, communications, currency and coinage, banking and customs) with respect to which the Union Parliament has exclusive power to make laws. The State legislature has exclusive power to make laws with respect to the 66 subjects in list II, the State List; these include police and public order, agriculture and irrigation, education, public health and local government. The powers to make laws with respect to the 47 subjects (including economic and social planning, legal questions and labour and price control) in list III, the Concurrent List, are held by both Union and State governments, though the former prevails. But Parliament may legislate with respect to any subject in the State List in circumstances when the subject assumes national importance or during emergencies.

Fundamental Rights

Two chapters of the constitution deal with fundamental rights and 'Directive Principles of State Policy'. 'Untouchability' is abolished, and its practice in any form is punishable. The fundamental rights can be enforced through the ordinary courts of law and through the Supreme Court of the Union. The directive principles cannot be enforced through the courts of law; they are nevertheless fundamental in the governance of the country.

Citizenship

Under the Constitution, every person who was on the 26 Jan. 1950 domiciled in India and (a) was born in India or (b) either of whose parents was born in India or (c) who has been ordinarily resident in the territory of India for not less than five years immediately preceding that date became a citizen of India. Special provision is made for migrants from Pakistan and for Indians resident abroad. The right to vote is granted to every person who is a citizen of India and who is not less than 18 years of age on a fixed date and is not otherwise disqualified.

Parliament

Parliament and the state legislatures are organized according to the following schedule (figures show distribution of seats in July 2005 for the Lok Sabha, the Rajya Sabha and the State Legislatures):

	Parliament		*State Legislatures*	
	House of the People (Lok Sabha)	*Council of States (Rajya Sabha)*	*Legislative Assemblies (Vidhan Sabhas)*	*Legislative Councils (Vidhan Parishads)*
States:				
Andhra Pradesh	42	18	295[1]	—
Arunachal Pradesh	2	1	60	—
Assam	14	7	126	—
Bihar	40	16	243	96
Chhattisgarh	11	5	90	—
Goa	2	1	40	—
Gujarat	26	11	182	—
Haryana	9	5	90	—
Himachal Pradesh	4	3	68	—
Jammu and Kashmir	6	4	89[2, 3]	36[4]
Jharkhand	14	6	81	—
Karnataka	28	12	225[1]	75
Kerala	19	9	141[1]	—
Madhya Pradesh	29	11	231[1]	—
Maharashtra	47	19	289[1]	78
Manipur	2	1	60	—
Meghalaya	2	1	60	—
Mizoram	1	1	40	—
Nagaland	1	1	60	—
Orissa	21	10	147	—
Punjab	13	7	117	—
Rajasthan	25	10	200	—
Sikkim	1	1	32	—
Tamil Nadu	39	18	235[1]	—
Tripura	2	1	60	—
Uttar Pradesh	80	31	404[1]	100
Uttarakhand	5	3	70	—
West Bengal	42	16	295[1]	—
Union Territories:				
Andaman and Nicobar Islands	1	—	—	—
Chandigarh	1	—	—	—
Dadra and Nagar Haveli	1	—	—	—
Daman and Diu	1	—	—	—
Delhi	7	3	70	—
Lakshadweep	1	—	—	—
Puducherry	1	1	30	—
Nominated by the President under Article 80 (1) (a) of the Constitution	—	11	—	—
Total	542[5]	244	4,130[6]	393

[1]Includes one nominated member.
[2]Includes two nominated members.
[3]Excludes 24 seats for Pakistan-occupied areas of the State which are in abeyance.
[4]Excludes seats for the Pakistan-occupied areas.
[5]Includes two nominated members to represent Anglo-Indians.
[6]Includes ten nominated members.

The number of seats allotted to the scheduled castes and the scheduled tribes in the House of the People is 79 and 41 respectively. Of the 4,120 elective seats in the state Legislative Assemblies, 570 are reserved for the scheduled castes and 532 for the scheduled tribes.

Language

The Constitution provides that the official language of the Union shall be Hindi in the Devanagari script. Hindi is spoken by over 30% of the population. It was originally provided that English should continue to be used for all official purposes until 1965. But the Official Languages Act 1963 provides that, after the expiry of this period of 15 years from the coming into force of the Constitution, English might continue to be used, in addition to Hindi, for all official purposes of the Union for which it was being used immediately before that day, and for the transaction of business in Parliament. According to the Official Languages (Use for official purposes of the Union) Rules 1976, an employee may record in Hindi or in English without being required to furnish a translation thereof in the other language and no employee possessing a working knowledge of Hindi may ask for an English translation of any document in Hindi except in the case of legal or technical documents.

The 58th amendment to the Constitution (26 Nov. 1987) authorized the preparation of a constitution text in Hindi.

The following 22 languages are included in the Eighth Schedule to the Constitution (with 2003 estimate of speakers): Assamese (16·5m.), Bengali (87·6m.), Bodo (1·5m.), Dogri (2·7m.), Gujarati (51·2m.), Hindi (424·7m.), Kannada (41·2m.), Kashmiri (5·0m.), Konkani (2·2m.), Maithili (9·8m.), Malayalam (38·3m.), Manipuri (1·6m.), Marathi (78·7m.), Nepali (2·6m.), Oriya (35·3m.), Punjabi (29·4m.), Sanskrit (fewer than 1m.), Santhali (6·6m.), Sindhi (2·7m.), Tamil (66·7m.), Telugu (83·1m.), Urdu (54·7m.). It is estimated that over 850 different languages are spoken throughout the country.

Thakur, R., *The Government and Politics of India*. 1995

National Anthem

'Jana-gana-mana' ('Thou art the ruler of the minds of all people'); words and tune by Rabindranath Tagore.

GOVERNMENT CHRONOLOGY

Prime Ministers since 1947. (BJP = Bharatiya Janata Party; BLD = Indian People's Party/Bharatiya Lok Dal; INC = Indian National Congress (a.k.a. Indian Congress Party); INC(i) = Indian National Congress-Indira Gandhi faction; JD = People's Party/Janata Dal; JD(s) = Janata Dal-Chandra Shekhar faction; JP = People's Party/Janata Dal; UPA = United Progressive Alliance)

1947–64	INC	Jawaharlal Nehru
1964	INC	Gulzarilal Nanda
1964–66	INC	Lal Bahadur Shastri
1966	INC	Gulzarilal Nanda
1966–77	INC	Indira Gandhi
1977–79	JP	Morarji Desai
1979–80	JP/BLD	Charan Singh
1980–84	INC(i)	Indira Gandhi
1984–89	INC(i)	Rajiv Gandhi
1989–90	JD	Vishwanath Pratap Singh
1990–91	JD(s)	Chandra Shekhar
1991–96	INC(i)	Pamulaparti Venkata Narasimha Rao
1996	BJP	Atal Bihari Vajpayee
1996–97	JD	Haradanahalli Dodde Deve Gowda
1997–98	JD	Inder Kumar Gujral
1998–04	BJP	Atal Bihari Vajpayee
2004–	INC, UPA	Manmohan Singh

Presidents of the Union since 1950.

1950–62	Rajendra Prasad
1962–67	Sarvepalli Radhakrishnan
1967–69	Zakir Husain
1969–74	Varahgiri Venkata Giri
1974–77	Fakhruddin Ali Ahmed
1977–82	Neelam Sanjiva Reddy
1982–87	Zail Singh
1987–92	Ramaswamy Iyer Venkataraman
1992–97	Shankar Dayal Sharma
1997–2002	Kocheril Raman Narayanan
2002–07	Avul Pakir Jainulabdeen Abdul Kalam
2007–	Pratibha Patil

RECENT ELECTIONS

Presidential elections were held on 21 July 2007. Pratibha Patil (backed by the ruling United Progressive Alliance) was elected by federal and state legislators, with 638,116 votes (65·8%), against 331,306 (34·2%) for incumbent vice-president Bhairon Singh Shekhawat.

Parliamentary elections were held in five phases between 16 April and 13 May 2009. Turnout was an estimated 60%. The Indian National Congress (INC) and its allies were just ten seats short of a majority after they gained 262 seats (217 seats in 2004), with the INC winning 206 seats; the National Democratic Alliance (NDA) gained 159 seats (185 seats in 2004), with the Bharatiya Janata Party (BJP) winning 116 seats; the Third Front won 79 seats, with the Left Front (LF) winning 24; the Fourth Front won 27 seats, with the Samajwadi Party (SP) winning 23; other parties and independents won 16 seats.

Singh, V. B., *Elections in India: Data Handbook on Lok Sabha Elections, 1986–91*. 1994

CURRENT ADMINISTRATION

President: Pratibha Patil; b. 1934 (sworn in 25 July 2007).

Vice-President: Hamid Ansari.

After the 2004 elections, despite emotional appeals from her supporters, Congress President Sonia Gandhi declined the premiership on 18 May. Manmohan Singh became India's first Sikh prime minister on 22 May.

In March 2010 the INC-led coalition government (known as the United Progressive Alliance) was composed as follows:

Prime Minister and Minister of Personnel, Public Grievances and Pensions, Planning, Atomic Energy, Space and Culture: Manmohan Singh; b. 1932 (INC; sworn in 22 May 2004).

Minister of Finance: Pranab Mukherjee (INC). *Agriculture, Consumer Affairs, Food and Public Distribution:* Sharad Pawar (Nationalist Congress Party). *Defence:* A. K. Antony (INC). *Home Affairs:* Palaniappan Chidambaram (INC). *Railways:* Mamata Banerjee (All India Trinamool Congress). *External Affairs:* S. M. Krishna (INC). *Steel:* Virbhadra Singh (INC). *Heavy Industries and Public Enterprises:* Vilasrao Deshmukh (INC). *Health and Family Welfare:* Ghulam Nabi Azad (INC). *Power:* Sushil Kumar Shinde (INC). *Law and Justice:* M. Veerappa Moily (INC). *New and Renewable Energy:* Dr Farooq Abdullah (Jammu and Kashmir National Conference). *Urban Development:* S. Jaipal Reddy (INC). *Road Transport and Highways:* Kamal Nath (INC). *Overseas Indian Affairs:* Vayalar Ravi (INC). *Textiles:* Dayanidhi Maran (Dravida Progressive Federation). *Communications and Information Technology:* A. Raja (Dravida Progressive Federation). *Petroleum and Natural Gas:* Murli Deora (INC). *Information and Broadcasting:* Ambika Soni (INC). *Labour and Employment:* Mallikarjun Kharge (INC). *Human Resource Development:* Kapil

Sibal (INC). *Mines and Development of the North Eastern Region:* Bijoy Krishna Handique (INC). *Commerce and Industry:* Anand Sharma (INC). *Rural Development and Panchayati Raj:* C. P. Joshi (INC). *Housing, Urban Poverty Alleviation and Tourism:* Kumari Selja (INC). *Food Processing Industries:* Subodh Kant Sahay (INC). *Youth Affairs and Sports:* M. S. Gill (INC). *Shipping:* G. K. Vasan (INC). *Parliamentary Affairs and Water Resources:* Pawan K. Bansal (INC). *Social Justice and Empowerment:* Mukul Wasnik (INC). *Tribal Affairs:* Kantilal Bhuria (INC). *Chemicals and Fertilizers:* M. K. Alagiri (Dravida Progressive Federation).

Office of the Prime Minister of India: http://www.pmindia.nic.in

CURRENT LEADERS

Pratibha Patil

Position
President

Introduction
Pratibha Patil was sworn in as India's first female president in July 2007. Backed by the ruling United Progressive Alliance (UPA) and the Left Front, she won nearly two-thirds of the votes cast in state assemblies and in India's parliament.

Early Life
Pratibha Patil was born on 19 Dec.1934 in Nadgaon, Maharashtra. She graduated with a Masters degree in political science and economics from Mooljee Jaitha College, Jalgaon and then studied at the Government Law College in Mumbai. She worked at the Jalgaon District Court before entering politics in 1962 when she successfully contested a seat in the Maharashtra State Assembly, representing the Indian National Congress (INC) party. Following re-election in 1967 she was appointed deputy minister working in the offices of public health, prohibition, tourism, housing and parliamentary affairs. From 1972–77 she held several cabinet portfolios including social welfare, public health and prohibition, rehabilitation and cultural affairs.

When the INC split in 1977 after Indira Gandhi's electoral defeat in the wake of the Indian Emergency, Patil remained loyal to Gandhi. She protested the arrest of Gandhi in Dec. 1977 and was herself arrested and imprisoned for ten days. Patil was appointed minister for education in 1978 and became leader of the opposition in the state assembly in July 1979 when Congress (Urs), a breakaway faction of the INC, came to power. The INC returned to power in 1980 and Patil was a frontrunner for the post of chief minister of Maharashtra but ultimately lost out to A. R. Antulay. She returned to the Maharashtra state assembly where she was minister for urban development and housing from 1982–83, then minister for civil supplies and social welfare from 1983–85.

In 1985 Patil was elected as an INC representative to the Rajya Sabha, parliament's upper house. Between 1986–88 she was variously deputy chairperson of the house, a member of the business advisory committee and chairman of the committee of privileges. Following a rift with Prabha Rau, president of the Maharashtra Pradesh Congress Committee (MPCC), Patil was chosen by Rajiv Gandhi as Rau's replacement in 1988, holding the post until 1990. In the elections of 1991 Patil was elected to the 10th Lok Sabha, the lower house of parliament, where she was chairperson of the House Committee. Having completed her term in April 1996 she did not stand for re-election.

In Nov. 2004 Patil became the first female governor of Rajasthan. In this capacity she refused to sign the contentious Rajasthan Freedom of Religion Bill in 2006, which had been introduced by the Bharatiya Janata Party-led state government and sought to ban forced religious conversion. Patil held that clauses in the bill infringed fundamental rights, including freedom of speech and freedom to practise and propagate religion.

Patil was announced as the United Progressive Alliance (UPA)–Left Front presidential candidate on 14 June 2007, the result of a last-minute compromise between the UPA and Left Front. Her campaign was marred by a series of allegations against her, including claims of a murder cover-up and financial irregularities. However, the allegations were not substantiated and she became president on 21 July 2007.

Career in Office
Though chiefly a ceremonial role, as president Patil has to navigate and reconcile the frequently bitter divides of party politics. A keen supporter of rights for women and the poor, she continues to champion the spread of education to all Indian children and has pledged to tackle abuses such as female infanticide.

Manmohan Singh

Position
Prime Minister

Introduction
After three decades as a civil servant, the quietly-spoken former academic and economist was sworn in as India's first Sikh prime minister on 22 May 2004. His appointment followed the general election victory of the Indian National Congress over the Bharatiya Janata Party (BJP; Indian People's Party) and Sonia Gandhi's unexpected rejection of the top job. A low-profile technocrat and adviser throughout the 1970s and 1980s, Singh came to the fore in 1991 when he was appointed finance minister in the cabinet of P. V. Narasimha Rao. India was in severe financial crisis and Manmohan Singh is credited with bringing about a fundamental change of direction, becoming known as the 'architect of India's economic reform'. His coalition won an emphatic victory at the 2009 elections, coming close to winning an absolute majority in parliament.

Early Life
Manmohan Singh was born in Gah, West Punjab (now in Pakistan), on 26 Sept. 1932, the son of a shopkeeper. He was educated at Punjab University in the newly-established city of Chandigarh (built to replace Lahore as the capital of the Indian state of Punjab following the formation of Pakistan in 1947). He also attended the universities of Cambridge and Oxford in England on scholarships and won Cambridge's prestigious Adam Smith Prize in 1956. Returning to India as an economics lecturer, he remained at Punjab University before being made professor in 1963. Three years later he joined UNCTAD (the UN Conference on Trade and Development) at the United Nations Secretariat in New York, as economic affairs officer. In 1969 Singh returned to India and joined the School of Economics at the University of Delhi as professor of international trade.

Cutting short his academic career in 1971, Singh joined Indira Gandhi's New Congress Party-led government to serve as an economic adviser to the ministry of foreign trade and, from 1972–76, as chief economic adviser in the finance ministry. Stronger ties with the USSR, which influenced Indian economic policy and brought in new aid agreements, marked this period. In 1976 Singh became director of the Reserve Bank of India, a post he held for four years. From 1982–85 he was governor of the Reserve Bank of India and then deputy chairman of the Planning Commission from 1985–87, undertaking various assignments at the International Monetary Fund and the Asian Development Bank. He was first selected for the Rajya Sabha (the upper house of parliament) in 1991, representing the Congress.

In 1991, with India in financial crisis, Singh was appointed finance minister in P. V. Narasimha Rao's cabinet. Foreign exchange reserves were nearly exhausted and the country was close to defaulting on its international debt. In his maiden speech as finance minister, Singh quoted Victor Hugo—'No power on earth can stop an idea whose time has come'—and brought in an ambitious and unprecedented economic reform programme. He slashed red tape, simplified the tax system and ended the 'license Raj' regulations that forced businesses to get government approval for most decisions. He also devalued the rupee, cut subsidies for domestically produced goods, and privatized some state-run companies. Singh spoke of wanting to 'release the innovative, entrepreneurial spirit which was always there in India in such a manner that our economy would grow at a much faster pace, sooner than most people believed.' The recipe worked; industry picked up, inflation was checked, and growth rates remained consistently high through the 1990s (his policies were broadly continued by the BJP-led coalition after they were elected in 1996).

Career in Office

When Singh was sworn in as prime minister on 22 May 2004, he took on a healthy economy: GDP growth was at 7%, foreign exchange reserves were comfortable at US$118bn. and inflation stood at just 4%. However, hundreds of millions of Indians were still living in poverty and Singh faced a tough task in bringing about improvements in living standards, while balancing the demands of leftist and communist parties in the coalition. His first address as prime minister called for 'economic reforms with a human face' stressing the need to achieve friendly relations with neighbouring countries, especially Pakistan. Although Singh has a reputation for honesty and even-handedness, there were some questions about his lack of election-winning political experience—he failed to win a seat in the Lok Sabha (Lower House) elections for South Delhi in 1999.

While India's economy continued to perform strongly, Singh's early premiership had to contend with the devastating effects of a number of severe natural disasters, including the tsunami across the Indian Ocean in Dec. 2004 which hit coastal communities in the south of the country and the Andaman and Nicobar Islands, floods and landslides in Maharashtra in July 2005 and an earthquake in Kashmir in Oct. 2005.

Terrorism has remained a serious problem for the government. Bomb attacks on commuter trains and railway stations in Mumbai in July 2006 killed about 200 people. This atrocity, blamed by India on Pakistan's intelligence services, threatened to undermine previous improvements in the volatile relations between the two nuclear-armed neighbours. A further terrorist bomb attack in Feb. 2007 on a train travelling from New Delhi to Lahore in Pakistan killed about 70 people. Terrorist incidents continued in 2008, particularly in Nov. when suspected Islamic extremists launched a co-ordinated series of attacks on prominent landmarks in India's commercial capital, Mumbai, killing civilians with grenades and machine guns and taking foreign hostages before being overcome by the security forces. The slaughter, in which some 190 people died, led to the resignation of the home affairs minister. India blamed militants from Pakistan for the atrocity, leading Singh's government to lodge a formal protest.

Although India is not party to the Nuclear Non-Proliferation Treaty, Singh and the then US president, George W. Bush, signed a controversial agreement in March 2006 giving India access to US civilian nuclear energy technology in return for having its nuclear sites inspected. The deal was approved by the US Congress in Dec. 2006, but was then stalled by political opposition within the Indian parliament. In July 2008 left-wing parties withdrew their parliamentary support for Singh's government, but it survived a no-confidence vote that cleared the way for it to try and finalize the agreement. In the USA the deal was signed into law by President Bush in Oct.

Also in Oct., Singh signed a security co-operation agreement with Japan during a visit to Tokyo. Following the victory at the general election in April and May 2009 of the United Progressive Alliance (of which the Indian National Congress won nearly 80% of the vote), Singh became only the second Indian prime minister after Indira Gandhi to hold office for two consecutive terms.

DEFENCE

The Supreme Command of the Armed Forces is vested in the president. As well as armed forces of 1,325,000 personnel in 2006, there are 1,721,000 active paramilitary forces including 208,000 members of the Border Security Force based mainly in the troubled Jammu and Kashmir region. Military service is voluntary but, under the amended constitution, it is regarded as a fundamental duty of every citizen to perform National Service when called upon. Defence expenditure in 2008 was US$30,030m. (US$25 per capita and 2·5% of GDP), a real-term increase of 5% on the previous year. In 2007 defence spending represented 2·5% of GDP. In the period 2004–08 India's spending on major conventional weapons was second only to that of China, at US$8·2bn. In Sept. 2003 India announced that it would be buying 66 Hawk trainer fighter jets, with delivery expected by 2011. In Oct. 2003 agreement was reached for India to purchase Israel's sophisticated US$1bn. Phalcon early-warning radar system.

Nuclear Weapons

India's first nuclear test was in 1974. Its most recent tests were a series of five carried out in May 1998. According to the Stockholm International Peace Research Institute, India's nuclear arsenal was estimated to consist of a minimum of 60–70 nuclear warheads in Jan. 2009. India, known to have a nuclear weapons programme, has not signed the Comprehensive Nuclear-Test-Ban-Treaty, which is intended to bring about a ban on any nuclear explosions. According to *Deadly Arsenals*, published by the Carnegie Endowment for International Peace, India has chemical weapons and has a biological weapons research programme. In 2006 the USA and India announced a civil nuclear co-operation initiative. Under the terms of the deal, India was exempted from a ban on nuclear energy sales that had previously covered non-signatories of the international non-proliferation treaty, of which India is one. In return India agreed to open up 14 of its 22 nuclear installations to international inspections. However, the deal has yet to be ratified.

Army

The Army is organized into six commands covering different areas, which in turn are subdivided into sub-areas, plus a training command.

The strength of the Army in 2006 was 1·1m. There are four 'RAPID' divisions, 18 infantry divisions, ten mountain divisions, three armoured divisions and two artillery divisions. Each division consists of several brigades. Officers are trained at the Indian Military Academy, Dehra Dun (Uttarakhand). Army reserves number 300,000 with a further 500,000 personnel available as a second-line reserve force. There is a volunteer Territorial Army of 40,000. There are numerous paramilitary groups including the Ministry of Defence *Rashtriya Rifles* (numbering 57,000), the Indo-Tibetan Border Police (36,300), the State Armed Police (450,000), the Civil Defence (500,000), the Central Industrial Security Force (94,000) and the Ministry of Home Affairs Assam Rifles (63,900). An Army Aviation Corps was established in 1986.

Navy

The Navy has three commands; Eastern (at Visakhapatnam), Western (at Mumbai) and Southern (at Kochi), the latter a training and support command. The fleet is divided into two elements, Eastern and Western; and well-trained, all-volunteer personnel operate a mix of Soviet and western vessels. In May 2003 India held joint naval exercises with Russia in the Arabian Sea for the first time since the collapse of the Soviet Union.

The principal ship is the light aircraft carrier, *Viraat*, formerly HMS *Hermes*, of 29,000 tonnes, completed in 1959 and transferred to the Indian Navy in 1987 after seeing service in the Falklands War. In 2003 India began construction of another aircraft carrier and began negotiations to purchase a third from the Russian navy. The fleet includes 12 Soviet-built diesel submarines and four new German-designed submarines. There are also 25 destroyers and frigates. The Naval Air force was 7,000-strong in 2006; equipment includes 34 combat aircraft. Main bases are at Mumbai (main dockyard), Goa, Visakhapatnam and Kolkata on the sub-continent and Port Blair in the Andaman Islands.

Naval personnel in 2006 numbered 55,000 including 5,000 Naval Air Arm and 1,200 marines.

Air Force

Units of the IAF are organized into five operational commands—Central at Allahabad, Eastern at Shillong, Southern at Thiruvananthapuram, South-Western at Gandhinagar and Western at Delhi. There is also a training command and a maintenance command. The air force has 170,000 personnel.

Equipment includes more than 850 combat aircraft. Major combat types include Su-30s, MiG-21s, MiG-23s, MiG-27s, MiG-29s, *Jaguars* and Mirage 2000s. Air Force reserves numbered 140,000 in 2006.

INTERNATIONAL RELATIONS

India is a member of the UN, World Bank, IMF and several other UN specialized agencies, WTO, BIS, Commonwealth, IOM, Asian Development Bank, Colombo Plan, SAARC and Antarctic Treaty.

ECONOMY

Agriculture accounted for 18·3% of GDP in 2006, industry 29·3% and services 52·4%.

Since the late 1990s a divide has become increasingly pronounced between the south and west, where a modern economy is booming in cities such as Bangalore, Hyderabad and Chennai, and the poorer and politically volatile areas in the north and east.

Overview

After independence India adopted a policy of import substituting industrialization (ISI). Protected from international competition by tariffs, a broad industrial base was built that initially generated strong growth. However, inefficient bureaucracy and the absence of competition hindered sustained productivity growth. In 1991 a balance of payments and foreign currency reserve crisis prompted market reforms that have helped India to become one of the world's fastest-growing economies. A 2007 report by Goldman Sachs suggested that if current growth patterns continued, India could have the second largest economy in the world by 2050, behind China and ahead of the USA.

Industrial licensing (determining how much entrepreneurs could manufacture) was abolished and trade barriers lowered after India joined the World Trade Organization in 1995. Foreign direct investment rose from almost nothing to over US$41bn. in 2008. Liberalization has contributed to increased foreign participation and growth in durable consumer goods production, including cars, scooters, consumer electronics, computer systems and white goods. The service sector has become the economy's most dynamic sector, with India a world leader in telecommunications, IT and pharmaceuticals. It is also an international centre for business outsourcing services, particularly for the USA. A large proportion of heavy industry is publicly-owned and inefficient state-owned enterprises, chiefly in the banking sector, hinder growth. Excessive regulation remains a deterrent to many businesses.

Two-thirds of the workforce is in agriculture, which accounts for one-quarter of the country's total output. Yields per hectare are low by international standards, with many workers at subsistence level. The high numbers employed in unproductive agriculture significantly limits the potential for non-agricultural demand and the development of other sectors. Poverty declined from 36% of the population in 1993–94 to 26% in the early 2000s and social indicators have improved but there are still over 250m. poor in the country according to the World Bank. Human development indicators are among the lowest in the world, especially in rural areas. The high growth rates in recent years have increased inequalities, with India's richest states now having incomes five times higher than those of the poorest. Inequalities between skilled and unskilled workers have also risen, and some 90% of India's labour force remains in low-productivity jobs in the informal sector. Sustained poverty reduction will be difficult until agricultural productivity is raised and the rural infrastructure developed.

But with an already worrisome level of fiscal deficits, increases in social and infrastructure expenditure are problematic. In Nov. 2005 the government approved the establishment of the India Infrastructure Finance Company to raise funds in financial markets for mega infrastructure projects. Economic data released by the Central Statistical Organisation in 2005 showed an encouraging surge in manufacturing production. The Economist Intelligence Unit argues, however, that unless the large fiscal deficits, rigid labour laws and weak regulatory system are tackled, the economy will continue to grow below potential.

India achieved growth of over 8% on average between 2004 and 2008, at the same time as reducing poverty. However, the country has not escaped the global financial crisis. Although India's economy was among the world's fastest growing (at 6·1%) in the second quarter of 2009, it still experienced a substantial decline from previous high rates. At the request of the government the World Bank approved four loans worth US$4·3bn. in Sept. 2009.

Currency

The unit of currency is the *Indian rupee* (INR) of 100 *paise*. Foreign exchange reserves were US$261,247m. in Aug. 2009 and gold reserves 11·50m. troy oz. Inflation rates (based on IMF statistics):

1999	*2000*	*2001*	*2002*	*2003*	*2004*	*2005*	*2006*	*2007*	*2008*
4·7%	4·0%	3·8%	4·3%	3·8%	3·8%	4·2%	6·2%	6·4%	8·3%

India's 2008 inflation rate was the highest since 1998. The official exchange rate was abolished on 1 March 1993; the rupee now has a single market exchange rate and is convertible. The pound sterling is the currency of intervention. Total money supply in July 2009 was Rs 12,133·0bn.

Budget

Central government revenues in 2004–05 (fiscal year beginning 1 April 2004) totalled 3,875,600m. rupees; expenditures totalled 4,822,000m. rupees in 2004–05.

Principal sources of revenue in 2004–05 were: taxes on income, profits and capital gains, 1,320,300m. rupees; taxes on goods and services, 1,151,200m. rupees; taxes on international trade and transactions, 576,100m. rupees. Main items of expenditure by economic type in 2004–05 were: grants, 1,426,800m. rupees; interest, 1,236,600m. rupees; compensation of employees, 428,000m. rupees.

VAT was introduced on 1 April 2005, at 12·5% (reduced rates, 4% and 1%).

Performance

India has one of the fastest-growing economies in Asia. Real GDP growth rates (based on IMF statistics):

2000	*2001*	*2002*	*2003*	*2004*	*2005*	*2006*	*2007*	*2008*
5·7%	3·9%	4·6%	6·9%	7·9%	9·2%	9·8%	9·4%	7·3%

Recent years have seen a growing disparity between the performance of India's richest states, mainly in the south and the west, and the poorest states, generally in the east and the north.

Total GDP in 2008 was US$1,217·5bn.

Banking and Finance

The Reserve Bank, the central bank for India, was established in 1934 and started functioning on 1 April 1935 as a shareholder's bank; it became a nationalized institution on 1 Jan. 1949. It has the sole right of issuing currency notes. The *Governor* is Duvvuri Subbarao. The Bank acts as adviser to the government on financial problems and is the banker for central and state governments, commercial banks and some other financial institutions. It manages the rupee public debt of central and state governments and is the custodian of the country's exchange reserve. The Bank has extensive powers of regulation of the banking system, directly under the Banking Regulation Act, 1949, and indirectly by the use of variations in Bank rate, variation in reserve ratios, selective credit controls and open market operations.

Scheduled commercial banks are categorized in five different groups according to their ownership and/or nature of operation: the State Bank of India and its six associates; 19 nationalized banks; regional rural banks; foreign banks; and other scheduled commercial banks (in the private sector). Total deposits in commercial banks, March 2007, stood at Rs 26,970,000m. The State Bank of India acts as the agent of the Reserve Bank for transacting government business as well as undertaking commercial functions. In 2008 India received a record US$41·6bn. worth of foreign direct investment. FDI inflows in 2008 were more than double those of 2006 and 15 times the level of 1998.

There are stock exchanges in Ahmedabad, Chennai, Delhi, Kolkata, Mumbai and 18 other centres.

Weights and Measures

The metric system is official but Imperial measurements are still used in commerce. Frequent use is made in figures of the terms *lakh* (=100,000) and *crore* (= 10m.).

ENERGY AND NATURAL RESOURCES

Environment

India's carbon dioxide emissions from the consumption and flaring of fossil fuels in 2008 accounted for 4·9% of the world total (the fourth highest after China, the USA and Russia). However, this was equivalent to just 1·3 tonnes per capita, well below the global average and the lowest figure for any major industrial country. An *Environmental Performance Index* compiled in 2008 ranked India 120th in the world out of 149 countries analysed, with 60·3%. The index examined various factors in six areas—air pollution, biodiversity and habitat, climate change, environmental health, productive natural resources and water resources.

Electricity

Installed capacity in 2004 was 114m. kW. In 2002 nearly 520,000 villages out of 600,000 had electricity. Production of electricity in 2005–06 was 623·8bn. kWh, of which 81·1% came from thermal stations, 16·3% from hydro-electric stations and 2·8% from nuclear stations. In 2008 there were 17 nuclear reactors in use. An additional six reactors were under construction. Electricity consumption per capita in 2005–06 was 631 kWh. Electricity demand exceeds supply, making power surges and cuts frequent. India aims to have electricity in every household by 2012.

Oil and Gas

Oil and Natural Gas Corporation Ltd and Oil India Ltd are the only producers of crude oil. Production 2008, 36·1m. tonnes. The main fields are in Assam and Gujarat and offshore in the Gulf of Cambay (the Mumbai High field). India imports 70% of its annual oil requirement. There were proven reserves of 5·8bn. bbls in 2008. Oil refinery capacity, 2008, was 3·0m. bbls daily. Natural gas production in 2008 was 30·6bn. cu. metres with 1,090bn. cu. metres of proven reserves.

Water

By 2005–06, 82·62m. ha. of irrigation potential had been created of which 60·19m. ha. was utilized. Irrigation projects have formed an important part of all the Five-Year Plans. The possibilities of diverting rivers into canals being nearly exhausted, the emphasis is now on damming the monsoon surplus flow and diverting that. Ultimate potential of irrigation is assessed at 110m. ha. by 2025, total cultivated land being 185m. ha.

A Ganges water-sharing accord was signed with Bangladesh in 1997, ending a 25-year dispute which had hindered and dominated relations between the two countries.

Minerals

The coal industry was nationalized in 1973. Production, 2004, 383m. tonnes; recoverable reserves were estimated at 56bn. tonnes (2005). Production of other minerals (in 1,000 tonnes): iron ore (2005), 140,000; lignite (2004), 30,337; salt (2002), 14,800; bauxite (2005), 11,957; chromite (2002), 1,900; manganese ore (2002–03), 1,662; aluminium (2005), 898; silver (2005), 31,900 kg; gold (2005), 3,200 kg. Other important minerals are lead, zinc, limestone, apatite and phosphorite, dolomite, magnesite and uranium. Value of mineral production, 2002–03, Rs 635,403·5m.; mineral fuels produced Rs 513,172·4m., metallic minerals Rs 45,405·8m. and non-metallic Rs 22,081·0m.

Agriculture

About 60% of the people are dependent on the land for their living. The farming year runs from July to June through three crop seasons: kharif (monsoon), rabi (winter) and summer. In 2002 there were 161,715,000 ha. of arable land and 8,400,000 ha. of permanent cropland. 57,198,000 ha. were irrigated in 2002. There were 1,525,000 tractors and 4,200 harvester-threshers in 2002. The average size of holdings for the whole of India is estimated at 1·4 ha.

Agricultural production, 2003 (in 1,000 tonnes): sugarcane, 289,630; rice, 132,013; wheat, 65,129; potatoes, 23,161; bananas, 16,450; maize, 14,800; millet, 10,700; mangoes, 10,500; coconuts, 9,500; aubergines, 8,200; sorghum, 8,000; groundnuts, 7,500; tomatoes, 7,420; cassava, 7,100; soybeans, 6,800; seed cotton, 6,300; cabbage, 6,100; onions, 5,000; cauliflowers, 4,800; cottonseed, 4,199; chick-peas, 4,130; rapeseed, 3,842; pumpkins and squash, 3,500; dry beans, 3,000. Jute is grown in West Bengal (70% of total yield), Bihar and Assam: total yield, 1,976,000 tonnes. The coffee industry is growing: the main cash varieties are Arabica and Robusta (main growing areas Karnataka, Kerala and Tamil Nadu). India is the world's leading producer of a number of agricultural crops, including mangoes, millet, bananas and chick-peas.

The tea industry is important, with production concentrated in Assam, West Bengal, Tamil Nadu and Kerala. India is the world's largest tea producer. The 2003 crop was 885,000 tonnes; exports in 2001–02, 180,100 tonnes, valued at US$360m.

Livestock (2003): cattle, 185·2m.; goats, 124·4m.; buffaloes, 97·9m.; sheep, 61·5m.; pigs, 13·5m.; horses and ponies, 751,000; donkeys, 650,000; camels, 632,000; poultry, 489m. There are more cattle and buffaloes in India than in any other country.

Fertilizer use in 2004–05 was 18·4m. tonnes.

Opium

By international agreement the poppy is cultivated under licence, and all raw opium is sold to the central government. Opium, other than for wholly medical use, is available only to registered addicts.

Forestry

The lands under the control of the state forest departments are classified as 'reserved forests' (forests intended to be permanently maintained for the supply of timber, etc., or for the protection of water supply, etc.), 'protected forests' and 'unclassed' forest land. In 2005 the total forest area was 67·70m. ha. (22·8% of the land area). Main types are teak and sal. About 16% of the area is inaccessible, of which about 45% is potentially productive. In 2007, 330·21m. cu. metres of roundwood were produced, making

India the second largest producer after the USA (9·2% of the world total in 2007). Most states have encouraged planting small areas around villages.

Fisheries

Total catch in 2005–06 was 6·5m. tonnes (3·76m. tonnes marine, 2·81m. tonnes inland). Fishing provides a livelihood for over 14m. people, contributing about 1% of total GDP and 5·3% of the GDP from the agriculture sector. Some 190 traditional fish landing centres, 60 minor fishing harbours and six major harbours serve 280,000 fishing craft, comprising 181,000 traditional craft, 45,000 motorized traditional craft and 54,000 mechanized boats. 551,000 tonnes of fish were exported in 2005–06.

INDUSTRY

The leading companies by market capitalization in India in March 2009 were: Reliance Industries, a chemical production company (US$47·2bn.); Oil and Natural Gas Corporation Ltd (ONGC), US$32·9bn.; and National Thermal Power (US$29·3bn.).

The information technology industry has become increasingly important; its contribution to GDP rose from 1·2% in 1998–99 to 5·2% by 2007–08. The National Association of Software and Services Companies (NASSCOM) estimated that in 2007–08 the IT industry registered a growth rate of 28% and revenues of US$52bn. (up from US$40bn. in 2006–07).

There is expansion in petrochemicals, based on the oil and associated gas of the Mumbai High field, and gas reserves offshore in the Krishna Godavari basin and the Bassein field, and onshore in Andhra Pradesh, Assam and Gujarat.

In 2006–07 there were an estimated 12·8m. micro and small enterprises, accounting for about 39% of the gross value of output in the manufacturing sector.

Industrial production (2006–07, in 1,000 tonnes): cement, 154,746; finished steel, 50,196; sugar, 24,187; nitrogenous and phosphate fertilizers, 16,153; petrol (2005–06), 10,502; kerosene (2005–06), 9,078; sulphuric acid, 7,156; paper and paperboard, 6,129; pig iron, 4,550; caustic soda, 1,929; jute goods (2003–04), 1,424. Other products (2006–07): 8,436,186 motorcycles, mopeds and scooters; 3,171,000 diesel engines; 1,238,737 cars; 520,000 commercial vehicles; 85·8bn. cigarettes.

Labour

In 2007 the workforce numbered 516·4m. (compared to 402·5m. at the 2001 census) and the unemployment rate was estimated at 7·2%. Workdays lost by industrial disputes through strikes and lockouts, 2005, 23·27m.

Companies

The total number of companies limited by shares at work as on 31 March 2002 was 589,246; estimated paid-up capital was Rs 3,870,239m. Of these, 76,279 were public limited companies with an estimated paid-up capital of Rs 2,587,149m., and 512,967 private limited companies (Rs 1,283,090m.).

During 2001–02 there were 21,059 new limited companies registered in the Indian Union under the Companies Act 1956 with a total authorized capital of Rs 53,156m.; 14 were government companies (Rs 5,781m.). There were 479 companies with unlimited liability and 3,007 companies with liability limited by guarantee and association not for profit also registered in 2001–02. During 2001–02, 760 non-government companies with an aggregate paid-up capital of Rs 144·7m. went into liquidation or were struck off the register.

On 31 March 2002 there were 1,261 government companies at work with a total paid-up capital of Rs 1,099,155m.; 658 were public limited companies and 603 were private limited companies. There were 587,985 non-government companies at work on 31 March 2002. Of these 75,621 were public limited companies and 512,364 were private limited companies.

On 31 March 2002, 1,285 companies incorporated elsewhere were reported to have a place of business in India; 241 were of UK and 286 of US origin.

Co-operative Movement

In 2001–02 there were 390,080 co-operative societies (146,206 credit, 243,874 non-credit) with a total membership of 209·3m. These included Primary Co-operative Marketing Societies, State Co-operative Marketing Federations and the National Agricultural Co-operative Marketing Federation of India. There were also State Co-operative Commodity Marketing Federations and Special Commodities Marketing Federations.

There were, in 2001–02, 368 Central Co-operative Banks, 94,825 Primary Agricultural Credit Societies, 770 Primary Land Development Banks and 1,047 banks and societies which provide long-term credits. There are 31 State Co-operative Banks.

Trade Unions

In 2004 there were 30,391 registered trade unions. The Indian National Trade Union Congress (INTUC) has a total membership of about 8m.

INTERNATIONAL TRADE

Foreign investment is encouraged by a tax holiday on income up to 6% of capital employed for five years. There are special depreciation allowances, and customs and excise concessions, for export industries. Proposals for investment ventures involving up to 51% foreign equity require only the Reserve Bank's approval under new liberalized policy. In Feb. 1991 India resumed trans-frontier trade with China, which had ceased in 1962.

Foreign debt was US$123,123m. in 2005.

Imports and Exports

The external trade of India (excluding land-borne trade with Tibet and Bhutan) was as follows (in Rs 100,000):

	Imports	*Exports and Re-exports*
2002–03	29,720,587	25,513,728
2003–04	35,910,766	29,336,675
2004–05	50,106,454	37,533,953
2005–06	66,040,890	45,641,786
2006–07	84,050,631	57,177,929

The main trading partners were as follows in the year ended 31 March 2007 (in Rs 100,000):

Countries	*Value of Imports*
Australia	3,171,090
Belgium	1,874,160
China	7,900,861
France	1,905,933
Germany	3,414,675
Hong Kong	1,123,930
Indonesia	1,886,486
Italy	1,210,172
Japan	2,079,488
Korea (Republic of)	2,174,700
Malaysia	2,395,876
Russia	1,090,284
Saudi Arabia	6,056,150
Singapore	2,483,997
South Africa	1,118,414
Switzerland	4,128,317
UAE	3,917,494
UK	1,888,930
USA	5,310,541
Countries	*Value of Exports*
Bangladesh	736,597
Belgium	1,572,170
China	3,752,978
France	950,601
Germany	1,800,723

Countries	Value of Exports
Hong Kong	2,117,938
Indonesia	917,697
Italy	1,621,243
Japan	1,295,361
Korea (Republic of)	1,137,901
Netherlands	1,208,248
Saudi Arabia	1,171,137
Singapore	2,746,161
South Africa	1,016,528
Spain	849,693
Sri Lanka	1,020,638
UAE	5,444,497
UK	2,542,129
USA	8,536,849

In 2006–07 the main import suppliers (percentage of total trade) were: China, 9·4%; Saudi Arabia, 7·2%; USA, 6·3%; Switzerland, 4·9%; United Arab Emirates, 4·7%. Main export markets in 2006–07 were: USA, 14·9%; United Arab Emirates, 9·5%; China, 6·6%; Singapore, 4·8%; UK, 4·4%.

The value (in Rs 100,000) of the leading articles of merchandise was as follows in the year ended 31 March 2007:

Imports	Value
Artificial resins, plastic materials, etc.	1,169,600
Chemical materials and products	598,000
Coal, coke and briquettes, etc.	2,071,000
Dying, tanning and colouring materials	269,500
Electronic goods	7,227,500
Fertilizers, crude and manufactured	1,373,200
Gold and silver	7,154,000
Iron and steel	2,907,100
Machine tools	670,300
Machinery (electrical and non-electrical)	7,154,000
Medicinal and pharmaceutical products	586,600
Metalliferous ores and metal scrap	3,776,400
Newsprint	240,700
Non-ferrous metal	1,178,700
Organic and inorganic chemicals	3,543,300
Pearls, precious and semi-precious stones	3,388.100
Petroleum, crude oil and related products	25,857,200
Professional instruments, optical equipment, etc.	1,059,300
Project goods	812,600
Pulp and waste paper	289,300
Textile yarn, fabrics and finished articles	940,000
Transport equipment	4,270,900
Vegetable oils (fixed)	954,000
Wood and wood products	468,400
Exports	*Value*
Basic chemicals	4,958,800
Carpet products	419,900
Cashew nuts	249,100
Coffee	196,900
Cotton yarn, fabrics and finished articles	1,908,900
Electronic goods	1,291,400
Engineering goods	11,987,500
Fruit and vegetables	361,100
Gems and jewellery	7,229,500
Handicrafts (excluding handmade carpets)	198,200
Iron ore	1,765,600
Jute manufacturing including floor coverings	117,800
Leather including garments and goods	1,327,800
Man-made yarn, fabrics and finished articles	997,500
Marine products	800,100
Mica, coal and other ores and minerals including processed minerals	1,403,000
Oil meals	550,400
Petroleum products	8,452,000
Plastics and linoleum	1,471,800
Ready-made garments, including clothing accessories of all textile materials	4,023,700
Rice	703,600
Spices	315,800
Tea	197,000
Tobacco	168,500

Technology industries have become increasingly important in recent years; the software and services exports sector grew by 29% in 2007–08 to register revenues of US$40·4bn. (up from US$31·4bn. in 2006–07).

COMMUNICATIONS

Roads

In 2006 there were 3·32m. km of roads, including 200 km of motorway. Roads are divided into six main administrative classes, namely: national highways, state highways, other public works department (PWD) roads, *Panchayati Raj* roads, urban roads and project roads. The national highways (198,489 km in 2006) connect capitals of states, major ports and foreign highways. The national highway system is linked with the UN Economic and Social Commission for Asia and the Pacific international highway system. The state highways are the main trunk roads of the states, while the other PWD roads and *Panchayati Raj* roads connect subsidiary areas of production and markets with distribution centres, and form the main link between headquarters and neighbouring districts. A ten-year highway plan, the National Highways Development Project, is currently under way; it aims to link India's main cities, ports and regions through the construction of new highways and the widening of existing ones by 2015.

In 2006 there were 11,526,000 passenger cars, 64,743,000 motorcycles and scooters, 992,000 buses and coaches, and 4,436,000 lorries and vans. In 2007 there were 476,219 road accidents resulting in 114,444 deaths.

Rail

The Indian railway system is government-owned (under the control of the Railway Board). Following reconstruction there are 16 zones, seven of which were created in 2002:

Zone	Headquarters	Year of Creation
Central	Mumbai	1951
Southern	Chennai	1951
Western	Mumbai	1951
Eastern	Kolkata	1952
Northern	Delhi	1952
North Eastern	Gorakhpur	1952
South Eastern	Kolkata	1955
North East Frontier	Guwahati	1958
South Central	Secunderabad	1966
East Central	Hajipur	2002
East Coast	Bhubaneswar	2002
North Central	Allahabad	2002
North Western	Jaipur	2002
South East Central	Bilaspur	2002
South Western	Hubli	2002
West Central	Jabalpur	2002

The total length of the Indian railway network is 63,000 km (14,600 electrified), with the Northern zone having the longest network, at 11,040 km.

The Konkan Railway (760 km of 1,676 mm gauge) linking Roha and Mangalore opened in 1996. It is operated as a separate entity.

Principal gauges are 1,676 mm (40,620 km) and 1 metre (18,501 km), with networks also of 762 mm and 610 mm gauge (3,794 km).

Passenger-km travelled in 2002–03 came to 515·0bn. and freight tonne-km to 353·2bn. Revenue (2002–03) from passengers, Rs 125,754m. (including the Kolkata Metro, which is part of Indian Railways); from goods, Rs 262,315m.

There are metros in Chennai (15·5 km), Delhi (23·0 km) and Kolkata (16·5 km).

Civil Aviation

The main international airports are at Chennai, Delhi (Indira Gandhi), Kolkata, Mumbai and Thiruvananthapuram, with some international flights from Ahmedabad, Amritsar, Bangalore,

Calicut, Goa and Hyderabad. Air transport was nationalized in 1953 with the formation of two Air Corporations: Air India for long-distance international air services, and Indian Airlines for air services within India and to adjacent countries. Domestic air transport has been opened to private companies, the largest of which is Jet Airways. All operational airports handled a total of 116·9m. passengers (87·1m. domestic and 29·8m. international) in the year to 31 March 2008. Total aircraft movements reached 1·31m. and freight volumes increased to over 1·7m. tonnes.

In 2003 Air India operated routes to Africa (Dar es Salaam and Nairobi); to Mauritius; to Europe (Frankfurt, London, Moscow, Paris, Vienna and Zürich); to western Asia (Abu Dhabi, Al Ain, Bahrain, Damman, Doha, Dubai, Jeddah, Kuwait, Muscat and Riyadh); to east Asia (Bangkok, Hong Kong, Jakarta, Kuala Lumpur, Osaka, Seoul, Singapore and Tokyo); and to North America (Chicago and New York). Indian Airlines (subsequently renamed Indian) operated international flights in 2003 to Almaty, Bahrain, Bangkok, Bishkek, Colombo, Dhaka, Doha, Dubai, Fujairah, Kathmandu, Kuala Lumpur, Kuwait, Malé, Muscat, Rangoon (Yangon), Ras-al-Khaimah, Sharjah and Singapore. Flights from Delhi to Lahore were restored in Jan. 2004. Air India and Indian merged in Aug. 2007, with the new airline keeping the name Air India. India's first budget airline, Air Deccan, began operations in 2003.

In 2007 Mumbai was the busiest airport, handling 25·2m. passengers, followed by Delhi, with 23·3m. passengers. They were ranked the world's 55th and 61st busiest airports respectively for the year 2006. Plans have been announced for the modernization and privatization of both Mumbai and Delhi airports.

Shipping

In Dec. 2006 the merchant fleet comprised 776 vessels totalling 8·4m. gross registered tonnage (GRT), including 370 dry cargo ships, 97 dry cargo bulk carriers, 135 tankers and 87 offshore supply vessels. Cargo traffic of major ports, 2001–02, was as follows:

Port	*Total (1m. tonnes)*	*Unloaded (1m. tonnes)*	*Loaded (1m. tonnes)*	*Transshipment (1m. tonnes)*
Chennai	36·46	23·22	13·14	0·10
Cochin	12·21	10·15	2·07	0·00
Haldia	25·12	18·50	6·62	0·01
Jawaharlal Nehru	24·09	12·18	11·01	0·91
Kandla	37·85	28·52	7·77	1·57
Mormugao	22·93	4·60	18·31	0·02
Mumbai	26·71	16·14	9·21	1·38
New Mangalore	17·51	8·77	8·75	0·00
Paradip	21·13	6·66	14·48	0·00
Tuticorin	13·23	9·91	3·32	0·00
Visakhapatnam	44·37	17·87	16·91	9·57

There are about 3,700 km of major rivers navigable by motorized craft, of which 2,000 km are used. Canals, 4,300 km, of which 900 km are navigable by motorized craft.

Telecommunications

The telephone system is in the hands of the Telecommunications Department, except in Delhi and Mumbai, which are served by a public corporation. In 2008 there were 37·9m. main (fixed) telephone lines. In the same year mobile phone subscribers numbered 346·9m. (293·6 per 1,000 persons). The number of mobile phone subscribers more than doubled between 2006 and 2008, while the number of fixed line subscribers has been gradually falling since 2003. There were 30·9m. PCs in use in 2006 and an estimated 51·8m. internet users in 2008.

Postal Services

In 2003 there were 155,618 post offices. India has more post offices than any other country. In 2003 a total of 9,126m. pieces of mail were processed, or nine items per person.

SOCIAL INSTITUTIONS

Justice

All courts form a single hierarchy, with the Supreme Court at the head, which constitutes the highest court of appeal. Immediately below it are the High Courts and subordinate courts in each state. Every court in this chain administers the whole law of the country, whether made by Parliament or by the state legislatures.

The states of Andhra Pradesh, Assam (in common with Nagaland, Meghalaya, Manipur, Mizoram, Tripura and Arunachal Pradesh), Bihar, Gujarat, Himachal Pradesh, Jammu and Kashmir, Karnataka, Kerala, Madhya Pradesh, Maharashtra (in common with Goa and the Union Territories of Daman and Diu, and Dadra and Nagar Haveli), Orissa, Punjab (in common with the state of Haryana and the Union Territory of Chandigarh), Rajasthan, Tamil Nadu (in common with the Union Territory of Puducherry), Uttar Pradesh, West Bengal and Sikkim each have a High Court. There is a separate High Court for Delhi. For the Andaman and Nicobar Islands the Calcutta High Court, for Puducherry the High Court of Madras and for Lakshadweep the High Court of Kerala are the highest judicial authorities. The Allahabad High Court has a Bench at Lucknow, the Bombay High Court has Benches at Nagpur, Aurangabad and Panaji, the Gauhati High Court has Benches at Kohima, Aizwal, Imphal and Agartala, the Madhya Pradesh High Court has Benches at Gwalior and Indore, the Patna High Court has a Bench at Ranchi and the Rajasthan High Court has a Bench at Jaipur. Judges and Division Courts of the Guwahati High Court also sit in Meghalaya. Similarly, judges and Division Courts of the Calcutta High Court also sit in the Andaman and Nicobar Islands. High Courts have also been established in the new states of Chhattisgarh, Jharkhand and Uttarakhand. Below the High Court each state is divided into a number of districts under the jurisdiction of district judges who preside over civil courts and courts of sessions. There are a number of judicial authorities subordinate to the district civil courts. On the criminal side magistrates of various classes act under the overall supervision of the High Court.

In Oct. 1991 the Supreme Court upheld capital punishment by hanging. In 2004 there were two executions, the first ones since 1995 (although there have been none since).

The population in penal institutions in Dec. 2006 was 373,271 (33 per 100,000 of national population).

Police

The states control their own police forces. The Home Affairs Minister of the central government co-ordinates the work of the states. The Indian Police Service provides senior officers for the state police forces. The Central Bureau of Investigation functions under the control of the Cabinet Secretariat.

The cities of Ahmedabad, Bangalore, Chennai, Delhi, Hyderabad, Kolkata, Mumbai, Nagpur and Pune have separate police commissionerates.

Education

Adult literacy was 64·8% in 2001 (75·3% among males and 53·7% among females). Of the states and territories, Kerala and Mizoram have the highest rates.

Educational Organization. Education is the concurrent responsibility of state and Union governments. In the Union Territories it is the responsibility of the central government. The Union government is also directly responsible for the central universities and all institutions declared by parliament to be of national importance; the promotion of Hindi as the federal language and co-ordinating and maintaining standards in higher education, research, science and technology. Professional education rests with the Ministry or Department concerned. There is a Central Advisory Board of Education to advise the Union and the State governments on any educational question which may be referred to it.

School Education. The school system has four stages: primary, middle, secondary and senior secondary.

Primary education is imparted either at independent primary (or junior basic) schools or primary classes attached to middle or secondary schools. The period of instruction varies from four to five years and the medium of instruction is in most cases the mother tongue of the child or the regional language. Free primary education is available for all children. Legislation for compulsory education has been passed by some state governments and Union Territories but it is not practicable to enforce compulsion when the reasons for non-attendance are socio-economic. There are residential schools for country children. The period for the middle stage varies from two to three years. In 2005, 47·2% of children who enrolled in the first grade went on to finish the eighth grade. In the same year it was estimated that 42m. children aged 6–14 were not attending school. In Aug. 2009 legislation was passed making education free and compulsory for all children between the ages of six and 14.

School statistics for 2004–05:

Type of recognized institution	No. of institutions	No. of students on rolls	No. of teachers[1]
Primary/junior basic schools	767,520	130,800,000	2,161,000
Middle/senior basic schools	274,731	51,200,000	1,589,000
High/higher secondary schools	152,049	37,100,000	2,083,000

[1]Provisional.

Higher Education. Higher education is given in arts, science or professional colleges, universities and all-India educational or research institutions. In 2005–06 there were 19,753 higher education institutions, comprising: 350 universities, institutions deemed to be universities and institutions of national importance; 12,751 general education colleges (including arts, science and commerce colleges); 5,179 professional education colleges (including engineering, technology, architecture, medical and teacher training colleges); and 1,473 other institutions (including research institutions). Total enrolment at universities, 2004–05, 10,481,000, of which 4,234,000 were women.

Adult Education. The Directorate of Adult Education, established in 1971, is the national resource centre.

There is also a National Literacy Mission.

Expenditure. Total budgeted central expenditure on revenue account of education and other departments for 2004–05 was estimated at Rs 96,694m. Total public expenditure on education during the Tenth (2002–07) Plan, Rs 438,250m. (Rs 138,250m. on secondary and higher education, Rs 300,000m. on elementary education and literacy). In 2004–05 total expenditure on education came to 3·4% of GDP and 12·1% of total government spending.

Health

Medical services are primarily the responsibility of the states. The Union government has sponsored major schemes for disease prevention and control which are implemented nationally.

Total public expenditure on health and family welfare during the Tenth (2002–07) Plan, Rs 373,530m. In 2002 there were 15,741 hospitals and 607,100 doctors. In 2002 there were 15 beds per 10,000 inhabitants.

In the period 2001–03, 20% of the population were undernourished. In 1979, 38% of the population had been undernourished. In 2004–05, 27·5% of the population lived below the poverty line, compared to 38·9% in 1987–88.

Approximately 2·5m. Indians are HIV-infected, a number only exceeded in South Africa and Nigeria.

RELIGION

India is a secular state; any worship is permitted, but the state itself has no religion. The principal religions in 2001 were: Hindus, 828m. (80% of the population); Muslims, 138m. (13%); Christians, 24m.; Sikhs, 19m.; Buddhists, 8m.; Jains, 4m. In addition to having the largest Hindu population of any country, India has the third highest number of Muslims, after Indonesia and Pakistan. In Feb. 2010 the Roman Catholic church had six cardinals.

CULTURE

World Heritage Sites

There are 27 sites under Indian jurisdiction that appear on the UNESCO World Heritage List. They are (with year entered on list): Ajanta Caves (1983), Ellora Caves (1983), Agra Fort (1983), Taj Mahal (1983), Sun Temple, Konârak (1984), Monuments at Mahabalipuram (1984), Kaziranga National Park (1985), Manas Wildlife Sanctuary (1985), Keoladeo National Park (1985), Churches and Convents of Goa (1986), Monuments at Khajuraho (1986), Monuments at Hampi (1986), Fatehpur Sikri (1986), Monuments at Pattadakal (1987), Elephanta Caves (1987), Great Living Chola Temples (1987 and 2004), Sundarbans National Park (1987), Nanda Devi National Park (1988 and 2005), Buddhist Monuments at Sanchi (1989), Humayan's Tomb, Delhi (1993), Qutb Minar and its Monuments, Delhi (1993), Mountain Railways of India (1999, 2005 and 2008), Mahabodhi Temple Complex at Bodh Gaya (2002), the Rock Shelters of Bhimbetka (2003), Champaner-Pavagadh Archaeological Park (2004), the Chhatrapati Shivaji Terminus—formerly Victoria Terminus—in Mumbai (2004) and the Red Fort Complex, Delhi (2007).

Broadcasting

The national television (Doordarshan) and radio (All India Radio, or Akashwani) networks are state-owned. Doordarshan operates 21 national, regional and local services. Private cable and satellite stations have proliferated since the monopoly of state television ended in 1992. Prominent satellite broadcasters include AajTak, Star and Zee TV. Commercial radio was sanctioned in 2000, although only All India Radio may broadcast news programmes. There were 151·2m. TV sets (colour by PAL) and 61m. cable subscribers in 2005.

Cinema

In 2004 there were 10,500 cinema screens with a total attendance of 3·6bn. A total of 934 Indian feature films were certified for release in 2004 (including 245 in Hindi, 208 in Telugu and 130 in Tamil).

Press

There were 58,469 registered newspapers in March 2004, with a total circulation of 133·1m. In 2002 there were 402 dailies with a total circulation of 31·1m. Hindi papers have the highest number and circulation, followed by English, then Urdu, Bengali and Marathi. The newspaper with the highest circulation is the *Times of India* (daily average of 2·1m. copies in 2002). In 2002 a total of 17,038 book titles were published.

Tourism

In 2005 there were 3,919,000 foreign tourists. Of these, 1,435,000 were from Europe, 842,000 from Southern Asia and 804,000 from the Americas. Tourist receipts amounted to US$4·13bn. in 2003.

Calendar

The Indian National Calendar, adopted in 1957, is dated from the Saka era (Indian dynasty beginning AD 78). It uses the same year-length as the Gregorian calendar (also used for administrative and informal purposes) but begins on 22 March. Local and religious variations are also used.

DIPLOMATIC REPRESENTATIVES

Of India in the United Kingdom (India House, Aldwych, London, WC2B 4NA)
High Commissioner: Nalin Surie.

Of the United Kingdom in India (Chanakyapuri, New Delhi 110021)
High Commissioner: Sir Richard Stagg, KCMG.

Of India in the USA (2107 Massachusetts Ave., NW, Washington, D.C., 20008)
Ambassador: Meera Shankar.

Of the USA in India (Shanti Path, Chanakyapuri, New Delhi 110021)
Ambassador: Tim Roemer.

Of India to the United Nations
Ambassador: Hardeep Singh Puri.

Of India to the European Union
Ambassador: Jaimini Bhagwati.

FURTHER READING

Bhambhri, C. P., *The Political Process in India, 1947–91.* 1991
Bose, S. and Jalal, A. (eds.) *Nationalism, Democracy and Development: State and Politics in India.* 1997
Brown, J., *Modern India: The Origins of an Asian Democracy.* 2nd ed. 1994
Fernandes, Edna, *Holy Warriors: A Journey into the Heart of Indian Fundamentalism.* 2007
Gandhi, Rajmohan, *Gandhi: The Man, His People and the Empire.* 2007
Guha, Ramachandra, *India After Gandhi: The History of the World's Largest Democracy.* 2007
Gupta, D. C., *Indian Government and Politics.* 3rd ed. 1992
Gupta, S. P., *Globalisation, Economic Reforms and Employment Strategy in India.* 2007
Hardgrave, Robert L. and Kochanek, Stanley A., *India: Government and Politics in a Developing Nation.* 7th ed. 2007
Jaffrelot, C. (ed.) *L'Inde Contemporain de 1950 à nos Jours.* 1996
James, L., *Raj: The Making and Unmaking of British India.* 1997
Joshi, V. and Little, I. M. D., *India's Economic Reforms, 1991–2000.* 1996
Kamdar, Mira, *Planet India: The Turbulent Rise of the World's Largest Democracy.* 2007
Keay, John, *India: A History.* 2000
Khan, Yasmin, *The Great Partition: The Making of India and Pakistan.* 2007
Khilnani, S., *The Idea of India.* 1997
King, R., *Nehru and the Language Politics of India.* 1997
Metcalf, Barbara D. and Metcalf, Thomas R., *A Concise History of India.* 2001
Mohan, C. Raja, *Crossing the Rubicon: The Shaping of India's New Foreign Policy.* 2003
New Cambridge History of India. 2nd ed. 5 vols. 1994–96
Nilekani, Nandan, *Imagining India: The Idea of a Renewed Nation.* 2009
Panagariya, Arvind, *India: The Emerging Giant.* 2008
Paul, T. V., *The India-Pakistan Conflict: An Enduring Rivalry.* 2005
Rajadhyaksha, Niranjan, *The Rise of India: Its Transformation from Poverty to Prosperity.* 2006
Robb, Peter, *A History of India.* 2002
SarDesai, D. R., *India: The Definitive History.* 2008
Tseng, Wanda and Cowen, David, *India's and China's Recent Experience with Reform and Growth.* 2007
Vohra, R., *The Making of India: A Historical Survey.* 1997
Von Tunzelmann, Alex, *Indian Summer: The Secret History of the End of an Empire.* 2007

National library: Belvedere, Kolkata 700027. *Director:* Dr R. Ramachandran.

National Statistical Office: Ministry of Statistics and Programme Implementation, Computer Centre, East Block-10, RK Puram, New Delhi 110066.

Website: http://mospi.nic.in

Census India Website: http://www.censusindia.net

Other more specialized titles are listed under CONSTITUTION AND GOVERNMENT *and* RECENT ELECTIONS *above.*

STATES AND TERRITORIES

GENERAL DETAILS

The Republic of India is composed of the following 28 States and seven centrally administered Union Territories:

States	*Capital*	*States*	*Capital*
Andhra Pradesh	Hyderabad	Maharashtra	Mumbai
Arunachal Pradesh	Itanagar	Manipur	Imphal
Assam	Dispur	Meghalaya	Shillong
Bihar	Patna	Mizoram	Aizawl
Chhattisgarh	Raipur	Nagaland	Kohima
Goa	Panaji	Orissa	Bhubaneswar
Gujarat	Gandhinagar	Punjab	Chandigarh
Haryana	Chandigarh	Rajasthan	Jaipur
Himachal Pradesh	Shimla	Sikkim	Gangtok
Jammu and Kashmir	Srinagar	Tamil Nadu	Chennai
Jharkhand	Ranchi	Tripura	Agartala
Karnataka	Bangalore	Uttar Pradesh	Lucknow
Kerala	Thiruvananthapuram	Uttarakhand	Dehra Dun
Madhya Pradesh	Bhopal	West Bengal	Kolkata

Union Territories. Andaman and Nicobar Islands; Chandigarh; Dadra and Nagar Haveli; Daman and Diu; Delhi; Lakshadweep; Puducherry.

Andhra Pradesh

KEY HISTORICAL EVENTS

Constituted a separate state on 1 Oct. 1953, Andhra Pradesh was the undisputed Telugu-speaking area of Madras. To this region was added, on 1 Nov. 1956, the Telangana area of the former Hyderabad State, comprising the districts of Hyderabad, Medak, Nizamabad, Karimnagar, Warangal, Khammam, Nalgonda and Mahbubnagar, parts of the Adilabad district, some taluks of the Raichur, Gulbarga and Bidar districts and some revenue circles of the Nanded district. On 1 April 1960, 221·4 sq. miles in the Chingleput and Salem districts of Madras were transferred to Andhra Pradesh in exchange for 410 sq. miles from Chittoor district. The district of Prakasam was formed on 2 Feb. 1970. Hyderabad was split into two districts on 15 Aug. 1978 (Ranga Reddy and Hyderabad). A new district, Vizianagaram, was formed in 1979.

TERRITORY AND POPULATION

Andhra Pradesh is in south India and is bounded in the south by Tamil Nadu, west by Karnataka, north and northwest by Maharashtra, northeast by Chhattisgarh and Orissa and east by the Bay of Bengal. The state has an area of 275,069 sq. km and a population (2001 census) of 76,210,007; density, 277 per sq. km. The principal language is Telugu. Cities with over 250,000 population (2001 census), *see* INDIA: Territory and Population. Other large cities (2001): Anantapur, 243,143; Ramagundam, 237,686; Karimnagar, 218,302; Eluru, 215,804; Khamman, 198,620; Vizianagaram, 195,801; Machilipatnam, 179,353; Chirala, 166,294; Adoni, 162,458; Nandyal, 157,120; Ongole, 153,829; Tenali, 153,756; Chittoor, 152,654; Proddutur, 150,309; Bheemavaram, 142,064; Mahbubnagar, 139,662; Adilabad, 129,403; Hindupur, 125,074; Mancherial, 118,195; Srikakulam, 117,320; Guntakal, 117,103; Gudivada, 113,054; Nalgonda, 111,380; Madanapalle, 107,449; Kottagudem, 105,266; Dharmavaram, 103,357; Tadepalligudem, 102,622.

SOCIAL STATISTICS

Growth rate 1991–2001, 14·59%.

CONSTITUTION AND GOVERNMENT

Andhra Pradesh has a unicameral legislature; the Legislative Council was abolished in June 1985. The Legislative Assembly consists of 295 members (one of which is nominated). For administrative purposes there are 23 districts in the state. The capital is Hyderabad.

RECENT ELECTIONS

At the State Assembly elections held on 20 and 26 April 2004 the Congress Alliance won 226 seats—of which 185 (38·2% of the vote) for the INC, 26 (6·6%) for Telangana Rashtra Samithi, 9 (2·0%) for the CPI-M and 6 (1·5%) for the CPI. The Telugu Desam Party won 47 seats (37·1%) and the BJP 2 (2·6%). Four other parties received a total of 8 seats and 11 independents were elected.

CURRENT ADMINISTRATION

Governor: E. S. L. Narasimhan; b. 1945 (since 27 Dec. 2009—acting until 22 Jan. 2010).

Chief Minister: Konijeti Rosaiah; b. 1933 (since 3 Sept. 2009).

ECONOMY

Budget

Budget estimate, 2002–03: receipts on revenue account, Rs 256,747·9m.; expenditure, Rs 281,205·0m. Annual plan, 2002–03: Rs 112,995·0m.

ENERGY AND NATURAL RESOURCES

Electricity

There are 13 hydro-electric plants, 11 thermal stations and two gas-based units. Installed capacity, Oct. 2008, 11,911 MW; power generated (1999) 6,480m. kWh. In Sept. 2008 all 26,613 inhabited villages had electricity.

Oil and Gas

Crude oil is refined at Visakhapatnam in Andhra Pradesh. Oil/gas structures are found in Krishna-Godavari basin which encompasses an area of 20,000 sq. km on land and 21,000 sq. km up to 200 metres isobath off-shore. In 2001, 1,604m. cu. metres of natural gas were produced. Reserves of the land basin are estimated at 760 metric tonnes of oil and oil equivalent of gas.

Water

In 2000 more than 120 irrigation projects had created irrigation potential of 6m. ha. The Telugu Ganga joint project with Tamil Nadu, begun in the early 1980s, will eventually irrigate about 233,000 ha., besides supplying drinking water to Chennai city (Tamil Nadu).

Minerals

The state is an important producer of asbestos and barytes. The Cuppadah basin is a major source of uranium and other minerals. Other important minerals are copper ore, coal, iron and limestone, steatite, mica and manganese.

Agriculture

There were (1999) about 10·7m. ha. of cropped land, of which 6·8m. ha. were under foodgrains. Irrigated area, 2000, 6m. ha. Production in 1999 (in tonnes): bananas, 13·73m.; pulses, 10·94m.; foodgrains, 10·37m. (rice, 8·51m.); oil seeds, 1·3m.; sugarcane, 0·2m.

Livestock (2003): sheep, 21·38m.; buffaloes, 10·63m.; cattle, 9·30m.; goats, 6·28m.; poultry, 102·28m.

Forestry

In 1999 it was estimated that forests occupy 15·7% of the total area of the state, or 43,290 sq. km; main forest products are teak, eucalyptus, cashew, casuarina, softwoods and bamboo.

Fisheries

Production 2001–02, 578,000 tonnes of marine and freshwater fish and crustaceans. This represents 10% of India's catch. The state has a coastline of 974 km. In 2005 there were 289,500 people engaged in fishing and allied activities.

INDUSTRY

The main industries are textile manufacture, sugar-milling, machine tools, pharmaceuticals (Andhra Pradesh commands 40% of India's pharmaceuticals industry), electronic equipment, heavy electrical machinery, aircraft parts and paper-making. There is an oil refinery at Visakhapatnam, where India's major shipbuilding yards are situated. A major steel plant at Visakhapatnam and a railway repair shop at Tirupati are functioning. At 31 March 1997 there were 1,536 large and medium industries employing 644,480 persons, and 124,209 small-scale industries employing 1m. There are cottage industries and sericulture. District Industries Centres have been set up to promote small-scale industry. Tourism is growing; the main centres are Hyderabad, Nagarjunasagar, Warangal, Arakuvalley, Horsley Hills and Tirupati.

COMMUNICATIONS

Roads

In 2002 there were 198,000 km of roads in the state including national roads. Number of vehicles as of 31 March 1997 was 2,783,220, including 2,287,029 motorcycles and scooters, 187,863 goods vehicles and 177,516 cars and jeeps.

Rail

There are 5,073 route-km of railway.

Civil Aviation

There are airports at Hyderabad, Tirupati, Vijayawada and Visakhapatnam, with regular scheduled services to Mumbai, Delhi, Kolkata, Bangalore, Chennai and Bhubaneswar. International flights are operated from Hyderabad to Bangkok, Dubai, Jeddah, Kuala Lumpur, Kuwait, Muscat, Sharjah and Singapore. A new Hyderabad airport (Rajiv Gandhi International Airport, located at Shamshabad) opened in March 2008.

Shipping

The chief port is Visakhapatnam, which handles 44·6m. tonnes of cargo annually. There are minor ports at Kakinada, Machilipatnam, Bheemunipatnam, Narsapur, Krishnapatnam, Nizampatnam, Vadarevu and Kalingapatnam.

SOCIAL INSTITUTIONS

Justice

The high court of Judicature at Hyderabad has a Chief Justice and a sanctioned strength of 39 judges.

Education

In 2001, 60·5% of the population were literate (70·3% of men and 50·4% of women). There were, in 1999, 51,836 primary schools (6,237,700 students); 8,713 upper primary (2,440,000); 8,819 high schools (3,732,000). Education is free for children up to 14.

In 1995–96 there were 1,818 junior colleges (676,455 students). In 1996–97 there were 805 degree colleges (427,652 students); 46 oriented colleges and 18 universities: Osmania University, Hyderabad; Andhra University, Waltair; Sri Venkateswara University, Tirupati; Kakatiya University, Warangal; Nagarjuna University, Guntur; Sri Jawaharlal Nehru Technological University, Hyderabad; Hyderabad University, Hyderabad; N. G. Ranga Agricultural University, Hyderabad; Sri Krishnadevaraya University, Anantapur; Smt. Padmavathi Mahila Vishwavidyalayam (University for Women), Tirupati; Dr B. R. Ambedkar Open University, Hyderabad; Patti Sriramulu Telugu University, Hyderabad; N. T. R. University of Health Science, Vijayawada; Moulana Azad National Urdu University, Hyderabad; Dravidian University, Chittoor; Rashtriya Sanskrit

Vidyapeeth, Tirupati; Sri Satya Sai Institute of Higher Learning, Prashanti Nilayam; National Academy of Legal Studies and Research University, Hyderabad.

Health
There were (1996) 1,947 allopathic hospitals and dispensaries, 550 Ayurvedic hospitals and dispensaries, 193 Unani and 283 homoeopathy hospitals and dispensaries. There were also 181 nature cure hospitals and (in 1999) 1,360 primary health centres. Number of beds in hospitals was 32,116.

RELIGION
At the 2001 census Hindus numbered 67,836,651; Muslims, 6,986,856; Christians, 1,181,917.

Arunachal Pradesh

KEY HISTORICAL EVENTS
Before independence the North East Frontier Agency of Assam was administered for the viceroy by a political agent working through tribal groups. After independence it became the North East Frontier Tract, administered for the central government by the Governor of Assam. In 1972 the area became the Union Territory of Arunachal Pradesh; statehood was achieved in Dec. 1986.

TERRITORY AND POPULATION
The state is in the extreme northeast of India and is bounded in the north by China, east by Myanmar, west by Bhutan and south by Assam and Nagaland. It has 13 districts and comprises the former frontier divisions of Kameng, Tirap, Subansiri, Siang and Lohit; it has an area of 83,743 sq. km and a population (2001 census) of 1,097,968; density, 13 per sq. km.

The state is mainly tribal; there are 106 tribes using about 50 tribal dialects. The official languages are English and Hindi.

SOCIAL STATISTICS
Growth rate 1991–2001, 27·00%.

CONSTITUTION AND GOVERNMENT
There is a Legislative Assembly of 60 members. The capital is Itanagar (population, 2001, 35,022).

RECENT ELECTIONS
At the State Assembly elections held on 13 Oct. 2009 the India National Congress Party won 42 seats; the Nationalist Congress Party, 6; the All Indian Trinamool Congress, 5; the Bharatiya Janata Party, 3; others, 4. Turnout was 72%.

CURRENT ADMINISTRATION
Governor: Joginder Jaswant Singh; b. 1945 (since 27 Jan. 2008).

Chief Minister: Dorjee Khandu; b. 1955 (since 9 April 2007).

ECONOMY

Budget
Total estimated receipts, 2000–01, Rs 11,843m.; total estimated expenditure, Rs 11,451m. Plan outlay, 2000–01, Rs 6,400m.

ENERGY AND NATURAL RESOURCES

Electricity
Total installed capacity (Oct. 2008), 180 MW. Power generated (1999): 66·28m. units. In Sept. 2008, 2,195 out of 3,863 inhabited villages had electricity.

Oil and Gas
Production, 2001, 31,000 tonnes of crude oil and 23m. cu. metres of gas. Crude oil reserves are estimated at nearly 30m. tonnes.

Minerals
Coal reserves are estimated at 90·23m. tonnes; dolomite, 154·13m. tonnes; limestone, 409·35m. tonnes.

Agriculture
Production of foodgrains, 1999, 204,000 tonnes.

Forestry
Area under forest, 51,540 sq. km; revenue from forestry (1995–96) Rs 402m.

INDUSTRY
In 1996 there were 18 medium and 3,306 small industries, 80 craft or weaving centres and 225 sericulture centres. Most of the medium industries are forest-based. Industries include coal, textiles, jute, iron and steel, chemicals, tea and leather.

COMMUNICATIONS

Roads
Total length of roads in the state, 12,280 km of which 9,855 km are surfaced. There were 14,821 vehicles in 1995–96. The state had 393 km of national highway in 2000. Four towns are linked by air services.

SOCIAL INSTITUTIONS

Education
In 2001, 54·3% of the population were literate (63·8% of men and 43·5% of women). There were (1996–97) 1,256 primary schools with 147,676 students, 301 middle schools with 42,197 students, 157 high and higher secondary schools with 24,951 students, six colleges and two technical schools. Arunachal University, established in 1985, had four colleges and 3,240 students in 1994–95.

Health
There were (2004) 14 hospitals, 19 community health centres, 58 primary health centres and 273 sub-centres. In 1996 there were two TB hospitals and 11 leprosy and other hospitals. Total number of beds (2002), 2,641.

RELIGION
At the 2001 census Hindus numbered 379,935; Christians, 205,548; Buddhists, 143,028.

FURTHER READING
Bose, M. L., *History of Arunachal Pradesh*. 1997

Assam

KEY HISTORICAL EVENTS
Assam first became a British Protectorate at the close of the first Burmese War in 1826. In 1832 Cachar was annexed; in 1835 the Jaintia Hills were included in the East India Company's dominions, and in 1839 Assam was annexed to Bengal. In 1874 Assam was detached from Bengal and made a separate chief commissionership. On the partition of Bengal in 1905, it was united to the Eastern Districts of Bengal under a Lieut.-Governor. From 1912 the chief commissionership of Assam was revived, and in 1921 a governorship was created. On the partition of India almost the whole of the predominantly Muslim district of Sylhet was merged with East Bengal (Pakistan). Dewangiri in North Kamrup was ceded to Bhutan in 1951. The Naga Hill district,

administered by the Union government since 1957, became part of Nagaland in 1962. The autonomous state of Meghalaya within Assam, comprising the districts of Garo Hills and Khasi and Jaintia Hills, came into existence on 2 April 1970, and achieved full independent statehood in Jan. 1972, when it was also decided to form a Union Territory, Mizoram (now a state), from the Mizo Hills district.

TERRITORY AND POPULATION

Assam is in northeast India, almost separated from central India by Bangladesh. It is bounded in the west by West Bengal, north by Bhutan and Arunachal Pradesh, east by Nagaland, Manipur and Myanmar, south by Meghalaya, Bangladesh, Mizoram and Tripura. The area of the state is now 78,438 sq. km. Population (2001 census) 26,655,528; density, 340 per sq. km. Cities with over 250,000 population (2001 census), *see* INDIA: Territory and Population. Other large cities (2001): Silchar, 184,105; Jorhat, 137,814; Dibrugarh, 137,661; Nagaon, 123,265; Tinsukia, 108,123; Tezpur, 105,377. The principal language is Assamese.

The central government is constructing a boundary fence to prevent illegal entry from Bangladesh.

SOCIAL STATISTICS

Growth rate 1991–2001, 18·92%.

CONSTITUTION AND GOVERNMENT

Assam has a unicameral legislature of 126 members. The capital is Dispur. The state has 23 districts.

RECENT ELECTIONS

In the elections of 3 and 10 April 2006 the Indian National Congress (INC) took 53 of 126 seats, Asom Gana Parishad 24, Bharatiya Janata Party (BJP) 10, Assam United Democratic Front 10 and ind. 22 with a number of smaller parties winning one or two seats each.

CURRENT ADMINISTRATION

Governor: Janaki Ballabh Patnaik; b. 1927 (took office on 11 Dec. 2009).

Chief Minister: Tarun Gogoi; b. 1936 (took office on 18 May 2001).

ECONOMY

Budget

The budget estimates for 2001 showed receipts of Rs 91,576m. and expenditure of Rs 100,124m.

ENERGY AND NATURAL RESOURCES

Electricity

In Oct. 2008 there was an installed capacity of 980 MW. In Sept. 2008, 19,741 out of 25,124 inhabited villages had electricity.

Oil and Gas

Assam contains important oilfields and produces about 16% of India's crude oil. Production (1999): crude oil, 5·00m. tonnes; gas (1999), 1,333m. cu. metres.

Minerals

Coal production (2002–03), 633,000 tonnes. The state also has limestone, refractory clay, dolomite and corundum.

Agriculture

Assam produces 50% of India's tea—in 2003 there were 1,196 registered tea estates in the state. Production in 1998 was 425·4m. kg. 82% of the cultivable area is used. Over 72% of the cultivated area is under food crops, of which the most important is rice. Total foodgrains, 1997, 3·53m. tonnes. Main cash crops: tea, jute, cotton, oilseeds, sugarcane, fruit and potatoes. Wheat production, 100,000 tonnes in 2000; rice, 3·9m. tonnes; pulses, 64,688 tonnes. Cattle are important.

Forestry

In 2000 there were 17,420 sq. km of reserved forests under the administration of the Forest Department and 6,000 sq. km of unclassed forests, altogether about 39% of the total area of the state. Revenue from forests, in 1999, Rs 9,590m.

INDUSTRY

Sericulture and hand-loom weaving, both silk and cotton, are important home industries together with the manufacture of brass, cane and bamboo articles. The main heavy industry is petrochemicals; there are four oil refineries in the region. Other industries include manufacturing paper, nylon, electronic goods, cement, fertilizers, sugar, jute and plywood products, rice and oil milling.

There were 23,218 small-scale industries in 2000. In 1999, 1·1m. persons were employed in state-run enterprises.

COMMUNICATIONS

Roads

In 1998 there were 33,064 km of road maintained by the Public Works Department. There were 2,034 km of national highway in 1999. There were 373,962 motor vehicles in the state in 1998–99.

Rail

The route-km of railways in 1999 was 3,722 km, of which 2,392 km was broad gauge.

Civil Aviation

Daily scheduled flights connect the principal towns with the rest of India. There are airports at Guwahati, Tezpur, Jorhat, North Lakhimpur, Silchar and Dibrugarh.

Shipping

Water transport is important in Lower Assam; the main waterway is the Brahmaputra River. Cargo carried in 1998 was 50,334 tonnes.

SOCIAL INSTITUTIONS

Justice

The seat of the High Court is Guwahati. It has a Chief Justice and Justice and a sanctioned strength of 19 judges.

Education

In 2001, 63·3% of the population were literate (71·3% of men and 54·6% of women). In 1999–2000 there were 31,888 primary/junior basic schools with 3,293,835 students; 8,019 middle/senior basic schools with 1,406,818 students; 4,514 high/higher secondary schools with 1,465,518 students. There were 247 colleges for general education, six medical colleges, three engineering and one agricultural, 24 teacher-training colleges, and a fisheries college at Raha. There were five universities: Assam Agricultural University, Jorhat; Dibrugarh University, Dibrugarh with 86 colleges and 55,982 students (1992–93); Gauhati University, Guwahati with 128 colleges and 80,363 students (1992–93); and two central universities, at Silchar and Tezpur.

Health

In 2000 there were 164 hospitals (12,900 beds), 618 primary health centres and 323 dispensaries.

RELIGION

At the 2001 census Hindus numbered 17,296,455; Muslims, 8,240,611; Christians, 986,589; Buddhists, 51,029.

FURTHER READING

Baruah, Sanjib, *India Against Itself: Assam and the Politics of Nationality*. 1999

Bihar

KEY HISTORICAL EVENTS

Bihar was part of Bengal under British rule until 1912 when it was separated together with Orissa. The two were joined until 1936 when Bihar became a separate province. As a state of the Indian Union it was enlarged in 1956 by the addition of land from West Bengal.

The state contains the ethnic areas of North Bihar, Santhal Pargana and Chota Nagpur. In 1956 some areas of Purnea and Manbhum districts were transferred to West Bengal. In 2000 the state of Jharkhand was carved from the mineral-rich southern region of Bihar, substantially reducing the state's revenue-earning power.

TERRITORY AND POPULATION

Bihar is in north India and is bounded north by Nepal, east by West Bengal, south by the new state of Jharkhand, southwest and west by Uttar Pradesh. After the formation of Jharkhand the area of Bihar is 94,163 sq. km (previously 173,877 sq. km). Population (2001 census), 82,998,509, with a density of 881 per sq. km. Population of principal towns, *see* INDIA: Territory and Population. Other large towns (2001): Biharsharif, 232,071; Arrah, 203,380; Purnea, 197,211; Katihar, 190,873; Munger, 188,050; Chapra, 179,190; Sasaram, 131,172; Saharsa, 125,167; Hajipur, 119,412; Dehri, 119,057; Bettiah, 116,670; Siwan, 109,919; Motihari, 108,428; Begusarai, 107,623.

The state is divided into 37 districts. The capital is Patna.

The official language is Hindi (spoken by 80·9% at the 2001 census), the second, Urdu (9·9%), and the third, Bengali (2·9%).

SOCIAL STATISTICS

Growth rate 1991–2001, 28·62%.

CONSTITUTION AND GOVERNMENT

Bihar has a bicameral legislature. The Legislative Assembly consists of 243 elected members, and the Council 96.

RECENT ELECTIONS

In elections held on 18 and 26 Oct., and 13 and 19 Nov. 2005 the Janata Dal (United) won 88 of 243 seats; Bharatiya Janata Party, 55; the ruling Rashtriya Janata Dal, 54; Lok Janshakti Party, 10; Indian National Congress, 9; Communist Party of India (Marxist-Leninist) (Liberation), 5; Bahujan Samaj Party, 4; Communist Party of India, 3; Samajwadi Party, 2; Akhil Jan Vikas Dal, 1; Communist Party of India (Marxist), 1; Nationalist Congress Party, 1; ind., 10.

CURRENT ADMINISTRATION

Governor: Devanand Konwar (took office on 29 June 2009).

Chief Minister: Nitish Kumar; b. 1951 (took office for a second time on 24 Nov. 2005).

ECONOMY

Budget

The budget estimates for 2001–02 showed total receipts of Rs 68,020m. and expenditure of Rs 66,806m. The creation of Jharkhand in 2000 removed two-thirds of Bihar's revenue.

ENERGY AND NATURAL RESOURCES

Electricity

Installed capacity (Oct. 2008) 1,970 MW. In Sept. 2008, 20,620 out of 39,015 inhabited villages had electricity.

Minerals

Before the creation of the new state of Jharkhand, Bihar was very rich in minerals. The truncated state has only deposits of bauxite, mica, glass sand and salt.

Agriculture

(Including Jharkhand). The irrigated area was 4·13m. ha. in 1993–94. Cultivable land, 11·6m. ha., of a total area of 17·4m. ha. Total cropped area, 1991–92, 9·79m. ha. Production (1995–96): rice, 6·91m. tonnes; wheat, 4·18m.; total foodgrains, 13·07m. Other food crops are maize and pulses. Main cash crops are jute, sugar-cane, oilseeds, tobacco and potatoes.

Forestry

Forests in 1995 covered 26,561 sq. km. There are 12 protected forests.

INDUSTRY

(Including Jharkhand). Iron, steel and aluminium are produced and there is an oil refinery. Other important industries are heavy engineering, machine tools, fertilizers, electrical engineering, manufacturing drugs and fruit processing. There were 500 large and medium industries and 163,000 small and handicraft units in 1996–97.

COMMUNICATIONS

Roads

(Including Jharkhand). In March 1997 the state had 87,836 km of roads, including 2,118 km of national highway, 4,192 km of state highway and 15,526 km of district roads. Passenger transport has been nationalized. There were 1,329,709 motor vehicles registered in March 1996.

Rail

(Including Jharkhand). The North Eastern, South Eastern and Eastern railways traverse the state; route-km, 1995–96, 5,283 km.

Civil Aviation

There are airports at Patna and Gaya with regular scheduled services to Kolkata and Delhi.

Shipping

(Including Jharkhand). The length of waterways open for navigation is 1,300 km.

SOCIAL INSTITUTIONS

Justice

There is a High Court (constituted in 1916) at Patna with a Chief Justice, 31 puisne judges and four additional judges.

Police

The police force is under a Director General of Police; in 1990 there were 1,097 police stations.

Education

At the census of 2001, 47·0% of the population were literate (59·7% of males and 33·1% of females). There were, 1996–97, 53,652 primary schools with 9·63m. pupils, 13,834 middle schools with 2·42m. pupils and 4,149 high and higher secondary schools with 1·08m. pupils. Education is free for children aged 6–11.

There are 12 universities: Patna University (founded 1917) with 14,699 students (1994–95); Babasaheb Bhimrao Ambedkar Bihar University, Muzaffarpur (1952) with 95 colleges, and 84,873 students (1989–90); Tilka Manjhi Bhagalpur University (1960) with 140,718 students (1990–91); Kameshwara Singh Darbhanga Sanskrit University (1961); Magadh University, Gaya (1962) with 186 colleges and 122,019 students (1994–95); Rajendra Agricultural University, Samastipur (1970); Lalit Narayan Mithila University (1972), Darbhanga; Nalanda Open University, Nalanda (1987); Jai Prakash University, Chapra (1990); BN Mandal University, Madhepura (1992); Mazrul Haque Arabi-Farsi University, Patna; and Veer Kunwar Singh University, Arrah. Including Jharkhand, there were 742 degree colleges, 11 engineering colleges, 31 medical colleges and 15 teacher training colleges in 1996–97. Ranchi University, Bisra Agricultural College and Sidhu Kanhu University, all formerly in Bihar, are now part of Jharkhand.

Health
(Including Jharkhand). In 2000 there were 1,636 hospitals and dispensaries with 12,123 beds.

RELIGION
At the 2001 census Hindus numbered 69,076,919, Muslims 13,722,048 and Christians 53,137.

CULTURE
Tourism
The main tourist centres are Bodh Gaya, Patna, Nalanda, Sasaram, Rajgir and Vaishali.

Chhattisgarh

KEY HISTORICAL EVENTS
Created from sixteen mainly tribal districts of Madhya Pradesh, the state became the twenty-sixth state of India on 1 Nov. 2000. Chhattisgarh has been under the administrative control of many different rulers during its history, which can be traced back to the 4th century. Originally known as South Kosala, archaeological excavations made in recent times indicate that the region was a hive of artistic and cultural experimentation in ancient times. During the Sarabhapuriyas, Nalas, Pandavamsis and Kalchuris dynasties between the 6th and 8th centuries many brick temples were built in the area. The British took control from the Mahrattas in the early 19th century. Despite possessing its own cultural identity Chhattisgarh was constantly swallowed up by other regions and in 1956, as a direct result of the Indian Union of 1949, it was made part of the new region of Madhya Pradesh. Protestors maintained that the revenue generated by their region, from rice and minerals, was insufficiently reinvested in the area. In 2000 the National Democratic Alliance negotiated the passage of a bill through both houses of the Indian parliament which carved out three new Indian states, Chhattisgarh among them.

TERRITORY AND POPULATION
Chhattisgarh is in central eastern India and is bounded by the new state of Jharkhand to the east, Orissa to the southeast, Andhra Pradesh to the south and Maharashtra and Madhya Pradesh to the west. Chhattisgarh has an area of 135,191 sq. km. Population (2001 census) 20,833,803; density, 154 per sq. km. The principal language is Hindi.

Cities with over 250,000 population, *see* INDIA: Territory and Population. Other large cities (2001): Rajnandgaon, 143,770; Raigarh, 115,908; Jagdalpur, 103,123.

SOCIAL STATISTICS
Growth rate 1991–2001, 18·27%.

CONSTITUTION AND GOVERNMENT
Chhattisgarh is the twenty-sixth state of India. In creating Chhattisgarh it was decided that the 90 members of the Madhya Pradesh Legislative Assembly from Chhattisgarhi districts would become the members of the new state's legislative assembly. For administrative purposes the region is divided into 16 districts. The council of ministers consists of 15 cabinet ministers and eight ministers of state.

The capital and seat of government is at Raipur.

RECENT ELECTIONS
At elections in Nov. 2008 the Bharatiya Janata Party won 50 seats and the Congress (I) Party took 38. Other parties won two seats.

CURRENT ADMINISTRATION
Governor: Sekhar Dutt; b. 1945 (took office 23 Jan. 2010).

Chief Minister: Dr Raman Singh; b. 1952 (took office 7 Dec. 2003).

ENERGY AND NATURAL RESOURCES
Electricity
In Sept. 2008, 18,877 out of 19,744 inhabited villages had electricity. There was an installed capacity of 3,528 MW in Oct. 2008.

Water
1·21m. ha. of land is under irrigation. 44,750 residential areas have sufficient drinking water supplies while 7,315 residential areas only have partial supplies and 2,751 areas have insufficient supplies. In total there were 102,063 hand pumps in the state and 701 water fulfilment plans in place in 1999.

Minerals
The state has extensive mineral resources including (1999 estimates): over 27,000m. tonnes of tin ore, 2,000m. tonnes of iron ore, 525m. tonnes of dolomite (accounting for 24% of India's entire share) and 73m. tonnes of bauxite. There are also significant deposits of limestone, copper ore, rock phosphate, corundum, tin, coal and manganese ore. Deobogh in the Raipur district contains deposits of diamonds.

Agriculture
Agriculture is the occupation for 1·7m. of the population (around 80%). 5·8m. ha. of land is agricultural and the area provides food grain for over 600 rice mills. The great plains of Chhattisgarh produce 10,000 varieties of rice. Other crops include maize, millet, groundnuts, soybeans and sunflower. More than 25% of the land in Chhattisgarh is double cropped.

COMMUNICATIONS
Roads
Total length of roads (1999) was 33,182 km. State highways connect Raipur to neighbouring states and to Jagdalpur and Kondagaon in the south of Chhattisgarh and Durg and Rajnandgaon in the west.

Rail
Raipur is at the centre of the state's railway network, linking Chhattisgarh to the states of Orissa and Madhya Pradesh.

SOCIAL INSTITUTIONS
Education
In 2001, 64·7% of the population were literate (77·4% of men and 51·9% of women). There are three universities in Chhattisgarh. Ravishankar University (founded 1964), at Raipur, had 89 affiliated colleges (1992–93); Indira Gandhi Krishi Vishwavidyalaya, Raipur, a music and fine arts institution (founded in 1956); and Guru Ghasidas University, Bilaspur which had 58 colleges and 34,717 students (1992–93).

Health
In 2004 there were 138 hospitals with 5,565 beds and 285 doctors.

RELIGION
At the 2001 census Hindus numbered 19,729,670; Muslims, 409,615; Christians, 401,035; Sikhs, 69,621; Buddhists, 65,267; Jains, 56,103.

Goa

KEY HISTORICAL EVENTS

The coastal area was captured by the Portuguese in 1510 and the inland area was added in the 18th century. In Dec. 1961 Portuguese rule was ended and Goa incorporated into the Indian Union as a Territory together with Daman and Diu. Goa was granted statehood on 30 May 1987. Daman and Diu remained Union Territories.

TERRITORY AND POPULATION

Goa, bounded on the north by Maharashtra and on the east and south by Karnataka, has a coastline of 105 km. The area is 3,702 sq. km. Population (2001 census) 1,347,668; density, 364 per sq. km. Marmagao is the largest town; population (urban agglomeration, 2001) 104,758. The capital is Panaji; population (urban agglomeration, 2001) 99,677. The state has two districts. There are 183 village Panchayats. The languages spoken are Konkani (official language; 51·5%), Marathi 33·4%, Kannada 4·6%, Hindi and English.

SOCIAL STATISTICS

Growth rate 1991–2001, 15·21%.

CONSTITUTION AND GOVERNMENT

The Indian Parliament passed legislation in March 1962 by which Goa became a Union Territory with retrospective effect from 20 Dec. 1961. On 30 May 1987 Goa attained statehood. There is a Legislative Assembly of 40 members. In March 2005 the state was put under president's rule following a controversy over a vote of confidence in the Legislative Assembly. It was lifted in June 2005 after Pratapsingh Rane was sworn in as the new chief minister.

RECENT ELECTIONS

Of the 40 seats available at the elections for the State Assembly on 2 June 2007 the Indian National Congress won 16; Bharatiya Janata Party, 14; Nationalist Congress Party, 3; Maharashtrawadi Gomantak Party, 2; Save Goa Front, 2; United Goans Democratic Party, 1. Two independents were elected.

CURRENT ADMINISTRATION

Governor: Shivinder Singh Sidhu; b. 1929 (took office on 21 July 2008).

Chief Minister: Digambar Kamat; b. 1954 (took office on 8 June 2007).

ECONOMY

Budget

The total budget for 2001–02 was Rs 21,377m.; receipts, Rs 22,125m.

ENERGY AND NATURAL RESOURCES

Electricity

In Oct. 2008 installed capacity was 352 MW, but Goa receives most of its power supply from the states of Maharashtra and Karnataka. In Sept. 2008 all 347 inhabited villages had electricity.

Minerals

Resources include bauxite, ferro-manganese ore and iron ore, all of which are exported. Iron ore production (2002–03) 17,502,000 tonnes. There are also reserves of limestone and clay.

Agriculture

Agriculture is the main occupation, important crops being rice, pulses, ragi, mango, cashew and coconuts. Area under rice (2001) 57,207 ha.; production, 128,100 tonnes. Area under pulses 13,250 ha., sugarcane 1,250 ha., cashew nuts 53,767 ha. Total production of foodgrains, 2001, 138,000 tonnes.

Government poultry and dairy farming schemes produced 94m. eggs and 29m. litres of milk in 1992–93. Poultry (2003), 566,000; pigs (2003), 87,000; cattle (2003), 76,000.

Forestry

Forests covered 1,250 sq. km in 1995.

Fisheries

Fish is the state's staple food. In 2005 there were 5,900 people engaged in fishing and allied activities. In 1995–96 the catch of seafish was 84,210 tonnes. There is a coastline of about 104 km.

INDUSTRY

In 2001 there were 891 factories registered with a workforce of 39,938. There were 6,127 small-scale industries registered employing 43,312 persons. Production included: automotive components, electronic goods, fertilizers, footwear, nylon fishing nets, pesticides, pharmaceuticals, ready made clothing, shipbuilding and tyres.

COMMUNICATIONS

Roads

There were 7,419 km of roads in 1993–94 (National Highway, 224 km). Motor vehicles numbered 211,756 in March 1996.

Rail

In 1995–96 there were 79 km of route. In 2003 plans were announced for a monorail system.

Civil Aviation

An airport at Dabolim is connected with Agatti, Bangalore, Chennai, Delhi, Kochi, Kozhikode, Mumbai and Pune. It also receives international charter flights and scheduled flights from Kuwait and Sharjah.

Shipping

There are seaports at Panaji, Marmagao and Margao.

SOCIAL INSTITUTIONS

Justice

There is a bench of the Bombay High Court at Panaji.

Education

In 2001, 82·0% of the population were literate (88·4% of men and 75·4% of women). In 2001 there were 1,268 primary schools (97,457 students), 440 middle schools (72,726 students) and 445 high and higher secondary schools (85,217 students). In 1996–97 there were also two engineering colleges, four medical colleges, two teacher-training colleges, 21 other colleges and six polytechnic institutes. Goa University, Taleigao (1985) had 33 colleges and 16,977 students in 1994–95.

Health

In 2001 there were 120 hospitals (4,865 beds), 201 rural medical dispensaries, health and sub-health centres and 268 family planning units.

RELIGION

At the 2001 census Hindus numbered 886,551; Christians, 359,568; Muslims, 92,210.

FURTHER READING

Hutt, A., *Goa: A Traveller's Historical and Architectural Guide.* 1988

Gujarat

KEY HISTORICAL EVENTS

The Gujarati-speaking areas of India were part of the Moghul empire, coming under Mahratta domination in the late 18th century. In 1818 areas of present Gujurat around the Gulf of Cambay were annexed by the British East India Company. The remainder consisted of a group of small principalities, notably Baroda, Rajkot, Bhavnagar and Nawanagar. British areas became part of the Bombay Presidency.

At independence the area now forming Gujarat became part of Bombay State except for Rajkot and Bhavnagar which formed the state of Saurashtra until incorporated into Bombay in 1956. In 1960 Bombay State was divided and the Gujarati-speaking areas became Gujarat.

In early 2002 at least 800 people, mostly Muslims, were killed in Gujarat in ethnic violence.

TERRITORY AND POPULATION

Gujarat is in western India and is bounded in the north by Pakistan and Rajasthan, east by Madhya Pradesh, southeast by Maharashtra, south and west by the Indian ocean and Arabian sea. The area of the state is 196,024 sq. km and the population (2001 census) 50,671,017; density, 258 per sq. km. The chief cities, *see* INDIA: Territory and Population. Other important towns (2001 census) are: Navsari (232,411), Surendranagar (219,585), Anand (218,486), Porbandar (197,382), Nadiad (196,793), Gandhinagar (195,985), Morbi (178,055), Bharuch (176,364), Veraval (158,032), Gandhidham (151,693), Valsad (145,592), Mehesana (141,453), Bhuj (136,429), Godhra (131,172), Palanpur (122,300), Patan (113,749), Anklesvar (112,643), Dahod (112,026), Kalol (112,013), Jetpur (104,312), Botad (100,194). Gujarati and Hindi in the Devanagari script are the official languages.

SOCIAL STATISTICS

Growth rate 1991–2001, 22·66%.

CLIMATE

Summers are intensely hot: 33–45°C. Winters: 7–13°C. Monsoon season: 22–36°C. Annual rainfall varies from 35 cm to 189 cm.

CONSTITUTION AND GOVERNMENT

Gujarat has a unicameral legislature, the *Legislative Assembly*, which has 182 elected members.

The capital is Gandhinagar. There are 25 districts.

RECENT ELECTIONS

In elections held in Dec. 2007 the Bharatiya Janata Party retained power with a slightly reduced majority, winning 117 seats against 59 for Congress, with ind. and others winning six seats.

CURRENT ADMINISTRATION

Governor: Dr Kamla Beniwal; b. 1927 (took office on 27 Nov. 2009).

Chief Minister: Shri Narendrabhai Modi; b. 1950 (took office on 7 Oct. 2001).

ECONOMY

Budget

The budget estimates for 2004–05 showed revenue receipts of Rs 208,136·7m. and revenue expenditure of Rs 237,863·3m.

Banking and Finance

At March 2004 there were 3,668 branches of commercial banks in the State with combined deposits of Rs 846,810m. Total credit advanced was Rs 366,820m.

ENERGY AND NATURAL RESOURCES

Electricity

In Oct. 2008 total installed capacity was 11,591 MW. In Sept. 2008, 18,014 out of 18,066 inhabited villages had electricity.

Oil and Gas

There are large crude oil and gas reserves. Production, 2002–03: crude oil, 6·0m. tonnes; gas, 3,324m. cu. metres.

Water

Water resources are limited. In 2003 irrigation potential was 6·49m. ha.

Minerals

Chief minerals produced in 2006–07 (in tonnes) included limestone (22·5m.), lignite (9·8m.), bauxite (3·5m.), quartz and silica (1·2m.), bentonite (896,000), crude china clay (469,000), dolomite (325,000) and fire clay (232,000). Value of production (2005–06) Rs 60,325m.

Agriculture

3·5m. ha. of the cropped area was irrigated in June 2003.

Production of principal crops, 2002–03: foodgrains, 3·6m. tonnes (wheat, 0·86m. tonnes); rice, 0·6m. tonnes from 481,000 ha.; pulses, 327,000 tonnes; cotton, 1·69m. bales of 170 kg. Tobacco and groundnuts are important cash crops.

Livestock (2003): buffaloes, 7·14m.; other cattle, 7·42m.; sheep and goats, 6·60m.; pigs, 351,000; poultry, 8·15m.

Forestry

Forests covered 18,940 sq. km in March 2003 (9·66% of total area). The State has four National Parks and 21 sanctuaries.

Fisheries

There were 158,000 people engaged in fisheries in 2005. In 2006–07 there were 31,370 fishing vessels; the total catch was 754,000 tonnes.

INDUSTRY

Gujarat ranks among India's most industrialized states. In 2005 there were 306,646 small-scale units and (2002) 19,661 factories including 3,720 chemical and chemical products factories, 2,560 textile factories, 2,072 food products and beverages factories, 2,064 non-metallic mineral products factories, 1,983 machinery and equipment factories and 1,897 fabricated metal products factories. There were 251 industrial estates in 2002–03. Principal industries are textiles, general and electrical engineering, oil-refining, fertilizers, petrochemicals, machine tools, automobiles, heavy chemicals, pharmaceuticals, dyes, sugar, soda ash, cement, man-made fibres, salt, sulphuric acid, paper and paperboard.

In 2002 state production of soda-ash was 1·88m. tonnes, salt production was 13·08m. tonnes and cement production 10·78m. tonnes.

COMMUNICATIONS

Roads

At March 2002 there were 74,018 km of roads. Gujarat State Road Transport Corporation operated 18,507 routes. Number of vehicles at the end of March 2004, 7,087,490.

Rail

In 2002–03 the state had 5,186 route-km of railway line.

Civil Aviation

Sardar Vallabhbhai Patel International Airport at Ahmedabad is the main airport. There are some international flights and regular internal services between Ahmedabad and Delhi, Jaipur and Mumbai, and within Gujarat between Ahmedabad and Bhavnagar, Bhuj, Rajkot and Vadodara (Baroda). There are five other airports: Jamnagar (which also has some international flights), Kandla, Keshod, Porbandar and Surat.

Shipping
The largest port is Kandla. There are 40 other ports. Cargo handled at the ports in 2003–04 totalled 130·9m. tonnes (41·5m. tonnes at Kandla).

Telecommunications
There were 2,775,500 telephone connections and 2,073,035 mobile phone connections in the state at the end of March 2004.

Postal Services
There were 9,023 post offices and 1,258 telegraph offices at the end of March 2004.

SOCIAL INSTITUTIONS

Justice
The High Court of Judicature at Ahmedabad has a Chief Justice and 30 puisne judges.

Education
In 2001, 69·1% of the population were literate (79·7% of males and 57·8% of females). Primary and secondary education up to Standard XII are free. Education above Standard XII is free for girls. In 2006–07 there were 39,064 primary schools with 8·28m. students and 7,967 secondary schools with 2·67m. students.

There are 11 universities in the state. Gujarat University, Ahmedabad, founded in 1950, is teaching and affiliating; it has 154 affiliated colleges and 143,692 students (all student figures for 1998–99). The Maharaja Sayajirao University of Vadodara (1949) is residential and teaching; it has 12 colleges and 26,511 students. The Sardar Patel University, Vallabh-Vidyanagar (1955), has 20 constituent and affiliated colleges and 17,913 students. Saurashtra University at Rajkot (1968) has 113 affiliated colleges and 72,234 students. South Gujarat University at Surat (1967) has 58 colleges and 59,600 students. Bhavnagar University (1978) is residential and teaching with 15 affiliated colleges and 11,195 students. North Gujarat University was established at Patan in 1986 and has 73 colleges and 54,720 students. Gujarat Vidyapith at Ahmedabad is deemed a university under the University Grants Commission Act. There are also Gujarat Agricultural University, Banaskantha, Gujarat Ayurved University, Jamnagar and Dr Babasaheb Ambedkar Open University, Ahmedabad.

There were 903 higher education institutions in 2006–07, with a total of 409,000 students enrolled.

Health
At March 2006 there were 273 community health centres, 1,072 primary health centres and 7,274 sub-centres. In 2003–04, 41·3m. patients were treated.

RELIGION
At the 2001 census Hindus numbered 45,143,074; Muslims, 4,592,854; Jains, 525,305; Christians, 284,092.

CULTURE

Press
At June 2004 there were 2,445 newspapers and periodicals of which 2,255 were published in Gujarati, 85 in English and 75 in Hindi.

Tourism
There are many sights of religious pilgrimage as well as archaeological sights, attractive beaches, the Lion Sanctuary of Gir Forest and the Wild Ass Sanctuary in Kachchh. Mahatma Gandhi's birthplace at Porbandar is also a popular tourist attraction.

FURTHER READING
Desai, I. F., *Untouchability in Rural Gujarat*. 1977
Sharma, R. N., *Gujarat Holocaust (Communalism in the Land of Gandhi)*. 2002

Haryana

KEY HISTORICAL EVENTS
The state of Haryana, created on 1 Nov. 1966 under the Punjab Reorganization Act, 1966, was formed from the Hindi-speaking parts of the state of Punjab (India). It comprises the districts of Ambala, Bhiwani, Faridabad, Fatehabad, Gurgaon, Hisar, Jhajjar, Jind, Kaithal, Karnal, Kurukshetra, Mahendragarh, Panchkula, Panipat, Rewari, Rohtak, Sirsa, Sonipat and Yamunanagar.

TERRITORY AND POPULATION
Haryana is in north India and is bounded north by Himachal Pradesh, east by Uttar Pradesh, south and west by Rajasthan and northwest by Punjab. Delhi forms an enclave on its eastern boundary. The state has an area of 44,212 sq. km and a population (2001 census) of 21,144,564; density, 478 per sq. km. Principal cities, *see* INDIA: Territory and Population. Other large towns (2001) are: Gurgaon (228,820), Sonipat (225,074), Karnal (221,236), Bhiwani (169,531), Ambala Sadar (168,316), Sirsa (160,735), Panchkula Urban Estate (140,925), Ambala (139,279), Jind (135,855), Bahadurgarh (131,925), Thanesar (122,319), Kaithal (117,285), Palwal (100,722), Rewari (100,684). The principal language is Hindi.

SOCIAL STATISTICS
Growth rate 1991–2001, 28·43%.

CONSTITUTION AND GOVERNMENT
The state has a unicameral legislature with 90 members. The capital (shared with Punjab) is Chandigarh. Its transfer to Punjab, intended for 1986, has been postponed. There are 19 districts.

RECENT ELECTIONS
In the elections of 13 Oct. 2009 the Indian National Congress won 40 seats, the Indian National Lok Dal 32, the Haryana Janhit Congress 6, the Bharatiya Janata Party 4 and others 8. Turnout was 69·4%.

CURRENT ADMINISTRATION
Governor: Jagannath Pahadia; b. 1932 (took office on 27 July 2009).

Chief Minister: Bhupinder Singh Hooda; b. 1947 (took office on 5 March 2005).

ECONOMY

Budget
Budget estimates for 2002–03 show revenue income of Rs 104,091·4m. and revenue expenditure of Rs 114,057·9m.

ENERGY AND NATURAL RESOURCES

Electricity
Installed capacity (Oct. 2008) was 4,590 MW. In Sept. 2008 all 6,764 inhabited villages had electricity.

Minerals
Minerals include placer gold, barytes, tin and rare earths. Value of production, 2002–03, Rs 1,487m.

Agriculture
Haryana has sandy soil and erratic rainfall, but the state shares the benefit of the Sutlej-Beas scheme. Agriculture employs over 82% of the working population; in 1995–96 there were about 1·7m. holdings (average 2·1 ha.), and the gross irrigated area was 2·05m. ha. in 1993–94. Area under foodgrains, 1995–96, 4·02m. ha. Foodgrain production, 1999–2000, 10·36m. tonnes (rice 2·59m.

tonnes in 2000, wheat 7·35m. tonnes in 1995–96); pulses, 416,400 tonnes in 1995–96; cotton, 1·5m. bales of 170 kg in 1995–96; sugar (gur) and oilseeds are important. Haryana produces a surplus of wheat and rice.

Forestry

Forests covered 603 sq. km in 1995.

INDUSTRY

Haryana has a large market for consumer goods in neighbouring Delhi. In 1996–97 there were 916 large and medium scale industries and 138,759 small units providing employment to about 1m. persons, and 56,012 rural industrial units. The main industries are cotton textiles, agricultural machinery and tractors, woollen textiles, scientific instruments, glass, cement, paper and sugar milling, cars, tyres and tubes, motorcycles, bicycles, steel tubes, engineering goods, electrical and electronic goods. An oil refinery at Panipat was commissioned in 1999 and includes a diesel hydro desulphurization plant.

COMMUNICATIONS

Roads

There were (2002) 29,524 km of metalled roads—including 656 km of national highways, 3,135 km of state highways and 1,587 km of district highways—linking all villages. Road transport is nationalized. There were 954,563 motor vehicles in 1995–96. Haryana roadways carried 1·75m. passengers daily in 2002 with a fleet of 3,411 buses.

Rail

The state is crossed by lines from Delhi to Agra, Ajmer, Ferozepur and Chandigarh. Route km, 1995–96, 1,452 km. The main stations are at Ambala and Kurukshetra.

Civil Aviation

There is no airport within the state but Delhi is on its eastern boundary.

SOCIAL INSTITUTIONS

Justice

Haryana shares the High Court of Punjab and Haryana at Chandigarh.

Education

In 2001, 67·9% of the population were literate (78·5% of men and 55·7% of women). In 1996–97 there were 5,651 primary schools with 1,981,993 students, 3,233 high and higher secondary schools with 511,377 students, 1,631 middle schools with 832,886 students and 129 colleges of arts, science and commerce, nine engineering and technical colleges and ten medical colleges. There are four universities: Haryana Agricultural University, Hisar; Kurukshetra University, Kurukshetra with 70 colleges and 80,000 students (1999); Maharshi Dayanand University, Rohtak; and Guru Jambeshwar University, Hisar.

Health

In 2003 there were 49 hospitals, 64 community health centres, 402 primary health centres and 2,299 health sub-centres. A further 12 primary health centres were under construction.

RELIGION

At the 2001 census Hindus numbered 18,655,925; Muslims, 1,222,916; Sikhs, 1,170,622; Jains, 57,167.

FURTHER READING

Yadav, K. C., *Modern Haryana: History and Culture.* 2002

Himachal Pradesh

KEY HISTORICAL EVENTS

Thirty small hill states were merged to form the Territory of Himachal Pradesh in 1948; the state of Bilaspur was added in 1954 and parts of the Punjab in 1966. The whole territory, a Himalayan area of hill-tribes, rivers and forests, became a state in Jan. 1971. Its main component areas are Chamba, a former principality, dominated in turn by Moghuls and Sikhs before coming under British influence in 1848; Bilaspur, an independent Punjab state until it was invaded by Gurkhas in 1814 (the British East India Company forces drove out the Gurkhas in 1815); Simla district around the town built by the Company near Bilaspur on land reclaimed from Gurkha troops (the summer capital of India from 1865 until 1948); Mandi, a principality until 1948 and Kangra and Kullu districts, originally Rajput areas which had become part of the British-ruled Punjab. These were all incorporated into Himachal Pradesh in 1966 when the Punjab was reorganized.

TERRITORY AND POPULATION

Himachal Pradesh is in north India and is bounded north by Kashmir, east by Tibet, southeast by Uttarakhand, south by Haryana, southwest and west by Punjab. The area of the state is 55,673 sq. km and the population (2001 census) 6,077,900; density, 109 per sq. km. Principal languages are Hindi and Pahari. The capital is Shimla, population (2001 census) of the urban agglomeration, 144,975.

SOCIAL STATISTICS

Growth rate 1991–2001, 17·54%.

CONSTITUTION AND GOVERNMENT

Full statehood was attained, as the 18th State of the Union, on 25 Jan. 1971. On 1 Sept. 1972 districts were reorganized and three new districts created, Solan, Hamirpur and Una, making a total of 12.

There is a unicameral *Legislative Assembly.*

RECENT ELECTIONS

Elections were held on 14 Nov. and 19 Dec. 2007. The opposition Bharatiya Janata Party won 41 seats; the Indian National Congress, 23; the Bahujan Samaj Party, 1; ind., 3.

CURRENT ADMINISTRATION

Governor: Urmila Singh; b. 1946 (took office on 25 Jan. 2010).

Chief Minister: Prem Kumar Dhumal; b. 1944 (took office for a second time on 30 Dec. 2007).

ECONOMY

Budget

Budget estimates for 2000–01 showed receipts of Rs 39,854m. and expenditure of Rs 48,860m.

ENERGY AND NATURAL RESOURCES

Electricity

In Sept. 2008, 17,183 out of 17,495 inhabited villages had electricity. The state has huge hydropower potential—there is an estimated potential of 20,376 MW (14·5% of India's potential). In Oct. 2008 there was an installed capacity of 1,896 MW. The Nathpa Jhakri project is India's largest hydroelectric power plant. The plant, which incorporates a 28 km power tunnel, came online in Oct. 2003. Electricity generated (1999), 1,485m. kWh.

Water

An artificial confluence of the Sutlej and Beas rivers has been made, directing their united flow into Govind Sagar Lake.

Minerals
The state has rock salt, slate, gypsum, limestone, barytes, dolomite, pyrites, copper, gold and sulphur. However, Himachal Pradesh supplies only 0·2% of the national mineral output.

Agriculture
Agriculture employed 69% of the workforce in 2001. Irrigated area is 19% of the area sown. Main crops are seed potatoes, off season vegetables, wheat, maize, rice, flowers and fruits such as apples, peaches, apricots, hops, kiwi fruit and strawberries; 695,517 tonnes of fruits were produced in 2005–06.

Production (2005–06): foodgrains 1,453,000 tonnes (of which wheat 550,000 tonnes, maize 543,000 tonnes and rice 112,000 tonnes), plus vegetables 930,000 tonnes and ginger 1,600 tonnes.

Livestock (2003 census): cattle, 2·20m.; goats, 1·12m.; sheep, 906,000; buffaloes, 773,000.

Forestry
Himachal Pradesh forests cover 66·2% of the state and supply the largest quantities of coniferous timber in northern India. The forests also ensure the safety of the catchment areas of the Yamuna, Sutlej, Beas, Ravi and Chenab rivers. Commercial felling of green trees has been totally halted and forest working nationalized. Area under forests, 37,033 sq. km.

INDUSTRY
The main sources of employment are the forests and their related industries; there are factories making turpentine and rosin. The state also makes fertilizers, cement, electronic items, TV sets, watches, computer parts, electronic toys and video cassettes. Sericulture is a major industry. There is a foundry and a brewery. Other industries include salt production and handicrafts, including weaving. The state has 173 large and medium units, 27,000 small scale units (providing employment for 140,000 people), seven industrial estates and 21 industrial areas. 300 mineral based industries have also been established.

COMMUNICATIONS

Roads
The national highway from Chandigarh runs through Shimla; other main highways from Shimla serve Kullu, Manali, Kangra, Chamba and Pathankot. The rest are minor roads. Pathankot is also on national highways from Punjab to Kashmir. Length of roads (2005–06), 29,011 km; number of vehicles (2003–04), 288,042.

Rail
There is a line from Chandigarh to Shimla, and the Jammu-Delhi line runs through Pathankot. A Nangal-Talwara rail link has been approved by the central government. There are two narrow gauge lines, from Shimla to Kalka (96 km) and Jogindernagar to Pathankot (103 km), and a broad gauge line from Una to Nangal (16 km). Route-km in 2003, 256 km.

Civil Aviation
The state has airports at Bhuntar near Kullu, at Jubbarhatti near Shimla and at Gaggal in Kangra district. There are also 12 state-run helipads across the state.

SOCIAL INSTITUTIONS

Justice
The state has its own High Court at Shimla with eight judges.

Education
In 2001, 76·5% of the population were literate (85·3% of men and 67·4% of women). There were (2004–05) 10,613 primary schools with 565,700 students, 2,012 middle schools with 366,200 students, 2,341 high and senior secondary schools with 383,800 students, and 69 colleges with 79,200 students. The universities are: Himachal Pradesh University, Shimla (1970) with 65 affiliated colleges and 32,773 students (1992–93); Himachal Pradesh Agricultural University, Palampur (1978); Dr Y. S. Parmar University of Horticulture and Forestry, Solan (1985); and Jaypee University of Information Technology, Solan (2002). There were also, in 2004–05, three medical colleges, 23 general education colleges, 20 Sanskrit institutions, 12 teaching training schools, six polytechnic institutions and four dental colleges.

Health
There were (2005) 50 hospitals (8,832 beds), 505 primary and community health centres and 2,068 sub-health centres.

RELIGION
At the 2001 census Hindus numbered 5,800,222, Muslims 119,512, Buddhists 75,859 and Sikhs 72,355.

FURTHER READING
Verma, Vishwashwar, *The Emergence of Himachal Pradesh: A Survey of Constitutional Development.* 1995

Jammu and Kashmir

KEY HISTORICAL EVENTS
The state of Jammu and Kashmir was brought into being in 1846 at the close of the First Sikh War. By the Treaty of Amritsar, Gulab Singh, *de facto* ruler of Jammu and Ladakh, added Kashmir to his existing territories, in return for paying the indemnity imposed by the British on the defeated Sikh empire. Of the state's three component parts, Ladakh and Kashmir were ancient polities, Ladakh having been an independent kingdom since the tenth century AD until its conquest by Gulab Singh's armies in 1834–42. Kashmir lost its independence to the Mughal empire in 1586, and was conquered in turn by the Afghans (1756) and the Sikhs (1819). Jammu was a collection of small principalities until consolidated by Gulab Singh and his brothers in the early nineteenth century.

British supremacy was recognized until the Indian Independence Act, 1947, when all states decided on accession to India or Pakistan. Kashmir asked for standstill agreements with both. Pakistan agreed, but India wanted further discussion with the government of Jammu and Kashmir State. Meantime the state was subject to armed attack from Pakistan. The Maharajah acceded to India on 26 Oct. 1947. India approached the UN in Jan. 1948, and the conflict ended by ceasefire in Jan. 1949. The major part of the state remained with India after territory in the north and west went to Pakistan. Hostilities between the two countries broke out in 1965 and again in 1971, but notwithstanding bilateral agreements—the Tashkent Declaration (Jan. 1966) and the Simla Agreement (July 1972)—the issue remains unresolved. With Muslims in the majority, both India and Pakistan regard the state as a touchstone of their divergent political raisons d'être—Pakistan as a Muslim nation, and India a secular one—and hence their position as non-negotiable. Intermittent violence between nationalistic factions has led to further negotiations between India and Pakistan with both sides pledging a peaceful solution. In Dec. 2002 the new provincial government promised to open talks with separatist groups.

TERRITORY AND POPULATION
The state is in the extreme north and is bounded north by China, east by Tibet, south by Himachal Pradesh and Punjab and west by Pakistan. The area is 101,387 sq. km and the population (2001 census) 10,143,700; density, 100 per sq. km. Srinagar (population, 2001, 988,210) is the summer and Jammu (612,163) the winter capital. The official language is Urdu; other commonly spoken

languages are Kashmiri, Hindi, Dogri, Gujri, Pahari, Ladakhi and Punjabi.

SOCIAL STATISTICS

Growth rate 1991–2001, 29·98%.

CONSTITUTION AND GOVERNMENT

The Maharajah's son, Yuvraj Karan Singh, took over as Regent in 1950 and, on the ending of hereditary rule (17 Oct. 1952), was sworn in as Sadar-i-Riyasat. On his father's death (26 April 1961) Yuvraj Karan Singh was recognized as Maharajah by the Indian government. The permanent Constitution of the state came into force in part on 17 Nov. 1956 and fully on 26 Jan. 1957. There is a bicameral legislature; the Legislative Council has 36 members and the Legislative Assembly has 89 (two of which are nominated). Since the 1967 elections the six representatives of Jammu and Kashmir in the central House of the People are directly elected; there are four representatives in the Council of States. There was a period of President's rule in 1977, and since then President's rule has been imposed on four further occasions—in 1986, from 1990–96, in 2002 and in 2008–09.

The state has 14 districts.

RECENT ELECTIONS

Elections to the State Assembly were held in between 17 Nov. and 24 Dec. 2008. The ruling pro-India Jammu and Kashmir National Conference won 28 of the 87 seats (28 in 2002); the People's Democratic Party won 21 (16 in 2002); the Indian National Congress, 17 (20 in 2002); the Bharatiya Janata Party, 11 (1 in 2002); and the Jammu and Kashmir National Panthers Party, 3 (0 in 2002). Despite ongoing violence and calls from Kashmiri separatist groups to boycott the elections, turnout was 61%. Following the elections, a coalition government was formed by the National Conference and the Indian National Congress.

CURRENT ADMINISTRATION

Governor: Narinder Nath Vohra; b. 1936 (since 25 June 2008).

Chief Minister: Omar Abdullah; b. 1970 (took office on 5 Jan. 2009).

ECONOMY

Budget

Budget estimates for 2000–01 show total receipts of Rs 57,158m. and total expenditure of Rs 77,483m.

ENERGY AND NATURAL RESOURCES

Electricity

The state has exploitable hydropower potential of about 15,000 MW. The gas turbine station at Srinagar is an important contributor. Installed capacity (Oct. 2008) 2,009 MW. In Sept. 2008, 6,304 out of 6,417 villages had electricity.

Minerals

Minerals include coal, bauxite and gypsum.

Agriculture

About 80% of the population are supported by agriculture. Rice, wheat and maize are the major cereals. The total area under foodgrains (1998–99) was estimated at 908,000 ha. Total foodgrains produced, 1998–99, 1·45m. tonnes (rice, 0·55m. tonnes; wheat, 0·43m. tonnes); pulses, 17,000 tonnes. Fruit is important: production, 1994–95, 0·9m. tonnes; exports, 0·76m. tonnes.

Irrigated area, 1993–94, 442,000 ha.

Livestock (2003): cattle, 3·08m.; buffaloes, 1·04m.; goats, 2·06m.; sheep, 3·41m.; poultry, 5·57m.

Forestry

Forests cover about 20,443 sq. km (1995), forming an important source of revenue, besides providing employment to a large section of the population.

INDUSTRY

There are two central public sector industries and 30 medium-scale. There are 35,576 small units (1994–95) employing over 125,000. There are industries based on horticulture; traditional handicrafts are silk spinning, wood-carving, papier mâché and carpet-weaving. 750 tonnes of silk cocoons were produced in 1994–95.

The handicraft sector employed 0·26m. persons and had a production turnover of Rs 2,500m. in 1995–96.

COMMUNICATIONS

Roads

Kashmir is linked with the rest of India by the motorable Jammu–Pathankot road. The Jawahar Tunnel, through the Banihal mountain, connects Srinagar and Jammu, and maintains road communication with the Kashmir Valley during the winter months. In 2000 there were 13,093 km of roads.

There were 195,125 motor vehicles in 1995–96.

Rail

Kashmir is linked with the Indian railway system by the line between Jammu and Pathankot; route-km of railways in the state, 2002, 77 km.

Civil Aviation

Major airports are at Srinagar and Jammu. There is a third airport at Leh. There are services connecting Jammu with Amritsar, Chandigarh, Delhi and Srinagar; and services connecting Srinagar with Ahmedabad, Amritsar, Chandigarh, Delhi, Jammu, Leh and Mumbai.

Telecommunications

There were 328,700 telephones in 2004 of which 40,100 were mobile phones.

Postal Services

There were 1,665 post offices at 31 March 2001.

SOCIAL INSTITUTIONS

Justice

The High Court, at Srinagar and Jammu, has a Chief Justice and four puisne judges.

Education

The proportion of literate people was 55·5% in 2001 (66·6% of men and 43·0% of women). Education is free. There were (1996–97) 1,351 high and higher secondary schools with 227,699 students, 3,104 middle schools with 405,598 students and 10,483 primary schools with 893,005 students. Jammu University (1969) has five constituent and 13 affiliated colleges, with 15,278 students (1992–93); Kashmir University (1948) has 18 colleges (17,000 students, 1992–93); there are two other universities: Sher-E-Kashmir University of Agricultural Sciences and Technology and Hemwati Nandan Bahuguna Garhwal University at Srinagar. There are four medical colleges, two engineering and technology colleges, four polytechnics, eight oriental colleges and an Ayurvedic college, 34 arts, science and commerce colleges and four teacher training colleges.

Health

In 2001 there were 43 hospitals with (2000) 2,076 beds, 337 primary health centres and 1,700 sub-centres, and 53 community health centres. There is a National Institute of Medical Sciences.

RELIGION

The majority of the population, except in Jammu, are Muslims (making it the only Indian state to have a Muslim majority). At the 2001 census Muslims numbered 6,793,240, Hindus 3,005,349, Sikhs 207,154 and Buddhists 113,787.

FURTHER READING

Behera, Navnita Chadha, *Demystifying Kashmir.* 2007
Hewitt, Vernon, *Towards the Future?: Jammu and Kashmir in the 21st Century.* 2001
Lamb, A., *Kashmir: a Disputed Legacy, 1846–1990.* 1991
Wirsing, R. G., *India, Pakistan and the Kashmir Dispute: on Regional Conflict and its Resolution.* 1995

Jharkhand

KEY HISTORICAL EVENTS

The state was carved from Bihar to become the twenty-eighth state of India on 15 Nov. 2000. Located in the plateau regions of eastern India, Jharkhand (literally land of forests) is mentioned in ancient Indian texts as an area inaccessible to the rest of India owing to its unforgiving terrain and the warring forest tribes. The Mughals attacked the region in 1385 and again in 1616, imprisoning the King of Jharkhand while they collected money from local chieftains. In the 17th century Jharkhand was a part of the Mughal empire and spread over areas of present-day Madhya Pradesh and Bihar. The East India Company was granted revenue-collecting power in 1765 and the permanent settlement of 1796 increased the company's grip on the area. In 1858 sovereignty was transferred to the English crown. From 1793 until 1915 there were periodic tribal rebellions throughout Jharkhand. In 1912 Jharkhand was constituted as part of the province of Bihar and Orissa after the former was separated from West Bengal. In 1995 the Jharkhand Party submitted a request to the State Reorganisation Committee for Jharkhand to become a separate state. In 2000 Jharkhand came into being after legislation initiated by the National Democratic Alliance.

TERRITORY AND POPULATION

Jharkhand is in central eastern India and is bounded by Bihar to the north, West Bengal to the east, Orissa to the south and the new state of Chhattisgarh to the west. Jharkhand has an area of 79,714 sq. km. Population (2001 census) 26,945,829; density: 338 per sq. km. Cities with over 250,000 population, *see* INDIA: Territory and Population. Other large cities (2001): Phusro (174,402), Hazaribag (135,473), Deogar (112,525), Ramgarh (110,496), Chirkunda (106,227), Giridih (105,634). The principal language is Hindi.

SOCIAL STATISTICS

Growth rate 1991–2001, 23·36%.

CONSTITUTION AND GOVERNMENT

Jharkhand is the twenty-eighth state of India. After the region was carved from Bihar it was decided that the 81 Members of the Legislative Assembly (MLAs) from Jharkhandi districts would become the members of the new state's legislative assembly. For administrative purposes the region is divided into 18 districts.

The capital and seat of government is at Ranchi.

Presidential rule was imposed on 19 Jan. 2009 following the resignation of Chief Minister Shibu Soren but was lifted on 30 Dec. 2009.

RECENT ELECTIONS

In elections held on 27 Nov., and 2, 8, 12 and 18 Dec. 2009 the Bharatiya Janata Party won 18 of 81 seats; Jharkhand Mukti Morcha, 18; the Indian National Congress, 14; Jharkhand Vikas Morcha (Prajatantrik), 11; Rashtriya Janata Dal, 5; Janata Dal (United), 2; ind. and other parties, 13.

CURRENT ADMINISTRATION

Governor: M. O. Hasan Farook Maricar; b. 1937 (took office on 22 Jan. 2010).

Chief Minister: Shibu Soren; b. 1944 (took office on 30 Dec. 2009).

ECONOMY

Budget

Budget estimates for Jharkhand in 2002 showed it had receipts of Rs 37,070m. and expenditure of Rs 36,560m. The formation of Jharkhand in 2000 substantially weakened the economy of Bihar, which lost 55% of its revenue but only 45% of its population. Jharkhand's annual plan of outlay for 2001–02 was Rs 19,000m.

ENERGY AND NATURAL RESOURCES

Electricity

In Sept. 2008, 9,119 out of 29,354 inhabited villages had electricity (equivalent to 31%—the lowest proportion of any state). Installed capacity was 2,153 MW in Oct. 2008.

Minerals

Jharkhand is very rich in minerals, with about 40% of national production, including 90% of the country's cooking coal deposits, 40% of its copper, 37% of known coal reserves and 2% of iron ore. Other important minerals: bauxite, quartz, building stones and ceramics, graphite, limestone, kyanite, manganese, lead and silver. The state has 176 coal mines with an annual production of 78·7m. tonnes. Annually the state mines 8·6m. tonnes of iron ore, 1·2m. tonnes of copper ores, 1·0m. tonnes of bauxite, 50,000 tonnes of fire clays and 18,700 tonnes of manganese.

INDUSTRY

There is a major engineering corporation in Jharkhand as well as India's largest steel plant at Bokaro. Other important industries are aluminium and copper plants, forging, explosives, refractories and glass production. Jharkhand contains large thermal plants at Patratu, Tenughat, Chandrapura and Bokaro.

COMMUNICATIONS

Roads

National highways connect Ranchi to the neighbouring states of Bihar in the north, West Bengal to the east and Orissa to the south. State highways connect to the new state of Chhattisgarh in the west. Jharkhand has a total length of about 6,450 km of state highways, 1,660 km of national highways and 400 km of district highways.

Rail

Ranchi and the steel city of Bokaro are at the hub of the state's railway network linking Jharkhand to its neighbouring states as well as to Kolkata.

SOCIAL INSTITUTIONS

Education

In 2001, 53·6% of the population were literate (67·3% of men and 38·9% of women). There are five universities: Ranchi University (founded 1960), with 106 colleges and 55,731 students (1994–95); Bisra Agricultural University at Ranchi (1980); Sidhu Kanhu University at Dumka; Binova Bhave University at Hazaribag; B. I. T. Mesra University at Ranchi (formerly Birla Institute of Technology). There are two law colleges, two agricultural colleges, five engineering colleges and ten medical colleges.

Health

There were 83 hospitals in 2003.

RELIGION

At the 2001 census Hindus numbered 18,475,681; Muslims, 3,731,308; Christians, 1,093,382; Sikhs, 83,358.

CULTURE

Tourism

The main tourist centre is Ranchi.

FURTHER READING

Corbridge, Stuart, Jewitt, Sarah and Kumar, Sanjay, *Jharkhand: Environment, Development, Ethnicity.* 2004

Karnataka

KEY HISTORICAL EVENTS

The state of Karnataka, constituted as Mysore under the States Reorganization Act, 1956, brought together the Kannada-speaking people distributed over five states. It consists of the territories of the old states of Mysore and Coorg, the Bijapur, Kanara and Dharwar districts and the Belgaum district (except one taluk) in former Bombay, the major portions of the Gulbarga, Raichur and Bidar districts in former Hyderabad, the South Kanara district (apart from the Kasaragod taluk) and the Kollegal taluk of the Coimbatore district in Madras. The state was renamed Karnataka in 1973.

TERRITORY AND POPULATION

The state is in south India and is bounded north by Maharashtra, east by Andhra Pradesh, south by Tamil Nadu and Kerala, west by the Indian ocean and northeast by Goa. The area of the state is 191,791 sq. km, and its population (2001 census), 52,850,562; density, 276 per sq. km. Principal cities, *see* INDIA: Territory and Population. The capital is Bangalore. Other large towns (2001) are: Tumkur (248,929), Raichur (207,421), Bidar (174,257), Hospet (164,240), Bhadravati (160,662), Robertson Pet (157,084), Gadag (154,982), Hassan (133,262), Mandya (131,179), Udupi (127,124), Chitradurga (125,170), Kolar (113,907), Gangawati (101,392), Chikmagalur (101,251).

Kannada is the language of administration and is spoken by about 66% of the people. Other languages include Urdu (9%), Telugu (8·2%), Marathi (4·5%), Tamil (3·6%), Tulu and Konkani.

SOCIAL STATISTICS

Growth rate 1991–2001, 17·51%.

CONSTITUTION AND GOVERNMENT

Karnataka has a bicameral legislature. The Legislative Council has 75 members. The Legislative Assembly consists of 225 members (one of which is nominated).

The state has 27 districts grouped in four divisions: Bangalore, Belgaum, Gulbarga and Mysore.

RECENT ELECTIONS

At the state elections on 10, 16 and 22 May 2008 the BJP won 110 seats; the INC 80; the Janata Dal (Secular) 28. Six independents were elected. Turnout was 65·1%.

CURRENT ADMINISTRATION

Governor: Hans Raj Bhardwaj; b. 1937 (took office on 29 June 2009).

Chief Minister: B. S. Yeddyurappa; b. 1943 (took office on 30 May 2008).

ECONOMY

Budget

Budget estimates, 2000–01: revenue receipts, Rs 200,252m.; revenue expenditure, Rs 200,615m.

ENERGY AND NATURAL RESOURCES

Electricity

In Oct. 2008 the state's installed capacity was 9,116·7 MW. Electricity generated, 1994–95, 16,830m. kWh. In Sept. 2008, 27,126 out of 27,481 inhabited villages had electricity.

Minerals

Karnataka is an important source of gold and silver. The state produces 84% of India's gold. The estimated reserves of high grade iron ore are 8,798m. tonnes. These reserves are found mainly in the Chitradurga belt. The National Mineral Development Corporation of India has indicated total reserves of nearly 332m. tonnes of magnesite and iron ore (with an iron content ranging from 25 to 40) which have been found in Kudremukh Ganga-Mula region in Chikmagalur District. Value of production (2002–03) Rs 10,580m. The estimated reserves of manganese are over 320m. tonnes.

Limestone is found in many regions; production (2002–03) was about 12·2m. tonnes.

Karnataka is the largest producer of chromite. It is one of only two states in India producing magnesite. The other minerals of industrial importance are corundum and garnet. Karnataka produces 63% of India's moulding sand annually and 57% of the country's quartzite, and is the only producer of felsite.

Agriculture

Agriculture forms the main occupation of more than three-quarters of the population. Physically, Karnataka divides into four regions—the coastal region, the southern and northern plains, comprising roughly the districts of Bangalore, Tumkur, Chitradurga, Kolar, Bellary, Mandya and Mysore, and the hill country, comprising the districts of Chikmagalur, Hassan and Shimoga. Rainfall is heavy in the hill country, and there is dense forest. The greater part of the plains are cultivated. Coorg district is essentially agricultural.

The main food crops are rice paddy and jowar, and ragi which is also about 30% of the national crop. Total foodgrains production (1998–99), 8·80m. tonnes (including rice 3·33m. tonnes); pulses 0·48m. tonnes. Sugar, groundnut, castor-seed, safflower, mulberry silk and cotton are important cash crops. The state grows about 70% of the national coffee crop.

Production, 1998–99: sugarcane, 28·33m. tonnes; cotton, 985,000 tonnes.

Livestock (2003): cattle, 9·54m.; sheep, 7·26m.; goats, 4·48m.; buffaloes, 3·99m.

Forestry

Total forest in the state (2000) is 38,284 sq. km, producing sandalwood, bamboo and other timbers.

Fisheries

The catch in 1998 totalled 140,000 tonnes. Catches are declining rapidly owing to overfishing and pollution. In 2005, 83,400 people were working in fishing and related activities.

INDUSTRY

There were 7,765 factories, 125 industrial estates and 5,176 industrial sheds employing 818,000 in March 1994. In 1994–95, 163,524 small industries employed 1,076,312 persons. The Vishveshwaraiah Iron and Steel Works is situated at Bhadravati, while at Bangalore are national undertakings for the manufacture of aircraft, machine tools, telephones, light engineering and electronics goods. The Kudremukh iron ore project is of national importance. An oil refinery is in operation at Mangalore. Other industries include textiles, vehicle manufacture, cement, chemicals, sugar, paper, porcelain and soap. In addition, much of the world's sandalwood is processed, the oil being one of the most valuable products of the state. Sericulture is a more important cottage industry giving employment, directly or indirectly, to about 2·7m. persons; production of raw silk, 2000, 9,000 tonnes, over two-thirds of national production.

COMMUNICATIONS

Roads

In 1999 the state had 137,520 km of roads, including 2,000 km of national highway and 73,000 km of state highway. There were (31 March 1996) 2,249,890 motor vehicles.

Rail

In 1999 there were 3,192 km of railway (including 149 km of narrow gauge) in the state.

Civil Aviation

There are airports at Bangalore, Hubli, Mysore, Mangalore, Bellary and Belgaum, with regular scheduled services to Chennai, Delhi, Kolkata and Mumbai. Bangalore is being upgraded to an international airport—the present airport already receives international flights from a number of destinations. A new Bangalore international airport has been constructed at Devanahalli, 34 km from the city, and opened in May 2008.

Shipping

Mangalore is a deep-water port for the export of mineral ores. Karwar is being developed as an intermediate port.

SOCIAL INSTITUTIONS

Justice

The seat of the High Court is at Bangalore. It has a Chief Justice and 42 puisne judges.

Education

In 2001, 66·6% of the population were literate (76·1% of men and 56·9% of women). In 1996–97 the state had 22,870 primary schools with 6,507,805 students, 18,485 middle schools with 2,158,487 students, 7,644 high and higher secondary schools with 1,270,794 students, 172 polytechnic and 125 medical colleges, 49 engineering and technology colleges, 761 arts, science and commerce colleges, 12 universities and the National Law School of India. Education is free up to pre-university level.

Universities: Mysore (1916); Karnataka (1949) at Dharwar; University of Agricultural Sciences (1964) at Hebbal, Bangalore; Bangalore; Gulbarga; Kannada; Mangalore; University of Agricultural Sciences, Dharwar; Kuvempu University, Shimoga; Karnataka State Open University, Mysore; Rajiv Gandhi University of Health Sciences, Bangalore; and Visveswaraiah Technological University, Nehrunagar.

Mysore has six university and 125 affiliated colleges; Karnataka, five and 240; Bangalore, 204 affiliated; Hebbal, eight constituent colleges.

The Indian Institute of Science, Bangalore and the Manipal Academy of Higher Education have the status of a university.

Health

There were in 2003, 293 hospitals, 622 primary health units and dispensaries, 1,297 primary health centres and 7,793 health subcentres. Total number of beds in 2003, about 50,000.

RELIGION

At the 2001 census Hindus numbered 44,321,279; Muslims, 6,463,127; Christians, 1,009,164; Buddhists, 393,300.

Kerala

KEY HISTORICAL EVENTS

The state of Kerala was created in 1956, bringing together the Malayalam-speaking areas. It includes most of the former state of Travancore-Cochin and small areas from the state of Madras. Cochin, a safe harbour, was an early site of European trading in India. In 1795 the British took it from the Dutch and British influence remained dominant. Travancore was a Hindu state which became a British protectorate in 1795, having been an ally of the British East India Company for some years. Cochin and Travancore were combined as one state in 1947, and reorganized and renamed Kerala in 1956.

TERRITORY AND POPULATION

Kerala is in south India and is bounded north by Karnataka, east and southeast by Tamil Nadu, southwest and west by the Indian ocean. The state has an area of 38,863 sq. km. The 2001 census showed a population of 31,841,374; density, 819 per sq. km. Chief cities, *see* INDIA: Territory and Population. Other principal towns (2001): Palakkad (197,369), Kottayam (172,878), Malappuram (170,409), Cherthala (141,558), Guruvayur (138,681), Kanhangad (129,367), Vadakara (124,083).

Languages spoken in the state are Malayalam, Tamil and Kannada.

SOCIAL STATISTICS

The growth rate during the period 1991–2001, at 9·43%, was the lowest of any Indian state.

CONSTITUTION AND GOVERNMENT

The state has a unicameral legislature of 141 members (one of which is nominated) including the Speaker.

The state has 14 districts. The capital is Thiruvananthapuram.

RECENT ELECTIONS

At the elections of 22 and 29 April and 3 May 2006 the Communist Party of India (Marxist) won 61 seats, followed by the Indian National Congress with 24, the Communist Party of India 17, the Muslim League Kerala State Committee 7, the Kerala Congress (Mani) 7, Janata Dal (Secular) 5, ind. (Left Democratic Front) 4, KEC 4 and Revolutionary Socialist Party 3 with eight smaller parties taking one seat each.

CURRENT ADMINISTRATION

Governor: Ramkrishnan Suryabhan Gavai; b. 1929 (took office on 10 July 2008).

Chief Minister: V. S. Achuthanandan; b. 1923 (took office on 18 May 2006).

ECONOMY

Budget

Budget estimates for 2000–01 showed revenue receipts of Rs 135,665m.; expenditure Rs 135,761m.

ENERGY AND NATURAL RESOURCES

Electricity

Installed capacity (Oct. 2008), 3,514 MW. Much of the state's electricity is produced by the Idukki hydro-electric plant and the Sabarigiri scheme. The state had a power deficit until the inauguration of the Kayamkulam thermal power plant in 1999. In Sept. 2008 all 1,364 inhabited villages had electricity.

Minerals

The beach sands of Kerala contain monazite, ilmenite, rutile, zircon, sillimanite, etc. There are extensive white clay deposits; other minerals of commercial importance include titanium, copper, magnesite, china clay, limestone, quartz sand and lignite. Iron ore has been found at Kozhikode (Calicut).

Agriculture

Area under irrigation in 2000–01 was 458,000 ha. The chief agricultural products are rice, tapioca, coconut, arecanut, cashew nuts, oilseeds, pepper, sugarcane, rubber, tea, coffee and cardamom. About 98% of Indian black pepper and about 95% of Indian rubber is produced in Kerala. Production of principal crops, 2002–03: total rice, 688,859 tonnes (from 310,521 ha.); tapioca, 2,413,217 tonnes; rubber, 594,917 tonnes; pepper, 67,358 tonnes; cashew nuts, 66,087 tonnes; coffee, 63,322 tonnes; tea, 53,480 tonnes; ginger, 32,412 tonnes; sugarcane, 31,283 tonnes; coconuts, 5,709m. nuts.

Livestock (2003): cattle, 2·12m.; goats, 1·21m.; poultry, 12·22m. In 2001–02 milk production was 2·73m. tonnes; egg production, 2,055m. units.

Forestry

Forest occupied 10,815 sq. km in 2000, including teak, sandalwood, ebony and blackwood and varieties of softwood. Net forest revenue, 1995–96, Rs 1,607·7m.

Fisheries

The total catch in 1995–96 was 582,000 tonnes (of which marine, 532,000 tonnes). In 2005 there were 211,300 people working in fishing and allied activities.

INDUSTRY

There are numerous cashew and coir factories. Important industries are rubber, tea, coffee, tiles, automotive tyres, watches, electronics, oil, textiles, ceramics, fertilizers and chemicals, pharmaceuticals, zinc-smelting, sugar, cement, rayon, glass, matches, pencils, monazite, ilmenite, titanium oxide, rare earths, aluminium, electrical goods, paper, shark-liver oil, etc. The state has a refinery and a shipyard at Kochi (Cochin).

The number of factories registered under the Factories Act 1948 in 2000 was 18,340, with daily average employment of 0·41m. There were 20,006 small-scale units in 2000; 0·78m. persons were employed in small-scale units on 31 March 1996.

COMMUNICATIONS

Roads

In 2000 there were 21,730 km of roads in the state (national and state highways, 4,113 km; district roads, 4,992 km). There were 1·91m. motor vehicles in 2000.

Rail

There is a coastal line from Mangalore in Karnataka which connects with Tamil Nadu. In 1995–96 there were 1,053 route-km of track.

Civil Aviation

There are airports at Kozhikode, Kochi and Thiruvananthapuram with regular scheduled internal services to Chennai, Delhi and Mumbai. In addition Kochi has international flights to a number of destinations in the Gulf states plus Colombo and Singapore, and Kozhikode and Thiruvananthapuram also have flights to the Gulf.

Shipping

Port Kochi, administered by the central government, is one of India's major ports; in 1983 it became the out-port for the Inland Container Depot at Coimbatore in Tamil Nadu. There are 12 other ports and harbours.

SOCIAL INSTITUTIONS

Justice

The High Court at Ernakulam has a Chief Justice and 29 puisne judges.

Education

Kerala is the most literate Indian state, with 25·49m. literate people at the 2001 census (90·9%; 94·2% of men and 87·7% of women). Education is free up to the age of 14.

In 2000 there were 6,726 primary schools with 2·79m. students, 2,968 upper primary schools with 1·84m. students and 3,511 high and higher secondary schools with 1·07m. students. There were 169 junior colleges in 1996–97 with 210,074 pupils.

Kerala University (established 1937) at Thiruvananthapuram is affiliating and teaching; in 1995–96 it had 52 affiliated colleges with 113,569 students. The University of Kochi is federal, and for post-graduate studies only. The University of Calicut (established 1968) is teaching and affiliating and has 95 affiliated colleges with 122,343 students (1995–96). Kerala Agricultural University (established 1971) has seven constituent colleges. Mahatma Gandhi University at Kottayam was established in 1983 and has 64 affiliated colleges with 112,992 students (1995–96). There are two other universities, Sree Sankaracharya University at Ernakulam and Kannur (formerly Malabar) University. There were also (2000) seven medical colleges, 20 pharmacy colleges, three dental colleges, four homeopathy colleges, 32 engineering colleges, 59 technology colleges, three nursing colleges, 19 teacher training colleges and 191 arts and science colleges.

Health

In 2000 there were 1,425 hospitals and health centres, including 113 Ayurvedic hospitals and 30 homeopathic hospitals. There were 41,462 hospital beds plus 2,604 beds in Ayurvedic hospitals and 970 beds in homeopathic clinics and hospitals.

RELIGION

At the 2001 census Hindus numbered 17,883,449; Muslims, 7,863,842; Christians, 6,057,427.

FURTHER READING

Jeffrey, R., *Politics, Women and Well-Being: How Kerala Became a Model.* 1992

Tharamangalam, Joseph, (ed.) *Kerala: The Paradoxes of Public Action and Development.* 2006

Madhya Pradesh

KEY HISTORICAL EVENTS

The state was formed in 1956 to bring together the Hindi-speaking districts including the 17 Hindi districts of the old Madhya Pradesh, most of the former state of Madhya Bharat, the former states of Bhopal and Vindhya Pradesh and a former Rajput enclave, Sironj. This was an area which the Mahrattas took from the Moghuls between 1712 and 1760. The British overcame the Mahrattas in 1818 and established their own Central Provinces. Nagpur became the Province's capital and was also the capital of Madhya Pradesh until, in 1956, boundary changes transferred it to Maharashtra. The present capital, Bhopal, was the centre of a Muslim princely state from 1723. Bhopal, an ally of the British against the Mahrattas, with neighbouring small states, became a British-protected agency in 1818. After independence Bhopal acceded to the Indian Union in 1949. In 1956 the states of Madhya Bharat and Vindhya Pradesh were combined with Bhopal and Sironj and renamed Madhya Pradesh. In 2000 sixteen mainly tribal districts were carved from Madhya Pradesh to form the new state of Chhattisgarh.

TERRITORY AND POPULATION

The state is in central India and is bounded north by Uttar Pradesh, east by the new state of Chhattisgarh, south by Maharashtra, and west by Gujarat and Rajasthan. Owing to the creation of Chhattisgarh, Madhya Pradesh is no longer the largest Indian state in size. Its revised area is 308,245 sq. km (previously 443,446 sq. km), making it the second largest state in the country (after Rajasthan). Population (2001 census), 60,348,023 (31,443,652 males); density, 196 per sq. km.

Cities with over 250,000 population, *see* INDIA: Territory and Population. Other large cities (2001): Ratlam, 234,419; Dewas, 231,672; Satna, 229,307; Burhanpur, 193,725; Murwara, 187,029; Singrauli, 185,190; Rewa, 183,274; Khandwa, 172,242; Bhind, 153,752; Chhindwara, 153,552; Morena, 150,959; Shivpuri, 146,892; Guna, 137,175; Damoh, 127,967; Vidisha, 125,453; Mandsaur, 117,555; Nimach, 112,852; Chhatarpur, 109,078; Itarsi, 107,831; Khargone, 103,448.

Hindi, Marathi, Urdu and Gujarati are spoken. In April 1990 Hindi, which predominates in the state, became the sole official language.

SOCIAL STATISTICS

Growth rate 1991–2001, 24·26%.

CONSTITUTION AND GOVERNMENT

Madhya Pradesh is one of the nine states for which the Constitution provides a bicameral legislature, but the Vidhan Parishad or Upper House (to consist of 90 members) has yet to be formed. The Vidhan Sabha or Lower House has 231 members (one of which is nominated).

For administrative purposes the state has been split into nine revenue divisions with a Commissioner at the head of each; the headquarters of these are located at Bhopal, Gwalior, Hoshangabad, Indore, Jabalpur, Morena, Rewa, Sagar and Ujjain. There are 22,029 *gram* (village) panchayats, 313 *janpad* (intermediate) panchayats and 45 *zila* (district) panchayats, following the creation of 16 new districts in administrative reforms of 1999 and the creation of Chhattisgarh in 2000.

The seat of government is at Bhopal.

RECENT ELECTIONS

At the election in Nov. 2008 the Bharatiya Janata Party (BJP) held power with 142 seats (173 in 2003). The Indian National Congress (INC) won 72 seats (38 in 2004). Other parties won 16 seats.

CURRENT ADMINISTRATION

Governor: Rameshwar Thakur; b. 1927 (took office on 30 June 2009).

Chief Minister: Shivraj Singh Chauhan; b. 1959 (took office on 29 Nov. 2005).

ECONOMY

Budget

Budget estimates for 2001–02 showed revenue receipts of Rs 125,184m. and expenditure of Rs 162,770m. Annual plan, 2002–03, Rs 48,209m.

ENERGY AND NATURAL RESOURCES

Electricity

Madhya Pradesh is rich in low-grade coal suitable for power generation, and also has immense potential for hydro-electric energy. Total installed capacity, 2008–09, 3,051 MW. Power generated, 16,315m. kWh in 2007–08. There are eight hydro-electric power stations of 747·5 MW installed capacity. In Sept. 2008, 50,218 out of 52,117 inhabited villages had electricity.

Water

Major irrigation projects include the Chambal Valley scheme, the Tawa project in Hoshangabad district, the Barna and Hasdeo schemes, the Mahanadi canal system and schemes in the Narmada valley at Bargi and Narmadasagar. Area under irrigation, 2007–08, 5·87m. ha.

Minerals

Much of the state's extensive mineral deposits were in the area that has now become the new state of Chhattisgarh. In 2004–05 the output of diamonds was 78,315 carats; Madhya Pradesh is India's only diamond producer. Production of other minerals included: 52·68m. tonnes of coal, 24·94m. tonnes of limestone, 2·05m. tonnes of copper ore (making Madhya Pradesh India's largest copper ore producer), 447,000 tonnes of manganese ore, 201,000 tonnes of iron ore and 186,000 tonnes of bauxite. In 2004–05 value of production was Rs 36,996m.

Agriculture

The creation in 2000 of the new state of Chhattisgarh, previously known as the 'rice bowl' of Madhya Pradesh, had serious implications for the state. Agriculture is the mainstay of the state's economy and 76·8% of the people are rural. 43·7% of the land area is cultivable, of which 30·5% is irrigated. Production of principal crops, 2004–05 (in tonnes): foodgrains, 7·83m.; pulses, 3·35m.; cotton, 0·32m. bales of 170 kg.

Livestock (2003): cattle, 18·91m.; buffaloes, 7·58m.; goats, 8·14m.; sheep, 546,000.

Forestry

The forested area totals 94,700 sq. km, or about 30·7% of the state. The forests are chiefly of sal, saja and teak species. They are the chief source in India of best-quality teak; they also provide firewood for about 60% of domestic fuel needs, and form valuable watershed protection.

INDUSTRY

The major industries are steel, aluminium, paper, cement, motor vehicles, ordnance, textiles and heavy electrical equipment. Other industries include electronics, telecommunications, sugar, fertilizers, straw board, vegetable oil, refractories, potteries, textile machinery, steel casting and rerolling, industrial gases, synthetic fibres, drugs, biscuit manufacturing, engineering, optical fibres, plastics, tools, rayon and art silk. The number of heavy and medium industries in the state is 805; the number of small-scale establishments in production is 497,000.

There are 23 'growth centres' in operation, and five under development. The Government of India has proposed setting up a Special Economic Zone at Indore.

COMMUNICATIONS

Roads

Total length of roads is 68,100 km. The length of national highways is 4,720 km and state highway 6,500 km. In March 2002 there were 3,173,000 motor vehicles.

Rail

The main rail route linking northern and southern India passes through Madhya Pradesh. Bhopal, Bina, Gwalior, Indore, Itarsi, Jabalpur, Katni, Khandwa, Ratlam and Ujjain are important junctions for the central, south, eastern and western networks. Route length (1998–99), 5,764·8 km.

Civil Aviation

There are domestic airports at Bhopal, Gwalior, Indore and Khajuraho with regular scheduled services to Agra, Delhi, Mumbai, Raipur and Varanasi.

SOCIAL INSTITUTIONS

Justice

The High Court of Judicature at Jabalpur has a Chief Justice and 29 puisne judges. Its benches are located at Gwalior and Indore. A National Institute of Law and a National Judicial Academy have been set up at Bhopal.

Education

In 2001, 63·7% of the population were literate (76·1% of men and 50·3% of women). Education is free for children aged up to 14.

In 2001 there were 97,273 government schools (63,712 pre-primary and primary schools, 25,090 middle schools, 8,471 high and higher secondary schools) and 22,620 private schools (10,473 pre-primary and primary schools, 7,474 middle schools, 4,673 high and higher secondary schools). Total enrolment in 2001: pre-primary and primary schools, 8·44m.; middle schools, 2·69m.; high and higher secondary schools, 1·52m.

Madhya Pradesh has ten universities (with towns): Barkatullah University (Bhopal) has 56 government colleges; Dr Harisingh Gour University (Sagar), 47 government colleges; Jiwaji Univeristy (Gwalior), 46 government colleges; Devi Ahilya University (Indore), 42 government colleges; Awadhesh Pratap Singh University (Rewa), 41 government colleges; Rani Durgavati University (Jabalpur), 40 government colleges; Vikram University (Ujjain), 40 government colleges; Mahatma Gandhi Gramodaya Vishwavidyalaya University (Chitrakoot); National Law Institute University (Bhopal); M. P. Bhoj Open University (Bhopal). There are a total of 312 colleges affiliated to the state's universities: 228 undergraduate and 84 postgraduate. Students studying in Madhya Pradesh totalled 272,296 in 2005–06 (of which arts students, 128,442; commerce, 73,211; science, 57,128).

Health

In 2001–02 there were 45 district hospitals, 57 urban civil hospitals, 1,194 primary health centres, 8,835 sub-health centres, 229 community health centres, seven TB hospitals and two TB sanatoriums.

RELIGION

At the 2001 census Hindus numbered 55,004,675; Muslims, 3,841,449; Jains, 545,446; Buddhists, 209,322; Christians, 170,381; Sikhs, 150,772.

Maharashtra

KEY HISTORICAL EVENTS

The Bombay Presidency region grew in the early 17th century from a collection of British East India Company trading posts. The island of Bombay was a Portuguese possession until it came under the control of Charles II of England on his marriage to Catherine of Braganza in 1661. It was then leased to the British East India Company in 1668 for £10 per annum. The Presidency expanded, overcoming the surrounding Mahratta chiefs until Mahratta power was finally conquered in 1818. After independence Bombay State succeeded to the Presidency; its area was altered in 1956 by adding Kutch and Saurashtra and the Marathi-speaking areas of Hyderabad and Madhya Pradesh, while taking away Kannada-speaking areas (which were added to Mysore). In 1960 the Bombay Reorganization Act divided Bombay State between Gujarati and Marathi areas, the latter becoming Maharashtra. The state of Maharashtra consists of the following districts of the former Bombay State: Ahmadnagar, Akola, Amravati, Aurangabad, Bhandara, Bhir, Buldana, Chanda, Dhulia (West Khandesh), Greater Mumbai, Jalgaon (East Khandesh), Kolaba, Kolhapur, Nagpur, Nanded, Nashik, Osmanabad, Parbhani, Pune, Ratnagiri, Sangli, Satara, Sholapur, Thane, Wardha, Yeotmal; certain portions of Thane and Dhulia districts have become part of Gujarat.

TERRITORY AND POPULATION

Maharashtra is in central India and is bounded north by Madhya Pradesh, east by Chhattisgarh, south by Andhra Pradesh, Karnataka and Goa, west by the Indian ocean and northwest by Daman and Gujarat. The state has an area of 307,577 sq. km. The population in 2001 (census) was 96,878,627; density, 315 per sq. km. In 2001 the area of Greater Mumbai was 603 sq. km and its population 16·4m. For other principal cities, *see* INDIA: Territory and Population. Other large towns (2001): Jalna (235,795), Bhusawal (187,564), Nalasopara (184,538), Vasai (174,396), Yavatmal (139,835), Bid (138,196), Kamthi (136,491), Gondia (120,902), Virar (118,928), Wardha (111,118), Satara (108,048), Achalpur (107,316), Barsi (104,785), Panvel (104,058).

The official language is Marathi.

SOCIAL STATISTICS

Growth rate 1991–2001, 22·73%.

CONSTITUTION AND GOVERNMENT

Maharashtra has a bicameral legislature. The Legislative Council has 78 members. The Legislative Assembly has 288 elected members and one member nominated by the Governor to represent the Anglo-Indian community.

The Council of Ministers consists of the Chief Minister, 16 other Ministers and 19 Ministers of State.

The capital is Mumbai (Bombay). The state has 35 districts.

RECENT ELECTIONS

At the elections held on 13 Oct. 2009 the Indian National Congress won 82 of the 288 seats, the Nationalist Congress Party 62, the Bharatiya Janata Party 46, Shiv Sena 44, the Maharashtra Navnirman Sena 13, Republican Left Democratic Front 9, other parties 7 and ind. 25. Turnout was approximately 60%.

CURRENT ADMINISTRATION

Governor: Kateekal Sankaranarayanan; b. 1932 (took office on 22 Jan. 2010).

Chief Minister: Ashok Chavan; b. 1958 (took office on 8 Dec. 2008).

ECONOMY

Budget

Budget estimates, 2000–01: revenue receipts, Rs 374,303m.; revenue expenditure, Rs 366,869m.

ENERGY AND NATURAL RESOURCES

Electricity

Installed capacity, Oct. 2008, 20,036 MW. In Sept. 2008, 36,296 out of 41,095 inhabited villages had electricity. Output, 2001, 53,013m. kWh.

Oil and Gas

Mumbai High (offshore) produced 14·25m. tonnes of crude oil and 17,200,000 cu. metres of natural gas in 2001. Oil production has declined by one-third since the early 1990s. A recovery plan for the ageing field began in 2000. Phase one of this plan was completed in 2006; by 2030 it is expected to yield an additional 23·25m. tonnes of crude oil and 6·10bn. cu. metres of natural gas. Phase two was announced in 2009 and will focus on drilling 73 new wells. The project is scheduled for completion in 2012.

Minerals

The state has coal, silica sand, dolomite, kyanite, chromite, limestone, iron ore, manganese and bauxite. Value of mineral production, 2001, Rs 21,340m. of which 94% is contributed by coal. Coal production in 2000–01 was 28·8m. tonnes. Manganese is the second most valuable mineral.

Agriculture

3·3m. ha. of the cropped area of 21·4m. ha. are irrigated. In normal seasons the main food crops are rice, wheat, jowar, bajra and pulses. Main cash crops: cotton, sugarcane, groundnuts. Production, 2000–01 (in tonnes): sugarcane, 36·5m.; foodgrains, 11·9m. (rice, 2·4m.; wheat, 1·11m.); pulses, 1·7m.; groundnuts, 0·6m.; cotton, 476,000.

Livestock (2003 census, in 1,000): buffaloes, 6,145; other cattle, 16,303; sheep and goats, 13,778; poultry, 37,968.

Forestry

Forests occupied 64,300 sq. km in 1995–96. Value of forest products in 1996–97, Rs 2,820m.

Fisheries
In 2000–01 the marine fish catch was estimated at 403,000 tonnes and the inland fish catch at 123,000 tonnes. In 2005 there were 153,900 people engaged in fishing and allied activities.

INDUSTRY
Industry is concentrated mainly in Mumbai, Nashik, Pune and Thane. The main groups are chemicals and products, textiles, electrical and non-electrical machinery, petroleum and products, aircraft, rubber and plastic products, transport equipment, automobiles, paper, electronic items, engineering goods, pharmaceuticals and food products. The state industrial development corporation invested Rs 77,020m. in 21,452 industrial units in 1994–95. In June 1995 there were 26,642 working factories employing 1·2m. people. In Dec. 1996 there were 203,882 small scale industries employing 1·63m. people.

COMMUNICATIONS
Roads
In 2001 there were 260,000 km of roads, of which nearly 200,000 km were surfaced. There were 7,194,000 motor vehicles on 1 Jan. 2001, of which about 25% were in Greater Mumbai. Passenger and freight transport has been nationalized.

Rail
The total length of railway in 2001 was 5,459 km; 66% was broad gauge, 14% metre gauge and 20% narrow gauge. The main junctions and termini are Mumbai, Dadar, Manmad, Akola, Nagpur, Pune and Sholapur.

Civil Aviation
The main airport is Mumbai, which has national and international flights. Nagpur airport is on the route from Mumbai to Kolkata and there are also airports at Pune and Aurangabad.

Shipping
Maharashtra has a coastline of 720 km. Mumbai is the major port, and there are 48 minor ports.

SOCIAL INSTITUTIONS
Justice
The High Court has a Chief Justice and 60 judges. The seat of the High Court is Mumbai, but it has benches at Nagpur, Aurangabad and Panaji (Goa).

Education
The number of literate people, according to the 2001 census, was 63·97m. (76·9%; 86·0% of men and 67·0% of women). In 2001 there were 10,225 high and 3,981 higher secondary schools with (1995) 2,795,567 pupils; 15,070 middle schools with (1995) 4,753,257 pupils; and 66,369 primary schools with (1995) 11,685,598 pupils. There are 111 engineering and technology colleges, 156 medical colleges (including dental and Ayurvedic colleges), 244 teacher training colleges, 152 polytechnics and 820 arts, science and commerce colleges.

The University of Mumbai, founded in 1857, is mainly an affiliating university. It has 276 colleges with a total (1993–94) of 234,469 students. Nagpur University (1923) is both teaching and affiliating. It has 258 colleges with 95,664 students. Pune University, founded in 1948, is teaching and affiliating; it has 167 colleges and 151,990 students. The SNDT Women's University had 33 colleges with a total of 33,343 students. Dr B. R. Ambedkar Marathwada University, Aurangabad was founded in 1958 as a teaching and affiliating body to control colleges in the Marathwada or Marathi-speaking area, previously under Osmania University; it has 190 colleges and 195,806 students. Shivaji University, Kolhapur, was established in 1963 to control affiliated colleges previously under Pune University. It has 205 colleges and 115,553 students. Amravati University has 130 colleges and 74,484 students. Other universities are: Marathwada Krishi Vidyapeeth, Parbhani; Y. Chavan Maharashtra Open University, Nashik; North Maharashtra University, Jalgaon, with 101 colleges and 66,092 students; Mahatma Phule Krishi University, Rahuri; Dr Punjabrao Deshmukh Krishi University, Akola; Konkan Krishi University, Dapoli; Dr Babasaheb Ambedkar Technological University, Lonere; Swami Ramanand Teerth Marathwad University, Nanded; Tilak Maharashtra Vidyapeeth, Pune; Bharati Vidyapeeth, Pune; Gokhale Institute of Politics and Economics, Pune; Deccan College, Pune; Indian Institute of Technology, Mumbai; Indira Gandhi Institute of Developmental Research, Mumbai; International Institute for Population Sciences, Mumbai; Tata Institute of Social Sciences, Mumbai. The Central Institute of Fisheries Education in Mumbai also has university-equivalent status.

Health
There were 3,446 hospitals with 99,062 beds in 2000; there were also 1,768 primary health centres, 9,725 sub-health centres and 351 community health centres in 2001.

RELIGION
At the 2001 census Hindus numbered 77,859,385; Muslims, 10,270,485; Buddhists, 5,838,710; Jains, 1,301,843; Christians, 1,058,313; Sikhs, 215,337.

FURTHER READING
Waite, Louise, *Embodied Working Lives: Work and Life in Maharashtra.* 2005

Manipur

KEY HISTORICAL EVENTS
Formerly a state under the political control of the government of India, Manipur entered into interim arrangements with the Indian Union on 15 Aug. 1947 and the political agency was abolished. Under a merger agreement, the administration was taken over by the government of India on 15 Oct. 1949 to be centrally administered by the government of India through a Chief Commissioner. In 1950–51 an Advisory government was introduced. In 1957 this was replaced by a Territorial Council of 30 elected and two nominated members. Later, in 1963, a Legislative Assembly of 30 elected and three nominated members was established under the government of Union Territories Act 1963. Because of the unstable party position in the Assembly, it had to be dissolved on 16 Oct. 1969 and president's rule introduced. The status of the administrator was raised from Chief Commissioner to Lieut.-Governor from 19 Dec. 1969. On 21 Jan. 1972 Manipur became a state and the status of the administrator was changed from Lieut.-Governor to Governor. In June 2001 Manipur was placed under central rule, but returned to self government after the 2002 elections.

TERRITORY AND POPULATION
The state is in northeast India and is bounded north by Nagaland, east by Myanmar, south by Myanmar and Mizoram, and west by Assam. Manipur has an area of 22,327 sq. km and a population (2001 census) of 2,166,788; density, 97 per sq. km. The valley, which is about 1,813 sq. km, is 800 metres above sea-level. The largest city is Imphal with a population of 250,234 (2001 census). The hills rise in places to 3,000 metres, but are mostly about 1,500–1,800 metres. The average annual rainfall is 165 cm. The hill areas are inhabited by various hill tribes who constitute about one-third of the total population of the state. There are about 30 tribes and sub-tribes falling into two main groups of Nagas and

Kukis. Manipuri and English are the official languages. A large number of dialects are spoken.

SOCIAL STATISTICS

Growth rate 1991–2001, 24·56%.

CONSTITUTION AND GOVERNMENT

Manipur has a Legislative Assembly of 60 members, of which 19 are from reserved tribal constituencies. There are nine districts. The capital is Imphal.

RECENT ELECTIONS

Elections were held in Feb. 2007. The Indian National Congress party won 30 seats; Manipur People's Party, 5; Nationalist Congress Party, 5; Communist Party of India, 4; Rashtriya Janata Dal, 3; National People's Party, 3; ind., 10.

CURRENT ADMINISTRATION

Governor: Gurbachan Jagat; b. 1942 (took office on 23 July 2008).

Chief Minister: Okram Ibobi Singh; b. 1948 (took office on 7 March 2002).

ECONOMY

Budget

Budget estimates for 2000–01 show revenue of Rs 12,220·2m. and expenditure of Rs 12,453·3m.

ENERGY AND NATURAL RESOURCES

Electricity

Installed capacity (Oct. 2008) was 158 MW. In Sept. 2008, 1,979 out of 2,315 inhabited villages had electricity.

Water

The main power, irrigation and flood-control schemes are the Loktak Lift Irrigation scheme (irrigation potential, 40,000 ha.); the Singda scheme (potential 4,000 ha., and improved water supply for Imphal); the Thoubal scheme (potential 34,000 ha.); and four other large projects. By 1994–95, 59,100 ha. had been irrigated.

Minerals

Chromite is the only significant mineral resource—it is extracted from a single mine.

Agriculture

Rice is the principal crop; with wheat, maize and pulses. Total foodgrains, 1998, 365,000 tonnes (rice, 352,000 tonnes).

Agricultural workforce, 453,040. Only 0·21m. ha. are cultivable, of which 158,000 ha. are under paddy. Fruit and vegetables are important in the valley, including pineapples, oranges, bananas, mangoes, pears, peaches and plums. Soil erosion, produced by shifting cultivation, is being halted by terracing. Fruit production in 1993–94, 0·11m. tonnes.

Forestry

Forests occupied about 17,418 sq. km in 1998. The main products are teak, jurjan and pine; there are also large areas of bamboo and cane, especially in the Jiri and Barak river drainage areas, yielding about 0·3m. tonnes annually. Total revenue from forests, 1990–91, Rs 9·95m.

INDUSTRY

Handloom weaving is a cottage industry. Manipur is one of the least industrialized states of India. Location, limited infrastructure and insufficient power hold back industrial development. Larger-scale industries include the manufacture of bicycles and TV sets, sugar, cement, starch, vegetable oil and glucose. Sericulture produces about 45 tonnes of raw silk annually. Estimated non-agricultural workforce, 229,000.

COMMUNICATIONS

Roads

Length of road (1995), 7,003 km; number of vehicles (1996–97) 65,223. A national highway from Kaziranga (Assam) runs through Imphal to the border with Myanmar. The total length of national highway in 2000 was 954 km.

Rail

A railway link was opened in 1990, linking Karong with the Assamese railway system.

Civil Aviation

There is an airport at Imphal with regular scheduled services to Delhi and Kolkata.

SOCIAL INSTITUTIONS

Education

In 2001, 70·5% of the population were literate (80·3% of men and 60·5% of women). In 1996–97 there were 2,548 primary schools with 230,230 students, 555 middle schools with 106,200 students, 553 high and higher secondary schools with 66,160 students, 50 colleges, one medical college, two teacher training colleges, three polytechnics, Manipur University with 62 colleges and 52,352 students (1997–98) and an agricultural university (Central Agricultural University, Imphal).

Health

In 2001 there were 85 hospitals and public health centres, 28 dispensaries, 16 community health centres, 420 sub-centres and 26 other facilities.

RELIGION

At the 2001 census Hindus numbered 46% of the population; Christians, 34%; Muslims, 9%.

Meghalaya

KEY HISTORICAL EVENTS

The state was created under the Assam Reorganization (Meghalaya) Act 1969 and inaugurated on 2 April 1970. Its status was that of a state within the State of Assam until 21 Jan. 1972 when it became a fully-fledged state of the Union. It consists of the former Garo Hills district and United Khasi and Jaintia Hills district of Assam.

TERRITORY AND POPULATION

Meghalaya is bounded in the north and east by Assam, south and west by Bangladesh. The area is 22,429 sq. km and the population (2001 census) 2,318,822; density, 103 per sq. km. The people are mainly of the Khasi, Jaintia and Garo tribes. The main languages of the state are Khasi, Garo and English.

SOCIAL STATISTICS

Growth rate 1991–2001, 30·65%.

CONSTITUTION AND GOVERNMENT

Meghalaya has a unicameral legislature. The Legislative Assembly has 60 seats.

There are seven districts. The capital is Shillong (population, 2001 census, 267,662 in the urban agglomeration).

Presidential rule was imposed on 18 March 2009 despite the state government winning a tightly contested confidence vote a day earlier. It was lifted on 8 May after the Indian National Congress managed to form an alliance with the United Democratic Party.

RECENT ELECTIONS

In elections held on 7 March 2008 the Indian National Congress won 25 seats; Nationalist Congress Party, 14; United Democratic Party, 11; Hill State People's Democratic Party, 2; Bharatiya Janata Party, 1; Khun Hynnieutrip National Awakening Movement, 1; ind., 5.

CURRENT ADMINISTRATION

Governor: Ranjit Shekhar Mooshahary (took office on 1 July 2008).

Chief Minister: D. D. Lapang (took office for a fourth time on 13 May 2009).

ECONOMY

Budget

Budget estimates for 2001–02 showed revenue receipts of Rs 13,211·3m. and expenditure of Rs 13,548·3m.

ENERGY AND NATURAL RESOURCES

Electricity

Total installed capacity (Oct. 2008) was 288 MW. In Sept. 2008, 3,428 out of 5,782 inhabited villages had electricity.

Minerals

The Khasi Hills, Jaintia Hills and Garo Hills districts produce coal, sillimanite (95% of India's total output), limestone, fire clay, dolomite, feldspar, quartz and glass sand. The state also has deposits of coal (estimated reserves 600m. tonnes), limestone (3,000m.), fire clay (6m.) and sandstone which are so far virtually untapped. Coal production in 2000–01 was 5,149,000 tonnes; limestone production in 2000–01 was 585,000 tonnes.

Agriculture

About 71% of the people depend on agriculture. Principal crops are rice, maize, potatoes, cotton, oranges, ginger, tezpata, areca nuts, jute, mesta, bananas and pineapples. Production 2000–01 (in tonnes) of principal crops: rice, 179,000; potatoes, 144,000; ginger, 45,000; jute, 36,000; citrus fruits, 32,000; maize, 24,000; cotton, 8,000; rape and mustard, 5,000. Poultry and cattle are the principal livestock.

Forestry

Forests covered 9,496 sq. km in 2002. Forest products are one of the state's chief resources.

INDUSTRY

Apart from agriculture the main source of employment is the extraction and processing of minerals; there are also important timber processing mills and cement factories. Other industries include electronics, tantalum capacitors, beverages and watches. The state has five industrial estates, two industrial areas and one growth centre. In 1995–96 there were 58 registered factories and 2,533 small-scale industries. In 2000, 17,800 workers were involved in manufacturing and processing. There were also, in 2001–02, 1,812 sericultural villages, six sericultural farms, eight silk units and nine weaving centres. In 2000 there were more than 5,400 *khadi* and village industrial units.

COMMUNICATIONS

Roads

Three national highways run through the state for a distance of 520 km. In 2000–01 there were 7,598 km of surfaced and unsurfaced roads, of which 3,523 km were surfaced. Total number of motor vehicles in 2000–01 was 67,076, including 13,464 trucks, 12,853 private cars and 2,463 buses.

Rail

The state has only 1 km of railways, but this does not connect the state with the national network. The nearest station is 103 km outside the state. There is a plan to extend the national network to Byrnihat, 20 km inside Meghalaya.

Civil Aviation

Umroi airport (35 km from Shillong) connects the state with main air services. There are regular flights to Kolkata. Umroi is to be upgraded to receive larger aircraft. However, the main airport serving the state is Borjhar, at Guwahati, 21 km across the state border but only 124 km from Shillong. Guwahati has air links with several major north Indian cities.

SOCIAL INSTITUTIONS

Justice

The Guwahati High Court is common to Assam, Meghalaya, Nagaland, Manipur, Mizoram, Tripura and Arunachal Pradesh—there are 19 judges. There is a bench of the Guwahati High Court at Shillong.

Education

In 2001, 62·6% of the population were literate (65·4% of men and 59·6% of women). In 2000–01 the state had 4,685 primary and middle schools with 445,443 students, and 1,613 senior middle, secondary and higher secondary schools with 181,068 students. There were 35 colleges and other institutions of higher education including ten teacher training schools, one college and one polytechnic, with a total enrolment of 31,975 students. The North Eastern Hill University started functioning at Shillong in 1973; in 1993–94 it had 41 colleges and 54,803 students.

Health

In 2000–01 there were ten government hospitals, 88 primary health centres and 12 additional health centres, 38 government dispensaries and 413 sub-centres. Total beds (hospitals and health centres), 2,377. There were 389 doctors, 384 staff nurses and 915 paramedics.

RELIGION

At the 2001 census Christians numbered 1,628,986; Hindus, 307,822; Muslims, 99,169.

Mizoram

KEY HISTORICAL EVENTS

On 21 Jan. 1972 the former Mizo Hills District of Assam was created a Union Territory. A long dispute between the Mizo National Front (originally Separatist) and the central government was resolved in 1986. Mizoram became a state by the Constitution (53rd Amendment) and the State of Mizoram Acts, July 1986.

TERRITORY AND POPULATION

Mizoram is one of the easternmost Indian states, lying between Bangladesh and Myanmar, and having on its northern boundaries Tripura, Assam and Manipur. There are eight districts. The area is 21,087 sq. km and the population (2001 census) 888,573; density, 42 per sq. km. The main languages spoken are Mizo and English.

SOCIAL STATISTICS

Growth rate 1991–2001, 28·82%.

CONSTITUTION AND GOVERNMENT

Mizoram has a unicameral Legislative Assembly with 40 seats. The capital is Aizawl (population, 2001, 228,280).

RECENT ELECTIONS

In the elections of Dec. 2008 distribution of seats was: Indian National Congress, 32; Mizo National Front, 3; Mizoram People's

Conference, 2; Zoram Nationalist Party, 2; Maraland Democratic Front, 1.

CURRENT ADMINISTRATION
Governor: M. M. Lakhera; b. 1937 (took office on 25 July 2006).

Chief Minister: Lal Thanhawla; b. 1942 (took office on 11 Dec. 2008).

ECONOMY
Budget
Budget estimates for 2000–01 show revenue receipts of Rs 9,227m. and expenditure of Rs 9,848m.

ENERGY AND NATURAL RESOURCES
Electricity
Installed capacity (Oct. 2008), 119 MW. In Sept. 2008, 570 out of 707 inhabited villages had electricity.

Agriculture
About 60% of the people are engaged in agriculture, either on terraced holdings or in shifting cultivation. Principal crop production, 2007–08 (in tonnes): bananas, 151,519; turmeric, 83,500; ginger, 57,010; passion fruit, 44,720; oranges, 41,567; squash, 26,418; rice, 15,688.

Forestry
State forest area, 2007–08, 7,406 sq. km.

INDUSTRY
Handloom weaving and other cottage industries are important. There were 205 registered small-scale businesses in 2007–08.

COMMUNICATIONS
Roads
Aizawl is connected by road with Silchar in Assam. Total length of roads in 2008, 7,592 km including 328 km of national highways, 700 km of state highways, 944 km classed as major roads and 1,075 km as village roads. 341 of Mizoram's 764 villages are served by all-weather roads, although 85 villages do not have any roads. There were 29,353 motor vehicles in 2000 of which 767 were buses, 12,847 private cars, and 357 tractors and trailers.

Rail
There is a metre-gauge rail link at Bairabi, 130 km from Aizawl.

Civil Aviation
Lengpui Airport, Aizawl is connected by air with Silchar in Assam and with Kolkata three days a week.

SOCIAL INSTITUTIONS
Education
In 2001, 88·8% of the population were literate (90·7% of men and 86·7% of women). In 2007–08 there were 1,752 primary schools with 134,656 students, 1,090 middle schools with 57,399 students, and 590 high and higher secondary schools with 56,491 students; there was one university, 22 colleges, one teacher training college, two polytechnics and twelve other training institutes.

Health
In 2007–08 there were ten hospitals, 66 health centres and 366 health sub-centres. Total beds, over 1,700. The state pays particular attention to immunization programmes.

RELIGION
At the 2001 census Christians numbered 772,809 and Buddhists 70,494.

Nagaland

KEY HISTORICAL EVENTS
The state was created in 1961, effective 1963. It consisted of the Naga Hills district of Assam and the Tuensang Frontier Agency. The agency was a British-supervised tribal area on the borders of Myanmar. Its supervision passed to the government of India at independence, and in 1957 Tuensang and the Naga Hills became a Centrally Administered Area, governed by the central government through the Governor of Assam.

A number of Naga leaders fought for independence until a settlement was reached with the Indian government at the Shillong Peace Agreement of 1975. However, calls for a greater Naga state, potentially incorporating parts of neighbouring Manipur, Arunachal Pradesh and Assam, continued to be voiced, notably through the National Socialist Council of Nagaland (NSCN), which had been active since 1954. The national government and NSCN met in Delhi in early Jan. 2003 to hold their first joint talks in 37 years, after which the NSCN declared 'the war is over'.

TERRITORY AND POPULATION
The state is in the northeast of India and is bounded in the north by Arunachal Pradesh, west by Assam, east by Myanmar and south by Manipur. Nagaland has an area of 16,579 sq. km and a population (2001 census) of 1,990,036; density, 120 per sq. km. The major towns are the capital, Kohima (2001 population, 77,030) and Dimapur (98,096). Other towns include Wokha, Mon, Zunheboto, Mokokchung and Tuensang. The chief tribes in numerical order are: Angami, Ao, Sumi, Konyak, Chakhesang, Lotha, Phom, Khiamngan, Chang, Yimchunger, Zeliang-Kuki, Rengma, Sangtam and Pochury. The official language of the state is English; Nagamese, a variant language form of Assamese and Hindi, is the most widely spoken language.

SOCIAL STATISTICS
Growth rate 1991–2001, 64·53% (the highest rate of any Indian state).

CONSTITUTION AND GOVERNMENT
An Interim Body (Legislative Assembly) of 42 members elected by the Naga people and an Executive Council (Council of Ministers) of five members were formed in 1961, and continued until the State Assembly was elected in Jan. 1964. The Assembly has 60 members. The Governor has extraordinary powers, which include special responsibility for law and order. Presidential rule was imposed in Jan. 2008 after the dismissal of the government but revoked in March 2008.

The state has eight districts (Dimapur, Kohima, Mon, Zunheboto, Wokha, Phek, Mokokchung and Tuensang). The capital is Kohima.

RECENT ELECTIONS
At the elections to the State Assembly on 8 March 2008 the Nagaland People's Front won 26 seats (19 in 2003); Indian National Congress party won 24 seats (20 in 2003); BJP, 2; Nationalist Congress Party, 2; ind., 6.

CURRENT ADMINISTRATION
Governor: Nikhil Kumar; b. 1941 (took office on 15 Oct. 2009).

Chief Minister: Neiphiu Rio; b. 1950 (since 12 March 2008, having previously been in office March 2003–Jan. 2008).

ECONOMY
Budget
Budget estimates for 2000–01 showed total receipts of Rs 15,283m. and expenditure of Rs 14,998m.

ENERGY AND NATURAL RESOURCES

Electricity

Installed capacity (Oct. 2008) 103 MW. In Sept. 2008, 823 out of 1,278 inhabited villages had electricity.

Oil and Gas

Oil has been located in three districts. Reserves are estimated at 600m. tonnes.

Minerals

In addition to oil, other minerals include: coal, limestone, marble, chromite, magnesite, nickel, cobalt, chromium, iron ore, copper ore, clay, glass sand and slate.

Agriculture

90% of the people derive their livelihood from agriculture. The Angamis, in Kohima district, practise a fixed agriculture in the shape of terraced slopes, and wet paddy cultivation in the lowlands. In the other two districts a traditional form of shifting cultivation (*jhumming*) still predominates, but some farmers have begun tea and coffee plantations and horticulture. About 61,000 ha. were under terrace cultivation and 74,040 ha. under *jhumming* in 1994–95. Production of rice (1999) was 187,000 tonnes, total foodgrains 227,300 tonnes and pulses 13,000 tonnes.

Forestry

Forests, including open forests, covered 14,221 sq. km in 1999, of which forest area excluding open forest was 8,630 sq. km.

INDUSTRY

There is a forest products factory at Tijit; a paper-mill (100 tonnes daily capacity) at Tuli, a distillery unit and a sugar-mill (1,000 tonnes daily capacity) at Dimapur, and a cement factory (50 tonnes daily capacity) at Wazeho. Bricks and TV sets are also made, and there are 1,850 small units. There is a ceramics plant and sericulture is also important.

COMMUNICATIONS

Roads

There is a national highway from Kaziranga (Assam) to Kohima and on to Manipur. There are state highways connecting Kohima with the district headquarters. Total length of roads in 1999, over 15,500 km, of which 365 km are national highway and 1,094 km state highway. There were 95,020 motor vehicles registered in 1994–95.

Rail

Dimapur has a rail-head. Railway route-km in 2000, 60 km.

Civil Aviation

There are scheduled services from Dimapur to Guwahati, Imphal and Kolkata.

SOCIAL INSTITUTIONS

Justice

A permanent bench of the Guwahati High Court has been established in Kohima. There are 19 judges.

Education

In 2001, 66·6% of the population were literate (71·2% of men and 61·5% of women). In 1996–97 there were 1,414 primary schools with 271,932 students, 416 middle schools with 63,437 students, 244 high and higher secondary schools with 24,547 students, 36 colleges, two teacher training colleges and two polytechnics. The North Eastern Hill University opened at Kohima in 1978. Nagaland University was established in 1994.

Health

In 2005 there were eight hospitals (1,300 beds), 93 primary and 21 community health centres, 16 dispensaries, 412 sub-centres, ten TB centres and 36 leprosy centres.

RELIGION

At the 2001 census Christians numbered 1,790,349 and Hindus 153,162.

FURTHER READING

Aram, M., *Peace in Nagaland*. 1974

Orissa

KEY HISTORICAL EVENTS

Orissa was divided between Mahratta and Bengal rulers when conquered by the British East India Company, the Bengal area in 1757 and the Mahratta in 1803. The area which now forms the state then consisted of directly controlled British districts and a large number of small princely states with tributary rulers. The British districts were administered as part of Bengal until 1912 when, together with Bihar, they were separated from Bengal to form a single province. Bihar and Orissa were separated from each other in 1936. In 1948 a new state government took control of the whole state, including the former princely states (except Saraikella and Kharswan which were transferred to Bihar, and Mayurbhanj which was not incorporated until 1949).

In Oct. 1999 Orissa was hit by a devastating cyclone which resulted in more than 10,000 deaths.

TERRITORY AND POPULATION

Orissa is in eastern India and is bounded north by Jharkhand, northeast by West Bengal, east by the Bay of Bengal, south by Andhra Pradesh and west by Chhattisgarh. The area of the state is 155,707 sq. km, and its population (2001 census), 36,804,660; density 236 per sq. km. Cities with over 250,000 population at 2001 census, *see* INDIA: Territory and Population. Other large cities (2001): Sambalpur, 226,469; Puri, 157,837; Baleshwar, 156,430; Baripada, 100,651. The principal and official language is Oriya.

SOCIAL STATISTICS

Growth rate 1991–2001, 16·25%.

CONSTITUTION AND GOVERNMENT

The Legislative Assembly has 147 members.

There are 30 districts. The capital is Bhubaneswar (18 miles south of Cuttack).

RECENT ELECTIONS

At the state elections of 20 and 26 April 2004 the Biju Janata Dal won 61 seats (with 27·4% of the vote); the INC, 38 (34·8%); the BJP, 32 (17·1%); the Jharkhand Mukti Morcha, 4 (1·8%); and the Orissa Gana Parishad, 2 (1·3%). Eight independents were elected and two other parties received one seat each.

CURRENT ADMINISTRATION

Governor: Murlidhar Chandrakant Bhandare; b. 1928 (took office on 21 Aug. 2007).

Chief Minister: Naveen Patnaik; b. 1946 (took office on 5 March 2000).

ECONOMY

Budget

Budget estimates, 2000–01, showed total receipts of Rs 124,216m. and total expenditure of Rs 121,046m.

ENERGY AND NATURAL RESOURCES

Electricity

The Hirakud Dam Project on the river Mahanadi irrigates 628,000 acres. The Upper Indravati Hydro Electric Project has an installed capacity of 600 MW. Hydro-electric power is now serving a large part of the state. Total installed capacity (Oct. 2008) 4,072 MW. In Sept. 2008, 26,535 out of 47,529 inhabited villages had electricity.

Minerals

Orissa is India's leading producer of chromite (97% of national output), graphite (80%), bauxite (71%), dolomite (50%), fire-clay (34%), iron ore (33% of national reserves), manganese ore (32%), limestone (20%), quartz-quartzite (18%) and iron ore (16%). Kaliapani is the centre of chromite mining and processing. Daitari is the major centre for iron production. Production in 2002–03 (1,000 tonnes): coal, 52,229; iron ore, 21,518; bauxite, 4,904; chromite, 3,047; limestone, 2,362; dolomite, 959; manganese ore, 616. Value of production in 2002–03 was Rs 33,560m.

Agriculture

The cultivation of rice is the principal occupation of about 80% of the workforce, and only a very small amount of other cereals is grown. Production of foodgrains (1998–99) totalled 6·35m. tonnes from 4·7m. ha. (rice 6·2m. tonnes, wheat 60,000 tonnes); pulses, 0·28m. tonnes; oilseeds, 0·21m. tonnes; sugarcane, 1,114,000 tonnes. Turmeric is cultivated in the uplands of the districts of Ganjam, Phulbani and Koraput, and is exported.

Livestock (2003): buffaloes, 1·39m.; other cattle, 13·90m.; sheep, 1·62m.; goats, 5·80m.; poultry, 17·61m.

Forestry

Forests occupied 58,135 sq. km in 1999 (37·3% of the state). The most important species are sal, teak, kendu, sandal, sisu, bija, kusum, kongada and bamboo.

Fisheries

There were, in 2005, 641 fishing villages. Fish production in 2002 was 1·3m. tonnes of marine fish (including crustaceans) and 140,000 tonnes of freshwater fish. Hundreds of fishing boats are engaged in illegal shrimp fishing. The state has four fishing harbours. In 2005 there were 273,800 people working in fishing and allied activities.

INDUSTRY

289 large and medium industries are in operation (1995–96), mostly based on minerals: steel, pig iron, ferrochrome, ferromanganese, ferrosilicon, aluminium, cement, automotive tyres and synthetic fibres.

Other industries of importance are caustic soda, fertilizers, glass, heavy machine tools, industrial explosives, paper, salt, sugar, a coach-repair factory, a rerolling mill, textile mills and electronics. There is an oil refinery. In the past decade there has been much investment and expansion in biotechnology, electronics, leather and marine-based industries. Also, there were 49,611 small-scale industries in 1995–96 employing 349,800 persons, and 1,342,561 artisan units providing employment to 2·33m. persons. Handloom weaving and the manufacture of baskets, wooden articles, hats and nets, silver filigree work and hand-woven fabrics are particularly significant.

COMMUNICATIONS

Roads

On 31 March 1996 length of roads was: state highway, 4,360 km; national highway, 1,625 km; other roads, 212,490 km. There were 658,401 motor vehicles in 1995–96. A 144-km expressway, part national highway, connects the Daitari mining area with Paradip Port.

Rail

The route-km of railway in 2001 was 2,261 km, of which 143 km was narrow gauge.

Civil Aviation

There is an airport at Bhubaneswar with regular scheduled services to Bangalore, Delhi, Hyderabad, Kolkata, Mumbai and Raipur.

Shipping

Paradip was declared a 'major' port in 1966; it handled 23·9m. tonnes of traffic in 2002–03. There are minor ports at Bahabalpur and Gopalpur.

SOCIAL INSTITUTIONS

Justice

The High Court of Judicature at Cuttack has a Chief Justice and 16 puisne judges.

Education

The percentage of literate people in the population in 2001 was 63·1% (males, 75·3%; females, 50·5%).

In 1996–97 there were 42,104 primary schools with 3·95m. students, 12,096 middle schools with 1·3m. students and 6,198 high and higher secondary schools with 945,000 students. There are ten engineering and technology colleges, 20 medical colleges, 13 teacher training colleges, 15 engineering schools/polytechnics, 497 arts, science and commerce colleges and 440 junior colleges.

Utkal University was established in 1943 at Cuttack and moved to Bhubaneswar in 1962; it is both teaching and affiliating. It has 368 affiliated colleges and 14,000 students (1993–94). Berhampur University has 33 affiliated colleges with 33,755 students, and Orissa University of Agriculture and Technology has eight constituent colleges with 641 students. Sambalpur University has 97 affiliated colleges and 43,982 students. Sri Jagannath Sanskrit Viswavidyalaya at Puri was established in 1981 for oriental studies.

Health

There were (1999–2000) 180 hospitals, 150 dispensaries, 1,351 primary health centres and units, and 5,929 health subcentres, with a total of 13,786 beds. There were also 462 homeopathic and 519 Ayurvedic dispensaries.

RELIGION

At the 2001 census Hindus numbered 34,726,129; Christians, 897,861; Muslims, 761,985.

CULTURE

Tourism

Tourist traffic is concentrated mainly on the 'Golden Triangle' of Konark, Puri, and Bhubaneswar and its temples. Tourists also visit Gopalpur, the Similipal National Park, Nandankanan and Chilka Lake, Bhiar-Kanika and Ushakothi Wildlife Sanctuary.

Punjab (India)

KEY HISTORICAL EVENTS

The Punjab was constituted an autonomous province of India in 1937. In 1947 it was partitioned between India and Pakistan as East and West Punjab. The name of East Punjab was changed to Punjab (India). On 1 Nov. 1956 Punjab and Patiala and East Punjab States Union (PEPSU) were integrated to form the state of Punjab. On 1 Nov. 1966, under the Punjab Reorganization Act, 1966, the state was reconstituted as a Punjabi-speaking state comprising the districts of Gurdaspur (excluding Dalhousie), Amritsar, Kapurthala, Jullundur, Ferozepur, Bhatinda, Patiala and Ludhiana; parts of Sangrur, Hoshiarpur and Ambala districts; and part of Kharar tehsil. The remaining area comprising 47,000 sq. km and an estimated (1967) population of 8·5m. was shared between the new state of Haryana and the Union Territory of Himachal Pradesh. The existing capital of Chandigarh was made joint capital of Punjab and Haryana; its transfer to Punjab alone (scheduled for 1986) has been delayed while the two states seek agreement as to which Hindi-speaking districts shall be transferred to Haryana.

TERRITORY AND POPULATION

The Punjab is in north India and is bounded at its northernmost point by Jammu and Kashmir, northeast by Himachal Pradesh, southeast by Haryana, south by Rajasthan, west and northwest by Pakistan. The area of the state is 50,362 sq. km, with a population (2001 census) of 24,358,999; density, 484 per sq. km. Cities with over 250,000 population at 2001 census, *see* INDIA: Territory and Population. Other principal towns (2001): Bathinda (217,256); Pathankot (168,485); Hoshiarpur (149,668); Batala (147,872); Moga (135,279); Abohar (124,339); S.A.S. Nagar (123,484); Maler Kotla (107,009); Khanna (103,099); Phagwara (102,253). The official language is Punjabi.

SOCIAL STATISTICS

Growth rate 1991–2001, 20·10%.

CONSTITUTION AND GOVERNMENT

Punjab (India) has a unicameral legislature, the Legislative Assembly, of 117 members. Presidential rule was imposed in May 1987 after outbreaks of communal violence. In March 1988 the Assembly was officially dissolved. Presidential rule was lifted in Feb. 1992.

There are 17 districts. The capital is Chandigarh.

RECENT ELECTIONS

Legislative Assembly elections were held on 13 Feb. 2007. The Shiromani Akali Dal (SAD) won 48 seats, the Congress Party (INC) 44, the Bharatiya Janata Party (BJP) 19, ind. 5. One seat was vacant.

CURRENT ADMINISTRATION

Governor: Shivraj Patil; b. 1935 (took office on 22 Jan. 2010).

Chief Minister: Parkash Singh Badal; b. 1927 (took office on 2 March 2007 for the fourth time, having previously been chief minister from March 1970–June 1971, June 1977–Feb. 1980 and Feb. 1997–Feb. 2002).

ECONOMY

Budget

Budget estimates, 2000–01, showed revenue receipts of Rs 159,597m. and revenue expenditure of Rs 159,725m.

ENERGY AND NATURAL RESOURCES

Electricity

Installed capacity, Oct. 2008, was 6,780 MW. In Sept. 2008 all 12,278 inhabited villages had electricity. The per capita consumption of electricity in Punjab is higher than in any other Indian state, at 821 units (kWh) per annum in 2000–01.

Agriculture

About 75% of the population depends on agriculture, which is technically advanced. The irrigated area rose from 2·2m. ha. in 1950–51 to 4·2m. ha. in 1996–97. 95·1% of cropland in Punjab is irrigated. In 2001 wheat production was 15·5m. tonnes; potatoes, 10·0m.; rice, 9·1m.; kinnow, 0·2m.; plus large amounts of chillies, mangoes, grapes, pears, peaches and lemons. Total foodgrains, 24·90m. tonnes; sugarcane, 1·3m. tonnes; oilseeds, 61,000 tonnes. Cotton, 1·91m. bales of 170 kg, representing 12·4% of India's cotton. Punjab contributes 22·6% of India's wheat. Agriculture in Punjab is more advanced and mechanized than in most other parts of India. Emphasis has recently been on diversification with new crops including hyola seeds, soybeans, sunflower, spring maize and floriculture, and the use of bio-fertilizers.

Livestock (2003 census): buffaloes, 5,995,000; other cattle, 2,039,000; sheep and goats, 498,000; poultry, 10,535,000.

Forestry

In 1999 there were 1,387 sq. km of forest land.

INDUSTRY

In March 2001 the number of registered industrial units was 202,356, employing about 1,184,550 people. In 2001 there were 620 large and medium industries and 201,736 small industrial units, investment Rs 43,310m. The chief manufactures are metals, textiles (especially hosiery and fabrics), yarn, sports goods, hand tools, sugar, bicycles, electronic goods, machine tools, hand tools, automobiles and vehicle parts, surgical goods, vegetable oils, tractors, chemicals and pharmaceuticals, fertilizers, food processing, electronics, railway coaches, paper and newsprint, cement, engineering goods and telecommunications items. There is an oil refinery.

COMMUNICATIONS

Roads

The total length of roads in 2001 was 50,389 km, including 1,729 km national highways—seven national highways pass through the state. All villages in the state are connected to metalled roads. State transport services cover 1·9m. effective km daily with a fleet of 3,426 buses carrying a daily average of over 1·2m. passengers. Coverage by private operators is estimated at 40%. There were 1,915,059 vehicles in 1995–96.

Rail

The Punjab possesses an extensive system of railway communications, served by the Northern Railway. Route-km (1995–96), 2,121 km.

Civil Aviation

There is an airport at Amritsar, and Chandigarh airport is on the northeastern boundary; both have regular scheduled services to Delhi, Jammu, Srinagar and Leh. There are also Vayudoot services to Ludhiana. Amritsar is now an international airport with charter flights from Europe and from several Middle East destinations.

SOCIAL INSTITUTIONS

Justice

The Punjab and Haryana High Court exercises jurisdiction over the states of Punjab and Haryana and the territory of Chandigarh. It is located in Chandigarh. In 2003 it consisted of a Chief Justice and 40 puisne judges.

Education

Compulsory education was introduced in April 1961; at the same time free education was introduced up to 8th class for boys and 9th class for girls as well as fee concessions. The aim is education for all children of 6–11. In 2001, 69·7% of the population were literate (75·2% of men and 63·4% of women).

In 1996–97 there were 12,590 primary schools with 2,081,965 students, 2,545 middle schools with 968,762 students, 2,159 high schools with 490,888 students and 1,134 higher secondary schools with 259,718 students.

Punjab University was established in 1882 at Lahore as an examining, teaching and affiliating body. It divided in 1947 with the Indian part moving to Shimla, and in 1956 moved again to Chandigarh (in 1993–94 it had 94 colleges and 77,868 students). In 1962 Punjabi University was established at Patiala (it had 66 colleges with 40,712 students) and Punjab Agricultural University at Ludhiana. Guru Nanak Dev University was established at Amritsar in 1969 to mark the 500th anniversary celebrations for Guru Nanak Dev, first Guru of the Sikhs (it had 85 colleges and

80,330 students, 1992–93). The Thapar Institute of Engineering and Technology, at Patiala, has university status and there is also the Baba Farid University of Health Science, at Faridkot. Altogether there are 293 affiliated colleges.

Health

There were (2000) 207 hospitals, 12 hospitals/health centres, 55 community health centres, 38 community primary health centres, 446 primary health centres, and 1,470 dispensaries and clinics. There were six Ayurvedic hospitals and 507 Ayurvedic dispensaries, plus one homeopathic hospital and 105 homeopathic dispensaries. There were over 25,000 hospital beds in 2000.

RELIGION

At the 2001 census Sikhs numbered 14,592,387; Hindus, 8,997,942; Muslims, 382,045; Christians, 292,800.

FURTHER READING

Singh, Khushwant, *A History of the Sikhs.* 2 vols. 1999

Rajasthan

KEY HISTORICAL EVENTS

The state is in the largely desert area formerly known as Rajputana. The Rajput princes were tributary to the Moghul emperors when they were conquered by the Mahrattas' leader, Mahadaji Sindhia, in the 1780s. In 1818 Rajputana became a British protectorate and was recognized during British rule as a group of princely states including Jaipur, Jodhpur and Udaipur. After independence the Rajput princes surrendered their powers and in 1950 were replaced by a single state government. In 1956 the state boundaries were altered; small areas of the former Bombay and Madhya Bharat states were added, together with the neighbouring state of Ajmer. Ajmer had been a Moghul power base; it was taken by the Mahrattas in 1770 and annexed by the British in 1818. In 1878 it became Ajmer-Merwara, a British province, and survived as a separate state until 1956.

TERRITORY AND POPULATION

Rajasthan is in northwest India and is bounded north by Punjab, northeast by Haryana and Uttar Pradesh, east by Madhya Pradesh, south by Gujarat and west by Pakistan. Since the area of Madhya Pradesh was reduced by the creation of Chhattisgarh in 2000, Rajasthan has become the largest Indian state in size, with an area of 342,239 sq. km. Population (2001 census), 56,507,188; density 165 per sq. km. For chief cities, *see* INDIA: Territory and Population. Other major towns (2001): Ganganagar (222,858), Bharatpur (205,235), Pali (187,641), Sikar (185,925), Tonk (135,689), Hunumangarh (129,556), Beawar (125,981), Kishangarh (116,222), Gangapur (105,396), Sawai Madhopur (101,997), Churu (101,874), Jhunjhunun (100,485). The main languages spoken are Rajasthani and Hindi.

SOCIAL STATISTICS

Growth rate 1991–2001, 28·41%.

CONSTITUTION AND GOVERNMENT

There is a unicameral legislature, the Legislative Assembly, having 200 members. The capital is Jaipur. There are 32 districts.

RECENT ELECTIONS

After the election in Dec. 2008 the Indian National Congress Party came to power. Congress (I) won 96 seats; Bharatiya Janata Party (BJP), 78; Bahujan Samaj Party (BSP), 6; ind. and others, 20.

CURRENT ADMINISTRATION

Governor: Prabha Rau; b. 1935 (since 2 Dec. 2009—acting until 25 Jan. 2010).

Chief Minister: Ashok Gehlot; b. 1951 (took office on 13 Dec. 2008, having previously been chief minister from Dec. 1998–Dec. 2003).

ECONOMY

Budget

The budget estimates for 2000–01 showed total revenue receipts of Rs 172,340m., and expenditure of Rs 172,403m.

ENERGY AND NATURAL RESOURCES

Electricity

Installed capacity in Oct. 2008, 6,426 MW. In Sept. 2008, 27,162 out of 39,753 inhabited villages had electricity.

Minerals

There are 64 different minerals mined in the state. It is the sole producer of garnet and jasper in India, and by far the leading producer of zinc, calcite, gypsum and asbestos. Others include silver, tungsten, granite, marble, kaolin (44% of India's production), dolomite, lignite, lead (80% of India's production), fluorite (59% of India's production), emeralds, soapstone, feldspar (70% of India's production), copper, barytes (53% of India's production), limestone and salt. Total revenue from minerals in 2002, Rs 3,000m. Four blocs are being explored for mineral oils and gas.

Agriculture

The state has suffered drought and encroaching desert for several years. The cultivable area is (1999) about 25·6m. ha., of which 4·65m. ha. is irrigated. Production of principal crops (in tonnes), 1999: pulses, 2·64m.; total foodgrains, 11·40m. (wheat, 6·7m.; rice, 190,000); cotton, 868,000 tonnes.

The total irrigable area of the state is 13·6m. ha., which is 53% of the cultivable area. The Indira Gandhi Nahar Canal—India's largest irrigation project—is the main canal system, of which 189 km of main canal, 204 km of feeder and more than 3,400 km of distributors have been built. There were 37,560 villages with full or partial drinking water facilities in Jan. 2004, out of 37,889 villages.

Livestock (2003): buffaloes, 10·41m.; other cattle, 10·85m.; sheep, 10·05m.; goats, 16·81m.; camels, 498,000; poultry, 6·19m.

Forestry

Forests covered 13,353 sq. km in 1999, of which 9,632 sq. km was protected.

INDUSTRY

In 2001 there were 221,369 small industrial units with an investment of Rs 31,160·6m. and employment of 857,000. Of these units 45,705 were agro-based, 26,842 forest-based, 27,397 metal-working and 24,861 textiles. There were 212 industrial estates in 2001. 10,244 medium-size and large factories were recorded in 2001. Total capital investment (1993–94) Rs 13,160m. Chief manufactures are textiles, dyeing, printing cloth, cement, glass, sugar, sodium, oxygen and acetylene units, pesticides, insecticides, dyes, caustic soda, calcium, carbide, synthetic fibres, fertilizers, shaving equipment, automobiles and automobile components, tyres, watches, nylon tyre cords and refined copper. The state is a major textile centre and is the leading producer of polyester and viscose yarns in India and the second largest producer of suiting material; out of 862 spinning mills in India, 69 are in Rajasthan.

COMMUNICATIONS

Roads

In 2001 there were 150,870 km of roads in Rajasthan including 61,520 km of good and surfaced roads. The state government gives a road length of 85,008 km in 1999 for surfaced roads—there were 4,453 km of national highways and 8,898 km of state highways. A total of 12 national highways crossed the state. Motor vehicles numbered 3·6m. in 2003.

Rail
Jodhpur, Marwar, Udaipur, Ajmer, Jaipur, Kota, Bikaner and Sawai Madhopur are important junctions of the northwestern network. Route km (2003) 5,924. The major cities of the state are integrated with the national broad-gauge network.

Civil Aviation
There are airports at Jaipur (Sanganer Airport), Jodhpur, Kota and Udaipur with regular scheduled services to Ahmedabad, Delhi and Mumbai. Sanganer has been upgraded and now receives charter international flights as well as scheduled flights from Dubai and other gulf destinations.

SOCIAL INSTITUTIONS

Justice
The seat of the High Court is at Jodhpur. There is a Chief Justice and 32 puisne judges. There is also a bench of High Court judges at Jaipur.

Education
In 2001, 60·4% of the population were literate (75·7% of men and 43·9% of women).

There were 35,015 primary schools with 7,540,000 students in 2001, 16,336 middle schools with 2,327,000 students, 4,124 high schools and 1,923 higher secondary schools with 1,560,000 students between them. Elementary education is free but not compulsory.

In 2001 there were 280 colleges. Rajasthan University, established at Jaipur in 1947, is teaching and affiliating; in 1993–94 it had 135 colleges and 160,000 students. There are 11 other universities: Rajasthan Agricultural University, Bikaner; Mohanlal Sukhadia University, Udaipur; Maharishi Dayanand Saraswati University, Ajmer; Jai Narayan Vyas University, Jodhpur; Kota Open University, Kota; National Law University, Jodhpur; Rajasthan Sanskrit University, Jaipur; Birla Institute of Science and Technology, Pilani; Jain Vishwa Bharti, Ladnu; Rajasthan Vidyapeeth, Udaipur; Vanasthali Vidyapeeth, Vanasthali. There are also 280 colleges: 111 government colleges (including teacher-training colleges and 27 polytechnics), 75 government colleges and research institutes, 92 non-aided colleges and two other institutes.

Health
In 2001 there were 113 hospitals with 17,459 beds, 263 community health centres, 1,674 primary health centres and 9,926 sub-centres.

RELIGION
At the 2001 census Hindus numbered 50,151,452; Muslims, 4,788,227; Sikhs, 818,420; Jains, 650,493.

FURTHER READING

Balzani, Marzia, *Modern Indian Kingship: Tradition, Legitimacy and Power in Rajasthan.* 2003

Sharma, S. K. and Sharma, Usha (eds.) *History and Geography of Rajasthan.* 2000

Sikkim

KEY HISTORICAL EVENTS
A small Himalayan kingdom between Nepal and Bhutan, Sikkim was independent in the 1830s although in continual conflict with larger neighbours. In 1839 the British took the Darjeeling district. British political influence increased in the 19th century, when Sikkim was a buffer between India and Tibet. However, Sikkim remained an independent kingdom ruled by the 14th-century Namgyal dynasty. In 1950 a treaty was signed with the government of India, declaring Sikkim an Indian Protectorate. Indian influence increased from then on. Political unrest coming to a head in 1973 led to the granting of constitutional reforms in 1974. Agitation continued until Sikkim became a 'state associated with the Indian Union' later that year. In 1975 the king was deposed and Sikkim became an Indian state, a change approved by referendum.

TERRITORY AND POPULATION
Sikkim is in the Eastern Himalayas and is bounded north by Tibet, east by Tibet and Bhutan, south by West Bengal and west Nepal. Area, 7,096 sq. km. It is inhabited chiefly by the Lepchas, a tribe indigenous to Sikkim, the Bhutias, who originally came from Tibet, and the Nepalis, who entered from Nepal in large numbers in the late 19th and early 20th century. Population (2001 census), 540,851; density, 76 per sq km. The capital is Gangtok (population of 29,354 at the 2001 census).

English is the principal language. Lepcha, Bhutia, Nepali and Limboo also have official status.

SOCIAL STATISTICS
Growth rate 1991–2001, 33·06%.

CONSTITUTION AND GOVERNMENT
The Assembly has 32 members.

The official language of the government is English. Lepcha, Bhutia, Nepali and Limboo have also been declared official languages.

Sikkim is divided into four districts for administration purposes, Gangtok, Mangan, Namchi and Gyalshing being the headquarters for the Eastern, Northern, Southern and Western districts respectively.

RECENT ELECTIONS
At the State Assembly election of 10 May 2004 the Sikkim Democratic Front won 31 seats (71·1% of the vote) and the INC took one seat (26·1%).

CURRENT ADMINISTRATION
Governor: Balmiki Prasad Singh; b. 1942 (took office on 9 July 2008).

Chief Minister: Pawan Kumar Chamling; b. 1950 (took office on 12 Dec. 1994).

ECONOMY

Budget
Budget estimates for 2000–01 showed receipts of Rs 114,360m. and expenditure of Rs 116,300m.

ENERGY AND NATURAL RESOURCES

Electricity
Installed capacity (Oct. 2008) 193 MW. There are four hydro-electric power stations. In Sept. 2008, 425 out of 450 inhabited villages had electricity.

Minerals
Copper, zinc and lead are mined.

Agriculture
There are 70,000 ha. of cultivable land. The economy is mainly agricultural; main crops are apples, barley, buckwheat, cardamom, ginger, maize, mandarin oranges, millet, potatoes, rice and wheat. Foodgrain production, 1999, 98,000 tonnes (maize, 56,000; rice, 21,000 tonnes; wheat, 14,000 tonnes);

potatoes, 28,000 tonnes; pulses, 6,000 tonnes. Tea is grown. Medicinal herbs are exported. Sericulture produces 179 kg of silk per annum.

Forestry

Forests occupied about 3,127 sq. km in 1995 and the potential for a timber and wood-pulp industry is being explored.

INDUSTRY

Small-scale industries include cigarettes, distilling, tanning, fruit preservation, carpets and watchmaking. Local crafts include carpet weaving, making handmade paper, wood carving and silverwork. The State Trading Corporation of Sikkim stimulates trade in indigenous products.

COMMUNICATIONS

Roads

There are 2,376 km of roads, all on mountainous terrain. Of these 40 km are national highways and 678 km state highways. 1,445 km are surfaced and 931 km unsurfaced. There are 18 major bridges. Public transport and road haulage is nationalized. There were 8,997 motor vehicles in 1995–96.

Rail

The nearest railhead is at Shiliguri (115 km from Gangtok).

Civil Aviation

The nearest airport is at Bagdogra (128 km from Gangtok), linked to Gangtok by helicopter service.

Telecommunications

At 31 Dec. 2002 there were 33,884 telephone subscribers.

SOCIAL INSTITUTIONS

Education

In 2001, 68·8% of the population were literate (76·0% of men and 60·4% of women). Sikkim had (1999) 739 pre-primary schools with 23,538 students, 335 primary schools with 84,986 students, 122 junior high schools with 23,949 students, 72 high schools with 3,331 students and 27 higher secondary schools with 1,484 students. Education is free up to class XII; text books are free up to class V. There are 500 adult education centres. There is also a training institute for primary teachers, two degree colleges and a teacher training college.

Health

In 2002 there was one state hospital, four community health centres, 24 primary health centres and 147 sub-primary health centres, with a total of 920 beds. Some 28,244 patients were treated in 2000–01.

RELIGION

At the 2001 census Hindus numbered 329,548 and Buddhists 152,042.

Tamil Nadu

KEY HISTORICAL EVENTS

The first trading establishment made by the British in the Madras State was at Peddapali (now Nizampatnam) in 1611 and then at Masulipatnam. In 1639 the British were permitted to create a settlement at the place which is now Chennai, and Fort St George was founded. By 1801 the whole of the country from the Northern Circars to Cape Comorin (with the exception of certain French and Danish settlements) had been brought under British rule.

Under the provisions of the States Reorganization Act, 1956, the Malabar district (excluding the islands of Laccadive and Minicoy) and the Kasaragod district taluk of South Kanara were transferred to the new state of Kerala; the South Kanara district (excluding Kasaragod taluk and the Amindivi Islands) and the Kollegal taluk of the Coimbatore district were transferred to the new state of Mysore; and the Laccadive, Amindivi and Minicoy Islands were constituted a separate Territory. Four taluks of the Trivandrum district and the Shencottah taluk of Quilon district were transferred from Travancore-Cochin to the new Madras State. On 1 April 1960, 1,049 sq. km from the Chittoor district of Andhra Pradesh were transferred to Madras in exchange for 844 sq. km from the Chingleput and Salem districts. In Aug. 1968 the state was renamed Tamil Nadu.

TERRITORY AND POPULATION

Tamil Nadu is in south India and is bounded north by Karnataka and Andhra Pradesh, east and south by the Indian Ocean and west by Kerala. Area, 130,058 sq. km. Population (2001 census), 62,405,679; density 480 per sq. km. Tamil is the principal language and has been adopted as the state language with effect from 14 Jan. 1958. For the principal towns, *see* INDIA: Territory and Population. Other large towns (2001 census): Tuticorin (243,415), Thanjavur (215,314), Nagercoil (208,179), Dindigul (196,955), Kanchipuram (188,733), Kumbakonam (160,767), Cuddalore (158,634), Karur (153,365), Neyveli (138,035), Tiruvannamalai (130,567), Pollachi (128,458), Arcot (126,671), Karaikkudi (125,717), Rajapalaiyam (122,307), Sivakasi (121,358), Pudukkottai (109,217), Bhavani (104,646), Vaniyambadi (103,950), Coonoor (101,490), Gudiyatham (100,115). The capital is Chennai (Madras).

SOCIAL STATISTICS

Growth rate 1991–2001, 11·72%.

CONSTITUTION AND GOVERNMENT

There is a unicameral legislature; the Legislative Assembly has 235 members (one of which is nominated). There are 30 districts.

RECENT ELECTIONS

In elections held on 8 May 2006 the Dravida Munnetra Kazhagam won 96 seats, the All India Anna Dravida Munnetra Kazhagam 61, the Indian National Congress 34, the Pattali Makkal Katchi 18, Communist Party of India (Marxist) 9, Communist Party of India 6, Marumalarchi Dravida Munnetra Kazhagam 6, Dalit Panthers of India (DPI) 2, Desiya Murpokku Dravida Kazhagam 1 and ind. 1.

CURRENT ADMINISTRATION

Governor: Surjit Singh Barnala; b. 1925 (since 3 Nov. 2004; in office for the second time).

Chief Minister: Kalaignar Muthuvel Karunanidhi; b. 1924 (since 13 May 2006; in office for the fourth time).

ECONOMY

Budget

2003–04 revenue receipts, Rs 228,505·3m.; expenditure, Rs 265,500·4m. Annual plan outlay, 2003–04, Rs 70,000m. Budget estimates for 2004–05: revenue receipts, Rs 247,923m.; revenue expenditure, Rs 281,287m.

ENERGY AND NATURAL RESOURCES

Electricity

Installed capacity in Jan. 2005 was 10,139 MW, of which 1,995 MW was hydro-electric, 6,424 MW thermal, 1,362 MW wind powered and 358 MW nuclear (the Kalpakkam nuclear power plant became operational in 1983). In Sept. 2008 all 15,400 inhabited villages had electricity.

Minerals
The state has magnesite, lignite, bauxite, limestone, manganese, fireclay and feldspar.

Agriculture
The land is a fertile plain watered by rivers flowing east from the Western Ghats, particularly the Cauvery and the Tambaraparani. Temperature ranges between 6°C and 40°C, rainfall between 442 mm and 934 mm. Of the total land area (13m. ha.), 6,519,000 ha. were cropped and 349,000 ha. of wasteland were cultivable in 1999–2000. Total area under irrigation in 2000–01, 3·49m. ha. The staple food crops grown are paddy, maize, jowar, bajra, pulses and millets. Important commercial crops are sugarcane, oilseeds, cotton, tobacco, coffee, rubber and pepper. In 2003–04, 3·2m. tonnes of paddy, 1·76m. tonnes of sugarcane, 918,000 tonnes of groundnuts, 888,000 tonnes of millets and other cereals, and 201,000 tonnes of pulses were produced.

Livestock (2003): buffaloes, 1·66m.; other cattle, 9·14m.; sheep, 5·59m.; goats, 8·18m.; poultry, 86·59m.

Forestry
Forest area, 2000, 22,871 sq. km. Products include timber, teak, wattle, sandalwood, pulp wood and sapwood.

Fisheries
In 2003–04 marine production totalled 381,148 tonnes and inland production 77,304 tonnes. In 2005 there were 314,400 people engaged in fishing and related activities.

INDUSTRY
In 2002–03 there were 448,905 registered small-scale industrial units, employing 3,142,335 workers; the number of working factories totalled 25,000, with 1,238,000 workers. The biggest central sector project is Salem steel plant. Textiles constitute one of the major industries; in 2003 Tamil Nadu produced nearly 40% of India's cotton textiles and accounted for 42% of Indian leather exports. Other important industries are automobile ancillaries (constituting 27·5% of exports from India as at mid-2003), chemicals and petrochemicals, agricultural and food processing, biotechnology and computer software (accounting for about 17% of India's software exports).

Trade Unions
In 2004 there were 9,685 registered trade unions.

COMMUNICATIONS

Roads
In March 2003 the state had 178,545 km of national and state highways, major and other district roads; there were 6,752,473 registered motor vehicles.

Rail
In March 2003 there were 4,016 route-km. Chennai and Madurai are the main centres.

Civil Aviation
There are airports at Chennai, Coimbatore, Tiruchirapalli and Madurai, with regular scheduled services to Delhi, Kolkata and Mumbai. Chennai is an international airport and the main centre of airline routes in south India. In 2003–04 Chennai handled 2,054,043 international passengers, 2,501,778 domestic passengers and 154,123 tonnes of freight.

Shipping
Chennai, Tuticorin and Ennore are the chief ports. Important minor ports are Cuddalore and Nagapattinam.

Telecommunications
In 2003–04 there were 3,871,900 telephones in use, with 123,706 public call facilities; there were 521,690 cellular phones.

Postal Services
Post offices numbered 8,692 in 2003–04.

SOCIAL INSTITUTIONS

Justice
There is a High Court at Chennai with a Chief Justice and 26 judges.

Police
In 2003–04 the strength of the police force was 95,412, with 1,217 police stations.

Education
At the 2001 census 73·5% of the population were literate (82·4% of men and 64·4% of women).

Education is free up to pre-university level. In 2003–04 there were 32,242 primary schools with 4·3m. students, 6,825 middle schools with 2·2m. students, 4,859 high schools with 1·9m. students and 4,136 higher secondary schools with 4·5m. students. There were 18 universities in 2003–04: Madras University (founded in 1857); Annamalai University, Annamalainagar (1929); Gandhigram Rural Institute, Gandhigram (1956); Madurai Kamaraj University, Palkalainagar (1966); Tamil Nadu Agricultural University, Coimbatore (1971); Anna University, Chennai (1978); Tamil University, Thanjavur (1981); Bharathidasan University, Tiruchirapalli (1982); Bharathiyar University, Coimbatore (1982); Mother Teresa Women's University, Kodaikanal (1984); Alagappa University, Karaikkudi (1985); Sri Ramachandra Medical College and Research Institute, Chennai (1985); Tamil Nadu Dr M. G. R. Medical University, Chennai (1987); Avinashilingam Institute for Home Science and Higher Education for Women, Coimbatore (1988); Tamil Nadu Veterinary and Animal Sciences University, Chennai (1989); Manonmaniam Sundaranar University, Tirunelveli (1990); Sri Chandrasekarendra Saraswathi Viswa Mahavidyalaya University, Enathur (1993); Thanthai Periyar University, Salem (1997).

Health
In 2002 there were 408 hospitals and 512 dispensaries, with about 61,000 beds.

RELIGION
At the 2001 census Hindus numbered 54,985,079; Christians, 3,785,060; Muslims, 3,470,647.

CULTURE

Press
In 2002–03 there were 3,093 newspapers and periodicals.

Tourism
In 2004, 1,058,012 foreign tourists visited the state.

FURTHER READING
Statistical Information: The Department of Statistics (Fort St George, Chennai) was established in 1948 and reorganized in 1953. Main publications: *Annual Statistical Abstract; Decennial Statistical Atlas; Season and Crop Report; Quinquennial Wages Census; Quarterly Abstract of Statistics.*

Tripura

KEY HISTORICAL EVENTS
Tripura is a Hindu state of great antiquity having been ruled by the Maharajahs for 1,300 years before its accession to the Indian Union on 15 Oct. 1949. With the reorganization of states on 1 Sept. 1956 Tripura became a Union Territory, and was so declared on 1 Nov. 1957. The Territory was made a State on 21 Jan. 1972.

TERRITORY AND POPULATION

Tripura is bounded by Bangladesh, except in the northeast where it joins Assam and Mizoram. The major portion of the state is hilly and mainly jungle. It has an area of 10,486 sq. km. Population, 3,199,203 (2001 census); density, 305 per sq. km.

The official languages are Bengali and Kokborok. Manipuri is also spoken.

SOCIAL STATISTICS

Growth rate 1991–2001, 16·03%.

CONSTITUTION AND GOVERNMENT

The territory has four districts, namely Dhalai, North Tripura, South Tripura and West Tripura. The capital is Agartala (population, 2001, 189,998).

The Legislative Assembly has 60 members.

RECENT ELECTIONS

The Communist Party of India (Marxist) won the Legislative Assembly elections on 23 March 2008 with 46 seats; Congress won 10; Revolutionary Socialist Party, 2; Communist Party of India, 1; Indigenous National Party of Tripura (INPT), 1.

CURRENT ADMINISTRATION

Governor: Dnyandeo Yashwantrao Patil; b. 1935 (took office on 27 Nov. 2009).

Chief Minister: Manik Sarkar; b. 1949 (took office on 11 March 1998).

ECONOMY

Budget

Budget estimates, 2004–05, showed expenditure of Rs 31,829m. and receipts of Rs 30,972m.

ENERGY AND NATURAL RESOURCES

Electricity

Installed capacity in 2005 was 220·46 MW, of which 76·11 MW were hydro-electric and 144·35 MW were thermal. In Sept. 2008, 491 out of 858 inhabited villages had electricity.

Oil and Gas

The state has significant natural gas resources in non-associate form, with established reserves of 31bn. cu. metres.

Agriculture

About 24% of the land area is cultivable. The tribes practise shifting cultivation, but this is being replaced by modern methods. The main crops are rice, wheat, jute, mesta, potatoes, oilseeds and sugarcane. In 2002–03 there were 246,000 ha. under cereal cultivation. In 2001 tea gardens covered 6,700 ha.

Forestry

Forests covered 6,293 sq. km in 2000, 3,588 sq. km of which were reserved and 509 sq. km protected. Commercial rubber plantation is being encouraged and in 2001–02 the state produced 12,000 tonnes of natural rubber.

INDUSTRY

Main small industries: aluminium utensils, rubber, saw-milling, soap, piping, fruit canning, handloom weaving and sericulture. In 1999–2000 there were 1,363 registered factories which employed 31,250 persons and 500 notified factories with 2,000 workers. 384,000 persons were employed in handloom and handicrafts industries in 2003–04.

COMMUNICATIONS

Roads

Total length of roads (2003–04), 10,242 km. In March 2002 vehicles registered totalled 57,428, of which 1,985 were buses and 5,775 were goods vehicles.

Rail

There is a railway between Kumarghat and Kalkalighat (Assam). Route-km in 2003–04, 66 km.

Civil Aviation

There is one airport and three airstrips. The airport (Agartala) has regular scheduled services to Kolkata.

SOCIAL INSTITUTIONS

Education

In 2001, 73·2% of the population were literate (81·0% of men and 64·9% of women). In Sept. 2003 there were 1,776 primary schools (451,731 pupils), 1,001 middle schools (186,651), and 652 high and higher secondary schools (118,006). There were 14 colleges of general education, two engineering and technical institutes, and five professional and other colleges. Tripura University, established in 1987, has 20 affiliated colleges.

Health

There were (2002) 27 hospitals, with 2,000 beds. There were 58 primary health centres, 539 sub-centres and 11 community health centres in 2001.

RELIGION

At the 2001 census Hindus numbered 2,739,310; Muslims, 254,442; Christians, 102,489; Buddhists, 98,922.

Uttar Pradesh

KEY HISTORICAL EVENTS

In 1833 the then Bengal Presidency was divided into two parts, one of which became the Presidency of Agra. In 1836 the Agra area was styled the North-West Province and placed under a Lieut.-Governor. In 1877 the two provinces of Agra and Oudh came under one administrator, Lieut.-Governor of the North-West Province and Chief Commissioner of Oudh. In 1902 the name was changed to 'United Provinces of Agra and Oudh', under a Lieut.-Governor, and the Lieut.-Governorship was altered to a Governorship in 1921. In 1935 the name was shortened to 'United Provinces'. On independence, the states of Rampur, Banaras and Tehri-Garwhal were merged with United Provinces. In 1950 the name of the United Provinces was changed to Uttar Pradesh. In 2000 the new state of Uttaranchal (officially renamed Uttarakhand on 1 Jan. 2007) was carved from the northern, mainly mountainous, region of Uttar Pradesh.

TERRITORY AND POPULATION

Uttar Pradesh is in north India and is bounded north by Uttarakhand and Nepal, east by Bihar and Jharkhand, south by Madhya Pradesh and Chhattisgarh and west by Rajasthan, Haryana and Delhi. After the formation of Uttarakhand the area of Uttar Pradesh is 240,928 sq. km (previously 294,411 sq. km). Population (2001 census), 166,197,921; density, 690 per sq. km. Despite the decline in the population caused by the creation of Uttarakhand, Uttar Pradesh still has the highest population of any of the Indian states. If Uttar Pradesh were a separate country it would have the sixth highest population in the world (after China, India, USA, Indonesia and Brazil). Cities with more than 250,000 population, *see* INDIA: Territory and Population. Other important towns (2001 census): Farrukhabad (242,997), Maunath Bhanjan (212,657), Hapur (211,983), Etawah (210,453), Faizabad (208,162), Mirzapur (205,053), Sambhal (182,478), Bulandshahr (176,425), Rae Bareli (169,333), Bahraich (168,323), Amroha (165,129), Jaunpur (160,055), Fatehpur (152,078), Sitapur (151,908), Budaun (148,029), Unnao (144,662), Modinagar

(139,929), Banda (139,436), Orai (139,318), Hathras (126,355), Pilibhit (124,245), Lakhimpur (121,486), Loni (120,945), Gonda (120,301), Mughal Sarai (116,308), Hardoi (112,486), Lalitpur (111,892), Basti (107,601), Etah (107,110), Mainpuri (104,851), Deoria (104,227), Chandausi (103,749), Ghazipur (103,298), Ballia (101,465), Sultanpur (100,065). The sole official language has been Hindi since April 1990.

SOCIAL STATISTICS

Growth rate 1991–2001, 25·85%.

CONSTITUTION AND GOVERNMENT

Uttar Pradesh has had an autonomous system of government since 1937. There is a bicameral legislature. The Legislative Council has 108 members; the Legislative Assembly has 404 (one of which is nominated).

There are 17 administrative divisions, each under a Commissioner, and 70 districts.

The capital is Lucknow.

RECENT ELECTIONS

Elections were held in April–May 2007. The Bahujan Samaj Party (BSP) won 206 seats; the Samajwadi Party (SP), 97; the Bharatiya Janata Party (BJP), 51; the Indian National Congress (INC), 22; ind. and others, 26.

CURRENT ADMINISTRATION

Governor: Banwari Lal Joshi; b. 1936 (took office on 28 July 2009).

Chief Minister: Mayawati; b. 1956 (took office for a fourth time on 13 May 2007).

ECONOMY

Budget

Budget estimates for 2004–05 showed revenue receipts of Rs 372,590m.; expenditure, Rs 427,860m.

ENERGY AND NATURAL RESOURCES

Electricity

Installed capacity in Jan. 2005 was 8,102·6 MW, of which 829·6 MW were hydro-electric, 7,135·0 MW thermal and 138·0 MW nuclear. In Sept. 2008, 86,450 out of 97,942 inhabited villages had electricity.

Minerals

The state's minerals include magnesite, granite, dolomite, coal, marble, limestone, bauxite, uranium and silica sand. In 2003–04, 15·8m. tonnes of coal were produced.

Agriculture

In 2003–04 Uttar Pradesh had almost 19·2m. ha. of land under foodgrain cultivation. It is India's largest producer of foodgrains: production (2002–03), 38·3m. tonnes (wheat, 23·7m. tonnes; rice, 9·6m. tonnes). The state is also one of India's main producers of sugar and potatoes: 2002–03 production of sugarcane, 120·9m. tonnes; and potatoes, 10·2m. tonnes.

Forestry

Forests covered 16,887 sq. km in 2002, 11,078 sq. km of which were reserved and 2,425 sq. km protected. In 1995 forests had accounted for 51,663 sq. km, but much of this area is now in Uttarakhand.

INDUSTRY

Sugar production is important; other industries include cement, vegetable oils, textiles, cotton yarn, jute and glassware. In 2003–04 there were 10,618 registered factories employing 359,267 workers.

COMMUNICATIONS

Roads

Total length of roads in 2004, 244,442 km, of which 182,057 km were surfaced. In March 2003 vehicles registered totalled 5,928,395, of which 4,488,426 were two-wheelers.

Rail

Lucknow is the main junction of the northern network; other important junctions are Agra, Kanpur, Allahabad, Mughal Sarai and Varanasi. Route-km in 2005–06, 8,546 km.

Civil Aviation

The main airports are at Lucknow, Kanpur, Varanasi, Allahabad, Agra and Gorakhpur.

SOCIAL INSTITUTIONS

Justice

The High Court of Judicature at Allahabad (with a bench at Lucknow) has a Chief Justice and 63 puisne judges including additional judges. The state is divided into 46 judicial districts.

Education

At the 2001 census 75·72m. people were literate (56·3%; 68·8% of men and 42·2% of women). In 2002–03 there were 98,220 primary schools with 15·60m. students, 23,696 middle schools with 5·54m. students and 11,524 higher secondary schools with 3·87m. students.

Universities: Allahabad University (founded 1887); the Banaras Hindu University, Varanasi (1916); Aligarh Muslim University (1920); Lucknow University (1921); Agra University (1927); Gorakhpur University (1957); Sampurnanand Sanskrit Vishwavidyalaya, Varanasi (1958); Ch. Charan Singh University (1966); Kanpur University (1966); Bundelkhand University, Jhansi (1975); C. S. Azad University of Agriculture and Technology, Kanpur (1975); Dr Ram Manohar Lohia Awadh, Faizabad (1975); Narendra Deva University of Agriculture and Technology, Faizabad (1975); Rohilkhand University, Bareilly (1975); Purvanchal University, Jaunpur (1987).

In 2005 there were also four institutions with university status: Indian Veterinary Research Institute; Central Institute of Higher Tibetan Studies; Sanjai Gandhi Post Graduate Institute of Medical Sciences; and Dayal Bagh Educational Institute. In 2004–05 there were 34 medical colleges, 42 veterinary colleges, 69 engineering colleges, eight agricultural colleges, two law colleges, 21 teacher training colleges and 1,009 arts, science and commerce colleges. There were 491 oriental learning colleges in 2000–01.

Health

In 2007 there were 4,595 allopathic, 2,362 Ayurvedic and Unani and 1,482 homoeopathic hospitals and dispensaries. There were 3,660 primary health centres, 20,521 sub-centres and 386 community health centres in 2006–07. In Dec. 2003 there were 44,927 doctors registered with the state medical council.

RELIGION

At the 2001 census Hindus numbered 133,979,263; Muslims, 30,740,158; Sikhs, 678,059; Buddhists, 302,031; Christians, 212,578; Jains, 207,111.

FURTHER READING

Hasan, Z., *Quest for Power: Oppositional Movements and Post-Congress Politics in Uttar Pradesh.* 1998

Kudaisya, Gyanesh, *Region, Nation, 'Heartland': Uttar Pradesh in India's Body Politic.* 2006

Lieten, G. K. and Srivastava, R., *Unequal Partners: Power Relations, Devolution and Development in Uttar Pradesh.* 1999

Misra, S., *A Narrative of Communal Politics, Uttar Pradesh, 1937–39.* 2001

Uttarakhand

KEY HISTORICAL EVENTS

The state was carved from Uttar Pradesh and became the twenty-seventh state of India on 9 Nov. 2000. It is located in the hilly and mountainous region of the northern border of the Indian subcontinent. The regions of Kumaon and Garhwal contained in the new state were referred to as Uttarakhand in ancient Hindu scriptures. The Chinese suppression of revolt in Tibet in 1959 saw a rapid influx of Tibetan exiles to the region and the Indo-Chinese conflict of 1962 persuaded the Indian government to initiate a modernization programme throughout the Indian Himalayas that resulted in the development of roads and communication networks in the previously backward region. From the 1970s the hill people began to agitate for their districts to be separated from Uttar Pradesh, which had been established in 1950. On 1 Aug. 2000 the Uttar Pradesh Reorganisation bill was passed, allowing for a separate state, called Uttaranchal (officially renamed Uttarakhand on 1 Jan. 2007), to incorporate 12 hill districts and, controversially, the lowland area of Udham Singh Nagar.

TERRITORY AND POPULATION

Uttarakhand is located in northern India and is bounded in the northeast by China and in the east by Nepal. The state of Uttar Pradesh is to the southwest, Haryana to the west and Himachal Pradesh to the northwest. Uttarakhand has an area of 53,483 sq. km. Population (2001 census), 8,489,349; density, 159 per sq. km. The principal languages are the Hindi dialects of Garhwali and Kumaoni. Cities with over 250,000 population, *see* INDIA: Territory and Population. Other large cities (2001 census): Hardwar (220,767), Haldwani (158,896), Roorkee (115,278).

SOCIAL STATISTICS

Growth rate 1991–2001, 20·41%.

CONSTITUTION AND GOVERNMENT

Uttarakhand is the twenty-seventh state of India. After the region was carved from Uttar Pradesh it was decided that the 22 members of the Legislative Assembly from Uttarakhandi districts would become the members of the new state's Legislative Assembly. Subsequently this was increased to 30 when the provisional assembly was established, and to 70 as a result of the elections to the Legislative Assembly of Feb. 2002. For administrative purposes the region is divided into 13 districts.

The interim capital and seat of government is at Dehra Dun.

RECENT ELECTIONS

On the formation of the new state the Bharatiya Janata Party (BJP) was the single largest party with 17 seats, enabling them to form a majority administration in the 23-seat assembly with Nityanand Swamy becoming the state's first chief minister.

State assembly elections were held on 21 Feb. 2007. The Bharatiya Janata Party (BJP) won 34 seats; the Indian National Congress party (INC) 21; the Bahujan Samaj Party (BSP), 8; the Uttarakhand Kranti Dal (UKKD), 3; ind. 3. One seat was vacant.

CURRENT ADMINISTRATION

Governor: Margaret Alva; b. 1942 (took office on 6 Aug. 2009).

Chief Minister: Ramesh Pokhriyal; b. 1958 (took office on 27 June 2009).

ENERGY AND NATURAL RESOURCES

Electricity

In Oct. 2008 the state had an installed capacity of 2,383 MW. In Sept. 2008, 15,213 out of 15,761 inhabited villages had electricity.

Water

Uttarakhand suffers from an acute shortage of water for drinking and irrigation. Only 10% of the water potential is currently utilized.

Minerals

There are deposits of limestone, gypsum, iron ore, graphite and copper.

Agriculture

Agriculture is the occupation for approximately 50% of the population. Subsistence farming is the norm, as only 9% of the land in the state is cultivable.

Forestry

Approximately 65%–70% of the state's area is covered in forest.

INDUSTRY

Tourism is by far the most important industry. The state can offer ski resorts, adventure tourism, mountaineering, hiking and several areas of religious interest. Other industries include: horticulture, floriculture, fruit-processing and medicine production. In the Terai region there are around 350 industrial units and 130 in the Doon Valley.

COMMUNICATIONS

Roads

There are 23 km of roads for every 100 sq. km of land in the state. State highways link Uttarakhand to the neighbouring states of Himachal Pradesh, Haryana and Uttar Pradesh. The state remains inaccessible in parts.

Rail

Four main railway lines in the south of the state link several districts to Uttar Pradesh and Himachal Pradesh. Railways along the foothills connect Dehra Dun, Hardwar, Rishikesh, Roorkee, Kotdwaar, Ram Nagar, Kathgodam and Tanakpur. The rest of the state is not connected to the rail network.

Civil Aviation

There are airports at Dehra Dun and Udham Singh Nagar.

SOCIAL INSTITUTIONS

Education

In 2001, 71·6% of the population were literate (83·3% of men and 59·6% of women).

RELIGION

At the 2001 census Hindus numbered 7,212,260, Muslims 1,012,141 and Sikhs 212,025.

West Bengal

KEY HISTORICAL EVENTS

Bengal was under the overlordship of the Moghul emperor and ruled by a Moghul governor (*nawab*) who declared himself independent in 1740. The British East India Company based at Calcutta was in conflict with the *nawab* from 1756 until 1757 when British forces defeated him at Plassey and installed their own *nawab* in 1760. The French were also in Bengal; the British captured their trading settlement at Chandernagore in 1757 and in 1794, restoring it to France in 1815.

The area of British Bengal included modern Orissa and Bihar, Bangladesh and (until 1833) Uttar Pradesh. Calcutta was the capital of British India from 1772 until 1912.

The first division into East and West took place in 1905–11 and was not popular. However, at Partition in 1947 the East (Muslim) chose to join what was then East Pakistan (now Bangladesh), leaving West Bengal as an Indian frontier state and promoting a steady flow of non-Muslim Bengali immigrants from the East. In 1950 West Bengal incorporated the former princely state of Cooch Behar and, in 1954, Chandernagore. Small areas were transferred from Bihar in 1956.

TERRITORY AND POPULATION

West Bengal is in northeast India and is bounded north by Sikkim and Bhutan, east by Assam and Bangladesh, south by the Bay of Bengal, southwest by Orissa, west by Jharkhand and Bihar and northwest by Nepal. The total area of West Bengal is 88,752 sq. km. Population (2001 census), 80,176,197; density, 903 per sq. km. The capital is Kolkata (Calcutta). Population of chief cities, *see* INDIA: Territory and Population. Other major towns (2001): Habra, 239,209; Ingraj Bazar (English Bazar), 224,415; Raiganj, 175,047; Haldia, 170,673; Baharampur, 170,322; Medinipur, 149,769; Krishnanagar, 148,194; Ranaghat, 145,285; Balurghat, 143,321; Santipur, 138,235; Bankura, 128,781; Navadvip, 125,341; Birnagar, 115,127; Alipur Duar, 114,035; Puruliya, 113,806; Basirhat, 113,159; Darjiling (Darjeeling), 108,830; Cooch Behar, 103,008; Bangaon, 102,163; Chakdaha, 101,320; Jalpaiguri, 100,348.

The principal language is Bengali.

SOCIAL STATISTICS

Growth rate 1991–2001, 17·77%.

CONSTITUTION AND GOVERNMENT

The state of West Bengal came into existence as a result of the Indian Independence Act, 1947. The territory of Cooch-Behar State was merged with West Bengal on 1 Jan. 1950, and the former French possession of Chandernagore became part of the state on 2 Oct. 1954. Under the States Reorganization Act, 1956, certain portions of Bihar State (an area of 3,157 sq. miles with a population of 1,446,385) were transferred to West Bengal.

The Legislative Assembly has 295 seats (294 elected and one nominated).

For administrative purposes there are three divisions (Jalpaiguri, Burdwan and Presidency), under which there are 18 districts, including Kolkata. The Kolkata Metropolitan Development Authority has been set up to co-ordinate development in the metropolitan area (1,350 sq. km). For the purposes of local self-government there are 16 *zilla parishads* (district boards) excluding Darjeeling, 328 *panchayat samities* (regional boards), one *siliguri mahakuma parishad* and 3,247 *gram* (village) *panchayats*. There are 113 municipalities, six Corporations and 11 Notified Areas. The Kolkata Municipal Corporation is headed by a mayor in council.

RECENT ELECTIONS

In elections held on 17, 22 and 27 April and 3 and 8 May 2006 the Communist Party of India (Marxist) won 176 seats, the All India Trinamool Congress 29, the All India Forward Bloc 23, the Indian National Congress 21, the Revolutionary Socialist Party 20, the Communist Party of India 9, the West Bengal Socialist Party 4, the Gorkha National Liberation Front 3, ind. and others 9. In winning the election the Communists retained power for a seventh consecutive term.

CURRENT ADMINISTRATION

Governor: Mayankote Kelath Narayanan; b. 1934 (since 24 Jan. 2010).

Chief Minister: Buddhadeb Bhattacharjee; b. 1944 (since 6 Nov. 2000).

ECONOMY

Budget

2003–04 revenue receipts, Rs 174,045m.; expenditure, Rs 267,800·7m. Budget estimates for 2004–05: revenue receipts, Rs 204,981·3m.; expenditure, Rs 277,984·4m.

ENERGY AND NATURAL RESOURCES

Electricity

Installed capacity as at Jan. 2005 was 6,762 MW, of which 261 MW were hydro-electric, 6,499 MW thermal and 2 MW wind powered. In Sept. 2008, 36,462 out of 37,945 inhabited villages had electricity.

Water

The largest irrigation and power scheme under construction is the Teesta Barrage (irrigation potential, 533,520 ha.). Other major irrigation schemes are the Mayurakshi Reservoir, Kangsabati Reservoir, Mahananda Barrage and Aqueduct and Damodar Valley. In 2000–01, 1·4m. ha. of land were under irrigation from tubewells and other wells, 434,000 ha. from canals and 523,000 ha. from other sources.

Minerals

Value of production, 2002–03, Rs 23,933m. The state has coal (the Raniganj field is one of the three biggest in India) including coking coal. Coal production (2002–03), 20·48m. tonnes.

Agriculture

About 5·84m. ha. were under rice-paddy in 2002–03. Total foodgrain production, 2002–03, 15·52m. tonnes (rice 14·39m. tonnes, wheat 887,000 tonnes, pulses 167,000 tonnes). Other principal crops (2002–03): potatoes, 6·9m. tonnes; sugarcane, 1·28m. tonnes; oilseeds, 476,000 tonnes; jute, 8·5m. bales of 180 kg (76·3% of the national output). The state produces around 200,000 tonnes of tea each year.

Livestock (2003): 18,913,000 cattle; 1,086,000 buffaloes; 1,525,000 sheep; 18,774,000 goats; 60,656,000 poultry.

Forestry

Forests covered 11,879 sq. km in 2000, 7,054 sq. km of which were reserved and 3,772 sq. km protected.

Fisheries

Fish production, 2007–08, 1,447,000 tonnes, of which inland 1,264,000 tonnes. In 2005 there were 128,500 people working in fishing and allied activities. The state is the largest inland fish producer in India.

INDUSTRY

In 2008 there were 14,389 factories (provisional) employing a daily average of 927,282 workers. There are 100 coal mines.

There is a large automobile factory at Uttarpara, and an aluminium rolling-mill at Belur. There is a steel plant at Burnpur (Asansol) and a spun pipe factory at Kulti. Durgapur has a large steel plant and other industries under the state sector—a thermal power plant, coke oven plant, fertilizer factory, alloy steel plant and ophthalmic glass plant. There is a locomotive factory at Chittaranjan and a cable factory at Rupnarayanpur. A refinery and fertilizer factory are operating at Haldia. Other industries include chemicals, engineering goods, electronics, textiles, automobile tyres, paper, cigarettes, distillery, aluminium foil, tea, pharmaceuticals, carbon black, graphite, iron foundry, silk and explosives.

Small industries are important; 361,051 units were registered in March 2007, employing some 2m. persons.

COMMUNICATIONS

Roads

Total length of roads in 1999: 79,255 km, of which 44,970 km were surfaced. As at 31 March 2008 there were 3,584,901 registered vehicles, including 671,248 cars, 74,338 taxis, 7,793 buses, 289,018 goods vehicles and 2,359,613 two-wheelers.

Rail

The route-km of railways within the state was 4,545 km in 2007–08. The main centres are Asansol, Burdwan, Howrah, Kharagpur, New Jalpaiguri and Sealdah. There is a metro in Kolkata (16·5 km).

Civil Aviation

The main airport is Kolkata, which has national and international flights. In 2001 it handled 2,549,965 passengers (1,990,746 on domestic flights) and 55,089 tonnes of freight. The second airport is at Bagdogra in the extreme north, which has regular scheduled services to Delhi and Kolkata.

Shipping

Kolkata is the chief port: a barrage has been built at Farakka to control the flow of the Ganges and to provide a rail and road link between North and South Bengal. A second port has been developed at Haldia, between the present port and the sea, which is intended mainly for bulk cargoes. West Bengal has about 800 km of navigable canals.

SOCIAL INSTITUTIONS

Justice

The High Court of Judicature at Kolkata has a Chief Justice and 45 puisne judges. The Andaman and Nicobar Islands come under its jurisdiction.

Police

In 2001 the police force numbered 83,466, under a director-general and an inspector-general. Kolkata has a separate force under a commissioner directly responsible to the government; its strength was about 26,000 in 2002.

Education

In 2001, 68·6% of the total population were literate (men, 77·0%; women, 59·6%). There were 52,426 primary schools, 2,883 junior high schools and 9,620 high and higher secondary schools in 2001 with (1998–99) 1,881,226 students. Education is free up to higher secondary stage.

In 2001 there were nine universities: the University of Calcutta (founded 1857); University of Jadavpur, Kolkata (1955); Burdwan University (1960); Kalyani University (1960); University of North Bengal (1962); Rabindra Bharati University (1962); Vidyasagar University, Medinipur (1981); Bengal Engineering College (deemed to have university status from 1992); Netaji Subhas Open University (1998). The enrolment of students in universities for 2001 totalled 37,461. There were 36 government degree colleges and institutes in 2001 and 370 non-government colleges and institutes; enrolment of students, 550,989.

Health

As at 1 Jan. 2002 there were 411 hospitals with 55,279 beds. There were 1,262 primary health centres, 8,126 sub-centres and 99 community health centres in 2001.

RELIGION

At the 2001 census Hindus numbered 58,104,835; Muslims, 20,240,543; Christians, 515,150; Buddhists, 243,364; Sikhs, 66,391; Jains, 55,223.

FURTHER READING

Bagchi, Jasodhara, (ed.) *The Changing Status of Women in West Bengal, 1970–2000: The Challenge Ahead.* 2005

Chatterjee, P., *The Present History of West Bengal: Essays in Political Criticism.* 1997

UNION TERRITORIES

Andaman and Nicobar Islands

GENERAL DETAILS

The Andaman and Nicobar Islands are administered by the President of the Republic of India acting through a Lieut.-Governor. There is a 30-member Pradesh Council, five members of which are selected by the Administrator as advisory counsellors. The seat of administration is at Port Blair, which is connected with Kolkata (1,255 km away) and Chennai (1,190 km) by steamer service which calls about every ten days; there are air services from Kolkata and Chennai. Roads in the islands, 733 km black-topped and 48 km others. There are two districts.

The population (2001 census) was 356,152. The area is 8,248 sq. km and the density 43 per sq. km. Growth rate 1991–2001, 26·90%. Port Blair (2001), 99,984.

The climate is tropical, with little variation in temperature. Heavy rain (125" annually) is mainly brought by the southwest monsoon. Humidity is high. The islands were severely affected by the tsunami of 26 Dec. 2004.

Budget figures for 2002–03 show total revenue receipts of Rs 885m., and total expenditure on revenue account of Rs 3,850m.

There is installed capacity of 38,805 KW. In Sept. 2008, 331 out of 501 inhabited villages had electricity.

In 2001, 26,524 ha. were under cultivation, of which 10,885 ha. were under rice. 48,167 tonnes of rice were grown. There were 70,923 goats, 60,180 cattle and 42,836 pigs in 2001.

In 2002, 25,561 tonnes of fish were landed. There were 1,966 registered fishing boats in 2002 and 2,721 fishermen.

There are 7,171 sq. km of forests, of which 4,242 sq. km are protected. In 2002, 4,712 cu. metres of sawn timber were extracted.

There are 1,502 km of paved roads and 45 km of other roads.

In 2003 there were 48 factories and 1,479 small-scale industrial units, employing 5,032 people.

In 2001 there were 207 primary schools with 43,000 students, 56 middle schools with 23,000 students, 45 high schools with 11,000 students and 48 higher secondary schools with 4,000 students. There is a teacher training college, two polytechnics and two colleges. Literacy (2001 census), 81·3% (86·3% of men and 75·2% of women).

In 2003 there were three hospitals, 28 health centres and 107 primary health sub-centres.

At the 2001 census Hindus numbered 246,589; Christians, 77,178.

Lieut.-Governor: Bhopinder Singh; b. 1946 (since 29 Dec. 2006).

The **Andaman Islands** lie in the Bay of Bengal, 193 km from Cape Negrais in Myanmar, 1,255 from Kolkata and 1,190 from Chennai. Five large islands grouped together are called the Great Andamans, and to the south is the island of Little Andaman. There are some 239 islets and a total of 572 islands, islets and rocks, the two principal groups being the Ritchie Archipelago and the Labyrinth Islands. The Great Andaman group is about 467 km long and, at the widest, 51 km broad.

The original inhabitants live in the forests by hunting and fishing. The total population of the Andaman Islands (including about 430 aboriginals) was 240,089 in 1991. Main aboriginal tribes: Andamanese, Onges, Jarawas and Sentinelese.

The Great Andaman group, densely wooded (forests covered 7,615 sq. km in 1995), contains hardwood and softwood and supplies the match and plywood industries. Annually the Forest Department export about 25,000 tonnes of timber to the mainland. Coconut, coffee and rubber are cultivated. The islands are slowly being made self-sufficient in paddy and rice, and now grow approximately half their annual requirements. Livestock (1997, including Nicobar Islands): 60,180 cattle, 14,208 buffaloes, 70,919 goats and 42,835 pigs. Fishing is important. There is a sawmill at Port Blair and a coconut-oil mill. Little Andaman has a palm-oil mill.

The islands possess a number of harbours and safe anchorages, notably Port Blair in the south, Port Cornwallis in the north and Elphinstone and Mayabandar in the middle.

The **Nicobar Islands** are situated to the south of the Andamans, 121 km from Little Andaman. The Danes were in possession 1756–1869, and then the British until 1947. There are 19 islands, seven uninhabited; total area, 1,841 sq. km. The islands are usually divided into three sub-groups (southern, central and northern), the chief islands in each being respectively Great Nicobar, Camotra with Nancowrie and Car Nicobar. There is a harbour between the islands of Camotra and Nancowrie, Nancowrie Harbour.

The population numbered, in 1991, 39,208, including about 22,200 of Nicobarese and Shompen tribes. The coconut and areca nut are the main items of trade, and coconuts are a major item in the people's diet.

FURTHER READING

Dhingra, Kiran, *The Andaman and Nicobar Islands in the Twentieth Century: A Gazetteer.* 2006

Chandigarh

On 1 Nov. 1966 the city of Chandigarh and the area surrounding it was constituted a Union Territory. Population (2001), 900,635; density, 7,900 per sq. km; growth rate 1991–2001, 40·28%. Area, 114 sq. km. It serves as the joint capital of both Punjab (India) and the state of Haryana, and is the seat of a High Court. The city, which had a population of 808,515 inhabitants at the 2001 census, will ultimately be the capital of just the Punjab; joint status is to last while a new capital is built for Haryana.

Budget for 2000–01 showed revenue of Rs 4,730m. and expenditure of Rs 6,327m.

In Sept. 2008 all 23 inhabited villages had electricity.

There is some cultivated land and some forest (27·5% of the territory).

In 2001 there were 280 factories, of which 15 were large and medium scale factories and about 2,100 small scale industries, employing 24,000 people.

In 1996–97 there were 44 primary schools (60,012 students), 33 middle schools (34,095 students), 50 high schools (18,510 students) and 47 higher secondary schools (16,710 students). There were also two engineering and technology colleges, 12 arts, science and commerce colleges, two polytechnic institutes and a university (Panjab University). Other institutes have university status: Chandigarh College of Architecture; the Chandigarh Government College of Art; Chandigarh Institute of Postgraduate Medicinal Education and Research; Punjab Engineering College.

In 2001, 81·9% of the population were literate (86·1% of men and 76·5% of women).

In 2000 there were 43 dispensaries, 16 general hospitals and 72 private hospitals with a total of 2,530 beds.

At the 2001 census Hindus numbered 707,978 and Sikhs 145,175.

Administrator: Shivraj Patil; b. 1935 (took office as Governor of Punjab on 22 Jan. 2010).

Dadra and Nagar Haveli

GENERAL DETAILS

Formerly Portuguese, the territories of Dadra and Nagar Haveli were occupied in July 1954 by nationalists, and a pro-India administration was formed; this body made a request for incorporation into the Union on 1 June 1961. By the 10th amendment to the constitution the territories became a centrally administered Union Territory with effect from 11 Aug. 1961, forming an enclave at the southernmost point of the border between Gujarat and Maharashtra, approximately 30 km from the west coast. Area 491 sq. km; population (census 2001), 220,490; density 449 per sq. km; growth rate 1991–2001, 59·22%. There is an Administrator appointed by the government of India. The day-to-day business is done by various departments, co-ordinated by the Secretaries, Assistant Secretary, Collector and Resident Deputy Collector. The capital is Silvassa, which had a population of 21,893 at the 2001 census. 78·82% of the population is tribal and organized in 140 villages. Languages used are dialects classified under Bhilodi (91·1%), Bhilli, Gujarati, Marathi and Hindi.

CURRENT ADMINISTRATION

Administrator: Satya Gopal.

ECONOMY

Budget

The budget for 2001–02 shows revenue receipts of Rs 1,178·3m. and revenue expenditure of Rs 507 was Rs 1,212·2m.; budget estimate was Rs 552·8m. under Plan Sector and Rs 3,688·4m. under Non-Plan Sector.

ENERGY AND NATURAL RESOURCES

Electricity

In Sept. 2008 all 70 inhabited villages had electricity. A major sub-station at Kharadpada village has been completed. Installed capacity was 79 MW in Oct. 2008.

Minerals

There are few natural mineral resources although there is some ordinary sand and quarry stone.

Agriculture

Farming is the chief occupation, and 22,352 ha. were under net crop in 2001–02. Much of the land is terraced and there is a 100% subsidy for soil conservation. The major food crops are rice and ragi; wheat, small millets and pulses are also grown. There is a coverage of lift irrigation over 6,736 ha. During 2001–02 the administration distributed 152 tonnes of high-yielding paddy and wheat seed and 1,574 tonnes of manures and fertilizers.

Forestry

20,359 ha. or 40·8% of the total area is forest, mainly of teak, sadad and khair. In 1985 a moratorium was imposed on commercial felling to preserve the environmental function of the forests and ensure local supplies of firewood, timber and fodder. The tribals have been given exclusive right to collect minor forest produce from the reserved forest area for domestic use. 92 sq. km of reserved forest was declared a wildlife sanctuary in 2000.

INDUSTRY

There is no heavy industry, and the Territory is a 'No Polluting Industry District'. Industrial estates for small and medium scales have been set up at Pipariya, Masat and Khadoli. In March 2002 there were 1,317 small scale and 383 medium scale units employing 37,297 people.

Labour

The Labour Enforcement Office ensures the application of the Monitoring of Minimum Wages Act (1948), the Industrial Disputes Act (1947), the Contract Labour (Regulation and Abolition) Act (1970) and the Workmen's Compensation Act (1923). During 2001–02, 81 cases under the Industrial Disputes Act were settled. Under the Contract Labour (Regulation and Abolition) Act (1970), 53 certificates of registration and 56 licences were issued to the industrial establishment. 19 cases under the Workman's Compensation Act (1923) were settled.

COMMUNICATIONS

Roads

In 2002 there were 580 km of road of which 545 km were surfaced. Out of 72 villages, 68 are connected by all-weather road. There were 27,300 motor vehicles in 2001–02. The National Highway no. 8 passes through Vapi, 18 km from Silvassa.

Rail

Although there are no railways in the territory the line from Mumbai to Ahmedabad runs through Vapi, 18 km from Silvassa.

Civil Aviation

The nearest airport is at Mumbai, 180 km from Silvassa.

SOCIAL INSTITUTIONS

Justice

The territory is under the jurisdiction of the Bombay (Maharashtra) High Court. There is a District and Sessions Court and one Junior Division Civil Court at Silvassa.

Education

Literacy was 57·6% of the population at the 2001 census (71·2% of men and 40·2% of women). In 2001–02 there were 195 primary and middle schools (35,637 students) and 17 high and higher secondary schools (8,887 students).

Health

The territory had (2001–02) a civil hospital, 6 primary health centres, 36 sub-centres, three dispensaries and a mobile dispensary. A Community Health Centre has been established at Khanvel, 20 km from Silvassa. The Pulse Polio Immunisation programme was organized in 1999 and 54,128 polio doses were provided to children below five years of age. There has been a sharp fall in the incidence of malaria, especially cerebral malaria, owing to the sustained efforts of the administration. Hepatitis B vaccination of all inmates in the social welfare hostels was completed with the co-operation of voluntary organizations. A blood testing centre has been established for HIV testing.

Welfare

The Social Welfare Department implements the welfare schemes for poor Scheduled castes, Scheduled tribes, women and physically disabled persons, etc.

RELIGION

Numbers of religious followers (2001 census): Hindus, 206,203 (94% of the population), with some Muslims and Christians.

CULTURE

Press

One weekly newspaper and two fortnightly news magazines are published.

Tourism

The territory is a rural area between the industrial centres of Mumbai and Surat-Vapi. The Tourism Department is developing areas of natural beauty to promote eco-friendly tourism. Several gardens and the Madhuban Dam are among the tourist sites. A lion safari park has been set up at Vasona over 20 ha. About 380,000 visitors came to Dadra and Nagar Haveli during 2000.

Daman and Diu

GENERAL DETAILS

Daman (Damão) on the Gujarat coast, 100 miles (160 km) north of Mumbai, was seized by the Portuguese in 1531 and ceded to them (1539) by the Shar of Gujarat. The island of Diu, captured in 1534, lies off the southeast coast of Kathiawar (Gujarat); there is a small coastal area. Former Portuguese forts on either side of the entrance to the Gulf of Cambay, in Dec. 1961 the territories were occupied by India and incorporated into the Indian Union; they were administered as one unit together with Goa, to which they were attached until 30 May 1987, when Goa was separated from them and became a state.

TERRITORY AND POPULATION

The territory has an area of 112 sq. km and a population of 158,204 at the 2001 census. Density, 1,413 sq. km. Daman has an area of 72 sq. km, population (2001) 113,989; Diu, 40 sq. km, population 44,215. Daman is the capital of the territory. The main language spoken is Gujarati.

The chief towns are (with 2001 populations) Daman (35,770) and Diu (21,578).

Daman and Diu have been governed as parts of a Union Territory since Dec. 1961, becoming the whole of that Territory on 30 May 1987. There are two districts.

SOCIAL STATISTICS

Growth rate 1991–2001, 55·73%.

CURRENT ADMINISTRATION

Administrator: Satya Gopal.

ECONOMY

The main activities are tourism, fishing and tapping the toddy palm (preparing palm tree sap for consumption). In Daman there is rice-growing, some wheat and dairying. Diu has fine tourist beaches, grows coconuts and pearl millet, and processes salt.

Budget

The budget for 2000–01 shows revenue receipts of Rs 713·0m. and revenue expenditure of Rs 553·5m.

ENERGY AND NATURAL RESOURCES

Electricity

In Sept. 2008 all 23 inhabited villages had electricity. There was an installed capacity of 69 MW in Oct. 2008.

SOCIAL INSTITUTIONS

Education

In 2001, 78·2% of the population were literate (86·8% of men and 65·6% of women). In 1996–97 there were 53 primary schools with

14,531 students, 20 middle schools with 6,834 students, 20 high schools with 3,220 students and 3 higher secondary schools with 1,202 students. There is a degree college and a polytechnic.

RELIGION

Numbers of religious followers (2001 census): Hindus, 141,901 (90% of the population), with some Muslims and Christians.

Delhi

GENERAL DETAILS

Delhi became a Union Territory on 1 Nov. 1956 and was designated the National Capital Territory in 1995.

TERRITORY AND POPULATION

The territory forms an enclave near the eastern frontier of Haryana and the western frontier of Uttar Pradesh in north India. Delhi has an area of 1,483 sq. km. Its population (2001 census) is 13,850,507 (density per sq. km, 9,340). Growth rate 1991–2001, 47·02%. In the rural area of Delhi there are 231 villages and 27 census towns. They are distributed in five community development blocks.

CONSTITUTION AND GOVERNMENT

The Lieut.-Governor is the Administrator. Under the New Delhi Municipal Act 1994 New Delhi Municipal Council is nominated by central government and replaces the former New Delhi Municipal Committee.

RECENT ELECTIONS

Elections for the 70-member Legislative Assembly were held on 29 Nov. 2008. The Indian National Congress won 42 seats (47 in 2003); Bharatiya Janata Party, 23 (20 in 2003); Bahujan Samaj Party, 2 (none in 2003); others, 2 (three in 2003). The INC won a by-election held on 13 Dec. 2008, bringing their total to 43 seats.

CURRENT ADMINISTRATION

Lieut.-Governor: Tejendra Khanna (took office on 9 April 2007).
Chief Minister: Sheila Dikshit (took office on 3 Dec. 1998).

ECONOMY

Budget

Estimates for 2003–04 show revenue receipts of Rs 98,000m. and expenditure of Rs 98,000m.

ENERGY AND NATURAL RESOURCES

Electricity

In Sept. 2008 all 158 inhabited villages had electricity. The installed capacity was 3,677 MW in Oct. 2008.

Minerals

The Union Territory has deposits of kaolin (china clay), quartzite and fire clay.

Agriculture

The contribution to the economy is not significant. In 2003–04 about 41,500 ha. were cropped (of which 22,700 ha. were irrigated). Animal husbandry is increasing and mixed farms are common. Chief crops are wheat, bajra, paddy, sugarcane, gram, jowar and vegetables. Buffaloes are kept as a source of milk; pigs and goats are kept for meat.

INDUSTRY

The modern city is the largest commercial centre in northern India and an important industrial centre. Since 1947 a large number of industrial units have been established; these include factories for the manufacture of razor blades, sports goods, electronic goods, bicycles and parts, plastic and PVC goods including footwear, textiles, chemicals, fertilizers, medicines, hosiery, leather goods, soft drinks and hand tools. The largest single industry is the manufacture of garments. There are also metal forging, casting, galvanizing, electro-plating and printing enterprises. The number of industrial units functioning was about 126,000 in 1996–97; average number of workers employed was 1·14m. Production was worth Rs 63,100m. and investment was about Rs 25,240m. in 1996–97.

Some traditional handicrafts, for which Delhi was formerly famous, still flourish; among them are ivory carving, miniature painting, gold and silver jewellery and papier mâché work. The handwoven textiles of Delhi are particularly fine; this craft is being successfully revived.

Delhi is a major market for manufactures, imports and agricultural goods; there are specialist fruit and vegetable, food grain, fodder, cloth, bicycle, hosiery, dry fruit and general markets.

COMMUNICATIONS

Roads

Five national highways pass through the city. There were (2000–01) 3,456,579 registered motor vehicles. There were 41,483 buses in 2000–01.

Rail

Delhi is an important rail junction with three main stations: New Delhi, Delhi Junction and Hazrat Nizamuddin. There is an electric ring railway for commuters (route-km in 1995–96, 214). The first of three lines of the Delhi metro system opened in 2002: when complete it will consist of 34·5 km subway, 35·5 km elevated and 111 km surface running.

Civil Aviation

Indira Gandhi International Airport operates international flights; Palam airport operates internal flights.

SOCIAL INSTITUTIONS

Education

The proportion of literate people to the total population was 81·7% at the 2001 census (87·3% of males and 74·7% of females). In 2003–04 there were 2,126 primary schools with 924,493 students and 22,930 teachers, 681 middle schools with 230,362 students and 9,192 teachers, 1,678 high schools and higher secondary schools with 1,747,884 students and 59,064 teachers. In 1996–97 there were nine engineering and technology colleges, nine medical colleges and 25 polytechnics.

The University of Delhi was founded in 1922; it had 78 affiliated colleges in 2002–03 and 189,332 students in 1994–95. There are also Jawaharlal Nehru University, Indira Gandhi National Open University, the Jamia Millia Islamia University, the Guru Gobind Singh Indraprastha University, Jamia Hamdard University and Shri Lal Bahadur Shastri Rashtriya Sanskrit Vidyapeeth University; the Indian Institute of Technology at Hauz Khas; the Indian Agricultural Research Institute at Pusa; the All India Institute of Medical Science at Ansari Nagar and the Indian Institute of Public Administration are the other important institutions.

Health

In 2001 there were 11 government hospitals plus 71 private hospitals, 167 government dispensaries plus 489 other dispensaries, 73 mobile health clinics and 64 school health clinics.

RELIGION

At the 2001 census Hindus numbered 11,358,049; Muslims, 1,623,520; Sikhs, 555,602; Jains, 155,122; Christians, 130,319.

CULTURE

Press

Delhi publishes major daily newspapers, including the *Times of India*, *Hindustan Times*, *The Hindu*, *Indian Express*, *National Herald*, *Patriot*, *Economic Times*, *The Pioneer*, *The Observer of Business and Politics*, *Financial Express*, *Statesman*, *Asian Age* and *Business Standard* (all in English); *Nav Bharat Times*, *Rashtriya Sahara*, *Jansatta* and *Hindustan* (all in Hindi); and three Urdu dailies.

Lakshadweep

The territory consists of an archipelago of 36 islands (ten inhabited), about 300 km off the west coast of Kerala. It was constituted a Union Territory in 1956 as the Laccadive, Minicoy and Amindivi Islands, and renamed in Nov. 1973. The total area of the islands is 32 sq. km. The northern portion is called the Amindivis. The remaining islands are called the Laccadives (except Minicoy Island). The inhabited islands are: Androth (the largest), Amini, Agatti, Bitra, Chetlat, Kadmat, Kalpeni, Kavaratti, Kiltan and Minicoy. Androth is 4·8 sq. km, and is nearest to Kerala. An Advisory Committee associated with the Union Home Minister and an Advisory Council to the Administrator assist in the administration of the islands; these are constituted annually. Population (2001 census), 60,650, nearly all Muslims. Density, 1,895 per sq. km; growth rate 1991–2001, 17·23%. The language is Malayalam, but the language in Minicoy is Mahl. Budget for 2000–01 showed revenue of Rs 90·3m. and expenditure of Rs 1,370m. Installed electric capacity (1998) 8,120 kW. In Sept. 2008 all eight inhabited villages had electricity. A solar power plant is under construction at Kadmat and wind generated plants at Kavaratti and Agatti. Guaranteeing supplies of potable water is problematic in most of the islands. Rain water harvesting schemes have been introduced as well as desalination plants. There are several small factories processing fibre from coconut husks: in 2002 these employed 316 workers. There are two handicraft training centres. The major industry is fishing—in 1999 there were 375 registered fishing boats. The principal catches are tuna and shark. Tuna is canned at a factory at Minicoy. There is an experimental pearl culture scheme at the uninhabited island of Bangarem. In 2001, 86·7% of the population were literate (92·5% of men and 80·5% of women). There were, in 1996–97, nine high schools (2,043 students) and nine nursery schools (1,197 students), 19 junior basic schools (9,015 students), four senior basic schools (4,797 students) and two junior colleges. There are two hospitals and four primary health centres plus 14 health sub-centres. At the 2001 census Muslims numbered 57,903 (95% of the population). The staple products are copra and fish; coconut is the only major crop. Headquarters of administration, Kavaratti, population 10,113 (2001 census), on Kavaratti Island. An airport, with Vayudoot services, opened on Agatti Island in April 1988. The islands are also served by ship from the mainland and have helicopter inter-island services. There are two catamaran-type high-speed inter-island ferries and four barges. The islands have 253 km of roads, of which 124 km have paved surfaces. The islands have great tourist potential.

Administrator: B. V. Selvaraj (took office on 22 Dec. 2006).

Puducherry

GENERAL DETAILS

Formerly the chief French settlement in India, Puducherry (known as Pondicherry until 2006) was founded by the French in 1673, taken by the Dutch in 1693 and restored to the French in 1699. The English took it in 1761, restored it in 1765, retook it in 1778, restored it a second time in 1785, retook it a third time in 1793 and finally restored it to the French in 1816. Administration was transferred to India on 1 Nov. 1954. A Treaty of Cession (together with Karaikal, Mahé and Yanam) was signed on 28 May 1956; instruments of ratification were signed on 16 Aug. 1962 from which date (by the 14th amendment to the Indian Constitution) Pondicherry, comprising the four territories, became a Union Territory.

TERRITORY AND POPULATION

The territory is composed of enclaves on the Coromandel Coast of Tamil Nadu and Andhra Pradesh, with Mahé forming two enclaves on the coast of Kerala. The total area of Puducherry is 480 sq. km, divided into 11 enclaves that are grouped into four Districts. On Tamil Nadu coast: Puducherry (290 sq. km; population, 2001 census, 735,332), Karaikal (161; 170,791). On Kerala coast: Mahé (9; 36,828). On Andhra Pradesh coast (although the enclave lies back from the shore but at no point does its territory touch the coast): Yanam (20; 31,394). Total population (2001 census), 974,345; density, 2,030 per sq. km. Puducherry Municipality had (2001) 220,865 inhabitants and the urban agglomeration had 505,959 inhabitants. The principal languages spoken are Tamil, Telugu, Malayalam, French and English.

SOCIAL STATISTICS

Growth rate 1991–2001, 20·62%. In 2001 the birth rate was 17·9 per 1,000 and the infant mortality rate was 23 per 1,000 live births.

CONSTITUTION AND GOVERNMENT

By the government of Union Territories Act 1963 Puducherry is governed by a Lieut.-Governor, appointed by the President, and a Council of Ministers responsible to a Legislative Assembly.

RECENT ELECTIONS

In the elections of 3 and 8 May 2006 the Indian National Congress won 10 seats, followed by the Dravida Munnetra Kazhagam with 7, the All India Anna Dravida Munnetra Kazhagam 3, the Pudhucherry Munnetra Congress 3, Pattali Makkal Katchi 2, Communist Party of India 1, Marumalarchi Dravida Munnetra Kazhagam 1 and ind. 3.

CURRENT ADMINISTRATION

Lieut.-Governor: Iqbal Singh; b. 1945 (took office on 27 July 2009).

Chief Minister: V. Vaithilingam; b. 1950 (took office on 4 Sept. 2008).

ECONOMY

Budget

Budget estimates for 2000–01 showed expenditure of Rs 8,534·7m. Total expenditure Rs 8,304·2m.

ENERGY AND NATURAL RESOURCES

Electricity

Power is bought from neighbouring states. In Sept. 2008 all 92 inhabited villages had electricity. There was an installed capacity of 257 MW in Oct. 2008.

Agriculture
Nearly 45% of the population is engaged in agriculture and allied pursuits; 90% of the cultivated area is irrigated. The main food crop is rice. Foodgrain production, 58,785 tonnes in 2003. Rice production, 2003, 57,514 tonnes from 24,142 ha. Principal cash crops are sugarcane (209,496 tonnes in 2003) and groundnuts; minor food crops include cotton, ragi, bajra and pulses.

Fisheries
In 2003 the marine catch was 40,105 tonnes. There was also a prawn catch of 4,310 tonnes. In 2005 there were 20,400 people working in fishing and related activities.

INDUSTRY
In March 2003 there were 55 large and 139 medium-scale enterprises manufacturing items such as textiles, sugar, cotton yarn, spirits and beer, potassium chlorate, rice bran oil, vehicle parts, soap, amino acids, paper, plastics, steel ingots, washing machines, glass and tin containers and bio polymers. These factories employed 25,095 people. There were also 6,876 small industrial units (2003) engaged in varied manufacturing.

COMMUNICATIONS
Roads
There were (2002–03) 2,498 km of roads of which 2,114 km were surfaced. Motor vehicles (March 2003) 293,248.

Rail
Puducherry is connected to Villupuram Junction. Route-km in 2001, 38 km.

Civil Aviation
The nearest main airport is Chennai.

SOCIAL INSTITUTIONS
Education
In 2001, 81·2% of the population were literate (88·6% of men and 73·9% of women). There were, in 2000–01, 223 pre-primary schools (22,462 pupils), 337 primary schools (38,405), 110 middle schools (34,034), 128 high schools (65,451) and 65 higher secondary schools (76,726). There were (2000–01) eight general education colleges, three medical colleges, a law college, five engineering colleges, an agricultural college and a dental college, and five polytechnics. Pondicherry University had around 1,600 students in 2005.

Health
There were 14 hospitals in 2004 (with 3,064 beds); and 39 primary health centres, 75 sub-centres and four community health centres in 2001.

RELIGION
At the 2001 census Hindus numbered 845,449; Christians, 67,688; Muslims, 59,358.

INDONESIA

Republik Indonesia
(Republic of Indonesia)

Capital: Jakarta
Population estimate, 2010: 232·52m.
GDP per capita, 2007: (PPP$) 3,712
HDI/world rank: 0·734/111

KEY HISTORICAL EVENTS

The Indonesian archipelago was populated from the north from around 3000 BC. Indian scholars described the Dvipantera civilization of Java and Sumatra as early as 200 BC and Indian-influenced Hindu kingdoms began to appear in the west of the archipelago from the 1st century AD. Small maritime trading settlements evolved into Srivijaya, a Buddhist Malay kingdom centred on southeast Sumatra. The Srivijaya empire controlled trade between India and China through the Melaka strait and by the late 7th century it had expanded to encompass much of Sumatra, the Malay peninsula and western Java. Other Indianized kingdoms developed in central Java, including Mataram (8th–10th centuries) and Mahayana (9th century).

Power shifted to east Java, culminating in the Majapahit empire (founded by Wijaya in 1293 and developed by Gaja Mada), which controlled much of present-day Indonesia. Islam was brought to northern Sumatra by Arab merchants from the 7th century but spread only gradually until the rise of the sultanate of Melaka from the early 15th century. The north Javanese coastal kingdoms that converted to Islam competed with the Majapahit empire, contributing to its decline by the early 16th century.

Portuguese forces, led by Afonso de Albuquerque, having conquered the sultanate of Melaka in 1511 attempted to control the spice trade, although local powers including Aceh (north Sumatra) and Makassar (Sulawesi) competed by opening new routes. Dutch mariners arrived in west Java in 1596 and Jan Pietersoon Coen established a base on Java (Batavia, which became Jakarta) in 1619. The capture of Melaka in 1641 heralded 150 years of Dutch control of the spice trade through its United East India Company (VOC).

Following the VOC's collapse at the end of the 18th century and after a short period of British rule under Thomas Stamford Raffles, the Dutch state took control of the archipelago. The Anglo-Dutch Treaty of 1824 delineated the border between British Malaya and the Dutch East Indies. Between 1825–50 the Dutch suppressed a rebellion on Java, initially led by Prince Diponegoro, and partly fuelled by opposition to the 'Cultivation System' whereby locals had to devote a percentage of their land to cultivating government-approved export crops. The Sarekat Islam (Islamic Union), founded in 1912, was the country's first major nationalist movement. In March 1942 Japanese forces invaded and began to dismantle the Dutch power base. The Indonesian nationalist leaders Sukarno and Mohammad Hatta worked with the Japanese occupiers whilst pushing for independence. On 17 Aug. 1945, two days after Japan's surrender, Sukarno and Hatta proclaimed an independent republic with Sukarno as its president, although the Netherlands did not concede unconditional sovereignty until 27 Dec. 1949.

In 1960 President Sukarno dismissed parliament after a dispute over the government's budget and dissolved political parties. In their place he set up the National Front and the Provisional People's Consultative Assembly. On 11–12 March 1966 the military commanders under the leadership of Lieut.-Gen. Suharto seized executive power, leaving President Sukarno as head of state. The Communist party, which had twice attempted to overthrow the government, was outlawed. On 22 Feb. 1967 Sukarno handed over all his powers to Gen. Suharto. Re-elected president at five-year intervals, on the final occasion on 10 March 1998, Suharto presided over a booming economy but one that was characterized by corruption and cronyism.

These weaknesses became apparent in 1997 when a failure of economic confidence spread from Japan across Asia. By May 1998 food prices had trebled and riots broke out in Jakarta. The risk of society fragmenting along ethnic and religious lines was emphasized by the sufferings of the Chinese community. President Suharto was forced to stand down on 21 May 1998 and was succeeded by his vice-president, Bacharuddin Jusuf Habibie, who promised political and economic reforms. Continuing protest centred on the Suharto family, which still exercised control over large parts of the economy. In Aug. 1999 Timor-Leste, the former Portuguese colony that Indonesia invaded in 1975, voted for independence, a move that was eventually approved by the Indonesian parliament after violent clashes between independence supporters and pro-Indonesian militia groups. It gained independence on 20 May 2002.

Abdurrahman Wahid was elected president by the People's Consultative Assembly in Oct. 1999. He oversaw some reform and economic growth but was forced to step down amid allegations of corruption on 29 Jan 2001. His vice-president, Megawati

Sukarnoputri, took control and assumed the presidency on 23 July 2001. In Oct. 2002 around 200 people died in a car-bomb explosion outside a nightclub in Bali. Jemaah Islamiyah, an extremist group with alleged links to Al-Qaeda, was implicated.

Indonesia's first direct presidential election took place in Sept. 2004 and Susilo Bambang Yudhoyono beat Megawati in a runoff vote. On 26 Dec. 2004 northwest Sumatra was hit by a devastating tsunami. The death toll in Indonesia was put at 166,000, mostly in Aceh. However, the disaster revived the peace process, initiated in late 2002 between the government and the separatist Free Aceh Movement (GAM). Accords signed in Helsinki, Finland in Aug. 2005 created a framework for a military stand-down on both sides.

TERRITORY AND POPULATION

Indonesia, with a land area of 1,890,754 sq. km (730,020 sq. miles), consists of 17,507 islands (6,000 of which are inhabited) extending about 3,200 miles east to west through three time-zones (East, Central and West Indonesian Standard time) and 1,250 miles north to south. The largest islands are Sumatra, Java, Kalimantan (Indonesian Borneo), Sulawesi (Celebes) and Papua, formerly West Papua (the western part of New Guinea). Most of the smaller islands except Madura and Bali are grouped together. The two largest groups of islands are Maluku (the Moluccas) and Nusa Tenggara (the Lesser Sundas). On the island of Timor, Indonesia is bounded in the east by Timor-Leste.

Population at the 2000 census was 206,264,595; density, 109·1 per sq. km. Indonesia has the fourth largest population in the world, after China, India and the USA. In 2005, 51·9% of the population were rural

The UN gives an estimated population for 2010 of 232·52m.; density, 123 per sq. km.

Area, population and chief towns of the provinces, autonomous districts and major islands:

	Area (in sq. km)	*Population (2000 census)*	*Chief town*	*Population (2000 census)*
Bali	5,633	3,151,162	Denpasar	533,252
Nusa Tenggara Barat	20,153	4,009,261	Mataram	317,374
Nusa Tenggara Timur	47,351	3,952,279	Kupang	237,000[1]
Bali and Nusa Tenggara	73,137	11,112,702		
Banten	8,651	8,098,780	Serang	—[2]
DKI Jakarta[3]	664	8,389,443	Jakarta	8,389,443
Jawa Barat	34,597	35,729,537	Bandung	2,138,066
Jawa Tengah	32,549	31,228,940	Semarang	1,427,207
Jawa Timur	47,922	34,783,640	Surabaya	2,610,477
Yogyakarta[3]	3,186	3,122,268	Yogyakarta	397,431
Java	127,569	121,352,608		
Kalimantan Barat	146,807	4,034,198	Pontianak	473,360
Kalimantan Selatan	43,546	2,985,240	Banjarmasin	530,908
Kalimantan Tengah	153,564	1,857,000	Palangkaraya	160,572
Kalimantan Timur	230,277	2,455,120	Samarinda	523,119
Kalimantan	574,194	11,331,558		
Maluku	46,975	1,205,539	Ambon	205,664
Maluku Utara	30,895	785,059	Ternate	152,000[1]
Papua[4]	365,466	2,220,934	Jayapura	166,201
Papua Barat[4]	—	—	Manokwari	—[2]
Maluku and Papua	443,336	4,211,532		
Gorontalo	12,215	835,044	Gorontalo	135,087
Sulawesi Barat[5]	—	—	Mamuju	—[2]
Sulawesi Selatan[5]	62,365	8,059,627	Makassar	1,101,933
Sulawesi Tengah	63,678	2,218,435	Palu	264,000[1]
Sulawesi Tenggara	38,140	1,821,284	Kendari	200,000[1]
Sulawesi Utara	15,273	2,012,098	Menado	382,451
Sulawesi	191,671	14,946,488		
Aceh[3, 6]	51,937	3,930,905	Banda Aceh	215,542
Bangka-Belitung	16,171	900,197	Pangkalpinang	125,835
Bengkulu	19,789	1,567,432	Bengkulu	281,605
Jambi	53,437	2,413,846	Jambi[7]	417,568
Kepulauan Riau[8]	—	—	Tanjung Pinang	—[2]
Lampung	35,384	6,741,439	Bandar Lampung	743,127
Riau[8]	94,560	4,957,627	Pakanbaru	587,842
Sumatera Barat	42,899	4,248,931	Padang	716,283
Sumatera Selatan	93,083	6,899,675	Palembang	1,458,664
Sumatera Utara	73,587	11,649,655	Medan	1,911,997
Sumatra	480,847	43,309,707		

[1]Estimate. [2]Province created since 2000 census. [3]Autonomous District. [4]Papua Barat (previously named Irian Jaya Barat), formerly part of Papua, was created in 2003. [5]Sulawesi Barat, formerly part of Sulawesi Selatan, was created in 2004. [6]The population of Aceh was reduced by about 166,000 as a result of the tsunami that struck Indonesia on 26 Dec. 2004. [7]Formerly Telanaipura. [8]Kepulauan Riau, formerly part of Riau, was created in 2002.

The capital, Jakarta, had an estimated population of 8·84m. in 2005. Other major cities (2005 estimates in 1m.): Surabaya, 2·61; Bandung, 2·29; Medan, 2·03; Bekasi, 1·94; Tangerang, 1·45; Semarang, 1·35.

The principal ethnic groups are the Acehnese, Bataks and Minangkabaus in Sumatra, the Javanese and Sundanese in Java, the Madurese in Madura, the Balinese in Bali, the Sasaks in Lombok, the Menadonese, Minahasans, Torajas and Buginese in Sulawesi, the Dayaks in Kalimantan, the Irianese in Papua and the Ambonese in the Moluccas. There were some 6m. Chinese resident in 1991.

Bahasa Indonesia (Indonesian) is the official language; Dutch is spoken as a colonial inheritance.

SOCIAL STATISTICS

Estimated births, 2001, 4,620,000; deaths, 1,533,000. 2001 birth rate, 22·0 per 1,000 population; death rate, 7·3. Life expectancy in 2007 was 68·5 years for men and 72·5 for women. Annual population growth rate, 1992–2002, 1·4%. Infant mortality, 2005, 28 per 1,000 live births; fertility rate, 2004, 2·3 births per woman.

CLIMATE

Conditions vary greatly over this spread of islands, but generally the climate is tropical monsoon, with a dry season from June to Sept. and a wet one from Oct. to April. Temperatures are high all the year and rainfall varies according to situation on lee or windward shores. Jakarta, Jan. 78°F (25·6°C), July 78°F (25·6°C). Annual rainfall 71" (1,775 mm). Padang, Jan. 79°F (26·1°C), July 79°F (26·1°C). Annual rainfall 177" (4,427 mm). Surabaya, Jan. 79°F (26·1°C), July 78°F (25·6°C). Annual rainfall 51" (1,285 mm).

On 26 Dec. 2004 an undersea earthquake centred off Sumatra caused a huge tsunami that flooded large areas along the coast of northwestern Indonesia resulting in 166,000 deaths. In total there were more than 225,000 deaths in 14 countries.

CONSTITUTION AND GOVERNMENT

The constitution originally dates from Aug. 1945 and was in force until 1949; it was restored on 5 July 1959.

The political system is based on *pancasila*, in which deliberations lead to a consensus. There is a 560-member *Dewan Perwakilan Rakyat* (House of People's Representatives), with members elected for a five-year term by proportional representation in multi-member constituencies. The constitution was changed on 10 Aug. 2002 to allow for direct elections for the president and the vice-president.

There is no limit to the number of presidential terms. Although predominantly a Muslim country, the constitution protects the religious beliefs of non-Muslims.

National Anthem

'Indonesia, tanah airku' ('Indonesia, our native land'); words and tune by W. R. Supratman.

GOVERNMENT CHRONOLOGY

Presidents since 1949. (Golkar = Party of the Functional Groups; PD = Democratic Party; PDIP = Indonesian Democratic Party–Struggle; PKB = National Awakening Party; PNI = Indonesian National Party)

1949–67	PNI	(Ahmed) Sukarno
1967–98	Golkar	(Mohamed) Suharto
1998–99	Golkar	Bacharuddin Jusuf Habibie
1999–2001	PKB	Abdurrahman Wahid
2001–04	PDIP	Megawati Sukarnoputri
2004–	PD	Susilo Bambang Yudhoyono

RECENT ELECTIONS

Elections to the House of People's Representatives were held on 9 April 2009. The Democrat Party (PD) won 20·9% of the vote (148 of 560 seats), the Party of the Functional Groups (Golkar) 14·5% (108), the Indonesian Democratic Party–Struggle (PDIP) 14·0% (93), the Prosperous Justice Party 7·9% (59), the National Mandate Party 6·0% (42), the United Development Party 5·3% (39), the National Awakening Party 4·9% (26), the Great Indonesia Movement Party 4·5% (30) and the People's Conscience Party 3·8% (15).

In the presidential election of 8 July 2009 incumbent Susilo Bambang Yudhoyono (PD) won 60·8% of the vote, former president Megawati Sukarnoputri (PDIP) 26·8% and vice-president Jusuf Kalla (Golkar) 12·4%.

CURRENT ADMINISTRATION

President: Susilo Bambang Yudhoyono; b. 1949 (PD; sworn in 20 Oct. 2004).

Vice-President: Boediono.

In March 2010 the cabinet was composed as follows:

Co-ordinating Ministers: (Political, Legal and Security Affairs) Djoko Suyanto; *(Economic Affairs)* Hatta Radjasa; *(People's Welfare)* Agung Laksono.

Minister of Agriculture: Suswono. *Culture and Tourism:* Jero Wacik. *Defence:* Purnomo Yusgiantoro. *Energy and Mineral Resources:* Darwin Zahedy Saleh. *Finance:* Sri Mulyani Indrawati. *Foreign Affairs:* Marty Natalegawa. *Forestry:* Zulkifli Hasan. *Health:* Endang Rahayu Setyaningsih. *Home Affairs:* Gamawan Fauzi. *Industry:* Mohamad Suleman Hidayat. *Justice and Human Rights:* Patrialis Akbar. *Manpower and Transmigration:* Abdul Muhaimin Iskandar. *Maritime Affairs and Fisheries:* Fadel Muhammad. *National Education:* Mohammad Nuh. *Public Works:* Joko Kirmanto. *Religious Affairs:* Suryadharma Ali. *Social Affairs:* Salim Segaf Al Jufrie. *State Secretary:* Sudi Silalahi. *Trade:* Mari Elka Pangestu. *Transportation:* Freddy Numberi.

Government Website: http://www.indonesia.go.id

CURRENT LEADERS

Susilo Bambang Yudhoyono

Position
President

Introduction
Retired general Susilo Bambang Yudhoyono, known widely by his acronym SBY, succeeded Megawati Sukarnoputri as president of Indonesia on 20 Oct. 2004. In the country's first direct presidential election he polled 61% of an estimated 125m. votes and he became the first incumbent to be re-elected in July 2009.

Early Life
Susilo Bambang Yudhoyono was born on 9 Sept. 1949 in the small town of Pacitan, in the east of the Indonesian island of Java. His family were observant Muslims and he attended a traditional *pesantren* (Muslim boarding school). He graduated from Indonesia's military academy in 1973 and joined the army, which was then, with Gen. Suharto as president, the country's dominant authority. He served as a senior officer in Indonesia's 1975 invasion of Timor-Leste, then a Portuguese colony. Gen. Suharto's 'New Order' political system was characterized by a strongly anti-communist foreign policy and relatively good relations with the USA. Yudhoyono travelled to the USA in 1976 and 1982, attending military training programmes at Fort Benning, Georgia. He later took a masters degree in business management from Webster University in Missouri and has since described the USA as his 'second home'. Between 1984–87 Yudhoyono returned to Timor-Leste and commanded Battalion 744 in the city of Dili. By the mid-1990s he had risen through the ranks to become chief-of-staff in the Jakarta command. Questions have been asked about his knowledge of a raid by security forces on the Jakarta offices of the Indonesian Democratic Party (PDI) on 27 July 1996 (then chaired by Megawati Sukarnoputri), which left five dead and 23 missing.

In 1996 Yudhoyono served as chief military observer with the United Nations force in Bosnia. Two years later, with Indonesia in turmoil following the ousting of President Suharto in March 1998, he left the army and was appointed the minister for mining and energy in the administration of Abdurrahman Wahid. When the Muslim cleric was succeeded as president in 2001 by Mrs Megawati, daughter of former president Sukarno, Yudhoyono joined her cabinet as chief security minister. He was praised for the way he handled the aftermath of the Oct. 2002 Bali bombing that killed 202 people. He subsequently helped draft Indonesia's first counter-terrorist law and attempted to broker a peace agreement with separatist rebels in the historically troubled province of Aceh in Sumatra in 2003, which collapsed in May of that year. In March 2004 Yudhoyono resigned from Megawati's increasingly unpopular cabinet to establish the Democratic Party (PD). In the first round of elections in early April (for choosing the members of parliament and three tiers of local officials) the PD had a strong showing. On 5 July, when Yudhoyono, along with his running mate Jusuf Kalla—a business tycoon with ties to many of the country's Islamic clerics—fought in the country's first direct presidential elections, no candidate won more than 50% of the vote. This forced a run-off election between Yudhoyono and Megawati on 20 Sept. which Yudhoyono won with 60·9% of the vote. He was officially sworn in as president on 20 Oct. 2004.

Career in Office

In interviews with the international media Yudhoyono vowed to fight terrorism and eradicate corruption in his five-year term. He also promised to restore Indonesian institutions and the rule of law and to rebuild the economy. The president set himself the goal of creating jobs for 50m. unemployed Indonesians. He also pledged to repair the often fractious relationship with Australia. In the aftermath of the Indian Ocean tsunami of 26 Dec. 2004, which is estimated to have killed some 166,000 people on the Indonesian island of Sumatra, Yudhoyono was quick to accept aid and expertise from the international community. Handling relief and reconstruction was an opportunity for him to be a more decisive and approachable leader than his predecessor. It was also an opportunity for him to improve relations between Jakarta and Aceh—the region worst-affected by the tsunami—and in Aug. 2005 his government signed a peace agreement with separatist leaders granting greater political autonomy to the province. Elections for a provincial governor and district officials in Aceh took place in Dec. 2006.

Yudhoyono's government was also confronted by renewed terrorism, as suicide bombers again targeted the tourist resort of Bali in Oct. 2005 killing 19 people, and by further natural disasters. An earthquake in May 2006 and another tsunami in July killed around 6,500 people on Java, floods in Jakarta in Feb. 2007 left an estimated 340,000 people homeless, another earthquake in Sumatra the following month killed more than 50 and, in Sept. 2009, an earthquake off the coast of Sumatra left more than 1,000 dead. In Nov. 2008 three Islamic terrorists convicted for their part in the Bali bombing in 2002 were executed by firing squad. However, extremist activity has continued, notably the launching of suicide bomb attacks in July 2009 on two luxury hotels in Jakarta which killed nine people and injured at least 50 more.

By 2008 Yudhoyono's political popularity was being undermined by continuing unemployment, rising prices and a cut in fuel subsidies, despite increased spending on anti-poverty programmes and significant progress in his anti-corruption drive. Nevertheless, in parliamentary elections in April 2009 his Democrat Party emerged as the largest party and in July he was returned to office with 60·8% of the vote in the presidential poll.

Following a final report in July 2008 by a joint investigative commission that blamed Indonesia for human rights violations in the run-up to Timor-Leste's independence in 2002, Yudhoyono expressed the Indonesian government's deep regret but did not apologize.

DEFENCE

There is selective conscription for two years. Defence expenditure in 2006 totalled US$3,645m. (US$16 per capita), representing 1·0% of GDP. Real-term military spending was cut by 7% in 2008.

Army

Army strength in 2007 was estimated at 233,000 with a strategic reserve (KOSTRAD) of 40,000 and further potential mobilizable reserves of 400,000.

There is a paramilitary police some 280,000 strong; and a part-time local auxiliary force, KAMRA (People's Security), which numbers around 40,000.

Navy

The Navy in 2007 numbered about 45,000, including some 20,000 marines and around 1,000 in Naval Aviation. Combatant strength in 2007 included two diesel submarines and 11 frigates.

The Navy's principal command is split between the Western Fleet, at Teluk Ratai (Jakarta), and the Eastern Fleet, at Surabaya.

Air Force

Personnel (2007) 24,000. There were 94 combat capable aircraft, including A-4s, F-16s, F-5s and British Aerospace *Hawks*.

INTERNATIONAL RELATIONS

Indonesia was in dispute with Malaysia over sovereignty of two islands in the Celebes Sea. Both countries agreed to accept the Judgment of the International Court of Justice which decided in favour of Malaysia in Dec. 2002.

Indonesia is a member of the UN, World Bank, IMF and several other UN specialized agencies, WTO, Islamic Development Bank, OIC, Asian Development Bank, APEC, ASEAN, Mekong Group and Colombo Plan.

ECONOMY

Agriculture accounted for 12·9% of GDP in 2006, industry 47·0% and services 40·1%.

Overview

In the 1970s the economy was based on agriculture, fishing and forestry. Its main exports consisted of a few primary products such as crude oil, natural rubber, coconut oil, copra and tin. The fall of oil prices after 1983 encouraged industrialization. From the mid-1980s the strongest growth was in manufacturing which averaged 13% real annual growth in the half decade from 1984–88, according to the Economist Intelligence Unit (EIU). In 1991 the manufacturing share of GDP moved ahead of agriculture for the first time. The mining sector also grew strongly during this period, exploiting the country's vast mineral resources. Services grew in importance too, led by a push to develop tourism. By the first half of the 2000s the growth rates of the various sectors converged, with the EIU estimating that mining and manufacturing output grew between 6–7% and services and agriculture near 4% in 2004. However, an estimated 42·1% of the labour force was still employed in agriculture in 2006. Main export commodities are oil and gas and electrical appliances.

Indonesia was the country worst hit by the Asian financial crisis that began in 1997. The dual banking and foreign exchange crisis caused real GDP to contract by over 13% in 1998 while inflation surged by close to 60% and the debt-to-GDP ratio jumped. In response the Indonesian Bank Restructuring Agency (IBRA) was established to recapitalize state banks. Interest rates were increased radically to reduce inflation while regulatory, institutional and other reforms helped regain investor confidence. In 1999 the economy stabilized and in 2000 it resumed growth at a solid pace. Despite a strong recovery, growth performance did not match the 7·6% annual average in the half decade from 1992–96 or the 8·9% average in the half decade from 1987–91. However, the economy witnessed above 5% growth in 2004–06 and over 6%

in 2007 and 2008. As a consequence of the global financial crisis, growth slowed in 2009 but was still 4·5%. Domestic consumption has ensured growth despite the world crisis, albeit at a slower pace.

The IMF has urged Indonesia to accelerate privatization and financial sector reform in order to boost investment. It also encourages tax and labour market reforms, as well as the upgrading of infrastructure and the strengthening of the legal framework. Corruption is rife but there are encouraging signs, with major institutional reforms in the areas of governance and financial supervision and an investment law introduced in early 2007. In the last five years, public and external debt has been reduced by half.

Currency

The monetary unit is the *rupiah* (IDR) notionally of 100 *sen*. Inflation rates (based on IMF statistics):

1999	*2000*	*2001*	*2002*	*2003*	*2004*	*2005*	*2006*	*2007*	*2008*
20·7%	3·8%	11·5%	11·8%	6·8%	6·1%	10·5%	13·1%	6·0%	9·8%

In Aug. 2009 foreign exchange reserves were US$55,440m., gold reserves were 2·35m. troy oz and total money supply was 490,111bn. rupiahs.

Budget

The fiscal year used to start 1 April but since 2001 has been the calendar year. Revenue in 2005 was 495,444bn. rupiahs (tax revenue, 70·0%) and expenditure was 509,419bn. rupiahs (current expenditure, 58·5%).

The standard rate of VAT is 10% (reduced rate, 5%).

Performance

Real GDP growth rates (based on IMF statistics):

1999	*2000*	*2001*	*2002*	*2003*	*2004*	*2005*	*2006*	*2007*	*2008*
0·8%	5·4%	3·6%	4·5%	4·8%	5·0%	5·7%	5·5%	6·3%	6·1%

Real GDP growth in 2009 was 4·5% according to the Central Bureau of Statistics. The Asian economic crisis of 1997 affected Indonesia more than any other country, leading to a recession in 1998 when the economy shrank by 13·1%. In 2008 total GDP was US$514·4bn.

Banking and Finance

The Bank Indonesia, successor to De Javasche Bank established by the Dutch in 1828, was made the central bank of Indonesia on 1 July 1953. Its *Acting Governor* is Darmin Nasution. It had an original capital of 25m. rupiahs, a reserve fund of 18m. rupiahs and a special reserve of 84m. rupiahs. In Jan. 2000 independent auditors declared that the bank was technically bankrupt. In response the IMF stated that future loans would probably depend on recapitalization and an internal reorganization.

In 2003 there were 138 commercial banks, 26 regional government banks, 76 private national banks and 31 foreign banks and joint banks. The leading banks are Bank Mandiri (with assets of US$25·6bn. in June 2005), Bank Central Asia and Bank Rakyat Indonesia. All state banks are authorized to deal in foreign exchange.

The government owns one Savings Bank, Bank Tabungan Negara, and 1,000 Post Office Savings Banks. There are also over 3,500 rural and village savings banks and credit co-operatives. At least 16 banks closed in the wake of the 1997 financial crisis.

There is a stock exchange in Jakarta.

ENERGY AND NATURAL RESOURCES

Environment

Indonesia's carbon dioxide emissions from the consumption and flaring of fossil fuels in 2008 were the equivalent of 1·8 tonnes per capita.

Electricity

Installed capacity in 2004 was 26·1m. kW and production in 2003 totalled 101·38bn. kWh (11·07bn. kWh hydro-electric). Consumption per capita was 472 kWh in 2003. Indonesia's first nuclear power plant is scheduled to become operational by 2016.

Oil and Gas

The importance of oil in the economy is declining. The 2008 output of crude oil was 49·1m. tonnes, down from 76·5m. tonnes in 1995. Proven reserves in 2008 totalled 3·7bn. bbls. With domestic demand having surpassed production, Indonesia became a net importer of oil in 2005.

Natural gas production, 2008, was 69·7bn. cu. metres with 3,180bn. cu. metres of proven reserves. In Jan. 2001 a 640-km gas pipeline linking Indonesia's West Natuna field with Singapore came on stream. It is expected to provide Singapore with US$8bn. worth of natural gas over a 20-year period.

Minerals

The high cost of extraction means that little of the large mineral resources outside Java is exploited; however, there is copper mining in Papua, nickel mining and processing on Sulawesi, and aluminium smelting in northern Sumatra. Open-cast coal mining has been conducted since the 1890s, but since the 1970s coal production has been developed as an alternative to oil. Reserves are estimated at 28,000m. tonnes. Coal production (2004), 119·7m. tonnes. Other minerals: bauxite (2004), 1,331,000 tonnes; copper (2006), 818,000 tonnes (metal content); salt (2005 estimate), 680,000 tonnes; nickel (2006), 150,000 tonnes (metal content); tin (2006), 117,500 tonnes (metal content); silver (2005), 329 tonnes; gold (2005), 167 tonnes.

Agriculture

There were approximately 22·0m. ha. of arable land in 2007 and 15·5m. ha. of permanent crops. 7·89m. ha. were irrigated in 2005. Production (2003, in 1,000 tonnes): rice, 52,079; sugarcane, 25,600; cassava, 18,474; coconuts, 15,630; maize, 10,910; bananas, 4,312; palm kernels, 2,187; sweet potatoes, 1,998; natural rubber, 1,792; cabbage, 1,450; groundnuts, 1,377; copra, 1,272; potatoes, 851; onions, 780; oranges, 733; mangoes, 731; coffee, 702; soybeans, 672; green beans, 620; chillies and green peppers, 553. Annual nutmeg production is 6,000 tonnes, more than two-thirds of the world total. Indonesia is the world's largest producer of coconuts.

Livestock (2003): goats, 13·28m.; cattle, 11·40m.; sheep, 8·13m.; pigs, 6·35m.; buffaloes, 2·46m.; chickens, 1·29bn.; ducks, 48m. Only China has more chickens.

Forestry

In 2005 the area under forests was 88·50m. ha., or 48·8% of the total land area. The annual loss of 1,871,000 ha. between 2000 and 2005 was exceeded during the same period only in Brazil. In 2007, 103·42m. cu. metres of roundwood were cut.

Fisheries

In 2005 total catch was 4,381,260 tonnes, of which 4,049,640 tonnes were sea fish. Indonesia's fish catch was the fourth highest in 2005, behind China, Peru and the USA.

INDUSTRY

The largest companies in Indonesia by market capitalization in Feb. 2009 were: Telekom Indonesia (US$10·6bn.); Bank Central Asia (US$4·8bn.); and Bank Rakyat Indonesia (US$3·8bn.).

There are shipyards at Jakarta Raya, Surabaya, Semarang and Ambon. There are textile factories, large paper factories, match factories, automobile and bicycle assembly works, large construction works, tyre factories, glass factories, a caustic soda and other chemical factories. Production (2004 unless otherwise indicated, in 1,000 tonnes): cement (2000), 22,789; distillate fuel oil, 14,623; residual fuel oil, 10,995; petrol, 9,398; kerosene, 7,341; fertilizers (2002), 7,038; paper and paperboard (2001), 6,995;

palm oil (2000), 6,900; sugar (2002), 1,902; plywood (2001), 7·3m. cu. metres; 4,937,000 radio sets (1999); 804,000 TV sets (1998); 342,500 cars and lorries; 254·3bn. cigarettes (1999). Indonesia is the third largest producer of plywood after the USA and China.

Labour
In 2001 the labour force was 98,812,000. 43·8% of employed persons worked in agriculture, forestry, hunting and fisheries, 19·2% in trade, restaurants and hotels, 13·3% in manufacturing and 12·1% in community, social and personal services. National daily average wage, 1996, 4,073 rupiahs. Unemployment in 2001 was 8·1%.

Trade Unions
Workers have a constitutional right to organize and under a law passed in Feb. 2003 have a right to be paid during lawful strikes. Until the fall of Suharto in 1998 unions were expected to affiliate to the All Indonesia Trade Union (SPSI), which enjoyed government approval and was affiliated to the ruling party. Between 1994 and 1996 there were more than 2,000 strikes involving 1m. workers. In Feb. 2003 the Indonesian Trade Union Congress (KSPI), supported by the International Confederation of Free Trade Unions, was inaugurated. It represents 3·1m. members and encompasses 12 industrial federations.

INTERNATIONAL TRADE
Since 1992 foreigners have been permitted to hold 100% of the equity of new companies in Indonesia with more than US$50m. part capital, or situated in remote provinces. Foreign debt was US$138,300m. in 2005.

Pressure on Indonesia's currency and stock market led to an appeal to the IMF and World Bank for long-term support funds in Oct. 1997. A bail-out package worth US$38,000m. was eventually agreed on condition that Indonesia tightened financial controls and instituted reforms, including the establishment of an independent privatization board, liberalizing foreign investment, cutting import tariffs and phasing out export levies.

Imports and Exports
Imports and exports in US$1m.:

	2002	*2003*	*2004*	*2005*	*2006*
Imports f.o.b.	35,652	39,546	50,615	69,462	73,868
Exports f.o.b.	59,165	64,109	70,767	86,995	103,514

Principal import items: machinery and transport equipment, basic manufactures and chemicals. Principal export items: gas and oil, forestry products, manufactured goods, rubber, coffee, fishery products, coal, copper, tin, pepper, palm products and tea. Main import suppliers, 2004: Japan, 14·2%; Singapore, 11·2%; China, 9·5%. Main export markets, 2004: Japan, 15·9%; USA, 13·6%; Singapore, 9·3%.

COMMUNICATIONS
Roads
In 2006 there were 324,150 km of classified roads (27,668 km of highways or main roads), of which 54% was surfaced. Motor vehicles, 2005: passenger cars, 5,494,034; buses and coaches, 1,184,918; trucks and vans, 2,920,828; motorcycles, 28,556,498. There were 11,451 fatalities in road accidents in 2005.

Rail
In 2005 the national railways totalled 6,482 km of 1,067 mm gauge, comprising 3,012 km on Java (of which 565 km electrified), 1,348 km on Sumatra and 2,122 km which was non-operational. Passenger-km travelled in 2002 came to 21·3bn. and freight tonne-km to 5·0bn.

Civil Aviation
Garuda Indonesia is the state-owned national flag carrier. Merpati Nusantara Airlines is their domestic subsidiary. There are international airports at Jakarta (Sukarno-Hatta), Denpasar (on Bali), Medan (Sumatra), Pekanbaru (Sumatra), Ujung Pandang (Sulawesi), Manado (Sulawesi), Solo (Java) and Surabaya Juanda (Java). Jakarta is the busiest airport, in 2001 handling 11,192,000 passengers (6,685,000 on domestic flights) and 280,900 tonnes of freight. Denpasar handled 4,431,000 passengers in 2001 and Surabaya Juanda 2,380,000. In 2003 scheduled airline traffic of Indonesia-based carriers flew 211m. km, carrying 20,358,000 passengers (1,984,000 on international flights).

Shipping
There are 16 ports for ocean-going ships, the largest of which is Tanjung Priok, which serves the Jakarta area and has a container terminal. In 2002 cargo traffic at Tanjung Priok totalled 39·3m. tonnes. The national shipping company Pelajaran Nasional Indonesia (PELNI) maintains inter-island communications. Jakarta Lloyd maintains regular services between Jakarta, Amsterdam, Hamburg and London. In 1995 the merchant marine comprised 535 ocean-going ships totalling 4·13m. DWT. 95 vessels (36·22% of total tonnage) were registered under foreign flags. In 2002 total tonnage registered came to 3·72m. GRT, including oil tankers 827,000 GRT. In 2002 vessels totalling 361,246,000 net registered tons entered ports and vessels totalling 86,554,000 NRT cleared.

Telecommunications
In 2008 there were 30,378,000 main (fixed) telephone lines; mobile phone subscribers numbered 140,578,000 in 2008 (618·3 per 1,000 persons). There were 4·5m. PCs in use in 2006. Indonesia had 18·0m. internet users in 2008, up from 400,000 in 2000.

Postal Services
In 2003 there were 20,073 post offices.

SOCIAL INSTITUTIONS
Justice
There are around 250 district courts of first instance, 20 high courts of appeal and a Supreme Court of Justice (Mahkamah Agung) for the whole of Indonesia in Jakarta. Religious sharia courts with limited jurisdiction are also in place to handle civil cases between Muslim spouses.

The current legal system is a mixture of 'adat' (customary) law, Dutch colonial law and the national law that was brought in following independence in 1945. As in Dutch civil law, the rule of precedence does not apply.

The present criminal law has been in force since 1915 and is codified and based on European penal law. The death penalty is still in use; there were ten executions in 2008 (although none in 2009).

The population in penal institutions in mid-2005 was 99,946 (45 per 100,000 of national population).

Education
Adult literacy in 2004 was 90·4%. In 2007 there were 29,796,705 pupils and 1,583,589 teaching staff at primary schools, and 18,716,929 pupils and 1,434,874 teachers at secondary schools. There were 3,755,187 students in higher education in 2007 and 265,527 academic staff. The University of Indonesia in Jakarta, founded in 1849, is the leading institution in the tertiary sector. Other prominent institutions include the Gadjah Mada University (Universitas Gadjah Mada) in Yogyakarta, the Parahyangan Catholic University (Universitas Katolik Parahyangan) in Bandung, the Bandung Insitute of Technology (Institut Teknologi Bandung) and the Bogor Agricultural Institute (Institut Pertanian Bogor).

In 2007 public expenditure on education came to 3·6% of GNI and 17·5% of total government spending.

Health

In 2000 there were 34,347 doctors, 92,371 nurses, 11,547 midwives and 2,406 dentists. There were 1,162 hospitals in 2002, with a provision of six beds per 10,000 population.

Welfare

There are currently no unemployment benefits or family allowance programmes. Establishments with at least ten employees (or a monthly payroll of 1m. rupiahs or more) are obliged to contribute towards old-age, sickness and maternity benefits for employees with contracts of more than three months.

RELIGION

Religious liberty is granted to all denominations. In 2001 there were 185·1m. Muslims (making Indonesia the world's biggest Muslim country), 12·8m. Protestants and 7·6m. Roman Catholics. There were also significant numbers of Hindus and Buddhists. In Feb. 2010 there was one cardinal.

CULTURE

World Heritage Sites

There are seven UNESCO World Heritage sites in Indonesia (the first four inscribed in 1991): Borobudur Temple Compounds, Ujung Kulon National Park, Komodo National Park, Prambanan Temple Compounds, Sangiran Early Man Site (1996), Lorentz National Park (1999) and the Tropical Rainforest Heritage of Sumatra (2004).

Broadcasting

Government-controlled Radio Republik Indonesia (RPI) operates six public national radio networks, as well as regional and local stations and the external Voice of Indonesia service. There are a number of private radio stations. The public television broadcaster, Televisi Republik Indonesia (TVRI), runs two networks. Commercial services include Surya Citra Televisi Indonesia (SCTV), Rajawali Citra TV Indonesia (RCTI) and Televisi Pendidkan Indonesia (TPI). There were 36·4m. television-equipped households (colour by PAL) in 2005.

Cinema

There were 929 cinema screens in 2006. 60 feature films were produced in 2006.

Press

In 2002 there were 176 daily newspapers (total average circulation of 4,665,000 at a rate of 22 per 1,000 inhabitants). In 2002 a total of 3,823 book titles were published.

Tourism

In 2005 there were 5,002,000 foreign tourists, spending US$4·5bn. In Feb. 2004 the government introduced a US$25 fee for a 30-day visa and a US$10 fee for a 3-day visa.

Festivals

Independence from the Dutch is celebrated on 17 Aug. with musical and theatrical performances, carnivals and sporting events. The military parades on Armed Forces Day (5 Oct.) and women are celebrated on Kartini Day (21 April) in memory of Raden Ajeng Kartini, a symbol of female emancipation. In Bali the Hindu new year is marked by a day of silence, Nyepi, followed by a day of feasting. Muslim, Hindu, Buddhist and Christian festivals are marked throughout the country.

DIPLOMATIC REPRESENTATIVES

Of Indonesia in the United Kingdom (38 Grosvenor Sq., London, W1K 2HW)
Ambassador: Yuri Octavian Thamrin.

Of the United Kingdom in Indonesia (Jalan M.H. Thamrin 75, Jakarta 10310)
Ambassador: Martin Hatfull.

Of Indonesia in the USA (2020 Massachusetts Ave., NW, Washington, D.C., 20036)
Ambassador: Vacant.
Chargé d'Affaires a.i.: Salman Al Farisi.

Of the USA in Indonesia (Medan Merdeka Selatan 5, Jakarta)
Ambassador: Cameron Hume.

Of Indonesia to the United Nations
Ambassador: Vacant.
Chargé d'Affaires a.i.: Hasan Kleib.

Of Indonesia to the European Union
Ambassador: Nadjib Riphat Kesoema.

FURTHER READING

Central Bureau of Statistics. *Statistical Yearbook of Indonesia.—Monthly Statistical Bulletin: Economic Indicator.*

Cribb, R., *Historical Dictionary of Indonesia.* 1993.
Cribb, R. and Brown, C., *Modern Indonesia: a History since 1945.* 1995
Day, Tony, (ed.) *Identifying with Freedom: Indonesia after Suharto.* 2007
Elson, R. E., *Suharto; a Political Biography.* 2001
Forrester, Geoff, (ed.) *Post-Soeharto Indonesia: Renewal or Chaos?* 1999
Forrester, Geoff and May, R. J. (eds.) *The Fall of Soeharto.* 1999
Friend, Theodore, *Indonesian Destinies.* 2003
Glassburner, Bruce, (ed.) *The Economy of Indonesia: Selected Readings.* 2007
Holt, Claire, (ed.) *Culture and Politics in Indonesia.* 2007
Kingsbury, Damien, *The Politics of Indonesia.* 2nd ed. 2002
Ricklefs, M. C., *A History of Modern Indonesia since c. 1200.* 4th ed. 2008
Schwarz, Adam, *A Nation in Waiting: Indonesia's Search for Stability.* Revised ed. 1999
Schwarz, Adam and Paris, Jonathan, (eds.) *The Politics of Post-Suharto Indonesia.* 1999
Vatikiotis, M. R. J., *Indonesian Politics under Suharto: Order, Development and Pressure for Change.* 2nd ed. 1994

National Statistical Office: Central Bureau of Statistics, Jl. Dr. Sutomo 6–8, Jakarta, 10710.
Website: http://www.bps.go.id

IRAN

Jomhuri-e-Eslami-e-Iran
(Islamic Republic of Iran)

Capital: Tehran
Population estimate, 2010: 75·08m.
GDP per capita, 2007: (PPP$) 10,955
HDI/world rank: 0·782/88

KEY HISTORICAL EVENTS

Neolithic farmers established settlements in the Zagros mountains, in the west of modern Iran, from 6000 BC. From around 2700 BC the southwestern region of Khuzestan was inhabited by Elamite societies, a formative influence on the first Persian empire, established by Cyrus the Great in 550 BC. His Achaemenian dynasty lasted until around 320 BC and was ruled from Persepolis. Persia was subsequently controlled by the Parthian and Sassanian dynasties, during which the Zoroastrian religion took hold. Arabians arriving in the 7th century AD spread the Islamic faith. Their armies defeated the Sassanians at Nahavand in 641, ushering in a period of control by Arab caliphs and, from the 10th century, Seljuk Turks. Persia came under the control of Ghengis Khan's Mongol armies in the 1220s and was then ruled by Timur from 1370.

The Safavid dynasty (1502–1736) was founded by Shah Ismail, who restored internal order and established the Shia sect of Islam as the state religion. The dynasty reached its zenith in the reign of Shah Abbas I (1587–1628), during which Esfahan became the Persian capital. In 1779, following the death of Mohammad Karim Khan Zand, Agha Mohammad Khan, a leader of the Qajars (a Turkmen tribe from modern Azerbaijan), attempted to reunify Persia. He regained Persian control over much of the Caucasus and established his capital at Tehran.

The Qajars fought with an expansionist Russia during the early 1800s and in 1828 Fath Ali Shah was forced to sign the Treaty of Turkmanchai, acknowledging Russian sovereignty over present-day Armenia and Azerbaijan. The reign of Naser o-Din Shah (1848–96) saw a period of modernization and the increasing influence of the Russian and British empires in Persia, which continued after the adoption of the first constitution and the establishment of a national assembly in Aug. 1906. The discovery of oil in Khuzestan province in 1908 led to further British and Russian jockeying for control in the region.

Following a bloodless coup in 1921, Reza Khan began his rise to power. He was crowned Reza Shah Pahlavi on 12 Dec. 1925 and set about a programme of reforms, encouraging the development of industry, education and a modern infrastructure. Responding to Iran's support for Germany in the Second World War, the Allies occupied the country and forced Reza Shah to abdicate in favour of his son, Muhammad Reza Shah, who was sworn in on 17 Sept. 1941.

The British-controlled oil industry was nationalized in March 1951 in line with the policy of the National Front Party, whose leader, Dr Muhammad Mussadeq, became prime minister in April 1951. He was opposed by the Shah, who fled the country until Aug. 1953, when Mussadeq was deposed in an Anglo-American sponsored monarchist coup. The Shah's policy, which included the redistribution of land to small farmers and the enfranchisement of women, was opposed by Shia religious scholars. Despite economic growth, unrest was caused by the Shah's repressive measures and his extensive use of the *Savak* (secret police). The opposition, led by Ayatollah Ruhollah Khomeini, the Shia Muslim spiritual leader who had been exiled in 1965, was increasingly successful. Following intense civil unrest in Tehran, the Shah left Iran with his family on 17 Jan. 1979 (and died in Egypt on 27 July 1980).

The Ayatollah Khomeini returned from exile on 1 Feb. 1979, the Shah's government resigned and parliament dissolved itself on 11 Feb. Following a referendum in March, an Islamic Republic was proclaimed. The Constitution gave supreme authority to a religious leader (*wali faqih*), a position held by Ayatollah Khomeini until his death in 1989. Ayatollah Ali Khamenei then became the nation's supreme leader. In Sept. 1980 border fighting with Iraq escalated into full-scale war. A UN-arranged ceasefire came into effect on 20 Aug. 1988, and in Aug. 1990, following Iraq's invasion of Kuwait, Iraq offered peace terms and began the withdrawal of troops from Iranian soil. 30,000 political opponents of the regime are believed to have been executed shortly after the end of the war.

In 1997 the election of Mohammad Khatami as president signalled a shift away from Islamic extremism. A clampdown on Islamic vigilantes who were waging a violent campaign against Western 'decadence' was evidence of a cautiously liberal integration of the constitution. However, the conservative faction led by Ayatollah Ali Khamenei retained considerable power, including the final say on defence and foreign policy.

In July 1999 riot police fought pitched battles with pro-democracy students in Tehran in the worst unrest since the 1979 revolution. Islamic leaders remain divided on the degree of overlap between politics and religion.

The election of Mahmoud Ahmadinejad as president in June 2005 was seen by some analysts as signalling a return to the extreme conservatism that preceded Khatami's tenure. Ahmadinejad's anti-Israeli rhetoric caused international concern. Under his leadership, Iran recommenced uranium conversion research. Despite Tehran's insistence that the research programme was for peaceful purposes only, increasing international disquiet culminated with the International Atomic Energy Agency reporting Iran to the UN Security Council in

Feb. 2006. In April 2006 President Ahmadinejad announced that Iran had successfully enriched uranium.

The country witnessed an upsurge of civil unrest in June 2009 following the presidential election in which incumbent president Mahmoud Ahmadinejad was declared the victor by a large majority.

TERRITORY AND POPULATION

Iran is bounded in the north by Armenia, Azerbaijan, the Caspian Sea and Turkmenistan, east by Afghanistan and Pakistan, south by the Gulf of Oman and the Persian Gulf, and west by Iraq and Turkey. It has an area (including inland water) of 1,648,195 sq. km (636,368 sq. miles), but a vast portion is desert. Population (2006 census): 70,472,846 (2005, 66·9% urban). Population density: 43 per sq. km.

The UN gives an estimated population for 2010 of 75·08m.

In 2007 Iran had 964,000 refugees. Only Pakistan and Syria have more refugees.

The areas, populations and capitals of the 30 provinces *(ostan)* are:

Province	*Area (sq. km)*	*Census Oct. 1996*	*Census Oct. 2006*	*Capital*
Ardabil	17,881	1,168,011	1,225,348	Ardabil
Azarbayejan, East	45,481	3,325,540	3,603,456	Tabriz
Azarbayejan, West	37,463	2,496,320	2,873,459	Orumiyeh
Bushehr	23,168	743,675	886,267	Bushehr
Chahar Mahal and Bakhtyari	16,201	761,168	857,910	Shahr-e-Kord
Esfahan	107,027	3,923,255	4,559,256	Esfahan
Fars	121,825	3,817,036	4,336,878	Shiraz
Gilan	13,952	2,241,896	2,404,861	Rasht
Golestan	20,893	1,426,288	1,617,087	Gorgan
Hamadan	19,547	1,677,957	1,703,267	Hamadan
Hormozgan	71,193	1,062,155	1,403,674	Bandar-e-Abbas
Ilam	20,150	487,886	545,787	Ilam
Kerman	181,714	2,004,328	2,652,413	Kerman
Kermanshah	24,641	1,778,596	1,879,385	Kermanshah
Khuzestan	63,213	3,746,772	4,274,979	Ahvaz
Kohgiluyeh and Boyer Ahmad	15,563	544,356	634,299	Yasuj
Kordestan	28,817	1,346,383	1,438,543	Sanandaj
Lorestan	28,392	1,584,434	1,716,527	Khorramabad
Markazi	29,406	1,228,812	1,349,590	Arak
Mazandaran	23,833	2,602,008	2,920,657	Sari
North Khorasan[1]	28,434	—	811,572	Bojnurd
Qazvin	15,491	968,257	1,143,200	Qazvin
Qom	11,237	853,044	1,040,681	Qom
Razavi Khorasan[1]	144,681	—	5,593,079	Mashhad
Semnan	96,816	501,447	589,742	Semnan
Sistan and Baluchestan	178,431	1,722,579	2,405,742	Zahedan
South Khorasan[1]	69,555	—	636,420	Birjand
Tehran	19,196	10,343,965	13,413,348	Tehran
Yazd	128,811	750,769	990,818	Yazd
Zanjan	21,841	900,890	964,601	Zanjan

[1]Created from the former province of Khorasan in Sept. 2004.

At the 2006 census the populations of the principal cities were:

	Population		*Population*
Tehran	7,797,520	Hamadan	479,640
Mashhad	2,427,316	Arak	446,760
Esfahan	1,602,110	Yazd	432,194
Tabriz	1,398,060	Ardabil	418,262
Karaj	1,386,030	Bandar-e-Abbas	379,301
Shiraz	1,227,331	Eslamshahr	357,389
Ahvaz	985,614	Qazvin	355,338
Qom	959,116	Zanjan	349,713
Kermanshah	794,863	Khorramabad	333,945
Orumiyeh	583,255	Sanandaj	316,862
Zahedan	567,449	Gorgan	274,438
Rasht	557,366	Sari	261,293
Kerman	515,991	Kashan	253,509

The official language is Farsi or Persian, spoken by 45·6% of the population in 2003. 28·5% spoke related languages, including Kurdish (9·1%) and Luri in the west, Gilaki and Mazandarami in the north, and Baluchi in the southeast; 22·3% speak Turkic languages (particularly Azeri), primarily in the northwest. Iranians, who are Persians, not Arabs, are less emotionally connected to the plight of the Arab Palestinians than people in other parts of the Middle East.

SOCIAL STATISTICS

2003 births, 1,171,573; deaths, 368,518. Rates (2003, per 1,000 population): birth, 17·6; death, 5·3. Abortion is illegal, but a family planning scheme was inaugurated in 1988. Expectation of life at birth, 2007, 72·5 years for females and 69·9 years for males. Infant mortality, 2005, 31 per 1,000 live births. Annual population growth rate, 2000–05, 1·5%; fertility rate, 2004, 2·1 births per woman. Iran has had one of the largest reductions in its fertility rate of any country in the world over the past 30 years, having had a rate of 6·4 births per woman in 1975. The suicide rate is 25 for every 100,000 people—more than twice the world average.

CLIMATE

Mainly a desert climate, but with more temperate conditions on the shores of the Caspian Sea. Seasonal range of temperature is considerable, as is rain (ranging from 2" in the southeast to 78" in the Caspian region). Winter is normally the rainy season for the whole country. Abadan, Jan. 54°F (12·2°C), July 97°F (36·1°C). Annual rainfall 8" (204 mm). Tehran, Jan. 36°F (2·2°C), July 85°F (29·4°C). Annual rainfall 10" (246 mm).

CONSTITUTION AND GOVERNMENT

The Constitution of the Islamic Republic was approved by a national referendum in Dec. 1979. It was revised in 1989 to expand the powers of the presidency and eliminate the position of prime minister. It gives supreme authority to the *Spiritual Leader (wali faqih)*, a position which was held by Ayatollah Khomeini until his death on 3 June 1989. Ayatollah Seyed Ali Khamenei was elected to succeed him on 4 June 1989. Following the death of the previous incumbent, Ayatollah Ali Khamenei was proclaimed the *Source of Knowledge (Marja e Taghlid)* at the head of all Shia Muslims in Dec. 1994.

The 86-member *Assembly of Experts* was established in 1982. It is popularly elected every eight years. Its mandate is to interpret the constitution and select the Spiritual Leader. Candidates for election are examined by the *Council of Guardians*.

The *Islamic Consultative Assembly* has 290 members, elected for a four-year term in single-seat constituencies. All candidates have to be approved by the 12-member *Council of Guardians*.

The *President* of the Republic is popularly elected for not more than two four-year terms and is head of the executive; he appoints Ministers subject to approval by the *Islamic Consultative Assembly (Majlis)*. The president is Iran's second highest-ranking official.

Legislative power is held by the Islamic Consultative Assembly, directly elected on a non-party basis for a four-year term by all citizens aged 17 or over. A new law passed in Oct. 1999 raised the voting age from 16 to 17, thus depriving an estimated 1·5m. young people from voting. Two-thirds of the electorate is under 30. Voting is secret but ballot papers are not printed; electors must write the name of their preferred candidate themselves. Five seats are reserved for religious minorities. All legislation is subject to approval by the *Council of Guardians* who ensure it is in accordance with the Islamic code and with the Constitution. The Spiritual Leader appoints six members, as does the judiciary.

National Anthem

'Sar zad az ofogh mehr-e khavaran' ('Rose from the horizon the affectionate sun of the East'); words by a group of poets, tune by Dr Riahi.

GOVERNMENT CHRONOLOGY

Spiritual Leaders of the Islamic Republic since 1980.

1980–89	Ayatollah Seyed Ruhollah Mousavi Khomeini
1989–	Ayatollah Seyed Mohammad Ali Hoseyn Khamenei

Heads of State since 1941.

Emperor (Shah)

1941–79	Mohammad Reza Pahlavi

Leader of the Revolution (Rahbar-e Enqelab)

1979–80	Ayatollah Seyed Ruhollah Mousavi Khomeini

President of the Republic

1980–81	Abolhasan Bani-Sadr

Interim Presidential Commission

1981

President of the Republic

1981	Mohammad Ali Rajai

Interim Presidential Commission

1981

Presidents of the Republic

1981–89	Ayatollah Seyed Mohammad Ali Hoseyn Khamenei
1989–97	Ali Akbar Hashemi Rafsanjani Hodjatoleslam Seyed
1997–2005	Mohammad Khatami
2005–	Mahmoud Ahmadinejad

RECENT ELECTIONS

In presidential elections held on 12 June 2009 official results indicated that incumbent president Mahmoud Ahmadinejad took 62·6% of the vote ahead of Mir-Hossein Mousavi with 33·8%, Mohsen Rezaee with 1·7% and Mehdi Karroubi with 0·9%. However, there were widespread accusations against the government of vote rigging and international observers also expressed doubt about the legitimacy of the results. Mir-Hossein Mousavi called for the result to be annulled. There were mass protests and civil unrest in the capital, with several deaths. The official turnout was put at 85%.

Elections to the Islamic Consultative Assembly were held on 14 March and 25 April 2008. In the first round of elections conservatives won 132 seats, reformists 31 and ind. 40. In the second round conservatives won 38 of 82 seats, reformists 15 and ind. 29. Five seats are reserved for religious minorities.

Elections to the Assembly of Experts were held on 15 Dec. 2006. 68 of the 86 available seats went to representatives of the conservative Combatant Clergy Association.

CURRENT ADMINISTRATION

In March 2010 the cabinet was composed as follows:

President: Mahmoud Ahmadinejad; b. 1956 (sworn in 6 Aug. 2005 and re-elected 12 June 2009).

First Vice-President: Mohammad Reza Rahimi.

Head of Presidential Office: Esfandiar Rahim Mashaie. *Vice-President and Head of National Atomic Energy Organization:* Ali Akbar Salehi. *Vice-President and Head of Cultural Heritage and Tourism Organization:* Hamid Baqai. *Vice-President and Head of Environmental Protection Organization:* Mohammad-Javad Mohammadizadeh. *Vice-President and Head of Foundation for Martyrs and Veterans' Affairs:* Masoud Zaribafan. *Vice-President for Parliamentary Affairs:* Mohammad Reza Mir Tajedini. *Vice-President and Head of Physical Education Organization:* Ali Saeedlou. *Vice-President for Planning and Strategic Supervision:* Dr Ebrahim Azizi. *Vice-President and Head of National Youth Organization:* Mehrdad Bazrpash. *Vice-President for Science and Technology:* Nasrin Soltankhah.

Minister of Foreign Affairs: Manouchehr Mottaki. *Oil:* Masoud Mirkazemi. *Interior:* Mostafa Mohammad Najjar. *Economy and Finance:* Shamseddin Hosseini. *Agriculture Jihad:* Sadeq Khalilian. *Commerce:* Mahdi Qazanfari. *Energy:* Majid Namjou. *Roads and Transportation:* Hamid Behbahani. *Industry and Mines:* Ali-Akbar Mehrabian. *Housing and Urban Development:* Ali Nikzad. *Labour and Social Affairs:* Abdolreza Sheikholeslami. *Health and Medical Education:* Marzieh Vahid Dastjerdi. *Education:* Hamid Reza Haji Babaie. *Science, Research and Technology:* Kamran Daneshjoo. *Justice:* Morteza Bakhtiari. *Defence and Logistics:* Ahmad Vahidi. *Culture and Islamic Guidance:* Mohammad Hosseini. *Co-operatives:* Mohammad Abbasi. *Intelligence and Security:* Heidar Moslehi. *Communications and Information Technology:* Reza Taqipour. *Welfare and Social Affairs:* Sadeq Mahsouli.

Speaker of the Islamic Consultative Assembly (Majlis): Ali Larijani.

Presidency Website: http://www.president.ir

CURRENT LEADERS

Ayatollah Seyed Ali Khamenei

Position

Spiritual Leader (wali faqih)

Introduction

Seyed Ali Khamenei succeeded Ayatollah Khomeini as Iran's supreme spiritual leader on the latter's death in June 1989, having previously served from 1981 as the third president of the Islamic Republic.

Early Life

Khamenei was born in Mashhad on 15 July 1939. He attended theological colleges in Qom, where he was a pupil of Ayatollah Khomeini, and Mashhad. From 1963 he was involved with the Islamic opposition to the regime of the Shah, for which he spent three years in prison and a year in exile. Active in the Islamic revolution of 1979, Khamenei was appointed to the Revolutionary Council and became deputy minister of defence. He was also leader of the Friday congregational prayers in Tehran from mid-1980 and, from Aug. 1981, was appointed secretary-general of the Islamic Republican Party (IRP), dissolved in 1987. He was injured in a bomb blast in June 1986.

Career in Office

On 2 Oct 1981, as the IRP candidate, Khamenei was the first cleric to be elected as president, with 95% of the popular vote. Ayatollah Khomeini had previously barred the clergy from the office. He succeeded Mohammad Ali Radjai who had been assassinated in Aug. In Aug. 1985 he was re-elected, again overwhelmingly, for a second four-year term. On the death of Khomeini, Khamenei was elected to succeed him on 4 June 1989 by an Assembly of Experts. Previously a middle-ranking cleric (Hojatolislam), he assumed the title of Ayatollah, a constitutional precondition of appointment to the Islamic republic's spiritual leadership. In Dec. 1994 he was proclaimed the Marja e Taghlid (Source of Knowledge) at the head of all Shia Muslims.

The standoff between President Khatami's reformist government and the hard-line conservative Council of Guardians reached a critical point in the run-up to the Feb. 2004 parliamentary elections. The Council's disqualification of over 2,000 reformist candidates provoked threats of resignations in government and boycott in the electorate. Khamenei intervened in Jan. 2004 on state television, calling for review of the Council's decisions and backing the 83 Majlis deputies whose candidacies had been rejected. However, over a third of the Majlis' deputies resigned in protest on 1 Feb. 2004 and in the subsequent election religious conservatives regained parliamentary control.

Khamenei has since presided over a deterioration in relations with the Western powers over Iran's uranium enrichment activities and its alleged ambitions to acquire nuclear weapons.

He has nevertheless maintained Iran's right to continue developing nuclear technology for peaceful purpose. Western concerns were further heightened by the election in June 2005 of the hard-line Islamic conservative Mahmoud Ahmadinejad as state president and his formal endorsement by Khamenei. There was some speculation about Khamenei's continued loyalty to the state president after he reportedly criticized Ahmadinejad's economic stewardship and inflammatory foreign policy rhetoric. However, he upheld the latter's disputed re-election in June 2009, dismissed calls for the poll to be rerun and endorsed the ensuing security crackdown on opposition to the regime.

Mahmoud Ahmadinejad

Position
President

Introduction
Mahmoud Ahmadinejad won the run-off in Iran's presidential election on 24 June 2005. The ultra-conservative former Revolutionary Guard and mayor of Tehran promised to tackle domestic poverty and corruption, and analysts expected an end to the fragile social reforms made under his predecessor, President Mohammad Khatami. In foreign policy he hardened Iran's stance towards the West, particularly over its nuclear programme, and engaged in anti-Israeli rhetoric, which heightened international tensions. Signs of internal dissension during his first term were reflected in his hotly disputed re-election in June 2009, which provoked waves of opposition protests and repressive government retaliation for the rest of the year and into 2010. He meanwhile maintained his uncompromising position on Iran's nuclear development activities and suspicion of the USA.

Early Life
The son of a blacksmith, Mahmoud Ahmadinejad was born in 1956 in the village of Aradan in northern Iran. The family moved to Tehran a year later. In 1976 he took up a place to study civil engineering at the Iran University of Science and Technology (IUST). As a conservative student, he was supportive of Ayatollah Khomeini's Islamic revolution in 1979. Some of the 52 Americans who were held hostage in the US embassy after the revolution allege that Ahmadinejad was among those who captured them, though he strongly denies the claim. He remained at the IUST until the late 1980s, taking a masters degree in civil engineering, followed by a PhD in traffic and transportation engineering and planning, and then winning a professorship.

Ahmadinejad was drawn into the long-running Iran–Iraq war in 1986, when he joined the Islamic Revolutionary Guards and fought on the Iraqi border near Kirkuk. When the war ended in 1988, he worked as an engineer in the local government offices of Maku and Khvoy in the province of West Azarbayejan. In 1993 he became governor of the northwestern province of Ardabil until he was ousted following the election of the reform-minded President Mohammad Khatami in 1997. Returning to Tehran, Ahmadinejad rejoined the IUST's civil engineering faculty, where he remained until May 2003.

Ahmadinejad was elected mayor of Tehran on 3 May 2003, and pursued conservative policies. He closed down some fast-food restaurants and banned an advertising campaign that featured a Western celebrity. His views were at odds with President Khatami, who barred him from attending cabinet meetings, a privilege normally accorded to mayors of the capital. With the backing of conservative groups, Ahmadinejad contested the June 2005 presidential elections. His campaign was aimed at the poor and disadvantaged, as well as religious hardliners. He emphasized his working-class upbringing and promised to redistribute the country's income from oil. In a run-off against the former president, Ali Akbar Hashemi Rafsanjani, on 24 June 2005, Ahmadinejad emerged victorious, with 63·4% of the vote, although there were complaints of voting irregularities.

Career in Office
On 3 Aug. Ahmadinejad received the formal approval of the Supreme Leader, Ayatollah Khamenei, and he became president on 6 Aug. 2005. In his inaugural address, he called for unity and the building of a model state based on principles of 'modern, advanced, and strong Islamic government'. However, he quickly caused consternation both at home and abroad.

Within Iran, Ahmadinejad instituted a purge of various branches of government, state economic agencies and the diplomatic service, drawing accusations that he was exceeding his constitutional powers. By the end of 2006 there were signs of domestic opposition to his policies. In Dec. his hard-line supporters fared badly in elections to local councils and to the powerful Assembly of Experts. Iran's economic malaise under his management incurred parliamentary rebuke in Jan. 2007, reportedly supported by Supreme Leader Khamenei, and in June 2007 his government introduced petrol rationing, provoking public protests. There was also increasing evidence in 2007 of an unpopular crackdown on civil liberties. However, in parliamentary elections in March–April 2008 (in which many pro-reform candidates were barred from standing) there was a strong showing by the president's conservative supporters.

On the international stage, Iran's resumption of uranium enrichment at its Esfahan plant from Aug. 2005 intensified Western concerns over nuclear weapon proliferation. Ahmadinejad nevertheless maintained a belligerent stance on Iran's refusal to suspend enrichment, resulting in punitive sanctions by the United Nations Security Council and also unilateral sanctions by the USA (although new US intelligence disclosed in Dec. 2007 deemed Iran to have abandoned its nuclear weapons programme in 2003). Meanwhile, an anti-Israeli speech by Ahmadinejad in Oct. 2005 provoked international condemnation, and he has also denounced the Holocaust as a myth. In July 2008 Iran test-fired a long-range missile believed to be capable of reaching Israeli cities. In March–April 2007 a dispute erupted between Iran and the UK as 15 British sailors patrolling the Iraqi coast were seized by the Iranian navy and detained for nearly two weeks before their release. In March 2008 Ahmadinejad made an unprecedented official visit to Iraq, where he called on all foreign forces to leave.

The June 2009 presidential election saw Ahmadinejad win 62·6% of the vote ahead of his nearest rival Mir-Hossein Mousavi with 33·8%. However, the opposition challenged the official results and accused the government of election rigging, resulting in violent clashes between police and demonstrators. Opposition unrest continued over the following months and was met with a repressive backlash by security forces, including many arrests and, in Feb. 2010, two executions. The government meanwhile claimed that outside interference was responsible for fomenting the upheaval.

International concerns over Iran's nuclear ambitions were further heightened in Sept. 2009 by the identification of a secret uranium enrichment plant near the city of Qom and by Iran's test-firing of missiles capable of reaching targets across the Middle East. In Nov., despite a resolution by the International Atomic Energy Agency condemning Iran's nuclear programme, Ahmedinejad's government maintained its defiance by announcing plans to build ten more enrichment facilities. In Feb. 2010, Ahmedinejad ordered Iran's atomic energy authority to begin enriching its uranium stockpile to a higher level—so edging towards the ability to make weapons-grade fuel and prompting moves by the UN Security Council to consider further punitive sanctions.

DEFENCE

16 to 17 months' military service is compulsory. Military expenditure totalled US$7,160m. in 2006 (equivalent to US$110 per capita), representing 3·3% of GDP, compared to 7·7% in 1985.

Iran has on a number of occasions successfully tested Shahab-3 medium-range ballistic missiles, initially with a range of 1,300 km, and most recently in Sept. 2009 an upgraded version that reportedly has a range of 2,000 km. In Nov. 2008, and again in Dec. 2009, it tested a new missile, the Sajil, which also reportedly has a range of 2,000 km. Unlike the Shahab-3, the Sajil is a solid fuel missile.

Nuclear Weapons
Although Iran is a member of the Non-Proliferation Treaty (NPT), United Nations inspectors have found enriched uranium in environmental samples, increasing US suspicion that Iran is developing nuclear weapons. In Aug. 2005 Iran rejected proposals from France, Germany and the UK for economic incentives in return for an indefinite suspension of uranium enrichment and resumed nuclear conversion activities at its plant in Esfahan.

According to *Deadly Arsenals*, published by the Carnegie Endowment for International Peace, Iran has a chemical and biological weapons programme.

Army
Strength (2006), 350,000 (about 220,000 conscripts). Reserves are estimated to be around 350,000, made up of ex-service volunteers.

Revolutionary Guard (*Pasdaran Inqilab*)
Numbering some 125,000, the Guard is divided between ground forces (100,000), naval forces (some 20,000) and marines (5,000). It controls the Basij, a volunteer 'popular mobilization army' of about 300,000, which can number 1m. strong in wartime.

Navy
The fleet includes six submarines (including three ex-Soviet *Kilo* class) and three ex-UK frigates. Personnel numbered 18,000 in 2006 including 6,000 in Naval Aviation and 2,600 marines.

The Naval Aviation wing operated 21 aircraft and 30 helicopters in 2006.

The main naval bases are at Bandar-e-Abbas, Bushehr and Chah Bahar.

Air Force
In 2006 there were 281 combat aircraft including US F-14 Tomcat, F-5E Tiger II and F-4D/E Phantom II fighter-bombers, and a number of MiG-29 interceptors and Su-24 strike aircraft. The serviceability of the aircraft varies with only 60–80% operational.

Strength (2006) estimated at 52,000 personnel (about 15,000 air defence).

INTERNATIONAL RELATIONS

Currently there is a standoff between Iran and the international community on the question of nuclear development.

Iran is a member of the UN, World Bank, IMF and several other UN specialized agencies, IOM, Islamic Development Bank, OIC, Colombo Plan, ECO and OPEC.

ECONOMY

Agriculture accounted for 10·4% of GDP in 2006, industry 44·6% and services 45·0%.

Overview
Iran's macroeconomic performance has been strong in recent years. Between 2000 and 2005 GDP grew by an average annual rate of 5·5% as a result of rising oil prices and strong private sector growth. Manufacturing and construction are key growth sectors, along with the wholesale and retail trade, and restaurants and hotels sectors. According to the World Bank, the private sector has reacted positively to structural reforms implemented by the government of Mohammad Khatami. However, in 2009 falling oil prices prompted an economic slowdown.

The economy remains over-reliant on oil and the Ahmadinejad government's commitment to pushing through further structural reform is uncertain. Inconsistent implementation of privatization (a major programme was announced in 2006) and liberalization reforms slowed the growth of the private sector, while price subsidies and controls are distorting the economy. State-owned enterprises produce over 60% of the manufacturing sector's output and state-owned banks dominate the financial sector. A programme of investment reforms was announced in 2008. Unemployment remains in double digits, with approximately 750,000 Iranians entering the job market each year. Sustained high growth rates will be required to create more jobs and reduce inflation.

Currency
The unit of currency is the *rial* (IRR) of which 10 = 1 *toman*. Total money supply in April 2008 was 440,095bn. rials. Inflation rates (based on IMF statistics) for fiscal years:

2000	*2001*	*2002*	*2003*	*2004*	*2005*	*2006*	*2007*	*2008*
12·8%	11·3%	15·7%	15·6%	15·3%	10·4%	11·9%	18·4%	25·4%

Budget
The financial year runs from 21 March. Revenues in 2005–06 totalled 503,765bn. rials and expenditures 484,332bn. rials. Petroleum and natural gas revenues accounted for 71·8% of all revenues and taxes 20·4%. Current expenditure accounted for 68·3% of all expenditures.

Performance
Real GDP growth rates (based on IMF statistics):

1999	*2000*	*2001*	*2002*	*2003*	*2004*	*2005*	*2006*	*2007*	*2008*
1·9%	5·1%	3·7%	7·5%	7·2%	5·1%	4·7%	5·8%	7·8%	2·5%

Total GDP in 2008 was US$385·1bn.

Banking and Finance
The Central Bank is the note issuing authority and government bank. Its *Governor* is Mahmud Bahmani. All other banks and insurance companies were nationalized in 1979, and reorganized into new state banking corporations. In April 2000 the government announced that it would permit the establishment of private banks for the first time since the revolution in 1979, ending the state monopoly on banking. The first private bank since the revolution came into existence in Aug. 2001 with the creation of Bank Eghtesad Novin (Modern Economic Bank). A further five private banks have opened in the meantime. In 2002 there were 11 commercial banks, two development banks, one housing bank and around 30 foreign banks.

A stock exchange reopened in Tehran in 1992.

ENERGY AND NATURAL RESOURCES

Environment
Iran's carbon dioxide emissions from the consumption and flaring of fossil fuels were the equivalent of 7·8 tonnes per capita in 2008.

Electricity
Total installed capacity in 2003 was 39·6m. kW; production (2004), 164·48bn. kWh (153·85bn. kWh thermal and 10·63bn. kWh hydro-electric). Consumption per capita in 2004 was 2,460 kWh. Iran's first nuclear reactor has been built by Russia at Bushehr and is expected to become operational in the course of 2010.

Oil and Gas

Oil is Iran's chief source of revenue. The main oilfields are in the Zagros Mountains where oil was first discovered in 1908. Oil companies were nationalized in 1979 and operations of crude oil and natural gas exploitation are now run by the National Iranian Oil Company. Iran produced 209·8m. tonnes of oil in 2008 (5·3% of the world total oil output); in 2008 it had reserves amounting to 137·6bn. bbls. In 1999 the most important discovery in more than 30 years was made, with the Azadegan oilfield in the southwest of the country being found to have reserves of approximately 26bn. bbls. In 2001 revenue from oil exports amounted to US$14bn. (US$19bn. in 2000). Iran depends on oil for some 86% of its exports, but domestic consumption has been increasing to such an extent that it is now as high as exports.

Iran has 16% of proven global gas reserves. Natural gas reserves in 2008 were 29,610bn. cu. metres, the second largest behind Russia. Natural gas production was 116·3bn. cu. metres in 2008, the fourth highest in the world. In Dec. 1997 the first natural gas pipeline linking Iran with the Caspian Sea via Turkmenistan was opened. The 200-km line links gas fields in western Turkmenistan to industrial markets in northern Iran.

Minerals

Production (in 1,000 tonnes), 2004: iron ore, 18,205; gypsum, 12,594; decorative stone, 6,450; salt, 1,791; coal, 1,246; bauxite, 366; zinc, 244; aluminium, 213; copper, 190; chromite, 139; manganese, 129. It was announced in Feb. 2003 that uranium deposits had been discovered in central Iran. In Nov. 2003 the International Atomic Energy Agency announced that Iran had admitted to enriching uranium at an electric plant outside Tehran.

Agriculture

There were an estimated 15·02m. ha. of arable land in 2002 and 2·07m. ha. of permanent crops. Around 7·5m. ha. were irrigated in 2002. Crop production (2002, in 1,000 tonnes): wheat, 12,450; sugar beets, 6,098; tomatoes, 4,109; potatoes, 3,756; sugarcane, 3,712; melons and watermelons, 3,388; barley, 3,085; rice (paddy), 2,888; grapes, 2,704. Livestock (2002): 53·9m. sheep; 25·8m. goats; 8·7m. cattle; 1·6m. asses; 270m. chickens.

Forestry

Approximately 6·8% of Iran was forested (11·08m. ha.) in 2005, much of it in the Caspian region. Timber production in 2007 was 865,000 cu. metres.

Fisheries

In 2005 the total catch was 410,558 tonnes (343,492 tonnes from sea fishing).

INDUSTRY

Major industries: petrochemical, automotive, food, beverages and tobacco, textiles, clothing and leather, wood and fibre, paper and cardboard, chemical products, non-metal mining products, basic materials, machinery and equipment, copper, steel and aluminium. The textile industry uses local cotton and silk; carpet manufacture is an important industry. The country's steel industry is the largest in the Middle East; crude steel production in 2002 totalled 7·3m. tonnes.

Production includes: residual fuel oil (2004), 25·8m. tonnes; cement (2001), 24·8m. tonnes; distillate fuel oil (2004), 23·8m. tonnes; petrol (2004), 10·8m. tonnes; crude steel (2002), 7·3m. tonnes; kerosene (2004), 6·8m. tonnes; naphthas (2001–02), 2·6m. tonnes; cottonseed oil (1998), 994,000 tonnes; sugar (2001), 911,000 tonnes; stockings (2000), 18·5m. pairs; building bricks (2000), 10,077m. units.

Labour

The economically active population numbered 20m. in 2002, of which 17·6m. were employed. Approximately 12·2% of the workforce are unemployed and 800,000 Iranians enter the workforce every year.

INTERNATIONAL TRADE

There had been a limit on foreign investment, but legislation of 1995 permits foreign nationals to hold more than 50% of the equity of joint ventures with the consent of the Foreign Investment Board. Foreign debt was US$21,260m. in 2005.

Imports and Exports

In 2005–06 imports totalled US$40,969m. and exports US$60,013m. Main imports: machinery and motor vehicles, iron and steel, chemicals, pharmaceuticals, food. Main exports: oil, carpets, pistachios, leather and caviar. Crude oil exports (2003): 2,396,300 bbls a day. Oil exports account for more than 80% of hard currency earnings. Carpet exports are the second largest hard currency earner. Main import suppliers, 1998–99: Germany, 11·6%; Italy, 8·3%; Japan, 7·0%; Belgium, 6·3%; United Arab Emirates, 5·3%; Argentina, 4·4%. Main export markets in 1998–99: UK, 16·8%; Japan, 15·7%; Italy, 8·6%; United Arab Emirates, 6·7%; Greece, 5·0%; South Korea, 5·0%.

COMMUNICATIONS

Roads

In 2006 the total length of roads was 174,301 km, of which 1,429 km were motorways, 27,256 km main roads, 41,129 km secondary regional roads and 104,487 km other local roads. In 2007 there were 920,100 passenger cars; 862,600 motorcycles and mopeds; 179,700 vans and lorries; 4,900 buses and coaches. In 2006 there were 165,130 road accidents resulting in 6,380 deaths.

Rail

The State Railways totalled 7,172 km in 2005, of which 148 km were electrified. The railways carried 16·1m. passengers in 2004 and 28·7m. tonnes of freight in 2005. An isolated 1,676 mm gauge line (94 km) in the southeast provides a link with Pakistan Railways. A rail link to Turkmenistan was opened in May 1996. A metro system was opened in Tehran in 1999.

Civil Aviation

There are international airports at Tehran (Mehrabad), Shiraz and Bandar-e-Abbas. Tehran is the busiest airport, in 2000 handling 8,474,000 passengers (6,473,000 on domestic flights). The Imam Khomeini International Airport, construction of which began in 1977 before being halted in 1979, was inaugurated in Feb. 2004. The first flight arrived at the airport in May 2004 but it was then shut down by Iran's Revolutionary Guard, citing breaches of security by the foreign operators. The state-owned IranAir is the flag-carrying airline. In 2003 scheduled airline traffic of Iranian-based carriers flew 89m. km, carrying 11,664,000 passengers (2,282,000 on international flights).

Shipping

In 2002 the merchant fleet totalled 4·13m. GRT, including oil tankers totalling 2·14m. GRT. In 2005 vessels totalling 99,689,000 NRT entered ports.

Telecommunications

In 2008 there were 24·8m. main (fixed) telephone lines. In the same year mobile phone subscribers numbered 43·0m. (586·5 per 1,000 persons). There were 7·4m. PCs in use in 2006 and 23·0m. internet users in 2008.

Postal Services

In 2003 there were 5,843 post offices. 521m. pieces of mail were processed during the year, or seven items per person.

SOCIAL INSTITUTIONS

Justice

A legal system based on Islamic law (*Sharia*) was introduced by the 1979 constitution. A new criminal code on similar principles was introduced in Nov. 1995. The President of the Supreme Court and the public Prosecutor-General are appointed by the Spiritual Leader. The Supreme Court has 16 branches and 109 offences carry the death penalty. To these were added economic crimes in 1990. The population in penal institutions in Aug. 2007 was 158,351 (222 per 100,000 of national population). Amnesty International reported that there were at least 388 executions in 2009. Executions are frequently held in public.

Police

Women rejoined the police force in 2003 for the first time since the 1979 revolution.

Education

Adult literacy in 2003 was 77·0% (83·5% among males and 70·4% among females). Most primary and secondary schools are state schools. Elementary education in state schools and university education is free; small fees are charged for state-run secondary schools. In 2007 there were 7,152,492 pupils and 372,859 teaching staff at primary schools; and in 2005, 9,942,201 pupils and 530,190 teaching staff at secondary schools.

In 2007 there were 2,828,528 pupils and 133,484 academic staff at institutions of higher education. The University of Tehran, established in 1851 and with university status since 1934, is the largest and oldest institute of tertiary education in Iran. Other leading universities include Sharif University of Technology, in Tehran, and Esfahan University of Technology.

In 2007 public expenditure on education came to 5·6% of GNI and represented 19·5% of total government expenditure.

Health

There were 717 hospitals in 2001, with 109,152 beds. In 2001 medical personnel totalled 295,325 of which 152,396 were paramedics. There were 25,988 nurses and 8,105 midwives.

Welfare

The official retirement ages are 60 years (men) or 55 (women) with at least 16 years of contributions; age 50 (men) or 45 (women) with at least 30 years of contributions; and at any age with at least 35 years of contributions or between 20 and 25 years of work in an unhealthy or physically demanding natural environment. The pension is equal to 1/30th of the insured's average earnings during the last 24 months multiplied by the number of years of contributions. The minimum old-age pension is 2,196,000 rials a month (the minimum wage of an unskilled labourer).

RELIGION

The official religion is the Shia branch of Islam. Adherents numbered approximately 85% of the population in 2001; 5% were Sunni Muslims. However, less than 2% of the population now attend Friday prayers.

CULTURE

World Heritage Sites

There are ten UNESCO World Heritage sites in Iran: Tchogha Zanbil (inscribed on the list in 1979), the ruins of the holy city of the kingdom of Elam founded around 1250 BC; Persepolis (1979), the palace complex founded by Darius I in 518 BC and capital of the Achaemenid empire (the first Persian empire); Meidan Imam (1979), the square built in Esfahan by Abbas I in the early 17th century, which is bordered on all sides by monumental buildings linked by a series of arcades; Takht-e Soleyman (2003), a Sasanian royal residence with important Zoroastrian religious architecture and decoration; Bam and its Cultural Landscape (2004 and 2007), a fortified medieval town where 26,000 people lost their lives in the earthquake of 2003; Pasargadae (2004), the first dynastic capital of the great multicultural Achaemenid Empire in Western Asia; Soltaniyeh (2005), the capital of the Ilkhamid dynasty that stands as a monument to Persian and Islamic architecture; Bisotun (2006), an ancient town on the trade route that linked the Iranian high plateau with Mesopotamia; the Armenian Monastic Ensembles (2008), three monastic buildings dating back to the 7th century; and Shushtar Historical Hydraulic System (2009), a homogeneous hydraulic system, designed globally and completed in the 3rd century AD.

Broadcasting

Broadcasting is state-controlled through the Islamic Republic of Iran Broadcasting (IRIB). It operates four national television networks, eight national radio networks and provincial and international services (including a Koran service and the external Voice of the Islamic Republic of Iran). Satellite dishes were banned in 1995 but tolerated for many years before security forces launched a crackdown against them in 2006. A 24-hour English-language news channel, Press TV, was launched in July 2007. There were 11·6m. television receivers (colour by SECAM H) in 2003.

Press

In 2005 there were 177 daily newspapers and more than 2,500 non-dailies. Approximately 80% of the Iranian press is printed in Farsi; much of the remaining 20% is in English or Arabic.

In 1999 a total of 14,783 book titles were published.

Tourism

There were 1,659,000 foreign tourists in 2004, spending US$1,305m.

Calendar

The Iranian year is a solar year starting on varying dates between 19 and 22 March. The current solar year is 1389 (20 March 2010 to 20 March 2011). The Islamic *hegira* (AD 622, when Mohammed left Makkah for Madinah) year 1431 corresponds to 18 Dec. 2009–7 Dec. 2010, and is the current lunar year.

Festivals

Iran celebrates Revolution Day on 11 Feb. to mark the anniversary of the overthrow of the Shah in 1979. Nowruz (New Year's Day) falls on 21 March while Constitution Day is on 5 Aug. The feast of Shab-e Yelda, held to mark the longest night of the year, is in Dec.

DIPLOMATIC REPRESENTATIVES

Of Iran in the United Kingdom (16 Prince's Gate, London, SW7 1PT)
Ambassador: Rasoul Movahedian.

Of the United Kingdom in Iran (198 Ferdowsi Ave., Tehran 11344)
Ambassador: Simon Gass, CMG, CVO.

The USA does not have diplomatic relations with Iran, but Iran has an Interests Section in the Pakistani Embassy in Washington, D.C., and the USA has an Interests Section in the Swiss Embassy in Tehran.

Of Iran to the United Nations
Ambassador: Mohammad Khazaee.

Of Iran to the European Union
Ambassador: Aliasghar Khaji.

FURTHER READING

Abrahamian, E., *Khomeinism: Essays on the Islamic Republic.* 1993
Amuzegar, J., *Iran's Economy Under the Islamic Republic.* 1992

Ansari, Ali M., *Modern Iran Since 1921: The Pahlavis and After*. 2003
Coughlin, Con, *Khomeini's Ghost: Iran Since 1979*. 2009
Daneshvar, P., *Revolution in Iran*. 1996
Ehteshami, A., *After Khomeini: the Iranian Second Republic*. 1994
Ehteshami, A. and Zweiri, M., *Iran and the Rise of its Neoconservatives: The Politics of Tehran's Silent Revolution*. 2007
Fuller, G. E., *Centre of the Universe: Geopolitics of Iran*. 1992
Goodarzi, Jubin, *Syria and Iran: Diplomatic Alliance and Power Politics in the Middle East*. 2006
Hunter, S. T., *Iran after Khomeini*. 1992
Kamrava, M., *Political History of Modern Iran: from Tribalism to Theocracy*. 1993
Kinzer, Stephen, *All the Shah's Men: an American Coup and the Roots of Middle East Terror*. 2003
Martin, Vanessa, *Creating an Islamic State: Khomeini and the Making of a New Iran*. 2000
Mir-Hosseini, Ziba, *Islam and Gender: The Religious Debate in Contemporary Iran*. 1999
Modaddel, M., *Class, Politics and Ideology in the Iranian Revolution*. 1992
Moin, Baqer, *Khomeini: Life of the Ayatollah*. 1999
Omid, H., *Islam and the Post-Revolutionary State in Iran*. 1994
Rahnema, A. and Behdad, S. (eds.) *Iran After the Revolution: the Crisis of an Islamic State*. 1995

National Statistical Office: Statistical Centre of Iran, Dr Fatemi Avenue, Tehran 1414663111, Iran.
Website: http://www.sci.org.ir

IRAQ

Jumhouriya al 'Iraqia
(Republic of Iraq)

Capital: Baghdad
Population estimate, 2010: 31·47m.
GNI per capita, 2007: US$725

KEY HISTORICAL EVENTS

Around 3000 BC the Sumerian culture flourished in Mesopotamia—the part of the Fertile Crescent between and around the Tigris and Euphrates rivers. Incursions from Semitic peoples of the Arabian Peninsula led to Akkadian supremacy after the victory of Sargon the Great (*c.* 2340 BC). The Sumerian cities, such as Ur, reasserted their independence until 1700 BC, when King Hammurabi established the first dynasty of Babylon. Hammurabi and his son, Samsu-iluna, presided over the political and cultural apogee of Babylon; it was a time of great prosperity and relative peace. Babylonia was challenged by the Anatolian Hittites, who sacked Babylon in 1595 BC. A weakened Babylonia fell to the Kassites from the Zagros mountains, who held sway for over 400 years. The power-vacuum in northern Babylonia was filled by the Hurrian kingdom of Mitanni until Assyria's dominance in the 13th century BC. The Semitic Assyrians built an empire that stretched from Tarsus on the Mediterranean to Babylon, which they sacked in 1240 BC.

Elamite invasions in the 12th century BC allowed the establishment of a second Babylonian dynasty—Isin, or Pashe—but the assertiveness of its king, Nebuchadnezzar I, provoked Assyrian retaliation. Assyrian control of Babylonia was regained but tempered by massive immigration of Aramaeans from Upper Mesopotamia and Syria. Nevertheless, the Assyrians achieved considerable imperial expansion under Ashurnasirpal II in the early ninth century BC. Assyrian decline and revival was repeated in the eighth century. Babylon was recaptured in 729 BC and most of the Fertile Crescent, from the Nile Delta to the Persian Gulf, was subjugated. However, the empire soon crumbled after the death of the great King Ashurbanipal in 627 BC. Revolts in Babylonia were led by the Chaldeans, who had settled in the south from the ninth century. An alliance of old enemies—the Medes and the Scythians—ravaged the Assyrian Empire and in 612 BC, the capital, Nineveh, fell to the Medes.

Babylonia, known at this time as Chaldea, assumed control of much of the Fertile Crescent. In 586 BC, Nebuchadnezzar II conquered Phoenicia and Judah, destroying Jerusalem and deporting 15,000 Judaeans as labourers for Babylon. This Babylonian revival withered under his successors, who were defeated by Achaemenid Persia. Cyrus the Great captured Babylon in 539 BC. His rule was strengthened by his self-association with the Babylonian throne and by his religious tolerance; the Babylonian deity Bel-Marduk was restored and the Temple of Jerusalem rebuilt. Xerxes I (485–465 BC) styled himself the Persian Emperor and seized the Bel-Marduk statue, provoking several Babylonian rebellions.

Alexander

The last of the Achaemenids, Darius III, was defeated at the Battle of Gaugamela (near Mosul) in 331 BC by Alexander the Great of Macedon, who established the Hellenistic Age of the Near East. Having assumed the Persian throne, he died at Babylon in 323 BC. His empire was split in four; Seleucus took control of Mesopotamia and Persia and declared himself king in 305 BC. Babylon was soon eclipsed by a new capital at Seleucia on the Tigris and was abandoned during the third century. Parthia, Bactria and Anatolia were lost by Seleucus' successors until Antiochus III (223–187 BC) reasserted his lordship over the lost provinces. However, his foray into Greece was repulsed by Rome, which forced a heavy indemnity on the Seleucid Empire. Rapid territorial losses to Rome, Ptolemaic Egypt and local rebellions led to a Parthian invasion of Babylonia in 129 BC.

The Parthian Empire, with its winter capital at Ctesiphon on the Tigris, reached its territorial zenith under Mithridates II (123–88 BC), who defeated Armenia and repelled the Scythians. Though a looser political unit than the Seleucid state, Mithridates' empire was a conscious inheritor of the great traditions—Persian, Babylonian and Hellenistic—in culture, language and symbolism. Intrigue over its nominal vassal, Armenia, brought Parthia into conflict with Rome. At Carrhae the Parthians inflicted a crushing defeat on a Roman army under Crassus in 53 BC. Several wars followed until Vologases I achieved a settlement with Emperor Nero over the Armenian buffer-state in AD 63. Dynastic disputes bedevilled Parthia and its vassal kingdoms. The invasion of Armenia by Osroes I (AD 109–129) sparked a Roman invasion in AD 113 under Trajan, who annexed Armenia and occupied most of Mesopotamia. Roman control ended after Trajan's death but Vologases IV was forced to cede western Mesopotamia to Rome. However, Mesopotamia remained a battleground, such as the AD 195 invasion by the Emperor Severus, who looted Ctesiphon, further weakening the Parthian state. In AD 224 Artabanus IV, the last of the Parthian kings, was defeated by Ardashir (Artaxerxes), ruler of Persia and founder of the Sassanid Dynasty.

The Sassanian Persians emulated the Achaemenids and attempted to regain their empire, leading to inevitable conflict with Rome. Ardashir's son, Shapur I, continued his father's expansion in the east and attacked Rome's Levantine provinces. Syria and Armenia were overrun and the Roman Emperor Valerian captured at Edessa in 259. Shapur II (309–379) consolidated Sassanid power, defeating threats from Arabia and Central Asia and wresting control of the Tigris and Armenia from the Romans. The religious policies of the Zoroastrian Sassanids fluctuated from tolerance to persecution. Khosrau I (531–579) revived imperial expansion; his grandson, Khosrau II, was restored to the throne by the Byzantine Emperor Maurice, who was rewarded with Armenia and northeastern Mesopotamia. However, Khosrau retook Mesopotamia after Maurice's murder, beginning a Persian rampage through the Byzantine East. The sack and pillage of Jerusalem provoked Emperor Heraclius, who struck the Persian heartland. In 627 Heraclius entered Ctesiphon and destroyed the palace of Khosrau, who was murdered. Sassanid Persia, exhausted by conflict with Rome, quickly fell to the Arab invasion.

Led by Sa'd ibn Abi Waqqas, the Arab forces of Islam defeated the Sassanians at the Battle of Al-Qadisiyyah (*c.* 636) on the Euphrates and at Nahavand, western Iran, in 642. By 639 most of Iraq (*Erak*, 'lower Iran'), comprising the centre and south of modern republic, had been conquered; as had Al-Jazirah ('The Island'), the area north of Tikrit. Mass Arab immigration saw the establishment of garrison towns at Kufa (near Babylon) and Al-Basrah and later at Mosul. After the first four caliphs, the Caliphate effectively became hereditary under the Ummayads, based at Damascus. However, their rule was disputed, especially in Iraq. The death of Ali's second son, Husayn, at Karbala in 680 left a body of opposition, the Shias, or 'partisans' of Ali. Iraq was controlled by a governor and, from the 690s, Arabic became the language of administration.

Rise of Baghdad

In 743 civil war came to the Caliphate. Having failed to resolve the tensions between rival Arab military groups, the Umayyads succumbed to the rebellion of the Abbasids, who called for a return to strong Islamic leadership. In 750 the last Ummayad caliph, Marwan II, was deposed by Abu al-'Abbas (As-Saffah), supported by Iranian and Iraqi Shias. However, As-Saffah installed himself as caliph, rejecting a Shia imam. In 754 he was succeeded by his brother Al-Mansur, who moved the capital to Baghdad on the Tigris. This move symbolized the end of the hegemony of Syrian and Yemeni Arabs over the Caliphate. Nevertheless, an overburdened Iraq provided numerous threats to Abbasid authority; Al-Mansur had to quell Shia revolts in Iraq in 763. Caliph Al-Mu'tasim moved his capital to Samarra in 836 to remove his Turkic Mamluk soldiers from Baghdad. The suppression of the Zanj Revolt (869–879) of African slaves around Al-Basrah prompted the return to Baghdad.

Rapid political fragmentation in the 930s broke the Caliphate. The Shia Buyids took Iraq in 946, depriving the Abbasid caliphs of temporal power. From the 970s, Egypt was ruled by a rival caliphate, the Ismaili Fatimids. Baghdad was taken by the Seljuk Turks under Toghrül, the Sultan of Iran, in 1055. Despite the Seljuk territories fragmenting after Malik Shah I died in 1092, Iraq remained under Seljuk authority until the Mongol invasion. In 1258 Baghdad was sacked by the Mongol Hulagu Khan; the city was ravaged, its people slaughtered and its Grand Library destroyed. The sack ended the Abbasid Caliphate and Baghdad's role as a major cultural centre. Hulagu established the Il-Khanid Dynasty of Iran. Buddhism and Nestorian Christianity flourished under the patronage of Hulagu's successors until the conversion of Khan Ghazan to Sunni Islam in 1292. The Il-Khanate fragmented in the 1330s and Iraq was ruled by the Mongol Jalayirids.

Ottoman Rule

In 1401 Baghdad was sacked in by Timur. His death in 1405 allowed the Black Sheep Turkmen (Kara Koyunlu) to overthrow their Jalayirid masters. However, their rapid expansion ended in defeat in 1466 at the hands of the White Sheep Turkmen (Ak Koyunlu). Rivalry with the Ottoman Turks in Anatolia weakened the White Sheep Turkmen, who were forced to withdraw from Iraq by the Turkic Safavid rulers of Iran. Shah Ismail I took Baghdad in 1509 and made Shi'ism the state religion; all other creeds were banned. However, Iraq soon fell to the Sunni Ottomans, with Sultan Suleyman the Magnificent taking Baghdad in 1534. Shah Abbas reclaimed Iraq for Iran in 1603, brutally suppressing a major Kurdish rebellion in 1610. Ottoman authority was reimposed by Sultan Murad IV, who led his army into Baghdad in 1638.

Centuries of neglect and war had devastated the irrigation systems and agricultural wealth of Iraq. The Ottomans treated Iraq as a buffer state against Iran and allowed Kurdish and Bedouin tribes to dominate. Mamluks asserted their power in Iraq until 1831, when Baghdad was devastated by flooding. Serious administrative reform (*tanzimat*) came in 1869 with the appointment of Midhat Pasha as governor of Baghdad, with great improvements in the army, the law and education. The Young Turks revolution of 1908 gave Iraq limited political representation.

British Mandate

Anglo-German rivalry led to a British invasion of southern Iraq in Nov. 1914. Although Al-Basrah fell in 1915, the British suffered a major defeat at Al-Kut in 1916. Nevertheless, Baghdad was taken in March 1917. After the First World War the Allies entrusted Iraq to Britain under the Sykes-Picot Agreement, which protected British oil interests in the region. The State of Iraq became a League of Nations mandate under British Control in Nov. 1920. Rebellions in Kurdish and southern areas were suppressed with bombing campaigns. A Hashemite monarchy was installed, under Amir Faysal ibn Husayn from Mecca, a wartime ally, and an indigenous army created. The monarchy was supported by a plebiscite in 1921. Kurdish-dominated Mosul province—vital for its massive oil reserves—was granted to Iraq by the League of Nations in 1925. Britain's mandate ended in 1932. Rebellions followed in Kurdish areas, led by Mustafa Barzani until he fled to the USSR in 1945. Rejecting the partition of Palestine, Iraq went to war with Israel in 1948, leading to the emigration of 120,000 Iraqi Jews.

The monarchy was overthrown in a military coup on 14 July 1958. King Faisal II and Nuri al Said, the prime minister, were killed. A republic was established, controlled by a military-led Council of Sovereignty under Gen. Abdul Karim Qassim. In 1963 Qassim was overthrown and Gen. Abdul Salam Aref became president, with a partial return to a civilian government, but on 17 July 1968 a successful coup was mounted by the Pan-Arabist Ba'ath Party. Gen. Ahmed Al Bakr became president, prime minister, and chairman of a newly established nine-member Revolutionary Command Council. In July 1979 Saddam Hussein, the vice-president and a Sunni Muslim, became president in a peaceful transfer of power.

The 1979 Iranian Revolution was perceived as a threat to the delicate Sunni-Shia balance in Iraq. In Sept. 1980 Iraq invaded Iran, ostensibly over territorial rights in the Shatt-al-Arab waterway. The war claimed over a million lives and saw the use of chemical weapons by the Iraqi army. The al-Anfal campaign (1986–89) countered Kurdish rebellions, killing 182,000 Kurds. Chemical weapons were prominent, most notably at Halabja, where 5,000 died in one day. A UN-arranged ceasefire took place on 20 Aug. 1988 and UN-sponsored peace talks continued in 1989. On 15 Aug. 1990 Iraq accepted the pre-war border and withdrew troops from Iranian soil.

1991 War

On 2 Aug. 1990 Iraqi forces invaded and rapidly overran Kuwait, on the pretext of alleged Kuwaiti 'slant-drilling' across the Iraqi border. The UN Security Council voted to impose economic sanctions on Iraq until it withdrew from Kuwait and the USA sent a large military force to Saudi Arabia. Further Security Council resolutions included authorization for the use of military force if Iraq did not withdraw by 15 Jan. 1991. On the night of 16–17 Jan. coalition forces (US and over 30 allies) began an air attack on strategic targets in Iraq. A land offensive followed on 24 Feb. The Iraqi army was routed and Kuwait City was liberated on 28 Feb.

Iraq agreed to the conditions of a provisional ceasefire, including withdrawal from Kuwait. Subsequent Kurdish and Shia rebellions were brutally suppressed.

In June 1991 UNSCOM, the United Nations Special Commission, conducted its first chemical weapons inspection in Iraq in accordance with UN Resolution 687. In Sept. a UN Security Council resolution permitted Iraq to sell oil worth US$1,600m. to pay for food and medical supplies. In Oct. the Security Council voted unanimously to prohibit Iraq from all nuclear activities. Imports of materials used in the manufacture of nuclear, biological or chemical weapons were banned, and UN weapons inspectors received wide powers to examine and retain data throughout Iraq.

In Aug. 1992 the USA, UK and France began to enforce air exclusion zones over southern and northern Iraq in response to the government's persecution of Shias and Kurds. Following Iraqi violations of this zone and incursions over the Kuwaiti border, US, British and French forces made air and missile attacks on Iraqi military targets in Jan. 1993. On 10 Nov. 1994 Iraq recognized the independence and boundaries of Kuwait. In the first half of 1995 UN weapons inspectors secured information on an extensive biological weapons programme. At the beginning of Sept. 1996 Iraqi troops occupied the town of Arbol in a Kurdish safe haven in support of the Kurdish Democratic Party faction which was at odds with another Kurdish faction, the Patriotic Union of Kurdistan. On 3 Sept. 1996 US forces fired missiles at targets in southern Iraq and extended the no-fly area northwards to the southern suburbs of Baghdad.

Weapons Inspection

Relations with the USA deteriorated still further in 1997 when Iraq refused co-operation with UN weapons inspectors. The USA and the UK threatened retaliatory action and a renewal of hostilities looked probable until late Feb. 1998 when Kofi Annan, the UN Secretary General, forged an agreement in Baghdad allowing for 'immediate, unconditional and unrestricted access' to all suspected weapons sites. In Aug. 1998 Saddam Hussein engineered another stand-off with the UN arms inspectors, demanding a declaration that Iraq had rid itself of all weapons of mass destruction. This was refused by the UN chief inspector. In Nov. all UN personnel left Iraq as the USA threatened air strikes unless Iraq complied with UN resolutions. Russia and France urged further diplomatic efforts, but on 16 Dec. the USA and Britain launched air and missile attacks aimed at destroying Saddam Hussein's suspected arsenal of nuclear, chemical and biological weapons.

In Feb. 2000 the UN Security Council nominated Sweden's Hans Blix to head the new arms inspectorate to Iraq but he was refused entry into the country. In Feb. 2001 the USA and Britain launched a further series of air attacks on military targets in and around Baghdad. A new UN Security Council resolution was passed in May 2002. Constituting the biggest change since the introduction in 1966 of a UN-administered Oil-for-Food scheme to alleviate the suffering among the civilian population, the new resolution limited import restrictions to a number of specific sensitive goods. In Nov. 2002 the UN Security Council adopted Resolution 1441, holding Iraq in 'material breach' of disarmament obligations. Weapons inspectors, under the leadership of Hans Blix, returned to Iraq four years after their last inspections, but US and British suspicion that the Iraq regime was failing to comply led to increasing tension, resulting in the USA, the UK and Spain reserving the right to disarm Iraq without the need for a further Security Council resolution. Other Security Council members, notably China, France, Germany and Russia, opposed the proposed action.

Fall of Saddam

On 20 March 2003 US forces, supported by the UK, began a war aimed at 'liberating Iraq'. UK troops entered Iraq's second city, Al-Basrah, on 6 April. On 9 April 2003 American forces took control of central Baghdad, effectively bringing an end to Saddam Hussein's rule. Widespread looting and disorder followed the fall of the capital. The bloodless capture of Tikrit, Saddam Hussein's hometown, on 14 April marked the end of formal Iraqi resistance. An interim government was planned until democratic elections could be held. On 22 May the UN Security Council voted to lift economic sanctions against Iraq and to support the US and UK occupation 'until an internationally recognized, representative government is established by the people of Iraq'. Only Syria opposed the resolution by boycotting the session. A 25-man Iraqi-led governing council (IGC) met in Baghdad for the first time in July 2003.

Resistance to the occupying forces increased from late summer. Bomb attacks in Aug. targeted the UN's Baghdad office, killing the UN special representative. Ayatollah Mohammed Baqr al-Hakim, the most senior Shia cleric in Iraq, was assassinated with 100 others in Najaf. Saddam Hussein was captured by American forces at Al-Dawr, near Tikrit, on 13 Dec. 2003. His trial for crimes against humanity, war crimes and genocide began in July 2004. In Feb. 2004 over 100 Kurds were killed in attacks in Irbil and the Shia community suffered 270 deaths in Baghdad and Karbala. In May 2004 accusations surfaced of abuse of Iraqi prisoners by American and British soldiers.

On 30 Jan. 2005 the first democratic elections to a Transitional National Assembly were won by the Shia-dominated United Iraqi Alliance. Jalal Talabani became the country's new president on 6 April 2005, and on 3 May 2005 Iraq's first democratically elected government under Prime Minister Ibrahim al-Jaafari was sworn in. In Oct. 2005 a new federal constitution was approved in a nationwide referendum (although without the support of the Sunni community) and the trial of former dictator Saddam Hussein for mass murder opened in Baghdad. Despite the political advances, insurgent violence has continued against foreign troops, domestic security forces and civilians. In Dec. 2005 a general election for a new parliament was won by the United Iraqi Alliance. In April 2006 after months of deadlock Nouri al-Maliki was appointed the new prime minister. Insurgent violence continues against foreign troops, domestic security forces and civilians. Nobody can be certain how many Iraqis have been killed since the start of the US-led invasion in March 2003. Estimates vary from 96,000 (to Feb. 2010) by Iraq Body Count and the Oxford Research Group on the basis of media reports through to about 600,000 in a John Hopkins University study of 2006 funded by the Massachusetts Institute of Technology based on interviews of households. In Nov. 2006 Saddam Hussein was sentenced to death. His execution on 30 Dec. 2006 drew mixed reaction both in Iraq and abroad.

In Jan. 2007 President Bush announced a 'troop surge' in Iraq, with 21,500 extra troops to be deployed to assist the Iraqi army in fighting insurgents and al-Qaeda forces. 4,000 US troops were stationed in Al-Anbar province, with the remainder sent to Baghdad. Iraqi forces gradually took control of internal security, with responsibility for Al-Basrah (Basra) province from Dec. 2007 and Al-Anbar from Sept. 2008. A US-Iraq Status of Forces Agreement (SOFA) that came into effect on 1 Jan. 2009 agreed on the withdrawal of the US army by the end of 2011. UK combat operations ended in April 2009 and in June US troops withdrew from Iraqi towns and cities.

TERRITORY AND POPULATION

Iraq is bounded in the north by Turkey, east by Iran, southeast by the Persian Gulf, south by Kuwait and Saudi Arabia, and west by Jordan and Syria. In April 1992 the UN Boundary Commission redefined Iraq's border with Kuwait, moving it slightly northwards in line with an agreement of 1932. Area, 434,128 sq. km. Population, 1997 census, 22,046,244; density, 50·8 per sq. km. Estimate, 2007, 29,682,100. In 2000, 67·9% of the population lived in urban areas.

The UN gives an estimated population for 2010 of 31·47m.

The areas, populations and capitals of the governorates:

Governorate	Area in sq. km	Population 1997 census	Capital
Al-Anbar	138,501	1,023,776	Ar-Ramadi
Babil (Babylon)	6,468	1,181,751	Al-Hillah
Baghdad	734	5,423,964	Baghdad
Al-Basrah	19,070	1,556,445	Al-Basrah
Dahuk	6,553	402,970	Dahuk
Dhi Qar	12,900	1,184,796	An-Nasiriyah
Diyala	19,076	1,135,223	Ba'qubah
Irbil	14,471	1,095,992	Irbil
Karbala	5,034	594,235	Karbala
Maysan	16,072	637,126	Al-Amarah
Al-Muthanna	51,740	436,825	As-Samawah
An-Najaf	28,824	775,042	An-Najaf
Ninawa (Nineveh)	37,323	2,042,852	Mosul
Al-Qadisiyah	8,153	751,331	Ad-Diwaniyah
Salah ad-Din	24,751	904,432	Tikrit
As-Sulaymaniyah	17,023	1,362,739	As-Sulaymaniyah
Ta'mim	10,282	753,171	Kirkuk
Wasit	17,153	783,614	Al-Kut

The most populous cities are Baghdad (the capital), population of 4,689,000 in 1999, Irbil and Mosul. Other large cities included Kirkuk, Al-Basrah, As-Sulaymaniyah and An-Najaf.

The population is approximately 80% Arab, 17% Kurdish (mainly in the north of the country) and 3% Turkmen, Assyrian, Chaldean or other. Shia Arabs (predominantly in the south of the country) constitute approximately 60% of the total population and Sunni Arabs (principally in the centre) 20%.

The official language is Arabic. Other languages spoken are Kurdish (official in Kurdish regions), Assyrian and Armenian.

SOCIAL STATISTICS

2000 estimates: births, 792,000; deaths, 177,000; marriages, 171,000. Birth and death rates, 2000 (per 1,000 population): births, 34·1; deaths, 7·6. Life expectancy at birth, 2007, was 64·2 years for men and 71·8 years for women. Annual population growth rate, 2000–05, 3·0%. Infant mortality, 2003: 107 per 1,000 live births. Fertility rate, 2004: 4·7 births per woman. Maternal mortality rate per 10,000 live births, 2003: 29·4.

CLIMATE

The climate is mainly arid, with limited and unreliable rainfall and a large annual range of temperature. Summers are very hot and winters are cold. Al-Basrah, Jan. 55°F (12·8°C), July 92°F (33·3°C). Annual rainfall 7" (175 mm). Baghdad, Jan. 50°F (10°C), July 95°F (35°C). Annual rainfall 6" (140 mm). Mosul, Jan. 44°F (6·7°C), July 90°F (32·2°C). Annual rainfall 15" (384 mm).

CONSTITUTION AND GOVERNMENT

Until the fall of Saddam Hussein, the highest state authority was the Revolutionary Command Council (RCC) but some legislative power was given to the 220-member *National Assembly*. The only legal political grouping was the National Progressive Front (founded 1973) comprising the Arab Socialist Renaissance (Ba'ath) Party and various Kurdish groups, but a law of Aug. 1991 legalized political parties provided they were not based on religion, racism or ethnicity.

In July 2003 a 25-man Iraqi-led governing council met in Baghdad for the first time since the US-led war in an important staging post towards full self-government. The temporary Coalition Provisional Authority was dissolved on 28 June 2004. Power was handed over to the interim Iraqi government which assumed full sovereign powers for governing Iraq. It became a transitional government after elections in Jan. 2005. The 275-member Transitional National Assembly approved a draft new constitution on 29 Aug. 2005, 14 days after the original deadline. It was approved in a nationwide referendum held on 15 Oct., with 78·6% of votes cast in favour. Shias and Kurds generally supported the constitution. Most Sunnis opposed it because of its reference to federalism and the risk that Iraq could ultimately break up, as Iraq's oil resources are in the Shia and Kurdish areas. The constitution states that Iraq is a democratic, federal, representative republic and a multi-ethnic, multi-religious and multi-sect country. Islam is the official religion of the state and a basic source of legislation. Elections were held in Dec. 2005 for the new 275-member *Council of Representatives*. It is expected to determine the composition of a proposed upper chamber. In Dec. 2009 the number of seats was increased from 275 to 325 ahead of the 2010 elections.

National Anthem

'Mawtini' ('My Homeland'); words by I. Touqan, tune by M. Fuliefil.

RECENT ELECTIONS

In parliamentary elections to the permanent Iraqi National Assembly held on 7 March 2010 the Iraqi National Movement coalition won 25·9% of the vote, taking 91 of 325 seats, ahead of the State of Law Coalition with 25·8% and 89 seats, the National Iraqi Alliance (19·4% and 70), the Kurdistan List (15·3% and 43) and the Movement for Change (4·4% and 8). Four parties claimed 16 seats with less than 3% of the vote each and eight seats were taken by minority parties.

CURRENT ADMINISTRATION

President: Jalal Talabani; b. 1933 (sworn in 7 April 2005).

Vice Presidents: Adil Abdel-Mahdi; Tariq al-Hashemi.

In March 2010 the cabinet consisted of:

Prime Minister: Nouri al-Maliki; b. 1950 (sworn in 20 May 2006).

Deputy Prime Ministers: Rafi Hiyad al-Issawi; Dr Rozh Shaways.

Minister of Defence: Abdul-Qader al-Mifraji. *Foreign Affairs:* Hoshyar Zebari. *Interior:* Jawad Polani. *Justice:* Dara Nur al-Din. *Finance:* Bayan Jabr. *Health:* Salih al-Hasnawi. *Telecommunications:* Farooq Abdulqadir Abdulrahman. *Environment:* Nermin Othman. *Housing:* Bayan Dizayee. *Human Rights:* Wejdan Mikhail. *Municipalities and Public Works:* Ryad Ghraib. *Science and Technology:* Raed Fahmi Jahed. *Planning:* Ali Baban. *Trade:* Vacant. *Youth and Sport:* Jassem Jaafar. *Agriculture:* Ali al-Bahadili. *Displacement and Migration:* Abdelsamad Rahman Sultan. *Water Resources:* Abdul Latif Rasheed. *Labour and Social Affairs:* Mahmud Muhammad Jawad Al Radi. *Transportation:* Amer Abdul Jabbar Ismail. *Education:* Khudair al-Khuzai. *Higher Education:* Abed Diab Al-Oujaili. *Culture:* Maher Dalli Ibrahim Al-Hadithi. *Industry:* Fawzi Al-Hariri. *Oil:* Hussein Sharistani. *Electricity:* Karim Wahid.

Government Website (Arabic only): http://www.cabinet.iq

CURRENT LEADERS

Jalal Talabani

Position

President

Introduction

Jalal Talabani, an experienced Iraqi Kurdish politician, was named state president of Iraq on 6 April 2005 by the Iraqi National Assembly. He was elected by parliament to a second term on 22 April 2006. He was previously the founder and secretary general of one of the main Iraqi Kurdish political parties, the Patriotic Union of Kurdistan (PUK), and later a prominent member of the Iraqi Governing Council which was established following the US-led invasion of Iraq in 2003.

Early Life

Jalal Talabani was born in the village of Kelkan, Irbil province in Iraqi Kurdistan in 1933, the year after Britain surrendered its mandate over Iraq. Talabani joined the Kurdistan Democratic Party (KDP) at the age of 14 and was elected to its central committee six years later. He attended secondary schools in Irbil and Kirkuk and the Law College in Baghdad from 1952 to 1955, when he was forced to leave the college because of his political activities. Following the Iraqi revolution in 1958, when the monarchy was overthrown by a military coup led by Abdul Karim Qassim, Talabani rejoined the college, and graduated in 1959. He subsequently served in the Iraqi army before working as a journalist for various Kurdish publications.

When the Kurdish north launched an armed uprising against the Iraqi government in Sept. 1961, Talabani joined the forces led by Mulla Mustafa al-Barzani (the *peshmerga*) and fought in the Kirkuk and As-Sulaymaniyah areas. He also led Kurdish diplomatic delegations to Europe and the Middle East and negotiated with the leftist, secular Ba'ath party, whose members dominated Iraq's governing council following a coup led by Abdul Salam Aref in Feb. 1963.

By 1964, when profound disagreements were emerging within the KDP, Talabani established a more secular, urban and left-leaning faction, criticizing al-Barzani for 'conservative and tribal' politics. Factional divisions throughout the late 1960s and early 1970s occasionally erupted into armed confrontations. Although deals that secured some autonomy for the Kurds were struck between the KDP and the ruling Ba'ath party, arguments broke out over access to the region's oil supplies and whether Kurds could maintain an army. When the Kurdish revolt collapsed in 1975 (partly as a result of Iran withdrawing its support), Talabani formed a new party, the Patriotic Union of Kurdistan (PUK), based in As-Sulaymaniyah.

The PUK bitterly opposed the Ba'ath party's enforced resettlement of Kurds to Arab areas of Iraq in the late 1970s, and there were also numerous armed confrontations with the KDP. In 1983, while the KDP was fighting Saddam Hussein's Ba'ath party, Talabani was prepared to negotiate. However, hostilities were resumed by the PUK in 1985, after Saddam failed to implement an agreement. In the aftermath of Saddam's chemical weapons attack that killed around 5,000 Kurds at Halabja in 1988 and the subsequent military action that led to more than 100,000 Kurds fleeing to Turkey, Talabani made efforts to bring unity to Kurdish politics. He improved relations between the PUK and the KDP (then led by Mas'ud al-Barzani) and later formed the Iraqi Kurdistan Front, seeking international support for Kurdish autonomy.

Following elections in the haven created for Kurds by the Western alliance after the first Gulf War, a PUK-KDP joint administration was formed in 1992. However, tensions resurfaced and led to serious confrontations between the two groups in 1994. Both parties signed a peace deal in Washington, D.C. in 1998 and the accord was cemented in Oct. 2002 when the regional parliament reconvened in a session attended by both parties' MPs.

Following the US-led invasion of Iraq and the fall of Saddam in April 2003, Talabani joined the US-appointed Iraqi Governing Council (IGC), distancing himself from the movement for Kurdish independence and pledging to support Iraqi federalism. In the Iraqi elections on 30 Jan. 2005, a Shia alliance won a slim majority in parliament and the Kurdish coalition came second in the polls. For over two months, with the country under sustained attacks from insurgents, both groups argued about the formation of the new government before electing Talabani as the president (a largely ceremonial role) on 6 April 2005.

Career in Office

A presidential council of Talabani and two vice-presidents appointed Ibrahim al-Jaafari, a conservative from the majority Shia community, as prime minister on 7 April 2005. Talabani promised as president to represent all the country's ethnic and religious groups and to reach out to Iraq's Arab and Islamic neighbours. In a letter to the then UK prime minister, he wrote: 'We honour those who sacrificed their lives for our liberation. We are determined out of respect to create a tolerant and democratic Iraq, an Iraq for all the Iraqi people. It will take time and much patience, but I can assure you it will be worthwhile, not only for Iraq, but for the whole of the Middle East.'

Against a backdrop of continuing violence in Iraq, many analysts questioned the strength of the Shia-Kurdish alliance, given that the two groups had little previous common ground beyond resistance against Saddam Hussein. In Oct. 2005 a new Iraqi constitution was approved narrowly in a national referendum, heralding fresh parliamentary elections on 15 Dec. 2005. After months of political deadlock, Iraq's parliament convened on 22 April 2006 to fill the top leadership posts and Talabani was elected by parliament to a second presidential term. On the same day he appointed the Shia politician Nouri al-Maliki as prime minister designate after the latter was nominated by his Shia coalition, the United Iraqi Alliance (UIA).

Following the restoration of Iraqi-Syrian diplomatic ties in Nov. 2006, Talabani became the first Iraqi head of state to visit Damascus for 30 years in Jan. 2007. While in Syria, Talabani urged other Arab countries to send their diplomats back to Iraq and pledged to provide protection for them.

Talabani underwent successful heart surgery in the USA in Aug. 2008. Earlier, in May, his wife had escaped unhurt after a bomb exploded near her motorcade in Baghdad.

Nouri al-Maliki

Position

Prime Minister

Introduction

Nouri al-Maliki was appointed Iraq's prime minister designate by the president, Jalal Talabani, on 22 April 2006. He succeeded his ally and fellow member of the conservative Shia Muslim al-Dawa group, Ibrahim al-Jaafari, who had been unable to curb the violent insurgency or create alliances with Sunni and Kurdish factions since elections in Dec. 2005. Al-Maliki, who once commanded Shia forces against Saddam Hussein's regime from exile in Syria, promised an inclusive government. The new government took office in May, but there was to be no respite from the insurgency and sectarian bloodshed, which led in Jan. 2007 to the announcement by President George W. Bush of a further US troop deployment to Iraq. Al-Maliki's government struggled to achieve the basis for a lasting political consensus, although levels of violence did subside and in Nov. 2008 parliament approved an agreement with the USA that all US troops leave the country by the end of 2011. Al-Maliki's State of Law alliance came second at elections in March 2010 but he remained in office while a workable coalition was established.

Early Life

Nouri Kamel al-Maliki was born in Hindiyah, southern Iraq in 1950. While studying Arabic at Baghdad University in the early 1970s he joined al-Dawa, which was opposed to the secularism of the ruling Ba'ath party. In 1980 he was forced into exile, initially in Iran and from 1990 in Syria.

Following the US-led invasion of Iraq in March 2003 and the fall of Saddam Hussein, al-Maliki returned home. In July 2003 he was selected as a member of the US-backed Interim Governing Council, serving as deputy chairman of a committee formed to purge Saddam's Ba'athist allies from political life. The committee was widely criticized for heavy-handedness and many Sunni Muslims resented what they saw as a Shia plot to deny them a role in post-Saddam Iraq. As a senior member of al-Dawa, al-Maliki worked closely with party leader al-Jaafari to forge a coalition of Shia parties, called the United Iraqi Alliance (UIA). The coalition won a parliamentary majority (140 of 275 available seats) in elections of 30 Jan. 2005.

Elected to the transitional National Assembly, al-Maliki became the senior Shia member of the committee charged with drafting the new constitution. In protracted negotiations, he resisted efforts by Sunnis to reduce the autonomy given to Kurds in the north and Shias in the south. Attempts by Prime Minister al-Jaafari to form a broad-based coalition government to reflect the results of the elections on 15 Dec. 2005 became deadlocked and he stepped down on 21 April 2006. Al-Maliki emerged as the UIA's premiership candidate and was named prime minister designate on 22 April 2006.

Career in Office

Calling for an end to sectarian divisions, in late June al-Maliki announced a national reconciliation plan, including a conditional amnesty for insurgents and intra-communal dialogue between political leaders, clerics, armed militias and civil society representatives. However, sectarian violence continued to inflict a high daily death toll. Sunni Muslim opinion was further inflamed by the widely criticized conduct of Saddam Hussein's execution for crimes against humanity at the end of Dec. 2006. In Jan. 2007 President Bush announced that he would send 21,000 extra US troops to Iraq to reassert the authority of al-Maliki's government. By the end of 2007 there were signs that the US military was quelling the insurgency in Baghdad and other centres. Meanwhile, al-Maliki remained under pressure to find a political consensus on divisive ethnic and sectarian issues, an impasse aggravated by the withdrawal from the national unity government of radical Shia members, secular-leaning Iraqis and the main Sunni coalition group (who rejoined in July 2008).

In Dec. 2007 the UK military contingent in Iraq handed control of Basra province to Iraqi forces, which in March 2008 launched a crackdown on radical Shia Mahdi Army militia. Also in March, Iranian President Mahmoud Ahmadinejad made an unprecedented two-day visit to Iraq for talks with al-Maliki, who returned the visit in June. The following month he first raised the prospect of a timetable for a US withdrawal, leading in Nov. to the approval by Iraq's parliament of a security pact under which all troops would leave the country by the end of 2011.

On 1 Jan. 2009 the Iraqi government took control of Baghdad's fortified Green Zone from US forces and assumed authority over foreign troops in the country. In the same month al-Maliki's allies did well in provincial elections. British troops formally ended their combat mission in Iraq in April and in June the Iraqi government declared a holiday to mark National Sovereign Day as US combat troops completed their withdrawal from towns and cities.

In Oct. 2009 al-Maliki announced the formation of a multiconfessional nationalist State of Law grouping to contest the forthcoming general election after a split in the broad Shia coalition that won the 2005 polls. Unexpectedly, his alliance was narrowly defeated at elections in March 2010 by the Iraqi National Movement of former prime minister Iyad Allawi, although al-Maliki challenged the result. He remained in office during the drawn-out process of negotiating a coalition.

DEFENCE

Following the downfall of Saddam Hussein, recruitment began in July 2003 for a new professional army run by the US military. Saddam Hussein's forces numbered 400,000 at their peak. Foreign troops in Iraq in Aug. 2009 numbered 128,000 (all American, following the withdrawal of the last British troops). In Nov. 2008 Iraq's parliament approved a plan whereby all American troops will leave by the end of 2011.

Army

A New Iraqi Army is being developed to replace Saddam's army with a professional force. In Nov. 2007 personnel numbered an estimated 163,500. In July 2004 the Civil Defense Corps (23,100 personnel in April 2004) was disbanded and converted into a National Guard. It was in turn merged into the Army in Jan. 2005.

Navy

A 1,100-strong (2007) Iraqi Navy (initially called the Coastal Defense Force) has been re-established since the 2003 war. It began operations in Oct. 2004.

Air Force

An Iraqi Air Force (initially called the Army Air Corps) has been reconstructed since 2003. There were a total of 1,200 personnel in Nov. 2007, with 22 aircraft and 37 helicopters.

INTERNATIONAL RELATIONS

Iraq is a member of the UN, World Bank, IMF and several other UN specialized agencies, Islamic Development Bank, OIC, League of Arab States and OPEC.

ECONOMY

The oil sector accounted for 76·1% of GDP in 2001; agriculture accounted for 7·8%, manufacturing 1·6% and services 13·8%.

Iraq featured among the ten most corrupt countries in the world in a 2009 survey of 180 countries carried out by the anti-corruption organization *Transparency International*.

Overview

The military victory of the US-led coalition in 2003 led to the shutdown of much of Iraq's administrative structure. World Bank estimates indicate that GDP declined by 30% in 2003. In Nov. 2004 the Paris Club of official creditors agreed to write off 80% of Iraq's external debt, to be achieved in three stages. Recently, progress has been made in implementing structural reforms but insecurity continues to hamper oil production and economic prospects, while inflation remains high.

Currency

From 15 Oct. 2003 a new national currency, the new *Iraqi dinar* (NID), was introduced to replace the existing currencies in circulation in the south and north of the country. Inflation was 30·8% in 2007, falling sharply to 2·7% in 2008.

Budget

Estimated revenue, 2006, ID61,650bn. (ID49,505bn. in 2005); expenditure, 2006, ID53,480bn. (ID44,497bn. in 2005). Petroleum revenues accounted for 76·4% of all revenues in 2006; current expenditure accounted for 79·8% of all expenditures.

Performance

Real GDP growth was 1·5% in 2007 and 9·5% in 2008. Total GDP in 2007 was US$69·7bn.

Banking and Finance

All banks were nationalized in 1964. Following the Gulf War in 1991 the formation of private banks was approved, although they were prohibited from conducting international transactions. A new post-Saddam banking law in Oct. 2003 authorized private banks to process international payments, remittances and foreign currency letters of credit. The Trade Bank of Iraq has been established as an export credit agency to facilitate trade financing. The independent Central Bank of Iraq is the sole bank of issue; its *Governor* is Dr Sinan Mohammed Rida Al-Shabibi. All domestic interest rates were liberalized on 1 March 2004.

ENERGY AND NATURAL RESOURCES

Environment

Iraq's carbon dioxide emissions from the consumption and flaring of fossil fuels were the equivalent of 3·6 tonnes per capita in 2008.

Electricity

Before the war in March–April 2003 installed capacity was 4,400 MW. Despite post-war looting and sabotage, production had recovered and by Oct. 2003 the generating capacity was back to pre-war levels. The estimated available power generating capacity in 2005 was about 6,000 MW.

Oil and Gas

Proven oil reserves in 2008 totalled 115·0bn. bbls. Oil production in 2008 totalled 119·3m. tonnes, the highest total since 2001.

In 2008 Iraq had natural gas reserves of 3,170bn. cu. metres.

Minerals

The principal minerals extracted are phosphate rock (100,000 tonnes in 2002) and sulphur (98,000 tonnes in 2002).

Agriculture

There were around 5·75m. ha. of arable land in 2002 and 0·34m. ha. of permanent crops. An estimated 3·53m. ha. were irrigated in 2002. Production (2003 estimates, in 1,000 tonnes): wheat, 2,553; barley, 1,316; tomatoes, 1,000; dates, 910; potatoes, 625; melons and watermelons, 575; cucumbers and gherkins, 350; oranges, 310; grapes, 300; rice, 125.

Livestock (2003 estimates): cattle, 1·5m.; sheep, 6·2m.; goats, 1·6m.; asses, 380,000; chickens, 23m.

Forestry

In 2005 forests covered 822,000 ha., representing 1·9% of the land area. Timber production in 2007 was 117,000 cu. metres.

Fisheries

Catches in 2005 totalled 20,100 tonnes, of which about 98% from inland waters.

INDUSTRY

Iraq remains under-developed industrially. Production figures (2004, in 1,000 tonnes): residual fuel oil, 8,257; distillate fuel oil, 4,906; petrol, 3,278; cement, 2,515; kerosene, 1,127; jet fuel, 607.

Labour

In 1996 the labour force was 5,573,000 (75% males). Unemployment was 33% in Aug. 2005, down from 55% in Aug. 2003. In Sept. 2003 the US civil administrator signed an order implementing a new 11-tier salary scale for all public employees, replacing a temporary scale in effect since the collapse of the Saddam regime.

Trade Unions

The Iraqi Federation of Workers' Trade Unions was formed in May 2003. There is also a Federation of Workers' Councils and Unions in Iraq, founded in Dec. 2003.

INTERNATIONAL TRADE

Imports and Exports

In 2007 imports amounted to US$18,289m. and exports to US$39,590m. Manufactures and food are the main import commodities. Crude oil is the main export commodity. Imports and exports have both increased significantly since the Saddam era.

COMMUNICATIONS

Roads

In 2002 there were an estimated 44,900 km of roads, of which 84·3% were paved. Vehicles in use in 2002 included 637,500 passenger cars and 375,000 lorries and vans. In 1996 there were 1,338 road accidents resulting in 1,573 deaths. Considerable post-war road reconstruction since 2003 reflects heavy military use and lack of maintenance.

Rail

In 2005 railways comprised 2,032 km of 1,435 mm gauge route. Passenger-km travelled in 2004 came to 24m. and freight tonne-km to 90m. In 2003, five main lines were in operation, serving 107 stations.

Civil Aviation

In 2000 there were international flights for the first time since the 1991 Gulf War, with air links being established between Iraq and Egypt, Jordan and Syria. Since 2003 the two international airports at Baghdad and Al-Basrah have undergone post-war reconstruction. Major domestic airports are at Mosul, Kirkuk and Irbil.

Shipping

The merchant fleet in 2002 had a total tonnage of 188,000 GRT, including oil tankers 59,000 GRT. A 565-km canal was opened in 1992 between Baghdad and the Persian Gulf for shipping, irrigation, the drainage of saline water and the reclamation of marsh land. Iraq has three oil tanker terminals at Al-Basrah, Khor Al-Amaya and Khor Al-Zubair. Its single deep-water port is at Umm Qasr.

Telecommunications

In 2004 there were 1,608,200 telephone subscribers (62·2 per 1,000 population), including 574,000 mobile phone subscribers. Mobile phones were banned during the Saddam Hussein era. Internet users in 2004 numbered 36,000. The Coalition Provisional Authority awarded three regional mobile telecommunications licences in Oct. 2003.

Postal Services

In 2003 there were 331 post offices.

SOCIAL INSTITUTIONS

Justice

Up until the war in March–April 2003, for civil matters: the court of cassation in Baghdad; six courts of appeal at Al-Basrah, Baghdad (2), Babil (Babylon), Mosul and Kirkuk; 18 courts of first instance with unlimited powers and 150 courts of first instance with limited powers, all being courts of single judges. In addition, six peace courts had peace court jurisdiction only. 'Revolutionary courts' dealt with cases affecting state security.

For religious matters: the Sharia courts at all places where there were civil courts, constituted in some places of specially appointed Qadhis (religious judges) and in other places of the judges of the civil courts. For criminal matters: the court of cassation; six sessions courts (two being presided over by the judge of the local court of first instance and four being identical with the courts of appeal). Magistrates' courts at all places where there were civil courts, constituted of civil judges exercising magisterial powers of the first and second class. There were also a number of third-class magistrates' courts, powers for this purpose being granted to municipal councils and a number of administrative officials.

The death penalty was introduced for serious theft in 1992; amputation of a hand for theft in 1994. It is believed that during the Saddam era there were hundreds of executions annually. The death penalty was suspended in April 2003 after the fall of Saddam, but reinstated in Aug. 2004. Amnesty International reported that there were at least 120 executions in 2009.

In the immediate aftermath of the war, the justice system was idle but by July 2003 an estimated 100 courts were functioning. All Baghdad criminal court functions were consolidated into two operational courthouses. In Dec. 2003 the Governing Council established the Iraqi Special Tribunal to try senior members of the Saddam regime for war crimes, crimes against humanity and genocide.

The population in penal institutions in April 2004 was approximately 15,000 (60 per 100,000 of national population).

Police

A new post-war national police force has been established and numbered about 135,000 in Nov. 2007. The personnel includes both former officers who are being retrained and new recruits.

Education

Primary education became compulsory in 1976. Primary school age is 6–11. Secondary education is for six years, of which the first three are termed intermediate. The medium of instruction is Arabic; Kurdish is used in primary schools in northern districts.

In 2005 there were 92,769 pre-primary school children with 5,981 teaching staff; 4·43m. primary school children with 215,795 teaching staff; and 1·75m. secondary school pupils with 93,219 teaching staff. Adult literacy rate was 56% in 2000 (male, 68%; female, 43%). Most schools were closed in March–April 2003 when UNICEF estimates that 200 were destroyed and a further 2,750 looted. By Oct. 2003 all 22 universities and 43 technical institutes and colleges were open, as were nearly all primary and secondary schools. There were 424,908 students and 19,231 academic staff in tertiary education in 2005. Expenditure on education in 2003 was an estimated US$384·5m.

Health

According to the World Health Organization, in 2003 there were (per 10,000 population): 6·3 physicians, 1·2 dentists, 1·0 pharmacists, 13·1 hospital beds, and 12·1 nurses and midwifery personnel. There are approximately 240 hospitals and 1,200 primary health care clinics operating in post-war Iraq.

RELIGION

The constitution proclaims Islam the state religion, but also stipulates freedom of religious belief and expression. In 2001 the population was 97% Muslim; there were also 750,000 Christians, although their numbers have declined since then to 500,000. In Feb. 2010 there was one Roman Catholic cardinal. *See also* TERRITORY AND POPULATION *above*.

CULTURE

World Heritage Sites

Iraq has three UNESCO World Heritage sites: Hatra (inscribed on the list in 1985), a large fortified city of the Parthian (Persian) Empire; Ashur (Qal'at Sherqat) (2003), the first capital and the religious centre of the Assyrians from the 14th to the 9th centuries BC; and Samarra Archaeological City (2007), the site of the capital of the former Abbasid Empire.

Broadcasting

In 2000 there were 1·88m. TV receivers (colour by SECAM H). The Iraqi Public Broadcasting Service is a publicly-funded broadcaster. Satellite television has become widely available in the post-Saddam Hussein era. Kurdish areas in the north of the country run their own broadcasting services.

Press

In 2005 there were more than 200 newspapers regularly published, the most popular of which, Al-Sabah ('The Morning'), had an average circulation of 50,000.

Tourism

In 2001 there were 127,000 foreign tourists.

DIPLOMATIC REPRESENTATIVES

Of Iraq in the United Kingdom (3 Elvaston Pl., London, SW7 5QH)
Ambassador: Vacant.
Chargé d'Affaires a.i.: Abdulmuhaiman Al-Oreibi.

Of the United Kingdom in Iraq (International Zone, Baghdad)
Ambassador: Dr John Jenkins, CMG, LVO.

Of Iraq in the USA (1801 P St., NW, Washington., D.C., 20036)
Ambassador: Samir Shakir Mahmood Sumaidaie.

Of the USA in Iraq (APO AE 09316, Baghdad)
Ambassador: Christopher R. Hill.

Of Iraq to the United Nations
Ambassador: Hamid Al-Bayati.

Of Iraq to the European Union
Ambassador: Jawad Al-Doreky.

FURTHER READING

Aburish, S. K., *Saddam Hussein: The Politics of Revenge.* 2000

Allawi, Ali A., *The Occupation of Iraq: Winning the War, Losing the Peace.* 2007

Blix, Hans, *Disarming Iraq: The Search for Weapons of Mass Destruction.* 2004

Butler, R., *Saddam Defiant: The Threat of Weapons of Mass Destruction and the Crisis of Global Security.* 2000

Herring, Eric and Rangwala, Glen, *Iraq in Fragments: The Occupation and Its Legacy.* 2006

Mackey, Sandra, *The Reckoning: Iraq and the Legacy of Saddam Hussein.* 2002

Marr, Phebe, *The Modern History of Iraq.* 2003

Polk, William R., *Understanding Iraq: The Whole Sweep of Iraqi History, from Genghis Khan's Mongols to the Ottoman Turks to the British Mandate to the American Occupation.* 2006

Shahid, Anthony, *Night Draws Near: Iraq's People in the Shadow of America's War.* 2005

Sluglett, Marion Farouk and Sluglett, Peter, *Iraq Since 1958: From Revolution to Dictatorship.* 3rd ed. 2001

Stansfield, Gareth, *Iraq: People, History, Politics.* 2007

Stiglitz, Joseph E. and Bilmes. Linda J., *The Three Trillion Dollar War: The True Cost of the Iraq Conflict.* 2008

Tripp, Charles, *A History of Iraq.* 2nd ed. 2002

National Statistical Office: Central Organization of Statistics & Information Technology, Baghdad.
Website: http://cosit.gov.iq

Kurdistan

The Kurdistan Region of Iraq ('Iraqi Kurdistan') is the only area of Kurdistan to be recognized officially as an autonomous federal entity. After decades of insurgency Iraq granted limited independence in 1970. *De facto* independence was established following the Kurdish uprising at the end of the Gulf War in 1991. This led to the creation of the Kurdistan Regional Government by the Iraqi Kurdistan Front a year later. Self-governance was disrupted in 1994 by civil war between the Kurdistan Democratic Party (KDP) and the Patriotic Union of Kurdistan (PUK). Rival administrations were set up in Irbil and As-Sulaymaniyah. Peace was restored in Sept. 1998 with the signing of the US-mediated Washington Agreement. The region was acknowledged officially in the 2005 Iraqi constitution and power-sharing began in 2006.

Area, 40,643 sq. km (15,692 sq. miles); population (2002 estimate), 3,757,058. The region comprises three governorates, Irbil, As-Sulaymaniyah and Dahuk, and claims territory in other Kurdish areas although borders remain a contentious issue with Iraq. The unified government has been based at the capital, Irbil, since 2006.

In presidential elections held on 25 July 2009 Massoud Barzani was re-elected with 69·6% of the vote against 25·3% for Kamal Mirawdily. In parliamentary elections held on the same day the Kurdistani List won 57·3% of the vote and 59 of 111 seats, the Change List 23·8% (25 seats) and the Service and Reform List 12·8% (13 seats). Barham Ahmad Salih (PUK) was sworn in as prime minister on 28 Oct. 2009.

Oil and gas are set to become a major source of revenue although exploitation has been hindered over rights' disputes with the Baghdad government. Oil exports began in June 2009 with Baghdad receiving 88% of revenues under current agreements. There are airports at As-Sulaymaniyah and Irbil.

IRELAND

Éire

Capital: Dublin
Population estimate, 2010: 4·59m.
GDP per capita, 2007: (PPP$) 44,613
HDI/world rank: 0·965/5

KEY HISTORICAL EVENTS

Ireland was first inhabited around 7500 BC by Mesolithic hunter-gatherers who travelled across the land bridge that connected southwest Scotland with the northern part of Ireland (it was submerged around 6700 BC). The earliest settlement, at Mount Sandel near Coleraine, has been dated to 5935 BC. Farmers from the Middle-East arrived in Ireland around 3500 BC. Their elaborate graves are also a feature of Neolithic communities in Brittany and the Iberian peninsula. From the sixth century BC, the island was invaded by waves of Celtic tribes from central Europe, including the Gaels, who established pastoral communities within massive stone forts. By AD 200 the Gaels dominated the island, though there was no central control: society was based on a complex structure of hundreds of small kingdoms. The Romans, who dominated much of northern Europe, never reached Ireland. The Gaels traded with other Celtic peoples and sent raiding parties to form settlements in Scotland (Dál Riata) and west Wales.

Christian missionaries reached Ireland during the third century AD. St Patrick, born on the west coast of Britain, was consecrated as a bishop in Gaul and lived and preached in Ireland from *c.* 432 until his death *c.* 465. Monasteries were founded and, in an overwhelmingly agrarian society, they became important centres of learning and the dissemination of the written word. In contrast to much of northern Europe, ravaged by fragmentary forces following the collapse of the Roman Empire, Christianity found a haven in Ireland. Later, Irish missionaries took Celtic Christianity to Britain and continental Europe. By the fifth century AD there were five leading Gaelic kingdoms, which roughly correspond to the latter-day provinces of Ulster, Leinster, Munster and Connacht (the fifth kingdom occupied land in the modern counties of Meath and Westmeath). Each kingdom was dominated by one or two families—the Uí Néill clan was especially powerful in the north and east. The south (Munster) was dominated by the Eóganachta family.

Nordic Invasion

Viking longboats first appeared off the Irish coast in the late seventh century. 795 saw a full-scale Viking invasion, which heralded more than two hundred years of Scandinavian influence. The Vikings were great traders and established the first towns along the east and south coasts—the towns of Wexford, Waterford, Cork and Limerick became prosperous centres of manufacturing and commerce. Dublin, said to be founded in 841 by the Norse king Thurgesius, became a key outpost in a Viking diaspora stretching as far as Sicily and Russia. Gaelic kings made military alliances with the Viking settlers to support their struggles with neighbouring dynasties. In 976 the warrior Brian Boru (Bóruma) became king of Munster following a series of victories against the powerful Eóganachta. Following Boru's defeat of the Leinster groups and their Norse allies at Clontarf in 1014 he seemed destined to be the first high king of all Ireland, but was murdered shortly after his famous victory.

In the mid-12th century the Pope gave his blessing to an expedition of Anglo-Normans to Ireland. They were sent by the English King Henry II, who had been approached for military support by the deposed king of Leinster, Dermot MacMurrough (Díarmait Mac Murchada). Returning to Ireland in 1169 with Norman barons and Welsh mercenaries, MacMurrough recovered part of his former territories and captured Dublin. Richard de Clare (Strongbow), a powerful Norman invader, became MacMurrough's heir after marrying his daughter. During the 13th century various Anglo-Norman adventurers began to establish themselves in Ireland. Dublin Castle was built in 1204 on the site of a Norse fort and the first parliament sat there in 1264. After his decisive defeat of English forces at the Battle of Bannockburn in 1314, Edward Bruce, the brother of Robert Bruce, king of Scotland, dreamed of establishing a Celtic kingdom. In 1315 he landed in Ulster and attempted to overthrow the English. Within a year he controlled most of Ireland north of Dublin, but his troops left a trail of destruction and soon lost support. Bruce was defeated and killed at Dundalk in 1317 by a Norman-Irish army reinforced from England under orders from King Edward II.

The descendants of the Anglo-Norman settlers gradually became identified with the native Irish, whose language, habits, and laws they adopted. To counteract this, the Anglo-Irish Parliament passed the Statute of Kilkenny in 1366, decreeing heavy penalties against all who allied themselves with the Irish. This statute, however, remained inoperative; although Richard II went to Ireland in 1394 and 1399 to reassert royal authority, he failed to achieve any practical result. During the subsequent Wars of the Roses in England the authority of the English crown became limited to the Pale, a coastal district around Dublin.

King Edward IV, of the House of York, came to the English throne in 1461 and appointed Gerald (Gearóid Mór) FitzGerald, 8th earl of Kildare as viceroy of Ireland. The FitzGeralds were wealthy Yorkists, well-connected to a network of Anglo-Norman and Gaelic families. Gearóid Mór wielded considerable power, and managed to hold onto it even after the return of the Lancastrians in 1485. He was eventually replaced in 1494 by Sir

Edward Poynings, who, representing English interests, brought in legislation providing for the reduction of the power of the Anglo-Irish lords. The Poynings Laws removed the legal rights of the Irish parliament to legislate independently.

Henry VII reappointed Gearóid Mór as viceroy in 1496. For the next 38 years the FitzGeralds (Geraldines) ruled Ireland from Maynooth Castle, paying deference to the English crown. Henry VIII was determined to centralize power and reduce the influence of provincial magnates. He introduced the Reformation to Ireland in 1537 and began to dissolve the monasteries with little resistance.

Ulster Rebellion

Elizabeth I, through her deputy in Ireland, Sir Henry Sidley, removed the Irish chiefdoms from their positions of power. An uprising in Munster in the early 1570s was quickly suppressed and only Ulster now provided a stumbling block to Tudor domination. It was from Ulster that Hugh O'Neill and Red Hugh O'Donnell launched an open rebellion. In 1598 O'Neill ambushed and defeated a government force of over 4,000 at the Battle of Yellow Ford near Armagh. Spoken of as 'Prince of Ireland', his ambitions were thwarted by the arrival of 20,000 troops under Lord Mountjoy in 1600. Reinforcements of Spanish soldiers in 1601 were insufficient and O'Neill left for the Continent with his followers in the 1607 'Flight of the Earls'.

The Earls' lands were seized by the English crown and in 1609 Ulster-Scottish and English settlers were invited to colonize. Swathes of land were cleared of farms and woodland, and 23 walled new towns were created, including Belfast. By the early 1620s the Anglo-Scottish population of Ulster was more than 20,000. English politics in the 1630s was dominated by struggles between the crown and parliament (the Puritans) and the Irish in Ulster took advantage, rebelling against the planters in late 1641 in a series of vicious attacks in which thousands of Protestants were killed. The following year Owen Roe O'Neill, who had fled to Spain with his uncle Hugh in 1607, returned to Ireland and led the Confederate forces. A provisional government was established at Kilkenny and by the end of 1642 O'Neill controlled the whole island apart from Dublin and parts of Ulster.

Victory for the English parliamentarians under Oliver Cromwell and the execution of Charles I in 1649 had a profound impact on Ireland. Cromwell was determined to avenge the 1641 massacre of the Ulster planters. With his New Model Army, Cromwell stormed Drogheda and murdered its garrison of 2,000 men. Wexford then fell, and by 1652 all of Ireland was in Cromwellian hands. Hundreds of thousands of acres of land were confiscated and given to a new wave of Protestant settlers.

Following the restoration of the English monarchy in 1660, Catholics in Ireland hoped to be rewarded for their former loyalty, but Charles II restored only a small number of Catholic estates. King James II, however, was a declared Catholic and under his viceroy in Ireland, Richard Talbot, earl of Tyrconnel, Catholics were advanced to positions of state and placed in control of the military. Protestant power was on the wane in England and the Protestant aristocracy invited William of Orange (the Dutch husband of James II's daughter Mary) to claim the English crown. James II fled to France, then travelled to Ireland with French soldiers. They moved north, aiming to subjugate Protestant Ulster. In the spring of 1689 only the walled towns of Derry/Londonderry and Enniskillen remained in Protestant hands. Derry/Londonderry was besieged, but it held out for 15 weeks until the arrival of William's forces, which defeated James at the Battle of the Boyne. The Jacobites retreated to Limerick, where they negotiated the Treaty of Limerick of 1691. Catholics were permitted some religious freedom, and the restoration of their lands. However, the treaty was not honoured by the English parliament and 11,000 Irish Jacobites set sail to join the French army.

Religious Divide

The defeat of the Catholic cause was followed by more confiscation of land and the introduction of the Penal Laws, which prevented Catholics from buying freehold land, holding public office or bearing arms. During the American revolution, fear of a French invasion led Irish Protestants to form the Protestant Volunteer army. Led by Henry Grattan, they used their military strength to extract concessions from Britain. Trade concessions were granted in 1779 and the Poynings Laws repealed three years later. However, Catholics continued to be denied the right to hold political office.

The principles of the French Revolution found their most powerful expression in Ireland in the Society of United Irishmen, which, led by the protestant lawyer Theobald Wolfe Tone, mounted a rebellion in 1798. Without the expected French assistance, the rebellion was crushed by crown troops led by Gen. Lake. The British prime minister, William Pitt, was convinced that the 'Irish problem' could be solved by the abolition of the Irish parliament, legislative union with Britain and Catholic emancipation. The first two goals were achieved in 1801, but the opposition of George III and British Protestants prevented the enactment of the Catholic Emancipation act until 1829, when it was accomplished largely through the efforts of Daniel O'Connell.

After 1829 the Irish representatives in the British Parliament, led by O'Connell, sought a repeal of the Act of Union. Calls for land reforms were drowned out by a disastrous potato famine. Between 1845–49 a blight wiped out the potato crop, the staple food of the Irish population and resulted in mass starvation. Of a population of 8·5m. almost 1m. died and well over 1m. emigrated, mostly to the United States. Irish Catholics in the United States formed the secret Fenian movement, dedicated to achieving full Irish independence.

Home Rule Campaign

Charles Parnell, a Home Rule League MP, came to the fore of the nationalist movement in 1877 as president of the Home Rule Confederation of Great Britain. Parnell led parliamentary obstruction in response to the House of Lords' rejection of limited land reform in Ireland. Parnell's Irish Land League saw limited gains in Gladstone's 1881 Land Act but Parnell, voicing continuing discontent, was imprisoned in Dublin. His release in 1882 and the subsequent Kilmainham Treaty, granting more concessions to tenants, was seen by London as the quickest solution to an increasingly anarchic Ireland.

The Home Rule Party, led by Parnell, brought down the Conservative government at Westminster by voting with the Liberals, allowing William Gladstone to form a government in 1886. Gladstone attempted to resolve the 'Irish problem' by introducing a Home Rule Bill—seen as Parnell's greatest achievement—which would give the Irish Parliament the right to appoint the executive of Ireland. However, Home Rule was greatly opposed in Ulster and England and failed at Westminster in 1886 and 1893. Parnell's domination of Irish politics came to end with the disclosure of his affair with Kitty O'Shea in 1890. After Gladstone rejected him, he lost control of the Irish parliamentarians and was condemned by the Catholic clergy.

During the 1880s a new pride in traditional Irish culture took root, symbolized by the establishment of the Gaelic Athletic Association in 1884 and the Gaelic League in 1893, which successfully campaigned for the return of the Irish language to the school curriculum. Though not political organizations, they provided a link between the conservative Catholic church and the Fenians (nationalists). In 1905 the Irish political leader and journalist Arthur Griffith founded Sinn Féin ('we ourselves') to promote Irish economic welfare and achieve complete political independence. However, at the time the dominant nationalist group remained the Home Rule party of John Redmond.

A Home Rule Bill was finally passed in 1914 but the act was suspended for the duration of the First World War. Redmond pledged the support of Ireland to the British war effort, which angered some nationalists. The Irish Republican Brotherhood (IRB) plotted a rebellion while Britain was at war, soliciting German support. On Easter Monday 1916 the IRB seized the General Post Office in Dublin and Patrick Pearse read out the proclamation of the Republic of Ireland. Though the Easter Rising was over in under a week, the emotional impact was heightened when the British executed 16 of the rebel leaders. Sinn Féin, linked in the Irish public's mind with the rising, scored a dramatic victory in the parliamentary elections of 1918. Its members refused to take their seats in Westminster, declared the *Dáil Éireann* ('Diet of Ireland') and proclaimed the Irish republic. The British outlawed Sinn Féin and the Dáil, which went underground and associated military groups including the Irish Republican Army (IRA) engaged in guerrilla warfare against the local authorities representing the Union. The British sent police reinforcements (the Black and Tans) who further inflamed the situation.

Civil War

A new Home Rule Bill was passed in 1920, establishing two parliaments, one in Belfast and the other in Dublin. The Unionists of the six counties accepted this scheme, and a Northern Parliament was duly elected in May 1921. Sinn Féin rejected the plan, but in autumn 1921 British Prime Minister Lloyd George negotiated with Griffith and Michael Collins of the Dáil a treaty granting Catholic Ireland dominion status within the British Empire. Collins managed to gain approval in the Dáil by a slim majority. The Republicans in the Dáil, led by Éamon de Valera, rejected the treaty, which had divided Ireland and fell short of full independence. A brutal civil war ensued; Collins, who had assumed command of the army, was assassinated in Aug. 1922 by anti-treaty rebels. The treaty supporters emerged as victors and the Irish Free State was established in Jan. 1922. William Cosgrave became the first prime minister and his Fine Gael party led for ten years. In 1932 de Valera, leader of the Fianna Fáil party, became prime minister (*taoiseach*). Five years later he brought in a new constitution establishing the sovereign nation of Ireland and abolishing the oath of allegiance sworn by Irish parliamentarians to the British crown.

Independence

Ireland remained neutral in the Second World War, though in the harsh economic conditions of the time tens of thousands of people emigrated to Britain for work and many thousands joined the war effort. In 1948 Prime Minister John Costello demanded total independence from Britain and reunification with the six counties of Northern Ireland. Independence came the following year and in 1955 the Republic of Ireland was admitted to the United Nations, but nothing came of the claim to the six Ulster counties under British rule. Economic relations between the Republic and Northern Ireland improved in the 1950s and '60s, though both decades were marked by large-scale emigration from the Republic, chiefly to the United States. Trouble in the North flared up in the late '60s over Catholic demands for civil rights and equality in the allocation of housing. Confrontation between the two religious communities intensified and in 1969 British troops were deployed to keep the peace. The British military soon lost the confidence of the Catholic community, the IRA increased its activity and more violence ensued. In 1972 the Unionist government in Belfast resigned and direct rule from London was imposed.

On 1 Jan. 1973 the Republic of Ireland became a member state of the European Economic Community. Jack Lynch led Fianna Fáil into power in 1977, though over the next decade there were party splits while general elections were held against a backdrop of soaring unemployment. Emigration increased, especially among young people, reaching a peak of 44,000 in 1989 under Charles Haughey's premiership. The 1990s were marked by an economic upturn, buoyed by EU subsidies and foreign investment. The legalization of divorce in 1995 symbolized the Irish Republic's embrace of modern European values. In the north, a ceasefire between the IRA and Protestant militias in 1994 formed the basis for the signing of the Good Friday Agreement in April 1998. On 2 Dec. 1999 the Irish constitution was amended to remove the articles laying claim to Northern Ireland. Prime Minister Bertie Ahern, who came to power in the 1997 general election, took Ireland into the single European currency in Jan. 2002. In Oct. 2002 the Northern Irish Assembly was suspended for the fourth time in its history over allegations of IRA spying at the Northern Ireland Office. Direct rule from London was subsequently reimposed. In May 2007 a devolved Northern Ireland government replaced direct rule from London.

TERRITORY AND POPULATION

The Republic of Ireland lies in the Atlantic Ocean, separated from Great Britain by the Irish Sea to the east, and bounded in the northeast by Northern Ireland (UK). In 2005, 60·5% of the population lived in urban areas. The population at the 2006 census was 4,239,848 (2,118,677 females), giving a density of 60·3 persons per sq. km. The census population in 2006 was the highest figure since 1861 when the census recorded a population of 4·40m.

The UN gives an estimated population for 2010 of 4·59m.

The capital is Dublin (Baile Átha Cliath). Town populations, 2006: Greater Dublin, 1,045,769; Cork, 190,384; Limerick, 90,757; Galway, 72,729; Waterford, 49,213.

		Population, 2006		
Counties and Cities[1]	*Area in ha*[2]	*Males*	*Females*	*Totals*
Province of Leinster				
Carlow	89,655	25,611	24,738	50,349
Dublin City	11,758	248,087	258,124	506,211
Dun Laoghaire-Rathdown	12,638	92,899	101,139	194,038
Fingal	45,467	119,200	120,792	239,992
Kildare	169,540	94,190	92,145	186,335
Kilkenny	207,289	44,263	43,295	87,558
Laois	171,990	34,409	32,650	67,059
Longford	109,116	17,573	16,818	34,391
Louth	82,613	55,335	55,932	111,267
Meath	234,207	82,651	80,180	162,831
Offaly	200,117	35,937	34,931	70,868
South Dublin	22,364	122,371	124,564	246,935
Westmeath	183,965	39,819	39,527	79,346
Wexford	236,685	66,070	65,679	131,749
Wicklow	202,662	62,905	63,289	126,194
Total of Leinster	1,980,066	1,141,320	1,153,803	2,295,123
Province of Munster				
Clare	345,004	56,048	54,902	110,950
Cork City	3,953	58,449	60,969	119,418
Cork	746,042	182,365	179,512	361,877
Kerry	480,689	70,641	69,194	139,835
Limerick City	2,087	25,698	26,841	52,539
Limerick	273,504	66,982	64,534	131,516
Tipperary, N. R.	204,627	33,568	32,455	66,023
Tipperary, S. R.	225,845	42,250	40,971	83,221
Waterford City	4,103	22,622	23,126	45,748
Waterford	181,556	31,310	30,903	62,213
Total of Munster	2,467,410	589,933	583,407	1,173,340
Province of Connacht				
Galway City	5,057	34,848	37,566	72,414
Galway	609,820	81,628	77,628	159,256
Leitrim	159,003	14,903	14,047	28,950
Mayo	558,605	62,636	61,203	123,839
Roscommon	254,819	30,178	28,590	58,768
Sligo	183,752	30,257	30,637	60,894
Total of Connacht	1,771,056	254,450	249,671	504,121

Counties and Cities[1]	Area in ha[2]	Population, 2006 Males	Females	Totals
Province of Ulster (part of)				
Cavan	193,177	32,915	31,088	64,003
Donegal	486,091	73,970	73,294	147,264
Monaghan	129,508	28,583	27,414	55,997
Total of Ulster (part of)	808,776	135,468	131,796	267,264
Total	7,027,308	2,121,171	2,118,677	4,239,848

[1]Cities were previously known as County Boroughs.
[2]Area details provided by Ordnance Survey.

The official languages are Irish (the national language) and English; according to the 2006 census, Irish is spoken by 1·66m. persons in the Republic of Ireland (41·9% of the population, down from 42·8% in 2002). It is a compulsory subject at school.

SOCIAL STATISTICS

Statistics for five calendar years:

	Births	Marriages	Deaths
2003	61,529	20,302	29,074
2004	61,972	20,619	28,665
2005	61,372	21,355	28,260
2006	64,237	21,841	27,479
2007	70,620	22,544	28,050

2007 rates (per 1,000 population): birth, 16·3; death, 6·5; marriage, 5·2. Annual population growth rate, 2000–05, 1·7%. Expectation of life at birth, 2006, 76·8 years for males and 81·6 years for females.

In 2005 the suicide rate per 100,000 population was 11·6 (men, 18·5; women, 4·8). Infant mortality in 2005, 4 per 1,000 live births; fertility rate (2004), 1·9 births per woman.

At a referendum on 24 Nov. 1995 on the legalization of civil divorce the electorate was 1,628,580; 818,852 votes were in favour, 809,728 against. In 2005 Ireland received 4,324 asylum applications, equivalent to 1·0 per 1,000 inhabitants.

The number of immigrants in the year to April 2006 was 107,800 while emigrants numbered 36,000 in the same period. Preliminary figures suggested that immigration peaked in 2006–07 and that it had almost halved by 2009. 44% of emigrants in 2005–06 went to countries other than the EU and the USA, while only 22% of all immigrants originated from outside the EU and USA.

A UNICEF report published in 2005 showed that 15·7% of children in Ireland live in poverty (in households with income below 50% of the national median), compared to 2·4% in Denmark.

CLIMATE

Influenced by the Gulf Stream, there is an equable climate with mild southwest winds, making temperatures almost uniform over the whole country. The coldest months are Jan. and Feb. (39–45°F, 4–7°C) and the warmest July and Aug. (57–61°F, 14–16°C). May and June are the sunniest months, averaging 5·5 to 6·5 hours each day, but over 7 hours in the extreme southeast. Rainfall is lowest along the eastern coastal strip. The central parts vary between 30–44" (750–1,125 mm), and up to 60" (1,500 mm) may be experienced in low-lying areas in the west. Dublin, Jan. 40°F (4°C), July 59°F (15°C). Annual rainfall 30" (750 mm). Cork, Jan. 42°F (5°C), July 61°F (16°C). Annual rainfall 41" (1,025 mm).

CONSTITUTION AND GOVERNMENT

Ireland is a sovereign independent, democratic republic. Its parliament exercises jurisdiction in 26 of the 32 counties of the island of Ireland. The first Constitution of the Irish Free State came into operation on 6 Dec. 1922. Certain provisions which were regarded as contrary to the national sentiments were gradually removed by successive amendments, with the result that at the end of 1936 the text differed considerably from the original document. On 14 June 1937 a new constitution was approved by Parliament and enacted by a plebiscite on 1 July 1937. This constitution came into operation on 29 Dec. 1937. Under it the name Ireland (Éire) was restored. In its original form the Irish Constitution provided that the territory of Ireland comprised the whole island, and thus included that of Northern Ireland. This position was modified by referendum in 1998 following the Good Friday Agreement of that year. The former territorial claim has now been replaced with a statement that, while it is the aspiration of the Irish nation to unite the peoples of the island and the current territory of Ireland is not final, unification shall not take place without the consent of majorities in both jurisdictions.

The head of state is the *President*, whose role is largely ceremonial, but who has the power to refer proposed legislation which might infringe the Constitution to the Supreme Court.

The *Oireachtas* or National Parliament consists of the President, a House of Representatives (*Dáil Éireann*) and a Senate (*Seanad Éireann*). The *Dáil*, consisting of 166 members, is elected by adult suffrage on the Single Transferable Vote system in constituencies of three, four or five members. Of the 60 members of the Senate, 11 are nominated by the *Taoiseach* (Prime Minister), six are elected by the universities and the remaining 43 are elected from five panels of candidates established on a vocational basis, representing the following public services and interests: (1) national language and culture, literature, art, education and such professional interests as may be defined by law for the purpose of this panel; (2) agricultural and allied interests, and fisheries; (3) labour, whether organized or unorganized; (4) industry and commerce, including banking, finance, accountancy, engineering and architecture; (5) public administration and social services, including voluntary social activities. The electing body comprises members of the *Dáil*, Senate, county boroughs and county councils.

A maximum period of 90 days is afforded to the Senate for the consideration or amendment of Bills sent to that House by the *Dáil*, but the Senate has no power to veto legislative proposals.

No amendment of the Constitution can be effected except with the approval of the people given at a referendum.

National Anthem

'Amhrán na bhFiann' ('The Soldier's Song'); words by P. Kearney, tune by P. Heeney and P. Kearney.

GOVERNMENT CHRONOLOGY

(FF = Fianna Fáil; FG = Fine Gael; n/p = non-partisan)

Presidents since 1938.

1938–45	FF	Douglas Hyde
1945–59	FF	Séan Thomas O'Kelly
1959–73	FF	Éamon de Valera
1973–74	FF	Erskine Hamilton Childers
1974–76	FF	Cearbhall O'Dalaigh
1976–90	FF	Patrick John Hillery
1990–97	n/p	Mary Terese Robinson
1997–	FF	Mary Patricia McAleese

Prime Ministers.

1932–48	FF	Éamon de Valera
1948–51	FG	John Aloysius Costello
1951–54	FF	Éamon de Valera
1954–57	FG	John Aloysius Costello
1957–59	FF	Éamon de Valera
1959–66	FF	Séan Francis Lemass

1966–73	FF	John (Jack) Mary Lynch
1973–77	FG	Liam Thomas Cosgrave
1977–79	FF	John (Jack) Mary Lynch
1979–81	FF	Charles James Haughey
1981–82	FG	Garret Michael FitzGerald
1982	FF	Charles James Haughey
1982–87	FG	Garret Michael FitzGerald
1987–92	FF	Charles James Haughey
1992–94	FF	Albert Reynolds
1994–97	FG	John Gerard Bruton
1997–2008	FF	Bartholomew (Bertie) P. Ahern
2008–	FF	Brian Cowen

RECENT ELECTIONS

A general election was held on 24 May 2007: Fianna Fáil (FF) gained 78 seats with 42·0% of votes cast (in 2002, 81 seats); Fine Gael (FG), 51 with 27·4% (31); Labour Party (L), 20 with 10·3% (21); Green Party (G), 6; Sinn Féin, 4; Progressive Democrats (PD), 2; ind., 5.

Following elections to the Senate in July 2007, FF held 28 of the 60 seats, FG had 14, L had 6, PD had 2, G had 2, Sinn Féin had 1 and independents held 7 seats.

Presidential elections would have taken place on 22 Oct. 2004, but incumbent Mary McAleese (FF) was reappointed unopposed as no other candidates secured the necessary backing for an election to take place.

European Parliament

Ireland has 12 (13 in 2004) representatives. At the June 2009 elections turnout was 58·6% (58·6% in 2004). Fine Gael won 4 seats with 29·1% of votes cast (political affiliation in European Parliament: European People's Party); Fianna Fáil, 3 with 24·1% (Alliance of Liberals and Democrats for Europe); Labour Party, 3 with 13·9% (Progressive Alliance of Socialists and Democrats); Socialist Party, 1 with 2·8% (European United Left/Nordic Green Left). One independent was elected, with 4·6% (Alliance of Liberals and Democrats for Europe).

CURRENT ADMINISTRATION

President: Mary McAleese (b. 1951; FF), elected out of five candidates on 30 Oct. 1997 and inaugurated 11 Nov. 1997, and appointed for a second term on 1 Oct. 2004.

Following the 2007 election a new coalition government was formed between Fianna Fáil (FF), the Green Party and the Progressive Democrats (PD). In March 2010 it was composed as follows:

Taoiseach (Prime Minister): Brian Cowen; b. 1960 (FF; in office since 7 May 2008).

Tánaiste (Deputy Prime Minister) and Minister for Education and Skills: Mary Coughlan (b. 1965; FF). *Finance:* Brian Lenihan (b. 1959; FF). *Health and Children:* Mary Harney (b. 1953; PD). *Transport:* Noel Dempsey (b. 1953; FF). *Justice, Equality and Law Reform:* Dermot Ahern (b. 1955; FF). *Foreign Affairs:* Micheál Martin (b. 1960; FF). *Social and Family Affairs:* Éamon Ó Cuív (b. 1952; FF). *Arts, Sport and Tourism:* Mary Hanafin (b. 1959; FF). *Environment, Heritage and Local Government:* John Gormley (b. 1959; Green). *Communications, Energy and Natural Resources:* Éamon Ryan (b. 1963; Green). *Agriculture, Fisheries and Food:* Brendan Smith (b. 1956; FF). *Enterprise, Trade and Innovation:* Batt O'Keeffe (b. 1945; FF). *Community, Equality and Gaeltacht Affairs:* Pat Carey (b. 1947, FF). *Defence:* Tony Killeen (b. 1952; FF).

There are 15 Ministers of State.

Attorney General: Paul Gallagher.

Chairman of Dáil Éireann: John O'Donoghue.

Government Website: http://www.gov.ie

CURRENT LEADERS

Mary McAleese

Position
President

Introduction
Mary McAleese became Ireland's president in 1997, the first person from Northern Ireland to fill the post. A lawyer by profession, she is a devout Catholic with a conservative stance on social issues. Her campaign for the presidency was dogged by claims that she was a supporter of the nationalist Sinn Féin movement, allegations she strongly refuted.

Early Life
Mary McAleese (*née* Leneghan) was born in Belfast on 27 June 1951. Her father was a pub landlord in Catholic West Belfast. The outbreak of sectarian violence in the late 1960s resulted in the family moving to County Down.

In 1973 she graduated in law from Queen's University, Belfast, and was called to the Bar the following year. In 1975 she took up a law professorship at Trinity College Dublin. She stayed in this position until 1987, although between 1979–81 she worked as a television broadcaster and journalist.

In 1987 she unsuccessfully stood as a Fianna Fáil candidate for a Dublin seat at the general election. In 1994 she was appointed pro-vice chancellor of Queen's University, the first female to hold the post. Three years later she was selected by Fianna Fáil to stand in the presidential elections, defeating former prime minister Albert Reynolds for the candidacy. Unpopular with many unionists, she was accused of having links to Sinn Féin, the political arm of the paramilitary Irish Republican Army (IRA). Having denied the accusations, she presented herself as a 'builder of bridges' and won an overwhelming majority at the polls.

Career in Office
McAleese was inaugurated as president on 11 Nov. 1997. Her role is largely ceremonial and non-partisan. A practising Catholic, she is opposed to abortion and aligns herself with the Vatican on such issues as divorce and contraception. She has voiced support for peace-making in Northern Ireland and for continued cross-border co-operation. In Oct. 2004 she was appointed unopposed for a second presidential term.

Brian Cowen

Position
Prime Minister

Introduction
A member of the Dáil since 1984, Brian Cowen took over as *taoiseach* (prime minister) in May 2008 following the resignation of Bertie Ahern. He is strongly pro-European, regarding close ties with the EU as vital for Ireland's economy. Having presided over increases in public spending as finance minister, he took office facing the challenges of an economic downturn.

Early Life
Brian Cowen was born on 10 Jan. 1960 in Clara, Co. Offaly, the son of Fianna Fáil politician Bernard Cowen. He was educated at Clara National School, Ard Scoil Naomh Chiaráin and the Cistercian College of Mount St Joseph. He then studied law at University College Dublin and the Incorporated Law Society of Ireland, qualifying as a solicitor. In 1984 he contested the Laois–Offaly by-election, caused by the death of his father, and succeeded him as the Fianna Fáil representative. Aged 24, he was the Dáil's youngest member. In the same year he was also elected to Offaly County Council.

Cowen served as a backbench MP for seven years, gaining a reputation as a tough, outspoken politician. He opposed Fianna

Fáil's decision to enter into a coalition government with the Progressive Democrats in 1989 and in Nov. 1991 he supported Albert Reynolds' campaign for the party leadership. Reynolds became *taoiseach* the following year and in Feb. 1992 appointed Cowen minister for labour.

Following the inconclusive election of Nov. 1992, Cowen was active in negotiating a coalition between Fianna Fáil and the Labour Party. In Jan. 1993 he was appointed minister for transport, energy and communications. After Fianna Fáil was defeated in the 1994 general election, Cowen became opposition spokesman on agriculture, food and forestry under the new party leader, Bertie Ahern. In 1997 he was named spokesman for health. After the June 1997 general election he became minister for health and children in the governing Fianna Fáil–Progressive Democrat coalition. His handling of this newly expanded portfolio raised his profile and he was increasingly viewed as a possible successor to Ahern. In Jan. 2000 he was appointed minister for foreign affairs and his influence in the party was strengthened when he became its deputy leader in 2002.

As minister of foreign affairs, Cowen oversaw Ireland's term in 2002 as a non-permanent member of the United Nations Security Council and was closely involved in the Northern Ireland peace process. A firm supporter of the EU, he backed Ireland's conversion to the euro in 2002. During Ireland's presidency of the European Council in 2004, Cowen helped the EU prepare for expansion.

As minister for finance from 2004–08, he introduced tax reforms and directed funds to public services and welfare, introducing a new childcare package and increased pension allowances. In June 2007, following Fianna Fáil's success in the general election, Cowen became deputy prime minister as well as minister of finance. Ahern announced his resignation in April 2008 amid controversy over his personal financial affairs. Cowen was elected unopposed as leader of Fianna Fáil on 9 April 2008 and took office as *taoiseach* on 7 May 2008.

Career in Office

Despite coming to office in a period of economic uncertainty, Cowen pledged to maintain public investment while controlling borrowing. He also signalled his continuing belief in the importance of the EU to Ireland's long-term prospects. Although voters in Ireland in a referendum in June 2008 rejected the Lisbon Treaty (signed in Dec. 2007) on EU institutional and administrative reform, this setback was reversed in a further referendum in Oct. 2009 after Cowen had secured assurances that Ireland would retain a permanent representative on the European Commission and that its strict anti-abortion laws and policy of neutrality would not be undermined. Meanwhile, the economy had deteriorated markedly into recession in the second half of 2008 in the wake of the global financial crisis, prompting a dramatic decline in public support for Cowen's government. Having announced plans in Feb. 2009 to rescue two of the country's largest banks, tough budgetary measures to address the widening deficit in the public finances and Ireland's declining credit rating status, including tax increases and public sector pay cuts, were introduced by the government in April 2009 and again in Dec.

DEFENCE

Supreme command of the Defence Forces is vested in the President. Exercise of the supreme command is regulated by law (Defence Act 1954). Military Command is exercised by the government through the Minister for Defence, who is the overall commander of the Defence Forces.

The Defence Forces comprise the Permanent Defence Force (the regular Army, the Air Corps and the Naval Service) and the Defence Reserve (comprising a First Line Reserve of members who have served in the Permanent Defence Force, a second-line Territorial Army Reserve and a second-line Naval Reserve).

The total strength of the Permanent Defence Force in Oct. 2005 was 10,541 (including 524 women). The total strength of the Reserve in Aug. 2005 was 11,218. In Dec. 2005, 768 Defence Forces personnel were involved in 19 peace-support missions throughout the world.

Defence expenditure in 2006 totalled US$1,113m. (US$274 per capita), representing 0·5% of GDP.

Army

The Army strength in Oct. 2005 was 8,623 personnel with 10,810 reservists. There is a Training Centre at the Curragh, Co. Kildare and a Logistics Base, with elements located at the Curragh and Dublin for force level logistical support.

Navy

The Naval Service is based at Haulbowline in Co. Cork. The strength in Oct. 2005 was 1,061 with 408 reservists. It operates eight patrol vessels.

Air Corps

The Air Corps has its headquarters at Casement Aerodrome, Baldonnel, Co. Dublin. The Air Corps is a stand-alone Corps which does not form an intrinsic part of the new Army Brigade structure. The Air Corps strength in Oct. 2005 was 857 personnel. The Corps operates 18 fixed-wing aircraft and 12 helicopters.

INTERNATIONAL RELATIONS

Ireland is a member of the UN, World Bank, IMF and several other UN specialized agencies, WTO, EU, Council of Europe, OSCE, BIS, IOM, OECD and Asian Development Bank.

On 12 June 2008 Ireland became the first European Union member to reject the Treaty of Lisbon when it held a national referendum in which 53·4% of votes cast were against the reform treaty and only 46·6% in favour. Turnout was 53·1%. However, at a second referendum on 2 Oct. 2009, the treaty was approved by 67·1% to 32·9% (turnout, 59·0%). Parliamentary ratification followed on 23 Oct. 2009.

ECONOMY

Agriculture accounted for 2% of GDP in 2005, industry 36% and services 62%.

According to the anti-corruption organization *Transparency International*, Ireland ranked equal 14th in the world in a 2009 survey of the countries with the least corruption in business and government. It received 8·0 out of 10 in the annual index.

Overview

Historically one of Western Europe's least developed economies, Ireland entered the new millennium as the region's second richest per capita after Luxembourg. The chief engine of growth has been the high-tech export sector (chiefly chemicals and computer hardware and software). US investors have been attracted by Ireland's favourable corporate tax environment for manufacturers and its skilled, English-speaking labour force. Net inflows of foreign direct investment (FDI) accelerated significantly in 1998, reaching US$25·8bn. in 2000. 2007 saw FDI rise to a new record high of US$30·6bn.

Growth during the decade had been robust until late 2007 when the global credit crunch began to have a severe impact. Ireland became the first eurozone economy to fall into recession in 2008 as housing construction decelerated. In Sept. 2008 the government moved to stabilize the domestic financial system with a €400bn. plan to protect all deposits, bonds and debts in six banks and building societies for two years. By Feb. 2009 the state had nationalized Anglo Irish Bank and provided emergency funding to Allied Irish Banks and the Bank of Ireland. The economy contracted by 7·1% in 2009 and while the pace of decline has reduced, recovery is expected to be slow and weak. In Dec. 2009 the government announced €4bn. of savings to reduce the budget deficit, including public sector wage cuts, but sustained adjustment efforts over several years will be required to contain the high public debt.

Currency

On 1 Jan. 1999 the euro (EUR) became the legal currency in Ireland at the irrevocable conversion rate of 0·787564 Irish pounds to 1 euro. The euro, which consists of 100 cents, has been in circulation since 1 Jan. 2002. There are seven euro notes in different colours and sizes denominated in 500, 200, 100, 50, 20, 10 and 5 euros, and eight coins denominated in 2 and 1 euros, then 50, 20, 10, 5, 2 and 1 cents. On the introduction of the euro there was a 'dual circulation' period before the Irish pound ceased to be legal tender on 9 Feb. 2002. Euro banknotes in circulation on 1 Jan. 2002 had a total value of €6·8bn.

Inflation rates (based on OECD statistics):

1999	*2000*	*2001*	*2002*	*2003*	*2004*	*2005*	*2006*	*2007*	*2008*
2·5%	5·3%	4·0%	4·7%	4·0%	2·3%	2·2%	2·7%	2·9%	3·1%

The Central Bank has the sole right of issuing legal tender notes; token coinage is issued by the Minister for Finance through the Bank. Gold reserves were 176,000 troy oz in Sept. 2009 and foreign exchange reserves US$574m. Total money supply was €83,181m. in Aug. 2009.

Budget

Current revenue and expenditure (in €1m.):

Current revenue	*2007*	*2008*
Customs duties	266	248
Excise duties	5,838	5,443
Capital taxes	3,498	1,762
Stamp duties	3,186	1,651
Income tax	13,572	13,177
Corporation tax	6,391	5,066
Value-added tax	14,497	13,430
Levies	3	1
Non-tax revenue	638	847
Total	47,887	41,624
Current expenditure		
Industry and labour	1,499	1,547
Agriculture	1,363	1,446
Fisheries, Forestry, Tourism	214	267
Health	14,281	15,356
Education	7,891	8,465
Social Welfare	15,498	17,807
Security	3,475	3,746
Other	4,386	4,749
Gross current	48,607	53,384
Less: Receipts, e.g. social security	11,647	12,626
Net total (including non-voted central fund)	36,960	40,758

VAT is 21·0% (reduced rates of 13·5% and 4·8%).

The general government debt at the end of 2008 was estimated at €80bn., or 44% of GDP, and is forecast to rise to 78% by the end of 2010.

Performance

Real GDP growth rates (based on OECD statistics):

1999	*2000*	*2001*	*2002*	*2003*	*2004*	*2005*	*2006*	*2007*	*2008*
10·7%	9·4%	5·8%	6·5%	4·4%	4·6%	6·2%	5·4%	6·0%	–3·0%

During the late 1990s Ireland had the fastest-growing economy in the European Union, with real GDP growth in 2000 of 9·4% following growth averaging 9·8% over the previous five years. From a GDP per head of only 69% of the EU average in 1987, it was estimated to have risen to 148% of the EU average by 2007. However, the Central Statistics Office reported negative GDP growth of 7·1% in 2009. Total GDP in 2008 was US$281·8bn.

Banking and Finance

The Central Bank (founded in 1943) replaced the Currency Commission as the note-issuing authority. In 2003 the Central Bank was renamed the Central Bank and Financial Services Authority of Ireland (CBFSAI). The CBFSAI has two component entities: the Central Bank and the Irish Financial Services Regulatory Authority. It has the power of receiving deposits from banks and public authorities, of rediscounting Exchequer bills and bills of exchange, of making advances to banks against such bills or against government securities, of fixing and publishing rates of interest for rediscounting bills, or buying and selling certain government securities and securities of any international bank or financial institution formed wholly or mainly by governments. The CBFSAI also collects and publishes information relating to monetary and credit matters.

The Board of Directors of the Central Bank consists of a Governor, appointed for a seven-year term by the President on the advice of the government, and twelve directors, all appointed by the Minister for Finance. The *Governor* is Patrick Honohan. In 2003 the Bank's net profit was €60·04m.; €321·73m. was paid to the Exchequer.

In 2004 the Irish Financial Services Regulatory Authority was responsible for the regulation of 80 credit institutions (including branches).

At 30 April 2004 total assets of within-the-State offices of all credit institutions amounted to €629·5bn.

Anglo Irish Bank, the country's third largest bank, was nationalized in Jan. 2009.

There is a stock exchange in Dublin.

ENERGY AND NATURAL RESOURCES

Environment

Ireland's carbon dioxide emissions from the consumption and flaring of fossil fuels in 2008 were the equivalent of 10·7 tonnes per capita.

Electricity

The total generating capacity in 2004 was 5,592 MW, as averaged on a daily basis. This included wind generation, small renewable and small Combined Heat and Power (CHP). In 2003 there were approximately 1,804,680 customers connected to the network consuming 22,286 GWh.

Oil and Gas

Oil accounts for 56% of primary energy demand in Ireland while gas makes up 25% of demand. Over 0·6m. sq. km of the Irish continental shelf has been designated an exploration area for oil and gas; at the furthest point the limit of jurisdiction is 520 nautical miles from the coast. In the offshore there is a vast Continental Shelf in which a number of major basins and troughs have been identified. Much of the shelf remains unexplored but since 1971 a total of 166 wells have been drilled (121 offshore exploration wells and 45 appraisal/development wells), and since 1965 a total of 381 offshore surveys have been carried out.

Natural gas reserves in 2007 totalled 10bn. cu. metres. Output in 2006 was 510m. cu. metres and consumption 4·6bn. cu. metres. 91% of natural gas supplies for the Irish Market are imported through the two sub-sea interconnectors connecting Ireland with Scotland and the remaining 9% is supplied from the Kinsale Head gas field, about 50 km off the south coast of Ireland. Deliveries from the Corrib gas field, about 80 km off the west coast, are scheduled to start in 2011.

Natural gas transmission and distribution is currently carried out by Bord Gáis Éireann (Irish Gas Board). The gradual liberalization of the Irish gas market, which started in July 2004, was completed in July 2007 when domestic as well as business users became free to select any licensed natural gas supplier.

Peat

The country has very little indigenous coal, but possesses large reserves of peat, the development of which is handled largely by Bord na Móna (Peat Board). To date, the Board has acquired and developed 85,000 ha. of bog and has 27 locations around the country. In 2006–07 the Board sold 2·4m. tonnes of milled peat for use in three milled peat electricity generating stations. 231,000 tonnes of briquettes were produced for sale to the domestic heating market. Bord na Móna also sold 1·8m. cu. metres of horticultural peat, mainly for export.

Minerals

Ireland has three zinc-lead mines, which in 2004 produced a combined total of 438,000 tonnes of zinc in concentrate and 64,000 tonnes of lead in concentrate, together with some silver (in lead). Ireland is Europe's leading zinc mine producer (44% of European output in 2004) and ranks seventh in the world for total zinc production. The total value of production in 2003 was €260m. Production of gypsum is significant and the aggregates sector has expanded dramatically in recent years. Aggregate production in 2004 was an estimated 120m. tonnes. About 30 companies hold 285 prospecting licences; a total of €8m. was spent on exploration in 2003. The main target is base metals but there is also interest in gold.

Agriculture

The Central Statistics Office's Quarterly National Household Survey showed in the quarter of March–May 2003 that there were 113,200 people whose primary source of income was from agriculture. A total of 240,100 people worked on farms on a regular basis. There were 136,500 farm holdings in Ireland, almost all of which were family farms. Average farm size was 32·0 ha. 43% of farms were under 20 ha. 13% of farmers were under 35 and 41% were over 55. In 2005 there were 1·15m. ha. of arable land in Ireland and 1,810 ha. of permanent crops.

Agriculture, fisheries and forestry represented 3·5% of GDP in 2002 (provisional). 90% of the agricultural area was devoted to grass in 2002. In 2003 beef and milk production accounted for 57% of goods output at producer prices.

In 2005: barley accounted (in ha.) for 164,500; wheat, 94,700; sugar beets, 31,000; oats, 16,500; potatoes, 12,200. Production figures (in 1,000 tonnes): sugar beets, 1,395; barley, 1,025; wheat, 798; potatoes, 422; oats, 111.

Goods output at producer prices including changes in stock for 2003 was estimated at €4·7bn.; operating surplus (aggregate income) was €2·5bn. Direct income payments, financed or co-financed by the EU, amounted to €1·6bn. It is estimated that net subsidies (subsidies on products plus subsidies on production less taxes on products and taxes on production) represented 63% of aggregate income. Livestock: (2005) 6,191,700 cattle; 4,257,000 sheep; 1,678,000 pigs; 13,208,400 poultry (2002).

Forestry

Total forest area in 2005 was 669,000 ha. (9·7% of total land area). Timber production in 2007 was 2·71m. cu. metres.

Fisheries

In 2004 approximately 14,800 people were engaged full- or part-time in the sea fishing industry; in 2004 the fishing fleet consisted of 1,425 vessels. The quantities and values of fish landed in 2004 were: wetfish, 256,170 tonnes, value €106·2m.; shellfish, 62,331 tonnes, value €80·1m. Total quantity (2004): 318,501 tonnes; total value, €186·4m. The main types of fish caught in 2004 were mackerel (63,000 tonnes), blue whiting (49,000 tonnes), horse mackerel (37,000 tonnes) and herring (29,000 tonnes). More than 98% of fish caught is from sea fishing.

INDUSTRY

The leading companies by market capitalization in Ireland in March 2009 were: CRH plc, a building materials company (US$14·7bn.); Ryanair Holdings (US$5·7bn.); and Kerry Group, a chilled food manufacturer (US$3·5bn.).

Enterprise Ireland. Enterprise Ireland was established in 1998 to provide an integrated development package specifically for indigenous firms. Its mission is 'to accelerate the development of world-class Irish companies to achieve strong positions in global markets resulting in increased national and regional prosperity'. Enterprise Ireland brings together the key marketing, technology, enterprise development, business training and science and innovation initiatives through which the government supports the growth of Irish manufacturing and internationally traded sectors.

County Enterprise Boards. The 35 County and City Enterprise Boards (CEBs), established in Oct. 1993, are locally based enterprise development agencies established in each county and local urban authority area in Ireland. The function of the Boards is to develop indigenous enterprise potential and to stimulate economic activity at a local level. This is primarily achieved through the provision of both financial and non-financial assistance to micro-enterprises (ten employees or less) in the form of grants, repayable loans, and management development training and mentoring.

IDA Ireland. IDA Ireland, founded in 1949 as the Industrial Development Authority, is an autonomous Irish government agency with responsibility for the attraction of foreign direct investment into Ireland and the development of the existing base of more than 1,000 IDA-supported overseas companies.

IDA Ireland's success in attracting leading global companies from all business sectors has led to Ireland being acknowledged as one of the world's leading locations for higher-value, knowledge-intensive and skills-driven activities in biopharmaceutical, pharmaceutical, ICT, international services and financial services, in all areas of business including innovative R&D, high-value manufacturing, leading-edge international services and financial services.

Shannon Development. Shannon Development, which was established in 1959, is the regional economic development company responsible for industrial, tourism and rural development in the Shannon region. Its regional mandate covers Counties Clare, Limerick, North Tipperary, South Offaly and North Kerry.

Forfás. Forfás is the national policy advisory and co-ordination board for industrial development and science and technology. It is the statutory agency through which powers are delegated to Enterprise Ireland for the promotion of indigenous enterprise and to IDA Ireland for the promotion of inward investment. Science Foundation Ireland was established as a third agency of Forfás in 2003.

The main functions of Forfás are to advise the Minister on matters relating to industrial policy, to advise on the development and co-ordination of policy for Enterprise Ireland, IDA Ireland and Science Foundation Ireland, and encourage the development of industry, technology, marketing and human resources.

The Chairman of Forfás is Eoin O'Driscoll and its Chief Executive is Jane Williams.

The census of industrial production for 2005 gives the following details of the values (in €1m.) of gross and net output for the principal manufacturing industries.

	Gross output	*Net output*
Mining and quarrying	1,436	742
Manufacture of food products, beverages and tobacco	18,226	10,187
Manufacture of textiles and textile products	507	277
Manufacture of leather and leather products	27	13
Manufacture of wood and wood products	1,061	417

	Gross output	*Net output*
Manufacture of pulp, paper and paper products; publishing and printing	13,661	12,219
Manufacture of chemicals, chemical products and man-made fibres	28,943	23,914
Manufacture of rubber and plastic products	1,356	634
Manufacture of other non-metallic mineral products	2,027	1,004
Manufacture of basic metals and fabricated metal products	2,050	881
Manufacture of machinery and equipment n.e.c.	1,784	871
Manufacture of electrical and optical equipment	29,371	12,910
Manufacture of transport equipment	1,128	553
Manufacturing n.e.c.	2,573	665
Electricity, gas and water supply	5,425	2,873
Total (all industries)	109,576	68,160

In 2004 gross output was €103,751m. and net output €66,289m.

Labour

The total labour force for 2003 was estimated to be 1,859,700, of which 81,400 were out of work. With the birth rate having peaked around 1980 there is currently a marked increase in the numbers entering the workforce. The unemployment rate in 2008 was 6·0%, down from nearly 16% in 1993. However, in 2009 it rose to 11·8% as a consequence of the global economic crisis, standing at 13·3% in Dec. Of those at work in 2003, 1,172,600 were employed in the services sector, 492,600 in the industrial sector and 113,200 in the agricultural sector. Employment rose by approximately 51% between 1991 and 2001—more than twice as much as in any other industrialized country. Ireland, along with the UK and Sweden, decided to open its labour market to nationals of the new EU member states in May 2004. Poles in particular went to Ireland following the EU expansion and by 2006 had become the second largest ethnic minority after the British; there were 63,000 Polish citizens in Ireland at the time of the 2006 census. The retirement age is 65 years.

Trade Unions

The number of trade unions affiliated to the Irish Congress of Trade Unions and based exclusively in Ireland was 31 in 2005; total membership, 557,000. There were also approximately 40,000 union members unaffiliated to the Congress. The six largest unions accounted for 68% of total membership in 2002. A series of three-year social pacts, which, in addition to covering a range of economic and social policy measures, include provision for pay increases, have been negotiated between the government, trade unions and employees' organizations since 1987. The fifth such agreement concluded in Feb. 2000, the Programme for Prosperity and Fairness (PPF), provided pay increases of 15% of basic pay in the public and private sectors of the economy over the period of the agreement, 2000–02. Owing to escalating inflation a further compensatory 1% lump sum payment was negotiated, for payment in March 2001. The third phase increase (4%) in the public service was not to be paid earlier than Oct. 2002 and was dependent on the establishment of performance indicators by April 2001 and the achievement of sectoral targets by April 2002.

The PPF agreement expired for some workers in the private sector in Dec. 2002; depending on start dates, for others the agreement continued into 2003. The PPF pay element expired in Oct. 2003 for the public service. The successor agreement, Sustaining Progress, was in operation between 1 Jan. 2003 and 31 Dec. 2005. The programme allowed for a cumulative increase in actual pay of 13·6%, in six separate increases, over that period.

INTERNATIONAL TRADE

Imports and Exports

Value of imports and exports of merchandise for calendar years (in €1m.):

	2002	*2003*	*2004*	*2005*	*2006*
Imports	55,628	47,865	51,105	57,465	60,857
Exports	93,675	82,076	84,409	86,732	86,772

The values of the chief imports and total exports are shown in the following table (in €1m.):

	Imports		*Exports*	
	2001	*2002*	*2001*	*2002*
Animal and vegetable oils and waxes	123	115	24	28
Beverages and tobacco	679	757	985	1,001
Chemicals	6,341	6,998	32,281	39,313
Live animals and food	3,116	3,135	5,801	5,679
Machinery and transport equipment	30,224	27,892	37,607	32,759
Manufactured articles	6,300	6,068	8,969	8,068
Manufactured goods	4,391	4,290	1,955	1,839
Mineral fuels and lubricants	2,219	1,740	297	361
Raw materials	799	788	953	855

Ireland is one of the most trade-dependent countries in the world. Exports constitute an increasing share of the economy's output of goods and services. In 2002 the total value of merchandise exports amounted to just over €93·7bn. (the highest ever level), which generated a trade surplus of €38·4bn. In 2002 merchandise imports from other European Union countries accounted for 59·4% of total imports while merchandise exports to other EU countries accounted for 63·7% of total exports. Information technology has become increasingly important, and by 1999 Ireland had become the largest exporter of software products in the world.

Import and export totals for Ireland's top ten export markets in 2001 and 2002 (€1m.):

	Imports		*Exports*	
	2001	*2002*	*2001*	*2002*
Belgium	864	791	4,431	3,519
France	2,752	2,252	5,532	4,668
Germany	3,521	3,533	11,671	6,744
Italy	1,185	1,092	3,309	3,593
Japan	1,991	2,012	3,261	2,642
Netherlands	1,860	1,822	4,237	3,410
Spain	646	676	2,283	2,231
Switzerland	530	557	2,706	3,121
United Kingdom	20,481	19,860	22,630	22,431
United States of America	8,700	8,504	15,694	16,385

In 2002 exports accounted for 94% of GDP (both merchandise and service). This showed a slight decrease on the 2001 level which was just over 96% of GDP.

COMMUNICATIONS

Roads

At 31 Dec. 2003 there were 95,811 km of public roads, consisting of 2,746 km of National Primary Roads (including 176 km of motorway), 2,685 km of National Secondary Roads, 11,607 km of Regional Roads and 78,773 km of Local Roads.

Number of licensed motor vehicles at 31 Dec. 2007: private cars, 1,882,901; public-service vehicles, 35,105; goods vehicles, 345,874; agricultural and industrial vehicles, 80,239; motorcycles, 37,178; other vehicles, 60,267. In 2007 a total of 338 people were killed in road accidents.

Rail

The total length of railway open for traffic in 2004 was 1,919 km (52 km electrified), all 1,600 mm gauge. A massive investment in public transport infrastructure is taking place in Ireland. The second National Development Plan that runs from Jan. 2007 to Dec. 2013 allows for €12·9bn. to be invested in public transport, particularly in the Greater Dublin area.

Railway statistics for years ending 31 Dec.	2005	2006
Passengers (journeys)	37,700,000	43,300,000
Receipts (€1)	181,860,000	227,696,000
Expenditure (€1)	446,785,000	439,113,000

A light railway system was launched in Dublin in 2004.

Civil Aviation

Aer Lingus and Ryanair are the two major airlines operating in Ireland.

Aer Lingus was founded in 1936 as a State-owned enterprise. Its principal business is the provision of passenger and cargo services to the UK, Europe and the USA. It was privatized in 2006, with Ryanair now holding a 29·8% stake in the company and the government a 25·1% stake. Ryanair began operations in 1985 and now operates to a range of destinations in the UK and Europe. In 2005 Ryanair carried 33·4m. passengers (all on international flights); passenger-km totalled 31·2bn. The total number of passengers carried by Ryanair on international flights in 2005 was the second highest of any airline, behind Lufthansa. However, it has in the meantime overtaken Lufthansa to become the airline carrying the highest number of international passengers.

In addition to Aer Lingus and Ryanair, there are 16 other independent air transport operators. The main operators in this group are Aer Arann Express and Cityjet.

The principal airports (Dublin, Shannon and Cork) are operated by the Dublin Airport Authority plc. In 2006 Dublin handled 21·2m. passengers (an increase of 14·9% on 2005) and 150,000 tonnes of freight. Shannon handled 3·6m. passengers (increase of 10·2%) and 45,015 tonnes of freight. Cork was the third busiest, with 3·0m. passengers (increase of 10·3%) and 8,300 tonnes of freight.

There are six privately owned regional airports. The government part funds the scheduled services from Dublin to five of these airports and to the City of Derry airport in Northern Ireland to ensure efficient and speedy access to the more isolated regions of the state for both business and tourist travellers. The principal focus of growth during 2003 was the European market with the Dublin–London air route amongst the busiest in Europe.

Shipping

The merchant fleet totalled 269,693 GRT in 2002. Total cargo traffic passing through the country's ports amounted to 44,919,000 tonnes in 2002. Dublin handled 22·2m. tonnes of cargo in 2002 and Cork 9·4m. tonnes.

Inland Waterways

The principal inland waterways open to navigation are the Shannon Navigation (270 km), which includes the Shannon-Erne Waterway (Ballinamore/Ballyconnell Canal), and the Grand Canal and Barrow Navigation (249 km). Merchandise traffic has now ceased and navigation is confined to pleasure craft operated either privately or commercially. The Royal Canal (146 km) from Dublin to Mullingar (53 km) was reopened for navigation in 1995.

Telecommunications

The Minister for Public Enterprise, a member of the government, has overall policy responsibility for the development of the sector. Among the key elements of the government's policy is the objective of creating a fully open and competitive telecommunications market that will stimulate investment in advanced information infrastructure and services in Ireland and develop Ireland as a global leader in the growth of internet-based industries and electronic commerce.

The Director of Telecommunications Regulation, established by legislation as an independent officer with a separate office and staff in June 1997, is responsible for licensing of operators, allocation of numbers and radio frequency spectrum, supervision of network interconnection arrangements and other regulatory functions.

Ireland's telecommunications sector has been fully liberalized with effect from 1 Dec. 1998 when the last remaining elements of Telecom Éireann's (now called eircom) exclusive privilege were removed. All elements of the market are now open to competition from other licensed operators. The three licensed mobile telephone operators are Vodafone, O2 and Meteor.

The Government has also sold the state's entire remaining stake of 50·1% in eircom by way of an initial public offering of shares in the company. The sale took place in July 1999.

eircom plc—Operational Information

The dominant operator in the telecommunications sector is eircom plc (previously Telecom Éireann). Telecom Éireann was a statutory body set up under the Postal and Telecommunications Services Act, 1983. In 1996, 20% of the State's holding was sold to KPN/Telia, a Dutch–Swedish consortium, who had an option of a further 15%, which was taken up in July 1999. In 1998 the government concluded an Employee Share Ownership Scheme under which 14·9% of the company was to be made available to employees and also held an Initial Public Offer (IPO) of shares in the company in July 1999. In Oct. 1999 the newly-privatized Telecom Éireann became eircom plc.

The level of network digitalization is 100%. In 2008 there were 2,204,000 main (fixed) telephone lines. In the same year mobile phone subscribers numbered 5,357,000 (1,207·4 per 1,000 persons). In 2004 Irish mobile phone subscribers sent 3·74bn. text messages in total (89 messages per subscriber per month). There were 2·48m. PCs in use in 2006. Ireland had 2·78m. internet users in 2008. The broadband penetration rate stood at 19·1 subscribers per 100 inhabitants in June 2008.

Postal Services

Postal services are provided by An Post, a statutory body established under the Postal and Telecommunications Services Act, 1983. In 2003 there were 1,658 post offices. A total of 830m. pieces of mail were handled during 2003, equivalent to 183 per person. An Post also offers a range of services to the business community through a dedicated unit, Special Delivery Services, and subsidiaries PostGEM, PrintPost and Precision Marketing Information. A range of services are provided through the Post Office network including Savings and Investments, passport applications, bill payments, National Lottery products and the payment of Social Welfare benefits on an agency basis for the State.

SOCIAL INSTITUTIONS

Justice

The Constitution provides that justice shall be administered in public in Courts established by law by Judges appointed by the President on the advice of the government. The jurisdiction and organization of the Courts are dealt with in the Courts (Establishment and Constitution) Act, 1961, the Courts (Supplemental Provisions) Acts, 1961–91, and the Courts and Court Officers Acts, 1995–2002. These Courts consist of Courts of First Instance and a Court of Final Appeal, called the Supreme Court. The Courts of First Instance are the High Court with full original jurisdiction and the Circuit and the District Courts with local and limited jurisdictions. A judge may not be removed from office except for stated misbehaviour or incapacity and then only on resolutions passed by both Houses of the Oireachtas. Judges of the Supreme Court and High Court are appointed from among practising barristers or solicitors of not less than 12 years standing or by the elevation of an existing member of the judiciary. Judges of the Circuit Court are appointed from among practising barristers or solicitors of not less than ten years standing or a County Registrar who has practised as a barrister or solicitor for not less than ten years before being appointed to that post or by the elevation of a District Court Judge. Judges of the District Court are appointed from among practising barristers or solicitors of not less than ten years standing.

The Supreme Court, which consists of the Chief Justice (who is *ex officio* an additional judge of the High Court) and seven ordinary judges, may sit in two Divisions and has appellate jurisdiction from all decisions of the High Court. The President may, after consultation with the Council of State, refer a Bill, which has been passed by both Houses of the Oireachtas (other than a money bill and certain other bills), to the Supreme Court for a decision on the question as to whether such Bill or any provision thereof is repugnant to the Constitution.

The High Court, which consists of a President (who is *ex officio* an additional Judge of the Supreme Court) and 31 ordinary judges (or 32 when a High Court Judge is appointed as a Commissioner of the Law Reform Commission, as is currently the case), has full original jurisdiction in and power to determine all matters and questions, whether of law or fact, civil or criminal. In all cases in which questions arise concerning the validity of any law having regard to the provisions of the Constitution, the High Court alone exercises original jurisdiction. The High Court on Circuit acts as an appeal court from the Circuit Court.

The Court of Criminal Appeal consists of the Chief Justice or an ordinary Judge of the Supreme Court, together with either two ordinary judges of the High Court or the President and one ordinary judge of the High Court. It deals with appeals by persons convicted on indictment where the appellant obtains a certificate from the trial judge that the case is a fit one for appeal, or, in case such certificate is refused, where the court itself, on appeal from such refusal, grants leave to appeal. The decision of the Court of Criminal Appeal is final, unless that court, the Attorney-General or the Director of Public Prosecutions certifies that the decision involves a point of law of exceptional public importance, in which case an appeal is taken to the Supreme Court.

The Offences against the State Act, 1939 provides in Part V for the establishment of Special Criminal Courts. A Special Criminal Court sits without a jury. The rules of evidence that apply in proceedings before a Special Criminal Court are the same as those applicable in trials in the Central Criminal Court. A Special Criminal Court is authorized by the 1939 Act to make rules governing its own practice and procedure. An appeal against conviction or sentence by a Special Criminal Court may be taken to the Court of Criminal Appeal. On 30 May 1972 Orders were made establishing a Special Criminal Court and declaring that offences of a particular class or kind (as set out) were to be scheduled offences for the purposes of Part V of the Act, the effect of which was to give the Special Criminal Court jurisdiction to try persons charged with those offences.

The High Court exercising criminal jurisdiction is known as the Central Criminal Court. It consists of a judge or judges of the High Court, nominated by the President of the High Court. The Court tries criminal cases which are outside the jurisdiction of the Circuit Court.

The Circuit Court consists of a President (who is *ex officio* an additional judge of the High Court) and 33 ordinary judges. The country is divided into eight circuits. The jurisdiction of the court in civil proceedings is subject to a financial ceiling, save by consent of the parties, in which event the jurisdiction is unlimited. In criminal matters it has jurisdiction in all cases except murder, treason, piracy, rape, serious and aggravated sexual assault and allied offences. The Circuit Court acts as an appeal court from the District Court. The Circuit Court also has jurisdiction in the Family Law area such as divorce.

The District Court, which consists of a President and 54 ordinary judges, has summary jurisdiction in a large number of criminal cases where the offence is not of a serious nature. In civil matters the Court has jurisdiction in contract and tort (except slander, libel, seduction, slander of title and false imprisonment) where the claim does not exceed €6,348·69; in proceedings founded on hire-purchase and credit-sale agreements, the jurisdiction is also €6,348·69. The District Court also has jurisdiction in Family Law matters such as maintenance, custody, access and the issuing of barring orders. The District Court also has jurisdiction in a large number of licensing (intoxicating liquor) matters.

All criminal cases, except those of a minor nature, and those tried in the Special Criminal Court, are tried by a judge and a jury of 12. Generally, a verdict need not be unanimous in a case where there are not fewer than 11 jurors if ten of them agree on the verdict.

The Courts Service Act, 1998, provided for the transfer of responsibility for the day to day management of the Courts from the Minister for Justice, Equality and Law Reform to a new body known as the Courts Service. The Board of the Courts Service consists of 17 members including members of the judiciary, the legal profession, staff and trade union representatives, a representative of court users, a person with commercial/financial experience and a Chief Executive Officer. The Courts Service was formally established on 9 Nov. 1999. While the Minister retains political responsibility to the Oireachtas, the courts are now administered independently by the Board and CEO.

At 31 Dec. 2003 the police force, the Garda Síochána, had a total staff of 12,210. There were 103,360 headline offences recorded in 2003, of which 37,184 were detected, and non-headline offences resulted in proceedings against 292,279 persons; there were 45 murders in 2003 (1·24 per 100,000 population). The National Juvenile Office received 19,915 referrals relating to 17,043 individual children during 2003. The population in penal institutions in Sept. 2003 was 3,366 (85 per 100,000 of national population).

Education

Education is compulsory from six to 16 years of age. In 2005 public expenditure on education came to 4·8% of GDP and 13·9% of total government spending. The adult literacy rate is at least 99%.

Elementary. Elementary education is free and was given in about 3,283 national schools (including 128 special schools) in 2002–03. The total number of pupils on rolls in 2002–03 was 443,720, including pupils in special schools and classes; the number of teachers of all classes was about 24,700 in 2002–03, including remedial teachers and teachers of special classes. The total expenditure for first level education during the financial year ended 31 Dec. 2003 was €2,119·7m. The total salaries for teachers for 2003, including superannuation etc., was €1,509·0m.

Special. Special provision is made for children with disabilities in special schools which are recognized on the same basis as primary schools, in special classes attached to ordinary schools and in certain voluntary centres where educational services appropriate to the needs of the children are provided. Integration of children with disabilities in ordinary schools and classes is encouraged wherever possible, if necessary with special additional support. There are also part-time teaching facilities in hospitals, child guidance clinics, rehabilitation workshops, special 'Saturday-morning' centres and home teaching schemes. Special schools (2002–03) numbered 128 with approximately 6,807 pupils. There were also some 9,384 pupils enrolled in about 1,001 special classes within ordinary schools. There is a National Education Officer for travelling children.

Secondary. Voluntary secondary schools are under private ownership and are conducted in most cases by religious orders. These schools receive grants from the State and are open to inspection by the Department of Education. The number of recognized secondary schools during the school year 2002–03 was 410, and the number of pupils in attendance was 189,093. There were 12,447 teachers in 2002–03.

Vocational Education Committee schools provide courses of general and technical education. Pupils are prepared for State examinations and for entrance to universities and institutes of further education. The number of vocational schools during the school year 2002–03 was 247, the number of full-time students in attendance was 98,233 and the number of teachers 5,933. These schools are controlled by the local Vocational Education Committees; they are financed mainly by State grants and also by contributions from local rating authorities and Vocational Education Committee receipts. These schools also provide adult education facilities for their own areas.

Comprehensive and Community Schools. Comprehensive schools which are financed by the State combine academic and technical subjects in one broad curriculum so that pupils may be offered educational options suited to their needs, abilities and interests. Pupils are prepared for State examinations and for entrance to universities and institutes of further education. The number of comprehensive and community schools during the school year 2002–03 was 89 and the number of students in attendance was 51,905. These schools also provide adult education facilities for their own areas and make facilities available to voluntary organizations and to the adult community generally.

The total current expenditure from public funds for second level and further education for 2003 was €2,304·8m.

Third-Level Education. Traditionally, the third-level education system in Ireland has comprised the university sector, the technical and technological colleges and the colleges of education, all of which are substantially funded by the State and are autonomous. In the mid- and late 1990s a number of independent private colleges came into existence, offering a range of mainly business-related courses conferring professional qualifications and, in some instances, recognized diplomas and certificates. Numbers in third-level education have expanded dramatically since the mid-1960s, from 21,000 full-time students in 1965 to over 129,000 in 2002–03.

University education is provided by the National University of Ireland, founded in Dublin in 1908, by the University of Dublin (Trinity College), founded in 1592, and by the Dublin City University and the University of Limerick established in 1989. The National University comprises four constituent universities—NUI Dublin, NUI Cork, NUI Galway and NUI Maynooth.

St Patrick's College, Maynooth, Co. Kildare is a national seminary for Catholic priests and a pontifical university with the power to confer degrees up to doctoral level in philosophy, theology and canon law.

Besides the University medical schools, the Royal College of Surgeons in Ireland (a long-established independent medical school) provides medical qualifications which are internationally recognized. Courses to degree level are available at the National College of Art and Design, Dublin.

There are five Colleges of Education for training primary school teachers. For degree awarding purposes, three of these colleges are associated with Trinity College, one with Dublin City University and one with the University of Limerick. There are also two Home Economics Colleges for teacher training, one associated with Trinity College and the other with the National University of Ireland, Galway.

Institutes of Technology in 14 centres (Athlone, Blanchardstown, Carlow, Cork, Dundalk, Dun Laoghaire, Galway, Letterkenny, Limerick, Sligo, Tallaght, Tipperary, Tralee and Waterford) provide vocational and technical education and training for trade and industry from craft to professional level through certificate, diploma and some degree courses. These colleges (with the exception of Blanchardstown, Dun Laoghaire and Tipperary) were established on a statutory basis on 1 Jan. 1993. Prior to this they operated under the aegis of the Vocational Education Committees (VECs) for their areas. Dun Laoghaire College of Art and Design was designated under the RTC Act 1992, from 1 April 1997. The Dublin Institute of Technology (DIT) was also established on a statutory basis on 1 Jan. 1993. Prior to this it operated under the aegis of City of Dublin VEC. The DIT provides certificate, degree and diploma level courses in engineering, architecture, business studies, catering, music, etc. The Hotel and Catering College in Killybegs continues to operate under the aegis of Co. Donegal VEC.

Total full-time enrolments in the Institutes of Technology/Other Technological Colleges in the 2002–03 academic year were approximately 51,507. The Higher Education and Training Awards Council (HETAC) was established by the Government on 11 June 2001, under the Qualifications (Education and Training) Act 1999. HETAC is the qualifications awarding body for third-level educational and training institutes outside the university sector. It is the successor to the National Council for Educational Awards (NCEA).

The total full-time enrolment at third-level in institutions aided by the Department of Education and Science in 2002–03 was 129,283. Whereas in the late 1970s only one in five school leavers went on to university, now at least six out of ten are doing so.

The total current expenditure from public funds on third-level education during the financial year ended 31 Dec. 2003 was approximately €1,388·3m.

Agricultural. Teagasc, the Agriculture and Food Development Authority, is the State agency responsible for providing advisory, training, research and development services for the agriculture and food industries. Full-time instruction in agriculture is provided for all sections of the farming community. Training for young entrants, adult farmers, rural dwellers and the food industry is provided from eight colleges, local training centres and research centres.

Health

Health boards are responsible for administering health services in Ireland. There are currently ten health boards established: three area health boards located in the eastern region under the guidance of the Eastern Regional Health Authority (ERHA) and seven regional health boards covering the rest of the country. Each health board is responsible for the provision of health and social services in its area. The boards provide many of the services directly and they arrange for the provision of other services by health professionals, private health service providers, voluntary hospitals and voluntary/community organizations.

A health service reform programme is currently being implemented which will result in the most significant structural changes in the Irish health services in recent decades. The existing health boards will be replaced by a single Health Service Executive (HSE) with four regional administrative areas. A Health Information and Quality Authority (HIQA) will also be established.

Everybody ordinarily resident in Ireland has either full or limited eligibility for the public health services.

A person who satisfies the criteria of a means test receives a medical card, which confers Category 1 or full eligibility on them and their dependants. This entitles the holder to the full range of public health and hospital services, free of charge, i.e. family doctor, drugs and medicines, hospital and specialist services as well as dental, aural and optical services. Maternity care and infant welfare services are also provided.

The remainder of the population has Category 2 or limited eligibility. Category 2 patients receive public consultant and public hospital services subject to certain charges. Persons in Category 2 are liable for a hospital in-patient charge of €75 per night up to a maximum of €750 in any 12 consecutive months. Persons in Category 2 are liable for a charge of €100 if they attend the Accident and Emergency Department of a hospital or receive out-patient services without a letter from a General Practitioner.

The Long Term Illness Scheme entitles persons to free drugs and medicines, which are prescribed in respect of 15 specific illnesses. The needs of individuals with significant or ongoing medical expenses are met by a range of other schemes, which provide assistance towards the cost of prescribed drugs and medicines. The *Drug Payment Scheme* was introduced on 1 July 1999 and replaced the Drug Cost Subsidisation Scheme (DCSS) and the Drug Refund Scheme (DRS). Under this scheme no individual or family will have to pay more than €120 in any calendar month for approved prescribed drugs, medicines and appliances for use by the person or his/her family in that month.

Services for People with Disabilities: The Department of Health and Children provides, through the health boards and the Eastern Regional Health Authority, a wide range of services for people with disabilities. These include day care, home support (including personal assistance services), therapy services, training, employment, sheltered work and residential respite care. The following allowances and grants for eligible people with disabilities come under the aegis of the Department of Health and Children and are administered by the health boards and the Eastern Regional Health Authority:

Disability Allowance—payable to persons who have an injury, disease, illness or disability that substantially restricts their capacity to work. The full rate of €196·00 per week has, since Jan. 2007, also been made available to long-term residents in institutions.

Blind Welfare Allowance—provides supplementary financial support to unemployed blind persons who are not maintained in an institution and who are in receipt of a Department of Social, Community and Family Affairs payment, such as Disability Allowance, Blind Pension or Old Age Pension.

Rehabilitative Training Bonus—payable to persons who are attending approved rehabilitative training programmes. The payment of €31·80 replaced the Disabled Persons Rehabilitation Allowance (DPRA) from 1 Aug. 2001.

Domiciliary Care Allowance (DCA)—provides home care for severely disabled or mentally handicapped children up to the age of 16. The maximum rate of DCA in Jan. 2010 was €309·50 per month.

Infectious Diseases Maintenance Allowance (IDMA)—payable to a person who is unable to make reasonable and proper provision for their own maintenance or the maintenance of their dependants because they are undergoing treatment for one of the infectious diseases specified in the IDMA regulations. The maximum personal adult rate in Jan. 2010 was €196·00 per week.

Mobility Allowance—provides assistance to severely disabled persons who are unable to walk or use public transport in order to finance the occasional use of taxis. At Jan. 2010 the monthly higher rate, payable only to those who do not benefit from the 'Disabled Drivers and Disabled Passengers Scheme', was €208·50. The lower rate was €104·25.

Motorized Transport Grant—provides financial assistance to disabled persons who require a car to obtain or retain employment or who have transport needs because they live in very isolated areas. The maximum grant in Jan. 2009 was €5,020·50.

Respite Care Grant (RCG)—an annual payment of €1,700 (per person cared for) to help carers obtain respite care.

Health Contributions—A health contribution of 2% of income is payable by those with Category 2 eligibility. Employers meet the levy in respect of those employees who have a medical card.

In 2003 there were 59 publicly funded acute hospitals in operation with an 85% occupancy rate. The average number of in-patient beds available for use over the year was 12,300. There were 96,499 wholetime equivalent numbers employed in health board/regional authority and voluntary/joint board hospitals and homes for the mentally handicapped at 31 Dec. 2003. Of these 6,792 were medical/dental staff, 12,690 were health and social care professionals and 33,766 were nursing staff. In 2007 Ireland spent 7·6% of its GDP on health.

Welfare

The Department of Social and Family Affairs is responsible for the day-to-day administration and delivery of social welfare schemes and services through a network of local, regional and decentralized offices. The Department's local delivery of services is structured on a regional basis. There are a total of ten regions, with offices in Waterford, Cork, Limerick, Galway, Longford, Sligo, Dundalk and three in the Dublin area.

Social Welfare Schemes. The social welfare supports can be divided into three categories:

—*Social Insurance (Contributory)* payments made on the basis of a Pay Related Social Insurance (PRSI) record. Such payments are funded by employers, employees and the self-employed. Any deficit in the fund is met by Exchequer subvention.

Contributory pensions are available to those aged 66 who have social insurance coverage beginning before 56 years of age. To obtain the full pension, claimants must have 260 weeks of paid contributions, with an annual average of at least 48 weeks worth of contributions (since 5 April 1979, up to the end of the last tax year) before turning 66. To qualify for the lowest pension rate, claimants must have 260 weeks of paid contributions, with an average of 10 weeks worth of contributions per year. There is also a means-tested non-contributory pension available to citizens aged 66 or older with limited means.

—*Social Assistance (Non Contributory)* payments made on the basis of satisfying a means test. These payments are financed entirely by the Exchequer.

—*Universal payments* such as Child Benefit or Free Travel which do not depend on PRSI or a means test.

The Social Welfare Appeals Office (SWAO) is an independent office responsible for determining appeals against decisions on social welfare entitlements.

There are, in addition, five statutory agencies under the aegis of the Department:

—*the Combat Poverty Agency* which has responsibilities in the areas of advice to the Minister, research, action programmes and public information in relation to poverty.

—*the Pensions Board* which has the function of promoting the security of occupational pensions, their development and the general issue of pensions coverage.

—*Comhairle* which has the function of ensuring that all citizens have easy access to the highest quality of information, advice and advocacy on social services.

—*Family Support Agency* which aims to support families, promote the continuity of stability in family life, prevent marital breakdown and foster a supportive community environment for families at a local level.

—*Office of the Pensions Ombudsman* which investigates and decides complaints and disputes involving occupational pension schemes and Personal Retirement Savings Accounts (PRSAs). The Ombudsman is independent of the Minister and the Department in the performance of his functions.

In 2003 social welfare expenditure accounted for 9·6% of GNP.

RELIGION

According to the census of population taken in 2002 the principal religious professions were as follows:

	Leinster	Munster	Connacht	Ulster (part of)	Total
Roman Catholics	1,828,097	995,728	424,019	214,762	3,462,606
Church of Ireland (including Protestants)	67,877	26,183	9,773	11,778	115,611
Other Christian religion n.e.c.	13,892	5,036	1,672	803	21,403
Presbyterians	8,447	2,056	1,086	8,984	20,582
Muslims (Islamic)	13,233	3,683	1,731	500	19,147
Methodists	5,778	2,574	812	869	10,033
Orthodox	7,570	1,884	657	326	10,437
Other stated religions	24,803	10,003	3,599	1,621	40,026
Not stated or no religion	135,882	53,458	20,947	7,071	217,358

Seán Brady (b. 1939) is the Roman Catholic Cardinal of Armagh and Primate of All Ireland. In Feb. 2010 there were two cardinals.

In May 1990 the General Synod of the Church of Ireland voted to ordain women.

CULTURE

World Heritage Sites

There are two UNESCO sites in Ireland: Archaeological Ensemble of the Bend of the Boyne (inscribed in 1993), the three principal sites of the Brúna Bóinne Complex, a major centre of prehistoric megalithic art; Skellig Michael (1996), a monastic complex on a craggy island from the 7th century.

Broadcasting

Public service broadcasting is provided by Radio Telefís Éireann (RTÉ), which operates two TV channels (RTÉ One and RTÉ Two) and four public radio networks including an Irish-language station. A public Irish-language TV channel, TG4, was launched in 1996. In 2004 a total of 1,241,381 TV licences were issued. Commercial broadcasting is regulated by the Broadcasting Commissioner of Ireland. TV3 (which began in 1998) and Today FM are national commercial television and radio services. There are also numerous local commercial and community radio stations. There were 3·01m. TV receivers (colour by PAL) in 2006. By Sept. 2004 there were 857,000 subscribers to pay TV via cable/MMDS and satellite, 55% of whom subscribed to digital TV. Legislation in 2007 set out a licensing framework for the development of digital terrestrial broadcasting.

Cinema

As at April 2004 there were 321 cinema screens. 12 feature films were produced in 2005.

Press

In 2004 there were six weekday newspapers and six Sunday newspapers (all in English) with a combined circulation of 1,492,099 for Jan. to June 2004.

Tourism

Total number of overseas tourists in 2008 was 7,839,000, compared to 8,012,000 in 2007 (a 2·2% decrease). In 2008 earnings from all visits to Ireland, including cross-border visits, amounted to €4,781m. 49% of visits in 2008 were from Great Britain. Irish residents made 7,877,000 visits abroad in 2008 (a 2·1% increase on 2007).

Festivals

Ireland's national holiday, St Patrick's Day (17 March), is celebrated annually.

Libraries

In 2003 there were 32 public library authorities with 365 service points open to the public (including 29 mobile libraries). They held 13·2m. items of stock. Total registered membership stood at 843,000. 12·3m. visits were made to public libraries in 2003 and 14·3m. items were borrowed. There were 52 academic libraries in 2003 including seven university libraries. There is one national library—the National Library of Ireland.

DIPLOMATIC REPRESENTATIVES

Of Ireland in the United Kingdom (17 Grosvenor Pl., London, SW1X 7HR)
Ambassador: Bobby McDonagh.

Of the United Kingdom in Ireland (29 Merrion Rd, Ballsbridge, Dublin 4)
Ambassador: Julian King, CMG.

Of Ireland in the USA (2234 Massachusetts Ave., NW, Washington, D.C., 20008)
Ambassador: Michael Collins.

Of the USA in Ireland (42 Elgin Rd, Ballsbridge, Dublin 4)
Ambassador: Daniel M. Rooney.

Of Ireland to the United Nations
Ambassador: Anne Anderson.

Of Ireland to the European Union
Permanent Representative: Rory Montgomery.

FURTHER READING

Central Statistics Office. *National Income and Expenditure* (annual), *Statistical Abstract* (annual), *Census of Population Reports* (quinquennial), *Census of Industrial Production Reports* (annual), *Trade and Shipping Statistics* (annual and monthly), *Trend of Employment and Unemployment, Reports on Vital Statistics* (annual and quarterly), *Statistical Bulletin* (quarterly), *Labour Force Surveys* (annual), *Trade Statistics* (monthly), *Economic Series* (monthly).

Adshead, Maura and Tonge, Jonathan, *Politics in Ireland: Convergence and Divergence in a Two-Polity Island.* 2009
Ardagh, J., *Ireland and the Irish: a Portrait of a Changing Society.* 1994
Chubb, B., *Government and Politics in Ireland.* 3rd ed. 1992
Cronin, Mike, *A History of Ireland.* 2001
Cronin, Mike, Gibbons, Luke and Kirby, Peadar, (eds.) *Reinventing Ireland: Culture, Society and the Global Economy.* 2002
Delanty, G. and O'Mahony, P., *Rethinking Irish History: Nationalism, Identity and Ideology.* 1997
Foster, R. F., *The Oxford Illustrated History of Ireland.* 1991
Gallagher, Michael and Marsh, Michael, (eds.) *How Ireland Voted 2007: The Full Story of Ireland's General Election.* 2007
Garvin, T., *1922 The Birth of Irish Democracy.* 1997
Harkness, D., *Ireland in the Twentieth Century: a Divided Island.* 1995
Institute of Public Administration, *Ireland: a Directory.* Annual
Kostick, C., *Revolution in Ireland – Popular Militancy 1917–1923.* 1997
Laffan, Brigid and O'Mahony, Jane, *Ireland and the European Union.* 2008
Lalor, Brian, (ed.) *The Encyclopedia of Ireland.* 2003
O'Beirne Ranelagh, J., *A Short History of Ireland.* 2nd ed. 1999
O'Sullivan, Michael J., *Ireland and the Global Question.* 2006
Patterson, Henry, *Ireland Since 1939: The Persistence of Conflict.* 2006
Vaughan, W. E. (ed.) *A New History of Ireland,* 6 vols. 1996
Wyndham, Andrew Higgins, (ed.) *Re-Imagining Ireland.* 2006

National Statistical Office: Central Statistics Office, Skehard Road, Cork. *Director-General:* Gerry O'Hanlon.
Website: http://www.cso.ie

ISRAEL

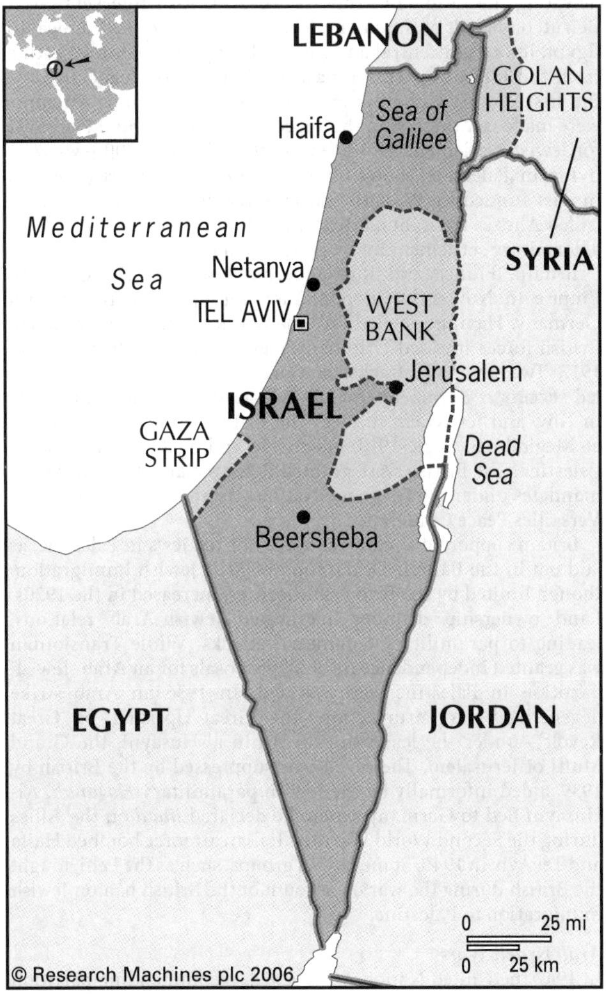

Medinat Israel
(State of Israel)

Capital: Jerusalem
Population estimate, 2010: 7·29m.
GDP per capita, 2007: (PPP$) 26,315
HDI/world rank: 0·935/27

KEY HISTORICAL EVENTS

A settled agricultural community by 6000 BC, the oasis of Jericho is possibly the world's oldest continuously inhabited settlement. Canaan—probably derived from 'Land of Purple', from the purple sea snail dye—described the Eastern Mediterranean coast and hinterland from the 3rd millennium BC. As part of the Fertile Crescent, it became an important caravan route between Egypt and Mesopotamia. 'Canaanite' has come to be associated with the Semitic group of languages and peoples of the pre-Classical Levant.

In the reign of Pharaoh Pepi I (*c.* 2313–2279 BC), Canaan was invaded five times by Egyptian forces. Egyptian authority collapsed in the 17th century, marking the end of the Middle Kingdom. Egyptian control was re-established with the reunification of Egypt in the 16th century. Thutmose III (1479–1425 BC), campaigning against the Mitanni Kingdom in Syria, defeated a Canaanite coalition at the Battle of Megiddo, subjugating Canaan and deporting thousands to Egypt. Egyptian power was challenged by the Hittites of Anatolia until Ramesses II concluded a peace treaty (the first recorded in the world) with the Hittite King Hattusilis III in 1258 BC, setting the border in northern Canaan.

The Israelite (or Hebrew) group occupied the hills of southern Canaan by the late 13th century. Around 1200 BC the Eastern Mediterranean littoral was attacked by the 'Sea Peoples' (probably including the Philistines), who destroyed coastal cities and settled on the coastal plain. The Israelite kingdom was formed from tribes supposedly returned from captivity in Egypt. In the late 11th century, Saul became king but it was his successor, David, who greatly expanded the Israelite state over most of southern Canaan. With Hittite and Egyptian power at low ebb, David conquered the trans-Jordanian states of Ammon, Edom and Moab, subjected Aram (lower Syria) to vassalage and made Jerusalem his capital. After the reign of Solomon (mid-10th century), who built the Temple of Jerusalem, the kingdom split into two: Judah in the south and the more populous Israel, centred on Samaria, in the north.

Having refused to pay tribute, Israel was conquered by Assyria's Sargon II in 722 BC and many of its people were deported; subsequent inhabitants of the Assyrian province of 'Samerina' became known as Samaritans, a mixed race of Israelites and immigrants from Mesopotamia and Persia. Sargon also besieged Jerusalem but was distracted by a Babylonian uprising. The resurgent Babylonians conquered Judah in 586 BC, having utterly destroyed Philistia in 605 to clear access to Egypt. Nebuchadnezzar II had taken Jerusalem the previous year, deporting much of the Judaean (Jewish) nobility to Babylon. Having conquered Babylon in 539 BC, Cyrus II of Persia allowed the return of the Jews to Jerusalem, as Persian vassals, and the rebuilding of the Temple. Persia's defeat by Alexander the Great of Macedon brought the region, by then known as Palestine (derived from Philistia), under Hellenistic control. The Hellenistic period saw an influx of Arab groups, including the Nabataeans, who replaced the Edomites south of the Dead Sea.

Roman Rule

A revolt against the religious intolerance of the Seleucid King Antiochus IV began in 167 BC, led by Judas Maccabaeus, who established the Hasmonean Dynasty in Judaea. Relations with the Samaritans, who also followed the Torah (the first five books of the Hebrew bible), deteriorated when the Hasmonean King John Hyrcanus destroyed the Samaritan Temple at Mount Gerizim in 128 BC. The entire region was conquered for Rome by Pompey in 67 BC; Judaea, including Samaria, was administered as a client kingdom. After the Parthian invasion of Judaea in 40 BC, an Idumaean, Herod, was installed by Rome as king of Judaea. On Herod's death in 4 BC, the kingdom was split amongst three of his sons, who ruled as tetrarchs. Herod's grandson, Herod Agrippa, was granted a reunited Judaea by Emperor Claudius in AD 41, as a reward for supporting Claudius' claim to the imperial throne. However, Herod Agrippa was assassinated in AD 44 and Judaea placed under a Roman procurator. Jewish resentment against loss of autonomy grew until the Great Jewish Revolt (AD 66–73), which was brutally suppressed. Jerusalem was destroyed and hundreds of thousands were massacred or sold into slavery. Jewish rebellions across the East in 115 (the Kitos War) were quickly suppressed. Emperor Hadrian's attempts to enforce cultural uniformity across the Empire included rebuilding Jerusalem as Aelia Capitolina and forbidding Jewish custom. Simon Bar Kokhba, supported by the Sanhedrin (Jewish sages), led a major revolt in AD 132 and established a Jewish government in Jerusalem. However, Roman armies prevailed in 135, with the death of around half a million Jews. Hadrian reacted to the rebellion by suppressing Judaism, banning Jews from Aelia Capitolina, deporting large numbers as slaves and renaming the province *(Syria) Palaestina*; the province was split in three around 390.

Christianity

Under the Christian Byzantine Empire, Palestine became a centre of Christianity (Jerusalem was recognized as a patriarchate in 451), bringing pilgrims and prosperity. It also received lavish imperial patronage, such as Constantine's Church of the Holy Sepulchre (*c.* 326). The Samaritans made a bid for independence in 529 but were crushed by Justinian I and the Ghassanid Arabs. Persecuted by Christians, Jews and later by Muslims, Samaritan numbers dwindled over the following centuries. Byzantine administration of Palestine ended temporarily during the Persian occupation of 614–28; Jerusalem was sacked, its churches burned and the city turned over to the Jews. A spectacular campaign in 628, led by Emperor Heraclius, forced the Persians to cede Palestine and Syria. However, Byzantine rule ended permanently after the Arabs conquered the region; Jerusalem was taken in 638.

The Arabs retained the existing system of administration in the provinces of Jund Filastine (the south) and Jund Urdunn (the north). Taxes and restrictions on religious practice and office-holding imposed on non-Muslims caused large-scale conversions. The Ummayad caliphs moved the capital to Damascus and built the Dome of the Rock on the site of the Jewish Temple in Jerusalem in the 690s. The Christian and Jewish communities of Palestine were partly administered by their own religious leaders. Under the Ummayads' successors, the Abbasids, the capital moved to Baghdad in 762, drawing Asian trade away from Palestine. Fragmentation of the Caliphate in the 9th century saw Egyptian independence under the Tulunids, who seized Palestine and Syria in 878. Although Palestine was retaken in 906 for the Caliphate, in 935 it again fell to Egypt, this time under the Ikhshid Dynasty and, in 970, to its successors, the Fatimids.

Crusades

1070 saw the arrival of the Seljuk Turks, who rapidly overran the Byzantine East. Seljuk restrictions on Christian pilgrimage led to the European Crusader invasions of Palestine and Syria in the 12th century. Having been wrested from the Seljuks by the Fatimids in 1098, Jerusalem was taken the following year by a Crusader army, which massacred the population. Baldwin, count of Edessa, became king of Jerusalem in 1100. Responding to Crusader threats to Mecca (Makkah), Saladin (Salah ad-Din), the Kurdish sultan of Egypt, recaptured Jerusalem in 1187, bringing Palestine under the Ayyubid Dynasty. A treaty in 1192 with Richard I of England allowed Christian pilgrimage to Jerusalem and secured the rump Crusader states along the coast. A treaty of 1229 gave much of Palestine (the Kingdom of Jerusalem) to the Holy Roman Emperor, Frederick II, though Jerusalem was destroyed by Central Asian Khwarezmians in 1244, on behalf of the Ayyubids. The fall of Acre (Akko) to the Mamluks, rulers of Egypt, in 1291 ended Crusader rule in the Holy Land.

Under Mamluk suzerainty, Palestine was administered by Muslim emirates. Economic decline was exacerbated by the arrival of the Black Death in 1351. Although the Mamluk sultanate successfully held off Mongol invasions, Palestine fell to the Ottomans in 1516, bringing it (as part of the Damascus-Syria province) and most of the Islamic world under the rule of Turkish İstanbul. Suleyman the Magnificent rebuilt Jerusalem's walls in 1537.

Zionism

Palestine was briefly invaded in 1799 by Napoleon Bonaparte of France, who had occupied Egypt. Muhammad Ali, the renegade Ottoman viceroy of Egypt, invaded Palestine and Syria in 1831, defeating the Ottoman army. However, British intervention at Beirut, on behalf of the sultan, forced the viceroy's withdrawal to Egypt. Jews from central and eastern Europe arrived in Palestine from the 1880s as part of a nascent Zionist movement. In 1897 the first Zionist Congress met in Basle, Switzerland. Attempts were made in vain to gain the approval of Sultan Abdul Hamid II for Jewish settlement. However, by 1914, about 85,000 Jews were living in Palestine, many on agricultural collectives (*kibbutz*), in part funded by Western Europe's Jewry. Tel Aviv (originally called Ahuzat Bayit 'homestead') was founded by Jews in 1909 as a dormitory settlement for workers in Jaffa.

Britain, France and Russia declared war on the Ottoman Empire in Nov. 1914, in retaliation for its co-operation with Germany. Having repelled Ottoman attacks on the Suez Canal, British forces invaded Ottoman Palestine, seizing Rafah in Jan. 1917. Two abortive attacks on Gaza were followed by British-led success at Beersheba in Oct. 1917, leading to the fall of Gaza in Nov. and Jerusalem in Dec. The British won a major victory at Megiddo in Sept. 1918, effectively ending Ottoman rule in Palestine. The British were granted Palestine and Transjordan as mandates under the League of Nations, established in 1919 at the Versailles Peace Conference.

Britain supported a 'national home' for the Jews in Palestine, as laid out in the Balfour Declaration of 1917. Jewish immigration, though limited by the British authorities, increased in the 1920s. Land ownership disputes aggravated Jewish-Arab relations, leading to paramilitary communal attacks. While Transjordan was granted independence in 1928, proposals for an Arab–Jewish partition in Palestine were rejected. In 1936 an Arab strike degenerated into insurrection—the 'Great Uprising' or 'Great Revolt'—under the leadership of Amin al-Husayni, the Grand Mufti of Jerusalem. The revolt was suppressed by the British by 1939, aided informally by the Jewish paramilitary *Haganah*. Al-Husayni fled to Germany, where he declared *jihad* on the Allies during the Second World War. The Italian air force bombed Haifa and Tel Aviv in 1940. Some Jewish groups, such as the Lehi, fought the British during the war on account of the British ban on Jewish immigration to Palestine.

Arab Israeli Wars

In 1947 the United Nations intervened, recommending partition of Palestine and an international administration for Jerusalem. The plan was accepted by the Jewish Agency (not representative of all Jewish groups) but rejected by the Palestinian Arab leadership; inter-communal war followed. On 14 May 1948 the British Government terminated its mandate and the Jewish leaders proclaimed the State of Israel. No independent Arab state was established in Palestine. Instead the neighbouring Arab states invaded Israel on 15 May 1948. The Jewish state defended itself successfully, and the ceasefire in Jan. 1949 left Israel with one-third more land than had been originally assigned by the UN.

In 1956 Israel was subject to international criticism for its involvement in the Suez Crisis. When Egypt nationalized the Suez Canal, France and the UK resorted to military action. Under the premiership of David Ben-Gurion, Israel joined forces with the European powers and agreed to lead an initial attack on the Egyptian-controlled Gaza Strip and the Sinai Peninsula. The plan was that the UK and France would offer to intervene in the conflict and reoccupy the areas. Nasser's expected refusal of the offer would be the pretext for an invasion that would reclaim the Canal. The Israeli incursions began in late Oct. 1956 but amid widespread international condemnation, most damagingly from the USA, the three nations were forced into a humiliating withdrawal by Dec. Nasser promoted the affair as a victory for pan-Arabism.

In 1967, following some years of uneasy peace, local clashes on the Israeli–Syrian border were followed by Egyptian mass concentration of forces on the borders of Israel. Israel struck out at Egypt on land and in the air on 5–9 June 1967. Jordan joined in the conflict which spread to the Syrian borders. By 11 June the Israelis had occupied the Gaza Strip and the Sinai peninsula as far as the Suez Canal in Egypt, West Jordan as far as the Jordan valley and the heights east of the Sea of Galilee, including the Syrian city of Quneitra, which was destroyed during the conflict.

A further war broke out on 6 Oct. 1973 when Egyptian and Syrian offensives were launched. Following UN Security Council resolutions a ceasefire came into force on 24 Oct. In Sept. 1978 Egypt and Israel agreed on frameworks for peace in the Middle East. A treaty was signed in Washington on 26 March 1979 whereby Israel withdrew from the Sinai Desert in two phases; part was achieved on 26 Jan. 1980 and the final withdrawal by 26 April 1982.

In June 1982 Israeli forces invaded the Lebanon. On 16 Feb. 1985 the Israeli forces started a withdrawal, leaving behind an Israeli trained and equipped Christian Lebanese force to act as a buffer against Muslim Shia or Palestinian guerrilla attacks.

Peace Process

In 1993, following declarations by Prime Minister Yitzhak Rabin recognizing the Palestine Liberation Organization (PLO) as representative of the Palestinian people, and by Yasser Arafat, leader of the PLO, renouncing terrorism and recognizing the State of Israel, an agreement was signed in Washington providing for limited Palestinian self-rule in the Gaza Strip and Jericho. Negotiations on the permanent status of the West Bank and Gaza began in 1996. On 4 Nov. 1995 Yitzhak Rabin was assassinated by a Jewish religious extremist. In the subsequent election, a right-wing coalition led by Binyamin Netanyahu took office. Peace talks with the Palestinians then stalled. In Oct. 1998 Israel accepted partial withdrawal from the West Bank on condition that the Palestinians cracked down on terrorism. The following month, 2% of the West Bank was handed over to Palestinian control. Further moves were put on hold after the collapse of the Netanyahu coalition and the announcement of early elections.

In Sept. 1999 Ehud Barak provided the first evidence that the Middle East peace process was back on track by releasing nearly 200 Palestinian prisoners and by handing over 430 sq. km of land on the West Bank. In May 2000 Israel completed its withdrawal from south Lebanon, 22 years after the first invasion. By Oct. 2000 violence had broken out again between Israelis and Palestinians, fuelled by the conflict over control of Jerusalem, with terrorist acts a daily occurrence, leading to heavy casualties on both sides. With peace talks stalled once again, Barak called for a nationwide vote of confidence by putting himself up for re-election as prime minister. Defeated by the right-wing Ariel Sharon in Feb. 2001, he retired from politics. As violence escalated, in Dec. 2001 Israel ended all contact with Yasser Arafat, besieging his compound at Ramallah and putting him under virtual house arrest. Israeli incursions into Palestinian-controlled areas of the West Bank and the Gaza Strip, and suicide attacks by Palestinians, continued unabated in early 2002 with heavy loss of life. In June 2002 Israel began constructing a barrier to cut off the West Bank, with the aim of shielding the country from suicide bombers. Arafat died on 11 Nov. 2004 and was succeeded by Mahmoud Abbas in Jan. 2005. In Feb. 2005 Israeli prime minister Ariel Sharon and Mahmoud Abbas agreed to a 'cessation of hostilities' between the two peoples, a move which encouraged hopes of a resumption of the peace process. In Aug. 2005 Israeli troops and police evicted the 8,500 Jewish settlers from the Gaza Strip in accordance with an agreement between Israel and the Palestinians. This was the first time Israel had withdrawn from Palestinian land captured in the 1967 war.

In July 2006, after Hizbollah forces in Lebanon had captured two Israeli soldiers, Israel launched a large-scale military campaign against Lebanon with a series of bombing raids, destroying large parts of the civilian infrastructure.

In Dec. 2008 Israel began a military assault on Gaza aimed at destroying Hamas strongholds responsible for rocket and mortar attacks on Israeli targets. Three weeks of air and ground operations resulted in many Palestinian civilian deaths and the destruction of much of Gaza's civilian infrastructure. Israel's action was widely criticized, particularly after the bombardment of the UN's relief and works headquarters. The UN Security Council called for an immediate ceasefire, with all members voting in favour of the motion bar the USA.

TERRITORY AND POPULATION

The area of Israel, including the Golan Heights (1,154 sq. km) and East Jerusalem, is 22,072 sq. km (8,522 sq. miles), of which 21,643 sq. km (8,357 sq. miles) are land. The population in 2005 was estimated to be 6·99m., including East Jerusalem, the Golan Heights and Israeli settlers in the occupied territories. Population density, 313 per sq. km.

The UN gives an estimated population for 2010 of 7·29m.

In 2005, 91·6% of the population lived in urban areas.

Population by place of origin as of 2005: former USSR, 938,000; Morocco, 156,500; Romania, 108,700; North America and Oceania, 80,000; Ethiopia, 71,100; Iraq, 69,100; Poland, 62,500; Iran, 49,100.

The Jewish Agency, which, in accordance with Article IV of the Palestine Mandate, played a leading role in establishing the State of Israel, continues to organize immigration.

Israel is administratively divided into six districts:

District	*Area (sq. km)*	*Population, 2005*	*Chief town*
Northern	4,473	1,185,400	Nazareth
Haifa	866	858,000	Haifa
Central	1,294	1,649,800	Ramla
Tel Aviv	172	1,190,000	Tel Aviv
Jerusalem[1]	653	851,400	Jerusalem
Southern	14,185	1,002,400	Beersheba

[1]Includes East Jerusalem.

On 23 Jan. 1950 the Knesset proclaimed Jerusalem the capital of the State and on 14 Dec. 1981 extended Israeli law into the Golan Heights. Population of the main towns (2006): Jerusalem, 729,100; Tel Aviv/Jaffa, 382,500; Haifa, 267,000; Rishon le-Ziyyon, 221,500; Ashdod, 203,300; Beersheba, 185,300; Petach Tikva, 182,800; Netanya, 173,300; Holon, 167,100; Bene Berak, 147,100; Bat Yam, 129,700; Ramat Gan, 129,400.

The official languages are Hebrew and Arabic.

SOCIAL STATISTICS

2001 births, 136,638; deaths, 37,173; marriages, 38,924; divorces, 11,164. 2001 crude birth rate per 1,000 population of Jewish population, 18·3; Non-Jewish: Muslims, 36·8; Christians, 20·0; Druzes, 26·2. Crude death rate per 1,000 (2001), Jewish, 6·6; Muslims, 2·8; Christians, 4·7; Druzes, 3·0. Infant mortality rate per 1,000 live births (2001–04), Jewish, 3·6; Muslims, 8·6; Christians, 3·1; Druzes, 5·9. Life expectancy, 2007, 78·5 years for males and 82·7 for females. Average annual population growth rate, 2000–05, 1·9%. Fertility rate, 2004, 2·8 births per woman.

Immigration

The following table shows the numbers of immigrants entering Palestine/Israel.

1997	66,221	1999	76,766	2001	43,580
1998	56,730	2000	60,192	2002	33,567

There were 199,516 immigrants in 1990 and 176,100 in 1991 following the fall of communism in eastern Europe and the break-up of the former Soviet Union.

CLIMATE

From April to Oct., the summers are long and hot, and almost rainless. From Nov. to March, the weather is generally mild, though colder in hilly areas, and this is the wet season. Jerusalem, Jan. 12·8°C, July 28·9°C. Annual rainfall, 657 mm. Tel Aviv, Jan. 17·2°C, July 30·2°C. Annual rainfall, 803 mm.

CONSTITUTION AND GOVERNMENT

Israel is an independent sovereign republic, established by proclamation on 14 May 1948.

In 1950 the Knesset (*Parliament*), which in 1949 had passed the Transition Law dealing in general terms with the powers of the Knesset, President and Cabinet, resolved to enact from time to time fundamental laws, which eventually, taken together, would form the Constitution. The eleven fundamental laws that have been passed are: the Knesset (1958), Israel Lands (1960), the President (1964), the State Economy (1975), the Army (1976), Jerusalem, capital of Israel (1980), the Judicature (1984), the State Comptroller (1988), Human Dignity and Liberty (1992), Freedom of Occupation (1994) and the Government (2001).

The *President* (head of state) is elected by the Knesset by secret ballot by a simple majority; his term of office is seven years. He may only serve for one term.

The Knesset, a one-chamber Parliament, consists of 120 members. It is elected for a four-year term by secret ballot and universal direct suffrage. Under the system of election introduced in 1996, electors vote once for a party and once for a candidate for Prime Minister. To be elected Prime Minister, a candidate must gain more than half the votes cast, and be elected to the Knesset. If there are more than two candidates and none gain half the vote, a second round is held 15 days later. The Prime Minister forms a cabinet (no fewer than eight members and no more than 18) with the approval of the Knesset.

National Anthem

'Hatikvah' ('The Hope'); words by N. H. Imber; folk-tune.

GOVERNMENT CHRONOLOGY

Prime Ministers since 1948. (Avoda = Labour Party; Herut = Freedom Movement; Kadima = 'Forward'; Likud = 'Consolidation'; Mapai = Israeli Workers' Party)

1948–53	Mapai	David Ben-Gurion
1953–55	Mapai	Moshe Sharett
1955–63	Mapai	David Ben-Gurion
1963–69	Mapai	Levi Eshkol
1969–74	Avoda	Golda Meir
1974–77	Avoda	Yitzhak Rabin
1977–83	Herut/Likud	Menahem Begin
1983–84	Herut/Likud	Yitzhak Shamir
1984–86	Avoda	Shimon Peres
1986–92	Likud	Yitzhak Shamir
1992–95	Avoda	Yitzhak Rabin
1995–96	Avoda	Shimon Peres
1996–99	Likud	Binyamin Netanyahu
1999–2001	Avoda	Ehud Barak
2001–06	Likud, Kadima	Ariel Sharon
2006–09	Kadima	Ehud Olmert
2009–	Likud	Binyamin Netanyahu

RECENT ELECTIONS

In the parliamentary (Knesset) elections on 10 Feb. 2009, Kadima won 28 of 120 seats with 22·5% of votes cast, Likud 27 (21·6%), Yisrael Beytenu 15 (11·7%), Labour 13 (9·9%), Shas 11 (8·5%), United Torah Judaism 5 (4·4%), the United Arab List 4 (3·4%), the National Union 4 (3·3%), Hadash 4 (3·3%), New Movement-Meretz 3 (3·0%), the Jewish Home 3 (2·9%) and Balad 3 (2·5%). Turnout was 64·7%.

In a parliamentary vote for the presidency on 13 June 2007, Shimon Peres was elected in the second round with 86 votes in favour and 23 against after his two opponents from the first round had withdrawn.

CURRENT ADMINISTRATION

President: Shimon Peres; b. 1923 (since 15 July 2007).

The government is formed by a coalition of Likud, Jewish Home, Labour, Shas and Yisrael Beytenu. In March 2010 the cabinet was composed as follows:

Prime Minister and Minister for Economic Strategy, Health, and Pensioner Affairs: Binyamin Netanyahu; b. 1949 (Likud; since 31 March 2009, having previously held office from June 1996–July 1999).

Vice-Prime Minister and Minister for Strategic Affairs: Moshe Ya'alon (Likud). *Vice-Prime Minister and Minister for Regional Development and the Development of the Negev and Galil:* Silvan Shalom (Likud).

Deputy Prime Minister and Minister of Defence: Ehud Barak (Labour). *Deputy Prime Minister and Minister of Foreign Affairs:* Avigdor Lieberman (Yisrael Beytenu). *Deputy Prime Minister and Minister of Intelligence and Atomic Energy:* Dan Meridor (Likud). *Deputy Prime Minister and Minister of Interior:* Eliyahu Yishai (Shas).

Minister of Agriculture and Rural Development: Shalom Simhon (Labour). *Communications:* Moshe Kahlon (Likud). *Culture and Sport:* Limor Livnat (Likud). *Education:* Gideon Sa'ar (Likud). *Environmental Protection:* Gilad Erdan (Likud). *Finance:* Yuval Steinitz (Likud). *Housing and Construction:* Ariel Atias (Shas). *Immigrant Absorption:* Sofa Landver (Yisrael Beytenu). *Improvement of Government Services:* Michael Eitan (Likud). *Industry, Trade and Labour:* Binyamin Ben-Eliezer (Labour). *Information and Diaspora:* Yuli-Yoel Edelstein (Likud). *Internal Security:* Yitzhak Aharonovitch (Yisrael Beytenu). *Justice:* Yaakov Neeman (ind.). *Minorities:* Avishay Braverman (Labour). *National Infrastructure:* Uzi Landau (Yisrael Beytenu). *Religious Affairs:* Yakov Margi (Shas). *Science and Technology:* Daniel Hershkowitz (Jewish Home). *Tourism:* Stas Misezhnikov (Yisrael Beytenu). *Transportation and Road Safety:* Yisrael Katz (Likud). *Welfare and Social Services:* Isaac Herzog (Labour). *Ministers without Portfolio:* Ze'ev Binyamin Begin (Likud), Meshulam Nahari (Shas), Yossi Peled (Likud).

Office of the Prime Minister: http://www.pmo.gov.il

CURRENT LEADERS

Binyamin Netanyahu

Position
Prime Minister

Introduction
Despite Likud coming second to Kadima in the general election of 10 Feb. 2009, Likud's leader Binyamin Netanyahu was asked to form a government by President Shimon Peres. Netanyahu's coalition consists of centre-right, centre-left and far-right parties and was approved in the Knesset in April 2009. Netanyahu, who was also premier from 1996–99, vowed to lead Israel through the economic downturn and the ongoing conflict with the Palestinians.

Early Life
Binyamin Netanyahu was born on 21 Oct. 1949 in Tel Aviv. He spent most of his adolescence in the USA before returning to Israel for military service. He served with the Sayeret Matkal reconnaissance unit, becoming a captain before he was discharged in 1972. Netanyahu returned to the USA to study at the Massachusetts Institute of Technology and then Harvard. He worked for a series of business consulting and management firms

and in 1982 joined the Israeli diplomatic service in Washington, D.C. as deputy chief of mission, serving as Israel's ambassador to the UN from 1984–88.

In 1988 Netanyahu was elected to the Knesset for the Likud party and named deputy minister of foreign affairs. From 1991–92 he served as deputy minister in the Prime Minister's Office before succeeding Yitzhak Shamir in 1993 as chairman of Likud and leader of the opposition. Sceptical of the Sept. 1993 Oslo Accords agreed by Yasser Arafat, Yitzhak Rabin and US President Bill Clinton, Netanyahu played on Israeli fears over security at a time of escalating Palestinian violence. He oversaw a slim victory at the elections of May 1996, exposing the deep divisions within Israel over the future direction of the peace process.

Although there was a failure to implement the provisions of the Oslo agreements during Netanyahu's tenure, negotiations with the Palestinians continued sporadically. Despite Netanyahu's previous refusal to give up Israel-controlled land, most of Hebron was placed under Palestinian jurisdiction. Netanyahu was defeated in the 1999 general election by Labour's Ehud Barak and subsequently lost the Likud leadership to Ariel Sharon.

Netanyahu returned to politics in 2002 as foreign minister and in 2003 was put in charge of the finance portfolio in Sharon's new cabinet. Although his policies to liberalize the economy met with heavy criticism, reforms to the banking system spurred GDP growth. In Aug. 2005 Netanyahu resigned over the Gaza disengagement plan. On 20 Dec. 2005 he retook the Likud party leadership, claiming 47% of the vote, and once again became opposition leader following parliamentary elections in 2006.

At the Feb. 2009 elections Netanyahu claimed victory, despite winning 27 seats to Kadima's 28, on the basis that his right-wing coalition partners had won the majority of the vote. In an attempt to form a broad centrist coalition, Netanyahu invited Kadima and Labour to join his government, although only Labour accepted.

Career in Office

Netanyahu's efforts at centrist government resulted in one of the largest cabinets in Israel's history. However, the policy divisions between coalition partners led to doubts about the long-term viability of his administration. Among his primary challenges are the sharp economic downturn, the continuing crisis with the Palestinians and concerns over Iran's nuclear ambitions.

In June 2009 Netanyahu expressed for the first time his acceptance of a two-state solution for Israel and Palestine, provided that the Palestinian state was demilitarized and that the Palestinians recognized Israel as the state of the Jewish people. There appeared to be a broad Israeli consensus in favour of the two-state policy and Netanyahu's domestic approval ratings rose sharply in response. A decline in terror attacks against Israelis also helped raise his popularity. Substantive progress in the peace process has nevertheless been elusive. At a three-way meeting in New York in Sept. between US President Obama, Netanyahu and Palestinian President Abbas at the UN General Assembly session, all sides agreed on the need to relaunch talks, but the divisive issue of Jewish settlement building in the West Bank and East Jerusalem remains a major obstacle. Having resisted early diplomatic pressure from the Obama administration to stop all settlement building on Palestinian land, Netanyahu announced in Nov. 2009 a plan for a ten-month freeze in the West Bank (but not East Jerusalem) in a bid to restart negotiations. Although welcomed by the USA, the move was rejected as not going far enough by the Palestinians and, as of Feb. 2010, President Abbas was refusing to countenance further negotiations.

Addressing the UN General Assembly in Sept. 2009, Netanyahu stated that Iran posed a threat to world peace and that it must be prevented from acquiring nuclear weapons. He also condemned the Iranian president's denial of the Holocaust. Such antagonism has fuelled speculation about future Israeli military intentions towards Iran.

DEFENCE

Conscription (for Jews and Druze only) is three years (usually four years for officers; two years for women). The Israel Defence Force is a unified force, in which army, navy and air force are subordinate to a single chief-of-staff. The Minister of Defence is *de facto* C.-in-C.

Defence expenditure in 2006 totalled US$11,031m., representing 7·9% of GDP. Expenditure per capita in 2006 was US$1,737, a figure exceeded only by the United Arab Emirates, Qatar and the USA.

Nuclear Weapons

Israel has an undeclared nuclear weapons capability. Although known to have a nuclear bomb, it pledges not to introduce nuclear testing to the Middle East. According to the Stockholm International Peace Research Institute, the nuclear arsenal was estimated to have about 100 warheads in Jan. 2009. Israel is one of three countries not to have signed the Nuclear Non-Proliferation Treaty (the others being India and Pakistan). Israel has never admitted possessing biological or chemical weapons, but according to *Deadly Arsenals*, published by the Carnegie Endowment for International Peace, it does have a chemical and biological weapons programme.

Army

Strength (2006) 125,000 (conscripts 105,000). There are also 380,000 reservists available on mobilization. In addition there is a paramilitary border police of about 8,000.

Navy

The Navy, tasked primarily for coastal protection and based at Haifa, Ashdod and Eilat, includes three small diesel submarines and three corvettes.

Naval personnel in 2006 totalled about 8,000 (including a Naval Commando of 300) of whom 2,500 are conscripts. There are also 11,500 naval reservists available on mobilization.

Air Force

The Air Force (including air defence) has a personnel strength (2006) of 35,000, with 402 combat aircraft, all jets, of Israeli and US manufacture including F-15s and F-16s, and 95 armed helicopters. There are 24,500 Air Force reservists.

INTERNATIONAL RELATIONS

Israel is a member of the UN, World Bank, IMF and several other UN specialized agencies, WTO, IOM and Inter-American Development Bank. It is the largest recipient of foreign aid in absolute terms, in 2002 receiving US$2·8bn., representing around US$435 per person.

ECONOMY

Services account for about 82% of GDP, industry 16% and agriculture 2%.

Overview

Israel's economy is diversified relative to its neighbours. Over the past two decades electronics manufacturing has replaced traditional industries such as footwear and clothing. Until the 1990s traditional industries benefited from protectionist policies but have since undergone structural changes, including outsourcing to regional neighbours with lower wages. As a result manufacturers have focused on product design and on trade agreements with the USA and the EU.

In 2000 the government opened the telecommunications sector to foreign competition. High-tech industries have been boosted over the years by Israel's high standard of education and its investment in military research and development. The 1990s saw strong growth and in 2000 the economy grew by 8·9%. However, in 2001 and 2002 Israel experienced its worst recession in 50 years, a result of high security costs arising from the second *intifada*, a sharp decline in tourism and difficulties in the high-tech sector. The collapse of the US financial markets, especially the NASDAQ, hurt Israel's technology sectors which relied on US market financing.

The economy rebounded and since 2004 real GDP has grown between 4–6% each year thanks to improved internal security, strong external demand, sound financial conditions and prudent macroeconomic policies. Nonetheless, key challenges remain, notably the high public debt ratio which stands at roughly 90% of GDP and constrains policy manoeuverability. Investor flight from risk and geopolitical uncertainties remain significant downside threats.

Currency

The unit of currency is the *shekel* (ILS) of 100 *agorot*. Foreign exchange reserves were US$58,426m. in Sept. 2009. Gold reserves have been negligible since 1998. Total money supply in Nov. 2008 was 83,131m. shekels.

Inflation rates (based on IMF statistics):

1999	*2000*	*2001*	*2002*	*2003*	*2004*	*2005*	*2006*	*2007*	*2008*
5·2%	1·1%	1·1%	5·7%	0·7%	–0·4%	1·4%	2·1%	0·5%	4·6%

Budget

In 2005 revenues were 263·0bn. shekels and expenditures 276·0bn. shekels. Tax revenue accounted for 67·3% of revenues in 2005; social security and welfare accounted for 24·4% of expenditures, defence 17·2% and education 15·2%.

VAT is 16%.

Performance

Real GDP growth rates (based on IMF statistics):

1999	*2000*	*2001*	*2002*	*2003*	*2004*	*2005*	*2006*	*2007*	*2008*
3·3%	9·2%	0·0%	–0·7%	1·5%	5·0%	5·1%	5·3%	5·2%	4·0%

Total GDP was US$199·5bn. in 2008.

Banking and Finance

The Bank of Israel was established by law in 1954 as Israel's central bank. Its Governor is appointed by the President on the recommendation of the Cabinet for a five-year term. The *Governor* is Prof. Stanley Fischer. Central bank reserves in Dec. 2002 were US$24·1bn. As part of a government scheme several banks were privatized in the years 1993–2006.

In 2001 there were 23 commercial banks headed by Bank Leumi le-Israel, Bank Hapoalim and Israel Discount Bank, two merchant banks, three foreign banks, eight mortgage banks and nine lending institutions specifically set up to aid industry and agriculture.

There is a stock exchange in Tel Aviv.

Weights and Measures

The metric system is in general use. The (metrical) *dunam* = 1,000 sq. metres.

ENERGY AND NATURAL RESOURCES

Environment

Carbon dioxide emissions from the consumption and flaring of fossil fuels in 2008 were the equivalent of 9·9 tonnes per capita.

Electricity

Installed capacity in 2004 was 10·3m. kW. Electric power production amounted to 49·03bn. kWh in 2004; consumption per capita was 6,924 kWh in 2004.

Oil and Gas

The only significant hydrocarbon is oil shale. Crude petroleum reserves in 2004 were 2m. bbls.

Minerals

The most valuable natural resources are the potash, bromine and other salt deposits of the Dead Sea. Production figures in 1,000 tonnes: phosphate rock (2004), 2,947; potash (2004), 2,060; lignite (2004), 439; salt (2004 estimate), 398.

Agriculture

In the coastal plain mixed farming, poultry raising, citriculture and vineyards are the main agricultural activities. The Emek (the Valley of Jezreel) is the main agricultural centre of Israel. Mixed farming is to be found throughout the valleys; the sub-tropical Beisan and Jordan plainlands are also centres of banana plantations and fish breeding. In Galilee mixed farming, olive and tobacco plantations prevail. The Hills of Ephraim are a vineyard centre; many parts of the hill country are under afforestation.

There were about 338,000 ha. of arable land in 2002 and 86,000 ha. of permanent crops. Production, 2002 (in 1,000 tonnes): melons and watermelons, 405; potatoes, 394; tomatoes, 383; grapefruit and pomelos, 256; wheat, 179; oranges, 159; cucumbers and gherkins, 144; apples, 126; bananas, 111; chillies and green peppers, 111.

Livestock (2003 estimates): 395,000 sheep; 390,000 cattle; 190,000 pigs; 63,000 goats; 35m. poultry.

Types of rural settlement: (1) the *Kibbutz* and *Kvutza* (communal collective settlement), where all property and earnings are collectively owned and work is collectively organized (117,700 people lived in 267 *Kibbutzim* in 2005). (2) The *Moshav* (workers' co-operative smallholders' settlement) which is founded on the principles of mutual aid and equality of opportunity between the members, all farms being equal in size (213,600 in 402 *Moshavim* in 2005). (3) The *Moshav Shitufi* (co-operative settlement), which is based on collective ownership and economy as in the *Kibbutz*, but with each family having its own house and being responsible for its own domestic services (17,000 in 40 *Moshavim Shitufi'im* in 2005). (4) Other rural settlements in which land and property are privately owned and every resident is responsible for his own well-being. In 2005 there were a total of 240 non-cooperative villages with a population of 159,400.

Forestry

In 2005 forests covered 171,000 ha. or 8·3% of the total land area. Timber production was 27,000 cu. metres in 2007.

Fisheries

Catches in 2005 totalled 4,151 tonnes, of which 2,755 tonnes were from marine waters.

INDUSTRY

The leading companies by market capitalization in Israel in March 2009 were: Teva Pharmaceutical Industries Ltd (US$39·8bn.); and Israel Chemicals Ltd (US$10·3bn.).

Products include chemicals, metal products, textiles, tyres, diamonds, paper, plastics, leather goods, glass and ceramics, building materials, precision instruments, tobacco, foodstuffs, electrical and electronic equipment.

Labour

The economically active workforce was 2,270,500 in 2001 (1,236,200 males). The principal areas of activity were: manufacturing, mining and quarrying, 394,200; wholesale and retail trade/repair of motor vehicles, motorcycles and personal and household goods, 299,800; education, 283,700; and real estate, renting and business activities, 277,200. Unemployment was 10·5% in 2002, up from 6·4% in 1996.

Trade Unions

New Histadrut (The New General Federation of Workers), founded in 1920 as Histadrut, had 700,000 members in 2006. Several trades unions also exist representing other political and religious groups.

INTERNATIONAL TRADE

Imports and Exports

External trade, in US$1m., for calendar years:

	2000	2001	2002	2003	2004
Imports f.o.b.	34,059	31,014	31,229	32,338	38,473
Exports f.o.b.	31,188	27,967	27,535	30,098	36,585

Main imports in 2002 were: machinery and apparatus, 23·7%; diamonds, 21·7%; chemicals and chemical products, 9·6%; petroleum, 7·7%; road vehicles, 5·7%. Main import suppliers in 2002: USA, 18·5%; Belgium, 9·1%; Germany, 7·1%; UK, 6·7%.

The main exportable commodities are citrus fruit and by-products, fruit juices, flowers, wines and liquor, sweets, polished diamonds, chemicals, tyres, textiles, metal products, machinery, electronic and transportation equipment. The main exports in 2002 were: cut diamonds, 28·2%; telecommunications equipment, 9·2%; rough diamonds, 6·5%; organic chemicals, 3·9%; electronic microcircuits, 3·6%. In 2002 the main export markets were: USA, 40·2%; Belgium, 6·3%; Hong Kong, 4·7%; UK, 3·9%.

COMMUNICATIONS

Roads

There were 17,870 km of paved roads in 2007, including 344 km of motorway. Motor vehicles in use in 2007 totalled 1,805,400 passenger cars, 362,200 lorries and vans, 94,800 motorcycles and mopeds, and 21,300 buses and coaches. There were 398 fatalities as a result of road accidents in 2007.

Rail

There were 909 km of standard gauge line in 2005. 26·8m. passengers and 7·5m. tonnes of freight were carried in 2005. One of the smallest metro systems in the world (1,800 metres) was opened in Haifa in 1959.

Civil Aviation

There are international airports at Tel Aviv (Ben Gurion), Eilat (J. Hozman), Haifa and Ovda. Tel Aviv is the busiest airport, in 2001 handling 8,305,950 passengers (7,864,200 on international flights) and 296,054 tonnes of freight. El Al is the state-owned airline. In 2005 scheduled airline traffic of Israeli-based carriers flew 97·9m. km and carried 4,382,200 passengers. In 2003 services (mainly domestic) were also provided by another Israeli airline, Arkia, and by over 40 international carriers.

Shipping

Israel has three commercial ports—Haifa, Ashdod and Eilat. In 2002, 5,984 ships departed from Israeli ports; 45,810,000 tonnes of freight and 137,000 passengers were handled. The merchant fleet totalled 765,000 GRT in 2002.

Telecommunications

In 2008 there were 3,224,000 main (fixed) telephone lines. In the same year mobile phone subscribers numbered 8,982,000 (1,273·8 per 1,000 persons). There were 3·3m. internet users in 2007.

Postal Services

The Ministry of Communications supervises the postal service. In 2003 there were 668 post offices, or one for every 9,630 persons.

SOCIAL INSTITUTIONS

Justice

Law. Under the Law and Administration Ordinance, 5708/1948, the first law passed by the Provisional Council of State, the law of Israel is the law which was obtaining in Palestine on 14 May 1948 in so far as it is not in conflict with that Ordinance or any other law passed by the Israel legislature and with such modifications as result from the establishment of the State and its authorities.

Capital punishment was abolished in 1954, except for support given to the Nazis and for high treason.

The law of Palestine was derived from Ottoman law, English law (Common Law and Equity) and the law enacted by the Palestine legislature, which to a great extent was modelled on English law.

Civil Courts. Municipal courts, established in certain municipal areas, have criminal jurisdiction over offences against municipal regulations and bylaws and certain specified offences committed within a municipal area. Magistrates courts, established in each district and sub-district, have limited jurisdiction in both civil and criminal matters. District courts, sitting at Jerusalem, Tel Aviv and Haifa, have jurisdiction, as courts of first instance, in all civil matters not within the jurisdiction of magistrates courts, and in all criminal matters, and as appellate courts from magistrates courts and municipal courts. The 14-member Supreme Court has jurisdiction as a court of first instance (sitting as a High Court of Justice dealing mainly with administrative matters) and as an appellate court from the district courts (sitting as a Court of Civil or of Criminal Appeal).

In addition, there are various tribunals for special classes of cases. Settlement Officers deal with disputes with regard to the ownership or possession of land in settlement areas constituted under the Land (Settlement of Title) Ordinance.

Religious Courts. The rabbinical courts of the Jewish community have exclusive jurisdiction in matters of marriage and divorce, alimony and confirmation of wills of members of their community and concurrent jurisdiction with the civil courts in all other matters of personal status of all members of their community with the consent of all parties to the action.

The courts of the several recognized Christian communities have a similar jurisdiction over members of their respective communities.

The Muslim religious courts have exclusive jurisdiction in all matters of personal status over Muslims who are not foreigners, and over Muslims who are foreigners, if under the law of their nationality they are subject in such matters to the jurisdiction of Muslim religious courts.

Where any action of personal status involves persons of different religious communities, the President of the Supreme Court will decide which court shall have jurisdiction, and whenever a question arises as to whether or not a case is one of personal status within the exclusive jurisdiction of a religious court, the matter must be referred to a special tribunal composed of two judges of the Supreme Court and the president of the highest court of the religious community concerned in Israel.

In 2001 government expenditure on public security and justice totalled 7,238m. shekels. The population in penal institutions in Jan. 2002 was 10,164 (163 per 100,000 of national population).

Education

The adult literacy rate in 2003 was 96·9% (male, 98·3%; female, 95·6%). There is free and compulsory education from five to 18 years. There is a unified state-controlled elementary school system with a provision for special religious schools. The standard curriculum for all elementary schools is issued by the Ministry with a possibility of adding supplementary subjects comprising not more than 25% of the total syllabus.

In 2004–05 there were 1,614,000 Hebrew pupils and 436,000 Arab pupils in the education system. In primary schools and kindergartens in 2004–05 there were 888,000 Hebrew children and 302,000 Arab children. There were 57,000 Hebrew teachers and 16,000 Arab teachers in primary education in 2004–05. In post-primary education there were 472,000 Hebrew pupils and 132,000 Arab pupils in 2004–05, with 64,000 Hebrew teachers and 11,000 Arab teachers. In special education there were 11,180 pupils in 2004–05. In post-secondary education, such as colleges, universities and vocational institutions, there were 255,000 pupils, of which 253,000 were Hebrew.

The Hebrew University of Jerusalem, founded in 1925, comprises faculties of the humanities, social sciences, law, science, medicine and agriculture. In 2004–05 it had 21,985 students. The Technion in Haifa had 12,810 students. The Weizmann Institute of Science in Rehovoth, founded in 1949, had 960 students in 2004–05.

Tel Aviv University had 28,740 students in 2004–05. The religious Bar-Ilan University at Ramat Gan, opened in 1965, had 25,025 students, the Haifa University had 16,270 students and the Ben Gurion University had 18,640 students.

In 2003 public expenditure on education came to 7·0% of GDP and accounted for 13·7% of total government spending.

Health

In 2002 there were 367 hospitals with 61 beds per 10,000 inhabitants. There were 24,140 physicians, 7,387 dentists, 38,029 nurses, 4,176 pharmacists and 1,108 midwives in 2001. In 2001 government expenditure on health totalled 12,960m. shekels.

Welfare

The National Insurance Law of 1954 provides for old-age pensions, survivors' insurance, work-injury insurance, maternity insurance, family allowances and unemployment benefits. In 2001 recipients of allocations from the National Insurance Institute included (monthly averages): child allowances, 2,154,735; old age pensions, 571,200; general disability allowances, 142,440; income support benefits, 142,011; maternity grants, 129,089; survivors' pensions, 105,818; unemployment benefits, 104,707.

RELIGION

Religious affairs are under the supervision of a special Ministry, with departments for the Christian and Muslim communities. The religious affairs of each community remain under the full control of the ecclesiastical authorities concerned: in the case of the Jews, the Ashkenazi and Sephardi Chief Rabbis, in the case of the Christians, the heads of the various communities, and in the case of the Muslims, the Qadis. The Druze were officially recognized in 1957 as an autonomous religious community.

In 2001 there were: Jews, 4,960,000; Muslims, 930,000; others (mainly Christians and Druze), 360,000.

The Chief Rabbis are Yona Metzger (Ashkenazi) and Shlomo Amar (Sephardi).

CULTURE

World Heritage Sites

There are six UNESCO sites in Israel: Masada and the old city of Acre were both inscribed in 2001. Masada was built as a palace complex and fortress by Herod the Great. It was the site of the mass suicide of about 1,000 Jewish patriots in the face of a Roman army in the 1st century AD and is a symbol of the ancient kingdom of Israel. The port city of Acre preserves remains of its medieval Crusader buildings beneath the existing Muslim fortified town dating from the 18th and 19th centuries. The White City of Tel Aviv—the Modern Movement (2003) is an example of early 20th century town planning, based on the plan of Sir Patrick Geddes. The Biblical Tels, a series of prehistoric settlement mounds with biblical connections, and the Incense Route, four Nabatean towns along the spice and incense trail, were added to the list in 2005. The Bahá'i Holy Places in Haifa and the Western Galilee (2008) is a complex of buildings including the Shrine of Bahá'u'lláh in Acre and the Shrine of the Báb in Haifa that are visited as part of the Bahá'i pilgrimage.

Broadcasting

The Israel Broadcasting Authority is responsible for public television (Channel 1) and radio services. Channel 2 and Israel 10 are independent national TV networks. Commercial radio services began in 1995. Satellite and cable services are also available. There were 2·29m. TV sets (colour by PAL) in 2005.

Press

In 2006 there were 13 daily newspapers. Combined circulation was 930,000. The newspaper with the highest circulation is Yedioth Ahronoth (Latest News), which sold a daily average of 300,000 copies.

Tourism

In 2005 there were 1,903,000 foreign tourists, spending US$3·41bn.

Calendar

The Jewish year 5770 corresponds to 19 Sept. 2009–8 Sept. 2010; 5771 corresponds to 9 Sept. 2010–28 Sept. 2011.

DIPLOMATIC REPRESENTATIVES

Of Israel in the United Kingdom (2 Palace Green, Kensington, London, W8 4QB)
Ambassador: Ron Prosor.

Of the United Kingdom in Israel (192 Hayarkon St., Tel Aviv 63405)
Ambassador: Tom Phillips, CMG.

Of Israel in the USA (3514 International Dr., NW, Washington, D.C., 20008)
Ambassador: Michael Oren.

Of the USA in Israel (71 Hayarkon St., Tel Aviv)
Ambassador: James B. Cunningham.

Of Israel to the United Nations
Ambassador: Gabriela Shalev.

Of Israel to the European Union
Ambassador: Ran Curiel.

FURTHER READING

Central Bureau of Statistics. *Statistical Abstract of Israel.* (Annual)—*Statistical Bulletin of Israel.* (Monthly)

Beitlin, Y., *Israel: a Concise History.* 1992
Bregman, Ahron, *History of Israel.* 2002
Freedman, R. (ed.) *Israel Under Rabin.* 1995
Garfinkle, A., *Politics and Society in Modern Israel: Myths and Realities.* 1997
Gelvin, James L., *The Israel-Palestine Conflict: One Hundred Years of War.* 2005
Gilbert, Martin, *Israel: A History.* 1998
Kershner, Isabel, *Barrier: The Seam of the Israeli-Palestinian Conflict.* 2005
Sachar, H. M., *A History of Israel: From the Rise of Zionism to Our Time.* 3rd ed. 2007
Segev, T., *1949: The First Israelis.* 1986
Shulman, David, *Dark Hope: Working for Peace in Israel and Palestine.* 2007
Smith, Charles D., *Palestine and the Arab-Israeli Conflict.* 2007
Thomas, Baylis, *How Israel Was Won: A Concise History of the Arab–Israeli Conflict (1900–1999).* 2000
Wasserstein, Bernard, *Israel and Palestine: Why They Fight and Can They Stop?* 2003

Other more specialized titles are entered under PALESTINIAN-ADMINISTERED TERRITORIES.

National library: The Jewish National and University Library, Edmond Safra Campus, Givat Ram, Jerusalem.
National Statistical Office: Central Bureau of Statistics, Prime Minister's Office, POB 13015, Jerusalem 91130.
Website: http://www.cbs.gov.il

Palestinian-Administered Territories

KEY HISTORICAL EVENTS

Under the Israeli-Palestinian agreement of 28 Sept. 1995 the Israeli army withdrew from six of the seven largest Palestinian towns in the West Bank and from 460 smaller towns and villages. In April 1996 an 82-member *Palestinian Council* was elected and also a head (*Rais*) of the executive authority of the Council. The rest of the West Bank stayed under Israeli army control with further withdrawals at six-month intervals, although Palestinian civil affairs here too were administered by the Palestinian Council. Negotiations on the permanent status of the West Bank and Gaza began in May 1996. Issues to be resolved include the position of 0·17m. Israelis in the West Bank and 0·18m. in East Jerusalem, the status of Jerusalem, military locations and water supplies.

Following the opening of an archaeological tunnel in Jerusalem, armed clashes broke out at the end of Sept. 1996 between demonstrators and Israeli troops. On 18 Nov. 1996 the Israeli Minister of Defence approved plans for an expansion of Jewish settlement in the West Bank. Under an agreement brokered by King Hussein of Jordan and signed by the Prime Minister of Israel and the President of the Palestinian Authority on 15 Jan. 1997, Israeli troop withdrawals from 80% of Hebron and all rural areas of the West Bank were scheduled to take place in three phases between 28 Feb. 1996 and 31 Aug. 1998.

The Israeli decision in Feb. 1997 to continue to promote Jewish settlement in the Jerusalem suburb of Har Homa was seen by the Palestinian authorities as a hostile move and caused a setback to peace negotiations. In 1998 an American proposal that Israel should withdraw from 13·1% of the West Bank was not agreed, but at a meeting in the USA in Oct. Israel accepted partial withdrawal on condition that the Palestinians cracked down on terrorism.

Prime Minister Netanyahu's defeat by Ehud Barak in Israel's 1999 elections led to improved relations with the Palestine Liberation Organization. Israel and the PLO signed the Sharm el-Sheikh Memorandum in Sept. 1999 which established a time-frame for the implementation of outstanding commitments from earlier Palestinian-Israeli agreements. Israel conducted two more phases of redeployment from the West Bank in Sept. 1999 and Jan. 2000. The permanent status negotiations, having commenced in May 1996, began in earnest in Nov. 1999. In March 2000 Yasser Arafat accepted Israel's plan for a further expansion of self-rule in the West Bank, involving the transfer of another 6·1% of the West Bank to the control of the Palestinian Authority. As a result, 39·8% of the West Bank came under full or partial Palestinian control. But violence escalated, and in Dec. 2001 Israel ended all direct contact with Yasser Arafat, besieging his compound and putting him under virtual house arrest. In March 2002 the UN Security Council endorsed a Palestinian state for the first time. Israeli incursions into Palestinian-controlled areas of the West Bank and the Gaza Strip, and suicide attacks by Palestinians, continued unabated in early 2002 with heavy loss of life.

In March 2003 the Palestinian parliament approved the creation of the post of prime minister. Mahmoud Abbas was nominated the Palestinian Authority's first premier, resulting in Yasser Arafat losing many of his powers. Yasser Arafat died on 11 Nov. 2004. Mahmoud Abbas was elected president in Jan. 2005. In Feb. 2005 he and Israeli prime minister Ariel Sharon agreed to a 'cessation of hostilities' between the two peoples, a move which encouraged hopes of a resumption of the peace process. In Aug. 2005 Israeli troops and police evicted the 8,500 Jewish settlers from the Gaza Strip in accordance with an agreement between Israel and the Palestinians. This was the first time Israel had withdrawn from Palestinian land captured in the 1967 war. Although representing less than 0·5% of the population of the Gaza Strip the Jewish settlers had occupied around a fifth of the total area.

In Jan. 2006 the legislative elections were won by the militant party Change and Reform (Hamas), which does not recognize Israel and has called for its destruction. Western aid was suspended as a result. In Dec. 2006, amid increasing tensions following months of deadlock between Fatah and Hamas over attempts to form a national unity government, President Abbas called for new elections.

Tensions between Fatah and Hamas climaxed in June 2007, with Hamas seizing control of the Gaza Strip while the West Bank remained under the control of Fatah. In response President Abbas established a new independent government, recognized by Fatah and Israel but not by Hamas, under the premiership of Salam Fayyad. While Fayyad runs the West Bank, Hamas remains the *de facto* power in the Gaza Strip.

In Dec. 2008 Israel began a military assault in Gaza aimed at destroying Hamas strongholds responsible for rocket and mortar attacks on Israeli targets. The international community called for a ceasefire amid concerns about the high number of civilian deaths and infrastructural damage. On 8 Jan. 2009 the UN Security Council called for an immediate ceasefire, with 14 Council members voting in favour and the USA abstaining.

On 13 Jan. 2009 the UN relief and works headquarters in Gaza was bombed by Israeli forces. Israel apologized for the attack, claiming their forces had been fired on by militants who had taken refuge in the complex. On 18 Jan. Israel and Hamas announced unilateral ceasefires. An estimated 1,300 Palestinians and 13 Israelis were killed during the three-week offensive, while 4,000 buildings were destroyed and a further 20,000 badly damaged. 50,000 people were displaced and 400,000 were left without running water.

TERRITORY AND POPULATION

The 2007 census population of the Palestinian territory was 3,767,126 (2,895,683 in 1997). In 2005, 71·6% of the population was urban. Life expectancy at birth, 2007, was 74·9 years for females and 71·7 years for males. The UN gives an estimated population for 2010 of 4·41m.

The West Bank (preferred Palestinian term, Northern District) has an area of 5,655 sq. km; the 2007 census population was 2,350,583, in addition to 275,000 Jewish settlers and 10,000 troops deployed there. 99·8% of the population in 1997 were Palestinians. In 2001 there were 1,860,000 Muslims, 230,000 Jews and 200,000 Christians and others. By 2009 the number of Jewish settlers had risen to 280,000. In 2006 there was a Palestinian diaspora of 5·0m. The birth rate in 2004 was estimated at 39·6 per 1,000 population and the death rate 4·8 per 1,000. In 1995–99 the infant mortality rate was 24·4 per 1,000 live births. The fertility rate in 1999 was 5·5 births per woman. In 2003 there were 31,646 private cars and 14,521 commercial vehicles and trucks registered. There were (2003–04) 542,520 pupils in basic stage education and 59,909 in secondary stage. In 1998–99 there were 36,224 students in institutions of higher education. In 2003 there were 54 hospitals.

The Gaza Strip (preferred Palestinian term, Gaza District) has an area of 365 sq. km; the 2007 census population was 1,416,543. The population doubled between 1975 and 1995. Crude birth rate in 2004 was 43·7 per 1,000 population. The death rate was estimated at 3·9 per 1,000 population. The fertility rate in 1999 was 6·8 births per woman. Infant mortality, 1995–99, 27·3 per 1,000 live births. Agricultural production, 2002 estimates, in 1,000 tonnes: oranges, 105; tomatoes, 48; potatoes, 35; cucumbers and gherkins, 18; grapefruit and pomelos, 10. Total fish catch in 2005 for the Palestinian-Administered Territories was 1,805 tonnes. In 2003–04 there were 374,713 students in basic stage education, 41,185 in secondary stage and 30,058 students in higher education (1998–99). In 2003 there were 17 hospitals.

The chief town is Gaza itself. Over 98% of the population are Arabic-speaking Muslims. In 1995 an estimated 94·2% of the population lived in urban areas. In 2003 there were 38,677 private cars and 9,392 commercial vehicles and trucks registered. Gaza International Airport, at the southern edge of the Gaza Strip, opened in Nov. 1998. Telecommunications development has been rapid, the number of fixed line telephone subscribers more than trebling between 1997 and 2000. In 2003 there were 243,494 subscribers. In 2003 life expectancy at birth was 71·7 years.

CONSTITUTION AND GOVERNMENT

In April 1996 the Palestinian Council removed from its Charter all clauses contrary to its recognition by Israel, including references to armed struggle as the only means of liberating Palestine, and the elimination of Zionism from Palestine. The *President* is directly elected and heads the executive organ, the Palestinian National Authority, one fifth of whose members he appoints, while four fifths are elected by the *Legislative Council*. The latter comprises 132 members (88 until 2005), of which 66 members are chosen by district voting and the other 66 by proportional representation. The Palestinian Authority was created by agreement of the PLO and Israel as an interim instrument of self-rule for Palestinians living on the West Bank and Gaza Strip. The failure of the PLO and Israel to strike a permanent status agreement has resulted in the Authority retaining its powers. It is entitled to establish ministries and subordinate bodies as required to fulfil its obligations and responsibilities. It possesses legislative and executive powers within the functional areas transferred to it in the 1995 Interim Agreement. Its territorial jurisdiction is restricted to Areas A and B in the West Bank and approximately two-thirds of the Gaza Strip.

Following an Israeli-Palestinian agreement on customs duties and VAT in Aug. 1994 the Palestinians set up their own customs and immigration points into Gaza and Jericho. Israel collects customs dues on Palestinian imports through Israeli entry points and transfers these to the Palestinian treasury.

A special committee is working on drafting a new Palestinian constitution. In March 2003 parliament approved the creation of the position of prime minister. Yasser Arafat nominated Mahmoud Abbas, the PLO Secretary General, to be the first premier. The president may dismiss the prime minister but parliament has to approve any new government.

There is a Palestinian *Council for Reconstruction and Development*.

RECENT ELECTIONS

Legislative Council elections were held on 25 Jan. 2006. Change and Reform (Hamas) won 74 seats; Fatah Movement, 45; Popular Front for the Liberation of Palestine, 3; the Alternative, 2; Independent Palestine, 2; Third Way, 2; ind. and others, 4. Turnout was 74·6%.

Presidential elections were held on 9 Jan. 2005. Mahmoud Abbas was elected president by 67·4% of votes cast, ahead of Mustafa Barghouti with 21·0%. There were five other candidates.

CURRENT ADMINISTRATION

President of the Palestinian Authority: Mahmoud Abbas (Fatah); b. 1935.

Prime Minister: Salam Fayyad (Third Way); b. 1952.

De Facto Prime Minister in Gaza Strip: Ismail Haniya (Hamas); b. 1963.

ECONOMY

Overview

Since the beginning of the second *intifada* in Sept. 2000, economic conditions in the Palestinian-Administered Territories have deteriorated severely. Real GDP in 2007 was predicted to be around 18% lower than its peak in 1999 as a result of access restrictions. Public and private consumption have remained constant in recent years owing to increased aid, borrowing and remittances, but in the last two years public investment has been almost non-existent, increasing dependency on aid and further limiting the Territories' already poor productive base. Unemployment increased to 23% in 2005 from a level of 10% in 2000, comprising 33% of the active working population in Gaza and 19% in the West Bank. Poverty is rising. Following Hamas' takeover of Gaza in 2006 the economic gap with the West Bank has widened according to the World Bank.

Currency

Israeli currency is in use.

Performance

The total GDP of the West Bank and the Gaza Strip was US$4·0bn. in 2007.

Banking and Finance

Banking is regulated by the Palestinian Monetary Authority. Palestine's leading bank is Arab Bank. A securities exchange, the Palestine Securities Exchange, opened in Nablus in Feb. 1997.

ENERGY AND NATURAL RESOURCES

Environment

Carbon dioxide emissions from the consumption and flaring of fossil fuels in 2008 were the equivalent of 0·8 tonnes per capita.

COMMUNICATIONS

Telecommunications

In 2005 there were 1,443,600 telephone subscribers (equivalent to 390·0 per 1,000 inhabitants), including 1,094,600 mobile phone subscribers. There were 169,000 PCs in use (45·9 per 1,000) in 2004 and 243,000 internet users in 2005.

SOCIAL INSTITUTIONS

Justice

The Palestinian police consists of some 15,000; they are not empowered to arrest Israelis, but may detain them and hand them over to the Israeli authorities. There were five executions in 2005.

Education

Adult literacy was 91·9% in 2003 (96·3% among males and 87·4% among females).

CULTURE

Tourism

In 2001 there were 7,000 foreign visitors; receipts from tourism totalled US$9m.

FURTHER READING

Chehab, Zaki, *Inside Hamas: The Untold Story of the Militant Islamic Movement.* 2007

Gelvin, James L., *The Israel-Palestine Conflict: One Hundred Years of War.* 2005

Hilal, Jamil, *Where Now for Palestine?: The Demise of the Two-State Solution.* 2007

Kershner, Isabel, *Barrier: The Seam of the Israeli-Palestinian Conflict.* 2005

Kimmerling, B. and Migdal J. S., *Palestinians: the Making of a People.* 1994.—*The Palestinian People: A History.* 2003

Mishal, Shaul and Sela, Avraham, *The Palestinian Hamas: Vision, Violence, and Coexistence.* 2006

Pappe, Ilan, *A History of Modern Palestine: One Land, Two Peoples.* 2003

Rubin, B., *Revolution Until Victory? The Politics and History of the PLO.* 1994

Segev, T., *One Palestine, Complete.* 2000

Smith, Charles D., *Palestine and the Arab-Israeli Conflict.* 2007

Stendel, O., *The Arabs in Israel.* 1996

Wasserstein, Bernard, *Israel and Palestine: Why They Fight and Can They Stop?* 2003

Statistical office: Palestinian Central Bureau of Statistics.
Website: http://www.pcbs.gov.ps

ITALY

Repubblica Italiana
(Italian Republic)

Capital: Rome
Population estimate, 2010: 60·10m.
GDP per capita, 2007: (PPP$) 30,353
HDI/world rank: 0·951/18

KEY HISTORICAL EVENTS

Excavations at Isernia have uncovered remains of Palaeolithic Neanderthal man that date back 70,000 years. New Stone Age settlements have been found across the Italian peninsula and at the beginning of the Bronze Age there were several Italic tribes, including the Ligurians, Veneti, Apulians, Siculi and the Sardi. The Etruscans were established in Italy by around 1200 BC. Their highly civilized society flourished between the Arno and Tiber valleys, with other important settlements in Campania, Lazio and the Po valley. The Etruscans were primarily navigators and travellers competing for the valuable trading routes and markets with the Phoenicians and Greeks. During the 8th century BC the Greeks had begun to settle in southern Italy and presented a challenge to Etruscan domination of sea trade routes. Greek settlements were established along the southern coast, on the island of Ischia in the Bay of Naples and in Sicily where the Corinthians founded the city of Syracuse. These colonies were known as *Magna Graecia* and flourished for six centuries. Magna Graecia eventually succumbed to the growing power of Rome where the impact of the Hellenic culture had already been felt.

According to legend, Rome was founded on 21 April 753 BC by Romulus (a descendant of Aeneas, a Trojan) who, after killing his twin brother, Remus, declared himself the first king of Rome. The Etruscan dynasty of Tarquins gained control in 616 BC and expanded Roman agriculture and trade to rival the Greeks. The Romans overthrew the Tarquins in 510 BC and the first Roman Republic was born.

With the Republic came the establishment of the 'Roman Code', a collection of principles of political philosophy that enshrined the sovereign rights of Roman citizens. The early Roman Senate was dominated by a few patrician families, who held a monopoly on public office with the *equites* (the highest class of non-noble rich).

With the exception of the Greek city-states, Italy was unified by the Romans, who then set their sights on the Mediterranean, controlled by Carthage. Between 264–146 BC Carthage and Rome fought three wars (the Punic Wars) for supremacy of the Mediterranean trade routes. At the start Carthage was the more powerful, with a colonial empire that stretched as far as Morocco and included Sicily, Corsica, Sardinia and parts of Spain. Rome was also inexperienced in maritime war. In 218 BC the second Punic War started when Hannibal crossed the Alps and marched south, defeating the Romans in a series of battles in Italy. Without taking Rome itself, he crossed over to Zama in North Africa where he was finally defeated by Scipio in 202 BC. But by the end of the third Punic War in 146 BC the destruction of Carthage was total and Macedonian Greece was added to Rome's provinces. Rome incorporated Spain into her colonies and became the dominant power in the Mediterranean.

This dominance of trade routes led to great riches for Rome and the ensuing corruption among the upper ruling classes gave rise to social unrest. Sulla, a patrician general, marched on Rome in 82 BC, took the city in a bloody coup and instituted a new constitution. Nine years later Spartacus, an escaped slave, led 70,000 of his fellow slaves in a rampage throughout the peninsula. Out of the ensuing chaos, Julius Caesar emerged as leader. He had already conquered Gaul and declared southern Britain a part of Rome in 54 BC. His disregard for the Senate led to his legions being disbanded but he remained popular and returned to Rome a hero. His strength and charisma led to his assassination by members of the Senate on the Ides of March 44 BC. After his death, various rival successors fought to gain control, including Mark Anthony (Marcus Antonius), Marcus Junius Brutus and Gaius Cassius. But it was Caesar's nephew Octavian, having defeated Mark Anthony in 31 BC, who was crowned the first emperor of Rome in 27 BC, assuming the title Augustus.

Roman Domination

Augustus reigned for 45 years. With the aid of a professional army and an imperial bureaucracy he established the *Pax Romana* while extending the empire and disseminating its laws and civic culture. The arts thrived with writers, dramatists and philosophers such as Cicero, Plautus, Terence, Virgil, Horace and Ovid developing Latin into an expressive and poetic language. In 100 BC Rome itself had more than 1·5m. inhabitants and the Roman Empire was a unified diversity of many races and creeds. It had more than 100,000 km of paved roads, a complex of sophisticated aqueducts, and an efficient army and administrative system.

In AD 14 Augustus was succeeded by his stepson, Tiberius, who ruled in an era that saw the rise of Christianity. Successive emperors tried to suppress the new religion, which spread quickly throughout the empire. The deranged and corrupt Emperor Nero, who came to power in AD 54, initiated violent persecution of the Christians and was accused of setting Rome on fire. His death in AD 68 brought the Julio-Claudian dynasty to a close and, after a period of instability, Vespasian, the son of a provincial civil servant, took the throne and began some of the most ambitious building projects the Empire had seen. He started the Colosseum (completed by his son Titus) and the Arco di Tito (where the Via Sacra joins the Forum).

In AD 98 the Senate elected Trajan as emperor. Beginning a century of successful rule by the Antonine dynasty, he expanded the empire with the conquests of Dacia (Romania), Mesopotamia, Persia, Syria and Armenia. By the end of his reign the Roman Empire stretched from the Persian Gulf to Britain, from the Caspian Sea to Morocco and from the Sahara to the Danube. Trajan was responsible for several great architectural projects. A huge column depicting his Dacian campaigns served as his tomb in Rome. Trajan's successor, Hadrian, continued this programme of huge constructions, including Hadrian's Wall in Britain. After his death in 138, his tomb was converted into the fortress of Castel Sant'Angelo on the banks of the Tiber.

Under pressure from Teutonic tribes along the Danube and as a result of the increasingly strong influence of the Eastern religions, Rome began to lose control of its empire at the start of the 3rd century. In 306 Constantine became emperor. After he converted to Christianity in 313 his Edict of Milan established Rome as the headquarters of the Christian religion. A new building programme of Christian cathedrals and churches began throughout Italy. At the same time, Constantine cultivated the wealthy eastern regions of the Empire and, in 324, he moved his capital to Constantinople (now İstanbul). The decline of the Roman Empire continued when, after the death of Constantine, two brothers, Valens and Valentian, divided the Empire. The west and east gradually became alienated, separated by invaders, language and religious interpretation. 'Rome' endured in the east as the Byzantine Empire, the most powerful medieval state in the Mediterranean.

Fall of Rome

The western half of the Roman Empire, having embraced Christianity as the state religion, came under repeated attacks from Central European ('Barbarian') tribes. The Germanic Vandals had cut off Rome's corn supplies from North Africa, and the Visigoths, a Teutonic tribe, controlled the northern Mediterranean coast and northern Italy. In 452 Attila the Hun, from the steppes of Central Asia, invaded and forced the people of northeastern Italy onto a lagoon haven that became Venice. Rome was captured and sacked in 455 by the Vandals and in 476 a Germanic mercenary captain, Odovacar, deposed Romulus Augustus, the last of the Western Roman Emperors. This date is generally accepted as the end of the Roman Empire in the West.

In 493 Odovacar was succeeded by Theodoric, an Ostrogoth who had acquired a taste for Roman culture. Theodoric ruled from Ravenna and by the time he died in 527 he had managed to restore peace to Italy. On his death, Italy was reconquered by an emperor of the Eastern Roman Empire, Justinian, who together with his wife Theodora laid the foundations of the Byzantine period. Although the Lombards drove back the Justinian conquest, Byzantine emperors managed to retain control of parts of southern Italy until the 11th century.

In the mid-5th century Attila the Hun had been persuaded not to attack Rome by Pope Leo I ('The Great'). This and a document known as the 'Donation of Constantine' secured the Western Roman Empire for the Catholic Church. In 590 Gregory I became pope and set about an extensive programme of reforms, including improved conditions for slaves and the distribution of free bread in Rome. He oversaw the Christianization of Britain, repaired Italy's network of aqueducts and created the foundations for Catholic services and rituals and church administration.

The invasion of Italy by the Lombards began before Gregory became pope and, although they eventually penetrated as far south as Spoleto and Benevento, they were unable to take Rome. They settled around Milan, Pavia and Brescia and abandoned their own language and customs in favour of the local culture. However, they were sufficiently threatening to cause the pope to invite the Franks under King Pepin to invade. In 756 the Franks overthrew the Lombards and established the Papal States (which survived until 1870). Pepin issued his 'Donation of Pepin', which gave the land still controlled by the Byzantine Empire to Pope Stephen II, proclaiming him and future popes the heirs of the Roman emperors. Pepin's son, Charlemagne, succeeded him and was crowned emperor on Christmas Day 800 by Pope Leo III in St Peter's Basilica in Rome. The installation of a 'Roman' emperor in the West—what was to become the Holy Roman Empire—endorsed the separation between Rome and Byzantium and moved the seat of European political power north of the Alps.

After Charlemagne's death it proved impossible to keep the enormous Carolingian Empire intact. In the period of anarchy that followed, many small independent rival states were established while in Rome the aristocratic families fought over the Papacy. Meanwhile, southern Italy was prospering under Muslim rule. By 831 Muslim Arabs had invaded Sicily and made Palermo their capital. Syracuse fell to them in 878. They created a Greek style civilization with Muslim philosophers, physicians, astronomers, mathematicians and geographers. Cotton, sugarcane and citrus fruits appeared for the first time in Italy and taxes were lowered. Hundreds of mosques were built and all over the region centres of academic and medical learning sprang up. Southern Italy lived harmoniously under Arab influence for more than 200 years while the north remained unsettled. After the collapse of the Carolingian Empire, warfare broke out between local rulers, forcing many people to take refuge in fortified hill towns. In 962 Otto I, a Saxon, was crowned Holy Roman Emperor, the first of a succession of Germanic emperors that was to continue until 1806.

At the beginning of the 11th century the Normans began to enter southern Italy in great numbers, where they had originally been recruited to fight the Arabs. Establishing themselves in Apulia and Calabria, they assimilated much of the eastern culture, coexisting peacefully with the Arabs. The architecture of churches and cathedrals built during this period shows the merging of the two cultural and religious influences. Roger II of Sicily (reigned 1112–54), nephew of the adventurer Robert Guiscard, extended Norman Hauteville power over southern Italy and his navy was dominant in the Mediterranean. He presided over a famous court of scholars and artists, many from the Muslim world, making Palermo a model of tolerance and learning.

North South Divide

Meanwhile, the delicate relationship between the Holy Roman Empire based in the north of Europe and the Papacy in the south was maintained by a common desire to recapture the Holy Land from the Muslims. Crusades were launched, mostly from the northern states, but achieved little. Germanic claims to the southern territories grew and after Frederick I (known as Barbarossa) was crowned Holy Roman Emperor in 1155, he married off his son Henry to the heir to the Norman throne in Sicily. Frederick II, Barbarossa's grandson, came to the throne of Sicily as a child in 1197 and was crowned Holy Roman Emperor in 1220. An enlightened and tolerant ruler, he was known as '*Stupor Mundi*' ('Wonder of the World'). An accomplished warrior, he valued scholarship and the Arab culture and allowed Muslims and Jews freedom to follow their own religions. He founded the University of Naples in 1224 with the intention of producing a generation of administrators for his kingdom and moved the court of the Holy Roman Empire to the newly built octagonal masterpiece, Castel del Monte, in Apulia.

During this period a new middle class emerged; with the seat of government so far south, some of the northern cities began to free themselves from feudal control and set themselves up as autonomous states under the protection of either the pope or the emperor. Milan, Cremona, Bologna, Florence, Pavia, Modena, Parma and Lodi were the most important of these new states, each dominated by a powerful family, exercising governmental power in the form of *signorie*. These states functioned autonomously within larger regional areas: Veneto, Lombardy, Tuscany, the Papal States and the Southern Kingdom. In 1265 Charles of Anjou (a Frenchman who had beheaded Frederick II's grandson) was crowned king of Sicily. Greatly increased taxes, especially on rich landowners, made him unpopular despite his programme of road building, reform of the monetary system, improvement of the ports and the opening of silver mines. In 1282 an uprising known as the Sicilian Vespers was sparked off by a French soldier assaulting a Sicilian woman. As a consequence of the opposition to the French in southern Italy, Palermo declared itself an independent republic while supporting the Spaniard Peter of Aragon as king. By 1302 the Anjou dynasty had established itself in Naples.

Plague

The Black Death (La Peste), the deadly plague that swept throughout Europe towards the end of the 13th century, ravaged the populations of the major cities, which were already struggling with famine after years of war. Despite this, the strength of the northern and central Italian city-states was increasing. The rival maritime republics of Venice and Genoa had their own fleets. Venice had added the ports of Dalmatia, the Peloponnese and Cyprus to its possessions and Genoa's influence stretched as far as the Black Sea. Meanwhile, the pope and the Church turned their crusading zeal from the East towards European heretics. Pope Boniface, elected in 1294, came from Italian nobility and was determined to safeguard the interests of his own family. He claimed papal supremacy in worldly and spiritual affairs with his Papal Bull (*Unam Sanctam*) in 1302.

Meanwhile, a rival Papacy had appeared in Avignon, where John XXII was based. Rome had lost most of her former glory and had become little more than a battleground for the power struggles between the Orsini and Colonna families. The Papal claim to be temporal rulers of Rome was under threat and the Papal States began to fall apart. The period 1305–77, when seven successive popes ruled in Avignon, became known as the 'Babylonian Captivity'. In 1377 Pope Gregory XI returned to Rome after Cardinal Egidio d'Albornoz managed to restore the Papal States with his Egidian Constitutions. Rome was in such a ruined state that Gregory was obliged to set up his court in the Vatican, which was fortified and protected by the proximity of the Castel Sant'Angelo. Gregory died a year later and the Roman cardinals elected one of their own, Urban VI, as his successor. Urban's unpopularity was such that the French cardinals rebelled, electing their own pope, Clement VII, who set up his rival claim in Avignon. Yet another rival pope set himself in Pisa and thus began the Great Schism that would separate the papacy from Rome for nearly half a century.

Renaissance

In 1418 the Great Schism was brought to an end by the Council of Constance and Rome began to recapture her previous glory. Italy was at the forefront of the Renaissance, a flowering of artistic and intellectual humanist expression in the city-states. After the Peace of Lodi in 1454, the powerful ruling families—among others the Medici in Florence, the Gonzaga in Mantua and the d'Este in Ferrara—were at leisure to sponsor the Renaissance and Rome became again the centre of Italian political, cultural and intellectual life. In Florence the Signoria was taken over by a wealthy merchant, Cosimo de Medici. His nephew, Lorenzo II Magnifico, became one of the great patrons of the arts. Feudal lords like Lorenzo de Medici frequently switched allegiance between the popes and the emperors, becoming wealthy bankers and captains of adventure in the process. Having defeated its arch-rival, Genoa, in 1381, Venice grew enormously, transforming its commercial maritime empire into a territorial empire that stretched almost to Milan.

The peace was shattered in 1494 by the invasion of Charles VIII, king of France. Encouraged to pursue his claim to the crown of Naples by Ludovico Sforza, duke of Milan, Charles shocked the Italian cities into an alliance to expel his army. As cities competed to become the richest and most cultured, a Dominican monk, Girolamo Savonarola, preached against humanism in Florence. He persuaded Charles VIII to overthrow the Medici family and declare a Florentine republic. Although he was eventually excommunicated, hanged and burned at the stake, Savonarola exerted a lasting influence on Florentine politics. The Venetian expansion, through diplomatic and military guile, had alienated Venice's neighbours, who formed in 1508 the League of Cambrai, which came close to eradicating the Venetian Republic.

The appearance of Spanish power in Naples began the Habsburg-Valois wars that used Italy as a battlefield until the Peace of Cateau-Cambrésis in 1559. These Italian Wars radically altered the political landscape of the peninsula, leaving Spain dominant in Italy. Florence's time as a republic was brief. The Emperor Charles V, who had sacked Rome in 1527, reinstated the Medici, who went on to rule Florence for the next 210 years.

By the second half of the 16th century, the Church of Rome was obliged to respond to the rise of the Protestant movement (the Reformation), inspired in Germany by Martin Luther. During the Counter-Reformation, the Inquisition, backed by Catholic Spain, was used to suppress heresy. Spain succeeded in dominating Italy during the second half of the 16th century but when Charles II (the last of the Spanish Habsburgs) died in 1700, the War of the Spanish Succession saw Italy become a prize for the dominant European powers. Italy was divided amongst the Austrian Habsburgs, the Spanish Bourbons, Savoy and the independent states. The papacy became less influential, the Jesuits were expelled from Portugal, France and Spain and, thanks to intermarriage between many of the ruling houses of Europe and new trading laws, many national barriers were broken down. The 18th century Age of Enlightenment gave Italy some of its greatest thinkers and writers as well as liberal legal reforms.

Unification

In 1796 Napoleon Bonaparte invaded Italy and declared an Italian Republic under his personal rule. In creating a single political entity, he laid the basis for modern Italy. The Congress of Vienna, which met after the defeat of Napoleon in 1815, reinstated Italy's former rulers. Secret societies, made up of disillusioned middle class intellectuals, fought for a new constitution to reunify the country. One such was founded in 1830 by a Genoan, Giuseppe Mazzini. His 'Young Italy' was committed to liberating the country from foreign dominance and to establishing a unified state under a republican government, a campaign that came to be known as *Il Risorgimento*. During the 1830s and 1840s Mazzini instigated a series of unsuccessful uprisings until he was exiled. By 1848 revolutionary uprisings were taking place all over Europe and the Italian Nationalist movement was gaining ground. Two supporters of the Nationalist cause, Cesare Balbo and Count Camillo Benso di Cavour, published a document—*Statuto*—that proposed a bicameral legislature and would become the basis of a new Italian constitution.

As nationalist feeling increased, Giuseppe Garibaldi, whose terrorist activities for Young Italy had obliged him to flee to South America, returned to Italy and allied himself with the Italian National Society. Cavour, the prime minister of Sardinia-Piedmont, attempted to remove Austria from Italy with French help but it was not until Garibaldi and 1,000 volunteers (the Red Shirts) took Sicily and Naples from the Bourbons in 1860 that unification became a real possibility. Garibaldi handed over these kingdoms to Victor Emmanuel II, king of Sardinia-Piedmont. This was to the relief of Cavour, who had feared that Garibaldi might institute a rival republican government in the south. Although Italy was declared a kingdom in 1861 under Victor Emmanuel II, the country was still not unified. Venice was in the hands of the Austrians while France held Rome. In 1866 the Italians took the Veneto from the Prussians and in 1870 Rome was recaptured from the French. Only the Papal troops resisted the advance of the Italian army in 1870 and Pope Pius IX refused to recognize the Kingdom of Italy. In retaliation, the government stripped the pope of his temporal powers. Thus Italy was fully unified.

Twentieth Century

The turn of the 20th century saw popular support fluctuate between left-wing socialist and right-wing imperialist political parties. When the First World War broke out in 1914, Italy remained neutral although the State was associated with the British, French and Russian allies while the Papacy declared for Catholic Austria. In 1919 Benito Mussolini founded the Italian Fascist Party, whose black shirts and Roman salutes were to become the symbols of aggressive nationalism in Italy for the next two decades. In the elections of 1921 the Fascist Party won 35 of the 135 seats in the Italian parliament. A year later, Mussolini raised a militia of 40,000 'Black Shirts' and marched on Rome to 'liberate' it from the socialists. In 1922 the king asked Mussolini to form a government. His Fascist party won the elections of 1924 and Mussolini assumed the title *Il Duce*. By the end of 1925 Mussolini had expelled all opposition parties from parliament and gained control of the trade unions. Four years later, he signed a pact with Pope Pius XI declaring Catholicism the sole religion of Italy and recognizing the Vatican as an independent state. In return, the pope finally recognized the United Kingdom of Italy.

Mussolini's aggressive foreign policy resulted in disputes with Greece over Corfu and military campaigns in the Italian colony of Libya. In 1935 Italy invaded Abyssinia (now Ethiopia) and captured Addis Ababa. The newly formed League of Nations condemned this action and imposed sanctions. In the face of international isolation, Mussolini formed an alliance with the German dictator, Adolf Hitler, and in 1936 the Rome-Berlin Axis was formed. Having annexed Albania in April 1939, Italy entered the Second World War in June 1940. Mussolini's armies invaded Greece from Albania in Oct. 1940 but were repelled, forcing Hitler to invade Yugoslavia and Greece in April 1941. This diversion of German troops has been seen as a critical factor in the ultimate failure of the invasion of the USSR, delayed from May to June 1941. The Italian colonies of East Africa were lost in 1941 and Italian forces in North Africa surrendered in May 1943. The Allied armies landed in Sicily in July 1943 and, in the face of diminishing popular support for fascism and Hitler's refusal to assign more troops to the defence of Italy, the king led a coup against Mussolini and had him arrested. In the 45 days that followed, Italy exploded in a series of uprisings against the war. The king signed an armistice with the Allies and declared war on Germany but Nazi troops had already overrun northern Italy. The Germans rescued Mussolini from prison and installed him as a puppet ruler. In 1945 after trying to flee the country, Mussolini was recaptured by Italian partisans and shot. After the Italian Resistance suffered huge losses against the Germans, the allies liberated northern Italy in May 1945.

Post-War Period

In the years following the end of the Second World War, Italy's political forces attempted to regroup. The Marshall Plan, America's post-war aid programme, exerted considerable political and economic influence. The constitutional monarchy was abolished in 1946 by referendum and a republic was formed with a president (elected for a seven-year term by an electoral college), a two-chamber parliament and a separate judiciary. Initially the newly formed Christian Democrats under Alcide De Gasperi were in power with both the Communist Party and the Socialist Party, participating in a series of coalition governments until they were both excluded by De Gasperi in 1947. More than 300 separate political factions have struggled for power throughout the post-war era and no government has lasted longer than four years. Despite this instability, the war-damaged Italian economy began to pick up in the early 1950s. The industrialized northern regions thrived while the less industrialized south remained underdeveloped. The Cassa per il Mezzogiorno (a state fund for the South) was founded to try to redress the balance but with limited success.

In 1957 Italy became a founder member of the European Economic Community (EEC). The rapid growth of the motor industry, most notably Fiat in Turin, saw huge migrations of peasants from the south to work in the factories. By the mid-1960s the Communist Party, which had been gradually increasing its share of the poll at each election, had more card carrying members than the Christian Democrats and was exerting considerable influence over Italian politics without actually managing to participate in government. Social unrest was commonplace and in 1969 a series of strikes, demonstrations and riots followed on the heels of unrest elsewhere in Europe. Various terrorist groups were active including the extreme left-wing socialist group, the Red Brigade, founded in 1970. Extreme right-wing neo-fascist terrorists were also in action, and in the less developed south, the Mafia, a loose coalition of crime 'families', flourished. Most of Italy's social, economic and political structures were manipulated by these unofficial organizations.

In 1963 Aldo Moro, a Christian Democrat, was appointed prime minister (a post he held until 1968) and invited the Socialists into his government. Later on, in the 1970s, he was working towards a compromise to allow the Communists to enter government when he was captured, held hostage and finally murdered by the Red Brigade. This national outrage prompted the government to appoint Carabinieri Gen. Carlo Alberto dalla Chiesa to wipe out the terrorist groups. He instituted a system of *pentiti* (informants) who, in return for collaboration, would receive greatly reduced prison sentences. In 1980 he was asked to expand his area of operations to include the Mafia but was assassinated in Palermo a few months later. Throughout the 1970s Italy experienced radical social and political change. The country was divided into regional administrative areas with their own elected governments. Divorce became legal, women's rights were expanded (Italian women only achieved full suffrage after the Second World War) and abortion was legalized. In 1983 the minority Christian Democratic government handed the premiership to the Socialists under Bettino Craxi.

Italy was well on its way to becoming one of the world's leading economic powers but the 1990s brought fresh crises in the economic and political arenas. Unemployment and inflation rose sharply which, combined with a huge national debt and unstable lira, led to instability. On the political front, the Communist Party split with the hard-liners forming the Rifondazione Communista, led by Fausto Bernotti, while the more moderate members set up the Democratic Party of the Left. In early 1992 the arrest of a Socialist Party worker on charges of accepting bribes in exchange for public works contracts sparked off Italy's largest ever political corruption scandal. Investigations into '*Tangentopoli*' ('kick-back city') implicated thousands of politicians, public officials and businessmen. Former Prime Minister Bettino Craxi was forced to resign as party secretary after he came under investigation for bribery. Allied to Italy's humiliating exit from Europe's Exchange Rate Mechanism (ERM), the old political establishment was driven out of office. In the April 1992 elections, the Christian Democrat share of the vote dropped by 5% while the Lega Nord (the Northern League), under Umberto Bossi, took 9% of the vote on an anti-corruption, federalist platform. Oscar Luigi Scalfaro was elected president on a promise to set about reforming electoral laws and clearing up the Tangentopoli scandal. Investigations into corruption continued, despite reprisals from the Mafia. Craxi was convicted *in absentia* while Giulio Andreotti, who was prime minister three times between 1972 and 1992, was brought to trial in 1995 on charges of dealing with the Sicilian Mafia.

In the 1994 elections a right-wing coalition was elected. The Freedom Alliance, including the neo-fascist National Alliance and the federalist Northern League, was led by Silvio Berlusconi, a multi-millionaire media tycoon. Berlusconi lost his majority when the Northern League withdrew after nine months. Under mounting criticism for his failure to disassociate himself from his business interests and after receiving a vote of no confidence, Berlusconi resigned. After leaving the Freedom Alliance, the Northern League became more fanatical, advocating a 'Northern Republic of Padania', a separation of the rich northern regions from the poorer southern ones. The 1996 elections brought to power the centre-left 'Olive Tree' alliance with Romano Prodi as prime minister. Prodi aimed to balance the budget and create a stable political environment. He gained his first objective with a succession of economic measures that prepared the way for Italy's entry into EMU.

Prodi was succeeded by Massimo D'Alema in 1998 who, in turn, was replaced by Giuliano Amato in 2000. By the time of the 2001 elections Berlusconi's popularity had revived and he formed a new centre-right coalition. He introduced the first major constitutional reforms in 55 years, allowing the nation's 20 regions increased responsibility for their own tax, education and environmental programmes.

Berlusconi's tenure was dogged by questions over his private business interests. In Oct. 2002 parliament passed new criminal reform legislation that critics claimed was partly designed to allow Berlusconi to escape charges of corruption. He nonetheless stood trial in May 2003 on corruption charges related to his business dealings in the 1980s but the trial was halted the following month when the new law granted the prime minister immunity from prosecution. The legislation was declared void by the constitutional court in Jan. 2004 and his trial resumed three months later, culminating in his acquittal in Dec. 2004.

The proposed EU constitution was approved by parliament in April 2005, shortly before Berlusconi's government collapsed after a poor showing in regional elections. He was then asked by the president to form a new government but was beaten by Prodi in the general election of April 2006. The following month Giorgio Napolitano was elected president. Prodi resigned in Feb. 2007 when his foreign policy failed to gain Senate backing but resumed his premiership after winning confidence votes in both the upper and lower houses.

In early 2008 Prodi's coalition split when a minor partner withdrew its support. Despite surviving a vote of no confidence in the lower house, Prodi lost a similar vote in the Senate. Parliament was dissolved in Feb. 2008 and Prodi was asked to remain as caretaker prime minister ahead of a general election in April 2008, in which Silvio Berlusconi was returned to power.

TERRITORY AND POPULATION

Italy is bounded in the north by Switzerland and Austria, east by Slovenia and the Adriatic Sea, southeast by the Ionian Sea, south by the Mediterranean Sea, southwest by the Tyrrhenian Sea and Ligurian Sea and west by France.

The area is 301,277 sq. km. Populations at successive censuses (in 1,000) were as follows:

10 Feb. 1901	33,778	15 Oct. 1961	50,624
10 June 1911	36,921	24 Oct. 1971	54,137
1 Dec. 1921	37,856	25 Oct. 1981	56,557
21 April 1931	41,043	20 Oct. 1991	56,778
21 April 1936	42,399	21 Oct. 2001	56,996
4 Nov. 1951	47,516		

Population estimate, 31 Dec. 2008, 60,045,068 (30,892,645 females). Density: 199 per sq. km.

The UN gives an estimated population for 2010 of 60·10m.

In 2005, 67·6% of the population lived in urban areas.

The following table gives area and population of the Autonomous Regions (censuses 1991 and 2001):

Regions	*Area in sq. km*	*Resident pop. census, 1991*	*Resident pop. census, 2001*	*Density per sq. km, 2001*
Piedmont (Piemonte)	25,399	4,302,565	4,214,677	166
Valle d'Aosta[1]	3,262	115,938	119,548	37
Lombardy (Lombardia)	23,857	8,856,074	9,032,554	379
Trentino-Alto Adige[1]	13,618	890,360	940,016	69
Bolzano-Bozen	7,400	440,508	462,999	63
Trento	6,218	449,852	477,017	77
Veneto	18,364	4,380,797	4,527,694	247
Friuli-Venezia Giulia[1]	7,845	1,197,666	1,183,764	151
Liguria	5,418	1,676,282	1,571,783	290
Emilia Romagna	22,123	3,909,512	3,983,346	180
Tuscany (Toscana)	22,992	3,529,946	3,497,806	152
Umbria	8,456	811,831	825,826	98
Marche	9,693	1,429,205	1,470,581	152
Lazio	17,203	5,140,371	5,112,413	297
Abruzzi	10,794	1,249,054	1,262,392	117
Molise	4,438	330,900	320,601	72
Campania	13,595	5,630,280	5,701,931	419
Puglia	19,348	4,031,885	4,020,707	208
Basilicata	9,992	610,528	597,768	60
Calabria	15,080	2,070,203	2,011,466	133
Sicily (Sicilica)[1]	25,709	4,966,386	4,968,991	193
Sardinia (Sardegna)[1]	24,090	1,648,248	1,631,880	68

[1]With special statute.

Communes of more than 100,000 inhabitants, with population resident at the census of 21 Oct. 2001:

Rome (Roma)	2,546,804	Parma	163,457
Milan (Milano)	1,256,211	Livorno	156,274
Naples (Napoli)	1,004,500	Foggia	155,203
Turin (Torino)	865,263	Perugia	149,125
Palermo	686,722	Reggio nell'Emilia	141,877
Genoa (Genova)	610,307	Salerno	138,188
Bologna	371,217	Ravenna	134,631
Florence (Firenze)	356,118	Ferrara	130,992
Bari	316,532	Rimini	128,656
Catania	313,110	Syracuse (Siracusa)	123,657
Venice (Venezia)	271,073	Sassari	120,729
Verona	253,208	Monza	120,204
Messina	252,026	Pescara	116,286
Trieste	211,184	Bergamo	113,143
Padua (Padova)	204,870	Forli	108,335
Taranto	202,033	Latina	107,898
Brescia	187,567	Vicenza	107,223
Reggio di Calabria	180,353	Terni	105,018
Modena	175,502	Trento	104,946
Prato	172,499	Novara	100,910
Cagliari	164,249	Ancona	100,507

The official language is Italian, spoken by 92·8% of the population in 2003. There are 0·3m. German-speakers in Bolzano and 30,000 French-speakers in Valle d'Aosta.

In addition to Sicily and Sardinia, there are a number of other Italian islands, the largest being Elba (363 sq. km), and the most distant Lampedusa, which is 205 km from Sicily but only 113 km from Tunisia.

SOCIAL STATISTICS

Vital statistics (and rates per 1,000 population), 2008: births, 576,659 (9·6); deaths, 585,126 (9·8). Marriages in 2007, 250,360 (4·2); divorces in 2006, 49,534 (0·8). Infant mortality rate, 2005 (up to one year of age): 4 per 1,000 live births. Expectation of life, 2007: females, 84·0 years; males, 78·1. In 2005, 19·7% of the population was over 65—one of the highest percentages in the world.

Annual population growth rate, 2000–05, 0·6%; fertility rate, 2004, 1·3 births per woman. With only 14·9% of births being to unmarried mothers in 2004 (albeit up from 8·1% in 1995), Italy has one of the lowest rates of births out of marriage in Europe.

In 2006 there were 3,701 suicides; 76·8% were men.

At 1 Jan. 2007 there were 2,938,922 foreigners living in Italy, up from 2,670,514 a year earlier. In 2005, 53,931 people emigrated from Italy and there were 304,960 immigrants into the country (compared to 440,301 immigrants in 2003). Italy received 8,613 asylum applications in 2006, equivalent to 0·1 per 1,000 inhabitants. New legislation was introduced in 2002 to tighten up immigration rules.

CLIMATE

The climate varies considerably with latitude. In the south, it is warm temperate, with little rain in the summer months, but the north is cool temperate with rainfall more evenly distributed over the year. Florence, Jan. 47·7°F (8·7°C), July 79·5°F (26·4°C). Annual rainfall 33" (842 mm). Milan, Jan. 38·7°F (3·7°C), July 73·4°F (23·0°C). Annual rainfall 38" (984 mm). Naples, Jan. 50·2°F (10·1°C), July 77·4°F (25·2°C). Annual rainfall 36" (935 mm). Palermo, Jan. 52·5°F (11·4°C), July 78·4°F (25·8°C). Annual rainfall 35" (897 mm). Rome, Jan. 53·4°F (11·9°C), July 76·3°F (24·6°C). Annual rainfall 31" (793 mm). Venice, Jan. 43·3°F (6·3°C), July 70·9°F (21·6°C). Annual rainfall 32" (830 mm).

CONSTITUTION AND GOVERNMENT

The Constitution dates from 1948. Italy is 'a democratic republic founded on work'. Parliament consists of the *Chamber of Deputies* and the *Senate*. The Chamber is elected for five years by universal and direct suffrage and consists of 630 deputies. The Senate is elected for five years on a regional basis by electors over the age of 25, each Region having at least seven senators. The total number of senators is 315. The Valle d'Aosta is represented by one senator only, the Molise by two. The President of the Republic can nominate 11 senators for life from eminent persons in the social, scientific, artistic and literary spheres. The President may become a senator for life. The *President* is elected in a joint session of Chamber and Senate, to which are added three delegates from each Regional Council (one from the Valle d'Aosta). A two-thirds majority is required for the election, but after a third indecisive scrutiny the absolute majority of votes is sufficient. The President must be 50 years or over; term of office, seven years. The Speaker of the Senate acts as the deputy President. The President can dissolve the chambers of parliament, except during the last six months of the presidential term. An attempt to create a new constitution, which had been under consideration for 18 months, collapsed in June 1998.

There is a *Constitutional Court* that consists of 15 appointed judges, five each by the President, Parliament (in joint session) and the highest law and administrative courts. The Court can decide on the constitutionality of laws and decrees, define the powers of the State and Regions, judge conflicts between the State and Regions and between the Regions, and try the President and Ministers.

The revival of the Fascist Party is forbidden. Direct male descendants of King Victor Emmanuel are excluded from all public offices and have no right to vote or to be elected; their estates are forfeit to the State. For 56 years they were also banned from Italian territory until the constitution was changed in 2002 to allow them to return from exile. Titles of nobility are no longer recognized, but those existing before 28 Oct. 1922 are retained as part of the name.

A referendum was held in June 1991 to decide whether the system of preferential voting by indicating four candidates by their listed number should be changed to a simpler system, less open to abuse, of indicating a single candidate by name. The electorate was 46m. Turnout was 62·5% (there was a 50% quorum). 95·6% of votes cast were in favour of the change. As a result, an electoral reform of 1993 provides for the replacement of proportional representation by a system in which 475 seats in the Chamber of Deputies are elected by a first-past-the-post single-round vote and 155 seats by proportional representation in a separate single-round vote on the same day. There are 27 electoral regions. There is a 4% threshold for entry to the Chamber of Deputies.

At a further referendum in April 1993, turnout was 77%. Voters favoured the eight reforms proposed, including a new system of election to the Senate and the abolition of some ministries. 75% of the Senate is now elected by a first-past-the-post system, the remainder by proportional representation; no party may present more than one candidate in each constituency. In July 1997 an all-party parliamentary commission on constitutional reform proposed a directly elected president with responsibility for defence and foreign policy, the devolving of powers to the regions, a reduction in the number of seats in the Senate and in the lower house and the creation of a third chamber to speak on behalf of the regions.

National Anthem

'Fratelli d'Italia' ('Brothers of Italy'); words by G. Mameli, tune by M. Novaro, 1847.

GOVERNMENT CHRONOLOGY

Presidents of the Council of Ministers (Prime Ministers) since 1944. (DC = Christian Democrats; DS = Democrats of the Left-Party of the European Socialism; FI = Forza Italia; PA = Action Party; PdL = People of Freedom; PRI = Italian Republican Party; PSI = Italian Socialist Party; Ulivo = Olive Tree; n/p = non-partisan)

1944–45	n/p	Ivanoe Bonomi
1945	PA	Ferruccio Parri
1945–53	DC	Alcide De Gasperi
1953–54	DC	Giuseppe Pella
1954	DC	Amintore Fanfani
1954–55	DC	Mario Scelba
1955–57	DC	Antonio Segni
1957–58	DC	Adone Zoli
1958–59	DC	Amintore Fanfani
1959–60	DC	Antonio Segni
1960	DC	Fernando Tambroni
1960–63	DC	Amintore Fanfani
1963	DC	Giovanni Leone
1963–68	DC	Aldo Moro
1968	DC	Giovanni Leone
1968–70	DC	Mariano Rumor
1970–72	DC	Emilio Colombo
1972–73	DC	Giulio Andreotti
1973–74	DC	Mariano Rumor
1974–76	DC	Aldo Moro
1976–79	DC	Giulio Andreotti
1979–80	DC	Francesco Cossiga
1980–81	DC	Arnaldo Forlani
1981–82	PRI	Giovanni Spadolini
1982–83	DC	Amintore Fanfani
1983–87	PSI	Benedettino Craxi
1987	DC	Amintore Fanfani
1987–88	DC	Giovanni Giuseppe Goria
1988–89	DC	Ciriaco De Mita
1989–92	DC	Giulio Andreotti
1992–93	PSI	Giuliano Amato
1993–94	n/p	Carlo Azeglio Ciampi
1994–95	FI	Silvio Berlusconi
1995–96	n/p	Lamberto Dini
1996–98	n/p	Romano Prodi
1998–2000	DS	Massimo D'Alema
2000–01	n/p	Giuliano Amato
2001–06	FI	Silvio Berlusconi

2006–08	Ulivo	Romano Prodi
2008–	PdL	Silvio Berlusconi

RECENT ELECTIONS

Parliamentary elections were held on 13–14 April 2008 following the dissolution of Romano Prodi's government. The centre-right coalition led by Silvio Berlusconi (comprised of the newly created People of Freedom party, the Northern League and the Movement for Autonomy) won 344 seats in the Chamber of Deputies and 174 in the Senate, against Walter Veltroni's centre-left alliance (comprised of the Democratic Party and the Italy of Values Party) with 246 and 132 seats respectively. Turnout was 80·5%.

Giorgio Napolitano was elected president on 10 May 2006 by 1,009 legislators and regional representatives. He received 543 votes in the fourth round of voting after three rounds on 8 and 9 May had failed to produce a clear result.

European Parliament

Italy has 72 (78 in 2004) representatives. At the June 2009 elections turnout was 65·1% (71·7% in 2004). People of Freedom won 29 seats with 35·3% of votes cast (political affiliation in European Parliament: European People's Party); Democratic Party, 21 with 26·1% (Progressive Alliance of Socialists and Democrats); the Northern League, 9 with 10·2% (Europe of Freedom and Democracy); Italy of Values, 7 with 8·0% (Alliance of Liberals and Democrats for Europe); the Union of Christian and Centre Democrats, 5 with 6·5% (European People's Party); South Tyrolean People's Party, 1 with 0·5% (European People's Party).

CURRENT ADMINISTRATION

President: Giorgio Napolitano; b. 1925 (sworn in 15 May 2006).

In March 2010 the government comprised:

President of the Council of Ministers (Prime Minister): Silvio Berlusconi; b. 1936 (People of Freedom; sworn in 8 May 2008 having previously held office from May 1994–Jan. 1995 and June 2001–May 2006).

Minister of Interior: Roberto Maroni (Northern League). *Foreign Affairs:* Franco Frattini (People of Freedom). *Justice:* Angelino Alfano (People of Freedom). *Education, Universities and Research:* Mariastella Gelmini (People of Freedom). *Labour, Health and Social Policy:* Maurizio Sacconi (People of Freedom). *Defence:* Ignazio La Russa (People of Freedom). *Agriculture:* Luca Zaia (Northern League). *Environment:* Stefania Prestigiacomo (People of Freedom). *Infrastructure and Transport:* Altero Matteoli (People of Freedom). *Finance:* Giulio Tremonti (People of Freedom). *Culture:* Sandro Bondi (People of Freedom). *Economic Development:* Claudio Scajola (People of Freedom). *Minister without Portfolio Responsible for Federal Reform:* Umberto Bossi (Northern League). *Minister without Portfolio Responsible for Relations with Parliament:* Elio Vito (People of Freedom). *Minister without Portfolio Responsible for Simplification:* Roberto Calderoli (Northern League). *Minister without Portfolio Responsible for Government Programme Implementation:* Gianfranco Rotondi (Movement for Autonomy). *Minister without Portfolio Responsible for Regional Affairs:* Raffaele Fitto (People of Freedom). *Minister without Portfolio Responsible for Youth Policies:* Giorgia Meloni (People of Freedom). *Minister without Portfolio Responsible for Equal Opportunities:* Mara Carfagna (People of Freedom). *Minister without Portfolio Responsible for European Affairs:* Andrea Ronchi (People of Freedom). *Minister without Portfolio Responsible for Innovation:* Renato Brunetta (People of Freedom).

Government Website (Italian only): http://www.governo.it

CURRENT LEADERS

Silvio Berlusconi

Position

Prime Minister

Introduction

Silvio Berlusconi is serving his third term as prime minister. His first government in 1994 lasted less than eight months. He was returned to power as the head of Italy's government on 14 May 2001. His appointment was controversial, with many protesting that his position as the owner of the country's three main private television networks meant that he was able to unfairly influence the outcome of the election. Nevertheless, his centre-right coalition achieved a convincing majority in both the Senate and the lower house. In April 2005 the coalition collapsed, triggering a brief political crisis before another centre-right coalition under his premiership won a vote of confidence. His term ended in 2006 when his government lost parliamentary elections to Romano Prodi's Union coalition. However, after Prodi's own coalition collapsed in Feb. 2008, Berlusconi emerged victorious from the general election held in April. Legal inquiries into Berlusconi's business dealings remain controversial, as do reports concerning his private life.

Early Life

The son of a bank clerk, Silvio Berlusconi was born in Milan on 29 Sept. 1936. After graduating from the University of Milan he embarked on a career in property development, acquiring a large personal fortune by the early 1970s. In 1974 he founded a cable television company, *Telemilano*, which was later at the forefront of his campaign to end the state's monopoly on national television. By the end of the decade Berlusconi had established the country's first commercial television network, *Canale 5*. By this time he had also amassed stock in retail outlets, cinemas, AC Milan football club and publishing. These holdings were consolidated under a new umbrella organization that Berlusconi dubbed Fininvest. The conglomerate expanded throughout the 1980s and at its peak controlled over 150 separate businesses.

In Jan. 1994 a series of high profile corruption and bribery scandals engulfed the government and prompted demands for reforms. It was in this atmosphere that Berlusconi entered the political arena. He founded a new party, Forza Italia, which attracted floating voters disenchanted with politics after the demise of the Christian Democrats and Socialists. Forza Italia proclaimed its agenda as one of justice, economic liberalization and the reduction of bureaucracy and government intervention in commerce and industry. To secure power, the party allied itself with the right-wing Northern League and the neo-Fascist National Alliance. Called House of Freedoms (Casa delle Libertà), this coalition won a majority of seats in the Chamber of Deputies on 28 March 1994. Berlusconi, as the leader of the largest party in the alliance, was sworn in as prime minister in May.

Career in Office

Berlusconi's first term of office was short-lived. He immediately became entangled in a legal battle against political opponents who accused him of corruption and conflicts of interest. In Dec. 1994 an official investigation began into his past business dealings, prompting a no confidence vote. He resigned on 22 Dec. 1994. In the 1996 elections Berlusconi lost to Romano Prodi's centre-left Olive Tree coalition. Prodi left office in 1998 when he himself lost a no confidence vote.

Despite the popularity of the Olive Tree government, its leader in the 2001 elections, Francesco Rutelli, was unable to muster enough support to return the coalition to power. By this time Berlusconi's reputation had recovered. The centre-right won 368 seats in the Chamber of Deputies (a gain of 65 seats) compared to the Olive Tree's 242. In the Senate the centre-right coalition secured 177 of 315 seats, while the centre-left won just 125. This performance was enough to ensure Berlusconi the premiership.

Berlusconi pledged to cut taxes, raise pensions and create 1·5m. new jobs. He also promised to form a stable government that would remain in power for the full five-year term. However, his term was marred by efforts to prosecute him for corruption and financial wrongdoing. Although his convictions for illegal party financing, false accounting and bribery were quashed, he stood trial in early 2003 for bribing the judiciary and business malpractice. However, in June 2003 parliament passed a law granting immunity from prosecution for leading government figures while they held office and Berlusconi's trial was dropped. Two of his smaller coalition partners threatened to leave government until the justice minister announced in Aug. 2003 that a judicial enquiry into Berlusconi's commercial affairs would still go ahead. Nevertheless, in Dec. 2004 he was cleared by the courts of a charge relating to his business affairs in the 1980s and another charge was dropped by virtue of the statute of limitations.

Meanwhile, in the aftermath of the attacks on the USA on 11 Sept. 2001, Berlusconi gave firm support to the US war on terror, backing military action in Afghanistan and Iraq, where Italian troops were deployed in the multinational forces.

On 20 April 2005 the centre-right coalition collapsed following a poor showing in regional elections. Berlusconi was forced to resign, but was reappointed a few days later by President Ciampi and formed a new coalition of all the parties in the previous administration. In April 2006 parliamentary elections were held, with House of Freedoms losing to Romano Prodi's centre-left coalition, Union. The results of the elections were close and disputed by Berlusconi, who claimed electoral fraud. He then called for a grand coalition government and for a House of Freedoms speaker in the Senate, where Union gained 158 seats to House of Freedoms' 156. He finally tendered his resignation on 2 May 2006, three weeks after his defeat. He remained in office as caretaker until Prodi was sworn in and formed the new government on 17 May 2006.

In Feb. 2008 Prodi's coalition collapsed and elections were called for April. Berlusconi announced he would stand for a third term, with the intention of completing the reform programme started during his previous tenure. Attacking the left for 'bringing Italy to its knees', he steered an alliance of centre-right parties to victory in the April elections and, in March 2009, oversaw the inaugural congress of the alliance (but excluding the independent Northern League) as a single People of Freedom (PdL) party.

His government has since been confronted by Italy's slide into economic recession under the shadow of its huge public debt and in the wake of the global financial crisis. In Oct. 2009 Italy's Constitutional Court overturned the law granting Berlusconi immunity from prosecution while in office. The ruling meant that he could face trial in two possible court actions. Also in 2009, the prime minister came under increasing media and opposition scrutiny over a series of allegations about his conduct in his private life. On 13 Dec. 2009 he sustained facial injuries in an assault by a single assailant after addressing a rally in Milan.

DEFENCE

Head of the armed forces is the Defence Chief of Staff. Conscription was abolished at the end of 2004 with the military becoming all-professional from 2005. In Aug. 1998 the government voted to allow women into the armed forces.

In 2008 defence expenditure totalled US$40·6bn. (US$689 per capita). In 2007 defence spending represented 1·8% of GDP.

Army

Strength (2006) 110,000 (about 2,000 conscripts). Equipment includes 120 *Leopard,* 300 *Centauro* and 200 *Ariete* tanks. There are 35,500 Army reserves.

The paramilitary Carabinieri (police force with military status) number 111,400.

Navy

The principal ship of the Navy is the light aircraft carrier *Giuseppe Garibaldi*. The combatant forces also include six diesel submarines, five destroyers and 12 frigates. The Naval Air Arm, 2,000 strong, operates 15 combat aircraft and 63 armed helicopters.

Main naval bases are at La Spezia, Brindisi, Taranto and Augusta. The personnel of the Navy numbered 33,100 in 2006. There were 21,000 naval reservists.

Air Force

Control is exercised through two regional headquarters near Taranto and Milan.

Air Force strength in 2006 was about 44,000 (1,200 conscripts). There were 234 combat aircraft in operation in 2006 including Typhoons and Tornados.

INTERNATIONAL RELATIONS

Italy is a member of the UN, World Bank, IMF and several other UN specialized agencies, WTO, EU, Council of Europe, WEU, OSCE, CERN, CEI, BIS, IOM, NATO, OECD, Inter-American Development Bank, Asian Development Bank and Antarctic Treaty. Italy is a signatory to the Schengen accord of June 1990 which abolishes border controls between Italy, Austria, Belgium, Czech Republic, Denmark, Estonia, Finland, France, Germany, Greece, Hungary, Iceland, Latvia, Lithuania, Luxembourg, Malta, Netherlands, Norway, Poland, Portugal, Slovakia, Slovenia, Spain, Sweden and Switzerland.

ECONOMY

Agriculture accounted for 2% of GDP, industry 27% and services 71% in 2007.

Overview

Italy has a diversified industrial base with average income levels on a par with those of other leading economies. However, since 1988 economic performance has trailed that of other developed countries. The economic structure is similar to that of other advanced OECD economies, with a small and diminishing primary sector and a large gross value added contribution by the service sector. But with the exceptions of design and tourism, Italy is not internationally competitive in most service sectors.

Economic growth recovered to 1·9% in 2006 following years of stagnant performance. However, in 2008 the economy was significantly affected by the global financial crisis and in 2009 annual growth was negative for the first time in over a decade, following five consecutive quarterly contractions. Growth returned in the third quarter of 2009 and improved financial conditions have helped boost confidence and bolster domestic demand. The OECD forecasts growth to reach just over 1% in 2010 as recovery in world trade provides further support to exports. That the financial system largely weathered the global turbulence reflects Italy's relatively safe risk profile.

Nonetheless, OECD research shows that Italian exports have declined 20% in terms of value compared to the mid-1990s. This has resulted from specialization in slow-growing sectors of world demand, comparatively weak FDI and little investment in research and development. Manufacturing has been a key sector for the economy, accounting for 90% of total merchandise exports and 25% of GDP.

Small and medium-sized family-owned companies are the strongest component of the economy, producing high-quality consumer goods such as clothing, furniture and white goods. These companies have resisted becoming publicly funded but face pressure from global economic integration and competition and are vulnerable to acquisition by foreign firms. A few large companies play an important role in the economy, including Fiat (still controlled by the Agnelli family), Pirelli, Telecom Italia (controlled by Marco Tronchetti Provera, heir to the Pirelli family) and Mediaset (controlled by the family of Prime Minister Silvio Berlusconi). These families have cross-shareholding pacts with industrial and financial allies that allow them to maintain control of companies even with small direct shareholdings.

The northeast is Italy's most dynamic region and where most value added production is concentrated. Despite progress in the *Mezzogiorno* (the south and Sicily and Sardinia) the economic gap between north and south remains. Unemployment rates in the north are low while the south faces some of the highest rates in the EU. Prior to the economic crisis of 2008, Italy had been enjoying improvements in job creation and a fall in unemployment.

In addition to regional imbalance, Italy's economy suffers from other structural weaknesses. Public debt has been reduced from over 120% in the mid-1990s to under 110% but it is still among the highest in the world. The fiscal deficit exceeded the 3% euro zone limit in 2006 but was reduced to 1·9% of GDP in 2007. However, against the backdrop of the global financial crisis, cyclically weak revenues resulted in the deficit exceeding 5% of GDP and debt is forecast to increase to 120% of GDP by 2011. Significant fiscal consolidation plans will be required to reduce the level of debt once growth picks up. Decline in productivity growth over the past decade remains a further major economic challenge. The IMF has emphasized the importance of reducing regulation, increasing competition and improving the business environment to raise Italy's productivity and growth potential.

Public pensions account for around 15% of GDP (nearly twice as high as the EU average) and 40% of public sector spending. Although reforms have aimed to stabilize state pension spending, they are expected to encounter union resistance. Italy also faces an unfavourable demographic situation, with low birth rates and a high and rising ratio of people over 65. The IMF predicts that population ageing will increase annual pension spending by approximately 2% of GDP over the coming years and annual health spending by 3% per year. Pension reforms in 2004, which increased the effective retirement age from 2008, may improve long-term fiscal sustainability by helping to raise the very low elderly worker participation rates. It is also hoped further scheduled pension reforms may reduce costs associated with an ageing population. Since 1993 privatization has reduced the state's direct involvement in the economy and enhanced competition but the OECD notes that further regulatory reform and liberalization are needed in the electricity, transportation, road freight, professional services and retail trade sectors.

Currency

On 1 Jan. 1999 the euro (EUR) became the legal currency in Italy at the irrevocable conversion rate of 1,936·27 lire to 1 euro. The euro, which consists of 100 cents, has been in circulation since 1 Jan. 2002. There are seven euro notes in different colours and sizes denominated in 500, 200, 100, 50, 20, 10 and 5 euros, and eight coins denominated in 2 and 1 euros, then 50, 20, 10, 5, 2 and 1 cents. On the introduction of the euro there was a 'dual circulation' period before the lira ceased to be legal tender on 28 Feb. 2002. Euro banknotes in circulation on 1 Jan. 2002 had a total value of €97·4bn.

Inflation rates (based on OECD statistics):

1999	*2000*	*2001*	*2002*	*2003*	*2004*	*2005*	*2006*	*2007*	*2008*
1·7%	2·6%	2·3%	2·6%	2·8%	2·3%	2·2%	2·2%	2·0%	3·5%

In Sept. 2009 gold reserves were 78·83m. troy oz and foreign exchange reserves US$35,474m. Total money supply in Aug. 2009 was €711,993m.

Budget

In 2006 central government revenues totalled €550·40bn. (€507·11bn. in 2005) and expenditures €602·43bn. (€559·11bn. in 2005). Principal sources of revenue in 2006: taxes on income, profits and capital gains, €188·45bn.; social security contributions, €188·32bn.; taxes on goods and services, €122·27bn. Main items of expenditure by economic type in 2006: social benefits, €251·42bn.; grants, €102·83bn.; compensation of employees, €93·22bn.

Italy's budget deficit has been in excess of the EU stability pact ceiling of 3% of GDP every year since 2003.

VAT is 20% (reduced rates, 10% and 4%).

The public debt at 31 Dec. 2006 totalled €1,256,946m.

Performance

Real GDP growth rates (based on OECD statistics):

1999	*2000*	*2001*	*2002*	*2003*	*2004*	*2005*	*2006*	*2007*	*2008*
1·4%	3·9%	1·7%	0·5%	0·1%	1·4%	0·8%	2·1%	1·5%	–1·0%

According to the National Institute of Statistics, real GDP growth contracted by 5·1% in 2009 (the lowest rate since the Institute was established in 1971). Italy's average economic growth rate since 1998 has been the slowest in the EU. Total GDP was US$2,293·0bn. in 2008.

Banking and Finance

The bank of issue is the Bank of Italy (founded 1893). It is owned by public-sector banks. Its *Governor* (Mario Draghi) is selected without fixed term by the 13 directors of the Bank's non-executive board. In 1991 it received increased responsibility for the supervision of banking and stock exchange affairs, and in 1993 greater independence from the government.

The number of banks has gradually been declining in recent years, from 1,176 in 1990 to 807 (32,818 branches) in 2007. Of these, 439 were mutual banks and 39 were co-operative banks. Italy's largest bank in terms of assets is UniCredito (until May 2008 known as UniCredito Italiano). In June 2005 UniCredito Italiano finalized an agreement to acquire Germany's HypoVereinsbank in Europe's biggest cross-border banking takeover. In 2006 it had Italian assets of €282bn. (€752bn. including assets from its German and eastern European operations). In Aug. 2006 Italy's second and third largest banks, Banca Intesa and Sanpaolo IMI, agreed to merge. The merger was approved in Dec. 2006, creating the largest Italian bank, Intesa Sanpaolo, with assets of €541bn.

The 'Amato' law of July 1990 gave public sector banks the right to become joint stock companies and permitted the placing of up to 49% of their equity with private shareholders. In 1999 the last state-controlled bank was sold off.

On 31 Dec. 2005 banks had total deposits of €690,746m.

Legislation reforming stock markets came into effect in Dec. 1990. In 1996 local stock exchanges, relics of pre-unification Italy, were closed, and stock exchange activities concentrated in Milan.

ENERGY AND NATURAL RESOURCES

Environment

Italy's carbon dioxide emissions from the consumption and flaring of fossil fuels in 2008 were the equivalent of 7·8 tonnes per capita.

Electricity

In 2005 installed capacity was 88,345 MW and the total power generated was 309·0bn. kWh (13·9% hydro-electric). Consumption in 2005 was 309·8bn. kWh, of which: industry, 153·7bn. kWh; services, 83·8bn. kWh; domestic use, 66·9bn. kWh; agriculture, 5·4bn. kWh. Consumption per capita was 5,273 kWh in 2005. Italy has four nuclear reactors in permanent shutdown, the last having closed in 1990.

Oil and Gas

Oil production, 2008, 5·2m. tonnes. Proven oil reserves in 2008 were 0·8bn. bbls. In 2008 natural gas production was 8·4bn. cu. metres with proven reserves of 120bn. cu. metres.

Minerals

Fuel and mineral resources fail to meet needs. Only sulphur and mercury yield a substantial surplus for exports.

Production of metals and minerals (in tonnes) was as follows:

	1998	1999	2000	2001	2002
Sulphur	3,413,522	3,338,162	3,339,761	—	—
Feldspar	2,503,541	2,493,846	2,851,289	3,240,457	3,159,569
Bentonite	580,209	562,674	636,589	579,029	463,231
Lead	10,102	9,734	5,961	4,016	4,709
Zinc	5,242	—	—	—	—

Agriculture

In 2000, 1,120,000 persons were employed in agriculture, of whom 451,000 were dependent (148,000 female); independently employed were 669,000 (203,000 female). At the fifth agricultural census, held on 22 Oct. 2000, there were 13,212,652 sq. km of agricultural and forest lands, distributed as follows (in 1,000 ha.): woods, 4,711; cereals, 4,052; forage and pasture, 3,414; olive trees, 1,081; vines, 676; leguminous plants, 66. In 2002 there were 8·29m. ha. of arable land and 2·78m. ha. of permanent crops. In 2003 organic crops were grown in an area covering 1·17m. ha. (the third largest area after Australia and Argentina), representing 8·0% of all farmland.

At the 2000 census agricultural holdings numbered 2,593,090 and covered 19,607,094 ha. 2,457,960 owners (95·7%) farmed directly 13,868,478 ha. (70·3%); 132,935 owners (3·9%) worked with hired labour on 5,706,993 ha. (29·1%); the remaining 2,195 holdings (0·4%) of 31,623 ha. (0·6%) were operated in other ways. 97,307 share-croppers tilled 1,445,826 ha. Only 13,212,652 sq. km was in active agricultural use.

Agriculture and fishing accounted for 1·5% of exports and 3·4% of imports in 2001.

In 2005, 3,069,599 tractors were in use and 27,445 harvester-threshers.

Output of principal crops (in 1,000 tonnes) in 2005: sugar beets, 14,156; maize, 10,428; wheat, 7,717; grapes, 6,892; tomatoes, 6,640; olives, 3,775; oranges, 2,261; apples, 2,192; potatoes, 1,756; peaches and nectarines, 1,693; rice, 1,445; barley, 1,214.

Wine production in 2006 totalled 52,036,000 hectolitres (18·4% of the world total). Italy was the second largest wine producer in the world in 2006 after France. Wine consumption in Italy has declined considerably in recent times, from more than 110 litres per person in 1966 to 48·8 litres per person in 2004.

Livestock, 2005: cattle, 6,251,925; sheep and goats, 8,900,062; pigs, 9,200,270; horses, 278,471; buffaloes, 205,093; chickens, 90,387,988. Livestock products, 2003 (in 1,000 tonnes): cow's milk, 11,000; sheep's milk, 790; buffalo's milk, 140; goat's milk, 112; pork, bacon and ham, 1,587; poultry meat, 1,156; beef and veal, 1,125; cheese, 1,099; butter, 130; eggs, 672. Italy is the second largest producer of sheep's milk, after China.

Forestry

In 2005 forests covered 9·98m. ha. or 33·9% of the total land area. Timber production was 8·12m. cu. metres in 2007.

Fisheries

The fishing fleet comprised, in 2002, 16,045 motor boats of 215,247 gross tonnes. The catch in 2005 was 298,373 tonnes, of which more than 98% were from marine waters.

INDUSTRY

The leading companies by market capitalization in Italy in March 2009 were: Eni, an integrated oil company (US$77·7bn.); Intesa Sanpaolo, the country's largest bank (US$34·4bn.); and Enel, an electricity and gas company (US$29·7bn.).

The value added at factor cost in 2001 was €1,098,992m. The percentage of industrial value at factor cost by activity sector was: agriculture, forestry and fishing: 2·93%; construction: 4·92%; financial activity, currency and real activities: 26·13%; strictly industry: 22·74%; trade, transport, hotels and restaurants: 24·21%; other services: 19·07%. Main strictly industry items (% of overall total) in 2001 were: metal production and metallic products: 2·69%; machines and mechanical apparatus: 2·50%; textiles and clothing: 2·40%; electric energy—production and distribution: 2·20%; food, beverages and tobacco: 2·10%; electric machines, electric apparatus and optical instruments: 1·74%; chemicals and synthetic fibres: 1·70%.

Production, 2001 unless otherwise stated: cement (2004 estimate), 40·0m. tonnes; crude steel (2004 estimate), 15·2m. tonnes; pig iron (2004 estimate), 10·0m. tonnes; polyethylene resins, 1,100,114 tonnes; artificial and synthetic fibres (including staple fibre and waste), 627,482 tonnes; motor vehicles, 1,272,000 units; TV sets, 1,208,000 units.

Labour

In 2003 the workforce was 24,150,000 (69·3% males and 42·7% females) of whom 21,829,000 were employed. 2,096,000 were unemployed and looking for work. Until the summer of 2007 the unemployment rate had been declining steadily for some years; it was 7·7% in 2005, 6·8% in 2006 and 6·1% in 2007 as a whole, down from 10·8% in 2000. However, it rose to 6·8% in 2008 and climbed steadily throughout 2009 to reach 8·5% in Dec. In 2002, 63·2% of the workforce were in services, 31·8% in industry and 5·0% in agriculture. There are strong indications of labour markets having become less rigid, especially in the north. In the northeast unemployment was 3·3% in 2003, in the northwest 4·4% and in the centre 6·6%; in the south it was 18·3%. In 2006 the difference in the unemployment rates in the north and in the south was more than 8%, compared to a difference of just 2% in the 1960s. Nearly 60% of Italy's jobless have been out of work for more than a year, the highest rate in any industrialized country. Pensionable retirement age rose from 57 to 58 in 2008, and is set to rise to 61 by 2013. In 2002 the rate of employment among people aged 55–64 was just 4·1%.

In 1997 parliament approved the so-called 'Treu Package', which involves a large number of institutional changes regarding working hours and apprenticeships, mainly for young people from the south, and the introduction of employment agencies. As a consequence, the share of temporary workers over total employees had grown from 6·2% in 1993 to 9·9% in 2002.

Trade Unions

There are three main groups: the Confederazione Generale Italiana del Lavoro (CGIL; formerly Communist-dominated), the Confederazione Italiana Sindacati Lavoratori (CISL; Catholic) and the Unione Italiana del Lavoro (UIL). Membership (2002): CGIL, 5·5m.; CISL, 4·2m.; UIL, 1·6m. In referendums held in June 1995 the electorate voted to remove some restrictions on trade union representation, end government involvement in public sector trade unions and end the automatic deduction of trade union dues from wage packets.

INTERNATIONAL TRADE

Imports and Exports

The following table shows the value of Italy's foreign trade (in US$1bn.):

	2003	2004	2005	2006	2007
Imports c.i.f.	297·4	355·3	384·8	442·6	504·6
Exports f.o.b.	299·5	353·5	373·0	417·2	492·1

Percentage of trade with other EU countries in 2006: imports, 55·2%; exports, 58·0%. Principal import suppliers, 2007 (% of total trade): Germany, 16·7%; France, 9·0%; China, 5·9%; Netherlands, 5·2%. Principal export markets: Germany, 12·8%; France, 11·4%; Spain, 7·3%; USA, 6·8%.

Imports/exports by category, 2007 (in US$1bn.):

	Imports	Exports
Animal and vegetable oils and fats	3·2	2·0
Beverages and tobacco	4·7	6·7
Chemicals and related products	63·4	49·7
Food and live animals	32·2	22·1
Inedible crude materials, excluding fuels	21·3	5·4
Machinery and transport equipment	143·1	186·1
Manufactured goods and articles	139·5	188·0
Mineral fuels and lubricants	60·4	18·8
Other products	36·9	13·3

COMMUNICATIONS

Roads

Roads totalled 175,430 km in 2005, of which 6,542 km were motorways, 21,524 km were highways and main roads, and 147,364 km were regional and provincial roads. In 2005 there were 47,104,048 motor vehicles, including: passenger cars, 34,882,476 (594 per 1,000 inhabitants); buses and coaches, 96,477; vans and trucks, 3,982,001. There were 5,426 fatalities in road accidents in 2005.

Rail

The length of state-run railway (*Ferrovie dello Stato*) in 2005 was 16,225 km (11,364 km electrified). In 2005 the railways carried 759·9m. passengers and 89·8m. tonnes of freight. There are metros in Milan (76·0 km), Rome (38·0 km), Naples (29·8 km), Turin (9·6 km), Genoa (5·3 km) and Catania (3·8 km), and tram/light rail networks in Genoa, Messina, Milan, Naples, Padua, Rome, Sassari, Trieste and Turin.

Civil Aviation

There are major international airports at Bologna (G. Marconi), Genoa (Cristoforo Colombo), Milan (Linate and Malpensa), Naples (Capodichino), Pisa (Galileo Galilei), Rome (Leonardo da Vinci/Fiumicino), Turin (Caselle) and Venice (Marco Polo). A number of other airports have a small selection of international flights. Alitalia commenced operations in Jan. 2009 as a privately-owned company (25%-owned by Air France-KLM), having taken over the name, landing rights and significant assets of the former national carrier (also Alitalia, which went bankrupt in 2008) and having merged with rival airline Air One. There are a number of other Italian airlines, notably Meridiana. In 2003 scheduled airline traffic of Italian-based carriers flew 398m. km, carrying 36,077,000 passengers (13,613,000 on international flights). The busiest airport for passenger traffic is Rome (Fiumicino), which in 2001 handled 24,331,558 passengers (12,244,136 on international flights), plus 381,956 passengers in transit and 169,648 tonnes of freight. Milan Malpensa was the second busiest for passengers, handling 18,457,037 (14,169,573 on international flights), plus 109,652 passengers in transit, but the busiest for freight, with 289,382 tonnes. Linate, which handled 7,131,604 passengers in 2001 (4,995,000 on domestic flights), plus 738 passengers in transit, had been the principal Milan airport and for many years Italy's second busiest for passenger traffic, but in 1998 a new terminal was opened at Malpensa with many foreign operators subsequently using it instead of Linate.

Shipping

The mercantile marine in 2004 totalled 10·96m. GRT, including oil tankers 1·47m. GRT. In 2004 vessels totalling 278,306,000 NRT entered ports and vessels totalling 191,187,000 NRT cleared. 39,277,00 passengers embarked and 39,476,000 departed in 2005. The chief ports are Taranto (47,869,000 tonnes in 2005), Trieste, Genoa, Augusta, Venice, Gioia Tauro, Ravenna and Livorno.

Telecommunications

In 2008 there were 21,246,000 main (fixed) telephone lines. In May 1999 Olivetti bought a controlling stake in the telephone operator Telecom Italia, and in July 2001 Pirelli, backed by the Benetton clothing empire, in turn paid €7bn. (US$6·1bn.) to take over control of Telecom Italia. In 2008 mobile phone subscribers numbered 90,341,000, equivalent to 1,515·7 per 1,000 persons (among the highest penetration rates in the world). TIM (Telecom Italia Mobile) is the largest operator, with a 34% share of the market, just ahead of Vodafone Italia, which has a 33% share. There were 21·5m. PCs in use in 2005 and 25·0m. internet users in 2008. There were 18·2 broadband subscribers per 100 inhabitants in June 2008.

Postal Services

In 2003 there were 13,728 post offices, or one for every 4,180 persons.

SOCIAL INSTITUTIONS

Justice

Italy has one court of cassation, in Rome, and is divided for the administration of justice into 29 appeal court districts, subdivided into 164 tribunal *circondari* (districts). There are also 93 first degree assize courts and 29 assize courts of appeal. For civil business, besides the magistracy above mentioned, *Giudici di pace* have jurisdiction in petty plaints.

2,231,550 crimes were reported in 2002; 768,771 persons were indicted in 2002. On 31 Dec. 2002 there were 55,670 persons in prison (2,469 females). There were 16,788 foreigners in prison (1,008 females). In 1947 the re-established democracy rewrote the Legislative Order; the constitution of the Italian Republic abolished the death penalty sanctioned in 1930 by Codice Penale, commonly known as Codice Rocco. Although the death penalty was abolished for ordinary crimes in 1947, it was not until 1994 that it was abolished for all crimes.

Education

Five years of primary and five years of secondary education are compulsory from the age of six. In 2005–06 there were 24,845 pre-school institutions with 1,662,139 children and 140,687 teachers (state and non-state schools); 18,218 primary schools with 2,790,254 pupils and 293,091 teachers (state and non-state schools); 7,886 compulsory secondary schools (*scuole secondarie primo grado*) with 1,764,230 pupils and 211,093 teachers (state and non-state schools); and 6,565 higher secondary schools with 2,691,713 pupils and 305,383 teachers (state and non-state schools).

Higher secondary education is subdivided into classical (*ginnasio* and classical *liceo*), scientific (scientific *liceo*), language lyceum, professional institutes and technical education: agricultural, industrial, commercial, technical, nautical institutes, institutes for surveyors, institutes for girls (five-year course) and teacher-training institutes (five-year course).

In 2005–06 there were 98 universities (79 state and 19 non-state), of which two are universities of Italian studies for foreigners, three specialized universities (commerce; education; Roman Catholic), three polytechnical university institutes; seven specialized university institutes (architecture; bio-medicine; modern languages; naval studies; oriental studies; social studies; teacher training). In 2005–06 there were 1,823,886 university students and 61,097 academic staff.

Adult literacy rate, 2004, 98·4% (male 98·8%; female 98·0%).

In 2004 public expenditure on education came to 4·6% of GDP and 9·6% of total government spending.

Health

The provision of health services is a regional responsibility, but they are funded by central government. Medical consultations are free, but a portion of prescription costs are payable. In 2003 the National Health Service included 1,367 hospitals of which 746 were public with 184,796 beds and 621 private hospitals with 55,059 beds. In 2003 there were 104,091 doctors and 258,615 auxiliary medical personnel. A survey published by the World

Health Organization in June 2000 to measure health systems in all of the sovereign countries and find which country has the best overall health care ranked Italy in second place, behind France. In 2007 Italy spent 8·7% of its GDP on health.

Welfare

Social expenditure is made up of transfers which the central public departments, local departments and social security departments make to families. Payment is principally for pensions, family allowances and health services. Expenditure on subsidies, public assistance to various classes of people and people injured by political events or national disasters are also included.

In Jan. 2008 the minimum retirement age was raised from 57 to 58 (or after 36 years of work, whichever comes first). It is set to rise to 60 in 2011 and 61 in 2013. The age restriction will not apply in the case of workers who have made 40 years of pension contributions. Those in 'arduous' professions, which encompasses 6% of the population, will be able to retire at 57. The average age for Italian men to stop work is 60 years 8 months, among the youngest in the EU. Pensions account for around 15% of GDP.

Citizens who have entered the workforce since 1996 will not qualify for this seniority pension, but will receive an old-age pension instead. There are three categories of pension. The first is for people who have joined the workforce since 1996, and is available to claimants aged 57 or above with at least five years of contributions. The second category is for men aged at least 65 or women aged at least 60, with under 18 years of contributions as of 1995. The third category is for men aged at least 65 or women aged at least 60, with at least 18 years of contributions as of 1995. It is paid at a rate of 0·9%–2% of earnings multiplied by number of years of contributions, up to a maximum of 40.

Public pensions are indexed to prices; 23,257,480 pensions were paid in 2005, with payments totalling €214,881·3m. (including 16,875,341 private sector, with payments totalling €152,483·5m.). The average annual pension in 2005 was €9,239. Social contributions in 2005 totalled €184,642m.

RELIGION

The treaty between the Holy See and Italy of 11 Feb. 1929, confirmed by article 7 of the Constitution of the republic, lays down that the Catholic Apostolic Roman Religion is the only religion of the State. Other creeds are permitted, provided they do not profess principles, or follow rites, contrary to public order or moral behaviour.

The appointment of archbishops and of bishops is made by the Holy See; but the Holy See submits to the Italian government the name of the person to be appointed in order to obtain an assurance that the latter will not raise objections of a political nature. In Feb. 2010 there were 39 cardinals.

Catholic religious teaching is given in elementary and intermediate schools. Marriages celebrated before a Catholic priest are automatically transferred to the civil register. Marriages celebrated by clergy of other denominations must be made valid before a registrar.

There were 46,260,000 Roman Catholics in 2001, 680,000 Muslims, 1,350,000 adherents of other religions and 9,600,000 non-religious and atheists.

CULTURE

World Heritage Sites

Italy has 44 sites that have been included on UNESCO's World Heritage List. They are listed here in the order in which they were designated world heritage sites: the Rock Drawings in Valcamonica near Brescia (1979); Santa Maria delle Grazie with 'The Last Supper' by Leonardo da Vinci (1980); San Paolo Fuori le Mura Historic Centre of Florence (1982); Venice and its Lagoon (1987); Piazza del Duomo, Pisa (1987 and 2007); Historic Centre of San Gimignano (1990); I Sassi di Matera (1993); Vicenza, the City of Palladio and the Villas of the Veneto (1994 and 1996); Historic Centre of Siena (1995); Historic Centre of Naples (1995); Ferrara and its Po Delta (1995 and 1999); Crespi d'Adda (1995); Castel del Monte (1996); Trulli of Alberobello (1996); Early Christian Monuments and Mosaics of Ravenna (1996); Historic Centre of the City of Pienza (1996); The 18th-Century Royal Palace at Caserta with the Park, the Aqueduct of Vanvitelli and the San Leucio Complex (1997); Residences of the Royal House of Savoy (1997); Botanical Garden (Orto Botanico), Padua (1997); Cathedral, Torre Civica and Piazza Grande, Modena (1997); Archaeological Areas of Pompeii, Ercolano and Torre Annunziata (1997); Villa Romana del Casale (1997); Su Nuraxi di Barumini (1997); Portovenere, Cinque Terre and the Islands (Palmaria, Tino and Tinetto) (1997); The Costiera Amalfitana (1997); Archaeological Area of Agrigento (1997); Cilento and Vallo di Diano National Park (1998); Historic Centre of Urbino (1998); Archaeological Area and the Patriarchal Basilica of Aquileia (1998); Villa Adriana (1999); Aeolian Islands (2000); Assisi (2000); the City of Verona (2000); Villa d'Este, Tivoli (2001); the Late Baroque Towns of the Val di Noto (2002); and Sacri Monti of Piedmont and Lombardy (2003); Val d'Orcia (2004), part of the agricultural hinterland of Siena; the Etruscan Necropolises of Cerveteri and Tarquinia (2004); Syracuse and the Rocky Necropolis of Pantalica (2005); Genoa (2006), featuring the Strade Nuove and the system of the Palazzi dei Rolli; Mantua and Sabbioneta (2008); and the Dolomites (2009).

The Historic Centre of Rome, the properties of the Holy See in that city enjoying extraterritorial rights (1980 and 1990), is shared with Vatican City State. The Rhaetian Railway in the Albula/Bernina Landscapes (2008) is shared with Switzerland.

Broadcasting

RAI, the public broadcasting company, operates public television channels RAI 1, RAI 2 and RAI 3, a 24-hour news station, and cable and satellite services. It also runs several national radio networks. Mediaset, the main independent TV broadcaster, produces three commercial channels: Canale 5, Italia 1 and Rete 4. There are about 2,500 commercial radio stations. There were 22·3m. TV-equipped households in 2006. Colour is by PAL. In 2006, 16,466,148 television licences were bought.

Cinema

In 2005 there were 3,280 cinema screens and 105·6m. admissions. In 2005 gross box office receipts came to €602m. and 98 full-length films were made (of which 70 entirely national and 28 co-productions).

Press

There were, in 2006, 91 paid-for dailies with a combined circulation of 5·6m. copies and ten free dailies with a combined circulation of 4·7m. copies. Several of the papers are owned or supported by political parties. The church and various economic groups exert strong right of centre influence on editorial opinion. Most newspapers are regional but Corriere della Sera (which has the highest circulation of any Italian newspaper), La Repubblica, Il Sole 24 Ore and La Stampa are the most important of those papers that are nationally circulated. In 2004 a total of 52,760 book titles were published in 243m. copies.

Tourism

In 2005, 36,513,000 foreigners visited Italy; receipts from tourism in 2005 were US$38·26bn. Only France, Spain, the USA and China receive more foreign tourists.

Festivals

One of the most traditional festivals in Italy is the Carnival di Ivrea which lasts for a week in late Feb. or early March. Among the famous arts festivals is the Venice Film Festival in Sept. Venice also plays host, in the ten days before Ash Wednesday, to a large carnival. Major music festivals are the Maggio Musicale Fiorentino in Florence (May–June), the Ravenna Festival (June–

July), the Spoleto Festival (June–July), the Rossini Opera Festival at Pesaro (Aug.) and the Verona Summer Opera Festival (July–Sept.).

Libraries

In 2006 there were 12,381 libraries of which 51·2% belonged to local authorities, 16·9% to universities and 10·2% to religious institutions. There are two national libraries. There are 47 state libraries, which had 32,484,941 volumes in 2005.

Museums and Galleries

In 2002 there were 192 museums and galleries and 198 archaeological sites. There were 31,041,436 visitors, up from 29,543,020 in 2001.

DIPLOMATIC REPRESENTATIVES

Of Italy in the United Kingdom (14 Three Kings Yard, Davies St., London, W1K 4EH)
Ambassador: Giancarlo Aragona, KCVO.

Of the United Kingdom in Italy (Via XX Settembre 80A, 00187, Rome)
Ambassador: Edward Chaplin, CMG, OBE.

Of Italy in the USA (3000 Whitehaven St., NW, Washington, D.C., 20008)
Ambassador: Giulio Terzi di Sant'Agata.

Of the USA in Italy (Via Vittorio Veneto 119/A, Rome)
Ambassador: David H. Thorne.

Of Italy to the United Nations
Ambassador: Cesare Maria Ragaglini.

Of Italy to the European Union
Permanent Representative: Ferdinando Nelli Feroci.

FURTHER READING

Istituto Nazionale di Statistica. *Annuario Statistico Italiano.—Compendio Statistico Italiano* (Annual).—*Italian Statistical Abstract* (Annual).—*Bollettino Mensile di Statistica* (Monthly).

Absalom, R., *Italy since 1880: a Nation in the Balance?* 1995
Baldassarri, M. (ed.) *The Italian Economy: Heaven or Hell?* 1993
Bufacchi, Vittorio and Burgess, Simon, *Italy since 1989.* 1999
Burnett, Stanton H. and Mantovani, Luca, *The Italian Guillotine: Operation 'Clean Hands' and the Overthrow of Italy's First Republic.* 1999
Cotta, Maurizio and Verzichelli, Luca, *Political Institutions of Italy.* 2007
Di Scala, S. M., *Italy from Revolution to Republic: 1700 to the Present.* 1995
Doumanis, Nicholas, *Italy: Inventing the Nation.* 2001
Duggan, Christopher, *A Concise History of Italy.* 1994.—*The Force of Destiny: A History of Italy Since 1796.* 2007
Foot, John, *Modern Italy.* 2003
Frei, M., *Italy: the Unfinished Revolution.* 1996
Furlong, P., *Modern Italy: Representation and Reform.* 1994
Gilbert, M., *Italian Revolution: the Ignominious End of Politics, Italian Style.* 1995
Ginsborg, Paul, *Italy and its Discontents, 1980–2001.* 2002.—*A History of Contemporary Italy: Society and Politics, 1943–1988.* 2003
Gundie, S. and Parker, S. (eds.) *The New Italian Republic: from the Fall of the Berlin Wall to Berlusconi.* 1995
Plant, Margaret, *Venice: Fragile City 1797–1997.* 2002
Putnam, R., *et al.*, *Making Democracy Work: Civic Traditions in Modern Italy.* 1993
Richards, C., *The New Italians.* 1994
Smith, D. M., *Modern Italy: A Political History.* 1997
Volcanasek, Mary L., *Constitutional Politics in Italy.* 1999

National library: Biblioteca Nazionale Centrale, Vittorio Emanuele II, Viale Castro Pretorio, Rome.
National Statistical Office: Istituto Nazionale di Statistica (ISTAT), 16 Via Cesare Balbo, 00184 Rome.
Website (limited English): http://www.istat.it

JAMAICA

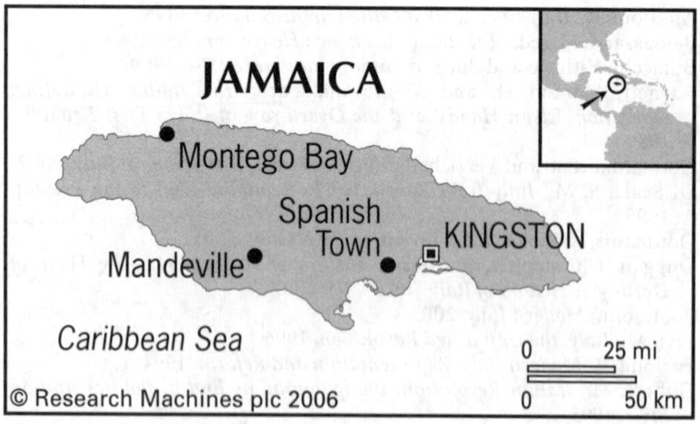

Capital: Kingston
Population estimate, 2010: 2·73m.
GDP per capita, 2007: (PPP$) 6,079
HDI/world rank: 0·766/100

KEY HISTORICAL EVENTS

Jamaica was discovered by Columbus in 1494 and was occupied by the Spaniards from 1509 until 1655 when the island was captured by the English. In 1661 a representative constitution was established consisting of a governor, privy council, legislative council and legislative assembly. The slavery introduced by the Spanish was augmented as sugar production increased in value and extent in the 18th century. The plantation economy collapsed with the abolition of the slave trade in the late 1830s. The 1866 Crown Colony government was introduced with a legislative council. In 1884 a partially elective legislative council was instituted. Women were enfranchised in 1919. By the late 1930s, demands for self-government increased and the constitution of Nov. 1944 stated that the governor was to be assisted by a freely-elected house of representatives of 32 members, a legislative council (the upper house) of 15 members, and an executive council. In 1958 Jamaica joined with Trinidad, Barbados, the Leeward Islands and the Windward Islands to create the West Indies Federation. In 1959 internal self-government was achieved. Jamaica withdrew from the West Indies Federation in 1961 and became an independent state within the British Commonwealth in 1962.

TERRITORY AND POPULATION

Jamaica is an island in the Caribbean Sea about 150 km south of Cuba. The area is 10,991 sq. km (4,244 sq. miles). The population at the census of Sept. 2001 was 2,607,632, distributed on the basis of the 13 parishes of the island as follows: Kingston and St Andrew, 651,880; St Catherine, 482,308; Clarendon, 237,024; Manchester, 185,801; St James, 175,127; St Ann, 166,762; St Elizabeth, 146,404; Westmoreland, 138,947; St Mary, 111,466; St Thomas, 91,604; Portland, 80,205; Trelawny, 73,066; Hanover, 67,037. 2001 density: 237 per sq. km. There is a worldwide Jamaican diaspora of more than 2m.

The UN gives an estimated population for 2010 of 2·73m.

Chief towns (in 1,000), 2001: Kingston (metropolitan area), 579; Portmore, 156; Spanish Town, 132; Montego Bay, 96; May Pen, 57.

In 2005, 53·1% of the population were urban. The population is about 92% of African ethnic origin. The official language is English. Patois, a combination of English and African languages, is widely spoken.

SOCIAL STATISTICS

Vital statistics (2006): births, 46,277 (17·4 per 1,000 population); deaths, 16,317 (6·1); marriages, 23,181 (8·7); divorces, 1,768 (0·7). There were 17,100 emigrants in 2006, mainly to the USA. Expectation of life at birth, 2007, 68·3 years for males and 75·1 years for females. Annual population growth rate, 2000–05, 0·5%; infant mortality, 2005, 17 per 1,000 live births; fertility rate, 2004, 2·4 births per woman.

CLIMATE

A tropical climate but with considerable variation. High temperatures on the coast are usually mitigated by sea breezes, while upland areas enjoy cooler and less humid conditions. Rainfall is plentiful over most of Jamaica, being heaviest in May and from Aug. to Nov. The island lies in the hurricane zone. Kingston, Jan. 76°F (24·4°C), July 81°F (27·2°C). Annual rainfall 32" (800 mm).

CONSTITUTION AND GOVERNMENT

Under the constitution of Aug. 1962 the Crown is represented by a Governor-General appointed by the Crown on the advice of the Prime Minister. The Governor-General is assisted by a Privy Council of six appointed members. The Legislature comprises the *House of Representatives* and the *Senate*. The Senate consists of 21 senators appointed by the Governor-General, 13 on the advice of the Prime Minister, eight on the advice of the Leader of the Opposition. The House of Representatives (60 members) is elected by universal adult suffrage for a period not exceeding five years. Electors and elected must be Jamaican or Commonwealth citizens resident in Jamaica for at least 12 months before registration.

National Anthem

'Eternal Father, bless our land'; words by H. Sherlock, tune by R. Lightbourne.

RECENT ELECTIONS

In parliamentary elections held on 2 Sept. 2007 the opposition Jamaica Labour Party (JLP) took 33 of the 60 seats with 50·1% of votes cast (up from 26 in 2002) and the People's National Party (PNP) 27 with 49·8% (down from 34 in 2002). Turnout was 60·4%.

CURRENT ADMINISTRATION

Governor-General: Patrick Allen.

In March 2010 the cabinet comprised:

Prime Minister and Minister of Defence, Planning, Development, Information and Telecommunications: Bruce Golding; b. 1947 (JLP; sworn in 11 Sept. 2007).

Deputy Prime Minister and Minister of Foreign Affairs and Foreign Trade: Kenneth Baugh.

Minister of Agriculture and Fisheries: Christopher Tufton. *Education:* Andrew Holness. *Finance and Public Service:* Audley Shaw. *Health and Environment:* Rudyard Spencer. *Industry, Commerce and Investment:* Karl Samuda. *Justice and Attorney General:* Dorothy Lightbourne. *Labour and Social Security:* Pearnel Charles. *Mining and Energy:* James Robertson. *National Security:* Dwight Nelson. *Tourism:* Edmund Bartlett. *Transport and Works:* Michael Henry. *Water and Housing:* Horace Chang. *Youth, Sport and Culture:* Olivia Grange. *Ministers without Portfolio:* Daryl Vaz; Don Wehby.

Cabinet Website: http://www.cabinet.gov.jm

CURRENT LEADERS

Bruce Golding

Position
Prime Minister

Introduction
Bruce Golding was sworn in as prime minister on 11 Sept. 2007 after the Jamaica Labour Party (JLP) had claimed victory at polls earlier that month. Winning 33 of 60 parliamentary seats, the JLP came back to government after 18 years in opposition.

Early Life
Bruce Golding was born on 5 Dec. 1947, the son of Tacius Golding, an MP for 22 years. Golding graduated from the University of the West Indies in 1969 with a degree in economics and was elected to the central executive of the JLP immediately afterwards. In 1970 he co-founded Young Jamaica, the party's youth affiliate, before winning the seat of West St Catherine in the 1972 general election.

In 1974 Golding was elected general secretary of the JLP but lost his constituency seat in the 1976 general election. A year later he was appointed to the senate and when the JLP returned to power in 1980, he was appointed minister of construction. In 1983 he won the seat of South Central St Catherine and was elected JLP chairman in 1984. Following his party's failure at the 1989 polls, Golding became shadow minister of finance and chairman of the public accounts committee.

In the early 1990s Golding's attempts to bring about change to the country's political practices met with resistance from his own party. He left the JLP to establish the National Democratic Movement (NDM) in 1995. However, he resigned from the NDM in 2001 and returned to the JLP in Sept. 2002 where he once again sat in the senate. He was given the post of shadow minister of foreign affairs and foreign trade. In Nov. 2003 Golding was elected unopposed as party chairman and on 20 Feb. 2005 became its leader. He won the seat of West Kingston in a by-election on 13 April 2005 and became leader of the opposition on 21 April 2005. He led the JLP to electoral victory in Sept. 2007, becoming the first JLP prime minister since 1989.

Career in Office
Golding promised an active first hundred days in office, prioritizing the tackling of crime, poverty and unemployment. He abolished tuition fees in secondary schools and established an independent body to investigate police corruption. However, his tenure has been marred by allegations of inappropriate use of executive power and crime remains a serious problem. Jamaica's murder rate is one of the highest in the world, in response to which parliament has voted to retain the death penalty and Golding has pledged to resume executions.

DEFENCE

In 2006 defence expenditure totalled US$57m. (US$21 per capita), representing 0·6% of GDP.

Army
The Jamaica Defence Force consists of a Regular and a Reserve Force. Total strength (Army, 2005): 3,377, including 877 reservists.

Navy
The Coast Guard, numbering 250 in 2005 including 60 reservists, operates nine patrol craft based at Port Royal and Pedro Cays.

Air Force
The Air Wing of the Jamaica Defence Force was formed in July 1963 and has since been expanded and trained successively by the British Army Air Corps and Canadian Air Force personnel. There are no combat aircraft. Personnel (2005), 156 (including 16 reservists).

INTERNATIONAL RELATIONS

Jamaica is a member of the UN, World Bank, IMF and several other UN specialized agencies, WTO, Commonwealth, IOM, ACS, CARICOM, Inter-American Development Bank, SELA, OAS and is an ACP member state of the ACP-EU relationship.

ECONOMY

Agriculture accounted for 5·7% of GDP in 2005, industry 33·1% and services 61·2%.

Overview
Jamaica has a small, open economy dominated by the service sector. Tourism is the most significant source of domestic employment and foreign exchange. Worker remittances also account for a large part of national income, roughly equalling the tourist sector in importance. From 2000–05 total remittances to the country grew from US$892m. to US$1,623m.

Industry (as opposed to the agricultural and service sectors) as a percentage of GDP has fallen significantly from 45·9% in 1990 to 33·1% in 2005. Leading exports are alumina, bauxite, bananas and sugar. After experiencing spiky but strong growth in the early part of the 1990s the economy fell into recession in 1997. Since then growth has been muted but positive. A rise in fixed income investment, resulting from large foreign investment in tourism and mining, has been a key contributor to growth, and the country has benefited from a pick-up in agriculture, construction and the goods-producing sectors.

Export growth has been recently outpaced by import growth, with foreign investment contributing to the increase in imports. Consumer price inflation picked up in the first half of the decade but peaked in 2005 and has since fallen. Jamaica scores relatively well in human development indicators but suffers from a persistently high crime rate linked primarily to drug trafficking. Private sector development is hampered by poor quality infrastructure and significant corruption, and government consumption is constrained by large debt-servicing obligations.

Currency
The unit of currency is the *Jamaican dollar* (JMD) of 100 *cents*. The Jamaican dollar was floated in Sept. 1990. Inflation was 9·3% in 2007, rising to 22·0% in 2008. Foreign exchange reserves were US$2,423m. in July 2005 and total money supply was J$68,141m.

Budget
Budgetary central government revenue and expenditure for fiscal years ending 31 March (in J$1m.):

	2004	*2005*	*2006*
Revenue	172,798	186,684	211,310
Expenditure	188,382	192,250	224,505

The chief items of current revenue are income taxes, consumption taxes and customs duties. The chief items of current expenditure are public debt, education and health.

VAT is 16·5%.

Performance
After suffering major economic difficulties with negative growth in 1996, 1997 and 1998, Jamaica's economy recovered slightly, with growth of 2·7% in 2006 and 1·5% in 2007. However, there was again negative growth in 2008, of –1·0%. Total GDP in 2008 was US$15·1bn.

Banking and Finance
The central bank and bank of issue is the Bank of Jamaica. The *Governor* is Bryan Wynter.

In 2002 there were five commercial banks, three development banks and two other banks (National Export-Import Bank of Jamaica and the National Investment Bank of Jamaica). Total assets of commercial banks at March 2006 were J$385,759·5m.; deposits were J$255,315·4m.

There is a stock exchange in Kingston, which participates in the regional Caribbean exchange.

ENERGY AND NATURAL RESOURCES

Environment

In 2008 carbon dioxide emissions from the consumption and flaring of fossil fuels were the equivalent of 4·7 tonnes per capita.

Electricity

The Jamaica Public Service Co. is the public supplier. Total installed capacity was an estimated 1·3m. kW in 2004. Production in 2004 totalled 7·22bn. kWh; consumption per capita in 2004 was 2,697 kWh.

Oil and Gas

There is an oil refinery in Kingston.

Minerals

Jamaica is ranks among the world's largest producers of bauxite. Ceramic clays, marble, silica sand and gypsum are also commercially viable. Production in 2005 (in tonnes): bauxite ore, 14·1m.; limestone, 2·6m.; sand and gravel, 2·4m.; gypsum, 302,066.

Agriculture

In 2007 there were an estimated 174,000 ha. of arable land and 110,000 ha. of permanent crops.

2003 production (in 1,000 tonnes): sugarcane, 2,400; coconuts, 170; yams, 151; oranges, 140; bananas, 130; grapefruit and pomelos, 42; pumpkins and squash, 36; cabbage, 29; plantains, 29.

Livestock (2003 estimates): goats, 440,000; cattle, 430,000; pigs, 180,000; chickens, 11m. Livestock products, 2003 estimates (in 1,000 tonnes): beef and veal, 14; pork, bacon and ham, 5; poultry meat, 81.

Forestry

Forests covered 339,000 ha. in 2005, or 31·3% of the total land area. Timber production was 834,000 cu. metres in 2007.

Fisheries

Catches in 2005 totalled 13,096 tonnes, of which 97% were sea fish.

INDUSTRY

Alumina production, 2005, 4·1m. tonnes. Output of other products (2004 unless otherwise indicated, in tonnes): cement (2005), 844,840; residual fuel oil, 370,000; sugar (2002), 174,949; distillate fuel oil, 129,000; petrol, 95,000; molasses (2003), 72,631; wheat flour (2002), 32,000; fertilizer (2002), 22,400; cigarettes (2003), 889m. units; rum (2003), 25·5m. litres. In 2005 industry accounted for 33·1% of GDP, with manufacturing contributing 13·6%.

Labour

Total labour force (2003), 1·10m., of whom 957,300 were employed. In 2003, 257,000 were employed in community, social and personal services; 210,000 in wholesale and retail trade, restaurants and hotels; 188,000 in agriculture, hunting, forestry and fishing; and 90,000 in construction. In 2005 the unemployment rate was 10·0%.

INTERNATIONAL TRADE

Foreign debt was US$6,511m. in 2005.

Imports and Exports

Value of imports and domestic exports for calendar years (in US$1m.):

	2002	*2003*	*2004*	*2005*	*2006*
Imports f.o.b.	3,179·6	3,328·2	3,546·1	4,245·5	5,077·1
Exports f.o.b.	1,309·1	1,385·6	1,601·6	1,664·3	2,133·6

Principal imports in 2006 (% of total): petroleum and petroleum products 23·6%, machinery and transport equipment 22·6%, manufactured goods 13·9%, food and live animals 12·5% and chemicals and related products 11·3%.

Principal domestic exports in 2006 (% of total): crude materials (excluding fuels) 63·3%, petroleum oils 13·5%, cane sugar 4·5%, alcoholic beverages 4·2% and chemicals 3·7%.

Main import suppliers, 2006: USA, 36·8%; Trinidad and Tobago, 11·5%; Venezuela, 10·7%; Japan, 4·2%; China, 4·1%. Main export markets, 2006: USA, 30·4%; Canada, 15·6%; China, 15·1%; UK, 10·3%; Netherlands, 7·0%.

COMMUNICATIONS

Roads

In 2007 the island had 22,121 km of roads, including 44 km of motorway and 4,922 km of main roads. In 2006 there were 373,700 passenger cars in use and 29,100 motorcycles and mopeds. There were 350 fatalities in traffic accidents in 2007.

Rail

Passenger traffic ceased in 1992 but there are plans to revive passenger services. Freight transport continues on a limited basis, mainly for carrying bauxite to docks.

Civil Aviation

International airlines operate through the Norman Manley and Sangster airports at Palisadoes and Montego Bay. Sangster International is the busiest for passenger traffic, handling 3,378,000 passengers in 2006–07. Norman Manley airport is busier for freight, handling 16,136 tonnes of freight in 2006 but only 1,715,078 passengers. Air Jamaica, originally set up in conjunction with BOAC and BWIA in 1966, became a new company, Air Jamaica (1968) Ltd. In 1969 it began operations as Jamaica's national airline. In 2003 scheduled airline traffic of Jamaica-based carriers flew 48m. km and carried 1,838,000 passengers.

Shipping

In 2002 the merchant marine totalled 75,000 GRT, including oil tankers 2,000 GRT. In 2001 there were 3,574 visits to all ports; 15·6m. tonnes of cargo were handled. In 2002 Kingston had 2,520 visits and handled 11·1m. tonnes. In 1997 vessels totalling 12,815,000 NRT entered ports and vessels totalling 6,457,000 NRT cleared.

Telecommunications

In 2005 there were 3,042,000 telephone subscribers (1,147·5 per 1,000 population), of which 2,700,000 were mobile phone subscribers. There were 166,000 PCs in use (62·0 for every 1,000 persons) in 2004 and 1,067,000 internet users.

Postal Services

In 2003 there were 624 post offices, or one for every 4,250 persons.

SOCIAL INSTITUTIONS

Justice

The Judicature comprises a Supreme Court, a court of appeal, resident magistrates' courts, petty sessional courts, coroners' courts, a traffic court and a family court which was instituted in 1975. The Chief Justice is head of the judiciary. Jamaica was one of ten countries to sign an agreement in Feb. 2001 establishing a Caribbean Court of Justice to replace the British Privy Council as the highest civil and criminal court. In the meantime the number of signatories has risen to twelve. The court was inaugurated at Port-of-Spain, Trinidad on 16 April 2005.

In 1995, 54,595 crimes were reported, of which 33,889 were solved. The daily average prison population, 1995, was 3,289. In 2005 there were 1,669 murders. The rate of 63 per 100,000 persons is more than eleven times that of the USA and ranks among the highest in the world.

The population in penal institutions in Nov. 2003 was 4,744 (176 per 100,000 of national population).

Police

The Constabulary Force in 2005 stood at approximately 8,011 officers, sub-officers and constables (men and women).

Education

Adult literacy was 87·6% in 2003 (91·4% among females but only 83·8% among males).

Education is free in government-operated schools. Enrolment in 2007 in primary institutions was 310,021; in secondary institutions, 257,186; and in tertiary institutions (2003), 45,770. Numbers of teaching staff: primary (2005), 11,793; secondary (2007), 13,006; tertiary (2003), 2,006.

The University of the West Indies, which was founded in 1948 and has its main campus at Kingston, is the oldest, fully regional institution of higher learning in the Commonwealth Caribbean. In 2006 there were two public universities and two private universities as well as six teacher training colleges, five community colleges, and several technical/vocational training institutes and specialist colleges. Large numbers of educated Jamaicans have left the island over the past 30 years, but in the early part of the 21st century there are signs that young professionals are increasingly returning to Jamaica. However, 72% of Jamaican graduates live in OECD member countries.

In 2005 public expenditure on education came to 5·6% of GNI and 8·8% of total government spending.

Health

In 2001 there were 27 hospitals with 4,606 beds. There were 2,253 physicians, 4,374 nurses and midwives, and 212 dentists in 2003.

Welfare

The official retirement age is 65 years (men) or 60 years (women). The old-age pension is made up of a basic benefit of J$900 a week (reduced to J$675 a week with annual average contributions of between 26 and 38 weeks; J$450 with 13 weeks to 25 weeks), plus an earnings-related benefit of J$0·06 a week for every J$13 of employer-employee contributions paid during the working lifetime.

Jamaica's social welfare projects also cover disability and survivor benefits, sickness and maternity, and work injury. Jamaica has no unemployment programmes.

RELIGION

Freedom of worship is guaranteed under the Constitution. The main Christian denominations are Anglican, Baptist, Roman Catholic, Methodist, Church of God, United Church of Jamaica and Grand Cayman (Presbyterian-Congregational-Disciples of Christ), Moravian, Seventh-Day Adventist, Pentecostal, Salvation Army and Quaker. Pocomania is a mixture of Christianity and African survivals. Non-Christians include Hindus, Jews, Muslims, Bahai followers and Rastafarians.

CULTURE

Broadcasting

The main terrestrial television services are TVJ (previously the Jamaica Broadcasting Corporation until privatization in 1997) and the independent CVM Television station (colour by NTSC); there is also a religious channel. Radio services, particularly Radio Jamaica Ltd (RJR) operating three networks, are similarly commercial. There were 536,000 TV-equipped households in 2005.

Press

In 2006 there were three daily newspapers with a combined circulation of 115,000.

Tourism

In 2006 there were a record 1,678,905 staying visitors and a record 1,336,994 cruise passenger arrivals. Tourism receipts in 2005 totalled US$1,783m.

DIPLOMATIC REPRESENTATIVES

Of Jamaica in the United Kingdom (1–2 Prince Consort Rd, London, SW7 2BZ)
High Commissioner: Burchell Anthony Whiteman.

Of the United Kingdom in Jamaica (28 Trafalgar Rd, Kingston 10)
High Commissioner: Howard Drake, OBE.

Of Jamaica in the USA (1520 New Hampshire Ave., NW, Washington, D.C., 20036)
Ambassador: Anthony Johnson.

Of the USA in Jamaica (142 Old Hope Rd, Kingston 6)
Ambassador: Vacant.
Chargé d'Affaires a.i.: Isiah Parnell.

Of Jamaica to the United Nations
Ambassador: Raymond Wolfe.

Of Jamaica to the European Union
Ambassador: Marcia Yvette Gilbert-Roberts.

FURTHER READING

Planning Institute of Jamaica. *Economic and Social Survey, Jamaica.* Annual.—*Survey of Living Conditions.* Annual
Statistical Institute of Jamaica. *Statistical Abstract.* Annual.—*Demographic Statistics.* Annual.—*Production Statistics.* Annual

Boyd, D., *Economic Management, Income Distribution, and Poverty in Jamaica.* 1988
Hart, R., *Towards Decolonisation: Political, Labour and Economic Developments in Jamaica 1938–1945.* 1999
Henke, H. W. and Mills, D., *Between Self-Determination and Dependency: Jamaica's Foreign Relations 1972–1989.* 2000

National library: National Library of Jamaica, 12 East Street, Kingston.
National Statistical Office: Statistical Institute of Jamaica (STATIN), 7 Cecelio Ave., Kingston 10. *Director General:* Sonia Jackson.
Website: http://www.statinja.com

JAPAN

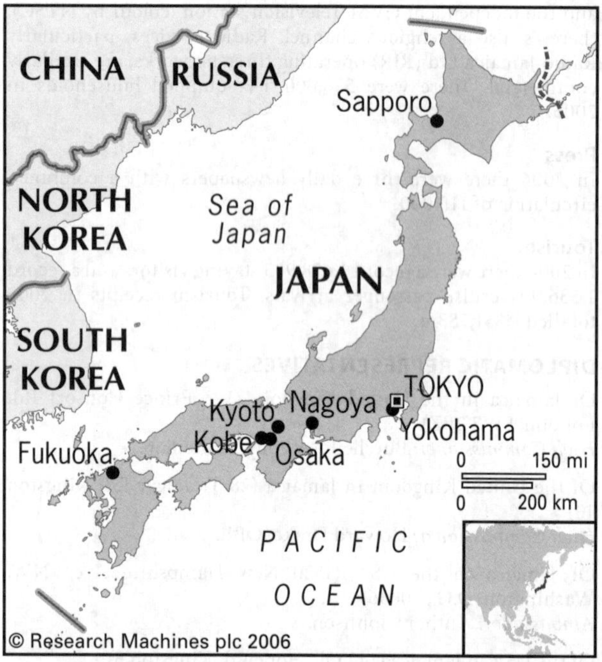

Nihon (or Nippon[1]) Koku
(Land of the Rising Sun)

Capital: Tokyo
Population estimate, 2010: 127·00m.
GDP per capita, 2007: (PPP$) 33,632
HDI/world rank: 0·960/10

KEY HISTORICAL EVENTS

When the last ice sheets covered much of Asia, the sea level fell low enough for a land bridge to appear between Japan and the Asian mainland. This route was taken by hunter-gatherers from Asia who crossed into previously uninhabited Japan. By 10,000 BC the first pottery was produced in Japan and there was some cultivation. Rice was introduced, probably from Korea, by about 400 BC, and the use of metals around a century later, but agriculture and fixed settlements were confined to the south for a long period. During this time waves of migrants came from mainland Asia, bringing with them skills and technologies, including the Chinese characters for writing.

Religion, too, came from China: both Buddhism and Confucianism entered Japan, the former gaining a large following. In time traditional beliefs consolidated into Shintoism, which became the national religion. But, until the first millennium AD, there was no Japanese nation, although the legends of Japan tell us otherwise. According to myth, the first Japanese emperor was Jimmu around 600 BC, said to be a descendant of the sun goddess, Amaterasu.

In the first century BC, another wave of migrants entered Japan from Korea. The first Japanese state appeared in the central region of Honshu in the 7th century. This state soon controlled most of the west and centre of the island. In 710 the first permanent Japanese capital was established in Nara by Empress Genmei. In 794 the seat of power moved to Heian-kyo (present-day Kyoto).

Following the court and government tradition of China, Japan cut itself off from the outside world. As the imperial office became increasingly religious the day-to-day power passed into the hands of powerful nobles, such as the Fujiwara clan. Fujiwara Yoshifusa (804–872) was a powerful regent of Japan from 857 until his death, and by the 11th century the Fujiwaras were unchallenged rulers of the country. In the 12th century, however, Japan entered into a period of anarchy. The country passed under the control of barons, the *daimyo*, who exercised power through the warrior class known as the *samurai*.

Shogun

The anarchy ended when Taira Kiyamori seized power and made himself dictator. A civil war, the Gempei War, followed (1180–85). When Taira was defeated, power passed to Minamoto Yoritomo (1147–99), a distant descendant of the imperial family. Yoritomo established a new office, the *shogun*. For the next 700 years Japan was ruled by a military dictator, the shogun, while the emperor lived reclusively as a religious and national symbol.

At first the shogunate was seated in Kamakura, near modern Tokyo. Nine shoguns ruled during the Kamakura epoch (1185–1333) although latterly the Kamakura shogun was a puppet of the Hojo clan. In 1274 and 1281 Mongol attempts to invade Japan were unsuccessful: in 1281 the invasion was thwarted by a sudden typhoon that became known as the 'divine wind' (kami-kaze).

In 1334 a brief restoration of power to the emperor was ended by Ashikaga Takauji (1305–58), who established a strong military government. Subsequent members of the Ashikaga family ruled as shoguns based in Kyoto. Eventually this system, too, collapsed into anarchy, the victim of the ambitions of rival warlords. From 1467 to 1603 Japan suffered the Fighting Principalities (*Sengokujidai*). It was when the country was at its weakest that another powerful outside influence began to exert itself.

From 1543 Portuguese traders and missionaries arrived on the southern and western coasts. At first, trade was welcomed. Christianity, too, made converts after the Spanish Jesuit missionary St Francis Xavier landed in Japan in 1549. Along with western ideas and religion, the Portuguese, and later the Dutch, brought firearms. Three warlords in turn used western weapons to seize power and reunite the country. The last of this trio was Tokugawa Ieyasu (1542–1616), who held power from 1600. Ieyasu ordered the nobles to destroy their fortifications, except their principal residences, and encouraged the arts and learning as a preferred alternative to warfare.

Isolation

As the true rulers of Japan until 1869, the Tokugawa shogunate established itself at Edo (present-day Tokyo). They ruled harshly, subduing the warring lords by holding members of their families hostages. The Tokugawa perceived foreign influences as unsettling and a danger to their supremacy. For this reason, they decreed that Japan should become a closed society. In 1636 Japanese were forbidden to emigrate. Europeans were expelled, except for a single Dutch trading post in Nagasaki, which—after 1639—became Japan's only contact with the outside world. Christianity was suppressed and the ownership of firearms, except by the central authorities, was made illegal. Japan entered 220 years of self-imposed isolation.

Cut off from outside influences, Japan gained stability and a strong sense of national identity. Yet this isolation came at a

[1]Both forms are valid, and derive from different pronunciations of a Chinese character.

price. In 1853 a US fleet led by Commodore Matthew C. Perry appeared off the Japanese coast. Japan was forced to open up to international trade through the threat of invasion. Other western nations followed the American example. Japan was thrust into a modern world for which it was ill suited. The voices for reform grew and the Tokugawa shogunate, humiliated by Perry's mission, collapsed. Reformers seized Kyoto and parts of the west, but they needed a national symbol to legitimize their rule. In 1869 the shadowy figure of the emperor was called out of his cloistered life. His city, Edo, had by then been renamed Tokyo, meaning 'eastern capital'. The emperor surprised the country by his zeal for modernization which led to a period of rapid reform and transformed Japan into a modern nation.

But while a constitution was introduced, the resemblance to a western democracy was skin deep. Though the peasants were freed from serfdom, power remained in the hands of the nobility. Priority was given to developing industry and modern technology. Japan's rise as an industrial state began.

Rise of the Military

Much emphasis was given to modernizing the armed forces. A revitalized Japan defeated China in the First Sino-Japanese War in 1894–95 and gained Taiwan. In 1900 Japan intervened alongside the western powers against the Boxer Rebellion in China. An even greater shock was Japan's victory against Russia in 1903–04 in a war over Korea and Manchuria. Having contained Russian land forces in Manchuria, the Japanese decisively defeated the Russian Baltic Fleet in the Tsushima Strait. Russia's influence in the region faded and Japan received half of Sakhalin and the Kurile Islands. Later, with Russia removed from the scene, Japan annexed Korea (1910) and took control of parts of Manchuria.

In 1902 Japan made an alliance with Britain. To emphasize Japan's western credentials, Tokyo entered the First World War against Germany in 1914. Japanese forces took the German island colonies in the north and central Pacific and received these archipelagoes as a League of Nations Trust Territory in 1919. But greater rewards for their efforts in the war had been expected and Tokyo's disillusion with the west began. The collapse of world trade at the end of the 1920s brought hardship and helped the rise of political extremism and nationalism.

Japan began a phase of aggressive expansionism. In 1931 Japan invaded Manchuria and, two years later, installed the deposed last emperor of China as puppet emperor of Manchukuo. From 1932 Japanese forces entered various coastal and border areas of China, and in 1937 there was a full-scale war with China. Japanese forces took Shanghai in 1937, Guangzhou in 1938 and Nanjing in 1940. By the end of 1940 Japan had occupied French Indochina and formed a triple alliance (or Axis) with Nazi Germany and Fascist Italy.

Pearl Harbor

Under premier Gen. Tojo Hideki (1884–1948), Japan attacked the US fleet in Pearl Harbor, Hawaii in Dec. 1941. This action brought the United States into the Second World War (1939–45) and ranged Japan against forces that were superior in size and technology. Nevertheless, the war was initially in Japan's favour. Japanese forces swept through the Pacific and into Malaya and the Dutch East Indies (now Indonesia). The speed of Japan's ruthless advance overwhelmed the Allied powers as British and American positions were surrendered. The tide turned with the American victory at Midway in late 1942, but by the time Germany surrendered in May 1945 Japanese forces were still in control of large areas of the Pacific and Southeast Asia. In Aug. 1945 US planes dropped atomic bombs on the Japanese cities of Hiroshima and Nagasaki, devastating the two cities and causing more than 200,000 deaths. The emperor Hirohito (1926–89) surrendered.

The war had cost Japan dearly. Not only had two cities suffered the horror of atomic warfare, but many more Japanese had died in combat. Nearly 2m. Japanese were abandoned in China, most of whom were shipped to Siberia as prisoners. Japan was to be reformed by the occupying US forces under Gen. MacArthur. In 1945 Shintoism, which had become associated with aggressive nationalism, ceased to be the state religion. In the following year, the emperor renounced his divinity.

A new liberal constitution was introduced in 1946. Japan signed a peace treaty in 1951 at San Francisco and the American occupation of Japan ended in April 1952 when the country regained its independence. A separate peace treaty was concluded later between Japan and China. There was, however, no agreement with the Soviet Union, which, at American behest, had declared war against Japan in the closing days of the Second World War. Soviet forces occupied Sakhalin and the Kurile islands to which Japan still lays claim.

The new Japan remained a monarchy, albeit one in which the emperor was a figurehead. Japan renounced war and the threat or use of force, but retained 'Self Defence Forces'. Japanese cities and industry were rebuilt. An astonishing economic recovery was led by an aggressive export policy. Huge investment in new technology gave the country a dominant position in many industries including motor vehicles, shipbuilding, electrical goods, electronics and computers. Japan grew to be the world's second biggest economy. This success is owed, in part, to the protection of domestic markets.

The power of Japanese industry was reflected in the political power of a small number of major corporations. From 1955 until 1993 the political scene was dominated by the centre-right pro-business Liberal Democrats (LDP). However, a series of major financial scandals broke the party's monopoly and coalition governments followed. By 2000 the LDP had resumed its dominant role.

In recent years, Japan has shown more confidence in international relations. The country is a major donor of aid to developing countries. In 1992 the Diet (parliament) approved the contribution of Japanese military personnel and equipment to UN peacekeeping missions and in 2002 Japan contributed naval support vessels to the US-led intervention in Afghanistan. However, the country faces severe economic problems. A heavy international debt and domestic deflation left the Japanese economy in the doldrums at the turn of the century.

TERRITORY AND POPULATION

Japan consists of four major islands, Honshu, Hokkaido, Kyushu and Shikoku, and many small islands, with an area of 377,915 sq. km. Census population of 1 Oct. 2005 (2000 census in brackets), 127,767,994 (126,925,843); of which males, 62,348,977 (62,110,764), females, 65,419,017 (64,815,079); population density, 343 per sq. km (340 per sq. km).

The UN gives an estimated population for 2010 of 127·00m. The population started to decline in 2007; the UN projects that by 2050 it will only be 101·66m.

In 2005, 65·8% of the population lived in urban areas. Foreigners registered on 31 Dec. 2007 were 2,152,973: including 606,889 Chinese, 593,489 Koreans, 316,967 Brazilians, 202,592 Filipinos, 59,696 Peruvians, 51,851 Americans, 41,384 Thais, 36,860 Vietnamese, 25,620 Indonesians, 20,589 Indians, 17,328 British, 11,459 Canadians, 11,255 Bangladeshis, 11,033 Australians, 9,332 Pakistanis and 1,573 stateless persons. In 2008 Japan accepted 57 asylum seekers (54 of whom were from Myanmar).

Japanese overseas, Oct. 2007, 1,085,671; of these 374,732 lived in the USA, 127,905 in China, 63,526 in the UK, 63,459 in Australia, 61,527 in Brazil, 47,376 in Canada, 42,736 in Thailand, 32,755 in Germany, 29,279 in France and 25,969 in Singapore.

The official language is Japanese.

A law of May 1997 'on the promotion of Ainu culture' marked the first official recognition of the existence of an ethnic minority in Japan. The Ainu were recognized as a people in their own right through a resolution passed by parliament in June 2008.

Japan is divided into 43 prefectures, one metropolis (Tokyo), one territory (Hokkaido) and two urban prefectures (Kyoto and Osaka). The areas, populations and chief cities are:

Prefecture	*Sq. km*	*Census pop. 2005*	*Chief city*
Aichi	5,164	7,254,704	Nagoya
Akita	11,612	1,145,501	Akita
Aomori	9,607	1,436,657	Aomori
Chiba	5,157	6,056,462	Chiba
Ehime	5,677	1,467,815	Matsuyama
Fukui	4,189	821,592	Fukui
Fukuoka	4,976	5,049,908	Fukuoka
Fukushima	13,783	2,091,319	Fukushima
Gifu	10,621	2,107,226	Gifu
Gumma	6,363	2,024,135	Maebashi
Hiroshima	8,478	2,876,642	Hiroshima
Hokkaido	83,456	5,627,737	Sapporo
Hyogo	8,395	5,590,601	Kobe
Ibaraki	6,096	2,975,167	Mito
Ishikawa	4,185	1,174,026	Kanazawa
Iwate	15,279	1,385,041	Morioka
Kagawa	1,876	1,012,400	Takamatsu
Kagoshima	9,188	1,753,179	Kagoshima
Kanagawa	2,416	8,791,597	Yokohama
Kochi	7,105	796,292	Kochi
Kumamoto	7,405	1,842,233	Kumamoto
Kyoto	4,613	2,647,660	Kyoto
Mie	5,777	1,866,963	Tsu
Miyagi	7,286	2,360,218	Sendai
Miyazaki	7,735	1,153,042	Miyazaki
Nagano	13,562	2,196,114	Nagano
Nagasaki	4,095	1,478,632	Nagasaki
Nara	3,691	1,421,310	Nara
Niigata	12,583	2,431,459	Niigata
Oita	6,339	1,209,571	Oita
Okayama	7,113	1,957,264	Okayama
Okinawa	2,275	1,361,594	Naha
Osaka	1,894	8,817,166	Osaka
Saga	2,440	866,369	Saga
Saitama	3,797	7,054,243	Saitama
Shiga	4,017	1,380,361	Otsu
Shimane	6,708	742,223	Matsue
Shizuoka	7,780	3,792,377	Shizuoka
Tochigi	6,408	2,016,631	Utsunomiya
Tokushima	4,145	809,950	Tokushima
Tokyo	2,187	12,576,601	Tokyo
Tottori	3,507	607,012	Tottori
Toyama	4,247	1,111,729	Toyama
Wakayama	4,726	1,035,969	Wakayama
Yamagata	9,323	1,216,181	Yamagata
Yamaguchi	6,112	1,492,606	Yamaguchi
Yamanashi	4,465	884,515	Kofu

The leading cities, with population in 2005 (in 1,000), are:

Akashi	291	Ichihara	280
Akita	333	Ichikawa	467
Amagasaki	463	Ichinomiya	372
Aomori	312	Iwaki	354
Asahikawa	355	Kagoshima	604
Chiba	924	Kakogawa	267
Fujisawa	396	Kanazawa	455
Fukui	269	Kashiwa	381
Fukuoka	1,401	Kasugai	296
Fukushima	291	Kawagoe	334
Fukuyama	459	Kawaguchi	480
Funabashi	570	Kawasaki	1,327
Gifu	413	Kitakyushu	994
Hachioji	560	Kobe	1,525
Hakodate	294	Kochi	333
Hamamatsu	804	Koriyama	339
Higashiosaka	514	Koshigaya	316
Himeji	536	Kumamoto	670
Hirakata	404	Kurashiki	469
Hiratsuka	259	Kure	251
Hiroshima	1,154	Kurume	306
Ibaraki	268	Kyoto	1,475
Machida	406	Sasebo	258
Maebashi	319	Sendai	1,025
Matsudo	473	Shimonoseki	291
Matsuyama	515	Shizuoka	714
Mito	263	Suita	354
Miyazaki	367	Takamatsu	418
Morioka	301	Takasaki	340
Nagano	379	Takatsuki	352
Nagaoka	283	Tokorozawa	336
Nagasaki	455	Tokushima	268
Nagoya	2,215	Tokyo	8,490
Naha	312	Toyama	421
Nara	370	Toyohashi	372
Niigata	814	Toyonaka	387
Nishinomiya	465	Toyota	412
Oita	462	Tsu	289
Okayama	675	Utsunomiya	458
Okazaki	364	Wakayama	376
Osaka	2,629	Yamagata	256
Otsu	324	Yao	273
Sagamihara	668	Yokkaichi	304
Saitama	1,176	Yokohama	3,580
Sakai	831	Yokosuka	426
Sapporo	1,881		

The Tokyo conurbation, with a population in 2005 of 35·2m., is the largest in the world, having overtaken New York around 1970.

SOCIAL STATISTICS

Statistics (in 1,000) for calendar years:

	2001	*2002*	*2003*	*2004*	*2005*	*2006*	*2007*
Births	1,171	1,154	1,124	1,111	1,063	1,093	1,090
Deaths	970	982	1,015	1,029	1,084	1,084	1,108

Birth rate of Japanese nationals in present area in 2007, 8·6 per 1,000 population (1947: 34·3); death rate, 8·8. Marriage rate in 2007 (per 1,000 persons), 5·7; divorce rate, 2·0. In 2007 the mean age at first marriage was 30·1 for males and 28·3 for females. The infant mortality rate per 1,000 live births, 2·6 (2007), is one of the lowest in the world. Life expectancy at birth was 86·0 years for women and 79·0 years for men in 2007. Japan's life expectancy is the highest of any sovereign country. The World Health Organization's *World Health Statistics 2009* put the Japanese in first place in a 'healthy life expectancy' list, with an expected 76 years of healthy life for babies born in 2007. Japan has a very quickly ageing population, stemming from a sharply declined fertility rate and one of the highest life expectancies in the world. In 2007 the total fertility rate was 1·34 births per woman (compared to 1·36 in 2000, 1·91 in 1975 and 3·65 in 1950). The percentage of the population over 65 rose from 10% in 1985 to more than 21% in 2007. Japan had an estimated 40,400 centenarians (35,000 women) in Sept. 2009—an increase of over 4,000 from Sept. 2008, and the 39th consecutive year the number has risen. In 2008 the population fell by 0·1%

There was a total of 33,093 suicides in 2007, a rate of 35·8 males per 100,000 and 13·7 females per 100,000. The rate among women is one of the highest in the world.

A UNICEF report published in 2005 showed that 14·3% of children in Japan live in poverty (in households with income below 50% of the national median), compared to just 2·4% in Denmark.

CLIMATE

The islands of Japan lie in the temperate zone, northeast of the main monsoon region of southeast Asia. The climate is temperate with warm, humid summers and relatively mild winters except in the island of Hokkaido and northern parts of Honshu facing the Sea of Japan. There is a month's rainy season in June–July, but the best seasons are spring and autumn, although Sept. may bring typhoons. Tokyo, Jan. 5·8°C, July 25·4°C. Annual rainfall 1,467 mm. Hiroshima, Jan. 5·3°C, July 26·9°C. Annual rainfall 1,541 mm. Nagasaki, Jan. 6·8°C, July 26·6°C. Annual rainfall 1,960 mm. Osaka, Jan. 5·8°C, July 27·2°C. Annual rainfall 1,306 mm. Sapporo, Jan. –4·1°C, July 20·5°C. Annual rainfall 1,128 mm.

CONSTITUTION AND GOVERNMENT

The Emperor is Akihito (b. 23 Dec. 1933), who succeeded his father, Hirohito on 7 Jan. 1989 (enthroned, 12 Nov. 1990); married 10 April 1959, to Michiko Shoda (b. 20 Oct. 1934). *Offspring:* Crown Prince Naruhito (Hironomiya; b. 23 Feb. 1960); Prince Akishino (Akishinomiya; b. 30 Nov. 1965); Princess Sayako (Norinomiya; b. 18 April 1969). Prince Naruhito married Masako Owada (b. 9 Dec. 1963) 9 June 1993. *Offspring:* Princess Aiko (b. 1 Dec. 2001). Prince Fumihito (henceforth to adopt his new title Prince Akishino) married Kawashima Kiko (b. 11 Sept. 1966) 29 June 1990. *Offspring:* Princess Mako (23 Oct. 1991); Princess Kako (29 Dec. 1994); Prince Hisahito (6 Sept. 2006). Princess Sayako married Yoshiki Kuroda (b. 17 April 1965) 15 Nov. 2005 and gave up her imperial title in doing so as required by law. The succession to the throne is fixed upon the male descendants. Prince Hisahito was the first male born into the imperial family since 1965. The 1947 constitution supersedes the Meiji constitution of 1889. In it the Japanese people pledge themselves to uphold the ideas of democracy and peace. The Emperor is the symbol of the unity of the people. Sovereign power rests with the people. The Emperor has no powers related to government. Fundamental human rights are guaranteed.

Legislative power rests with the *Diet*, which consists of the *House of Deputies* (Shugi-in), elected by men and women over 20 years of age for a four-year term, and an upper house, the *House of Councillors* (Sangi-in) of 242 members (96 elected by party list system with proportional representation according to the d'Hondt method and 146 from prefectural districts), one-half of its members being elected every three years. The number of members has been reduced in recent years. There had been 252 members until 2001 and 247 members from 2001 until elections of July 2004.

The number of members in the House of Deputies was reduced from 500 to 480 for the election of June 2000, of whom 300 were to be elected from single-seat constituencies, and 180 by proportional representation on a base of 11 regions. There is a 2% threshold to gain one of the latter seats. Donations to individual politicians are to be supplanted over five years by state subsidies to parties.

A new electoral law passed in Oct. 2000 gives voters a choice between individual candidates and parties when casting ballots for the proportional representation seats in the *House of Councillors*.

On becoming prime minister in April 2001 Junichiro Koizumi established a panel to consider introducing the direct election of prime ministers by popular vote.

National Anthem

'Kimigayo' ('The Reign of Our Emperor'); words 9th century, tune by Hayashi Hiromori. On 9 Aug. 1999 a law on the national flag and the national anthem was enacted. The law designates the Hinomaru and 'Kimigayo' as the national flag and national anthem of Japan. The 'Kimi' in 'Kimigayo' indicates the Emperor who is the symbol of the State and of the unity of the people, deriving his position from the will of the people with whom resides sovereign power; 'Kimigayo' depicts the state of being of the country as a whole.

GOVERNMENT CHRONOLOGY

Prime ministers since 1945. (DPJ = Democratic Party of Japan; JSP = Japan Socialist Party; Jt = Liberal Party; LDP = Liberal Democratic Party; Mt = Democratic Party; NSt = Japan New Party; SDP = Social Democratic Party; SSt = Renewal Party; n/p = non party)

1945	military	Kantaro Suzuki
1945	military	Naruhito Kigashi-Kuni
1945–46	n/p	Kijuro Shidehara
1946–47	Jt	Shigeru Yoshida
1947–48	JSP	Tetsu Katayama
1948	Mt	Hitoshi Ashida
1948–54	Jt	Shigeru Yoshida
1954–56	LDP	Ichiro Hatoyama
1956–57	LDP	Tanzan Ishibashi
1957–60	LDP	Nobusuke Kishi
1960–64	LDP	Hayato Ikeda
1964–72	LDP	Eisaku Sato
1972–74	LDP	Kakuei Tanaka
1974–76	LDP	Takeo Miki
1976–78	LDP	Takeo Fukuda
1978–80	LDP	Masayoshi Ohira
1980	LDP	Masayoshi Ito
1980–82	LDP	Zenko Suzuki
1982–87	LDP	Yasuhiro Nakasone
1987–89	LDP	Noboru Takeshita
1989	LDP	Sosuke Uno
1989–91	LDP	Toshiki Kaifu
1991–93	LDP	Kiichi Miyazawa
1993–94	NSt	Morihiro Hosokawa
1994	SSt	Tsutomu Hata
1994–96	SDP	Tomiichi Murayama
1996–98	LDP	Ryutaro Hashimoto
1998–2000	LDP	Keizo Obuchi
2000	LDP	Michio Aoki
2000–01	LDP	Yoshiro Mori
2001–06	LDP	Junichiro Koizumi
2006–07	LDP	Shinzo Abe
2007–08	LDP	Yasuo Fukuda
2008–09	LDP	Taro Aso
2009–	DPJ	Yukio Hatoyama

RECENT ELECTIONS

Elections to the House of Deputies were held on 30 Aug. 2009. Turnout was 69·3%. The opposition Democratic Party of Japan (DPJ; Minshuto), won 308 seats (with 42·4% of the vote); the ruling Liberal Democratic Party (LDP; Jiyu Minshuto), 119 (26·7%); New Clean Government Party (New Komeito), 21 (11·5%); Communist Party of Japan (Nihon Kyosanto), 9 (7·0%); Social Democratic Party (SDP; Shakai Minshuto), 7 (4·3%); Your Party (Minna no To), 5 (4·3%); People's New Party (Kokumin Shinto), 3 (1·7%). Non-partisans took 8 seats. Only 54 (a record high) of the 480 elected MPs were women. The DPJ's victory brought to an end 13 years of LDP rule. Apart from a short period of time in 1993 and 1994 the LDP had been in power continuously since 1954.

Elections to 121 seats of the House of Councillors were held on 29 July 2007. The opposition Democratic Party of Japan gained 60 seats, LDP 37, New Komeito 9, Communist Party of Japan 3, People's New Party 2, SDP 2, New Party Nippon 1 and ind. 7. As a result the Democratic Party held 109 seats, LDP 83, New Komeito 20, Communist Party of Japan 7, Social Democratic Party 5, People's New Party 4, New Party Nippon 1 and ind. 13. As a result the LDP lost its majority in the upper house for the first time since its inception in 1947.

CURRENT ADMINISTRATION

Prime Minister: Yukio Hatoyama; b. 1947 (DPJ; sworn in 16 Sept. 2009).

In March 2010 the coalition government consisting of the Democratic Party of Japan, the Social Democratic Party and the People's New Party comprised:

Deputy Prime Minister, Minister of Finance and Minister of State for Economic and Fiscal Policy: Naoto Kan. *Minister of Internal Affairs and Communications and Minister of State for the Promotion of Local Sovereignty:* Kazuhiro Haraguti. *Justice:* Keiko Chiba. *Foreign Affairs:* Katsuya Okada. *Education, Culture, Sports, Science and Technology and Minister of State for Science and Technology Policy:* Tatsuo Kawabata. *Health, Labour and Welfare and Minister of State for Pension Reform:* Akira Nagatsuma. *Agriculture, Forestry and Fisheries:* Hirotaka Akamatsu. *Economy, Trade and Industry:* Masayuki Naoshima. *Land, Infrastructure, Transport and Tourism and Minister of State for Okinawa and Northern Territories Affairs:* Seiji Maehara. *Environment:* Sakihito Ozawa. *Defence:* Toshimi Kitazawa.

Chief Cabinet Secretary: Hirofumi Hirano. *Chairman of the National Commission on Public Safety and Minister of State for Disaster Management and the Abduction Issue:* Hiroshi Nakai. *Minister of State for Financial Services and Postal Reform:* Shizuka Kamei. *Minister of State for Consumer Affairs and Food Safety, Social Affairs and Gender Equality:* Mizuho Fukushima. *Minister of State for Government Realization, Civil Service Reform and National Policy:* Yoshito Sengoku.

Office of the Prime Minister: http://www.kantei.go.jp

CURRENT LEADERS

Yukio Hatoyama

Position
Prime Minister

Introduction
Yukio Hatoyama became prime minister in Sept. 2009, leading the Democratic Party of Japan into government for the first time. A centre-left politician, Hatoyama has moved to strengthen Japan's ties with other Asian countries, while signalling a more independent relationship with the United States. Domestically he favours redirecting public money from large infrastructure projects into tax cuts, pensions and welfare, but may be stymied by a weak economy.

Early Life
Yukio Hatoyama was born on 11 Feb. 1947 in Bunkyo, Tokyo. His grandfather had been prime minister and his father served as foreign minister, while his mother is heir to the founder of the Bridgestone Corporation tyre company. Brought up and educated in Tokyo, Hatoyama graduated from Tokyo University in 1969 with a degree in engineering and continued his studies at Stanford University, USA, where he was awarded a PhD in engineering in 1976. Returning to Japan, he worked at Senshu University, becoming an assistant professor in 1981. In 1983 he left academe to become private secretary to his father, Iichiro Hatoyama, in the House of Representatives.

In 1986 he was elected to the House of Representatives as a member of the ruling Liberal Democratic Party (LDP), representing his father's former seat in Hokkaido. In 1990 he became parliamentary vice minister of the Hokkaido Development Agency. In June 1993 he left the LDP and co-founded New Party Sakigake which, as part of a coalition, defeated the LDP in general elections that year. He served as deputy chief cabinet secretary under Prime Minister Morihiro Hosokawa until the government fell in 1994. In 1996 Hatoyama co-founded the centrist Democratic Party of Japan (DPJ) with his brother Kunio Hatoyama and, two years later, steered the party into a merger with three other opposition parties, becoming deputy secretary general of the enlarged DPJ in April 1998 and its president in 1999.

In 2002, following confusion arising from rumours that he was planning a merger with Ichiro Ozawa's Liberal Party, Hatoyama resigned from the leadership. The merger duly occurred in 2003. The DPJ campaigned for more open and accountable policy-making and advocated redirecting public money to improve welfare. It performed strongly in elections in 2003 and 2004, while Hatoyama served as shadow minister for internal affairs. In Sept. 2004 he became shadow minister for foreign affairs and secretary general of the DPJ. Having worked closely with Ozawa after the latter took over party leadership in 2006, Hatoyama regained the DPJ presidency in May 2009 when Ozawa resigned over financial scandals.

Hatoyama led the DPJ into the 2009 general election on a reformist platform. The party promised to address deepening economic problems by cutting funding for large infrastructure projects and boosting welfare provision. It advocated changing government procedures to shift policy-making powers from the civil service to ministers. It also argued for a more Asia-focused foreign policy and a re-evaluation of the relationship with the USA. In the general election of Aug. 2009 the DPJ decisively defeated the LDP, winning 308 seats to the LDP's 119, bringing to an end half a century of almost unbroken LDP rule.

Career in Office
Hatoyama took office on 16 Sept. 2009. He made early moves to strengthen Japan's relations with its Asian neighbours, initiating a series of visits. In Nov. 2009 he announced plans to boost the economy by developing a market in environmentally-friendly products and renewable power, and targeted 2020 for establishing a free trade zone in Asia. He also began renegotiating with the USA over the future of its military bases on the island of Okinawa. However, economic conditions have hampered his attempts to introduce promised spending reforms. His popularity further suffered from rumours of financial impropriety surrounding his mother's donations to the DPJ. The economy is likely to remain a major challenge, along with the need to reinvigorate Japan's professional sector and address the needs of an ageing population.

DEFENCE

Japan has renounced war as a sovereign right and the threat or the use of force as a means of settling disputes with other nations. Its troops had not previously been able to serve abroad, but in 1992 the House of Representatives voted to allow up to 2,000 troops to take part in UN peacekeeping missions. A law of Nov. 1994 authorizes the Self-Defence Force to send aircraft abroad in rescue operations where Japanese citizens are involved. Following the attacks on New York and Washington of 11 Sept. 2001, legislation was passed allowing Japan's armed forces to take part in operations in the form of logistical support assisting the US-led war on terror. The legislation permits troops to take part in limited overseas operations but not to engage in combat. In May 2003 parliament passed a series of measures in response to North Korea's nuclear programme. Central government won increased control over the military which now has greater freedom to requisition civilian property in the event of attack.

In Jan. 1991 Japan and the USA signed a renewal agreement under which Japan pays 40% of the costs of stationing US forces and 100% of the associated labour costs. US forces in Japan totalled 38,660 in 2006.

Total armed forces in 2006 numbered 260,250.

Defence expenditure in 2008 totalled US$46,296m. (US$361 per capita). In 2007 defence spending represented 0·9% of GDP.

Army

The 'Ground Self-Defence Force' is organized in five regional commands and in 2006 had a strength of 148,200. Equipment includes 980 main battle tanks.

Navy

The 'Maritime Self-Defence Force' is tasked with coastal protection and defence of the sea lanes to 1,000 nautical miles range from Japan. The main elements of the fleet are organized into four escort flotillas based at Yokosuka, Kure, Sasebo, Maizuru and Ominato. The submarines are based at Yokosuka and Kure.

Personnel in 2006 numbered 44,400. The combatant fleet, all home-built, includes 18 diesel submarines, 45 destroyers and nine frigates. The Air Arm operated 80 combat aircraft in 2006. Air Arm personnel was estimated at 9,800 in 2006.

Air Force

An 'Air Self-Defence Force' was inaugurated on 1 July 1954. Its equipment includes (2006) F-15 *Eagles*, F-4E *Phantoms* and Mitsubishi F-1 fighters.

Strength (2006) 45,600 operating 300 combat aircraft.

INTERNATIONAL RELATIONS

Japan is a member of the UN, World Bank, IMF and several other UN specialized agencies, WTO, BIS, IOM, OECD, Inter-American Development Bank, Asian Development Bank, APEC, Colombo Plan and Antarctic Treaty.

In terms of total aid given, Japan was the fifth most generous country in the world in 2007 after the USA, Germany, France and the UK, donating US$7·7bn. in international aid in the course of the year (although down from US$11·2bn. in 2006). However, this represented only 0·17% of its GNI (compared to the UN target of 0·7%).

ECONOMY

In 2007 services accounted for 68·4% of GDP, industry 30·2% and agriculture, forestry and fisheries 1·4%.

According to the anti-corruption organization *Transparency International*, Japan ranked equal 17th in the world in a 2009 survey of the countries with the least corruption in business and government. It received 7·7 out of 10 in the annual index.

Overview

Japan is the world's second largest economy at market exchange rates after the USA and a major donor of global aid, capital and credit. Japan enjoyed its longest economic recovery since the Second World War from 2002–08. Export demand drove expansion with its share of GDP rising from 10·6% to 16·5%. In 2008 the economy fell into recession amid global financial turmoil.

Japan suffered from weak economic performance in the 1990s and early 2000s following on from the monetary policies of the 1980s, problems in the banking sector, weak competition and outdated regulations. Lax monetary policies caused a bubble economy and in its aftermath there was deflation, low wages and declining investment. Output per capita, measured on purchasing power parity terms, fell from 83% of the US level in the early 1990s to less than 75% in 2004. Growth in the five years after 2002 was robust, with exports the initial driving force before momentum shifted to strong domestic demand and private investment.

The IMF attributed the strengthening of the economy to reforms in labour and product markets, success in bank balance sheet restructuring and corporate efforts to eliminate excess capacity and debt. The traditional system of lifetime employment, limiting labour market flexibility, is slowly being replaced by more flexible contracts. Meanwhile, the system of *keiretsu* (closely knit production chains linking manufacturers, suppliers and distributors) is being eroded. Foreign direct investment nearly tripled between 1998–2002, reaching record levels in 2007 despite negative inflows in 2006 (although its level as a percentage of GDP remains the lowest in the OECD).

Labour productivity is more than 30% below that of the USA. In the OECD area Japan has the highest proportion of working age population with at least a secondary school education. R&D expenditure runs at 3% of GDP (the third highest in the OECD) and growth in capital investment is 4·5% (second highest in the OECD). Gross fixed investment was 25% of GDP in 2005, considerably above that of other G7 countries.

The Long-Term Trade Agreement (LTTA) led to Japan becoming China's most important trading partner in the late 1970s, with Japan particularly interested in close ties with a regional oil supplier. Since the adoption of market policies in China, domestic demand for energy has increased rapidly, constraining the export market and causing friction between the two countries. Expanding international ties has been a priority of the Chinese government, leading to Japan's relative decline as a major trading partner. Sensitivity to past Japanese aggressions has mounted since 2004.

Although monetary easing, with short term interest rates of around 0%, failed to end the deflationary period which began in 1999, it succeeded in boosting the monetary base by 60% between 2002–05. The key rate rose to 0·5% in Feb. 2007, an eight-year high, to counter likely inflation sparked by healthy corporate earnings and increasing property prices. However, by Dec. 2008 the Bank of Japan was forced to cut interest rates to 0·1% as it sought to battle the effects of the global financial crisis.

Japanese households retain a high level of net wealth relative to other OECD countries. 85% of the population has savings with Japan Post. With assets of over US$3trn., it is one of the largest financial institutions in the world and the largest life insurer in Japan. Privatization of the postal service, approved in 2005, split it into four separate units for savings, insurance, postal services and personnel and property management.

A fall in bank lending since 1998 has reduced total bank credit by 30% of GDP. Lending continued to drop in 2005 despite increased mortgage loans from banks taking the place of government housing loans. The banking system has been strengthened by tighter regulation introduced in the Program for Financial Revival (PFR). The combination of the PFR and corporate sector improvements halved non-performing loans to below 3% of total loans in major banks in 2005, although the progress of regional banks has been weaker. Despite sectoral improvements, bank profitability remains low by OECD standards, with small profit margins and greater vulnerability to shocks and losses. Nonetheless, the banking system has remained relatively well insulated from the global financial crisis as a result of its low exposure to toxic securities and bad debts. Commercial banks have increased lending to firms as credit has dried up, helped by government guarantees for small and medium-sized businesses.

The economy experienced four consecutive quarters of contraction during 2008 and 2009 owing to a collapse in overseas demand compounded by a strong yen. Difficulties were accentuated by a reliance on manufactured exports, notably cars and consumer technology, for which demand fell particularly quickly. The economy emerged from recession in the second quarter of 2009 on the back of a rebound in exports and fiscal stimulus measures put forward by the government. However, significant problems remain; production is well below capacity, deflation has re-emerged with consumer prices falling since early 2009, and unemployment is likely to persist at a level of around 5·5% until 2011. With interest rates already near zero there is limited scope to use monetary policy to boost the economy. The economy shrank by 5·2% in 2009, although growth is set to pick up in 2010 and 2011 in line with a recovery in the global economy.

In 2004 public debt stood at 166% of GDP, the highest level in the OECD, following a decade of high deficits. Since long-term interest rates are greater than nominal GDP growth, the size of public debt relative to GDP has continued to rise. Government revenue stands at 30% of GDP and is among the lowest in the OECD. The budget deficit peaked at 8% in 2002 and 2003, attributable to a 5% rise in spending and a decline in revenues of 3% owing to weak growth. With tax cuts and persistently slow economic growth in the recent past, the share of tax revenue in GDP is the second lowest in the OECD.

Japan's fiscal position has worsened as a result of the global financial crisis but the return of growth combined with the already high budget deficit and public debt means further fiscal stimulus is unlikely. The IMF and OECD assert that a comprehensive medium-term fiscal consolidation plan will now be required to set the debt ratio on a downward path and should include expenditure cuts and tax reforms, as well as structural reforms to improve living standards in the face of an ageing population.

The ratio of elderly to young people is increasing more rapidly than in other OECD countries. Japan is one of the few OECD countries where the working-age population started declining in the early 2000s. Pension expenditure has doubled from 6% to 12% of national income, putting further pressure on public finances.

Currency

The unit of currency is the *yen* (JPY). Inflation rates (based on OECD statistics):

1999	*2000*	*2001*	*2002*	*2003*	*2004*	*2005*	*2006*	*2007*	*2008*
−0·3%	−0·5%	−0·8%	−0·9%	−0·2%	0·0%	−0·6%	0·2%	0·1%	1·4%

Japan's foreign exchange reserves totalled US$1,002·6bn. in Sept. 2009 (US$203·2bn. in 1998)—second only to those of China. Gold reserves in Sept. 2009 were 24·60m. troy oz. In Dec. 2006 the currency in circulation consisted of 79,837,000m. yen Bank of Japan notes and 4,529,000m. yen subsidiary coins.

Budget

Ordinary revenue and expenditure for fiscal year ending 31 March 2006 balanced at 79,686,000m. yen.

Of the proposed revenue (in yen) in 2006, 45,878,000m. was to come from taxes and stamps, 29,973,000m. from public bonds. Main items of expenditure (in yen): social security, 20,574,000m.; local government, 13,742,000m.; public works, 7,201,000m.; education, 5,267,000m.; defence, 4,814,000m.

The outstanding national debt incurred by public bonds was estimated in March 2006 to be 670,579,000m. yen.

The estimated 2006 budgets of the prefectures and other local authorities forecast a total revenue of 83,151,000m. yen, to be made up partly by local taxes and partly by government grants and local loans.

VAT is 5%.

Performance

Real GDP growth rates (based on OECD statistics):

1999	*2000*	*2001*	*2002*	*2003*	*2004*	*2005*	*2006*	*2007*	*2008*
−0·1%	2·9%	0·2%	0·3%	1·4%	2·7%	1·9%	2·0%	2·3%	−0·7%

GDP growth in 2009 was −5·2% according to the Cabinet Office, the sharpest drop on record. In 2008 Japan's total GDP was US$4,909·3bn., the second highest in the world after the USA (although the USA's economy is nearly three times larger than that of Japan).

Banking and Finance

The Nippon Ginko (Bank of Japan), founded 1882, finances the government and the banks, its function being similar to that of a central bank in other countries. The Bank undertakes the management of Treasury funds and foreign exchange control. Its *Governor* is Masaaki Shirakawa (appointed April 2008 for a five-year term). Its gold bullion and cash holdings at 31 Dec. 2002 stood at 638,000m. yen.

There were in Feb. 2004, six city banks, 64 regional banks, 27 trust banks, two long-term credit banks, 50 member banks of the second association of regional banks, 309 Shinkin banks (credit associations), 185 credit co-operatives, 72 foreign banks and six others. There is also a public corporation Japan Post handling postal savings which amounted to 229,938,100m. yen in Sept. 2003. Total savings by individuals, including insurance and securities, stood at 1,209,453,100m. yen on 30 Sept. 2003, and about 61% of these savings were deposited in banks and the post office. In 1999 a number of important mergers were announced in the banking sector, most notably the proposed merger of the Industrial Bank of Japan, Dai-Ichi Kangyo and Fuji Bank, which in Sept. 2000 created Mizuho Financial Group, at the time the world's biggest bank in terms of assets, at over 135,000bn. yen (US$1·3trn.). The second and fourth biggest banks, the Mitsubishi Tokyo Financial Group and UFJ Holdings, announced in Aug. 2004 that they had reached a basic agreement to merge to create Japan's largest bank. The new bank, named Bank of Tokyo–Mitsubishi UFJ, came into existence in Jan. 2006 with assets of 190,000bn. yen (US$1·6trn.). In Oct. 2007 the newly-created Japan Post Bank became the world's largest bank by assets, at US$3·1trn.

Japan's banks are in a situation where many of them would be insolvent if they admitted the market value of the loans, shares and property they hold. At 31 March 2003 it was estimated that the banking system's bad loans amounted to 21,441bn. yen.

Foreign direct investment rose to US$24·4bn. in 2008 following negative inflows in 2006.

There are five stock exchanges, the largest being in Tokyo.

ENERGY AND NATURAL RESOURCES

Environment

Japan's carbon dioxide emissions from the consumption and flaring of fossil fuels in 2008 accounted for 4·0% of the world total and were equivalent to 9·5 tonnes per capita. An *Environmental Performance Index* compiled in 2008 ranked Japan 21st in the world, with 86·3%. The index examined various factors in six areas—air pollution, biodiversity and habitat, climate change, environmental health, productive natural resources and water resources.

Electricity

Japan is poor in energy resources, and nuclear power generation is important in reducing dependence on foreign supplies. In 2006 Japan had a nuclear generating capacity of 47,700 MW. Total installed generating capacity was 274·5m. kW in 2006. Electricity produced in 2005–06 was 1,157,911m. kWh. In 2006 there were 55 nuclear reactors; in 2002 nuclear reactors produced approximately 39% of electricity. In 2006–07, ten regional publicly-held supply companies produced 70·7% of output. There is one reactor under construction with a further 12 reactors planned. Consumption per capita in 2004 was an estimated 8,459 kWh.

Oil and Gas

Output of crude petroleum, 2005, was 917,725 kilolitres, almost entirely from oilfields on the island of Honshu, but 249·0m. kilolitres of crude oil had to be imported. Output of natural gas, 2005, 3,120m. cu. metres; with reserves of 40bn. cu. metres.

Minerals

Production in tonnes: zinc (2005), 41,452; lead (2005), 3,437; copper (2002), 1,519; iron (2005), 736; silver (2005), 54,098 kg; gold (2005), 8,319 kg. Output of other minerals (2005 unless otherwise indicated, in 1,000 tonnes): limestone, 165,240; quartzite, 12,600; gypsum (2004), 5,865; silica sand, 4,549; dolomite, 3,534; coal (2004), 1,339; salt (2004), 1,225.

Agriculture

The agricultural population was 4·08m. in 2004 (of whom 2·17m. were economically active), compared to 12·98m. in 1980. Land under cultivation in 2004 was 4·7m. ha., down from 6·1m. ha. in 1961. In 2002 Japan had 0·34m. ha. of permanent crops. Average farm size was 1·6 ha. in 2002. In 2002 there were 2,028,000 tractors and 1,042,000 harvester-threshers.

Rice is the staple food, but its consumption is declining. Rice cultivation accounted for 1,706,000 ha. in 2005. Output of rice (in 1,000 tonnes) was 10,748 in 1995, 9,490 in 2000 and 9,074 in 2005.

Production in 2005 (in 1,000 tonnes) of sugar beets was 4,201; potatoes, 2,752; cabbage, 1,364; sugarcane, 1,214; onions, 1,087; wheat, 875; tomatoes, 759; cucumbers, 675; carrots, 615; lettuce, 552; aubergines, 396; spinach, 298; pumpkins and squash, 234;

soybeans, 225; yams, 204. Sweet potatoes, which in the past mitigated the effects of rice famines, have, in view of rice over-production, decreased from 4,955,000 tonnes in 1965 to 1,053,000 tonnes in 2005. Domestic sugar production accounted for only 36·7% of consumption in 2006. 1·31m. tonnes were imported, of which 42·0% from Australia, 39·9% from Thailand and 13·8% from South Africa.

Fruit production, 2005 (in 1,000 tonnes): oranges, 1,207; apples, 819; watermelons, 450; pears, 394; persimmons, 286; grapes, 220.

Livestock (2006): 9·62m. pigs, 4·39m. cattle (including about 1·64m. milch cows), 284m. chickens; and (2003) 34,000 goats, 20,000 horses and 11,000 sheep. Livestock products, 2005 (in 1,000 tonnes): milk, 8,285; meat (2003), 2,991; eggs, 2,481.

Forestry

Forests covered 24·87m. ha. in 2005, or 68·2% of the land area. The forestry industry employed 60,000 people in 2005. Timber production was 17·75m. cu. metres in 2007.

Fisheries

The catch in 2005 was 5,765,000 tonnes, excluding whaling. More than 98% of fish caught are from marine waters. Japan is the leading importer of fishery commodities, with imports in 2003 totalling US$12·40bn.

INDUSTRY

The leading companies by market capitalization in Japan in March 2009 were: the Toyota Motor Corporation (US$108·9bn.); NTT DoCoMo, a mobile telecommunications company (US$59·5bn.); and Nippon Telegraph and Telephone Corporation (US$59·4bn.).

The industrial structure is dominated by corporate groups (*keiretsu*) either linking companies in different branches or linking individual companies with their suppliers and distributors.

Japan's industrial capacity, 2004, numbered 246,603 plants of all sizes, employing 8·11m. production workers.

Output in 2003 included: watches, 523·5m.; personal computers (2007), 8·35m.; television sets, 3·05m.; refrigerators, 2·86m.; radio sets, 1·86m. The chemical industry ranks fourth in shipment value after machinery, metals and food products. Production, 2003, included (in tonnes): sulphuric acid, 6·53m.; caustic soda, 4·37m.; ammonium sulphate (2007), 1·46m.; compound fertilizers (2007), 1·25m. A total of 11,564,000 motor vehicles were manufactured in Japan in 2008, making it the world's largest vehicle producer. It is also the largest producer of passenger cars (9,916,000 in 2008).

Output, in 1,000 tonnes, 2006: crude steel, 116,226; pig iron, 84,270; ordinary rolled steel, 81,314; cement (2004), 67,376.

2004 production (in 1,000 tonnes): distillate fuel oil, 57,059; petrol, 42,647; residual fuel oil, 31,004; kerosene, 22,014.

In 2005 paper production was 18·90m. tonnes; paperboard, 12·05m. tonnes.

Output of woven fabrics, 2007, 1,699m. sq. metres. Output of cotton yarn, 2007, 71,669 tonnes; and of cotton woven fabrics, 368m. sq. metres. Output, 2007, 3,870 tonnes of woollen yarns and 68m. sq. metres of wool fabrics. Output, 2007, of synthetic woven fabrics, 1,096m. sq. metres; rayon woven fabrics, 38·9m. sq. metres; silk fabrics, 14·3m. sq. metres.

3,959m. litres of beer were produced in 2003–04; 13,649m. litres of soft drinks and mineral water in 2003; 800,000 tonnes of sugar in 2006.

Shipbuilding orders in 2005 totalled 8,698,000 GRT. In 2007, 17,240,220 GRT were launched of which 5,284,893 GRT were tankers.

Labour

Total labour force, 2006, was 66·57m., of which 11·61m. were in manufacturing, 11·13m. in wholesale and retail trade, 9·38m. in services, 5·71m. in health and welfare, 5·59m. in construction, 3·37m. in hotels and restaurants, 3·24m. in transport, 2·87m. in education and 2·50m. in agriculture and forestry. Retirement age is being raised progressively from 60 years to reach 65 by 2013. However, in 2002 the average actual retirement age was 69.

In July 2009 unemployment stood at 5·7%, the highest rate on record (up from 3·9% in 2007 and 4·0% in 2008 as a whole). In the second half of 2009 the rate fell gradually to 5·1% in Dec. In 2005, 5,629 working days were lost in industrial stoppages (down from 9,755 in 2004). Between 1996 and 2005 strikes cost Japan an average of just one day per 1,000 employees a year—one of the lowest rates in the industrialized world. In 2006 the average working week was 38·38 hours.

Trade Unions

In 2002 there were 10,801,000 workers organized in 65,642 unions. In Nov. 1989 the 'Japanese Private Sector Trade Union Confederation' (Rengo), which was organized in 1987, was reorganized into the 'Japanese Trade Union Confederation' (Rengo) with the former 'General Council of Japanese Trade Unions' (Sohyo) and other unions, and was the largest federation with 6,595,000 members in 2006. The 'National Confederation of Trade Unions' (Zenroren) had 787,000 members in 2002 and the 'National Trade Union Council' (Zenrokyo) 169,000 members.

INTERNATIONAL TRADE

Imports and Exports

Trade (in US$1m.):

	2003	*2004*	*2005*	*2006*
Imports	414,404	477,603	483,273	565,850
Exports	509,556	593,595	557,169	632,246

In 2004 Japanese imports accounted for 4·8% of the world total imports, and exports 6·2% of the world total exports.

Distribution of trade by countries (customs clearance basis) (US$1m.):

	Imports		*Exports*	
	2005	*2006*	*2005*	*2006*
Australia	22,963	27,291	11,626	12,209
China	101,621	115,818	74,991	90,695
Germany	16,701	18,032	17,464	19,964
Hong Kong	1,468	1,487	33,681	35,618
Korea, Republic of	22,870	26,703	43,669	49,146
Saudi Arabia	26,909	36,340	3,912	4,537
Taiwan	16,921	19,872	40,809	43,113
Thailand	14,579	16,502	21,028	22,392
UAE	23,719	30,854	4,540	5,915
USA	60,030	66,471	125,636	142,286

China has in the meantime overtaken the USA as Japan's leading trading partner. In 2005 machinery and transport equipment accounted for 26·6% of Japan's imports and 65·6% of exports; chemicals, manufactured goods classified chiefly by material and miscellaneous manufactured articles 32·0% of imports and 32·1% of exports; mineral fuels, lubricants and related materials 25·5% of imports and 0·7% of exports; food, live animals, beverages and tobacco 9·8% of imports and 0·5% of exports; inedible crude materials, and animal and vegetable oil and fats 6·1% of imports and 1·1% of exports.

The importation of rice was prohibited until the emergency importation of 1m. tonnes from Australia, China, Thailand and the USA in 1993–94 to offset a poor domestic harvest. The prohibition was lifted in line with WTO agreements. Until 2000 rice imports had limited access; the market is now fully open.

COMMUNICATIONS

Roads

The total length of roads (including urban and other local roads) was 1,185,590 km at 1 April 2005. There were 54,265 km of national roads of which 48,900 km were paved. In 2006, 79·2% of all roads were paved. Motor vehicles, at 31 Dec. 2006, numbered

79,236,000, including 42,229,000 passenger cars and 7,014,000 trucks. In 2007 there were 5,353,648 new vehicle registrations. In 2006 there were 6,352 road deaths (10,679 in 1995).

The world's longest undersea road tunnel, spanning Tokyo Bay, was opened in Dec. 1997. The Tokyo Bay Aqualine, built at a cost of 1·44trn. yen (US$11·3bn.), consists of a 4·4 km (2·7 mile) bridge and a 9·4 km tunnel that allows commuters to cross the bay in about 15 minutes.

Rail

The first railway was completed in 1872, between Tokyo and Yokohama (29 km). Most railways are of 1,067 mm gauge, but the high-speed 'Shinkansen' lines are standard 1,435 mm gauge. In April 1987 the Japanese National Railways was reorganized into seven private companies, the Japanese Railways (JR) Group—six passenger companies and one freight company. Total length of railways in March 2006 was 27,634 km, of which the JR had 20,011 km and other private railways 7,444 km. In 2005 the JR carried 8,683m. passengers (other private, 13,280m.) and 37m. tonnes of freight (other private, 16m.). An undersea tunnel linking Honshu with Hokkaido was opened to rail services in 1988.

There are metros/rapid transit systems in Tokyo (two metro systems, total 316·6 km in 2007; and a rapid transit system of 12·2 km), Fukuoka (29·8 km), Hiroshima (18·4 km), Kobe (38·2 km—a metro of 30·6 km and a rapid transit system of 7·6 km), Kyoto (28·8 km), Nagoya (89·1 km), Osaka (137·8 km), Sapporo (48·0 km), Sendai (14·8 km) and Yokohama (44·5 km—a metro of 40·4 km and a rapid transit system of 4·1 km). There are also tram/light rail networks in 19 cities.

Japan was ranked second only to Switzerland for quality of rail infrastructure in the World Economic Forum's *Global Competitiveness Report 2009–2010*.

Civil Aviation

The main international airports are at Fukuoka, Hiroshima, Kagoshima, Nagoya, Naha, Niigata, Osaka (Kansai International), Sapporo, Sendai and two serving Tokyo—at Narita (New Tokyo International) and Haneda (Tokyo International). The principal airlines are Japan Airlines International (JAL), formed when Japan Airlines and Japan Air System merged in 2001, and All Nippon Airways. In Jan. 2010 JAL filed for bankruptcy protection after making a single-quarter loss of nearly 100bn. yen. The move prompted a restructuring of the company and the expected loss of 15,600 jobs. In the financial year 2005 Japanese companies carried 94·42m. passengers on domestic services and 17·91m. passengers on international services. JAL flew 361·8m. km in 2002 and carried 33,525,752 passengers, All Nippon Airways flew 259·1m. km and carried 43,680,438 passengers, and Japan Air System flew 106·9m. km and carried 21,426,817 passengers.

In 2007 Narita handled 35,478,146 passengers (mainly on international flights) and 2,254,421 tonnes of freight (making it the 7th busiest airport in the world for freight). Tokyo Haneda is mainly used for domestic flights, but handled 66,823,414 passengers in 2007 (making it the 4th busiest airport in the world for overall traffic volume).

Shipping

In 2007 the merchant fleet consisted of 4,622 vessels of 100 GRT and over; total tonnage 11m. GRT; there were 2,096 cargo ships (4,671,000 GRT) and 1,237 tankers (5,420,000 GRT). In 2004 vessels totalling 494,187,000 NRT entered ports. The busiest ports are Chiba (158,929,000 freight tons handled in 2002), Nagoya, Yokohama, Osaka and Kitakyushu.

Coastguard

The 'Japan Coast Guard' consists of one main headquarters, 11 regional headquarters, 66 offices, one maritime guard and rescue office, 53 stations, six info-communication management centres, seven traffic advisory service centres, 14 air stations, one transnational organized crime strike force station, one special security station, one special rescue station, one national strike team station, five district communications centres, four hydrographic observatories, one Loran navigation system centre and 39 aids-to-navigation offices (with 5,604 aids-to-navigation facilities); and controlled 52 large patrol vessels, 44 medium patrol vessels, 23 small patrol vessels, 233 patrol craft, 13 hydrographic service vessels, five large firefighting boats, four medium firefighting boats, 87 special guard and rescue boats, one aids-to-navigation evaluation vessel, four buoy tenders and 50 aids-to-navigation tenders in the financial year 2003. Personnel numbered 12,258. The 'Japan Coast Guard' aviation service includes 29 fixed-wing aircraft and 46 helicopters.

Telecommunications

Telephone services have been operated by private companies (NTT and others) since 1985. In 2008 there were 48,427,000 main (fixed) telephone lines. In the same year mobile phone subscribers numbered 110,395,000 (867·3 per 1,000 persons). There were 69·2m. PCs in use in 2004 (541·5 per 1,000 persons). In 2008 there were an estimated 96·0m. internet users—a figure exceeded only in China and the USA. Approximately 70% of internet users are men. Internet commerce, or e-commerce, amounted to 1·97trn. yen (US$17·07bn.) in 2007. The broadband penetration rate in June 2008 was 23·0 subscribers per 100 inhabitants.

Postal Services

There were 24,631 post offices in 2005, handling a total of 22,666m. items of domestic mail, and foreign items of mail numbering 66m. out of and 203m. into Japan. Privatization of Japan Post was begun in Oct. 2007 under the former government. However, the current government froze the plans in Dec. 2009 pending a re-examination by the minister of state for financial services and postal reform.

SOCIAL INSTITUTIONS

Justice

The Supreme Court is composed of the Chief Justice and 14 other judges. The Chief Justice is appointed by the Emperor, the other judges by the Cabinet. Every ten years a justice must submit himself to the electorate. All justices and judges of the lower courts serve until they are 70 years of age.

Below the Supreme Court are eight regional higher courts, district courts in each prefecture (four in Hokkaido) and the local courts.

The Supreme Court is authorized to declare unconstitutional any act of the Legislature or the Executive which violates the Constitution.

Jury trials were reintroduced in Aug. 2009 for the first time since the Second World War.

In 2005, 3,125,216 penal code offences were reported, including 1,392 homicides. The death penalty is authorized; there were seven executions in 2009 (down from 15 in 2008). The average daily population in penal institutions in 2005 was 79,055 (62 per 100,000 population).

Education

Education is compulsory and free between the ages of six and 15. Almost all national and municipal institutions are co-educational. In May 2006 there were 13,835 kindergartens with 110,807 teachers and 1,727,000 pupils; 22,533 elementary schools with 417,858 teachers and 7,187,000 pupils; 10,921 lower secondary schools with 248,280 teachers and 3,602,000 pupils; 5,272 upper secondary schools with 247,804 teachers and 3,495,000 pupils; 468 junior colleges with 11,278 teachers and 202,000 pupils; and 64 technical colleges with 6,726 teachers and 59,380 pupils. There were also 919 special schools for children with physical disabilities (67,725 teachers, 104,592 pupils).

Japan has seven main state universities: Tokyo University (1877); Kyoto University (1897); Tohoku University, Sendai

(1907); Kyushu University, Fukuoka (1910); Hokkaido University, Sapporo (1918); Osaka University (1931); and Nagoya University (1939). In addition, there are various other state and municipal as well as private universities. There are 744 colleges and universities altogether with (May 2006) 2,859,000 students and 328,238 teaching staff (164,473 full-time).

In 2004 expenditure on education came to 3·7% of GDP and 9·8% of total government spending.

The adult literacy rate is at least 99%.

Health

Hospitals on 1 Oct. 2005 numbered 9,026 with 1,631,473 beds. The hospital bed provision of 128 per 10,000 population was one of the highest in the world. Physicians in 2004 numbered 270,371; dentists, 95,197. In 2006 Japan spent 8·1% of its GDP on health, with public spending accounting for 81·3% of total expenditure on health and private spending 18·7%.

Welfare

There are various types of social security schemes in force, such as health insurance, unemployment insurance and age pensions. The old age pension system in Japan is made up of a two-tiered public benefit. The first tier of the public pension is the basic pension which is payable from age 65 with 25 years' contributions. To receive the full benefit amount, 40 years' contributions to the system are necessary. There is an earnings floor for contributions at approximately 28% of average earnings. The monthly premium of the National Pension is uniformly fixed (13,300 yen in fiscal year 2004). The full basic pension was a flat amount of 804,200 yen per annum in fiscal year 2002, paid in two-monthly instalments. A reduced early pension is available between the ages 60–64, while pensions may also be deferred up to age 69. There were a total of 45·5m. pensioners in 2004.

14 weeks maternity leave is statutory.

Social security expenditure in 2006–07 was 89,109·8bn. yen, including 47,325·3bn. yen on pensions and 28,102·7bn. on medical care. In 2006, 18,166,704 persons and 12,909,835 households received some form of regular public assistance. A proposed reform of the pension system involves the public making higher payments for lower benefits.

RELIGION

State subsidies have ceased for all religions, and all religious teachings are forbidden in public schools. In Dec. 2005 Shintoism claimed 107·25m. adherents, Buddhism 91·26m.; these figures overlap. Christians numbered 2·60m.

CULTURE

World Heritage Sites

Japan has 14 sites on the UNESCO World Heritage List (date of inscription on the list in brackets): the Buddhist Monuments in the Horyu-ji Area (1993); Himeji-jo (1993); Yakushima (1993); Shirakami-Sanchi (1993); the Historic Monuments of Ancient Kyoto (Kyoto, Uji and Otsu Cities) (1994), including 13 of Kyoto's Buddhist temples, three Shinto shrines and one castle—temples include Byōdo-in, Daigo-ji, Enryaku-ji, Ginkaku-ji, Kinkaku-ji, Kiyomizu-dera, Kōzan-ji, Ninna-ji, Nishi Hongan-ji, Ryōan-ji, Saihō-ji, Tenryū-ji and Tō-ji; the Historic Villages of Shirakawa-go and Gokayama (1995); Hiroshima Peace Memorial (Genbaku Dome) (1996); Itsukushima Shinto Shrine (1996); the Historic Monuments of Ancient Nara (1998), including five Buddhist temples—Tōdai-ji, Kōfuku-ji, Gango-ji, Yakushi-ji and Tōshōdai-ji—and three listed shrines—Kasuga Taisha, Kasuga Yama Primeval Forest and the remains of Heijō-kyō Palace; Shrines and Temples of Nikko (1999); Gusuku Sites and Related Properties of the Kingdom of Ryukyu (2000); Sacred sites and pilgrimage routes in the Kii mountain range (2004); marine and land ecosystems at Shiretoko (2005); and the Iwami Ginzan Silver Mine and its cultural landscape (2007).

Broadcasting

Broadcasting is under the aegis of the public Japan Broadcasting Corporation (Nippon Hoso Kyokai—NHK) and the National Association of Commercial Broadcasters. NHK operates two national television networks, two satellite channels and a high-definition TV (HDTV) network. It also runs three national radio stations and an external service, Radio Japan. In 2005 there were 127 commercial television companies operating on terrestrial broadcasting waves. TV Asahi, Fuji TV, Nippon TV and Tokyo Broadcasting System are national terrestrial commercial television networks. Major commercial radio stations include Inter FM, Tokyo FM and TBS radio. There were 37·55m. TV equipped households in 2006 (colour by NTSC) and 24·68m. cable TV subscribers in 2003. In 2007 there were a total of 74,841 facilities providing cable TV broadcasting services.

Cinema

In 2006 cinemas numbered 3,062 with an annual attendance of 164m. (1960: 1,014m.). Of 821 new films shown in 2006, 417 were Japanese.

Press

In 2007 daily newspapers numbered 121 with aggregate circulation of 68·44m. including four major English-language newspapers. The newspapers with the highest circulation are Yomiuri Shimbun (daily average of 10·0m. copies in 2005) and Asahi Shimbun (daily average of 8·1m. copies in 2005). They are also the two most widely read newspapers in the world. Japan has one of the highest circulation rates of daily newspapers in the world, at 633 per 1,000 adult inhabitants in 2005.

In 2005, 78,304 book titles were published.

Tourism

In 2007, 9,152,186 foreigners visited Japan, 2,845,556 of whom came from South Korea, 1,428,873 from Taiwan and 1,140,419 from mainland China. Japanese travelling abroad totalled 17,294,935. Tourism receipts in 2004 totalled US$14·3bn.

Festivals

Japan has a huge number of annual festivals, among the largest of which are the Sapporo Snow Festival (Feb.); Hakata Dontaku, Fukuoka City (May); the Sanja Festival of Asakusa Shrine, Tokyo (May); the Tanabata Festival in Hiratsuka City (July) and Sendai City (Aug.); the Nebuta Festival in Aomori City (Aug.); and Jidai Matsuri, Kyoto (Oct.).

Libraries

In 2005 public libraries numbered 2,979 (including one National Diet Library), holding 340m. books. In addition the 716 university libraries held 187m. Japanese and 93m. foreign books.

Theatre and Opera

In 2003 there were five national theatres: National Theatre (traditional Japanese performances); Nogakudo (Noh Theatre); Bunraku Theatre (Japanese puppet show); New National Theatre (Opera House); and National Theatre Okinawa.

Museums and Galleries

In 2005 there were 1,196 museums. These included 405 historical, 423 fine arts and 156 general museums. There were 117,854,000 visitors in 2004.

DIPLOMATIC REPRESENTATIVES

Of Japan in the United Kingdom (101–104 Piccadilly, London, W1J 7JT)
Ambassador: Shin Ebihara.

Of the United Kingdom in Japan (1 Ichiban-cho, Chiyoda-ku, Tokyo 102-8381)
Ambassador: David Warren.

Of Japan in the USA (2520 Massachusetts Ave., NW, Washington, D.C., 20008)
Ambassador: Ichiro Fujisaki.

Of the USA in Japan (10–5, Akasaka 1-chome, Minato-ku, Tokyo)
Ambassador: John V. Roos.

Of Japan to the United Nations
Ambassador: Yukio Takasu.

Of Japan to the European Union
Ambassador: Nobutake Odano.

FURTHER READING

Statistics Bureau of the Prime Minister's Office (up to 2000) and Statistics Bureau of the Ministry of Internal Affairs and Communications (from 2001): *Statistical Yearbook* (from 1949).—*Statistical Handbook* (from 1958).—*Monthly Statistics of Japan* (from 1947–2006; online only since 2006 as *Japan Monthly Statistics*).—*Historical Statistics* (from 1868–2002)

Economic Planning Agency (up to 2000) and Economic and Social Research Institute (from 2001) of the Cabinet Office: *Economic Survey* (annual), *Economic Statistics* (monthly), *Economic Indicators* (monthly)

Ministry of International Trade and Industry (up to 2000) and the Ministry of Economy, Trade and Industry (from 2001): *Foreign Trade of Japan* (annual)

Allinson, G. D., *Japan's Postwar History.* 1997

Argy, V. and Stein, L., *The Japanese Economy.* 1996

Bailey, P. J., *Post-war Japan: 1945 to the Present.* 1996

Beasley, W. G., *The Rise of Modern Japan: Political, Economic and Social Change Since 1850.* 2nd ed. 1995

Buruma, Ian, *Inventing Japan: 1853–1964.* 2003

The Cambridge Encyclopedia of Japan. 1993

Cambridge History of Japan. Vols. 1–5. 1990–93

Campbell, A. (ed.) *Japan: an Illustrated Encyclopedia.* 1994

Clesse, A., *et al.*, (eds.) *The Vitality of Japan: Sources of National Strength and Weakness.* 1997

Gordon, A., *Postwar Japan as History.* 1993

Henshall, K. G., *A History of Japan: From Stone Age to Superpower.* 2nd ed. 2004

Ito, T., *The Japanese Economy.* 1992

Jain, P. and Inoguchi, T., *Japanese Politics Today.* 1997

Japan: an Illustrated Encyclopedia. 1993

Johnson, C., *Japan: Who Governs? The Rise of the Developmental State.* 1995

McCargo, Duncan, *Contemporary Japan.* 2nd ed. 2004

McClain, James, *Japan: A Modern History.* 2001

Morton, W. Scott and Olenik, J. Kenneth, *Japan: Its History and Culture.* 2004

Nakano, M., *The Policy-making Process in Contemporary Japan.* 1996

Okabe, M. (ed.) *The Structure of the Japanese Economy: Changes on the Domestic and International Fronts.* 1994

Perren, R., *Japanese Studies From Pre-History to 1990.* 1992

Schirokauer, C., *Brief History of Japanese Civilization.* 1993

Stockwin, J., *Dictionary of the Modern Politics of Japan.* 2003

Takao, Yasuo, *Reinventing Japan: From Merchant Nation to Civic Nation.* 2008

Woronoff, J., *The Japanese Economic Crisis.* 2nd ed. 1996

Yoda, Tomiko, *Japan After Japan: Social and Cultural Life from the Recessionary 1990s to the Present.* 2006

National library: The National Diet Library, 1-10-1 Nagata-cho, Chiyoda-ku, Tokyo 100-8924.

National Statistical Office: Statistics Bureau, Ministry of Internal Affairs and Communications, 19-1 Wakamatsu-cho, Shinjuku-ku, Tokyo 162-8668.

Website: http://www.stat.go.jp

JORDAN

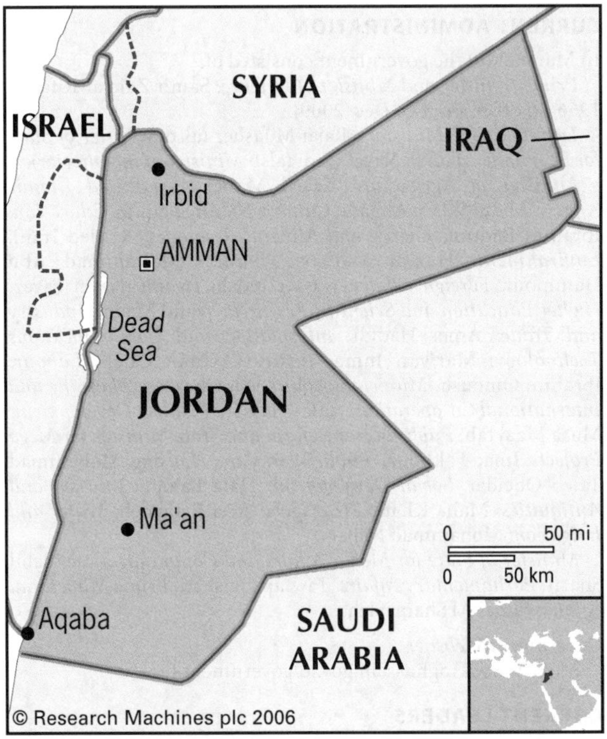

Al-Mamlaka Al-Urduniya Al-Hashemiyah (Hashemite[1] Kingdom of Jordan)

Capital: Amman
Population estimate, 2010: 6·47m.
GDP per capita, 2007: (PPP$) 4,901
HDI/world rank: 0·770/96

KEY HISTORICAL EVENTS

Egyptian control was established over Semitic Amorite tribes in the Jordan valley in the 16th century BC. However, Egypt's conflict with the Hittite Empire allowed the development of autonomous kingdoms such as Edom, Moab, Gilead and Ammon (centred on modern Amman). The Israelites settled on the east bank of the Jordan in the 13th century and crossed into Canaan. David subjugated Moab, Edom and Ammon in the 10th century but the Assyrians wrested control in the 9th century, remaining until 612 BC. Nabataea expanded in the south during the Babylonian and Persian periods until conquered for Rome by Pompey in the 1st century BC. After Trajan's campaign of AD 106, the Jordan area was absorbed as Arabia Petraea.

Rome (later Byzantium) and Sassanid Persia clashed over the area but a Muslim army under Khalid ibn al-Walid defeated Byzantium in 636 at the Yarmuk River. After the fall of the Umayyad Caliphate in 750, the centre of power moved from Damascus to Baghdad and Jordan was neglected. The principality of Oultre Jourdain, established by the Christian crusader kingdom of Jerusalem in the early 12th century, was destroyed by Saladin in 1187. The Mamluk Empire held power until the advent of the Turkish Ottoman Empire in the 16th century.

The Arabs of the Ottoman Damascus province rebelled with British support in 1916. The Hashemite Prince Faisal ibn Husayn took Aqaba in 1917 and the British took Amman and Damascus in 1918. The First World War victors decreed two mandates—British Palestine and French Syria. Britain created the Transjordan Emirate in 1922, ruled semi-autonomously by Faisal's brother, Abdullah. Full independence was achieved on 25 May 1946 as the Hashemite Kingdom of Transjordan (Jordan from 1949).

Transjordan declared war on the Israeli state in May 1948, taking the West Bank and East Jerusalem, an occupation supported only by Britain. Palestinian resistance to the annexation culminated in King Abdullah's assassination in 1951. Talal, his son and successor, was deemed mentally unfit in 1952 and Hussein Bin Talal was installed in 1953. After an attempted coup in 1957, instigated by West Bank Palestinians, King Hussein banned political parties and ended Palestinian representation. A brief union with Iraq, ruled by his cousin, ended after an Iraqi republican coup in 1958. Hussein turned to Britain and the USA for military and financial support.

Fatah and the Palestine Liberation Organization (PLO) maintained terrorist attacks on Israel from Jordan, provoking Israeli retaliation in the West Bank. Despite secret co-operation with Israel over containing the Palestinians, Hussein allied with Syria and Egypt in the war of June 1967. Israel repelled Jordanian forces from the West Bank, moving the *de facto* border to the River Jordan. This devastated the Jordanian economy but removed Palestinian opposition to the Hashemite regime. However, Jordan's relations with the Palestinians deteriorated; in Sept. 1970 four airliners were destroyed by Palestinian extremists in the Jordanian desert. Jordan, with US and British assistance, repelled a Syrian invasion and evicted the PLO. Relations with Israel also worsened from 1977 with the Jewish settlement programme in the West Bank.

On 31 July 1988 Hussein dissolved Jordan's legal and administrative ties with the West Bank in reaction to the *intifada*, which he saw as a threat to his regime. Elections in 1989 led the way to the suspension of martial law—in place from 1967–91. Hussein, constrained by Jordan's economic and political ties with Iraq, refused to abandon Saddam Hussein in the 1991 Gulf War, creating a rift with Jordan's Western partners. Multi-party elections were held in 1993, giving Hussein parliamentary support. He signed a peace treaty with Israel in 1994. In Jan. 1999 Hussein replaced as crown prince his brother, Hassan, with his son, Abdullah, who succeeded on his father's death a month later.

TERRITORY AND POPULATION

Jordan is bounded in the north by Syria, east by Iraq, southeast and south by Saudi Arabia and west by Israel. It has an outlet to an arm of the Red Sea at Aqaba. Its area is 89,342 sq. km. The 2004 census population was 5,103,639; density 57·1 per sq. km. The United Nations population estimate for 2004 was 5,400,000.

The UN gives an estimated population for 2010 of 6·47m.

In 2005, 82·3% of the population lived in urban areas. Populations of the 12 governorates:

Governorate	*Census 2004*	*Governorate*	*Census 2004*
Ajloun	118,725	Aqaba	102,097
Amman	1,942,066	Balqa	346,354

[1]'Hashemite' denotes a descendant of the prophet Mohammed.

Governorate	Census 2004	Governorate	Census 2004
Irbid	928,292	Madaba	129,960
Jerash	153,602	Mafraq	244,188
Karak	204,185	Tafilah	75,267
Ma'an	94,253	Zarqa	764,650

The largest towns, with 2004 census population, are: Amman, the capital, 1,036,330; Zarqa, 395,227; Irbid, 250,645.

Jordan's population includes an estimated 2·8m. Palestinian refugees. About 750,000 Iraqi refugees have entered Jordan since the start of the war in 2003.

The official language is Arabic.

SOCIAL STATISTICS

Births, 2003, 148,294; deaths, 16,937. Rates, 2003 per 1,000 population: birth, 27·1; death, 3·1. Annual population growth rate, 2000–05, 2·4%. Life expectancy at birth in 2007; 70·7 years for men, 74·3 for women. Infant mortality, 2005, 22 per 1,000 live births; fertility rate, 2004, 3·4 births per woman.

CLIMATE

Predominantly a Mediterranean climate, with hot dry summers and cool wet winters, but in hilly parts summers are cooler and winters colder. Those areas below sea-level are very hot in summer and warm in winter. Eastern parts have a desert climate. Amman, Jan. 46°F (7·5°C), July 77°F (24·9°C). Annual rainfall 13·4" (340·6 mm). Aqaba, Jan. 61°F (16°C), July 89°F (31·5°C). Annual rainfall 1·4" (36·7 mm).

CONSTITUTION AND GOVERNMENT

The Kingdom is a constitutional monarchy headed by H. M. King **Abdullah Bin Al Hussein** II, born 30 Jan. 1962, married H. M. Queen Rania (Rania Al-Yassin, b. 31 Aug. 1970) on 10 June 1993. He succeeded on the death of his father, H. M. King Hussein, on 7 Feb. 1999. *Sons:* Hussein, b. 28 June 1994; Hashem, b. 30 Jan. 2005; *daughters:* Iman, b. 27 Sept. 1996; Salma, b. 26 Sept. 2000.

The Constitution ratified on 8 Dec. 1952 provides that the Cabinet is responsible to Parliament. It was amended in 1974, 1976 and 1984. The legislature consists of a *Senate* of 55 members appointed by the King and a *Chamber of Deputies* of 110 members (six are reserved for women elected by an electoral college) elected by universal suffrage. Nine seats are reserved for Christians, and three for Circassians or Chechens. A law of 1993 restricts each elector to a single vote.

The lower house was dissolved in 1976 and elections postponed because no elections could be held in the West Bank under Israeli occupation. Parliament was reconvened on 9 Jan. 1984. By-elections were held in March 1984 and six members were nominated for the West Bank, bringing Parliament to 60 members. Women voted for the first time in 1984. On 9 June 1991 the King and the main political movements endorsed a national charter which legalized political parties in return for the acceptance of the constitution and monarchy. Movements linked to, or financed by, non-Jordanian bodies are not allowed.

National Anthem

'Asha al Malik' ('Long Live the King'); words by A. Al Rifai, tune by A. Al Tanir.

GOVERNMENT CHRONOLOGY

Kings since 1946.

1946–51	Abdullah Bin Al Hussein Al Hashimi I
1951–52	Talal Bin Abdullah Al Hashimi
1953–99	Hussein Bin Talal Al Hashimi
1999–	Abdullah Bin Al Hussein Al Hashimi II

RECENT ELECTIONS

Elections to the Chamber of Deputies were held on 20 Nov. 2007. 104 of the 110 seats were won by independents loyal to the king. The Islamic Action Front won six seats. Turnout was 54%.

CURRENT ADMINISTRATION

In March 2010 the government consisted of:

Prime Minister and Minister of Defence: Samir Zaid al-Rifai; b. 1966 (in office since 14 Dec. 2009).

Deputy Prime Ministers: Rajai Muasher (also *Minister of State for Economic Affairs*); Nayef Qadi (also *Minister of the Interior*).

Minister of Agriculture: Saeed Masri. *Awqaf and Islamic Affairs:* Abdul Salam Abbadi. *Culture:* Nabih Shoqum. *Education:* Ibrahim Badran. *Energy and Mineral Resources:* Khaled Irani. *Environment:* Hazim Malhas. *Finance:* Mohammad Abu Hammour. *Foreign Affairs:* Nasser Judeh. *Health:* Nayef Fayez. *Higher Education and Scientific Research:* Walid Maani. *Industry and Trade:* Amer Hadidi. *Information and Communications Technology:* Marwan Juma. *Justice:* Ayman Odeh. *Labour:* Ibrahim Omoush. *Municipal Affairs:* Ali Ghazawi. *Planning and International Co-operation:* Jaafar Hassan. *Political Development:* Musa Maaytah. *Public Sector Reform and State Minister for Mega Projects:* Imad Fakhouri. *Public Works and Housing:* Mohammad Taleb Obeidat. *Social Development:* Hala Latouf. *Tourism and Antiquities:* Maha Khatib. *Transport:* Aref Batayneh. *Water and Irrigation:* Mohammad Najjar.

Minister of State for Media Affairs and Communication: Nabil Sharif. *Parliamentary Affairs:* Tawfiq Kreishan. *Prime Ministerial Affairs:* Jamal Al Shamayleh.

Government Website:
http://www.kinghussein.gov.jo/government.html

CURRENT LEADERS

Abdullah Bin Al Hussein II

Position
King

Introduction
Abdullah came to the throne of the Hashemite Kingdom in Feb. 1999 on the death of his father, Hussein Bin Talal. He had been declared Crown Prince and heir by his father the previous month, replacing his uncle, Prince Hassan, who had served in that capacity since 1965. Abdullah has maintained the moderate policies of his late father. He has aimed to reconcile the domestically unpopular 1994 peace agreement with Israel and friendly relations with the USA with the need to appease Jordan's more militant Arab neighbours and its own large Palestinian population.

Early Life
Born in Amman on 30 Jan. 1962, Abdullah was educated at St Edmund's School in Surrey, England, then Eaglebrook School in Massachusetts and Deerfield Academy in the USA. With his uncle holding office as Crown Prince, Abdullah focused on the military, enrolling in the Royal Military Academy Sandhurst, England in 1980. Having then attended Oxford University and Georgetown University in Washington, D.C., for studies in international relations, he moved up through the ranks of Jordan's armed forces to become Major-Gen. in May 1998.

Career in Office
Abdullah became Crown Prince on 25 Jan. 1999 after King Hussein had rescinded the 1965 constitutional amendment in favour of his younger brother Hassan. Two weeks later, on 7 Feb. 1999, Hussein died and Abdullah assumed the throne. Consistent with the policy of his father, Abdullah has deterred Islamic militancy (particularly the activities of the radical Palestinian Hamas group), while extending economic liberalization. He

revived the privatization programme, oversaw Jordan's admission to the World Trade Organization and concluded a free trade accord with the USA.

Abdullah has supported the wider Arab-Israeli peace process and maintains a close affinity with the USA. He also backs Palestinian statehood in the West Bank, a policy that takes account of Jordan's large Palestinian population. He made early overtures towards Jordan's moderate Arab neighbours, visiting Egypt, Saudi Arabia, Oman and the United Arab Emirates in the first few months of his reign, and also tried to forge closer relations with Syria, a traditional antagonist. Relations with Iran have wavered since Abdullah's accession. In 2003 Abdullah backed the US intervention in Iraq, a decision not wholly popular with Jordanian citizens. The subsequent insurgency in Iraq spilled over into Jordan in Nov. 2005 when nearly 70 people were killed in the capital, Amman, in co-ordinated suicide bomb attacks apparently perpetrated by an Iraqi wing of the al-Qaeda terrorist network. Nevertheless, in Aug. 2008 Abdullah became the first leader of an Arab state to visit Iraq since the 2003 US invasion in a move signifying a rapprochement across the confessional Sunni-Shia divide and also growing international confidence in the Iraqi government.

Although Abdullah retains the power to rule by decree, there is an elected Chamber of Deputies to which a large majority of non-partisan candidates loyal to the King were returned in polling in Nov. 2007. Abdullah subsequently appointed Nader Dahabi as the new prime minister, replacing Marouf al-Bakhit who had been in office since Nov. 2005. In Nov. 2009 the King unexpectedly dissolved the Chamber only halfway through its four-year term and called for early elections. No official reason was given, but the assembly had reportedly been accused of inaction and inept handling of legislation.

DEFENCE

Defence expenditure in 2006 totalled US$1,115m. (US$189 per capita), representing 7·9% of GDP.

Army

Total strength (2007) 88,000. In addition there were 60,000 army reservists, a paramilitary Public Security Directorate of approximately 10,000 and a civil militia 'People's Army' of approximately 35,000.

Navy

The Royal Naval Force numbered an estimated 500 in 2007 and operates 13 patrol and coastal combatants, all based at Aqaba.

Air Force

Strength (2007) 12,000 personnel, 100 combat capable aircraft (including F-5Es, F-16As and Mirage F1s) and some 20 attack helicopters.

INTERNATIONAL RELATIONS

A 46-year-old formal state of hostilities with Israel was brought to an end by a peace agreement on 26 Oct. 1994.

Jordan is a member of the UN, World Bank, IMF and several other UN specialized agencies, WTO, IOM, Islamic Development Bank, OIC and League of Arab States.

ECONOMY

Services accounted for 67·4% of GDP in 2006, industry 29·5% and agriculture 3·1%.

Overview

Classified by the World Bank as a small, lower middle-income country, Jordan lacks a sufficient supply of water and, unlike many of its neighbours, has limited energy supplies. Jordan imported most of its oil from Iraq prior to 2003 but in recent years has depended more on other Gulf countries. Aside from potash and phosphate there are few natural resources. Development relies on human capital, as well as remittances from abroad and one of the world's highest levels of unilateral financial transfers.

The country compares favourably to other middle-income economies in human development indicators, particularly in education and female access to public services. It also has a strong record of recent reform. Authorities have focused on opening up the economy to the private sector and foreign trade and much work has been done to build modern regulatory institutions. Since 2004 the economy has grown 6–7% per year on average, the sizable foreign debt has been reduced and the current account balance has narrowed. Exports have grown significantly since the signing of a free trade accord with the USA in 2000 and the development of Jordanian Qualifying Industrial Zones, where exports are allowed duty free to the USA.

The country is highly urbanized, with about 80% of the population living in cities, and has one of the youngest populations among middle-income countries. Challenges include generating the employment growth to meet the needs of a growing working-age population, reducing debt and current account deficits, dealing with rising energy costs and coping with the investment impact of volatility in the region. The economy is also vulnerable to a decline in foreign grants.

Currency

The unit of currency is the *Jordan dinar* (JOD), usually written as JD, of 1,000 *fils*, pegged to the US dollar since 1995 at a rate of one dinar = US$1·41. Inflation was 5·4% in 2007, rising to 14·9% in 2008. Foreign exchange controls were abolished in July 1997. Foreign exchange reserves were US$5,601m. and gold reserves 411,000 troy oz in July 2005. Total money supply in May 2005 was JD 3,487m.

Budget

Revenue and expenditure over a six-year period (in JD 1m.):

	1998	*1999*	*2000*	*2001*	*2002*	*2003*
Revenue	1,574·9	1,732·1	1,815·9	1,968·0	2,020·8	2,381·2
Expenditure	2,087·7	2,039·5	2,054·1	2,192·3	2,296·7	2,542·6

There is a sales tax of 16%.

Performance

Total GDP was US$20·0bn. in 2008. Real GDP growth in 2008 was 7·9% (8·9% in 2007).

Banking and Finance

The Central Bank of Jordan was established in 1964 (*Governor*, Dr Umayya Toukan). In 2002 there were nine national banks, seven foreign banks and 11 specialized credit institutions. Assets and liabilities of the banking system (including the Central Bank, commercial banks, the Housing Bank and investment banks) totalled JD 8,430·4m. in 1995.

There is a stock exchange in Amman (Amman Financial Market).

Weights and Measures

The metric system is in force. Land area is measured in *dunums* (1 dunum = 0·1 ha.).

ENERGY AND NATURAL RESOURCES

Environment

Carbon dioxide emissions in 2008 were the equivalent of 3·6 tonnes per capita.

Electricity

Installed capacity was 2·1m. kW in 2004. Production (2004) 8·97bn. kWh; consumption per capita was 1,738 kWh.

Oil and Gas

Natural gas reserves in 2007 totalled 6bn. cu. metres, with production (2004) 267m. cu. metres.

Water
99% of the total population and 100% of the urban population has access to safe drinking water.

Minerals
Phosphate ore production in 2003 was 6·47m. tonnes; potash, 1·96m. tonnes.

Agriculture
The country east of the Hejaz Railway line is largely desert; northwestern Jordan is potentially of agricultural value and an integrated Jordan Valley project began in 1973. In 2007 there were 81,090 ha. of irrigated land. The agricultural cropping pattern for irrigated vegetable cultivation was introduced in 1984 to regulate production and diversify the crops being cultivated. In 1986 the government began to lease state-owned land in the semi-arid southern regions for agricultural development by private investors, mostly for wheat and barley. In 2007 there were 142,958 ha. of arable land and 99,484 ha. of permanent crops. There were 5,357 tractors in 2007 and 76 harvester-threshers.

Production in 2007 (in 1,000 tonnes): tomatoes, 617; cucumbers and gherkins, 154; olives, 125; watermelons, 116; potatoes, 97; pumpkins and squash, 55; cauliflowers, 44; cabbage, 36; bananas, 34; apples, 32; lemons and limes, 22.

Livestock (2007): 2·5m. sheep; 559,600 goats; 88,200 cattle; 9,600 asses; 8,000 camels; 36m. chickens. Total meat production was 154,300 tonnes in 2007; milk, 344,980 tonnes.

Forestry
Forests covered 83,000 ha. in 2005, or 0·9% of the land area. In 2007, 281,000 cu. metres of roundwood were cut.

Fisheries
Fish landings in 2005 totalled 510 tonnes, mainly from inland waters.

INDUSTRY
The largest company by market capitalization in Jordan in Feb. 2009 was Arab Bank (US$9·0bn.).

The number of industrial establishments in 2006 was 20,214, employing 174,368 persons. The principal industrial concerns are the production or processing of phosphates, potash, fertilizers, cement and oil.

Production in 1,000 tonnes (2007 unless otherwise indicated): cement, 4,051; residual fuel oil (2004), 1,402; distillate fuel oil (2004), 1,187; fertilizers, 831; phosphoric acid, 480.

Labour
The workforce in 2004 was 2,000,900. In 2002, 692,070 persons worked in social and public administration, 150,922 in commerce, 122,741 in mining and manufacturing, and 31,095 in transport and communications. In 2003 approximately 10% of the total labour force worked in agriculture. Unemployment was officially 12% in Oct. 2000 but was estimated by economists to be more than 20%. In 2000 Jordan had more than 600,000 foreign workers, many of them Iraqis.

INTERNATIONAL TRADE
Foreign debt was US$7,696m. in 2005. Legislation of 1995 eases restrictions on foreign investment and makes some reductions in taxes and customs duties.

Imports and Exports
Imports (f.o.b.) in 2006 totalled US$10,260·2m. and exports (f.o.b.) US$5,204·4m. Major exports are phosphate, potash, fertilizers, foodstuffs, pharmaceuticals, clothes, cement, fruit and vegetables, textiles and plastics.

Principal imports in 2004 were from: Saudi Arabia, 19·9%; China, 8·4%; Germany, 6·8%; and USA, 6·7%. Main exports in 2004 were to: USA, 26·2%; Iraq, 18·8%; Free zones, 7·6%; and India, 6·5%. In 2000 Jordan became the first Arab country to sign a free trade agreement with the USA.

COMMUNICATIONS

Roads
Total length of roads, 2007, 7,768 km, of which 3,206 km were main roads. In 2007 there were 536,700 passenger cars (94 per 1,000 inhabitants), 2,800 motorcycles and mopeds, 17,200 coaches and buses, and 230,800 lorries and vans. There were 992 deaths in road accidents in 2007 (388 in 1992).

Rail
The 1,050 mm gauge Hejaz Jordan and Aqaba Railway runs from the Syrian border at Nassib to Ma'an and Naqb Ishtar and Aqaba Port (total, 504 km). Passenger-km travelled in 2004 came to 0·9m. Freight tonne-km travelled amounted to 521m. on the Aqaba Railway in 2005 and 2m. on the Hejaz Railway in 2004.

Civil Aviation
The Queen Alia International airport is at Zizya, 30 km south of Amman. There are also international flights from Amman's second airport. Queen Alia International handled 2,231,806 passengers in 2001 (2,209,168 on international flights) and 87,679 tonnes of freight. The national carrier, Royal Jordanian, sold 71% of its shares in Dec. 2007; shares sold to non-Jordanian investors are not to exceed 49%. In 2003 scheduled airline traffic of Jordanian-based carriers flew 36m. km, carrying 1,353,000 passengers (all on international flights).

Shipping
In 2002 sea-going shipping totalled 69,000 GRT. Vessels totalling 2,789,000 NRT entered ports in 2002. The main port is Aqaba.

Telecommunications
There were 2,211,900 telephone subscribers in 2004, or 394·1 per 1,000 persons, of which 1,624,100 were mobile phone subscribers. In 2000 the government sold a 40% stake in Jordan Telecommunications Company (Jordan Telecom) to France Télécom. In 2006 France Télécom became the majority shareholder when it purchased a further 11% of Jordan Telecom from the government. Jordan Telecom's monopoly on fixed-line services ended on 1 Jan. 2005. There were 300,000 PCs (53·4 for every 1,000 persons) in 2004 and 629,500 internet users.

Postal Services
In 2003 there were 393 post offices.

SOCIAL INSTITUTIONS

Justice
The legal system is based on Islamic law (Sharia) and civil law, and administers justice in cases of civil, criminal or administrative disputes. The constitution guarantees the independence of the judiciary. Courts are divided into three tiers: regular courts (courts of first instance, magistrate courts, courts of appeal, Court of Cassation/High Court of Justice); religious courts (Sharia courts and Council of Religious Communities); special courts (e.g. police court, military councils, customs court, state security court).

The death penalty is authorized, and was last used in 2006. The murder rate in 2007 stood at 1·7 per 100,000 population. The population in penal institutions in April 2008 was approximately 7,500 (123 per 100,000 of national population).

Education
Adult literacy in 2007 was 91·1% (male, 95·7%; female, 88·4%). Basic primary and secondary education is free and compulsory. In 2006–07 there were 1,267 kindergartens (1,259 private) with 4,834 teachers and 93,236 pupils; 2,996 basic schools (706 private) with 66,075 teachers and 1,294,075 pupils; 1,268 secondary schools (160 private) with 17,771 teachers and 184,663 pupils; and

27 vocational schools with 3,581 teachers and 31,432 pupils. In 2006–07 there were ten state and 15 private universities. 16,753 Jordanians were studying abroad in 2007.

In 1999–2000 total expenditure on education came to 5·0% of GNP and 20·6% of total government spending.

Health
There were 10,623 physicians, 14,251 nurses and midwives, 2,850 dentists and 4,975 pharmacists in 2001. In 2007 there were a total of 11,029 hospital beds in 103 hospitals.

Welfare
There are numerous government organizations involved in social welfare projects. The General Union of Voluntary Societies finances and supports the Governorate Unions, voluntary societies, and needy individuals through financial and in-kind aid. There are also 240 day care centres run by non-governmental organizations.

RELIGION
About 94% of the population are Sunni Muslims.

CULTURE
World Heritage Sites
There are three sites on the World Heritage List: the rose-red rock-carved city of Petra and Quseir Amra (both entered on the list in 1985) and Um er-Rasas (2004). Petra is over 2,000 years old and contains more than 800 monuments, some built but most carved out of the natural rock. Quseir Amra is the best preserved of Jordan's 'desert castles' and is noted for its frescoes. Um er-Rasas (Kastron Mefa'a) is an archaeological site largely unexcavated, containing remains from the Roman, Byzantine and Early Muslim periods.

Broadcasting
The Jordan Radio and Television Corporation transmits two national radio services (one in English), a Koran service and an external service, Radio Jordan. There are two television services (colour by PAL). There were 1·21m. TV sets in use in 2006.

Press
In 2006 there were seven daily newspapers with a combined circulation of 120,000. Newspapers were denationalized in 1990, although government institutions still hold majority ownership. In 2002 a total of 791 book titles were published.

Tourism
Tourism accounts for 8·5% of GDP. In 2005 there were 2,987,000 non-resident tourists; spending by tourists totalled US$1,759m.

DIPLOMATIC REPRESENTATIVES
Of Jordan in the United Kingdom (6 Upper Phillimore Gdns, Kensington, London, W8 7HA)
Ambassador: Dr Alia Bouran.

Of the United Kingdom in Jordan (PO Box 87, Abdoun, Amman 11118)
Ambassador: James Watt, CVO.

Of Jordan in the USA (3504 International Dr., NW, Washington, D.C., 20008)
Ambassador: Prince Zeid Raad Al-Hussein.

Of the USA in Jordan (Al-Omawyeen, Abdoun, Amman 11118)
Ambassador: R. Stephen Beecroft.

Of Jordan to the United Nations
Ambassador: Mohammed F. Al-Allaf.

Of Jordan to the European Union
Ambassador: Ahmad K. Masa'deh.

FURTHER READING
Department of Statistics. *Statistical Yearbook*
Central Bank of Jordan. *Monthly Statistical Bulletin*

Dallas, R., *King Hussein, The Great Survivor.* 1998
George, Alan, *Jordan: Living in the Crossfire.* 2006
Lucas, Russell E., *Institutions and the Politics of Survival in Jordan: Domestic Responses to External Challenges, 1988–2001.* 2006
Rogan, E. and Tell, T. (eds.) *Village, Steppe and State: the Social Origins of Modern Jordan.* 1994
Salibi, Kamal, *The Modern History of Jordan.* 1998
Satloff, R. B., *From Abdullah to Hussein: Jordan in Transition.* 1994
Wilson, M. C., *King Abdullah, Britain and the Making of Jordan.* 1987

National Statistical Office: Department of Statistics, P. O. Box 2015, Amman.
Website: http://www.dos.gov.jo

KAZAKHSTAN

Qazaqstan Respūblīkasy
(Republic of Kazakhstan)

Capital: Astana
Population estimate, 2010: 15·75m.
GDP per capita, 2007: (PPP$) 10,863
HDI/world rank: 0·804/82

KEY HISTORICAL EVENTS

Turkestan (part of the territory now known as Kazakhstan) was conquered by the Russians in the 1860s. In 1866 Tashkent was occupied, followed in 1868 by Samarkand. Subsequently further territory was conquered and united with Russian Turkestan. In the 1870s Bokhara was subjugated, with the amir, by an agreement of 1873, recognizing Russian suzerainty. In the same year Khiva became a vassal state to Russia. Until 1917 Russian Central Asia was divided politically into the Khanate of Khiva, the Emirate of Bokhara and the Governor-Generalship of Turkestan. In the summer of 1919 the authority of the Soviet Government extended to these regions. The Khan of Khiva was deposed in Feb. 1920, and a People's Soviet Republic was set up, the medieval name of Khorezm being revived. In Aug. 1920 the Amir of Bokhara suffered the same fate and a similar regime was set up in Bokhara. The former Governor-Generalship of Turkestan was constituted an Autonomous Soviet Socialist Republic within the RSFSR on 11 April 1921.

In the autumn of 1924 the Soviets of the Turkestan, Bokhara and Khiva Republics decided to redistribute their territories on a nationality basis; at the same time Bokhara and Khiva became Socialist Republics. The redistribution was completed in May 1925, when the new states of Uzbekistan, Turkmenistan and Tajikistan were accepted into the USSR as Union Republics. The remaining districts of Turkestan populated by Kazakhs were united with Kazakhstan which was established as an Autonomous Soviet Republic in 1925 and became a constituent republic in 1936. Independence was declared on 16 Dec. 1991 when Kazakhstan joined the CIS. Nursultan Nazarbaev became president, and legislation has been introduced to award him privileges for life. Over a million of the country's ethnic Russians and Germans have returned to their homelands in the last ten years. Kazakhstan has been focusing on border disputes with China and Uzbekistan and fighting fundamentalism along with other Central Asian governments.

TERRITORY AND POPULATION

Kazakhstan is bounded in the west by the Caspian Sea and Russia, in the north by Russia, in the east by China and in the south by Uzbekistan, Kyrgyzstan and Turkmenistan. The area is 2,724,900 sq. km (1,052,090 sq. miles). The 1999 census population was 14,953,126 (density of 5·5 per sq. km), of whom Kazakhs accounted for 53·4% and Russians 30·0%. There are also Ukrainians, Uzbeks, Germans, Tatars, Uigurs and smaller minorities. In 1999 the population was 51·8% female; it was 57·3% urban in 2005. During the 1990s some 1·5m. people left Kazakhstan—mostly Russians and Germans returning to their homelands. Approximately 10·8m. Kazakhs live abroad.

The UN gives an estimated population for 2010 of 15·75m.; density, 6 per sq. km.

Kazakhstan's administrative divisions consist of 14 provinces and three cities as follows, with area and population:

	Area (sq. km)	*Population (1999)*
Almaty[1]	224,000	1,558,500
Almaty City	300	1,129,400
Aqmola[2]	146,200	836,300
Aqtöbe	300,600	682,600
Astana City	700	319,300
Atyraū[3]	118,600	440,300
Batys Qazaqstan	151,300	616,800
Bayqonyr (city)	(6,700)	—[4]
Mangghystaū	165,600	314,700
Ongtüstik Qazaqstan	117,300	1,978,300
Pavlodar	124,800	807,000
Qaraghandy	428,000	1,410,200
Qostanay	196,000	1,017,700
Qyzylorda	226,000	596,200
Shyghys Qazaqstan	283,200	1,531,000
Soltüstik Qazaqstan	98,000	726,000
Zhambyl[5]	144,300	988,800

[1]Formerly Alma-Ata. [2]Formerly Tselinograd and then Akmola. [3]Formerly Gurev. [4]As the space base of Bayqonyr is under Russian administration, its 6,700 sq. km and estimated 70,000 inhabitants are excluded from overall Kazakhstan figures. The lease was extended until 2050 in 2004. [5]Formerly Dzhambul.

In Dec. 1997 the capital was moved from Almaty to Aqmola, which was renamed Astana in May 1998 (the name of the province remained as Aqmola). Astana has a population of 313,000 (2000). Other major cities, with 2000 populations: Almaty (1,129,000); Qaraghandy (437,000); Shymkent (360,000).

The official languages are Kazakh and Russian; Russian is more widely spoken.

SOCIAL STATISTICS

2007: births, 321,963; deaths, 158,297; marriages, 146,379; divorces, 36,107. Rates, 2007 (per 1,000 population): birth, 20·8; death, 10·2; marriage, 9·5; divorce, 2·3. Suicides in 2007 numbered 4,168 (rate of 26·9 per 100,000 population). Annual population growth rate, 2000–05, 0·4%. Expectation of life at birth, 2007, 59·1 years for males and 71·2 years for females. Infant mortality, 2005, 27 per 1,000 live births; fertility rate, 2004, 1·9 births per woman.

CLIMATE

The climate is generally fairly dry. Winters are cold but spring comes earlier in the south than in the far north. Almaty, Jan. –4°C, July 24°C. Annual rainfall 598 mm.

CONSTITUTION AND GOVERNMENT

Relying on a judgement of the Constitutional Court that the 1994 parliamentary elections were invalid, President Nazarbaev dissolved parliament on 11 March 1995 and began to rule by decree. A referendum on the adoption of a new constitution was held on 30 Aug. 1995. The electorate was 8·8m.; turnout was 80%. 89% of votes cast were in favour. The Constitution thus adopted allowed the President to rule by decree and to dissolve parliament if it holds a no-confidence vote or twice rejects his nominee for Prime Minister. It established a parliament consisting of a 39-member Senate (two selected by each of the elected assemblies of Kazakhstan's 16 principal administrative divisions plus seven appointed by the president); and a lower house (*Majlis*) of 77 (67 popularly elected by single mandate districts, with ten members elected by party-list vote). The constitution was amended in Oct. 1998 to provide for a seven-year presidential term. It was amended again in May 2007 to lift the term-limit clause on the president, reduce the presidential term to five years with effect from 2012, oblige the president to consult with parliament when choosing a prime minister and adopt proportional representation for the lower house. The amendment also raised from seven to 15 the number of senators appointed by the president (increasing the total number of senators to 47) and from 77 to 107 the number of lower house deputies (with 98 elected by proportional representation from party lists and nine elected by the Assembly of the People of Kazakhstan—a body comprising the various ethnic groups in the country, which itself is appointed by the president).

A Constitutional Court was set up in Dec. 1991 and a new constitution adopted on 28 Jan. 1993, but President Nazarbaev abolished the Constitutional Court in 1995. In June 2000 a bill to provide President Nazarbaev with life-long powers and privileges was passed into law.

National Anthem

'Mening Qazaqstan' ('My Kazakhstan'); words by Z. Nazhimedenov and N. Nazarbaev, tune by S. Kaldayakov.

GOVERNMENT CHRONOLOGY

Presidents since 1991.
1991– Nursultan Abishuly Nazarbaev

RECENT ELECTIONS

At the presidential elections of 4 Dec. 2005 Nursultan Nazarbaev was re-elected with 91·2% of votes cast against four other candidates. Turnout was 76·8%.

National Assembly elections were held on 18 Aug. 2007. President Nursultan Nazarbaev's Nur Otan (Light of the Fatherland) Party won all the available 98 seats, with 88·1% of the vote. Six other parties participated but all received less than 5% of the vote and failed to win any seats. Turnout was 64·6%. There were widespread allegations that the elections were fraudulent and failed to meet international standards.

CURRENT ADMINISTRATION

President: Nursultan Nazarbaev; b. 1940 (elected in 1991 and re-elected in 1999 and 2005).

In March 2010 the government comprised:

Prime Minister: Karim Massimov; b. 1965 (sworn in 10 Jan. 2007).

First Deputy Prime Minister: Umirzak Shukeev. *Deputy Prime Ministers:* Serik Akhmetov; Yerbol Orynbayev.

Minister of Agriculture: Akylbek Kurishbayev. *Culture and Information:* Mukhtar Kul-Mukhammed. *Defence:* Adilbek Dzhaksybekov. *Economy and Budget Planning:* Bakhyt Sultanov. *Education and Science:* Zhanseit Tuimebayev. *Emergency Situations:* Vladimir Bozhko. *Energy and Mineral Resources:* Sauat Mynbayev. *Environmental Protection:* Nurgali Ashimov. *Finance:* Bolat Zhamishev. *Foreign Affairs:* Kanat Saudabayev. *Health:* Zhaksylyk Doskaliyev. *Industry and Trade:* Aset Isekeshev. *Internal Affairs:* Serik Baymagambetov. *Justice:* Gen. Rashid Tusupbekov. *Labour and Social Security:* Gulshara Abdykalikova. *Tourism and Sport:* Temirkhan Dosmukhanbetov. *Transport and Communications:* Abelgazi Kusainov.

Chairman, Senate (Upper House): Kassym-Jomart Tokaev.

Chairman, Majlis (Lower House): Ural Mukhamedzhanov.

Government Website: http://www.government.kz

CURRENT LEADERS

Nursultan Abishuly Nazarbaev

Position
President

Introduction
Nursultan Nazarbaev, leader of the Nur Otan (Light of the Fatherland) Party, was elected president of Kazakhstan in 1991, leading the country to independence after the collapse of the USSR. He has sought to exploit the nation's rich mineral resources although much of the population remains poor. He has also sought close ties with southern regional neighbours as well as Russia, China and the West. His regime, however, has been widely accused of corruption and human rights abuses.

Early Life
Nursultan Nazarbaev was born on 6 July 1940 in Chemolgan in the Almaty region. He was employed by the Karagandy metallurgical works in 1960 and graduated in engineering from a higher technical college in 1967. Having joined the Soviet Communist Party in 1962, he became secretary of the party's regional committee in 1977 and rose through the ranks to the central committee. In 1984 he was appointed chairman of the Republic's council of ministers and became a full member of the Politburo five years later. In the same year Nazarbaev was named first secretary of the Kazakh Communist party. In April 1990 he was chosen by the Supreme Soviet as president of the Republic of Kazakhstan.

Career in Office
Nazarbaev spoke out in support of Soviet leader Mikhail Gorbachev during a coup attempt in Moscow in Aug. 1991. Nevertheless, Kazakhstan seceded from the USSR in Dec. 1991 to join the Commonwealth of Independent States (CIS). In the same month Nazarbaev's position as head of state was consolidated in presidential elections. Earlier in the year he had closed the country's most important nuclear test ground at Semipalatinsk.

In 1992 Nazarbaev secured Kazakhstan's membership of the UN and of the Conference on Security and Co-operation in Europe (the precursor of the OSCE). Despite parliamentary opposition, he implemented a series of economic reforms, including a programme of privatization. He sought close co-operation with his CIS partners and signed up Kazakhstan to the strategic arms reduction treaty and the treaty on the non-proliferation of nuclear weapons. Two years later he signed an agreement on economic and military co-operation with Russia. In the same year his term of office was extended by referendum to 2000 amid accusations that he was becoming increasingly autocratic.

In 1997 Nazarbaev announced the transfer of the national capital from Almata to Aqmola (renamed Astana in 1998) to take advantage of Aqmola's central location and its seismatically less sensitive position. He won presidential elections brought forward to Jan. 1999 with 79·8% of the vote, but earned international criticism for the disqualification of the leading opposition figure, Akezhan Kazhegeldin, from the polls. Kazhegeldin was accused of corruption, went into exile and was sentenced *in absentia* to ten years imprisonment. Parliamentary elections held later in the year were criticized by the OSCE.

Nazarbaev implemented heightened security measures against Islamist militants following increased activity in the region in 2000. In June 2001 Kazakhstan joined the Shanghai Co-operation

Organization (along with China, Russia, Kyrgyzstan, Uzbekistan and Tajikistan) to bolster regional co-operation in economics and against ethnic and religious activism. In the aftermath of the 11 Sept. attacks on Washington and New York in 2001, Nazarbaev met US President George W. Bush to consolidate relations between the two countries.

Nazarbaev's autocratic style of governance has regularly been the focus of international attention. In 2000 the government passed constitutional amendments granting him wide-ranging influence once he has retired from office. In Nov. 2001 he purged his government of founding members of Democratic Choice, a group seeking to reduce presidential powers. Leading Democratic Choice figures were subsequently imprisoned on a variety of disputed charges, as were journalists critical of his regime. In 2002 Nazarbaev was accused of siphoning state monies into a personal bank account, but he denied any wrongdoing.

In Feb. 2003 the government announced plans to work with Russia to develop a national nuclear energy programme. In June 2003 the prime minister, Imangali Tasmagambetov, resigned in protest at land reforms allowing private ownership for the first time in the nation's history. Nazarbaev's Otan Party (the predecessor of the Nur Otan Party) won a majority of National Assembly seats in parliamentary elections in 2004, and on 4 Dec. 2005 he was re-elected overwhelmingly as president with 91% of the votes cast. There was some movement towards further democratization, including the establishment in March 2006 of a new state commission chaired by the president to oversee a widening of the powers of legislative bodies, strengthening of the judiciary and law enforcement agencies, and constitutional development. Kazakhstan also ratified two international covenants on civil, political, economic and cultural rights. However, the political opposition has remained sceptical about these moves in the light of parliament's vote in May 2007 to allow Nazarbaev to stay in office for an unlimited number of terms and the legislative elections later in the year which returned all the seats to his Nur Otan Party.

After almost a decade of average annual growth of around 10%, Kazakhstan's economy started to slow markedly in 2008 in the wake of the global credit crisis. This prompted Nazarbaev in Oct. to announce a US$10bn. injection of reserves from the National Fund (established in 2000 to accumulate revenues from the expanding oil and gas sector) into the economy, with a further US$5bn. in support for struggling local banks.

In April 2009, responding to an earlier initiative by the International Atomic Energy Agency, Nazarbaev announced his country's readiness to host an international nuclear fuel bank to ensure other countries do not need to develop their own sources and to curtail nuclear proliferation.

DEFENCE

Defence expenditure in 2006 totalled US$648m. (US$43 per capita), representing 0·8% of GDP.

Army

Personnel, 2007, 30,000. Paramilitary units: Presidential Guard (2,000), Government Guard (500), Internal Security Troops (approximately 20,000), State Border Protection Forces (approximately 9,000).

Navy

A 3,000-strong Maritime Border Guard operates on the Caspian Sea. Kazakhstan hopes to have a fully-fledged navy by 2013.

Air Force

In 2007 there were 12,000 personnel (including Air Defence) with 163 combat capable aircraft, including MiG-29, MiG-31 and Su-27 interceptors and Su-24 and Su-25 strike aircraft.

INTERNATIONAL RELATIONS

In Jan. 1995 agreements were reached for closer integration with Russia, including the combining of military forces, currency convertibility and a customs union.

Kazakhstan is a member of the UN, World Bank, IMF and several other UN specialized agencies, OSCE, CIS, IOM, Islamic Development Bank, NATO Partnership for Peace, OIC, Asian Development Bank and ECO. In 1998 President Nazarbaev signed major treaties with Russia and China, Kazakhstan's neighbours to the north, west and east, in the hope of improving relations with both countries. In Jan. 2010 Kazakhstan joined the newly established Customs Union, together with Russia and Belarus. The three countries are now looking to enter the WTO as a single customs territory.

ECONOMY

Agriculture accounted for 5·9% of GDP in 2006, industry 42·1% and services 52·0%.

Overview

Kazakhstan's economy shrunk dramatically after the break-up of the Soviet Union. From 1991–95 both GDP and GDP per capita fell before stabilizing over the latter half of the 1990s. Economic reform and privatization schemes implemented during this period prompted a strong recovery in the 2000s.

In recent years real GDP growth has averaged over 10% per year, driven by expansion in construction and financial services. Per capita income levels have surpassed the average for ex-Soviet republics and have converged on the world average. The country is a net energy exporter and industry is heavily geared towards the exploitation of its vast natural resources. Exports are strong but so too is dependence on imports. Government policy has been geared toward increasing output in other industrial areas but has so far had little impact on import levels. Despite strong growth, vulnerabilities are emerging, particularly within the banking sector where external debt doubled to 41% in 2006. Inflation remains relatively high.

Currency

The unit of currency is the *tenge* (KZT) of 100 *tiyn*, which was introduced on 15 Nov. 1993 at 1 tenge = 500 roubles. It became the sole legal tender on 25 Nov. 1993. Inflation was running at nearly 1,880% in 1994, but dropped dramatically and remained relatively stable for several years before it rose again to 10·8% in 2007 and further still to 17·2% in 2008. In July 2005 foreign exchange reserves were US$6,953m. and gold reserves amounted to 1·88m. troy oz. Total money supply was 876,981m. tenge in June 2005.

Budget

In 2004 revenues were 1,441bn. tenge and expenditures 1,289bn. tenge. Tax revenue accounted for 90·7% of revenues in 2004; social security accounted for 21·2% of expenditures, education 14·8% and health 10·2%.

Performance

The break-up of the Soviet Union triggered an economic collapse as orders from Russian factories for Kazakhstan's metals and phosphates, two mainstays of the economy, dried up. Real GDP growth was –1·9% in 1998 but there was a slight recovery in 1999, with growth of 2·7%. Growth was an impressive 9·8% in 2000 and an even more spectacular 13·5% in 2001. Driven by increased oil production, the economy continued to expand, with growth of 8·9% in 2007 and 3·2% in 2008. Total GDP in 2008 was US$132·2bn.

Banking and Finance

The central bank and bank of issue is the National Bank (*Governor*, Grigorii Marchenko). In 2001 there were 44 domestic banks, with assets totalling US$5·3bn. The largest bank is Kazkommertsbank

(KKB), with assets of US$1·8bn. in Dec. 2002. The other major banks are Bank TuranAlem and Halyk Bank. In 2001 there were also 12 branches or representative offices of foreign banks. Foreign direct investment amounted to US$2·8bn. in 2001, more than double the 2000 total.

ENERGY AND NATURAL RESOURCES

Environment
Carbon dioxide emissions from the consumption and flaring of fossil fuels in 2008 were the equivalent of 13·0 tonnes per capita.

Electricity
Installed capacity was an estimated 16·3m. kW in 2004. Output in 2004 was 66·9bn. kWh. There is one nuclear power station. Consumption per capita was 4,320 kWh in 2004.

Oil and Gas
Proven oil reserves in 2008 were 39·8bn. bbls. The onshore Tengiz field has estimated oil reserves between 6bn. and 9bn. bbls; the onshore Karachaganak field has oil reserves of 2bn. bbls, and gas reserves of 600bn. cu. metres. Output in 2008 of oil, 72·0m. tonnes; natural gas, 30·2bn. cu. metres with proven reserves of 1,820bn. cu. metres. The first major pipeline for the export of oil from the Tengiz field was opened in March 2001, linking the Caspian port of Atyraū with the Russian Black Sea port of Novorossiisk. In Sept. 1997 Kazakhstan signed oil agreements with China worth US$9·5bn.; although only a small portion of that investment ever materialized. However, a 962-km oil pipeline linking Atasu in Kazakhstan and Alashankou in China opened in Dec. 2005. Oil and gas investment by foreign companies is now driving the economy. In 1997 oil production sharing deals were concluded with two international consortia to explore the North Caspian basin and to develop the Karachaganak gas field. A huge new offshore oilfield in the far north of the Caspian Sea, known as East Kashagan, was discovered in early 2000. The field could prove to be the largest find in the last 30 years, and estimates suggest that it may contain 50bn. bbls of oil. Commercial production is expected to begin in 2011. Oil production is expected to triple in the next ten years.

It is believed that there may be as much as 14bn. tonnes of oil and gas reserves under Kazakhstan's portion of the Caspian Sea.

A state-owned national company, KazMunaiGaz, was created in 2002 to manage the oil and natural gas industries.

Minerals
Kazakhstan is extremely rich in mineral resources, including coal, bauxite, cobalt, vanadium, iron ores, chromium, phosphates, borates and other salts, copper, lead, manganese, molybdenum, nickel, tin, gold, silver, tungsten and zinc. Production figures (2003 unless otherwise indicated), in tonnes: coal (2004), 86·00m.; iron ore, 19·28m.; bauxite, 4·74m.; lignite (2004), 3·95m.; copper, 485,000; zinc, 394,000; uranium, 3,300; silver, 827·4; gold, 19·3.

Agriculture
Kazakh agriculture has changed from primarily nomad cattle breeding to production of grain, cotton and other industrial crops. In 2006 agriculture accounted for 6% of GDP. There were 21·54m. ha. of arable land and 0·14m. ha. of permanent crops in 2001. 2·35m. ha. were irrigated in 2001. In 1993, 181·3m. ha. were under cultivation, of which private subsidiary agriculture accounted for 0·3m. ha. and commercial farming 6·3m. ha. in 16,300 farms. Around 60,000 private farms have emerged since independence.

Tobacco, rubber plants and mustard are also cultivated. Kazakhstan has rich orchards and vineyards. Kazakhstan is noted for its livestock, particularly its sheep, from which excellent quality wool is obtained. Livestock (2003): 4·56m. cattle (down from 9·57m. in 1993), 9·79m. sheep (down from 33·63m. in 1993), 1·49m. goats, 1·23m. pigs, 1·02m. horses and 23·79m. chickens.

Output of main agricultural products (in 1,000 tonnes) in 2003: wheat, 11,537; potatoes, 2,308; barley, 2,154; watermelons, 604; tomatoes, 448; maize, 438; sugar beets, 424; cabbage, 328; onions, 320; sunflower seeds, 293; rice, 273. Livestock products, 2002 (in 1,000 tonnes): cow's milk, 4,110; meat, 676; eggs, 117. Kazakhstan is a major exporter of grain to Russia, but in recent years there has been a significant reduction in the quantity exported as a result of low crop yields coupled with the need to meet domestic demand.

Forestry
Forests covered 3·34m. ha. in 2005, or 1·2% of the land area. In 2007, 852,000 cu. metres of timber were cut.

Fisheries
Catches in 2004 totalled 33,896 tonnes, exclusively freshwater fish.

INDUSTRY
Kazakhstan was heavily industrialized in the Soviet period, with non-ferrous metallurgy, heavy engineering and the chemical industries prominent. Output was valued at 2,000bn. tenge in current prices in 2001, up from 1,798bn. tenge in 2000. Production, 2003 (in 1,000 tonnes) includes: crude steel, 5,069; pig iron, 4,138; distillate fuel oil (2004), 2,888; residual fuel oil (2004), 2,708; cement, 2,581; wheat flour, 2,123; petrol (2004), 1,928; ferroalloys (2002), 1,241; cotton woven fabrics (2002), 14m. sq. metres; leather footwear (2002), 250,000 pairs; TV sets (2001), 347,000 units.

Labour
In 2002 the economically active labour force numbered 6,708,900, with the main areas of activity as follows: agriculture, hunting and forestry, 2,366,700; trade, restaurants and hotels, 1,007,200; industry, 824,000; education, 589,000; transport, storage and communications, 503,700. In 2003 the unemployment rate was 8·8% (down from 13·5% in 1999).

INTERNATIONAL TRADE
In Jan. 1994 an agreement to create a single economic zone was signed with Kyrgyzstan and Uzbekistan. Since Jan. 1992 individuals and enterprises have been able to engage in foreign trade without needing government permission, except for goods 'of national interest' (fuel, minerals, mineral fertilizers, grain, cotton, wool, caviar and pharmaceutical products) which may be exported only by state organizations. Foreign debt was US$43,354m. in 2005.

Imports and Exports
In 2006 imports (f.o.b.) were valued at US$24,120·4m. (compared to US$7,944·4m. in 2001) and exports (f.o.b.) at US$38,762·1m. (US$8,927·8m. in 2001). In 2003, 39·0% of imports came from Russia, 8·7% from Germany, 6·2% from China and 5·6% from the USA. Main export markets in 2003 were Bermuda, 17·0%; Russia, 15·2%; Switzerland, 13·0%; China, 12·8%. Main imports: machinery, mechanical appliances and electrical equipment, transportation equipment, and mineral products. Main exports: mineral products, ferrous and non-ferrous metals, and vegetable products. Oil and gas account for 70% of exports.

COMMUNICATIONS

Roads
In 2007 there were 93,123 km of roads, of which 23,507 were highways, main or national roads. Passenger cars in use in 2007 numbered 2,183,100, and there were also 359,200 lorries and vans, 83,400 buses and coaches, and 45,200 motorcycles and mopeds. There were 4,365 fatalities as a result of road accidents in 2007. With 28·2 deaths per 100,000 population in 2007, Kazakhstan has among the highest death rates in road accidents of any country.

Rail

In 2005 there were 14,195 km of 1,520 mm gauge railways. Passenger-km travelled in 2003 came to 10·7bn. and freight tonne-km to 147·7bn.

Civil Aviation

The national carrier is Air Astana. There is an international airport at Almaty. In 2005 scheduled airline traffic of Kazakhstan-based carriers flew 93·3m. km, carrying 583,600 passengers.

Shipping

There is one large port, Aktau. In 1993, 1·2m. passengers and 4m. tonnes of freight were carried on inland waterways. Merchant shipping totalled 11,845 GRT and 20 vessels in 2002.

Telecommunications

Telephone subscribers numbered 5,258,900 in 2004, or 354·4 per 1,000 persons, including 2,758,900 mobile phone subscribers. Kazakhstan had 400,000 internet users in 2004.

Postal Services

In 2003 there were 3,791 post offices.

SOCIAL INSTITUTIONS

Justice

Jury trials for serious offences were introduced in Jan. 2007. In 1994, 201,796 crimes were reported; in 1996 there were 2,986 murders. The population in penal institutions in April 2001 was 84,000 (522 per 100,000 of national population—one of the highest rates in the world).

Education

In 2007, 330,897 children were attending pre-school institutions, there were 947,807 pupils at primary schools, 1,874,213 pupils at secondary schools and 772,600 students in tertiary education. Adult literacy rate is more than 99%.

In 2007 public government expenditure on education came to 3·2% of GNI.

Health

In 2002 there were 894 hospitals with a provision of 65 beds per 10,000 inhabitants. There were 51,289 physicians, 4,337 dentists, 88,140 nurses, 2,672 pharmacists and 8,094 midwives in 2001.

Welfare

In Jan. 1994 there were 2·1m. age and 0·9m. other pensioners. Pension contributions are 20% of salary and are payable to the State Pension Fund.

RELIGION

There were some 4,000 mosques in 1996 (63 in 1990). An Islamic Institute opened in 1991 to train imams. A Roman Catholic diocese was established in 1991. In 2001 there were 6,988,000 Muslims, 1,216,000 Russian Orthodox and 318,000 Protestants. The remainder of the population followed other religions or were non-religious.

CULTURE

World Heritage Sites

Kazakhstan has three sites on the UNESCO World Heritage List: the Mausoleum of Khoja Ahmed Yasawi (inscribed on the list in 2003), an excellent and well preserved example of late 14th century Timurid architecture; Petroglyphs within the Archaeological Landscape of Tamgaly (2004), a concentration of some 5,000 rock carvings; and Saryarka-Steppe and the Lakes of Northern Kazakhstan (2008), 450,344 ha. of wetlands that contain the Naurzum State Nature Reserve and the Korgalzhyn State Nature Reserve and are of outstanding importance for migratory water birds.

Broadcasting

Broadcasting is the responsibility of the Kazakh Television and Radio Broadcasting Corporation. Kazakh TV is the state-owned television channel. Private networks include Khabar TV, Kazakh Commercial TV and Channel 31 TV. State-owned Kazakh Radio transmits in Kazakh and Russian. Among numerous private radio stations are Europa Plus, Khabar Hit FM and Russkoye Radio. There were 5·11m. television receivers (colour by SECAM) in 2003.

Press

There were 1,202 newspapers in 2005. The leading newspapers are the Kazakh-language Egemen Kazakhstan and Zhas Alash, and the Russian-language Kazakhstanskaya Pravda. There is frequent harassment of independent journalists. In 2002 a total of 1,005 book titles were published.

Tourism

In 2005 there were 3,143,000 non-resident tourists; spending by tourists totalled US$809m.

DIPLOMATIC REPRESENTATIVES

Of Kazakhstan in the United Kingdom (33 Thurloe Sq., London, SW7 2DS)
Ambassador: Kairat Abusseitov.

Of the United Kingdom in Kazakhstan (62 Kosmonavtov St., Renco Building, 6th Floor, Astana 010000)
Ambassador: David Moran.

Of Kazakhstan in the USA (1401 16th St., NW, Washington, D.C., 20036)
Ambassador: Erlan Idrissov.

Of the USA in Kazakhstan (22–23 Str., No. 3, Ak Bulak 4, Astana)
Ambassador: Richard E. Hoagland.

Of Kazakhstan to the United Nations
Ambassador: Byrganym Aitimova.

Of Kazakhstan to the European Union
Ambassador: Yerik Utembayev.

FURTHER READING

Alexandrov, M., *Uneasy Alliance: Relations Between Russia and Kazakhstan in the Post-Soviet Era, 1992–1997.* 1999

Cummings, Sally, *Kazakhstan: Power and the Elite.* 2005

Nazpary, J., *Post-Soviet Chaos: Violence and Dispossession in Kazakhstan.* 2001

Olcott, Marta Brill, *The Kazakhs.* 1987.—*Kazakhstan: Unfilled Promise.* 2001

National Statistical Office: Agency of Kazakhstan on Statistics, 125 Abay Ave., 480008 Almaty, Kazakhstan.
Website: http://www.stat.kz

KENYA

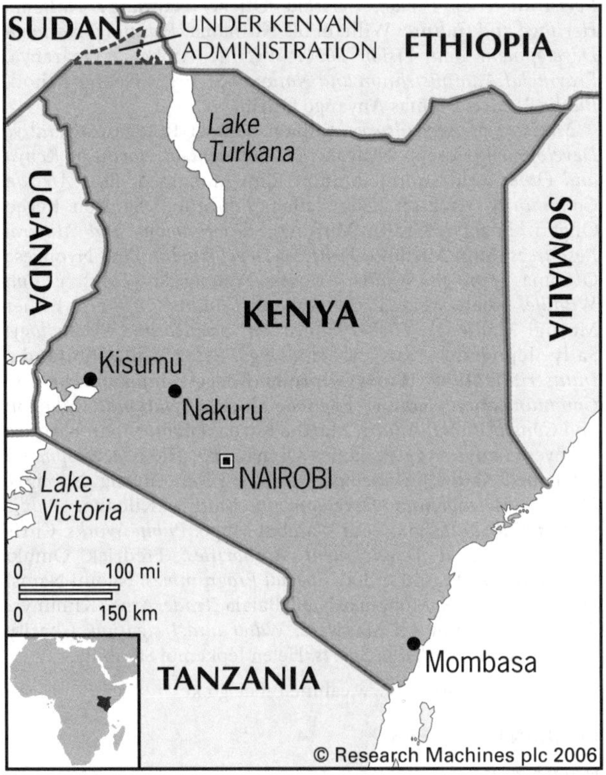

Jamhuri ya Kenya
(Republic of Kenya)

Capital: Nairobi
Population estimate, 2010: 40·86m.
GDP per capita, 2007: (PPP$) 1,542
HDI/world rank: 0·541/147

KEY HISTORICAL EVENTS

Prior to colonialism, the area comprised African farming communities, notably the Kikuyu and the Masai. From the 16th century through to the 19th, they were loosely controlled by the Arabic rulers of Oman. In 1895 the British declared part of the region the East Africa Protectorate, which from 1920 was known as the Colony of Kenya. The influx of European settlers was resented by Africans not only for the whites' land holdings but also for their exclusive political representation in the colonial Legislative Council. A state of emergency existed between Oct. 1952 and Jan. 1960 during the period of the Mau Mau uprising. Over 13,000 Africans and 100 Europeans were killed. The Kenya African Union was banned and its president, Jomo Kenyatta, imprisoned. The state of emergency ended in 1960. Full internal self-government was achieved in 1962 and in Dec. 1963 Kenya became an independent member of the Commonwealth. In 1982 Kenya became a one-party state and in 1986 party preliminary elections were instituted to reduce the number of parliamentary candidates at general elections. Only those candidates obtaining over 30% of the preliminary vote were eligible to stand. On the death of Kenyatta in Aug. 1978 Daniel T. arap Moi, the vice-president, became acting president and was elected in 1979, and then re-elected in 1983, 1988, 1992 and 1997. An attempted coup in 1982 was unsuccessful. A multi-party election was permitted in 1992 and again in 1997, the first genuinely competitive elections since 1963. In the 2002 elections the opposition united behind Mwai Kibaki, who won a landslide victory against Moi's successor Uhuru Kenyatta. Kibaki became the first non-Kenya African National Union president of independent Kenya. In Nov. 2005 a new draft constitution was rejected amid criticism that it gave too much power to the president. In Dec. 2007 Kibaki claimed victory in the presidential election, although the opposition and international observers alleged irregularities, prompting a wave of civil unrest that claimed around 1,500 lives. In Feb. 2008 Kibaki and the opposition leader, Raila Odinga, agreed to a power-sharing deal.

TERRITORY AND POPULATION

Kenya is bounded by Sudan and Ethiopia in the north, Uganda in the west, Tanzania in the south and Somalia and the Indian Ocean in the east. The total area is 582,646 sq. km, of which 581,677 sq. km is land area. The 1999 census gave a population of 28,686,607 (14,481,018 females). In 2005, 79·3% of the population were rural. In 2006 more than 30,000 Somali refugees entered Kenya to escape the fighting that escalated in Somalia the course of the year.

The UN gives an estimated population for 2010 of 40·86m.; density, 70 per sq. km.

Kenya is divided into seven provinces and one national capital area (Nairobi). The land areas, populations and capitals are:

Province	*Sq. km*	*Census 1999*	*Capital*	*Census 1999*
Rift Valley	173,868	6,987,036	Nakuru	219,366
Eastern	159,891	4,631,779	Embu	31,500
Nyanza	16,162	4,392,196	Kisumu	322,734
Central	13,176	3,724,159	Nyeri	98,908
Western	8,360	3,358,776	Kakamega	73,607
Coast	83,603	2,487,264	Mombasa	655,018
Nairobi	684	2,143,254		
North-Eastern	126,902	962,143	Garissa	50,955

Other large towns (1999): Eldoret (167,016), Thika (82,665), Ruiru (79,741).

Most of Kenya's 26·44m. people belong to 13 tribes, the main ones including Kikuyu (about 22% of the population), Luhya (14%), Luo (13%), Kalenjin (12%), Kamba (11%), Gusii (6%), Meru (5%) and Mijikenda (5%).

Swahili and English are both official languages, but people belonging to the different tribes have their own language as their mother tongue.

SOCIAL STATISTICS

2000 births (estimates), 1,042,000; deaths, 419,000. Estimated birth rate in 2000 was 34·1 per 1,000 population; estimated death rate, 13·7. Annual population growth rate, 2000–05, 3·1%. Expectation of life at birth in 2007 was 53·2 years for males and 54·0 years for females. Infant mortality, 2005, 78 per 1,000 live births. Fertility rate, 2004, 5·0 births per woman. In 2005, 46% of Kenyans lived below the poverty line (down from 52% in 1997).

CLIMATE

The climate is tropical, with wet and dry seasons, but considerable differences in altitude make for varied conditions between the hot, coastal lowlands and the plateau, where temperatures are very much cooler. Heaviest rains occur in April and May, but in some parts there is a second wet season in Nov. and Dec. Nairobi, Jan. 65°F (18·3°C), July 60°F (15·6°C). Annual rainfall 39" (958 mm). Mombasa, Jan. 81°F (27·2°C), July 76°F (24·4°C). Annual rainfall 47" (1,201 mm).

CONSTITUTION AND GOVERNMENT

There is a unicameral *National Assembly*, which until the Dec. 1997 elections had 200 members, comprising 188 elected by universal suffrage for a five-year term, ten members appointed by the President, and the Speaker and Attorney-General *ex officio*. Following a review of constituency boundaries, the National Assembly now has 210 elected members, 12 members appointed and the two *ex officio* members, making 224 in total. The President is also directly elected for five years; he appoints a Vice-President and other ministers to a cabinet over which he presides. A constitutional amendment of Aug. 1992 stipulates that the winning presidential candidate must receive a nationwide majority and also the vote of 25% of electors in at least five of the eight provinces. The sole legal political party had been the Kenya African National Union (KANU), but after demonstrations by the pro-reform lobby which led to extreme violence, KANU agreed to legalize opposition parties. A Constitutional Review Commission was established in 1997 to amend the Constitution before elections that were scheduled for 2002. In Sept. 2002 the Commission recommended changes to Kenya's system of government, including the curbing of presidential powers and the introduction of an executive prime ministerial position. However, in Oct. 2002 President Daniel arap Moi announced the dissolution of parliament before the Commission had completed its task, preventing a new constitution from being in place in time for the elections. A proposed new constitution was rejected at a referendum held in Nov. 2005, with 57% of votes cast against and only 43% in favour. The new constitution would have introduced the post of prime minister, dealt with land reform and provided greater rights for women.

National Anthem

'Ee Mungu nguvu yetu' ('Oh God of all creation'); words by a collective, tune traditional.

GOVERNMENT CHRONOLOGY

President since 1964. (DP = Democratic Party; KANU = Kenya African National Union; NARC = National Rainbow Coalition; PNU = Party of National Unity)

1964–78	KANU	Jomo Kenyatta
1978–2002	KANU	Daniel arap Moi
2002–	NARC/DP, PNU	Mwai Kibaki

RECENT ELECTIONS

In presidential elections held on 27 Dec. 2007 incumbent Mwai Kibaki of the Party of National Unity (PNU) won 46·4% of the vote, Raila Odinga of the Orange Democratic Movement (ODM) 44·1% and Kalonzo Musyoka of the Orange Democratic Movement-Kenya (ODM-Kenya) 8·9%. There were six other candidates.

In parliamentary elections also held on 27 Dec. 2007 ODM won 99 of 207 seats, the Party of National Unity (PNU) 43, ODM-Kenya 16 and KANU 14. The remaining 35 seats were shared amongst 19 parties. The ODM and its allies received a total of 102 seats and the PNU and its allies 78.

CURRENT ADMINISTRATION

President: Mwai Kibaki; b. 1931 (PNU; sworn in 30 Dec. 2002 and re-elected in Dec. 2007).

Following the elections of Dec. 2007 and a subsequent power-sharing agreement in Feb. 2008 a new coalition cabinet was formed, composed in March 2010 as follows:

Prime Minister: Raila Amollo Odinga; b. 1945 (ODM; since 17 April 2008).

Vice President and Minister for Home Affairs: Stephen Kalonzo Musyoka; b. 1953 (ODM-Kenya; sworn in 9 Jan. 2008).

Deputy Prime Minister and Minister for Local Government: Wycliffe Musalia Mudavadi. *Deputy Prime Minister and Minister for Finance:* Uhuru Kenyatta.

Minister of State for Defence: Yusuf Haji. *Immigration and Registration of Persons:* Gerald Otieno Kajwang'. *National Heritage and Culture:* William ole Ntimama. *Planning, National Development and Vision 2030:* Wycliffe Ambetsa Oparanya. *Provincial Administration and National Security:* George Saitoti. *Public Service:* Dalmas Anyango Otieno.

Minister of Agriculture: William Samoei Ruto. *Co-operative Development:* Joseph Nyagah. *Development of Northern Kenya and Other Arid Lands:* Ibrahim Elmi Mohamed. *East African Community:* Amason Kingi Jeffah. *Education:* Samson Kegeo Ongeri. *Energy:* Kiraitu Murungi. *Environment and Mineral Resources:* John Michuki. *Fisheries Development:* Paul Nyongesa Otuoma. *Foreign Affairs:* Moses Wetangula. *Forestry and Wildlife:* Noah Wekesa. *Gender and Children's Affairs:* Esther Murugi Mathenge. *Higher Education, Science and Technology:* Sally Jepngetich Kosgey. *Housing:* Peter Soita Shitanda. *Industrialization:* Henry Kiprono Kosgey. *Information and Communication:* Samuel Poghisio. *Justice, National Cohesion and Constitutional Affairs:* Martha Karua. *Labour:* John Kiyonga Munyes. *Lands:* Aggrey James Orengo. *Livestock Development:* Mohamed Abdi Kuti. *Medical Services:* Peter Anyang' Nyong'o. *Nairobi Metropolitan Development:* Mutula Kilonzo. *Public Health and Sanitation:* Beth Wambui Mugo. *Public Works:* Chris Obure. *Regional Development Authorities:* Fredrick Omulo Gumo. *Roads:* Franklin Bett. *Special Programmes:* Naomi Namsi Shabani. *Tourism:* Mohamed Najib Balala. *Trade:* Amos Kimunya. *Transport:* Chirau Ali Makwere. *Water and Irrigation:* Charity Kaluki Ngilu. *Youth and Sports:* Helen Jepkemoi Sambili.

Cabinet Office: http://www.cabinetoffice.go.ke

CURRENT LEADERS

Mwai Kibaki

Position
President

Introduction
Economist and former vice president Mwai Kibaki was first elected president in Dec. 2002. Representing a coalition of opposition parties (the National Rainbow Coalition, or NARC) in a bid to oust the KANU party, which had ruled the country since independence in 1963, he successfully campaigned on an anti-corruption ticket to end Daniel arap Moi's 24 year-presidency. However, Kibaki's government itself became widely tainted by corruption scandals and allegations. His controversial re-election in Dec. 2007 was violently disputed by supporters of Raila Odinga, the leader of the opposition ODM, before a power-sharing agreement was negotiated in Feb. 2008.

Early Life
Kibaki was born on 15 Nov. 1931 in Othaya, Nyeri District. In 1950 he joined the youth section of the pro-independence Kenyan African Union. In 1954 he graduated in economics, history and political science at Makerere University, Uganda, before further studies at the London School of Economics in the UK (1956–59).

Along with the subsequent presidents Jomo Kenyatta and Daniel arap Moi, Kibaki became involved in the fight for independence from British colonial rule, which was finally achieved in 1963. He contributed to the creation of the new constitution and was among the original members of the KANU party (Kenyan African National Union). He served as the party's chief executive officer from 1961–63 before being elected representative of Bahati, Nairobi in 1963. From 1963–66 he worked for the finance ministry heading an economic planning commission, after which he was appointed commerce and industry minister. From 1970–81 he served as finance minister. Vice president under Kenyatta and then his successor Moi, he also served as home affairs minister (1982–88) and health minister (1988–91).

A one-party state from 1964, the ban on opposition parties was finally lifted in 1991. In 1992 Kibaki and other party members left KANU to form the Democratic Party, criticizing endemic government corruption. In the country's first multi-party presidential elections that year, Kibaki took third place with around 20% of votes as Moi retained the presidency despite alleged irregularities. In 1997 he again stood against Moi, coming second with 30·9% of votes.

In 2002 he was chosen to head the National Rainbow Coalition (NARC), a coalition of opposition parties. The ruling party was split when Moi announced his chosen successor to be Uhuru Kenyatta, son of the country's first independent president Jomo Kenyatta. Several KANU members joined NARC. Kibaki's campaign focused on corruption within the ruling party and growing discontent with Moi's presidency. In the Dec. 2002 elections Kibaki won a landslide victory with 62·2% to Kenyatta's 31·3%, ending nearly forty years of KANU rule.

Career in Office

On election, Kibaki prioritized the fight against corruption, which had deterred international aid donors and investors since 1997. All public figures, including civil servants, were obliged to declare their wealth confidentially to the anti-corruption police. Kibaki also outlined plans to pass a new constitution and vowed to provide free universal primary school education and improve healthcare. In July 2003 the World Bank announced a resumption of loans to the Kenyan government.

In Oct. 2003 Kibaki suspended over 20 judges and 80 magistrates and appointed tribunals to investigate them over allegations of unethical conduct. Later that month he also extended his anti-corruption drive to forestry officers accused of complicity in illegal logging. Nevertheless, corruption remained an endemic problem throughout Kibaki's first presidential term.

Standing for re-election in Dec. 2007 as leader of the newly-created Party of National Unity (PNU), Kibaki claimed a narrow victory in the presidential poll. However, the opposition ODM rejected the result, alleging fraud that sparked widespread political and ethnic violence. The turmoil, which claimed about 1,500 lives, continued until Kibaki and Odinga agreed a power-sharing deal in Feb. 2008 (with the latter becoming prime minister) following protracted negotiations brokered by former United Nations Secretary-General Kofi Annan. A new national unity cabinet took office in April 2008 but the power-sharing arrangement has since been unstable, with Odinga accusing Kibaki of undermining it and attempting to sideline ODM ministers.

In Oct. 2008 an independent report into the post-election clashes called for an international tribunal to try those implicated in the violence. However, in July 2009 the cabinet announced that it would use local courts instead—a decision criticized by the visiting US state secretary.

In Nov. 2009 the government published a draft constitution, subject to a planned referendum, which would reduce presidential power and make the prime minister responsible for routine government business.

DEFENCE

In 2006 defence expenditure totalled US$355m. (US$10 per capita), representing 1·6% of GDP.

Army

Total strength (2007) 20,000. In addition there is a paramilitary Police General Service Unit of 5,000.

Navy

The Navy, based in Mombasa, consisted in 2007 of 1,620 personnel (including 120 marines).

Air Force

An air force, formed on 1 June 1964, was built up with RAF assistance. Personnel (2007) 2,500, with 29 combat capable aircraft and 11 attack helicopters although their serviceability is in doubt.

INTERNATIONAL RELATIONS

Kenya is a member of the UN, World Bank, IMF and several other UN specialized agencies, WTO, Commonwealth, IOM, African Development Bank, African Union, COMESA, EAC, Intergovernmental Authority on Development and is an ACP member state of the ACP-EU relationship.

In Nov. 1999 a treaty was signed between Kenya, Tanzania and Uganda to create a new East African Community as a means of developing East African trade, tourism and industry and laying the foundations for a future common market and political federation.

ECONOMY

Agriculture contributed 27·1% of GDP in 2006, industry 18·8% and services 54·1%.

Overview

Following independence in 1963 Kenya was among the leading East African economies, with average annual GDP growth of 6·5%. But economic performance declined from 1974. Kenya used to have one of the strongest economies in Africa but years of mismanagement and corruption have had a detrimental effect, made worse in 2000 by one of the longest droughts in living memory. Up to US$1bn. in international aid was frozen during the Moi era because Kenya failed to pass anti-corruption legislation. From 2003, under the presidency of Mwai Kibaki, GDP has increased, driven by the agriculture and service sectors. Flowers, fruits and vegetables lead Kenya's exports to Europe (its largest export market) along with coffee, tea and petroleum goods. In the service sectors, telecommunications and tourism have taken off while economic growth has stimulated the domestic construction industry.

In Dec. 2007 President Kibaki won his second term amid claims that the election results were rigged in his favour. Mass unrest across the country resulted in hundreds of casualties and the displacement of over 200,000 Kenyans. The finance ministry estimates that the unrest has cost the economy US$1bn. while the effect on import-export links has had serious ramifications for neighbouring countries.

Currency

The monetary unit is the *Kenya shilling* (KES) of 100 *cents*. The currency became convertible in May 1994. The shilling was devalued by 23% in April 1993. The annual rate of inflation was 13·1% in 2008. Foreign exchange reserves were US$1,653m. in July 2005, total money supply was K Sh 222,558m. and gold reserves were 1,000 troy oz.

Budget

In 2004–05 revenues totalled K Sh 304,705m. and expenditures K Sh 303,705m. Tax revenue accounted for 79·7% of revenues; recurrent expenditure accounted for 85·0% of expenditures. The fiscal year ends on 30 June.

Performance

Real GDP growth was 1·7% in 2008. Total GDP in 2008 was US$34·5bn.

Banking and Finance

The central bank and bank of issue is the Central Bank of Kenya (*Governor*, Njuguna Ndung'u). There are 43 banks, two non-banking financial institutions and a couple of building societies. In Dec. 2003 their combined assets totalled K Sh 567,600m. In 1998 the government offloaded 25% of its stake in the Kenya

Commercial Bank, which lowered its shareholding to 35%. In 2004 it further lowered its shareholding, to 25%.

There is a stock exchange in Nairobi.

ENERGY AND NATURAL RESOURCES

Environment

Kenya's carbon dioxide emissions from the consumption and flaring of fossil fuels in 2008 were the equivalent of 0·3 tonnes per capita.

Electricity

Installed generating capacity was an estimated 1·22m. kW in 2004, mostly provided by hydropower from power stations on the Tana river with some from oil-fired power stations and by geothermal power. Production in 2004 was 5·89bn. kWh, with consumption per capita 179 kWh. In 1999 it was decided to encourage the private sector to take part in electricity generation alongside the state-owned Kenya Electricity Generating Company as a means of bringing to an end the shortage of power and the frequent blackouts. In June 2000 a rationing scheme was introduced in much of the country restricting the power supply to 12 hours a day, and sometimes less.

Minerals

Production, 2005 (in 1,000 tonnes): lime and limestone (estimate), 1,085; soda ash, 360; fluorite, 97. Other minerals include gold (616 kg exported in 2005), raw soda, diatomite, garnets, salt and vermiculite.

Agriculture

As agriculture is possible from sea-level to altitudes of over 2,500 metres, tropical, sub-tropical and temperate crops can be grown and mixed farming is pursued. In 2006 there were around 5·31m. ha. of arable land and 444,000 ha. of permanent crop land. 14,000 ha. were irrigated in 2006. There were 26 tractors and two harvester-threshers per 10,000 ha. of arable land in 2006. Four-fifths of the country is range-land which produces mainly livestock products and the wild game which is a major tourist attraction.

Tea, coffee and horticultural products, particularly flowers, are all major foreign exchange earners.

Kenya has about 131,450 ha. under tea production, and is the world's fourth largest producer and largest exporter of tea. The production is high quality tea, raised in near-perfect agronomic conditions. In 2003 production was 294,000 tonnes; exports were worth US$434m.

Coffee output in 2003 was 55,000 tonnes; 170,000 ha. is under coffee production. Some 75% of the total hectarage under coffee is cultivated by smallholders, although their production has been in decline in recent years. Other major agricultural products (2003 estimates, in 1,000 tonnes): sugarcane, 4,500; maize, 2,300; potatoes, 900; plantains, 830; cassava, 600; pineapples, 600; sweet potatoes, 520; cabbage, 270; tomatoes, 260; dry beans, 255.

Livestock (2003): cattle, 12·8m.; goats, 11·5m.; sheep, 9·5m.; camels, 863,000; pigs, 337,000; chickens, 28·6m.

More than half the agricultural labour force is employed in the livestock sector, accounting for 10% of GDP.

Forestry

Forests covered 3·52m. ha. in 2005 (6·2% of the land area). There are coniferous, broad-leaved, hardwood and bamboo forests. Timber production was 27·65m. cu. metres in 2007.

Fisheries

Catches in 2005 totalled 148,124 tonnes, of which 141,020 tonnes were freshwater fish (mostly from Lake Victoria). Marine fishing has not reached its full potential, despite a coastline of 680 km. Fish landed from the sea totals less than 8,000 tonnes annually, but there is an estimated potential of 200,000 tonnes in tuna and similar species.

INDUSTRY

In 2006 industry accounted for 18·8% of GDP, with manufacturing contributing 11·5%. In 2003 there were 579 manufacturing firms employing more than 50 persons. The main products are textiles, chemicals, vehicle assembly and transport equipment, leather and footwear, printing and publishing, food and tobacco processing and oil refining. Production (2003) included (in tonnes): cement, 1,658,073; residual fuel oil (2005), 549,000; sugar, 448,489; distillate fuel oil (2005), 374,000; petrol (2004), 275,000; wheat flour, 179,866; maize meal, 120,942; cattle feed, 99,616; kerosene (2004), 95,000.

Labour

The labour force in 1998–99 was 12,326,000. In 1998–99 the unemployment level was estimated to be 1·8m.

INTERNATIONAL TRADE

Foreign debt was US$6,169m. in 2005.

Imports and Exports

Imports in 2006 totalled US$6,768·4m. and exports US$3,502·0m. Principal imports in 2003: machinery and transport equipment, 26·1%; petroleum, 23·3%; chemicals, 15·9%; manufactured goods, 13·4%. Exports: horticultural produce, 26·7%; tea, 24·1%; chemicals, 5·2%; coffee, 4·6%. Main import suppliers, 2003: United Arab Emirates, 11·3%; Saudi Arabia, 8·6%; South Africa, 8·3%; UK, 7·0%. Main export markets, 2003: Uganda, 16·7%; UK, 11·6%; Tanzania, 8·0%; Netherlands, 7·7%.

COMMUNICATIONS

Roads

In 2004 there were 63,265 km of roads (6,527 km of highways, national and main roads). There were, in 2007, 562,400 passenger cars in use, 210,900 vans and lorries, 180,800 motorcycles and mopeds, and 20,100 buses and coaches. There were 2,893 fatalities as a result of road accidents in 2007.

Rail

In 2002 route length was 2,597 km of metre-gauge. Passenger-km travelled in 2002 came to 288m. and freight tonne-km to 1,538m. A South African-led consortium signed agreements with the Kenyan and Ugandan governments in Nov. 2005 to take over the management of the Kenya-Uganda railway linking Mombasa to the Ugandan capital, Kampala.

Civil Aviation

There are international airports at Nairobi (Jomo Kenyatta International) and Mombasa (Moi International). The national carrier is the now privatized Kenya Airways. KLM has a 26% share of Kenya Airways. In 2003 scheduled airline traffic of Kenyan-based carriers flew 41m. km and carried 1,732,000 passengers (1,250,000 on international flights). In 2000 Jomo Kenyatta International handled 2,734,108 passengers and 135,619 tonnes of freight, and Moi International 853,944 passengers and 2,716 tonnes of freight.

Shipping

The main port is Mombasa, which handled 12·8m. tonnes of cargo in 2002. Container traffic has doubled since 1990 to 246,731 TEUs (twenty-foot equivalent units) in 2001. The merchant marine totalled 19,000 GRT in 2002, including oil tankers 5,000 GRT. In 2001 vessels totalling 10,600,000 NRT entered ports.

Telecommunications

Kenya had 4,893,700 telephone subscribers in 2005, or 142·9 per 1,000 persons. The government aims to improve telephone availability in rural areas from 0·16 lines per 100 persons in 1997 to one line per 100 by 2015, and in urban areas from four lines to 20 lines per 100 persons. In 2005 mobile phone subscribers numbered 4,612,000. There were 300,000 PCs in 2003 (9·5 per 1,000 persons) and 1,054,900 internet users in 2004.

Postal Services
In 2003 there were 877 post offices, or one for every 36,500 persons.

SOCIAL INSTITUTIONS

Justice
The courts of Justice comprises the court of Appeal, the High Court and a large number of subsidiary courts. The court of Appeal is the final Appellant court in the country and is based in Nairobi. It comprises seven Judges of Appeal. In the course of its Appellate duties the court of Appeal visits Mombasa, Kisumu, Nakuru and Nyeri. The High court with full jurisdiction in both civil and criminal matters comprises a total of 28 puisne Judges. Puisne Judges sit in Nairobi (16), Mombasa (two), Nakuru, Kisumu, Nyeri, Eldoret, Meru and Kisii (one each).

The Magistracy consists of approximately 300 magistrates of various cadres based in all provincial, district and some divisional centres. In addition to the above there are the Kadhi courts established in areas of concentrated Muslim populations: Mombasa, Nairobi, Malindi, Lamu, Garissa, Kisumu and Marsabit. They exercise limited jurisdiction in matters governed by Islamic Law.

There were 17,589 criminal convictions in 1993; the prison population was 35,278 in 2002 (111 per 100,000 of national population).

Education
The adult literacy rate in 2003 was 73·6% (77·7% among males and 70·2% among females). Free primary education was introduced in 2003. In 2007 there were 1,691,093 children in pre-primary schools with 76,323 teaching staff, 6,687,510 pupils were in primary schools with 146,796 teaching staff and 2,729,040 pupils in secondary schools with 102,449 teaching staff. There were 139,524 students in higher education in 2007.

In 2005 public expenditure on education came to 7·3% of GNI and 17·9% of total government spending.

Health
In 2003 there were 4,813 physicians, 772 dentists, 40,081 nurses and 1,881 pharmacists. There were 526 hospitals (with 63,407 beds), 649 health centres and 3,382 sub-centres and dispensaries in 2003. Free medical service for all children and adult out-patients was launched in 1965.

RELIGION
In 2001 there were 6·78m. Roman Catholics, 6·40m. African Christians, 6·17m. Protestants, 2·90m. Anglicans and 2·24m. Muslims. Traditional beliefs persist. In Feb. 2010 there was one Roman Catholic cardinal.

CULTURE

World Heritage Sites
Kenya has four sites on the UNESCO World Heritage List: Mount Kenya National Park/Natural Forest (1997), including the second highest peak in Africa; Lake Turkana National Parks (1997 and 2001), a breeding ground for Nile crocodiles and hippopotami; Lamu Old Town (2001), the oldest and best-preserved Swahili settlement in East Africa; and the Sacred Mijikenda Kaya Forests (2008), 11 separate forest sites containing the remains of numerous fortified villages.

Broadcasting
Broadcasting is the responsibility of the state-owned Kenya Broadcasting Corporation (KBC). KBC transmits the following public radio services: National Kiswahili, National English, Regional Central (four languages), Regional Western (eight languages) and Regional Eastern (five languages). It also provides television programmes, mainly in English and Swahili. There are several private television stations, including Kenya Television Network, Stella TV, Nation TV and Citizen TV. Independent radio services include Capital FM, East FM and Radio Citizen. The BBC and Voice of America relay broadcasts on the FM frequency. Number of TV-equipped households (2006): 2·0m.

Press
In 2006 there were five daily papers with a total circulation of 215,000. In May 2002 the Kenyan parliament passed a law making it illegal to sell books, newspapers or magazines that had not been submitted to the government for review.

Tourism
In 2005 there were 1,536,000 foreign visitors (1,199,000 in 2004). In 2005 receipts from tourism amounted to US$579m., up from US$486m. in 2004. Tourism is the country's leading source of hard currency.

DIPLOMATIC REPRESENTATIVES
Of Kenya in the United Kingdom (45 Portland Pl., London, W1B 1AS)
High Commissioner: Ephraim Waweru Ngare.

Of the United Kingdom in Kenya (Upper Hill Rd, Nairobi)
High Commissioner: Robert Macaire.

Of Kenya in the USA (2249 R. St., NW, Washington, D.C., 20008)
Ambassador: Peter Nicholas Rateng Oginga Ogego.

Of the USA in Kenya (United Nations Ave., Gigiri, Nairobi)
Ambassador: Michael E. Ranneberger.

Of Kenya to the United Nations
Ambassador: Zachary Dominic Muburi-Muita.

Of Kenya to the European Union
Ambassador: Marx G. N. Kahende.

FURTHER READING

Anderson, David, *Histories of the Hanged: The Dirty War in Kenya and the End of Empire.* 2005
Elkins, Caroline, *Britain's Gulag.* 2005; US title: *Imperial Reckoning: The Untold Story of the End of Empire in Kenya.* 2005
Haugerud, A., *The Culture of Politics in Modern Kenya.* 1995
Kyle, Keith, *The Politics of the Independence of Kenya.* 1999
Miller, N. N., *Kenya: the Quest for Prosperity.* 2nd ed. 1994
Murunga, Godwin R. and Nasong'o, Shadrack W., *Kenya: The Struggle for Democracy.* 2007
Ogot, B. A. and Ochieng, W. R. (eds.) *Decolonization and Independence in Kenya, 1940–93.* 1995
Throup, David and Hornsby, Charles, *Multi-Party Politics in Kenya.* 1999

National Statistical Office: Kenya National Bureau of Statistics, PO Box 30266—00100 GPO, Nairobi.
Website: http://www.knbs.or.ke

KIRIBATI

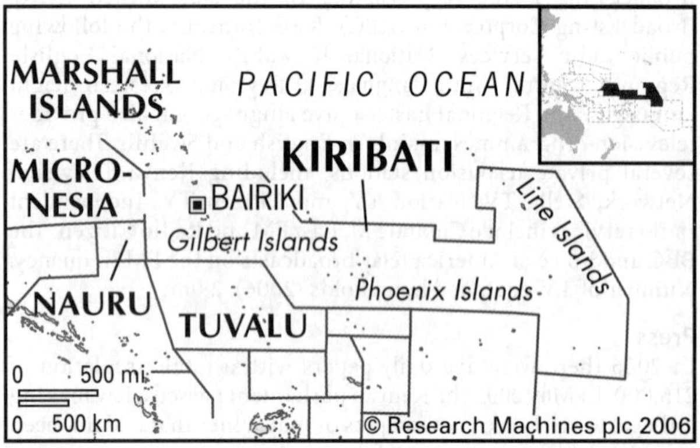

Ribaberikin Kiribati
(Republic of Kiribati)

Capital: Bairiki (Tarawa)
Population, 2005: 93,000
GDP per capita, 2007: (PPP$) 1,295

KEY HISTORICAL EVENTS

The islands that now constitute Kiribati were first settled by early Austronesian-speaking peoples long before the 1st century AD. Fijians and Tongans arrived about the 14th century and subsequently merged with the older groups to form the traditional I-Kiribati Micronesian society and culture. The Gilbert and Ellice Islands were proclaimed a British protectorate in 1892 and annexed at the request of the native governments as the Gilbert and Ellice Islands Colony on 10 Nov. 1915. On 1 Oct. 1975 the Ellice Islands severed constitutional links with the Gilbert Islands and took on a new name, Tuvalu. The Gilberts achieved full independence as Kiribati in 1979. Internal self-government was obtained on 1 Nov. 1976 and independence on 12 July 1979 as the Republic of Kiribati.

TERRITORY AND POPULATION

Kiribati (pronounced Kiribahss) consists of three groups of coral atolls and one isolated volcanic island, spread over a large expanse of the Central Pacific with a total land area of 811 sq. km (313 sq. miles). It comprises **Banaba** or Ocean Island (6 sq. km), the 16 **Gilbert Islands** (280 sq. km), the eight **Phoenix Islands** (29 sq. km), and eight of the 11 **Line Islands** (496 sq. km), the other three Line Islands (Jarvis, Palmyra Atoll and Kingman Reef) being uninhabited dependencies of the USA. The capital is the island of Bairiki in Tarawa. The gradual rise in sea levels in recent years is slowly reducing the area of the islands. Most of the land is less than 3 metres above sea level.

Population, 2005 census, 92,533 (46,921 females); density, 114 per sq. km.

In 2005 an estimated 56·4% of the population lived in rural areas.

The population distribution at the 2005 census was 46·9% in the Outer Islands, 43·6% in South Tarawa (urban area) and 9·6% in the Line and Phoenix Islands. Banaba, all 16 Gilbert Islands, Kanton (or Abariringa) in the Phoenix Islands and three atolls in the Line Islands (Teraina, Tabuaeran and Kiritimati—formerly Washington, Fanning and Christmas Islands respectively) are inhabited; their populations in 2005 (census) were as follows:

Banaba (Ocean Is.)	301	Tabiteuea	4,898
Makin	2,385	North Tabiteuea	3,600
Butaritari	3,280	South Tabiteuea	1,298
Marakei	2,741	Beru	2,169
Abaiang	5,502	Nikunau	1,912
Tarawa	45,989	Onotoa	1,644
North Tarawa	5,678	Tamana	875
South Tarawa	40,311	Arorae	1,256
Maiana	1,908	Kanton	41
Abemama	3,404	Teraina	1,155
Kuria	1,082	Tabuaeran	2,539
Aranuka	1,158	Kiritimati	5,115
Nonouti	3,179		

The remaining 12 atolls have no permanent population; the seven Phoenix Islands comprise Birnie, Rawaki (formerly Phoenix), Enderbury, Manra (formerly Sydney), Orona (formerly Hull), McKean and Nikumaroro (formerly Gardner), while the others are Malden and Starbuck in the Central Line Islands, and Millennium Island (formerly Caroline), Flint and Vostok in the Southern Line Islands. The population is almost entirely Micronesian.

English is the official language; I-Kiribati (Gilbertese) is also spoken.

SOCIAL STATISTICS

2005 estimates: births, 2,460; deaths, 810. Rates, 2005 estimates (per 1,000 population): births, 26·6; deaths, 8·7. Infant mortality rate (2005), 48 per 1,000 live births; life expectancy (2005), 61·0 years. Annual population growth rate, 2000–05, 1·8%; fertility rate, 2004, 4·1 births per woman.

CLIMATE

The Line Islands, Phoenix Islands and Banaba have a maritime equatorial climate, but the islands further north and south are tropical. Annual and daily ranges of temperature are small; mean annual rainfall ranges from 50" (1,250 mm) near the equator to 120" (3,000 mm) in the north. Typhoons are prevalent (Nov.–March) and there are occasional tornadoes. Tarawa, Jan. 83°F (28·3°C), July 82°F (27·8°C). Annual rainfall 79" (1,977 mm).

CONSTITUTION AND GOVERNMENT

Under the constitution founded on 12 July 1979 the republic has a unicameral legislature, the *House of Assembly* (Maneaba ni Maungatabu), comprising 46 members, 44 of whom are elected by popular vote, and two (the Attorney-General *ex officio* and a representative from the Banaban community) appointed for a four-year term. The *President* is both Head of State and government. Presidential candidates are initially selected by members of parliament before facing a popular vote.

National Anthem

'Teirake kain Kiribati' ('Stand up, Kiribatians'); words and tune by U. Ioteba.

RECENT ELECTIONS

The last House of Assembly elections were held on 22 and 30 Aug. 2007. Boutokanto Koaava (BK; 'Pillars of Truth') won 18 seats and Maneaban te Mauri (MTM; 'Protect the Maneaba') won 7, with 19 going to independents.

On 17 Oct. 2007 Anote Tong (BK) was re-elected president by parliament with 64·3% of the vote, defeating Nabuti Mwemwenikarawa who took 33·4%, Patrick Tatireta with 1·5% and Timon Aneri with 0·8%.

CURRENT ADMINISTRATION

President and Minister of Foreign Affairs and Immigration: Anote Tong (elected 4 July 2003).

In March 2010 the government comprised:

Vice President and Minister of Commerce, Industry and Co-operatives: Teima Onorio.

Minister of Communications, Transport and Tourism Development: Temate Ereateiti. *Education, Youth and Sport Development:* James Taom. *Environment, Lands and Agricultural Development:* Tetabo Nakara. *Finance and Economic Development:* Naatan Teewe. *Fisheries and Marine Resources Development:* Taberannang Timeon. *Health and Medical Services:* Dr Kautu Tenaua. *Internal and Social Affairs:* Amberoti Nikora. *Labour and Human Resources Development:* Ioteba Redfern. *Line and Phoenix Islands:* Tawita Temoku. *Public Works and Utilities:* Kouraiti Beniato.

Parliament Website: http://www.parliament.gov.ki

CURRENT LEADERS

Anote Tong

Position
President

Introduction
Anote Tong became president of the Pacific Ocean republic in July 2003 and was re-elected in Oct. 2007. The president is chief of state and head of government.

Early Life
Anote Tong was born in the British Gilbert and Ellice Islands colony in 1952, the son of a Chinese father and a Gilbertian mother. He was an undergraduate at the University of Canterbury, Christchurch, New Zealand and graduated in 1988 with an MSc from the London School of Economics.

He entered politics in 1976 as an assistant secretary in the ministry of education, then served in the ministry of communications and works during the 1980s. Between 1994–96 he was minister of environment and natural resources in the government of President Teburoro Tito, after which he represented Maiana Island in parliament. When Tito lost a parliamentary confidence motion shortly after being elected to serve for a third term, the speaker, Taomati Iuta, led an interim government until presidential elections in July 2003. Anote Tong stood for the opposition Boutokanto Koaava party (Pillars of Truth) against his older brother, the government candidate Dr Harry Tong. Anote won by 13,500 to 12,500 votes.

Career in Office
Following Tong's election his brother mounted a court challenge alleging electoral fraud but in Oct. 2003 an Australian judge ruled in President Tong's favour. During his campaign the president had promised to review the lease on a satellite-tracking base used by China. Within six months of taking office the president established relations with Taiwan, which had paid a large sum for fishing rights in Kiribati's territorial waters. China severed relations with Kiribati and abandoned the satellite-tracking base.

During 2004 the political scene was dominated by a dispute between the president and his brother over the extent of Taiwanese influence in Kiribati affairs. The government was also faced by high unemployment and rising sea levels caused by climate change, a pressing threat to the 33-island archipelago, whose land rises only a few metres above sea level. In March 2006 the government created a large marine reserve, banning fishing around the Phoenix Islands.

Following parliamentary elections in Aug. 2007, Tong was returned in Oct. for another presidential term. He has continued to publicize the threat posed to Kiribati by rising sea levels and the prospect that the population may eventually need to be resettled elsewhere.

INTERNATIONAL RELATIONS

Kiribati is a member of the UN, World Bank, ILO, IMF, Commonwealth, Asian Development Bank, Pacific Islands Forum and SPC and is an ACP member state of the ACP-EU relationship.

ECONOMY

Agriculture accounted for 7·1% of GDP in 2006, industry 6·6% and services 86·4%.

Overview

Following independence in 1979, the economy experienced moderate growth from the mid-1980s until 2003. Growth has been driven by fishing licence fees from its Exclusive Economic Zone, drawings from the Revenue Equalization Reserve Fund (which constitutes pre-1979 revenues accrued from phosphate mining), passport fees and foreign aid (including remittances from Kiribati seamen). The economy has a narrow production base with exports limited to copra, seaweed and fish from which around 80% of households make a living. The public sector dominates the economy, accounting for nearly 80% of employment.

Limited resources and geographic isolation make transport and communications costly. The country is also one of the most vulnerable to climate change and sea-level rise. However, public finances remain sound, with the fiscal deficit declining to 13·3% of GDP in 2008 from 16% the previous year, while improvements have been made in revenue administration. Financial stability will support the capitalization of Kiribati's marine and natural resources, with growth opportunities in fishing and tourism.

Currency

The currency in use is the Australian *dollar*. After three years of deflation consumer prices rose by 4·2% in 2007 and 11·0% in 2008.

Budget

Foreign financial aid, mainly from the UK and Japan, has amounted to 25–50% of GDP in recent years. Revenues in 2005 totalled $A182·4m. and expenditures $A78·6m.

Performance

Following negative growth of –0·5% in 2007 the economy grew by 3·4% in 2008. Total GDP in 2008 was US$131m.

Banking and Finance

The Bank of Kiribati is 25% government-owned and 75% owned by ANZ Bank. In 1999 it had total assets of $A46·3m. There is also a Development Bank of Kiribati and a network of village lending banks and credit institutions.

ENERGY AND NATURAL RESOURCES

Environment

Carbon dioxide emissions from the consumption and flaring of fossil fuels were the equivalent of 0·4 tonnes per capita in 2008.

Electricity

Installed capacity (2004 estimate), 3,000 kW; production (2004), 10m. kWh.

Agriculture

In 2007 there were about 2,000 ha. of arable land and 35,000 ha. of permanent crops. Copra and fish represent the bulk of production and exports. The principal tree is the coconut; other food-bearing trees are the pandanus palm and the breadfruit. The only vegetable which grows in any quantity is a coarse calladium (alocasia) with the local name 'bwabwai', which is cultivated in pits; taro and sweet potatoes are also grown. Coconut production

(2003), 99,000 tonnes; copra, 7,000 tonnes; bananas, 5,000 tonnes; taro, 2,000 tonnes. Principal livestock: pigs (12,000 in 2003).

Fisheries

Tuna fishing is an important industry; licenses are held by the USA, Japan and the Republic of Korea. Catches in 2005 totalled an estimated 34,000 tonnes, exclusively from sea fishing.

INDUSTRY

Industry is concentrated on fishing and handicrafts.

Labour

The economically active population classified as cash workers (not including village workers engaged in subsistence activities) totalled 13,133 in 2005. In 2005, 52·9% of cash workers were employed in public administration, 11·2% in transport and communication, 9·0% in retail trade, and 7·1% in agriculture and fishing. 6·1% of the labour force were unemployed in 2005; the unemployment rate in 2005 including village workers was 64·5%.

INTERNATIONAL TRADE

Imports and Exports

Total imports (2005), US$74·0m.; exports, US$3·6m. Main import sources in 2005: Australia, 35·5%; Fiji Islands, 20·9%; Japan, 17·0%; New Zealand, 5·4%. Main export markets in 2005: Free zones, 33·3%; Australia, 22·2%; Fiji Islands, 16·7%; Hong Kong, 8·3%. Principal exports: copra, seaweed, fish; imports: foodstuffs, machinery and equipment, manufactured goods and fuel.

COMMUNICATIONS

Roads

In 2002 there were 670 km of roads. There were 634 motorcycles, 610 cars and 502 trucks in 2004.

Civil Aviation

There were 20 airports in 2002. In 2003 there were scheduled services from Tarawa (Bonriki) to the Marshall Islands, Nauru and the Fiji Islands.

Shipping

The main port is at Betio (Tarawa). Other ports of entry are Banaba, English Harbor and Kanton. There is also a small network of canals in the Line Islands. The merchant marine fleet totalled 4,000 GRT in 2002.

Telecommunications

In 2008 there were 4,000 main (fixed) telephone lines. There were 1,000 PCs in use in 2004 (11·8 per 1,000 persons) and 2,000 internet users.

Postal Services

In 2003 there were 25 post offices.

SOCIAL INSTITUTIONS

Justice

Kiribati's police force is under the command of a Commissioner of Police who is also responsible for prisons, immigration, fire service (both domestic and airport) and firearms licensing. There is a Court of Appeal and High Court, with judges at all levels appointed by the President.

The population in penal institutions in May 2007 was 88 (equivalent to 82 per 100,000 of national population).

Education

In 2005 there were 16,133 pupils and 654 teachers at primary schools and 7,487 pupils in general secondary education with 665 teachers. 51·6% of males and 49·5% of females had received secondary or higher education in 2005 compared to 27·1% of males and 20·6% of females in 1995. There is a regional campus of the University of the South Pacific on Tarawa. Other post-secondary institutions include a teachers' training college, a marine training centre, a fisheries training centre, a school of nursing and and a technical institute.

Health

The government maintains free medical and other services. In 1998 there were 26 physicians, four dentists and 208 nurses. There was one hospital on Tarawa in 1990 with 283 beds, and dispensaries on other islands.

RELIGION

In 2005, 55% of the population were Roman Catholic and 36% Kiribati Protestant; there are also small numbers of Seventh-Day Adventists, Latter-day Saints (Mormons), Bahais and Church of God.

CULTURE

Broadcasting

Radio Kiribati, a division of the Broadcasting and Publications Authority, transmits daily in English and I-Kiribati from Tarawa. There is no domestic television service. A satellite link to Australia was established in 1985. There were 4,000 TV receivers in 2003.

Cinema

There are no cinemas. There is a private-owned projector with film shows once a week in every village on South Tarawa.

Press

In 2003 there were two newspapers: the government-owned Te Uekera and the independent weekly Kiribati Newstar.

Tourism

There were 5,687 visitors to Kiribati in 2007.

DIPLOMATIC REPRESENTATIVES

Of Kiribati in the United Kingdom
Acting High Commissioner: Makurita Baaro (resides in Kiribati).
Honorary Consul: Michael Walsh (The Great House, Llanddewi Rhydderch, Monmouthshire, NP7 9UY).

Of the United Kingdom in Kiribati
High Commissioner: Mac McLachlan, MBE (resides in Suva, Fiji Islands).

Of the USA in Kiribati
Ambassador: C. Steven McGann (resides in Suva, Fiji Islands).

FURTHER READING

Tearo, T., *Coming of Age.* 1989

National Statistical Office: Kiribati Statistics Office, PO Box 67, Bairiki.
Website: http://www.spc.int/prism/Country/ki/Stats

KOREA, NORTH

Chosun Minchu-chui Inmin Konghwa-guk
(Democratic People's Republic of Korea)

Capital: Pyongyang
Population estimate, 2010: 23·99m.
GDP per capita: not available
GNI per capita, 2007: US$600

KEY HISTORICAL EVENTS

The Korean peninsula was first settled by tribal peoples from Manchuria and Siberia who provided the basis for the modern Korean language. By 3000 BC agriculture-based communities had emerged. The earliest known colony in the region was established at Pyongyang in the 12th century BC. Among the most prominent agricultural communities was Old Choson, which by 194 BC had evolved into a league of tribes ruled by Wiman or 'Wei Man', a leader widely held to have defected from China, although he may have been a native of the Choson region. His realm was taken over by the Han empire of China in 108 BC and replaced by four Chinese colonies.

The rest of the peninsula developed into tribal states; Puyo in the north and Chin south of the Han River. Chin was itself split into three tribal states (Mahan, Chinhan and Pyonhan); these states then evolved into three rival kingdoms (Koguryo, Paekche and Silla). Three powerful figures, King T'aejo (AD 53–146) of Koguryo, King Koi (AD 234–86) of Paekche and King Naemul (AD 356–402) of Silla, established hereditary monarchies while powerful aristocracies developed from tribal chiefdoms.

With China's support Silla conquered the other two kingdoms; Paekche in 660 and Koguryo in 668. In 676 Silla drove out the Chinese and gained complete control of the peninsula. Survivors from Koguryo established Parhae, under the leadership of Tae Cho-yong, in the northern region. After a period of conflict with Silla, Parhae grew into a prosperous state in its own right before being taken over by northern nomadic peoples. In Silla an absolute monarchy replaced the council of nobles (its former decision making body) with a central administrative body called the chancellery (*Chipsabu*), thus undermining aristocratic power. Meanwhile, the capital Kumsong (now Kyongju in South Korea) was developed. The state was divided into administrative units by province (*chu*), prefecture (*kun*), and county (*hyon*), and five provincial capitals prospered as cultural centres. Avatamsaka Buddhism was the dominant religion.

Divisions within the aristocracy in the 8th century led to the restoration of the Council of Nobles and the overthrow of the monarchy. Forced to pay taxes to powerful provincial families and central government, the peasants rebelled. Two provincial leaders, Kyonhwon and Kungye, established the Later Paekche (892) and Later Koguryo (901) as rivals to Silla.

National Unity

The powerful leader Wang Kon founded Koryo (now Kaesong, North Korea) in 918, and established a unified kingdom in the Korean peninsula in 936. Three chancelleries and the royal secretariat formed the supreme council of state and governed the kingdom. Koryo's leaders were then largely aristocratic, and the political system greatly favoured those in the top five tiers of the nine hierarchical levels. That the military was not eligible for any hierarchical position above the second level and received little land, led to a military coup in 1170. Gen. Ch'oe Ch'ung-hon established a military regime which held power for the next sixty years. Zen Buddhism and the allied ideology of Confucianism had grown popular but were suppressed under the Ch'oe regime. Many monks fled to the mountains, where they formed what became Korean Buddhism, the *Chogye*.

In 1231 the Mongols invaded Koryo but were resisted by the Ch'oe leaders for nearly three decades, until a peasant uprising saw the Ch'oe overthrown. A power-sharing agreement between the rebels and the Mongols came into force in 1258. Despite some interference from the Mongols, Koryo retained its identity as a unified state. The aristocracy established seats of power throughout the country, encouraging peasants to seek protection as serfs. This, however, led to reduced tax revenues and when the government did not have sufficient resources to reward its bureaucratic class, a rebellion ensued. Led by General Yi Song-gye, and with the help of the Ming dynasty in China, government officials seized power in 1392 and established a new system of land distribution, thus ending the Koryo dynasty.

Gen. Yi named the state Choson, designating Hanyang (now Seoul, South Korea) as the capital. Buddhism was dropped in favour of a new Chinese-influenced Confucian ethical system and the state was governed by a hereditary aristocracy (the *yangban*), who controlled all aspects of Korean society. In 1420 the Hall of Worthies (*Chiphyonjon*) was established for scholars, and after 1443 the Korean phonetic alphabet (*hangul*) developed. Later in the period, a centralized yangban government was formed and the country divided into eight administrative regions, with standardized laws and a central decision-making and judicial body.

In 1592 Japan, newly unified under the command of Toyotomi Hideyoshi, sent an army to Korea supposedly as part of an invasion of China. Korea's naval forces, under Admiral Yi Sun-shin, were able to repel the invaders. Swelling anti-Japanese sentiment prompted Koreans from all hierarchical divisions to fight in the war alongside troops dispatched from Ming China. However, Japanese forces did not withdraw completely until Toyotomi's death in 1598, leaving Korea in ruins.

Despite joint efforts by China and Korea to stem the advances of the nomadic Manchu in the early 17th century, Seoul was captured in 1636. The Manchu established the Ch'ing dynasty several years later and demanded tribute from Korea.

During the 17th and 18th centuries, Korea's agriculture developed as irrigation improved and rice, tobacco and ginseng became increasingly important crops. By the late 18th century many Korean scholars had turned to Roman Catholicism, leading to government suppression of Christianity in a bid to preserve the dominance of Confucianism. However, European priests maintained strong links in the country.

Japanese Influence

In the 19th century, a succession of monarchs yet to attain the age of majority undermined national stability. In 1864 Taewon'gun, the father of the child-king Kojong, took power and pursued a programme of controversial political reform that increasingly isolated Korea from the outside world. When Taewon'gun was eventually forced to step down, Korea came under pressure from Japan to open up its ports. Nervous of growing Japanese influence, China placed troops in Korea following a failed coup attempt by pro-Taewon'gun forces. There followed a trade agreement which greatly benefited Chinese commercial interests. Further treaties with France, Germany, Russia, the UK and the USA followed in the 1880s. As foreign influence increased, Korea's ruling elite divided between moderates and radicals. The radicals carried out a coup in 1884 but were quickly defeated by Chinese troops. An agreement to maintain a balance of power in the region was signed by Japan and China the following year.

As modernization gathered pace, government spending increased, adding to the burden of reparations payments to Japan. The peasants turned to *Tonghak* ('Eastern Learning'), a new religion established by an old yangban scholar and based on traditional beliefs. A Tonghak rebellion in 1894 caused China to send in troops. Japan responded by sending its own forces and war broke out. By the following year Japan had secured control of the peninsula.

Korea declared neutrality at the outbreak of war between Japan and Russia in 1904 but was pressured by Japan into allowing use of Korean territory. Japan achieved victory in 1905 and made Korea a protectorate. An unsuccessful appeal to the international peace conference at The Hague further undermined relations between Japan and Korea. Anti-Japanese guerrilla fighters in the southern provinces were active during 1908–09 but were crushed the following year when Korea was annexed by Japan.

Japan established a government in Korea and implemented a programme designed to supplant the Korean identity. There were restrictions on freedom of speech, press and assembly and the language and history of Japan was taught in schools at the expense of those of Korea. Many Koreans were dispossessed of their land as Japan built new transport and communications infrastructures. When the Japanese brutally suppressed a 2m.-strong demonstration in 1919, independence leaders established a provisional government in Shanghai and named Syngman Rhee as president. Hoping to calm dissent, Japan lifted certain press restrictions and replaced the gendarmerie with an ordinary police force, but uncompromising colonial rule remained in place.

Korea became a market for Japanese goods and attracted much capital investment but at the expense of agriculture, leading to a long-term shortage of rice. Tokyo reimposed military rule in 1931 when war broke out between Japan and China and attempted to quash all manifestations of a separate Korean identity over the following decade. Magazines, newspapers and academic organisations operating in the Korean language were banned and hundred of thousands of Koreans were made to fight in the Japanese army or work in Japanese mines and factories in order to support Japan's military efforts during the Second World War. The Shanghai provisional government, having moved to Chungking in southwest China, declared war on Japan in Dec. 1941. An army of resistance fighters joined the Allied forces in China and fought with them until the Japanese surrender in 1945.

Korea Divided

Korea was promised independence by China, Britain and the USA at the Cairo conference of 1943 but at the end of the war, after Japan's collapse, Korea was divided in two along the 38° Parallel. Initially the USA and the USSR had agreed informally to a four-way power share in Korea, involving Britain and the Republic of China. However, in order to hasten a Japanese surrender, US troops controlled the south of the country while the USSR took command of the north. The Soviet forces helped to establish a Communist-led provisional government under Kim Il Sung. As relations between the USA and the Soviet Union worsened, trade ceased between the two zones, causing economic hardship because industry was concentrated in the north and agriculture in the south.

In Sept. 1947 the United Nations reviewed the question of Korean reunification and general elections in Korea were proposed. However, a commission to oversee voting was denied entry by Soviet troops. Rhee was elected in the South while the North appointed Kim Il Sung as leader. In 1948 the southern Republic of Korea (with Seoul as the capital) and the northern Democratic People's Republic of Korea (with Pyongyang as capital) formally came into being.

Soviet and US troops left the peninsula in 1949 and war broke out between the North and South in June 1950. A US-led UN force under Gen. Douglas MacArthur entered South Korea and pushed back the North Korean forces. The UN pressed on into North Korea and established a commission for the reunification and rehabilitation of Korea. China, which at that point had no representation in the United Nations, entered the war and contributed 1·2m. troops to the North Korean side. Negotiations to end the war began in 1951 and a new international boundary and demilitarized zone were declared in 1953. The USA offered South Korea financial support and signed a mutual security pact with Rhee, who had been reluctant to accept the division of the country. The issue of prisoner returns, particularly of North Koreans unwilling to return to the communist state, remained a point of contention. The war left 4m. people dead or injured.

In the aftermath, Kim set about tightening his grip on his country by purging potential rivals. He established a dictatorship based on a personality cult and introduced his philosophy of *Juche*, by which the country was to develop without any help from outside. Industrialization and military spending gathered pace in the later 1950s and the 1960s despite North Korea's international isolation. However, by the late 1970s North Korea had fallen far behind its southern neighbour and a period of stagnation began.

Kim maintained close relations with China and the Soviet Union, although his allegiance wavered between the two as Sino-Soviet relations deteriorated from the 1960s onwards. When the Soviet Union collapsed in 1990–91, North Korea went into an economic crisis that included widespread famine. Attempts to improve relations with South Korea in the early 1990s faltered over the North's alleged nuclear capacity although in 1994 North Korea agreed to shut down controversial reactors in return for aid and oil. Kim died in 1994 and power passed to his son, Kim Jong Il, who, like his father, has received international condemnation for civil rights abuses.

Under the younger Kim the economy has collapsed to subsistence level although spending on the military remains high. In 1997 the UN World Food Programme estimated that 2m. North Koreans faced starvation. More than 5% of the population starved to death during the 1990s. In 2000 Kim received South Korean President Kim Dae-jung as relations between the North and South appeared to be thawing. The two leaders agreed that reunification was the eventual aim of both Koreas but relations had again deteriorated by 2002 after a naval battle in the Yellow Sea between North and South forces killed four South Korean and around 30 North Korean sailors. Kim Jong Il blamed the USA and South Korea for the attack. South Korean president Kim

Dae-jung suspended rice shipments to the north and demanded an apology.

Relations with the USA worsened during 2002 and 2003 after the USA claimed that North Korea had a secret nuclear programme. US president George W. Bush accused North Korea of forming part of what he called the 'Axis of Evil' along with Iraq and Iran. North Korea subsequently reactivated a nuclear plant and demanded the withdrawal of inspectors from the UN International Atomic Energy Agency. Pyongyang claimed it had been forced to reopen the reactor in response to US plans for a pre-emptive nuclear strike. North Korea then announced its withdrawal from the nuclear non-proliferation treaty, although it denied any intention to produce nuclear weapons. Many observers suggested Kim carried out these manoeuvres to pressurize the USA into direct talks with a view to signing a mutual non-aggression pact. North Korea's nuclear programme has in turn unsettled relations with regional neighbours including South Korea and Japan. In Feb. 2005 North Korea publicly admitted for the first time that it possessed nuclear weapons. On 9 Oct. 2006 it conducted its first test of a nuclear weapon, carrying out an underground explosion. In Feb. 2007 at talks between North Korea, South Korea, Japan, Russia, China and the USA, Pyongyang agreed to close its chief nuclear reactor in return for fuel aid. In Oct. 2007 it agreed to close a further three installations and was scheduled to surrender its nuclear stockpile in 2008. However, Pyongyang missed a Dec. 2007 deadline to disclose full details of all of its nuclear facilities. Also in Oct. 2007 North and South Korea issued a joint declaration calling for a permanent peace on the peninsula to replace the armistice in place since the end of the Korean War.

TERRITORY AND POPULATION

North Korea is bounded in the north by China, east by the Sea of Japan (East Sea of Korea), west by the Yellow Sea and south by South Korea, from which it is separated by a demilitarized zone of 1,262 sq. km. Its area is 122,762 sq. km.

The census population in 2008 was 24,052,231; density 195·9 per sq. km.

The UN gives an estimated population for 2010 of 23·99m.

The area, 2008 census population (in 1,000) of the provinces and Pyongyang (directly governed city):

	Area in sq. km	*Population*	*Chief Town*
Chagang	16,968	1,300	Kanggye
North Hamgyong[1]	17,570	2,327	Chongjin
South Hamgyong	18,970	3,066	Hamhung
North Hwanghae[2]	9,262	2,114	Sariwon
South Hwanghae	8,002	2,310	Haeju
Kangwon[3]	11,152	1,478	Wonsan
North Pyongan[4]	12,191	2,729	Sinuiju
South Pyongan	12,330	4,052	Pyongsong
Pyongyang (directly governed city)	2,000	3,255	
Yanggang	14,317	719	Hyesan

[1]Area and population include Rason directly governed city.
[2]Area and population include Kaesong industrial region.
[3]Area and population include Kumgangsan tourist region.
[4]Area and population include Sinuiju special administrative region.

Pyongyang, the capital, had a 2008 census population of 2,581,076. Other large towns (census, 2008): Hamhung (703,610); Chongjin (614,892); Sinuiju (334,031).

The official language is Korean.

SOCIAL STATISTICS

1995 births, 477,000; deaths, 122,000. 1995 birth rate, 21·6 per 1,000 population; death rate, 5·5. Annual population growth rate, 1990–99, 1·6%. Marriage is discouraged before the age of 32 for men and 29 for women. Life expectancy at birth, 2007, was 64·9 years for men and 69·1 years for women. Infant mortality, 2005, 42 per 1,000 live births; fertility rate, 2004, 2·0 births per woman. It was estimated in 1999 that up to 300,000 North Korean food-seeking refugees had gone to China to escape the famine. 27% of the population is classified as 'hostile' by the regime and 45% as 'unstable'.

CLIMATE

There is a warm temperate climate, though winters can be very cold in the north. Rainfall is concentrated in the summer months. Pyongyang, Jan. 18°F (–7·8°C), July 75°F (23·9°C). Annual rainfall 37" (916 mm).

CONSTITUTION AND GOVERNMENT

The political structure is based upon the constitution of 27 Dec. 1972. Constitutional amendments of April 1992 delete references to Marxism-Leninism but retain the Communist Party's monopoly of rule. The Constitution provides for a 687-seat *Supreme People's Assembly* elected every five years by universal suffrage. Citizens of 17 years and over can vote and be elected. The government consists of the *Administration Council* directed by the Central People's Committee.

The head of state is the *President*, elected for four-year terms. On the death of Kim Il Sung on 8 July 1994 his son and designated successor, Kim Jong Il (b. 1942), assumed all his father's posts. On 5 Sept. 1998 he took over as President and 'Supreme Leader'.

Party membership was 2m. in 1995. There are also the puppet religious Chongu and Korean Social Democratic Parties and various organizations combined in a Fatherland Front.

National Anthem

'A chi mun bin na ra i gang san' ('Shine bright, o dawn, on this land so fair'); words by Pak Se Yong, tune by Kim Won Gyun.

RECENT ELECTIONS

Elections to the Supreme People's Assembly were held on 8 March 2009. Only the list of the Democratic Front for the Reunification of the Fatherland (led by the Korean Workers' Party) was allowed to participate. 687 deputies were elected unopposed.

CURRENT ADMINISTRATION

President: Kim Jong Il. He also holds the posts of *Supreme Commander of the Korean People's Army* and *Chairman of the National Defence Commission.*

In March 2010 the government comprised:

Prime Minister: Kim Yong-il; b. 1944 (appointed 11 April 2007).

Vice Prime Ministers: Kwak Pom-ki, Ro Tu-chol, Pak Myong-son, O Su-yong, Pak Su-gil (also *Minister of Finance*).

Minister of Agriculture: Kim Chang-sik. *Capital City Construction:* Kim Ung-gwan. *Chemical Industry:* Yi Mu-yong. *Coal Industry:* Kim Hyong-sik. *Commerce:* Kim Pong-chol. *Construction and Building Materials Industry:* Tong Chong-ho. *Culture:* Kang Nung-su. *Education:* Kim Yong-chin. *Electronic Industry:* Han Kwang-bok. *Extractive Industries:* Kang Min-chol. *Fisheries:* Pak Thae-won. *Food Procurement and Administration:* Mun Ung-jo. *Foodstuffs and Daily Necessities Industry:* Jong Yon-gwa. *Foreign Affairs:* Pak Ui-chun. *Foreign Trade:* Ri Ryong-nam. *Forestry:* Kim Kwang-yong. *Labour:* Jong Yong-su. *Land and Environment Protection:* Pak Song-nam. *Land and Marine Transport:* Ra Tong-hui. *Light Industry:* Yi Chu-o. *Machine-Building Industry:* Jo Pyong-ju. *Metal Industry:* Kim Tae-bong. *Oil:* Kim Hui-yong. *People's Security:* Ju Sang-song. *Post and Telecommunications:* Ryu Yong-sop. *Power Industry:* Ho Taek. *Public Health:* Choe Chang-sik. *Railways:* Chon Kil-su. *State Construction Control:* Pae Tal-chun. *State Inspection:* Kim Ui-sun. *Urban Management:* Hwang Hak-won.

President, Supreme People's Assembly Praesidium: Kim Yong-nam. *Vice Presidents:* Yang Hyong-sop, Kim Yong-dae.

In addition there is one minister who is not in the cabinet. *Minister of the People's Armed Forces:* Kim Yong-chun.

In practice the country is ruled by the Korean Workers' (i.e. Communist) Party which elects a Central Committee that in turn appoints a Politburo.

Government Website: http://www.korea-dpr.com

CURRENT LEADERS

Kim Jong Il

Position
President

Introduction
Kim Jong Il is the second ruler of the world's only Communist dynasty. Groomed to succeed his father, Kim Il Sung, the founder of the Democratic People's Republic of Korea (North Korea), Kim junior is commonly known to his countrymen as the 'Dear Leader'. Despite some thawing in foreign relations, North Korea's nuclear weapons programme has continued to cause international unease, particularly since Oct. 2006 when the country claimed to have carried out its first nuclear test. Multilateral talks with the USA, China, Russia, Japan and South Korea on disabling the North's nuclear facilities have since made stuttering progress, but suspicions remain about the true ambitions of Kim's secretive regime, which has concurrently presided over the collapse of the country's economy to subsistence level.

Early Life
According to some accounts, Kim Jong Il was born on 16 Feb. 1941 on Paekdusan, the highest mountain in Korea, although it is probable he was born in the Siberian city of Khabarovsk, where his father was based at the time and where he spent his first four years.

Kim Jong Il returned with his family to Korea after World War II, only to be sent to China for safety at the outbreak of the Korean War (1950–53). Thereafter, he grew up in North Korea, where he has since lived apart from a brief period in East Germany training to be a pilot. On his return he studied at the Kim Il Sung University in Pyongyang.

From the early 1960s Kim Jong Il was groomed to succeed his father. In the mid-1960s he helped his father purge the (Communist) Korean Workers' Party (KWP) and held a variety of posts within the party. In 1973, Kim Jong Il was placed in charge of party propaganda and organization. In 1980 he was named as his father's heir. During the 1970s and 1980s he was appointed to various high offices, beginning with election to the KWP Politburo in 1974. In Dec. 1991 he took over the country's armed forces and three years later, on his father's death, he became president.

Career in Office
Kim Jong Il did not immediately assume any of his father's offices of state. He became general secretary of the KWP in 1997 and chairman of the National Defence Commission, a role that is now effectively head of state. He maintained spending on the military, considered the base of his support, and encouraged the development of a missile programme. His regime was widely perceived to have nuclear ambitions and in Jan. 2002 US President George Bush labelled North Korea part of an 'Axis of Evil' with Iraq and Iran.

In 2000 he received South Korean President Kim Dae-jung on an unprecedented visit. Although the two leaders agreed that reunification was the eventual aim of both Koreas, relations deteriorated in June 2002 after a naval engagement in the Yellow Sea between North and South forces. Kim Jong Il blamed the USA and South Korea for the attack.

In Sept. 2002 some progress was made in ending North Korea's isolation when the Japanese prime minister Junichiro Koizumi visited the president in a move to re-establish diplomatic relations, although Kim was forced to admit to, and apologize for, the kidnapping of 11 Japanese citizens in 1970s and 1980s. In Oct. 2002 North Korea admitted to developing nuclear technology in contravention of an agreement signed with the USA in 1994. In late Nov. 2002 the EU, Japan and South Korea suspended fuel oil shipments to North Korea. The crisis between Kim's regime and the USA intensified in Dec. 2002 and Jan. 2003 when North Korea reactivated a nuclear plant and demanded the withdrawal of inspectors from the UN International Atomic Energy Agency (IAEA). Pyongyang claimed it had been forced to reopen the reactor in response to US plans for a pre-emptive nuclear strike. North Korea then announced its withdrawal from the Nuclear Non-Proliferation Treaty, although it denied any intention to produce nuclear weapons. President Bush responded with proposals for a 'tailored containment' strategy, potentially involving economic sanctions. South Korea opposed attempts to isolate the North Korean economy and sent diplomats to China and Russia, two of North Korea's traditional allies, in a bid to exert pressure on Pyongyang to reconsider its nuclear policy.

Relations with the international community deteriorated further in early 2003. The IAEA formally reported North Korea to the UN Security Council for failing to comply with nuclear non-proliferation accords. Pyongyang responded by asserting its capability to attack US interests throughout the world if provoked. The following month Pyongyang launched two short-range anti-ship missiles in the direction of the Sea of Japan. Kim then withdrew from border liaison negotiations with US officials and the North Korean parliament increased its defence budget. Pyongyang had earlier claimed that joint military exercises between the USA and South Korea, which coincided with the invasion of Iraq, were a sign that the USA intended to launch strikes on the North's nuclear establishments. Pyongyang also accused Japan of a 'hostile act' after it launched two spy satellites. In April 2003 Chinese-brokered talks with the USA ended acrimoniously and the following month Pyongyang announced its withdrawal from a 1992 accord with South Korea guaranteeing the Korean peninsula as a nuclear weapon-free zone.

In July 2003 Pyongyang claimed to have produced enough plutonium to start making nuclear bombs. Over the next three years there followed several rounds of inconclusive negotiations between North Korea and the USA, together with South Korea, Japan, China and Russia. During this period Kim's regime admitted publicly in Feb 2005 that it had built nuclear weapons for self-defence before agreeing in principle in Sept. 2005 to give up its development programme in return for aid and security guarantees. However, that accord was almost immediately undermined when North Korea then demanded the delivery of civil nuclear equipment. In July 2006 North Korea test-fired seven missiles in defiance of international warnings, and on 9 Oct. announced that it had carried out its first nuclear test. Reflecting worldwide condemnation, the UN Security Council voted to impose punitive sanctions, which Kim's regime called an act of war. However, as the crisis threatened to escalate further, Pyongyang announced at the end of Oct. that it would rejoin multilateral negotiations with the USA, China, Russia, Japan and South Korea, on dismantling its nuclear programme.

The talks resumed in Dec. 2006 and in Feb. 2007 North Korea agreed to shut its nuclear facilities at Yongbyon in return for fuel aid. Although implementation of the agreement was initially delayed, due to the freezing of North Korean funds under US-instigated international sanctions, inspectors were able to verify in July that Yongbyon had been shut down. There were further grounds for optimism in Oct. 2007 when Kim Jong Il met the South Korean president in Pyongyang for only the second-ever summit between the leaders of the divided peninsula since the Korean War. At the same time, at further multilateral talks in Beijing, North Korea agreed to declare all its nuclear development programmes by the end of 2007. However, Kim Jong Il failed to honour this commitment, giving no explanation for missing the deadline.

In early 2008 relations between the two Koreas deteriorated markedly as the South's new conservative president made aid conditional on the North's nuclear disarmament and progress on human rights and the North test-fired short-range missiles. In June Pyongyang submitted its overdue declaration of nuclear assets, but fresh concerns over its intentions were triggered in Sept. by its threat to resume plutonium reprocessing. However, in Oct. the USA agreed to remove the North from its list of states that sponsor terrorism in return for full access for IAEA inspectors to nuclear sites. Meanwhile, Kim Jong Il's absence from public events fuelled speculation from mid-2008 over the state of his health, with press reports claiming that he had suffered a stroke.

International tensions increased again from late 2008 and in April 2009 North Korea walked out of negotiations on its nuclear activities. The following month a second underground nuclear weapon test was conducted, prompting worldwide condemnation, and the government declared that it would no longer be bound by the armistice that ended the Korean War in 1953. In response, the UN Security Council voted unanimously in June to impose new sanctions on the North. Some optimism was generated in Oct. when Pyongyang indicated that it might be willing to resume the international talks on the nuclear issue. However, in Jan. 2010 there was further friction following renewed military exchanges between North and South Korean forces near their disputed maritime border.

In parliamentary elections in the North in March 2009, the 687 candidates nominated by the Democratic Front for the Reunification of the Fatherland (led by the Korean Workers' Party) were returned unopposed, and the following month the Supreme People's Assembly confirmed Kim Jong Il as Chairman of the National Defence Commission.

In a rare public apology to the people by the Pyongyang regime, in Feb. 2010 the prime minister acknowledged that a redenomination of the *won* in Nov. 2009 had led to a currency collapse, triggering steep price rises and threatening famine. In the same month lavish celebrations marked Kim Jong Il's birthday, although rumours of his declining health continued to circulate.

DEFENCE

The Supreme Commander of the Armed Forces is Kim Jong Il. Military service is compulsory at the age of 16 for periods of 5–12 years in the Army, 5–10 years in the Navy and 3–4 years in the Air Force, followed by obligatory part-time service in the Pacification Corps to age 40. Total armed forces troops were estimated to number 1,106,000 in 2007, up from 840,000 in 1986 although down from 1,160,000 in 1997. Around 70% of the troops are located along or near the Demilitarized Zone between North and South Korea.

Defence expenditure in 2003 totalled US$5,500m. (US$243 per capita), and represented 25·0% of GDP.

In 1998 North Korea tested a medium-range nuclear-capable Taepo Dong-1 missile. It has also developed a shorter-range No-Dong ballistic missile in addition to Scud B and Scud C missiles, and is developing a longer-range inter-continental ballistic missile, the two-stage Taepo Dong-2, which experts believe could reach Alaska and the westernmost Hawaiian islands. A first unsuccessful test was carried out in July 2006.

Nuclear Weapons

North Korea was for many years suspected of having a secret nuclear-weapons programme, and perhaps enough material to build two warheads. In Oct. 2002 it revealed that it had developed a nuclear bomb in violation of an arms control pact agreed with the USA in 1994. North Korea has not signed the Comprehensive Nuclear-Test-Ban-Treaty, which is intended to bring about a ban on any nuclear explosions. It ratified the Nuclear Non-Proliferation Treaty in 1985 but withdrew in 2003. In Feb. 2005 it declared that it had manufactured nuclear weapons and stated that it would not re-enter multilateral negotiations on its disarmament. It carried out its first test of a nuclear weapon in Oct. 2006. In July 2007 Pyongyang closed the Yongbyon nuclear complex in return for international aid and in Oct. pledged to disable a further three facilities, ahead of surrendering its nuclear stockpile in 2008. However, Pyongyang missed a Dec. 2007 deadline to give a full account of all of its nuclear facilities although it eventually did so in June 2008. The following day North Korea destroyed Yongbyon's cooling tower. Further dismantling of its nuclear facilities was postponed after the USA refused to remove North Korea from its list of state sponsors of terrorism until Pyongyang produced verification of its nuclear downgrading. North Korea was removed from the list in Oct. 2008 and pledged to resume dismantling the Yongbyon reactor.

In April 2009 North Korea was accused by South Korea and the UN of testing long-range nuclear missile technology. North Korea responded by walking out of international talks to wind up its nuclear programme. The following month Pyongyang claimed it had successfully completed underground nuclear tests. In June the UN imposed new sanctions, with Pyongyang stating its intent to weaponize plutonium supplies.

Army

One of the world's biggest, the Army was estimated at 950,000 personnel in 2007 with 600,000 reserves. There is also a paramilitary worker-peasant Red Guard of some 3·5m. and a ministry of public security force of 189,000 including border guards.

Equipment includes some 3,500 T-34, T-54/55, T-62 and Type-59 main battle tanks.

Navy

The Navy, principally tasked to coastal patrol and defence, comprises 63 diesel submarines, three small frigates and five corvettes. Personnel in 2007 totalled about 46,000 with 65,000 reserves.

Air Force

The Air Force had a total of 590 combat capable aircraft and 110,000 personnel in 2007. Combat capable aircraft include J-5/6/7s (Chinese built versions of MiG-17/19/23s), MiG-23s, MiG-29s, Su-7s and Su-25s.

INTERNATIONAL RELATIONS

In 2005 North Korea received US$81m. in foreign aid.

North Korea is a member of the UN and Antarctic Treaty.

ECONOMY

Agriculture is estimated to account for approximately 25% of GDP, industry 60% and services 15%.

Overview

In Dec. 1993 it was officially recognized that the third seven-year plan had failed to achieve its industrial targets following the disappearance of communist markets and aid. Policy now concentrates on the development of agriculture, light industry and foreign trade but progress is impeded by an all-powerful bureaucracy and a reluctance to depart from the Marxist-Stalinist line. In July 2002 a repeal of the rationing system for rice and large increases in prices for food, electricity and housing prompted hopes of an upturn but food shortages became critical in 2003 after the deterioration of relations with international donors. In Oct. 2005 the government announced a reversal of some of the 2002 reforms with a return to centralized food rationing and a ban on private grain sales. Resumption of US food assistance began in June 2008 following concerns over a major shortfall in food supplies.

Currency

The monetary unit is the *won* (KPW) of 100 *chon*. Banknotes were replaced by a new issue in July 1992. Exchanges of new for old notes were limited to 500 won. In Nov. 2009 the government readjusted the value of the won, with 100 old won worth one new won. Officially the won trades at 135 per US dollar but unofficially it can sometimes trade at up to 3,000 per dollar. Inflation was an estimated 5% in 1998.

Budget

Estimated revenue, 1999, 19,801m. won; expenditure, 20,018m. won.

Performance

The real GDP growth rate was 6·2% in 1999 following a decade of negative growth. This was followed in 2000 by growth of 1·3%, rising in 2001 to 3·7%. In both 2002 and 2003 there was growth of 0·8%. GDP per head was put at US$494 in 2003, or less than a twentieth of that of South Korea.

Banking and Finance

The bank of issue is the Central Bank of Korea (*President*, Ri Kwang Gon). In 2002 there were seven state banks, seven joint venture banks and two foreign investment banks.

Weights and Measures

While the metric system is in force traditional measures are in frequent use. The *jungbo* = one ha; the *ri* = 3,927 metres.

ENERGY AND NATURAL RESOURCES

Environment

Carbon dioxide emissions from the consumption and flaring of fossil fuels in 2008 were the equivalent of 3·1 tonnes per capita.

Electricity

There are three thermal power stations and four hydro-electric plants. Installed capacity was an estimated 9·5m. kW in 2004. Production in 2004 was 21·97bn. kWh. Consumption per capita was 968 kWh in 2004. Hydro-electric potential exceeds 8m. kW. A hydro-electric plant and dam under construction on the Pukhan River near Mount Kumgang has been denounced as a flood threat by the South Koreans, who constructed a defensive 'Peace Dam' in retaliation. American aid to increase energy supply slowed after evidence that North Korea had broken its promise to freeze its nuclear weapons programme. But in Oct. 1998 Japan agreed to contribute US$1bn. towards building two nuclear power stations and the US Congress agreed to funds to supply fuel oil on condition that North Korea abandons its nuclear ambitions. In Aug. 2002 work began on the construction of the two western-designed light-water nuclear reactors. In Feb. 2003 North Korea reactivated its nuclear reactor at Yongbyon that had been dormant since 1994. It was again shut down in July 2007 in exchange for economic aid and political concessions following negotiations with China, Japan, Russia, South Korea and the USA.

Oil and Gas

Oil wells went into production in 1957. An oil pipeline from China came on stream in 1976. China's supplies account for 70% of North Korea's oil consumption. Refinery distillation output amounted to 2·5m. tonnes in 1998.

Minerals

North Korea is rich in minerals. Estimated reserves in tonnes: coal, 11,990m.; manganese, 6,500m.; iron ore, 3,300m.; uranium, 26m.; zinc, 12m.; lead, 6m.; copper, 2·15m. 22·8m. tonnes of coal were mined in 2004, 7·3m. tonnes of lignite in 2004, 5m. tonnes of iron ore in 2006, 500,000 tonnes of salt in 2006 and 12,000 tonnes of copper in 2006. 2006 production of silver was 20 tonnes; gold, 2,000 kg.

Agriculture

In 2007 there were approximately 2·8m. ha. of arable land and 200,000 ha. of permanent crop land. An estimated 3·12m. persons were economically active in agriculture in 2007.

Collectivization took place between 1954 and 1958. 90% of the cultivated land is farmed by co-operatives. Land belongs either to the State or to co-operatives, and it is intended gradually to transform the latter into the former, but small individually-tended plots producing for 'farmers' markets' are tolerated as a 'transition measure'.

There is a large-scale tideland reclamation project. In 2002 around 1·46m. ha. were under irrigation, making possible two rice harvests a year. There were an estimated 64,000 tractors in 2002. The technical revolution in agriculture (nearly 95% of ploughing, etc., is mechanized) has considerably increased the yield of wheat (sown on 58,000 ha.). Areas harvested of other major crops, 2003: rice, 593,000 ha.; maize, 495,000 ha.; potatoes, 188,000 ha. Production (2003, in 1,000 tonnes): rice, 2,284; potatoes, 2,023; maize, 1,725; cabbage, 680; apples, 660; soybeans, 360; sweet potatoes, 350; dry beans, 300; melons and watermelons, 224.

Livestock, 2003: pigs, 3·18m.; goats, 2·72m.; cattle, 576,000; sheep, 171,000; 20m. chickens.

A chronic food shortage has led to repeated efforts by UN agencies to stave off famine. In Jan. 1998 the UN launched an appeal for US$378m. for food for North Korea, the largest ever relief effort mounted by its World Fund Programme.

Forestry

Forest area in 2005 was 6·19m. ha. (51·4% of the land area). Timber production was 7·37m. cu. metres in 2007.

Fisheries

In 2005 total catch was approximately 205,000 tonnes, of which 98% were sea fish.

INDUSTRY

Industries were intensively developed by the Japanese occupiers, notably cotton spinning, hydro-electric power, cotton, silk and rayon weaving, and chemical fertilizers. Production: pig iron (2002), 800,000 tonnes; cement (2002), 5·3m. tonnes; crude steel (2000), 1·11m. tonnes; textile fabrics (1994), 350m. metres; TV sets (1995), 240,000 units; cars (2000), 6,600 units; ships (1995), 50,000 GRT. Industrial production is estimated to have halved between 1990 and 2000.

Labour

The labour force totalled 11,881,000 (55% males) in 1996. Nearly 29% of the economically active population in 2002 were engaged in agriculture.

INTERNATIONAL TRADE

Joint ventures with foreign firms have been permitted since 1984. A law of Oct. 1992 revised the 1984 rules: foreign investors may now set up wholly-owned facilities in special economic zones, repatriate part of profits and enjoy tax concessions. In 1996 foreign debt was estimated at US$11,830m. The USA imposed sanctions in Jan. 1988 for alleged terrorist activities. Since June 1995 South Korean businesses and individuals have been permitted to make investments and set up branch offices in North Korea.

Imports and Exports

Imports in 2001 were US$1,847m.; exports, US$826m. In 2001 China was the biggest import supplier (31%), followed by Japan (13%) and South Korea (12%); Japan was the main export destination (27%), ahead of South Korea (21%) and China (20%). The chief imports are machinery and petroleum products, the chief exports metal ores and products.

COMMUNICATIONS

Roads

There were around 31,200 km of road in 2002, of which 2,000 km were paved. There were 262,000 passenger cars in 2000. The first of two planned cross-border roads between the two Koreas opened in Feb. 2003.

Rail

The railway network totalled 8,533 km in 1990, of which 3,250 km were electrified. In 1990, 38·5m. tonnes of freight and 35m. passengers were carried. In June 2000 it was agreed to start consultations to restore the railway from Sinuiju, on the North Korean/Chinese border, to Seoul by rebuilding an 8 km long stretch from Pongdong-ni to Changdan, on the North Korean/South Korean border, and a 12 km long stretch in South Korea. Two passenger trains crossed the border between North and South Korea on 17 May 2007 (one northbound and one southbound), completing the first cross-border journey in more than 50 years. Regular freight services between the two Koreas were resumed in Dec. 2007.

There is a metro and two tramways in Pyongyang.

Civil Aviation

There is an international airport at Pyongyang (Sunan). There were flights in 2003 to Bangkok, Beijing, Khabarovsk, Macao, Shenyang and Vladivostok. The national carrier is Air Koryo.

Shipping

The leading ports are Chongjin, Wonsan and Hungnam. Pyongyang is connected to the port of Nampo by railway and river. In 2002 the ocean-going merchant fleet totalled 870,000 GRT, including oil tankers 16,000 GRT.

The biggest navigable river is the Yalu, 698 km up to the Hyesan district.

Telecommunications

There were 1,180,000 main (fixed) telephone lines in 2008. A mobile phone service was introduced in Dec. 2008 four years after a previous service had been shut down without explanation. In March 2009 there were 20,000 subscribers.

SOCIAL INSTITUTIONS

Justice

The judiciary consists of the Supreme Court, whose judges are elected by the Assembly for three years; provincial courts; and city or county people's courts. The procurator-general, appointed by the Assembly, has supervisory powers over the judiciary and the administration; the Supreme Court controls the judicial administration.

In Jan. 1999 approximately 200,000 political prisoners were being held at ten detention camps in the country. North Korea does not divulge figures on its use of the death penalty; however, Amnesty International reported that there were at least 15 executions in 2008.

Education

Free compulsory universal technical education lasts 11 years: one pre-school year, four years primary education starting at the age of six, followed by six years secondary. In 1994–95 there were 37 universities, 31 specialized universities and 108 specialized colleges.

The adult literacy rate in 2004 was 98·0%.

Health

Medical treatment is free. In 2003 there were 74,597 doctors (one per 312·5 population), 87,330 nurses and 6,084 midwives. In 2002 there were 214,647 hospital beds (92 per 10,000 population). 6·3% of GDP was spent on health care in 2004.

North Korea has been one of the least successful countries in the battle against undernourishment in the past 15 years. The proportion of undernourished people rose from 18% of the population in the period 1990–92 to 35% in 2001–03.

RELIGION

The Constitution provides for 'freedom of religion as well as the freedom of anti-religious propaganda'. In 2001 there were 3·0m. Chondoists. Another 3·4m. followed traditional beliefs. There were also significant numbers of Christians and Buddhists.

CULTURE

World Heritage Sites

There is one UNESCO site in North Korea: the Complex of Koguryo Tombs (2004).

Broadcasting

The government-run Korean Central Broadcasting Station and Korean Central Television control all radio and TV output in the country. Voice of Korea is the state-run external service. There were 3·56m. TV sets in 2003 (colour by PAL).

Press

There were three national daily newspapers and 12 regional dailies in 2004 with a combined circulation of 4·5m. The party newspaper is Nodong (or Rodong) Sinmun (Workers' Daily News).

Tourism

A 40-year ban on non-Communist tourists was lifted in 1986. In 2002 there were 400,000 foreign tourists. On 19 Nov. 1998 North Korea received its first tourists from South Korea, on a cruise and tour organized by the South Korean firm Hyundai.

Calendar

A new yearly calendar was announced on 9 July 1997 based on Kim Il Sung's birthday on 15 April 1912. Thus 1912 became *Juche* year 1; 2010 is *Juche* 99.

DIPLOMATIC REPRESENTATIVES

Of North Korea in the United Kingdom (73 Gunnersbury Ave., London, W5 4LP)
Ambassador: Ja Song Nam.

Of the United Kingdom in North Korea (Munsu Dong Diplomatic Compound, Pyongyang)
Ambassador: Peter Hughes.

Of North Korea to the United Nations
Ambassador: Sin Son Ho.

Of North Korea to the European Union
Ambassador: Vacant.

FURTHER READING

Becker, Jasper, *Rogue Regime: Kim Jong Il and the Looming Threat of North Korea.* 2005
Cha, Victor D. and Kang, David C., *Nuclear North Korea: A Debate on Engagement Strategies.* 2003
Cumings, Bruce, *North Korea: Another Country.* 2004
Harrison, S., *Korean Endgame: A Strategy for Reunification and US Disengagement.* 2002
Hunter, H., *Kim Il-Song's North Korea.* 1999
Kleiner, J., *Korea: a Century of Change.* 2001
Oh, K. and Hassig, R. C., *North Korea Through the Looking Glass.* 2000
O'Hanlon, Michael E. and Mochizuki, Mike, *Crisis on the Korean Peninsula: How to Deal with a Nuclear North Korea.* 2003
Sigal, L. V., *Disarming Strangers: Nuclear Diplomacy with North Korea.* 1999
Smith, H., *et al.*, (eds.) *North Korea in the New World Order.* 1996

National Statistical Office: Central Statistics Bureau, Pyongyang.

KOREA, SOUTH

Daehan Minguk
(Republic of Korea)

Capital: Seoul
Population estimate, 2010: 48·50m.
GDP per capita, 2007: (PPP$) 24,801
HDI/world rank: 0·937/26

KEY HISTORICAL EVENTS

The Korean peninsula was first settled by tribal peoples from Manchuria and Siberia who provided the basis for the modern Korean language. By 3000 BC agriculture-based communities had emerged. The earliest known colony in the region was established at Pyongyang in the 12th century BC. Among the most prominent agricultural communities was Old Choson, which by 194 BC had evolved into a league of tribes ruled by Wiman or 'Wei Man', a leader widely held to have defected from China, although he may have been a native of the Choson region. His realm was taken over by the Han empire of China in 108 BC and replaced by four Chinese colonies.

The rest of the peninsula developed into tribal states; Puyo in the north and Chin south of the Han River. Chin was itself split into three tribal states (Mahan, Chinhan and Pyonhan); these states then evolved into three rival kingdoms, Koguryo, Paekche, and Silla. Three powerful figures, King T'aejo (AD 53–146) of Koguryo, King Koi (AD 234–86) of Paekche and King Naemul (AD 356–402) of Silla, established hereditary monarchies while powerful aristocracies developed from tribal chiefdoms.

With China's support Silla conquered the other two kingdoms; Paekche in 660 and Koguryo in 668. In 676 Silla drove out the Chinese and gained complete control of the peninsula. Survivors from Koguryo established Parhae, under the leadership of Tae Cho-yong, in the northern region. After a period of conflict with Silla, Parhae grew into a prosperous state in its own right before being taken over by northern nomadic peoples. In Silla an absolute monarchy replaced the council of nobles (its former decision making body) with a central administrative body called the chancellery (*Chipsabu*), thus undermining aristocratic power. Meanwhile, the capital Kumsong (now Kyongju in South Korea) was developed. The state was divided into administrative units by province (*chu*), prefecture (*kun*), and county (*hyon*), and five provincial capitals prospered as cultural centres. Avatamsaka Buddhism was the dominant religion.

Divisions within the aristocracy in the 8th century led to the restoration of the Council of Nobles and the overthrow of the monarchy. Forced to pay taxes to powerful provincial families and central government, the peasants rebelled. Two provincial leaders, Kyonhwon and Kungye, established the Later Paekche (892) and Later Koguryo (901) as rivals to Silla.

National Unity

The powerful leader Wang Kon founded Koryo (now Kaesong, North Korea) in 918, and established a unified kingdom in the Korean peninsula in 936. Three chancelleries and the royal secretariat formed the supreme council of state and governed the kingdom. Koryo's leaders were then largely aristocratic, and the political system greatly favoured those in the top five tiers of the nine hierarchical levels. That the military was not eligible for any hierarchical position above the second level and received little land, led to a military coup in 1170. Gen. Ch'oe Ch'ung-hon established a military regime which held power for the next sixty years. Zen Buddhism and the allied ideology of Confucianism had grown popular but were suppressed under the Ch'oe regime. Many monks fled to the mountains, where they formed what became Korean Buddhism, the *Chogye*.

In 1231 the Mongols invaded Koryo but were resisted by the Ch'oe leaders for nearly three decades, until a peasant uprising saw the Ch'oe overthrown. A power-sharing agreement between the rebels and the Mongols came into force in 1258. Despite some interference from the Mongols, Koryo retained its identity as a unified state. The aristocracy established seats of power throughout the country, encouraging peasants to seek protection as serfs. This, however, led to reduced tax revenues and when the government did not have sufficient resources to reward its bureaucratic class, a rebellion ensued. Led by General Yi Song-gye, and with the help of the Ming dynasty in China, government officials seized power in 1392 and established a new system of land distribution, thus ending the Koryo dynasty.

Gen. Yi named the state Choson, designating Hanyang (now Seoul, South Korea) as the capital. Buddhism was dropped in favour of a new Chinese-influenced Confucian ethical system and the state was governed by a hereditary aristocracy (the *yangban*), who controlled all aspects of Korean society. In 1420 the Hall of Worthies (*Chiphyonjon*) was established for scholars, and after 1443 the Korean phonetic alphabet (*hangul*) developed. Later in the period, a centralized yangban government was formed and the country divided into eight administrative regions, with standardized laws and a central decision-making and judicial body.

In 1592 Japan, newly unified under the command of Toyotomi Hideyoshi, sent an army to Korea supposedly as part of an invasion of China. Korea's naval forces, under Admiral Yi Sun-shin, were able to repel the invaders. Swelling anti-Japanese sentiment prompted Koreans from all hierarchical divisions to fight in the war alongside troops dispatched from Ming China. However, Japanese forces did not withdraw completely until Toyotomi's death in 1598, leaving Korea in ruins.

Despite joint efforts by China and Korea to stem the advances of the nomadic Manchu in the early 17th century, Seoul was captured in 1636. The Manchu established the Ch'ing dynasty several years later and demanded tribute from Korea.

During the 17th and 18th centuries, Korea's agriculture developed as irrigation improved and rice, tobacco and ginseng became increasingly important crops. By the late 18th century many Korean scholars had turned to Roman Catholicism, leading to government suppression of Christianity in a bid to preserve the dominance of Confucianism. However, European priests maintained strong links in the country.

Japanese Influence

In the 19th century, a succession of monarchs yet to attain the age of majority undermined national stability. In 1864 Taewon'gun, the father of the child-king Kojong, took power and pursued a programme of controversial political reform that increasingly isolated Korea from the outside world. When Taewon'gun was eventually forced to step down, Korea came under pressure from Japan to open up its ports. Nervous of growing Japanese influence, China placed troops in Korea following a failed coup attempt by pro-Taewon'gun forces. There followed a trade agreement which greatly benefited Chinese commercial interests. Further treaties with France, Germany, Russia, the UK and the USA followed in the 1880s. As foreign influence increased, Korea's ruling elite divided between moderates and radicals. The radicals carried out a coup in 1884 but were quickly defeated by Chinese troops. An agreement to maintain a balance of power in the region was signed by Japan and China the following year.

As modernization gathered pace, government spending increased, adding to the burden of reparations payments to Japan. The peasants turned to *Tonghak* ('Eastern Learning'), a new religion established by an old yangban scholar and based on traditional beliefs. A Tonghak rebellion in 1894 caused China to send in troops. Japan responded by sending its own forces and war broke out. By the following year Japan had secured control of the peninsula.

Korea declared neutrality at the outbreak of war between Japan and Russia in 1904 but was pressured by Japan into allowing use of Korean territory. Japan achieved victory in 1905 and made Korea a protectorate. An unsuccessful appeal to the international peace conference at The Hague further undermined relations between Japan and Korea. Anti-Japanese guerrilla fighters in the southern provinces were active during 1908–09 but were crushed the following year when Korea was annexed by Japan.

Japan established a government in Korea and implemented a programme designed to supplant the Korean identity. There were restrictions on freedom of speech, press and assembly and the language and history of Japan was taught in schools at the expense of those of Korea. Many Koreans were dispossessed of their land as Japan built new transport and communications infrastructures. When the Japanese brutally suppressed a 2m.-strong demonstration in 1919, independence leaders established a provisional government in Shanghai and named Syngman Rhee as president. Hoping to calm dissent, Japan lifted certain press restrictions and replaced the gendarmerie with an ordinary police force, but uncompromising colonial rule remained in place.

Korea became a market for Japanese goods and attracted much capital investment but at the expense of agriculture, leading to a long-term shortage of rice. Tokyo reimposed military rule in 1931 when war broke out between Japan and China and attempted to quash all manifestations of a separate Korean identity over the following decade. Magazines, newspapers and academic organisations operating in the Korean language were banned. Hundreds of thousands of Koreans were made to fight in the Japanese army, or work in Japanese mines and factories in order to support Japan's military efforts during the Second World War. The Shanghai provisional government, having moved to Chungking in southwest China, declared war on Japan in Dec. 1941. An army of resistance fighters joined the Allied forces in China and fought with them until the Japanese surrender in 1945.

Korea Divided

Korea was promised independence by China, Britain and the USA at the Cairo conference of 1943 but at the end of the war, after Japan's collapse, Korea was divided in two along the 38° Parallel. Initially the USA and the USSR had agreed informally to a four-way power share in Korea, involving Britain and the Republic of China. However, in order to hasten a Japanese surrender, US troops controlled the south of the country while the USSR took command of the north. The Soviet forces helped to establish a Communist-led provisional government under Kim Il Sung. As relations between the USA and the Soviet Union worsened, trade ceased between the two zones, causing economic hardship because industry was concentrated in the north and agriculture in the south.

In Sept. 1947 the United Nations urged elections in both sectors. However, a commission to oversee voting in the North was denied entry by Soviet troops. Rhee was elected in the South while the North appointed Kim Il Sung as leader. In 1948 the southern Republic of Korea (with Seoul as the capital) and the northern Democratic People's Republic of Korea (with Pyongyang as capital) came into being.

Soviet and US troops left the peninsula in 1949 and war broke out between the North and South in June 1950. A US-led UN force under Gen. Douglas MacArthur entered South Korea and pushed back the North Korean forces. The UN pressed on into North Korea and established a commission for the reunification and rehabilitation of Korea. China, which at that point had no representation in the United Nations, entered the war and contributed 1·2m. troops to the North Korean side. Negotiations to end the war began in 1951 and a new international boundary and demilitarized zone were declared in 1953. The USA offered South Korea financial support and signed a mutual security pact with Rhee, who had been reluctant to accept the division of the country. The issue of prisoner returns, particularly of North Koreans unwilling to return to the communist state, remained a point of contention. The war left 4m. people dead or injured.

Traditionally an agricultural region, South Korea faced severe economic problems after partition. Limited resources, war damage and a flood of refugees from North Korea all pointed towards economic disaster, and the country became dependent on foreign aid, particularly from the USA.

The authoritarian rule of President Rhee, marred by corruption, received widespread condemnation. The elections of 1960 were blighted by violence and fraud and when the police shot 125 students during a demonstration, the government was forced to step down. Rhee was exiled. Subsequent leaders failed to solve the country's problems and in May 1961 Gen. Park Chung-hee led a military coup. As leader of the Democratic Republican Party, he was elected president in 1963, 1967 and, following a constitutional amendment to allow a third term in office, 1971.

Park's government was powerful and efficient, reviving the economy through the development of manufacturing for export and attracting increased foreign investment, especially from America. In 1972 Park proclaimed martial law and abolished the national assembly. In 1979 he was assassinated and the country collapsed into chaos. Chun Doo-hwan became leader in 1980 in another military coup and, as leader of the Democratic Justice Party (DJP), revived the national assembly. Dissatisfaction with the government grew, however, and a new constitution in 1987 stipulated that the president be elected by popular vote and his term of office reduced to five years.

Roh Tae-woo was elected president in 1988 as leader of the DJP and later of the Democratic Liberal Party. Fighting rising inflation, he established diplomatic relations with China and the Soviet Union and developed a better relationship with opposition parties in his own country. North and South Korea met several times during the 1980s in a bid to improve relations. In 1991 the two countries signed a treaty of non-aggression, with each country promising not to interfere in the internal affairs of the other.

In 1992 Kim Young-sam, the former opposition leader who had merged his party with Roh's, became the first civilian to be elected president since the Korean War. He launched an anti-corruption campaign and continued to pursue closer relations with North Korea. During the financial crisis that affected East Asia in 1997 South Korea was forced to ask the International Monetary Fund for help, though it largely avoided long-term economic damage and remains one of Asia's most affluent countries.

In Dec. 1997 Kim Dae-jung, a pro-democracy dissident during the years of military dictatorship, was elected president. Kim forged a 'sunshine policy' aimed at closer ties with the North and received the Nobel peace prize for his efforts. The two Koreas have subsequently undertaken a series of joint commercial and infrastructural projects. Constitutionally disqualified from standing for the presidency again in 2002, Kim was replaced by Roh Moo-hyun who continued the 'sunshine policy', despite North Korea's declining relationship with the USA.

In Oct. 2007 South and North Korea jointly called for a permanent peace on the peninsula to replace the armistice in place since the end of the Korean War.

TERRITORY AND POPULATION

South Korea is bounded in the north by the demilitarized zone (separating it from North Korea), east by the Sea of Japan (East Sea), south by the Korea Strait (separating it from Japan) and west by the Yellow Sea. The area is 99,585 sq. km. The population (census, 1 Nov. 2005) was 47,278,951; density, 474·76 per sq. km (one of the highest in the world). In 2005 the urban population was 80·8%.

The UN gives an estimated population for 2010 of 48·50m.

The official language is Korean. In July 2000 the Korean government introduced a new Romanization System for the Korean Language to romanize Korean words into English.

There are nine provinces (*do*) and seven metropolitan cities with provincial status. Area and population in 2005:

Province	*Area (in sq. km)*	*Population (in 1,000)*
Gyeonggi	10,135	10,415
Gyeongsangnam	10,516	3,056
Gyeongsangbuk	19,024	2,608
Chungcheongnam	8,586	1,889
Jeollanam	11,987	1,820
Jeollabuk	8,050	1,784
Gangwon	16,502	1,465
Chungcheongbuk	7,432	1,460
Jeju	1,846	532
Seoul (city)	606	9,820
Busan (city)	760	3,524
Incheon (city)	965	2,531
Daegu (city)	886	2,465
Daejeon (city)	540	1,443
Gwangju (city)	501	1,418
Ulsan (city)	1,056	1,049

Cities with over 500,000 inhabitants (census 2005):

Seoul	9,820,171	Ulsan	1,049,177	Cheongju	642,805
Busan	3,523,582	Suwon	1,044,113	Bucheon	838,801
Incheon	2,531,280	Seongnam	934,984	Jeonju	623,298
Daegu	2,464,547	Goyang	866,846	Anyang	612,423
Daejeon	1,442,856	Yongin	689,691	Cheonan	521,887
Gwangju	1,417,716	Ansan	681,590	Changwon	501,705

SOCIAL STATISTICS

2008: births, 465,900; deaths, 246,100; marriages, 327,700; divorces, 116,500. Rates per 1,000 population in 2008: birth, 9·7; death, 5·1; marriage, 6·8; divorce, 2·4. Suicides numbered 10,688 in 2006. Expectation of life at birth, 2007, 82·4 years for females and 75·8 for males. Life expectancy had been 47 in 1955 and 62 in 1971. Infant mortality, 2005, six per 1,000 live births; fertility rate, 2004, 1·2 births per woman (one of the lowest rates in the world). Annual population growth rate, 2000–05, 0·5%. In 2001 the average age of first marriage was 29·6 for men and 26·8 for women, with 28·0 years being the average age that women had their first child. South Korea has one of the most rapidly ageing populations in the world, partly owing to an ever-decreasing birth rate. In 2002, 7·9% of the population were over 65, up from 2·9% in 1960. There were 14·31m. households in 2000, with on average 3·1 members per household. 11,584 South Koreans emigrated in 2001, down from 15,307 in 2000. Between 1962 and 1998 a total of 847,714 Koreans emigrated, 77·8% of them to the USA. 5·65m. Koreans lived abroad in 2001, including 2·1m. in the USA, 1·9m. in China and 640,000 in Japan.

CLIMATE

The country experiences continental temperate conditions. Rainfall is concentrated in the period April to Sept. and ranges from 40" (1,020 mm) to 60" (1,520 mm). Busan, Jan. 36°F (2·2°C), July 76°F (24·4°C). Annual rainfall 56" (1,407 mm). Seoul, Jan. 23°F (–5°C), July 77°F (25°C). Annual rainfall 50" (1,250 mm).

CONSTITUTION AND GOVERNMENT

The 1988 constitution provides for a *President*, directly elected for a single five-year term, who appoints the members of the *State Council* and heads it, and for a *National Assembly* (*Gukhoe*), currently of 299 members, directly elected for four years (243 from constituencies and 56 from party lists in proportion to the overall vote). The current constitution created the Sixth Republic. The minimum voting age is 20.

National Anthem

'Aegukga' ('A Song of Love for the Country'); words anonymous, tune by Ahn Eaktay.

GOVERNMENT CHRONOLOGY

Heads of State of South Korea since 1948. (DJP = Democratic Justice Party; DLP = Democratic Liberal Party; DP = Democratic Party; DRP = Democratic Republican Party; GNP = Grand National Party; LP = Liberal Party; MDP = Millennium Democratic Party; NCNP = National Congress for New Politics; NDP = New Democratic Party; NKP = New Korea Party; UD = Uri Party)

Presidents

1948–60	LP	Syngman Rhee
1960–62	DP, NDP	Yun Po-sun

Chairman of the Supreme Council for National Reconstruction

1962–63	military	Park Chung-hee

Presidents

1963–79	DRP	Park Chung-hee
1979–80	DRP	Choi Kyu-hah
1980–88	military, DJP	Chun Doo-hwan
1988–93	DJP, DLP	Roh Tae-woo
1993–98	DLP, NKP	Kim Young-sam
1998–2003	NCNP, MDP	Kim Dae-jung
2003–08	MDP, UD	Roh Moo-hyun
2008–	GNP	Lee Myung-bak

RECENT ELECTIONS

Presidential elections were held on 19 Dec. 2007. Lee Myung-bak of the Grand National Party (GNP) won with 48·7% of votes cast, ahead of Chung Dong-young of the United New Democratic Party with 26·1%, Lee Hoi-chang (ind.) with 15·1% and seven other candidates. Turnout was 63·0%.

Elections to the National Assembly were held on 9 April 2008. Turnout was 46·0%. The GNP won 153 out of 299 seats with 37·4% of votes cast; Uri Party (UD) won 81 with 25·1%; the Liberty Forward Party (LFP) 18 with 6·8%; the Park Geun-hye Coalition 14 with 13·1%; the Democratic Labour Party (MDD) 5 with 5·6%; the Renewal of Korea Party (CKP) 3 with 3·8%. 25 seats went to non-partisans.

CURRENT ADMINISTRATION

President: Lee Myung-bak; b. 1946 (Grand National Party; sworn in 25 Feb. 2008).

In March 2010 the cabinet comprised:

Prime Minister: Chung Un-chan; b. 1946 (Grand National Party; since 22 Sept. 2009).

Minister of Culture, Sport and Tourism: You In-chon. *Education, Science and Technology:* Ahn Byong-man. *Environment:* Lee Man-eui. *Food, Agriculture, Forestry and Fisheries:* Jang Tae-pyoung. *Foreign Affairs and Trade:* Yu Myung-hwan. *Gender Equality:* Paik Hee-young. *Health, Welfare and Family Affairs:* Jeon Jae-hee. *Justice:* Lee Kwi-nam. *Knowledge Economy:* Choi Kyoung-hwan. *Labour:* Yim Tae-hee. *Land, Transport and Maritime Affairs:* Chung Jong-hwan. *National Defence:* Kim Tae-young. *Public Administration and Security:* Lee Dal-gon. *Special Affairs:* Joo Ho-young. *Strategy and Finance:* Yoon Jeung-hyun. *Unification:* Hyun In-taek.

National Assembly Speaker: Kim Hyong-o.

Government Website: http://www.korea.net

CURRENT LEADERS

Lee Myung-bak

Position
President

Introduction
Lee Myung-bak made his name by playing a key role in establishing Hyundai among the world's leading industrial firms. He was swept to power as president in Dec. 2007, promising to revitalize the economy and resurrect close ties with the USA. However, his first years in office have proved difficult amid financial and currency turmoil and turbulent relations with North Korea.

Early Life
Lee Myung-bak was born on 19 Dec. 1941 near Osaka, Japan, where his Korean parents worked as farm labourers. The family moved to Pohang in the newly liberated southern Korea in 1946, with Lee attending Dongji Commercial High School. He studied business administration at Korea University in Seoul, financed in part by his work as a street cleaner.

A politically active student, Lee served a short prison term for demonstrating against the normalization of South Korea's diplomatic links with Japan. As a result, he struggled to find employment but was taken on by a then small manufacturing company, Hyundai Engineering. He became its youngest chief executive officer at the age of 35 and was chairman at 46. Known as 'the Bulldozer', Lee pushed through a range of large-scale construction projects that underpinned the country's transformation from a poor agricultural economy to a major industrial power. Hyundai became one of the region's most powerful conglomerates, with around 160,000 staff by the time Lee left in 1992. During the boom years of the 1970s and 1980s, Lee became a wealthy property owner.

Lee entered political life at the 1992 parliamentary elections with the then ruling conservative New Korea Party, the predecessor of the Grand National Party (GNP, formed in 1997). He contested the mayorship of Seoul in 1995 but lost to the former prime minister, Chung Wong-sik. Lee subsequently spent a year as a visiting professor at George Washington University in the USA.

On his return to South Korea, Lee established several companies specializing in internet-based financial services. In 2002 he returned to public life when he was elected mayor of Seoul. Over the next five years he earned plaudits for his campaigns to regenerate the city by investing in parks and open spaces and public transport. The restoration of the Cheonggye stream, which had been submerged by concrete in the 1970s, provoked protest but has become one of Seoul's most popular attractions. In 2007 he was named a 'hero of the environment' by *Time* magazine.

In May 2007 Lee declared his intention to run for the presidency for the right-leaning opposition GNP. Three months later he defeated Park Guen-hye in the party's primary. His campaign centred on economic issues, including the ambitious '747' plan aiming to achieve 7% annual GDP growth and to double average GDP per head to US$40,000 to advance South Korea from the world's eleventh to seventh largest economy over the next decade.

Lee's fondness for large-scale infrastructure projects was underlined by plans to build a canal between Seoul and the port of Busan, which he has claimed would create 300,000 jobs, improve and diversify the transport system and revitalize the country's interior. He also floated a plan to create a Korean high-tech version of Silicon Valley in the central region of Chungcheongnam. Much of his campaign was dogged by allegations of involvement in stock market price manipulation in 2001. He denied the charges and was formally cleared of fraud in Feb. 2008 after an investigation by an independent counsel. Lee won a landslide victory in the presidential election of 19 Dec. 2007, defeating Chung Dong-young of the United New Democratic Party.

Career in Office
Lee was sworn in as president on 25 Feb. 2008. He promised to slash economic regulations, initiate tax reforms, streamline government and attract foreign investment. He also pledged to strengthen ties with the USA and hinted at a tougher line than his predecessor, Roh Moo-hyun, in relations with North Korea. In April 2008 Lee's GNP won an overall parliamentary majority in elections to the National Assembly. However, his poll ratings then fell markedly in the wake of his unpopular agreement to resume US beef imports (suspended since 2003 on health grounds) and also the impact of the global credit crisis which led the government to announce a US$130bn. intervention package in Oct. 2008 to support the banking system and stabilize financial markets. In Feb. 2009 the central bank reduced interest rates to a record low as the economy faced its first contraction in over a decade, and in April the GNP suffered a crushing defeat in parliamentary by-elections. In Sept. Lee replaced his prime minister in a cabinet reshuffle and also removed the defence minister, with whom he had clashed over military spending.

Meanwhile, relations with North Korea remained unpredictable and volatile. In Jan. 2009 the North announced that it was abandoning all military and political agreements signed with South Korea because of the latter's 'hostile intent'. Then in May the North conducted its second nuclear weapon test and declared that it was no longer bound by the armistice that ended the Korean War, heightening tensions further. However, later in the year Pyongyang made some conciliatory gestures towards Lee's government, including agreeing to resume a programme of family reunions suspended since 2008 and indicating a willingness to return to multilateral talks on its nuclear programme. But in Jan. 2010 hostilities again threatened to reignite as forces from both sides exchanged artillery fire near their disputed maritime border.

DEFENCE

Peacetime operational control, which had been transferred to the United Nations Command (UNC) under a US general in July 1950 after the outbreak of the Korean War, was restored to South Korea on 1 Dec. 1994. In the event of a new crisis, operational control over the Korean armed forces will revert to the Combined Forces Command (CFC). However, in Feb. 2007 it was agreed that in 2012 South Korea would resume wartime command of its military. Conscription is 24 months in the Army, 26 months in the Navy and 24 months in the Air Force. In Sept. 2007 it was announced that the length of conscription will be gradually reduced and that conscientious objectors will be allowed to choose community service in place of military service. In 2004 the USA and South Korea agreed to the redeployment of 12,500 US personnel in three phases that would continue until 2008. In April 2008 the number of troops had been reduced to 28,000 from 37,000 in 2002.

Defence expenditure in 2008 totalled US$24,172m. (US$501 per capita). In 2007 defence spending represented 2·7% of GDP. In the period 2004–08 South Korea's spending on major conventional weapons, at US$6·9bn., was the fourth highest behind China, India and the United Arab Emirates (although in both 2007 and 2008 South Korea's spending was the highest of any country).

Army

Strength (2007) 560,000 (140,000 conscripts). Paramilitary Civilian Defence Corps, 3·5m. The armed forces reserves numbered 4·5m.

Navy

In 2007 the Navy had a substantial force of 63,000 (around 19,000 conscripts), including 28,000 marine corps troops. In 2007 the fleet included 12 submarines, seven destroyers, nine frigates, 28 corvettes and around 75 patrol and coastal combatants. Naval Aviation operated eight combat capable aircraft. The fleet headquarters is at Jinhae.

Air Force

In 2007 the Air Force had a strength of 64,000 men and 555 combat capable aircraft (F-4s, F-5s, F-15s and F-16s).

INTERNATIONAL RELATIONS

Defections to South Korea from North Korea totalled a record 2,809 in 2008 (1,387 in 2005, 312 in 2000 and 9 in 1990).

South Korea is a member of the UN, World Bank, IMF and several other UN specialized agencies, WTO, BIS, IOM, OECD, Inter-American Development Bank, Asian Development Bank, APEC, Colombo Plan and Antarctic Treaty.

The aim of Korea's foreign policy is to secure international support for peace and stability in Northeast Asia, including a means to reunify the Korean Peninsula without confrontation.

ECONOMY

Agriculture accounted for 3% of GDP in 2008, industry 37% and services 60%.

Overview

South Korea has seen rapid economic development since the 1950s, when it was ranked amongst the poorest nations. It is now among the top 15 richest countries. Economic convergence with the developed world came only in the late 1980s. With few natural resources, imports were focused on raw materials and technology at the expense of consumer goods. Furthermore, domestic savings and investment were encouraged over consumption, resulting in an extremely high fixed-investment expenditure share of GDP.

Korea's development model was based on export-oriented industrialization. Export production has been dominated by *chaebol* (conglomerates such as Samsung, Hyundai and LG), controlled by founding families with close government ties. Subsidization of businesses (and the careers of the associated bureaucrats) were contingent on export success. Textile manufacturing was the first internationally competitive sector but the country is now competitive in electronics, automobiles, shipbuilding, chemicals and steel. According to the World Bank, Korea ranks 19th out of 183 economies for the ease of doing business. Korea is a key long-term destination for Japanese foreign direct investment.

Korea's manufacturing sector has benefited from the transfer of technological know-how as well as capital equipment. Despite spending a relatively large share of GDP (around 3%) on research and development, the OECD notes that research is concentrated in a few companies and market segments.

The 1997 Asian financial crisis exposed weaknesses in the development model. High debt-to-equity ratios, heavy foreign borrowing and an undisciplined financial sector with a significant amount of non-performing loans weighed heavily on the economy. IMF-designed reforms to strengthen competition and the financial sector helped growth rebound in 1999. Strong domestic demand, spurred by a credit card boom, helped weather the global slowdown in 2001–02 but a credit card crisis hit in 2003, with 3·7m. people defaulting by the end of the year. Although household consumption accelerated in 2005, many households remain heavily indebted. Since 1997 government reforms and large-scale bankruptcies have changed the role of the *chaebol*. Daewoo, a once-major *chaebol*, was dismantled by the Korean government in 1999 following a massive bankruptcy, while only half of the 30 largest *chaebol* recorded in 1995 remained by 2003.

Reliance on oil makes the economy vulnerable to fluctuations in the oil price. China, a major export and FDI destination, poses an increasingly competitive threat to many of Korea's leading industries. Nonetheless, real GDP performance was positive before the global financial crisis that started in 2007, with growth in 2006 at its highest level for four years as a result of robust exports and stronger domestic demand. GDP growth was above 5% in 2006 and 2007 before the effects of the global financial crisis hit hard in 2008. Exports slumped and capital left the country at a higher rate than during the Asian crisis. GDP growth declined to 2·2% in 2008 before recovery—one of the earliest and strongest in the OECD— started in early 2009.

Average incomes and productivity have converged with the OECD average over the last two decades but catch-up growth has faded and levels remain well below those of other leading economies. The OECD has highlighted service sector reform as essential for further growth, especially since the country will soon face a shrinking labour force. Population ageing poses risks to future growth as the old age dependency ratio is expected to increase to 65% by 2050, potentially a major strain on fiscal resources.

Currency

The unit of currency is the *won* (KRW). Inflation rates (based on OECD statistics):

1999	*2000*	*2001*	*2002*	*2003*	*2004*	*2005*	*2006*	*2007*	*2008*
0·8%	2·3%	4·1%	2·7%	3·6%	3·6%	2·8%	2·2%	2·5%	4·7%

Foreign exchange reserves were US$240,915m. in Aug. 2009 (US$51,963m. in 1998) and gold reserves 463,000 troy oz. Total money supply in June 2009 was 103,242bn. won.

Budget

In 2006 budgetary central government revenue was 148,907bn. won and expenditure 133,164bn. won. Principal sources of revenue in 2006: taxes on income, profits and capital gains, 60,367bn. won; taxes on goods and services, 54,996bn. won. Main items of expenditure by economic type in 2006: grants, 67,473bn. won; compensation of employees, 20,220bn. won.

VAT is 10%.

Performance
Real GDP growth rates (based on OECD statistics):

1999	*2000*	*2001*	*2002*	*2003*	*2004*	*2005*	*2006*	*2007*	*2008*
9·5%	8·5%	4·0%	7·2%	2·8%	4·6%	4·0%	5·2%	5·1%	2·2%

Total GDP in 2008 was US$929·1bn.

Banking and Finance
The central bank and bank of issue is the Bank of Korea (*Governor*, Lee Seong-tae). In Oct. 2002 bank deposits totalled 498,886bn. won, of which 447,329bn. won were savings and time deposits.

In Dec. 2001 there were 20 national and provincial commercial banks. The largest bank is Kookmin Bank, with assets in Sept. 2002 of 204,337bn. won (US$171·47bn.). Other major banks are the National Agricultural Cooperative Federation (NACF) and Woori (formerly Hanvit) Bank. There were 40 foreign banks in Dec. 2002. In Dec. 2001 non-bank financial institutions included 44 insurance companies, 45 securities companies and three merchant banks. The use of real names in financial dealings has been required since 1994.

South Korea has started to open up once protected industries to foreign ownership, and in 2008 attracted US$7·6bn. in foreign direct investment.

There is a stock exchange in Seoul.

Weights and Measures
The metric system is in use alongside traditional measures. 1 *gwan* = 3·75 kg. 1 *pyeong* = 3·3 sq. metres.

ENERGY AND NATURAL RESOURCES

Environment
South Korea's carbon dioxide emissions from the consumption and flaring of fossil fuels in 2008 were the equivalent of 11·2 tonnes per capita.

Electricity
Installed capacity in 2004 was 65·7m. kW. Electricity generated (2004) was 371,011m. kWh (thermal, 234,085m. kWh; nuclear, 130,715m. kWh; hydro-electric, 5,861m. kWh; geothermal, 350m. kWh). There were 20 nuclear reactors in use in 2008. Consumption per capita in 2004 was 7,716 kWh.

Oil and Gas
In 2001 the imports of petroleum products amounted to 1,099m. bbls, of which crude oil was 859·4m. bbls. The output of petroleum products was 892·8m. bbls; consumption 743·6m. bbls and the volume of exports 295·0m. bbls. In 2001, 873·4m. bbls of crude oil were imported. In Sept. 1999 a massive crude oil terminal was opened at Yeosu, Jeollanam-do. It has a capacity to store more than 30m. bbls.

In 2001 imports of natural gas totalled 16·1m. tonnes, consumption 16·0m. tonnes. The total output of city gas in 2001 was 12,657m. cu. metres as was consumption, of which 8,964m. cu. metres was used for household purposes, 3,376m. cu. metres for industrial use and 1,761m. cu. metres for commercial use. In April 1999 a large underwater gas deposit was discovered off the southeastern coast of the country, which was estimated to contain up to 60bn. cu. metres of natural gas.

Water
Water consumption in 2000 was 33,100m. cu. metres, of which 15,800m. cu. metres was for agricultural purposes, 7,300m. cu. metres was supplied to households and 2,900m. cu. metres was for industrial use. Of the total population, 87·8% had tap water in 2001 and per capita supply was 374 litres per day. As of 2001 there were 1,206 dams with walls higher than 15 metres and containing a total of 17·96bn. cu. metres of water.

Minerals
In 2001, 599 mining companies employed 12,103 people. Output, 2001, included (in tonnes): limestone, 82m.; anthracite coal, 3·82m.; iron ore, 0·2m.; zinc ore, 10,259; lead ore, 1,975; gold, 28,595 kg; silver, 664,533 kg. The largest gold deposits in South Korea were discovered in Suryun Mine near Daegu in June 1999. The mine contained an estimated 9·9 tonnes of gold, worth approximately US$81m. Salt production averages 500,000 tonnes a year.

Agriculture
Cultivated land was 1·88m. ha. in 2001, of which 1·15m. ha. were rice paddies. In 2002 there were 1·68m. ha. of arable land and 193,000 ha. of permanent crops. In 2001 the farming population was 3·93m. and there were 1·35m. farms. The agricultural workforce was 2·1m. in 2001. There were 206,371 tractors in 2002.

In 2003, 1·02m. ha. were sown to rice. Production (2003, in 1,000 tonnes): rice, 6,068; cabbage, 2,576; melons and watermelons, 1,087; onions, 933; potatoes, 666; tangerines and mandarins, 666; cucumbers and gherkins, 464; apples, 433; grapes, 422; garlic, 391; pears, 386; chillies and green peppers, 381; sweet potatoes, 317; barley, 300.

Livestock in 2003 (in 1,000): pigs, 8,912; cattle, 1,935; goats, 435; chickens, 98,000.

Livestock products in 2003 (in 1,000 tonnes): pork, bacon and ham, 1,153; beef and veal, 185; poultry meat, 425; milk, 2,363; eggs (2002), 537.

Forestry
Forest area was 6·40m. ha. in 2005 (64% of the land area). Total stock was 489·0m. cu. metres. In 2004, 62% of the total forest area was privately owned. Timber production was 5·15m. cu. metres in 2007.

Fisheries
In 2001 there were a total of 94,835 boats (864,853 gross tonnes). 482 deep-sea fishing vessels were operating overseas as of Dec. 2002. The fish catch was 1,639,069 tonnes in 2005, mainly from marine waters.

INDUSTRY
The leading companies by market capitalization in South Korea in March 2009 were: Samsung Electronics Company Ltd (US$65·7bn.); Pohang Iron and Steel Company (POSCO), US$23·0bn.; and Korea Electric Power (US$11·8bn.).

Manufacturing industry is concentrated primarily on oil, petrochemicals, chemical fibres, construction, iron and steel, mobile phones, cement, machinery, chips, shipbuilding, automobiles and electronics. Tobacco manufacture is a semi-government monopoly. Industry is dominated by giant conglomerates (*chaebol*). There were 3·19m. businesses in 2004, of which 263,128 were incorporated. 878,294 businesses were in wholesale and retail trades, 643,773 in hotels and restaurants, 331,458 in transport and communications and 328,338 in manufacturing. The leading *chaebol* are Samsung, with assets in April 2002 of 72·4trn. won; LG, with assets of 54·5trn. won; and SK, with assets of 46·8trn. won.

Production in 2005: petroleum products, 922·9m. bbls; mobile phones, 201·2m. units; refrigerators, 6·92m. units; TV sets, 5·85m. units; cars, 3·70m. units; cigarettes, 107·2bn. units. Production (2005) in 1,000 tonnes: cement, 51,391; crude steel, 47,770; residual fuel oil (2004), 30,509; distillate fuel oil (2004), 29,383; pig iron (2004), 27,556; beer (2004), 2,016m. litres.

Shipbuilding orders totalled 21·96m. GT in 2005.

Labour
In 2005 the population of working age (15 to 59 years) was 31·84m.; the economically active population was 23·74m. (13·88m. males and 9·89m. females). At Nov. 2002, 13·9m. persons were employed in services, 4·2m. in manufacturing, 2·2m. in agriculture, fisheries

and forestry, 1·8m. in construction and 19,000 in mining. 6·34m. persons were self-employed in Nov. 2002. Unemployment was 3·5% in Dec. 2009—one of the lowest rates in the industrialized world. An annual legal minimum wage is set by the *Minimum Wage Act* (enforced from 1988), which applies to all industries. In Jan. 2009 it was increased to 4,000 won per hour and 32,000 won per eight-hour day. In Dec. 2001 the average monthly wage was 1·75m. won. In 2001 the working week averaged 47 hours (including a half day on Saturdays). In July 2004 the working week in the civil service, for financial and insurance firms, and for employers with 1,000 or more staff, was reduced from 44 to 40 hours. A five-day working week for smaller companies is being gradually phased in; employers with fewer than 20 workers do not have to introduce the shorter working week until 2011. Workers in South Korea put among the longest hours in the industrialized world. In 2008 full- and part-time workers put in an average of 2,256 hours (although this has been declining every year since 2000 when the average was 2,520 hours).

Trade Unions

At Dec. 2001 there were 6,150 unions with a total membership of 1,568,723. 877,827 workers belong to the government-recognized Federation of Korean Trade Unions. Since 1997 unions have been permitted to engage in political activities. The Korean Confederation of Trade Unions had 644,000 members in 2002.

INTERNATIONAL TRADE

Total external foreign debt was US$110,109m. in 2001. In May 1998 the government removed restrictions on foreign investment in the Korean stock market. It also began to allow foreign businesses to engage in mergers and acquisitions. From July 1998 foreigners were allowed to buy plots of land for both business and non-business purposes. Since Aug. 1990 South Korean businesses and individuals have been permitted to make investments and set up branch offices in North Korea, on an approval basis. According to the Unification Ministry, the overall volume of inter-Korean trade was US$641m. in 2002 (US$342m. in business transactions and US$298m. in non-profit transactions), a 59·3% increase on 2001.

Imports and Exports

Imports (c.i.f.) and exports (f.o.b.) for calendar years in US$1m.:

	2003	*2004*	*2005*	*2006*	*2007*
Imports	178,825·9	224,460·9	261,235·6	309,379·5	356,841·0
Exports	193,817·3	253,844·6	284,418·2	325,457·2	371,477·1

Both imports and exports almost doubled between 2003 and 2007.

Leading import sources in 2007 were: China, 17·7%; Japan, 15·8%; USA, 10·5%; Saudi Arabia, 5·9%. The principal export markets in 2007 were: China, 22·1%; USA, 12·4%; Japan, 7·1%; Hong Kong, 5·0%.

In 2004 machinery and transport equipment accounted for 33·6% of imports and 63·0% of exports; chemicals, manufactured goods classified chiefly by material and miscellaneous manufactured articles 33·4% of imports and 30·7% of exports; mineral fuels, lubricants and related materials 22·4% of imports and 4·1% of exports; inedible crude materials, and animal and vegetable oil and fats 6·3% of imports and 1·0% of exports; and food, live animals, beverages and tobacco 4·4% of imports and 1·2% of exports.

Rice imports were prohibited until 1994, but following the GATT Uruguay Round the rice market opened to foreign imports in 1995.

Trade Fairs

In 2001 there were about 100 trade fairs hosted by COEX and 30 hosted by BEXCO (Busan). 3,187 Korean companies participated in 145 trade fairs held in other countries supported by KOTRA, the Korea Trade-Investment Agency.

COMMUNICATIONS

Roads

In 2007 there were 102,061 km of roads, comprising 3,103 km of motorways, 14,225 km of highways and main roads and 84,733 km of secondary roads; 77·6% of roads (79,189 km) were paved. In 2006, 97,854m. passenger-km were travelled by road and 12,545m. tonne-km of freight were moved. In 2007 motor vehicles in use included 12,020,700 passenger cars, 4,189,000 vans and lorries, 182,100 buses and coaches, and 1,821,300 motorcycles and mopeds. In 2007 there were 6,166 fatalities as a result of road accidents (9,353 in 2000). The first of two planned cross-border roads between the two Koreas opened in Feb. 2003.

Rail

In 2005 the National Railroad totalled 3,374 km of 1,435 mm gauge (1,385 km electrified). In 2004 passenger-km travelled came to 28·6bn. and freight tonne-km to 10·6bn. In June 2000 it was agreed to start consultations to restore the railway from Seoul to Sinuiju, on the North Korean/Chinese border, by rebuilding a 12 km long stretch from Munsan, in South Korea, to Jangdan, on the South Korean/North Korean border, and an 8 km long stretch in North Korea. Work on the restoration began in Sept. 2000 but has been delayed in part because of the diplomatic crisis between North Korea and the USA, which escalated in Oct. 2002.

Two passenger trains crossed the border between North and South Korea on 17 May 2007 (one northbound and one southbound), completing the first cross-border journey in more than 50 years. Regular freight services between the two Koreas were resumed in Dec. 2007.

There are metros in Seoul (287 km), and smaller ones in Busan (95 km), Daegu (54 km), Daejeon (23 km), Gwangju (12 km) and Incheon (25 km).

Civil Aviation

There are six international airports in South Korea: at Seoul (Incheon), Busan (Gimhae), Daegu, Jeju, Yangyang and Cheongju. The new Incheon airport, 50 km to the west of Seoul, built on reclaimed land made up of four small islands, opened in March 2001 and is the largest airport in Asia. It has replaced Gimpo Airport as Seoul's International Airport. The national carrier is Korean Air. In 2005 Korean Air carried 22·0m. passengers (11·0m. on international flights); passenger-km totalled 50·3bn. The other main Korean carrier is Asiana Airlines. In 2001, 28·5m. passengers and 423,692 tonnes of cargo were carried on domestic routes and 19·7m. passengers and 1·8m. tonnes of cargo on international routes.

In 2001 Seoul's Gimpo airport handled 22,041,099 passengers (17,743,235 on domestic flights) and 588,938 tonnes of freight. Busan handled 9,168,089 passengers (7,662,429 on domestic flights) and 167,024 tonnes of freight. Jeju handled 9,320,337 passengers (8,968,107 on domestic flights) and 285,648 tonnes of freight.

Shipping

In 2005 there were 52 ports (28 for international trade), including Busan, Incheon, Gunsan, Mokpo, Yeosu, Pohang, Donghae, Jeju, Masan, Ulsan, Daesan and Kwangyang. In Jan. 2003 the merchant marine comprised 828 vessels of 300 GRT and over totalling 10·36m. DWT. Vessels totalling 819,677,000 NRT entered South Korean ports in 2002, and vessels totalling 828,211,000 NRT cleared. The busiest port is Busan, which was visited by 48,343 vessels of 354,350,000 GRT in 2005. Freight handled in 2004 totalled 219,760,000 revenue tons.

In 2005, 11,099,554 domestic passengers and 2,104,939 international passengers took ferries and other ocean-going vessels. There were 7,119 registered vessels accounting for a tonnage of 10,068,379.

Telecommunications

In 2008 there were 21,325,000 main (fixed) telephone lines. In the same year mobile phone subscribers numbered 45,607,000 (947·1 per 1,000 persons). The largest operator, SK Telecom, has 46% of the market share, ahead of KT, with 29%. There were 26·1m. PCs in use in 2006 and 36·8m. internet users in 2008. The broadband penetration rate in June 2008 was 31·2 subscribers per 100 inhabitants.

Postal Services

In 2003 there were 3,702 post offices operating, with each *myon* (administrative unit comprising several villages) having one or more post offices. In 2002 the mail volume totalled 4,498m. items.

SOCIAL INSTITUTIONS

Justice

Judicial power is vested in the Supreme Court, High Courts, District Courts and Family Court, as well as the Administrative Court and Patent Court. The single six-year term Chief Justice is appointed by the President with the consent of the National Assembly. The other 13 Justices of the Supreme Court are appointed by the President with the consent of the National Assembly, upon the recommendation of the Chief Justice, for renewable six-year terms; the Chief Justice appoints other judges. There has been an unofficial moratorium on executions since 1998—the death penalty was last used in Dec. 1997. In Jan. 2002 there were 1,508 judges, 1,134 prosecutors and about 3,800 private practising lawyers.

The population in penal institutions in Oct. 2002 was 60,721 (128 per 100,000 of national population).

Education

The Korean education system consists of a six-year elementary school, a three-year middle school, a three-year high school and college and university (two to four years). Elementary education for 6–11 year olds and middle school education are compulsory. Mandatory middle school education began in 2002.

The total number of schools has increased sixfold from 3,000 in 1945 to 19,586 in 2005, with 11,934,863 enrolled students. In 2005 there were 8,275 kindergartens with 541,603 pupils and 31,033 teachers; 5,646 elementary schools with 4,023,806 pupils and 160,143 teachers; 2,010,704 pupils and 103,835 teachers at 2,935 middle schools; and 2,095 high schools with 1,762,896 pupils and 116,411 teachers. In 2005 there were 158 colleges and universities with 1,859,639 students and 49,200 teachers; 11 universities of education with 25,141 students and 798 teachers; 1,051 graduate schools with 282,225 students; and 18 industrial universities with 188,753 students and 2,658 teachers. In 2005, 5·6% of the population was enrolled in tertiary education, up from just 0·6% in 1970. Around 214,000 South Koreans were studying abroad in 2005.

In 2005 public expenditure on education came to 4·3% of GDP and 15·3% of total government spending. Total expenditure on tertiary education in 2005 was among the highest in the world at 2·4% of GDP. Private spending on education in 2005 came to 2·9% of GDP, the highest share of any industrialized country. The adult literacy was 97·9% in 2001 (99·2% of males and 96·6% of females).

According to the OECD's 2006 PISA (Programme for International Student Assessment) study, 15-year-olds in Korea rank first in reading and fourth in mathematics. The three-yearly study compares educational achievement of pupils in the major industrialized countries.

Health

In 2004 there were 282 general hospitals (with 117,323 beds), 25,346 other hospitals and clinics (189,044 beds), 9,303 oriental medical hospitals and clinics (9,585 beds) and 15,406 dental hospitals and clinics. In 2004 there were 81,998 physicians (587 people per doctor), 15,406 oriental medical doctors, 21,344 dentists, 8,626 midwives, 202,012 nurses and 53,492 pharmacists. In 2007 South Korea spent 6·3% of its GDP on health, with public spending accounting for 54·9% of total expenditure on health and private spending 45·1%. In 2003, 64·9% of all adult men smoked (the highest proportion in any country in the world), but only 3·8% of women were smokers.

Welfare

In Dec. 2001, 16·3m. persons were covered by the National Pension System introduced in 1988. Employers and employees make equal contributions; persons joining by choice or in rural areas pay their own contributions. The System covers age pensions, disability pensions and survivors' pensions.

Under a system of unemployment insurance introduced in July 1995, workers laid off after working at least six months for a member employer are entitled to benefits averaging 50% of their previous wage for a period of 90 up to 240 days.

RELIGION

Traditionally, Koreans have lived under the influence of shamanism, Buddhism (introduced AD 372) and Confucianism, which was the official faith from 1392 to 1910. Catholic converts from China introduced Christianity in the 18th century, but a ban on Roman Catholicism was not lifted until 1882. The Anglican Church was introduced in 1890 and became an independent jurisdiction in 1993 under the Archbishop of Korea. In 1998 it had 110 churches, 175 priests and some 65,000 faithful. Religious affiliations of the population in 2001: Buddhism, 23·3%; Protestantism, 19·8%; Roman Catholicism, 6·7%; Confucianism, 0·5%; others, 0·8%; no religion, 49·6%. In Feb. 2010 there was one Roman Catholic cardinal.

CULTURE

World Heritage Sites

There are nine sites in South Korea that appear on the UNESCO World Heritage List. They are (with year entered on list): the Sokkuram Grotto and Pulguksa Temple (1995), the Temple of Haeinsa (1995), Chongmyo Shrine (1995), Changdeokgung Palace, Seoul (1997), Hwasong Fortress, Suwon (1997), the dolmens of Gochang, Hwasun and Ganghwa (2000), Gyeongju historic area (2000), Jeju volcanic island and lava tubes (2007) and the Royal Tombs of the Joseon Dynasty (2009).

Broadcasting

The Korean Broadcasting System (KBS) is a public corporation operating six domestic radio networks, two terrestrial television channels, cable channels, an external radio service and an international satellite TV channel (KBS World, launched in 2003). KBS has also pioneered the distribution of TV via mobile devices and digital multimedia broadcasting (DMB). Munhwa Broadcasting Corporation (MBC) and Education Broadcasting System (EBS) are also public service TV operators. Cable and satellite TV stations are widely available. There were 20·1m. TV sets (colour by NTSC) in 2006.

Cinema

In 2004 there were 302 cinemas with a seating capacity of 297,584. 82 full-length films were produced in 2004.

Press

There were 123 dailies in 2001 and 6,913 periodicals. The main dailies are Chosun Ilbo (average circulation of 2·4m. per issue), JoongAng Ilbo (average circulation of 2·1m. per issue) and Dong-A Ilbo (average circulation of 2·0m. per issue).

A total of 36,185 book titles and 118m. books were published in 2002.

Tourism

6,155,000 foreign nationals visited South Korea in 2006 (6,023,000 in 2005). In 2006 tourist revenues from foreign visitors totalled US$5·8bn.; overseas travel expenditure by Koreans going abroad totalled US$18·9bn. On 18 Nov. 1998 the first South Korean tourists to visit North Korea went on a cruise and tour organized by the South Korean firm Hyundai.

Libraries

There were 9,337 libraries in 2001, including one national library, one congressional, 420 public, 420 university and 7,918 libraries at primary, middle and high schools. There were also 578 specialized and professional libraries.

Theatre and Opera

There are 316 theatres nationwide. 47 have 1,200 seats that can accommodate large-scale dramas, operas, dances and musicals. The Seoul Arts Centre has an opera house.

Museums and Galleries

In 2001 there were 249 museums, including 25 national museums, 36 public museums, 107 private museums and 81 university museums. There were an estimated 500 art galleries in 2001.

DIPLOMATIC REPRESENTATIVES

Of the Republic of Korea in the United Kingdom (60 Buckingham Gate, London, SW1E 6AJ)
Ambassador: Chun Yung-woo.

Of the United Kingdom in the Republic of Korea (Taepyeongno 40, 4 Jeong-dong, Jung-gu 100-120, Seoul)
Ambassador: Martin Uden.

Of the Republic of Korea in the USA (2450 Massachusetts Ave., NW, Washington, D.C., 20008)
Ambassador: Han Duck-soo.

Of the USA in the Republic of Korea (32 Sejongno, Jongno-gu 110-710, Seoul)
Ambassador: Kathleen D. Stephens.

Of the Republic of Korea to the United Nations
Ambassador: Park In-kook.

Of the Republic of Korea to the European Union
Ambassador: Park Joon-woo.

FURTHER READING

National Bureau of Statistics. *Korea Statistical Yearbook*
Bank of Korea. *Economic Statistics Yearbook*

Castley, R., *Korea's Economic Miracle.* 1997
Cumings, B., *Korea's Place in the Sun: A Modern History.* 1997
Eckert, C. J., *et al., Korea Old and New: a History.* 1991
Kang, M.-H., *The Korean Business Conglomerate: Chaebol Then and Now.* 1996
Kim, D.-H. and Tat, Y.-K. (eds.) *The Korean Peninsula in Transition.* 1997
Simons, G., *Korea: the Search for Sovereignty.* 1995
Smith, H., *Industry Policy in Taiwan and Korea in the 1980s.* 2000
Song, P.-N., *The Rise of the Korean Economy.* 2nd ed. 1994
Tennant, R., *A History of Korea.* 1996

National Statistical Office: National Bureau of Statistics, Ministry of Finance and Economy, Seoul
Website: http://kostat.go.kr

KUWAIT

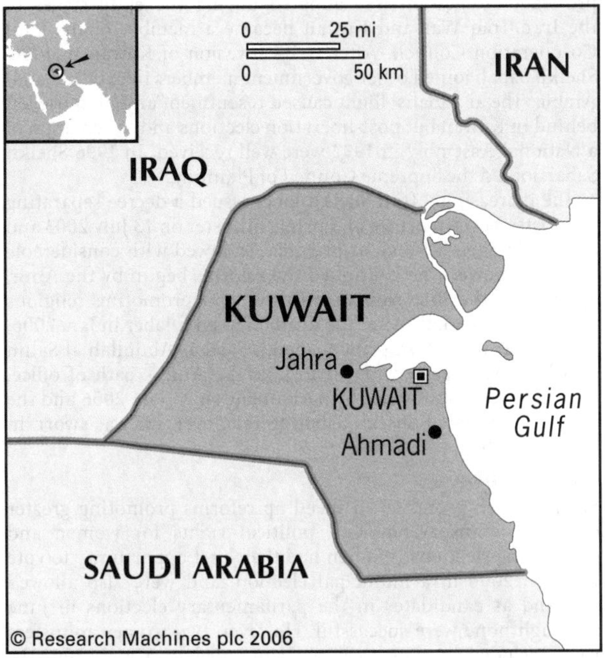

Dowlat al Kuwait
(State of Kuwait)

Capital: Kuwait
Population estimate, 2010: 3·05m.
GDP per capita, 2005: (PPP$) 26,321
HDI/world rank: 0·916/31

KEY HISTORICAL EVENTS

The ruling dynasty was founded by Sheikh Sabah al-Awwal, who ruled from 1756 to 1772. In 1899 Sheikh Mubarak concluded a treaty with Great Britain wherein, in return for the assurance of British protection, he undertook to support British interests. In 1914 the British Government recognized Kuwait as an independent government under British protection. On 19 June 1961 an agreement reaffirmed the independence and sovereignty of Kuwait and recognized the Government of Kuwait's responsibility for the conduct of internal and external affairs. On 2 Aug. 1990 Iraqi forces invaded the country. Following the expiry of the date set by the UN for the withdrawal of Iraqi forces, an air offensive was launched by coalition forces, followed by a land attack on 24 Feb. 1991. Iraqi forces were routed and Kuwait City was liberated on 26 Feb. On 10 Nov. 1994 Iraq recognized the independence and boundaries of Kuwait. In 2006 Sheikh Jaber, who had been Amir since 1977, died and was replaced by Sheikh Sabah.

TERRITORY AND POPULATION

Kuwait is bounded in the east by the Persian Gulf, north and west by Iraq and south and southwest by Saudi Arabia, with an area of 17,818 sq. km. In 1992–93 the UN Boundary Commission redefined Kuwait's border with Iraq, moving it slightly northwards in conformity with an agreement of 1932. The population at the 2005 census (provisional) was 2,213,403; density, 124 per sq. km. The United Nations population estimate for 2005 was 2,700,000. At the 1995 census about 58·5% were non-Kuwaitis. In 2005, 98·3% of the population were urban.

The UN gives an estimated population for 2010 of 3·05m.

The country is divided into six governorates: the capital (comprising Kuwait City, Kuwait's nine islands and territorial and shared territorial waters) (2004 population, 439,030); Farwaniya (686,116); Hawalli (565,767); Ahmadi (449,716); Jahra (322,783); Mubarak Al-Kabir (175,167). The capital city is Kuwait, with a population in 1995 of 28,747. Other major cities are (1995 populations): as-Salimiya (129,775), Qalib ash-Shuyukh (102,169), Hawalli (82,154), Hitan-al-Janubiyah (62,241).

The Neutral Zone (Kuwait's share, 2,590 sq. km), jointly owned and administered by Kuwait and Saudi Arabia from 1922 to 1966, was partitioned between the two countries in May 1966, but the exploitation of the oil and other natural resources continues to be shared.

Over 78% speak Arabic, the official language. English is also used as a second language.

SOCIAL STATISTICS

Births, 2003, 43,982; deaths, 4,424. The birth rate was 17·6 per 1,000 population. Kuwait's 2003 death rate, at 1·8 per 1,000 population, was the lowest in the world. Expectation of life at birth, 2007, was 76·0 years for males and 79·8 years for females. Infant mortality, 2005, ten per 1,000 live births. Annual population growth rate, 2000–05, 2·8%.

Fertility rate, 2004, 2·3 births per woman. Kuwait has had one of the largest reductions in its fertility rate of any country in the world over the past 30 years, having had a rate of 7·2 births per woman in 1975. Kuwait has a young population, with 40·7% of the population being under 15 in 2004.

CLIMATE

Kuwait has a dry, desert climate which is cool in winter but very hot and humid in summer. Rainfall is extremely light. Kuwait, Jan. 56°F (13·5°C), July 99°F (36·6°C). Annual rainfall 5" (125 mm).

CONSTITUTION AND GOVERNMENT

The ruler is HH Sheikh Sabah al-Ahmed al-Jaber al-Sabah, the 15th Amir of Kuwait, who succeeded on 29 Jan. 2006. *Crown Prince:* Sheikh Nawwaf al-Ahmed al-Sabah (b. 1937). The present constitution was approved and promulgated on 11 Nov. 1962.

In 1990 the *National Council* was established, consisting of 50 elected members and 25 appointed by the Amir. It was replaced by a *National Assembly* or *Majlis al-Umma* in 1992, consisting of 50 elected members. The franchise extends to Kuwaiti citizens who are 21 or older, with the exception of those who are serving in the armed forces and citizens who have been naturalized for fewer than 30 years. In May 1999 the cabinet approved a draft law giving women the right to vote and run for parliament. However, in Dec. 1999 parliament rejected the bill allowing women to vote by a margin of 32 to 20. Women were granted the right to vote and run for office in May 2005 when parliament voted in favour of amending the election law by a margin of 35 votes to 23. Women were eligible to stand for election and to vote in a council by-election held in April 2006 and in the full parliamentary election held in June 2006.

Executive authority is vested in the *Council of Ministers.*

National Anthem

'Watanil Kuwait salemta lilmajdi, wa ala jabeenoka tali ossaadi,' ('Kuwait, my fatherland! May you be safe and glorious! May you always enjoy good fortune!'); words by Moshari al-Adwani, tune by Ibrahim Nassar al-Soula.

GOVERNMENT CHRONOLOGY

Amirs since 1950.

1950–65 Sheikh Abdullah al-Salem al-Sabah
1965–77 Sheikh Sabah al-Salem al-Sabah
1977–2006 Sheikh Jaber al-Ahmed al-Jaber al-Sabah
2006– Sheikh Sabah al-Ahmed al-Jaber al-Sabah

RECENT ELECTIONS

National Assembly elections were held on 16 May 2009. Of the 50 available seats the Sunni Islamic Bloc gained 13, liberals 7, Shia Islamists 6, the Popular Bloc 3 and ind. 21. On 16 May 2005 the National Assembly passed legislation granting women the right to vote, as a result of which women participated for the first time in a National Assembly poll in the June 2006 election. In May 2009, four women became the first female candidates to be elected to parliament.

CURRENT ADMINISTRATION

In March 2010 the government comprised:

Prime Minister: Sheikh Nasser Muhammad Al-Ahmad Al-Sabah; b. 1941 (appointed 7 Feb. 2006).

First Deputy Prime Minister and Minister of Defence: Sheikh Jabir Mubarak Al-Hamad Al-Sabah. *Deputy Prime Minister and Minister of Foreign Affairs:* Sheikh Muhammad Sabah Al-Salem Al-Sabah. *Deputy Prime Minister for Economic Affairs and State Minister for Housing and Development:* Sheikh Ahmad Fahad Al-Sabah. *Deputy Prime Minister for Legal Affairs and Minister for Religious Endowments and Islamic Affairs, and Justice:* Rashed Al-Hammad.

Minister of Commerce and Industry: Ahmad Al-Harun. *Communications:* Mohammad Al-Baseeri. *Education and Higher Education:* Mudhi Al-Humoud. *Electricity and Water:* Bader Al-Azemi. *Finance:* Mustafa Al-Shamali. *Health:* Helal Al-Sayer. *Interior:* Sheikh Jaber Al-Khaled Al-Sabah. *Oil and Information:* Sheikh Ahmad Abdullah Al-Sabah. *Public Works and Municipalities:* Fadhel Safar. *Social Affairs and Labour:* Mohammad Al-Afasai. *State Minister for Cabinet Affairs:* Roudhan al-Roudhan.

Government Website: http://www.da.gov.kw

CURRENT LEADERS

Sheikh Sabah al-Ahmed al-Jaber al-Sabah

Position

Amir

Introduction

Sheikh Sabah became Amir of Kuwait in Jan. 2006, ending a brief constitutional crisis in the wake of the death of Sheikh Jaber. As foreign minister for over 40 years, Sheikh Sabah oversaw the positioning of Kuwait as a key Western ally in the Gulf, allowing the USA to use the country as a launch pad for its invasion of Iraq in 2003.

Early Life

Sabah IV al-Ahmed al-Jaber al-Sabah was born in 1929 in Kuwait, then a British protectorate. He is the fourth son of Sheikh Ahmed al-Jaber al-Sabah, the founder of modern Kuwait and its leader from 1921–50. Educated at al Mubarakya School and by tutors, Sheikh Sabah became a member of the central committee municipality council in 1954. He also served as a member of the building and construction council at a time when the Amir, Sheikh Abdullah al-Salem al-Sabah, was pumping much of the state's new oil wealth into an ambitious public works programme.

From 1956–62 Sheikh Sabah chaired the printing and publishing authority and was then appointed minister of information in the first post-independence cabinet. He was promoted to foreign minister in 1963 and headed Kuwait's inaugural delegation to the UN later that year. He presided over a generally low-profile, neutralist foreign policy. Palestinian rights received strong support; Fatah was founded in Kuwait.

On 16 Feb. 1978 Sheikh Sabah was appointed deputy prime minister while keeping the foreign affairs portfolio. A broadly pro-Iraqi orientation was adopted during the early stages of the Iran–Iraq War and Kuwait became a member of the Gulf Co-operation Council. After Iraq's invasion of Kuwait in 1990, Sheikh Sabah joined other government members in exile in Saudi Arabia. The al-Sabahs' flight caused resentment among those left behind in Kuwait but post-liberation elections and the creation of a National Assembly in 1992 were well received. In 1996 Sheikh Sabah joined the Supreme Council of Planning.

The increasingly frail Sheikh Jaber issued a decree separating the posts of crown prince and prime minister on 13 July 2003 and appointed Sheikh Sabah as premier. Endowed with considerable executive powers, he continued the reforms begun by the Amir, appointing the first woman minister and promoting religious tolerance in schools. After the death of Sheikh Jaber in Jan. 2006, the 76-year old crown prince, Sheikh Saad al-Abdullah al Salim al-Sabah, was deemed too ill to take the Amir's oath of office. He was voted out of office by parliament on 24 Jan. 2006 and the cabinet nominated Sheikh Sabah to take over. He was sworn in on 29 Jan. 2006.

Career in Office

Sheikh Sabah promised to speed up reforms promoting greater economic transparency, full political rights for women and democratic elections. Women had their first opportunity to vote in April 2006 in a municipal election, and were also allowed to stand as candidates in the parliamentary elections in June although none were successful. However, two women ministers were included in a new cabinet appointed in March 2007. In March 2008 Sheikh Sabah dissolved parliament and called fresh elections in May, in which Islamists won 30 of the 50 National Assembly seats. Women candidates were again unsuccessful. A year later he dissolved parliament again when the cabinet resigned on 16 March 2009 to prevent questioning of the Amir's nephew, Prime Minister Sheikh Nasser Muhammad Al-Ahmad Al-Sabah, on charges of misuse of public funds. Sheikh Nasser was subsequently reappointed prime minister following elections held on 16 May in which four women candidates were returned as parliamentary members for the first time.

DEFENCE

In Sept. 1991 the USA signed a ten-year agreement with Kuwait to store equipment, use ports and carry out joint training exercises. US troops are deployed in Kuwait as part of Operation *New Dawn* (formerly *Iraqi Freedom*).

Defence expenditure in 2006 totalled US$3,497m. (US$1,446 per capita), representing 3·4% of GDP. The expenditure per capita in 2006 was one of the highest in the world.

Army

Strength (2007) 11,000. In addition there is a National Guard of around 6,600.

Navy

Personnel in 2007 numbered an estimated 2,000, including 500 Coast Guard personnel.

Air Force

From a small initial combat force the Air Force has grown rapidly, although it suffered heavy losses after the Iraqi invasion of 1990–91. Equipment includes F/A-18 *Hornet* strike aircraft and BAe *Hawks*. Personnel strength was estimated (2007) at 2,500, with 50 combat capable aircraft and 16 attack helicopters.

INTERNATIONAL RELATIONS

Kuwait is a member of the UN, World Bank, IMF and several other UN specialized agencies, WTO, Islamic Development Bank, OIC, Gulf Co-operation Council, League of Arab States and OPEC.

ECONOMY

Industry accounted for 59·7% of GDP in 2003 and services 40·3%.

Overview

After the liberation that followed invasion by Iraq in 1991, the economy achieved relative stability. The economy is dominated by oil production, accounting for 80% of government revenue. High oil prices since 2003 have produced large trade surpluses and growth has been strong, although inflationary pressures have emerged as a result of higher imported food prices and domestic rents. Recent OPEC decisions resulted in a decline of oil production by 2·6% in 2007.

However, non-oil activity (particularly within the financial, transportation and communication services) grew by nearly 9%, thanks to a boost in investment and expansionary macroeconomic policies. With high earnings from oil and with a small population, the government has maintained a generous welfare system. Government-initiated structural reforms are seeking to create a dynamic private sector-driven open economy, with Kuwait Airways, the oldest airline operating in the Gulf, set to be the country's first major privatization.

Currency

The unit of currency is the *Kuwaiti dinar* (KWD), usually written as KD, of 1,000 *fils*. Inflation was 5·5% in 2007 and 10·5% in 2008. Foreign exchange reserves were US$7,544m. in July 2005, monetary gold reserves were 2·54m. troy oz and total money supply was KD 3,581m.

In 2001 the six Gulf Arab states—Kuwait, along with Bahrain, Oman, Qatar, Saudi Arabia and the United Arab Emirates—signed an agreement to establish a single currency by 2010. In June 2009 it was agreed to postpone the implementation of the new currency, the *khaleeji*, until 2013. Both Oman and the United Arab Emirates have now withdrawn from the scheme, in 2007 and 2009 respectively.

Budget

The fiscal year begins on 1 April. Budgetary central government revenue in 2006–07 totalled KD 15,304m. and expenditure KD 11,192m. Oil accounts for 94% of government revenues. Expenditure by function in 2006–07 (in KD 1m.): social protection, 2,964; economic affairs, 1,405; defence, 1,060; general public services, 1,030.

Performance

Real GDP growth was 2·5% in 2007 and 6·3% in 2008. Total GDP in 2007 was US$112·1bn.

Banking and Finance

The *Governor* of the Central Bank is Sheikh Salem Abdulaziz Al-Sabah. There is also the Kuwait Finance House. In 2002 there were eleven national banks and one Islamic banking firm. The combined assets of banks operating in Kuwait totalled KD 18,818m. in Dec. 2003. Foreign banks were not permitted until 2005.

There is a stock exchange, linked with those of Bahrain and Oman.

ENERGY AND NATURAL RESOURCES

Environment

Kuwait's carbon dioxide emissions from the consumption and flaring of fossil fuels were the equivalent of 31·6 tonnes per capita in 2008.

Electricity

There are six power stations with an estimated total installed capacity of 9·4m. kW in 2004. Production in 2004 was 41·3bn. kWh; consumption per capita was 15,423 kWh.

Oil and Gas

Oil production in 2008, 137·3m. tonnes. Kuwait had reserves in 2008 amounting to 101·5bn. bbls. Most of the oil is in the Great Burgan area (reserves of approximately 70bn. bbls), comprising the Burgan, Maqwa and Ahmadi fields located south of Kuwait City. Natural gas production was 12·8bn. cu. metres in 2008, with 1,780bn. cu metres of proven reserves.

Water

The country depends upon desalination plants. In 1993 there were four plants with a daily total capacity of 216m. gallons. Fresh mineral water is pumped and bottled at Rawdhatain. Underground brackish water is used for irrigation, street cleaning and livestock. Production, 2003, 127,185m. gallons (95,174m. gallons fresh, 32,011m. gallons brackish). Consumption, 2003, 119,521m. gallons (94,987m. gallons fresh, 24,534m. gallons brackish).

Agriculture

There were 10,400 ha. of arable land in 2003 and 2,100 ha. of permanent crops. Production of main crops, 2003 (in 1,000 tonnes): tomatoes, 64; cucumbers and gherkins, 35; potatoes, 21; dates, 16; aubergines, 15; chillies and green peppers, 8; pumpkins and squash, 8; cauliflowers, 7.

Livestock (2003): sheep, 481,000; goats, 194,000; cattle, 27,000; poultry, 30m. Milk production (2003), 43,000 tonnes.

Forestry

Forests covered 6,000 ha. in 2005, or 0·3% of the land area.

Fisheries

The total catch in 2005 was 4,895 tonnes, exclusively from sea fishing. In the space of a month in 2001 more than 2,000 tonnes of dead fish were washed ashore. Some experts claimed the cause was the alleged pumping of raw sewage into the Gulf while others attributed it to waste from the oil industry. Shrimp fishing was important, but has declined since the 1990–91 war through oil pollution of coastal waters. Before the discovery of oil, pearls were at the centre of Kuwait's economy, but today pearl fishing is only on a small scale.

INDUSTRY

Industries, apart from oil, include boat building, fishing, food production, petrochemicals, gases and construction. Production figures in 2004 (in 1,000 tonnes): distillate fuel oil, 12,038; residual fuel oil, 9,589; kerosene, 4,636; liquefied petroleum gas, 4,598; jet fuel, 2,258; petrol, 1,914; cement (2003), 1,863.

Labour

In June 2004 the labour force totalled 1,551,342 (81·3% non-Kuwaitis). Of the total labour force, 52·1% worked in social, community and personal services, 15·2% in trade, hotels and restaurants, 7·2% in construction and 5·8% in manufacturing. Registered unemployment in June 2004 was 1·7%. Approximately 95% of nationals work for the government, with around 95% of private jobs being filled by expatriates.

Trade Unions

There is a Kuwaiti Trade Union Federation, but in 2002 only 5·6% of the workforce belonged to a union or labour group.

INTERNATIONAL TRADE

Kuwait, along with Bahrain, Oman, Qatar, Saudi Arabia and the United Arab Emirates entered into a customs union in Jan. 2003.

Imports and Exports

Imports (f.o.b.) were valued at US$14,350m. in 2006 and exports (f.o.b.) at US$58,638m. Oil accounts for 91% of revenue from exports, and oil exports account for approximately 46% of GDP. The main non-oil export is chemical fertilizer. Main import suppliers, 2003: Germany, 10·3%; Japan, 9·9%; USA, 1·6%. Main export markets, 2003: Saudi Arabia, 13·7%; Iraq, 10·8%; UAE, 10·0%.

COMMUNICATIONS

Roads

There were 5,749 km of roads in 2004, 85% of which were paved. There were 750,600 passenger cars in use in 2007 (282 per 1,000 inhabitants), 573,200 lorries and vans, and 27,300 buses and coaches. There were 45,376 road accidents in 2003 involving injury with 1,704 fatalities.

Civil Aviation

There is an international airport (Kuwait International). The national carrier is the state-owned Kuwait Airways. Kuwait's first low-cost airline, Jazeera Airways, began operations in Oct. 2005. In 2005 scheduled airline traffic of Kuwait-based carriers flew 50·7m. km and carried 1,944,200 passengers. Kuwait International airport handled 4,260,136 passengers in 2003 and 144,727 tonnes of freight.

Shipping

The port of Kuwait formerly served mainly as an entrepôt, but this function is declining in importance with the development of the oil industry. The largest oil terminal is at Mina Ahmadi. Three small oil ports lie to the south of Mina Ahmadi: Mina Shuaiba, Mina Abdullah and Mina Al-Zor. The merchant fleet totalled 2,256,000 GRT in 2002, of which 1,628,000 GRT were oil tankers. In 2002 vessels totalling 2,052,000 NRT entered ports and vessels totalling 1,178,000 NRT cleared.

Telecommunications

Kuwait had 2,890,100 telephone subscribers in 2005, or 1,075·6 per 1,000 population, of which 2,379,800 were mobile phone subscribers. There were 600,000 PCs in use (223·3 for every 1,000 persons) in 2005 and 700,000 internet users.

Postal Services

In 2003 there were 113,000 post office boxes, 96,301 rented. There were 31,943 outgoing telegrams and 26,482 incoming.

SOCIAL INSTITUTIONS

Justice

In 1960 Kuwait adopted a unified judicial system covering all levels of courts. These are: Courts of Summary Justice, Courts of the First Instance, Supreme Court of Appeal, Court of Cassation and a Constitutional Court. Islamic Sharia is a major source of legislation. The death penalty is still in use. There was one confirmed execution in 2007 but none in 2008.

The population in penal institutions in 2003 was approximately 3,700 (148 per 100,000 of national population).

Education

Education is free and compulsory from six to 14 years. In 2007 there were 211,576 pupils in primary schools with 22,016 teaching staff, and 247,233 pupils in secondary schools with 26,050 teaching staff. In 2006 there were 37,521 students in tertiary education and 1,986 academic staff. There are two state-supported higher education institutions, Kuwait University and the Public Authority for Applied Education and Training. There were approximately 28,000 students at Kuwait University in 2009. There are also a number of private universities and colleges, a teacher training college, a music academy and several Quranic schools. The Arab Open University which opened in Nov. 2002 is based in Kuwait and has branches in several other Middle Eastern countries. There were around 17,000 enrolments in 2003–04. Adult literacy rate in 2003 was 93·4% (97·7% among men and 89·3% among women). In 2005 public expenditure on education came to 4·7% of GDP and accounted for 12·7% of total government spending.

Health

Medical services are free to all residents. In 2003 there were 15 hospitals and sanatoria, with a provision of 4,712 beds (19 per 10,000 population). There were 3,643 doctors (15 per 10,000 population), 613 dentists, 8,997 nurses and 532 pharmacists in 2003. There were 74 clinics and other health centres and 1,569,549 people were admitted to public hospitals in 2003.

RELIGION

In 2001, 1,020,000 people were Sunni Muslims, 680,000 Shia Muslims, 230,000 other Muslims and 340,000 other (mostly Christian and Hindu).

CULTURE

Broadcasting

State-run Kuwaiti TV runs three networks and a satellite channel. Al-Rai was launched in 2004 as the first private satellite TV station. Government-controlled Radio Kuwait transmits programmes in Arabic and English. Marina FM, launched in 2006, is the first private radio station. In 2005 there were 480,000 TV-equipped households. Colour is by PAL.

Press

In 2006 there were eight daily newspapers, with a combined circulation of 430,000. Formal press censorship was lifted in Jan. 1992.

Tourism

There were 94,000 foreign tourists in 2003, bringing revenue of US$98m. There were 38 hotels providing 5,063 beds in 2003.

Libraries

In 2003 there were 11 non-specialized and 27 public libraries, stocking 461,000 books for 12,500 registered users. The number of school libraries was 585 in 2002–03.

Museums and Galleries

There were three museums attracting 38,000 visitors in 2003.

DIPLOMATIC REPRESENTATIVES

Of Kuwait in the United Kingdom (2 Albert Gate, London, SW1X 7JU)
Ambassador: Khaled Al-Duwaisan, GCVO.

Of the United Kingdom in Kuwait (Arabian Gulf St., Dasman, Kuwait)
Ambassador: Frank Baker, OBE.

Of Kuwait in the USA (2940 Tilden St., NW, Washington, D.C., 20008)
Ambassador: Salem Abdulla Al-Jaber Al-Sabah.

Of the USA in Kuwait (Al-Masjed Al-Aqsa St., Bayan, Kuwait)
Ambassador: Deborah K. Jones.

Of Kuwait to the United Nations
Ambassador: Vacant.
Chargé d'Affaires a.i.: Khalaf Bu Dhhair.

Of Kuwait to the European Union
Ambassador: Nabeela Abdulla Al-Mulla.

FURTHER READING

Al-Yahya, M.A., *Kuwait: Fall and Rebirth.* 1993

Boghardt, Lori Plotkin, *Kuwait Amid War, Peace and Revolution: 1979–1991 and New Challenges.* 2007

Crystal, J., *Kuwait: the Transformation of an Oil State.* 1992

Finnie, D. H., *Shifting Lines in the Sand: Kuwait's Elusive Frontier with Iraq.* 1992

National Statistical Office: Statistics and Census Sector, Ministry of Planning.

Website (limited English): http://mopweb4.mop.gov.kw

KYRGYZSTAN

Kyrgyz Respublikasy
(Kyrgyz Republic)

Capital: Bishkek
Population estimate, 2010: 5·55m.
GDP per capita, 2007: (PPP$) 2,006
HDI/world rank: 0·710/120

KEY HISTORICAL EVENTS

Kyrgyzstan became part of Soviet Turkestan, which itself became a Soviet Socialist Republic within the Russian Soviet Federal Socialist Republic (RSFSR) in April 1921. In 1924, when Central Asia was reorganized territorially on a national basis, Kyrgyzstan was separated from Turkestan. In Dec. 1936 Kyrgyzstan was proclaimed one of the constituent Soviet Socialist Republics of the USSR. With the collapse of the Soviet Empire, the republic asserted its claim to sovereignty in 1990 and declared independence in Sept. 1991. Askar Akayev became president in 1990 and subsequently expanded presidential powers. Kyrgyzstan became a member of the CIS in Dec. 1991.

Incursions into Kyrgyz territory by Islamic rebels and border skirmishes in the Fergana Valley are a cause for concern for all Central Asian governments. Kyrgyzstan tripled its defence budget for 2001 to combat terrorism. Allegations of widespread government corruption and disputed parliamentary elections in Feb. 2005 led to widespread popular protests. The Supreme Court declared the elections void and Kurmanbek Bakiyev was appointed prime minister and acting president. Akayev, in exile in Russia, resigned as president in April 2005. Bakiyev was confirmed as president by winning the elections held in July 2005. His tenure was marked by elections that fell below accepted international standards, concerns over civil liberties and growing popular resentment at his failure to address corruption. The doubling of household utility costs in Jan. 2010 sparked a wave of protests that resulted in Bakiyev stepping down in April 2010 with Roza Otunbayeva, previously foreign minister, heading an interim government.

TERRITORY AND POPULATION

Kyrgyzstan is situated on the Tien-Shan mountains and bordered in the east by China, west by Kazakhstan and Uzbekistan, north by Kazakhstan and south by Tajikistan. Area, 199,900 sq. km (77,180 sq. miles). Population (census 1999), 4,822,938 (2,442,473 females); density, 24 per sq. km. In 2007, 65·3% of the population lived in rural areas.

The UN gives an estimated population for 2010 of 5·55m.; density, 28 per sq. km.

The republic comprises seven provinces (Batken, Djalal-Abad, Issyk-Kul, Naryn, Osh, Talas and Chu) plus the city of Bishkek, the capital (formerly Frunze; 1999 census population, 750,327; 2008 estimate, 827,100). Other large towns are Osh (208,520 in 1999), Djalal-Abad (70,401), Karakol (formerly Przhevalsk, 64,322), Tokmak (59,409), Karabalta (47,159), Balykchy (41,342) and Naryn (40,050).

The Kyrgyz are of Turkic origin and formed 69·2% of the population in 2008; the rest included Uzbeks (14·5%), Russians (8·7%) and Dungans (1·2%).

The official languages are Kyrgyz and Russian. After the break-up of the Soviet Union, Russian was only the official language in provinces where Russians are in a majority. However, in May 2000 parliament voted to make it an official language nationwide, mainly in an attempt to stem the ever-increasing exodus of skilled ethnic Russians. The Cyrillic alphabet is still used although the reintroduction of the Roman alphabet (in use 1928–40) remains a source of political debate.

SOCIAL STATISTICS

2003 births, 105,490; deaths, 35,941; marriages, 34,266. Rates, 2003 (per 1,000 population): birth, 20·9; death, 7·1; infant mortality (per 1,000 live births, 2005), 58. Life expectancy, 2007, 63·9 years for males and 71·4 for females. In 2003 the most popular age for marrying was 20–24 for females and 25–29 for males. Annual population growth rate, 2000–05, 0·9%; fertility rate, 2004, 2·6 births per woman.

CLIMATE

The climate varies from dry continental to polar in the high Tien-Shan, to sub-tropical in the southwest (Fergana Valley) and temperate in the northern foothills. Bishkek, Jan. 9°F (–13°C), July 70°F (21°C). Annual rainfall 14·8" (375 mm).

CONSTITUTION AND GOVERNMENT

A new constitution was adopted on 8 Nov. 2006. The constitution reduced the president's power, gave to the party that has the most seats in parliament rather than the president the right to form the government and enlarged the parliament from 75 to 90 deputies. However, further amendments in Jan. 2007 restored much of the power that the president had earlier surrendered, notably the authority to form the government. In a referendum of 22 Oct. 2007, 75·0% of voters supported further reforms that would increase the number of deputies and alter the election process from a single-constituency system to a proportional all-party list. The Presidency is directly elected for renewable five-year terms. At a referendum on 30 Jan. 1994, 96% of votes cast favoured President Akayev's serving out the rest of his term of office; turnout was 95%. At a referendum on 22–23 Oct. 1994 turnout was 87%. 75% of votes cast were in favour of instituting referendums as a constitutional mechanism, and 73% were in favour of establishing a new bicameral parliament (*Jogorku Kenesh*), with a 35-member directly-elected legislature (Legislative Assembly), and a 70-member upper house (Assembly of People's Representatives) elected on a regional basis and meeting twice a year. At a referendum in Feb. 2003 it was decided to revert to a unicameral parliament of 75 members (since increased to 90). 94·5% of votes cast at a referendum on 10 Feb. 1996 were in favour of giving the President the right to appoint all ministers except the Prime Minister without reference to parliament.

National Anthem

'Ak möngülüü aska yoolor, talaalar' ('High mountains, valleys and fields'); words by D. Sadykov and E. Kuluev, tune by N. Davlyesov and K. Moldovasanov.

RECENT ELECTIONS

Parliamentary elections were held on 16 Dec. 2007 in which 71 of 90 seats were won by Ak Zhol (Bright Path), 11 by the Social Democratic Party of Kyrgyzstan and eight by the Party of Communists of Kyrgyzstan. Turnout was 71·9%.

Presidential elections were held on 23 July 2009. Incumbent President Kurmanbek Bakiyev won with 76·1% of the vote, ahead of former prime minister Almazbek Atambayev with 8·4% and Temir Sariev with 6·7%. There were three other candidates. Reported turnout was 79·3%. The elections were marred by controversy with Atambayev withdrawing his candidature after polls opened in protest against alleged government attempts to rig the voting. OSCE also raised concerns as to the transparency of the elections.

CURRENT ADMINISTRATION

In April 2010 the Kyrgyz government was overthrown following a political uprising sparked by the country's weak economy, rising fuel tariffs and media censorship by the government. An interim opposition government led by Roza Otunbayeva took over, pledging to remain in power until new elections could be called in six months' time. President Kurmanbek Bakiyev fled the country but refused to resign or recognize the new administration. In April 2010 the interim government comprised:

Head of Interim Government: Roza Otunbayeva; b. 1950 (Social Democratic Party; in office since 7 April 2010).

Deputy Prime Ministers: Almaz Atambayev (*in Charge of Economy*); Omurbek Tekebayev (*in Charge of Constitutional Reform*); Temir Sariyev (*in Charge of Finance*); Azimbek Beknazarov (*in Charge of Security*).

Minister of Agriculture: Kubat Kaseyinov. *Cultural Affairs Agency:* Ryskeldy Mombekov. *Defence:* Ismail Isakov. *Foreign Affairs:* Ruslan Kazakbayev. *General Prosecutor:* Baitemir Ibrayev. *Health:* Damira Niyazaliyeva. *Interior:* Bolot Sherniyazov. *Justice:* Aida Salyanova. *State Security Service:* Keneshbek Dushebayev.

CURRENT LEADERS

Roza Otunbayeva

Position

Head of Interim Government

Introduction

Roza Otunbayeva became the head of an interim government established on 8 April 2010 following anti-government protests that forced incumbent president, Kurmanbek Bakiyev, to flee the capital. A former ally of the ousted president, Otunbayeva is a veteran opposition politician who has served as foreign minister and ambassador to the UK and the USA.

Early Life

Otunbayeva was born on 23 Aug. 1950 in Osh, in the south of what was then the Kyrgyz Soviet Socialist Republic. Graduating from the faculty of philosophy at Moscow State University in 1972, she completed a postgraduate course at the same institution three years later, then went on to spend six years as head of the philosophy department of the Kyrgyz State National University.

Otunbayeva entered politics in 1981 as second secretary of the Lenin Regional Council of Frunze (now Bishkek). She later served as vice-chairman of the Republic's council of ministers and in 1992 became the recently independent Kyrgyzstan's first ambassador to the USA and Canada. After two years she was appointed the country's first and thus far only female foreign minister, before requesting a posting to the UK in 1997 to become Kyrgyzstan's first post-Soviet ambassador in London.

Between 2002 and 2004 Otunbayeva was the deputy special representative of the UN secretary-general on the Georgian-Abkhazian settlement. She was present during the 'Rose Revolution' of 2003 that deposed President Eduard Shevardnadze. In Dec. 2004, on returning from Georgia, Otunbayeva founded an opposition movement, Ata-Szhurt ('Fatherland'), to contest forthcoming parliamentary elections. In Jan. 2005 her candidate registration was rejected on the grounds that she had not been resident in Kyrgyzstan for all of the preceding five years.

Otunbayeva was one of the senior opposition figures during the 'Tulip Revolution' of March 2005. In the aftermath of President Askar Akayev's deposition, she was named acting foreign minister under the interim administration of Kurmanbek Bakiyev. However, when Bakiyev became president Otunbayeva failed to secure parliamentary backing to win the post on a permanent basis. In Dec. 2007 she was elected to the Kyrgyz parliament as a representative of the Social Democratic Party and became party leader in Oct. 2009.

On 8 April 2010, after violent protests had driven the incumbent president from Bishkek, the Krygyz opposition elected Otunbayeva to head an interim 'government of people's trust'.

Career in Office

On coming to power Otunbayeva announced that her temporary government would put together a new constitution to establish a parliamentary democracy. She promised that elections would be held within six months but, as of April 2010, argued that it was too early to say whether she would run for president.

DEFENCE

Conscription is for 18 months. Defence expenditure in 2006 totalled US$36m. (US$7 per capita), representing 1·3% of GDP. The USA opened a military base in Kyrgyzstan in 2001 to aid the war in Afghanistan against the Taliban. The base was scheduled to close by the end of Aug. 2009 after an eviction notice was served on 20 Feb. 2009 giving the US military 180 days to vacate the site. However, on 23 June 2009 the Kyrgyz and US governments agreed a new deal that allowed a one-year extension of the lease. It was subsequently extended indefinitely in April 2010. In Sept. 2003 Kyrgyzstan agreed to allow Russia to open an air force base in the country.

Army

Personnel, 2007, 8,500. In addition there are 5,000 border guards, 3,500 interior troops and a National Guard of 1,000.

Air Force

Personnel, 2007, 2,400, with 52 combat capable aircraft (mainly MiG-21 fighters) and nine attack helicopters.

INTERNATIONAL RELATIONS

Kyrgyzstan is a member of the UN, World Bank, IMF and several other UN specialized agencies, WTO, OSCE, CIS, Islamic Development Bank, NATO Partnership for Peace, IOM, OIC, Asian Development Bank and ECO.

ECONOMY

Agriculture accounted for 33·0% of GDP in 2006, industry 20·1% and services 46·9%.

Overview

Following independence from the Soviet Union in 1991, the loss of trade preferences and Soviet subsidies caused a major downturn in Kyrgyzstan's economy with declining GDP, hyperinflation and widespread poverty. Economic performance and macroeconomic stability improved after the 1998 Russian financial crisis, with GDP growth averaging 5% per year. Traditionally, agriculture and mining have been the leading sectors but in recent years growth has stemmed from the construction, power, and transportation, trade and communication services sectors.

Recent growth has been fairly robust despite a challenging political environment. Following a slight contraction in 2005, real GDP growth rebounded in 2006. The overall fiscal deficit fell to 3·2% of GDP in 2006 from a level of 5% in 2003, while public debt fell to 58% of GDP in 2007 from a level of nearly 100% in 2004. There has been a decline in the poverty rate, particularly for those in extreme poverty. Inflation threatens to become entrenched in the economy. Following a period in which it remained in the 3–5% range, a global rise in food and energy prices led to an inflation surge in late 2007. According to the IMF, tighter monetary and fiscal policy should hold down prices while protecting medium-term growth prospects.

Currency

On 10 May 1993 Kyrgyzstan introduced its own currency unit, the *som* (KGS), of 100 *tyiyn*, at a rate of 1 som = 200 roubles. Inflation was 10·2% in 2007, rising to 24·5% in 2008. Gold reserves totalled 83,000 troy oz in July 2005, foreign exchange reserves US$509m. and total money supply 13,884m. soms.

Budget

Budgetary central government revenue totalled 32,670·1m. soms in 2007 and expenditure 25,666·4m. soms. Tax revenues in 2007 were 23,266·0m. soms. Main items of expenditure by economic type in 2007 were: compensation of employees (6,845·1m. soms) and use of goods and services (6,370·6m. soms).

VAT is 20%.

Performance

The economy shrank by 0·2% in 2005, but it then recovered with growth of 8·5% in 2007 and 7·6% in 2008. Total GDP in 2008 was US$4·4bn.

Banking and Finance

The central bank and bank of issue is the National Bank (*Acting Governor,* Manas Zhakypov). There were 22 commercial banks, including three foreign banks, in 2002. There is a stock exchange in Bishkek.

ENERGY AND NATURAL RESOURCES

Environment

Kyrgyzstan's carbon dioxide emissions from the consumption and flaring of fossil fuels were the equivalent of 1·1 tonnes per capita in 2008.

Electricity

Installed capacity was 4·0m. kW in 2004. Production in 2004 was 15·15bn. kWh, of which 93·1% hydro-electric; consumption per capita was 2,320 kWh.

Oil and Gas

Output of oil, 2003, 69,500 tonnes; natural gas, 2003, 27·1m. cu. metres.

Minerals

In 2004 lignite production totalled 397,000 tonnes and coal production 64,000 tonnes. Some gold is mined.

Agriculture

Kyrgyzstan is famed for its livestock breeding, in particular the small Kyrgyz horse. In 2004 there were 2,882,000 sheep, 1,003,000 cattle, 795,000 goats, 340,000 horses and 2m. chickens. Yaks are bred as meat and dairy cattle, and graze on high altitudes unsuitable for other cattle. Crossed with domestic cattle, hybrids give twice the yield of milk.

There were 1·34m. ha. of arable land in 2003 and 67,000 ha. of permanent crops. Number of peasant farms (2003), 255,822.

Principal crops include wheat, barley, corn and vegetables. Fodder crops for livestock are grown, particularly lucerne; also sugar beets, cotton, tobacco and medicinal herbs. Sericulture, fruit, grapes and vegetables are major branches.

Output of main agricultural products (in 1,000 tonnes) in 2003: potatoes, 1,308; wheat, 1,014; sugar beets, 812; corn for grain, 399; barley, 198; tomatoes, 144; carrots, 126; raw cotton, 106; cabbage, 104; onions, 104; cucumbers, 50. Livestock products, 2003, in 1,000 tonnes: beef and veal, 94; mutton and goat meat, 44; milk, 1,192; eggs, 268m. units.

Forestry

In 2003 forests covered 1,057,000 ha., or 5·3% of the land area. Timber production in 2007 was 27,000 cu. metres.

Fisheries

The catch in 2004 was seven tonnes, entirely from freshwater fishing.

INDUSTRY

Industrial enterprises include food, timber, textile, engineering, metallurgical, oil and mining. There are also sugar refineries, tanneries, cotton and wool-cleansing works, flour-mills and a tobacco factory. In 2006 industry accounted for 20·1% of GDP, with manufacturing contributing 12·9%. In 2003 output was valued at 48,940·1m. soms at current prices.

Production, 2003: cement, 757,300 tonnes; carpets, 13·4m. sq. metres; cotton woven fabrics, 1m. sq. metres; footwear, 238,000 pairs.

Labour

Out of 1,837,000 people in employment in 2003, 951,200 were engaged in agriculture, hunting and forestry; 205,800 in wholesale and retail trade/repair of motor vehicles, motorcycles and personal and household goods; 151,900 in education; and 113,700 in manufacturing. In 2004 the unemployment rate was 2·9%.

INTERNATIONAL TRADE

In Jan. 1994 an agreement to create a single economic zone was signed with Kazakhstan and Uzbekistan. In March 1996 Kyrgyzstan joined a customs union with Russia, Kazakhstan and Belarus. Total external debt was US$2,032m. in 2005.

Imports and Exports

Imports (f.o.b.) were valued at US$1,792·3m. in 2006 and exports (f.o.b.) at US$810·8m. Principal imports in 2004: machinery and transport equipment, 19·9%; petroleum and petroleum products, 17·6%; chemicals and related products, 14·4%; food and livestock, 7·9%. Principal exports in 2004: gold, 44·7%; petroleum and petroleum products, 8·2%; textile fibres, 7·9%; machinery and transport equipment, 7·5%.

Main import suppliers in 2003: Russia, 24·6%; Kazakhstan, 23·8%; China, 10·8%; USA, 6·7%; Uzbekistan, 5·5%; Germany, 5·3%. Main export markets, 2003: United Arab Emirates, 24·8%; Switzerland, 20·3%; Russia, 16·7%; Kazakhstan, 9·8%; Canada, 5·3%; China, 4·0%.

COMMUNICATIONS

Roads

There were 34,000 km of roads in 2007. Passenger cars in use in 2007 numbered 229,700 (44 per 1,000 inhabitants). There were 1,252 road accident fatalities in 2007.

Rail

In the north a railway runs from Lugovaya through Bishkek to Rybachi on Lake Issyk-Kul. Towns in the southern valleys are linked by short lines with the Ursatyevskaya–Andizhan railway in Uzbekistan. Total length of railway, 2005, 424 km. Passenger-km travelled in 2003 came to 49·8m. and freight tonne-km to 562m.

Civil Aviation
There is an international airport at Bishkek (Manas). The national carrier is Kyrgyzstan Airlines. In 2003 Bishkek handled 217,576 passengers (112,487 on international flights) and 1,978 tonnes of freight. In 2003 scheduled airline traffic of Kyrgyzstan-based carriers flew 6m. km, carrying 206,000 passengers (103,000 on international flights).

Shipping
The total length of inland waterways was 460 km in 2003. In 2003, 38,700 tonnes of freight were carried.

Telecommunications
There were 979,800 telephone subscribers in 2005, equivalent to 186·2 for every 1,000 persons, including 541,700 mobile phone subscribers. There were 100,000 PCs in use (19·0 per 1,000 inhabitants) in 2005 and internet users numbered 280,000.

Postal Services
In 2003 there were 920 post offices.

SOCIAL INSTITUTIONS

Justice
In 2004, 32,616 crimes were reported, including 419 murders and attempted murders. The population in penal institutions in March 2008 was 8,427 (156 per 100,000 of national population). The new constitution that came into force in Jan. 2007 abolished the death penalty.

Education
In 2003 there were 417 pre-primary schools for 47,464 pupils; in 2004 there were 143 primary schools with 11,769 pupils, 160 basic schools with 32,192 pupils, 1,778 secondary schools with 1,084,922 pupils and 13,337 university level lecturers for 218,273 students. There were 49 higher educational institutions and 75 secondary professional education establishments in 2004–05. Kyrgyz University had 20,855 students in 2004–05. Adult literacy was 98·7% in 1999.

In 2005 public expenditure on education came to 4·9% of GDP.

Health
In 2003 there were 13,608 physicians, 1,076 dentists, 21,120 nurses and 2,663 midwives; in 2003 there were 151 hospitals.

Welfare
In Dec. 2007 there were 529,000 pensioners.

RELIGION
In 2001, 75% of the population was Sunni Muslim. There were 1,784 mosques, 359 Christian congregations, one synagogue and one Buddhist temple in 2008.

CULTURE

World Heritage Sites
Sulaiman-Too Sacred Mountain in the Fergana Valley was inscribed on the UNESCO World Heritage List in 2009. Situated at the crossroads of important routes on the Central Asian Silk Roads system, Sulaiman-Too is the site of numerous ancient places of worship and caves with petroglyphs.

Broadcasting
The state-run Kyrgyz National TV and Radio Broadcasting Corporation operates two television (colour by SECAM) and two radio networks. Private television services include Kyrgyz Public Educational TV, NTS, Independent Bishkek TV and Osh TV. There are also several private radio stations, mostly based in Bishkek. There were 1·19m. television receivers in 2006.

Cinema
In 2007 there were 51 cinemas with an annual attendance of 211,000.

Press
There were three national daily newspapers in 2006, with a combined circulation of 35,000.

Tourism
In 2005 there were 315,000 non-resident tourists; spending by tourists totalled US$94m.

DIPLOMATIC REPRESENTATIVES
Of Kyrgyzstan in the United Kingdom (Ascot House, 119 Crawford St., London, W1U 6BJ)
Ambassador: Dr Kuban Mambetaliev.

Of the United Kingdom in Kyrgyzstan
Ambassador: David Moran (resides in Astana, Kazakhstan).

Of Kyrgyzstan in the USA (1732 Wisconsin Ave., NW, Washington, D.C., 20007)
Ambassador: Zamira Sydykova.

Of the USA in Kyrgyzstan (171 Prospekt Mira, Bishkek 720016)
Ambassador: Tatiana Gfoeller.

Of Kyrgyzstan to the United Nations
Ambassador: Nurbek Jeenbaev.

Of Kyrgyzstan to the European Union
Ambassador: Jyrgalbek Kumarovich Azylov.

FURTHER READING
Abazov, Rafis, *Historical Dictionary of Kyrgyzstan.* 2004
Anderson, J., *Kyrgyzstan: Central Asia's Island of Democracy?* 1999
Marat, Erica, *The Tulip Revolution: Kyrgyzstan One Year After.* 2006
National Statistical Office: National Statistical Committee of the Kyrgyz Republic, 374 Frunze Street, Bishkek City 720033.
Website (Russian only): http://www.stat.kg

LAOS

Sathalanalath Pasathipatai Pasasonlao
(Lao People's Democratic Republic)

Capital: Vientiane
Population estimate, 2010: 6·44m.
GDP per capita, 2007: (PPP$) 2,165
HDI/world rank: 0·619/133

KEY HISTORICAL EVENTS

The Kingdom of Laos, once called Lanxang (the Land of a Million Elephants), was founded in the 14th century. In 1893 Laos became a French protectorate and in 1907 acquired its present frontiers. In 1945, after French authority had been suppressed by the Japanese, an independence movement known as Lao Issara (Free Laos) set up a government which collapsed with the return of the French in 1946. Under a new constitution of 1947 Laos became a constitutional monarchy under the Luang Prabang dynasty and in 1949 became an independent sovereign state within the French Union. An almost continuous state of war began in 1953 between the Royal Lao Government, supported by American bombing and Thai mercenaries, and the Patriotic Front Pathet Lao, supported by North Vietnamese troops. Peace talks resulted in an agreement on 21 Feb. 1973 providing for the formation of a provisional government of national union and the withdrawal of foreign troops. A provisional coalition government was duly formed in 1974. However, after the Communist victories in neighbouring Vietnam and Cambodia in April 1975, the Pathet Lao took over the running of the whole country, maintaining only a façade of a coalition. On 29 Nov. 1975 HM King Savang Vatthana abdicated and the People's Congress proclaimed a People's Democratic Republic of Laos on 2 Dec. 1975. Since then the country has been run by a regime with zero tolerance for dissent and a fierce distrust of foreigners.

TERRITORY AND POPULATION

Laos is a landlocked country of 236,800 sq. km (91,428 sq. miles) bordered on the north by China, the east by Vietnam, the south by Cambodia and the west by Thailand and Myanmar. Apart from the Mekong River plains along the border of Thailand, the country is mountainous, particularly in the north, and in places densely forested.

The population (2005 census) was 5,621,982 (2,821,431 females); density, 24 per sq. km. In 2005, 79·4% of the population lived in rural areas.

The UN gives an estimated population for 2010 of 6·44m.

There are 16 provinces and one prefecture divided into 141 districts and one special region (*khetphiset*). Area, population and administrative centres in 2005:

Province	*Sq. km*	*Population (in 1,000)*	*Administrative centre*
Attopeu	10,320	112·1	Samakhi Xai
Bokeo	6,196	145·3	Ban Houei Xai
Bolikhamxai	14,863	225·3	Paksan
Champassak	15,415	607·4	Pakse
Houa Phan	16,500	280·9	Xam Neua
Khammouane	16,315	337·4	Thakhek
Luang Namtha	9,325	145·3	Luang Namtha
Luang Prabang	16,875	407·0	Luang Prabang
Oudomxai	15,370	265·2	Muang Xai
Phongsali	16,270	165·9	Phongsali
Salavan	10,691	324·3	Salavan
Savannakhet	21,774	825·9	Shanthabouli
Sayabouri	16,389	338·7	Sayabouri
Sekong	7,665	85·0	Sekong
Vientiane	18,526	388·9	Phonghong
Vientiane[1]	3,920	698·3	Vientiane
Xaisomboun	4,506	39·4	Ban Muang Cha
Xieng Khouang	15,880	229·6	Phonsavanh

[1]Prefecture.

The capital and largest town is Vientiane, with a population of (2005 estimate) 570,000. Other important towns are Savannakhet, Pakse, Xam Neua and Luang Prabang.

The population is divided into three groups: about 67% Lao-Lum (Valley-Lao); 17% Lao-Theung (Lao of the mountain sides); and 7·4% Lao-Sung (Lao of the mountain tops), who comprise the Hmong and Yao (or Mien). Lao is the official language. French and English are spoken.

SOCIAL STATISTICS

2004 estimates: births, 203,000; deaths, 70,000. Rates, 2004 estimates (per 1,000 population): birth, 35; death, 12; infant mortality, 62 per 1,000 live births (2005). Life expectancy, 2007: 63·2 years for men and 65·9 for women. Annual population growth rate, 2000–05, 1·7%. Fertility rate, 2004, 4·7 births per woman.

CLIMATE

A tropical monsoon climate, with high temperatures throughout the year and very heavy rains from May to Oct. Vientiane, Jan. 70°F (21·1°C), July 81°F (27·2°C). Annual rainfall 69" (1,715 mm).

CONSTITUTION AND GOVERNMENT

In Aug. 1991 the National Assembly adopted a new constitution. The head of state is the President, elected by the National

Assembly, which consists of 115 members (109 prior to the elections of April 2006).

Under the constitution the People's Revolutionary Party of Laos (PPPL) remains the 'central nucleus' of the 'people's democracy'; other parties are not permitted. The PPPL's Politburo comprises 11 members, including Choummaly Sayasone (PPPL, *President*).

National Anthem

'Xatlao tangtae dayma lao thookthuana xeutxoo sootchay' ('For the whole of time the Lao people have glorified their Fatherland'); words by Sisana Sisane, tune by Thongdy Sounthonevichit.

RECENT ELECTIONS

The Sixth Legislature of the National Assembly elected Choummaly Sayasone as president on 8 June 2006. Bouasone Bouphavanh was elected prime minister on the same day.

There were parliamentary elections on 30 April 2006 in which the People's Revolutionary Party of Laos (PPPL) won 113 of 115 seats. Only two (approved) non-partisan candidate won seats.

CURRENT ADMINISTRATION

President: Lieut.-Gen. Choummaly Sayasone; b. 1936 (PPPL; elected on 8 June 2006).

Vice President: Boungnang Volachit.

In March 2010 the government consisted of:

Prime Minister: Bouasone Bouphavanh; b. 1954 (PPPL; elected on 8 June 2006).

Deputy Prime Ministers: Maj. Gen. Asang Laoli (also *Chairman of State Control Commission*); Thongloun Sisoulit (also *Minister of Foreign Affairs*); Lieut.-Gen. Douangchai Phichit (also *Minister of Defence*); Somsavat Lengsavad.

Minister of Agriculture and Forestry: Sitaheng Latsaphone. *Communications, Transport, Posts and Construction:* Sommad Pholsena. *Education:* Somkot Mangnormek. *Energy and Mining:* Soulivong Dalavong. *Finance:* Somdy Duangdy. *Industry and Commerce:* Nam Vignaket. *Information and Culture:* Mounkeo Ouraboun. *Justice:* Chaleuan Yapaoher. *Labour and Social Welfare:* Onechanh Thammavong. *Public Health:* Ponemek Daraloy. *Public Security:* Thongbanh Sengaphone. *Ministers in the Prime Minister's Office:* Bounpheng Mounphosay; Onneua Phommachanh; Kham-Ouane Boupha; Saysengly Tengbliacheua; Bouasy Lovansay; Douangsavath Souphanouvong; Phouthong Seng Akhom; Khampheng Pholsena.

National Assembly Website: http://www.na.gov.la

CURRENT LEADERS

Choummaly Sayasone

Position

President

Introduction

Choummaly Sayasone was appointed president in June 2006, succeeding his long-time mentor, Khamtay Siphandone. Part of the Lao ruling elite for decades, Sayasone had previously served as vice president and minister of national defence.

Early Life

Born on 6 March 1936 into a farming family in Vat Neua village, Attopeu province, Sayasone took up arms with the revolutionary Pathet Lao guerrilla forces in 1954. While fighting in Houaphan province in 1955, he joined the People's Revolutionary Party. A successful soldier, Sayasone became deputy head of a regiment of Pathet Lao forces in 1959. He also held a variety of posts within the party hierarchy and was appointed head of the military department in 1972.

When the Pathet Lao took over government in 1975, he worked as a close ally of Khamtay Siphandone, minister of national defence and deputy prime minister. Sayasone became Siphandone's deputy at the defence ministry in 1982 and was promoted to minister of national defence in 1991. Sayasone became vice president in 2001 and on 21 March 2006 he was elected secretary general of the People's Revolutionary Party of Laos. On Siphandone's retirement as president the national assembly chose Sayasone as his successor in June 2006.

Career in Office

Sayasone has continued his predecessor's policies, including the banning of rival political parties and tight control of the media. Some economic liberalization has been under way since Laos joined ASEAN in 1997.

DEFENCE

Military service is compulsory for a minimum of 18 months. Defence expenditure in 2006 totalled US$13m. (US$2 per capita), representing 0·4% of GDP.

Army

There are four military regions. Strength (2007) about 25,000. In addition there are local defence forces totalling over 100,000.

Navy

There is an Army Marine Section of about 600 personnel (2007).

Air Force

The Air Force has 22 combat capable aircraft, including MiG-21 fighters, although serviceability is in doubt. Personnel strength, 3,500 in 2007.

INTERNATIONAL RELATIONS

Laos is a member of the UN, World Bank, IMF and several other UN specialized agencies, International Organization of the Francophonie, Asian Development Bank, ASEAN, Mekong Group and Colombo Plan.

ECONOMY

In 2006 agriculture accounted for 42·0% of GDP, industry 32·5% and services 25·5%.

Overview

The economy has achieved impressive growth in recent years, owing in large part to the enhanced role of export-oriented mining and hydropower projects. GDP has grown at an average of 6·5% per year since 2001. There are high levels of FDI for the production of gold, copper and export-oriented hydropower. Meanwhile, large mineral and hydro resources remain untapped.

Inflation has fallen to record lows reflecting favourable oil and food prices, although pressures from the resources sector may affect exchange rate appreciation. Tourism is the fastest growing industry which, together with strong resource exports, has offset imports of petroleum products and construction materials.

The number of poor households fell from 45% in 1992–93 to 31% in 2005. The National Socio-Economic Development Plan (NSEDP), which has received World Bank backing, aims to sustain economic growth and to reduce poverty while promoting modernization and safeguarding environmental resources. The sixth five-year plan (2006–10) aims to remove Laos from the UN list of least developed countries by 2020.

Currency

The unit of currency is the *kip* (LAK). Inflation was 128·4% in 1999 but has since fallen steeply, and in 2008 stood at 7·6%. Foreign exchange reserves were US$199m. in March 2005 and gold reserves were 117,000 troy oz. Total money supply was 1,364·1bn. kip in Feb. 2005.

Budget

The fiscal year begins on 1 Oct. Revenues in 2005–06 were 4,962bn. kip (tax revenue, 73·4%) and expenditures 6,205bn. kip (current expenditure, 50·3%).

VAT is 10%.

Performance
Real GDP growth was 7·5% in 2007 and 7·2% in 2008. Total GDP in 2008 was US$5·2bn.

Banking and Finance
The central bank and bank of issue is the State Bank (*Governor*, Phouphet Khamphounvong). There were 17 commercial banks in 2002 (seven foreign; branches only permitted). Total savings and time deposits in 1991 amounted to 4,075m. kip.

ENERGY AND NATURAL RESOURCES

Environment
In 2008 carbon dioxide emissions from the consumption and flaring of fossil fuels were the equivalent of 0·2 tonnes per capita.

Electricity
Total installed capacity in 2004 was an estimated 284,000 kW, of which around 266,000 kW was hydro-electric. In 2004 production was about 1,295m. kWh, almost exclusively hydro-electric. Consumption per capita was an estimated 126 kWh; approximately 750m. kWh were exported.

Minerals
2002 output (in tonnes): gypsum, 160,000; salt, 22,100; tin, 510; coal (2004 estimate), 290.

Agriculture
In 2002, 76·1% of the economically active population were engaged in agriculture. There were an estimated 920,000 ha. of arable land in 2002 and 81,000 ha. of permanent crop land. The chief products (2002 estimates in 1,000 tonnes) are: rice, 2,416; sugarcane, 222; sweet potatoes, 194; maize, 124; melons and watermelons, 116; cassava, 83; bananas, 53; pineapples, 36; potatoes, 35; coffee, 32; oranges, 29; tobacco, 27.

Livestock (2003 estimates): pigs, 1·65m.; cattle, 1·20m.; buffaloes, 1·08m.; chickens, 20m.

Livestock products (2003 estimates, in 1,000 tonnes): pork, bacon and ham, 36; beef and veal, 22; poultry, 18; milk, 6; eggs, 13.

Forestry
Forests covered 12·44m. ha. in 2002, or 47% of the land area, down from 13·18m. ha. in 1990. They produce valuable woods such as teak. Timber production, 2007, 6·14m. cu. metres.

Fisheries
The catch in 2005 was approximately 29,800 tonnes, entirely from inland waters.

INDUSTRY
Production in 2002: cement, 201,000 tonnes; iron bars, 13,000 tonnes; detergent, 650 tonnes; nails, 650 tonnes; corrugated iron, 2·8m. sheets; plywood, 2·1m. sheets; mineral water, 235m. litres; beer, 60·49m. litres; soft drinks, 13·15m. litres; oxygen, 21,500 cylinders; cigarettes, 38·3m. packets; lumber, 155,000 cu. metres.

Labour
The working age is 16–55 for females and 16–60 for males. In 2003 the labour force totalled 2,672,900. 82·2% of the employed population were engaged in agriculture in 2003.

INTERNATIONAL TRADE
Since 1988 foreign companies have been permitted to participate in Lao enterprises. Total foreign debt was US$2,690m. in 2005.

Imports and Exports
Imports were estimated at US$534·60m. in 2002 (US$528·27m. in 2001) and exports at US$319·60m. (US$324·89m. in 2001). The main imports in 2000 were: consumption goods, 50·6%; mineral fuels, 13·9%; materials for garment assembly, 10·6%. Main exports: electricity, 32·0%; garments, 26·1%; wood products, 24·8%. Main import suppliers, 2001: Thailand, 52·0%; Vietnam, 26·5%; China, 5·7%; Singapore, 3·3%. Main export markets, 2001: Vietnam, 41·5%; Thailand, 14·8%; France, 6·1%; Germany, 4·6%.

COMMUNICATIONS

Roads
In 2006 there were 29,811 km of roads, of which 13·5% were paved. In 2007 there were 12,800 passenger cars (two per 1,000 inhabitants), 109,000 lorries and vans, 6,400 buses and coaches, and 506,500 motorcycles and mopeds. There were 5,198 traffic accidents with 608 fatalities in 2006. A bridge over the River Mekong, providing an important north-south link, was opened in 1994.

Rail
The Thai railway system extends to Nongkhai, on the Thai bank of the Mekong River.

Civil Aviation
There are three international airports at Vientiane (Wattay), Pakse and Luang Prabang. The national carrier is Lao Airlines, which in 2005 operated domestic services and international flights to Bangkok, Chiang Mai, Hanoi, Ho Chi Minh City, Kunming, Phnom Penh and Siem Reap (Cambodia). In 2003 scheduled airline traffic of Laos-based carriers flew 3m. km, carrying 219,000 passengers (58,000 on international flights).

Shipping
The River Mekong and its tributaries are an important means of transport. 898,000 tonnes of freight were carried on inland waterways in 1995. Merchant shipping totalled 2,000 GRT in 2002.

Telecommunications
In 2005 there were 713,500 telephone subscribers (120·4 per 1,000 persons), with 638,200 mobile phone subscribers. Laos had 25,000 internet users in 2005 and 100,000 PCs in use (16·9 for every 1,000 persons).

Postal Services
There were 342 post offices in 2003.

SOCIAL INSTITUTIONS

Justice
Criminal legislation of 1990 established a system of courts and a prosecutor's office. Polygamy became an offence.

Education
In 2007 there were 891,807 pupils in primary schools with 29,604 teaching staff, and 403,833 pupils and 17,110 teaching staff at secondary level.

There are eight teacher training institutes (four teacher training colleges and four teacher training schools) and one college of Pali. In June 1995 the National University of Laos (NUOL) was established by merging nine existing higher education institutes and a centre of agriculture. NUOL comprises faculties in agriculture, pedagogy, political science, economics and management, forestry, engineering and architecture, medical science, humanities and social science, science, and literature. In 2007 there were 75,003 students in higher education and 3,030 academic staff.

Adult literacy in 2003 was 68·7% (male, 77·0%; female, 60·9%). Laos has only a small educated elite.

In 2007 public expenditure on education came to 3·6% of GNI and 15·8% of total government spending.

Health
In 2003 there were 24 hospitals (with 2,711 beds), 125 district-level hospitals and 662 primary health care centres. In 2003 there were 1,283 physicians, 83 dentists and 5,291 nurses. Only 37% of the population had access to safe drinking water in 2000.

RELIGION

In 2001 some 2·75m. were Buddhists (Hinayana), but about 40% of the population follow tribal religions.

CULTURE

World Heritage Sites

Laos has two sites on the UNESCO World Heritage List: the Town of Luang Prabang (inscribed on the list in 1995), a unique blend of Lao and European colonial architecture; and Vat Phou and Associated Ancient Settlements within the Champasak Cultural Landscape (2001), including a Khmer era Hindu temple complex.

Broadcasting

Lao National Radio and Lao National TV (TVNL) are government-owned. AM broadcasting has been relayed around the country by satellite since Aug. 1999 and FM broadcasting (two channels) since April 2000. There were 279,900 television equipped households in 2005 (colour by PAL).

Press

In 2005 there were five national dailies (two in English) with a combined circulation of 21,000.

Tourism

There were 895,000 foreign visitors in 2004 (including 730,000 from elsewhere in Asia and Oceania, 116,000 from Europe and 47,000 from the Americas); revenue from tourism amounted to US$119m.

DIPLOMATIC REPRESENTATIVES

Of Laos in the United Kingdom
Ambassador: Soutsakhone Pathammavong (resides in Paris).

Of the United Kingdom in Laos
Ambassador: Quinton Quayle (resides in Bangkok).

Of Laos in the USA (2222 S. St., NW, Washington, D.C., 20008)
Ambassador: Phiane Philakone.

Of the USA in Laos (Rue Bartholonie, Vientiane)
Ambassador: Ravic Huso.

Of Laos to the United Nations
Ambassador: Kanika Phommachanh.

Of Laos to the European Union
Ambassador: Southam Sakonhninhom.

FURTHER READING

National Statistical Centre. *Basic Statistics about the Socio-Economic Development in the Lao P.D.R.* Annual.

Evans, Grant, *A Short History of Laos: The Land in Between.* 2002

Stuart-Fox, M., *Laos: Politics, Economics and Society.* 1986—*History of Laos.* 1997

National Statistical Office: National Statistical Centre, Committee for Planning and Investment, Luang Prabang Road, Vientiane.

LATVIA

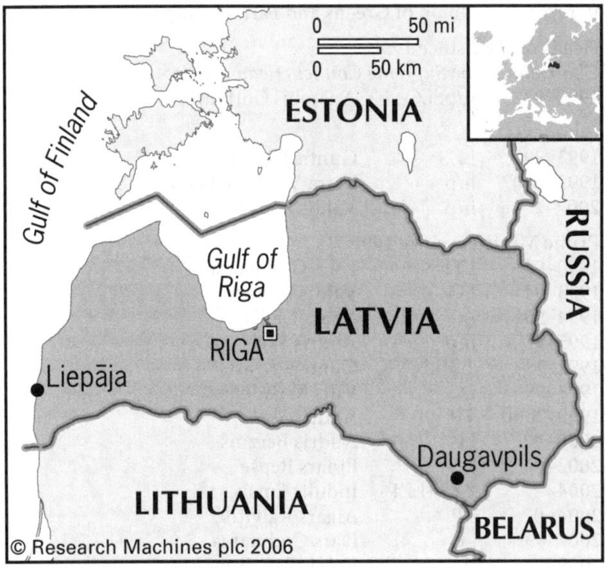

Latvijas Republika
(Republic of Latvia)

Capital: Riga
Population estimate, 2010: 2·24m.
GDP per capita, 2007: (PPP$) 16,377
HDI/world rank: 0·866/48

KEY HISTORICAL EVENTS

The name Latvia derives from *latvis*, a 'forest clearer'. Human inhabitation dates from around 9000 BC and the Balts (or proto-Balts) probably arrived around 2000 BC. In addition to the Finnic predecessors of the Estonians and Livs, four Baltic tribal groups emerged during the Iron Age: the Couronians (Kurši), Selonians (Sēļi), Semigallians (Zemgaļi) and Latgallians (Latgaļi). Linguistic evidence points to the habitation of central Latvia by Latgallians and Lithuanians while coastal areas were populated by Couronians, Semigallians, Selonians and Prussians. The north of the country, occupied mainly by Finnic Livs, was separated by sparsely inhabited areas, which accounts for the lack of cultural mixing between the ethnic groupings.

Scandinavian settlements were established after 650 AD, disappearing abruptly around 850. In the 10th century the Baltic tribes came under attack from Varangians (Swedish Vikings), attracted in part by amber which was traded up the Daugava River to Russia and south to Byzantium. Slavic incursions from the east were hampered by primeval forest and marshes.

The region was transformed by German colonization in the 13th century. The Archbishop of Bremen ordered the Christian conquest of the Eastern Baltic sending his nephew Albert, who founded Riga in 1201 and became its bishop. He also created the Sword Brothers (or Livonian Order), a small military order that carved out a feudal state ruled mainly by German aristocracy. It subdued Livonia (southern Estonia and northeastern Latvia), Courland and Zemgale, forming the Livonian Confederation. In 1237 the weakened Sword Brothers were incorporated as an autonomous order into the Order of the Teutonic Knights, which completed the conquest of modern-day Latvia. Riga joined the Hanseatic League in 1282.

The Teutonic Knights were defeated in 1410 at the Battle of Grünwald (Tannenberg) by a Polish-Lithuanian army. Russian Tsar Ivan IV invaded in 1558 in an attempt to gain access to the Baltic Sea. The Livonian War ended with the disbandment of the Livonian Order and the partition of Livonia in 1561. The north went to Lithuania, while Courland became a Lithuanian fief. During the early 17th century Latvia was a theatre of war between Sweden and the Commonwealth of Lithuania-Poland. In 1605 the small hussar army of Jan Karol Chodkiewicz destroyed a much larger Swedish force at the Battle of Kircholm (Salaspils), near Riga. However, Sweden had taken control of Livonia by 1621 and its empire in the Baltic did not end until the signing of the Treaty of Nystad in 1721. The Livonian territory of Vidzeme passed to Russia which acquired Latgale (Latgallia) in 1772 from Poland, and Courland in 1795.

The German landowners remained within the Russian Empire, bolstered by unification with other Germans in the Baltic. The abolition of serfdom in 1817 created new tensions between the Latvian and German communities, though there were German elements who supported land reform which duly arrived in 1847. Nascent Latvian nationalism in the 1860s prompted the Russian authorities to centralize power away from the German aristocracy. Tensions between the communities erupted during the 1905 Russian Revolution when attacks on hundreds of German settlements precipitated a wave of German emigration.

After the German occupation of 1915 demands for the creation of a Latvian state grew until the 1917 Russian Revolution. Soviet rule was proclaimed in Dec. 1917 but was overthrown when the Germans reinvaded in Feb. 1918, with Russia ceding its claims on Latvia by the Treaty of Brest-Litovsk. After the armistice, Latvia declared independence but the Soviets reasserted power following the German withdrawal in Dec. 1918. The Soviets were again overthrown between May–Dec. 1919 by combined British naval and German military forces and a democratic government was established.

In the wake of economic depression, the democratic regime fell in a May 1934 coup when Prime Minister Kārlis Ulmanis dissolved parliament and, in 1936, merged his office with that of the president. When the secret protocol of the Soviet–German agreement of 23 Aug. 1939 assigned Latvia to the Soviet sphere of interest, most of the ancient Baltic German community emigrated. Formal annexation came in 1940 and over 15,000 Latvians were deported to Siberia. The German occupation of 1941–45 caused the deaths of over 90,000 Latvians, mostly Jews. Violent resistance to Soviet reoccupation led to the deportation of another 43,000 Latvians to Siberia and substantial Soviet immigration followed.

The Latvian Supreme Soviet declared sovereignty in July 1989 and on 4 May 1990, having declared the 1940 Soviet occupation illegal, re-established the 1922 constitution. This was annulled by Soviet President Mikhail Gorbachev, sparking violent protest and police crackdowns. Following a referendum, independence was declared on 21 Aug. 1991 and recognized in Sept. by the USSR. With independence, issues of ethnic identity came to the fore, with the large Russian minority initially disadvantaged by new citizenship and language laws (later repealed). President Vaira Vīķe-Freiberga was elected as the former Communist bloc's first female president in 1999. Latvia became a member of NATO and the European Union in 2004.

TERRITORY AND POPULATION

Latvia is situated in northeastern Europe. It is bordered by Estonia on the north and by Lithuania on the southwest, while on the east there is a frontier with the Russian Federation and to the southeast with Belarus. Territory, 64,589 sq. km (larger than Denmark, the Netherlands, Belgium and Switzerland). Population (2000 census), 2,377,383; density, 37 per sq. km. The estimated population on 1 Jan. 2009 was 2,261,294.

The UN gives an estimated population for 2010 of 2·24m.

In 2006, 68·0% of the population were urban. Major ethnic groups in 2006: Latvians 59·0%, Russians 28·5%, Belarusians 3·8%, Ukrainians 2·5%, Poles 2·4%, Lithuanians 1·4%, Jews 0·4%, Roma 0·4%, Germans 0·2%, Estonians 0·1%.

There are 26 districts *(apriņķis)* and seven municipalities *(lielpilsētas)* with separate status. The capital is Riga (727,578, or nearly a third of the country's total population, at Jan. 2006); other principal towns, with Jan. 2006 populations, are Daugavpils (109,482), Liepāja (85,915), Jelgava (66,087), Jurmala (55,602) and Ventspils (43,806).

The official language is Latvian. Latgalian is also spoken.

SOCIAL STATISTICS

2005: births, 21,497 (rate of 9·3 per 1,000 population); deaths, 32,777 (14·2 per 1,000 population); marriages, 12,544 (5·5 per 1,000 population); divorces, 6,341 (2·8 per 1,000 population); infant mortality, eight per 1,000 live births (2005). In 2007 life expectancy was 67·1 years for males but 77·1 years for females. In 2005 the most popular age range for marrying was 25–29 for males and 20–24 for females. The annual population growth rate in the period 2000–05 was –0·6%. Fertility rate, 2004, 1·3 births per woman. The suicide rate was 24·3 per 100,000 population in 2004 (rate among males, 42·9). In 2005 there were 1,886 immigrants and 2,450 emigrants.

CLIMATE

Owing to the influence of maritime factors, the climate is relatively temperate but changeable. Average temperatures in Jan. range from –2·8°C in the western coastal town of Liepāja to –6·6°C in the inland town of Daugavpils. The average summer temperature is 20°C.

CONSTITUTION AND GOVERNMENT

The Declaration of the Renewal of the Independence of the Republic of Latvia dated 4 May 1990, and the 21 Aug. 1991 declaration re-establishing *de facto* independence, proclaimed the authority of the Constitution *(Satversme)*. The Constitution was fully re-instituted as of 6 July 1993, when the fifth Parliament *(Saeima)* was elected.

The head of state in Latvia is the *President*, elected by parliament for a period of four years.

The highest legislative body is the one-chamber parliament comprised of 100 deputies and elected in direct, proportional elections by citizens 18 years of age and over. Deputies serve for four years and parties must receive at least 5% of the national vote to gain seats in parliament.

In a referendum on 3 Oct. 1998, 53% of votes cast were in favour of liberalizing laws on citizenship, which would simplify the naturalization of the Russian-speakers who make up nearly a third of the total population and who were not granted automatic citizenship when Latvia regained its independence from the former Soviet Union in 1991. Around half of the 650,000 ethnic Russians in Latvia have not taken out Latvian citizenship. Ethnic Russians who are not Latvian citizens do not have the right to vote. A seven-member *Constitutional Court* was established in 1996 with powers to invalidate legislation not in conformity with the constitution. Its members are appointed by parliament for ten-year terms.

Executive power is held by the *Cabinet of Ministers*.

National Anthem

'Dievs, svēti Latviju' ('God bless Latvia'); words and tune by Kārlis Baumanis.

GOVERNMENT CHRONOLOGY

(JL = New Era; LC = Latvian Way; LTF = Latvian Popular Front; LZP = Latvian Green Party; LZS = Latvian Farmers' Alliance; TB/LNNK = Fatherland and Freedom Union; TP = People's Party; ZZS = Union of Greens and Farmers; n/p = non-partisan)

Heads of State since 1990.

Chairman of the Supreme Council/Head of State

1990–93	n/p, LC	Anatolijs Gorbunovs

Presidents

1993–99	LZS	Guntis Ulmanis
1999–2007	n/p	Vaira Vīķe-Freiberga
2007–	n/p	Valdis Zatlers

Prime Ministers since 1990.

1990–93	LTF	Ivars Godmanis
1993–94	LC	Valdis Birkavs
1994–95	LC	Māris Gailis
1995–97	n/p	Andris Šķēle
1997–98	TB/LNNK	Guntars Krasts
1998–99	LC	Vilis Krištopāns
1999–2000	TP	Andris Šķēle
2000–02	LC	Andris Bērziņš
2002–04	JL	Einars Repše
2004	ZZS (LZP)	Indulis Emsis
2004–07	TP	Aigars Kalvītis
2007–09	LC	Ivars Godmanis
2009–	JL	Valdis Dombrovskis

RECENT ELECTIONS

Valdis Zatlers was elected president by parliament on 31 May 2007, defeating Aivars Endziņš by 58 votes to 39.

Parliamentary elections were held on 7 Oct. 2006. The People's Party (Tautas partija; TP) won 23 seats with 19·6% of votes cast; Union of Greens and Farmers (Zaļo un Zemnieku savienība; ZZS), 18 with 16·7%; New Era (Jaunais laiks; JL) 18 with 16·4%; Harmony Centre (Saskanas Centrs; SC), 17 with 14·4%; Latvia's First Party/Latvian Way Party (Latvijas Pirmā Partija/Savienība 'Latvijas ceļš'; LPP/LC), 10 with 8·6%; Fatherland and Freedom Alliance/LNNK (Apvienība 'Tēvzemei un Brīvībai'; TB/LNNK), 8 with 6·9%; For Human Rights in a United Latvia (Par cilvēka tiesībām vienotā Latvijā; PCTVL) 6 with 6·0%. Turnout was 62·2%.

European Parliament

Latvia has 8 (9 in 2004) representatives. At the June 2009 elections turnout was 53·7% (41·3% in 2004). The Civic Union (Pilsoniskā savienība) won 2 seats with 24·3% of votes cast (political affiliation in European Parliament: European People's Party); SC, 2 with 19·6% (one with Progressive Alliance of Socialists and Democrats and one with European United Left/Nordic Green Left); PCTVL, 1 with 9·7% (Greens/European Free Alliance); LPP/LC, 1 with 7·5% (Alliance of Liberals and Democrats for Europe); TB/LNNK, 1 with 7·5% (European Conservatives and Reformists); JL, 1 with 6·7% (European People's Party).

CURRENT ADMINISTRATION

President: Valdis Zatlers; b. 1955 (sworn in 8 July 2007).

Prime Minister and Minister for Children and Family Affairs and Integration Affairs: Valdis Dombrovskis; b. 1971 (JL; took office on 12 March 2009). In April 2010 the People's Party (TP) quit the cabinet; subsequently the coalition government comprised:

Minister for Defence: Imants Viesturs Lieģis (Pilsoniskā savienība/Civic Union). *Finance:* Einars Repše (JL). *Foreign Affairs:* Aivis Ronis (ind). *Economics:* Artis Kampars (JL). *Interior, and Health (acting):* Linda Mūrniece (JL). *Education and Science:* Tatjana Koķe (ZZS). *Culture:* Ints Dālderis (ind.). *Environment, and Regional Development and Local Government (acting):* Raimonds Vējonis (ZZS). *Agriculture:* Jānis Dūklavs (ind.). *Transport:* Kaspars Gerhards (TB/LNNK). *Welfare, and Justice (acting):* Uldis Augulis (ZZS).

Office of the President: http://www.president.lv

CURRENT LEADERS

Valdis Zatlers

Position
President

Introduction
Valdis Zatlers was elected president by Latvia's parliament, the Saeima, in May 2007. He began his four-year term in July, taking over from Vaira Vīķe-Freiberga. The president's role is principally ceremonial with limited legislative powers.

Early Life
Zatlers was born on 22 March 1955 in Riga. He attended secondary school before going on to the Riga Institute of Medicine in 1973 to train as a surgeon. He graduated in 1979 in orthopaedic and trauma surgery and began working at Riga Hospital No. 2. From 1985–94 he was head of the hospital's traumatology unit. His initial foray into politics saw him join the Popular Front of Latvia in 1988, shortly before the first significant protests against Soviet rule. In 1990–91 Zatlers completed six months of medical training at the universities of Yale and Syracuse in the USA, returning to Latvia as it won its independence.

From 1994–98 he was director of the State Orthopaedic and Traumatology Hospital, during which time he worked with patients suffering the effects of the 1996 Chernobyl disaster. He left the hospital in 2007, having been accused of malpractice over the purchasing of medical supplies and of accepting undeclared payments from patients, but was cleared of wrongdoing in both cases. Though a signatory of the People's Party's 1998 founding manifesto, Zatlers was not affiliated to any party before his election to the presidency on 31 May 2007, when he defeated Aivars Endziņš.

Career in Office
Zatlers' election by the ruling coalition was viewed as a compromise deal by the major parties. He has since sought to strengthen Latvia's bilateral economic relations through state visits and by raising the country's profile in the United Nations.

After anti-government demonstrations in Oct. and Nov. 2007 forced the resignation of Prime Minister Aigars Kalvītis, Zatlers appointed the interior minister, Ivars Godmanis, as premier. In Dec. 2007 the Schengen Treaty abolishing border controls between certain EU member states came into force in Latvia. With the country under increasing economic pressure, Godmanis' administration collapsed in Feb. 2009. Valdis Dombrovskis formed a new government the following month.

Valdis Dombrovskis

Position
Prime Minister

Introduction
Valdis Dombrovskis became prime minister in March 2009 following the resignation of Ivars Godmanis. The former finance minister's tenure is likely to be dominated by austerity measures to solve the country's economic crisis.

Early Life
Dombrovskis was born on 5 Aug. 1971 in Riga, while Latvia was part of the USSR. He studied physics and economics at the University of Latvia in Riga and the Riga Technological University. He was employed as a laboratory assistant at Germany's University of Mainz and at the University of Latvia's Institute of Solid-State Physics. In 1998 he was a research assistant at Maryland University in the USA.

Later that year he began working for the Bank of Latvia, leaving in 2002 after a year as chief economist. A member of the centre-right New Era party, he joined its governing board in 2002 and was also elected to parliament, serving until 2004 as finance minister in Einars Repše's government. From 2003–04 he was Latvia's observer at the Council of the European Union and became a member of the European Parliament (MEP) in 2004, sitting with the European People's Party–European Democrats.

Against the backdrop of global economic turmoil, Latvia's economy crashed in 2008. The economy shrank by almost 5% and international credit rating agency Standard & Poor's predicted a further 12% shrinkage in 2009. In Dec. 2008, having nationalized the country's second biggest bank, Prime Minister Ivars Godmanis turned to the IMF, World Bank and European Union for a US$9·5bn. bail-out package. In return he was forced to accept public spending cuts and tax increases. After an anti-government riot in Riga in Jan. 2009, his coalition fell the following month. President Valdis Zatlers nominated Dombrovskis to form a new administration.

Career in Office
Having resigned as an MEP, Dombrovskis formed a six-party coalition and won parliamentary approval for his premiership on 12 March 2009. His principal task has been to reverse the economic collapse. In Aug. 2009 his government reached agreement with unions and employers on deep spending cuts and tax rises aimed at staving off bankruptcy and persuading the IMF and EU to release further tranches of loans. Subsequently, as a condition for these disbursements, the government committed to further cuts in fiscal expenditures to contain the budget deficit.

DEFENCE

The National Armed Forces (NAF) were created in 1994 and comprise the Land Forces, which are based on an infantry brigade and the National Guard, the Naval Forces, the Air Forces, the Logistic Command, the Training Doctrine Command and the National Defence Academy. Compulsory military service was abolished in Jan. 2007.

In 2006 military expenditure totalled US$279m. (US$122 per capita), representing 1·4% of GDP.

Army

The Land Forces were 1,526 strong in 2007. There is a National Guard reserve numbering 10,483 in 2007.

Navy

The Naval Forces, based at Riga and Liepāja, numbered 603 in 2007. Latvia, Estonia and Lithuania have established a joint naval unit 'BALTRON' (Baltic Naval Squadron), with bases at Liepāja, Riga and Ventspils in Latvia, Tallinn in Estonia and Klaipėda in Lithuania.

Air Force

Personnel numbered 480 in 2007. There are no combat capable aircraft.

INTERNATIONAL RELATIONS

Latvia is a member of the UN, World Bank, IMF and several other UN specialized agencies, WTO, EU, Council of Europe, OSCE, Council of the Baltic Sea States, BIS, IOM, NATO and is an associate partner of the WEU. Latvia held a referendum on EU membership on 20 Sept. 2003, in which 67·4% of votes cast were in favour of accession, with 32·6% against. It became a member of NATO on 29 March 2004 and the EU on 1 May 2004.

In Dec. 2007 Latvia acceded to the Schengen accord, which abolishes border controls between Latvia, Austria, Belgium, Czech Republic, Denmark, Estonia, Finland, France, Germany, Greece, Hungary, Iceland, Italy, Lithuania, Luxembourg, Malta, Netherlands, Norway, Poland, Portugal, Slovakia, Slovenia, Spain, Sweden and Switzerland.

ECONOMY

Agriculture accounted for 3·7% of GDP in 2006, industry 21·5% and services 74·8%.

The Latvian Privatization Agency, established in 1994 to oversee the privatization process, has adopted a case-by-case approach. 97% of all state enterprises have been assigned for privatization. In 2003 the private sector constituted 70% of GDP and 76% of employment.

Overview

With Latvia's transition from communism in the early 1990s, the economy suffered from raw material and energy shortages, the loss of Soviet export markets and weak international competitiveness. After independence, market reforms were introduced including privatization, price liberalization, land reforms and the establishment of a local currency and an independent central bank.

After joining the EU in May 2004, growth accelerated to double-digit figures driven by private sector capital inflows and EU funds. However, by mid-2006 the economy showed signs of overheating as credit and domestic demand grew excessively, inflation accelerated and the current account deficit peaked at over 20% of GDP. In 2008 the global financial crisis led to a slowdown in lending driven by the withdrawal of funds from foreign banks. In Dec. 2008 Latvia accepted a US$9·5bn. IMF-led bail-out, causing widespread social turmoil and the resignation of the ruling coalition in Feb. 2009.

In July 2009 the new coalition government agreed a series of spending cuts, including reductions of up to 40% in public sector pay and 10% in pensions in order to meet IMF targets to reduce the budget deficit. The economy is estimated to have contracted by around 18% in 2009 and unemployment was the highest in the EU at nearly 21%. However, the current account moved into surplus and growth is expected to return in 2010.

Currency

The unit of currency is the *lats* (LVL) of 100 *santims*. The lats is pegged to the euro at a rate of one euro to 0·7028 lats. Inflation, which reached a high of 109·1% in 1993, was 10·1% in 2007 and 15·3% in 2008. Gold reserves were 249,000 troy oz in July 2005, foreign exchange reserves US$2,076m. and total money supply 1,736m. lats.

Budget

The financial year is the calendar year.

Government revenue and expenditure (in 1m. lats), year ending 31 Dec.:

	2000	*2001*	*2002*	*2003*
Revenue	1,264·5	1,340·5	1,529·2	1,715·5
Expenditure	1,335·8	1,373·2	1,597·1	1,735·7

The standard rate of VAT is 21·0% (reduced rate, 10·0%).

Performance

In 2007 real GDP growth was 10·0% (the second highest rate in the European Union). However, in 2008 the economy contracted by 4·6% (the second lowest rate in the world). Latvia has the lowest GDP per capita of any of the ten countries that joined the EU in May 2004. Total GDP was US$33·8bn. in 2008.

Banking and Finance

The Bank of Latvia both legally and practically is a completely independent institution. Governor of the Bank and Council members are appointed by Parliament for office for six years (present *Governor*, Ilmars Rimševičs). In 2002 there were 22 banks in Latvia, including the Riga branches of Société Générale and Vereinsbank. In 1999 the transitional period which had been given for banks to ensure they had capital of €5m. ended with 14 banks fulfilling the requirement. Latvia's largest bank is Parex Bank, with deposits in 2001 of 592·5m. lats. Foreign direct investment inflows in 2003 totalled US$360m. The accumulated FDI at the end of 2002 reached US$2·75bn.

There is a stock exchange in Riga.

ENERGY AND NATURAL RESOURCES

Environment

Latvia's carbon dioxide emissions from the consumption and flaring of fossil fuels in 2008 were the equivalent of 4·4 tonnes per capita. An *Environmental Performance Index* compiled in 2008 ranked Latvia eighth in the world, with 88·8%. The index examined various factors in six areas—air pollution, biodiversity and habitat, climate change, environmental health, productive natural resources and water resources.

Electricity

Electricity production in 2004 totalled 4·68bn. kWh. Consumption per capita in 2004 was 2,923 kWh. 66% of electrical power produced in Latvia is generated in hydro-electric power stations. The largest consumers are industry (34%) and private users (23%). Installed capacity was about 2·1m. kW in 2004.

Oil and Gas

Latvia produces virtually no oil and is dependent on imports, although the Latvian Development Agency estimates that there are 733m. bbls of offshore reserves in the Latvian areas of the Baltic Sea. Oil consumption was 43,000 bbls per day in 2001. All Latvia's natural gas supplies are imported from Russia. Consumption in 2004 totalled 1·6bn. cu. metres.

Minerals

Peat deposits extend over 645,000 ha. or about 10% of the total area, and it is estimated that total deposits are 3bn.–4bn. tonnes. Peat output in 2005 totalled 829,865 tonnes.

Production of other minerals (2005, in 1,000 tonnes): silica and construction sand, 3,242; gravel, pebbles, shingle and flint, 2,817; crude dolomite, 1,676; crushed stone for concrete aggregate, 587. Clays, gypsum and limestone are also produced.

Agriculture

In 2001 there were 1·84m. ha. of arable land and 29,000 ha. of permanent crops. Cattle and dairy farming are the chief agricultural occupations. Oats, barley, rye, potatoes and flax are the main crops.

In 2001 there were 174,459 farms. 43% of farms have fewer than 5 ha. There were 56,300 tractors and 6,200 harvester-threshers in 2001. Large state and collective farms have been converted into shareholding enterprises; the remainder have been divided into small private holdings for collective farm workers or former owners. In 2001, 14·7% of the economically active population were employed in agriculture.

Output of crops (in 1,000 tonnes), 2002: potatoes, 768; sugar beets, 622; wheat, 520; barley, 262; rye, 102; oats, 80; cabbage, 62; apples, 50; rapeseeds, 33; carrots, 23. Livestock, 2003: pigs, 453,000; cattle, 388,000; sheep, 32,000; poultry, 4m. Livestock products (2003, in 1,000 tonnes): meat, 68; milk, 820; eggs, 30.

Forestry

In 2005 Latvia's total forest area was 2·94m. ha., or 47·4% of the land area. The overall resources of wood amount to 502m. cu. metres (an increase of 118m. cu. metres since 1984), including 304m. cu. metres of softwood. Private forests account for 44·2% or 1·3m. ha. and comprise about 153,000 holdings. Timber production in 2007 was 12·17m. cu. metres.

The share of the forest sector in gross industrial output is between 13 and 15%. Timber and timber products exports account for 37–38% of Latvia's total exports.

To provide the protection of forests there are three forest categories: commercial forests, 70·4%; restricted management forests, 18·6%; protected forests, 11·0%.

Fisheries

In 2005 the total catch was 150,618 tonnes, of which marine fish 150,262 tonnes. The main types of fish caught are sprat, Baltic herring, cod and salmon. The Latvian fishing fleet consists of almost 400 vessels.

INDUSTRY

Industry accounted for 22·6% of GDP in 2004, with manufacturing contributing 13·4%.

Industrial output in 1,000 tonnes: crude steel (2004), 554; steel products (2000), 549; cement (2004), 284; sugar (2002), 77; sawnwood (2005), 3·71m. cu. metres; wood-based panels (2003), 358,000 cu. metres; plywood (2003), 179,000 cu. metres; beer (2005), 129·3m. litres.

Labour

The total labour force in 2005 numbered 1,134,700. In 2005 there were 1,033,700 persons in employment in Latvia (excluding those in compulsory military service). The leading areas of activity were: wholesale and retail trade/repair of motor vehicles, motorcycles and personal and household goods, 157,700; manufacturing, 154,100; agriculture, hunting, forestry and fishing, 122,300. In 2005 women constituted 48% of the workforce. In 2006 there was a monthly minimum wage of 90 lats. Average gross monthly salary was 246 lats in 2005. The unemployment rate in Feb. 2010 was 21·7% (13·2% in Feb. 2009), making it the highest in the EU. The average gross monthly salary in the public sector in 2005 was 285 lats.

Trade Unions

The Free Trade Union Federation of Latvia, LBAS (*President:* Pēteris Krīgers) was established in 1990. In 2003 there were 28 branch trade unions and professional employee unions representing more than 250,000 members.

INTERNATIONAL TRADE

State debt, as a proportion of GDP, has increased from 14·7% in 2000 to 15·4% in 2001, 16·6% in 2002 and 19·5% in 2003. Total external debt was US$14,283m. in 2005.

Imports and Exports

Imports (f.o.b.) were valued at US$11,271m. in 2006 and exports (f.o.b.) at US$6,140m. The leading imports are machinery and mechanical appliances (21·2%), products of chemical and allied industries (10·5%), mineral products (9·7%), metals and products thereof (8·4%). The main exports are wood and wood products (33·6%), base metals and articles of base metals (13·2%), textiles and textile articles (12·8%). Main import suppliers (2006): Germany, 15·5%; Lithuania, 13·0%; Russia, 7·8%; Estonia, 7·7%; Poland, 7·2%. Main export markets (2006): Lithuania, 14·7%; Estonia, 12·7%; Germany, 10·1%; Russia, 8·9%; UK, 7·8%.

COMMUNICATIONS

Roads

In 2005 there were 66,319 km of roads, including 20,182 km of national roads. Public road transport totalled 2,869m. passenger-km in 2005 and freight 8,547m. tonne-km. There were 442 fatalities in traffic accidents in 2005. With 19·2 deaths per 100,000 population in 2005 Latvia has one of the highest death rates in road accidents of any industrialized country. Passenger cars in 2005 numbered 742,447 (324 per 1,000 inhabitants), in addition to which there were 113,113 trucks and vans, 25,193 motorcycles, 7,284 mopeds and 10,644 buses and coaches.

Rail

In 2005 there were 2,270 km of 1,520 mm gauge route (257 km electrified). In 2003, 48·4m. tonnes of cargo and 23·0m. passengers were carried by rail. The main groups of freight transported are oil and oil products, mineral fertilizers, ferrous metals and ferrous alloys.

Civil Aviation

There is an international airport at Riga. A new national carrier, Air Baltic, assumed control of Latavio and Baltic International Airlines in Aug. 1995 and began flying in Oct. 1995. It went on to become eastern Europe's first low-cost airline; in 2006 it carried 1·42m. passengers. In 2003 it operated scheduled services to Berlin, Copenhagen, Hamburg, Helsinki, Kyiv, Moscow, Prague, Stockholm, Tallinn, Vilnius and Warsaw. It is 52·6% state-owned, with SAS owning 47·2% and Transaero the remaining 0·2%. In 2005 Riga handled 1,877,461 passengers and 15,963 tonnes of freight.

Shipping

There are three large ports (with 51·1m. tonnes of cargo handled, 2002): Ventspils (29m.), Riga (18m.) and Liepāja (4m.). 7,100 ships in all docked at the three ports in 2002. A total of 47·7m. tonnes were loaded at the three ports in 2002 and 3·4m. tonnes unloaded. In 2002 the merchant marine totalled 89,000 GRT, including oil tankers 4,000 GRT (oil tankers 279,000 GRT in 1996 out of a total of 723,000 GRT).

Ventspils can handle up to 100,000 containers a year and it is estimated that it will be able to handle 250,000 a year when the second stage of a US$70m. development project is completed. This project will change Ventspils from a port principally designed for the export of oil and other products from Russia to one which is also a major import centre.

Telecommunications

Telecommunications are conducted by companies in which the government has a 51% stake, under the aegis of the state-controlled Lattelecom. In 2005 telephone subscribers numbered 2,511,700 (1,088·7 per 1,000 inhabitants), of which 1,871,600 were mobile phone subscribers. There were 501,000 PCs in use (219·2 per 1,000 persons) in 2004 and 1,030,000 internet users in 2005.

Postal Services

In 2003 there were 964 post offices.

SOCIAL INSTITUTIONS

Justice

A new criminal code came into force in 1998. Judges are appointed for life. There is a Supreme Court, regional and district courts and administrative courts. The death penalty is retained but has been subject to a moratorium since Oct. 1996; it was abolished for peacetime offences in 1999. In 2003, 51,773 crimes were reported, 48·8% of which were solved; 13,586 people were convicted for offences. There were 220 murders in 2003 (a 6·3% increase on 2002). In June 2003 there were 8,156 people in penal institutions, giving a prison population rate of 352 per 100,000 population.

Education

Adult literacy rate in 2003 was 99·7% (99·8% among males and 99·7% among females). The Soviet education system has been restructured on the UNESCO model. Education begins with two years of compulsory attendance at pre-primary schools. From the age of six or seven education is compulsory for nine years in comprehensive schools. This may be followed by three years in special secondary school or one to six years in art, technical or vocational schools. In 2003–04 there were 1,044 schools with 327,358 pupils.

State-financed education is available in Latvian and eight national minority languages (Russian, Polish, Hebrew, Ukrainian, Estonian, Lithuanian, Roma and Belarusian), although the use of Latvian in the classroom is being increased. A bilingual curriculum had to be implemented by all minority primary schools from the start of the 2002–03 school year. Secondary schools started to implement minority education curricula with an increased Latvian-language component (60% of all teaching) from Sept. 2004. In 2003–04, 230,212 pupils were taught solely in

Latvian, 95,841 received instruction in Russian and 1,305 in other minority languages.

In 2002 there were 37 higher education institutions, with 118,944 students. Courses at state-financed universities are conducted in Latvian. A number of private educational institutions have languages of instruction other than Latvian.

Public expenditure on education in 2004 came to 5·1% of GDP and accounted for 14·2% of total government expenditure.

Health

In 2003 there were 7,900 physicians and dentists. In 2001 there were 11,954 nurses and 501 midwives. There were 131 hospitals in 2003 with a provision of 78 beds per 10,000 persons.

Welfare

The official retirement age is age 62 years for men and women. In 2008 the minimum pension was just over the state social security allowance of 45 lats a month at 49·50 lats. The minimum pension is increased by 1·1% for an insurance period of at least 20 years, by 1·3% for an insurance period of 20 to 30 years and by 1·5% and for an insurance period of more than 30 years. In Dec. 2007 there were 567,400 pension recipients.

The government runs an unemployment benefit scheme in which the amount awarded is determined by the number of insurance contributions and the length of previous employment.

RELIGION

In order to practise in public, religious organizations must be licensed by the Department of Religious Affairs attached to the Ministry of Justice. New sects are required to demonstrate loyalty to the state and its traditional religions over a three-year period. Traditionally Catholics and Lutherans constitute the largest churches, with about 500,000 and 400,000 members respectively in 2002. Congregations in Feb. 2003: Lutherans, 307; Roman Catholics, 252; Russian Orthodox, 117; Baptists, 90; Old Believers, 67; Adventists, 47; Jews, 13; others, 47. In Feb. 2010 the Roman Catholic church had one cardinal.

CULTURE

World Heritage Sites

Latvia has two sites on the UNESCO World Heritage List: the Historic Centre of Riga (inscribed on the list in 1997), a late-medieval Hanseatic centre; and the Struve Geodetic Arc (2005). The Arc is a chain of survey triangulations spanning from Norway to the Black Sea that helped establish the exact shape and size of the earth and is shared with nine other countries.

Broadcasting

Broadcasting is overseen by the National Broadcasting Council of Latvia (NRTP), a public body established under legislation in 1995. Latvijas Radio operates four national networks. There are numerous commercial radio stations. Latvijas Televīzija, the national public broadcaster, transmits on two networks (colour by PAL). The main commercial networks are LNT, TV3 Latvia and TV5. There were 1·99m. television receivers in 2003.

Press

Latvia had 26 daily newspapers in 2005 with a combined circulation of 429,200 (187 per 1,000 inhabitants). The leading newspapers in terms of readership are Diena and Latvijas Avize.

Tourism

In 2005 there were 1,116,000 non-resident tourists; tourist spending totalled US$446m. In 2003 there were 2·3m. border crossings by Latvian travellers returning from abroad (mainly visitors to neighbouring countries for short-stay shopping trips and visits to friends and relatives). In 2006 there were 393 hotels and other accommodation facilities.

Festivals

There is an annual Riga Opera Festival in June. The National Song Festival (held every five years) will next be held in 2013.

DIPLOMATIC REPRESENTATIVES

Of Latvia in the United Kingdom (45 Nottingham Place, London, W1U 5LY)
Ambassador: Eduards Stiprais.

Of the United Kingdom in Latvia (5 Alunana iela, Riga, LV 1010)
Ambassador: Richard Moon.

Of Latvia in the USA (2306 Massachusetts Ave., NW, Washington, D.C., 20008)
Ambassador: Andrejs Pildegovičs.

Of the USA in Latvia (7 Raina Blvd, Riga, LV 1510)
Ambassador: Judith G. Garber.

Of Latvia to the United Nations
Ambassador: Normans Penke.

Of Latvia to the European Union
Permanent Representative: Normunds Popens.

FURTHER READING

Central Statistical Bureau. *Statistical Yearbook of Latvia.—Latvia in Figures.* Annual.

Dreifeld, J., *Latvia in Transition.* 1997

Lieven, A., *The Baltic Revolution: Estonia, Latvia, Lithuania and the Path to Independence.* 2nd ed. 1994

Misiunas, R. J. and Taagepera, R., *The Baltic States: the Years of Dependence, 1940–91.* 2nd ed. 1993

O'Connor, Kevin, *The History of the Baltic States.* 2003

Smith, David J., Purs, Aldis, Pabriks, Artis and Lane, Thomas, (eds.) *The Baltic States: Estonia, Latvia and Lithuania.* 2002

Who is Who in Latvia. 2007–08

National Statistical Office: Central Statistical Bureau, Lāčplēša ielā 1, 1301 Riga.

Website: http://www.csb.lv

LEBANON

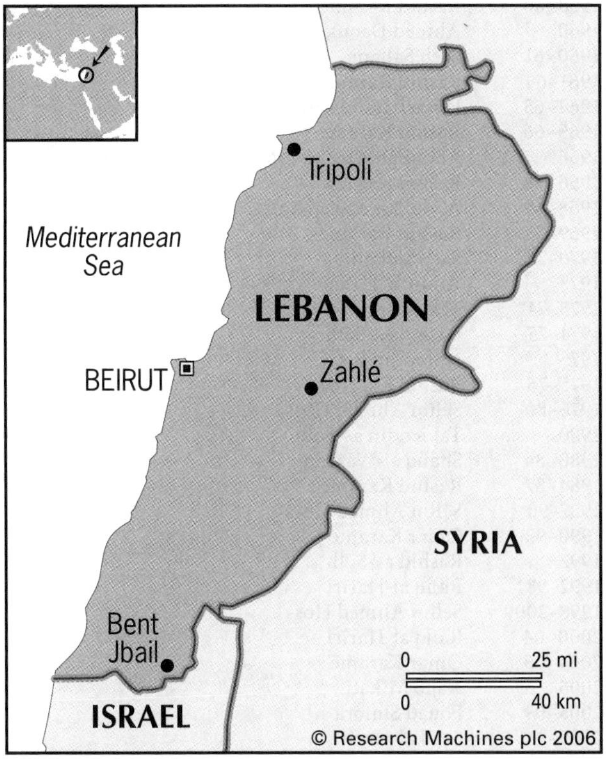

Jumhouriya al-Lubnaniya
(Republic of Lebanon)

Capital: Beirut
Population estimate, 2010: 4·26m.
GDP per capita, 2007: (PPP$) 10,109
HDI/world rank: 0·803/83

KEY HISTORICAL EVENTS

The Ottomans invaded Lebanon, then part of Syria, in 1516–17 and held nominal control until 1918. After 20 years' of French mandatory regime, Lebanon was proclaimed independent on 26 Nov. 1941. In early May 1958 the Muslim opposition to President Chamoun rose in insurrection and for five months the Muslim quarters of Beirut, Tripoli, Sidon and the northern Bekaa were in insurgent hands. On 15 July the US Government landed army and marines who re-established Government authority. Internal problems were exacerbated by the Palestinian problem. An attempt to regulate the activities of Palestinian fighters through the secret Cairo agreement of 1969 was frustrated both by the inability of the Government to enforce its provisions and by an influx of battle-hardened fighters expelled from Jordan in Sept. 1970. From March 1975 Lebanon was beset by civil disorder bringing the economy to a virtual standstill.

By Nov. 1976 large-scale fighting had been brought to an end by the intervention of the Syrian-dominated Arab Deterrent Force. Large areas of the country, however, remained outside governmental control, including West Beirut, which was the scene of frequent conflict between opposing militia groups. In March 1978 there was an Israeli invasion following a Palestinian attack inside Israel. Israeli troops eventually withdrew in June, but instead of handing over all their positions to UN Peacekeeping Forces, they installed Israeli-controlled Christian Lebanese militia forces in border areas. In June 1982 Israeli forces once again invaded, this time in massive strength, and swept through the country, eventually laying siege to and bombing Beirut. In Sept. Palestinian forces, together with the PLO leadership, evacuated Beirut. Israeli forces started a withdrawal on 16 Feb. 1985 but it was not until the end of 1990 that the various militias which had held sway in Beirut withdrew. A new Government of National Reconciliation was announced on 24 Dec. 1990. The dissolution of all militias was decreed by the National Assembly in April 1991, but the Shia Muslim militia Hizbollah was allowed to remain active. Following a 17-day Israeli bombardment of Hizbollah positions in April 1996, a US-brokered unsigned 'understanding' of 26 April 1996 guaranteed that Hizbollah guerrillas and Palestinian radical groups would cease attacks on civilians in northern Israel and granted Israel the right to self-defence. Hizbollah maintained the right to resist Israel's occupation of Lebanese soil. In May 2000 Israel completed its withdrawal from south Lebanon, 22 years after the first invasion.

On 14 Feb. 2005 former Prime Minister Rafiq al-Hariri was assassinated in a bomb attack on his car, sparking international condemnation of the murder and massive public protests at the continued presence of Syrian soldiers in the country. Soon afterwards Syria began withdrawing and redeploying its 14,000 troops and intelligence agents from Beirut. By the end of April 2005 all Syrian troops had been withdrawn from Lebanon. In July 2006, after Hizbollah forces in Lebanon had captured two Israeli soldiers, Israel launched a large-scale military campaign against Lebanon with a series of bombing raids, destroying large parts of the civilian infrastructure. More than 1,200 Lebanese, the majority of them civilians, were killed during the conflict. Following the resignation of five Shia Muslim cabinet ministers and the assassination of industry minister Pierre Gemayel in Nov. 2006 there were anti-government demonstrations in Beirut in which over 800,000 protesters—nearly a quarter of the population of Lebanon—demanded the resignation of Prime Minister Fouad Siniora.

TERRITORY AND POPULATION

Lebanon is mountainous, bounded on the north and east by Syria, on the west by the Mediterranean and on the south by Israel. The area is 10,452 sq. km (4,036 sq. miles). Population (2005 estimate), 4·01m.; density, 384 per sq. km. The last census was in 1932. In 2005, 86·6% of the population were urban.

The UN gives an estimated population for 2010 of 4·26m.

The principal towns, with estimated population (1998), are: Beirut (the capital), 1·5m.; Tripoli, 160,000; Zahlé, 45,000; Saida (Sidon), 38,000.

The official language is Arabic. French and, increasingly, English are widely spoken in official and commercial circles. Armenian is spoken by a minority group.

SOCIAL STATISTICS

2001 estimates: births, 86,000; deaths, 19,000. Estimated rates, 2001 (per 1,000 population): births, 24·3; deaths, 5·4. Infant mortality was 27 per 1,000 live births in 2005; expectation of life (2007), 69·8 years for males and 74·1 for females. Annual population growth rate, 1992–2002, 2·3%; fertility rate, 2004, 2·3 births per woman.

CLIMATE

A Mediterranean climate with short, warm winters and long, hot and rainless summers, with high humidity in coastal areas.

Rainfall is largely confined to the winter months and can be torrential, with snow on high ground. Beirut, Jan. 55°F (13°C), July 81°F (27°C). Annual rainfall 35·7" (893 mm).

CONSTITUTION AND GOVERNMENT

The first Constitution was established under the French Mandate on 23 May 1926. It has since been amended in 1927, 1929, 1943 (twice), 1947 and 1990. It is based on a separation of powers, with a President, a single-chamber *National Assembly* elected by universal suffrage at age 21 in 12 electoral constituencies, and an independent judiciary. The President serves a six-year term, although in both 1995 and 2004 the terms of office of the then Presidents were extended from six to nine years through 'exceptional' constitutional amendments. The executive consists of the President and a Prime Minister and Cabinet appointed after consultation between the President and the National Assembly. The system is adapted to the communal balance on which Lebanese political life depends by an electoral law which allocates deputies according to the religious distribution of the population, and by a series of constitutional conventions whereby, e.g. the President is always a Maronite Christian, the Prime Minister a Sunni Muslim and the Speaker of the Assembly a Shia Muslim. There is no party system. In Aug. 1990, and again in July 1992, the National Assembly voted to increase its membership, and now has 128 deputies with equal numbers of Christians and Muslims (although Muslims make up a clear majority of the population).

On 21 Sept. 1990 President Haraoui established the Second Republic by signing constitutional amendments which had been negotiated at Taif (Saudi Arabia) in Oct. 1989. These institute an executive collegium between the President, Prime Minister and Speaker, and remove from the President the right to recall the Prime Minister, dissolve the Assembly and vote in the Council of Ministers.

National Anthem

'Kulluna lil watan lil 'ula lil 'alam' ('All of us for our country, flag and glory'); words by Rashid Nakhlé, tune by W. Sabra.

GOVERNMENT CHRONOLOGY

Presidents since 1943.

1943–52	Béchara Khalil El-Khoury
1952–58	Camille Nemr Chamoun
1958–64	Fouad Abdallah Chehab
1964–70	Charles Alexandre Hélou
1970–76	Soleiman Kabalan Franjieh
1976–82	Elias Sarkis
1982–88	Amine Pierre Gemayel
1989	René Anis Moawad
1989–98	Elias Khalil Haraoui
1998–2007	Emile Geamil Lahoud
2007–08	Fouad Siniora (acting)
2008–	Gen. Michel Suleiman

Prime Ministers since 1943.

1943–45	Riyad as-Solh
1945	Abdulhamid Karame
1945–46	Abd' Rashin Sami as-Solh
1946	Saadi al-Munla
1946–51	Riyad as-Solh
1951	Hussein al-Oweini
1951–52	Abdullah Aref al-Yafi
1952	Abd Rashin Sami as-Solh
1952	Nazim al-Akkari
1952	Saeb Sallam
1952	Abdullah Aref al-Yafi
1952–53	Amir Khalid Chehab
1953	Saeb Sallam
1953–54	Abdullah Aref al-Yafi
1954–55	Abd Rashin Sami as-Solh
1955–56	Rashid Karame
1956	Abdullah Aref al-Yafi
1956–58	Abd Rashin Sami as-Solh
1958	Khalil al-Hibri
1958–60	Rashid Karame
1960	Ahmed Daouk
1960–61	Saeb Sallam
1961–64	Rashid Karame
1964–65	Hussein al-Oweini
1965–66	Rashid Karame
1966	Abdullah Aref al-Yafi
1966–68	Rashid Karame
1968–69	Abdullah Aref al-Yafi
1969–70	Rashid Karame
1970–73	Saeb Sallam
1973	Amin al-Hafez
1973–74	Takieddin as-Solh
1974–75	Rashid as-Solh
1975	Nureddin Rifai
1975–76	Rashid Karame
1976–80	Sélim Ahmed Hoss
1980	Takieddin as-Solh
1980–84	Shafiq al-Wazzan
1984–87	Rashid Karame
1987–90	Sélim Ahmed Hoss
1990–92	Omar Karame
1992	Rashid as-Solh
1992–98	Rafiq al-Hariri
1998–2000	Sélim Ahmed Hoss
2000–04	Rafiq al-Hariri
2004–05	Omar Karame
2005	Najib Mikati
2005–09	Fouad Siniora
2009–	Saad al-Hariri

RECENT ELECTIONS

Elections were held on 7 June 2009. The ruling anti-Syrian 14 March Alliance—including the Movement of the Future, the Progressive Socialist Party, the Lebanese Forces, the Kataeb Party and their allies—won 71 of 128 seats; Hizbollah, Amal and their allies, 29 seats; and the Free Patriotic Movement and its allies, 28.

The presidential election, originally scheduled for 25 Sept. 2007, was put back repeatedly amid continued deadlock between rival political leaders. At the 20th attempt on 25 May 2008 Gen. Michel Suleiman was elected president, receiving 118 of 127 votes in parliament.

CURRENT ADMINISTRATION

President: Gen. Michel Suleiman; b. 1948 (took office 25 May 2008).

In March 2010 the government comprised:

Prime Minister: Saad al-Hariri; b. 1970 (took office 9 Nov. 2009).

Deputy Prime Minister and Minister of Defence: Elias al-Murr.

Minister of Agriculture: Hussein Hajj Hassan. *Culture:* Salim Wardeh. *Displaced Persons:* Akram Chehayeb. *Economy and Trade:* Mohammad Safadi. *Education:* Hassan Mneimneh. *Energy and Water:* Gebran Bassil. *Environment:* Mohammad Rahhal. *Finance:* Rayya al-Haffar al-Hassan. *Foreign Affairs:* Ali Shami. *Health:* Mohammad Jawad Khalifa. *Industry:* Abraham Dedeyan. *Information:* Tarek Mitri. *Interior:* Ziad Baroud. *Justice:* Ibrahim Najjar. *Labour:* Boutros Harb. *Public Works:* Ghazi Aridi. *Social Affairs:* Salim Sayegh. *Telecommunications:* Charbel Nahhas. *Tourism:* Fadi Abboud. *Youth and Sport:* Ali Abdullah.

President's Website: http://www.presidency.gov.lb

CURRENT LEADERS

Michel Suleiman

Position
President

Introduction
Gen. Michel Suleiman was sworn into office on 25 May 2008, filling a power vacuum created when Emile Lahoud's term ended in Nov. 2007. Suleiman was appointed as a 'compromise candidate' after negotiations between the Western-backed government and the Hizbollah-led opposition.

Early Life
Michel Suleiman was born in Amsheet on 21 Nov. 1948 to a prominent Maronite Christian family. He joined the armed forces in 1967 and graduated from Lebanon's Military Academy as a second lieutenant in 1970. He went on to complete a degree in political and administrative sciences at the Lebanese University.

Suleiman rose rapidly through the ranks of the armed forces at a time when Syria played a dominant role in Lebanon's military. On 21 Dec. 1998 he was appointed commander of the armed forces when Emile Lahoud left the post to take over the presidency. During his tenure Suleiman managed to maintain the military's non-partisan status and built good relationships with all sides. In the days following the Feb. 2005 assassination of Rafiq al-Hariri, Suleiman refused to crack down on anti-Syrian demonstrations or sanction military intervention. His stance is credited with paving the way to Syria's withdrawal from Lebanese politics. Suleiman also ensured that the military stood back when Hizbollah and Israel fought a 34-day war in 2006 and oversaw a successful operation against Fatah al-Islam militants at the Nahr el-Bared refugee camp in 2007.

On 25 May 2008 Suleiman won the presidency when he received 118 of 127 parliamentary votes after Qatari-brokered talks on Lebanon's political future. His appointment put an end to six months of political deadlock, with the government and opposition agreeing to a power-sharing deal.

Career in Office
Suleiman reappointed pro-Western Fouad Siniora as prime minister on 28 May 2008 and invited him to form a national unity cabinet. In Sept. 2008 Suleiman launched a national dialogue for reconciliation, an initiative aimed at ending Lebanon's internal conflicts. In Oct. 2008 Lebanon and Syria established diplomatic ties. However, Suleiman still faced formidable challenges, including the implementation of the UN Security Council resolution calling for all militias in Lebanon to be disarmed. Following general elections in June 2009 in which the pro-Western 14 March Alliance won a majority of seats in the National Assembly, Suleiman designated as the new prime minister Alliance leader Saad al-Hariri, who eventually succeeded in forming a national unity government in Nov.

Saad al-Hariri

Position
Prime Minister

Introduction
Saad al-Hariri was appointed premier by President Michel Suleiman on 27 June 2009, after his pro-Western coalition, the March 14 Alliance, defeated a Hezbollah-led alliance in the June 2009 elections.

Early Life
Al-Hariri was born on 18 April 1970. He is the second son of Rafiq al-Hariri, the former prime minister assassinated in 2005, a year after resigning from office. Al-Hariri graduated from Georgetown University in 1992 with a degree in international business.

The assassination of his father on 14 Feb 2005 prompted a chain of demonstrations in Lebanon known as the Cedar Revolution. After his father's death, al-Hariri assumed the leadership of the Movement for the Future, a majority Sunni Muslim group. Protesters demanded that Syrian troops withdraw from Lebanon and that a new government be formed, independent of Syrian influence. On 28 Feb. the government of pro-Syrian Prime Minister Omar Karami resigned but was reappointed on 8 March following pro-Syrian Hezbollah demonstrations. On 10 March 2005 the last remaining Syrian troops left Lebanon, with the last Syrian agents crossing the border on 26 April.

Despite Karami's pleas for opposition parties to take part in Lebanon's government until elections were called, he failed to form a government and resigned on 13 April 2005. Ahead of elections scheduled from 29 May to 19 June 2005, al-Hariri formed an anti-Syrian coalition (the March 14 Alliance) that subsequently won 72 of 128 National Assembly seats. He himself became an MP and several of his allies were appointed to key posts. However, the 2006 Israeli–Hezbollah war and the 2007 and 2008 Lebanese conflicts highlighted the nation's continuing instability. In 2008 al-Hariri's house was blockaded by pro-Hezbollah protesters after the government accused the group of preparing a terrorist attack.

Career in Office
Following former army commander Suleiman's election to the presidency in 2008, parliamentary elections were held on 7 June 2009. The March 14 Alliance won 45% of the vote but with a majority of seats, allocated among religious groups. However, several leaders subsequently left the Alliance and in Sept. 2009 al-Hariri resigned as prime minister designate when the Alliance rejected his proposed cabinet. He was reappointed by Suleiman on 16 Sept.

After five months of negotiations over the make-up of his cabinet, al-Hariri formed a national unity government in Nov. 2009. Fifteen ministers came from the March 14 Alliance, ten from the opposition March 8 Alliance and five were nominated by President Suleiman.

On 20 Dec. 2009 al-Hariri met Syrian President Bashar al-Assad in Damascus to attempt to ease tensions between the countries. Al-Hariri said that both leaders wanted the truth concerning his father's assassination and that investigations were in the hands of the international community. In Feb. 2010 al-Hariri restated his concern over the hostile relationship between Israel, Syria and Lebanon.

DEFENCE

There were 14,000 Syrian troops in the country in early 2005, but in March 2005 Lebanon and Syria agreed that the troops would be redeployed to the Bekaa Valley in the east of the country. They were subsequently all withdrawn from Lebanon. The United Nations Interim Force in Lebanon (UNIFIL), created in 1978, had a strength of 1,990 in June 2006. Following the conflict between Israel and Lebanon of July–Aug. 2006 the Security Council established UNIFIL II, a more powerful peacekeeping force deployed to maintain the ceasefire, support the Lebanese armed forces and aid humanitarian efforts. In Dec. 2009 UNIFIL II comprised 11,862 military personnel.

Conscription was reduced from 12 months to six in 2005, and was finally abolished in Feb. 2007.

Defence expenditure in 2006 totalled US$589m. (US$152 per capita), representing 2·8% of GDP.

Army

The strength of the Army was 53,900 in 2007 and includes a Presidential Guard and five special forces regiments. There is an internal security force, run by the Ministry of the Interior, some 20,000 strong.

Navy

A force of 1,100 personnel (2007) operate 21 patrol and coastal combatants. An additional seven inshore patrol craft are operated by customs.

Air Force

The Air Force had (2007) 1,000 personnel. There are no combat capable aircraft although eight attack helicopters were in operation in 2007.

INTERNATIONAL RELATIONS

A Treaty of Brotherhood, Co-operation and Co-ordination with Syria of May 1991 provides for close relations in the fields of foreign policy, the economy, military affairs and security. The treaty stipulates that Lebanese government decisions are subject to review by six joint Syrian-Lebanese bodies.

Lebanon is a member of the UN, World Bank, IMF and several other UN specialized agencies, International Organization of the Francophonie, Islamic Development Bank, OIC and League of Arab States.

ECONOMY

Agriculture accounted for 6·7% of GDP in 2006, industry 23·7% and services 69·6%.

Overview

Prior to Lebanon's civil war the country was a model for economic development in the Middle East, displaying impressive growth, strong investment and high social indicators. After the civil war Lebanon found itself with heavy reconstruction costs and little foreign aid, leaving the country with US$35bn. in debt and the second highest debt-to-GDP ratio in the world in 1991. The economy recovered, however, and growth rates were strong until the country fell back into recession in 1999. Austerity measures helped the economy recover strongly from 2001–04. In 2005 the economy stalled after the assassination of former prime minister Rafiq al-Hariri.

Despite signs of recovery in the first half of 2006 the IMF's forecast for the country in June 2006 suggested that its debt ratio would grow from 175% of GDP to 210% by 2011 and that Lebanon could face a vicious cycle of increasing debt, rising interest rates and subdued growth. In July–Aug. 2006 Israeli bombing shook the Lebanese economy, with the government putting the cost from lost income and damage at US$6·5bn. International donors initially pledged nearly US$1bn. in recovery and reconstruction assistance, with a further US$7·5bn. promised in Jan. 2007.

Political troubles hampered economic activity until an agreement was reached in May 2008. Since then, political stability has boosted investment and tourism. However, preliminary figures suggest growth slowed in 2009 as a result of the global financial crisis. Another concern is the large public debt, which stands at around 162% of GDP.

Currency

The unit of currency is the *Lebanese pound* (LBP) of 100 *piastres*. Inflation was 4·1% in 2007 and 10·8% in 2008. In July 2005 foreign exchange reserves totalled US$10,627m., gold reserves were 9·22m. troy oz and total money supply was £Leb.3,005·7bn. The Lebanese pound has been pegged to the US dollar since Sept. 1999 at £Leb.1,507·5 = 1 US$.

Budget

The fiscal year is the calendar year.

In 2007 budgetary central government revenue totalled £Leb.8,390bn. and expenditure £Leb.11,816bn. Tax revenues in 2007 were £Leb.5,593bn. Main items of expenditure by economic type in 2007 were interest (£Leb.4,695bn.) and compensation of employees (£Leb.3,198bn.).

VAT of 10% was introduced in 2002.

Performance

Total GDP was US$28·7bn. in 2008. Real GDP growth was 7·5% in 2007 and 8·5% in 2008.

Banking and Finance

The Bank of Lebanon (*Governor*, Riad Salameh) is the bank of issue. In 1994 there were 52 domestic banks, 14 subsidiaries and 12 foreign banks, with 590 branches in all. Commercial bank deposits in June 1998 totalled £Leb.41,836,800m. There is a stock exchange in Beirut (closed 1983–95).

ENERGY AND NATURAL RESOURCES

Environment

Lebanon's carbon dioxide emissions from the consumption and flaring of fossil fuels in 2008 were the equivalent of 3·6 tonnes per capita.

Electricity

Installed capacity in 2004 was approximately 2·5m. kW. Production in 2004 was 10·19bn. kWh and consumption per capita 2,691 kWh.

Minerals

There are no commercially viable deposits.

Agriculture

In 2002 there were around 170,000 ha. of arable land and 143,000 ha. of permanent crop land. Crop production (in 1,000 tonnes), 2002: potatoes, 397; tomatoes, 270; olives, 184; oranges, 155; apples, 150; cucumbers and gherkins, 132; wheat, 119; grapes, 102; melons and watermelons, 100.

Livestock (2002): goats, 409,000; sheep, 298,000; cattle, 88,000; pigs, 21,000; chickens, 33m.

Forestry

The forests of the past have been denuded by exploitation and in 2005 covered 136,000 ha., or 13·3% of the total land area. Timber production was 87,000 cu. metres in 2007.

Fisheries

The catch in 2005 was 3,798 tonnes, of which 3,523 tonnes were sea fish.

INDUSTRY

In 2001 industry accounted for 21·9% of GDP, with manufacturing contributing 10·3%. Industrial production, 2001 (in 1,000 tonnes): cement, 2,890; flour, 420; sulphuric acid, 357; mineral water, 276·8m. litres.

Labour

The workforce was some 650,000 in 1995, of whom 72,000 worked in agriculture. Following considerable labour unrest, an agreement on wage increases and social benefits was concluded between the government and the General Confederation of Lebanese Workers (GCLW) in Dec. 1993.

Trade Unions

The main unions are the General Confederation of Lebanese Workers and the General Confederation of Sectoral Unions.

INTERNATIONAL TRADE

Foreign and domestic trade is the principal source of income. Foreign debt was US$22,373m. in 2005.

Imports and Exports

Imports, 2006: US$8,547m.; exports, US$2,792m. Major imports in 2004 were: mineral products, 22·0%; electrical equipment, 11·8%; food and live animals, 10·4%; transportation equipment, 9·0%. Major exports in 2004 were: precious metal jewellery and stones, 16·4%; electrical equipment, 15·7%; base metals, 13·0%; chemicals and chemical products, 8·5%.

In 2004 the main export markets were: Iraq, 14·6%; Switzerland, 10·7%; Syria, 8·3%; UAE, 7·7%. Main import suppliers: Italy, 9·9%; France, 7·8%; Germany, 7·8%; China, 7·6%.

COMMUNICATIONS

Roads

There were 6,970 km of roads in 2005, including 170 km of motorway. Passenger cars in 2002 numbered 1,253,700, and there were also 97,200 trucks and vans; in 1997 there were 61,470 motorcycles and mopeds and 6,830 buses and coaches. In 2007 there were 4,281 road accidents resulting in 487 deaths.

Rail

Railways are state-owned. There is 222 km of standard gauge track.

Civil Aviation

Beirut International Airport was served in 2003 by nearly 30 airlines. It handled 2,373,056 passengers (all on international flights) in 2001 and 62,789 tonnes of freight. The national airline is the state-owned Middle East Airlines. In 2003 scheduled airline traffic of Lebanese-based carriers flew 20m. km, carrying 935,000 passengers (all on international flights).

Shipping

Beirut is the largest port, followed by Tripoli, Jounieh and Saida (Sidon). Total GRT in 2002 was 229,000, including oil tankers 1,000 GRT.

Telecommunications

Lebanon had 1,980,000 telephone subscribers in 2005, or 553·5 per 1,000 persons, of which 990,000 were mobile phone subscribers. There were 409,000 PCs in use (114·5 for every 1,000 persons) in 2005 and 700,000 internet users.

Postal Services

In 2003 there were 349 post offices.

SOCIAL INSTITUTIONS

Justice

The population in penal institutions in March 2003 was 6,382 (172 per 100,000 of national population). The death penalty is still in force. There were three confirmed executions in 2004, the first since 1998.

Education

There are state and private primary and secondary schools. In 2007 there were 450,566 pupils with 32,412 teaching staff at primary schools; and 368,359 pupils with 40,919 teaching staff in secondary education. There are 13 universities, including two American and one French, and ten other institutions of higher education. In 2007 there were 187,055 students in tertiary education and 21,778 academic staff. Adult literacy was 86·5% in 2001 (92·4% among males and 81·0% among females). In 2007 public expenditure on education came to 2·7% of GNI and 9·6% of total government spending.

There is an Academy of Fine Arts.

Health

There were 153 hospitals in 1995 (provision of 22 beds per 10,000 population), and in 2001 there were 11,505 physicians, 4,283 dentists, 4,157 nurses and 3,359 pharmacists.

RELIGION

In 2001 it was estimated that the population was 56·6% Muslim (34·8% Shia and 21·8% Sunni), 36·0% Christian (mainly Maronite) and 7·4% Druze. In 1996 there were 119 Roman Catholic bishops. In Feb. 2010 there was one cardinal.

CULTURE

World Heritage Sites

There are five UNESCO sites in Lebanon. Four were entered on the list in 1984: the ruins of Anjar, a city founded by the Muslim Arab caliph Walid I at the beginning of the 8th century; Baalbek, the most impressive ancient site in Lebanon and one of the most important Roman ruins in the Middle East; Byblos, the site of multi-layered ruins of one of the most ancient cities of Lebanon, dating back to Neolithic times; and Tyre, which has important archaeological remains, principally from Roman times. The Qadisha Valley and Bcharre district, inscribed in 1998, has been the site of monastic communities since the earliest years of Christianity. Its cedar trees, among the most highly prized building materials of the ancient world, are survivors of a sacred forest.

Broadcasting

Lebanon was the first Arab country to legalize private broadcasting. The Lebanese Broadcasting Corporation was launched in 1985 as the first private television service. Future Television and (pro-Hizbollah) Al-Manar TV are the other main commercial channels. Télé-Liban and Radio Liban remain state-run services. Voice of Lebanon is an established private radio station. Regulatory legislation was introduced in the 1990s to restrict unlicensed private broadcasting. Colour is by SECAM H. There were 1·40m. TV sets in 2006.

Press

In 2006 there were 14 paid-for daily newspapers with a combined circulation of 240,000, and two free dailies. The newspapers with the highest circulation are An-Nahar and Assafir.

Tourism

In 2005 there were 1,140,000 non-resident tourists (excluding Syrian nationals), spending US$5,869m.

Festivals

Major annual cultural events are the Al Bustan Festival of music, dance and theatre in Feb.–March; Baalbek International Festival, which reopened in 1997 after an absence of 23 years; Hamra Festival in June; Beiteddine Festival in July–Aug.; Tyre Festival; Byblos Festival; and the Beirut Film Festival.

DIPLOMATIC REPRESENTATIVES

Of Lebanon in the United Kingdom (21 Palace Garden Mews, London, W8 4RB)
Ambassador: Inaam Osseiran.

Of the United Kingdom in Lebanon (Embassies Complex, Army St., Zkak Al-Blat, Serail Hill, PO Box 11–471, Beirut)
Ambassador: Frances Guy.

Of Lebanon in the USA (2560 28th St., NW, Washington, D.C., 20008)
Ambassador: Antoine Chedid.

Of the USA in Lebanon (PO Box 70-840, Antelias, Beirut)
Ambassador: Michele J. Sison.

Of Lebanon to the United Nations
Ambassador: Nawaf Salam.

Of Lebanon to the European Union
Ambassador: Adnan Mansour.

FURTHER READING

Choueiri, Y. M., *State and Society in Syria and Lebanon.* 1994
Fisk, R., *Pity the Nation: Lebanon at War.* 3rd ed. 2001
Gemayel, A., *Rebuilding Lebanon.* 1992
Harris, William, *The New Face of Lebanon: History's Revenge.* 2005
Hiro, D., *Lebanon Fire and Embers: a History of the Lebanese Civil War.* 1993

National library: Dar el Kutub, Parliament Sq., Beirut.
National Statistical Office: Service de Statistique Générale, Beirut.
Website: http://www.cas.gov.lb

LESOTHO

Muso oa Lesotho
(Kingdom of Lesotho)

Capital: Maseru
Population estimate, 2010: 2·08m.
GDP per capita, 2007: (PPP$) 1,541
HDI/world rank: 0·514/156

KEY HISTORICAL EVENTS

The Basotho nation was constituted in the 19th century under the leadership of Moshoeshoe I, bringing together refugees from disparate tribes scattered by Zulu expansionism in southern Africa. After war with land-hungry Boer settlers in 1856 (and again in 1886), Moshoeshoe appealed for British protection. This was granted in 1868, and in 1871 the territory was annexed to the Cape Colony (now Republic of South Africa), but in 1883 it was restored to the direct control of the British government through the High Commissioner for South Africa. In 1965 full internal self-government was achieved under King Moshoeshoe II. On 4 Oct. 1966 Basutoland became an independent and sovereign member of the British Commonwealth as the Kingdom of Lesotho. Chief Leabua Jonathan, leader of the Basotho National Party and prime minister from 1965, suspended the constitution when the elections of 1970 were declared invalid. On 20 Jan. 1986, after a border blockade by the Republic of South Africa, Chief Jonathan was deposed in a bloodless military coup led by Maj.-Gen. Justin Lekhanya who granted significant powers to the king. King Moshoeshoe II was deposed in Nov. 1990 and replaced by King Letsie III. Lekhanya was deposed in May 1991. A democratic constitution was promulgated in April 1993. The elections in May 1998 were won by the ruling Lesotho Congress for Democracy. In Sept. 1998 an army mutiny prompted intervention from South Africa to support the government.

TERRITORY AND POPULATION

Lesotho is an enclave within South Africa. The area is 30,355 sq. km (11,720 sq. miles).

The census in 2006 showed a total population of 1,876,633 (963,835 females); density, 61·8 per sq. km. In 2006 the population was 77·2% rural.

The UN gives an estimated population for 2010 of 2·08m.

There are ten districts, all named after their chief towns, except Berea (chief town, Teyateyaneng). Area and population:

Region	*Area (in sq. km.)*	*2006 census population*
Berea	2,222	250,006
Butha-Buthe	1,767	110,320
Leribe	2,828	293,369
Mafeteng	2,119	192,621
Maseru	4,279	431,998
Mohale's Hoek	3,530	176,928
Mokhotlong	4,075	97,713
Qacha's Nek	2,349	69,749
Quthing	2,916	124,048
Thaba-Tseka	4,270	129,881

In 2006 the capital, Maseru, had a population of 197,907. Other major towns (with 2006 census population) are: Teyateyaneng, 61,475; Mafeteng, 32,148; Maputsoe, 30,800 (estimate); Mohale's Hoek, 28,310.

The official languages are Sesotho and English.

The population is more than 98% Basotho. The rest is made up of Xhosas, approximately 3,000 expatriate Europeans and several hundred Asians.

SOCIAL STATISTICS

1995 births, 76,000; deaths, 21,000. Rates, 1995: birth (per 1,000 population), 37; death, 10. Annual population growth rate, 1992–2002, 1·1%. Life expectancy at birth in 2007 was 43·9 years for males and 45·5 years for females. Life expectancy has declined dramatically over the last 15 years, largely owing to the huge number of people in the country with HIV. In 2007, 23·2% of all adults between 15 and 49 were infected with HIV. Infant mortality, 2005, 102 per 1,000 live births; fertility rate, 2004, 3·5 births per woman.

CLIMATE

A healthy and pleasant climate, with variable rainfall, but averaging 29" (725 mm) a year over most of the country. The rain falls mainly in the summer months of Oct. to April, while the winters are dry and may produce heavy frosts in lowland areas and frequent snow in the highlands. Temperatures in the lowlands range from a maximum of 90°F (32·2°C) in summer to a minimum of 20°F (–6·7°C) in winter.

CONSTITUTION AND GOVERNMENT

Lesotho is a constitutional monarchy with the King as Head of State. Following the death of his father, Moshoeshoe II, **Letsie III** succeeded to the throne in Jan. 1996.

The 1993 constitution provided for a *National Assembly* comprising an elected 80-member lower house and a *Senate* of 22 principal chiefs and 11 members nominated by the King. For the elections of May 2002 a new voting system was introduced, increasing the number of seats in the National Assembly to 120, elected for a five-year term as before, but with 80 members in single-seat constituencies and 40 elected by proportional representation.

National Anthem

'Lesotho fatsela bontat'a rona' ('Lesotho, land of our fathers'); words by F. Coillard, tune by L. Laur.

RECENT ELECTIONS

Following the elections of May 1998 the King swore allegiance to a new constitution and the Military Council was dissolved.

Parliamentary elections were held on 17 Feb. 2007. The ruling Lesotho Congress for Democracy (LCD) won 61 seats (all in single-seat constituencies), National Independent Party 21 (all through proportional representation), All Basotho Convention 17, Lesotho Workers' Party 10, Alliance of Congress Parties 4, Basotho National Party 3, Basotho Democratic National Party 1, Basotho Batho Democratic Party 1, Popular Front for Democracy 1.

CURRENT ADMINISTRATION

In March 2010 the Council of Ministers comprised:

Prime Minister, Minister of Defence and National Security: Pakalitha Bethuel Mosisili; b. 1945 (LCD; sworn in 29 May 1998).

Deputy Prime Minister and Minister for Home Affairs, Public Safety and Parliamentary Affairs: Archibald Lesao Lehola. *Minister for Justice and Human Rights, and Law and Constitutional Affairs:* Mpeo Mahase. *Education and Training:* Mamphono Khaketla. *Foreign Affairs:* Mohlabi Tsekoa. *Finance and Development Planning:* Timothy Thahane. *Employment and Labour:* Refiloe Masemene. *Local Government:* Dr Pontso Suzan Matumelo Sekatle. *Gender, Youth and Sports:* Mathabiso Lepono. *Industry, Trade and Marketing:* Popane Lebesa. *Health and Social Welfare:* Dr Mphu Ramatlapeng. *Tourism and Culture:* Lebohang Ntsinyi. *Communications, Science and Technology:* Mothejoa Metsing. *Natural Resources:* Monyane Moleleki. *Public Service:* Semano Sekatle. *Public Works and Transport:* Tsele Chakela. *Agriculture and Food Security:* Lesole Mokoma. *Forestry and Land Reclamation:* Ralechate 'Mokose. *Minister in the Prime Minister's Office:* Motloheloa Phooko.

The *College of Chiefs* settles the recognition and succession of Chiefs and adjudicates cases of inefficiency, criminality and absenteeism among them.

Government Website: http://www.lesotho.gov.ls

CURRENT LEADERS

Pakalitha Bethuel Mosisili

Position

Prime Minister

Introduction

Pakalitha Bethuel Mosisili became prime minister in May 1998 after leading the Lesotho Congress for Democracy (LCD) to electoral victory. The win was contested by the opposition, resulting in widespread protests and rioting. At the elections of May 2002 Mosisili was confirmed as prime minister despite a parliamentary split led by former deputy Kelebone Maope. The LCD also won the election of Feb. 2007.

Early Life

Pakalitha Bethuel Mosisili was born on 14 March 1945 in the Qacha's Nek District in Lesotho. He attended the University of Botswana, Lesotho and Swaziland (UBLS) from 1966–70, gaining a BA and a teaching qualification. He studied for an MA at the University of Wisconsin from 1975–76, before claiming a further BA from the University of South Africa (1977–78). In 1982 he gained a masters in education from the Simon Fraser University in Canada.

In 1967, whilst at UBLS, Mosisili joined the Basutoland Congress Party (BCP) and was an active member of its youth league. In 1970 he was detained under emergency regulations and sent to a maximum-security prison for 16 months.

Mosisili's political career began in 1993 when he was elected to parliament representing Qacha's Nek. He was appointed minister of education and training, sports, culture and youth affairs. In Feb. 1995 he became deputy prime minister following the death of Selometsi Baholo the previous year. He took responsibility for the home affairs and local government portfolios, a role he retained until the 1998 elections. In Feb. 1998 he succeeded Prime Minister Dr Ntsu Mokhele as leader of the LCD.

Career in Office

The victory of the LCD at the elections of May 1998 led to opposition accusations of vote rigging. Mass rioting culminated in protesters seizing the palace grounds. Mosisili called on the Southern African Development Community (SADC) for military assistance to prevent a coup and troops remained in Lesotho until May 1999. In 2001 the government charged 33 protest leaders with treason. The SADC continued to provide military support and was again called in when, following the LCD's re-election in 2002, the Basotho National Party (BNP) contested the government's legitimacy and stability. In April 2004 the first local elections since independence were held but were boycotted by the opposition in protest at Mosisili's rule.

Mosisili pledged to tackle Lesotho's severe food shortages, high unemployment rates and rapidly escalating HIV/AIDS problem. However, poverty remained far reaching and food output was affected by deaths of farmers from AIDS and by long periods of severe weather. In Feb. 2004 Mosisili declared a state of emergency and requested international food aid, announcing that hundreds of thousands faced shortages following three years of drought. In March 2004 the first phase of the Lesotho Highlands Water Project was opened, with the long-term aim of supplying water to large areas of southern Africa. During its building, Mosisili called for charges of corruption to be brought against several Western construction companies accused of bribery.

Mosisili has aimed to tackle unemployment by encouraging foreign investment, emphasizing Lesotho's low corporate tax rates and eager work-force. However, thousands were left unemployed when the textile industry collapsed after the WTO scrapped the global textile quota system in Jan. 2005. He has also sought to diversify the economy, focusing on mining and electronics and industrial equipment manufactures.

In 2003, Lesotho hosted an SADC conference on the problem of AIDS in southern Africa. Mosisili campaigned for nationwide testing (taking a public test himself in 2004), the establishment of regional anti-retroviral clinics and a national AIDS commission. In Sept. 2005 he called on the UN to give the same attention to southern Africa's HIV/AIDS plight as to global security.

In April 2005 the government, unable to finance home connections to the national electricity network, decided to privatize the electricity system. The decision followed the government's privatization of its telecommunications system in 2000.

In Nov. 2006 Mosisili dissolved parliament following a split in the ruling LCD in which some 18 parliamentary deputies left the party to form an opposition All Basotho Convention (ABC). The LCD won the election of Feb. 2007, although with a smaller majority than in 2002.

In April 2009 Mosisili survived an apparent assassination attempt by gunmen in the capital, Maseru.

DEFENCE

South African and Batswanan troops intervened after a mutiny by Lesotho's armed forces in Sept. 1998. The foreign forces were withdrawn in May 1999.

The Royal Lesotho Defence Force has about 2,000 personnel. Defence expenditure totalled US$33m. in 2006 (US$16 per capita), representing 2·3% of GDP.

INTERNATIONAL RELATIONS

Lesotho is a member of the UN, World Bank and several other UN specialized agencies, WTO, the Commonwealth, African

Development Bank, African Union, SADC and is an ACP member state of the ACP-EU relationship.

ECONOMY

In 2006 agriculture accounted for 16·3% of GDP, industry 43·2% and services 40·5%.

Overview

Lesotho's economy is heavily integrated with that of South Africa. Its only significant natural resource is water, exported to South Africa via the Lesotho Highlands Water Project. Subsistence agriculture dominates the economy and the garment sector also has a significant role in generating employment and exports. Imports account for roughly 90% of GDP, with the economy heavily dependent on Southern African Customs Union (SACU) receipts and workers' remittances. Lesotho is a member of the Common Monetary Area together with South Africa, Namibia and Swaziland.

Following several sluggish years, recent macroeconomic growth has been strong, with real GDP rising by 7·2% in 2006, owing to booming diamond production, a recovery in the garment sector and positive performance in the agriculture and service industries. Inflation has been rising since late 2006 as a consequence of rising fuel and food prices but was still in single figures in Aug. 2008. High SACU receipts have resulted in a record fiscal surplus, an improved current account, lower public debt and an increase in international reserves to the equivalent of five months of imports.

Although the outlook is positive there are uncertainties over the continued level of SACU revenues and remittances. The economy needs sustained and broad-based growth and the acceleration of structural reforms to help reduce poverty (57% of households in 2002–03).

Currency

The unit of currency is the *loti* (plural *maloti*) (LSL) of 100 *lisente*, at par with the South African rand, which is legal tender. Total money supply in July 2005 was 1,659m. maloti and foreign exchange reserves were US$539m. Inflation was 8·0% in 2007 and 10·7% in 2008.

Budget

The fiscal year is 1 April–31 March. Revenues in 2004–05 were 4,080m. maloti and expenditures 3,762m. maloti.

VAT of 14% was introduced in 2003.

Performance

Real GDP growth was 5·1% in 2007 and 3·5% in 2008. Total GDP in 2008 was US$1·6bn.

Banking and Finance

The Central Bank of Lesotho (*Governor*, Moeketsi Senaoana) is the bank of issue, founded in 1982 to succeed the Lesotho Monetary Authority. There are three commercial banks (Lesotho Bank, Nedbank Lesotho, Standard Bank Lesotho) and one development bank (Lesotho Building Finance Corp.). Savings deposits totalled 342·8m. maloti in 1993.

ENERGY AND NATURAL RESOURCES

Environment

Lesotho's carbon dioxide emissions from the consumption and flaring of fossil fuels in 2008 were the equivalent of 0·1 tonnes per capita.

Electricity

Capacity (1993) 13,400 kW (98% supplied by South Africa). Consumption in 1996 was 335m. kWh.

Minerals

Diamonds are the main product; 2003 output was about 2,099 carats. Gravel and crushed rock production, 389,695 cu. metres (2003).

Agriculture

Agriculture employs two-thirds of the workforce. The chief crops were (2002 production in 1,000 tonnes): maize, 108; potatoes, 90; wheat, 45; sorghum, 38; dry beans, 7. Soil conservation and the improvement of crops and pasture are matters of vital importance. In 2002 there were an estimated 330,000 ha. of arable land and 4,000 ha. of permanent crop land. There were 2,000 tractors in 2002.

Livestock (2003 estimates): sheep, 850,000; cattle, 540,000; goats, 650,000; asses, 154,000; horses, 100,000; chickens, 2m.

Forestry

In 2005 Lesotho's total forest area was 8,000 ha., or 0·3% of the land area. Timber production was 2·07m. cu. metres in 2007.

Fisheries

The catch in 2005 was 45 tonnes, exclusively from inland waters.

INDUSTRY

Important industries are food products, beverages, textiles and chemical products.

Labour

The labour force in 1996 was 847,000 (63% males). In 1998, 76,100 were working in mines in South Africa.

INTERNATIONAL TRADE

Lesotho is a member of the Southern African Customs Union (SACU) with Botswana, Namibia, South Africa and Swaziland. Foreign debt was US$690m. in 2005.

Imports and Exports

In 2006 imports (f.o.b.) were valued at US$1,360·8m. and exports (f.o.b.) at US$693·6m.

Principal exports in 1993 (in 1,000 maloti): machinery and transport equipment, 25,540; wool, 16,853; manufactures, 13,426; cattle, 8,409; mohair, 5,131; canned vegetables, 2,275; wheat flour, 1,717.

The bulk of international trade is with South Africa. In 2001 SACU member countries accounted for 82·8% of imports and 37·0% of exports.

COMMUNICATIONS

Roads

The road network in 2002 totalled 7,091 km, of which 19·8% were paved. In 2002 there were 4,800 passenger cars (2·1 per 1,000 inhabitants) plus 13,000 trucks and vans. In 2007 there were 402 deaths as a result of road accidents.

Rail

A branch line built by the South African Railways, one mile long, connects Maseru with the Bloemfontein–Natal line at Marseille for transport of cargo.

Civil Aviation

There are direct flights from Maseru to Johannesburg. In 2000 Maseru handled 28,613 passengers (28,503 on international flights).

Telecommunications

Lesotho had 293,000 telephone subscribers in 2005, or 163·2 for every 1,000 persons. Mobile phones have been available since 1996 and in 2005 there were 245,100 subscribers. There were 43,000 internet users in 2004.

Postal Services

In 2003 there were 153 post offices.

SOCIAL INSTITUTIONS

Justice

The legal system is based on Roman-Dutch law. The Lesotho High Court and the Court of Appeal are situated in Maseru, and there are Magistrates' Courts in the districts. 5,888 criminal offences were reported in 1993.

The population in penal institutions in 2002 was 3,000 (143 per 100,000 of national population).

Education

Education levels: pre-school, 3 to 5 years; first level (elementary), 6 to 12; second level (secondary or teacher training or technical training), 7 to 13; third level (university or teacher training college). Free primary education was introduced in 2000. Lesotho has the highest proportion of female pupils at secondary schools in Africa, with 56% in 2007. In 2006 there were 424,855 pupils in primary schools with 10,513 teaching staff, 93,996 pupils in secondary schools with 3,725 teaching staff, and 8,500 students in higher education with 638 academic staff. The National University of Lesotho was established in 1975 at Roma; enrolment in 2006–07, 8,566 students. There are eight government-supported technical and vocational training institutions as well as a teacher-training college, the Lesotho College of Education. The adult literacy rate in 2003 was 81·4% (73·7% among males but 90·3% among females). Lesotho has the biggest difference in literacy rates between the sexes in favour of females of any country in the world, and the highest female literacy rate in Africa.

In 2005 public expenditure on education came to 13·8% of GDP and 29·8% of total government spending (one of the highest percentages of any country).

Health

In 1995 there were 105 physicians, 10 dentists, 1,169 nurses and 914 midwives. There were 2,400 hospital beds, equivalent to one bed per 765 persons, in 1992.

RELIGION

In 2001 there were 0·82m. Roman Catholics, 0·28m. Protestants, 0·26m. African Christians and the remainder followed other religions.

CULTURE

Broadcasting

Radio Lesotho and Lesotho Television (LTV) are the national state-owned stations. The broadcasting authority is the Lesotho National Broadcasting Service. The first licenses for private radio transmissions were issued in 1998. In 2003 there were 80,000 TV sets (colour by PAL).

Press

There were 15 non-daily newspapers and periodicals in 2005. There are no daily newspapers.

Tourism

In 2005 there were 304,000 non-resident visitors; spending by tourists totalled US$30m. (excluding passenger transport).

Festivals

The Morija Arts & Cultural Festival is held annually at Morija, where missionaries first arrived in Lesotho in 1833.

DIPLOMATIC REPRESENTATIVES

Of Lesotho in the United Kingdom (7 Chesham Pl., Belgravia, London, SW1 8HN)
High Commissioner: Prince Seeiso Bereng Seeiso.

Of the United Kingdom in Lesotho (High Commission in Maseru closed in Aug. 2005)
High Commissioner: Dr Nicola Brewer (resides in Pretoria, South Africa).

Of Lesotho in the USA (2511 Massachusetts Ave., NW, Washington, D.C., 20008)
Ambassador: David Mohlomi Rantekoa.

Of the USA in Lesotho (254 Kingsway Ave., Maseru 100)
Ambassador: Robert Nolan.

Of Lesotho to the United Nations
Ambassador: Motlatsi Ramafole.

Of Lesotho to the European Union
Ambassador: Mamoruti Tiheli.

FURTHER READING

Bureau of Statistics. *Statistical Reports.* [Various years]

Haliburton, G. M., *A Historical Dictionary of Lesotho.* 1977
Machobane, L. B. B. J., *Government and Change in Lesotho, 1880–1966: A Study of Political Institutions.* 1990
Rosenberg, Scott, Weisfelder, Richard F. and Frisbie-Fulton, Michelle, (eds.) *Historical Dictionary of Lesotho.* 2003

National Statistical Office: Bureau of Statistics, PO Box 455, Maseru 100.
Website: http://www.bos.gov.ls

LIBERIA

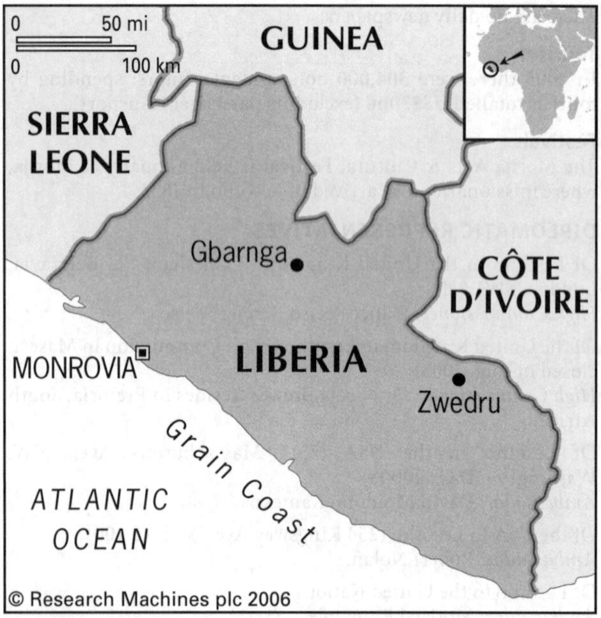

Republic of Liberia

Capital: Monrovia
Population estimate, 2010: 4·10m.
GDP per capita, 2007: (PPP$) 362
HDI/world rank: 0·442/169

KEY HISTORICAL EVENTS

The Republic of Liberia was created on the Grain Coast for freed American slaves. In 1822 a settlement was formed near the spot where Monrovia now stands. On 26 July 1847 the state was constituted as the Free and Independent Republic of Liberia.

On 12 April 1980 President Tolbert was assassinated and his government overthrown in a coup led by Master-Sergeant Samuel Doe. At the beginning of 1990 rebel forces entered Liberia from the north and fought their way successfully southwards to confront President Doe's forces in Monrovia. The rebels comprised the National Patriotic Front of Liberia (NPFL) led by Charles Taylor, and the hostile breakaway Independent National Patriotic Front led by Prince Johnson. A peacekeeping force dispatched by the Economic Community of West African States (ECOWAS) disembarked at Monrovia on 25 Aug. 1990. On 9 Sept. President Doe was assassinated by Johnson's rebels. ECOWAS installed a provisional government led by Amos Sawyer. Charles Taylor declared himself president, as did the former vice-president, Harry Moniba. A succession of ceasefires was negotiated and broken. An ECOWAS-sponsored peace agreement was signed on 17 Aug. 1996 in Abuja, providing for the disarmament of all factions by the end of Jan. 1997 and the election of a president on 31 May 1997. By the end of Jan. 1997 some 20,000 out of approximately 60,000 insurgents had surrendered their arms. It is estimated that up to 200,000 people died in the civil war and up to 1m. were made homeless. Charles Taylor was elected president in July 1997. In Feb. 2002 Taylor declared a state of emergency after an attack by a group of rebels on the town of Kley, where thousands of refugees from Sierra Leone were encamped.

In Aug. 2003 the UN called for the immediate deployment of an ECOWAS peacekeeping force, to be replaced by a full UN force on 1 Oct. Nigerian peacekeepers arrived on 4 Aug. 2003. Taylor relinquished power to his vice-president, Moses Blah, and to a transitional government on 11 Aug. In Nov. 2005 Ellen Johnson-Sirleaf won presidential elections to become Africa's first elected female head of state.

TERRITORY AND POPULATION

Liberia is bounded in the northwest by Sierra Leone, north by Guinea, east by Côte d'Ivoire and southwest by the Atlantic ocean. The total area is 97,036 sq. km. At the last census, in 2008, the population was 3,476,608; density, 36 per sq. km. The United Nations population estimate for 2008 was 3,793,000.

The UN gives an estimated population for 2010 of 4·10m.

In 2007, 59·5% of the population lived in urban areas. English is the official language spoken by 20% of the population. The rest belong in the main to three linguistic groups: Mande, West Atlantic and the Kwa. These are in turn subdivided into 16 ethnic groups: Bassa, Bella, Gbandi, Mende, Gio, Dey, Mano, Gola, Kpelle, Kissi, Krahn, Kru, Lorma, Mandingo, Vai and Grebo.

The population of Monrovia the capital was 970,824 in 2008 including its suburbs.

There are 15 counties, whose areas, populations and capitals are as follows:

County	*Sq. km*	*2008 population*	*Chief town*
Bomi	1,942	84,119	Tubmanburg
Bong	8,769	333,481	Gbarnga
Gbarpolu	9,685	83,388	Bepolu
Grand Bassa	7,932	221,693	Buchanan
Grand Cape Mount	5,160	127,076	Robertsport
Grand Gedeh	10,480	125,258	Zwedru
Grand Kru	3,894	57,913	Barclayville
Lofa	9,978	276,863	Voinjama
Margibi	2,615	209,923	Kakata
Maryland	2,296	135,938	Harper
Montserrado	1,908	1,118,241	Bensonville
Nimba	11,546	462,026	Saniquillie
River Cess	5,592	71,509	Cesstos City
River Gee	5,110	66,789	Fish Town
Sinoe	10,133	102,391	Greenville

SOCIAL STATISTICS

1997 births, estimate, 110,000; deaths, 30,000. 1997 rates (per 1,000 population), estimate: birth, 42·3; death, 11·5. Annual population growth rate, 1992–2002, 4·3% (the highest of any sovereign country). Life expectancy at birth (2007): 56·5 years for men and 59·3 years for women. Infant mortality in 2005 was among the highest in the world, at 157 per 1,000 live births. Fertility rate, 2004, 6·8 births per woman.

CLIMATE

An equatorial climate, with constant high temperatures and plentiful rainfall, although Jan. to May is drier than the rest of the year. Monrovia, Jan. 79°F (26·1°C), July 76°F (24·4°C). Annual rainfall 206" (5,138 mm).

CONSTITUTION AND GOVERNMENT

A constitution was approved by referendum in July 1984 and came into force on 6 Jan. 1986. Under it the National Assembly consisted of a 26-member Senate and a 64-member House of Representatives. For the elections of Oct. 2005 the number of seats in the Senate was increased to 30.

National Anthem

'All hail, Liberia, hail!'; words by President Daniel Warner, tune by O. Luca.

RECENT ELECTIONS

Presidential and parliamentary elections were held on 11 Oct. 2005. In the presidential elections George Weah of the Congress for Democratic Change (CDC) received 28·3% of the votes cast, ahead of Ellen Johnson-Sirleaf of the Unity Party (UP) with 19·8%, Charles Brumskine of the Liberal Party (LP) with 13·9%, Winston Tubman of the National Democratic Party of Liberia with 9·2% and Varney Sherman of the Coalition for the Transformation of Liberia (COTOL) with 7·8%. There were 17 other candidates. Turnout was 74·9%. As a result a second round run-off was needed, in which Ellen Johnson-Sirleaf received 59·6% of the vote on 8 Nov. 2005 against 40·4% for George Weah. Turnout was 61·0%.

In the elections to the House of Representatives on 11 Oct. 2005 the CDC won 15 of 64 seats, and 3 of 30 Senate seats. The LP won 9 seats (and 3 in the Senate); the UP 8 (3 in the Senate), COTOL 8 (7 in the Senate), the Alliance for Peace and Democracy (APD) 5 (3 in the Senate), and the National Patriotic Party (NPP) 4 (4 in the Senate). Other parties won three seats or fewer in the House of Representatives and two seats or fewer in the Senate.

CURRENT ADMINISTRATION

President: Ellen Johnson-Sirleaf; b. 1938 (Unity Party; sworn in 16 Jan. 2006).

In March 2010 the government comprised:

Vice President: Joseph Boakai.

Minister of Agriculture: Florence Chenoweth. *Commerce:* Miatta Beysolow. *Defence:* Brownie Samukai. *Education:* Dr Joseph Korto. *Finance:* Augustine Kpehe Ngafuan. *Foreign Affairs:* Olubanke King-Akerele. *Gender Development:* Varbah Gayflor. *Health and Social Welfare:* Dr Walter Gwenigale. *Information, Culture and Tourism:* Vacant. *Internal Affairs:* Vacant. *Justice:* Christiana Tah. *Labour:* Taiwon Gongloe. *Land, Mines and Energy:* Dr Eugene Shannon. *National Security:* Vacant. *Planning and Economic Affairs:* Amara Konneh. *Posts and Telecommunications:* Jeremiah Sulunteh. *Public Works:* Samuel Kofi Woods. *Transport:* Alphonso Gaye. *Youth and Sports:* Etmonia Tarpeh.

Government Website: http://www.emansion.gov.lr

CURRENT LEADERS

Ellen Johnson-Sirleaf

Position
President

Introduction
Ellen Johnson-Sirleaf became Africa's first elected female president in Jan. 2006, having defeated the former footballer, George Weah, in a run-off. A US-educated economist, she returned from exile to attempt to resurrect Liberia's shattered economy after 14 years of civil war.

Early Life
Ellen Johnson-Sirleaf was born in Monrovia, Liberia on 29 Oct. 1938. She was educated at the College of West Africa in Monrovia from 1948–55, before graduating in accountancy in 1964 from the University of Wisconsin in the USA. From 1967 she served as special assistant to the secretary of the treasury in Liberia before undertaking an MA in public administration at America's Harvard University from 1969–71. Returning to Liberia, Johnson-Sirleaf became assistant minister of finance in the administration of William R. Tolbert, Jr. Following public criticisms of Tolbert's presidency she resigned and left the country, taking up a post as a loan officer for several Latin American countries at the World Bank. In 1977 she was invited to return home to become deputy minister of finance for fiscal and banking affairs. In Aug. 1979 she replaced James T. Philips as minister of finance.

Shortly after a coup d'état and Tolbert's assassination on 12 April 1980, the new military leader, Sgt Samuel Doe, appointed Johnson-Sirleaf president of the Liberia Bank for Development and Investment. However, she resigned in Dec. 1980 and returned to the World Bank, before becoming vice president of Citibank in Nairobi, Kenya in mid-1981. She stood in Liberia's general elections in Oct. 1985, at which Doe was controversially elected president. Johnson-Sirleaf was elected senator but was sentenced to ten years in jail as part of Doe's crackdown on 'opponents' following a failed coup in Nov. 1985. Pardoned and released in June 1986, she again left Liberia for the USA, where she worked for the Equator Bank in Washington, D.C., followed by the UN Development Programme (UNDP) in New York.

While in the USA, Johnson-Sirleaf joined other Liberian exiles in criticizing Doe and helped raise funds for a fellow exile, Charles Taylor, to lead the National Patriotic Front of Liberia (NPFL) into Liberia from the Côte d'Ivoire in 1989. It triggered a devastating civil war that led to the deaths of over 200,000 people by the time a ceasefire was declared in Aug. 1996. Disillusioned with Taylor, Johnson-Sirleaf resigned as director of the UNDP's Bureau for Africa (a post she held from July 1992) and stood against him on behalf of the Unity Party in presidential elections in 1997. She received only 10% of the vote (against 75% for Taylor) and was later charged with treason by him. Forced into exile again, she became active in various humanitarian projects, including investigations into the 1994 Rwandan genocide for the Organization for African Unity and serving on the board of the International Crisis Group and the Nelson Mandela Foundation. Liberia again descended into civil war but Johnson-Sirleaf returned after Taylor was forced into exile in Aug. 2003. She headed the governance reform commission until resigning in March 2005 to enter the presidential race.

During her campaign, Johnson-Sirleaf criticized the transitional government's inability to fight corruption. She went through to a run-off against George Weah, a former World Footballer of the Year who was representing the Congress for Democratic Change, and on 11 Nov. the national elections commission declared Johnson-Sirleaf the winner. Although Weah accused her of fraud, her victory was confirmed on 23 Nov. Independent observers declared the vote to be free, fair and transparent and her inauguration took place on 16 Jan. 2006.

Career in Office
In her inaugural speech, Johnson-Sirleaf vowed to wage a war on corruption, promising that leading civil servants and ministers would have to declare their assets. She also pledged to work towards reconciliation by bringing former opponents into a government of national unity, and spoke of establishing peaceful relations with neighbouring West African states. She appointed a number of women to ministerial positions and controversially nominated a Nigerian soldier to head Liberia's army. While rebuilding the country's shattered economy—with a road network in ruins, no national telephone network, no national electricity grid and no piped water—has remained a major challenge, the World Bank and other international bodies have praised her government's efforts in office. A Truth and Reconciliation Commission was inaugurated with a mandate to investigate human rights abuses during the long civil war, and she has made progress in confronting poor governance and corrupt officialdom.

DEFENCE

In June 2003 UN Secretary-General Kofi Annan called for an international peacekeeping force to restore peace after fighting broke out between government forces and Liberians United for Reconciliation and Democracy (LURD). An ECOWAS peacekeeping force of over 3,000 troops was deployed initially, but this has been replaced by the UN Peacekeeping Mission in Liberia (UNMIL), totalling 10,947 uniformed personnel in Dec. 2009.

The Armed Forces of Liberia were created in 2007 to replace the Liberian Army, which was demobilized in 1999. In 2009 there were approximately 2,100 troops although they are not expected to be fully operational until late 2010.

Defence expenditure totalled US$45m. in 2003 (US$13 per capita), representing 11·4% of GDP.

INTERNATIONAL RELATIONS

Liberia is a member of the UN, World Bank, IMF and several other UN specialized agencies, IOM, African Development Bank, African Union, ECOWAS and is an ACP member state of the ACP-EU relationship.

ECONOMY

Agriculture accounted for 54% of GDP in 2007 (one of the highest proportions of any country), industry 19% and services 27%.

Overview

After years of civil war when much of the economy's human and physical capital was destroyed, post-war reconstruction has accelerated. On the basis of its Poverty Reduction Strategy Paper, the government has made progress in repaying long-standing arrears to the World Bank and African Development Bank, strengthening public revenues and public finance management and improving institutional governance. The international community has provided financial support, estimated by the IMF at US$85–100 per capita.

Real GDP growth rose to 9·5% in 2007 from a level of 8% in 2006, supported by continued recovery in agriculture as well as mining and other services. However, the country remains one of the world's poorest (per capita GDP was estimated at US$195 per capita in 2007) with growth still below pre-war levels. Short-term prospects are favourable but with downside risks arising from a fall in global commodity prices. Inflation remains high and the external current account deficit large.

Currency

US currency is legal tender. There is a *Liberian dollar* (LRD), in theory at parity with the US dollar. Between 1993 and March 2000 different notes were in use in government-held Monrovia and the rebel-held country areas, but on 27 March 2000 a set of new notes went into circulation to end the years of trading in dual banknotes. Inflation was 13·7% in 2007 and 17·5% in 2008. Total money supply was L$4,316m. in July 2005 and foreign exchange reserves were US$21m.

Budget

Revenue in 2007 was L$10,222m.; expenditure was L$9,498m. Customs and excise duties accounted for 44·3% of revenues in 2007; general administration accounted for 41·5% of expenditures.

Performance

Real GDP growth was 9·4% in 2007 and 7·1% in 2008. Total GDP was US$0·9bn. in 2008.

Banking and Finance

The National Bank of Liberia opened on 22 July 1974 to act as a central bank. The *Governor* of the bank is Joseph Mills Jones. There were only three banks in operation in Jan. 2004.

ENERGY AND NATURAL RESOURCES

Environment

Liberia's carbon dioxide emissions from the consumption and flaring of fossil fuels were the equivalent of 0·2 tonnes per capita in 2008.

Electricity

Installed capacity in 2004 was estimated at 0·2m. kW. Production in 2004 was 330m. kWh. Consumption per capita in 2004 was 118 kWh.

Minerals

2005 estimates: gold production 16 kg and diamond production 30,000 carats.

Agriculture

In 2007 the agricultural population was approximately 2·31m., of which about 853,000 were economically active. There were an estimated 385,000 ha. of arable land in 2007 and 215,000 ha. of permanent crops. Principal crops (2003 estimates) in 1,000 tonnes: cassava, 480; sugarcane, 255; bananas, 110; rice, 110; rubber, 108; palm oil, 42; plantains, 40; taro, 26; yams, 20. Coffee, cocoa and palm kernels are produced mainly by the traditional agricultural sector.

Livestock (2003 estimates): cattle, 36,000; pigs, 130,000; sheep, 210,000; goats, 220,000; chickens, 6m.

Livestock products (2003 estimates) in tonnes: meat, 23,000; milk, 1,000; eggs, 4,000.

Forestry

Forest area was 3·15m. ha. (32·7% of the land area) in 2005. In 2007, 6·62m. cu. metres of roundwood were cut. There are rubber plantations.

Fisheries

Fish landings in 2004 were 10,359 tonnes, of which approximately 61% from sea fishing.

INDUSTRY

There are a number of small factories. Production of cement, cigarettes, soft drinks, palm oil and beer are the main industries.

Labour

In 1996 the labour force was 977,000 (61% males).

INTERNATIONAL TRADE

Foreign debt was US$2,581m. in 2005.

Imports and Exports

Imports in 2004 were US$268·1m. and exports US$103·8m. Main import sources in 2004 were South Korea, 38·1%; Japan, 21·9%; Singapore, 12·6%. Major export destinations in 2004 were the USA, 61·4%; Belgium, 29·5%; China, 5·3%.

Main imports are food and live animals, petroleum and petroleum products, and machinery and transport equipment. Main exports are rubber, and logs and timber.

COMMUNICATIONS

Roads

There were about 10,600 km of roads in 2002 (only 6·2% of which were paved). In 2007 there were 7,400 passenger cars in use and 2,800 lorries and vans.

Rail

There is a total of 490 km single track. A 148-km freight line connects iron mines to Monrovia. There is a line from Bong to Monrovia (78 km). The railways were out of use for many years because of the civil wars but there is now some traffic, both freight and passenger. However, large sections of track have been dismantled.

Civil Aviation

There are two international airports (Roberts International and Sprigg Payne), both near Monrovia. In 2003 there were services to Abidjan, Accra, Brussels, Freetown and Lagos.

Shipping

There are ports at Buchanan, Greenville, Harper and Monrovia. Over 2,000 vessels enter Monrovia each year. The Liberian government requires only a modest registration fee and an almost nominal annual charge and maintains no control over the operation of ships flying the Liberian flag. In 2004 shipping registered totalled 53·90m. GRT (second only to Panama), including oil tankers 21·09m. GRT. In 2000 the fleet consisted of 1,557 vessels of 100 GRT or over, including 585 tankers.

Telecommunications

In 2008 Liberia had just 2,000 main (fixed) telephone lines, but there were 732,000 mobile phone subscribers. No other country has such a high ratio of mobile phone subscriptions to fixed telephone lines. There were 20,000 internet users in 2007.

Postal Services

In 2006 there were 18 post offices.

SOCIAL INSTITUTIONS

Justice

Liberia is governed by a dual system of statutory law. The modern sector is regulated by Anglo-American common law with the indigenous sector following customary law based on unwritten tribal practices. Following a 2003 proposal by UNMIL (United Nations Mission in Liberia), a scheme to rebuild the post civil war justice system was introduced. However, reforms are progressing at a slow rate and the judiciary remains severely dysfunctional.

Education

Schools are classified as: (1) Public schools, maintained and run by the government; (2) Mission schools, supported by foreign Missions and subsidized by the government, and operated by qualified Missionaries and Liberian teachers; (3) Private schools, maintained by endowments and sometimes subsidized by the government.

Adult literacy in 2004 was 51·9%.

Health

In 2004 there were 103 physicians (approximately one for every 33,300 inhabitants), 13 dentists, 613 nurses, 422 midwives and 35 pharmacists. The John F. Kennedy Memorial Hospital in Monrovia is the country's leading health care institution.

RELIGION

There were (2001) about 1·27m. Christians and 520,000 Sunni Muslims, plus 1·39m. followers of traditional beliefs.

CULTURE

Broadcasting

There is one state-run radio service and several private television and community radio stations. In 2001 there were 69,000 television receivers (colour by PAL).

Press

There were six paid-for daily newspapers in 2006 with a combined circulation of 50,000.

DIPLOMATIC REPRESENTATIVES

Of Liberia in the United Kingdom (23 Fitzroy Sq., London, W1T 6EW)
Ambassador: Wesley Momo Johnson.

Of the United Kingdom in Liberia
Ambassador: Ian Hughes (resides in Freetown, Sierra Leone).

Of Liberia in the USA (5201 16th St., NW, Washington, D.C., 20011)
Ambassador: Milton Nathaniel Barnes.

Of the USA in Liberia (111 United Nations Drive, Mamba Point, Monrovia)
Ambassador: Linda Thomas-Greenfield.

Of Liberia to the United Nations
Ambassador: Marjon V. Kamara.

Of Liberia to the European Union
Ambassador: Youngor Telewoda.

FURTHER READING

Daniels, A., *Monrovia Mon Amour: a Visit to Liberia.* 1992
Sawyer, A., *The Emergence of Autocracy in Liberia: Tragedy and Challenge.* 1992

National Statistical Office: The Liberia Institute of Statistics and Geo-Information Services (LISGIS), 9th Street, Sinkor, Monrovia.
Website: http://www.lisgis.org

LIBYA

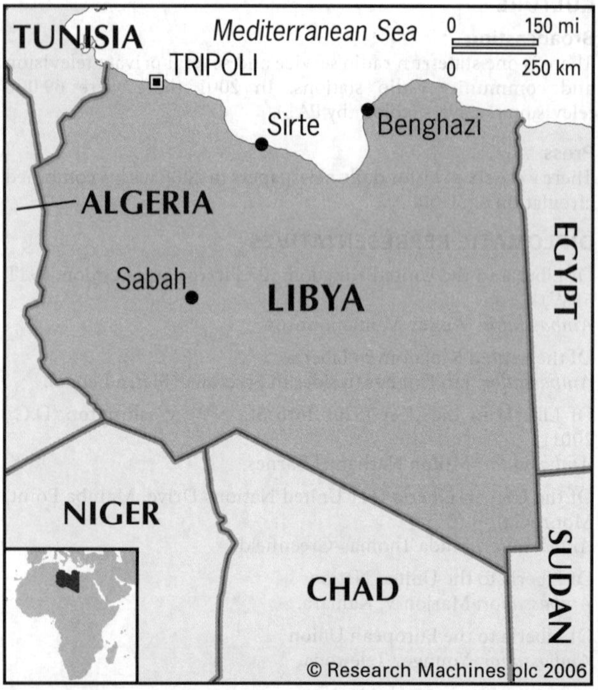

Jamahiriya Al-Arabiya Al-Libiya Al-Shabiya Al-Ishtirakiya Al-Uzma
(Great Socialist People's Libyan Arab Jamahiriya)

Capital: Tripoli
Population estimate, 2010: 6·55m.
GDP per capita, 2007: (PPP$) 14,364
HDI/world rank: 0·847/55

KEY HISTORICAL EVENTS

Libya's earliest inhabitants were the semi-nomadic Berbers, whose descendants still live throughout North Africa's Atlas Mountains. Phoenician merchants from the Levant began to settle in what is today Libya from around 1000 BC and they founded Carthage in what is now Tunisia in 814 BC. Carthage became the leading port in the western Mediterranean, extending its influence over Libya and most of coastal North Africa for the next five centuries. The port of Oea (now Tripoli) was founded by Phoenicians around 500 BC. Greek traders settled in the Cyrenaica region (eastern Libya) in the seventh century BC, founding Cyrene in 630 BC. Roman settlements appeared in Libya in the third century BC, growing in importance following Rome's sacking of Carthage in 146 BC. The port of Leptis Magna was founded in Tripolitania in the first century AD, becoming a major centre of commerce until it fell to the Vandals early in the fifth century.

The first of several waves of Arab conquerors arrived in 630, spreading the Islamic faith, initially along the coastal fringes. Libya became part of the powerful Umayyad and Abbasid Caliphates, the latter centred on Baghdad where it reached its apotheosis under Harun al Rashid (786–809). From 971 until 1045 Libya, along with present-day Algeria and Tunisia, were ruled by the Zirid amirs who were loyal to the Fatimid Caliphs of the Nile Valley. Bedouin Arabs from the Nile Valley, known as the Banu Hilal, entered the region in around 1000 spreading Islam and the Arabic language throughout Libya over the next three centuries.

By the beginning of the 15th century the Libyan, or Barbary, coast had become infamous as a haven for pirates. Habsburg Spain occupied Tripoli in 1510 but it fell to Ottoman corsairs in 1551. Direct control from Istanbul was superseded by rule through local Turkish governors (known as beys). In 1711 Ahmed Karamanli, an Ottoman cavalry officer, seized power and declared Libyan independence. Direct Ottoman rule was re-established in 1835 when Sultan Mahmud II made Libya a province of the Sublime Ports.

On 29 Sept. 1911 Italy declared war on the ailing Ottoman Empire and occupied Tripoli four days later. Italian control was confirmed following the signing of the Treaty of Ouchy in 1912 but local resistance, particularly by the Sanusi Order in Cyrenaica, confined Italian power to the coastal cities of Tripoli, Benghazi, Tobruk and Derna.

During the Second World War the British army expelled the Italians and their German allies, placing Tripolitania and Cyrenaica under British military administration and Fezzan under French control. This continued under a UN directive until 1951 when Libya gained independence. The former Amir of Cyrenaica, Muhammad Idris al Senussi, was crowned king.

The discovery of oil in 1959 brought rapid economic growth but resentment grew as wealth remained in the hands of the elite. Idris was deposed in Sept. 1969 by a group of army officers, 12 of whom formed the Revolutionary Command Council which, chaired by Col. Muammar Qadhafi, proclaimed the Libyan Arab Republic. In 1977 the Revolutionary Command Council was superseded by a more democratic People's Congress, though Qadhafi remained head of state. Throughout the 1980s Libya found itself at odds with its neighbours while deteriorating relations with the USA and other Western countries culminated in the US bombing of Tripoli in April 1986, a punishment for Qadhafi's alleged support of international terrorism. A US trade embargo was also enforced that year.

In 1992 the UN imposed sanctions after Libya refused to surrender suspects in the 1988 bombing of a Pan Am flight over Lockerbie in Scotland. In April 1999 Libya handed over two suspects to face trial under Scottish law in the Netherlands. In Jan. 2001 Abdelbaset Ali Mohmed Al-Megrahi was found guilty of murder and sentenced to life imprisonment. The UN suspended sanctions in 1999 but they were not lifted formally until Sept. 2003. The USA lifted its remaining sanctions in Sept. 2004 after Col. Qadhafi pledged to end his weapons of mass destruction programme. Libya's auction of oil and gas exploration licences in Jan. 2005 led to the return of US energy companies and full diplomatic ties between the two countries were resumed in May 2006.

TERRITORY AND POPULATION

Libya is bounded in the north by the Mediterranean Sea, east by Egypt and Sudan, south by Chad and Niger and west by Algeria and Tunisia. The area is 1,759,540 sq. km. The population at the 2006 census was 5,657,692; density, 3·2 per sq. km. The United Nations population estimate for 2006 was 6,045,000. In 2005, 84·8% of the population lived in urban areas. Ethnic composition, 2000: Libyan Arab and Berber, 64%; other (mainly Egyptians, Sudanese and Chadians), 36%.

The UN gives an estimated population for 2010 of 6·55m.

Libya is divided into 22 municipalities (*sha'biyat*). Capitals and populations (2006 census) were as follows:

	Capital	Population
Al Butnan	Tubruq	157,747
Al Jabal al Akhdar	Al Bayda	206,180
Al Jabal al Gharbi	Gharyan	302,705
Al Jifarah	Al' Aziziyah	451,175
Al Jufrah	Hun	52,092
Al Kufrah	Al Jawf	48,328
Al Marj	Al Marj	184,531
Al Marqab	Al Hums	427,886
Al Wahah	Ajdabiya	179,155
An Nuqat al Khams	Zuwarah	287,359
Ash Shati'	Birat	78,563
Az Zawiyah	Az Zawiyah	290,637
Benghazi	Benghazi	674,951
Darnah	Darnah	162,857
Ghat	Ghat	23,199
Misratah	Misratah	543,129
Murzuq	Murzuq	78,772
Nalut	Nalut	93,896
Sabha	Sabha	133,206
Surt	Surt	141,495
Tarabulus (Tripoli)	Tarabulus (Tripoli)	1,063,571
Wadi al Hayat	Awbari	76,258

The two largest cities are Tripoli, the capital (population of 1,063,571 in 2006), and Benghazi (912,000 in 2000).

The official language is Arabic.

SOCIAL STATISTICS

Estimates, 2001: births, 99,000; deaths, 18,000. Estimated rates, 2001 (per 1,000 population): births, 18·6; deaths, 3·4. Life expectancy (2007), 71·6 years for men and 76·8 for women. Annual population growth rate, 1992–2002, 2·0%; infant mortality, 2005, 18 per 1,000 live births; fertility rate, 2004, 2·9 births per woman.

CLIMATE

The coastal region has a warm temperate climate, with mild wet winters and hot dry summers, although most of the country suffers from aridity. Tripoli, Jan. 52°F (11·1°C), July 81°F (27·2°C). Annual rainfall 16" (400 mm). Benghazi, Jan. 56°F (13·3°C), July 77°F (25°C). Annual rainfall 11" (267 mm).

CONSTITUTION AND GOVERNMENT

The present constitution came into force on 11 Dec. 1969. In 1977 a new form of direct democracy, the state of the masses, was promulgated and the name of the country was changed to Great Socialist People's Libyan Arab Jamahiriya. Under this system, every adult is supposed to be able to share in policy making through the Basic People's Congresses of which there are some 2,000. These Congresses appoint People's Committees to execute policy. Provincial and urban affairs are handled by People's Committees responsible to Municipality People's Congresses, of which there are 22, now called *sha'biyat*. Officials of these Congresses and Committees form at national level the 2,700-member General People's Congress which normally meets for about a week early each year (usually in March). This is the highest policy-making body in the country. The General People's Congress appoints its own General Secretariat and the General People's Committee, whose members (the equivalents of ministers elsewhere) head the government departments which execute policy at national level.

Until 1977 Libya was ruled by a Revolutionary Command Council (RCC) headed by Col. Muammar Qadhafi. Upon its abolition in that year the five surviving members of the RCC became the General Secretariat of the General People's Congress, still under Qadhafi's direction. In 1979 they stood down to be replaced by officials elected by the Congress. Since then, Col. Qadhafi has retained his position as Leader of the Revolution. Neither he nor his former RCC colleagues have any formal posts in the present administration, although they continue to wield considerable authority.

National Anthem

'Allah Akbar' ('God is Great'); words by Abdullah Al-Din, tune by Mahmoud Al-Sharif.

GOVERNMENT CHRONOLOGY

Leaders since 1951.

1951–69 (King) Muhammad Idris I al Senussi

1969– Col. Muammar Abu Minyar al-Qadhafi (Chairman of the Revolutionary Command Council until 1977; General Secretary of the General People's Congress until 1979; *de facto* leader since 1979)

CURRENT ADMINISTRATION

Leader: Col. Muammar Abu Minyar al-Qadhafi; b. 1942 (came to power 1 Sept. 1969).

In March 2010 the Secretariat for the General People's Congress was headed by Mohamed Abdul Quasim al-Zwai.

In March 2010 the General People's Committee comprised:

Secretary: Al-Baghdadi Al-Mahmoudi. *Agriculture, Animal Resources and Marine Resources:* Abou Bakr Mansouri. *Education and Research:* Abdul Kabir Fakhri. *Foreign Liaison and International Co-operation:* Mussa Kussa. *Health and Environment:* Mahmoud Mohammed Hijazi. *Industry, Economy and Trade:* Mohammed Huwaji. *Justice:* Mustapha Abdeljelil. *National Planning:* Bashir Ali Zimbil. *Planning and Finance:* Abdulhafid Mahmoud Zlitni. *Public Security:* Abdel Fatah Yunis Al-Ubaydi. *Public Utilities:* Maatouq M. Maatouq. *Social Affairs:* Ibrahim Cherif. *Transport:* Mohamed Ali Zidan. *Treasury:* Ali Hessnawi.

Government Website (Arabic only): http://www.gpc.gov.ly

CURRENT LEADERS

Col. Muammar Abu Minyar al-Qadhafi

Position
Leader of the Revolution

Introduction
Muammar Qadhafi took power in a military coup against the monarchy in 1969, espousing radical Arab nationalism and Islamic socialist policies. His revolutionary fervour has frequently brought him into conflict with the Western powers, which have held him responsible for acts of international terrorism. There have been improvements in diplomatic and business relations since 2003 as Qadhafi settled the Lockerbie bombing claims and agreed to stop developing weapons of mass destruction.

Early Life
Born into a Bedouin family near Sirte in June 1942, Qadhafi's education was strongly religious and he remains a devout and austere Muslim. He was also influenced in his early life by the Arab nationalist ideology of President Nasser and the Egyptian revolution. In 1965 Qadhafi graduated from the Royal Libyan Military Academy in Benghazi. As he and other officers of like mind rose through the ranks, their radicalism was fuelled by the humiliating defeat of Arab forces by Israel in the Six Day War of 1967. Qadhafi and others in a Revolutionary Command Council (RCC) deposed King Idris on 1 Sept. 1969 in a bloodless coup.

Career in Office
The RCC, with Qadhafi as chairman, instigated a programme of revolutionary reform. British and US military bases in Libya were closed in 1970, foreign-owned oil companies were nationalized and extended welfare provision was funded from oil export revenues. Assuming increasingly dictatorial powers, Qadhafi pursued wider Arab unity, initiating a series of unsuccessful schemes for merging Libya with other Arab countries (including Egypt, Syria, Tunisia, Chad, Morocco and Algeria), while maintaining implacable opposition to Israel. His Islamic socialist ideology was

published in *The Green Book*, and in 1977 he promulgated a new constitution. This established the Great Socialist People's Libyan Arab Jamahiriya, which vested power in the masses through the General People's Congress (GPC). In 1979 Qadhafi relinquished his formal posts in the administration but remained Libya's undisputed leader.

With a reputation in international circles for erratic and unpredictable moves, Qadhafi mobilized Libya's oil wealth in support of revolutionary and terrorist groups around the world, intervening militarily in neighbouring states, particularly Chad. Accusing Qadhafi of sponsoring terrorism, the USA and UK bombed Tripoli and Benghazi in April 1986 in a reprisal air operation. In 1992 United Nations sanctions were imposed on Libya to force the extradition of two Libyan nationals implicated in an aircraft bombing atrocity over Lockerbie in Scotland in Dec. 1988. Qadhafi eventually relented and in 1999 surrendered the two principal suspects for trial in the Netherlands. One of the accused was convicted and sentenced in 2001. In 2003 Libya signed an agreement to compensate families of the Lockerbie bombing victims. Once the Libyan leader formally took responsibility for the atrocity, the UN Security Council voted to lift sanctions. In March 2004 the UK prime minister, Tony Blair, met with Qadhafi following the latter's promise to abandon programmes to develop weapons of mass destruction and to allow weapons inspectors into Libya. Diplomatic links with the USA were restored in May 2006.

In 2006 his unpredictable regime again came under international scrutiny as Libyan courts upheld death sentences on six foreign medical workers charged controversially with infecting hundreds of Libyan children with AIDS. However, the sentences were later commuted to imprisonment before the detainees were freed in July 2007 following diplomatic intervention by the European Union.

Libya's international rehabilitation progressed further in 2008 as the country took over the one-month rotating presidency of the UN Security Council in Jan. and the US Secretary of State made the highest-level US visit to Libya since 1953 in Sept. In Feb. 2009 Qadhafi was elected to chair of the African Union for the year and in June made his first state visit to Italy.

In Aug. 2009 Abdelbaset Ali al-Megrahi, a Libyan national convicted in 2001 for the Lockerbie bombing, was released from prison in Scotland on compassionate grounds (he was suffering from a terminal illness). However, the decision was denounced by the US government and his triumphal return to Libya provoked outrage among the families of the victims of the atrocity.

In Sept. there were national celebrations to mark Qadhafi's 40 years in power in Libya.

DEFENCE

There is selective conscription for one–two years. Defence expenditure in 2006 totalled US$593m. (US$100 per capita), representing 1·1% of GDP.

Nuclear Weapons

In Dec. 2003 Col. Muammar Qadhafi agreed to dismantle his weapons of mass destruction programmes. He also agreed unconditionally to allow inspectors from international organizations to enter Libya.

Army

Strength (2007) 50,000 (including an estimated 25,000 conscripts). In addition there is a People's Militia of some 40,000 that acts as a reserve force.

Navy

The fleet, a mixture of Soviet and West European-built ships, includes two diesel submarines, two frigates and one corvette although serviceability is in doubt. There is a small Naval Aviation wing operating seven helicopters.

Personnel in 2007 totalled 8,000, including coastguard. The main naval bases are at Tripoli, Benghazi, Tubruq and Al Hums.

Air Force

The Air Force has 374 combat capable aircraft, including MiG-21s, MiG-23s, MiG-25s and Mirage F1s, but many are in storage. Personnel total (2007) 18,000.

INTERNATIONAL RELATIONS

Libya is a member of the UN, World Bank, IMF and several other UN specialized agencies, IOM, Islamic Development Bank, OIC, African Development Bank, African Union, COMESA, League of Arab States and OPEC. Libya has declared its desire to join the WTO.

ECONOMY

Petroleum and natural gas accounted for 71·6% of GDP in 2007; public administration, defence and services 6·9%; finance, insurance and real estate 6·2%; and construction 4·3%.

Overview

Libya's economy has struggled to achieve solid growth. The production of hydrocarbons accounts for the majority of the government's revenues and the country's export earnings. Oil accounts for roughly a quarter of GDP although the benefits have not been evenly distributed.

During the first half of the 2000s the economy posted its most solid growth performance in recent history. In 2003 UN sanctions were lifted after Libya admitted complicity in the 1988 Lockerbie aircraft bombing. In 2004 the USA lifted almost all its unilateral sanctions after Libya agreed to give up its nuclear weapons programmes. Libya's improved international standing has allowed investment to flow back into the oil sector.

In Nov. 2003 the government announced a three-part privatization scheme (including the mineral and chemical industries). Since then, real GDP growth has been reasonably robust, reaching 5·6% in 2006. There has been greater contribution from non-oil industries resulting from increased government spending and liberalization of the trade, tourism and service sectors (including the abolition of most of its import monopolies). The authorities' decision to loosen fiscal conditions in the 2007 budget, including an 80% wage increase in the civil service, poses a threat to future macroeconomic stability.

Currency

The unit of currency is the *Libyan dinar* (LYD) of 1,000 *millemes*. The dinar was devalued 15% in Nov. 1994, and alongside the official exchange rate a new rate was applied to private sector imports. Foreign exchange reserves were US$29,315m. in June 2005. Total money supply in May 2005 was 11,552m. dinars. There was inflation of 6·2% in 2007 and 10·4% in 2008.

Budget

In 2005 revenues totalled 37,433m. dinars and expenditures 18,319m. dinars. Oil accounts for 92·9% of government revenues.

Performance

GDP growth was 7·5% in 2007 and 3·4% in 2008. Total GDP in 2008 was US$99·9bn.

Banking and Finance

A National Bank of Libya was established in 1955; it was renamed the Central Bank of Libya in 1972. The *Governor* is Farhat Bengdara. All foreign banks were nationalized by Dec. 1970. In 1972 the government set up the Libyan Arab Foreign Bank whose function is overseas investment and to participate in multinational banking corporations. The Agricultural Bank has been set up to give loans and subsidies to farmers to develop their land and to assist them in marketing their crops. There were 19 banks in total in 2007.

Weights and Measures

Although the metric system has been officially adopted and is obligatory for all contracts, the following weights and measures are still used: *oke* = 1·282 kg; *kantar* = 51·28 kg; *draa* = 46 cm; *handaza* = 68 cm.

ENERGY AND NATURAL RESOURCES

Environment

Libya's carbon dioxide emissions from the consumption and flaring of fossil fuels in 2008 were the equivalent of 9·3 tonnes per capita.

Electricity

Installed capacity in 2004 was an estimated 4·7m. kW. Production was 20·20bn. kWh in 2004 and consumption per capita 3,147 kWh.

Oil and Gas

Oil accounts for 30% of Libya's GDP. Oil production in 2008 totalled 86·2m. tonnes. Proven reserves (2008) 43·7bn. bbls. Some analysts believe total reserves may be as high as 100bn. bbls. The National Oil Corporation (NOC) is the state's organization for the exploitation of oil resources. Libya's first oilfields were discovered in 1959, but the offshore sector remains relatively unexplored although the decision to abandon programmes for developing weapons of mass destruction in 2003 led to greatly increased interest among foreign oil companies. Oil export revenues more than doubled between 1998 and 2003. Production increased by a third between 2002 and 2008.

Proven natural gas reserves totalled 1,540bn. cu. metres in 2008. Agip, the Italian oil company, is investing US$3bn. in a project to export natural gas to Europe. Production (2008), 15·9bn. cu. metres.

Water

Since 1984 a US$20bn. project has been under way to bring water from aquifers underlying the Sahara to the inhabited coastal areas of Libya. This scheme, called the 'Great Man-Made River', is intended, on completion, to bring 6,000 cu. metres of water a day along some 4,000 km of pipes. Phase I was completed in Aug. 1991; Phase II of the project (covering the west of Libya) was completed in Sept. 1996. The river is providing Libya's main centres of population with clean water as well as making possible the improvement and expansion of agriculture. The whole project is more than three-quarters complete.

Minerals

Iron ore deposits have been found in the south.

Agriculture

Only the coastal zone, which covers an area of about 17,000 sq. miles, is really suitable for agriculture. Of some 25m. acres of productive land, nearly 20m. are used for grazing and about 1m. for static farming. Agriculture employs around 17% of the workforce. The sub-desert zone produces the alfalfa plant. The desert zone and the Fezzan contain some fertile oases. In 2002 there were around 1·82m. ha. of arable land and 0·34m. ha. of permanent crops. 470,000 ha. were irrigated in 2002. There were about 40,000 tractors in 2002 and 3,400 harvester-threshers.

Cyrenaica has about 10m. acres of potentially productive land and is suitable for grazing. Certain areas are suitable for dry farming; in addition, grapes, olives and dates are grown. About 143,000 acres are used for settled farming; about 272,000 acres are covered by natural forests. The Agricultural Development Authority plans to reclaim 6,000 ha. each year for agriculture. In the Fezzan there are about 6,700 acres of irrigated gardens and about 297,000 acres are planted with date palms.

Production (2003 estimates, in 1,000 tonnes): watermelons, 218; potatoes, 195; onions, 180; tomatoes, 160; olives, 150; dates, 140; wheat, 125; barley, 80; oranges, 42.

Livestock (2003 estimates): 4·1m. sheep, 1·3m. goats, 130,000 cattle, 47,000 camels, 25m. chickens.

Forestry

Forest area in 2005 was 217,000 ha. (0·1% of the land area). In 2007, 1·03m. cu. metres of roundwood were cut

Fisheries

The catch in 2005 was approximately 46,073 tonnes, entirely from marine waters.

INDUSTRY

Industry employs nearly 30% of the workforce. Small-scale private sector industrialization in the form of partnerships is permitted. Output (2004, in 1,000 tonnes): distillate fuel oil, 4,782; residual fuel oil, 4,597; cement (2002 estimate), 3,300; petrol, 1,991.

Labour

The labour force in 1996 was 1,601,000 (79% males).

INTERNATIONAL TRADE

In 1986 the USA applied a trade embargo on the grounds of Libya's alleged complicity in terrorism. Many of the economic sanctions were suspended in April 2004, and in June 2006 Libya was removed from Washington's list of state sponsors of terror. In 1992 UN sanctions were imposed for Libya's refusal to deliver suspected terrorists for trial in the UK or USA, but these were formally lifted in 2003. In Feb. 1989 Libya signed a treaty of economic co-operation with the four other Maghreb countries: Algeria, Mauritania, Morocco and Tunisia.

Imports and Exports

In 2006 imports were valued at US$13·2bn. and exports at US$37·5bn. Some 80% of GDP derives from trade. Oil accounts for over 95% of exports. Main import suppliers in 2000 were Italy (24%), Germany (12%), Tunisia (9%) and the UK (7%); main export markets were Italy (33%), Germany (24%), Spain (10%) and France (5%).

COMMUNICATIONS

Roads

There were 100,024 km of roads in 2002 (57·2% paved). In 2007 there were 1,388,200 passenger cars in use (225 per 1,000 inhabitants), plus 310,500 lorries and vans. There were 1,080 deaths as a result of road accidents in 1996.

Rail

A 4,800 km trans-African rail line has been proposed, scheduled to run through Libya from Tunisia to Egypt.

Civil Aviation

The UN ban on air traffic to and from Libya enforced since April 1992 was lifted in April 1999 following the handing over for trial of two suspected Lockerbie bombers. Libyan Arab Airlines provides both international and domestic services. In 2003 scheduled airline traffic of Libya-based carriers flew 8m. km, carrying 742,000 passengers.

Shipping

Sea-going vessels totalled 165,000 GRT in 2002, including oil tankers 7,000 GRT.

Telecommunications

In 2003 telephone subscribers numbered 877,000 (158·6 per 1,000 population), including 127,000 mobile phone subscribers. The national operator is the state-run General Posts and Telecommunications Company (GPTC). There are two mobile phone companies, Al-Madar and Libyana, both of which are state-owned. In Nov. 2009 the government announced plans to sell small stakes in both companies as part of a wider plan to sell off state-owned corporations. There were 205,000 internet users in 2004.

Postal Services

In 2003 there were 351 post offices, or one for every 15,800 persons.

SOCIAL INSTITUTIONS

Justice

The Civil, Commercial and Criminal codes are based mainly on the Egyptian model. Matters of personal status of family or succession matters affecting Muslims are dealt with in special courts according to the Muslim law. All other matters, civil, commercial and criminal, are tried in the ordinary courts, which have jurisdiction over everyone.

There are civil and penal courts in Tripoli and Benghazi, with subsidiary courts at Misratah and Darnah; courts of assize in Tripoli and Benghazi, and courts of appeal also in Tripoli and Benghazi.

The population in penal institutions in July 2004 was 11,790 (207 per 100,000 of national population). The death penalty is in force; Amnesty International reported that there were at least four executions in 2009.

Education

In 2006 there were 755,338 primary school pupils and 732,614 secondary level pupils. In 2009 the government launched a five-year US$9bn. plan to reform higher education and scientific research through strengthening international ties and improving the information technology network as well as creating a National Authority for Scientific Research. There are 12 state universities in Libya (of which Al Fateh University in Tripoli and Garyounis University in Benghazi are the largest), eight other higher education institutions and eight oil/bank training centres/petroleum training and qualifying institutes. In 2003 there were 375,028 tertiary level students and 15,711 academic staff. Adult literacy in 2004 was 84·2%.

Health

There were 6,092 physicians in 1997 and 619 dentists, 17,136 nurses and 1,095 pharmacists in 1996. Provision of hospital beds in 1991 was 41 per 10,000 population.

RELIGION

Islam is declared the State religion, but the right of others to practise their religion is provided for. In 2001, 92% were Sunni Muslims.

CULTURE

World Heritage Sites

Libya has five sites on the UNESCO World Heritage List: the Archaeological Site of Leptis Magna (inscribed on the list in 1982); the Archaeological Site of Sabratha (1982); the Archaeological Site of Cyrene (1982); the Rock-art Sites of Tadrart Acacus (1985); and the Old Town of Ghadamès (1986).

Broadcasting

Broadcasting is controlled by the government Libyan Jamihiriya Broadcasting Corporation. The first private television station, Al-Libiyah (a satellite service), was launched in 2007. There is an external service, Voice of Africa. In 2000 there were 717,000 TV receivers (colour by SECAM H).

Press

In 2006 there were four daily newspapers with a combined circulation of 70,000.

Tourism

In 2004 there were 149,000 foreign tourists (excluding day-visitors); spending by tourists totalled US$261m.

DIPLOMATIC REPRESENTATIVES

Of Libya in the United Kingdom (15 Knightsbridge, London, SW1X 7LY)
Ambassador: Vacant.
Chargé d'Affaires a.i.: Omar R. Jelban.

Of the United Kingdom in Libya (PO Box 4206, Tripoli)
Ambassador: Sir Vincent Fean, KCVO.

Of Libya in the USA (2600 Virginia Ave., NW, Suite 705, Washington, D.C., 20037)
Ambassador: Ali Aujali.

Of the USA in Libya (Ben Ashor Area, Jaraba St., Tripoli)
Ambassador: Gene A. Cretz.

Of Libya to the United Nations
Ambassador: Abdul Rahman Mohammad Shalgam.

Of Libya to the European Union
Ambassador: Alhadi Ahmed Hadeiba.

FURTHER READING

Simons, G., *Libya: the Struggle for Survival.* 1993.—*Libya and the West: From Independence to Lockerbie.* 2004

Vandewalle, D. (ed.) *Qadhafi's Libya, 1969–1994.* 1995.—*A History of Modern Libya.* 2006.—*Libya Since 1969: Qadhafi's Revolution Revisited.* 2008

Afghanistan · Albania · Algeria · Andorra · Angola · Antigua and Barbuda · Argentina

Armenia · Australia · Austria · Azerbaijan · Bahamas · Bahrain · Bangladesh

Barbados · Belarus · Belgium · Belize · Benin · Bhutan · Bolivia

Bosnia and Herzegovina · Botswana · Brazil · Brunei · Bulgaria · Burkina Faso · Burundi

Cambodia · Cameroon · Canada · Cape Verde · Central African Republic · Chad · Chile

China, People's Republic of · Colombia · Comoros · Congo, Democratic Republic of · Congo, Republic of · Costa Rica · Côte d'Ivoire

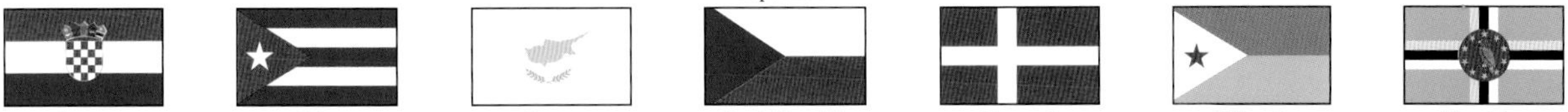

Croatia · Cuba · Cyprus · Czech Republic · Denmark · Djibouti · Dominica

Dominican Republic · Ecuador · Egypt · El Salvador · Equatorial Guinea · Eritrea · Estonia

Ethiopia · Fiji Islands · Finland · France · Gabon · The Gambia · Georgia

Germany · Ghana · Greece · Grenada · Guatemala · Guinea · Guinea-Bissau

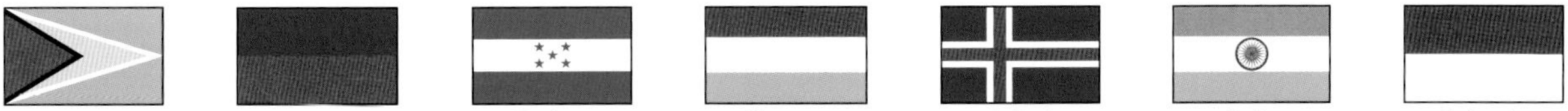

Guyana · Haiti · Honduras · Hungary · Iceland · India · Indonesia

Iran · Iraq · Ireland · Israel · Italy · Jamaica · Japan

Jordan · Kazakhstan · Kenya · Kiribati · Korea, North · Korea, South · Kuwait

Kyrgyzstan · Laos · Latvia · Lebanon · Lesotho · Liberia · Libya

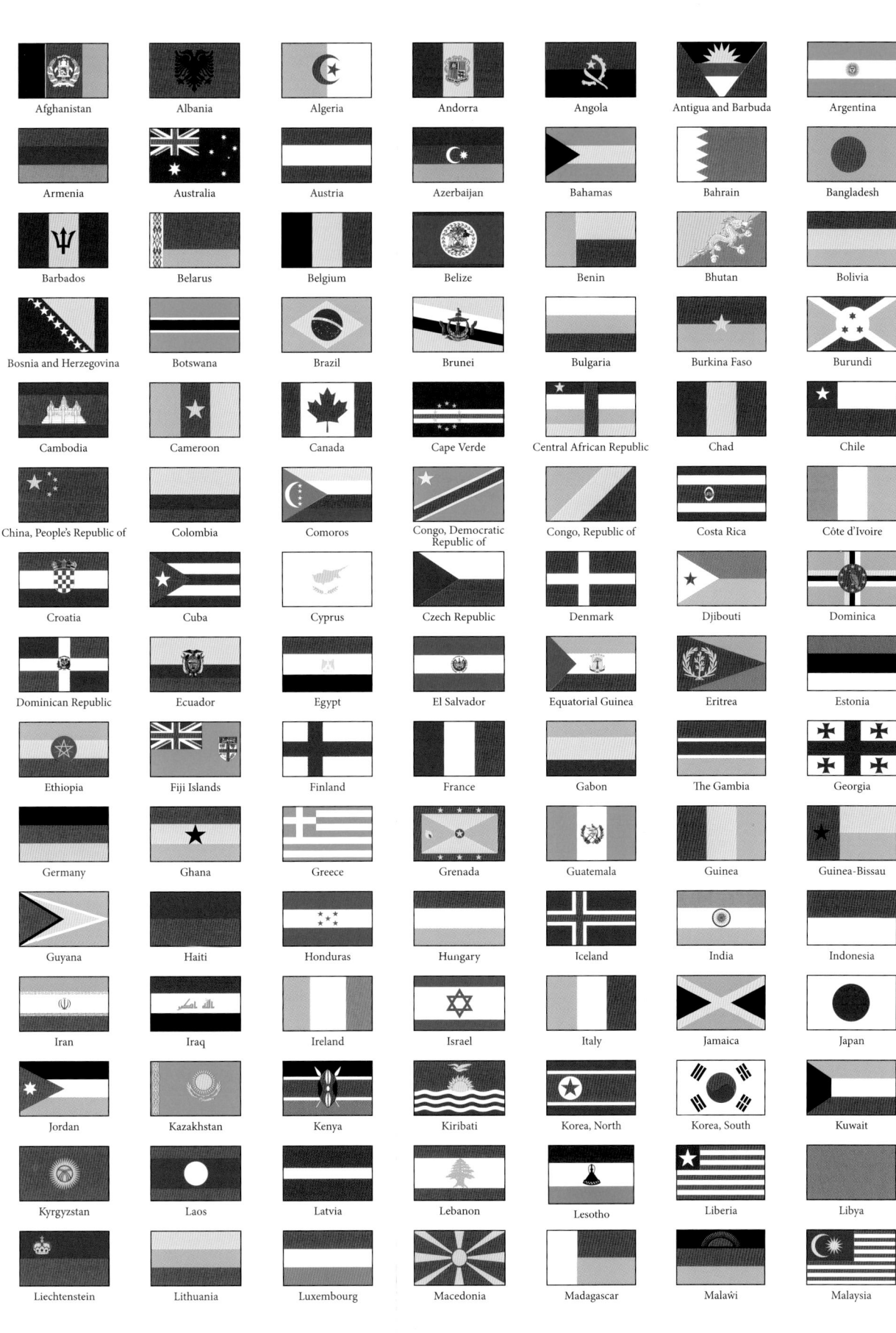

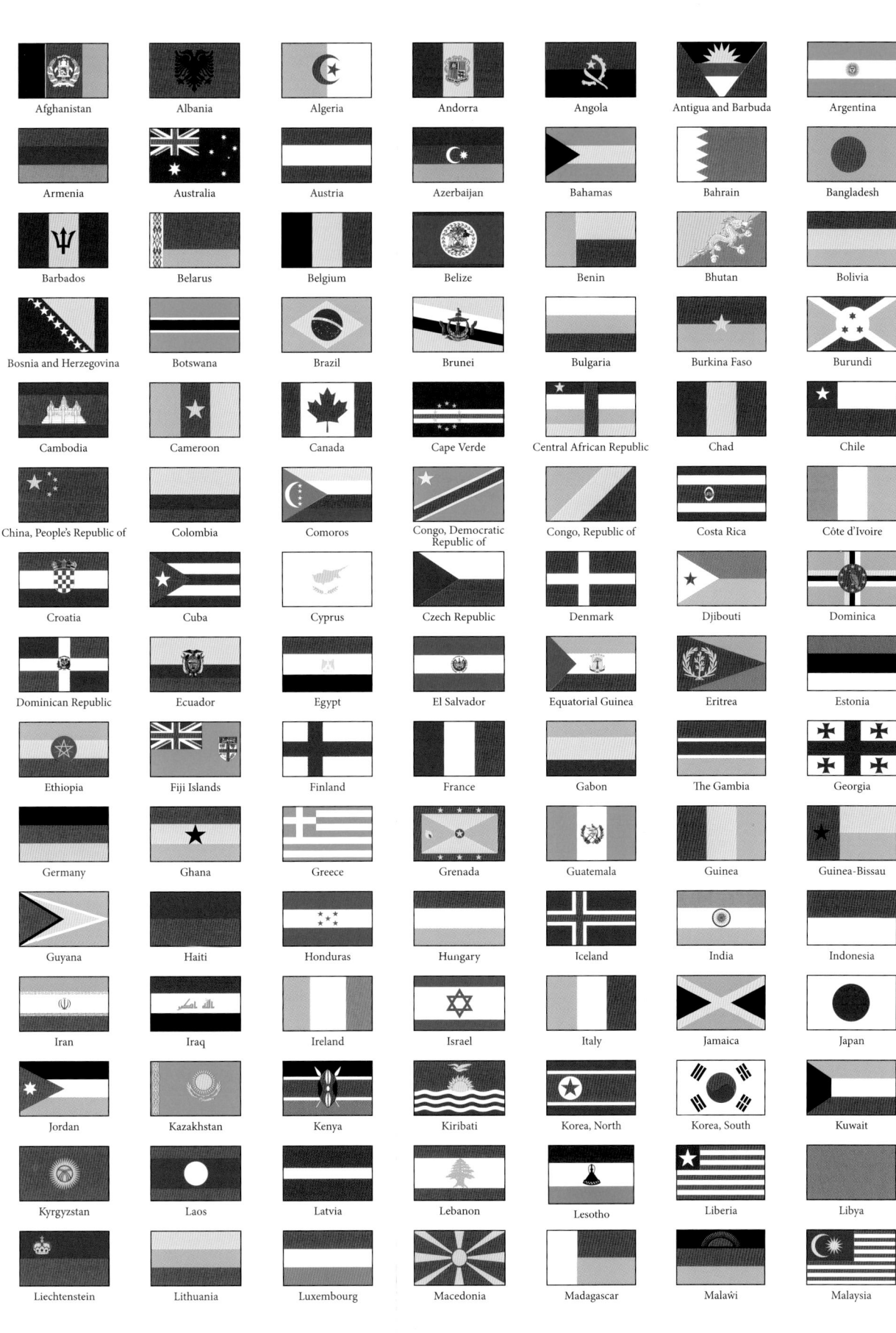

Liechtenstein · Lithuania · Luxembourg · Macedonia · Madagascar · Malaŵi · Malaysia

ical World

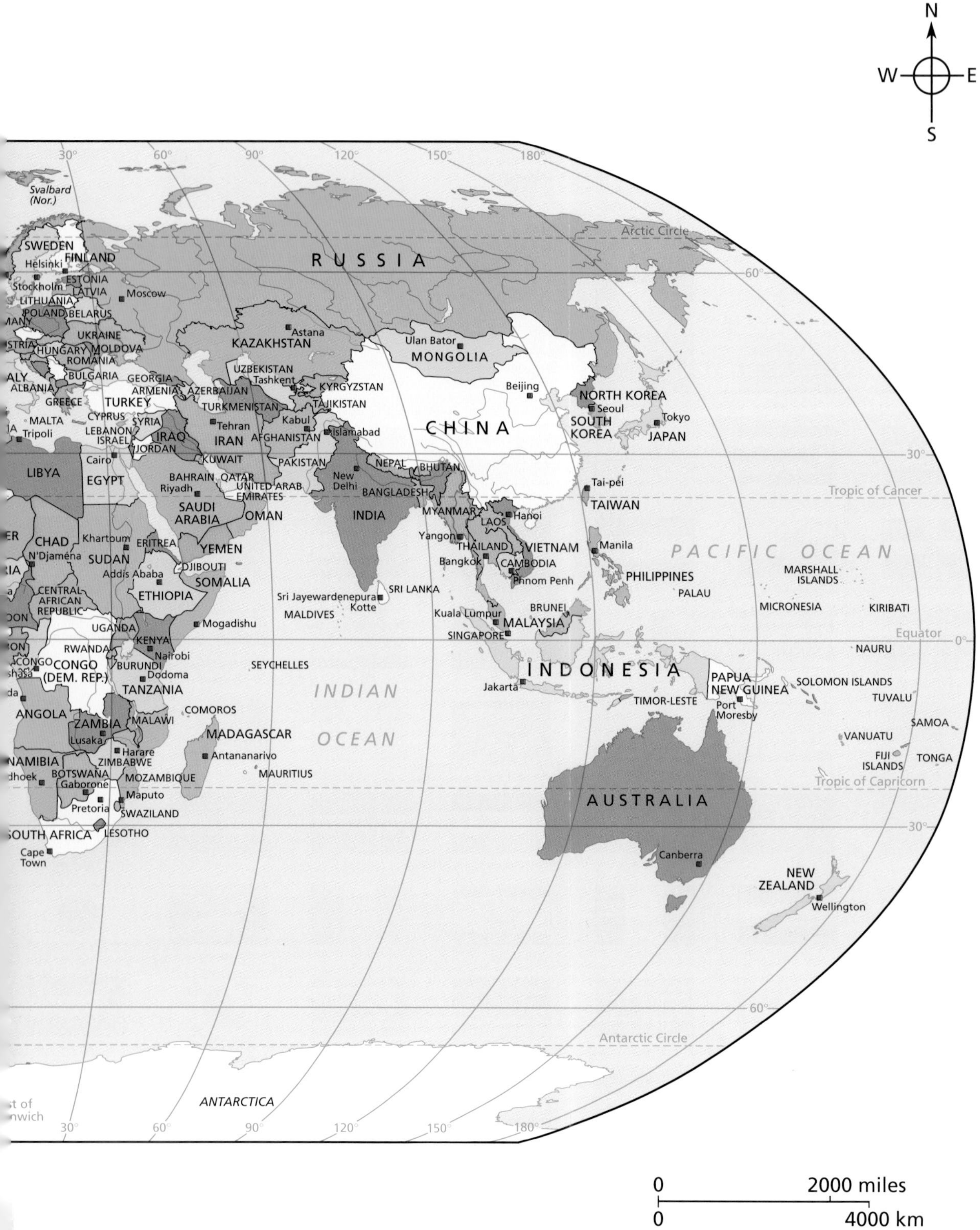
N
W
E
S
RUSSIA
KAZAKHSTAN
MONGOLIA
CHINA
INDIA
JAPAN
NORTH KOREA
SOUTH KOREA
INDONESIA
AUSTRALIA
NEW ZEALAND
PACIFIC OCEAN
INDIAN OCEAN
ANTARCTICA
Arctic Circle
Tropic of Cancer
Equator
Tropic of Capricorn
Antarctic Circle
0
2000 miles
0
4000 km

The Politi

Key

—— International border

▪ Capital city

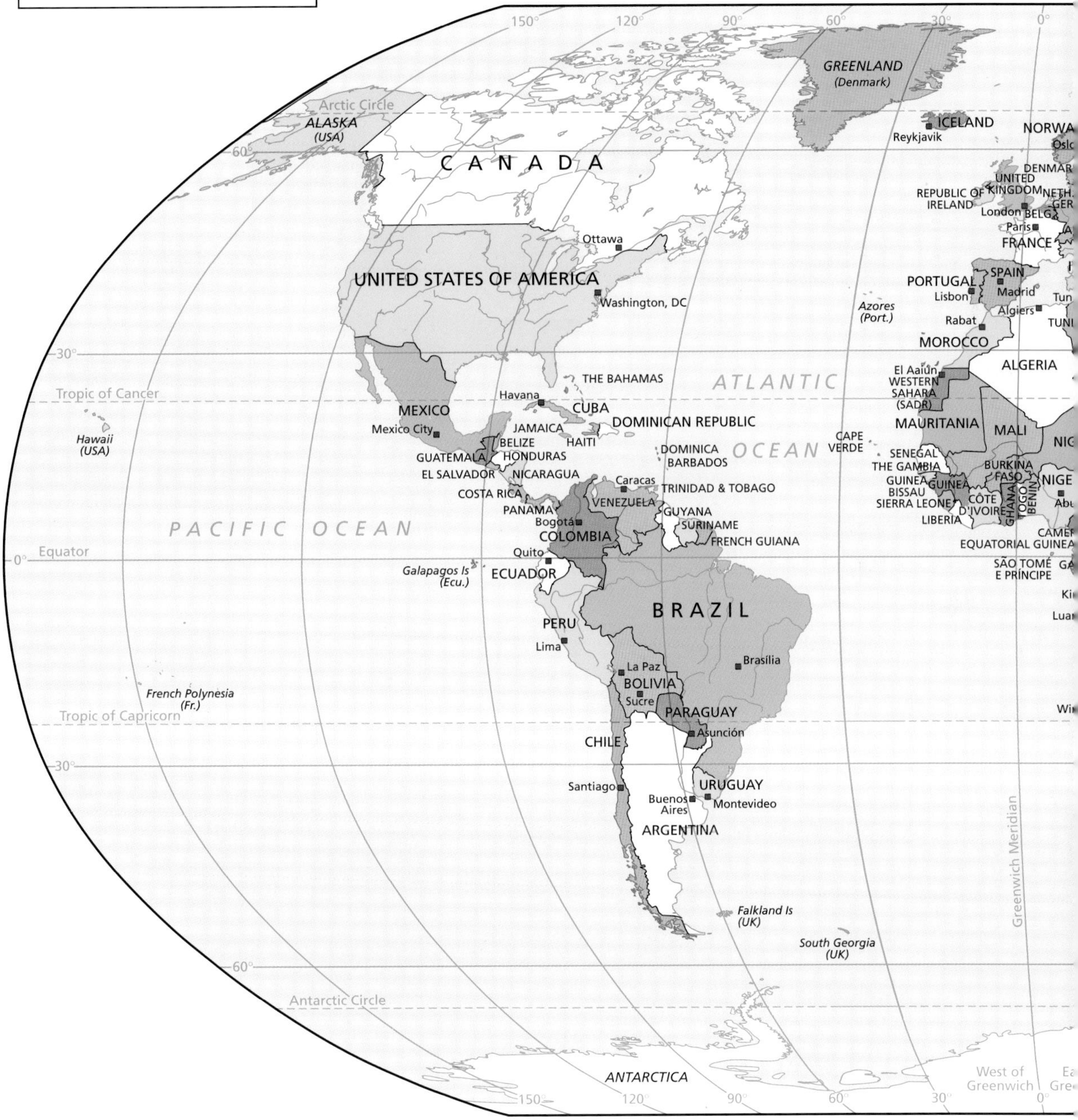

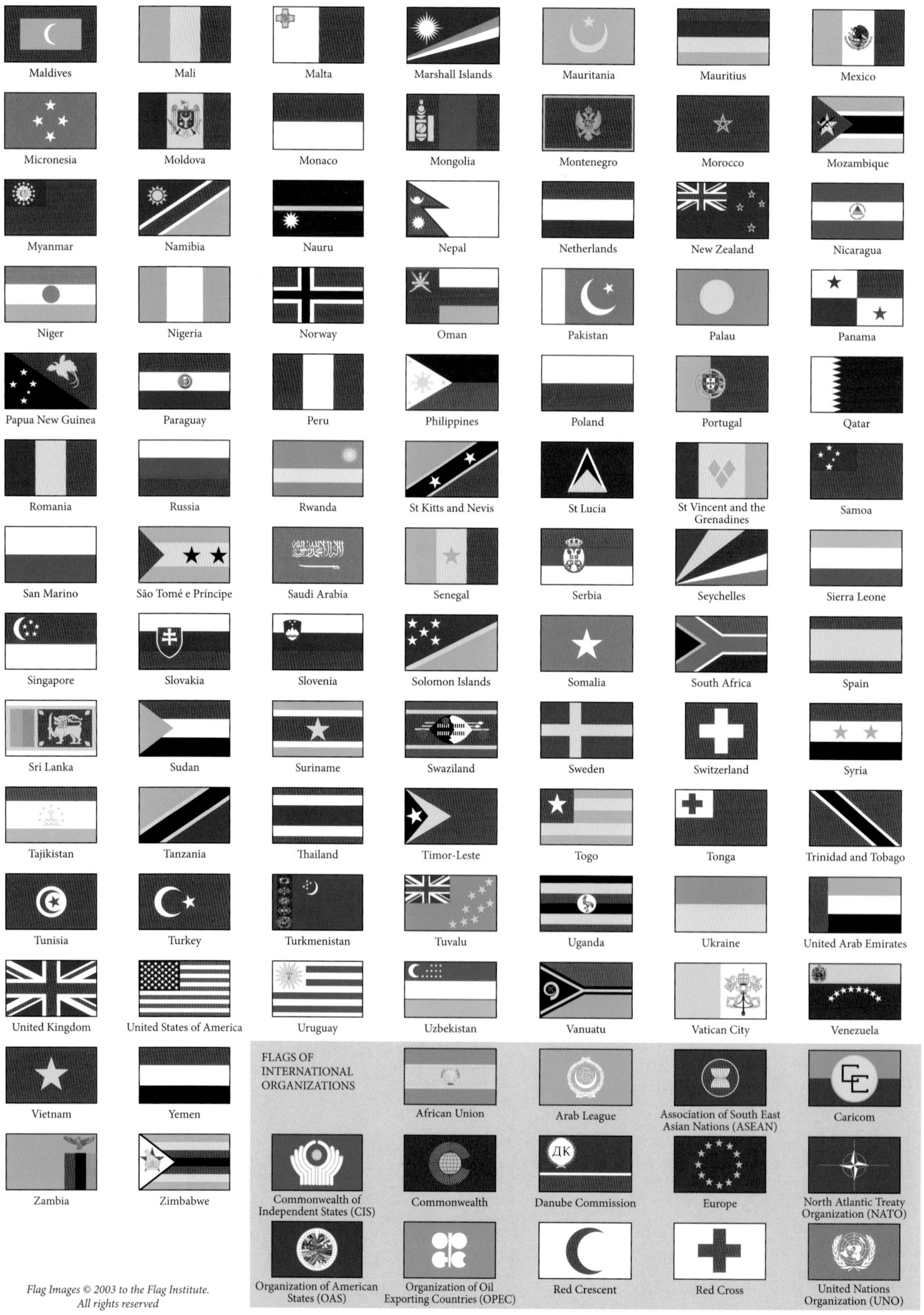
Maldives
Mali
Malta
Marshall Islands
Mauritania
Mauritius
Mexico
Micronesia
Moldova
Monaco
Mongolia
Montenegro
Morocco
Mozambique
Myanmar
Namibia
Nauru
Nepal
Netherlands
New Zealand
Nicaragua
Niger
Nigeria
Norway
Oman
Pakistan
Palau
Panama
Papua New Guinea
Paraguay
Peru
Philippines
Poland
Portugal
Qatar
Romania
Russia
Rwanda
St Kitts and Nevis
St Lucia
St Vincent and the Grenadines
Samoa
San Marino
São Tomé e Príncipe
Saudi Arabia
Senegal
Serbia
Seychelles
Sierra Leone
Singapore
Slovakia
Slovenia
Solomon Islands
Somalia
South Africa
Spain
Sri Lanka
Sudan
Suriname
Swaziland
Sweden
Switzerland
Syria
Tajikistan
Tanzania
Thailand
Timor-Leste
Togo
Tonga
Trinidad and Tobago
Tunisia
Turkey
Turkmenistan
Tuvalu
Uganda
Ukraine
United Arab Emirates
United Kingdom
United States of America
Uruguay
Uzbekistan
Vanuatu
Vatican City
Venezuela
Vietnam
Yemen
FLAGS OF INTERNATIONAL ORGANIZATIONS
African Union
Arab League
Association of South East Asian Nations (ASEAN)
Caricom
Zambia
Zimbabwe
Commonwealth of Independent States (CIS)
Commonwealth
Danube Commission
Europe
North Atlantic Treaty Organization (NATO)
Organization of American States (OAS)
Organization of Oil Exporting Countries (OPEC)
Red Crescent
Red Cross
United Nations Organization (UNO)

LIECHTENSTEIN

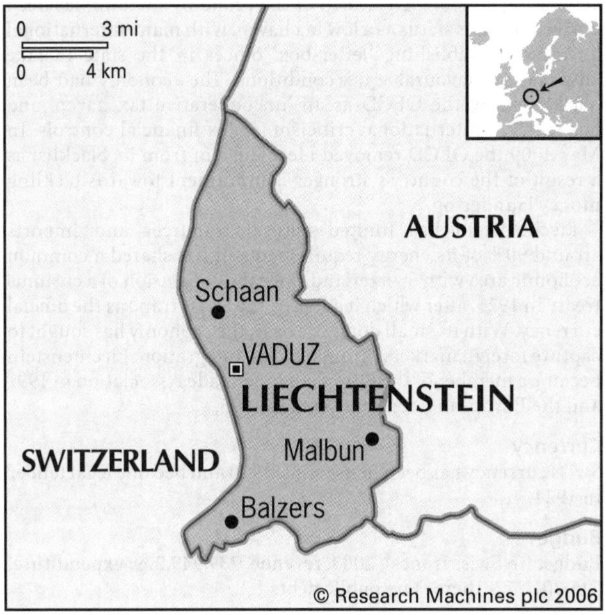

Fürstentum Liechtenstein
(Principality of Liechtenstein)

Capital: Vaduz
Population, 2008: 36,000
GDP per capita: not available
GNI per capita, 2007: US$106,550
HDI/world rank: 0·951/19

KEY HISTORICAL EVENTS

Liechtenstein is a sovereign state with a history dating back to 1342 when Count Hartmann III became ruler of the county of Vaduz. Additions were later made to the count's domains and by 1434 the territory reached its present boundaries. On 23 Jan. 1719 the Emperor Charles VI constituted the two counties as the Principality of Liechtenstein. In 1862 the constitution established an elected diet. After the First World War, Liechtenstein was represented abroad by Switzerland. Swiss currency was adopted in 1921. On 5 Oct. 1921 a new constitution based on that of Switzerland extended democratic rights, but in March 2003 the people of Liechtenstein voted in a referendum to give their prince the power to govern without reference to elected representatives.

TERRITORY AND POPULATION

Liechtenstein is bounded on the east by Austria and the west by Switzerland. Total area 160 sq. km (61·8 sq. miles). The population (Dec. 2008) was 35,589 (17,998 females), including 11,770 resident foreigners, giving a density of 222 per sq. km.

The population of Liechtenstein is predominantly rural. Population of Schaan (2008), 5,758; Vaduz (2008), 5,111.

The official language is German.

SOCIAL STATISTICS

In 2003 there were 347 births and 217 deaths (rates of 10·2 per 1,000 population and 6·4 respectively). The annual population growth rate was 1·2% over the period 2000–05.

CLIMATE

There is a distinct difference in climate between the higher mountains and the valleys. In summer the peaks can often be foggy while the valleys remain sunny and warm, while in winter the valleys can often be foggy and cold whilst the peaks remain sunny and comparatively warm. Vaduz, Jan. 0°C, July 20°C. Annual rainfall 1,090 mm.

CONSTITUTION AND GOVERNMENT

Liechtenstein is a constitutional monarchy ruled by the princes of the House of Liechtenstein.

The reigning Prince is **Hans-Adam II**, b. 14 Feb. 1945; he succeeded his father Prince Francis Joseph, 13 Nov. 1989 (he exercised the prerogatives to which the Sovereign is entitled from 26 Aug. 1984); married on 30 July 1967 to Countess Marie Kinsky von Wchinitz und Tettau. *Offspring:* Hereditary Prince Alois (b. 11 June 1968), married Duchess Sophie of Bavaria on 3 July 1993 (*offspring:* Prince Joseph Wenzel, b. 24 May 1995; Marie Caroline, b. 17 Oct. 1996; Georg Antonius, b. 20 April 1999; Nikolaus Sebastian, b. 6 Dec. 2000); Prince Maximilian (b. 16 May 1969), married Angela Brown on 29 Jan. 2000 (*offspring:* Alfons, b. 18 May 2001); Prince Constantin (b. 15 March 1972), married Countess Marie Kálnoky de Köröspatak on 17 July 1999 (*offspring:* Moritz, b. 27 May 2003; Georgina, b. 23 July 2005; Benedikt, b. 18 May 2008); Princess Tatjana (b. 10 April 1973), married Philipp von Lattorff on 5 June 1999 (*offspring:* Lukas, b. 13 May 2000; Elisabeth, b. 25 Jan. 2002; Marie Teresa, b. 18 Jan. 2004; Camilla Maria, b. 4 Nov. 2005). The monarchy is hereditary in the male line.

The present constitution of 5 Oct. 1921 provided for a unicameral parliament (*Landtag*) of 15 members elected for four years, but this was amended to 25 members in 1988. Election is on the basis of proportional representation. The prince can call and dismiss the parliament, and following a referendum held on 16 March 2003, dismiss the government and veto bills. On parliamentary recommendation, he appoints the ministers. According to the constitution, the Government is a collegial body consisting of five ministers including the prime minister. Each minister has an Alternate who takes part in the meetings of the collegial Government if the minister is unavailable. Any group of 1,000 persons or any three communes may propose legislation (initiative). Bills passed by the parliament may be submitted to popular referendum. A law is valid when it receives a majority approval by the parliament and the prince's signed concurrence. The capital is Vaduz.

National Anthem

'Oben am jungen Rhein' ('Up above the young Rhine'); words by H. H. Jauch; tune, 'God save the Queen'.

RECENT ELECTIONS

At the elections on 7 and 8 Feb. 2009 the opposition Patriotic Union (VU) gained 13 seats (47·6% of votes cast); the Progressive Citizens' Party (FBP), 11 (43·5% of votes); the Free List (FL), 1 (8·9% of votes). Turnout was 84·6%.

CURRENT ADMINISTRATION

Head of Government, and Minister for Family and Equal Opportunity, Finance and General Government Affairs: Klaus Tschütscher; b. 1967 (VU; sworn in 25 March 2009).

In March 2010 the cabinet comprised:

Deputy Head of Government, and Minister for Construction and Public Works, Economic Affairs and Transport: Martin Meyer. *Environmental Affairs, Land-Use Planning, Agriculture and Forestry, Public Health and Social Affairs:* Renate Müssner. *Education, Home Affairs and Sport:* Hugo Quaderer. *Cultural Affairs, Foreign Affairs and Justice:* Aurelia Frick.

Princely House Website: http://www.fuerstenhaus.li

CURRENT LEADERS

Hans-Adam II

Position
Prince

Introduction
Hans-Adam II succeeded his father, Francis Joseph II, as Prince of Liechtenstein in 1989. A successful banker with a large personal fortune, in March 2003 he was granted extensive legal rights which effectively made him Europe's only absolute monarch. He handed day-to-day responsibility for running the country to his son, Crown Prince Alois, in 2004.

Early Life
Hans-Adam, whose full name is Johannes Adam Pius Ferdinand Alois Josef Maria Marko d'Aviano von und zu Liechtenstein, was born on 14 Feb. 1945. The eldest son of the ruling Prince Francis Joseph II, he was brought up with his three brothers and one sister in Vaduz castle. He was schooled in Austria and Vienna, worked for a short while at a London bank and studied at the St Gallen School of Economics and Social Sciences, graduating with a masters degree in 1969.

In 1970 he was named head of the Prince of Liechtenstein Foundation, a position he retained until 1984. In 1972 his father put him in charge of running the royal estate, during which time he won a reputation for sound management and an interest in the wider economic sphere. In Aug. 1984 Franz Joseph transferred much of his executive power to Hans-Adam, who formally acceded to the throne on his father's death in Nov. 1989.

Career in Office
Hans-Adam has striven to maintain Liechtenstein's strong economy, consolidating its position as a major tax haven. In 1990 he successfully concluded membership talks with the United Nations. A year later, despite having previously declared his support for European unity, he ruled out a bid for membership of the European Union.

In March 2003 Hans-Adam called a national referendum on constitutional amendments which would award him the right to dissolve the government, appoint judges and unilaterally veto legislation. In return he proposed that his right to rule by emergency decree would be reduced to six months, his entitlement to nominate government officials be terminated and that the future of the monarchy be subject to referendum. He threatened to leave for Vienna if the proposals were rejected, a move many Liechtensteiners feared would severely diminish the country's economic standing. Despite the presence of a strong pro-democracy group within Liechtenstein and the threat that the nation might lose its membership of the Council of Europe if the motion was passed, the reforms won 64·3% backing.

In Aug. 2004 Hans-Adam formally transferred responsibility for day to day affairs to his son, Alois. However, he reiterated he had no intention of abdicating the throne.

INTERNATIONAL RELATIONS

Liechtenstein is a member of the UN, WTO, Council of Europe, OSCE and EFTA.

ECONOMY

Liechtenstein is one of the world's richest countries with a well diversified economy. Low taxes and bank secrecy laws have made Liechtenstein a successful financial centre.

Overview

Liechtenstein is a diversified and highly industrialized economy. Industry and manufacturing comprises the largest sector, producing mainly capital- and research-intensive products and generating 40% of GDP. Much of the economy's wealth has been derived from its status as a low tax haven, with many international businesses establishing 'letter-box' offices in the state to take advantage of favourable tax conditions. The economy had been blacklisted by the OECD as an 'uncooperative tax haven' and has received international criticism for lax financial controls. In May 2009 the OECD removed Liechtenstein from its blacklist as a result of the country's stronger commitment towards tackling money laundering.

Liechtenstein has limited natural resources and imports around 90% of its energy requirements. It has shared a common economic area with Switzerland since the conclusion of a customs treaty in 1923, after which it adopted the Swiss franc as the official currency. With its small domestic base, the economy has sought to capture foreign markets through global integration. Liechtenstein became a member of the European Free Trade Association in 1991 and the European Economic Area in 1995.

Currency

Swiss currency has been in use since 1920 and became legal tender in 1924.

Budget

Budget (in Swiss francs), 2003: revenue, 739,949,279; expenditure, 745,201,777. There is no public debt.

Performance

Real GDP growth was 3·9% in 2004. Total GDP was 4,296m. Swiss francs in 2004.

Banking and Finance

There were 16 banks in 2003. Combined total assets were 34,908·3m. Swiss francs in 2003.

ENERGY AND NATURAL RESOURCES

Electricity

In 2003 the consumption of electricity was 329,582 MWh (imported 270,333 MWh; produced in Liechtenstein 59,249 MWh).

Agriculture

In 2001 there were 962 ha. of arable land (agricultural land 2001: 3,750 ha.). In 2003 approximately 1,000 ha. (26% of all agricultural land—the highest proportion of any country) was set aside for organic farming. The rearing of cattle on the Alpine pastures is highly developed. In 2003 there were 5,314 cattle (including 2,737 milch cows), 3,070 sheep, 1,979 pigs, 408 horses, 241 goats. Total production of dairy produce in 2003 was 13,499 tonnes.

Forestry

In 2003 there were 6,700 ha. of forest (42% of the land area). Timber production in 2007 was 22,000 cu. metres.

INDUSTRY

Liechtenstein has a broadly diversified economic structure with a significant emphasis on industrial production. The most important branches of the heavily export-oriented industry are mechanical engineering, plant construction, manufacturing of precision instruments, dental technology and the food-processing industry.

Labour

The farming population went down from 70% in 1930 to 1·3% in 2003. The rapid change-over has led to the immigration of foreign workers (Austrians, Germans, Italians, Swiss). The workforce was 29,055 in 2003, including employees commuting from abroad (13,413 in 2003).

INTERNATIONAL TRADE

Liechtenstein has been in a customs union with Switzerland since 1923.

Imports and Exports

Imports in 2003 amounted to 1,490m. Swiss francs. Exports of home produce in 2003, for member companies affiliated to the Chamber of Industry and Commerce, amounted to 4,646m. Swiss francs: 595m. Swiss francs (12·8%) went to Switzerland, 2,000m. Swiss francs (43·1%) went to EFTA countries and 2,051m. Swiss francs (44·1%) went to other countries.

COMMUNICATIONS

Roads

There are 400 km of roads. Postal buses are the chief means of public transportation within the country and to Austria and Switzerland. There were 24,293 cars in 2006. There were 420 road accidents in 2007 (none fatal).

Rail

The 10 km of main railway passing through the country is operated by Austrian Federal Railways.

Telecommunications

In 2007 there were 19,518 main telephone lines. There were 32,013 mobile phone subscribers in 2007 and 23,500 internet users in 2008.

Postal Services

Post and telegraphs are administered by Switzerland. There were 12 post offices in 2004.

SOCIAL INSTITUTIONS

Justice

The principality has its own civil and penal codes. The lowest court is the county court, *Landgericht*, presided over by one judge, which decides minor civil cases and summary criminal offences. The criminal court, *Kriminalgericht*, with a bench of five judges is for major crimes. Another court of mixed jurisdiction is the court of assizes (with three judges) for misdemeanours. Juvenile cases are treated in the Juvenile Court (with a bench of three judges). The superior court, *Obergericht*, and Supreme Court, *Oberster Gerichtshof*, are courts of appeal for civil and criminal cases (both with benches of five judges). An administrative court of appeal from government actions and the State Court determines the constitutionality of laws.

The death penalty was abolished in 1989. Some persons convicted by Liechtenstein are held in Austrian prisons.

Police

The principality has no army. 2003: police force 103, auxiliary police 35.

Education

In 2004 there were 16 primary, three upper, seven secondary and two grammar schools, with approximately 4,300 pupils and 550 teachers. Other schools include an evening technical school and a music school.

Health

There is an obligatory sickness insurance scheme. In 2003 there was one hospital, but Liechtenstein has an agreement with the Swiss cantons of St Gallen and Graubünden and the Austrian Federal State of Vorarlberg that her citizens may use certain hospitals. In 2003 there were 64 physicians, 26 dentists and two pharmacists.

RELIGION

In 2003, 80·4% of the population was Roman Catholic and 7·1% Protestant; 12·5% belonged to other religions.

CULTURE

Broadcasting

Foreign satellite broadcasters provide most television and radio services. In 2006 there were 18,700 TV sets.

Cinema

There were three cinemas in 2003.

Press

In 2003 there were two daily newspapers with a total circulation of 17,652, and one weekly with a circulation of 32,658. Liechtenstein has among the highest circulation rates of daily newspapers in the world, at 515 per 1,000 inhabitants in 2003.

Tourism

In 2003, 50,207 tourists visited Liechtenstein.

DIPLOMATIC REPRESENTATIVES

In 1919 Switzerland agreed to represent the interests of Liechtenstein in countries where it has diplomatic missions and where Liechtenstein is not represented in its own right. In so doing Switzerland always acts only on the basis of mandates of a general or specific nature, which it may either accept or refuse, while Liechtenstein is free to enter into direct relations with foreign states or to set up its own additional diplomatic missions.

Of the United Kingdom in Liechtenstein
Ambassador: Sarah Gillett, CMG, MVO (resides in Berne).

Of Liechtenstein to the USA (2900 K. St. NW, Washington, D.C., 20007)
Ambassador: Claudia Fritsche.

Of the USA in Liechtenstein
Ambassador: Donald S. Beyer, Jr (resides in Berne).

Of Liechtenstein to the United Nations
Ambassador: Christian Wenaweser.

Of Liechtenstein to the European Union
Ambassador: Prince Nikolaus of Liechtenstein.

FURTHER READING

Amt für Volkswirtschaft. *Statistisches Jahrbuch.* Vaduz
Rechenschaftsbericht der Fürstlichen Regierung. Vaduz. Annual, from 1922
Jahrbuch des Historischen Vereins. Vaduz. Annual since 1901
National library: Landesbibliothek, Vaduz

Beattie, David, *Liechtenstein: A Modern History.* 2004

National Statistical Office: Amt für Volkswirtschaft, Gerberweg 5, 9490 Vaduz.
Website (limited English): http://www.llv.li/amtsstellen/llv-as-home.htm

LITHUANIA

Lietuvos Respublika
(Republic of Lithuania)

Capital: Vilnius
Population estimate, 2010: 3·26m.
GDP per capita, 2007: (PPP$) 17,575
HDI/world rank: 0·870/46

KEY HISTORICAL EVENTS

Lithuania has been inhabited since the 10th millennium BC, with agriculture developing in the 3rd millennium BC. Baltic tribes settled in the area around 2000 BC. In the 13th century AD their lands came under threat from two German religious orders, the Teutonic Knights and the Livonian Brothers of the Sword, prompting several of the tribes to establish a defensive union. The union defeated the Livonians in 1236 and in 1250 its leader, Mindaugas, signed a peace treaty with the Teutonic Order.

In 1253 Lithuania was proclaimed a state, with Mindaugas its crowned head. In the second half of the 13th century the Grand Duchy of Lithuania suffered internal unrest and was repeatedly raided by the Turks and Mongols of the Golden Horde. In the 14th century, led by Grand Duke Gediminas, Lithuania repulsed the threat from the Golden Horde and expanded eastwards. Gediminas established relations with the Christian church while retaining pagan beliefs.

In 1386 Lithuania's ruler Jogaila married Jadwiga, queen of Poland, and became king of Poland. During the 14th century Lithuania was Christianized. Lithuania continued its expansion and by 1430 extended from the Baltic to the Black Sea. Lithuania and Poland became permanently allied in 1447 and from 1501 they shared the same leader. In 1569 the Lublin Union legislated for a Lithuanian-Polish commonwealth. Polish culture was increasingly influential and Polish became the official state language in 1696. The constitution promulgated on 3 May 1791 is generally regarded as Europe's first national constitution (and the world's second after the USA). However, its democratic and egalitarian tone provoked Prussia and Russia.

During partitions of the Polish-Lithuanian Commonwealth by Russia, Prussia and Austria in 1772, 1793 and 1795, Lithuania was divided between Russia and Prussia. From 1795 Russia ruled most of Lithuania, including its capital, Vilnius. Uprisings were quelled in 1831 and 1863. In the second half of the 19th century, a cultural awakening interacted with an independence movement. On 5 Dec. 1905 at the Great Seimas (Congress) of Vilnius, Lithuanian representatives demanded political autonomy within the Russian Empire. The demand failed but in its aftermath pro-independence political parties were formed.

During the First World War Lithuania was occupied by Germany. Following the Russian revolution, heavy fighting occurred between Soviet Russian, German, Polish and Lithuanian forces in Feb. 1918. In Nov. 1918, after Germany's surrender, Lithuania declared full independence. In April 1919 the Soviets withdrew and the reformed Lithuanian government established a democratic republic. Lithuanian independence was recognized by the Treaty of Versailles later that year. Territorial disputes led to Lithuania supporting an uprising in the Memelland (under French jurisdiction from 1920) in Jan. 1923. In May 1924 Memelland became an autonomous part of Lithuania. There was also continued conflict with Poland over ownership of Vilnius. Following the establishment of a Polish-controlled mini-state around the city in 1922, Lithuania maintained a formal state of war with Poland.

In Dec. 1926 an internal coup deposed Lithuania's elected government and a non-democratic regime was installed. In 1938, under Polish pressure, diplomatic relations with Poland were restored. The secret protocol of the Soviet–German non-aggression pact of 1939 assigned the greater part of Lithuania to the Soviet sphere of influence. Soviet troops occupied Lithuania in June 1940 and it became part of the USSR on 3 Aug. 1940. Following the German invasion of the USSR in 1941, Lithuania was occupied by Germany. Lithuanian armed groups fought against or with German troops, according to regional and ideological loyalties. Pogroms took place against the Jewish population, which had risen to 250,000 following influxes of refugees from Poland. In 1944 the USSR reclaimed Lithuania as a Soviet Republic, with the agreement of the USA and Britain. An estimated 350,000 Lithuanians were deported to Siberia. In 1949 the Soviets closed most Lithuanian churches. More deportations occurred in 1956, when Poles and Russians were encouraged to move to Vilnius.

In 1988 the Lithuanian Movement for Reconstruction (Sajudis) was formed and drew up a programme of democratic and national rights. In the same year the ruling communists relaxed anti-nationalist measures and legalized a multi-party system. On 11 March 1990 the newly-elected Lithuanian Supreme Soviet declared independence, a move rejected by the USSR. Initially despatched to Vilnius to enforce conscription, Soviet army units occupied key buildings in the face of mounting popular unrest. On 13 Jan. 1991 the army fired on demonstrators. A referendum held in Feb. 1991 produced a 90·5% vote in favour of independence. The USSR recognized Lithuania's independence on 6 Sept. 1991, with all Russian troops withdrawn by Aug. 1993. The 1992 Lithuanian constitution provided for a presidency and Algirdas Brazauskas won the first presidential elections the following year. Lithuanian became the official language in Jan 1995, prompting protests from some Polish and Russian speakers. Lithuania joined NATO on 29 March 2004 and became a member of the EU on 1 May 2004.

TERRITORY AND POPULATION

Lithuania is bounded in the north by Latvia, east and south by Belarus, and west by Poland, the Russian enclave of Kaliningrad and the Baltic Sea. The total area is 65,200 sq. km (25,212 sq. miles) and the population (2001 census) 3,483,972 (1,854,824 females); density, 53·4 per sq. km. The estimated population in Jan. 2009 was 3,349,872. The United Nations population estimate for 2009 was 3,287,000. In 2005, 66·6% of the population lived in urban areas. Of the 2001 census population, Lithuanians accounted for 83·5%, Poles 6·7%, Russians 6·3% (9·4% in 1989), Belarusians 1·2%, Ukrainians 0·7% and Jews 0·1%.

The UN gives an estimated population for 2010 of 3·26m.

There are ten counties (with capitals of the same name): Alytus; Kaunas; Klaipėda; Marijampolė; Panevėžys; Šiauliai; Tauragė; Telšiai; Utena; Vilnius.

The capital is Vilnius (Jan. 2007 population, 542,782). Other large towns are Kaunas (358,111), Klaipėda (185,936), Šiauliai (128,397) and Panevėžys (114,582).

The official language is Lithuanian, but ethnic minorities have the right to official use of their language where they form a substantial part of the population. All residents who applied by 3 Nov. 1991 received Lithuanian citizenship, requirements for which are ten years' residence and competence in Lithuanian.

SOCIAL STATISTICS

2002: births, 30,014; deaths, 41,072; marriages, 16,151; divorces, 10,579; infant deaths, 238. Rates (per 1,000 population): birth, 8·6; death, 11·8; marriage, 4·7; divorce, 3·1. The population started to decline in 1993, a trend which is set to continue. Annual population growth rate, 2000–05, –0·5%. In 2002, 8,386 births were registered to unmarried mothers and there were 18,907 legally induced abortions. Life expectancy at birth in 2007 was 65·9 years for males and 77·7 years for females. In 2002 the most popular age range for marrying was 20–24 for both males and females. Infant mortality, 2005, seven per 1,000 live births; fertility rate, 2004, 1·3 births per woman. In 2002 there were 7,086 emigrants and 5,110 immigrants.

Lithuania has one of the world's highest suicide rates, at 30·4 per 100,000 inhabitants in 2007 (a rate of 53·9 among males but only 9·8 among women).

CLIMATE

Vilnius, Jan. –2·8°C, July 20·5°C. Annual rainfall 520 mm. Klaipėda, Jan. –0·6°C, July 19·4°C. Annual rainfall 770 mm.

CONSTITUTION AND GOVERNMENT

A referendum to approve a new constitution was held on 25 Oct. 1992. Parliament is the 141-member *Seimas*. Under a new electoral law passed in July 2000, 71 of the parliament's 141 members will defeat rivals for their seats if they receive the most votes in a single round of balloting. Previously they had to win 50% of the votes or face a run-off against the nearest competitor. The parliament's 70 other seats are distributed according to the proportional popularity of the political parties at the ballot box.

The *Constitutional Court* is empowered to rule on whether proposed laws conflict with the constitution or existing legislation. It comprises nine judges who serve nine-year terms, one third rotating every three years.

National Anthem

'Lietuva, tėvyne mūsų' ('Lithuania, our fatherland'); words and tune by V. Kurdirka.

GOVERNMENT CHRONOLOGY

(LDDP = Democratic Labour Party of Lithuania; LDP = Liberal Democratic Party; LKP = Communist Party of Lithuania; LLS = Lithuanian Liberal Union; LSDP = Lithuanian Social Democratic Party/Social Democratic Party of Lithuania; Sajūdis = 'Unity'/Reform Movement of Lithuania; TS(LK) = Homeland Union (Conservatives of Lithuania); TS-LKD = Homeland Union-Lithuanian Christian Democrats; n/p = non-partisan)

Heads of State since 1990.

Chairman of the Supreme Council

1990–92	Sajūdis	Vytautas Landsbergis

Chairman of the Seimas (Parliament)

1992–93	LDDP	Algirdas Brazauskas

Presidents of the Republic

1993–98	LDDP	Algirdas Brazauskas
1998–2003	n/p	Valdas Adamkus
2003–04	LDP	Rolandas Paksas
2004–09	n/p	Valdas Adamkus
2009–	n/p	Dalia Grybauskaitė

Prime Ministers since 1990.

1990–91	LKP/LDDP	Kazimiera Prunskienė
1991	Sajūdis	Albertas Simenas
1991–92	Sajūdis	Gediminas Vagnorius
1992	n/p	Aleksandras Abišala
1992–93	LDDP	Bronislovas Lubys
1993–96	LDDP	Adolfas Šleževičius
1996	LDDP	Mindaugas Stankevičius
1996–99	TS(LK)	Gediminas Vagnorius
1999	TS(LK)	Rolandas Paksas
1999–2000	TS(LK)	Andrius Kubilius
2000–01	LLS	Rolandas Paksas
2001–06	LSDP	Algirdas Brazauskas
2006–08	LSDP	Gediminas Kirkilas
2008–	TS-LKD	Andrius Kubilius

RECENT ELECTIONS

Presidential elections were held on 17 May 2009. Dalia Grybauskaitė, Lithuania's European Union commissioner, won 69·1% of the vote, ahead of Algirdas Butkevičius with 11·8%, Valentinas Mazuronis 6·2%, Valdemar Tomaševski 4·7%, former prime minister Kazimiera Prunskienė 3·9%, Loreta Graužinienė 3·6% and Česlovas Jezerskas 0·6%. Turnout was 51·7%.

Parliamentary elections were held in two rounds on 12 and 26 Oct. 2008. The opposition Homeland Union-Lithuanian Christian Democrats won 44 of the 141 seats (with 19·7% of the votes cast), of which 26 were in single-member constituencies and 18 through proportional representation; Social Democratic Party of Lithuania 26 (with 11·7%), of which 16 were in single-member constituencies and 10 through proportional representation; National Resurrection Party 16 (15·1%); former president Rolandas Paksas' coalition 'Order and Justice' 15 (12·7%); Liberals' Movement of the Republic of Lithuania 11 (5·7%); Labour Party and Youth 10 (9·0%); Liberal and Centre Union 8 (5·3%); Lithuanian Poles' Electoral Action 3 (4·8%); Union of Lithuanian Peasants and Peoples 3 (3·7%); New Union 1 (3·6%). Four seats went to independents. Turnout for the first round was 48·6% and for the second round 32·3%.

European Parliament

Lithuania has 12 (13 in 2004) representatives. At the June 2009 elections turnout was 21·0% (48·4% in 2004). The Homeland Union-Lithuanian Christian Democrats won 4 seats with 26·9% of votes cast (political affiliation in European Parliament: European People's Party); Social Democratic Party of Lithuania, 3 with 18·6% (Progressive Alliance of Socialists and Democrats); 'Order and Justice' coalition, 2 with 12·2% (Europe of Freedom and Democracy); Labour Party, 1 with 8·8% (Alliance of Liberals and Democrats for Europe); Lithuanian Poles' Electoral Action, 1 with 8·4% (European Conservatives and Reformists); Liberals' Movement of the Republic of Lithuania, 1 with 7·4% (Alliance of Liberals and Democrats for Europe).

CURRENT ADMINISTRATION

President: Dalia Grybauskaitė; b. 1956 (took office on 12 July 2009).

Prime Minister: Andrius Kubilius; b. 1956 (TS-LKD; in office since 9 Dec. 2008, having previously been prime minister from Nov. 1999 to Oct. 2000).

In March 2010 the four-party coalition government comprised:

Minister of Foreign Affairs: Audronius Ažubalis. *National Defence:* Rasa Juknevičienė. *Finance:* Ingrida Šimonytė. *Economy:* Dainius Kreivys. *Energy:* Arvydas Sekmokas. *Social Security and Labour:* Donatas Jankauskas. *Interior:* Raimundas Palaitis. *Health:* Raimondas Šukys. *Justice:* Remigijus Šimašius. *Agriculture:* Kazys Starkevičius. *Environment:* Gediminas Kazlauskas. *Transport and Communications:* Eligijus Masiulis. *Culture:* Remigijus Vilkaitis. *Education and Science:* Gintaras Steponavičius.

Seimas Speaker: Irena Degutienė.

Government of the Republic of Lithuania: http://www.lrvk.lt

CURRENT LEADERS

Dalia Grybauskaitė

Position
President

Introduction
Dalia Grybauskaitė was sworn in as the first female president of Lithuania on 12 July 2009 after a landslide election victory. Grybauskaitė left her job as EU commissioner for financial programming and budget to stand as an independent candidate, backed by the incumbent centre-right government. Renowned as a tough negotiator and skilled economist, she took office during the worst economic crisis since the dissolution of the Soviet Union.

Early Life
Grybauskaitė was born on 1 March 1956 in Vilnius, the then capital of the Lithuanian Soviet Socialist Republic, and went on to study political and economic science at Zhdanov University (now St Petersburg State University).

After graduating, Grybauskaitė returned to Lithuania and embarked on a career as a lecturer at the department of political economy at Vilnius Higher Party School, in which role she worked for seven years. She received her doctorate in economic sciences from the Moscow Academy of Social Sciences in 1988.

Following the dissolution of the USSR and Lithuanian independence, Grybauskaitė completed a special course for leaders at Georgetown University in Washington in 1991. She subsequently entered government, going on to head departments in the ministries of international economic relations and foreign affairs between 1991 and 1994. She was Lithuania's representative when it entered into the European Union Free Trade Agreement in 1993.

She continued her involvement with the EU in 1994, when she was appointed envoy extraordinary and minister plenipotentiary at the Lithuanian mission to the EU. In this role she worked as a senior negotiator on the Treaty of Europe. She continued her diplomatic work when she moved to the Lithuanian embassy in the USA.

In 1999 Grybauskaitė was appointed vice-minister of finance and foreign affairs in the cabinet of Prime Minister Andrius Kubilius. In this role she was responsible for conducting negotiations with international institutions including the World Bank and the IMF. In 2001 she was made minister of finance in the government of Algirdas Brazauskas.

Lithuania acceded to the EU on 1 May 2004, with Grybauskaitė appointed EU commissioner responsible for managing the EU budget and embarking on an ambitious programme of reform. In 2005 she criticized the UK's presidency of the EU, stating that the 'main obstacle' to reaching agreement on budgetary reform was Britain's insistence that it retain its rebate.

On 26 Feb. 2009 Grybauskaitė ended months of speculation by announcing her intention to stand in the forthcoming presidential elections. A popular figure across party lines, her entry into the race rendered the election a foregone conclusion, with opposition candidates either withdrawing or remaining in the race only to develop support ahead of elections to the European parliament. In the event, Grybauskaitė gained 69·1% of the vote, against 11·8% for her nearest challenger, Algirdas Butkevičius.

Career in Office
Grybauskaitė's victory was broadly popular, with several media commentators comparing the optimism that her election inspired with that seen in the United States on the inauguration of President Obama. In her inaugural address she promised to invest in local government and to narrow the gap between rich and poor in Lithuanian society. She has been a supporter of austerity measures to reduce the long-term impact of the economic crisis.

Despite her close association with the EU, Grybauskaitė has promised that greater integration into Europe will not come at the price of deteriorating bilateral relations with Russia. She has promised a more considered, less confrontational approach to issues of international relations. She sparked a parliamentary inquiry in Nov. 2009 after conceding that she harboured 'indirect suspicions' that the CIA had used a Lithuanian riding school as a secret jail for the detention of suspected Al-Qaeda militants captured in Afghanistan.

She has described the reinforcement of Lithuania's energy security as among her top priorities and met with Herman Van Rompuy in Dec. 2009, before he began his spell as president of the European Council, to secure the provision of extra funds from the EU to develop energy links with the West, thus reducing dependence on Russia.

Andrius Kubilius

Position
Prime Minister

Introduction
Andrius Kubilius became prime minister for the second time after his nomination by President Valdas Adamkus was approved by parliament on 27 Nov. 2008. He had previously served as premier from 1999–2000. His centre-right coalition government is faced with tackling Lithuania's economic crisis.

Early Life
Andrius Kubilius was born on 8 Dec. 1956 in Vilnius. In 1979 he graduated in physics from Vilnius University, where he remained for a further 11 years to pursue an academic career. In 1988 he became involved in the pro-independence movement and joined Sąjūdis ('Unity'/Reform Movement of Lithuania). He was appointed executive secretary of its council in 1990, serving for two years until he was elected to the Seimas (parliament).

In 1993 Kubilius joined the newly-established conservative Homeland Union party and was re-elected to the Seimas in 1996, becoming its vice chairman. In Oct. 1999 he was named prime minister by President Valdas Adamkus following the resignation of Rolandas Paksas. Kubilius' appointment was approved by the Seimas by a vote of 82 to 20. His term lasted from Nov. 1999–Oct. 2000. Policy priorities included reform of the Soviet-era bureaucracy and economic liberalization.

In the Oct. 2000 general election Kubilius won re-election to the Seimas despite the Homeland Union suffering a heavy defeat. He served as the party's first deputy chairman from 2000 until 2003, when he became party leader. In Oct. 2006 he was appointed deputy speaker of the Seimas and chair of the parliamentary committee on European affairs.

After gaining a lead in the first round of voting at the Oct. 2008 general election, the Homeland Union-Lithuanian Christian Democrats (TS-LKD), which had formed in May 2008 following a merger between the two parties, won 44 of a possible 141 seats, providing a mandate to form a coalition government. The Homeland Union joined with three smaller centre-right parties, jointly controlling 79 seats.

Career in Office
Kubilius' principal challenge has been to tackle the country's worsening economic crisis. Hours after being sworn into office he won parliamentary approval for tax reforms, cuts to public spending and measures to support businesses. However, there was widespread public discontent at tax increases following election promises that they would be cut. He has proposed adoption of the EU's single currency (euro) by 2011, but that target is likely to be missed in light of the economic downturn. Over the medium term, a return to growth depends on banks' ability to restart lending and on a recovery of external demand.

Kubilius' government oversaw the decommissioning of the Ignalina power plant at the end of 2009 as part of Lithuania's EU accession agreement. However, the closure of the plant has raised the spectre of dependency on Russian gas, a situation Kubilius is keen to avoid. An electricity bridge between Sweden and Lithuania that could solve the country's energy problem has yet to be built.

DEFENCE

Conscription ended on 1 July 2009. In 2006 military expenditure totalled US$349m. (US$97 per capita), representing 1·2% of GDP.

Army
The Land Forces numbered 7,800 in 2007 and included one motorized infantry brigade ('Iron Wolf'). Reserves numbered 6,700 in 2007 and there were also 4,700 active reservists in the National Defence Voluntary Forces. There was a paramilitary riflemen union numbering 9,600 and a state border guard service of 5,000 operates under the ministry of internal affairs.

A joint Polish/Lithuanian battalion (LITPOLBAT), which was a component of the EU's rapid reaction forces, was disbanded in 2007. However, plans are under way to replace it with a Lithuanian/Polish/Ukrainian Brigade (LITPOLUKRBRIG), which is expected to become operational in 2011.

Navy
In 2007 the Navy numbered 450 personnel (150 conscripts). It operates several vessels including one frigate. Lithuania, Estonia and Latvia have established a joint naval unit 'BALTRON' (Baltic Naval Squadron), with bases at Klaipėda in Lithuania, Tallinn in Estonia, and Liepāja, Riga and Ventspils in Latvia.

In addition there is a 540-strong Coast Guard.

Air Force
The Air Force consisted of 900 personnel (100 conscripts) in 2007. There are no combat capable aircraft.

The joint Baltic Regional Air Surveillance Network (BALTNET), established in co-operation between the air forces of Estonia, Latvia and Lithuania, has its co-ordination centre in Karmėlava in Lithuania.

INTERNATIONAL RELATIONS

Lithuania is a member of the UN, World Bank, IMF and several other UN specialized agencies, WTO, EU, Council of Europe, OSCE, EBRD, Council of the Baltic Sea States, BIS, IOM, NATO and is an associate partner of the WEU. Lithuania held a referendum on EU membership on 10–11 May 2003, in which 91·0% of votes cast were in favour of accession, with 9·0% against. It became a member of NATO on 29 March 2004 and the EU on 1 May 2004.

In Dec. 2007 Lithuania acceded to the Schengen accord, which abolishes border controls between Lithuania, Austria, Belgium, Czech Republic, Denmark, Estonia, Finland, France, Germany, Greece, Hungary, Iceland, Italy, Latvia, Luxembourg, Malta, Netherlands, Norway, Poland, Portugal, Slovakia, Slovenia, Spain, Sweden and Switzerland.

ECONOMY

Agriculture accounted for 5·1% of GDP in 2006, industry 33·7% and services 61·2%.

Overview
Lithuania's recession in the early years of its transition from a command economy to a market economy was more pronounced than that of its Baltic neighbours, partly because the country's export sector had closer ties to the Russian market. From 1995 to 1998 the economy grew at a strong and stable rate but the country fell back into recession in 1999 following the 1998 Russian financial crisis. In 2000 Lithuania rebounded and enjoyed one of the highest annual growth rates of any transition economy.

The country has privatized most enterprises, maintaining a stable macroeconomic policy and encouraging economic relations with foreign countries. Whilst not as successful as fellow Baltic State Estonia, Lithuania has been able to attract foreign investment from EU members, particularly the Nordic countries. Russia's share of Lithuanian exports fell from roughly 30% in 1997 to under 8% in 2000. Lithuania is a member of the World Trade Organization and joined the EU in May 2004. According to the World Bank, Lithuania ranks 26th out of 183 economies for the ease of doing business.

Core exports are mineral products (27·5% of total exports in 2005), machinery and equipment (12·4%), textiles (9·2%) and transportation equipment (8·3%). Unemployment fell from 17·4% in 2001 to 4·3% in 2007. Thriving exports and domestic consumer demand ensured average growth of 8% per year in the four years before the 2008 financial crisis. Between 1998 and 2008 real per capita incomes rose from about two-fifths to two-thirds of the EU average, principally driven by strong exports.

The downturn following the global financial crisis has been the worst since independence and among the most severe in the region. A large contraction in domestic demand was compounded by Lithuania's main export partners also being in recession. The economy is estimated to have shrunk by 15·0% in 2009, although a slight recovery is envisaged for 2010.

During the boom years a large structural deficit was accumulated, putting current government finances under considerable strain. Debt threatened to amount to over 90% of GDP by the end of 2014. With its currency fixed against the euro and lending from the international bond markets unforthcoming, the government implemented a package of austerity measures in Dec. 2009. Public spending was cut by 30%, public sector wages fell by between 20–30%, pensions were cut by up to 11%, VAT rose from 18% to 21%, corporate tax went from 15% to 20% and there were significant tax rises on alcohol and pharmaceuticals. The measures resulted in savings equivalent to 9% of GDP without calling on the assistance of the IMF.

Currency
The unit of currency is the *litas* (plural *litai*) (LTL) of 100 *cents*, which was introduced on 25 June 1993 and became the sole legal tender on 1 Aug. The litas was pegged to the US dollar on 1 April 1994 at US$1 = four litai, but since 2 Feb. 2002 it has been pegged to the euro at 3·4528 litai = one euro. Inflation, which reached a high of 1,161% in the early 1990s, was 3·8% in 2006, 5·8% in 2007 and 11·1% in 2008.

Total money supply was 13,884m. litai in July 2005, foreign exchange reserves were US$3,411m. and gold reserves 186,000 troy oz.

Budget
Budgetary central government revenue and expenditure (in 1m. litai):

	2005	2006	2007[1]
Revenue	13,770	16,286	19,543
Expenditure	13,280	15,433	18,012

[1]Provisional.

Principal sources of revenue in 2006: taxes on goods and services, 8,828m. litai; taxes on income, profits and capital gains, 4,328m. litai; grants, 1,818m. litai. Main items of expenditure by economic type in 2006: compensation of employees, 4,415m. litai; grants, 3,683m. litai; use of goods and services, 2,986m. litai.

VAT is 21%.

Performance
Among the wealthiest provinces of the former Soviet Union, Lithuania has weathered the economic crisis overspilling from Russia. In 1999 Lithuania experienced a recession, with the economy shrinking by 1·5%. However, between 2000 and 2006 growth averaged 7·3%. In 2007 and 2008 the economy continued to grow, by 8·9% and 3·0% respectively, although Lithuania was then one of the countries most affected by the economic crisis in 2009, with real GDP growth estimated at –15·0%. Total GDP in 2008 was US$47·3bn. At Nov. 2003 total public debt stood at €3·8bn., of which €2·6bn. was foreign debt.

Banking and Finance
The central bank and bank of issue is the Bank of Lithuania (*Governor*, Reinoldijas Šarkinas). A programme to restructure and privatize the state banks was started in 1996. In 2007 there were 11 commercial banks and foreign bank branches, the central credit union of Lithuania and 66 credit unions in operation. The largest private bank in Lithuania is SEB Vilniaus bankas, which controls approximately 36% of the total banking assets in the country. In 2006 it was estimated that total assets of domestic commercial banks amounted to 59bn. litai.

A stock exchange opened in Vilnius in 1993. In Nov. 2007 its capitalization was €6·8bn. The trading turnover in 2006 was €1·6bn.

ENERGY AND NATURAL RESOURCES

Environment
According to Lithuania's Ministry of Environment, carbon dioxide emissions were the equivalent of 5·1 tonnes per capita in 2008.

Electricity
Installed capacity was 6·57m. kW in 2003; production was 19·27bn. kWh in 2004. A nuclear power station (with two reactors) in Ignalina was responsible for 78·4% of total output in 2004, and there are also two large hydro-electric, five public and five autoproducer thermal plants. At the time no other country had such a high percentage of its electricity generated through nuclear power. However, as a condition of entry into the European Union the government agreed to close down Ignalina. The process to close the first reactor began on 31 Dec. 2004. The whole facility was shut down on 31 Dec. 2009. Electricity consumption per capita in 2004 was 3,505 kWh.

Oil and Gas
Oil production started from a small field at Kretinga in 1990. In Jan. 2003 remaining recoverable reserves were estimated at 3·25m. tonnes; potential recoverable resources, 60–80m. tonnes. Oil production in 2004 was 2·2m. bbls. Lithuania relies on Russia for almost all of its oil and gas.

Minerals
Output of minerals in 2006 (1,000 cu. metres): dolomite, 1,600; limestone, 900; peat, 400. Quarrying of gravel, clay and sand totalled 8·7m. cu. metres in 2006.

Agriculture
In 2002 agriculture employed about 17·2% of the workforce. As of 1 Jan. 2003 the average farm size was 15·2 ha., one of the lowest in eastern Europe; the agricultural land area was 3,956,200 ha. In 2002 there were 2·93m. ha. of arable land and 59,000 ha. of permanent crops. In 2002, 242,000 persons were employed in agriculture and forestry.

Output of main agricultural products (in 1,000 tonnes) in 2002: potatoes, 1,531; wheat, 1,218; sugar beets, 1,052; barley, 871; rye, 170; rapeseed, 105; cabbage, 98; oats, 97. Value of agricultural production, 2002 (in 1m. litai), was 4,303·3, of which from individual farm holdings, 3,396·2; and from agricultural partnerships and enterprises, 907·1.

Livestock, Jan. 2003 (in 1,000): cattle, 779·1 (of which milch cows, 443·3); pigs, 1,061·0; sheep and goats, 35·6; horses, 60·7; poultry, 6,848·1. There were 103,000 tractors in use in 2002. Animal products, 2002 (in 1,000 tonnes): meat, 173·6; milk, 770·9; eggs, 779m. units.

Forestry
In 2002 forests covered 2·0m. ha., or 30·6% of Lithuania's territory, and consist of conifers, mostly pine. Timber production in 2007, 5·86m. cu. metres.

Fisheries
In Jan. 2004 the fishing fleet comprised 90 vessels averaging 872 GRT. Total catch in 2005 amounted to 139,785 tonnes (mainly from sea fishing), compared to 57,477 tonnes in 1995.

INDUSTRY
Industrial output in 2006 included (in 1,000 tonnes): petrol, 2,303; cement, 1,100; sulphuric acid, 730; sugar, 97; woollen fabrics, 22·5m. sq. metres; cotton fabrics, 20·4m. cu. metres; linen, 12·8m. sq. metres; television picture tubes, 1,240,000 units; TV sets, 711,300 units; bicycles, 330,000 units.

Labour
In 2002 the workforce was 1·6m. (69·9% in private enterprises and 30·1% in the public sector). Employed population by activity (as a percentage): manufacturing, 18·6; wholesale and retail trade, 15·0; education, 9·9; health and social work, 6·7; construction, 6·6; transport and communications, 6·2; real estate, 3·9. Employment skills, 33·2% with tertiary education, 52·5% with upper secondary education, 11·8% with lower secondary. In 2002 the average monthly wage was 1,013·9 litai.

In 2002 old age pension for men started at 62 years and for women at 58. Average number of persons entitled to pensions in 2001 was 636,900. The unemployment rate in the fourth quarter of 2009 was 15·8% (8·1% in the fourth quarter of 2008).

Trade Unions
On 1 Jan. 2001 there were 655 registered unions (339 in operation) affiliated with four federations: the Lithuanian Trade Union Centre (LPSC); the Lithuanian Trade Union Unification (LPSS); the Lithuanian Workers Union (LDS); the Lithuanian Labour Federation (LDF). The LPSC and the LPSS merged on 1 May 2002 to form the Lithuanian Trade Union Confederation (LPSK), now Lithuania's largest trade union organization with 120,000 members.

INTERNATIONAL TRADE
Foreign investors may purchase up to 100% of the equity companies in Lithuania. By mid-2003, €4·06bn. of foreign capital had been invested. Leading source nations of foreign investment were Denmark, Sweden, Estonia, Germany and the USA.

Total foreign debt was US$11,201m. in 2005.

Individual laws on three free economic zones (namely the laws on Šiauliai, Klaipėda and Kaunas) have been cleared by Lithuania's Parliament, the Seimas.

Imports and Exports

Imports and exports for calendar years in US$1m.:

	2002	2003	2004	2005	2006
Imports f.o.b.	7,343·3	9,362·0	11,688·9	14,690·4	18,291·0
Exports f.o.b.	6,028·4	7,657·8	9,306·3	11,774·4	14,122·3

Leading import suppliers, 2006: Russia, 24·2%; Germany, 14·9%; Poland, 9·5%; Latvia, 4·8%. Principal export markets, 2006: Russia, 12·8%; Latvia, 11·1%; Germany, 8·6%; Estonia, 6·5%.

Main imports are machinery and apparatus, crude petroleum, road vehicles, and chemicals and chemical products. Main exports are mineral products, electrical equipment, textiles and textile articles, transport equipment, TV sets, chemical products and prepared foodstuffs.

COMMUNICATIONS

Roads

In 2007 there were 80,715 km of roads (including 309 km of motorways), of which 28·6% were paved. There were 1,587,900 passenger cars in use in 2007 (470 per 1,000 inhabitants), plus 14,000 buses and coaches, 14,500 lorries and vans, and 35,300 motorcycles and mopeds. There were 6,448 traffic accidents in 2007, with 740 fatalities.

Rail

In 2005 there were 1,817 km of railway track in operation in Lithuania. The majority of rail traffic was diesel propelled, although 122 km of track was electrified. In 2003, 6·7m. passengers and 43·5m. tonnes of freight were carried.

Civil Aviation

The main international airport is based in the capital, Vilnius. Other international airports are at Kaunas, Palanga and Šiauliai. FlyLAL–Lithuanian Airlines, formerly Lithuania's largest airline, ceased operations in Jan. 2009. In 2008 a number of international airlines ran regular scheduled flights to Lithuania. Vilnius was the busiest airport for passenger traffic in 2003, handling 719,850 passengers, but Kaunas (which handles approximately 6,700 tonnes per annum) was the busiest for freight.

Shipping

The ice-free port of Klaipėda plays a dominant role in the national economy and Baltic maritime traffic. It has the second largest tonnage in the Baltic region and a cargo capacity of 30m. tonnes per annum. A 412 ha. site at the port is dedicated a Free Economic Zone, which offers attractive conditions to foreign investors.

In 2003 the merchant fleet numbered 67 ships totalling 362,103 GRT, including eight bulkers, 35 general cargo ships, three tankers and 17 reefers. The turnover of the port in 2003 was 21m. tonnes (up from 12·7m. in 1995).

In 2003 there were 902·3 km of inland waterways, of which 467·7 km were used for carrying freight and passengers. The inland fleet comprised 142 working vessels.

Telecommunications

A majority stake in Lithuanian Telecom (the only fixed telephone service provider) was sold to the Finnish and Swedish consortium SONERA in 1998 and by Jan. 2003 the telecommunications market was fully liberalized. There were 5,154,600 telephone subscribers in 2005 (1,504·8 per 1,000 population), including 4,353,400 mobile phone subscribers (1,271·0 per 1,000 population—among the highest penetration rates in the world). In 2004 there were 533,000 PCs in use (154·7 per 1,000 persons) and 968,000 internet users.

Postal Services

In 2004 there were 955 post offices.

SOCIAL INSTITUTIONS

Justice

The general jurisdiction court system consists of the Supreme Court, the Court of Appeal, five county courts and 54 district courts. Specialized administrative courts were established in 1999. In 2006 there were 732 judges: 469 in district courts, 144 in county courts, 27 in the Court of Appeal, 34 in the Supreme Court, 43 in the administrative county courts and 15 in the High Administrative Court.

75,474 crimes were reported in 2006, of which 43% were solved. In 2006 there were 294 murders. 14,717 persons were convicted of offences in 2006. There were 8,079 prisoners in 2006, 7,082 of whom had been convicted. The death penalty was abolished for all crimes in 1998.

Education

Education is compulsory from seven to 16. In 2002–03 there were 686 pre-school establishments with 90,860 pupils and 2,172 general schools with 49,286 teachers and 594,313 pupils, in the following categories:

Type of School	*No. of Schools*	*No. of Pupils*
Nursery	148	12,219
Primary	683	35,819
Junior	25	2,326
Basic	645	118,415
Special	67	7,212
Secondary	574	400,566
Adult	27	17,318

119,548 students (70,777 females) attended 19 institutions of higher education and 22,367 (13,735 females) attended vocational colleges in 2002–03. The adult literacy rate in 2003 was 99·6% (99·6% for both males and females).

In 2006 public expenditure on education represented 5·0% of GNI and 14·4% of total government expenditure.

Health

In 2002 there were 13,856 physicians, 2,309 dentists and 26,918 nurses. There were 196 hospitals with 31,031 beds in 2002, and 2,238 pharmacists.

Welfare

The social security system is financed by the State Social Insurance Fund. In 2002, 625,000 persons were eligible for retirement pensions, 188,000 for disability provisions and 219,000 for widow's/widower's pensions. In 2002 the average state social insurance old age pension was 323 litai (monthly).

RELIGION

Under the Constitution, the state recognizes traditional Lutheran churches and religious organizations, as well as other churches and religious organizations if their teaching and rituals do not contradict the law. In 2001, 79% of the population was Roman Catholic. As of 2006 there were 677 Roman Catholic churches with 710 priests, and 50 Orthodox parishes with 47 priests. In 2007 the Lutheran Church had 54 parishes and 20 pastors headed by a bishop. In Feb. 2010 there was one cardinal.

CULTURE

World Heritage Sites

Lithuania has four sites (two shared) on the UNESCO World Heritage List: Vilnius Historic Centre (inscribed on the list in 1994) and Kernavė Archaeological Site (2004).

Lithuania shares the Curonian Spit (2000) with the Russian Federation as a UNESCO site. A sand-dune spit between Zelenogradsk, Kaliningrad Region, and Klaipėda, Lithuania, the Spit was subject to massive protective engineering in the 19th century. Lithuania also shares the Struve Geodetic Arc (2005). The Arc is a chain of survey triangulations spanning from Norway to the Black Sea that helped establish the exact shape and size of the earth and is shared with nine other countries.

Broadcasting
Lithuanian Radio and TV (LRT) is the public broadcaster, operating two national television stations and two national radio networks. There are an increasing number of competing national and local commercial TV and radio stations. There were 1·34m. television-equipped households in 2005 (colour by PAL).

Cinema
There were 68 cinemas in 2003; attendance, 1,342,535; gross box office receipts came to 14·4m. litai.

Press
In 2003 there were 337 newspapers (306 in Lithuanian, 19 in Russian, four in Polish, three in English, three in German, one in Yiddish and one in Belarusian) and 391 magazines. 4,859 book titles were published in 2002.

Tourism
There were 4,458,700 foreign visitors in 2008; tourism receipts in 2005 amounted to US$975m.

Festivals
The Lithuanian Song and Dance Celebration is held every four years, focusing international attention on the country's culture. There is also a Kaunas Jazz Festival and the Pažaislis Classical Music Festival (also in Kaunas). Major film festivals include Cinema Spring in Vilnius and the Kaunas International Film Festival. The annual Klaipėda Sea Festival attracts nearly half a million visitors each year.

DIPLOMATIC REPRESENTATIVES
Of Lithuania in the United Kingdom (84 Gloucester Place, London, W1U 6AU)
Ambassador: Oskaras Jusys.

Of the United Kingdom in Lithuania (Antakalnio str. 2, 10308 Vilnius)
Ambassador: Simon Butt.

Of Lithuania in the USA (2622 16th St., NW, Washington, D.C., 20009)
Ambassador: Audrius Brūzga.

Of the USA in Lithuania (Akmenu 6, 03106 Vilnius)
Ambassador: John A. Cloud.

Of Lithuania to the United Nations
Ambassador: Dalius Čekuolis.

Of Lithuania to the European Union
Permanent Representative: Rytis Martikonis.

FURTHER READING

Department of Statistics to the Government. *Statistical Yearbook of Lithuania*. Annual. *Economic and Social Development in Lithuania*. Monthly.

Hood, N., *et al.*, (eds.) *Transition in the Baltic States.* 1997
Lieven, A., *The Baltic Revolution: Estonia, Latvia, Lithuania and the Path to Independence.* 2nd ed. 1994
Misiunas, R. J. and Taagepera, R., *The Baltic States: the Years of Dependence, 1940–91.* 2nd ed. 1993
O'Connor, Kevin, *The History of the Baltic States.* 2003
Smith, David J., Purs, Aldis, Pabriks, Artis and Lane, Thomas, (eds.) *The Baltic States: Estonia, Latvia and Lithuania.* 2002
Vardys, V. S. and Sedaitis, J. B., *Lithuania: the Rebel Nation.* 1997

National Statistical Office: Department of Statistics to the Government, Gedimino Pr. 29, LT 01 500 Vilnius. *Acting Director General:* Vilija Lapėnienė.
Website: http://www.stat.gov.lt

LUXEMBOURG

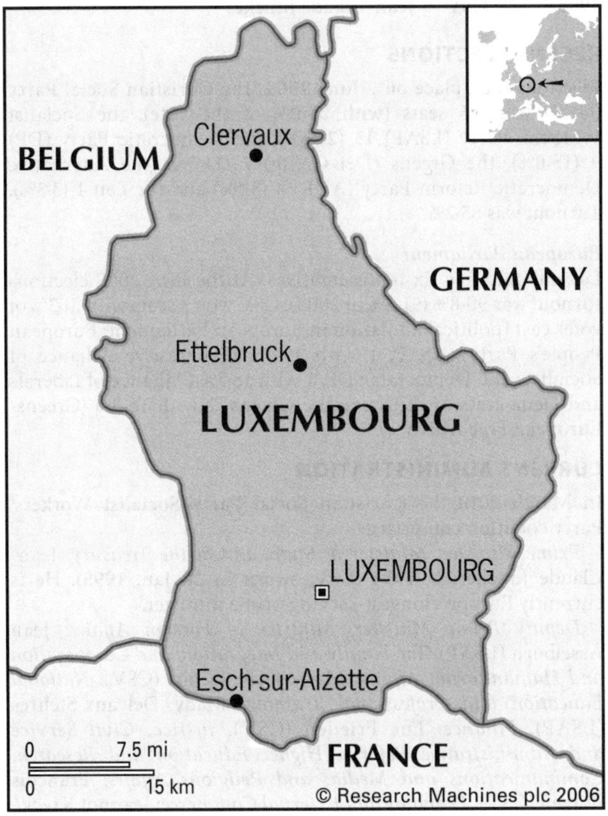

Grand-Duché de Luxembourg
(Grand Duchy of Luxembourg)

Capital: Luxembourg
Population estimate, 2010: 492,000
GDP per capita, 2007: (PPP$) 79,485
HDI/world rank: 0·960/11

KEY HISTORICAL EVENTS

Celtic tribes, with origins in the Danube basin, settled in the Ardennes hills and surrounding plains from at least 1000 BC. The Romans advanced north into the region (then part of Gaul) from around 50 BC and controlled much of it over the next five centuries from garrisons such as that at Trier. Frankish clans from the middle Rhine valley spread across present-day Luxembourg from around the 5th century AD and intermarried with the Gallo-Romans. Anglo-Saxon missionaries were active in the region during the 7th century, and a Benedictine monastery was founded at Echternach in 698. From the early 9th century the region was controlled by Charlemagne, the Roman Emperor in the West, who ruled from Hungary to the Atlantic Ocean. The empire's division, following the signing of the Treaty of Verdun in 843, enabled the rise of several feudal states, one of which became Luxembourg; the castle of Lutzilinburhurch was founded by Count Sigefroi in 963 on an outcrop overlooking the river Alzette.

Subsequent Counts of Luxembourg became powerful and influential in the wider European arena. From 1353, under Wenzel I, Luxembourg expanded to its greatest extent, covering four times the area of the present state. The House of Luxembourg subsequently went into decline and from 1443 was ruled by the Burgundians from their capital, Brussels. In 1477 Luxembourg became one of the 17 provinces of the Netherlands to come under Habsburg rule, initially under Maximillian of Austria and later under Charles of Ghent, who became the King of Spain in 1516 and Holy Roman Emperor in 1520. Luxembourg was ruled as part of the Spanish Netherlands for much of the next 200 years, although there were brief periods of French dominance under Louis XIV in the 1680s and 1690s. The transfer of the Spanish Netherlands to Austrian rule in 1715 heralded a period of relative tranquility for Luxembourg, which lasted until the territory was occupied by French revolutionary forces in the 1790s.

The 1815 Congress of Vienna made Luxembourg a grand duchy, which subsequently came under the jurisdiction of the house of Orange-Nassau, the ruling house of the Netherlands. At the same time it became part of the German Confederation. In 1839 the Walloon-speaking area was joined to Belgium, which had achieved independence in 1831, giving the Lëtzebuergesch-speaking provinces autonomy. At the London Conference of 1867 the European powers declared Luxembourg a neutral territory and in 1890 the union with the Netherlands was ended. Full independence was confirmed in the same year when Adolf of Nassau-Weilburg became grand duke, founding the present line of rulers.

Luxembourg was invaded and occupied by Germany in both the First and Second World Wars. In June 1942 the Grand Duchy became the only Nazi-occupied country to stage a general strike against the occupation. In 1948 a Benelux customs union formed by Belgium, the Netherlands and Luxembourg allowed for standardization of prices, taxes and wages and the free movement of labour among the three countries. Luxembourg joined NATO in 1949 and became one of the six founding countries of the European Economic Community in 1957. On 24 Dec. 1999 Prime Minister Jean-Claude Juncker announced Grand Duke Jean's decision to abdicate the throne on 7 Oct. 2000. He was succeeded by Prince Henri who assumed the title of Grand Duke.

TERRITORY AND POPULATION

Luxembourg has an area of 2,586 sq. km (999 sq. miles) and is bounded on the west by Belgium, south by France, east by Germany. A census took place on 15 Feb. 2001; the population was 439,539 (including 162,285 foreigners). At 1 Jan. 2008 the population was an estimated 483,800 (including 205,900 foreigners); density, 187 per sq. km. The percentage of foreigners living in Luxembourg has increased dramatically in recent years, from 26% in 1986 to 43% in 2008. The main countries of origin of foreigners living in Luxembourg are Portugal (76,600 in Jan. 2008), France (26,600) and Italy (19,100).

In 2005, 82·8% of the population were urban. The capital, Luxembourg, has (Jan. 2008 estimate) 85,500 inhabitants; Esch-sur-Alzette, the centre of the mining district, 29,500; Differdange, 20,400; Dudelange, 18,100; Pétange, 15,200; Sanem, 14,200; and Hesperange, 12,400.

The UN gives an estimated population for 2010 of 492,000.

Lëtzebuergesch is spoken by most of the population, and since 1984 has been an official language with French and German.

SOCIAL STATISTICS

Statistics (figures in parentheses indicate births and deaths of resident foreigners):

	Births	Deaths	Marriages	Divorces
2001	5,459 (2,736)	3,719 (531)	1,983	1,029
2002	5,345 (2,653)	3,744 (628)	2,022	1,092
2003	5,303 (2,782)	4,053 (632)	2,001	1,026
2004	5,452 (2,919)	3,578 (571)	1,999	1,055

2004 rates per 1,000 population; birth, 12·0; death, 8·9; marriage, 4·3; divorce, 2·3. Nearly half of annual births are to foreigners. In 2003 the most popular age range for marrying was 25–29 for both males and females. Life expectancy at birth in 2007 was 76·5 years for males and 82·0 years for females. Annual population growth rate, 2000–05, 0·9%. Infant mortality, 2005, four per 1,000 live births; fertility rate, 2004, 1·7 births per woman. In 2004 Luxembourg received 1,578 asylum applications.

A UNICEF report published in 2005 showed that 9·1% of children in Luxembourg live in poverty (in households with income below 50% of the national median), compared to just 2·4% in Denmark.

CLIMATE

In general the country resembles Belgium in its climate, with rain evenly distributed throughout the year. Average temperatures are Jan. 0·8°C, July 17·5°C. Annual rainfall 30·8" (782·2 mm).

CONSTITUTION AND GOVERNMENT

The Grand Duchy of Luxembourg is a constitutional monarchy.

The reigning Grand Duke is **Henri**, b. 16 April 1955, son of the former Grand Duke Jean and Princess Joséphine-Charlotte of Belgium; succeeded 7 Oct. 2000 on the abdication of his father; married Maria Teresa Mestre 14 Feb. 1981. *Offspring:* Prince Guillaume, b. 11 Nov. 1981; Prince Felix, b. 3 June 1984; Prince Louis, b. 3 Aug. 1986 (married Tessy Antony, b. 28 Oct. 1985, on 29 Sept. 2006; *offspring,* Gabriel, b. 12 March 2006; Noah, b. 21 Sept. 2007); Princess Alexandra, b. 16 Feb. 1991; Prince Sebastian, b. 16 April 1992.

The constitution of 17 Oct. 1868 was revised in 1919, 1948, 1956, 1972, 1983, 1988, 1989, 1994, 1996 and 1998.

The separation of powers between the legislature and the executive is not very strong, resulting in much interaction between the two bodies. Only the judiciary is completely independent.

The 12 cantons are divided into four electoral districts: the South, the East, the Centre and the North. Voters choose between party lists of candidates in multi-member constituencies. The parliament is the *Chamber of Deputies*, which consists of a maximum of 60 members elected for five years. Voting is compulsory and there is universal suffrage. Seats are allocated according to the rules of proportional representation and the principle of the smallest electoral quote. There is a *Council of State* of 21 members appointed by the Sovereign. Membership is for a maximum period of 15 years, with retirement compulsory at the age of 72. It advises on proposed laws and any other question referred to it.

The head of state takes part in the legislative power, exercises executive power and has a part in the judicial power. The constitution leaves to the sovereign the right to organize the government, which consists of a Minister of State, who is Prime Minister, and of at least three Ministers. Direct consultation by referendum is provided for in the Constitution.

National Anthem

'Ons Hemecht' ('Our Homeland'); words by M. Lentz, tune by J. A. Zinnen.

GOVERNMENT CHRONOLOGY

Prime Ministers since 1937. (CSV = Christian Social Party; DP = Democratic Party)

1937–53	CSV	Pierre Dupong
1953–58	CSV	Joseph Bech
1958–59	CSV	Pierre Frieden
1959–74	CSV	Pierre Werner
1974–79	DP	Gaston Thorn
1979–84	CSV	Pierre Werner
1984–95	CSV	Jacques Santer
1995–	CSV	Jean-Claude Juncker

RECENT ELECTIONS

Elections took place on 7 June 2009. The Christian Social Party (CSV) won 26 seats (with 38·0% of the vote), the Socialist Workers' Party (LSAP) 13 (21·6%), the Democratic Party (DP) 9 (15·0%), the Greens (Déi Gréng) 7 (11·7%), the Alternative Democratic Reform Party (ADR) 4 (8·1%) and the Left 1 (3·3%). Turnout was 85·2%.

European Parliament

Luxembourg has six representatives. At the June 2009 elections turnout was 90·8% (91·4% in 2004). CSV won 3 seats with 31·3% of votes cast (political affiliation in European Parliament: European People's Party); LSAP, 1 with 19·4% (Progressive Alliance of Socialists and Democrats); DP, 1 with 18·7% (Alliance of Liberals and Democrats for Europe); the Greens, 1 with 16·8% (Greens/European Free Alliance).

CURRENT ADMINISTRATION

In March 2010 the Christian Social Party–Socialist Workers' Party coalition comprised:

Prime Minister, Minister of State, and of the Treasury: Jean-Claude Juncker; b. 1954 (CSV; sworn in 20 Jan. 1995). He is currently Europe's longest-serving prime minister.

Deputy Prime Minister, Minister of Foreign Affairs: Jean Asselborn (LSAP). *The Family and Integration, and Co-operation and Humanitarian Affairs:* Marie-Josée Jacobs (CSV). *National Education and Professional Training:* Mady Delvaux-Stehres (LSAP). *Finance:* Luc Frieden (CSV). *Justice, Civil Service and Administrative Reform, Higher Education and Research, Communications and Media, and Religious Affairs:* François Biltgen (CSV). *Economy and External Commerce:* Jeannot Krecké (LSAP). *Health and Social Security:* Mars Di Bartolomeo (LSAP). *Interior and Defence:* Jean-Marie Halsdorf (CSV). *Sustainable Development and Infrastructure:* Claude Wiseler (CSV). *Labour, Employment and Immigration:* Nicholas Schmit (LSAP). *Culture, Parliamentary Relations, and Administrative Simplification:* Octavie Modert (CSV). *Housing:* Marco Schank (CSV). *Middle Classes and Tourism, and Equal Opportunities:* Françoise Hetto-Gaasch (CSV). *Agriculture, Viticulture and Rural Development, and Sport:* Romain Schneider (LSAP).

The *Speaker* is Laurent Mosar.

Government Website (French only): http://www.gouvernement.lu

CURRENT LEADERS

Jean-Claude Juncker

Position

Prime Minister

Introduction

Jean-Claude Juncker was appointed prime minister in Jan. 1995, replacing Jacques Santer who became president of the European Commission. He is the leader of the Christian Social Party (CSV). Having been re-elected as prime minister in 1999, 2004 and 2009, he is currently Europe's longest-serving head of government. He is committed to European integration, and played an important role in the decisions leading up to the creation of the EU's single currency (euro).

Early Life

Juncker was born in Redange-sur-Attert on 9 Dec. 1954. He obtained his primary and secondary education in Luxembourg and Belgium. Having studied law at the University of Strasbourg, he was admitted to the Bar of Luxembourg in Feb. 1980. He was an active member of the CSV and chaired its youth organization from 1979–84. Juncker was appointed state secretary for employment and social affairs in 1982. In 1984 he was elected to Parliament for the first time as minister of labour, minister of social security and minister in charge of the budget. When Luxembourg held the presidency of the European Community in 1985, Juncker chaired the council of ministers for social affairs and the budget. In 1990 he was elected party leader of the CSV. As president of the EC Economic and Finance Council in 1991, Juncker was among the core co-authors of the Treaty of Maastricht. He was a governor of the World Bank from 1989–95, and since 1995 has been the country's governor of the European Investment Bank and the International Monetary Fund.

Career in Office

Juncker concurrently holds the position of prime minister, minister of state and of the Treasury. In Oct. 2000 his government oversaw the abdication of the King, Grand Duke Jean, in favour of his son Prince Henri. In Feb. 2002 Juncker was awarded the Légion d'Honneur by French President Jacques Chirac. Following his re-election in mid-2004, he formed a new CSV coalition government with the Socialist Workers' Party. From Jan.–June 2005 he led Luxembourg's six-month presidency of the European Union. In Dec. 2008 Luxembourg's parliament voted to amend the constitution so that bills no longer need the approval of Grand Duke Henri before passing into law following a controversy over proposed euthanasia legislation. In the June 2009 elections the CSV increased its vote share and its representation in the Chamber of Deputies and Juncker began his fourth term as prime minister at the head of the CSV–LSAP coalition.

DEFENCE

There is a volunteer light infantry battalion of (2004) 1,000, of which only the career officers are professionals. In recent years Luxembourg soldiers and officers have been actively participating in peacekeeping missions, mainly in the former Yugoslavia. There is also a Gendarmerie of 612. In 2000 the Gendarmerie and the police force merged to form the Police grand-ducale. NATO maintains a squadron of E-3A *Sentries.*

In 2006 military expenditure totalled US$254m. (US$535 per capita), representing 0·6% of GDP.

INTERNATIONAL RELATIONS

Luxembourg is a member of the UN, World Bank, IMF and several other UN specialized agencies, WTO, EU, Council of Europe, WEU, OSCE, IOM, International Organization of the Francophonie, NATO, OECD and Asian Development Bank. The Schengen accord of June 1990 abolished border controls between Luxembourg, Austria, Belgium, Czech Republic, Denmark, Estonia, Finland, France, Germany, Greece, Hungary, Iceland, Italy, Latvia, Lithuania, Malta, Netherlands, Norway, Poland, Portugal, Slovakia, Slovenia, Spain, Sweden and Switzerland.

Luxembourg gave US$376m. in international aid in 2007, which at 0·91% of GNI made it the third most generous developed country as a percentage of its gross national income, behind Norway and Sweden. Luxembourg was one of only five countries to exceed the UN target of 0·7% in 2007.

ECONOMY

Services accounted for 85% of GDP in 2007 and industry 14%.

According to the anti-corruption organization *Transparency International*, Luxembourg ranked 12th in the world in a 2009 survey of the countries with the least corruption in business and government. It received 8·2 out of 10 in the annual index.

Overview

Luxembourg's post-World War Two economic growth was based primarily upon its highly productive steel industry. The small industrial sector has since diversified to include chemical, rubber and other manufactured products. The main engine of recent growth has been the financial services sector, particularly investment fund management. The government is looking to diversify into other financial services. Financial and business services accounted for 43·8% of total gross added value in 2000, well above the developed country norm, while its agricultural and manufacturing sectors accounted for 0·7% and 12·1% respectively, well below the OECD norm.

Other dynamic sectors of the economy include telecommunications, audio-visual and multimedia, industrial plastics and air transport. The strength of the economy has allowed Luxembourg to absorb a significant amount of foreign labour while maintaining low unemployment, although the inflow has put a strain on infrastructure. In the half-decade before the global slowdown of 2001, Luxembourg's economy grew faster than its neighbours at an annual average of over 7%. The economy was hit by the slowdown but proved comparatively resilient. Luxembourg is the second richest country in the world when measured by per capita GDP. The economy grew 4–6% per year between 2004 and 2007 but has slowed as a result of the international financial crisis.

Currency

On 1 Jan. 1999 the euro (EUR) became the legal currency in Luxembourg at the irrevocable conversion rate of 40·3399 Luxembourg francs to 1 euro. The euro, which consists of 100 cents, has been in circulation since 1 Jan. 2002. There are seven euro notes in different colours and sizes denominated in 500, 200, 100, 50, 20, 10 and 5 euros, and eight coins denominated in 2 and 1 euros, then 50, 20, 10, 5, 2 and 1 cents. On the introduction of the euro there was a 'dual circulation' period before the Luxembourg franc ceased to be legal tender on 28 Feb. 2002. Euro banknotes in circulation on 1 Jan. 2002 had a total value of €5·6bn.

Inflation rates (based on OECD statistics):

1999	*2000*	*2001*	*2002*	*2003*	*2004*	*2005*	*2006*	*2007*	*2008*
1·0%	3·8%	2·4%	2·1%	2·5%	3·2%	3·8%	3·0%	2·7%	4·1%

Foreign exchange reserves were US$285m. in Sept. 2009 (none in 2002) and gold reserves 73,000 troy oz. Total money supply was €84,140m. in March 2009.

Budget

Revenue and expenditure for calendar years in €1m.:

	2005	*2006*	*2007*
Revenue	8,499	9,213	10,015
Expenditure	8,883	9,455	9,727

Public debt in 2007 was €532·0m.

VAT is 15%, with reduced rates of 12%, 6% and 3%. Income taxes and business taxes have been reduced to preserve competitiveness in the international environment. The normal tax rate for companies at 1 Jan. 2006 was 29·63%, compared with 40·3% in 1996.

Performance

In terms of GDP per head, Luxembourg ranks among the richest countries in the world with a per capita PPP (purchasing power parity) GDP of US$81,222 in 2007.

Real GDP growth rates (based on OECD statistics):

1999	*2000*	*2001*	*2002*	*2003*	*2004*	*2005*	*2006*	2007	2008
8·4%	8·4%	2·5%	4·1%	1·6%	4·4%	5·4%	5·5%	6·5%	0·0%

Total GDP in 2008 was US$54·3bn.

Banking and Finance

Luxembourg's Central Bank (formerly the Monetary Institute) was established in July 1998 (*Director-General*, Yves Mersch). In Dec. 2004 there were 162 banks. German banks make up nearly a third of all the banks. Total deposits in 2004 were €560·7bn.; net assets in unit trusts, €504·0bn.; net assets in investment companies, €600·3bn. There is a stock exchange.

In 2004 the financial sector accounted for 18·1% of gross added value at basic prices and the banks showed a net profit of €2·9bn. The total number of approved insurance companies in 2004 was 95, with reinsurance companies numbering 271; the amount of premiums due was €8,737·5m.

ENERGY AND NATURAL RESOURCES

Environment

Carbon dioxide emissions from the consumption and flaring of fossil fuels in 2008 were the equivalent of 23·9 tonnes per capita (compared to the European average of 7·8 tonnes per capita).

Electricity

Apart from hydro-electricity and electricity generated from fossil fuels, Luxembourg has no national energy resources. Installed capacity in 2003 was 1·6m. kW. Production was 4,136m. kWh in 2004 and consumption per capita 16,630 kWh.

Agriculture

The contribution of agriculture, viticulture and forestry to the economy has been gradually declining over the years, accounting for only 0·5% of gross added value at basic prices in 2004. However, the actual output of this sector has nearly tripled during the past 30 years, a trend common to many EU countries. There were 4,975 workers engaged in agricultural work (including wine-growing and forestry) in 2004. In 2007 there were 2,303 farms with an average area of 63·4 ha.; 130,884 ha. were under cultivation in 2007.

Production, 2007 (in tonnes) of main crops: grassland and pasturage, 749,101; maize, 197,508; forage crops, 129,096; bread crops, 77,435; potatoes, 19,968; colza (rape), 18,302. Production, 2007 (in 1,000 tonnes) of meat, 26·8; milk, 274·2. In 2007–08, 142,000 hectolitres of wine were produced. Total tractors and other agriculture vehicles, 2008: 15,238.

Livestock (15 May 2007): 4,334 horses, 191,928 cattle, 83,255 pigs, 9,339 sheep.

Forestry

In 2003 there were 89,785 ha. of forests, which in 2004 produced 128,500 cu. metres of broadleaved and 124,200 cu. metres of coniferous wood.

INDUSTRY

In 2004 there were 3,038 industrial enterprises, of which 1,972 were in the building industry. Production, 2007 (in tonnes): rolled steel products, 2,933,000; steel, 2,858,000. The world's largest steel producer, ArcelorMittal, has its headquarters in Luxembourg. Created in June 2006 through the merger of Arcelor and Mittal Steel, it produces in excess of 100m. tonnes of steel annually and accounts for approximately 10% of world steel output. The steel industry mainly relies on imported ore.

Labour

In 2004 the estimated total workforce was 301,000. The government fixes a legal minimum wage. Retirement is at 65. Employment creation was 3·2% in 2004–05. In Dec. 2009 the unemployment rate was 6·2%. The minimum wage in Jan. 2005 was €8·48 an hour.

Between 1996 and 2005 strikes cost Luxembourg an average of just one days per 1,000 employees a year.

There was a 2·6% increase in employment in 2004. Of the new jobs created, around two-thirds went to so-called *frontaliers*, workers living in surrounding countries who commute into Luxembourg to work. More than 100,000 people cross into Luxembourg every day from neighbouring France, Germany and Belgium to work, principally in the financial services industry.

Trade Unions

The main trade unions are the OGB-L (Socialist) and the LCGB (Christian-Social). Other sectoral unions include ALEBA (the banking sector), FNCTTFEL (railworkers) and FEP (private employers). In Nov. 2008 employees chose representatives to the 60-member Chamber of Employees from trade union candidate lists. The elections are held every five years.

INTERNATIONAL TRADE

Luxembourg is in the process of turning itself into a centre for electronic commerce, the world's fastest-growing industry.

Imports and Exports

Imports in 2007 (provisional figures) totalled €16,262·2m. and exports €11,823·0m. In 2005 exports reached 158% of GDP. In 2007, 90·5% of imports were from other EU member countries and 85·9% of exports went to other EU member countries.

Principal imports and exports by standard international trade classification (provisional figures) in €1m.:

	Imports 2007	*Exports* 2007
Food and live animals	1,120·7	539·2
Beverages and tobacco	425·3	195·0
Crude materials, oils, fats and waxes	1,297·9	251·3
Mineral fuels and lubricants	2,076·4	91·9
Chemicals and related products	1,568·2	798·7
Manufactured goods in metals	1,250·8	1,821·1
Other manufactured goods classified chiefly by material	1,789·4	3,928·5
Machinery	2,547·1	2,136·0
Transport equipment	2,602·4	885·7
Other manufactured goods	1,583·9	1,175·6
Total	16,262·2	11,823·0

Trade with selected countries (provisional figures) in €1m.:

	Imports 2007	*Exports* 2007
Austria	137·8	243·1
Belgium	5,496·3	1,481·2
Czech Republic	79·4	124·0
France	1,899·8	1,993·0
Germany	4,800·0	3,124·1
Italy	356·6	641·7
Netherlands	1,002·6	644·9
Poland	109·0	196·1
Spain	168·9	413·5
Sweden	112·9	172·7
UK	282·1	553·7
(Total EU	14,722·7	10,154·4)
Canada	151·6	62·3
China	95·1	194·4
Hong Kong	119·2	46·4
Russia	44·1	147·2
Switzerland	152·2	144·7
Turkey	39·9	129·7
USA	623·2	298·7
Total (including others)	16,262·2	11,823·0

Trade Fairs

The *Foires Internationales de Luxembourg* occur twice a year, and there are a growing number of specialized fairs.

COMMUNICATIONS

Roads

On 1 Jan. 2008 there were 2,894 km of roads of which 147 km were motorways. Motor vehicles registered at 1 Jan. 2008 numbered

394,917 including 321,520 passenger cars, 27,043 trucks, 1,455 coaches and 14,946 motorcycles. In 2005 there were 46 fatalities in road accidents (the lowest in a year since 1950).

Rail
In 2004 there were 275 km of railway (standard gauge) of which 261 km were electrified; 14·1m. passengers were carried in 2005.

Civil Aviation
Findel is the airport for Luxembourg. 1,643,000 passengers and 856,450 tonnes of freight were handled in 2007. The national carrier is Luxair, 26·85% state-owned. Cargolux has developed into one of the major international freight carriers. In 2003 scheduled airline traffic of Luxembourg-based carriers flew 74m. km, carrying 854,000 passengers (all on international flights).

Shipping
A shipping register was set up in 1990; 143 vessels were registered in Dec. 2006.

Telecommunications
In 2006 there were 362,722 main (fixed) telephone lines. In 2008 active mobile phone subscribers numbered 707,000 (1,471·1 per 1,000 persons). There were 318,000 PCs in use in 2006 and an estimated 387,000 internet users in 2008. The broadband penetration rate in June 2008 was 28·3 subscribers per 100 inhabitants.

Postal Services
In 2003 there were 108 post offices. In 2003 a total of 177·8m. items of mail were processed.

SOCIAL INSTITUTIONS

Justice
The Constitution makes the Courts of Law independent in performing their functions, restricting their sphere of activity, defining their limit of jurisdiction and providing a number of procedural guarantees. The Constitution has additionally laid down a number of provisions designed to ensure judges remain independent of persons under their jurisdiction, and to ensure no interference from the executive and legislative organs. All judges are appointed by Grand-Ducal order and are irremovable.

The judicial organization comprises three Justices of the Peace (conciliation and police courts). The country is, in addition, divided into two judicial districts—Luxembourg and Diekirch. District courts deal with matters such as civic and commercial cases. Offences which are punishable under the Penal Code or by specific laws with imprisonment or hard labour fall within the jurisdiction of the criminal chambers of District Courts, as the Assize Court was repealed by law in 1987. The High Court of Justice consists of a Supreme Court of Appeal and a Court of Appeal.

The judicial organization of the Grand-Duchy does not include the jury system. A division of votes between the judges on the issue of guilt/innocence may lead to acquittal. Society before the Courts of Law is represented by the Public Prosecutor Department, composed of members of the judiciary directly answerable to the government.

In 1999 a new Administrative Tribunal, Administrative Court and Constitutional Court were established.

The population in penal institutions in Dec. 2004 was 455.

Education
The adult literacy rate in 2004 was 100%. Education is compulsory for all children between the ages of four and 15 (including two years of pre-primary school attendance). In 2006–07 there were 13,672 children in pre-primary school (pre-nursery education, 3,671; nursery education, 10,001) with 1,227 teachers; 33,136 pupils in primary schools; 34,970 pupils in secondary schools. In higher education (2003–04) the Higher Institute of Technology (IST) had 358 students and there were 401 students in teacher training. In 2006–07 the University Centre of Luxembourg had 3,180 students. Many students go abroad, predominantly to France, Germany and Belgium. In 2006–07, 7,222 students pursued university studies abroad.

In 2005 public expenditure on education came to 3·8% of GDP.

Health
In 2004 there were 1,591 doctors (411 GPs and 840 specialists) and 340 dentists. There were 17 hospitals and 3,045 hospital beds in 2004. In 2005 Luxembourg spent 7·7% of its GDP on health, with public expenditure accounting for 90·2% of the total.

Welfare
The official retirement age is 65 years for both men and women. To be eligible, a pensioner must have paid 120 months contributions. The maximum old-age pension is €5,130·08 per month. The minimum pension is €1,108·10 per month if insured for 40 years, reduced by 1/40 for each year less than 40. A minimum pension is not payable if the person has been insured for less than 20 years.

Unemployment benefit is 80% (85% if the insured has a dependant child) of the basis salary during the previous three months, up to 2·5 times the social minimum wage. Recent graduates receive 70% of the social minimum wage whereas self-employed persons receive 80% of the social minimum wage.

RELIGION

The population was 91% Roman Catholic in 2001. There are small Protestant, Jewish, Greek Orthodox, Russian Orthodox and Muslim communities as well.

CULTURE

World Heritage Sites
Luxembourg has one site on the UNESCO World Heritage List: the City of Luxembourg—its Old Quarters and Fortifications (inscribed on the list in 1994).

Broadcasting
The major broadcaster is RTL Group, Europe's largest TV, radio and production company, alongside other private local and regional networks that emerged following liberalizing legislation in 1991. In 2006 there were 186,000 TV-equipped households.

Cinema
In 2005 there were 24 cinema screens throughout the country. Cinema attendances in 2004 totalled 1,357,000.

Press
There were six paid-for daily newspapers in 2006 with an average circulation of 114,000 and nine paid-for non-dailies with an average circulation of 87,000. There were also six free non-dailies in 2006. The German-language *Luxemburger Wort* has the highest circulation, with an average of 74,000 copies in 2005.

Tourism
In 2004 there were 933,000 tourists, and 7,424 hotel rooms and 1,279,000 overnight stays. Tourists spent US$3,883m. in 2004. Camping is widespread, and weekend and short-stay tourism accounts for many tourists. There were 1,141,000 overnight stays at campsites in 2004.

Festivals
The Festival International Echternach (May–June) and the Festival of Wiltz (June–July) are annual events. Both feature a variety of classical music, jazz, theatre and recitals.

Libraries
In Dec. 2005 there were 21 public libraries, one national library and six university libraries (which are also open to non-students).

In 2004 these libraries held around 2·5m. volumes in total; there were 2,587,201 library loans.

Theatre and Opera

There are several theatres in Luxembourg City, including the *Grand Théâtre de la Ville*, *Théâtre des Capucins*, *Théâtre du Centaure* and *Philharmonie du Luxembourg—Salle de Concerts Grande-Duchesse Joséphine Charlotte*. There are also a number of smaller theatres elsewhere, notably in Esch/Alzette and Echternach.

Museums and Galleries

In 2007 there were 45 museums that received 455,826 visitors. The main museums in Luxembourg City are the *Musée d'Histoire de la Ville*, the *Villa Vauban*, the *Musée National d'Histoire Naturelle*, the *Musée National d'Histoire et d'Art*, the *Musée d'Art Moderne Grand-Duc Jean*, the *Musée de la Forteresse* and the *Casino Luxembourg—Forum d'Art Contemporain*. There are smaller museums in the rest of the country.

DIPLOMATIC REPRESENTATIVES

Of Luxembourg in the United Kingdom (27 Wilton Cres., London, SW1X 8SD)
Ambassador: Hubert Wurth.

Of the United Kingdom in Luxembourg (5 Boulevard Joseph II, L-1840 Luxembourg)
Ambassador: Peter Bateman.

Of Luxembourg in the USA (2200 Massachusetts Ave., NW, Washington, D.C., 20008)
Ambassador: Jean-Paul Senninger.

Of the USA in Luxembourg (22 Blvd. Emmanuel Servais, L-2535 Luxembourg)
Ambassador: Cynthia Stroum.

Of Luxembourg to the United Nations
Ambassador: Sylvie Lucas.

Of Luxembourg to the European Union
Permanent Representative: Christian Braun.

FURTHER READING

STATEC. *Annuaire Statistique 2008.*

Newcomer, J., *The Grand Duchy of Luxembourg: The Evolution of Nationhood, 963 AD to 1983.* 2nd ed. 1995

National library: 37 Boulevard Roosevelt, Luxembourg City.
National Statistical Office: Service Central de la Statistique et des Études Économiques (STATEC), CP 304, Luxembourg City, L-2013 Luxembourg. *Director:* Serge Allegrezza.
Website: http://www.statec.public.lu

MACEDONIA

Republika Makedonija
(The Republic of Macedonia)
(Former Yugoslav Republic of Macedonia)

Capital: Skopje
Population estimate, 2010: 2·04m.
GDP per capita, 2007: (PPP$) 9,096
HDI/world rank: 0·817/72

KEY HISTORICAL EVENTS

The history of Macedonia can be traced to the reign of King Karan (808–778 BC), but the country was at its most powerful at the time of Philip II (359–336 BC) and Alexander the Great (336–323 BC). At the end of the 6th century AD Slavs began to settle in Macedonia. There followed a long period of internal fighting but the spread of Christianity led to consolidation and the creation of the first Macedonian Slav state, the Kingdom of Samuel, 976–1018. In the 14th century it fell to Serbia, and in 1355 to the Turks. After the Balkan wars of 1912–13 Turkey was ousted and Serbia received part of the territory, the rest going to Bulgaria and Greece. In 1918 Yugoslav Macedonia was incorporated into Serbia as South Serbia, becoming a republic in the Socialist Federal Republic of Yugoslavia. Claims to the historical Macedonian territory have long been a source of contention with Bulgaria and Greece. Macedonia declared its independence on 18 Sept. 1991. In April 1999 the Kosovo crisis which led to NATO air attacks on Yugoslavian military targets set off a flood of refugees into Macedonia, although most returned home after the end of the crisis.

In March 2001 there were a series of clashes between government forces and ethnic Albanian separatists near the border between Macedonia and Kosovo. As violence escalated Macedonia found itself on the brink of civil war. In May 2001 the new national unity government gave ethnic Albanian rebels a 'final warning' to end their uprising. As the crisis worsened, a stand-off within the government between the Macedonian and the ethnic Albanian parties was only resolved after the intervention of Javier Solana, the EU's foreign and security policy chief. A number of Macedonian soldiers were killed in clashes with the rebels, and following reverses in the military campaign the commander of the Macedonian army, Jovan Andrevski, resigned in June 2001. In Aug. 2001 a peace accord was negotiated.

TERRITORY AND POPULATION

Macedonia (often referred to as the Former Yugoslav Republic of Macedonia) is bounded in the north by Serbia, in the east by Bulgaria, in the south by Greece and in the west by Albania. Its area is 25,713 sq. km. According to the 2002 census final results, the population on 1 Nov. 2002 was 2,022,547. The main ethnic groups in 2002 were Macedonians (1,297,981), Albanians (509,083), Turks (77,959), Romas (53,879), Serbs (35,939) and Vlachs (9,695). Estimate, 31 Dec. 2008, 2,048,619. Ethnic Albanians predominate on the western side of Macedonia. Minorities are represented in the Council for Inter-Ethnic Relations. In Dec. 2004 density was 79 per sq. km. In 2005, 68·9% of the population lived in urban areas.

The UN gives an estimated population for 2010 of 2·04m.

Macedonia is divided into 84 municipalities. The major cities (with 2002 census population) are: Skopje, the capital, 506,926; Kumanovo, 76,275; Bitola, 74,550; Prilep, 69,704; Tetovo, 52,915.

The official language is Macedonian, which uses the Cyrillic alphabet. Around 25% of the population speak Albanian.

SOCIAL STATISTICS

In 2004: births, 23,361; deaths, 17,944; marriages, 14,073; divorces, 1,645; infant deaths, 308. Rates (per 1,000 population): birth, 11·5; death, 8·8; marriage, 6·9; divorce, 0·8. Infant mortality, 2005 (per 1,000 live births), 15. Expectation of life at birth in 2007 was 71·7 years for males and 76·5 years for females. Annual population growth rate, 2000–05, 0·1%. In 2004 the most popular age range for marrying was 25–29 for males and 20–24 for females. Fertility rate, 2004, 1·5 births per woman.

Migration within the Republic of Macedonia, 2004: 9,326. International (external) migration: emigrated persons, 669; immigrated persons 1,381. Net migration in 2004 was 712.

CLIMATE

Macedonia has a mixed Mediterranean-continental type climate, with cold moist winters and hot dry summers. Skopje, Jan. –0·4°C, July 23·1°C.

CONSTITUTION AND GOVERNMENT

At a referendum held on 8 Sept. 1991 turnout was 74%; 99% of votes cast were in favour of a sovereign Macedonia. On 17 Nov. 1991 parliament promulgated a new constitution which officially proclaimed Macedonia's independence. This was replaced by a constitution adopted on 16 Nov. 2001 which for the first time included the recognition of Albanian as an official language. It also increased access for ethnic Albanians to public-sector jobs.

The *President* is directly elected for five-year terms. Candidates must be citizens aged at least 40 years. The parliament is a 120-member single-chamber *Assembly* (*Sobranie*), elected by universal suffrage for four-year terms. There is a *Constitutional Court* whose members are elected by the assembly for non-renewable eight-year terms, and a *National Security Council* chaired by the President. Laws passed by the Assembly must be countersigned by the President, who may return them for reconsideration, but cannot veto them if they gain a two-thirds majority.

Political Parties

The Law on Political Parties makes a distinction between a political party and an association of citizens. The signatures of 500 citizens with the right to vote must be produced for a party to be legally registered. As of 2002 the country had 89 legally registered parties.

National Anthem

'Denes nad Makedonija se radja novo sonce na slobodata' ('Today a new sun of liberty appears over Macedonia'); words by V. Maleski, tune by T. Skalovski.

RECENT ELECTIONS

Parliamentary elections were held on 1 June 2008. Following violent disruptions on election day a partial revote was held in 187 polling stations on 15 June 2008, and in 15 polling stations on 29 June. The final results saw the For a Better Macedonia coalition, led by the Internal Macedonian Revolutionary Organization-Democratic Party for Macedonian National Unity (VMRO-DPMNE), win 63 seats with 48·8% of votes cast. The Sun–Coalition for Europe took 27 seats with 23·7% of the vote, the Democratic Union for Integration (BDI) 18 with 12·8%, the Democratic Party of Albanians (DPA) 11 with 8·5% and the Party for European Future 1 with 1·5%. Turnout was 57·4%.

Presidential elections were held on 22 March 2009. Gjorgje Ivanov (VMRO-DPMNE), took 35·1% of the vote, Ljubomir Frčkoski (Social Democratic Union of Macedonia/SDSM) 20·5%, Imer Selmani (New Democracy) 15·0%, Ljube Boškoski (ind.) 14·9%, Agron Buxhaku (BDI) 7·5%, Nano Ružin (Liberal Democratic Party) 4·1%, and Mirushe Hoxha (DPA) 3·1%. In the run-off on 5 April Ivanov won with 63·1% against Frčkoski with 36·9%. Turnout was an estimated 56·4% in the first round and 42·6% in the second.

CURRENT ADMINISTRATION

President: Gjorgje Ivanov; b. 1960 (VMRO-DPMNE; sworn in 12 May 2009).

Prime Minister: Nikola Gruevski; b. 1970 (VMRO-DPMNE; in office since 27 Aug. 2006).

Following elections in July 2006 a multi-party coalition government was formed. In March 2010 it was composed as follows:

Deputy Prime Minister and Minister of Finance: Zoran Stavrevski. *Deputy Prime Minister for European Affairs:* Vasko Naumovski. *Deputy Prime Minister in Charge of Implementation of the Ohrid Agreement:* Abdulakim Ademi. *Deputy Prime Minister for Economic Affairs:* Vladimir Pesevski.

Minister of Agriculture, Forestry and Water Supply: Ljupcho Dimovski. *Culture:* Elizabeta Kanceska Milevska. *Defence:* Zoran Konjanovski. *Economy:* Fatmir Besimi. *Education and Science:* Nikola Todorov. *Environment and Physical Planning:* Nexhati Jakupi. *Foreign Affairs:* Antonio Milososki. *Health:* Bujar Osmani. *Information Society:* Ivo Ivanovski. *Interior:* Gordana Jankulovska. *Justice:* Mihajlo Manevski. *Labour and Social Policy:* Xhelil Bajrami. *Local Self-Government:* Musa Xhaferi. *Transport and Communications:* Mile Janakieski. *Ministers without Portfolio:* Vele Samak; Hadi Neziri; Nezdet Mustafa.

Government Website: http://www.vlada.mk

CURRENT LEADERS

Gjorgje Ivanov

Position

President

Introduction

Gjorgje Ivanov was sworn into office on 12 May 2009 after winning the second round of the presidential election on 5 April with more than 60% of the vote. Although his duties during his five-year term will be largely ceremonial, Ivanov is supreme commander of the army and has decision-making powers on foreign policy and the judiciary.

Early Life

Gjorgje Ivanov was born on 2 May 1960 in Valandovo. He graduated in law from Ss. Cyril and Methodius University of Skopje in 1982 and was appointed assistant law professor in 1995. In 1998 he became an associate professor in political theory and political philosophy at the same time as completing his doctorate.

In 1999 Ivanov was made a professor of post-graduate studies at the University of Athens before joining the political science departments of the University of Bologna and the University of Sarajevo the following year. He returned to his alma mater in 2001 to take up the post of director of political studies. In 2008 Ivanov received his political science professorship and was appointed as chair of the Macedonian Higher Education Accreditation Council.

On 25 Jan. 2009 the ruling conservative VMRO-DPMNE announced Ivanov as its presidential candidate for the 2009 election. In the first round of voting on 22 March 2009 he received 35% of the vote and claimed 63% in a second round to claim the presidency.

Career in Office

With critics attacking his lack of political experience, Ivanov has pledged to continue Macedonia's campaign for EU and NATO membership. He also promised to seek out a resolution to the dispute with Greece over the country's name (*see* GREECE: Key Historical Events on page 549) and aims to diffuse ongoing tensions with Macedonia's ethnic Albanian minority.

DEFENCE

The President is the C.-in-C. of the armed forces. Compulsory national military service was abolished in 2006.

Defence expenditure in 2006 totalled US$134m. (US$65 per capita), representing 2·2% of GDP.

The European Union's first ever peacekeeping force (EUFOR) officially started work in Macedonia on 1 April 2003, replacing the NATO-led force that had been in the country since 2001. EUFOR left the country in Dec. 2003.

Army

Army strength was 9,760 in 2007. There is a paramilitary police force of 7,600.

Navy

In 2007 the Marine Wing operated four river patrol craft.

Air Force

The Army Air Force numbered 1,130 in 2007, and had four combat capable aircraft (in storage) and ten attack helicopters.

INTERNATIONAL RELATIONS

On 13 Sept. 1995 under the auspices of the UN, Macedonia and Greece agreed to normalize their relations.

Macedonia is a member of the UN, World Bank, IMF and several other UN specialized agencies, WTO, Council of Europe, OSCE, Central European Initiative, BIS, the International Organization of the Francophonie and NATO Partnership for Peace.

ECONOMY

Agriculture accounted for 12·7% of GDP in 2006, industry 29·5% and services 57·8%.

Overview

Fighting in 2001 between the government and ethnic Albanian rebels interrupted a period of positive growth but the economy has gradually recovered its pre-conflict levels, with GDP growing at around 3% per year. Disciplined fiscal policy has seen large fiscal and external imbalances corrected. Inflation is low, despite a 30% expansion of bank credit, and foreign interest in the banking system continues to rise. In order to improve growth prospects, unemployment (which is amongst the highest in the region) and high poverty levels need to be addressed. Greater international integration may promote foreign investment and enhance the business climate but uncertainty over the region's stability continues to undermine investor confidence.

Currency
The national currency of Macedonia is the *denar* (MKD), of 100 *deni*. Foreign exchange reserves were US$910m. in July 2005, gold reserves 197,000 troy oz and total money supply was 29,745m. denars. Inflation was 8·3% in 2008 (2·3% in 2007).

Budget
In 2005 revenues totalled 92,805m. denars and expenditures 92,228m. denars.

Performance
In 2001 the political turmoil in the country resulted in the economy contracting by 4·5%. There was then a slight recovery in 2002, with a growth rate of 0·9%. The economy continued to expand with real GDP growth rates of 5·9% in 2007 and 4·9% in 2008. Total GDP in 2008 was US$9·5bn.

Banking and Finance
The central bank and bank of issue is the National Bank of Macedonia. Its *Governor* is Petar Goshev (since May 2004). Privatization of the banking sector was completed in 2000. In 2001 there were 20 commercial banks, six of which were majority foreign-owned. As of 31 Dec. 1998 commercial banks' total non-government deposits were 23,136m. denars, and non-government savings deposits were 15,095m. denars. The largest banks are Stopanska Banka, followed by Komercijalna Banka; between them they control more than half the total assets of all banks in Macedonia.

A stock exchange opened in Skopje in 1996.

ENERGY AND NATURAL RESOURCES

Environment
Macedonia's carbon dioxide emissions from the consumption and flaring of fossil fuels were the equivalent of 3·6 tonnes per capita in 2008.

Electricity
Installed capacity in 2004 was an estimated 1·5m. kW. Output in 2004: 6·67bn. kWh, of which 1·48bn. kWh were from hydro-electric plants. Consumption per capita was 3,863 kWh in 2004.

Oil and Gas
A 230-km long pipeline bringing crude oil to Macedonia from Thessaloniki in Greece opened in July 2002. Built at a cost of over US$130m., it has the capacity to provide Macedonia with 2·5m. tonnes of crude oil annually.

Minerals
Macedonia is relatively rich in minerals, including lead, zinc, copper, iron, chromium, nickel, antimony, manganese, silver and gold. Output in 2003, unless otherwise indicated (in tonnes): lignite (2004), 7,245,000; copper ore, 1,200,000; lead-zinc ore, 40,000; copper concentrate, 15,000; lead concentrates, 5,000; silver, 10.

Agriculture
In 2002 the agricultural population numbered 833,000 persons, of whom 109,000 were economically active. In 2004 there were 560,264 ha. of arable land, 703,830 ha. of pasture and 44,000 ha. of permanent crops. In 2004, 101,004 ha. of arable land were owned by agricultural organizations and 459,260 ha. by individual farmers. There were 65,338 tractors in use in 2004.

Crop production, 2004 (in 1,000 tonnes): wheat, 356; grapes, 194; potatoes (2003), 175; barley, 149; wine, 142; maize (2003), 141; watermelons, 115; chillies and green peppers (2003), 111; tomatoes (2002), 109; lucerne, 98; apples, 82; cabbage (2002), 71; sugar beets, 47; onions (2003), 31; cucumbers and gherkins, 27; plums, 26. In 2004, 119,000 tonnes of wine were produced.

Livestock, 2004 (in 1,000): sheep, 1,432; cattle, 255; pigs, 158; horses, 40; chickens, 2,725. Livestock products, 2004 (in 1,000 tonnes): beef, 9; pork, bacon and ham, 9; mutton, 7; poultry, 3; cow's milk, 213m. litres; sheep's milk, 49m. litres; eggs (total), 340m.

Forestry
Forests covered 947,653 ha. in 2004, chiefly oak and beech. 752,000 cu. metres of timber were cut in 2007.

Fisheries
Total catch in 2004 was 1,271 tonnes, entirely from inland waters.

INDUSTRY

In 1999 there were 94,404 enterprises (90,426 private, 1,112 public, 1,257 co-operative, 1,577 mixed and 32 state-owned). Production, 2004 (in tonnes): cement, 585,000; distillate fuel oil, 359,000; residual fuel oil, 282,000; petrol, 146,377; sulphuric acid (2001), 101,058; ferroalloys, 72,082; detergents, 14,507.

Labour
In April 2004 there were 522,995 employed persons, including: 116,300 in manufacturing; 87,608 in agriculture, hunting and forestry; 74,218 in wholesale and retail trade/repair of motor vehicles, motorcycles and personal and household goods; and 33,635 in education. The number of unemployed persons in 2004 was 309,286, giving an unemployment rate of 37·2%.

INTERNATIONAL TRADE

The foreign debt of Macedonia, including debt taken over from the former Yugoslavia, was US$2,243m. in 2005.

Imports and Exports
In 2004 imports (f.o.b.) were valued at US$2,903·4m. (US$2,306·4m. in 2003) and exports (f.o.b.) at US$1,673·5m. (US$1,367·0m. in 2003).

Main import suppliers, 2003: Germany (12·6%), Greece (9·7%), Russia (8·7%), Serbia and Montenegro (8·4%) and Bulgaria (7·2%). Main export markets, 2003: Serbia and Montenegro (20·8%), Germany (18·9%), Greece (13·7%), Italy (8·0%) and the USA (4·3%).

COMMUNICATIONS

Roads
In 2004 there were 906 km of main roads, 3,801 km of regional roads and 8,417 km of local roads: 1,224 km of roads were paved and 6,939 km asphalted. 9·3m. passengers and 10·5m. tonnes of freight were transported. In 2007 there were 248,800 passenger cars in use, 2,300 buses and coaches, and 26,600 lorries and vans. In 2004 there were 1,988 road accidents with 155 fatalities.

Rail
In 2004 there were 696 km of railways (233 km electrified). 0·9m. passengers and 2·6m. tonnes of freight were transported.

Civil Aviation
There are international airports at Skopje and Ohrid. A new Macedonia-based carrier, Aeromak, has been established to replace MAT Macedonian Airlines, the former flag carrier which ceased operations in 2009. In 2004 Skopje handled 489,942 passengers (all on international flights) and 1,749 tonnes of freight. Ohrid handled 32,497 passengers (all on international flights) and 21 tonnes of freight.

Telecommunications
In 2004 there were 1,522,600 telephone subscribers (749·9 per 1,000 inhabitants), including 985,600 mobile phone subscribers. There were 159,900 internet users in 2005 and 451,000 PCs in use (221·7 per 1,000 inhabitants). In 2002 the Hungarian firm Matav acquired a 51% stake in MakTel, the state monopoly

telecommunications provider, in the most significant economic development in the country's history. The deal, worth €618·2m. (US$568·4m.) over two years, is the biggest foreign investment to date.

Postal Services

In 2003 there were 317 post offices.

SOCIAL INSTITUTIONS

Justice

Courts are autonomous and independent. Judges are tenured and elected for life on the proposal of the *Judicial Council*, whose members are themselves elected for renewable six-year terms. The highest court is the Supreme Court. There are 27 courts of first instance and three higher courts.

The population in penal institutions in March 2008 was 2,200 (107 per 100,000 of national population).

Education

The literacy rate was 96·1% in 2003 (98·2% among males and 94·1% among females). Education is free and compulsory for nine years. In 2004, 36,392 children attended 51 pre-school institutions and 486 infant schools of elementary education. In 2004–05 there were 227,254 pupils enrolled in 1,012 primary schools, 95,268 in 96 secondary schools and (2001–02) 343,587 students in higher education. There are universities at Skopje (Cyril and Methodius, founded in 1949; 36,509 students and 1,314 academic staff in 2004–05) and Bitola (founded 1979; 10,043 students and 233 academic staff in 2004–05). There are two private universities at Skopje (1,075 students and 41 academic staff in 2004–05) and Tetovo (1,737 students and 86 academic staff in 2004–05).

In 2002 public expenditure on education came to 3·5% of GDP.

Health

In 2004 there were 4,490 doctors, 1,134 dentists, 322 pharmacologists and 63 hospitals with 9,699 beds.

Welfare

In 2004 social assistance was paid to 67,260 households. Child care and special supplements went to 46,203 children, and 16,970 underage and 95,053 adults received social benefits. There were 260,075 pensioners in 2004.

RELIGION

Macedonia is traditionally Orthodox but the church is not established and there is freedom of religion. In 2001 there were 1·21m. Serbian (Macedonian) Orthodox and 580,000 Sunni Muslims. In 1967 an autocephalous Orthodox church split off from the Serbian. Its head is the Archbishop of Ohrid and Macedonia whose seat is at Skopje. It has five bishoprics in Macedonia and representatives in USA, Canada and Australia. It has some 300 priests.

The Muslim Religious Union has a superiorate at Skopje. The Roman Catholic Church has a seat at Skopje.

CULTURE

World Heritage Sites

The Former Yugoslav Republic of Macedonia has one site on the UNESCO World Heritage List: Ohrid Region with its Cultural and Historic Aspect and its Natural Environment (inscribed on the list in 1979 and 1980), a rich repository of Byzantine art and architecture.

Broadcasting

State-owned Macedonian Radio and Television operates three national television channels, radio channels and satellite services. In 2004 there were also 29 local public broadcasting enterprises (state-owned), 18 of which transmitted only radio programmes while the other 11 transmitted radio and TV programmes (colour by PAL). In 2004 there were 69 private radio and 54 private TV stations. In 2005 there were 558,000 TV-equipped households.

Cinema

There were 19 cinemas and 302,653 admissions in 2004; gross box office receipts came to 27m. denars. One full-length film was made in 2004.

Press

There were ten daily newspapers and 11 weeklies in 2004, and 207 other newspapers and periodicals published in Macedonian, Albanian, Turkish, English and other languages.

There are two news agencies in Macedonia, the Macedonian Information Agency (national) and Makfax (privately owned).

Tourism

In 2004 tourists numbered 465,015 spending 1·86m. nights in Macedonia. Total tourist expenditure was US$92m. in 2005.

DIPLOMATIC REPRESENTATIVES

Of Macedonia in the United Kingdom (Suites 2·1 and 2·2, Buckingham Court, 75–83 Buckingham Gate, London, SW1E 6PE)
Ambassador: Marija Efremova.

Of the United Kingdom in Macedonia (Salvador Aljende 73, 1000 Skopje)
Ambassador: Andrew Key.

Of Macedonia in the USA (2129 Wyoming Ave., NW, Washington, D.C., 20008)
Ambassador: Zoran Jolevski.

Of the USA in Macedonia (ul. Samoilova 21, 1000 Skopje)
Ambassador: Philip T. Reeker.

Of Macedonia to the United Nations
Ambassador: Slobodan Tašovski.

Of Macedonia to the European Union
Ambassador: Blerim Reka.

FURTHER READING

Danforth, L. M., *The Macedonian Conflict: Ethnic Nationalism in a Transnational World.* 1996
Phillips, John, *Macedonia: Warlords and Rebels in the Balkans.* 2004
Poulton, H., *Who Are the Macedonians?* 1996

National Statistical Office: State Statistical Office, Dame Gruev 4, Skopje. *Director:* Blagica Novkovska.
Website: http://www.stat.gov.mk

MADAGASCAR

Repoblikan'i Madagasikara
(Republic of Madagascar)

Capital: Antananarivo
Population estimate, 2010: 20·15m.
GDP per capita, 2007: (PPP$) 932
HDI/world rank: 0·543/145

KEY HISTORICAL EVENTS

The island was settled by people of African and Indonesian origin when it was visited by the Portuguese explorer, Diego Diaz, in 1500. The island was unified under the Imérina monarchy between 1797 and 1861. A French protectorate was established in 1895. Madagascar became a French colony on 6 Aug. 1896 and achieved independence on 26 June 1960.

In Feb. 1975 Col. Richard Ratsimandrava, head of state, was assassinated. The 1975 constitution instituted a 'Democratic Republic' in which only a single political party was permitted. After six months of anti-government unrest an 18-month transitional administration was agreed. A new constitution instituted the Third Republic in Sept. 1992.

Following the presidential election of Dec. 2001 the opposition candidate Marc Ravalomanana claimed victory, although the High Constitutional Court called for a run-off. On 22 Feb. 2002 Ravalomanana declared himself president and imposed a state of emergency. However, incumbent Didier Ratsiraka and his government set up a rival capital in Toamasina. In April 2002 both men agreed to a recount of votes to solve the dispute. Ravalomanana was declared president.

Re-elected in 2006, the suppression of political opponents led to an army mutiny against Ravalomanana in early 2009. As civil unrest increased, he resigned the presidency and handed power to the military which installed Andry Rajoelina, Ravalomanana's chief political rival, as president.

TERRITORY AND POPULATION

Madagascar is situated 400 km (250 miles) off the southeast coast of Africa, from which it is separated by the Mozambique channel. Its area is 587,041 sq. km (226,658 sq. miles). At the 1993 census the population was 12,092,157 (50·45% female); density, 20·6 per sq. km. 73·2% of the population lived in rural areas in 2005.

The UN gives an estimated population for 2010 of 20·15m.; density, 34 per sq. km.

Province	*Area in sq. km*	*Population (1993 census)*	*Chief town*	*Population (1993 census)*
Antananarivo	58,283	3,483,236	Antananarivo	1,432,000[1]
Antsiranana	43,046	942,410	Antsiranana	54,418[2]
Fianarantsoa	102,373	2,671,150	Fianarantsoa	99,005
Mahajanga	150,023	1,330,612	Mahajanga	100,807
Toamasina	71,911	1,935,330	Toamasina	127,441
Toliary	161,405	1,729,419	Toliary	61,460[2]

[1]1999 figure. [2]1990 estimate.

Following a referendum held in April 2007 the six provinces were to be dissolved and replaced as the main administrative sub-division by 22 existing regions. The divisional changes were scheduled to take effect by 4 Oct. 2009 but have been delayed owing to political unrest.

The indigenous population is of Malayo-Polynesian stock, divided into 18 ethnic groups of which the principal are Merina (24%) of the central plateau, the Betsimisaraka (13%) of the east coast and the Betsileo (11%) of the southern plateau. Foreign communities include Europeans (mainly French), Indians, Chinese, Comorians and Arabs.

Malagasy, French and (since 2007) English are all official languages.

SOCIAL STATISTICS

2000 estimates: births, 663,000; deaths, 211,000. Rates, 2000 estimates (per 1,000 population): births, 41·5; deaths, 13·2. Infant mortality, 2005 (per 1,000 live births), 74. Expectation of life in 2007 was 58·3 years for males and 61·5 for females. Annual population growth rate, 2000–05, 3·2%. Fertility rate, 2004, 5·3 births per woman.

CLIMATE

A tropical climate, but the mountains cause big variations in rainfall, which is very heavy in the east and very light in the west. Antananarivo, Jan. 70°F (21·1°C), July 59°F (15°C). Annual rainfall 54" (1,350 mm). Toamasina, Jan. 80°F (26·7°C), July 70°F (21·1°C). Annual rainfall 128" (3,256 mm).

CONSTITUTION AND GOVERNMENT

Following a referendum, a constitution came into force on 30 Dec. 1975 establishing a Democratic Republic. It provided for a National People's Assembly elected by universal suffrage from the single list of the *Front National pour la Défense de la Révolution Socialiste Malgache.* Executive power was vested in the President with the guidance of a Supreme Revolutionary Council.

Under a convention of 31 Oct. 1991 the powers of the National People's Assembly and the Supreme Revolutionary Council were delegated to a High State Authority for a Provisional government. Following a referendum on 19 Aug. 1992 at which turnout was 77·68% and 75·44% of votes cast were in favour, a new constitution was adopted on 21 Sept. 1992 establishing the Third Republic. The *National Assembly* has 127 members elected to four-year terms (down from 160 for the 2002 election). There is also a *Senate* of 90 members.

A referendum on 17 Sept. 1995 was in favour of the President appointing and dismissing the Prime Minister, hitherto elected by parliament. The electorate was 6m.; turnout was 50%. The National Assembly and Senate were suspended in March 2009 and a High Transitional Authority created to act as an emergency parliament following the political upheaval of Feb. 2009.

National Anthem

'Ry tanindrazanay malala ô!' ('O our beloved Fatherland'); words by Pastor Rahajason, tune by N. Raharisoa.

RECENT ELECTIONS

Presidential elections were held on 3 Dec. 2006. Incumbent president Marc Ravalomanana won with 54·8% of the vote, ahead of Jean Lahiniriko with 11·7%, former president Roland Ratsiraka with 10·1% and Herizo Razafimahaleo with 9·0%. There were ten other candidates who each took less than 5% of the vote. Turnout was 61·5%.

In parliamentary elections held on 23 Sept. 2007 President Marc Ravalomanana's I Love Madagascar party won 105 of the 127 seats, independents 11 and Fanjava Velogno 2 with nine smaller parties each winning one seat.

CURRENT ADMINISTRATION

Interim President: Andry Rajoelina; b. 1974 (Young Malagasies Determined/TGV, assumed office 17 March 2009 and sworn in 21 March 2009).

In April 2010 the cabinet was composed as follows:

Prime Minister and Minister of the Armed Forces: Col. Albert Camille Vital (ind.; sworn in 20 Dec. 2009).

Vice Prime Minister and Minister of Foreign Affairs: Hyppolite Ramaroson. *Vice Prime Minister and Minister of Health:* Alain Tehindrazanavelo. *Vice Prime Minister and Minister of Interior:* Cécile Manorohanta.

Minister of Agriculture: Jaona Mamitiana. *Civil Service, Work and Social Laws:* Noëlson William. *Commerce:* Jean-Claude Rakotonirina. *Communications:* Nathalie Rabe. *Culture and Heritage:* Gilbert Raharizatovo. *Decentralization and Land Management:* Hajo Andrianainarivelo. *Economy and Industry:* Richard Fienena. *Energy:* Jean-Rodolphe Ramanantsoa. *Environment and Forests:* Col. Randriamiandrisoa Calixte. *Finance and Budget:* Hery Rajaonarimampianina. *Fisheries and Fishing Resources:* Alain Andriamiseza. *Higher Education and Scientific Research:* Athanase Tongavelo. *Internal Security:* Rémy Sylvain Organes Rakotomiantarizaka. *Justice:* Christine Harijaona Razanamahasoa. *Livestock:* Maharante Jean de Dieu. *Mines and Hydrocarbons:* Mamy Ratovomalala. *National Education:* Julien Razafimananjato. *Population and Social Affairs:* Nadine Ramaroson. *Public Works and Meteorology:* Éric Razafimandimby. *Sports:* Virapin Ramamonjisoa. *Telecommunications, Post and New Technologies:* Augustin Andriamananoro. *Tourism and Handicrafts:* Irène Victoire Andréas. *Transport:* Rolland Ranjatoelina. *Water:* Nirhy Lanto Andriamahazo. *Youth and Leisure:* Serge Ranaivo.

Government Website (French only):
http://www.madagascar.gov.mg

CURRENT LEADERS

Andry Rajoelina

Position
President

Introduction
Andry Rajoelina was sworn in as president of the High Transition Authority of Madagascar government on 21 March 2009. He was installed by the military after the former president, Marc Ravalomanana, ceded power following three months of political turmoil. On assuming power Rajoelina suspended parliament and set up two transitional bodies to run the country. Although his authority is not universally recognized by the international community, Rajoelina is expected to serve until the expiry of his predecessor's term in 2011. Rajoelina was mayor of Antananarivo until his dismissal by President Ravalomanana in Feb. 2009.

Early Life
Rajoelina was born on 30 May 1974 into the wealthy family of a colonel in the Malagasy army. He rose to prominence as a disc jockey in the capital city of Antananarivo, before going on to set up the TV and radio station, Viva, and running a successful advertising company. Rajoelina's brash personality earned him the nickname TGV, after the French high-speed train. The initials went on to serve as the acronym for his political movement, Tanora malaGasy Vonona (Young Malagasies Determined). He harnessed his public profile to win the Antananarivo mayoral election in Dec. 2007.

In Dec. 2008 and Jan. 2009 Rajoelina's Viva radio and TV networks were shut down by the government, which accused them of 'inciting civil disobedience'. Rajoelina reacted by calling a general strike, resulting in widespread disorder. On 17 March Ravalomanana stepped down under pressure from military chiefs who immediately announced the installation of Rajoelina as his successor. The African Union denounced the change of government as a coup and suspended Madagascar's membership. Rajoelina's ascent to power was also condemned by the European Union and the USA.

Career in Office
Aged 34 when he assumed power, Rajoelina was the youngest president in Madagascar's history, although the constitution stipulates that presidential candidates must be at least 40 years of age. Rajoelina promised a new constitution and elections within two years. One of his first acts as president was to cancel a contract with South Korean conglomerate Daewoo that had granted a large swathe of Madagascan territory to the firm for agricultural development.

On 17 April 2009 Rajoelina issued a warrant for the arrest of Ravalomanana, who was then tried in absentia (having fled to South Africa) and sentenced in June to four years in prison for abuse of office. In Aug. 2009 a power-sharing agreement, sponsored by international mediators, was signed between the rival Rajoelina and Ravalomanana political camps with the aim of establishing a transitional unity government. However, continued disputes prevented its effective implementation and in Dec. Rajoelina announced that he was abandoning the agreement and calling a general election for March 2010 (although it was subsequently postponed until May).

DEFENCE

There is conscription (including civilian labour service) for 18 months. Defence expenditure totalled US$298m. in 2006 (US$16 per capita), representing 5·4% of GDP.

Army

Strength (2007) approximately 12,500 and gendarmerie 8,100.

Navy
In 2007 the Navy had a strength of 500 (including some 100 marines).

Air Force
Personnel (2007) 500. There are no combat capable aircraft.

INTERNATIONAL RELATIONS
Madagascar is a member of the UN, World Bank, IMF and several other UN specialized agencies, WTO, IOM, International Organization of the Francophonie, African Development Bank, COMESA, SADC and is an ACP member state of the ACP-EU relationship.

ECONOMY
In 2006 agriculture contributed 27·5% of GDP, industry 15·3% and services 57·2%.

Overview
Economic decline over several decades has seen Madagascar's per capita income fall from US$473 in 1970 to US$290 in 2005. Key commodities such as vanilla and oil are highly susceptible to both external price and weather-related shocks. Nonetheless, GDP growth has been above 4% per year since 2002, with tourism prospering. Tourist arrivals in 2005 were 21% higher than in 2004. Improved rice productivity and public investment have also boosted GDP performance, while the mining sector has benefited from foreign direct investment. However, upward pressure on the exchange rate poses a challenge to macroeconomic stability, already constrained by ineffective monetary policy and the central bank's weak position.

Currency
In July 2003 President Marc Ravalomanana announced that the *Ariary* (MGA) would become the official currency, replacing the *Malagasy franc* (MGFr). The Ariary became legal tender on 1 Aug. 2003 at a rate of 1 *Ariary* = 5 *Malagasy francs*. The Ariary is subdivided into five *Iraimbilanja*.

In July 2005 foreign exchange reserves were US$435m. and total money supply was 1,324·0bn. ariarys. Inflation was 10·4% in 2007 and 9·2% in 2008.

Budget
Revenues totalled 1,685·1bn. ariarys in 2005 (1,656·8bn. ariarys in 2004) and expenditures 1,114·7bn. ariarys (1,027·6bn. ariarys in 2004).

VAT is 18%.

Performance
Total GDP in 2008 was US$9·0bn. There was a recession in 2002 with the economy contracting by 12·4% as a result of the six-month long political crisis, but a recovery followed in 2003 and 2004 with real GDP growth of 9·8% and 5·3% respectively. The recovery continued with growth of 6·2% in 2007 and 7·1% in 2008.

Banking and Finance
A Central Bank, the Banque Centrale de Madagascar, was formed in 1973, replacing the former Institut d'Émission Malgache as the central bank of issue. The *Governor* is Frédéric Rasamoely. All commercial banking and insurance was nationalized in 1975 and privatized in 1988. Of the six other banks, the largest are the Bankin'ny Tantsaha Mpamokatra and the BNI—Crédit Lyonnais de Madagascar.

ENERGY AND NATURAL RESOURCES

Environment
Madagascar's carbon dioxide emissions from the consumption and flaring of fossil fuels in 2008 were the equivalent of 0·1 tonnes per capita.

Electricity
Installed capacity was around 0·2m. kW in 2004. Production in 2004 was 990m. kWh, with consumption per capita 56 kWh.

Oil and Gas
Several oil blocks both on land and offshore were discovered in 2005.

Minerals
Mining production in 2005 included: chromite, 141,000 tonnes; salt (estimate), 65,000 tonnes; graphite (2004), 8,000 tonnes. There have also been discoveries of precious and semi-precious stones in various parts of the country, in particular sapphires, topaz and garnets. Madagascar is believed to have the world's largest reserves of sapphires.

Agriculture
75–80% of the workforce is employed in agriculture. There were an estimated 2·95m. ha. of arable land in 2007 and 0·6m. ha. of permanent crops. 890,000 ha. were irrigated in 2007. The principal agricultural products in 2003 were (in 1,000 tonnes): rice, 2,800; cassava, 2,367; sugarcane, 2,236; sweet potatoes, 509; potatoes, 298; bananas, 290; mangoes, 210; tomatoes, 210; taro, 200; maize, 181; coconuts, 84; oranges, 83; dry beans, 70. Rice is produced on some 40% of cultivated land. Madagascar is the world's largest producer of vanilla.

Cattle breeding and agriculture are the chief occupations. There were, in 2003, 10·5m. cattle, 1·6m. pigs, 1·2m. goats, 650,000 sheep and 24m. chickens.

Forestry
In 2005 the area under forests was 12·84m. ha., or 22·1% of the total land area. The forests contain many valuable woods, while gum, resins and plants for tanning, dyeing and medicinal purposes abound. Timber production was 13·35m. cu. metres in 2007.

Fisheries
The catch of fish in 2005 was 136,400 tonnes (78% from marine waters).

INDUSTRY
Industry, hitherto confined mainly to the processing of agricultural products, is now extending to cover other fields.

Labour
In 2003 the economically active population totalled 7,573,900 (50·5% males). In 2002 approximately 82·2% of the economically active population were engaged in agriculture, hunting and forestry.

INTERNATIONAL TRADE
Foreign debt was US$3,465m. in 2005.

Imports and Exports
In 2005 imports (f.o.b.) were valued at US$1,427m. and exports (f.o.b.) at US$834m. The principal imports in 2004 were machinery and transport equipment (30·7%), petroleum and petroleum products (22·9%), food and livestock (9·8%) and chemicals and related products (8·6%). Principal exports in 2004 were vanilla (27·8%), shellfish (13·9%), printed matter (10·0%) and cloves (6·3%). Main import suppliers, 2004: France, 15·3%; China, 10·3%; Bahrain, 8·9%; South Africa, 7·3%. Main export markets, 2004: France, 35·8%; USA, 20·6%; Mauritius, 5·7%; Singapore, 5·6%.

COMMUNICATIONS

Roads
In 2002 there were about 65,663 km of roads, 11·6% of which were paved. There were 52,200 passenger cars in 2002, 39,400 trucks and vans and (1996) 4,850 buses and coaches. 25 people died in road accidents in 1995.

Rail
In 2005 there were 854 km of railways, all metre gauge. In 2005, 100,000 passengers and 300,000 tonnes of freight were transported.

Civil Aviation
There are international airports at Antananarivo (Ivato) and Mahajanga (Amborovy). The national carrier is Air Madagascar, which is 90·6% state-owned. In 2003 scheduled airline traffic of Madagascar-based carriers flew 9m. km, carrying 452,000 passengers (140,000 on international flights). In 2001 Antananarivo handled 699,074 passengers (348,238 on domestic flights) and 15,499 tonnes of freight.

Shipping
The main ports are Toamasina, Mahajanga, Antsiranana and Toliara. In 2002 the merchant marine totalled 35,000 GRT, including oil tankers 5,000 GRT. In 2000 vessels totalling 4,842,000 NRT entered ports.

Telecommunications
Madagascar had 571,600 telephone subscribers in 2005, equivalent to 30·7 per 1,000 persons, of which 504,700 were mobile phone subscribers. There were 91,000 PCs were in use (5·0 per 1,000 persons) in 2004 and 90,000 internet users.

Postal Services
There were 957 post offices in 2003, or one for every 18,200 persons.

SOCIAL INSTITUTIONS

Justice
The Supreme Court and the Court of Appeal are in Antananarivo. In most towns there are Courts of First Instance for civil and commercial cases. For criminal cases there are ordinary criminal courts in most towns.

The population in penal institutions in 2003 was approximately 19,000 (109 per 100,000 of national population).

Education
Education is compulsory from six to 14 years of age. In 2007 there were 78,743 teaching staff for 3,837,343 pupils in primary schools, 835,539 pupils at secondary level with 34,320 teaching staff and 58,313 students at tertiary level with 3,032 academic staff. Adult literacy rate in 2003 was 70·6% (male, 76·4%; female, 65·2%). In 2007 public expenditure on education came to 3·4% of GNI and 16·4% of total government spending.

Health
There were nine hospital beds per 10,000 population in 1990. In 2001 there were 1,428 physicians, 76 dentists, 3,088 nurses, 1,472 midwives and eight pharmacists. In 1996 government expenditure on health totalled MGFr191,300m.

Welfare
In 1996 government expenditure on social security and welfare totalled MGFr26,000m.

RELIGION
About 48% of the population practise the traditional religion, 43% are Christians (of whom approximately half are Roman Catholic and half are Protestant, mainly belonging to the Fiangonan'i Jesosy Kristy eto Madagasikara) and 9% are followers of other religions (predominantly Islam).

CULTURE

World Heritage Sites
Tsingy de Bemaraha Strict Nature Reserve joined the UNESCO World Heritage List in 1990. The undisturbed forests, lakes and mangrove swamps are the habitat for rare and endangered lemurs and birds. The Royal Hill of Ambohimanga was added in 2001, a royal city and burial site and a symbol of Malagasy identity. The rainforests of Atsinanana, comprising six national parks in the eastern part of the island, were inscribed on the list in 2007.

Broadcasting
State-owned Radio-Télévision Malagasy is responsible for national television and radio broadcasting, but there are hundreds of independent local TV and radio stations. Major private networks include MBS TV and Radio MBS, both owned by President Ravalomanana's Malagasy Broadcasting System. In 2006 there were 710,000 TV sets (colour by PAL).

Press
In 2006 there were 14 daily newspapers with a total circulation of 110,000.

Tourism
There were 277,000 tourists in 2005. Receipts totalled US$62m.

DIPLOMATIC REPRESENTATIVES
Of Madagascar in the United Kingdom (8–10 Hallam St., London, W1W 6JE)
Ambassador: Vacant.
Chargé d'Affaires a.i.: Iary Berthine Ravaoarimanana.

Of the United Kingdom in Madagascar (embassy in Antananarivo closed in 2005)
Ambassador: Dr John Murton (resides in Port Louis, Mauritius).

Of Madagascar in the USA (2374 Massachusetts Ave., NW, Washington, D.C., 20008)
Ambassador: Jocelyn Radifera.

Of the USA in Madagascar (14–16 rue Rainitovo, Antsahavola, Antananarivo)
Ambassador: R. Niels Marquardt.

Of Madagascar to the United Nations
Ambassador: Zina Andrianarivelo.

Of Madagascar to the European Union
Ambassador: Jeannot Rakotomalala.

FURTHER READING
Banque des Données de l'État. *Bulletin Mensuel de Statistique*

Allen, P. M., *Madagascar.* 1995

National Statistical Office: Institut National de la Statistique (INSTAT), BP 485 Anosy, Antananarivo 101.
Website (French only): http://www.instat.mg

MALAŴI

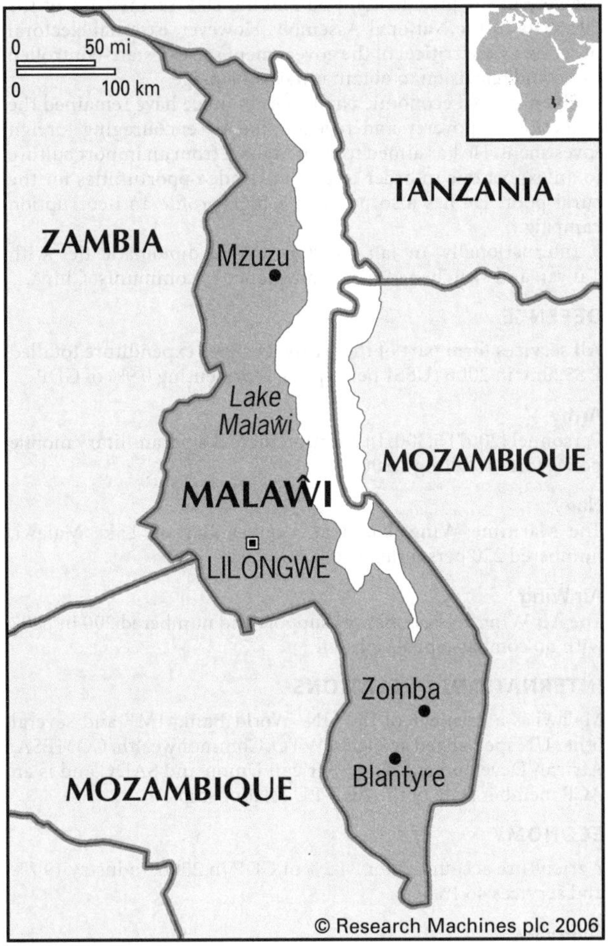

Dziko la Malaŵi
(Republic of Malaŵi)

Capital: Lilongwe
Population estimate, 2010: 15·69m.
GDP per capita, 2007: (PPP$) 761
HDI/world rank: 0·493/160

KEY HISTORICAL EVENTS

The explorer David Livingstone reached Lake Nyasa, now Lake Malaŵi, in 1859 and it was the land along the lake's western shore that became, in 1891, the British Protectorate of Nyasaland. In 1884 the British South Africa Company applied for a charter to trade. Pressure on land, the colour bar and other grievances generated Malaŵian resistance. In 1953 Nyasaland was joined with Southern Rhodesia (Zimbabwe) and Northern Rhodesia (Zambia) to form the Federation of Rhodesia and Nyasaland, under British control. This union was dissolved in 1963. Nyasaland was self-governing until on 6 July 1964 it became independent, adopting the name Malaŵi. In 1966 Malaŵi was declared a republic and Dr Hastings Banda became the first president, establishing a one party dictatorship which lasted for 30 years. In 1994 Malaŵi returned to multi-party democracy.

TERRITORY AND POPULATION

Malaŵi lies along the southern and western shores of Lake Malaŵi (the third largest lake in Africa), and is otherwise bounded in the north by Tanzania, south by Mozambique and west by Zambia. Area (including the inland water areas of Lake Malombe, Chilwa, Chiuta and the Malaŵi portion of Lake Malaŵi, which total 24,208 sq. km), 118,484 sq. km (45,747 sq. miles).

Census population (2008), 13,077,160 (6,718,227 females); density, 110·4 per sq. km. The United Nations population estimate for 2008 was 14,846,000. In 2005, 82·8% of the population was rural.

The UN gives an estimated population for 2010 of 15·69m.

Population of main towns (2008): Lilongwe, 674,448; Blantyre, 661,256; Mzuzu, 133,968; Zomba, 88,314. Population of the regions (2008): Northern, 1,708,930; Central, 5,510,195; Southern, 5,858,035.

The official languages are Chichewa, spoken by over 58% of the population, and English.

SOCIAL STATISTICS

2001 estimates: births, 556,000; deaths, 222,000. Estimated rates, 2001 (per 1,000 population): births, 47·8; deaths, 19·1. Annual population growth rate, 2000–05, 3·3%. Expectation of life at birth in 2007 was 51·3 years for males and 53·4 for females. Infant mortality, 2005, 78 per 1,000 live births; fertility rate, 2004, 6·0 births per woman.

CLIMATE

The tropical climate is marked by a dry season from May to Oct. and a wet season for the remaining months. Rainfall amounts are variable, within the range of 29–100" (725–2,500 mm), and maximum temperatures average 75–89°F (24–32°C), and minimum temperatures 58–67°F (14·4–19·4°C). Lilongwe, Jan. 73°F (22·8°C), July 60°F (15·6°C). Annual rainfall 36" (900 mm). Blantyre, Jan. 75°F (23·9°C), July 63°F (17·2°C). Annual rainfall 45" (1,125 mm). Zomba, Jan. 73°F (22·8°C), July 63°F (17·2°C). Annual rainfall 54" (1,344 mm).

CONSTITUTION AND GOVERNMENT

The *President* is also head of government. Malaŵi was a one-party state, but following a referendum on 14 June 1993, in which 63% of votes cast were in favour of reform, a new constitution was adopted on 17 May 1994 which ended Hastings Banda's life presidency and provided for the holding of multi-party elections. At these Bakili Muluzi was elected president with 47·16% of votes cast, beating President Banda and two other opponents. There is a *National Assembly* of 193 members, elected for five-year terms in single-seat constituencies.

National Anthem

'O God Bless our Land of Malaŵi'; words and tune by M.-F. Sauka.

RECENT ELECTIONS

At parliamentary elections of 19 May 2009 the Democratic Progressive Party (DPP) won 114 seats, the Malaŵi Congress Party (MCP—formerly the only legal party) 27 and the United Democratic Front (UDF) 17. Independents took 32 seats and others three.

At the concurrent presidential elections incumbent Bingu wa Mutharika (DPP) won with 66·0% of the vote, ahead of John Tembo (MCP) with 30·7%. There were five other candidates who all received less than 1% of the vote.

CURRENT ADMINISTRATION

President and Minister of Agriculture and Food Security: Dr Bingu wa Mutharika; b. 1934 (Democratic Progressive Party; sworn in 24 May 2004).

President Mutharika was sworn into office despite protests from his two main opponents in the May elections. In Feb. 2005 he left the UDF after a power struggle with its chairman, former president Bakili Muluzi, and launched a new party, the Democratic Progressive Party. The government consisted of the following in March 2010:

Vice President: Joyce Banda.

Minister of Development, Planning and Co-operation: Abbie Shaba. *Education, Science and Technology:* Dr George Chaponda. *Finance:* Ken Kandodo. *Foreign Affairs:* Etta Banda. *Gender, Child Development and Community Development:* Patricia Kaliati. *Health:* Moses Chirambo. *Home Affairs and Internal Security:* Aaron Sangala. *Industry and Trade:* Eunice Kazembe. *Information and Civic Education:* Leckford Mwanza. *Irrigation and Water Development:* Richie Muheya. *Justice and Constitutional Affairs:* Peter Mutharika. *Labour:* Yunus Mussa. *Lands, Housing and Urban Development:* Peter Mwanza. *Local Government and Rural Development:* Goodall Gondwe. *National Defence:* Sidik Mia. *Natural Resources, Energy and the Environment:* Grain Malunga. *Persons with Disabilities and the Elderly:* Rene Kachere. *Tourism, Wildlife and Culture:* Anna Kachikho. *Transport and Public Infrastructure:* Khumbo Kachali. *Youth Development and Sports:* Lucious Kanyumba.

CURRENT LEADERS

Dr Bingu wa Mutharika

Position
President

Introduction
Dr Bingu wa Mutharika became president of Malaŵi following elections in May 2004, having been nominated by former president (and his former political foe), Bakili Muluzi, who retired after two consecutive terms in office. He was re-elected in May 2009.

Early Life
Bingu wa Mutharika was born in Thyolo, Malaŵi on 24 Feb. 1934. The son of a Catholic primary school teacher, he gained a masters degree in economics from the University of Delhi, India, before studying for a PhD in development economics at Pacific Western University in Los Angeles, USA. He then went to work for the Malaŵian civil service and later for the Zambian government.

In 1978 Mutharika joined the UN, motivated by his opposition to the regime of Hastings Banda, Malaŵi's self-declared 'President for Life'. He was given the post of director for trade and development finance for Africa. In 1991 he became secretary-general of the Common Market for Eastern and Southern Africa (COMESA).

Mutharika was a founding member of the United Democratic Front (UDF), the party led by Muluzi that went on to win Malaŵi's first multi-party elections in 1994. The two became adversaries when Mutharika opposed Muluzi's economic policies. Mutharika left the UDF to form the United Party (UP) in 1997. However, after unsuccessfully contesting the presidency in 1999, he disbanded the UP and returned to the UDF, where he was made minister of economic planning and development in 2002.

Career in Office
In Feb. 2005, following a series of clashes with Muluzi and an alleged assassination attempt in Jan. by UDF members, Mutharika again resigned from the party, subsequently forming the Democratic Progressive Party (DPP). In June 2005 he survived an impeachment motion backed by the UDF. In April 2006 Vice President Chilumpha was charged with treason and in July Muluzi was arrested on corruption charges. In May 2008 several opposition figures were arrested after Mutharika accused Muluzi of plotting to overthrow him. Mutharika retained power following elections in May 2009 in which he received 66% of the vote in the presidential poll and his DPP secured 114 of the 193 seats in the National Assembly. However, external electoral observers were critical of the government's use of state-controlled radio and television to obtain unfair advantage.

His principal economic challenges in office have remained the reduction of poverty and regeneration by encouraging foreign investment. He has aimed to turn Malaŵi from an import culture to an export one in order to provide trade opportunities for the rural poor. He has also pursued a high-profile anti-corruption campaign.

Internationally, in Jan. 2008 he ended diplomatic ties with Taiwan and switched Malaŵi's allegiance to communist China.

DEFENCE

All services form part of the Army. Defence expenditure totalled US$20m. in 2006 (US$1 per capita), representing 0·9% of GDP.

Army

Personnel (2007) 5,300. In addition there is a paramilitary mobile police force totalling 1,500.

Navy

The Maritime Wing, based at Monkey Bay on Lake Malaŵi, numbered 220 personnel in 2007.

Air Wing

The Air Wing acts as infantry support and numbered 200 in 2007 with no combat capable aircraft.

INTERNATIONAL RELATIONS

Malaŵi is a member of the UN, World Bank, IMF and several other UN specialized agencies, WTO, Commonwealth, COMESA, African Development Bank, African Union and SADC and is an ACP member state of the ACP-EU relationship.

ECONOMY

Agriculture accounted for 34·2% of GDP in 2006, industry 19·7% and services 46·1%.

Overview

Malaŵi has improved macroeconomic performance in recent years. The economy reached the Heavily Indebted Poor Countries (HIPC) completion point in Aug. 2006 and enjoyed levels of growth double the average annual 3% in the period 1996–2005. The IMF expected real GDP growth to reach 7% in 2007 on the back of a strong harvest, while inflation was predicted to fall below 10%.

Heavy dependence on agriculture (which accounts for 80% of export earnings and supports 85% of the population) makes the economy prone to weather shocks. Tobacco, tea, cotton, coffee and sugar are the primary exports, with tobacco accounting for more than half of exports. Social indicators are poor, with poverty high and HIV/AIDS an increasing problem. Malaŵi depends on assistance from the World Bank, IMF and other international donors. The government now faces the challenge of consolidating macroeconomic stability, translating gains into improved social indicators and reducing domestic debt to below 10% of GDP in order to free up resources for the private sector.

Currency

The unit of currency is the *kwacha* (MWK) of 100 *tambala*. Foreign exchange reserves were US$119m. in June 2005, gold reserves 13,000 troy oz and total money supply was K.29,579m. Foreign exchange controls were abolished in Feb. 1994. Inflation fell from 83·1% in 1995 to 7·9% in 2007, before rising slightly to 8·7% in 2008.

Budget
The fiscal year runs from 1 July–30 June. In 2005 revenues were K.103·30bn. and expenditures K.110·94bn. Tax revenue accounted for 52·9% of revenues in 2005; current expenditure accounted for 76·3% of expenditures.

VAT is 16·5%.

Performance
Since shrinking by 4·1% during a recession in 2001 the economy has recovered, with real GDP growth rates of 8·6% in 2007 and 9·7% in 2008. Total GDP was US$4·3bn. in 2008.

Banking and Finance
The central bank and bank of issue is the Reserve Bank of Malaŵi (founded 1964). The *Governor* is Perks Ligoya. In 2002 there were four commercial banks, one development bank, three merchant banks and a savings bank.

There is a stock exchange in Blantyre.

ENERGY AND NATURAL RESOURCES

Environment
Carbon dioxide emissions from the consumption and flaring of fossil fuels in 2008 were the equivalent of 0·1 tonnes per capita.

Electricity
The Electricity Supply Commission of Malaŵi is the sole supplier. Installed capacity was about 0·2m. kW in 2004. Production was approximately 1,270m. kWh in 2004; consumption per capita was an estimated 100 kWh. Only 4% of the population has access to electricity.

Oil and Gas
In 1997 Malaŵi and Mozambique came to an agreement on the construction of an oil pipeline between the two countries.

Minerals
Mining operations have been limited to small-scale production of coal, limestone, rubies and sapphires, but companies are now moving in to start exploration programmes. Bauxite reserves are estimated at 29m. tonnes and there are proven reserves of clays, diamonds, glass and silica sands, graphite, limestone, mercurate, phosphates, tanzanite, titanium and uranium. Output in 2004: limestone, 21,224 tonnes; gemstones, 1,820 kg.

Agriculture
Malaŵi is predominantly an agricultural country. Agricultural produce contributes 90% of export earnings. There were an estimated 3·0m. ha. of arable land in 2007 and 120,000 ha. of permanent crops. Maize is the main subsistence crop and is grown by over 95% of all smallholders. Tobacco is the chief cash crop, employing 12% of the workforce and generating a quarter of tax earnings. Also important are groundnuts, cassava, millet and rice. There are large plantations which produce sugar, tea and coffee. Production (2003 estimates, in 1,000 tonnes): maize, 1,901; sugarcane, 1,900; cassava, 1,774; potatoes, 1,100; plantains, 200; groundnuts, 158; dry beans, 94; bananas, 93; rice, 87; tobacco, 70; sorghum, 45; tea, 45.

Livestock in 2003: goats, 1·7m.; cattle, 750,000; pigs, 456,000; sheep, 115,000; chickens, 15m.

Forestry
In 2005 the area under forests was 3·40m. ha., or 36·2% of the total land area. Timber production in 2007 was 5·76m. cu. metres.

Fisheries
Landings in 2005 were 58,783 tonnes, entirely from inland waters.

INDUSTRY
Index of industrial production in 2001 (1984 = 100): total general industrial production, 101·9; of this goods for the domestic market were at 73·2 and export goods were at 101·5. Electricity and water were at 231·7.

Labour
The labour force in 1996 was 4,807,000 (51% males). Approximately 85% of the economically active population in 1995 were engaged in agriculture, fisheries and forestry.

INTERNATIONAL TRADE
External debt was US$3,155m. in 2005.

Imports and Exports
In 2004 imports (c.i.f.) amounted to US$477·6m. and exports (f.o.b.) US$483·3m. Major imports, 2004 (in US$1m.): road vehicles, 49·1; textile yarn, fabrics and finished articles, 31·7. Major exports, 2004 (in US$1m.): tobacco and tobacco products, 221·4 (46% of the total); sugar, sugar preparations and honey, 75·6.

Main sources of imports in 2004 were South Africa (35·6%), UK (6·7%), India (6·6%) and Zimbabwe (5·9%). Principal destinations in 2004 for exports were South Africa (14·6%), USA (11·3%), UK (9·9%) and Germany (7·6%).

Trade Fairs
The annual Malaŵi International Trade Fair takes place in Blantyre, the commercial capital.

COMMUNICATIONS

Roads
The road network consisted of 15,451 km in 2003, of which 45·0% were paved. There were 16,300 passenger cars (1·4 per 1,000 inhabitants) and 19,100 commercial vehicles in use in 2002.

Rail
In 2005 Malaŵi Railways operated 797 km on 1,067 mm gauge, providing links to the Mozambican ports of Beira and Nacala. In 2004 passenger-km travelled came to 29·5m. and freight tonne-km to 26·1m.

Civil Aviation
The national carrier is Air Malaŵi. It flies to a number of regional centres in Ethiopia, Kenya, South Africa, Zambia and Zimbabwe. In 2003 scheduled airline traffic of Malaŵi-based carriers flew 4m. km, carrying 109,000 passengers (68,000 on international flights). There are international airports at Lilongwe (Lilongwe International Airport) and Blantyre (Chileka). In 2000 Lilongwe handled 175,915 passengers (120,575 on international flights) and 4,182 tonnes of freight, and Blantyre had 101,809 passengers (53,426 on international flights) and 680 tonnes of freight.

Shipping
In 1995 lake ships carried 169,000 passengers and 6,000 tonnes of freight.

Telecommunications
Malaŵi had 532,000 telephone subscribers in 2005, or 41·3 for every 1,000 population, including 429,300 mobile phone subscribers. Internet users numbered 52,500 in 2005 and 25,000 PCs were in use (1·9 per 1,000 persons).

Postal Services
In 2003 there were 324 post offices.

SOCIAL INSTITUTIONS

Justice
Justice is administered in the High Court and in the magistrates' courts. Traditional courts were abolished in 1994. Appeals from magistrates' courts lie to the High Court, and appeals from the High Court to Malaŵi's Supreme Court of Appeal.

The population in penal institutions in Nov. 2003 was 8,566 (70 per 100,000 of national population).

Education
The adult literacy rate in 2001 was 61·0% (75·0% among males and 47·6% among females). Fees for primary education were abolished in 1994. In 2007 the number of pupils in primary schools was 2,943,248 (44,048 teaching staff). The primary school course is of eight years' duration, followed by a four-year secondary course. In 2007 there were 574,003 pupils in secondary schools. English is taught from the 1st year and becomes the general medium of instruction from the 4th year.

The University of Malaŵi (consisting of four colleges and one polytechnic) had 6,257 students and 676 academic staff in 2007. A university at Mzuzu opened in 1998 and provides courses for secondary school teachers. In 2007 there were 6,458 students in higher education and 861 academic staff.

In 2003 public expenditure on education came to 4·3% of GNI.

Health
In 2003 there were 187 doctors, giving a provision of one doctor for every 64,775 persons—the lowest ratio in the world. In 2003 there were 3,094 nurses, four dentists and 39 pharmacists. In 1998 there were 82 hospitals with 10,251 beds.

RELIGION
2001 estimates: 2,600,000 Roman Catholic; 2,070,000 Protestant (mostly Presbyterian); 1,770,000 African Christian; 1,560,000 Muslim; 820,000 traditional beliefs. The remainder follow other religions.

CULTURE
World Heritage Sites
Malaŵi has two sites on the UNESCO World Heritage List: Lake Malaŵi National Park (inscribed on the list in 1984); and the Chongoni Rock-Art area (2006).

Broadcasting
Radio is the most widely available medium: television was not introduced until 1999. The Malaŵi Broadcasting Corporation, a statutory body, runs two national radio networks. Television Malaŵi (TVM) is also state-run. Private radio stations have been operating since 1997. There were 135,000 TV sets in 2004.

Press
There are more than 16 newspapers in circulation, the main ones being: *The Daily Times* (English, Monday to Friday), 17,000 copies daily; *The Nation* (English, Monday to Friday), 16,000 copies daily; *Malaŵi News* (English and Chichewa, Saturdays), 23,000 copies weekly; and *Weekend Nation* (English and Chichewa, Saturdays), 16,000 copies weekly. In addition there is Odini (English and Chichewa), 8,500 copies fortnightly; Boma Lathu (Chichewa), 150,000 copies monthly; Za Alimi (English and Chichewa), 10,000 copies monthly.

Tourism
There were 438,000 non-resident tourists in 2005, spending US$36m.

DIPLOMATIC REPRESENTATIVES
Of Malaŵi in the United Kingdom (70 Winnington Rd, London, N2 0TX)
High Commissioner: Dr Francis Moto.

Of the United Kingdom in Malaŵi (PO Box 30042, Lilongwe 3)
High Commissioner: Fergus Cochrane-Dyet.

Of Malaŵi in the USA (1156 15th St., NW, Suite 320, Washington, D.C., 20005)
Ambassador: Hawa Olga Ndilowe.

Of the USA in Malaŵi (Area 40, Plot 24, Kenyatta Rd, Lilongwe 3)
Ambassador: Peter W. Bodde.

Of Malaŵi to the United Nations
Ambassador: Steve Dick Tennyson Matenje.

Of Malaŵi to the European Union
Ambassador: Brave Rona Ndisale.

FURTHER READING

National Statistical Office. *Monthly Statistical Bulletin*
Ministry of Economic Planning and Development. *Economic Report.* Annual

Crosby, Cynthia A., *Historical Dictionary of Malawi.* 2001
Kalinga, O. J. M. and Crosby, C. A., *Historical Dictionary of Malawi.* 1993
Sindima, Harvey J., *Malawi's First Republic: An Economic and Political Analysis.* 2002

National Statistical Office: National Statistical Office, POB 333, Zomba.
Website: http://www.nso.malawi.net

MALAYSIA

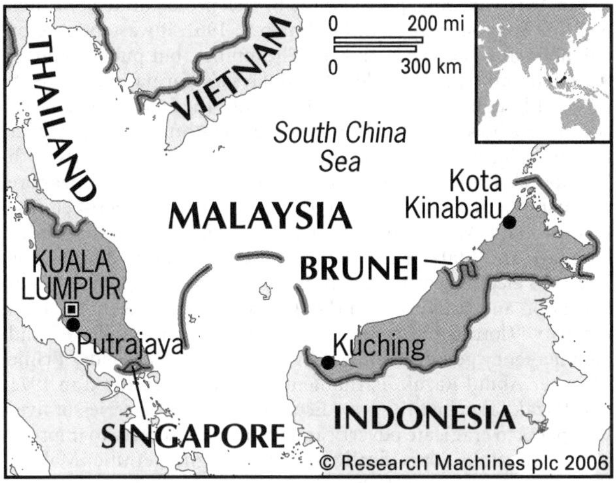

Persekutuan Tanah Malaysia
(Federation of Malaysia)

Capitals: Putrajaya (Administrative),
Kuala Lumpur (Legislative and Financial)
Population estimate, 2010: 27·91m.
GDP per capita, 2007: (PPP$) 13,518
HDI/world rank: 0·829/66

KEY HISTORICAL EVENTS

Excavations at Niah in Sarawak, East Malaysia have uncovered evidence of human settlement from 38,000 BC (the oldest relic of *homo sapiens* in southeast Asia). There are numerous sites in the north of Peninsular Malaysia where evidence of hunter-gatherers has been dated to around 10,000 BC. These Hoabinhians were spread across the region from present-day Myanmar to southern China between 12,000 and 3,000 BC. After 3,000 BC Mon-Khmer speaking immigrants moved south into Peninsular Malaysia and introduced a more advanced Neolithic culture, engaging in rudimentary farming. The indigenous people known as Orang Asli, who still live in the remoter, mountainous areas of the northern Malay Peninsula, are considered to be descendents of the Neolithic farmers. Indian traders first visited the Malay Peninsula in the 1st century BC and introduced political ideas, art forms and the Sanskrit language. Hinduism and Buddhism gained a foothold and were practised alongside traditional animist beliefs.

Various Hinduized city-states were established, one of which was located in Kedah. In the 7th century AD Kedah came under the control of the Hinduized Srivijaya empire, centred on Palembang in Sumatra. Srivijaya rule ended in the late 13th century when Sumatra fell to a Javan invasion, after which the king of Sukothai sent forces south into the Malay Peninsula. The Sumatran kingdom of Melayu next ruled over the southern part of the Peninsula, followed by the Madjapahit, the last Hindu empire of Java. In the mid-15th century Melaka emerged as the key trading port in the region—it was host to indigenous Malays, Sumatrans, Javans, Gujaratis, Arabs, Persians, Filipinos and Chinese—and grew rapidly in prosperity. A pattern of government was established in Melaka that became the basis of Malay identity and it was emulated by subsequent Malay kingdoms. Gujarati sailors introduced Islam to the region through Melaka in the 15th century. In 1511 the port was captured by the Portuguese navigator Alfonso de Albuquerque (who had seized Goa in western India the previous year), and who sought to dominate the route by which precious spices were shipped to Europe.

The sultan of Melaka fled to Johor and some of the Muslim mercantile elite relocated to Brunei in northwest Borneo. Sultanates also emerged in Pahang and Perak, which subsequently received large numbers of immigrants from Indonesian islands, notably Acehnese, Bugis and Minangkabau settlers, who displaced the Orang Asli from their coastal communities and drove them to the Malay Peninsula's interior. Conflict arose between the sultanates of Johor and Aceh and the Portuguese as they vied for control over the Straits of Melaka. In the late 16th century the northern Peninsular states of Kedah, Kelantan and Terengganu came under the control of the Thai state of Phetburi. The early 17th century saw the arrival of Dutch traders in the strait of Melaka. As part of the United Netherlands East India Company (Vereenigde Oostindische Compagnie, VOC) they made an alliance with Johor to besiege Melaka, capturing it in 1641. The Dutch brokered a peace deal between Aceh and Johor in the same year, ushering in an era of relative peace and prosperity for Johor under Laksamana Tun Abdul Jamil.

In the late 17th century the Malay Peninsula came under the influence of Bugis merchants from the Indonesian island of Sulawesi, who began settling in Selangor to trade in tin. The Bugis were formidable warriors, renowned for their navigational and commercial skills. By the 1740s they controlled many of the key shipping routes across the Indonesian archipelago and influenced all areas of government in Johor and the Riau archipelago, although Sultan Suliaman was permitted to remain as a figurehead.

British Influence

In the mid-18th century Johor and Melaka became entrepôts for the trade in tea between China and Europe. Ships owned by the British East India Company (EIC) began plying the Melaka straits in greater numbers. The British foothold in India allowed them to expand eastwards, and their control of India's poppy fields enabled them to dominate the lucrative opium trade. In 1786 Francis Light of the EIC leased the island of Penang from the Sultan Abdullah of Kedah, who hoped the British would provide protection against attacks from Siam or Burma. Penang grew swiftly, luring trade away from Melaka (which remained in Dutch control) and Johor-Riau. The British sought to increase their control over the maritime route to China and Sir Thomas Stamford Raffles was ordered to establish an entrepôt in the southern reaches of the Melaka Straits. In 1819 he signed a treaty with Sultan Husein Syah of Johor and founded Singapore. Five years later the British formally acquired Melaka from the Dutch. From 1826 Penang, Singapore and Melaka were ruled by the British authorities in India under a joint administration known as the Straits Settlements. By 1831 the population of Singapore had reached 18,000 (a large proportion were Chinese immigrants) and the following year the port replaced Penang as the capital of the Straits Settlements. Meanwhile, the northern provinces of Kedah and Perak came under the influence of the Siamese Chakri dynasty.

The discovery of tin deposits at Larut (western Malay Peninsula) in the 1850s led to large-scale immigration by Chinese miners and labourers. They organized themselves into *hui* (brotherhoods), which eventually became powerful political and economic organizations. Vast profits could be made from tin and there were clashes between rival developers. At the same time, piracy was on the increase in the Melaka straits, and merchants asked the British to intervene and restore order. A series of agreements in 1874 introduced the British Residential system to Perak, Selangor and Sungei Ujung. In each region, a British Resident functioned as an adviser to the Malay Sultan on all aspects of administration apart from matters relating to the Islamic faith and Malay tradition.

Colonial Rule

In 1896 the three states and Pahang were grouped together as the Federated Malay States, presided over by a British Resident-General at Kuala Lumpur in the heart of the tin-mining district. By the end of the century, a British colonial infrastructure was taking shape, in the form of public buildings, municipal services, rubber plantations and road and rail construction, which required a stream of low-cost workers. Tamils from south India and Sri Lanka arrived as indentured (and later as licensed) labourers. Negotiations between the British and Siamese in the early years of the 20th century led to British control over the northern states of Kedah, Perlis, Kelantan and Terengganu. Between 1905–08 Malaysia experienced a rubber boom, in line with the expansion of the motor car industry in Europe and North America. Rubber plants, originally from the forests of Brazil and introduced to Malaysia in the 1880s, were planted in every state in Malaysia by 1908 and by 1913 rubber had eclipsed tin as the country's chief export.

Sabah, Sarawak and Brunei, which had come under the control of the North Borneo Chartered Company and was granted protectorate status in 1888, experienced slower economic development than British Malaya but gold, antimony and coal were mined and oil was discovered at Miri in 1910. The colony was hit hard by the global depression of 1929–31 and widespread unemployment in the mines and plantations caused the repatriation of Chinese and Indian workers. Rubber, tin and oil made Malaya a focus for Imperial Japan from early in the Second World War. When Pearl Harbor and Hong Kong came under attack from Japanese forces in Dec. 1941, other Japanese divisions came ashore at Kota Bharu and Miri. British forces retreated south to Singapore, but the 'impregnable' island capitulated within a few weeks, on 15 Feb. 1942. Japanese troops quickly took over from British colonial officers and controlled Malaya from Singapore (Shonan), meting out harsh treatment to the Chinese population. Thailand allied itself with Japan and was granted control of the northern Malay states in 1943.

Post-War Period

When the British returned in 1946 they reorganized the colony into the Malayan Union. The Malay elite, fearing an end to their privileges as a consequence of equal rights for Chinese and Indian subjects, campaigned via the United Malays National Organization (UMNO, led by Datuk Onn) to demand the continuation of individual sultanates. The British were forced to compromise and established the Federation of Malaya in Feb. 1948, consisting of the nine Malay states, Melaka and Penang and administered by a High Commissioner in Kuala Lumpur. Within months the Federation was under attack by the Malayan Communist Party (MCP). The Chinese-dominated MCP had grown in strength during the Japanese occupation, when it controlled various anti-Japanese National Salvation Organizations. The High Commissioner Sir Henry Gurney responded to guerrilla attacks by the MCP by putting Malaya on a war-footing in 1950: tightening security, recruiting soldiers from other colonies and dispersing the Chinese squatter settlements that harboured much of the MCP's support. More than 500,000 Chinese were resettled by the mid-1950s. The Communist insurrection, known by the British as 'the Emergency', hastened the transition to Malayan independence and local elections were held in Penang in late 1951. Four years later the first federal-level election was held and won convincingly by the Alliance Party, a loose coalition of Malay, Chinese and Indian parties, led by Tuanku (Prince) Abdul Rahman. On 31 Aug. 1957 the Federation of Malaya became an independent state with Tuanku Abdul Rahman as the first prime minister.

The concept of Malaysia, as a broader federation including Sabah, Sarawak, Singapore and the British protectorate of Brunei, was first suggested by Abdul Rahman in 1961. It was opposed by neighbouring Indonesia and the Philippines, but public support in Sabah and Sarawak led to Malaysia's formation in Sept. 1963, although Brunei declined to join. The new nation faced continuing hostility from Indonesia, led by Ahmed Sukarno, over the sovereignty of Borneo. There were also disagreements with Singapore's Prime Minister Lee Kuan Yew, leading to Singapore declaring independence in 1965. Tension arose between the Chinese and Malay communities over the use of the Malay language and Malay fears about Chinese economic dominance. The 1969 elections were fought on the highly emotional issues of education and language and the Alliance party failed to obtain a majority. Rioting and serious inter-ethnic violence followed and an emergency government was brought in, led by Deputy Prime Minister Abdul Razak. Parliamentary rule was restored in 1971 and Razak launched the New Economic Policy—a series of five-year plans to eradicate poverty and restructure society to improve ethnic relations, specifically by encouraging ethnic Malays, the *bumiputera*, to shift from subsistence agriculture into the mainstream economy.

Mahathir Mohamad was the first non-royal or non-aristocrat to become prime minister of Malaysia, winning the 1981 elections for the UMNO and leading the National Front coalition to further victories in 1986, 1990, 1995 and 1999. Mahathir shifted the economy away from dependence on commodities and towards manufacturing, services and tourism, aided by substantial Japanese and east Asian investment in manufacturing. The prolonged spell of economic growth and stability was broken by the 1997–98 recession but Mahathir refused to accept financial aid from the International Monetary Fund. In Sept. 1998 Mahathir dismissed Anwar Ibrahim, his finance minister, deputy prime minister and heir apparent. Anwar was found guilty of corruption charges in 1999 and sentenced to prison for six years. In 2002 Mahathir announced that he would resign from the presidency of UMNO and he stepped down as prime minister on 31 Oct. 2003, to be succeeded by Abdullah Ahmad Badawi. Badawi won a landslide victory in the March 2004 general elections for the National Front. In Sept. 2004 Anwar was unexpectedly released after being acquitted by the Federal Court.

TERRITORY AND POPULATION

The federal state of Malaysia comprises the 13 states and three federal territories of Peninsular Malaysia, bounded in the north by Thailand, and with the island of Singapore as an enclave on its southern tip; and, on the island of Borneo to the east, the state of Sabah (which includes the federal territory of the island of Labuan), and the state of Sarawak, with Brunei as an enclave, both bounded in the south by Indonesia and in the northwest and northeast by the South China and Sulu Seas.

The area of Malaysia is 329,847 sq. km (127,354 sq. miles) and the population (2000 census) 23,274,690; density, 70·6 per sq. km. The estimated population in July 2008 was 27,728,700. Malaysia's national waters cover 515,256 sq. km. In 2005, 67·3% of the population lived in urban areas.

The UN gives an estimated population for 2010 of 27·91m.

The growth of the population has been:

Year	*Peninsular Malaysia*	*Sarawak*	*Sabah/ Labuan*	*Total Malaysia*
1980	11,426,613	1,307,582	1,011,046	13,745,241
1991	14,797,616	1,718,380	1,863,659	18,379,655
2000	18,523,632	2,071,506	2,679,552	23,274,690

The areas, populations and chief towns of the states and federal territories are:

Peninsular states	Area (in sq. km)	Population (2000 census)	Chief town	Population (1991 census)
Johor	18,987	2,740,625	Johor Bharu	328,436
Kedah	9,425	1,649,756	Alor Star	124,412
Kelantan	15,024	1,313,014	Kota Bharu	219,582
Kuala Lumpur[1]	243	1,379,310	Kuala Lumpur	1,145,342[1]
Melaka	1,652	635,791	Melaka	75,909
Negeri Sembilan	6,644	859,924	Seremban	182,869
Pahang	35,965	1,288,376	Kuantan	199,484
Perak	21,005	2,051,236	Ipoh	382,853
Perlis	795	204,450	Kangar	14,247
Pulau Pinang	1,031	1,313,449	Penang (Georgetown)	219,603
Putrajaya[1]	50	—[2]	Putrajaya	—
Selangor	7,910	4,188,876[2]	Shah Alam	102,019
Terengganu	12,955	898,825	Kuala Terengganu	228,119
Other states				
Labuan[1]	92	76,067	Victoria	—
Sabah	73,619	2,603,485	Kota Kinabalu	76,120
Sarawak	124,450	2,071,506	Kuching	148,059

[1]Federal territory. [2]Putrajaya figure included in population of Selangor.

Other large cities (1997 estimate): Petaling Jaya (254,350), Kelang (243,355), Taiping (183,261), Sibu (126,381), Sandakan (125,841) and Miri (87,167).

Putrajaya, a planned new city described as an 'intelligent garden city', became the administrative capital of Malaysia in 1999 and was created a federal territory on 1 Feb. 2001.

Bahasa Malaysia (Malay) is the official language of the country—53% of the population are Malays. The government promotes the use of the national language to foster national unity. However, the people are free to use their mother tongue and other languages. English as the second language is widely used in business. In Peninsular Malaysia Chinese dialects and Tamil are also spoken. In Sabah there are numerous tribal dialects and Chinese (Mandarin and Hakka dialects predominate). In Sarawak Mandarin and numerous tribal languages are spoken. In addition to Malays, 26% of the population are Chinese, 12% other indigenous ethnic groups, 8% Indians and 1% others.

SOCIAL STATISTICS

2002 births, 482,600; deaths, 105,900. 2002 rates (per 1,000 population): birth, 19·7; death, 4·3. Life expectancy, 2007: males, 71·9 years; females, 76·6 years. Annual population growth rate, 2000–05, 2·1%. Infant mortality, 2005, ten per 1,000 live births; fertility rate, 2004, 2·8 births per woman. Today only 6% of Malaysians live below the poverty line, compared to 50% in the early 1970s.

CLIMATE

Malaysia lies near the equator between latitudes 1° and 7° North and longitudes 100° and 119° East. Malaysia is subject to maritime influence and the interplay of wind systems which originate in the Indian Ocean and the South China Sea. The year is generally divided into the South-East and the North-East Monsoon seasons. The average daily temperature throughout Malaysia varies from 21°C to 32°C. Humidity is high.

CONSTITUTION AND GOVERNMENT

The Constitution of Malaysia is based on the Constitution of the former Federation of Malaya, but includes safeguards for the special interests of Sabah and Sarawak. It was amended in 1983. The Constitution provides for one of the Rulers of the Malay States to be elected from among themselves to be the *Yang di-Pertuan Agong* (Supreme Head of the Federation). He holds office for a period of five years. The Rulers also elect from among themselves a Deputy Supreme Head of State, also for a period of five years. In Feb. 1993 the Rulers accepted constitutional amendments abolishing their legal immunity.

Supreme Head of State (Yang di-Pertuan Agong). HRH Sultan Mizan Zainal Abidin ibni al-Mahrum Sultan Mahmud, b. 1962, acceded 13 Dec. 2006.

Raja of Perlis. HRH Tuanku Syed Sirajuddin ibni al-Marhum Syed Putra Jamalullail, b. 1943, acceded 17 April 2000.

Sultan of Kedah. HRH Tuanku Haji Abdul Halim Mu'adzam Shah ibni Al-Marhum Sultan Badlishah, b. 1927, acceded 14 July 1958.

Sultan of Johor. HRH Tuanku Ibrahim Ismail ibni al-Marhum Sultan Iskandar, b. 1958, acceded 23 Jan. 2010.

Sultan of Perak. HRH Sultan Azlan Shah Muhibbuddin Shah ibni Al-Marhum Sultan Yussuf Izzuddin Ghafarullahu-luhu Shah, b. 1928, acceded 3 Feb. 1984.

Yang Di-Pertuan Besar Negeri Sembilan. HRH Tuanku Muhriz ibni Al-Marhum Tuanku Munawir, b. 1948, acceded 29 Dec. 2008.

Sultan of Kelantan. HRH Sultan Ismail Petra ibni Al-Marhum Sultan Yahya Petra, b. 1949, appointed 29 March 1979.

Sultan of Terengganu. HRH Sultan Mizan Zainal Abidin ibni al-Mahrum Sultan Mahmud Al-Muktafi Billah Shah, b. 1962, acceded 15 May 1998.

Sultan of Pahang. HRH Sultan Haji Ahmad Shah Al-Musta'in Billah ibni Al-Marhum Sultan Abu Bakar Ri'Ayatuddin Al-Mu'Adzam Shah, b. 1930, acceded 8 May 1975.

Sultan of Selangor. HRH Sharafuddin Idris Shah ibni al-Marhum Sultan Salehuddin Abdul Aziz Shah, b. 1945, appointed 22 Nov. 2001.

Yang di-Pertua Negeri Pulau Pinang. HE Datuk Abdul Rahman Haji Abbas, b. 1938, appointed 1 May 2001.

Yang di Pertua Negeri Melaka. HE Tan Sri Khalil Yaakob, b. 1937, appointed 4 June 2004.

Yang di-Pertua Negeri Sarawak. HE Tun Datuk Patinggi Abang Mohamad Salaheddin, b. 1921, acceded 4 Dec. 2000.

Yang di-Pertua Negeri Sabah. HE Datuk Ahmad Shah Abdullah, b. 1946, acceded 1 Jan. 2003.

The federal parliament consists of the *Yang di-Pertuan Agong* and two *Majlis* (Houses of Parliament) known as the *Dewan Negara* (Senate) of 70 members (26 elected, two by each state legislature; and 44 appointed by the *Yang di-Pertuan Agong*) and the *Dewan Rakyat* (House of Representatives) of 222 members. Appointment to the Senate is for three years. The maximum life of the House of Representatives is five years, subject to its dissolution at any time by the *Yang di-Pertuan Agong* on the advice of his Ministers.

National Anthem

'Negaraku' ('My Country'); words collective, tune by Pierre de Béranger.

GOVERNMENT CHRONOLOGY

Supreme Heads of State since 1957.

1957–60	Tuanku Abdul Rahman ibni al-Marhum
1960	Tuanku Hisamuddin Alam Shah ibni al-Marhum
1960–65	Syed Harun Petra ibni al-Marhum
1965–70	Tuanku Ismail Nasiruddin Shah ibni al-Marhum
1970–75	Tuanku Abdul Halim Muadzam Shah ibni al-Marhum
1975–79	Tuanku Yahaya Petra ibni al-Marhum
1979–84	Tuanku Ahmad Shah al-Mustain Billah ibni al-Marhum
1984–89	Tuanku Mahmud Iskandar ibni al-Marhum
1989–94	Tuanku Azlan Muhibuddin Shah ibni al-Marhum

1994–99	Tuanku Jaafar ibni al-Marhum
1999–2001	Tuanku Salehuddin Abdul Aziz Shah ibni al-Marhum
2001–06	Syed Sirajuddin ibni al-Marhum
2006–	Tuanku Mizan Zainal Abidin ibni al-Marhum Sultan Mahmud

Prime Ministers since 1957. (UMNO = United Malays National Organization)

1957–59	UMNO	Tunku Abdul Rahman Putra
1959	UMNO	Tun Abdul Razak bin Hussein (acting)
1959–70	UMNO	Tunku Abdul Rahman Putra
1970–76	UMNO	Tun Abdul Razak bin Hussein
1976–81	UMNO	Hussein bin Onn
1981–2003	UMNO	Mahathir bin Mohamad
2003–09	UMNO	Abdullah bin Haji Ahmad Badawi
2009–	UMNO	Najib Tun Razak

RECENT ELECTIONS

Elections to the *Dewan Rakyat* and 13 state assemblies were held on 8 March 2008. The 14-party National Front Coalition (BN; Barisan Nasional) gained 140 seats, obtaining 50·3% of the votes cast (the predominant partner, the United Malays National Organization (UMNO), won 79 seats). Opposition parties won 82 seats of which the People's Justice Party (Parti Keadilan Rakyat) won 31 (18·6%), the Democratic Action Party (Parti Tindakan Deomkratik) won 28 (13·8%) and the Islamic Party of Malaysia (PAS) won 23 (14·1%). The National Front Coalition gained a majority in eight of the 13 state assemblies. Previously it had held every state except Kelantan.

CURRENT ADMINISTRATION

In March 2010 the government comprised:

Prime Minister and Minister of Finance: Dato' Sri Haji Mohd Najib bin Tun Haji Abdul Razak; b. 1953 (UMNO; took office on 3 April 2009).

Deputy Prime Minister and Minister of Education: Tan Sri Dato' Haji Muhiyiddin bin Mohamed Yassin. *Minister of Transport:* Dato' Sri Ong Tee Keat. *Plantation Industries and Commodities:* Tan Sri Bernard Giluk Dompok. *Home Affairs:* Dato' Seri Hishammuddin bin Tun Hussein. *Information, Communications, Arts and Culture:* Dato' Seri Utama Dr Rais Yatim. *Energy, Green Technology and Water:* Datuk Peter Chin Fah Kui. *Rural and Regional Development:* Dato' Seri Haji Mohd Shafie bin Haji Apdal. *Higher Education:* Dato' Seri Mohamed Khaled bin Nordin. *International Trade and Industry:* Dato' Mustapa bin Mohamed. *Science, Technology and Innovation:* Datuk Dr Maximus Johnity Ongkili. *Natural Resources and the Environment:* Datuk Douglas Uggah Embas. *Tourism:* Dato' Sri Dr Ng Yen Yen. *Agriculture and Agro-Based Industry:* Dato' Haji Noh bin Omar. *Defence:* Dato' Seri Dr Ahmad Zahid bin Hamidi. *Works:* Dato' Shaziman bin Abu Mansor. *Health:* Dato' Sri Liow Tiong Lai. *Youth and Sports:* Dato' Ahmad Shabery Cheek. *Human Resources:* Datuk Dr S. Subramaniam. *Domestic Trade and Consumer Affairs:* Dato' Sri Ismail Sabri bin Yaakob. *Housing and Local Government:* Dato' Kong Cho Ha. *Women, Family and Community Development:* Dato' Seri Shahrizat Abdul Jalil. *Foreign Affairs:* Datuk Anifah bin Haji Aman. *Federal Territories:* Dato' Raja Nong Chik bin Dato' Raja Zainal Abidin. *Second Minister of Finance:* Dato' Haji Ahmad Husni bin Mohamad Hanadzlah. *Ministers in Prime Minister's Department:* Tan Sri Dr Koh Tsu Koon; Dato' Seri Mohamad Nazri bin Abdul Aziz; Tan Sri Nor Mohamed bin Yakcop; Dato' Maj.-Gen. Jamil Khir bin Baharom.

Office of the Prime Minister: http://www.pmo.gov.my

CURRENT LEADERS

Tuanku Mizan Zainal Abidin ibni al-Marhum Sultan Mahmud

Position
King (Yang di-Pertuan Agong)

Introduction
Tuanku Mizan Zainal Abidin, sultan of the oil rich state of Terengganu, was sworn in as the 13th Yang di-Pertuan Agong (supreme head of state, popularly referred to as king) on 13 Dec. 2006. He is serving a five-year term, having been elected by the conference of rulers from among the nine hereditary state rulers. His role is largely ceremonial within a system of constitutional monarchy.

Early Life
Tuanku Mizan Zainal Abidin was born on 2 Jan. 1962, the son of Sultan Mahmud Al-Muktafi Billah Shah. He was schooled in Terengganu before going to Geelong Grammar School in Melbourne, Australia. From Nov. 1982 to Dec. 1983 Tuanku Mizan Zainal Abidin was engaged in military courses including a course at the Royal Military Academy, Sandhurst in the UK. He was commissioned as an honorary lieutenant in March 1984, serving in the Royal Cavalry. He graduated in international relations from the US International University-Europe (London) in 1988.

On his return to Malaysia he served as an officer at the Kuala Terengganu land and district office and later at the state economic planning unit. Mizan was appointed crown prince of Terengganu on 6 Nov. 1979 and was crowned sultan on 15 May 1998 following the death of his father. On 26 April 1999 he was appointed deputy Yang di-Pertuan Agong and became acting Yang di-Pertuan Agong when Tuanku Salahuddin Abdul Aziz Shah died in 2001. He was reappointed deputy Yang di-Pertuan Agong on 12 Dec. 2001, with Syed Sirajuddin ibni al-Marhum taking the more senior position. Tuanku Mizan Zainal Abidin succeeded him for a five-year term of office in Dec. 2006.

Career in Office
Although the Yang di-Pertuan Agong is mainly a ceremonial figurehead, royal assent is necessary for the appointment of members of the cabinet and judiciary and for laws passed by parliament. He stands as the nominal commander-in-chief and is the symbolic Islamic head to the large population of Malay Muslims.

Dato' Sri Haji Mohd Najib bin Tun Haji Abdul Razak

Position
Prime Minister

Introduction
Dato' Sri Haji Mohd Najib bin Tun Haji Abdul Razak became prime minister on 3 April 2009, replacing Abdullah bin Haji Ahmad Badawi, who left office following the poor showing of the Barisan Nasional (National Front Coalition) at the general election of March 2008. Najib had replaced Badawi as head of the United Malays National Organization (UMNO), the senior party in the coalition, in March 2009.

Early Life
Najib was born on 23 July 1953 in Kuala Lipis, Pahang into a political family. His father was independent Malaysia's second prime minister and his uncle was its third. Najib was educated at St John's Institution, Kuala Lumpur, and at Malvern College in England before graduating from the University of Nottingham in 1974 with a bachelor's degree in industrial economics.

In 1976 he became Malaysia's youngest member of parliament when he stood uncontested for his late father's seat of Pekan, the constituency he still represents. In his first year as an MP Najib was appointed deputy minister of energy, telecommunications and posts. He was later appointed deputy minister of education and deputy minister of finance. In 1981 he joined UMNO's Supreme Council and the following year became the Menteri Besar (Chief Executive) of Pahang state, after winning the State Assembly seat of Pekan.

Najib became vice president of UMNO Youth in 1982, a post he also held from 1987–93. Having lost his parliamentary seat, he regained it at the elections of 1986 and was appointed minister of culture, youth and sports. He went on to hold several other cabinet portfolios including defence and education. On 7 Jan. 2004 Najib was selected as Badawi's deputy and given the defence portfolio. In July 2004 he stood unopposed for the vice presidency of UMNO.

Although Barisan Nasional won the election of 2008, it was with a much reduced majority. Badawi named Najib as his likely successor and on 17 Sept. 2008 Najib was handed the finance portfolio as part of a gradual power transfer. On 26 March 2009 he stood unopposed for the UMNO presidency, ensuring him the post of prime minister when Badawi resigned on 2 April 2009.

Career in Office

Najib took office promising reform and change but faced the immediate challenges of a severe economic downturn, a divided UMNO and the increasing unpopularity of the ruling coalition that opponents accused of corruption and complacency. Najib slimmed the cabinet from 32 ministers to 28 but a financial stimulus of RM60bn. was met with a lukewarm response. He has also faced ongoing personal controversies including allegations of a political conspiracy against former deputy prime minister Anwar Ibrahim, the murder of a Mongolian woman in which several associates of Najib (including his wife) were implicated and problems with the national service programme that he devised and in which several conscripts have died.

DEFENCE

The Constitution provides for the Head of State to be the Supreme Commander of the Armed Forces who exercises his powers in accordance with the advice of the Cabinet. Under their authority, the Armed Forces Council is responsible for all matters relating to the Armed Forces other than those relating to their operational use. The Ministry of Defence has established bilateral defence relations with countries within as well as outside the region. Malaysia is a member of the Five Powers Defence Arrangement with Australia, New Zealand, Singapore and the UK.

The Malaysian Armed Forces has participated in 16 UN peacekeeping missions in Africa, the Middle East, Indo-China and Europe. Five of the operations are military contingents, the remainder are Observer Groups.

Since 2004 a lottery system has been in place to choose conscripts to serve three months of national service. In 2006 defence expenditure totalled US$3,206m. (US$131 per capita), representing 2·1% of GDP.

Army

Strength (2007) about 80,000. There is a paramilitary Police General Operations Force of 18,000 and a People's Volunteer Corps of 240,000 of which some 17,500 are armed.

Navy

The Royal Malaysian Navy is commanded by the Chief of the Navy from the integrated Ministry of Defence in Kuala Lumpur. The main base is at Lumut, with other bases at Kuantan, Labuan, Sandakan, Semporna, Sepanggar and Tanjung Pengelih. Further bases are under construction at Langkawi and Sejingkat. The peacetime tasks include fishery protection and anti-piracy patrols. The fleet includes three frigates and eight corvettes. A Naval aviation squadron operates six helicopters although serviceability is in doubt.

Navy personnel in 2007 totalled 14,000 including 160 Naval Air personnel. There were 1,000 naval reserves.

In addition, there is a maritime enforcement agency some 4,500 strong and 2,100 marine police.

Air Force

Formed on 1 June 1958, the Royal Malaysian Air Force is equipped primarily to provide air defence and air support for the Army, Navy and Police. Its secondary role is to render assistance to government departments and civilian organizations.

Personnel (2007) totalled 15,000, with 68 combat capable aircraft including F-5Es, MiG-29s and British Aerospace *Hawks*. There were 600 Air Force reserves.

INTERNATIONAL RELATIONS

Malaysia was in dispute with Indonesia over sovereignty of two islands in the Celebes Sea. Both countries agreed to accept the Judgment of the International Court of Justice which decided in favour of Malaysia in Dec. 2002.

Malaysia is a member of the UN, World Bank, IMF and several other UN specialized agencies, WTO, BIS, Commonwealth, Islamic Development Bank, OIC, APEC, ASEAN, Mekong Group, Colombo Plan and Asian Development Bank.

ECONOMY

In 2006 agriculture accounted for 8·7% of GDP, industry 49·9% and services 41·3%.

Overview

Malaysia has transformed itself from an economy dependent on mineral production and agriculture into an industrialized, manufacturing-based economy. In the decade prior to the 1997 Asian financial crisis, the economy grew consistently at an annual rate of 7–10%. In 1998 the economy was hit hard by twin currency and banking crises, shrinking by 7·4%. In response, the government sought to boost growth via spending on large infrastructure projects. The Badawi government has since brought spending levels down and has pledged to reduce fiscal deficits.

Manufacturing exports have been the main engine of economic growth, with the Economist Intelligence Unit (EIU) estimating that in 2004 electronic manufacturing accounted for 37·9% of the country's total exports, making Malaysia vulnerable to fluctuations in global electronics demand. When global recession cut demand in 2001, the country managed to avoid recession by introducing a US$1·9bn. fiscal stimulus package. Despite continued weak global demand and the outbreak of SARS, the economy rebounded in 2002 with growth of 4·4%. According to the EIU, in 2004 Malaysia's total factor productivity grew at 4·8%, its highest rate since 1988. A rebound in the global economy and electronics demand buoyed the economy in 2004–05.

Growth has averaged above 5% since 2003, touching 6% in 2006 as private consumption remained buoyant and private investment continued its recovery. The exchange rate has become more flexible since the depegging of the *ringgit* from the dollar in July 2005, seen as an important step toward broad-based growth. It strengthened by roughly 7% against the US dollar in 2006. Despite positive near-term prospects, the economy will need to broaden its base to protect against competition from emerging low-cost economies.

Currency

The unit of currency is the Malaysian *ringgit* (RM) of 100 *sen*. For seven years it was pegged to the US dollar at 3·8 ringgit = 1 US$, but since the revaluation of the Chinese yuan on 21 July 2005 it has been allowed to operate in a managed float. Foreign exchange reserves were US$92,217m. and gold reserves 1·17m. troy oz in Sept. 2009. Inflation rates (based on IMF statistics):

1999	2000	2001	2002	2003	2004	2005	2006	2007	2008
2·7%	1·6%	1·4%	1·8%	1·1%	1·4%	3·0%	3·6%	2·0%	5·4%

Total money supply in April 2009 was RM179,274m.

Budget
In 2007 revenues were RM139,885m. and expenditures RM163,648m. Tax revenue accounted for 68·0% of revenues in 2007; current expenditure accounted for 75·2% of expenditures.

There is a sales tax of 10%.

Performance
Malaysia was badly affected by the Asian financial crisis, with the economy contracting by 7·4% in 1998. The country also narrowly avoided a recession in 2001. Real GDP growth rates (based on IMF statistics):

2000	2001	2002	2003	2004	2005	2006	2007	2008
8·7%	0·5%	5·4%	5·8%	6·8%	5·3%	5·8%	6·2%	4·6%

The real GDP growth rate in 2009 according to Bank Negara Malaysia (Malaysia's central bank) was –1·7%. Total GDP in 2008 was US$194·9bn.

Banking and Finance
The central bank and bank of issue is the Bank Negara Malaysia (*Governor*, Dr Zeti Akhtar Aziz). In 2002 there were 47 domestic commercial banks, merchant banks and finance companies. Total deposits of commercial banks, finance companies and merchant banks at 31 Dec. 2005 were RM140·6bn. In Jan. 2006 there were 54 banks licensed by the Labuan Offshore Financial Services Authority (LOFSA).

There is a stock exchange at Kuala Lumpur, known as BSKL.

ENERGY AND NATURAL RESOURCES

Environment
Malaysia's carbon dioxide emissions from the consumption and flaring of fossil fuels in 2008 were the equivalent of 6·4 tonnes per capita.

Electricity
Installed capacity in 2004, 22·9m. kW. In 2004, 82,282m. kWh were generated. Consumption per capita in 2004 was 3,476 kWh.

Oil and Gas
Oil reserves, 2008, 5·5bn. bbls. Oil production, 2008, was 34·3m. tonnes. Natural gas reserves, 2008, 2,390bn. cu. metres. Production of natural gas in the same year was 62·5bn. cu. metres. In April 1998 Malaysia and Thailand agreed to share equally the natural gas jointly produced in an offshore area (the Malaysian-Thailand Joint Development Area) which both countries claim as their own territory.

Minerals
In 2004 mining contributed 7·0% of GDP. Production in 2004 (in tonnes): aggregate, 51,236,000; limestone, 19,968,000; sand and gravel, 18,371,000; iron ore, 663,732; silica sand, 631,402; coal, 389,176; kaolin, 326,928; ilmenite concentrate, 61,471; gold, 4,221 kg.

Agriculture
In 2002 agriculture contributed 9·2% of GDP. There were an estimated 1·80m. ha. of arable land in 2002 and 5·79m. ha. of permanent crops. In 2002 approximately 365,000 ha. were irrigated. Production in 2003 (in 1,000 tonnes): palm kernels, 3,550; rice, 2,145; sugarcane, 1,600; coconuts, 740; rubber, 589; bananas, 500; cassava, 370; pineapples, 255. Livestock (2002): pigs, 1·82m.; cattle, 748,000; goats, 248,000; sheep, 118,000; buffaloes, 154,000; chickens, 161m. Oil palms account for 75% of Malaysia's agricultural area. Malaysia's output of palm kernels is the highest of any country.

Forestry
In 2005 there were 20·89m. ha. of forests, or 63·6% of the total land area. Timber production in 2007 was 25·15m. cu. metres.

Fisheries
Total catch in 2005 amounted to 1,214,183 tonnes, almost entirely from sea fishing.

INDUSTRY
The leading companies by market capitalization in Malaysia in Feb. 2009 were: Sime Darby, a diversified industrial conglomerate (US$9·16bn.); Public Bank (US$8·62bn.); and MISC Berhard, a shipping company (US$8·58bn.).

In 2001 industry accounted for 48·3% of GDP, with manufacturing contributing 30·5%. Production figures for 2001 (in 1,000 tonnes): cement, 13,820; palm oil (2002), 11,909; distillate fuel oil (2004), 9,463; petrol (2004), 4,496; residual fuel oil (2004), 1,828; refined sugar, 1,210; wheat flour, 664; plywood (2002), 4,341,000 cu. metres; cigarettes, 25·6bn. units; radio sets, 28·8m. units; pneumatic tyres, 13·1m. units; TV sets, 9·5m. units.

Labour
In 2001 the workforce was 9,892,000 (46·7% female in 2000), of whom 9,535,000 were employed (22·6% in manufacturing, 14·2% in agriculture, forestry and fishing, 10·5% in government services and 8·9% in construction). Unemployment was 3·8% in 2002. It is estimated that Malaysia has some 500,000 illegal workers.

Trade Unions
Membership was 784,881 in 2001, of which the Malaysian Trades Union Congress, an umbrella organization of 235 unions, accounted for 0·5m. Number of unions was 578.

INTERNATIONAL TRADE
Privatization policy permits foreign investment of 25–30% generally; total foreign ownership is permitted of export-oriented projects. External debt was US$50,981m. in 2005.

Imports and Exports
In 2006 imports totalled US$124,144m. and exports US$160,842m. The trade surplus in 2006 was US$36·7bn., up from US$18·1bn. in 2002.

Main imports, 2006: electrical machinery, apparatus and appliances, 31·9%; manufactured goods, 11·6%; petroleum and petroleum products, 8·3%; chemicals and related products, 7·8%. Chief exports, 2006: electrical machinery, apparatus and appliances, 21·3%; office machines and computers, etc., 17·4%; telecommunications, sound recording and reproducing equipment, 9·0%; petroleum and petroleum products, 8·9%.

The principal import sources in 2006 were: Japan (13·2%), USA (12·5%), China (12·1%), Singapore (11·7%). The leading export markets were: USA (18·8%), Singapore (15·4%), Japan (8·9%), China (7·2%).

COMMUNICATIONS

Roads
Total road length in 2004 was 109,333 km, of which 82·8% were paved. In 2006 there were 7,024,000 passenger cars in use, 60,000 buses and coaches, 836,600 lorries and vans, and 7,458,100 motorcycles and mopeds. There were 6,287 deaths as a result of road accidents in 2006, which at 24·1 per 100,000 people ranks among the highest rates in the world.

Rail
Length of route in 2004, 1,667 km, of which 150 km were electrified. The Malayan Railway carried 34·6m. passengers and

4·1m. tonnes of freight in 2005; the Sabah State Railway carried 347,000 passengers and 500,000 tonnes of freight. A railway from Kuala Lumpur to the international airport opened in 2002 and carried 10m. passengers in 2003. There are two metro systems in Kuala Lumpur with a combined length of 56 km.

Civil Aviation

There are a total of 19 airports of which five are international airports and 14 are domestic airports at which regular public air transport is operated. *International airports;* Kuala Lumpur, Penang, Kota Kinabalu, Kuching and Langkawi. *Domestic airports;* Johor Bharu, Alor Star, Ipoh, Kota Bharu, Kuala Terengganu, Kuantan, Melaka, Sandakan, Lahad Datu, Tawau, Labuan, Bintulu, Sibu and Miri. There are 39 Malaysian airstrips of which ten are in Sabah, 15 in Sarawak and 14 in peninsular Malaysia.

In 2003, 40 international airlines operated through Kuala Lumpur (KLIA-Sepang). Malaysia Airlines, the national airline, is 69% state-owned, and operates domestic flights within Malaysia and international flights to nearly 40 different countries. A new long-haul budget airline, Air Asia X, began operations in March 2009. In 2005 scheduled airline traffic of Malaysian-based carriers flew 282·7m. km, carrying 23,026,000 passengers. In 2001 Kuala Lumpur handled 14,208,055 passengers (10,044,013 on international flights) and 423,712 tonnes of freight. Kota Kinabalu handled 2,912,802 passengers in 2001 and Kuching 2,544,502.

Shipping

The major ports are Port Kelang, Pulau Pinang, Johor Pasir Gudang, Tanjung Beruas, Miri, Rajang, Pelabuhan Sabah, Port Dickson, Kemaman, Teluk Ewa, Kuantan, Kuching and Bintulu. Port Kelang, the busiest port, handled 82,271,000 freight tons of cargo in 2002. In 1996 there were 2,429 marine vessels including 118 oil tankers (0·73m. GRT), 198 passenger carriers (0·03m. GRT) and 426 general cargo ships (0·76m. GRT), with a total GRT of 4·27m. In 1996, 167·9m. tonnes of cargo were loaded and unloaded. Total container throughput in 2002 was 8,716,463 TEUs (twenty-foot equivalent units). In 2002 merchant shipping totalled 5,394,000 GRT, including oil tankers 767,000 GRT.

Telecommunications

In 2008 there were 4,292,000 main (fixed) telephone lines. In the same year mobile phone subscribers numbered 27,713,000 (1,025·9 per 1,000 persons). There were 6,040,000 PCs in use in 2006 and 15,074,000 internet users in 2008.

Postal Services

Postal services are the responsibility of the Ministry of Information, Communications, Arts and Culture. In 2003 there were 1,211 post offices.

SOCIAL INSTITUTIONS

Justice

The highest judicial authority and final court of appeal is the Federal Court. There are also two High Courts, one for Peninsular Malaysia and one for the States of Sabah and Sarawak, as well as a system of subordinate courts (comprising Magistrate Courts and Sessions Courts).

The Federal Court comprises the Chief Justice—the head of the Malaysian judiciary—the President of the Court of Appeal, the Chief Judges of the two High Courts and four other judges. It has jurisdiction to determine the validity of any law made by Parliament or by a State legislature and disputes between States or between the Federation and any State. It also has jurisdiction to hear and determine appeals from the High Courts.

The death penalty is authorized, and was reportedly used in 2009. The population in penal institutions in 2007 was 50,305 (192 per 100,000 of national population).

Education

School education is free; tertiary education is provided at a nominal fee. There are six years of primary schooling starting at age seven, three years of universal lower secondary, two years of selective upper secondary and two years of pre-university education. During the Seventh Plan period (1996–2000), a number of major changes were introduced to the education and training system with a view to strengthening and improving the system. These efforts were aimed at improving the quality of output to meet the manpower needs of the nation, particularly in the fields of science and technology. In addition, continued emphasis will be given to expand educational opportunities for those in the rural and remote areas. Under the Seventh Plan, the Education Ministry allocated RM8,437,200 on this education programme and RM1,661,600 for training purposes.

In 2005 there were 3,133,399 pupils at primary schools with 194,872 teaching staff, 2,489,117 pupils with 146,503 teaching staff at secondary schools and (2006) 749,165 students and 39,809 academic staff at higher education institutions.

Adult literacy was 88·7% in 2003 (92·0% among males and 85·4% among females).

In 2006 public expenditure on education came to 4·7% of GNI.

Health

In 2001 there were 15,619 doctors, 2,144 dentists, 31,129 nurses and 2,333 pharmacists. In 2001 the Ministry of Health ran a total of 855 health clinics and 1,744 dental clinics. In 2002 there were 323 hospitals (provision of 16 beds per 10,000 inhabitants).

Welfare

The Employment Injury Insurance Scheme (SOCSO) provides medical and cash benefits and the Invalidity Pension Scheme provides protection to employees against invalidity as a result of disease or injury from any cause. Other supplementary measures are the Employees' Provident Fund, the pension scheme for all government employees, free medical benefits for all who are unable to pay and the provision of medical benefits particularly for workers under the Labour Code. In 1998 there were 49 welfare service institutions with capacity for 7,170.

RELIGION

Malaysia has a multi-racial population divided between Islam, Buddhism, Taoism, Hinduism and Christianity. Under the Federal constitution, Islam is the official religion of Malaysia but there is freedom of worship. In 2001 there were an estimated 10·77m. Muslims, 5·45m. adherents of Chinese traditional religions, 1·88m. Christians, 1·66m. Hindus and 1·50m. Buddhists.

CULTURE

World Heritage Sites

There are three sites in Malaysia that appear on the UNESCO World Heritage List: the Gunung Mulu National Park (inscribed on the list in 2000) with its limestone caves; Kinabalu Park/ Mount Kinabalu (2000); and the historic cities of Melaka and Georgetown (2008) in the Straits of Malacca.

Broadcasting

The government-controlled Radio Television Malaysia operates the national TV1 and TV2 networks, around 30 radio stations and an external service, Voice of Malaysia. TV3, ntv7 and 8TV are commercial networks; MiTV and Fine TV are pay-television operators. There are numerous private radio stations broadcasting in Malay, Tamil, Chinese and English. There were 5·30m. television-equipped households (colour by PAL) in 2005.

Cinema

In 2006 there were 68 cinemas. 28 feature films were produced in 2006. English, Malay, Chinese, Hindi and Indonesian films are shown.

Press

The Malaysian Media Agencies are comprised of the press, magazine and press agencies/local media, which are further divided into home and foreign news. In 2002 there were 32 daily newspapers with a combined circulation of 2,334,000. A total of 5,123 book titles were published.

Tourism

In 2005 there were 16,431,000 non-resident tourists, spending US$10,389m.

Festivals

National Day (31 Aug.) is celebrated in Kuala Lumpur at the Dataran Merdeka and marks Malaysia's independence.

Libraries

The National Library of Malaysia is strong on information technology. The 14 state public libraries and 31 ministry and government department libraries are linked in a Common User Scheme called *Jaringan Ilmu* (Knowledge Network).

Theatre and Opera

Performances by the National Budaya Group include premiere theatre staging, dance drama, national choir concerts, national symphony orchestra, chamber music, and traditional and folk music. Local theatre groups regularly stage contemporary Asian and western dramas, dance dramas and the *bangsawan* (traditional Malay opera).

Museums and Galleries

There is a National Museum for preserving, restoring and imparting knowledge on the historical and cultural heritage of Malaysia. The National Art Gallery promotes Malaysian visual arts through exhibitions, competitions and support programmes which are held locally and abroad.

DIPLOMATIC REPRESENTATIVES

Of Malaysia in the United Kingdom (45 Belgrave Sq., London, SW1X 8QT)
High Commissioner: Dato'Abd Aziz bin Mohammed.

Of the United Kingdom in Malaysia (185 Jalan Ampang, 50450 Kuala Lumpur)
High Commissioner: Boyd McCleary.

Of Malaysia in the USA (3516 International Court, NW, Washington, D.C., 20008)
Ambassador: Dr Jamaludin Jarjis.

Of the USA in Malaysia (376 Jalan Tun Razak, Kuala Lumpur)
Ambassador: James R. Keith.

Of Malaysia to the United Nations
Ambassador: Datuk Hamidon Ali.

Of Malaysia to the European Union
Ambassador: Dato' Hussein Haniff.

FURTHER READING

Department of Statistics: Kuala Lumpur. *Yearbook of Statistics, Malaysia* (2008); *Yearbook of Statistics, Sabah* (2008); *Yearbook of Statistics, Sarawak* (2008); *Vital Statistics, Malaysia* (2008).

Prime Minister's Department: Economic Planning Unit. *Malaysian Economy in Figures.* Annual, 2009.

Andaya, B. W. and Andaya, L. Y., *A History of Malaysia.* 2nd ed. 2001

Drabble, J., *An Economic History of Malaysia, c. 1800–1990.* 2001

Kahn, J. S. and Wah, F. L. K., *Fragmented Vision: Culture and Politics in Contemporary Malaysia.* 1992

Stockwell, A. J., *Making of Malaysia.* I. B. 2005

Swee-Hock, Saw, *Malaysia: Recent Trends and Challenges.* 2006

BNM: Kuala Lumpur. *Bank Negara Malaysia, Annual Report.* 2008

National Statistical Office: Department of Statistics, Block C6, Parcel C, Federal Government Administrative Centre, 62514 Putrajaya.
Website: http://www.statistics.gov.my

MALDIVES

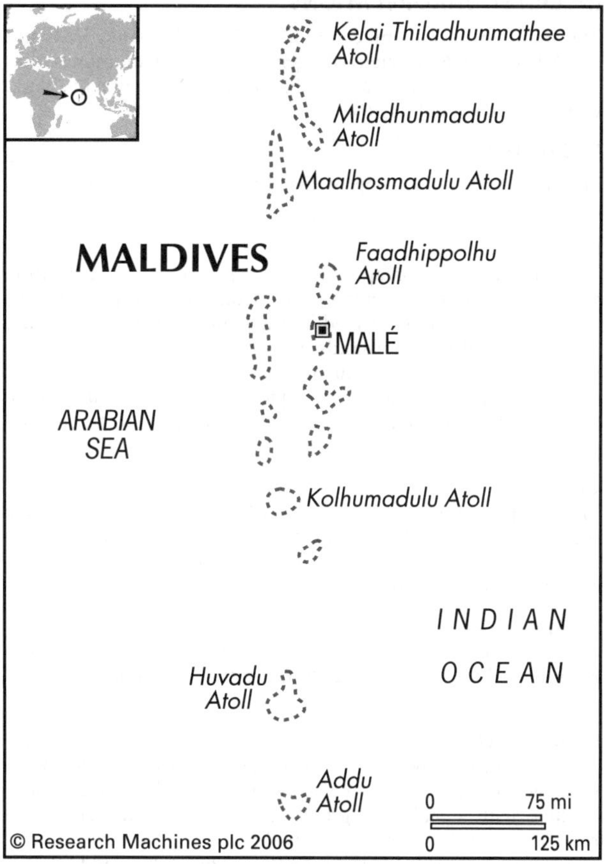

Divehi Raajjeyge Jumhooriyyaa
(Republic of the Maldives)

Capital: Malé
Population estimate, 2010: 314,000
GDP per capita, 2007: (PPP$) 5,196
HDI/world rank: 0·771/95

KEY HISTORICAL EVENTS

Divehi-speaking people (a language related to Sinhalese) have lived on the Maldives since at least AD 400. Visited by Middle Eastern merchants from around AD 1000, the archipelago became an Islamic sultanate in 1153. Portuguese explorers occupied the island of Malé (the modern capital) from 1558 until they were expelled by Muhammad Thakurufaanu Al-Azam in 1573. The Dutch, who replaced the Portuguese as the dominant power in Ceylon in the mid-1600s, controlled Maldivian affairs until 1796, although the sultanate held sway over local administration. Thereafter the Maldives came under British protection (formalized in an agreement in 1887) until complete independence was achieved on 26 July 1965. A republic was declared on 11 Nov 1968.

TERRITORY AND POPULATION

The republic, some 650 km to the southwest of Sri Lanka, consists of 1,192 low-lying (the highest point is 2·4 metres above sea-level) coral islands, grouped into 20 atolls and one city. 199 are inhabited. Area 298 sq. km (115 sq. miles). At the 2006 census the population was 298,968; density, 1,003·2 per sq. km.

The UN gives an estimated population for 2010 of 314,000.

In 2005, 70·4% of the population lived in rural areas. Capital, Malé (2006 population, 92,555).

The official and spoken language is Divehi.

SOCIAL STATISTICS

2006 births, 5,827; deaths, 1,084. Birth rate, 2006, per 1,000 population, 19·5; death rate, 3·6. Annual population growth rate, 2000–05, 1·6%. Life expectancy at birth in 2007 was 69·7 years for males and 72·7 years for females. Infant mortality, 2005, 33 per 1,000 live births. The fertility rate dropped from 5·8 births per woman in 1994 to 4·1 births per woman in 2004.

CLIMATE

The islands are hot and humid, and affected by monsoons. Malé: average temperature 81°F (27°C), annual rainfall 59" (1,500 mm).

CONSTITUTION AND GOVERNMENT

The present constitution came into effect on 1 Jan. 1998. There is a Citizens' *Majlis* (Parliament) which consists of 77 members all of whom are directly elected for a term of five years. Political parties were not permitted until the introduction of a multiparty system in June 2005. In a referendum held on 18 Aug. 2007 voters supported the retention of a presidential system, with 62·0% of votes cast in favour and 38·0% for a switch to a parliamentary system. The President of the Republic is elected by the Citizens' Majlis.

National Anthem

'Gavmii mi ekuverikan matii tibegen kuriime salaam' ('In national unity we salute our nation'); words by M. J. Didi, tune by W. Amaradeva.

RECENT ELECTIONS

The Maldives' first multi-party presidential elections were held on 8 and 29 Oct. 2008. Turnout in the first round was 85·4%. Incumbent president Maumoon Abdul Gayoom (Dhivehi Rayyithunge Party; DRP) won 40·3% of the vote, Mohamed Nasheed ('Anni') (Maldivian Democratic Party; MDP) 24·9%, Hassan Saeed (ind.) 16·7%, Qasim Ibrahim (Jumhooree Party) 15·2%, Umar Naseer (Islamic Democratic Party) 1·4% and Ibrahim Ismail (Social Liberal Party) 0·8%. A second round run-off was held on 29 Oct. 2008 which Mohamed Nasheed won with 54·2% of the vote against 45·8% for Maumoon Abdul Gayoom. Turnout was 86·6%.

Legislation passed in 2005 allowed political parties to stand for the first time in elections to the Majlis held on 9 May 2009. The DRP won 28 seats, the MDP 26, the People's Alliance 7, the Dhivehi Qaumee Party 2 and the Justice Party 1. 13 seats went to independents.

CURRENT ADMINISTRATION

The multi-party coalition government is led by the Maldivian Democratic Party. In March 2010 the government consisted of:

President: Mohamed Nasheed ('Anni'); b. 1967 (MDP; in office since 11 Nov. 2008).

Vice-President: Dr Mohamed Waheed Hassan Manik.

Minister of Agriculture and Fisheries: Dr Ibrahim Didi. *Civil Aviation and Communication:* Mahmood Razee. *Defence and National Security:* Ameen Faisal. *Economic Development:* Mohamed Rasheed. *Education:* Dr Musthafa Luthfy. *Finance and Treasury:* Ali Hashim. *Foreign Affairs:* Dr Ahmed Shaheed. *Health and Family:* Dr Aminath Jameel. *Home Affairs:* Mohamed Shihab. *Housing, Transport and Environment:* Mohamed Aslam. *Human Resources, Youth and Sport:* Hassan Latheef. *Islamic Affairs:* Dr Abdul Majeed Abdul Bari. *Tourism, and Arts and Culture:* Ahmed Ali Sawad. *Attorney General:* Husnu Suood.

Speaker of Citizens' Majlis: Abdulla Shahid.

Office of the President: http://www.presidencymaldives.gov.mv

CURRENT LEADERS

Mohamed Nasheed ('Anni')

Position
President

Introduction
Mohamed Nasheed, popularly known as 'Anni', became the Maldives' first democratically elected president in Oct. 2008. Anni, a former political prisoner, defeated incumbent Maumoon Abdul Gayoom, who had held office for 30 years, on a reform platform.

Early Life
Mohamed Nasheed was born on 17 July 1967 in Malé. He went to school in Sri Lanka and England before graduating from Liverpool John Moores University with a degree in maritime studies in 1989.

In 1990 Anni became a journalist in the Maldives with a current affairs magazine, *Sandhaanu*, where he earned a reputation for anti-government commentaries at a time when such criticism was rare. *Sandhaanu* was banned the following year and Anni was arrested, the first of 13 detentions for his opposition to Gayoom's administration. Amnesty International declared him a prisoner of conscience.

He was elected to the Citizens' Majlis (Parliament) in 2000 as the member for Malé, which was to become his central power base. In 2001, six months after his election, he was arrested and sentenced to two-and-a-half-years imprisonment for the theft of unspecified 'government property'. His supporters claimed the charge was politically motivated. After his release in 2003 Anni went into exile, firstly in Sri Lanka and then in Britain where, in Nov. 2003, he formed the Maldivian Democratic Party (MDP) with Mohamed Latheef. Anni was granted political asylum by the British government in 2004 but returned to Malé in April 2005.

On 12 Aug. 2005 he was arrested during a protest to mark the first anniversary of Black Friday (when anti-government protests ended in violent conflict with security forces). Anni was charged under the Terrorism Act but released in Sept. 2006 without trial following a British-brokered deal between the government and the MDP. Anni had been named chairperson of the MDP in absentia on 20 Dec. 2005.

He resigned as chairperson in Feb. 2008 to make a successful run for the MDP presidential candidature in the party's primary elections. In the first round of the presidential election on 8 Oct. 2008 Anni was placed second behind Gayoom, with 25% of the vote. With the support of the four defeated candidates in the run-off on 28 Oct. 2008, he received 54% of the vote and was sworn into office on 11 Nov. 2008.

Career in Office
On taking office Anni committed US$350m. to improve the quality of life of Maldivians and to create a 'sovereign wealth fund' to buy a new homeland should the country disappear as sea levels rise. He also made a surprise announcement that he would hold a 'mid-term' election. Anni's challenges include maintaining the lucrative tourist trade, ensuring a fairer distribution of wealth and tackling the youth drugs culture.

In multi-party elections in May 2009, Anni's MDP narrowly came second to the opposition DRP, taking 26 of 77 parliamentary seats.

DEFENCE

In 2006 military expenditure totalled US$56m. (US$156 per capita), representing 6·1% of GDP.

INTERNATIONAL RELATIONS

The Maldives is a member of the UN, World Bank, IMF and several other UN specialized agencies, WTO, Commonwealth, Islamic Development Bank, OIC, Asian Development Bank, Colombo Plan and SAARC.

ECONOMY

Fisheries accounts for approximately 7% of GDP, industry 15% and services 78%.

Overview

Tourism accounts for approximately 28% of total GDP, while 60% of government revenues derive from imports and tourism. The region was badly affected by the tsunami of Dec. 2004 that left many dead and thousands displaced. GDP growth has been variable in recent years. In 2005 growth was at –5·1% (the result of the tsunami), then in 2006 jumped to 23·5%, concurrent with the revival of tourism and the construction of new resorts. In 2007 growth stabilized at 7·2%.

Currency

The unit of currency is the *rufiyaa* (MVR) of 100 *laari*. There was inflation in 2008 of 11·9%. Gold reserves were 2,000 troy oz in July 2005, foreign exchange reserves were US$218m. and total money supply was 3,163m. rufiyaa.

Budget

In 2005 budgetary central government revenue totalled 4,577·9m. rufiyaa (including taxes, 1,722·8m. rufiyaa); expenditure totalled 4,643·3m. rufiyaa.

Performance

After shrinking by 4·6% in 2005 as a consequence of the devastation wreaked by the tsunami, the economy rebounded spectacularly in 2006 with a real GDP growth rate of 18·0%, driven by the return of tourists, reconstruction efforts and new development. The recovery continued with growth of 7·2% in 2007 and 5·8% in 2008. Total GDP in 2008 was US$1·3bn.

Banking and Finance

The Maldives Monetary Authority (*Governor*, Fazeel Najeeb), established in 1981, is endowed with the regular powers of a central bank and bank of issue. There is one domestic commercial bank (Bank of Maldives) and branches of four foreign banks.

There is a stock exchange in Malé.

ENERGY AND NATURAL RESOURCES

Environment

Carbon dioxide emissions from the consumption and flaring of fossil fuels were the equivalent of 2·3 tonnes per capita in 2008.

Electricity

Installed capacity was 49,000 kW in 2004. Production in 2004 was 160m. kWh; consumption per capita in 2004 was 539 kWh. Utilization in Malé was 97m. kWh in 2003.

Minerals

Inshore coral mining has been banned as a measure against the encroachment of the sea.

Agriculture

There were approximately 4,000 ha. of arable land in 2007 and 8,000 ha. of permanent crops. Principal crops in 2003 (estimates, in 1,000 tonnes): coconuts, 36; copra, 6; bananas, 3; tree nuts, 2.

Fisheries

The total catch in 2005 was 185,980 tonnes. The Maldives has the highest per capita consumption of fish and fishery products of any country in the world. In the period 2001–03 the average person consumed 191 kg (420 lb) a year, or more than 11 times the average for the world as a whole.

INDUSTRY

The main industries are fishing, tourism, shipping, lacquerwork and garment manufacturing.

Labour

In 2005 the economically active workforce totalled 99,000 of whom 96,000 were employed. More than two-thirds of the working population are engaged in tourism.

INTERNATIONAL TRADE

Total foreign debt amounted to US$562m. in 2007.

Imports and Exports

In 2006 imports (f.o.b.) were valued at US$815·3m. (US$655·5m. in 2005) and exports (f.o.b.) at US$215·9m. (US$152·3m. in 2005). Tuna is the main export commodity. It is exported principally to Thailand, Sri Lanka, Japan and some European markets. Main import suppliers in 2003 were Singapore (24·9%), Sri Lanka (13·7%), India (10·1%), Malaysia (7·7%), UAE (7·6%). Leading export destinations were the USA (23·3%), Thailand (16·4%), Sri Lanka (13·6%), Japan (10·3%), UK (9·7%).

COMMUNICATIONS

Roads

In 2007 there were 3,060 passenger cars in use (10 per 1,000 inhabitants), 26,780 motorcycles and mopeds, 2,870 lorries and vans, and 74 buses and coaches.

Civil Aviation

The former national carrier Air Maldives collapsed in April 2000 with final losses in excess of US$50m. In 2003 there were 1,833,620 passenger arrivals, 21m. pieces of cargo and 100,352 pieces of mail handled at Malé's international airport. There are four domestic airports. In 2001 scheduled airline traffic of Maldives-based carriers flew 7m. km, carrying 367,000 passengers (226,000 on international flights).

Shipping

The Maldives Shipping Line operated ten vessels in 1992. In 2000 merchant shipping totalled 58,000 GRT.

Telecommunications

In Oct. 2004 telephone subscribers numbered 31,300 (108 fixed lines per 1,000 inhabitants) and mobile phone users 98,300. Landline and mobile usage combined gives an overall density of 447 telephones per 1,000 inhabitants. At the end of 2003 the number of PCs in use was estimated at 25,000. There were approximately 15,000 internet users in 2003.

Postal Services

In Nov. 2004 there were 197 agency post offices and nine sub-post offices. There are a total of 300 employees.

SOCIAL INSTITUTIONS

Justice

Justice is based on the Islamic Sharia.

Education

Adult literacy in 2003 was 97·2% (male, 97·3%; female, 97·2%). Education is not compulsory. In 2004 there were 81 government schools (57,139 pupils), 176 community schools (38,043 pupils) and 337 private schools (104,214 pupils) with a total of 5,239 teachers. In 2005 public expenditure on education came to 7·8% of GDP and 15·0% of total government spending.

Health

In 2003 there were 236 beds at the Indira Gandhi Memorial Hospital in Malé, six regional hospitals (226 beds) and 27 health centres. In 2003 there were 315 doctors and 785 nurses, 251 pharmacists and 409 midwives.

RELIGION

The State religion is Islam.

CULTURE

Broadcasting

Voice of Maldives radio and Television Maldives are government-controlled. The first private radio station began transmission in 2007. In 2003 there were 41,000 television sets (colour by PAL).

Press

In 2005 there were 18 newspapers and 77 magazines.

Tourism

Tourism is the major foreign currency earner. There were a record 616,716 visitors in 2004, spending US$471m.

DIPLOMATIC REPRESENTATIVES

Of the Maldives in the United Kingdom (22 Nottingham Pl., London, W1U 5NJ)
High Commissioner: Dr Farahanaz Faizal.

Of the United Kingdom in the Maldives
High Commissioner: Dr Peter Hayes (resides in Colombo, Sri Lanka).

Of the Maldives in the USA (800 2nd Ave., Suite 400E, New York, NY 10017)
Ambassador: Abdul Ghafoor Mohamed.

Of the USA in the Maldives
Ambassador: Patricia A. Butenis (resides in Colombo, Sri Lanka).

Of the Maldives to the United Nations
Ambassador: Abdul Ghafoor Mohamed.

Of the Maldives to the European Union
Ambassador: Mohamed Asim.

FURTHER READING

Gayoom, M. A., *The Maldives: A Nation in Peril.* 1998

National Statistical Office: Statistics Section, Ministry of Planning and National Development.
Website: http://www.planning.gov.mv

MALI

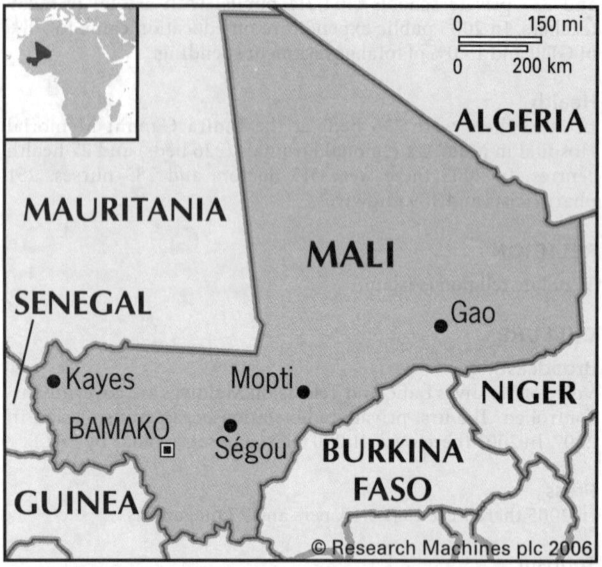

République du Mali
(Republic of Mali)

Capital: Bamako
Population estimate, 2010: 13·32m.
GDP per capita, 2007: (PPP$) 1,083
HDI/world rank: 0·371/178

KEY HISTORICAL EVENTS

Mali's power reached its peak between the 11th and 13th centuries when its gold-based empire controlled much of the surrounding area. The country was annexed by France in 1904. As French Sudan it was part of French West Africa. The country became an autonomous state within the French Community on 24 Nov. 1958, and on 4 April 1959 joined with Senegal to form the Federation of Mali. The Federation achieved independence on 20 June 1960, but Senegal seceded on 22 Aug. and Mali proclaimed itself an independent republic on 22 Sept. There was an army coup on 19 Nov. 1968, which brought Moussa Traoré to power. Ruling the country for over 22 years, he wrecked the economy. A further coup followed in March 1991.

In Jan. 1991 a ceasefire was signed with Tuareg insurgents in the north and in April 1992 a national pact was concluded providing for a special administration for the Tuareg north.

Under President Alpha Oumar Konaré, two elections for the National Assembly were held. The first (April 1997) was cancelled by the Constitutional Court and the second, in July 1997, was boycotted by opposition parties. Amadou Toumani Touré, a former military ruler, won presidential elections held in April and May 2002. In July 2005 severe food shortages led to more than 1m. people facing starvation.

TERRITORY AND POPULATION

Mali is bounded in the west by Senegal, northwest by Mauritania, northeast by Algeria, east by Niger and south by Burkina Faso, Côte d'Ivoire and Guinea. Its area is 1,248,574 sq. km (482,077 sq. miles) and it had a population of 14,517,176 at the 2009 census (provisional); density, 11·6 per sq. km. In 2005, 69·5% of the population were rural.

The UN gives an estimated population for 2010 of 13·32m.

The areas, populations and chief towns of the regions are:

Region	*Sq. km*	*2009 census population (provisional)*	*Chief town*
Gao	170,572	544,120	Gao
Kayes	119,743	1,996,812	Kayes
Kidal	151,430	67,638	Kidal
Koulikoro	95,848	2,418,305	Koulikoro
Mopti	79,017	2,037,330	Mopti
Ségou	64,821	2,336,255	Ségou
Sikasso	70,280	2,625,919	Sikasso
Tombouctou	496,611	681,691	Tombouctou
Capital District	252	1,809,106	Bamako

In 1999 the capital, Bamako, had an estimated population of 1,083,000.

In 2000 the principal ethnic groups were: Bambara, 30·6%; Senufo, 10·5%; Fulani, 9·6%; Soninke, 7·4%; Tuareg, 7·0%; Maninka, 6·6%; Songhai, 6·3%; Dogon, 4·3%. The official language is French; Bambara is spoken by about 68% of the population.

SOCIAL STATISTICS

2000 estimates: births, 590,000; deaths, 206,000. Rates, 2000 estimates (per 1,000 population): births, 49·6; deaths, 17·3. Infant mortality, 2005 (per 1,000 live births), 120. Expectation of life in 2007 was 47·4 years for males and 48·8 for females. Annual population growth rate, 1992–2002, 2·8%; fertility rate, 2004, 6·8 children per woman.

CLIMATE

A tropical climate, with adequate rain in the south and west, but conditions become increasingly arid towards the north and east. Bamako, Jan. 76°F (24·4°C), July 80°F (26·7°C). Annual rainfall 45" (1,120 mm). Kayes, Jan. 76°F (24·4°C), July 93°F (33·9°C). Annual rainfall 29" (725 mm). Tombouctou, Jan. 71°F (21·7°C), July 90°F (32·2°C). Annual rainfall 9" (231 mm).

CONSTITUTION AND GOVERNMENT

A constitution was approved by a national referendum in 1974; it was amended by the National Assembly on 2 Sept. 1981. The sole legal party was the *Union démocratique du peuple malien* (UDPM).

A national conference of 1,800 delegates agreed a draft constitution enshrining multi-party democracy in Aug. 1991, and this was approved by 99·76% of votes cast at a referendum in Jan. 1992. Turnout was 43%.

The *President* is elected for not more than two terms of five years.

There is a *National Assembly*, consisting of 147 deputies (formerly 116) plus 13 Malinese living abroad.

A *Constitutional Court* was established in 1994.

National Anthem

'A ton appel, Mali' ('At your call, Mali'); words by S. Kouyate, tune by B. Sissoko.

RECENT ELECTIONS

Presidential elections were held on 29 April 2007. Amadou Toumani Touré was re-elected with 71·2% of votes cast, against Ibrahim Boubacar Keita (19·2%) and five other candidates. Turnout was 36·2%. The Front for Democracy and the Republic, the coalition backing Keita, refused to accept the result, alleging widespread fraud. However, foreign observers declared it mostly fair.

Parliamentary elections were held in two rounds on 1 and 22 July 2007. The Alliance for Democracy in Mali (ADEMA) won 51 seats (67 in 2002), Union for the Republic and Democracy 34, Rally for Mali 11, Patriotic Movement for Renewal 8, National Congress for Democratic Initiative 7, Party for National Rebirth 4, African Solidarity for Democracy and Independence 4, Union of Democrats for Citizenship and Development 3, Movement for the Independence, Renaissance and Integration of Africa 2, Popular Party for Progress 2 and Alternation Bloc for Renewal, Integration and African Co-operation 2. Four other parties won a single seat each and 15 seats went to independents. The Alliance for Democracy and Progress, a coalition that supports President Touré and includes the Alliance for Democracy in Mali and the Union for the Republic and Democracy, won 113 of the 147 seats. The opposition coalition, the Front for Democracy and the Republic (which includes Rally for Mali), won 15 seats. Turnout was about 33% in the first round and about 11% in the second.

CURRENT ADMINISTRATION

President: Amadou Toumani Touré; b. 1948 (sworn in 8 June 2002 and re-elected 29 April 2007, having previously been president from March 1991–June 1992 following a coup).

In March 2010 the government comprised:

Prime Minister: Modibo Sidibé; b. 1952 (sworn in 3 Oct. 2007).

Minister for Agriculture: Agatham Ag Alassane. *Basic Education, Literacy and National Languages:* Sidibé Aminata Diallo. *Communications and Information Technology:* Diarra Mariam Flantié Diallo. *Culture:* Mohamed El Moctar. *Defence and Veterans:* Natié Pleah. *Economy and Finance:* Sanoussi Touré. *Employment and Professional Training:* Ibrahima N'Diaye. *Energy and Water Resources:* Mamadou Diarra. *Environment and Decontamination:* Tiemoko Sangaré. *Equipment and Transport:* Hamed Diané Sémega. *Foreign Affairs and International Co-operation:* Moctar Ouane. *Handicrafts and Tourism:* N'Diaye Bah. *Health:* Ibrahim Oumar Touré. *Housing and Urbanization:* Gakou Salimata Fofana. *Internal Security and Civil Protection:* Col. Sadio Gassama. *Investment, Industry and Commerce:* Ahmadou Abdoulaye Diallo. *Justice and Keeper of the Seals:* Maharam Ba Traoré. *Labour, Civil Service and State Reform:* Abdoul Wahab Berthé. *Livestock and Fishing:* Diallo Madeleine Bâ. *Malians Abroad and African Integration:* Badra Alou Macalou. *Mines:* Aboubacar Traoré. *Promotion of Women, Children and the Family:* Maiga Sina Damba. *Relations with Institutions and Government Spokesperson:* Diabaté Fatoumata Guindo. *Secondary and Higher Education and Scientific Research:* Siby Ginette Belgade. *Social Development, Solidarity and the Aged:* Sekou Diakité. *Territorial Administration and Local Collectivities:* Gen. Kafougouna Koné. *Youth and Sports:* Hamane Niang.

Office of the President (French only): http://www.koulouba.pr.ml

CURRENT LEADERS

Amadou Toumani Touré

Position
President

Introduction
In 2002 Amadou Toumani Touré won Mali's election to become the country's second democratically-elected president. He had previously acted as head of state in 1991 when, as an army general, he overthrew military leader Moussa Traoré. He was re-elected in April 2007.

Early Life
Amadou Toumani Touré was born on 4 Nov. 1948 in Mopti. From 1966–69 he studied at Badalabougou Standard Secondary School in Bamako with the intention of becoming a teacher. However, he abandoned teaching in favour of military training and joined the army, enrolling at the Kita-Inter Military College. He then trained in the former USSR and France before joining the parachute corps as a commander in 1984.

Touré led a coup in 1991 against Moussa Traoré after the latter's security forces killed more than a hundred pro-democracy demonstrators. In 1992 Touré handed power back to the newly-elected president Alpha Oumar Konaré, ending 23 years of military dictatorship and earning himself the nickname 'Soldier of Democracy'.

Having retired from the army in Sept. 2001, he decided to return to politics as an independent presidential candidate in 2002, beating Soumaïla Cissé in the second round of elections.

Career in Office
Touré took office with the support of 22 minor parties and a number of other groups. He pledged to promote education and youth employment and has created a children's foundation. He also pledged to ease poverty and improve the health system. In Aug. 2005 he launched the food security website, developed in conjunction with the Malian food security commission, designed to monitor and improve the country's food distribution. Touré was returned for a second term in April 2007 and the ruling pro-president Alliance for Democracy and Progress coalition won parliamentary elections in July.

In June 2006 his government signed an Algerian-brokered peace agreement with Tuareg rebels seeking greater autonomy for the north of the country. Despite these peace overtures, however, attacks involving suspected Tuareg insurgents continued until early 2009 when the government claimed to have taken control of Tuareg bases and some 700 rebels surrendered their weapons.

DEFENCE

In 2006 military expenditure totalled US$132m. (US$11 per capita), representing 2·2% of GDP.

Army

Strength (2007) 7,350. There are also paramilitary forces of 4,800.

Navy

There is a Navy of around 50 operating three patrol craft although their serviceability is in doubt.

Air Force

Personnel (2007) total 400. There were around 16 combat capable aircraft.

INTERNATIONAL RELATIONS

Mali is a member of the UN, World Bank, IMF and several other UN specialized agencies, WTO, IOM, International Organization of the Francophonie, Islamic Development Bank, OIC, African Development Bank, African Union, ECOWAS and is an ACP member state of the ACP-EU relationship.

ECONOMY

Agriculture accounted for 36·9% of GDP in 2006, industry 24·0% and services 39·1%.

Overview

One of the world's poorest nations, Mali is rated 178th out of 182 on the UN Human Development Index. The economy is heavily dependent on agriculture. Real GDP growth has averaged over 5% per year since 1994 and reached 6·1% in 2005. Exports are concentrated in the primary sector, including gold, but reliance on cotton and livestock makes the economy vulnerable to drought.

Per capita income rose from US$240 in 1994 to US$380 in 2005. Slowing inflation, which was negative in both 2003 and 2004, and improving external balances resulting from high gold prices have contributed to recent positive performance. State fiscal management has improved, with targets reached for net domestic financing, external debt terms, the wage bill, payment arrears and the basic balance in 2005. However, over 70% of the population is estimated to be living below the poverty line.

Currency

The unit of currency is the *franc CFA* (XOF), which replaced the Mali franc in 1984. It has a parity rate of 655·957 francs CFA to one euro. Total money supply in June 2005 was 573,692m. francs CFA and foreign exchange reserves were US$827m. Inflation was 1·5% in 2007 and 9·1% in 2008.

Budget

Revenues for 2006 were 694·3bn. francs CFA and expenditures 795·1bn. francs CFA.

VAT is 18%.

Performance

Real GDP growth was 4·3% in 2007 and 5·1% in 2008. Total GDP in 2008 was US$8·7bn.

Banking and Finance

The bank of issue and the central bank is the regional Central Bank of West African States (BCEAO). The *Governor* is Philippe-Henri Dacoury-Tabley. In 2002 there were eight commercial and two development banks.

There is a stock exchange in Bamako.

ENERGY AND NATURAL RESOURCES

Environment

Carbon dioxide emissions from the consumption and flaring of fossil fuels were the equivalent of 0·1 tonnes per capita in 2008. An *Environmental Performance Index* compiled in 2008 ranked Mali 145th in the world out of 149 countries analysed, with 44·3%. The index examined various factors in six areas—air pollution, biodiversity and habitat, climate change, environmental health, productive natural resources and water resources.

Electricity

Installed capacity in 2004 was estimated at 0·1m. kW. Production in 2004 totalled about 455m. kWh, approximately 53% of it hydro-electric. Consumption per capita was an estimated 41 kWh in 2004.

Minerals

Gold (51,957 kg in 2006) is the principal mineral produced. There are also deposits of iron ore, uranium, diamonds, bauxite, manganese, copper, salt, limestone, phosphate, gypsum and lithium.

Agriculture

About 80% of the population depends on agriculture, mainly carried on by small peasant holdings. Mali is second only to Egypt among African cotton producers. In 2002 there were an estimated 4·66m. ha. of arable land and 40,000 ha. of permanent cropland. There were around 2,600 tractors in 2002 and 650 harvester-threshers. Production in 2003 included (estimates, in 1,000 tonnes): millet, 815; rice, 693; sorghum, 650; seed cotton, 464; maize, 365; sugarcane, 300; cotton lint, 250; cottonseed, 185; groundnuts, 170; sweet potatoes, 74, tomatoes, 50.

Livestock, 2003 estimates: goats, 11·46m.; sheep, 7·97m.; cattle, 7·31m.; asses, 700,000; camels, 470,000; horses, 170,000; chickens, 29m.

Livestock products, 2003 estimates (in 1,000 tonnes): beef and veal, 113; goat meat, 46; lamb and mutton, 36; poultry meat, 34; goat's milk, 227; cow's milk, 179; sheep's milk, 117; eggs, 10.

Approximately 138,000 ha. were irrigated in 2002.

Forestry

In 2005 forests covered 12·57m. ha., or 10·3% of the total land area. Timber production in 2007 was 5·56m. cu. metres.

Fisheries

In 2005 approximately 100,000 tonnes of fish were caught, exclusively from inland waters.

INDUSTRY

The main industries are food processing, followed by cotton processing, textiles and clothes. Cement and pharmaceuticals are also produced.

Labour

There were 2,491,800 employed persons (58·4% males) in 2004. In 2003 approximately 79·0% of the total labour force were engaged in agriculture. Large numbers of Malians emigrate temporarily to work abroad, principally in Côte d'Ivoire.

INTERNATIONAL TRADE

Foreign debt was US$2,969m. in 2005.

Imports and Exports

In 2005 imports (f.o.b.) were valued at US$1,245·5m. and exports (f.o.b.) at US$1,100·9m. Principal import commodities are machinery and equipment, foodstuffs, construction materials, petroleum and textiles. Principal export commodities are cotton and livestock (between them accounting for three-quarters of Mali's annual exports) and gold. The main import suppliers are France and its former colonies (in particular Côte d'Ivoire), western Europe and China. Main export markets are also France and its former colonies, western Europe and China.

COMMUNICATIONS

Roads

There were 18,709 km of roads in 2004, of which 18·0% were paved. In 2007 there were 87,000 passenger cars (seven per 1,000 inhabitants), 26,800 lorries and vans, and 10,000 motorcycles and mopeds.

Rail

Mali has a railway from Kayes to Koulikoro by way of Bamako, a continuation of the Dakar–Kayes line in Senegal; total length, 2005, 643 km (metre-gauge). In 2005, 179,000 passengers and 1·7m. tonnes of freight were transported.

Civil Aviation

There is an international airport at Bamako (Senou), which handled 312,000 passengers (305,000 on international flights) and 4,400 tonnes of freight in 2001. In 2003 Trans African Airlines operated services to Abidjan, Brazzaville, Cotonou, Dakar, Lomé and Pointe-Noire. There were also international flights to Accra, Addis Ababa, Banjul, Bobo-Dioulasso, Casablanca, Conakry, Douala, Kano, Lagos, Libreville, N'Djaména, Niamey, Nouakchott, Ouagadougou, Paris and Tripoli. In 2001 scheduled airline traffic of Mali-based carriers flew 1m. km, carrying 46,000 passengers (all on international flights).

Shipping

For about seven months in the year small steamboats operate a service from Koulikoro to Tombouctou and Gao, and from Bamako to Kouroussa.

Telecommunications

In 2008 there were 81,100 main (fixed) telephone lines; mobile phone subscribers numbered 3,439,000 in 2008 (27·1 per 100 persons). There were 45,000 PCs in use in 2005 and an 200,000 internet users in 2008.

Postal Services

In 2002 there were 117 post offices.

SOCIAL INSTITUTIONS

Justice

The Supreme Court was established at Bamako in 1969 with both judicial and administrative powers. The Court of Appeal is also at Bamako, at the apex of a system of regional tribunals and local *juges de paix*.

The population in penal institutions in 2004 was 4,407 (33 per 100,000 of national population).

Education
The adult literacy rate in 2003 was 24·0%. In 2007 there were 1,510 teaching staff for 54,591 children in pre-primary schools, 33,230 teaching staff for 1,716,956 pupils in primary schools, 15,013 teaching staff for 533,849 secondary school pupils and 50,787 students in tertiary education with 976 academic staff. During the period 1990–95 only 19% of females of primary school age were enrolled in school but by 2007 this had risen to 56%.

In 2005 public expenditure on education came to 4·1% of GDP.

Health
In 2001 there were 17 hospitals. In 2000 there were 529 physicians, 1,501 nurses and 284 midwives.

RELIGION
The state is secular, but predominantly Sunni Muslim. About 15% of the population follow traditional animist beliefs and there is a small Christian minority.

CULTURE

World Heritage Sites
Mali has four sites on the UNESCO World Heritage List: Old Towns of Djenné (inscribed in 1988), a market centre established in 250 BC and an important Islamic centre in the 16th century—its buildings are all mudbrick, plastered annually with adobe; Tomboctou (1988), an important Islamic centre containing the Koranic Sankore University and the famous Djingareyber Mosque; the Cliff of Bandiagara (Land of the Dogons) (1989), for its natural and architectural wonders; and the Tomb of Askia (2004).

Broadcasting
Public broadcasting is the responsibility of the Office de la Radiodiffusion Télévision du Mali (ORTM). There are also private television and radio stations. Number of TV sets (2006): 450,000 (colour by SECAM).

Press
In 2005 there were 12 daily newspapers with a combined circulation of 40,000.

Tourism
There were 113,000 foreign tourists in 2004 (including 64,000 from Europe and 29,000 from other African countries), bringing in revenue of US$130m.

DIPLOMATIC REPRESENTATIVES

Of Mali in the United Kingdom
Ambassador: Ibrahim Bocar Ba (resides in Brussels).

Of the United Kingdom in Mali (embassy in Bamako closed in May 2003)
Ambassador: Christopher Trott (resides in Dakar, Senegal).

Of Mali in the USA (2130 R. St., NW, Washington, D.C., 20008)
Ambassador: Vacant.
Chargé d'Affaires a.i.: Mohamed Ouzouna Maiga.

Of the USA in Mali (ACI 2000, Rue 243, Porte 297, Bamako)
Ambassador: Gillian A. Milovanovic.

Of Mali to the United Nations
Ambassador: Oumar Daou.

Of Mali to the European Union
Ambassador: Ibrahim Bocar Ba.

FURTHER READING

Bingen, R. James, *Democracy and Development in Mali.* 2000

National Statistical Office: Direction National de la Statistique et de l'Informatique, BP 12 rue Archinard, Porte 233.
Website (French only): http://instat.gov.ml

MALTA

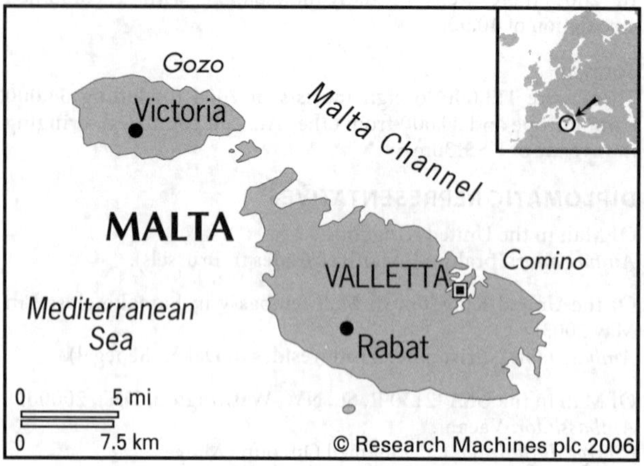

Repubblika ta' Malta
(Republic of Malta)

Capital: Valletta
Population estimate, 2010: 410,000
GDP per capita, 2007: (PPP$) 23,080
HDI/world rank: 0·902/38

KEY HISTORICAL EVENTS

Malta was held in turn by Phoenicians, Carthaginians and Romans, and was conquered by Arabs in 870. From 1090 it was subject to the same rulers as Sicily until 1530, when it was handed over to the Knights of St John, who ruled until dispersed by Napoleon in 1798. The Maltese rose in rebellion against the French and the island was blockaded by the British, aided by the Maltese from 1798 to 1800. The Maltese people freely requested the protection of the British Crown in 1802 on condition that their rights and privileges be preserved. The island was finally annexed to the British Crown by the Treaty of Paris in 1814. Malta became independent on 21 Sept. 1964 and a republic within the Commonwealth on 13 Dec. 1974. On 1 May 2004 Malta became a member of the European Union.

TERRITORY AND POPULATION

The three Maltese islands and minor islets lie in the Mediterranean 93 km (at the nearest point) south of Sicily and 288 km east of Tunisia. The area of Malta is 246 sq. km (94·9 sq. miles); Gozo, 67 sq. km (25·9 sq. miles) and the virtually uninhabited Comino, 3 sq. km (1·1 sq. miles); total area, 316 sq. km (121·9 sq. miles). The census population in 2005 was 404,962 (Malta island, 373,955; Gozo and Comino, 31,007). Density, 1,282 per sq. km.

The UN gives an estimated population for 2010 of 410,000.

In 2005, 95·3% of the population were urban. Chief town and port, Valletta, population 6,300 (2005) but the southern harbour district, 81,047. Other towns: Birkirkara, 21,858; Mosta, 18,735; Qormi, 16,559; Zabbar, 14,671; St Paul's Bay, 13,412.

The constitution provides that the national language and language of the courts is Maltese, but both Maltese and English are official languages. Italian is also spoken.

SOCIAL STATISTICS

2002: births, 3,805; deaths, 3,031; marriages, 2,240; emigrants, 96; returned emigrants, 382. 2002 rates per 1,000 population: birth, 9·9; death, 7·8; marriage, 5·8. Divorce and abortion are illegal. In 2002 the most popular age range for marrying was 25–29 for males and 20–24 for females. Life expectancy at birth in 2007: 77·7 years for males and 81·3 years for females. Annual population growth rate, 2000–05, 1·1%. Infant mortality in 2005: 5 per 1,000 live births; fertility rate, 2004, 1·5 births per woman.

CLIMATE

The climate is Mediterranean, with hot, dry and sunny conditions in summer and very little rain from May to Aug. Rainfall is not excessive and falls mainly between Oct. and March. Average daily sunshine in winter is six hours and in summer over ten hours. Valletta, Jan. 12·8°C (55°F), July 25·6°C (78°F). Annual rainfall 578 mm (23").

CONSTITUTION AND GOVERNMENT

Malta is a parliamentary democracy. The constitution of 1964 provides for a *President*, a *House of Representatives* of members elected by universal suffrage and a Cabinet consisting of the Prime Minister and such number of Ministers as may be appointed. The Constitution makes provision for the protection of fundamental rights and freedom of the individual, and for freedom of conscience and religious worship, and guarantees the separation of executive, judicial and legislative powers. The House of Representatives currently has 65 members directly elected on a plurality basis.

National Anthem

'Lil din l'art helwa, l'omm li tatna isimha' ('Guard her, O Lord, as ever Thou hast guarded'); words by Dun Karm Psaila, tune by Dr Robert Samut.

RECENT ELECTIONS

At the elections of 8 March 2008 the electorate was 315,357; turnout was 93·3%. The Nationalist Party (NP) gained 31 seats with 49·3% of votes cast; the Labour Party (MLP), 34 with 48·8%. However, constitutional law dictates that in a two-party parliament the winner of the popular vote must hold a parliamentary majority, so the Nationalist Party was awarded a further four seats, giving them a total of 35 out of 69.

European Parliament
Malta has five representatives. At the June 2009 elections turnout was 78·8% (82·4% in 2004). The MLP won 3 seats with 54·8% of votes cast (political affiliation in European Parliament: Progressive Alliance of Socialists and Democrats); and the NP 2 with 40·5% (European People's Party).

CURRENT ADMINISTRATION

President: George Abela; b. 1948 (MLP; sworn in 4 April 2009).

In March 2010 the government comprised:

Prime Minister: Dr Lawrence Gonzi; b. 1953 (NP; sworn in 23 March 2004 and re-elected in March 2008).

Deputy Prime Minister and Minister for Foreign Affairs: Dr Tonio Borg. *Education, Employment and Family:* Dolores Cristina. *Finance, Economy and Investment:* Tonio Fenech. *Gozo:* Giovanna Debono. *Health, the Elderly and Community Care:* Dr Joe Cassar. *Infrastructure, Transport and Communications:* Dr Austin Gatt. *Justice and Home Affairs:* Dr Carmelo Mifsud Bonnici. *Resources and Rural Affairs:* George Pullicino. *Social Policy:* John Dalli.

Speaker: Louis Galea.

Government Website: http://www.gov.mt

CURRENT LEADERS

George Abela

Position
President

Introduction
George Abela was sworn in as president on 4 April 2009. He was nominated by Prime Minister Lawrence Gonzi, the first time a president has been appointed from the opposition (having been a member of the MLP before renouncing political affiliation to take up the office). He was also the first president to be elected with the unanimous approval of parliament.

Early Life
Abela was born in Qormi, a small town in central Malta, in April 1948. The son of a postal worker, he was educated at the University of Malta, gaining a degree in English, Maltese and History before graduating as a lawyer in 1975. He subsequently took up private legal practice specializing in civil, commercial and industrial law. For 25 years he was the legal consultant for Malta's General Workers' Union, representing its membership in negotiations including the 2002 Air Malta rescue plan.

In 1982, having previously served as treasurer and president of his hometown football team, Abela was appointed president of the Maltese Football Association, a position he held for ten years. He also sat as an arbitrator at the Court of Arbitration for Sport in Lausanne. In 1992 he was elected deputy leader of the MLP, resigning in 1998 in protest at then leader Alfred Sant's call for an early election. Abela served as the Labour Party representative on the Malta–EU Steering and Action Committee (MEUSAC), having been involved in pre-accession talks regarding Malta's bid for European Union membership. He has also served as director of the Central Bank of Malta. In June 2008 he was defeated in a bid for the MLP leadership by Joseph Muscat.

Career in Office
Abela will attempt to harness the political unity evidenced by his unanimous election to the presidency, a largely ceremonial role. A devout Catholic, he has emphasized the importance of family values.

Dr Lawrence Gonzi

Position
Prime Minister

Introduction
Appointed Malta's prime minister on 23 March 2004, Lawrence Gonzi oversaw the nation's accession to the EU six weeks later. Leading the right-of-centre Nationalist Party (NP), he has advocated seizing the opportunities for trade and investment afforded by Malta's EU membership, including adoption of the single European currency.

Early Life
Lawrence Gonzi was born on 1 July 1953 in Valletta, Malta. He attended St Joseph's school, St Aloysious College and The Archbishop's Seminary, and went on to study law at the University of Malta, graduating in 1975, the year after Malta became a fully independent republic (having achieved independence from Great Britain in 1964). Gonzi took up employment as a junior solicitor in a private firm and later worked as a company lawyer with the Mizzi Organization. From 1976 he was engaged in the voluntary sector, working with people with disabilities and mental health problems. He was also the general president of the Malta Catholic Action Movement between 1976 and 1986.

Gonzi entered politics in 1986, contesting the 1987 general election as a candidate for the Nationalist Party. Duly elected, he served in the government of the new Nationalist prime minister, Edward Fenech Adami. Gonzi was elected speaker of the House of Representatives on 10 Oct. 1988. The NP took up a pro-Western stance and argued for integration into the European Community. It also embarked on a programme to stimulate business, increase tourism and reduce the role of the government in the economy. The party held on to power in the 1992 general election, but lost the Oct. 1996 poll to a rejuvenated MLP, led by Alfred Sant.

Gonzi retained his parliamentary seat in the 1996 election and, a month later, was appointed opposition party whip, secretary to the parliamentary group and shadow minister for social policy. The following year he was elected secretary general of the Nationalist Party, subsequently playing a central role in achieving an NP electoral victory after just 22 months of the Labour administration. Gonzi was appointed minister for social policy and leader of the House of Representatives. The appointment of Prof. Guido de Marco as president of the republic on 2 May 1999 prompted Gonzi to contest the election for the deputy leadership of the NP. He was successful, and shortly afterwards was made deputy to Prime Minister Adami.

During his years at the social policy ministry, Gonzi is remembered for reforms to the industrial relations legislation, his zero-tolerance policy towards benefit fraud and for overseeing the restructuring of Malta's shipyards. In March 2003 Malta's population voted in favour of EU membership in a referendum, and the following month the NP was returned to power in a general election. Adami stepped down as NP leader in March 2004, and in the subsequent leadership contest, Gonzi emerged victorious. On 23 March 2004 he took office as prime minister (and minister of finance) of Malta.

Career in Office
In his first media briefing in April 2004, Prime Minister Gonzi announced his government's intention to adopt the euro 'when it is advantageous to Malta'. He also proposed to boost tourism (the nation's most important source of income), create favourable conditions for investment, restructure the public finances and improve Malta's competitiveness in the international market. In Nov. 2005 Gonzi hosted the Commonwealth Heads of Government Meeting (CHOGM). In Dec. 2007 his government signed the Lisbon treaty on streamlining the operation of the European Union and from 1 Jan. 2008 Malta adopted the single currency.

Gonzi's NP won a third successive term by narrowly winning the popular vote in parliamentary elections in March 2008, with Gonzi being sworn in for a second prime ministerial term (but relinquishing the finance portfolio) on 11 March. In an address to the nation he said that his government would concentrate particularly on sustainable development, with an emphasis on the environment.

In April 2009 the Maltese government refused to accept 140 illegal African migrants aboard a cargo ship that had rescued them in rough waters near the island of Lampedusa, claiming that they were Italy's responsibility.

DEFENCE

The Armed Forces of Malta (AFM) are made up of a Headquarters and three Regiments. In 2007 they had a strength of 1,609 personnel. An Emergency Volunteer Reserve Force was introduced in 1998 on a small scale (40 in 2007). There were also 50 individuals reserves in 2007. In addition to infantry and light air defence artillery weapons, the AFM are equipped with helicopters, light fixed wing and trainer aircraft. There is no conscription.

Apart from normal military duties, AFM are also responsible for Search and Rescue, airport security, surveillance of Malta's territorial and fishing zones, harbour traffic control and anti-pollution duties.

In 2006 military expenditure totalled US$46m. (US$114 per capita), representing 0·7% of GDP.

Navy
There is a maritime squadron that operated nine patrol and coastal combatants in 2007.

Air Force
The Air Wing had four combat capable aircraft in 2007 although they were in storage.

INTERNATIONAL RELATIONS
Malta is a member of the UN, World Bank, IMF and several other UN specialized agencies, EU, Council of Europe, OSCE, Commonwealth, IOM, Inter-Parliamentary Union and NATO Partnership for Peace. Malta held a referendum on EU membership on 9 March 2003, in which 53·6% of votes cast were in favour of accession, with 46·4% against. It became a member of the EU on 1 May 2004.

In Dec. 2007 Malta acceded to the Schengen accord, which abolishes border controls between Malta, Austria, Belgium, Czech Republic, Denmark, Estonia, Finland, France, Germany, Greece, Hungary, Iceland, Italy, Latvia, Lithuania, Luxembourg, Netherlands, Norway, Poland, Portugal, Slovakia, Slovenia, Spain, Sweden and Switzerland.

ECONOMY
Services accounted for 71% of GDP in 2002, industry 26% and agriculture 3%.

Overview
GDP per capita is above the EU average but limited domestic resources have left the economy heavily reliant on foreign trade, manufacturing and tourism as sources of growth.

Since joining the EU in 2004 Malta has restructured the public-enterprise sector (PES) and liberalized trade. GDP growth has been ignited by a public investment boom largely financed by EU grants. Fiscal policy is directed towards reducing the budget deficit which had expanded to 56% of GDP by the late 1990s. By 2006 the government had brought the general deficit down to 2·5% of GDP, below the 3% threshold required for eurozone membership. It joined the European Monetary Union (EMU) on 1 Jan. 2008.

Exports currently make up 83% of total GDP, with tourism and electronics comprising a third of GDP and half of exports. Although both sectors remain under competitive pressure, they have recently made positive strides following years of difficulty. Ongoing structural changes, notably in the financial services and gaming industries, should help Malta remain competitive within the EMU.

Currency
On 1 Jan. 2008 the euro (EUR) replaced the Maltese lira (MTL) as the legal currency of Malta at the irrevocable conversion rate of Lm0·4293 to one euro. Inflation was 2·5% in 2005, 2·6% in 2006, 0·7% in 2007 and 4·7% in 2008. Foreign exchange reserves stood at US$2,390m. in March 2005, gold reserves were 4,000 troy oz in May 2005 and total money supply was Lm1,413m. in July 2005.

Budget
Revenue and expenditure (in Lm1m.):

	1998	*1999*	*2000*	*2001*	*2002*
Revenue	659·1	721·9	642·3	797·4	771·0
Expenditure	666·0	691·0	716·2	766·7	819·3

The most important sources of revenue are Customs and Excise tax, customs and excise duties, income tax, VAT, social security and receipts from the Central Bank of Malta. Also significant in certain years are proceeds from the sale of Government shares, foreign grants and foreign and local loans.

The standard rate of VAT is 18·0% (reduced rate, 5%).

Performance
Real GDP growth was 4·1% in 2005, 4·4% in 2006, 3·7% in 2007 and 2·1% in 2008. Total GDP in 2007 was US$7·4bn.

Banking and Finance
The Central Bank of Malta (*Governor*, Michael C. Bonello) was founded in 1968. In Jan. 2004 there were 16 licensed credit institutions carrying out domestic and international banking activities. In addition 13 local financial institutions licensed in terms of the Financial Institutions Act 1994 also provide services that range from exchange bureau related business to merchant banking.

There is a stock exchange in Valletta.

ENERGY AND NATURAL RESOURCES

Environment
Malta's carbon dioxide emissions from the consumption and flaring of fossil fuels in 2008 were the equivalent of 7·9 tonnes per capita.

Electricity
Electricity is generated at two interconnected thermal power stations located at Marsa (267 MW) and Delimara (304 MW). The primary transmission voltages are 132,000, 33,000 and 11,000 volts while the low-voltage system is 400/230V, 50Hz with neutral point earthed. Installed capacity was 571,000 kW in 2006. Production in 2004 was 2·22bn. kWh; consumption per capita was 5,542 kWh.

Oil and Gas
Malta enjoys a large offshore area, which represent geological extensions of southeast Sicily, east Tunisia and northwest Libya where significant hydrocarbon reserves and production exists. Active exploration is at present being carried out by TGS-Nopec, Pancontinental Oil & Gas and TM Services Ltd in offshore areas. Discussions are also under way with oil companies with a view to awarding new licences. The policy of Malta in the oil and gas sector is to intensify exploration by offering oil companies competitive terms and returns that are commensurate with the risk undertaken.

Water
The demand for water in 2003 was 34m. cu. metres. Seawater desalination (Reverse Osmosis Plants) provides 54% of the total potable water requirements.

Agriculture
Malta is self-sufficient in fresh vegetables, pig meat, poultry, eggs and fresh milk. The main crops are potatoes (the spring crop being the country's primary agricultural export), vegetables and fruits, with some items such as tomatoes serving as the main input in the local canning industry. In 2001 there were about 1,524 full-time farmers and 12,589 part-time. There were around 11,959 agricultural holdings and 943 intensive livestock farm units. In 2001 there were 9,000 ha. of arable land and 1,000 ha. of permanent crops.

Agriculture contributes around 2·6% of GDP annually. 2001 production figures (in 1,000 tonnes): potatoes, 25; tomatoes, 18; melons, 12; wheat, 10; onions, 7; cauliflowers, 6.

Livestock in 2001: cattle, 18,417; pigs, 80,481; sheep, 10,376; chickens, 1·9m.

Livestock produce accounted for 60·7% of the total value of agricultural production during 2001.

Fisheries
In 2001 the fishing industry employed 1,747 power-propelled fishing boats, engaging around 365 full time and 1,598 part-time fisherman. The catch for 2005 was 1,435 tonnes. It is estimated that during 2001 the local aquaculture industry produced a total of about 1,235 tonnes of sea bass and bream. 95% of the local

production was exported to EU countries in 2001, especially to Italy.

INDUSTRY

Besides manufacturing (food, clothing, chemicals, electrical machinery parts and electronic components and products), the mainstays of the economy are ship repair and shipbuilding, agriculture, small crafts units, tourism and the provision of other services such as the freeport facilities. The majority of state-aided manufacturing enterprises operating in Malta are foreign-owned or with foreign interests. The Malta Development Corporation is the government agency responsible for promoting investment, while the Malta Export Trade Corporation serves as a catalyst to the export of local products.

Labour

The labour supply in Dec. 2002 was 144,016 (females, 40,185), including 35,571 in private direct production (agriculture and fisheries, 2,203; manufacturing, 28,970; oil drilling, construction and quarrying, 6,398), 50,059 in private market services, 47,992 in the public sector (including government departments, armed forces, revenue security corps, independent statutory bodies and companies with government majority shareholding) and 1,206 in temporary employment. There were 7,188 registered unemployed (5·0% of labour supply).

Trade Unions

In 2003 there were 33 Trade Unions with a total membership of 86,061 and 23 employers' associations with a total membership of 8,960. In 2003 the largest union was the General Workers' Union with a total membership of 47,254.

INTERNATIONAL TRADE

Imports are being liberalized. Marsaxlokk is an all-weather freeport zone for transhipment activities. The Malta Export Trade Corporation promotes local exports. External debt was US$1,531m. in 2001.

Imports and Exports

In 2002 imports (f.o.b.) were valued at Lm1,222·3m. (Lm1,225·1m. in 2001) and exports (f.o.b.) at Lm905·4m. (Lm880·6m. in 2001). In 2002 the principal items of imports were: machinery and transport equipment, Lm596·3m.; semi-manufactures, Lm151·0m.; manufactures, Lm116·8m.; foodstuffs, Lm109·8m.; fuels, Lm103·0m.; chemicals, Lm96·4m. Of domestic exports: machinery and transport equipment, Lm517·7m.; manufactures, Lm166·8m.; semi-manufactures, Lm50·9m.; foodstuffs, Lm21·4m.; chemicals, Lm13·4m.

In 2000 imports valued at Lm281·9m. came from France; Lm249·7m. from Italy; Lm158·5m. from the USA; Lm122·1m. from Germany; Lm119·7m. from the UK. Main export markets: USA, Lm286·5m.; Singapore, Lm164·7m.; Germany, Lm96·7m.; France, Lm84·1m.; UK, Lm70·0m.; Italy, Lm33·1m.

Trade Fairs

The Malta Trade Fairs Corporation organizes the International Fair of Malta (early July).

COMMUNICATIONS

Roads

In 2004 there were 3,096 km of roads, including 185 km of highways. 87·5% of roads are paved. Malta has one of the densest road networks in the world. Motor vehicles in use in 2007 included 203,900 passenger cars, 23,600 vans and lorries, 10,600 motorcycles and mopeds, and 690 buses and coaches. There were 1,209 casualties in traffic accidents in 2007, including 14 fatalities (equivalent to 3·4 fatalities per 100,000 population, giving Malta the lowest death rate in road accidents of any industrialized country).

Civil Aviation

The national carrier is Air Malta, which is 96·4% state-owned. There were scheduled services in 2003 to around 30 different countries. In 2001 there were 32,652 commercial aircraft movements at Malta International Airport. 2,806,013 passengers and 12,925 tonnes of freight/mail were handled. In 2003 scheduled airline traffic of Maltese-based carriers flew 22m. km and carried 1,309,000 passengers (all on international flights).

Shipping

There is a car ferry between Malta and Gozo. The number of vessels registered on 30 Sept. 2003 was 3,365 totalling 26,702,959 GT, a total only exceeded by Panama, Liberia, the Bahamas and Greece. Ships entering harbour in the period Oct. 2002–Sept. 2003 totalled 9,043. A total of 410 cruise vessels put in during the same period.

The Malta Freeport plays an important role in the economy as it is effectively positioned to act as a distribution centre in the Mediterranean. Apart from providing efficient transhipment operations to the major shipping lines, the Freeport offers warehouse facilities and the storage and blending of oil products.

Telecommunications

The Maltacom plc group is Malta's leading telecommunications and ancillary services provider. Malta's national network consist of 12 AXE10 Ericsson Digital Exchanges and one Siemens EWSD Exchange. Maltacom provides various data services including packet switching, frame relay and high-speed leased lines. The company has an optical fibre-based SDH backbone and large companies are connected to the Network. Maltacom's International Network includes two fully digital gateways, two satellite Standard B Earth Stations (one transmitting to the Atlantic Ocean Region and the other to the Indian Ocean Region) and an optic fibre submarine cable linking Malta to Sicily (Italy) and terrestrially extending to Palermo which is the hub of international submarine cables passing through the Mediterranean.

In 2008 there were 241,100 main (fixed) telephone lines; mobile phone subscribers numbered 385,600 in 2008 (94·6 per 100 persons). There were 198,800 internet users in the same year.

Postal Services

In 2003 there were 50 post offices operated by Maltapost plc. Airmail dispatches are forwarded twice daily to the UK, Canada, Australia, USA and Italy. Airmails from most countries are received daily or every other day. There are branch post offices and sub post offices in most towns and villages in Malta and Gozo.

SOCIAL INSTITUTIONS

Justice

The number of persons arrested between 1 Jan. 2001 and 31 Oct. 2001 was 5,451; those found guilty numbered 2,180. 184 persons were committed to prison.

In Jan. 2003 total police strength was 1,841 including 107 officers (92 males and 15 females) and 1,734 other ranks (250 females).

Malta abolished the death penalty for all crimes in 2000.

Education

Adult literacy rate, 2001, 92·3% (male, 91·5%; female, 93·0%).

Education is compulsory between the ages of 5 and 16 and free in government schools from kindergarten to university. Kindergarten education is provided for three- and four-year old children. The primary school course lasts six years. In 2003 there were 19,300 children enrolled in 77 state primary schools. There are education centres for children with special needs, but they are taught in ordinary schools if possible.

Secondary schools, trade schools and junior lyceums provide secondary education in the state sector. At the end of their primary education, pupils sit the 11+ examination to start a secondary education course. Pupils who qualify are admitted in the junior lyceum, while the others attend secondary schools. In 2003–04, 11 junior lyceums had a total of 9,700 students (5,600 girls and 4,100 boys). About 8,200 pupils attend secondary schools. Five centres providing secondary education for under-performing students have a registered student population of about 900, of which 500 are boys. Secondary schools and junior lyceums offer a five-year course leading to the Secondary Education Certificate and the General Certificate of Education, Ordinary Level.

At the end of the five-year secondary course, students may opt to follow a higher academic or technical or vocational course of from one to four years. The academic courses generally lead to Intermediate and Advanced Level examinations set by the British universities. The Matriculation Certificate, which qualifies students for admission to university, is a broad-based holistic qualification covering—among others—the humanities and the sciences, together with systems of knowledge.

About 35% of the student population attend non-state schools, from kindergarten to higher secondary level. In Oct. 2003 there were about 25,700 pupils attending non-state schools, 800 of whom were at post-compulsory secondary level, 17,100 were in schools run by the Roman Catholic Church, while 8,500 students were attending private schools. Under an agreement between the government and the Church, the government subsidizes Church schools and students attending these schools do not pay any fees. During 2001 the government introduced tax rebates for parents whose children attended independent schools.

More than 9,800 students (including 750 from overseas) were following courses at the University in 2003. University students receive a stipend.

A post-compulsory vocational college, the Malta College of Arts, Science and Technology, provides vocational and technical courses up to degree level. In Oct. 2003 about 9,000 students (47% of which were females) were following post-compulsory education in state colleges and institutes.

In 2004 public expenditure on education came to 4·9% of GDP.

Health

In 2003 there were 1,254 doctors, 169 dentists, 799 pharmacists, 1,060 paramedics, 365 midwives and 5,220 nursing personnel. There were eight hospitals (three private) with 2,122 beds. There are also nine health centres.

Welfare

Legislation provides a national contributory insurance scheme and also for the payment of non-contributory allowances, assistances and pensions. It covers the payment of marriage grants, maternity benefits, child allowances, parental allowances, disabled child allowance, family bonus, sickness benefit, injury benefits, disablement benefits, unemployment benefit, contributory pensions in respect of retirement, invalidity and widowhood, and non-contributory medical assistance, free medical aids, social assistance, a carers' pension and pensions for the visually impaired, disabled or severely disabled persons and the aged.

Malta's average actual retirement age is just 53 years, compared to the EU average of 57.

RELIGION

98% of the population belong to the Roman Catholic Church, which is established by law as the religion of the country, although full liberty of conscience and freedom of worship are guaranteed.

CULTURE

World Heritage Sites

Malta has three sites on the UNESCO World Heritage List (all inscribed on the list in 1980): Hal Saflieni Hypogeum, a prehistoric underground necropolis; the City of Valletta, a highly concentrated centre marked by the influences of Romans, Byzantines and Arabs and the Knights of St John; and the Megalithic Temples of Malta (reinscribed in 1992), seven temples on Malta and Gozo containing Bronze Age structures.

Broadcasting

Radio and TV services are under the control of the Broadcasting Authority, an independent statutory body. The government-owned Public Broadcasting Services Ltd was set up in 1991 and operates three radio stations and a TV station (TVM—colour by PAL). Legislation of 1991 introduced private commercial broadcasting. The first private licences were granted to the Malta Labour Party, the Nationalist Party and the Catholic Church. In 2003 there were 11 radio and four TV services and a cable TV network. In 2005 television-equipped households numbered 126,000.

Cinema

In 2004 there were eight cinemas.

Press

In 2004 there were two English dailies (the Times and the Malta Independent) and two Maltese dailies (In-Nazzjon and L-Orizzont), five Maltese and three English weeklies and two financial weeklies in English.

Tourism

Tourism is the major foreign currency earner, and accounts for more 35% of Malta's GDP.

In 2005, 1·17m. non-resident tourists visited Malta, spending US$923m. Cruise passenger visits totalled 320,104 in 2005. Over 40% of tourists are from the UK.

Festivals

Major festivals include the Malta Song Festival; Carnival Festivals at Valletta (Feb.); History and Elegance Festival at Valletta (April); National Folk Singing; Malta International Arts Festival; Malta Jazz Festival; International Food and Beer Festival (June/July); Festa Season (June–Sept.); Malta International Choir Festival (Nov.).

Libraries

The National Library, housed in one of Valletta's 18th-century buildings, is Malta's foremost research Library, founded in 1763. There is a Central Public Library in Floriana, Branch Libraries in government schools in most towns and villages, and the University of Malta Library.

Theatre and Opera

The Manoel Theatre (built 1731) is Malta's National Theatre. There is also the Mediterranean Conference Centre in Valletta, and the Astra Theatre in Victoria, Gozo.

Museums and Galleries

In Valletta: National Museum of Archaeology, National Museum of Fine Arts, Palace Armoury, War Museum (Fort St. Elmo). Mdina and Rabat: National Museum of Natural History, Museum of Roman Antiquities, St Paul's Catacombs, the Cathedral Museum. Paula: Hal Saflieni Hypoguem. Qrendi: Hagar Qim and Mnajra Megalithic Temples. Birzebbuga: Ghar Dalam Cave and Museum. Vittoriosa: Maritime Museum. Gozo (Victoria): Museum of Archaeology, Natural Science Museum, Folklore Museum. Xaghra: Ggantija Megalithic Temples.

DIPLOMATIC REPRESENTATIVES

Of Malta in the United Kingdom (36–38 Piccadilly, London, W1J 0LE)
High Commissioner: Joseph Zammit Tabona.

Of the United Kingdom in Malta (Whitehall Mansions, Ta'Xbiex Seafront, Ta'Xbiex XBX 1026)
High Commissioner: Louise Stanton.

Of Malta in the USA (2017 Connecticut Ave., NW, Washington, D.C., 20008)
Ambassador: Mark Miceli-Farrugia.

Of the USA in Malta (Development House, St Anne St., Floriana)
Ambassador: Douglas W. Kmiec.

Of Malta to the United Nations
Ambassador: Saviour F. Borg.

Of Malta to the European Union
Permanent Representative: Richard Cachia Caruana.

FURTHER READING

National Statistics Office (Lascaris, Valletta). *Abstract of Statistics*, a quarterly digest of statistics, quarterly and annual trade returns, annual vital statistics and annual publications on shipping and aviation, education, agriculture, industry, National Accounts and Balance of Payments. *Malta in Figures 2009.*

Department of Information (3 Castille Place, Valletta). *The Malta Government Gazette, Malta Information, Economic Survey [year], Reports on the Working of Government Departments, Business Opportunities on Malta, Acts of Parliament and Subsidiary Legislation, Laws of Malta, Constitution of Malta 1992.*

Central Bank of Malta. *Annual Reports.*

Chamber of Commerce (annual). *Trade Directory.*

Berg, W. G., *Historical Dictionary of Malta*. 1995

Pace, Roderick, *The European Union's Mediterranean Enlargement: Cyprus and Malta*. 2006

The Malta Year Book. Annual

National Statistical Office: National Statistics Office, Lascaris, Valletta CMR 02.
Website: http://www.nso.gov.mt

MARSHALL ISLANDS

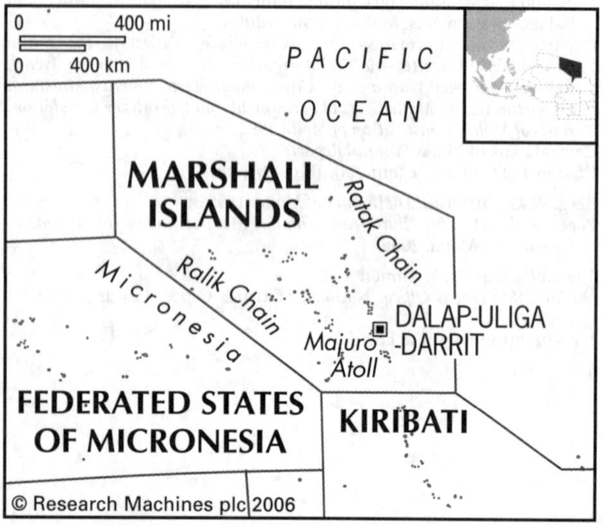

Republic of the Marshall Islands

Capital: Dalap-Uliga-Darrit
Population, 2003: 56,000
GDP per capita: not available
GNI per capita, 2007: US$3,247

KEY HISTORICAL EVENTS

The Pacific archipelago was populated by emigrants from southeast Asia from around 2000 BC and first documented by Portuguese mariners in 1528. The islands owe their name to the English seafarer, John Marshall, who visited in 1788. They became part of the protectorate of German New Guinea in 1886 and administrative affairs were managed by private German and Australian interests. Japan seized control in 1914 and received a League of Nations mandate over the islands in 1919. The Marshall Islands were occupied by Allied forces in 1944 and became part of the UN Trust Territory of the Pacific Islands on 18 July 1947 (administered by the USA). On 21 Oct. 1986 the islands gained independence. A Compact of Free Association with the USA that came into force at the time was extended by 20 years in May 2004.

TERRITORY AND POPULATION

The Marshall Islands lie in the North Pacific Ocean north of Kiribati and east of Micronesia, and consist of an archipelago of 31 coral atolls, five single islands and 1,152 islets strung out in two chains, eastern and western. Of these, 25 atolls and islands are inhabited. The land area is 181 sq. km (70 sq. miles). At the 1999 census the population was 50,840 (26,026 males); density, 281 per sq. km. 2003 estimate: 56,000. The capital is Dalap-Uliga-Darrit (1999 population, 15,486) on Majuro Atoll in the eastern chain. The largest atoll in the western chain is Kwajalein, containing the only other town, Ebeye (1999 population, 9,345). The two archipelagic island chains of Bikini and Enewetak are former US nuclear test sites; Kwajalein is now used as a US missile test range. The islands lay claim to the US territory of Wake Island. In 2000 the population was 65·8% urban. About 88% of the population are Marshallese, a Micronesian people.

English is universally spoken and is the official language. Two major Marshallese dialects from the Malayo-Polynesian family, and Japanese, are also spoken.

SOCIAL STATISTICS

2001 births, estimate, 1,511; deaths, 271. 2001 rates per 1,000 population, estimates: birth, 28·0; death, 5·0. Infant mortality rate, 2005, 51 per 1,000 live births; life expectancy, 2000, 68·4 years. Annual population growth rate, 1999–2003, 2·5%; fertility rate, 2004, 4·4 births per woman.

CLIMATE

Hot and humid, with wet season from May to Nov. The islands border the typhoon belt. Jaluit, Jan. 81°F (27·2°C), July 82°F (27·8°C). Annual rainfall 161" (4,034 mm).

CONSTITUTION AND GOVERNMENT

Under the constitution which came into force on 1 May 1979, the Marshall Islands form a republic with a *President* as head of state and government, who is elected for four-year terms by the parliament. The parliament consists of a 33-member *House of Assembly* (Nitijela), directly elected by popular vote for four-year terms. There is also a 12-member appointed *Council of Chiefs* (Iroij) which has a consultative and advisory capacity on matters affecting customary law and practice.

National Anthem

'Forever Marshall Islands'; words and tune by Amata Kabua.

RECENT ELECTIONS

Following the ousting of Litokwa Tomeing after he lost a parliamentary no-confidence vote, former speaker Jurelang Zedkaia was elected president by parliament on 26 Oct. 2009, defeating Kessai Note. At the House of Assembly elections on 19 Nov. 2007 the United People's Party (UPP) won 15 of 33 seats, United Democratic Party (UDP) 14 and independents 4.

CURRENT ADMINISTRATION

President: Jurelang Zedkaia; (UDP; took office on 2 Nov. 2009).

In March 2010 the government comprised:

Minister of Assistance to the President: Ruben Zackhras. *Education:* Nidel Lorak. *Finance:* Jack Ading. *Foreign Affairs:* John Silk. *Health:* Amenta Matthew. *Internal Affairs:* Norman Matthew. *Justice:* Brenson Wase. *Natural Resources and Development:* Mattlan Zackhras. *Public Works:* Maynard Alfred. *Transportation and Communications:* Kenneth Kedi.

Office of the President: http://www.rmigovernment.org/index.jsp

CURRENT LEADERS

Jurelang Zedkaia

Position
President

Introduction
Jurelang Zedkaia was elected president in Oct. 2009. Having represented the capital, Majuro, in parliament for 19 years, Zedkaia has vowed to unite the nation after two years of political tumult.

Early Life
Iroji Jurelang Zedkaia was born on 13 July 1950 on Majuro Atoll, the administrative centre of the Marshall Islands, then part of the US-controlled Trust Territory of the Pacific Islands. He attended local schools and the Calvary Bible Institute (1967–69) before employment in the health service.

In the mid-1980s Zedkaia joined the Majuro Atoll's local authority, looking after the health, education and social affairs portfolios. First elected to represent Majuro in the *Nitijela* (the lower house of the legislature) in 1991, he held his seat in 1994 and was elected vice speaker for the *Nitijela* in 1997. He was returned as Majuro's representative for the Aelon Kein Ad (Our Islands) Party in the 2000 general election and again in Nov. 2007, when the United People's Party (UPP) eventually emerged as victors. After the results were tested in the courts, the new president, Litokwa Tomeing, appointed Zedkaia as speaker in Jan. 2008.

The controversy surrounding the Nov. 2007 general election ushered in a power struggle between Tomeing and the defeated former president, Kessai Note. Against a backdrop of the global financial crisis, numerous party defections and new alliances, Tomeing weathered two motions of no confidence. However, in a third vote held on 21 Oct. 2009, a majority voted to oust Tomeing and trigger a presidential election. Zedkaia narrowly defeated Note by 17 votes to 15 and he was sworn in to office on 2 Nov. 2009.

Career in Office

In his inaugural address, Zedkaia called for the country to put aside political divisions. He has prioritized improvement of the health care and education systems and improving conditions for outer islanders, as well as forming closer relations with other countries. He attended the UN summit on climate change in Dec. 2009 and pledged to support the Copenhagen Accord while pushing for a legally binding treaty to protect island nations vulnerable to rising seas.

DEFENCE

The Compact of Free Association gives the USA responsibility for defence in return for US assistance. In 2003 the US lease of Kwajalein Atoll, a missile testing site, was extended by 50 years.

INTERNATIONAL RELATIONS

The Marshall Islands are a member of the UN, World Bank, ILO, IMF, ITU, Asian Development Bank, Pacific Islands Forum and SPC.

ECONOMY

Agriculture accounts for approximately 15% of GDP, industry 13% and services 72%.

Overview

The 1986 Compact of Free Association with the USA was renegotiated from 1999–2003 to allow for an increase in aid. This led to seven years of continuous growth. However, growth has slowed since 2005–06, while inflation has been volatile and rising, reflecting higher electricity costs and the rising price of food and fuel. Unemployment, particularly among young people, remains high, contributing to increased emigration to the USA, made easier under the Compact agreement.

The economy is highly vulnerable to external shocks owing to its geographical isolation, narrow production base and reliance on foreign aid. The planned steady decline in Compact grants means fiscal consolidation and structural reforms will be needed to ensure long-term fiscal sustainability. The IMF suggests expenditure cuts and revenue-raising policies. Structural reforms should aim to stimulate the private sector so that it may replace the government as the primary engine of growth.

Currency

US currency is used. The average annual inflation rate during the period 1990–96 was 6·4%.

Budget

Revenue in 2005 was US$83·9m.; expenditure was US$86·9m. Under the terms of the Compact of Free Association, the USA provides approximately US$65m. a year in aid. The fiscal year begins on 1 Oct.

Performance

Total GDP in 2008 was US$158m.; GDP per capita in 2006 was US$2,770. Real GDP growth was 1·0% in 2005–06.

Banking and Finance

There are three banks: the Bank of Marshall Islands, the Marshall Islands Development Bank and the Bank of Guam.

ENERGY AND NATURAL RESOURCES

Electricity

Total installed capacity (1997), 20,200 kW. Production (2004), 81m. kWh.

Minerals

High-grade phosphate deposits are mined on Ailinglaplap Atoll. Deep-seabed minerals are an important natural resource.

Agriculture

A small amount of agricultural produce is exported: coconuts, tomatoes, melons and breadfruit. Other important crops include copra, taro, cassava and sweet potatoes. Pigs and chickens constitute the main livestock. In 2007 there were approximately 2,000 ha. of arable land and 8,000 ha. of permanent crop land.

Fisheries

Total catch in 2005 amounted to 56,664 tonnes. There is a commercial tuna-fishing industry with a canning factory on Majuro. Seaweed is cultivated. Fisheries offer some of the best opportunities for economic growth.

INDUSTRY

The main industries are copra, fish, tourism, handicrafts (items made from shell, wood and pearl), mining, manufacturing, construction and power.

Labour

In 2004 the labour force was estimated at 17,342. Approximately 34% were unemployed in 2004. In 1994 agriculture accounted for 16% of the working population; industry, 14%; services, 70%.

INTERNATIONAL TRADE

The Compact of Free Association with the USA is the major source of income for the Marshall Islands, and accounts for about 70% of total GDP.

Imports and Exports

Imports (mainly oil) were US$54·7m. in 2000; exports, US$9·1m. Main import suppliers in 2000: USA, 56·7%; Australia, 10·0%; Japan, 9·3%; Hong Kong, 5·9%. The USA accounted for approximately 71·0% of exports in 2000. Main exports: coconut oil, copra cake, chilled and frozen fish, pet fish, shells and handicrafts.

COMMUNICATIONS

Roads

There are paved roads on major islands (Majuro, Kwajalein); roads are otherwise stone-, coral- or laterite-surfaced. In 2004 there were 1,555 passenger cars and 159 trucks and buses.

Civil Aviation

There were two international airports and 30 airfields on 24 atolls and islands in 2004. The main airport is Majuro International. In 2003 there were flights to Guam, Honolulu, Johnston Island, Kiribati and Micronesia as well as domestic services. Efforts are being made to re-establish the national carrier, Air Marshall Islands, after it was forced to suspend services in early 2009.

Shipping

Majuro is the main port. In 2000 merchant shipping consisted of 302 vessels totalling 9,745,000 GRT, including oil tankers

5,462,000 GRT. The ship's register of the Marshall Islands is a flag of convenience register.

Telecommunications
In 2008 there were 4,400 main (fixed) telephone lines. There is a US satellite communications system on Kwajalein and two Intelsat satellite earth stations (Pacific Ocean). The National Telecommunications Authority provides domestic and international services. Mobile phone subscribers numbered 1,000 in 2008 (1·7 per 100 persons) and there were 2,200 internet users (3·6 per 100 persons).

Postal Services
Postal services are available on the main island of Majuro and also in Ebeye.

SOCIAL INSTITUTIONS

Justice
The Supreme Court is situated on Majuro. There is also a High Court, a District Court and 23 Community Courts. A Traditional Court deals with disputes involving land properties and customs.

Education
In 2003–04 there were 10,991 pupils with 703 teachers in 100 primary schools, and 3,153 pupils with 207 teachers in 16 secondary schools. There is a College of the Marshall Islands, and a subsidiary of the University of the South Pacific, on Majuro. In 2004 public expenditure on education came to 11·8% of GDP.

Health
There were two hospitals in 2003, with a total of 140 beds. There were 31 doctors, 189 nurses and four dentists in 2003; and two pharmacists in 2000.

RELIGION
The population is mainly Protestant, with Roman Catholics next. Other Churches and denominations include Latter-day Saints (Mormons), Jehovah's Witnesses, Baptists, Bahais, Seventh Day Adventists and Assembly of God.

CULTURE

Broadcasting
MBC TV and V7AB are the state-run television and radio services. There are also some private radio stations and US military broadcasting services.

Press
There is a publication called Micronitor (The Marshall Islands Journal).

Tourism
In 2007 there were 6,959 foreign tourists. Tourism offers one of the best opportunities for economic growth.

Festivals
Custom Day and the Annual Canoe Race are the main festivals.

Libraries
There is one public library.

DIPLOMATIC REPRESENTATIVES

Of the United Kingdom in the Marshall Islands
Ambassador: Stephen Lillie (resides in Manila, Philippines).

Of the Marshall Islands in the USA (2433 Massachusetts Ave., NW, Washington, D.C., 20008)
Ambassador: Banny DeBrum.

Of the USA in the Marshall Islands (Oceanside Mejen Weto, Long Island, Majuro)
Ambassador: Martha Campbell.

Of the Marshall Islands to the United Nations
Ambassador: Phillip Muller.

Of the Marshall Islands to the European Union
Ambassador: Vacant.

FURTHER READING

Barker, Holly, *Bravo for the Marshallese: Regaining Control in a Post-Nuclear, Post-Colonial World.* 2003

MAURITANIA

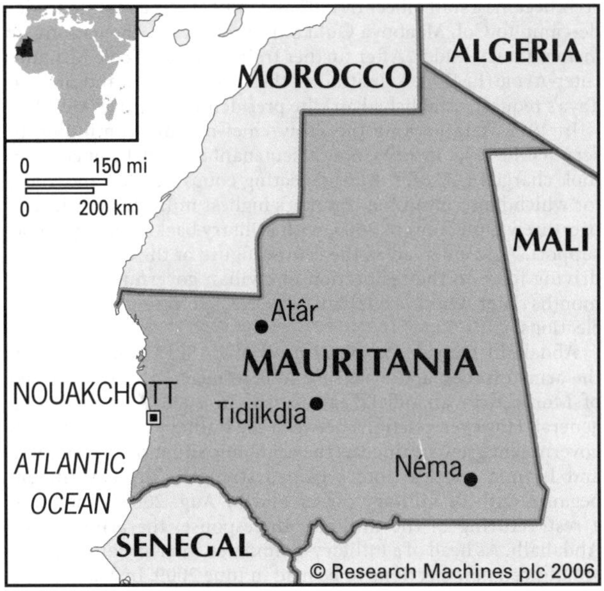

Al-Jumhuriyah al-Islamiyah al-Muritaniyah
(Islamic Republic of Mauritania)

Capital: Nouakchott
Population estimate, 2010: 3·37m.
GDP per capita, 2007: (PPP$) 1,927
HDI/world rank: 0·520/154

KEY HISTORICAL EVENTS

Mauritania became a French protectorate in 1903 and a colony in 1920. It achieved full independence on 28 Nov. 1960. Mauritania became a one-party state in 1964.

The 1980s were marked by territorial disputes with Morocco and Senegal. Seizing power in 1984, Lieut.-Col. Maaouya Ould Sid'Ahmed Taya prepared the way for a new constitution allowing for a multi-party political system, which also gave extensive powers to the president. A coup attempt against Ould Taya failed in June 2003. But in Aug. 2005, while out of the country, he was overthrown in a bloodless coup by a group of army officers who set up a Military Council for Justice and Democracy. Under the leadership of Col. Ely Ould Mohammed Vall, the Council pledged to hold democratic elections within two years. In June 2006 a new constitution was approved, limiting the president to two five-year terms. Sidi Mohamed Ould Cheikh Abdallahi won presidential elections in March 2007 but was ousted in a coup in Aug. 2008.

TERRITORY AND POPULATION

Mauritania is bounded west by the Atlantic Ocean, north by Western Sahara, northeast by Algeria, east and southeast by Mali, and south by Senegal. The total area is 1,030,700 sq. km (398,000 sq. miles) of which 47% is desert, and the population at the census of 2000 was 2,508,159; density, 2·4 per sq. km. In 2005, 59·6% of the population lived in rural areas.

The UN gives an estimated population for 2010 of 3·37m.

Area (in sq. km), population (at the 2000 census) and chief towns of the Nouakchott Capital District and 12 regions:

Region	*Area*	*Population*	*Chief town*
Açâba	36,600	242,265	Kiffa
Adrar	215,300	69,542	Atâr
Brakna	33,800	247,006	Aleg
Dakhlet Nouâdhibou	22,300	79,516	Nouâdhibou
Gorgol	13,600	242,711	Kaédi
Guidimaka	10,300	177,707	Sélibaby
Hodh ech-Chargui	182,700	281,600	Néma
Hodh el-Gharbi	53,400	212,156	Aïoun el Atrouss
Inchiri	46,800	11,500	Akjoujt
Nouakchott District	1,000	558,195	Nouakchott
Tagant	95,200	76,620	Tidjikdja
Tiris Zemmour	252,900	41,121	Zouérate
Trarza	67,800	268,220	Rosso

Principal towns (1999 population): Nouakchott, 881,000 including the suburbs of Nouâdhibou and Kaédi.

In 2000 there were also 0·23m. nomads.

The major ethnic groups are (with numbers in 1993): Moors (of mixed Arab, Berber and African origin), 1,513,400; Wolof, 147,000; Tukulor, 114,600; Soninke, 60,000.

Arabic is the official language. French no longer has official status. Pulaar, Soninke and Wolof are national languages.

SOCIAL STATISTICS

2000 estimates: births, 109,000; deaths, 34,000. 2000 rates, estimate (per 1,000 population): births, 42·9; deaths, 13·4. Expectation of life at birth in 2007 was 54·7 years for males and 58·5 for females. Annual population growth rate, 2000–05, 1·9%. Infant mortality, 2005, 78 per 1,000 live births; fertility rate, 2004, 5·7 births per woman.

CLIMATE

A tropical climate, but conditions are generally arid, even near the coast, where the only appreciable rains come in July to Sept. Nouakchott, Jan. 71°F (21·7°C), July 82°F (27·8°C). Annual rainfall 6" (158 mm).

CONSTITUTION AND GOVERNMENT

A referendum was held on 25 June 2006 to approve a new constitution. Turnout was 76·5%; 96·99% of votes cast were in favour.

The new constitution imposes a limit of two five-year terms for a president, to be elected by popular vote. It also sets a maximum age of 75 for a president. There is a 56-member *Senate* (53 elected and three appointed) and a 95-member *National Assembly.*

Following the coup d'état in Aug. 2008 a transitional government took power, headed by an 11-member High Council of State (all of whom came from the military). Nonetheless, the junta has retained the constitution and vowed to protect the country's democratic institutions. In April 2009 Gen. Mohamed Ould Abdel Aziz stood down as head of government to run in the presidential elections of July 2009.

National Anthem

'Kun lil-ilahi nasiran' ('Be a helper for God'); words by Baba Ould Cheikh, tune by Tolia Nikiprowetzky.

RECENT ELECTIONS

Presidential elections originally scheduled for 6 June 2009 were held on 18 July 2009. Mohamed Ould Abdel Aziz, the leader of the 2008 coup, received 52·6% of votes cast, Messaoud Ould Boulkheir 16·3%, Ahmed Ould Daddah 13·7%, Mohamed Jemil Ould Mansour 4·8%, Ibrahima Moctar Sarr 4·6% and Ely Ould Mohamed Vall 3·8%. There were four other candidates. Turnout was 65·1%. The opposition contested the results but the appeal was rejected in the Constitutional Court.

Elections for the National Assembly—the first since the coup in Aug. 2005 that ended 20 years of authoritarian rule—were held on 19 Nov. and 3 Dec. 2006. An 11-member Coalition of Forces for Democratic Change, comprising groups opposed to former President Taya, won 41 of the 95 seats; the parties supporting the former president, 13 (comprising the Republican Party for Renewal and Democracy 7, the Rally for Democracy and Unity 3 and the Union for Democracy and Progress 3); Alternative (Mauritania), 1; the Union of the Democratic Centre, 1; the National Rally for Liberty, Democracy and Equality, 1; ind., 38. In the Senate elections of 21 Jan. and 4 Feb. 2007 Coalition of Forces for Democratic Change won 15 seats; Republican Party for Democracy and Renewal, 3; Union for Democracy and Progress, 1; ind., 34.

CURRENT ADMINISTRATION

President: Gen. Mohamed Ould Abdel Aziz; b. 1956 (since 5 Aug. 2009).

Prime Minister: Moulaye Ould Mohamed Laghdaf; b. 1957 (ind.; in office since 14 Aug. 2008).

In March 2010 the government comprised:

Minister of Justice: Abidine Ould El Khaire. *Foreign Affairs and Co-operation:* Naha Mint Mouknass. *National Defence:* Hamadi Ould Hamadi. *Interior and Decentralization:* Mohamed Ould Boilil. *Economic Affairs and Development:* Sidi Ould Tah. *Finance:* Ahmed Ould Moualaye Ahmed. *Primary Education:* Ahmedou Ould Idey Ould Mohamed Radhi. *Secondary and Higher Education:* Ahmed Ould Baya. *Islamic Affairs and Basic Education:* Ahmed Ould Neini. *Civil Service and Administrative Modernization:* Maty mint Hamadi. *Employment and Professional Training, and New Technologies:* Mohamed Ould Khouna. *Health:* Cheikh El Moctar Ould Horma Ould Babana. *Oil and Energy:* Wane Ibrahima Lamine. *Fisheries and Maritime Economy:* Ghdafna Ould Eyih. *Trade, Handicrafts and Tourism:* Bomba Ould Daramane. *Housing, Town Planning and Land Management:* Ismail Ould Bedde Ould Cheikh Sidiya. *Rural Development:* Brahim Ould M'Bareck Ould Mohamed El Moctar. *Equipment and Transport:* Camara Moussa Seydi Boubou. *Water Supply and Sanitation:* Mohamed Lemine Ould Aboye. *Industry and Mining:* Mohamed Abdallahi Ould Oudaa. *Culture, Youth and Sports:* Cissé Mint Cheikh Ould Boyde. *Communications and Relations with Parliament:* Hamdy ould Mahjoub. *Social Affairs, Children and Family:* Moulaty Mint El Moctar.

Government Website (French and Arabic only): http://www.mauritania.mr

CURRENT LEADERS

Gen. Mohamed Ould Abdel Aziz

Position
President

Introduction
Gen. Mohamed Ould Abdel Aziz was elected president of Mauritania in July 2009, having called elections after seizing power in a coup against his predecessor Sidi Mohamed Ould Cheikh Abdallahi in Aug. 2008. Aziz led the country at the head of a governing council until April 2009.

Early Life
Ould Abdel Aziz was born on 20 Dec. 1956 in Akjoujt, Mauritania, half way between the costal capital and the Sahara desert. He was born into the Oulad Bou Sbaa Berber-Arab tribe, from which a number of powerful Mauritanian figures have emerged. In 1977 he attended officer training at the Royal Military Academy in Meknès, Morocco. After a stint in the army, he returned to the Military Academy in 1980 to receive training in logistics.

From 1978 Mauritania had a string of *de facto* governments following the overthrow of the civilian president Ould Daddah. Aziz became a staff officer in 1982 and in 1984 was appointed aide-de-camp to Col. Maaouya Ould Sid'Ahmed Taya, the nation's *de facto* military leader. After further training at the École Militaire Inter-Arme (EMIA), Aziz attained the rank of captain and, at Ould Taya's request, established an elite presidential guard (BASEP).

In 1992 Aziz became the army chief of staff, continuing to serve Ould Taya. In 1998, now a lieutenant colonel, he once again took charge of BASEP. After defeating coups in 2003 and 2004, for which he received the country's highest military award, Aziz overthrew Ould Taya in 2005, with military backing and popular support. Aziz emerged as the central figure of the coup and as a driving force to the restoration of civilian government. Twenty months later Ould Abdallahi was elected president in open elections.

Abdallahi named Aziz (still head of BASEP) commander of the armed forces, and even sent Aziz to meet King Mohammed of Morocco in an official state visit. In 2008 Aziz became a general. However, relations between the military and the civilian government grew strained as the economic situation deteriorated and Islamic political forces gained strength. The government began a curb of military power and in Aug. 2008 announced a restructuring of the military. In response, the army ousted Abdahalli. As head of a military-dominated interim council, Aziz announced new elections to be held in June 2009. In March 2009 Aziz announced his intention to run for president in the elections, rescheduled for July.

Career in Office
His assumption of office in Aug. 2009 was attacked by France, the former colonial power, the African Union, the USA and Algeria. But Aziz was received warmly in neighbouring Morocco and Libya.

The African Union continued to impose sanctions at the beginning of 2010, including a travel ban in AU countries for military personnel who had supported the coup and a seizure of their assets in AU banks. Aziz's electoral pledges included re-establishing civilian governance, improving national unity and consolidating republican institutions.

DEFENCE

Conscription is authorized for two years. Defence expenditure in 2006 totalled US$18m. (US$6 per capita), representing 0·6% of GDP.

Army

There are six military regions. Army strength was 15,000 in 2007. In addition there was a Gendarmerie of about 3,000 and a National Guard of 2,000.

Navy

The Navy, some 620 strong in 2007, has bases at Nouâdhibou and Nouakchott.

Air Force

Personnel (2007), 250 with 18 aircraft (none combat capable).

INTERNATIONAL RELATIONS

Mauritania is a member of the UN, World Bank, IMF and several other UN specialized agencies, WTO, IOM, International Organization of the Francophonie, Islamic Development Bank, OIC, African Development Bank, African Union, League of Arab States and is an ACP member state of the ACP-EU relationship.

ECONOMY

In 2006 agriculture accounted for 13·1% of GDP, industry 47·8% and services 39·1%.

Overview

Mauritania is a developing economy that has limited agrarian resources but extensive mineral deposits and rich fishing grounds. Its dependence on mining and fisheries for export earnings makes it vulnerable to external shocks. The economy has experienced strong growth in recent years, owing in part to the discovery of crude oil reserves in 2001 and the commencement of oil production in 2006. Growth increased from an average of 4·8% between 2001–04 to 11·4% in 2006.

Social indicators are poor but have improved under the IMF's Poverty Reduction and Growth Facility (PRGF). Poverty reduction spending has exceeded programme targets and the incidence of poverty is estimated to have fallen from 51% to 47% between 2000 and 2004. However, the economy is ranked in the bottom layer of the World Bank's 'Doing Business' rankings. Long-term growth prospects rely on oil revenues being used to stimulate non-oil growth.

Currency

The monetary unit is the *ouguiya* (MRO) which is divided into five *khoums*. The ouguiya was devalued in Oct. 1992 by 28% and again in July 1998 by 18%. Inflation was 7·3% in both 2007 and 2008. Total money supply in March 2004 was 34,318m. ouguiya, foreign exchange reserves were US$390m. and gold reserves 12,000 troy oz.

Budget

Revenues were 131·3bn. ouguiya in 2005 and expenditures 166·1bn. ouguiya.

VAT is 18%.

Performance

Real GDP growth was 1·0% in 2007 and 2·2% in 2008. Mauritania's total GDP in 2008 was US$2·9bn.

Banking and Finance

The Central Bank (created 1973) is the bank of issue (*Governor*, Sid'Ahmed Ould Raiss). In 2002 there were seven commercial banks and two Islamic banks. Bank deposits totalled 12,304m. ouguiya in 1992.

ENERGY AND NATURAL RESOURCES

Environment

In 2008 carbon dioxide emissions from the consumption and flaring of fossil fuels were the equivalent of 0·9 tonnes per capita. An *Environmental Performance Index* compiled in 2008 ranked Mauritania 146th in the world out of 149 countries analysed, with 44·2%. The index examined various factors in six areas—air pollution, biodiversity and habitat, climate change, environmental health, productive natural resources and water resources.

Electricity

Installed capacity was an estimated 0·2m. kW in 2004. Production in 2004 was around 240m. kWh; consumption per capita was an estimated 80 kWh.

Oil and Gas

Oil was discovered off the coast of Mauritania in 2001. Production began in Feb. 2006, initially with 75,000 bbls a day.

Minerals

There are reserves of copper, gold, phosphate, gypsum, platinum and diamonds. Iron ore, 11·2m. tonnes of which were mined in 2006, accounts for about 69% of exports. Prospecting licences have also been issued for diamonds.

Agriculture

Only 1% of the country receives enough rain to grow crops, so agriculture is mainly confined to the south, in the Senegal river valley. In 2007 the agricultural population numbered 1,598,000 of whom 674,000 were economically active. There were an estimated 450,000 ha. of arable land in 2007 and 12,000 ha. of permanent crops. Production (2006, in 1,000 tonnes): sorghum, 84; rice, 70; dates, 20; maize, 17; dry beans, 10 (estimate); dry peas, 10 (estimate); yams, 3 (estimate); millet, 2; potatoes, 2 (estimate).

Herding is the main occupation of the rural population and accounted for 11% of GDP in 2005. In 2003 there were 7·01m. sheep and goats; 1·51m. camels; 1·36m. cattle; 4m. chickens (estimate).

Forestry

There were 267,000 ha. of forests in 2005 covering 0·3% of the land area, chiefly in the southern regions, where wild acacias yield the main product, gum arabic. In 2007, 1·71m. cu. metres of roundwood were cut.

Fisheries

Total catch in 2005 was 247,577 tonnes, of which 98% came from marine waters. Mauritania's coastal waters are among the world's most abundant fishing areas, earning it significant amounts of hard currency through licensing agreements. Fishing-related fees account for an estimated 15% of Mauritania's national budget.

INDUSTRY

Output, 2002 (in tonnes): residual fuel oil, 364,000; petrol, 235,000; distillate fuel oil, 155,000; frozen and chilled fish (2001), 27,000; hides and skins (2001), 5,400.

Labour

In 1996 the workforce was 1,072,000 (56% males). In 1994, 430,000 people worked in agriculture, forestry and fishing, 177,000 in services and 80,000 in industry.

INTERNATIONAL TRADE

Total foreign debt was US$2,281m. in 2005. In Feb. 1989 Mauritania signed a treaty of economic co-operation with the four other Maghreb countries—Algeria, Libya, Morocco and Tunisia.

Imports and Exports

In 2002 imports were valued at US$418·0m. and exports at US$330·3m. Main imports are foodstuffs, consumer goods, petroleum products and capital goods. Main exports are iron ore (68·6% of total exports) and fish (24·7%). Main import suppliers in 2002 were France (20·8%), Belgium-Luxembourg (8·8%), Spain (6·7%) and Germany (5·6%). Principal export markets in 2002 were Italy (14·8%), France (14·4%), Spain (12·1%) and Germany (10·8%).

COMMUNICATIONS

Roads

There were about 11,066 km of roads in 2006, of which 26·8% were paved. In 2002 there were 7,100 passenger cars and 5,700 commercial vehicles.

Rail

A 704-km railway links Zouérate with the port of Point-Central, 10 km south of Nouâdhibou, and is used primarily for iron ore exports. In 2005 it carried 10·8m. tonnes of freight.

Civil Aviation

There are international airports at Nouakchott, Nouâdhibou and Néma. Air Mauritanie provides domestic services, and in 2003 operated international services to Abidjan, Bamako, Bissau, Casablanca, Cotonou, Dakar, Las Palmas and Paris. In 2003 scheduled airline traffic of Mauritania-based carriers flew 1m. km, carrying 116,000 passengers (14,000 on international flights).

Shipping

In 2002 the merchant fleet totalled 48,000 GRT. The major ports are at Point-Central (for mineral exports), Nouakchott and Nouâdhibou.

Telecommunications
In 2008 there were 76,400 main (fixed) telephone lines; mobile phone subscribers numbered 2,092,000 in 2008 (65·1 per 100 persons). There were 79,000 PCs in use in 2005 and 60,000 internet users in 2008.

Postal Services
In 2004 there were 26 post offices.

SOCIAL INSTITUTIONS
Justice
There are courts of first instance at Nouakchott, Atâr, Kaédi, Aïoun el Atrouss and Kiffa. The Appeal Court and Supreme Court are situated in Nouakchott. Islamic jurisprudence was adopted in 1980.

The population in penal institutions in Dec. 2005 was 815 (26 per 100,000 of national population).

Education
Basic education is compulsory for all children between the ages of six and 14. In 2007 there were 483,776 pupils and 11,379 teaching staff in primary schools, 102,130 secondary level pupils with 3,843 teaching staff and 11,794 tertiary level students with (2006) 353 academic staff. The University of Nouakchott, founded in 1981, is the leading tertiary education institution. Adult literacy rate in 2003 was 51·2% (male, 59·5%; female, 43·4%).

Public expenditure on education came to 2·8% of GNI in 2006.

Health
In 1990 there were 16 hospitals with a provision of seven beds per 10,000 persons. There were 323 physicians, 47 dentists, 1,461 nurses and 267 midwives in 1995.

In 2000 only 37% of the population had access to safe drinking water.

RELIGION
Over 99% of Mauritanians are Sunni Muslim, mainly of the Qadiriyah sect.

CULTURE
World Heritage Sites
Mauritania has two sites on the UNESCO World Heritage List: Banc d'Arguin National Park (inscribed on the list in 1989), a coastal park of dunes and swamps; and the Ancient Ksour of Ouadane, Chinguetti, Tichitt and Oualata (1996), Islamic trading and religious centres in the Sahara.

Broadcasting
Radio Mauritanie and Mauritanian TV are state-owned and controlled by the Office de Radiodiffusion-Télévision de Mauritanie (ORTM). Private broadcasting is not licensed. There were 145,000 TV sets (colour by SECAM) in 2006.

Press
In 2006 there were four daily newspapers with a circulation of 9,000.

Tourism
There were 30,000 foreign tourists in 2000; spending by tourists totalled US$25m.

DIPLOMATIC REPRESENTATIVES
The Mauritanian Embassy in London closed on 30 Sept. 2007.

Of the United Kingdom in Mauritania
Ambassador: Timothy Morris (resides in Rabat, Morocco).

Of Mauritania in the USA (2129 Leroy Pl., NW, Washington, D.C., 20008)
Ambassador: Vacant.
Chargé d'Affaires a.i.: Mohamed El Moctar Ould Youba.

Of the USA in Mauritania (Rue Abdallaye, Nouakchott)
Ambassador: Mark M. Boulware.

Of Mauritania to the United Nations
Ambassador: Abderrahim Ould Hadrami.

Of Mauritania to the European Union
Ambassador: Moulaye Ould Mohamed Laghdaf.

FURTHER READING
Belvaud, C., *La Mauritanie.* 1992

National Statistical Office: Office National de la Statistique, BP240, Nouakchott.
Website (French only): http://www.ons.mr

MAURITIUS

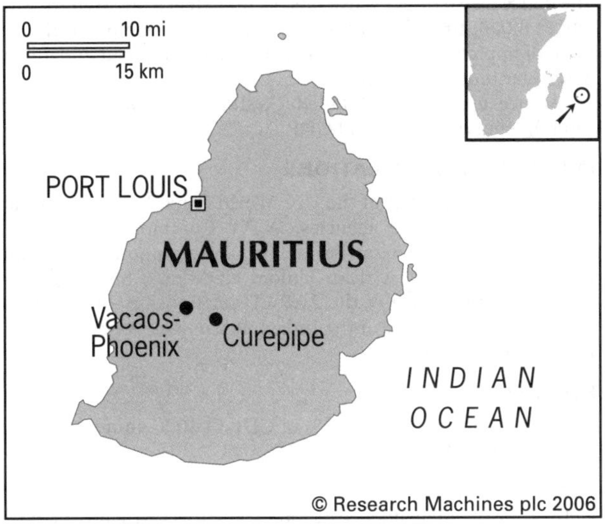

Republic of Mauritius

Capital: Port Louis
Population estimate, 2010: 1·30m.
GDP per capita, 2007: (PPP$) 11,296
HDI/world rank: 0·804/81

KEY HISTORICAL EVENTS

Mauritius was visited by Middle Eastern and Malay merchants from around AD 1000 and documented by Portuguese seafarers between 1507 and 1512. In 1598 the Dutch admiral, Van Warwyck, established a settlement and named the island after Prince Maurice of Nassau, the stadtholder of Holland and Zeeland. French forces settled the island in 1722, renamed it Isle de France and brought African slaves to cultivate sugarcane. The British occupied the island in 1810 and it was formally ceded to Great Britain by the Treaty of Paris in 1814. Following the abolition of slavery in 1835, indentured labourers were transported from India. Independence was attained within the Commonwealth on 12 March 1968. Mauritius became a republic on 12 March 1992.

TERRITORY AND POPULATION

Mauritius, the main island, lies 800 km (500 miles) east of Madagascar. Rodrigues is 560 km (350 miles) east. The outer islands are Agalega and the St Brandon Group. Area and population:

Island	*Area in sq. km*	*2008 mid-year population*
Mauritius	1,865	1,230,995
Rodrigues	104	37,570
Outer Islands	71	289
Total	2,040	1,268,854

Port Louis is the capital (148,877 inhabitants in 2007). Other towns: Beau Bassin-Rose Hill, 109,411; Vacoas-Phoenix, 106,574; Curepipe, 83,557; Quatre Bornes, 80,542. In 2005, 57·6% of the population were rural.

The UN gives an estimated population for 2010 of 1·30m.

Ethnic composition, 2000: Indo-Pakistani, 67·0%; Creole, 27·4%; Chinese, 3·0%.

The official language is English, although French is widely used. Creole and Bhojpuri are vernacular languages.

SOCIAL STATISTICS

2007: births, 17,034 (rate of 13·5 per 1,000 population); deaths, 8,498 (6·7 per 1,000); marriages, 11,547 (9·2 per 1,000); divorces, 1,302 (1·0 per 1,000). In 2007 the suicide rate was 15·7 per 100,000 population among men and 4·7 per 100,000 among women. Population growth rate in 2007 was 0·65%. In 2007 the most popular age range for marrying was 25–29 for males and 20–24 for females. Life expectancy at birth in 2007 was 69·1 years for males and 75·8 for females. Infant mortality, 2007, 15 per 1,000 live births; fertility rate, 2007, 2·0 births per woman.

CLIMATE

The sub-tropical climate is humid. Most rain falls in the summer. Rainfall varies between 40" (1,000 mm) on the coast to 200" (5,000 mm) on the central plateau, though the west coast only has 35" (875 mm). Mauritius lies in the cyclone belt, whose season runs from Nov. to April, but is seldom affected by intense storms. Port Louis, Jan. 73°F (22·8°C), July 81°F (27·2°C). Annual rainfall 40" (1,000 mm).

CONSTITUTION AND GOVERNMENT

The present constitution came into effect on 12 March 1968 and was amended on 12 March 1992. The head of state is the *President*, elected by a simple majority of members of the National Assembly. The role of *President* is largely a ceremonial one.

The 70-seat *National Assembly* consists of 62 elected members (three each for the 20 constituencies of Mauritius and two for Rodrigues) and eight additional seats in order to ensure a fair and adequate representation of each community within the Assembly. The government is headed by the *Prime Minister* and a Council of Ministers. Elections are held every five years on the basis of universal adult suffrage.

National Anthem

'Glory to thee, Motherland'; words by J. G. Prosper, tune by P. Gentille.

RECENT ELECTIONS

Parliamentary elections were held on 3 July 2005. The Social Alliance won 42 seats with 48·8% of votes cast, followed by the coalition of the Militant Socialist Movement (MSM) and the Mauritian Militant Movement (MMM) with 24 seats (42·6% of votes cast). The Organization of the People of Rodrigues and the Rodrigues Movement won two seats each. Turnout was 81·5%.

CURRENT ADMINISTRATION

President: Sir Anerood Jugnauth (MSM); b. 1930 (sworn in 7 Oct. 2003 and re-elected 19 Sept. 2008; prime minister from June 1982 to Dec. 1995 and Sept. 2000 to Sept. 2003).

Vice-President: Angidi Chettiar.

In March 2010 the cabinet was composed as follows:

Prime Minister, Minister of Defence and Home Affairs: Navin Ramgoolam (Social Alliance); b. 1947 (took office 5 July 2005, having previously been prime minister from Dec. 1995 to Sept. 2000).

Deputy Prime Minister and Minister of Renewable Energy and Public Utilities: Ahmed Rashid Beebeejaun.

Minister of Agro-Industry, Food Production and Safety: Satya Veyash Faugoo. *Civil Service and Administrative Reform:*

Balkissoon Hookoom. *Consumer Protection and Citizens Charter:* Sylvio Tang Wah Hing. *Education, Culture and Human Resources:* Vasant Kumer Bunwaree. *Environment and National Development Unit:* Lormus Bundhoo. *Finance and Economic Development:* Rama Krishna Sithanen. *Foreign Affairs, Regional Integration and International Trade:* Arvin Boolell. *Health and Quality of Life:* Rajeshwar Jeetah. *Housing and Lands:* Abu Kasenally. *Industry, Science and Research:* Dharambeer Gokhool. *Information Technology and Telecommunications:* Asraf Dulull. *Labour, Industrial Relations and Employment:* Jean-François Chaumière. *Public Infrastructure, Land Transport and Shipping:* Anil Bachoo. *Regional Administration, Rodrigues and Outer Islands:* Hervé Aimée. *Security, National Solidarity, Senior Citizen Welfare and Institutional Reform:* Sheilabai Bappoo. *Small and Medium Enterprises, Commerce and Co-operatives:* Mahendra Gowressoo. *Tourism, Leisure and External Communications:* Xavier-Luc Duval. *Women's Rights, Child Development and Family Welfare:* Indranee Seebun. *Youth and Sports:* Satyaprakash Ritoo. *Attorney General:* Jayarama Valayden.

Government Website: http://www.gov.mu

CURRENT LEADERS

Navin Ramgoolam

Position
Prime Minister

Introduction
Navin Ramgoolam was returned as prime minister at the elections of July 2005, defeating Paul Bérenger, leader of the Mauritian Militant Movement. Ramgoolam had previously held the post from Dec. 1995 to Sept. 2000, when he lost to former Mauritian president Sir Anerood Jugnauth.

Early Life
Navin Ramgoolam was born in Mauritius on 14 July 1947, the son of Seewoosagur Ramgoolam, the country's first president following independence in 1968. The younger Ramgoolam studied sciences at the Royal College at Curepipe in Mauritius before moving to Dublin, Ireland to train as a doctor at the Royal College of Surgeons in 1968. He gained full registration with the UK General Medical Council in 1977. Over the next ten years he worked as a senior medical officer and as a general practitioner in Mauritius, also holding the post of resident medical officer at the Yorkshire Clinic in the UK.

In 1987 Ramgoolam abandoned medicine to study for a masters degree in law at the London School of Economics. However, he subsequently abandoned a legal career in favour of politics, becoming leader of the Mauritius Labour Party in 1991. He went on to succeed Sir Anerood Jugnauth as prime minister in 1995.

Career in Office
In 2000, towards the end of Ramgoolam's first period in office, Mauritius secured a temporary seat on the United Nations Security Council. Having lost the premiership to his predecessor, Jugnauth, at elections later that year, he then formed the Social Alliance, a coalition led by the Mauritian Labour Party and including the Mauritian Party of Xavier-Luc Duval, the Mauritian Social Democrat Party, the Greens, the Republican Movement and the Mauritian Militant Socialist Movement (MMSM).

At the election of July 2005 the Social Alliance won 42 of a possible 70 seats, giving Ramgoolam a further term as prime minister. On coming to power he announced plans to tackle rising inflation and high levels of unemployment, and sought trade agreements to protect Mauritian exports, particularly sugar and textiles. By 2008 he had overseen a reduction in both unemployment and the budget deficit and the attraction of increasing levels of foreign investment. However, as Mauritius imports most of its food and energy, rising world prices for these commodities have pushed up inflation. Also, recession in the developed world has posed a threat to the country's tourism industry and export potential.

DEFENCE

The Police Department is responsible for defence. Its strength was (2008) 8,000. In addition there is a special mobile paramilitary force of approximately 1,400, a Coast Guard of about 700 and a helicopter unit of about 100.

Defence expenditure totalled US$18m. in 2006 (US$15 per capita), representing 0·3% of GDP.

INTERNATIONAL RELATIONS

Mauritius is a member of the UN, World Bank, IMF and several other UN specialized agencies, WTO, Commonwealth, IOM, International Organization of the Francophonie, African Development Bank, African Union, COMESA, SADC and is an ACP member state of the ACP-EU relationship. Mauritius is also a founder member of the Indian Ocean Rim Association for Regional Co-operation.

ECONOMY

Agriculture accounted for 5·6% of GDP in 2006, industry 26·9% and services 67·6%.

Overview

At the time of independence in 1968 Mauritius had a low-income, agro-based economy but has subsequently developed into an upper middle income economy with the second highest GDP per capita in Africa.

This growth has largely derived from the preferential trade status for textiles and sugar with the USA and the EU, with the EU accounting for over 95% of total sugar exports in 2004. However, the phasing out of preferential agreements for sugar exports to the EU, the expiration of textile quotas at the end of 2004 and the loss of Mauritius' 'developing economy' status are likely to impact on the economy in the near future. The sugar sector accounts for 3·5% of total GDP while the mainly textile-based export processing zone (EPZ) accounts for 7·5%. Nearly 90% of EPZ exports go to signatory countries of the WTO agreement on textiles and clothing.

In 2006 GDP growth was 3·5%, slightly higher than 2005 levels but significantly lower than during its earlier 'miracle years'. Inflation rose in 2006 for the fourth consecutive year and inflationary pressures are building as a result of high public debt, rising oil prices and a widening current account deficit. Government policy is aimed at downsizing traditional industries such as sugar and textiles, expanding offshore entities and local financial institutions, and attracting FDI to modernize the domestic telecommunications and IT sectors. Tourism is strong, with the industry growing by 10% between 2000 and 2004.

Currency

The unit of currency is the *Mauritius rupee* (MUR) of 100 *cents*. There are Bank of Mauritius notes, cupro-nickel coins, nickel-plated steel coins and copper-plated steel coins. Inflation was 9·1% in 2007 and 8·8% in 2008. In July 2005 foreign exchange reserves were US$1,365m. and gold reserves totalled 62,000 troy oz. Total money supply was Rs 22,646m. in June 2005.

Budget

For years ending 30 June: government recurrent revenue in 2004 (revised estimates) was Rs 32,155m. (Rs 29,488m. in 2003). Capital revenue in 2004 (revised estimates) was Rs 7,193m. (Rs 3,153m. in 2003). Recurrent and capital expenditure in 2004 were Rs 36,700m. and Rs 8,500m. respectively (Rs 33,529m. and Rs 8,407m. in 2003). Principal sources of recurrent revenue, 2003–04 (revised estimates): direct taxes, Rs 6,310m.; indirect taxes, Rs 22,505m.; receipts from public utilities, Rs 190m.; receipts from public services, Rs 946m.; rental of government property,

Rs 130m.; interest and royalties, Rs 1,826m.; reimbursement, Rs 238m.; miscellaneous income, Rs 10m.

VAT is 15%.

Performance

Real GDP growth was 4·2% in 2007 and 6·6% in 2008. Total GDP in 2008 was US$8·7bn. Thanks to tourism, financial services and the traditional industries of sugar and textiles, Mauritius is now one of Africa's richest and most developed countries.

Banking and Finance

The Bank of Mauritius (founded 1967) is the central bank. The *Governor* is Rundheersing Bheenick. In 2007 there were 19 commercial banks and one development bank. Since 2005 there has been no distinction between onshore and offshore banks. Non-bank financial intermediaries are the Post Office Savings Bank, the State Investment Corporation Ltd, the Mauritius Leasing Company, the National Mutual Fund, the National Investment Trust and the National Pension Fund. Other financial institutions are the Mauritius Housing Company and the Development Bank of Mauritius. There is also a stock exchange in Port Louis.

ENERGY AND NATURAL RESOURCES

Environment

Carbon dioxide emissions were the equivalent of 3·6 tonnes per capita in 2008.

Electricity

Installed capacity was 0·65m. kW in 2004. Production (2004) was 2·17bn. kWh. Consumption per capita in 2004 was 1,775 kWh.

Agriculture

68,523 ha. were planted with sugarcane in 2007; yield in 2007 was 4,235,849 tonnes. Main secondary crops (2007, in 1,000 tonnes): potatoes, 15; tomatoes, 11; bananas, 9; tea, 8; pumpkins and squash, 7; cucumbers, 6; onions, 6; pineapples, 6. In 2003 there were 100,000 ha. of arable land and 6,000 ha. of permanent cropland; 21,619 ha. were irrigated.

Livestock, 2007: cattle, 7,000; goats and sheep, 26,000; pigs, 17,000.

Livestock products (2003) in tonnes: beef and veal, 2,580; pork, bacon and ham, 1,040; milk, 4,000; eggs, 12,500.

Forestry

The total forest area was 37,000 ha. in 2005 (18·2% of the land area). In 2007 timber production totalled 15,000 cu. metres.

Fisheries

The catch in 2005 totalled 10,048 tonnes, exclusively sea fish.

INDUSTRY

Manufacturing includes: sugar, textile products, footwear and other leather products, diamond cutting, jewellery, furniture, watches and watchstraps, sunglasses, plastic ware, chemical products, electronic products, pharmaceutical products, electrical appliances, ship models and canned food. There were eight sugar mills in 2007 producing 435,972 tonnes of sugar. Production figures for other leading commodities: beer and stout (2007), 33·8m. litres; rum (2003), 7·0m. litres; animal feeds (2007), 144,000 tonnes; molasses (2007), 130,917 tonnes.

Labour

In 2007 the labour force was estimated at 548,900. Manufacturing employed the largest proportion, with 30·8% of total employment; agriculture, forestry and fishing, 7·2%; wholesale and retail trade, 6·3%. In 2007 the unemployment rate was 8·5%.

Trade Unions

In 2007 there were 349 registered trade unions with a total membership of about 100,000.

INTERNATIONAL TRADE

External debt was US$857m. at June 2007.

Imports and Exports

In 2007 imports were valued at Rs 121,037m. and exports at Rs 69,708m. In 2003 Rs 8,068m. of the imports came from South Africa, Rs 7,841m. from France, Rs 5,539m. from China and Rs 5,438m. from India. In 2003 Rs 15,915m. of the exports went to the UK, Rs 9,403m. to France, Rs 8,772m. to the USA and Rs 3,184m. to Madagascar.

Major imports in 2003 included manufactured goods (paper, textiles, iron and steel), Rs 18,863m.; machinery and transport equipment, Rs 14,241m.; food and live animals, Rs 10,308m. Major exports (2003) included articles of apparel and clothing, Rs 26,759m.; sugar, Rs 8,775m.; fish and fish preparations, Rs 3,167m.; textile yarns, fabrics and finished articles, Rs 2,055m.

COMMUNICATIONS

Roads

In 2007 there were 75 km of motorway, 962 km of main roads and 991 km of secondary and other roads. In 2007 there were 144,400 passenger cars, 142,600 motorcycles and mopeds, 40,900 lorries and vans, and 4,000 buses and coaches. In 2007 there were 140 deaths as a result of road accidents.

Civil Aviation

In 2007, 2,412,200 passengers were handled at Sir Seewoosagur Ramgoolam International Airport. The national carrier is Air Mauritius, which is partly state-owned. In 2003 scheduled airline traffic of Mauritius-based carriers flew 33m. km, carrying 1,043,000 passengers (929,000 on international flights).

Shipping

A free port was established at Port Louis in Sept. 1991. In 2002 merchant shipping totalled 58,000 GRT. In 2003 vessels totalling 8,309,000 NRT entered ports and vessels totalling 8,843,000 NRT cleared.

Telecommunications

In 2008 there were 364,500 main (fixed) telephone lines; mobile phone subscribers numbered 1,033,300 in 2008 (80·7 per 100 persons). Communication with other parts of the world is by satellite and microwave links. There were 220,000 PCs in use in 2006 and 282,000 internet users in 2008.

Postal Services

In 2007 there were 102 post offices.

SOCIAL INSTITUTIONS

Justice

There is an Ombudsman. The death penalty was abolished for all crimes in 1995.

The population in penal institutions in April 2003 was 2,565 (210 per 100,000 of national population).

Education

The adult literacy rate in 2003 was 84·3% (88·2% among males and 80·5% among females). Primary and secondary education is free, primary education being compulsory. Almost all children aged 5–11 years attend schools. In 2008 there were 114,007 pupils in 286 primary schools and 112,995 pupils in 175 secondary schools in the island of Mauritius, and 5,015 pupils in 13 primary schools and 3,508 in six secondary schools in Rodrigues. In 2007, 3,945 teachers were enrolled for training at the Mauritius Institute of Education.

In 2007–08 there were 7,794 students and 487 academic staff at the University of Mauritius.

In 2007–08 total expenditure on education came to 3·2% of GDP and 12·7% of total government spending.

Health

In 2007 there were 1,444 physicians, 228 dentists, 3,300 nurses and midwives, and 327 pharmacists. There were 12 hospitals in 2006 with a provision of 28 beds per 10,000 inhabitants.

RELIGION

In 2001 there were 610,000 Hindus, 330,000 Roman Catholics and 190,000 Muslims.

CULTURE

World Heritage Sites

Mauritius has two sites on the UNESCO World Heritage List: Aapravasi Ghat (inscribed on the list in 2006), the site where the modern indentured labour diaspora began; and Le Morne cultural landscape (2008), a rugged mountain jutting into the Pacific Ocean that was used by runaway slaves (maroons) as a shelter in the 18th and 19th centuries.

Broadcasting

Television and radio transmission is controlled by the state-owned Mauritius Broadcasting Corporation. Private radio stations were licensed in 2002. There were 465,000 television sets (colour by SECAM V) in 2006.

Cinema

In 2004 there were 28 cinemas.

Press

In 2006 there were four daily papers with a combined circulation of 110,000. There were also 12 weeklies (two in Chinese, one in English and the rest in French).

Tourism

In 2004 there were 719,000 visitors (including 477,000 from Europe and 175,000 from other African countries), bringing in US$1,156m. in tourist revenue.

Festivals

Independence Day is marked by an official celebration at the Champ de Mars racecourse on 12 March. The Hindu festival of Cavadee is celebrated by the Tamil community at the beginning of the year; the major three-day Hindu festival of Maha Shivarati takes place around Feb./March. Other Hindu festivals include Divali and Ganesh Chaturhi, which is celebrated around Aug./Sept. The Spring Festival is celebrated on the eve of the Chinese New Year; Ougadi, the Telegu new year, is celebrated in March; the Tamil new year, Varusha Pirappu, takes place in April. Muslim festivals include Eid El Fitr and Eid El Adha. On 9 Sept. pilgrims visit the grave of the 19th century missionary Père Laval who is regarded as a national saint.

DIPLOMATIC REPRESENTATIVES

Of Mauritius in the United Kingdom (32–33 Elvaston Pl., London, SW7 5NW)
High Commissioner: Abhimanu Mahendra Kundasamy.

Of the United Kingdom in Mauritius (Les Cascades Bldg, Edith Cavell St., Port Louis)
High Commissioner: Dr John Murton.

Of Mauritius in the USA (1709 N. St., NW, Washington, D.C., 20036)
Ambassador: Vacant.
Chargé d'Affaires a.i.: Joyker Nayeck.

Of the USA in Mauritius (Rogers House, John Kennedy St., Port Louis)
Ambassador: Vacant.
Chargé d'Affaires a.i.: R. Barrie Walkley.

Of Mauritius to the United Nations
Ambassador: Somduth Soborun.

Of Mauritius to the European Union
Ambassador: Sutiawan Gunessee.

FURTHER READING

Central Statistical Information Office. *Bi-annual Digest of Statistics.*

Bowman, L. W., *Mauritius: Democracy and Development in the Indian Ocean.* 1991

National Statistical Office: Central Statistics Office, LIC Building, President John Kennedy Street, Port Louis.
Website: http://www.gov.mu/portal/site/cso

MEXICO

Estados Unidos Mexicanos
(United States of Mexico)

Capital: Mexico City
Population estimate, 2010: 110·65m.
GDP per capita, 2007: (PPP$) 14,104
HDI/world rank: 0·854/53

KEY HISTORICAL EVENTS

The first settlers of the New World arrived in Alaska from Asia about 15,000 years ago. From about 2000 BC the people of Ancient Mexico began to settle in villages and to cultivate maize and other crops. From about 1000 BC the chief tribes were the Olmec on the Gulf Coast, the Maya in the Yucatán peninsula and modern day Chiapas, the Zapotecs and Mixtecs in Oaxaca, the Tarascans in Michoacán and the Toltecs in central Mexico. One of the largest and most powerful cities in ancient Mexico was Teotihuacán, which in the 6th century AD was one of the six largest cities in the world. By the time the Spanish *conquistadores* arrived in 1519, the dominant people were the Mexica, more commonly known as the Aztecs, whose capital Tenochtitlán became Mexico City after the conquest.

Hernán Cortés landed on the Gulf Coast in 1519 and by 1521 his small band of Spaniards, assisted by an army of indigenous peoples, had destroyed the Aztec state. The land conquered by Cortés was named New Spain, and was ruled by the Spanish Crown for three centuries. The new colony was the personal property of the King, whose representative, the Viceroy, was charged with extracting the maximum income for the Crown. The mainstays of the colonial economy were silver and land. Rich silver mines were discovered and large estates (*haciendas*) were formed. Spain controlled trade with the colonies and discouraged manufacturing to maximize profits for the King. Acapulco became Spain's sole port for trade with Asia.

One early result of the Conquest was a collapse of the indigenous population caused by social dislocation and European diseases. In 1520 the native population was probably 20m. By 1540 it had fallen to 6·5m. and by 1650 the figure was just over 1m.

The beginning of the end of Spanish rule came on 16 Sept. 1810 when the parish priest of Dolores, Miguel Hidalgo y Costilla, called for independence (the 'grito de Dolores') and led a popular army against the Spaniards. Hidalgo's revolution failed as did that of the insurrectionary José María Morelos y Pavón. Independence from Spain was declared in the Plan of Iguala on 24 Feb. 1821 when Agustín de Iturbide proclaimed himself Emperor of Mexico. He ruled for two years.

There followed half a century of coups and counter coups. Spain invaded Tampico in 1829. Texas declared secession in 1836. The Mexican dictator Antonio de Santa Anna marched north but was defeated by the Texans. France invaded Veracruz in 1838 (the 'Pastry War'). In 1846 the USA declared war on Mexico. The war was ended in 1848 by the Treaty of Guadalupe which forced Mexico to cede a huge swathe of its territory to the USA. Liberals and conservatives fought the War of the Reform from 1858–61. The liberal government of Benito Juárez abolished the *fueros* (clerical and military privileges) and hereditary titles, confiscated the church's lands and attempted far-reaching land reform. This was followed by the French Intervention (1862–67), which installed the Habsburg Archduke Maximilian of Austria as Emperor of Mexico. The French were resisted stubbornly by President Juárez but the republicans were forced into the resource-poor and sparsely populated north. Napoleon III withdrew his troops from Mexico in 1867 despite a pledge to support Maximilian, allowing the republicans to take back the country virtually unopposed. Asserting Mexico's independence, Juárez ordered the execution of Maximilian.

From 1876–1910, a period known as the *porfiriato*, Mexico was ruled (with one interlude from 1880–84) by Gen. Porfirio Díaz. Díaz imposed a degree of stability and order. He encouraged foreign investment, which funded a rapid expansion of the railways and an export-led economic boom. The economy faltered in the first decade of the 20th century. Díaz was deposed in 1911 by Francisco Madero, whose Plan of San Luís Potosí launched the Mexican Revolution.

Madero was deposed and assassinated in 1913. There followed a civil war fought by the armies of Venustiano Carranza, Pancho Villa and Emiliano Zapata. A new constitution was written in 1917. Zapata was ambushed and killed in 1919 and Carranza was assassinated in 1920. Villa retired the same year but was assassinated in 1923.

In the 1920s Mexico was ruled by Alvaro Obregón and Plutarco Elías Calles. Obregón's assassination in 1928 led to the formation of the Natural Revolutionary Party (PRN), later the Institutional Revolutionary Party (PRI), which ruled Mexico for the rest of the century. Lázaro Cárdenas was president from 1934–40. He nationalized the oil industry and accelerated the distribution of land to the peasantry. The election of Miguel Alemán in 1946 was opposed unsuccessfully by the last military rebellion in Mexico's history. Alemán's pro-business administration began a long period of relative economic prosperity, the 'Mexican Miracle'.

However, by the late 1960s the Mexican economic and political system was under increasing strain. An uprising led by students ended in a bloody massacre in the Tlatelolco district of Mexico City in 1968. Successive PRI presidents made gestures towards democratization and effective opposition gradually developed. Financial and economic problems in the 1980s increased the pressure on the political system. The crisis came in 1988 when the PRI candidate, Carlos Salinas de Gortari, defeated Cuauhtémoc Cárdenas, son of the former president and candidate of the Democratic Revolutionary Party (PRD), in a rigged election. Salinas took Mexico into the North American Free Trade Agreement (NAFTA) with the USA and Canada in 1992. Salinas' choice as the PRI's presidential candidate, Luís Donaldo Colosio, was assassinated in Tijuana on 23 March 1994. He was replaced by Ernesto Zedillo. In the same year the Zapatista National Liberation Army (EZLN) led an uprising in Chiapas, which is ongoing.

In 2000 Vicente Fox Quesada of the National Action Party (PAN) was elected to the presidency. Fox attempted to address two key issues: Mexico's economic and financial weakness and illegal migration to the USA. However, the PRI majority in Congress blocked Fox's fiscal reforms and the Bush administration was unwilling to support Fox's proposal to liberalize immigration. In the 2006 presidential elections the conservative Felipe Calderón and the socialist Andrés Manuel López Obrador both claimed victory. Calderón was finally declared the winner more than two months after the election, but in Nov. López Obrador proclaimed himself the 'legitimate' president. Nevertheless, Calderón was sworn in as scheduled in Dec. 2006.

TERRITORY AND POPULATION

Mexico is bounded in the north by the USA, west and south by the Pacific Ocean, southeast by Guatemala, Belize and the Caribbean Sea, and northeast by the Gulf of Mexico. It comprises 1,964,375 sq. km (758,464 sq. miles), including uninhabited islands (5,127 sq. km) offshore.

Population at recent censuses: 1970, 48,225,238; 1980, 66,846,833; 1990, 81,249,645; 2000, 97,483,412; 2005, 103,263,388 (53,013,433 females). Population density, 52·6 per sq. km (2005). 76·0% of the population were urban in 2005.

The UN gives an estimated population for 2010 of 110·65m.

Area, population and capitals of the Federal District and 31 states:

	Area (Sq. km)	*Population (2005 census)*	*Capital*
Federal District	1,499	8,720,916	Mexico City
Aguascalientes	5,589	1,065,416	Aguascalientes
Baja California Norte	70,113	2,844,469	Mexicali
Baja California Sur	73,677	512,170	La Paz
Campeche	51,833	754,730	Campeche
Chiapas	73,887	4,293,459	Tuxtla Gutiérrez
Chihuahua	247,087	3,241,444	Chihuahua
Coahuila de Zaragoza	151,571	2,495,200	Saltillo
Colima	5,455	567,996	Colima
Durango	119,648	1,509,117	Victoria de Durango
Guanajuato	30,589	4,893,812	Guanajuato
Guerrero	63,794	3,115,202	Chilpancingo de los Bravo
Hidalgo	20,987	2,345,514	Pachuca de Soto
Jalisco	80,137	6,752,113	Guadalajara
México	21,461	14,007,495	Toluca de Lerdo
Michoacán de Ocampo	59,864	3,966,073	Morelia
Morelos	4,941	1,612,899	Cuernavaca
Nayarit	27,621	949,684	Tepic
Nuevo Léon	64,555	4,199,292	Monterrey
Oaxaca	95,364	3,506,821	Oaxaca de Juárez
Puebla	33,919	5,383,133	Heroica Puebla de Zaragoza
Querétaro Arteaga	11,769	1,598,139	Santiago de Querétaro
Quintana Roo	50,350	1,135,309	Chetumal
San Luis Potosí	62,848	2,410,414	San Luis Potosí
Sinaloa	58,092	2,608,442	Culiacán Rosales
Sonora	184,934	2,394,861	Hermosillo
Tabasco	24,661	1,989,969	Villahermosa
Tamaulipas	79,829	3,024,238	Ciudad Victoria
Tlaxcala	3,914	1,068,207	Tlaxcala de Xicohténcatl
Veracruz-Llave	72,815	7,110,214	Xalapa-Enríquez
Yucatán	39,340	1,818,948	Mérida
Zacatecas	75,040	1,367,692	Zacatecas
Total	1,967,183	103,263,388	

The *de facto* official language is Spanish, the mother tongue of over 93% of the population (2005), but there are some indigenous language groups (of which Náhuatl, Maya, Zapotec, Otomi and Mixtec are the most important) spoken by 6,011,202 persons over five years of age (census 2005).

The populations (2005 census) of the largest cities (250,000 and more) were:

Mexico City	8,463,906	Tuxtla Gutiérrez	490,455
Ecatepcec de Morelos	1,687,549	Cuautitlán Izcalli	477,872
Guadalajara	1,600,894	San Nicolás de los Garza	476,761
Heroica Puebla de Zaragoza	1,399,519	Ciudad López Mateos	471,904
		Toluca de Lerdo	467,712
Juárez	1,301,452	Victoria de Durango	463,830
Tijuana	1,286,187	Veracruz	444,438
León de los Aldama	1,137,465	Heroica Matamoros	422,711
Ciudad Nezahualcoyotl	1,136,300	Apodaca	393,195
Monterrey	1,133,070	Xalapa-Enríquez	387,879
Zapopan	1,026,492	Tonalá	374,258
Naucalpan de Juárez	792,226	Mazatlán	352,471
Chihuahua	748,518	Nuevo Laredo	348,387
Mérida	734,153	Irapuato	342,561
Guadalupe	691,434	Villahermosa	335,778
San Luis Potosí	685,934	Cuernavaca	332,197
Tlalnepantla	674,417	Xico	331,321
Aguascalientes	663,671	Celaya	310,413
Mexicali	653,046	Tampico	303,635
Hermosillo	641,791	Tepic	295,204
Saltillo	633,667	Escobedo	295,131
Acapulco de Juárez	616,394	Ixtapaluca	290,076
Morelia	608,049	San Francisco Coacalco	285,822
Culiacán Rosales	605,304	Ciudad Victoria	278,455
Santiago de Querétaro	596,450	Ciudad Obregón	270,992
Torreón	548,723	Pachuca de Soto	267,751
Tlaquepaque	542,051	Ensenada	260,075
Cancún	526,701	Ciudad Santa Catarina	259,202
Chimalhuacan	524,223	Oaxaca de Juárez	258,008
Reynosa	507,998		

SOCIAL STATISTICS

Statistics for calendar years:

	Births	*Deaths*	*Marriages*	*Divorces*
2001	2,767,610	443,127	596,984	53,789
2002	2,699,084	459,687	616,654	60,641
2003	2,655,894	472,140	584,142	64,248
2004	2,625,056	473,417	600,563	67,575
2005	2,567,906	495,240	595,713	70,184

Rates per 1,000 population, 2003: births, 25·6; deaths, 4·6. In 2003 the most popular age range for marrying was 20–24 for both males and females. Infant mortality was 22 per 1,000 live births in 2005. Life expectancy at birth in 2007 was 73·6 years for males and 78·5 years for females. Annual population growth rate, 2000–05, 1·1%. Fertility rate, 2004, 2·3 births per woman. Much of the population still lives in poverty, with the gap between the modern north and the backward south constantly growing.

CLIMATE

Latitude and relief produce a variety of climates. Arid and semi-arid conditions are found in the north, with extreme temperatures, whereas in the south there is a humid tropical climate, with temperatures varying with altitude. Conditions on the shores of the Gulf of Mexico are very warm and humid. In general, the rainy season lasts from May to Nov. Mexico City, Jan. 55°F (12·9°C), July 61°F (16·2°C). Annual rainfall 31" (787·6 mm). Guadalajara, Jan. 63°F (17·0°C), July 72°F (22·1°C). Annual rainfall 39" (987·6 mm). La Paz, Jan. 62°F (16·8°C), July 86°F (29·9°C). Annual rainfall 7" (178·3 mm). Mazatlán, Jan. 68°F (20·0°C), July 84°F (29·0°C). Annual rainfall 32" (822·1 mm). Mérida, Jan. 73°F (23·0°C), July 81°F (27·4°C). Annual rainfall 39" (990·0 mm). Monterrey, Jan. 58°F (14·3°C), July 83°F (28·1°C). Annual rainfall 23" (585·4 mm). Puebla de Zaragoza, Jan. 52°F (11·4°C), July 62°F (16·9°C). Annual rainfall 36" (900·8 mm).

CONSTITUTION AND GOVERNMENT

A new Constitution was promulgated on 5 Feb. 1917 and has occasionally been amended. Mexico is a representative, democratic and federal republic, comprising 31 states and a federal district, each state being free and sovereign in all internal affairs, but united in a federation established according to the principles of the Fundamental Law. The head of state and supreme executive authority is the *President*, directly elected for a non-renewable six-year term. The constitution was amended in April 2001, granting autonomy to 10m. indigenous peoples. The amendment was opposed both by the National Congress of Indigenous Peoples and Zapatista rebels who claimed it would leave many indigenous people worse off.

There is complete separation of legislative, executive and judicial powers (Art. 49). Legislative power is vested in a General Congress of two chambers, a *Chamber of Deputies* and a *Senate*. The Chamber of Deputies consists of 500 members directly elected for three years, 300 of them from single-member constituencies and 200 chosen under a system of proportional representation. In 1990 Congress voted a new Electoral Code. This established a body to organize elections (IFE), an electoral court (TFE) to resolve disputes, new electoral rolls and introduce a voter's registration card. Priests were enfranchised in 1991.

The Senate comprises 128 members. In each of the 31 states and the Federal District the party coming first wins two seats and the party coming second wins one seat, making 96 in total. An additional 32 seats are filled through proportional representation from national party lists. Members of both chambers are not immediately re-eligible for election. Congress sits from 1 Sept. to 31 Dec. each year; during the recess there is a permanent committee of 15 deputies and 14 senators appointed by the respective chambers.

National Anthem

'Mexicanos, al grito de guerra' ('Mexicans, at the war-cry'); words by F. González Bocanegra, tune by Jaime Nunó.

GOVERNMENT CHRONOLOGY

Presidents since 1940. (PRI = Institutional Revolutionary Party; PAN = National Action Party)

1940–46	PRI	Manuel Ávila Camacho
1946–52	PRI	Miguel Alemán Valdés
1952–58	PRI	Adolfo Ruiz Cortines
1958–64	PRI	Adolfo López Mateos
1964–70	PRI	Gustavo Díaz Ordaz Bolaños
1970–76	PRI	Luis Echeverría Álvarez
1976–82	PRI	José López Portillo y Pacheco
1982–88	PRI	Miguel de la Madrid Hurtado
1988–94	PRI	Carlos Salinas de Gortari
1994–2000	PRI	Ernesto Zedillo Ponce de León
2000–06	PAN	Vicente Fox Quesada
2006–	PAN	Felipe de Jesús Calderón Hinojosa

RECENT ELECTIONS

In the presidential elections of 2 July 2006 Felipe Calderón of the Partido Acción Nacional (National Action Party/PAN) won 35·9% of the vote, Andrés Manuel López Obrador of the Partido de la Revolución Democrática (Party of the Democratic Revolution/PRD) 35·3%, Roberto Madrazo of the Partido Revolucionario Institucional (Institutional Revolutionary Party/PRI) 22·3%, Patricia Mercado Castro of the Partido Alternativa Socialdemócrata y Campesina (Social Democratic and Peasant Alternative Party/ASC) 2·7% and Roberto Campa Cifrián of the Partido Nueva Alianza (New Alliance Party/PNA) 1·0%. Turnout was 58·6%. López Obrador claimed electoral irregularities and refused to concede defeat. After mass protests in support of the leftist López Obrador and nearly two months of deadlock, the Federal Electoral Tribunal rejected the allegations of systematic fraud and on 5 Sept. 2006 declared Calderón the winner.

In elections to the Chamber of Deputies held on 5 July 2009 the Institutional Revolutionary Party (PRI) won 241 seats (36·7% of the vote), the National Action Party (PAN) 147 (28·0%), the Party of the Democratic Revolution (PRD) 72 (12·2%), the Ecologist Green Party of Mexico (PVEM) 17 (6·7%), the Labor Party (PT) 9 (3·7%), the New Alliance Party (PNA) 8 (3·4%) and Convergence 6 (2·5%).

CURRENT ADMINISTRATION

President: Felipe Calderón; b. 1962 (National Action Party; sworn in 1 Dec. 2006).

In March 2010 the government comprised:

Head of the Presidential Office: Patricia Flores Elizondo. *Minister of Interior:* Fernando Francisco Gómez-Mont Urueta. *Foreign Affairs:* Patricia Espinosa Cantellano. *Defence:* Gen. Guillermo Galván Galván. *Naval Affairs:* Adm. Mariano Francisco Saynez Mendoza. *Finance and Public Credit:* Ernesto Cordero Arroyo. *Social Development:* Heriberto Félix Guerra. *Energy:* Georgina Kessel Martínez. *Economy:* Gerardo Ruiz Mateos. *Agriculture, Livestock, Rural Development, Fisheries and Food:* Francisco Javier Mayorga Castañeda. *Communication and Transport:* Juan Molinar Horcasitas. *Public Education:* Alonso Lujambio Irazábal. *Health:* José Ángel Córdoba Villalobos. *Public Security:* Genaro García Luna. *Labour and Social Welfare:* Javier Lozano Alarcón. *Agrarian Reform:* Abelardo Escobar Prieto. *Tourism:* Gloria Guevara Manzo. *Environment and Natural Resources:* Juan Rafael Elvira Quesada. *Civil Service:* Salvador Vega Casillas. *Attorney General:* Arturo Chávez Chávez.

Presidency Website: http://www.presidencia.gob.mx

CURRENT LEADERS

Felipe Calderón

Position
President

Introduction
Felipe Calderón of the centre-right National Action Party (PAN) became president after winning the election of July 2006 by a margin of less than 1 percent. When his closest rival, López Obrador, disputed the result there were mass protests. Calderón pledged to reduce rising crime and to tackle poverty by creating incentives for foreign investment.

Early Life
Felipe de Jesús Calderón Hinojosa was born on 18 Aug. 1962 in Morelia, Michoacán. He studied law at the Escuela Libre de Derecho in Mexico City and economics at the Instituto Tecnológico Autónomo de México, before gaining a Masters in public administration from Harvard University in the USA.

From a young age Calderón was a member of PAN, which his father had helped to found in 1939. Calderón became the organization's national youth leader in 1986 and served in the federal chamber of deputies from 1991–94. In 1993 he was elected the party's secretary-general when his mentor, Carlos Castillo Peraza, assumed the party presidency. Calderón succeeded Peraza in 1996 and during three years as leader maintained control of 14 state capitals.

However, Vicente Fox was selected to succeed him as party president in late 1999 and went on to contest the 2000 national elections. Fox forged a centre-right alliance (the Alliance for Change) with the Ecologist Green Party of Mexico and won elections to end 71 years of continuous rule by the Institutional Revolutionary Party (PRI).

Calderón was appointed parliamentary co-ordinator of PAN and president of the council of political co-ordination. He also served as a director of the state-owned development bank, Banco Nacional de Obras y Servicios Públicos (BANOBRAS), and in 2002 joined the cabinet as energy secretary. He resigned in 2004 in protest at Fox's support for Santiago Creel as PAN's presidential candidate. In a series of party primaries in late 2005, Calderón decisively defeated Creel and another contender, Alberto Cardenas.

During the election campaign he initially trailed Andrés Manuel López Obrador of the left-wing Party of the Democratic

Revolution but closed the gap with promises of job creation and a clampdown on crime and corruption. In the election of 2 July 2006 both Calderón and López Obrador claimed victory before Calderón was declared victor by 0·56% four days later. López Obrador's claims of voting irregularities and electoral fraud resulted in large-scale public protests. A partial recount saw the result upheld but López Obrador continued to protest and formed a 'parallel administration'. Calderón was sworn in on 1 Dec. 2006 inside a barricaded parliament building.

Career in Office

During his first year in office Calderón introduced significant reforms of public sector pensions and the tax system, and launched an employment programme giving cash incentives to companies taking on new employees. He also agreed to an electoral reform law put forward by the opposition. However, his campaign against drugs cartels has proved ineffective, despite the establishment of a new federal police force and the deployment of troops in an anti-trafficking drive. In the first 18 months of his presidency more than 4,000 people were killed in drug-related violence and kidnapping, including about 450 police officers, soldiers and prosecutors, prompting mass protest marches throughout Mexico in Aug. 2008. In addition, a US Justice Department report in Dec. 2008 stated that Mexican drug traffickers posed the largest organized crime threat to the USA. Despite government measures, drug-related violence continued to rise in 2009 with an estimated 6,500 killings in Mexico over the year.

The economy was hit hard by the global downturn in 2008, forcing the government to respond with a package of emergency measures in Jan. 2009. Approval ratings for the president and the PAN slumped, and in mid-term congressional elections in July 2009 the opposition PRI made large gains to become the main force in the Chamber of Deputies.

DEFENCE

Conscription is for 12 months. In 2006 defence expenditure totalled US$3,229m. (US$30 per capita), representing 0·4% of GDP.

Army

Enlistment into the regular army is voluntary, but there is also one year of conscription (four hours per week) by lottery. Strength of the regular army (2007) 178,000. There are reserve forces numbering 39,899 in 2007. In addition there is a rural defence militia of 18,000.

Navy

The Navy is primarily equipped and organized for offshore and coastal patrol duties. It includes one destroyer and six frigates. Naval Aviation, 1,250 strong, operates eight combat capable aircraft.

Naval personnel in 2007 totalled 46,400, including Naval Aviation. In addition there were 12,600 marines.

Air Force

The Air Force had (2007) a strength of 11,700 with 78 combat capable aircraft, including PC-7s and F-5Es.

INTERNATIONAL RELATIONS

Mexico is a member of the UN, World Bank, IMF and several other UN specialized agencies, WTO, BIS, IOM, OECD, ACS, Inter-American Development Bank, SELA, LAIA, OAS, APEC and North American Free Trade Agreement. A free trade agreement was signed with the European Union in 1999.

ECONOMY

Agriculture accounted for 3·9% of GDP in 2006, industry 26·7% and services 69·4%.

Overview

Mexico ranks among the dozen largest economies in the world. Average income levels are the highest in Latin America but remain well below the OECD average. There is a high degree of income inequality, with the World Bank estimating that the richest 10% of the population earns over 40% of total income while the poorest 10% accounts for only 1·1%. The economy suffered from poor macroeconomic management and economic crises in the 1980s while in 1994–95 a currency crisis threw millions into poverty. Yet economic performance during the 1990s compared favourably with that of the previous decade, with inflation significantly reduced and public debt brought down from 115% in 1986 to 22% in 1999.

Since 1995 macroeconomic management has been on a sound footing. The labour market and banking system have been reformed and privatization has reduced the state's direct involvement in the economy. The economy is buoyed by increasing stability, low inflation and low interest rates that have been falling since late 2005. External debt has been reduced to 7% of GDP and there has been a steady rise in foreign direct investment. Capital inflows from the energy sector have made possible increased spending on infrastructure projects. Growth in the domestic property and construction sectors as well as remittances from Mexicans working in the USA have also helped. Nonetheless, recent growth is considered to be well below the country's potential and insufficient to reduce poverty significantly.

Until 1985 oil was the principal export and Mexico was still the world's fifth largest producer in 2004. Manufactured goods now make up over 80% of total exports while oil accounts for 15%. The transfer to manufactured exports started with the economic liberalization of the 1980s and was accelerated by membership of the North American Free-Trade Agreement in 1994. Nearly half of the country's total exports are produced in *maquiladoras* (in-bond assembly plants for re-export). The mining sector was estimated to account for only 1·4% of GDP in 2003 but this understates the importance of oil production, although oil output was projected to fall by 3·8% and oil exports by 8·6% in 2009.

The USA is Mexico's main trading partner, accounting for 80% of exports. Mexico has benefited from a shift in industrial production in the USA to south of the border. Nonetheless, industrial production has slowed, as evidenced by a 0·2% year-on-year fall in mid-2008. The global economic turmoil of 2008 led to a deep recession in 2009, reflecting falling demand from the USA. Meanwhile, Mexico must meet the challenge of increasingly efficient competitors, including China.

The OECD recommends further structural reform and economic liberalization. Other priorities include educational reform (Mexico's human capital is the lowest in the OECD) and public finance reform. The OECD proposes that more oil revenue be saved or spent on education, infrastructure, health and poverty alleviation, and that alternative revenue sources should be tapped by tax reforms.

Currency

The unit of currency is the *Mexican peso* (MXN) of 100 *centavos*. A new peso was introduced on 1 Jan. 1993: 1 new peso = 1,000 old pesos. The peso was devalued by 13·94% in Dec. 1994. Foreign exchange reserves were US$82,023m. and gold reserves 288,000 troy oz in Sept. 2009. Inflation rates (based on OECD statistics):

1999	2000	2001	2002	2003	2004	2005	2006	2007	2008
16·6%	9·5%	6·4%	5·0%	4·5%	4·7%	4·0%	3·6%	4·0%	5·1%

Total money supply in Aug. 2009 was 1,391·5bn. new pesos.

Budget

Government revenue and expenditure (in 1m. new pesos), year ending 31 Dec.:

	2002	*2003*	*2004*	*2005*	*2006*
Revenue	989,353	1,132,985	1,270,211	1,412,305	1,558,808
Expenditure	1,124,451	1,232,942	1,373,362	1,513,210	1,739,467

VAT is 16% (11% in the frontier region).

Performance

Real GDP growth rates (based on OECD statistics):

1999	*2000*	*2001*	*2002*	*2003*	*2004*	*2005*	*2006*	*2007*	*2008*
3·9%	6·6%	–0·2%	0·8%	1·4%	4·0%	3·2%	5·1%	3·3%	1·4%

According to the Instituto Nacional de Estadística, real GDP growth in 2009 was –6·5%. In 2008 total GDP was US$1,086·0bn.

Banking and Finance

The Bank of Mexico, established 1 Sept. 1925, is the central bank of issue (*Governor*, Agustín Carstens Carstens). It gained autonomy over monetary policy in 1993. Exchange rate policy is determined jointly by the bank and the Finance Ministry. Banks were nationalized in 1982, but in May 1990 the government approved their reprivatization. The state continues to have a majority holding in foreign trade and rural development banks. In 1999 Congress approved the removal of regulations limiting foreign holdings to 49%.

In 2007 there were 38 commercial banks (including seven development banks) and 81 representative offices of foreign banks. In 2001 the American financial services company Citigroup bought Mexico's largest financial group, Banacci, and its second largest bank, Banamex, for US$12·5bn., but retained the name Banamex. The new Banamex is now Mexico's largest bank. Most of Mexico's leading banks are now foreign-owned.

Mexico received US$22·0bn. worth of foreign direct investment in 2008, down from US$27·3bn. in 2007.

There is a stock exchange in Mexico City.

ENERGY AND NATURAL RESOURCES

Environment

Mexico's carbon dioxide emissions from the consumption and flaring of fossil fuels in 2008 were the equivalent of 4·0 tonnes per capita.

Electricity

Installed capacity, 2004, 51·9m. kW. Output in 2004 was 224·08bn. kWh and consumption per capita 2,130 kWh. In 2003 there were two nuclear reactors in operation.

Oil and Gas

Oil production was 157·4m. tonnes in 2008. Mexico produced 4·0% of the world total oil output in 2008, and had reserves amounting to 11·9bn. bbls. Revenues from oil exports provide about a third of all government revenues. Natural gas production was 54·9bn. cu. metres in 2008 with 500bn. cu. metres in proven reserves.

Minerals

Output (in 1,000 tonnes): iron ore (2006), 14,568; salt (2005), 9,508; lignite (2004), 8,147; gypsum and anhydrite (2006), 6,076; silica (2005), 2,121; coal (2004), 1,735; sulphur (2005), 1,590; fluorite (2005), 876; aluminium (2005), 574; zinc (2005), 476; copper (2005), 429; feldspar (2005), 373; barite (2005), 269; lead (2005), 134; manganese (2005), 133; silver (2005), 2·9; gold (2005), 30,356 kg. Mexico is the biggest producer of silver in the world.

Agriculture

In 2007 Mexico had an estimated 24·5m. ha. of arable land and around 2·4m. ha. of permanent cropland. There were 5·4m. ha. of irrigated land in 2006. There were 238,830 tractors and some 22,500 harvester-threshers in 2007. In 2007 agriculture, fishing and forestry contributed 3·6% of GDP. In 1992 the Mexican constitution was amended to permit the voluntary privatization of *ejidos*, communal land in which each member farms an independent plot, to combat the low productivity resulting from the fragmentation of farming units, some 58% of which were less than 5 ha. in 1991.

Sown areas, 2003 (in 1,000 ha.) included: maize, 7,781; beans, 1,948; sorghum, 1,879; coffee beans, 744; wheat, 627; sugarcane, 639; barley, 384; chick-peas, 150; chillies and green peppers, 141; safflower seeds, 85; rice, 50. Production in 2003 (in 1,000 tonnes): sugarcane, 45,126; maize, 19,652; sorghum, 6,462; oranges, 3,970; wheat, 3,000; tomatoes, 2,148; bananas, 2,027; chillies and green peppers, 1,854; lemons and limes, 1,825; potatoes, 1,735; mangoes, 1,503; beans, 1,400; barley, 1,109; avocados, 1,040.

Livestock (2003): cattle, 30·80m.; sheep, 6·56m.; pigs, 18·10m.; goats, 9·50m.; horses, 6·26m.; mules, 3·28m.; asses, 3·26m.; chickens, 540m. Production, 2003 (in 1,000 tonnes): beef and veal, 1,496; pork, bacon and ham, 1,043; horse, 79; goat meat, 42; lamb and mutton, 40; poultry meat, 2,204; cow's milk, 9,842; goat's milk, 148; eggs, 1,882; cheese, 130; honey, 56.

Forestry

Forests extended over 64·24m. ha. in 2005, representing 33·7% of the land area, containing pine, spruce, cedar, mahogany, logwood and rosewood. There are 14 forest reserves (nearly 0·8m. ha.) and 47 national park forests of 0·75m. ha. Timber production was 44·91m. cu. metres in 2007.

Fisheries

The total catch in 2005 was 1,304,830 tonnes, of which 1,204,949 tonnes came from sea fishing.

INDUSTRY

The leading companies by market capitalization in Mexico in March 2009 were: América Móvil S.A. de C.V. (a mobile phone company), US$29·0bn.; Wal-Mart de México S.A.B. de C.V. (general retailers, formerly Cifra), US$19·8bn.; and Telecomunicaciones de México (TELECOMM-TELÉGRAFOS), US$11·6bn.

In 2001 the manufacturing industry provided 19·6% of GDP. Output (in 1,000 tonnes): cement (2004), 34,992; residual fuel oil (2004), 21,089; petrol (2004), 19,855; crude steel (2004), 16,730; distillate fuel oil (2004), 16,057; sugar (2002), 5,073; pig iron (2004), 4,278; wheat flour (2001), 2,611; cigarettes (2001), 56·1bn. units; soft drinks (2001), 13,005·0m. litres; beer (2001), 6,163·2m. litres. Car production has increased from 857,000 in 1994 to 1,098,000 in 2006.

Labour

In the period March–June 2001 the employed population totalled 39,004,300. The principal areas of activity were (in 1,000): wholesale and retail trade/repair of motor vehicles, motorcycles and personal and household goods, 8,839·2; manufacturing, 7,373·0; agriculture, hunting and forestry, 6,920·7; construction, 2,396·9; hotels and restaurants, 1,982·2; education, 1,971·6. Unemployment rate, Dec. 2009, 5·4%. The daily minimum wage at Jan. 2009 ranged from 51·95 new pesos to 54·80 new pesos.

Trade Unions

The Mexican Labour Congress (CTM) is incorporated into the Institutional Revolutionary Party, and is an umbrella organization numbering some 5m. A breakaway from CTM took place in 1997 when rebel labour leaders set up the National Union of Workers (UNT) to combat what they saw as a sharp drop in real wages.

INTERNATIONAL TRADE

In Sept. 1991 Mexico signed the free trade Treaty of Santiago with Chile, envisaging an annual 10% tariffs reduction from Jan. 1992. The North American Free Trade Agreement (NAFTA), between Canada, Mexico and the USA, was signed on 7 Oct. 1992 and came into effect on 1 Jan. 1994. A free trade agreement was signed with Costa Rica in March 1994. Some 8,300 products were free from tariffs, with others to follow over ten years. The Group of

Three (G3) free trade pact with Colombia and Venezuela came into effect on 1 Jan. 1995. Total foreign debt was US$167,228m. in 2005.

Imports and Exports

Trade for calendar years in US$1m.:

	2003	2004	2005	2006	2007
Imports c.i.f.	170,546	196,809	221,819	256,086	281,927
Exports f.o.b.	164,907	187,980	214,207	249,961	271,821

Of total imports in 2007, 49·6% came from the USA, 10·6% from China, 5·8% from Japan, 4·5% from South Korea and 3·8% from Germany. Of total exports in 2007, 82·2% went to the USA, 2·4% to Canada, 1·5% to Germany, 1·4% to Spain and 1·1% to Colombia. In 2004 exports to the USA accounted for 24% of GDP.

The in-bond (*maquiladora*) assembly plants generate the largest flow of foreign exchange. Although originally located along the US border when the programme was introduced in the 1960s, they are now to be found in almost every state. In 2009 there were over 5,200 'foreign to Mexico' manufacturing companies, employing more than 1·6m. people. Manufactured goods account for 90% of trade revenues.

COMMUNICATIONS

Roads

The total road length in 2007 was 360,075 km, of which 6,565 km were motorways, 40,631 km other main roads, 73,874 km secondary roads and 239,005 km other roads. In 2005 there were 14,074,669 passenger cars, 7,111,172 trucks and vans and 264,726 buses and coaches. There were 5,398 fatalities as a result of road accidents in 2007.

Rail

The National Railway, *Ferrocarriles Nacionales de México*, was split into four companies in 1995 as a preliminary to privatization. It ceased operations in 1999. The rail network comprises 26,677 km of 1,435 mm gauge. In 2007, 99·9m. tonnes of freight were transported. Passenger traffic declined dramatically between 1997 and 2008, when a suburban rail network was opened between Mexico City and Cuautitlán in the state of México. There is a 202 km metro in Mexico City with 11 lines. There are light rail lines in Guadalajara (24 km) and Monterrey (32 km).

Civil Aviation

There is an international airport at Mexico City (Benito Juárez) and 55 other international and 29 national airports. Each of the larger states has a local airline which links it with main airports. The national carriers are Aeroméxico, Mexicana and Aviacsa; Aeroméxico and Mexicana, both privatized in the late 1980s, are the main ones. In 2005 scheduled airline traffic of Mexican-based carriers flew 366·7m. km and carried 20,218,800 passengers. In 2001 Mexico City handled 20,599,064 passengers (13,711,141 on domestic flights). Cancún was the second busiest airport for passengers in 2001, with 7,640,007 (5,905,813 on international flights). Guadalajara handled 5,020,631 passengers (3,337,339 on domestic flights).

Shipping

Mexico had 114 ports and terminals in 2007 (66 ocean navigation), of which the most important are Altamira, Progreso, Tampico, Tuxpan and Veracruz on the Gulf coast and Manzanillo on the Pacific coast. Mexico's busiest port is Manzanillo, which handled 21·21m. tonnes of cargo in 2007 (7·53m. tonnes loaded and 13·68m. tonnes discharged). A law to privatize port operations was passed in 1993.

In 2007 the merchant marine numbered 2,387 vessels with a total tonnage of 1,727,000 GRT. In 2005 vessels totalling 60,527,000 NRT entered ports and vessels totalling 144,652,000 NRT cleared.

Telecommunications

Telmex (Teléfonos de México), a former state-run company privatized in 1991, is the leading provider of fixed line telephone services and broadband. In 2008 there were 20,668,000 fixed telephone lines and 75,305,000 mobile phone subscribers (693·7 per 1,000 persons). There were 15·0m. PCs in use in 2006 and 23·6m. internet users in 2008. There were 4·7 broadband subscribers per 100 inhabitants in June 2008.

Postal Services

There were 8,681 post offices in 2003 (local administration, offices, agencies), equivalent to one for every 11,900 persons.

SOCIAL INSTITUTIONS

Justice

Magistrates of the Supreme Court are appointed for six years by the President and confirmed by the Senate; they can be removed only on impeachment. The courts include the Supreme Court with 21 magistrates, 12 collegiate circuit courts with three judges each and nine unitary circuit courts with one judge each, and 68 district courts with one judge each.

The penal code of 1 Jan. 1930 abolished the death penalty, except for the armed forces. Mexico abolished the death penalty for all crimes in Dec. 2005—the last execution had been in 1961.

There were 11,558 murders in 2006 (a rate of 11·0 per 100,000 population). The population in penal institutions in Aug. 2006 was 214,450 (196 per 100,000 of national population). Following the collapse of the main Colombian drug cartels in the 1990s, Mexican cartels are estimated to control 70% of illicit foreign drugs entering the US market. Since 2006 President Calderón has spearheaded a 'war' on the cartels, engaging 45,000 military and police personnel in often bloody battles.

Education

Adult literacy was 90·3% in 2003 (male, 92·0%; female, 88·7%). Primary and secondary education is free and compulsory, and secular, although religious instruction is permitted in private schools.

In 2002–03 there were:

	Establishments	*Teachers*	*Students (in 1,000)*
Pre-school	74,758	163,282	3,636
Primary	99,463	557,278	14,857
Secondary	29,749	325,233	5,660
Baccalaureate	9,668	202,161	2,936
Vocational training	1,659	31,683	359
Medium/Professional	664	17,280	167
Higher education	2,539	192,593	1,932
Postgraduate education	1,283	21,685	138

In 2006 public expenditure on education came to 4·8% of GDP and 22·0% of total government spending (the highest share in the OECD).

Health

In 2003 there were 3,039 hospitals, with a total provision of 73,446 beds. In 2001 there were 172,266 physicians, 9,669 dentists and 222,389 nurses. In 2007 Mexico spent 5·9% of its GDP on health.

Welfare

As of 1 July 1997 all workers had to join the private insurance system, while the social insurance system was being phased out. At retirement, employees covered by the social insurance system before 1997 can choose to receive benefits from either the social insurance system or the private insurance system. The official retirement age is 65 years but to be eligible, a pensioner must have paid 1,250 weeks of contributions. The guaranteed minimum pension is equal to the minimum salary in July 1997 indexed to prices. On social insurance, the minimum monthly pension is

100% of the minimum monthly salary in Mexico City (1,357·20 new pesos in 2004).

Unemployment benefit exists under a labour law which requires employers to pay a dismissed employee a lump sum equal to three months' pay plus 20 days' pay for each year of service. Social security pays an unemployment benefit of between 75% and 95% of the old-age pension for unemployed persons aged 60 to 64.

RELIGION

In 2001 an estimated 91% of the population was Roman Catholic, down from 98% in 1950. In Feb. 2010 there were four cardinals. The Church is separated from the State, and the constitution of 1917 provided strict regulation of this and all other religions. In Nov. 1991 Congress approved an amendment to the 1917 constitution permitting the recognition of churches by the state, the possession of property by churches and the enfranchisement of priests. Church buildings remain state property. In 2001 there were estimated to be 3·82m. Protestants, plus followers of various other religions. There were 811,000 Latter-day Saints (Mormons) in 1998.

CULTURE

World Heritage Sites

Mexico has 29 UNESCO World Heritage sites. They are (with year entered on list): the Sian Ka'an nature reserve; the historic centre of Mexico City and the canal and island network of Xochimilco; Puebla's historic centre; the pre-Hispanic city of Teotihuacán, now a major archaeological site; the Historic Centre of Oaxaca and archaeological site of Monte Alban; and Palenque—lying in the foothills of the Altos de Chiapas, the Maya ruins of Palenque are surrounded by waterfalls, rainforest and fauna (all 1987); the historic town of Guanajuato and adjacent disused silver mines; and the pre-Hispanic city of Chichen-Itza, Yucatan (both 1988); the historic centre of Morelia, on the southern Pacific coast (1991); the pre-Hispanic city of El Tajin, Veracruz (1992); the El Vizcaino whale sanctuary; the historic centre of Zacatecas, once a major silver mining centre; and the Sierra de San Francisco rock paintings (all 1993); the 14 early 16th-century monasteries on Popocatépetl, to the southeast of Mexico City (1994); the Maya town of Uxmal, Yucatán, with its preserved pyramids and sculptures; and the historic monuments zone of Querétaro (both 1996); the Hospicio (Hospice) Cabañas, Guadalajara (1997); the historic monuments zone of Tlacotalpan; and the archaeological zone of Paquimé, Casas Grandes in Chihuahua (both 1998); the historic fortified town of Campeche; and Xochicalco's archaeological monuments zone, Morelos state (both 1999); the Ancient Maya City of Calakmul, Campeche (2002); the Franciscan Missions in the Sierra Gorda of Querétaro (2003); Luis Barragán House and Studio in Mexico City (2004); the islands and protected areas of the Gulf of California (2005 and 2007); the Agave landscape and ancient industrial facilities of Tequila (2006); the Central University City Campus of the Universidad Nacional Autónoma de México (2007); the Monarch Butterfly Biosphere Reserve (2008); and the fortified town of San Miguel and Sanctuary of Jesús Nazareno de Atotonilco (2008).

Broadcasting

Television is dominated by Televisa (which operates four networks) and Televisión Azteca (with two), but there is increasing competition from foreign satellite and cable services. Local and regional radio stations number around 1,400. There were 25·2m. TV sets (colour by NTSC) in 2006.

Cinema

In 2004 there were 3,248 cinema screens and 165m. admissions.

Press

In 2002 there were 299 daily newspapers with a circulation of 8,734,000, equivalent to 88 per 1,000 inhabitants. In 2002 a total of 7,306 book titles were published.

Tourism

There were 21·92m. non-resident tourists in 2005; tourist spending amounted to US$12,801m. in 2005.

DIPLOMATIC REPRESENTATIVES

Of Mexico in the United Kingdom (16 St George St., Hanover Sq., London, W1S 1LX)
Ambassador: Juan Bremer de Martino, CVO.

Of the United Kingdom in Mexico (Rio Lerma 71, Col. Cuauhtémoc, 06500 México, D.F.)
Ambassador: Judith Macgregor.

Of Mexico in the USA (1911 Pennsylvania Ave., NW, Washington, D.C., 20006)
Ambassador: Arturo Sarukhán Casamitjana.

Of the USA in Mexico (Paseo de la Reforma 305, 06500 México, D.F.)
Ambassador: Carlos Pascual.

Of Mexico to the United Nations
Ambassador: Claude Heller Rouassant.

Of Mexico to the European Union
Ambassador: Sandra Fuentes-Beráin.

FURTHER READING

Instituto Nacional de Estadística, Geografía e Informática. *Anuario Estadístico de los Estados Unidos Mexicanos. Mexican Bulletin of Statistical Information.* Quarterly.

Aspe, P., *Economic Transformation: the Mexican Way.* 1993
Bartra, R., *Agrarian Structure and Political Power in Mexico.* 1993
Bethell, L. (ed.) *Mexico since Independence.* 1992
Camp, R. A., *Politics in Mexico.* 2nd ed. 1996
Hamnett, Brian R., *A Concise History of Mexico.* 1999
Krauze, E., *Mexico, Biography of Power: A History of Modern Mexico, 1810–1996.* 1997
Levy, Daniel C., *Mexico: The Struggle for Democratic Development.* 2006
Mentinis, Mihalis, *Zapatistas: The Chiapas Revolt and What it Means for Radical Politics.* 2006
Philip, G. (ed.) *The Presidency in Mexican Politics.* 1991
Randall, Laura, *Changing Structure of Mexico: Political, Social and Economic Prospects.* 2005
Rodríguez, J. E., *The Evolution of the Mexican Political System.* 1993
Ruíz, R. E., *Triumphs and Tragedy: a History of the Mexican People.* 1992
Snyder, Richard, *Politics After Neoliberalism: Reregulation in Mexico.* 2006
Whiting, V. R., *The Political Economy of Foreign Investment in Mexico: Nationalism, Liberalism, Constraints on Choice.* 1992

National Statistical Office: Instituto Nacional de Estadística, Geografía e Informática (INEGI), Aguascalientes.
Website (Spanish only): http://www.inegi.org.mx

MICRONESIA

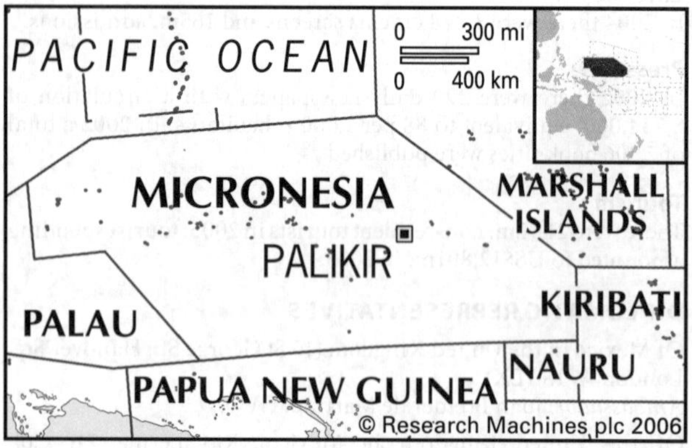

Federated States of Micronesia

Capital: Palikir
Population estimate, 2010: 111,000
GDP per capita, 2007: (PPP$) 2,802

KEY HISTORICAL EVENTS

Spain acquired sovereignty over the Caroline Islands in 1886 but sold the archipelago to Germany in 1899. Japan occupied the Islands at the beginning of the First World War and in 1921 they were mandated to Japan by the League of Nations. Captured by Allied Forces in the Second World War, the Islands became part of the UN Trust Territory of the Pacific Islands created on 18 July 1947 and administered by the USA. The Federated States of Micronesia came into being on 10 May 1979. American trusteeship was terminated on 3 Nov. 1986 by the UN Security Council and on the same day Micronesia entered into a 15-year Free Association with the USA. An amended 20-year Compact of Free Association was signed into law on 17 Dec. 2003, guaranteeing US$1·8bn. to Micronesia in grants for a government trust fund.

TERRITORY AND POPULATION

The Federated States lie in the North Pacific Ocean between 137° and 163° E, comprising 607 islands with a total land area of 701 sq. km (271 sq. miles). The population (2000 census) was 107,008; density, 153 per sq. km.

The UN gives an estimated population for 2010 of 111,000.

In 2000 an estimated 71·5% of the population lived in rural areas.

The areas and populations of the four major groups of island states (east to west) are as follows:

State	*Area (sq. km)*	*Population (2000 census)*	*Headquarters*
Kosrae	110	7,686	Tofol
Pohnpei	345	34,486	Kolonia
Chuuk	127	53,595	Weno
Yap	119	11,241	Colonia

Kosrae consists of a single island. Its main town is Lelu (2,591 inhabitants in 2000). Pohnpei comprises a single island (covering 334 sq. km) and eight scattered coral atolls. Kolonia (5,681 inhabitants in 2000) was the national capital until 1989. The new capital, Palikir (6,444 inhabitants in 2000), lies approximately 10 km southwest in the Palikir valley. Chuuk consists of a group of 14 islands within a large reef-fringed lagoon (44,000 inhabitants in 1994); the state also includes 12 coral atolls (8,000 inhabitants), the most important being the Mortlock Islands. The chief town is Weno (13,802 inhabitants in 2000). Yap comprises a main group of four islands (covering 100 sq. km with 7,000 inhabitants in 1994) and 13 coral atolls (4,000 inhabitants), the main ones being Ulithi and Woleai. Colonia is its chief town (3,216 inhabitants in 2000).

English is used in schools and is the official language. Trukese, Pohnpeian, Yapese and Kosrean are also spoken.

SOCIAL STATISTICS

2004 estimates: births, 3,400; deaths, 700. Rates, 2004 estimates (per 1,000 population): birth, 31; death, 6. Infant mortality rate (2005), 34 per 1,000 live births. 2007 life expectancy, 67·6 years for men and 69·2 years for women. Annual population growth rate, 1992–2002, 0·7%; fertility rate, 2004, 4·3 births per woman.

CLIMATE

Tropical, with heavy year-round rainfall, especially in the eastern islands, and occasional typhoons (June–Dec.). Kolonia, Jan. 80°F (26·7°C), July 79°F (26·1°C). Annual rainfall 194" (4,859 mm).

CONSTITUTION AND GOVERNMENT

Under the Constitution founded on 10 May 1979, there is an executive presidency and a 14-member *National Congress*, comprising ten members elected for two-year terms from single-member constituencies of similar electorates, and four members elected one from each State for a four-year term by proportional representation. The *Federal President* and *Vice-President* first run for the Congress before they are elected by members of Congress for a four-year term.

National Anthem

'Patriots of Micronesia'; words anonymous, tune adapted from J. Brahms' 'Academic Festival Overture'.

RECENT ELECTIONS

The last election for Congress was held on 3 March 2009. Only non-partisans were elected. Immanuel Mori was elected President by Congress on 11 May 2007, defeating incumbent Joseph Urusemal. Alik K. Alik was elected Vice-President.

CURRENT ADMINISTRATION

President: Immanuel 'Manny' Mori; b. 1948 (took office 11 May 2007).

Vice-President: Alik L. Alik.

In March 2010 the government comprised:

Minister of Education: Casiano Shoniber. *Finance and Administration:* Finley Perman. *Foreign Affairs:* Lorin Robert. *Health and Social Affairs:* Dr Vita Skilling. *Justice:* Maketo Robert. *Resources and Development:* Peter Christian. *Transportation, Communications and Infrastructure:* Francis Itimai. *Chief Public Defender:* Julius Joey Sapelalut.

Speaker of the Congress: Isaac V. Figir.

Government Website: http://www.fsmgov.org

CURRENT LEADERS

Immanuel Mori

Position
President

Introduction
Immanuel 'Manny' Mori became the seventh president of the Federated States of Micronesia (FSM) on 11 May 2007. He is the second president to come from the state of Chuuk. The president,

who is both head of state and of the unicameral government, serves for a four-year term.

Early Life
Mori was born on 25 Dec. 1948 in Sapore on the island of Fefan, Chuuk. He spent his childhood in Fefan and attended the Xavier High School in Chuuk's capital, Weno. From 1969–73 he studied at the University of Guam, graduating in business management. He joined Citycorp Credit as a management intern, becoming assistant manager at the Saipan branch.

Mori returned to the FSM in 1976 and joined the Trust Territory social security office. In 1979 he became responsible for Chuuk's tax and revenue office. From 1981–83 he served as comptroller of the Development Bank of the FSM before being appointed its president and CEO. He held the post until Feb. 1997, when the bank's board ousted him in an attempt to encourage reform. He was subsequently named vice-president.

Mori's political career began in July 1999 when he was elected a Chuuk congressman. He held several positions including chair of the ways and means committee and vice-chair of the committee on judiciary and government operation. He also sat on the committees for resource and development and for health and social affairs. In 2003 he was elected senator-at-large for Chuuk for a four-year term. In this capacity Mori served on the task force for national government restructuring and on the planning council of the College of Micronesia. He also served as a CEO of the Chuuk Public Utility Corporation and on the board of the Pacific Island Development Bank.

In May 2007 parliament selected Mori to replace Joseph Urusemal as president. Alik L. Alik was chosen as vice-president.

Career in Office
Under a Compact of Free Association Micronesia is guaranteed US aid until 2023. Chief among Mori's challenges is to prepare for economic self-reliance and to reinvigorate the stagnant private sector.

INTERNATIONAL RELATIONS

Micronesia is a member of the UN, World Bank, IMF, Asian Development Bank, Pacific Islands Forum and SPC.

ECONOMY

Overview
Following independence in 1986, the region signed a Compact of Free Association with the USA, providing it with grants upon which it relies heavily. A renegotiated Compact Agreement with the USA effective since 2004 steadily lowers aid payments to the economy until 2023. In addition, stricter rules have been placed on reporting, auditing and the use of grants, which the islands have been unable to meet. As a result of this, the economy has experienced a contraction of growth for five years running, among the worst returns of Pacific Island nations. Compact-related spending cuts have reduced public sector employment, stimulating migration to the USA where citizens can work without a visa. Higher fuel and food import costs have put further pressure on state finances.

Medium-term growth prospects are poor owing to declining aid revenues and the need for fiscal consolidation. The IMF has recommended reducing the large public sector wage bill and strengthening tax administration to improve long-term finances, alongside reforms to ease the cost of doing business and to stimulate private sector growth and employment. Owing to the global economic crisis, the near-term outlook is negative with the prospect of declining tourist arrivals, remittances, exports and foreign investment.

Currency
US currency is used. Foreign exchange reserves were US$50m. and total money supply was US$23m. in June 2005.

Budget
US compact funds are an annual US$100m. Revenue (2001–02), US$160m.; expenditure, US$155m. The financial year runs from 1 Oct.–30 Sept.

Performance
In 2008 total GDP was US$247m.; real GDP growth in 2005–06 was negative, at –2·3%.

Banking and Finance
There are three commercial banks: Bank of Guam, Bank of Hawaii and Bank of the Federated States of Micronesia. There is also a Federated States of Micronesia Development Bank and a regulatory Banking Board.

ENERGY AND NATURAL RESOURCES

Electricity
Electricity production in 2002 was 192m. kWh.

Minerals
The islands have few mineral deposits except for high-grade phosphates.

Agriculture
Agriculture consists mainly of subsistence farming: coconuts, breadfruit, bananas, sweet potatoes and cassava. A small amount of crops are produced for export, including copra, tropical fruits, peppers and taro. Production (2003 estimates, in 1,000 tonnes): coconuts, 140; copra, 18; cassava, 12; sweet potatoes, 3; bananas, 2. Livestock (2003 estimates): pigs, 32,000; cattle, 14,000; goats, 4,000. In 2007 there were approximately 2,500 ha. of arable land and 18,000 ha. of permanent crops.

Forestry
The total forest area was 63,000 ha. in 2005 (90·6% of the land area).

Fisheries
In 2005 the catch amounted to approximately 29,336 tonnes, almost entirely from marine waters. Fishing licence fees were US$20m. in 1993 and are a primary revenue source.

INDUSTRY

The chief industries are construction, fish processing, tourism and handicrafts (items from shell, wood and pearl).

Labour
Two-thirds of the labour force are government employees. In 1994, 8,092 people worked in public administration and 7,375 in agriculture, fisheries and farming out of a total labour force of 27,573. The unemployment rate was 15·2%.

INTERNATIONAL TRADE

Imports and Exports
Total imports (2005), US$130·2m.; exports, US$13·0m. Main import suppliers, 2002: USA (excluding Guam), 42·2%; Guam, 20·2%; Japan, 10·6%. Main export markets, 2002: USA (excluding Guam), 29·0%; Japan, 18·7%; Guam, 7·9%. The main imports are foodstuffs and beverages, manufactured goods, machinery and equipment. Main exports: copra, bananas, black pepper, fish and garments.

COMMUNICATIONS

Roads
In 2000 there were 240 km of roads (42 km paved).

Civil Aviation
There are international airports on Pohnpei, Chuuk, Yap and Kosrae. Services are provided by Continental Airlines. In 2003 there were international flights to Guam, Honolulu, Manila, the Marshall Islands and Palau in addition to domestic services. There were five airports in 1996 (four paved).

Shipping
The main ports are Kolonia (Pohnpei), Colonia (Yap), Lepukos (Chuuk), Okat and Lelu (Kosrae). In 2002 merchant shipping totalled 13,000 GRT.

Telecommunications
Micronesia had 36,100 telephone subscribers in total in 2007, or 325·2 per 1,000 population. Mobile phone subscribers numbered 27,400 in 2007. The islands are interconnected by shortwave radiotelephone. There are four earth stations linked to the Intelsat satellite system. There were 15,000 internet users in 2007.

Postal Services
All four states have postal services.

SOCIAL INSTITUTIONS

Justice
There is a Supreme Court headed by the Chief Justice with two other judges, and a State Court in each of the four states with 13 judges in total.

Education
In 2007 there were 18,512 pupils in primary schools with 1,113 teaching staff; and 14,742 pupils in secondary schools. The College of Micronesia in Pohnpei, initially founded as the Micronesian Teacher Education Center in 1963, is the only institute of higher education and now has campuses on all four major island groups, including the Fisheries and Maritime Institute on the Yap Islands.

In 2001–02 total expenditure on education came to 6·7% of GNP.

Health
In 1994 there were four hospitals with 325 beds. There were 76 physicians, 16 dentists and 368 nurses in 1999.

RELIGION
The population is predominantly Christian. Yap is mainly Roman Catholic; Protestantism is prevalent elsewhere.

CULTURE

Broadcasting
There are radio stations on the four island states and television stations on Pohnpei, Chuuk and Yap. There were 2,800 TV receivers (colour by NTSC) in 2004.

Tourism
In 2005 there were 19,000 visitors, bringing in US$17m. in tourist revenue.

DIPLOMATIC REPRESENTATIVES
Of the United Kingdom in Micronesia
Ambassador: Stephen Lillie (resides in Manila, Philippines).

Of Micronesia in the USA (1725 N St., NW, Washington, D.C., 20036)
Ambassador: Yosiwo P. George.

Of the USA in Micronesia (POB 1286, Kolonia, Pohnpei)
Ambassador: Peter A. Prahar.

Of Micronesia to the United Nations
Ambassador: Masao Nakayama.

FURTHER READING
Wuerch, W. L. and Ballendorf, D. A., *Historical Dictionary of Guam and Micronesia.* 1995

National Statistical Office: FSM Statistics Division, P.O. Box PS 253, Palikir, Pohnpei, FM 96941.
Website: http://www.spc.int/prism/country/fm/stats

MOLDOVA

Republica Moldova
(Republic of Moldova)

Capital: Chişinău
Population estimate, 2010: 3·58m.
GDP per capita, 2007: (PPP$) 2,551
HDI/world rank: 0·720/117

KEY HISTORICAL EVENTS

In Dec. 1991 Moldova became a member of the Commonwealth of Independent States, a decision ratified by parliament in April 1994. Fighting took place in 1992 between government forces and separatists in the (largely Russian and Ukrainian) area east of the River Nistru (Transnistria). An agreement signed by the presidents of Moldova and Russia on 21 July 1992 brought to an end the armed conflict and established a 'security zone' controlled by peacekeeping forces from Russia, Moldova and Transnistria. On 21 Oct. 1994 a Moldo-Russian agreement obliged Russian troops to withdraw from the territory of Moldova over three years but the agreement was not ratified by the Russian Duma. On 8 May 1997 an agreement between Transnistria and the Moldovan government to end the separatist conflict stipulated that Transnistria would remain part of Moldova as it was territorially constituted in Jan. 1990. In 1997 some 7,000 Russian troops were stationed in Transnistria. In the autumn of 1999 Ion Sturza's centre-right coalition collapsed, along with privatization plans for the wine and tobacco industries. Communist President Vladimir Voronin, who was elected in 2001, has proposed giving the Russian language official status and joining the Russia–Belarus union.

In Aug. 2009 the Communist government fell to a coalition of four opposition parties after earlier disputed elections and a failure to elect a new president.

TERRITORY AND POPULATION

Moldova is bounded in the east and south by Ukraine and on the west by Romania. The area is 33,848 sq. km (13,067 sq. miles). At the last census, in 2004, the population was 3,938,679 (52·2% female).

The UN gives an estimated population for 2010 of 3·58m.

In 2005, 53·3% of the population lived in rural areas. Ethnicity (2004): Moldovans accounted for 69·6%, Ukrainians 11·3%, Russians 9·3%, Gagauz 3·9%, Bulgarians 2·0%, Roma (Gypsy) 1·9%, and others 2·0%.

Apart from Chişinău, the capital (population of 644,204 in 2004), major towns are Tiraspol (158,069 in 2004), Bălţi (122,669 in 2004) and Tighina (97,027 in 2004). The official Moldovan language (i.e. Romanian) was written in Cyrillic prior to the restoration of the Roman alphabet in 1989. It is spoken by 62% of the population; the use of other languages (Russian, Gagauz) is safeguarded by the Constitution.

SOCIAL STATISTICS

2007: births, 37,973; deaths, 43,050. Rates, 2007 (per 1,000 population): births, 10·6; deaths, 12·0. In 2004 the most popular age range at first marriage was 20–24 for both males and females. Life expectancy at birth in 2007 was 65·0 years for males and 72·6 years for females. Annual population growth rate, 2000–05, –0·2%. Infant mortality, 2005, 14 per 1,000 live births; fertility rate, 2004, 1·2 births per woman (one of the lowest rates in the world). In 2004, 27% of the population were classified as living in absolute poverty, down from 73% in 1999.

CLIMATE

The climate is temperate, with warm summers, crisp, sunny autumns and cold winters with snow. Chişinău, Jan. –7°C, July 20°C. Annual rainfall 677 mm.

CONSTITUTION AND GOVERNMENT

A declaration of republican sovereignty was adopted in June 1990 and in Aug. 1991 the republic declared itself independent. A new constitution came into effect on 27 Aug. 1994, which defines Moldova as an 'independent, democratic and unitary state'. At a referendum on 6 March 1994 turnout was 75·1%; 95·4% of votes cast favoured 'an independent Moldova within its 1990 borders'. The referendum (and the Feb. parliamentary elections) were not held by the authorities in Transnistria. In a further referendum on 4 June 1999, on whether to switch from a parliamentary system to a presidential one, turnout was 58% with the majority of the votes cast being in favour of the change.

Parliament (*Parlamentul*) has 101 seats and is elected for four-year terms. There is a 4% threshold for election; votes falling below this are redistributed to successful parties. The *President* is now elected for four-year terms by parliament, after the constitution had been amended to abolish direct presidential elections.

The 1994 constitution makes provision for the autonomy of Transnistria and the Gagauz (Gagauzi Yeri) region. Work began in July 2003 on the drafting of a new constitution to resolve the conflict between Moldova and Transnistria.

Transnistria. In the predominantly Russian-speaking areas of Transnistria a self-styled 'Dniester Republic' was established in Sept. 1991, and approved by a local referendum in Dec. 1991. A Russo-Moldovan agreement of 21 July 1992 provided for a special statute for Transnistria and a guarantee of self-determination should Moldova unite with Romania. The population at the 2004 census was 555,347. Romanian here is still written in the Cyrillic alphabet. At a referendum on 24 Dec. 1995, 81% of votes cast were in favour of adopting a new constitution proclaiming independence.

On 17 June 1996 the Moldovan government granted Transnistria a special status as 'a state-territorial formation in the form of a republic within Moldova's internationally recognized border'.

At elections to the Supreme Council held on 11 Dec. 2005, which were not internationally recognized as legitimate, the Renovation Party and its allies won 29 of 43 seats and the Republic Party 13. In a referendum held on 17 Sept. 2006, 97·2% of votes cast were in favour of independence and possible future union with Russia, although no international organization or foreign country recognized the referendum. Elections for president were held on 10 Dec. 2006. Turnout was 66·1%. Igor Smirnov (b. 1941) was re-elected for a fourth five-year term against three opponents, winning 82·4% of votes cast.

Gagauz Yeri. This was created an autonomous territorial unit by Moldovan legislation of 13 Jan. 1995. In 2004 the census population was 155,646. There is a 35-member *Popular Assembly* directly elected for four-year terms and headed by a *Governor*, who is a member of the Moldovan cabinet. At the elections of 16 and 30 March 2008 turnout was 60·5%.

Governor: Mihail Formuzal; b. 1959.

National Anthem

The Romanian anthem was replaced in 1994 by a traditional tune, 'Lîmbă noastră' ('Our Tongue'); words by Alexei Mateevici, tune by Alexandru Cristi.

RECENT ELECTIONS

On 10 Nov. 2009 the only presidential candidate, Marian Lupu, failed to obtain the requisite 61 votes from parliament to be elected after the communist opposition walked out before the ballot was held. Lupu was also rejected in a second round of voting on 7 Dec.

In April 2009 the ruling Party of Communists of the Republic of Moldova (PCRM) were returned to power in disputed elections but, having failed to elect a new president, snap parliamentary elections were called for 29 July 2009. The PCRM won 48 seats with 44·7% of the vote (down from 61 seats at the elections in April 2009), the Liberal Democratic Party of Moldova 18 with 16·5%, the Liberal Party 15 with 14·6%, the Democratic Party 13 with 12·5% and the Party Alliance Our Moldova 7 with 7·3%. Turnout was 58·8%. The latter four parties agreed to form a coalition in Aug. 2009, taking power from the PCRM.

CURRENT ADMINISTRATION

In March 2010 the government comprised:

President (acting): Mihai Ghimpu; b. 1951 (Liberal Party; since 11 Sept. 2009).

Prime Minister: Vladimir Filat; b. 1969 (Liberal Democratic Party of Moldova; since 25 Sept. 2009).

Deputy Prime Ministers: Iurie Leancă (also *Minister of Foreign Affairs and European Integration*); Valeriu Lazăr (also *Minister of the Economy*); Ion Negrei; Victor Osipov.

Minister of Agriculture and Food Industries: Valeriu Cosarciuc. *Construction and Regional Development*: Marcel Răducan. *Culture*: Boris Focşa. *Defence*: Vitalie Marinuta. *Education*: Leonid Bujor. *Environment*: Gheorghe Şalaru. *Finance*: Veaceslav Negruţă. *Health*: Dr Vladimir Hotineanu. *Information Technologies and Communications*: Alexandru Oleinic. *Internal Affairs*: Victor Catan. *Justice*: Alexandru Tănase. *Labour, Social Protection and Family*: Valentina Buliga. *Transport and Road Infrastructure*: Anatol Şalaru. *Youth and Sports*: Ion Cebanu.

Government Website: http://www.gov.md

CURRENT LEADERS

Mihai Ghimpu

Position

Acting President

Introduction

Mihai Ghimpu was appointed acting president in Sept. 2009 by the newly-installed pro-Western coalition government. A leading figure in the former Soviet Republic's independence movement, he once supported unification with Romania.

Early Life

Mihai Ghimpu was born in Coloniţa, Chişinău county, in the Moldavian SSR on 19 Nov. 1951. He attended secondary school in Chişinău, followed by military service in the Soviet army. He graduated in law in 1978 from Moldova State University and became a legal adviser to various state enterprises. In the era of *glasnost* ('openness'), Ghimpu became a leading figure in the democratic movement. He co-founded the Popular Front of Moldova (FPM) in May 1989 with a manifesto calling for independence and for Moldovan (with a Romanized script) to be the official language.

In 1990 Ghimpu won a seat for the FPM in Moldova's Supreme Soviet. With 27% of elected members the party broke the Communist monopoly. Independence followed on 27 Aug. 1991. The FPM subsequently suffered from internal disputes and support for a proposed union with Romania dwindled. Ghimpu switched allegiance to the Congress of Intellectuals ahead of Moldova's first multiparty elections in Feb. 1994, winning a seat in parliament. However, he failed to be returned at the 1998 election, when he stood for the Party of Reform.

Ghimpu subsequently rebranded the Party of Reform as the Liberal Party (PL) and became its chairman. In 2007 he was elected to the Chişinău city council, where his nephew was mayor. He played a key role in opposing the ruling Party of Communists of the Republic of Moldova (PCRM) in the run-up to the April 2009 parliamentary election and was re-elected to parliament, where the Communists held a narrow majority. Accusations of electoral fraud led to clashes between demonstrators and police in Chişinău, leaving three dead and 300 injured. In a re-run election on 29 July 2009 a four-party pro-Western coalition (including the PL) won 53 of the 101 available seats. Ghimpu was elected speaker in Aug. 2009 and, following the resignation of the PCRM-backed President Voronin on 11 Sept., he was appointed as his acting successor.

Career in Office

Ghimpu's caretaker tenure stretched into 2010 following the governing coalition's failure to secure the three-fifths majority required to elect a successor to Voronin. In Oct. 2009 Ghimpu said that EU accession was a long-term goal but that his priority was to rescue the ailing economy. He blamed mismanagement and corruption by the Communist Party for the deficit of €500m. A 'substantial assistance package' was promised by the European Commission once an agreement has been signed with the IMF.

DEFENCE

Conscription is for 12 months (three months for higher education graduates). In 2006 military expenditure totalled US$10m. (US$2 per capita), representing 0·3% of GDP.

Russian troops remained in Transnistria after Moldova gained independence, but in Nov. 1999 the Organization for Security and Co-operation in Europe (OSCE) passed a resolution at its summit requiring Russia to withdraw its troops to Russia by Dec. 2002, unconditionally and under international observation. This deadline was extended to Dec. 2003 but around 1,200 troops remained in the region in 2009.

Army
Personnel, 2007, 5,150 (3,479 conscripts). There is also a paramilitary Interior Ministry force of 2,379, riot police numbering 900 and combined forces reserves of 66,000.

Air Force
Personnel (including air defence), 2007, 850.

INTERNATIONAL RELATIONS
Moldova is a member of the UN, World Bank, IMF and several other UN specialized agencies, WTO, Council of Europe, OSCE, CEI, BSEC, Danube Commission, CIS, IOM, International Organization of the Francophonie and NATO Partnership for Peace.

ECONOMY
Agriculture accounted for 18·1% of GDP in 2006, industry 15·1% and services 66·8%.

Overview
Despite poor performance through most of the 1990s, Moldova has recovered since 2000, with real GDP growth averaging 6·6% per year since 2001. In spite of economic shocks (such as a 200% price increase for imported natural gas and a Russian ban on wine imports in 2006), growth has remained robust in recent years and was expected to accelerate in 2008.

Growth in recent years has been consumption-led and driven by workers' remittances, an issue which the government is seeking to address through structural reforms aimed at an improved investment climate and more efficient management of public resources. Inflation is high for the region, standing at over 13%. Other areas of concern include high rural poverty (which has increased since 2003), reliance on energy imports and continued large-scale emigration by the economically active population.

Currency
A new unit of currency, the *leu* (MDL), replaced the rouble in Nov. 1993. Inflation was 12·7% in 2008, down from a peak of 2,198% in the early 1990s. Foreign exchange reserves were US$506m. in July 2005. Total money supply in June 2005 was 6,523m. lei.

Budget
Budgetary central government revenue and expenditure in 1m. lei (years ending 31 Dec.):

	2005	*2006*	*2007*
Revenue	7,941	9,823	14,059
Expenditure	7,031	9,121	12,164

Principal sources of revenue in 2007 were: taxes 10,900m. lei; grants, 967m. lei. Main items of expenditure by economic type in 2007: grants, 4,597m. lei; compensation of employees, 2,634m. lei; subsidies, 1,262m. lei.

VAT is 20%.

Performance
Moldova's economy has been in dire straits although until the global economic downturn of 2009 it was making a strong recovery. Economic growth was negative in 1998 at –6·5% and again in 1999, at –3·4%. However, more recently there has been growth of 3·0% in 2007 and 7·2% in 2008.

In 2002 the level of GDP was estimated to be only 38% of that in 1989. Total GDP was US$6·0bn. in 2008 (excluding Transnistria). The private sector accounts for over 50% of official GDP. Moldova ranks among the countries most reliant on remittances from abroad, which accounted for 36·5% of total GDP in 2007.

Banking and Finance
The central bank and bank of issue is the National Bank (*Governor*, Dorin Drăguţanu). At June 2002 there were 21 commercial banks and one savings bank. There is a stock exchange in Chişinău.

ENERGY AND NATURAL RESOURCES

Environment
Moldova's carbon dioxide emissions from the consumption and flaring of fossil fuels in 2008 were the equivalent of 1·7 tonnes per capita.

Electricity
Installed capacity in 2004 was estimated at 1·0m. kW. Production was 3·62bn. kWh in 2004; consumption per capita in 2004 was 1,554 kWh.

Minerals
There are deposits of lignite, phosphorites, gypsum and building materials.

Agriculture
There were 387,400 people employed in agriculture in 2008. Land under cultivation in 2008 was 2·5m. ha., of which 0·3m. ha. was accounted for by private subsidiary agriculture and 668,600 ha. by farms. In 2008 there were 1·82m. ha. of arable land and 303,000 ha. of permanent crops. The agricultural and food sector accounts for 38% of Moldova's total exports.

Output of main agricultural products (in 1,000 tonnes) in 2008: maize, 1,479; wheat, 1,286; sugar beets, 961; grapes, 636; sunflower seeds, 372; barley, 353; potatoes, 271.

Livestock (2008): 853,000 sheep and goats, 299,000 pigs, 232,000 cattle, 17m. chickens.

Livestock products, 2008 (in 1,000 tonnes): milk, 542; meat, 78; eggs, 541m. units.

Forestry
In 2005 forests covered 329,000 ha., or 10·0% of the total land area. Timber production in 2007 was 188,000 cu. metres.

Fisheries
The catch in 2005 (exclusively freshwater fish) was 531 tonnes.

INDUSTRY
There are canning plants, wine-making plants, woodworking and metallurgical factories, a factory of ferro-concrete building materials, footwear, dairy products and textile plants. Manufacturing accounted for 14·8% of GDP in 2007. Production (in tonnes): crude steel (2004), 1,011,000; cement (2004), 440,000; flour (2007), 113,300; canned fruit and vegetables (2007), 94,000; granulated sugar (2007), 74,000; footwear (2007), 3·8m. pairs; 5·0bn. cigars and cigarettes (2007); wine (2004), 302·6m. litres.

Labour
In 2007 the labour force totalled 1,314,000. A total of 1,247,000 persons were in employment in 2007, including 409,000 engaged in agriculture, hunting, forestry and fisheries, 250,000 in public administration, education, heath and social work, 198,000 in wholesale and retail trade/hotels and restaurants and 128,000 in manufacturing. In 2007 the unemployment rate was 5·1%.

INTERNATIONAL TRADE
Foreign debt was US$2,053m. in 2005.

Imports and Exports
Imports and exports for calendar years in US$1m.:

	2002	*2003*	*2004*	*2005*	*2006*
Imports f.o.b.	1,037·5	1,428·1	1,748·2	2,296·1	2,644·4
Exports f.o.b.	659·7	805·1	994·1	1,104·6	1,053·0

Chief import sources in 2006 were: Ukraine, 19·2%; Russia, 15·5%; Romania, 12·8%; Germany, 7·9%. Main export markets in 2006 were: Russia, 17·3%; Romania, 14·8%; Ukraine, 12·2%; Italy, 11·1%.

Moldova's leading imports are mineral products and fuel, machinery and equipment, chemicals and textiles. The main export commodity is wine, ahead of tobacco. Fruit and vegetables, textiles and footwear, and machinery are also significant exports.

COMMUNICATIONS

Roads

There were 9,343 km of public roads in 2009 (94·3% hard surfaced). Registered passenger cars (including taxis) in 2008 numbered 366,351, there were 115,967 goods vehicles and 21,491 buses and minibuses. In 2005 there were 2,289 road accidents resulting in 391 deaths.

Rail

Total length in 2005 was 1,026 km of 1,520 mm gauge. Passenger-km travelled in 2005 came to 355m. and freight tonne-km to 2,980m.

Civil Aviation

The main Moldovan-based airline is Air Moldova, which had flights in 2003 to Amman, Amsterdam, Athens, Bucharest, İstanbul, Larnaca, Moscow, Paris, Prague, Rome and Vienna. In 2000 the airport at Chişinău handled 254,234 passengers (all on international flights) and 2,159 tonnes of freight. In 2003 scheduled airline traffic of Moldovan-based carriers flew 5m. km, carrying 179,000 passengers (all on international flights).

Shipping

In 2008, 0·11m. passengers and 0·20m. tonnes of freight were carried on inland waterways.

Telecommunications

There were 2,962,700 telephone subscribers in total in 2007 (781·0 per 1,000 persons). There were 1,882,800 mobile phone subscribers in 2007—up from 338,200 in 2002—and 700,000 internet users.

Privatization of the state-owned telecommunications company, Moldtelecom, is a priority for the government. A majority stake offer from MGTS, Moscow's main telephone company, failed in Nov. 2002.

Postal Services

In 2003 there were 1,270 post offices.

SOCIAL INSTITUTIONS

Justice

A total of 24,362 crimes were recorded in 2007. The population in penal institutions in Sept. 2007 was 8,130 (227 per 100,000 of national population). The death penalty was abolished for all crimes in 1995.

Education

In 2007 there were 103,811 children and 10,517 teaching staff in pre-schools; 160,528 pupils and 9,876 teaching staff in primary schools; and 367,636 pupils and 30,376 teaching staff in secondary schools. There were 148,449 students (8,570 academic staff) in tertiary education in 2007. In 2006 there were 16 public and 15 private higher education institutions. Adult literacy rate in 2003 was 96·2% (male, 97·5%; female, 95·0%).

In 2007 public expenditure on education came to 7·3% of GNI and represented 19·8% of total government expenditure.

Health

In 2007 there were 83 hospitals with 21,892 beds, a provision of 61 per 10,000 inhabitants. In 2007 there were 12,733 physicians (11% private sector), 1,566 dentists, 20,868 nurses and 2,834 pharmacists (2006).

Welfare

There were 469,600 age pensioners and 169,800 other pensioners in 2008.

RELIGION

Religious affiliation in 2001: Romanian Orthodox, 1·26m.; Russian (Moldovan) Orthodox, 342,000.

CULTURE

World Heritage Sites

Moldova has one site on the UNESCO World Heritage List: the Struve Geodetic Arc (inscribed in 2005). The Arc is a chain of survey triangulations spanning from Norway to the Black Sea that helped establish the exact shape and size of the earth and is shared as a UNESCO site with nine other countries.

Broadcasting

Teleradio Moldova (formerly Radioteleviziunea Nationala) is the state-owned national broadcaster operating the Moldova One television channel, Radio Moldova and an external service (Radio Moldova International). In 2003 around 20 radio stations and 30 television stations operated commercially. Romanian and Russian channels are also broadcast. There were 1·3m. television receivers in 2006 (colour by SECAM D/K).

Press

In 2005 there were seven daily newspapers and 120 non-dailies with a combined circulation of 988,000.

Tourism

In 2005 there were 23,000 non-resident tourists, spending US$163m.

DIPLOMATIC REPRESENTATIVES

Of Moldova in the United Kingdom (5 Dolphin Sq., Edensor Rd, Chiswick, London, W4 2ST)
Ambassador: Natalia Solcan.

Of the United Kingdom in Moldova (18 Nicolae Iorga St., Chişinău MD-2012)
Ambassador: Keith Shannon.

Of Moldova in the USA (2101 S St., NW, Washington, D.C., 20008)
Ambassador: Vacant.
Chargé d'Affaires a.i.: Andrei Galbur.

Of the USA in Moldova (103 Strada Alexei Matveevici, Chişinău)
Ambassador: Dr Asif J. Chaudhry.

Of Moldova to the United Nations
Ambassador: Alexandru Cujba.

Of Moldova to the European Union
Ambassador: Daniela Cujba.

FURTHER READING

Gribincea, M., *Agricultural Collectivization in Moldavia.* 1996
King, C., *Post-Soviet Moldova: A Borderland in Transition.* 1997.—*The Moldovans: Romania, Russia, and the Politics of Culture.* 2000
Kolsto, Pal, *National Integration and Violent Conflict in Post-Soviet Societies: The Cases of Estonia and Moldova.* 2002
Mitrasca, M., *Moldova: A Romanian Province Under Russian Rule: Diplomatic History from the Archives of the Great Powers.* 2002

National Statistical Office: National Bureau of Statistics of Moldova, MD-2019, Chişinău mun., 106 Grenoble St.
Website: http://www.statistica.md

MONACO

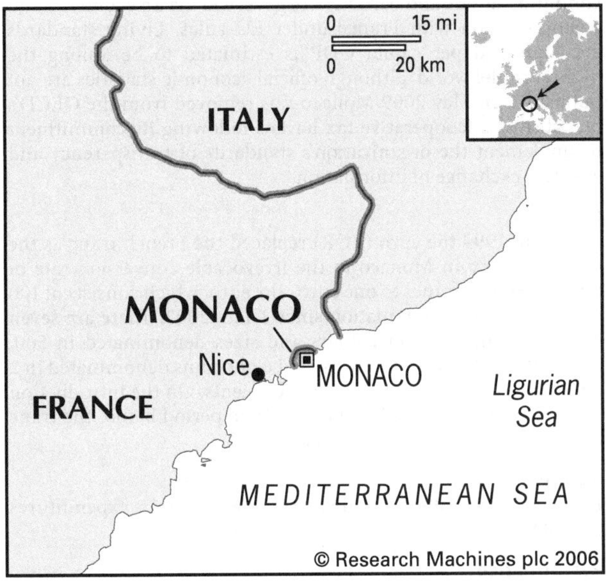

Principauté de Monaco
(Principality of Monaco)

Capital: Monaco
Population, 2008: 31,000
GDP per capita: not available
GNI per capita, 2007: US$183,151

KEY HISTORICAL EVENTS

Monaco's natural harbour was settled by Phoenicians, Greeks and Ligurians and later by Saracens. A fortress, built where the palace now stands, was captured by the Grimaldi family of Genoa in 1297. It was passed on through the male line until 1731, when control of Monaco passed to Louise Hippolyte, daughter of Antoine I and wife of Jacques de Goyon Matignon, who took the name of Grimaldi. The Principality was placed under the protection of the Kingdom of Sardinia by the Treaty of Vienna in 1815, and under that of France in 1861. A constitution, signed in 1911, was the first move away from an absolute monarchy. Prince Rainier III succeeded his grandfather, Louis II, in 1949 and ruled the Principality until his death on 6 April 2005.

TERRITORY AND POPULATION

Monaco is bounded in the south by the Mediterranean and elsewhere by France (Department of Alpes Maritimes). The area is 197 ha. (1·97 sq. km). The Principality is divided into four districts: Monaco-Ville, la Condamine, Monte-Carlo and Fontvieille. Population (2008 census), 31,109; there were 6,687 Monegasques (22%), 8,785 French (28%) and 5,778 Italian (19%).

The official language is French.

SOCIAL STATISTICS

2004: births, 825; deaths, 525; marriages, 171; divorces, 82. Rates per 1,000 population, 2000: birth, 23·7; death, 17·1; marriage, 5·0; divorce, 2·6. Annual population growth rate, 2000–04, 0·9%; fertility rate, 2004, 1·9 births per woman. Infant mortality per 1,000 live births (2005), 3.

CLIMATE

A Mediterranean climate, with mild moist winters and hot dry summers. Monaco, Jan. 50°F (10°C), July 74°F (23·3°C). Annual rainfall 30" (758 mm).

CONSTITUTION AND GOVERNMENT

On 17 Dec. 1962 a new constitution was promulgated which maintains the hereditary monarchy.

The reigning Prince is **Albert II**, b. 14 March 1958, son of Prince Rainier III, 1923–2005, and Grace Kelly, 1929–1982. Prince Albert succeeded his father Rainier III, who died on 6 April 2005.

Sisters of the Prince. Princess Caroline Louise Marguerite, b. 23 Jan. 1957; married Philippe Junot on 28 June 1978, divorced 9 Oct. 1980; married Stefano Casiraghi on 29 Dec. 1983 (died 3 Oct. 1990); married Prince Ernst of Hanover on 23 Jan 1999. *Offspring:* Andrea, b. 8 June 1984; Charlotte, b. 3 Aug. 1986; Pierre, b. 7 Sept. 1987; Alexandra, b. 20 July 1999. Princess Stéphanie Marie Elisabeth, b. 1 Feb. 1965, married Daniel Ducruet on 1 July 1995, divorced 4 Oct. 1996; married Adans López Peres on 12 Sept. 2003; separated 2004. *Offspring:* Louis, b. 27 Nov. 1992; Pauline, b. 4 May 1994; Camille, b. 15 July 1998.

Prince Rainier III renounced the principle of divine right. Executive power is exercised jointly by the Prince and a five-member *Council of government*, headed by a Minister of State (a French citizen). A 24-member *National Council* is elected for five-year terms.

The constitution can be modified only with the approval of the National Council. Laws of 1992, 2003 and 2005 permit Monegasque women to give their nationality to their children.

National Anthem

'Principauté Monaco ma patrie' ('Principality of Monaco my fatherland'); words by T. Bellando de Castro, tune by C. Albrecht.

RECENT ELECTIONS

In parliamentary elections held on 3 Feb. 2008 the ruling Union for Monaco won 21 of 24 seats against 3 for the Rally and Issues for Monaco. Turnout was 76·9%.

CURRENT ADMINISTRATION

Chief of State: Prince Albert II.

In March 2010 the cabinet comprised:

Minister of State: Michel Roger; b. 1949 (sworn in 29 March 2010).

Minister of Equipment, Environmental Affairs and Town Planning: Gilles Tonelli. *External Relations, Economic Affairs and International Finance:* Franck Biancheri. *Finance and Economics:* Sophie Thévenoux. *Interior:* Paul Masseron. *Social Affairs and Health:* Stéphane Valeri.

President of the National Council: Jean-François Robillon.

Government Website: http://www.monaco.gouv.mc

CURRENT LEADERS

Albert II

Position
Prince

Introduction
Albert II became ruler of Monaco on 6 April 2005 following the death of his father, Prince Rainier III, who had ruled the principality for 56 years. Albert II has maintained the status quo, upholding the low-tax regime that has made Monaco a haven for the super-rich.

Early Life

Albert Alexandre Louis Pierre Grimaldi was born in Monaco on 14 March 1958, the second child and only son of Prince Rainier III and Grace Kelly, a US cinema actress. He attended the Lycée Albert Ier, then the principality's sole secondary school, where he developed a passion for sport. Having received his baccalaureate diploma in 1976, Albert enrolled the following year at Amherst College in Massachusetts, USA, and graduated with a degree in political science in 1981. From Sept. 1981–April 1982 he served in the French Navy as a sub-lieutenant on the aircraft carrier *Jeanne d'Arc*. On 14 Sept. 1982 his mother was killed in a car crash in the mountains near Monaco. Subsequently, he became vice-president of the Princess Grace-USA Foundation, which grants scholarships to talented young musicians, actors and dancers. In the same year he also became president of the Monaco Red Cross.

During the mid-1980s Albert undertook work experience at an investment bank and an international law firm in New York, as well as the French luxury goods group, Moet-Hennessy, in Paris. Back in Monaco he chaired the principality's prestigious Yacht Club, the International Television Festival and Monaco's Athletic Federation. Albert also became increasingly involved in the Olympic movement, both as an administrator (as a member of the International Olympic Committee in 1985 and president of Monaco's Olympic Committee in 1993) and competitor (in the principality's bobsleigh team at four Winter Olympics between 1988 and 2002).

During the 1990s he began to increase his involvement in the day-to-day administration of Monaco. In 1997 he organized the 700th anniversary celebrations of the Grimaldi family's control over the principality. He also assisted his father and the government in preparing reports that strongly denied allegations by French parliamentarians in 2000 that Monaco's lax policies had facilitated money laundering.

Long described in the press as the world's 'most eligible bachelor', Albert's unmarried status became a matter of political concern, casting doubt on the succession of the Grimaldi family and the independence of the principality. A change to the constitution was formulated in April 2002, however, allowing the throne to continue through the female line. On 31 March 2005 the Palace of Monaco announced that Albert would take over the duties of his father as Regent, after Prince Rainier III, who had been admitted to hospital, was no longer able to rule. Following the death of his father on 6 April 2005, he became Sovereign Prince of Monaco, and was enthroned on 12 July.

Career in Office

In his first public statement as Prince Albert II, he said that the death of his father, who had governed for 56 years, had left the people of the principality feeling orphaned and united in a profound sense of loss. He did not make reference to the future direction of policy, but analysts expected him to retain the famously low-tax regime and continue to develop tourism, as well as nurturing Monaco's precision engineering, fish canning, banking and pharmaceutical industries. He was also expected to rule in a more consensual style than his father.

INTERNATIONAL RELATIONS

Monegasque relations with France are based on conventions of 1963. French citizens are treated as if in France. Monaco is a member of the UN, Council of Europe, OSCE, International Organization of the Francophonie and Antarctic Treaty.

ECONOMY

Overview

A tiny economy with sparse natural resources, Monaco is primarily geared towards tourism, finance and commerce. Tourism provides one of the main sources of income thanks to the climate and Monte Carlo's famed gambling casino opened in 1856. The economy is a major banking centre attracting many foreign companies drawn by its low corporate taxes and has thrived as a tax haven for individuals and businesses.

Although not a member of the EU, it is closely associated with its economic structures. Customs, postal services, telecommunications and banking are governed via an economic and customs union with France under EU rules. Living standards are high and per capita GDP is estimated to be among the highest in the world, although official economic statistics are not published. In May 2009 Monaco was removed from the OECD's blacklist of uncooperative tax havens following its commitment to implement the organization's standards of transparency and effective exchange of information.

Currency

On 1 Jan. 1999 the euro (EUR) replaced the French franc as the legal currency in Monaco at the irrevocable conversion rate of 6·55957 French francs to one euro. The euro, which consists of 100 cents, has been in circulation since 1 Jan. 2002. There are seven euro notes in different colours and sizes denominated in 500, 200, 100, 50, 20, 10 and 5 euros, and eight coins denominated in 2 and 1 euros, then 50, 20, 10, 5, 2 and 1 cents. On the introduction of the euro there was a 'dual circulation' period before the franc ceased to be legal tender on 17 Feb. 2002.

Budget

Revenues in 2004 totalled €636·18m. and expenditures €694·84m.

Performance

Monaco does not publish annual income information. However, the principality's turnover increased from €9,194·42m. in 2003 to €9,815·20m. in 2004, a growth rate of 6·75%.

Banking and Finance

There were 43 banks in 2004 of which 19 were Monegasque banks.

ENERGY AND NATURAL RESOURCES

Electricity

Electricity is imported from France. 503 GWh were supplied to 24,178 customers in 2004. In 2001 output capacity was 83 MW.

Oil and Gas

In 2004, 61 GWh of gas were supplied to 3,935 customers; output capacity was 21 MW.

Water

Total consumption (2004), 5·38m. cu. metres.

INDUSTRY

The main industry is tourism. There is some production of cosmetics, pharmaceuticals, glassware, electrical goods and precision instruments.

Labour

There were 42,637 persons employed in Jan. 2004. 38,773 worked in the private sector; 3,864 in the public sector. 26,017 French citizens worked in Monaco in 2004.

INTERNATIONAL TRADE

Imports and Exports

There is a customs union with France. Imports for 2004 totalled €512m.; exports, €528m. Main imports: pharmaceuticals, perfume, clothing, paper, synthetic and non-metallic products, and building materials.

COMMUNICATIONS

Roads

There were 77 km of roads in 2007. In 2004 there were 33,275 vehicles. Monaco has the densest network of roads of any country in the world. In 2004, 5,141,964 people travelled by bus.

Rail
The 1·7 km of main line passing through the country are operated by the French National Railways (SNCF). In 2004, 3,953,859 people arrived at or departed from Monaco railway station.

Civil Aviation
There are helicopter flights to Nice with Heli Air Monaco and Heli Inter. Helicopter movements (2004) at the Heliport of Monaco (Fontvieille), 37,521; the number of passengers carried was 112,379. The nearest airport is at Nice in France.

Shipping
In 2004 there were 3,829 vessels registered, of which 12 were over 100 tonnes. 2,636 yachts put in to the port of Monaco and 1,193 at Fontvieille in 2004. 178 liners put in to port in Monaco; 10,581 people embarked, 10,195 disembarked and 104,202 were in transit.

Telecommunications
In 2004 there were 33,400 land-based telephone lines and 16,261 mobile phone subscribers. Internet users numbered 22,000 in 2008.

Postal Services
24·19m. items were posted and 27·59m. items were delivered by the Post Office in 2004.

SOCIAL INSTITUTIONS

Justice
There are the following courts: *Tribunal Suprème*, *Cour de Révision*, *Cour d'Appel*, a Correctional Tribunal, a Work Tribunal, a Tribunal of the First Instance, two Arbitration Commissions for Rents (one commercial, one domestic), courts for Work-related Accidents and Supervision, a *Juge de Paix*, and a Police Tribunal. There is no death penalty.

Police
In 2004 the police force (Sûreté Publique) comprised 516 personnel. Monaco has one of the highest number of police per head of population of any country in the world.

Education
In 2004, in the public sector, there were six pre-school institutions (*écoles maternelles*) with 750 pupils; four elementary schools with 1,367 pupils; two secondary schools with 2,359 pupils. There were 277 primary teachers and 150 secondary school teachers in total in 2004. In the private sector there were two pre-schools and three primary schools with 179 and 481 pupils respectively; and one secondary school with 700 pupils. In 2005 the government allocated 5·2% of its total budget to education.

The University of Southern Europe in Monaco had 250 students in 2004.

Health
In 2005 the government allocated 6·4% of its total budget to public health. There were 191 doctors and 19 dentists in 2004 and 19 childcare nurses in 2002. There were 503 hospital beds in 2002. Monaco has the highest provision of hospital beds of any country: in 2002 there were 162 per 10,000 population.

RELIGION
90% of the resident population are Roman Catholic. There is a Roman Catholic archbishop.

CULTURE

Broadcasting
The Radio Monte Carlo networks broadcast in French and Italian. Monte Carlo Doualiya is an Arabic-speaking station operated by Radio France Internationale. Riviera Radio is a private English-language station. Télé Monte-Carlo (TMC) broadcasts programmes in French, Italian and English (colour by SECAM H). There are also cable services. There were 25,500 television receivers in 2006.

Press
Monaco had one newspaper in 2004 with a circulation of 8,000, equivalent to 247 per 1,000 inhabitants. There was one weekly magazine in 2004, one monthly newspaper, two monthly magazines, one bimonthly magazine and two quarterly magazines.

Tourism
In 2004, 250,159 foreign visitors spent a total of 695,265 nights in Monaco. The main visitors are Italians, followed by French and Americans. 58,521 people attended 389 congresses in 2004. There are three casinos run by the state, including the one at Monte Carlo attracting 0·4m. visitors a year.

DIPLOMATIC REPRESENTATIVES
British Consul-General (resident in France): Vacant.
British Honorary Consul: Eric G. F. Blair.

Consul-General for Monaco in London: Evelyne Genta (7 Upper Grosvenor St., London, W1K 2LX).

Of Monaco in the USA (2314 Wyoming Ave., NW, Washington, D.C., 20008)
Ambassador: Gilles Noghès.

Of Monaco to the United Nations
Ambassador: Isabelle Picco.

Of Monaco to the European Union
Ambassador: José Badia.

FURTHER READING
Journal de Monaco. Bulletin Officiel. 1858 ff.

MONGOLIA

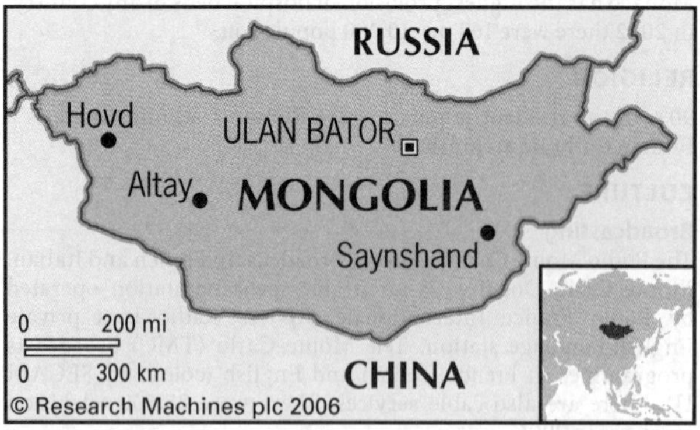

Mongol Uls

Capital: Ulan Bator
Population estimate, 2010: 2·70m.
GDP per capita, 2007: (PPP$) 3,236
HDI/world rank: 0·727/115

KEY HISTORICAL EVENTS

Temujin became khan of Hamag Mongolia in 1190. Having united by conquest various Tatar and Mongolian tribes he was confirmed as 'Universal' ('Genghis', 'Chingiz') khan in 1206. The expansionist impulse of his nomadic empire (Beijing captured in 1215; Samarkand in 1220) continued after his death in 1227. Tamurlaine (died 1405) was the last of the conquering khans. In 1368 the Chinese drove the Mongols from Beijing, and for the next two centuries Sino-Mongolian relations alternated between war and trade. In 1691 Outer Mongolia accepted Manchu rule. The head of the Lamaist faith became the symbol of national identity, and his seat ('Urga', now Ulan Bator) was made the Mongolian capital. When the Manchu dynasty was overthrown in 1911 Outer Mongolia declared its independence under its spiritual ruler and turned to Russia for support against China. Soviet and Mongolian revolutionary forces set up a provisional government in March 1921. On the death of the spiritual ruler a people's republic and new constitution were proclaimed in May 1924. With Soviet help Japanese invaders were fended off during the Second World War. The Mongols then took part in the successful Soviet campaign against Inner Mongolia and Manchuria. On 5 Jan. 1946 China recognized the independence of Outer Mongolia. Until 1990 sole power was in the hands of the (Communist) Mongolian People's Revolutionary Party (MPRP), but an opposition Mongolian Democratic Party, founded in Dec. 1989, achieved tacit recognition and held its first congress in Feb. 1990. Following demonstrations and hunger-strikes, on 12 March the entire MPRP Politburo resigned and political opposition was legalized.

TERRITORY AND POPULATION

Mongolia is bounded in the north by the Russian Federation, and in the east and south and west by China. Area, 1,565,008 sq. km (604,250 sq. miles). Population (2000 census), 2,373,493 (1,195,512 females). Density, 2000, 1·5 per sq. km. In 2005, 56·7% of the population were urban.

The UN gives an estimated population for 2010 of 2·70m.

The population is predominantly made up of Mongolian peoples (81·5% Khalkh). There is a Turkic Kazakh minority (4·3% of the population) and 20 Mongol minorities. The official language is Khalkh Mongol.

The republic is administratively divided into four municipalities (*hot*)—Ulan Bator, the capital (2000 population, 760,077), Darhan-Uul (83,271 in 2000), Orhon (71,525 in 2000) and Govisumber (12,230 in 2000)—and 18 provinces *(aimag)*. The provinces are sub-divided into 334 districts or counties *(suums)*.

SOCIAL STATISTICS

Births, 2005, 45,326; deaths, 16,480. 2001 rates: birth, 17·8 per 1,000 population; death, 6·5 per 1,000; marriage, 5·9 per 1,000; divorce, 0·6 per 1,000. Annual population growth rate, 2000–05, 1·3%. Infant mortality rate, 2005, 39 per 1,000 live births. Expectation of life in 2007 was 63·0 years for males and 69·6 for females. Fertility rate, 2004, 2·4 births per woman.

CLIMATE

A very extreme climate, with six months of mean temperatures below freezing, but much higher temperatures occur for a month or two in summer. Rainfall is very low and limited to the months from mid-May to mid-Sept. Ulan Bator, Jan. –14°F (–25·6°C), July 61°F (16·1°C). Annual rainfall 8" (208 mm).

CONSTITUTION AND GOVERNMENT

The constitution of 12 Feb. 1992 abolished the 'People's Democracy', introduced democratic institutions and a market economy and guarantees freedom of speech.

The *President* is directly elected for renewable four-year terms.

Since June 1992 the legislature has consisted of a single-chamber 76-seat parliament, the *Great Hural (Ulsyn Ich-Chural)*, which elects the Prime Minister.

National Anthem

'Darkhan manai khuvsgalt uls' ('Our sacred revolutionary country'); words by Tsendiyn Damdinsüren, tune by Bilegin Damdinsüren and Luvsanjamts Murjorj.

RECENT ELECTIONS

At the parliamentary elections of 29 June 2008 turnout was 74·3%. Preliminary results declared that the Mongolian People's Revolutionary Party (MPRP) gained 47 of the 76 available seats, the Motherland Democracy (EOA, comprising the Democratic Party and two smaller parties—the Civic Will Republican Party and the Mongol Democratic New Socialist Party) 26 seats. Three seats went to independents. However, the Democratic Party (DP) refused to accept the results and protests leading to violence followed. After consultations between the main parties and recounts in some constituencies the MPRP had 44 seats, EOA 27 and independents one with the remaining seats still to be declared.

In presidential elections on 24 May 2009 former prime minister Tsakhiagiin Elbegdorj (Democratic Party) won with 51·2% of the vote against incumbent Nambaryn Enkhbayar (Mongolian People's Revolutionary Party) with 47·4%. Turnout was 73·5%.

CURRENT ADMINISTRATION

President: Tsakhiagiin Elbegdorj; b. 1963 (Democratic Party; sworn in 18 June 2009).

In March 2010 the MPRP-DP coalition government comprised:

Prime Minister: Sukhbaataryn Batbold, b. 1963 (Mongolian People's Revolutionary Party; sworn in 29 Oct. 2009).

First Deputy Prime Minister: Norovyn Altankhuyag.

Deputy Prime Minister: Miyegombo Enkhbold.

Minister of Defence: Luvsanvandan Bold. *Education, Culture and Science:* Yondon Otgonbayar. *Environment and Tourism:* Luimed Gansukh. *Finance:* Sangajav Bayartsogt. *Food, Agriculture and Light Industry:* Tunjin Badamjunai. *Foreign Affairs:* Gombojav Zandanshatar. *Health:* Sanbuu Lambaa. *Justice and the Interior:* Tsendiin Nyamdorj. *Mineral Resources and Energy:* Dashdorj Zorigt. *Roads, Transportation, Construction and Urban Development:* Khaltmaa Battulga. *Social Welfare and Labour:* Tugsjargal Gandi. *Chief of the Cabinet Secretariat:* Chimed Khurelbaatar.

Office of the President: http://www.president.mn

CURRENT LEADERS

Tsakhiagiin Elbegdorj

Position
President

Introduction
Tsakhiagiin Elbegdorj took office on 18 June 2009, becoming the first president not to have been a member of the Mongolian People's Revolutionary Party (MPRP). Campaigning on a platform of change and anti-corruption that appealed to urban voters, he won the election with over 51% of the vote on 24 May 2009, beating MPRP candidate and incumbent president Nambaryn Enkhbayar.

Early Life
Elbegdorj was born on 30 March 1963 in the district of Zereg. In 1988 he graduated in military journalism from the Military Political Institute in the Ukraine (then part of the USSR). He went on to attain his master's degree in public administration from Harvard University.

Elbegdorj played an active role in the in the fight against communism and in 1989 co-established the Mongolian Democratic Union. On 10 Dec. 1989 he opened the first pro-democracy demonstration, marking the birth of a recognized democracy movement. The following year he founded Mongolia's first independent newspaper, *Democracy*. A few months later he was elected to government and was a key figure in drafting a new constitution, adopted in Jan. 1992. In 1996, as leader of the Democratic Party (DP), Elbegdorj led the Democratic Union Coalition to victory in parliamentary elections, paving the way for the country's first peaceful power transition.

Elbegdorj was elected prime minister in April 1998 but a banking scandal forced his resignation shortly afterwards. After the 2004 elections he was again appointed to the premiership, heading a fragile MPRP-DP coalition. During his tenure, he announced a 'Plan of Action' to boost tourism, reorganized domestic political structures, loosened control of the news media and saw English replace Russian as Mongolia's second language. In Jan. 2006 he was forced to resign when the MPRP withdrew from the coalition, sparking public demonstrations in Ulan Bator.

At elections in May 2009 Elbegdorj won by a narrow margin over the incumbent president, Nambaryn Enkhbayar. The MPRP's acceptance of the result produced a peaceful outcome after fears of a repeat of the violence that followed the DP's claims of fraud at the 2008 parliamentary elections.

Career in Office
Elbegdorj faces the challenge of working with a parliament dominated by the MPRP. He must also strive to tackle high levels of corruption and unemployment. He aims to spread the profits of Mongolia's mineral wealth more widely. On the foreign stage, he is expected to cultivate Western ties to counterbalance the influence of Russia and China.

Sukhbaataryn Batbold

Position
Prime Minister

Introduction
Sukhbaataryn Batbold became prime minister in Oct. 2009 after his predecessor, Sanj Bayar, resigned because of ill health. Batbold's appointment was approved with 62 of 66 votes cast in a plenary session of the Great Hural. His initial tenure is scheduled to last until parliamentary elections in 2012.

Early Life
Batbold was born in 1963 in Ulan Bator. He was educated at the University of Moscow, graduating from its School of International Relations in 1986. He joined the ministry of economic foreign relations and was appointed head of the Mongol Impex Cooperative in 1988. After returning to higher education, he graduated from the London School of Business in 1991. In 1992 he joined Altai Trading LLC as its director general, a post he held until 2000.

He was appointed deputy minister of foreign affairs after the return to power of the Mongolian People's Revolutionary Party (MPRP) in 2000. From 2004–06 he served as minister of trade and industry and in 2008 was named minister of foreign affairs. During his tenure he hosted UN Secretary General Ban Ki-moon's visit to Ulan Bator to discuss climate change in Mongolia and stood in for Bayar at a Council of Heads of State meeting of the Shanghai Cooperation Organisation.

On 26 Oct. 2009 parliament accepted Bayar's resignation and Batbold was immediately nominated by the MPRP as his successor. His appointment was approved on 29 Oct. 2009.

Career in Office
Batbold's government undertook a review of strategies to take advantage of Mongolia's largely untapped natural resources without falling prey to 'Dutch Disease', where a sudden surge of wealth hampers long term growth. He is also keen to loosen economic reliance on Russia and China by developing relationships with the USA and Canada, while at the same time ensuring Mongolia does not alienate her powerful neighbours.

DEFENCE

Conscription is for one year for males aged 18–25 years. Defence expenditure in 2006 totalled US$19m. (US$7 per capita), representing 0·8% of GDP.

Army
Strength (2007) 7,500 (3,300 conscripts). There is a border guard of 6,000, 1,200 internal security troops and 300 Construction Troops.

Air Force
The Air Force had a strength of 800 in 2007 with 11 attack helicopters and nine aircraft.

INTERNATIONAL RELATIONS

Mongolia is a member of the UN, World Bank, IMF and several other UN specialized agencies, WTO, IOM, Asian Development Bank and Colombo Plan.

ECONOMY

In 2006 agriculture accounted for 21·9% of GDP, industry 42·3% and services 35·9%.

Overview
Traditionally a nomadic pastoral economy, substantial progress has been made in the past decade towards a private sector-led open economy. The country is rich in mineral resources, especially copper and gold. Growth has averaged 9% per year since 2004, driven initially by developments in the mining sector but spreading to other sectors including construction and financial

services. Strong growth has reduced Mongolia's vulnerability to extreme weather shocks and changes in terms of trade. Medium-term growth prospects are positive, with plans to exploit large untapped mineral resources, while the economy continues to benefit from low debt and healthy international reserves. However, inflation, resulting from heavy government spending and higher prices for imported oil and food, threaten short-term growth and macroeconomic stability.

Currency

The unit of currency is the *tugrik* (MNT) of 100 *möngö*. The tugrik was made convertible in 1993. In March 2005 foreign exchange reserves were US$276m. and gold reserves totalled 112,000 troy oz. Total money supply was 222,085m. tugriks in Dec. 2004. Inflation, which reached a high of 268% in 1993, was just 0·9% in 2002, although it rose to 26·8% in 2008.

Budget

In 2006 revenues were 1,360·4bn. tugriks and expenditures 1,237·0bn. tugriks; taxes accounted for 83·0% of revenue and economic services 26·1% of expenditure.

VAT was reduced from 15% to 10% as of 1 Jan. 2007.

Performance

Real GDP growth was 10·2% in 2007 and 8·9% in 2008. Total GDP in 2008 was US$5·3bn.

Banking and Finance

The Mongolian Bank (established 1924) is the bank of issue, being also a commercial, savings and development bank: the *Governor* is Lhanaasuren Purevdorj. It has 21 main branches. There were 25 other banks in 2002. The largest bank is the state-owned Trade and Development Bank.

A stock exchange opened in Ulan Bator in 1992.

ENERGY AND NATURAL RESOURCES

Environment

In 2008 carbon dioxide emissions from the consumption and flaring of fossil fuels in Mongolia were the equivalent of 2·4 tonnes per capita.

Electricity

Installed capacity was 0·8m. kW in 2004. There are six thermal electric power stations. Production, 2004, 3·30bn. kWh; consumption per capita in 2004 was 1,260 kWh.

Minerals

There are large deposits of copper, gold, nickel, zinc, molybdenum, phosphorites, tin, wolfram and fluorspar; production of the latter in 2005, 367,000 tonnes. There are major coalmines near Ulan Bator and Darhan. In 2004 lignite production was 5·75m. tonnes; coal production, 1·12m. tonnes. Copper production, 2003, 130,270 tonnes; gold production, 2003, 11,119 kg.

Agriculture

The prevailing Mongolian style of life is pastoral nomadism. Livestock production comprises 79·5% of the total agricultural production. In 2003 there were 10·8m. sheep, 2·0m. horses, 1·8m. cattle and 257,000 camels. The number of goats rose from 5·5m. to 10·7m. between 1992 and 2003 as production of cashmere has increased along with the market economy. In late 1999 and early 2000 approximately 3m. animals died as a result of extreme weather and overgrazing, and in late 2000 and early 2001 more than 1·3m. animals died.

In 2007 there were around 851,000 ha. of arable land and 2,000 ha. of permanent crop land. In 2003 output of major crops was 165,000 tonnes of wheat (down from 607,000 in the period 1989–91) and 79,000 tonnes of potatoes (down from 128,000 in 1989–91). Vegetables produced in 2003 included (in tonnes): turnips, 25,000; cabbage, 15,000; carrots, 10,000. Livestock products, 2003 (in 1,000 tonnes): milk, 292; meat, 153. There were 48 tractors and seven harvester-threshers per 10,000 ha. of arable land in 2006.

Forestry

Forests, chiefly larch, cedar, fir and birch, occupied 10·25m. ha. in 2005 (6·5% of the land area). Timber production was 791,000 cu. metres in 2007.

Fisheries

The catch in 2005 was 366 tonnes, entirely from inland waters.

INDUSTRY

Industry is still small in scale and local in character. The food industry accounts for 25% of industrial production. The main industrial centre is Ulan Bator; others are at Darhan and Erdenet. Production figures: cement (2002), 148,000 tonnes; lime (2002), 41,000 tonnes; bread (2003), 22,000 tonnes; carpets (2003), 663,000 sq. metres; sawnwood (2002), 300,000 cu. metres.

Labour

Out of 870,800 people in employment in Dec. 2002, 381,400 were engaged in agriculture, hunting, fishing and forestry; 104,500 in wholesale and retail trade/repair of motor vehicles, motorcycles and personal and household goods; 59,300 in education; and 55,600 in manufacturing. In July 2003 there were 37,300 registered unemployed persons.

Trade Unions

Most union members are affiliated with the Confederation of Mongolian Trade Unions, although some belong to the Association of Free Trade Unions. They had a combined 430,000 members in 1999.

INTERNATIONAL TRADE

Mongolia is dependent on foreign aid. Total foreign assistance to Mongolia exceeds US$300m. annually. Japan is the largest bilateral donor. Foreign debt was US$1,327m. in 2005.

Imports and Exports

In 2006 imports (f.o.b.) were valued at US$1,356·7m. and exports (f.o.b.) at US$1,545·2m. Main exports, 2006: copper concentrate, 42·7%; gold, 18·1%; refined copper, 7·2%. Principal import suppliers in 2006: Russia, 36·9%; China, 27·2%; Japan, 6·6%; South Korea, 5·6%. Main export markets, 2006: China, 67·8%; Canada, 11·1%; USA, 7·7%; Russia, 2·9%.

COMMUNICATIONS

Roads

The total road network covered 49,250 km in 2002, including 11,121 km of highway. There are 1,185 km of surfaced roads running around Ulan Bator, from Ulan Bator to Darhan, at points on the frontier with the Russian Federation and towards the south. Truck services run where there are no surfaced roads. Vehicles in use in 2007 included 110,200 passenger cars and 37,300 lorries and vans. In 2003 passenger transport totalled 557m. passenger-km and freight 242m. tonne-km. In 2007 there were 562 fatalities as a result of road accidents.

Rail

The Trans-Mongolian Railway (1,815 km of 1,520 mm gauge in 2005) connects Ulan Bator with the Russian Federation and China. There are spur lines to Erdenet and to the coalmines at Nalayh and Sharyn Gol. A separate line connects Choybalsan in the east with Borzaya on the Trans-Siberian Railway. Passenger-km travelled in 2004 came to 1,228m. and freight tonne-km to 11,700m.

Civil Aviation

MIAT-Mongolian Airlines operates internal services, and in 2003 flew from Ulan Bator to Beijing, Berlin, Frankfurt, Hohhot, Irkutsk, Moscow, Seoul and Tokyo. In 2003 scheduled airline traffic of Mongolian-based carriers flew 9m. km, carrying 289,000 passengers (139,000 on international flights). In 2001 Ulan Bator handled 285,399 passengers and 2,660 tonnes of freight.

Shipping

There is a steamer service on the Selenge River and a tug and barge service on Hövsgöl Lake. 1,800 tonnes of freight were carried in 2003.

Telecommunications

In 2008 there were 200,500 main (fixed) telephone lines; mobile phone subscribers numbered 1,763,200 in 2008 (66·8 per 100 persons). There were 360,100 PCs in use in 2006 and 330,000 internet users in 2008.

Postal Services

There were 385 post offices in 2003.

SOCIAL INSTITUTIONS

Justice

The Procurator-General is appointed, and the Supreme Court elected, by parliament for five years. There are also courts at province, town and district level. Lay assessors sit with professional judges. The death penalty is in force and was reportedly used in 2008, although not in 2009.

The population in penal institutions in 2006 was 6,593 (244 per 100,000 of national population).

Education

Adult literacy was 97·8% in 2003 (male, 98·0%; female, 97·5%). Schooling begins at the age of seven. In 2007 there were 94,702 children in pre-primary education and 3,262 teaching staff; 239,262 pupils and 7,572 teaching staff in primary education; and 328,009 pupils and 16,605 teaching staff in secondary schools. There were 142,411 students in tertiary education in 2007 and 8,754 academic staff. In 2003 there were eight state and three private universities, and 38 public and 134 private institutes and colleges.

In 2007 public expenditure on education came to 5·2% of GNI.

Health

In 2003 there were 385 state hospitals with the equivalent of 73 beds per 10,000 inhabitants. There were 6,823 physicians, 469 dentists, 612 midwives and 7,802 nurses in 2002.

RELIGION

Tibetan Buddhist Lamaism is the prevalent religion; the Dalai Lama is its spiritual head. In 1995 there were about 100 monasteries and 2,500 monks.

CULTURE

World Heritage Sites

Mongolia has two sites (one shared) on the UNESCO World Heritage List: the Orkhon Valley Cultural Landscape (inscribed on the list in 2004), an extensive area on both banks of the Orkhon River including the archaeological remains of Kharkhorum, the 13th and 14th century capital of Genghis Khan's vast Empire. The second site falls under joint Mongolian and Russian jurisdiction: Uvs Nuur Basin (2003), an important saline lake system supporting a rich wildlife, especially the snow leopard and Asiatic ibex.

Broadcasting

MNB (Mongolian National Broadcaster) is the national public-service television provider. UBS TV is also publicly financed through the Ulan Bator municipal authority. Mongolian Radio is the national public radio broadcaster. There are also private TV and radio stations, together with cable and satellite services. Number of TV sets (2006): 189,240 (colour by SECAM D).

Press

In 2003 there were five daily newspapers, including Onoodor (10,000 regular subscribers) and Udriin Sonin (Daily News), and two English-language weeklies, the UB Post and the government's Mongol Messenger.

Tourism

In 2005 there were 338,000 non-resident tourists; spending by tourists totalled US$223m.

DIPLOMATIC REPRESENTATIVES

Of Mongolia in the United Kingdom (7 Kensington Ct, London, W8 5DL)
Ambassador: Bulgaa Altangerel.

Of the United Kingdom in Mongolia (30 Enkh Taivny Gudamzh, Bayanzurkh District, Ulan Bator 13381)
Ambassador: Bill Dickson.

Of Mongolia in the USA (2833 M St., NW, Washington, D.C., 20007)
Ambassador: Behkbat Khasbazar.

Of the USA in Mongolia (Micro Region 11, Big Ring Rd, Ulan Bator)
Ambassador: Mark C. Minton.

Of Mongolia to the United Nations
Ambassador: Enkhtsetseg Ochir.

Of Mongolia to the European Union
Ambassador: Avirmed Battur.

FURTHER READING

State Statistical Office: *Mongolian Economy and Society in [year]: Statistical Yearbook.— National Economy of the MPR, 1924–1984: Anniversary Statistical Collection.* Ulan Bator, 1984

Akiner, S. (ed.) *Mongolia Today.* 1992
Becker, J., *The Lost Country.* 1992
Bruun, O. and Odgaard, O. (eds.) *Mongolia in Transition.* 1996
Griffin, K. (ed.) *Poverty and the Transition to a Market Economy in Mongolia.* 1995
Hanson, Jennifer L., *Mongolia.* 2003
Rossabi, Morris, *Modern Mongolia: From Khans to Commissars to Capitalists.* 2005

National Statistical Office: Government Building-III, Bagatoiruu-44, Ulan Bator-11.

MONTENEGRO

Republika Crna Gora
(Republic of Montenegro)

Capital: Podgorica
Population estimate, 2010: 626,000
GDP per capita, 2007: (PPP$) 11,699
HDI/world rank: 0·834/65

KEY HISTORICAL EVENTS

Montenegro emerged as a separate entity on the break-up of the Serbian Empire in 1355. Owing to its mountainous terrain, it was never effectively subdued by Turkey. It was ruled by Bishop Princes until 1851, when a royal house was founded. The Treaty of Berlin (1828) recognized the independence of Montenegro and doubled the size of the territory.

The assassination of Archduke Franz Ferdinand of Austria in Sarajevo on 28 June 1914 precipitated the First World War. In the winter of 1915–16 the Serbian army was forced to retreat to Corfu, where the government aimed at a centralized, Serb-run state. But exiles from Croatia and Slovenia wanted a South Slav federation. This was accepted by the victorious Allies as the basis for the new state. The Croats were forced by the pressure of events to join Serbia and Montenegro on 1 Dec. 1918. From 1918–29 the country was known as the Kingdom of the Serbs, Croats and Slovenes. The remains of King Nicholas I, who was deposed in 1918, were returned to Montenegro for reburial in Oct. 1989.

A constitution of 1921 established an assembly but the trappings of parliamentarianism could not bridge the gulf between Serbs and Croats. The Croat peasant leader Radić was assassinated in 1928; his successor, Vlatko Maček, set up a separatist assembly in Zagreb. On 6 Jan. 1929 the king suspended the constitution and established a royal dictatorship, redrawing provincial boundaries without regard for ethnicity. In Oct. 1934 he was murdered by a Croat extremist while on an official visit to France.

During the regency of Prince Paul, the government pursued a pro-fascist line. On 25 March 1941 Paul was persuaded to adhere to the Axis Tripartite Pact. On 27 March he was overthrown by military officers in favour of the boy king Peter. Germany invaded on 6 April. Within ten days Yugoslavia surrendered; king and government fled to London. Resistance was led by a royalist group and the communist-dominated partisans of Josip Broz, nicknamed Tito. Having succeeded in liberating Yugoslavia, Tito set up a Soviet-type constitution but he was too independent for Stalin, who sought to topple him. However, Tito made a *rapprochement* with the west and it was the Soviet Union under Khrushchev that had to extend the olive branch in 1956. Yugoslavia was permitted to evolve its 'own road to socialism'. Collectivization of agriculture was abandoned; and Yugoslavia became a champion of international 'non-alignment'. A collective presidency came into being with the death of Tito in 1980.

Dissensions in Kosovo between Albanians and Serbs, and in parts of Croatia between Serbs and Croats, reached crisis point after 1988. On 25 June 1991 Croatia and Slovenia declared independence. Fighting began in Croatia between Croatian forces and Serb irregulars from Serb-majority areas of Croatia. On 25 Sept. the UN Security Council imposed a mandatory arms embargo on Yugoslavia. A three-month moratorium agreed at EU peace talks on 30 June having expired, both Slovenia and Croatia declared their independence from the Yugoslav federation on 8 Oct. After 13 ceasefires had failed, a fourteenth was signed on 23 Nov. under UN auspices. A Security Council resolution of 27 Nov. proposed the deployment of a UN peacekeeping force if the ceasefire was kept. Fighting, however, continued. On 15 Jan. 1992 the EU recognized Croatia and Slovenia as independent states. Bosnia and Herzegovina was recognized on 7 April 1992 and Macedonia on 8 April 1993. A UN delegation began monitoring the ceasefire on 17 Jan. and the UN Security Council on 21 Feb. voted to send a 14,000-strong peacekeeping force to Croatia and Yugoslavia. On 27 April 1992 Serbia and Montenegro created a new federal republic of Yugoslavia.

On 30 May, responding to further Serbian military activities in Bosnia and Croatia, the UN Security Council voted to impose sanctions. In mid-1992 NATO committed air, sea and eventually land forces to enforce sanctions and protect humanitarian relief operations in Bosnia. At a joint UN-EC peace conference on Yugoslavia held in London on 26–27 Aug. some 30 countries and all the former republics of Yugoslavia endorsed a plan to end the fighting in Croatia and Bosnia, install UN supervision of heavy weapons, recognize the borders of Bosnia and Herzegovina and return refugees. At a further conference at Geneva on 30 Sept. the Croatian and Yugoslav presidents agreed to make efforts to bring about a peaceful solution in Bosnia, but fighting continued. Following the Bosnian-Croatian-Yugoslav (Dayton) agreement all UN sanctions were lifted in Nov. 1995.

In July 1997 Slobodan Milošević switched his power base to become president of federal Yugoslavia. The former Yugoslav foreign minister, Milan Milutinović, succeeded Milošević as Serbian President. Meanwhile, in Montenegro, the pro-western Milo Đukanović succeeded a pro-Milošević president.

Following the break-up of Yugoslavia, in March 1998 a coalition government was formed between the Socialist Party of Slobodan Milošević and the ultra-nationalist Serb Radical Party.

Kosovo

In 1998 unrest in Kosovo, with its largely Albanian population, led to a bid for outright independence. Violence flared resulting in what a US official described as 'horrendous human rights violations', including massive shelling of civilians and destruction of villages. A US-mediated agreement to allow negotiations to proceed during an interim period of autonomy allowed for food and medicine to be delivered to refugees; American support for a degree of autonomy (short of independence), accepted in principle by President Milošević, lifted the immediate threat of NATO air strikes. Further outbreaks of violence in early 1999 were followed by the departure of the 800-strong team of international 'verifiers' of the fragile peace. Peace talks in Paris broke down without a settlement though subsequently Albanian freedom fighters accepted terms allowing them broad autonomy. The sticking point on the Serbian side was the international insistence on having 28,000 NATO-led peacemakers in Kosovo to keep apart the warring factions. Meanwhile, the scale of Serbian repression in Kosovo persuaded the NATO allies to take direct action. On the night of 24 March 1999 NATO aircraft began a bombing campaign against Yugoslavian military targets. Further Serbian provocation in Kosovo caused hundreds of thousands of ethnic Albanians to seek refuge in neighbouring countries. On 9 June after 78 days of air attacks NATO and Yugoslavia signed an accord on the Serb withdrawal from Kosovo, and on 11 June NATO's peacekeeping force, KFOR, entered Kosovo.

When the general election held on 24 Sept. 2000 resulted in a victory for the opposition democratic leader Vojislav Koštunica, President Milošević demanded a second round of voting. A strike by miners at the Kolubara coal mine on 29 Sept. was followed by a mass demonstration in Belgrade on 5 Oct. when the parliament building was set on fire and on 6 Oct. Slobodan Milošević accepted defeat. He was arrested on 1 April 2001 after a 30-hour confrontation with the authorities. On 28 June he was handed over to the United Nations War Crimes Tribunal in the Hague to face charges of crimes against humanity. Prime Minister Zoran Žižić resigned the next day. On 12 Feb. 2002 the trial of Slobodan Milošević, on charges of genocide and war crimes in the Balkans over a period of nearly ten years, began at the International Criminal Tribunal in The Hague. Milošević defended himself and questioned the legitimacy of the court but died in March 2006 before his trial had ended.

On 14 March 2002 Montenegro and Serbia agreed to remain part of a single entity called Serbia and Montenegro, thus relegating the name Yugoslavia to history. The agreement was ratified in principle by the federal parliament and the republican parliaments of Serbia and Montenegro on 9 April 2002. The new union came into force on 4 Feb. 2003. Most powers in this loose confederation were divided between the two republics. After 4 Feb. 2006 Serbia and Montenegro had the right to vote for independence. Following a referendum held on 21 May 2006, Montenegro declared independence on 3 June and was recognized as such by Serbia on 15 June. Montenegro became the 192nd member state of the United Nations on 28 June 2006.

TERRITORY AND POPULATION

Montenegro is a mountainous country which opens to the Adriatic in the southwest. It is bounded in the west by Croatia, northwest by Bosnia and Herzegovina, in the northeast by Serbia and in the southeast by Albania. The capital is Podgorica (population, 2003, 136,473), although some capital functions have been transferred to Cetinje, the historic capital of the former kingdom of Montenegro. Its area is 13,812 sq. km. Population at the 2003 census was 620,145 (314,920 females), of which the predominating ethnic groups were Montenegrins (267,669), Serbs (198,414) and Albanians (31,163). Estimate, 1 Jan. 2007, 626,188. Population density per sq. km (2003), 44·9.

The UN gives an estimated population for 2010 of 626,000.

The official language is the Serbian language of the Iekavian dialect. The Roman and Cyrillic alphabets have equal status.

SOCIAL STATISTICS

Statistics for calendar years:

	Live births	*Deaths*	*Marriages*	*Divorces*
2001	8,839	5,431	3,893	492
2002	8,499	5,513	3,794	506
2003	8,344	5,704	4,050	494
2004	7,849	5,707	3,440	505

Life expectancy, 2007, 71·6 years for men and 76·5 years for women. Infant mortality per 1,000 births (2005), 9.

CLIMATE

Mostly a central European type of climate, with cold winters and hot summers. Podgorica, Jan. 2·8°C, July 26·5°C. Annual rainfall 1,499 mm.

CONSTITUTION AND GOVERNMENT

The *President* is elected by direct vote to serve a five-year term. There is an 81-member single-chamber *National Assembly*, elected through a party list proportional representation system to serve four-year terms. The *Prime Minister* is nominated by the President and has to be approved by the National Assembly.

A referendum was held on 29 Feb.–1 March 1992 to determine whether Montenegro should remain within a common state, Yugoslavia, as a sovereign republic. The electorate was 412,000, of whom 66% were in favour. The then president, Milo Đukanović, had pledged a referendum on independence in May 2002, but this was postponed with the announcement of the creation of the new entity of Serbia and Montenegro, which came into being on 4 Feb. 2003.

Montenegro held a referendum on 21 May 2006 in which 55·5% voted for independence. The margin required for victory was 55·0%. Turnout was 86·6%.

RECENT ELECTIONS

In presidential elections held on 6 April 2008 incumbent president Filip Vujanović won 51·9% of the vote against Andrija Mandić with 19·5% and Nebojša Medojević with 16·6%. Turnout was 68·2%.

Milo Đukanović was elected prime minister by Parliament on 29 Feb. 2008 by 41 votes to none, with thirty abstentions.

Parliamentary elections were held on 29 March 2009. The ruling Coalition for European Montenegro (consisting of the Democratic Party of Socialists of Montenegro/DPS CG, the Social Democratic Party of Montenegro, the Croatian Civic Initiative and the Bosniak Party) won 48 of 81 seats (51·9% of votes cast), the Socialist People's Party 16 (16·8%), New Serb Democracy 8 (9·2%), the Movement for Change 5 (6·0%), New Democratic Power 1 (1·9%), the Democratic Union of Albanians 1 (1·5%), the Albanian List 1 (0·9%) and the Albanian Coalition-Perspective 1 (0·8%). Turnout was 66·2%.

CURRENT ADMINISTRATION

President: Filip Vujanović; b. 1954 (DPS CG; sworn in 22 May 2003 and re-elected in April 2008).

In March 2010 the coalition cabinet comprised:

Prime Minister: Milo Đukanović; b. 1962 (DPS CG; sworn in 29 Feb. 2008 having previously been prime minister from Feb. 1991–Feb. 1998 and Jan. 2003–Nov. 2006).

Deputy Prime Minister and Minister in Charge of Economic Policy, the Financial System and an Information Society: Vujica Lazović. *Deputy Prime Minister and Minister in Charge of International Economic Co-operation and Structural Reform:* Igor Lukšić. *Deputy Prime Minister and Minister in Charge of the Political System, Internal and External Affairs:* Svetozar Marović.

Minister of Agriculture, Forestry and Water Management: Milutin Simović. *Culture, Sports and Media:* Branislav Mićunović.

Defence: Boro Vučinić. *Economy:* Branko Vujović. *Education and Science:* Sreten Škuletić. *European Integration:* Gordana Đurović. *Foreign Affairs:* Milan Roćen. *Health:* Miodrag Bobo Radunović. *Human and Minority Rights:* Ferhat Dinoša. *Interior and Public Administration:* Ivan Brajović. *Justice:* Miraš Radović. *Labour and Social Welfare:* Suad Numanović. *Maritime Affairs, Transport and Telecommunications:* Andrija Lompar. *Spatial Planning and Environmental Protection:* Branimir Gvozdenović. *Tourism:* Predrag Nenezić. *Ministers without Portfolio:* Rafet Husović; Slovoljub Stijepović.

Government Website: http://www.montenegro.yu

CURRENT LEADERS

Filip Vujanović

Position
President

Introduction
Filip Vujanović became Montenegro's president following independence in June 2006. He had served as president of Montenegro within the confederation of Serbia and Montenegro for the previous three years. Economic and structural reforms have included a programme of privatization, while closer links have been pursued with the European Union including the presentation in Dec. 2008 of an official application for EU membership.

Early Life
Born on 1 Sept. 1954 in Belgrade, then the capital of Yugoslavia, Filip Vujanović was educated in Nikšić and studied law at the University of Belgrade. After graduating in 1978 he worked at a municipal court and then as an official at the Belgrade District Court. In 1981 he moved south to Podgorica.

Following a period as secretary to the Podgorica district court, Vujanović worked as an attorney from 1981–93. Following the break-up of the Yugoslav Federation, Serbia and Montenegro formed the Federal Republic of Yugoslavia in 1992. In March 1993 the Montenegrin Prime Minister Đukanović appointed Vujanović as minister for justice. He served for two years, becoming a close ally of Đukanović, who adopted a pro-independence and pro-European stance. In May 1995 Vujanović took over as minister of the interior. When the ruling Democratic Party of Socialists (DPS CG) split into two factions in 1996, Vujanović backed Đukanović against his rival Momir Bulatović, a former ally of Serbian leader Slobodan Milošević.

In 1997 Đukanović was elected president of Montenegro and in Feb. 1998 Vujanović took up the premiership. While supporting Montenegro's independence campaign, he continued to maintain good relations with Serbia. He offered his resignation in April 2002 during a constitutional crisis over ratification of a looser federation between Serbia and Montenegro.

Following legislative elections in Oct. 2002 Vujanović was appointed parliamentary speaker and stood as the DPS CG candidate for Montenegro's presidency. He won the first round with 86% of the vote in Dec. 2002 and a second round with 81% in Feb. 2003 but the result was declared invalid as less than 50% of the electorate voted. Parliament subsequently abolished the minimum turnout rule and Vujanović became president in March 2003 with 63% of the vote.

Career in Office
Vujanović identified Montenegro's accession to the EU and entry into NATO's Partnership for Peace programme as priorities. To these ends, he oversaw the privatization of key parts of the economy, including the banking sector and Kombinat Aluminijuma Podgorica, the country's largest industrial company. He also introduced social and judicial reforms and made a start in combating organized crime. A long-time advocate of cross-border co-operation, he opened talks on joint commercial ventures with neighbouring states including Croatia, Slovenia and Serbia.

On 3 June 2006, following a referendum, Montenegro declared independence and on 28 June 2006 became a member of the United Nations. The country has since joined the World Bank and International Monetary Fund, and signed a stabilization and association agreement with the EU.

Vujanović was re-elected for a further five-year term in the presidential election of April 2008.

DEFENCE

The all-professional Military of Montenegro was formed from part of the Armed Forces of Serbia and Montenegro when the two countries became independent in 2006.

Defence expenditure in 2006 totalled US$54m. (US$80 per capita), representing 2·4% of GDP.

Army
Strength (2007) 2,500. There are paramilitary forces numbering around 10,100.

Navy
Strength (2007) 3,300 including 900 marines.

INTERNATIONAL RELATIONS

Montenegro is a member of the UN, World Bank, IMF and several other UN specialized agencies, Council of Europe, OSCE, CEI, IOM and NATO Partnership for Peace. In Dec. 2008 it applied to join the European Union.

ECONOMY

In 2006 agriculture accounted for 10·0% of GDP, industry 17·6% and services 72·4%.

Overview
An independent state since June 2006, the economy has experienced strong growth and expansion in recent years. Real GDP growth was over 10% in 2007, with the country's significant tourism potential bringing large inflows of FDI and generating strong construction activity. The contribution of tourism to GDP rose from 15% in 2004 to 21% in 2007.

While the potential growth outlook is strong, the economy shows signs of overheating, with inflationary pressures growing despite the adoption of the euro. Wages have increased rapidly, while the current account deficit has soared and is expected to continue to do so, driven by high investment and low savings. Given the limits of monetary policy following the adoption of the euro, the IMF recommends fiscal measures to stem overheating, ease credit growth and boost structural reforms to improve competitiveness.

Currency
On 2 Nov. 1999 the pro-Western government decided to make the Deutsche Mark legal tender alongside the dinar. Subsequently it was made the sole official currency, and consequently the euro (EUR) became the currency of Montenegro on 1 Jan. 2002. Inflation was 9·0% in 2008 (3·5% in 2007).

Budget
In 2004 total revenue was €77,568m. and total expenditure was €75,839m.

VAT is 17% (reduced rate, 7%).

Performance
Total GDP in 2008 was US$4·5bn. Real GDP growth was 10·7% in 2007 and 7·5% in 2008.

Banking and Finance
The Central Bank of Montenegro (*President of the Council*, Ljubisa Krgović) was established in Nov. 2000. Montenegro has 11 commercial banks.

ENERGY AND NATURAL RESOURCES

Electricity

Electricity production in 2006 was 2·95bn. kWh.

Minerals

Lignite production in 2006 totalled 1,502,000 tonnes; bauxite production was 659,370 tonnes.

Agriculture

In 2004 the cultivated area was 188,766 ha. Yields (2004, in 1,000 tonnes): potatoes, 117; grapes, 43; maize, 10; oranges and tangerines, 7; plums, 6; wheat, 3. Livestock (15 Jan. 2005, 1,000 head): poultry, 800; sheep, 254; cattle, 169; pigs, 27.

Forestry

Timber cut in 2007: 457,000 cu. metres.

INDUSTRY

Production (2006, in 1,000 tonnes): alumina, 237; steel bars, 137; bread, 24; steel ingots, 20; wheat flour, 17; cigarettes, 433m. units; beer, 51·7m. litres.

Labour

In 2004 there were 143,485 people employed, including 26,277 in manufacturing; 24,105 in wholesale and retail trade, repair of vehicles, personal and household goods; 14,146 in transport, storage and communications; 13,098 in education; 11,606 in health and social work; 9,563 in hotels and restaurants; and 9,337 in public administration and compulsory social security. In Oct. 2004 there were 49,266 employees and 31,328 self-employed persons. Average monthly salary in 2004 was €302·81. Unemployment was running at 27·7% in Oct. 2004.

COMMUNICATIONS

Roads

In 2004 there were 7,314 km of roads. Passenger-km in 2004 were 100·6m.; tonne-km of freight carried, 64·5m.

Rail

In 2004 there were 250 km of railway. 1,066,000 passengers and 1,006,000 tonnes of freight were carried in 2004.

SOCIAL INSTITUTIONS

Justice

There is a Supreme Court, two High Courts, 15 Municipal Courts, two Commercial Courts, one Appellate Court and one Administrative Court. In 2005 the Supreme Court had 14 judges, the High Courts 40, the Municipal Courts 147, the Commercial Courts 24, the Appellate Court 9 and the Administrative Court 8.

Education

In 2004–05 there were: 82 pre-schools with 11,761 pupils and 673 teachers; 457 primary schools with 74,205 pupils and 4,796 teachers; and 47 secondary schools with 32,078 pupils and 2,245 teachers. A total of 11,011 students were enrolled at the University of Montenegro at the beginning of the 2004–05 academic year.

Health

In 2005 there were eight general hospitals with 1,743 beds. A total of 54,332 patients were admitted in 2005.

RELIGION

The Serbian Orthodox Church is the official church in Montenegro. The Montenegrin church was banned in 1922, but in Oct. 1993 a breakaway Montenegrin church was set up under its own patriarch.

CULTURE

World Heritage Sites

There are two sites on the UNESCO World Heritage List: the Natural and Culturo-Historical Region of Kotor (inscribed on the list in 1979); and Durmitor National Park (1980 and 2005).

Broadcasting

State-funded TV Montenegro and Radio Montenegro operate across the public broadcasting networks. There are also commercial television and radio stations.

Cinema

In 2005 there were 20 cinemas with 7,000 seats, with attendances totalling 92,000.

Press

In 2006 there were four daily newspapers with a combined circulation of 55,000.

Tourism

There were 703,484 tourist arrivals in 2004, staying for a total of 4,561,094 nights. Domestic visitors accounted for 73% of the total.

Libraries

In 2004 there were 34 libraries (20 public and 14 professional and scientific). The public libraries had 893,000 books in 2004, with 1,914,000 in the professional and scientific libraries.

DIPLOMATIC REPRESENTATIVES

Of Montenegro in the United Kingdom (11 Callcott Pl., London, W8 7SU)
Ambassador: Dr Dragiša Burzan.

Of the United Kingdom in Montenegro (Ulcinjska 8, Gorica C, 81000 Podgorica)
Ambassador: Catherine Knight-Sands.

Of Montenegro in the USA (1610 New Hampshire Ave., Washington, D.C., 20009)
Ambassador: Miodrag Vlahović.

Of the USA in Montenegro (Ljubljanska bb, 81000 Podgorica)
Ambassador: Roderick W. Moore.

Of Montenegro to the United Nations
Ambassador: Nebojša Kaludjerović.

Of Montenegro to the European Union
Ambassador: Slavica Milačić.

FURTHER READING

Bieber, Florian, *Montenegro in Transition: Problems of Identity and Statehood.* 2003
Fleming, Thomas, *Montenegro: The Divided Land.* 2002
Roberts, Elizabeth, *Realm of the Black Mountain: A History of Montenegro.* 2007
Stevenson, Francis Seymour, *A History of Montenegro.* 2002
Treadway, J. D., *The Falcon and the Eagle: Montenegro and Austria-Hungary, 1908–1914.* 1998

National Statistical Office: Statistical Office of the Republic of Montenegro, IV Proleterske No. 2, 81000 Podgorica.
Website: http://www.monstat.org

MOROCCO

Mamlaka al-Maghrebia
(Kingdom of Morocco)

Capital: Rabat
Population estimate, 2010: 32·38m.
GDP per capita, 2007: (PPP$) 4,108
HDI/world rank: 0·654/130

KEY HISTORICAL EVENTS

The native people of Morocco are the Berbers, an ancient race who have suffered the attention of a succession of invaders. When the city of Carthage fell to Rome in the second century BC, the African Mediterranean coast was under Roman dominance for almost six hundred years. When the Roman Empire in turn fell into decline, the area was invaded first by the Vandals in AD 429 and later by Byzantium in AD 533. An Arab invasion of Morocco in AD 682 marked the end of Byzantium dominance and the first Arab rulers, the Idrisid dynasty, ruled for 150 years. Arab and Berber dynasties succeeded the Idrisids until the 13th century when the country was plunged into bitter civil war between Arab and Berber factions. The reign of Ahmed I al-Man-sur in the first Sharifian dynasty stabilized and unified the country between 1579 and 1603. Moors and Jews expelled from Spain settled in Morocco during this time and the country flourished. In 1415 the Moroccan port of Ceuta was captured by Portugal. Moroccan forces defeated the Portuguese in 1578 and by 1700 had regained control of many coastal towns which had previously been in Portuguese hands. During the 18th and early 19th centuries the Barbary Coast became the scene of widespread piracy.

As part of the *Entente Cordiale*, Britain recognized Morocco as a French sphere of influence and in 1904 Morocco was divided between France and Spain, with the former receiving the larger area. From 1912 to 1956 Morocco was divided into a French protectorate, a Spanish protectorate, and the international zone of Tangiers which was established by France, Great Britain and Spain in 1923. On 29 Oct. 1956 the international status of the Tangiers Zone was abolished and Morocco became a kingdom on 18 Aug. 1957, with the Sultan taking the title Mohammed V. Succeeding his father on 3 March 1961, King Hassan tried to combine the various parties in government and established an elected House of Representatives but political unrest led him to discard any attempt at a parliamentary government and to rule autocratically from 1965 to 1977. In 1977 a new Chamber of Representatives was elected and under the constitution Morocco became a constitutional monarchy with a single elected chamber.

TERRITORY AND POPULATION

Morocco is bounded by Algeria to the east and southeast, Mauritania to the south, the Atlantic Ocean to the northwest and the Mediterranean to the north. Excluding the Western Saharan territory claimed and retrieved since 1976 by Morocco, the area is 458,730 sq. km. The population at the 2004 census (including Western Sahara) was 29,891,708; density (including Western Sahara), 42·1 per sq. km. At the 2004 census Western Sahara had an area of 252,120 sq. km and a population of about 356,000. The Moroccan superficie is 710,850 sq. km. The population was 58·7% urban in 2005.

The UN gives an estimated population for 2010 of 32·38m.

Morocco has 16 states (*wilaya'at*) divided further into 71 prefectures and provincial units. Areas of the states and census populations in 2004:

State	*Area in sq. km*	*Population*
Chaouia-Ouardigha	16,760	1,655,660
Doukkala-Abda	13,285	1,984,039
Fès-Boulemane	19,795	1,573,055
Gharb-Chrarda-Béni Hssen	8,805	1,859,540
Grand Casablanca	1,615	3,631,061
Guelmin-Es Semara	71,970	462,410
Laâyoune-Boujdour-Sakia El Hamra[1]	—	256,152
Marrakesh-Tensift-Al Haouz	31,160	3,102,652
Meknès-Tafilalet	79,210	2,141,527
Oriental	82,820	1,918,094
Oued Eddahab-Lagouira[1]	—	99,367
Rabat-Salé-Zemmour-Zaer	9,580	2,366,494
Souss Massa-Draâ	70,880	3,113,653
Tadla-Azilal	17,125	1,450,519
Tangier-Tétouan	11,570	2,470,372
Taza-Al Hoceima-Taounate	24,155	1,807,113

[1]Laâyoune-Boujdour-Sakia El Hamra and Oued Eddahab-Lagouira correspond roughly to Western Sahara.

The chief cities (with populations in 1,000, 2004) are as follows:

Casablanca	2,934	Tangiers (Tanger)	670	Tétouan	321
Rabat	1,623	Meknès	536	Safi	285
Fès (Fez)	947	Oujda	401	Mohammedia	189
Marrakesh	823	Kénitra	359	Khouribga	166
Agadir	679			Béni Mellal	163

The official language is Arabic, spoken by 65% of the population. Berber languages, including Tachelhit (or Soussi), Tamazight and Tarafit (or Rifia), are spoken by about half the population. French (widely used for business), Spanish (in the north) and English are also spoken.

SOCIAL STATISTICS

2002 estimates: births, 632,000; deaths, 169,000. Estimated rates, 2002 (per 1,000 population): birth, 21·0; death, 5·6. Annual population growth rate, 2000–05, 1·0%. Life expectancy at birth in 2007 was 68·8 years for males and 73·3 years for females. Infant mortality, 2005, 36 per 1,000 live births; fertility rate, 2004, 2·7 births per woman.

CLIMATE

Morocco is dominated by the Mediterranean climate which is made temperate by the influence of the Atlantic Ocean in the northern and southern parts of the country. Central Morocco is continental while the south is desert. Rabat, Jan. 55°F (12·9°C), July 72°F (22·2°C). Annual rainfall 23" (564 mm). Agadir, Jan. 57°F (13·9°C), July 72°F (22·2°C). Annual rainfall 9" (224 mm). Casablanca, Jan. 54°F (12·2°C), July 72°F (22·2°C). Annual rainfall 16" (404 mm). Marrakesh, Jan. 52°F (11·1°C), July 84°F (28·9°C). Annual rainfall 10" (239 mm). Tangiers, Jan. 53°F (11·7°C), July 72°F (22·2°C). Annual rainfall 36" (897 mm).

CONSTITUTION AND GOVERNMENT

The ruling King is **Mohammed VI**, born on 21 Aug. 1963, married to Salma Bennani on 21 March 2002; succeeded on 23 July 1999, on the death of his father Hassan II, who reigned 1961–99. *Offspring:* Hassan, b. 8 May 2003; Khadija, b. 28 Feb. 2007. The King holds supreme civil and religious authority, the latter in his capacity of Emir-el-Muminin or Commander of the Faithful. He resides usually at Rabat, but occasionally in one of the other traditional capitals, Fès (founded in 808), Marrakesh (founded in 1062), or at Skhirat.

A new constitution was approved by referendum in March 1972 and amendments were approved by referendum in May 1980 and Sept. 1992. The Kingdom of Morocco is a constitutional monarchy. Parliament consists of a *Chamber of Representatives* composed of 325 deputies directly elected for five-year terms. For the Sept. 2002 elections a series of measures were introduced, including a new proportional representation voting system and a national list reserved for women candidates to ensure that at least 10% of new MPs are females.

A referendum on 13 Sept. 1996 established a second *Chamber of Counsellors,* composed of 270 members serving nine-year terms, of whom 162 are elected by local councils, 81 by chambers of commerce and 27 by trade unions. One third are renewed every three years. The Chamber of Counsellors has power to initiate legislation, issue warnings of censure to the government and ultimately to force the government's resignation by a two-thirds majority vote. The electorate was 12·3m. and turnout was 82·95%. The King, as sovereign head of state, appoints the Prime Minister and other Ministers, has the right to dissolve Parliament and approves legislation.

A new electoral code of March 1997 fixed voting at 20 and made enrolment on the electoral roll compulsory. In Dec. 2002 King Mohammed VI announced that the voting age was to be lowered from 20 to 18.

National Anthem

'Manbit al Ahrah, mashriq al anwar' ('Fountain of freedom, source of light'); words by Ali Squalli Houssaini, tune by Leo Morgan.

GOVERNMENT CHRONOLOGY

Kings since 1955.

1955–61	Mohammed V ibn Yusuf (sultan from 1955–57)
1961–99	Hassan II ibn Mohammed
1999–	Mohammed VI ibn al-Hasan

RECENT ELECTIONS

Elections to the Chamber of Representatives took place on 7 Sept. 2007. The Parti de l'Indépendance/Istiqlal (Independence Party) gained 52 seats (10·7% of the vote), the Islamist Parti de la Justice et du Développement (Party of Justice and Development) 46 (10·9%), Mouvement Populaire (MP/Popular Movement) 41 (9·3%), Rassemblement National des Indépendants (RNI/National Rally of Independents) 39 (9·7%), Union Socialiste des Forces Populaires (USFP/Socialist Union of Popular Forces) 38 (8·9%), Union Constitutionnelle (Constitutional Union) 27 (7·3%), Parti du Progrès et du Socialisme (Party of Progress and Socialism) 17 (5·4%) and Parti National-Démocrate/Al-Ahd (National Democrat Party/The Covenant) 14 (5·5%). A further 12 parties and independents obtained fewer than ten seats each. Turnout was 37·0%.

In indirect elections to the Chamber of Counsellors on 3 Oct. 2009 Parti Authenticité et Modernité (Authenticity and Modernity Party) gained 22 of 90 available seats, Istiqlal 17, MP 11, USFP 10 and RNI 9 with the remaining seats going to 11 other parties.

CURRENT ADMINISTRATION

In March 2010 the five-party coalition government comprised:

Prime Minister: Abbas El Fassi; b. 1940 (Istiqlal; in office since 19 Sept. 2007).

Ministers of State: Mohamed El Yazghi; Mohand Laenser.

Minister for Justice: Mohamed Naciri. *Interior:* Taib Cherkaoui. *Foreign Affairs and Co-operation:* Taieb Fassi Fihri. *'Habous' and Islamic Affairs:* Ahmed Toufiq. *Relations with Parliament:* Driss Lachguer. *Economy and Finance:* Salaheddine Mezouar. *Equipment and Transport:* Karim Ghellab. *Housing, Town Planning and Development:* Ahmed Taoufiq Hejira. *Tourism and Handicrafts:* Yassir Znagui. *Energy, Mines, Water and Environment:* Amina Benkhadra. *Health:* Yasmina Baddou. *Youth and Sports:* Moncef Belkhayat. *Agriculture and Sea Fisheries:* Aziz Akhenouch. *National and Higher Education, Management Training and Scientific Research:* Ahmed Akhchichine. *Communications and Government Spokesperson:* Khalid Naciri. *Employment and Professional Training:* Jamal Aghmani. *Industry, Commerce and New Technologies:* Ahmed Chami. *Foreign Trade:* Abdellatif Maâzouz. *Social Development, Family and Solidarity:* Nouzha Skalli. *Culture:* Bensalem Himmich. *Secretary General of the Government:* Driss Dahak.

Office of the Prime Minister (French and Arabic only): http://www.pm.gov.ma

CURRENT LEADERS

Mohammed VI ibn al-Hasan

Position
King

Introduction
Mohammed VI ibn al-Hasan was crowned King in July 1999 after the death of his father, King Hassan II. Less austere than his father, he pledged to improve Morocco's democratic institutions and encourage private investment in key economic sectors.

Early Life
King Mohammed VI was born on 21 Aug. 1963 in Rabat, Morocco. In 1985 he graduated from the College of Law in the Rabat Mohammed V University. In 1987 he took a degree in political science and in 1993 was awarded a law doctorate from the French University of Nice-Sophia Antipolis.

Mohammed undertook his first official royal duty, standing in for his father at a commemorative ceremony for French President Georges Pompidou, when he was 11. He was made honorary president of the Socio-Cultural Association of the Mediterranean Basin in 1979 and by the time he was 20 he had led a Moroccan delegation to the Franco-African conference and negotiated with the Organization of African Unity (now the African Union) over the Western Sahara conflict.

Appointed head of the general staff of the Royal Armed Forces in 1985, he succeeded to the throne in 1999.

Career in Office
Mohammed voiced support for developing a market economy and urged increased private sector investment in tourism, sea fishing, agro-industries and handicrafts. However, economic liberalization

has not significantly alleviated Morocco's widespread poverty nor reduced unemployment. Also, despite expectations of greater democratization, political power remains concentrated in the monarchy.

In foreign policy, he has co-operated with the USA in its anti-terror initiatives since the Sept. 2001 attacks. However, Morocco has itself been targeted by terrorist violence, including co-ordinated suicide bombings in Casablanca in May 2003 and further incidents in 2007. Elsewhere, Mohammed has expressed support for Palestinian claims to their own independent state and spoken out against the use of heavy-handed military force by Israel.

In 2002 the King came into conflict with the Spanish government when Moroccan forces landed on the small, uninhabited island of Perejil (a Spanish possession since 1668), 200 metres off the Moroccan coast. Spain quickly retook the island in a bloodless counter-assault, before withdrawing its troops on the understanding that neither country would occupy the island. In Jan. 2006 Prime Minister Rodríguez Zapatero became the first Spanish leader in 25 years to make an official visit to the enclaves of Melilla and Ceuta. However, a subsequent visit to the territories by Spain's King Juan Carlos in Nov. 2007 was criticized by Mohammed.

DEFENCE

Compulsory national military service was abolished in 2006. Defence expenditure in 2006 totalled US$2,161m. (US$65 per capita), representing 3·8% of GDP.

Army

The Army is deployed in two commands: Northern Zone and Southern Zone. There is also a Royal Guard of 1,500. Strength (2007), 175,000 (100,000 conscripts). There is also a Royal Gendarmerie of 20,000, an Auxiliary Force of 30,000 and reserves of 150,000.

Navy

The Navy includes three frigates, 27 patrol and coastal combatants and four amphibious craft.

Personnel in 2007 numbered 7,800, including 1,500 marines. Bases are located at Casablanca, Agadir, Al Hoceima, Dakhla and Tangiers.

Air Force

Personnel strength (2007) about 13,000, with 89 combat capable aircraft, including F-5s and Mirage F-1s.

INTERNATIONAL RELATIONS

Morocco is a member of the UN, World Bank, IMF and several other UN specialized agencies, WTO, IOM, International Organization of the Francophonie, Islamic Development Bank, OIC, African Development Bank and League of Arab States.

ECONOMY

Agriculture accounted for 15·7% of GDP in 2006, industry 27·8% and services 56·5%.

Overview

Morocco has achieved strong macroeconomic growth since 2001, with growth averaging 5·4% per year thanks to the diversification of the non-agricultural sector. As a result, unemployment and poverty rates have begun to fall, though poverty remains at around 15%. The implementation of broad-based structural reforms has seen an increase in foreign direct investment, containment of inflation and a reduction in financial sector vulnerabilities. However, further significant reductions in poverty and unemployment will require sustained growth rates of above 6% per year.

Trade is focused on the EU, which in 2005 accounted for 75% of exports and 56% of imports. The government is abolishing tariffs in preparation for the 2012 implementation of its three-stage free trade association agreement with the EU. This will liberalize the market for industrialized goods. In 2004 Morocco signed free trade agreements with the USA, Turkey, Egypt, Jordan and Tunisia.

Currency

The unit of currency is the *dirham* (MAD) of 100 *centimes*, introduced in 1959. Foreign exchange reserves were US$14,710m. in July 2005, gold reserves 708,000 troy oz and total money supply was DH353,598m. Since 1993 the dirham has been convertible for current account operations. Inflation was 2·0% in 2007 and 3·9% in 2008.

Budget

Revenues in 2007 totalled DH167,904m. and expenditures DH168,959m. The main revenue items were VAT (29·6%), corporate taxes (18·1%) and income tax (16·5%). Current expenditure accounted for 78·5% of total expenditures and capital expenditure 16·3%.

VAT is 20%.

Performance

Real GDP growth was 2·7% in 2007 and 5·6% in 2008. Total GDP in 2008 was US$86·3bn.

Banking and Finance

The central bank is the Bank Al Maghrib (*Governor*, Abdellatif Jouahri) which had assets of DH161,873m. in Dec. 2004. There were 12 other banks in 2002 and three development banks, specializing respectively in industry, housing and agriculture.

There is a stock exchange in Casablanca.

ENERGY AND NATURAL RESOURCES

Environment

Carbon dioxide emissions from the consumption and flaring of fossil fuels in 2008 were the equivalent of 1·3 tonnes per capita.

Electricity

Installed capacity was 4·9m. kW in 2004. Production was 18·24bn. kWh (approximately 90% thermal) in 2004 and consumption per capita 652 kWh.

Oil and Gas

Natural gas reserves in 2007 were 1·6bn. cu. metres; output (2004), 45m. cu. metres.

Minerals

The principal mineral exploited is phosphate (Morocco has the largest reserves in the world), the output of which was 27·24m. tonnes in 2006. Other minerals (in tonnes, 2006) are: barytine, 628,400; salt, 506,700; zinc, 148,700; lead, 59,100; iron, 35,500; copper, 17,800; manganese, 4,815; silver, 246.

Agriculture

Agricultural production is subject to drought; about 1·35m. ha. were irrigated in 2002. 85% of farmland is individually owned. Only 1% of farms are over 50 ha.; most are under 3 ha. There were 8·40m. ha. of arable land in 2002 and 887,000 ha. of permanent crops. Main land usage, 2003 (in 1,000 ha.): wheat, 2,989; barley, 2,267; maize, 247. There were 43,226 tractors in 2001 and 3,763 harvester-threshers. Production in 2003 (in 1,000 tonnes): wheat, 5,147; sugar beets, 3,428; barley, 2,620; potatoes, 1,435; tomatoes, 1,004; melons and watermelons, 944; sugarcane, 899; oranges, 822; onions, 684. Livestock, 2002: sheep, 16·34m.; goats, 5·09m.; cattle, 2·67m.; asses, 982,000; chickens, 137m. Livestock products in 2003 included (in 1,000 tonnes): milk, 1,311; meat, 598.

Forestry

Forests covered 4·36m. ha. in 2005, or 9·8% of the total land area. Produce includes firewood, building and industrial timber and some cork and charcoal. Timber production was 1·04m. cu. metres in 2007.

Fisheries

Total catch in 2005 was 932,704 tonnes (sea fish, 931,814 tonnes). Morocco's annual catch is the highest of any African country.

INDUSTRY

The largest company in Morocco by market capitalization in March 2009 was Itissalat Al-Maghrib (a fixed line telecommunications company), US$16·0bn.

In 2006 industry contributed 27·8% of GDP, with manufacturing accounting for 16·5%. Production in 1,000 tonnes (2004 unless otherwise indicated): cement, 9,828; residual fuel oil, 2,264; distillate fuel oil, 2,254; sugar (2003), 487; petrol, 257; paper and paperboard (2003), 129; olive oil (2004–05), 50.

Labour

Of 9,927,728 persons in employment in 2006, 43·3% were engaged in agriculture, fishing and forestry, 12·4% in commerce, 12·3% in industry (including handicrafts), 8·0% in construction and public works, 5·4% in general administration and public services, 4·0% in transport and communication and 14·5% in other services. The unemployment rate in 2006 was 9·7%. In Nov. 2006 the minimum hourly wage for non-agricultural workers was DH9·66. The minimum wage for agricultural workers is set at DH50 per day.

Trade Unions

In 1996 there were six trade unions: UMT (Union Marocaine de Travail), CDT (Confédération Démocratique du Travail), UGTM (Union Générale des Travailleurs Marocaine), UNTM (National Union of Moroccan Workers), USP (Union of Popular Workers) and the SNP (National Popular Union).

INTERNATIONAL TRADE

In 1989 Morocco signed a treaty of economic co-operation with the four other Maghreb countries: Algeria, Libya, Mauritania and Tunisia. Morocco is an active participant in the Euromed process, which aims to create a Euro-Mediterranean Free Trade Area in the course of 2010. Foreign debt was US$16,846m. in 2005.

Imports and Exports

Imports (f.o.b.) in 2006 were US$21,332m. and exports (f.o.b.) US$11,916m. Imports in 2006 included: machinery and transport equipment, 27·7%; mineral fuels, 21·6%; chemicals and related products, 9·7%; food and live animals, 7·0%; iron and steel, 5·2%. Exports included: apparel and clothing accessories, 25·8%; machinery and transport equipment, 17·2%; chemicals and related products, 13·4%; fish and seafood, 9·3%; fruit and vegetables, 6·8%. Main import suppliers in 2006: France, 16·5%; Spain, 11·6%; Saudi Arabia, 6·8%; Italy, 6·4%; China, 5·4%. Leading export markets in 2006: France, 28·4%; Spain, 20·8%; UK, 6·0%; Italy, 4·9%; India, 4·3%.

COMMUNICATIONS

Roads

In 2007 there were 57,799 km of classified roads, including 813 km of motorways and 11,251 km of main roads. There are motorways linking Rabat to Casablanca, Fès and Tangiers, and Casablanca to Marrakesh and El Jadida. In 2007 freight transport totalled 697m. tonne-km. In 2007 there were 1,644,500 passenger cars in use, 525,300 lorries and vans and 22,800 motorcycles and mopeds. There were 58,924 road accidents in 2007 (3,838 fatalities).

Rail

In 2005 there were 1,907 km of railways, of which 1,003 km were electrified. Passenger-km travelled in 2004 came to 2·65bn. and freight tonne-km to 5·54bn. In 2003 the construction of two 40 km-long rail tunnels under the Straits of Gibraltar was agreed with Spain at an estimated cost of US$30m.

Civil Aviation

The national carrier is Royal Air Maroc. The major international airport is Mohammed V at Casablanca; there are eight other airports. Casablanca handled 3,457,209 passengers in 2001 (2,612,998 on international flights) and 41,140 tonnes of freight; Marrakesh (Menara) handled 1,371,851 passengers and 2,471 tonnes of freight and Agadir (Al Massira) 1,052,181 passengers and 2,351 tonnes of freight. In July 1997 Morocco launched its first private air company, Regional Air Lines, to serve the major regions of the kingdom, in addition to southern Spain and the Canary Islands. In 2005 scheduled airline traffic of Moroccan-based carriers flew 70·3m. km, carrying 4,423,100 passengers.

Shipping

The busiest ports are Casablanca, Mohammedia, Nador, Tanger Med and Tangiers. 1·56m. passengers were handled in the ports in 1994 and 56·1m. tonnes of freight in 2003. In 2002 sea-going shipping totalled 502,000 GRT, including oil tankers 4,000 GRT.

Telecommunications

In 2008 there were 2,991,200 main (fixed) telephone lines; mobile phone subscribers numbered 22,815,700 in 2008 (72·2 per 100 persons). French media group Vivendi Universal bought a 35% stake in the state-run operator Maroc Telecom in 2000. It increased its holding to 51% in Jan. 2005 and to 53% in Oct. 2007. There were 920,000 PCs in use in 2006 and 10,442,500 internet users in 2008.

Postal Services

In 2003 there were 1,623 main post offices.

SOCIAL INSTITUTIONS

Justice

The legal system is based on French and Islamic law codes. There are a Supreme Court, 21 courts of appeal, 65 courts of first instance, 196 centres with resident judges and 706 communal jurisdictions for petty offences.

The population in penal institutions in Dec. 2006 was 53,580 (167 per 100,000 of national population). On ascending to the throne in July 1999, King Mohammed VI pardoned and ordered the release of 7,988 prisoners and reduced the terms of 38,224 others.

Education

The adult literacy rate in 2004 was 52·3% (65·7% among males and 39·6% among females). Education in Berber languages has been permitted since 1994; Berber languages were officially added to the syllabus in 2003. Education is compulsory from the age of six to 14 but is expected to be extended to 15 by 2015. In 2004 pre-primary schools had 39,443 teachers for 684,783 pupils. In 2003–04 there were 135,663 teachers at primary schools for 4,070,182 pupils, 89,892 teachers in secondary schools for 1,764,787 pupils and 10,413 teaching staff at universities for 277,632 students. There is an English-language university at Ifrane.

In 2007 public expenditure on education came to 5·1% of GNP.

Health

In 2006 there were 18,269 physicians, 3,473 dentists, 27,658 paramedical personnel and 8,002 pharmacists. There were 133 public hospitals in 2006 with about 27,000 beds, a provision of 87 beds per 100,000 inhabitants.

RELIGION

Islam is the established state religion. 98% of the population are Sunni Muslims of the Malekite school and 0·2% are Christians, mainly Roman Catholic, and there is a small Jewish community.

CULTURE

World Heritage Sites

Morocco has eight sites on the UNESCO World Heritage List: the Medina of Fès (inscribed on the list in 1981); the Medina of Marrakesh (1985); the Ksar of Ait-Ben-Haddou (1987); the Historic City of Meknès (1996); the Archaeological Site of Volubilis (1997 and 2008); the Medina of Tétouan (1997); the Medina of Essaouira/Magador (2001); and the Portuguese City of Mazagan, now part of the city of El Jadida (2004).

Broadcasting

Government-controlled Radiodiffusion Télévision Marocaine (RTM) and 2M (which is partly-state-owned) operate the two public television networks. RTM also broadcasts regional and national radio services. There are a growing number of private TV and radio operators, as well as access to foreign stations via satellite. There were 5·35m. TV sets in 2006 (colour by SECAM V).

Press

In 2004 there were 355 paid-for daily newspapers. The leading dailies are the Arabic-language Assabah and Al-Ahdath al-Maghrebia and the French-language Le Matin du Sahara et du Maghreb.

Tourism

There were 5,843,000 foreign tourists in 2005, spending US$5·4bn. The tourism sector employs some 600,000 people, equivalent to 5·8% of the workforce.

DIPLOMATIC REPRESENTATIVES

Of Morocco in the United Kingdom (49 Queen's Gate Gdns, London, SW7 5NE)
Ambassador: HH Princess Lalla Joumala Alaoui.

Of the United Kingdom in Morocco (28 avenue S.A.R. Sidi Mohammed, Souissi, Rabat)
Ambassador: Timothy Morris.

Of Morocco in the USA (1601 21st St., NW, Washington, D.C., 20009)
Ambassador: Aziz Mekouar.

Of the USA in Morocco (2 Ave. de Mohamed el Fassi, Rabat)
Ambassador: Samuel L. Caplan.

Of Morocco to the United Nations
Ambassador: Mohammed Loulichki.

Of Morocco to the European Union
Ambassador: Menouar Alem.

FURTHER READING

Direction de la Statistique. *Annuaire Statistique du Maroc.—Conjoncture Économique.* Quarterly *Bulletin Official.*

Bourqia, Rahma and Gilson Miller, Susan (eds.) *In the Shadow of the Sultan: Culture, Power and Politics in Morocco.* 2000

Pennell, C. R., *Morocco: From Empire to Independence.* 2003

National library: Bibliothèque Générale et Archives, 5 Avenue Ibn Batouta, BP 1003, Rabat.
National Statistical Office: Direction de la Statistique, Haut-Commissariat au Plan, BP 178, Rabat.
Website (French only): http://www.hcp.ma

Western Sahara

GENERAL DETAILS

The Western Sahara was designated by the United Nations in 1975, its borders having been marked as a result of agreements made between France, Spain and Morocco in 1900, 1904 and 1912. Sovereignty of the territory is in dispute between Morocco and the Polisario Front (Popular Front for the Liberation of the Saguia el Hamra and Rio de Oro), which formally proclaimed a government-in-exile of the Sahrawi Arab Democratic Republic (SADR) in Feb. 1976. According to a UN Security Council resolution adopted in July 2003, Western Sahara should be a semi-autonomous region of Morocco for five years. There would then be a referendum to decide whether it should remain part of Morocco or becomes a separate state. However, the Moroccan government rejected the plan.

Area 252,120 sq. km (97,346 sq. miles). Around 356,000 inhabitants (2004 estimate) are within Moroccan jurisdiction. Another estimated 196,000 Sahrawis live in refugee camps around Tindouf in southwest Algeria. The main towns are El-Aaiún (Laâyoune), the capital (183,691 inhabitants in 2004), Dakhla and Es-Semara.

Life expectancy at birth (1997 est.) male, 46·7 years; female, 50·0 years. Birth rate (1997 est.) per 1,000 population: 46·1; death rate: 17·5. The UN gives an estimated population for 2010 of 530,000.

The population is Arabic-speaking, and almost entirely Sunni Muslim.

President: Mohammed Abdelaziz.
Prime Minister: Abdelkader Taleb Oumar.

Rich phosphate deposits were discovered in 1963 at Bu Craa. Morocco holds 100% of the shares of the former Spanish state-controlled company Phosboucraa. Production reached 5·6m. tonnes in 1975, but exploitation has been severely reduced by guerrilla activity. After a nearly complete collapse, production and transportation of phosphate resumed in 1978, ceased again, and then resumed in 1982. Installed electrical capacity was an estimated 58,000 kW in 2004, with production in 2004 of 90m. kWh. Carbon dioxide emissions from the consumption and flaring of fossil fuels in 2008 were the equivalent of 0·8 tonnes per capita. There are about 6,100 km of motorable tracks, but only about 500 km of paved roads. There are airports at El-Aaiún and Dakhla. As most of the land is desert, less than 19% is in agricultural use, with about 2,000 tonnes of grain produced annually. There were 56,000 radio receivers and 6,000 television sets in 1997. In 1994 there were 100 physicians, equivalent to one per 2,504 inhabitants.

FURTHER READING

Sheley, Toby, *Endgame in the Western Sahara: What Future for Africa's Last Colony?* 2004

Zoubir, Y. H. and Volman, D. (eds.) *The International Dimensions of the Western Sahara Conflict.* 1993

MOZAMBIQUE

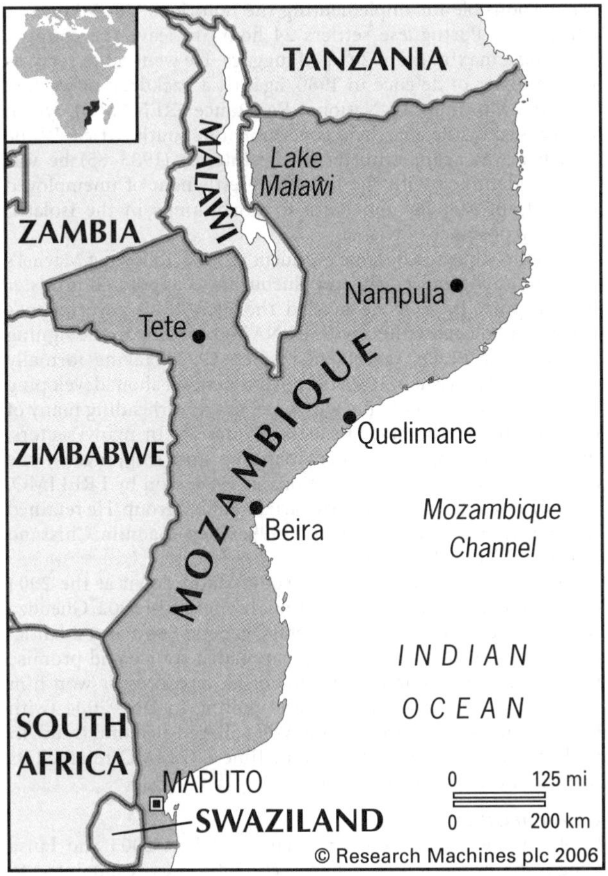

República de Moçambique
(Republic of Mozambique)

Capital: Maputo
Population estimate, 2010: 23·41m.
GDP per capita, 2007: (PPP$) 802
HDI/world rank: 0·402/172

KEY HISTORICAL EVENTS

Mozambique was at first ruled as part of Portuguese India but a separate administration was created in 1752. Following a decade of guerrilla activity, independence was achieved on 25 June 1975. A one-party state dominated by the Liberation Front of Mozambique (FRELIMO) was set up but armed insurgency led by the Mozambican National Resistance (RENAMO) continued until 4 Oct. 1992. The peace treaty provided for all weapons to be handed over to the UN and all armed groups to be disbanded within six months. In 1994 the country held its first multi-party elections. In early 2000 some 700 people died in the floods which made thousands homeless.

TERRITORY AND POPULATION

Mozambique is bounded east by the Indian ocean, south by South Africa, southwest by Swaziland, west by South Africa and Zimbabwe and north by Zambia, Malaŵi and Tanzania. It has an area of 799,380 sq. km (308,642 sq. miles) and a population, according to the 2007 census, of 20,226,296, giving a density of 25·3 per sq. km. Up to 1·5m. refugees abroad and 5m. internally displaced persons during the Civil War have begun to return home.

The UN gives an estimated population for 2010 of 23·41m.

In 2005, 65·5% of the population were rural. The areas, populations and capitals of the provinces are:

Province	*Sq. km*	*2007 census*	*Capital*
Cabo Delgado	82,625	1,605,649	Pemba
Gaza	75,709	1,226,272	Xai-Xai
Inhambane	68,615	1,252,479	Inhambane
Manica	61,661	1,412,029	Chimoio
City of Maputo	300	1,094,315	
Province of Maputo	26,058	1,205,553	Maputo
Nampula	81,606	3,985,285	Nampula
Niassa	129,056	1,169,347	Lichinga
Sofala	68,018	1,642,636	Beira
Tete	100,724	1,783,967	Tete
Zambézia	105,008	3,848,274	Quelimane

The capital is Maputo (2007 provisional population, 1,099,102). Other large cities (with 2007 provisional populations) are Matola (675,422), Nampula (477,900) and Beira (436,240).

The main ethnolinguistic groups are the Makua/Lomwe (52% of the population), the Tsonga/Ronga (24%), the Nyanja/Sena (12%) and Shona (6%).

Portuguese remains the official language, but vernaculars are widely spoken throughout the country. English is also widely spoken.

SOCIAL STATISTICS

2001 estimates: births, 753,000; deaths, 331,000. Estimated rates per 1,000 population, 2001: births, 41·7; deaths, 18·3. Infant mortality per 1,000 live births, 2005, 100. Life expectancy at birth, 2007, was 46·9 years for males and 48·7 years for females. Annual population growth rate, 2000–05, 1·9%; fertility rate, 2004, 5·4 births per woman.

CLIMATE

A humid tropical climate, with a dry season from June to Sept. In general, temperatures and rainfall decrease from north to south. Maputo, Jan. 78°F (25·6°C), July 65°F (18·3°C). Annual rainfall 30" (760 mm). Beira, Jan. 82°F (27·8°C), July 69°F (20·6°C). Annual rainfall 60" (1,522 mm).

CONSTITUTION AND GOVERNMENT

On 2 Nov. 1990 the People's Assembly unanimously voted a new constitution, which came into force on 30 Nov. This changed the name of the state to 'Republic of Mozambique', legalized opposition parties, provided for universal secret elections and introduced a bill of rights including the right to strike, press freedoms and *habeas corpus*. The head of state is the *President*, directly elected for a five-year term. Parliament is a 250-member *Assembly of the Republic*, elected for a five-year term by proportional representation.

National Anthem

'Patria Amada' ('Beloved Motherland'); words and tune by J. Sigaulane Chemane.

RECENT ELECTIONS

In the parliamentary elections of 28 Oct. 2009 the Liberation Front of Mozambique (FRELIMO) won 191 of the 250 seats with 74·7% of the vote, the Mozambican National Resistance (RENAMO) 51 with 17·7% and the Democratic Movement of Mozambique 8 with 3·9%.

In the presidential election, also held on 28 Oct. 2009, incumbent Armando Guebuza of FRELIMO took 75·0% of the vote against 16·4% for RENAMO's Afonso Marceta Macacho Dhlakama and 8·6% for Daviz Simango of the Democratic Movement of Mozambique. Turnout was 44·6%.

CURRENT ADMINISTRATION

President: Armando Guebuza; b. 1943 (FRELIMO; sworn in 2 Feb. 2005 and re-elected in Oct. 2009).

In March 2010 the government comprised:

Prime Minister: Aires Bonifácio Ali; b. 1955 (took office on 16 Jan. 2010).

Minister of Agriculture: Soares Nhaca. *Culture:* Armando Artur João. *Defence:* Filipe Jacinto Nhussi. *Development and Planning:* Aiuba Cuereneia. *Education:* Zeferino Martins. *Energy:* Salvador Namburete. *Environmental Action Co-ordinator:* Alcinda Abreu. *Finance:* Manuel Chang. *Fisheries:* Victor Borges. *Foreign Affairs and Co-operation:* Oldemiro Balói. *Health:* Paulo Ivo Garrido. *Industry and Commerce:* António Fernando. *Interior:* José Pacheco. *Justice:* Maria Benvinda Levi. *Labour:* Helena Taípo. *Mineral Resources:* Esperança Bias. *Public Service:* Vitória Dias Diogo. *Public Works and Housing:* Cadmiel Muthemba. *Science and Technology:* Venâncio Massingue. *State Administration:* Caremelita Namashalua. *Tourism:* Fernando Sumbana. *Transport and Communications:* Paulo Zucula. *Veterans' Affairs:* Mateus Óscar Kida. *Women's and Social Affairs:* Iolanda Cintura. *Youth and Sport:* Pedrito Caetano. *Minister of Civilian Affairs (President's Office):* António Correia Sumbana. *Minister of Parliamentary, Municipal and Provincial Affairs (President's Office):* Adelaide Amurane. *Minister of Social Affairs (President's Office):* Feliciano Salomão Gundana.

Government Website (Portuguese only):
http://www.mozambique.mz

CURRENT LEADERS

Armando Guebuza

Position

President

Introduction

Armando Guebuza, a veteran of Mozambique's fight for independence and one of the nation's wealthiest businessmen, was chosen as the ruling party's candidate for the 2004 presidential elections. Having won a large majority, he took office in Feb. 2005 and was re-elected for a second term in Oct. 2009.

Early Life

Armando Emílio Guebuza was born on 20 Jan. 1943 in Murrupula, in the northern province of Nampula. Politically active from an early age, he was elected in 1963 as president of the Mozambican Centre of African Students, a group created by Eduardo Mondlane, then the leader of Mozambique's fight for independence from Portugal. Later that year Guebuza joined the Liberation Front of Mozambique (FRELIMO) and in 1965 was elected to the organization's central and executive committees. Having undergone military training in Tanzania, Guebuza was involved in guerrilla fighting against the Portuguese administration in northern Mozambique. Following Mondlane's assassination in 1969, FRELIMO was led by Uria Simango and then Samora Machel. Under Machel it grew to include over 7,000 guerrillas and by the early 1970s had control over much of northern and central Mozambique. Guebuza became a general and was also an inspector of the schools run by FRELIMO.

When Marcello Caetano was overthrown in a military coup in Portugal on 25 April 1974, independence was assured for Mozambique. Following the signing of the Lusaka Agreements later in 1974, Guebuza was appointed to the transitional government that led the country to full independence in June 1975. He then served as minister of the interior in the single-party Marxist government led by President Machel. Guebuza was responsible for implementing the notorious '20–24' decree, which gave Portuguese settlers 24 hours to leave the country, carrying a maximum of 20 kg of luggage. He went on to serve as vice minister of defence in 1980, against a backdrop of warfare with the Mozambican National Resistance (RENAMO), which was backed by the apartheid government in South Africa. While Guebuza was again minister of the interior (1983–85) he was heavily identified with the forcible resettlement of unemployed residents of Maputo and Beira to work-camps in the isolated northern province of Niassa.

Joaquim Chissano became president in 1986, following Machel's death in an aircraft crash, and Guebuza was appointed minister of transport. In 1990 he headed the FRELIMO government's delegation to negotiations with RENAMO, leading to the signing of the Rome Peace Agreement in Oct. 1992. Having formally renounced Marxism in 1989, the government set about developing a market-oriented economy with Guebuza spearheading many of the reforms. He developed business interests in many sectors, including brewing, investment banking and shipping. In the country's first multi-party elections in 1994, won by FRELIMO, Guebuza was elected head of its parliamentary group. He retained that position in the elections of 1999, when Joaquim Chissano again led FRELIMO to victory.

Chissano announced that he would stand down at the 2004 elections. During FRELIMO's national congress in 2002, Guebuza was elected the party's secretary-general and presidential candidate. His uncompromising nationalist stance and promise to continue the economic reforms of his predecessor won him a large majority in the presidential polling in Dec. 2004 (with 63·7% of the vote), although RENAMO alleged electoral fraud. In parliamentary elections at the same time FRELIMO retained its majority in the National Assembly.

Career in Office

Guebuza was sworn in as president on 2 Feb. 2005 and Lúisa Diogo, the prime minister since Feb. 2004, was reappointed to head the government. Guebuza pledged to fight poverty and tackle corruption, and to seek further foreign investment to build infrastructure. In mid-2005 a trade and investment agreement was signed with the USA, whose officials cited Mozambique as 'a positive model because of its impressive track record on democracy, political stability, economic growth, openness to foreign direct investment and expanding exports'. In July 2006 the World Bank cancelled most of the country's debt under a scheme backed by the Group of Eight (G-8) major industrialized nations.

In May 2008 the Mozambique government began a repatriation of many of its citizens working legally in South Africa following a wave of violence directed against African migrants there.

Guebuza and FRELIMO increased their respective vote shares in the presidential and parliamentary elections in Oct. 2009.

DEFENCE

The President of the Republic is C.-in-C. of the armed forces. Defence expenditure totalled US$57m. in 2006 (US$3 per capita), representing 0·8% of GDP.

Army

Personnel numbered around 9–10,000 in 2007.

Navy

Naval personnel in 2007 were believed to total 200.

Air Force

Personnel (2007) 1,000 (including air defence units). There were four attack helicopters although their serviceability was in doubt but no combat capable aircraft.

INTERNATIONAL RELATIONS

Mozambique is a member of the UN, World Bank, IMF and several other UN specialized agencies, WTO, Commonwealth, Islamic Development Bank, OIC, African Development Bank, African Union, SADC and is an ACP member state of the ACP-EU relationship.

Formerly very heavily dependent on foreign assistance, in 2004 official aid made up only 12% of GDP.

ECONOMY

Agriculture accounted for 27·6% of GDP in 2006, industry 26·6% and services 45·8%.

Overview

A privatization programme launched in 1989 resulted in the partial or total privatization of over 1,200 enterprises by 2002. Following the end of its civil war in 1992, Mozambique has performed exceptionally well with several years of annual GDP growth in excess of 10%. Although heavy flooding in 2000 devastated the economy and infrastructure, growth had fully recovered by 2001. The economy has benefited from the IMF's Poverty Reduction and Growth Facility (PRGF) programme, including a low-interest lending facility for low-income countries that has helped maintain macroeconomic stability, strengthen the economy against external shocks, reduce inflation and provide a sustainable fiscal and external position. The number in extreme poverty fell by around 3m. between 1997 and 2003, though an HIV/AIDS infection rate of 16% is a long-term concern.

Currency

The unit of currency is the *new metical* (MZN) of 100 *centavos*, which replaced the *metical* (MZM) in July 2006. The currency was revalued at a rate of 1 new metical = 1,000 meticais. Inflation was 10·3% in 2008. Foreign exchange reserves were US$979m. in July 2005 and total money supply was 18,258·3bn. meticais.

Budget

In 2004 revenues were 26,891bn. meticais and expenditures 32,602bn. meticais.

Performance

GDP growth has averaged 8·4% since 2001, making Mozambique one of Africa's fastest-expanding economies. There was real GDP growth of 7·0% in 2007 and 6·8% in 2008. Total GDP in 2008 was US$9·7bn.

Banking and Finance

Most banks had been nationalized by 1979. The central bank and bank of issue is the Bank of Mozambique (*Governor*, Ernesto Gouveia Gove) which hived off its commercial functions in 1992 to the newly-founded Commercial Bank of Mozambique. In 1998 the Commercial Bank of Mozambique had 35% of deposits. In 2002 there were ten commercial banks, three foreign banks and a credit fund for agricultural and rural development. The new Mozambique Stock Exchange opened in Maputo in Oct. 1999. By the late 1990s financial services had become one of the fastest-growing areas of the economy.

ENERGY AND NATURAL RESOURCES

Environment

Carbon dioxide emissions from the consumption and flaring of fossil fuels in 2008 were the equivalent of 0·1 tonnes per capita.

Electricity

Installed capacity was 2·4m. kW in 2004. Production in 2004 was 11·71bn. kWh; consumption per capita was 545 kWh.

Oil and Gas

Natural gas finds are being explored for potential exploitation, and both onshore and offshore foreign companies are prospecting for oil. In 2007 natural gas reserves were 127bn. cu. metres; output (2004), 1·2bn. cu. metres. Some river basins, especially the Rovuma, Zambezi and Limpopo, are of interest to oil prospectors.

Water

Although the country is rich in water resources, the provision of drinking water to rural areas remains a major concern.

Minerals

There are deposits of pegamite, tantalite, graphite, apatite, tin, iron ore and bauxite. Other known reserves are: nepheline, syenite, magnetite, copper, garnet, kaolin, asbestos, bentonite, limestone, gold, titanium and tin. Output in 2005 (in 1,000 tonnes): aluminium, 554; sea salt (estimate), 80; bauxite, 10; coal, 3.

Agriculture

All land is owned by the state but concessions are given. There were an estimated 4·2m. ha. of arable land in 2002 and 0·24m. ha. of permanent crops. Around 107,000 ha. were irrigated in 2002. There were about 5,750 tractors in 2002. Production in 1,000 tonnes (2003): cassava, 6,150; maize, 1,248; sugarcane, 400; sorghum, 314; coconuts, 265; rice, 200; groundnuts, 110. Livestock, 2003 estimates: 1·32m. cattle, 392,000 goats, 180,000 pigs, 125,000 sheep, 28m. chickens.

Forestry

In 2005 there were 19·26m. ha. of forests, or 24·6% of the land area, including eucalyptus, pine and rare hardwoods. In 2007 timber production was 18·03m. cu. metres.

Fisheries

The catch in 2005 was 42,473 tonnes, of which 29,466 tonnes were from sea fishing. Prawn and shrimp are the major exports at 10,000 tonnes per year. The potential sustainable annual catch is estimated at 500,000 tonnes of fish (anchovies 300,000 tonnes, the rest mainly mackerel).

INDUSTRY

Although the country is overwhelmingly rural, there is some substantial industry in and around Maputo (steel, engineering, textiles, processing, docks and railways). A huge aluminium smelter, Mozal, was constructed in two phases—the last phase was completed in 2003. Production exceeds its theoretical annual capacity of 506,000 tonnes and is a focal point in the country's strategy of attracting foreign investment.

Labour

The labour force in 1996 totalled 9,221,000 (52% males). In 1998, 83% of the economically active population were engaged in agriculture, 8% in industry and 9% in services. Women represent 48% of the total labour force.

Trade Unions

The main trade union confederation is the Organização dos Trabalhadores de Moçambique, but several unions have broken away.

INTERNATIONAL TRADE

Foreign debt was US$5,121m. in 2005.

Imports and Exports

Imports (c.i.f.) totalled US$1,849·7m. in 2004 (US$1,648·1m. in 2003). Exports (f.o.b.) totalled US$1,503·9m. in 2004 (US$1,043·9m. in 2003). Principal imports in 2003: mineral fuels, 16·5%; machinery and apparatus, 16·2%; foodstuffs, 12·3%; transport equipment, 9·0%. Principal exports in 2003: aluminium, 54·4%; electricity, 10·9%; prawns, 7·3%; cotton, 3·1%. Main import suppliers in 2003: South Africa, 37·3%; Australia, 12·1%; USA, 5·9%; India, 4·2%. Main export markets in 2003: Belgium, 43·5%; South Africa, 16·2%; Spain, 6·7%; Portugal, 3·7%.

COMMUNICATIONS

Roads

In 2002 there were estimated to be 30,400 km of roads, of which 18·7% were paved. Passenger cars numbered 86,500 in 2002. There were 4,748 road accidents in 1997, with 805 fatalities. The flooding of early 2000 washed away at least one fifth of the country's main road linking the north and the south.

Rail

The state railway consists of three separate networks, with principal routes on 1,067 mm gauge radiating from the ports of Maputo, Beira and Nacala. Total length in 2002 was 2,072 km, mainly on 1,067 mm gauge with some 762 mm gauge lines. In 2005 passenger-km travelled on the Mozambique Ports and Railways network came to 172m. and freight tonne-km to 768m.

Civil Aviation

There are international airports at Maputo and Beira. The national carrier is the state-owned Linhas Aéreas de Moçambique (LAM). It provides domestic services and in 2003 operated international routes to Comoros, Dar es Salaam, Durban, Harare, Johannesburg and Lisbon. In 2001 Maputo handled 394,671 passengers (213,612 on international flights) and Beira 106,586 (98,590 on domestic flights). In 2003 scheduled airline traffic of Mozambique-based carriers flew 6m. km, carrying 281,000 passengers.

Shipping

The principal ports are Maputo, Beira, Nacala and Quelimane. In 2002 the merchant fleet had a total displacement of 37,000 GRT.

Telecommunications

Telephone subscribers numbered 2,406,300 in 2006 (119·4 per 1,000 persons). There were 2,339,300 mobile phone subscribers in 2006, up from just 254,800 in 2002, and 200,000 internet users in 2007.

Postal Services

In 2003 there were 272 post offices. Postal services in Mozambique are provided by a public company, Correios de Moçambique, E.P.

SOCIAL INSTITUTIONS

Justice

The 1990 constitution provides for an independent judiciary, *habeas corpus*, and an entitlement to legal advice on arrest. The death penalty was abolished in Nov. 1990. The judiciary is riddled with bribery and extortion.

The population in penal institutions in Dec. 2004 was approximately 10,000 (51 per 100,000 of national population).

Education

The adult literacy rate in 2002 was 46·5% (62·3% among males but only 31·4% among females).

In 2007 there were 4,563,633 pupils with 70,389 teaching staff in primary schools; and 444,926 pupils with 12,064 teaching staff at secondary schools. Private schools and universities were permitted to function in 1990. There were 28,298 students and 3,009 academic staff in higher education in 2005. The largest higher education institution is the Eduardo Mondlane University, founded in 1962 and granted university status in 1968.

In 2006 public expenditure on education came to 5·8% of GNI and 21·0% of total government spending.

Health

There were (2004) 46 hospitals, 722 health centres and 479 medical posts. There were two psychiatric hospitals. In 2000 there were 435 doctors, 1,414 midwives, 3,664 nursing personnel, 136 dentists and 419 pharmacists. Private health care was introduced alongside the national health service in 1992.

RELIGION

About 55% of the population follow traditional animist religions. In 2001 there were 6·18m. Christians (mainly Roman Catholic) and 2·04m. Muslims. In Feb. 2010 there was one cardinal.

CULTURE

World Heritage Sites

Mozambique has one site on the UNESCO World Heritage List: the Island of Mozambique (inscribed on the list in 1991), a Portuguese trading post with a style of architecture unchanged since the 16th century.

Broadcasting

State-run Televisão de Moçambique (TVM) and Radio Moçambique operate the sole national television network, the Antena Nacional radio network and provincial and local radio services. Soico TV (STV) is the main private television station. Independent FM radio stations operate in most urban areas. There were 390,000 TV receivers (colour by PAL) in 2004.

Press

There were two well-established daily newspapers in 2006 (Notícias and Diário in Maputo and Beira respectively) with a combined circulation of 17,000.

Tourism

Tourism is a potential growth area for the country. There were 578,000 non-resident tourists in 2005, spending US$138m.

DIPLOMATIC REPRESENTATIVES

Of Mozambique in the United Kingdom (21 Fitzroy Sq., London, W1T 6EL)
High Commissioner: António Gumende.

Of the United Kingdom in Mozambique (Ave. Vladimir I. Lenine 310, Maputo)
High Commissioner: Andrew Soper.

Of Mozambique in the USA (1990 M. St., NW, Washington, D.C., 20036)
Ambassador: Amélia Matos Sumbana.

Of the USA in Mozambique (Ave. Kenneth Kaunda 193, Maputo)
Ambassador: Vacant.
Chargé d'Affaires a.i.: Todd C. Chapman.

Of Mozambique to the United Nations
Ambassador: Daniel António.

Of Mozambique to the European Union
Ambassador: Maria Manuela dos Santos Lucas.

FURTHER READING

Alden, Chris, *Mozambique and the Construction of the New African State: From Negotiations to Nation Building.* 2001

Andersson, H., *Mozambique: a War against the People.* 1993

Cabrita, João M., *Mozambique: The Tortuous Road to Democracy.* 2001

Finnegan, W., *A Complicated War: the Harrowing of Mozambique.* 1992

Manning, Carrie L., *The Politics of Peace in Mozambique: Post-Conflict Democratization, 1992–2000.* 2002

Newitt, M., *A History of Mozambique.* 1996

Pitcher, M. Anne, *Transforming Mozambique: The Politics of Privatization, 1975–2000.* 2002

National Statistical Office: Instituto Nacional de Estatística, Av. Ahmed Sekou Touré, No. 21.
Website: http://www.ine.gov.mz

MYANMAR

Myanmar Naingngandaw
(Union of Myanmar)

Capitals: Naypyidaw/Pyinmana (Administrative and Legislative), Yangon/Rangoon (Commercial)
Population estimate, 2010: 50·50m.
GDP per capita: not available
GNI per capita, 2007: US$375
HDI/world rank: 0·586/138

KEY HISTORICAL EVENTS

After Burma's invasion of the kingdom of Assam, the British East India Company retaliated in defence of its Indian interests and in 1826 drove the Burmese out of India. Territory was annexed in south Burma but the kingdom of Upper Burma, ruled from Mandalay, remained independent. A second war with Britain in 1852 ended with the British annexation of the Irrawaddy Delta. In 1885 the British invaded and occupied Upper Burma. In 1886 all Burma became a province of the Indian empire. There were violent uprisings in the 1930s and in 1937 Burma was separated from India and permitted some degree of self-government. Independence was achieved in 1948. In 1958 there was an army coup, and another in 1962 led by Gen. Ne Win, who installed a Revolutionary Council and dissolved parliament.

The Council lasted until March 1974 when the country became a one-party socialist republic. On 18 Sept. 1988 the Armed Forces seized power and set up the State Law and Order Restoration Council (SLORC). Since then civil unrest has cost more than 10,000 lives. On 19 June 1989 the government changed the name of the country in English to the Union of Myanmar. Aung San Suu Kyi, leader of the National League for Democracy, was put under house arrest in July 1989. In spite of her continuing detention, her party won the 1990 election by a landslide, but the military junta refused to accept the results. She was eventually freed in July 1995, only to be placed under house arrest for a second time in Sept. 2000; she was again released in May 2002, and then again detained in May 2003.

In Aug. 2007 the government implemented fuel price hikes that prompted public protests, led chiefly by students and political activists. Despite the authorities taking a hard line, the demonstrations were given renewed force when several thousand monks came out in support in mid-Sept. The government crackdown, during which thousands of monks were reportedly rounded up and several protesters killed, brought condemnation from the international community.

In May 2008 the Irrawaddy delta suffered a cyclone that caused massive damage, claimed an estimated 145,000 lives and left 1m. people displaced. Nonetheless, the following week the government proceeded with a referendum on a new constitution.

TERRITORY AND POPULATION

Myanmar is bounded in the east by China, Laos and Thailand, and west by the Indian Ocean, Bangladesh and India. Three parallel mountain ranges run from north to south; the Western Yama or Rakhine Yama, the Bagu Yama and the Shaun Plateau. The total area of the Union is 676,577 sq. km (261,228 sq. miles). At the last census, in 1983, the population was 35,307,913. In 2005, 69·4% of the population lived in rural areas.

The UN gives an estimated population for 2010 of 50·50m.; density, 75 per sq. km.

The administrative capital is Naypyidaw (Pyinmana), with an estimated population of 97,400 in 2005. The largest city is Yangon (Rangoon); its population was 3,874,000 in 2003. Other leading towns are Mandalay, Naypyidaw, Moulmein, Bago (Pegu), Bassein, Sittwe (Akyab), Taunggye and Monywa. In Nov. 2005 the government began relocating from Yangon to a new administrative and legislative capital, Pyinmana, subsequently renamed Naypyidaw. The move was completed in Feb. 2006.

The population of the seven states and seven administrative divisions (2000 estimates): Ayeyarwady (Irrawaddy) Division, 6,779,000; Bago (Pegu) Division, 5,099,000; Magway Division, 4,548,000; Mandalay Division, 6,574,000; Sagaing Division, 5,488,000; Tanintharyi Division, 1,356,000; Yangon (Rangoon) Division, 5,560,000; Chin State, 480,000; Kachin State, 1,272,000; Kayah State, 266,000; Kayin (Karen) State, 1,489,000; Mon State, 2,502,000; Rakhine (Arakan) State, 2,744,000; Shan State, 4,851,000. Myanmar is inhabited by many ethnic nationalities. There are as many as 135 national groups with the Bamars, comprising about 68% of the population, forming the largest group. The Shan and the Karen account for 9% and 7% of the population respectively.

The official language is Burmese; English is also in use.

SOCIAL STATISTICS

2000 estimates: births, 1,165,000; deaths, 550,000. Estimated birth rate in 2002 was 23·7 per 1,000 population; estimated death rate, 11·2. Annual population growth rate, 1992–2002, 1·5%. Life expectancy at birth, 2007, was 59·0 years for males and 63·4 years for females. Infant mortality, 2005, 74 per 1,000 live births; fertility rate, 2004, 2·3 births per woman.

CLIMATE

The climate is equatorial in coastal areas, changing to tropical monsoon over most of the interior, but humid temperate in the extreme north, where there is a more significant range of temperature and a dry season lasting from Nov. to April. In coastal parts, the dry season is shorter. Very heavy rains occur in the monsoon months May to Sept. Yangon, Jan. 77°F (25°C), July 80°F (26·7°C). Annual rainfall 104" (2,616 mm). Sittwe, Jan. 70°F (21·1°C), July 81°F (27·2°C). Annual rainfall 206" (5,154 mm). Mandalay, Jan. 68°F (20°C), July 85°F (29·4°C). Annual rainfall 33" (828 mm).

CONSTITUTION AND GOVERNMENT

In May 2008 an army-drafted constitution won 92·5% support in a referendum. The constitution specified that multi-party elections should be scheduled for 2010 (although none had been arranged by April 2010); 25% of parliamentary seats were automatically allocated to the military. It also laid out rules that would ban opposition leader Aung San Suu Kyi from holding public office. The constitution was formally adopted on 30 May 2008. The previous constitution, dating from 3 Jan. 1974, had been suspended since 1988.

In May 1991, 48 members of the National League for Democracy (NLD) were given prison sentences on charges of treason. In July 1991 opposition members of the People's Assembly were unseated for alleged offences ranging from treason to illicit foreign exchange dealing. Such members, and unsuccessful candidates in the May 1990 elections, are forbidden to stand in future elections.

On 28 Nov. 1995 the government reopened a 706-member Constitutional Convention in which the NLD was given 107 places. The NLD withdrew on 29 Nov.

In Nov. 1997 the country's ruling generals changed the name of the government to the State Peace and Development Council (SPDC) and reshuffled the cabinet. In Dec. 1997, following a period when the national currency fell to a record low, there were further changes to the cabinet, while corruption investigations were begun against some former ministers.

National Anthem

'Gba majay Bma' ('We shall love Burma for ever'); words and tune by Saya Tin.

RECENT ELECTIONS

In elections in May 1990 the opposition National League for Democracy (NLD), led by Aung San Suu Kyi (b. 1945), won 392 of the 485 People's Assembly seats contested with some 60% of the valid vote. Turnout was 72%, but 12·4% of ballots cast were declared invalid. The military ignored the result and refused to hand over power.

CURRENT ADMINISTRATION

In March 2010 the government comprised:

Chairman of the State Peace and Development Council (SPCD) and Minister of Defence: Senior Gen. Than Shwe; b. 1933 (in office since 23 April 1992).

Prime Minister: Lieut.-Gen. Thein Sein.

Secretary-1 of the SPDC and Minister of Military Affairs: Lieut.-Gen. Tin Aung Myint Oo. *Secretary-2 of the SPDC:* Lieut.-Gen. Ye Myint.

Minister of Agriculture and Irrigation: Maj.-Gen. Htay Oo. *Industry (No. 1):* Aung Thaung. *Industry (No. 2):* Soe Thein. *Foreign Affairs:* Maj. Gen. Nyan Win. *National Planning and Economic Development:* Soe Tha. *Transport:* Maj.-Gen. Thein Swe. *Culture:* Maj.-Gen. Khin Aung Myint. *Co-operatives:* Maj.-Gen. Tin Htut. *Rail Transportation:* Maj.-Gen. Aung Min. *Energy:* Brig.-Gen. Lun Thi. *Education:* Chan Nyein. *Health:* Dr Khaw Myint. *Commerce:* Brig.-Gen. Tin Naing Thein. *Hotels and Tourism:* Maj.-Gen. Soe Naing. *Communications, Posts and Telegraphs:* Brig.-Gen. Thein Zaw. *Finance and Revenue:* Maj. Gen. Hla Tun. *Religious Affairs:* Brig.-Gen. Thura Myint Maung. *Social Welfare, Relief and Resettlement:* Maj.-Gen. Maung Maung Swe. *Labour:* Maj.-Gen. Aung Kyi. *Science and Technology:* U Thaung. *Information:* Brig.-Gen. Kyaw Hsan. *Progress of Border Areas, National Races and Development Affairs:* Col. Thein Nyunt. *Electric Power (No. 1):* Col. Zaw Min. *Construction, and Electric Power (No. 2):* Maj.-Gen. Khin Maung Myint. *Sports:* Brig.-Gen. Thura Aye Myint. *Forestry:* Brig.-Gen. Thein Aung. *Home Affairs, and Immigration and Population:* Maj.-Gen. Maung Oo. *Mines:* Brig.-Gen. Ohn Myint. *Livestock and Fisheries:* Brig.-Gen. Maung Maung Thein.

CURRENT LEADERS

Senior Gen. Than Shwe

Position

Chairman of the State Peace and Development Council

Introduction

Than Shwe became Myanmar's head of state and government in 1992, succeeding Saw Maung as leader of the military junta. Political oppression and widespread civil rights abuses have resulted in international condemnation and the nation's isolation. The economy is blighted by corruption and bad management and a reliance on the black market.

Early Life

Than Shwe was born on 2 Feb. 1933 in Kyaukse, Myanmar. He joined the army when he was 20 and had a decorated career, holding several high-profile positions including chief of staff at the ministry of defence and vice chief of staff of the army. In 1990 he was appointed deputy commander-in-chief of the defence services and deputy chairman of the State Law and Order Restoration Council (SLORC). In April 1992 Than Shwe succeeded Saw Maung as chairman of the SLORC, prime minister and minister of defence.

Career in Office

Than Shwe's legitimacy as head of state and government has been challenged by the presence of Aung San Suu Kyi, who led the National League for Democracy (NLD) to a handsome victory in the free elections of 1990 (Myanmar's first since the 1960s). Saw Maung and the army refused to recognize the result, but international dissatisfaction was reflected in 1991 when Aung San Suu Kyi received the Nobel Peace Prize. Put under house arrest after the elections, she was released in 1995 but the Than Shwe regime continued its oppression of the NLD. In Nov. 1997 the SLORC reconstituted itself as the State Peace and Development Council (SPDC).

In 2000 Aung San Suu Kyi began secret negotiations with the SPDC. However, despite Than Shwe authorizing the release of several hundred political prisoners, Myanmar's reputation for human rights abuses worsened. Amnesty International reported the increased use of torture, and critics suggested that prisoner releases were motivated by the hope of foreign aid rather than the desire to create a more transparent political infrastructure. Myanmar attracted further international condemnation when the International Labour Organization highlighted the use of forced adult and child labour. In June 2001 several opposition parties were allowed to resume operations and in May 2002 Aung San Suu Kyi was released from the house arrest which had been reimposed in 2000. However, she was again put under 'protective custody' in May 2003 after clashes between NLD supporters and government forces.

Than Shwe has meanwhile overseen the continued decline of the economy, with inflation spiralling and export revenues shrinking. Much of Myanmar's commerce has relied on the black market, with heroin among the country's leading revenue earners. Military control of many key industrial sectors has resulted in corruption and bad management.

In foreign policy, the oppressive nature of Than Shwe's regime has seen Myanmar increasingly isolated. However, there were some successes, notably acceptance into ASEAN in 1997 and the visit of China's President Jiang Zemin in 2001. Relations with neighbouring Thailand have been changeable. Tensions rose in 2001 when conflict between Myanmese troops and Shan separatist rebels spilled onto Thai territory, but subsequent meetings between the two countries helped restrengthen ties. Relations with Bangladesh have been strained since the early 1990s when up to 250,000 Muslim Rohingya refugees entered Bangladesh from Myanmar. However, there was some improvement when, in 2001, Than Shwe abandoned a proposed dam on the Naf River, shared by the two countries, which Bangladesh had claimed would cause widespread damage. In Dec. 2002 talks between Than Shwe and Bangladeshi Prime Minister Khaleda Zia resulted in accords on closer economic co-operation and improved road and shipping links. The first authorized sea route between the two countries was opened in Feb. 2003 and the following month Khaleda Zia made the first official visit to Myanmar by a Bangladeshi prime minister.

In 2002 the international community expressed concern at Than Shwe's deal with Russia to develop nuclear facilities. The USA, EU, China and IAEA all raised doubts about Myanmar's ability to ensure the safety of such enterprises while the NLD suggested that it could lead to the development of nuclear arms.

The renewed detention of Aung San Suu Kyi in May 2003 provoked further hostility from the international community and unprecedented public criticism from ASEAN. Malaysia's then prime minister, Mahathir Mohamad, suggested that Myanmar could be expelled from ASEAN as a last resort, although the then Thai prime minister, Thaksin Shinawatra, emphasized the importance of Myanmar's continued membership for the promotion of democracy in the country. Fresh sanctions were imposed by the USA and the EU, but neither banned all investment in Myanmar and large oil companies have continued to operate there.

In Aug. 2003 the head of intelligence, Gen. Khin Nyunt, was appointed prime minister and unveiled a seven-point road map to democracy. At that time, his appointment suggested a step closer to negotiations with the NLD, and from May–July 2004 a national convention was reconvened for the first time since 1996 to draw up a new constitution for Myanmar. However, in Oct. 2004 Khin Nyunt was removed from office and arrested on charges of corruption. The national convention met again intermittently between Feb. 2005–Jan. 2006 and a further session began in Oct. 2006, but without the participation of the main opposition and ethnic minority groups independent observers continued to question the validity of the process. In Nov. 2005 the ruling junta announced that the country's seat of government was moving from Yangon to Naypyidaw in central Myanmar. In Nov. 2006 a senior United Nations official visited Myanmar and was allowed to see Aung San Suu Kyi. At the same time, however, the junta ordered the closure of humanitarian operations in the country by the International Committee of the Red Cross. UN concern about the junta's policies prompted the preparation of a critical Security Council resolution, but this was vetoed by China and Russia in Jan. 2007.

In Sept. 2007 the government declared that constitutional talks were complete and closed the national convention. Buddhist monks then led a series of pro-democracy demonstrations in Yangon and other cities that provoked a violent response from the authorities and the mass detention of protesters. The United Nations Security Council condemned the military crackdown and the EU adopted tighter sanctions against the generals. In April 2008 the government published the proposed new constitution, which reserved 25% of parliamentary seats for the military and banned Aung San Suu Kyi from holding office. In a subsequent national referendum in May, the government claimed that 93% of voters endorsed the constitution. Aung San Suu Kyi's house arrest was also renewed at that time.

The constitutional referendum took place amid a humanitarian crisis, brought about by a cyclone that hit southern Myanmar at the beginning of May. By the end of the month about 145,000 people were thought to have died, with thousands more made homeless. The effects of the disaster were exacerbated by restrictions imposed on international relief efforts by Than Shwe and the government, who played down the scale of the devastation and insisted that the authorities did not need foreign help.

In Aug. 2009 tougher sanctions were imposed on Myanmar by the international community after Aung San Suu Kyi was convicted of having broken the terms of her confinement and the period of her detention was extended by an additional 18 months. In Oct., however, she met with a minister from the military government in the first such contact for two years and was also allowed to meet Western diplomats.

DEFENCE

Military expenditure in 2006 totalled US$6,920m. (US$147 per capita), representing 18·7% of GDP.

Army

The strength of the Army was reported to be about 375,000 in 2007. The Army is organized into 12 regional commands. There are three paramilitary units: People's Police Force (72,000), People's Militia (35,000) and People's Pearl and Fishery Ministry (approximately 250).

Navy

Personnel in 2007 totalled about 16,000 including 800 naval infantry.

Air Force

The Air Force is intended primarily for internal security duties. Personnel (2007) approximately 15,000 operating 125 combat capable aircraft, including F-7s.

INTERNATIONAL RELATIONS

Myanmar is a member of the UN, World Bank, IMF and several other UN specialized agencies, WTO, Asian Development Bank, ASEAN, Mekong Group and Colombo Plan.

ECONOMY

Agriculture accounted for 48·3% of GDP in 2004–05, trade 22·3%, manufacturing 11·6% and transport and communications 10·3%.

Myanmar featured among the ten most corrupt countries in the world in a 2009 survey of 180 countries carried out by the anti-corruption organization *Transparency International*.

Overview

Myanmar is subject to sanctions from the EU and the USA, which were expanded after a state crackdown on popular protests in 2007. That event also effected tourism, prompting a sharp decrease in visitor numbers. The 2004 tsunami and Cyclone Nargis in 2008 further contributed to the country's economic woes.

Agriculture employs 70% of the labour force and contributes 48% of GDP. Oil and gas reserves attract much-needed foreign investment. Further inward investment is limited owing to an inefficient and corrupt business environment which supports a black market.

Currency

The unit of currency is the *kyat* (MMK) of 100 *pyas*. Total money supply was K.1,742,810m. in June 2005. Foreign exchange reserves were US$691m. and gold reserves 231,000 troy oz in May 2005.

Inflation was 32·9% in 2007 and 22·5% in 2008. Since 1 June 1996 import duties have been calculated at a rate US$1 = K.100.

Budget
In 2002–03 revenues were K.279,377m. and expenditures K.353,389m. Non-tax revenue accounted for 59·6% of revenues in 2002–03; economic affairs accounted for 31·4% of expenditures, public services 23·4% and defence 21·5%. The fiscal year begins on 1 April.

Performance
Real GDP growth was 11·9% in 2007 and 4·0% in 2008.

Banking and Finance
The Central Bank of Myanmar was established in 1990. Its *Governor* is U Than Nyein. In 2002 there were two state banks (Myanma Economic Bank and Myanma Foreign Trade Bank), two development banks (Myanma Agricultural and Rural Development Bank and Myanma Investment and Commercial Bank) and 17 private banks. Since 1996 foreign banks with representative offices (there were 31 in 1996) have been permitted to set up joint ventures with Myanmese banks. The foreign partner must provide at least 35% of the capital. The state insurance company is the Myanmar Insurance Corporation. Deposits in savings banks were K.30,963m. in 1994.

Before being delisted in Oct. 2006, Myanmar was the only country named in a report in June 2006 as failing to co-operate in the fight against international money laundering. The Financial Action Task Force on Money Laundering was set up by the G7 group of major industrialized nations.

A stock exchange opened in Yangon in 1996.

Weights and Measures
The British Imperial and metric systems are used but in the markets traditional measurements are common: one *tical* (*kyat-tha*) = 16·33 grams; one *viss* (*peit-tha*) = 100 ticals.

ENERGY AND NATURAL RESOURCES

Environment
Myanmar's carbon dioxide emissions from the consumption and flaring of fossil fuels in 2008 were the equivalent of 0·3 tonnes per capita.

Electricity
Total electricity generated, 2004, 6·44bn. kWh; consumption per capita in 2004 was 129 kWh. Installed capacity was approximately 1·2m. kW in 2004.

Oil and Gas
Production (2004) of crude oil was 7·1m. bbls; natural gas (2008), 12·4bn. cu. metres. There were proven natural gas reserves of 490bn. cu. metres in 2008.

Minerals
Myanmar's mineral resources include antimony, coal, copper, lead, limestone, marble, precious stones, tin, tungsten and zinc. Production (in tonnes unless otherwise indicated): hard coal (2007), 283,703; lignite (2004), 213,000; gypsum (2004), 71,155; copper (2004), 31,756; jade (2004), 12,408, ruby, sapphire and spinel (2004), 6,198,915 carats. 90% of the world's rubies are mined in Myanmar.

Agriculture
In 1995–96, 4·5m. peasant families cultivated 10·1m. ha. In 2001 there were 10·0m. ha. of arable land and 635,000 ha. of permanent crops.

Liberalization measures of 1990 permit farmers to grow crops of their choice. 1·99m. ha. were irrigated in 2001. Production (2000, in 1,000 tonnes): rice, 20,000; sugarcane, 5,147; dry beans, 1,229; groundnuts, 640; onions, 507; plantains, 354; maize, 349; sesame seeds, 302; sunflower seeds, 270; coconuts, 263; potatoes, 245. Opium output was 1,097 tonnes in 2001, falling to 312 tonnes in 2005 before rising back up to 460 tonnes in 2007. Myanmar's opium production is second only to that of Afghanistan.

Livestock (2000): cattle, 10·96m.; buffaloes, 2·44m.; pigs, 3·91m.; goats, 1·39m.; sheep, 390,000; chickens, 44m. There were 6·8m. draught cattle in 1997. In 2001 there were 10,304 tractors and 21,562 harvester-threshers.

Forestry
Forest area in 2005 was 32·22m. ha., covering 49·0% of the total land area. Teak resources cover about 6m. ha. (15m. acres). In 2007, 42·55m. cu. metres of roundwood were cut.

Fisheries
In 2005 the total catch was 1,742,956 tonnes (1,204,286 tonnes from sea fishing). Aquacultural fish production was 79,851 tonnes in 1995–96. Cultured pearls and oyster shells are produced.

INDUSTRY
Production in 1,000 tonnes: cement (2004), 519; sawnwood (2002), 381; sugar (2000), 75; fertilizers (2001), 60; paper and paperboard (2002), 42; cigarettes (2001), 2,650m. units; clay bricks (2001), 77m. units; bicycles (1995–96), 35,042 units.

Labour
In 1998 the civilian workforce in employment numbered 18,359,000. The leading areas of activity (in 1,000) were: agriculture, hunting, forestry and fishing, 11,507; wholesale and retail trade/repair of motor vehicles, motorcycles and personal and household goods, 1,781; manufacturing, 1,666. In 2001 there were 398,300 persons aged 18 years and over registered as unemployed.

INTERNATIONAL TRADE
In Aug. 1991 the USA imposed trade sanctions in response to alleged civil rights violations. Foreign debt was US$6,645m. in 2005. A law of 1989 permitted joint ventures, with foreign companies or individuals able to hold 100% of the shares.

Imports and Exports
Since 1990, in line with market-oriented measures, firms have been able to participate directly in trade.

Imports (f.o.b.) in 2004 totalled US$1,998·7m. and exports (f.o.b.) US$2,926·6m. Main imports, 1997–98: machinery and transport equipment, 28·6%; intermediate raw materials, 19·9%; basic manufactures, 15·8%; capital construction material, 12·3%; consumer durable goods, 4·3%. Leading import suppliers in 2001 were China, 21·8%; Singapore, 16·6%; Thailand, 13·9%; South Korea, 9·1%. Main exports in 1997–98: pulses and beans, 22·3%; teak, 11·1%; fish and fish products, 4·6%; hardwood, 2·5%; rubber, 2·1%. Main export markets, 2001: Thailand, 20·6%; USA, 16·2%; India, 10·2%; China, 5·0%.

COMMUNICATIONS

Roads
There were 27,000 km of roads in 2005, of which 11·9% were surfaced. In 2005 there were 194,411 passenger cars, 54,482 vans and lorries, 17,985 buses and coaches, and 640,313 motorcycles and mopeds. There were 1,638 deaths as a result of road accidents in 2007.

Rail
In 2005 there were 4,809 km of route on metre gauge. Passenger-km travelled in 2003 came to 4,708m. and freight tonne-km to 1,163m.

Civil Aviation
Myanmar Airways International operates domestic services and in 2003 had international flights to Bangkok, Kuala Lumpur and

Singapore. In 2003 scheduled airline traffic of Myanmar-based carriers flew 16m. km, carrying 1,117,000 passengers (691,000 on international flights).

Shipping

There are nearly 100 km of navigable canals. The Irrawaddy is navigable up to Myitkyina, 1,450 km from the sea, and its tributary, the Chindwin, is navigable for 630 km. The Irrawaddy delta has approximately 3,000 km of navigable water. The Salween, the Attaran and the G'yne provide about 400 km of navigable waters around Moulmein. In 2002 merchant shipping totalled 402,000 GRT.

In 1995–96, 24·5m. passengers and 1·03m. tonnes of freight were carried on inland waterways. The ocean-going fleet of the state-owned Myanma Five Star Line in 1995 comprised 11 liners, four short-haul vessels and three coastal passenger/cargo vessels. In 1995–96, 60,000 passengers and 1,030,000 tonnes of freight were transported coastally and overseas. In 2000 vessels totalling 4,545,000 NRT entered ports and vessels totalling 2,252,000 NRT cleared. The port is Yangon.

Telecommunications

Myanmar had 632,600 telephone subscribers in 2005 (12·5 per 1,000 persons). In 2005 mobile phone subscribers numbered 128,700 and in 2007 there were 40,000 internet users.

Postal Services

In 2003 there were 1,314 post offices.

SOCIAL INSTITUTIONS

Justice

The highest judicial authority is the Chief Judge, appointed by the government. In 2004 there were approximately 60,000 people (120 per 100,000 of national population) held in prisons. Amnesty International reported in 2007 that, before the protests against the government that resulted in hundreds more arrests, there were around 1,150 political prisoners in the country's jails.

Education

Education is free in primary, middle and vocational schools; fees are charged in senior secondary schools and universities. In 2007 there were 5,013,582 pupils at primary schools with 172,209 teaching staff; and 2,686,198 pupils at secondary schools with 81,943 teaching staff. In 1995–96 there were 1,578 monastic primary schools (permitted since 1992) with 80,863 pupils. There were 507,660 students and 10,669 academic staff in tertiary education in 2007.

In higher education in 1995–96 there were 12 teacher training schools with 315 teachers and 2,067 students, five teacher training institutes with 304 teachers and 2,170 students, 17 technical high schools with 498 teachers and 7,145 students, 11 technical institutes with 668 teachers and 12,080 students, ten agricultural high schools with 100 teachers and 1,053 students, seven agricultural institutes with 162 teachers and 1,844 students, 41 vocational schools with 369 teachers and 6,532 students, six universities with 3,050 teachers and 154,680 students, six degree colleges with 705 teachers and 53,362 students, and ten colleges with 629 teachers and 40,327 students.

There was also a University for the Development of the National Races of the Union and institutes of medicine (3), dentistry, paramedical science, pharmacy, nursing, veterinary science, economics, technology (2), agriculture, education (2), foreign languages, computer science and forestry. An institute of remote education maintains a correspondence course at university level.

The adult literacy rate was 89·7% in 2003 (93·7% among males and 86·2% among females).

In 2001 public expenditure on education came to 1·3% of GDP.

Health

In 1996 there were 737 hospitals with a provision of seven beds per 10,000 inhabitants. In 2000 there were 14,356 physicians, 12,642 nurses, 10,307 midwives and 871 dentists (1999). Public spending on health is less than 0·2% of GDP.

Welfare

In 1995–96 contributions to social security totalled (K.1m.) 117·5 (from employers, 73·2; from employees, 43·9). Benefits paid totalled 82·6, and included: sickness, 12·9; maternity, 3·9; disability, 3·7; survivors' pensions, 1·3.

RELIGION

About 89·3% of the population—mainly Bamars, Shans, Mons, Rakhines and some Kayins—are Buddhists, while the rest are Christians, Muslims, Hindus and Animists. The Christian population is composed mainly of Kayins, Kachins and Chins. There are about 400,000 monks. Islam and Hinduism are practised mainly by people of Indian origin.

CULTURE

Broadcasting

All media outlets are tightly controlled by the military government, which operates the main TV Myanmar and Radio Myanmar networks. There were 373,000 television receivers (colour by NTSC) in 2005.

Press

There were eight daily newspapers in 2006, with a combined circulation of 550,000. The three largest newspapers were all government-owned.

Tourism

In 2005 there were 232,000 non-resident tourists; spending by tourists totalled US$98m. in 2004.

DIPLOMATIC REPRESENTATIVES

Of Myanmar in the United Kingdom (19A Charles St., London, W1J 5DX)
Ambassador: U Nay Win.

Of the United Kingdom in Myanmar (80 Strand Rd, Yangon)
Ambassador: Andrew Heyn.

Of Myanmar in the USA (2300 S. St., NW, Washington, D.C., 20008)
Ambassador: Vacant.
Chargé d'Affaires a.i: Kyaw Win.

Of the USA in Myanmar (110 University Ave., Yangon)
Ambassador: Vacant.
Chargé d'Affaires a.i.: Larry M. Dinger.

Of Myanmar to the United Nations
Ambassador: U Than Swe.

FURTHER READING

Aung San Suu Kyi, *Freedom from Fear and Other Writings*. 1991
Carey, P. (ed.) *Burma: The Challenge of Change in a Divided Society*. 1997
Hiaing, Kyaw Yin, *Myanmar: Beyond Politics to Social Imperatives*. 2005
Metraux, Daniel A., *Burma's Modern Tragedy*. 2005
Myint, S., *Burma File: A Question of Democracy*. 2004
Seekins, Donald M., *Historical Dictionary of Burma*. 2006
Skidmore, Monique, *Burma at the Turn of the Twenty-First Century*. 2005
Smith, Martin, *Burma: Insurgency and the Politics of Ethnicity*. 1999
Steinberg, David I., *Burma: The State of Myanmar*. 2002
Thant Myint-U, *The Making of Modern Burma*. 2001.—*The River of Lost Footsteps: Histories of Burma*. 2007
Tucker, Shelby, *Burma: The Curse of Independence*. 2001

National Statistical Office: Ministry of National Planning and Economic Development, Yangon.
Website: http://www.csostat.gov.mm

NAMIBIA

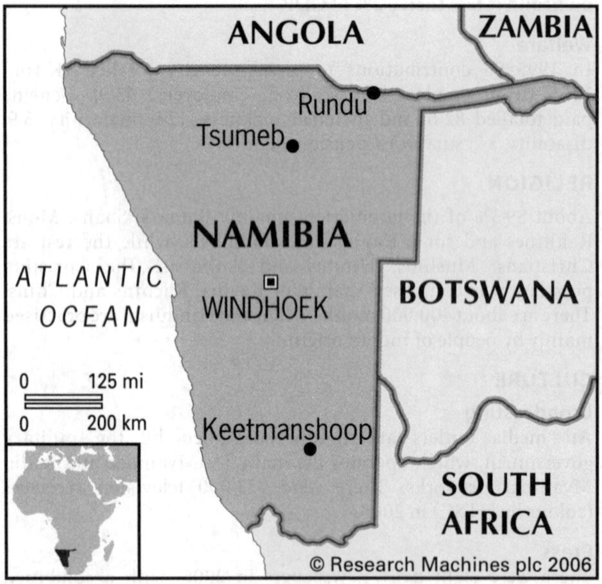

Republic of Namibia

Capital: Windhoek
Population estimate, 2010: 2·21m.
GDP per capita, 2007: (PPP$) 5,155
HDI/world rank: 0·686/128

KEY HISTORICAL EVENTS

Namibia was first settled by people from the Khoisan language group. The earliest, the nomadic San people, were followed about 2000 years ago by the pastoral Nama, who became dominant in the south. In the 9th century AD the Damara settled the central grasslands (known as Damaraland). Other clans followed and by the 19th century three Bantu peoples were established: the Herero in northeastern and central Namibia (Kaokoland); the Ovambo around the Kunene River in the north; and the Kavango people in the east. In the far east, the Barotse expanded from Zambia to settle the Caprivi Strip while the Tswana (from Botswana) settled the edges of the Kalahari desert.

European traders and settlers arrived in the late 18th century. Walvis Bay came under Dutch (1793) then British (1797) control, and European settlement began on the coast. In the 1830s the Oorlans, from South Africa, expanded into Nama and Damara territory, becoming dominant under the leadership of Jonker Afrikaner.

In 1884 the area then known as South West Africa became a German protectorate. From 1904–08 conflict between German troops and the Herero and Nama peoples saw the deaths of 80% of the Herero population and 50% of the Nama. In the aftermath, Germany introduced racial segregation and used forced labour for diamond mines. In 1915 the Union of South Africa occupied German South West Africa and on 17 Dec. 1920 the League of Nations entrusted the territory as a Mandate to the Union of South Africa. After the Second World War South Africa applied unsuccessfully to annex the territory, continuing to administer it in defiance of the UN. Indigenous opposition to South African rule became organized in the 1950s: the Ovamboland Peoples' Organization was founded in 1958 (known as the South West Africa Peoples' Organization, or SWAPO, from 1960) and the South West Africa National Union (SWANU) in 1959.

In 1968 the UN changed the territory's name to Namibia. Following widespread strikes in 1971–72, negotiations took place between South Africa and the UN and in 1973 a multi-racial advisory council was appointed in preparation for independence. However, attempts at organizing free elections failed. In 1988, after military defeat in Angola, South Africa withdrew. UN-supervised elections took place in Nov. 1989, delivering a victory for SWAPO. After independence on 21 March 1990, Namibia joined the Commonwealth.

In April 1990 Namibia joined the UN and in June 1990 the Organization of African Unity, forerunner of the African Union. In 2004 the country suffered major flooding. It continues to face a serious AIDS epidemic, with around 20% of adults infected, though in 2007 the rate fell for the first time.

TERRITORY AND POPULATION

Namibia is bounded in the north by Angola and Zambia, west by the Atlantic Ocean, south and southeast by South Africa and east by Botswana. The Caprivi Strip (Caprivi Region), about 300 km long, extends eastwards up to the Zambezi river, projecting into Zambia and Botswana and touching Zimbabwe. The area, including the Caprivi Strip and Walvis Bay, is 825,112 sq. km. South Africa transferred Walvis Bay to Namibian jurisdiction on 1 March 1994. Census population, 1991, 1,409,920 (723,593 females; urban, 32·76%). 2001 census population, 1,830,330 (density 2·2 per sq. km). In 2005, 64·9% of the population were rural.

The UN gives an estimated population for 2010 of 2·21m.

Population by ethnic group at the censuses of 1970 and 1981 and estimates for 1991:

	1970	*1981*	*1991*
Ovambos	342,455	506,114	665,000
Kavangos	49,577	95,055	124,000
Damaras	64,973	76,179	100,000
Hereros	55,670	76,296	100,000
Whites	90,658	76,430	85,000
Namas	32,853	48,541	64,000
Caprivians	25,009	38,594	50,000
Coloureds	28,275	42,254	—
Bushmen	21,909	29,443	—
Basters	16,474	25,181	—
Tswanas	4,407	6,706	—
Other	—	12,403	—
	732,260	1,033,196	1,401,711

Namibia is administratively divided into 13 regions. Area, population and chief towns in 2001:

Region	*Area (in sq. km)*	*Population*	*Chief town*
Caprivi (Liambezi)	19,532	79,826	Katima Mulilo
Erongo	63,719	107,663	Swakopmund
Hardap	109,888	68,249	Mariental
Karas	161,324	69,329	Keetmanshoop
Khomas	36,804	250,262	Windhoek
Kunene	144,254	68,735	Opuwo
Ohangwena	10,582	228,348	Oshikango
Okavango	43,417	202,694	Rundu
Omaheke	84,731	68,039	Gobabis
Omusati	13,637	228,842	Outapi
Oshana	5,290	161,916	Oshakati
Oshikoto	26,607	161,007	Tsumeb
Otjozondjupa	105,327	135,384	Grootfontein

Towns with populations over 5,000 (2001): Windhoek, 233,529; Walvis Bay, 43,611; Rundu, 36,964; Oshakati, 28,255; Swakopmund, 23,808; Katima Mulilo, 22,134; Rehoboth, 21,308; Otjiwarongo, 19,614; Keetmanshoop, 15,778; Tsumeb, 14,929; Grootfontein, 14,249; Okahandja, 14,039; Gobabis, 13,856; Lüderitz, 13,295; Ongwediva, 10,742; Mariental, 9,836; Outjo, 6,013; Khorixas, 5,890; Opuwo, 5,101.

English is the official language. Afrikaans and German are also spoken.

SOCIAL STATISTICS

Estimates, 2000: births, 68,000; deaths, 35,000. Estimated birth rate in 2000 was 34·5 per 1,000 population; estimated death rate, 17·8. Expectation of life, 2007: males, 59·3 years; females, 61·2. Annual population growth rate, 1992–2002, 2·7%; infant mortality, 2005, 46 per 1,000 live births. The fertility rate dropped from 5·5 births per woman in 1994 to 3·8 births per woman in 2004.

CLIMATE

The rainfall increases steadily from less than 50 mm in the west and southwest up to 600 mm in the Caprivi Strip. The main rainy season is from Jan. to March, with lesser showers from Sept. to Dec. Namibia is the driest African country south of the Sahara.

CONSTITUTION AND GOVERNMENT

On 9 Feb. 1990 with a unanimous vote the Constituent Assembly approved the Constitution which stipulated a multi-party republic, an independent judiciary and an executive *President* who may serve a maximum of two five-year terms. The constitution became effective on 12 March 1990 and was amended in 1999 to allow President Sam Nujoma to stand for a third term in office. The bicameral legislature consists of a 78-seat *National Assembly*, 72 members of which are elected for five-year terms by proportional representation and up to six appointed by the president by virtue of position or special expertise, and a 26-seat *National Council* consisting of two members from each Regional Council elected for six-year terms.

National Anthem

'Namibia, land of the brave'; words and tune by Axali Doeseb.

RECENT ELECTIONS

Presidential and parliamentary elections were held on 27–28 Nov. 2009. Hifikepunye Pohamba (South West Africa People's Organization/SWAPO) was elected president with 75·3% of votes cast followed by Hidipo Hamutenya (Rally for Democracy and Progress/RDP) with 10·9%, Katuutire Kaura (Democratic Turnhalle Alliance/DTA) with 3·0%, Kuaima Riruako (National Unity Democratic Organization/NUDO) with 2·9% and Chief Justus Garoëb (United Democratic Front/UDF) with 2·4%. There were seven other candidates. Turnout was an estimated 75%. In the parliamentary elections SWAPO won 54 of the available 72 seats with 74·3% of the vote; the RDP, 8 with 11·2%; DTA, 2 with 3·1%; NUDO, 2 with 3·0%; UDF, 2 with 2·4%; All People's Party, 1 with 1·3%; Republican Party, 1 with 0·8%; Congress of Democrats, 1 with 0·7%; South West Africa National Union, 1 with 0·6%.

CURRENT ADMINISTRATION

President: Hifikepunye Pohamba; b. 1935 (SWAPO; sworn in 21 March 2005 and re-elected in Nov. 2009).

In March 2010 the government comprised:

Prime Minister: Nahas Angula; b. 1943 (SWAPO; sworn in 21 March 2005).

Deputy Prime Minister: Marco Hausiku.

Minister of Home Affairs and Immigration: Rosalia Ngidinwa. *Presidential Affairs and Attorney General:* Albert Kawana. *Foreign Affairs:* Utoni Nujoma. *Defence:* Maj.-Gen. Charles Namoloh. *Finance:* Saara Kuugongelwa-Amadhila. *Education:* Abraham Iyambo. *Health:* Richard Kamwi. *Mines and Energy:* Isak Katali. *Justice:* Pendukeni Iivula-Iithana. *Regional and Local Government, Housing and Rural Development:* Jerry Ekandjo. *Agriculture, Water and Forests:* John Mutorwa. *Trade and Industry:* Hage Geingob. *Environment and Tourism:* Netumbo Nandi-Ndaitwah. *Works and Transport:* Erkki Nghimtina. *Lands and Rehabilitation:* Alpheus Naruseb. *Fisheries and Marine Resources:* Bernard Esau. *Safety and Security:* Nangolo Mbumba. *Youth, National Service, Sport and Culture:* Kazenambo Kazenambo. *Gender Equality and Child Welfare:* Doreen Sioka. *Labour and Social Protection:* Immanuel Ngatjizeto. *Information and Information Technology:* Joel Kaapanda. *Veterans' Affairs:* Nickey Iyambo.

Office of the Prime Minister: http://www.opm.gov.na

CURRENT LEADERS

Hifikepunye Pohamba

Position
President

Introduction
Lucas Hifikepunye Pohamba, representing the ruling South West Africa People's Organization (SWAPO), won a landslide victory at presidential elections in Nov. 2004 and took office in March 2005. He succeeded Namibia's 'founding father' and former president, Sam Nujoma, and has continued with the same broad political programme. He was re-elected in Nov. 2009.

Early Life
Pohamba was born on 18 Aug. 1935 at Okanghudi in South West Africa (modern Namibia) and educated at the Holy Cross Mission School at Onamunama. He worked in the Tsumeb copper mines and joined SWAPO in April 1959. He joined Nujoma in exile in Dar es Salaam (Tanzania) and became a leading figure in SWAPO, representing it in Zambia and Algeria and raising funds. In 1969 he was appointed to SWAPO's central committee and in 1975 became secretary for finance and administration. From 1979 until the late 1980s he was based in Luanda, Angola.

Following Nujoma's victory in the country's first presidential elections on 7 Nov. 1989, Pohamba was appointed as minister of home affairs. In 1995 he became minister for fisheries and marine resources until 2001, when he took responsibility for lands, resettlement and rehabilitation. As such, he pushed ahead with Namibia's controversial 'land reform' scheme, involving the compulsory purchase of land owned by white farmers for distribution to black citizens.

Career in Office
Since his inauguration on 21 March 2005 Pohamba has pursued established policies, including development of education, the rural water supply and the infrastructure network. He has also continued the controversial compulsory land purchases scheme. In elections in Nov. 2009, Pohamba was returned to the presidency with about 75% of the vote and SWAPO retained its majority of parliamentary seats with a similar vote share.

DEFENCE

In 2006 defence expenditure totalled US$197m. (US$96 per capita), representing 3·0% of GDP.

Army

Personnel (2007), 9,000. There is also a 6,000-strong paramilitary police force.

Navy

A force of around 200 (2007) is based at Walvis Bay.

Air Force

The Army has a small air wing that operates two combat capable aircraft.

INTERNATIONAL RELATIONS

Namibia is a member of the UN, World Bank, IMF and several other UN specialized agencies, WTO, Commonwealth, IOM, African Development Bank, African Union, SADC and is an ACP member state of the ACP-EU relationship.

ECONOMY

Agriculture accounted for 10·9% of GDP in 2006, industry 30·6% and services 58·5%.

The Namibian economy is heavily dependent on mining and fisheries.

Overview

Although the country is dependent on uranium, diamonds, silver, tin and zinc, the majority of the population is employed in agriculture and few benefit from the mineral wealth. The mining sector accounts for 50% of exports, with exports in turn accounting for nearly 40% of GDP.

80% of the manufacturing sector comprises food-related industries. GDP growth is volatile because of the heavy reliance on mineral exports but nevertheless remains robust and has exceeded many neighbouring economies. Inflation is moderate and exhibits similar trends to South Africa. Since 1990 the government's role in the economy has expanded to include control of the electricity and water utilities, the national airline and a telecommunications company. There is strong potential for tourism growth.

Namibia is a member of the Southern African Customs Union, which has a 12% common external tariff. The country promotes foreign investment but favours domestic and foreign partnerships. Trade is closely linked to South Africa, although the EU is the core export market. Unemployment (including underemployment) is near 60%. A history of apartheid policies has led to one of the world's most unequal income distribution patterns and there is a shortage of skilled labour.

Currency

The unit of currency is the *Namibia dollar* (NAD) of 100 *cents*, introduced on 14 Sept. 1993 and pegged to the South African rand. The rand is also legal tender at parity. Inflation was 7·1% in 2008. In May 2005 foreign exchange reserves were US$333m. Total money supply in Dec. 2003 was N$7,851m.

Budget

The financial year runs from 1 April. Budgetary central government revenue and expenditure (in N$1m.):

	2001	*2002*	*2003*
Revenue	7,894	8,953	10,349
Expenditure	7,476	8,724	9,474

Performance

Real GDP growth was 2·9% in 2008; total GDP in 2008 was US$8·6bn.

Banking and Finance

The Bank of Namibia is the central bank. Its *Governor* is Tom Alweendo. Commercial banks in 2002 included First National Bank of Namibia, Namibia Banking Corporation, Standard Bank Namibia, Commercial Bank of Namibia, Bank Windhoek (the only locally-owned bank) and City Savings and Investment Bank. There is a state-owned Agricultural Bank and a merchant bank, UAL-Namibia. Total assets of commercial banks were R2,383·2m. at 31 Dec. 1991.

There are two building societies with total assets (31 March 1990) R424·9m. A Post Office Savings Bank was established in 1916. In March 1991 its total assets were R21·8m. A stock exchange (NSE) is in operation in Windhoek.

ENERGY AND NATURAL RESOURCES

Environment

Carbon dioxide emissions from the consumption and flaring of fossil fuels were the equivalent of 1·5 tonnes per capita in 2008.

Electricity

In 2002 electricity production was 1·4bn. kWh. Namibia also imports electricity from South Africa (1·0bn. kWh in 2002). Consumption per capita in 2002 was 1,236 kWh.

Oil and Gas

Natural gas reserves in 2007 totalled 62bn. cu. metres.

Minerals

There are diamond deposits both inshore and off the coast, with production equally divided between the two. Some 3bn. carats of diamonds are believed to be lying in waters off Namibia's Atlantic coast. Namibia produced 2·0m. carats in 2004, exclusively of gem quality. Output in 2005 (in tonnes): salt, 573,248; zinc (metal content), 69,368; lead (metal content), 14,320; copper (metal content), 10,157; uranium (metal content), 2,855; silver (metal content), 34; gold (metal content), 2,649 kg.

Agriculture

Namibia is essentially a stock-raising country, the scarcity of water and poor rainfall rendering crop-farming, except in the northern and northeastern parts, almost impossible. There were an estimated 800,000 ha. of arable land in 2007 and 5,000 ha. of permanent crops. There were 39 tractors per 10,000 ha. of arable land in 2006. Generally speaking, the southern half is suited for the raising of small stock, while the central and northern parts are more suited for cattle. Guano is harvested from the coast, converted into fertilizer in South Africa and most of it exported to Europe. In 2007 the agricultural population was an estimated 905,000, of which some 252,000 were economically active.

Principal crops (2003, in tonnes): millet, 51,000; maize, 33,000; wheat, 8,000; grapes, 6,000; seed cotton, 5,000; sorghum, 5,000. Livestock (2003 estimates): 2·51m. cattle, 2·37m. sheep, 1·78m. goats, 3m. chickens. In 2003 an estimated 105,000 tonnes of milk and 83,000 tonnes of meat were produced.

Forestry

Forests covered 7·66m. ha. in 2005, or 9·3% of the land area.

Fisheries

Pilchards, mackerel and hake are the principal fish caught. The catch in 2005 was 552,695 tonnes, of which more than 99% came from marine waters. Conservation policies are in place. The policy aims at ensuring that the country's fisheries resources are utilized on a sustainable basis and also aims to ensure their lasting contribution to the country's economy.

INDUSTRY

Of the estimated total of 400 undertakings, the most important branches are food production (accounting for 29·3% of total output), metals (12·7%) and wooden products (7%). The supply of specialized equipment to the mining industry, the assembly of goods from predominantly imported materials and the manufacture of metal products and construction material play an important part. Small industries (including home industries, textile mills, leather and steel goods) have expanded. Products manufactured locally include chocolates, beer, cement, leather shoes, delicatessen meats and game meat products.

Labour

Of 431,800 people in employment in 2000, 126,500 were engaged in agriculture, hunting and forestry; 46,300 in community, social and personal service activities; 39,300 in real estate, renting and business activities; and 38,900 in wholesale and retail trade/repair of motor vehicles, motorcycles and personal and household goods. In 2000 the unemployment rate was 33·8%.

INTERNATIONAL TRADE

Total foreign debt was US$140m. in 1996. Export Processing Zones were established in 1995 to grant companies with EPZ status some tax exemptions and other incentives. The Offshore Development Company (ODC) is the flagship of the Export Processing Zone regime. The EPZ regime does not restrict; any investor (local or foreign) enjoys the same or equal advantages in engaging themselves in any choice of business (allowed by law).

Imports and Exports

In 2007 imports (c.i.f.) were valued at US$4,026·0m. and exports (f.o.b.) at US$4,040·3m. Exports in 2007 (in US$1m.) included diamonds (705), zinc (624), fish (432), uranium ores and concentrates (350), machinery and transport equipment (280), meat products (153). The largest import supplier in 2006 was South Africa with 82·4%; largest export markets: UK, 25·6%; South Africa, 24·6%.

COMMUNICATIONS

Roads

In 2002 the total road network covered 42,237 km, including 4,550 km of national roads. In 2008 there were 107,800 passenger cars in use and 117,400 lorries and vans. There were 368 deaths as a result of road accidents in 2007.

Rail

The Namibia system connects with the main system of the South African railways at Ariamsvlei. The total length of the line inside Namibia was 2,628 km of 1,065 mm gauge in 2005. In 2002–03 railways carried 150,000 passengers and 1·9m. tonnes of freight.

Civil Aviation

The national carrier is the state-owned Air Namibia. In 2001 the major airport, Windhoek's Hosea Kutako International, handled 379,000 passengers (363,000 on international flights). Eros is used mainly for domestic flights. In 2003 scheduled airline traffic of Namibian-based carriers flew 11m. km, carrying 266,000 passengers (222,000 on international flights).

Shipping

The main port is Walvis Bay. During 1997–98, 808 ships called and 1,156,143 tonnes of cargo were landed. There is a harbour at Lüderitz which handles mainly fishing vessels. In 2002 merchant shipping totalled 69,000 GRT.

Telecommunications

Telecom Namibia is the responsible corporation. In 2008 there were 140,000 main (fixed) telephone lines; mobile phone subscribers numbered 1,052,000 in 2008 (49·4 per 100 persons). There were 400,000 PCs in use in 2006 and 113,500 internet users in 2008.

Postal Services

The national postal service is run by Namibia Post. In 2003 there were 118 post offices, or one for every 16,800 persons.

SOCIAL INSTITUTIONS

Justice

There is a Supreme Court, a High Court and a number of magistrates' and lower courts. An Ombudsman is appointed. Judges are appointed by the president on the recommendation of the Judicial Service Commission.

The population in penal institutions in Dec. 2001 was 4,814 (267 per 100,000 of national population).

Education

Literacy was 85·0% in 2003 (male, 86·8%; female, 83·5%). Primary education is free and compulsory. In 2007 there were 409,508 pupils at primary schools, 158,162 at secondary schools and (2006) 13,185 students at institutions of higher education.

In 2003 public expenditure on education came to 6·9% of GDP.

Health

In 1992 there were 47 hospitals (four private) and 238 clinics and health centres. There were 495 physicians, 67 dentists, 2,817 nurses and 1,954 midwives in 1997.

RELIGION

About 75% of the population is Christian (mainly Protestant).

CULTURE

World Heritage Sites

Namibia has one site on the UNESCO World Heritage List: a large collection of rock engravings at Twyfelfontein (added to the list in 2007).

Broadcasting

The Namibian Broadcasting Corporation is the state broadcaster, providing a national television and radio service. There is a private TV station operating from Windhoek and several independent radio stations. International TV channels can be received via satellite and cable. In 2004 there were 154,000 TV-equipped households (colour by PAL).

Press

There were four daily newspapers in 2006 with a combined circulation of 28,000.

Tourism

In 2005 there were 778,000 visitors who spent US$348m.

DIPLOMATIC REPRESENTATIVES

Of Namibia in the United Kingdom (6 Chandos St., London, W1G 9LU)
High Commissioner: George Mbanga Liswaniso.

Of the United Kingdom in Namibia (116 Robert Mugabe Ave., 9000 Windhoek)
High Commissioner: Mark Bensberg.

Of Namibia in the USA (1605 New Hampshire Ave., NW, Washington, D.C., 20009)
Ambassador: Patrick Nandago.

Of the USA in Namibia (14 Lossen St., Private Bag 12029, Windhoek)
Ambassador: G. Dennise Mathieu.

Of Namibia to the United Nations
Ambassador: Kaire Munionganda Mbuende.

Of Namibia to the European Union
Ambassador: Hanno Burkhard Rumpf.

FURTHER READING

Herbstein, D. and Evenston, J., *The Devils are Among Us: the War for Namibia.* 1989

Kaela, L. C. W., *The Question of Namibia.* 1996

Melber, Henning, *Re-examining Liberation in Namibia: Political Cultures Since Independence.* 2003

Sparks, D. L. and Green, D., *Namibia: the Nation after Independence.* 1992

National Statistical Office: National Planning Commission.
Website: http://www.npc.gov.na/cbs/index.htm

NAURU

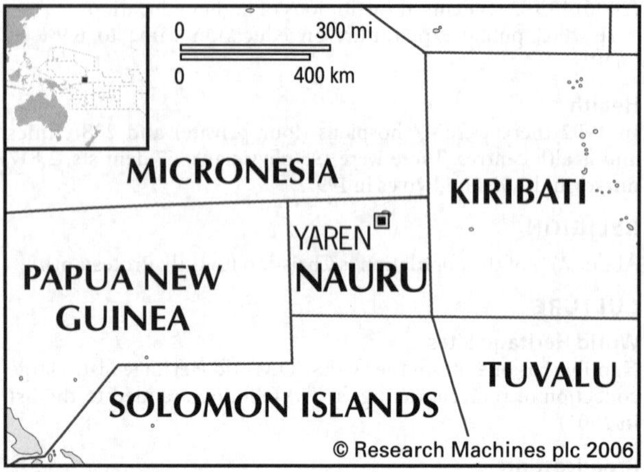

Ripublik Naoero
(Republic of Nauru)

Population, 2002: 10,000
GDP per capita: not available
GNI per capita, 2007: US$3,270

KEY HISTORICAL EVENTS

Nauru was originally settled by Melanesians and Polynesians. Tradition holds that among the earliest settlers were castaways from another island, probably Kiribati. The name 'Nauru' is a European corruption of 'A-nao-ero', which means 'I am going to the beach to lay my bones'. The island has had little contact with its neighbours, enabling its distinctive language to survive. By the 18th century the society was organized into 12 matrilineal tribes, each headed by a different chief.

The island was discovered by a British captain, John Fearn, in 1798 but was avoided by most ships in subsequent decades because of the region's notoriety for piracy. In the 1830s European whaling ships began using Nauru as a supply port and European settlers arrived. Though small in number, they had a profound impact by introducing alcohol, firearms and disease. An escalation in tribal conflict resulted in a war from 1878–88, killing 500 people or one third of the population. Germany annexed the island in 1888 to protect its trading interests and in the early 1900s agreed a deal to allow the British Pacific Phosphate Company to mine newly discovered phosphates.

Nauru was surrendered to Australian forces in 1914. In 1920 its administration was formally passed to the UK under a League of Nations mandate but in practice Australia continued to run the island. Australia, Britain and New Zealand set up and jointly ran the British Phosphate Commission, which controlled the phosphate mining industry. During the Second World War Japanese forces occupied from 1942–45, deporting 1,200 Nauruans to Truk (now Chuuk, in present-day Micronesia) as forced labour. Only 737 of the deportees returned. In 1947 Nauru became a UN trust, with Australia, New Zealand and the UK as trustees.

On 31 Jan. 1968 the country gained independence. The government of President Hammer DeRoburt took over the phosphate industry, continuing to run it as a communal trust. Phosphate prices rose and the country enjoyed a boom throughout the 1970s, achieving one of the world's highest rates of GDP per capita. However, mismanagement of the revenues, poor investment decisions and a lack of political accountability led to problems when prices fell in 1988. In 1993 Australia and the UK paid US$73m. compensation for environmental damage done during mining. Nauru developed an offshore banking industry in the 1990s but was accused of money-laundering by the international community. In the mid-1990s the economic crisis deepened with the collapse of the Bank of Nauru and in 2000 the OECD's financial watchdog (Financial Action Task Force on Money Laundering, or FATF) blacklisted the country. In 2001 Nauru agreed to hold detained asylum seekers on behalf of Australia and has subsequently relied heavily on Australian aid.

The 21st century has seen much political turmoil. During 2003 there were six changes of president and in Sept. 2004 President Ludwig Scotty declared a state of emergency. Following regulatory tightening of the offshore banking industry, Nauru was removed from the FATF blacklist in 2005. The island continues to face severe challenges, including a health crisis arising from the world's highest obesity rate.

TERRITORY AND POPULATION

Nauru is a coral island surrounded by a reef situated 0° 32' S. lat. and 166° 56' E. long. Area, 21·2 sq. km. At the 2002 census the population totalled 10,065 (5,136 males), of whom 7,572 were indigenous Nauruans. Population density, 475 per sq. km. The *de facto* capital is Yaren.

Nauruan is the official language, although English is widely used for government purposes.

SOCIAL STATISTICS

2002 births, 219; deaths, 75. Birth rate in 2002 was 17·8 per 1,000 population; death rate, 6·1. Infant mortality (2005), 25 (per 1,000 live births). Annual population growth rate, 1992–2002, 2·5%; fertility rate, 2004, 3·8 births per woman.

CLIMATE

A tropical climate, tempered by sea breezes, but with a high and irregular rainfall, averaging 82" (2,060 mm). Average temperature, Jan. 81°F (27·2°C), July 82°F (27·8°C). Annual rainfall 75" (1,862 mm).

CONSTITUTION AND GOVERNMENT

A Legislative Council was inaugurated on 31 Jan. 1966. The constitution was promulgated on 29 Jan. 1968 and was amended on 17 May 1968. An 18-member Parliament is elected on a three-yearly basis.

National Anthem

'Nauru bwiema, ngabena ma auwe' ('Nauru our homeland, the country we love'); words by M. Hendrie, tune by L. H. Hicks.

RECENT ELECTIONS

At the parliamentary elections of 26 April 2008, President Marcus Stephen's supporters won 12 of the 18 seats. On 29 April 2008 Stephen was re-elected by parliament, having first taken office on 19 Dec. 2007.

CURRENT ADMINISTRATION

In March 2010 the government comprised:

President and Minister of Public Service, Home Affairs, Police, Prisons and the Emergency Services and the Nauru Phosphate Royalties Trust: Marcus Stephen; b. 1969 (sworn in 19 Dec. 2007).

Minister Assisting the President and Minister for Foreign Affairs and Trade, and Finance and Sustainable Development: Dr Kieren

Keke. *Commerce, Industry and Natural Resources:* Frederick Pitcher. *Telecommunications and Transport:* Sprent Dabwido. *Education and Fisheries:* Roland Kun. *Health, Sports and Justice:* Matthew Batsiua.

Speaker: Riddell Akua.

CURRENT LEADERS

Marcus Stephen

Position
President

Introduction
Marcus Stephen became president in Dec. 2007 after a vote of no confidence against the previous incumbent, Ludwig Scotty. Stephen had served as education and finance minister from 2003–04 and represented Nauru on the International Whaling Commission (IWC) from 2005.

Early Life
Born in Nauru on 1 Oct. 1969, Marcus Stephen attended secondary school and university in Australia. After completing his education, he returned to Nauru and played Australian rules football before switching to weightlifting. His success in the sport led to the establishment of the Nauru Weightlifting Federation in 1989. Stephen subsequently represented Nauru in the 1996 and 2000 Olympics, won a series of gold and silver medals in four successive Commonwealth Games and was a runner-up in the 1999 World Championship. He was appointed treasurer of the Nauru Olympic Committee in 1997. On 3 May 2003 he was elected to parliament, representing the constituency of Ewa and Anetan.

Stephen served as education and finance minister in the government of René Harris from Aug. 2003–June 2004. He was re-elected to parliament in Oct. 2004, when he served under President Ludwig Scotty. When Nauru joined the IWC in June 2005, Stephen was nominated as a delegate for Nauru. Following parliamentary elections in Aug. 2007, he stood as a presidential candidate but lost out to Scotty. Allegations of corruption within the Scotty government led to a vote of no confidence in Nov. 2007, supported by Stephen. Scotty survived the vote but on 19 Dec. 2007 a second vote forced his resignation, paving the way for Stephen to become president.

Career in Office
Stephen took office promising transparency in public affairs. Dr Kieren Keke, who had been instrumental in bringing the votes of no confidence against Scotty, was appointed foreign minister. Early indications suggested Stephen was likely to maintain the financial reform programme and tighter banking regulations brought in by Scotty. The beginning of 2008 saw a deterioration in the economic climate when a controversial Australian immigrants' detention centre was closed. The island had hosted the centre, which generated 20% of GDP, for seven years. Replacing this income source is an urgent priority. Longer term challenges include a fundamental rebuilding of the economy and reparation of the environment. In April 2008 a snap parliamentary election called by Stephen resulted in a win for his supporters, and at the parliament's first sitting he was re-elected as president.

INTERNATIONAL RELATIONS

Nauru is a member of the UN, Asian Development Bank, Commonwealth, Pacific Islands Forum and SPC.

ECONOMY

Overview
The exhaustion of phosphate deposits has seen GDP per capita recede since peaking in the 1970s and 1980s. The economy is now dependent on external aid and imports owing to its narrow resource base. Attempts to diversify the economy into offshore banking during the 1990s proved unsuccessful and the country became a haven for money laundering, resulting in blacklisting by international bodies (including the Financial Action Task Force) until 2005. In 2001 Nauru signed an agreement with Australia to house asylum seekers on the island, generating millions of dollars in revenue. However this agreement was terminated in 2008.

New phosphate contracts came into force in 2008 resulting in the resumption of growth-driving exports. Mining of deeper, secondary reserves has commenced and the long-term future of the economy depends on the conversion of this mineral wealth into alternative sources of income. Further challenges include reducing public debt and promoting sound public and private investment.

Currency
The Australian dollar is in use.

Budget
The fiscal year is 1 July–30 June. Revenues in 2005–06 were \$A27·0m. and expenditures \$A26·4m.

Performance
Real GDP growth was 0·9% in 2002 and 2·5% in 2003.

Banking and Finance
The Bank of Nauru is a state bank and there is a commercial bank, Hampshire Bank and Trust Inc.

Nauru was one of three countries named in a report in June 2005 as failing to co-operate in the fight against international money laundering. In Oct. 2005 Nauru was delisted and its formal monitoring was ended a year later. The Financial Action Task Force on Money Laundering was set up by the G7 group of major industrialized nations.

ENERGY AND NATURAL RESOURCES

Environment
Carbon dioxide emissions from the consumption and flaring of fossil fuels were the equivalent of 14·7 tonnes per capita in 2008.

Electricity
Installed capacity in 2004 was an estimated 10,000 kW; production was estimated at 32m. kWh in 2004.

Minerals
A central plateau contained high-grade phosphate deposits. The interests in the phosphate deposits were purchased in 1919 from the Pacific Phosphate Company by the UK, Australia and New Zealand. In 1967 the British Phosphate Corporation agreed to hand over the phosphate industry to Nauru for approximately \$A20m. over three years. Nauru took over the industry in July 1969, and the profits from the mining meant that Nauru had, for a brief period, one of the highest rates of GDP per capita in the world. However, production declined (from 1·67m. tonnes in 1985–86 to 162,000 tonnes in 2001–02) and the primary reserves were exhausted in 2003. Mining of a deeper layer of secondary phosphate began in 2006, and it is hoped that this development might resuscitate Nauru's ailing economy. Production was an estimated 84,000 tonnes in 2006. In May 1989 Nauru filed a claim against Australia for environmental damage caused by the mining. In Aug. 1993 Australia agreed to pay compensation of \$A73m. In March 1994 New Zealand and the UK each agreed to pay compensation of \$A12m.

Agriculture
In 2007 about 1,000 people were economically active in agriculture. In 2003 the crop of coconuts was an estimated 2,000 tonnes. Livestock (2003 estimates): pigs, 3,000.

Fisheries
The catch in 2005 was 39 tonnes.

INTERNATIONAL TRADE

Imports and Exports

Imports are food, building construction materials, machinery for the phosphate industry and medical supplies. Phosphate accounts for virtually all of Nauru's exports.

Imports, 2005, A$33·7m.; exports, A$5·0m. The leading import sources in 2005 were Korea, Australia and the USA; the main export markets in 2005 were Korea, Canada and the UK.

COMMUNICATIONS

Roads

In 2002 there were 30 km of roads, 24 km of which were paved.

Civil Aviation

There is an airfield on the island capable of accepting medium size jet aircraft. The national carrier, Our Airline (formerly Air Nauru), is a wholly-owned government subsidiary. It has one aircraft. In 2006 it flew to Brisbane, Honiara, Tarawa and Majuro. In 2003 Our Airline flew 3m. km, carrying 156,000 passengers (all on international flights).

Shipping

Deep offshore moorings can accommodate medium-size vessels. Shipping coming to the island consists of vessels under charter to the phosphate industry or general purpose vessels bringing cargo by way of imports.

Telecommunications

There were 1,800 main telephone lines in operation in 2008.

SOCIAL INSTITUTIONS

Justice

The highest Court is the Supreme Court of Nauru. It is the Superior Court of record and has the jurisdiction to deal with constitutional matters in addition to its other jurisdiction. There is also a District Court which is presided over by the Resident Magistrate who is also the Chairman of the Family Court and the Registrar of Supreme Court. The laws applicable in Nauru are its own Acts of Parliament. A large number of British statutes and much common law has been adopted insofar as is compatible with Nauruan custom.

Education

Attendance at school is compulsory between the age of six and 16. In 2003 there were 588 children in pre-primary schools with 44 teachers, 1,375 pupils in primary schools with 63 teachers and 645 pupils in secondary schools with 34 teachers. There is also a trade school with four instructors and an enrolment of 88 trainees. Scholarships are available for Nauruan children to receive secondary and higher education and vocational training in Australia and New Zealand.

In 2000–01 total expenditure on education came to 7·0% of total government spending.

Health

In 1995 there were 17 physicians and 62 nurses.

Nauru has the highest percentage of overweight people of any country, with 94% overweight or obese according to a 2006 World Health Organization survey.

RELIGION

The population is mainly Roman Catholic or Protestant.

CULTURE

Broadcasting

The government-owned Nauru Broadcasting Service relays programmes from Radio Australia and the BBC. Nauru Television broadcasts programmes from New Zealand. There were 800 television receivers in 2002.

DIPLOMATIC REPRESENTATIVES

Of Nauru in the United Kingdom
Honorary Consul: Martin W. L. Weston (Romshed Courtyard, Underriver, Nr Sevenoaks, Kent, TN15 0SD).

Of the United Kingdom in Nauru
High Commissioner: Mac McLachlan, MBE (resides in Suva, Fiji Islands).

Of Nauru in the USA and to the United Nations (800 Second Ave., New York, NY 10017)
Ambassador: Marlene Inemwin Moses.

Of the USA in Nauru
Ambassador: C. Steven McGann (resides in Suva, Fiji Islands).

FURTHER READING

McDaniel, Carl N., *Paradise for Sale: Back to Sustainability.* 2000
Weeremantry, C., *Nauru: Environmental Damage under International Trusteeship.* 1992

National Statistical Office: Nauru Bureau of Statistics, Ministry of Finance, Government Offices, Yaren District.
Website: http://www.spc.int/prism/country/nr/stats

NEPAL

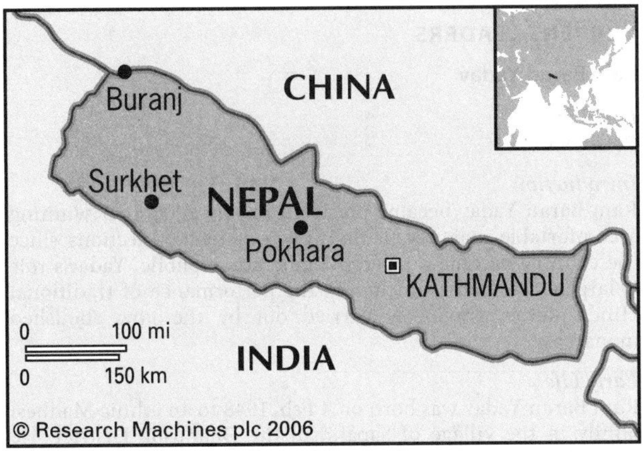

Sanghiya Loktantrik Ganatantra Nepal
(Federal Democratic Republic of Nepal)

Capital: Kathmandu
Population estimate, 2010: 29·85m.
GDP per capita, 2007: (PPP$) 1,049
HDI/world rank: 0·553/144

KEY HISTORICAL EVENTS

Nepal is an independent Himalayan Kingdom located between India and the Tibetan region of China. From the 8th to the 11th centuries many Buddhists fled to Nepal from India, which had been invaded by Muslims. In the 18th century Nepal was a collection of small principalities (many of Rajput origin) and the three kingdoms of the Malla dynasty: Kathmandu, Patan and Bhadgaon. In central Nepal lay the principality of Gurkha (or Gorkha); its ruler after 1742 was Prithvi Narayan Shah, who conquered the small neighbouring states. Fearing his ambitions, in 1767 the Mallas requested armed support from the British East India Company. In 1769 these forces were withdrawn and Gurkha was then able to conquer the Malla kingdoms and unite Nepal as one state with its capital at Kathmandu. In 1846 the Rana family became the effective rulers of Nepal, establishing the office of prime minister as hereditary. In 1860 Nepal reached agreement with the British in India whereby Nepali independence was preserved and the recruitment of Gurkhas to the British army was sanctioned.

In 1950 the Shah royal family allied itself with Nepalis abroad to end the power of the Ranas. The last Rana prime minister resigned in Nov. 1951, the king having proclaimed a constitutional monarchy in Feb. 1951. A new constitution, approved in 1959, led to confrontation between the king and his ministers; it was replaced by one less liberal in 1962. In Nov. 1990 the king relinquished his absolute power. The Maoists abandoned parliament in 1996 and launched a 'people's war' in the aim of turning the kingdom into a republic. This has resulted in more than 13,000 deaths.

In June 2001 the king and queen, along with six other members of the royal family, were shot dead by their son and heir to the throne, Crown Prince Dipendra, allegedly following a dispute over his choice of bride. Prince Dipendra then shot himself. The former monarch's younger brother, Gyanendra, was crowned king. In Nov. 2001 King Gyanendra declared a state of emergency and ordered troops to contain a fresh outbreak of Maoist violence. The government lifted the state of emergency in Aug. 2002. In Jan. 2003 the government and Maoist rebels reached a ceasefire agreement, seen as a first step towards bringing to an end the rebels' seven-year insurgency. In Feb. 2005 King Gyanendra dismissed his government and once more declared a state of emergency, taking control of the country and suspending democracy for three years. He lifted the state of emergency on 29 April 2005. In April 2006 he agreed to a return to parliamentary democracy after more than two weeks of unrest. On 21 Nov. 2006 a peace agreement was signed between the government and the country's Maoist rebels, bringing a formal end to the decade-long insurgency. In Dec. 2007 an agreement was made to abolish the monarchy and establish Nepal as a republic. On 28 May 2008 the newly-elected Constituent Assembly officially inaugurated the Federal Democratic Republic of Nepal and began the process of creating a new constitution.

TERRITORY AND POPULATION

Nepal is bounded in the north by China (Tibet) and the east, south and west by India. Area 147,181 sq. km; population census 2001, 23,151,423 of which 11,587,502 were female; density 157·3 per sq. km. In 2005, 84·2% of the population were rural.

The UN gives an estimated population for 2010 of 29·85m.

The country is divided into five developmental regions and 75 administrative districts. Area, population and administrative centres are:

Region	*Sq. km*	*Population (2001 census)*	*Administrative centre*
Central Region	27,410	8,031,629	Kathmandu
East Region	28,456	5,344,476	Dhankuta
West Region	29,398	4,571,013	Pokhara
Mid-West Region	42,378	3,012,975	Surkhet
Far West Region	19,539	2,191,330	Dipayal

Capital, Kathmandu; population (2001) 671,846. Other towns include (2001 census population): Biratnagar, 166,674; Lalitpur, 162,991; Pokhara, 156,312.

The indigenous people are of Tibetan origin with a considerable Hindu admixture. The Gurkha clan became predominant in 1559 and has given its name to men from all parts of Nepal. There are 18 ethnic groups, the largest being: Newars, Indians, Tibetans, Gurungs, Mogars, Tamangs, Bhotias, Rais, Limbus and Sherpas. The official language is Nepalese but there are 20 new languages divided into numerous dialects.

SOCIAL STATISTICS

2002 estimates: births, 790,000; deaths, 247,000. Estimated rates per 1,000 population, 2002: births, 32·0; deaths, 10·0. Annual population growth rate, 2000–05, 2·0%. Expectation of life was 65·6 years for males and 66·9 years for females in 2007. Infant mortality, 2005, 56 per 1,000 live births; fertility rate, 2004, 3·6 births per woman.

CLIMATE

Varies from cool summers and severe winters in the north to sub-tropical summers and mild winters in the south. The rainfall is high, with maximum amounts from June to Sept., but conditions are very dry from Nov. to Jan. Kathmandu, Jan. 10°C, July, 25°C. Average annual rainfall, 1,424 mm.

CONSTITUTION AND GOVERNMENT

Following years of political turbulence an interim constitution was approved in Dec. 2006, effectively removing King Gyanendra as the head of the state.

On 23 Dec. 2007 the interim government declared the establishment of the Federal Democratic Republic of Nepal, with the abolition of the monarchy approved by parliament five days later. This change entered into force on 28 May 2008 at the first meeting of a 601-member *Constituent Assembly* (with 240 seats filled on a first-past-the-post system, 335 filled through proportional representation and 26 nominated by the cabinet). The Constituent Assembly is charged with drafting a new constitution.

National Anthem

'Sayaun thunga phoolka hami eutai mala Nepali' ('From hundreds of flowers, we are one garland Nepali'); words by Byakul Maila, tune by Ambar Gurung.

RECENT ELECTIONS

In elections to the Constituent Assembly held on 10 April 2008 the Communist Party of Nepal/Maoist (CPN-M) won 220 of the 575 elected seats (26 seats are reserved for nominated members). Nepali Congress won 110 seats, the Communist Party/Unified Marxist-Leninist 103, the Madhesi Jana Adhikar Forum/Madhesi People's Rights Forum 52 and the Tarai-Madhesh Loktantrik Party 20. The remaining 70 seats were shared among fringe parties and independents.

Ram Baran Yadav (Nepali Congress) was elected president by the Constituent Assembly in a second round of voting on 21 July 2008, defeating Ram Raja Prasad Singh (Communist Party of Nepal/Maoist) by 308 votes to 282.

CURRENT ADMINISTRATION

President: Ram Baran Yadav; b. 1948 (Nepali Congress; sworn in 23 July 2008).

Vice President: Parmanand Jha.

In March 2010 the cabinet comprised:

Prime Minister: Madhav Kumar Nepal; b. 1953 (Communist Party of Nepal/Unified Marxist-Leninist; sworn in 25 May 2009).

Deputy Prime Minister and Minister for Physical Planning and Works: Bijay Kumar Gachchhadar (Madhesi People's Rights Forum).

Minister of Agriculture and Co-operatives: Mrigendra Kumar Singh Yadav (Madhesi People's Rights Forum). *Commerce and Supplies:* Rajendra Mahto (Sadbhavana Party). *Defence:* Bidhya Bhandari (Communist Party of Nepal/Unified Marxist-Leninist). *Education:* Sarbendra Nath Shukla (Tarai-Madesh Loktantrik Party). *Energy:* Prakash Sharan Mahat (Nepali Congress). *Environment, Science and Technology:* Thakur Sharma (Communist Party of Nepal/Unified Marxist-Leninist). *Federal Affairs, Constituent Assembly Affairs, Parliamentary Affairs and Culture:* Minendra Prasad Rijal (Nepali Congress). *Finance:* Surendra Pande (Communist Party of Nepal/Unified Marxist-Leninist). *Foreign Affairs:* Sujata Koirala (Nepali Congress). *Forestry and Soil Conservation:* Deepak Bohara (Rastriya Prajatantra Party). *General Administration:* Rabindra Shrestha (Communist Party of Nepal/Unified Marxist-Leninist). *Health and Population:* Umakanta Chaudhary (Nepali Congress). *Home Affairs:* Bhim Bahadur Rawal (Communist Party of Nepal/Unified Marxist-Leninist). *Industry:* Mahendra Prasad Yadav (Tarai-Madesh Loktantrik Party). *Information and Communications:* Shankar Pokheral (Communist Party of Nepal/Unified Marxist-Leninist). *Irrigation:* Bal Krishna Khana (Nepali Congress). *Labour and Transport:* Mohamad Aftab Aalam (Nepali Congress). *Land Reform and Management:* Dambar Shrestha (Communist Party of Nepal/Unified Marxist-Leninist). *Law and Justice:* Prem Bahadur Singh (Samajbadi Prajatantrik Janata Party). *Local Development:* Purna Kumar Serma Limbu (Nepali Congress). *Peace and Reconstruction:* Rakam Chemjong (Communist Party of Nepal/Unified Marxist-Leninist). *Tourism and Civil Aviation:* Sharat Singh Bhandari (Madhesi People's Rights Forum). *Women, Children and Social Welfare:* Sarbadev Prasad Ojha (Madhesi People's Rights Forum). *Youth and Sports:* Ganesh Tiwari Nepali (Tarai-Madesh Loktantrik Party). *Minister without Portfolio:* Laxman Lal Karna (Sadbhavana Party).

Office of the Prime Minister and Council of Ministers: http://www.opmcm.gov.np

CURRENT LEADERS

Ram Baran Yadav

Position
President

Introduction
Ram Baran Yadav became president in July 2008 after winning a comfortable majority in the first presidential elections since the country became a federal democratic republic. Yadav's role is largely ceremonial, including the performance of traditional Hindu duties previously carried out by the now abolished monarchy.

Early Life
Ram Baran Yadav was born on 4 Feb. 1948 to an ethnic Madhesi family in the village of Sapahi, in the Dhanusha District. He studied medicine at the School of Tropical Medicine (Kolkata) and the Calcutta Medical College. He obtained his postgraduate degree from the Institute of Medical Education and Research in Chandigarh, India. Upon returning to Nepal, Yadav ran his own medical practice in Janakpur.

While in India, Yadav had become involved in the Nepali pro-democracy movement and in 1980 he joined the Nepali Congress (NC) party. He participated in the 1990 Jana Andolan (People's Movement) but was arrested and jailed for three months until the implementation of a democratic constitution. Yadav was elected to parliament as an NC candidate in 1991 and served as minister of health for three years in the administration of Girija Prasad Koirala.

At the 1999 general election Yadav was re-elected and continued as health minister, establishing a healthcare system in rural Nepal. He then became general secretary of the NC. He won the seat of Dhanusa-5 at elections for the constituent assembly in April 2008.

Yadav contested the presidential election of July 2008 on an NC ticket but fell four votes short of the 298 needed to win a simple majority. In a second round of voting he won 308 of 590 votes cast. Yadav's victory came as an upset to the Communist Party of Nepal/Maoist (CPN-M) who were seeking to form the government after their win in the April 2008 Constituent Assembly election. Yadav was sworn into office on 23 July 2008.

Career in Office
Yadav has prioritized the drafting of a new democratic constitution in a bid to end Nepal's long track-record of political violence, and has been keen to maintain friendly ties with both India and China. However, he faced opposition from the CPN-M whose leader, Pushpa Kamal Dahal (Prachanda), led a coalition government from Aug. 2008 until May 2009 when he resigned in protest at Yadav's blocking of his controversial attempt to dismiss the country's army head. Madhav Kumar Nepal of the Communist Party/Unified Marxist-Leninist was sworn in as the prime minister of a new coalition, excluding the CPN-M, later in the month. The CPN-M has since demanded a return to power, claiming that Yadav had acted unconstitutionally, and organized a general strike in Dec.

Madhav Kumar Nepal

Position
Prime Minister

Introduction
Madhav Kumar Nepal became prime minister on 25 May 2009 when he was elected by parliament to replace Pushpa Kamal

Dahal, who had resigned. The former general secretary of the Communist Party of Nepal/Unified Marxist-Leninist, Madhav Nepal heads a 22-party coalition.

Early Life

Madhav Nepal was born on 6 March 1953 in the southern Nepalese district of Rautahat. He studied at Sitamarhi in Bihar and graduated in commerce from Tribhuvan University in 1973. He joined the underground Marxist Leninist communist movement in 1969, and in 1971 became a district committee member of the Nepal Revolutionary Coordinating Committee (Marxist Leninist), otherwise known as the ANCRCC (ML). He pursued a career in banking and then in the civil service before taking up politics full-time.

In 1978 the ANCRCC (ML) legitimized itself as the Communist Party of Nepal/Unified Marxist-Leninist (CPN-UML), with Madhav Nepal elected to its politburo. From 1991–99 he was the CPN-UML leader of the opposition and served as deputy prime minister in the CPN-UML minority government of 1994–95. He argued against mobilizing the army during the civil war and in 2005 he campaigned against the king's usurpation of executive powers. At the 2008 election Madhav Nepal lost the Kathmandu seat and his home town seat of Rautahat to Maoist candidates, prompting him to resign as party general secretary.

In May 2009 the Maoist premier, Pushpa Kamal Dahal, resigned in protest at the president's refusal to accept his dismissal of the army chief. Madhav Nepal was chosen by parliament to replace Dahal in an unopposed poll, boycotted by the opposition.

Career in Office

Since becoming prime minister, he has all but officially revoked the previous government's dismissal of the army chief. Attempts to pass the budget were obstructed by opposition parties unhappy with Madhav Nepal's lack of commitment to spending on agriculture and infrastructure. Meanwhile, he has agreed to negotiations towards some level of independence for the Madhesi region in the south of the country. The premier has succeeded in clearing Kathmandu of much of its street rubbish problem and he has instigated plans to erect a monument to the republic.

He faces three key challenges: to establish a new constitution; to reintegrate and resettle ex-Maoist combatants (19,000 of whom were in UN-monitored cantonments in early 2010); and to ensure adherence to the comprehensive peace accord. In March 2010 the Maoist opposition was showing signs that it would not co-operate with the government and there was speculation that a motion of no confidence was under preparation.

DEFENCE

The King was formerly commander-in-chief of the armed forces, but he was stripped of the position in May 2006. The cabinet now has the power to appoint the army chief.

Defence expenditure in 2006 totalled US$158m. (US$6 per capita), representing 2·0% of GDP.

As at Oct. 2009, 4,348 personnel (3,451 troops, 839 police and 58 military observers) were deployed in UN peacekeeping operations.

Army

Strength (2007) 69,000, and there is also a 62,000-strong paramilitary police force (15,000 armed).

Air Force

The Army's air wing has no combat capable aircraft. Personnel, 2007, 320.

INTERNATIONAL RELATIONS

Nepal is a member of the UN, World Bank, IMF and several other UN specialized agencies, WTO, IOM, Asian Development Bank, Colombo Plan and SAARC.

ECONOMY

Agriculture accounted for 35·1% of GDP in 2006, industry 17·4% and services 47·5%.

Overview

Since the early 1990s the government has encouraged trade and foreign investment by simplifying business licenses and registration requirements. The production of textiles and carpets accounts for over two-thirds of foreign exchange earnings. Apart from agricultural land and forests, exploitable natural resources include mica, hydropower and tourism. Agriculture remains the economy's principal area of activity, employing around 80% of the workforce and accounting for roughly 40% of GDP.

In recent years the economy has underperformed as a result of political tensions and internal unrest. According to the IMF, real GDP growth averaged only 2% between 2000–01 and 2004–05 compared to 5% in the 1990s. Tourism, an important source of earnings, has also suffered with the number of visitors below peak levels of the late 1990s. Monetary and exchange rate policies are geared towards supporting the exchange rate peg to the Indian rupee, which has helped to contain inflation. Social indicators are poor; Nepal is ranked 144th of 182 countries on the UN Human Development Index, although poverty levels have fallen markedly from a level of 42% in 1995–96 to just over 30% in 2003–04. The IMF states that critical reform of the financial sector, public enterprises and governance are required in order to reduce poverty and restore growth.

Currency

The unit of currency is the *Nepalese rupee* (NPR) of 100 *paisas*. 50 *paisas* = 1 *mohur*. Inflation was 6·4% in 2007 and 7·7% in 2008. Foreign exchange reserves were US$1,478m. in July 2005 and gold reserves totalled 129,000 troy oz. Total money supply in March 2009 was NRs 177,682m.

Budget

Budgetary central government revenue totalled NRs 102,188m. in 2006–07 (NRs 84,100m. in 2005–06) and expenditure NRs 116,606m. (NRs 94,881m. in 2005–06). Main sources of revenue, 2006–07 (NRs 1m.): taxes, 71,127 (including: taxes on goods and services, 36,434; taxes on international trade and transactions, 16,708); grants, 15,801. Major items of expenditure, 2006–07 (NRs 1m.): general public services, 27,151; economic affairs, 26,571; education, 21,388; defence, 10,958.

VAT is 13%.

Performance

Real GDP growth was 3·2% in 2007 and 4·7% in 2008. Nepal's total GDP in 2008 was US$12·6bn.

Banking and Finance

The Central Bank is the bank of issue (*Governor*, Bijaya Nath Bhattarai). In 2002 there were four domestic commercial banks (Kumari Bank; Nepal Bank; Nepal Industrial and Commercial Bank; Rastriya Banijya Bank), ten joint-venture banks and four development finance organizations (Agricultural Development Bank; Nepal Development Bank; Nepal Housing Development Finance Corporation; Nepal Industrial Development Corporation).

There is a stock exchange in Kathmandu.

ENERGY AND NATURAL RESOURCES

Environment

Nepal's carbon dioxide emissions from the consumption and flaring of fossil fuels in 2008 were the equivalent of 0·1 tonnes per capita.

Electricity

Installed capacity was approximately 0·4m. kW in 2004. Production in 2004 was an estimated 2·35bn. kWh (over 99% hydro-electric), with consumption per capita 86 kWh.

Minerals
Production (in tonnes), 2005: limestone, 263,701; red clay, 35,484; agricultural lime (2003), 13,025; coal, 9,289; talc, 5,832; salt, 2,000.

Agriculture
Agriculture is the mainstay of the economy, providing a livelihood for over 90% of the population and accounting for 39% of GDP. In 2002 there were about 3·2m. ha. of arable land and 94,000 ha. of permanent crops. Cultivated land accounts for 26·5% of land use; forest and woodland 42·4%. Crop production (2003, in 1,000 tonnes): rice, 4,155; sugarcane, 2,250; potatoes, 1,480; maize, 1,441; wheat, 1,344; millet, 288.

Livestock (2002); cattle, 6·98m.; goats, 6·61m.; buffaloes, 3·70m.; pigs, 934,000; sheep, 840,000; chickens, 21m.

Livestock products (2003 estimates, in 1,000 tonnes): buffalo meat, 130; beef and veal, 48; goat meat, 39; poultry meat, 15; buffalo's milk, 816; cow's milk, 353; goat's milk, 64; eggs, 27.

Forestry
In 2005 the area under forests was 3·64m. ha., or 25·4% of the total land area. There are eight national parks, covering 1m. ha., five wildlife reserves (170,490 ha.) and two conservation areas (349,000 ha.). Timber production was 13·88m. cu. metres in 2007, mainly for use as fuelwood and charcoal. Expansion of agricultural land has led to widespread deforestation.

Fisheries
The catch in 2005 was 19,983 tonnes, exclusively from inland waters.

INDUSTRY
In 2002 industry accounted for 20·9% of GDP, with manufacturing contributing 8·1%. Production (2001–02 unless otherwise stated): cement, 215,000 tonnes; sugar, 65,000 tonnes; soap, washing powder and detergents, 55,100 tonnes; animal feed, 22,000 tonnes; paper and paperboard, 13,000 tonnes; tea (1994), 2,351 tonnes; synthetic textiles (1994), 14·7m. metres; electrical cable (1994), 9·3m. metres; cotton woven fabrics, 2·5m. metres; leather (1994), 1,369,750 sq. metres; shoes, 0·71m. pairs; beer (2003), 23·1m. litres; cigarettes, 6,979m. units. Brewing is one of the successes of Nepal's economy, accounting for some 3% of GDP.

Labour
The labour force in 1996 totalled 10,179,000 (60% males). In 1992, 84% of the economically active population were engaged in agriculture, forestry or fisheries.

INTERNATIONAL TRADE
External debt was an estimated US$3,285m. in 2005.

Imports and Exports
The following table shows the value of Nepal's imports (f.o.b.) and exports (f.o.b.) for calendar years in US$1m.:

	2000	*2001*	*2002*	*2003*	*2004*
Imports	1,590·1	1,485·7	1,425·4	1,665·9	1,812·5
Exports	776·1	720·5	632·0	703·2	763·6

The main import suppliers in 2004 were: India (43·0%), China (10·0%), UAE (10·0%), Saudi Arabia (4·4%). The leading export markets in 2004 were: India (48·8%), USA (22·3%), Germany (8·5%), UK (2·8%).

Principal import commodities are petroleum products, transport equipment and parts, chemical fertilizer and raw wool. Principal export commodities are carpets, clothing, leather goods, pulses, raw jute and jute goods, and handicrafts. Hand-knotted woollen carpets are the largest overseas export item constituting almost 32% of foreign exchange earnings.

COMMUNICATIONS

Roads
In 2006 there were 16,834 km of roads, of which 17% were paved.

Rail
101 km (762 mm gauge) connect Jayanagar on the North Eastern Indian Railway with Janakpur and thence with Bizalpura (54 km). 653,000 passengers and 9,151 tonnes of freight were carried in 1994.

Civil Aviation
There is an international airport (Tribhuvan) at Kathmandu. The national carrier is the state-owned Royal Nepal Airlines. It operates domestic services and in 2003 flew to Bangalore, Bangkok, Delhi, Dubai, Hong Kong, Kuala Lumpur, Mumbai, Osaka, Shanghai and Singapore. In 2004 Kathmandu handled 2,066,950 passengers (1,140,660 on international flights) and 15·3m. tonnes of freight. In 2003 scheduled airline traffic of Nepali-based carriers flew 8m. km, carrying 356,000 passengers (279,000 on international flights).

Telecommunications
In 2008 there were 805,100 main (fixed) telephone lines in Nepal and mobile phone subscribers numbered 4,200,000 (14·6 per 100 persons). There were 132,000 PCs in use in 2005 and 499,000 internet users in 2008.

Postal Services
In 2000 there were 4,012 post offices.

SOCIAL INSTITUTIONS

Justice
The Supreme Court Act established a uniform judicial system, culminating in a supreme court of a Chief Justice and no more than six judges. Special courts to deal with minor offences may be established at the discretion of the government. The king previously had the power to appoint the Chief Justice, but this power passed to the prime minister under the temporary constitution signed in Dec. 2006.

The death penalty was abolished in 1997. The population in penal institutions in Jan. 2008 was approximately 6,700 (24 per 100,000 of national population).

Education
The adult literacy rate in 2003 was 48·6% (62·7% among males but only 34·9% among females). Only Yemen has a bigger difference in literacy rates between the sexes.

In 2007 there were there were 4,515,059 pupils and 112,827 teaching staff in primary schools and 1,998,990 pupils in secondary schools with (in 2003) 52,528 teaching staff. There were 320,844 students in tertiary education in 2007 with 9,932 academic staff. The oldest and largest university in Nepal is Tribhuvan University, which was established in 1959.

In 2003 public expenditure on education came to 3·1% of GNI and 14·9% of total government spending.

Health
There were 1,259 physicians and 6,216 nurses in 2001. In 2000 there were 133 hospitals, 180 primary health care centres and 711 health posts.

RELIGION
Nepal is a Hindu state. Hinduism was the religion of 82·8% of the people in 2001. Buddhists comprise 8·9% and Muslims 4·2%. Christian missions are permitted, but conversion is forbidden.

CULTURE

World Heritage Sites
Nepal has four sites on the UNESCO World Heritage List: Sagarmatha National Park (inscribed on the list in 1979);

Kathmandu Valley (1979 and 2006); Royal Chitwan National Park (1984); and Lumbini, the Birthplace of the Lord Buddha (1997).

Broadcasting

State-run Nepal Television Corporation (NTV) and Radio Nepal are the national broadcasters. The private television and radio sector has been expanding under political liberalization. In 2006 there were 590,000 TV sets (colour by PAL).

Press

In 2003 there were 251 daily newspapers, including the official English-language *Rising Nepal*, 14 bi-weeklies, 1,304 weeklies and 167 fortnightlies. Press censorship was relaxed in June 1991, but following the imposition of a state of emergency in Feb. 2005 the press was subjected to total censorship.

Tourism

Foreign tourists visiting Nepal numbered 361,200 in 2001, down from 463,600 in 2000, largely as a consequence of the massacre of the royal family and an upsurge in Maoist rebel violence. They have since returned to and surpassed former levels with 526,700 tourists in 2007, an increase of 37·2% on 2006. Gross foreign exchange earnings came to US$230·6m. in 2007, an increase of 41·7% on the previous year. In 2007, 24,700 hotel beds were available. Tourism accounts for approximately 4% of GDP.

Festivals

Hindu, Buddhist and traditional festivals crowd the Nepali lunar calendar. Dasain (Sept./Oct.) is the longest and most widely observed festival in Nepal. The 15 days of celebration include Dashami, when family elders are honoured. Tihar (Oct./Nov.) celebrates the Hindu goddess Laxmi. During the first three days crows, dogs and cows are worshipped, followed by the spirit, or self. It concludes with Bhai Tika ('Brother's Day'). Buddha Jayanti (May/June) remembers the birth, enlightenment and death of the Buddha. Sherpas gather at Tengboche Monastery near Mount Everest in May to observe Mani Rimdu with meditation, mask dances and Buddhist ceremonies.

DIPLOMATIC REPRESENTATIVES

Of Nepal in the United Kingdom (12A Kensington Palace Gdns, London, W8 4QU)
Ambassador: Vacant.
Chargé d'Affaires a.i: Jhabindra P. Aryal.

Of the United Kingdom in Nepal (Lainchaur, Kathmandu, POB 106)
Ambassador: Dr Andrew Hall, OBE.

Of Nepal in the USA (2131 Leroy Pl., NW, Washington, D.C., 20008)
Ambassador: Shankar Prasad Sharma.

Of the USA in Nepal (Maharajguni, Kathmandu)
Ambassador: Vacant.
Chargé d'Affaires a.i.: Donald Camp.

Of Nepal to the United Nations
Ambassador: Gyan Chandra Acharya.

Of Nepal to the European Union
Ambassador: Pramesh Kumar Hamal.

FURTHER READING

Central Bureau of Statistics. *Statistical Pocket Book.* [Various years]

Borre, O., *et al., Nepalese Political Behaviour.* 1994
Ghimire, K., *Forest or Farm? The Politics of Poverty and Land Hunger in Nepal.* 1993
Hutt, Michael, (ed.) *Himalayan 'People's War' Nepal's Maoist Rebellion.* 2004
Lawoti, Mahendra, *Towards a Democratic Nepal: Inclusive Political Institutions for a Multicultural Society.* 2005
Sanwal, D. B., *Social and Political History of Nepal.* 1993
Thapa, Deepak, *A Kingdom Under Siege: Nepal's Maoist Insurgency, 1996 to 2004.* 2005
Whelpton, John, *A History of Nepal.* 2005

National Statistical Office: Central Bureau of Statistics, National Planning Commission Secretariat, Kathmandu.
Website: http://www.cbs.gov.np

THE NETHERLANDS

Koninkrijk der Nederlanden
(Kingdom of the Netherlands)

Capital: Amsterdam
Seat of government: The Hague
Population estimate, 2010: 16·65m.
GDP per capita, 2007: (PPP$) 38,694
HDI/world rank: 0·964/6

KEY HISTORICAL EVENTS

Flint tools found in the Maastricht area have been estimated to be 250,000 years old. The first definable culture (*c.* 3000 BC) was the Late Stone Age 'Funnel-neck Beaker' culture, named after the objects made by a people known for their monolithic burial monuments. The environment of the 'Low Countries' affected the behaviour of its earliest inhabitants, as demonstrated by the *terpen*—islands of earth and clay—built by the autochthonous Frisians (Frisii) *c.* 500 BC as protection from the sea.

The Romans encountered Celtic tribes to the west and south of the Rhine and Germanic tribes, such as the Frisii, to the north and east. In the 1st century BC Julius Caesar attested to the resistance of the Celtic Eburones and Aduatuci. Roman power beyond the Rhine was limited to isolated forts and client kingdoms.

In the 3rd century AD the stagnant Roman borders began to crumble as military posts were abandoned. Among the most prominent of the encroaching Germanic tribes were the Franks, who settled at first in Toxandria (modern Brabant). Like many 'barbarian' tribes, the Franks entered into agreements with Rome, settling and guarding the border region and assimilating Roman culture. The Frisians became important traders, holding strategic territory between the German (North) Sea and the Meuse and Rhine rivers. With the collapse of Roman government in Gaul and the Rhine in the 5th century, the Franks extended their power, centred on Austrasia (the central Rhine region). The spread of Christianity in the 7th century, first from the bishoprics of Arras, Tournai and Cambrai, assisted Frankish expansion into the northern Low Countries, where the missionary bishopric of Utrecht was established.

Viking raids on the North Sea coast devastated the flourishing Frisian economy. The Frisian trading centre of Dorestad was destroyed four times between 834–37 by raiders seeking Carolingian silver. Frisia came under Frankish domination during the reign of Pippin the Short, the founder of the Carolingian Empire.

The High Middle Ages saw the development of independent and semi-autonomous principalities, both secular and ecclesiastical. Great landlords established the large counties (Flanders, Hainault, Namur and Holland and Zeeland) and duchies (Brabant, Limburg and Guelders), increasing their authority and size through dynastic alliances and inheritance. The majority fell broadly under the authority of the German king, heirs to the Eastern Frankish realm, though the feudal relationship allowed the growth of a tradition of independence that became a defining characteristic of Dutch politics. The growth of population and its pressure on the land increased the need for land reclamation. Dykes were built from Friesland to Flanders to drain the bogs and marshes for pasturage and, later, agrarian use. The development of urban centres outside the feudal structure was encouraged by the strength of trade and the merchant classes.

The Burgundian era in the Low Countries was born of a series of dynastic matches, most importantly that of Duke Philip II (the Bold) of Burgundy and Margaret, Countess of Flanders and Artois in 1369. Their son, Philip III (the Good), brought most of the northern Low Countries under one lord by inheriting Brabant and Hainault-Holland in the 1430s as well as Luxembourg in 1443. Although the dukes attempted to rule through new centralized bodies, the Burgundian Low Countries were held in a personal union and did not constitute a state. The duke appointed *stadhouders* (stadtholders) and governors to represent him in each of his territories. The summoning of the Estates in 1464 in Brugge (Bruges) represented the first parliamentary assembly in the Low Countries and the importance of the *Nederlands* in the Burgundian realm.

Burgundian Rule

The reign of Charles the Bold, or Rash (1467–77), saw the brief land connection of the realm (by the acquisition of Lorraine) and the first explicit attempt to create a unitary kingdom—an echo of the Middle Frankish Kingdom, Lotharingia. Charles failed in his bid to make himself regent of this kingdom in 1473 and his death at the Battle of Nancy left his domains to his daughter, Mary. The duchess was soon stripped of the Duchy of Burgundy by the French king and was forced to concede privileges to the provinces. Her marriage to Maximilian of Habsburg, the future Holy Roman Emperor, brought the Low Countries into personal union with Austria and, later, Spain. Mary's son, Philip the Handsome, inherited the Spanish throne through his wife, Juana the Mad, forging a massive and disparate empire of kingdoms, principalities and lordships. Philip's son, Charles V, though born in Ghent, spent little time in the Low Countries after succeeding to the Spanish throne. They were administered by governors-general, normally taken from the ruler's family. Centralization, though consistently opposed, continued to be pressed on the inhabitants of the Low Countries. The 17 provinces were brought together formally in 1548 as the 'Burgundian *Kreis*' and the sovereign succession regulated by Pragmatic Sanction the following year. Brussels became the centre of government, being the location of the court and most organs of government.

Philip (II of Spain) imposed a new ecclesiastical hierarchy, sanctioned by papal bull in 1559, in an attempt to use the church as a centralizing force. The traditional resistance of the towns and provinces was given added fervour by the religious controversies attributable to the Reformation. Erasmus, a leading Dutch humanist, openly attacked the abuses and corruptions of the Church but rejected the theology of the reformers such as Martin Luther. However, the works of the radical Jean Calvin arrived in Antwerp in 1545, spreading throughout the region rapidly after their translation in 1560. Calvinism appealed to the intellectual middle classes, as well as the artisans, whose work ethic it extolled. The government focused its repressive efforts on the Anabaptists, whose refusal to swear allegiance to the prince was an affront to temporal and spiritual authority. The iconoclastic purges of 1566 provoked Philip to send the duke of Alba to restore his authority, thereby sparking full-scale revolt and the Eighty Years War (1568–1648).

The causes of the Dutch Revolt were numerous; religious tensions, resentment towards 'Spanish' authority, the heavy burden of taxes and absolutist government and the perceived desecration of traditional privileges were combined with years of hardship caused by climatic conditions and wars with France. However, in the earlier years of the revolt, the 'legitimate' *casus belli* claimed by the Dutch was the influence of 'evil advisers' around the prince—few openly rejected Philip's sovereignty. The *Geuzen*, an army of beggars, pillaging and pirating in the name of William of Orange, took the port of Brielle in 1572. This began the expulsion of Spanish authority from the northern provinces, a process completed by 1574.

The conversion of William (the Silent) to Calvinism in 1572, in response to his selection as stadtholder of Holland and Zeeland, was a political move to gain support for a united Netherlands of Catholics and Protestants. The 1576 Pacification of Ghent brought together predominantly Catholic and Protestant provinces in the face of bloody repression meted out by Alba's Council of Troubles (Council of Blood) and the notorious 'Spanish Fury' massacre in Antwerp. The mainly Catholic southern provinces were largely regained for Philip by the brilliant Alessandro Farnese, duke of Parma in 1578, forcing a 'closer union'—the Union of Utrecht—in the north in 1579, committed to resisting the Spanish. This marked the birth of the United Provinces of the Netherlands, or the 'Dutch Republic', with power concentrated in the hands of the stadtholders, nominally representing the hereditary prince. Philip's refusal to compromise led to his 'forfeiture of sovereignty' in the States-General Act of Abjuration in 1581, on the grounds of persistent tyranny.

The constitutional position of the Republic was unclear. The House of Orange was recognized as the traditional stadtholders of each province, though the lordship of the territories was tendered to both France and England in the 1580s. Maurice of Nassau, the son of William of Orange, was named stadtholder of Holland and Zeeland in 1587. Maurice's victories over Farnese came to be called the 'closing of the garden', giving the United Provinces the approximate borders it has maintained to the modern day. With recognition from England and France, the government negotiated the Twelve Year Truce in 1609 with Spain, which recognized the independence of the United Provinces.

The Calvinist church divided between the followers of two prominent clerics, Jacobus Arminius (the Remonstrants) and Franciscus Gomarus (the Contra-Remonstrants). The Arminians, championed by the elite of Holland and the towns, objected to the repressive orthodoxy of the Gomarists and demanded an inclusive reformed church to protect trade and foreign relations. The execution of the Remonstrant Johan van Oldenbarnvelt, the Advocate of Holland, signified the triumph of Maurice's Contra-Remonstrants and made permanent peace with Spain impossible. After initial Spanish success at Breda in 1621, Maurice's successor, Frederick Henry, turned the tide, taking Maastricht in the far south. Ending the persecution of the Remonstrants, Frederick Henry augmented the authority of his princely house, even earning an honorific royal title from the French King. Lasting peace with Spain was finally won at the 1648 Treaty of Münster, which formally recognized the Dutch Republic.

Independence and the Golden Age

The 17th century has traditionally been called the Golden Age of the Dutch. From the Twelve Year Truce, the Dutch economy expanded massively, principally through trade in the Baltic and with France, Iberia and the colonies of the West and East Indies. The United East Indies Company, chartered in 1602, held quasi-sovereign authority over its colonies in Sri Lanka, India and Indonesia. Dutch banking financed the northern European markets, chiefly through foreign government bonds. The increase of wealth stimulated the arts. Prosperous life in Dutch towns was painted by Jan Vermeer and Amsterdam's burghers by Rembrandt. Although Calvinism had been officially adopted, Catholics were left unmolested but public worship was prohibited.

After the death of Frederick Henry's bellicose son, William II, in 1650, the republic experienced its first 'stadtholderless' period when the prosperous province of Holland dominated the Netherlands. Relations with Republican England deteriorated because of the execution of Charles I, who was closely related to the House of Orange. More importantly, competition for trade and shipping between the two great maritime powers caused skirmishes in America and Europe and a series of Anglo-Dutch Wars, conducted at sea. The destruction of the English fleet at Chatham in 1667 destroyed relations with Charles II, who had supported Orangist interests in the Netherlands.

The House of Orange reassumed the leadership of the Netherlands when William III took the stadtholdership of Holland in 1672 and defeated the French and the English in naval encounters. The Dutch supported William in his invasion of England—the Glorious Revolution—in 1688, claiming the throne with his wife, Mary Stuart. His death without issue in 1702 heralded the second stadtholderless period, when the councillor pensionaries of Holland asserted the province's leadership. However, the oligarchic nature of government attracted little support, especially during Dutch humiliations at the hands of the French in the War of the Austrian Succession (1740–48). William IV of Orange was elected to all provinces in 1747, the House of Orange being seen as the natural leaders of the Dutch people.

Both William IV and William V resisted calls for a more relaxed rule. The Patriot Movement took advantage of the Dutch defeat in the Fourth Anglo-Dutch War of the 1780s to depose William V. However, Prussia's intervention restored the stadtholder and many Patriots fled to France, then on the brink of revolution.

Revolutionary France's invasion of Belgium (the Spanish Netherlands) in 1794 was soon extended to the United Provinces. William V fled to England and the Patriots, supported by the French, assumed control of government. The new 'Batavian Republic', styled after the supposedly original inhabitants, was in reality a protectorate of France. This truly republican period enabled political modernization, much of which has lasted to the modern day. An elected national assembly was instituted (though the franchise was retained by property owners only), with new electoral constituencies to replace the old provinces. Religious toleration was adopted, with all denominations awarded equal treatment. However, the economy declined, partly because of the seizure of the Dutch colonies in the name of William V by Great Britain, which had declared war on France.

Napoleon

The republic was ended in 1806 when Napoleon incorporated the Netherlands into his empire. He installed his brother, Louis, as king of Holland. Louis adopted the cause of his new subjects, frequently defying his brother's orders in favour of Dutch interests. Napoleon ended his brother's reign in 1810 and brought his kingdom under French rule. Gijsbert Karel van Hogendorp, who drew up the new constitution after the French withdrawal in 1813, led the opposition to France. The new constitution provided for a constitutional monarchy, with William V's son proclaimed king (William I), as demanded by the Congress of Vienna. The northern provinces were united with Belgium and Luxembourg under the Kingdom of the Netherlands.

William I saw the revival of the economy as the first priority. Using his personal resources as well as the treasury, he invested heavily in the re-establishment of Dutch shipping, especially to the restored colonies. Domestically, William was not so successful. In 1830 Belgium proclaimed its independence, rejecting a common identity with the predominantly Protestant north—the declaration of Dutch as the sole official language had alienated the French-speaking Walloons in Brussels. Though defeated by the Dutch army, the Belgians gained their independence in 1839 thanks to French and British intervention in 1832.

In response to the European revolutions of 1848, the king granted a liberal constitution. Support for the king was bolstered by the patriotic reaction in the northern provinces to the Belgian secession. The reintroduction of the Catholic hierarchy in 1853 won over a community which made up over a third of the population.

Dutch imperialism was consolidated in the second half of the 19th century. Having lost numerous colonies in the Americas, southern Africa and India, attention focused on the Indonesian archipelago. War with Aceh in northern Sumatra, famous for its piracy, was long and bloody but secured the archipelago for the Netherlands. The division of New Guinea was settled with Germany and Great Britain in 1875. Personal union with Luxembourg came to an end on the accession of Wilhelmina in 1890, barred by Salic Law from inheriting the Grand Duchy.

European War

In 1917 universal male suffrage was granted in return for the secular parties' acceptance of funding for religious schools, thus concluding the thirty-year School Conflict. Female suffrage followed in 1922. Wilhelmina, though less active in government than her father, William III, strongly advocated neutrality in the conflicts of the early 20th century, keeping the Netherlands out of the First World War. The German Kaiser, Wilhelm II, was granted asylum in the Netherlands.

The inter-war years were a period of social and political continuity. The *zuilen* system expanded, cementing what has been described as a bourgeois consensus, though worldwide depression hit the Netherlands hard in the 1930s. In 1932 the IJsselmeer dam was completed, transforming the Zuider Zee, an inlet of the North Sea, into a freshwater lake, the IJsselmeer.

The neutrality of the Netherlands was not respected by Germany in the Second World War, despite assurances from Hitler after the invasion of Poland. Control of the Netherlands and Belgium was seen as essential to protect the industrial centres of the Ruhr and to gain broader access to the North Sea. The Dutch armed forces were overwhelmed within a week in May 1940. The queen and government went into exile in London. Persecution of the Jews began in Oct. 1941. The first transports left in July 1942, mostly to Auschwitz. 107,000 Dutch Jews died. Dutch resistance took the form of civilian sabotage and the hiding of Jews and *onkerduikers* ('underdivers')—underground military operatives.

The Netherlands saw some of the bitterest fighting near the close of the war when Allied troops made airborne incursions—Arnhem Bridge in Sept. 1944—to speed victory over Germany. By the end of the war the Dutch were on the brink of famine. The destruction of the economy and much of the infrastructure caused large-scale emigration. In 1947 the Netherlands accepted US$1bn. for reconstruction from the Marshall Plan and entered the Benelux Economic Union with Belgium and Luxembourg (fully established in 1958). The Netherlands abandoned its neutrality when it joined NATO in 1949, the year it granted Indonesia independence. Further changes to Dutch overseas possessions took place in 1954 under the *Statute for the Kingdom*, which gave the territories in the West Indies equal status. Dutch New Guinea (Irian Jaya) was ceded to Indonesia in 1963 and Suriname was given its independence in 1974.

Dutch politics saw several important changes in the post-war years, such as the introduction of proportional representation in elections. From the end of the war until 1958, a coalition of Catholic and labour parties held power, taking the Netherlands into the Korean War in 1950. The Netherlands was a founder member of the European Coal and Steel Community (ECSC) in 1951, which later merged with the European Economic Community (EEC).

The economy grew rapidly in the late 1950s when the welfare state was greatly expanded. Social unrest in the 1960s was led by youth and labour groups. Social changes in the '70s included the demise of the traditional *zuilen* and the creation of new political parties across religious divides; most notable of these was the Christian Democratic Appeal (CDA). Newspapers, the voice of the *zuilen*, disassociated themselves from religious denominations, becoming independent commercial enterprises. The decriminalization of personal cannabis use in the 1970s indicated a policy towards drug use and abuse that focused on rehabilitation (for hard drug users) as opposed to punishment. Vocal youth action was seen most clearly in the confrontations between the police and the *krakers*—squatters demanding affordable housing.

Opposition to nuclear weapons grew in the 1980s, sparked by the support given by Prime Minister Andreas van Agt to placing US cruise missiles on Dutch soil. In 1986 the pressures of the Netherlands' population density led to creation of the 12th province, Flevoland, from four polders reclaimed from the IJsselmeer.

The Netherlands joined the coalition forces in the 1991 Gulf War, providing two naval frigates. Serious flooding in Gelderland and the threat of worse to come led to the evacuation of 240,000 people from the province in 1995. In 2000 the Netherlands became the first country to legalize euthanasia.

Social liberalization has continued in the Netherlands in recent years. In addition to euthanasia, homosexual marriage and adoption were legalized in 2000. In April 2002, Prime Minister Wim Kok's government resigned in the wake of a report that criticized Dutch inaction in preventing the massacre at Srebrenica in 1995. During the subsequent election campaign, the right-wing politician Pim Fortuyn was assassinated by an animal-rights activist who opposed Fortuyn's anti-immigration policies. The coalition government led by Jan Peter Balkenende, formed in July, collapsed in Oct., necessitating fresh elections. Balkenende formed a new government in May 2003.

TERRITORY AND POPULATION

The Netherlands is bounded in the north and west by the North Sea, south by Belgium and east by Germany. The area is 41,528 sq. km, of which 33,756 sq. km is land. Projects of sea-flood control and land reclamation (polders) by the construction of dams and drainage schemes have continued since 1920. More than a quarter of the country is below sea level.

The population was 13,060,115 at the census of 1971 and 16,405,399 on 1 Jan. 2008 (8,293,326 females). Population growth in 2007, 0·3%.

The UN gives an estimated population for 2010 of 16·65m.

Ongoing 'rolling' censuses have replaced the former decennial counts.

Area, estimated population and density, and chief towns of the 12 provinces on 1 Jan. 2007:

	Area 2003 (in sq. km)	Population 2007	Density 2007 per sq. km land area	Provincial capital
Groningen	2,967·90	573,614	246	Groningen
Friesland	5,740·87	642,209	192	Leeuwarden
Drenthe	2,680·37	486,197	184	Assen
Overijssel	3,420·86	1,116,374	336	Zwolle
Flevoland	2,412·30	374,424	264	Lelystad
Gelderland	5,136·51	1,979,059	398	Arnhem
Utrecht	1,449·12	1,190,604	860	Utrecht
Noord-Holland	4,091·76	2,613,070	978	Haarlem
Zuid-Holland[1]	3,403·38	3,455,097	1,228	The Hague
Zeeland	2,933·89	380,497	213	Middelburg
Noord-Brabant	5,081·76	2,419,042	492	's-Hertogenbosch
Limburg	2,209·22	1,127,805	524	Maastricht
Total	41,527·94	16,357,992	485	

[1]Since 29 Sept. 1994 includes inhabitants of the municipality of The Hague formerly registered in the abolished Central Population Register.

In 2005, 80·2% of the population lived in urban areas.

Population of municipalities with over 50,000 inhabitants on 1 Jan. 2007:

Alkmaar	94,174	Hilversum	83,669
Almelo	72,096	Hoogeveen	54,383
Almere	180,924	Hoorn	68,174
Alphen a/d Rijn	71,100	Katwijk	61,111
Amersfoort	139,054	Leeuwarden	92,342
Amstelveen	78,945	Leiden	117,485
Amsterdam	742,884	Leidschendam-Voorburg	72,824
Apeldoorn	155,564	Lelystad	72,252
Arnhem	142,569	Maastricht	119,038
Assen	64,391	Nieuwegein	61,365
Barneveld	50,953	Nijmegen	160,907
Bergen op Zoom	65,400	Oosterhout	53,295
Breda	170,349	Oss	76,652
Capelle a/d Ijssel	65,374	Purmerend	77,955
Delft	95,379	Roermond	54,248
Deventer	96,617	Roosendaal	77,450
Doetinchem	56,238	Rotterdam	584,058
Dordrecht	118,541	Schiedam	75,162
Ede	107,500	Sittard-Geleen	96,245
Eindhoven	209,699	Smallingerland	54,956
Emmen	108,832	Spijkenisse	73,885
Enschede	154,476	Terneuzen	55,268
Gouda	70,953	Tilburg	201,259
Groningen	181,613	Utrecht	288,401
Haarlem	146,960	Veenendaal	61,706
Haarlemmermeer	138,255	Velsen	67,635
The Hague (Den Haag)	473,941	Venlo	92,091
Hardenberg	58,105	Vlaardingen	71,461
Heerlen	90,537	Westland	98,869
Den Helder	58,227	Zaanstad	141,402
Helmond	86,061	Zeist	60,326
Hengelo	81,429	Zoetermeer	118,024
's-Hertogenbosch	135,648	Zwolle	114,635

Urban agglomerations as at 1 Jan. 2007: Amsterdam, 1,022,487; Rotterdam, 985,950; The Hague, 619,414; Utrecht, 423,153; Eindhoven, 322,633; Leiden, 249,480; Dordrecht, 244,846; Tilburg, 223,343; Heerlen, 207,762; Groningen, 200,422; Haarlem, 189,563; Breda, 170,349; Amersfoort, 167,664; Nijmegen, 160,907; 's-Hertogenbosch, 160,887; Apeldoorn, 155,564; Enschede, 154,476; Arnhem, 144,096; Sittard-Geleen, 139,293; Maastricht, 119,038; Zwolle, 114,635.

Dutch is the official language. Frisian, spoken as a first language by 2·2% of the population, is also recognized as an official language in the northern province of Friesland.

SOCIAL STATISTICS

Vital statistics for calendar years:

	Live births Total	Live births Outside marriage	Marriages	Divorces	Deaths
2002	202,083	58,525	85,808	33,179	142,355
2003	200,297	61,439	80,427	31,479	141,936
2004	194,007	63,029	73,441	31,098	136,553
2005	187,910	65,563	72,263	31,905	136,402
2006	185,057	68,575	72,369	31,734	135,372
2007	181,336	71,559	72,485	31,983	133,022

2007 rates per 1,000 population: birth, 11·1; death, 8·1. Annual population growth rate, 2000–05, 0·5%. In 2004 the suicide rate per 100,000 population was 9·3 (men, 12·7; women, 6·0). In 2004 the average age of marrying was 35·4 years for males and 32·3 for females. Expectation of life, 2007, was 77·6 years for males and 81·9 for females. Infant mortality, 2004, 4·4 per 1,000 live births; fertility rate, 2004, 1·7 births per woman. Percentage of population by age in 2005: 0–19 years, 24·5%; 20–64, 61·5%; 65 and over, 14·0%. In 2004 the Netherlands received 9,782 asylum applications, equivalent to 0·6 per 1,000 inhabitants. In 2000 the Netherlands became the first country to legalize same-sex marriage.

CLIMATE

A cool temperate maritime climate, marked by mild winters and cool summers, but with occasional continental influences. Coastal temperatures vary from 37°F (3°C) in winter to 61°F (16°C) in summer, but inland the winters are slightly colder and the summers slightly warmer. Rainfall is least in the months Feb. to May, but inland there is a well-defined summer maximum in July and Aug.

The Hague, Jan. 37°F (2·7°C), July 61°F (16·3°C). Annual rainfall 32·8" (820 mm). Amsterdam, Jan. 36°F (2·3°C), July 62°F (16·5°C). Annual rainfall 34" (850 mm). Rotterdam, Jan. 36·5°F (2·6°C), July 62°F (16·6°C). Annual rainfall 32" (800 mm).

CONSTITUTION AND GOVERNMENT

According to the Constitution (promulgated 1815; last revision, 2002), the Kingdom consists of the Netherlands, Aruba and the Netherlands Antilles. Their relations are regulated by the 'Statute' for the Kingdom, which came into force on 29 Dec. 1954. Each part enjoys full autonomy; they are united, on a footing of equality, for mutual assistance and the protection of their common interests.

The Netherlands is a constitutional and hereditary monarchy. The royal succession is in the direct female or male line in order of birth. The reigning Queen is **Beatrix Wilhelmina Armgard**, born 31 Jan. 1938, daughter of Queen Juliana and Prince Bernhard; married to Claus von Amsberg on 10 March 1966 (born 6 Sept. 1926, died 6 Oct. 2002); succeeded to the crown on 30 April 1980, on the abdication of her mother. *Offspring:* Prince Willem-Alexander, born 27 April 1967, married to Máxima Zorreguieta on 2 Feb. 2002 (*offspring:* Catharina-Amalia, born 7 Dec. 2003; Alexia, born 26 June 2005; Ariane, born 10 April 2007); Prince Johan Friso, born 25 Sept. 1968, married to Mabel Wisse Smit on 24 April 2004 (*offspring:* Luana, born 26 March 2005; Zaria, born 18 June 2006); Prince Constantijn, born 11 Oct. 1969, married to Laurentien Brinkhorst on 19 May 2001 (*offspring:* Eloise, born 8 June 2002; Claus-Casimir, born 21 March 2004; Leonore, born 3 June 2006).

The Queen receives an allowance from the civil list. This is €5,102,000 in 2010; and that of Crown Prince Willem-Alexander, €1,376,000. Princess Máxima also receives allowances from the civil list (€624,000 in 2010).

Sisters of the Queen. Princess Irene Emma Elisabeth, born 5 Aug. 1939, married to Prince Charles Hugues de Bourbon-Parma on 29 April 1964, divorced 1981 (*sons:* Prince Carlos Javier Bernardo, born 27 Jan. 1970; Prince Jaime Bernardo, born 13

Oct. 1972; *daughters:* Princess Margarita Maria Beatriz, born 13 Oct. 1972; Princess Maria Carolina Christina, born 23 June 1974); Princess Margriet Francisca, born in Ottawa, 19 Jan. 1943, married to Pieter van Vollenhoven on 10 Jan. 1967 (*sons:* Prince Maurits, born 17 April 1968; Prince Bernhard, born 25 Dec. 1969; Prince Pieter-Christiaan, born 22 March 1972; Prince Floris, born 10 April 1975); Princess Maria Christina, born 18 Feb. 1947, married to Jorge Guillermo on 28 June 1975 (*sons:* Bernardo, born 17 June 1977; Nicolas, born 6 July 1979; *daughter:* Juliana, born 8 Oct. 1981).

The central executive power of the State rests with the Crown, while the central legislative power is vested in the Crown and Parliament (the *States-General*), consisting of two Chambers. The upper *First Chamber* is composed of 75 members, elected by the members of the Provincial States. The 150-member *Second Chamber* is directly elected by proportional representation for four-year terms. Members of the States-General must be Netherlands subjects of 18 years of age or over. The Hague is the seat of the Court, government and Parliament; Amsterdam is the capital.

The *Council of State*, appointed by the Crown, is composed of a vice-president and not more than 28 members. The monarch is president, but the day-to-day running of the Council is in the hands of the vice-president. The Council has to be consulted on all legislative matters. The Sovereign has the power to dissolve either Chambers, subject to the condition that new elections take place within 40 days, and the new Chamber be convoked within three months. Both the government and the Second Chamber may propose Bills; the First Chamber can only approve or reject them without inserting amendments. The meetings of both Chambers are public, although each of them may by a majority vote decide on a secret session. A Minister or Secretary of State cannot be a member of Parliament at the same time.

The Constitution can be revised only by a Bill declaring that there is reason for introducing such revision and containing the proposed alterations. The passing of this Bill is followed by a dissolution of both Chambers and a second confirmation by the new States-General by two-thirds of the votes. Unless it is expressly stated, all laws concern only the realm in Europe, and not the overseas part of the kingdom, Aruba and the Netherlands Antilles.

National Anthem

'Wilhelmus van Nassaue' ('William of Nassau'); words by Philip Marnix van St Aldegonde, tune anonymous.

GOVERNMENT CHRONOLOGY

Prime Ministers since 1940. (ARP = Anti-Revolutionary Party; CDA = Christian Democratic Appeal; KVP = Catholic People's Party; PvdA = Labour Party; VDB = Liberal Democratic League)

1940–45	ARP	Pieter Sjoerds Gerbrandy
1945–46	VDB/PvdA	Willem Schermerhorn
1946–48	KVP	Louis Jozef Maria Beel
1948–58	PvdA	Willem Drees
1958–59	KVP	Louis Jozef Maria Beel
1959–63	KVP	Jan Eduard de Quay
1963–65	KVP	Victor Gérard Marie Marijnen
1965–66	KVP	Joseph Maria Laurens Theo (Jo) Cals
1966–67	ARP	Jelle Zijlstra
1967–71	KVP	Petrus Josephus Sietse (Piet) de Jong
1971–73	ARP	Barend Willem Biesheuvel
1973–77	PvdA	Johannes Marten (Joop) den Uyl
1977–82	CDA	Andreas Maria (Andries) van Agt
1982–94	CDA	Rudolphus Frans Marie (Ruud) Lubber
1994–2002	PvdA	Willem (Wim) Kok
2002–	CDA	Jan Peter Balkenende

RECENT ELECTIONS

Party affiliation in the First Chamber as elected on 25 May 2003: Christian Democratic Appeal (CDA), 23 seats; Labour Party (PvdA), 19; People's Party for Freedom and Democracy (VVD), 15; Green Left (GL), 5; Socialist Party (SP), 4; Democrats '66 (D66), 3; Christian Union (CU), 2; Political Reformed Party (SGP), 2; List Pim Fortuyn party (LPF), 1; Independent Group in the Senate—Frisian National Party, 1.

Elections to the Second Chamber were held on 22 Nov. 2006. The CDA won 41 seats with 26·5% of votes cast (44 seats at the 2003 election); PvdA, 33 seats and 21·2% (42 in 2003); SP, 25 seats and 16·6% (9); VVD, 22 seats and 14·6% (28); Party for Freedom (PVV), 9 seats and 5·9% (0); GL, 7 seats and 4·6% (8); CU, 6 seats and 4·0% (3); D66, 3 seats and 2·0% (6); Party for the Animals, 2 seats and 1·8% (0); SGP, 2 seats and 1·6% (2). Turnout was 80·4%.

Parliamentary elections were scheduled to take place on 9 June 2010.

European Parliament

The Netherlands has 25 (27 in 2004) representatives. At the June 2009 elections turnout was 36·8% (39·3% in 2004). The CDA won 5 seats with 20·1% of votes cast (political affiliation in European Parliament: European People's Party); PVV, 4 with 17·0% (non-attached); PvdA 3 with 12·1% (Progressive Alliance of Socialists and Democrats); VVD, 3 with 11·4% (Alliance of Liberals and Democrats for Europe); D66, 3 with 11·3% (Alliance of Liberals and Democrats for Europe); Green Left, 3 with 8·9% (Greens/European Free Alliance); SP, 2 with 7·1% (European United Left/Nordic Green Left); Christian Union-Political Reformed Party, 2 with 6·8% (one with European Conservatives and Reformists and one with Europe of Freedom and Democracy).

CURRENT ADMINISTRATION

A coalition government of CDA, PvdA and CU was sworn in 22 Feb. 2007. Following the resignation of the PvdA ministers in March 2010 the caretaker government comprised:

Prime Minister and Minister of General Affairs: Jan Peter Balkenende; b. 1956 (CDA).

Deputy Prime Minister and Minister of Youth and Family: André Rouvoet (CU).

Minister of Foreign Affairs and Development Co-operation: Maxime Verhagen (CDA). *Justice, Interior and Kingdom Relations:* Ernst Hirsch Ballin (CDA). *Finance:* Jan Kees de Jager (CDA). *Defence, and Housing, Communities and Integration:* Eimert van Middelkoop (CU). *Environment and Spatial Planning:* Tineke Huizinga-Heringa (CU). *Transport, Public Works and Water Management:* Camiel Eurlings (CDA). *Economic Affairs:* Maria van der Hoeven (CDA). *Agriculture, Nature and Food Quality:* Gerda Verburg (CDA). *Social Affairs and Employment:* Piet Hein Donner (CDA). *Health, Welfare and Sport:* Ab Klink (CDA). *State Secretary for the Interior and Kingdom Relation:* Ank Bijleveld-Schouten (CDA). *State Secretary for Education, Culture and Science:* Marja van Bijsterveldt-Vliegenthart (CDA). *State Secretary for Defence:* Jack de Vries (CDA).

Office of the Prime Minister: http://www.minaz.nl

CURRENT LEADERS

Jan Peter Balkenende

Position

Prime Minister

Introduction

Jan Peter Balkenende, head of the Christian Democratic Appeal (CDA), succeeded Wim Kok as Dutch prime minister following the elections of May 2002. He briefly led a right-of-centre coalition which included the People's Party for Freedom and Democracy (VVD) and List Pim Fortuyn (LPF) until Oct. 2002, when LPF in-fighting forced the collapse of the government. Balkenende then led the CDA to victory at the elections of Jan.

2003 and formed a new coalition with the VVD and Democrats '66 (D66). Following the Nov. 2006 elections, in which the CDA was again returned as the largest party but lost ground, Balkenende remained prime minister as he formed a new coalition government.

Early Life

Balkenende was born on 7 May 1956 in Kapelle. He graduated in history and law from the Amsterdam Free University. Between 1982 and 1984 he was a legal affairs policy officer for the Netherlands Universities Council before joining the policy institute of the CDA, where he stayed until 1998. Between 1993 and 2002 he held a professorship of Christian social thought on society and economics at the Amsterdam Free University. An alderman for Amstelveen, he won a parliamentary seat at the elections of 1998.

When Jaap de Hoop Scheffer resigned the party leadership in late 2001 there was a divisive contest to replace him. Balkenende came under fire for his lack of experience and perceived weak leadership skills, but eventually emerged victorious. In the build-up to the 2002 elections he refused to rule out a coalition with any party, including List Pim Fortuyn, although he distanced himself from some of its extremist policies.

Career in Office

Following the May 2002 elections Balkenende headed a coalition of the CDA, LPF and VVD. His cabinet was sworn in nine weeks later. He pledged to tighten up immigration policy, reduce taxes and reduce the number of people receiving disability benefits. In addition, he sought a review of the Netherlands' liberal drugs and euthanasia legislation. However, his government was plagued by the instability of the LPF, whose leader, Mat Herben, resigned in Aug. 2002. LPF in-fighting was caused by a personality clash between two of its ministers, Eduard Bomhoff and Herman Heinsbroek, both of whom resigned in Oct. 2002. The CDA and VVD were unable to continue alone and the government resigned on 21 Oct. 2002. Balkenende agreed to remain in place in a caretaker capacity until new elections.

At elections to the Second Chamber in Jan. 2003, the CDA took 44 seats, two ahead of the Labour Party (PvdA). In May 2003, after months of negotiations, Balkenende was sworn in as head of a coalition government comprising the CDA, VVD and D66. His government's policies proved unpopular. In Oct. 2004 more than 200,000 people turned out in Amsterdam to protest against public spending cuts and welfare reform, and in June 2005 the electorate voted decisively against the proposed new European Union constitution in a national referendum.

In July 2006 Balkenende formed a temporary minority administration pending fresh elections. This resulted from the collapse of the previous coalition on the withdrawal of D66 in a row over immigration (a highly-charged issue in Dutch politics). The CDA lost support in the elections in Nov. 2006 but remained the largest parliamentary party with 41 seats. Balkenende eventually formed a new three-party centrist coalition in Feb. 2007. His government eased immigration legislation in 2007 and increased public spending on health care and education.

In Sept. 2008, as crisis in the credit system spread through continental Europe, the governments of the Netherlands, Belgium and Luxembourg partly nationalized Fortis, a large regional retail bank, amid uncertainty about its financial stability.

The CDA remained the largest Dutch party in the June 2009 polling for the European Parliament, taking five of 25 seats allocated to the Netherlands, but conceded electoral ground to the far-right Party for Freedom (PVV), which won four seats. However, Balkenende's preparations for the general election of June 2010 suffered a setback in Feb. 2010 when the PvdA left his coalition, causing the collapse of the cabinet. He remained in office as caretaker prime minister.

DEFENCE

Conscription ended on 30 Aug. 1996.

The total strength of the armed forces in 2007 was 45,608. Reserves, 32,200. In 2006 defence expenditure totalled US$9,904m. (US$601 per capita), representing 1·5% of GDP.

Army

The core fighting element of the Royal Netherlands Army is divided into two mechanized brigades and one airborne brigade. The 1st Netherlands Army Corps merged with a German corps to become 1 German/Netherlands Corps in 1995. It is based in Münster, Germany and is a certified NATO Response Force.

Personnel in 2007 numbered 18,266. The core fighting element of the Army consists of a single element divided into two mechanized brigades and one airborne brigade. Some units in the Netherlands may be assigned to the UN as peacekeeping forces. The army is responsible for the training of these units.

There is a paramilitary Royal Military Constabulary, 6,800 strong. In addition there are 22,200 army reservists.

Navy

The principal headquarters and main base of the Royal Netherlands Navy is at Den Helder, with a minor base at Curaçao (Netherlands Antilles). Command and control in home waters is exercised jointly with the Belgian Naval Component (submarines excepted).

The combatant fleet includes four diesel submarines, four destroyers and four frigates. In 2007 personnel totalled 10,401 including 3,100 in the Royal Netherlands Marine Corps.

Air Force

The Royal Netherlands Air Force (RNLAF) had 10,141 personnel in 2007. It had 105 combat capable aircraft in 2007 (F-16s) and 24 attack helicopters. All squadrons are operated by Tactical Air Command.

INTERNATIONAL RELATIONS

The Netherlands is a member of the UN, World Bank, IMF and several other UN specialized agencies, WTO, EU, Council of Europe, WEU, OSCE, CERN, BIS, IOM, NATO, OECD, Inter-American Development Bank, Asian Development Bank and Antarctic Treaty. The Netherlands is a signatory of the Schengen accord which abolishes border controls between the Netherlands and Austria, Belgium, Czech Republic, Denmark, Estonia, Finland, France, Germany, Greece, Hungary, Iceland, Italy, Latvia, Lithuania, Luxembourg, Malta, Norway, Poland, Portugal, Slovakia, Slovenia, Spain, Sweden and Switzerland.

On 1 June 2005 the Netherlands became the second European Union member after France to reject the proposed EU constitution, with 61·54% of votes cast in a referendum against the constitution and only 38·46% in favour.

The Netherlands gave US$6·2bn. in international aid in 2007, which at 0·81% of GNI made it the equal fourth most generous developed country as a percentage of its gross national income. The Netherlands was one of only five countries to exceed the UN target of 0·7% in 2007.

The Hague is the seat of several international organizations, including the International Court of Justice.

ECONOMY

Services accounted for 74% of GDP in 2007, industry 24% and agriculture 2%.

According to the anti-corruption organization *Transparency International*, the Netherlands ranked equal sixth in the world in a 2009 survey of the countries with the least corruption in business and government. It received 8·9 out of 10 in the annual index.

Overview

The Dutch economy has one of the world's highest levels of average income and relatively low income inequality. Given its small domestic market, a location at the heart of northwest Europe's economy and favourable harbour facilities, the economy is among the most open and outward-looking. The Netherlands is one of the leading donors of international aid and has committed itself to poverty reduction in Africa.

Economic vitality depends on an international trade which accounted for 70% of GDP in 2007. Rotterdam is Europe's largest port and generates annual added value equal to nearly 10% of total GDP. Trade dependency is even stronger because of the scarcity of industrial raw materials while industry is geared towards processing.

In 2006 the government introduced tax cuts and a programme of moderate expenditure, resulting in increased economic activity, rising employment rates, modest wage rises and favourable fiscal conditions. Private consumption also rose. However, the global economic crisis of 2008 saw the economy fall into its worst recession for several decades. A fall in domestic as well as foreign demand reduced production in the manufacturing sector. Nonetheless, in Nov. 2009 the IMF predicted growth to resume in 2010, although at a slow pace.

Annual budget deficits between 2000 and 2008 averaged roughly 1% compared to 3·7% over the previous half decade, despite weaker growth. The government was projected to run a deficit of 4·5% in 2009, increasing to 6% of GDP in 2010. Public debt had been reduced from over 70% of GDP in the mid-1990s to 44·9% in 2007, but surged in 2008–09 and was expected to approach 65% of GDP by 2010.

The Netherlands is among the most competitive destinations for global foreign direct investment (FDI). A favourable tax environment for multinationals has attracted many foreign companies and significant FDI inflows. FDI was strong in the period 1998–2001 when inflows averaged over €48bn. per year—greater than those to much larger countries including France and China. Although FDI declined over the next five years, it recovered to reach a record high in 2007.

Relative to the European Big Four, the manufacturing sector share of GDP is small compared to its agricultural and service sectors. The Netherlands is a leader in horticulture and is a competitive meat and dairy product exporter.

Industrial relations are stable with an emphasis on consensus and pragmatism. The Social Economic Council, a broad-based association representing employers, trade unions and appointees of the central government, is central to policy-making and has been the main force behind wage moderation over the last two decades. The welfare system and labour market institutions follow the German model, with extensive welfare provisions and worker influence at the corporate level. The state's pension liabilities are substantial. An ageing population is a significant challenge and the chief reason for the aggressive strengthening of public finances in recent years.

Currency

On 1 Jan. 1999 the euro (EUR) became the legal currency in the Netherlands at the irrevocable conversion rate of 2·20371 guilders to 1 euro. The euro, which consists of 100 cents, has been in circulation since 1 Jan. 2002. There are seven euro notes in different colours and sizes denominated in 500, 200, 100, 50, 20, 10 and 5 euros, and eight coins denominated in 2 and 1 euros, then 50, 20, 10, 5, 2 and 1 cents. On the introduction of the euro there was a 'dual circulation' period before the guilder ceased to be legal tender on 28 Jan. 2002. Euro banknotes in circulation on 1 Jan. 2002 had a total value of €29·7bn.

Inflation rates (based on OECD statistics):

1999	*2000*	*2001*	*2002*	*2003*	*2004*	*2005*	*2006*	*2007*	*2008*
2·0%	2·3%	5·1%	3·9%	2·2%	1·4%	1·5%	1·7%	1·6%	2·2%

Gold reserves were 19·69m. troy oz in Sept. 2009 and foreign exchange reserves US$10,102m. Total money supply was €217,793m. in Aug. 2009.

Budget

In 2005 central government revenues totalled €202,045m. (€191,867m. in 2004) and expenditures €201,573m. (€198,280m. in 2004). Principal sources of revenue in 2005: social security contributions, €66,477m.; taxes on goods and services, €56,729m.; taxes on income, profits and capital gains, €52,640m. Main items of expenditure by economic type in 2005: social benefits, €88,631m.; grants, €61,067m.; compensation of employees, €16,993m.

VAT is 19·0% (reduced rate, 6·0%).

Performance

Real GDP growth rates (based on OECD statistics):

1999	*2000*	*2001*	*2002*	*2003*	*2004*	*2005*	*2006*	*2007*	*2008*
4·7%	3·9%	1·9%	0·1%	0·3%	2·2%	2·0%	3·4%	3·6%	2·0%

Real GDP growth in 2009 was –4·0% according to Statistics Netherlands. In 2008 total GDP was US$860·3bn.

Banking and Finance

The central bank and bank of issue is the Netherlands Bank (*President*, Arnout Wellink), founded in 1814 and nationalized in 1948. Its Governor is appointed by the government for seven-year terms. The capital amounted to €500m. in 2002. In 2002 there were 18 leading commercial banks. The largest banks in 2007 were ABN Amro Holding NV (assets in 2007 of €1,025·2bn.) and ING Bank NV (assets in 2007 of €994·1bn.). In Oct. 2007 ABN Amro and a consortium led by the UK's Royal Bank of Scotland (and including Santander from Spain and the Belgian-Dutch company Fortis) agreed a merger worth US$98·5bn., representing Europe's largest banking takeover. The Dutch part of Fortis was nationalized in Oct. 2008 and its shares in ABN Amro were also transferred to the Dutch government. There is a stock exchange in Amsterdam; it is a component of Euronext, which was created in Sept. 2000 through the merger of the Amsterdam, Brussels and Paris bourses.

ENERGY AND NATURAL RESOURCES

Environment

Carbon dioxide emissions from the consumption and flaring of fossil fuels in 2008 were the equivalent of 15·9 tonnes per capita.

The Netherlands is one of the world leaders in recycling. In 2003, 50% of all household waste was recycled, including 78% of glass.

Electricity

Installed capacity was 21·7m. kW in 2004. Production of electrical energy in 2004 was 100·77bn. kWh (approximately 4% nuclear); consumption per capita was 7,196 kWh. There was one nuclear reactor in operation in 2003.

Oil and Gas

Production of natural gas in 2008, 67·5bn. cu. metres. Reserves in 2008 were 1,390bn. cu. metres. The Groningen gas field in the north of the country is the largest in continental Europe. In 2005 crude oil production was 2·5m. tonnes; reserves were 100m. bbls in 2007.

Wind

There were 2,048 wind turbines and an installed capacity of 2,216 MW at the end of 2008.

Minerals

In 2005, 5·0m. tonnes of salt were produced. Aluminium production in 2005 totalled 341,000 tonnes.

Agriculture

The Netherlands is one of the world's largest exporters of agricultural produce. There were 83,885 farms in 2004.

Agriculture accounted for 11·6% of exports and 7·6% of imports in 2005. The agricultural sector employs 2·8% of the workforce. In 2002 there were 916,000 ha. of arable land and 33,000 ha. of permanent crops. The total area of cultivated land in 2004 was 1,926,000 ha.: grassland, 983,000 ha.; arable crops, 825,000 ha.; open ground horticultural and permanent crops, 107,000 ha.; glasshouse horticulture, 10·5 ha. In 2004, 230,000 people were employed in agriculture (of which family workers, 168,000; non-family workers, 62,000).

The yield of the more important arable crops, in 1,000 tonnes, was as follows:

Crop	*2003*	*2004*	*2005*[1]
Potatoes	6,469	7,488	6,777
Sugarbeets	6,210	6,292	5,931
Wheat	1,130	1,224	1,175
Sown onions	809	1,225	983
Barley	349	288	307

[1]Provisional.

Other major fruit and vegetable production in 2004 included (in 1,000 tonnes): tomatoes, 655; apples, 436; cucumbers, 435; carrots, 342; sweet peppers, 318; mushrooms, 260; pears, 210.

Cultivated areas of main flowers (2004) in 1,000 ha.: tulips, 11·0; lilies, 4·5; daffodils, 1·8; gladioli, 1·4; hyacinths, 1·1.

Livestock, 2004 (in 1,000) included: 11,153 pigs; 3,767 cattle; 1,236 sheep; 168 milk goats; 85,816 chickens.

Animal products in 2002 (in 1,000 tonnes) included: pork, bacon and ham, 1,420; beef and veal, 464; poultry, 774; milk, 10,842; cheese, 637; butter, 119; hens' eggs, 583.

Forestry

Forests covered 365,000 ha. in 2005, or 10·8% of the land area. In 2007, 1·02m. cu. metres of roundwood were cut.

Fisheries

Total catch in 2005 was 549,208 tonnes (chiefly scad, herring, mackerel and plaice), of which 547,108 tonnes were from marine waters. There were 932 fishing vessels in 2002.

INDUSTRY

In March 2009 the leading companies by market capitalization were: Unilever (Dutch/British), a consumer goods firm (US$54·5bn.); ArcelorMittal, the world's largest steel producer (US$29·4bn.); and KPN, a telecommunications company (US$22·9bn.).

At 1 Jan. 2001 there were 1,524 enterprises in the manufacturing industry (with 100 employees or more), of which 772 had 100–199 employees and 249 had 500 employees or more; total annual sales of these enterprises for 2001 were 133,568m. euros.

The three largest industrial sectors are chemicals, food processing and metal, mechanical and electrical engineering. The food, drink and tobacco industry employed 123,000 people in 2002 (annual sales for 2002 in €1m., 42,411); basic metal and metal products, 118,000 (11,318); machinery and equipment, 86,000 (8,690); electrical and optical equipment, 83,000 (16,766); publishing and printing, 73,000 (6,806); chemical products, 68,000 (31,460); transport equipment, 48,000 (9,028); rubber and synthetic products, 33,000 (3,256).

Labour

The total labour force in 2005 was 7,401,000 persons (3,182,000 women) of whom 483,000 (245,000) were unemployed. By education level, the 2005 employed labour force included (in 1,000): primary education, 331; junior secondary education, 463; junior vocational training, 825; senior secondary education, 608; senior vocational training; 2,448; higher professional education, 1,370; university education, 840.

The unemployment rate was 4·0% in Dec. 2009, the lowest in the EU. Although the Netherlands has a very low unemployment rate, for every 100 people below the age of 65 who are active in the labour market, 35 are not. In 2003 the average age for retirement among males was 61.

At 31 Dec. 2004 the weekly working hours (excluding overtime) of employees were 35·2. In 2004 employees' working hours (excluding overtime) totalled 1,340; full-time employees totalled 1,723. Workers in the Netherlands put in among the shortest hours of any industrialized country. In 2004 part-time work accounted for approximately 35% of all employment in the Netherlands—the highest percentage in any major industrialized country. 76·0% of part-time workers in 2004 were women. Average annual earnings of employees in 2004 totalled €27,400, with average hourly earnings of €18·18 (men, €19·59; women, €15·81). By type of employment, hourly earnings at 31 Dec. 2004 ranged from €11·96 in hotels and restaurants to €23·98 in energy and water companies and €27·71 in mineral extraction.

Trade Unions

Trade unions are grouped in three central federations: Dutch Trade Union Federation (FNV), Christian National Trade Union Confederation (CNV) and Trade Union Confederation for Middle and Higher Management (MHP). Total membership was 1·94m. in 2003, approximately a quarter of waged employees. In Nov. 1993 an agreement on wage restraint was concluded between the trade unions and the employers' federations, in return for an enhancement of the roles of works committees and professional training for employees.

INTERNATIONAL TRADE

On 5 Sept. 1944 and 14 March 1947 the Netherlands signed agreements with Belgium and Luxembourg for the establishment of a customs union. On 1 Jan. 1948 this union came into force and the existing customs tariffs of the Belgium–Luxembourg Economic Union and of the Netherlands were superseded by the joint Benelux Customs Union Tariff. It applied to imports into the three countries from outside sources, and exempted from customs duties all imports into each of the three countries from the other two.

Imports and Exports

In 2005 imports totalled €248,827m. (€228,247m. in 2004); exports, €280,743m. (€255,660m. in 2004).

Value of trade with major partners (in €1m.):

Region/Country	*Imports 2005*	*Exports 2005*	*Imports (% change on 2004)*	*Exports (% change on 2004)*
Europe	154,904	233,413	+6	+9
Belgium	26,708	33,328	+7	+13
France	12,352	25,834	0	+5
Germany	47,345	66,311	+6	+9
Italy	6,424	15,940	+8	+2
Russia	8,345	4,145	+36	+29
UK	15,610	25,985	+6	+1
Africa	6,453	5,510	+49	+19
Americas	30,010	18,747	+13	+16
USA	19,949	13,789	+9	+16
Asia	56,696	20,083	+11	+9
China	19,207	2,514	+32	+9
Japan	6,126	2,221	–9	+2
Australia and Oceania	764	2,988	+1	+15

The main imports in 2005 (in €1m.) were machines and transport equipment, 88,845; mineral fuels, 36,485; chemical products, 32,709; manufactured goods, 28,361; food and live animals, 18,963; inedible raw materials except fuel, 9,789; beverages and tobacco, 2,719. Main exports in 2005 (in €1m.) were machines and transport equipment, 89,365; chemical products, 47,757; food and live animals, 32,618; mineral fuels, 30,786; manufactured goods, 27,209; inedible raw materials except fuels, 15,737; beverages and tobacco, 5,699.

COMMUNICATIONS

Roads

In 2004 the total length of the Netherlands road network was 133,383 km (including 2,585 km of dual carriageway). Number of private cars (2004), 6·91m.; trucks and vans, 0·95m.; motorcycles, 517,000. There were 750 fatalities as a result of road accidents in 2008, equivalent to 4·6 fatalities per 100,000 population (one of the lowest death rates in road accidents of any industrialized country).

Rail

All railways are run by the mixed company 'N.V. Nederlandse Spoorwegen'. Route length in 2004 was 2,807 km. Passengers carried (2002), 320m.; goods transported (2004), 30·4m. tonnes. There is a metro (44 km) and tram/light rail network (154 km) in Amsterdam and in Rotterdam (76 km and 67 km). Tram/light rail networks operate in The Hague (128 km) and Utrecht (22 km).

Civil Aviation

There are international airports at Amsterdam (Schiphol), Rotterdam, Maastricht and Eindhoven. The Royal Dutch Airlines (KLM) was founded on 7 Oct. 1919. In Oct. 2003 it merged with Air France to form Air France-KLM, in which the French state owns a 17·9% stake. In 2005 KLM carried 21·5m. passengers (21·4m. on international flights); passenger-km totalled 68·3bn. Services were provided in 2003 by around 80 foreign airlines. In 2004 Amsterdam handled 42,425,000 passengers. Rotterdam is the second busiest airport, handling 1,097,000 passengers in 2004, followed by Maastricht, with 228,000 in 2004. 1,466,000 tonnes of freight were transported via Dutch airports in 2004.

Sea-going Shipping

Survey of the Netherlands mercantile marine as at 1 Jan. (capacity in 1,000 GRT):

Ships under Netherlands flag	*2001* Number	*2001* Capacity	*2002* Number	*2002* Capacity
Passenger ships	17	644	19	734
Freighters (100 GRT and over)	514	3,225	511	3,444
Tankers	61	517	57	477
	592	4,386	587	4,655

In 2002, 42,057 sea-going ships (including 7,575 Dutch-registered ships) of 622·95m. gross tons entered Netherlands ports.

Total goods traffic by sea-going ships in 2004 (with 2003 figures in brackets), in 1m. tonnes, amounted to 351 (329) unloaded and 113 (102) loaded; total seaborne goods loaded and unloaded in 2002 (and 2001) at Rotterdam was 319·8 (319·6) and at Amsterdam 48·5 (42·1).

The number of containers (including flats) at Dutch ports in 2002 (and 2001) was: unloaded from ships, 2,100,000 (1,982,000); and 2,043,000 (1,893,000) loaded into ships.

The Netherlands was ranked third in the World Economic Forum's *Global Competitiveness Report 2009–2010* for the quality of its port facilities.

Inland Shipping

The total length of navigable rivers and canals is 5,046 km, of which 2,398 km is for ships with a capacity of 1,000 and more tonnes. On 1 Jan. 2002 the inland fleet used for transport (with carrying capacity in 1,000 tonnes) was composed as follows:

	Number	*Capacity*
Self-propelled barges	3,636	3,879
Dumb barges	549	275
Pushed barges	666	1,347
	4,851	5,501

In 2002, 227·6m. tonnes of goods were transported on rivers and canals, of which 132·0m. tonnes was by international shipping. Goods transport on the Rhine across the Dutch–German frontier near Lobith in 2002 amounted to 149·1m. tonnes.

Telecommunications

In 2008 there were 7,317,000 main (fixed) telephone lines. In the same year mobile phone subscribers numbered 20,627,000 (1,248·0 per 1,000 persons). There were 14·9m. PCs in 2006 and 14·3m. internet users in 2008. The Netherlands has the third highest broadband penetration rate (after Bermuda and Denmark), at 35·5 subscribers per 100 inhabitants in June 2008.

Postal Services

In 2003 there were 2,577 post offices, equivalent to one for every 6,270 persons.

SOCIAL INSTITUTIONS

Justice

Justice is administered by the High Court (Court of Cassation), by five courts of justice (Courts of Appeal), by 19 district courts and by 61 cantonal courts. The Cantonal Court, which deals with minor offences, comprises a single judge; more serious cases are tried by the district courts, comprising as a rule three judges (in some cases one judge is sufficient); the courts of appeal are constituted of three and the High Court of five judges. All judges are appointed for life by the Sovereign (the judges of the High Court from a list prepared by the Second Chamber of the States-General). They can be removed only by a decision of the High Court.

At the district court the juvenile judge is specially appointed to try children's civil cases and at the same time charged with administration of justice for criminal actions committed by young persons between 12 and 18 years old, unless imprisonment of more than six months ought to be inflicted; such cases are tried by three judges.

The population in penal institutions at 30 Sept. 2004 was 16,500, of which 7,100 were convicted. 1,324,600 crimes were reported in 2004.

Police

The police force is divided into 25 regions. There is also a National Police Service which includes the Central Criminal Investigation Office, which deals with serious crimes throughout the country, and the International Criminal Investigation Office, which informs foreign countries of international crimes.

Education

Statistics for the academic year 2004–05:

	Schools	*Full-time pupils/students (in 1,000)* Total
Primary education	6,986	1,549
Special primary education	328	50
Expertise centres	324	56
Secondary education	668	938
Senior vocational secondary education	68	332
Apprenticeship training	67	143
Vocational colleges	54	346
University education	13	199

In 2004–05 there were 199,900 students enrolled in Dutch universities (of which female, 49·7%). Enrolment by subject in 2004–05 (with total students): social sciences (46,600); business and administration (31,800); humanities and arts (25,300); law (24,400); health and welfare (23,500); science (19,200); engineering, manufacturing and construction (18,000); education (7,900); agriculture and veterinary science (2,400); services (800).

In 2007 there were 29,104 Open University students and 752 staff. There are 12 study centres in the Netherlands and three support centres, plus six study centres in Belgium.

In 2006 public expenditure on education came to 5·4% of GNI and 12·0% of total government spending. The adult literacy rate is at least 99%.

Health

There were 8,673 general practitioners on 1 Jan. 2007; 2,825 pharmacists and 2,197 midwives on 1 Jan. 2006; and 16,346 specialists and 13,355 physiotherapists on 1 Jan. 2005. There were 7,994 dentists in 2005. At 1 Jan. 2006 there were 117 hospitals and 50,209 licensed hospital beds (excluding mental hospitals). The 1919 Opium Act (amended in 1928 and 1976) regulates the production and consumption of 'psychoactive' drugs. Personal use of cannabis is effectively decriminalized and the sale of soft drugs through 'coffee shops' is not prosecuted provided certain conditions are met. Euthanasia became legal when the First Chamber (the Senate) gave its formal approval on 10 April 2001 by 46 votes to 28. The Second Chamber had voted to make it legal by 104 votes to 40 in Nov. 2000. The law came into effect on 1 April 2002. In 2007 euthanasia organizations recorded 2,120 instances of doctors helping patients to die. The Netherlands was the first country to legalize euthanasia. In 2007 the Netherlands spent 8·9% of its GDP on health.

Welfare

The General Old Age Pension Act (AOW) entitles everyone to draw an old age pension from the age of 65. At 31 Dec. 2005 there were 2,554,000 persons entitled to receive an old age pension, and 138,000 a pension under the Surviving Relatives Insurance; 1,915,000 parents were receiving benefits under the General Family Allowances Act. In 2005 there were 899,000 persons claiming labour disablement benefits and 305,000 persons claiming benefits under the Unemployment Act.

RELIGION

Entire liberty of conscience is granted to the members of all denominations. The royal family belong to the Dutch Reformed Church.

Population aged 12 years and over in 2004 was: Roman Catholics, 30%; Dutch Reformed Church, 11%; Calvinist, 6%; other creeds, 12%; no religion, 42%. On 1 July 1992 the Dutch Reformed Church had one synod, nine provincial districts, 75 classes, about 160 districts and about 2,000 parishes. Their clergy numbered 1,735. It merged with the Reformed Churches in the Netherlands and the Evangelical Lutheran Church in the Kingdom of the Netherlands in May 2004 to form the Protestant Church in the Netherlands—now the second largest church body in the country. The Roman Catholic Church had, Jan. 1992, one archbishop (of Utrecht), six bishops, four assistant bishops and about 1,750 parishes and rectorships. In Feb. 2010 there was one Roman Catholic cardinal. The Old Catholic Church of the Netherlands has one Archbishop (of Utrecht), one Bishop (of Haarlem) and 26 parishes. The Jews had, in 2008, 30 communities. As at 1 Jan. 2002 there were an estimated 890,000 Muslims (5·5% of the population) and 95,000 Hindus (0·6%).

CULTURE

World Heritage Sites

The Kingdom of the Netherlands has eight sites on the UNESCO World Heritage List: Schokland and its surroundings (inscribed on the list in 1995); the defence line at Amsterdam (1996); the mill network at Kinderdijk-Elshout (1997); the historic area of Willemstad, the inner city and harbour in Curaçao (Netherlands Antilles) (1997); the D. F. Wouda steam pumping station (1998); Droogmakerij de Beemster (Beemster Polder) (1999); and the Rietveld Schröder house (2000).

The Netherlands shares the Wadden Sea (2009) with Germany.

Broadcasting

Public broadcasting programmes are provided by broadcasting associations representing clearly identifiable social or religious ideals or groupings. The associations work together in the Netherlands Broadcasting Corporation (Nederlandse Omroepprogramma Stichting—NOS), which oversees the three national public television networks and several radio stations. In addition there is a wide range of commercial broadcasters, as well as access to foreign services (particularly through cable links). RTL is a major commercial operator. There were 7·08m. TV receivers (colour by PAL) in 2006.

Cinema

In 2005 there were 628 cinema screens, with admissions totalling 20·65m. In 2004, 27 feature films were made.

Press

In 2006 there were 32 daily newspapers with a combined circulation of 4,769,000. The most widely read daily is De Telegraaf, with an average daily circulation of 723,000 copies in2006.

Tourism

Tourism is a major sector of the economy. In 2005 tourist spending (excluding passenger transport) came to US$10,383m. A total of 10,383,000 non-resident tourists stayed in holiday accommodation in 2005.

Festivals

Floriade, a world-famous horticultural show, takes place every ten years and is the largest Dutch attraction, being attended by 2·3m. people in 2002. The Maastricht Carnival in April attracts many visitors. The Flower Parade from Noordwijk to Haarlem occurs in late April. Koninginnedag on 30 April is a nationwide celebration of Queen Beatrix's birthday. The Oosterparkfestival, a cultural celebration of that district of Amsterdam, runs for three days in the first week of May. Liberation Day is celebrated every five years on 5 May, with the next occurrence being in 2015. An international music festival, the Holland Festival, is held in Amsterdam throughout June each year and the Early Music Festival is held in Utrecht. The North Sea Jazz Festival, the largest in Europe, takes place in The Hague. Each year the most important Dutch and Flemish theatre productions of the previous season are performed at the Theatre Festival in Amsterdam and Antwerp (Belgium). The Holland Dance Festival is held every other year in The Hague and the Springdance Festival in Utrecht annually. Film festivals include the Rotterdam Film Festival in Feb., the World Wide Video Festival in April, the Dutch Film Festival in Sept. and the International Documentary Film Festival of Amsterdam in Dec.

DIPLOMATIC REPRESENTATIVES

Of the Netherlands in the United Kingdom (38 Hyde Park Gate, London, SW7 5DP)
Ambassador: Pieter Willem Waldeck.

Of the United Kingdom in the Netherlands (Lange Voorhout 10, 2514 ED The Hague)
Ambassador: Paul Arkwright.

Of the Netherlands in the USA (4200 Linnean Ave., NW, Washington, D.C., 20008)
Ambassador: Renée Jones-Bos.

Of the USA in the Netherlands (Lange Voorhout 102, The Hague)
Ambassador: Fay Hartog Levin.

Of the Netherlands to the United Nations
Ambassador: Herman Schaper.

Of the Netherlands to the European Union
Permanent Representative: T. J. A. M. De Bruijn.

FURTHER READING

Centraal Bureau voor de Statistiek. *Statistical Yearbook of the Netherlands.* From 1923/24.—*Statistisch Jaarboek.* From 1899/1924.—*CBS Select (Statistical Essays).* From 1980.—*Statistisch Bulletin.* From 1945; weekly.—*Maandschrift.* From 1944; monthly bulletin.—*90 Jaren Statistiek in Tijdreeksen* (historical series of the Netherlands 1899–1989)
Nationale Rekeningen (National Accounts). From 1948–50.—*Statistische onderzoekingen.* From 1977.—*Regionaal Statistisch Zakboek* (Regional Pocket Yearbook). From 1972
Staatsalmanak voor het Koninkrijk der Nederlanden. Annual from 1814
Staatsblad van het Koninkrijk der Nederlanden. From 1814
Staatscourant (State Gazette). From 1813
Andeweg, Rudy B. and Irwin, Galen A., *Governance and Politics of the Netherlands.* 3rd ed. 2009
Cox, R. H., *The Development of the Dutch Welfare State: from Workers' Insurance to Universal Entitlement.* 1994
Gladdish, K., *Governing from the Centre: Politics and Policy-Making in the Netherlands.* 1991

National library: De Koninklijke Bibliotheek, Prinz Willem Alexanderhof 5, The Hague.
National Statistical Office: Centraal Bureau voor de Statistiek, Netherlands Central Bureau of Statistics, POB 4000, 2270 JM Voorburg.
Statistics Netherlands Website: http://www.cbs.nl

Aruba

KEY HISTORICAL EVENTS

Discovered by Alonzo de Ojeda in 1499, the island of Aruba was claimed for Spain but not settled. It was acquired by the Dutch in 1634, but apart from garrisons, was left to the indigenous Caiquetious (Arawak) Indians until the 19th century. From 1828 it formed part of the Dutch West Indies and, from 1845, part of the Netherlands Antilles with which, on 29 Dec. 1954, it achieved internal self government. Following a referendum in March 1977 the Dutch government announced on 28 Oct. 1981 that Aruba would proceed to independence separately from the other islands. Aruba was constitutionally separated from the Netherlands Antilles from 1 Jan. 1986, and full independence promised by the Netherlands after a ten-year period. However, an agreement with the Netherlands government in June 1990 deletes references to eventual independence at Aruba's request.

TERRITORY AND POPULATION

The island, which lies in the southern Caribbean 32 km north of the Venezuelan coast and 68 km west of Curaçao, has an area of 180 sq. km (75 sq. miles) and a population at the last census in Dec. 2000 of 90,506; density 503 inhabitants per sq. km. Dec. 2008 estimate, 106,050, giving a density of 589 per sq. km. The UN gives an estimated population for 2010 of 107,000. The chief towns are Oranjestad, the capital (2000 population, 26,000) and San Nicolas. Dutch is the official language, but the language usually spoken is Papiamento, a creole language. Over half the population is of Indian stock, with the balance of Dutch, Spanish and mestizo origin.

SOCIAL STATISTICS

Population growth rate, 2008, 1·5%. Life expectancy in the period 2000–05 was 71 years for males and 77 years for females. Birth rate per 1,000 population (2008), 11·6; death rate, 4·9; infant mortality, 1·6.

CLIMATE

Aruba has a tropical marine climate, with a brief rainy season from Oct. to Dec. Oranjestad (1998), Jan. 28°C (82°F), July 29·4°C (85°F). The annual rainfall in 2000 was 551 mm.

CONSTITUTION AND GOVERNMENT

Under the separate constitution inaugurated on 1 Jan. 1986, Aruba is an autonomous part of the Kingdom of the Netherlands with its own legislature, government, judiciary, civil service and police force. The Netherlands is represented by a Governor appointed by the monarch. The unicameral legislature *(Staten)* consists of 21 members elected for a four-year term of office.

RECENT ELECTIONS

Elections were held on 25 Sept. 2009. The Aruban People's Party (AVP) won with 12 out of 21 seats (48·1% of the vote), against 8 seats (35·9%) for the People's Electoral Movement (MEP) and 1 seat (5·7%) for the Real Democracy Party (PDR). Turnout was 86·3%.

CURRENT ADMINISTRATION

Governor: Fredis Refunjol; b. 1950 (took office on 11 May 2004).

Prime Minister: Mike Eman; b. 1961 (sworn in on 30 Oct. 2009).

Government Website: http://www.aruba.com

ECONOMY

Currency

Since 1 Jan. 1986 the currency has been the *Aruban florin* (AWG), at par with the Netherlands Antilles guilder. Inflation was 3·8% in 2005. Total money supply in July 2005 was 1,030m. Aruban florins, foreign exchange reserves were US$297m. and gold reserves were 100,000 troy oz.

Budget

In 2005 revenues totalled 907·3m. Aruban florins and expenditures 1,032·2m. Aruban florins. Tax revenue accounted for 85·7% of revenues in 2005; wages accounted for 29·5% of expenditures and goods and services 14·8%.

Performance

There was a recession in 2002, with the economy shrinking by 3·8%. GDP per capita was 35,966 Aruban florins in 2002.

Banking and Finance

There were six domestic and Dutch banks, and one foreign bank, in 2000. There is a special tax regime for offshore banks. The *President* of the Central Bank of Aruba is Jane Semeleer.

ENERGY AND NATURAL RESOURCES

Environment

Carbon dioxide emissions from the consumption and flaring of fossil fuels were the equivalent of 10·9 tonnes per capita in 2008.

Electricity

In 2004 consumption of electricity was 816,000 MWh.

Fisheries

In 2004 the catch totalled 162 tonnes.

INDUSTRY

The government has established six industrial sites at Oranjestad harbour. The quantity of oil refined in 2001 was 64m. bbls.

Labour

The working age population (15–64 yrs) grew between 1991–2000 from 45,563 to 62,637 persons. The economically active population in 2000 numbered 44,384 persons of which 41,286 were employed and 3,098 unemployed. The employment rate for women grew from 52·8% to 59·2% during the 1990s.

Trade Unions

There are four trade unions: COC, Chambers of Commerce; ATIA, Aruba Trade and Industrial Association; ORMA, Oranjestad Retail and Merchants Association; SNBA, San Nicolas Business Association.

EXTERNAL ECONOMIC RELATIONS

There are two Free Zones at Oranjestad.

Imports and Exports

2006: imports, US$3,838m.; exports, US$3,952m. Leading import suppliers are the USA, Netherlands, Venezuela and the Netherlands Antilles. Leading export destinations are the USA, Colombia, Netherlands and the Netherlands Antilles.

COMMUNICATIONS

Roads

In 1984 (latest data available) there were 380 km of surfaced highways. In 2000 there were 39,995 passenger cars and 5,443 commercial vehicles. There were 439 passenger cars per 1,000 inhabitants.

Civil Aviation

There is an international airport (Aeropuerto Internacional Reina Beatrix). There were flights in 2003 to Amsterdam, Atlanta, Barranquilla, Bogotá, Bonaire, Boston, Caracas, Charlotte, Chicago, Curaçao, Harrisburg, Hartford, Las Piedras, Manchester, Maracaibo, Miami, Minneapolis, New York, Paramaribo, Philadelphia, Pittsburgh, Raleigh/Durham, San Juan, Santo Domingo and Washington, D.C. In Dec. 2003 a new airline, Royal Aruban Airlines was launched, with flights to Curaçao and Fort Lauderdale. In 2002 Aruba handled 13,761 commercial landings and 3,113 non-commercial landings. In total 759,285 passengers arrived by air, 751,106 departed and 153,663 were in transit.

Shipping

Oranjestad has a container terminal and cruise ship port. The port at Barcadera services the offshore and energy sector and a deep-water port at San Nicolas services the oil refinery.

Telecommunications

Aruba had 184,400 telephone subscribers in 2007, or 1,775·3 per 1,000 inhabitants. There were 145,800 mobile phone subscribers in 2007 and 24,000 internet users.

Postal Services

In 2003 there were five post offices.

SOCIAL INSTITUTIONS

Justice

There is a Common Court of Justice with the Netherlands Antilles. Final Appeal is to the Supreme Court in the Netherlands. The population in penal institutions in Jan. 2005 was 231 (equivalent to 324 per 100,000 population).

Education

In 2007 there were 2,713 pupils in pre-primary schools, 9,511 in primary schools, 2,950 in junior high schools, 2,372 in high schools and 2,192 in technical or vocational schools. Literacy rate (2000 census), 97·3%. In 2007 public spending on education amounted to 4·0% of GDP and 11·4% of total government expenditure.

Health

In 2000 there were 123 doctors, 29 dentists, 18 pharmacists and one hospital with 305 beds.

Welfare

All citizens are entitled to an old age pension at the age of 60.

RELIGION

In 2000, 86·2% of the population were Roman Catholic.

CULTURE

Broadcasting

In 2000 there were 18 radio stations and three commercial television stations (colour by NTSC). In 2001 there were 20,000 TV sets.

Press

In 2006 there were four daily newspapers with a combined circulation of 54,000. Aruba has among the highest circulation rates of daily newspapers in the world, at 667 per 1,000 adult inhabitants in 2006.

Tourism

In 2008 there were 826,774 tourists staying 6,264,689 nights and 556,090 cruise passenger visitors. In 2003 tourist receipts were US$861m. The majority of tourists are from the USA (65·3%) and Venezuela (13·6%).

FURTHER READING

Central Bureau of Statistics Website: http://www.cbs.aw

The Netherlands Antilles

De Nederlandse Antillen

KEY HISTORICAL EVENTS

With Aruba, the islands formed part of the Dutch West Indies from 1828, and the Netherlands Antilles from 1845, with internal self-government being granted on 29 Dec. 1954. The Netherlands Antilles is to be disbanded on 10 Oct. 2010, with Curaçao and Sint Maarten becoming states associated with the Netherlands, while Bonaire, Saba and Sint Eustatius will become special municipalities of the Netherlands.

TERRITORY AND POPULATION

The Netherlands Antilles comprise two groups of islands, the Leeward group (Curaçao and Bonaire) being situated 100 km north of the Venezuelan coast and the Windward group (Saba, Sint Eustatius and the southern portion of Sint Maarten) situated 800 km away to the northeast, at the northern end of the Lesser Antilles. The total area is 800 sq. km (308 sq. miles) and the UN gives an estimated population for 2010 of 201,000. An estimated 69·6% of the population were urban in 2001. Willemstad is the capital and had a 2001 population of 125,000.

The areas, populations and chief towns of the islands are (as at 1 Jan.):

Island	*Sq. km*	*2009 population*	*Chief town*
Bonaire	288	12,877	Kralendijk
Curaçao	444	141,766	Willemstad
Saba	13	1,601	The Bottom
Sint Eustatius	21	2,768	Oranjestad
Sint Maarten[1]	43	40,917	Philipsburg

[1]The northern portion (St Martin) belongs to France.

Dutch, Papiamento (derived from Dutch, Spanish and Portuguese) and English are all official languages (the latter two since March 2007).

SOCIAL STATISTICS

2004, live births, 2,357; deaths, 1,412; marriages, 710; divorces, 513. Population growth rate, 2004, 0·7%. Expectation of life at birth, 1998–2002, was 72·1 years for males and 78·7 for females. Infant mortality, 2004, 8·5 per 1,000 live births; fertility rate, 2004, 2·1 births per woman.

CLIMATE

All the islands have a tropical marine climate, with very little difference in temperatures over the year. There is a short rainy season from Oct. to Jan. Willemstad, Feb. 27·7°C, Aug. 29·0°C. Annual rainfall 499 mm.

CONSTITUTION AND GOVERNMENT

On 29 Dec. 1954 the Netherlands Antilles became an integral part of the Kingdom of the Netherlands but are fully autonomous in internal affairs, and constitutionally equal with the Netherlands and Aruba. The Sovereign of the Kingdom of the Netherlands is Head of State and Government, and is represented by a Governor.

The executive power in internal affairs rests with the *Governor* and the *Council of Ministers*. The Ministers are responsible to a unicameral legislature *(States)* consisting of 22 members, elected for a four-year term in three multi-seat constituencies and two single-seat constituencies. The executive power in external affairs is vested in the Council of Ministers of the Kingdom, in which the Antilles is represented by a Minister Plenipotentiary with full voting powers.

At a non-binding referendum in Curaçao on 8 April 2005, 68% of votes cast favoured Curaçao seceding from the Netherlands Antilles and becoming a territory of the Netherlands in its own right. At a contemporaneous referendum in Sint Eustatius, 76% voted to remain within the Netherlands Antilles but subject to a federal restructure. In Sept. 2004, 56% of voters in Bonaire voted for direct administration by the Dutch government, as did 86% in Saba in Nov. 2004. Sint Maarten voted for outright autonomy in 2000.

By July 2007 the Netherlands had concluded agreements with each of the islands to dissolve the Netherlands Antilles by 15 Dec. 2008. Curaçao and Sint Maarten will become associated states within the Kingdom of the Netherlands, independent in all respects excepting defence, while Bonaire, Saba and Sint Eustatius will become special municipalities of the Netherlands. After the original Dec. 2008 deadline was missed, 10 Oct. 2010 was scheduled for the formal dissolution of the Netherlands Antilles.

RECENT ELECTIONS

In elections held on 22 Jan. 2010 the Party for the Restructured Antilles (PAR) won 6 seats, the List of Change coalition 5, the National Alliance 3, Sovereign People 2, the Bonaire Patriotic Union 2, with 1 seat each going to four other parties.

CURRENT ADMINISTRATION

Governor: Frits Goedgedrag; b. 1951 (took office on 1 July 2002).

Prime Minister: Emily de Jongh-Elhage; b. 1946 (took office on 26 March 2006).

Government Website (Dutch only): http://www.gov.an

ECONOMY

Currency

The unit of currency is the *Netherlands Antilles guilder, gulden* (ANG) or *florin* (NAfl.) divided into 100 *cents*. The NA guilder is pegged to the US dollar at US$1 = 1·79 NA guilder. In 2004 inflation was 1·5%. Total money supply in July 2005 was 1,615m. NA guilders, foreign exchange reserves were US$499m. and gold reserves totalled 421,000 troy oz.

Budget

In 2006 revenues were 822·6m. NA guilders and expenditures 910·6m. NA guilders.

Performance

Real GDP growth was 1·7% in 2003 but there then followed a recession, with the economy shrinking by 0·1% in 2004.

Banking and Finance

At 31 Dec. 2005 the Bank of Netherlands Antilles (*President*, Emsley D. Tromp) had total assets and liabilities of 1,507·9m. NA guilders; commercial banks, 6,939·9m. NA guilders.

ENERGY AND NATURAL RESOURCES

Environment

Carbon dioxide emissions from the consumption and flaring of fossil fuels were the equivalent of 54·5 tonnes per capita in 2008 (compared to the world average of 4·5 tonnes per capita).

Electricity

Installed capacity in 2004 was an estimated 0·2m. kW. Production in 2004 totalled 1·07bn. kWh and consumption per capita was 4,885 kWh.

Oil and Gas

The economy was formerly based largely on oil refining at the Shell refinery on Curaçao, but following an announcement by Shell that closure was imminent, this was sold to the Netherlands Antilles government in Sept. 1985, and leased to Petróleos de Venezuela to operate on a reduced scale. The refinery has a capacity of 470,000 bbls a day, but output has not reached this for several years.

Minerals

Production of salt (2004 estimate): 450,000 tonnes.

Agriculture

Livestock (2002): cattle, 1,000; goats, 13,000; pigs, 2,000; sheep, 8,000; asses, 3,000.

Fisheries

Total catch estimate (2005), approximately 2,422 tonnes.

INDUSTRY

Curaçao has an oil refinery and a large ship-repair dry docks. Bonaire has a textile factory and a modern equipped salt plant. Sint Maarten's industrial activities are primarily based on a rum factory and a fishing factory.

Labour

In the 2001 census there were 69,682 employed persons, of which 12,380 worked in wholesale and retail trade, 6,622 in hotels and restaurants, 5,997 in public administration, 5,781 in real estate, renting and business activities and 5,410 in transport, storage and communication. In 2001 the unemployment rate was 14·6% (Curaçao: unemployment rate, 15·9%).

EXTERNAL ECONOMIC RELATIONS

Imports and Exports

In 2005 imports totalled US$2,285·2m. and exports US$971·1m. In 2002 crude petroleum made up 59·7% of imports, refined petroleum 8·7% and food 6·4%. 94·7% of exports in 2002 was refined petroleum. Principal import suppliers in 2000: USA, 25·8%; Mexico, 20·7%; Gabon, 6·6%; Italy, 5·8%. Main export markets, 2000: USA, 35·9%; Guatemala, 9·4%; Venezuela, 8·7%; France, 5·4%. There is a Free Zone on Curaçao.

COMMUNICATIONS

Roads

In 2004 there were 75,248 registered vehicles on Curaçao (60,590 passenger cars) and 6,766 on Bonaire (4,139 passenger cars).

Civil Aviation

There are international airports on Curaçao (Curaçao-Hato Airport), Bonaire (Flamingo Airport) and Sint Maarten (Princess Juliana Airport). In 2005 Sint Maarten handled 1,663,226 passengers, Curaçao handled 840,581 and Bonaire 552,417. There are smaller airports on Sint Eustatius and Saba.

Shipping

The largest harbour is Curaçao; in 2005, 2,826 ships (totalling 46,554,000 GRT) entered the port. Merchant shipping in 2002 totalled 1,391,000 GRT.

Telecommunications
Number of main telephone lines in 2008 was 88,000 (450·7 per 1,000 population). There were 200,000 mobile phone subscribers in 2003.

SOCIAL INSTITUTIONS

Justice
There is a Court of First Instance, which sits in each island, and a Court of Appeal in Willemstad. The population in penal institutions in Sept. 2004 was 539.

Education
In 2000–01 there were 22,140 pupils in primary schools, 2,337 pupils in special schools, 12,174 pupils in general secondary schools, 3,710 pupils in junior and senior secondary vocational schools, and 928 students in vocational colleges and universities.

In 2000–01 total expenditure on education came to 13·6% of total government spending.

Health
In 2001 there were 12 hospitals with 1,343 beds. There were 333 physicians, 60 dentists, 1,198 nurses, 47 pharmacists (2004) and nine midwives in 2001.

RELIGION
In 2001 about 70% of the population were Roman Catholics and 10% were Protestants (Sint Maarten and Sint Eustatius being primarily Protestant).

CULTURE

World Heritage Sites
The Netherlands Antilles has one site on the UNESCO World Heritage List: the Historic Area of Willemstad, Inner City and Harbour (inscribed on the list in 1997), established on the island of Curaçao in 1634 by Dutch traders.

Broadcasting
In 2006 there were 53 radio transmitters (including 28 on Curaçao) and each island had one cable television station, broadcasting in Papiamento, Dutch, English and Spanish. Broadcasting is administered by Landsradio, Telecommunication Administration and Tele Curaçao. In 1999 there were 71,000 TV sets (colour by NTSC) in use. In addition, Radio Nederland and Trans World Radio have powerful relay stations operating on medium- and short-waves from Bonaire.

Press
In 2006 there were three daily newspapers (combined circulation of 30,000).

Tourism
In 2001 there were 677,000 foreign visitors. Spending by tourists totalled US$821m. in 2001 (excluding Saba and Sint Eustatius). In 2005 Bonaire handled 40,077 cruise ship passengers, Curaçao handled 267,217 and Sint Maarten 1,488,461.

DIPLOMATIC REPRESENTATIVES
US Consul-General: Timothy J. Dunn (J. B. Gorsiraweg 1, Curaçao).

FURTHER READING

Central Bureau of Statistics. *Statistical Yearbook of the Netherlands Antilles*

Bank of the Netherlands Antilles. *Annual Report.*

Statistical office: Central Bureau of Statistics, Fort Amsterdam Z/N, Curaçao.

Website: http://www.central-bureau-of-statistics.an

NEW ZEALAND

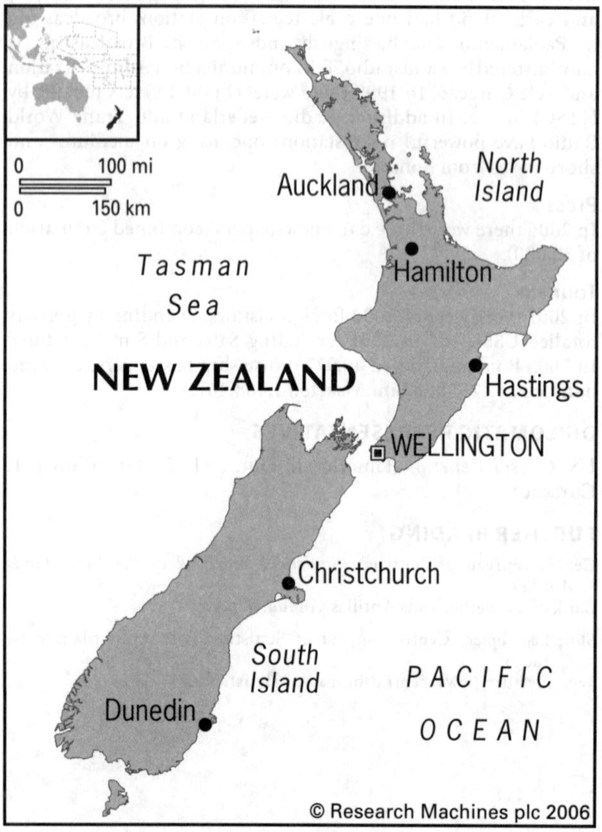

Aotearoa

Capital: Wellington
Population estimate, 2010: 4·30m.
GDP per capita, 2007: (PPP$) 27,336
HDI/world rank: 0·950/20

KEY HISTORICAL EVENTS

The earliest settlers of New Zealand are thought to have originated from eastern Polynesia, around the turn of the first millennium though some estimates suggest as early as AD 650 or as late as 1400. Maori oral traditions point to discovery of the country by Kupe, who gave New Zealand its first name, Aotearoa, or 'Land of the Long White Cloud'. Oral tradition also refers to seven waka leaving a homeland known as Hawaiiki in a Great Fleet. The waka are still remembered in the names of significant tribal groupings and descent lines: *Aotea*, *Kurahaupo*, *Mataatua*, *Tainui*, *Takitimu*, *Te Arawa*, and *Tokomaru*.

By Capt. James Cook's arrival in 1769, substantial settlements existed throughout the North Island, with smaller settlements in the South Island. Despite kinship links, sporadic warfare was common as tribes, or 'iwi', fought for resources and status, or 'mana'.

The first recorded European contact was Dutch explorer Abel Tasman's arrival in 1642. Believing the South Island to be the beginning of a mythical continent connected to Southern Africa, he bequeathed the name 'Staten Land'. A Dutch cartographer corrected Tasman's reasoning, giving the name New Zealand to compliment the larger New Holland, as Australia was known at the time. Tasman had one lasting impact, naming Murderer's Bay after several crew were cannibalized by local Maori. Earlier on the same voyage Tasman had landed on an island off Australia which he named Van Diemen's Land but which was later called Tasmania in his honour.

Intensive contact between Maori and Europeans, or 'Pakeha', followed Cook's journeys to New Zealand and mapping of the coastline, opening the way for sealing and whaling stations. Coastal trade grew throughout the first decades of the 19th century and trade routes were established between Maori and the new colony of New South Wales as early as the 1820s. The Maori adapted quickly to both a market economy—selling provisions, timber and flax—and to new technologies (notably the musket). Pakeha settlement in the decades following Cook's arrival was often on Maori terms and was used by Maori in the traditional pursuit of mana in the eyes of rivals and neighbours. Mission stations soon appeared: the Church Missionary Society established three stations in the Bay of Islands between 1814 and 1823, and were joined by a Wesleyan Missionary Society station in the Hokianga in the 1820s.

British Ascendancy

With greater contact both Maori and Pakeha saw the need to regulate Pakeha settlement. The Colonial Office in London appointed a Resident, James Busby, in 1833; in 1835, prompted by Busby, thirty-five chiefs signed a Declaration of Independence and announced themselves the heads of state of a 'United Tribes of New Zealand'. Colonial Office acknowledgement of the declaration signalled an official but non-interventionist policy. Relations between Maori and Pakeha were formalized by the signing of the Treaty of Waitangi in 1840. In principle—or at least in the Maori text—this treaty guaranteed Maori chieftainship, or 'rangatiratanga', while granting governorship, or 'kawanatanga', to Queen Victoria. Until 1860 Maori outnumbered Pakeha but in practice—and in the English text—sovereignty was transferred, allowing greater British settlement and control.

Established in 1840, Auckland was chosen as the colony's capital by its first governor, Capt. William Hobson. Planned migration occurred through the New Zealand Company with settlements at Wellington and Wanganui (1840), New Plymouth (1841), and Nelson (1842). Scottish immigrants founded Dunedin (1848); and Edward Gibbon Wakefield made plans for a model English settlement—unrealized, he felt, by the New Zealand Company—at Christchurch (1851). In 1852 representative government was established with a constitution providing for a House of Representatives and Legislative Council, as well as six provincial councils. The governor at the time, Sir George Grey, retained the right of veto and was responsible for 'Native' policy. At first the provincial councils exercised extensive powers over what were effectively separate settlements; their abolition in 1876 marked the beginnings of central government. The Legislative Council was disbanded in 1950 leaving New Zealand with a single-tier parliament.

Initially, voting was based on individual land ownership and excluded Maori who traditionally owned land collectively. Participation was extended to Maori in 1867 through four Maori seats. Maori representation in parliament came later: James Carroll, Apirana Ngata, Maui Pomare, and Peter Buck (Te Rangi Hiroa) were all prominent: Carroll was the first Maori to hold the posts of minister of native affairs and later acting prime minister; all made important contributions to Maori policy on issues such as health, education and land development.

Settlement was not always peaceful: war broke out in the 1840s and 1860s in the central and western North Island between settlers, represented by the British army, and Maori opposed to further settlement. British troops fought alongside local militia and friendly Maori, facing some of the earliest forms of trench and guerrilla warfare. Land and the willingness of tribes to provide larger and more productive hinterlands for the growing townships was one issue. Attempts at pan-Maori unity were another: the King movement in the Waikato gained prominence, and the Kotahitanga met as a Maori parliament during the second half of the 19th century.

Confiscating land belonging to tribes who fought against the government was one way in which the Pakeha gained wider possession. They were also helped by the Native Land Court, formed in 1865, to determine the ownership of Maori land according to Pakeha law. Where Maori land and user rights existed communally among a tribe, the Court sought to define parcels of land owned individually, thereby facilitating land sales.

Economic Boom

Earlier land speculation had fuelled an agricultural boom in the 1840s and 1850s providing the colony's first sustainable export commodity. New Zealand provided 8·6% of Britain's wool imports in 1861 and had 8·5m. sheep by 1867. The development of refrigerated shipping in the 1880s bolstered the pastoral economy through meat exports. Gold rushes in the 1860s and 1870s in Otago, the west coast of the South Island, and in Coromandel also contributed to the economy. Gold exports totalled £46m. by 1890. Wealth brought progress; the 1870s administrations of Julius Vogel and Harry Atkinson borrowed heavily to fund work schemes to encourage immigration and settlement. 1,100 miles of rail track were laid by 1879, and telegraphs linked all the main towns. The population had doubled to 500,000 by 1881.

The 1880s saw the beginnings of party politics. Grey's 1879 attempt to form a Liberal party, with policies of 'one man, one vote' and the compulsory purchase of large estates, was popular and succeeded in extending suffrage to all men. Robert Stout and John Ballance's leasehold land policies in the mid-1880s were similarly popular. A Liberal Party was eventually formed in 1889 and, backed by unions and the landless, won the 1890 election with Ballance as its leader. The Conservatives formed the first genuine opposition. Richard John Seddon took over the Liberal leadership in 1892 and remained Premier until his death in 1906. Among the Liberal's achievements were the Land and Income Tax Act 1891 and the Advance to Settlers Act 1894, which assisted 17,000 people on to the land by 1912. Suffrage was extended to women in 1893, New Zealand being the first country to do so. Other reforms included William Pember Reeves' Industrial Conciliation and Arbitration Act of 1894, one of the most radical and extensive labour systems of its time; and one of the world's first pension schemes.

In 1901 New Zealand declined the offer to join the Commonwealth of Australia and remained a British colony until 1907 when it gained Dominion status. Parliament remained subordinate to the British parliament until the adoption in 1947 of the Statute of Westminster under which New Zealand became fully sovereign with the British monarch as head of state. New Zealand exercised its own colonial interests, annexing the Cook Islands in 1901, and being granted administration of Western Samoa at the Treaty of Versailles after capturing it from Germany in the First World War. It administered Samoa until the 1960s. Two world wars tested the spirit of the Australian and New Zealand Army Corps. Both countries saw a duty to fight for the homeland of Britain. New Zealand contributed around 100,000 soldiers in the First World War from a population of little more than a million; nearly 17,000 did not return. Nearly 9,000 New Zealanders died in the influenza epidemic spread by returning soldiers, with a Maori mortality rate six times that of Pakeha. New Zealand's Second World War contribution was even greater; around 200,000 joined Allied forces from a population of 1·6m.

Twentieth Century

Class-based political divisions intensified in the early twentieth century. Worker's unions, early supporters of the Liberal Party, rallied around an embryonic Labour movement while farmers and employers favoured William 'Farmer Bill' Massey's Reform Party. Amid industrial unrest in 1912, the Liberal government fell to a vote of no confidence. Reform took power, introducing anti-union legislation. Strikes in Waihi, Wellington and Huntly were quelled by Massey's 'Cossacks', police forces specially enlisted for the task. Reform governed until 1928, assisted at first by a wartime coalition with the Liberals, and then by tacit Liberal support. Their policies broadly followed the dictates of farmers, creating a national Meat Board (1922) and Dairy Board (1923).

A United–Reform coalition government (1931–35) fought the effect of world recession. Employment reached 12%; the national income fell from an estimated £150m. to £90m., and the value of exports fell by 40%. To balance the budget, cuts were made to pensions, education, health and public works. In the absence of an unemployment benefit, men were sent to rural relief camps to work on low-capital, high-labour tasks. Measures such as creating a Reserve Bank and currency devaluation in 1933 helped farmers but did not address the broader social distress.

Welfare State

Michael Joseph (Micky) Savage's first Labour government (1935–49) reclaimed for New Zealand its title of social laboratory of the world, first bestowed during the Liberal era of the 1890s. Its legacy would be a welfare state which survived until the 1980s. It introduced one of the world's most comprehensive social welfare systems—incorporating pensions, health, education and family benefits—and increased state housing; introduced state guaranteed prices for farm produce to protect farmers from international price fluctuations; and nationalized the Reserve Bank, making it an instrument of state economic policy. By the late 1940s, state finances were healthy enough to allow a £10m. gift to post-war Britain.

Labour lost rural support which rallied around a National Party formed in 1936 from remnants of the United–Reform coalition. Labour retained power in part owing to the support of the four Maori seats, all held by the Ratana Party. The National Party won in 1949, promising to increase spending power and curb creeping socialism in the form of union power and economic controls. 1951 saw militant unions again taking on a conservative government, and losing. National retained power for most of the post-war boom years; brief Labour administrations under Walter Nash (1957–60) and Norman Kirk (1972–75) coincided with unfavourable economic conditions. Keith Holyoake's National government (1960–72) was dominated by international affairs, joining the IMF in 1961 and manoeuvring around Britain's anticipated entry to the EEC. Notable domestic policy included the Equal Pay Act (1972) to address gender-based pay discrimination and the creation of state-funded workplace injury compensation.

Maori demands for recognition of the Treaty of Waitangi grew in the 1970s. The 1975 Land March saw tens of thousands march on parliament and the occupation of Bastion Point in 1977–78 centred on land compulsorily acquired by the government in 1951. Both raised public awareness of disaffection with the way the Treaty had been interpreted. Labour established the Waitangi Tribunal in 1975 to hear Maori claims of Treaty breaches. It lacked authority until 1985 when the next Labour government made its powers retrospective to 1840. Tribunal recommendations have formed the basis for settling several large claims through negotiations between the Crown and tribal authorities.

Britain's entry into the EEC in 1973 was a set-back for an economy dependent on exports to Britain. Robert Muldoon's National government (1975–84) tried to ameliorate the effects through tariff protection, wage and price freezes, and increased borrowing for 'Think Big' public works. Muldoon won a narrow victory in the 1981 election following civil unrest during the 'Springbok' rugby tour. Riot police faced massive demonstrations as many New Zealanders opposed sporting links with the South African apartheid regime. The country found a new direction in the free market policies of David Lange's Labour government, which came to power in 1984. The economic direction of Roger Douglas, 'Rogernomics', radically altered the socio-economic landscape, reducing trade barriers and selling state assets to fund debt recovery.

In international affairs the Labour government was truer to its left-wing support, passing the New Zealand Nuclear Free Zone, Disarmament, and Arms Control Act 1987, which declared the country nuclear free. The legislation—supported by all political parties—led to the end of New Zealand's involvement in the ANZUS military agreement with Australia and the USA. Nuclear issues were high in popular consciousness. In 1973 Australia and New Zealand had tried to halt French nuclear testing in the Pacific through the International Court of Justice, and New Zealand sent two frigates to Mururoa Atoll in protest. The 1985 bombing of the *Rainbow Warrior* in Auckland harbour by French secret service agents reopened the issue.

Internal wrangling over economic direction caused the collapse of the Labour leadership in the late 1980s. Lange resigned and was replaced by Geoffrey Palmer in 1989, who in turn resigned shortly before the 1990 election. He was succeeded by Mike Moore. Labour lost the 1990 election to a National Party led by Jim Bolger who was determined to carry on free market reforms. Social welfare reform, cuts in tertiary education funding and reform of accident compensation legislation cut back state intervention. The Employment Contracts Act (1991) outlawed compulsory union membership and introduced individual contracts, weakening union power. Jenny Shipley led a leadership coup in 1997 and became the country's first female prime minister, though not the first elected female prime minister; that landmark was reserved for Helen Clark who led the Labour Party to victory in the 1999 election. In 2008 John Key led National back to power after nine years of Labour government under Helen Clark.

Electoral reform in the 1990s saw New Zealand move from a first-past-the-post system to proportional representation under the mixed-member-proportional system (MMP). Despite the debacle of the first MMP election in 1996 where a minor party (New Zealand First, formed by disgruntled National supporters) played National off against Labour for two months before forming a coalition with National, the system has provided greater representation for minority interests.

TERRITORY AND POPULATION

New Zealand lies southeast of Australia in the south Pacific, Wellington being 1,983 km from Sydney. There are two principal islands, the North and South Islands, besides Stewart Island, Chatham Islands and small outlying islands, as well as the territories overseas.

New Zealand (i.e. North, South and Stewart Islands) extends over 1,750 km from north to south. Area, excluding territories overseas, 270,534 sq. km: comprising North Island, 115,777 sq. km; South Island, 151,215 sq. km; Stewart Island, 1,746 sq. km; Chatham Islands, 963 sq. km. The minor islands (total area, 829 sq. km or 320 sq. miles) included within the geographical boundaries of New Zealand (but not within any local government area) are the following: Kermadec Islands (34 sq. km), Three Kings Islands (8 sq. km), Auckland Islands (606 sq. km), Campbell Island (114 sq. km), Antipodes Islands (62 sq. km), Bounty Islands (1 sq. km), Snares Islands (3 sq. km), Solander Island (1 sq. km). With the exception of meteorological station staff on Raoul Island in the Kermadec Group and Campbell Island there are no inhabitants.

The Kermadec Islands were annexed to New Zealand in 1887, have no separate administration and all New Zealand laws apply to them. Situation, 29° 10' to 31° 30' S. lat., 177° 45' to 179° W. long., 1,600 km NNE of New Zealand. The largest of the group is Raoul or Sunday Island, 29 sq. km, smaller islands being Macaulay and Curtis, while Macaulay Island is 5 km in circuit.

Growth in census population, exclusive of territories overseas:

	Total population	*Average annual increase (%)*		*Total population*	*Average annual increase (%)*
1858	115,461	—	1945[1,2]	1,702,329	0·83
1874	344,985	—	1951[1]	1,939,473	2·37
1878	458,007	7·33	1956[1]	2,174,061	2·31
1881	534,030	5·10	1961[1]	2,414,985	2·12
1886	620,451	3·06	1966[1]	2,676,918	2·11
1891	668,652	1·50	1971[1]	2,862,630	1·35
1896	743,214	2·13	1976[1]	3,129,384	1·80
1901[1]	815,862	1·90	1981[1]	3,175,737	0·29
1906	936,309	2·75	1986[1]	3,307,083	0·82
1911	1,058,313	2·52	1991[1]	3,434,949	0·76
1916[1]	1,149,225	1·50	1996[1]	3,681,546	1·40
1921	1,271,667	2·27	2001[1]	3,820,749	0·74
1926	1,408,140	2·06	2006[1]	4,143,279	1·63
1936[2]	1,573,812	1·13			

[1]Excluding members of the Armed Forces overseas.
[2]The census of New Zealand is quinquennial, but the census falling in 1931 was abandoned as an act of national economy, and owing to war conditions the census due in 1941 was not taken until 25 Sept. 1945.

The latest census took place on 7 March 2006. Of the 4,143,279 people counted, 4,027,947 were usually resident in the country and 115,332 were overseas visitors.

In 2005, 86·2% of the population lived in urban areas. Density, 14·5 per sq. km (2001).

The usually-resident populations of the 12 regional councils, four unitary authorities and one special territorial authority (all data conforms with boundaries redrawn after the 1989 reorganization of local government) in 2001 and 2006:

Local Government Region	*Total Population 2001 census*	*2006 census*	*Percentage change 2001–06 (%)*
Northland	140,133	148,470	5·9
Auckland	1,158,891	1,303,068	12·4
Waikato	357,726	382,713	7·0
Bay of Plenty	239,412	257,379	7·5
Gisborne[1]	43,974	44,499	1·2
Hawke's Bay	142,947	147,783	3·4
Taranaki	102,858	104,124	1·2
Manawatu-Wanganui	220,089	222,423	1·1
Wellington	423,765	448,959	5·9
Total North Island	2,829,798	3,059,418	8·1
Tasman[1]	41,352	44,625	7·9
Nelson[1]	41,568	42,891	3·2
Marlborough[1]	39,558	42,558	7·6
West Coast	30,303	31,326	3·4
Canterbury	481,431	521,832	8·4
Otago	181,542	193,800	6·8
Southland	91,005	90,876	–0·1
Total South Island	906,753	967,908	6·7
Area outside region[2]	726	618	–14·9
Total New Zealand	*3,737,277*	*4,027,947*	*7·8*

[1]Unitary Authorities.
[2]Special Territorial Authority—Chatham Islands.

The UN gives an estimated population for 2010 of 4·30m.

Between 1996 and 2006 the number of people who identified themselves as being of European ethnicity dropped from 83·1% to 77·6%. Pacific Island people made up 6·9% of the population in 2006 (5·8% in 1996); Asian ethnic groups went from 5·0% in 1996 to 9·2% in 2006. Permanent and long-term arrivals in 2001 totalled 81,094, including 16,844 from the UK, 12,186 from Australia, 11,107 from the People's Republic of China, 4,249 from India and 3,920 from Japan. Permanent and long-term departures in 2001 totalled 71,368, including 36,033 to Australia, 14,852 to the UK, 3,151 to the USA and 1,874 to Japan.

Maori population: 1896, 42,113; 1936, 82,326; 1945, 98,744; 1951, 115,676; 1961, 171,553; 1971, 227,414; 1981, 279,255; 1986, 294,201; 1991, 324,000; 1996, 523,374; 2001, 526,281; 2006, 565,329 (14·6% of the total population compared with 15·1% in 1996). In the 2006 census, 157,100 New Zealanders said they could hold a conversation about everyday matters in Maori. In 2001, one in four people of Maori ethnicity claimed to speak the language.

From the 1970s organizations were formed to pursue Maori grievances over loss of land and resources. The Waitangi Tribunal was set up in 1975 as a forum for complaints about breaches of the Treaty of Waitangi, and in 1984 empowered to hear claims against Crown actions since 1840. Direct negotiations with the Crown have been offered to claimants and a range of proposals to resolve historical grievances launched for public discussion in Dec. 1994. These proposals specify that all claims are to be met over ten years with treaty rights being converted to economic assets. There have been four recent major treaty settlements: NZ$170m. each for Tainui and Ngai Tahu, the NZ$150m. Sealord fishing agreement and NZ$40m. for Whakatohea in the Bay of Plenty. The Maori Land Court has jurisdiction over Maori freehold land and some general land owned by Maoris under the Te Ture Whenue Maori Act 1993.

Resident populations of main urban areas at the 2006 census were as follows:

North Island		Wanganui	38,988
Auckland	1,208,094	Wellington	360,624
Gisborne	32,529	Whangarei	49,080
Hamilton	184,905		
Kapiti	37,347	*South Island*	
Napier	118,404	Christchurch	360,765
New Plymouth	49,281	Dunedin	111,000
Palmerston North	76,029	Invercargill	46,773
Rotorua	53,766	Nelson	56,367
Tauranga	108,882		

English and Maori are the official languages.

SOCIAL STATISTICS

Statistics for calendar years:

	Total live births	*Deaths*	*Marriages*	*Divorces (decrees absolute)*
2002	54,021	28,065	20,690	10,292
2003	56,134	28,010	21,419	10,491
2004	58,073	28,419	21,006	10,609
2005	57,745	27,034	20,470	9,972
2006	59,193	28,245	21,423	10,065
2007	64,044	28,522	21,494	9,650

Birth rate, 2007, 15·14 per 1,000 population; death rate, 6·74 per 1,000 population; infant mortality, 2005, 5 per 1,000 live births. Annual population growth rate, 2000–05, 1·2%. In 2005 there were 514 suicides (382 males). Expectation of life, 2006: males, 78·0 years; females, 82·2. Fertility rate, 2007, 2·2 births per woman.

In 2007 there were 82,572 permanent and long-term immigrants (78,963 in 2005) and 77,081 permanent and long-term emigrants (71,992 in 2005).

CLIMATE

Lying in the cool temperate zone, New Zealand enjoys very mild winters for its latitude owing to its oceanic situation, and only the extreme south has cold winters. The situation of the mountain chain produces much sharper climatic contrasts between east and west than in a north-south direction. Mean daily maximum temperatures and rainfall figures:

	Jan (°C)	*July (°C)*	*Annual rainfall (mm) in 2004*
Auckland	23·3	14·5	1,331
Christchurch	22·5	11·3	643
Dunedin	18·9	9·8	765
Wellington	20·3	11·4	1,447

The highest extreme temperature recorded in 2004 was 38·4°C, recorded at Darfield on 1 Jan., and the lowest –12·0°C, at Fairlie on 16 Aug.

CONSTITUTION AND GOVERNMENT

Definition was given to the status of New Zealand by the (Imperial) Statute of Westminster of Dec. 1931, which had received the antecedent approval of the New Zealand Parliament in July 1931. The Governor-General's assent was given to the Statute of Westminster Adoption Bill on 25 Nov. 1947.

The powers, duties and responsibilities of the Governor-General and the Executive Council are set out in Royal Letters Patent and Instructions thereunder of 11 May 1917. In the execution of the powers vested in him the Governor-General must be guided by the advice of the Executive Council.

At a referendum on 6 Nov. 1993 a change from a first-past-the-post to a proportional representation electoral system was favoured by 53·9% of votes cast.

Parliament is the *House of Representatives*, consisting of 122 members (for the 2008 election 63 were general seats, 52 party list seats and seven Maori seats), elected by universal adult suffrage on the mixed-member-proportional system (MMP) for three-year terms. The seven Maori electoral districts cover the whole country. Maori and people of Maori descent are entitled to register either for a general or a Maori electoral district. As at Oct. 2008 there were 229,666 persons on the Maori electoral roll.

Joseph, P. A., *Constitutional Law in New Zealand.* 1993.—(ed.) *Essays on the Constitution.* 1995
McGee, D. G., *Parliamentary Practice in New Zealand.* 2nd ed. 1994
Ringer, J. B., *An Introduction to New Zealand Government.* 1992
Vowles, J. and Aimer, P. (eds.) *Double Decision: the 1993 Election and Referendum in New Zealand.* 1994

National Anthem

'God Defend New Zealand'; words by T. Bracken, tune by J. J. Woods. There is a Maori version, 'Aotearoa', words by T. H. Smith. The UK national anthem has equal status.

GOVERNMENT CHRONOLOGY

Prime Ministers since 1940. (Lab = Labour; Nat = National)

1940–49	Lab	Peter Fraser
1949–57	Nat	Sidney Holland
1957	Nat	Keith Jacka Holyoake
1957–60	Lab	Walter Nash
1960–72	Nat	Keith Jacka Holyoake
1972	Nat	John Ross Marshall
1972–74	Lab	Norman Eric Kirk
1974	Lab	Hugh Watt (acting)
1974–75	Lab	Wallace Edward Rowling
1975–84	Nat	Robert David Muldoon
1984–89	Lab	David Lange
1989–90	Lab	Geoffrey Palmer
1990	Lab	Mike Moore
1990–97	Nat	Jim Bolger
1997–99	Nat	Jenny Shipley
1999–2008	Lab	Helen Clark
2008–	Nat	John Key

RECENT ELECTIONS

At parliamentary elections on 8 Nov. 2008 turnout was 78·7%. The opposition National Party won 59 seats with 45·5%; the ruling Labour Party 43 with 33·8%; the Green Party 8 with 6·4%; ACT New Zealand 5 with 3·7%; the Maori Party 5 with 2·2%; the Progressive Party 1 with 0·9%; and United Future New Zealand 1 with 0·9%.

CURRENT ADMINISTRATION

Governor-General: Anand Satyanand (b. 1944; sworn in 23 Aug. 2006).

In March 2010 the cabinet consisted of:

Prime Minister and Minister of Tourism: John Key; b. 1961 (National Party; in office since 19 Nov. 2008).

Deputy Prime Minister, Minister of Finance, and Infrastructure: Bill English.

Minister of Agriculture, Biosecurity, and Forestry: David Carter. *Conservation, Labour, and Food Safety:* Kate Wilkinson. *Courts, Pacific Islands, and Disarmament and Arms Control:* Georgina te Heuheu. *Defence, and Research, Science and Technology:* Dr Wayne Mapp. *Economic Development, and Energy and Resources:* Gerry Brownlee. *Education:* Anne Tolley. *Environment, Climate Change Issues and the ACC (Accident Compensation Corporation):* Dr Nick Smith. *Ethnic Affairs, and Women's Affairs:* Pansy Wong. *Fisheries, and Housing:* Phil Heatley. *Foreign* Affairs, Sport and Recreation, and the Rugby World Cup: Murray McCully. *Health, and State Services:* Tony Ryall. *Immigration, and Broadcasting:* Dr Jonathan Coleman. *Justice, State Owned Enterprises, and Commerce:* Simon Power. *Police, Corrections, and Veterans' Affairs:* Judith Collins. *Social Development and Employment, and Youth Affairs:* Paula Bennett. *Trade:* Tim Groser. *Transport, Communications and Information Technology, and Tertiary Education:* Steven Joyce. *Treaty of Waitangi Negotiations, Arts, Culture and Heritage, and Attorney General:* Christopher Finlayson.

In addition there are eight ministers who are not in the cabinet. *Minister of Building and Construction, Small Business, Customs, Land Information and Statistics:* Maurice Williamson (National Party). *Civil Defence, Senior Citizens, and Racing:* John Carter (National Party). *Community and the Voluntary Sector, and Disability Issues:* Tariana Turia (Maori Party). *Consumer Affairs:* Heather Roy (ACT New Zealand). *Internal Affairs:* Nathan Guy (National Party). *Local Government, and Regulatory Reform:* Rodney Hide (ACT New Zealand). *Maori Affairs:* Dr Pita Sharples (Maori Party). *Revenue:* Peter Dunne (United Future New Zealand).

Office of the Prime Minister: http://newzealand.govt.nz

CURRENT LEADERS

John Key

Position

Prime Minister

Introduction

John Key, a former currency trader, was elected prime minister in Nov. 2008. Leading the National Party to electoral victory, he ended nine years of Labour government under Helen Clark.

Early Life

John Phillip Key was born on 9 Aug. 1961 in Auckland, where his British father and Austrian–Jewish mother ran a restaurant. When his father died in 1967 the family were left with large debts and lived in state housing in a suburb of Christchurch. After finishing at Burnside School, he graduated in accounting from the University of Canterbury. He then studied management at Harvard University in the USA.

In 1982 Key began working as an auditor, subsequently joining a clothing manufacturer as a project manager. In 1985 he joined Elders Merchant Finance in Wellington, starting his career in foreign exchange (forex) trading just as the NZ dollar was floated on currency markets. Within two years he had become its head forex trader. In 1988 he was recruited by the Bankers Trust in Auckland as head of their forex dealing team, remaining there until 1995.

Key then joined Merrill Lynch as managing director of the Asia forex group in Singapore. Later in the year he was appointed head of Merrill's global forex group in London. In 2001 he moved to Sydney as head of the institution's debt markets. In 2008 Key was listed in the National Business Review's rich list with an estimated wealth of NZ$50m., owning properties in Auckland, Wellington, Omaha (on the coast north of Auckland), London and Hawaii.

In 2001 he joined the National Party, winning the seat for Helensville, a newly-created constituency in northwest Auckland. He won re-election in 2005, a year after joining the opposition front benches as finance spokesman, and again in 2008. In 2006 Key became party leader following the resignation of Don Brash. He led the party to victory at the general election of 8 Nov. 2008 and was sworn in as prime minister 11 days later

Career in Office

Following the election, the National Party signed deals with ACT New Zealand, the Maori Party and United Future, offering ministerial positions outside the cabinet. Key has guaranteed the continuation of a number of Maori-specific parliamentary seats. He has a reputation as a pragmatic centrist and favours privatization, but his first year in office was largely overshadowed by the longest economic recession in the country's history. In Feb. 2009 he launched an NZ$480m. strategy to help small businesses, including a 90-day probation period for workers, the lowering of provisional tax and the relaxing of tax penalties for businesses with incorrect tax returns. The plan also provided for short-term export credit and the fast-tracking of several government building projects.

In foreign affairs, there has been a diplomatic rift with the Fiji Islands over alleged interference by New Zealand in Fijian affairs, leading to the mutual expulsion of high commissioners.

DEFENCE

The control and co-ordination of defence activities is obtained through the Ministry of Defence. New Zealand forces serve abroad in Australia, Iraq and Singapore, and with UN peacekeeping missions.

Defence expenditure in 2006 totalled US$1,544m. (US$379 per capita), representing 1·5% of GDP.

Army

Personnel total in 2007: 4,580, plus reserves numbering 1,762.

Navy

The Navy includes three frigates. The main base and Fleet headquarters is at Auckland.

The Royal New Zealand Navy personnel totalled 2,034 uniformed plus 291 reserve personnel in 2007.

Air Force

Squadrons are based at RNZAF Base Auckland and RNZAF Base Ohakea. Flying training is conducted at Ohakea and Auckland. Ground training is carried out at RNZAF Base Woodbourne.

The uniform strength in 2007 was 2,437 with 190 reserves. There were six combat capable aircraft.

INTERNATIONAL RELATIONS

New Zealand is a member of the UN, World Bank, IMF and several other UN specialized agencies, WTO, Commonwealth, IOM, OECD, Asian Development Bank, APEC, Colombo Plan, Pacific Islands Forum, SPC and Antarctic Treaty.

ECONOMY

Agriculture accounted for 8% of GDP in 2001, industry 23% and services 69%.

According to the anti-corruption organization *Transparency International*, New Zealand ranked first in a 2009 survey of the countries with the least corruption in business and government. It received 9·4 out of 10 in the annual index.

Overview

The economy is heavily reliant on agriculture, fishing and forestry. Prior to the 1980s the economy was one of the most regulated and protected in the developed world. With liberalization, the economy has grown every year since 1991 despite the 1997 Asian crisis, periods of drought and the global slowdown which followed the 11 Sept. attacks in the USA.

In the early 2000s real GDP and per capita income growth rates were greater than the OECD average, though per capita income remains below the developed world average. Following an economic downturn in late 2005, domestic demand has regained momentum, aided by a recovery in the housing market and improved business and consumer confidence. Inflation has crept above the 1–3% target range set by the Bank of New Zealand while the current account deficit peaked at over 9% of GDP in mid-2006. However, the current period of lower-than-expected growth should help reduce inflationary pressures and aid the narrowing of the current account.

With the economy at full capacity, the country has experienced skilled and unskilled labour shortages and infrastructure bottlenecks. There have been strong capital inflows from international investors borrowing in low interest-rate areas to invest in high interest-rate economies like New Zealand. The New Zealand dollar suffered a fall following the Feb. 2006 króna collapse in Iceland, a country which has also attracted recent significant capital inflows.

Currency

The monetary unit is the *New Zealand dollar* (NZD), of 100 *cents*. The total value of notes and coins on issue from the Reserve Bank in Dec. 2002 was NZ$2,451m. Inflation rates (based on OECD statistics):

1999	*2000*	*2001*	*2002*	*2003*	*2004*	*2005*	*2006*	*2007*	*2008*
−0·1%	2·6%	2·6%	2·7%	1·8%	2·3%	3·0%	3·4%	2·4%	4·0%

In Aug. 2009 foreign exchange reserves were US$11,783m. and total money supply was NZ$33,640m. Gold reserves are negligible.

Budget

The fiscal year begins 1 April. Total central government revenue for 2005–06 was NZ$76,581m. (NZ$67,065m. in 2004–05). Central government expenditure in 2005–06 was NZ$65,084m. (NZ$60,910m. in 2004–05).

2002–03 tax revenue was NZ$39,785m. and NZ$2,763m. was earned through levies, fees, fines and penalties. Direct income tax totalled NZ$26,778m. in 2002–03 (including income tax on individuals, NZ$19,669m.; and corporate tax, NZ$5,940m.). Indirect income tax totalled NZ$13,007m. in 2002–03 (including goods and services tax, NZ$8,738m.).

The gross public debt at June 2003 was NZ$38,285m., of which NZ$24,380m. was held in New Zealand currency, NZ$6,697m. in foreign currency and NZ$7,208m. in non-sovereign-guaranteed debt.

There is a Goods and Services Tax (GST) of 12·5%.

Performance

Real GDP growth rates (based on OECD statistics):

1999	*2000*	*2001*	*2002*	*2003*	*2004*	*2005*	*2006*	*2007*	*2008*
4·7%	3·8%	2·4%	4·7%	4·3%	4·4%	2·8%	2·7%	2·9%	−1·1%

Total GDP was US$130·7bn. in 2008.

Banking and Finance

The central bank and bank of issue is the Reserve Bank (*Governor*, Dr Alan Bollard).

The financial system comprises a central bank (the Reserve Bank of New Zealand), registered banks and other financial institutions. Registered banks include banks from abroad, which have to satisfy capital adequacy and managerial quality requirements. Other financial institutions include the regional trustee banks, now grouped under Trust Bank, building societies, finance companies, merchant banks and stock and station agents. The number of registered banks was 18 in 2003 of which only four were operating in New Zealand before 1986. Around 99% of the assets of the New Zealand banking system were under the ownership of a foreign bank parent.

The primary functions of the Reserve Bank are the formulation and implementation of monetary policy to achieve the economic objectives set by the government, and the promotion of the efficiency and soundness of the financial system, through the registration of banks, and supervision of financial institutions. Since 1996 supervision has been conducted on a basis of public disclosure by banks of their activities every quarter.

On 30 June 2003 the assets of the Reserve Bank were NZ$11,543m. (including government securities totalling NZ$3,300m. and marketable securities totalling NZ$3,137m.).

The stock exchange in Wellington conducts on-screen trading, unifying the three former trading floors in Auckland, Christchurch and Wellington. There is also a stock exchange in Dunedin.

ENERGY AND NATURAL RESOURCES

Environment

New Zealand's carbon dioxide emissions from the consumption and flaring of fossil fuels were the equivalent of 9·4 tonnes per capita in 2008. An *Environmental Performance Index* compiled in 2008 ranked New Zealand seventh in the world, with 88·9%. The index examined various factors in six areas—air pollution, biodiversity and habitat, climate change, environmental health, productive natural resources and water resources.

Electricity

On 1 April 1987 the former Electricity Division of the Ministry of Energy became a state-owned enterprise, the Electricity Corporation of N.Z. Ltd, which has since been split into two state-owned enterprises causing a competitive wholesale electricity market to be established. Around 68% of the country's electricity is generated by renewable sources. Hydro-electric plants, mainly based in the South Island, account for some 61% with geothermal power, generated in the North Island, accounting for around 7%. The rest comes from natural gas (25%), coal, wind and landfill gas. Electricity generating capacity, 2004, 8·8m. kW. Consumption per capita was 10,238 kWh in 2004.

Electricity consumption statistics (in GWh) for years ended 31 March are:

	Residential	*Commercial*	*Industrial*	*Total consumption*
1999	11,290	7,334	14,010	32,635
2000	11,057	6,919	14,759	32,735
2001	11,306	6,819	15,142	33,267
2002	11,660	6,965	14,525	33,150

New Zealand also has eight wind farms.

Oil and Gas

Crude oil production was 7·4m. bbls in 2004. Around 75% of production is exported. 119,700 bbls per day were imported in 2001. Proven reserves were estimated at 53m. bbls in 2007.

In 2008 gasfields produced 3·8bn. cu. metres. Gas reserves are estimated to last until about 2014. In 2007 proven natural gas reserves were estimated at 25·0bn. cu. metres.

Minerals

Coal production in 2004 was 2·53m. tonnes. Of the 45 mines operating in 2002, 29 were opencast and 16 underground, responsible for 79·6% and 20·3% of total coal production respectively. Only 12 mines produced over 200,000 tonnes of coal and 14 operations had an output of less than 10,000 tonnes. Around 60% of New Zealand's exported coal goes to India and Japan.

While New Zealand's best known non-fuel mineral is gold (producing about 9·77 tonnes in 2002 worth NZ$212m.) there is also production of silver, ironsand, aggregate, limestone, clay, aluminium, dolomite, pumice, salt, serpentinite, zeolite and bentonite. In addition, there are resources or potential for deposits of titanium (ilmenite beach sands), platinum, sulphur, phosphate, silica and mercury.

Agriculture

Two-thirds of the land area is suitable for agriculture and grazing. The total area of farmland in use in 2002 was 15,640,000 ha. There were 11,967,000 ha. of grazing, arable, fodder and fallow land, 110,000 ha. of land for horticulture and 1,879,000 ha. of plantations of exotic timber. In 2001 there were 1·5m. ha. of arable land and 1·87m. ha. of permanent crops.

The largest freehold estates are held in the South Island. The number of occupied holdings as at 30 June 2002 were as follows:

Regional Council	*No. of farms*	*Total area of farms (1,000 ha.)*
Auckland	5,500	302
Bay of Plenty	5,700	600
Gisborne	1,300	653
Hawke's Bay	3,900	962
Manawatu-Wanganui	6,500	1,545
Northland	5,800	836
Taranaki	3,900	496
Waikato	12,000	1,730
Wellington	2,500	504
Total North Island	*47,000*	*7,627*
Canterbury	10,000	3,151
Marlborough	1,700	723
Nelson	190	21
Otago	4,100	2,368
Southland	4,300	1,198
Tasman	1,900	277
West Coast	830	225
Total South Island	*23,000*	*8,013*
Total New Zealand	*70,000*	*15,640*

Production of main crops (2000, in 1,000 tonnes): potatoes, 500; apples, 482; wheat, 360; barley, 281; maize, 174; pumpkins and squash, 155; tomatoes, 85; carrots, 80; grapes, 80; cauliflower, 63.

Livestock, 2002: sheep, 39·54m.; cattle, 9·65m.; pigs, 344,000; goats, 153,000; deer, 1·64m.; chickens, 13m. (2000). Total meat produced in 2002 was 1·40m. tonnes (including 576,000 tonnes of beef and veal, and 521,000 tonnes of lamb and mutton). Meat industry products are New Zealand's second largest export income earner, accounting for about 14% of merchandise exports. New Zealand's main meat exports are lamb, mutton and beef. About 65% of lamb, 61% of beef and 51% of mutton produced in New Zealand in 2001–02 was exported overseas. The domestic market absorbs over 99% of the pigmeat and poultry produced in New Zealand. 54% of the world's exported sheepmeat comes from New Zealand.

Production of wool for the year 2002–03 was 173,000 tonnes. Milk production for 2000–01 totalled a record 12,322m. litres. In 1999–2000 butter production totalled 254,639 tonnes and cheese production 296,745 tonnes.

Forestry

Forests covered 8·0m. ha. in 2002 (30% of New Zealand's land area), up from 7·67m. ha. in 1990. Of this, about 6·2m. ha. are indigenous forest and 1·8m. ha. planted productive forest. New planting and restocking was 65,900 ha. in 2002. Introduced pines form the bulk of the large exotic forest estate and among these radiata pine is the best multi-purpose tree, reaching log size in 25–30 years. Other species planted are Douglas fir and Eucalyptus species. Total roundwood production in 2002–03 was 23·10m. cu. metres. The table below shows production of rough sawn timber in 1,000 cu. metres for years ending 31 March:

	Indigenous			*Exotic*			*All Species*
	Rimu and Miro	*Beech*	*Total*	*Radiata Pine*	*Douglas Fir*	*Total*	*Total*
1998	28	5	38	2,995	105	3,157	3,195
1999	30	4	38	2,996	143	3,188	3,226
2000	22	6	30	3,583	134	3,776	3,806
2001	17	8	28	3,625	136	3,820	3,848
2002	13	13	28	3,678	124	3,836	3,864

In 2002–03 forest industries consisted of approximately 360 sawmills, seven plywood and 11 veneer plants, four particle board mills, eight wood pulp mills (four of which also produced paper and paperboard) and six fibreboard mills.

The basic products of the pulp and paper mills are mechanical and chemical pulp which are converted into newsprint, kraft and other papers, paperboard and fibreboard. Production of wood pulp in the year ending 31 March 2002 amounted to 1,523,730 tonnes and of paper (including newsprint paper and paperboard) to 846,727 tonnes.

Fisheries

In 2005 the total catch was 535,394 tonnes, almost entirely from sea fishing. The total value of New Zealand fisheries exports in 2002 was NZ$1,530m., of which hoki exports constituted NZ$314·7m.

INDUSTRY

The leading companies in New Zealand in Feb. 2009 by market capitalization were the Telecom Corporation of New Zealand (TCNZ), US$2·2bn.; and Fletcher Building (US$1·3bn.).

Statistics of manufacturing industries (in NZ$1m.):

Production year	*Salaries and wages paid*	*Closing stocks of raw materials*	*Closing stocks of finished goods*	*Operating income*	*Purchases and other operating expenses*
2001–02	8,961	2,618	4,945	63,396	47,163
2002–03	9,523	2,595	6,954	65,146	47,770

The following is a statement of the value of the products (including repairs) of the principal industries for the year 2002–03 (in NZ$1m.):

Industry group	*Salaries and wages paid*	*Closing stocks of raw materials*	*Closing stocks of finished goods*	*Operating income*	*Purchases and other operating expenses*
Dairy and meat products	1,481	261	3,015	16,057	13,777
Other food	869	213	651	6,939	5,063
Beverage, malt and tobacco	292	154	423	2,926	2,060

Industry group	Salaries and wages paid	Closing stocks of raw materials	Closing stocks of finished goods	Operating income	Purchases and other operating expenses
Textile and apparel	579	205	296	3,069	2,092
Wood products	674	107	381	4,245	3,227
Paper and paper products	407	110	206	2,870	2,002
Printing, publishing and recorded media	796	84	84	3,392	2,001
Petroleum and industrial chemical	267	195	192	3,202	2,154
Rubber, plastic and other chemical products	728	218	513	4,144	2,840
Non-metallic mineral products	295	52	137	2,041	1,364
Basic metal	314	108	161	2,041	1,524
Structural, sheet and fabricated metal products	780	195	214	4,112	2,849
Transport equipment manufacturing	499	212	145	2,244	1,488
Machinery and equipment	1,138	357	429	5,876	4,010
Furniture and other manufacturing	405	124	106	1,984	1,317

According to the World Bank's *Doing Business 2010* New Zealand is the easiest country in which to start a business and the second easiest country in which to do business (after Singapore).

Labour

There were an estimated 1,928,300 persons employed in the quarter ending Sept. 2003. The largest number of employed people worked in the community, social and personal services area (27·4%); followed by wholesale and retail trade, restaurants and hotels (22·9%); and manufacturing (14·7%). Unemployment total for the quarter ending Sept. 2003 was estimated to be 86,300. The unemployment rate for the quarter ending Dec. 2009 was 7·2% of the workforce.

The weekly average wage in the quarter ended June 2003 was NZ$857 for men, NZ$685 for women. A minimum wage is set by the government annually. As of 1 April 2004 it was NZ$9·00 an hour; a youth rate of NZ$7·20 per hour applies for 16–17 year-olds. In 2002 there were 46 work stoppages (42 in 2001) with 34,398 person-days of work lost (54,440 in 2001).

Trade Unions

In 2000, 19 industrial unions of workers (representing 80% of all union members) were affiliated to the Council of Trade Unions, NZCTU (*President*, Helen Kelly). Compulsory trade union membership was made illegal in 1991, and the national wage award system was replaced by local wage agreements under the Employment Contracts Act 1991. In Dec. 2002 there were 174 unions in total with a combined membership of 334,783.

INTERNATIONAL TRADE

Total overseas debt was NZ$130,615m. in June 2003. In 1990 New Zealand and Australia completed the Closer Economic Relations Agreement (initiated in 1983), which provides for mutual free trade in goods.

Imports and Exports

Trade in NZ$1m. for recent years ending 30 June:

	Imports (c.i.f.)	Exports, including re-exports (f.o.b.)	Balance of Merchandise Trade
2001	31,927	32,000	73
2002	31,811	32,332	521
2003	32,161	29,291	–2,870
2004	33,378	29,864	–3,514
2005	35,793	30,618	–5,175

The principal imports for the 12 months ended 30 June 2003 were:

Commodity	Value (NZ$1m. v.f.d.)
Vehicles, parts and accessories	4,985
Mechanical machinery and equipment	4,333
Mineral fuels	3,152
Electrical machinery and equipment	2,699
Plastics and plastic articles	1,279
Optical, medical and measuring equipment	967
Paper, paperboard and paper articles	924
Aircraft and parts	804
Pharmaceutical products	747
Iron or steel articles	491
Iron and steel	481
Apparel (not knitted or crocheted)	446

The principal exports for the 12 months ended 30 June 2003 were:

Commodity	Value (NZ$1m. f.o.b.)
Dairy produce, eggs and honey	4,714
Meat and edible offal	4,111
Wood and articles of wood	2,386
Machinery and mechanical appliances	1,356
Fish, crustaceans and molluscs	1,215
Albuminoidal substances; modified starches; glues; enzymes	1,148
Fruits and nuts (edible)	1,032
Aluminium and aluminium articles	980
Wool, fine or coarse animal hair	943
Electrical machinery, equipment and parts	938

The principal import suppliers in 2002–03 (imports v.f.d., in NZ$1m.) were: Australia, 7,278; USA, 4,067; Japan, 3,876; China, 2,687; Germany, 1,713; UK, 1,120; Malaysia, 864. The leading export destinations in 2002–03 (exports and re-exports f.o.b., in NZ$1m.) were: Australia, 6,050; USA, 4,366; Japan, 3,354; China, 1,457; UK, 1,361; Republic of Korea, 1,178; Germany, 855.

COMMUNICATIONS

Roads

Total length of roads in 2007 was 93,748 km (65·4% paved), including 172 km of motorways. There were 10,893 km of highways, main or national roads. At 30 June 2008 motor vehicles licensed numbered 4,125,932, of which 2,788,938 were passenger cars and vans. In addition there were 577,684 trailers and caravans, 519,992 commercial vehicles, and 130,213 motorcycles and mopeds. In 2007 there were 422 deaths in road accidents.

In 2008 there were 34,590 persons employed in road transport. Total expenditure on roads (including infrastructure) by the central government and local authorities combined amounted to NZ$1,751m. in 2008.

Rail

KiwiRail Holdings is the national rail operator. Previously called New Zealand Rail, it was privatized in 1994 and renamed Tranz Rail Ltd in 1995. In 2003 Tranz Rail was bought by Toll Holdings of Australia and became Toll New Zealand. Under the terms of the takeover, the following year Toll NZ sold the network back to the government for NZ$1 and exclusive operating rights, trading under the name ONTRACK. In July 2008 Toll NZ was bought by the government for NZ$690m. and renamed KiwiRail.

In 1994 a 24-hour freight link was introduced between Auckland and Christchurch. There were, in 2002, 3,898 km of 1,067 mm gauge railway open for traffic (506 km electrified). In 2003 Tranz Rail carried 14·8m. tonnes of freight and 12·3m. passengers. Total revenue in the financial year 1999–2000 was NZ$594·5m.

At 30 June 2003 Tranz Rail track and rolling stock included 322 diesel, electric and shunting locomotives, 4,048 freight wagons, 177 passenger carriages and commuter units, three rail/road ferries (linking the North and South Islands) and plant and support equipment. After renationalization Tranz Rail was renamed Toll NZ and subsequently KiwiRail.

Civil Aviation

There are international airports at Wellington, Auckland and Christchurch, with Auckland International being the main airport. The national carrier is Air New Zealand, which was privatized in 1989 but then renationalized in 2001. Trans-Tasman air travel is subject to agreement between Air New Zealand and Qantas.

New Zealand has one of the highest ratios of aircraft to population in the world with 3,530 aircraft in the year to March 2003. Since 1992 air transport flights have increased by about 9% per year. In 2005 scheduled airline traffic of New Zealand-based carriers flew 243·0m. km, carrying 11,402,400 passengers. In 2002 there were 113 airports, of which 46 had paved runways.

Shipping

In 2002 merchant shipping totalled 180,000 GRT, including oil tankers 50,000 GRT. In 2003 there were 1,069 km of waterway.

Telecommunications

The provision of telecommunication services is the responsibility of the Telecom Corporation of New Zealand, formed in 1987 and privatized in 1990; and CLEAR Communications, which began operations in Dec. 1990. In 2008 there were 1,750,000 main (fixed) telephone lines. In the same year mobile phone subscribers numbered 4,620,000 (1,092·2 per 1,000 persons). There were 2·2m. PCs in use in 2006 and 3·0m. internet users in 2008. The broadband penetration rate was 20·4 subscribers per 100 inhabitants in June 2008.

Postal Services

On 1 April 1998 the Postal Services Act removed New Zealand Post's former statutory monopoly on the carriage of letters and opened the postal market to full competition. To carry out a business involving the carriage of letters, a person or company must be registered as a postal operator with the Ministry of Commerce.

In 2003 there were 315 post shops, 697 post centre franchises and 2,735 stamp resellers.

SOCIAL INSTITUTIONS

Justice

The judiciary consists of the Supreme Court, the Court of Appeal, the High Court and District Courts. All exercise both civil and criminal jurisdiction. The Supreme Court replaced the Privy Council in London as the court of final appeal in 2004. Special courts include the Maori Land Court, the Maori Appellate Court, Family Courts, the Youth Court, Environment Court and the Employment Court. In 2003 there were 5,826 sentenced inmates of whom 274 were women. Of male inmates in 2001, 53% (some 2,499) identified themselves as Maori only compared to 29% who identified themselves as European only. There were 170,999 convictions, including 14,537 for violent offences, in 2002. The death penalty for murder was replaced by life imprisonment in 1961.

The Criminal Injuries Compensation Act, 1963, which came into force on 1 Jan. 1964, provided for compensation of persons injured by certain criminal acts and the dependants of persons killed by such acts. However, this has now been phased out in favour of the Accident Compensation Act, 1982, except in the residual area of property damage caused by escapees. The Offenders Legal Aid Act 1954 provides that any person charged or convicted of any offence may apply for legal aid which may be granted depending on the person's means and the gravity of the offence etc. Since 1970 legal aid in civil proceedings (except divorce) has been available for persons of small or moderate means. The Legal Services Act 1991 now brings together in one statute the civil and criminal legal aid schemes.

Police

The police are a national body maintained by the central government. In June 2003 there were 7,257 full-time equivalent sworn officers (16% female).

Ombudsmen

The office of Ombudsman was created in 1962. From 1975 additional Ombudsmen have been authorized. There are currently two. Ombudsmen's functions are to investigate complaints under the Ombudsman Act, the Official Information Act and the Local Government Official Information and Meetings Act from members of the public relating to administrative decisions of central, regional and local government. During the year ended 30 June 2003 a total of 4,418 complaints were received. A total of 27 complaints were sustained during the year and 729 were still under investigation

Education

Education is compulsory between the ages of 6 and 16. Children aged three and four years may enrol at the 606 free kindergartens maintained by Free Kindergarten Associations, which receive government assistance. There are also 492 play centres which also receive government subsidy. In 2002 there were 45,169 and 14,879 children on the rolls respectively. There were also 1,612 care centres in 2002 with 76,246 children, 545 *te kohanga reo* (providing early childhood education in the Maori language) with 10,389 children, and a number of other smaller providers of early childhood care and education.

In 2002 there were 2,132 state primary schools (including intermediate and state contributing schools), with 411,850 pupils; the number of teachers was 19,329. A correspondence school for children in remote areas and those otherwise unable to attend school had 7,872 primary and secondary pupils and 242 teachers. In 2003 there were 45 registered private primary and intermediate schools with 6,106 pupils. In 2002 there were 534 teachers at private primary and intermediate schools.

In 2002 there were 320 state secondary schools with 14,577 full-time teachers and 212,426 pupils. There were also 58 state composite area schools with 4,831 scholars in the secondary division. In 2003 there were 2,280 full-time secondary pupils taught by 282 secondary teachers at the Correspondence School. There were 17 registered private secondary schools with 615 teachers and 8,498 pupils in 2002.

New Zealand has eight universities—the University of Auckland, Auckland University of Technology, University of Waikato (at Hamilton), Victoria University of Wellington, Massey University (at Palmerston North), the University of Canterbury (at Christchurch), the University of Otago (at Dunedin) and Lincoln University (near Christchurch). The number of equivalent full-time students attending universities in 2002 was 100,772. There were four teachers' training colleges with 6,338 equivalent full-time students in 2002, and 63,741 equivalent full-time students were enrolled in polytechnic courses in 2002.

Total budgeted expenditure estimated in 2003 on education was NZ$8·2bn. (16·8% of government expenses). The universities are autonomous bodies. All state-funded primary and secondary schools are controlled by boards of trustees. Education in state schools is free for children under 19 years of age. All educational institutions are reviewed every three years by teams of educational reviewers.

A series of reforms is being implemented by the government following reports of 18 working groups on tertiary education. These include a new funding system, begun in 1991 and based solely on student numbers.

The adult literacy rate is at least 99%.

Health

In 2003 there were 10,355 practising doctors. In 2002 there were 85 public hospitals with 12,484 beds and 360 private hospitals with 11,341 beds. In 2007 New Zealand spent 9·0% of its GDP on health. Total budgeted expenditure on health in 2003–04 was NZ$9·6bn.

Welfare

Non-contributory old-age pensions were introduced in 1898. Large reductions in welfare expenditure were introduced by the government in Dec. 1990.

From 1 Oct. 1998 anyone receiving unemployment benefit, sickness benefit, a training benefit, a 55 plus benefit, or a young job seekers allowance has received a benefit called the Community Wage. In return for receiving the Community Wage, recipients are expected to search for work, meet with Work and Income New Zealand when asked, take a suitable work offer and take part in activities that would improve their chances of finding a job.

In the budget of July 1991 it was announced that current rates of Guaranteed Retirement Income Scheme (GRI) payment would be frozen until 1 April 1993, thereafter to be on the previous year's consumer price index. On 1 April 1992 GRI was replaced by the national superannuation scheme which is income-tested. Eligibility has been gradually increased to 65 years. Universal eligibility is available at 70 years. At 1 April 2008 a married couple received NZ$439·80 per week, a single person living alone NZ$285·87 per week.

Social Welfare Benefits

Benefits	*Number in force at 30 June 2003*	*Total expenditure 2003 (NZ$1,000)*
Community Wage—Job Seeker	111,906	1,287,730
Community Wage—Training	4,291	37,942
Community Wage—Sickness	39,902	460,209
Invalids' Benefit	68,507	926,515
Domestic Purposes' Benefit	109,295	1,634,477
Orphans' Benefit/ Unsupported Child's Benefit	6,789	47,081
Widows' Benefit	8,659	90,265
Transitional Retirement Benefit	2,110	42,013
New Zealand Superannuation	457,278	5,798,873
Veterans' Pension	7,872	87,625
War Pension	22,271	108,862
Total Income Support	838,880	10,521,592

Reciprocity with Other Countries. New Zealand has overseas social security agreements with the United Kingdom, the Netherlands, Greece, Ireland, Australia, Jersey and Guernsey, Denmark and Canada. The main purpose of these agreements is to encourage free movement of labour and to ensure that when a person has lived or worked in more than one country, each of those countries takes a fair share of the responsibility for meeting the costs of that person's social security coverage. New Zealand also pays people eligible for New Zealand Superannuation or veterans' pensions who live in the Cook Islands, Niue or Tokelau.

RELIGION

No direct state aid is given to any form of religion. For the Church of England the country is divided into seven dioceses, with a separate bishopric (Aotearoa) for the Maori. The Presbyterian Church is divided into 23 presbyteries and the Maori Synod. The Moderator is elected annually. The Methodist Church is divided into ten districts; the President is elected annually. The Roman Catholic Church is divided into four dioceses, with the Archbishop of Wellington as Metropolitan Archbishop. In Feb. 2010 there was one cardinal.

Adherents of leading religions at the 2001 census were as follows:

Religious denomination	*Adherents*
Anglican	584,793
Catholic	486,012
Presbyterian	417,453
Methodist	120,708
Baptist	51,426
Ratana	48,975
Buddhist	41,664
Latter-day Saints (Mormons)	39,915
Hindu	39,876
Pentecostal	30,222
Islam/Muslim	23,637
Brethren	20,406
Jehovah's Witnesses	17,826
Assemblies of God	16,023
Salvation Army	12,618
Seventh-day Adventist	12,600
All other religious affiliations	398,847
No religion	1,028,052
Object to state	239,241
Not specified	211,638
Total	3,841,932[1]

[1]Where a person reported more than one religious affiliation, they have been counted in each applicable group.

CULTURE

World Heritage Sites

There are three UNESCO World Heritage sites under New Zealand jurisdiction. Te Wahipounamu on South Island was listed in 1990; Tongariro National Park, on North Island, was listed in 1990 and 1993; the Sub-Antarctic Islands, consisting of the Auckland Islands, Antipodes Islands, Bounty Islands, Campbell Island and the Snares, were inscribed on the list in 1998.

Broadcasting

State-owned Television New Zealand operates two main channels, TV1 and TV2. The Maori Television and TVNZ6 channels are also government-owned. Radio New Zealand broadcasts on three national networks: Radio New Zealand International is an external service. There are a number of competing commercial television and radio services at national and local level. In 2006 there were 2·50m. television sets (colour by PAL).

Cinema

Cinema admissions totalled 18·3m. in 2003, up from 6·1m. in 1991. Gross box office receipts came to NZ$156·1m. in 2003. In 1999 there were 315 cinema screens.

Press

In 2003 there were 24 daily newspapers with a combined daily average circulation of 740,763, giving a rate of 185 per 1,000 inhabitants. The *New Zealand Herald*, published in Auckland, had the largest daily circulation in 2003, with an average of 210,910 copies. Other major dailies are *The Dominion Post* and *The Press*, with circulations of over 90,000 copies.

There are two Sunday newspapers, *Sunday Star-Times* and *Sunday News*, both published by Fairfax New Zealand Limited and distributed nationwide. The *Sunday Star-Times* is a broadsheet and circulates about 204,000 copies while the *Sunday News* is a tabloid and circulates 115,000 (2000) copies every Sunday.

Tourism

There were 2,400,719 tourists in the year to March 2009 (down from a record 2,496,994 in the year to March 2008) of whom 975,870 were from Australia, 263,733 were from the UK, 196,655 were from the USA and 113,465 were from China. Tourism receipts excluding passenger transport totalled US$4·98bn. in 2005.

Festivals

The biennial New Zealand Festival takes place in Wellington in Feb./March in even-numbered years. The biennial Christchurch Arts Festival takes place in July/Aug. in odd-numbered years.

DIPLOMATIC REPRESENTATIVES

Of New Zealand in the United Kingdom (New Zealand House, Haymarket, London, SW1Y 4TQ)
High Commissioner: Derek Leask.

Of the United Kingdom in New Zealand (44 Hill St., Wellington, 6011)
High Commissioner: George Fergusson.

Of New Zealand in the USA (37 Observatory Cir., NW, Washington, D.C., 20008)
Ambassador: Roy Ferguson.

Of the USA in New Zealand (29 Fitzherbert Terr., Wellington)
Ambassador: David Huebner.

Of New Zealand to the United Nations
Ambassador: Jim McLay.

Of New Zealand to the European Union
Ambassador: Peter Kennedy.

FURTHER READING

Statistics New Zealand. *New Zealand Official Yearbook.—Key Statistics: a Monthly Abstract of Statistics.—Profile of New Zealand.*

Belich, James, *Making Peoples: a History of the New Zealanders from Polynesian Settlement to the End of the Nineteenth century.* 1997.—*Paradise Reforged: A History of New Zealanders from the 1880s to the Year 2000.* 2002

Harland, B., *On Our Own: New Zealand in a Tripolar World.* 1992

Harris, P. and Levine, S. (eds.) *The New Zealand Politics Source Book.* 2nd ed. 1994

Massey, P., *New Zealand: Market Liberalization in a Developed Economy.* 1995

Mein Smith, Philippa, *A Concise History of New Zealand.* 2005

Miller, Raymond, *Political Leadership in New Zealand.* 2006

Rowe, James E., *Economic Development in New Zealand.* 2005

Sinclair, K. (ed.) *The Oxford Illustrated History of New Zealand.* 2nd ed. 1994

For other more specialized titles see under CONSTITUTION AND GOVERNMENT above.

National Statistical Office: Statistics New Zealand, POB 2922, Wellington, 1.
Website: http://www.stats.govt.nz

TERRITORIES OVERSEAS

Territories Overseas coming within the jurisdiction of New Zealand consist of Tokelau and the Ross Dependency.

Tokelau

Tokelau is situated some 500 km to the north of Samoa and comprises three dispersed atolls—Atafu, Fakaofo and Nukunonu. The land area is 12 sq. km and the population at the 2004 census was 1,609, giving a density of 134 per sq. km.

The British government transferred administrative control of Tokelau to New Zealand in 1925. Formal sovereignty was transferred to New Zealand in 1948 by act of the New Zealand Parliament. New Zealand statute law, however, does not apply to Tokelau unless it is expressly extended to Tokelau.

Under a programme agreed in 1992, the role of Tokelau's political institutions is being better defined and expanded. The process under way enables the base of Tokelau government to be located within Tokelau's national level institutions rather than as before, within a public service located largely in Samoa. In 1994 the Administrator's powers were delegated to the *General Fono* (the national representative body), and when the *General Fono* is not in session, to the *Council of Faipule*. The Tokelau Amendment Act 1996 conferred on the *General Fono* a power to make rules for Tokelau, including the power to impose taxes. There are no parties—in elections of 18 and 19 Jan. 2008, 20 independents were elected to the *General Fono*.

Administrator: David Payton.
Head of Government: Foua Toloa.

Coconuts (the source of copra) are the only cash crop. Pulaka, breadfruit, papayas, the screw-pine and bananas are cultivated as food crops. Livestock comprises pigs, poultry and goats.

Tokelau affirmed to the United Nations in 1994 that it had under active consideration both the Constitution of a self-governing Tokelau and an act of self-determination. It also expressed a strong preference for a future status of free association with New Zealand. A referendum on self-determination took place in Feb. 2006 with 60% voting in favour of the proposal, short of the two-thirds majority needed for the referendum to succeed. Another referendum in Oct. 2007 showed 64% in favour, still short of the required two-thirds majority. In May 2008 Ban Ki-moon, secretary general of the UN, reiterated his desire that the process of 'decolonizing' all of the 16 non-self-governing regions around the world be accelerated.

Ross Dependency

By Imperial Order in Council, dated 30 July 1923, the territories between 160° E. long. and 150° W. long. and south of 60° S. lat. were brought within the jurisdiction of the New Zealand government. The region was named the Ross Dependency. From time to time laws for the Dependency have been made by regulations promulgated by the Governor-General of New Zealand.

The mainland area is estimated at 400,000–450,000 sq. km and is mostly ice-covered. In Jan. 1957 a New Zealand expedition under Sir Edmund Hillary established a base in the Dependency. In Jan. 1958 Sir Edmund Hillary and four other New Zealanders reached the South Pole.

The main base—Scott Base, at Pram Point, Ross Island—is manned throughout the year, about 12 people being present during winter. The annual activities of 200–300 scientists and support staff are managed by a crown agency, Antarctica New Zealand, based in Christchurch.

SELF-GOVERNING TERRITORIES OVERSEAS

The Cook Islands

KEY HISTORICAL EVENTS

The Cook Islands, which lie between 8° and 23° S. lat., and 156° and 167° W. long., were made a British protectorate in 1888, and on 11 June 1901 were annexed as part of New Zealand. In 1965 the Cook Islands became a self-governing territory in 'free association' with New Zealand.

TERRITORY AND POPULATION

The islands fall roughly into two groups—the scattered islands towards the north (Northern group) and the islands towards the south (Southern group). The islands with their populations at the census of 2001:

Southern Group—	*Area sq. km*	*Population*
Aitutaki	18·3	1,946
Atiu	26·9	623
Mangaia	51·8	744
Manuae and Te au-o-tu	6·2	—
Mauke (Parry Is.)	18·4	470
Mitiaro	22·3	230
Rarotonga	67·1	12,188
Northern Group—	*Area sq. km*	*Population*
Manihiki (Humphrey)	5·4	515
Nassau	1·3	72
Palmerston (Avarua)	2·1	48
Penrhyn (Tongareva)	9·8	357
Pukapuka (Danger)	1·3	664
Rakahanga (Reirson)	4·1	169
Suwarrow (Anchorage)	0·4	1
Total	235·4	18,027

Population density in 2001 was 76 per sq. km. In 2001 an estimated 67·6% of the population lived in urban areas. The 2001 total population (18,027) and the resident population (15,017) have both fallen since 1996, when the total population at the time of the census was 19,103 and the resident population 18,071.

SOCIAL STATISTICS

2005: births, 278; deaths, 86. Birth rate (2005, per 1,000 population), 22·4; death rate, 6·9. Life expectancy was estimated in 2003 at: males, 68·0 years; females 74·0. Fertility rate, 2004, 2·6 births per woman.

CLIMATE

Oceanic climate where rainfall is moderate to heavy throughout the year, with Nov. to March being particularly wet. Weather can be changeable from day to day and can end in rainfall after an otherwise sunny day. Rarotonga, Jan. 26°C, July 20°C. Annual rainfall 2,060 mm.

CONSTITUTION AND GOVERNMENT

The Cook Islands Constitution of 1965 provides for internal self-government but linked to New Zealand by a common Head of State and a common citizenship, that of New Zealand. It provides for a ministerial system of government with a Cabinet consisting of a Prime Minister and not more than eight nor fewer than six other Ministers. There is also an advisory council composed of hereditary chiefs, the 15-member House of Ariki, without legislative powers. The New Zealand government is represented by a New Zealand Representative and the Queen, as head of state, by the Queen's Representative. The capital is Avarua on Rarotonga.

The bicameral *Parliament* comprises a Legislative Assembly (or lower house) of 25 members (including one representing overseas voters) elected for a term of five years and a House of Ariki (or upper house) that has an advisory role only and is made up of chiefs.

RECENT ELECTIONS

At the elections of 26 Sept. 2006 the centrist Democratic Party won 15 of the 24 seats, the Cook Islands Party 7 seats and ind. 1 seat. A subsequent by-election for a tied seat was won by the Cook Islands Party, giving them eight in total.

CURRENT ADMINISTRATION

Acting High Commissioner: Nicola Ngawati.
Prime Minister: Jim Marurai.

Government Website: http://www.cook-islands.gov.ck

ECONOMY

Overview

A package of economic reforms including privatization and deregulation was initiated in July 1996 to deal with a national debt of US$141m., 120% of GDP.

Currency

The Cook Island *dollar* was at par with the New Zealand *dollar*, but was replaced in 1995 by New Zealand currency.

Budget

Revenue, 2003–04, NZ$81·4m.; expenditure, NZ$83·9m. Grants from New Zealand, mainly for medical, educational and general administrative purposes, totalled NZ$10·0m. in 2003–04.

Performance

Real GDP growth was 3·7% in 2002 and 1·5% in 2003.

Banking and Finance

There are four banks in the Cook Islands. The Cook Islands Savings Bank is state-owned and has deposit services throughout the islands. The Cook Islands Development Bank is a state-owned corporation funded in part by loans from the Asian Development Bank. The two remaining banks are subsidiaries of the Australia and New Zealand Banking Group Limited and the Westpac Bank, which are both Australian-owned and major banks in Australasia.

ENERGY AND NATURAL RESOURCES

Environment

Carbon dioxide emissions from the consumption and flaring of fossil fuels in 2008 were the equivalent of 7·4 tonnes per capita.

Electricity

Production in 2004 was 30m. kWh. Installed capacity was an estimated 8,000 kW in 2004.

Minerals

The islands of the Cook group have no significant mineral resources. However, the seabed, which forms part of the exclusive economic zone, has some of the highest concentrations of manganese nodules in the world. Manganese nodules are rich in cobalt and nickel.

Agriculture

In 2002 there were approximately 4,000 ha. of arable land and 2,000 ha. of permanent crops. Production estimates (2002, in 1,000 tonnes): coconuts, 5; cassava, 3; mangoes, 3. Livestock (2002): 40,000 pigs, 2,000 goats.

Forestry

Timber production was 5,000 cu. metres in 2007.

Fisheries

In 2005 the total catch was 3,737 tonnes, entirely from sea fishing.

INDUSTRY

Labour

In 2001 there were 5,928 employed persons in the Cook Islands and 892 unemployed. Of those employed, 3,386 were men and 2,542 were women.

INTERNATIONAL TRADE

Imports and Exports

Exports (f.o.b.) were valued at NZ$7·1m. in 2007. Main items exported are fish and pearls. Imports (c.i.f.) totalled NZ$144·7m.

In 2004 the main import suppliers were (in NZ$1m.): New Zealand, 92·4; Fiji Islands, 7·9; Australia, 4·7. Main export markets in 2004 (in NZ$1m.): Japan, 4·2; New Zealand, 2·0; USA, 0·5.

COMMUNICATIONS

Roads

In 1992 there were 320 km of roads and, in 1991, 5,015 vehicles.

Civil Aviation

New Zealand has financed the construction of an international airport at Rarotonga which became operational for jet services in 1973. There are nine useable airports. Domestic services are provided by Air Rarotonga, and in 2003 there were also services to Auckland, Honolulu, Los Angeles, the Fiji Islands, French Polynesia and Vancouver.

Shipping

A fortnightly cargo shipping service is provided between New Zealand, Niue and Rarotonga. In 2002 merchant shipping totalled 8,000 GRT.

Telecommunications

In 2008 there were 6,700 main telephone lines in service. There were 6,700 mobile phone subscribers in 2008 and 5,000 internet users.

Postal Services

A full range of postal services are offered and there are post agents in all inhabited islands.

SOCIAL INSTITUTIONS

Justice

There is a High Court and a Court of Appeal, from which further appeal is to the Privy Council in the UK.

The population in penal institutions in April 2005 was 27 (equivalent to 126 per 100,000 population).

Education

In March 1998 there were 28 primary schools with 140 teachers and 2,711 pupils, 23 secondary schools with 129 teachers and 1,779 pupils, and 26 pre-schools with 30 teachers and 460 pupils.

In 1998–99 total expenditure on education came to 13·1% of total government spending.

Health

A user pay scheme was introduced in July 1996 where all Cook Islanders pay a fee of NZ$5·00 for any medical or surgical treatment including consultation. Those under the age of 16 years or over the age of 60 years are exempted from payment of this charge. The dental department is privatized except for the school dental health provision. This service continues to be free to all schools.

The Rarotonga Hospital, which is the referral hospital for the outer islands, consists of 80 beds. The hospital has eight doctors, 33 registered nurses and 11 hospital aides.

RELIGION

From the census of 2001, 55% of the population belong to the Cook Islands Christian Church; about 17% are Roman Catholics, and the rest are Seventh-Day Adventists and Latter-day Saints and other religions.

CULTURE

Broadcasting

In 1997 there were approximately 4,000 TV receivers. There are two radio stations (AM and FM) operating in the Cook Islands.

Press

The *Cook Islands News* (circulation 2,000 in 2006) is the sole daily newspaper. The *Cook Islands Star*, which is published fortnightly, is sold in the Cook Islands and in New Zealand.

Tourism

In 2008 there were 94,152 tourist arrivals.

FURTHER READING

Local statistical office: Ministry of Finance and Economic Management, P.O. Box 41, Rarotonga, Cook Islands.
Statistical office: Cook Islands Statistics Office, PO Box 41, Avarua, Rarotonga.
Website: http://www.stats.gov.ck

Niue

KEY HISTORICAL EVENTS

Capt. James Cook sighted Niue in 1774 and called it 'Savage Island'. Christian missionaries arrived in 1846. Niue became a British Protectorate in 1900 and was annexed to New Zealand in 1901. Internal self-government was achieved in free association with New Zealand on 19 Oct. 1974, with New Zealand taking responsibility for external affairs and defence. Niue is a member of the South Pacific Forum. In Jan. 2004 Cyclone Heta destroyed the capital, Alofi, and a state of emergency was declared, although it was lifted a month later.

TERRITORY AND POPULATION

Niue is the largest uplifted coral island in the world. Distance from Auckland, New Zealand, 2,161 km; from Rarotonga, 933 km. Area, 260 sq. km; height above sea level, 67 metres. The population has been declining steadily, from around 6,000 in the 1960s to 1,625 recorded in the 2006 census, giving a population density of 6 per sq. km. Migration to New Zealand is the main factor in population change. The capital is Alofi.

SOCIAL STATISTICS

Annual growth rate, 1992–2002, –1·2%. In the period 1997–2001 average number of births registered was 29 per year; average number of deaths, 16. Fertility rate, 2004, 2·8 births per woman.

CLIMATE

Oceanic, warm and humid, tempered by trade winds. May to Oct. are cooler months. Temperatures range from 20°C to 28°C.

CONSTITUTION AND GOVERNMENT

There is a Legislative Assembly (*Fono*) of 20 members, 14 elected from 14 constituencies and six elected by all constituencies.

RECENT ELECTIONS

Parliamentary elections were held on 7 June 2008. Of the 14 seats in parliament allocated to representatives of the villages, nine were uncontested. Three of the six common assembly members were re-elected.

CURRENT ADMINISTRATION

High Commissioner: Brian Smythe.

Prime Minister: Toke Talagi (ind.; took office in June 2008).

Government Website: http://www.gov.nu

ECONOMY

Budget

Financial aid from New Zealand, 2006–07, totalled NZ$9·1m.

ENERGY AND NATURAL RESOURCES

Electricity

Production in 2004 was about 3m. kWh; installed capacity was estimated at 1,000 kW in 2004.

Agriculture
In 2002 there were approximately 4,000 ha. of arable land and 3,000 ha. of permanent crops. The main commercial crops of the island are coconuts, taro and yams.

In 2002 there were 2,000 pigs.

Fisheries
In 2005 the total catch was approximately 200 tonnes, exclusively from marine waters.

INTERNATIONAL TRADE

Imports and Exports
Imports, 2002, NZ$3·25m.; exports, NZ$0·14m.

COMMUNICATIONS

Civil Aviation
Weekly commercial air services link Niue with New Zealand, Sydney and Samoa.

Telecommunications
There is a wireless station at Alofi, the port of the island. Main telephone lines (2008) 1,000. There were 1,000 internet users in 2008 and 600 mobile phone subscribers in 2003.

SOCIAL INSTITUTIONS

Justice
There is a High Court under a Chief Justice, with a right of appeal to the New Zealand Supreme Court.

Education
In 2002 there was one primary school with 17 teachers and 251 pupils, and one secondary school with 29 teachers and 240 pupils. There is also the University of the South Pacific.

Health
In 2003 there were four doctors, two dentists, three midwives and 14 nursing personnel. The 24-bed hospital at Alofi was destroyed by Cyclone Heta in Jan. 2004.

RELIGION

At the 1991 census, 1,487 people belonged to the Congregational (Ekalesia Niue); Latter-day Saints (213), Roman Catholics (90), Jehovah's Witness (47), Seventh Day Adventists (27), other (63), no religion (34), not stated (1).

CULTURE

Press
A weekly newspaper is published in English and Niuean; circulation about 400.

Tourism
In 2007 there were 3,463 visitor arrivals.

FURTHER READING

Statistical Office: Statistics Niue, Economic Planning Development & Statistics, Premier's Department, Utuko, Alofi.

Website: http://www.spc.int/prism/country/nu/stats

NICARAGUA

República de Nicaragua
(Republic of Nicaragua)

Capital: Managua
Population estimate, 2010: 5·82m.
GDP per capita, 2007: (PPP$) 2,570
HDI/world rank: 0·699/124

KEY HISTORICAL EVENTS

There is evidence of settlement by Paleo-Indians in the region around 4000 BC. Spanish explorers, led by Gil González de Ávila, arrived in the west of present-day Nicaragua in 1523. They made contact with the Niquirano and the Chorotegano tribes, thought to have been linked to the Aztec civilization in Mexico, and the Chontal, who shared cultural traits with the Honduran Maya people. Government up to this point was through tribal monarchies and each grouping had distinct customs. In 1524 Francisco Hernández de Córdoba established Granada on Lake Nicaragua and León on Lake Managua. Many indigenous Indians were killed, died of introduced diseases or were enslaved. Estimates suggest the population fell from 1m. to less than 100,000.

In 1538 the Vice Royalty of New Spain was established, spanning Mexico and most of Central America. In 1570 present-day Nicaragua came under the authority of the Captaincy General of Guatemala. A conservative landholding elite developed around Granada, whilst León was associated with the colonial government. British pirates and adventurers took control of parts of the Mosquito Coast during the 17th century. After it declared independence from Spain in 1821, Nicaragua briefly came under the influence of the Mexican Empire, ruled by Agustín de Iturbide. From 1825–38 it was part of the Central American Federation, which unsuccessfully attempted to build a democratic union along US lines.

The 1840s and '50s saw escalating conflict between the elites of Conservative Granada and Liberal León. In 1855 the American mercenary, William Walker, arrived with 57 men to support the Liberal cause. Having defeated the national Nicaraguan army, he took Granada and proclaimed himself the country's ruler. However, his rule was short-lived and he was driven out of office by Honduran forces, with British assistance, two years later. There followed 30 years of relative stability under Conservative rule.

José Santos Zelaya's defeat of the Conservatives in 1893 led to a Liberal dictatorship, which became synonymous with economic decline. Civil war erupted in 1912, prompting the arrival of US forces. The Bryan–Chamarro Treaty of 1914 entitled the USA to a permanent option for a canal route through Nicaragua, a 99-year option for a naval base in the Bay of Fonseca on the Pacific coast and occupation of the Corn Islands on the Atlantic coast. The treaty was not abrogated until 1970 when the Corn Islands returned to Nicaragua.

The Somoza family dominated Nicaragua from 1933 to 1979. Imposing a brutal dictatorship, they plundered a large share of the national wealth. In 1962 the Sandanista National Liberation Front (FLSN; named after the murdered Liberal general, Augusto César Sandino, who fought against the US military presence in the 1920s) was formed to overthrow the Somozas. After 17 years of civil war the Sandanistas triumphed. On 17 July 1979 President Somoza fled into exile. The USA made efforts to unseat the revolutionary government by supporting the Contras (counter-revolutionary forces). It was not until 1988 that the state of emergency was lifted as part of the Central American peace process. Rebel anti-Sandanista activities had ceased by 1990 and the last organized insurgent group negotiated an agreement with the government in April 1994. In Oct. 1998 Hurricane Mitch devastated the country, killing 3,800. In Nov. 2006 presidential elections were won by Daniel Ortega of the FLSN, returning him to power after 16 years in opposition.

TERRITORY AND POPULATION

Nicaragua is bounded in the north by Honduras, east by the Caribbean, south by Costa Rica and west by the Pacific. Area, 131,812 sq. km (121,428 sq. km dry land). The coastline runs 450 km on the Atlantic and 305 km on the Pacific. The census population in May 2005 was 5,142,098 (density, 39·0 per sq. km). The United Nations population estimate for 2005 was 5,455,000. 59·0% of the population were urban in 2005.

The UN gives an estimated population for 2010 of 5·82m.

15 administrative departments and two autonomous regions are grouped in three zones. Areas (in sq. km), populations at the 2005 census and chief towns:

	Area	*Population*	*Chief town*
Pacific Zone	18,429	2,778,257	
Carazo	1,050	166,073	Jinotepe
Chinandega	4,926	378,970	Chinandega
Granada	929	168,186	Granada
León	5,107	355,779	León
Managua	3,672	1,262,978	Managua
Masaya	590	289,988	Masaya
Rivas	2,155	156,283	Rivas
Central-North Zone	35,960	1,647,605	
Boaco	4,244	150,636	Boaco
Chontales	6,378	153,932	Juigalpa
Estelí	2,335	201,548	Estelí
Jinotega	9,755	331,335	Jinotega
Madriz	1,602	132,459	Somoto
Matagalpa	8,523	469,172	Matagalpa
Nueva Segovia	3,123	208,523	Ocotal
Atlantic Zone	67,039	716,236	
Atlántico Norte[1]	32,159	314,130	Puerto Cabezas
Atlántico Sur[1]	27,407	306,510	Bluefields
Río San Juan	7,473	95,596	San Carlos

[1]Autonomous region.

The capital is Managua with (2005 census population) 908,892 inhabitants. Other cities (2005 populations): León, 139,433; Chinandega, 95,614; Masaya, 92,598; Estelí, 90,294; Tipitapa, 85,948; Matagalpa, 80,228; Granada, 79,418; Ciudad Sandino, 72,501; Juigalpa, 42,763.

The population is of Spanish and Amerindian origins with an admixture of Afro-Americans on the Caribbean coast. Ethnic groups in 2000: Mestizo (mixed Amerindian and White), 63%; White, 14%; Black, 8%; Amerindian, 5%. The official language is Spanish.

SOCIAL STATISTICS

2002 estimates: births, 175,000; deaths, 28,000. Estimated rates (per 1,000 population), 2002: births, 32·8; deaths, 5·2. Annual population growth rate, 2000–05, 1·3%. 2007 life expectancy: male 69·8 years, female 75·9. Infant mortality, 2005, 30 per 1,000 live births; fertility rate, 2004, 3·2 births per woman. A law prohibiting abortion was passed in Nov. 2006.

CLIMATE

The climate is tropical, with a wet season from May to Jan. Temperatures vary with altitude. Managua, Jan. 81°F (27°C), July 81°F (27°C). Annual rainfall 38" (976 mm).

CONSTITUTION AND GOVERNMENT

A new Constitution was promulgated on 9 Jan. 1987 and underwent reforms in 1995 and 2000. It provides for a unicameral 92-seat *National Assembly* comprising 90 members directly elected by proportional representation for a five-year term, together with one seat for the previous president and one seat for the runner-up in the previous presidential election. Citizens are entitled to vote at the age of 16.

The *President* and *Vice-President* are directly elected for a five-year term commencing on the 10 Jan. following their date of election. At present the President may stand for a second term, but not consecutively—however, incumbent president Daniel Ortega is trying to abolish term limits in order to seek re-election in 2011.

National Anthem

'Salve a ti Nicaragua' ('Hail to thee, Nicaragua'); words by S. Ibarra Mayorga, tune by L. A. Delgadillo.

RECENT ELECTIONS

Presidential and parliamentary elections took place on 5 Nov. 2006. In the presidential elections José Daniel Ortega Saavedra of the Sandinista National Liberation Front (FSLN) was elected with 38·1% of votes cast, defeating Eduardo Montealegre Rivas (29·0%), José Rizo Castellón (26·2%), Edmundo Jarquín Calderón (6·4%) and Edén Pastora Gómez (0·3%). At the parliamentary elections the Sandinista National Liberation Front won 38 seats, Constitutional Liberal Party 25, the Nicaraguan Liberal Alliance 22 and the Sandinista Renewal Movement 5.

CURRENT ADMINISTRATION

President: José Daniel Ortega Saavedra; b. 1945 (FSLN; in office since 10 Jan. 2007, having previously been president from Jan. 1985–April 1990).

Vice President: Jaime Morales Carazo.

In March 2010 the government comprised:

Minister of Agriculture and Forestry: Ariel Bucardo. *Defence:* Ruth Esperanza Tapia Roa. *Education, Culture and Sports:* Miguel de Castilla Urbina. *Environment and Natural Resources:* Juana Argeñal. *Family:* Rosa Adilia Vizcaya. *Finance:* Alberto Guevara. *Foreign Affairs:* Samuel Santos López. *Health:* Dr Guillermo González. *Industry, Commerce and Development:* Orlando Solórzano Delgadillo. *Interior:* Ana Isabel Morales Mazún. *Labour:* Jeaneth Chávez Gómez. *Transportation and Infrastructure:* Pablo Martínez.

Office of the President (Spanish only):
http://www.presidencia.gob.ni

CURRENT LEADERS

Daniel Ortega

Position
President

Introduction
Daniel Ortega began his second five-year term as president of Nicaragua in Jan. 2007. An iconic figure of the Sandinista movement since the late 1970s, he first served as president from 1985–90.

Early Life
Ortega was born in Nov. 1945 in La Libertad, Chontales to a middle-class family who opposed the Somoza family's dictatorship. After briefly attending the University of Central America in Managua, Ortega joined the Sandinista National Liberation Front (FSLN) in 1963. In 1967 he was convicted of staging a bank robbery to raise money for arms. He was released in 1974 in exchange for FSLN-held hostages and spent a brief spell in Cuba.

He led the FSLN in Somoza Debayle's overthrow in 1979 and joined the governing junta of national reconstruction. The Sandinistas dominated the junta and established a national constitution and democratic elections, which Ortega won in 1984. His presidency was marked by conflict with the US-backed Contras, resulting in tens of thousands of deaths. US sanctions and high inflation weakened the economy.

At the end of his term Ortega enacted the 'Piñata' laws by which large estates were appropriated and handed to FSLN supporters. In the 1990 elections Ortega suffered a surprise defeat to a US-supported coalition of anti-Sandinista groups led by Violeta de Chamorro. Ortega retained the leadership of the FSLN but was again defeated at the 1996 elections. He survived several damaging scandals, including allegations, in 1998, by his step-daughter of sexual abuse, followed in 1999 by a furore over an immunity pact with then president Miguel Aleman, who was facing charges of corruption. Ortega again made an unsuccessful bid for office in 2001.

Ortega publicly apologized for excesses during his first presidency. His politics moderated and he increasingly embraced Catholicism. The USA openly opposed his candidacy for the 2006 presidential election but he emerged victorious from the polls in Nov. 2006.

Career in Office
Ortega campaigned on a platform of 'unity and reconciliation', symbolized by his appointment of former Contra leader Jaime Morales as vice president. He announced plans to address the effects of poverty, which plagues 80% of the population, while at the same time addressing soaring inflation, crippling interest payments on public debt, a national energy shortage and endemic corruption. In Nov. 2006 the FSLN came out in support of a strict anti-abortion law.

On the international stage Ortega sought to reassure foreign investors and the private sector, many of whom feared further deterioration in US–Nicaraguan relations. His tenure received an early boost when the Inter-American Development Bank confirmed its commitment to an assistance loan of US$100m. promised to the previous government.

Ortega committed Nicaragua to the Bolivarian Alternative for the Americas (ALBA) while guaranteeing active membership of a free trade agreement with the USA (CAFTA). He pledged to maintain good relations with the USA while simultaneously strengthening links with Iran, Cuba and China. He also signed off a major natural gas deal with Bolivia. Venezuela pledged US$60m. in debt relief and donations for social development and helped establish a 40% Nicaraguan-owned and 60% Venezuelan-owned oil company, Albanic. In Oct. 2007 the Nicaraguan and Honduran governments accepted an International Court of

Justice ruling settling a long-running territorial dispute between their two countries.

In 2008 doubts about Ortega's democratic credentials resurfaced, and in municipal elections in Nov. opposition parties denounced the Sandinista victory (in 94 of 146 mayorships, including the capital Managua) as rigged. He has also sought to circumvent a constitutional barrier to his standing for re-election in polling scheduled for 2011. In Oct. 2009 the Supreme Court overturned the ban on consecutive re-election and on serving more than two presidential terms although the opposition declared the ruling illegal.

DEFENCE

In 2006 defence expenditure totalled US$35m. (US$6 per capita), representing 0·7% of GDP.

Army

There are six regional commands. Strength (2007) around 12,000.

Navy

The Nicaraguan Navy was some 800 strong in 2007.

Air Force

The Air Force has been semi-independent since 1947. Personnel (2007) 1,200, with no combat capable aircraft.

INTERNATIONAL RELATIONS

Nicaragua is a member of the UN, World Bank, IMF and several other UN specialized agencies, WTO, IOM, ACS, Central American Common Market, Inter-American Development Bank, SELA and OAS.

ECONOMY

In 2006 agriculture accounted for 19·7% of GDP, industry 29·5% and services 50·8%.

Overview

Nicaragua, one of Latin America's poorest countries, suffers from low productivity, high current account deficit, high unemployment and a severe external debt. Natural disasters have hampered opportunities for growth. Although positive strides have been made since 2002 the economy is dependent on foreign aid which amounts to 20% of GDP.

Coffee and meat account for around 40% of exports and tourism is thriving. Leading trading partners include the USA, the members of the Central American Common Market and the EU. In May 2004 Nicaragua signed the Central America-Dominican Republic-United States Free Trade Agreement (CAFTA-DR) to promote regional trade. Structural reforms are focused on government procurement, the reform of social security and privatization. The unemployment rate is 8–10%. Half the population lives in poverty and about 17% fall below the extreme poverty line. Corruption is a major problem.

Currency

The monetary unit is the *córdoba* (NIO), of 100 *centavos*, which replaced the córdoba oro in 1991 at par. Inflation was 11·1% in 2007 and 19·9% in 2008. In July 2005 Nicaragua had foreign exchange reserves of US$628m. In June 2005 total money supply was 4,746m. córdobas.

Budget

In 2004 revenues were 12,251m. córdobas and expenditures 16,698m. córdobas. Tax revenue accounted for 96·3% of revenues in 2004; current expenditure accounted for 58·4% of expenditures.

The standard rate of VAT is 15%.

Performance

Real GDP growth was 3·2% in both 2007 and 2008. Total GDP in 2008 was US$6·6bn.

Banking and Finance

The Central Bank of Nicaragua came into operation on 1 Jan. 1961 as an autonomous bank of issue, absorbing the issue department of the National Bank. The *President* is Antenor Rosales. There were seven private commercial banks in 2000.

There is a stock exchange in Managua.

ENERGY AND NATURAL RESOURCES

Environment

Nicaragua's carbon dioxide emissions from the consumption and flaring of fossil fuels in 2008 were the equivalent of 0·9 tonnes per capita.

Electricity

Installed capacity in 2004 was 0·7m. kW. In 2004, 2·82bn. kWh were produced; consumption per capita in 2004 was 525 kWh.

Minerals

Production in 2005: gold, 3,674 kg; silver, 2,999 kg. Calcium carbonate, gypsum and limestone are also mined.

Agriculture

In 2002 there were an estimated 1·93m. ha. arable land and 236,000 ha. permanent cropland. Approximately 94,000 ha. were irrigated in 2002. Production (in 1,000 tonnes) in 2003: sugarcane, 3,603; maize, 524; rice, 291; dry beans, 203; sorghum, 99; groundnuts, 82; oranges, 70; coffee, 60; bananas, 59; cassava, 52; pineapples, 48; plantains, 40.

In 2003 there were 3·5m. cattle, 440,000 pigs, 260,000 horses and 16m. chickens. Livestock products (in 1,000 tonnes), 2003: beef and veal, 66; poultry meat, 62; milk, 281; eggs, 22.

Forestry

The forest area in 2005 was 5·19m. ha., or 42·7% of the land area. Timber production was 6·10m. cu. metres in 2007.

Fisheries

In 2005 the catch was 30,914 tonnes (29,567 tonnes from sea fishing).

INDUSTRY

Industry contributed 26·0% of GDP in 2001, with manufacturing accounting for 14·4%. Important industries include chemicals, textiles, metal products, oil refining and food processing. Production (in 1,000 tonnes): cement (2000), 568; residual fuel oil (2004), 432; raw sugar (2000), 398; distillate fuel oil (2004), 215; petrol (2004), 98; wheat flour (2001), 60; vegetable oil (2001), 21; rum (1998), 7·7m. litres; sawnwood (2002), 45,000 cu. metres.

Labour

The workforce in 2001 was 1,900,400 (1,315,000 males). In 2001, 1,701,700 persons were in employment, of whom 739,000 were engaged in agriculture, hunting, forestry and fishing; 294,300 in community, social and personal services; 279,800 in wholesale and retail trade, and restaurants and hotels; and 131,600 in manufacturing. There were 159,500 unemployed in 2005, a rate of 7·2%.

INTERNATIONAL TRADE

In 2004 Nicaragua signed the Central America-Dominican Republic-United States Free Trade Agreement (CAFTA-DR), along with Costa Rica, the Dominican Republic, El Salvador, Guatemala, Honduras and the USA. The agreement entered into force for Nicaragua on 1 April 2006. Foreign debt was US$5,144m. in 2005.

Imports and Exports

Imports and exports in US$1m.:

	2003	2004	2005	2006	2007
Imports c.i.f.	1,904·6	2,249·7	2,535·6	2,740·7	3,538·0
Exports f.o.b.	605·2	759·8	866·0	758·6	1,194·5

Main imports in 2006 were: petroleum and petroleum products, 24·3%; machinery and transport equipment, 22·9%; chemicals and related products, 16·7%; food and live animals, 9·7%. Principal exports were: coffee, 26·5%; beef, 10·3%; seafood, 9·5%; gold, 7·7%, cane sugar, 6·6%.

Main import suppliers, 2006: USA, 22·8%; Mexico, 14·8%; China, 7·6%; Venezuela, 6·8%; Costa Rica, 5·4%. Main export markets, 2006: USA, 46·5%; Mexico, 6·9%; Canada, 6·0%; Spain, 4·5%; Honduras, 4·4%.

COMMUNICATIONS

Roads

Road length in 2004 was 18,669 km, of which 5,117 km were main roads. In 2007 there were 101,900 passenger cars (18 per 1,000 inhabitants), 7,700 buses and coaches, 179,900 lorries and vans and 61,200 motorcycles and mopeds. 522 fatalities were caused by road accidents in 2007.

Civil Aviation

In 1999 scheduled airline traffic of Nicaragua-based carriers flew 0·8m. km, carrying 59,000 passengers (all on international flights). The Augusto Sandino international airport at Managua handled 754,000 passengers in 2001 (608,000 on international flights) and 20,000 tonnes of freight.

Shipping

The merchant marine totalled 4,000 GRT in 2002. The Pacific ports are Corinto (the largest), San Juan del Sur and Puerto Sandino through which pass most of the external trade. The chief eastern ports are El Bluff (for Bluefields) and Puerto Cabezas.

Telecommunications

In 2008 there were 312,000 main (fixed) telephone lines; mobile phone subscribers numbered 3,108,000 in 2008 (54·8 per 100 persons). There were 220,000 PCs in use in 2005 and 185,000 internet users in 2008.

Postal Services

In 2002 there were 215 post offices.

SOCIAL INSTITUTIONS

Justice

The judicial power is vested in a Supreme Court of Justice at Managua, five chambers of second instance and 153 judges of lower courts.

The population in penal institutions in Oct. 2004 was 5,610 (100 per 100,000 of national population).

Education

Adult literacy rate in 2003 was 76·7% (male, 76·8%; female, 76·6%). In 2007 there were 952,964 primary school pupils (31,188 academic staff), 470,520 secondary school pupils (15,126 academic staff) and (2003) 103,577 students at tertiary level with 6,757 academic staff. The largest university is the National Autonomous University of Nicaragua, established in 1812.

In 2003 public expenditure on education came to 3·3% of GNI.

Health

In 2003 there were 32 hospitals, with a provision of nine beds per 10,000 population. There were 8,986 physicians, 1,585 dentists and 5,862 nurses in 2003.

RELIGION

The prevailing form of religion is Roman Catholicism (3·59m. adherents in 2001), but religious liberty is guaranteed by the Constitution. There were also 810,000 Protestants in 2001. There is one arch-bishopric, seven bishoprics and one cardinal.

CULTURE

World Heritage Sites

Nicaragua has one site on the UNESCO World Heritage List: the Ruins of León Viejo (inscribed on the list in 2000), a 16th century Spanish settlement.

Broadcasting

Broadcasting is predominantly commercial, incorporating over 100 radio stations and several television services. There were 710,000 television sets (colour by NTSC) in 2005.

Press

In 2005 there were six daily newspapers in Managua, with a total circulation of 180,000.

Tourism

In 2005 there were 712,000 non-resident tourists, spending US$211m.

DIPLOMATIC REPRESENTATIVES

Of Nicaragua in the United Kingdom (Suite 31, Vicarage House, 58–60 Kensington Church St., London, W8 4DP)
Ambassador: Vacant.
Chargé d'Affaires a.i: Alicia Sandino.

Of the United Kingdom in Nicaragua (embassy in Managua closed in March 2004)
Ambassador: Tom Kennedy (resides in San José, Costa Rica).

Of Nicaragua in the USA (1627 New Hampshire Ave., NW, Washington, D.C., 20009)
Ambassador: Vacant.
Chargé d'Affaires a.i.: Alcides Montiel.

Of the USA in Nicaragua (Km. 5½ Carretera Sur, Managua)
Ambassador: Robert J. Callahan.

Of Nicaragua to the United Nations
Ambassador: María Rubiales de Chamorro.

Of Nicaragua to the European Union
Ambassador: Lester Mejía Solis.

FURTHER READING

Baracco, Luciano, *Nicaragua: The Imagining of a Nation—From Nineteenth-Century Liberals to Twentieth-Century Sandinistas.* 2005

Cruz, Consuelo, *Political Culture and Institutional Development in Costa Rica and Nicaragua: World-making in the Tropics.* 2005

Dijkstra, G., *Industrialization in Sandinista Nicaragua: Policy and Party in a Mixed Economy.* 1992

Horton, Lynn, *Peasants in Arms: War and Peace in the Mountains of Nicaragua, 1979–94.* 1998

Jones, Adam, *Beyond the Barricades: Nicaragua and the Struggle for the Sandinista Press, 1979–1998.* 2002

National Statistical Office: Dirección General de Estadística y Censos, Managua.

Website (Spanish only): http://www.inide.gob.ni

NIGER

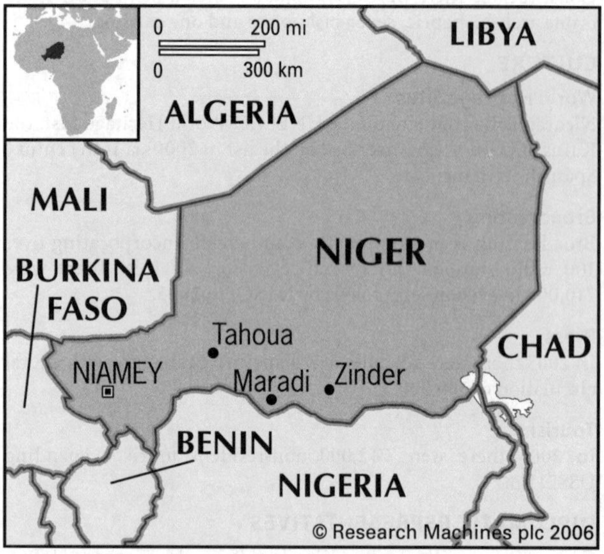

République du Niger
(Republic of Niger)

Capital: Niamey
Population estimate, 2010: 15·89m.
GDP per capita, 2007: (PPP$) 627
HDI/world rank: 0·340/182

KEY HISTORICAL EVENTS

Niger has been settled for at least 6,000 years. Early cattle-herding and agricultural economies developed in the Sahara and by the 14th century AD the Hausa people had established city-states in the south of the region. Meanwhile Berbers dominated trade routes in the north, which came under the control of the Songhai Empire around 1515. After the fall of the Songhai Empire in the late 16th century the Bornu Empire expanded into the centre and east of the region, while the Hausa people retained the south and the Tuareg were prominent in the north. The Djerma people later became established in the southwest.

In the 19th century Fulani Muslims vied for power with the Hausas and Bornus. French forces took control of the region at the end of the century, creating the military district of Niger as part of the larger territory of Haut-Sénégal et Niger. Tuareg resistance led to a major uprising during the First World War, which was put down by combined French and British forces. France formally designated Niger as a colony in 1922.

Gradual decentralization of power began in 1946. Niger became an autonomous state in 1958 and on 3 Aug. 1960 it obtained independence, with Hamani Diori as its first president. In 1968 severe drought culminated in civil unrest. Diori was deposed in a 1974 military coup and Lieut. (later Col.) Seyni Kountché took power. Kountché gradually replaced the military government with civilians, surviving several coup attempts in the process. He was succeeded in 1987 by Ali Seibou, whose National Movement for the Development Society (MNSD), became Niger's only legal political party. A new constitution was approved in 1989 and in the early 1990s Seibou responded to pro-reform demonstrations by legalizing opposition parties.

In 1990 conflict broke out in the north of the country between government forces and the Tuaregs, who demanded autonomy. Relations with Libya deteriorated as the Niger government suspected its neighbour of encouraging the insurgency. In 1995 a ceasefire established land rights for the Tuaregs and formalized their relationship with government. The agreement has largely held despite sporadic conflict.

In July 1991 a constitutional conference removed Seibou's powers and established a transitional government under André Salifou. Multi-party elections were held in 1993 and, following victory for the Alliance of the Forces of Change, Mahamane Ousmane was elected president. However, the MNSD won back control of the national assembly in 1995 and tensions mounted between President Ousmane and the government. In Jan. 1996 Ousmane was deposed in a military coup and replaced by Col. Ibrahaim Baré Mainassara (known as Baré).

Strict military rule was eventually relaxed and in July 1996 Baré claimed decisive victory in a disputed election. In April 1999 Baré was killed by his bodyguards and Major Daoude Wanké took power with military backing. Under international pressure, multi-party elections were held in Oct. 1999 and were declared by independent observers to be largely fair. Tandja Mamadou of the MNSD was elected president and his party won control of the national assembly. Niger held its first local elections in July 2004, with most seats being won by parties supporting the president. The new national assembly established amnesties for those involved in the 1996 and 1999 coups. In Dec. 2004 Mamadou Tandja won a second term as president, with Hama Amadou as prime minister.

Niger continues to suffer severe economic problems. In 2005 the government increased tax on basic goods (including food), leading to widespread protests and strikes until the government granted exemptions on some staples. Drought and locust infestations the previous year devastated harvests. After UN World Food Programme warnings that millions faced severe malnutrition, an international relief effort staved off the worst of the disaster but thousands still died of diseases associated with hunger and poverty. In June 2006 unions organized a national strike to protest against rising prices. In response to allegations of corruption by aid donors, several ministers were dismissed from the government.

In 2006 the International Court of Justice settled a land dispute with Benin by awarding Niger most of the river islands along the shared border. In April 2009 the government reached a peace agreement with the rebel Movement of Niger People for Justice after several years of troubles. The following month President Mamadou Tandja dismissed parliament and suspended the constitution after a constitutional court ruling against his attempt to hold a referendum on his running for a third presidential term. In Aug. 2009 the referendum, criticized for lacking legitimacy, supported Tandja's candidacy but elections in Oct. were boycotted by opponents. Tandja claimed a landslide victory but was removed from office in a coup in Feb. 2010, with power falling to a military junta.

TERRITORY AND POPULATION

Niger is bounded in the north by Algeria and Libya, east by Chad, south by Nigeria, southwest by Benin and Burkina Faso, and west by Mali. Area, 1,186,408 sq. km, with a population at the 2001 census of 11,060,291; density, 9·3 per sq. km. Estimate, 2008, 14,297,000. In 2005, 83·2% of the population were rural.

The UN gives an estimated population for 2010 of 15·89m.

The country is divided into the capital, Niamey, an autonomous district, and seven departments. Area, population and chief towns at the 2001 census:

Department	Sq. km	Population	Chief town	Population
Agadez	634,209	321,639	Agadez	78,289
Diffa	140,216	346,595	Diffa	23,409
Dosso	31,002	1,505,864	Dosso	43,561
Maradi	38,581	2,235,748	Maradi	148,017
Niamey	670	707,951	Niamey	707,951
Tahoua	106,677	1,972,729	Tahoua	73,002
Tillabéry	89,623	1,889,515	Tillabéry	16,683
Zinder	145,430	2,080,250	Zinder	170,575

The population is composed chiefly of Hausa (53%), Djerma-Songhai (21%), Fulani (10%), Tuareg (10%) and Kanuri-Manga (4%). The official language is French. Hausa, Djerma and Fulani are national languages.

SOCIAL STATISTICS

Estimates, 2000: births, 593,000; deaths, 205,000. Estimated birth rate in 2000 was 55·2 per 1,000 population (the highest in the world); estimated death rate, 19·1. Niger has one of the youngest populations of any country, with 49% of the population under the age of 15. Infant mortality, 2005, 150 per 1,000 live births. Annual population growth rate, 2000–05, 3·7%. Expectation of life at birth, 2007, 50·0 years for males and 51·7 for females. Fertility rate, 2004, 7·8 children per woman (along with Timor-Leste the highest anywhere in the world).

CLIMATE

Precipitation determines the geographical division into a southern zone of agriculture, a central zone of pasturage and a desert-like northern zone. The country lacks water, with the exception of the southwestern districts, which are watered by the Niger and its tributaries, and the southern zone, where there are a number of wells. Niamey, 95°F (35°C). Annual rainfall varies from 22" (560 mm) in the south to 7" (180 mm) in the Sahara zone. The rainy season lasts from May until Sept., but there are periodic droughts.

CONSTITUTION AND GOVERNMENT

In May 2009 former president Mamadou Tandja dissolved the 113-member *National Assembly*, allowing a constitutional referendum to be pushed through. At the referendum on 4 Aug. 2009, 92·5% of votes cast were in favour of abolishing the two-term limit that had existed under the constitution of 1999, although both the opposition and the international community condemned the poll. A coup followed in Feb. 2010 with the military junta suspending the constitution and dissolving the cabinet. In March 2010 the military leadership announced it had formed a transitional government of 20 ministers and promised to return Niger to democracy, although no date was set for fresh elections.

National Anthem

'Auprès du grand Niger puissant' ('By the banks of the mighty great Niger'); words by M. Thiriet, tune by R. Jacquet and N. Frionnet.

RECENT ELECTIONS

In the first round of presidential elections held on 16 Nov. 2004 incumbent Tandja Mamadou won 40·7% of the votes followed by former prime minister Mahamadou Issoufou with 24·6%; former president Mahamane Ousmane with 17·4%; a second former prime minister, Amadou Cheiffou, with 6·4%; former foreign minister Moumouni Adamou Djermakoye with 6·1%; and a third former prime minister, Hamid Algabid, with 4·9%. Turnout was 48·3%. In the run-off on 4 Dec. 2004 Tandja Mamadou won 65·5% of the vote with Mahamadou Issoufou taking 34·5%. Turnout was 45·0%.

Parliamentary elections were held on 20 Oct. 2009. The National Movement for the Development Society (MNSD) won 76 seats; the Social Democratic Rally, 15; and the Rally for Democracy and Progress, 7. The Nigerien Self-Management Party, the Rally of Nigerien Patriots, the Workers' Movement Party-Albarka and the Union of Independent Nigeriens all took one seat each and 11 independents were elected. Opposition parties boycotted the election. Turnout was 51·3%.

CURRENT ADMINISTRATION

In Feb. 2010 the government led by President Tandja Mamadou was overthrown in a military coup. A new ruling body headed by Salou Djibou calling itself the Supreme Council for the Restoration of Democracy was established to provide a transitional government until the next elections.

President of the Supreme Council for the Restoration of Democracy: Salou Djibo, b. 1965 (in office since 18 Feb. 2010).

Prime Minister: Mahamadou Danda.

In March 2010 the transitional government comprised:

Minister of Agriculture and Livestock: Malick Sadelher. *Civil Service and Labour:* Yahaya Chaibou. *Commerce, Industry and Promotion of Young Entrepreneurs:* Hamid Hamed. *Communication, New Information Technologies and Culture:* Takoubakoye Aminata Boureima. *Defence:* Gen. Mamadou Ousseini. *Economy and Finance:* Anou Badamassi. *Equipment:* Col. Amadou Diallo. *Foreign Affairs, African Integration and Nigeriens Abroad:* Touré Aminatou. *Interior, Security, Decentralization and Religious Affairs:* Cissé Ousmane. *Justice, Human Rights and Keeper of the Seals:* Abdoulaye Djibo. *Mines and Energy:* Souleymane Mamadou Abba. *National Education:* Sidibé Maman Dioula Fadjimata. *Population, the Promotion of Women and Child Protection:* Tchimadem Hadattan Sanady. *Professional Training and Literacy:* Tidjani Harouna Dembo. *Public Health:* Nounou Hassan. *Secondary and Higher Education, Scientific Research and Government Spokesperson:* Mahaman Laouali Dan Dah. *Transport, Tourism and Handicrafts:* Col. Mohamed Ahmed. *Urban Affairs, Housing and Land Management:* Djibo Salamatou Gourouza Magagi. *Water, Environment and the Fight Against Desertification:* Gen. Abdou Kaza. *Youth and Sports:* Gen. Mai Manga Oumara.

CURRENT LEADERS

Salou Djibo

Position

Chairman of the Supreme Council for the Restoration of Democracy

Introduction

Salou Djibo came to power in Feb. 2010 after a military coup. An army squadron leader, he was one of a faction that objected to President Mamadou Tandja's law change allowing him to extend his term of office. Despite a low public profile, Djibo was named leader of the Supreme Council for the Restoration of Democracy by fellow coup members. He has pledged to prepare the country for democratic elections.

Early Life

Salou Djibo was born on 15 April 1965 in the village of Namaro on the River Niger, in western Niger. He joined the army in 1987, serving in several divisions before training as an officer in Bouaké, Côte d'Ivoire. He rose through the ranks, becoming second lieutenant in 1997, lieutenant in 1998, captain in 2003 and squadron leader in 2006. During this period he became a specialist in artillery warfare, participating in training programmes in China and Morocco. He served on two UN peacekeeping missions, in Côte d'Ivoire in 2004 and in the Democratic Republic of the Congo in 2006, after which he returned to Niger to take command of a garrison in Niamey.

Following President Tandja's amendment of the constitution to extend his term of rule, Djibo joined an army faction opposed to his actions in late 2009. Against a background of domestic protests and growing international pressure, during which Niger was suspended from the Economic Community of West African States, a group of senior officers—including Djibo, Col. Adamou Harouna and Col. Djibrilla Hamidou Hima—planned a takeover. On 18 Feb. 2010 troops stormed the presidential palace and seized control of government, imprisoning Tandja. Djibo was named leader of the Supreme Council for the Restoration of Democracy and announced that he was forming a transitional government.

Career in Office

On taking power Djibo dissolved the constitution and put government business under the control of regional and ministerial leaders. On 24 Feb. 2010 he appointed Mahamadou Danda, a civilian and former spokesman of Niger's 1999 transitional government, as temporary prime minister. In March 2010 Djibo acknowledged that Niger would suffer famine later in the year. His government also announced a review of uranium contracts in a bid to ensure transparency. After enjoying initial widespread public support and cautious cooperation from the international community, Djibo insisted that the military-led government would work towards holding general elections and that no member of the junta would be allowed to stand in the presidential election.

DEFENCE

Selective conscription for two years operates. Defence expenditure totalled US$38m. in 2006 (US$3 per capita), representing 1·1% of GDP.

Army

There are three military districts. Strength (2007) 5,200. There are additional paramilitary forces of 5,400.

Air Force

In 2007 the Air Force had 100 personnel. There are no combat capable aircraft.

INTERNATIONAL RELATIONS

Niger is a member of the UN, World Bank, IMF and several other UN specialized agencies, WTO, IOM, International Organization of the Francophonie, Islamic Development Bank, OIC, African Development Bank, Lake Chad Basin Commission and is an ACP member state of the ACP-EU relationship.

ECONOMY

Agriculture, forestry and fishing accounted for 43·0% of GDP in 2006; trade and hotels 14·7%; services 8·8%; and finance and real estate 7·6%.

Overview

Niger is among the poorest countries in the world, ranking last out of 182 countries in the UN Human Development Index. Long-term GDP growth has been low and volatile, averaging 1·7% between 1970 and 2005. The economy is dominated by agriculture and is susceptible to droughts. Drought and a locust plague resulted in a 12% decline in agricultural production in 2004. However, inflation is low as a result of effective management by the regional central bank and future growth prospects are encouraging. Agriculture has benefited from good rainfall in recent years while mining, construction and telecommunications have been buoyant. Nonetheless, poverty remains a major problem with over 60% of the population living on less than a dollar a day.

Niger has received enhanced debt relief since Dec. 2000 under the IMF programme for Heavily Indebted Poor Countries (HIPC) and qualifies for the Multilateral Debt Relief Initiative (MDRI), which covers large fiscal and external current account deficits.

Currency

The unit of currency is the *franc CFA* (XOF) with a parity of 655·957 francs CFA to one euro. In June 2005 total money supply was 170,798m. francs CFA and foreign exchange reserves were US$177m. Inflation was just 0·1% in 2007, rising sharply to 11·3% in 2008.

Budget

In 2003 revenue (in 1,000m. francs CFA) was 221·3 and expenditure 272·2. Taxes accounted for 69·3% of revenues, and external aids and gifts 29·2%. Current expenditures accounted for 57·6% of expenditure.

Performance

Real GDP growth was 3·3% in 2007 and 9·5% in 2008; total GDP in 2008 was US$5·4bn.

Banking and Finance

The regional Central Bank of West African States (BCEAO)—*Governor*, Philippe-Henri Dacoury-Tabley—functions as the bank of issue. There were six commercial banks in 2002, three development banks and a savings bank.

There is a stock exchange in Niamey.

ENERGY AND NATURAL RESOURCES

Environment

In 2008 Niger's carbon dioxide emissions from the consumption and flaring of fossil fuels were the equivalent of 0·1 tonnes per capita. An *Environmental Performance Index* compiled in 2008 ranked Niger 149th in the world out of 149 countries analysed, with 39·1%. The index examined various factors in six areas—air pollution, biodiversity and habitat, climate change, environmental health, productive natural resources and water resources.

Electricity

Installed capacity was approximately 0·1m. kW in 2004. Production in 2004 amounted to about 247m. kWh, with consumption per capita an estimated 40 kWh.

Minerals

Large uranium deposits are mined at Arlit and Akouta. Uranium production (2006), 3,434 tonnes. Niger's uranium production is exceeded only by that of Canada, Australia and Kazakhstan. Phosphates are mined in the Niger valley, and coal reserves are being exploited by open-cast mining (production of hard coal in 2004 was an estimated 178,000 tonnes). Salt production in 2006 was an estimated 1,300 tonnes.

Agriculture

There were an estimated 4·49m. ha. of arable land in 2002 and 13,000 ha. of permanent crops. About 66,000 ha. were irrigated in 2002. There were about 130 tractors in 2002. Production estimates in 2003 (in 1,000 tonnes): millet, 2,500; sorghum, 797; onions, 270; sugarcane, 220; cabbage, 120; cassava, 105; groundnuts, 100; tomatoes, 100. Livestock (2003 estimates): goats, 6·9m.; sheep, 4·5m.; cattle, 2·3m.; asses, 580,000; camels, 420,000; chickens, 25m. Livestock products (in 1,000 tonnes), 2003 estimates: milk, 305; meat, 130; cheese, 15; eggs, 11.

Forestry

There were 1·27m. ha. of forests in 2005 (1·0% of the land area). Timber production in 2007 was 9·63m. cu. metres, mainly for fuel.

Fisheries

There are fisheries on the River Niger and along the shores of Lake Chad. In 2005 the catch was 50,018 tonnes, exclusively from inland waters.

INDUSTRY

Some small manufacturing industries, mainly in Niamey, produce textiles, food products, furniture and chemicals. Output of cement in 2004 (estimate), 55,000 tonnes.

Labour
The economically active population in 2001 totalled 4,073,300 (68% males). Nearly 90% of the economically active population in 1994 were engaged in agriculture, fisheries and forestry.

Trade Unions
The national confederation is the Union Syndicale des Travailleurs du Niger, which has 15,000 members in 31 unions.

INTERNATIONAL TRADE
Foreign debt was US$1,972m. in 2005.

Imports and Exports
In 2005 imports were valued at US$769·5m. and exports at US$477·6m. Main imports in 2003: machinery and transport goods, 19·6%; petroleum and petroleum products, 14·5%; cereal and cereal preparations, 10·6%. Main exports in 2003: uranium ores and concentrates, 54·0%; livestock, 19·5%; cotton fabrics, 5·6%; fruit and vegetables (particularly onions), 5·6%. Main import suppliers in 2003 (as % of total): France, 14·6; Côte d'Ivoire, 13·4; China, 9·4; USA, 8·2. Main export destinations in 2003: France, 36·5; Nigeria, 27·5; Japan, 14·9; USA, 4·5.

COMMUNICATIONS

Roads
In 2007 there were 18,949 km of roads including 3,912 km of paved roads. Niamey and Zinder are the termini of two trans-Sahara motor routes; the Hoggar–Aïr–Zinder road extends to Kano and the Tanezrouft–Gao–Niamey road to Benin. A 648-km 'uranium road' runs from Arlit to Tahoua. There were, in 2005, 57,732 passenger cars, 11,261 vans, 2,613 buses and 1,035 lorries. In 2007 there were 676 road accidents resulting in 265 fatalities.

Civil Aviation
There is an international airport at Niamey (Diori Hamani Airport), which handled 108,000 passengers in 2006 and 2,300 tonnes of freight. In 2003 there were international flights to Abidjan, Bamako, Casablanca, Dakar, Khartoum, Libreville, Ouagadougou, Paris and Tripoli. In 1999 scheduled airline traffic of Niger-based carriers flew 3·0m. km, carrying 84,000 passengers (all on international flights).

Shipping
Sea-going vessels can reach Niamey (300 km inside the country) between Sept. and March.

Telecommunications
Niger had 347,800 telephone subscribers in 2005 (24·9 per 1,000 population), including 323,900 mobile phone subscribers. Internet users numbered 40,000 in 2006.

Postal Services
In 2003 there were 52 post offices, or one for every 230,000 persons.

SOCIAL INSTITUTIONS

Justice
There are Magistrates' and Assize Courts at Niamey, Zinder and Maradi, and justices of the peace in smaller centres. The Court of Appeal is at Niamey.

The population in penal institutions in May 2006 was 5,709 (46 per 100,000 of national population).

Education
In 2007 there were 31,131 teaching staff for 1,235,065 primary school pupils and 7,852 teaching staff for 213,991 secondary school pupils. There were 11,208 students in tertiary education (1,095 academic staff) in 2006. There is a university and an Islamic university.

Adult literacy in 2003 was 14·4% (male, 19·6%; female, 9·4%), among the lowest in the world.

In 2006 public expenditure on education came to 3·3% of GNI and 17·6% of total government spending.

Health
In 1998 there were 1·2 hospital beds per 10,000 inhabitants. There were 427 physicians, 28 dentists, 1,988 nurses, 500 midwives and 22 pharmacists in 2008.

RELIGION
In 2001 there were 9·39m. Sunni Muslims. There are some Roman Catholics, and traditional animist beliefs are widespread.

CULTURE

World Heritage Sites
Niger has two sites on the UNESCO World Heritage List: the Aïr and Ténéré Natural Reserves (inscribed on the list in 1991), part of the largest protected area in Africa (7·7m. ha.); and the 'W' National Park of Niger (1996), a savannah and forested area of biodiversity.

Broadcasting
La Voix du Sahel and Télé-Sahel, controlled by the government's Office de Radiodiffusion Télévision du Niger, are the national radio and TV services (colour by PAL). There are also private television stations based in Niamey and a growing number of independent radio stations. In 2005 there were 170,000 TV sets.

Press
In 2005 there was one government-owned daily newspaper and around 15 weekly and monthly newspapers.

Tourism
In 2005 there were 63,000 non-resident tourists; spending by tourists totalled US$32m. in 2004.

DIPLOMATIC REPRESENTATIVES
Of Niger in the United Kingdom
Ambassador: Adamou Seydou (resides in Paris).

Of the United Kingdom in Niger
Ambassador: Dr Nicholas Westcott, CMG (resides in Accra, Ghana).

Of Niger in the USA (2204 R. St., NW, Washington, D.C., 20008)
Ambassador: Aminata Maiga Djibrilla Touré.

Of the USA in Niger (BP 11201, Rue des Ambassades, Niamey)
Ambassador: Bernadette Mary Allen.

Of Niger to the United Nations
Ambassador: Aboubacar Ibrahim Abani.

Of Niger to the European Union
Ambassador: Abdou Agbarry.

FURTHER READING
Miles, W. F. S., *Hausaland Divided: Colonialism and Independence in Nigeria and Niger.* 1994

National Statistical Office: Institut National de la Statistique, 182 rue de la Sirba, BP 13416, Niamey.
Website (French only): http://www.stat-niger.org

NIGERIA

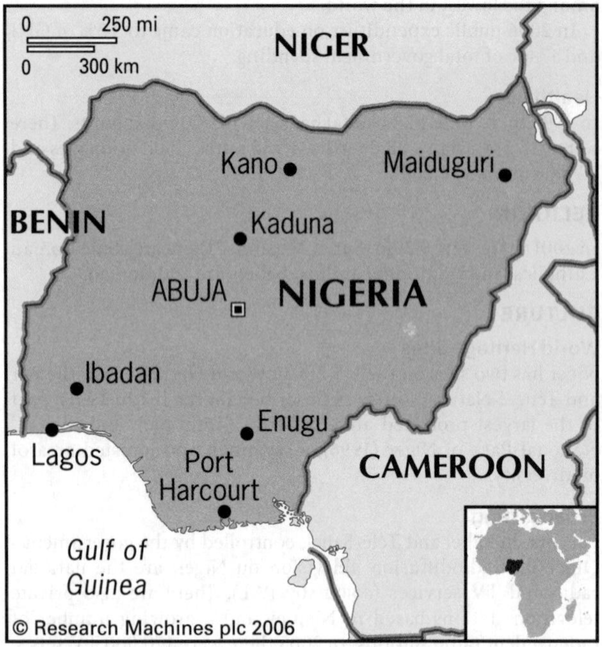

Federal Republic of Nigeria

Capital: Abuja

Population estimate, 2010: 158·26m.

GDP per capita, 2007: (PPP$) 1,969

HDI/world rank: 0·511/158

KEY HISTORICAL EVENTS

The earliest evidence of human settlement in Nigeria dates from 9000 BC and by 2000 BC its inhabitants were cultivating crops and domestic animals. However, the first organized society was of the Nok people, from around 800 BC to AD 200. Traces of Nok influence are visible in Nigerian art today, particularly in areas such as Igbo, Ukwe, Esie and Benin City. By AD 1000, Nok had given way to the Kanem, thanks to the trans-Saharan trade route that ran from West Africa to the Mediterranean.

In the 11th century northern Nigeria split into seven independent Hausa city-states, Biram, Daura, Gobir, Kano, Katsina, Rano and Zaria. By the 14th century, two states had developed in the south, Oyo and Benin, with the Igbo people of the southeast living in small village communities. South of the Hausa states and west of the Niger, the Ife flourished between the 11th and 15th centuries. The importance of the Ife civilization is evident today; all Yoruba states claim that their leaders are descended from the Ife as a way of establishing legitimacy, and its ritual is imitated in their modern public ceremonies.

Most of the north was held by the Songhai empire by the early 16th century, only to be taken later in the century by Kanem-Bornu, allowing the Hausa states to retain their autonomy. At the end of the 18th century, Fulani religious groups waged war in the north, merging states to create the single Islamic state of the Sokoto Caliphate.

In the late 15th century Portuguese navigators, following the demise of the spice trade, began to purchase slaves from middlemen in the region. They were followed by British, French and Dutch traders. Wealthy traders established towns such as Bonny, Owome and Okrika. Slave trading had a profound effect on Nigeria. From the 1650s until the 1860s, it caused a forced migration of around 3·5m. people. Within Nigeria itself, the defensive measures adopted to avoid enslavement led to the reinforcement of ethnic distinctions and of the north-south divide.

After the abolition of the slave trade in Britain in 1807, attempts to find a lucrative alternative and to discourage the predominance of slavery in Nigeria (other countries continued to trade in slaves until 1875) led to a large-scale campaign to encourage the production of palm oil for export. This itself caused the development of an internal slave trade, involving slaves in the collection and manufacture of palm fruits, as well as the transportation of the oil. The British also took over the mines at Jos at the expense of the livelihoods of independent tin producers. When heavy reliance on mining exports resulted in the neglect of agricultural work, Nigeria experienced its first food shortage.

Religious missions were active at this time, with Presbyterians, Methodists, Baptists and the Church Missionary Society (CMS) operating in Lagos, Abeokuta, Ibadan, Oyo and Ogbomosho. The CMS pioneered trade on the Niger by encouraging merchants to run steamboats, partially as a means of travel for the missionaries but also to ship goods.

In 1804 Usuman dan Fodio began a 'Holy war' to reform the practice of Islam in the north, conquering the Hausa city-states, though Kanem-Bornu retained its independence. However, by the late 19th century Kanem-Bornu's power was in decline. Usuman's son, Muhammed Bello, established a state centred at Sokoto, controlling most of northern Nigeria for the rest of the century. In the south, the Oyo region was troubled by civil wars, only brought to a close when the British intervened and the Oyo Empire collapsed. Britain took Lagos as its colony in 1861.

In 1879 Sir George Goldie gained all British firms trading on the Niger, and in the 1880s took over French companies trading there, signing treaties with African leaders and enabling Britain's domination of southern Nigeria in 1884–85. In 1887, Jaja, an African trader based in the Niger Delta, was deported following his fierce opposition to European competition. Goldie's firm received a British Royal Charter as the Royal Niger Company to administer the Niger River and north Nigeria, and this monopoly of trade on the river angered Africans and Europeans alike. The Royal Niger Company also lacked sufficient power to control north Nigeria. In 1900 its charter was revoked and British forces moved in, taking Sokoto in 1903. By 1906 Britain controlled Nigeria as the Colony (Lagos), the Protectorate of Southern Nigeria and the Protectorate of Northern Nigeria, amalgamating the regions in 1914 to establish the Colony and Protectorate of Nigeria. The administration was based on existing leadership systems. Yet the appointment of African officials failed to gain wide acceptance from Nigeria's people. The British governor made all major decisions, and the traditional authority of African rulers was weakened irreparably.

British dominance met with major resistance from the Nigerian people. In the south, the tribal Yoruba group, the Ijebu, fought against colonial rule in 1892, as did the Aro in the east and the Aniocha (both Igbo groups) in the west. There were also rebellions in the north. The British forces responded with brutality, destroying the homes of many Nigerians in order to secure their capitulation.

British colonial rule brought development in the transportation and communications systems and a shift towards cash crops. Western and Christian influences prevailed, including widespread use of the English language. This influence spread far more rapidly in the south, where British control had been secure over a longer period, and this added to the growing disparity between north and south. Nigerian forces helped defeat the German army in Cameroon during the First World War, involved in an arduous campaign until 1916.

Growing unrest and widespread anticolonialism became focused in the 1920s as demands for African representation increased. In 1923 Herbert Macaulay, grandson of the first Nigerian to be ordained, established the first Nigerian political party, the Nigerian National Democratic Party. In 1944 he united the party with several others to form the National Council of Nigeria and the Cameroons (NCNC). In response to this activity, the British attempted to quell demands for an end to colonial rule by granting some political reforms. In 1947 they announced a new constitution that they claimed would give traditional authorities a stronger voice. This met with resistance, and in 1951 the British agreed to form a new constitution that would provide for elected representation on a regional basis.

Three political parties developed, the National Council of Nigeria and the Cameroons (later the National Convention of Nigerian Citizens), largely supported by the Igbo, the Action Group, with mostly Yoruba membership, and the Northern People's Congress (NPC). When the constitution failed in 1952, a new one divided Nigeria into three regions, Eastern, Western and Northern, plus the federal territory of Lagos. In 1956 the Western and Eastern regions became self-governing, as did the Northern region in 1959.

In 1960 Nigeria declared independence. Elections failed to elect any one party by a majority, and the NPC and the NCNC formed a coalition government, with Abukar Tafawa Balewa (NPC) as prime minister. Nnamdi Azikiwe, who had helped Herbert Macaulay to establish the NCNC in 1944, was governor-general. When Nigeria became a republic in 1963 Azikiwe became president.

Continuing conflict between north and south undermined the new republic. In 1966 fighting culminated in a military coup that installed Maj.-Gen. Aguiyi-Ironsi, an Igbo, as head of a military government. Another coup later in the year placed Lieut.-Col. Yakubu Gowon in power and saw many northern Igbo massacred. In May 1967 the Igbo people of the south declared their region independent from the rest of the country, naming the breakaway republic Biafra. Civil war raged for three years until federal Nigeria triumphed at the price of 1m. dead and widespread famine and destruction.

This was followed by a period of relative prosperity as oil prices rose. Foreign interest and investment flourished but government overspending and high levels of corruption and crime led to social chaos. In the 1980s recession sent oil prices down, and Nigeria found itself struggling with major debt, rising inflation and mass unemployment.

Gowon's regime was overthrown in 1975 by Gen. Murtala Muhammed whose plans for a new capital to be built at Abuja drained the economy. He was assassinated in 1976, to be succeeded by Gen. Olusegun Obasanjo who oversaw the transition to civilian rule, while juggling the need for Western aid with his support for African nationalist movements.

In 1979 elections brought Alhaji Shehu Shagari to power. Shagari's government came under popular attack for alleged corruption but he was re-elected in 1983, amidst rumours of voting irregularities. Under Shagari relations with the USA improved, heralded by a visit from President Jimmy Carter. However, dogged by worsening economic problems, Shagari was ousted in a military coup in 1983 and replaced by Gen. Muhammadu Buhari. Buhari's regime quickly fell out of favour with the public when it arrested not only the politicians blamed for the country's social and economic problems, but also journalists and academics.

A bloodless coup in 1985 brought to power Maj.-Gen. Ibrahim Babangida, who promulgated a new constitution with the aim of returning to civilian government. Babangida, however, clung to power and refused to accept electoral defeat in 1990, 1992 and 1993. Unrest eventually forced his resignation, but after just three months of rule by an interim leader, one of Babangida's long-term allies, Gen. Sani Abacha, became president and closed down all unions and political institutions. He extended his military rule for a further three years in 1995, proposing a return to civilian rule after this period. To this end five political parties were formed in 1996. However, the Abacha regime attracted international controversy when it executed writer Ken Saro-Wiwa and eight other human rights activists for alleged seditious political activity. Nigeria was suspended from the Commonwealth as a result. Further outrage followed with the arrest of former leader Obasanjo and the murder of the wife of leading political dissident, Chief Moshood Abiola, who had claimed victory at the presidential elections of 1993. Rioting and civil unrest broke out across Nigeria and Abacha's family was accused of siphoning off US$4bn. of national assets.

Abacha died in office in 1998. Maj.-Gen. Abdusalam Abubakar came to power and brought about a return to civilian rule, scrapping plans that would have extended Abacha's rule and releasing political prisoners. Abiola was scheduled to be freed as part of this process but died the day before his scheduled release. In Feb. 1999 Nigeria chose Obasanjo, the 62-year-old retired general and previous military leader, to be president.

This transition of power greatly improved Nigeria's international standing and the country was readmitted to the Commonwealth. However, tribal and religious conflict continued and fighting between the Igbo Christians and Hausa Muslims over the implementation of Islamic law has left thousands dead. Obasanjo's re-election in 2003 was accompanied by violence and rumours of ballot-rigging and bribery.

In July 2005 the Paris Club (an informal grouping of wealthy nations) wrote off around US$20bn. of Nigeria's debt. Assisted by high oil prices, Nigeria had paid off the remaining US$10bn. by April 2006, the first African nation to fully service its Paris Club debt. In April 2007 Umaru Yar'Adua won disputed presidential elections. In March 2008 Nigeria and Cameroon reached agreement on the long-running dispute over sovereignty of the Bakassi Peninsula.

TERRITORY AND POPULATION

Nigeria is bounded in the north by Niger, east by Chad and Cameroon, south by the Gulf of Guinea and west by Benin. It has an area of 923,768 sq. km (356,667 sq. miles). For sovereignty over the Bakassi Peninsula *see* CAMEROON: Territory and Population. Census population, 2006, 140,431,790 (69,086,302 females); population density, 152·0 per sq. km. Nigeria is Africa's most populous country. In 2005, 51·8% of the population were rural.

The UN gives an estimated population for 2010 of 158·26m.

There were 36 states and a Federal Capital Territory (Abuja) in 2006.

Area, population and capitals of these states:

State	*Area (in sq. km)*	*Population (2006 census)*	*Capital*
Adamawa	36,917	3,178,950	Yola
Bauchi	45,837	4,653,066	Bauchi
Benue	34,059	4,253,641	Makurdi
Borno	70,898	4,171,104	Maiduguri
Gombe	18,768	2,365,040	Gombe
Jigawa	23,154	4,361,002	Dutse
Kaduna	46,053	6,113,503	Kaduna
Kano	20,131	9,401,288	Kano
Katsina	24,192	5,801,584	Katsina
Kebbi	36,800	3,256,541	Birnin-Kebbi
Kogi	29,833	3,314,043	Lokoja
Kwara	36,825	2,365,353	Ilorin

State	Area (in sq. km)	Population (2006 census)	Capital
Nassarawa	27,117	1,869,377	Lafia
Niger	76,363	3,954,772	Minna
Plateau	30,913	3,206,531	Jos
Sokoto	25,973	3,702,676	Sokoto
Taraba	54,473	2,294,800	Jalingo
Yobe	45,502	2,321,339	Damaturu
Zamfara	39,762	3,278,873	Gusau
Federal Capital Territory	7,315	1,406,239	Abuja
Total North	*730,885*	*75,269,722*	
Abia	6,320	2,845,380	Umuahia
Akwa Ibom	7,081	3,902,051	Uyo
Anambra	4,844	4,177,828	Awka
Bayelsa	10,773	1,704,515	Yenagoa
Cross River	20,156	2,892,988	Calabar
Delta	17,698	4,112,445	Asaba
Ebonyi	5,670	2,176,947	Abakaliki
Edo	17,802	3,233,366	Benin City
Ekiti	6,353	2,398,957	Ado Ekiti
Enugu	7,161	3,267,837	Enugu
Imo	5,530	3,927,563	Owerri
Lagos	3,345	9,113,605	Ikeja
Ogun	16,762	3,751,140	Abeokuta
Ondo	14,606	3,460,877	Akure
Osun	9,251	3,416,959	Oshogbo
Oyo	28,454	5,580,894	Ibadan
Rivers	11,077	5,198,716	Port-Harcourt
Total South	*192,883*	*65,162,068*	

Abuja replaced Lagos as the federal capital and seat of government in Dec. 1991.

Estimated population of the largest cities, 1995:

Lagos	1,484,000[1]	Ikorodu	180,300
Ibadan	1,365,000	Ilawe-Ekiti	179,900
Ogbomosho	711,900	Owo	178,900
Kano	657,300	Ikirun	177,000
Oshogbo	465,000	Calabar	170,000
Ilorin	464,000	Shaki	169,700
Abeokuta	416,800	Ondo	165,400
Port Harcourt	399,700	Akure	158,200
Zaria	369,800	Gusau	154,000
Ilesha	369,000	Ijebu-Ode	152,500
Onitsha	362,700	Effon-Alaiye	149,300
Iwo	353,000	Kumo	144,400
Ado-Ekiti	350,500	Shomolu	144,100
Abuja (capital)	339,100	Oka	139,600
Kaduna	333,600	Ikare	137,300
Mushin	324,900	Sapele	135,800
Maiduguri	312,100	Deba Habe	135,400
Enugu	308,200	Minna	133,600
Ede	299,500	Warri	122,900
Aba	291,600	Bida	122,500
Ife	289,500	Ikire	120,200
Ila	257,400	Makurdi	120,100
Oyo	250,100	Lafia	119,500
Ikerre	238,500	Inisa	116,800
Benin City	223,900	Shagamu	114,300
Iseyin	211,800	Awka	108,400
Katsina	201,500	Gombe	105,200
Jos	201,200	Ejigbo	103,300
Sokoto	199,900	Igboho	103,300
Ilobu	194,400	Agege	100,300
Offa	192,300	Ugep	100,000

[1]Greater Lagos had a population of 12,763,000 in 1999.

There are about 250 ethnic groups. The largest linguistic groups are the Yoruba (17·5% of the total) and the Hausa (17·2%), followed by Igbo (13·3%), Fulani (10·7%), Ibibio (4·1%), Kanuri (3·6%), Egba (2·9%), Tiv (2·6%), Bura (1·1%), Edo (1·0%) and Nupe (1·0%). The official language is English, but 50% of the population speak Hausa as a *lingua franca*.

SOCIAL STATISTICS

2000 estimates: births, 4,530,000; deaths, 1,530,000. Rates, 2000 estimates (per 1,000 population): births, 39·5; deaths, 13·3. Infant mortality, 2005, 101 (per 1,000 live births). Annual population growth rate, 2000–05, 3·0%. Life expectancy at birth, 2007, was 47·2 years for males and 48·2 years for females. Fertility rate, 2004, 5·7 children per woman.

CLIMATE

Lying wholly within the tropics, temperatures everywhere are high. Rainfall varies greatly, but decreases from the coast to the interior. The main rains occur from April to Oct. Lagos, Jan. 81°F (27·2°C), July 78°F (25·6°C). Annual rainfall 72" (1,836 mm). Ibadan, Jan. 80°F (26·7°C), July 76°F (24·4°C). Annual rainfall 45" (1,120 mm). Kano, Jan. 70°F (21·1°C), July 79°F (26·1°C). Annual rainfall 35" (869 mm). Port Harcourt, Jan. 79°F (26·1°C), July 77°F (25°C). Annual rainfall 100" (2,497 mm).

CONSTITUTION AND GOVERNMENT

The constitution was promulgated on 5 May 1999, and entered into force on 29 May. Nigeria is a federation, comprising 36 states and a federal capital territory. The constitution includes provisions for the creation of new states and for boundary adjustments of existing states. The legislative powers are vested in a *National Assembly*, comprising a *Senate* and a *House of Representatives.* The 109-member Senate consists of three senators from each state and one from the federal capital territory, who are elected for a term of four years. The House of Representatives comprises 360 members, representing constituencies of nearly equal population as far as possible, who are elected for a four-year term. The *President* is elected for a term of four years and must receive not less than one-quarter of the votes cast at the federal capital territory. A president may not serve more than two consecutive four-year terms. In 2006 Olusegun Obasanjo sought to alter the constitution to allow him to run for a third term, but he failed to win backing for the amendment.

National Anthem

'Arise, O compatriots, Nigeria's call obey'; words by a collective, tune by B. Odiase.

GOVERNMENT CHRONOLOGY

(NCNC = National Council of Nigeria and the Cameroons; NPN = National Party of Nigeria; PDP = People's Democratic Party; n/p = non-partisan)

Heads of State since 1963.

President of the Republic
1963–66 NCNC Benjamin Nnamdi Azikiwe

Heads of the Military Government
1966 military Johnson Aguiyi-Ironsi
1966–75 military Yakubu Gowon
1975–76 military Murtala Ramat Muhammed
1976–79 military Olusegun Obasanjo

President of the Republic
1979–83 NPN Shehu Shagari

Head of the Federal Military Government
1983–85 military Muhammadu Buhari

Chairman of the Armed Forces Ruling Council, then Chairman of the National Defence and Security Council
1985–93 military Ibrahim Babangida

Head of the Interim National Government
1993 n/p Ernest Shonekan

Chairmen of the Provisional Ruling Council
1993–98 military Sani Abacha
1998–99 military Abdulsalam Abubakar

President of the Republic

1999–2007	PDP	Olusegun Obasanjo
2007–10	PDP	Umaru Yar'Adua
2010–	PDP	Goodluck Jonathan (acting for Umaru Yar'Adua)

RECENT ELECTIONS

Presidential elections were held on 21 April 2007. Umaru Yar'Adua, the candidate for the ruling People's Democratic Party (PDP), won against 23 opponents with 70·0% of the votes cast. His main opponent, Muhammadu Buhari of the All Nigeria People's Party (ANPP), received 18·7%, and outgoing vice president Atiku Abubakar 7·2%. International observers denounced the result, alleging widespread fraud.

In elections to the House of Representatives on the same day the PDP won 262 seats, the ANPP 62 seats, Action Congress 32 seats, the Progressive People's Alliance (PPA) 3 seats and the Labour Party 1 seat. However, the European Union Election Observation Mission said that 'in view of the lack of transparency and evidence of fraud, there can be no confidence in the results'.

In the Senate elections held on 21 April 2007 with polls in six districts on 26 April, 85 seats went to the PDP, 16 to the ANPP, 6 to Action for Change, 1 to the PPA and 1 to Accord.

CURRENT ADMINISTRATION

President (acting) and Minister of Power: Goodluck Jonathan; b. 1957 (PDP; since 9 Feb. 2010).

In April 2010 the government comprised:

Minister of Agriculture: Sheikh Ahmed Abdullah. *Aviation:* Fidelia Njeze. *Commerce and Industry:* Jibril Martins Kuye. *Culture and Tourism:* Abubakar Sadiq A. Mohammed. *Defence:* Adetokunbo Kayode. *Education:* Ruqayyatu A. Rufa'i. *Environment:* John Odey. *Federal Capital Territory:* Bala Muhammed. *Finance:* Olusegun Olutoyin Aganga. *Foreign Affairs:* Henry Odein Ajumogobia. *Health:* Vacant. *Information and Communications:* Dora Akunyili. *Internal Affairs:* Emmanuel Iheanacho. *Justice and Attorney General:* Mohammed Bello Adoke. *Labour and Productivity:* Chukwuemeka Ngozichineke Wogu. *Lands, Housing and Urban Development:* Nduese Essien. *Mines and Steel Development:* Musa Mohammed Sada. *National Planning Commission:* Shamsudeen Usman. *National Sports Commission:* Ibrahim Isa Bio. *Niger Delta:* Peter Godsday Orubebe. *Petroleum Resources:* Dieziani Alison-Madueke. *Police Affairs:* Alhaji Adamu Waziri. *Science and Technology:* Muhammed K. Abubakar. *Special Duties:* Earnest Olubolade. *Transport:* Yusuf Sulaiman. *Water Resources:* Vacant. *Women's Affairs:* Josephine Anenih. *Works:* Sanusi M. Dagash. *Youth Development:* Akinlabe Olasunkanmi.

Nigerian Parliament: http://www.nigeriacongress.org

CURRENT LEADERS

Goodluck Ebele Jonathan

Position

Acting President

Introduction

The National Assembly appointed Goodluck Jonathan as acting president in Feb. 2010, replacing President Umaru Yar'Adua, who has been undergoing medical treatment since Nov. 2009. An academic and former governor of Bayelsa State, Jonathan had been vice-president since Nov. 2007 and is expected to hold office for the remaining year of Yar'Adua's tenure.

Early Life

Jonathan was born on 20 Nov. 1957 in Otueke, Bayelsa State, in the oil-rich Niger Delta. A member of the indigenous Ijaw people, he was raised as a Pentecostal Christian by his father, a canoe builder and fisherman. After attending local primary schools Jonathan went to Mater Dei High School in Imiringi. He graduated in zoology from Port Harcourt University in 1981.

After completing military service Jonathan pursued an academic career, gaining an MSc in hydrobiology and fisheries in 1985 and a PhD in zoology ten years later, both from Port Harcourt University. He worked as a lecturer, education inspector and environmental protection officer before entering politics in 1998 with the People's Democratic Party (PDP). He was appointed deputy governor of Bayelsa State in 1999 and again in 2003. When state governor Diepriye Alamieyeseigha was charged with corruption in the UK in 2005, Jonathan replaced him.

In Dec. 2006, months after his wife Patience Faka was accused of but not charged with money laundering, Jonathan was elected vice-presidential running mate to Yar'Adua for the 2007 elections. The pair won although opponents questioned the legitimacy of the vote and Jonathan's house in Bayelsa was bombed shortly after.

Jonathan's knowledge of the Niger Delta region helped Yar'Adua secure a ceasefire and disarmament from Delta rebels, generally considered the biggest achievement of his time in office. In Nov. 2009 Yar'Adua left Nigeria for medical treatment in Saudi Arabia without designating an interim presidential replacement. Jonathan was granted presidential powers after much wrangling by a parliamentary resolution of 9 Feb. 2010, though its constitutional validity was questioned. Yar'Adua returned to Nigeria in Feb. 2010 but remained out of public view, fuelling speculation about his condition.

Career in Office

On becoming acting president, Jonathan made moves to secure his tenuous position. In a government reshuffle he replaced two-thirds of Yar'Adua's appointments, including the justice minister and the national security adviser. He selected a London-based Goldman Sachs banker as finance minister and named the first female oil minister.

Jonathan has vowed to calm militancy in the Delta region and address electricity shortages. He met with major oil corporations in Feb. 2010 after one of the main rebel groups renewed its campaign against the oil infrastructure in Dec. 2009. In April 2010 he dismissed the head of the state-run Nigerian National Petroleum Corporation. In March there was renewed conflict between Christians and Muslims in the northern city of Jos.

DEFENCE

In 2006 defence expenditure totalled US$768m., equivalent to US$6 per capita and representing 0·7% of GDP.

Nigeria's armed forces have over 3,000 personnel in peacekeeping missions in other African countries, notably Liberia and Sierra Leone.

Army

Strength (2007) 62,000.

Navy

The Navy includes one frigate with a helicopter and one corvette. There is a small aviation element. Naval personnel in 2007 totalled 8,000, including Coastguard. The main bases are at Apapa (Lagos) and Calabar.

Air Force

Personnel (2007) total 10,000 although the force has a very limited operational capacity. There were 75 combat capable aircraft in 2007 including MiG-21s and Aero L-39s, but the serviceability of much of the equipment is in doubt. In addition there were five attack helicopters in 2007.

INTERNATIONAL RELATIONS

Nigeria is a member of the UN, World Bank, IMF and several other UN specialized agencies, WTO, IOM, Islamic Development Bank, OIC, African Development Bank, African Union,

ECOWAS, Lake Chad Basin Commission, OPEC and is an ACP member state of the ACP-EU relationship.

ECONOMY

Agriculture accounted for 32·0% of GDP in 2006, industry 41·9% and services 26·1%.

Overview

The economy is highly dependent on oil, which accounts for 33% of GDP, 76% of government revenues and 95% of export revenues. Since independence in 1960, weak and corrupt government has damaged the economy. GDP per capita is low (at approximately US$1,168 in 2007), while poverty is widespread (55% based on a 2004 household survey compared to 43% in 1985). The black market economy constitutes 77% of the country's official GDP, one of the highest percentages in the world.

A ten-year rift with the IMF ended with an agreement in Jan. 1999 on a Fund-monitored economic reform programme, which includes provisions for abolishing the dual exchange rate, ending the subsidy on local fuel and increasing privatization. Nigeria is currently well-positioned to build a prosperous economy. Real GDP growth is strong (at over 5% in 2006), predominantly based on the agricultural sector.

Oil output has fallen owing to instability in the Niger Delta region but could increase by 50% in the medium-term, benefiting from the recently completed West African gas pipeline. Inflation has eased while external debt is low following successful negotiations with the Paris and London Clubs to eradicate its major foreign arrears. According to the IMF, continued prudent policy-making is required in order to protect macroeconomic stability and realize the economy's strong potential, while reducing poverty and achieving its Millennium Development Goals. It recommends agreements with constituent states to delink spending from oil revenue flows.

Currency

The unit of currency is the *naira* (NGN) of 100 *kobo*. Foreign exchange reserves were US$44,786m. in May 2009 (US$7,100m. in 1998) and gold reserves were 687,000 troy oz. Inflation rates (based on IMF statistics):

1999	*2000*	*2001*	*2002*	*2003*	*2004*	*2005*	*2006*	*2007*	*2008*
6·6%	6·9%	18·0%	13·7%	14·0%	15·0%	17·9%	8·2%	5·4%	11·6%

In June 2009 total money supply was ₦4,247·6bn.

Budget

The financial year is the calendar year. 2003 revenue, ₦2,752,107m. (tax revenue 37·4%; non-tax revenue 62·6%); expenditure, ₦2,853,918m. (including state and local governments, 40·5%; and current expenditure, 32·0%).

VAT was raised from 5% to 10% in May 2007, but as a result of a general strike in protest against the increase was lowered back to 5% a month later.

Performance

Real GDP growth rates (based on IMF statistics):

2000	*2001*	*2002*	*2003*	*2004*	*2005*	*2006*	*2007*	*2008*
5·3%	8·2%	21·2%	10·3%	10·6%	5·4%	6·2%	7·0%	6·0%

Before the discovery of oil in the early 1970s Nigeria's GDP per head was around US$200. By the early 1980s it had reached around US$800, but has now declined to some US$300. Total GDP in 2008 was US$212·1bn.

Banking and Finance

The Central Bank of Nigeria (CBN) is the bank of issue (*Governor*, Lamido Sanusi).

A banking crisis resulted in a decline in the number of banks to 74 at March 1999. In 2004 a major banking reform was announced. However, despite attempts to strengthen the banking sector, the financial condition of the banks deteriorated. Subsequently the CBN requested technical assistance from the IMF to strengthen the banking system. The leading banks are Intercontinental Bank, Oceanic Bank, United Bank for Africa and Zenith Bank. In 2002 there were 12 merchant banks and two development banks. In 2004 bank reserves at the CBN totalled ₦187bn. and CBN net foreign assets amounted to ₦2,250bn.

Nigeria was one of three countries and territories named in a report in June 2005 as failing to co-operate in the fight against international money laundering. In June 2006 Nigeria was delisted and its formal monitoring was ended a year later. The Financial Action Task Force on Money Laundering was set up by the G7 group of major industrialized nations.

The Nigerian Stock Exchange is in Lagos.

ENERGY AND NATURAL RESOURCES

Environment

Nigeria's carbon dioxide emissions from the consumption and flaring of fossil fuels were the equivalent of 0·7 tonnes per capita in 2008.

Electricity

Installed capacity, 2004 estimate, 5·9m. kW. Production, 2004, 20·22bn. kWh (34% kWh hydro-electric); consumption per capita was 157 kWh in 2004. Power cuts are frequent, with both businesses and homes having to rely on generators as demand for electricity far outweighs supply.

Oil and Gas

Oil accounts for around 97% of Nigeria's exports. The cumulative income from oil over more than 30 years exceeds US$330,000m. Nigeria's oil production, though declining, is the largest of any African country and amounted to 105·3m. tonnes in 2008. Reserves in 2008 totalled 36·2bn. bbls. There are four refineries. Oil income in 1998 was around US$1bn. a month, representing more than 75% of government revenue, but unrest that threatened to escalate into civil war caused production to be cut by around a third. Most of Nigeria's oil wealth comes from onshore wells, but there are also large untapped offshore deposits.

Natural gas reserves, 2008, were 5,220bn. cu. metres; production, 35·0bn.cu. metres. In March 2007 the 678-km West Africa Gas pipeline was completed to supply natural gas to Benin, Ghana and Togo. After a series of delays resulting from vandalism and fuel quality problems, it was restarted in March 2010 and should help to reduce Nigeria's dependence on oil for government revenue. In Dec. 2002 the African Development Bank, six Nigerian banks and 19 international banks announced plans to invest US$1bn. in the Nigeria Liquefied Natural Gas company (NLNG) to exploit exports to the USA and Europe.

It was announced in Aug. 2007 that the state-owned Nigerian National Petroleum Corporation was to be abolished and broken up into five independent units. The process, overseen by the newly created National Energy Council, was to take six months but has been delayed for the foreseeable future.

Minerals

Production, 2005 estimates (in tonnes): limestone, 2·10m.; kaolin, 200,000; marble, 149,000. There are large deposits of iron ore, coal (reserves estimate 245m. tonnes), lead and zinc. There are small quantities of gold and uranium. Lead production was 5,000 tonnes in 2002. Tin is also mined.

Agriculture

Of the total land mass, 75% is suitable for agriculture, including arable farming, forestry, livestock husbandry and fisheries. In 2001, 28·5m. ha. were arable and 2·7m. ha. permanent cropland. 0·23m. ha. were irrigated in 2001. 90% of production was by smallholders with less than 3 ha. in 2000, and less than 1% of farmers had access to mechanized tractors. Main food crops are millet and sorghum in the north, plantains and oil palms in the south, and maize, yams, cassava and rice in much of the country. The north is, however, the main food producing area. Cocoa is the crop that contributes most to foreign exchange earnings. Output, 2000 (in 1,000 tonnes): cassava, 32,697; yams, 25,873; sorghum, 7,520; millet, 5,960; maize, 5,476; taro, 3,835; rice, 3,277; groundnuts, 2,783; plantains, 1,902; sweet potatoes, 1,662; palm oil, 896; pineapples, 881; tomatoes, 879. Nigeria is the biggest producer of yams, accounting for more than two-thirds of the annual world output. It is also the leading cassava and taro producer and the second largest millet producer.

Livestock, 2000: cattle, 19·83m.; sheep, 20·50m.; goats, 24·30m.; pigs, 4·86m.; chickens, 126m. Products (in 1,000 tonnes), 2000: beef and veal, 298; goat meat, 154; mutton and lamb, 91; pork, bacon and ham, 78; poultry meat, 172; milk, 386; eggs, 435.

Forestry
There were 11·09m. ha. of forests in 2005, or 12·2% of the land area. Timber production in 2007 was 71·42m. cu. metres.

Fisheries
The total catch in 2005 was 523,182 tonnes, of which 285,131 tonnes came from sea fishing.

INDUSTRY
In 2001 industry accounted for 35·5% of GDP, with manufacturing contributing 4·2%. Production, 2004 unless otherwise indicated (in 1,000 tonnes): cement (2001), 3,000; residual fuel oil, 1,866; distillate fuel oil, 1,179; palm oil (2001), 903; petrol, 534; kerosene, 441; paper and products (1998), 57; cigarettes (1995), 256m. units. Also plywood (2001), 55,000 cu. metres.

Labour
The labour force in 2004 totalled an estimated 55·67m. There were 33 work stoppages in 2003–04 with 407,000 working days lost (233·5m. working days lost in 1994–95).

Trade Unions
All trade unions are affiliated to the Nigerian Labour Congress.

INTERNATIONAL TRADE
Nigeria's external debt was US$22,178m. in 2005.

Imports and Exports
Imports (c.i.f.) in 2006 totalled US$22,903m.; exports (f.o.b.) US$59,215m. Principal imports in 2003 were: machinery and transport equipment, 38·0%; manufactured goods, 16·0%; food and livestock, 14·0%; petroleum and petroleum products, 12·3%. In 2003 crude oil amounted to 96·4% of exports by value. Other exports included ships and boats, and natural gas.

In 2006 the main import suppliers were: USA, 15·7%; China, 13·8%; UK, 11·8%; Germany, 5·6%. Leading export destinations in 2006 were: USA, 45·0%; India, 9·3%; Spain, 8·0%; France, 5·7%.

COMMUNICATIONS
Roads
The road network covered 193,200 km in 2004, including 15,688 km of main roads. In 2007 there were 4,560,000 passenger cars in use and 3,040,000 motorcycles and mopeds. There were 14,279 road accidents with 5,351 fatalities in 2004.

Rail
In 2003 there were 3,505 route-km of track (1,067 mm gauge). There are plans to convert the entire network to 1,435 mm gauge. Passenger-km travelled in 2003 came to 973m. and freight tonne-km to 39m.

Civil Aviation
Lagos (Murtala Muhammed) is the major airport, and there are also international airports at Port Harcourt and Kano (Mallam Aminu Kano Airport). The main carrier is Nigerian Eagle Airlines, established in 2004 as Virgin Nigeria Airways and rebranded in Sept. 2009. It operated direct flights in Sept. 2009 to Abidjan, Accra, Banjul, Cotonou, Dakar, Douala, Libreville and Monrovia as well as providing domestic services. In 2001 Lagos handled 2,735,000 passengers (1,485,000 on domestic flights) and, in 1998, 15,100 tonnes of freight. Nigeria Airways, the former national airline, flew 2·7m. km in 1999, carrying 109,200 passengers (30,300 on international flights).

Shipping
In 2002 the merchant marine totalled 411,000 GRT, including oil tankers 285,000 GRT. In 1997 vessels totalling 2,464,000 NRT entered ports and vessels totalling 2,510,000 NRT cleared. The principal ports are Lagos and Port Harcourt. There is an extensive network of inland waterways.

Telecommunications
In 2008 there were 1,308,000 main (fixed) telephone lines. In the same year mobile phone subscribers numbered 62,989,000 (416·6 per 1,000 persons), up from 18,587,000 in 2005. The largest mobile phone company is MTN Nigeria Communications. There were 1·2m. PCs in use in 2006 and 24·0m. internet users in 2008, up from 5·0m. users in 2005.

Postal Services
In 2003 there were 4,228 post offices. A total of 62m. pieces of mail were processed in 2003.

SOCIAL INSTITUTIONS
Justice
The highest court is the Federal Supreme Court, which consists of the Chief Justice of the Republic, and up to 15 Justices appointed by the government. It has original jurisdiction in any dispute between the Federal Republic and any State or between States; and to hear and determine appeals from the Federal Court of Appeal, which acts as an intermediate appellate Court to consider appeals from the High Court.

High Courts, presided over by a Chief Justice, are established in each state. All judges are appointed by the government. Magistrates' courts are established throughout the Republic, and customary law courts in southern Nigeria. In each of the northern States of Nigeria there are the Sharia Court of Appeal and the Court of Resolution. Muslim Law has been codified in a Penal Code and is applied through Alkali courts. The northern province of Zamfara introduced *sharia*, or Islamic law, in Oct. 1999, as have the other 11 predominantly Muslim northern provinces in the meantime. The death penalty is in force and was used in 2006.

The population in penal institutions in Jan. 2007 was 39,438 (28 per 100,000 of national population).

Education
The adult literacy rate was 69·1% in 2004. Free, compulsory education for nine years is provided for all children from the age of six. In 2006 there were 22·86m. pupils and 565,646 teaching staff in primary schools; 6·44m. pupils and 202,082 teaching staff in secondary schools; and (2005) 1·39m. students in tertiary education with 37,031 academic staff.

Among the leading institutions of higher education are Ahmadu Bello University in Zaria—Nigeria's largest university—with around 35,000 students, and the University of Ibadan—the country's oldest university—founded in 1948.

Health
Health personnel, 2000: 30,885 doctors, 2,180 dentists and 8,642 pharmacists.

Nigeria has made significant progress in the reduction of undernourishment in the past 25 years. In the period 2001–03 only 9% of the population was undernourished, one of the lowest rates in sub-Saharan Africa.

An estimated 2·9m. people in Nigeria are living with HIV/AIDS, a total exceeded only in South Africa.

RELIGION

Muslims and Christians both constitute about 45% of the population; traditional animist beliefs are also widespread. Northern Nigeria is mainly Muslim; southern Nigeria is predominantly Christian and western Nigeria is evenly divided between Christians, Muslims and animists. Far more Nigerians consider their religion to be of prime importance rather than their nationality. In Feb. 2010 the Roman Catholic church had two cardinals.

CULTURE

World Heritage Sites

The Sukur Cultural Landscape, a hilly area in Adamawa State (northeastern Nigeria), was entered on the UNESCO World Heritage list in 1999. Osun Sacred Grove is one of the last remnants of primary high forest in southern Nigeria and was inscribed in 2005.

Broadcasting

The Federal Radio Corporation of Nigeria, a statutory body, broadcasts Radio Nigeria from the cities of Abuja, Enugu, Ibadan, Kaduna and Lagos, and also the external Voice of Nigeria service. The government-owned Nigerian Television Authority transmits national and regional services. Nearly all states run their own radio and television stations. By 2005 nearly 300 broadcasting licences had been awarded to private operators. In 2005 there were 7m. TV-equipped households.

Cinema

Nigeria has the third largest film industry in the world, producing more than 1,000 feature films a year and bringing in US$250m. in revenues.

Press

In 2005 there were 26 daily newspapers with a combined circulation of 820,000.

Tourism

In 2004 there were 2,646,000 foreign visitors (including 1,825,000 from other African countries and 483,000 from Europe); spending by tourists totalled US$49m.

DIPLOMATIC REPRESENTATIVES

Of Nigeria in the United Kingdom (Nigeria House, 9 Northumberland Ave., London, WC2N 5BX)
High Commissioner: Dr Dahaltu S. Tafida.

Of the United Kingdom in Nigeria (Dangote House, Aguyi Ironsi St., Wuse, Abuja)
High Commissioner: Robert Dewar, CMG.

Of Nigeria in the USA (3519 International Court, NW, Washington, D.C., 20008)
Ambassador: Vacant.
Chargé d'Affaires a.i.: Baba Gana Wikil.

Of the USA in Nigeria (Plot 1075, Diplomatic Drive, Central District Area, Abuja)
Ambassador: Robin Sanders.

Of Nigeria to the United Nations
Ambassador: U. Joy Ogwu.

Of Nigeria to the European Union
Ambassador: Usman Alhaji Baraya.

FURTHER READING

Forrest, T., *Politics and Economic Development in Nigeria.* 1993
Maier, K., *This House Has Fallen: Midnight in Nigeria.* 2000
Miles, W. F. S., *Hausaland Divided: Colonialism and Independence in Nigeria and Niger.* 1994
Okafor, Victor Oguejiofor, *A Roadmap for Understanding African Politics.* 2006

National Statistical Office: National Bureau of Statistics, Plot 762, Independence Ave., Central Business District, Garki, P.M.B. 127, Abuja.
Website: http://www.nigerianstat.gov.ng

NORWAY

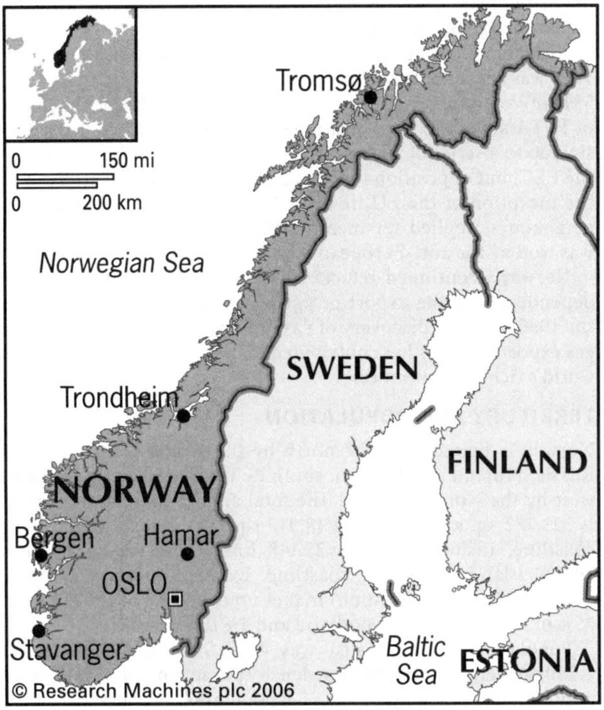

Kongeriket Norge
(Kingdom of Norway)

Capital: Oslo
Population estimate, 2010: 4·86m.
GDP per capita, 2007: (PPP$) 53,433
HDI/world rank: 0·971/1

KEY HISTORICAL EVENTS

The first settlers arrived at the end of the Ice Age, as the glaciers retreated north. Archaeological remains in Finnmark in the north and in Rogaland in the southwest of Norway date from between 9500 to 8000 BC and suggest coastal, hunting-fishing communities. By 2500 BC a new influx of settlers brought cattle and crop farming and gradually replaced the earlier hunting-fishing communities. Although there is little evidence of the impact of the bronze and iron ages on Norway as its people had not yet found ways to exploit their natural resources for trade, links with Roman-occupied Gaul in the first four centuries AD were strong. By the time of the collapse of the Roman Empire, tribal groups had started to develop and by AD 800 had each established their own legislative and adjudicatory assemblies, known as *things*.

In the ninth century communities from the Vik, an area between the south coasts of Norway and Sweden, gave their name to the people collectively known as Vikings. The Norwegian Vikings sailed to the Atlantic islands, England, France, Scotland and Ireland, and also colonized Iceland. One of the many whose exploits were faithfully recorded by the saga writers was Eric the Red, who discovered Greenland. His son, Leif Erikson, voyaged across the Davis Strait, to America, becoming possibly the first European to do so.

The first steps towards centralized rule were taken by Harold Fairhair who extended his rule along the coastal region of Norway. Battles with rival chieftains culminated in about 900 when Harold was proclaimed king of the Norwegians. His successors were less assertive and by the mid-tenth century the country was effectively under the suzerainty of Harold Bluetooth, king of Denmark and Skåne. Bluetooth's grandson, Canute the Great, fought successfully to incorporate England into his North Sea Empire before setting his sights on Sweden. But the limitations of royal authority were shown on the death of Canute when the English, unchallenged, simply chose their own king while the Danish and Norwegian nobles decided that whichever of their own monarchs lived longest should take power in both countries, an agreement which for a time resulted in a Norwegian ruler for Denmark.

Viking Strength

The Viking's territorial expansion came to an end with the Norwegian King Harald Hardrada's defeat at the battle of Stamford Bridge in England in 1066. Supported by the English church, the Norwegian monarchy gained strength. By the 12th century the balance of power between the church and monarchy had become a source of civil conflict which was only resolved when Håkon IV became King in 1217. Thus began Norway's 'Golden Age' in which the unity of the kingdom was solidly established. Blood feuds were prohibited, a royal council was created, and primogeniture was introduced to secure the continuity of the monarchic line. Under Håkon's rule, both Greenland and Iceland ceded control to Norway. It was Håkon's son, Magnus VI, known as the Lawmender, who oversaw the codification of a national law system between 1274–76, elements of which have survived to this day. Under Erik II, Magnus' son, much of the royal power was divested to wealthy magnates. His succession by his brother Håkon V in 1299 marked a renewed effort to strengthen the monarchy and also a movement of political power to Oslo.

Union with Sweden came in 1319 with the coronation of Magnus VII, the son of Håkon's daughter and Duke Erik of Sweden. This was to last until 1355, when the Swedish crown passed to Magnus' son. Between 1349–50 Norway fell victim to the Black Death which killed around two-thirds of its population. The effects of this were to dramatically reduce the strength of the nobility and to undermine the cohesion of the government, as many official positions were taken up by Danes and Swedes. Newly vulnerable to the threat of encroachment by the Germans, the incentive for all three Scandinavian kingdoms to unite was strong. When the Danish king died in 1375 his widow, Margaret, claimed the throne on behalf of her five-year-old son, Olav. Acting for her son, Margaret became regent of Denmark and, on the death of Håkon, regent of Norway. Confirmed as regent of Denmark and Norway, Margaret defeated Albrecht, the German claimant to the Swedish throne, thus clearing the way to a Nordic union. With the death of her son in 1387 and unable to take the triple crown for herself, she nominated her five-year-old nephew, Erik of Pomerania, as king of all three countries. His election was formalized at Kalmar in 1397.

From 1450 the Norwegian government was based in Copenhagen and many administrative positions were taken by Germans and Danes. An attempt by the Norwegian council to gain independence in 1523 led to civil war between 1534–36 and the council's subsequent abolition. Norway was then to remain a province of Denmark, with limited control over internal affairs, until the 19th century.

In the Napoleonic Wars, Denmark and Norway were allied with Napoleon I. Napoleon's defeat at the battle of Leipzig in 1813 was followed by a successful attack on Denmark from Sweden which resulted in the Treaty of Kiel (Jan. 1814). With the signing of the treaty Norway was conceded to the Swedish throne and, despite Denmark's continued resistance, its newly written constitution came into force in Nov. 1814. Although the arrangement meant the regency and foreign policy were to be shared with Sweden, the new constitution gave Norway control over internal affairs, with a newly established political base at Christiana.

The economic damage of the Napoleonic Wars was remedied by the rapid expansion of the fishing industry and, from the 1850s onwards, agriculture. In the latter half of the century, the merchant navy grew to become the third largest in the world after the United States and Great Britain.

Independence

From the 1880s, successive steps towards self-government within the union culminated in a referendum in which the overwhelming majority of Norwegians voted for separation. In Oct. 1905 Oscar II renounced his title to the western provinces and a month later a Danish prince was confirmed as Håkon VII of free Norway. Reigning for 52 years, he was succeeded by his son.

At the outset of the First World War Norway declared its neutrality. This did not prevent the loss of almost half of its merchant navy and damage to the economy as a result of trade embargos. But despite the hardships of the 1930s' depression, industrial expansion continued.

From 1940 to 1944, during the Second World War, Norway was occupied by the Germans who set up a pro-German government under Vidkun Quisling. Apart from this wartime episode, the Labour Party held office, and the majority in the *Storting* (parliament), from 1935 to 1965. Norway's first post-war prime minister, Einar Gerhardsen, had spent four years in a concentration camp. He had been vice-chairman of Oslo city council until he became leader of the underground anti-Nazi movement in the early days of the occupation. As recently elected social democrat leader he was the natural choice to head the 1945 caretaker government.

The action needed to restore Norway's prosperity was self evident: to make good the heavy losses in the merchant fleet; to increase the output of hydro-electricity; and to develop new industries. The chief worry for the social democrats was the likely impact of communists who had gained credit for leading the resistance. Talks on a possible merger of the parties were as unproductive as parallel negotiations in Denmark, but the electoral results of each party's going its own way were markedly different in the two countries. More confident of their purpose, the Norwegian social democrats took the electorate by storm, increasing their share of the popular vote in the 1945 election by close on 10%. Their advance gave them the one prize that eluded their colleagues everywhere else in Scandinavia—an absolute majority and the freedom to govern without always looking over their shoulder.

The government was supported wholeheartedly by the trade unions. In return for price controls and food subsidies which stabilized the cost of living for almost five years, and the guarantee of full employment, the unions accepted compulsory arbitration for all wage disputes. Returned in 1949 with an increased majority, the social democrats were able to point to a rise in productivity and living standards well beyond that achieved by most other Western countries. But the general increase in world prices triggered by the Korean War meant that Norway had to pay much more for essential imports. The use of subsidies to counteract price increases reached its limit when they became the largest item in the national budget. In 1950 food prices were allowed to get closer to their market level and the cost of living started on an upward curve, leading to a 30% increase over three years. Industrial investment suffered a sharp cutback.

The social democrats held on to power until the mid-sixties when a centre right coalition took over led by Per Borten. By 1969 the social democrats had recovered much of their lost ground. The centre right coalition government struggled on with a majority of two until the EEC issue broke through the normally placid surface of Norwegian politics.

Although Norway's application for membership in the EEC in 1969 was successful, a referendum held in 1972 found more than 53% of voters opposed to joining. Norway had been a member of EFTA since that organization's foundation, and continued to sign up to a series of bilateral free-trade treaties with members of the EEC, but opposition to joining the EEC remained strong. On the inception of the EU in 1992, Norway, like its Scandinavian neighbours, applied for membership. But, again, a referendum was won by the anti-European lobby.

Norway's continued reluctance to join the EU hinges on its dependence on the export of petroleum and natural gas. Since the 1960s and the discovery of vast off-shore deposits, the oil and gas export industry has contributed to making Norway one of the world's richest economies.

TERRITORY AND POPULATION

Norway is bounded in the north by the Arctic Ocean, east by Russia, Finland and Sweden, south by the Skagerrak Straits and west by the Norwegian Sea. The total area of mainland Norway is 323,782 sq. km, including 18,312 sq. km of fresh water. Total coastline, including fjords, 25,148 km. There are more than 50,000 islands along the coastline. Exposed mountain (either bare rock or thin vegetation) makes up over 70% of the country. 25% of the land area is woodland and 4% tilled land.

Population (2001 census) was 4,520,947 (2,240,281 males; 2,280,666 females); population density per sq. km, 14·8. Estimated population, 1 Jan. 2009, 4,799,252; population density, 15·7. With the exception of Iceland, Norway is the most sparsely populated country in Europe.

The UN gives an estimated population for 2010 of 4·86m.

There were 19 counties (*fylke*) in Jan. 2009. Land area, population and densities:

	Land area (sq. km)	*Population (2001 census)*	*Population (2009 estimate)*	*Density per sq. km 2009*
Østfold	3,922	252,520	268,584	68
Akershus	4,620	476,440	527,625	114
Oslo (City)	427	512,093	575,475	1,348
Hedmark	26,244	187,878	190,071	7
Oppland	23,878	183,302	184,288	8
Buskerud	13,870	239,591	254,634	18
Vestfold	2,157	216,333	229,134	106
Telemark	13,894	165,732	167,548	12
Aust-Agder	8,353	102,848	107,359	13
Vest-Agder	6,706	157,697	168,233	25
Rogaland	8,605	377,579	420,574	49
Hordaland	14,554	411,100	469,681	32
Sogn og Fjordane	17,709	107,261	106,457	6
Møre og Romsdal	14,614	243,888	248,727	17
Sør-Trøndelag	17,909	266,098	286,729	16
Nord-Trøndelag	20,881	127,444	130,708	6
Nordland	36,194	237,561	235,380	7
Troms Romsa	24,950	151,646	155,553	6
Finnmark	45,984	73,936	72,492	2
Mainland total	305,470[1]	4,520,947	4,799,252	16

[1] 117,943 sq. miles.

The Arctic territories of Svalbard and Jan Mayen have an area of 61,397 sq. km. Persons staying on Svalbard and Jan Mayen are registered as residents of their home Norwegian municipality.

At Jan. 2008, 78·6% of the population lived in urban areas.

Population of the principal urban settlements on 1 Jan. 2008:

Oslo	856,915	Ålesund	45,902
Bergen	223,593	Haugesund	42,112
Stavanger/Sandnes	185,913	Sandefjord	40,596
Trondheim	156,776	Moss	40,309
Fredrikstad/Sarpsborg	100,458	Bodø	36,073
Drammen	94,901	Arendal	32,103
Porsgrunn/Skien	86,342	Hamar	29,808
Kristiansand	66,532	Larvik	23,577
Tromsø	54,070	Halden	22,688
Tønsberg	46,862		

The official language is Norwegian, which has two versions: Bokmål (or Riksmål) and Nynorsk (or Landsmål).

The Sami, the indigenous people of the far north, number some 40,000 and form a distinct ethnic minority with their own culture and language.

SOCIAL STATISTICS

Statistics for calendar years:

	Births	*Still-born*	*Outside marriage*	*Deaths*	*Marriages*	*Divorces*
2004	56,951	210	29,252	41,200	22,354	11,045
2005	56,756	182	29,374	41,232	22,392	11,040
2006	58,545	201	31,056	41,253	21,721	10,598
2007	58,459	241	31,849	41,954	23,471	10,280
2008	60,497	221	33,302	41,712	25,125	10,158

Rates per 1,000 population, 2008, birth, 12·7; death, 8·7; marriage, 5·3; divorce, 2·1. Average annual population growth rate, 1998–2008, 0·76% (2008, 1·31%). In 2006 there were 529 suicides, giving a rate of 11·4 per 100,000 population (men, 16·8 per 100,000; women, 6·0).

Expectation of life at birth, 2008, was 78·3 years for males and 83·0 years for females. Infant mortality, 2008, 2·7 per 1,000 live births; fertility rate, 2008, 1·96 births per woman. 55% of births are to unmarried mothers. In 2007 the average age at marriage was 37·2 years for males and 33·7 years for females (33·7 years and 30·8 years respectively for first marriages).

At 1 Jan. 2009 the immigrant population totalled 508,199, including 44,482 from Poland, 30,161 from Pakistan, 28,730 from Sweden and 24,505 from Iraq. In 2008 Norway received 14,431 asylum applications. Most were from Iraq (3,138), Eritrea (1,806), Afghanistan (1,371) and Somalia (1,293).

A UNICEF report published in 2005 showed that 3·4% of children in Norway live in poverty (in households with income below 50% of the national median), the third lowest percentage of any country behind Denmark and Finland.

In the Human Development Index, or HDI (measuring progress in countries in longevity, knowledge and standard of living), Norway was ranked first in the 2007 rankings published in the annual Human Development Report.

CLIMATE

There is considerable variation in the climate because of the extent of latitude, the topography and the varying effectiveness of prevailing westerly winds and the Gulf Stream. Winters along the whole west coast are exceptionally mild but precipitation is considerable. Oslo, Jan. 24·3°F (–4·3°C), July 61·5°F (16·4°C). Annual rainfall 30·0" (763 mm). Bergen, Jan. 34·3°F (1·3°C), July 57·7°F (14·3°C). Annual rainfall 88·6" (2,250 mm). Trondheim, Jan. 26°F (–3·5°C), July 57°F (14°C). Annual rainfall 32·1" (870 mm). Bergen has one of the highest rainfall figures of any European city. The sun never fully sets in the northern area of the country in the summer and even in the south the sun rises at around 3 a.m. and sets at around 11 p.m.

CONSTITUTION AND GOVERNMENT

Norway is a constitutional and hereditary monarchy.

The reigning King is **Harald V**, born 21 Feb. 1937, married on 29 Aug. 1968 to Sonja Haraldsen. He succeeded on the death of his father, King Olav V, on 21 Jan. 1991. *Offspring:* Princess Märtha Louise, born 22 Sept. 1971 (married Ari Behn, b. 30 Sept. 1972, on 24 May 2002; *offspring*, Maud Angelica, b. 29 April 2003; Leah Isadora, b. 8 April 2005); Crown Prince Haakon Magnus, born 20 July 1973 (married Mette-Marit Tjessem Høiby, b. 19 Aug. 1973, on 25 Aug. 2001; *offspring*, Ingrid Alexandra, b. 21 Jan. 2004; Sverre Magnus, b. 3 Dec. 2005; *offspring* of Crown Princess Mette-Marit from previous relationship, Marius, b. 13 Jan. 1997). The king and queen together receive an annual personal allowance of 9·0m. kroner from the civil list, and the Crown Prince and Crown Princess together 7·5m. kroner. Princess Märtha Louise relinquished her allowance in 2002. Women have been eligible to succeed to the throne since 1990. There is no coronation ceremony. The royal succession is in direct male line in the order of primogeniture. In default of male heirs the King may propose a successor to the *Storting*, but this assembly has the right to nominate another, if it does not agree with the proposal.

The Constitution, voted by a constituent assembly on 17 May 1814 and modified at various times, vests the legislative power of the realm in the *Storting* (Parliament). The royal veto may be exercised; but if the same Bill passes two Stortings formed by separate and subsequent elections it becomes the law of the land without the assent of the sovereign. The King has the command of the land, sea and air forces, and makes all appointments.

The 169-member Storting (increased from 165 for the 2005 election) is directly elected by proportional representation. The country is divided into 19 districts, each electing from 4 to 15 representatives.

The Storting, when assembled, divides itself by election into the *Lagting* and the *Odelsting*. The former is composed of one-fourth of the members of the Storting, and the other of the remaining three-fourths. Each Ting (the Storting, the Odelsting and the Lagting) nominates its own president. Most questions are decided by the Storting, but questions relating to legislation must be considered and decided by the Odelsting and the Lagting separately. In the event of the Odelsting and the Lagting disagreeing the Bill is considered by the Storting in plenary sitting, with a majority of two-thirds of the votes required for a new law to be passed. The same majority is required for alterations of the Constitution, which can only be decided by the Storting in plenary sitting. The Storting elects five delegates, whose duty it is to revise the public accounts. The Lagting and the ordinary members of the Supreme Court of Justice (the *Høyesterett*) form a High Court of the Realm (the *Riksrett*) for the trial of ministers, members of the *Høyesterett* and members of the Storting. The impeachment before the *Riksrett* can only be decided by the Odelsting.

The executive is represented by the King, who exercises his authority through the Cabinet. Cabinet ministers are entitled to be present in the Storting and to take part in the discussions, but without a vote.

National Anthem

'Ja, vi elsker dette landet' ('Yes, we love this land'); words by B. Bjørnson, tune by R. Nordraak.

GOVERNMENT CHRONOLOGY

Prime Ministers since 1945. (DNA = Labour Party; H = Conservative Party; KrF = Christian People's Party; Sp = Center Party)

1945–51	DNA	Einar Henry Gerhardsen
1951–55	DNA	Oscar Fredrik Torp
1955–63	DNA	Einar Henry Gerhardsen
1963	H	John Fyrstenberg Lyng

1963–65	DNA	Einar Henry Gerhardsen
1965–71	Sp	Per Borten
1971–72	DNA	Trygve Martin Bratteli
1972–73	KrF	Lars Korvald
1973–76	DNA	Trygve Martin Bratteli
1976–81	DNA	Odvar Nordli
1981	DNA	Gro Harlem Brundtland
1981–86	H	Kåre Isaachsen Willoch
1986–89	DNA	Gro Harlem Brundtland
1989–90	H	Jan Peder Syse
1990–96	DNA	Gro Harlem Brundtland
1996–97	DNA	Thorbjørn Jagland
1997–2000	KrF	Kjell Magne Bondevik
2000–01	DNA	Jens Stoltenberg
2001–05	KrF	Kjell Magne Bondevik
2005–	DNA	Jens Stoltenberg

RECENT ELECTIONS

At the elections for the Storting held on 14 Sept. 2009 the following parties were elected: the ruling Labour Party (DNA), winning 64 out of 169 seats (with 35·4% of the vote, up from 61 and 32·7% in 2005); Progress Party (FrP), 41 (22·9%); Conservative Party (H), 30 (17·2%); Socialist Left Party (SV), 11 (6·2%); Centre Party (Sp), 11 (6·2%); Christian People's Party (KrF), 10 (5·5%); Liberal Party (V), 2 (3·9%). Turnout was 75·7%.

CURRENT ADMINISTRATION

In March 2010 the coalition government comprised:

Prime Minister: Jens Stoltenberg; b. 1959 (Labour Party/DNA; sworn in 17 Oct. 2005 and re-elected in Sept. 2009, having previously held office from March 2000 to Oct. 2001).

Minister of Agriculture and Food: Lars Peder Brekk (Sp). *Children, Equality and Social Inclusion:* Audun Lysbakken (SV). *Culture:* Anniken Huitfeldt (DNA). *Defence:* Grete Faremo (DNA). *Education:* Kristin Halvorsen (SV). *Environment and International Development:* Erik Solheim (SV). *Finance:* Sigbjørn Johnsen (DNA). *Fisheries and Coastal Affairs:* Lisbeth Berg-Hansen (DNA). *Foreign Affairs:* Jonas Gahr Støre (DNA). *Health and Care Services:* Anne-Grete Strøm-Erichsen (DNA). *Justice, Police and Immigration:* Knut Storberget (DNA). *Labour:* Hanne Bjurstrøm (DNA). *Local Government and Regional Development:* Liv Signe Navarsete (Sp). *Petroleum and Energy:* Terje Riis-Johansen (Sp). *Reform and Church Affairs and Nordic Co-operation:* Rigmor Aasrud (DNA). *Research and Higher Education:* Tora Aasland (SV). *Trade and Industry:* Trond Giske (DNA). *Transport and Communication:* Magnhild Meltveit Kleppa (Sp). *Minister at the Office of the Prime Minister:* Karl Eirik Schjøtt-Pedersen (DNA).

Office of the Prime Minister: http://www.regjeringen.no

CURRENT LEADERS

Jens Stoltenberg

Position

Prime Minister

Introduction

Jens Stoltenberg became prime minister of Norway for a second time on 17 Oct. 2005, following the victory of his centre-left coalition in parliamentary elections a month earlier. He had previously held the office from 2000–01. He pledged to use Norway's oil wealth to improve education, health and care for the elderly. He was returned to power in elections in Sept. 2009.

Early Life

Jens Stoltenberg was born in Oslo on 16 March 1959, the son of Thorvald Stoltenberg, a former foreign minister, and Karin Stoltenberg, also a politician. Having attended a Steiner school in Oslo, he studied economics at Oslo University. Here he became an active member of the Norwegian Labour Party (Det Norske Arbeiderpartiet, DNA) and was appointed leader of the Labour Youth League in 1985, having served on its central board for six years. Between 1985–89 he was vice president of the International Union of Socialist Youth. He worked for a brief spell at the national statistics office and was an economics lecturer at the University of Oslo before serving for two years as leader of the Oslo Labour Party (1990–92). He was also a state secretary at the department of the environment at this time.

Elected a member of the Storting (parliament) for Oslo in the Sept. 1993 general election, Stoltenberg served as minister of trade and energy from 1993–96 in Gro Harlem Brundtland's administration and oversaw Norway's accession to the European Economic Area in 1994. The government had applied for full EU membership in 1992 but the Norwegian electorate rejected the treaty in a referendum in Nov. 1994.

When Brundtland resigned in Oct. 1996 her successor, Thorbjørn Jagland, made Stoltenberg minister of finance, a post he held for a year until the DNA lost power to the conservative Christian People's Party, led by Kjell Magne Bondevik. Bondevik, who attempted to govern with a coalition which held a slim majority, resigned in March 2000 and Stoltenberg (by now deputy leader of the DNA) was asked to form a government. On 17 March 2000 he was sworn in to become the youngest prime minister in Norway's history.

Career in Office

Stoltenberg kept up Norway's reputation as an international peace-broker by mediating between Tamil separatists and the government of Sri Lanka. More controversially, he ushered in reforms to the welfare state that included the part-privatization of several state-owned services. In the parliamentary elections of Sept. 2001 the party suffered a heavy defeat, gaining only 24% of the vote. Bondevik returned as prime minister of a centre-right coalition. A DNA party leadership battle between Stoltenberg and Jagland (leader since 1992) ensued with Stoltenberg emerging victorious.

Thanks to burgeoning oil and gas exports and high international prices, the economy prospered under Bondevik but Stoltenberg tapped into people's dissatisfaction with the welfare system. The DNA's campaign in the run-up to the Sept. 2005 parliamentary elections centred on increased funding for education, health and care of the elderly. In partnership with the Socialist Left Party and the Centre Party, the DNA took 87 of 169 seats. Stoltenberg was sworn in to office on 17 Oct. 2005.

Stoltenberg vowed to reform the welfare system while creating conditions for Norway to develop as a knowledge-based economy. He also pledged sustainable management of the country's fish and energy resources. In 2006 his administration approved the expansion of oil exploration in the Barents Sea and also the huge merger (agreed in Dec.) of Norway's two largest energy companies, Statoil and Norsk Hydro (with the government having a controlling stake in the combined group). Stoltenberg withdrew the small contingent of Norwegian troops from Iraq, but promised to increase the country's participation in United Nations peacekeeping missions elsewhere in the world.

In Sept. 2009 his centre-left coalition was returned to power in parliamentary elections, with the DNA marginally increasing its share of the vote.

DEFENCE

Conscription is for 12 months, with four to five refresher training periods.

In 2006 defence spending totalled US$5,015m. (US$1,088 per capita), representing 1·5% of GDP. Expenditure per capita was the highest of any European country in 2006.

Army

Strength (2007) 6,700 (including 3,500 conscripts). The Army fast mobilization reserve numbers 83,000.

Navy

The Royal Norwegian Navy has three components: the Navy, Coast Guard and Coastal Artillery. Main naval combatants include six German-built Ula class submarines and five frigates.

The personnel of the Navy totalled 4,100 in 2007, of whom 2,000 were conscripts. 721 (400 conscripts) served in the Coast Guard. The main naval base is at Bergen (Håkonsvern), with a subsidiary base at Ramsund.

Air Force

The Air Force consists of seven air stations, two control and reporting centres, ten squadrons with aircraft and helicopters, and two surface-to-air battalions. Total strength (2007) is 5,000 personnel, including 3,200 conscripts. There were 52 combat capable aircraft in operation including F-16A/Bs.

Home Guard

The Home Guard is organized in small units equipped and trained for special tasks. Service after basic training is one week a year. The Home Guard consists of the Land Home Guard (strength, 2007, 46,000 reservists in mobilization), Naval Home Guard (1,800) and Anti-Air Home Guard (2,500).

INTERNATIONAL RELATIONS

Norway is a member of the UN, World Bank, IMF and several other UN specialized agencies, WTO, Council of Europe, OSCE, EFTA, CERN, Nordic Council, Council of the Baltic Sea States, BIS, IOM, NATO, OECD, Inter-American Development Bank, Asian Development Bank, Antarctic Treaty and is an associate member of WEU. Norway has acceded to the Schengen accord abolishing border controls between Norway, Austria, Belgium, Czech Republic, Denmark, Estonia, Finland, France, Germany, Greece, Hungary, Iceland, Italy, Latvia, Lithuania, Luxembourg, Malta, Netherlands, Poland, Portugal, Slovakia, Slovenia, Spain, Sweden and Switzerland.

In a referendum on 27–28 Nov. 1994, 52·2% of votes cast were against joining the EU. The electorate was 3,266,182; turnout was 88·9%.

Norway gave US$3·7bn. in international aid in 2007, which at 0·95% of GNI made it the most generous developed country as a percentage of its gross national income and one of only five countries to exceed the UN target of 0·7%.

ECONOMY

Services accounted for 56% of GDP in 2007, industry 43% and agriculture 1%.

Transparency International, the anti-corruption organization, ranked Norway 11th in the world in a survey of the countries with the least corruption in business and government in 2009. It received 8·6 out of 10 in the annual index.

Overview

Norway has one of the world's highest levels of GDP per capita and one of the lowest levels of income inequality. It is the second-largest supplier of natural gas to continental Europe and in 2008 was the 11th largest oil producer and 6th largest oil exporter in the world. Oil and gas account for about a quarter of GDP and a quarter of total investment. Norway is well endowed with other natural resources including hydropower, fish, forests and minerals.

Oil revenues allow Norway to run large fiscal surpluses, which averaged 11·5% of GDP per year from 2000–04. In 2008 the current account surplus was 19%. Fiscal guidelines effective since the 2002 budget hold the central government non-oil deficit to 4 percent of the assets of the Government Pension Fund–Global (formerly the Government Petroleum Fund). Revenue from oil production is transferred to this fund. After being hard hit by the financial crisis in 2008, the fund reported record growth of 13·5% in the third quarter of 2009.

The economy combines free market capitalism and an advanced welfare state. Since emerging as a major oil and gas exporter in the mid-1970s, Norway has enjoyed solid growth linked to global oil prices. In 2002 and 2003 growth was below average as a result of falling oil prices but recovered and entered a cyclical upswing in mid-2003 that continued through to 2007. GDP growth slowed to 2·1% in 2008 as a result of lower oil prices and the global financial crisis. Norway went into recession with two quarters of negative growth in the first half of 2009, but a recovery started in the second half of the year. Unemployment is low, standing at 3·2% in Oct. 2009.

A significant policy issue is how to finance pensions for an ageing population. The 2007 budget projected pension spending to rise by 10% of GDP by 2060. IMF calculations suggest that income from the Government Pension Fund–Global will cover only about two percentage points of the gap. Parliament agreed on a pension reform package in 2007.

Currency

The unit of currency is the *Norwegian krone* (NOK) of 100 *øre*. After Oct. 1990 the krone was fixed to the ecu in the EMS of the EU in the narrow band of 2·25%, but it was freed in Dec. 1992. Inflation rates (based on OECD statistics):

1999	*2000*	*2001*	*2002*	*2003*	*2004*	*2005*	*2006*	*2007*	*2008*
2·3%	3·1%	3·0%	1·3%	2·5%	0·5%	1·5%	2·3%	0·7%	3·8%

Foreign exchange reserves were US$42,214m. in Aug. 2009. Gold reserves are negligible. On 30 Sept. 2009 the nominal value of notes and coins in circulation was 49,798m. kroner.

Budget

Central government current revenue and expenditure (in 1m. kroner) for years ending 31 Dec.:

	2004	*2005*	*2006*	*2007*	*2008*
Revenue	832,027	948,922	1,100,931	1,153,967	1,313,738
Expenditure	627,408	655,031	700,452	738,531	802,218

The standard rate of VAT is 25·0% (reduced rates of 14% and 8%).

Performance

Real GDP growth rates (based on OECD statistics):

1999	*2000*	*2001*	*2002*	*2003*	*2004*	*2005*	*2006*	*2007*	*2008*
2·0%	3·3%	2·0%	1·5%	1·0%	3·9%	2·7%	2·3%	3·1%	2·1%

According to Statistics Norway, GDP growth in 2009 was –1·5%. Major oil discoveries on the Norwegian continental shelf coincided with the 1974 and 1979 oil shocks, resulting in a pronounced upswing in the mainland economy which lasted until the 1986 oil price collapse. Norway only began to recover from the subsequent slump in the economy in 1993. The strong performance of the Norwegian economy in 1993–98 lifted mainland GDP by 20%, but there was a significant slowdown in 1998 when the oil price collapsed at a time when the labour market was overheated. Norway's total GDP in 2008 was US$450·0bn.

Banking and Finance

Norges Bank is the central bank and bank of issue. Supreme authority is vested in the Executive Board consisting of seven members appointed by the King and the Supervisory Council consisting of 15 members elected by the Storting. The *Governor* is Svein Gjedrem. Total assets and liabilities at 31 Dec. 2007 were 2,426,791m. kroner.

Norway's largest commercial bank is DnB NOR bank (with assets at 30 June 2007 of 1,437bn. kroner); the second largest bank is Nordea Bank Norge. There were 16 commercial banks in 2007 (with total assets of 1,799bn. kroner) and 121 savings banks in 2007 (with total assets of 1,993bn. kroner).

There is a stock exchange in Oslo.

ENERGY AND NATURAL RESOURCES

Environment

Norway's carbon dioxide emissions from the consumption and flaring of fossil fuels in 2008 were the equivalent of 8·7 tonnes per capita. An *Environmental Performance Index* compiled in 2008 ranked Norway third in the world behind Switzerland and Sweden, with 93·1%. The index examined various factors in six areas—air pollution, biodiversity and habitat, climate change, environmental health, productive natural resources and water resources.

In 2008 there were 29 national parks (total area, 2,677,416 ha.), 1,872 nature reserves (472,638 ha.), 184 landscape protected areas (1,521,745 ha.) and 406 other areas with protected flora and fauna (42,664 ha.).

Norway is one of the world leaders in recycling. In 2008, 52% of all household waste was sent for recovery.

Electricity

Norway is the sixth largest producer of hydropower in the world and the largest in Europe. The potential total hydro-electric power was estimated at 205,732m. kWh in 2008. Installed electrical capacity in 2007 was 30·5m. kW, 95% of it hydro-electric. Production, 2007, was 137,164m. kWh (98% hydro-electric). Consumption per capita in 2006, at 26,289 kWh, was one of the highest in the world. In 1991 Norway became the first country in Europe to deregulate its energy market. Norway is a net importer of electricity.

Oil and Gas

There are enormous oil reserves in the Norwegian continental shelf. In 1966 the first exploration well was drilled. Production of crude oil, 2008, 114·2m. tonnes. Norway ranks among the world's biggest oil exporters, with net oil exports of around 2·2m. bbls a day in 2008. It had proven reserves of 7·5bn. bbls in 2008. In March 1998 Norway announced that it would reduce its output for the year by 100,000 bbls per day as part of a plan to cut global crude production. In June 2001 the Norwegian government sold a 17·5% stake in Statoil, the last major state-owned oil company in western Europe. In Oct. 2007 Statoil and the oil and gas division of Norsk Hydro (a Norwegian energy and metals company) merged to form StatoilHydro, as a result creating the world's largest offshore oil and natural gas producer.

Output of natural gas, 2008, 99·2bn. cu. metres with proven reserves in 2008 of 2,910bn. cu. metres.

Minerals

Production in 2006 unless otherwise indicated (in tonnes): coal (2007), 4,073,000; aluminium, 1,422,000; ilmenite concentrate, 850,000; iron ore, 620,000; zinc, 160,700; nickel, 82,000; refined copper, 39,700.

Agriculture

Norway is barren and mountainous. The arable area is in strips in valleys and around fjords and lakes.

In 2007 the agricultural area was 1,032,100 ha., of which 665,100 ha. were meadow and pasture, 140,700 ha. were sown to barley, 91,200 ha. to wheat, 72,400 ha. to oats and 14,500 ha. to potatoes. Production in 2008 (in 1,000 tonnes, provisional): hay, 2,711; barley, 530; wheat, 460; potatoes, 400; oats, 310.

Livestock, 2007, 905,515 cattle (314,309 milch cows), 894,483 sheep (one year and over), 99,216 pigs for breeding, 41,161 dairy goats, 3,542,094 hens, 168,000 silver fox, 161,000 blue and silver blue fox, 812,000 mink and 241,500 tame reindeer.

Forestry

In 2006 the total area under forests was 9·12m. ha., or 29·7% of the total land area. Productive forest area, 2006, approximately 7·4m. ha. About 80% of the productive area consists of conifers and 20% of broadleaves. In 2006, 7·28m. cu. metres of roundwood were cut.

Fisheries

The total number of fishermen in 2008 was 12,904, of whom 2,597 had another chief occupation. In 2008 the number of registered fishing vessels (all with motor) was 6,790.

The catch in 2007 totalled 2,393,259 tonnes, almost entirely from sea fishing. The catch of herring in 2007 totalled 884,593 tonnes, saithe 225,299 tonnes and cod 217,788 tonnes. 14,043 seals were caught in 2007 (13,981 harp seals plus 62 hooded seals for scientific purposes). Commercial whaling was prohibited in 1988, but recommenced in 1993: 592 whales were caught in 2007. Norway is the second largest exporter of fishery commodities, after China. In 2007 exports were valued at US$6·23bn.

INDUSTRY

The leading companies by market capitalization in Norway in March 2009 were: Statoil, US$56·2bn.; Telenor Group, a telecommunications company (US$9·5bn.); and Orkla, an industrial conglomerate (US$7·0bn.).

Industry is chiefly based on raw materials. Paper and paper products, industrial chemicals and basic metals are important export manufactures. In the following table figures are given for industrial establishments in 2007. The values are given in 1m. kroner.

Industries	*Establishments*	*Number of employees*	*Gross value of production*	*Value added (in market prices)*
Coal and peat	15	427	2,097	713
Metal ores	8	429	776	421
Other mining and quarrying	628	3,677	8,898	3,103
Food products	2,069	44,408	139,074	31,897
Beverages and tobacco	75	4,671	14,590	8,988
Textiles	639	3,886	4,901	1,749
Clothing, etc.	587	1,579	2,186	779
Leather and leather products	46	267	377	99
Wood and wood products	1,828	16,440	28,900	8,676
Pulp, paper and paper products	102	6,169	20,098	4,100
Printing and publishing	2,914	25,174	43,105	17,336
Refined petroleum products and basic chemicals	95	9,095	101,214	15,997
Other chemical products	190	5,738	17,554	7,575
Rubber and plastic products	407	5,698	10,515	3,495
Other non-metallic mineral products	881	10,915	25,094	8,282
Basic metals	157	11,848	81,489	15,001
Metal products, except machinery/equipment	2,488	23,353	37,715	14,238
Machinery and equipment	2,386	26,086	72,791	21,425
Office machinery and computers	15	120	650	122
Electrical machinery and apparatus	443	8,031	20,319	6,337
Radio, television and communication equipment	128	4,079	11,099	4,080
Medical, precision and optical instruments	605	7,946	18,319	6,329
Oil platforms	129	22,089	60,244	16,929
Motor vehicles and trailers	133	4,783	9,081	2,476

Industries	Establish-ments	Number of employees	Gross value of production	Value added (in market prices)
Other transport equipment	1,050	16,717	46,173	9,095
Other manufacturing industries	1,787	12,189	19,594	6,780
Total	19,805	275,814	769,852	216,023

Labour

Norway has a tradition of centralized wage bargaining. Since the early 1960s the contract period has been for two years with intermediate bargaining after 12 months, to take into consideration such changes as the rate of inflation.

The labour force averaged 2,591,000 in 2008 (1,222,000 females). The total number of employed persons in 2008 averaged 2,524,000 (1,192,000 females), of whom 1,845,000 were in full-time employment, 674,000 in part-time employment and 5,000 working unspecified hours. Distribution of employed persons by occupation in 2006 showed 477,100 in health and social work; 350,700 in trade; 279,300 in business services; 277,100 in manufacturing; 182,000 in education; 168,700 in construction; 161,300 in transport; 150,500 in public administration and defence; 74,600 in hotels and restaurants; 62,000 in agriculture.

The unemployment rate in Oct. 2009 was 3·2% (2·5% in 2008 as a whole).

There were ten work stoppages in 2008 (four in 2007): 62,568 working days were lost (3,954 in 2007).

Trade Unions

There were 1,621,073 union members at the end of 2008.

INTERNATIONAL TRADE

Imports and Exports

Total imports and exports in calendar years (in 1m. kroner):

	2004	2005	2006	2007	2008
Imports	326,102	357,657	411,755	468,918	497,379
Exports	554,896	668,760	782,943	795,366	957,834

Norway's trade surplus was a record 460,456m. kroner in 2008. Major import suppliers in 2008 (value in 1m. kroner): Sweden, 70,868·5; Germany, 66,676·6; Denmark, 34,208·8; China, 32,089·3; UK, 29,727·7; USA, 26,893·9; Netherlands, 20,466·8; France, 18,114·7; Finland, 16,786·2; Italy, 16,478·6. Imports from economic areas: EU, 337,946·6; Nordic countries, 123,896·2; OECD, 397,910·4.

Major export markets in 2008 (value in 1m. kroner): UK, 265,909·8; Germany, 123,004·8; Netherlands, 95,899·0; France, 89,647·6; Sweden, 59,918·9; USA, 41,190·6; Denmark, 31,642·5; Italy, 29,804·1; Belgium, 24,292·9; Canada, 22,465·0. Exports to economic areas: EU, 801,664·3; Nordic countries, 109,352·0; OECD, 892,161·7.

Principal imports in 2008 (in 1m. kroner): motor vehicles, 44,439·3 (including passenger cars and station wagons, 21,941·0); transport equipment excluding motor vehicles, 32,217·7; general industrial machinery and equipment, 30,395·6; metalliferous ores and metal scrap, 26,421·9; electrical machinery, apparatus and appliances, 24,701·5; manufactures of metals, 23,140·0; specialized machinery for particular industries, 21,344·5; petroleum, petroleum products and related materials, 21,126·9; telecommunications, sound recording and similar appliances, 18,614·6.

Principal exports in 2008 (in 1m. kroner): petroleum, petroleum products and related materials, 413,013·3 (including crude petroleum, 370,206·3); natural and manufactured gas, 239,687·1 (including natural gas, 214,364·2); non-ferrous metals, 48,274·6 (including aluminium, 32,130·2); fish, crustaceans and molluscs, and preparations thereof, 37,390·8; general industrial machinery and equipment, 21,607·4; iron and steel, 17,797·2; transport equipment excluding road vehicles, 15,333·3; electrical machinery, apparatus and appliances, 13,886·7; specialized machinery for particular industries, 13,780·5.

COMMUNICATIONS

Roads

In Jan. 2009 the length of public roads (including roads in towns) totalled 93,247 km. Total road length in Jan. 2009 included: national roads, 27,469 km; provincial roads, 27,262 km; local roads, 38,516 km. Number of registered motor vehicles, 2008, included: 2,197,193 passenger cars (including station wagons and ambulances), 379,343 vans, 248,463 tractors and special purpose vehicles, 161,662 mopeds, 134,721 motorcycles, 84,350 goods vehicles (including lorries), 59,657 combined vehicles and 23,324 buses. In 2008, 10,868 injuries were sustained in road accidents, with 255 fatalities. Norway has one of the lowest death rates in road accidents of any industrialized country, at 5·3 deaths per 100,000 people in 2008.

Rail

The length of state railways in 2008 was 4,114 km (2,552 km electrified). In 2007 passenger-km travelled came to 2,622m. and freight tonne-km to 2,444m. Sales and other operating income totalled 10,329m. kroner in 2008.

There is a metro (104 km) and a tram network (146 km) in Oslo.

Civil Aviation

The main international airports are at Oslo (Gardermoen), Bergen (Flesland), Trondheim (Værnes) and Stavanger (Sola). Kristiansand (Kjevik) and Torp also have a few international flights. Norway's largest airline is SAS Norge, a wholly-owned subsidiary of the Scandinavian Airlines System (SAS) Group. It was established in 2004 as SAS Braathens through the merger of the Norwegian part of SAS and Braathens, and was renamed SAS Norge in 2007. SAS Norge carries around 10m. passengers a year to 55 Norwegian and European destinations.

In 2008 Oslo (Gardermoen) handled 19,344,459 passengers (10,188,497 on domestic flights) and 89,770 tonnes of freight. Bergen is the second busiest airport for passenger traffic, with 4,808,419 passengers in 2008 (3,431,821 on domestic flights); and Stavanger the second busiest for freight, with 9,667 tonnes in 2008.

Shipping

The Norwegian International Ship Register was set up in 1987. At 31 Dec. 2008, 577 ships were registered (385 Norwegian) totalling 15,099,000 GRT. 276 tankers accounted for 8,270,000 GRT. There were also 770 ships totalling 2,306,000 GRT on the Norwegian Ordinary Register. These figures do not include fishing boats, tugs, salvage vessels, icebreakers and similar special types of vessels. In 2006 Norway's merchant fleet represented 3·9% of total world tonnage. In 2007, 41m. passengers travelled on internal ferries. The warm Gulf Stream ensures ice-free harbours throughout the year.

Telecommunications

In 2008 there were 1,896,000 main (fixed) telephone lines. In the same year mobile phone subscribers numbered 5,251,000 (1,101·6 per 1,000 persons). There were 2·9m. PCs in 2006 and 3·9m. internet users in 2008. Since 2000 the government has been reducing its interest in Telenor, the country's largest telecommunications operator, and in March 2004 lowered its stake to 54·0%.

Postal Services
In 2001 post offices began to be converted to Post in Shops. 452 post offices were replaced by 519 Post in Shops. The final target, set in 2001, was for a minimum of 1,150 Post in Shops, 300 post offices and 20 Business Centres. By 2005 there were 1,201 Post in Shops, 303 post offices and 25 Business Centres. In 2003 a total of 2,750m. items of mail were processed, or 603 per person.

SOCIAL INSTITUTIONS

Justice
The judicature is common to civil and criminal cases; the same professional judges preside over both. These judges are state officials. The participation of lay judges and jurors, both summoned for the individual case, varies according to the kind of court and kind of case.

The 96 city or district courts of first instance are in criminal cases composed of one professional judge and two lay judges, chosen by ballot from a panel elected by the local authority. In civil cases two lay judges may participate. These courts are competent in all cases except criminal cases where the maximum penalty exceeds six years imprisonment. In every community there is a Conciliation Board composed of three lay persons elected by the district council. A civil lawsuit usually begins with mediation by the Board which can pronounce judgement in certain cases.

The five high courts, or courts of second instance, are composed of three professional judges. Additionally, in civil cases two or four lay judges may be summoned. In serious criminal cases, which are brought before high courts in the first instance, a jury of ten lay persons is summoned to determine whether the defendant is guilty according to the charge. In less serious criminal cases the court is composed of two professional and three lay judges. In civil cases, the court of second instance is an ordinary court of appeal. In criminal cases in which the lower court does not have judicial authority, it is itself the court of first instance. In other criminal cases it is an appeal court as far as the appeal is based on an attack against the lower court's assessment of the facts when determining the guilt of the defendant. An appeal based on any other alleged mistakes is brought directly before the Supreme Court.

The Supreme Court *(Høyesterett)* is the court of last resort. There are 18 Supreme Court judges. Each individual case is heard by five judges. Some major cases are determined in plenary session. The Supreme Court may in general examine every aspect of the case and the handling of it by the lower courts. However, in criminal cases the Court may not overrule the lower court's assessment of the facts as far as the guilt of the defendant is concerned.

The Court of Impeachment *(Riksretten)* is composed of five judges of the Supreme Court and ten members of Parliament.

All serious offences are prosecuted by the State. The Public Prosecution Authority consists of the Attorney General, 18 district attorneys and legally qualified officers of the ordinary police force. Counsel for the defence is in general provided for by the State.

The population in penal institutions in Aug. 2006 was 3,048 (66 per 100,000 of national population).

Education
Free compulsory schooling in primary and lower secondary schools was extended to 10 years from 9, and the starting age lowered to 6 from 7, in July 1997. All young people between the ages of 16 and 19 have the statutory right to three years of upper secondary education. In 2007 there were 6,622 kindergartens (children up to six years old) with 249,815 children and 76,089 staff. There were 616,388 pupils at primary and lower secondary schools in 2007; 228,363 pupils at upper secondary schools; and 10,264 students at folk high schools and vocational schools.

There are seven universities: Oslo (founded 1811), with 27,341 students in 2007; Bergen (1948), with 14,057 students; Tromsø (1972), with 5,424 students; the Norwegian University of Science and Technology (1996, formerly the University of Trondheim and the Norwegian Institute of Technology), with 19,351 students; Stavanger (2005, formerly Stavanger University College), with 8,050 students; Norwegian University of Life Sciences (1859, university since 2005—formerly the Agricultural University of Norway), with 2,817 students; and Agder (2007, formerly Agder University College), with 7,801 students. There are also 24 state university colleges and a number of private colleges. In 2007 the universities had 84,841 students and the state university colleges 85,415 students. The University of Tromsø is responsible for Sami language and studies.

In 2006 public expenditure on education came to 6·6% of GNI and 16·2% of total government spending. The adult literacy rate is at least 99%.

Health
The health care system, which is predominantly publicly financed (mainly by a national insurance tax), is run on both county and municipal levels. Persons who fall ill are guaranteed medical treatment, and health services are distributed according to need. In 2007 there were the equivalent of 8,729 full-time doctors, 24,614 nurses and 4,442 auxiliary nursing personnel. On 31 Dec. 2007 there were 15,945 hospital beds (excluding those in psychiatric institutions). In 2007 Norway spent 8·9% of its GDP on health. In 2005–06, 25% of men and 24% of women aged 16–74 smoked on a daily basis. The rate among women is one of the highest in the world.

Welfare
Expenditure on social assistance in 2007 totalled 4,262m. kroner. There were 642,815 old age pensioners in 2007 (369,846 women) and 295,225 disability pensioners (167,950 women). Maternity leave is either for 44 weeks on 100% of previous salary or 54 weeks on 80% of previous salary; unused portions may pass to the father. In Dec. 2008, 40,730 children aged one to three received cash benefit (34% of all children between one and three years of age).

RELIGION
There is freedom of religion, the Church of Norway (Evangelical Lutheran), however, being the national church, endowed by the State. Its clergy are nominated by the King. Ecclesiastically Norway is divided into 11 dioceses, 100 deaneries and 1,298 parishes. About 86% of Norwegians belong to the Church of Norway (which had 3,873,847 members in 2007) and approximately 77% of infants were baptised in the Church in 2004. There were 403,909 members of registered and unregistered religious communities outside the Church of Norway in 2007, subsidized by central government and local authorities, including 225,507 Christians and 79,068 Muslims. The Roman Catholics are under a Bishop at Oslo, a Vicar Apostolic at Trondheim and a Vicar Apostolic at Tromsø.

CULTURE

World Heritage Sites
Norway's UNESCO heritage sites (with year listed) are: the 12–13th century wooden church in Sogn og Fjordane on the west coast, the Urnes Stave Church (1979), a testimony to the city's key role in the Hanseatic League trading route between the 14–16th centuries; the 58 wooden buildings in Bergen's wharf of Bryggen (1979); the wooden houses of the copper mining village of Røros (1980), active between the 17–20th centuries; the pre-historic Rock Drawings of Alta (1995) in the Alta Fjord, near the Arctic Circle, dating from 4200 to 500 BC; Vegaøyan—the Vega Archipelago (2004), a cluster of dozens of islands centred on Vega, just south of the Arctic Circle; the West Norwegian Fjords—Geirangerfjord and Naerøyfjord (2005); and the Struve Geodetic Arc (2005). The Arc is a chain of survey triangulations spanning from Norway to

the Black Sea that helped establish the exact shape and size of the earth and is shared with nine other countries.

Broadcasting

The Norwegian Broadcasting Corporation (Norsk Rikskringkasting—NRK) is a non-commercial enterprise operated by an independent public foundation. It operates four national television channels (new third and fourth channels having been launched in Sept. and Dec. 2007), three national radio stations and local services. There are also commercial terrestrial and satellite services, notably TV2 (NRK's main television competitor) and the P4 private radio station. There were 2·0m. television-equipped households in 2006 (colour by PAL).

Cinema

There were 427 cinemas in 2008, with a seating capacity of 79,998. Attendances totalled 11·8m. In 2007, 27 full-length feature films were made.

Press

There were 74 paid-for daily newspapers with a combined average net circulation of 2·19m. in 2008, and in 2007 there were 151 non-dailies with a circulation of 623,000. Norway has among the highest circulation rates of daily newspapers in the world, at 580 per 1,000 adult inhabitants in 2007. In 2006 a total of 7,041 book titles were published.

Tourism

In 2006 there were 3,004,000 foreign holiday and leisure visitors (excluding day-visitors) who stayed an average of 7·2 nights each, totalling 21,652,000 nights. The main countries of origin were Sweden (758,000), Germany (493,000), Denmark (408,000) and the UK (240,000). In 2008 there were 1,108 hotels and 797 camping sites. Spending by foreign tourists totalled 28·4bn. kroner in 2006.

Festivals

The Bergen International Festival, Norway's oldest festival, is held annually in May/June and includes music, dance and theatre. The biennial Ibsen Festival (theatre) is held in Oslo in Aug./Sept. in even-numbered years. CODA (the Oslo International Dance Festival) runs for three weeks every Sept./Oct.

Libraries

In 2007 there were 807 public libraries, 2,783 school libraries, 18 county libraries and 322 special and research libraries (one national).

Theatre and Opera

There were 9,268 theatre and opera performances attended by 1,792,395 people at 30 theatres in 2007.

Museums and Galleries

There were 173 museums in 2007 (including 103 social history museums, 20 art museums and nine natural history museums), with 10,193,903 visitors.

DIPLOMATIC REPRESENTATIVES

Of Norway in the United Kingdom (25 Belgrave Sq., London, SW1X 8QD)
Ambassador: Bjarne Lindstrøm.

Of the United Kingdom in Norway (Thomas Heftyesgate 8, 0264 Oslo)
Ambassador: David Powell.

Of Norway in the USA (2720 34th St., NW, Washington, D.C., 20008)
Ambassador: Wegger Christian Strommen.

Of the USA in Norway (Henrik Ibsens Gate 48, 0244 Oslo)
Ambassador: Barry B. White.

Of Norway to the United Nations
Ambassador: Morten Wetland.

Of Norway to the European Union
Ambassador: Oda Helen Sletnes.

FURTHER READING

Statistics Norway (formerly Central Bureau of Statistics). *Statistisk Årbok; Statistical Yearbook of Norway.—Economic survey* (annual, from 1935; with English summary from 1952, now published in *Økonomiske Analyser*, annual).—*Historisk Statistikk; Historical Statistics.—Statistisk Månedshefte* (with English index)
Norges Statskalender. From 1816; annual from 1877

Archer, Clive, *Norway and an Integrating Europe.* 2004
Petersson, O., *The Government and Politics of the Nordic Countries.* 1994

National library: The National Library of Norway, Drammensveien 42b, 0255 Oslo.
National Statistical Office: Statistics Norway, PB 8131 Dep., N-0033 Oslo.
Website: http://www.ssb.no

Svalbard

An archipelago situated between 10° and 35° E. long. and between 74° and 81° N. lat. Total area, 61,020 sq. km (23,560 sq. miles). The main islands are Spitsbergen, Nordaustlandet, Edgeøya, Barentsøya, Prins Karls Forland, Bjørnøya, Hopen, Kong Karls Land and Kvitøya. The Arctic climate is tempered by mild winds from the Atlantic.

The archipelago was probably discovered by Norsemen in 1194 and rediscovered by the Dutch navigator Barents in 1596. In the 17th century whale-hunting gave rise to rival Dutch, British and Danish-Norwegian claims to sovereignty; but when in the 18th century the whale-hunting ended, the question of the sovereignty of Svalbard lost its significance. It was again raised in the 20th century, owing to the discovery and exploitation of coalfields. By a treaty, signed on 9 Feb. 1920 in Paris, Norway's sovereignty over the archipelago was recognized. On 14 Aug. 1925 the archipelago was officially incorporated in Norway.

Total population on 1 Jan. 2008 was 2,449, of whom 1,821 were Norwegians, 620 Russians and eight Poles. Coal is the principal product. There are two Norwegian and two Russian mining camps. 2,904,301 tonnes of coal were produced from Norwegian mines in 2004 valued at 1,304m. kroner.

There were 3,349 motor vehicles and trailers registered at 31 Dec. 2004, including 1,468 snow scooters. There are research and radio stations, and an airport near Longyearbyen (Svalbard Lufthavn) opened in 1975.

Greve, T., *Svalbard: Norway in the Arctic.* 1975
Hisdal, V., *Geography of Svalbard.* Rev. ed., 1984

Jan Mayen

This bleak, desolate and mountainous island of volcanic origin and partly covered by glaciers is situated at 71° N. lat. and 8° 30' W. long., 300 miles north-northeast of Iceland. The total area is 377 sq. km (146 sq. miles). Beerenberg, its highest peak, reaches a height of 2,277 metres. Volcanic activity, which had been dormant, reactivated in Sept. 1970.

There exist several unverified and inconclusive reports of the island's discovery. Its present name derives from the Dutch whaling captain Jan Jacobsz May, who mapped the island in 1614. Jan Mayen was subsequently established as a whaling base for the Dutch Noordsche Compagnie. The island was abandoned in 1638 owing to the near extinction of the local whale population, and remained uninhabited, though occasionally visited by seal hunters and trappers, until 1921 when Norway established a radio and meteorological station. On 8 May 1929 Jan Mayen was officially proclaimed as incorporated into the Kingdom of Norway. Its relation to Norway was finally settled by law of 27 Feb. 1930. A LORAN station (1959) and a CONSOL station (1968) have been established.

Bouvet Island

Bouvetøya

This uninhabited volcanic island, mostly covered by glaciers and situated at 54° 25' S. lat. and 3° 21' E. long., was discovered in 1739 by a French naval officer, Jean Baptiste Loziert Bouvet, but no flag was hoisted until, in 1825, Capt. Norris raised the Union Jack. In 1928 Great Britain waived its claim to the island in favour of Norway, which in Dec. 1927 had occupied it. A law of 27 Feb. 1930 declared Bouvetøya a Norwegian dependency. The area is 49 sq. km (19 sq. miles). Since 1977 Norway has had an automatic meteorological station on the island.

Peter I Island

Peter I Øy

This uninhabited island, situated at 68° 48' S. lat. and 90° 35' W. long., was sighted in 1821 by the Russian explorer, Admiral von Bellingshausen. The first landing was made in 1929 by a Norwegian expedition which hoisted the Norwegian flag. On 1 May 1931 Peter I Island was placed under Norwegian sovereignty, and on 24 March 1933 it was incorporated as a dependency. The area is 156 sq. km (60 sq. miles).

Queen Maud Land

Dronning Maud Land

On 14 Jan. 1939 the Norwegian Cabinet placed that part of the Antarctic Continent from the border of Falkland Islands dependencies in the west to the border of the Australian Antarctic Dependency in the east (between 20° W. and 45° E.) under Norwegian sovereignty. The territory had been explored only by Norwegians and hitherto been ownerless. In 1957 it was given the status of a dependency.

OMAN

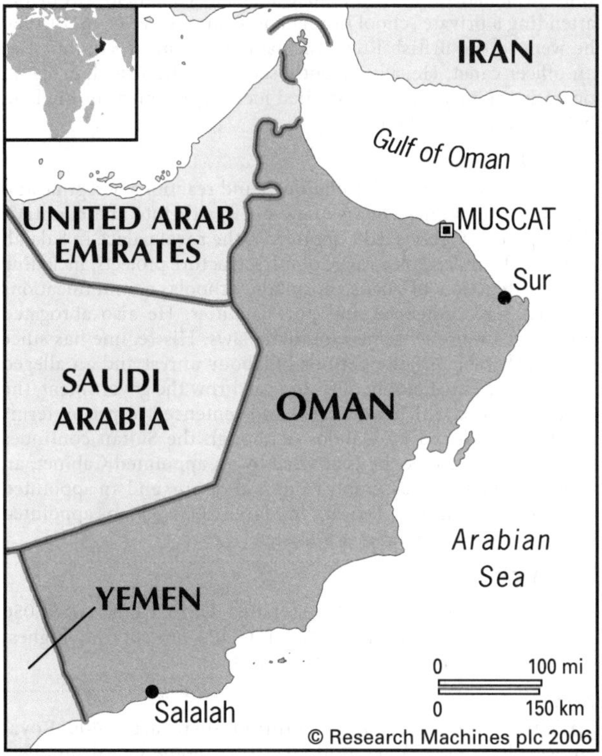

Saltanat 'Uman
(Sultanate of Oman)

Capital: Muscat
Population estimate, 2010: 2·91m.
GDP per capita, 2004: (PPP$) 15,259
HDI/world rank: 0·846/56

KEY HISTORICAL EVENTS

The ancestors of present day Oman are believed to have arrived in two waves of migration, the first from Yemen and the second from northern Arabia. In the 9th century maritime trade flourished and Sohar became the greatest sea port in the Islamic world. In the early 16th century the Portuguese occupied Muscat. The Ya'aruba dynasty introduced a period of renaissance in Omani fortunes both at home and abroad, uniting the country and bringing prosperity; but, on the death in 1718 of Sultan bin Saif II, civil war broke out over the election of his successor. Persian troops occupied Muttrah and Muscat but failed to take Sohar which was defended by Ahmad bin Said, who expelled the Persians from Oman after the civil war had ended. In 1744 the Al bu Said family assumed power and has ruled to the present day. Oman remained largely isolated from the rest of the world until 1970 when Said bin Taimur was deposed by his son Qaboos in a bloodless coup.

TERRITORY AND POPULATION

Situated at the southeast corner of the Arabian peninsula, Oman is bounded in the northeast by the Gulf of Oman and southeast by the Arabian Sea, southwest by Yemen and northwest by Saudi Arabia and the United Arab Emirates. There is an enclave at the northern tip of the Musandam Peninsula. An agreement of April 1992 completed the demarcation of the border with Yemen, and an agreement of March 1990 finalized the border with Saudi Arabia.

With a coastline of 1,700 sq. km from the Strait of Hormuz in the north to the borders of the Republic of Yemen, the Sultanate is strategically located overlooking ancient maritime trade routes linking the Far East and Africa with the Mediterranean.

The Sultanate of Oman occupies a total area of 309,500 sq. km and includes different terrains that vary from plain to highlands and mountains. The coastal plain overlooking the Gulf of Oman and the Arabian Sea forms the most important and fertile plain in Oman.

The **Kuria Muria** islands were ceded to the UK in 1854 by the Sultan of Muscat and Oman. On 30 Nov. 1967 the islands were retroceded to the Sultan of Muscat and Oman, in accordance with the wishes of the population. They are now known as the **Halaniyat Islands**.

In 2003 the census population was 2,340,815 (density 7·6 per sq. km.), chiefly Arabs, and including 0·6m. foreign workers. Estimate, 2007, 2,743,000.

The UN gives an estimated population for 2010 of 2·91m.

In 2005, 71·5% of the population lived in urban areas. The census population of the capital, Muscat, in 2003 was 632,073.

The official language is Arabic; English is in commercial use.

SOCIAL STATISTICS

2002 estimates: births, 71,000; deaths, 10,000. Estimated rates, 2002 (per 1,000 population): births, 25·7; deaths, 3·5. Consequently Oman has a young population, with approximately a third of the population under the age of 15. Expectation of life at birth, 2007, was 74·1 years for males and 77·3 years for females. Average annual population growth rate, 2000–05, 0·9%. Fertility rate, 2004, 3·6 births per woman, down from 7·8 in 1988.

Oman has achieved some of the most rapid advances ever recorded. Infant mortality declined from 200 per 1,000 live births in 1960 to ten per 1,000 live births in 2005, and as recently as 1970 life expectancy was just 40. In the Human Development Index, or HDI (measuring progress in countries in longevity, knowledge and standard of living), Oman's index has improved the most of any country during the past 30 years, rising from 0·487 in 1975 to 0·846 in 2007.

CLIMATE

Oman has a desert climate, with exceptionally hot and humid months from April to Oct., when temperatures may reach 47°C. Light monsoon rains fall in the south from June to Sept., with highest amounts in the western highland region. Muscat, Jan. 28°C, July 46°C. Annual rainfall 101 mm. Salalah, Jan. 29°C, July 32°C. Annual rainfall 98 mm.

CONSTITUTION AND GOVERNMENT

Oman is a hereditary absolute monarchy. The Sultan legislates by decree and appoints a Cabinet to assist him. The Basic Statute of the State was promulgated on 6 Nov. 1996.

The present Sultan is **Qaboos bin Said Al Said** (b. Nov. 1940).

In 1991 a new consultative assembly, the *Majlis al-Shura*, replaced the former State Consultative Chamber. The Majlis consists of 84 elected members. It debates domestic issues, but has no legislative or veto powers. There is also an upper house, the *Majlis al-Dawla*, which consists of 72 appointed members; it too has advisory powers only.

In Dec. 2002 the Sultan of Oman extended voting rights to all citizens over the age of 21.

National Anthem
'Ya Rabbana elifidh lana jalalat al Saltan' ('O Lord, protect for us his majesty the Sultan'); words by Rashid bin Aziz, tune by Rodney Bashford.

GOVERNMENT CHRONOLOGY
Sultans since 1932.
1932–70 Said bin Taimur Al Said
1970– Qaboos bin Said Al Said

RECENT ELECTIONS
The last elections to the *Majlis al-Shura* were on 27 Oct. 2007. No parties are allowed. 84 legislators were chosen for four-year terms from among 631 candidates, including 21 women (although no women were elected).

CURRENT ADMINISTRATION
The Sultan is nominally Prime Minister and Minister of Foreign Affairs, Defence and Finance.

In March 2010 the other Ministers were:

Special Representative of the Sultan: Thuwayni bin Shihab Al Said.

Deputy Prime Minister for Cabinet Affairs: Fahd bin Mahmud Al Said. *Minister Responsible for Defence Affairs:* Sayyid Badr bin Saud bin Harib Al Busaidi. *Minister Responsible for Foreign Affairs:* Yusuf bin Alawi bin Abdallah. *Agriculture:* Salim bin Hilal bin Ali Al Khalili. *Awqaf and Religious Affairs:* Abdallah bin Muhammad bin Abdallah Al Salimi. *Civil Service:* Sheikh Mohammed bin Abdullah Al Harthi. *Commerce and Industry:* Maqbul bin Ali bin Sultan. *Education:* Yahya bin Saud bin Mansour Al Suleimi. *Environment and Climate Change:* Sayyid Hamoud bin Faisal Al Busaidi. *Fisheries:* Sheikh Mohammed bin Ali Al Qatabi. *Health:* Dr Ali bin Muhammad bin Musa. *Higher Education:* Rawya bint Saud Al Busaidi. *Housing:* Sheikh Saif bin Mohammed bin Saif Al Shabibi. *Information:* Hamad bin Mohammed bin Mohsin Al Rashdi. *Interior:* Saud bin Ibrahim bin Saud Al Busaidi. *Justice:* Muhammad bin Abdallah bin Zahir Al Hinai. *Legal Affairs:* Muhammad bin Ali bin Nasir Al Alawi. *Manpower:* Abdullah bin Nasser Al Bakri. *National Economy:* Ahmad bin Abd Al Nabi Al Makki. *National Heritage and Culture:* Sayyid Haitham bin Tariq Al Said. *Oil and Gas:* Muhammad bin Hamad bin Seif Al Rumhi. *Regional Municipalities and Water Resources:* Abdullah bin Salem bin Amer Al Rawas. *Social Development:* Sharifa bint Khalfan bin Nasser Al Yahyaeyah. *Sport:* Ali bin Masoud bin Ali Al Sunaidi. *Tourism:* Rajiha bint Abdul Amir bin Ali. *Transportation and Communications:* Khamis bin Mubarak bin Issa Al Alawi. *Diwan of the Royal Court:* Said Ali bin Hamoud Al Busaidi. *Royal Office:* Gen. Ali bin Majid Al Mamari. *Minister of State and Governor of the Capital:* Sayyid Al Mutassim bin Hamoud Al Busaidi. *Minister of State and Governor of Dhofar:* Shaikh Mohammed bin Marhoon bin Ali Al Maamari. *Secretary General of the Council of Ministers:* Sayyid Khalid bin Hilal bin Saud bin Harib Al Busaidi.

CURRENT LEADERS

Qaboos bin Said

Position
Sultan

Introduction
Qaboos has been the Sultan since 23 July 1970 when he deposed his father, Said bin Taimur. He has carried out an ambitious social and economic modernization programme, opening Oman to the outside world through accession to the League of Arab States, Gulf Co-operation Council and United Nations and pursuing a moderate regional foreign policy while preserving a longstanding political and military relationship with the United Kingdom. He is currently prime minister, minister of defence, minister of foreign affairs, minister of finance and chairman of the central bank.

Early Life
Born in Salalah on 18 Nov. 1940, Qaboos was taught locally before attending a private school in England from the age of 16. In 1960 he went to the British Royal Military Academy at Sandhurst as an officer cadet. He subsequently served in the British army on operational duty and then studied local government in England before returning to Oman.

Career in Office
Concerned at his father's isolationist and reactionary regime and inability to channel Oman's new oil wealth into the country's development, Qaboos led a coup from the royal palace in Salalah in 1970. He undertook a range of infrastructure projects, including the construction of roads, hospitals, schools, communications systems, and industrial and port facilities. He also abrogated his father's more extreme moralistic laws. His regime has since remained stable despite periods of labour unrest and an alleged Islamist extremist plot in 2005 to overthrow the government, the perpetrators of which were tried and sentenced to prison terms but then pardoned by Qaboos. Although the Sultan continues to legislate by decree, he is advised by an appointed Cabinet, an elected consultative assembly (*Majlis al-Shura*) and an appointed upper house (*Majlis al-Dawla*). In March 2004 Qaboos appointed Oman's first female Cabinet minister.

DEFENCE
Military expenditure in 2006 totalled US$3,276m. (US$1,056 per capita), representing 9·0% of GDP—one of the highest percentages of any country in the world.

Army
Strength (2007) 25,000. In addition there are 6,400 Royal Household troops. A paramilitary tribal home guard numbers 4,000.

Navy
The main naval base is at Wudam. Naval personnel in 2007 totalled 4,200.

The wholly separate Royal Yacht Squadron consists of a yacht, a support ship with helicopter and troop-carrying capability, and a dhow.

Air Force
The Air Force, formed in 1959, has 64 combat capable aircraft including F-16s, Jaguars and Hawks.

Personnel (2007) 5,000.

INTERNATIONAL RELATIONS
A 1982 Memorandum of Understanding with the UK provided for regular consultations on international and bilateral issues.

Oman is a member of the UN, World Bank, IMF and several other UN specialized agencies, WTO, Islamic Development Bank, OIC, Gulf Co-operation Council and League of Arab States.

ECONOMY
Oil and natural gas accounted for 48% of GDP in 2006; trade, restaurants and hotels 12%; manufacturing 10%; and services 8%.

Overview
Oman is diversifying its economy by increasing investment in tourism, shipping and infrastructure. Nonetheless, crude oil still accounts for over two-thirds of total exports. Growth since 2006 has been strong, averaging over 6%, supported by high oil prices and accelerated growth of non-hydrocarbon sectors including petrochemicals, trade, and transport and communications. Higher global commodity prices, domestic demand growth

(prompted by fiscal stimuli) and strong private sector credit growth have placed upward pressure on inflation. The economy continues to register strong fiscal and external surpluses that support infrastructure investment and consumption. The current account surplus narrowed in 2007 to 10% of GDP (down from 12% in 2006).

The Seventh Five-Year Development Plan from 2006 allows for the expansion of liquefied natural gas output capacity, the development of gas-based and non-hydrocarbon industries such as manufacturing and tourism, and the creation of new employment opportunities for the rapidly growing population. Medium-term growth prospects are positive, so long as energy prices remain favourable and progress is made in diversification. The banking sector reflects well-capitalized and profitable institutions. However, unemployment is a major concern, with authorities prioritizing education and training to raise the productivity of the labour force.

Currency

The unit of currency is the *Rial Omani* (OMR). It is divided into 1,000 *baiza*. The rial is pegged to the US dollar. In July 2005 foreign exchange reserves were US$4,511m. and gold reserves totalled 1,000 troy oz (291,000 troy oz in April 2002). Total money supply was RO 1,067m. in May 2005. Inflation was 1·9% in 2005, rising to 3·4% in 2006, 5·9% in 2007 and further still to 12·6% in 2008.

In 2001 the six Gulf Arab states—Oman, along with Bahrain, Kuwait, Qatar, Saudi Arabia and the United Arab Emirates—signed an agreement to establish a single currency by 2010. However, Oman withdrew from the scheme in 2007.

Budget

Budget revenue and expenditure (in RO 1m.):

	2001	*2002*	*2003*	*2004*	*2005*
Revenue	2,539·8	3,009·5	3,305·3	4,062·4	4,556·9
Expenditure	2,860·2	2,939·5	3,188·9	3,809·9	4,207·6

In 2005 approximately 80% of total revenue came from oil.

Performance

Real GDP growth was 4·9% in 2005, 6·0% in 2006, 7·7% in 2007 and 7·8% in 2008. Total GDP in 2006 was US$35·7bn.

Banking and Finance

The bank of issue is the Central Bank of Oman, which commenced operations in 1975 (*President*, Hamood Sangour Al Zadjali). All banks must comply with BIS capital adequacy ratios and have a minimum capital of RO 20m. (minimum capital requirement for foreign banks established in Oman is RO 3m.). In 2002 there were 15 commercial banks (of which nine were foreign) and three specialized banks. The largest bank is BankMuscat SAOG, with assets of RO 1·3bn. It was created in 2000 following a merger between BankMuscat and the Commercial Bank of Oman.

There is a stock exchange in Muscat, which is linked with those in Bahrain and Kuwait.

ENERGY AND NATURAL RESOURCES

Environment

Oman's carbon dioxide emissions from the consumption and flaring of fossil fuels in 2008 were the equivalent of 13·2 tonnes per capita.

Electricity

Installed capacity was 3·0m. kW in 2004. Production in 2004 was 11·50bn. kWh, with consumption per capita 5,079 kWh.

Oil and Gas

The economy is dominated by the oil industry. Oil in commercial quantities was discovered in 1964 and production began in 1967. Production in 2008 was 36·0m. tonnes. In 2000 exports of oil stood at 29·5m. tonnes. Total proven reserves in 2008 were 5·6bn. bbls. It was announced in Aug. 2000 that two new oilfields in the south of the country had been discovered, with a potential combined daily production capacity of 12,200 bbls. Earlier in 2000 oil began to be pumped from two further recently-discovered oilfields.

Gas is likely to become the second major source of income for the country. Oman's proven natural gas reserves were 980bn. cu. metres in 2008 (570bn. cu. metres in 1998). Natural gas production was 24·1bn. cu. metres in 2008 (5·2bn. cu. metres in 1998).

Water

Oman relies on a combination of aquifers and desalination plants for its water, augmented by a construction programme of some 60 recharge dams. Desalination plants at Ghubriah and Wadi Adai provide most of the water needs of the capital area. In 2005 water production was 32,951m. gallons.

Minerals

Production in 2005 (in 1,000 tonnes): limestone, 1,000; gypsum (2002), 60; copper cathode, 25; chromite (2004), 19; salt (2002), 14; silver, 4,659 kg; gold, 323 kg. The mountains of the Sultanate of Oman are rich in mineral deposits; these include chromite, coal, asbestos, manganese, gypsum, limestone and marble. The government is studying the exploitation of gold, platinum and sulphide.

Agriculture

Agriculture and fisheries are the traditional occupations of Omanis and remain important to the people and economy of Oman to this day. The country now produces a wide variety of fresh fruit, vegetables and field crops. The country is rapidly moving towards its goal of self-sufficiency in agriculture with the total area under cultivation standing at over 70,000 ha. and total output more than 1m. tonnes. This has not been achieved without effort. In a country where water is a scarce commodity it has meant educating farmers on efficient methods of irrigation and building recharge dams to make the most of infrequent rainfall. In 2002 there were an estimated 38,000 ha. of arable land and 43,000 ha. of permanent crops. Approximately 62,000 ha. were irrigated in 2002. In 2002, 35·2% of the economically active population were engaged in agriculture.

The coastal plain (Batinah) northwest of Muscat is fertile, as are the Dhofar highlands in the south. In the valleys of the interior, as well as on the Batinah coastal plain, date cultivation has reached a high level, and there are possibilities of agricultural development. Agricultural products, 2004 estimates (in 1,000 tonnes): dates, 239; tomatoes, 43; bananas, 33; watermelons, 27. Vegetable and fruit production are also important, and livestock are raised in the south where there are monsoon rains. Camels (125,000 in 2004) are bred by the inland tribes. Other livestock, 2004: sheep, 355,000; cattle, 315,000; goats, 1m.; chickens, 3·4m.

Fisheries

The catch was 150,571 tonnes in 2005, exclusively sea fish. More than 80% is taken by some 85,000 self-employed fishermen.

INDUSTRY

Apart from oil production, copper smelting and cement production, there are light industries, mainly food processing and chemical products. The government gives priority to import substitute industries.

Labour

Males constituted 83·9% of the economically active population in 2000. In 2003 there were 482,632 employees in the private sector and 123,045 persons in government service. The employment of foreign labour is being discouraged following 'Omanization' regulations of 1994.

INTERNATIONAL TRADE

Total foreign debt was US$3,472m. in 2005. A royal decree of 1994 permits up to 65% foreign ownership of Omani companies with a five-year tax and customs duties exemption.

Oman, along with Bahrain, Kuwait, Qatar, Saudi Arabia and the United Arab Emirates entered into a customs union in Jan. 2003.

Imports and Exports

Imports and exports in US$1m.:

	2003	*2004*	*2005*	*2006*	*2007*
Imports c.i.f.	6,801	8,796	8,970	11,038	16,025
Exports f.o.b.	12,196	13,381	18,692	21,586	24,692

Main import suppliers, 2006: United Arab Emirates, 25·5%; Japan, 17·1%; India, 5·2%; USA, 5·2%. In 2004 crude oil exports made up approximately 68% of total exports. Main export markets in 2006 were: China, 26·5%; South Korea, 16·0%; Thailand, 12·4%; United Arab Emirates, 9·5%.

COMMUNICATIONS

Roads

A network of adequate graded roads links all the main sectors of population, and only a few mountain villages are not accessible by motor vehicles. In 2005 there were about 42,300 km of roads (16,500 km paved) including 953 km of dual carriageway. In 2007 there were 453,400 passenger cars in use (174 per 1,000 inhabitants), 113,300 vans and lorries, and 26,400 buses and coaches. In 2007 there were 8,816 road accidents and 798 deaths. With 30·7 deaths per 100,000 population in 2007, Oman has among the highest death rates in road accidents of any country.

Civil Aviation

The national airline is Oman Air, which in 2007 had 15 aircraft and served 26 destinations. Oman formerly had a 50% share in Gulf Air with Bahrain, but withdrew in May 2007. In 2002 Seeb International Airport (Muscat) handled 2,314,102 passengers and 50,008 tonnes of freight.

There are plans to expand Oman's two major airports, Seeb International and Salalah (mainly domestic flights).

Shipping

In Mutrah a deep-water port (named Mina Qaboos) was completed in 1974. The annual handling capacity is 1·5m. tonnes. Mina Salalah, the port of Salalah, has a capacity of 1m. tonnes per year. Sea-going shipping totalled 19,000 GRT in 2002.

Telecommunications

In 2008 there were 274,200 main (fixed) telephone lines in Oman; mobile phone subscribers numbered 3,219,300 in 2008 (115·6 per 100 persons). There were 180,000 PCs in use in 2006 and an estimated 557,000 internet users in 2008.

Postal Services

In 2003 there were 610 post offices. 32m. items of mail were processed in 2003.

SOCIAL INSTITUTIONS

Justice

The population in penal institutions in 2000 was 2,020 (81 per 100,000 of national population). The death penalty is in force, but has not been used since 2001.

Education

Adult literacy was 81·4% in 2003. In 2003–04 there were 1,022 schools. The total number of pupils in state education in 2003–04 was 576,472 (139,082 in basic education and 437,390 in general education) with 32,345 teachers (13,939 in basic education and 18,406 in general education). Oman's first university, the Sultan Qaboos University, opened in 1986 and in 2003–04 there were 12,437 students.

In 2006 public expenditure on education came to 4·2% of GNI and 31·1% of total government spending (the highest percentage of any country).

Health

In 2003 there were 49 hospitals with 4,501 beds. There were also 129 health centres. In 2002 there were 3,478 doctors, 297 dentists, 594 pharmacists and 8,004 nursing staff.

RELIGION

In 2001, 83·5% of the population were Muslim. There were also Hindu and Christian minorities.

CULTURE

World Heritage Sites

The four sites on the UNESCO World Heritage List under Omani jurisdiction are (with the year entered on the list): Bahla Fort (1987); the archaeological sites of Bat, Al-Khutm and Al-Ayn, a collection of settlements and necropolises of the 3rd millennium BC (1988); the Frankincense Trail, a group of archaeological sites representing the production and distribution of frankincense (2000); and the five ancient Aflaj irrigation systems (2006). A fifth site, the Arabian Oryx Sanctuary, was removed from the list after the Omani government decided to reduce the size of the protected area by 90%.

Broadcasting

Radio Oman (broadcasting in Arabic and English) and Oman TV are government-operated. Satellite services from neighbouring states are available. The first private radio station began transmitting in May 2007. Oman had the greatest increase in the number of TV receivers per 1,000 inhabitants (31 up to 563) of any country in the world between 1980 and 2000. In 2003 there were 307,000 TV-equipped households but 1·56m. TV sets. Colour is by PAL.

Press

In 2006 there were six daily newspapers with a combined circulation of 165,000.

Tourism

Non-resident tourists numbered 1,195,000 in 2004; spending by tourists in 2005 totalled US$679m. In 2005 there were 153 hotels with a total of over 7,200 rooms. Tourism accounts for 1% of GDP.

Festivals

National Day (18 Nov.); Spring Festival in Salalah (July–Aug.); Ramadan (Aug.–Sept. in 2010; Aug. in 2011).

Libraries

Three public libraries are run by the Royal Court of Diwan, the Islamic Institute and the Ministry of National Heritage.

Theatre and Opera

There is one national theatre.

Museums and Galleries

The main attractions are the Omani Museum (est. 1974) at Medinat al-Alam; the Omani-French Museum, Children's Museum and Bait al-Zubair (a historic house) at Muscat; the Natural History Museum at the Ministry of National Heritage and Culture; the National Museum; Salalah Museum; the Sultan's Armed Forces museum at Bait al-Falaj; the Oil & Gas Exhibition at Mina al-Fahal. There is also a museum in the historic fort at Sohar.

In 2005 total museum attendance was 92,000.

DIPLOMATIC REPRESENTATIVES

Of Oman in the United Kingdom (167 Queen's Gate, London, SW7 5HE)
Ambassador: Vacant.
Chargé d'Affaires a.i: Yousuf Ahmed Hamed Al Jabri.

Of the United Kingdom in Oman (PO Box 185, Mina Al Fahal, Postal Code 116, Muscat)
Ambassador: Dr Noel Guckian, OBE.

Of Oman in the USA (2535 Belmont Rd, NW, Washington, D.C., 20008)
Ambassador: Hunaina Sultan Ahmed Al-Mughairi.

Of the USA in Oman (PO Box 202, Medinat Qaboos, Muscat)
Ambassador: Richard J. Schmierer.

Of Oman to the United Nations
Ambassador: Fuad Mubarak Al-Hinai.

Of Oman to the European Union
Ambassador: Sheikh Ghazi Bin Said Al-Bahar Al-Rawas.

FURTHER READING

Ghubash, Hussein, *Oman: The Islamic Democratic Tradition.* 2005
Manea, Elham, *Regional Politics in the Gulf: Saudi Arabia, Oman and Yemen.* 2005
Oman. A Country Study. 2004
Owtram, Francis, *A Modern History of Oman: Formation of the State since 1920.* 2002
Skeet, I., *Oman: Politics and Development.* 1992

National Statistical Office: Ministry of National Economy, Information and Documentation Centre, POB 881, Muscat 113.
Website: http://www.mone.gov.om

PAKISTAN

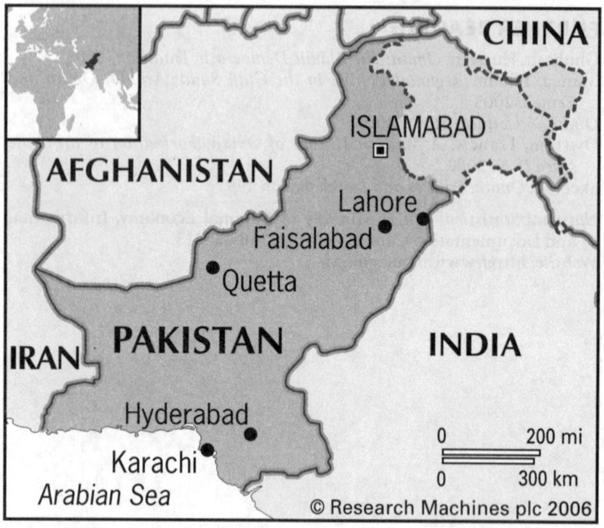

Islami Jamhuriya e Pakistan
(Islamic Republic of Pakistan)

Capital: Islamabad
Population estimate, 2010: 184·75m.
GDP per capita, 2007: (PPP$) 2,496
HDI/world rank: 0·572/141

KEY HISTORICAL EVENTS

The Neolithic settlement of Mehrgarh in Balochistan, western Pakistan dates from around 7000 BC. Continuously occupied for over 4,000 years, it was a precursor to the Indus Valley civilization, which flourished between 3300 and 1700 BC. Indus Valley settlements spread across much of present-day Pakistan and northwest India, from the Arabian Sea to the foothills of the Himalayas, centring on the cities of Mohenjo-Daro and Harappa. The civilization's decline coincided with the arrival of Indo-European-speaking tribes, including the Aryans, from central Asia. Taxila in northern Pakistan became a centre for the development of Vedic/Hindu culture from the 6th century BC.

Under the influence of the Persian Achaemenid Empire from around 550 BC, most of present-day Pakistan was ruled by Darius the Great from Persepolis after 515 BC. Alexander the Great, conqueror of the Persian Empire, invaded northern Pakistan in 326 BC but was superseded by the Maurya dynasty from around 300 BC. Its emperor, Ashoka the Great, ruled over central Asia and much of the Indian sub-continent between 273 and 232 BC. The Indus Valley came under Greco-Bactrian control from around 180 BC, bringing about a fusion of classical Greek culture and Buddhism. Invasions by Scythians and Parthians were followed by the arrival of the Yuechi from the steppes of western China. They established the Buddhist Kushan dynasty in the first century AD. Centred on Peshawar, it linked the Silk Road with the Arabian Sea and the Ganges Valley.

Arab settlers introduced Islam early in the 8th century. In 712 Muhammad ibn Qasim conquered Sindh province and incorporated it into the Umayyad Caliphate, ruled from Baghdad. Over the next three centuries the southern provinces of Multan and Balochistan were also absorbed. In 1005 Peshawar was conquered by the Turkic-Afghan warlord, Sultan Mahmud of Ghazni, who went on to take Punjab, Kashmir and Balochistan. The Ghaznavid Dynasty made Lahore one of its key cities—the easternmost outpost of Islam—though it was destroyed during Genghis Khan's Mongol invasion of 1219.

In the late 13th century northern and eastern Pakistan came under the influence of Islamic sultanates. Centred on Delhi, they gradually gained control of most of the Indian subcontinent. Timur-i Lang seized Persia, Afghanistan and western Pakistan in the 1380s, absorbing them into a vast central Asian empire. Babur, the founder of the Moghul dynasty in the early 16th century, initially made Kabul his capital, before power transferred to Lahore, Delhi and Agra. While most of the Indian sub-continent remained part of a united Moghul empire between the 16th and 19th centuries, the northwestern fringe was attacked by Persians in the 1730s and Sindh and Punjab were incorporated into Ahmad Shah Durrani's Afghan state from 1747.

The British, who established a protectorate in Bengal in 1757 and subsequently controlled much of the sub-continent, attempted to secure the anarchic northwest against Russian expansion in the first Afghan War (1838–42). Although Sindh and the Punjab were absorbed into British India in the 1840s, Balochistan and Afghanistan remained independent. Following Britain's failure to win these mountainous regions in the second Afghan War (1878–80), the North-West Frontier Province was created in 1901 as a semi-autonomous region.

Hindu–Muslim tensions escalated and in the 1930s the poet Muhammad Iqbal proposed a separate Muslim nation, an idea taken up by Muhammad Ali Jinnah, leader of the Muslim League. Following the League's victories in most of the majority-Muslim constituencies in the 1946 elections, the British agreed to the formation of East and West Pakistan under the 1947 Independence of India Act. Jinnah became West Pakistan's governor-general in the new capital, Karachi.

The partition of India saw 14m. people leaving their homes, with violence claiming 500,000 lives on both sides of the border. The signing over to India of Kashmir in Oct. 1947 was disputed by Pakistan. War broke out until a UN-brokered ceasefire and temporary border was agreed in 1949. In 1951 Pakistan's first prime minister, Liaquat Ali Kahn, was assassinated. The popularity of the Muslim League declined and Pakistan became increasingly unstable.

1958 saw the first of several periods of martial law, followed by the rule of Field Marshal Mohammad Ayub Khan (until 1969) and Gen. Agha Mohammad Yahya Khan (until 1971). Discontent in East Pakistan with the federal government led to calls by the Awami League for full autonomy. Following East Pakistan's declaration of independence as Bangladesh in March 1971, West Pakistan sent in troops, sparking civil war. Hundreds of thousands died and 10m. refugees fled to India. The surrender of Pakistan's forces to the Indian army in Dhaka on 16 Dec. 1971 cleared the way to an independent Bangladesh.

A new constitution in 1973 provided for a federal parliamentary government with a president and prime minister. Zulfiquar Ali Bhutto, representing the Pakistan People's Party (PPP), became premier. Considered by traditionalists to be insufficiently Islamic, in July 1977 Gen. Mohammad Zia ul-Haq led an army coup against Ali Bhutto, who was hanged for conspiracy to murder. His daughter, Benazir, led the PPP to victory in the elections in 1988 but was dismissed on charges of corruption and incompetence in 1990. Reinstated as prime minister following elections in 1993, President Farooq Leghari overthrew her administration in 1996.

Indo–Pakistani relations have foundered over Kashmir. In May 1998 Pakistan carried out five nuclear tests in the deserts of Balochistan in response to India's tests earlier in the month.

US President Bill Clinton invoked sanctions but Pakistan carried out a sixth test. On 11 June, following India's example, Pakistan announced a unilateral moratorium on nuclear tests. On 12 Oct. 1999 Gen. Pervez Musharraf seized power in a coup, overthrowing the democratically-elected government of Nawaz Sharif after Sharif tried to dismiss Musharraf as army chief of staff. Sharif was convicted of corruption and sentenced to life imprisonment.

Negotiations with India over Kashmir began in July 1999. In May 2001 India ended its six-month long ceasefire but invited Pakistan for further talks, prompting hopes of avoiding more violence. Following the attacks on New York and Washington of 11 Sept. 2001 Pakistan found itself central to the war against terrorism. Neighbouring Afghanistan was believed to be sheltering Osama bin Laden and the USA persuaded Musharraf to allow its forces to use Pakistani air bases. In return the USA lifted its remaining sanctions. In Dec. 2001 suicide bombers attacked the Indian parliament. Although no-one claimed responsibility, the Indian authorities suspected Kashmiri separatists, heightening Indo-Pakistani tensions. Musharraf's subsequent crackdown on militants helped to reduce tension between the two countries.

An attack on an Indian army base in Indian-occupied Kashmir in May 2002, killing 31, was linked to terrorists infiltrating from Pakistan. Musharraf drew widespread criticism for failing to combat terrorism in the region. In Nov. 2003 Pakistan and India agreed to another ceasefire along Kashmir's Line of Control. Relations gradually improved and in April 2005 bus services resumed across the divided territory for the first time in 60 years.

In Oct. 2005 Pakistan-administered Kashmir was struck by an earthquake which killed 73,300 people and left 3m. homeless. In 2006 there was an upsurge in violence by tribal groups in Balochistan demanding greater autonomy. Bomb blasts rocked Karachi and Islamabad in early 2007 and 68 passengers were killed in an explosion on a train travelling between Lahore and New Delhi. Musharraf's decision to suspend the chief justice of the Supreme Court, Iftikhar Mohammad Chaudhry, for alleged abuse of power in March 2007 sparked riots in Karachi.

In July 2007 security forces stormed Islamabad's Red Mosque, considered to have close links with militant groups. At the end of a week-long siege, over 100 people were killed and 250 injured. In Oct. 2007 Musharraf won the presidential election, though the Supreme Court refused to confirm the result until it had ruled on Musharraf's eligibility to stand while still head of the army. The court dismissed challenges to the result the following month. Meanwhile, fighting intensified in Waziristan, a stronghold of Islamic militant groups.

The assassination of leading opposition figure Benazir Bhutto in Dec. 2007 ahead of elections in Jan. 2008 threw the already fragile political climate into turmoil. The election was rescheduled for Feb. when the leading opposition parties, including Bhutto's, won a resounding victory against pro-Musharraf parties and formed a coalition government. Musharraf's presidency was severely weakened as a result and he eventually resigned in Aug. 2008. In Sept. 2008 Asif Ali Zardari was elected his successor. His term in office has seen continued fighting between government forces and Islamic militant groups linked with several high-profile attacks including the Mumbai bombings of Nov. 2008 and an assault on the visiting Sri Lankan cricket team in March 2009. In Oct. 2009 the military launched an offensive against Taliban forces in the South Waziristan region. Since then more than 500 civilians have been killed in terrorist attacks throughout the country.

TERRITORY AND POPULATION

Pakistan is bounded in the west by Iran, northwest by Afghanistan, north by China, east by India and south by the Arabian Sea. The area (excluding the disputed area of Kashmir) is 796,096 sq. km (307,374 sq. miles); population (1998 census, excluding the autonomous states Azad-Kashmir and Gilgit-Baltistan), 132,352,279 (68,873,686 males). In 2005, 65·1% lived in rural areas. There were 2·0m. refugees in 2007, mostly from Afghanistan, the highest number in any country in the world.

The UN gives an estimated population for 2010 of 184·75m.; density, 232 per sq. km.

The population of the principal cities is as follows:

1998 census					
Karachi	9,339,023	Multan	1,197,384	Peshawar	982,816
Lahore	5,143,495	Hyderabad	1,166,894	Quetta	565,137
Faisalabad	2,008,861	Gujranwala	1,132,509	Islamabad	529,180
Rawalpindi	1,409,768				

Population of the four provinces and two territories (census of 1998):

	Area (sq. km)	*1998 census population (in 1,000) Total*	*Male*	*Female*	*Urban*	*Density per sq. km*
North-West Frontier Province[1]	74,521	17,744	9,089	8,655	2,994	238
Federally Administered Tribal Areas[2]	27,220	3,176	1,652	1,524	85	117
Federal Capital Territory Islamabad[2]	906	805	434	371	529	889
Punjab[1]	205,345	73,621	38,094	35,527	23,019	359
Sindh[1]	140,914	30,440	16,098	14,342	14,840	216
Balochistan[1]	347,190	6,566	3,507	3,059	1,569	19

[1]Province. [2]Territory.

English, the official language, is used in business, higher education and in central government; Urdu is the national language and the *lingua franca*, although only spoken as a first language by about 8% of the population. Around 48% of the population speak Punjabi.

SOCIAL STATISTICS

Estimates, 2002: births, 4,310,000; deaths, 1,230,000. Estimated birth rate in 2002 was 28·7 per 1,000 population; estimated death rate, 8·2. Infant mortality (per 1,000 live births), 80 (2005). Formal registration of marriages and divorces has not been required since 1992. Expectation of life in 2007 was 65·9 years for men and 66·5 years for women. Annual population growth rate, 2000–05, 2·0%. Fertility rate, 2004, 4·1 births per woman.

CLIMATE

A weak form of tropical monsoon climate occurs over much of the country, with arid conditions in the north and west, where the wet season is only from Dec. to March. Elsewhere, rain comes mainly in the summer. Summer temperatures are high everywhere, but winters can be cold in the mountainous north. Islamabad, Jan. 50°F (10°C), July 90°F (32·2°C). Annual rainfall 36" (900 mm). Karachi, Jan. 61°F (16·1°C), July 86°F (30°C). Annual rainfall 8" (196 mm). Lahore, Jan. 53°F (11·7°C), July 89°F (31·7°C). Annual rainfall 18" (452 mm). Multan, Jan. 51°F (10·6°C), July 93°F (33·9°C). Annual rainfall 7" (170 mm). Quetta, Jan. 38°F (3·3°C), July 80°F (26·7°C). Annual rainfall 10" (239 mm).

CONSTITUTION AND GOVERNMENT

Under the 1973 constitution, the *President* was elected for a five-year term by a college of parliamentary deputies, senators and members of the Provincial Assemblies. Parliament is bicameral, comprising a *Senate* of 100 members and a *National Assembly* of 342. In the *Senate*, each of the four provinces is allocated 14 seats, while the federally administered tribal areas and the federal capital are assigned eight and two seats respectively. In addition, each province is conferred four seats for technocrats and four for women. Two seats, one for technocrats and another for women, are reserved for the federal capital. The *National Assembly* is directly elected for five-year terms. 272 members are elected in single-seat constituencies, there are ten seats for non-Muslim minorities and 60 seats for women.

Following the 1999 coup Gen. Musharraf announced that the Constitution was to be held 'in abeyance' and issued a 'Provisional Constitution Order No. 1' in its place. In Aug. 2002 he unilaterally amended the constitution to grant himself the right to dissolve parliament.

During the period of martial law from 1977–85 the Constitution was also in abeyance, but not abrogated. In 1985 it was amended to extend the powers of the President, including those of appointing and dismissing ministers and vetoing new legislation until 1990. Legislation of 1 April 1997 abolished the President's right to dissolve parliament, appoint provincial governors and nominate the heads of the armed services.

Gen. Pervez Musharraf, Chief of the Army Staff, assumed the responsibilities of the chief executive of the country following the removal of Prime Minister Nawaz Sharif on 12 Oct. 1999. He formed a National Security Council consisting of six members belonging to the armed forces and a number of civilians with expertise in various fields. A Federal Cabinet of Ministers was also installed working under the guidance of the National Security Council. Also formed was the National Reconstruction Bureau, a think tank providing institutional advice and input on economic, social and institutional matters. The administration declared that it intended to first restore economic order before holding general elections to install a civilian government. The Supreme Court of Pakistan allowed the administration a three-year period, which expired on 12 Oct. 2002, to accomplish this task. Elections were held on 10 Oct. 2002. On 30 April 2002 a referendum was held in which 97·7% voted in favour of extending Musharraf's rule by a further five years. Turnout was around 50%. He amended the constitution in Aug. 2002 to formally extend his mandate by five years. The constitution was further amended in Dec. 2003 to enhance Musharraf's power and allow a vote of confidence in his presidency.

In March 2007 Musharraf announced his intention to stand for a five-year presidential term. The Supreme Court rejected his candidacy while opposition parties challenged his constitutional right to hold the presidency and head the military. In Sept. 2007 the Supreme Court's earlier judgement was overturned and the following month Musharraf was granted a further term of office by the national parliament and provincial assemblies. However, the Supreme Court refused to sanction the appointment until the surrounding legal questions had been resolved. In Nov. 2007 Musharraf suspended the constitution and imposed martial rule. Several prominent members of the judiciary and opposition leaders, including Benazir Bhutto and Imran Khan, were arrested or jailed. The Constitution was reinstated in Dec. but judicial freedom was severely compromised by the dismissal of senior court officials. Amendments were introduced to extend the military's power to try citizens and facilitate the arrest of political opponents. Following Musharraf's resignation in Aug. 2008, ousted Chief Justice Iftikhar Chaudry was reinstated in March 2009. The 2007 amendments to the constitution were subsequently revoked in July 2009 and in Aug. the Supreme Court ruled that Musharraf's actions had been illegal.

National Anthem

'Pak sarzamin shadbad' ('Blessed be the sacred land'); words by Abul Asr Hafeez Jaulandhari, tune by Ahmad G. Chaagla.

GOVERNMENT CHRONOLOGY

Heads of State since 1947. (ML = Muslim League; n/p = non partisan; PML-N = Pakistan Muslim League-Nawaz Sharif; PML-Q = Pakistan Muslim League (Quaid-e-Azam); PPP = Pakistan People's Party; RP = Republican Party)

Governors-General

1947–48	ML	Mohammad Ali Jinnah
1948–51	ML	Khwaja Nazimaddin
1951–55	ML	Ghulam Mohammad
1955–56	military	Iskander Ali Mirza

Presidents of the Republic

1956–58	RP	Iskander Ali Mirza
1958–69	military	Mohammad Ayub Khan
1969–71	military	Agha Mohammad Yahya Khan
1971–73	PPP	Zulfiqar Ali Bhutto
1973–78	PPP	Fazal Elahi Chaudhry
1978–88	military	Mohammad Zia ul-Haq
1988–93	n/p	Ghulam Ishaq Khan
1993–97	PPP	Farooq Ahmed Khan Leghari
1998–2001	PML-N	Mohammad Rafiq Tarar
2001–08	military	Pervez Musharraf
2008	PML-Q	Mohammadmian Soomro (acting)
2008–	PPP	Asif Ali Zardari

RECENT ELECTIONS

Parliamentary elections were held on 18 Feb. 2008 having been delayed following the assassination of Benazir Bhutto, the leader of the Pakistan People's Party (PPP), in Dec. 2007. Turnout was 44·5%. The PPP gained 87 of the National Assembly's 272 elected seats and received 30·6% of votes cast; the Pakistan Muslim League-N (PML-N, led by ex-prime minister Nawaz Sharif) won 67 seats and received 19·6% of the vote; the pro-Musharraf Pakistan Muslim League (Quaid-e-Azam) (PML-Q) gained 42 seats and 23·0% of the vote; and the United National Movement (MQM) 19 seats with 7·4% of the vote. The remaining seats went to smaller parties and non-partisans. After the election, allocation of seats to women and minority representatives was carried out in accordance with the constitution resulting in the PPP having 121 seats, the PML-N 91 seats, the PML-Q 54 and the MQM 25. On 21 Feb. 2008 the PPP, the PML-N and the Awami National Party agreed to form a coalition government; the PPP's Yousaf Raza Gilani was elected prime minister on 24 March 2008.

In indirect elections held on 6 Sept. 2008 Asif Ali Zardari (PPP) was elected president by federal and provincial lawmakers, winning 481 votes against 153 for Saeeduz Zaman Siddique (PML-N) and 44 for Mushahid Hussain Syed (PML-Q).

CURRENT ADMINISTRATION

President: Asif Ali Zardari; b. 1955 (Pakistan People's Party; since 9 Sept. 2008).

In March 2010 the government comprised:

Prime Minister: Yousaf Raza Gilani; b. 1952 (Pakistan People's Party; sworn in 25 March 2008).

Minister for Commerce: Makhdoom Ameen Faheem. *Communications:* Arbab Alamgir Khan. *Defence:* Chaudhry Ahmed Mukhtar. *Defence Production:* Abdul Qayyum Khan Jatoi. *Education:* Sardar Aseff Ahmed Ali. *Environment:* Hameedullah Jan Afridi. *Finance, Revenue, Planning and Development:* Vacant. *Food and Agriculture:* Nazar Muhammad Gondal. *Foreign Affairs:* Shah Mehmood Qureshi. *Health:* Makhdoom Shahabuddin. *Housing and Works:* Rehmatullah Kakar. *Human Rights:* Syed Mumtaz Alam Gilani. *Industries and Production:* Mir Hazar Khan Bijarani. *Information and Broadcasting:* Qamar Zaman Kaira. *Interior:* Rehman Malik. *Inter-Provincial Co-ordination:* Pir Aftab Hussain Shah Gilani. *Kashmir Affairs and Gilgit-Baltistan:* Mian Manzoor Ahmad Wattoo. *Labour and Manpower:* Syed Khursheed Ahmed Shah. *Law, Justice and Parliamentary Affairs:*

Dr Zaheeruddin Babar Awan. *Livestock and Dairy Development:* Humayun Aziz Kurd. *Local Government and Rural Development:* Abdul Razzaq Thahim. *Minorities:* Shahbaz Bhatti. *Narcotics Control:* Vacant. *Overseas Pakistanis:* Farooq Sattar. *Population Welfare:* Dr Firdous Ashiq Awan. *Ports and Shipping:* Syed Babur Ghauri. *Postal Services:* Mir Israr Ullah Zehri. *Privatization:* Waqar Ahmed Khan. *Railways:* Ghulam Ahmed Bilour. *Religious Affairs:* Syed Hamid Saeed Kazmi. *Social Welfare and Special Education:* Samina Khalid Ghurki. *Special Initiatives:* Lal Muhammad Khan. *Sports:* Mir Aijaz Hussain Jakhrani. *States and Frontier Regions:* Najmuddin Khan. *Textile Industry:* Rana Muhammad Farooq Saeed Khan. *Tourism:* Maulana Atta ur-Rahman. *Water and Power:* Raja Pervaiz Ashraf. *Youth Affairs:* Shahid Hussain Bhutto. *Zakat and Ushr:* Noorul Haq Qadri.

Office of the President: http://www.president.gov.pk

CURRENT LEADERS

Asif Ali Zardari

Position
President

Introduction
Asif Ali Zardari became Pakistan's president in Sept. 2008 following the resignation of Pervez Musharraf. He has been co-chairman of the Pakistan's People's Party (PPP), the largest grouping in the National Assembly, since the assassination of his wife, Benazir Bhutto, in Dec. 2007. A controversial figure, he has struggled to maintain a stable coalition government.

Early Life
Born on 26 July 1955 in Nawabshah, Zardari was brought up and educated in Karachi. He established a career in business and property and in 1983 unsuccessfully contested local elections in Nawabshah. In 1987 Zardari married Benazir Bhutto, then leader-in-exile of the PPP in London. The following year Bhutto became prime minister when the PPP won the general election.

During Bhutto's first term of office Zardari prospered amid rumours of corruption. In 1990 Bhutto was ousted by President Ghulam Ishaq Khan, and Zardari was arrested and jailed on corruption and blackmail charges although never brought to trial. He claimed the action was politically motivated. While in prison Zardari was elected to the National Assembly and in 1993, when Bhutto won a second term as prime minister, the charges against him were dropped. He then served as minister for the environment from 1993–96 and as minister for investment from 1995–96.

In 1996 Bhutto was again removed from office and Zardari was arrested on charges of murder and corruption. He was detained for eight years, during which time he and Bhutto appealed against a Swiss court conviction for money laundering. With Bhutto in exile in Dubai, Zardari continued to deny all charges and claimed political persecution. In 2004 he was freed and the charges against him in Pakistan were dropped. From 2004–07 he lived primarily in the USA, where he received medical treatment for several conditions.

In Nov. 2007 President Musharraf introduced a measure to cancel criminal charges against National Assembly members, clearing the way for Zardari and Bhutto to return to Pakistan. Following Bhutto's assassination during a PPP rally on 27 Dec. 2007, Zardari assumed joint chairmanship of the party with his 19-year-old son, Bilawal. In Feb. 2008 the PPP won the general election in coalition with the Pakistan Muslim League-Nawaz Sharif (PML-N). Zardari and Sharif sought to establish a coalition government and made preparations to impeach Musharraf, who was refusing to relinquish power. Musharraf finally resigned on 18 Aug. 2008 and four days later the PPP nominated Zardari as their presidential candidate. However, on 25 Aug. Sharif took his party out of the coalition, protesting at the concentration of executive power in Zardari's hands and claiming that he had reneged on a promise to reinstate 60 Supreme Court judges. Zardari was elected president on 6 Sept. 2008.

Career in Office
Zardari's first eighteen months in office were marked by political tensions, both domestic and with neighbouring states. In March 2009 he defused mounting friction with the Pakistani judiciary and the PML-N by announcing the reinstatement of former chief justice Iftikhar Chaudhry—sacked by Musharraf in 2007 and since championed by Sharif—in response to widespread popular protests. Zardari had also pledged to reduce some of the powers invested in the presidency, and in Nov. 2009 relinquished his control of the country's nuclear weapons to the prime minister in an apparent effort to deflect growing opposition. This gesture, however, was overshadowed in Dec. as the Supreme Court quashed an earlier legal amnesty protecting Zardari and several political allies from corruption charges, prompting calls for his resignation.

Meanwhile, Zardari's attempt to improve relations with India suffered when militants involved in the Nov. 2008 terrorist attacks in Mumbai were found to have come from Pakistan. He also faced an increasing domestic security threat from Islamic extremists, especially in the volatile northwest region of the country. In response to a series of attacks, government forces launched major military offensives against Taliban militants from April 2009 in the Swat valley and from Oct. in the tribal area of South Waziristan. However, suicide bombings by militants continued unabated in most of Pakistan's major cities into early 2010, further undermining Zardari's political authority.

DEFENCE

A *Council for Defence and National Security* was set up in Jan. 1997, comprising the President, the Prime Minister, the Ministers of Defence, Foreign Affairs, Interior, Finance and the military chiefs of staff. The Council advised the government on the determination of national strategy and security priorities, but was disbanded in Feb. 1997. The Council was revived in Oct. 1999 following the change of government but was to have a wider scope and not restrict itself to defence matters.

Defence expenditure in 2006 totalled US$4,156m. (US$25 per capita), representing 3·2% of GDP. However, following the return of civilian government in March 2008, the 2008–09 defence budget was reduced. Expenditure is also increasingly targeted at developing counter-insurgency capabilities as a result of the threat from Taliban forces along the border with Afghanistan.

As at Oct. 2009 Pakistan had 10,605 personnel serving in UN peacekeeping operations (the largest contingent of any country).

Nuclear Weapons
Pakistan began a secret weapons programme in 1972 to reach parity with India, but was restricted for some years by US sanctions. The Stockholm International Peace Research Institute estimates that Pakistan possesses a minimum of 60 nuclear weapons. In May 1998 Pakistan carried out six nuclear tests in response to India's tests earlier in the month. Pakistan, known to have a nuclear weapons programme, has not signed the Comprehensive Nuclear-Test-Ban-Treaty, which is intended to bring about a ban on any nuclear explosions. According to *Deadly Arsenals*, published by the Carnegie Endowment for International Peace, Pakistan has both chemical and biological weapon research programmes.

Army

Strength (2007) 550,000. There were also about 304,000 personnel in paramilitary units: National Guard, Frontier Corps and Pakistan Rangers.

Most armoured equipment is of Chinese origin including over 2,450 main battle tanks. There is an air wing with fixed-wing aircraft and 26 attack helicopters.

Navy

The combatant fleet includes five French-built diesel submarines, three midget submarines for swimmer delivery and six ex-British frigates. The Naval Air wing operates 16 combat capable aircraft.

The principal naval base and dockyard are at Karachi. There are secondary bases at Gwadar and Ormara. Naval personnel in 2007 totalled 24,000 (including an estimated 1,400 marines and some 2,000 Marine Security Agency personnel).

Air Force

The Pakistan Air Force came into being on 14 Aug. 1947. It has its headquarters at Peshawar and is organized within three air defence sectors, in the northern, central and southern areas of the country. There is an Air Force Academy at Risalpur, which includes a College of Aeronautical Engineering .

Total strength in 2007 was 360 combat capable aircraft and 45,000 personnel. Equipment included Mirage IIIs, Mirage 5s, F-16s, Q-5s and J-7s.

INTERNATIONAL RELATIONS

Pakistan is a member of the UN, World Bank, IMF and several other UN specialized agencies, WTO, Commonwealth (not 1972–89), IOM, Inter-Parliamentary Union, Islamic Development Bank, OIC, Asian Development Bank, Colombo Plan, Economic Co-operation Organization and SAARC. Following Gen. Musharraf's coup in Oct. 1999, Pakistan was suspended from the Commonwealth's councils although the suspension was ended in May 2004. Pakistan was again suspended in Nov. 2007 after President Musharraf declared emergency rule but it was readmitted in May 2008.

ECONOMY

Agriculture accounted for 19·4% of GDP in 2006, industry 27·2% and services 53·4%.

Overview

Agriculture contributes around a quarter of GDP. Pakistan is one of the world's largest producers of raw cotton but historically the country's textile exports have added little value. Chiefly grown in Punjab province, cotton is crucial to the success of the yarn-spinning industry concentrated around Karachi. In recent years Pakistan has enjoyed increased US quotas for higher added value textile products, largely as a result of Pakistan's support for US military action in Afghanistan.

The economy grew strongly in 2004 and 2005, with the agricultural sector posting above-average output. Broad-based growth was supported by sound macroeconomic management and progress in implementing structural reforms and privatization. The health of the financial sector has improved and all but one of Pakistan's public-sector banks have been privatized. However, recent political instabilities have hampered economic performance. 2008 projections suggested real GDP growth of 5% a year for at least four years, fuelled by investment and private consumption, while the economy will continue to rely on textiles, services and manufacturing.

In an uncertain political environment, the focus of the State Bank is on containing inflation. The size of fiscal deficits in the first half of the 2000s, averaging 3·6% of GDP, compares favourably with the 7–8% levels seen throughout the previous two decades. Public debt was also reduced from 75·1% of GDP in 2001 to 50·6% in 2007.

The Oct. 2005 earthquake in northern Pakistan had little impact on Pakistan's total production. However, the cost of reconstruction has put major strain on the public finances and has adversely affected the current-account balance.

Currency

The monetary unit is the *Pakistan rupee* (PKR) of 100 *paisas*. Gold reserves in Sept. 2009 were 2·10m. troy oz; foreign exchange reserves, US$10,418m. Inflation rates (based on IMF statistics):

1999	*2000*	*2001*	*2002*	*2003*	*2004*	*2005*	*2006*	*2007*	*2008*
5·7%	3·6%	4·4%	2·5%	3·1%	4·6%	9·3%	7·9%	7·8%	12·0%

The rupee was devalued by 3·65% in Sept. 1996, 8·5% in Oct. 1996 and 8·7% in Oct. 1997, and by 4·2% in June 1998 in response to the financial problems in Asia. In June 2008 total money supply was Rs3,359·3bn.

Budget

The financial year ends on 30 June. Central government revenues totalled Rs1,066·2bn. in 2005–06 (Rs863·4bn. in 2004–05); expenditures totalled Rs1,162·3bn. in 2005–06 (Rs950·5bn. in 2004–05). Taxes accounted for 75·8% of total revenues in 2005–06.

There is a general sales tax of 16%.

Performance

Real GDP growth rates (based on IMF statistics):

1999	*2000*	*2001*	*2002*	*2003*	*2004*	*2005*	*2006*	*2007*	*2008*
3·7%	4·3%	1·9%	3·2%	4·9%	7·4%	7·7%	6·1%	5·6%	2·0%

Pakistan's total GDP in 2008 was US$168·3bn.

Banking and Finance

The State Bank of Pakistan is the central bank (*Governor*, Syed Salim Raza); it came into operation as the Central Bank on 1 July 1948 and was nationalized in 1974 with other banks. Private commercial bank licences were reintroduced in 1991.

The State Bank of Pakistan is the issuing authority of domestic currency, custodian of foreign exchange reserves and bankers for the federal and provincial governments and for scheduled banks. It also manages the rupee public debt of the federal and provincial governments. The National Bank of Pakistan acts as an agent of the State Bank where the State Bank has no offices of its own.

In Feb. 1994 the State Bank of Pakistan was granted more autonomy to regulate the monetary sector of the economy.

In Dec. 1999 the Supreme Court ruled that Islamic banking methods, whereby interest is not permitted, had to be used from 1 July 2001. However, the decision was rescinded in June 2002. The State Bank offered three options for the implementation of Islamic banking practices: i) banks to establish an independent Islamic bank; ii) the opening of subsidiaries of existing commercial banks; iii) the establishment of new branches to execute Islamic banking procedures.

In Sept. 2003 total assets of public sector commercial banks amounted to Rs980,300m., total assets of local private banks to Rs1,122,400m., total assets of foreign banks to Rs276,900m. and total assets of all commercial banks amounted to Rs2,379,600m. In Dec. 2005 total deposits of scheduled banks (stocks) equalled Rs2,661,697m. and net foreign assets amounted to Rs523,044m.

There were 37 commercial banks in Sept. 2003 (five state-owned and 15 foreign) with assets Rs2,380bn. In 2002 there were 45 leasing banks, operating in accordance with Sharia demands. There is a Federal Bank for Co-operatives.

Foreign direct investment was US$5,438m. in 2008, down from a record high of US$5,590m. in 2007 but up from US$4,273m. in 2006. The total stock of FDI at the end of 2008 was US$31·06bn.

There are stock exchanges in Islamabad, Karachi and Lahore.

ENERGY AND NATURAL RESOURCES

Environment

Pakistan's carbon dioxide emissions from the consumption and flaring of fossil fuels were the equivalent of 0·9 tonnes per capita in 2008.

Electricity
Installed capacity in 2003 was 17·79m. kW, of which 12·29m. kW was thermal, 5·05m. kW was hydro-electric and 0·46m. kW was nuclear. In 2003 there were two nuclear reactors in use. Production in 2004 was 85·70bn. kWh, of which 67% was thermal and 30% was hydro-electric. Consumption per capita in 2004 was 564 kWh.

Oil and Gas
Crude petroleum production in 2004 was 24m. bbls. Reserves in 2007 were 289m. bbls. Exploitation is mainly through government incentives and concessions to foreign private sector companies. Natural gas production in 2008 was 37·5bn. cu. metres with 850bn. cu. metres of proven reserves. The French oil company Total agreed a US$3bn. deal with the government in July 2003 for exploration in the Arabian Sea.

Water
Pakistan's Indus Basin irrigation system is the largest and oldest in the world. It includes a network of 43 independent canal systems and two storage reservoirs. Total length of main canals is 58,000 km which serve 35m. acres of cultivatable land.

Currently three major surface water projects are under way, as are flood control schemes and programmes to check the problems of waterlogging and salinity.

Minerals
Production (tonnes, 2005): limestone, 14·86m.; coal, 3·37m.; rock salt, 1·65m.; gypsum, 552,496; fire clay, 253,501; dolomite, 199,653; chromite, 46,359; barytes, 42,087; china clay, 37,732; fuller's earth, 17,001; bauxite, 6,504. Other minerals of which useful deposits have been found are magnesite, sulphur, marble, antimony ore, bentonite, celestite, fluorite, phosphate rock, silica sand and soapstone.

Agriculture
The north and west are covered by mountain ranges. The rest of the country consists of a fertile plain watered by five big rivers and their tributaries. Agriculture is dependent almost entirely on the irrigation system based on these rivers. Area irrigated, 2002, about 17·80m. ha. Agriculture employs around half of the workforce. In 2002 there were an estimated 21·45m. ha. of arable land and 672,000 ha. of permanent crops.

Pakistan is self-sufficient in wheat, rice and sugar. Areas harvested, 2003: wheat, 8·07m. ha.; seed cotton, 3·00m. ha.; rice, 2·21m. ha.; chick-peas, 1·68m. ha.; sugarcane, 1·09m. ha.; maize, 0·88m. ha. Production, 2003 (1,000 tonnes): sugarcane, 52,056; wheat, 19,210; rice, 6,751; seed cotton, 5,071; cottonseed, 3,337; potatoes, 1,946; cotton lint, 1,690; onions, 1,400; oranges, 1,400; maize, 1,275; mangoes, 1,036; chick-peas, 672; dates, 650.

A Land Reforms Act of 1977 reduced the upper limit of land holding to 100 irrigated or 200 non-irrigated acres. A new agricultural income tax was introduced in 1995, from which holders of up to 25 irrigated or 50 unirrigated acres are exempt. Of about 5m. farms, 12% are of less than 10 ha.

Livestock, 2003 (in 1m.): goats, 52·8; buffaloes, 24·8; sheep, 24·6; cattle, 23·3; asses, 4·1; camels, 0·8; chickens, 155·0.

Livestock products, 2003 (in 1,000 tonnes): beef and veal, 445; poultry meat, 375; goat meat, 373; mutton and lamb, 174; buffalo's milk, 18,520; cow's milk, 8,620; goat's milk, 640; eggs, 354; wool, 40.

Forestry
The area under forests in 2005 was 1·90m. ha., some 2·5% of the total land area. Timber production in 2007 totalled 29·22m. cu. metres.

Fisheries
In 2005 the catch totalled 434,473 tonnes, 78% from marine waters and the rest from inland waters.

INDUSTRY
The leading companies by market capitalization in Feb. 2009 were Oil & Gas Development (US$3·0bn.) and the National Bank of Pakistan (US$0·8bn.).

Industry is based largely on agricultural processing, with engineering and electronics. Government policy is to encourage private industry, particularly small businesses. The public sector, however, is still dominant in large industries. Steel, cement, fertilizer and vegetable ghee are the most valuable public sector industries.

Production in tonnes (in 1998–99 unless otherwise stated): cement (2000–01), 9,674,000; distillate fuel oil (2004), 3,603,000; sugar (2002), 3,334,000; residual fuel oil (2004), 3,132,000; petrol (2004), 1,326,000; cotton yarn, 895,000; pig iron, 735,000; vegetable ghee, 615,000; coke, 443,000; paper and board, 256,000; steel billets, 212,000; soda ash, 186,000; caustic soda, 82,000; jute textiles, 63,000; sulphuric acid (2001), 57,000; cotton cloth, 443m. sq. metres; bicycles, 409,000 items; jeeps and cars, 28,815 items.

Labour
Out of 45·29m. economically active people in 2005, 37·81m. were males. The rate of unemployment in 2005 was 6·8%. In 2005 a total of 17·18m. persons were engaged in agriculture, forestry and fishing, 6·67m. in manufacturing, 6·50m. in community, social and personal services and 6·29m. in wholesale and retail trade, restaurants and hotels.

In 2001 there were four industrial disputes and 7,078 working days were lost.

Trade Unions
In 1997 there were 7,355 trade unions with a membership of 1,022,275.

INTERNATIONAL TRADE
Foreign debt was US$33,675m. in 2005. Most foreign exchange controls were removed in Feb. 1991. Tax exemptions are available for companies set up before 30 June 1995.

Imports and Exports
Trade in US$1m.:

	2000	*2001*	*2002*	*2003*	*2004*
Imports f.o.b.	9,896	9,741	10,428	11,978	16,735
Exports f.o.b.	8,739	9,131	9,832	11,869	13,352

Major imports in 2004 (as % of total value): machinery and transport equipment, 27·0; petroleum and petroleum products, 20·6; chemicals and related products, 18·6; manufactured goods, 10·3. Major exports in 2004: textile yarn, fabrics and finished articles, 45·8; clothing and apparel, 22·6; rice, 5·1; machinery and transport equipment, 3·9.

Major import suppliers in 2004 (as % of total): Saudi Arabia, 11·5; UAE, 10·0; USA, 9·6; China, 8·3; Japan, 6·4. Major export markets in 2004: USA, 23·3; UAE, 7·9; UK, 7·2; Germany, 5·0; Hong Kong, 4·4.

COMMUNICATIONS

Roads
In 2006 there were 260,420 km of roads. There are ten motorways providing links between Pakistan's major cities. These include the M-1 from Islamabad to Peshawar, the M-2 from Islamabad to Lahore, the M-4 from Faisalabad to Multan and the M-9 from Karachi to Hyderabad. In 2007 there were 1,440,100 passenger cars in use, 187,100 vans and lorries, 170,400 buses and coaches and 2,684,300 motorcycles. There were 10,466 road accidents involving injury in 2007, with 5,465 fatalities.

All traffic in Pakistan drives on the left. All cars must be insured and registered. Minimum age for driving: 18 years.

Rail
In 2005 Pakistan Railways had a route length of 7,791 km (of which 305 km electrified) mainly on 1,676 mm gauge, with some metre gauge line. Passenger-km travelled in 2004–05 came to 24·2bn. and freight tonne-km to 5·0bn.

Civil Aviation
There are international airports at Karachi, Islamabad, Lahore, Peshawar and Quetta.

The national carrier is the state-owned Pakistan International Airlines, or PIA. It operates scheduled services to 46 international and 24 domestic destinations. In 2006, 88,302,000 revenue-km were flown. The revenue passengers carried totalled 5·73m. in 2006 and revenue tonne-km came to 1,801m. Operating revenues of the corporation stood at Rs70,587m. in 2006 and operating expenditure at Rs79,164m.

Shipping
In 2002 ocean-going shipping totalled 247,000 GRT, including oil tankers 50,000 GRT. The busiest port is Karachi. In 2001–02 cargo traffic totalled 25,852,000 tonnes (6,244,000 tonnes loaded and 19,608,000 tonnes discharged). In 1998–99, 1,262 international vessels were handled at the port of Karachi. There is also a port at Port Qasim.

Telecommunications
The telephone system is government-owned. In 2008 there were 4,416,000 main (fixed) telephone lines. In the same year mobile phone subscribers numbered 88,020,000 (497·4 per 1,000 persons). There were 18·5m. internet users in 2008.

Postal Services
In 2003 there were 15,035 post offices.

SOCIAL INSTITUTIONS

Justice
The Federal Judiciary consists of the Supreme Court of Pakistan, which is a court of record and has three-fold jurisdiction; original, appellate and advisory. There are four High Courts in Lahore, Peshawar, Quetta and Karachi. Under the Constitution, each has power to issue directions of writs of *Habeas Corpus, Mandamus, Certiorari* and others. Under them are district and sessions courts of first instance in each district; they have also some appellate jurisdiction. Below these are subordinate courts and village courts for civil matters and magistrates for criminal matters.

The Constitution provides for an independent judiciary, as the greatest safeguard of citizens' rights. There is an Attorney-General, appointed by the President, who has right of audience in all courts and the Parliament, and a Federal Ombudsman.

A Federal Sharia Court at the High Court level has been established to decide whether any law is wholly or partially un-Islamic. In Aug. 1990 a presidential ordinance decreed that the criminal code must conform to Islamic law (Sharia), and in May 1991 parliament passed a law incorporating it into the legal system.

378,301 crimes were reported in 2001. Execution of the death penalty for murder, in abeyance since 1986, was resumed in 1992. According to Amnesty International there were at least 36 executions in 2008 but none in 2009. There were 9,528 murders in 2001. The population in penal institutions in 2002 was 87,000 (59 per 100,000 of national population).

Education
The National Education Policy (1998–2010) was launched in March 1998. The major aim was the eradication of illiteracy and the spread of a basic education. The policy stresses vocational and technical education, disseminating a common culture based on Islamic ideology. The principle of free and compulsory primary education has been accepted as the responsibility of the state. The adult literacy rate in 2003 was 48·7% (61·7% among males and 35·2% among females). Adult literacy programmes are being strengthened.

In 2007 there were 17·98m. primary schools pupils (450,027 teaching staff), 9·15m. secondary school pupils (197,082 teaching staff in 2004) and 955,000 students in tertiary education (52,245 academic staff). There are 70 public and 58 private universities of which Quaid-i-Azam University in Islamabad and the University of the Punjab in Lahore are considered to be the most prestigious.

Public expenditure on education came to 2·8% of GNI and 11·2% of total government spending in 2007.

Health
In 2002 there were 906 hospitals and 4,590 dispensaries (with a total of 98,264 beds) and 862 maternity and child welfare centres. There were 102,541 doctors, 44,520 nurses, 23,084 midwives, 5,057 dentists and 45,390 pharmacists (2001).

Welfare
The official retirement age is 60 (men) or 55 (women and miners). To qualify for a pension, 15 years of contributions are needed. The minimum old age and survivor pension is Rs700 per month (as of Nov. 2001).

Medical services, provided mainly through social security facilities, cover cash and medical benefits such as general medical care, specialist care, medicines, hospitalization, maternity care and transportation.

RELIGION
Pakistan was created as a Muslim state. The Muslims are mainly Sunni, with an admixture of 15–20% Shia. Religious groups: Muslims, 93%; Christians, 2%; Hindus, Parsees, Buddhists, Qadianis and others. Pakistan has the second highest number of Muslims, after Indonesia. There is a Minorities Wing at the Religious Affairs Ministry to safeguard the constitutional rights of religious minorities.

CULTURE
There is a Pakistan National Council of the Arts, a cultural organization to promote art and culture in Pakistan and abroad.

World Heritage Sites
There are six sites under Pakistani jurisdiction which appear on the UNESCO World Heritage List. They are (with year entered on list): the archaeological ruins at Moenjodaro (1980), Taxila (1980), the Buddhist ruins at Tahkt-i-Bahi and the neighbouring city remains at Sahr-i-Bahlol (1980), Thatta (1981), the Fort and Shalamar Gardens in Lahore (1981) and Rohtas Fort (1997).

Broadcasting
The state-owned Pakistan Broadcasting Corporation (PBC) operates more than 20 domestic radio stations, a world service for Pakistanis overseas, an external service and its FM 101 service (in major urban areas). The network of PBC transmitters covers 96·5% of the population and 80% of the total area of the country. A separate government authority, Azad Kashmir Radio, broadcasts in Kashmir. TV services transmitted by the state-run Pakistan Television Corporation (PTV) include PTV Home, PTV News, PTV Bolan, PTV National (a satellite channel), PTV Global and AJK TV (a Kashmiri channel). There has been an expansion of commercial satellite television services (although there are no private terrestrial stations), some of which were critical of the Musharraf government, and FM radio stations. Number of TV sets in use (2003): 12·23m. TV colour is by PAL.

Cinema
There were 139 cinemas in 2007. 35 films were released in 2008 in Urdu, Punjabi and Pushto. The KaraFilm Festival is held annually in Karachi.

Press
In 2004 there were 291 paid-for dailies and 988 paid-for non-daily periodicals. Average combined circulation of all dailies in 2004 was 7,818,000. The most popular daily paper in 2004 was Jang, with a circulation of 775,000.

Tourism
In 2005 there were 798,000 non-resident tourists. More than half of foreign tourist arrivals in 2006 were for the purpose of visiting friends and relatives, followed by business (21·4%) and holidays and recreation (14·7%). Tourist receipts totalled US$827m. in 2005.

Festivals
Pakistan is rich in culture. Famous festivals include the Eid Festival, Eid-e-Milad un Nabi (Birthday of Prophet Muhammad), the Basnat Festival, Shab-e-Baraat Festival and the Independence Day Festival.

Libraries
The National Library of Pakistan is located in Islamabad and contains some 130,000 volumes. Other notable institutions include the Liaquat National Memorial Library in Karachi, the Baitul Quran at Lahore which is exclusively devoted to the manuscripts of the Holy Koran and the libraries of the Punjab University, Karachi University and the Quaid-e-Azam library in Lahore which together hold a combined 700,000 volumes. The Islamic Research Institute Library at Islamabad also has an important collection on Islam.

Theatre and Opera
There are regular theatrical productions in the major cities. There are fully equipped theatre halls in Rawalpindi, Lahore, Karachi and Peshawar, and traditional street theatre is still prominent.

Museums and Galleries
There are dozens of galleries and museums in Islamabad, Lahore, Karachi, Peshawar and Quetta. Amongst the most famous are the National Art Gallery, Shakir Ali Museum, Choukandi Art Gallery, Karachi Art Council, Tasneen Art Gallery, the Lahore Art Museum, the National Heritage Museum and the National Archives.

DIPLOMATIC REPRESENTATIVES

Of Pakistan in the United Kingdom (35–36 Lowndes Sq., London, SW1X 9JN)
High Commissioner: Wajid Shamsul Hasan.

Of the United Kingdom in Pakistan (Diplomatic Enclave, Ramna 5, Islamabad)
High Commissioner: Adam Thomson, CMG.

Of Pakistan in the USA (3517 International Court, NW, Washington, D.C., 20008)
Ambassador: Husain Haqqani.

Of the USA in Pakistan (Diplomatic Enclave, Ramna, 5, Islamabad)
Ambassador: Anne W. Patterson.

Of Pakistan to the United Nations
Ambassador: Abdullah Hussain Haroon.

Of Pakistan to the European Union
Ambassador: Shafkat Saeed.

FURTHER READING

Federal Bureau of Statistics.—*Pakistan Statistical Yearbook.—Statistical Pocket Book of Pakistan.* (Annual)

Ahmed, A. S., *Jinnah, Pakistan and Islamic Identity: The Search for Saladin.* 1997
Ahsan, A., *The Indus Saga and the Making of Pakistan.* 1997
Akhtar, R., *Pakistan Year Book.*
Bhutto, B., *Daughter of the East.* 1988
Cohen, Stephen Philip, *The Idea of Pakistan.* 2006
James, W. E. and Roy, S. (eds.) *The Foundations of Pakistan's Political Economy: Towards an Agenda for the 1990s.* 1992
Joshi, V. T., *Pakistan: Zia to Benazir.* 1995
Khan, Hamid, *Constitutional and Political History of Pakistan.* 2005
Malik, I. H., *State and Civil Society in Pakistan: the Politics of Authority, Ideology and Ethnicity.* 1996
Paul, T. V., *The India-Pakistan Conflict: An Enduring Rivalry.* 2005
Talbot, Ian, *Pakistan: A Modern History.* 1999
Ziring, Lawrence, *Pakistan in the 20th Century: A Political History.* 2004

National library: National Library of Pakistan, Constitution Avenue, Islamabad.
National Statistical Office: Federal Bureau of Statistics, 5-SLIC Bldg., F-6/4, Blue Area, Islamabad.
Website: http://www.statpak.gov.pk

PALAU

Beluu er a Belau
(Republic of Palau)

Capital: Melekeok
Population, 2005: 20,000
GDP per capita: not available
GNI per capita, 2007: US$8,493

KEY HISTORICAL EVENTS

Spain acquired sovereignty over the Palau Islands in 1886 but sold the archipelago to Germany in 1899. Japan occupied the islands in 1914 and in 1921 they were mandated to Japan by the League of Nations. Captured by Allied Forces in 1944, the islands became part of the UN Trust Territory of the Pacific Islands created on 18 July 1947 and administered by the USA. Following a referendum in July 1978 in which Palauans voted against joining the new Federated States of Micronesia, the islands became autonomous from 1 Jan. 1981. A referendum in Nov. 1993 favoured a Compact of Free Association with the USA. Palau became an independent republic on 1 Oct. 1994.

TERRITORY AND POPULATION

The archipelago lies in the western Pacific and has a total land area of 488 sq. km (188 sq. miles). It comprises 26 islands and over 300 islets. Only nine of the islands are inhabited, the largest being Babelthuap (396 sq. km), but most inhabitants live on the small island of Koror (18 sq. km) to the south. In Oct. 2006 the capital moved from Koror to Melekeok, a newly-built town in eastern Babelthuap. The total population of Palau at the time of the 2005 census was 19,907, giving a density of 40·8 per sq. km. Koror's population according to the 2005 census was 12,676. In 2000 approximately 70% of the population were Palauans.

In 2000 an estimated 69·5% of the population lived in urban areas. Some 6,000 Palauans live abroad. The local language is Palauan; both Palauan and English are official languages.

SOCIAL STATISTICS

2005 births, 279; deaths, 134. Rates, 2005 (per 1,000 population): births, 14·0; deaths, 6·7; infant mortality (2005), ten per 1,000 live births. Annual population growth rate, 1992–2002, 2·3%. Expectation of life: males, 69 years; females, 73. Fertility rate, 2004, 1·4 births per woman.

CLIMATE

Palau has a pleasantly warm climate throughout the year with temperatures averaging 81°F (27°C). The heaviest rainfall is between July and Oct.

CONSTITUTION AND GOVERNMENT

The Constitution was adopted on 2 April 1979 and took effect from Jan. 1981. The Republic has a bicameral legislature, the *Olbiil Era Kelulau* (National Congress), comprising a 13-member *Senate* and a 16-member *House of Delegates* (one from each of the Republic's 16 states), both elected for a term of four years as are the *President* and *Vice-President.* Customary social roles and land and sea rights are allocated by a matriarchal 16-clan system.

National Anthem

'Belau loba klisiich er a kelulul' ('Palau is coming forth with strength and power'); words anonymous, tune Y. O. Ezekiel.

RECENT ELECTIONS

At the elections on 4 Nov. 2008 Johnson Toribiong was elected president with 51·1% of votes cast against 48·9% for Elias Camsek Chin. At the legislative elections that were also held on 4 Nov. 2008 only non-partisans were elected.

CURRENT ADMINISTRATION

President: Johnson Toribiong; b. 1946 (in office since 15 Jan. 2009).

Vice-President and Minister of Finance: Kerai Mariur.

In April 2010 the cabinet consisted of:

Minister of Community and Cultural Affairs: Faustina Rehuher-Marugg. *Education:* Masa-Aki Emesiochl. *Health:* Dr Stevenson Kuartei. *Justice:* Johnny Gibbons. *Natural Resources, Environment and Tourism:* Harry Fritz. *Public Infrastructure, Industries and Commerce:* Jackson Ngiraingas. *Minister of State:* Dr Victor Yano.

Government Website: http://www.palaugov.net

CURRENT LEADERS

Johnson Toribiong

Position
President

Introduction
Johnson Toribiong assumed the presidency on 15 Jan. 2009 following victory in the presidential election of Nov. 2008. A prominent attorney, Toribiong is a former ambassador to Taiwan.

Early Life
Toribiong was born in Airai village in 1946. He was given his Christian name in honour of US troops who were stationed on the island in the Second World War.

Adopted by his paternal grandmother, Toribiong grew up in Ngiaul in a traditional family. In 1972 he graduated from the University of Washington, School of Law, from where he also gained a master's degree the following year. In 1999, when he was appointed to succeed his uncle as chief of Airai village, he expressed his determination to preserve the Palauan heritage.

In 2005, while serving as Palau's ambassador to Taiwan, Toribiong refused to attend a Taiwanese court hearing to answer allegations that he was involved in investment fraud linked to the sale of funds to Taiwan by a Palauan bank. He was granted diplomatic immunity and did not face charges.

Career in Office
Toribiong campaigned for the presidency on a platform of government transparency and increased spending on public health. He also promised sustainable economic growth. While Toribiong was in Taiwan for his first state visit, the Taiwanese president, Ma Ying-jeou, described Palau as Taiwan's 'closest ally'. Toribiong is expected to continue to campaign for international recognition for Taiwan and has pledged to reduce Palau's dependence on US aid.

INTERNATIONAL RELATIONS

Palau is a member of the UN, World Bank, IMF, Asian Development Bank, Pacific Islands Forum and SPC.

ECONOMY

Currency
US currency is used.

Budget
The fiscal year begins on 1 Oct. Revenues for 2005–06 were US$83·7m. and expenditures US$87·6m.

Performance
Total GDP in 2008 was US$182m. Real GDP growth was 5·3% in 2005.

Banking and Finance
The National Development Bank of Palau is situated in Koror. Other banks include the Bank of Guam, the Bank of Hawaii, Bank Pacific, Melekeok Government Bank and the Pacific Savings Bank.

ENERGY AND NATURAL RESOURCES

Electricity
Electricity production was about 171m. kWh in 2004; installed capacity was about 62,000 kW in 2004.

Agriculture
The main agricultural products are bananas, coconuts, copra, cassava and sweet potatoes. In 2007 approximately 2,000 people were economically active in agriculture. In 2007 there were about 1,000 ha. of arable land and 2,000 ha. of permanent crop land.

Forestry
Forests covered 40,000 ha. in 2005, or 87·6% of the land area.

Fisheries
In 2005 the catch totalled 932 tonnes, mainly tuna.

INDUSTRY

There is little industry, but the principal activities are food-processing and boat-building.

Labour
In 2000 the total labour force numbered 9,607 (61·9% males), of whom 9,383 were employed.

INTERNATIONAL TRADE

Imports and Exports
Imports (2006–07) US$91·3m.; exports (2006–07) US$10·1m. The main trading partner is Japan for exports and the USA for imports.

COMMUNICATIONS

Roads
There were 61 km of roads in 1996 of which 36 km are paved.

Civil Aviation
The main airport is on Koror (Airai). In 2003 there were scheduled flights to Guam, Manila, Yap (Micronesia) and Taipei.

Shipping
There is a port at Malakal. In 1995 over 280 vessels called there, delivering cargo totalling in excess of 70,000 tonnes.

Telecommunications
In 2008 there were 7,400 main (fixed) telephone lines and 12,200 mobile phone subscribers.

SOCIAL INSTITUTIONS

Justice
There is a Supreme Court and various subsidiary courts. The population in penal institutions in Feb. 2003 was 103 (523 per 100,000 national population).

Education
In 2007 there were 1,544 pupils at primary schools and 2,448 at secondary schools. In 2004 there were 23 primary schools and six secondary schools. There were 727 students at Palau Community College in 2002–03. The adult literacy rate is 92%.

In 2002 government expenditure on education came to an estimated 10·3% of GDP.

Health
In 1998 there was one hospital, 20 physicians, two dentists, 26 nurses and one midwife.

RELIGION

The majority of the population is Roman Catholic.

CULTURE

Broadcasting
Palau has no television stations but cable services are available (rebroadcasting satellite TV and US channels). T8AA is a government-run national radio station; WWFM and KRFM are private stations.

Press
There were three weekly newspapers in 2006: Tia Belau and Palau Horizon, published in English, and Roureur Belau, published in Palauan.

Tourism
Tourism is a major industry, particularly marine-based. There were 83,114 foreign tourists in 2008.

DIPLOMATIC REPRESENTATIVES

Of the United Kingdom in Palau
Ambassador: Stephen Lillie (resides in Manila, Philippines).

Of Palau in the USA (1800 K St., NW, Suite 400, Washington, D.C., 20006)
Ambassador: Hersey Kyota.

Of the USA in Palau (PO Box 6028, PW 96940, Koror)
Ambassador: Vacant.

Of Palau to the United Nations
Ambassador: Stuart Beck.

FURTHER READING

National Statistical Office: Bureau of Planning and Budget, P.O. Box 6011, Melekeok PW 96940.
Website: http://www.palaugov.net/stats

PANAMA

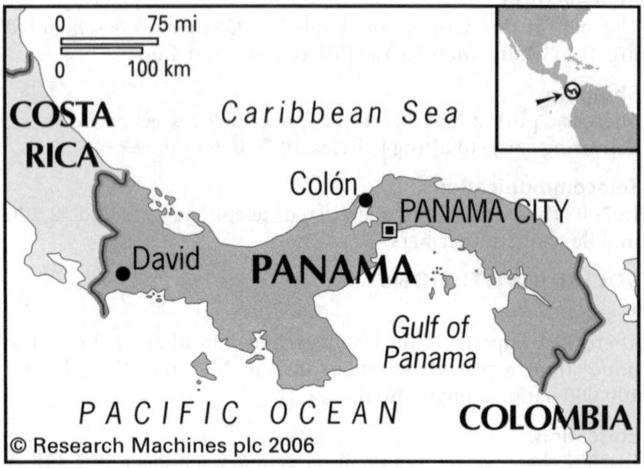

República de Panamá
(Republic of Panama)

Capital: Panama City
Population estimate, 2010: 3·51m.
GDP per capita, 2007: (PPP$) 11,391
HDI/world rank: 0·840/60

KEY HISTORICAL EVENTS

A revolution, inspired by the USA, led to the separation of Panama from the United States of Colombia and the declaration of its independence on 3 Nov. 1903. This was followed by an agreement making it possible for the USA to build and operate a canal connecting the Atlantic and Pacific oceans through the Isthmus of Panama. The treaty granted the USA in perpetuity the use, occupation and control of a Canal Zone, in which the USA would possess full sovereign rights. In return the USA guaranteed the independence of the republic. The Canal was opened on 15 Aug. 1914.

The US domination of Panama provoked frequent anti-American protests. In 1968 Col. Omar Torrijos Herrera took power in a coup and attempted to negotiate a more advantageous treaty with the USA. Two new treaties between Panama and the USA were agreed on 10 Aug. and signed on 7 Sept. 1977. One dealt with the operation and defence of the Canal until the end of 1999 and the other guarantees permanent neutrality.

Torrijos vacated his position as chief of government in 1978 but maintained his power as head of the National Guard until his death in an air crash in 1981. Subsequently, Gen. Manuel Noriega, Torrijos' successor as head of the National Guard, became the strong man of the regime. His position was threatened by some internal political opposition and economic pressure applied by the USA but in Oct. 1989 a US-backed coup attempt failed. On 15 Dec. Gen. Noriega declared a 'state of war' with the USA. On 20 Dec. the USA invaded. Gen. Noriega surrendered on 3 Jan. 1990. Accused of drug dealing he was convicted by a court in Miami and is now serving a 40-year jail sentence. All remaining US troops left the country when the Panama Canal was handed back to Panama at the end of 1999.

TERRITORY AND POPULATION

Panama is bounded in the north by the Caribbean Sea, east by Colombia, south by the Pacific Ocean and west by Costa Rica. The area is 75,001 sq. km. Population at the census of 2000 was 2,839,177 (1,432,566 males); density, 37·6 per sq. km. The population was 70·8% urban in 2005.

The UN gives an estimated population for 2010 of 3·51m.

The largest towns (2000) are Panama City, the capital, on the Pacific coast (469,307); its suburb San Miguelito (293,745); Tocumen (82,419); and David (77,057).

The areas and populations of the nine provinces and the five indigenous districts were:

Province	*Sq. km*	*Census 2000*	*Capital*
Bocas del Toro	4,601	89,269	Bocas del Toro
Chiriquí	6,477	368,790	David
Coclé	4,927	202,461	Penonomé
Colón	4,891	204,208	Colón
Darién	11,091	39,151	La Palma
Emberá[1]	4,398	8,246	Cirilo Guainora
Herrera	2,341	102,465	Chitré
Kuna de Madungandí[1]	2,319	3,305	—
Kuna de Wargandí[1]	775	1,133	—
Kuna Yala[1]	2,393	32,446	El Porvenir
Los Santos	3,805	83,495	Las Tablas
Ngöbe-Buglé[1]	6,673	110,080	Chichica
Panamá	9,633	1,385,052	Panama City
Veraguas	10,677	209,076	Santiago

[1]Indigenous district.

The population is a mix of African, American, Arab, Chinese, European and Indian immigrants. The official language is Spanish.

SOCIAL STATISTICS

2006 births, 65,764; deaths, 14,358; marriages, 10,747; divorces, 2,866. Birth rate, 2006 (per 1,000 population), 20·0; death rate, 4·4. Annual population growth rate, 2000–05, 2·5%. Expectation of life at birth, 2007, was 73·0 years for males and 78·2 years for females. In 2006 the most popular age range for marrying was 25–29 for both males and females. Infant mortality, 2006, 15 per 1,000 live births; fertility rate, 2006, 2·4 births per woman.

CLIMATE

Panama has a tropical climate, unvaryingly with high temperatures and only a short dry season from Jan. to April. Rainfall amounts are much higher on the north side of the isthmus. Panama City, Jan. 79°F (26·1°C), July 81°F (27·2°C). Annual rainfall 70" (1,770 mm). Colón, Jan. 80°F (26·7°C), July 80°F (26·7°C). Annual rainfall 127" (3,175 mm). Balboa Heights, Jan. 80°F (26·7°C), July 81°F (27·2°C). Annual rainfall 70" (1,759 mm). Cristóbal, Jan. 80°F (26·7°C), July 81°F (27·2°C). Annual rainfall 130" (3,255 mm).

CONSTITUTION AND GOVERNMENT

The 1972 constitution, as amended in 1978, 1983, 1994 and 2004, provides for a *President*, elected for five years, two *Vice-Presidents* and a 72-seat *Legislative Assembly* (since reduced to 71 seats) to be elected for five-year terms by a direct vote. As a result of the amendment of 2004 there has only been one *Vice-President* since the election of May 2009. To remain registered, parties must have attained at least 50,000 votes at the last election. A referendum held on 15 Nov. 1992 rejected constitutional reforms by 64% of votes cast. Turnout was 40%. In a referendum on 30 Aug. 1998 voters rejected proposed changes to the constitution which would allow for a President to serve a second consecutive term.

National Anthem

'Alcanzamos por fin la victoria' ('We achieve victory in the end'); words by J. de la Ossa, tune by Santos Jorge.

GOVERNMENT CHRONOLOGY

(CD = Democratic Change; CNP = National Patriotic Coalition; PA = Arnulfist Party; PL = Liberal Party; PLN = National Liberal Party; PP = Panameñista Party; PR = Republican Party; PRA = Authentic Revolutionary Party; PRD = Revolutionary Democratic Party; n/p = non-partisan)

Heads of State since 1941.

Presidents of the Republic

1941–45	n/p	Ricardo Adolfo de la Guardia Arango
1945–48	PL	Enrique Adolfo Jiménez Brin
1948–49	PL	Domingo Díaz Arosemena
1949	PL	Daniel Chanis Pinzón
1949–51	PRA	Arnulfo Arias Madrid
1951–52	PRA	Alcibíades Arosemena Quinzada
1952–55	CNP	José Antonio Remón Cantera
1955–56	CNP	Ricardo Manuel Arias Espinosa
1956–60	CNP	Ernesto de la Guardia Navarro
1960–64	PLN	Roberto Francisco Chiari Remón
1964–68	PLN	Marco Aurelio Robles Méndez
1968	PP	Arnulfo Arias Madrid

Chairmen of the Provisional Junta of Government

1968–69	military	José María Pinilla Fábrega
1969–72	n/p	Demetrio Basilio Lakas Bahas

Presidents of the Republic

1972–78	n/p	Demetrio Basilio Lakas Bahas
1978–82	n/p	Arístides Royo Sánchez
1982–84	n/p	Ricardo de la Espriella Toral
1984	n/p	Jorge Enrique Illueca Sibauste
1984–85	PRD	Nicolás Ardito Barletta Vallarino
1985–88	PR	Eric Arturo Delvalle Cohen-Henríquez
1989–94	PA	Guillermo David Endara Galimany
1994–99	PRD	Ernesto Pérez Balladares González
1999–2004	PA	Mireya Elisa Moscoso de Arias
2004–09	PRD	Martín Erasto Torrijos Espino
2009–	CD	Ricardo Martinelli Berrocal

De facto rulers from 1968–89.

1968–81	military	Omar Efraín Torrijos Herrera
1982–83	military	Rubén Darío Paredes del Río
1983–89	military	Manuel Antonio Noriega Moreno

RECENT ELECTIONS

In the presidential election on 3 May 2009 Ricardo Martinelli of Democratic Change (CD) won 60·3% of the vote, against 37·3% for Balbina Herrera of the ruling Revolutionary Democratic Party (PRD) and 2·4% for Guillermo Endara (Moral Vanguard of the Fatherland).

At the parliamentary elections, also held on 3 May 2009, the PRD won 26 seats; the Panameñista Party won 21 seats; CD, 15; Patriotic Union Party, 4; Nationalist Republican Liberal Movement (Molirena), 2; independents, 2; People's Party, 1. Turnout was 70·1%.

CURRENT ADMINISTRATION

President: Ricardo Martinelli; b. 1952 (Democratic Change; sworn in 1 July 2009).

Vice-President and Minister of Foreign Affairs: Juan Carlos Varela Rodríguez.

In March 2010 the government comprised:

Minister of Government and Justice: José Raúl Mulino. *Education:* Lucinda Molinar. *Public Works:* Federico José Suárez. *Health:* Franklin Vergara. *Labour and Work Development:* Alma Lorena Cortés Aguilar. *Commerce and Industry:* Roberto Henríquez. *Housing:* Carlos Alberto Duboy Sierra. *Agricultural Development:* Víctor Manuel Pérez Batista. *Canal Affairs:* Rómulo Roux. *Social Development:* Guillermo Antonio Ferrufino Benítez. *Economy and Finance:* Alberto Vallarino Clément. *Tourism:* Salomón Shamah Zuchin. *Micro, Small and Medium-sized Business Authority:* Giselle de Calcagno. *Minister of the Presidency:* Demetrio Papadimitriu.

Office of the President (Spanish only):
http://www.presidencia.gob.pa

CURRENT LEADERS

Ricardo Martinelli Berrocal

Position
President

Introduction
Businessman Ricardo Martinelli became president in May 2009. He led the Democratic Change party to a landslide victory, ending 40 years of bipartisan government.

Early Life
Ricardo Martinelli was born in March 1952 in Panama City to parents of Italian and Spanish descent. He was schooled in Panama City before attending Staunton Military Academy in Virginia, USA. In 1973 he graduated in business administration from Arkansas University and subsequently obtained a master's in the same subject from the Central American Institute of Business Administration in Costa Rica.

He returned to Panama to embark on a business career, first at Citibank before joining the retail company Almacen 99 in 1981. By 1985 he had set up the Super 99 supermarket chain and variously headed the Panamanian Chamber of Commerce, the Italian-Panamanian Chamber of Commerce and the governing association of retail companies. In 1991 he set up the Ricardo Martinelli Foundation, which grants scholarships to several thousand poor students each year. From 1993–96 Martinelli was involved with the Revolutionary Democratic Party (PRD) and was briefly head of the National Social Security Institute (CSS).

After two years out of the political spotlight, Martinelli established his own party in 1998, called Democratic Change (CD). In 1999 he allied himself with Mireya Moscoso in a conservative coalition against the PRD. When Moscoso went on to win the presidency, CD was rewarded with the ministry for the Panama Canal, just as management of the Canal was being handed over to Panama by the USA. Martinelli was a strong advocate for expansion of the Canal but progress was slow and in 2003 he resigned to stand for the presidency in 2004. Martinelli started with a strong base in local and international commerce, insurance, banking, food, the agricultural and chemical industries, and the media.

Although his 2004 campaign was unsuccessful, it positioned him in the public eye ahead of his second run in 2009. He stood as the candidate for the CD-led Alliance for Change coalition campaigning on a platform of change and fighting corruption. He won with over 60% of the vote.

Career in Office
Martinelli's election bucked the left-leaning trend in neighbouring El Salvador and Nicaragua. Among the policies he has advocated are Panama's exit from the Central American Parliament (Parlacen), increased police wages, a monthly stipend of 100 balboas for the unpensioned elderly and the eradication of corruption. In 2009 he appointed the ex-military Gustavo Pérez as head of police and pledged to tackle the 'wild capitalism' of Panama. Martinelli also plans to reform the tax system and to overhaul Panama City's transport system with the construction of a metro network.

DEFENCE

The armed forces were disbanded in 1990 and constitutionally abolished in 1994. Divided between both coasts, the National

Maritime Service, a coast guard rather than a navy, numbered around 600 personnel in 2007. In addition there is a paramilitary police force of 11,000 and a paramilitary national air service of 400 with no combat capable aircraft. In 2006 defence expenditure totalled US$171m. (US$54 per capita), representing 1·0% of GDP. For Police *see* JUSTICE *below*.

INTERNATIONAL RELATIONS

Panama is a member of the UN, World Bank, IMF and several other UN specialized agencies, WTO, IOM, ACS, Inter-American Development Bank, SELA and OAS.

ECONOMY

Agriculture accounted for 8·2% of GDP in 2006, industry 18·6% and services 73·2%.

Overview

Panama boasts one of the fastest-growing GDP rates in Latin America, averaging over 9·5% between 2006–08, although provisional figures suggested a much lower growth rate for 2009. It has buoyant transportation, commerce and tourism sectors and a sound banking system. However, 28·6% of the population lived in poverty in 2006 and inequality is very high, despite the government of Martín Torrijos that was in power from 2004 to 2009 setting a goal of reducing poverty by 20% by 2009.

As the link between North and South America, Panama benefits from its strategic importance for shipping and trade. About 80% of GDP is derived from related service sectors such as transportation, packaging, shipping, importing and exporting. The sector is centred around the Canal and the Colón Free Zone, at the Canal's Atlantic entrance. An expansion of the Canal, begun in 2007 and scheduled to be completed by 2014, is expected to boost the economy.

The banking system is highly integrated with international markets. The national currency is pegged to the US dollar, making it vulnerable to global trends.

Currency

The monetary unit is the *balboa* (PAB) of 100 *centésimos*, at parity with the US dollar. The only paper currency used is that of the USA. US coinage is also legal tender. Inflation was 2·5% in 2006, 4·2% in 2007 and 8·8% in 2008. In July 2005 foreign exchange reserves were US$1,018m. and total money supply was 1,587m. balboas.

Budget

Revenues in 2004 were 2,042m. balboas (tax revenue, 59·2%) and expenditures 2,810m. balboas (current expenditure, 83·8%).

VAT is 5%.

Performance

Real GDP growth was 8·5% in 2006, 11·5% in 2007 and 9·2% in 2008. Total GDP in 2008 was US$23·1bn.

Banking and Finance

There is no statutory central bank. Banking is supervised and promoted by the Superintendency of Banks (formerly the National Banking Commission); the *Superintendent* is Alberto Diamond. Government accounts are handled through the state-owned Banco Nacional de Panama. In 2007 there were two other state banks, 39 banks operating under general licence, 34 under international licence and 11 as representative offices. In Aug. 2007 the combined assets of those banks operating under general and international licences totalled US$50,500m.; their combined deposits were US$36,500m.

There is a stock exchange in Panama City.

Weights and Measures

The US and metric system are used.

ENERGY AND NATURAL RESOURCES

Environment

Panama's carbon dioxide emissions from the consumption and flaring of fossil fuels in 2008 were the equivalent of 4·6 tonnes per capita.

Electricity

In 2004 capacity was 1·6m. kW. Production was 5·9bn. kWh in 2004, with consumption per capita 1,807 kWh.

Minerals

Limestone, clay and salt are produced. There are known to be copper deposits.

Agriculture

In 2002, 19·3% of the economically active population were engaged in agriculture. In 2002 there were approximately 548,000 ha. of arable land and 147,000 ha. of permanent crops. Production in 2002 (in 1,000 tonnes): sugarcane, 1,441; bananas, 500; rice, 245; plantains, 105; maize, 76; melons and watermelons, 63; oranges, 47; potatoes, 26; yams, 26; pineapples, 23; tomatoes, 21; cassava, 20.

Livestock (2003 estimates): 1,550,000 cattle, 305,000 pigs, 175,000 horses and 14m. chickens.

Livestock products (2002, in 1,000 tonnes): beef and veal, 54; pork, bacon and ham, 18; poultry meat, 89; milk, 178; eggs, 26.

Forestry

Forests covered 4·29m. ha. in 2005 (57·7% of the land area). There are great timber resources, notably mahogany. Production in 2007 totalled 1·35m. cu. metres.

Fisheries

In 2005 the catch totalled 214,737 tonnes (mainly shrimp), almost entirely from sea fishing.

INDUSTRY

The main industry is agricultural produce processing. Other areas include chemicals and paper-making. Cement production (2004), 1,042,200 tonnes; sugar (2005), 157,280 tonnes.

Labour

In Aug. 2003 a total of 1,145,982 persons were in employment, with principal areas of activity as follows: agriculture, hunting and forestry, 228,305; wholesale and retail trade/repair of motor vehicles, motorcycles and personal and household goods, 196,418; manufacturing, 105,830; transport, storage and communications, 85,883. In Aug. 2003 the unemployment rate was 13·1%.

Trade Unions

There are three major trade union confederations: Convergencia Sindical (CS), with 75,000 members in 2006; Confederación General de Trabajadores de Panamá (CGTP), with 53,250 members in 2006; and Confederación de Trabajadores de la República de Panamá (CTRP), with 40,000 members in 2006.

INTERNATIONAL TRADE

The Colón Free Zone, the largest free zone in the Americas, is an autonomous institution set up in 1953. More than 2,500 companies were operating there in 2007. Foreign debt was US$9,765m. in 2005.

Imports and Exports

Imports and exports in US$1m.:

	2002	*2003*	*2004*	*2005*	*2006*
Imports f.o.b.	3,035·3	3,122·3	3,592·2	4,152·8	4,817·7
Exports f.o.b.	759·6	805·0	891·1	963·2	1,021·8

Main imports: machinery and apparatus, mineral fuels, chemicals and chemical products. Main exports: marine products, bananas, melons.

Chief import suppliers, 2006: USA, 27%; Curaçao, 10%; Costa Rica, 5%; Japan, 5%. Principal export markets, 2006: USA, 39%; Spain, 8%; Netherlands, 7%; Sweden, 6%.

COMMUNICATIONS

Roads

In 2006 there were 13,365 km of roads, of which 34·1% were paved. The road from Panama City westward to the cities of David and Concepción and to the Costa Rican frontier, with several branches, is part of the Pan-American Highway. The Trans-Isthmian Highway connects Panama City and Colón. In 2007 there were 436,200 passenger cars, 174,500 lorries and vans and 20,100 buses and coaches. There were 425 road accident fatalities in 2007.

Rail

The 1,435 mm gauge Ferrocarril de Panama, which connects Ancón on the Pacific with Cristóbal on the Atlantic along the bank of the Panama Canal, is the principal railway. Traffic in 2004 amounted to 77,000 passengers and 700,000 tonnes of freight. The United Brands Company runs 376 km of railway, and the Chiriquí National Railroad 171 km.

Civil Aviation

There is an international airport at Panama City (Tocumén International). The national carrier is COPA, which flew to 15 different countries in 2003. In 2003 scheduled airline traffic of Panama-based carriers flew 43m. km and carried 1,313,000 passengers (all on international flights). In 2005 Tocumén International handled 2,710,857 passengers and 100,063 tonnes of freight.

Shipping

Panama, a nation with a transcendental maritime career and a strategic geographic position, is the shipping world's preferred flag for ship registry. The Ship Registry System equally accepts vessels of local or international ownership, as long as they comply with all legal parameters. Ship owners also favour Panamanian registry because fees are low. Today, the Panamanian fleet is the largest in the world with 6,838 ships registered and 141·8m. GT in 2006.

All the international maritime traffic for Colón and Panama runs through the Canal ports of Cristóbal, Balboa and Manzanillo International.

Panama Canal

The Panama Canal Commission is concerned primarily with the operation of the Canal. In Oct. 2002 a new toll structure was adopted based on ship size and type.

Although most of the world's shipping fleet can use the Canal the percentage that is able to is gradually declining as many new ships are too wide for the Canal. A referendum was held in Oct. 2006 on whether to expand the canal and double its capacity. The US$5·25bn. plan was approved by 78% of voters. The expansion work began in Sept. 2007 and expected to be completed in 2014.

Administrator of the Panama Canal Authority: Alberto Alemán Zubieta.

Particulars of the ocean-going commercial traffic through the Canal are given as follows:

Fiscal year ending 30 Sept.	*No. of vessels transiting*	*Cargo in long tons*	*Tolls revenue (in US$1)*
2002	11,790	187,815,000	587,567,000
2003	11,634	188,273,000	664,667,000

Most numerous transits by flag (2003): Panama, 2,740; Liberia, 1,347; Bahamas, 922; Cyprus, 697; Malta, 565.

Statistical Information: The Panama Canal Authority Corporate Communications Division

Annual Reports on the Panama Canal, by the Administrator of the Panama Canal

Rules and Regulations Governing Navigation of the Panama Canal. The Panama Canal Authority

Major, J., *Prize Possession: the United States and the Panama Canal, 1903–1979.* 1994

Telecommunications

Panama had 3,505,900 telephone subscribers in 2007, or 1,048·6 per 1,000 persons, including 3,010,600 mobile phone subscribers. There were 745,300 internet users in 2007, including 143,900 broadband subscribers.

Postal Services

In 2003 there were 125 post and telegraph offices.

SOCIAL INSTITUTIONS

Justice

The Supreme Court consists of nine justices appointed by the executive. There is no death penalty. The police force numbered 11,000 in 2007, and includes a Presidential Guard.

The population in penal institutions in March 2003 was 10,630 (354 per 100,000 of national population).

Education

Adult literacy was 91·9% in 2003 (male, 92·5%; female, 91·2%). Elementary education is compulsory for all children from six to 14 years of age. In 2007 there were 446,176 pupils with 18,183 teaching staff at primary schools and 260,694 pupils with 16,847 teaching staff at secondary schools. In 2006 there were 130,838 students and 11,528 academic staff in tertiary education. The University of Panama (Universidad de Panamá), founded in 1935 in Panama City, is the leading higher education institution.

In 2004 public expenditure on education came to 4·1% of GNI and 8·9% of total government spending.

Health

In 2002 there were 61 hospitals with a provision of 25 beds per 10,000 persons. There were 4,203 physicians, 897 dentists, 3,451 nurses and 612 pharmacists.

RELIGION

80% of the population is Roman Catholic, 14% Protestant. The remainder of the population follow other religions (notably Islam). There is freedom of religious worship and separation of Church and State. Clergymen may teach in the schools but may not hold public office.

CULTURE

World Heritage Sites

Panama has five sites on the UNESCO World Heritage List: the Fortifications on the Caribbean side of Panama: Portobelo-San Lorenzo (inscribed on the list in 1980); Darien National Park (1981); the Archaeological Site of Panamá Viejo and the Historic District of Panamá (1997 and 2003); and the Coiba National Park (2005).

Panama shares a UNESCO site with Costa Rica: the Talamanca Range-La Amistad Reserves (1983 and 1990), an important cross-breeding site for North and South American flora and fauna.

Broadcasting

Broadcasting is predominantly commercial, with around 100 radio stations and several television networks (including TVN, RPC, Telemetro and the educational FETV channel). In 2006 there were 720,000 TV sets in use. Colour is by NTSC.

Press
In 2005 there were seven dailies with a combined circulation of 191,000.

Tourism
In 2006 there were 843,000 non-resident tourists (702,000 in 2005); spending by tourists totalled US$1,450m. in 2006 (US$1,108m. in 2005).

Festivals
Leading festivals include: the National Folkloric Festival, held annually (Sept.) in Guararé since 1949; the Panama Jazz Festival (Jan.); the International Fair of the Sea, held in Bocas del Toro province in Sept.; and the International Fair of Changuinola, also in Bocas del Toro in Sept.

DIPLOMATIC REPRESENTATIVES
Of Panama in the United Kingdom (40 Hertford St., London, W1J 7SH)
Ambassador: Gilberto Arias.

Of the United Kingdom in Panama (MMG Tower, Calle 53, Apartado/POB 0816-07946, Panama City)
Ambassador: Richard Austen, MBE.

Of Panama in the USA (2862 McGill Terr., NW, Washington, D.C., 20008)
Ambassador: Jaime Eduardo Alemán.

Of the USA in Panama (Edificio 783, Avenida Demetrio Basilio Lakas, Panama City 5)
Ambassador: Barbara J. Stephenson.

Of Panama to the United Nations
Ambassador: Pablo Antonio Thalassinos.

Of Panama to the European Union
Ambassador: Pablo Garrido Araúz.

FURTHER READING
Statistical Information: The Controller-General of the Republic (Contraloria General de la República, Calle 35 y Avenida 6, Panama City) publishes an annual report and other statistical publications.

Lindsay-Poland, John, *Emperors in the Jungle.* 2003
McCullough, D. G., *The Path Between the Seas: The Creation of the Panama Canal, 1870–1914.* 1999
Sahota, G. S., *Poverty Theory and Policy: a Study of Panama.* 1990

Other titles are listed under Panama Canal, *above.*

National library: Biblioteca Nacional, Departamento de Información, Av. Balboa y Federico Boyd, Ciudad de Panamá.
Website (Spanish only): http://www.contraloria.gob.pa

PAPUA NEW GUINEA

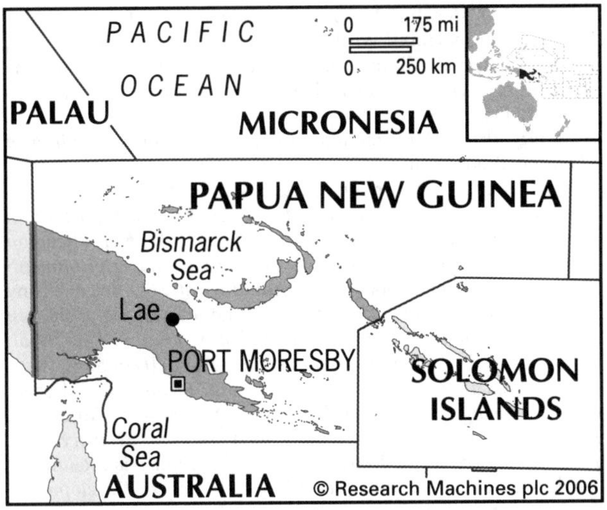

Capital: Port Moresby
Population estimate, 2010: 6·89m.
GDP per capita, 2007: (PPP$) 2,084
HDI/world rank: 0·541/148

KEY HISTORICAL EVENTS

The region was settled by Asian peoples around 50,000 years ago, when New Guinea was still part of the main Australian landmass. 10,000 years ago, at the end of the last ice age, the waters of the Torres Straight cut off New Guinea from Australia, giving rise to separate development of the indigenous peoples. Plant-based agriculture developed about 9,000 years ago in the New Guinea highlands. 2,500 years ago a large migration of Austronesian-speaking peoples settled the coastal areas. These communities developed animal husbandry, pottery and fishing and there is evidence of trade with the southeast Asian mainland. The rugged topography meant that contact between communities was limited and they retained their separate languages and customs. This heterogeneity continued down the centuries, so that today Papua New Guinea has an estimated 1,000 different cultural groups. Spanish and Portuguese explorers reached the island in the early 16th century and the Portuguese are thought to have introduced the kaukau (sweet potato), which became a staple crop. Spain laid claim to the western half of the island in 1545, naming it 'New Guinea' because of the supposed resemblance of its inhabitants to the people of Africa's Guinea coast.

From the late 18th century the British and Dutch competed for control of the island. In 1828 the Dutch claimed the western half as part of the Dutch East Indies, while the eastern half came under British influence. Following an abortive annexation attempt by Australian colonists, Britain declared a protectorate over the southern coast and islands adjacent to the eastern half of New Guinea on 6 Nov. 1884. Germany colonized the northern portion of the eastern half, along with New Britain, New Ireland and Bougainville, an arrangement formalized by the 1885 Anglo-German Agreement.

In 1888 Britain formally annexed the area under its control as British New Guinea and passed its administration to Australia in 1902. On 1 Sept. 1906 the Australian administration renamed it the Territory of Papua, Papua being a Malay word used to describe the Melanesian inhabitants' curly hair. The northeastern section of the island remained a German colony until the outbreak of the First World War in 1914, when Australian armed forces occupied it. For the next seven years it was under their administration and remained so after 1921, when it became a League of Nations mandated territory. In the Second World War, Allied and Japanese forces fought a prolonged military campaign on the island. It began with a Japanese victory at the Battle of Rabaul, New Britain in Feb. 1942 and continued throughout the war, with Japanese troops in occupation for much of the time until the Allies' victory in Aug. 1945.

In 1947 the northeastern part of the island became the UN Trust Territory of New Guinea, before merging in 1949 with the Territory of Papua to become the Territory of Papua New Guinea. A legislative council was established in 1953, succeeded by a house of assembly in 1964. On 1 Dec. 1973 Australia granted Papua New Guinea self-government. After a vigorous debate over questions of land-reform and citizenship, a constitution was passed and on 16 Sept. 1975 Papua New Guinea became fully independent. It also became a member of the Commonwealth, recognizing the British monarch as its own. In the same year the new state ignored a unilateral declaration of independence by the island of Bougainville and suppressed its campaign of civil disobedience. In 1988 an armed campaign by tribes claiming traditional land rights against the Australian owner of the massive Panguna copper field escalated into a civil war for Bougainville's secession. Fighting lasted nine years and cost an estimated 20,000 lives before a permanent truce was signed in April 1998. Bougainville gained autonomy in 2005 and is expected to hold a referendum on full independence in the future.

Political volatility caused frequent changes of government in Papua New Guinea during its first three decades of independence. In 2002, following violence in the general election, the electoral system was changed to encourage stable government. The deployment of Australian police on the island in 2003 caused resentment and from 2005, under a new agreement between the two governments, they operated in smaller numbers and with reduced powers. Despite its considerable mineral resources, the country's economy has stagnated in recent years; the difficulty of establishing land ownership has contributed to this, as has the need to protect the environment in what remains a largely subsistence culture. In 2006 the United Nations downgraded Papua New Guinea's status to least developed nation.

TERRITORY AND POPULATION

Papua New Guinea extends from the equator to Cape Baganowa in the Louisiade Archipelago to 11° 40' S. lat. and from the border of West Irian to 160° E. long. with a total area of 462,840 sq. km. According to the 2000 census the population was 5,190,786 (2,691,744 males); density, 11·2 per sq. km.

The UN gives an estimated population for 2010 of 6·89m.

In 2005, 86·6% of the population lived in rural areas. In 1999 population of Port Moresby (National Capital District) was 293,000. Population of other main towns (1990 census): Lae, 80,655; Madang, 27,057; Wewak, 23,224; Goroka, 17,855; Mount Hagen, 17,392; Rabaul, 17,022. The areas, populations and capitals of the provinces are:

Provinces	*Sq. km*	*Census 2000*	*Capital*
Bougainville	9,300	175,160	Arawa
Central	29,500	183,983	Port Moresby
Chimbu	6,100	259,703	Kundiawa
East New Britain	15,500	220,133	Rabaul
East Sepik	42,800	343,181	Wewak

Provinces	Sq. km	Census 2000	Capital
Eastern Highlands	11,200	432,972	Goroka
Enga	12,800	295,031	Wabag
Gulf	34,500	106,898	Kerema
Madang	29,000	365,106	Madang
Manus	2,100	43,387	Lorengau
Milne Bay	14,000	210,412	Alotau
Morobe	34,500	539,404	Lae
National Capital District	240	254,158	—
New Ireland	9,600	118,350	Kavieng
Oro	22,800	133,065	Popondetta
Sandaun	36,300	185,741	Vanimo
Southern Highlands	23,800	546,265	Mendi
West New Britain	21,000	184,508	Kimbe
Western	99,300	153,304	Daru
Western Highlands	8,500	440,025	Mount Hagen

Tok Pisin (or Pidgin, a creole of English), Hiri Motu and English are all official languages.

SOCIAL STATISTICS

Estimates, 2003: births, 177,000; deaths, 53,000. Rates, 2003 estimates (per 1,000 population): births, 31·2; deaths, 9·3. Expectation of life at birth in 2007 was 58·7 years for males and 63·0 years for females. Annual population growth rate, 1992–2002, 2·6%. Infant mortality, 2005, 54 per 1,000 live births; fertility rate, 2004, 3·9 births per woman.

CLIMATE

There is a monsoon climate, with high temperatures and humidity the year round. Port Moresby is in a rain shadow and is not typical of the rest of Papua New Guinea. Jan. 82°F (27·8°C), July 78°F (25·6°C). Annual rainfall 40" (1,011 mm).

CONSTITUTION AND GOVERNMENT

The constitution took effect on 16 Sept. 1975. The head of state is the British sovereign, who is represented by a *Governor-General*, nominated by parliament for six-year terms. A single legislative house, known as the *National Parliament*, is made up of 109 members: 89 district representatives and 20 provincial representatives (MPs). The members are elected by universal suffrage; elections are held every five years. All citizens over the age of 18 are eligible to vote and stand for election. Voting is by secret ballot and follows the limited preferential system. The *Prime Minister*, nominated by parliament and appointed by the Governor-General, selects ministers for the National Executive Council. The government cannot be subjected to a vote of no confidence in the first 18 months of office. The 20 provincial assemblies, comprising elected national MPs, appointed members and elected local government representatives, are headed by a Governor, normally the provincial representative in the National Parliament.

National Anthem

'Arise, all you sons of this land'; words and tune by T. Shacklady.

RECENT ELECTIONS

Parliamentary elections were held between 30 June and 14 July 2007. Sir Michael Somare's National Alliance Party won 27 out of 109 seats; Papua New Guinea Party, 8 seats; People's Action Party, 6; Pangu Party, 5; People's Democratic Movement, 5; United Resources Party, 5; People's Progress Party, 4; New Generation Party, 4; People's National Congress Party, 4; Rural Development Party, 4; People's Party, 3; Melanesian Liberal Party, 2; People's Labour Party, 2; PNG Country Party, 2; United Party, 2; Melanesian Alliance Party, 1; National Advance Party, 1; People's First Party, 1; PNG Conservative Party, 1; PNG Labour Party, 1; PNG National Party, 1; ind. 20.

Sir Paulias Matane was elected governor-general by parliament on 27 May 2004.

CURRENT ADMINISTRATION

Governor-General: Sir Paulias Matane; b. 1931 (took office on 29 June 2004).

In March 2010 the government comprised:

Prime Minister and Minister for Autonomy and Autonomous Regions, Transport and Works: Sir Michael Somare, GCMG, CH; b. 1936 (National Alliance Party; sworn in 5 Aug. 2002 for the third time, having previously been prime minister from 1975 to 1980 and from 1982 to 1985).

Deputy Prime Minister and Minister of Lands and Physical Planning: Puka Temu.

Minister of Agriculture and Livestock: John Hickey. *Commerce and Industry:* Gabriel Kapris. *Communication and Information:* Patrick Tammur. *Community Development, Women, Religion and Sports:* Dame Carol Kidu. *Conservation and Environment:* Benny Allan. *Correctional and Administrative Services:* Tony Aimo. *Defence:* Bob Dadae. *Education:* James Marabe. *Fisheries:* Ben Semri. *Foreign Affairs, Trade and Immigration:* Sam Abal. *Forestry:* Belden Namah. *Health, and HIV/AIDS:* Sasa Zibe. *Higher Education, Research, Science and Technology:* Michael Ogio. *Housing and Urban Development:* Andrew Kumbakor. *Inter-Government Relations:* Job Pomat. *Internal Security:* Sani Rambe. *Justice:* Allan Marat. *Labour and Industrial Relations:* Mark Maipakai. *National Planning and District Development:* Paul Tiensten. *Petroleum and Energy:* William Duma. *Public Enterprise:* Arthur Somare. *Public Service:* Peter O'Neill. *Tourism, Culture and the Arts, and Civil Aviation:* Charles Abel. *Treasury and Finance:* Patrick Pruaitch. *Minister of State Assisting the Prime Minister on Constitutional Matters:* Philemon Embel.

Office of the Prime Minister: http://www.pm.gov.pg

CURRENT LEADERS

Sir Michael Somare

Position

Prime Minister

Introduction

Sir Michael Somare GCMG, CH was the first prime minister of independent Papua New Guinea, having negotiated its independence from Australia. His reputation for surrounding himself with able ministers did not prevent him from being twice toppled by close associates, a common occurrence in Papua New Guinean politics. Returning in 2002 to serve his third term 17 years after his second, Somare faced a depressed economy and the ramifications of the Bougainville peace agreement. Nevertheless, he was returned for a second consecutive term as premier following elections in mid-2007. Relations with his country's most important neighbour, Australia, have been strained and Somare has pressed for closer ties with East Asia and the Pacific. He was knighted by Queen Elizabeth II of the UK in 1990 and was honoured with a pontifical knighthood by Pope John Paul II in 1992.

Early Life

Michael Somare was born on 9 April 1936 in Rabaul, East New Britain, the eldest child of Kambe Somare and Ludwig Somare Sana, a policeman from East Sepik province. During the Second World War Somare received his early education at a Japanese-run school in Karau, the family village in East Sepik, where he learnt Japanese. He left Sogari High School in 1957 to teach until returning to Sogari for further training in 1962. After two years as deputy headmaster of Talidig Primary School in Madang he moved into radio journalism.

Removed from his position for his political views, Somare was elected to the House of Assembly in 1968 as regional MP for East Sepik. The previous year Somare had helped to found the Papua New Guinea United Party (Pangu Party) and became its parliamentary leader and leader of the opposition. Re-elected with an independence agenda in 1972, Somare became Papua New Guinea's first chief minister. Peaceful negotiations with Australia's prime minister, Gough Whitlam, led to self-rule in 1973 and full independence from Australia in Sept. 1975.

Career in Office

Constitutional issues dominated Somare's first term of office. Setting up the Constitutional Development Committee (CPC), he brought together a coalition to produce a 'home-grown' constitution. Influenced by Fiji's prime minister, Ratu Sir Kamisese Mara, Somare promoted a Melanesian attitude towards politics, attempting to gain co-operation across tribal and linguistic lines. He expressed his nationalist pride and belief in traditional practices by training to succeed his father as *sana* (peacemaker) of his village.

Negotiations with Australia, although mostly cordial, were complicated by territorial uncertainties, finally settled by the Torres Strait Treaty of Dec. 1978. The treaty established a Protected Zone for the coastal peoples of southern Papua and the Torres Strait Islanders, allowing them free movement across the new sea border for traditional practices.

Having won the 1977 elections, Somare's coalition with the People's Progress Party collapsed when its leader, Julius Chan, toppled him with a vote of no confidence in 1980. After two years of Chan's premiership, Somare returned as prime minister with an electoral mandate. In Nov. 1985 he was again forced from office by a vote of no confidence, this time led by his successor, Paias Wingti. Somare stepped down as Pangu leader in May 1988 and was succeeded by Rabbie Namaliu, who formed a government in July 1988. Serving as Namaliu's foreign minister, Somare courted the Association of South East Asian Nations (ASEAN), to which Papua New Guinea held observer status, signing a Treaty of Amity and Co-operation in 1989. Urging less dependence on Australia, Papua New Guinea's largest aid donor and importer, Somare persuaded Namaliu's government to reduce foreign control of the mining industry, causing a dent in exports.

The 1990s saw deteriorating relations between Somare and his party. In 1992 he regained the Pangu leadership but resigned in 1993. Somare again left Pangu only to rejoin in 1994. His attention turned to regional politics between 1995–99 when he served as governor of East Sepik after the passing of the Organic Law on Provincial and Local-level Governments, which gave more power to national MPs in their constituencies. His relationship with Pangu ended in 1997 when he was ejected by the Pangu MPs. Forming his own party, the National Alliance—drawing support in the Islands and Momase, his home region—he was re-elected to parliament in 1997. Despite initial support from Bill Skate of the People's National Congress and his coalition partners, Somare lost to Skate in the vote for prime minister. Following the early termination of Skate's premiership in 1999, Somare was appointed to Sir Mekere Morauta's government and given the foreign affairs and Bougainville portfolios. As foreign minister Somare implemented the rejection of Skate's diplomatic recognition of Taiwan, restoring good relations with the People's Republic of China, a major aid donor. Instead, Somare proposed reciprocal investment and trading relations with Taiwan while adhering to the 'One China' principle. Morauta dismissed him in Dec. 2000, accusing him of disloyalty, whereupon Somare became leader of the opposition. In Aug. 2001 Somare accompanied former US president Jimmy Carter to observe Timor-Leste's first parliamentary elections.

The elections of 2002 were the country's most violent and unpredictable. About 70% of MPs were ousted, irregularities were rife and over 30 people died. Somare managed to install Skate as speaker, strengthening his own chances of being elected prime minister. Surrounded by a police cordon, Parliament unanimously voted for Somare. Changes in the electoral system, pushed through by Morauta, tightened up party rules, ensuring MPs remained loyal, thus giving Somare better prospects for stable government. Somare pleased MPs by adopting his old approach of inclusive government, appointing ministers regardless of political affiliations, including former prime minister Sir Rabbie Namaliu.

The success of the National Alliance was partly attributed to the perilous state of the economy, then in its third year of recession. Somare accused Morauta's government of reckless spending, leading to high inflation and a deficit of US$50m. in the first half of 2002, compared to a US$3·5m. surplus for the first six months of 2001. Spending cuts stabilized the currency, the *kina*, which had fallen dramatically during the previous three administrations from a value of US$1·25 in June 1995 to US$0·25 by Aug. 2002.

Australian Prime Minister John Howard's belief that Morauta had been Papua New Guinea's last hope promised difficult relations with the new government. Despite threats to turn away from Australia, in Sept. 2003 Somare agreed to a deal involving operational duties for Australian policemen and professionals within Papua New Guinea's administration, a step beyond the advisory roles previously agreed. This caused unrest in Somare's coalition, with Sir Julius Chan warning against confrontation with Australia. Following a Supreme Court ruling in May 2005 that the Australian deployment violated the country's constitution, the policemen left Papua New Guinea. However, a further agreement was reached in Aug. 2005 whereby a reduced Australian contingent would return to help train the Papuan police and tackle corruption.

During the state visit of Malaysia's outgoing prime minister, Dr Mahathir Mohamad, in Oct. 2003, Somare pressed for full membership of ASEAN, as part of a shift towards Asia for aid and investment.

In Aug. 2006 the government declared a state of emergency in Southern Highlands. Accusing the provincial government of corruption, Somare ordered the deployment of soldiers and police to restore law, order and good governance in the energy-rich territory, which is also key to a proposed gas pipeline link between Papua New Guinea and Queensland in Australia.

It was reported in Sept. 2006 that nearly 2% of Papua New Guinea's population was believed to be suffering from HIV/AIDS, with infection rates in double figures in some areas, and that Somare was directly overseeing a co-ordinated approach to tackling the crisis.

Following the 2007 parliamentary elections, in which more than 2,000 troops and police were deployed in an attempt to prevent a repeat of the violence in 2002, Somare became prime minister again at the head of a National Alliance-led coalition government.

DEFENCE

The Papua New Guinea Defence Force had a total estimated strength of 3,100 in 2007 consisting of land, maritime and air elements. The Navy is based at Port Moresby and Manus. Personnel numbered around 400 in 2007. There is an air force, 200 strong in 2007, but it does not possess any combat capable aircraft.

Defence expenditure in 2006 totalled US$30m. (US$5 per capita), representing 0·6% of GDP.

INTERNATIONAL RELATIONS

Papua New Guinea is a member of the UN, World Bank, IMF and several other UN specialized agencies, WTO, Commonwealth, Asian Development Bank, APEC, Colombo Plan, Pacific Islands Forum, SPC, Antarctic Treaty and is an observer at ASEAN and an ACP member state of the ACP-EU relationship.

ECONOMY

Agriculture accounted for 19·1% of GDP in 2006, industry 45·2% and services 35·7%.

Overview

Papua New Guinea has experienced sound growth and macroeconomic stability since 2002. The country has large deposits of oil, gas, gold, copper, timber and silver. The formal economy is focused on large-scale export of natural resources, while the informal sector consists of subsistence activities by a large proportion of the rural population.

In recent years, higher prices for key export commodities (such as petroleum, gold and copper) plus expanding mineral production have helped strengthen the fiscal and external positions. The outlook for growth in the near-term is favourable. However, GDP per capita has shown little improvement since independence in 1975 owing to a volatile mineral sector, high population growth and poor economic management. Non-mineral sectors have been underdeveloped while poor infrastructure, lack of governance and an unattractive business environment have further restricted growth.

GDP growth is expected to rise to over 4% in the near future as a result of increased production from new mines and increased government spending in the non-mineral sector. Poverty nonetheless remains high among those engaged in subsistence farming.

Currency

The unit of currency is the *kina* (PGK) of 100 *toea*. The kina was floated in Oct. 1994. Foreign exchange reserves were US$543m. in July 2005, gold reserves 63,000 troy oz and total money supply was K2,765m. Inflation was 0·9% in 2007, rising to 10·7% in 2008.

Budget

In 2005 revenues totalled K5,243·0m. (tax revenue, 71·4%) and expenditures K4,104·0m. (current expenditure, 69·0%).

VAT is 10%.

Performance

Papua New Guinea experienced a three-year recession at the start of the millennium, with the economy shrinking by 2·5% in 2000, 0·1% in 2001 and 0·2% in 2002. Since then there has been a recovery, with growth of 6·5% in 2007 and 7·0% in 2008. Total GDP in 2008 was US$8·2bn.

Banking and Finance

The Bank of Papua New Guinea (*Governor*, Loi Martin Bakani) assumed the central banking functions formerly undertaken by the Reserve Bank of Australia on 1 Nov. 1973. A national banking institution, the Papua New Guinea Banking Corporation, has been established. This bank has assumed the Papua New Guinea business of the Commonwealth Trading Bank of Australia.

In 2002 there were seven commercial banks (Australia and New Zealand Banking Group; Bank of Hawaii; Bank of South Pacific; Maybank; MBf Finance; Papua New Guinea Banking Corporation; Westpac Bank) and a Rural Development Bank.

Total commercial bank deposits, 1992, K1,318·2m. Total savings account deposits, 1992, K226·8m. In addition, the Agriculture Bank of Papua New Guinea had assets of K82·6m. in 1992, and finance companies and merchant banks had total assets of K198·4m.

There is a stock exchange in Port Moresby.

ENERGY AND NATURAL RESOURCES

Environment

Carbon dioxide emissions from the consumption and flaring of fossil fuels in 2008 were the equivalent of 0·8 tonnes per capita.

Electricity

Installed capacity was an estimated 0·5m. kW in 2004. Production in 2004 was estimated at 1·39bn. kWh, around 66% of it hydro-electric. Consumption per capita was an estimated 258 kWh.

Oil and Gas

Natural gas reserves in 2008 were 440bn. cu. metres; output in 2004 was 85m. cu. metres. Crude oil production (2004), 18m. bbls. Oil predominantly comes from the Iagifu field in the Southern Highlands. There were 240m. bbls of proven oil reserves in 2007.

Minerals

In 2004 the mineral sector produced 20·8% of GDP. Copper is the main mineral product. Gold, copper and silver are the only minerals produced in quantity. The Misima open-pit gold mine was opened in 1989 but its resources were depleted by the end of 2001. The Porgera gold mine opened in 1990 with an expected life of 20 years. Major copper deposits in Bougainville have proven reserves of about 800m. tonnes; mining was halted by secessionist rebel activity. Copper and gold deposits in the Star Mountains of the Western Province are being developed by Ok Tedi Mining Ltd at the Mt Fubilan mine. Production of gold commenced in 1984 and of copper concentrates in 1987. In 2005 Ok Tedi Mining Ltd produced 192,978 tonnes of copper and 16 tonnes of gold. Gold mining also began at Lihir in 1997. In 2005 total gold production was 67 tonnes; silver production in 2002 was 64 tonnes.

Agriculture

In 2002 agriculture employed 73% of the economically active population. In 2002 there were approximately 220,000 ha. of arable land and 650,000 ha. of permanent cropland. Minor commercial crops include pyrethrum, tea, peanuts and spices. Locally consumed food crops include sweet potatoes, maize, taro, bananas, rice and sago. Tropical fruits grow abundantly. There is extensive grassland. The sugar industry has made the country self-sufficient in this commodity while a beef-cattle industry is being developed.

Production (2002, in 1,000 tonnes): bananas, 860; coconuts, 513; sweet potatoes, 490; sugarcane, 370; palm oil, 316; yams, 280; taro, 250; cassava, 130.

Livestock (2003 estimates): pigs, 1·8m.; cattle, 90,000; chickens, 4m.

Forestry

The forest area totalled 29·44m. ha. in 2005 (65·0% of the land area). Timber production is important for both local consumption and export. Timber production was 7·24m. cu. metres in 2007.

Fisheries

Tuna is the major resource. In 2005 the fish catch was an estimated 250,280 tonnes (85% sea fish).

INDUSTRY

Secondary and service industries are expanding for the local market. The main industries are food processing, beverages, tobacco, timber products, wood and fabricated metal products. Industry accounted for 45·2% of GDP in 2006, with manufacturing contributing 6·1%. Production (2002): palm oil, 370,000 tonnes; copra, 110,000 tonnes; wood-based panels, 79,000 cu. metres; sawnwood, 70,000 cu. metres.

Labour

In 2000 there were 2,344,734 persons in employment (51·3% males). The rate of unemployment was 2·8%.

INTERNATIONAL TRADE

Australian aid amounts to an annual $A300m. The 'Pactra II' agreement of 1991 established a free trade zone with Australia and protects Australian investments. Foreign debt was US$1,849m. in 2005.

Imports and Exports

Imports in 2004 were US$1,567·2m. (US$1,302·4m. in 2003); exports were US$2,722·2m. (US$2,260·2m. in 2003).

The main imports in terms of value are machinery and transport equipment, manufactured goods, and food and live animals; and the main exports crude petroleum, gold and logs.

Of imports in 2001, Australia furnished 60·0%; Japan, 8·5%; Singapore, 7·8%; USA, 7·1%. Of exports in 2001, Singapore took 27·5%; Japan, 13·2%; Australia 10·6%; China, 4·4%.

COMMUNICATIONS

Roads

In 2002 there were 19,600 km of roads, only about 690 km of which were paved. There were 38,200 passenger cars in use in 2007 and 11,300 lorries and vans.

Civil Aviation

Jacksons International Airport is at Port Moresby. The state-owned national carrier is Air Niugini. In 2003 there were scheduled international flights to Brisbane, Cairns, Honiara, Manila, Singapore, Sydney and Tokyo. There are a total of 177 airports and airstrips with scheduled services.

Shipping

There are 12 entry and four other main ports served by five major shipping lines; the Papua New Guinea Shipping Corporation is state-owned. Sea-going shipping totalled 72,000 GRT in 2002, including oil tankers 2,000 GRT.

Telecommunications

In 2007 there were 360,000 telephone subscribers, or 56·9 for every 1,000 inhabitants. There were 300,000 mobile phone subscribers in 2007 and 110,000 internet users in 2006. In Dec. 2004 the government rejected a bid by a South African joint venture to acquire a 51% stake in the state-owned telecommunications company Telikom PNG.

Postal Services

The 1996 Postal Service Act created the government-owned Post PNG Limited. In 2004 its network consisted of 31 post offices, 26 agency post offices and two international mail exchange centres.

SOCIAL INSTITUTIONS

Justice

The judicial system consists of a Supreme Court, a National Court, and district and local courts. The Supreme Court sittings are usually held with three or five judges. In 2004 there were 64,709 court cases registered of which 16,459 were civil cases. The death penalty for wilful murder was abolished in 1970 but reintroduced in 1991, although there have not been any executions since 1954.

The population in penal institutions in April 2005 was 4,056 (69 per 100,000 of national population).

Education

Obligatory universal primary education is a government objective. In 1990 about two-thirds of eligible children were attending school. In 2001 there were 3,055 elementary and primary schools with 395,129 pupils and 11,307 teachers, 77,451 pupils in secondary schools (2,187 teachers) and 14,333 students in institutes of higher education. There are six universities: the University of Papua New Guinea (UPNG), Port Moresby; the Papua New Guinea University of Technology, Lae; Divine Word University, Madang; Pacific Adventist University, Boroko; the University of Goroka; and the University of Vudal, Rabaul. UPNG, founded in 1965, has two campuses in the capital, five provincial open campuses and 13 study centres. In 2002 there were also ten colleges, eight nursing schools and three academic institutes.

Adult literacy rate was 57·3% in 2003 (63·4% among males and 50·9% among females).

In 2000–01 total expenditure on education came to 2·4% of GNP and 17·5% of total government spending.

Health

In 2000 there were 275 physicians, 90 dentists and 2,841 nurses. Provision of hospital beds in 1993 was 34 per 10,000 persons.

RELIGION

At the 2000 census there were 4·93m. Christians: Roman Catholics made up 27·0%; Lutherans, 19·5%; United Church, 11·5%; Anglicans, 3·2%. In 1998 the Catholic Church had four archdioceses (Madang, Mount Hagen, Port Moresby and Rabaul), 14 dioceses, 340 parishes and 540 priests.

CULTURE

World Heritage Sites

There is one UNESCO site in Papua New Guinea: Kuk Early Agricultural Site (inscribed on the list in 2008).

Broadcasting

The state-run National Broadcasting Commission operates a national radio station and provincial services. EMTV is the country's only commercial radio station; TV reception is limited to Port Moresby and provincial urban centres. In 2003 television receivers (colour by PAL) numbered 130,000.

Press

In 2004 there were two daily newspapers (the *Post-Courier* and the *National*) and a number of weeklies and monthlies. The *Post-Courier* is the oldest (1969) and most widely read, with a daily circulation of 29,000.

Tourism

In 2004 there were 59,000 visitors; spending by tourists totalled US$6m.

Festivals

Alongside the major Christian festivals several cultural shows are held, in Enga (late July), at Mount Hagen (Western Highlands; late Aug.) and at Goroka (Eastern Highlands; mid-Sept.). Independence Day is celebrated on 16 Sept.

Libraries

The National Library Service was created in 1975 and the National Library opened in 1978. The University of Papua New Guinea's Michael Somare Library has over 450,000 volumes. The National Archives were established in 1957 at Waigani, National Capital District.

DIPLOMATIC REPRESENTATIVES

Of Papua New Guinea in the United Kingdom (3rd Floor, 14 Waterloo Pl., London, SW1Y 4AR)
High Commissioner: Jean Kekedo, CSM, OBE.

Of the United Kingdom in Papua New Guinea (Sec 411 Lot 1 and 2, Kiroki St., Waigani, Port Moresby)
High Commissioner: David Dunn.

Of Papua New Guinea in the USA (1779 Massachusetts Ave., NW, Washington, D.C., 20036)
Ambassador: Evan Paki.

Of the USA in Papua New Guinea (Douglas St., Port Moresby)
Ambassador: Teddy B. Taylor.

Of Papua New Guinea to the United Nations
Ambassador: Robert Aisi.

Of Papua New Guinea to the European Union
Ambassador: Isaac Lupari.

FURTHER READING

National Statistical Office. *Summary of Statistics.* Annual.—*Abstract of Statistics.* Quarterly.
Bank of Papua New Guinea. *Quarterly Economic Bulletin.*
Turner, A., *Historical Dictionary of Papua New Guinea.* 1995
Waiko, J. D., *Short History of Papua New Guinea.* 1993

National Statistical Office: National Statistical Office, PO Box 337, Waigani, National Capital District, Port Moresby.
Website: http://www.nso.gov.pg

Bougainville

The region of Bougainville, as part of New Guinea, became a United Nations Trust Territory in 1947 under the jurisdiction of Australia. Bougainville declared independence in 1975 but the uprising was suppressed and the islands became part of the North Solomons Province of the newly independent Papua New Guinea. Following tensions between landowners and Rio Tinto, the owners of the Panguna copper mine, conflict between separatists and Papua New Guinea began in 1989, lasting nearly a decade. A ceasefire was agreed in 1998, overseen by the United Nations. The Bougainville Peace Agreement was signed in Aug. 2001, allowing for the creation of an autonomous government and a referendum on full independence 10–15 years later. After the promulgation of a constitution, elections were held for the autonomous government in May–June 2005.

Area, 9,300 sq. km (3,600 sq. miles); population (2000), 175,160. The autonomous region consists of the main Bougainville island, Buka island and several smaller island groups. The government is currently based at Buka but the capital city will eventually revert to the former capital, Arawa.

In presidential elections held in Dec. 2008 James Tanis was elected with 54·7% of votes cast, defeating Sam Akoitai with 34·4%. Tanis took office on 6 Jan. 2009, succeeding acting president John Tabinaman. He ran for re-election in the elections that were scheduled for May 2010 at the end of the late president Joseph Kabui's term.

Agriculture is the mainstay of Bougainville's economy. Major crops include cocoa (production in 2006, 16,000 tonnes) and copra (12,472 tonnes). However, the region is still reliant on grants and donors, raising only 20% of its 2007 budget internally. New exploration for minerals is banned but the government is considering reopening Panguna. There is an airport at Buka.

PARAGUAY

República del Paraguay
(Republic of Paraguay)

Capital: Asunción
Population estimate, 2010: 6·46m.
GDP per capita, 2007: (PPP$) 4,433
HDI/world rank: 0·761/101

KEY HISTORICAL EVENTS

Paraguay was occupied by the Spanish in 1537 and became a Spanish colony as part of the viceroyalty of Peru. The area gained its independence, as the Republic of Paraguay, on 14 May 1811. Paraguay was then ruled by a succession of dictators. A devastating war fought from 1865 to 1870 between Paraguay and a coalition of Argentina, Brazil and Uruguay reduced Paraguay's population from about 600,000 to 233,000. Further severe losses were incurred during the war with Bolivia (1932–35) over territorial claims in the Chaco inspired by the unfounded belief that minerals existed in the territory. A peace treaty by which Paraguay obtained most of the area her troops had conquered was signed in July 1938.

A new constitution took effect in Feb. 1968 under which executive power is discharged by an executive president. Gen. Alfredo Stroessner Mattiauda was re-elected seven times between 1958 and 1988. Since then, Paraguay has had more or less democratic government. On 23 March 1999 Paraguay's vice-president Luis Maria Argaña was assassinated. The following day, Congress voted to impeach President Raúl Cubas who was said to be implicated in the murder. He then resigned. The victory of Fernando Lugo of the Patriotic Alliance for Change in the April 2008 presidential election brought to an end the 61-year rule of the Colorado Party, at the time the world's longest-ruling party.

TERRITORY AND POPULATION

Paraguay is bounded in the northwest by Bolivia, northeast and east by Brazil and southeast, south and southwest by Argentina. The area is 406,752 sq. km (157,042 sq. miles).

The 2002 census population was 5,163,198 (2,603,242 males), giving a density of 12·7 per sq. km. In 2005, 58·5% lived in urban areas.

The UN gives an estimated population for 2010 of 6·46m.

In 2002 the capital, Asunción, had a population of 512,112. Other major cities (2002 census populations) are: Ciudad del Este, 222,274; San Lorenzo, 204,356; Luque, 185,127.

There are 17 departments and the capital city. Area and population at the 2002 census:

Department	*Area in sq. km*	*Population*
Asunción (city)	117	512,112
Central	2,465	1,362,893
Alto Paraná	14,895	558,672
Itapúa	16,525	453,692
Caaguazú	11,474	435,357
San Pedro	20,002	318,698
Cordillera	4,948	233,854
Paraguari	8,705	221,932
Concepción	18,051	179,450
Guairá	3,846	178,650
Canendiyú	14,667	140,137
Caazapá	9,496	139,517
Amambay	12,933	114,917
Misiones	9,556	101,783
Neembucú	12,147	76,348
Oriental	*159,827*	*5,028,012*
Presidente Hayes	72,907	82,493
Boquerón[1]	91,669	41,106
Alto Paraguay[2]	82,349	11,587
Occidental	*246,925*	*135,186*

[1]Incorporates former department of Nueva Asunción.
[2]Incorporates former department of Chaco.

The population is mixed Spanish and Guaraní Indian. There are 89,000 unassimilated Indians of other tribal origin, in the Chaco and the forests of eastern Paraguay. The official languages are Spanish and Guaraní: 24·8% of the population speak only Guaraní; 51·5% are bilingual (Spanish/Guaraní); and 7·6% speak only Spanish.

Mennonites, who arrived in three groups (1927, 1930 and 1947), are settled in the Chaco and eastern Paraguay. There are also Korean and Japanese settlers.

SOCIAL STATISTICS

2006 births, 112,659; deaths, 19,298. Rates, 2006 (per 1,000 population): birth, 18·7; death, 3·2. Annual population growth rate, 2000–05, 2·0%. Expectation of life, 2007: 69·6 years for males and 73·8 for females. Infant mortality, 2005, 20 per 1,000 live births; fertility rate, 2004, 3·8 births per woman (along with Bolivia the highest in South America).

CLIMATE

A tropical climate, with abundant rainfall and only a short dry season from July to Sept., when temperatures are lowest. Asunción, Jan. 81°F (27°C), July 64°F (17·8°C). Annual rainfall 53" (1,316 mm).

CONSTITUTION AND GOVERNMENT

On 18 June 1992 a Constituent Assembly approved a new constitution. The head of state is the *President,* elected for a non-renewable five-year term. Parliament consists of an 80-member *Chamber of Deputies*, elected from departmental constituencies, and a 45-member *Senate*, elected from a single national constituency.

National Anthem

'Paraguayos, república o muerte!' ('Paraguayans, republic or death!'); words by F. Acuña de Figueroa, tune by F. Dupuy.

RECENT ELECTIONS

Parliamentary and presidential elections were held on 20 April 2008. Fernando Lugo of the Patriotic Alliance for Change (APC) was elected president with 42·3% of votes cast. Bianca Ovelar of the National Republican Association–Colorado Party (ANR), which had held power for the previous 61 years, won 31·8% and Lino Oviedo of the National Union of Ethical Citizens (UNACE) won 22·8%. Turnout was 65·6%.

In the parliamentary elections the ANR won 30 seats in the Chamber of Deputies, the Authentic Radical Liberal Party (PLRA) won 27 seats, the UNACE won 15, the Beloved Fatherland Movement (MPQ) 3, the APC 2, the Popular Movement Tekojoja 1, the Democratic Progressive Party (PDP) 1 and the Departmental Alliance Boquerón 1. In the Senate the ANR won 15 seats, the PLRA won 14, the UNACE 9, the MPQ 4, the Popular Movement Tekojoja 1, the PDP 1 and the Party for a Country of Solidarity (PPS) 1.

CURRENT ADMINISTRATION

President: Fernando Lugo; b. 1951 (APC; sworn in 15 Aug. 2008).

Vice-President: Federico Franco.

In March 2010 the cabinet comprised:

Minister of Agriculture and Livestock: Enzo Cardozo. *Defence:* Luis Bareiro Spaini. *Education and Culture:* Luis Alberto Riart. *Finance:* Dionisio Borda. *Foreign Affairs:* Héctor Lacognata. *Industry and Commerce:* Francisco Rivas. *Interior:* Rafael Filizzola. *Justice and Labour:* Humberto Blasco. *Public Health and Social Welfare:* Esperanza Martínez. *Public Works:* Efraín Alegre.

Office of the President (Spanish only):
http://www.presidencia.gov.py

CURRENT LEADERS

Fernando Armindo Lugo Mendes

Position

President

Introduction

Fernando Lugo was elected president in Aug. 2008 for a five-year term. A former bishop of San Pedro, he is leader of the Christian Democratic Party and head of a 12-party coalition, the Patriotic Alliance for Change (APC). He is the first president from a party other than the National Republican Association (ANR, or Colorado Party) since 1947.

Early Life

Fernando Lugo was born on 30 May 1951 in the San Pedro del Parana District of Itapúa. His parents were members of the ruling Colorado Party while Lugo's uncle, Epifanio Mendez Fleitas, was a Colorado Party dissident and the main rival of Gen. Alfredo Stroessner. During Stroessner's rule (1954–89), both Lugo's parents were arrested while his three brothers and uncle spent periods in exile.

In Oct. 1951 the Lugo family moved to Itapúa's capital, Encarnación, where Lugo completed his education and qualified as a teacher in 1969. He taught in the San Pedro department and in 1970 joined the Catholic Society of the Divine Word. In 1972 he took religious vows and in 1977 was ordained. He went as a missionary to Ecuador, where he spent five years and became influenced by liberation theology. Returning to Paraguay in 1982, the Church, under pressure from the Stroessner regime, sent Lugo to Rome to study at the Pontificia Università Gregoriana. In 1987 he graduated in sociology, specializing in Church social doctrine, and returned to Paraguay. He taught at the Superior Institute of Theology in Asunción, set up national and regional Episcopal commissions and, after Stroessner's fall in 1989, pressed for land reform. In 1992 he became vice president of the Confederation of Religious Leaders and in 1994 was made bishop of the diocese of San Pedro.

As internal rifts weakened the Colorado Party, Lugo's public profile rose. Nicknamed 'Bishop of the Poor,' he became a leading non-partisan critic of the government. He called for popular movements to rally against the government and resigned his bishopric in 2005. He led a high-profile march through the capital in 2006 and in Dec. of that year applied to be laicized to allow him to run for president. In Oct. 2007 he joined the Christian Democratic Party in a 12-party coalition and won the presidential election of April 2008. The Pope accepted his laicism in July 2008.

Career in Office

Having campaigned on a platform of social reform, Lugo needed to confront the country's widespread poverty and social inequality and promised to enact land reform, prompting conservatives to label him a leftist ally of President Hugo Chávez of Venezuela. In 2009 he initiated modest reforms in education and health care and negotiated an agreement with neighbouring Brazil to increase Paraguay's revenue from their jointly-controlled Itaipu hydroelectric plant. However, he encountered increasing hostility and resistance within Congress and from the armed forces, and had his moral authority undermined by paternity claims made against him by three women during the year.

DEFENCE

The army, navy and air forces are separate services under a single command. The President of the Republic is the active C.-in-C. Conscription is for 12 months (two years in the navy).

In 2006 defence expenditure totalled US$67m. (US$10 per capita), representing 0·7% of GDP.

Army

Strength (2007) 7,600 (1,500 conscripts). In addition there is a paramilitary Special Police Force numbering 14,800 (4,000 conscripts).

Navy

Personnel in 2007 totalled 1,950 (or which 850 conscripts) including 900 marines (of which 200 conscripts) and 100 naval aviation.

Air Force

The air force had a strength of 1,100 in 2007 (200 conscripts). There are ten combat capable aircraft including Lockheed T-33s.

INTERNATIONAL RELATIONS

Paraguay is a member of the UN, World Bank, IMF and several other UN specialized agencies, WTO, IOM, Inter-American Development Bank, SELA, LAIA, OAS, MERCOSUR and UNASUR.

ECONOMY

In 2006 agriculture accounted for 21·0% of GDP, industry 18·3% and services 60·7%.

Overview

In the 1990s growth was slow but steady until 1998 when the economy stagnated. In 2002 performance slumped again, partly as a knock-on from the recession in Argentina, leading to a request for IMF help. There has been steady growth since 2003, with restored confidence in public institutions, structural reform and debt reduction leading to fiscal account stability. Since 2004, economic growth has been at its highest level since the 1970s, boosted by strong exports.

There are few mineral resources and the economy is focused on agriculture, which contributed 21·0% of GDP in 2006. 42% of the population live in rural areas and agriculture (particularly meat and soy) accounts for nearly all registered exports. The country is also a major exporter of hydro-electric power.

Commercialization of the agricultural and timber production sectors has led to forest clearances. Combined with rising population levels, this has accelerated movement into urban areas. There is a large informal component of the economy and most enterprises are small. A growing concern is the lack of infrastructure to serve basic needs. Some 60% of the population is in poverty and only 35% of the rural population has access to drinking water. Owing to high food prices, absolute poverty increased in the period 2002–07. Other problems include endemic corruption and Paraguay's reputation as a centre for smuggling, organized crime and money laundering.

Currency

The unit of currency is the *guaraní* (PYG), notionally divided into 100 *céntimos*. In July 2005 total money supply was 4,733·6bn. guaranís and foreign exchange reserves were US$1,109m. Inflation was 10·2% in 2008 (8·1% in 2007).

Budget

Budgetary central government revenue and expenditure in 1bn. guaranís:

	2001	*2002*	*2003*
Revenue	4,972·0	5,078·1	6,065·6
Expenditure	4,530·1	4,918·7	5,215·1

Principal sources of revenue in 2003: taxes on goods and services, 2,278·4bn. guaranís; taxes on international trade and transactions, 665·1bn. guaranís; taxes on income, profits and capital gains, 623·9bn. guaranís. Main items of expenditure by economic type in 2003: compensation of employees, 2,724·0bn. guaranís; social benefits, 991·0bn. guaranís; grants, 593·4bn. guaranís.

VAT is 10% (reduced rate, 5%).

Performance

Real GDP growth was 6·8% in 2007 and 5·8% in 2008. Total GDP in 2008 was US$16·0bn.

Banking and Finance

The Central Bank is a state-owned autonomous agency with the sole right of note issue, control over foreign exchange and the supervision of commercial banks (*Governor*, Jorge Raúl Corvalán Mendoza). There is a Superintendencia de Bancos under Edgar Virgilio Paredes Álvarez. In 2002 there were five commercial banks and 11 foreign banks.

There is a stock exchange in Asunción.

ENERGY AND NATURAL RESOURCES

Environment

Paraguay's carbon dioxide emissions from the consumption and flaring of fossil fuels were the equivalent of 0·6 tonnes per capita in 2008.

Electricity

Installed capacity was 7·4m. kW in 2004. Output (2004), 51·92bn. kWh (almost exclusively hydro-electric); consumption per capita in 2004 was 1,141 kWh. Paraguay is the third largest exporter of electricity (after France and Germany), with 45·0bn. kWh in 2004.

Minerals

The country is poor in minerals. Limestone, gypsum, kaolin and salt are extracted. Deposits of bauxite, iron ore, copper, manganese and uranium exist. 2006 estimated output: kaolin, 66,000 tonnes; limestone, 16,000 tonnes.

Agriculture

In 2002, 33·4% of the economically active population were engaged in agriculture. In 2002 there were approximately 3·02m. ha. of arable land and 95,000 ha. of permanent crops.

Output (in 1,000 tonnes), 2002: cassava, 4,430; soybeans, 3,300; sugarcane, 3,210; maize, 867; wheat, 359; oranges, 207; seed cotton, 124; sweet potatoes, 124; watermelons, 115; rice, 105. *Yerba maté*, or strongly flavoured Paraguayan tea, continues to be produced but is declining in importance.

Livestock (2003 estimates): 8·81m. cattle, 3·25m. pigs, 410,000 sheep, 360,000 horses and 16m. chickens.

Forestry

The area under forests in 2005 was 18·48m. ha., or 46·5% of the total land area. Timber production was 10·30m. cu. metres in 2007.

Fisheries

In 2005 the catch totalled approximately 21,000 tonnes, exclusively from inland waters.

INDUSTRY

Paraguay is one of the least industrialized countries in Latin America. Industries include meat packing, sugar processing, cement, textiles, brewing, wood products and consumer goods. In 2006 industry accounted for 18·3% of GDP, with manufacturing contributing 11·8%.

Labour

The labour force in 2002 totalled 1,980,492 (67·9% males). In 2002, 27% of the economically active population were engaged in agriculture, fisheries, hunting and forestry.

Trade Unions

Trade unionists number about 30,000 (Confederación Paraguaya de Trabajadores and Confederación Cristiana de Trabajadores).

INTERNATIONAL TRADE

Foreign debt was US$3,120m. in 2005.

Imports and Exports

Trade in US$1m.:

	2003	*2004*	*2005*	*2006*	*2007*
Imports c.i.f.	2,227·5	3,097·4	3,714·9	5,878·8	5,844·7
Exports f.o.b.	1,241·5	1,625·7	1,687·8	1,906·4	2,784·7

Main imports in 2006: machinery and transport equipment, 46·9%; chemicals and chemical products, 12·2%; petroleum oils, 11·8%; metal tools, 2·6%. Main exports, 2006: soybeans, 23·0%; beef, 21·5%; maize, 8·7%; oilcake and other solid residues, 7·2%. Main import suppliers in 2006: China, 25·1%; Brazil, 19·0%; Argentina, 13·0%; USA, 6·0%. Main export markets, 2006: Uruguay, 22·0%; Brazil, 17·2%; Russia, 11·9%; Cayman Islands, 9·5%.

COMMUNICATIONS

Roads

In 2002 there were around 29,500 km of roads, of which 53·9% were paved. Passenger cars numbered 240,700 in 2007, there were 248,100 lorries and vans, 12,800 buses and coaches, and 134,900 motorcycles and mopeds. There were 845 fatalities as a result of road accidents in 2007.

Rail

The President Carlos Antonio López (formerly Paraguay Central) Railway runs from Asunción to Encarnación, on the Río Alto Paraná, with a length of 441 km (1,435 mm gauge), and connects with Argentine Railways over the Encarnación-Posadas bridge opened in 1989. In 2003 freight carried came to 210,000 tonnes.

Civil Aviation

There is an international airport at Asunción (Silvio Pettirossi). The main Paraguay-based carrier is TAM Airlines (formerly TAM Mercosur). In 2003 scheduled airline traffic of Paraguay-based carriers flew 6m. km, carrying 299,000 passengers (288,000 on international flights). In 2000 Asunción handled 466,000 passengers (422,000 on international flights) and 6,600 tonnes of freight.

Shipping

Asunción, the chief port, is 1,500 km from the sea. In 2002 ocean-going shipping totalled 47,000 GRT, including oil tankers 4,000 GRT.

Telecommunications

In 2008 there were 491,000 main (fixed) telephone lines; mobile phone subscribers numbered 5,954,400 in 2008 (95·5 per 100 persons). There were 460,000 PCs in use in 2005 and 894,200 internet users in 2008.

Postal Services

In 2003 there were 258 post offices.

SOCIAL INSTITUTIONS

Justice

The 1992 constitution confers a large measure of judicial autonomy. The highest court is the Supreme Court with nine members. Nominations for membership must be backed by six of the eight members of the Magistracy Council, which appoints all judges, magistrates and the electoral tribunal. The Council comprises elected representatives of the Presidency, Congress and the bar. There are special Chambers of Appeal for civil and commercial cases, and criminal cases. Judges of first instance deal with civil, commercial and criminal cases in six departments. Minor cases are dealt with by Justices of the Peace.

The Attorney-General represents the State in all jurisdictions, with representatives in each judicial department and in every jurisdiction.

The population in penal institutions in 2003 was 5,063 (86 per 100,000 of national population). The death penalty was abolished for all crimes in 1992.

Education

Adult literacy was 91·6% in 2003 (male, 93·1%; female, 90·2%). Education is free and nominally compulsory. In 2005 there were 933,995 pupils at primary schools (with 33,434 teaching staff in 2004) and 529,309 at secondary level (with 44,440 teaching staff in 2004). There were 156,167 students in tertiary education in 2005. Paraguay's leading institute of higher education is the National University of Asunción (Universidad Nacional de Asunción), the country's oldest university, founded in 1889.

In 2004 public expenditure on education came to 4·1% of GNI and 10·0% of total government spending.

Health

In 2003 there were 1,117 health establishments (including 84 hospitals) with 7,167 beds. There were 6,400 physicians, 1,947 dentists and 1,089 nurses in 2000.

RELIGION

Religious liberty was guaranteed by the 1967 constitution. Article 6 recognized Roman Catholicism as the official religion of the country. It had 3·5m. adherents in 2002. There are Mennonite, Anglican and other communities as well. In 2002 followers of other religions (mostly Protestants) totalled 322,000.

CULTURE

World Heritage Sites

Paraguay has one site on the UNESCO World Heritage List: the Jesuit Missions of La Santísima Trinidad de Paraná and Jesús de Tavarangue (inscribed on the list in 1993).

Broadcasting

Virtually all television and radio broadcasting is privately-operated. Red Guarani, Telefuturo, Paravision, SNT and El Trece provide the television services (colour by PAL M). Radio Nacional del Paraguay is a state-run radio station. In 2006 there were 1·25m. television-equipped households.

Cinema

There are 15 cinemas in Asunción.

Press

In 2006 there were four daily newspapers with a combined circulation of 130,000.

Tourism

In 2005 there were 341,000 foreign tourists, spending US$96m.

DIPLOMATIC REPRESENTATIVES

Of Paraguay in the United Kingdom (3rd Floor, 344 High St. Kensington, London, W14 8NS)
Ambassador: Vacant.
Chargé d'Affaires a.i.: José Emilio Gorostiaga Peña.

Of the United Kingdom in Paraguay (embassy in Asunción closed in April 2005)
Ambassador: Shan Morgan (resides in Buenos Aires, Argentina).

Of Paraguay in the USA (2400 Massachusetts Ave., NW, Washington, D.C., 20008)
Ambassador: Rigoberto Gauto.

Of the USA in Paraguay (1776 Mariscal López Ave., Asunción)
Ambassador: Liliana Ayalde.

Of Paraguay to the United Nations
Ambassador: José Antonio dos Santos.

Of Paraguay to the European Union
Ambassador: Raúl José Vera Bogado.

FURTHER READING

Gaceta Official, published by Imprenta Nacional, Estrella y Estero Bellaco, Asunción
Anuario Daumas. Annual
Anuario Estadístico de la República del Paraguay. Annual

Nickson, R. A. and Lambert, P. (eds.) *The Transition to Democracy in Paraguay.* 1997

National library: Biblioteca Nacional, Calle de la Residenta, 820 c/ Perú, Asunción.
National Statistical Office: Dirección General de Estadísticas, Encuestas y Censos.
Website (Spanish only): http://www.dgeec.gov.py

PERU

República del Perú
(Republic of Peru)

Capital: Lima
Population estimate, 2010: 29·50m.
GDP per capita, 2007: (PPP$) 7,836
HDI/world rank: 0·806/78

KEY HISTORICAL EVENTS

Hunter-gatherers lived in Peru from at least 9000 BC. Irrigation canals discovered recently in the Andean foothills of northern Peru date farming from around 3400 BC. The Chavin culture in central and northern Peru between 900 BC and 200 BC left monumental temples and intricate artwork across a wide area. The Paracas culture emerged on the southern coast in around 300 BC and evolved into the Nazca culture, famed for its exquisite textiles. Further north, the coastal Moche culture flourished between around 100 BC and 700 AD, producing distinctive metalwork and pottery. The following centuries saw the rise of inland, Andean cultures and powerful city states such as Chancay, Sipan and Cajamarca.

The Inca civilization is thought to have its origins in a Quechua-speaking tribe that settled in the Cusco Valley from about 1200. By the mid-15th century, under Emperor Tupac Yupanqui (1471–93) and subsequently under Huayna Capac, the empire stretched along the Andes from Ecuador to Chile. The Inca's road network was an engineering masterpiece, as were the terraced fields and cities such as the famed Machu Picchu.

The Spanish adventurer, Francisco Pizarro, landed on the Ecuadorian coast in 1532 and moved south. Relations between the Spanish and the Incas quickly soured and Emperor Atahualpa was captured following the battle of Cajamarca. He was executed in 1533 and a year later Pizarro conquered the city of Cusco. Lima was founded in 1535 and in 1542 it became the seat of the Viceroyalty of Peru, which for a time had jurisdiction over all the Spanish colonies in South America. The Spanish conquistadors amassed vast wealth and power by controlling the trade in Andean gold and silver, while the Incas became increasingly marginalized. Revolts against Spanish rule occurred in the 1780s but concerted demands for independence came only after the French Revolution and Napoleon's conquest of Spain in 1808.

José de San Martin of Argentina (who had ended Spanish rule in Chile in 1818) and Simón Bolívar of Venezuela proclaimed Peruvian independence on 28 July 1821 but it was only confirmed in Dec. 1824, when Antonio José de Sucre defeated Spanish troops at Ayacucho. After independence Peru and its neighbours engaged in various territorial disputes. Chile's victory over Peru and Bolivia in the War of the Pacific (1879–83) resulted in Peru ceding the department of Tarapaca and the provinces of Tacna and Arica to Chile. Gen. Andres A. Cacares became president in 1885 and tried to breathe life into the crippled economy by encouraging foreign management of the railways and guano (fertilizer) exports.

A businessman, Augusto Leguia, who became president for four years in 1908, pushed through economic reforms. He became increasingly authoritarian during his second term of office (1919–30), and in 1924 Dr Victor Raúl Haya de la Torre founded the Alianza Popular Revolucionaria Americana (APRA), which called for radical reform. The party was banned by Leguia and then outlawed by his successor, Sanchez Cerro, during the 1930s. Peru sided with the Allies during the Second World War and in 1945 Luis Bustamante y Rivero was elected president, with APRA backing. Splits soon emerged and Manuel Odria led a military coup three years later. An inconclusive election in 1962 enabled Gen. Ricardo Pérez Godoy to seize power, although he was deposed in a coup led by Gen. Nicolás Lindley López a year later. There followed a period of civilian rule but the military staged yet another coup in 1968. In 1978–79 a constituent assembly drew up a new constitution, after which a civilian government was installed.

Peru was plagued by political violence between the early 1980s and the late 1990s with 69,000 people killed by Maoist Shining Path insurgents, the smaller Tupac Amaru Revolutionary Movement and government forces. On 5 April 1992 President Alberto Fujimori suspended the constitution, dissolved parliament and implemented drastic economic reforms to tackle rampant inflation. A new constitution was promulgated on 29 Dec. 1993. But while Peru enjoyed stability and economic growth, continuing autocratic rule put some politicians above the law. Embroiled in a bribery and corruption scandal, President Fujimori's discredited administration came to an end in Nov. 2000 when he resigned while out of the country.

A caretaker government under Valentin Paniagua presided over new presidential and congressional elections in April 2001. A new government led by President Alejandro Toledo took office in July 2001. The Toledo government consolidated Peru's return to democracy and presided over a period of strong economic growth, although great inequalities persisted. Alan García, who had been president for five years in the second half of the 1980s, narrowly won a run-off election in April 2006 and was sworn in as president for a second term in July 2006.

TERRITORY AND POPULATION

Peru is bounded in the north by Ecuador and Colombia, east by Brazil and Bolivia, south by Chile and west by the Pacific Ocean. Area, 1,285,216 sq. km (including the area of the Peruvian part of Lake Titicaca).

For an account of the border dispute with Ecuador, *see* ECUADOR: Territory and Population.

Census population, 2007, 28,220,764 (adjusted for under-enumeration); density, 22·0 per sq. km. In 2005 the population was 75·9% urban.

The UN gives an estimated population for 2010 of 29·50m.

The country is administratively divided into 25 regions and an autonomous province of Lima (with capitals): Amazonas (Chachapoyas), Ancash (Huaráz), Apurímac (Abancay), Arequipa (Arequipa), Ayacucho (Ayacucho), Cajamarca (Cajamarca), Callao (Callao), Cusco (Cusco), Huancavelica (Huancavelica), Huánuco (Huánuco), Ica (Ica), Junín (Huancayo), La Libertad (Trujillo), Lambayeque (Chiclayo), Lima (Huacho), Lima province (Lima), Loreto (Iquitos), Madre de Dios (Puerto Maldonado), Moquegua (Moquegua), Pasco (Cerro de Pasco), Piura (Piura), Puno (Puno), San Martín (Moyobamba), Tacna (Tacna), Tumbes (Tumbes), Ucayali (Pucallpa).

The largest cities (with 2007 census populations) are: Lima, 8,472,935; Arequipa, 784,651; Trujillo, 682,834; Chiclayo, 524,442; Piura, 377,496; Iquitos, 370,962.

In 1991 there were some 100,000 Peruvians of Japanese origin. Indigenous peoples account for 47% of the population.

The official languages are Spanish (spoken by 83·9% of the population in 2007), Quechua (13·2%) and Aymara (1·8%).

SOCIAL STATISTICS

2004 estimates: births, 621,000; deaths, 168,000; infant deaths (under 1 year), 20,000. Rates per 1,000 population (2004 estimates): birth, 22·5; death, 6·1. Annual population growth rate, 2000–05, 1·5%; infant mortality, 2005, 23 per 1,000 live births. Life expectancy, 2007: males, 70·4 years; females, 75·8. Fertility rate, 2004, 2·8 births per woman.

CLIMATE

There is a very wide variety of climates, ranging from tropical in the east to desert in the west, with perpetual snow in the Andes. In coastal areas, temperatures vary very little, either daily or annually, though humidity and cloudiness show considerable variation, with highest humidity from May to Sept. Little rain is experienced in that period. In the Sierra, temperatures remain fairly constant over the year, but the daily range is considerable. There the dry season is from April to Nov. Desert conditions occur in the extreme south, where the climate is uniformly dry, with a few heavy showers falling between Jan. and March. Lima, Jan. 74°F (23·3°C), July 62°F (16·7°C). Annual rainfall 2" (48 mm). Cusco, Jan. 56°F (13·3°C), July 50°F (10°C). Annual rainfall 32" (804 mm). El Niño is the annual warm Pacific current that develops along the coasts of Peru and Ecuador. El Niño in 1982–83 resulted in agricultural production down by 8·5% and fishing output down by 40%. El Niño in 1991–94 was unusually long. El Niño in 1997–98 resulted in a sudden rise in the surface temperature of the Pacific by 9°F (5°C) and caused widespread damage and loss of life.

CONSTITUTION AND GOVERNMENT

The 1980 constitution provided for a legislative *Congress* consisting of a *Senate* and a *Chamber of Deputies*, and an Executive formed of the President and a Council of Ministers appointed by him. Elections were to be every five years with the President and Congress elected, at the same time, by separate ballots.

On 5 April 1992 President Fujimori suspended the 1980 constitution and dissolved Congress.

A referendum was held on 31 Oct. 1993 to approve the twelfth constitution, including a provision for the president to serve a consecutive second term. 52·24% of votes cast were in favour. The constitution was promulgated on 29 Dec. 1993. In Aug. 1996 Congress voted for the eligibility of the President to serve a third consecutive term of office.

Congress has 120 members, elected for a five-year term by proportional representation. All citizens over the age of 18 are eligible to vote. Voting is compulsory.

National Anthem

'Somos libres, seámoslo siempre' ('We are free, let us always be so'); words by J. De La Torre Ugarte, tune by J. B. Alcedo.

GOVERNMENT CHRONOLOGY

Heads of State since 1945. (AP = Popular Action; APRA = American Popular Revolutionary Alliance; FDN = National Democratic Front; MDP = Pradista Democratic Movement/Peruvian Democratic Movement; NM-C90 = New Majority/Change 90; PAP = Peruvian Aprista Party; PP = Peru Possible; PR = Restorer Party)

President of the Republic		
1945–48	FDN	José Luis Bustamante y Rivero
Chairmen of the Military Junta of Government		
1948–50	military	Manuel Apolinario Odría Amoretti
1950	military	Zenón Noriega Agüero
Presidents of the Republic		
1950–56	PR	Manuel Apolinario Odría Amoretti
1956–62	MDP	Manuel Prado y Ugarteche
Junta of Government/Joint Command of the Armed Forces		
1962–63	military	Ricardo Pío Pérez Godoy, Nicolás Lindley López, Juan Francisco Torres Matos, Pedro Vargas Prada Peirano
Presidents of the Republic		
1963–68	AP	Fernando Belaúnde Terry
1968–75	military	Juan Francisco Velasco Alvarado
1975–80	military	Francisco Morales Bermúdez
1980–85	AP	Fernando Belaúnde Terry
1985–90	APRA	Alan Gabriel Ludwig García Pérez
1990–2000	NM-C90	Alberto Keinya Fujimori Fujimori
2000–01	AP	Valentín Paniagua Corazao
2001–06	PP	Alejandro Celestino Toledo Manrique
2006–	PAP	Alan Gabriel Ludwig García Pérez

RECENT ELECTIONS

The first round of presidential elections were held on 9 April 2006. Ollanta Humala Tasso of the Union for Peru won 30·6% of the vote, followed by Alan García Pérez of the Peruvian Aprista Party (formerly the American Popular Revolutionary Alliance/APRA) with 24·3%, Lourdes Flores Nano of the National Unity Party with 23·8% and Martha Chávez Cossio of Alliance for the Future with 7·4%. There were 15 other candidates. The second round run-off held on 4 June 2006 was won by Alan García Pérez with 52·6% of the vote against 47·4% for Ollanta Humala Tasso. Turnout was 88·7% in the first round and 87·7% in the run-off.

In the congressional elections of 9 April 2006 the Union for Peru gained 45 seats with 21·2% of votes cast. The Peruvian Aprista Party came second with 36 seats (20·6%), ahead of the National Unity Party with 17 (15·3%), the Alliance for the Future 13 (13·1%), Centre Front 5 (7·1%), Peru Possible 2 (4·1%) and National Restoration 2 (4·0%). Other parties received 14·6% of the vote between them but won no seats.

CURRENT ADMINISTRATION

President: Alan García Pérez; b. 1949 (Peruvian Aprista Party; sworn in 28 July 2006, having previously been in office from July 1985–July 1990).

First Vice-President: Luis Giampietri Rojas. *Second Vice-President:* Lourdes Mendoza del Solar.

In March 2010 the government comprised:

President of the Council of Ministers (Prime Minister): Ángel Javier Velásquez Quesquén; b. 1959 (sworn in 12 July 2009).

Minister of Foreign Affairs: José Antonio García Belaúnde. *Defence:* Rafael Rey Rey. *Justice:* Aurelio Pastor Valdivieso. *Foreign Trade and Tourism:* Martín Pérez Monteverde. *Interior:* Octavio Edilberto Salazar Miranda. *Education:* José Antonio Chang Escobedo. *Health:* Óscar Ugarte Ubilluz. *Labour and Employment Promotion:* Manuela Esperanza García Cochagne. *Agriculture:* Dante Adolfo de Córdova Vélez. *Transport and Communications:* Enrique Cornejo Ramírez. *Economy and Finance:* Mercedes Rosalba Aráoz Fernández. *Energy and Mines:* Pedro Sánchez Gamarra. *Production:* José Nicanor Gonzales Quijano. *Women's Affairs and Social Development:* Nidia Vilchez Yucra. *Housing, Construction and Sanitation:* Juan Sarmiento. *Environment:* Antonio José Brack Egg.

President of the Council of Ministers (Spanish only): http://www.pcm.gob.pe

CURRENT LEADERS

Alan García Pérez

Position
President

Introduction
Head of the Peruvian Aprista Party (PAP; formerly known as the American Popular Revolutionary Alliance/APRA), Alan García is serving a second term as Peru's president. His first term in office, from 1985–90, was marked by hyperinflation and a rising national debt as he tried to invigorate the economy through spending. After a period of exile García returned to Peru in 2001 and won the 2006 presidential election, promising to fight poverty whilst pursuing more orthodox economic policies.

Early Life
Born on 23 May 1949 in Lima, García was raised in a family with strong ties to the APRA party. His father, Carlos García Ronceros, served as party secretary and was imprisoned during García's childhood for political militancy. García was educated at the Colegio Nacional José María Eguren in Lima and the Pontificia Universidad Católica, before completing a law degree at the National University of San Marcos in 1971. He pursued further studies in Europe, obtaining a doctorate in political science from the Universidad Complutense in Madrid and a degree in sociology from the University of Paris. In 1978, when civilian government was restored in Peru after a ten-year period of military rule, García returned to build a political career with APRA.

García won the April 1985 presidential election on a platform of alleviating poverty and implementing social justice. After his inauguration on 28 July 1985, he launched ambitious public spending programmes to combat the poverty rate of 41·6%. His government printed money to finance the policies, resulting in soaring inflation. The unit of currency, the sol, was replaced by the inti in 1985 at a rate of 1,000 intis to 1 sol but inflation continued to rise, reaching a rate of more than 2m. percent by 1991. García won some initial popularity at home by announcing that only 10% of Peru's export earnings would be devoted to debt repayments and by attempting to nationalize the banks in 1987. However, these policies alienated the IMF and international financial markets and added to the economic turmoil.

Insurgent groups, notably the Shining Path, carried out campaigns of political violence that were put down by government forces. The army was accused of human rights abuses, notably at Accomarco in Aug. 1985 and at Cayara in May 1988. By 1990 the numbers of people living in poverty had risen to 55%, per capita income had fallen to US$720 and the country had a deficit of US$900m. After losing the 1990 election to Alberto Fujimori, García faced allegations of corruption and left Peru under the threat of criminal charges. He lived for the next eight years in Colombia and France, returning in 2001 after Peru's Supreme Court ruled that any charges dating from his time in office had lapsed under the Statute of Limitations.

He fought the 2001 presidential election for APRA, losing narrowly to Alejandro Toledo of the Peru Possible party. From 2001–05 he was leader of the opposition. In the 2006 presidential election García fought a vigorous campaign, claiming that he had learned from past mistakes and would build international trade partnerships. He also exploited unease over the close connections between his main opponent, Ollanta Humala of the left-wing Union for Peru party, and Venezuelan president Hugo Chavéz. In the second round of voting on 4 June 2006 Humala conceded and García was voted in as president for the second time.

Career in Office
García signalled his willingness to work within prevailing economic orthodoxies by appointing a banker, Luis Carranza, as economic and finance minister, and renewing an aid package with the IMF. He accepted a free trade agreement with the USA and in Nov. 2006 signed 12 commercial agreements with Brazil. Also in late 2006 he allocated 968m. nuevos soles (US$300m.) to aid the poor. At the same time, he provoked protests from trade unions by announcing salary cuts for many state employees.

In April 2007 Congress agreed to give his government powers to legislate by decree in pursuit of its popular tough line against drug trafficking and organized crime. However, the failure of his economic policies to spread the benefits of growth more widely provoked violent demonstrations in July. In a speech marking the end of his first year in office, García asked Peruvians to show patience, promising that increased investment would reduce poverty before the end of his term. In 2008, despite an improvement in the economy and a high rate of growth, his popularity declined. By Oct., when he was obliged to replace members of the cabinet over a corruption scandal involving bribes for oil-exploration contracts, his approval rating among voters had fallen to only 20%.

His government was also criticized by environmental and human rights campaigners over plans to open up more Amazon forest territory to foreign energy companies. In June 2009 land ownership laws to this effect provoked violent demonstrations by indigenous groups in the area. Although the controversial decrees were subsequently repealed, this episode—along with a sharp decline in the economy in 2009 in the wake of the global downturn and opposition protests against his free-trade policies—contributed to a further steep fall in Garcia's political standing.

In late 2009 relations with Chile were strained by Chilean military activity near the two countries' disputed border and by accusations against a Peruvian officer of spying for the Chilean military.

DEFENCE

Conscription was abolished in 1999. In 2006 defence expenditure totalled US$1,108m. (US$39 per capita), representing 1·2% of GDP.

Army

There are four military regions. In 2007 the Army comprised 74,000 personnel and 188,000 reserves. In addition there is a paramilitary national police force of 77,000 personnel.

Navy

The principal ship of the Navy is the former Netherlands cruiser *Almirante Grau*, built in 1953. Other combatants include six diesel submarines (two in refit) and eight Italian-built frigates.

Callao is the main base, where the dockyard is located and most training takes place. Smaller bases exist at Iquitos, Paita, Puerto Maldonado, Puno, San Lorenzo Island and Talara.

Naval personnel in 2007 totalled 23,000 including 1,000 Coast Guards, about 800 Naval Air Arm and 4,000 Marines.

Air Force

The operational force is divided into five regions—North, Lima, South, Central and Amazon.

In 2007 there were some 17,000 personnel and 60 combat capable aircraft (including Su-25s, Mirage 2000s and MiG-29s) and 16 attack helicopters.

INTERNATIONAL RELATIONS

Peru is a member of the UN, World Bank, IMF and several other UN specialized agencies, WTO, IOM, Andean Community, Inter-American Development Bank, SELA, LAIA, OAS, UNASUR, APEC and Antarctic Treaty.

ECONOMY

Agriculture produced 6·8% of GDP in 2006, industry 37·5% and services 55·7%.

Overview

The economy has undergone a transformation since 1990 with the ending of hyperinflation and a debt crisis. Tax and pension reforms have accompanied a programme of liberalization and privatization. Inflation fell steadily in the 1990s and has since stayed under the central bank's inflation target, permitting a gradual reduction in interest rates. From 77·9% in 1986, annual consumer price growth fell to 11·5% in 1996 and has averaged less than 2% for over half a decade.

Recession between 1997 and 2001 was caused by a spillover from emerging market crises and commodity price weaknesses. The economy has since responded well to a policy of fiscal responsibility, job creation programmes and rising commodity prices. The government has overseen reforms to open the economy, reduce labour costs in the formal sector and improve the climate for private investment.

Following the difficulties of 1997–2001 the economy has grown at its most sustained pace since the 1950s with higher commodity prices, particularly for minerals and metals, as well as growth in agriculture, textiles, manufacturing and construction. GDP per capita has increased significantly and the country has a growing middle class. The poverty rate fell from 44·5% in 2006 to 36·2% in 2008, although poverty remains a concern.

Private investment has been concentrated in the natural resource sector while employment creation has been predominantly in the capital, Lima (home to roughly a third of the population), and the mining-intensive north coast region. The impoverished rural highlands have benefited little and remain without proper access to basic infrastructure and running water. Key challenges include improving the national infrastructure and investment climate. The economy remains vulnerable to fluctuation in world commodity prices.

The global economic crisis has led to a reduction in Peru's economic growth, with lower commodity prices and a weakened demand. The government has appealed for increased World Bank loans.

Currency

The monetary unit is the *nuevo sol* (PEN), of 100 *céntimos*, which replaced the *inti* in 1991 at a rate of 1m. intis = 1 nuevo sol. Inflation, which had been over 7,000% in 1990, was just 1·8% in 2007, although it then rose to 5·8% in 2008. Foreign exchange reserves were US$14,773m. in July 2005, gold reserves totalled 1·12m. troy oz and total money supply was 24,565m. nuevos soles.

Budget

Central government revenue and expenditure (in 1m. sols), year ending 31 Dec.:

	2001	2002	2003
Revenue	30,327	31,785	34,742
Expenditure	31,913	33,133	35,416

In Dec. 2005 the World Bank approved a US$150m. loan to assist with the government decentralization process and enhance competitiveness.

VAT is 19%.

Performance

Real GDP growth was 7·7% in 2006, rising to 8·9% in 2007 and still further to 9·8% in 2008. Peru's real GDP growth was above average for Latin America every year between 2002 and 2008 with the exception of 2004. Total GDP in 2008 was US$127·4bn.

Banking and Finance

The bank of issue is the Banco Central de Reserva (*President*, Julio Velarde Flores), which was established in 1922. The government's fiscal agent is the Banco de la Nación. In 2002 there were three other government banks (Banco Central Hipotecario del Perú, Banco de la Nación and Corporación Financiera de Desarrollo), ten commercial banks, one regional bank and three foreign banks. Legislation of April 1991 permitted financial institutions to fix their own interest rates and reopened the country to foreign banks. The Central Reserve Bank sets the upper limit.

There are stock exchanges in Lima and Arequipa.

ENERGY AND NATURAL RESOURCES

Peru lays claim to 84 of the world's 114 ecosystems; 28 of its climate types; 19% of all bird species; 20% of all plant species; and 25 conservation areas (seven national parks, eight national reserves, seven national sanctuaries and three historic sanctuaries).

Environment

Peru's carbon dioxide emissions from the consumption and flaring of fossil fuels in 2008 were the equivalent of 1·2 tonnes per capita.

Electricity

In 2004 output was 25·55bn. kWh. Total generating capacity was 6·0m. kW in 2004. Consumption per capita in 2004 was 927 kWh. Peru's reliance on hydro-generated electricity means that electricity production was affected by the drought brought on by the 1997–98 El Niño.

Oil and Gas

Proven oil reserves at the end of 2008 amounted to 1·1bn. bbls. Output, 2008, 5·3m. tonnes. Natural gas reserves in 2008 were 330bn. cu. metres; output in 2004 was 1,409m. cu. metres. Commercial development of the huge Camisea gas field began in late 2004.

Minerals

The mining and fuel sectors accounted for some 8·1% of GDP in 2005. Lead, copper, iron, silver, zinc and petroleum are the chief minerals exploited. Mineral production, 2004 (in 1,000 tonnes): iron, 4,315; zinc, 1,209; copper, 1,036; lead, 306; silver, 3·1; gold, 0·17. 16,000 tonnes of coal were produced in 2004. Early in 1998 Southern Peru Copper, the country's largest mining company, estimated that 3,000 tonnes of copper production had been lost as a result of flooding caused by El Niño.

Agriculture

There are four natural zones: the Coast strip, with an average width of 80 km; the Sierra or Uplands, formed by the coast range of mountains and the Andes proper; the Montaña or high wooded region which lies on the eastern slopes of the Andes; and the jungle in the Amazon Basin, known as the Selva. Legislation of 1991 permits the unrestricted sale of agricultural land. Workers in co-operatives may elect to form limited liability companies and become shareholders.

Production in 2003 (in 1,000 tonnes): sugarcane, 9,550; potatoes, 3,300; rice, 2,139; bananas and plantains, 1,600; maize, 1,471; cassava, 890; onions, 450; oranges, 295; lemons and limes, 255; sweet potatoes, 225.

Livestock, 2003 estimates: sheep, 14·1m.; cattle, 5·0m.; pigs, 2·9m.; alpacas, 2·5m.; goats, 2·0m.; poultry, 95m. Livestock products (in 1,000 tonnes), 2003 estimates: poultry meat, 635; beef and veal, 146; pork, bacon and ham, 85; mutton and lamb, 32; milk, 1,220.

In 2002 there were approximately 3·70m. ha. of arable land and 0·61m. ha. of permanent crops. About 1·2m. ha. were irrigated in 2002.

Coca was cultivated in 2005 on approximately 38,000 ha., down from 115,000 ha. in 1995.

Forestry
In 2005 the area covered by forests was 68·74m. ha., or 53·7% of the total land area. The forests contain valuable hardwoods; oak and cedar account for about 40%. In 2007 timber production was 9·45m. cu. metres.

Fisheries
Sardines and anchovies are caught offshore to be processed into fishmeal, of which Peru is a major producer. Fishing in deeper waters is being developed, subject to government conservation by the imposition of quotas and fishing bans. Total catch in 2005 was 9,388,662 tonnes, almost entirely from sea fishing. Peru's annual catch is the second largest in the world after that of China. In 2006 total exports of fish and seafood came to a value of US$1·77bn. Peru is the world's leading fishmeal producer with a 2007 output of 1·4m. tonnes or 28% of world production.

INDUSTRY
About 70% of industries are located in the Lima/Callao metropolitan area. Industry accounted for 29·7% of GDP in 2001, with manufacturing contributing 15·3%. Production (2004 unless otherwise indicated, in 1,000 tonnes): cement (2002), 4,120; residual fuel oil, 3,268; distillate fuel oil, 1,916; prepared animal feeds (2001), 1,508; petrol, 1,284; kerosene, 765; sugar (2001), 755; soft drinks (2002), 1,179·7m. litres; beer (2002), 618·0m. litres; cigarettes (2002), 3·8bn. units.

Labour
The labour force in 1996 totalled 8,652,000 (71% males). In 1993, 1,852,800 people worked in agriculture, 1,167,000 in commerce, 783,900 in manufacturing, 599,700 in services, 347,500 in transport, 255,000 in building, 72,200 in mining and 18,700 in electricity production. In 2002 an estimated 8·4% of the workforce was unemployed, up from 5·9% in 1991.

Trade Unions
Trade unions have about 2m. members (approximately 1·5m. in peasant organizations and 500,000 in industrial). The major trade union organization is the Confederación de Trabajadores del Perú, which was reconstituted in 1959 after being in abeyance for some years. The other labour organizations recognized by the government are the Confederación General de Trabajadores del Perú, the Confederación Nacional de Trabajadores and the Central de Trabajadores de la Revolución Peruana.

INTERNATIONAL TRADE
An agreement of 1992 gives Bolivia duty-free transit for imports and exports through a corridor leading to the Peruvian Pacific port of Ilo from the Bolivian frontier town of Desaguadero, in return for Peruvian access to the Atlantic via Bolivia's roads and railways. In April 2006 Peru and the USA signed a free trade agreement that eliminates tariffs on each other's goods; it took effect in Jan. 2009. Foreign debt was US$28,653m. in 2005.

Imports and Exports
Trade in US$1m.:

	2002	*2003*	*2004*	*2005*	*2006*
Imports f.o.b.	7,393	8,205	9,805	12,082	14,866
Exports f.o.b.	7,714	9,091	12,809	17,368	23,800

In 2004 the main import suppliers were: USA, 19·6%; Colombia, 7·7%; China, 7·6%; Brazil, 6·9%. Main export markets, 2004: USA, 29·0%; China, 9·9%; UK, 9·1%; Chile, 5·1%. Leading imports in 2004 were machinery and transport equipment (27·8%), chemicals and related products (16·7%), petroleum and petroleum products (16·6%) and manufactured goods (14·3%). Leading exports in 2004 were metalliferous ore and scrap metal (19·5%), gold (19·0%), copper (11·8%) and animal feeds (8·0%).

COMMUNICATIONS

Roads
In 2006 there were 78,986 km of roads, of which 13·9% were paved. In 2007 there were 917,100 passenger cars, 480,900 lorries and vans and 44,400 buses and coaches. There were 67,155 road accidents involving injury in 2006 with 3,481 fatalities.

Rail
Total length (2002), 2,121 km on 1,435- and 914-mm gauges. Passenger-km travelled in 2002 came to 98m. and freight tonne-km to 1,008m. A mass transit system opened in Lima in 2003.

Civil Aviation
There is an international airport at Lima (Jorge Chávez International). The main airline is the Chilean-owned Lan Perú. In 2003 services were also provided by the domestic airlines Aero Cóndor, AVIANDINA and Transportes Aéreos Nacionales de Selva, and by more than 20 international carriers. In 2003 scheduled airline traffic of Peruvian-based carriers flew 44m. km, carrying 2,226,000 passengers (547,000 on international flights). In 2001 Jorge Chávez International handled 4,089,914 passengers (2,128,872 on international flights) and 112,709 tonnes of freight.

Shipping
In 2004 there were 46 sea-going vessels and 651 lake and river craft. In 2002 sea-going shipping totalled 240,000 GRT (including oil tankers 15,000 GRT). In 2002 vessels totalling 8,260,000 net registered tons entered ports and vessels totalling 6,112,000 NRT cleared. Callao is the busiest port, handling 11,609,000 tonnes of cargo in 2002. There are also ports at Chimbote, Paita and Talara.

Telecommunications
In 2008 there were 2,878,200 main (fixed) telephone lines; mobile phone subscribers numbered 20,951,800 in 2008 (72·7 per 100 persons). There were 2·8m. PCs in use in 2005 and an estimated 4·6m. internet users.

Postal Services
In 2003 there were 1,771 post offices.

SOCIAL INSTITUTIONS

Justice
The judicial system is a pyramid at the base of which are the justices of the peace who decide minor criminal cases and civil cases involving small sums of money. The apex is the Supreme Court with a president and 12 members; in between are the judges of first instance, who usually sit in the provincial capitals, and the superior courts.

The police had 95,789 personnel in 2008. The population in penal institutions in Oct. 2004 was 32,129 (114 per 100,000 of national population).

Education
Adult literacy was 87·7% in 2003 (male, 93·5%; female, 82·1%). Elementary education is compulsory and free between the ages of six and 16; secondary education is also free. In 2007 there were 1,204,022 children in pre-school education with 58,177 teaching staff, 3,993,965 pupils in primary schools with 179,743 teaching staff and 2,861,313 pupils in secondary schools with 158,890 teaching staff. There were 952,437 students in tertiary education in 2006. The leading higher education institute is the National University of San Marcos (Universidad Nacional Mayor de San Marcos), founded in 1551, making it the oldest both in the country and in South America.

In 2007 public expenditure on education came to 2·7% of GNI and 16·4% of total government spending.

Health
There were 483 hospitals with 43,074 beds (provision of 16 beds per 10,000 inhabitants) in 2002. There were 29,138 physicians, 3,190 dentists and 21,351 nurses in 2002.

Peru has been one of the most successful countries in reducing undernourishment in the past 15 years. Between 1990–92 and 2001–03 the proportion of undernourished people declined from 42% of the population to 12%.

Welfare
An option to transfer from state social security (IPSS) to privately-managed funds was introduced in 1993.

RELIGION
Religious liberty exists, but the Roman Catholic religion is protected by the State, and since 1929 only Roman Catholic religious instruction is permitted in schools, state or private. There were 23·17m. Catholics in 2001 as well as 1·73m. Protestants and 1·19m. with other beliefs (mostly non-religious). In Feb. 2010 there was one cardinal.

CULTURE

World Heritage Sites
There are 11 sites in Peru appearing on the UNESCO World Heritage List. They are (with year entered on list) the City of Cusco (1983), the Historic Sanctuary of Machu Picchu (1983), Chavin Archaeological Site (1985), Huascarán National Park (1985), Chan Chan Archaeological Zone (1986), Manú National Park (1987), Historic Centre of Lima (1988 and 1991), Río Abiseo National Park (1990 and 1992), Lines and Geoglyphs of Nasca and Pampas de Jumana (1994), the Historical Centre of the City of Arequipa (2000) and the Sacred City of Caral-Supe (2009).

Broadcasting
Broadcasting is dominated by privately-run national, provincial and local stations. Televisión Nacional del Perú and Radio Nacional are state-owned national services. There were 4·71m. TV-equipped households in 2006 (colour by NTSC).

Press
There were 86 dailies in 2006. The leading daily, Trome, had a circulation of 207,000. A total of 2,286 book titles were published in 2002.

Tourism
There were 976,000 foreign visitors in 2003 (591,000 in 1996), bringing foreign exchange earnings of US$923m.

DIPLOMATIC REPRESENTATIVES
Of Peru in the United Kingdom (52 Sloane St., London, SW1X 9SP)
Ambassador: Ricardo V. Luna.

Of the United Kingdom in Peru (Torre Parque Mar, Piso 22, Avenida Jose Larco 1301, Miraflores, Lima)
Ambassador: Catherine Nettleton, OBE.

Of Peru in the USA (1700 Massachusetts Ave., NW, Washington, D.C., 20036)
Ambassador: Luis Valdivieso.

Of the USA in Peru (Avenida La Encalada Cdra 17-Monterrico, Lima)
Ambassador: P. Michael McKinley.

Of Peru to the United Nations
Ambassador: Gonzalo Gutiérrez.

Of Peru to the European Union
Ambassador: Jorge Valdez Carrillo.

FURTHER READING
Instituto Nacional de Estadística e Informática.—*Anuario Estadistico del Perú.—Perú: Compendio Estadístico.* Annual.—*Boletin de Estadistica Peruana.* Quarterly

Banco Central de Reserva. Monthly Bulletin.—*Renta Nacional del Perú.* Annual

Cameron, M. A., *Democracy and Authoritarianism in Peru: Political Coalitions and Social Change.* 1995

Carrion, Julio F., *The Fujimori Legacy: The Rise of Electoral Authoritarianism in Peru.* 2006

Daeschner, J., *The War of the End of Democracy: Mario Vargas Llosa vs. Alberto Fujimori.* 1993

Gorriti, Gustavo, (trans. Robin Kirk) *The Shining Path: A History of the Millenarian War in Peru.* 1999

Starn, Orin, *The Peru Reader: History, Culture, Politics.* 2005

Stokes, S. C., *Cultures in Conflict: Social Movements and the State in Peru.* 1995

Strong, S., *Shining Path.* 1993

Vargas Llosa, A., *The Madness of Things Peruvian: Democracy under Siege.* 1994

National Statistical Office: Instituto Nacional de Estadística e Informática, Av. Gral. Garzón 654–658, Jesús María, Lima.
Website (Spanish only): http://www.inei.gob.pe

PHILIPPINES

Republika ng Pilipinas
(Republic of the Philippines)

Capital: Manila
Population estimate, 2010: 93·62m.
GDP per capita, 2007: (PPP$) 3,406
HDI/world rank: 0·751/105

KEY HISTORICAL EVENTS

Pottery was being made on the Philippine archipelago from at least 3000 BC, probably by people of Malay origin, and metals were being worked by the first millennium BC. Merchants from south China reached the islands during the 10th century AD (T'ang Dynasty), heralding centuries of Chinese trade with the region. Arab traders brought Islam from the Malay peninsula via Borneo and the Sulu archipelago in the late 13th century, and by the 15th century Islamic influence had spread as far north as Luzon. Most islanders lived in barangays, communities of 30–100 households based largely on kinship.

The Portuguese explorer, Ferdinand Magellan, landed at Samar on 16 April 1521 during his Spanish-financed expedition round the world. Subsequent expeditions consolidated Spanish control over the islands, which were named after Philip II of Spain in 1542. Manila was established by Miguel Lopez de Legaspi in 1571 on the site of an existing Moro (Muslim Filipinos) settlement. By the end of the 16th century the Philippines had become a major trading centre with India, China and the East Indies. The islands came under Dutch control from around 1600.

The waning of the Spanish Empire during the 18th century saw a rise in the power base of the Jesuit orders, which caused resentment and stoked demands for independence. In 1896 revolution in the province of Cavite, led by Emilio Aguinaldo among others, spread through the major islands. However, in Dec. 1898, following the Spanish-American War, the Philippines were ceded to the United States. Aguinaldo fought a guerrilla campaign but was captured in 1901. The US granted the Philippines partial autonomy in 1916 and the Hare-Hawes-Cutting Act of 1932 set a timetable for full independence after a ten-year period of self-governance as a Commonwealth of the USA. Manuel Quezon was elected the first president in Sept. 1935.

In Dec. 1941 the islands were invaded by Japanese troops, who went on to take complete control in 1942. Quezon escaped to the USA and established a government-in-exile in Washington, D.C. Sergio Osmena succeeded Quezon in 1944 and returned to the Philippines with a US-backed liberation force in Oct. 1944. Manuel Roxas defeated Osmena in the election of April 1946, becoming president of the Republic of the Philippines when independence was achieved on 4 July 1946. The USA continued to play a key role in its former colony, particularly in economic policy. In return for assistance in rebuilding the country's war-torn infrastructure, the USA secured 99-year leases over several air and naval bases. Relations with neighbouring countries improved and in 1954 the Philippines joined the Southeast Asia Treaty Organization, precursor to the Association of South East Asian Nations (ASEAN).

Ferdinand Marcos was elected president in 1965 and re-elected four years later, although his rule became increasingly unpopular. In Sept. 1972 Marcos declared martial law and thousands of political opponents were arrested. In May 1980 Benigno Aquino, Jr, the leading opponent of Marcos, was released from prison to go to the USA for medical treatment. His assassination, on his return to the Philippines in 1983, led to growing US pressure for Marcos to restore democracy. In late 1985 he announced a snap presidential election. He was challenged by Aquino's widow, Corazón, who eventually emerged victorious from a controversial poll and was installed as president on 25 Feb. 1986. Marcos fled the country and a new constitution limiting the president to a single, six-year term in office was ratified in Feb. 1987.

More than twenty years of insurgency by the Moro National Liberation Front were ended by a peace agreement of 2 Sept. 1996, providing for a Muslim autonomous region in an area of Mindanao island. The rebellion left more than 120,000 people dead. In Oct. 2000 impeachment proceedings began against President Estrada who was alleged to have received more than US$10·8m. from gambling kickbacks. His impeachment trial collapsed in Jan. 2001 when he was forced from office by mass protests. Subsequently Estrada's supporters tried to overthrow his successor, Gloria Macapagal-Arroyo.

In Nov. 2001 the fragile peace between the government and Islamic militants was shattered. Since then violence has frequently erupted, notably in early 2005, when fighting on the southern island of Jolo left 90 dead and caused 12,000 people to flee. On 14 Feb. 2005 three bombs were detonated killing nine and injuring 130. In Feb. 2006 President Arroyo declared a week-long state of emergency after the military declared it had discovered a coup plot.

TERRITORY AND POPULATION

The Philippines is situated between 21° 25' and 4° 23' N. lat. and between 116° and 127° E. long. It is composed of 7,100 islands and islets, 3,144 of which are named. Approximate land area, 300,076 sq. km (115,859 sq. miles). The largest islands (in sq. km) are Luzon (104,688), Mindanao (94,630), Samar (13,080), Negros (12,710), Palawan (11,785), Panay (11,515), Mindoro (9,735), Leyte (7,214), Cebu (4,422), Bohol (3,865) and Masbate (3,269).

The census population in Aug. 2007 was 88,574,614; density, 295·2 per sq. km. In 2005, 62·7% of the population lived in urban areas.

The UN gives an estimated population for 2010 of 93·62m.

The area and population of the 17 regions (from north to south):

Region	*Sq. km*	*2007*
Ilocos	12,840	4,545,906
Cordillera[1]	18,294	1,520,743
Cagayan Valley	26,838	3,051,487
Central Luzon	21,470	9,720,982
National Capital	636	11,553,427
Calabarzon	16,229	11,743,110
Mimaropa	27,456	2,559,791
Bicol	17,632	5,109,798
Western Visayas	20,223	6,843,643
Central Visayas	14,951	6,398,628
Eastern Visayas	21,432	3,912,936
Northern Mindanao	17,125	3,952,437
Davao	19,672	4,156,653
Soccskargen	18,433	3,829,081
Zamboanga Peninsula	14,811	3,230,094
Muslim Mindanao[2]	12,695	4,120,795
Caraga	18,847	2,293,480

[1]Administrative region. [2]Autonomous region.

City populations (2007 census, in 1,000) are as follows; all on Luzon unless indicated in parenthesis.

Quezon City[1]	2,679	Muntinlupa[1]	453
Manila (the capital)[1]	1,661	General Santos (Mindanao)	443
Caloocan[1]	1,379	Bacoor	441
Cebu (Cebu)	798	San Jose del Monte	439
Davao (Mindanao)	786	Marikina[2]	425
Antipolo	634	Iloilo (Panay)	419
Pasig[1]	617	Pasay[1]	403
Taguig[2]	613	Zamboanga (Mindanao)	392
Valenzuela[2]	569	Malabon[2]	364
Dasmariñas	556	Calamba	360
Cagayan de Oro (Mindanao)	554	Mandaue (Cebu)	319
Parañaque[2]	553	Angeles	314
Las Piñas[2]	532	Mandaluyong[1]	306
Makati[1]	510	Baguio[1]	302
Bacolod (Negros)	499		

[1]City within Metropolitan Manila. Population of Metro Manila in 2007, 11,553,427. [2]Municipality within Metropolitan Manila.

Filipino (based on Tagalog) is spoken as a mother tongue by only 29·3%; among the 76 other indigenous languages spoken, Cebuano is spoken as a mother tongue by 23·3% and Ilocano by 9·3%. English, which along with Filipino is one of the official languages, is widely spoken.

In 2000 some 5·5m. Filipinos were living and working abroad, including 2m. in the USA, 850,000 in Saudi Arabia and 620,000 in Malaysia.

SOCIAL STATISTICS

Births, 2003, 1,669,442; deaths, 396,331. Divorce is illegal. Birth rate per 1,000 population (2003), 20·6; death rate, 4·9. Expectation of life at birth, 2007, was 69·4 years for males and 73·9 years for females. Annual population growth rate, 2000–05, 2·2%. Infant mortality, 2005, 25 per 1,000 live births; fertility rate, 2004, 3·1 births per woman.

CLIMATE

Some areas have an equatorial climate while others experience tropical monsoon conditions, with a wet season extending from June to Nov. Mean temperatures are high all year. Manila, Jan. 77°F (25°C), July 82°F (27·8°C). Annual rainfall 83·3" (2,115·9 mm).

CONSTITUTION AND GOVERNMENT

A new constitution was ratified by referendum in Feb. 1987 with the approval of 78·5% of voters. The head of state is the *President*, directly elected for a non-renewable six-year term.

Congress consists of a 24-member upper house, the *Senate* (elected for a six-year term from 'at large' seats covering the country as a whole, half of them renewed every three years), and a *House of Representatives* of not more than 250 members (unless otherwise fixed by law). In the *House of Representatives* 240 members are directly elected for a three-year term and the rest are chosen from party and minority-group lists.

A campaign led by the president at the time, Fidel Ramos, to amend the constitution to allow him to stand for a second term was voted down by the Senate by 23 to one in Dec. 1996.

National Anthem

'Land of the Morning', lyric in English by M. A. Sane and C. Osias, tune by Julian Felipe; 'Lupang Hinirang', Tagalog lyric by the Institute of National Language.

GOVERNMENT CHRONOLOGY

Presidents since 1946. (KBL = New Society Movement; Lakas-CMD = Lakas-Christian Muslim Democrats; LE-NUCD = People's Power-National Union of Christian Democrats; LMP = Struggle of the Philippine Masses; PL = Liberal Party; PN = Nationalist Party; UNIDO = Nationalist Democratic Organization)

1946–48	PL	Manuel Roxas y Acuña
1948–53	PL	Elpidio Quirino y Rivera
1953–57	PN	Ramon Magsaysay y del Fierro
1957–61	PN	Carlos Polestico García
1961–65	PL	Diosdado Pañgan Macapagal
1965–86	PN, KBL	Ferdinand Emmanuel Edralin Marcos
1986–92	UNIDO	Corazón Cojuangco Aquino
1992–98	LE-NUCD	Fidel Valdez Ramos
1998–2001	LMP	Joseph Marcelo Ejercito Estrada
2001–	Lakas-CMD	Gloria Macapagal-Arroyo

RECENT ELECTIONS

The presidential elections of 10 May 2004 were won by President Gloria Macapagal-Arroyo (Lakas-Christian Muslim Democrats) with 40·0% of the votes cast, ahead of Fernando Poe, Jr (Coalition of United Filipinos) with 36·5% of the vote and Panfilo Morena Lacson (Struggle of Democratic Filipinos) with 10·9%. There were two other candidates.

Elections to the House of Representatives were held on 14 May 2007. The Commission on Elections did not publish final results, but 92 seats went to Lakas-Christian Muslim Democrats, 49 to the Kabalikat ng Malayang Pilipino (KAMPI), 28 to the Nationalist People's Coalition, 16 to the Liberal Party and 8 to the Nacionalista Party. The remaining seats went to smaller parties. Senate elections were also most recently held on 14 May 2007, following which the Liberal Party had 4 seats, Nacionalista Party 4, Genuine Opposition 3, Lakas-Christian Muslim Democrats 3, Nationalist People's Coalition 2, Pwersa ng Masang Pilipino (Force of the Filipino Masses) 2 and non-partisans and others 5 with one vacant.

Presidential and parliamentary elections were scheduled to take place on 10 May 2010.

CURRENT ADMINISTRATION

President: Gloria Macapagal-Arroyo; b. 1947 (Lakas-Christian Muslim Democrats; sworn in 20 Jan. 2001 and elected on 10 May

2004). Her father, Diosdado Macapagal, had been president from 1961–65.

Vice-President: Noli de Castro (elected on 10 May 2004).

In March 2010 the government comprised:

Minister of Justice: Alberto Agra. *Trade and Industry:* Jesli Lapus. *Finance:* Margarito Teves. *National Defence:* Norberto Gonzales. *Agriculture:* Bernie Fondevilla. *Foreign Affairs:* Alberto Romulo. *Public Works and Highways:* Victor Domingo. *Energy:* Angelo Reyes. *Education:* Mona Valisno. *Labour and Employment:* Marianito Roque. *Health:* Dr Esperanza Cabral. *Agrarian Reform:* Nasser Pangandaman. *Tourism:* Joseph Durano. *Budget and Management:* Joaquin Lagonera. *Transport and Communications:* Leandro Mendoza. *Science and Technology:* Estrella Alabastro. *Environment and Natural Resources:* Eleazar Quinto. *Social Welfare and Development:* Celia Capadocia-Yangco. *Socioeconomic Planning:* Ralph Recto. *Interior and Local Government:* Ronaldo Puno.

Executive Secretary: Leandro Mendoza.

Speaker of the House of Representatives: Prospero Nograles.

Government Website: http://www.gov.ph

CURRENT LEADERS

Gloria Macapagal-Arroyo

Position
President

Introduction
Gloria Macapagal-Arroyo was swept to power in Jan. 2001 when her predecessor was forced from office by mass street protests. She is the daughter of Diosdado Macapagal, the president of the Philippines from 1961–65. Returned to power in elections in 2004, she then survived two parliamentary attempts to impeach her over alleged corruption, human rights abuses and electoral fraud, and a failed coup attempt during the ensuing six-year term.

Early Life
Gloria Macapagal was born on 5 April 1947 into a prominent Filipino political family. After education at a convent high school in the Philippines, she took a degree in commerce at Georgetown University in Washington, D.C., where the future US president Bill Clinton was one of her classmates. Returning to the Philippines, she studied for a master's degree and a PhD and then spent time teaching, during which period she married, becoming Mrs Arroyo, although in her subsequent political career she has used both her maiden and married names.

Prominent as an economist as well as a member of a political dynasty, Arroyo was appointed to the government of President Corazón Aquino in 1986 as assistant secretary of the department of trade and industry, rising to become under-secretary. She also held the post of executive director of the garments and textile export board. During her tenure the textile industry grew to become the country's top foreign-currency earner.

When Aquino's presidency ended in 1992, Arroyo stood for the Senate and was elected at her first attempt. Although she had held office in the outgoing government, Arroyo was still something of a political unknown, and her initial appeal to many voters was the memory of her popular father. However, when she stood for re-election in 1995 her own reputation won her nearly 16m. votes, the greatest number ever received by an individual in Philippine elections.

In 1998, Arroyo stood as a candidate for the vice-presidency. The presidency was won by Joseph Estrada, a former cinema actor, but in her electoral race, Arroyo received more votes than Estrada—12·7m., the most ever received by anyone in a Philippine presidential or vice-presidential contest.

President Estrada appointed her vice-president and secretary of social welfare and development. She resigned from the Cabinet in Oct. 2000, but retained her role as vice-president. By that time the Estrada government was in trouble, the president having been accused of cronyism and taking bribes from illegal gambling syndicates. Impeachment proceedings began. Arroyo led the calls for Estrada to resign. Mass street protests forced Estrada to flee the presidential palace and the Supreme Court declared the presidency to be vacant. On 20 Jan. 2001, Arroyo was sworn in as president.

Career in Office
The immediate challenge facing President Arroyo was reconciliation. Many supporters of Estrada initially refused to recognize the transfer of power. She took office at a difficult time for the country, politically and economically. Arroyo set economic recovery, including a privatization programme, and economic and social reform as her priorities. However, one of her main problems was Islamic terrorism and the continued guerrilla activity by separatists in the south of the country and by communist insurgents. In 2003 Arroyo negotiated a cessation of hostilities with the separatists pending formal peace talks, although clashes with government troops still took place. She meanwhile vowed to wipe out the Abu Sayyaf, an Islamic terrorist organization responsible for bombings and the kidnapping and murder of foreign tourists and others, which has been linked to al-Qaeda by the US government.

In July 2003 Ramon Cardenas, a former junior minister to ex-President Joseph Estrada, was arrested after leading a military uprising in Manila. Several hundred troops took possession of a shopping and residential complex but withdrew after accusing Arroyo's government of corruption. Standing for Lakas-Christian Muslim Democrats, Arroyo was returned to power in the presidential elections of May 2004, ahead of Fernando Poe, Jr of the Coalition of United Filipinos. Despite coming under intense pressure to resign in July 2005 over allegations of electoral vote-rigging, she survived an opposition attempt to impeach her in Sept. Arroyo declared a week-long state of emergency in Feb. 2006 after the military reported a plot to oust her in a coup. In July–Aug. 2006 a second opposition attempt to impeach her was blocked by her majority supporters in the House of Representatives, but her attempt later in the year to change the constitution and abolish the more independent Senate was withdrawn in Dec. in the face of popular protest.

Parliamentary elections in May 2007 were marred by violence, voter intimidation and irregularities. The opposition won the majority of the Senate seats while Arroyo's support in the lower house was strengthened. In July Arroyo set out a new agenda, pledging to create jobs, improve education, health and welfare, and bring peace to the troubled south. She also defended a controversial new anti-terrorism law. In Sept. former president Estrada was sentenced to life imprisonment for corruption, but was subsequently pardoned by Arroyo. In Nov. 2007 a coup attempt by renegade soldiers occupying a hotel in Manila was quashed by security forces.

In July 2008 the government reached an agreement with the Moro Islamic Liberation Front to extend self-government for the semi-autonomous Muslim region covering parts of Mindanao and nearby islands. However, the deal collapsed the following month after Christian communities raised objections and petitioned the Supreme Court, sparking renewed violence on Mindanao.

In Nov. 2009, 57 people were killed on the island of Mindanao in a massacre seemingly related to political rivalry between powerful local clans. Amid reports of her alleged links with the clan believed to be responsible, Arroyo quickly distanced herself from the outrage and its perpetrators and her government appointed an independent commission to oversee the disbanding of private armies in the country before the presidential, legislative and local elections that were scheduled for 10 May 2010. Under the constitution Arroyo was not eligible to stand in the presidential poll and was scheduled to leave office on 30 June.

DEFENCE

An extension of the 1947 agreement granting the USA the use of several Army, Navy and Air Force bases was rejected by the Senate in Sept. 1991. An agreement of Dec. 1994 authorizes US naval vessels to be repaired in Philippine ports. The Philippines is a signatory of the South-East Asia Collective Defence Treaty.

Defence expenditure in 2006 totalled US$909m. (US$10 per capita), representing 0·8% of GDP.

Army

The Army is organized into five area joint-service commands.

Strength (2007) 66,000, with reserves totalling 100,000. The paramilitary Philippines National Police numbered 40,500 in 2007 with 40,000 reservists.

Navy

The Navy consists principally of ex-US ships completed in 1944 and 1945, and serviceability and spares are a problem. The modernization programme in progress has been revised and delayed, but the first 30 inshore patrol craft of US and Korean design have been delivered. The present fleet includes one ex-US frigate.

Navy personnel in 2007 was estimated at 24,000 including 7,500 marines.

Air Force

The Air Force had an estimated strength of 16,000 in 2007, with 30 combat capable aircraft. There was one fighter squadron of Agusta S-211s.

INTERNATIONAL RELATIONS

The Philippines is a member of the UN, World Bank, IMF and several other UN specialized agencies, WTO, IOM, Asian Development Bank, APEC, ASEAN and Colombo Plan.

ECONOMY

Agriculture accounted for 14·2% of GDP in 2006, industry 31·6% and services 54·2%.

Overview

Market-oriented reforms have been implemented over the last two decades. Foreign investment and trade barriers have been dismantled and many industries deregulated. Most state industrial assets were privatized between 1992–95 and monopolies were dismantled in the telecommunications, oil, civil aviation, shipping, water and power industries.

President Arroyo was re-elected in 2004 on a platform of public debt reduction and has focused on addressing low government revenues (14·5% of GDP in 2004). Chronic public deficits have been significantly reduced, with public debt to GDP down by over a third since 2003. Tax collection has become more aggressive and VAT reform was implemented in early 2006. Fiscal reforms have emerged within an environment of sustained growth and falling inflation. GDP grew by nearly 5·5% in 2006, driven by strong private consumption and supported by a rise in remittances. However, with the reduction in the government deficit largely resulting from constrained spending following the failure of Congress to pass the 2006 budget, further tax and public sector reforms will be required to balance the budget.

Strong growth has not been translated into poverty reduction. Poverty prevalence rose from 30% to 33% between 2003–06, indicating a need for increased priority spending. Mounting global uncertainties pose further risks to growth in the medium-term.

Currency

The unit of currency is the *peso* (PHP) of 100 *centavos*. Inflation rates (based on IMF statistics):

1999	*2000*	*2001*	*2002*	*2003*	*2004*	*2005*	*2006*	*2007*	*2008*
6·4%	4·0%	6·8%	3·0%	3·5%	6·0%	7·7%	6·2%	2·8%	9·3%

Foreign exchange reserves were US$35,493m. in Aug. 2009 and gold reserves 5·08m. troy oz. Total money supply in Feb. 2008 was 836,709m. pesos.

Budget

In 2004 revenues totalled 757,945m. pesos and expenditures 899,990m. pesos.

VAT was introduced in 1988. The standard rate was raised from 10·0% to 12·0% in Feb. 2006.

Performance

Real GDP growth rates (based on IMF statistics):

1999	*2000*	*2001*	*2002*	*2003*	*2004*	*2005*	*2006*	*2007*	*2008*
3·4%	6·0%	1·8%	4·4%	4·9%	6·4%	5·0%	5·3%	7·1%	3·8%

Total GDP in 2008 was US$166·9bn.

Banking and Finance

The Central Bank (*Chairman*, Amando Tetangco, Jr) issues the currency, manages foreign exchange reserves and supervises the banking system. At 30 June 2003 there were 42 commercial banks (24 regular commercial banks and 18 universal banks), 93 thrift banks and 771 rural and co-operative banks. In June 2003 the total number of banking institutions was 6,414, with total assets of 3,529,128m. pesos.

There is a stock exchange in Manila.

The financial crisis that struck southeast Asia in 1997 led to the floating of the peso in July. It subsequently lost 36% of its value against the dollar.

Weights and Measures

The metric system is used but with some local units, including the *picul* (63·25 kg) for sugar and fibres, and the *cavan* (16·5 gallons) for cereals.

ENERGY AND NATURAL RESOURCES

Environment

Carbon dioxide emissions from the consumption and flaring of fossil fuels in 2008 were the equivalent of 0·8 tonnes per capita.

Electricity

Total installed capacity was 15·6m. kW in 2004. Production was 55·96bn. kWh in 2004. Consumption per capita was 686 kWh in 2004.

Oil and Gas

The largest natural gas field is the Camago-Malampaya gas field, discovered off the island of Palawan in 1992, with reserves initially put at 76bn. cu. metres but now increased to 85bn. cu. metres. The Philippines' total natural gas reserves in 2007 were 99bn. cu. metres.

Crude petroleum reserves were 139m. bbls in 2007.

Water

Water production in 1997 was 997m. cu. metres and water consumption 230m. cu. metres. Breakdown of water consumption: industrial, 89m. cu. metres; residential, 82m. cu. metres; and commercial, 59m. cu. metres.

Minerals

Mineral production in 2003, unless otherwise indicated (in tonnes): coal (2004), 2,482,000; salt, 429,160; silica sand, 372,200; copper, 80,920; chromite refractory ore (chromium content), 13,220; nickel bearing ore (2002), 26,532 (nickel content); gold, 37,840 kg; silver, 9,530 kg. Other minerals include rock asphalt, sand and gravel. Total value of mineral production, 2003, 139,597m. pesos.

Agriculture

Agriculture is a mainstay of the economy, contributing up to 30% of national output. In 2001 there were 5·65m. ha. of arable land and 5·0m. ha. of permanent crops. In 2001, 37·4% of the working population was employed in agriculture. In 2002 agricultural production grew by 2·6% (7·4% in 2001).

Output (in 1,000 tonnes) in 2002: sugarcane, 21,417; coconuts, 13,683; rice, 13,271; bananas, 5,275; maize, 4,319; copra, 2,010; pineapples, 1,639; cassava, 1,626. The output of copra is the highest of any country in the world. Minor crops are fruits, nuts, vegetables, coffee, cacao, peanuts, ramie, rubber, maguey, kapok, abaca and tobacco.

Livestock, 2003: pigs, 12·36m.; goats, 3·27m.; buffaloes, 3·18m.; cattle, 2·56m.; chickens, 128·51m.; ducks, 9·81m.

Forestry

Forests covered 7·16m. ha. (24·0% of the land area) in 2005. Timber production was 15·79m. cu. metres in 2007.

Fisheries

The catch in 2005 was 2,246,352 tonnes (94% from marine waters).

INDUSTRY

Leading sectors are foodstuffs, oil refining and chemicals. Production, 2002 (in 1,000 tonnes): cement, 11,396; residual fuel oil, 3,537; distillate fuel oil, 3,004; sugar, 1,988; petrol, 1,501; paper and paperboard, 1,056; plywood, 409,000 cu. metres.

Labour

In 2003 the total workforce was 34,635,000, of whom 30,418,000 were employed (19,263,000 in non-agricultural work). Employees by sector, 2003: 14·4m. in services; 11·2m. in agriculture, hunting, forestry and fisheries; 4·9m. in industry. 3·9m. persons were registered unemployed in 2004. 868,000 persons worked overseas in 2003 (652,000 land-based).

The unemployment rate in Oct. 2001 was 9·8%.

Trade Unions

In the third quarter of 2000 there were 10,217 unions with a total membership of 3,778,000.

INTERNATIONAL TRADE

Foreign debt totalled US$61,527m. in 2005. A law of June 1991 gave foreign nationals the right to full ownership of export and other firms considered strategic for the economy.

Imports and Exports

Imports (c.i.f.) in 2007 totalled US$57,995·7m. (US$54,078·0m. in 2006) and exports (f.o.b.) US$50,465·7m. (US$47,410·1m. in 2006).

Main imports: electronics and components, mineral fuels, lubricants and related materials, industrial machinery and equipment, telecommunications equipment, transport equipment. Principal exports: electronics, garments, machinery, transport equipment and apparatus, and processed foods. In 2001 electronics exports were worth US$21·4bn. and constituted 67% of all exports although this had shrunk to US$16·3bn. and 32% by 2007. In 1992 they had been worth just US$3bn.

Main sources of import in 2007: USA, 14·0%; Japan, 12·4%; Singapore, 11·1%; China, 7·3%. Main export markets, 2007: USA, 17·0%; Japan, 14·5%; Hong Kong, 11·5%; China, 11·4%.

COMMUNICATIONS

Roads

In 2003 roads totalled 200,037 km; of these, 28,266 km were national roads and 49,782 km were regional roads. In 2007 there were 937,600 passenger cars in use, 55,200 buses and coaches, 1,875,300 vans and lorries, and 2,647,500 motorcycles and mopeds. There were 6,240 road accidents involving injury in 2006 with 961 fatalities.

Rail

In 2005 the National Railways totalled 419 km (1,067 mm gauge). In 2003 passenger-km totalled 83·1m. There is a light metro railway in Manila.

Civil Aviation

There are international airports at Manila (Ninoy Aquino) and Cebu (Mactan International). In Sept. 1998 the Asian economic crisis that had started more than a year earlier forced the closure of the national carrier, Philippine Airlines, after it had suffered huge losses. However, it has since resumed its operations both internally and externally. In 2005 scheduled airline traffic of Philippine-based carriers flew 28·4m. km, carrying 6,610,400 passengers. In 2001 Manila handled 12,545,000 passengers (7,144,000 on international flights) and 356,700 tonnes of freight.

Shipping

The main ports are Cagayan de Oro, Cebu, Davao, Iloilo, Manila and Zamboanga. Manila, the leading port, handled 43,820,000 tonnes of cargo in 2002. In 2002 merchant shipping totalled 5,320,000 GRT, including oil tankers 146,000 GRT.

Telecommunications

In 2008 there were 4,076,000 main (fixed) telephone lines. In the same year mobile phone subscribers numbered 68,117,000 (753·9 per 1,000 persons). There were 6·3m. PCs in use in 2006 and 5·6m. internet users in 2008.

Postal Services

In 2003 there were 2,476 post offices.

SOCIAL INSTITUTIONS

Justice

There is a Supreme Court which is composed of a chief justice and 14 associate justices; it can declare a law or treaty unconstitutional by the concurrent votes of the majority sitting. There is a Court of Appeals, which consists of a presiding justice and 50 associate justices. There are 15 regional trial courts, one for each judicial region, with a presiding regional trial judge in each of its 720 branches. Municipal trial courts and municipal circuit trial courts are found in the municipalities of the Philippines. If the court covers one municipality it is a municipal trial court; if it covers two or more municipalities it is a municipal circuit trial court. In Metropolitan Manila the equivalents are metropolitan trial courts, and in the cities outside Metropolitan Manila the courts are known as municipal trial courts in cities.

The Supreme Court may designate certain branches of the regional trial courts to handle exclusively criminal cases, juvenile and domestic relations cases, agrarian cases, urban land reform cases which do not fall under the jurisdiction of quasijudicial bodies and agencies and/or such other special cases as the Supreme Court may determine. The death penalty, abolished in 1987, was officially restored in Dec. 1993 as punishment for 'heinous crimes'. In Feb. 1999 a rapist was executed, the first incident of capital punishment in the Philippines since 1976. The death penalty was abolished again for all crimes in 2006.

In 2003 there were 116,000 police. Local police forces are supplemented by the Philippine Constabulary, which is part of the armed forces.

In 2003 the prison population was 24,381.

Constabulary

Since 1990 public order has been maintained completely by the Philippine National Police. Qualified Philippine Constabulary personnel were absorbed by the PNP or were transferred to branches or services of the Armed Forces of the Philippines.

Education

Public elementary education is free and schools are established in virtually all parts of the country. The majority of secondary and post-secondary schools are private. Formal education consists of an optional one to two years of pre-school education; six years of elementary education; four years of secondary education; and four to five years of tertiary or college education leading to academic degrees. Three-year post-secondary non-degree technical/vocational education is also considered formal education. In 2007 there were 961,397 children in pre-school institutions with (2006) 27,742 teaching staff; 13,145,210 pupils in primary schools with 390,432 teaching staff; and 6,365,985 pupils in secondary schools with 181,193 teaching staff. In 2005 there were 2,402,649 students in tertiary education with 112,941 academic staff.

Non-formal education consists of adult literacy classes, agricultural and farming training programmes, occupation skills training, youth clubs, and community programmes of instructions in health, nutrition, family planning and co-operatives.

In 2004–05 there were 176 public higher education institutions including 111 state and 50 local universities and colleges, and 1,443 private higher education institutions including 340 religious institutions. The adult literacy rate in 2003 was 92·6% (92·5% among males and 92·7% among females).

Public expenditure on education in 2005 came to 2·3% of GNI and was equivalent to 15·2% of total government spending.

Health

In 2003 there were 1,723 hospitals (1,061 private) with 85,040 beds (1·1 beds per 1,000 inhabitants). In 2002 there were 91,408 physicians, 44,129 dentists, 347,349 nurses, 140,675 midwives and 47,463 pharmacists.

Welfare

The Social Security System (SSS) is a contributory scheme for employees. Disbursements in 2001 (in 1m. pesos): social security, 37,813 (1,775,996 recipients); employees' compensation, 1,201 (90,356 recipients).

RELIGION

82% of the population are Roman Catholics, 5% Protestants, 5% Muslims and 7% Buddhists or other religions. There were 181,500 Latter-day Saints (Mormons) in 2000.

The Roman Catholic Church has three cardinals, 23 archbishoprics, 91 bishoprics, 79 dioceses, 2,328 parishes and some 20,873 chapels or missions.

CULTURE

World Heritage Sites

The Philippines has five sites on the UNESCO World Heritage List: Tubbataha Reefs Natural Park (inscribed on the list in 1993 and 2009); the Baroque Churches of the Philippines (1993); the Rice Terraces of the Philippine Cordilleras (1995); the Historic Town of Vigan (1999); and Puerto-Princesa Subterranean River National Park (1999).

Broadcasting

In 2002 there were 952 (mostly commercial) AM and FM radio stations and 225 television stations (colour by NTSC). The two dominant service providers are the private ABS-CBN and GMA networks. There were 10·5m. TV-equipped households in 2005.

Cinema

In 2005 there were 810 cinemas; admissions in 2005 totalled 63·7m. 56 feature films were produced in 2005.

Press

There were 31 daily newspapers in 2003, with a combined circulation of 5,497,000. In 2002 a total of 1,510 book titles were published.

Tourism

In 2003, 1,907,000 foreign visitors brought foreign exchange receipts of US$1,740m.

DIPLOMATIC REPRESENTATIVES

Of the Philippines in the United Kingdom (8 Suffolk St., London, SW1Y 4HH)
Ambassador: Antonio M. Lagdameo.

Of the United Kingdom in the Philippines (120 Upper McKinley Rd, McKinley Hill, Taguig City 1634, Manila)
Ambassador: Stephen Lillie.

Of the Philippines in the USA (1600 Massachusetts Ave., NW, Washington, D.C., 20036)
Ambassador: Willy Calaud Gaa.

Of the USA in the Philippines (1201 Roxas Blvd, Manila)
Ambassador: Kristie A. Kenney.

Of the Philippines to the United Nations
Ambassador: Hilario G. Davide, Jr.

Of the Philippines to the European Union
Ambassador: Cristina Garcia Ortega.

FURTHER READING

National Statistics Office. *Philippine Statistical Yearbook.*

Abinales, Patricio N., *State and Society in the Philippines.* 2005

Boyce, J. K., *The Political Economy of Growth and Impoverishment in the Marcos Era.* 1993

Hamilton-Paterson, J., *America's Boy: The Marcoses and the Philippines.* 1998

Hedman, Eva-Lotta, *In the Name of Civil Society: From Free Election Movements to People Power in the Philippines.* 2005

Kerkvliet, B. J. and Mojares, R. B. (eds.) *From Marcos to Aquino: Local Perspectives on Political Transition in the Philippines.* 1992

Larkin, J. A., *Sugar and the Origins of Modern Philippine Society.* 1993

Vob, R. and Yap, J. T., *The Philippine Economy: East Asia's Stray Cat? Structure, Finance and Adjustment.* 1996

National Statistical Office: National Statistics Office, Solicarel Bldg., 1 Ramon Magsaysay Blvd., Sta Mesa, Manila 1008.
Website: http://www.census.gov.ph

POLAND

Rzeczpospolita Polska
(Polish Republic)

Capital: Warsaw
Population estimate, 2010: 38·04m.
GDP per capita, 2007: (PPP$) 15,987
HDI/world rank: 0·880/41

KEY HISTORICAL EVENTS

In the 7th and 8th centuries Slavic peoples first settled on the forest covered plains between the Odra and Vistula rivers. Poland takes its name from the Polanie ('plain dwellers'), whose ruler Mieszko I, first in line of the Piast dynasty, founded the Polish state in 966. Christianity came via Bohemia and Moravia to the Kraków region, and in 991 Mieszko I placed Poland under the Holy Roman See. His son and heir, Bolesław I the Brave (ruled 992–1025) continued his father's territorial expansionism until Poland's boundaries were much as they are today. He established an independent Polish Catholic Church in the year 1000 and was officially crowned the first king of Poland in 1024 with the support of Holy Roman Emperor Otto III. The growing power of the church stimulated economic activity ranging from the manufacture of parchment and glass to building and painting.

In the twelfth century, under the rule of Bolesław III, German infiltration and internecine struggles led to Bolesław's 1138 Testament which divided the kingdom between his three sons. Around this time, many Jewish immigrants from Western Europe were attracted by the offer of asylum. The General Charter of Jewish Liberties was published in 1264 by Bolesław V, the Duke of Kraków.

A series of Mongol invasions in 1241–42 laid waste much of Poland, and in 1308 the crusades of the Teutonic Knights captured Gdańsk, cutting off Poland's access to the sea. In 1320 Władysław I Łokietek (the Short) of Kraków reunited the majority of the Polish lands that had been divided in 1138 and was crowned king of a united Poland. His son Casimir III the Great (Kasimierz, ruled 1333–70) continued this work, and his reign brought prosperity and administrative efficiency. He negotiated a truce with the Teutonic Knights and fostered closer diplomatic relations with the neighbouring kingdoms of Bohemia and Hungary.

Casimir III was the last monarch in the Piast line, and when he died his nephew Louis of Anjou, simultaneously King Lajos I of Hungary, donned the Polish crown. His death led to a disjointed succession. After a brief civil war his eleven-year-old daughter Jadwiga married Jagiełło, the pagan Grand Duke of Lithuania, who converted to Catholicism. Their marital union in 1386 signalled the beginning of the Jagiełłonian dynasty which ruled over Lithuania and Poland, at the time the largest state in Europe. The Jagiełłonian period to 1572 is regarded as an economic and cultural 'golden age'. This joint, multi-ethnic power managed to quell opposition on its eastern and western fronts. Poland–Lithuania crushed the Tatars and in 1410 defeated an army of 27,000 Teutonic Knights at the Battle of Tannenberg. In 1454 the Polish–Teutonic war broke out. King Casimir IV (1427–92) led a successful campaign, taking control of Western Prussia. At the Peace of Toruń in 1466 Gdańsk was returned to the Polish crown. The city, granted autonomy in exchange for its efforts in the war, thrived on shipping trade with the Netherlands, Spain and England among others while the population outgrew that of Warsaw.

The link between Poland and Lithuania was further strengthened by the Union of Lublin in 1569, which was primarily signed to protect both parties from expansionist threats on the Eastern front from Russia's Tsar Ivan IV (the Terrible). Warsaw became the capital of the two kingdoms which were henceforth known as the Commonwealth of Poland–Lithuania.

The last Jagiełłonian, Zygmunt II, died in 1572, after which the nobility introduced an elective monarchy with powers limited by the Acta Henriciana, so called because the first elected king to whom it applied was Henri III de Valois. He was obliged to swear his allegiance to maintaining the elective monarchy, which consulted the nobles on tax and warfare, respected religious tolerance and held a bi-annual meeting of the Sejm, the bicameral assembly dating from 1493. In contrast to many other countries in Europe, the Commonwealth was sufficiently broadminded on religious issues to abide by the Statute of Toleration (1573), although Catholicism was still the official religion.

Polish Wars

During this period, many foreign leaders were elected, partly to neutralize external interests. In 1573 Catherine de Médicis of France organized the election of her third son, Henry, duke of Anjou, to the Polish crown. When he returned to France as king on his brother's death, he was succeeded by a Transylvanian, Prince István Bathory. He increased Poland–Lithuania's military strength—a necessity given Ivan the Terrible's bellicose claims. In campaigns throughout 1578–81 the latter was beaten with a huge loss of Russian lives, and the territories he had encroached upon were restored.

1587 marked the beginning of Vasa rule, with Swedish-born Sigismund III taking the throne. But his succession led to territorial claims from his native land. Disapproving of Sigismund's Catholic persuasion, Calvinist Sweden occupied Livonia and Pomerania. In alliance with Russia, King Karl X of Sweden mounted a full invasion of Poland–Lithuania, devastating Warsaw and Kraków. During the ensuing Polish–Swedish war of 1655–60, support for Poland–Lithuania came from the Netherlands and Denmark. The Poles fought back against the invaders, winning a major battle at Częstochowa, but were eventually defeated. King Jan Kazimiercz (John Casimir), the last in line of the Vasa dynasty, abdicated in 1668.

Hopes of salvation for the Commonwealth came with Jan III Sobieski's election to the throne in 1674. He fought off the Ottomans who were advancing onto Polish territory. But further invasions and wars weakened Poland. The Great Northern War of 1700–21 had Poland as the battleground for fierce fighting between Russia, Denmark–Norway and Saxony–Poland (also Prussia from 1715) on one side against Sweden on the other. Each of the warring factions occupied parts of Poland, which was also subject to internecine fighting. Russia played the dominant role in Polish affairs until Frederick II, king of an increasingly powerful Prussia, proposed the division of Poland between Russia, Prussia and Austria. The outcome was the first Partition of Poland, in 1772. Austria was awarded the Kingdom of Galicia–Lodomeria, with 2·5m. inhabitants. Russia took over an area with a population of over 1m. Prussia contented itself with 0·5m. new citizens, and the long-desired connection between Western Pomerania and East Prussia.

In 1791 Stanisław II, the last king of the remaining Poland–Lithuania, introduced a constitution which amounted to a bid for independence. The three surrounding superpowers nonetheless engaged in a second partition in 1793. A peasant uprising against Russian rule, led by Tadeusz Kościuszko, was crushed, along with Poland itself which lost control of all its territory to Austria, Prussia and Russia in the third partition (1795).

The territory remained a battleground, particularly during the Napoleonic wars. Napoleon established the Grand Duchy of Warsaw in 1807, which had a French-style constitution, but came under Saxon, and later Russian, administration. Polish legions, which fought on the French side against Prussia, incurred heavy losses. In 1815, when the victorious Allies redistributed the territory Napoleon had won, the 'Congress' Kingdom of Poland reappeared, this time under Russian rule, with the Tsar as its hereditary king.

Thereafter the Poles suffered by their colonizers' attempts to assimilate their culture. A series of uprisings against the Russians took place throughout the century. In the November Revolution of 1830 inexperienced military cadets were suppressed by Tsar Nicholas, who led a campaign of bloody reprisals. Around 8,000 Poles emigrated after this defeat—many of them intellectuals, and most headed for France. During the peasants' revolt in Galicia in 1846 up to 2,000 nobles were murdered and their land ravaged. There was a strong insurgent movement among the peasants, but in 1848 they failed once more to topple their oppressors, this time the Prussians.

The January Uprising against the Russians which began in 1863–64 and ended in the spring of 1865 again led to defeat. Wide-scale Russianization followed, though the abolition of serfdom marked a significant concession. As part of Bismarck's 'Kulturkampf'—the Germanization of the Prussian zones—German was introduced as the official language and Polish began to be taught in schools as a foreign language. Anti-Semitism became rife, and pogroms were not unusual. Many Jewish and Gentile Poles fled.

The Habsburg-dominated part of Poland, Galicia, was more tolerant of Polish nationalism which centred on Kraków. At one point the Austrian prime minister, finance minister and foreign minister were all Polish. Newly-formed parties began to gain ground, with the National Democrats under Roman Dmowski campaigning for autonomy and Józef Piłsudski's Socialists engaging in an underground struggle for independence. Piłsudski led an anti-Russian uprising in 1905, and was to take up arms against Russia in the First World War when Poland's territory again bore the brunt of much of the fighting between its three partitioners.

In 1917 a Polish National Committee, formed by Roman Dmowski in Paris, was recognized by the Allies. One of its members and US representative was the pianist Ignacy Jan Paderewski, who urged the Americans to support the cause for Polish independence. President Woodrow Wilson's 'Fourteen Points' for peace addressed the Polish issue, guaranteeing independence and access to the sea under point thirteen. A Polish army was formed in France in 1918. In Poland, Piłsudski set up the Polish legions and a rival government. Poland regained its independence under Piłsudski's leadership on 11 Nov. 1918.

But while the Paris Peace Conference recognized the republic, the question of its borders was highly contentious. Poland challenged Lithuania over Vilnius, the city changing hands more than once before the Second World War. Fighting also took place against Ukraine over the issue of Galicia. A war with Russia followed over the next two years, which Poland narrowly managed to win before signing the Soviet–Polish Peace Treaty in Riga in 1921. The Treaty established the borders between Russia, Ukraine and Belarus, the last two being swallowed up by the USSR the following year. Gdańsk was awarded the status of a free city, and the Polish Corridor was formed between German West and East Prussia and the rest of Germany.

Between the wars there were 16 palatinates, all centrally governed from Warsaw. The new republic was first headed by President Narutowicz, the representative of the left and centre parties, who served for only days before being assassinated by a right-wing fanatic, and replaced in 1922 by Stanisław Wojciechowski. A series of intra-party disputes and factionalisms led the way for Józef Piłsudski to mount a coup in May 1926, seizing the power he maintained under a dictatorship until his death in 1935.

Second World War

In foreign affairs Poland managed to maintain a balance between its two most intimidating neighbours, Germany and the USSR, signing a non-aggression pact with Germany in 1934. However, the Molotov–Ribbentrop non-aggression pact of Aug. 1939 secretly agreed to partition Poland between Germany and the Soviet Union in the event of war. British and French guarantees of Polish independence that had been agreed in April of the same year obliged them to declare war on Nazi Germany two days after Hitler's troops marched into Poland on 1 Sept. 1939.

The response of Britain and France signalled the start of the Second World War. The German army invaded Poland along the entire front from the Baltic Sea to Slovakia, annexing over half of the country within three weeks. Stalin's troops marched into Poland from the Eastern Front on 17 Sept., leaving the country occupied for most of the duration of the war. The Nazis undertook a policy of liquidation—not only of Jews and ethnic 'undesirables' but also of the intelligentsia, so as to avoid any possibility of a Polish leadership class. Many Polish children seen as racially pure were taken away from their parents to be brought up as Germans, while others were deported. A total of over 6m. Polish nationals, or 17% of the population, were killed in the war, half of them Jewish. Not all of the murders were attributable to the Nazis, however. In 1989 Soviet authorities finally admitted to having murdered 15,000 Polish officers who went missing in May 1940. The Soviet secret service had been equally keen to obliterate potential opposition leaders.

Polish forces regrouped on Allied soil under a government-in-exile headed by Gen. Władysław Sikorski, first in Paris and then, after 1940, in London. In Poland an underground national army, the AK, was formed under Gen. Komorowski to fight against the occupiers and to organize resistance. After Germany's invasion of the USSR in 1941, Poland was occupied solely by Nazi forces. Many of the largest concentration camps were built on Polish soil, including Auschwitz near Kraków.

In 1943 the exiled prime minister Gen. Sikorski was killed in a plane crash. He was replaced by Stanisław Mikołajczyk of the Polish Peasants' Party. The same year saw a Jewish uprising in the Warsaw ghetto, and in 1944 there was a second rebellion against the Nazi occupation in the capital which lasted for two months. The Red Army was on the threshold of Warsaw throughout the two month revolt, but did not intervene. 150,000 civilians and 18,000 members of the AK lost their lives with virtually the whole of the remaining urban population deported and 85% of the city destroyed. By the time of Warsaw's liberation in Jan. 1945, the Jewish population numbered 200. The decimated underground movement was forced to seek assistance from Moscow, and after a number of compromises the Soviets recognized the Polish Committee of National Liberation, or the 'Lublin Committee', which proclaimed itself the sole legal government when Lublin was liberated in July 1944.

Poland's post-war fate was decided by the Allies at the Yalta and Potsdam conferences. At Yalta, Stalin agreed that the Lublin government should be extended to include non-Communists from the exile government, a promise that he failed to keep. Stanisław Mikołajczyk and three other members joined the provisional cabinet in July 1945. Nonetheless, many Polish politicians left the country. The Potsdam conference set Poland's Western border along the Oder–Neisse line, with all former German territories east of these rivers handed to Poland. As a result, Poles and Germans had to be resettled.

The first post-war elections were held in Jan. 1947. The Stalinist Polish Workers' Party (PPR) managed to crush both official and underground opposition. A Communist-dominated coalition under the leadership of Władysław Gomułka, the 'Democratic Bloc', won over three-quarters of the votes. Bolesław Bierut, leader of the USSR-backed Polish Communist Party, was named president. Defeated, Stanisław Mikołajczyk fled the country. An independently minded politician, Gomułka entered into conflict with Stalin by opposing agricultural collectivization and by speaking out against the formation of Cominform (Communist Information Bureau) in 1947. As a result he was removed as Secretary General of the PPR in Sept. 1948. Expelled from the party in late 1949, he was put under house arrest in July 1951. In 1948 the Polish United Workers' Party (PZPR) was formed, with Bierut as first party secretary. The nationalization of industry, land expropriation and the restructuring of the economy to favour heavy industry, including arms production, were accompanied in 1952 by a Soviet-style constitution and the renaming of the country as the People's Republic of Poland. This 'Stalinization' also included political and religious suppression and persecution, which targeted the Catholic church in particular.

Post-War Reform

In 1955 Poland joined other Eastern bloc countries in signing the Warsaw Pact military treaty. Meanwhile, the planned economy was failing, leading to widespread public unrest as food prices spiralled. Workers' strikes and riots in Poznań in 1956 were brutally suppressed by the authorities resulting in the death of 53 people. At this time Gomułka, the opponent of Stalinism, gained popularity. Readmitted to the party in 1956, Gomułka was reinstated as first secretary of the Party.

He attempted to introduce reforms, winning public support for his pledges of a 'Polish way' to socialism. Gomułka cut the power of the secret police, halted agricultural collectivization and brought an end to attacks on the Catholic Church. However, the suppression of freedom of expression continued and the economy did not improve. Gomułka's popular appeal began to falter. Student riots sprang up throughout the 1960s. In the 'March events' of 1968, the campaign for intellectual freedom led to widespread student riots and a reactive Party campaign against intellectuals and Jews, many of whom were forced to flee abroad.

Unrest and dissatisfaction with the party remained. Increased food prices in Dec. 1970 resulted in riots and strikes in the shipyards of Gdańsk, Szczecin and Gdynia. These were met with armed opposition, the authorities firing into the masses and killing several demonstrators. Gomułka and other leaders subsequently resigned, although Gomułka at least had the satisfaction of procuring West Germany's recognition of the Oder–Neisse line as the official Western border of Poland in Dec. 1970.

Solidarity

Edward Gierek succeeded Gomułka as first secretary, and in the following years launched a reform programme which was chiefly financed by loans from Western banks. He was hoping for a Polish economic miracle, but lacked the will to push through the necessary reforms. Short term rewards were not enough to overcome the problems of a failing infrastructure, economic mismanagement of successive governments and a faltering world economy following the 1973–74 world oil crisis. Further demonstrations took place in several cities in 1976 to protest at more food price increases, and in Radom a Workers' Defence Committee was founded. While the government expressed disapproval, it did not act against the Committee.

In 1978 the election of Karol Wojtyła, Cardinal of Kraków, as Pope John Paul II boosted Poland's national self-esteem, celebrated in his trip to his native country the following year. Nonetheless, increased meat prices in July 1980 led to more waves of strikes, rippling out from the Ursus tractor plant near Warsaw across the country, and culminating in the Lenin shipyards in Gdańsk, where the Solidarity movement was born. The first independent trade union to be established in a communist country soon boasted a membership of 10m. Its leader, Lech Wałęsa, a shipyard electrician, set up a strike committee, the first of a succession across the country, and drew up a 21-point accord, demanding the right to strike and to form independent trade unions, the abolition of censorship, freedom of expression, the release of political prisoners and access to the media. Soviet and Polish communist efforts to curb Solidarity's popularity failed and the group was officially recognized after some government resistance.

The social unrest, coupled with failing health, led to Gierek's resignation in Sept. 1980. In Feb. 1981 Gen. Wojciech Jaruzelski, the defence minister, became prime minister. This brought the military into the political front line and in Dec. 1981 Jaruzelski imposed martial law. A Military Council of National Salvation was established and Solidarity was proscribed. Wałęsa was among the thousands of members who were arrested and imprisoned. Demonstrations and strikes provoked the government into even stricter controls with the banning of all independent trade unions, although martial law was dropped a year later.

New hope was given to Poland in 1983, by the Pope's second visit, and by the award of the Nobel Peace Prize to Lech Wałęsa. Economic difficulties continued throughout the 1980s, and when the government proposed unpopular economic reforms in 1987, support for Solidarity led to nationwide strikes during 1988. Jaruzelski was forced to embark on negotiations with Wałęsa and the Catholic Church. Agreement was reached in April 1989 and Solidarity was given legal status and freedom to fight the upcoming elections, whilst the previously ceremonial post of Presidency was vested with new legislative powers. In return, Solidarity agreed to compete for only 35% of the seats in the Sejm.

At the July 1989 elections Solidarity won virtually all the seats they contested but because of the 35% rule Jaruzelski was voted in as president. However, Solidarity refused to join the communists in a grand coalition and Jaruzelski had to appoint Tadeusz Mazowiecki, an official of Solidarity, to be Poland's first non-communist premier in over 40 years. Jaruzelski subsequently resigned.

The first round of presidential elections in Nov. 1990 pitted Lech Wałęsa against Tadeusz Mazowiecki. Wałęsa won 43% of the votes in the first round and 74% in the second round in Dec., when he was inaugurated. Mazowiecki resigned his premiership and was replaced by Jan Bielcki, whose government held office until Aug. 1991. Genuinely free parliamentary elections did not take place until Oct. 1991, when there was a surprisingly low electoral turnout. In the absence of a clear-cut winner, several parties combined to form a centre-right coalition headed by Jan Olszewski. Owing to disputes both within the party and with President Wałęsa, however, the government lasted only seven months. This factionalism and inability to make compromises was typical of Poland's early post-Communist years. The government formed under Hanna Suchocka, Poland's first female prime minister, fared no better.

As in other post-Communist states, the economic measures necessary for the transition to a profitable market economy were highly unpopular with the electorate, not least when industrial modernization led to unemployment. In 1990 the finance minister, Leszek Balcerowicz, had introduced a range of tight austerity measures, including price rises and currency devaluation in an attempt to stabilize the economy before opening it to market forces. The Polish economy prospered but Wałęsa's popular appeal diminished as his tenure progressed. His skills as Solidarity's leader revolved around his ability to speak for the common people, but in government his tone was often regarded as aggressive and his style of leadership autocratic. Solidarity's loyalties as a trade union were often incompatible with its responsibilities as a political party. The elections of 1993 saw the return of the left under Waldemar Pawlak of the Polish Peasants' Party. After a series of intra-party quarrels and accusations of corruption, Pawlak's premiership ended in Feb. 1995.

Pawlak was replaced by the Communist Józef Oleksy of the Democratic Left Alliance. The left gained further political clout when Wałęsa was ousted in the presidential elections of 1995 by Aleksander Kwaśniewski. Redundancies in the Gdańsk shipyards in 1997 saw a renewed outbreak of nationwide strikes. Revising its political agenda, Solidarity forged a coalition of 25 centre-right parties to create Solidarity Electoral Action. This party emerged as the strongest in the 1997 general election when Jerzy Buzek, a member of Solidarity since its inception, became prime minister. A new constitution came into effect, reducing the powers of the president and committing the country to a social market economy.

Kwaśniewski's communist heritage caused concern among many Western leaders, but he confirmed his intention to press for EU and NATO membership. Market reforms and privatization continued apace. In 1999, at a joint ceremony with Czech president Vaclav Havel, Kwaśniewski signed Poland into NATO. The following year Kwaśniewski secured a second term and in 2001 Buzek was succeeded by Leszek Miller. A former communist turned social democrat, Miller's key aim was to prepare Poland for entry into the EU. Facing a deteriorating economy, he cut the national debt by increases in taxation and spending cuts. On 1 May 2004 Poland became a member of the EU.

Lech Kaczyński succeeded Kwaśniewski in 2005, with his twin brother Jarosław Kaczyński, serving as prime minister in 2006–07. President Kaczyński was killed in April 2010 when his plane crashed over Russia on its way to a war memorial service. The head of the national bank, the entire command of the armed services and several senior government figures, MPs, clergy and academics also perished in the accident.

TERRITORY AND POPULATION

Poland is bounded in the north by the Baltic Sea and Russia, east by Lithuania, Belarus and Ukraine, south by the Czech Republic and Slovakia and west by Germany. Poland comprises an area of 312,685 sq. km (120,728 sq. miles).

At the census of 20 May 2002 the population was 38,230,080 (18·52m. males), giving a density of 122·3 per sq. km. Population estimate, Dec. 2007: 38,115,641. In 2005, 62·1% of the population lived in urban areas.

The UN gives an estimated population for 2010 of 38·04m.

The country is divided into 16 regions or voivodships (*wojewodztwo*), created from the previous 49 on 1 Jan. 1999 following administrative reform. Area (in sq. km) and population (in 1,000) in 2002 (density per sq. km in brackets).

Voivodship	*Area*	*Population*	
Dolnośląskie	19,948	2,907	(146)
Kujawsko-Pomorskie	17,970	2,069	(115)
Lubelskie	25,121	2,199	(88)
Lubuskie	13,981	1,009	(72)
Łódzkie	18,219	2,613	(143)
Małopolskie	15,190	3,232	(213)
Mazowieckie	35,559	5,124	(144)
Opolskie	9,412	1,065	(113)
Podkarpackie	17,844	2,104	(117)
Podlaskie	20,187	1,209	(60)
Pomorskie	18,293	2,180	(119)
Śląskie	12,331	4,743	(386)
Świętokrzyskie	11,708	1,297	(111)
Warmińsko-Mazurskie	24,192	1,428	(59)
Wielkopolskie	29,826	3,352	(112)
Zachodniopomorskie	22,896	1,698	(74)

Population (in 1,000) of the largest towns and cities (2002):

Warsaw (Warszawa)	1,671·7	Częstochowa	251·4
Łódź	789·3	Sosnowiec	232·6
Cracow (Kraków)	758·5	Radom	229·7
Wrocław	640·4	Kielce	212·4
Poznań	578·9	Toruń	211·2
Gdańsk	461·3	Gliwice	203·8
Szczecin	415·4	Zabrze	195·3
Bydgoszcz	373·8	Bytom	193·5
Lublin	357·1	Bielsko-Biała	178·0
Katowice	327·2	Olsztyn	173·1
Białystok	291·4	Rzeszów	160·4
Gdynia	253·5	Ruda Śląska	150·6

The population is 96·7% Polish. Minorities at the 2002 census included 173,153 Silesians, 152,987 Germans, 48,737 Belarusians and 30,957 Ukrainians. There are an estimated 300,000 people in Poland of Kashubian ethnicity (direct descendants of an early Slavic tribe of Pomeranians). They generally declare Polish nationality and consider themselves both Poles and Kashubians.

A movement for Silesian autonomy has attracted sufficient support to suggest that further moves towards decentralization may soon be considered. A Council of National Minorities was set up in March 1991. There is a large Polish diaspora, some 65% in the USA.

The official language is Polish.

SOCIAL STATISTICS

2005 (in 1,000): births, 364·4; deaths, 368·3; marriages, 206·9; divorces, 67·5; infant deaths, 2·3. Rates (per 1,000 population): birth, 9·5; death, 9·7; marriage, 5·4; divorce, 1·8; infant mortality (per 1,000 live births), 6·4. A law prohibiting abortion was passed in 1993, but an amendment of Aug. 1996 permits it in cases of hardship or difficult personal situation. The most popular age range for marrying in 2005 was 20–24 for females and 25–29 for males. Expectation of life at birth, 2007, was 71·3 years for males and 79·7 years for females. In 2005 there were 22,242 emigrants (including 12,317 to Germany) and 9,364 immigrants. 70% of Polish emigrants between 2000 and 2005 settled in Germany. Number of suicides, 2004, 6,071; the suicide rate per 100,000 population was 27·9 among males and 4·6 among females in 2004. Population growth rate, 2005, 0·1%; fertility rate, 2005, 1·2 births per woman (one of the lowest rates in the world).

CLIMATE

Climate is continental, marked by long and severe winters. Rainfall amounts are moderate, with a marked summer maximum. Warsaw, Jan. 24°F (–4·3°C), July 64°F (17·9°C). Annual rainfall 18·3" (465 mm). Gdańsk, Jan. 29°F (–1·7°C), July 63°F (17·2°C). Annual rainfall 22·0" (559 mm). Kraków, Jan. 27°F (–2·8°C), July 67°F (19·4°C). Annual rainfall 28·7" (729 mm). Poznań, Jan. 26°F (–3·3°C), July 64°F (17·9°C). Annual rainfall 21·0" (534 mm). Szczecin, Jan. 27°F (–3·0°C), July 64°F (17·7°C). Annual rainfall 18·4" (467 mm). Wrocław, Jan. 24°F (–4·3°C), July 64°F (17·9°C). Annual rainfall 20·7" (525 mm).

CONSTITUTION AND GOVERNMENT

The present Constitution was passed by national referendum on 25 May 1997 and became effective on 17 Oct. 1997. The head of state is the *President*, who is directly elected for a five-year term (renewable once). The President may appoint, but may not dismiss, cabinets.

The authority of the republic is vested in the *Sejm* (Parliament of 460 members), elected by proportional representation for four years by all citizens over 18. There is a 5% threshold for parties and 8% for coalitions, but seats are reserved for representatives of ethnic minorities even if their vote falls below 5%. 69 of the Sejm seats are awarded from the national lists of parties polling more than 7% of the vote. The Sejm elects a *Council of State* and a *Council of Ministers*. There is also an elected 100-member upper house, the *Senate*. The President and the Senate each has a power of veto which only a two-thirds majority of the Sejm can override. The President does not, however, have a veto over the annual budget. The *Prime Minister* is chosen by the President with the approval of the Sejm.

A *Political Council* consultative to the presidency consisting of representatives of all the major political tendencies was set up in Jan. 1991.

National Anthem

'Jeszcze Polska nie zginęla' ('Poland has not yet perished'); words by J. Wybicki, tune by M. Ogiński.

GOVERNMENT CHRONOLOGY

First Secretaries of the Polish United Workers' Party (1943–90) and Presidents of the Republic (since 1990). (PiS = Law and Justice Party; PO = Civic Platform; PZPR = Polish United Workers' Party; SdRP = Social Democracy of the Republic of Poland; SLD = Democratic Left Alliance; n/p = non-partisan)

First Secretaries of PZPR

1943–48	Władysław Gomułka
1948–52	Bolesław Bierut
1952–54	Hilary Minc
1954–56	Bolesław Bierut
1956	Edward Ochab
1956–70	Władysław Gomułka
1970–80	Edward Gierek
1980–81	Stanisław Kania
1981–89	Wojciech Jaruzelski (military)
1989–90	Mieczysław F. Rakowski

Presidents

1989–90	n/p	Wojciech Jaruzelski
1990–95	Solidarność	Lech Wałęsa
1995–2005	SdRP/SLD	Aleksander Kwaśniewski
2005–10	PiS	Lech Kaczyński
2010–	PO	Bronisław Komorowski (acting)

Prime Ministers since 1945. (AWS = Solidarity Electoral Action; KLD = Liberal Democratic Congress; PC = Centre Alliance; PiS = Law and Justice Party; PO = Civic Platform; PPR = Polish Workers' Party; PPS = Polish Socialist Party; PSL = Polish Peasants' Party; PZPR = Polish United Workers' Party; RS-AWS = Social Movement-Solidarity Electoral Action; SdRP = Social Democracy of the Republic of Poland; SLD = Democratic Left Alliance; UD = Democratic Union)

1945–47	PPS	Edward Osóbka-Morawski
1947–52	PPR, PZPR	Józef A. Z. Cyrankiewicz
1952–54	PZPR	Bolesław Bierut
1954–70	PZPR	Józef A. Z. Cyrankiewicz
1970–80	PZPR	Piotr Jaroszewicz
1980	PZPR	Edward Babiuch
1980–81	PZPR	Józef Pińkowski
1981–85	PZPR/military	Wojciech Jaruzelski
1985–88	PZPR	Zbigniew Messner
1988–89	PZPR	Mieczysław F. Rakowski
1989	PZPR	Czesław Kiszczak
1989–91	Solidarność, UD	Tadeusz Mazowiecki
1991	KLD	Jan Krzysztof Bielecki
1991–92	PC	Jan Olszewski
1992	PSL	Waldemar Pawlak
1992–93	UD	Hanna Suchocka
1993–95	PSL	Waldemar Pawlak
1995–96	SdRP/SLD	Józef Oleksy
1996–97	SdRP/SLD	Włodzimierz Cimoszewicz
1997–2001	RS-AWS/AWS	Jerzy Buzek
2001–04	SLD	Leszek Miller
2004–05	SLD	Marek Belka
2005–06	PiS	Kazimierz Marcinkiewicz
2006–07	PiS	Jarosław Kaczyński
2007–	PO	Donald Tusk

RECENT ELECTIONS

Parliamentary elections were held on 25 Oct. 2007. The opposition Civic Platform (PO) won 209 of 460 seats with 41·5% of the votes (up from 133 seats in 2005), ahead of the ruling Law and Justice Party (PiS), with 166 seats and 32·1%; Left and Democrats (LiD) won 53 seats with 13·2%; Polish Peasants' Party (PSL) won 31 with 8·9%; German Minority (MN), won one seat with 0·2%. In the Senate, the Civic Platform won Law and Justice Party won 60 seats, with the Law and Justice Party winning 39 and independents 1. Turnout was 53·9% (the highest in Poland since the collapse of socialism in 1989). Following the election a coalition government was formed between Civic Platform and the Polish Peasants' Party.

Presidential elections were held in two rounds on 9 and 23 Oct. 2005. In the first round 12 candidates stood; turnout was 49·7%. Donald Tusk of the Civic Platform (PO) gained 36·3% of votes cast, Lech Kaczyński of the Law and Justice Party (PiS) 33·1%, Andrzej Lepper of Self-Defence of the Polish Republic (SRP) 15·1% and Marek Borowski of the Democratic Party (PD) 10·3%. Other candidates obtained 2% or less. In the second round run-off Lech Kaczyński was elected president with 54·0% of the vote against 46·0% for Donald Tusk.

Presidential elections were scheduled to take place on 20 June 2010.

European Parliament

Poland has 50 (54 in 2004) representatives. At the June 2009 elections turnout was 24·5% (20·9% in 2004). The PO won 25 seats with 44·4% of votes cast (political affiliation in European Parliament: European People's Party); the PiS, 15 with 27·4% (European Conservatives and Reformists); the Democratic Left Alliance–Union of Labour, 7 with 12·3% (Progressive Alliance of Socialists and Democrats); the PSL, 3 with 7·0% (European People's Party).

CURRENT ADMINISTRATION

President (acting): Bronisław Komorowski; b. 1952 (PO; since 10 April 2010).

In March 2010 the coalition government consisted of:

Prime Minister: Donald Tusk; b. 1957 (PO; sworn in 16 Nov. 2007).

Deputy Prime Minister: Waldemar Pawlak (also *Minister of Economy*) (PSL).

Minister of Agriculture and Rural Development: Marek Sawicki (PSL). *Culture and National Heritage:* Bogdan Zdrojewski (PO). *Environment:* Andrzej Kraszewski (ind.). *Finance:* Jan Vincent-Rostowski (ind.). *Foreign Affairs:* Radosław Sikorski (PO). *Health:* Ewa Kopacz (PO). *Infrastructure:* Cezary Grabarczyk (PO). *Interior and Administration:* Jerzy Miller (PO). *Justice:* Krzysztof Kwiatkowski (PO). *Labour and Social Policy:* Jolanta Fedak (PSL). *National Defence:* Bogdan Klich (PO). *National Education:* Katarzyna Hall (ind.). *Regional Development:* Elżbieta Bieńkowska (ind.). *Science and Higher Education:* Barbara Kudrycka (PO). *Sport and Tourism:* Adam Giersz (ind.). *State Treasury:* Aleksander Grad (PO). *Minister, Member of the Council of Ministers:* Zbigniew Derdziuk (ind.).

Speaker of the Sejm: Bronisław Komorowski (PO).

Office of the Prime Minister: http://www.kprm.gov.pl

CURRENT LEADERS

Donald Tusk

Position

Prime Minister

Introduction

Donald Tusk became prime minister on 9 Nov. 2007 following his party's resounding victory in parliamentary elections. The former Solidarity activist has taken a pro-business stance and is keen to establish closer relations with EU neighbours.

Early Life

Donald Franciszek Tusk was born on 22 April 1957 in Gdańsk. His family is part of the city's long-established minority Kashubian community. Following his secondary education he attended the University of Gdansk where he studied history. A long-time critic of the communist administration, Tusk helped to establish the student committee of the Solidarity movement, which grew out of the nationwide industrial unrest centred on the Gdańsk shipyard during the summer of 1980. He subsequently co-founded the Independent Polish Students' Association (NZS). Following the authorities' crackdown on Solidarity in 1981, Tusk and other activists were forced into the shadows. He earned a living as a builder, an experience subsequently presented as evidence of his empathy with 'ordinary people'.

In the late 1980s Tusk left Solidarity to join the nascent liberal movement, developing close ties with Janusz Lewandowski and Jan Krzysztof Bielecki and forming Gdańsk's Liberal Congress. In 1991 he joined the Liberal Democratic Congress (KLD), which contested the first multi-party elections in Oct. 1991 on a free-market platform, calling for privatization, freedom of movement and accession to the EU. Tusk took one of the KLD's 37 seats in the Sejm. Although he was re-elected as a deputy in the 1993 elections, the KLD fared poorly and in March 1994 merged with the Democratic Union to form a new centre-right party, Freedom Union (UW). The party secured 13·4% of the vote in the 1997 elections, becoming the junior partner (with six ministries) in Jerzy Buzek's coalition government. Tusk was elected to the Senate, where from 1998–2001 he served as vice-speaker.

Having failed to win the chairmanship of the UW in 2000 (losing to Bronisław Geremek), Tusk resigned from the party. He joined Andrzej Olechowski (who had performed creditably in the 2000 presidential contest) and Maciej Płażyński in establishing the secular, liberal Civic Platform (PO) in early 2001, with Płażyński at the helm. The PO performed strongly in the 2001 elections, taking 65 seats in the Sejm and becoming the largest opposition party to Leszek Miller's government. In June 2003 Tusk became the PO's chairman. He was a vocal critic of the left-leaning SLD government, particularly its economic policies. His standing improved as the SLD became mired in corruption scandals but he failed in his 2005 bid for the presidency, losing to Lech Kaczyński of the socially conservative, nationalist Law and Justice Party. Later in 2005 the PO suffered further electoral defeat to Law and Justice, led by Jarosław Kaczyński (Lech's twin brother), who became prime minister.

Tusk remained leader of the PO and took a more aggressive approach in the run-up to the early election called for Oct. 2007. The election followed the collapse of the Law and Justice-led coalition amid allegations of corruption. Tusk accused Kaczyński of incompetence on international relations—notably deteriorating relations with Germany—and of failing to prevent the mass movement of Poles to Britain and Ireland in search of work. Tusk campaigned on a platform to speed up privatization, lower taxes and reduce business bureaucracy to encourage investors.

In parliamentary elections on 21 Oct. 2007 the PO emerged victorious, taking around 41% of the vote against 32% for Law and Justice. Tusk took office as prime minister on 16 Nov and his cabinet won a confidence vote in the Sejm on 24 Nov. 2007.

Career in Office

Tusk pledged to create jobs and promote economic development by cutting bureaucracy and regulation. However, the global financial downturn in 2008 threatened to undermine Poland's growth prospects, prompting the government to launch an economic stimulus programme in Dec. and to negotiate a one-year US$20·6bn. credit line with the International Monetary Fund which was approved in May 2009. On the international stage, he oversaw the withdrawal in Oct. 2008 of Poland's last troops stationed in Iraq, fulfilling a key electoral pledge. However, plans agreed in 2008 for Poland to host a controversial missile defence shield for the USA were effectively abandoned in Sept. 2009 when the US president announced the scrapping of key elements of the system. Despite the Polish government's disappointment at the decision, Tusk insisted that the USA and Poland would remain close allies.

DEFENCE

Poland is divided into two military districts: Pomeranian (North) and Silesian (South). In 2006 military expenditure totalled US$6,235m. (US$162 per capita), representing 1·8% of GDP.

Conscription ended on 1 Jan. 2010.

Army

Strength (2007) 79,000 (including 39,000 conscripts). In accordance with a programme of modernization of the armed forces, the strength has been gradually declining, from 230,000 in the socialist era in 1988 to 186,000 in 1995 and further to the current figure of under 80,000. In addition there were 188,000 Army reservists in 2007 and 14,100 border guards.

Navy

The fleet comprises four ex-Soviet and one ex-Norwegian diesel submarines, three frigates and five corvettes. There is a small Naval Aviation force.

Personnel in 2007 totalled 11,600 including 600 conscripts and 1,900 in Naval Aviation. Bases are at Gdynia, Hel, Świnoujście and Kolobrzeg.

Air Force

The Air Force had a strength (2007) of 28,466 (466 conscripts). There are two air defence corps (North and South) with 103 combat capable aircraft (including MiG-29s and Su-22s).

INTERNATIONAL RELATIONS

A treaty of friendship with Germany signed on 17 June 1991 renounced the use of force, recognized Poland's western border as laid down at the Potsdam conference of 1945 (the 'Oder–Neisse line') and guaranteed minority rights in both countries.

Poland is a member of the UN, World Bank, IMF and several other UN specialized agencies, WTO, EU, Council of Europe, OSCE, CERN, CEI, Council of the Baltic Sea States, BIS, IOM, NATO, OECD, Antarctic Treaty and is an associate member of WEU. A referendum held on 8 June 2003 approved accession to the EU, with 77·4% of votes cast for membership and 22·6% against. Poland became a member of the EU on 1 May 2004.

In Dec. 2007 Poland acceded to the Schengen accord, which abolishes border controls between Poland, Austria, Belgium, Czech Republic, Denmark, Estonia, Finland, France, Germany, Greece, Hungary, Iceland, Italy, Latvia, Lithuania, Luxembourg, Malta, Netherlands, Norway, Portugal, Slovakia, Slovenia, Spain, Sweden and Switzerland.

Poland's Senate approved the European Union's Treaty of Lisbon on 2 April 2008, the day after the *Sejm* had done so. However, then President Kaczyński did not ratify it until 12 Oct. 2009, following acceptance of the Treaty by Ireland in a referendum ten days earlier.

ECONOMY

Agriculture accounted for 4·4% of GDP in 2006, industry 31·7% and services 63·9%.

Overview

Under communism the economy was skewed towards heavy industry to the neglect of services. Since the collapse of the old regime in 1990 the service sector has gained, contributing 63·9% of GDP in 2006 compared to 31·7% for industry. Despite slow privatization in the manufacturing sector, the private sector accounted for 75% of GDP in 2003, up from 18% in 1989. Most of the banking sector has been privatized, as have many large industries. In 1990 and 1991 the economy shrank by 11·5% and 7·0% respectively but economic restructuring has since helped to achieve productivity gains.

The Economist Intelligence Unit estimates that from 1994–2003 total factor productivity grew at an annual average of over 3%. This resulted from sound macroeconomic management combined with a raft of transition policies, including price liberalization and lower import barriers. After accession to the EU in May 2004 growth was buoyant, following half a decade of below-par expansion. An unspectacular yet solid growth performance since the initial transition shock has helped raise living standards. Per capita income levels by 2004 had grown to over two-and-a-half times 1993 levels, reaching US$6,265 per annum.

The economic environment is friendly with transparent investment rules and equality for domestic and foreign firms. According to the World Bank, the main impediment to stronger growth is the public sector. Weak public finances, high fiscal deficits, administrative inefficiencies, weakness in the judicial system, low investment in public infrastructure and non-competitive state-led sectors are all ripe for reform. The privatization push that began in the 1990s has slowed significantly. The health care sector has proved difficult to reform and is a significant fiscal liability.

Unemployment declined steadily until the effects of the global crisis of 2008 began to be felt in Poland (from 19·8% in 2002 to 7·1% in 2008), although the rate had risen back up to 8·9% by Dec. 2009. Lowering the tax burden on labour, which is high in Poland compared to other EU members, would benefit employment. Unemployment is highest where state farms were once the rule (primarily in the northeast) while former industrial areas have proved dynamic. Agriculture has resisted structural change and continues to be dominated by small and inefficient farms. Though accounting for only 4·4% of GDP in 2006, agriculture accounts for a large share of total employment and is powerful politically. EU funding should help with restructuring and promoting investment in the rural infrastructure. Polish exporters have benefited from EU market integration.

The economy was significantly affected by the global downturn that began in 2007, though Poland fared better than many of its neighbours. Real GDP growth fell to 5·0% in 2008, down from 6·8% in 2007. In response the central bank cut the seven-day reference interest rate by 75 basis points to 4·25%. Output in the industrial sector fell by 4·4% year-on-year in Dec. 2008 and manufacturing output, which makes the largest contribution to industrial output, fell by 3·9%, mirroring a slowdown in the export market. Exports contracted by 30% year-on-year in the first quarter of 2009 and FDI fell by 50%.

In April 2009 the Polish government approached the IMF for US$20·5bn. from its flexible credit line (FCL) to shore up borrowing needs in the face of the financial crisis. This helped Poland to avoid recession in 2009, with the IMF predicting modest growth of about 1·5% in 2010 given improving global conditions.

Currency

The currency unit is the *złoty* (PLN) of 100 *groszy*. A new złoty was introduced on 1 Jan. 1995 at 1 new złoty = 10,000 old złotys. Inflation rates (based on OECD statistics):

1999	*2000*	*2001*	*2002*	*2003*	*2004*	*2005*	*2006*	*2007*	*2008*
7·2%	9·9%	5·4%	1·9%	0·7%	3·4%	2·2%	1·3%	2·5%	4·2%

Inflation, in single figures since 1999, had been nearly 250% in 1990. The złoty became convertible on 1 Jan. 1990. In 1995 the złoty was subject to a creeping devaluation of 1·2% per month; it was allowed to float in a 14% (+/–7%) band from 16 May 1995. In April 2000 Poland introduced a floating exchange rate. Foreign exchange reserves were US$72,280m. and gold reserves 3·31m. troy oz in Sept. 2009. In July 2009 total money supply was 363,655m. złotys.

Budget

Central government revenue and expenditure (in 1bn. złotys):

	2004	*2005*	*2006*
Revenue	290·85	319·42	346·03
Expenditure	340·89	356·68	380·06

VAT is 22·0% (reduced rates, 7% and 3%). Taxes accounted for 53·1% of revenues in 2006. Social benefits accounted for 44·6% of expenditures.

Performance

Real GDP growth rates (based on OECD statistics):

1999	*2000*	*2001*	*2002*	*2003*	*2004*	*2005*	*2006*	*2007*	*2008*
4·5%	4·3%	1·2%	1·4%	3·9%	5·3%	3·6%	6·2%	6·8%	5·0%

In 2009 real GDP growth was provisionally put at 1·7% by the Central Statistical Office, making Poland the only EU member country not to experience a recession and the only one with positive growth. Total GDP in 2008 was US$527·0bn. The private sector accounts for more than 70% of GDP.

Banking and Finance

The National Bank of Poland (established 1945) is the central bank and bank of issue (*Acting Governor*, Piotr Wiesiołek). There were 73 banks operating at the end of 2000, of which only seven were controlled—directly or indirectly—by the Polish government through its state treasury. Poland's leading banks are PKO Bank Polski with assets of 156·5bn. złotys in Dec. 2009, and Bank Pekao (assets of 130·6bn. złotys in Dec. 2009).

In 2008 Poland received US$16,533m. of foreign direct investment, down from US$22,612m. in 2007 although up from just US$4,870m. in 2003 and US$88m. in 1990. It receives the most foreign direct investment of any of the former socialist countries of central and eastern Europe. The total stock of FDI at the end of 2008 was US$161·4bn.

There is a stock exchange in Warsaw.

ENERGY AND NATURAL RESOURCES

Environment

Poland's carbon dioxide emissions from the consumption and flaring of fossil fuels in 2008 were the equivalent of 7·8 tonnes per capita.

Electricity

Installed capacity was 31·7m. kW in 2004. Production (2004) 154·16bn. kWh; consumption per capita was 3,793 kWh in 2004.

Oil and Gas

Total oil reserves (2007) amount to some 96m. bbls; natural gas reserves (2008), 110bn. cu. metres. Crude oil production was 6·6m. bbls in 2004; natural gas (2008), 4·1m. cu. metres. The largest oil distributor is Polski Koncern Naftowy ORLEN SA, created by the merger of Petrochemia Płock and Centrala Produktów Naftowych.

Minerals

Poland is a major producer of coal (reserves of some 14,000m. tonnes), copper (56m. tonnes) and sulphur. Production (in tonnes): coal (2004), 101·2m.; brown coal (2004), 61·2m.; salt (2006), 4·0m.; copper (2006), 497,000; silver (2006), 1,265.

Agriculture

In 2007, 15·2% of the economically active population were engaged in agriculture. In 2007 there were 11·87m. ha. of arable land. There were 2·6m. farms in 2007; private farms accounted for 89·1% of the total area of agricultural land and state-owned farms for 10·9%. In 2007 agriculture, hunting and forestry contributed 3·8% of GDP.

Output in 2007 (in 1,000 tonnes): sugar beets, 12,682; potatoes, 11,791; wheat, 8,317; barley, 4,008; rye, 3,126; rapeseed, 2,130; maize, 1,722; oats, 1,462; cabbage, 1,325; apples, 1,040; carrots, 938; onions, 752. Poland is the third largest producer of rye, after Russia and Germany.

Livestock, 2007: pigs, 18·13m.; cattle, 5·70m. (including cows, 2·79m.); sheep, 332,000; horses, 329,000; chickens, 124m.

Livestock products, 2007: pork, bacon and ham, 2,150,700 tonnes; beef and veal, 379,500 tonnes; poultry meat, 1,139,600 tonnes; milk, 12,096,000 tonnes; cheese (including soft cheese), 670,000 tonnes; eggs, 547,000 tonnes.

In 2007 there were 1,553,400 tractors in use.

Forestry

In 2005 forest area was 9·19m. ha. (predominantly coniferous), or 30·0% of the land area. 82% of Poland's forests are state-owned, with the balance being private or municipal. Timber production in 2007 was 35·93m. cu. metres.

Fisheries

The catch was 185,179 tonnes in 2007, of which 72% were sea fish. In 2007 there were 4,500 people employed in the fishing industry.

INDUSTRY

The leading companies by market capitalization in Poland in March 2009 were: Telekomunikacja Polska (US$7·3bn.); Pekao (US$6·2bn.), a banking company; and PKO Bank (US$6·0bn.).

In 2007 there were 572 state firms, 216,887 limited liability companies, 324,246 other companies and 18,128 co-operatives. Production in 2007 unless otherwise indicated (in 1,000 tonnes): cement, 17,000; crude steel, 10,631; distillate fuel oil (2004), 7,371; pig iron, 5,804; petrol (2004), 3,978; paper and paperboard, 2,992; fertilizers, 2,835; plastics in primary forms, 2,778; residual fuel oil (2004), 2,754; ammonia, 2,417; nitric acid, 2,270; sulphuric acid, 2,010; sugar, 1,857; soda ash, 1,215; paints and lacquers, 1,117; sulphur, 834; beer, 3,690m. litres; mineral water, 2,708m. litres; fruit and vegetable juice, 664m. litres; vodka, 93m. litres; cigarettes, 124bn. units; bricks, 839m. units; television receivers, 14,929,000 units; refrigerators and freezers, 2,305,000 units; washing machines, 1,938,000 units; telephone sets, 797,000 units; cars, 698,000 units; tractors, 7,400 units; public transport vehicles, 3,600 units.

Output of light industry in 2007: cotton woven fabrics, 142·9m. sq. metres; silk fabrics, 18·1m. sq. metres; woollen woven fabrics, 5·6m. sq. metres; shoes, 43·6m. pairs.

Since 1993 employment in the Polish mining industry has fallen by 40% and 23 mines have closed. For some time the Polish government had been trying to reduce employment further, but in 2006 the latest mining strategy suggested that the industry may face serious labour shortages by 2015. Around 125,000 jobs have been lost in the steel industry since the early 1990s; by 2003 it employed just 23,000 people. In 2002 the four largest state-owned steel enterprises were regrouped into one company, Polskie Huty Stali SA, which was privatized in 2003. It was bought by Mittal Steel (now ArcelorMittal) in 2004.

Labour

In 2003 a total of 13,617,000 persons were in employment. In Dec. 2002, 2,441,000 persons worked in industry, 1,998,000 in trade and repairs, 897,000 in property, renting and business activities, 895,000 in education, 852,000 in health and social services, 725,000 in transport, storage and communications, and 676,000 in construction. The unemployment rate increased steadily for several years peaking at 19·8% in 2002, compared to the EU average of 7·7%. It has declined considerably since then, and in Dec. 2009 stood at 8·9%. Unemployment among the under 25s is in excess of 20%. Workers made redundant are entitled to one month's wages after one year's service, two months after two years' service and three months after three or more years' service. A five-day working week was introduced in May 2001. The number of hours worked was reduced to 40 in 2003. Retirement age is 60 for women and 65 for men.

Trade Unions

In 1980 under Lech Wałęsa, Solidarity was an engine of political reform. Dissolved in 1982 it was relegalized in 1989 and successfully contested the parliamentary elections, but was defeated in 1993. It had 1·2m. members in 1998 and 780,000 in 2003. The official union in the 1980s, OPZZ, had 5m. members in 1990; there were also about 4,000 small unions not affiliated to it. In 2003 OPZZ had 800,000 members.

INTERNATIONAL TRADE

Foreign debt was US$98,821m. in 2005.

Imports and Exports

In 2007 imports (c.i.f.) totalled US$161·94bn. (US$124·73bn. in 2006); exports (f.o.b.), US$137·83bn. (US$109·33bn. in 2006). The main imports in 2005 were electrical equipment (14·4%); chemicals and chemical products (13·3%); transportation equipment (12·4%); mineral fuels (11·3%); machinery and apparatus (11·2%). Leading exports were transportation equipment (21·1%); base and fabricated metals (12·4%); electrical equipment (11·0%); food (8·4%); machinery and apparatus (8·4%).

Main import suppliers, 2006: Germany, 24·0%; Russia, 9·7%; Italy, 6·8%; China, 6·1%; France, 5·5%. Main export markets, 2006: Germany, 27·2%; Italy, 6·5%; France, 6·2%; United Kingdom, 5·7%; Czech Republic, 5·5%. In 2006 trade with the European Union accounted for 63·2% of Polish imports and 77·4% of Polish exports.

COMMUNICATIONS

Roads

In 2007 there were 258,910 km of roads, including 663 km of motorways. In 2006 there were 13,384,000 passenger cars, 2,393,000 lorries and vans, 84,000 buses and 784,000 motorcycles and mopeds. In 2006 public transport totalled 28,148m.

passenger-km and freight 136,490m. tonne-km. There were 5,583 road accident fatalities in 2007. With 14·7 deaths per 100,000 population in 2007, Poland has among the highest death rates in road accidents of any industrialized country.

Rail

In 2007 there were 20,107 km of railways in use managed by Polish State Railways (11,898 km electrified). Over 98% is standard 1,435 mm gauge with the rest broad gauge (1,520 mm). All narrow gauge lines (511 km in 2001) have been closed or sold to private or local authorities. In 2007 railways carried 279·7m. passengers and 245·3m. tonnes of freight. Passenger-km travelled in 2007 came to 19·9bn. and freight tonne-km to 54·3bn. Some regional railways are operated by local authorities. An 11 km metro opened in Warsaw in 1995, extended by 2007 to 18 km, and there are 14 tram/light rail networks with a total length of 930 km.

Civil Aviation

The main international airport is at Warsaw (Frederic Chopin), with some international flights from Kraków (John Paul II Balice International), Gdańsk, Katowice, Poznań, Szczecin and Wrocław. The national carrier is LOT-Polish Airlines (68·0% state-owned). It flew 95·7m. km in 2005, carrying 4,637,098 passengers (3,787,532 on international flights). In 2005 Warsaw handled 6,217,228 passengers (5,362,575 on international flights) and 51,712 tonnes of freight.

Shipping

The principal ports are Gdańsk, Szczecin, Świnoujście and Gdynia. 59·48 tonnes of cargo were handled at Polish ports in 2005. In 2005, 9·36m. tonnes of freight and 714,133 passengers were carried by the maritime transport fleet. In 2005 the merchant marine totalled 1,862,265 GRT. Ships with a capacity of 739,686 GRT were built in 2005. Vessels totalling 52,004,843 NRT entered ports in 2005 and vessels totalling 52,199,635 NRT cleared. In 2005 there were 3,638 km of navigable inland waterways. Inland barges carried 9·6m. tonnes of freight in 2005.

Telecommunications

In 2008 there were 9,711,000 main (fixed) telephone lines. In the same year mobile phone subscribers numbered 43,926,000 (1,152·8 per 1,000 persons). The privatization of Telekomunikacja Polska (TP SA), the former state telecom operator, was completed in 2001. France Télécom, the biggest foreign investor in Poland, now owns a 49·8% stake in the company. There were 6·5m. PCs in 2006 and 18·7m. internet users in 2008. There were 9·6 broadband subscribers per 100 inhabitants in June 2008.

Postal Services

In 2003 there were 8,304 post offices. A total of 2,553m. pieces of mail were handled in 2003, or 66 items per person.

SOCIAL INSTITUTIONS

Justice

The penal code was adopted in 1969. Espionage and treason carry the severest penalties. For minor crimes there is provision for probation sentences and fines. In 1995 the death penalty was suspended for five years; it had not been applied since 1988. A new penal code abolishing the death penalty was adopted in June 1997.

There exist the following courts: one Supreme Court, one high administrative court, 16 administrative courts of first instance, 11 appeal courts, 45 regional courts, 311 district courts, 67 family consultative centres and 35 juvenile courts. Judges and lay assessors are appointed. Judges for higher courts are appointed by the President of the Republic from candidatures proposed by the National Council of the Judiciary. Assessors are nominated by the Minister of Justice. Judges have life tenure. An ombudsman's office was established in 1987.

Family consultative centres were established in 1977 for cases involving divorce and domestic relations, but in 1990 divorce suits were transferred to ordinary courts. In 2005, 504,281 criminal sentences were passed. There were 835 ascertained homicides in 2005. The population in penal institutions in Dec. 2004 was 80,368 (211 per 100,000 of national population).

Education

Education from six to 18 is free and compulsory, although from 16 to 18 it may be part-time. Secondary education is then optional in general or vocational schools. In the 2005–06 school year there were: pre-primary schools, 17,229 with 839,996 pupils; primary schools, 14,582 with 2,602,120 pupils and 187,480 teachers; lower secondary schools, 7,455 with 1,614,669 pupils and 115,433 teachers; upper secondary schools, 12,868 with 2,010,654 pupils and 101,854 teachers; post-secondary schools, 3,618 with 290,284 pupils and 9,519 teachers; tertiary institutions, 558 with 1,977,032 students and 100,935 academic staff (excluding postgraduate and doctoral courses). In 2005 institutions of higher education included 18 universities, 22 technical universities, nine agricultural schools, 95 schools of economics, 13 theological schools, nine medical schools and 107 teacher training colleges. Since the early 1990s there has been a boom in private higher education—by 2006–07 more than 30% of all students in higher education were at private colleges.

The adult literacy rate in 2002 was 99·7%.

Religious (Catholic) instruction was introduced in all schools in 1990; for children of dissenting parents there are classes in ethics.

In 2005–06 total expenditure on education came to 4·1% of GDP and 13·0% of total government spending.

Health

Medical treatment is free and funded from the state budget. Medical care is also available in private clinics. In 2004 there were 781 general hospitals with a total of 183,280 beds. There were 83,372 physicians, 10,081 dentists, 177,501 nurses, 22,170 pharmacists and 21,090 midwives in 2004. In Jan. 1999 reform of the health care system was inaugurated. All citizens can now choose their own doctor, who is paid by one of the health-maintenance organizations which are financed directly from the state budget. The share of income tax paid by employers, equalling 7·5% of the amount earned by them, is assigned for the financing of the health care system. In 2007 Poland spent 6·4% of its GDP on health.

Welfare

Social security benefits are administered by the State Insurance Office and funded 45% by a payroll tax and 55% from the state budget. Pensions, disability payments, child allowances, survivor benefits, maternity benefits, funeral subsidies, sickness compensation and alimony supplements are provided. In 2003 social benefits totalling 133,064·5m. złotys were paid (including 112,980·2m. złotys in retirement pay and pensions). There were a total of 9,206,000 pensioners in 2003. Unemployment benefits are paid from a fund financed by a 3% payroll tax. It is indexed in various categories to the average wage and payable for 12 months.

In 2005 there were protests against proposed pension reforms that would make pensions available to men aged 65 and women aged 60, with no provision for early pensions. There had previously been early pensions for workers in selected occupations including mining, dancing, teaching and the aviation and maritime industries. Pension value is based on the value of contributions paid to the pension insurance scheme divided by average life expectancy at the age of retirement.

RELIGION

Church-State relations are regulated by laws of 1989 which guarantee religious freedom, grant the Church radio and TV programmes and permit it to run schools, hospitals and old age homes. The Church has a university (Lublin) and seminaries. On 28 July 1993 the government signed a Concordat with the Vatican regulating mutual relations. The religious capital is Gniezno. Its archbishop, Henryk Muszyński (b. 1933) is the primate of Poland. Kazimierz Nycz was appointed archbishop of Warsaw on 1 April 2007. In Oct. 1978 Cardinal Karol Wojtyła, archbishop of Kraków, was elected Pope as John Paul II. In Feb. 2010 there were eight cardinals.

Statistics of major churches as at Dec. 2008:

Church	*Congregations*	*Places of Worship*	*Clergy*	*Adherents*
Roman Catholic	10,108	13,662[1]	29,912	33,693,390
Uniate	134	98	74	55,000
Old Catholics	141	146	134	45,261
Polish Orthodox	232	409	404	504,150
Protestant (45 churches)	1,207	964	2,364	155,783
Muslim	17	16	33	2,665
Jewish	8	19	5	1,320
Jehovah's Witnesses	1,805	—	—	127,154

[1]1999.

CULTURE

World Heritage Sites

There are 13 UNESCO World Heritage sites in Poland. They are: Kraków's Historic Centre (inscribed on the list in 1978), Poland's former capital; Wieliczka Salt Mine (1978 and 2008), a mine since the 13th century; Auschwitz Concentration Camp (1979), the German concentration camp and nearby Birkenau death camp; Historic Centre of Warsaw (1980), celebrating the 20th century reconstruction of the city's 18th century heart decimated during World War II; Old City of Zamość (1992), a 16th century town; Medieval Town of Toruń (1997); Castle of the Teutonic Order in Malbork (1997), a medieval brick castle; Kalwaria Zebrzydowska: the Mannerist Architectural and Park Landscape Complex and Pilgrimage Park (1999); Churches of Peace in Jawor and Świdnica (2001), Europe's biggest timber-framed religious buildings; Wooden Churches of Southern Little Poland (2003); the Centennial Hall in Wrocław (2006).

Poland and Belarus are jointly responsible for Belovezhskaya Pushcha/Białowieża Forest (1979 and 1992), in the Baltic/Black Sea region; and Poland and Germany are jointly responsible for Muzkauer Park/Park Muzakowski (2004), a landscaped park astride the Neisse river.

Broadcasting

Broadcasting is regulated by the National Council of Radio Broadcasting and Television (established in 1992). Telewizja Polska is the public television broadcaster, providing two national stations, regional services and an international satellite channel. The public Polskie Radio operates national and regional radio services. The leading commercial television channels are TVN and Polsat. Colour programmes are transmitted by the PAL System. Polskie Radio dla Zagranicy/Polish Radio External Service is the public external service. TV sets in use in 2006, 15·7m.

Cinema

In 2006 there were 514 cinemas; admissions (2007), 32·6m. 37 feature films were made in 2006.

Press

In 2005 there were 42 daily newspapers with a combined daily circulation of 5,332,300 (140 per 1,000 inhabitants). The most popular newspapers are Fakt, Gazeta Wyborcza, Super Express and Rzeczpospolita. In 2005, 19,999 book titles were published (including 4,850 literature, 4,443 social sciences and 2,761 applied sciences).

Tourism

There were 15·2m. foreign visitors in 2005, bringing in revenue of US$7·1bn. Germans account for about 60% of all tourists to Poland.

Festivals

The most significant festivals are the International Chopin Festival at Duszniki Zdrój, held in Aug., and the Warsaw Autumn Festival, held in Sept.

Libraries

In 2005, 8,591 libraries housed 135·13m. books.

Theatre and Opera

The audience in 139 theatres in 2005 was 5·97m.; the 22 opera houses had a total audience of 1·22m. in 2005.

Museums and Galleries

There were 139 museums in 2005, with 18·49m. visitors; there were also 292 art galleries, with 2·31m. visitors.

DIPLOMATIC REPRESENTATIVES

Of Poland in the United Kingdom (47 Portland Pl., London, W1B 1JH)
Ambassador: Barbara Tuge-Erecińska.

Of the United Kingdom in Poland (ul. Kawalerii 12, 00-468, Warsaw)
Ambassador: Ric Todd.

Of Poland in the USA (2640 16th St., NW, Washington, D.C., 20009)
Ambassador: Robert Kupiecki.

Of the USA in Poland (Aleje Ujazdowskie 29/31, 00-540 Warsaw)
Ambassador: Lee Feinstein.

Of Poland to the United Nations
Ambassador: Andrzej Towpik.

Of Poland to the European Union
Permanent Representative: Jan Tombiński.

FURTHER READING

Central Statistical Office, *Rocznik Statystyczny*. Annual—*Concise Statistical Yearbook of Poland—Statistical Bulletin*. Monthly

Chodakiewicz, Marek Jan, *Poland's Transformation: A Work in Progress*. 2006

Lukowski, Jerzy and Zawadzki, Hubert, *A Concise History of Poland*. 2001

Mitchell, K. D. (ed.) *Political Pluralism in Hungary and Poland: Perspectives on the Reforms*. 1992

Prazmowska, Anita J., *History of Poland*. 2004

Sikorski, R., *The Polish House: An Intimate History of Poland*. 1997; US title: *Full Circle*. 1997

Slay, B., *The Polish Economy: Crisis, Reform and Transformation*. 1994

Staar, R. F. (ed.) *Transition to Democracy in Poland*. 1993

Wedel, J., *The Unplanned Society: Poland During and After Communism*. 1992

Zamoyski, Adam, *Poland: A History*. 2009

National library: Biblioteka Narodowa, al. Niepodległości 213, 02-086 Warsaw.

National Statistical Office: Central Statistical Office, Aleje Niepodległości 208, 00-925 Warsaw.

Website: http://www.stat.gov.pl

PORTUGAL

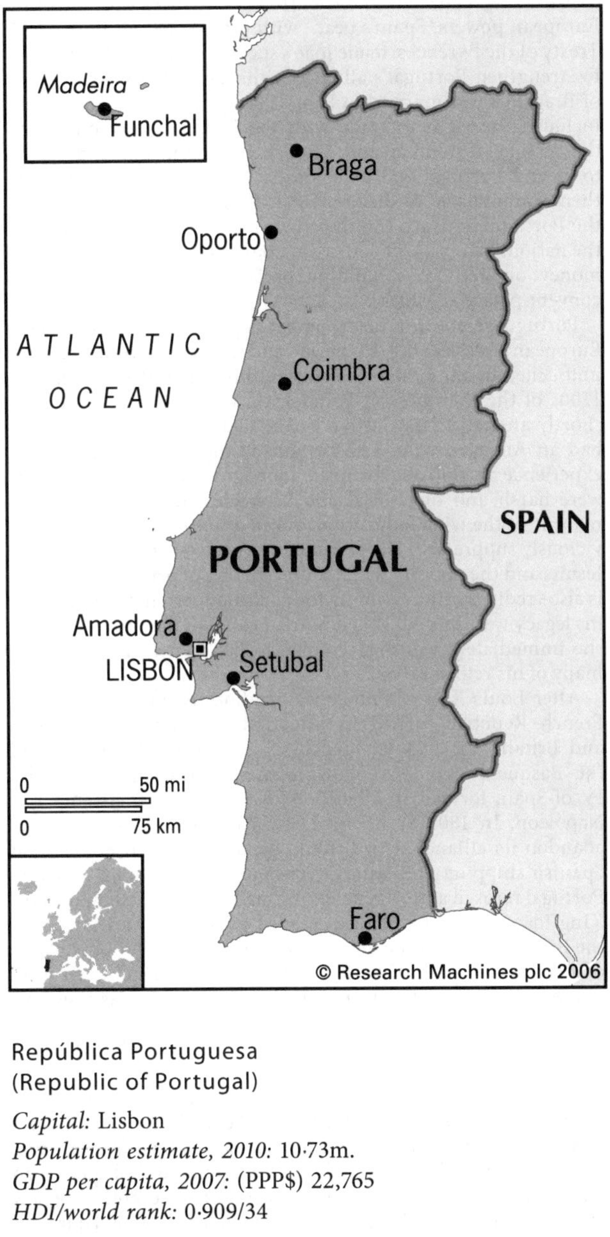

República Portuguesa
(Republic of Portugal)

Capital: Lisbon
Population estimate, 2010: 10·73m.
GDP per capita, 2007: (PPP$) 22,765
HDI/world rank: 0·909/34

KEY HISTORICAL EVENTS

The western fringe of the Iberian peninsula was inhabited from at least 8000 BC by Neolithic peoples known as Iberians. Archaeological evidence points to the arrival of Celtic tribes in the north and west of the peninsula in the first millennium BC and the establishment of Phoenician settlements in the southwest around Cádiz from around 800 BC. From 241 BC the Iberian peninsula came under the influence of Carthage, and then Rome after 206 BC. The Romans made their way north to what is now central Portugal and clashed with a Celtic federation, the Lusitanians. They resisted the Roman advance under their leader Viriathus until he was killed in 140 BC, after which the Romans were able to move north across the Douro river. In 25 BC Augustus founded Augustus Emirita (now Mérida) as the capital of Lusitania.

From AD 409, with the Roman Empire in decline, the Iberian Peninsula was invaded by Germanic tribes from central Europe, including the Suevi and Visigoths, who established Christian kingdoms. Southern Galicia was settled by the Suevi, who were converted to Christianity by St Martin of Braga in around AD 550. Following the arrival of Muslim armies in Iberia in 711, the southern part of what is now Portugal became part of the Muslim dominion of al-Andalus and absorbed its influences for five centuries. The northern and western fringes of Iberia remained largely agrarian, poor and Christian.

From 850 the Christians began to push southward: the region between the rivers Minho and Douro became known as Territorium Portugualense and was ruled by Mumadona Dias after 931. Fernando I, King of Castile, drove the Muslims from the city of Viseu in 1058 and reconquered Coimbra in 1064. Fernando's successor, Afonso VI of Leon, set up his power base in the town of Braga. His daughter, Teresa, who was married to Henry of Burgundy, then governed Portugal as regent for their son, Afonso Henriques. Teresa eventually lost the support of many of the powerful local barons, who united behind Afonso and made him the first king of Portugal in 1139.

Muslim chroniclers refer to Afonso I as 'the cursed of Allah'. He crusaded southwards through the Muslim strongholds, capturing Lisbon in 1147. However, the Portuguese reconquest was not completed for 150 years, when Afonso III finally took Algarve in the far south. Afonso III established the first Cortes (government) at Leiria in 1254. Large swathes of the newly conquered lands were given over to the army and monastic orders to ensure their protection. Afonso's son, Dinis (1279–1325), became one of the most celebrated of the Burgundian dynasty. He established trade links with other European powers and in 1317 worked with a Genoese admiral to establish a formal navy. Dinis made the vernacular, rather than Latin, the official language and founded the first university in Lisbon in 1290.

The later kings of the House of Burgundy were entangled in various marriage alliances with neighbouring Castile. Fernando I (1367–83) inherited the Portuguese crown as a battle raged in Castile between King Pedro 'the Cruel' and his half-brother Enrique de Trastámara. Both sides attempted to garner support from outside the kingdom, with the English supporting Pedro (Peter) and his heirs and the French backing Enrique (Henry) and his supporters. Enrique eventually prevailed, being crowned Enrique II of Castile in 1369. The new king offered his support to Fernando, who accepted, and Castilian rule was duly established in Portugal.

King Fernando ensured that his heiress, Beatriz, married Juan I of Castile but, though the entrenched nobility broadly supported Castilian rule, commoners in Portugal's coastal towns wanted independence and rebelled. Their choice for ruler was João of Avis, half brother of Fernando, and he was declared King João I in 1384. A year later, assisted by English archers, the Portuguese won a famous victory over Juan I and his Castilian army at the battle of Aljbarrota. This military success marked the beginning of a 200-year era of independence for Portugal, and the Anglo-Portuguese alliance was cemented by King João's marriage in 1387 to Philippa of Lancaster, sister of England's future King Henry IV.

Empire Building

Having made peace with Spain, João turned his attention overseas. The capture of the town of Ceuta on the north African coast in 1415 was the beginning of a remarkable era of discovery by Portuguese mariners, spearheaded by João's third son Henry who became known as Henry the Navigator. He founded a school of navigation at Sagres and organized numerous expeditions along the west coast of Africa. Madeira and the Azores were also discovered and settled during this period.

Relations with Castile deteriorated sharply during the reign of Afonso V (1438–81). Afonso married Juana, daughter of Enrique IV of Castile, and laid claim to the Castilian throne. Following the marriage of Fernando II and Isabella I of Castile and the merging of the powerful kingdoms of Aragon and Castile, Afonso's claim began to look increasingly untenable. There were lengthy battles for land in the Zamora and Toro regions, which Afonso eventually lost in 1476. Peace was established three years later by Afonso's heir, João II. During his reign overseas explorations were resumed, and Portugal became a haven for tens of thousands of Jews fleeing persecution in Spain.

In 1487 Bartolomeu Dias rounded the southern cape of Africa, but the Portuguese crown rejected Christopher Columbus' proposal for finding a new westward route to the Indies. He was backed instead by Fernando II and Isabella I of Castile and reached the New World in 1492. The two countries, with their fleets of sailing ships and entrepreneurial merchants, now had a stake in much of the rest of the world, and needed to divide their discoveries. The 1493 Treaty of Tordesillas gave the newly-unified Spain all lands west of a vertical line drawn 370 degrees west of the Cape Verde Islands. Land to the east was to be the property of Portugal, which happened to include Brazil, prompting speculation that Portuguese mariners already knew of its existence. In 1497, with backing from King Manuel I, Vasco da Gama set out from Lisbon in a fleet of purpose-built cargo ships known as *naus*. Two years later he returned, having mapped out a sea route to India. Indian spices were especially prized in Europe: they were used for preserving food, in the preparation of medicines and in glues, perfumes, dyes and varnishes. The Portuguese built an administrative capital at Goa, after seizing it in 1510, and by 1550 it was considered Portugal's second city.

Fortified trading posts were later established along the coast of East Africa and India, and commercial centres set up with the consent of native rulers further east. The vast profits generated by the spice trade made Manuel I 'the Fortunate' one of the wealthiest rulers in Europe. But such rapid expansion came at a price: Portugal suffered from a 'brain drain'—many of the nation's entrepreneurs had moved overseas, leaving the domestic economy weakened. The king was no longer dependent on taxes from the people, who then lost political influence. The Cortes did not meet for 23 years between 1502–25 and the expulsion of many of Manuel's Jewish subjects in 1496 (a condition of his marriage to Princess Isabella of Castile—daughter of Isabella I) dealt a heavy blow to the economy, depriving it of much of its financial expertise.

When King Sebastião inherited the throne in 1557, he was keen to establish Portuguese authority closer to home, and in 1568 he launched a disastrous crusade to eradicate Islam in the Maghreb. More than 10,000 Portuguese troops were killed, including Sebastião himself by superior Moroccan forces. The throne passed to the elderly and childless Cardinal Henrique, who soon died. The line of succession passed to the cardinal's nephew, Felipe II of Spain.

Spanish Rule

Felipe II saw his opportunity and annexed Portugal in 1580. The Spanish empire was at its height and Portuguese merchants saw the commercial advantages in forming an alliance with Spain. Portugal was granted virtual autonomy but this was gradually eroded. The Inquisition was established in Portugal and the ports of Lisbon and Porto (Oporto) were closed to English and Dutch ships, which then made their own way to the east and snatched control of the spice trade. The 'Spanish domination' of Portugal lasted for 60 years, though after 1621 Spain was considerably weakened by the cost of defending its empire against France and England. A rebellion in Catalonia spurred the Portuguese to stage their own revolution. They rallied round the duke of Bragança, who was crowned King João IV in 1640.

João IV was anxious to formalize new alliances with the other European powers. Spain's peace with France, set out in the 1659 Treaty of the Pyrenees, made João's successor, Afonso VI, anxious to strengthen Portugal's alliance with England. Thus Catherine of Bragança was married to King Charles II in 1662. Her dowry included the right to trade with the Portuguese colonies and the cession of Bombay and Tangier. In return, England agreed to defend Portugal and its colonies. In the late 1600s gold and then diamonds were discovered in Brazil. Money poured into the Portuguese court, but the crown's wealth did little to enrich the nation. João V (1706–50) aped Louis XIV of France, lavishing money on ambitious building projects, including a gigantic convent-palace at Mafra.

Portuguese political development lagged behind that of many European states during this period and it remained comparatively untouched by the Enlightenment until the emergence in the late 1700s of the Marquess of Pombal. He was made chief minister shortly after the great Lisbon earthquake in 1755. Pombal, who had an Austrian wife, had formulated many of his ideas from experience as ambassador in London and Vienna. His methods were harsh and dictatorial and he made enemies quickly: his reforms of the wine industry provoked a riot in Porto, which was viciously suppressed. His principal victims were the conservative Jesuits and the nobility with their vast array of privileges. Pombal is also credited with reforming the education system but ultimately his legacy was limited. When Maria I came to the throne in 1777, she immediately banished Pombal to his estates and rescinded many of his reforms.

After Louis XVI of France was guillotined in 1793, the new French Republic turned its attention to neighbouring Spain and Britain. In 1794–95 French forces invaded Catalonia and the Basque provinces. Following these defeats, King Charles IV of Spain formed an alliance with France under its emperor, Napoleon. In 1801 France and Spain demanded that Portugal abandon its alliance with Britain, open its ports to French and Spanish shipping and hand over some of its colonies to Spain. Portugal refused and a French army marched into Lisbon in 1807. King João VI and his family escaped to Brazil with the help of the British navy and the defence of Portugal was left in the hands of British Generals Wellesley and Beresford. The French were finally driven out of Portugal in 1811 and the British, as a reward, were granted free access to the Brazilian ports, a concession which damaged the Portuguese economy and stoked-up popular resentment.

After an army-backed revolution in Porto in 1820, an unofficial Cortes was set up to devise a new liberal constitution. The Cortes was to be a single chamber parliament elected by universal male suffrage, and feudal and clerical rights would be abolished. João VI returned from Brazil the following year and accepted the new constitution. Brazil declared its independence, with Pedro IV (João's elder son) as emperor.

Following João's death in 1826, Pedro became king of Portugal in defiance of the Brazilian constitution. Forced to abdicate in favour of his daughter, Maria II, then aged seven, he chose his brother Miguel as her steward and insisted Maria accept a new charter limiting royal authority and marry Miguel when she was old enough. But Miguel, a conservative by nature, seized the throne in 1828, defeating the liberals and repealing Pedro's constitution. Pedro IV returned to Portugal in 1832 to lead the liberals in the Miguelist Wars. Maria was eventually restored to the throne. As governments came and went, little was done to address the parlous state of the economy until 1852, when the duke of Saldanha introduced reforms. The late 1850s saw improvements in the nation's infrastructure under the new ministry of public works but by the start of the reign of Carlos I in 1889, Portugal was burdened with high unemployment, leading to strikes and public demonstrations. Explorations in Africa strengthened Portugal's hold on Angola and Mozambique but the British refused to give up territory which would have linked the two colonies. Carlos attempted to end inefficiency and corruption, establishing a dictatorship in 1906 under the conservative João Franco. Amidst growing public discontent, Carlos and his eldest son Prince Luís Filipe were assassinated in 1908. Manuel II succeeded to the throne but in 1910 a republican revolution forced his abdication and flight to Britain.

The first republican leader was Teófilo Braga but the change of rule did not cure Portugal's chronic economic problems. In the First World War Portugal was at first neutral, then joined the Allies in 1916. The economy deteriorated and insurrections of both the right and the left made conditions worse. In 1926 a military coup overthrew the government and Gen. Carmona became president. António de Oliveira Salazar was made finance minister in 1928 with a brief to reform the economy.

Dictatorship to Democracy

Salazar became prime minister in 1932. His *Estado Novo* (New State) had a strongly nationalist and dictatorial flavour. Political parties, unions and strikes were abolished and dissent was crushed by the notorious PIDE (Polícia Internacional e de Defesa do Estado) secret police force. Portugal was neutral in the Second World War but allowed the Allies to establish naval and air bases. Although the colony of Goa was seized by India in 1961, Salazar was determined to cling on to the African territories. Despite growing independence movements in Angola, Guinea-Bissau and Mozambique in the 1960s, by 1968 over 100,000 Portuguese were fighting in Africa. On the domestic front, censorship of the press and of cultural activities grew especially severe in the mid-1960s and student demonstrations were sternly repressed.

In 1968 Salazar suffered a stroke and was replaced by Marcello Caetano as premier. Under Caetano repression was eased but the unpopular wars in Africa continued. In 1974, amid mounting public discontent, a group of officers formed the Movement of Armed Forces and toppled the government in a bloodless coup known as 'the Revolution of the Carnations'. Gen. António de Spínola was appointed head of the ruling military junta. The secret police force was abolished. All political prisoners were released; full civil liberties, including freedom of the press and of all political parties, were restored and, in 1975, Angola, Mozambique, São Tomé e Príncipe and Cape Verde were granted independence. Timor-Leste was forcibly taken by Indonesia. Following an attempted revolt in late 1975, the military junta was dissolved and a Supreme Revolutionary Council ruled until a new constitutional government resumed the following year. During the late 1970s several moderate, Socialist-dominated governments tried unsuccessfully to stabilize the country. In 1982 a centre-right coalition revised the constitution, reducing presidential power and the right of the military to intervene in politics. From 1983 to 1985 a coalition government under Socialist leader Mário Soares began to make tangible progress in reducing the chaos and poverty that were the legacy of Salazar's long dictatorship.

In 1985 the centrist Social Democratic party under Aníbal Cavaco Silva won an undisputed majority in parliament. In 1986 Soares was elected to the presidency, and Portugal was admitted to the European Community. Political stability and economic reforms created a favourable business climate, especially for renewed foreign investment, and Portugal became one of the fastest-growing economies in Europe. The Socialists returned to power as a minority government after the 1995 parliamentary elections. Macao, Portugal's colony on the south coast of China, was handed back to China in 1999. Portugal joined the single European currency in 2001. In Jan. 2006 the centre-right candidate Aníbal Cavaco Silva was elected president, beginning a period of political 'cohabitation' alongside the Socialist prime minister, Jóse Sócrates.

TERRITORY AND POPULATION

Mainland Portugal is bounded in the north and east by Spain and south and west by the Atlantic Ocean. The Atlantic archipelagoes of the Azores and of Madeira form autonomous but integral parts of the republic, which has a total area of 91,947 sq. km. Population (2001 census), 10,356,117 (5,355,976 females).

Mainland Portugal is divided into five regions. At the time of the 2001 census the regions, with their populations, were: North (3,687,293); Central (1,783,596); Lisbon and Tagus Valley (3,467,483); Alentejo (535,753); Algarve (395,218). Population of the Azores, 241,763; Madeira, 245,011. Density (2001), 113 per sq. km (North, 173; Central, 75; Lisbon and Tagus Valley, 291; Alentejo, 20; Algarve, 79; Azores, 104; Madeira, 315). In 2002 Lisbon and Tagus Valley became a smaller Lisbon province, with Central and Alentejo increasing in size. The estimated population in Dec. 2008 was 10,627,250.

The UN gives an estimated population for 2010 of 10·73m.

In 2005, 57·6% of the population lived in urban areas. The populations of the districts and Autonomous Regions (2001 census):

Areas	*Population*	*Areas*	*Population*
North	*3,687,293*	Pinhal Interior Norte	138,535
Alto Trás os Montes	223,333	Pinhal Interior Sul	44,803
Ave	509,968	Pinhal Litoral	250,990
Cávado	393,063	Serra da Estrela	49,895
Douro	221,853	*Lisbon and Tagus Valley*[1]	*3,467,483*
Entre Douro e Vouga	276,812	Grande Lisboa	1,947,261
Grande Porto	1,260,680	Lezíria do Tejo[2]	240,832
Minho-Lima	250,275	Médio Tejo[3]	226,090
Tâmega	551,309	Oeste[3]	338,711
Central	*1,783,596*	Península de Setúbal	714,589
Baixo Mondego	340,309	*Alentejo*	*535,753*
Baixo Vouga	385,724	Alentejo Central	173,646
Beira Interior Norte	115,325	Alentejo Litoral	99,976
Beira Interior Sul	78,123	Alto Alentejo	127,026
Cova da Beira	93,579	Baixo Alentejo	135,105
Dão Lafões	286,313	*Algarve*	*395,218*

[1]Lisbon since 2002. [2]Now part of Alentejo. [3]Now part of Central.

In 2007, 401,612 foreigners were legally registered, with the leading nationalities as follows: Cape Verde, 61,110; Brazil, 55,665; Angola, 30,431; UK, 23,608; Guinea-Bissau, 22,174. 200,000 immigrants have come to Portugal from eastern Europe since 1999, mainly from Ukraine.

The capital is Lisbon (Lisboa), with a population of 489,562 in 2008 (metropolitan area population, 2,547,665 in 2001). Other major cities are Porto, 216,080 in 2008 (metropolitan area population, 1,509,958 in 2001), Amadora, Braga, Coimbra, Funchal (in Madeira) and Setúbal.

The official language is Portuguese.

The Azores islands lie in the mid-Atlantic Ocean, between 1,200 and 1,600 km west of Lisbon. They are divided into three widely separated groups with clear channels between, São Miguel (759 sq. km) together with Santa Maria (97 sq. km) being the most easterly; about 160 km northwest of them lies the central cluster of Terceira (382 sq. km), Graciosa (62 sq. km), São Jorge (246 sq. km), Pico (446 sq. km) and Faial (173 sq. km); still another 240 km to the northwest are Flores (143 sq. km) and Corvo (17 sq. km), the latter being the most isolated and undeveloped of the islands. São Miguel contains over half the total population of the archipelago.

Madeira comprises the island of Madeira (745 sq. km), containing the capital, Funchal; the smaller island of Porto Santo (40 sq. km), lying 46 km to the northeast of Madeira; and two groups of uninhabited islets, Ilhas Desertas (15 sq. km), being 20 km southeast of Funchal, and Ilhas Selvagens (4 sq. km), near the Canaries.

SOCIAL STATISTICS

2006: births, 105,449; deaths, 101,990; marriages, 47,857; divorces, 22,881. Rates per 1,000 population in 2006: birth, 9·9; death, 9·6; marriage, 4·5; divorce, 2·2. Annual population growth rate, 2000–05, 0·6%. In 2005 the most popular age range for marrying was 25–29 for both males and females. Expectation of life at birth, 2007, was 75·3 years for males and 81·8 years for females. Infant mortality in 2005 was four per 1,000 live births, down from 77 per 1,000 live births in 1960, representing the greatest reduction in infant mortality rates in Europe over the past half century. Around one in five babies are born outside marriage, up from one in 14 in 1970. Fertility rate, 2004, 1·5 births per woman.

On 11 Feb. 2007 a national referendum was held on whether to decriminalize abortion up until the 10th week of pregnancy. Turnout was low at 44%; 59·3% of voters approved the motion. Despite results only having to be legally binding if the turnout exceeded 50%, parliament voted overwhelmingly in favour on 9 March 2007. In 1998 the same question had been put in another referendum. 51% voted against the motion; turnout was 32%.

In 2006 Portugal received 130 asylum applications.

CLIMATE

Because of westerly winds and the effect of the Gulf Stream, the climate ranges from the cool, damp Atlantic type in the north to a warmer and drier Mediterranean type in the south. July and Aug. are virtually rainless everywhere. Inland areas in the north have greater temperature variation, with continental winds blowing from the interior. Lisbon, Jan. 52°F (11°C), July 72°F (22°C). Annual rainfall 27·4" (686 mm). Porto, Jan. 48°F (8·9°C), July 67°F (19·4°C). Annual rainfall 46" (1,151 mm).

CONSTITUTION AND GOVERNMENT

Portugal is governed under the constitution of April 1976, amended in 1982, 1989, 1992, 1997, 2001, 2004 and 2005. The 1982 revision abolished the (military) Council of the Revolution and reduced the role of the President under it. Portugal is a sovereign, unitary republic. Executive power is vested in the *President*, directly elected for a five-year term (for a maximum of two consecutive terms). Political parties may support a candidate in presidential elections but not actually field a candidate. The President appoints a Prime Minister and, upon the latter's nomination, other members of the Council of Ministers.

The 230-member *National Assembly* is a unicameral legislature elected for four-year terms by universal adult suffrage under a system of proportional representation. Women did not have the vote until 1976.

National Anthem

'Herois do mar, nobre povo' ('Heroes of the sea, noble breed'); words by Lopes de Mendonça, tune by Alfredo Keil.

GOVERNMENT CHRONOLOGY

(PS = Socialist Party; PSD = Social Democratic Party; UN = National Union; n/p = non-partisan)

Presidents since 1926.

1926–51	UN/military	António (Óscar de) Fragoso Carmona
1951–58	UN/military	Francisco (Higino de) Craveiro Lopes
1958–74	UN/military	Américo (de Deus Rodrigues) Thomaz
1974	National Salvation Junta (all military)	
1974	military	António (Sebastião Ribeiro) de Spinola
1974–76	military	Francisco da Costa Gomes
1976–86	military, n/p	(António dos Santos) Ramalho Eanes
1986–96	PS	Mário (Alberto Nobre Lopes) Soares
1996–2006	PS	Jorge (Fernando Branco de) Sampaio
2006–	PSD	Aníbal (António) Cavaco Silva

Prime Ministers since 1932.

1932–68	UN	António de Oliveira Salazar
1968–74	UN	Marcello (das Neves Alves) Caetano
1974	n/p	Adelino da Palma Carlos
1974–75	military	Vasco (dos Santos) Gonçalves
1975–76	military	José (Batista) Pinheiro de Azevedo
1976–78	PS	Mário (Alberto Nobre Lopes) Soares
1978	n/p	Alfredo (Jorge) Nobre da Costa
1978–79	n/p	Carlos (Alberto) da Mota Pinto
1980	PSD	Francisco (Manuel Lumbrales de) Sá Carneiro
1981–83	PSD	Francisco (José Pereira) Pinto Balsemão
1983–85	PS	Mário (Alberto Nobre Lopes) Soares
1985–95	PSD	Aníbal (António) Cavaco Silva
1995–2002	PS	António (Manuel de Oliveira) Guterres
2002–04	PSD	José Manuel Durão Barroso
2004–05	PSD	Pedro (Miguel de) Santana Lopes
2005–	PS	José Sócrates (Carvalho Pinto de Sousa)

RECENT ELECTIONS

At the presidential elections of 22 Jan. 2006, the centre-right former prime minister Aníbal Cavaco Silva won 50·5% of the vote, Manuel Alegre (ind.) 20·7%, former president Mário Soares 14·3%, Jerónimo de Sousa 8·6%, Francisco Louçã 5·3% and António Garcia Pereira 0·4%. Turnout was 62·6%.

At the parliamentary elections of 27 Sept. 2009 the ruling Socialist Party (PS) won 96 seats (36·6% of votes cast); the Social Democratic Party (PSD), 78 (29·1%); the Popular Party (CDS-PP), 21 (10·5%); the Left Bloc (BE), 16 (9·8%); and the Communist Party/Green Party coalition (Unitarian Democratic Coalition; UDC), 15 (7·9%). Turnout was 60·6%.

European Parliament

Portugal has 22 (24 in 2004) representatives. At the June 2009 elections turnout was 36·8% (38·6% in 2004). The PSD won 8 seats with 31·7% of votes cast (political affiliation in European Parliament: European People's Party); the PS 7 with 26·5% (Progressive Alliance of Socialists and Democrats); the BE, 3 with 10·7% (European United Left/Nordic Green Left); the UDC, 2 with 10·6% (European United Left/Nordic Green Left); CDS-PP, 2 with 8·4% (European People's Party).

CURRENT ADMINISTRATION

President: Aníbal Cavaco Silva; b. 1939 (ind.; sworn in 9 March 2006).

In March 2010 the Socialist Party government was composed as follows:

Prime Minister: José Sócrates; b. 1957 (PS; sworn in 12 March 2005).

Ministers of State: Fernando Teixeira dos Santos (also *Minister of Finance*); Luís Amado (also *Minister of Foreign Affairs*).

Minister of Agriculture, Rural Development and Fisheries: António Serrano. *Culture:* Gabriela Canavilhas. *Economy, Innovation and Development:* Vieira da Silva. *Education:* Isabel Alçada. *Environment and Spatial Planning:* Dulce Pássaro. *Health:* Ana Jorge. *Internal Affairs:* Rui Pereira. *Justice:* Alberto Martins. *Labour and Social Solidarity:* Helena André. *National Defence:* Augusto Santos Silva. *Parliamentary Affairs:* Jorge Lacão. *Public Works, Transportation and Communications:* António Mendonça. *Science, Technology and Higher Education:* Mariano Gago. *Minister for the Presidency:* Pedro Silva Pereira.

Government Website (Portuguese only):
http://www.portugal.gov.pt/en

CURRENT LEADERS

Aníbal Cavaco Silva

Position
President

Introduction
When Aníbal Cavaco Silva was elected president on 22 Jan. 2006 he became the first centre-right politician to fill the largely ceremonial post since the country's 1974 revolution. The free-market economist played a key role in preparing Portugal's entry to the EEC in 1986 and served as prime minister from 1985–95.

Early Life
Aníbal António Cavaco Silva was born in Boliqueime, Algarve, southern Portugal on 15 July 1939. Educated in Faro and Lisbon, he graduated in finance from the Technical University of Lisbon in 1964. He worked as a researcher for the Calouste Gulbenkian Foundation in Lisbon from 1967 to 1971 before studying for a PhD in economics at the University of York, UK.

Returning to Portugal in 1974, the year of the 'Revolution of Carnations' when the socialist Armed Forces Movement toppled Dr Marcello Caetano's dictatorship, Cavaco Silva taught economics at the Catholic University of Lisbon. He also joined the newly formed centre-right Popular Democratic Party (PPD), which became the Social Democratic Party (PSD) in 1976. From 1977 he worked as director of the research and statistics department of the Bank of Portugal. Elected to parliament for the PSD in Oct. 1980, Cavaco Silva served as minister of finance and planning, initially under PSD leader and prime minister, Francisco Sá Carneiro, and then under Francisco Balsemão.

A powerful advocate of free-market economics, Cavaco Silva's reforms, combined with a constitutional reduction in presidential power, paved the way for Portugal's entry into the EEC (later EU) in 1986. Elected head of the PSD on 2 June 1985, he led the party to victory in elections in Oct. 1985. He retained the position for ten years, the longest tenure of any democratically elected prime minister in Portuguese history. The PSD won a clear majority of seats in legislative elections in both 1987 and 1991, with analysts attributing Cavaco Silva's success to economic liberalization, tax cuts and the flow of funds from the EEC.

Cavaco Silva stepped down as leader of the PSD prior to the 1995 elections, which were won by the Socialist Party (PS). He stood in the 1996 presidential election but after losing to the Socialist candidate, Jorge Sampaio, he retired from politics, serving as an adviser to the board of the Bank of Portugal and teaching economics at the Catholic University of Portugal. In Oct. 2005 Cavaco Silva returned to the political fray and announced his candidacy for the forthcoming presidential election. He received 50·5% of the votes cast on 22 Jan. 2006, narrowly avoiding the need for a second round, and was sworn in on 9 March 2006.

Career in Office
Cavaco Silva's victory over the two Socialist candidates, Manuel Alegre and Mário Soares, was a setback for the Socialist prime minister, Jóse Sócrates, who had presided over a period of economic stagnation. The result ushered in a new era of 'cohabitation' in Portuguese politics, but analysts predicted that the two leaders would find common ground to implement economic reform. Although a Roman Catholic, Cavaco Silva endorsed new legislation in April 2007 liberalizing abortion and aligning Portuguese law with that of most other EU countries. In Oct. 2009, following parliamentary elections the previous month, Cavaco Silva invited Prime Minister Sócrates to form a new PS government.

José Sócrates

Position
Prime Minister

Introduction
José Sócrates was swept into power as Portugal's prime minister following a resounding victory for his Socialist Party (PS) in a snap parliamentary election on 20 Feb. 2005. The former civil engineer is a modernizer who has described himself as a 'market-oriented socialist'. Previously an environment minister, he is committed to sustainable development and sees educational reform and the development of high-tech industries as a way of reviving the country's flagging economy. His economic reforms have nevertheless been controversial, provoking public protests.

Early Life
José Sócrates Carvalho Pinto de Sousa was born in Vilar de Macada, Alijó, near the northern city of Porto, on 6 Sept. 1957. He attended secondary school in Covilhã in the district of Castelo Branco and went on to study at the Institute of Engineering in Coimbra, before completing a master's degree in medical engineering at the National School of Public Health. Sócrates then worked as a medical engineer for Castelo Branco's municipal authority. He joined the PS in 1981 and was first elected as a member of the Portuguese assembly in 1987, the year after the government—a Social Democratic Party (PSD)-led coalition—had taken the country into the European Community. In 1991 Sócrates became a member of the National Secretariat of the PS, and was spokesman for the environment.

Following the victory of the Socialists over the centre-right PSD in the 1995 general election, Sócrates held a range of portfolios under Prime Minister António Guterres. He served as secretary of state in the ministry of the environment and territorial planning for two years from 1995, before being made deputy minister to Guterres. In Oct. 1999, after Guterres had led the PS to another election win, Sócrates was promoted to minister for the environment, a post he held until the parliamentary elections of March 2002. He gained a reputation for boldness and determination, and is widely regarded as the man who brought the Euro 2004 football tournament to Portugal.

When the Socialists lost power to the PSD, led by José Manuel Durão Barroso, in March 2002, Sócrates remained in the spotlight by taking part in a weekly television debate against Pedro Santana Lopes, then the Social Democratic mayor of Lisbon. Following the resignation of Ferro Rodrigues as leader of the PS in 2004, Sócrates bid for the post of secretary-general, and won the vote of almost 80% of party members in Sept. 2004. Sócrates was again in direct opposition to Santana Lopes, who had taken over as prime minister and leader of the PSD in July 2004 when Barroso resigned to become head of the European Commission. Already unpopular at the time of Barroso's resignation, the PSD-led coalition struggled to improve Portugal's moribund economy. There was also a month-long delay to the start of the school year and disunity over Santana Lopes' plan to introduce tax cuts and public-sector pay rises. By Nov. loss of confidence in Santana Lopes' administration had reached the point where the president, Jorge Sampaio, felt obliged to dissolve parliament and call a snap general election, two years ahead of schedule.

Sócrates focused the PS' campaign on the promise to provide disciplined and transparent leadership and pledged to reform the country's education system, alleviate poverty and boost employment. The strategy proved successful—the PS gained 45% of the vote in the elections on 20 Feb. 2005, up from 38% in 2002. With 121 seats in Portugal's 230-seat parliament, it was the first time since the end of the Salazar-Caetano dictatorship in 1974 that the PS had received an outright majority. On 24 Feb. Sócrates was called on by President Sampaio to form a new government, which took office on 12 March 2005.

Career in Office

In his inaugural address as Portugal's prime minister, Sócrates pledged to restore confidence in the country and its institutions. He also vowed to increase the economy's competitiveness while cutting the budget deficit and fulfilling the requirements of the euro zone's stability and growth pact. Sócrates said his model for the country was a 'Nordic social democracy'—a society combining efficient capitalist enterprise with generous social services. Critics nevertheless described Sócrates' vision as unobtainable, pointing out that his economic reforms would lead to further job losses and suggesting that improvements to the education system to provide a labour force adapted to high-tech industries would take many years.

To comply with EU fiscal requirements, the 2006 budget included reforms to pension schemes and public administration wage structures. However, the government continued to struggle with the budget deficit in 2007 and in March there were mass demonstrations and industrial action against Sócrates' economic policies.

Portugal's six-month presidency of the European Union, which began in July 2007, culminated in the signature in Dec. by the heads of government of the Lisbon Treaty streamlining the institutional structure and operation of the enlarged EU. Parliament then ratified the treaty in April 2008.

Parliamentary elections in Sept. 2009 were contested against a background of economic contraction and uncertainty in the wake of the global financial crisis. The PS was returned as the largest single party but lost its overall majority in the National Assembly. Sócrates continued as prime minister for a second term, but at the head of a minority government which was sworn in on 26 Oct.

DEFENCE

Conscription was abolished in Nov. 2004. Portugal now has a purely professional army.

In 2006 defence expenditure totalled US$3,080m. (US$290 per capita), representing 1·6% of GDP.

Army

Strength (2007) 26,700. There are Army reserves totalling 210,000. Paramilitary forces include the National Republican Guard (26,100) and the Public Security Police (21,600).

Navy

In 2007 the combatant fleet comprised one French-built diesel submarine, 12 frigates and seven corvettes. Naval personnel in 2007 totalled 9,110 including 335 recalled reservists and 1,725 marines. There were 900 naval reserves.

Air Force

The Air Force in 2007 had a strength of 7,100. There were 25 combat capable aircraft (mainly F-16s).

INTERNATIONAL RELATIONS

Portugal is a member of the UN, World Bank, IMF and several other UN specialized agencies, WTO, EU, Council of Europe, WEU, OSCE, CERN, BIS, IOM, NATO, OECD and Inter-American Development Bank. Portugal is a signatory to the Schengen accord abolishing border controls between Portugal, Austria, Belgium, Czech Republic, Denmark, Estonia, Finland, France, Germany, Greece, Hungary, Iceland, Italy, Latvia, Lithuania, Luxembourg, Malta, Netherlands, Norway, Poland, Slovakia, Slovenia, Spain, Sweden and Switzerland.

The Community of Portuguese-Speaking Countries (CPLP, comprising Angola, Brazil, Cape Verde, Guinea-Bissau, Mozambique, Portugal and São Tomé e Príncipe) was founded in July 1996 with headquarters in Lisbon, primarily as a cultural and linguistic organization.

ECONOMY

Services accounted for about 73% of GDP in 2007, industry 24% and agriculture 3%.

Overview

The economy has become increasingly service-based since the 1980s. The agriculture and fishing sectors accounted for 3·8% of GDP in 2000, compared to 24% in 1960. Since joining the EC (as it was at the time) in 1986 Portugal has attracted foreign direct investment and income levels have approached the EU average. Convergence has stalled, however, and Eastern Europe has become a rival for foreign investment. Though its labour costs are the lowest in Western Europe, the liberalization of Eastern Europe means Portugal can no longer rely on labour costs alone for competitiveness.

Privatization and liberalization have proceeded steadily over the years. Export industries, such as clothing and textiles, have been modernized but industrial restructuring has been slow and the industrial base lacks economies of scale. Productivity remains well below the EU average, primarily because of poor management skills and a weak education system.

A serious violator of the euro zone's 3% deficit ceiling, Portugal's deficit rose from 2·8% in 2008 to 9·3% in 2009 as a result of a government stimulus package. While GDP increased by 1·9% in 2007 owing to buoyant export growth, it contracted by 2·7% in 2009 against the backdrop of the global economic crisis. Weak global macroeconomic conditions threaten the near-term outlook although moderate growth has been forecast for 2010.

Currency

On 1 Jan. 1999 the euro (EUR) became the legal currency in Portugal at the irrevocable conversion rate of 200·482 escudos to 1 euro. The euro, which consists of 100 cents, has been in circulation since 1 Jan. 2002. There are seven euro notes in different colours and sizes denominated in 500, 200, 100, 50, 20, 10 and 5 euros, and eight coins denominated in 2 and 1 euros, then 50, 20, 10, 5, 2 and 1 cents. On the introduction of the euro there was a 'dual circulation' period before the escudo ceased to be legal tender on 28 Feb. 2002. Euro banknotes in circulation on 1 Jan. 2002 had a total value of €10·6bn.

Inflation rates (based on OECD statistics):

1999	2000	2001	2002	2003	2004	2005	2006	2007	2008
2·2%	2·8%	4·4%	3·7%	3·3%	2·5%	2·1%	3·0%	2·4%	2·7%

Gold reserves were 12·30m. troy oz in Sept. 2009 and foreign exchange reserves US$774m. Total money supply was €52,659m. in Aug. 2009.

Budget

In 2006 central government revenues totalled €59,782m. and expenditures €65,569m. Taxes accounted for 57·3% of revenues in 2006 and social contributions 32·1%; social benefits accounted for 43·7% of expenditures and compensation of employees 27·7%.

The standard rate of VAT is 20·0% (reduced rates, 12% and 5%).

Performance

Real GDP growth rates (based on OECD statistics):

1999	2000	2001	2002	2003	2004	2005	2006	2007	2008
3·8%	3·9%	2·0%	0·8%	–0·8%	1·5%	0·9%	1·4%	1·9%	0·0%

In the years since Portugal joined the European Union its GDP per head has risen from being 53% of the EU average to 70% in 2006, although the 2006 GDP growth rate of 1·4% was the lowest in the EU. Portugal's total GDP in 2008 was US$242·7bn.

Banking and Finance

The central bank and bank of issue is the Bank of Portugal, founded in 1846 and nationalized in 1974. Its *Governor* is Vítor Manuel Ribeiro Constâncio.

In 2006 there were 5,039 branches of banks and savings banks and 676 branches of agricultural credit co-operatives. Deposits in all monetary establishments totalled €146·7bn. in 2006. The largest Portuguese bank is the state-owned Caixa Geral de Depósitos, with assets of €111·1bn. in 2008. Other major banks are Banco Comercial Português, Banco Espírito Santo and Banco Português de Investimento.

There are stock exchanges in Lisbon and Porto.

ENERGY AND NATURAL RESOURCES

Environment

Portugal's carbon dioxide emissions from the consumption and flaring of fossil fuels in 2008 were the equivalent of 5·4 tonnes per capita.

Electricity

Installed capacity was 12·7m. kW in 2004. Production in 2004 was 45·11bn. kWh; consumption per capita was 4,925 kWh.

Minerals

Portugal possesses considerable mineral wealth. Production in tonnes (2005): limestone, marl and calcite, 51,025,000; granite (2004), 30,311,000; marble, 752,000; salt, 597,945; kaolin, 164,072; copper, 89,541; tungsten, 816.

Agriculture

There were 274,563 agricultural holdings in 2007. The agricultural sector employs 11·6% of the workforce. In 2007 there were 1·08m. ha. of arable land and 796,000 ha. of permanent crops.

The following figures show the production (in 1,000 tonnes) of the chief crops:

Crop	*2005*	*2006*	*2007*	*Crop*	*2005*	*2006*	*2007*
Carrots and turnips[1]	150	160	170	Olive oil[2]	318	518	353
Fruits				Olives	212	373	375[1]
oranges	218	234	211	Onions[1]	118	118	121
apples	252	258	247	Potatoes	570	611	657
grapes	989	1,029	822	Rice	120	149	156
pears	130	175	141	Sugar beets	605	320	254
Lettuce and chicory[1]	95	100	100	Tomatoes	1,085	983	1,236
Maize	511	535	605	Wheat	82	250	102
				Wine[2]	7,064	7,338	5,842

[1]Estimates. [2]In 1,000 hectolitres.

Livestock (1,000 head):

	2005	*2006*	*2007*
Cattle	1,441	1,407	1,443
Goats	551	547	509
Pigs	2,344	2,295	2,374
Sheep	3,583	3,549	3,356
Poultry[1]	42,000	43,200	44,500

[1]Estimates.

Animal products in 2007 (1,000 tonnes): meat, 844·8; eggs, 121·6; cheese, 79·5; milk, 2,029m. litres.

Forestry

Forests covered 3·78m. ha. (41·3% of the land area) in 2005. Portugal is a major producer of cork. Estimated production, 2001, 158,000 tonnes; production of resin, 15,000 tonnes. Timber production was 10·80m. cu. metres in 2007.

Fisheries

The fishing industry is important, although much less so than in the past, and the Portuguese eat more fish per person than in any other European Union member country (more than twice the EU average). In 2006 there were 8,754 registered fishing vessels (7,153 with motors) and 17,261 registered fishermen. The catch was 141,683 tonnes in 2006 (almost exclusively from marine waters).

The 2006 fishing catch consisted of:

Species	*Tonnes*	*Value (in €1m.)*
Sardine	48,096	26,334
Mackerel	30,486	23,235
Shellfish	17,501	62,394
Other	45,600	132,337
Total	141,683	244,300

INDUSTRY

The leading companies by market capitalization in Portugal in March 2009 were: EDP—Energias de Portugal (US$12·7bn.); Galp Energia, SGPS, SA, an oil and gas company (US$9·2bn.); and Portugal Telecom (US$7·3bn.).

Output of major industrial products (in tonnes unless otherwise specified):

Product	*2001*	*2002*
Ready-mix concrete	25,658,038	25,567,852
Portland cement	10,162,310	9,760,964
Refined sugar	381,626	399,621
Preparation of animal food feeds	3,933,649	3,905,501
Beer (hectolitres)	6,829,719	7,124,710
Woven fabrics of synthetic staple fibres[1]	60,624	56,251
Footwear with leather uppers (1,000 pairs)	72,373	68,757
Wood pulp	1,784,347	1,806,403
Paper and cardboard	1,341,576	1,453,105
Petrol	2,619,805	2,484,639
Glass bottles (1,000)	3,663,323	3,890,782

[1]In 1,000 sq. metres.

Labour

The maximum working week was reduced from 44 hours to 40 in 1997. A minimum wage is fixed by the government. In 2004 the minimum wage was €365·60 a month. Retirement is at 65 years for men and 62 for women. In 2003, out of a working population of 5,460,300 (2,947,900 male), 5,118,000 (2,787,100 male) were employed. In Dec. 2009 the unemployment rate was 10·4%. Employment (in 1,000) by sector, 2003 (males in parentheses): services, 2,823·1 (1,283·6); industry, construction, energy and water, 1,652·8 (1,174·7); agriculture, forestry and fishing, 642·1 (328·7). The immigrant population makes up 10% of the labour force.

Trade Unions

There are two major trade union confederations in Portugal: the Confederação Geral dos Trabalhadores Portugueses—Intersindical Nacional (CGTP) and the União Geral de Trabalhadores (UGT). In 2002 there were 388 unions.

INTERNATIONAL TRADE

Imports and Exports

In 2006 imports (f.o.b.) totalled US$64·45bn. (US$59·07bn. in 2005); exports (f.o.b.), US$43·58bn. (US$38·24bn. in 2005).

In 2003 chemicals, manufactured goods classified chiefly by material and miscellaneous manufactured articles accounted for 40·6% of Portugal's imports and 50·2% of exports; machinery and transport equipment 33·9% of imports and 36·7% of exports; food, live animals, beverages and tobacco 11·3% of imports and 6·8% of exports; mineral fuels, lubricants and related materials 10·4% of imports and 2·5% of exports; inedible crude materials, and animal and vegetable oil and fats 3·8% of imports and 3·8% of exports.

Imports and exports to main trading partners, 2002 and 2003 (in US$1m.):

From or to	Imports 2002	Imports 2003	Exports 2002	Exports 2003
Spain	10,266·4	12,505·4	5,058·1	6,782·0
Germany	5,515·4	6,429·2	4,650·8	4,668·4
France	3,755·9	4,307·6	3,045·7	3,884·4
UK	1,917·5	2,131·4	2,628·0	3,322·2
Italy	2,346·0	2,765·5	1,179·8	1,472·8
Netherlands	1,697·9	1,963·6	944·2	1,151·2
Belgium/Luxembourg	1,202·0	1,418·5	1,159·3	1,434·6
USA	853·4	874·3	1,445·0	1,800·8

In 2003 fellow European Union members accounted for 76·0% of Portugal's imports and 78·5% of exports.

COMMUNICATIONS

Roads

In 2005 there were 2,613 km of motorways, 5,883 km of national roads, 4,406 km of secondary roads and 63,900 km of other roads. In 2006 the number of vehicles registered included 5,234,500 passenger cars, 535,300 motorcycles and mopeds, 119,000 lorries and vans and 29,700 buses and coaches. In 2007 there were 854 deaths in road accidents.

Rail

In 2002 total railway length was 3,600 km. Passenger-km travelled in 2002 came to 3·93bn. and freight tonne-km to 2·58bn. There is a metro (19 km) and tramway (94 km) in Lisbon. A new light rail system was opened in Porto in 2002.

Civil Aviation

There are international airports at Portela (Lisbon), Pedras Rubras (Porto), Faro (Algarve) and Funchal (Madeira). The national carrier is the state-owned TAP-Air Portugal, with some domestic and international flights being provided by Portugália. In 2003 scheduled airline traffic of Portuguese-based carriers flew 128m. km, carrying 7,590,000 passengers (4,994,000 on international flights). In 2007 Lisbon handled 13,393,000 passengers (11,249,000 on international flights) and 82,645 tonnes of freight. Faro was the second busiest in terms of passenger traffic, with 5,471,000 passengers, and Porto was the second busiest for freight, with 31,991 tonnes.

Shipping

In 2007, 15,226 vessels of 151·82m. tonnes entered all Portuguese ports; 367,391 passengers embarked and 368,095 disembarked during 2007. 21·17m. tonnes of cargo were loaded in 2007 and 47·05m. tonnes unloaded. In 2002 merchant ships totalled 1,100,000 GRT, including oil tankers 424,000 GRT.

Telecommunications

Portugal Telecom (PT) was formed from a merger of three state-owned utilities in 1994. It is now fully privatized. In 2008 there were 4,111,000 main (fixed) telephone lines. In the same year mobile phone subscribers numbered 14,910,000 (1,396·4 per 1,000 persons). There were 1·8m. PCs in use in 2006 and 4·5m. internet users in 2008. There were 14·8 broadband subscribers per 100 inhabitants in June 2008.

Postal Services

The number of post offices was 3,537 in 2003; a total of 1,082m. pieces of mail were processed during 2003.

SOCIAL INSTITUTIONS

Justice

There are four judicial districts (Lisbon, Porto, Coimbra and Evora) divided into 58 circuits. In 2007 there were 335 courts, including 329 common courts of first instance. There are also six higher courts (five courts of appeal and a Supreme Court in Lisbon).

Capital punishment was abolished completely in the constitution of 1976.

In 2006 there were 54 prisons with an inmate capacity of 12,115. The population in penal institutions in Nov. 2008 was 11,017 (104 per 100,000 of national population).

Education

Adult literacy rate was 93·8% in 2004. Compulsory education has been in force since 1911.

In 2007 there were 263,887 children in pre-school establishments with 16,599 teaching staff, 753,646 pupils in primary schools with 64,274 teaching staff and 680,338 pupils in secondary schools with 92,965 teaching staff.

In 2006 public tertiary education institutions included 14 universities and a non-integrated university institution; 15 polytechnics and a number of polytechnic schools integrated in universities; 9 non-integrated nursing schools; 4 university-level military schools; and 5 polytechnic military schools. In the private sector there were 34 university level institutions and 66 polytechnics as well as a Catholic university. Portugal's oldest university is the University of Coimbra (Universidade de Coimbra), initially established in Lisbon in 1290; its largest is the University of Porto (Universidade do Porto), with 27,184 students in 2007–08. In 2007 there were 366,729 students in higher education with 36,069 academic staff.

Public expenditure on education came to 5·5% of GNI in 2006 (11·3% of total government expenditure).

Health

There were 200 hospitals in 2006 with 36,563 beds, and 378 clinics. In 2007 there were 37,904 doctors, 5,629 dentists, 10,117 pharmacists and 54,079 nurses. In 2006 Portugal spent 9·9% of its GDP on health.

Welfare

In 2001, €25,817m. were paid in social security benefits. Cash payments in euros (and types) were: 9,984m. (old age); 8,070m. (sickness); 3,186m. (disability); 1,846m. (survivors); 1,458m. (family); 940m. (unemployment); 328m. (social exclusion); 6m. (housing).

Pensions are available to men and women aged at least 65 with 15 years of contributions. Pensions are available at a younger age to workers in specified industries including mining, dancing, and the maritime and aviation sectors. The pension value is 2% of the average lifetime salary for each year of contributions, up to 40 years. Until 2017 pensions may also be calculated using an older system (2% of average earnings for the best ten of the last 15 years, multiplied by the number of years of contributions).

RELIGION

There is freedom of worship, both in public and private, with the exception of creeds incompatible with morals and the life and physical integrity of the people. There were 9·52m. Roman Catholics in 2001. In Feb. 2010 there were two cardinals.

CULTURE

World Heritage Sites

(With year entered on list). In the Central Zone of the Town of Angra do Heroísmo in the Azores (1983) are the fortresses of San Sebastião and San Filipe, the latter built around 1590 on the orders of King Phillip II of Spain. The Monastery of the Hieronymites was built at the turn of the 16th century in Belém, Lisbon, while the capital's Tower of Belém was constructed as a monument to Vasco da Gama's explorations (1983 and 2008). The Monastery of Batalha (1983) near Leiria was built from 1388. The Convent of Christ in Tomar (1983) was originally built in 1160 as the centre of the Templar order. It was taken over by the Order of Christ in 1360 of which Henry the Navigator was made governor in 1418, and was greatly enriched in the 16th century. Other sites are the medieval walled Historic Centre of Évora (1988), the Gothic Cistercian 12th century Monastery of Alcobaça, north of Lisbon (1989), the Cultural Landscape of Sintra (1995), the Historic Centre of Porto (1996), the Upper Palaeolithic Rock-Art Sites in the Côa Valley (1998) and the Laurisilva of Madeira (1999), an area of biodiverse laurel forest. In 2001 two more sites were added: the Alto Douro Wine Region, famous for its port wine since the 18th century, and the Historic Centre of Guimarães, a town closely associated with the formation of Portuguese identity. The Landscape of the Pico Island Vineyard Culture followed in 2004.

Broadcasting

Radiotelevisão Portuguesa (RTP) and Radiodifusão Portuguesa (RDP) operate the public television and radio services. There are two RTP domestic television channels, while RDP runs three national radio networks, regional services and the external Radio Portugal. SIC and TVI are commercial television stations; multichannel cable and satellite services are also widely available. Colour is by PAL. There are some 300 private radio stations. In 2005 there were 3·55m. TV-equipped households and 1·40m. cable TV subscribers.

Press

In 2006 there were 35 daily newspapers (morning and evening editions) including seven in the Azores and two in Madeira, with a combined annual circulation of 671,329,640. In addition there were 2,019 periodicals in 2006 with a combined circulation of 223,765,806. In 2002 a total of 11,331 book titles were published.

Tourism

In 2007 there were 12,321,000 non-resident tourists (11,282,000 in 2006), including (in 1,000): from Spain, 2,661; UK, 2,326; France, 1,859; Germany, 1,212; Switzerland, 537; the Netherlands, 526. There were 2,031 hotel establishments with 264,747 beds in 2007. In 2005 tourist receipts totalled US$9,222m.

DIPLOMATIC REPRESENTATIVES

Of Portugal in the United Kingdom (11 Belgrave Sq., London, SW1X 8PP)
Ambassador: António Santana Carlos.

Of the United Kingdom in Portugal (Rua de São Bernardo 33, 1249-082 Lisbon)
Ambassador: Alexander Ellis.

Of Portugal in the USA (2125 Kalorama Rd, NW, Washington, D.C., 20008)
Ambassador: João de Vallera.

Of the USA in Portugal (Ave. das Forças Armadas, 1600 Lisbon)
Ambassador: Vacant.
Chargé d'Affaires a.i.: David Ballard.

Of Portugal to the United Nations
Ambassador: José Filipe Moraes Cabral.

Of Portugal to the European Union
Permanent Representative: Manuel Lobo Antunes.

FURTHER READING

Instituto Nacional de Estatística. *Anuário Estatístico de Portugal/Statistics Year-Book.— Estatísticas do Comércio Externo.* 2 vols. Annual from 1967

Birmingham, David, *A Concise History of Portugal.* 1993
Maxwell, K., *The Making of Portuguese Democracy.* 1995
Page, Martin, *The First Global Village: How Portugal Changed the World.* 2002
Saraiva, J. H., *Portugal: A Companion History.* 1997
Wheeler, D. L., *Historical Dictionary of Portugal.* 1994

National library: Biblioteca Nacional de Lisboa, Campo Grande 83, 1749-081 Lisbon.
National Statistical Office: Instituto Nacional de Estatística (INE), Avenida António José de Almeida, 1000-043 Lisbon.
Website: http://www.ine.pt

QATAR

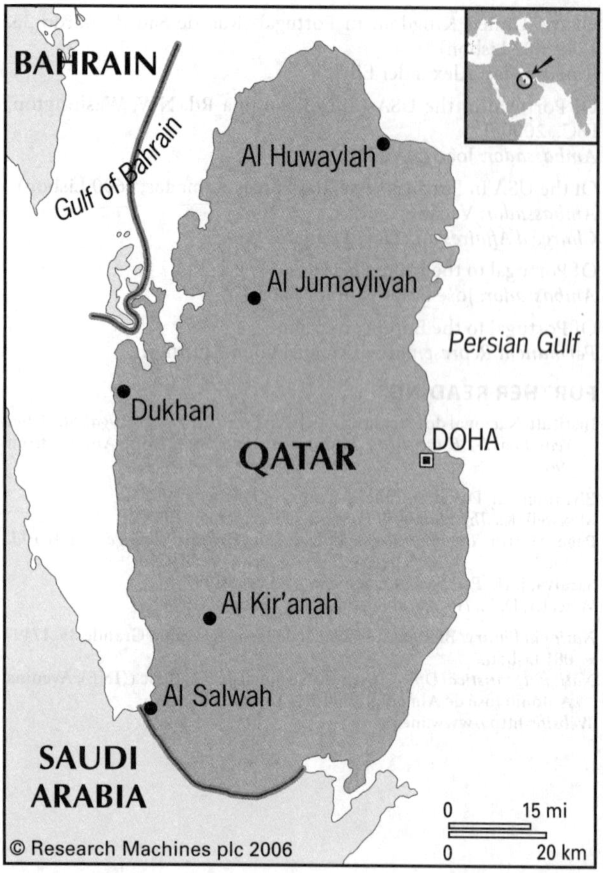

Dawlat Qatar
(State of Qatar)

Capital: Doha
Population estimate, 2010: 1·51m.
GDP per capita, 2006: (PPP$) 27,664
HDI/world rank: 0·910/33

KEY HISTORICAL EVENTS

Qatar has rock carvings, inscriptions and fragments of pottery dating from 4000 BC. The early population was swelled by seasonal migration of Arab tribes and the peninsula became a centre for fishing and pearls. Commercial activity declined in the Roman era, when trade was concentrated in the Red Sea, but recovered in the 3rd century AD.

Islam was established in Qatar in the mid-7th century AD. During the Abbasid period (750–1258) Qatar enjoyed strong relations with the Caliphs in Baghdad. After briefly coming under Portuguese influence in the early 16th century, Qatar fell under Ottoman sovereignty. For the next four centuries it was nominally part of the Ottoman Empire, though considerable power remained with local tribal sheikhs.

Pearling and trading settlements were established along the coast in the 18th century, which also saw the rise of the Al Thani family who were originally from Saudi Arabia. In the mid-19th century Sheikh Mohammed bin Thani moved the family to the growing coastal town of Doha and established control of the surrounding region. Territorial disputes with the Al Khalifa family in neighbouring Bahrain led to a war in 1867 in which Doha was almost destroyed. The British intervened to recognize the Al Thani family as rulers of Qatar and in 1878 Sheikh Mohammed was succeeded by his son, Sheikh Qassim, who became the first Amir. With the collapse of the Ottoman Empire during the First World War, Qatar came under British rule. Under the treaties of 1916 and 1934 Qatar ceded Britain control over its external affairs in return for British military protection.

Oil was discovered in 1939 and, after a delay caused by the Second World War, exports began in 1949. In Dec. 1961 Qatar joined the Organization of the Petroleum Exporting Countries (OPEC). In 1968 British troops left Qatar and in 1970 Qatar adopted a constitution confirming the emirate as an absolute monarchy. It led negotiations to establish a union of Arab emirates but terms could not be agreed. On 3 Sept. 1971 Qatar assumed full independence under the rule of Sheikh Ahmad and joined the Arab League and the United Nations. In 1972 Sheikh Ahmad was ousted in a coup and chief minister Sheikh Khalifa bin Hamad Al Thani assumed power.

The discovery in 1971 of a large offshore oil field gave further impetus to the economy and Qatar rapidly developed a modern infrastructure, building up its health and education services. In 1981 it was a founder member of the Gulf Co-operation Council (GCC) and in 1988 established diplomatic relations with the USSR and the People's Republic of China. Qatar allied itself with Saudi Arabia on many regional and international issues and in 1991 joined the US-led international alliance against Iraq following the invasion of Kuwait.

In Jan. 1992 pressure for political reform culminated in demands from 50 prominent Qataris for a consultative assembly. On 27 June 1995 Amir Sheikh Khalifa was ousted by his son, Sheikh Hamad, who announced plans to introduce democratic reforms. In 1996 he survived an assassination attempt, part of an abortive attempt to restore his father to power. In 1996 the Arabic-language news agency Al-Jazeera was established in Doha, with the Amir's personal support and state financial backing. The station has won widespread respect and influence, despite pressure from some powers to tone down what is seen as an anti-West bias.

In 2001 a long-standing territorial dispute between Qatar and Bahrain was settled by the International Court of Justice, with Qatar recognizing Bahrain's sovereignty over the Hamar Islands in return for Bahrain renouncing claims on parts of mainland Qatar. In 2003 Qatar supported the UN-backed, American- and British-led invasion of Iraq, with Doha hosting the coalition headquarters.

In recent years Qatar's economy has grown rapidly. In 2003 a referendum was held to approve the country's constitution, which provides for a parliament with 30 elected and 15 appointed members. In the same year Qatar's first female minister, Sheikha Ahmad Al Mahmoud, was appointed.

TERRITORY AND POPULATION

Qatar is a peninsula running north into the Persian Gulf. It is bounded in the south by Saudi Arabia. The territory includes a number of islands in the coastal waters of the peninsula, the most important of which is Halul, the storage and export terminal for the offshore oilfields. The area of Qatar is 11,493 sq. km. Population at the census of March 2004, 744,029 (496,382 males); density 64·7 per sq. km. In 2005, 95·4% of the population lived in urban areas.

The UN gives an estimated population for 2010 of 1·51m.

In March 2004 there were ten municipalities:

	2004 census population		2004 census population
Doha	339,847	Al Jumayliyah	10,303
Al Rayyan	272,860	Al Shamal	4,915
Al Wakra	31,441	Jarian Al Batnah	6,678
Umm Salal	31,605	Al Ghwayriyah	2,159
Al Khour	31,547	Mesaieed	12,674

In 2004 the number of municipalities was reduced from ten to seven. Al Jumayliyah, Jarian Al Batnah, Al Ghwayriyah and Mesaieed ceased to exist after they merged with other municipalities while a new municipality, Al Daayen, was created.

The capital is Doha, which is the main port, and had a census population in 2004 of 339,847. Other towns are Dukhan (the centre of oil production), Umm Said (the oil-terminal of Qatar), Ruwais, Wakra, Al-Khour, Umm Salal Mohammad and Umm-Bab.

About 40% of the population are Arabs, 18% Indian, 18% Pakistani and 10% Iranian. Other nationalities make up the remaining 14%.

The official language is Arabic.

SOCIAL STATISTICS

Births, 2002, 12,200; deaths, 1,220; marriages, 2,351; divorces, 732. 2002 rates per 1,000 population: births, 20·3; deaths, 2·0. Qatar's 2002 death rate was the second lowest in the world (only Kuwait's was lower). Infant mortality, 2005 (per 1,000 live births), 10. Expectation of life in 2007 was 74·8 years for males and 76·8 for females. Annual population growth rate, 2000–05, 5·1%. Fertility rate, 2004, 2·9 births per woman.

CLIMATE

The climate is hot and humid. Doha, Jan. 62°F (16·7°C), July 98°F (36·7°C). Annual rainfall 2·5" (62 mm).

CONSTITUTION AND GOVERNMENT

Qatar is ruled by an *Amir*. HH Sheikh Hamad bin Khalifa Al Thani, KCMG (b. 1952) assumed power after deposing his father on 27 June 1995. The heir apparent was Sheikh Hamad's third son, Sheikh Jasim bin Hamad Al Thani (b. 1978), but in Aug. 2003 he named his fourth son, Sheikh Tamim bin Hamad Al Thani (b. 1979), as heir apparent instead.

Qatar's first written constitution was approved in June 2004 and came into force on 9 June 2005. It allows for a 45-member *Consultative Assembly* or *Majlis al-Shura*, with 30 members directly elected and 15 appointed by the Amir.

A *Council of Ministers* is assisted by a 35-member nominated Advisory Council.

National Anthem

'As-Salam Al-Amiri' ('Peace for the Amir'); words by Sheikh Mubarak bin Saïf al-Thani, tune by Abdul Aziz Nasser Obaidan.

GOVERNMENT CHRONOLOGY

Amirs since 1971.

1971–72 Sheikh Ahmad bin Ali Al Thani
1972–95 Sheikh Khalifa bin Hamad Al Thani
1995– Sheikh Hamad bin Khalifa Al Thani

RECENT ELECTIONS

30 of the 45 members of the Consultative Assembly may be elected for a four-year term for the first time in the course of 2010.

CURRENT ADMINISTRATION

In March 2010 the government comprised:

Amir, Minister of Defence and C.-in-C. of the Armed Forces: HH Sheikh Hamad bin Khalifa Al Thani; b. 1952.

Prime Minister and Minister of Foreign Affairs: Sheikh Hamad bin Jasim bin Jabir Al Thani; b. 1959 (in office since 3 April 2007).

Deputy Prime Minister and Minister of Energy and Industry: Abdallah bin Hamad Al Attiyah. *Labour:* Hassan Dhabit Al Dousari. *Economy and Finance:* Yusif Husayn Al Kamal. *Business and Trade (acting):* Khalid bin Mohamed Al-Attiyah. *Education and Higher Education:* Saad bin Ibrahim Al Mahmoud. *Culture, Arts and Heritage:* Dr Hamad bin Abdul Aziz Al Kawari. *Justice:* Hasan bin Abdallah Al Ghanim. *Awqaf and Islamic Affairs:* Ahmed bin Abdullah Al Marri. *Municipal Affairs and Urban Planning:* Sheikh Abdul Rahman bin Khalifa bin Abdul Azziz Al Thani. *Public Health:* Abdallah bin Khaled Al Qahtani. *Environment:* Abdullah bin Mubarak bin Aaboud Al Midhadhi. *Social Affairs:* Nasser bin Abdullah Al Hemaidi. *Interior:* Abdullah bin Khalid Al Thani.

CURRENT LEADERS

Sheikh Hamad bin Khalifa Al Thani

Position
Amir

Introduction
Sheikh Hamad is the eighth member of the Al Thani family to rule Qatar, having seized power from his father, Sheikh Khalifa, on 27 June 1995.

Early Life
Born in Doha in 1952, Hamad graduated from the Royal Military Academy, Sandhurst in 1971. He then joined the Qatari military with the rank of major. In 1975 he was promoted to major-general and commander-in-chief of the armed forces. On his appointment as Crown Prince and heir apparent in May 1977, he also became minister of defence.

Career in Office
Having ousted his father in 1995, Hamad appointed himself prime minister. However, in Oct. 1996 he relinquished the premiership to his younger brother Sheikh Abdallah. The Amir is credited with initiating plans for an elected consultative council (through the new constitution which he approved in 2004 and which took effect in June 2005), giving women the right to vote in municipal elections (from 1999) and ending official media censorship. He has also encouraged foreign investment in Qatar's oil and natural gas industries. In foreign relations he has overseen the resolution of longstanding border disputes with Bahrain and Saudi Arabia. In Aug. 2003 he named his fourth son as his heir apparent, and in April 2007 appointed his foreign minister and cousin, Sheikh Hamad bin Jasim bin Jabir Al Thani, prime minister. In Jan. 2009 Qatar severed its trading links with Israel (having previously been the only Gulf state to have such ties) in protest at the Israeli military offensive in Gaza.

DEFENCE

Defence expenditure in 2006 totalled US$2,335m. (US$2,638 per capita), representing 4·5% of GDP. The expenditure per capita in 2006 was the second highest in the world after that of the UAE.

Army

Personnel (2007) 8,500.

Navy

Personnel in 2007 totalled 1,800 including Marine Police; the base is at Doha.

Air Force

The Air Force operates 18 combat capable aircraft (including Mirage 2000 fighters), 11 attack helicopters and 14 other helicopters. Personnel (2007) 1,500.

INTERNATIONAL RELATIONS

Qatar is a member of the UN, World Bank, IMF and several other UN specialized agencies, WTO, Islamic Development Bank, OIC, Gulf Co-operation Council, League of Arab States and OPEC.

In March 2001 the International Court of Justice ruled on a long-standing dispute between Bahrain and Qatar over the boundary between the two countries and ownership of certain islands. Both countries accepted the decision.

ECONOMY

Oil, natural gas and other mining accounted for 62% of GDP in 2006, public administration and defence 9%, finance and real estate 8% and manufacturing 7%.

Overview

Qatar is an oil and natural gas exporter, with an oil production capacity of 800,000 bbls a day and the world's third largest reserves of natural gas. Qatar has welcomed foreign investment in the development of its gas fields over the last decade and became the world's leading liquefied natural gas exporter in 2007. Considered to be one of the most competitive economies in the world, it is highly rated by credit agencies. The economy is open, barriers to trade are low and no income taxes are levied.

In recent years the economy has benefited from rising oil prices, with growth rates among the highest in the world (reaching double digits from 2006–08). In 2009 the oil and gas sector accounted for 61·7% of GDP, although the drop in oil prices in late 2008 and the global financial crisis held back growth. Nonetheless, investments aimed at diversification provided a boost in 2009. Manufacturing, construction and financial services have performed particularly well in recent years.

Tourism has also thrived, with the country aiming to rival Dubai as a destination. Construction in the emirate is booming and a large expansion of the Doha International Airport is under way. Qatar is looking to compete with Bahrain and Dubai in establishing itself as a regional financial centre. Additionally, it is home to branches of five leading universities, including Georgetown University, Carnegie Mellon University and Weill Cornell Medical College.

Currency

The unit of currency is the *Qatari riyal* (QAR) of 100 *dirhams*, introduced in 1973. Foreign exchange reserves were US$4,370m. in July 2005, gold reserves were 19,000 troy oz and total money supply was 19,159m. riyals. There was inflation of 13·8% in 2007 and 15·0% in 2008.

In 2001 the six Gulf Arab states—Qatar, along with Bahrain, Kuwait, Oman, Saudi Arabia and the United Arab Emirates—signed an agreement to establish a single currency by 2010. In June 2009 it was agreed to postpone the implementation of the new currency, the *khaleeji*, until 2013. Both Oman and the United Arab Emirates have now withdrawn from the scheme, in 2007 and 2009 respectively.

Budget

The fiscal year is 1 April–31 March. Revenue (2005–06) 64,984m. riyals; expenditure, 50,833m. riyals. Oil and natural gas account for about 67% of revenues.

Performance

In terms of GDP per head, Qatar ranks among the richest countries in the world with a per capita PPP (purchasing power parity) of US$85,371 in 2007. Qatar has been experiencing a period of rapid economic expansion, driven by rising oil prices and the increased exploitation of its natural gas reserves, the third largest in the world. Real GDP growth was 16·4% in 2008—the highest rate of any country—up from 9·2% in 2005, 15·0% in 2006 and 15·3% in 2007. Total GDP in 2006 was US$52·7bn.

Banking and Finance

The Qatar Monetary Agency, which functioned as a bank of issue, became the Central Bank in 1995 (*Governor*, Abdullah bin Saud Al-Thani). In 2003 there were eight commercial domestic banks and seven foreign banks. The largest bank is the Qatar National Bank, with assets in 2003 of 34·8bn. riyals.

A stock exchange was established in Doha by the Amir's decree in 1995, initially to trade only in Qatari stocks.

ENERGY AND NATURAL RESOURCES

Environment

Qatar's carbon dioxide emissions from the consumption and flaring of fossil fuels in 2008 were the equivalent of 74·1 tonnes per capita, the highest of any sovereign country.

Electricity

Installed capacity was an estimated 2·9m. kW in 2004. Production was 13·23bn. kWh in 2004; consumption per capita was 19,840 kWh.

Oil and Gas

Proven reserves of oil (2008) 27·3bn. bbls. Output, 2008, 60·8m. tonnes. Production rose by 13·2% in 2008 compared to 2007—the largest increase of any oil producing country.

The North Field, the world's biggest single reservoir of gas and containing 12% of the known world gas reserves, is half the size of Qatar itself. Development cost is estimated at US$25bn. In 2008 natural gas reserves were 25,460bn. cu. metres (the third largest after Russia and Iran); output in 2008 was 76·6bn. cu. metres.

Agriculture

In 2002, 1·2% of the economically active population were engaged in agriculture. Government policy aims at ensuring self-sufficiency in agricultural products. In 2002 an estimated 13,000 ha. were irrigated. There were approximately 18,000 ha. of arable land in 2002 and 3,000 ha. of permanent crops. Production (2002) in 1,000 tonnes: dates, 16; tomatoes, 11; pumpkins and squash, 8; aubergines, 5; barley, 5; cucumbers and gherkins, 5; melons and watermelons, 5; onions, 4.

Livestock (2003 estimates): sheep, 200,000; goats, 180,000; camels, 51,000; cattle, 15,000; chickens, 4m. Livestock products, 2003 estimates (in 1,000 tonnes): meat, 15; milk, 22; eggs, 4.

Fisheries

The catch in 2005 totalled 13,935 tonnes, entirely from sea fishing. The state-owned Qatar National Fishing Company has three trawlers and its refrigeration unit processes 10 tonnes of shrimp a day.

INDUSTRY

Production (2005, in 1,000 tonnes): urea, 2,979; ammonia, 2,134; petrol, 1,656; butane, 1,075; cement, 1,049; distillate fuel oil, 926; jet fuel, 905; steel bars, 791; ethylene, 544; residual fuel oil, 418; polyethylene, 415. There is an industrial zone at Umm Said.

Labour

In 2004 the economically active population totalled 444,100. Males constituted 85% of the labour force in 2004; foreigners make up 75% of the workforce.

INTERNATIONAL TRADE

Qatar, along with Bahrain, Kuwait, Oman, Saudi Arabia and the United Arab Emirates entered into a customs union in Jan. 2003.

Imports and Exports

Total imports and exports in calendar years (in US$1m.):

	2003	2004	2005	2006
Imports	4,897·4	6,004·6	10,060·9	16,440·1
Exports	13,382·6	18,685·1	25,762·5	34,051·3

The main imports are machinery and equipment, consumer goods, food and chemicals. Main exports are petroleum and petroleum products (52%) and liquefied natural gas (35%). Qatar is the world's largest exporter of liquefied natural gas. Principal import suppliers in 2004: France, 26·7%; USA, 9·6%; Saudi Arabia, 9·5%. Leading export markets, 2004: Japan, 41·6%; South Korea, 15·7%; Singapore, 9·1%.

COMMUNICATIONS

Roads

In 2007 there were about 7,790 km of roads. Vehicles in use in 2007 totalled 605,700. In 2007 there were 199 fatalities as a result of road accidents.

Civil Aviation

Gulf Air was formed as a partnership between Qatar, Bahrain, Oman and Abu Dhabi, but Qatar withdrew in 2002 (and Abu Dhabi and Oman have withdrawn in the meantime). In 2003 it operated services from Doha International to Abu Dhabi and Bahrain. A Qatari airline, Qatar Airways, operates on the same routes, and in 2003 additionally flew to Amman, Bangkok, Beirut, Cairo, Casablanca, Colombo, Damascus, Damman, Dhaka, Dubai, Frankfurt, Hyderabad, Islamabad, Jakarta, Jeddah, Karachi, Kathmandu, Khartoum, Kochi, Kuala Lumpur, Kuwait, Lahore, London, Malé, Manchester, Manila, Milan, Mumbai, Munich, Muscat, Paris, Peshawar, Riyadh, Salalah, Sana'a, Sharjah and Thiruvananthapuram. In June 2003 Qatar Airways commissioned 32 aircraft worth US$5·1bn. from Airbus SAS. Doha handled 2,759,000 passengers (all on international flights) and 64,000 tonnes of freight in 2001.

Shipping

In 2002 sea-going vessels totalled 623,000 GRT, including oil tankers 210,000 GRT. In 1993, 1,383 vessels with a total tonnage of 66,255,841 GRT and 2,697,629 tonnage of cargo was discharged.

Telecommunications

In 2008 there were 263,400 main (fixed) telephone lines; mobile phone subscribers numbered 1,683,000 in 2008 (131·4 per 100 persons). There were 157,000 PCs in use in 2006 and 436,000 internet users in 2008.

Postal Services

There were 53 post offices in 2003.

SOCIAL INSTITUTIONS

Justice

The Judiciary System is administered by the Ministry of Justice which comprises three main departments: legal affairs, courts of justice and land and real estate register. In 2004 a High Judicial Council was established to oversee the court system, which as a result of a new Judicial Authority Law that took effect at the same time comprises the Court of Cassation, the Court of Appeal and the Court of First Instance. The courts proclaim sentences in the name of HH the Amir. The death penalty is in force. There was one execution in 2003, but none since. The population in penal institutions in Dec. 2004 was 465 (55 per 100,000 of national population).

All issues related to personal affairs of Muslims under Islamic Law embodied in the Holy Koran and Sunna are decided by Sharia Courts.

Education

Adult literacy rate was 89·0% in 2004. There were, in 2007, 75,451 pupils at primary schools (with 6,639 teaching staff in 2006), 61,226 pupils at secondary schools (6,200 teaching staff in 2006) and 8,881 students with 1,153 academic staff in higher education. There were 265 Arab and foreign private schools with 56,183 pupils and 4,092 teachers in 2002–03. The University of Qatar had 7,867 students and 676 academic staff in 2003–04.

Students abroad (2003–04) numbered 374. In 2002–03, 2,009 men and 940 women attended night schools and literacy centres.

In 2005 public expenditure on education accounted for 19·6% of total government spending.

Health

There were three government and two private hospitals in 2002. In 2002 there were 1,204 government-employed doctors, 145 government-employed dentists, 279 government-employed pharmacists and 3,139 government-employed nurses.

RELIGION

The population is predominantly Muslim, although there is a small Christian minority among expatriates.

CULTURE

Broadcasting

The government operates the Qatar Broadcasting Service (transmitting radio programmes in Arabic, English, French and Urdu) and the Qatar Television Service (broadcasting an Arabic Service, an English channel, a satellite channel and a Koran service). Transmissions are received from Bahrain, the United Arab Emirates or Saudi Arabia. There are also satellite and cable broadcasters (Al-Jazeera Satellite Channel and Qatar Cable Vision). Al-Jazeera has a reputation for outspoken, independent reporting and has become increasingly high-profile since the attacks on the USA on 11 Sept. 2001. Al-Jazeera launched an English-language network, Al-Jazeera English, in Nov. 2006. There were 315,000 television receivers in use (colour by PAL) in 2004.

Press

There are three Arabic language daily newspapers—Al-Rayah, Al-Sharq and Al-Watan. The Gulf Times and Al-Jazeera (The Peninsula) are English dailies. In 2006 the combined circulation was 81,000.

Tourism

In 2005, 913,000 non-resident tourists stayed in hotels.

DIPLOMATIC REPRESENTATIVES

Of Qatar in the United Kingdom (1 South Audley St., London, WIK 1NB)
Ambassador: Khalid Rashid Salem Al-Homoudi Al-Mansouri.

Of the United Kingdom in Qatar (PO Box 3, Doha, Qatar)
Ambassador: John Hawkins.

Of Qatar in the USA (2555 M St., NW, Washington, D.C., 20037)
Ambassador: Ali bin Fahd al-Hajiri.

Of the USA in Qatar (22 February St., Doha)
Ambassador: Joseph LeBaron.

Of Qatar to the United Nations
Ambassador: Nassir Abdulaziz Al-Nasser.

Of Qatar to the European Union
Ambassador: Sheikh Meshal Bin Hamad Al-Thani.

FURTHER READING

Central Statistical Organization. *Annual Statistical Abstract.*

El-Nawawy, Mohammed and Iskandar, Adel, *Al-Jazeera: How the Free Arab News Network Scooped the World and Changed the Middle East.* 2002

National Statistical Office: Central Statistical Organization, Presidency of the Council of Ministers, Doha.
Website: http://www.qsa.gov.qa

ROMANIA

România

Capital: Bucharest
Population estimate, 2010: 21·19m.
GDP per capita, 2007: (PPP$) 12,369
HDI/world rank: 0·837/63

KEY HISTORICAL EVENTS

The foundation of the feudal 'Danubian Principalities' of Wallachia and Moldavia in the late 13th and early 14th centuries marks the beginning of modern Romania. The nobility acted as the Turks' agents until 1711 when, suspected of pro-Russian sentiments, they were replaced by Greek merchant adventurers, the Phanariots. The ruthless extortion and corruption of the Phanariot period was tempered by Russian influence. Between 1829 and 1834 the foundations of the modern state were laid but Russian interference soon became repressive. The Moldavian and Wallachian assemblies were fused in 1862. In 1866 Carol of Hohenzollern came to the throne and a constitution adopted based on that of Belgium of 1831. Romania was formally declared independent by the Treaty of Berlin of 1878.

This was a period of expansion for an economy controlled by land-owners and nascent industrialists. The condition of the peasantry remained miserable and the rebellion of 1907 demonstrated their discontent. Romania joined the First World War on the allied side in 1916. The spoils of victory brought Transylvania (with large Hungarian and German populations), Bessarabia, Bukovina and Dobrudja into the union with the 'Old Kingdom'. Hit by the world recession, Romania was drawn into Germany's economic orbit. Against this background the fascist Iron Guard assassinated the Liberal leader, Ion G. Duca, in 1933. Carol II adopted an increasingly totalitarian rule. Following Nazi and Soviet annexations of Romanian territory in 1940, he abdicated in favour of his son Mihai. The government of the fascist Ion Antonescu declared war on the USSR on 22 June 1941. On 23 Aug. 1944 Mihai, with the backing of a bloc of opposition parties, deposed Antonescu and switched sides.

The armistice of Sept. 1944 gave the Soviet army control of Romania's territory. This, and the 'spheres of influence' diplomacy of the Allies, predetermined the establishment of communism in Romania. Transylvania was restored to Romania (although it lost Bessarabia and Southern Dobrudja), and large estates were broken up for the benefit of the peasantry. Elections in Nov. 1946 were held in an atmosphere of intimidation and fraudulence. Mihai was forced to abdicate and a people's republic was proclaimed. The communist leader, Gheorghe Gheorghiu-Dej, purged his fellow leaders in the early 1950s. Under Nicolae Ceaușescu, who became the effective centre of power in 1965, Romania took a relatively independent stand in foreign affairs while becoming increasingly repressive and impoverished.

An attempt by the authorities on 16 Dec. 1989 to evict a Protestant pastor, László Tökés, from his home in Timișoara provoked a popular protest which escalated into a mass demonstration against the government. A state of emergency was declared but the Army went over to the rebels and Nicolae and Elena Ceaușescu fled the capital. A dissident group which had been active before the uprising, the National Salvation Front (FSN), proclaimed itself the provisional government. The Ceaușescus were captured and after a secret two hour trial by military tribunal, summarily executed on 25 Dec. The following day Ion Iliescu, leader of the FSN, was sworn in as President. But the Iliescu-led administration, while committed to reform, was inhibited by its communist origins. The economy stalled and the debts piled up. Iliescu was voted out of office and his government replaced by a four-party coalition led by President Emil Constantinescu. Iliescu returned as president in 2000. The economy continued to struggle but in 2004 Romania joined NATO. It became a member of the European Union on 1 Jan. 2007.

TERRITORY AND POPULATION

Romania is bounded in the north by Ukraine, in the east by Moldova, Ukraine and the Black Sea, south by Bulgaria, southwest by Serbia and northwest by Hungary. The area is 238,391 sq. km. Population (2002 census), 21,680,974; density, 90·9 per sq. km. In 2005, 53·7% of the population lived in urban areas. Romania's population has been falling at such a steady rate since 1990 that its population at the time of the 2002 census was the same as that in the late 1970s. The estimated population on 1 Jan. 2009 was 21,498,616.

The UN gives an estimated population for 2010 of 21·19m.

Romania is divided into 41 counties (*județ*) and the municipality of Bucharest (București).

County	*Area in sq. km*	*Population (2002 census)*	*Capital*	*Population (in 1,000) (2002)*
Bucharest (București)[1]	228	1,926,334		
Alba	6,242	382,747	Alba Iulia	66
Arad	7,754	461,791	Arad	173
Argeș	6,826	652,625	Pitești	168
Bacău	6,621	706,623	Bacău	176
Bihor	7,544	600,246	Oradea	207
Bistrița-Năsăud	5,355	311,657	Bistrița	81
Botoșani	4,986	452,834	Botoșani	115
Brăila	4,766	373,174	Brăila	216
Brașov	5,363	589,028	Brașov	285
Buzău	6,103	496,214	Buzău	134
Călărași	5,088	324,617	Călărași	70

County	Area in sq. km	Population (2002 census)	Capital	Population (in 1,000) (2002)
Caraş-Severin	8,520	333,219	Reşiţa	84
Cluj	6,674	702,755	Cluj-Napoca	318
Constanţa	7,071	715,151	Constanţa	310
Covasna	3,710	222,449	Sf. Gheorghe	62
Dâmboviţa	4,054	541,763	Tîrgovişte	90
Dolj	7,414	734,231	Craiova	303
Galaţi	4,466	619,556	Galaţi	299
Giurgiu	3,526	297,859	Giurgiu	69
Gorj	5,602	387,308	Tîrgu Jiu	97
Harghita	6,639	326,222	Miercurea-Ciuc	42
Hunedoara	7,063	485,712	Deva	69
Ialomiţa	4,453	296,572	Slobozia	53
Iaşi	5,476	816,910	Iaşi	321
Ilfov[1]	1,593	300,123	—	—
Maramureş	6,304	510,110	Baia Mare	138
Mehedinţi	4,933	306,732	Drobeta-Turnu Severin	105
Mureş	6,714	580,851	Tîrgu Mureş	150
Neamţ	5,896	554,516	Piatra-Neamţ	105
Olt	5,498	489,274	Slatina	79
Prahova	4,716	829,945	Ploieşti	233
Sălaj	3,864	248,015	Zalău	63
Satu Mare	4,418	367,281	Satu Mare	115
Sibiu	5,432	421,724	Sibiu	155
Suceava	8,553	688,435	Suceava	106
Teleorman	5,790	436,025	Alexandria	50
Timiş	8,697	677,926	Timişoara	318
Tulcea	8,499	256,492	Tulcea	92
Vâlcea	5,765	413,247	Râmnicu Vâlcea	108
Vaslui	5,318	455,049	Vaslui	71
Vrancea	4,857	387,632	Focşani	102

[1]Bucharest municipality and surrounding localities of Ilfov cover 1,821 sq. km.

At the 2002 census the following ethnic minorities numbered over 50,000: Hungarians, 1,431,807 (mainly in Transylvania); Roma (Gypsies), 535,140; Ukrainians, 61,098; Germans, 59,764. A *Council of National Minorities* made up of representatives of the government and ethnic groups was set up in 1993. The actual number of Roma is estimated to be nearer 2m. Romania has the largest Roma population of any country.

The official language is Romanian.

SOCIAL STATISTICS

2005: births, 221,020; deaths, 262,101; marriages, 141,832; divorces, 33,193. Rates, 2005 (per 1,000 population): live births, 10·2; deaths, 12·1; marriages, 6·6; divorces, 1·5. Infant mortality, 2005 (per 1,000 live births), 16. Expectation of life at birth, 2007, was 69·0 years for males and 76·1 years for females. In 2005 the most popular age range for marrying was 25–29 for males and 20–24 for females. Measures designed to raise the birth rate were abolished in 1990, and abortion and contraception legalized. The annual abortion rate, at approximately 41 per 1,000 women, ranks among the highest in the world. Annual population growth rate, 2000–05, –0·7%; fertility rate, 2004, 1·3 births per woman.

CLIMATE

A continental climate with an annual average temperature varying between 8°C in the north and 11°C in the south. Bucharest, Jan. 27°F (–2·7°C), July 74°F (23·5°C). Annual rainfall 23·1" (579 mm). Constanţa, Jan. 31°F (–0·6°C), July 71°F (21·7°C). Annual rainfall 15" (371 mm).

CONSTITUTION AND GOVERNMENT

A new constitution was approved by a referendum on 18–19 Oct. 2003. Turnout was 55·7%, and 89·7% of votes cast were in favour. The Constitution, which replaces the previous one from 1991, defines Romania as a republic where the rule of law prevails in a social and democratic state. Private property rights and a market economy are guaranteed. The new pro-European constitution was aimed at helping Romania achieve EU membership.

The head of state is the *President*, elected by direct vote for a maximum of two five-year terms. The president is not allowed to be affiliated with any political party while in office. The President appoints the *Prime Minister*, who then has to be approved by a vote in parliament. The President is empowered to veto legislation unless it is upheld by a two-thirds parliamentary majority. The National Assembly consists of a 334-member *Chamber of Deputies* and a 137-member *Senate*; both are elected for four-year terms from 43 constituencies through a proportional mixed member system. 18 seats in the Chamber of Deputies are reserved for ethnic minorities. There is a 3% threshold for admission to either house. Votes for parties not reaching this threshold are redistributed.

There is a *Constitutional Court.*

National Anthem

'Desteaptăte, Române, din somnul cel de moarte' ('Wake up, Romanians, from your deadly slumber'); words by A. Muresianu, tune by A. Pann.

GOVERNMENT CHRONOLOGY

(FDSN = Democratic National Salvation Front; FSN = National Salvation Front; PCR = Romanian Communist Party; PD = Democratic Party; PDSR = Party of Social Democracy in Romania; PD-L = Democratic Liberal Party; PNL = National Liberal Party; PNTCD = National Peasant Party Christian Democratic; PSD = Social Democratic Party)

Heads of State since 1940.

King

1940–47	Mihai I	

Presidents of the Presidium of the Grand National Assembly

1947–52	PCR	Constantin Ion Parhon
1958	PCR	Anton Moisescu
1958–61	PCR	Ion Gheorghe Maurer

Chairmen of the Council of State

1961–65	PCR	Gheorghe Gheorghiu-Dej
1965–67	PCR	Chivu Stoica
1967–74	PCR	Nicolae Ceauşescu

Presidents

1974–89	PCR	Nicolae Ceauşescu
1989–96	PCR, n/p, FSN, FDSN, PDSR	Ion Iliescu
1996–2000	PNTCD	Emil Constantinescu
2000–04	PDSR, PSD	Ion Iliescu
2004–07	PD	Traian Băsescu
2007	PSD	Nicolae Văcăroiu (acting for Traian Băsescu)
2007–	PD, PD-L	Traian Băsescu

Heads of Government since 1945.

Chairmen of the Council of Ministers

1945–52	PCR	Petru Groza
1952–55	PCR	Gheorghe Gheorghiu-Dej
1955–61	PCR	Chivu Stoica
1961–74	PCR	Ion Gheorghe Maurer
1974–79	PCR	Manea Mănescu
1979–82	PCR	Ilie Verdeţ
1982–89	PCR	Constantin Dăscalescu

Prime Ministers

1989–91	FSN	Petre Roman
1991–92	n/p	Teodor Stolojan
1992–96	n/p, PDSR	Nicolae Văcăroiu
1996–98	PNTCD	Victor Ciorbea

1998–99	PNTCD	Radu Vasile
1999–2000	n/p	Mugur Isărescu
2000–04	PDSR/PSD	Adrian Năstase
2004–08	PNL	Călin Popescu-Tăriceanu
2008–	PD-L	Emil Boc

RECENT ELECTIONS

Presidential elections were held in two rounds on 22 Nov. and 6 Dec. 2009. In the first round President Traian Băsescu of the Democratic Liberal Party (PD-L) received 32·4% of votes cast, Mircea Geoană of the Social Democratic Party (in alliance with the Conservative Party) (PSD-PC) 31·2%, Crin Antonescu of the National Liberal Party (PNL) 20·0% and Corneliu Vadim Tudor of the Greater Romania Party 5·6%. There were eight other candidates. In the second round run-off Băsescu retained the presidency with 50·3% of the vote against 49·7% for Geoană. However, the opposition contested the results and accused Băsescu of ballot-rigging.

In parliamentary elections held on 30 Nov. 2008 the PD-L took 115 seats (but only 32·4% of the vote) in the lower house and 51 (33·6% of the vote) in the Senate, the PSD-PC alliance 114 seats (but 33·1%) and 49 (34·2%), the PNL 65 seats (18·6%) and 28 (18·7%), and the Democratic Union of Hungarians in Romania (UDMR) 22 seats (6·2%) and 9 (6·4%). Turnout was 39·2%.

European Parliament

Romania has 33 (35 in 2007) representatives. In June 2009 elections, turnout was 27·7% (29·5% in 2007). The PSD-PC won 11 seats with 31·1% of the vote (political affiliation in European Parliament: Progressive Alliance of Socialists and Democrats), the PD-L 10 seats with 29·7% (European People's Party), the PNL 5 seats with 14·5% (Alliance of Liberals and Democrats for Europe), the UDMR 3 seats with 8·9% (European People's Party), Greater Romania Party 3 seats with 8·7% (non-attached) and independents 1 seat with 4·2% (European People's Party).

CURRENT ADMINISTRATION

President: Traian Băsescu; b. 1951 (Democratic Liberal Party; since 20 Dec. 2004, but suspended from 20 April–23 May 2007; re-elected 6 Dec. 2009).

In March 2010 the government comprised:

Prime Minister: Emil Boc; b. 1951 (Democratic Liberal Party; sworn in 22 Dec. 2008).

Vice Prime-Minister: Markó Béla.

Minister of Administration and Interior: Vasile Blaga. *Agriculture and Rural Environment:* Mihail Dumitru. *Communication and Information Society:* Gabriel Sandu. *Culture and National Heritage:* Kelemen Hunor. *Economy, Trade and the Business Environment:* Adriean Videanu. *Education, Research, Youth and Sports:* Daniel Funeriu. *Environment and Forests:* László Borbély. *Foreign Affairs:* Teodor Baconschi. *Health:* Cseke Attila. *Justice:* Cătălin Marian Predoiu. *Labour, Family and Social Protection:* Mihai Şeitan. *National Defence:* Gabriel Oprea. *Public Finance:* Sebastian Teodor Gheorghe Vlădescu. *Regional Development and Tourism:* Elena Udrea. *Transportation and Infrastructure:* Radu Berceanu.

Government Website: http://www.gov.ro

CURRENT LEADERS

Traian Băsescu

Position

President

Introduction

Traian Băsescu, a former ship's captain and the charismatic mayor of Bucharest, fought the country's 2004 presidential elections on a tough anti-corruption platform and emerged victorious. He took over from Ion Iliescu, who had served as president for much of the post-Communist period. Băsescu was suspended from office in April 2007 but resumed his role a month later after a national referendum supported his reinstatement. He was narrowly re-elected in Dec. 2009.

Early Life

Băsescu was born in the village of Basarabi near the Romanian port of Constanţa on 4 Nov. 1951. He studied at the Marine Institute in Constanţa, graduating in 1976 from the commercial section of the faculty of navigation. He then joined the merchant navy, controlled in Romania's Communist era by NAVROM, and worked his way through the ranks, becoming a captain in 1981. He went on to captain some of the country's largest merchant ships and was promoted to Admiral of Romania's merchant fleet by the mid-1980s. In 1987 Băsescu travelled to Antwerp, Belgium, to work as head of the NAVROM Agency. Two years later he returned to Bucharest and entered the political scene as general director of the State Inspectorate of Civic Navigation in the ministry of transport, in what turned out to be the final months of Nicolae Ceauşescu's 24-year grip on power. After the dramatic collapse of Ceauşescu's regime in Dec. 1989, Băsescu was promoted to deputy minister in the Ministry of Transport. He became minister of transport in 1991 in the government dominated by the National Salvation Front (FSN), which had received mass support in the first post-Communist elections on 20 May 1990.

Following a split in the FSN in 1992, Băsescu joined Petre Roman in the newly-established centre-left Democratic Party and, in 1996, he co-ordinated Roman's unsuccessful presidential campaign—the victor was Emil Constantinescu, a former rector of Bucharest University. Băsescu was re-elected as a Democratic Party MP in 1996 and served as minister of transport until 2000, when he stood as the Democratic Party candidate in the Bucharest mayoral election. He won and began co-ordinating the regeneration of large areas of the city, gaining praise for his direct approach—from cracking down on the notorious packs of stray dogs to improving traffic flow. When the government blocked his plans for a new bypass and improved municipal central heating systems, Băsescu asked citizens to sign a petition, and eventually managed to convince the officials to back down.

Following disagreements with Petre Roman, Băsescu replaced him as leader of the (opposition) Democratic Party in 2001. Two years later, in Sept. 2003, Băsescu became a co-chairman of the centre-right Justice and Truth Alliance (DA), forged between his Democratic Party and the National Liberal Party (PNL). Băsescu's energetic rule as mayor of Bucharest proved popular, and he was re-elected to the post in June 2004, easily beating his rival, Mircea Geoana.

Career in Office

Băsescu's first task as president was the formation of a new government, which became possible for his Justice and Truth Alliance when the small Humanist Party (since renamed the Conservative Party) pledged their support, in addition to the backing of the ethnic Hungarian Democratic Federation of Romania. Băsescu appointed the PNL leader and former minister of the economy Călin Popescu-Tăriceanu to the post of prime minister. In his inaugural address Băsescu said that fighting corruption would remain his priority and that he intended to steer Romania on a course to enter the European Union. This was achieved on 1 Jan. 2007 as Romania and Bulgaria became the EU's 26th and 27th member states. He also stressed the need to strengthen strategic partnerships with the USA and the UK, as well as to improve relations with Russia and the former Soviet states.

Although allied within the ruling Justice and Truth Alliance, Băsescu's relations with his prime minister, Călin Popescu-Tăriceanu, deteriorated to the point where, in April 2007, Popescu-Tăriceanu won a vote in parliament to suspend Băsescu for 'grave infringements of the constitution' and the Democratic

Party was excluded from the government. Former prime minister Nicolae Văcăroiu was appointed interim president. However, Băsescu returned to office on 23 May 2007 after he was backed by 74·5% of voters in a referendum on his leadership. He then promised to campaign for electoral reform to increase MPs' accountability to the electorate and for a lustration law that could be used to remove former senior officials of the Ceauşescu regime from their offices. In Dec. 2007 he called on Popescu-Tăriceanu to dismiss his justice minister because of corruption allegations. Also in Dec. 2007 the Democratic Party (PD) merged with the Liberal Democratic Party (PLD) to form the Democratic Liberal Party (PD-L). Concerns over high-level corruption also prompted the EU in Feb. 2008 to threaten sanctions against Romania if serious failings were not corrected. In April 2008 Băsescu hosted a summit meeting of NATO leaders in Bucharest.

Following inconclusive parliamentary elections in Nov. 2008, Băsescu nominated Theodor Stolojan, an economist and former prime minister, to head a new government. Stolojan soon withdrew his acceptance and Băsescu then asked Emil Boc, the leader of the Democratic Liberal Party, to form the new administration, which was approved by parliament in Dec. 2008. However, in Oct. 2009 this government lost a confidence vote, although Boc carried on in a caretaker capacity until the pending presidential elections as Băsescu's subsequent nominees for prime minister-designate were not acceptable to parliament.

Băsescu stood for re-election at the presidential elections of 22 Nov. 2009. Following a close first round of voting, a second round run-off between Băsescu and Geoană of the Social Democratic Party-Conservative Party alliance was held on 6 Dec. Băsescu narrowly defeated Geoană by 50·3% of votes cast to 49·7% but the victory was challenged by his opponent who claimed Băsescu was guilty of electoral fraud. Băsescu then turned again to Boc on 17 Dec. to form a new government, which was approved by parliament on 23 Dec.

Emil Boc

Position
Prime Minister

Introduction
Emil Boc succeeded Călin Popescu-Tăriceanu as prime minister in Dec. 2008. The former mayor of Cluj-Napoca, Boc comes from a centre-right background and is close to President Traian Băsescu. Following a closely fought general election in Nov. 2008 he headed a coalition charged with tackling a severe economic downturn. Following the collapse of this administration in Oct. 2009, Boc served in a caretaker capacity until Dec. when he formed a new centrist government endorsed by parliament.

Early Life
Boc was born in the village of Rachitele, northwestern Romania on 6 Sept. 1966. After graduating in law from Babeş-Bolyai University in Cluj-Napoca in 1991, he taught history in a secondary school and later at the university, where he undertook further study in political science. During the mid- to late-1990s Boc combined teaching and legal practice in Cluj-Napoca and as a visiting scholar to the Universities of Virginia and Michigan in the USA and the Université Libre de Bruxelles, Belgium.

Boc was elected to parliament for the centre-right Democratic Party (PD) in the Nov. 2000 general election. Within three years he was party leader and successfully stood as the PD candidate for the mayoralty of Cluj-Napoca. He oversaw rapid economic growth in the city, winning praise from local and foreign investors before securing re-election in 2008 with 76% of the vote.

A breakdown in relations between President Băsescu and Prime Minister Popescu-Tăriceanu precipitated the collapse of the ruling Justice and Truth Alliance (forged between the PD and the National Liberal Party/PNL) in Jan. 2007. The prime minister formed a minority government consisting of the PNL and the Hungarian Democratic Federation of Romania. Boc remained at the helm of the PD and in Dec. 2007 orchestrated a merger with the Liberal Democratic Party, headed by former prime minister, Teodor Stolojan, to form the Democratic Liberal Party (PD-L). Boc led the new centre-right party to a narrow victory in the general election of 30 Nov. 2008.

Băsescu initially nominated Stolojan for the premiership but when Stolojan rejected the post, Boc was offered it. He was sworn in on 22 Dec. 2008, heading a grand coalition of the PD-L and the Social Democratic Party (PSD) of Mircea Geoană. Under the coalition agreement Geoană became leader of the Senate, parliament's upper house.

Career in office
Boc had to confront a steep decline in Romania's economic fortunes amid the global economic slowdown. Priorities included tackling spiralling government and household debt, rising unemployment and a fast-devaluing currency. Tensions within the coalition soon emerged, with the PSD interior minister, Liviu Dragnea, resigning after 12 days. Sweeping cuts to public spending, including a U-turn on recently-promised public-sector wage increases, proved unpopular but Boc was forced to announce further austerity measures as economic conditions continued to worsen and Romania had to accept IMF support in March 2009.

Bad feeling between the coalition partners came to a head in Sept. 2009 when Boc sacked interior minister Dan Nica of the PSD after Nica accused the PD-L of plotting to rig the voting in the forthcoming presidential election. Nica's dismissal prompted the remaining PSD cabinet ministers to resign in protest and a subsequent parliamentary vote of no-confidence passed by 254 votes to 176 on 13 Oct. resulted in the collapse of Boc's government. Subsequent nominees for prime minister-designate failed to gain parliamentary approval until Dec. when, following his re-election, President Băsescu's reappointed Boc to head a new centrist coalition. The new government was endorsed by parliament and quickly announced an austerity budget for 2010, promising tough measures to meet conditions attached to IMF aid.

DEFENCE

Compulsory national military service was abolished in 2006.

In 2006 military expenditure totalled US$2,324m. (US$104 per capita), representing 1·9% of GDP.

Army

Strength (2007) 42,200. There is a joint reserve of 45,000. The Ministry of the Interior operates a paramilitary Border Guard (22,900 strong in 2007) and a Gendarmerie (around 57,000).

Navy

The fleet includes three frigates and four corvettes. There is also a naval infantry force.

The headquarters of the Navy is at Mangalia with the main base at Constanţa. The Danube flotilla is based at Brăila. Personnel in 2007 totalled 8,067.

Air Force

The Air Force numbered some 10,500 in 2007, with 74 combat capable aircraft (MiG-21s).

INTERNATIONAL RELATIONS

Romania is a member of the UN, World Bank, IMF and several other UN specialized agencies, WTO, EU, Council of Europe, OSCE, Central European Initiative, BSEC, Danube Commission, BIS, IOM, International Organization of the Francophonie, NATO, Antarctic Treaty and is an associate partner of WEU. At the European Union's Helsinki Summit in Dec. 1999 Romania, along with five other countries, was invited to begin full negotiations for membership in Feb. 2000. Romania joined the EU on 1 Jan. 2007. Romania became a member of NATO on 29 March 2004.

ECONOMY

Agriculture accounted for 10·5% of GDP in 2006, industry 37·9% and services 51·5%. The percentage of Romania's GDP coming from agriculture is the highest of any EU member country.

Overview

Having signed an accession treaty in 2005, Romania joined the EU in Jan. 2007, with the aim of adopting the euro by 2014. Economic growth averaged 6·2% annually in the period 2002–06. The economy had been on the brink of collapse in the late 1980s as the Soviet Union disintegrated. When Romania made the transition to a market economy in 1990 it attempted to create macroeconomic stability without structural reform. Negative economic growth followed and poverty doubled. In 2000 the state implemented structural reforms including tight monetary and fiscal policies, which brought macroeconomic stability and a fall in inflation.

The inflation increase in 2007 was caused by currency depreciation, a surge in the cost of energy and a nationwide drought affecting food prices. Previous strong growth has made little impact on levels of poverty while corruption and an overweight bureaucracy hinder business activity. The appreciation of the lei, Romania's currency, caused a trade imbalance in 2004. Income per capita was around 44% of the EU average in 2008. FDI was estimated to amount to about 5–6% of GDP in the 2000s.

After seven years of strong growth, economic activity declined in the last quarter of 2008 and continued to fall in 2009, with real GDP contracting by 7·6% in the first half of the year. In March 2009 Romania secured a €20bn. (US$27bn.) loan from the IMF, European Union and other lenders to help stabilize the economy in the wake of the financial crisis.

In Nov. 2009 the IMF predicted that stronger external demand would lead to growth of 1·3% in 2010 but further public sector and governance reforms are needed to reduce economic vulnerability.

Currency

The monetary unit has since 1 July 2005 been the *new leu*, pl. *new lei* (RON) notionally of 100 *bani*, which replaced the *leu* (ROL) at a rate of one new leu = 10,000 lei. Foreign exchange reserves were US$41,571m. and gold reserves 3·34m. troy oz in Sept. 2009. Inflation rates (based on IMF statistics):

1999	2000	2001	2002	2003	2004	2005	2006	2007	2008
45·8%	45·7%	34·5%	22·5%	15·3%	11·9%	9·0%	6·6%	4·8%	7·8%

Total money supply was 64,201m. new lei in Aug. 2009.

Budget

Central government revenue and expenditure (in 1m. new lei) for calendar years:

	2003	2004	2005
Revenue	49,324	61,301	72,243
Expenditure	46,448	57,371	69,238

VAT is 19% (reduced rate, 9%).

Performance

Real GDP growth rates (based on IMF statistics):

1999	2000	2001	2002	2003	2004	2005	2006	2007	2008
−1·2%	2·9%	5·6%	5·0%	5·3%	8·5%	4·1%	7·9%	6·2%	7·1%

Total GDP in 2008 was US$200·1bn.

Banking and Finance

The National Bank of Romania (founded 1880; nationalized 1946) is the central bank and bank of issue under the Minister of Finance. Its *Governor* is Dr Mugur Isărescu. In 2002 there were 31 banks, plus eight branches of foreign banks. Only one bank remains state-owned. The largest bank is Romanian Commercial Bank (Banca Comercială Română), with a market share of 20% and assets in 2008 of US$24·7bn.; the government sold a 61·9% stake to Austria's Erste Bank AG in Dec. 2005. The size of the government's share in the banking sector fell from over 80% in the mid-1990s to just over 40% in 2002.

A stock exchange reopened in Bucharest in 1995.

ENERGY AND NATURAL RESOURCES

Environment

Romania's carbon dioxide emissions from the consumption and flaring of fossil fuels were the equivalent of 4·6 tonnes per capita in 2008.

Electricity

In 2004 installed capacity was approximately 21·9m. kW; output in 2004 was 56·50bn. kWh (29% hydro-electric). Consumption per capita in 2004 was 2,548 kWh. A nuclear power plant at Cernavodă began working in 1996. A second reactor became operational there in 2007.

Oil and Gas

Oil production in 2008 was 4·7m. tonnes, but with annual consumption of more than twice as much a large amount has to be imported. There were 0·5bn. bbls of proven oil reserves in 2008. Romania was the first country to start oil exploration, and in the late 1850s was the world's leading oil producer, with an output of 200 tonnes a year. Natural gas production in 2008 totalled 11·5bn. cu. metres with 630bn. cu. metres in proven reserves.

The oil company Petrom, Romania's largest company, was privatized in 2004 when the government sold a 51% stake to the Austrian oil and gas group ÖMV.

Minerals

The principal minerals are oil and natural gas, salt, lignite, iron and copper ores, bauxite, chromium, manganese and uranium. Output, 2005 (in 1,000 tonnes): lignite, 31,070; salt, 2,420; iron ore, 265; zinc, 14.

Agriculture

Romania has the biggest agricultural area in eastern Europe after Poland. In 2002, 13·7% of the economically active population were engaged in agriculture. There were 13·94m. ha. of agricultural land in 2002 including 8·96m. ha. of arable land and 4·63m. ha. of permanent pasture. There were 3,081,000 ha. of irrigated land in 2001. There were 164,221 tractors and 27,051 harvester-threshers in 2001.

Production (2003, in 1,000 tonnes): maize, 9,577; potatoes, 3,947; wheat, 2,479; sunflower seeds, 1,506; grapes, 1,078; cabbage, 1,019; melons and watermelons, 1,000; tomatoes, 819; sugar beets, 764; wine, 546; barley, 541.

Livestock, 2002 (in 1,000): pigs, 8,229; sheep, 7,221; cattle, 2,865; horses, 909; goats, 737; poultry, 82,000.

A law of Feb. 1991 provided for the restitution of collectivized land to its former owners or their heirs up to a limit of 10 ha. Land could be resold, but there was a limit of 100 ha. on total holdings. In 2000 a law was passed allowing the restitution of state farm land for the first time (up to 50 ha. of farmland and 10 ha. of forest land per family).

Forestry

Total forest area was 6·37m. ha. in 2005 (27·7% of the land area). Timber production in 2007 was 15·34m. cu. metres.

Fisheries

The catch in 2005 totalled 6,068 tonnes (216,938 tonnes in 1988), of which 4,042 tonnes were from inland waters.

INDUSTRY

In 2001 industry accounted for 37·0% of GDP. Industrial output grew by 7·5% in 2001.

Output of main products (in 1,000 tonnes): cement (2001), 5,668; crude steel (2002), 5,500; distillate fuel oil (2004), 4,170; rolled steel (2000), 3,685; petrol (2004), 3,419; pig iron (2002), 2,500; fertilizers (2000), 1,931; lime (2001), 1,790; wheat flour (2001), 1,597; residual fuel oil (2004), 1,559; ammonia (2001), 1,155; steel tubes (2001), 665; caustic soda (2001), 661; soda ash (2001), 451; paper and paperboard (2002), 370.

Labour

The labour force in 2006 totalled 10·04m.; the employed population was 9·31m. In the civilian labour force 29·7% worked in agriculture and 26·7% in manufacturing and construction. In 2006, 46% of the employed workforce were women. The standard retirement age is 65 years for men and 60 for women. A minimum monthly wage was set in 1993; it is 600 new lei for full-time adult employees from 1 Jan. 2009. The average monthly wage was 762 new lei in 2005. Unemployment was 7·3% in 2006 (7·2% in 2005).

Trade Unions

In 2002 the National Confederation of Free Trade Unions-Fratia had 44 professional federations, 41 regional branches and 800,000 members; the other major confederations were the National Trade Union Bloc (375,000), Democratic Trade Union Confederation of Romania (345,000), Alfa Cartel (325,000 members) and Meridien (170,000).

INTERNATIONAL TRADE

Foreign debt was US$38,694m. in 2005.

Imports and Exports

Imports in 2007 were valued at US$69,946m. (US$24,003m. in 2003) and exports US$40,247m. (US$17,618m. in 2003). Principal imports are mineral fuels, machinery and transport equipment, and textiles; main export commodities are textiles, mineral products and chemicals.

Romania's main import sources in 2007 were: Germany (17·2%); Italy (12·8%); Hungary (6·9%); Russia (6·3%); France (6·3%). In 2007 Romania's main export markets were: Italy (17·2%); Germany (17·0%); France (7·7%); Turkey (7·0%).

COMMUNICATIONS

Roads

There were 198,817 km of roads in 2004, including 228 km of motorways, 14,809 km of highways, main and national roads and 36,010 km of secondary roads. Passenger cars in 2005 numbered 3,363,800 (156 per 1,000 inhabitants). In 2007 there were 2,712 fatalities as a result of road accidents.

Rail

Length of standard-gauge route in 2005 was 10,882 km, of which 3,929 km were electrified; there were 425 km of narrow-gauge lines and 57 km of 1,524 mm gauge. Freight carried in 2005, 55·3m. tonnes; passengers, 98·6m. There is a metro (62·4 km) and tram/light rail network (338 km) in Bucharest, and tramways in 13 other cities.

Civil Aviation

Tarom (*Transporturi Aeriene Române*) is the 95·0% state-owned airline. In 2002 it provided domestic services and international flights to Amman, Amsterdam, Ancona, Athens, Beijing, Beirut, Berlin, Bologna, Brussels, Budapest, Cairo, Chişinău, Copenhagen, Damascus, Dubai, Düsseldorf, Frankfurt, İstanbul, Larnaca, London, Luxembourg, Madrid, Milan, Moscow, Munich, New York, Paris, Prague, Rome, Sofia, Stuttgart, Tel Aviv, Thessaloniki, Treviso, Verona, Vienna, Warsaw and Zürich. Other Romanian airlines which operated international flights in 2007 were Blue Air, Carpatair, Chris Air, Ion Ţiriac Air, Jet Tran Air and Romavia. In 2003 scheduled airline traffic of Romanian-based carriers flew 26m. km, carrying 1,255,000 passengers (1,034,000 on international flights).

Bucharest's airports are at Baneasa (mainly domestic flights) and Otopeni (international flights). Constanţa, Cluj-Napoca, Oradea, Arad, Sibiu and Timişoara also have some international flights. Otopeni handled 1,981,508 passengers in 2001 and 11,410 tonnes of freight; Timişoara handled 161,000 passengers in 2001 and Baneasa 74,000.

Shipping

In 2001 the merchant marine comprised 163 vessels totalling 1·45m. DWT. The total GRT was 403,974, including oil tankers and container ships, in 2000. In 2001 vessels totalling 12,646,000 NRT entered ports and vessels totalling 13,817,000 NRT cleared. The main ports are Constanţa and Constanţa South Agigea on the Black Sea and Galaţi, Brăila and Tulcea on the Danube. In 2001 sea-going transport carried 0·38m. tonnes of freight. In 2001 the length of navigable inland waterways was 1,779 km including: Danube River, 1,075 km; Black Sea Canal, 64 km; Poarta Albă–Midia Năvodari Canal, 28 km. The Romanian inland waterway fleet comprised 169 tugs and pushers and 1,695 dumb and pushed vessels with a carrying capacity of 2·23m. tonnes. The freight carried by Romanian vessels was 383,700 tonnes. The traffic of goods in the Romanian inland ports amounted to 18·7m. tonnes.

Telecommunications

In 2008 there were 5,036,000 main (fixed) telephone lines. In the same year active mobile phone subscribers numbered 24,467,000 (1,145·4 per 1,000 persons). The telecommunications sector was fully liberalized on 1 Jan. 2003, ending the monopoly of the Greek-controlled operator Romtelecom. OTE, the major shareholder, increased its stake in Romtelecom to 54% in Jan. 2003, with the government retaining 46% of shares. There were 3·2m. PCs in use in 2006 and 6·2m. internet users in 2008.

Postal Services

There were 6,840 post offices in 2003.

SOCIAL INSTITUTIONS

Justice

The legal system is based on the Napoleonic code and the judiciary is constitutionally independent. The High Court of Cassation and Justice is the highest judicial authority, with its judges appointed by the president after consultation with the Superior Council of the Magistracy (an elected professional body). There is also a Constitutional Court.

Day-to-day hearings are administered through a system of local courts and 40 county courts (and the Bucharest Municipal Court), whose judgements may be challenged in any one of 15 courts of appeal. In 2006 there were 3,799 judges.

As a condition of EU accession and World Bank financing, Romania has been subject to a Judicial Reform Project aimed at increasing the efficiency of the court system, improving transparency and reducing corruption. This has included the implementation of four revised codes (the criminal code, civil code, criminal procedures code and civil procedures code).

The death penalty was abolished in Jan. 1990 and is forbidden by the 1991 constitution. The population in penal institutions in Sept. 2006 was 35,429 (164 per 100,000 of national population).

Education

Education is free and compulsory from the age of six. There is compulsory school attendance for ten years. Primary education comprises four years of study, secondary education comprises lower secondary education (organized in two cycles: grades 5th–8th in elementary schools and grades 9th–10th in high schools or vocational schools) and upper secondary education includes further education in high schools. Further secondary education is also available at *lycées*, professional schools or advanced technical schools.

In 2007 there were 648,862 children and 36,555 teaching staff in pre-primary schools; 917,829 pupils and 55,487 teaching staff in primary schools; and 1,954,077 pupils and 153,805 teaching staff in secondary schools. In 2002–03 primary and secondary education in Hungarian was given to 106,515 pupils, in German to 10,019 pupils and in other national minority languages to 1,536 pupils.

In 2007 there were 928,175 students in tertiary education and 30,583 academic staff. In 2002–03 there were 125 higher education institutions with 742 faculties, 30,000 teaching staff and 596,297 students (545,405 for long-term studies and 50,892 for short-term studies). The distribution of pupils and subjects studied was as follows: pedagogy, 30·3%; economics, 26·5%; technical subjects, 25·6%; law, 10·6%; medicine and pharmacy, 5·4%; arts, 1·5%.

Adult literacy rate in 2003 was 97·3% (male 98·4%; female 96·3%).

In 2005 public expenditure on education came to 3·6% of GNI and 14·3% of total government spending.

Health

In 2006 there were 419 public hospitals with 141,225 beds; there were 45,815 physicians and 4,360 dentists in the public sector in 2006.

Welfare

In Dec. 2004 pensioners comprised 3,050,500 old age and retirement, 1,441,800 retired farmers, 798,200 disability, 639,500 survivor allowance and 418,000 social assistance. These drew average monthly pensions ranging from 792,698 lei to 3,504,205 lei. The social security spending in 2002 was 10·4% of GDP.

RELIGION

The government officially recognizes 17 religions (which receive various forms of state support); the predominant one is the Romanian Orthodox Church. It is autocephalous, but retains dogmatic unity with the Eastern Orthodox Church. Its *Patriarch* is Daniel (enthroned 30 Sept. 2007). It is made up of five metropolitan sees, with 10 archdioceses and 13 dioceses, 158 deaneries and 10,987 parishes.

Religious affiliation at the 2002 census included: Romanian Orthodox, 18,817,975 (about 87% of the population); Roman Catholic, 1,026,429; Protestant Reformed Church, 701,077; Pentecostal, 324,462; Greek Catholics or Uniates, 191,556; Baptist, 126,639; Seventh Day Adventist, 93,670; Muslim, 67,257.

CULTURE

World Heritage Sites

Romania has seven sites on the UNESCO World Heritage List: the Danube Delta (inscribed on the list in 1991); the Villages with Fortified Churches in Transylvania (1993 and 1999); the Monastery of Horezu (1993); the Churches of Moldavia (1993); the Historic Centre of Sighişoara (1999); the Dacian Fortresses of the Orastie Mountains (1999); and the Wooden Churches of Maramureş (1999).

Broadcasting

The National Audiovisual Council, established in 1992, is responsible for granting broadcasting licences to private stations. By 2003 it had granted 3,318 cable licences, 260 television broadcasting licences, 422 radio broadcasting licences, 62 licences for satellite television stations and 15 licences for satellite radio stations. The public radio and TV stations have broadcasts in Romanian, and in Hungarian and German as well as other minority languages in Romania. TVR, the state broadcaster, operates two national TV networks and a pan-European satellite channel. The two major private stations are Pro TV and Antena 1. Cable TV is widely available. State-owned Radio Romania operates national and regional networks and Radio Romania International. Over 100 private stations have been launched since 1990. TV-equipped households (colour by PAL), 2006, 6·6m.

Press

In 2005 there were 48 daily papers with a combined circulation of 1,135,000. In 1999 there were 2,200 periodicals, including 200 periodicals in minority languages. 8,000 book titles were published in 1999.

Tourism

In 2005 there were 5,839,000 non-resident visitors, spending US$1,310m.

DIPLOMATIC REPRESENTATIVES

Of Romania in the United Kingdom (Arundel House, 4 Palace Green, London, W8 4QD)
Ambassador: Dr Ion Jinga.

Of the United Kingdom in Romania (24 Strada Jules Michelet, 010463 Bucharest)
Ambassador: Robin Barnett, CMG.

Of Romania in the USA (1607 23rd St., NW, Washington, D.C., 20008)
Ambassador: Adrian Cosmin Vieriţa.

Of the USA in Romania (7–9 Strada Tudor Arghezi, Bucharest)
Ambassador: Mark H. Gitenstein.

Of Romania to the United Nations
Ambassador: Simona-Mirela Miculescu.

Of Romania to the European Union
Permanent Representative: Mihnea Motoc.

FURTHER READING

Comisia Nationala pentru Statistica. *Anuarul Statistic al României/Romanian Statistical Yearbook.* Annual.—*Revista de Statistica.* Monthly

Carey, Henry F., *Romania since 1989: Politics, Economics and Society.* 2004

Gallagher, T., *Romania after Ceauşescu; the Politics of Intolerance.* 1995

Phinnemore, David, (ed.) *The EU and Romania: Accession and Beyond.* 2006

Rady, M., *Romania in Turmoil: a Contemporary History.* 1992

National Statistical Office: Comisia Nationala pentru Statistica, 16 Libertatii Ave., sector 5, Bucharest.
Website: http://www.insse.ro

RUSSIA

Rossiiskaya Federatsiya
(Russian Federation)

Capital: Moscow
Population estimate, 2010: 140·37m.
GDP per capita, 2007: (PPP$) 14,690
HDI/world rank: 0·817/71

KEY HISTORICAL EVENTS

Archaeological evidence points to the influence of Arabic and Turkic cultures prior to the 4th century AD. Avar, Goth, Hun and Magyar invasions punctuated the development of the East Slavs over the next five centuries, while trade with Germanic, Scandinavian and Middle Eastern regions began in the 8th century.

In 882 the Varangian prince Oleg of Novgorod took Kyiv and made it the capital of Kievan Rus, the first unified state of the East Slavs, uniting Finnish and Slavic tribes. During the 10th century, trade was extended between the Baltic and Black Seas, forming Kyiv's main economy. The Varangians, led by Rurik of Jutland, led attacks on Baghdad and Constantinople, subsequently establishing a trade link with the latter.

During the 13th century the area was invaded from the west by Teutonic Knights, Lithuanians and Swedes, and from the south by Mongol and Tatar tribes. In 1223 Genghis Khan's grandson, Batu Khan, conquered Kievan Rus. Despite the ruthless reign of the Mongols, trade flourished during the period and many cities were reinvigorated. The Mongols and Tatars created an ascendency known as the 'Golden Horde' around most of Western Russia and Central Asia and made Itil (near modern Astrakhan) the capital. Its dominance lasted until the 15th century when internal struggles finally forced the break-up of the empire.

Co-operation between Moscow's leader Ivan and the Mongol Öz Beg (ruled 1312–41), in addition to geographical advantages and natural resources, allowed Moscow to develop and prosper. The city was first consolidated under the Muscovite Grand Duke Ivan III (ruled 1462–1505), who adopted the Roman title of tsar and Byzantine ritual after marrying into Byzantine royalty. Ivan annexed the East Slavic regions, as well as Belarus and the Ukraine, conquered Novgorod in 1478 and opened up contacts with Western Europe.

The empire was strengthened and further expanded by his son Vasily III and reformed by Vasily's successor Ivan IV, a sickly and volatile ruler known as Ivan the Terrible (or 'Awesome', *Grozny*) who came to the throne at the age of 16 in 1547. Ivan's divisive and suppressive administration, *oprichnina*, led a reign of terror from 1566–72 in which thousands were executed (although it is believed that initially the Russian nobles, or boyars, had strong control over the throne and its direction, including local government reforms, a new law code and restrictions of hereditary rights). Ivan bolstered the military and led campaigns against the khanates of Kazan (1552), Astrakhan (1556) and the Crimea, extending Russia's territory towards Siberia and down to the Caspian Sea. But the costly war with Livonia (1558–82) drained Russia's resources. Ivan murdered his son in 1581 leaving a hereditary gap and a struggle for succession.

Russia was ruled nominally by Ivan's mentally subnormal brother Fyodor I—in actuality by Fyodor's brother-in-law Boris

Godunov, who succeeded Fyodor in 1598. But in 1601 False Dmitri claimed to be Ivan IV's son (Dmitri had died in 1591) and challenged Boris for the throne. With the backing of the boyars, the Cossacks and the Polish nobility, Dmitri succeeded Boris as tsar on the latter's death in 1605. There followed a chaotic period of instability as differing sides fought for control of the realm. The following year Dmitri was assassinated and the boyars crowned the rebel leader Vasily Shuysky in return for privileges. But soon a subgroup of boyars led by the Romanovs gave support to a second False Dmitri in 1608, establishing a shadow government just outside Moscow. Shuysky turned to Sweden for help, bargaining away territory and triggering Poland's invasion of Muscovy and the siege of Smolensk (1609). Both governments collapsed and a coalition government was formed. A peace treaty signed with Sweden in 1617 lost Russia Novgorod in exchange for Baltic control, while an armistice with Poland began the following year.

Romanovs

With the Polish occupiers ejected from Moscow, Mikhail Fyodorovich Romanov, the first of a dynasty that would rule until 1917, became tsar of a country ruined by war and with regions occupied by Swedish, Polish or rebel forces. But by avoiding involvement in the Thirty Years' War, in which Sweden and Poland were embroiled, he managed to restore some stability and to strengthen Russia's holdings in the southern regions. His son Aleksey inherited the throne as a child. Unpopular measures implemented by Aleksey's adviser, Boris Ivanovich Morozov, including a crippling salt tax, led to a riot in 1648 and rebellion in Novgorod and Pskov. Eastern Ukraine was annexed, while the support of a Cossack rebellion against Polish rule in the Ukraine degenerated into a costly war with Sweden and Poland over Ukrainian, Baltic and Belorussian territory. Russia consequently lost the Baltic coast to Sweden in 1661 and later Belarus and parts of the Ukraine to Poland. Sophia succeeded Aleksey to the disputed throne in 1682, followed seven years later by her half brother Peter the Great.

The reign of Peter I (1689–1725) signalled a new era for Russia that broke so far with Muscovy tradition as to be seen as the birth of modern Russia. The empire was expanded and strengthened and there was increased trade with Western Europe. His modest upbringing and travels to the West gave Peter a novel pro-European stance. The capital was transferred from Moscow to the newly built St Petersburg (1712), as part of a Europeanization programme. Peter introduced radical structural changes to the Russian body politic, converting it into the Western European mould. The tsardom of Muscovy became the Empire of All Russias and Peter became head of state as opposed to ruling patriarch. Administrative reforms divided Russia into eight main provinces, put the church under state control and introduced compulsory secular education for the nobility, although the rights of the peasantry were abolished and they were forced into serfdom. Peter expanded industry, created the navy, introduced army conscription and strengthened the southern border against the Crimean Tatars. He formed an alliance with Denmark, Poland and Saxony against Sweden, resulting in the Great Northern War (1700–21), which ended with Russia claiming Livonia in the Treaty of Nystad (1721). The expanded empire made Russia the leading Baltic power.

Catherine the Great

Despite Peter's rejection of hereditary rule in favour of appointing a successor, his choice was never named before his sudden death. The rest of the 18th century was marked by disputed succession. After Peter's death, his widow Catherine I was declared empress, though Peter's collaborator Prince Menshikov ruled in her name. A supreme privy council was established to distribute power; Peter's grandson, Peter II, ruled briefly before dying of smallpox. He was succeeded by Peter I's niece, Anna, the duchess of Courland (1730), then by her niece Anna Leopoldovna, before Peter I's daughter, Elizabeth, came to power in 1741 in a bloodless coup. During her 21-year reign, her father's reforms were consolidated and Western culture and literature flourished. She founded the University of Moscow and established the St Petersburg Academy of Arts. At the end of her reign Russia was involved in the Seven Years' War, occupying Berlin for a short time before Elizabeth's death in 1762. Russia's subsequent withdrawal saved Frederick the Great's Prussia from destruction.

Elizabeth's nephew, Peter III, proved an unpopular ruler. Childless, his politically ambitious wife, Catherine the Great, plotted to depose him, claiming the throne for herself soon after. Influenced by the Enlightenment, she attempted to implement legislative, educative and administrative reforms. But many of these, as well as the emancipation of the serfs, were blocked by the nobility. The imposed Russification of the Ukrainian, Polish and Baltic regions proved unpopular, while civil unrest led to the Pugachev Revolt (1773–75), in which peasants, Cossacks and workers rebelled against the aristocracy. Catherine's foreign policy was an aggressive expansion plan to the south and east to make Russia the leading European power at the expense of the Turks and Tatars. She forged a path through to the Mediterranean Sea to maximize maritime trade routes and developed close relations with Prussia and Austria with whom Poland was shared. But despite two wars with Turkey she failed to take Constantinople, as much an emotional as a political prize.

After Catherine's death in 1796, her son Paul's tyrannical rule led to his murder in 1801. His son Alexander I adopted more liberal policies in administration, science and education. War with France in 1805 led to a crushing defeat at Austerlitz, but when Napoleon invaded Russia in 1812 his army fell victim to the Russian winter. Alexander's death in 1825 provoked instability and uprisings which were quashed by military force. Russia was defeated by Britain, France and Turkey in the Crimean War (1853–56). Alexander II (ruled 1855–81), who followed Nicholas I (ruled 1825–55), implemented reforms, the most important of which was the partial emancipation of the serfs in 1861. Major judicial reform followed three years later and universal military service in 1874. But towards the end of his reign Alexander's increasingly conservative measures exacerbated the revolutionary mood of socialist-influenced university students and the peasantry. He was assassinated in 1881 and was succeeded by Alexander III (1881–94). Labour reforms introduced by Alexander III were harsh and restrictive and the peasants' lot failed to improve. The government's neglect of agricultural policy resulted in crop failure and widespread famine in 1891.

The Russian empire had expanded to the far reaches of Asia, to Afghanistan and into Central Europe. By the end of Alexander III's reign, only half the population spoke Russian or were members of the Orthodox Church.

Revolution

Nicholas II's reign (1894–1917) marked the end of Tsarist Russia. Like his father, he did little to improve social conditions for the masses, concentrating instead on military power. Industrial growth produced an unskilled urban working class whose living conditions fuelled revolutionary feeling. Socialism and Liberalism were also taking hold of the educated middle classes—doctors, teachers and engineers—as well as disaffected civil servants. In 1904 Nicholas embarked on and lost an unpopular war with Japan. The middle classes campaigned for a legislative assembly. In Jan. 1905 the priest, Georgy Gapon, led a protest of factory workers to St Petersburg's Winter Palace. Tsarist troops opened fire on the crowds killing over 100 people. Public outrage to 'Bloody Sunday' soon spread throughout the country. A general strike, paralysing most of Russia, led to violence between monarchists and insurgents well into 1907, while factions in the armed forces rebelled. Yielding to the pressure of the 1905 revolution, the tsar permitted the establishment of the first *Duma* (parliament), which convened in St Petersburg in 1906. But it lasted only 70 days. Violence continued into 1907.

In 1912 the two strands of the Social Democratic Workers' Party—the Bolsheviks (or majority) led by Vladimir Ilyich Ulianov (Lenin), and the Mensheviks (or minority)—split, the Bolsheviks pursuing revolution, the Mensheviks evolutionary change. The outbreak of the First World War in 1914 temporarily unified Russians in the war effort. The tsar took command of the armed forces in 1915, leaving an authoritarian vacuum that allowed the tsarina and the influential adviser Grigori Rasputin to implement various unpopular ministerial changes. Rasputin was assassinated by disgruntled nobles in 1916. Depleting military resources and social unrest caused by hardship forced the end of the tsar's reign. A succession of anti-tsar demonstrations culminated in a mass protest in St Petersburg. Soldiers deserted, allying themselves with the workers, a pattern repeated throughout the country. A provisional government comprising Menshevik and Bolshevik elements was established and Tsar Nicholas abdicated on 2 March 1917. The Royal Family was executed in July 1918.

Tension between moderate Mensheviks and radical Bolsheviks intensified and in Oct. 1917 the Bolsheviks led by Lenin, newly returned from exile, seized control. The new government headed by Lenin, the Council of People's Commissars, created the Soviet constitution the following year. Russia was declared the Soviet Republic of Workers, Soldiers and Peasants and the capital was moved back to Moscow. Russia eventually withdrew from the First World War in 1918 but its forced acceptance of the unfavourable Brest-Litovsk treaty led many to abandon the government. Between 1918–21 a civil war raged between the Bolshevik Red Army, led by Lenin's ally Leon Trotsky, and the White Army, formed by former imperial officers, Cossacks, anti-communists and anarchists. The government imposed 'war communism'—forced labour and expropriation of business and food supplies—to support its cause, and eventually overcame the White Army. Lenin instituted the New Economic Policy (NEP) in 1921 to replace War Communism, reintroducing a monetary system and private ownership of small-scale industry and agriculture. In 1922 the Union of Soviet Socialist Republics was established comprising Russia, the Ukraine, Belarus and Transcaucasia. The Turkmen and Uzbek republics were added two years later, and the Tadzhik republic joined in 1929.

Stalin

On Lenin's death in 1924, Joseph Stalin (Ioseb Dzhugashvili) became general secretary of the Communist Party. Stalin rejected the 'state capitalism' of the NEP, which had failed to provide enough food for the urban workforce. From 1928 Stalin pursued a programme of industrialization and from 1933 agricultural collectivization, which cost the lives of 10m. peasants through famine or persecution. Constructing a personality cult for Lenin and himself, Stalin reasserted his absolute authority in massive purges; in 1934 and 1937 the NKVD (political police) eliminated millions of political dissidents.

Despite a non-aggression pact signed with Germany in Aug. 1939, the USSR was forced into the Second World War (termed the Great Patriotic War) in 1941 when the Nazi's Plan Barbarossa targeted Kyiv, Moscow and Leningrad for invasion. Up to 20m. Soviet lives were lost, almost 1m. in the battle of Stalingrad alone (1942–43). Expansion before and during the war created 15 aligned republics. Transcaucasia was divided into Armenia, Georgia and Azerbaijan, Kazakh and Kirghiz Soviet Socialist Republics were formed, and, along with Latvia, Lithuania, Estonia and Moldavia, were incorporated into the USSR. Following the war, Stalin managed to gain Western acceptance of a Soviet sphere of influence in Eastern Europe. The Baltic States and large tracts of land from neighbouring countries were annexed, while puppet regimes established Poland, Czechoslovakia, East Germany, Hungary, Bulgaria and Romania as satellites of Moscow.

The blockade of West Berlin (1948–49) and the Soviet detonation of an atomic bomb in Aug. 1949 were major factors in the escalation of the Cold War, waged indirectly in the Korean War (1950–53). On Stalin's death, Nikita Khrushchev reversed many of Stalin's policies and condemned his predecessor. In reaction to the famine in his native Ukraine, he developed the vast wheatfields in Kazakhstan. Relaxing control in the Eastern Bloc allowed for some liberalization although the Hungarian Uprising and the Poznań Riots in Poland (both 1956) were brutally suppressed and the Berlin Wall built in 1961. Relations with the Soviet Union's great ideological ally, China, collapsed over differences in interpretation of Marxist doctrine and Chinese opposition to Khrushchev's attempts at détente with the West (which came to be known as 'peaceful co-existence'). The Cuban Missile Crisis of 1962 intensified hostilities with the West and led the world to the brink of nuclear war. Khrushchev's perceived failure in the crisis, coupled with food shortages, led to widespread discontent. He was forced out of office in a 1964 coup led by Leonid Brezhnev, who ruled until 1982.

Soviet Reform

By the 1970s, Russia's international status had reached its zenith. Along with the USA, it was perceived as one of two global superpowers, despite relative economic stagnation. But Brezhnev kept a tight grip on the Eastern Bloc, introducing his 'Brezhnev Doctrine' which permitted the Soviet Union to intervene in the Eastern Bloc countries if Communist rule was ever threatened. In Aug. 1968 the USSR invaded Czechoslovakia to suppress an increasingly liberal regime. Relations with the West were further strained when the Soviets invaded Afghanistan in 1979. By the end of his tenure Brezhnev's failing health mirrored the country's economic decline. The domestic price of Brezhnev's obsessive pursuit of prominence in the space race was the failure of the agricultural and consumer-goods sectors and the decline of living standards. From his death in 1982, the country was led by his aides Yuri Andropov, a short-lived reformer, then Konstantin Chernenko.

When the latter died in 1985, Mikhail Gorbachev became general secretary of the Communist Party. He launched *perestroika*, a policy of economic and structural reform. *Glasnost* ('openness') extended civil liberties, including freedom of the press, and led to official rejection of Stalinist-style totalitarianism. The political system was overhauled, with electoral processes made more democratic and some free-market principles introduced. Gorbachev sought warmer relations with both Communist and Western governments and withdrew troops from Afghanistan in 1989. In a rejection of the 'Brezhnev Doctrine', throughout 1989 and 1990 Gorbachev refused to intervene as one Communist regime after another fell in the Eastern Bloc. Within the USSR, the republics demanded independence. Initially rejected, ethnic tensions arose between and within the republics, with heavy fighting in the Caucasus. Suppressed for so long, the newfound freedom also brought chaos and Gorbachev was blamed. Nonetheless, he won the first USSR presidential elections. Opposition parties were legalized soon after, although he was reluctant to open up the economy to privatization. An attempted coup in Aug. 1991 led to Gorbachev's house arrest for three days and though the coup failed, largely owing to Russian president Boris Yeltsin's intervention (elected June 1991), Gorbachev's leadership was existing on borrowed time. In quick succession Gorbachev resigned his party membership, dismantled the central committee and took KGB and military control away from the Communists. On Christmas Day 1991 Gorbachev resigned as Soviet president and the Soviet Union was dissolved.

Yeltsin

A period of confrontation in 1992–93 between President Yeltsin and parliament climaxed when thousands of armed anti-Yeltsin demonstrators assembled on 3 Oct. 1993 and were urged to seize the Kremlin and television centre. On 4 Oct. troops took the parliament building by storm after a 10-hour assault in which 140 people died. Vice-President Rutskoi and Speaker Khasbulatov were arrested.

Boris Yeltsin was re-elected president in 1996. Many took this as a signal of confidence in the new, democratic Russia. But the reality was a state in which democratic institutions were weakened to the point of impotence by racketeering and bureaucratic dead-weight. Russia defaulted on its debt, the rouble halved in value, imports fell by 45% and oil revenues slumped. On 17 Aug. 1998 the government freed the rouble, in effect devaluing it, imposed currency controls and froze the domestic debt market.

In Aug. 1999 Boris Yeltsin appointed as prime minister Vladimir Putin, a former KGB colonel and director of the KGB's successor organization, the FSB. On 31 Dec. 1999, Yeltsin resigned the presidency, nominating Putin as his interim successor, a job he retained after a clear-cut victory in the presidential election of March 2000. Under Putin, Russia continued the war with separatist Chechnya that began in Dec. 1994. One of his primary aims has been to reduce the power of the business oligarchs and to fight corruption. Tax cuts have been introduced and in 2000 a programme of regional reform divided Russia's 89 regions into seven new districts run by Kremlin representatives.

Following the attacks on the USA in Sept. 2001, Putin made clear his support for the war on terrorism. In Oct. 2002 a group of Chechen rebels took control of a Moscow theatre and held hostage 800 people for three days before Russian troops stormed the building. An anaesthetic gas, used to combat the rebels, killed many of the hostages. The rebels had been demanding that Russia end the war in Chechnya. The new relationship with the USA faltered as a result of the war with Iraq, which Russia opposed. Russia's vulnerability to terrorism was highlighted in Sept. 2004 when hostage takers seized a school in Beslan, in the Russian republic of North Ossetia. A three-day standoff ended with more than 350 people killed, nearly half of them children. Chechen rebels claimed responsibility for the siege.

In 2006 Russia temporarily cut off oil and gas links to Ukraine, Georgia and Belarus ostensibly over pricing disputes. As well as incurring the wrath of those governments immediately involved, the knock-on effects to pipeline flows throughout Europe prompted official protests. The future of Chechnya continues to be a thorn in Moscow's side. Relations with Georgia took a downturn in 2006 over Russia's implicit support for the breakaway Georgian region of South Ossetia. They reached a new low in Aug. 2008 when Russian and Georgian troops fought each other for a week following the Georgian government's military attack on separatist forces in the region.

Putin's human and civil rights records have come under increasing international scrutiny. In the aftermath of the Beslan siege, Putin assumed responsibility for nominating regional governors who had previously been directly elected. Restrictions on press freedom have been criticized as has the absence of a credible opposition and an independent judiciary. Particularly controversial was the imprisonment of Mikhail Khordorkovsky, a multibillion dollar businessman and Putin critic who was sentenced to nine years in 2005 amid claims that the prosecution was politically motivated. In 2006 there was widespread concern at Putin's new powers to monitor non-governmental organizations and potentially expel foreign-based groups, some of which Putin accused of being 'led by puppeteers from abroad'.

In March 2008 Dmitry Medvedev won the presidential election, from which Putin was constitutionally barred. Medvedev named Putin his prime minister in May 2008.

TERRITORY AND POPULATION

Russia is bounded in the north by various seas (Barents, Kara, Laptev, East Siberian) which join the Arctic Ocean, and in which is a fringe of islands, some of them large. In the east Russia is separated from the USA (Alaska) by the Bering Strait; the Kamchatka peninsula separates the coastal Bering and Okhotsk Seas. Sakhalin Island, north of Japan, is Russian territory. Russia is bounded in the south by North Korea, China, Mongolia, Kazakhstan, the Caspian Sea, Azerbaijan, Georgia, the Black Sea and Ukraine, and in the west by Belarus, Latvia, Estonia, the Baltic Sea and Finland. Kaliningrad (the former East Prussia) is an exclave on the Baltic Sea between Lithuania and Poland in the west. Russia's area is 17,075,400 sq. km and it has 11 time zones. In 2007 Russia claimed control over 1·2m. sq. km of the Arctic Ocean bed, known to be rich in energy sources. Immediately disputed by the international community, the claim would require validation by the UN Commission on the Limits of the Continental Shelf. The 2002 census population was 145,166,731 (53·5% females); density, 8·6 per sq. km. The estimated population on 1 Jan. 2009 was 141,903,979. Ethnicity in 2002 showed 79·8% were Russians, 3·8% Tatars, 2·0% Ukrainians, 1·1% Bashkir and 1·1% Chuvash. There are also small numbers of Armenians, Avars, Belarusians, Chechens, Germans, Jews, Kazakhs, Mari, Mordovians and Udmurts.

In 2005, 73·0% of the population lived in urban areas.

The UN gives an estimated population for 2010 of 140·37m.

Russia's population has been declining since the break-up of the Soviet Union and will continue to do so in the future. By 2050 its population is projected to be the same as it was in the early 1950s.

The two principal cities are Moscow (Moskva), the capital, with a 2002 census population of 10·13m. and St Petersburg (formerly Leningrad), with 4·16m. Other major cities (with 2002 populations) are: Novosibirsk (1·43m.), Nizhny Novgorod (1·31m.), Ekaterinburg (1·29m.), Samara (1·16m.) and Omsk (1·13m.). In May 2000 President Putin signed a decree dividing Russia into seven federal districts (*okrug*), in the process creating a layer above the various federal subjects (*see* CONSTITUTION AND GOVERNMENT *below*). These, with their administrative centres and 2002 populations in brackets, are: Central (Moscow, 38·00m.), North-Western (St Petersburg, 13·97m.), Southern (Rostov-on-Don, 22·91m.), Volga (Nizhny Novgorod, 31·15m.), Ural (Ekaterinburg, 12·37m.), Siberian (Novosibirsk, 20·06m.) and Far-Eastern (Khaborovsk, 6·69m.). In Jan. 2010 President Medvedev created a new North Caucasus federal district (making eight now in total) by splitting the Southern federal district in two. The 2002 population in the area that constitutes the North Caucasus federal district was 8·93m. Its administrative centre is Pyatigorsk.

The official federal language is Russian, although there are several other officially-recognized languages within individual administrative units.

SOCIAL STATISTICS

2008 births, 1,717,500; deaths, 2,081,000; marriages, 1,178,700; divorces, 703,400. Rates, 2008 (per 1,000 population): birth, 12·1; death, 14·7; marriage, 8·3; divorce, 5·0. At the beginning of the 1970s the death rate had been just 9·4 per 1,000 population. Infant mortality, 2005 (per 1,000 live births), 11. There were 1,582,400 legal abortions in 2006. The annual abortion rate, at approximately 52 per 1,000 women, ranks among the highest in the world. The divorce rate is also among the highest in the world. The most popular age range for marrying in 2004 was 25–34 for males and 18–24 for females. Expectation of life at birth, 2007, was 59·9 years for males and 72·9 years for females. With a difference of 13·0 years, no other country has a life expectancy for females so high compared to that for males. The low life expectancy (down from 64·6 years for males and 74·0 years for females in the USSR as a whole in 1989) and the low birth rate (down from 17·6 per 1,000 population in the USSR in 1989) is causing a demographic crisis. Disease, pollution, poor health care and alcoholism are all contributing to a steady decline in the population. More than 35,000 Russians died of alcohol poisoning in 2005. In 2005, 16%

of Russians were living below the subsistence level (down from 27% in 2001). Annual population growth rate, 2000–05, –0·5%; fertility rate, 2004, 1·3 births per woman. The suicide rate, at 30·1 per 100,000 population in 2006, is one of the highest in the world. Among males it was 53·9 per 100,000 population in 2006.

CLIMATE

Moscow, Jan. -9·4°C, July 18·3°C. Annual rainfall 630 mm. Arkhangelsk, Jan. –15°C, July 13·9°C. Annual rainfall 503 mm. St Petersburg, Jan. –8·3°C, July 17·8°C. Annual rainfall 488 mm. Vladivostok, Jan. –14·4°C, July 18·3°C. Annual rainfall 599 mm.

CONSTITUTION AND GOVERNMENT

The Russian Soviet Federative Socialist Republic (RSFSR) adopted a declaration of republican sovereignty by 544 votes to 271 in June 1990. It became a founding member of the Commonwealth of Independent States (CIS) in Dec. 1991, and adopted the name 'Russian Federation'. A law of Nov. 1991 extended citizenship to all who lived in Russia at the time of its adoption and to those in other Soviet republics who requested it.

According to the 1993 constitution the Russian Federation is a 'democratic federal legally-based state with a republican form of government'. The Federation consists of 83 federal subjects (administrative units), of which 21 are republics, one autonomous region, four autonomous districts, nine territories, 46 regions and two federal cities. The state is secular. Individuals have freedom of movement within or across the boundaries of the Federation; there is freedom of assembly and association, and freedom to engage in any entrepreneurial activity not forbidden by law. The state itself is based upon a separation of powers and upon federal principles, including a Constitutional Court. The most important matters of state are reserved for the federal government, including socio-economic policy, the budget, taxation, energy, foreign affairs and defence. Other matters, including the use of land and water, education and culture, health and social security, are for the joint management of the federal and local governments, which also have the right to legislate within their spheres of competence. A central role is accorded to the *President*, who defines the 'basic directions of domestic and foreign policy' and represents the state internationally. The President is directly elected for a six-year term (since Dec. 2008—previously a four-year term), and for not more than two consecutive terms; he must be at least 35 years old, a Russian citizen, and a resident in Russia for the previous ten years. 2m. signatures are needed to validate a presidential candidate not affiliated to a party represented in the State Duma, no more than 2·5% of which may come from any one region or republic. The President has the right to appoint the prime minister, and (on his nomination) to appoint and dismiss deputy prime ministers and ministers, and may dismiss the government as a whole. In the event of the death or incapacity of the President, the Prime Minister becomes head of state.

Parliament is known as the *Federal Assembly* (Federalnoe Sobranie). The 'representative and legislative organ of the Russian Federation', it consists of two chambers: the *Federation Council* (Sovet Federatsii) and the *State Duma* (Gosudarstvennaya Duma). The Federation Council, or upper house, consists of 178 deputies. The State Duma, or lower house, consists of 450 deputies elected for a four-year term. Starting with the elections in Dec. 2007 all deputies to the State Duma are elected from party lists by proportional representation. There is a 7% threshold for the party-list seats. To qualify for candidacy an individual must be nominated by a registered political party. Incumbent parties are automatically included in the ballot; others must obtain a minimum of 200,000 supporting signatures of which no more than 5% may come from any one region. Alternatively, non-incumbent parties may put forward a deposit of 60m. roubles, which is returned if the party manages to win at least 4% of the popular vote. Parties which gain at least 35 seats may register as a faction, which gives them the right to join the Duma Council and chair committees. Any citizen aged over 21 may be elected to the State Duma, but may not at the same time be a member of the upper house or of other representative bodies. The Federation Council considers all matters that apply to the Federation as a whole, including state boundaries, martial law, and the deployment of Russian forces elsewhere. The Duma approves nominations for Prime Minister, and adopts federal laws (they are also considered by the Federation Council but any objection may be overridden by a two-thirds majority; objections on the part of the President may be overridden by both houses on the same basis). The Duma can reject nominations for Prime Minister but after the third rejection it is automatically dissolved. It is also dissolved if it twice votes a lack of confidence in the government, or if it refuses to express confidence in the government when the matter is raised by the Prime Minister.

A law was approved in June 2001 to reduce the proliferation of political parties (numbering some 200 in 2001). It took effect in July 2003. The new law introduced stricter registration criteria and obliging existing parties to reregister within two years. In order to register, political parties are required to have at least 50,000 members and (since Jan. 2006) more than 45 regional branches with a minimum membership of 500 each. Multiple party membership is banned.

There is a 19-member *Constitutional Court*, whose functions under the 1993 constitution include making decisions on the constitutionality of federal laws, presidential and government decrees, and the constitutions and laws of the subjects of the Federation. It is governed by a Law on the Constitutional Court, adopted in July 1994. Judges are elected for non-renewable 12-year terms.

National Anthem

In Dec. 2000 the Russian parliament, on President Putin's initiative, decided that the tune of the anthem of the former Soviet Union should be reintroduced as the Russian national anthem. Written by Alexander Alexandrov in 1943, the anthem was composed for Stalin. New words were written by Sergei Mikhalkov, who had written the original words for the Soviet anthem in 1943. The new anthem is 'Rossiya—svyashennaya nasha derzhava, Rossiya—lyubimaya nasha strana' ('Russia—our holy country, Russia—our beloved country'). Boris Yeltsin had introduced a new anthem during his presidency—'Patriotic Song', from an opera by Mikhail Glinka and arranged by Andrei Petrov.

GOVERNMENT CHRONOLOGY

General/First Secretaries of the Central Committee of the USSR (1922–91) and Presidents of Russia (1991–)

1922–53	Joseph Stalin
1953–64	Nikita Sergeyevich Khrushchev
1964–82	Leonid Ilyich Brezhnev
1982–84	Yuri Vladimirovich Andropov
1984–85	Konstantin Ustinovich Chernenko
1985–91	Mikhail Sergeyevich Gorbachev
1991–99	Boris Nikolayevich Yeltsin
1999–08	Vladimir Vladimirovich Putin
2008–	Dmitry Anatolyevich Medvedev

RECENT ELECTIONS

In the presidential elections held on 2 March 2008 Dmitry Medvedev, the candidate endorsed by outgoing president Vladimir Putin, won 70·3% of the votes cast. Gennady Zyuganov (Communist Party of the Russian Federation; KPRF) won 17·7% of the vote; Vladimir Zhirinovsky (Liberal Democratic Party; LDPR) 9·3%; and Andrei Baganov (ind.) 1·3%. Turnout was 69·7%.

Elections for the State Duma were held on 2 Dec. 2007. United Russia won 315 seats (with 64·1% of the vote); the KPRF 57 seats (11·6%); the LDPR 40 seats (8·2%); and Fair Russia 38 seats (7·8%).

Turnout was 62%. International observers described the poll as 'not free and fair'.

CURRENT ADMINISTRATION

President: Dmitry Medvedev; b. 1965 (sworn in 7 May 2008).

In March 2010 the government comprised:

Prime Minister: Vladimir Putin; b. 1952 (sworn in 7 May 2008).

First Deputy Prime Ministers: Igor Shuvalov; Viktor Zubkov (also *Minister of Fisheries*).

Deputy Prime Ministers: Sergei Sobyanin (also *Head of the Ministerial Apparatus*); Alexander Zhukov; Igor Sechin; Sergei Ivanov; Dmitry Kozak; Alexei Kudrin (also *Minister of Finance*).

Minister of Agriculture and Food: Yelena Skrynnik. *Culture:* Alexander Avdeyev. *Defence:* Anatoly Serdyukov. *Economic Development:* Elvira Nabiullina. *Education and Science:* Andrei Fursenko. *Emergency Situations:* Sergei Shoigu. *Energy:* Sergei Shmatko. *Foreign Affairs:* Sergei Lavrov. *Health and Social Development:* Tatyana Golikova. *Industry and Trade:* Viktor Khristenko. *Information and Mass Communication:* Igor Shchegolev. *Internal Affairs (MVD):* Rashid Nurgaliev. *Justice:* Alexander Konovalov. *Natural Resources and Ecology:* Yuri Trutnev. *Regional Development:* Viktor Basargin. *Sport, Tourism and Youth:* Vitaly Mutko. *Transportation and Communications:* Igor Levitin.

Chairman of the State Duma: Boris Gryzlov.

Government Website (Limited English): http://www.gov.ru

CURRENT LEADERS

Dmitry Anatolyevich Medvedev

Position

President

Introduction

After being named by Vladimir Putin as his preferred successor, Dmitry Medvedev was elected to the presidency by a landslide vote in March 2008. Medvedev's political career has been closely associated with Putin's since the mid-1990s and he is seen as a fellow modernizer. As chairman of Russia's giant gas company Gazprom he became a key figure in Russia's economy.

Early Life

Dmitry Medvedev was born in St Petersburg (then called Leningrad) on 14 Sept. 1965. Both his parents were university teachers. He grew up in the suburb of Kupchino and studied law at Leningrad State University, graduating in 1987. After obtaining a PhD in private law in 1990, he worked as an assistant professor at the university until 1999. In 1990 he also worked at the Leningrad Soviet of People's Deputies. From 1991–95 he served as legal adviser to the chairman of Leningrad city council and to the committee for external relations of the St Petersburg mayor's office, headed by Vladimir Putin. In Nov. 1993 he became legal affairs director of Ilim Pulp Enterprise and in 1998 he was elected to the board of governors of Bratskiy LPK paper mill.

Medvedev was appointed deputy head of the presidential administration by Putin in Dec. 1999. In 2000 he was promoted to the rank of first deputy chief of staff and during the 2000 election was in charge of the presidential campaign headquarters. In the same year Medvedev became chairman of the board of directors of Gazprom, Russia's largest company. From 2001 he served as deputy chairman until, in June 2002, he became chairman again. Under Medvedev, Gazprom acquired other energy companies and expanded overseas, increasing its significance both within the Russian economy and as an international supplier. In 2005–06 a dispute with neighbouring Ukraine over oil prices was seen by some observers as an attempt to influence the outcome of Ukraine's elections.

In 2003 Medvedev was appointed chief of staff of the presidential executive office and in Nov. 2005 Putin made him first deputy prime minister, giving him control of four national infrastructure projects: health care, education, housing and agriculture. Medvedev's initiatives included supporting foster families and developing pre-school education; he also attempted to reshape relationships between the Kremlin and Russia's billionaire oligarchs. In Dec. 2007, having served the constitutional maximum of two terms, Putin named Medvedev as his chosen successor. This was interpreted by many as an arrangement by which the two could continue to govern in partnership. Medvedev was elected president with 70% of the vote on 2 March 2008 and was sworn in on 7 May 2008.

Career in Office

As expected, Medvedev appointed Putin prime minister. Medvedev pledged to continue with Putin's policies, indicating that he would encourage a diversification of the economy to reduce reliance on gas revenues. He also signalled his support for a free press and free judiciary and spoke of limiting the influence of the security services. Early challenges internationally have included a deterioration in relations with NATO and Russian's western neighbours.

In Aug. 2008 he sent troops to South Ossetia and Abkhazia in Georgia, in response to Tbilisi's military attacks on separatist forces within the breakaway regions. A week of fierce fighting ended with a French-brokered peace deal. Russia's intervention received widespread international criticism, as did Medvedev's announcement of Russia's unilateral recognition of the independence of the two territories.

In his first state-of-the-nation address in Nov. 2008, Medvedev proposed a constitutional change to extend the presidential term of office from four to six years and that of parliament from four to five years, arguing that it was necessary to guarantee effective government. However, critics considered the move undemocratic and designed to perpetuate authoritarian rule from the Kremlin. In the same speech Medvedev threatened to deploy short-range missiles in Kaliningrad to counter the USA's proposed missile shield in central Europe (although a more conciliatory approach followed Barack Obama's assumption of the US presidency in Jan. 2009). He meanwhile claimed that the USA bore responsibility for the global financial crisis that had undermined the Russian banking system and destabilized markets. Also in Nov. 2008 Medvedev undertook a week-long overseas tour of Latin America and Cuba.

In April 2009 Medvedev ordered the end of the counter-terrorism operation against separatist rebels in Chechnya and instigated an inquiry into the killing of a leading human rights campaigner, Nataliya Estemirova, who was investigating alleged abuses by government-backed militias in the republic.

Russia's relations with the USA improved in 2009 following the installation of a new US administration under President Obama. Medvedev met Obama in July as the latter made his first official visit to Moscow and they agreed to negotiate cuts in their countries' nuclear weapon arsenals in a new initiative to supersede the 1991 Strategic Arms Reduction Treaty (START I). In Sept. Medvedev welcomed the US decision not to site controversial missile defence bases in Poland and the Czech Republic, the Russian military having earlier confirmed that plans to deploy short-range missiles in the Kaliningrad enclave were being shelved.

In his state of the nation address in Nov. 2009 Medvedev called for reform of the economy and emphasized the need for Russia to end its dependency on gas and oil exports. He also said that Russia's survival depended on rapid modernization, based on democratic institutions and an end to corruption.

Vladimir Vladimirovich Putin

Position
Prime Minister

Introduction
Vladimir Putin became prime minister in May 2008, having previously served two terms as state president. His appointment as president at the end of 1999 had been the culmination of a rapid political rise in the post-Communist era. Little known internationally, his KGB past aroused early concerns but he quickly gained respect within Russia as a modernizer and efficient administrator. He also made a determined effort to re-establish a more influential world role for his country. However, his handling of the Chechen war led to international criticism, while his opposition to the US war in Iraq from 2003 and to US plans to expand its missile defence systems into Eastern Europe strained relations with Washington. He nevertheless maintained a high approval rating among most Russian voters, although his style of government was perceived as authoritarian and imperial. Precluded from serving a third term under the constitution, he oversaw the election of his chosen successor, Dmitry Medvedev, to the presidency in March 2008 and he assumed the post of prime minister in May.

Early Life
Vladimir Putin was born in St Petersburg (then called Leningrad) on 7 Oct. 1952, the son of a war veteran who, with his wife, had survived the siege of Leningrad. Baptized into Russian Orthodoxy, he was an accomplished athlete, excelling at wrestling and martial arts. After graduating from law school in 1975, he began a 15-year career with the KGB's foreign intelligence arm, stationed in Leningrad and East Germany. When collapse threatened the Soviet Union, he retired as a colonel and embarked on a political career.

In the early 1990s Putin worked in local government in St Petersburg as an adviser to the city mayor, himself becoming deputy mayor in 1994, and chairman of the committee on external relationships. In 1996 President Yeltsin brought Putin to Moscow and appointed him deputy chief Kremlin administrator. He became the Kremlin's official in charge of relations with Russia's diverse regions and in 1998 head of the Federal Security Service (successor of the KGB) and secretary of the presidential Security Council. Putin was named acting prime minister in Aug. 1999 when Yeltsin sacked Russia's government for the fourth time in 17 months.

Career in Office
Putin became the acting president of Russia after Yeltsin's resignation on 31 Dec. 1999 and was officially elected president on 26 March 2000, taking 53% of the vote. His election programme prioritized a 'dictatorship of law' to combat high crime rates, as well as pledging to vanquish poverty and promote family values, patriotism and fair business conditions. One of his first public addresses as acting president underlined his support for 'freedom of speech, conscience and the press', which he propagated along with private property rights as tenets of a 'civilized society'.

He quickly set about exercising firm control over local government and the economy, with a stated aim of reducing corruption. In a bid to centralize power in Moscow, he restructured 89 legislative regions into seven districts, each with a government-approved leader (the majority of whom had military or security backgrounds). He reversed tax concessions that Yeltsin had brought in to assist the regions and reserved the right to dismiss any democratically-elected politician found to have broken the law.

Putin also removed several high-profile business and media figures from official positions. Yeltsin's daughter was dismissed as a Kremlin adviser but immunity was granted to Yeltsin himself, one of the more controversial moves of the then acting president. Putin appointed former finance minister and Yeltsin ally Mikhail Kasyanov as prime minister while placing other supporters in key Kremlin positions. Putin's economic policy was influenced by his allegiance to Anatoly Chubais, who led the wave of privatization in Russia in the early 1990s.

In April 2001 Putin's Unity party merged with the opposition Fatherland bloc, led by the mayor of Moscow, Yury Luzhkov. To pass legislation the president needed a simple majority of 226, with the merger giving him at least 132. In the summer of 2001 new laws on land, labour and pensions were proposed. These were opposed by the Communists whose leader Gennady Zyuganov called for a national demonstration against the reforms.

After Oct. 2001 Russians were free to buy residential and commercial land for the first time since the Bolsheviks took power in 1917. Farm land, making up 98% of the total, was not covered by the law. Critics feared that a privileged few would buy up the land much as they bought privatized businesses in the 1990s. Supporters maintained that it would attract foreign investment, speed up economic reform and stop the illegal sale of land.

Putin's image was dented by the sinking of the Kursk nuclear submarine in Aug. 2000 when all 118 Russian sailors on board died. He was widely condemned for inaction, refusing to return from his holiday and turning down offers of help from Norway and the UK. He was subsequently dogged by allegations of an official cover-up. The Kursk was finally raised in Aug. 2001, a salvage operation costing US$65m.

Putin meanwhile used the war with Chechnya to establish his 'strong man' credentials, although heavy Russian losses cost him some support and alleged human rights abuses led to a suspension of Russia's voting rights in the Council of Europe. In Oct. 2002 Chechen rebels took 800 people hostage inside a Moscow theatre, demanding the immediate withdrawal of Russian troops from Chechnya. The siege lasted three days before the Russian military stormed the building using an anaesthetic gas which killed the rebels but also over 100 hostages. In March 2003 Putin promised greater autonomy for Chechnya. This followed a referendum in the republic supporting a new constitution that would keep Chechnya within Russia but provide for a president and parliament. Moscow claimed 96% support for the proposals although no international observers were present and the referendum was opposed by separatist groups. In May 2003, following two suicide bomb attacks, Putin reaffirmed his determination to defeat Chechnya's rebel forces. He offered an amnesty for rebels who handed over their weapons by 1 Aug. 2003 and for Russian troops accused of human rights violations.

Following the 11 Sept. attacks on New York and Washington, D.C. there was a rapprochement between Russia and the USA. In 2001 Putin gave unprecedented support for UN military action in Afghanistan. His offers of military assistance to the Afghan Northern Alliance, the use of Russian airspace for humanitarian aid and his role in persuading Tajikistan and Uzbekistan to support the campaign were well received in the West where leaders were quick to downplay Russia's role in Chechnya. In May 2002 Putin and US President George W. Bush signed an anti-nuclear deal agreeing to reduce their respective strategic nuclear warheads by two-thirds over the next ten years.

However, tension between the two countries increased over the question of Iraq in late 2002. While President Bush attempted to garner support for military action in Iraq—with Russia holding a power of veto within the UN Security Council—he warned Putin at the same time that he would not support Russian military incursions into Georgia, which Russia claimed was tolerating Chechen activity in the Pankisi Gorge. Putin's political dealings with 'rogue' nations, including North Korea and Cuba, were also criticized, as was Russia's trading of nuclear fuel and weapons with India, Iran, Iraq and Syria.

When US-led forces began attacking Iraq in March 2003 Russia condemned the action and delayed ratifying the US-Russian strategic arms control treaty (*see above*) until the war was over. Putin refuted US accusations that Russia had breached UN sanctions by selling armaments, including anti-tank missiles and jamming equipment, to Iraq. When the UN agreed to reinstate Iraq's oil-for-food programme, halted at the outbreak of war, Russia was one of several UN Security Council members to emphasize that the resumption did not signify UN backing for the invasion. However, in May 2003 Russia voted to accept a UN resolution on Iraq's future jointly proposed by the USA, UK and Spain. In return for the immediate ending of sanctions, the UN was to co-operate with the occupying forces to form a new government. In addition Russia would be able to complete longstanding contracts with Iraq. Despite tension in Russia's relationship with the UK as a result of differences over Iraq, Putin made an official state visit to Britain, the first by a Russian leader for over a century.

Having previously avoided party politics, Putin publicly endorsed a pro-government party—United Russia—in the Dec. 2003 parliamentary elections. In the March 2004 presidential elections, he was criticized by the international press and by OSCE monitors for manipulating the Russian media to influence voting in his favour. He was re-elected in the poll, claiming 71% of the vote and leaving his closest rival, the Communist Nikolai Kharitonov, with less than 14%. In May 2004 Putin set out his goals for his second term—modernizing Russia and raising living standards while aiming for a more stable democracy able to pursue strategic interests abroad. The cutting of state benefits led to worker protests across Russia as many demanded further action against poverty.

Chechen violence had continued in 2003 with a suicide bombing at a rock music festival in July. Following a referendum in which Chechens agreed to a Moscow-approved constitution, Putin announced that a presidential vote would go ahead. In Oct. 2003, with a turnout of 85%, the pro-Moscow leader Akhmad Kadyrov was elected. In the wake of the killing of Akhmad Kadyrov in a bomb attack in Chechnya's capital in May 2004, Putin pledged to send extra troops to deal with the conflict. Alu Alkhanov was elected president of Chechnya on 29 Aug. 2004, and in Chechen parliamentary elections in Nov. 2005 the pro-Moscow United Russia party claimed about 60% of the popular vote.

In the aftermath of the bloodbath that ended the Beslan school siege in Sept. 2004, Putin controversially took control of the appointment of regional governors who had been directly elected for the previous decade. Critics saw the move as undermining democracy.

In May 2005 Mikhail Khodorkovsky, a billionaire former head of oil-exporting company Yukos, was sentenced to nine years' imprisonment for tax evasion and fraud. His conviction, following the effective renationalization of Yukos in 2004, was widely viewed as politically motivated, owing to his criticism of Putin's regime.

High oil and gas prices continued to underpin Russia's strong economic growth during Putin's presidency. There was increasing state influence over the energy industry, exercised through the giant gas monopoly Gazprom and through Rosneft (another state-run company that acquired the prime assets of Yukos in 2004). However, Russia's reputation as a reliable international energy trader has been tarnished. Several cuts in Russian oil and gas supplies to neighbouring countries since 2006—particularly Ukraine, and most recently in Jan. 2009—purportedly over pricing disputes but with suspected political overtones, have in turn disrupted pipeline flows to EU countries and prompted high-level protests.

There was meanwhile growing concern for civil and political freedoms in Putin's Russia, with foreign commentators citing increasing authoritarianism, the lack of a genuine opposition or independent judiciary and more general lawlessness, including violent xenophobia. The deaths in late 2006 of two prominent government critics—campaigning journalist Anna Politkovskaya and former intelligence officer Alexander Litvinenko—fuelled widespread suspicions of official involvement, although the government denied this. Litvinenko's poisoning in London in particular led to a sharp deterioration in Russian-UK relations. Putin's refusal to extradite a prime suspect in the affair to Britain resulted in the mutual imposition of diplomatic sanctions in July 2007.

Plans by the USA to expand its missile defences into the Eastern European member countries of NATO further soured Russian-US relations in Putin's second term of office. In Nov. 2007 he approved a law suspending Russia's participation in the 1990 Conventional Armed Forces in Europe (CFE) Treaty limiting military deployments.

In Dec. 2007 the pro-Putin United Russia party won a landslide victory in parliamentary elections. With his second term set to expire in 2008, Putin announced that he would nevertheless continue in politics as the next prime minister and that Dmitry Medvedev (the chair of Gazprom) would be his preferred successor as president after elections scheduled for March. Russian voters duly endorsed this political continuity at the polls and Putin and Medvedev were sworn into their respective posts in May 2008. Putin remains a pivotal figure in the Russian leadership, having an increasingly centralized grip on power and policy with President Medvedev.

In Oct. 2009 Putin's ruling United Russia party won a sweeping victory in nationwide regional and local elections. Opposition parties walked out of parliament, claiming that the vote had been rigged, and they threatened to demonstrate in protest. Also in Oct., Putin visited China to conclude trade deals worth US$3·5bn.

DEFENCE

The President of the Republic is C.-in-C. of the armed forces. Conscription was reduced to 18 months for those drafted in 2007 and was further reduced to one year for those drafted from 1 Jan. 2008.

A presidential decree of Feb. 1997 ordered a cut in the armed forces of 200,000 men, reducing them to an authorized strength of 1,004,000 in 1999. In 2007 armed forces totalled 1,027,000, plus 418,000 personnel in paramilitary forces. There were estimated to be around 20,000,000 reserves (all armed forces) in 2006 of whom 2,000,000 had seen service within the previous five years.

Military expenditure totalled an estimated US$58,600m. in 2008 (less than a tenth of that of the USA), equivalent to US$413 per capita. This made Russia the world's fifth biggest military spender. In the period 1999–2008 military expenditure rose by 173% in real terms. In 2007 defence spending represented 3·5% of GDP.

Nuclear Weapons

Russia's strategic warhead count is now shrinking and stood at 2,787 in Jan. 2009 according to the Stockholm International Peace Research Institute. There were also 2,047 defensive and non-strategic warheads in Jan. 2009, making a total of 4,834 deployed warheads. There are a further 8,800 warheads held in reserve or scheduled to be dismantled. Shortfalls in planned investments to replace current systems as they reach the end of their service lives means the number of strategic warheads will continue to decline.

At the height of the Cold War each side possessed over 10,000 nuclear warheads. The START I arms-control treaty, signed in 1991, limited to approximately 6,000 the number of nuclear warheads that Russia and the USA may each deploy on long-range, or 'strategic', land-based missiles, submarine-launched missiles and bombers. The 1993 START II treaty would have obliged both sides to reduce their stocks of strategic weapons to 3,500 nuclear warheads. However, instruments of ratification were never exchanged and the treaty lapsed. Russia retracted acceptance in June 2002 after the USA withdrew from the Anti-Ballistic Missile treaty. START I expired on 5 Dec. 2009. A replacement agreement, the Measures to Further Reduction and Limitation of Strategic Offensive Arms, was signed in April 2010. Under its terms, both Russia and the USA were limited to 1,550 warheads, a 30% drop on previous levels, to be implemented within seven years.

On 24 May 2002 the USA and Russia signed the Strategic Offensive Reductions Treaty (or Moscow Treaty) to reduce the number of US and Russian warheads to between 1,700 and 2,200 each by 2012.

Chemical and Biological Weapons

Russia has converted or destroyed its former chemical weapon production facilities and is currently working to complete destruction of its chemical weapon stockpile in accordance with the provisions of the 1993 Chemical Weapons Convention. Russia has the largest declared stockpile of chemical weapons, originally totalling 40,000 tonnes.

The Soviet Union had perhaps the world's largest biological weapon programme until at least the 1980s. Russia has reiterated its commitment to the 1972 Biological and Toxin Weapons Convention.

Arms Trade

Russia was the world's second largest exporter after the USA in 2006, with sales worth US$5,800m. or 21·5% of the world total.

Army

In 2006 Army personnel numbered around 395,000 (including about 190,000 conscripts). There were around 17,000 Russian troops stationed outside Russia in 2006, the majority in various states of the former USSR (including 7,800 in Tajikistan and 3,000 in the Caucasus).

The Army is deployed in six military districts and one Operational Strategic Group. Equipment includes some 23,000 main battle tanks (including T-55s, T-62s, T-64A/-Bs, T-72L/-Ms, T-80/-U/UD/UMs and T-90s) plus 150 light tanks (PT-76s).

Strategic Nuclear Ground Forces

In 2008 there were three rocket armies, which will fall to two by 2016. Each rocket army is divided into launcher groups with ten silos and one control centre. Inter-continental ballistic missiles numbered 506. Personnel, 40,000.

Navy

The Russian Navy continues to reduce steadily and levels of sea-going activity remain very low with activity concentrated on a few operational units in each fleet. The safe deployment and protection of the reduced force of ballistic missile submarines remains its first priority; and the defence of the Russian homeland its second. The strategic missile submarine force operates under command of the Strategic Nuclear Force commander whilst the remainder come under the Main Naval Staff in Moscow, through the Commanders of the fleets.

The Northern and Pacific fleets count the entirety of the ballistic missile submarine force, all nuclear-powered submarines, the sole operational aircraft carrier (the *Admiral Kuznetsov*) and most major surface warships. The Baltic Fleet organization is based in the St Petersburg area and in the Kaliningrad exclave. The Black Sea Fleet is based at facilities in the Crimea, Ukraine. Ukraine had stated that the lease on these three harbours for warships and two airfields would not be extended and that the fleet must leave the main base of Sevastopol by 2017. However, since being elected in Feb. 2010 Ukraine's president Viktor Yanukovych has suggested that he would allow Russia's fleet to remain in his country beyond 2017. There is a small Caspian Sea flotilla. In Nov. 2008 Russia held joint exercises with the Venezuelan Navy in the Caribbean Sea in what was widely perceived as an attempt to provoke the USA.

The material state of all the fleets is suffering from continued inactivity and lack of spares and fuel. The nuclear submarine refitting and refuelling operations in the Northern and Pacific Fleets remain in disarray, given the large numbers of nuclear submarines awaiting defuelling and disposal. The strength of the submarine force has now essentially stabilized, but there are still large numbers of decommissioned vessels awaiting their turn for scrapping in a steadily deteriorating state. In Jan. 2003 it was announced that up to a fifth of the fleet was to be scrapped.

In 2009 there were 12 operational nuclear-fuelled ballistic-missile submarines (five of Delta-III class, six Delta-IV, including two undergoing overhaul, and one unarmed Typhoon used as a test platform). There was a total of 276 sea-launched SS-N-9, -12, -19, -21 and -22s in Jan. 2009. A new submarine-launched ballistic missile 'Bulava' (SS-NX-30) has been developed, with a series of test launches since 2005. Depending on the outcome of further tests the missile could enter service before the end of 2010 with the Borei-class nuclear submarine, the first vessel of which was launched in April 2007.

The attack submarine fleet comprises a wide range of classes, from the enormous 16,250 tonne 'Oscar' nuclear-powered missile submarine to diesel boats of around 2,000 tonnes. The inventory of tactical nuclear-fuelled submarines comprises seven 'Oscar II', one former strategic 'Yankee'-class, eight 'Akula'-class, one 'Sierra'-class and four 'Victor III'-class submarines.

The diesel-powered 'Kilo' class, of which the Navy operates 14, is still building at a reduced rate mostly for export.

Cruisers are divided into two categories; those optimized for anti-submarine warfare (ASW) are classified as 'Large Anti-Submarine Ships' and those primarily configured for anti-surface ship operations are classified 'Rocket Cruisers'. The principal surface ships of the Russian Navy include the following classes:

Aircraft Carrier. The *Admiral Kuznetsov* of 67,500 tonnes was completed in 1989. It is capable of embarking 20 aircraft and 15–17 helicopters. All other aircraft carriers have been decommissioned or scrapped.

Cruisers. The ships of this classification are headed by the two ships of the Kirov-class, the largest combatant warships, apart from aircraft carriers, to be built since the Second World War. There are, in addition, three Slava-class and one of the Nikolaev ('Kara') class in operation.

Destroyers. There are seven Udaloy-class, the first of which entered service in 1981, one Udaloy II-class and six Sovremenny-class guided missile destroyers in operation. In addition there is a single remaining 'modified Kashin'-class ship in operation.

Frigates. There are seven frigates in operation including the first of a new class, the 'Gepard', one Neustrashimy class, three Krivak I-class and two Krivak II-class ships.

The Russian Naval Air Force operates some 266 combat aircraft including 58 Tu-22M bombers and 58 Su-24, 10 Su-25 and 49 Su-27 fighters. In 2006 there were an additional 161 armed helicopters in operation.

Total Naval personnel in 2006 numbered 142,000. Some 11,000 serve in the strategic submarine force, 35,000 in naval aviation and 9,500 naval infantry/coastal defence troops.

Air Force

Air Force personnel is estimated at 160,600 and equipment includes some 1,852 combat aircraft and about 2,000 helicopters.

The Air Force is organized into three main Commands: Long-Range Aviation (37th Air Army), Tactical Aviation and Military Transport Aviation. An air force base opened in Kyrgyzstan in Oct. 2003.

Equipment of the 37th Air Army includes 124 Tu-22Ms plus Tu-95s and Tu-160s.

Tactical Aviation comprised in 2006 (numbers in brackets) Su-24 (400) and Su-25 (275) fighter-bombers and MiG-29 (314), MiG-31 (279) and Su-27 (390) fighters. In addition MiG-25 and Su-24s are used for reconnaissance missions.

Military Transport Aviation Command comprises nine regiments and has some 293 aircraft. Funding shortages have reduced serviceability drastically.

INTERNATIONAL RELATIONS

Russia is a member of the UN (and a permanent member of its Security Council), World Bank, IMF and several other UN specialized agencies, Council of Europe, OSCE, BSEC, Council of the Baltic Sea States, Danube Commission, BIS, CIS, the NATO Partnership for Peace, APEC and Antarctic Treaty. On 16 May 1997 NATO ratified a 'Fundamental Act on Relations, Co-operation and Mutual Security' with Russia. In Jan. 2010 Russia joined the newly established Customs Union, together with Belarus and Kazakhstan. The three countries are now looking to enter the WTO as a single customs territory.

ECONOMY

Agriculture accounted for 5·1% of GDP in 2006, industry 38·0% and services 57·0%.

In Oct. 1991 a programme was launched to create a 'healthy mixed economy with a powerful private sector'. The prices of most commodities were freed on 2 Jan. 1992.

Privatization, which is overseen by the State Committee on the Management of State Property, began with small and medium-sized enterprises. A state programme of privatization of state and municipal enterprises was approved by parliament in June 1992, and vouchers worth 10,000 roubles each began to be distributed to all citizens in Oct. 1992. These could be sold or exchanged for shares. Employees had the right to purchase 51% of the equity of their enterprises. 25 categories of industry (including raw materials and arms) remained in state ownership. The voucher phase of privatization ended on 30 June 1994. A post-voucher stage authorized by presidential decree of 22 July 1994 provides for firms to be auctioned for cash following the completion of the sale of up to 70% of manufacturing industry for vouchers. The Ministry of Property Relations was established in 2000 with the mandate of overall federal policies on property issues and the management of state property, and in Dec. 2001 a new Federal Law on Privatization of State and Municipal Property was adopted. By that time a total of 129,811 enterprises had been sold. In 2004 only 36% of total employment was still in the public sector.

Overview

Russia experienced robust growth after the 1998 economic crisis, when the country defaulted on US$40bn. of domestic debt. With the world's fifth biggest gold and foreign exchange reserves, worth over US$206bn. in 2006, real growth averaged 6·8% between 1999–2004, just below the target rate of 7·25% to double GDP in a decade. In 2006 GDP growth was boosted by high oil and gas prices, strong domestic consumption (which increased by 11%) and a 9·8% increase in real wages. The poverty headcount has been reduced by over half to less than 14% since 1998.

Growth has been driven by export-orientated industries, notably the oil industry, which reacted to high oil prices by increasing output and investment. Large gains in terms of trade saw the export sector flourish and helped reduce unemployment from over 13% in the late 1990s to 6·1% by 2008. High investment in other sectors has spurred growth in total factor productivity and real wages, with growth increasingly driven by domestic demand. However, there is a large degree of inequality, with the bottom 10% of the population receiving only 1·9% of income in 2007, compared with 30·4% for the top 10%.

The global financial crisis that began in 2007 caused two shocks to the economy, with a collapse in oil prices and an abrupt reversal of capital flows. Alongside concerns over the conflict with Georgia, the Russian stock market fall by 70% in late 2008. A US$200bn. rescue package to support the stock market in Oct. 2008 was followed by a supplementary budget in April 2009 to prop up domestic demand, including increased spending on defence and security, tax reductions, support to strategic sectors and increased social assistance.

The economy contracted by nearly 8% in 2009. Losses in output and employment were larger than expected and poverty increased sharply. With an increase in oil prices and increased global demand, the economy began to turn around, with modest growth forecast for 2010. According to the World Bank, Russia's real GDP will return to pre-crisis levels in late 2012 but further structural reforms are needed to regain pre-crisis growth rates.

President Medvedev's long-term development strategy centres on creating a stronger investment climate, including reforms of the civil service and public administration, alongside proposals to tackle corruption. Plans to join the WTO may accelerate this reform momentum. A BRIC summit in 2008 indicated a growing alliance between Russia and the similarly fast-growing nations of Brazil, India and China.

Currency

The unit of currency is the *rouble* (RUB), of 100 *kopeks*. In Jan. 1998 the rouble was redenominated by a factor of a thousand. Foreign exchange reserves were US$383,664m. in Sept. 2009 and gold reserves 19·00m. troy oz. In Feb. 2005 Russia abandoned its *de facto* dollar peg and switched to a euro-dollar basket. Inflation rates (based on IMF statistics):

1999	*2000*	*2001*	*2002*	*2003*	*2004*	*2005*	*2006*	*2007*	*2008*
85·7%	20·8%	21·5%	15·8%	13·7%	10·9%	12·7%	9·7%	9·0%	14·1%

Inflation had been 2,510% in 1992. Total money supply in Dec. 2008 was 7,419·7bn. roubles. In Nov. 2000 then President Putin and President Lukashenka of Belarus agreed the introduction of a single currency, but plans to introduce the Russian rouble to Belarus have since been postponed indefinitely.

Budget

Budgetary central government revenue totalled 6,276·8bn. roubles in 2006 (5,125·8bn. roubles in 2005) and expenditure 3,763·7bn. roubles (3,242·4bn. roubles in 2005). Principal sources of revenue in 2006: taxes on international trade and transactions, 2,306·4bn. roubles; taxes on goods and services, 1,629·1bn. roubles; taxes on income, profits and capital gains, 509·9bn. roubles. Main items of expenditure by economic type in 2006: grants, 1,518·9bn. roubles; compensation of employees, 859·3bn. roubles; use of goods and services, 821·0bn. roubles.

VAT is 18% (reduced rate, 10%).

Performance

Real GDP growth rates (based on IMF statistics):

1999	*2000*	*2001*	*2002*	*2003*	*2004*	*2005*	*2006*	*2007*	*2008*
6·4%	10·0%	5·1%	4·7%	7·3%	7·2%	6·4%	7·7%	8·1%	5·6%

GDP growth in 2009 was –7·9% according to the Federal Statistics Service. Total GDP was US$1,607·8bn. in 2008. In June 2002 Russia was acknowledged as a market economy under United States trade law, symbolically underscoring the country's transformation from a state-planned economy.

Banking and Finance

The central bank and bank of issue is the State Bank of Russia (*Governor,* Sergey Mikhailovich Ignatiev). The Russian Bank for Reconstruction and Development and the State Investment Company were created in 1993 to channel foreign and domestic investment. Foreign bank branches have been operating since Nov. 1992.

By 1995 the number of registered commercial banks had increased to around 5,000 but following the Aug. 1997 liquidity crisis, owing to the ensuing bankruptcies, mergers and the Central Bank's revoking of licences, the number fell to 2,500. This has since fallen to 1,300. Approximately 80% of the commercial banks were state-owned through ministries or state enterprises. Sberbank is the leading bank with assets of US$220·86bn. in April 2009, followed by VTB Bank (formerly Vneshtorgbank) with assets of US$92·51bn. In 2001 there were around 1,300 credit institutions.

In the wake of one of the worst financial crises which Russia's market economy had experienced, the central bank tripled interest rates to 150% in May 1998 in an effort to restore stability to the financial system. In 2002 the banking sector in Russia was healthier than at any time since the collapse of the former Soviet Union.

In 2008 Russia received a record US$70·3bn. worth of foreign direct investment—more than double the 2006 total.

There are stock exchanges in Moscow, Novosibirsk, St Petersburg and Vladivostok.

ENERGY AND NATURAL RESOURCES

Environment

Russia's carbon dioxide emissions from the consumption and flaring of fossil fuels in 2008 accounted for 5·7% of the world total (the third highest after China and the USA), and were equivalent to 12·3 tonnes per capita. An *Environmental Performance Index* compiled in 2008 ranked Russia 28th in the world, with 86·3%. The index examined various factors in six areas—air pollution, biodiversity and habitat, climate change, environmental health, productive natural resources and water resources.

Electricity

In 2004 installed capacity was an estimated 212·8m. kW and electricity production 931·87bn. kWh. Consumption per capita was 6,425 kWh in 2004. The dominant electricity company is Unified Energy System of Russia. It generated 617·4bn. kWh in 2002 (69% of all electricity produced in Russia). It was broken up into several state-owned and private companies in two stages in 2007 and 2008—a process that was completed on 1 July 2008. There were 30 nuclear reactors in use in 2003.

Oil and Gas

Russia was the second largest oil producer in 2008 (after Saudi Arabia) and the second largest exporter (again, after Saudi Arabia). Russia consumes less than a third of the oil that it produces. Oil and gas account for 50% of Russia's export revenues. In 2008 there were proven crude petroleum reserves of 79·0bn. bbls, but they are expected to be exhausted by 2030. 2008 production of oil was 488·5m. tonnes (12·4% of the world total). Oil production rose every year between 1998 and 2007 but fell slightly in 2008. There is an extensive domestic oil pipeline system. The main export pipeline to Europe is the Druzhba pipeline (crossing Belarus before splitting into northern and southern routes). The main export terminal is at Novorossiisk on the Black Sea. Other export pipeline developments include the Baltic Pipeline System (the first stage of which became operational in Dec. 2001 with the opening of a new terminal at Primorsk) and the Caspian Pipeline Consortium's pipeline from Tengiz (Kazakhstan) to Novorossiisk, which was commissioned in March 2001.

Output of natural gas in 2008 was 601·7bn. cu. metres, making Russia the world's largest producer. It also has the largest reserves of natural gas—in 2008 it had proven reserves of 43,300bn. cu. metres (23% of the world total). There is a comprehensive domestic distribution system (run by state-owned Gazprom, in which the government has a 50·002% stake), as well as gas pipelines linking Russia with former Soviet republics. In Russia's biggest-ever takeover Gazprom agreed in Sept. 2005 to buy a 72·7% stake in Sibfneft, a leading oil company. The main export pipelines run from western Siberia through Ukraine and Belarus to European markets. Russia is seeking to diversify its gas export routes and a number of pipeline projects are under development. Russia is also looking to export its natural gas to Asian markets.

The oil and gas boom has meant that the sector's share in Russia's total GDP has risen from 12·7% in 1999 to 31·6% in 2007.

Minerals

Russia contains great mineral resources: coal (17% of the world's total reserves), iron ore, gold, platinum, copper, zinc, lead, tin and rare metals. Output (in tonnes): coal (2004), 189·8m.; iron ore (2004), 97m.; lignite (2004), 72·6m.; bauxite (2003), 5·4m.; aluminium (2004), 3·6m.; copper (2004), 675,000; chrome ore (2004), 320,200; nickel (2002), 310,000; zinc (2004), 179,000; tin (2004), 6,000; molybdenum (2004), 2,900; gold (2004), 169. Salt production, 2002 estimate: 2·8m. tonnes. Diamond production, 2005 estimate: 38·0m. carats. Only Australia produces more diamonds. Annual uranium production is nearly 3,000 tonnes.

Agriculture

A presidential decree of Dec. 1991 authorized the private ownership of land on a general basis, but excluded farmland. Nevertheless, large state and collective farms, inherited from the Soviet era, were forced officially to reorganize, with most becoming joint-stock companies. Farm workers could branch off as private farmers by obtaining a grant of land from their parent farm, although they lacked full ownership rights. In 2002 over 90% of Russia's 400m. ha. of farmland remained under the control of the state or former collectives. In Jan. 2003 a new law came into force regulating the possession, use and disposal of land plots designated as agricultural land. The law provides that: the authorities may confiscate farmland if its owners are using it for non-agricultural purposes; regional authorities will have the first option to purchase farmland from its owners; and farmland can only be sold to third parties if authorities refuse their option to buy. The law also deprives foreigners of the right to own agricultural land, although they may lease it for up to 49 years. In 2007 there were 121·57m. ha. of arable land and 1·79m. ha. of permanent crops. There were 4·4m. ha. of irrigated land in 2007.

Output in 2003 (in 1,000 tonnes) included: potatoes, 36,747; wheat, 34,062; sugar beets, 19,384; barley, 17,968; oats, 5,175; sunflower seeds, 4,871; cabbage, 4,441; rye, 4,151; maize, 2,113; tomatoes, 2,016; apples, 1,900; carrots, 1,735; onions, 1,561. Russia is the world's largest producer of oats and sunflower seeds, and the second largest producer of potatoes.

Livestock, 2003: cattle, 26·5m.; pigs, 17·3m.; sheep, 13·7m.; poultry, 339m. Livestock products in 2003 (in tonnes): beef and veal, 2·0m.; pork, bacon and ham, 1·7m.; poultry meat, 1·0m.; cow's milk, 32·8m.; goat's milk, 0·3m.; eggs, 2·0m.; cheese, 500,000.

Forestry

Russia has the largest area covered by forests of any country in the world, with 808·79m. ha. in 2005 (47·9% of the land area). In 2007 timber production was 207·0m. cu. metres. Russia was the world's largest exporter of roundwood in 2007, with 36·2% of the world total.

Fisheries

Total catch in 2005 was 3,190,946 tonnes (down from 8,211,516 tonnes in 1989). Approximately 93% of the fish caught are from marine waters.

INDUSTRY

As a result of Soviet central planning, Russian industry remains dominated by heavy industries, such as energy and metals. In 2001 fuels and energy production accounted for almost 20% of industrial output and metallurgy for 17%. Machine building and metalworking remained the largest processing industry, accounting for almost 20% of industrial production, followed by chemical manufacture. Light industry accounted for less than 2% of industrial output in 2001. Russia had fewer than 1m. small- and medium-sized enterprises at the end of 2001. Small- and medium-sized enterprises account for only 10–15% of GDP.

The leading companies by market capitalization in Russia in March 2009 were: Gazprom, a gas company (US$91·5bn.); Rosneft, an oil and gas field construction company (US$46·6bn.); and Lukoil Holding, an oil production company (US$32·3bn.).

Output (in tonnes) includes: crude steel (2004), 65·6m.; residual fuel oil (2004), 58·3m.; distillate fuel oil (2004), 55·4m.; rolled steel (2004), 53·8m.; pig iron (2004), 50·3m.; cement (2004), 45·6m.; petrol (2004), 30·5m.; jet fuel (2004), 9·6m.; sulphuric acid (2003), 8·7m.; bread (2001), 8·6m.; steel pipe (2004), 6·0m.; paper and paperboard (2002), 5·9m.; cellulose (2000), 5·0m.; sugar (2002), 1·8m.; caustic soda (2000), 1·2m.; biscuits, pastry and cakes (2001), 1·0m.; soap, washing powder and detergents (2000), 436,000; synthetic fibre (2000), 164,000; (in sq. metres) glass (2001), 33·8m.; (in units) bricks (2000), 10,700m.; passenger cars (2002), 981,000; tractors (1999), 15,417; combine harvesters (2001), 9,063; watches (2000), 6·5m.; refrigerators (2001), 1·5m.; televisions (2001), 1·0m.; washing machines (2001), 1·0m.; cigarettes (2001), 355·6bn.; beer (2001), 6,370m. litres; soft drinks (2001), 2,730·0m. litres; vodka and liquors (2000), 1,230m. litres; mineral water (2001), 1,220m. litres.

Labour

In 2004 the economically active population numbered 72·9m., of whom 67·1m. were in employment. The unemployment rate was 9·9% in May 2009—with 7·5m. people unemployed using ILO methodology—down from 10·2% in April 2009 although up from 6·1% in Oct. 2008. Average monthly wages were 6,831·8 roubles in 2004 (compared to 5,498·5 roubles in 2003 and 4,360·3 in 2002); the minimum wage from Oct. 2003 was 600 roubles (compared to 250 roubles in 2001 and 107·8 in 2000). In 2004, 25·5m. people, or 17·8% of the population, had an average per capita money income lower than the subsistence minimum. The state Federal Employment Service was set up in 1992. Unemployment benefits are paid by the Service for 12 months, payable at: 75% of the average monthly wage during the last two months preceding unemployment for the first three months; 60% for the next four months; and 45% for the last five months. Annual paid leave is 24 working days. The workforce was 65·90m. in 2004, of which 14·13m. worked in industry, 11·34m. in wholesale and retail trade and catering, 6·79m. in agriculture, 6·06m. in education, 5·14m. in construction, 4·78m. in public health, physical culture and social security, and 4·22m. in transport. In 2005, 85,900 working days were lost through strikes (6,000,500 in 1996). Retirement age is 55 years for women, 60 for men.

Trade Unions

The Federation of Independent Trade Unions (founded 1990) is the successor to the former Communist official union organization. In 2002 it comprised 78 regional and 48 sectoral trade unions, with a total membership of 40m. There are also free trade unions.

INTERNATIONAL TRADE

Foreign debt was US$229,042m. in 2005 (much of it inherited from the Soviet Union). Most CIS republics have given up claims on Soviet assets in return for Russia assuming their portion of foreign debt. A Foreign Investment Agency was set up in Dec. 1992.

Imports and Exports

Trade in US$1m.:

	2003	2004	2005	2006	2007
Imports c.i.f.	57,346	75,569	98,707	137,806	199,726
Exports f.o.b.	133,656	181,600	241,452	301,244	352,266

Germany provided 13·4% of imports in 2005, Ukraine 7·9%, China 7·4%, Japan 5·9% and Belarus 5·8%. In 2005 the Netherlands accounted for 10·2% of exports, Germany 8·2%, Italy 7·9%, China 5·4% and Ukraine 5·1%. In 2004, of imports, 35·4% by value was machinery and transport equipment, 13·1% food and livestock, 11·7% chemicals and related products, and 3·6% iron and steel. Of exports, 41·0% by value was petroleum and petroleum products, 11·5% natural gas, 8·2% iron and steel, and 5·9% machinery and transport equipment.

COMMUNICATIONS

Roads

There were 933,000 km of roads in 2006, of which 80·9% were hard surfaced. In 2007, 78bn. passenger-km were travelled by road. There were 29,249,000 passenger cars in use in 2007 plus 4,730,000 lorries and vans and 861,000 buses and coaches. In 2007 there were 33,300 road deaths.

Rail

Length of railways in 2002 was 86,200 km of 1,520 mm gauge (of which 40,300 km electrified), and 957 km of 1,067 mm gauge on Sakhalin island. In 2002, 1,270·9m. passengers and 1,084·2m. tonnes of freight were carried by rail; passenger-km travelled came to 153bn. and freight tonne-km to 1,508bn. There are metro services in Moscow (292 km), St Petersburg (105 km), Nizhny Novgorod (15 km), Novosibirsk (14 km), Samara (10 km), Ekaterinburg (9 km) and Kazan (7 km). Kazan's metro opened in 2005, making it the first metro to be opened in Russia since the breakup of the Soviet Union.

Civil Aviation

The main international airports are at Moscow (Sheremetevo) and St Petersburg (Pulkovo). The national carrier is Aeroflot International Russian Airlines (51·2% state-owned). Rossiya, S7 Airlines and Transaero also operate internationally.

In 2003 scheduled airline traffic of Russian-based carriers flew 602m. km, carrying 22,723,000 passengers (6,972,000 on international flights). Moscow Sheremetevo handled 11,513,739 passengers in 2001 (8,405,378 on international flights) and 100,203 tonnes of freight. Moscow Vnukovo is mainly used for internal flights and was the second busiest airport in 2001, handling 3,666,304 passengers (2,956,135 on domestic flights) and 56,583 tonnes of freight. St Petersburg was the third busiest in 2001 for passengers (2,866,471) and for freight (20,014 tonnes).

The state-owned airline Pulkovo merged with the Russia State Transport Company in 2006 to form a new airline, Rossiya.

Shipping

At the end of 2001 the merchant fleet comprised 4,727 vessels totalling 10,247,803 GRT. In Jan. 2005, 128 vessels (51% of tonnage) were registered under foreign flags. Vessels totalling 117,306,000 NRT entered ports in 2002 and vessels totalling 100,620,000 NRT cleared. In 2002, 31·1m. passengers and 115·7m. tonnes of freight were carried on 95,900 km of inland waterways. The busiest ports are Novorossiisk (which handled 63,291,000 tonnes in 2002) and St Petersburg (42,680,000 tonnes in 2002).

Telecommunications

In 2008 there were 44,897,000 main (fixed) telephone lines. In the same year mobile phone subscribers numbered 199,522,000 (1,411·1 per 1,000 persons). 19·0m. PCs were in use in 2006 and there were 45·3m. internet users in 2008.

Postal Services

In 2003 there were 40,314 post offices (one for every 3,550 persons).

SOCIAL INSTITUTIONS

Justice

The Supreme Court is the highest judicial body on civil, criminal and administrative law. The Supreme Arbitration Court deals with economic cases. The KGB, and the Federal Security Bureau which succeeded it, were replaced in Dec. 1992 by the Federal Counter-Intelligence Service. The legal system is, however, crippled by corruption.

A new civil code was introduced in 1993 to replace the former Soviet code. It guarantees the inviolability of private property and includes provisions for the freedom of movement of capital and goods.

12-member juries were introduced in a number of courts after Nov. 1993, but in the years that followed jury trials were not widely used. However, on 1 Jan. 2003 jury trials began to be phased in nationwide. A new criminal code came into force on 1 Jan. 1997, based on respect for the rights and freedoms of the individual and the sanctity of private property. A further new code that entered force on 1 July 2002 introduced new levels of protection for defendants and restrictions on law enforcement officials. The death penalty is retained for five crimes against the person. It is not applied to minors, women or men over 65.

In 2000, 2,952,400 crimes were recorded, including 28,904 murders, 132,393 robberies and 6,978 rapes. Russia's murder rate, at 19·9 per 100,000 population in 2000, ranks among the highest in the world. In 1996 there were 140 executions (86 in 1995; 1 in 1992). President Yeltsin placed a moratorium on capital punishment in 1996 when Russia joined the Council of Europe, but parliament has refused to abolish the death penalty. The last execution was in Aug. 1996. The prison population in Aug. 2003 was 865,000. Russia's prison population rate (606 per 100,000 population in Aug. 2003) is the second highest in the world after the USA. In 2003 there were 1,010 prison establishments and institutions.

Education

Adult literacy rate in 2003 was 99·4% (male, 99·7%; female, 99·2%). In 2004 there were 4·42m. children in 47,200 pre-school establishments, 16·17m. pupils in 63,182 primary and secondary day schools; 6·88m. students in 1,071 higher educational institutions (including correspondence students). In addition there were 708 private schools with 70,000 pupils.

In 2006 public expenditure on education came to 4·0% of GNI.

Russia's largest university is the M. V. Lomonosov Moscow State University. Founded in 1755, it now has 30 faculties and 15 research centres. It has an annual enrolment of 31,000 students. The Russian Academy of Sciences, founded in 1724 and reorganized in 1925 as the Academy of Sciences of the Union of Soviet Socialist Republics, was restored under its present name in 1991. It is the highest scientific self-governing institution in Russia and has 18 divisions on particular areas of science. The Academy also has three regional branches: the Urals Branch, the Siberian Branch and the Far East Branch.

Health

Doctors in 2003 numbered 609,043 and hospital beds 1·65m. There were 43 doctors per 10,000 people in 2003 and 97 hospital beds per 10,000 persons in 2005. There were 45,972 dentists, 1,153,683 nurses, 11,404 pharmacists and 67,403 midwives in 2003. Expenditure on health in 2004 was 6·0% of GDP. Russia has among the highest rates of growth of HIV cases in the world; by Dec. 2004 there were 298,000 registered cases. In 2005 there were 150 cases of tuberculosis per 100,000 people. In 2004, 35·8% of Russians aged 18 and over smoked (males, 61·3%; females, 15·0%).

Welfare

Russia is in the process of implementing a reform of its pensions system, the focus of which is to move away from a distributive system to an accumulating (funded) scheme. Instead of citizens paying 28% of their monthly salary into the state pension fund, since 2004 it has been possible to pay between 2% and 6% to private asset managers.

State welfare provision in 1999 included: old age, disability and survivor pensions; sickness and maternity benefits; work injury payments; unemployment benefits; and family allowances. In the period April–June 2002 the average monthly pension was 1,337 roubles. The subsistence level for pensioners was 1,383 roubles a month.

RELIGION

The Russian Orthodox Church is the largest religious association in the country. In early 2003 it had 128 dioceses (compared with 67 in 1989), over 19,000 parishes (6,893 in 1988) and about 480 monasteries (18 in 1980). There are also five theological academies, 26 seminaries, 29 pre-seminaries, two Orthodox universities, a theological institute, a women's pre-seminary and 28 icon-painting schools. In 2001 there were 23·6m. adherents. The total number of theological students is around 6,000. There are still many Old Believers, whose schism from the Orthodox Church dates from the 17th century. The Russian Church is headed by the Patriarch of Moscow and All Russia (Patriarch Kirill I—Metropolitan Kirill of Smolensk and Kaliningrad, b. 1946; elected Jan. 2009), assisted by the Holy Synod, which has seven members—the Patriarch himself and the Metropolitans of Krutitsy and Kolomna (Moscow), St Petersburg and Kyiv *ex officio*, and three bishops alternating for six months in order of seniority from the three regions forming the Moscow Patriarchate. The Patriarchate of Moscow maintains jurisdiction over 119 eparchies, of which 59 are in Russia; there are parishes of Russian Orthodox abroad, in Belarus, Ukraine, Kazakhstan, Moldova, Uzbekistan, the Baltic states, and in Damascus, Geneva, Prague, New York and Japan. There is a spiritual mission in Jerusalem, and a monastery at Mt Athos in Greece. A Russian Orthodox church was consecrated in Dublin in Ireland in Feb. 2003. Muslims represent the second largest religious community in Russia, numbering 19m. In Feb. 2010 the Supreme Co-ordinating Council of Russian Muslims was established to be co-chaired by the heads of the three major organizations—Talgat Tajuddin of the Central Spiritual Board of Muslims, Ravil Gainutdin of the Council of Muftis of Russia and Ismail Berdiyev of the Co-ordinating Muslim Council of the North Caucasus. There are an estimated 2m. Protestants, and Jewish communities, primarily in Moscow and St Petersburg, numbered 590,000 in 2001.

CULTURE

World Heritage Sites

Russia's World Heritage sites as classified by UNESCO (with year entered on list) are: the Historic Centre of St Petersburg (1990); the Kremlin and Red Square in Moscow (1990); Khizi Pogost (1990); the Historic Monuments of Novgorod and surroundings (1992); Cultural and Historic Ensemble of the Solovetsky Islands (1992); the White Monuments of Vladimir and Suzdal (1992); Architectural Ensemble of the Trinity Sergius Lavra in Sergiev Posad (1993); the Church of the Ascension, Kolomenskoye (1994); Virgin Komi Forests (1995); Lake Baikal (1996); Volcanoes of Kamchatka (1996, 2001); Golden Mountains of Altai (1998); Western Caucasus (1999); the Ensemble of Ferapontov Monastery (2000); Historic and Architectural Complex of the Kazan Kremlin (2000); Central Sikhote-Alin (2001); the Citadel, Ancient City and Fortress Buildings of Derbent (2003); Ensemble of the Novodevichy Convent in southwest Moscow (2004); Natural System of Wrangel Island Reserve (2004); the historical centre of the city of Yaroslavl (2005).

The Russian Federation also shares three UNESCO sites: the Curonian Spit with Lithuania (2000); Uvs Nuur Basin with Mongolia (2003); and the Struve Geodetic Arc (2005), a chain of survey triangulations spanning from Norway to the Black Sea that helped establish the exact shape and size of the earth, with nine other countries.

Broadcasting

Television broadcasting (colour by SECAM) is still largely state-controlled. There are three large national TV networks; RTR (owned by the Russian State Television and Radio Broadcasting Company), Channel One (majority state shareholding) and NTV (owned by state-run Gazprom). TVS, the only private national network, closed in 2003. A government-funded English-language satellite channel, Russia Today, was launched in 2005 as a news-based station. In 2003, 99% of the population could receive TV broadcasts. There are also local city channels. Access to cable TV varies with locality. In 2005 there were 49·8m. TV-equipped households. Radio Russia and Radio Mayak are state national radio networks. Voice of Russia is an external service. There are hundreds of commercial FM radio stations, many carrying relays from the state national networks. 96% of the population in 2002 could receive radio broadcasts.

Cinema

There were 1,532 cinema screens in 2007; admissions in 2008 totalled 123·9m. In 2004, 93 feature films were produced in Russia.

Press

In 2002 there were 436 daily newspapers with combined annual sales of 7,850m. There were 26,112 non-daily newspapers in 2006. The most popular daily newspaper in 2002 was Komsomolskaya Pravda, with a circulation of 674,000. A presidential decree of 22 Dec. 1993 brought the press agencies ITAR-TASS and RIA-Novosti under state control. In 2004 more than 90,000 new or revised books were published, a figure exceeded only by China, the UK, the USA and Germany. Revenue from book publishing in 2005 was around 55bn. roubles. Russia's media has become relatively independent, but press freedom has suffered setbacks since 2000 when Vladimir Putin became president.

Tourism

There were 19,940,000 non-resident tourists in 2005; tourist receipts amounted to US$7·40bn.

DIPLOMATIC REPRESENTATIVES

Of Russia in the United Kingdom (13 Kensington Palace Gdns, London, W8 4QX)
Ambassador: Yury V. Fedotov.

Of the United Kingdom in Russia (Smolenskaya Naberezhnaya 10, 121099 Moscow)
Ambassador: Anne Pringle.

Of Russia in the USA (2650 Wisconsin Ave., NW, Washington, D.C., 20007)
Ambassador: Sergei Kislyak.

Of the USA in Russia (8 Bolshoy Devyatinskiy Pereuulok, 121099 Moscow)
Ambassador: John R. Beyrle.

Of Russia to the United Nations
Ambassador: Vitaly Churkin.

Of Russia to the European Union
Ambassador: Vladimir A. Chizhov.

FURTHER READING

Rossiiskii Statisticheskii Ezhegodnik. Annual (title varies)

Acton, E., *et al.*, *Critical Companion to the Russian Revolution.* 1997

Aron, Leon, *Boris Yeltsin: A Revolutionary Life.* 2000

Aslund, Anders, (ed.) *Economic Transformation in Russia.* 1994.—*Building Capitalism: the Transformation of the Former Soviet Bloc.* 2002

Bacon, Edwin, *Securitising Russia: The Domestic Politics of Putin.* 2006.—*Contemporary Russia.* 2nd ed. 2010

Brady, Rose, *Kapitalizm: Russia's Struggle to Free its Economy.* 2000

Cambridge Encyclopedia of Russia and the Former Soviet Union. 1995

Dunlop, J., *Russia Confronts Chechnya: Roots of a Separatist Conflict, Vol. 1.* 1998

Evans, Alfred B., *Russian Civil Society: A Critical Assessment.* 2005

Fowkes, B. (ed.) *Russia and Chechnia: The Permanent Crisis, Essays on Russo-Chechen Relations.* 1998

Freeze, G. (ed.) *Russia: A History.* 1997

Gall, C. and de Waal, T., *Chechnya: Calamity in the Caucasus.* 1998

Gorbachev, Mikhail, *On My Country and the World*; translated from Russian. 2000

Granville, Brigitte and Oppenheimer, Peter (eds.) *Russia's Post-Community Economy.* 2001

Gustafson, Thane, *Capitalism Russian-Style.* 2000

Hollander, Paul, *Political Will and Personal Belief: The Decline and Fall of Soviet Communism.* 2000

Holmes, Stephen, *The State After Communism: Governance in the New Russia.* 2006

Hosking, Geoffrey, *Russia and the Russians, A History from Rus to the Russian Federation.* 2001

Kanet, Roger E. (ed.) *Russia: Re-Emerging Great Power.* 2007

Kochan, L., *The Making of Modern Russia.* 2nd ed., revised by R. Abraham. 1994

Kotkin, Stephen, *Armageddon Averted: the Soviet Collapse 1970–2000.* 2001

Lieven, A., *Chechnya: Tombstone of Russian Power.* 1998

Lloyd, J., *Rebirth of a Nation.* 1998

Marks, Steven, *How Russia Shaped the Modern World: From Art to Anti-Semitism, Ballet to Bolshevism.* 2002

Paxton, J., *Encyclopedia of Russian History.* 1993.—*Leaders of Russia and the Soviet Union.* Fitzroy Dearborn, London, 2004

Ponsard, Lionel, *Russia, NATO and Cooperative Security.* 2006

Putin, Vladimir, *First Person*; interviews, translated from Russian. 2000

Remington, Thomas F., *Politics in Russia.* 2005

Remnick, D., *Resurrection: The Struggle for a New Russia.* 1998

Riasanovsky, N. V., *A History of Russia.* 5th ed. 1993

Sakwa, R., *Russian Politics and Society.* 2nd ed. 1996

Service, Robert, *A History of Twentieth-Century Russia.* 1997.—*Lenin: A Biography.* 2000.—*Russia: Experiment with a People.* 2002

Shevtsova, Lilia, *Putin's Russia.* 2003

Shriver, G. (ed. and transl.) *Post-Soviet Russia, A Journey Through the Yeltsin Era.* 2000

Tsygankov, Andrei P., *Russia's Foreign Policy: Change and Continuity in National Identity.* 2006

Webber, Stephen L., *Military and Society in Post-Soviet Russia.* 2006

Westwood, J. N., *Endurance and Endeavour: Russian History, 1812–1992.* 4th ed. 1993

White, Stephen, *et al.*, *How Russia Votes.* 1997

White, Stephen, Sakwa, Richard and Hale, Henry E. (eds.) *Developments in Russian Politics 7.* 2009

Woodruff, David, *Money Unmade: Barter and the Fate of Russian Capitalism.* 2000

Yeltsin, B., *The View from the Kremlin* (in USA *The Struggle for Russia*). 1994

National Statistical Office: Federal State Statistics Service, 39 Myasnitskaya St., Moscow 103450.
Website: http://www.gks.ru

THE REPUBLICS

Status

The 21 republics that with Russia itself constitute the Russian Federation were part of the RSFSR in the Soviet period. On 31 March 1992 the federal government concluded treaties with the then 20 republics, except Checheno-Ingushetia and Tatarstan, defining their mutual responsibilities. The *Council of the Heads of the Republics* is chaired by the Russian President and includes the Russian Prime Minister. Its function is to provide an interaction between the federal government and the republican authorities.

Adygeya

Part of Krasnodar Territory. Area, 7,600 sq. km (2,950 sq. miles); population (2002 census), 477,109. Estimated population, 1 Jan. 2005, 444,400. Capital, Maikop (2002 census, 156,931). Established 27 July 1922; granted republican status in 1991.

President: Aslan Tkhakushinov, b. 1947 (in office since 13 Jan. 2007).

Prime Minister: Murat Kumpilov, b. 1973 (in office since 14 May 2008—acting until 28 May 2008).

Chief industries are timber, woodworking and food processing; there is some engineering and gas production. Agriculture consists primarily of crops (beets, wheat, maize), on partly irrigated land. Industry accounted for 15·2% of gross regional product in 2003 and agriculture 13·6%.

In 2004 there were 12,400 pupils in 126 pre-school institutions and 50,700 pupils in 175 primary and secondary day schools. There were 20,000 students at the two institutions of higher education, Adygeya State University and Maikop State Technological Institute.

In 2004 the rates of doctors and hospital beds per 10,000 population were 37·2 and 110 respectively.

Altai

Part of Altai Territory. Area, 92,600 sq. km (35,750 sq. miles); population (2002 census), 202,947. Estimated population, 1 Jan. 2005, 203,900. Capital, Gorno-Altaisk (2002 census, 53,538). Established 1 June 1922 as Oirot Autonomous Region; renamed 7 Jan. 1948; granted republican status in 1991 and renamed in 1992.

Chairman of the Government: Aleksandr Berdnikov (since 20 Jan. 2006).

Cattle breeding predominates. Chief industries are clothing and footwear, foodstuffs, gold mining, timber, chemicals and dairying. Industrial output was valued at 838m. roubles in 2004 and agricultural output at 2,972m. roubles. In 2000, 91,200 people were economically active, of whom 72,000 were in employment.

In 2004 there were 6,600 pupils in 130 pre-school institutions and 32,300 pupils in 202 primary and secondary day schools. There were 6,000 students at Gorno-Altaysk State University.

The rates of doctors and hospital beds per 10,000 population in 2004 were 38·0 and 123 respectively.

Bashkortostan

Area 143,600 sq. km (55,450 sq. miles), population (2002 census), 4,104,336. Estimated population, 1 Jan. 2005, 4,078,800. Capital, Ufa (2002 census population, 1,042,437). Bashkiria was annexed to Russia in 1557. It was constituted as an Autonomous Soviet Republic on 23 March 1919. A declaration of republican sovereignty was adopted in 1990, and a declaration of independence on 28 March 1992. A treaty of Aug. 1994 with Russia preserves the common legislative framework of the Russian Federation while defining mutual areas of competence. The main ethnic groups are Russians, Tatars and Bashkirs. There are also Chuvash and Mari minorities.

A constitution was adopted on 24 Dec. 1993. It states that Bashkiria conducts its own domestic and foreign policy, that its laws take precedence in Bashkiria, and that it forms part of the Russian Federation on a voluntary and equal basis.

President: Murtaza Gubaidullovich Rakhimov (since 17 Dec. 1993).

Prime Minister: Rail Sarbayev (since 10 April 2008).

Industrial production was valued at 354,000m. roubles in 2004 and agricultural output at 57,160m. roubles. The most important industries are oil and oil products; there are also engineering, glass and building materials enterprises. Agriculture specializes in wheat, barley, oats and livestock.

In 2004 there were 144,600 pupils in 1,904 pre-school institutions and 583,300 pupils in 3,187 primary and secondary day schools. There were 150,200 students in 17 institutions of higher education. There is a state university and a branch of the Academy of Sciences with eight learned institutions.

In 2004 the rates of doctors and hospital beds per 10,000 population were 41·9 and 104 respectively.

Buryatia

Area is 351,300 sq. km (135,650 sq. miles). The Buryat Republic, situated to the south of Sakha, adopted the Soviet system on 1 March 1920. This area was penetrated by the Russians in the 17th century and finally annexed from China by the treaties of Nerchinsk (1689) and Kyakhta (1727). Population (2002 census), 981,238. Estimated population, 1 Jan. 2005, 969,200. Capital, Ulan-Ude (2002 census population, 359,391). The main ethnic groups are Russians, followed by Buryats. There are also Ukrainian, Tatar and Belarusian minorities.

There is a 65-member parliament, the *People's Hural*.

President: Vyacheslav Nagovitsyn (in office since 10 July 2007).

The main industries are engineering, brown coal and graphite, timber, building materials, sheep and cattle farming. Industrial production was valued at 32,161m. roubles in 2004 and agricultural output at 8,352m. roubles.

In 2004 there were 30,100 pupils in 423 pre-school institutions and 139,000 pupils in 572 primary and secondary day schools. There were 31,900 pupils in five institutions of higher education.

In 2004 the rates of doctors and hospital beds per 10,000 population were 38·3 and 109 respectively. The level of poverty in Buryatia was 38·2% in 2003.

Chechnya

GENERAL DETAILS

The area of the Republic of Chechnya is 15,000 sq. km (5,800 sq. miles). The population at the 2002 census was 1,103,686. The estimated population at 1 Jan. 2005 was 1,141,300. Capital, Dzhohar (since March 1998; previously known as Grozny; 2002 census population, 210,720). The Chechens and Ingushes were conquered by Russia in the late 1850s. In 1920 each nationality were constituted areas within the Soviet Mountain Republic and the Chechens became an Autonomous Region on 30 Nov. 1922. In Jan. 1934 the two regions were united, and on 5 Dec. 1936 constituted as the Checheno-Ingush Autonomous Republic. This was dissolved in 1944 and the population was deported en masse, allegedly for collaboration with the German occupation forces. It was reconstituted on 9 Jan. 1957: 232,000 Chechens and Ingushes returned to their homes in the next two years.

In 1991 rebel leader Jokhar Dudayev seized control of Chechnya and won elections. In Nov. he declared an independent Chechen Republic. Ingush desire to separate from Chechnya led to fighting along the Chechen-Ingush border and a deployment of Russian troops. An agreement to withdraw was reached between Russia and Chechnya on 15 Nov. 1992. The separation of Chechnya and Ingushetia was formalized in Dec. 1992. In April 1993 President Dudayev dissolved parliament. Hostilities continued throughout 1994 between the government and forces loosely grouped under the 'Provisional Chechen Council'. The Russian government, which had never recognized the Chechen declaration of independence of Nov. 1991, moved troops and armour into Chechnya on 11 Dec. 1994. Grozny was bombed and attacked by Russian ground forces at the end of Dec. 1994 and the presidential palace was captured on 19 Jan. 1995, but fighting continued. On 30 July 1995 the Russian and Chechen authorities signed a ceasefire. However, hostilities, raids and hostage-taking continued; Dudayev was killed in April 1996 and a ceasefire was agreed on 30 Aug. 1996.

Fighting broke out again, however, in Sept. 1999 as Russian forces launched attacks on 'rebel bases'. Fighting intensified and more than 200,000 civilians were forced to flee, mostly to neighbouring Ingushetia. By Feb. 2000 much of Grozny had been destroyed and was closed by the Russians. In June 2000 Vladimir Putin declared direct rule. The conflict continues, with estimates of the number of deaths varying from 6,500 to 15,000. Over 4,000 Russian soldiers have been killed. However, on 18 Nov. 2001 the first official meeting between negotiators for the Russian government and Chechen separatists took place. In Oct. 2002 a group of Chechen rebels took control of a Moscow theatre and held hostage 800 people for three days, before Russian troops stormed the building. An anaesthetic gas, used to combat the rebels, also killed many of the hostages.

On 23 March 2003 a referendum was held on a new constitution that would keep Chechnya within Russia but give it greater autonomy, and provide a new president and parliament for the republic. Although 96% of votes cast were in favour of the new constitution there was criticism of the conduct of the referendum. Presidential elections held on 5 Oct. 2003 were won by the Kremlin-backed candidate Akhmad Kadyrov, with 80·8% of the vote, but there was widespread condemnation of the electoral process. President Kadyrov was assassinated on 9 May 2004. Presidential elections held on 29 Aug. 2004, widely seen as rigged, were won by the Kremlin-backed Alu Alkhanov with 73·5% of the vote, against 5·9% for Movsur Khamidov, head of the Chechen department of the Federal Security Service. There were five other candidates. Turnout was 85·2%. On 27 Nov. 2005 the first parliamentary elections took place since Russian troops restored Moscow's control over Chechnya in 1999. In the elections to the People's Assembly (lower chamber) the United Russia party won 19 of 38 seats with 60·7% of the vote, the Communist Party 3 with 12·2%, the Union of Rightist Forces 1 with 12·4%, the Eurasian Union 1 with 3·9%; independents won 14 seats. In the Council of the Republic (upper chamber), United Russia won 14 of 20 seats, the Communist Party 3 and the Union of Rightist Forces 3.

Separatist President Aslan Maskhadov was killed by Russian troops on 8 March 2005, as was his successor Abdul-Khalim Sadulayev on 17 June 2006.

Moscow-backed President: Ramzan Kadyrov; b. 1976.

Prime Minister: Odes Baisultanov; b. 1965.

Amir of the Caucasus Emirate (self-proclaimed): Doku Umarov; b. 1964.

Checheno-Ingushetia had a major oilfield, and a number of engineering works, chemical factories, building materials works and food canneries. There was a timber, woodworking and furniture industry. In 2003 oil production was 1·8m. tonnes. Chechnya's oil reserves are estimated at some 220m. bbls. Industrial output in the two republics was valued at 213,000m. roubles in 1993, agricultural output at 79,000m. roubles.

In 2004 there were 212,300 pupils in 460 primary and secondary day schools. There were 23,500 students in three institutions of higher education. In 1995 the rates of doctors and hospital beds per 10,000 population were 21·1 and 91 respectively.

FURTHER READING

Jagielski, Wojciech, *Towers of Stone: The Battle of Wills in Chechnya.* 2009

Lieven, A. and Bradner, H., *Chechnya: Tombstone of Russian Power.* 1999

Chuvashia

Area, 18,300 sq. km (7,050 sq. miles); population (2002 census), 1,313,754. Estimated population, 1 Jan. 2005, 1,229,300. Capital, Cheboksary (2002 census population, 440,621). The territory was annexed by Russia in the middle of the 16th century. On 24 June 1920 it was constituted as an Autonomous Region, and on 21 April 1925 as an Autonomous Republic. The main ethnic groups are Chuvash, followed by Russians. There are also Tatar and Mordovian minorities. Republican sovereignty was declared in Sept. 1990.

President: Nikolai Fedorov (in office since 21 Jan. 1994).

Prime Minister: Nina Suslonova (in office since 2 April 2010—acting until 8 April 2010).

The timber industry antedates the Soviet period. Other industries include railway repair works, electrical and other engineering industries, building materials, chemicals, textiles and food industries. Grain crops account for nearly two-thirds of all sowings and fodder crops for nearly a quarter. Chuvashia is Russia's main producer of hops and the republic has a significant brewing industry. Industrial output was valued at 49,826m. roubles in 2004 and agricultural output at 12,722m. roubles.

In 2004 there were 47,100 pupils at 433 pre-school institutions and 166,200 pupils in 619 primary and secondary day schools. There were 63,900 students in seven higher educational establishments.

In 2004 the rates of doctors and hospital beds per 10,000 population were 46·8 and 116 respectively.

Dagestan

Area, 50,300 sq. km (19,400 sq. miles); population (2002 census), 2,576,531. Estimated population, 1 Jan. 2005, 2,621,800. Capital, Makhachkala (2002 census population, 462,412). Over 30 nationalities inhabit this republic apart from Russians; the most numerous are Dagestanis and there are also Azerbaijani, Chechen and Jewish minorities. Annexed from Persia in 1723, Dagestan was constituted an Autonomous Republic on 20 Jan. 1921. In 1991 the Supreme Soviet declared the area of republican, rather than autonomous republican, status. Many of the nationalities who live in Dagestan have organized armed militias, and in May 1998 rebels stormed the government building in Makhachkala. In Aug. 1999 Dagestan faced attacks from Islamic militants who invaded from Chechnya. Although Russian troops tried to restore order and discipline, the guerrilla campaign has continued with a series of bombings targeting Russian military personnel.

President: Magomedsalam Magomedov (in office since 20 Feb. 2010).

Prime Minister: Magomed Abdulayev (in office since 25 Feb. 2010).

There are engineering, oil, chemical, woodworking, textile, food and other light industries. Agriculture is varied, ranging from wheat to grapes, with sheep farming and cattle breeding. Industrial output was valued at 6,568m. roubles in 2001 and agricultural output at 13,162m. roubles.

In 2004 there were 55,900 pupils in 593 pre-schools and 443,300 pupils in 1,683 primary and secondary day schools. There were 105,500 students in 15 institutions of higher education. There is a branch of the Russian Academy of Sciences with ten learned institutions.

In 2004 the rates of doctors and hospital beds per 10,000 population were 38·2 and 70 respectively.

Ingushetia

The history of Ingushetia is interwoven with that of Chechnya (*see above*). Ingush desire to separate from Chechnya led to fighting along the Chechen-Ingush border and a deployment of Russian troops. The separation of Ingushetia from Chechnya was formalized by an amendment of Dec. 1992 to the Russian Constitution. On 15 May 1993 an extraordinary congress of the peoples of Ingushetia adopted a declaration of state sovereignty within the Russian Federation. Skirmishes between Ingush refugees and local police broke out in Aug. 1999 and tensions remained high with the danger of further outbreaks of fighting. The Russian attacks on neighbouring Chechnya in Sept. 1999 led to thousands of Chechen refugees fleeing to Ingushetia. In April 2004 President Murat Zyazikov survived an assassination attempt, as did Prime Minister Ibragim Malsagov in Aug. 2005.

The capital is Magas (since 1999; formerly Nazran; 2002 census population, 125,066).

Area, 4,300 sq. km (1,700 sq. miles); population (2002 census), 467,294. Estimated population, 1 Jan. 2005, 481,600.

There is a 27-member parliament. On 27 Feb. 1994 presidential elections and a constitutional referendum were held. Turnout was 70%. At the referendum 97% of votes cast approved a new constitution stating that Ingushetia is a democratic law-based secular republic forming part of the Russian Federation on a treaty basis.

President: Yunus-bek Yevkurov.

Prime Minister: Aleksei Vorobyov.

Industry accounted for 14·6% of gross regional product in 2003 and agriculture 14·1%. A special economic zone for Russian residents was set up in 1994, and an 'offshore' banking tax haven in 1996.

In 2004 there were 2,500 pupils in 20 pre-school institutions and 64,600 pupils in 113 primary and secondary day schools. There were 9,400 students in five institutions of higher education.

In 2004 the rates of doctors and hospital beds per 10,000 population were 22·8 and 41 respectively.

Kabardino-Balkaria

Area, 12,500 sq. km (4,850 sq. miles); population (2002 census), 901,494. Estimated population, 1 Jan. 2005, 896,900. Capital, Nalchik (2002 census population, 274,974). Kabarda was annexed to Russia in 1557. The republic was constituted on 5 Dec. 1936. The main ethnic groups are Kabardinians, followed by Russians and Balkars. There are also Ukrainian, Ossetian and German minorities.

A treaty with Russia of 1 July 1994 defines their mutual areas of competence within the legislative framework of the Russian Federation. The recent history of Kabardino-Balkaria has been marked by the instability that has plagued the whole of the north Caucasus. In Oct. 2005 militants staged a large-scale assault on government buildings in Nalchik, an act for which Chechen rebel leader Shamil Besayev claimed responsibility. All mosques in the capital have been closed.

President: Arsen Kanokov (since 28 Sept. 2005).

Prime Minister (acting): Aleksandr Merkulov (since 21 Aug. 2009).

Main industries are ore-mining, timber, engineering, coal, food processing, timber and light industries, building materials. Grain, livestock breeding, dairy farming and wine-growing are the principal branches of agriculture. Agriculture accounted for 31·9% of gross regional product in 2003 and industry 14·2%.

In 2004 there were 26,100 pupils in 102 pre-school institutions and 123,400 pupils in 371 primary and secondary day schools. There were 28,500 students in four institutions of higher education. There is a branch of the Academy of Sciences with five learned institutions.

In 2004 the rates of doctors and hospital beds per 10,000 population were 41·3 and 101 respectively.

Kalmykia

Area, 76,100 sq. km (29,400 sq. miles); population (2002 census), 292,410. Estimated population, 1 Jan. 2005, 289,900. Capital, Elista (2002 census population, 104,254). The population is mainly Kalmyk and Russian, with small Chechen, Kazakh and German minorities.

The Kalmyks migrated from western China to Russia (Nogai Steppe) in the early 17th century. The territory was constituted an Autonomous Region on 4 Nov. 1920, and an Autonomous Republic on 22 Oct. 1935; this was dissolved in 1943. On 9 Jan. 1957 it was reconstituted as an Autonomous Region and on 29 July 1958 as an Autonomous Republic once more. In Oct. 1990 the republic was renamed the Kalmyk Soviet Socialist Republic; it was given its present name in Feb. 1992.

President: Kirsan Nikolaevich Ilyumzhinov (since April 1993).

Prime Minister: Vladimir Sengleyev (since Dec. 2007).

In April 1993 the Supreme Soviet was dissolved and replaced by a professional parliament consisting of 25 of the former deputies. On 5 April 1994 a specially-constituted 300-member constituent assembly adopted a 'Steppe Code' as Kalmykia's basic law. This is not a constitution and renounces the declaration of republican sovereignty of 18 Oct. 1990. It provides for a *President* elected for five-year terms with the power to dissolve parliament, and a 27-member parliament, the *People's Hural*, elected every four years. It stipulates that Kalmykia is an equal member and integral part of the Russian Federation, functioning in accordance with the Russian constitution.

Main industries are oil and gas production, canning and building materials. Cattle breeding and irrigated farming (mainly fodder crops) are the principal branches of agriculture. Overgrazing during the Soviet period has led to the desertification of Kalmykia's pastures and agricultural output has declined substantially in recent years. Agriculture accounted for 10·4% of gross regional product in 2003 and industry 6·4%.

In 2004 there were 9,500 pupils in 119 pre-school institutions and 44,900 pupils in 213 primary and secondary day schools. There were 10,000 students in two institutions of higher education. Chess forms part of the general school curriculum; President Kirsan Ilyumzhinov has been president of FIDE, the international chess federation, since Nov. 1995. In 2004 the rates of doctors and hospital beds per 10,000 population were 51·0 and 136 respectively. The main religion is Buddhism.

Karachai-Cherkessia

Area, 14,300 sq. km (5,500 sq. miles); population (2002 census), 439,470. Estimated population, 1 Jan. 2005, 434,500. Capital, Cherkessk (2002 census population, 116,244). A Karachai Autonomous Region was established on 26 April 1926 (out of a previously united Karachaevo-Cherkess Autonomous Region created in 1922), and dissolved in 1943. A Cherkess Autonomous Region was established on 30 April 1928. The present Autonomous Region was re-established on 9 Jan. 1957. The Region declared itself a Soviet Socialist Republic in Dec. 1990. Tension between the two ethnic groups increased after the first free presidential election in April 1999 was won by Vladimir Semyonov, an ethnic Karchayev. Despite numerous allegations of fraud the result was upheld by the Supreme Court. There were subsequently fears that the ethnic Cherkess opposition would attempt to set up breakaway government bodies.

President: Boris Ebzeyev, b. 1950 (took office on 4 Sept. 2008).

Prime Minister: Vladimir Kaishev, b. 1954 (took office on 17 Sept. 2008).

There are ore-mining, engineering, chemical and woodworking industries. The Kuban-Kalaussi irrigation scheme irrigates 200,000 ha. Livestock breeding and grain growing predominate in agriculture. Conflict in the north Caucasus has had a serious impact on the economy and the agricultural sector is supported by central government. Agriculture accounted for 19·4% of gross regional product in 2003 and industry 18·7%.

In 2004 there were 10,900 pupils in 99 pre-school institutions and 60,000 pupils in 190 primary and secondary day schools. There were 16,200 students in two institutions of higher education.

In 2004 the rates of doctors and hospital beds per 10,000 population were 33·9 and 101 respectively.

Karelia

The Karelian Republic, capital Petrozavodsk (2002 census population, 266,160), covers an area of 172,400 sq. km, with a 2002 census population of 716,281. Estimated population, 1 Jan. 2005, 703,100. Russians constitute the majority of the population, with some Karelians, Belarusians and Ukrainians.

Karelia (formerly Olonets Province) became part of the RSFSR after 1917. In June 1920 a Karelian Labour Commune was formed and in July 1923 this was transformed into the Karelian Autonomous Soviet Socialist Republic (one of the autonomous republics of the RSFSR). On 31 March 1940, after the Soviet-Finnish war, practically all the territory (with the exception of a small section in the neighbourhood of the Leningrad area) which had been ceded by Finland to the USSR was added to Karelia, and the Karelian Autonomous Republic was transformed into the Karelo-Finnish Soviet Socialist Republic as the 12th republic of the USSR. In 1946, however, the southern part of the republic, including its whole seaboard and the towns of Viipuri (Vyborg) and Keksholm, was attached to the RSFSR, reverting in 1956 to autonomous republican status within the RSFSR. In Nov. 1991 it declared itself the 'Republic of Karelia'.

Head of the Republic: Sergei Katanandov (since May 1998).

Prime Minister: Pavel Chernov (since Jan. 2003).

Karelia has a wealth of timber, some 70% of its territory being forest land. It is also rich in other natural resources, having large deposits of mica, diabase, spar, quartz, marble, granite, zinc, lead, silver, copper, molybdenum, tin, baryta and iron ore. Its lakes and rivers are rich in fish.

There are timber mills, paper-cellulose works, mica, chemical plants, power stations and furniture factories. Industrial output was valued at 512,000m. roubles in 2004. Over half of Karelia's production output is exported annually, principally to EU countries. Exports totalled US$842m. in 2004.

In 2004 there were 28,800 pupils in 496 pre-schools and 81,100 pupils in 293 primary and secondary day schools. There were 21,900 students in three institutions of higher education. There is a branch of the Russian Academy of Sciences with seven learned institutions.

In 2004 the rates of doctors and hospital beds per 10,000 population were 49·4 and 123 respectively.

Khakassia

Area, 61,900 sq. km (23,900 sq. miles); population (2002 census), 546,072. Estimated population, 1 Jan. 2005, 541,000. Capital, Abakan (2002 census population, 165,197). Established 20 Oct. 1930; granted republican status in 1991.

Chairman of the Government: Viktor Zimin (since 15 Jan. 2009).

There are coal- and ore-mining, timber and woodworking industries. The region is linked by rail with the Trans-Siberian line. Industrial output was valued at 25,651m. roubles in 2004 and agricultural output at 3,807m. roubles.

In 2004 there were 16,500 pupils in 157 pre-school institutions and 69,200 pupils in 289 primary and secondary day schools. There were 20,400 students in three higher education institutions.

In 2004 the rates of doctors and hospital beds per 10,000 population were 37·3 and 110 respectively.

Komi

Area, 415,900 sq. km (160,550 sq. miles); population (2002 census), 1,018,674. Estimated population, 1 Jan. 2005, 996,400. Capital, Syktyvkar (2002 census population, 230,011). Annexed by the princes of Moscow in the 14th century, the territory was constituted as an Autonomous Region on 22 Aug. 1921 and as an Autonomous Republic on 5 Dec. 1936. The largest ethnic group are Russians, followed by Komis, with Ukrainian and Belarusian minorities.

A declaration of sovereignty was adopted by the republican parliament in Sept. 1990, and the designation 'Autonomous' dropped from the republic's official name.

Head of the Republic: Vyacheslav Gayzer (since 15 Jan. 2010).

There are coal, oil, timber, gas, asphalt and building materials industries, and light industry is expanding. Livestock breeding (including dairy farming) is the main branch of agriculture. Industrial output was valued at 87·5bn. roubles in 2004 and agricultural output at 4·3bn. roubles.

In 2004 there were 47,700 pupils in 412 pre-schools and 128,300 pupils in 531 primary and secondary day schools. There were 35,400 students in seven institutions of higher education.

In 2004 the rates of doctors and hospital beds per 10,000 population were 43·9 and 116 respectively.

Mari-El

Area, 23,200 sq. km (8,950 sq. miles); population (2002 census), 727,979. Estimated population, 1 Jan. 2005, 716,900. Capital, Yoshkar-Ola (2002 census population, 256,719). The Mari people were annexed to Russia, with other peoples of the Kazan Tatar Khanate, when the latter was overthrown in 1552. On 4 Nov. 1920 the territory was constituted as an Autonomous Region, and on 5 Dec. 1936 as an Autonomous Republic. The republic renamed itself the Mari Soviet Socialist Republic in Oct. 1990, and adopted a new constitution in June 1995. In Dec. 1991 Vladislav Zotin was elected the first president. The main ethnic groups are Russians, followed by Maris, with some Tatars.

President: Leonid Markelov (since 14 Jan. 2001).

Coal is mined. The main industries are metalworking, timber, paper, woodworking and food processing. Crops include grain, flax, potatoes, fruit and vegetables. Industry accounted for 24·4% of gross regional product in 2003 and agriculture 16·5%.

In 2004 there were 25,700 pupils in 265 pre-school institutions and 88,600 pupils in 382 primary and secondary day schools. There were 28,500 students in five institutions of higher education.

In 2004 the rates of doctors and hospital beds per 10,000 population were 35·2 and 125 respectively.

Mordovia

Area, 26,200 sq. km (10,100 sq. miles); population (2002 census), 888,766. Estimated population, 1 Jan. 2005, 866,600. Capital, Saransk (2002 census population, 304,866). By the 13th century the Mordovian tribes had been subjugated by Russian princes. In 1928 the territory was constituted as a Mordovian Area within the Middle-Volga Territory, on 10 Jan. 1930 as an Autonomous Region and on 20 Dec. 1934 as an Autonomous Republic. The main ethnic groups are Russians, followed by Mordovians, with some Tatars.

President: Nikolai Merkushkin (since Jan. 1995).

Prime Minister: Vladimir Volkov (since Oct. 1995).

Industries include wood-processing and the production of building materials, furniture, textiles and leather goods. Agriculture is devoted chiefly to grain, sugar beet, sheep and dairy farming. Industrial output was valued at 29,117m. roubles in 2002.

In 2004 there were 23,900 pupils in 241 pre-school institutions and 97,300 students in 713 primary and secondary day schools. There were 42,900 students in four institutions of higher education.

In 2004 the rates of doctors and hospital beds per 10,000 population were 51·4 and 134 respectively.

North Ossetia (Alania)

Area, 8,000 sq. km (3,100 sq. miles); population (2002 census), 710,275. Estimated population, 1 Jan. 2005, 704,400. Capital, Vladikavkaz (2002 census population, 315,608). North Ossetia was annexed by Russia from Turkey and named the Terek region in 1861. On 4 March 1918 it was proclaimed an Autonomous Soviet Republic, and on 20 Jan. 1921 set up with others as the Mountain Autonomous Republic, with North Ossetia as the Ossetian (Vladikavkaz) Area within it. On 7 July 1924 the latter was constituted as an Autonomous Region and on 5 Dec. 1936 as an Autonomous Republic. In the early 1990s there was a conflict with neighbouring Ingushetia to the east, and to the south the decision of the Georgian government to disband the republic of South Ossetia led to ethnic war, with North Ossetia supporting the South Ossetians. Pressure for Ossetian reunification continues. In Sept. 2004 hostage takers seized a school in the town of Beslan. A three-day standoff ended with more than 350 people killed, nearly half of them children. Chechen rebels claimed responsibility for the siege.

A new constitution was adopted on 12 Nov. 1994 under which the republic reverted to its former name, Alania. Ossetians are the largest ethnic group, followed by Russians, with some Chechens, Armenians and Ukrainians.

Head of Republic: Taimuraz Mamsurov.

Prime Minister: Nikolay Khlyntsov.

The main industries are non-ferrous metals (mining and metallurgy), maize processing, timber and woodworking, textiles, building materials, distilleries and food processing. There is also a varied agriculture. Agriculture accounted for 16·8% of gross regional product in 2003 and industry 13·0%.

In 2004 there were 22,000 pupils in 216 pre-school institutions and 95,200 pupils in 218 primary and secondary day schools. There were 32,200 students in nine institutions of higher education.

In 2004 the rates of doctors and hospital beds per 10,000 population were 68·0 and 115 respectively.

Sakha

The area is 3,103,200 sq. km (1,197,750 sq. miles), making Sakha the largest republic in the Russian Federation; population (2002 census), 949,280. Estimated population, 1 Jan. 2005, 950,700. Capital, Yakutsk (2002 census population, 210,642). The Yakuts were subjugated by the Russians in the 17th century. The territory was constituted an Autonomous Republic on 27 April 1922. The largest ethnic group are Russians, followed by Yakuts, with Ukrainian and Tatar minorities.

President: Vyacheslav Shtyrov (since 27 Jan. 2002).

Prime Minister: Yegor Borisov (since 6 Feb. 2003).

The principal industries are mining (gold, tin, mica, coal) and livestock-breeding. Silver- and lead-bearing ores and coal are worked. Large diamond fields have been opened up; Sakha produces most of the Russian Federation's output. Timber and food industries are developing. Trapping and breeding of fur-bearing animals (sable, squirrel, silver fox) are an important source of income. Industry accounted for 41·1% of gross regional product in 2003 and agriculture 3·6%.

In 2004 there were 51,900 pupils in 697 pre-school institutions and 168,400 pupils in 692 primary and secondary day schools. There were 43,700 students in eight institutions of higher education.

In 2004 the rates of doctors and hospital beds per 10,000 population were 49·5 and 147 respectively.

Tatarstan

Area, 68,000 sq. km (26,250 sq. miles); population (2002 census), 3,779,265. Estimated population, 1 Jan. 2005, 3,768,500. Capital, Kazan (2002 census population, 1,105,289). From the 10th to the 13th centuries this was the territory of the Volga-Kama Bulgar State; conquered by the Mongols, it became the seat of the Kazan (Tatar) Khans when the Mongol Empire broke up in the 15th century, and in 1552 was conquered again by Russia. On 27 May 1920 it was constituted as an Autonomous Republic. The main ethnic groups are Tatars and Russians, with Chuvash, Ukrainian and Mordovian minorities.

In Oct. 1991 the Supreme Soviet adopted a declaration of independence. At a referendum in March 1992, 61·4% of votes cast were in favour of increased autonomy. A constitution was adopted in April 1992, which proclaims Tatarstan a sovereign state which conducts its relations with the Russian Federation on an equal basis. On 15 Feb. 1994 the Russian and Tatar presidents signed a treaty defining Tatarstan as a state united with Russia on the basis of the constitutions of both, but the Russian parliament has not ratified it.

President: Rustam Minnikhanov (since March 2010).

Prime Minister: Ildar Khalikov (since April 2010).

The republic has engineering, oil and chemical, timber, building materials, textiles, clothing and food industries. Industrial production was valued at 252,037m. roubles in 2003 and agricultural output at 43,639m. roubles. Tatarstan is one of the fastest-growing Russian republics.

In 2004 there were 149,900 pupils in 1,982 pre-school institutions and 472,900 pupils in 2,448 primary and secondary day schools. There were 207,100 students in 35 institutions of higher education. There is a branch of the Russian Academy of Sciences with four learned institutions. In 2004 the rates of doctors and hospital beds per 10,000 population were 44·9 and 109 respectively.

Tuva

Area, 170,500 sq. km (65,800 sq. miles); population (2002 census), 305,510. Estimated population, 1 Jan. 2005, 307,600. Capital, Kyzyl (2002 census population, 104,105). Tuva was incorporated in the USSR as an autonomous region on 11 Oct. 1944 and elevated to an Autonomous Republic on 10 Oct. 1961. The largest ethnic group are Tuvans, followed by Russians. Tuva renamed itself the 'Republic of Tuva' in Oct. 1991.

A new constitution was promulgated on 22 Oct. 1993 which adopts the name 'Tyva' for the republic. This constitution provides for a 32-member parliament (*Supreme Hural*), and a *Grand Hural* alone empowered to change the constitution, asserts the precedence of Tuvan law and adopts powers to conduct foreign policy. It was approved by 62·2% of votes cast at a referendum on 12 Dec. 1993.

Chairman of the Government: Sholban Kara-ool.

Tuva is well-watered and hydro-electric resources are important. The Tuvans are mainly herdsmen and cattle farmers and there is much good pastoral land. There are deposits of gold, cobalt and asbestos. The main exports are hair, hides and wool. There are mining, woodworking, garment, leather, food and other industries. Industrial production was valued at 1,700m. roubles in 2003 and agricultural output at 1,994m. roubles.

In 2004 there were 14,700 pupils in 217 pre-school institutions and 64,400 pupils in 176 primary and secondary day schools. There were 5,800 students at Tuva State University.

In 2004 the rates of doctors and hospital beds per 10,000 population were 42·7 and 178 respectively.

Udmurtia

Area, 42,100 sq. km (16,250 sq. miles); population (2002 census), 1,570,316. Estimated population, 1 Jan. 2005, 1,552,800. Capital, Izhevsk (2002 census population, 632,140). The Udmurts (formerly known as 'Votyaks') were annexed by the Russians in the 15th and 16th centuries. On 4 Nov. 1920 the Votyak Autonomous Region was constituted (the name was changed to Udmurt in 1932), and on 28 Dec. 1934 was raised to the status of an Autonomous Republic. The main ethnic group are Russians, followed by Udmurts, with Tatar, Ukrainian and Mari minorities.

A declaration of sovereignty and the present state title were adopted in Sept. 1990.

A new parliament was established in Dec. 1993 consisting of a 50-member upper house, the *Council of Representatives*, and a full-time 35-member lower house.

President: Alexander Alexandrovich Volkov (since April 1995).

Prime Minister: Yury Pitkevich (since Oct. 2000).

Heavy industry includes the manufacture of locomotives, machine tools and other engineering products, most of them for the defence industries, as well as timber and building materials. There are also light industries: clothing, leather, furniture and food. Industrial production was valued at 82,405m. roubles in 2004 and agricultural output at 16,662m. roubles.

In 2004 there were 73,900 pupils in 806 pre-school institutions and 185,400 pupils in 849 primary and secondary day schools. There were 73,300 students in eight institutions of higher education.

In 2004 the rates of doctors and hospital beds per 10,000 population were 56·4 and 131 respectively.

Autonomous Districts and Provinces

Chukot

Situated in Magadan region (Far East); area, 737,700 sq. km, population (2002 census), 53,824. Estimated population, 1 Jan. 2005, 50,700. Capital, Anadyr. Formed 1930. Population chiefly Russian, also Chukchi, Koryak, Yakut, Even. Minerals are extracted in the north, including gold, tin, mercury and tungsten.

Khanty-Mansi

Situated in Tyumen region (western Siberia); area, 523,100 sq. km, population (2002 census), 1,432,817. Estimated population, 1 Jan. 2005, 1,469,000, chiefly Russians but also Khants and Mansi. Capital, Khanty-Mansiisk. Formed 1930.

Nenets

Situated in Archangel region (Northern Russia); area, 176,700 sq. km, population (2002 census), 41,546. Estimated population, 1 Jan. 2005, 42,000. Capital, Naryan-Mar. Formed 1929.

Yamalo-Nenets

Situated in Tyumen region (western Siberia); area, 750,300 sq. km, population (2002 census), 507,006. Estimated population, 1 Jan. 2005, 523,400. Capital, Salekhard. Formed 1930.

Yevreyskaya (Jewish) Autonomous Oblast (Province)

Part of Khabarovsk Territory. Area, 36,000 sq. km (13,895 sq. miles); population (2002 census), 190,915. Estimated population, 1 Jan. 2005, 188,800, chiefly Russians, but also Ukrainians and Jews. Capital, Birobijan (2002 census population, 77,250). Established as Jewish National District in 1928. There is a Yiddish national theatre, newspaper and broadcasting service.

RWANDA

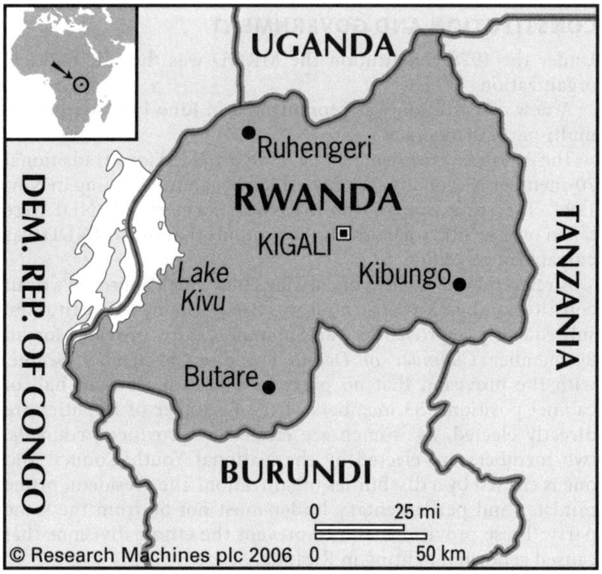

Republika y'u Rwanda
(Republic of Rwanda)

Capital: Kigali
Population estimate, 2010: 10·28m.
GDP per capita, 2007: (PPP$) 866
HDI/world rank: 0·460/167

KEY HISTORICAL EVENTS

The Twa—hunter-gatherer pygmies—were the first people to inhabit Rwanda. They now comprise 1% of the population. The Hutu were the next group to settle in Rwanda. They arrived at some point between AD 500 and 1100. They were small-scale agriculturalists, led by a king who ruled over clan groups. The final group to migrate to Rwanda was the Tutsi around 1400. Their ownership of cattle and their combat skills allowed them to gain economic and political control of the country. A feudalistic system developed where the Tutsi lent cows to the Hutu in return for labour and military service. At the apex was the Tutsi king, the *mwami* (pl., *abami*), who was believed to be of divine origin. The *abami* consolidated their power by centralizing the monarchy and reducing the power of neighbouring chiefs. Mwami Kigeri IV (reigned 1853–95) established the borders of Rwanda in the 19th century.

The Conference of Berlin in 1885 placed Rwanda under German control. However, no German actually reached the area until 1894 when Count von Götzen became the governor of German East Africa. The Belgians and British had ambitions in the area owing to its strategic position at the juncture of their separate empires. However, by 1910 German rule was accepted.

A consequence of German influence was the arrival of the Catholic Church through the mission of the White Fathers, who established schools and missions from 1899. Germany did not change the political structure of the country but made use of the mwami, Yuhi V (reigned 1896–1931), who accepted German overlordship. The victors of the First World War disrupted this relationship by stripping Germany of all her colonies. Rwanda was occupied by Belgian forces in 1916 and was declared a Belgian mandate in Aug. 1923 by the League of Nations. The Belgians ruled more directly than the Germans, curtailing the mwami's power and favouring the Tutsi minority on more explicitly racial grounds. From 1952 the UN ordered Belgium to integrate Rwandans into the political system. The Belgians continued their policy of favouring the fairer skinned Tutsi and placed them in a position of domination over the Hutu majority. Increasing civil unrest erupted into a civil war by 1959. A state of Ruanda-Urundi was established in 1960, under Belgian trusteeship, following an election. In 1961, while abroad, Mwami Kigeli V was exiled by the Belgians, who refused to allow him to return despite pressure from the UN. On 27 June 1962 the parliament voted to terminate the trusteeship and on 1 July 1962 Rwanda became independent.

Independence

The independent state of Rwanda was first governed by the Parmehutu party (a Hutu party representing the 85% Hutu population), led by Grégoire Kayibanda, but this was not accepted by some Tutsis. An attempted invasion in 1963 by Tutsis who had fled to Uganda and Burundi was repelled. In retaliation over 12,000 Tutsis in Rwanda were massacred by the Hutu. The next massacre in 1972–73 was partly in response to the persecution of Hutus in neighbouring Tutsi-dominated Burundi. An attempt by Kayibanda to revive his waning popularity, the violence instead spurred Maj.-Gen. Juvénal Habyarimana, a senior army commander, to launch a bloodless coup and take over government. In 1975 Habyarimana formed *le Mouvement Révolutionaire National pour le Développement* (MRND), and turned Rwanda into a one-party and tightly controlled police state, discriminating against the Tutsi in favour of the Hutu.

In 1990 the Rwandan Patriotic Front (RPF), of between 5,000 and 10,000 Tutsis, invaded Rwanda from Uganda, starting a civil war. A ceasefire was agreed on 29 March 1991 and on 14 July 1992 the Arusha Accords were signed. These allowed other political parties to stand for election and share power.

Many Hutus opposed Arusha. Multi-partyism led to the rise of far-right Hutu power groups who believed that the only solution to Hutu-Tutsi problems was the extermination of the Tutsi. The assassination of the first legitimately elected Hutu president of Burundi (21 Oct. 1993) by Tutsi army officers and the massacre of over 150,000 Hutus in Burundi served to further destabilize Rwanda. The assassination of Habyarimana in a plane crash on 6 April 1994, probably shot down by Hutu extremists, was the first step in a carefully premeditated genocide which killed around 1m. Rwandans in three months and forced over 2m. to flee to neighbouring countries.

Among the victims was the moderate Hutu prime minister, Agathe Uwilingiyimana. Gangs of *interahamwe* (civilian death squads) roamed the capital, Kigali, killing, looting and raping Tutsis and politically-moderate Hutus. When the RPF, led by Paul Kagame, reached Kigali the killings spread to other parts of the country. The UN sent a peacekeeping force (the United Nations Assistance Mission for Rwanda; UNAMIR) but a lack of resources, an unclear mandate and international apathy made it impotent as the genocide took hold. Eventually France dispatched 2,000 troops on a humanitarian mission on 22 June 1994 to maintain a 'safe zone'. Owing to France's affinity with the French-speaking Hutu former government, this zone served as an escape route for Hutu extremists to flee to Zaïre (now the Democratic Republic of the Congo).

The RPF declared the war over on 17 July 1994 and was quickly recognized as the new government. Genocide trials began in Arusha, Tanzania in Dec. 1996. In Sept. 1998 Jean Kambanda, the former prime minister (April–July 1994), was sentenced to life imprisonment.

Rwanda was destabilized by the presence of Hutu refugee camps on the Zaïre borders. Amongst the 1·1m. refugees were *interahamwe* who used the camps as bases for attacks on Rwanda. These were broken up by Laurent Kabila in May 1997, before he assumed power in Zaïre (later renamed the Democratic Republic of the Congo).

In April 2000 Paul Kagame (the Tutsi vice-president and defence minister) was elected president by parliament, replacing Pasteur Bizimungu, a Hutu who had been appointed by the RPF, in July 1994. Kagame was re-elected president in Aug. 2003 in Rwanda's first democratic elections since the atrocities.

TERRITORY AND POPULATION

Rwanda is bounded south by Burundi, west by the Democratic Republic of the Congo, north by Uganda and east by Tanzania. A mountainous state of 25,314 sq. km (9,774 sq. miles), its western third drains to Lake Kivu on the border with the Democratic Republic of the Congo and thence to the Congo river, while the rest is drained by the Kagera river into the Nile system.

The population was 7,164,994 at the 1991 census, of whom over 90% were Hutu, 9% Tutsi and 1% Twa (pygmy). 2002 census population, 8,128,553; density, 321·1 per sq. km.

The UN gives an estimated population for 2010 of 10·28m.

In 2005 the population was 80·7% rural, but urbanization is increasing rapidly.

At the time of the 2002 census there were 12 administrative divisions (11 provinces and Kigali City). Areas and populations were:

Province	*Area (in sq. km)*	*Population (2002 census)*
Butare	1,872	725,914
Byumba	1,694	707,786
Cyangugu	1,894	607,495
Gikongoro	1,974	489,729
Gisenyi	2,047	864,377
Gitarama	2,141	856,488
Kibungo	2,964	702,248
Kibuye	1,748	469,016
Kigali City	313	603,049
Kigali-Ngali	2,780	789,330
Ruhengeri	1,657	891,498
Umutara	4,230	421,623

Since Jan. 2006 Rwanda has been reorganized into five provinces (*intara*): Eastern, Northern, Southern, Western and Kigali City. Among the reasons given for the change were the reduction of ethnic divisions and the suppression of reminders of the 1994 genocide.

Kigali, the capital, had 603,049 inhabitants in 2002; other towns are Butare, Gisenyi, Gitarama and Ruhengeri.

Kinyarwanda, the language of the entire population, and English are the official languages (French having ceased to be an official language in Oct. 2008). Swahili is spoken in the commercial centres.

SOCIAL STATISTICS

2000 estimates: births, 325,000; deaths, 159,000. Estimated birth rate in 2000 was 42·1 per 1,000 population; estimated death rate, 20·6. Annual population growth rate, 1992–2002, 3·2%. Life expectancy at birth in 2007 was 51·4 years for females and 47·9 for males, up from 23·1 years for females and 22·1 years for males during the period 1990–95 (at the height of the civil war). Infant mortality, 2005, 118 per 1,000 live births; fertility rate, 2004, 5·6 births per woman.

CLIMATE

Despite the equatorial situation, there is a highland tropical climate. The wet seasons are from Oct. to Dec. and March to May. Highest rainfall occurs in the west, at around 70" (1,770 mm), decreasing to 40–55" (1,020–1,400 mm) in the central uplands and to 30" (760 mm) in the north and east. Kigali, Jan. 67°F (19·4°C), July 70°F (21·1°C). Annual rainfall 40" (1,000 mm).

CONSTITUTION AND GOVERNMENT

Under the 1978 constitution the MRND was the sole political organization.

A new constitution was promulgated in June 1991 permitting multi-party democracy.

The Arusha Agreement of Aug. 1994 provided for a transitional 70-member National Assembly, which began functioning in Nov. 1994. The seats won by the MRNDD (formerly MRND) were taken over by other parties on the grounds that the MRNDD was culpable of genocide.

A referendum was held on 26 May 2003 which approved a draft constitution by 93·4% (turnout was 87%). The new constitution, subsequently approved by the Supreme Court, provides for an 80-member *Chamber of Deputies* and a 26-member *Senate*, with the provision that no party may hold more than half of cabinet positions. 53 members of the Chamber of Deputies are directly elected, 24 women are elected by provincial councils, two members are elected by the National Youth Council and one is elected by a disabilities organization. The president, prime minister and parliamentary leader must not be from the same party. These provisions aim to prevent the ethnic divisions that caused genocidal fighting in Rwanda.

National Anthem

'Rwanda Nziza' ('Beautiful Rwanda'); words by F. Murigo, tune by Capt. J.-B. Hashakaimana.

RECENT ELECTIONS

In a popular election on 25 Aug. 2003 Paul Kagame was re-elected president for a seven-year term with 95·1% of the vote. Faustin Twagiramungu won 3·6% and Népomuscène Nayinzira won 1·3%. Turnout was 96·6%.

In parliamentary elections held on 15 Sept. 2008, President Kagame's Rwandan Patriotic Front (RPF) and its coalition won 78·8% of the vote. The RPF took 42 of the 53 directly elected seats, the Social Democratic Party 7 and the Liberal Party 4. Following the Sept. 2008 election, of the 80 Members of Parliament there were 45 women (56·25%) and 35 men (43·75%), making Rwanda the first country in the world to have a female majority in parliament (in part as a consequence of the adoption of quotas, which stipulate that at least 24 of the 80 seats must be filled by women).

Presidential elections were scheduled to take place on 9 Aug. 2010.

CURRENT ADMINISTRATION

President: Paul Kagame; b. 1957 (RPF—Tutsis; sworn in 22 April 2000 having been acting president since 24 March 2000 and re-elected in Aug. 2003).

In April 2010 the government comprised:

Prime Minister: Bernard Makuza; b. 1961 (ind.; sworn in 8 March 2000).

Minister of Agriculture: Agnes Kalibata. *Commerce and Industry:* Monique Nsanzabaganwa. *Culture and Sports:* Joseph Habineza. *Defence:* Gen. James Kabarebe. *East African Community:* Monique Mukaruliza. *Education:* Dr Charles Murigande. *Environment and Lands:* Stanislas Kamanzi. *Finance and Planning:* John Rwangombwa. *Foreign Affairs and Regional Co-operation:* Louise Mushikiwabo. *Forestry and Mines:* Christophe Bazivamo. *Gender and Family Promotion:* Jeannne d'Arc Mujawamariya. *Health:* Dr Richard Sezibera. *Infrastructure:* Vincent Karega. *Internal Security:* Musa Fazil Harerimana. *Justice:* Tharcisse Karugarama.

Local Government: James Musoni. *Public Service and Labour:* Anastase Murakezi. *Youth:* Protais Mitali. *Minister in Charge of Energy:* Albert Butare. *Minister in the President's Office:* Solina Nyirahabimana. *Minister in the Prime Minister's Office in Charge of Cabinet Affairs:* Protais Musoni.

Government Website: http://www.gov.rw

CURRENT LEADERS

Paul Kagame

Position
President

Introduction
Paul Kagame has long played a dominant role in Rwandan politics. He was elected president by the transitional National Assembly in April 2000, replacing Pasteur Bizimungu, and democratic elections in 2003 cemented his mandate. He is leader of the ruling Rwandan Patriotic Front (RPF) and the first member of the Tutsi minority to be president since Rwanda gained independence in 1962. Although a leading force in the country, he is a low-key public figure. He has openly criticized the United Nations, arguing it could have done more to avoid the genocide of 1994 when around 1m. Rwandans were killed, and also accused France of complicity.

Early Life
Kagame was born in Oct. 1957 in the Gitarama prefecture of central Rwanda. Following violence in Rwanda, his family fled to Uganda in 1960 where he grew up in a refugee camp. He received primary and secondary schooling in Uganda and then studied at Makerere University in Kampala. In 1979 Kagame joined the National Salvation Front (FRONASA), led by Yoweri Museveni, which took part in the Tanzanian removal of Idi Amin's regime in 1979. In 1980 he became a founding member of Museveni's National Resistance Army (NRA) and fought against the dictatorship of Milton Obote in Uganda. He became head of intelligence of the NRA in 1986 and the following year, together with Fred Rwigyema, established the Rwandan Patriotic Front (RPF) with support from Museveni.

The RPF first invaded Rwanda in 1990 when Kagame was on military training in Kansas, USA. After Rwigyema's death, Kagame returned and took over as military leader, leading the guerrilla war against Juvénal Habyarimana and his Hutu government. In 1993 a peace agreement was signed, but following the death of President Habyarimana in 1994 violence recurred with the Hutu massacres of the Tutsi. The RPF resumed the civil war and soon gained control over the country. The new government of national unity, formed in July 1994, was led by Pasteur Bizimungu, a Hutu, with Kagame as vice president and defence minister.

Career in Office
Rwanda's involvement in the Democratic Republic of the Congo (DRC; known as Zaïre until 1997) began covertly in 1996 with an agreement with Uganda to oust the Zaïrean president Mobutu Sese Seko. Kagame and Museveni sent troops back into the east of the DRC in 1998 to assist rebel groups against President Laurent Kabila and to eliminate the *interahamwe* (death squads from the 1994 genocide in Rwanda). In Nov. 1998 Kagame publicly admitted that Rwandese forces were active in the DRC for reasons of national security. Divisions appeared between the allied forces leading to support for different rebel groups and three confrontations in Kisangani, a major northern city. Kisangani's mineral wealth prompted allegations, categorically denied, that Uganda and Rwanda clashed over the allocation of spoils. Relations between Kagame and Museveni continued to sour, owing to the movement of dissidents taking refuge in each other's countries. The massive enlargement and reorganization of the Rwandese forces was interpreted as a direct threat by Museveni, who appealed to the British government in Aug. 2001 for financial support for increases in defence spending. The UK international development minister chaired talks between the two presidents in London in Nov. 2001, where once again they pledged not to support dissident groups.

In March 2000 President Bizimungu resigned, leaving Kagame as interim president. Bizimungu claimed that he and the prime minister, Pierre-Celéstin Rwigema, were hounded from office for being Hutus. Elected president by the transitional National Assembly in April 2000, Kagame relinquished the defence ministry to Col. Emmanuel Habyarimana, a Hutu, and promoted Nyamuasa Kayumba, the army chief, to Major-General, a rank only Kagame himself had held previously. Kagame has attempted to portray himself as a civilian and neutral president, calling for ethnic peace and reconciliation as a Rwandan rather than a Tutsi.

Following the assassination of Laurent Kabila (president of the DRC) in Jan. 2001, his son and successor, Joseph Kabila, met Kagame in Washington, D.C., ending the impasse. During the African Union summit in Durban in July 2002, Kagame again met with Kabila. Kagame accused the DRC of harbouring Hutu militias and was not willing to withdraw his troops until they were disarmed. Kabila blamed Rwanda for killing more than 3·5m. inhabitants of the DRC and refused to co-operate until Rwandan troops were withdrawn. However, on 30 July 2002 in Pretoria, South Africa, the two nations signed a peace deal under which the DRC agreed to disarm and arrest Hutu rebels and Rwanda withdrew its troops from the DRC in Oct. 2002.

Kagame was elected president by a popular democratic vote on 25 Aug. 2003. His massive win—with 95% of the vote—prompted allegations of irregularities from his main rival, Faustin Twagiramungu, although he accepted the win in Sept. Museveni's attendance at Kagame's inauguration ceremony demonstrated the easing of tensions between the two men. In 2007 Kagame authorized the release of several thousand prisoners accused of genocide. He also awarded a presidential pardon to Pasteur Bizimungu, who had served three years of a 15-year prison sentence for attempting to form a militia and for embezzlement. Parliamentary elections in Sept. 2008 returned the ruling coalition led by Kagame's RPF to power with almost 79% of the vote.

In Nov. 2006 a French investigative judge had accused Kagame of ordering the assassination of President Habyarimana in 1994. Kagame responded by cutting diplomatic links with France. Then, in Aug. 2008, a Rwandan report commissioned by Kagame made a counter-accusation of complicity by French politicians (including former president François Mitterrand) and army officers in the genocide. Relations were soured further when in Nov. 2008 one of Kagame's senior aides, Rose Kabuye, was arrested in Germany on a French extradition warrant. However, diplomatic ties were eventually restored in Nov. 2009.

From Aug. 2008 fighting in the DRC intensified between the army and the mainly Tutsi insurgents loyal to Laurent Nkunda. Kabila's government had for some time claimed that Kagame was giving Rwandan support to Nkunda. However, in an apparent reversal of Rwandan policy, troops from both countries launched a joint offensive in Jan. 2009 against Nkunda's headquarters in the DRC and the rebel leader was arrested when he fled into Rwanda. Since the operation, relations between Rwanda and the DRC have remained stable, with increased governmental contacts including a summit between Kagame and Kabila in Aug. 2009 in the border town of Goma.

In Nov. 2009 Rwanda was admitted to the Commonwealth despite (like Mozambique) not having had colonial or constitutional ties to the United Kingdom.

Bernard Makuza

Position
Prime Minister

Introduction
Bernard Makuza became prime minister of Rwanda in March 2000, nine days after the former prime minister, Pierre-Celéstin Rwigema, resigned amidst corruption allegations.

Early Life
Bernard Makuza was born in 1961. The former ambassador to Germany, Makuza returned to Rwanda to take up the post of prime minister. He was a former head of the predominately Hutu Republican Democratic Movement (MDR) but no longer belongs to a political party.

Career in Office
While the power of government resides with the president, the prime minister has a strong public image. In Jan. 2003 Makuza headed a national ceremony to mark the opening of rehabilitation centres for those who admitted taking part in the 1994 genocide. In Sept. 2004, alongside the then UN Secretary-General Kofi Annan and the Democratic Republic of the Congo's president, Joseph Kabila, Makuza was part of a UN-backed body created to resolve the civil unrest on the border between Rwanda and the DRC. In Oct. 2005 he opened the 6th African Congress on Savings and Credit Co-operatives; a two-day conference held in Kigali, it discussed the reduction of poverty in Africa via the management of co-operatives. Makuza has aimed to improve political, economic and trade relations with foreign countries and has forged a strong partnership with China.

DEFENCE

In 2006 defence expenditure totalled US$72m. (US$7 per capita), representing 2·4% of GDP.

Army

Strength (2007) about 32,000. There were local defence forces of some 2,000 in 2007.

INTERNATIONAL RELATIONS

Rwanda is a member of the UN, World Bank, IMF and several other UN specialized agencies, WTO, Commonwealth, IOM, International Organization of the Francophonie, African Development Bank, African Union, COMESA, EAC and is an ACP member state of the ACP-EU relationship.

ECONOMY

Agriculture accounted for 41·3% of GDP in 2006, industry 13·3% and services 45·4%.

Overview

In the past decade, Rwanda has seen strong economic growth while maintaining overall macroeconomic stability. Agriculture, which accounts for 40% of GDP and 90% of jobs, has been the primary economic driver. GDP growth averaged between 5–6% per year between 2002–06, buoyed by strong activity in the construction and service sectors. Inflation has remained below 10% in the last decade, although rising fuel prices led to increased transportation costs.

The economy is heavily dependent on foreign aid to finance development. A three-year Poverty Reduction and Growth Facility (PRGF) arrangement was agreed with the IMF in 2006 to maintain macroeconomic stability while allowing for growth. According to the OECD, strong growth has thus far had little significant impact on poverty reduction. An Economic Development and Poverty Reduction Strategy (EDPRS) aims to stimulate broad-based economic growth through better economic infrastructure and higher agricultural productivity.

Currency

The unit of currency is the *Rwanda franc* (RWF) notionally of 100 *centimes*. On 3 Jan. 1995, 500-, 1,000- and 5,000-Rwanda franc notes were replaced by new issues, demonetarizing the currency taken abroad by exiles. The currency is not convertible. Foreign exchange reserves were US$312m. in July 2005. Total money supply in Dec. 2003 was 82,305m. Rwanda francs. Inflation was 9·1% in 2007 and 15·4% in 2008.

Budget

In 2007 revenues were 472·3bn. Rwanda francs and expenditures 491·4bn. Rwanda francs.

VAT is 18%.

Performance

Real GDP growth was 35·2% in 1995, following five years of negative growth including a rate of –50·2% in 1994 at the height of the civil war. By 2000 the growth had slowed, but was still 6·0%. Real GDP growth was 7·9% in 2007 and 11·2% in 2008. Total GDP in 2008 was US$4·5bn.

Banking and Finance

The central bank is the National Bank of Rwanda (founded 1960; *Governor*, François Kanimba), the bank of issue since 1964. There are seven commercial banks (Banque de Kigali, Banque de Commerce et de Développement Industriel, Banque Continentale Africaine au Rwanda, Banque à la Confiance d'Or, Banque Commerciale du Rwanda, Caisse Hypothécaire du Rwanda and Compagnie Générale de Banque), one development bank (Rwandan Development Bank) and one credit union system (Rwandan Union of Popular Banks).

ENERGY AND NATURAL RESOURCES

Environment

Carbon dioxide emissions from the consumption and flaring of fossil fuels in 2008 were the equivalent of 0·1 tonnes per capita.

Electricity

Installed capacity was 31,000 kW in 2004. Production was estimated at 173m. kWh in 2004 and consumption per capita an estimated 31 kWh.

Oil and Gas

In 2007 proven natural gas reserves were 57bn. cu. metres.

Minerals

Production (2002): cassiterite, 197 tonnes; wolfram, 153 tonnes.

Agriculture

There were an estimated 1·2m. ha. of arable land in 2007 and 275,000 ha. of permanent crops. Production (2003, in 1,000 tonnes): bananas and plantains, 2,408; potatoes, 1,110; cassava, 1,003; sweet potatoes, 868; dry beans, 239; pumpkins and squash, 210; sorghum, 172; taro, 139; maize, 79; sugarcane, 40; rice, 28; dry peas, 18; tea, 15; wheat, 15.

In 2006 there were 1,330,000 goats, 997,000 cattle, 473,000 sheep, 327,000 pigs and 2m. chickens.

Forestry

Forests covered 480,000 ha. (19·5% of the land area) in 2005. Timber production in 2007 was 10·0m. cu. metres.

Fisheries

The catch in 2004 totalled 7,826 tonnes, entirely from inland waters.

INDUSTRY

There are about 100 small-sized modern manufacturing enterprises in the country. Food manufacturing is the dominant industrial activity (64%) followed by construction (15·3%) and mining (9%). There is a large modern brewery.

Labour
In 2005–06 there were 4,377,000 employed persons, with 79% of the economically active population engaged in agriculture, fisheries and forestry.

INTERNATIONAL TRADE
Rwanda, Burundi and the Democratic Republic of the Congo make up the Economic Community of the Great Lakes. Foreign debt was US$1,518m. in 2005.

Imports and Exports
In 2006 imports (f.o.b.) amounted to US$488m. (US$355m. in 2005); exports (f.o.b.) US$145m. (US$128m. in 2005). Leading imports are capital goods, food and energy products; major exports are coffee, tea and tin. Main import suppliers, 2006: Kenya, 26·1%; Uganda, 13·3%; Belgium, 6·9%; UAE, 6·9%. Main export markets, 2006: UK, 21·4%; Kenya, 21·3%; Belgium, 16·2%; Hong Kong, 10·7%.

COMMUNICATIONS
Roads
There were 14,008 km of roads in 2004, of which 19·0% were paved. There are road links with Burundi, Uganda, Tanzania and the Democratic Republic of the Congo. In 2006 there were 4,130 motorcycles, 1,813 cars and jeeps, and 1,270 trucks and pick-ups. There were 308 road deaths in 2007.

Civil Aviation
There is an international airport at Kigali (Gregoire Kayibanda), which handled 103,000 passengers (100,000 on international flights) in 2001. In 2003 there were scheduled flights to Addis Ababa, Brussels, Bujumbura, Douala, Entebbe, Johannesburg and Nairobi. A national carrier, Rwandair Express, began operations in 2003 flying to Entebbe and Johannesburg.

Telecommunications
Rwanda had 27,000 fixed telephone lines in 2006 and 268,000 mobile phone subscribers. Internet users numbered 100,000 in 2006.

Postal Services
In 2003 there were 25 post offices, or one for every 335,000 persons.

SOCIAL INSTITUTIONS
Justice
A system of Courts of First Instance and provincial courts refer appeals to Courts of Appeal and a Court of Cassation situated in Kigali. The death penalty was last used in 1998 and was abolished in 2007. A number of people were executed for genocide in the civil war in 1994, including 22 at five different locations throughout the country on 24 April 1998.

The population in penal institutions in Dec. 2007 was 58,598, of which around 39,000 were being held on suspicion of genocide.

Education
In 2003–04 there were 2,262 primary schools with 28,254 teachers for 1·8m. pupils; 230,909 secondary pupils with 7,750 teachers; and 27,243 students at university level with 1,909 academic staff. Adult literacy rate in 2003 was 64·0% (male, 70·5%; female, 58·8%).

In 2007 public expenditure on education came to 4·9% of GDP and accounted for 19·0% of total government spending.

Health
In 2005 there were 221 public sector physicians and dentists (148 in 2000), and 4,063 nurses (1,167 in 2000). There were 42 hospitals and 389 health centres in 2007.

There were 1·07m. reported cases of malaria in 2006.

RELIGION
In 2001 approximately 47% of the population were Roman Catholics, 19% Protestants and 7% Muslims. Some of the population follow traditional animist religions. Before the civil war there were nine Roman Catholic bishops and 370 priests. By the end of 1994, three bishops had been killed and three reached retiring age; 106 priests had been killed and 130 had sought refuge abroad.

CULTURE
Broadcasting
Radio is the principal medium and state-run Radio Rwanda is the most popular service. There are also several private radio stations. Télévision Rwandaise is the public TV service. In 2005 there were 58,000 television-equipped households. Colour is by SECAM V.

Press
There are no daily newspapers. The English-language *New Times* was published three times a week in 2006.

Tourism
In 2007 there were 826,374 tourist arrivals.

DIPLOMATIC REPRESENTATIVES
Of Rwanda in the United Kingdom (120–122 Seymour Place, London, W1H 1NR)
Ambassador: Claver Gatete.

Of the United Kingdom in Rwanda (Parcelle No. 1131, Blvd de l'Umuganda, Kacyira-Sud, PB 576, Kigali)
Ambassador: Nicholas Cannon, OBE.

Of Rwanda in the USA (1714 New Hampshire Ave., NW, Washington, D.C., 20009)
Ambassador: James Kimonyo.

Of the USA in Rwanda (2657 Ave. de la Gendarmerie, Kigali)
Ambassador: W. Stuart Symington.

Of Rwanda to the United Nations
Ambassador: Eugène-Richard Gasana.

Of Rwanda to the European Union
Ambassador: Joseph Bonesha.

FURTHER READING

Barnett, Michael, *Eyewitness to a Genocide: The United Nations and Rwanda.* 2003
Braeckman, C., *Rwanda: Histoire d'un Génocide.* 1994
Dallaire, Romeo, *Shake Hands with the Devil: The Failure of Humanity in Rwanda.* 2005
Dorsey, L., *Historical Dictionary of Rwanda.* 1995
Gourevitch, P., *We Wish to Inform You That Tomorrow We Will Be Killed With Our Families.* 1998
Melson, Robert, *Genocide and Crisis in Central Africa: Conflict Roots, Mass Violence and Regional War.* 2001
Melvern, Linda, *A People Betrayed: The Role of the West in Rwanda's Genocide.* 2000
Prunier, G., *The Rwanda Crisis: History of a Genocide.* 1995
Waugh, Colin M., *Paul Kagame and Rwanda: Power, Genocide and the Rwandan Patriotic Front.* 2004

National Statistical Office: National Institute of Statistics of Rwanda, B.P. 46, Kigali.
Website: http://www.statistics.gov.rw

ST KITTS AND NEVIS

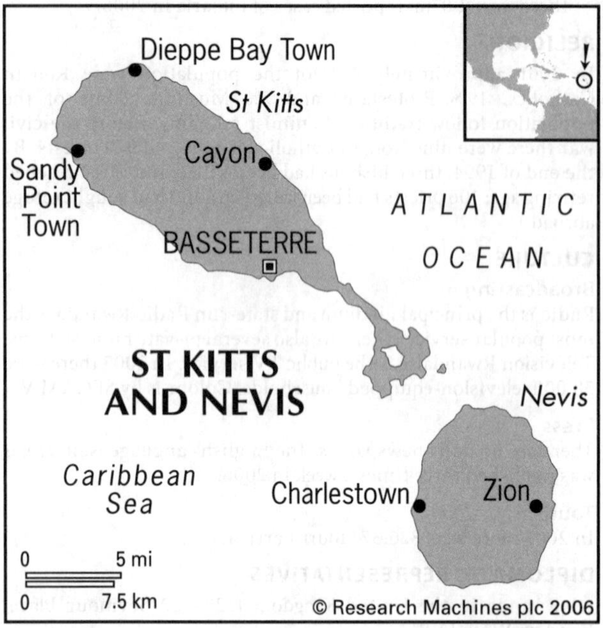

Federation of St Kitts and Nevis

Capital: Basseterre
Population, 2001: 46,000
GDP per capita, 2007: (PPP$) 14,481
HDI/world rank: 0·838/62

KEY HISTORICAL EVENTS

The islands of St Kitts (formerly St Christopher) and Nevis were discovered and named by Columbus in 1493. They were settled by Britain in 1623 and 1628, but ownership was disputed with France until 1783. In Feb. 1967 colonial status was replaced by an 'association' with Britain, giving the islands full internal self-government. St Kitts and Nevis became fully independent on 19 Sept. 1983. In Oct. 1997 the five-person Nevis legislature voted to end the federation with St Kitts. However, in a referendum held on 10 Aug. 1998 voters rejected independence, only 62% voting for secession when a two-thirds vote in favour was needed. In Sept. 1998 Hurricane Georges caused devastation, leaving 25,000 people homeless, with some 80% of the houses in the islands damaged.

TERRITORY AND POPULATION

The two islands of St Kitts and Nevis are situated at the northern end of the Leeward Islands in the eastern Caribbean. Nevis lies 3 km to the southeast of St Kitts. Population, 2001 census (provisional), 46,111. In 2005, 67·8% of the population were rural.

	Sq. km	*Census 1991*	*Census 2001 (provisional)*	*Chief town*	*Census 2001 (provisional)*
St Kitts	176·1	31,824	34,930	Basseterre	13,220
Nevis	93·3	8,794	11,181	Charlestown	1,820
	269·4	40,618	46,111		

In 2000, 90·4% of the population were Black. English is the official and spoken language.

SOCIAL STATISTICS

Births, 2001, 803; deaths, 352. Rates, 2001 (per 1,000 population): births, 17·4; deaths, 7·6. Infant mortality, 2005 (per 1,000 live births), 18. Life expectancy in 2004 was 70 years. Annual population growth rate, 1991–2001, 1·4%; fertility rate, 2004, 2·4 births per woman.

CLIMATE

Temperature varies between 21·4–30·7°C, with a sea breeze throughout the year and low humidity. Rainfall in 1999 was 1,706·9 mm.

CONSTITUTION AND GOVERNMENT

The British sovereign is the head of state, represented by a Governor-General. The 1983 constitution described the country as 'a sovereign democratic federal state'. It allowed for a unicameral Parliament consisting of 11 elected Members (eight from St Kitts and three from Nevis), three appointed Senators and one *ex officio* member. Nevis was given its own Island Assembly and the right to secession from St Kitts.

National Anthem

'O Land of beauty! Our country where peace abounds'; words and tune by K. A. Georges.

RECENT ELECTIONS

At the National Assembly elections on 25 Jan. 2010 the Labour Party gained 6 seats, the People's Action Movement 2, the Concerned Citizens Movement 2 and the Nevis Reformation Party 1. Turnout was 79·8%.

CURRENT ADMINISTRATION

Governor-General: Sir Cuthbert Montraville Sebastian, GCMG, OBE; b. 1921 (appointed 1 Jan. 1996).

In March 2010 the government comprised:

Prime Minister, Minister of Finance, Sustainable Development and Human Resource Development: Dr Denzil L. Douglas; b. 1936 (Labour Party; sworn in 7 July 1995 and re-elected in 2000, 2004 and 2010).

Deputy Prime Minister, Minister of Foreign Affairs, National Security, Immigration, Labour and Social Security: Sam Condor.

Minister of Education and Information: Nigel Carty. *Health, Social Services, Community Development, Culture and Gender Affairs:* Marcella Liburd. *International Trade, Industry, Commerce, Agriculture, Marine Resources, Consumer Affairs and Constituency Empowerment:* Timothy Harris. *Public Works, Utilities, Housing and Energy:* Dr Earl Asim Martin. *Tourism and International Transport:* Richard Skerritt. *Youth Empowerment, Sports, Information Technology, Telecommunications and Post:* Glenn Phillip. *Attorney General, Justice and Legal Affairs:* Patrice Nisbett.

The *Nevis Island* legislature comprises an Assembly of three nominated members and five elected members (one from each electoral district on the Island), and an Administration consisting of the Premier and two other persons appointed by the Deputy Governor-General.

The Premier of *Nevis* is Joseph Parry.

Government Website: http://www.gov.kn

CURRENT LEADERS

Dr Denzil L. Douglas

Position

Prime Minister

Introduction

Denzil Douglas has been prime minister of St Kitts and Nevis since 1995. In Jan. 2010 he was re-elected for his fourth consecutive term after his Labour Party secured six out of a possible eleven seats.

Early Life
Born in 1953, Denzil Llewellyn Douglas is a graduate of the University of the West Indies. He worked as a family physician before embarking on a career in politics. A Labour party activist from an early age, he became leader of the St Kitts and Nevis Labour Party in 1989. The 1995 election was called following drug smuggling allegations brought against the prime minister at the time, Kennedy Simmonds.

Career in Office
On becoming prime minister, Douglas sought to mend relations between the islands of St Kitts and Nevis. Nevertheless, in 1998 a referendum on secession was held after occupants of Nevis complained that the federal government in St Kitts was ignoring their needs. Although they failed to gain the two-thirds vote needed to break away, unrest remained. Douglas has since tried to tackle the differences through constitutional reform.

In Nov. 2004 Douglas chaired a CARICOM–UK conference aimed at reducing stigma and discrimination against those living with HIV and AIDS in the Caribbean. In May 2005 he chaired the first Caribbean Forum of Development, aimed at transforming the regional economy, and achieving international competitiveness and sustainable growth. He has also called for the cancellation of international debt, which has been crippling many Caribbean Islands.

While he has been widely praised for promoting poverty reduction and combating crime in Kitts and Nevis, he has been criticized for not reviving the islands' ailing sugar industry. In March 2005 the government effectively closed the 300 year-old industry after another loss-making harvest. Although the closure has had an adverse impact on government debt, economic activity was buoyed in 2006 and early 2007 by an expansion in tourism and construction spending related to the 2007 Cricket World Cup.

Re-elected for the third time in Jan. 2010, Douglas holds a number of ministerial posts in addition to the premiership.

INTERNATIONAL RELATIONS

St Kitts and Nevis is a member of the UN, World Bank, IMF and several other UN specialized agencies, WTO, Commonwealth, ACS, CARICOM, OECS, OAS and is an ACP member state of the ACP-EU relationship.

ECONOMY

Agriculture accounted for 3% of GDP in 2005, industry 28% and services 69%.

Overview

The economy is in transition following the government's closure of the sugar industry in 2005, a move encouraged by the EU and WTO after many years of heavy losses. The most important sources of revenue are service industries, offshore finance and tourism but the country is highly vulnerable to external shocks, such as natural disasters and shifts in the tourist market.

The Islands performed strongly in 2006 as output grew by 4%, driven by tourism, construction and communications. Fiscal accounts benefited as the government registered primary surpluses for four years in a row, while tax administration improved and wage restraint was implemented. However, public debt remains high (at 175% of GDP in 2008) and near-term growth prospects deteriorated following damage caused by Hurricane Omar in Oct. 2008. The global recession has put serious strains on the financial system, resulting from links with the troubled Trinidad and Tobago-based CL Financial Group.

Currency

The *East Caribbean dollar* (XCD) (of 100 *cents*) is in use. Inflation was 4·5% in 2007 and 5·4% in 2008. In July 2005 foreign exchange reserves were US$75m. Total money supply was EC$200m. in June 2005.

Budget

Total revenues in 2006 were EC$524·6m. and expenditures EC$551·2m. Tax revenue accounted for 71·3% of revenues in 2006; current expenditure accounted for 86·0% of expenditures.

Performance

Real GDP growth was 0·9% in 2007 and 2·4% in 2008. Total GDP was US$0·5bn. in 2008.

Banking and Finance

The East Caribbean Central Bank (*Governor*, Sir Dwight Venner) is located in St Kitts. It is a regional bank that serves the OECS countries. In 2002 there were four domestic commercial banks (Bank of Nevis, Caribbean Banking Corporation, Nevis Co-operative Bank and St Kitts-Nevis-Anguilla National Bank), three foreign banks and one development bank. Nevis has some 9,000 offshore businesses registered.

St Kitts and Nevis is a member of the Eastern Caribbean Securities Exchange, based in Basseterre.

ENERGY AND NATURAL RESOURCES

Environment

Carbon dioxide emissions from the consumption and flaring of fossil fuels in 2008 were the equivalent of 4·9 tonnes per capita.

Electricity

Installed capacity was 20,000 kW in 2003. Production in 2003 was 127m. kWh.

Agriculture

Main crops are coconuts, cotton, bananas, yams and molasses, and until 2005 sugarcane. The sugar industry was closed down following the 2005 harvest after years of losses at the state-run sugar company. In 2007 there were an estimated 4,000 ha. of arable land. Most of the farms are small-holdings and there are a number of coconut estates amounting to some 400 ha. under public and private ownership. Production, 2003 estimates (in 1,000 tonnes): sugarcane, 193; coconuts, 1.

Livestock (2003 estimates): goats, 14,000; sheep, 14,000; cattle, 4,000; pigs, 4,000.

Forestry

The area under forests in 2005 was 5,000 ha., or 14·7% of the total land area.

Fisheries

The catch in 2004 was approximately 484 tonnes.

INDUSTRY

There are three industrial estates on St Kitts and one on Nevis. Export products include electronics and data processing equipment, and garments for the US market. Other small enterprises include food and drink processing, and construction. Production of raw sugar (2001), 20,000 tonnes; molasses (1994), 6,000 tonnes.

Labour

In 1994 the economically active population numbered 16,608, of which 22·3% worked in services, finance and real estate, 20·3% in trade and restaurants, 16·5% in public administration and defence, and 10·5% in construction.

INTERNATIONAL TRADE

Foreign debt in 2007 amounted to US$274m.

Imports and Exports

Imports, 2005, US$185·21m.; exports, US$62·48m. The USA is by far the biggest trading partner. In 2005, 57·9% of imports were from the USA and 91·8% of exports went to the USA. Trinidad and Tobago is the second largest import supplier and the United Kingdom the second largest export destination. Main imports include machinery, manufactures, food and fuels. Major exports are machinery, food, electronics, beverages and tobacco.

COMMUNICATIONS

Roads

In 2002 there were about 383 km of roads, of which 42·5% were paved; and 6,900 passenger cars and 2,500 commercial vehicles.

Rail

In 2005 there were 50 km of railway, formerly operated by the sugar industry but now used for tourist purposes.

Civil Aviation

The main airport is the Robert Llewelyn Bradshaw International Airport (just over 3 km from Basseterre). In 2003 there were flights to Anguilla, Antigua, Barbados, British Virgin Islands, Dominica, Grenada, Jamaica, Netherlands Antilles, Nevis (Newcastle), Philadelphia, Puerto Rico, St Lucia, St Vincent, Trinidad and the US Virgin Islands.

Shipping

There is a deep-water port at Bird Rock (Basseterre). 202,000 tons of cargo were unloaded in 1999 and 24,000 tons loaded. The government maintains a commercial motor boat service between the islands.

Telecommunications

In 2008 there were 20,400 main (fixed) telephone lines; mobile phone subscribers numbered 80,000 in 2008 (156·7 per 100 persons). There were 16,000 internet users in 2008 (31·3 per 100 persons).

Postal Services

In 2003 there were seven post offices.

SOCIAL INSTITUTIONS

Justice

Justice is administered by the Supreme Court and by Magistrates' Courts. They have both civil and criminal jurisdiction. St Kitts and Nevis was one of ten countries to sign an agreement in Feb. 2001 establishing a Caribbean Court of Justice to replace the British Privy Council as the highest civil and criminal court. In the meantime the number of signatories has risen to twelve. The court was inaugurated at Port-of-Spain, Trinidad on 16 April 2005.

The death penalty is in force and was used in 2008 for the first time since 1998.

The population in penal institutions in Sept. 2003 was 195 (equivalent to 415 per 100,000 of national population).

Education

Adult literacy was 98% in 1998–99. Education is compulsory between the ages of 5 and 16. In 2007 there were 2,360 pupils in pre-primary schools with 357 teaching staff, 6,172 pupils with 372 teaching staff in primary schools and 4,522 pupils with 447 teaching staff in secondary schools.

The main post-secondary institution is the Clarence Fitzroy Bryant College (formerly the St Kitts and Nevis College of Further Education). There are six divisions: Adult and Continuing Education; Arts, Sciences and General Studies; Health Science; Hospitality Studies; Teacher Education; and Technical and Vocational Education and Management Studies.

In 2005 public expenditure on education came to 10·9% of GNI.

Health

In 1999 there were 46 doctors, 14 dentists, 184 nurses and 17 pharmacists; and four hospitals, with a provision of 49 beds per 10,000 population.

RELIGION

In 2001, 25·6% of the population were Anglican, 25·6% Methodist and 17·9% Pentecostal. There are also followers of other beliefs, including Roman Catholics, Baptists and Church of God.

CULTURE

World Heritage Sites

There is one site on the UNESCO World Heritage List: Brimstone Hill Fortress National Park (inscribed on the list in 1999), a well-preserved example of 17th and 18th century British military architecture.

Broadcasting

There are state-run television and radio networks, several commercial radio stations and multichannel cable TV services. There were 11,000 television sets (colour by NTSC) in 2001.

Press

In 2006 there was one daily newspaper with a circulation of 3,000. There were also four non-dailies.

Tourism

There were 91,769 tourists in 2004 and 150,429 cruise passenger arrivals (including arrivals by yacht) in 2003. In 2004, 57·0% of visitors came from the USA and 9·3% from the UK. Receipts from tourism in 2005 (excluding passenger transport) totalled US$107m.

DIPLOMATIC REPRESENTATIVES

Of St Kitts and Nevis in the United Kingdom (2nd Floor, 10 Kensington Ct, London, W8 5DL)
High Commissioner: James Williams.

Of the United Kingdom in St Kitts and Nevis
High Commissioner: Paul Brummell (resides in Bridgetown, Barbados).

Of St Kitts and Nevis in the USA (OECS Building, 3216 New Mexico Ave., NW, 3rd Floor, Washington, D.C., 20016)
Ambassador: Izben Cordinal Williams.

Of the USA in St Kitts and Nevis
Ambassador: Vacant (resides in Bridgetown, Barbados).
Chargé d'Affaires a.i.: D. Brendt Hardt.

Of St Kitts and Nevis to the United Nations
Ambassador: Delano Frank Bart.

Of St Kitts and Nevis to the European Union
Ambassador: Shirley Skerritt-Andrew.

FURTHER READING

Statistics Division. *National Accounts.* Annual.—*St Kitts and Nevis Quarterly.*

Dyde, Brian, *St Kitts: Cradle of the Caribbean.* 1999
Hubbard, Vince, *A History of St Kitts.* 2002

National library: Public Library, Burdon St., Basseterre.
National Statistical Office: Statistics Division, Ministry of Finance, Planning and Development, Church St., Basseterre.

ST LUCIA

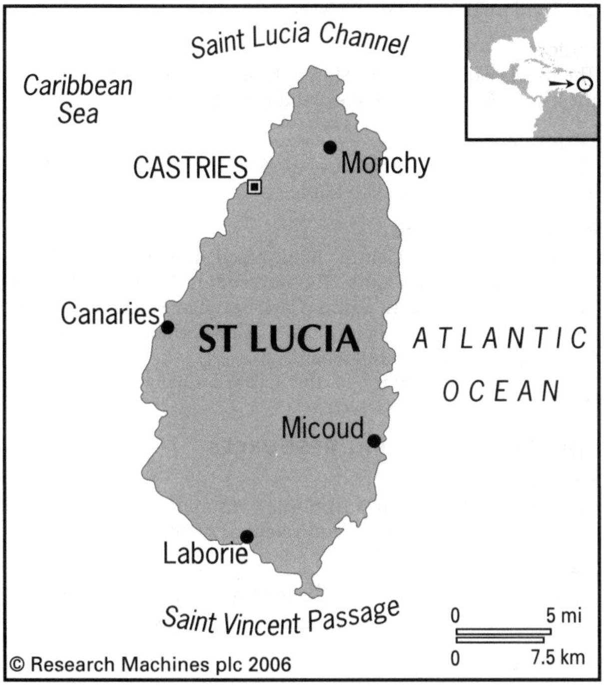

Capital: Castries
Population estimate, 2010: 174,000
GDP per capita, 2007: (PPP$) 9,786
HDI/world rank: 0·821/69

KEY HISTORICAL EVENTS

The island was probably discovered by Columbus in 1502. An unsuccessful attempt to colonize by the British took place in 1605 and again in 1638 when settlers were soon murdered by the Caribs who inhabited the island. France claimed the right of sovereignty and ceded it to the French West India Company in 1642. St Lucia regularly and constantly changed hands between Britain and France, until it was finally ceded to Britain in 1814 by the Treaty of Paris. Since 1924 the island has had representative government. In March 1967 St Lucia gained full control of its internal affairs while Britain remained responsible for foreign affairs and defence. On 22 Feb. 1979 St Lucia achieved independence, opting to remain in the British Commonwealth.

TERRITORY AND POPULATION

St Lucia is an island of the Lesser Antilles in the eastern Caribbean between Martinique and St Vincent, with an area of 617 sq. km (238 sq. miles). Population (2001 census) 158,076 (51% females); density, 255·7 per sq. km. In 2005 the population was 72·4% rural.

Areas and populations of the districts at the 2001 census were:

Districts	*Sq. km*	*Population*
Anse-la-Raye	31	6,495
Canaries	16	1,906
Castries	79	61,341
Choiseul	31	6,372
Dennery	70	12,773
Gros Inlet	101	19,816
Laborie	38	7,978
Micoud	78	17,153
Soufrière	51	7,328
Vieux Fort	44	16,329
Central Forest Reserve	78	—

The UN gives an estimated population for 2010 of 174,000.

The official language is English, but 80% of the population speak a French Creole.

In 2000, 50% of the population was Black, 44% were of mixed race and 3% of south Asian ethnic origin.

The capital is Castries (population, 1999, 57,000).

SOCIAL STATISTICS

2004 births, 2,322; deaths, 1,114. Rates, 2004 (per 1,000 population): births, 14·3; deaths, 6·9. Infant mortality, 2005 (per 1,000 live births), 13. Expectation of life in 2007 was 71·7 years for males and 75·5 for females. Annual population growth rate, 2000–05, 1·1%; fertility rate, 2004, 2·2 births per woman.

CLIMATE

The climate is tropical, with a dry season from Jan. to April. Most rain falls in Nov.–Dec.; annual amount varies from 60" (1,500 mm) to 138" (3,450 mm). The average annual temperature is about 80°F (26·7°C).

CONSTITUTION AND GOVERNMENT

The head of state is the British sovereign, represented by an appointed Governor-General. There is a 17-seat *House of Assembly* elected for five years and an 11-seat *Senate* appointed by the Governor-General.

National Anthem

'Sons and daughters of St Lucia'; words by C. Jesse, tune by L. F. Thomas.

RECENT ELECTIONS

At the elections of 11 Dec. 2006 the opposition United Workers' Party won 11 seats with 51·4% of votes cast against 6 for the St Lucia Labour Party (48·2%).

CURRENT ADMINISTRATION

Governor-General: Dame Pearlette Louisy; b. 1946 (appointed 17 Sept. 1997).

In March 2010 the government comprised:

Prime Minister and Minister of Finance, Economic Affairs, Economic Planning and National Development: Stephenson King (UWP; sworn in 9 Sept. 2007, having been acting prime minister since 1 May 2007).

Minister of Agriculture, Lands, Forestry and Fisheries: Ezechiel Joseph. *Commerce, Industry and Consumer Affairs:* Tessa Mangal. *Communications, Works, Transport and Public Utilities:* Guy Joseph. *Education and Culture:* Arsene James. *External Affairs, International Trade and Investment:* Rufus Bousquet. *Health, Wellness, Family Affairs, National Mobilization, Human Services and Gender Relations:* Keith Mondesir. *Home Affairs and National Security:* Guy Mayers. *Justice and Attorney General:* Nicholas Frederick. *Labour, Information and Broadcasting:* Edmund Estaphane. *Physical Planning, Housing, Urban Renewal, Local Government and Environment:* Richard Frederick. *Social Transformation, Public Service, Human Resource Department,*

Youth and Sports: Leonard 'Spider' Montoute. *Tourism and Civil Aviation:* Allen Chastanet.

Government Website: http://www.stlucia.gov.lc

CURRENT LEADERS

Stephenson King

Position
Prime Minister

Introduction
Stephenson King took office in Sept. 2007 to become St Lucia's ninth prime minister since independence in 1979. He succeeded Sir John Compton, who died in office.

Early Life
King was born on 13 Nov. 1958. He entered parliament in 1987, representing the United Workers Party (UWP), and was appointed minister for community development, social affairs, youth and sport. He held a range of portfolios in the governments of Sir John Compton in the 1990s including health, local government, and information and broadcasting. From 1997–2006 the UWP was in opposition, with King serving in various capacities, including party general secretary. After winning the Castries North seat for the UWP in the Dec. 2006 general election, King was appointed minister for health and labour relations.

Career in Office
From May to Sept. 2007 King served as acting prime minister as Compton's health went into decline. Compton died on 7 Sept. Amid rumours that two UWP MPs were withholding support of King to succeed Compton unless they were given cabinet posts, all ten UWP representatives in the House of Assembly finally agreed on his appointment. King was sworn in as prime minister by Governor-General Dame Pearlette Louisy on 9 Sept.

In his first cabinet, King appointed himself minister of finance (including international financial services), external affairs, home affairs and national security. Tackling gang culture and the drugs trade was his first priority. He has sought American investment for the proposed development of Castries into a major cruise ship and yachting destination. In late 2007, following wide-ranging price rises across the Caribbean, King announced price caps on certain food items. In Dec. 2007 the government launched a scheme to increase youth employment by providing private sector-driven training.

In Nov. 2007 a by-election candidate claimed that he was offered a position in the economics department if he suspended his campaign in favour of the daughter of the late Sir John Compton.

INTERNATIONAL RELATIONS

St Lucia is a member of the UN, World Bank, IMF and several other UN specialized agencies, WTO, Commonwealth, International Organization of the Francophonie, ACS, CARICOM, OECS, OAS and is an ACP member state of the ACP-EU relationship.

ECONOMY

In 2007 agriculture, forestry, hunting and fishing contributed 6·4% of GDP, industry 19·6% and services 76·8%.

Overview

GDP at PPP was US$1·85bn. in 2008. From 2005–06 GDP grew by nearly 5%, the result of a boost in the services sector centred on tourism, the economy's principal source of revenue. The government is also making efforts to boost banana production. The economy is vulnerable to trade shocks, especially in relation to oil imports and banana exports. High unemployment is an ongoing problem.

Currency

The *East Caribbean dollar* (XCD) (of 100 *cents*) is in use. US dollars are also normally accepted. Inflation was 2·2% in 2007, rising to 7·2% in 2008. Foreign exchange reserves were US$109m. in July 2005 and total money supply was EC$542m.

Budget

The fiscal year ends on 31 March. Revenues were EC$469·9m. in the fiscal year 1998–99 and expenditures EC$496·6m.

Performance

There was real GDP growth of 1·7% in 2007 and 0·7% in 2008. Total GDP in 2008 was US$1·0bn.

Banking and Finance

The East Caribbean Central Bank based in St Kitts and Nevis functions as a central bank. The *Governor* is Sir Dwight Venner. There are three domestic banks (Caribbean Banking Corporation, St Lucia Co-operative Bank, East Caribbean Financial Holding Company) and three foreign banks.

St Lucia is a member of the Eastern Caribbean Securities Exchange, based in Basseterre.

ENERGY AND NATURAL RESOURCES

Environment

Carbon dioxide emissions from the consumption and flaring of fossil fuels in 2008 were the equivalent of 2·6 tonnes per capita.

Electricity

Installed capacity in 2003 was 66,000 kW. Production in 2004 was 309m. kWh; consumption per capita in 2004 was 1,879 kWh.

Agriculture

In 2007 St Lucia had approximately 3,000 ha. of arable land and 7,000 ha. of permanent crops. Bananas, cocoa, breadfruit and mango are the principal crops, but changes in the world's trading rules and changes in taste are combining to depress the banana trade. Farmers are experimenting with okra, tomatoes and avocados to help make up for the loss. Production, 2003 estimates (in 1,000 tonnes): bananas, 120; mangoes, 28; coconuts, 14; yams, 4; grapefruit and pomelos, 3.

Livestock (2003 estimates): pigs, 15,000; cattle, 12,000; sheep, 12,000; goats, 10,000.

Forestry

In 2005 the area under forests was 17,000 ha. (27·9% of the total land area).

Fisheries

In 2005 the total catch was 1,409 tonnes.

INDUSTRY

The main areas of activity are clothing, assembly of electronic components, beverages, corrugated cardboard boxes, tourism, lime processing and coconut processing.

Labour

In the period April–June 2004 the labour force totalled 78,210. The unemployment rate was 21·0% in 2004.

INTERNATIONAL TRADE

Foreign debt in 2007 amounted to US$441m.

Imports and Exports

Imports and exports for calendar years in US$1m.:

	2003	*2004*	*2005*	*2006*
Imports c.i.f.	407·7	421·6	485·8	592·4
Exports f.o.b.	62·5	79·8	64·2	93·7

Main imports in 2006: machinery and transport equipment, 25·8%; food and live animals, 15·9%; petroleum and petroleum products, 12·1%; chemicals and related products, 6·9%. Main exports, 2006: petroleum and petroleum products, 21·7%; bananas, 19·0%; machinery and transport equipment, 18·2%; beer, 14·0%. Main import suppliers, 2006: USA, 39·2%; Trinidad and Tobago, 16·9%; UK, 6·9%; Japan, 6·3%. Main export markets, 2006: Trinidad and Tobago, 30·1%; UK, 20·7%; USA, 20·6%; Barbados, 6·6%.

COMMUNICATIONS

Roads

The island had about 1,210 km of roads in 2002, of which 150 km were main roads and a further 150 km secondary roads. Passenger cars numbered 13,100 in 2002.

Civil Aviation

There are international airports at Hewanorra (near Vieux-Fort) and Vigie (near Castries). In 2001 Vigie handled 378,000 (373,000 on international flights) and Hewanorra 301,000 passengers (291,000 on international flights).

Shipping

There are two ports, Castries and Vieux Fort. Merchant shipping in 1995 totalled 1,000 GRT. In 1997 vessels totalling 6,803,000 net registered tons entered the ports.

Telecommunications

Fixed telephone lines numbered 40,900 in 2008 (240·2 per 1,000 persons). There were 105,700 mobile phone subscribers in 2005. Internet users numbered 110,000 in 2007.

Postal Services

There were 27 post offices in 2003.

SOCIAL INSTITUTIONS

Justice

The island is divided into two judicial districts, and there are nine magistrates' courts. Appeals lie to the Eastern Caribbean Supreme Court of Appeal. St Lucia was one of ten countries to sign an agreement in Feb. 2001 establishing a Caribbean Court of Justice to replace the British Privy Council as the highest civil and criminal court. In the meantime the number of signatories has risen to twelve. The court was inaugurated at Port-of-Spain, Trinidad on 16 April 2005.

The population in penal institutions in Aug. 2003 was 460 (287 per 100,000 of national population).

Education

Primary education is free and compulsory. In 2002–03 there were 81 primary schools with 1,057 teachers for 27,175 pupils; and (1999–2000) 12,817 pupils and 645 teachers at secondary level. There is a community college. The adult literacy rate was 90·1% in 2003 (89·5% among males and 90·6% among females).

In 2006 public expenditure on education came to 6·9% of GNI and 19·1% of total government spending.

Health

In 2002 there were five hospitals (with 305 beds) and 35 health centres. There were 70 physicians, seven dentists and 302 nurses.

RELIGION

In 2001, 79% of the population was Roman Catholic.

CULTURE

World Heritage Sites

There is one UNESCO World Heritage site in St Lucia: Pitons Management Area (inscribed on the list in 2004). The site near the town of Soufrière includes the Pitons, two volcanic spires rising side by side from the sea, linked by the Piton Mitan ridge.

Broadcasting

In 2003 there were three television stations (colour by PAL) broadcasting locally and on satellite and a satellite network, Cablevision. The government-owned Radio St Lucia broadcasts in English and Creole. There were two other radio stations in 2003. There were 46,000 television receivers in 2001.

Press

In 2003 there were seven newspapers. The weekly *One Caribbean* had the highest circulation (7,500). *The Voice*, founded in 1885, has a thrice-weekly combined circulation of 15,000.

Tourism

The number of foreign tourists in 2005 was 318,000. Receipts in 2005 totalled US$345m. (excluding passenger transport).

DIPLOMATIC REPRESENTATIVES

Of St Lucia in the United Kingdom (1 Collingham Gdns, Earls Court, London, SW5 0HW)
High Commissioner: Eldridge Stephens.

Of the United Kingdom in St Lucia
High Commissioner: Paul Brummell (resides in Bridgetown, Barbados).

Of St Lucia in the USA (3216 New Mexico Ave., NW, Washington, D.C., 20016)
Ambassador: Michael Louis.

Of the USA in St Lucia
Ambassador: Vacant (resides in Bridgetown, Barbados).
Chargé d'Affaires a.i.: D. Brendt Hardt.

Of St Lucia to the United Nations
Ambassador: Donatus St Aimee.

Of St Lucia to the European Union
Ambassador: Shirley Skerritt-Andrew.

FURTHER READING

National Statistical Office: Central Statistical Office, Chreiki Building, Micoud Street, Castries.
Website: http://www.stats.gov.lc

ST VINCENT AND THE GRENADINES

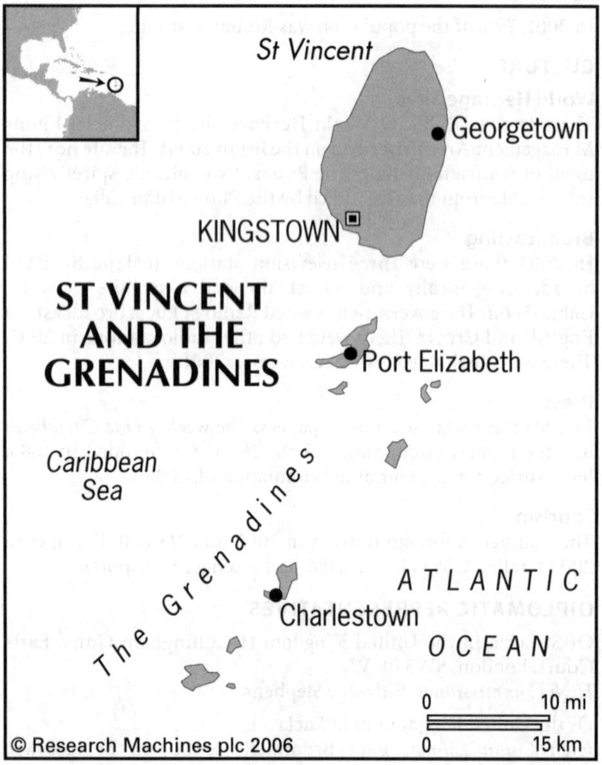

Capital: Kingstown
Population estimate, 2010: 109,000
GDP per capita, 2007: (PPP$) 7,691
HDI/world rank: 0·772/91

KEY HISTORICAL EVENTS

St Vincent was discovered by Columbus on 22 Jan. (St Vincent's Day) 1498. British and French settlers occupied parts of the islands after 1627. In 1773 the Caribs recognized British sovereignty and agreed to a division of territory between themselves and the British. Resentful of British rule, the Caribs rebelled in 1795, aided by the French, but the revolt was subdued within a year. On 27 Oct. 1969 St Vincent became an Associated State with the UK responsible for foreign policy and defence. On 27 Oct. 1979 the colony gained full independence as St Vincent and the Grenadines.

TERRITORY AND POPULATION

St Vincent is an island of the Lesser Antilles, situated in the eastern Caribbean between St Lucia and Grenada, from which latter it is separated by a chain of small islands known as the Grenadines. The total area of 389 sq. km (150 sq. miles) comprises the island of St Vincent itself (345 sq. km) and those of the Grenadines attached to it, of which the largest are Bequia, Mustique, Canouan, Mayreau and Union.

The population at the 2001 census was 106,253, of whom 97,638 lived on St Vincent; density, 273 per sq. km. In 2005, 54·1% of the population lived in rural areas.

The UN gives an estimated population for 2010 of 109,000.

The capital, Kingstown, had 25,307 inhabitants in 2004 (including suburbs). The population is mainly of Black (65·5%) and mixed (23·5%) origin, with small White, Asian and American minorities.

English is the official language, although French patois is widely spoken.

SOCIAL STATISTICS

Births, 2001, 1,967; deaths, 720. 2001 rates (per 1,000 population): births, 18·0; deaths, 6·6. Infant mortality, 2005, 17 per 1,000 live births. Life expectancy, 2007, was 69·4 years for males and 73·6 years for females. Annual population growth rate, 1992–2002, 0·6%; fertility rate, 2004, 2·2 births per woman.

CLIMATE

The climate is tropical marine, with northeast trades predominating and rainfall ranging from 150" (3,750 mm) a year in the mountains to 60" (1,500 mm) on the southeast coast. The rainy season is from June to Dec., and temperatures are equable throughout the year.

CONSTITUTION AND GOVERNMENT

The head of state is Queen Elizabeth II, represented by a Governor-General. Parliament is unicameral with a 22-member *House of Assembly* consisting of 15 members directly elected for a five-year term from single-member constituencies, six senators appointed by the Governor-General (four on the advice of the Prime Minister and two on the advice of the Leader of the Opposition) and one *ex officio* member.

National Anthem

'St Vincent, land so beautiful'; words by Phyllis Punnett, tune by J. B. Miguel.

RECENT ELECTIONS

At the elections to the House of Assembly on 7 Dec. 2005 the ruling Unity Labour Party (ULP, social democratic) won 12 of the 15 elected seats with 55·3% of the vote, against 3 (44·7%) for the opposition New Democratic Party (NDP, conservative).

CURRENT ADMINISTRATION

Governor-General: Sir Frederick Ballantyne (since 2 Sept. 2002).

In March 2010 the government comprised:

Prime Minister, Minister of Finance, Economic Planning, National Security, Legal Affairs, Grenadine Affairs, Public Service and Energy: Dr Ralph E. Gonsalves; b. 1946 (ULP; sworn in 29 March 2001 and re-elected in Dec. 2005).

Deputy Prime Minister and Minister of Foreign Affairs, Commerce and Trade: Louis Straker.

Minister of National Mobilization, Social Development, Relations with Non-Governmental Organizations, Family, Gender Affairs and Persons with Disabilities: Mike Browne. *Education:* Girlyn Miguel. *Rural Transformation, Information, Public Service and Ecclesiastical Affairs:* Selmon Walters. *Health and Environment:* Dr Douglas Slater. *Urban Development, Labour, Culture and Electoral Matters:* René Baptiste. *Transportation and Works:* Clayton Burgin. *Agriculture, Forestry and Fisheries:* Montgomery Daniel. *Telecommunications, Science, Technology and Industry:* Dr Jerrol Thompson. *Tourism, Youth and Sports:* Glen Beache. *Housing, Informal Human Settlements, Physical Planning, and Lands and Surveys:* Julian Francis. *Minister of State in the Prime Minister's Office:* Conrad Sayers.

CURRENT LEADERS

Dr Ralph E. Gonsalves

Position
Prime Minister

Introduction
Dr Ralph E. Gonsalves became prime minister in 2001 after his Unity Labour Party (ULP) won 12 of 15 seats in an election brought forward from 2003 following anti-government protests in 2000. He won a second term in Dec. 2005.

Early Life
'Comrade Ralph' was born in 1945. He studied at the University of the West Indies in Jamaica, gaining a PhD in political science. He later graduated in law from the University of the West Indies in Barbados, before returning home. In 1982 he founded the left-wing Movement for National Unity, which in 1994 amalgamated with the St Vincent Labour Party to form the ULP. Gonsalves succeeded the ULP's first leader, Vincent Beache, in 1998 and led the party to electoral victory in 2001, ending 15 years of New Democrat rule.

Career in Office
Gonsalves has sought to tackle the problems of money laundering, gun violence and drug-related crime. In June 2003 St Vincent and Grenadines was removed from a list of uncooperative countries in the fight against money laundering throughout the Caribbean islands. In Jan. 2005 death row prisoners were told they would face hanging once their appeals were exhausted. Gonsalves is the chairman of the Regional Security System council of ministers, put together to tackle security threats throughout the islands.

The country's economy is reliant on the banana trade and the government continues to pay large subsidies to farmers. However, a decline in banana prices and demand has led to some diversification. In June 2004 Gonsalves announced the launch of National Investments Promotions Incorporated to attract investment and boost exports, and the tourism sector has seen significant growth.

Gonsalves is committed to maintaining close ties with Taiwan and Cuba. In May 2005 Taiwan made a gift of computer equipment to his government to enhance efficiency. It also helped to build facilities for the 2007 Cricket World Cup. In Jan. 2005 Gonsalves met with Fidel Castro to announce that new diplomatic missions would be established in their respective countries. Castro also promised Cuban assistance to Gonsalves' campaign to increase national literacy rates.

Gonsalves is chairman of the national HIV/AIDS council and Feb. 2005 saw the launch of the World Bank-assisted HIV/AIDS prevention and control project, with the government expected to invest at least US$1·7m. over five years. In April 2005 he signed agreements with St Lucia and Dominica to introduce measures to combat climate change in the coastal areas of the three Windward Islands (with substantial funding from the USA and Japan). In May 2005 his government ratified the Kyoto protocol.

In parliamentary elections in Dec. 2005 the ULP retained their 12 seats. Gonsalves was sworn in for a new term and took over the national security portfolio. In May 2007 his government introduced VAT to increase public revenue (with a reduced rate for hotel accommodation to help protect the tourist industry). A referendum to adopt a new constitution and establish a republic, in which Gonsalves campaigned for acceptance, was rejected by 55% of voters in Nov. 2009.

In 2008 diplomatic relations were established with Iran.

INTERNATIONAL RELATIONS

St Vincent and the Grenadines is a member of the UN, World Bank, IMF and several other UN specialized agencies, WTO, Commonwealth, ACS, CARICOM, OECS, OAS and is an ACP member state of the ACP-EU relationship.

ECONOMY

Agriculture accounted for 8% of GDP in 2005, industry 25% and services 67%.

Overview
With the banana crop accounting for around a third of export earnings, the economy enjoyed vigorous growth in 2006 and 2007 at around 7% per annum, boosted by healthy construction activity and government services. With tourism increasingly important, an international airport is expected to raise the economy's medium-term growth potential. In Oct. 2007 an agreement was made with Italy to write off a debt obligation, reducing the public debt stock by around 10% of GDP. However, public debt-to-GDP ratio remains high at around 68%. In May 2007 the authorities introduced VAT, contributing to higher inflation for the year. The global slowdown is expected to reduce growth in the short term as tourist demand weakens and the construction sector loses dynamism.

Currency
The currency in use is the *East Caribbean dollar* (XCD). Inflation was 6·9% in 2007 and 10·1% in 2008. Foreign exchange reserves were US$66m. in July 2005. Total money supply was EC$319m. in June 2005.

Budget
In 2006 revenues totalled EC$399·2m. and expenditures EC$456·7m.

VAT is 15% (reduced rate, 10%).

Performance
Real GDP growth was just 0·9% in 2008, down from 7·0% in 2007. In 2008 total GDP was US$0·6bn.

Banking and Finance
The East Caribbean Central Bank is the bank of issue. The *Governor* is Sir Dwight Venner. There are branches of Barclays Bank PLC, the Caribbean Banking Corporation, FirstCaribbean International, the Canadian Imperial Bank of Commerce and the Bank of Nova Scotia. Locally-owned banks: First St Vincent Bank, Owens Bank, New Bank, the National Commercial Bank and St Vincent Co-operative Bank. The 'offshore' sector numbered over 11,000 organizations in 2001.

St Vincent and the Grenadines is a member of the Eastern Caribbean Securities Exchange, based in Basseterre.

ENERGY AND NATURAL RESOURCES

Environment
Carbon dioxide emissions from the consumption and flaring of fossil fuels were the equivalent of 2·1 tonnes per capita in 2008.

Electricity
Installed capacity was approximately 25,000 kW in 2004. Production in 2004 was an estimated 110m. kWh; consumption per capita in 2004 was around 939 kWh.

Agriculture
In 2007 the agricultural population was an estimated 23,000, of which 11,000 were economically active. There were an estimated 7,000 ha. of arable land and 5,000 ha. of permanent crops in 2007. The sugar industry was closed down in 1985 although some sugarcane is grown for rum production. Production (2003, in 1,000 tonnes): bananas, 50; coconuts, 3; copra, 2; maize, 2; oranges, 2; plantains, 2; sugarcane, 2; sweet potatoes, 2; yams, 2.

Livestock (2003, in 1,000): sheep, 12; pigs, 9; goats, 7; cattle, 5.

Forestry
Forests covered 11,000 ha. in 2005, or 27·4% of the land area.

Fisheries
Total catch, 2005, 2,745 tonnes (all from sea fishing).

INDUSTRY

Industries include assembly of electronic equipment, manufacture of garments, electrical products, animal feeds and flour, corrugated galvanized sheets, exhaust systems, industrial gases, concrete blocks, plastics, soft drinks, beer and rum, wood products and furniture, and processing of milk, fruit juices and food items. Rum production, 1994, 0·4m. litres.

Labour

The Department of Labour is charged with looking after the interest and welfare of all categories of workers, including providing advice and guidance to employers and employees and their organizations and enforcing the labour laws. In 1991 the total labour force was 41,682, of whom 33,355 (11,699 females) were employed.

INTERNATIONAL TRADE

Foreign debt was US$253m. in 2007.

Imports and Exports

Imports in 2005 totalled US$212·4m. and exports US$43·6m. Principal imports are basic manufactures, machinery and transport equipment, and food products. Principal exports are bananas, packaged flour and packaged rice. Main import suppliers, 2005: USA, 33·3%; Trinidad and Tobago, 23·6%; UK, 9·4%. Main export markets, 2005: UK, 26·8%; Barbados, 12·8%; Trinidad and Tobago, 12·3%.

COMMUNICATIONS

Roads

In 2002 there were 829 km of roads, of which 70% were paved. Vehicles in use (2008): 9,250 passenger cars, 12,900 vans and lorries, and 1,220 motorcycles and mopeds.

Civil Aviation

There is an airport (E. T. Joshua) on mainland St Vincent at Arnos Vale. An airport on Union also has regular scheduled services. In 1995 E. T. Joshua handled 185,000 passengers and 1,200 tonnes of freight.

Shipping

In 2000 the merchant navy had 1,366 vessels. Merchant shipping in 2002 totalled 6,584,000 GRT, including oil tankers 313,000 GRT. In 2001 vessels totalling 1,790,000 net registered tons entered and cleared ports.

Telecommunications

There were 133,400 telephone subscribers in 2007, equivalent to 1,108·1 for every 1,000 inhabitants, including 110,500 mobile phone subscribers. The telephone network has almost 100% geographical coverage. In 2007 there were 57,000 internet users.

Postal Services

There were 41 post offices in 1997.

SOCIAL INSTITUTIONS

Justice

Law is based on UK common law as exercised by the Eastern Caribbean Supreme Court on St Lucia. Final appeal lies to the UK Privy Council. In 1995 there were 4,700 criminal matters disposed of in the three magisterial districts which comprise 11 courts. 62 cases were dealt with in the Criminal Assizes in the High Court. St Vincent and the Grenadines was one of twelve countries to sign an agreement establishing a Caribbean Court of Justice to replace the British Privy Council as the highest civil and criminal court. The court was inaugurated at Port-of-Spain, Trinidad on 16 April 2005. Strength of police force (1995), 663 (including 19 gazetted officers).

The population in penal institutions in Oct. 2001 was 302 (270 per 100,000 of national population).

Education

In 2007 there were 3,894 children in pre-primary schools with 340 teaching staff, 15,928 pupils in primary schools with 933 teaching staff and (2005) 9,780 pupils in secondary schools. There is a community college. Adult literacy in 2004 was 88·1%.

In 2005 public expenditure on education came to 8·6% of GNI and 16·1% of total government spending.

Health

In 1997 there were 11 hospitals with a provision of 19 beds per 10,000 persons. In 1998 there were 59 physicians, six dentists and 267 nurses, and in 1991 there were 27 pharmacists.

RELIGION

In 2001 there were estimated to be 20,000 Anglicans, 17,000 Pentecostalists, 12,000 Methodists, 12,000 Roman Catholics and 52,000 followers of other religions.

CULTURE

Broadcasting

NBC Radio is a partly government-funded national FM service. There are several other radio stations and a television service (SVG TV). There were 26,000 TV sets (colour by NTSC) in 2000.

Press

In 2006 there was one daily newspaper, *The Herald*. There were also six weekly papers.

Tourism

In 2005 there were 95,505 staying visitors, 69,391 cruise passenger arrivals and 84,610 recorded yacht visitors. Tourism receipts (excluding passenger transport) in 2005 totalled US$105m.

DIPLOMATIC REPRESENTATIVES

Of St Vincent and the Grenadines in the United Kingdom (10 Kensington Ct, London, W8 5DL)
High Commissioner: Cenio Elwin Lewis.

Of the United Kingdom in St Vincent and the Grenadines (Francis Compton Building, 2nd Floor, Waterfront, Castries)
High Commissioner: Paul Brummell (resides in Bridgetown, Barbados).

Of St Vincent and the Grenadines in the USA (3216 New Mexico Ave., NW, Washington, D.C., 20016)
Ambassador: La Celia Aritha Prince.

Of the USA in St Vincent and the Grenadines
Ambassador: Vacant (resides in Bridgetown, Barbados).
Chargé d'Affaires a.i.: D. Brendt Hardt.

Of St Vincent and the Grenadines to the United Nations
Ambassador: Camillo Gonsalves.

Of St Vincent and the Grenadines to the European Union
Ambassador: Shirley Skerritt-Andrew.

FURTHER READING

Sutty, L., *St Vincent and the Grenadines*. 1993

SAMOA

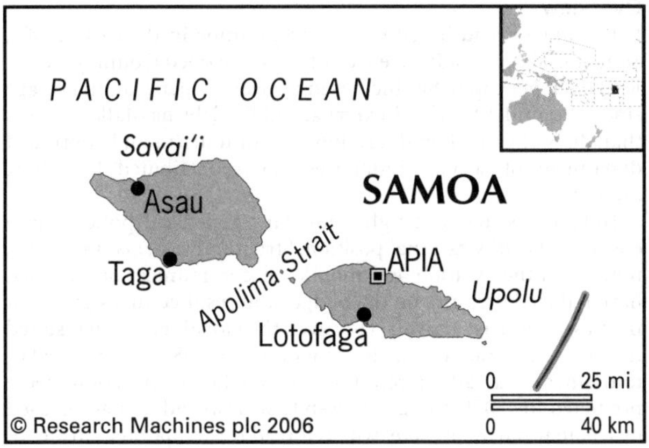

O le Malo Tutoatasi o Samoa
(Independent State of Samoa)

Capital: Apia
Population estimate, 2010: 179,000
GDP per capita, 2007: (PPP$) 4,467
HDI/world rank: 0·771/94

KEY HISTORICAL EVENTS

Polynesians settled in the Samoan group of islands in the southern Pacific from about 1000 BC. Although probably sighted by the Dutch in 1722, the first European visitor was French in 1768. Treaties were signed between the Chiefs and European nations in 1838–39. Continuing strife among the chiefs was compounded by British, German and US rivalry for influence. In the Treaty of Berlin 1889 the three powers agreed to Western Samoa's independence and neutrality. When unrest continued, the treaty was annulled and Western Samoa became a German protectorate until in 1914 it was occupied by a New Zealand expeditionary force. The island was administered by New Zealand from 1920 to 1961. On 1 Jan. 1962 Western Samoa gained independence. In July 1997 the country renamed itself the Independent State of Samoa.

TERRITORY AND POPULATION

Samoa lies between 13° and 15° S. lat. and 171° and 173° W. long. It comprises the two large islands of Savai'i and Upolu, the small islands of Manono and Apolima, and several uninhabited islets lying off the coast. The total land area is 2,830·8 sq. km (1,093·0 sq. miles), of which 1,707·8 sq. km (659·4 sq. miles) are in Savai'i, and 1,117·6 sq. km (431·5 sq. miles) in Upolu; other islands, 5·4 sq. km (2·1 sq. miles). The islands are of volcanic origin, and the coasts are surrounded by coral reefs. Rugged mountain ranges form the core of both main islands. The large area laid waste by lava-flows in Savai'i is a primary cause of that island supporting less than one-third of the population of the islands despite its greater size than Upolu.

Population at the 2001 census, 176,710. 2006 census population (provisional), 179,186. The population at the 2001 census was 134,024 in Upolu (including Manono and Apolima) and 42,824 in Savai'i. The capital and chief port is Apia in Upolu (population 38,836 in 2001). In 2005, 77·6% of the population lived in rural areas.

The UN gives an estimated population for 2010 of 179,000.

The official languages are Samoan and English.

SOCIAL STATISTICS

2003 estimates: births, 5,100; deaths, 1,000. Rates, 2003 estimates (per 1,000 population): births, 28·6; deaths, 5·5. Expectation of life in 2007 was 68·4 years for males and 74·7 for females. Annual population growth rate, 2000–05, was 1·4%. Infant mortality, 2005, 24 per 1,000 live births; fertility rate, 2004, 4·3 births per woman.

CLIMATE

A tropical marine climate, with cooler conditions from May to Nov. and a rainy season from Dec. to April. The rainfall is unevenly distributed, with south and east coasts having the greater quantities. Average annual rainfall is about 100" (2,500 mm) in the drier areas. Apia, Jan. 80°F (26·7°C), July 78°F (25·6°C). Annual rainfall 112" (2,800 mm).

CONSTITUTION AND GOVERNMENT

HH Malietoa Tanumafili II, who was Head of State for life, died on 11 May 2007. The Head of State is henceforth elected by the Legislative Assembly and holds office for five-year terms.

The executive power is vested in the *Head of State*, who swears in the *Prime Minister* (who is elected by the Legislative Assembly) and, on the Prime Minister's advice, the Ministers to form the Cabinet. The Constitution also provides for a *Council of Deputies* of three members, of whom the chairman is the Deputy Head of State.

The *Legislative Assembly* contains 49 members serving five-year terms. 47 are elected exclusively by *matai* (customary family heads) and the other two by non-Samoans on separate electoral rolls.

National Anthem

'Samoa, tula'i ma sisi ia laufu'a ('Samoa, Arise and Raise your Banner'); words and tune by S. I. Kuresa.

RECENT ELECTIONS

At the most recent elections, on 31 March 2006, the Human Rights Protection Party won 29 seats; the Samoan National Development Party, 12; and non-partisans, 8.

Tuiatua Tupua Tamasese Efi was elected head of state unanimously by the Legislative Assembly on 16 June 2007.

CURRENT ADMINISTRATION

Head of State: Tuiatua Tupua Tamasese Efi; b. 1938 (in office since 20 June 2007).

In March 2010 the cabinet was composed as follows:

Prime Minister and Minister of Foreign Affairs: Tuila'epa Sailele Malielegaoi; b. 1945 (Human Rights Protection Party; sworn in 23 Nov. 1998, and re-elected in March 2001 and March 2006).

Deputy Prime Minister and Minister of Commerce, Industry and Labour: Misa Telefoni Retzlaff. *Agriculture:* Taua Tavaga Kitiona Seuala. *Communication and Information Technology:* Safuneituuga Paaga Neri. *Education, Sports and Culture:* Toomata Alapati Poese Toomata. *Finance:* Niko Lee Hang. *Health:* Gatoloaifaana Amataga Alesana Gidlow. *Justice and Courts Administration:* Unasa Mesi Galo. *Natural Resources and Environment:* Faumuina Tiatia Liuga. *Police, Prisons and Fire Services:* Toleafoa Apulu Faafisi. *Revenue:* Tuuu Anasii Leota. *Women's Affairs, Community and Social Development:* Fiame Naomi Mataafa. *Works, Transportation and Infrastructure:* Tuisugaletaua Sofara Aveau.

Government Website: http://www.govt.ws

CURRENT LEADERS

Tuila'epa Sailele Malielegaoi

Position
Prime Minister

Introduction
Tuila'epa Sailele Malielegaoi became prime minister in Nov. 1998 and won further terms in March 2001 and March 2006. He is leader of the Human Rights Protection Party (HRPP), the traditional ruling party of Samoa since 1982.

Early Life
Tuila'epa Sailele Malielegaoi was born on 14 April 1945 in Lepa, Samoa. He was educated in Samoa and at New Zealand's Auckland University, graduating with a master's degree (the first Samoan to do so) in commerce in 1969.

In 1978 he moved to Brussels to work for the European Economic Community. He entered Samoa's parliament two years later while working as a partner in the accounting firm Coopers and Lybrand. He was elected to the premiership after former prime minister Tofilau Eti Alesana retired in 1998.

Career in Office
Malielegaoi has aimed to diversify an economy dependent on fishing and agriculture and susceptible to natural disasters, focusing particularly on the tourism industry. In Aug. 2004 his government introduced internet access to assist economic development.

Malielegaoi has also been keen to promote education in Samoa. There is a scholarship scheme offering study opportunities in New Zealand, Australia and the Fiji Islands, and in Jan. 2003 a new inter-denominational Christian secondary school was opened. The police and health sectors have also received increased funding. In Jan. 2004 parliament voted to abolish the death penalty and in the same year Australia provided $A7m. to fund training of Samoan security forces.

In foreign relations, Malielegaoi has pursued close relations with China. China agreed to help build an aquatic centre in Samoa for the 2007 South Pacific Games and has been aiding the construction of new buildings for the Samoan parliament and Justice Department. Japan has also invested in Samoa, providing funding for education and vocational training and for land redevelopment. In 2004 Samoa hosted the 35th Pacific Forum, which concentrated on regional economic and political co-operation and the Pacific-wide campaign to tackle HIV and AIDS.

Malielegaoi was re-elected for a third term when his Human Rights Protection Party won the March 2006 election. In May 2007 King Malietoa Tanumafili II died after 45 years on the throne, having been appointed king for life at independence in 1962. Under the constitution, his successor, Tuiatua Tupua Tamasese Efi, was appointed for a five-year term by the Legislative Assembly in June.

Opposition to controversial road traffic legislation by Malielegaoi (changing the driving side from right to left), which took effect in Sept. 2009, had earlier led to defections from the HRPP and to the formation in 2008 of two new political parties—the Tautua Samoa Party and the People's Party.

INTERNATIONAL RELATIONS

Samoa, as an independent state, deals directly with other governments and international organizations. It has diplomatic relations with a number of countries.

Samoa is a member of the UN, World Bank, IMF and several other UN specialized agencies, Commonwealth, Asian Development Bank, Pacific Islands Forum, SPC and is an ACP member state of the ACP-EU relationship.

ECONOMY

Agriculture accounted for 11·8% of GDP in 2006, industry 27·1% and services 61·2%.

Overview

Following a broad-based reform programme in the early 1990s, Samoa is about to advance from Less Developed Country status. Real GDP per capita has increased by over 3% per year on average since the mid-1990s and external public debt has fallen to less than 40% of GDP. Rapid development of tourism and continued dynamism of service industries have contributed to robust growth.

Inflation is low and tight monetary and fiscal policies have ensured a healthy external position. Structural reforms since 2005, notably in the aviation and mobile telecommunications sectors, have reduced pressure on the budget and resulted in a significant increase in tourist arrivals. However, the global recession resulted in a large contraction in the economy in 2008 through weaker tourism and a fall in remittances. Smaller contractions were predicted for 2009 and 2010, despite widespread damage caused by a tsunami in Sept. 2009 which forced the temporary closure of many tourist resorts.

Currency

The unit of currency is the *tala* (WST) of 100 *sene*. Inflation was 4·5% in 2007 and 6·2% in 2008. Foreign exchange reserves were US$94m. in July 2005. Total money supply was 133m. tala in June 2005.

Budget

The fiscal year begins on 1 July. For 2005–06 revenue was SA$387·2m. (tax revenue, 70·5%); expenditure, SA$391·7m. (current expenditure, 72·0%).

VAT is 12·5%.

Performance

Real GDP growth was 2·2% in 2007 and 4·8% in 2008. Total GDP in 2008 was US$0·5bn.

Banking and Finance

The Central Bank of Samoa (founded 1984) is the bank of issue. The *Governor* is Leasi Papali'i Tommy Scanlan. There is one development bank. Commercial banks include: ANZ, Industrial Bank, International Business Bank Corporation, National Bank of Samoa, Samoa Commercial Bank and Westpac Bank Samoa.

ENERGY AND NATURAL RESOURCES

Environment

Samoa's carbon dioxide emissions from the consumption and flaring of fossil fuels in 2008 were the equivalent of 0·8 tonnes per capita.

Electricity

Installed capacity in 2004 was around 29,000 kW. Production was about 110m. kWh. in 2004 and consumption per capita an estimated 619 kWh.

Agriculture

In 2002 there were 60,000 ha. of arable land and 69,000 ha. of permanent cropland. The main products (2002, in 1,000 tonnes) are coconuts (140), bananas (22), taro (17), copra (11) and pineapples (5).

Livestock (2003 estimates): pigs, 201,000; cattle, 29,000; asses, 7,000.

Forestry

Forests covered 171,000 ha. (60·4% of the land area) in 2005. Timber production was 131,000 cu. metres in 2007.

Fisheries

Fish landings in 2004 totalled approximately 4,719 tonnes.

INDUSTRY

Some industrial activity is being developed associated with agricultural products and forestry.

Labour

In 2001 the total labour force numbered 52,945 (36,739 males).

INTERNATIONAL TRADE

Total external debt was US$1,140m. in 2007.

Imports and Exports

In 2005 imports were valued at 647m. tala and exports at 236m. tala. Main imports are machinery and transport equipment, foodstuffs and basic manufactures. Principal exports are coconuts, palm oil, taro and taamu, coffee and beer. New Zealand is the principal import source, accounting for 39·2% of imports in 2004. Australia was the largest export market in 2004, accounting for 71·5% of exports. Australia is the second biggest supplier of imports and the USA the second biggest export market.

COMMUNICATIONS

Roads

In 2002 the road network covered 790 km, of which 235 km were main roads. In 2005 there were 5,920 passenger cars plus 4,600 lorries and vans in use.

Civil Aviation

There is an international airport at Apia (Faleolo), which handled 156,000 passengers (155,000 on international flights) in 2001. The national carrier is Polynesian Airlines. In 2003 it operated domestic services and international flights to American Samoa, Auckland, the Fiji Islands, Honolulu, Los Angeles, Niue, Sydney and Tonga.

Shipping

Sea-going shipping totalled 10,000 GRT in 2002. Samoa is linked to Japan, USA, Europe, the Fiji Islands, Australia and New Zealand by regular shipping services.

Telecommunications

There are three radio communication stations at Apia. Radio telephone service connects Samoa with American Samoa, the Fiji Islands, New Zealand, Australia, Canada, USA and UK. In 2008 there were 28,800 main (fixed) telephone lines; mobile phone subscribers numbered 124,000 in 2008 (69·3 per 100 persons). There were 4,200 PCs in use in 2006 and 9,000 internet users in 2008.

Postal Services

In 2003 there were 36 post offices.

SOCIAL INSTITUTIONS

Justice

The population in penal institutions in Nov. 2003 was 281 (158 per 100,000 of national population). The death penalty, not used in more than 50 years, was abolished in 2004.

Education

There were 30,199 pupils at primary schools in 2007 with 1,269 teaching staff and 24,242 pupils at secondary schools in 2005 with (2004) 1,141 teaching staff. The University of the South Pacific has a School of Agriculture in Samoa, at Apia. A National University was established in 1984. In 1994–95 it had 614 students and 30 academic staff. There is also a Polytechnic Institute which provides mainly vocational and training courses.

The adult literacy in 2004 was 98·6%.

In 2002 public expenditure on education came to 4·4% of GNI and 13·7% of total government spending.

Health

In 2002 there were 33 general hospitals (with 320 beds), one private hospital, 11 district hospitals and 12 primary health care centres. In 2002 there were 43 physicians, six dentists, 333 nurses and 13 midwives.

RELIGION

In 2001 there were 46,200 Latter-day Saints (Mormons), 44,000 Congregationalists, 38,100 Roman Catholics and 21,800 Methodists. The remainder of the population follow other beliefs.

CULTURE

Broadcasting

The Samoa Broadcasting Corporation is the state-run service provider. Other television and radio networks include O Lau TV, TV3, Magik FM and Talofa FM. In 2005 television sets numbered 22,500 (colour by NTSC).

Press

There are two dailies, plus a weekly, a fortnightly and a monthly. The most widely read newspaper is the independent *Samoa Observer*.

Tourism

In 2008 there were 122,163 foreign tourists.

DIPLOMATIC REPRESENTATIVES

Of Samoa in the United Kingdom and to the European Union
High Commissioner: Tuala Falani Chan Tung (resides in Brussels).
Honorary Consul: Prunella Scarlett, LVO (Church Cottage, Pedlinge, Nr Hythe, Kent, CT12 5JL).

Of the United Kingdom in Samoa
High Commissioner: George Fergusson (resides in Wellington).

Of Samoa in the USA and to the United Nations (800 Second Ave., Suite 400D, New York, NY, 10017)
Ambassador: Ali'ioaiga Feturi Elisaia.

Of the USA in Samoa
Ambassador: David Huebner (resides in Wellington).

FURTHER READING

National Statistical Office: Samoa Bureau of Statistics (SBS), Ministry of Finance, Level 1, Government Building (MFMII), P.O. Box 1151, Apia.
Website: http://www.spc.int/prism/Country/ws/stats

SAN MARINO

Repubblica di San Marino
(Republic of San Marino)

Capital: San Marino
Population, 2008: 31,000
GDP per capita: not available
GNI per capita, 2007: US$48,210

KEY HISTORICAL EVENTS

San Marino is a small republic situated on the Adriatic side of central Italy. According to tradition, St Marinus and a group of Christians settled there to escape persecution. By the 12th century San Marino had developed into a commune ruled by its own statutes and consul. Unsuccessful attempts were made to annex the republic to the papal states in the 18th century and when Napoleon invaded Italy in 1797 he respected the rights of the republic and even offered to extend its territories. In 1815 the Congress of Vienna recognized the independence of the republic. On 22 March 1862 San Marino concluded a treaty of friendship and co-operation, including a *de facto* customs union, with Italy, thus preserving its independence although it is completely surrounded by Italian territory.

TERRITORY AND POPULATION

San Marino is a land-locked state in central Italy, 20 km from the Adriatic. Area is 61·19 sq. km (23·6 sq. miles) and the population (Dec. 2008), 31,269; at Dec. 2008 some 12,487 citizens lived abroad.

In 2005 an estimated 93% of the population were urban. Population density, 511·0 per sq. km. The capital, San Marino, has 4,377 inhabitants (2008); the largest town is Serravalle (10,146 in 2008), an industrial centre in the north. The official language is Italian.

SOCIAL STATISTICS

Births, 2005, 284; deaths, 219; marriages, 223; divorces (2004), 62. Birth rate, 2005 (per 1,000 population), 10·6; death rate, 6·9. Annual population growth rate, 2000–05, 2·7%; fertility rate, 2004, 1·2 births per woman (one of the lowest rates in the world); infant mortality rate, 2005, 3 per 1,000 live births. The World Health Organization's *World Health Statistics 2009* put citizens of San Marino in equal second place in a 'healthy life expectancy' list (level with Switzerland and only behind Japan), with an expected 75 years of healthy life for babies born in 2007.

CLIMATE

Temperate climate with cold, dry winters and warm summers.

CONSTITUTION AND GOVERNMENT

The legislative power is vested in the *Great and General Council* of 60 members elected every five years by popular vote, two of whom are appointed every six months to act as *Captains Regent*, who are the heads of state.

Executive power is exercised by the ten-member *Congress of State*, presided over by the Captains Regent. The *Council of Twelve*, also presided over by the Captains Regent, is appointed by the Great and General Council to perform administrative functions.

National Anthem

No words, tune monastic, transcribed by F. Consolo.

RECENT ELECTIONS

In parliamentary elections on 9 Nov. 2008 the Pact for San Marino coalition won 35 of 60 seats, with 54·2% of the vote (Sammarinese Christian Democratic Party 31·9% and 22 seats, the Popular Alliance 11·5% and 7, Freedom List 6·3% and 4, Sammarinese Union of Moderates 4·2% and 2); the Reforms and Freedom coalition won 25 seats, with 45·8% (Party of Socialists and Democrats 32·0% and 18 seats, United Left 8·6% and 5, Democrats of the Centre 4·9% and 2). Turnout was 68·5%.

CURRENT ADMINISTRATION

Captains Regent: Marco Conti (since 1 April 2010); Glauco Sansovini (since 1 April 2010).

In March 2010 the Congress of State comprised:

Minister of Foreign and Political Affairs, Telecommunications and Transport: Antonella Mularoni. *Internal Affairs and Civil Protection:* Valeria Ciavatta. *Finance and Budget:* Gabriele Gatti. *Industry, Crafts and Commerce:* Marco Arzilli. *Tourism, Sport and Economic Co-operation:* Fabio Berardi. *Public Education, Universities, Culture and Youth Affairs:* Romeo Morri. *Territory, Environment and Agriculture:* Gian Carlo Venturini. *Health, Social Security, Welfare, Family and Social Affairs, and Equal Opportunities:* Claudio Podeschi. *Labour, Co-operation and Post:* Gian Marco Marcucci. *Justice, Information and Research:* Augusto Casali.

CURRENT LEADERS

Marco Conti

Position

Captain Regent

Introduction

A mechanical engineer, Marco Conti was sworn in for his first term as a captain regent on 1 April 2010.

Early Life

Born on 14 April 1969 in San Marino, Conti graduated in mechanical engineering from the University of Bologna, Italy. After completing further studies at the Technical Institute of

Rimini, he registered as a professional engineer. Conti joined the Sanmarinese Christian Democratic Party (PDCS) in 1992 and grew increasingly active in the political sphere. He was appointed director of the office of vehicle registration in 1995, a position he retained until March 2009, when he started work as head of San Marino's authority for civil aviation and maritime affairs.

Conti served as co-ordinator for internal affairs and civil protection from 2002–05 and in June 2006 he was elected to the Great and General Council when the PDCS won 21 seats and a third of the vote. Prior to the Nov. 2008 parliamentary election the PDCS joined forces with two other parties, Euro-Populars for San Marino and Arengo & Freedom, under the centre-right Pact for San Marino. Conti retained his seat in parliament, one of 22 captured by his party and its partners.

Career in Office
While captain regent, Conti continues to serve on the state council's commission of internal affairs.

Glauco Sansovini

Position
Captain Regent

Introduction
Glauco Sansovini, a retired businessman, was sworn in for his first term as a captain regent on 1 April 2010.

Early Life
Born on 20 May 1938 in Rocca San Casciano, near the Italian town of Forli, Sansovini worked as a logistics and distribution manager for various private enterprises in San Marino for 44 years until retiring in 2000. A political activist, in March 2001 he helped establish the right-wing National Alliance of San Marino (ANS), with links to Italy's National Alliance. In June 2001 he was elected the party's sole representative in the Great and General Council, winning re-election at the general elections of June 2006 and Nov. 2008. In the 2008 election the ANS entered into an alliance with the Sanmarinese Union of Moderates, necessitated by a new rule requiring an electoral threshold of 3·5%. The alliance won two seats with 4·2% of the vote. The Union is part of the majority centre-right coalition, the Pact for San Marino.

Career in Office
Glauco Sansovini is currently chairman of San Marino's Inter-Parliamentary Union and serves on the boards of the state committees for the environment and foreign affairs.

DEFENCE

Military service is not obligatory, but all citizens between the ages of 16 and 55 can be called upon to defend the State. They may also serve as volunteers in the Military Corps. There is a military Gendarmerie.

INTERNATIONAL RELATIONS

San Marino maintains a traditional neutrality, and remained so in the First and Second World Wars. It has diplomatic and consular relations with over 100 countries.

San Marino is a member of the UN, World Bank, IMF and several other UN specialized agencies, Council of Europe and OSCE.

ECONOMY

Overview

The economy is integrated with that of Italy via a monetary and customs union, close trade links and labour mobility. The economy relies principally on manufacturing and financial services, while tourism remains important despite stagnation in recent years.

The early 2000s saw the public finances in a precarious state but the economy has rebounded in recent years. Growth was estimated at around 5% in 2005, following a spate of reforms to improve competitiveness and resurgent growth in Italy. Growth and financial sector profitability have helped curtail budget deficits and reduce public debt. A reform of the pension system from 2006 together with tax cuts, declining balances of public enterprises and budget overspend will erode the budget surplus.

Currency

Since 1 Jan. 2002 San Marino has been using the euro (EUR). Italy has agreed that San Marino may mint a small part of the total Italian euro coin contingent with their own motifs. Inflation in 2001 was 3·3%. Total money supply in June 2005 was €906m.

Budget

Revenues totalled €504·8m. in 2005 and expenditures €433·1m. VAT accounted for 23·6% of revenue, social contributions 21·3% and income tax 20·2%; wages and salaries accounted for 35·4% of expenditure and social contributions 30·5%.

Performance

Real GDP growth was 4·5% in 2007. Total GDP was US$1·7bn. in 2007.

Banking and Finance

The Banca Centrale della Repubblica di San Marino (*President*, Biagio Bossone) was established in 2005 as an amalgamation of the Istituto di Credito Sammarinese and the Ispettorato per il Credito e le Valute (the Inspectorate for Credit and Currencies). Many of its functions have since been taken over by the European Central Bank and it has taken on a more supervisory role. Commercial banks include: Banca di San Marino, Credito Industriale Sammarinese, Cassa di Risparmio della Repubblica di San Marino and the Banca Agricola Commerciale della Repubblica di San Marino.

ENERGY AND NATURAL RESOURCES

Electricity

Electricity is supplied by Italy.

Agriculture

There were 1,000 ha. of arable land in 2006. Wheat, barley, maize and vines are grown.

INDUSTRY

Labour

Out of 20,530 people in employment in 2006, 6,247 worked in manufacturing and 2,901 in wholesale and retail trade. In 2006 there were 473 registered unemployed persons.

Trade Unions

There are two Confederations of Trade Unions: the Democratic Confederation of Sammarinese Workers and the Sammarinese Confederation of Labour.

INTERNATIONAL TRADE

Imports and Exports

Import commodities are a wide range of consumer manufactures and foodstuffs. Export commodities are building stone, lime, wine, baked goods, textiles, varnishes and ceramics. San Marino maintains a customs union with the European Union.

COMMUNICATIONS

Roads

A bus service connects San Marino with Rimini. There are 252 km of public roads and 40 km of private roads, and (2006) 32,263 passenger cars and 5,907 commercial vehicles.

Civil Aviation
The nearest airport is Rimini, 10 km to the east, which had scheduled flights in 2003 to Berlin, Düsseldorf, Frankfurt, Hamburg, Helsinki, Munich, Naples and Rome.

Telecommunications
San Marino had 21,300 main telephone lines in 2008 and 24,000 mobile phone subscribers. Internet users numbered 17,000 in 2008.

Postal Services
In 2006 there were 11 post offices.

SOCIAL INSTITUTIONS

Justice
Judges are appointed permanently by the Great and General Council; they may not be San Marino citizens. Petty civil cases are dealt with by a justice of the peace; legal commissioners deal with more serious civil cases, and all criminal cases and appeals lie to them from the justice of the peace. Appeals against the legal commissioners lie to two appeals judges as a court of third instance.

Education
Education is compulsory up to 16 years of age. In 2005 there were 15 nursery schools with 1,054 pupils and 141 teachers, 14 elementary schools with 1,497 pupils and 245 teachers, three junior high schools with 805 pupils and 144 teachers, and one high school with 1,289 pupils and 77 teachers. The University of San Marino began operating in 1988.

Health
In 2003 there were 139 hospital beds and 135 doctors. A survey published by the World Health Organization in June 2000 to measure health systems in all of the sovereign countries and find which country has the best overall health care ranked San Marino in third place.

RELIGION
The great majority of the population are Roman Catholic.

CULTURE

World Heritage Sites
There is one UNESCO World Heritage site in San Marino: San Marino Historic Centre and Mount Titano (inscribed on the list in 2008).

Broadcasting
San Marino RTV (colour by PAL) is the state broadcasting company. In 2006 television receivers numbered 10,300.

Press
San Marino had three daily newspapers in 2006 with a combined daily circulation of 2,000.

Tourism
In 2004, 2·81m. tourists visited San Marino.

DIPLOMATIC REPRESENTATIVES
Of San Marino in the United Kingdom
Ambassador: Contessa Marina Meneghetti de Camillo (resides in Rome).

Of the United Kingdom in San Marino
Ambassador: Edward Chaplin, CMG, OBE (resides in Rome).

Of San Marino in the USA (Honorary Consulate General at 1899 L St., NW, Suite 500, Washington D.C., 20036).
Ambassador: Paolo Rondelli.

Of the USA in San Marino
Ambassador: David H. Thorne (resides in Rome).

Of San Marino to the United Nations
Ambassador: Daniele Bodini.

Of San Marino to the European Union
Ambassador: Gian Nicola Filippi Balestra.

FURTHER READING
National Statistical Office: Ufficio Programmazione Economica e Centro Elaborazione Dati e Statistica, Via 28 Luglio, 192–47893 Borgo Maggiore.
Website (Italian only): http://www.upeceds.sm

SÃO TOMÉ E PRÍNCIPE

República Democrática de São Tomé e Príncipe
(Democratic Republic of São Tomé e Príncipe)

Capital: São Tomé
Population estimate, 2010: 165,000
GDP per capita, 2007: (PPP$) 1,638
HDI/world rank: 0·651/131

KEY HISTORICAL EVENTS

The islands of São Tomé and Príncipe off the west coast of Africa were colonized by Portugal in the fifteenth century. There may have been a few African inhabitants earlier but most of the population arrived during the centuries when the islands served as a slave-trading depot for South America. In the 19th century the islands became the first parts of Africa to grow cocoa. In 1876 Portugal officially abolished slavery but in practice it continued with many Angolans, Mozambicans and Cape Verdians brought in to work on the cocoa plantations. Because the slave-descended population was cut off from African culture, São Tomé had a higher proportion than other Portuguese colonies of *assimilados* (Africans acquiring full Portuguese culture and some rights). São Tomé saw serious riots against Portuguese rule in 1953. From 1960 a Movement for the Liberation of São Tomé e Príncipe operated from neighbouring African territories. In 1970 Portugal formed a 16-member legislative council and a provincial consultative council. Following the Portuguese revolution of 1974 a transitional government was formed. Independence came on 12 July 1975. Independent São Tomé e Príncipe officially proclaimed Marxist-Leninist policies but maintained a non-aligned foreign policy and has received aid from Portugal.

The government was overthrown by a coup on 16 July 2003 while President Fradique de Menezes and his foreign minister were abroad. The coup leader, Major Fernando Pereira, installed a junta but accepted a general amnesty from parliament on 24 July after agreeing to allow the ousted president to form a government of national unity.

TERRITORY AND POPULATION

The republic, which lies about 200 km off the west coast of Gabon, in the Gulf of Guinea, comprises the main islands of São Tomé (845 sq. km) and Príncipe and several smaller islets including Pedras Tinhosas and Rolas. It has a total area of 1,001 sq. km (387 sq. miles). Population (census, 2001) 137,599; density, 163 per sq. km. In 2005, 58·0% of the population were rural.

The UN gives an estimated population for 2010 of 165,000.

Areas and populations of the two provinces:

Province	*Sq. km*	*Census 2001*	*Chief town*	*Census 2001*
São Tomé	859	131,633	São Tomé	51,886
Príncipe	142	5,966	São António	1,040

The official language is Portuguese. Lungwa São Tomé, a Portuguese Creole, and Fang, a Bantu language, are the spoken languages.

SOCIAL STATISTICS

2006: births, 5,072; deaths, 1,111. Rates, 2006 (per 1,000 population): birth, 33·4; death, 7·3; infant mortality, 44 per 1,000 live births. Expectation of life, 2006, 63·5 years for males and 68·5 years for females. Annual population growth rate, 2000–05, 1·9%; fertility rate, 2004, 3·9 births per woman.

CLIMATE

The tropical climate is modified by altitude and the effect of the cool Benguela current. The wet season is generally from Oct. to May, but rainfall varies considerably, from 40" (1,000 mm) in the hot and humid northeast to 150–200" (3,800–5,000 mm) on the plateau. São Tomé, Jan. 79°F (26·1°C), July 75°F (23·9°C). Annual rainfall 38" (951 mm).

CONSTITUTION AND GOVERNMENT

The 1990 constitution was approved by 72% of votes at a referendum of March 1990 and became effective in Sept. 1990. It abolished the monopoly of the Movement for the Liberation of São Tomé e Príncipe (MLSTP). The *President* must be over 34 years old, and is elected by universal suffrage for one or two (maximum) five-year terms. He or she is also head of government and appoints a Council of Ministers. The 55-member *National Assembly* is elected for four years.

Since April 1995 **Príncipe** has enjoyed internal self-government, with a five-member regional government and an elected assembly.

National Anthem

'Independência total, glorioso canto do povo' ('Total independence, glorious song of the people'); words by A. N. do Espírito Santo, tune by M. de Sousa e Almeida.

RECENT ELECTIONS

At the presidential election on 30 July 2006 incumbent Fradique de Menezes (Force for Change Democratic Movement/MDFM) was re-elected, receiving 60·6% of votes cast, against Patrice Trovoada (Independent Democratic Action/ADI) with 38·8% and Nilo Guimarães (ind.) with 0·6%. Turnout was 64·9%.

At the National Assembly elections on 26 March 2006 the Force for Change Democratic Movement (MDFM) won 23 seats with 36·8% of votes cast, the Liberation Movement of São Tomé e Príncipe-Social Democratic Party (MLSTP-PSD) 20 (29·5%), Independent Democratic Action (ADI) 11 (20·0%) and the New Way Movement (MNR) 1 (4·7%).

CURRENT ADMINISTRATION

President, C.-in-C: Fradique Bandeira Melo de Menezes; b. 1942 (MDFM; sworn in 23 July 2003 and re-elected 30 July 2006, having previously held office from 3 Sept. 2001 to 16 July 2003).

In March 2010 the coalition government comprised:

Prime Minister: Rafael Branco; b. 1953 (MLSTP-PSD; in office since 22 June 2008).

Minister of Agriculture, Rural Development and Fisheries, and Natural Resources and the Environment: Xavier Mendes. *Commerce, Industry and Tourism:* Celestino Andrade. *Defence and Internal Order, and Justice, Public Administration, State Reform and Parliamentary Affairs:* Elsa Teixeira Pinto. *Education and Culture:* Jorge Bom Jesus. *Foreign Affairs and Community Co-operation:* Carlos Tiny. *Health:* Arlindo de Carvalho. *Internal Administration, Civil Protection and Territorial Administration:* António Paquete. *Labour, Solidarity, Family and Women's Affairs:* Carlos Gomes. *Planning and Finances:* Ângela Viegas. *Public Works, Infrastructure, Urban Development, Transportation and Communications:* Benjamin Vera Cruz. *Social Communication, Youth and Sports:* Maria de Cristo Carvalho.

Office of the President (Portuguese only):
http://www.presidencia.st

CURRENT LEADERS

Fradique Bandeira Melo de Menezes

Position

President

Introduction

First elected president in Sept. 2001 and re-elected in July 2006, Fradique de Menezes has weathered numerous political storms. Tensions have mounted since the discovery of large offshore oil reserves, revenue from which looks set to transform the archipelago.

Early Life

Fradique Bandeira Melo de Menezes was born in Madalena on the island of São Tomé in 1942, the son of a Portuguese father and a São Toméan mother. He attended school in both São Tomé and Portugal, before studying education and psychology at the Free University of Brussels, Belgium. De Menezes then completed postgraduate studies in international trade in the USA. In 1967 he took up work at Marconi Radio in Lisbon, before working for various US companies in Brussels.

He returned to São Tomé e Príncipe following the country's independence from Portugal in July 1975 and taught at the National High School. In the late 1970s he worked at the ministry of agriculture, under the Marxist-inspired Liberation Movement of São Tomé e Príncipe (MLSTP). De Menezes relocated to London in 1981, where he was director of São Tomé e Príncipe's Commercial Center. From 1983–86 he served as his country's ambassador to the European Community. When de Menezes returned to São Tomé in 1986 the MLSTP had begun to embrace economic and political reforms. He was appointed minister of foreign affairs but left politics to pursue business interests, establishing companies involved in shipping, agriculture (cocoa) and investment.

Following constitutional reform in 1990 and the country's first multi-party elections in Jan. 1991, de Menezes was elected to parliament. In the July 2001 presidential election, as the candidate of the centrist Independent Democratic Action (which had been founded in 1992), he ran against the former president, Manuel Pinto da Costa, and won in the first round with 56·3% of the vote. He was sworn in as president on 3 Sept. 2001.

Career in Office

Following his electoral success, de Menezes and his supporters set up a new party—the Force for Change Democratic Movement (MDFM). He promised to reverse the country's crippling economic crisis, although progress has since been slow. The discovery of substantial oil deposits offshore brought optimism but also raised the political temperature. While de Menezes was visiting Nigeria in July 2003 his government was toppled briefly in a military coup. International intervention led to an agreement with the coup leaders and he was reinstated on 23 July 2003. As political infighting continued, de Menezes dismissed the prime minister and appointed a new cabinet after a corruption scandal in Sept. 2004. There were further reshuffles in June 2005 and again in April 2006 following the resignation of the prime minister. Meanwhile, in Feb. 2005, São Tomé e Príncipe signed (jointly with Nigeria) its first offshore oil exploration and production-sharing agreement with international oil companies. In elections to the National Assembly in March 2006 the MDFM was returned as the largest party, and in July de Menezes was re-elected to the presidency as the MDFM representative.

In March 2007 the International Monetary Fund and World Bank cancelled most of São Tomé's foreign debt in the light of progress towards economic stability.

Criticism of worsening economic conditions and the government's handling of dissent among police officers led de Menezes to replace several ministers in late 2007. In Feb. 2008 he appointed Patrice Trovoada of the ADI as prime minister. However, Trovoada's coalition government collapsed after only three months, having lost a parliamentary vote of confidence, and de Menezes turned in June to the MLSTP-PSD leader Rafael Branco to form a new administration.

In Feb. 2009 it was reported that the authorities had foiled an attempted coup plot against Menezes and that over 30 people had been arrested.

INTERNATIONAL RELATIONS

São Tomé e Príncipe is a member of the UN, World Bank, IMF and several other UN specialized agencies, International Organization of the Francophonie, African Development Bank, African Union, CEEAC and is an ACP member state of the ACP-EU relationship.

ECONOMY

In 2005 agriculture accounted for 17% of GDP, industry 21% and services 63%.

Overview

Most branches of the economy were nationalized after independence, but economic liberalization began in 1985 and accelerated in the 1990s.

Currency

The unit of currency is the *dobra* (STD) of 100 *centimos*. From a rate of 69·0% in 1997 inflation had fallen to 9·2% in 2002 before rising to 18·5% in 2007 and 26·0% in 2008. In Dec. 2006 foreign exchange reserves were US$34m. Total money supply in Dec. 2004 was 172,817m. dobras (up from 23,683m. dobras in Dec. 1996).

Budget

In 2005 revenues totalled 972·1bn. dobras and expenditures 545·5bn. dobras.

Performance

Real GDP growth was 5·8% in 2008 (6·0% in 2007). In 2008 total GDP was US$175m.

Banking and Finance

In 1991 the Banco Central de São Tomé e Príncipe (*Governor*, Luís Fernando Moreira de Sousa) replaced the Banco Nacional as the central bank and bank of issue. A private commercial bank, the Banco Internacional de São Tomé e Príncipe, began operations in 1993.

ENERGY AND NATURAL RESOURCES

Environment

In 2008 carbon dioxide emissions from the consumption and flaring of fossil fuels were the equivalent of 0·6 tonnes per capita.

Electricity

Installed capacity, 2004 estimate, 5,000 kW. Production was about 18m. kWh in 2004, with consumption per capita an estimated 99 kWh.

Oil and Gas

There are large oil reserves around São Tomé e Príncipe that could greatly add to the country's wealth; the Joint Development Zone was set up with Nigeria to administer the exploitation because the reserves are located in shared waters. The first license to begin exploration was granted in April 2004.

Agriculture

After independence all landholdings over 200 ha. were nationalized into 15 state farms. These were partially privatized in 1985 by granting management contracts to foreign companies, and distributing some state land as small private plots. There were an estimated 9,000 ha. of arable land in 2007 and 47,000 ha. of permanent crops. Production (2003 estimates in 1,000 tonnes): bananas, 27; coconuts, 27; cassava, 6; palm kernels, 4; cocoa beans, 3; maize, 2; palm oil, 2. There were an estimated 5,000 goats, 4,000 cattle, 3,000 sheep and 2,000 pigs in 2003.

Forestry

In 2005 forests covered 27,000 ha., or 28·4% of the land area. In 2007, 9,000 cu. metres of timber were cut.

Fisheries

There are rich tuna shoals. The total catch in 2004 came to 4,141 tonnes.

INDUSTRY

Manufacturing contributed 4·2% of GDP in 2001. There are a few small factories in agricultural processing (including beer and palm oil production), timber processing, bricks, ceramics, printing, textiles and soap-making.

Labour

In 2001 the economically active population was 52,150. The unemployment rate was 15·7% in 2001.

INTERNATIONAL TRADE

Foreign debt was US$110m. in 2008, equivalent to 61% of São Tomé e Príncipe's GDP (but down from 265% in 2006).

Imports and Exports

Trade figures for 2006: imports, US$70·9m.; exports, US$3·8m. Cocoa accounts for two-thirds of all exports.

In 2006 the main import suppliers were Portugal (63·6%), Angola (18·3%) and Belgium (4·6%); main export markets were Portugal (33·3%), the Netherlands (27·1%) and Belgium (14·3%).

COMMUNICATIONS

Roads

There were 500 km of roads in 2009, 375 km of which were paved. Approximately 4,500 passenger cars, 2,183 motorcycles and over 1,800 trucks and vans were in use in 2008.

Civil Aviation

São Tomé airport had flights in 2003 to Cape Verde, Libreville, Lisbon and Luanda. In 2007 São Tomé handled 50,625 passengers. There is a light aircraft service to Príncipe.

Shipping

São Tomé is the main port, but it lacks a deep water harbour. Neves handles oil imports and is the main fishing port. Portuguese shipping lines run routes to Lisbon, Porto, Rotterdam and Antwerp. In 2002 merchant shipping totalled 86,000 GRT.

Telecommunications

In 2008 there were 7,700 main (fixed) telephone lines; mobile phone subscribers numbered 49,000 in 2008 (30·6 per 100 persons). There were 6,000 PCs in use in 2005 and an estimated 21,000 internet users.

Postal Services

In 2003 there were ten post offices.

SOCIAL INSTITUTIONS

Justice

Members of the Supreme Court are appointed by the National Assembly. There is no death penalty. The population in penal institutions in July 2006 was 160 (83 per 100,000 of national population).

Education

Adult literacy was 84·9% in 2001. Education is free and compulsory. In 2007–08 there were 90 primary schools and 32,616 pupils, and ten secondary schools and 8,380 pupils; 96% of primary age children were attending school in 2006. There are two institutions of higher education.

Health

In 2004 there were 81 physicians, 11 dentists, and 308 nurses and midwives.

RELIGION

In 2001, 81% of the population were Roman Catholic. There is a small Protestant church and a Seventh Day Adventist school.

CULTURE

Broadcasting

Broadcasting is dominated by the government-run Televisão Sãotomense (TVS) and Rádio Nacional. There were 12,000 TV-equipped households in 2004.

Press

In 2006 there was one daily newspaper. Two government-owned and six independent papers were also published irregularly.

Tourism

In 2005 there were 11,000 non-resident tourists.

DIPLOMATIC REPRESENTATIVES

Of São Tomé e Príncipe in the United Kingdom
Ambassador: Vacant (resides in Brussels).
Chargé d'Affaires a.i.: Armindo de Brito Fernandes.

Of the United Kingdom in São Tomé e Príncipe
Ambassador: Vacant (resides in Luanda, Angola).
Chargé d'Affaires a.i: Angela Trott.

Of São Tomé e Príncipe in the USA and to the United Nations
Ambassador: Ovídio Manuel Barbosa Pequeno.

Of the USA in São Tomé e Príncipe
Ambassador: Eunice Reddick (resides in Libreville, Gabon).

Of São Tomé e Príncipe to the European Union
Ambassador: Carlos Gustavo dos Anjos.

FURTHER READING

National Statistical Office: Instituto Nacional de Estatística, Largo das Alfândegas, Cx. Postal 256, São Tomé.
Website (Portuguese only): http://www.ine.st

SAUDI ARABIA

Al-Mamlaka al-Arabiya as-Saudiya
(Kingdom of Saudi Arabia)
Capital: Riyadh
Population estimate, 2010: 26·25m.
GDP per capita, 2007: (PPP$) 22,935
HDI/world rank: 0·843/59

KEY HISTORICAL EVENTS

Nomadic tribes have existed across the Arabian peninsula for thousands of years. The pre-Islamic period saw the development of civilizations based on trade in frankincense and spices, notably, from about the 12th century BC, the Minaeans in the southwest of what is now Saudi Arabia and Yemen. The Sabaean and Himyarite kingdoms flourished from around 650 BC and 115 BC respectively, their loose federations of city states lasting until the 6th century AD. Although increased trade brought these civilizations into contact with the Roman and Persian empires—the two great regional powers before the advent of Islam—they remained, for the most part, politically independent. The Nabataeans, an Aramaic people whose capital was at Petra, modern-day Jordan, spread into northern Arabia over a period covering the 1st century BC and the 1st AD before annexation of their territory by Rome. Persian influence was prevalent along Arabia's eastern coast, centred on Dilmun which covered parts of the mainland and the island of Bahrain.

By the 6th century AD the Hejaz region in northwestern Arabia was becoming increasingly powerful and an important link in the overland trade route from Egypt and the Byzantine Empire to the wider East. One of the principal cities of Hejaz was Makkah (Mecca), a staging post on the camel train routes and site of pilgrimage to numerous pre-Islamic religious shrines. The leading tribe in the city was the Quraysh, into which the Prophet Muhammad was born in 570. Muhammad and his followers (known as Muslims) took control of Makkah in 630. He had earlier declared himself a prophetic reformer, destroying the city's pagan idols and declaring it a centre of Muslim pilgrimage dedicated to the worship of Allah (God) alone. Muhammad died in AD 632, by then commanding the loyalty of almost all of Arabia.

The leaders who succeeded Muhammad, known as caliphs, spread the Islamic faith throughout and beyond the Arab world. However, Arabia itself began to fragment and by the latter part of the 7th century it had become a province of the Islamic realm, although the holy cities of Makkah and Madinah retained their spiritual focus. Meanwhile, increasingly remote from the main centres of Islamic authority under the Umayyad and Abbasid caliphate dynasties, Arabia became an arena for sectarian divisions—Shia, Sunni and Kharijite—which developed within the Islamic faith.

After 1269 most of the Hejaz region came under the suzerainty of the Egyptian Mameluks. The Ottoman Turks conquered Egypt in 1517 and, to counter the influence of the Christian Portuguese presence in the Gulf region, extended their nominal control over the whole Arabian Peninsula. Portuguese traders were followed by British, Dutch and French merchants during the 17th and 18th centuries, the British gradually securing political and commercial supremacy in the Gulf and southern Arabia through a system of protectorates and local treaties.

Saudi Arabia's origins as a political entity lay in the rise of the puritanical Wahhabi movement of the 18th century, which called for a return to the original principles of Islam and gained the allegiance of the powerful Al-Saud dynasty (founded in the 15th century) in the Nejd region of central Arabia. By 1811 the Al-Saud/Wahhabi armies controlled most of the peninsula and were seen as a threat to the Ottoman Turkish overlord. The Sultan called on his viceroy in Egypt, Mehmet Ali, to suppress the Wahhabis, who were defeated between 1811 and 1818. Nevertheless, the house of Al-Saud continued to hold sway over the interior of Arabia until 1891 when, after a long period of tribal warfare, the rival Al-Rashid family, with Ottoman support, seized control of the city of Riyadh.

The Al-Saud family was exiled to Kuwait but Abdulaziz Ibn Abdul Rahman (known to Europeans as Ibn Saud) restored Wahhabi fortunes, recapturing Riyadh in 1902 and reasserting Al-Saud control over Nejd by 1906. On the eve of the First World War Abdulaziz gained the al Hasa region east of Nejd on the Gulf from the Ottoman Turks. In 1920 he captured the Asir region and in 1921 added the Jebel Shammar territory (northwest of Nejd) of the Al-Rashid family. In 1925 Abdulaziz completed his conquest of Hejaz, overthrowing Hussein, Sharif of Makkah and a member of the Hashimi family. Abdulaziz became both Sultan of Nejd and King of the Hejaz. Britain recognized Abdulaziz as an independent ruler by the Treaty of Jeddah on 20 May 1927, and in 1932 Nejd and Hejaz were unified as the Kingdom of Saudi Arabia, ruled as an absolute monarchy under Islamic law.

Abdulaziz (died 9 Nov. 1953) concentrated on the political consolidation and modernization of the country. Oil was discovered in 1938 and its exploitation was developed with the support of the USA after the Second World War. Crown Prince Saud succeeded his father and ruled until Nov. 1964, when he was effectively deposed by his brother Faisal. During his reign Saudi relations with the pan-Arabist Nasser regime in Egypt deteriorated, most notably over the 1962 revolution in Yemen.

As king and prime minister, Faisal used oil production revenues to build up the country's economic base. In 1970 came the first of the five-year economic development programmes. Meanwhile, financial support was given to other Arab states in their conflict with Israel. Leading on from the Oct. 1973 Arab-Israeli war Arab producers, including Saudi Arabia, cut supplies to the USA and other Western countries, causing a fourfold increase in oil prices. However, Faisal subsequently adopted a more conciliatory stance than the more radical members of the Organization of Petroleum Exporting Countries (OPEC, founded in 1960) and the close Saudi economic relationship with the USA was reinforced with a co-operation agreement in 1974. In March 1975, when Faisal was assassinated by a nephew, believed to be mentally unstable, his half-brother Khalid became king.

Khalid continued Faisal's policies promoting Islamic solidarity and Arab unity in the wake of hostilities with Israel. In practice his moderate stance was in marked contrast to the militancy of many other Arab states, particularly over oil pricing by OPEC and opposition to Egypt's 1978 peace treaty with Israel. Khalid was also involved in early efforts to stop the civil war in Lebanon and, in 1981, he inaugurated the Gulf Co-operation Council (GCC). Domestically, he maintained his family's absolute political control and the conservative Islamic character of the country. However, opposition to his regime was demonstrated in Nov. 1979 when Sunni Muslim fundamentalists occupied the Grand Mosque at Makkah. A two-week siege ended with over 200 deaths. The second and third five-year development plans (1975–79 and 1980–84), both launched by Khalid, created much of the country's current economic infrastructure. Owing to Khalid's poor health throughout his reign much of his executive responsibility was assumed by his younger half-brother, Crown Prince Fahd.

Fahd succeeded to the throne on 13 June 1982. Like his predecessors, he maintained absolute power but broadened the process of political consultation and decision-making by setting up the Consultative Council (*Majlis Al-Shura*) of royal appointees from 1993. In 1986 he assumed the title of 'Custodian of the Two Holy Mosques' but the Saudi role in protecting religious pilgrims incurred international criticism in 1987 when 400 Iranian worshippers were killed in clashes in Makkah with security forces and again in 1994 when 270 pilgrims died in a stampede. Internationally, Fahd adopted a moderate policy on regional problems and closely allied the kingdom with the USA. Fahd was a key participant in diplomatic efforts to end the Iran-Iraq war in 1988 and, in 1989, he participated in the Taif reconciliation accord ending the 14-year Lebanese civil war. His pro-Western stance and co-operation in the 1990–91 Gulf crisis were crucial to the deployment and successful military operations of the US-led multinational force raised against Iraq following its invasion of Kuwait.

However, anti-Western disaffection among Saudi nationals has become more overt in recent years. In 1996 a bomb exploded at a US military complex at Dhahran, killing 19 and wounding over 300. In 2000 a series of bomb blasts, blamed by Saudi officials on British nationals engaged in criminal activity, was widely believed abroad to be the work of Saudi dissidents. Up to 15 Saudi nationals were involved in the attacks on New York and Washington, D.C. on 11 Sept. 2001, co-ordinated by Saudi dissident Osama bin Laden. In Nov. 2002 the Saudi government refused permission for the US to use its military facilities to attack Iraq, even if sanctioned by the United Nations. In May 2003 suicide bombers killed ten US citizens and many others at housing compounds for Western expatriate workers in Riyadh. In April 2003 the US agreed to pull out most of its troops from the kingdom, while stressing that the two countries would remain allies.

As King Fahd's health declined, his half brother, Crown Prince Abdullah Ibn Abdulaziz Al-Saud, assumed responsibility for government in 1996. When King Fahd died on 1 Aug. 2005, Crown Prince Abdullah was appointed his successor.

TERRITORY AND POPULATION

Saudi Arabia, which occupies nearly 80% of the Arabian peninsula, is bounded in the west by the Red Sea, east by the Persian Gulf, Qatar and the United Arab Emirates, north by Jordan, Iraq and Kuwait and south by Yemen and Oman. For the border dispute with Yemen *see* YEMEN: Territory and Population. The total area is 2,149,690 sq. km (829,995 sq. miles). Riyadh is the political, and Makkah (Mecca) the religious, capital.

The total population at the 2004 census was 22,678,262; density, 10·5 per sq. km. Estimate, 2007, 23,981,000. Approximately 73% of the population are Saudi nationals. In 2005, 81·0% of the population lived in urban areas.

The UN gives an estimated population for 2010 of 26·25m.

Principal cities with 2004 population estimates (in 1m.): Riyadh, 4·09; Jeddah, 2·80; Makkah, 1·29; Madinah, 0·92; Dammam, 0·74; Taif, 0·52.

The Neutral Zone (5,700 sq. km, 3,560 sq. miles), jointly owned and administered by Kuwait and Saudi Arabia from 1922 to 1966, was partitioned between the two countries in 1966, but the exploitation of the oil and other natural resources continues to be shared.

The official language is Arabic.

SOCIAL STATISTICS

2001 estimates: births, 715,000; deaths, 84,000. Birth rate (2001) was approximately 34 per 1,000 population; death rate, 4. 75% of the population is under the age of 30. Expectation of life at birth, 2007, was 70·8 years for males and 75·1 years for females. Annual population growth rate, 2000–05, 2·4%. Infant mortality, 2005, was 21 per 1,000 live births, down from 58 in the years 1980–85. Fertility rate, 2004, 3·9 births per woman.

CLIMATE

A desert climate, with very little rain and none at all from June to Dec. The months May to Sept. are very hot and humid, but winter temperatures are quite pleasant. Riyadh, Jan. 58°F (14·4°C), July 108°F (42°C). Annual rainfall 4" (100 mm). Jeddah, Jan. 73°F (22·8°C), July 87°F (30·6°C). Annual rainfall 3" (81 mm).

CONSTITUTION AND GOVERNMENT

The reigning King, **Abdullah Ibn Abdulaziz Al-Saud** (b. 1924), Custodian of the two Holy Mosques, succeeded in Aug. 2005, after King Fahd's death. *Crown Prince:* Prince Sultan Ibn Abdulaziz Al-Saud (b. 1926). The Saudi royal family is around 8,000-strong.

Constitutional practice derives from Sharia law. There is no formal constitution, but three royal decrees of 1 March 1992 established a Basic Law which defines the systems of central and municipal government, and set up a 60-man Consultative Council (*Majlis Al-Shura*) of royal nominees in Aug. 1993. The *Chairman* is Salih bin Abdullah bin Hemaid. In July 1997 the King decreed an increase of the Consultative Council to a chairman plus 90 members, selected from men of science and experience; in 2001 it was increased again to a chairman plus 120 members and in 2005 further to a chairman plus 150 members. The Council does not have legislative powers.

Saudi Arabia is an absolute monarchy; executive power is discharged through a *Council of Ministers,* consisting of the King, Deputy Prime Minister, Second Deputy Prime Minister and Cabinet Ministers.

The King has the post of *Prime Minister* and can veto any decision of the Council of Ministers within 30 days.

In Oct. 2003 the government announced that municipal elections would be held in 2004 for the first time, followed by city elections and partial elections to the *Majlis Al-Shura* in the following years.

National Anthem

'Sarei lil majd walaya' ('Onward towards the glory and the heights'); words by Ibrahim Khafaji, tune by Abdul Rahman al Katib.

GOVERNMENT CHRONOLOGY

Kings since 1932.

1932–53	Abdulaziz Ibn Abdul Rahman Al-Saud
1953–64	Saud Ibn Abdulaziz Al-Saud
1964–75	Faisal Ibn Abdulaziz Al-Saud
1975–82	Khalid Ibn Abdulaziz Al-Saud
1982–2005	Fahd Ibn Abdulaziz Al-Saud
2005–	Abdullah Ibn Abdulaziz Al-Saud

RECENT ELECTIONS

Saudi Arabia's first ever elections were held in three phases between Feb.–April 2005 to create 178 local municipal councils. Half of the 1,184 seats were elected by the people and the other half appointed. Women were not permitted to stand for election or to vote. There are no political parties, but most seats were won by candidates backed by conservative Muslim clerics.

CURRENT ADMINISTRATION

In March 2010 the Council of Ministers comprised:

Prime Minister: King Abdullah Ibn Abdulaziz Al-Saud; b. 1924.

First Deputy Prime Minister, Minister of Defence and Aviation and Inspector-General: Crown Prince Sultan Ibn Abdulaziz Al-Saud. *Second Deputy Prime Minister and Minister of Interior:* Prince Nayef Ibn Abdulaziz Al-Saud.

Minister of Municipal and Rural Affairs: Prince Meta'ab Ibn Abdul Aziz Al-Saud. *Foreign Affairs:* Prince Saud Al-Faisal Ibn Abdulaziz Al-Saud. *Agriculture:* Dr Fahd Ibn Abdulrahman Balghanaim. *Water and Electricity:* Abdul Rahman Al-Hussayen. *Civil Service:* Muhammad Ibn Ali Al-Fayez. *Education:* Prince Faisal Ibn Abdullah Ibn Muhammad Al-Saud. *Finance:* Dr Ibrahim Ibn Abdulaziz Al-Assaf. *Health:* Dr Abdullah Ibn Abdul Aziz Al-Rabeah. *Higher Education:* Dr Khalid Ibn Mohammed Al-Angary. *Commerce and Industry:* Abdallah Ibn Zainal ali Reza. *Culture and Information:* Abdul Aziz Ibn Mohieddin Khoja. *Islamic Affairs, Endowments, Call and Guidance:* Sheikh Saleh Ibn Abdulaziz Al-Ashaikh. *Justice:* Sheikh Dr Mohammed Ibn Abdulkarim Ibn Abdul Aziz Al-Issa. *Labour:* Dr Ghazi Ibn Abdulrahman Al-Qusaibi. *Social Affairs:* Yusuf Ibn Ahmed Al-Othaimeen. *Petroleum and Mineral Resources:* Ali Ibn Ibrahim Al-Naimi. *Pilgrimage:* Fouad Ibn Abdul-Salam Al-Farsi. *Economy and Planning:* Khalid Ibn Muhammad Al-Qusaibi. *Communications and Information Technology:* Muhammad Ibn Jameel Mulla. *Transport:* Dr Jubarah Ibn Eid Al-Suraiseri.

Majlis Website: http://www.shura.gov.sa

CURRENT LEADERS

King Abdullah Ibn Abdulaziz Al-Saud

Position

King

Introduction

King Abdullah administered Saudi Arabia on behalf of his half-brother, King Fahd Ibn Abdulaziz, between 1996 and Fahd's death on 1 Aug. 2005, following which he was named as successor. Abdullah has maintained the strict Islamic code of governance associated with the Wahhabi Saudis while attempting to rein in the excesses of the princely class. He has gained respect internationally for his efforts in the Middle East peace process but at times relations with the USA administration have been strained.

Early Life

Prince Abdullah Ibn Abdulaziz was born in Riyadh in 1924, the only son of Fahda bint Asi bin Shurayim Shammar, the eighth wife of Abdulaziz Ibn Abdul Rahman Al-Saud, then Sultan of Nejd, who founded the Kingdom of Saudi Arabia in 1932. Abdulaziz, known as Ibn Saud by Europeans, reared his massive family in the Bedouin tradition, educating his sons at court and instilling them with Islamic and Arab virtues.

Abdullah's career began in 1952 when he was given the command of the Saudi National Guard by his half-brother, King Saud, the first son to succeed Abdulaziz. The National Guard comprised descendants of Abdulaziz's Bedouin warriors who took part in the expansion of Saudi power. On his accession in 1975, King Khalid Ibn Abdulaziz appointed Abdullah second deputy prime minister. In this post Abdullah became involved in foreign policy, visiting the USA in 1976 to meet President Gerald Ford. On the accession of King Fahd in 1982, Abdullah was designated crown prince and first deputy prime minister.

Career in Office

The succession in Saudi Arabia is decided by the Saudi princes, who number over 4,000 (some sources claim an estimated 8,000). A crown prince is traditionally selected by seniority and ability. Since the death of the kingdom's founder, Abdulaziz, in 1953, only his sons have been considered suitable for the succession. Abdullah, who has only two full sisters and no full brothers, lacks a fraternal support base and relies on alliances forged with other factions within the family, most notably the sons of King Faisal, Prince Saud (foreign minister since 1975) and Prince Turki (head of Saudi intelligence).

Known as a devout Muslim, Abdullah has 14 sons and 20 daughters by six wives. His reputation for piety has earned him support from religious leaders. Having assumed the position of regent in 1996, he was soon considered the *de facto* ruler of Saudi Arabia on account of King Fahd's recurrent illnesses and absences from the country. It was likely that Abdullah consulted and, to some extent, ruled with Fahd's Sudairi brothers, Sultan and Salman, the second deputy prime minister and the governor of Riyadh respectively.

Hopes for political reform under Abdullah have been disappointed. However, he has attacked the corruption and profligacy of the princes. His insistence on budgetary accountability has been met with resistance by many of his extended family. In 1999 Prince Talal Ibn Abdulaziz, another half-brother, made a call for more openness in Saudi governance.

Abdullah's foreign policy has concentrated on improving relations within the Arab world and the Gulf region and encouraging the peace process in the Middle East. He has shown support for militant Islamic groups such as Hizbollah and condemned Israeli aggression in Lebanon. In early 2002 he proposed a peace plan for the Palestinian situation. In essence, the proposal was a restatement of the UN resolution for the Oslo peace process, which demanded the withdrawal of Israeli authority to the 1967 boundaries. However, his offer of normalization of relations with the Arab world in addition to recognition was seen as a greater incentive for Israeli compromise. Abdullah's subsequent retraction was explained as a reaction to the then Israeli prime minister Ariel Sharon's move to an 'unprecedented level' of violence against the Palestinians.

Abdullah is seen as less pro-Western than King Fahd. The attacks on New York, USA, in Sept. 2001, although condemned by Abdullah, created serious tensions owing to the high proportion of Saudi nationals among the perpetrators. He had declined a visit to the USA on two occasions before the attacks, complaining of US one-sidedness in the Palestinian issue, and his relations with President George W. Bush were also mixed. Abdullah stated that Bush was 'uninformed' about the Middle East and the plight of the Palestinians. Nevertheless, he maintained that the USA would remain a firm ally.

Internal reforms have been slow under Abdullah, but some key issues have been addressed. Female education, previously the preserve of the *ulema* (religious leaders), was placed under the jurisdiction of the ministry of education in 2002 and Abdullah has supported the increase of female employment. His visit to a Riyadh slum in Nov. 2002, wholly out of character for the Saudi royal family, heralded the establishment of a committee for the eradication of poverty in Saudi Arabia. The country's first ever elections in 2005, although with a limited franchise and only for local councils, were a partial response to pressure for political reform.

The issue of human rights has complicated external relations and provoked civil unrest in Saudi Arabia. Abdullah has rejected Western calls for the abolition of Sharia law and the emancipation of women, stating that it is 'absurd to impose on an individual or a society rights that are alien to its beliefs or principles'. However, in Aug. 2002 the justice ministry announced the licensing of lawyers in an attempt to moderate the Sharia system.

Saudi Arabia was gripped by widespread demonstrations against the regime's pro-US stance in 2002, causing open rifts in the Saudi family, particularly between the factions of Abdullah and Prince Sultan. Abdullah appointed a personal representative to Washington to balance the influence of the Saudi ambassador, Prince Bandar, son of Prince Sultan. These developments have been explained as an attempt by Abdullah to bypass Sultan, seen by many Saudis as corrupt.

Abdullah has been forced to focus on the issue of Islamic fundamentalism since the suicide bombings in Riyadh in May 2003. The attacks, which caused the death of 34 people including many foreign nationals, were blamed by the US administration and by the crown prince on a resurgent al-Qaeda. Further attacks by suspected al-Qaeda terrorists have since taken place, including those on the major oil-processing facility in Abqaiq in Feb. 2006 and on French tourists near the ruins of Madain Saleh in the northwest of the country in Feb. 2007.

Abdullah's age and state of health have meanwhile generated speculation about the issue of succession and internecine royal politics. In late 2006 he announced that a committee of senior princes would be formed to select the future crown prince and reduce the likelihood of family conflicts. The new committee would in theory have the power to remove a king if he was judged to be permanently incapacitated and would lead the country in a caretaker capacity until a successor was chosen.

In Dec. 2006 the UK government controversially suspended a fraud investigation into the 1980s al-Yamamah defence contract with Saudi Arabia, stating that diplomatic co-operation between the two countries was being put at risk (a decision subsequently confirmed as lawful by the British House of Lords in July 2008). In Sept. 2007 Saudi Arabia announced a £4·4bn. agreement with the UK to buy 72 Typhoon military jet aircraft.

In Oct. 2007 a law to reform the judicial system was enacted. This provided for new specialized courts and the introduction of a supreme court as a final court of appeal. Plans were also announced to curb the powers of the religious police, which had come under increasing criticism over deaths in custody.

In Nov. 2007 Pope Benedict XVI greeted Abdullah at the Vatican in the first such meeting between the head of the Roman Catholic Church and a Saudi monarch.

In Feb. 2009 Abdullah made extensive changes in government affecting top positions in the courts, the armed forces, the central bank, the health, education and information ministries, the religious police and the Consultative Council. He also appointed the country's first woman minister, Nora al-Fayez, as deputy minister responsible for girls' education.

In late 2009 the Saudi military was involved in clashes with rebels from neighbouring Yemen along the two countries' common border.

DEFENCE

Defence expenditure (including expenditure on public order and safety) in 2008 totalled US$38,223m. (US$1,511 per capita). In 2007 defence spending represented 9·3% of GDP.

5,000 US troops were stationed in Saudi Arabia after the 1991 Gulf War and were joined by a further 20,000 during the 2003 conflict. However, virtually all US troops have now been withdrawn. The Gulf Co-operation Council's Peninsular Shield Force previously comprised a standing force of 9,000 based in Saudi Arabia. In 2008 it changed to become a quick reaction unit that draws upon 22,000 troops based in their home countries.

Army

Strength (2007) was 75,000. There is a paramilitary Border Guard (10,500) and a National Guard (see below).

Navy

The Royal Saudi Naval Forces fleet includes seven frigates and four corvettes. Naval Aviation forces operate 15 armed helicopters.

The main naval bases are at Riyadh (HQ Naval Forces), Jeddah (Western Fleet) and Jubail (Eastern Fleet). Naval personnel in 2007 totalled 15,500, including 3,000 marines.

Air Force

Current combat units include F-15s, F-5Bs, F-5Fs, Tornado strike aircraft and Tornado interceptors. The Air Force operated 278 combat capable aircraft and numbered 20,000 personnel in 2007.

Air Defence Force

This separate Command was formerly part of the Army. In 2007 it operated surface-to-air missile batteries and had a strength of 4,000.

National Guard

The total strength of the National Guard amounted to 100,000 (75,000 active, 25,000 tribal levies) in 2007. The National Guard's primary role is the protection of the Royal Family and vital points in the Kingdom. It is directly under royal command. The UK provides small advisory teams to the National Guard in the fields of general training and communications.

Industrial Security Force

This force was established in 2007 to protect state oil facilities in response to attacks in 2006 on Abqaiq oil processing plant. Initial strength, 9,000.

INTERNATIONAL RELATIONS

Saudi Arabia is a member of the UN, World Bank, IMF and several other UN specialized agencies, WTO, BIS, Islamic Development Bank, OIC, Gulf Co-operation Council, League of Arab States and OPEC.

In April 2001 Saudi Arabia and Iran signed a security pact to fight drug trafficking and terrorism, 13 years after the two countries had broken off relations.

ECONOMY

Agriculture accounted for 2% of GDP in 2008, industry 70% and services 27%.

Overview

Saudi Arabia is the world's leading oil producer and exporter. The economy is dominated by the oil sector, accounting for roughly 35% of GDP, 75% of government revenue and 85% of exports since the end of the Gulf War in 1991 (Economist Intelligence Unit). However, reduced oil production led to oil accounting for only 35% of government revenue in 2009. In 1998 American and European oil companies were allowed to invest in the energy sector for the first time. The industrial sector is based on hydrocarbon resources. In 2003 petroleum refining accounted for 25·8% of manufacturing GDP. The country also has deposits of iron ore, phosphates, bauxite and copper.

Structural reforms were introduced in 1999 to attract foreign investment. The stock market was opened to foreign investors and tax and customs administrations were reformed. Improvements in the investment climate paved the way for full membership of the WTO in 2005. A tourism authority was also established.

In the 1980s the economy posted negative annual growth rates over five years. Nor was its 3·1% average annual growth rate in the 1990s particularly impressive relative to other developing countries, particularly in the Asia Pacific region. In 2001 and 2002 the Saudi economy barely grew at all. However, rising oil prices lifted the economy in 2003 and annual growth accelerated to 7·7%. Per capita GDP grew more robustly after the 2003 rise in oil prices, with the IMF putting the level at nearly US$15,500 in 2007.

The GDP growth rate was 4·4% in 2008, although provisional figures suggested a significant downturn in 2009 in the wake of the global financial crisis and a reduction in oil production. Non-oil sector growth was projected to be 3·3% for the year. The economy as a whole is predicted to recover to around 4% growth in 2010.

Inflation remains in single figures as a result of an open and flexible labour market and an open trade system. Over half of the 2004 fiscal surplus was used to reduce central government debt by 16% to 66% of GDP, while the rest was put into a fund to finance investment in priority areas over a five-year period. In 2008 high oil prices helped ensure record surpluses, some of which was used to repay debt which stood at 13·5% of GDP.

The post-2003 boom saw strong growth in the private sector and in non-oil segments of the economy. According to the World Bank, Saudi Arabia ranks 13th out of 183 economies for the ease of doing business. The weakness of the dollar in much of the first half of the 2000s caused the rial to depreciate, enhancing the competitiveness of non-oil exports. Further structural reforms, reduced corruption, more privatization and vigilant macroeconomic management will be necessary in order for the economy to remain buoyant. High unemployment, at 11·8% of males in 2008, is an ongoing concern.

Currency

The unit of currency is the *rial* (SAR) of 100 *halalah*. Foreign exchange reserves totalled US$27,637m. in Sept. 2009 and gold reserves were 4·60m. troy oz. Total money supply in June 2009 was SAR474,307m. Inflation rates (based on IMF statistics):

1999	2000	2001	2002	2003	2004	2005	2006	2007	2008
–1·3%	–1·1%	–1·1%	0·2%	0·6%	0·4%	0·6%	2·3%	4·1%	9·9%

In 2001 the six Gulf Arab states—Saudi Arabia, along with Bahrain, Kuwait, Oman, Qatar and the United Arab Emirates—signed an agreement to establish a single currency by 2010. In June 2009 it was agreed to postpone the implementation of the new currency, the *khaleeji*, until 2013. Both Oman and the United Arab Emirates have now withdrawn from the scheme, in 2007 and 2009 respectively.

Budget

In 1986 the financial year became the calendar year. 2007 budget: revenue, SAR642·8bn.; expenditure, SAR466·2bn. Oil revenues accounted for 87·5% of revenue in 2007; current expenditures accounted for 74·5% of expenditure.

Performance

Real GDP growth rates (based on IMF statistics):

1999	2000	2001	2002	2003	2004	2005	2006	2007	2008
–0·7%	4·9%	0·5%	0·1%	7·7%	5·3%	5·6%	3·2%	3·3%	4·4%

Total GDP in 2008 was US$467·6bn. Per capita GDP is now around half the level of 1980.

Banking and Finance

The Saudi Arabian Monetary Agency (*Governor*, Dr Muhammad Al-Jasser), established in 1953, functions as the central bank and the government's fiscal agent. In 2002 there were three national banks (the National Commercial Bank, the Al-Rajhi Banking and Investment Corporation and the Riyad Bank), five specialist banks, eight foreign banks and three government specialized credit institutions. The leading banks are National Commercial Bank (assets in 2005 of US$38·9bn.), Saudi-American (US$28·9bn. in 2005) and Riyad Bank (US$19·8bn. in 2004). Sharia (the religious law of Islam) forbids the charging of interest; Islamic banking is based on sharing clients' profits and losses and imposing service charges. In 2005 total assets of commercial banks were US$202·4bn.

A number of industry sectors are closed to foreign investors, including petroleum exploration, defence-related activities and financial services.

There is a stock exchange in Riyadh.

ENERGY AND NATURAL RESOURCES

Environment

Saudi Arabia's carbon dioxide emissions from the consumption and flaring of fossil fuels in 2008 were the equivalent of 16·6 tonnes per capita.

Electricity

By 1995 over 100 electricity producers had been amalgamated into four companies. Installed capacity was 30·5m. kW in 2004. All electricity is thermally generated. Production was 156·51bn. kWh in 2004; consumption per capita in 2004 was 6,902 kWh.

Oil and Gas

Proven oil reserves (2008) 264·1bn. bbls (the highest of any country and around 21% of world resources). Oil production began in 1938 by Aramco, which is now 100% state-owned and accounts for about 99% of total crude oil production. Output in 2008 totalled 515·3m. tonnes (494·2m. tonnes in 2007) and accounted for 13·1% of the world total oil output. In 2004 oil export revenues were US$106bn.

Production comes from 14 major oilfields, mostly in the Eastern Province and offshore, and including production from the Neutral Zone. The Ghawar oilfield, located between Riyadh and the Persian gulf, is the largest in the world, with estimated reserves of 70bn. bbls. Oil reserves are expected to run out in approximately 2075.

In 2008 natural gas reserves were 7,570bn. cu. metres; output in 2008 was 78·1bn. cu. metres. The gas sector has been opened up to foreign investment.

Water

Efforts are under way to provide adequate supplies of water for urban, industrial, rural and agricultural use. Most investment has gone into sea-water desalination. In 1996, 33 plants produced 1·9m. cu. metres a day, meeting 70% of drinking water needs. Total annual consumption was 18,200m. cu. metres in 1995. Irrigation for agriculture consumes the largest amount, from fossil reserves (the country's principal water source), and from surface water collected during seasonal floods. In 1996 there were 183 dams with a holding capacity of 450m. cu. metres. Treated urban waste water is an increasing resource for domestic purposes; in 1996 there were two recycling plants in operation.

Minerals

Production began in 1988 at Mahd Al-Dahab gold mine, the largest in the country. In 2003 total gold production was an estimated 8,769 kg. Deposits of iron, phosphate, bauxite, uranium, silver, tin, tungsten, nickel, chrome, zinc, lead, potassium ore and copper have also been found.

Agriculture

Land ownership is under the jurisdiction of the Ministry of Municipal and Rural Affairs.

Since 1970 the government has spent substantially on desert reclamation, irrigation schemes, drainage and control of surface water and of moving sands. Undeveloped land has been distributed to farmers and there are research and extension programmes. Large scale private investment has concentrated on wheat, poultry and dairy production.

In 2002 there were an estimated 3·60m. ha. of arable land and 194,000 ha. of permanent cropland. Approximately 1·62m. ha. were irrigated in 2002. In 2002, 8·5% of the economically active population were engaged in agriculture (19·1% in 1990).

Production of leading crops, 2002 (in 1,000 tonnes): wheat, 2,431; dates, 829; melons and watermelons, 450; tomatoes, 403; potatoes, 313; sorghum, 239; cucumbers and gherkins, 168; barley, 136; grapes, 117; pumpkins and squash, 101; onions, 80.

Livestock (2002): 8·17m. sheep, 2·50m. goats, 323,000 cattle, 260,000 camels and 130m. chickens. Livestock products (2003, in 1,000 tonnes): milk, 948; meat, 642; eggs, 130.

Forestry
The area under forests was 2·73m. ha. (1·3% of the land area) in 2005.

Fisheries
In 2005 the total catch was 60,403 tonnes, entirely from sea fishing.

INDUSTRY
The largest companies in Saudi Arabia by market capitalization in March 2009 were SABIC (Saudi Basic Industries), at US$33·4bn.; Saudi Telecom (US$21·3bn.); and Al-Rajhi Banking (US$20·7bn.).

In 2005 manufacturing accounted for 9·5% of GDP and construction 4·7%. The government encourages the establishment of manufacturing industries. Its policy focuses on establishing industries that use petroleum products, petrochemicals and minerals. Petrochemical and oil-based industries have been concentrated at eight new industrial cities, with the two principal cities at Jubail and Yanbu. Products include chemicals, plastics, industrial gases, steel and other metals. In 2004 there were 3,657 factories employing 340,000 workers.

Labour
The labour force in 2002 totalled 6,242,000. In 2002 females constituted 14% of the labour force—one of the lowest percentages of females in the workforce of any country. In 2001, 35·7% of the economically active population were engaged in wholesale and retail trade, 18·7% in manufacturing, 15·7% in construction, 6·7% in research, consultancy and recruitment. There are 6m. foreign workers, including over 1m. Egyptians and over 1m. Indians. Unemployment, which was less than 8% in 1999, reached 12% in 2002. Young people in particular are affected, with nearly a third unemployed.

INTERNATIONAL TRADE
Saudi Arabia, along with Bahrain, Kuwait, Oman, Qatar and the United Arab Emirates entered into a customs union in Jan. 2003.

Imports and Exports
Trade in US$1m.:

	2002	*2003*	*2004*	*2005*	*2006*
Imports f.o.b.	29,624	33,868	41,050	54,595	63,914
Exports f.o.b.	72,464	93,244	125,998	180,712	211,305

The principal export is crude oil; refined oil, petrochemicals, fertilizers, plastic products and wheat are other major exports. Saudi Arabia is the world's largest exporter of oil (8·7m. bbls per day), accounting for 85·4% of all the country's exports in 2006. Major import suppliers, 2006: USA, 14·5%; China, 8·6%; Germany, 8·1%; Japan, 8·1%. Main export destinations, 2006: Japan, 16·5%; USA, 15·1%; South Korea, 9·2%; China, 6·3%.

COMMUNICATIONS

Roads
In 2005 there was a total road network of 221,372 km (21·5% paved), including 3,891 km of motorway. A causeway links Saudi Arabia with Bahrain. Passenger cars in use in 2005 numbered 3,206,000 (415 per 1,000 inhabitants in 2004) and there were 1,127,900 lorries and vans. Women are not allowed to drive. In 2004–05 there were 293,281 road accidents resulting in 5,168 deaths.

Rail
In 2005, 1,394 km of 1,435 mm gauge lines linked Riyadh and Dammam with stops at Hofuf and Abqaiq. The network is to be extended by 2,000 km at an estimated cost of US$2·6bn., in four phases, consisting of links to Jeddah, the Jordanian border, Jubail, and Makkah and Madinah. In 2004 railways carried 1,124,000 passengers and 2,557,000 tonnes of freight.

Civil Aviation
The national carrier is the part-privatized Saudi Arabian Airlines, which in 2006 owned 139 aircraft and served 76 destinations. In 2005 scheduled airline traffic of Saudi-based carriers flew 117·1m. km and carried 11,126,300 passengers. There are four major international airports, at Jeddah (King Abdulaziz), Dhahran, Riyadh (King Khaled), and the newly constructed King Fahd International Airport at Dammam. There are also 22 domestic airports. In 2001 Jeddah handled 10,237,161 passengers (5,413,841 on international flights) and 188,386 tonnes of freight. Riyadh was the second busiest airport in 2001, handling 8,702,697 passengers (5,428,429 on domestic flights) and 155,245 tonnes of freight.

Shipping
The ports of Dammam and Jubail are on the Persian Gulf and Jeddah, Yanbu and Jizan on the Red Sea. There is a deepwater oil terminal at Ras Tanura, and 16 minor ports. In 2002 the ports handled 104·2m. tonnes of cargo. In 1995 the merchant marine comprised 110 vessels totalling 8·2m. DWT. In 2002 shipping totalled 1·47m. GRT, including oil tankers 664,000 GRT.

Telecommunications
In 2008 there were 4·1m. main (fixed) telephone lines. In the same year mobile phone subscribers numbered 36·0m. (1,428·5 per 1,000 persons). The government sold a 30% stake in Saudi Telecom Company (STC) in Dec. 2002. STC lost its monopoly in the mobile phone market in 2005 and in landline services in 2007. The number of internet users in 2008 was 7·8m. and there were 3·5m. PCs in use in 2006.

Postal Services
In 2003 there were 1,517 main post offices. A total of 636m. pieces of mail were processed in 2003.

SOCIAL INSTITUTIONS

Justice
The religious law of Islam (Sharia) is the common law of the land, and is administered by religious courts, at the head of which is a chief judge, who is responsible for the Department of Sharia Affairs. Sharia courts are concerned primarily with family inheritance and property matters. However, following judicial reforms of Oct. 2007 a newly-established Supreme Court replaced the Supreme Judiciary Council as the highest judicial authority. Specialized courts are also to be established to operate alongside the Sharia courts and there are plans to codify Sharia and introduce the principle of precedent into court practice. The Committee for the Settlement of Commercial Disputes is the commercial court. Other specialized courts or committees include one dealing exclusively with labour and employment matters; the Negotiable Instruments Committee, which deals with cases relating to cheques, bills of exchange and promissory notes; and the Board of Grievances, whose preserve is disputes with the government or its agencies and which also has jurisdiction in trademark-infringement cases and is the authority for enforcing foreign court judgments.

The death penalty is in force for murder, rape, sodomy, armed robbery, sabotage, drug trafficking, adultery and apostasy; executions may be held in public. There were 69 confirmed executions in 2009. The population in penal institutions in 2002 was 28,612 (132 per 100,000 of national population).

Education
The educational system provides students with free education, books and health services. General education consists of kindergarten, six years of primary school and three years each of intermediate and high school. In 2005–06 there were: 1,449 pre-primary schools with 10,150 teachers and 97,137 pupils; 13,163 primary schools with 213,355 teachers and 2,417,811 pupils; 7,086 intermediate schools with 104,675 teachers and 1,071,747 pupils; 4,215 secondary schools with 79,754 teachers and 954,141 pupils.

In 2002–03 there were 71 teacher training colleges with 4,253 teachers and 92,777 students. Students can attend either high schools offering programmes in arts and sciences, or vocational schools. Girls' education has traditionally been administered separately, but in Sept. 2009 the country's first mixed-gender university was opened and in Oct. 2009 a trial of mixed-gender education in 15 private elementary schools was launched. In 2005 there were 903 institutions for special needs pupils with 18,958 students. The adult literacy rate in 2003 was 79·4% (87·1% among males and 69·3% among females). Although Saudi girls were not even allowed to attend school until 1964 women now make up nearly 60% of Saudi Arabia's higher education students.

In 2005 there were 3,775 adult education centres. In 2005–06 there were 11 universities (including two Islamic universities and one university of petroleum and minerals); there were 603,767 students in total in higher education and 26,827 teachers.

Health

In 2005 there were 1,848 health care centres, 1,043 private dispensaries and 364 hospitals with 51,130 beds. Health personnel, 2005: 42,975 physicians, 78,587 nurses and 49,167 technical staff. At Jeddah there is a quarantine centre for pilgrims.

Welfare

The retirement age is 60 (men) or 55 (women), with eligibility based on 120 months of contributions. The minimum monthly old-age pension is SAR1,500, calculated as 2·5% of the average monthly wage during the previous two years multiplied by the number of years of contributions. A 1969 law requires employers with more than 20 employees to pay 100% of wages for the first 30 days of sick leave and 75% of wages for the next 60 days.

Workers' medical benefits include medical, dental and diagnostic treatment, hospitalization, medicines, appliances, transportation and rehabilitation.

RELIGION

In 2001, 90% of the total population were Sunni Muslims, 4% Shias, 4% Christians and 1% Hindus. The *Grand Mufti*, Sheikh Abdul Aziz bin Abdullah bin Mohammed Al-Sheikh, has cabinet rank. A special police force, the Mutaween, exists to enforce religious norms.

The annual *Hajj*, the pilgrimage to Makkah, takes place from the 8th to the 13th day of Dhu al Hijjah, the last month of the Islamic year. It attracts more than 1·8m. pilgrims annually. In the current Islamic year, 1431, the *Hajj* will begin on 15 Nov. 2010 in the Gregorian calendar.

CULTURE

World Heritage Sites

The archaeological site of Madain Salih (Al-Hijr) was inscribed on the UNESCO World Heritage List in 2008.

Broadcasting

The government-controlled Broadcasting Service of the Kingdom of Saudi Arabia is responsible for all broadcasting. Private radio and television stations may not operate from within the country, but pan-Arab satellite and pay-TV services can be accessed. Colour is by SECAM H. There were 6·6m. TV sets in 2004 and 3·9m. TV-equipped households in 2005.

Press

In 2006 there were 13 daily newspapers with a combined circulation of 1,397,000. The most widely read newspaper is Asharq Al-Awsat ('Middle East'), with an average daily circulation of 272,000 in 2006. In 1997 a total of 3,780 book titles were published.

Tourism

There were 8,037,000 foreign tourists in 2005; spending by tourists in 2005 totalled US$5·2bn.

Calendar

Saudi Arabia follows the Islamic *hegira* (AD 622, when Mohammed left Makkah for Madinah), which is based upon the lunar year of 354 days. The Islamic year 1431 corresponds to 18 Dec. 2009–7 Dec. 2010, and is the current lunar year.

Libraries

There was one national library in 1999 and 80 public libraries, with 1,883,120 volumes.

DIPLOMATIC REPRESENTATIVES

Of Saudi Arabia in the United Kingdom (30 Charles St., London, W1J 5DZ)
Ambassador: Prince Mohammed Bin Nawaf Bin Abdulaziz Al-Saud.

Of the United Kingdom in Saudi Arabia (PO Box 94351, Riyadh 11693)
Ambassador: Sir William Patey, KCMG.

Of Saudi Arabia in the USA (601 New Hampshire Ave., NW, Washington, D.C., 20037)
Ambassador: Adel bin Ahmed Al-Jubeir.

Of the USA in Saudi Arabia (PO Box 94309, Riyadh)
Ambassador: James B. Smith.

Of Saudi Arabia to the United Nations
Ambassador: Khalid Abdalrazaq Al-Nafisee.

Of Saudi Arabia to the European Union
Ambassador: Abdallah Y. Al-Moullimi.

FURTHER READING

Aarts, Paul, *Saudi Arabia in the Balance: Political Economy, Society, Foreign Affairs*. 2006
Al-Rasheed, Madawi, *A History of Saudi Arabia*. 2002
Al-Rasheed, Madawi and Vitalis, Robert (eds.) *Counter-Narratives: History, Contemporary Society, and Politics in Saudi Arabia and Yemen*. 2004
Azzam, H., *Saudi Arabia: Economic Trends, Business Environment and Investment Opportunities*. 1993
Bradley, John R., *Saudi Arabia Exposed*. 2005
Kostiner, J., *The Making of Saudi Arabia: from Chieftaincy to Monarchical State*. 1994
Mackey, Sandra, *The Saudis: Inside the Desert Kingdom*. Revised ed. 2003
Manea, Elham, *Regional Politics in the Gulf: Saudi Arabia, Oman and Yemen*. 2005
Peterson, J. E., *Historical Dictionary of Saudi Arabia*. 1994
Wright, J. W. (ed.) *Business and Economic Development in Saudi Arabia: Essays with Saudi Scholars*. 1996

National Statistical Office: Ministry of Economy and Planning, Central Department of Statistics and Information, Riyadh.
Website: http://www.cdsi.gov.sa

SENEGAL

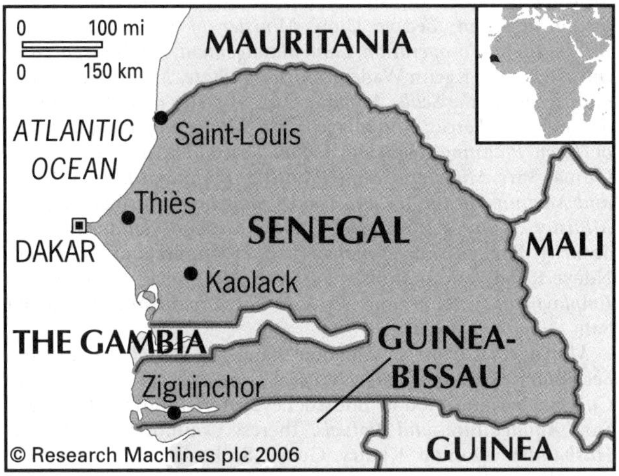

République du Sénégal
(Republic of Senegal)

Capital: Dakar
Population estimate, 2010: 12·86m.
GDP per capita, 2007: (PPP$) 1,666
HDI/world rank: 0·464/166

KEY HISTORICAL EVENTS

For much of the 1st millennium AD Senegal was under the influence of the gold-rich Ghana Empire of the Soninke people. In western Senegal the Takrur state was established in the 9th century. Islam was introduced in the 11th century by the Zenega Berbers of southern Mauritania, who gave their name to the region. The power of the Malinke (Madingo) in present-day Mali expanded in the 13th and 14th centuries, especially under Mansa Musa, who subjugated Takrur and the Tukulor in Senegal. The west was dominated by the Jolof empire, which fragmented into four kingdoms in the 16th century.

Portuguese trading colonies were established on Gorée Island and at Rufisque in around 1444, encouraging the growth of the slave trade. The Dutch took control of Senegalese trade in the 17th century, only to be evicted in 1677 by the French, based at Saint-Louis at the mouth of the Sénégal River. Inland, the Tukulor created a Muslim theocracy in Fouta Toro, usurping the Denianké Dynasty in 1776. Tukulor power grew in the 1850s under al-Hajj Umar Tal, whose *jihad* was contained by treaty with the French in 1857. Britain accepted French hegemony in the region in 1814 after half a century of colonial rivalry, while retaining the Gambia River. Railway construction in 1879 cemented French control over western Senegal and Dakar became the capital of French West Africa in 1904. Casamance and eastern Senegal were conquered in the 1890s.

Senegalese service in the French army in the First World War secured representation in Paris and French citizenship for Africans in certain communes. The colonial administration followed a moderate liberalization programme, including the right to form political parties and trade unions. However, the decline in the groundnut trade in the 1930s increased poverty in Senegal. The expansion of the vote after the Second World War gave support to the Democratic Bloc (BDS), which joined the Socialist Party to become the Progressive Union (UPS), dominating the 1959 elections in the newly-autonomous Senegal. Membership of the French Community lasted until independence on 20 June 1960 as part of the Federation of Mali with French Soudan (Mali); the Federation was dissolved on 20 Aug. 1960.

Leopold Sédar Senghor, the BDS founder and leader of the UPS, was elected president on 5 Sept. 1960. Relations with his prime minister, Mamadou Dia, deteriorated and Senghor had him arrested in Dec. 1962 after an attempted coup. Presidential power was augmented by referendum in 1963, allowing Senghor to ban all other parties in 1966. Senghor appointed Abdou Diouf prime minister in 1973 and began relaxing political restrictions. Abdoulaye Wade founded the Democratic Party (PDS) and a Marxist-Leninist party was formed. Recession and political agitation forced Senghor's resignation in Dec. 1980; Diouf succeeded and was confirmed by elections in 1983, 1988 and 1993.

Diouf pursued a vigorous foreign policy via the Organization of African Unity and the Economic Community of West African States. He reinstated the Gambian president, Sir Dawda Jawara, in 1981, creating the Senegambian confederation, which lasted until 1989. Unrest in the southern Casamance region escalated into secessionist civil war in the early 1990s. A skirmish on the Mauritanian border in 1989 resulted in the death of Senegalese and Mauritanians expatriates and the closing of the border, a dispute not resolved until 1994. The deterioration of the economy and the Casamance crisis led to electoral defeat in 2000. He conceded peacefully, handing power to his long-term rival, PDS leader Abdoulaye Wade. The coalition with Moustapha Niasse, his prime minister and key electoral ally, broke down in March 2001.

TERRITORY AND POPULATION

Senegal is bounded by Mauritania to the north and northeast, Mali to the east, Guinea and Guinea-Bissau to the south and the Atlantic to the west with The Gambia forming an enclave along that shore. Area, 196,722 sq. km. Population (2002 census), 9,858,482 (5,005,718 females). The United Nations population estimate for 2002 was 10,433,000, giving a density of 53·0 per sq. km. In 2005 the population was 58·4% rural.

The UN gives an estimated population for 2010 of 12·86m.

About 2m. Senegalese live abroad, particularly in France, Italy, Spain and the USA.

The areas, populations and capitals of the regions at the time of the 2002 census:

Region	*Area (in sq. km)*	*Population 2002 census*	*Capital*
Dakar	550	2,168,314	Dakar
Diourbel	4,359	1,051,941	Diourbel
Fatick	7,935	609,789	Fatick
Kaffrine[1]	—	—	Kaffrine
Kaolack[1]	16,010	1,070,203	Kaolack
Kédougou[2]	—	—	Kédougou
Kolda[3]	21,011	817,438	Kolda
Louga	29,188	677,264	Louga
Matam	25,083	423,967	Matam
Saint-Louis	19,044	694,652	Saint-Louis
Sédhiou[3]	—	—	Sédhiou
Tambacounda[2]	59,602	612,855	Tambacounda
Thiès	6,601	1,322,579	Thiès
Ziguinchor	7,339	409,480	Ziguinchor

[1]Kaffrine (11,853 sq. km), formerly part of Kaolack, was created in 2008. [2]Kédougou (16,896 sq. km), formerly part of Tambacounda, was created in 2008. [3]Sédhiou (7,293 sq. km), formerly part of Kolda, was created in 2008.

Dakar, the capital, had a provisional census population in 2002 of 1,983,093. Other large cities (with 2002 provisional census population) are: Thiès (237,849), Rufisque (179,797), Kaolack (172,305), Saint-Louis (154,555), Mbour (153,503) and Ziguinchor (153,269).

Ethnic groups are the Wolof (36% of the population), Fulani (16%), Serer (16%), Diola (9%), Tukulor (9%), Bambara (6%), Malinké (6%) and Sarakole (2%).

The official language is French; Wolof is widely spoken.

SOCIAL STATISTICS

2005 estimates: births, 430,000; deaths, 132,000. Rates, 2005 estimates (per 1,000 population): births, 39·4; deaths, 12·1. Annual population growth rate, 2000–05, 2·8%; infant mortality, 2005, 77 per 1,000 live births. Life expectancy in 2007 was 53·9 years for men and 56·9 for women. Fertility rate, 2004, 4·9 births per woman. 51% of the population were living in poverty in 2005.

CLIMATE

A tropical climate with wet and dry seasons. The rains fall almost exclusively in the hot season, from June to Oct., with high humidity. Dakar, Jan. 72°F (22·2°C), July 82°F (27·8°C). Annual rainfall 22" (541 mm).

CONSTITUTION AND GOVERNMENT

A new constitution was approved by a referendum held on 7 Jan. 2001. The head of state is the *President*, elected by universal suffrage for not more than two five-year terms (previously two seven-year terms). The *President* has the power to dissolve the National Assembly, without the agreement, as had been the case, of a two-thirds majority. The new constitution also abolished the upper house (the Senate), confirmed the status of the prime minister and for the first time gave women the right to own land. Senegal has a bicameral legislature. For the 150-member *National Assembly*, 90 members are elected by simple majority vote in single or multi-member constituencies for five years with 60 elected by a system of party-list proportional representation. The Senate was re-established in Jan. 2007 six years after being dissolved and has 100 members, of which 35 are indirectly elected and 65 are appointed by the president.

National Anthem

'Pincez tous vos koras, frappez les balafos' ('All pluck the koras, strike the balafos'); words by Léopold Sédar Senghor, tune by Herbert Pepper.

RECENT ELECTIONS

Presidential elections took place on 25 Feb. 2007. Incumbent Abdoulaye Wade was re-elected with 55·9% of the vote, ahead of Idrissa Seck with 14·9%, Ousmane Tanor Dieng with 13·6% and Moustapha Niasse with 5·9%. Turnout was 70·5%.

Parliamentary elections were held on 3 June 2007. Turnout was 34·7%. Coalition 'Sopi', a coalition led by President Abdoulaye Wade's Senegalese Democratic Party, took 131 seats with 69·2% of votes cast (including all 90 elected by majority vote), Takku Defaraat Senegal 3 with 5·0%, And Defar Senegal 3 with 4·9% and Waar-wi Coalition 3 with 4·4%. A number of smaller parties took either one or two seats. The leading opposition parties boycotted the elections.

In indirect elections to the Senate held on 19 Aug. 2007 the Senegalese Democratic Party won 34 of the available 35 seats, with one going to And-Jëf/African Party for Democracy and Socialism.

CURRENT ADMINISTRATION

President: Abdoulaye Wade; b. 1926 (PDS; sworn in 1 April 2000 and re-elected in Feb. 2007).

In March 2010 the government was composed as follows:

Prime Minister: Souleymane Ndéné Ndiaye; b. 1958 (ind.; sworn in 30 April 2009).

Minister of State, Minister of Economy and Finance: Abdoulaye Diop. *Minister of State, Minister of Environment, Protection of Nature, Retention Ponds and Artificial Lakes:* Djibo Leïty Kâ. *Minister of State, Minister of Foreign Affairs:* Madické Niang. *Minister of State, Minister of Interior, Local Collectivities and Decentralization:* Bécaye Diop. *Minister of State, Minister of International Co-operation, Land Management, Air Transport and Infrastructure:* Karim Wade. *Minister of State, Minister of Justice and Keeper of the Seals:* Amadou Sall. *Minister of State, Minister of the Armed Forces:* Abdoulaye Baldé. *Minister of State, Minister of Town Planning, Housing, Urban Hydraulics and Sanitation:* Oumar Sarr. *Minister of State, Minister of Mines, Industry, Small and Medium Businesses and Food Production:* Ousmane Ngom. *Minister of State, Minister of Family, National Solidarity, Food Security, Women's Entrepeneurship, Microfinance and Childhood:* Ndèye Khady Diop. *Minister of State, Minister of Civil Service, Employment, Labour and Professional Organizations:* Adama Sall.

Minister of Commerce: Amadou Niang. *Pre-school, Primary and Secondary Education, and National Languages:* Kalidou Diallo. *Culture:* Serigne Modou Bousso Lèye. *Agriculture:* Fatou Gaye Sarr. *Aquaculture, and Biofuels:* Thérèse Coumba Diop. *Animal Husbandry:* Oumou Khaïry Guèye Seck. *Scientific Research, and Higher Education and Universities:* Amadou Tidiane Bâ. *Health, Prevention of Disease and Public Hygiene:* Modou Diagne Fada. *Telecommunications, Information and Communication Technology, and Land Transportation and Railways:* Abdourahim Agne. *Energy:* Samuel Amète Sarr. *Senegalese Abroad:* Sada Ndiaye. *Handicrafts, Tourism and Private Sector Relations:* Thierno Lô. *Technical Education and Professional Training:* Moussa Sakho. *Maritime Economy, Fisheries and Shipping:* Khoureyssy Thiam. *Social Affairs and Parliamentary Relations:* Faustin Diatta. *Communication and Government Spokesman:* Moustapha Guirassy.

Government Website (French only): http://www.gouv.sn

CURRENT LEADERS

Abdoulaye Wade

Position

President

Introduction

A barrister, writer and newspaper editor, Abdoulaye Wade spent nearly 40 years in opposition before becoming president at his fifth attempt in 2000. His election marked the end of Senegal's socialist era. He was re-elected in Feb. 2007.

Early Life

Wade was born on 29 May 1926, in Kébémer. He was educated in Senegal and at the Sorbonne in Paris, France, where he studied law and economics. After practising as a barrister in France for some years, he returned to Senegal to take up an academic post at the University of Dakar.

In 1974 he created the liberal Parti Démocratique Sénégalais (PDS; Senegalese Democratic Party), one of the three parties allowed under the 1976 constitution. He unsuccessfully stood as a presidential candidate in the 1978 elections against Léopold Sédar Senghor. In the same year he entered the National Assembly.

He lost the 1988 presidential race against Abdou Diouf. The latter accused Wade of inflaming riots with his claims of election fraud and Wade was arrested. He spent several months in prison while Diouf declared a state of emergency. However, following his release Wade was appointed a minister in Diouf's government in 1991. He resigned the following year and in 1993 once more stood unsuccessfully for the presidency. He joined Diouf's government again in March 1995, resigning three years later.

By 2000 public dissatisfaction with Diouf's leadership was running high, yet he emerged with most votes after the first round of a presidential poll against Wade and six other candidates. Diouf and Wade went into a run-off, and Wade, benefiting from the absence of the other candidates (particularly Moustapha Niasse), won 58·5% of the vote. He was sworn in as the new president on 1 April 2000 and formed a coalition government with Niasse as prime minister.

Career in Office

Wade's election promises included boosting the economy and confronting growing poverty, while raising literacy and health levels. However, attempts to implement necessary reforms have been hampered by Senegal's crippling levels of international debt. In addition, Wade's popular standing was soon diminished by the resignation of Niasse in 2001, on whom he had relied for electoral victory. Nevertheless, his coalition won almost 75% of National Assembly seats in the 2001 elections. In Oct. 2002 the transport and armed forces ministers resigned following the death of around 1,000 people in the sinking of a state-operated ferry. The following month Wade dismissed Prime Minister Madior Boye (who on her appointment was Africa's only female leader) and her entire cabinet, replacing her with Idrissa Seck. He in turn was replaced in April 2004 by Macky Sall of the PDS (and subsequently detained from July 2005 until Feb. 2006 on charges of fraud and sedition). In April 2005, 14 PDS deputies in the National Assembly defected, protesting an increasing lack of democracy and transparency.

Negotiations between the government and the Casamance separatist movement culminated in a ceasefire in Dec. 2004 and the signing of a peace agreement in early 2005.

Wade was closely involved in the launch of the New Partnership for Africa's Development (NEPAD), an African-led strategy (endorsed by the then Organization of African Unity in July 2001) for economic recovery, good governance and sustainable growth.

He was elected to a further term in the presidential election of Feb. 2007 and his ruling coalition then increased its majority in legislative elections the following June, with Cheikh Hadjibou Soumaré replacing Macky Sall as prime minister. However, the parliamentary poll was boycotted by the main opposition parties. In local elections in March 2009 opposition parties made substantial gains, prompting the resignation of Soumaré as prime minister and his replacement by Souleymane Ndéné Ndiaye in April.

DEFENCE

There is selective conscription for two years. Defence expenditure totalled US$149m. in 2006 (US$12 per capita), representing 1·6% of GDP.

Army

There are four military zones. The Army had a strength of 11,900 (including conscripts) in 2007. There is also a paramilitary force of gendarmerie and customs of 5,000.

Navy

Personnel (2007) totalled 950, and bases are at Dakar and Casamance.

Air Force

The Air Force, formed with French assistance, has eight combat capable aircraft. Personnel (2007) 770.

INTERNATIONAL RELATIONS

Senegal is a member of the UN, World Bank, IMF and several other UN specialized agencies, WTO, IOM, International Organization of the Francophonie, Islamic Development Bank, OIC, African Development Bank, African Union, ECOWAS and is an ACP member state of the ACP-EU relationship.

A short section of the boundary with The Gambia is indefinite.

ECONOMY

Agriculture accounted for 13·4% of GDP in 2007, industry 23·6% and services 63·0%.

Overview

In contrast to many of its West African neighbours, Senegal enjoys relative social and political stability and is open to the outside world. Prompted by the devaluation of the CFA franc in 1994 and aggressive structural reforms, growth rates have been slow but steady, averaging 5% per year since the late 1990s. Nonetheless, poverty affects half the population and the unemployment rate is 48%. An estimated 24·1% of the tertiary educated population emigrated in 2000.

The service sector accounted for 63·0% of GDP in 2007, having grown rapidly during the 1990s (especially transportation and telecommunications). Agriculture and construction have also contributed to recent prosperity, although the agricultural sector is in long-term decline despite employing 77·5% of the labour force. In 2000 Senegal became eligible for the Heavily Indebted Poor Country (HIPC) initiative, which aims to cancel debts of US$800m.

The port of Dakar serves as an important centre of trade in West Africa. A 20-ha. dry port project was started in 2006 while Jafza International of Dubai is developing a Special Economic Zone adjacent to Dakar International Airport. Oil exploration in the Casamance region offers potential for future revenue streams, although work has been hampered by weak transportation links and civil unrest.

Foreign capital enters the country via Senegalese citizens living abroad. In 2006 remittances made up 17% of GDP.

Currency

The unit of currency is the *franc CFA* (XOF) with a parity of 655·957 francs CFA to one euro. In June 2005 total money supply was 930,246m. francs CFA and foreign exchange reserves totalled US$1,380m. Inflation was 5·8% in 2008.

Budget

Revenues in 2005 totalled 955·8bn. francs CFA (tax revenue, 89·0%) and expenditures 1,084·4bn. francs CFA (current expenditure, 58·0%).

VAT is 18%.

Performance

Real GDP growth was 4·7% in 2007, falling to 2·5% in 2008. Senegal's total GDP in 2008 was US$13·2bn.

Banking and Finance

The Banque Centrale des États de l'Afrique de l'Ouest is the bank of issue of the franc CFA for all the countries of the West African Economic and Monetary Union (Benin, Burkina Faso, Côte d'Ivoire, Mali, Niger, Senegal and Togo) but has had its headquarters in Dakar, the Senegalese capital, since 1973. Its *Governor* is Philippe-Henri Dacoury-Tabley. There are eight commercial banks, the largest including Banque Internationale pour le Commerce et l'Industrie and Banque de l'Habitat. There are also four development banks and an Islamic bank. Only about 5% of the population have bank accounts.

Senegal is affiliated to the regional BRVM stock exchange (serving the member states of the West African Economic and Monetary Union), based in Abidjan, Côte d'Ivoire.

ENERGY AND NATURAL RESOURCES

Environment

Senegal's carbon dioxide emissions from the consumption and flaring of fossil fuels in 2008 were the equivalent of 0·5 tonnes per capita.

Electricity

In 2004 installed capacity was an estimated 0·4m. kW. Production in 2004 was 2·35bn. kWh and consumption per capita 206 kWh.

Minerals

In 2003, 1·5m. tonnes of calcium phosphate were produced. Limestone production in 2003 totalled 1,588,000 tonnes. Annual gold production is approximately 600 kg. British, Canadian and Australian gold exploration companies are all active in the country.

Agriculture

Because of erratic rainfall 25% of agricultural land needs irrigation. Most land is owned under customary rights and holdings tend to be small. In 2007 the economically active population engaged in agriculture was an estimated 3,750,000. In 2006 approximately 2·99m. ha. were used as arable land and 52,000 ha. for permanent crops. An estimated 63,000 ha. were irrigated in 2006. There were about 700 tractors in use in 2006 and 155 harvester-threshers. Production, 2005–06 (in 1,000 tonnes): sugarcane, 829; groundnuts, 703; millet, 609; maize, 400; rice, 289; cassava, 281; watermelons, 241; tomatoes, 161; sorghum, 144; onions, 76; mangoes, 62.

Livestock (2006): 5·00m. sheep, 4·26m. goats, 3·14m. cattle, 518,000 horses, 415,000 asses, 318,000 pigs.

Meat production (2006, in 1,000 tonnes): beef and veal, 69; lamb and mutton, 17; goat meat, 12; pork, bacon and ham, and camel, 5. Milk production (2006, in 1,000 litres): cow's milk, 135; goat's milk, 46; sheep's milk, 31.

Forestry

Forests covered 8·67m. ha. in 2005 (45·0% of the land area). Roundwood production in 2007 amounted to 6·13m. cu. metres.

Fisheries

The fishing fleet comprises 167 vessels totalling 40,600 GRT. In 2005 the total catch was 405,070 tonnes, of which marine fish approximately 88% and freshwater fish 12%.

INDUSTRY

Predominantly agricultural and fish processing, phosphate mining, petroleum refining and construction materials.

Labour

In 2002 the economically active population numbered 3,699,859, of whom 208,135 were unemployed (5·6%).

Trade Unions

There are two major unions, the Union Nationale des Travailleurs Sénégalais (government-controlled) and the Confédération Nationale des Travailleurs du Sénégal (independent) which broke away from the former in 1969 and in 1994 comprised 75% of salaried workers.

INTERNATIONAL TRADE

Foreign debt was US$3,793m. in 2005.

Imports and Exports

In 2007 imports (f.o.b.) totalled US$4,871·4m. and exports (f.o.b.) US$1,546·3m. Chief imports: petroleum and petroleum products, food and live animals, and machinery and transport equipment. Chief exports: fish, petroleum and petroleum products, and chemicals and related products. Main import suppliers, 2007: France, 22·9%; Nigeria, 8·4%; Netherlands, 7·2%; China, 5·7%; Thailand, 5·3%. Main export markets, 2007: Mali, 24·0%; France, 9·5%; India, 6·7%; Bunkers and ships' stores, 5·5%; Gambia, 5·4%.

COMMUNICATIONS

Roads

The length of roads in 2006 was 14,805 km, of which 29·3% were paved. In 2008 there were 205,704 passenger cars, 56,795 trucks and vans and 15,982 coaches. There were 320 deaths as a result of road accidents in 2007.

Rail

There were previously four railway lines but the total length of the track has fallen from 1,034 km (metre gauge) in 1986 to 645 km in 2005. Only the Dakar-Kidira line (continuing in Mali) is still theoretically in service although traffic was suspended in 2003 and again in 2009 owing to the poor state of the track. There is also a suburban rail service linking Dakar and Rufisque. Passenger-km travelled in 2004 came to 122m. and freight tonne-km to 358m., much of which was for export.

Civil Aviation

The international airport is at Dakar/Yoff (Léopold Sédar Senghor), which handled 1,882,242 passengers and 21,816 tonnes of freight in 2008. Air Sénégal International was 49% state-owned and 51% owned by Royal Air Maroc (RAM). After an attempted takeover bid by the government to gain 75% of the shares, RAM pulled out of the airline and flights were suspended on 24 April 2009 owing to financial difficulties. Senegal Airlines was launched as a replacement national carrier in Oct. 2009 although it is to be privately controlled. Flights within Africa and to Europe are scheduled to commence in Sept. 2010.

Shipping

In 2002 the merchant marine totalled 47,000 GRT. 10·6m. tonnes of freight were handled in the port of Dakar in 2008. There is a river service on the Senegal from Saint-Louis to Podor (363 km) open throughout the year, and to Kayes (924 km) open from July to Oct. The Senegal River is closed to foreign flags. The Saloum River is navigable as far as Kaolack, the Casamance River as far as Ziguinchor.

Telecommunications

In 2008 there were 237,800 main (fixed) telephone lines; mobile phone subscribers numbered 5,389,100 in 2008 (44·1 per 100 persons). There were 250,000 PCs in use in 2005 and 1,020,000 internet users in 2008.

Postal Services

There were 137 post offices in 2003.

SOCIAL INSTITUTIONS

Justice

There are *juges de paix* in each *département* and a court of first instance in each region. Assize courts are situated in Dakar, Kaolack, Saint-Louis and Ziguinchor, while the Court of Appeal resides in Dakar. The death penalty, last used in 1967, was abolished in Dec. 2004.

The population in penal institutions in Dec. 2007 was 6,487 (55 per 100,00 of national population).

Education

The adult literacy rate in 2003 was 39·3% (51·1% among males and 29·2% among females). In 2007 there were 1,572,178 pupils (45,957 teaching staff) in primary schools; 505,097 pupils (20,007 teaching staff) in secondary schools; and 76,949 students in tertiary education. There are two public universities (Cheikh Anta Diop and Gaston Berger) and three private universities (Dakar Bourguiba, Sahel and Suffolk).

In 2006 public expenditure on education came to 4·9% of GNI and 26·3% of total government spending.

Health

In 2006 there were 22 hospitals, 68 health centres and 949 health posts. In 2004–05 medical personnel in government service included: 765 doctors, 64 dentists, 54 pharmacists, 546 midwives and 874 nurses. In 2003 there were 551 doctors and 567 midwives in the private sector. Senegal has been one of the most successful countries in Africa in the prevention of AIDS. Levels of infection have remained low, with the anti-AIDS programme having started as far back as 1986. The infection rate has been kept below 2%.

RELIGION

The population was 93% Sunni Muslim in 2001, the remainder being Christian (mainly Roman Catholic) or animist. There was one Roman Catholic cardinal in Feb. 2010.

CULTURE

World Heritage Sites

Gorée Island, off the coast of Senegal, was added to the UNESCO World Heritage List in 1978. It was formerly the largest slave trading centre on the African coast. The Djoudj Sanctuary in the Senegal River delta (added in 1981), protects 1·5m. birds, including the white pelican, the purple heron, the African spoonbill, the great egret and the cormorant. Niokolo-Koba National Park, along the banks of the Gambia River (added in 1981), is home to the Derby eland (largest of the antelopes), chimpanzees, lions, leopards and a large population of elephants as well as many birds, reptiles and amphibians. The Island of Saint-Louis joined the UNESCO list in 2000 (reinscribed in 2007), as a reminder of its status as the capital between 1872 and 1957.

Senegal shares a UNESCO site with The Gambia: the Stone Circles of Senegambia (added in 2006) are a collection of 93 stone circles, tumuli and burial mounds from between the 3rd century BC and the 16th century AD.

Broadcasting

The government-owned Office de Radiodiffusion Télévision Sénégalaise is the public broadcasting company, operating two television channels (colour by SECAM) and national and regional radio networks. Pay-TV services are available and there has been an increase in the number of private and community radio stations. In 2006, 550,000 households were equipped with televisions.

Press

In 2006 there were 26 daily newspapers with a total average circulation of 120,000 copies and 30 non-dailies.

Tourism

In 2004, 363,000 foreign tourists visited Senegal (including 243,000 from Europe and 90,000 from other African countries). Revenue in 2003 amounted to US$269m.

Festivals

The 3rd World Festival of Black Arts is scheduled to be held in Dakar in Dec. 2010.

DIPLOMATIC REPRESENTATIVES

Of Senegal in the United Kingdom (39 Marloes Rd, London, W8 6LA)
Ambassador: Abdou Sourang.

Of the United Kingdom in Senegal (20 Rue du Docteur Guillet, Dakar)
Ambassador: Christopher Trott.

Of Senegal in the USA (2112 Wyoming Ave., NW, Washington, D.C., 20008)
Ambassador: Amadou Lamine Ba.

Of the USA in Senegal (Ave. Jean XXIII, Dakar)
Ambassador: Marcia S. Bernicat.

Of Senegal to the United Nations
Ambassador: Paul Badji.

Of Senegal to the European Union
Ambassador: Mame Balla Sy.

FURTHER READING

Centre Français du Commerce Extérieur. *Sénégal: un Marché.* 1993

Adams, A. and So, J., *A Claim in Senegal, 1720–1994.* 1996
Gellar, Sheldon, *Democracy in Senegal: Tocquevillian Analytics in Africa.* 2005
Phillips, L. C., *Historical Dictionary of Senegal.* 2nd ed, revised by A. F. Clark. 1995

National Statistical Office: Direction de la Prévision et de la Statistique, BP 116, Dakar.
Website (French only): http://www.ansd.sn

SERBIA

Republika Srbija
(Republic of Serbia)

Capital: Belgrade
Population estimate, 2010: 9·86m.
GDP per capita: not available
GNI per capita, 2007: US$5,425
HDI/world rank: 0·826/67

KEY HISTORICAL EVENTS

The Serbs were converted to Orthodox Christianity by the Byzantines in 891, before becoming a prosperous independent state under Stevan Nemanja (1167–96). A Serbian Patriarchate was established at Peć during the reign of Stevan Dušan (1331–55). Dušan's attempted conquest of Constantinople failed and after he died many Serbian nobles accepted Turkish vassalage. The reduced Serbian state under Prince Lazar received the coup de grace at Kosovo on St Vitus' Day, 1389. However, Turkish preoccupations with a Mongol invasion and wars with Hungary delayed the incorporation of Serbia into the Ottoman Empire until 1459.

The Turks tolerated the Orthodox church though the Patriarchate was abolished in 1776. The native aristocracy was eliminated and replaced by a system of fiefdoms held in return for military or civil service. Local self-government based on rural extended family units (*zadruga*) continued. In its heyday the Ottoman system was no harder on the peasantry than the Christian feudalism it had replaced, but with the gradual decline of Ottoman power, corruption, oppression and reprisals led to economic deterioration and social unrest.

In 1804, murders carried out by mutinous Turkish infantry provoked a Serbian rising under Djordje Karadjordje. By the Treaty of Bucharest (1812) Russia agreed that Serbia, known as Servia until 1918, should remain Turkish. The Turks reoccupied Serbia with ferocious reprisals. A rebellion in 1815 was led by Miloš Obrenović who, with Russian support, won autonomy for Serbia within the Ottoman empire. Obrenović had Karadjordje murdered in 1817. After he was forced to grant a constitution establishing a state council he abdicated in 1839. In 1842 a coup overthrew the Obrenovićs and Alexander Karadjordjević was elected ruler. He was deposed in 1858.

During the reign of the western-educated Michael Obrenović (1860 until his assassination in 1868) the foundations of a modern centralized and militarized state were laid, and the idea of a 'Great Serbia', first enunciated in Prime Minister Garašanin's *Draft Programme* of 1844, took root. Milan Obrenović, adopting the title of king, proclaimed formal independence in 1882. He suffered defeats against Turkey (1876) and Bulgaria (1885) and abdicated in 1889. After Alexander Obrenović was assassinated in 1903 Peter Karadjordjević brought in a period of stable constitutional rule.

Serbia's aim to secure an outlet to the sea was thwarted by Austria. Annexing Bosnia in 1908, Austria forced the Serbs to withdraw from the Adriatic after the first Balkan war (1912).

The assassination of Archduke Franz Ferdinand of Austria in Sarajevo on 28 June 1914 precipitated the First World War. In the winter of 1915–16 the Serbian army was forced to retreat to Corfu, where the government aimed at a centralized, Serb-run state. But exiles from Croatia and Slovenia wanted a South Slav federation. This was accepted by the victorious Allies as the basis for the new state. The Croats were forced by the pressure of events to join Serbia and Montenegro on 1 Dec. 1918. From 1918–29 the country was known as the Kingdom of the Serbs, Croats and Slovenes.

A constitution of 1921 established an assembly but the trappings of parliamentary rule could not bridge the gulf between Serbs and Croats. The Croat peasant leader, Radić, was assassinated in 1928; his successor, Vlatko Maček, set up a separatist assembly in Zagreb. Faced with the threat of his kingdom's dissolution, on 6 Jan. 1929 the king suspended the constitution and established a royal dictatorship, redrawing provincial boundaries without regard for ethnicity and renaming the country Yugoslavia. In Oct. 1934 he was murdered by a Croat extremist while on an official visit to France.

During the regency of Prince Paul, the government pursued a pro-fascist line. On 25 March 1941 Paul was persuaded to adhere to the Axis Tripartite Pact. On 27 March he was overthrown by military officers in favour of the boy king Peter. Germany invaded on 6 April. Within ten days Yugoslavia surrendered; king and government fled to London. Resistance was led by a royalist group and the communist-dominated partisans of Josip Broz, nicknamed Tito. Having succeeded in liberating Yugoslavia, Tito set up a Soviet-type constitution but he was too independent for Stalin who sought to topple him. However, Tito made a *rapprochement* with the west and it was the Soviet Union under Khrushchev that had to extend the olive branch in 1956. Yugoslavia was permitted to evolve its 'own road to socialism'. Collectivization of agriculture was abandoned and Yugoslavia became a champion of international 'non-alignment'. A collective presidency came into being with the death of Tito in 1980.

Dissensions in Kosovo between Albanians and Serbs, and in parts of Croatia between Serbs and Croats, reached crisis point after 1988. In 1988 the Serbian presidency fell to the nationalist Slobodan Milošević, who aimed at the creation of an enlarged Serbian state. On 25 June 1991 Croatia and Slovenia declared independence. Fighting began in Croatia between Croatian forces and Serb irregulars from Serb-majority areas of Croatia. On 25 Sept. the UN Security Council imposed a mandatory arms embargo on Yugoslavia. A three-month moratorium agreed at EU peace talks on 30 June having expired, both Slovenia and Croatia declared their independence from the Yugoslav federation on 8 Oct. After 13 ceasefires had failed, a fourteenth was signed on 23 Nov. under UN auspices. A Security Council resolution of 27 Nov. proposed the deployment of a UN peacekeeping force if the ceasefire was kept. Fighting, however, continued. On 15 Jan. 1992 the EU recognized Croatia and Slovenia as independent states. Bosnia and Herzegovina was recognized on 7 April 1992 and Macedonia on 8 April 1993. A UN delegation began monitoring the ceasefire on 17 Jan. and the UN Security Council on 21 Feb. voted to send a 14,000-strong peacekeeping force to Croatia and Yugoslavia. On 27 April 1992 Serbia and Montenegro created a new federal republic of Yugoslavia.

On 30 May, responding to further Serbian military activities in Bosnia and Croatia, the UN Security Council voted to impose sanctions. In mid-1992 NATO committed air, sea and eventually land forces to enforce sanctions and protect humanitarian relief operations in Bosnia. At a joint UN-EC peace conference on Yugoslavia held in London on 26–27 Aug. some 30 countries and all the former republics of Yugoslavia endorsed a plan to end the fighting in Croatia and Bosnia, install UN supervision of heavy weapons, recognize the borders of Bosnia and Herzegovina and return refugees. At a further conference at Geneva on 30 Sept. the Croatian and Yugoslav presidents agreed to make efforts to bring about a peaceful solution in Bosnia, but fighting continued. Following the Bosnian-Croatian-Yugoslav (Dayton) agreement all UN sanctions were lifted in Nov. 1995.

In July 1997 Slobodan Milošević switched his power base to become president of federal Yugoslavia. The former Yugoslav foreign minister, Milan Milutinović, succeeded Milošević as Serbian President. Meanwhile, in Montenegro, the pro-western Milo Đukanović succeeded a pro-Milošević president.

Following the break-up of Yugoslavia, in March 1998 a coalition government was formed between the Socialist Party of Slobodan Milošević and the ultra-nationalist Serb Radical Party.

Kosovo

In 1998 unrest in Kosovo, with its largely Albanian population, led to a bid for outright independence. Violence flared resulting in what a US official described as 'horrendous human rights violations', including massive shelling of civilians and destruction of villages. A US-mediated agreement for negotiations to proceed during an interim period of autonomy allowed for food and medicine to be delivered to refugees. American support for a degree of autonomy (short of independence), accepted in principle by President Milošević, lifted the immediate threat of NATO air strikes. Further outbreaks of violence in early 1999 were followed by the departure of the 800-strong team of international 'verifiers' of the fragile peace. Peace talks in Paris broke down without a settlement though subsequently Albanian freedom fighters accepted terms allowing them broad autonomy. The sticking point on the Serbian side was the international insistence on having 28,000 NATO-led peacemakers in Kosovo to keep apart the warring factions. Meanwhile, the scale of Serbian repression in Kosovo persuaded the NATO allies to take direct action. On the night of 24 March 1999 NATO aircraft began a bombing campaign against Yugoslavian military targets. Further Serbian provocation in Kosovo caused hundreds of thousands of ethnic Albanians to seek refuge in neighbouring countries. On 9 June after 78 days of air attacks NATO and Yugoslavia signed an accord on the Serb withdrawal from Kosovo, and on 11 June NATO's peacekeeping force, KFOR, entered Kosovo.

When the general election held on 24 Sept. 2000 resulted in a victory for the opposition democratic leader Vojislav Koštunica, President Milošević demanded a second round of voting. A strike by miners at the Kolubara coal mine on 29 Sept. was followed by a mass demonstration in Belgrade on 5 Oct. when the parliament building was set on fire. On 6 Oct. Slobodan Milošević accepted defeat. He was arrested on 1 April 2001 after a 30-hour confrontation with the authorities. On 28 June he was handed over to the United Nations War Crimes Tribunal in The Hague to face charges of crimes against humanity. Prime Minister Zoran Žižić resigned the next day. On 12 Feb. 2002 the trial of Slobodan Milošević, on charges of genocide and war crimes in the Balkans over a period of nearly ten years, began at the International Criminal Tribunal in The Hague. However, Milošević's death in March 2006 from heart failure while in the custody of the Tribunal brought proceedings to a close.

On 14 March 2002 Serbia and Montenegro agreed to remain part of a single entity called Serbia and Montenegro, thus relegating the name Yugoslavia to history. The agreement was ratified in principle by the federal parliament and the republican parliaments of Serbia and Montenegro on 9 April 2002. The new union came into force on 4 Feb. 2003. The country's fragile political structures came under the spotlight on 12 March 2003 when the Serbian prime minister Zoran Đinđić, a key figure in the toppling of the Milošević regime, was shot dead on the stairway of Serbia's chief government building.

After 4 Feb. 2006 Serbia and Montenegro had the right to vote for independence. Following a referendum on 21 May 2006, Montenegro declared independence and was recognized as such by Serbia on 15 June. As a result of Montenegro's vote, Serbia's parliament formally proclaimed Serbia to be independent for the first time since 1918 on 5 June 2006.

TERRITORY AND POPULATION

Serbia is bounded in the northwest by Croatia, in the north by Hungary, in the northeast by Romania, in the east by Bulgaria, in the south by Macedonia and in the west by Albania, Montenegro and Bosnia and Herzegovina. According to the constitution it includes the two provinces of Kosovo and Metohija in the south and Vojvodina in the north. With these Serbia's area is 88,361 sq. km; without, 55,968 sq. km. Population at the 2002 census was (with Vojvodina but without Kosovo) 7,498,001, of which the predominating ethnic group was Serbs (6,212,838); population density per sq. km, 97·7. 2002 census population (without Kosovo and Vojvodina), 5,466,009, of which the predominating ethnic group was Serbs (4,891,031); population density per sq. km, 96·8.

The UN gives an estimated population for 2010 of 9·86m.

The capital is Belgrade (2002 census population, 1,120,092). Populations (2002 census) of principal towns:

Belgrade	1,120,092	Subotica	99,981
Priština	5,648,001[1]	Zrenjanin	79,773
Novi Sad	191,405	Pančevo	77,087
Niš	173,724	Čačak	73,217
Kragujevac	146,373	Leskovac	63,185

[1]2002 estimate.

The official language is Serbian.

SOCIAL STATISTICS

In 2008 there were a total of 69,083 live births in Serbia (without Kosovo and Metohija), a rate of 9·4 per 1,000 inhabitants. There were 102,711 deaths (14·0 per 1,000) and 38,285 marriages (5·2 per 1,000). Population growth rate, 2007, –0·4%. Life expectancy in 2007 was 71·6 years for men and 76·3 for women. Infant mortality was 6·7 per 1,000 live births in 2008.

CLIMATE

Most parts have a central European type of climate, with cold winters and hot summers. 2000, Belgrade, Jan. –1·0°C, July 23·5°C. Annual rainfall 367·7 mm.

CONSTITUTION AND GOVERNMENT

There is a 250-member single-chamber National Assembly. The *President* is elected by universal suffrage for not more than two five-year terms.

A new constitution was approved in a referendum held on 28–29 Oct. 2006, with 53·0% of the electorate (and 96·6% of those voting) supporting the proposed constitution. It declares the province of Kosovo and Metohija an integral part of Serbia and grants Vojvodina financial autonomy. Kosovo Albanians were not able to vote. Turnout was 54·9%.

National Anthem

'Bože pravde' ('God of Justice'); words by Jovan Đorđević, tune by Davorin Jenko.

RECENT ELECTIONS

Early parliamentary elections were held on 11 May 2008 after the incumbent government coalition was forced to dissolve owing to disagreements over the issues of Kosovan independence and membership of the European Union. The Za Evropsku Srbiju (For a European Serbia) coalition, comprising Demokratska Stranka (DS; Democratic Party), G17 Plus, the League of Social Democrats of Vojvodina and the Sanjak Democratic Party, won 102 seats (38·4% of the vote). The Srpska Radikalna Stranka (SRS; Serb Radical Party) won 78 seats (29·5% of the vote); Demokratska Stranka Srbije-Nova Srbije (DSS-NS; Democratic Party of Serbia-New Serbia), 30 (11·6%); Socijalisticka Partija Srbije (SPS; Serb Socialist Party), 20 (7·6%); Liberalno Demokratska Partija (LDP; Liberal Democratic Party and allies), 13 (5·2%). The Alliance of Vojvodina Hungarians won 4 seats, Bosniak List for a European Sanjak 2 and the Albanian Coalition from Preševo Valley 1. Turnout was 61·3%.

In the first round of presidential elections held on 20 Jan. 2008 Tomislav Nikolić (SRS) took 40·0% of the vote, followed by incumbent Boris Tadić (DS) with 35·4%, Velimir Ilić with 7·4% and Milutin Mrkonjic with 6·0%. There were five other candidates. In the run-off on 3 Feb. 2008 between the first two candidates, Tadić took 51·2%, defeating Nikolić with 48·8%. Turnout was 61·4% in the first round and 68·1% in the second.

CURRENT ADMINISTRATION

President: Boris Tadić; b. 1958 (DS; took office on 11 July 2004 and re-elected 3 Feb. 2008).

In March 2010 the government comprised:

Prime Minister: Mirko Cvetković; b. 1950 (ind.; took office on 7 July 2008).

First Deputy Prime Minister and Minister for the Interior: Ivica Dačić. *Deputy Prime Minister in Charge of European Integration and Minister for Science and Technological Development:* Božidar Đelić. *Deputy Prime Minister and Minister for the Economy and Regional Development:* Mlađan Dinkić. *Deputy Prime Minister in Charge of Social Affairs:* Jovan Krkobabić.

Minister of Agriculture, Forestry and Water: Saša Dragin. *Culture:* Nebojša Bradić. *Defence:* Dragan Šutanovac. *Diaspora:* Srdjan Srecković. *Education:* Žarko Obradović. *Energy and Mining:* Petar Škundrić. *Environmental Protection:* Oliver Dulić. *Finance:* Diana Dragutinović. *Foreign Affairs:* Vuk Jeremić. *Health:* Tomica Milosavljević. *Human Rights and Minorities:* Svetozar Čiplić. *Infrastructure:* Milutin Mrkonjić. *Justice:* Snežana Malović. *Kosovo and Metohija:* Goran Bogdanović. *Labour and Welfare:* Rasim Ljajić. *National Investments:* Verica Kalanović. *Public Administration and Local Self-Government:* Milan Marković. *Religion:* Bogoljub Šijaković. *Telecommunications and Information Technology:* Jasna Matić. *Trade:* Slobodan Milosavljević. *Youth and Sport:* Snežana Samardžić-Marković. *Minister without Portfolio:* Sulejman Ugljanin.

Government Website: http://www.srbija.gov.rs

CURRENT LEADERS

Boris Tadić

Position

President

Introduction

Boris Tadić became president of Serbia and Montenegro on 11 July 2004, having narrowly defeated the right-wing nationalist, Tomislav Nikolić, in a run-off. The pro-Western, reform-minded politician had been an anti-communist activist and was central to the opposition campaign to bring down Slobodan Milošević in the late 1990s. Advocating integration in the European Union and free market reforms, he was re-elected in Feb. 2008, again defeating Nikolić but only by a slim margin.

Early Life

Boris Tadić was born in Sarajevo in what was then Yugoslavia on 15 Jan. 1958, the son of the philosopher and dissident, Ljubomir Tadić. He attended school in Belgrade and graduated in psychology from the University of Belgrade's faculty of philosophy. During his student years Tadić was convicted for anti-communist political activities. He went on to undertake further study and research in psychology at the university and became a clinical psychologist in the army.

In 1990, amid the collapse of communism in Central and Eastern Europe, Yugoslavia was in deep economic recession and nationalism was growing among the constituent republics. Tadić joined the resuscitated centrist Democratic Party (DS), performing several roles including secretary of the general committee and party vice-president. He was a close ally of Zoran Đinđić, who became president of the party in 1993 following an internal power struggle. In the winter of 1996–97 Tadić and Đinđić helped organize the mass street demonstrations against the attempts of the Milošević administration to annul the victory of the Zajedno (Together) bloc in municipal elections across Serbia.

In 2002 Tadić became telecommunications minister in the Democratic Opposition of Serbia ruling coalition of the Federal Republic of Yugoslavia. It was led by Đinđić who had become prime minister in Dec. 2000 after Milošević's fall. Appointed minister of defence in the newly declared Serbia and Montenegro in March 2003 (days before Đinđić's assassination), Tadić became known for his sweeping army reforms and his plan (subsequently blocked by the UK, USA and the Netherlands) to send a Serbian contingent to Afghanistan in a bid to improve relations with NATO.

He took over the presidency of the DS in Feb. 2004 and stood in the first round of the presidential election, winning 27·6% of the vote. In his campaign he stood on a democratic, pro-European and reform-minded platform. He narrowly defeated the nationalist Tomislav Nikolić in the second round with 53·7% of the vote. He was sworn in on 11 July 2004.

Career in Office

At his inauguration Tadić expressed his hopes of leading the country into the EU, urging the Union to show its political and economic support by accelerating Serbia's much-delayed preparations for a stabilization and association agreement (SAA). He pledged to co-operate with the UN war crimes tribunal and said he was committed to the idea of a democratic, rational European solution for the province of Kosovo, based on UN Security Council resolution 1244. This resolution of 1999 recognized Kosovo as an autonomous constituent of

Yugoslavia (as it then was) while acknowledging its status as a UN protectorate.

Talks on an SAA with the EU finally began in Oct. 2005 but were suspended in early May 2006 after the country's repeated failures to hand over Ratko Mladić, the Bosnian Serb commander wanted on genocide charges for the 1995 massacre of 8,000 Muslims in Srebrenica. NATO, however, did admit Serbia to its Partnership for Peace programme in Dec. of that year, despite having earlier expressed similar reservations concerning war crime suspects.

Following Montenegro's declaration of independence on 4 June 2006, the government declared Serbia the legal successor to the union of Serbia and Montenegro. Shortly afterwards Tadić visited the Montenegrin president and prime minister and expressed his desire for mutual co-operation and friendship between the two countries.

Tadić's re-election as president in Feb. 2008 was welcomed by the EU, which pledged more support for his bid to join the Union. However, judgment of his second term would likely rest on a lasting settlement of the status of Kosovo. In Feb. 2008 the province unilaterally declared itself an independent state, but this move was denounced by Serb opinion and also by Russia. Disagreements within the Serbian coalition government over policy towards the EU in the wake of Kosovo's declaration led Tadić in March to accept calls for fresh parliamentary elections. After a bitter campaign, no party won an outright advantage in the elections in May. Tadić asked Mirko Cvetković, a pro-European independent, to try to form a government and in July his new coalition was approved by parliament and sworn in.

Also in July, the former Bosnian Serb leader Radovan Karadžić, who had been sought for war crimes for almost 13 years, was arrested in Belgrade and transferred to The Hague to stand trial.

In April 2008 the EU eventually signed an SAA with Serbia as a first step towards eventual membership, but implementation was hindered by a Dutch veto because of the continuing failure to arrest Mladić. In Dec. 2009 this veto was lifted (although the lack of further progress in detaining war criminals remained contentious), at which time Serbia submitted a formal application to join the Union.

Serbia's economy contracted sharply in the first half of 2009 in the wake of the global financial crisis. In response, the International Monetary Fund approved a stand-by arrangement in May worth almost €3bn. (covering more than two years), and in Oct. 2009 Russia granted a €1bn. loan to help cover Serbia's budget deficit.

Mirko Cvetković

Position
Prime Minister

Introduction
Following parliamentary elections, President Boris Tadić named Mirko Cvetković as prime minister on 27 June 2008. Cvetković leads a coalition of his pro-EU Democratic Party and the Serb Socialist Party. He has rejected Kosovan independence and has reasserted his commitment to Serbian accession to the EU. However, hopes of imminent membership were undermined by the impact on the economy of the global economic crisis.

Early Life
Mirko Cvetković was born in the city of Zaječar in eastern Serbia on 16 Aug. 1950, the son of an economist and a pharmacist. He graduated from the faculty of economics at the University of Belgrade, completing a doctorate before beginning his career at the Institute of Mining. He then worked for six years at the Institute of Economics and subsequently as an external consultant of the World Bank.

After the overthrow of Slobodan Milošević, Cvetković became deputy minister of economy and privatization in 2001 in the moderate government of Zoran Đinđić. In 2003–04 he was director of the Privatization Agency but when inconclusive parliamentary elections of 2003 led to Democratic Prime Minister Zoran Živković stepping down and the Socialist Party playing a key role in the coalition government, Cvetković withdrew from politics.

However, in 2007 he returned to government as finance minister in the newly-formed coalition of the main pro-reform parties. He held the position until snap elections in 2008 following a coalition split over EU policy in the wake of Kosovo's independence declaration. The May 2008 elections resulted in the Democratic Party entering into a surprise coalition with the Socialist Party. President Tadić subsequently nominated Cvetković in a move regarded as a necessary compromise to ensure the maintenance a working coalition.

Career in Office
Seen as a low-profile technocrat, Cvetković's chief task has been to improve the economy. In 2009 the government secured almost €3bn. in loans from the IMF and €1bn. from Russia to cover the budget deficit. Cvetković reiterated the government's opposition to Kosovan independence and he is committed to securing EU membership, overseeing the submission of Serbia's formal application in Dec. 2009. In March 2010 parliament passed a resolution expressing its apologies for the 1995 Srebrenica massacre of some 8,000 Bosnian Serbs.

DEFENCE

Conscription is for six months. In 2006 military expenditure totalled US$812m. (US$80 per capita), representing 2·5% of GDP.

Army
Strength (2007) 11,180 including 1,724 conscripts. The headquarters of the Army are at Niš. Equipment includes 224 main battle tanks.

Air Force
The Air Force and Air Defence is based at Zemun. Strength (2007) 4,155.

INTERNATIONAL RELATIONS

Serbia is a member of the UN, World Bank, IMF and several other UN specialized agencies, Council of Europe, OSCE, CEI, BSEC, Danube Commission, IOM and NATO Partnership for Peace. In Dec. 2009 it applied to join the European Union.

ECONOMY

Agriculture accounted for 13% of GDP in 2007, industry 28% and services 59%.

Overview
Since the democratic changes of 2000, Serbia has enjoyed strong growth and positive structural changes. GDP grew on average by 5·5% per year in the first five years after transition and has remained strong in subsequent years. Inflation has fallen significantly since the 1990s. Large scale privatization, a restructuring of the banking sector and improvements in the business environment have underpinned economic progress.

FDI has been strong in recent years as the economy becomes more attractive to investors. Averaging 6·7% of GDP in the period 2002–07 according to the World Bank, Serbia is a top target for European and South East Asian investment. However, political uncertainty has hindered progress and reform, while high unemployment (at around 20% of the labour force) is a concern. A large and expanding current account deficit and external debt makes the economy vulnerable to shocks, exacerbated by an expansionist fiscal policy.

EU accession is a major objective and in Dec. 2009 a formal application for membership was submitted. However, political issues—especially the status of Kosovo—are likely to impact on the timeframe for full membership, with knock-on effects for the economy.

Currency

The unit of currency of Serbia is the *dinar* (RSD) of 100 *paras*. On 1 Jan. 2001 Yugoslavia adopted a managed float regime. The National Bank of Yugoslavia began setting the exchange rate of the dinar daily in the foreign exchange market on the previous day. In Kosovo both the dinar and the euro are legal tender. Inflation was 6·5% in 2007, rising to 11·7% in 2008.

Budget

In 2003 total revenue was 366,504m. dinars; total expenditure was 353,329m. dinars. VAT at 18% (reduced rate 8%) was introduced on 1 Jan. 2005.

Performance

Real GDP growth was 5·4% in 2008 (6·9% in 2007). Total GDP was US$50·1bn. in 2008.

Banking and Finance

The National Bank is the bank of issue responsible for the monetary policy, stability of the currency of Serbia, the dinar, control of the money supply and prescribing the method of maintaining internal and external liquidity. The dinar became fully convertible in May 2002. The present *Governor* of the National Bank of Serbia is Radovan Jelašić.

There is a stock exchange in Belgrade.

ENERGY AND NATURAL RESOURCES

Electricity

Electricity production in 2004 was 33·87bn. kWh.

Minerals

(Excluding Kosovo and Vojvodina, in 1,000 tonnes). 2004: lignite, 33,753; copper ore, 5,495 tonnes.

Agriculture

(Excluding Kosovo and Vojvodina). In 2004 the cultivated area was an estimated 2,604,000 ha. Yields in 2004 (in 1,000 tonnes): maize, 2,843; wheat, 1,195; potatoes, 692; plums, 515; grapes, 343; cabbage and kale, 273; tomatoes, 128; sugar beets, 125. Livestock estimates (in 1,000): cattle, 867; pigs, 1,975; sheep, 1,381; poultry, 10,808.

Forestry

Timber cut in 2007: 2,981,000 cu. metres.

INDUSTRY

(Excluding Kosovo and Vojvodina). 2004: rolled steel, 1,543,453 tonnes; cement, 1,332,000 tonnes; pig iron, 959,019 tonnes; cotton fabrics, 5,852,000 sq. metres; woollen fabrics, 144,000 sq. metres; cars, 13,516 units; lorries, 647 units.

Labour

In Oct. 2004 there were 2,930,846 workers employed (without Kosovo and Metohija), including 700,681 in agriculture, forestry and water supply; 551,429 in manufacturing; 441,800 in wholesale and retail trade and repair; 170,861 in public administration and social insurance; 166,619 in health and social work; and 163,628 in transport, storage and communications. In Oct. 2004 there were 2,059,417 employees and 659,427 self-employed persons. Average annual salary in Sept. 2004 (without Kosovo and Metohija) was 21,085 dinars. Unemployment in Oct. 2004 was running at 18·5% with Vojvodina and 18·4% without.

INTERNATIONAL TRADE

Imports and Exports

In 2007 imports (c.i.f.) amounted to US$18,553·6m.; exports (f.o.b.) US$8,824·7m. The main imports are machinery and transport equipment, chemicals, petroleum, and iron and steel. Main exports are food and livestock, machinery and transport equipment, iron and steel, and chemicals,. The main import sources in 2007 were Russia (14·2%), Germany (11·8%), Italy (9·7%) and China (7·4%). Principal export markets in 2007 were Italy (12·4%), Bosnia and Herzegovina (11·8%), Montenegro (10·8%) and Germany (10·6%).

COMMUNICATIONS

Roads

The length of roads in 2007 was 39,184 km, including 374 km of motorway and 5,133 km of main roads. In 2007 there were 1,476,600 passenger cars in use, 162,900 lorries and vans, 24,900 motorcycles and mopeds, and 8,900 buses and coaches. There were 962 deaths as a result of road accidents in 2007.

Rail

Railways are operated by Železnice Srbije; total length of network in 2005 (excluding Kosovo and Metohija) was 3,809 km. In 2004, 15·3m. passengers and 12·3m. tonnes of freight were carried (without Kosovo and Metohija).

Civil Aviation

The national airline (and the former national carrier of Yugoslavia) is Jat Airways. In Jan. 2010 it flew to 30 destinations in 23 countries.

SOCIAL INSTITUTIONS

Justice

In 2002 there was one Supreme Court, 30 District Courts and 138 Communal Courts with 2,180 judges and 17 Economic Courts of Law with 237 judges.

Education

In 2003–04 there were: 1,804 kindergartens and pre-schools with 161,938 pupils; 3,592 primary schools with 664,577 pupils; 491 secondary schools with 303,596 pupils; and 223 high and higher schools with 218,368 students.

RELIGION

Serbia has been traditionally Orthodox. Muslims are found in the south as a result of the Turkish occupation. The Serbian Orthodox Church with its seat in Belgrade has 27 bishoprics within the boundaries of former Yugoslavia and 12 abroad (five in the USA and Canada, five in Europe and two in Australia). The Serbian Orthodox Church numbers about 2,000 priests. Its *Patriarch* is Irinej (enthroned 23 Jan. 2010).

CULTURE

World Heritage Sites

There are four sites on the UNESCO World Heritage List: Stari Ras and Sopočani (inscribed on the list in 1979); Studenica Monastery (1986); Medieval monuments in Kosovo (2004 and 2006); and Gamzigrad-Romuliana, the palace of Galerius (2007).

Broadcasting

The Republic Broadcasting Agency is the regulatory authority. Radio-Television Serbia (RTS) is the national public broadcaster. It has the largest audience of any broadcaster in the country, but is facing increased competition from new private TV and radio stations. In 2006 the regulator awarded national TV licences to several private operators (including B92, TV Pink and TV Avala) and also five national radio licences.

Press

In 2006 there were 11 daily newspapers. The two largest newspapers are Blic (readership of 650,000 in 2006) and Večernje novosti (636,000).

DIPLOMATIC REPRESENTATIVES

Of Serbia in the United Kingdom (28 Belgrave Sq., London, SW1X 8QB)
Ambassador: Dejan Popović.

Of the United Kingdom in Serbia (Resavska 46, 11000 Belgrade)
Ambassador: Stephen Wordsworth, LVO.

Of Serbia in the USA (2134 Kalorama Rd, NW, Washington, D.C., 20008)
Ambassador: Vladimir Petrović.

Of the USA in Serbia (Kneza Miloša 50, 11000 Belgrade)
Ambassador: Mary Warlick.

Of Serbia to the United Nations
Ambassador: Feodor Starčević.

Of Serbia to the European Union
Ambassador: Vacant.

FURTHER READING

Anzulovic, Branimir, *Heavenly Serbia: From Myth to Genocide*. 1999
Judah, Tim, *The Serbs: History, Myth and the Destruction of Yugoslavia*. 1997
Pavolwitch, Stevan K., *Serbia: The History of an Idea*. 2002
Stojanovic, Svetozar, *Serbia: The Democratic Revolution*. 2003
Thomas, Robert, *Serbia Under Milosevic: Politics in the 1990s*. 1999
Vladisavljević, Nebojša, *Serbia's Antibureaucratic Revolution: Milošević, the Fall of Communism and Nationalist Mobilization*. 2008

National Statistical Office: Statistical Office of the Republic of Serbia, 5 Milana Rakića St., 11000 Belgrade.
Website: http://webrzs.stat.gov.rs/axd/index.php

Kosovo and Metohija

KEY HISTORICAL EVENTS

Kosovo has a large ethnic Albanian majority. Following Albanian-Serb conflicts, the Kosovo and Serbian parliaments adopted constitutional amendments in March 1989 surrendering much of Kosovo's autonomy to Serbia. Renewed Albanian rioting broke out in 1990. The Prime Minister and six other ministers resigned in April 1990 over ethnic conflicts. In July 1990, 114 of the 130 Albanian members of the National Assembly voted for full republican status for Kosovo but the Serbian National Assembly declared this vote invalid and unanimously voted to dissolve the Kosovo Assembly. Direct Serbian rule was imposed causing widespread violence. Western demands for negotiations in granting Kosovo some kind of special status were rejected. Ibrahim Rugova, the leader of the main Albanian party, the Democratic League of Kosovo (LDK), declared himself 'president' demanding talks on independence. In 1998 armed conflict between Yugoslavia and the Kosovo Liberation Army led 200,000 people, or a tenth of the population of the province, to flee the fighting. Further repression by Serbian forces led to the threat of NATO direct action. Air strikes against Yugoslavian military targets began on 24 March 1999. Retaliation against Albanian Kosovars led to a massive exodus of refugees. On 9 June after 78 days of air attacks NATO and Yugoslavia signed an accord on the Serb withdrawal from Kosovo, and on 11 June NATO's peacekeeping force, KFOR, entered Kosovo. In Nov. 2001 the Organization for Security and Co-operation in Europe mounted elections for a provincial assembly that were deemed fair and democratic.

The worst fighting between Serbs and Albanians since the end of the war claimed 19 lives in March 2004. The following March President Ramush Haradinaj resigned when he was indicted to face charges of war crimes at the UN tribunal in The Hague. In 2006 the UN sponsored talks on the future status of Kosovo and ethnic Serbian and Kosovan leaders met for the first time since 1999. In Oct. 2006 Serbia held a referendum that approved a new constitution keeping Kosovo as an integral part of the country. However, the Kosovan Albanian majority rejected the poll. In Feb. 2007 the UN announced plans for Kosovo's eventual independence that were immediately rejected by Serbia and heavily revised in July 2007 after Russian protests.

In Nov. 2007 Hashim Thaçi's Democratic Party of Kosovo won elections that were boycotted by the Serb minority. On 17 Feb. 2008 Kosovo made a unilateral declaration of independence though international recognition was patchy. Independence was recognized by the USA and EU member countries including Germany, France and the UK. However, Serbia rejected the declaration as did Russia, while Spain refused to support it and China expressed 'grave concern'. As such, Kosovo lacks recognition as a sovereign country by the UN and the EU.

TERRITORY AND POPULATION

Area: 10,887 sq. km. The capital is Priština. The 1991 and 2002 censuses were not taken. According to the Statistical Office of Kosovo the population in 2007 was an estimated 2·1m., of whom 92% are Albanians; density, 192·9 per sq. km. About 5% of the population are Serbs, mostly in the north of the country. Population estimate of Priština, 2002, 564,800. Other major towns include Prizren, Peć and Kosovska Mitrovica.

SOCIAL STATISTICS

Statistics for 2004: live births, 33,897; deaths, 6,255; marriages, 16,938; divorces, 1,329.

CONSTITUTION AND GOVERNMENT

The constitution of Serbia defines the autonomous province of Kosovo and Metohija as an 'integral part' of the territory of Serbia with 'substantial autonomy'.

In April 2008 Kosovo's 120-member multi-ethnic parliamentary assembly (first convened on 10 Dec. 2001) approved a new constitution, which came into force on 15 June 2008. Its promulgation followed Kosovo's unilateral declaration of independence from Serbia in Feb. 2008 as the Republic of Kosovo. The constitution envisages a handover of executive power from the UN, which has been responsible for administration in the region since 1999, to the majority ethnic Albanian parliament, under the supervision of an EU team. It also specifies that Kosovo will 'have no territorial claim against, and shall seek no union with' any other state. However, the constitution was rejected by Serbia as it considers Kosovo to be part of its sovereign territory, while Russia claimed any EU involvement would be illegal as it had yet to be approved by the UN Security Council. In June 2008 an ethnic Serb assembly set up a rival administration in Mitrovica. The UN referred the declaration of independence to the International Court of Justice in Oct. 2008.

Kosovo came under interim international administration on 10 June 1999, in accordance with the terms of UN Security Council resolution 1244. The United Nations Interim Administration Mission in Kosovo (UNMIK) administered Kosovo following the arrival of KFOR (NATO-led peacekeeping force) and remained in place even after the Feb. 2008 declaration of independence. The unilateral declaration received a mixed response from the international community, with Serbia, Russia and Spain prominent among those nations who refused to recognize it. In Dec. 2008 EULEX, the European Union Rule of Law Mission in Kosovo, took over responsibility from the UN for policing, justice and customs services, with the agreement of Serbia.

There is a 120-member multi-ethnic parliamentary assembly, which first convened on 10 Dec. 2001. The new assembly brought together representatives of Kosovo's ethnic Albanian majority and its Serbian minority for the first time in more than a decade.

RECENT ELECTIONS

Parliamentary elections held on 17 Nov. 2007; turnout was 40·1%. The Democratic Party of Kosovo won 37 seats with 34·3% of the vote, the Democratic League of Kosovo 25 with 22·6%, the Alliance for New Kosovo 13 with 12·3%, the Democratic League of Dardania-Albanian Christian Democratic Party of Kosovo 11 with 10·1% and the Alliance for the Future of Kosovo 10 with 9·6%. Four contested seats were won by minorities and in addition 20 seats are reserved for minorities.

Dr Fatmir Sejdiu was re-elected president by parliament on 9 Jan. 2008. In a third round of voting he received 68 votes against 39 for Naim Maloku, with 11 void votes. On the same day parliament elected Hashim Thaçi prime minister by 85 votes to 22 against.

CURRENT ADMINISTRATION

President: Dr Fatmir Sejdiu; b. 1951 (Democratic League of Kosovo; since 10 Feb. 2006).

Prime Minister: Hashim Thaçi; b. 1969 (Democratic Party of Kosovo; since 9 Jan. 2008).

Head of EULEX Kosovo: Yves de Kermabon (France; since 16 Feb. 2008).

INTERNATIONAL RELATIONS

As at March 2010 Kosovo was recognized as an independent state by 65 of the 192 UN members.

Kosovo is a member of the World Bank and the IMF.

ECONOMY

Budget

Total revenue in 2003 was €835·3m., including €184·6m. in international aid. Total expenditure was €791·6m.

Banking and Finance

In Aug. 1999 the Deutsche Mark became legal tender alongside the Yugoslav dinar, and on 1 Jan. 2002 the euro became the official currency of Kosovo. The Serb dinar is also legal tender in Kosovo but is used only by ethnic Serbs.

ENERGY AND NATURAL RESOURCES

Electricity

Electricity production in 2004 was 3·48bn. kWh.

Minerals

Production (1997): lignite, 8,421,991 tonnes.

Agriculture

The cultivated area in 2004 was 264,340 ha. Yields in 2004 (in 1,000 tonnes): wheat, 197; maize, 92; potatoes, 56; peppers, 40; plums, 16. Livestock (in 1,000): cattle, 241; milch cows, 129; sheep, 124; pigs, 47; chickens, 1,617.

Forestry

Timber cut in 1997: 130,000 cu. metres.

INDUSTRY

Production (1997): cement, 89,528 tonnes; sulphuric acid, 26,900 tonnes.

Labour

In 1997 there were 120,763 workers in the public sector, including 54,223 in industry, 10,471 in education and culture, 9,245 in trade, catering and tourism, 8,933 in transport and communications, 7,880 in communities and organizations and 1,526 in commercial services. In Oct. 1997 in the private sector there were 35,869 self-employed and employed, including 15,113 in trade, 5,023 in catering and tourism, 4,364 in arts and crafts and 2,006 in transport and communications. Average monthly salary in Dec. 1998 was 1,066 dinars.

COMMUNICATIONS

Roads

In 2007 there were 1,924 km of main and regional roads in Kosovo. Total vehicle registrations in April 2003 were 234,297.

Rail

Total length of railways in 2007 was 430 km, of which 97 km were freight only. In 2005 the state-owned Kosovo Railways was established to take over the running of railways from the UN Mission in Kosovo.

Civil Aviation

There is an international airport at Priština, which handled 990,952 passengers in 2007.

Telecommunications

In 2003 there were 101,059 main telephone lines and 315,000 mobile phones.

SOCIAL INSTITUTIONS

Justice

In 2004 there were five district courts and 23 municipal courts.

Education

In 2002–03 there were: 465 pre-schools and nurseries with 1,018 teachers and 20,365 pupils; 992 primary schools with 15,733 teachers and 299,934 pupils; and 128 secondary schools with 5,439 teachers and 89,387 pupils. In 2001–02, 21,216 students attended the University of Priština.

RELIGION

The population of Kosovo is predominantly Muslim.

FURTHER READING

Judah, Tim, *Kosovo: War and Revenge.* 2000
King, Iain and Mason, Whit, *Peace at any Price: How the World Failed Kosovo.* 2006
Malcolm, N., *Kosovo: a Short History.* 2nd ed. 2002
Vickers, M., *Between Serb and Albanian: A History of Kosovo.* 1998

Vojvodina

KEY HISTORICAL EVENTS

After the Battle of Kosovo in 1389 Turkish attacks on the Balkans led to a mass migration of Serbians to Vojvodina. Turkish rule ended after their 1716–18 war with Austria and the Požarevac peace agreement. In exchange for acting as frontier protectors, the Austrians granted the people of Vojvodina religious autonomy. However, in 1848 a short-lived revolution led to a Serbian alliance with the Croats. Vojvodina was briefly declared an independent dukedom. After the First World War Vojvodina became part of the first Yugoslav state. In 1974 President Tito granted autonomy to Vojvodina, but this status was brought into question after Vojvodina's largely anti-Milošević provincial assembly resigned in 1988. In 1989 the Serbian government, led by Slobodan Milošević, stripped Vojvodina of most of its autonomous rights and secured Serbian control. After the fall of Milošević in 2000 there was a growing demand for autonomy, which was granted by statute in Dec. 2009.

TERRITORY AND POPULATION

Area: 21,506 sq. km. The capital is Novi Sad. Population of Vojvodina at the 2002 census, 2,031,992 (1,321,807 Serbs, 290,207 Hungarians); density, 94·5 per sq. km. Population of Novi Sad, 2002, 191,405. There are six official languages: Serbian, Hungarian, Slovak, Romanian, Croatian and Rusyn.

SOCIAL STATISTICS

In 2003 there were a total of 20,381 live births in Vojvodina, a rate of 9·9 per 1,000 inhabitants. There were 29,741 deaths (14·4 per 1,000) and 11,127 marriages (5·4 per 1,000). Rate of natural increase in 2003: –4·5 per 1,000.

CONSTITUTION AND GOVERNMENT

Vojvodina's autonomous status, rescinded by the Yugoslav government in 1990, was restored by statute in Dec. 2009. Novi Sad was defined as the province's chief administrative centre and Vojvodina is permitted to establish representative offices in Europe with the consent of the Serbian government.

RECENT ELECTIONS

In March 2010 the Assembly of Vojvodina comprised 120 deputies, of which For a European Vojvodina had 65 seats, the Serbian Radical Party 24, the Hungarian Coalition 9, the Democratic Party of Serbia 6, Citizens' Groups 6, Together for Vojvodina 5, the coalition of the Socialist Party of Serbia and the Party of United Pensioners 4 and the Liberal Democratic Party 1.

CURRENT ADMINISTRATION

President of the Assembly: Šandor Egereši; b. 1964 (in office since 16 July 2008).

Chairman of the Executive Council: Bojan Pajtić; b. 1970 (in office since 30 Oct. 2004).

Government Website: http://www.vojvodina.gov.rs

ECONOMY

Budget

In 2003 total revenue was 66,538m. dinars; total expenditure was 59,234m. dinars.

ENERGY AND NATURAL RESOURCES

Electricity

Electricity production in 2004 was 526m. kWh.

Agriculture

The cultivated area in 2004 was an estimated 1,648,000 ha. Yield (in 1,000 tonnes): maize, 3,726; sugar beets, 2,689; wheat, 1,563; potatoes, 283. Livestock estimates (in 1,000): cattle, 212; sheep, 195; pigs, 1,190; poultry, 5,823.

Forestry

Timber cut in 2004: 699,000 cu. metres.

INDUSTRY

Production (2004): cement, 908,000 tonnes; fertilizers, 651,166 tonnes; crude petroleum, 640,000 tonnes; plastics, 179,000 tonnes.

Labour

In Oct. 2004 there were 748,809 persons employed, including 175,673 in manufacturing; 163,738 in agriculture, forestry and water works supply; 114,868 in wholesale and retail trade and repair; 42,170 in construction; 40,979 in health and social work; and 38,176 in transport, storage and communications. In Oct. 2004 there were 569,488 employees and 154,801 self-employed persons. Unemployment was 18·8% in Oct. 2004.

SOCIAL INSTITUTIONS

Education

In 2003–04 there were: 620 kindergartens and pre-schools with 46,696 pupils; 535 primary schools with 178,905 pupils; 124 secondary schools with 78,008 pupils; and 50 high and higher schools with 46,273 students.

SEYCHELLES

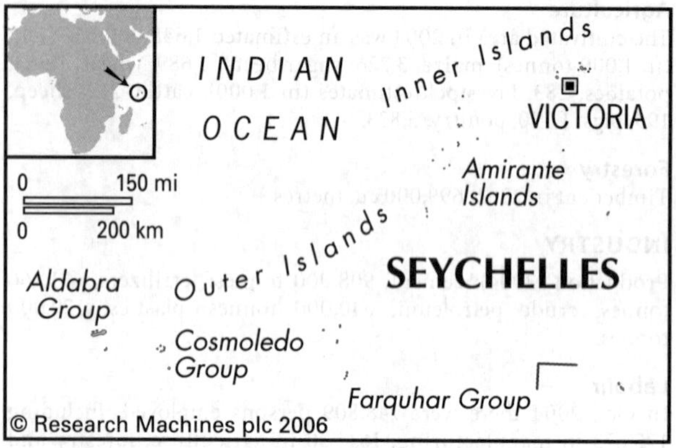

Republic of Seychelles

Capital: Victoria
Population, 2006: 85,000
GDP per capita, 2007: (PPP$) 16,394
HDI/world rank: 0·845/57

KEY HISTORICAL EVENTS

The Seychelles were colonized by the French in 1756 to establish spice plantations to compete with the Dutch monopoly. The islands were captured by the English in 1794. Subsequently, Britain offered to return Mauritius and its dependencies, which included the Seychelles, to France if that country would renounce all claims in India. France refused and the Seychelles were formally ceded to Britain as a dependency of Mauritius. In Nov. 1903 the Seychelles archipelago became a separate British Crown Colony. Internal self-government was achieved on 1 Oct. 1975 and independence as a republic within the British Commonwealth on 29 June 1976.

The first president, James Mancham, was deposed in a coup on 5 June 1977. Under the new constitution, the Seychelles People's Progressive Front became the sole legal party. There were several attempts to overthrow the regime but in 1979 and 1984 Albert René was the only candidate in the presidential elections. Under the new constitution approved in June 1993, President René was re-elected against two opponents. He stood down in 2004.

TERRITORY AND POPULATION

The Seychelles consist of 115 islands in the Indian Ocean, north of Madagascar, with a combined area of 455 sq. km (175 sq. miles) in two distinct groups and a population (2002 census) of 81,177; 2006 estimate, 84,600. The Granitic group of 40 islands cover 232 sq. km (90 sq. miles); the principal island is Mahé, with 153 sq. km (59 sq. miles) and 73,900 inhabitants (2006 estimate), the other inhabited islands of the group being Praslin, La Digue, Silhouette, Fregate, North and Denis, which together had an estimated 10,700 inhabitants in 2006.

The Outer or Coralline group comprises 75 islands spread over a wide area of ocean between the Mahé group and Madagascar, with a total land area of 223 sq. km (86 sq. miles). The main islands are the Amirante Isles (including Desroches, Poivre, Daros and Alphonse), Coetivy Island and Platte Island, all lying south of the Mahé group; the Farquhar, St Pierre and Providence Islands, north of Madagascar; and Aldabra, Astove, Assumption and the Cosmoledo Islands, about 1,000 km southwest of the Mahé group. Aldabra (whose lagoon covers 142 sq. km), Farquhar and Desroches were transferred to the new British Indian Ocean Territory in 1965, but were returned by Britain to the Seychelles on the latter's independence in 1976.

Victoria, the chief town, had a census population of 24,970 in 2002. In 2005, 52·9% of the population was urban.

The official languages are Creole, English and French but 91% of the population speak Creole.

SOCIAL STATISTICS

2006 births, 1,467; deaths, 664. 2006 rates per 1,000 population, birth, 17·3; death, 7·8; infant mortality (2005), 12 per 1,000 births. Annual population growth rate, 2000–05, 0·4%. Life expectancy at birth in 2003 was estimated to be 72 years (67 for males and 77 for females). Fertility rate, 2004, 2·1 births per woman.

CLIMATE

Though close to the equator, the climate is tropical. The hot, wet season is from Dec. to May, when conditions are humid, but southeast trades bring cooler conditions from June to Nov. Temperatures are high throughout the year, but the islands lie outside the cyclone belt. Victoria, Jan. 80°F (26·7°C), July 78°F (25·6°C). Annual rainfall 95" (2,287 mm).

CONSTITUTION AND GOVERNMENT

Under the 1979 constitution the Seychelles People's Progressive Front (SPPF) was the sole legal Party. There is a unicameral People's Assembly consisting of 34 seats, of which 25 are directly elected and nine are allocated on a proportional basis, and an executive president directly elected for a five-year term. A constitutional amendment of Dec. 1991 legalized other parties. A commission was elected in July 1992 to draft a new constitution. The electorate was some 50,000; turnout was 90%. The SPPF gained 14 seats on the commission, the Democratic Party, eight; the latter, however, eventually withdrew. At a referendum in Nov. 1992 the new draft constitution failed to obtain the necessary 60% approval votes. The commission was reconvened in Jan. 1993. At a further referendum on 18 June 1993 the constitution was approved by 73·6% of votes cast. The elections of 1993 were the first multiparty ones since 1974.

National Anthem

'Koste Seselwa' ('Come Together Seychellois'); words and tune by D. F. M. André and G. C. R. Payet.

RECENT ELECTIONS

In parliamentary elections held on 10–12 May 2007 the ruling Seychelles People's Progressive Front (SPPF) won 23 of the 34 seats with 56·2% of the vote, against 11 for the Seychelles National Party–Democratic Party (43·8%). Turnout was 85·9%. In presidential elections held on 28–30 July 2006 incumbent James Michel (Seychelles People's Progressive Front) won 53·7% of the vote against Wavel Ramkalawan (Seychelles National Party) with 45·7% and Philippe Boullé (ind.) with 0·6%. Turnout was 85·9%.

CURRENT ADMINISTRATION

On 14 April 2004 France-Albert René stepped down as president, a post he had held since 1977.

President: James Michel; b. 1944 (SPPF; took office on 14 April 2004 and then elected in July 2006). The President is *Minister of Defence, Police, Legal Affairs, Risk and Disaster Management, Information and Public Relations, and Foreign Affairs.*

Vice-President, Minister of Internal Affairs and Public Administration: Joseph Belmont.

In March 2010 the government comprised:

Minister of Community Development, Youth, Sports and Culture: Vincent Meriton. *Education:* Bernard Shamlaye. *Employment and Human Resources Development:* Macsuzy Mondon. *Environment, Natural Resources and Transport:* Joel Morgan. *Finance:* Danny Faure. *Health and Social Development:* Marie-Pierre Lloyd. *National Development:* Jacqueline Dugasse.

Government Website: http://www.egov.sc

CURRENT LEADERS

James Michel

Position
President

Introduction
Former Vice-President James Michel came to power in April 2004, handpicked by then president France-Albert René to succeed to the presidency on René's retirement after 27 years in power. Michel had been vice-president since 1996 and had previously held a variety of ministerial positions. He was elected to the post in July 2006.

Early Life
James Alix Michel was born in the Seychelles on 18 Aug. 1944. He was a teacher before deciding to pursue a career in politics. His profile rose in the mid-1970s because of his involvement in the country's booming tourism industry.

In 1976, just before independence, he joined René's left-of-centre Seychelles People's United Party (SPUP)—renamed the Seychelles People's Progressive Front (SPPF) in 1978. He was a member of the SPUP's central committee when the party staged a bloodless coup in 1977, overthrowing the country's first president, James Mancham, and replacing him with René. There followed a 16-year one-party socialist dictatorship, during which time Michel held a series of important ruling party and ministerial positions. For several periods he was in charge of the highly-regulated Seychellois economy. On René's retirement in April 2004, Michel was sworn in as president.

Career in Office
Despite his allegiance to René, Michel was under pressure to speed up the country's democratization process, which had begun with multi-party elections in 1993. He also pledged to introduce more open political dialogue, particularly over matters concerning the Seychellois economy, and to develop the private sector. In Jan. 2005 Michel granted the Emirates Group the rights to operate non-stop flights three times a week between the Seychelles and Dubai in order to enhance the tourism industry and to increase trade for the business and cargo communities.

In March 2005 Michel detailed his foreign policy, underpinned by a desire to cement stronger regional ties in the Indian Ocean region—particularly in light of the Seychelles' exit in July 2004 from the Southern African Development Community, ostensibly because of high membership fees. He particularly focused on strengthening relations with Mauritius, working alongside the then Mauritian prime minister, Paul Bérenger, to strengthen the Indian Ocean Commission. Michel has favoured increased promotion of the Seychelles as a high-quality and safe tourist resort, and sought to make the country a leader in environmental issues.

In June 2005 Michel announced plans for a new national pension fund and a scheme to set-up a savings account of R1,000 for every Seychellois child, both of which came into effect in Jan. 2006.

After a close electoral contest in July 2006 he retained the presidency, defeating his Seychelles National Party rival. In the May 2007 parliamentary elections the SPPF retained its majority. Michel brought the poll forward after opposition MPs had boycotted parliamentary proceedings over moves to ban political parties (and also religious groups) from owning radio stations.

Confronted by a balance of payments and public debt crisis in 2008, Michel launched an economic reform programme with the help of the International Monetary Fund, which approved a two-year US$26m. support arrangement in Nov. As part of the programme, the government floated the currency and lifted foreign exchange controls. In Jan. 2009 he appealed for debt relief from international creditors as the Seychelles economy was hit by reduced tourist traffic and the effects of the global financial crisis.

In response to the expansion of Somali piracy in the Indian Ocean, the Seychelles government entered into agreements with European Union countries and the USA to enhance naval and air patrol and surveillance to deter attacks on international shipping.

DEFENCE

The Defence Force comprises all services. Personnel (2007) Army, 200; paramilitary national guard, 250; paramilitary coastguard, 200 including 80 marines.

Defence expenditure totalled US$14m. in 2006 (US$172 per capita), representing 2·0% of GDP.

Coastguard

The Seychelles Coast Guard superseded the former navy and air force in 1992. Based at Port Victoria it operates nine patrol and coastal combatants.

INTERNATIONAL RELATIONS

The Seychelles are a member of the UN, World Bank, IMF and several other UN specialized agencies, Commonwealth, International Organization of the Francophonie, African Development Bank, African Union, COMESA, SADC and is an ACP member state of the ACP-EU relationship.

ECONOMY

Services accounted for 71·5% of GDP in 2006, industry 25·5% and agriculture 3·0%.

Overview

Since the early 1990s the government has tried to create a free market economy. Tourism forms the backbone of the economy followed by the fisheries sector, where tuna fishing dominates. More than 75% of earnings derive from tourism which employs 30% of the labour force. The government is making efforts to diversify the economy by encouraging agriculture and domestic (small-scale) industrial production. In recent years the Seychelles have attempted to develop an offshore sector as a third pillar of the economy and to position itself as a provider of business and financial services.

In 2006 and 2007 GDP grew by over 5%, reflecting increased tourism. The devaluation of the Seychelles rupee in 2006 has contributed to economic recovery.

Currency

The unit of currency is the *Seychelles rupee* (SCR) divided into 100 *cents*. In July 2005 foreign exchange reserves were US$44m. and total money supply was 1,220m. rupees. After a year of deflation in 2006, consumer prices rose by 5·3% in 2007 and 37·0% in 2008. Only Zimbabwe had a higher rate of inflation in 2008.

Budget

Fiscal budget in 1m. rupees, for calendar years:

	2003	*2004*	*2005*	*2006*
Total revenues and grants	1,867·2	1,891·1	2,167·6	2,476·2
Total expenditures	1,597·2	1,788·8	1,815·6	2,301·8

VAT is 12–15%.

Performance
There was a recession in both 2003 and 2004, with the economy contracting by 5·9% and 2·9% respectively. In 2005 the economy recovered to grow by 7·5%. Since then there has been growth of 8·3% in 2006 and 7·3% in 2007 but 2008 saw the economy shrink by 1·9%. Total GDP was US$0·8bn. in 2008.

Banking and Finance
The Central Bank of Seychelles (established in 1983; *Governor*, Pierre Laporte), which is the bank of issue, and the Development Bank of Seychelles provide long-term lending for development purposes. There are also six commercial banks, including two local banks (the Seychelles Savings Bank and the Seychelles International Mercantile Banking Co-operation or NOUVOBANQ), and four branches of foreign banks (Barclays Bank, Banque Française Commerciale, Habib Bank and Bank of Baroda).

ENERGY AND NATURAL RESOURCES

Environment
Carbon dioxide emissions from the consumption and flaring of fossil fuels were the equivalent of 12·4 tonnes per capita in 2008.

Electricity
Installed capacity on Mahé and Praslin combined was an estimated 95,000 kW in 2004. Production in 2004 was approximately 220m. kWh and consumption per capita about 2,716 kWh.

Water
There are two raw water reservoirs, the Rochon Dam and La Gogue Dam, which have a combined holding capacity of 1·05bn. litres.

Agriculture
Since the rise of the tourism industry in the 1970s there has been a general decline in the production of traditional cash crops, notably cinnamon bark, of which 158 tonnes were exported in 2002 (down from 289 tonnes in 1998). 261 tonnes of tea (green leaf) were produced in 2003. Other crops grown for local consumption include bananas, oranges, cassava, sweet potatoes, paw-paw, yams and vegetables. The staple food crop, rice, is imported from Asia. Livestock, 2003 estimates: 18,000 pigs, 5,000 goats, 1,000 cattle and 1m. chickens. In 2002 there were approximately 1,000 ha. of arable land and 6,000 ha. of permanent crop land.

Forestry
In 2005 forests covered 40,000 ha., or 88·9% of the total land area. The Ministry of Environment has a number of ongoing forestry projects which aim at preserving and upgrading the local system. There are also a number of terrestrial nature reserves including three national parks, four special reserves and an 'area of outstanding natural beauty'.

Fisheries
The fisheries sector is the Seychelles' largest foreign exchange earner. In 2006 it accounted for 52% of export revenue. Total catch in 2005 was 106,555 tonnes, exclusively from sea fishing. 2006 fisheries exports amounted to 1,096·8m. rupees, of which: canned tuna, 1,030·4m.; fish meal 25·1m.; frozen prawns, 23·7m. 2006 fish production (in tonnes) included: canned tuna, 40,222; fish landed, 4,050; crustaceans, 606.

INDUSTRY
Local industry is expanding, the major development in recent years being in tuna canning; in 2003 output totalled 36,436 tonnes, up from 7,500 tonnes in 1995. This is followed by brewing, with 7·1m. litres in 2003. Other main activities include production of cigarettes (50m. in 2003), dairy production, prawn production, paints and processing of cinnamon barks.

Labour
Some 41% of employed persons work in the services sector. In 2003, 7,195 people worked in trade, restaurants and hotels. In 2003, 17,425 were formally employed in the private sector, 11,973 in the public sector and 5,463 in the parastatal sector.

Trade Unions
There are two major trade unions, the National Workers' Union and the Forum for Progress.

INTERNATIONAL TRADE
Foreign debt totalled US$1,308m. in 2007.

Imports and Exports
In 2005 imports (c.i.f.) totalled 3,712·2m. rupees (2,731·8m. rupees in 2004); exports (f.o.b.), 1,868·6m. rupees (1,599·9m. rupees in 2004). Domestic exports constitute around two-thirds of exports and re-exports a third. Principal imports: mineral fuel; food and live animals; machinery and transport equipment; manufactured goods; chemicals. Principal origins of imports, 2005: Saudi Arabia (23·0%), Spain (7·8%), Singapore (7·6%), France (6·5%). Principal exports: canned tuna; petroleum products; medicaments and medical appliances; fish meal (animal feed); frozen prawns. Main export markets (for domestic exports), 2005: UK (45·4%), France (23·1%), Italy (12·4%), Germany (10·2%).

COMMUNICATIONS

Roads
In 2006 there were 502 km of roads, of which 96·0% were surfaced. There were 6,800 private cars in 2006 (80 per 1,000 inhabitants), 2,600 commercial vehicles, 300 taxis and 215 buses.

Rail
There are no railways in the Seychelles.

Civil Aviation
Seychelles International airport is on Mahé. In 2003 Air Seychelles flew on domestic routes and to Comoros, Dubai, Frankfurt, Johannesburg, London, Malé, Mauritius, Mumbai, Munich, Paris, Réunion, Rome, Singapore and Zürich. In 2003 scheduled airline traffic of Seychelles-based carriers flew 12m. km, carrying 413,000 passengers (187,000 on international flights). In 2001 Seychelles International handled 598,133 passengers (330,726 on international flights) and 5,607 tonnes of freight.

Shipping
The main port is Victoria, which is also a tuna-fishing and fuel and services supply centre. In 2002 merchant shipping totalled 65,000 GRT. In 2003 vessels totalling 1,332,000 net registered tons entered ports. Sea freight (2006) comprised: imports, 534,000 tonnes; exports, 4,604,000 TEUs (twenty foot equivalent units); transhipments (fish), 74,000 tonnes.

Telecommunications
There were 100,000 telephone subscribers in 2007, or 1,154·7 per 1,000 population. Mobile phone subscribers numbered 77,300 in 2007. There were 32,000 internet users (including 3,500 broadband subscribers) in 2007.

Postal Services
In 2003 there were five post offices. The central post office is in Victoria.

SOCIAL INSTITUTIONS

Justice
The death penalty was abolished for all crimes in 1993. The population in penal institutions in 2007 was 221 (270 per 100,000 of national population).

Education
Adult literacy was 91·9% in 2003 (91·4% among males and 92·3% among females). Education is free from five to 12 years in primary

schools, and 13 to 17 in secondary schools. There are three private schools providing primary and secondary education and one dealing only with secondary learning. Education beyond 18 years of age is funded jointly by the government and parents. The University of Seychelles opened in Sept. 2009. In 2007 there were 8,864 pupils and 711 teaching staff in primary schools, 7,816 pupils and 588 teaching staff in secondary schools and (2003) 1,652 students and 193 teaching staff at polytechnic level.

Public expenditure on education came to 6·6% of GNI in 2006 or 12·6% of total government spending.

Health
In 2003 there were 107 doctors, 16 dentists and 422 nurses. In 2003 there were seven hospitals with 419 beds. The health service is free.

Welfare
Social security is provided for people of 63 years and over, for the disabled and for families needing financial assistance. There is also assistance via means testing for those medically unfit to work and for mothers who remain out of work for longer than their designated maternity leave. Orphanages are also subsidized by the government.

RELIGION

87% of the inhabitants are Roman Catholic, the remainder of the population being followers of other religions (mainly Anglicans, with some 7th Day Adventists, Bahais, Muslims, Hindus, Pentecostalists, Jehovah's Witnesses, Buddhists and followers of the Grace and Peace church).

CULTURE

World Heritage Sites
Entered on the UNESCO World Heritage List in 1982, the four coral islands of Aldabra Atoll protect a shallow lagoon. A heritage site since 1983, the Vallée de Mai Nature Reserve is a natural palm forest on the small island of Praslin.

Broadcasting
The Seychelles Broadcasting Corporation (SBC) is the public broadcasting service. It operates two radio stations; the AM station, which hosts most programmes in Creole with frequent use of English and French, and Paradise FM which broadcasts mostly in English. The BBC and Radio France International also transmit programmes locally. There is only one local TV station directed by the SBC. International channels can be reached through satellite and cable TV. TV colour is by PAL. 22,200 households were equipped with TV sets in 2006.

Cinema
There is one cinema, based in Victoria.

Press
In 2006 there was one daily newspaper (circulation of 3,000), as well as three weekly papers.

Tourism
Tourism is the main foreign exchange earner. Visitor numbers were a record 161,273 in 2007; spending in 2005 totalled US$192m. Tourism accounts for 23% of GDP.

Festivals
There are numerous religious festivals including Kavadi, an annual procession organized by the Hindu Association of Seychelles. Secular festivals include the annual Youth Festival, Jazz Festival, Creole Festival, Kite Festival and the Subios Festival, a celebration of the underwater world.

Libraries
There is a national library in Victoria with branches on Praslin and La Digue Islands. It also provides a mobile service, and there are libraries in all educational institutions.

Theatre and Opera
There are three national theatres, all located on Mahé. The Mont Fleuri Theatre and the International Conference Centre serve central Mahé while the Anse Royale Theatre caters for the southern region of the island.

Museums and Galleries
There are four museums: the Historical Museum, the Natural History Museum, the National Heritage Museum and the Eco Musée, a museum of the country's economic activities. There is also a National Art Gallery, located in the National Library, and a number of smaller galleries exhibiting mostly local artists.

DIPLOMATIC REPRESENTATIVES

Of the Seychelles in the United Kingdom and to the European Union
High Commissioner: Claude Morel (resides in Paris).

Of the United Kingdom in the Seychelles (3rd Floor, Oliaji Trade Centre, Francis Rachel St., PO Box 161, Victoria, Mahé)
High Commissioner: Matthew Forbes.

Of the Seychelles in the USA and to the United Nations (800 2nd Ave., Suite 400C, New York, NY 10017)
Ambassador: Ronald Jean Jumeau.

Of the USA in the Seychelles
Ambassador: Vacant (resides in Port Louis, Mauritius)
Chargé d'Affaires a.i.: R. Barrie Walkley.

Of the Seychelles to the European Union
Ambassador: Barry Faure.

FURTHER READING

Scarr, D., *Seychelles Since 1970: History of a Slave and Post-Slavery Society.* 2000

National Statistical Office: Statistics and Database Administration Section (MISD), P. O. Box 206, Victoria, Mahé. *Seychelles in Figures*
Website: http://www.nsb.gov.sc

SIERRA LEONE

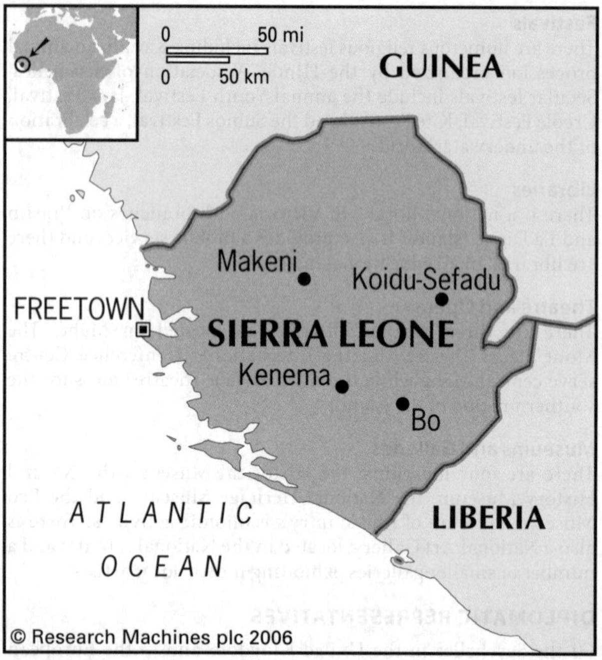

Republic of Sierra Leone

Capital: Freetown

Population estimate, 2010: 5·84m.

GDP per capita, 2007: (PPP$) 679

HDI/world rank: 0·365/180

KEY HISTORICAL EVENTS

The ancestors of the Bulom, Nalou, Baga and Krim people are thought to have been the earliest settlers in coastal Sierra Leone. The Kissi and Gola lived inland to the east and the Limba inhabited the foothills of the Wara Wara mountains from at least the 10th century AD. Following the break-up of the Malian empire in the late 14th century much of Sierra Leone was settled by the Mande whose domination and interaction with the original inhabitants gave rise to new ethnic groups, including the Vai and Loko.

The Portuguese mariner Alvaro Fernandez sailed into the Rokel estuary near present-day Freetown in 1447 and located a source of fresh water. The inlet became a trading post for Portuguese, Dutch, French and British explorers on their way to and from India. Having established plantations in America and the Caribbean, European colonists sought labour from the Atlantic slave trade, much of it centred on Sierra Leone. In 1672 British traders from the Royal African Company established trading forts along the coast, although they repeatedly came under attack from European rivals.

When Britain outlawed slavery in 1772 the government established Granville Town (later Freetown) as a home for freed slaves. In 1791 the Sierra Leone Company was founded as a trading concession, with Sierra Leone becoming a British crown colony in 1808. By 1850 more than 40,000 freed slaves, many of them from Nova Scotia and Jamaica, had settled in Freetown and surrounding areas, intermarrying with natives and Europeans to forge the 'Krio' culture. British administrators and Krio traders led expeditions inland in the late 19th century and on 21 Aug. 1896 the hinterland was declared a British protectorate, governed by Frederic Cardew. The early years of the 20th century saw the development of the country's interior while Lebanese merchants increasingly dominated business and trade.

Milton Margai became the prime minister in 1960 and led the country to independence on 27 April 1961. In 1967 Dr Siaka Stevens' All People's Congress (APC) came to power via the ballot box, despite an attempted military coup. Sierra Leone became a republic on 19 April 1971 with Stevens as executive president. Following a referendum in June 1978 a new constitution was instituted under which the ruling APC became the sole legal party.

On 28 Nov. 1985 Joseph Saidu Momoh succeeded Stevens as president. He presided over an economic collapse and the rise of the Revolutionary United Front (RUF). Under the leadership of Foday Sankoh (and with alleged links to the Liberian president, Charles Taylor), the RUF began taking control of diamond mines in the east of the country. President Momoh was overthrown in a military coup led by Valentine Strasser on 29 April 1992 and a National Provisional Ruling Council (NPRC) was set up, although it was unable to prevent the country's slide into civil war. By 1995 the RUF controlled much of the countryside and the NPRC sought assistance from foreign mercenaries.

The NPRC agreed to presidential and parliamentary elections in April 1996 to establish a civilian government. Ahmad Tejan Kabbah became president but was ousted in May 1997 by the Armed Forces Revolutionary Council, led by Maj. Johnny Paul Koroma. In Feb. 1998 a Nigerian-led intervention force (ECOMOG) launched an offensive against the military junta. On 10 March President Kabbah returned from exile in Guinea promising a 'new beginning' but in Jan. 1999 the country again erupted into civil war.

In July 1999 the government reached an agreement with the rebel movement to bring the civil war to an end. Under the terms of the accord, the RUF was to gain four key government posts along with control of the country's mineral resources in return for surrendering its weapons. However, civil war resumed in early 2000 and, responding to a government appeal, British forces were sent to back up the UN peacekeeping force (UNAMSIL). Foday Sankoh was captured and handed over to UN forces in May 2000. In July 2001 the RUF formally recognized the civil government of President Kabbah. In Jan. 2002 Kabbah declared the war over. Re-elected in May 2002, he has been at the forefront of reconstruction efforts although corruption remains an obstacle to progress. The last UN peacekeeping troops left Sierra Leone in Dec. 2005.

TERRITORY AND POPULATION

Sierra Leone is bounded on the northwest, north and northeast by Guinea, on the southeast by Liberia and on the southwest by the Atlantic Ocean. The area is 71,740 sq. km (27,699 sq. miles). Population (census 2004), 4,976,871; density, 69·4 per sq. km. In 2005, 59·3% of the population were rural.

The UN gives an estimated population for 2010 of 5·84m.

The capital is Freetown, with a 2004 census population of 772,873.

Sierra Leone is divided into three provinces and one area:

	Sq. km	*Census 2004*	*Capital*	*Census 2004*
Eastern Province	15,553	1,191,539	Kenema	128,402
Northern Province	35,936	1,745,553	Makeni	82,840
Southern Province	19,694	1,092,657	Bo	149,957
Western Area	557	947,122	Freetown	772,873

The provinces are divided into districts as follows: Bo, Bonthe, Moyamba, Pujehun (Southern Province); Kailahun, Kenema,

Kono (Eastern Province); Bombali, Kambia, Koinaduga, Port Loko, Toukolili (Northern Province).

The principal peoples are the Mendes (26% of the total) in the south, the Temnes (25%) in the north and centre, the Konos, Fulanis, Bulloms, Korankos, Limbas and Kissis. English is the official language; a Creole (Krio) is spoken.

SOCIAL STATISTICS

2000 estimates: births, 217,000; deaths, 103,000. Estimated birth rate in 2000 was 49·1 per 1,000 population; estimated death rate, 23·3. Annual population growth rate, 1992–2002, 1·5%. Expectation of life at birth in 2007 was 48·5 years for females and 46·0 years for males. The World Health Organization's *World Health Statistics 2009* ranked Sierra Leone in last place in a 'healthy life expectancy' list, with an expected 35 years of healthy life for babies born in 2007. Infant mortality was 165 per 1,000 live births in 2005 (the joint highest in the world with Afghanistan). Fertility rate, 2004, 6·5 births per woman.

CLIMATE

A tropical climate, with marked wet and dry seasons and high temperatures throughout the year. The rainy season lasts from about April to Nov., when humidity can be very high. Thunderstorms are common from April to June and in Sept. and Oct. Rainfall is particularly heavy in Freetown because of the effect of neighbouring relief. Freetown, Jan. 80°F (26·7°C), July 78°F (25·6°C). Annual rainfall 135" (3,434 mm).

CONSTITUTION AND GOVERNMENT

In a referendum in Sept. 1991 some 60% of the 2·5m. electorate voted for the introduction of a new constitution instituting multi-party democracy. The constitution has been amended several times since. The president, who is both head of state and head of government, is elected by popular vote for not more than two terms of five years. There is a 124-seat *National Assembly* (112 members elected by popular vote and 12 filled by paramount chiefs).

There is a *Supreme Council of State (SCS)*, and a *Council of State Secretaries.*

National Anthem

'High We Exalt Thee, Realm of the Free'; words by C. Nelson Fyle, tune by J. J. Akar.

RECENT ELECTIONS

Presidential and parliamentary elections were held on 11 Aug. 2007, with the presidential election having a second round on 8 Sept. 2007.

In the first round of presidential elections, Ernest Bai Koroma of the All People's Congress (APC) received 44·3% of the vote, Solomon Berewa of the ruling Sierra Leone People's Party (SLPP) 38·3%, Charles Margai of the People's Movement for Democratic Change (PMDC) 13·9%, Andrew Turay of the Convention People's Party (CPC) 1·6%, Amadu Jalloh of the National Democratic Alliance (NDA) 1·0%, Kandeh Baba Conteh of the Peace and Liberation Party (PLP) 0·6% and Abdul Kady Karim of the United National People's Party (UNPP) 0·4%. As no candidate received the 55% required to win outright a run-off was held, which Ernest Bai Koroma won with 54·6% of votes cast against 45·4% for Solomon Berewa. Turnout was 75·8% in the first round and 68·1% in the run-off.

In the parliamentary elections the opposition APC won 59 of 124 seats with 41·7% of votes cast, the SLPP 43 (39·5%) and the PMDC 10 (15·4%), with five smaller parties failing to win any seats; 12 seats are reserved for traditional chiefs.

CURRENT ADMINISTRATION

President: Ernest Bai Koroma; b. 1953 (APC; sworn in 17 Sept. 2007).

Vice-President: Samuel Sam-Sumana.

In March 2010 the government comprised:

Minister of Agriculture, Food Security and Forestry: Sam Sesay. *Defence:* Paulo Conteh. *Education, Youth and Sports:* Minkailu Bah. *Employment and Social Security:* Minkailu Mansaray. *Energy and Water Resources:* Ogunlade Davidson. *Finance and Development:* Samura Kamara. *Foreign Affairs:* Zainab Hawa Bangura. *Health and Sanitation:* Vacant. *Information and Communications:* Alhaji Ibrahim Ben Kargbo. *Internal Affairs, Local Government and Rural Development:* Dauda Sulaiman Kamara. *Justice and Attorney-General:* Abdul Serry Kamal. *Lands, Country Planning and Environment:* Dr Dennis Sandi. *Marine Resources and Fisheries:* Haja Afsatu Kabba. *Mineral Resources:* Alhaji Alpha Saahid Bakarr Kanu. *Presidential and Public Affairs:* Joseph Koroma. *Social Welfare, Gender and Children's Affairs:* Soccoh Kabia. *Tourism and Cultural Affairs:* Hindolo Trye. *Trade and Industry:* David Carew. *Transport and Aviation:* Allieu Pat Sowe. *Works, Housing and Infrastructural Development:* Alimamy Koroma.

Government Website:
http://www.sierra-leone.org/government.html

CURRENT LEADERS

Ernest Bai Koroma

Position
President

Introduction
Ernest Bai Koroma became president in Sept. 2007 following victory in the second round of elections. He had previously run unsuccessfully for the presidency in 2002.

Early Life
Koroma was born in 1953 in Bombali, northern Sierra Leone. Though the region is predominantly Muslim, Koroma is a Christian. He attended the local church primary school before going to secondary school in Tonkilili. In 1976 he graduated from Fourah Bay College, part of the University of Sierra Leone, in Freetown. He worked as a teacher before joining the National Insurance Company in 1978. In 1985 Koroma moved to the Reliance Insurance Trust Corporation (Ritcorps), becoming managing director in 1988 and holding the post for 14 years.

A latecomer to politics, Koroma was chosen as the APC's presidential candidate in March 2002 but was beaten into second place by Ahmad Tejan Kabbah of the Sierra Leone People's Party (SLPP). Under Koroma's leadership the APC grew in popularity and won a landslide victory in the 2004 local government elections, winning almost all seats in the densely-populated Western Area (which includes Freetown). In June 2005 Koroma was briefly stripped of his party leadership after the Supreme Court found him guilty of illegally altering his party's constitution. However, he was unanimously re-elected leader in Sept. 2005. Having spent most of his life in Freetown, his support base was strongest in the north though he also made in-roads in the south ahead of the 2007 presidential election. In a run-off in Sept. 2007 Koroma won against Solomon Berewa and was sworn in on 17 Sept.

Career in Office
Koroma took over an almost bankrupt country, at the time ranked 177th and last out of 177 in the Human Development Index world rankings. He has had to maintain the peace process that followed ten years of civil war which ended in 2001, and must handle the fallout from the trial in The Hague of former Liberian leader Charles Taylor, accused of war crimes relating to Sierra Leone's civil war. The day after his inauguration, Koroma visited neighbouring Guinea and Liberia, which subsequently granted citizenship to 2,600 Sierra Leonean refugees.

Key challenges facing Koroma's presidency included promoting economic development and rejuvenating energy and public services. He pledged a zero tolerance approach to corruption and in Nov. 2007 his government published a report detailing inadequacies in tax collection, health care and security services, as well as suspect loans.

Also in Nov. 2007 Koroma signed a commercial investment deal to double the country's rutile (titanium ore) production capacity and secured China's cancellation of US$22m. worth of debt.

DEFENCE

In 2006 military expenditure totalled US$24m. (US$4 per capita), representing 1·7% of GDP.

The UN peacekeeping force (UNAMSIL) left Sierra Leone in Dec. 2005 after monitoring the ceasefire for six years. It was replaced in Jan. 2006 by the United Nations Integrated Office (UNIOSIL), and this in turn was replaced by the United Nations Integrated Peacebuilding Office in Sierra Leone (UNIPSIL) in Aug. 2008. UNIPSIL was appointed to help support the continuing peace process; its current mandate runs until 30 Sept. 2010.

Army

Following the civil war, the Army has disbanded and a new National Army has been formed with a strength of 10,500.

Navy

Based in Freetown there is a small naval force of around 200 operating four patrol and coastal combatants.

INTERNATIONAL RELATIONS

Sierra Leone is a member of the UN, World Bank, IMF and several other UN specialized agencies, WTO, Commonwealth, IOM, Islamic Development Bank, OIC, African Development Bank, African Union, ECOWAS and is an ACP member state of the ACP-EU relationship.

ECONOMY

Agriculture accounted for 47·4% of GDP in 2006 (one of the highest percentages of any country), industry 25·5% and services 27·1%.

Overview

The economy has made substantial progress since the civil war ended in the early 2000s. Real GDP grew 7·3% in 2005 and 7·4% in 2006, aided by remittances and investments from citizens working abroad. Agriculture, mining, construction and the services sectors make up the bulk of the economy. External assistance and foreign aid have helped finance the current account deficit, presently standing at 3·8% of GDP. Programmes such as the Poverty Reduction and Growth Facility (2001–04) have improved public finance management. Inflation fell to 9·5% in 2006 from a level of above 14% two years earlier, reflecting a tight fiscal stance.

Growth is expected to remain strong in the medium-term following refurbishment investments in rutile and bauxite mining operations, growth in the services sector and a projected increase in gold exports. However, social indicators remain poor, with the economy ranked 180th out of 182 countries in the UNDP Human Development Index. Poverty is rife, particularly in rural areas.

Currency

The unit of currency is the *leone* (SLL) of 100 *cents*. Inflation was 14·8% in 2008. Exchange controls were liberalized in 1993. Total money supply in July 2005 was 346,027m. leones and foreign exchange reserves were US$94m.

Budget

In 2007 total revenue was 1,179bn. leones (42·7% grants and 21·8% import duties) and total expenditure 1,222bn. leones (63·4% current expenditures).

Performance

GNP per capita was US$183 in 2000 compared to US$536 in 1984, although it has since risen back up to US$322 in 2007. There was positive growth in 2000 for the first time since 1994, with a rate of 3·8%, rising to 18·2% in 2001 and further to 27·4% in 2002. Real GDP growth was 5·5% in 2008. Total GDP in 2008 was US$2·0bn. Sierra Leone is among the world's bottom five countries in income and life expectancy.

Banking and Finance

The bank of issue is the Bank of Sierra Leone which was established 1964 (*Governor*, Sheku Sambadeen Sesay). There are four commercial banks (two foreign).

ENERGY AND NATURAL RESOURCES

Environment

Carbon dioxide emissions from the consumption and flaring of fossil fuels in 2008 were the equivalent of 0·2 tonnes per capita. An *Environmental Performance Index* compiled in 2008 ranked Sierra Leone 147th in the world out of 149 countries analysed, with 40·0%. The index examined various factors in six areas—air pollution, biodiversity and habitat, climate change, environmental health, productive natural resources and water resources.

Electricity

Installed capacity was 0·1m. kW in 2004. Production in 2004 was around 85m. kWh; consumption per capita in 2004 was an estimated 15 kWh.

Minerals

The chief minerals mined are diamonds (estimated at 692,000 carats in 2005) and rutile (73,600 tonnes in 2006). There are also deposits of gold, iron ore and bauxite. The presence of rich diamond deposits partly explains the close interest of neighbouring countries in the politics of Sierra Leone.

Agriculture

In 2007 the agricultural population was an estimated 3·34m., of which approximately 1·26m. were economically active. Cattle production is important in the north. Production (2003 estimates, in 1,000 tonnes): cassava, 377; rice, 250; palm oil, 36; bananas and plantains, 30; sweet potatoes, 25; sugarcane, 24. In 2007 there were an estimated 900,000 ha. of arable land and 80,000 ha. of permanent crops.

Livestock (2003 estimates): cattle, 400,000; sheep, 375,000; goats, 220,000; pigs, 52,000; chickens, 8m.

Forestry

In 2005 forests covered 2,754,000 ha., or 38·5% of the total land area. Timber production in 2007 was 5·60m. cu. metres.

Fisheries

In 2005, 145,993 tonnes of fish were caught, of which marine fish 90% and freshwater fish 10%.

INDUSTRY

There are palm oil and rice mills; sawn timber, joinery products and furniture are produced.

Labour

The workforce was 1,610,000 in 1996 (64% males). In 1995 around two-thirds of the economically active population were engaged in agriculture, fisheries and forestry. 14,800 persons were registered unemployed in 1992.

INTERNATIONAL TRADE

Foreign debt was US$1,682m. in 2005.

Imports and Exports

Total trade for 2006: imports, US$351·2m.; exports, US$272·9m. Main exports are bauxite, diamonds, gold, coffee and cocoa. A

UN-mandated diamond export certification scheme is in force. The Security Council has commended Sierra Leone's government for its efforts in monitoring trade to prevent diamonds from becoming a future source of conflict. The main import suppliers in 2001 were the UK (25·3%), Netherlands (10·1%), USA (7·9%), Germany (6·3%). Principal export markets in 2001 were Belgium (40·6%), USA (9·1%), UK (8·5%), Germany (7·8%).

COMMUNICATIONS

Roads

There were 11,300 km of roads in 2007 (8% paved). Much of the damage to the road network as a result of the civil war has now been repaired. In 2007 there were 16,400 passenger cars in use and 14,100 vans and lorries. There were 71 deaths as a result of road accidents in 2007.

Civil Aviation

Freetown Airport (Lungi) is the international airport. In 2003 Sierra National Airlines flew to Banjul and London. Other international carriers operated flights to Abidjan, Accra, Brussels, Conakry, Dakar, Lagos and Monrovia. In 2003 scheduled airline traffic of Sierra Leone-based carriers flew 1m. km, carrying 14,000 passengers (all on international flights).

Shipping

The port of Freetown has one of the largest natural harbours in the world. Iron ore is exported through Pepel, and there is a small port at Bonthe. In 2002 the merchant fleet totalled 23,000 GRT. 2·31m. tonnes of cargo were loaded in 1993 and 0·59m. tonnes discharged.

Telecommunications

In 2008 Sierra Leone had 31,500 main (fixed) telephone lines. The country's telecommunications network was virtually destroyed during the civil war, but since then the sector has been one of Sierra Leone's main successes. The country's largest mobile phone operator is Zain, with a 46% share of the market. In 2007 internet users numbered 13,000. There were 1,009,000 mobile phone subscribers in 2008, up from 67,000 in 2002.

Postal Services

In 2002 there were 45 post offices.

SOCIAL INSTITUTIONS

Justice

The High Court has jurisdiction in civil and criminal matters. Subordinate courts are held by magistrates in the various districts. Native Courts, headed by court Chairmen, apply native law and custom under a criminal and civil jurisdiction. Appeals from the decisions of magistrates' courts are heard by the High Court. Appeals from the decisions of the High Court are heard by the Sierra Leone Court of Appeal. Appeal lies from the Sierra Leone Court of Appeal to the Supreme Court, which is the highest court.

The death penalty is in force, and was last used when 24 soldiers were executed on 19 Oct. 1998 for their part in the May 1997 coup.

Education

The adult literacy rate in 2003 was 29·6% (39·8% among males and 20·5% among females). Primary education is partially free but not compulsory. In 2004–05 there were 4,295 primary schools with 1,286,074 pupils and 19,316 teachers, and 282 secondary schools with 198,827 pupils and 6,622 teachers. There were also 196 technical/vocational establishments with 18,686 pupils and 918 staff. As a result of the 2005 Universities Act there are now two universities. The University of Sierra Leone comprises Fourah Bay College, the College of Medicine and Allied Health Sciences, and the Institute of Public Administration and Management. Njala University, until 2005 a constituent college of the University of Sierra Leone, is now an autonomous institution.

In 2005 public expenditure on education came to 3·9% of GNI.

Health

In 2000 there were 145 general practitioners, 1,331 nurses and five dentists. In 2000 there were 64 hospitals with 692 beds.

RELIGION

There were 2·49m. Muslims in 2001 (just under half the population). Traditional animist beliefs persist; there is also a Christian minority.

CULTURE

Broadcasting

The government-controlled Sierra Leone Broadcasting Service operates a limited terrestrial television service and two radio services. ABC TV is a private television station. There are several private radio stations, mainly in Freetown; the United Nations Mission in Sierra Leone also operates a radio network. There were 63,000 TV sets (colour by PAL) in 2003.

Press

In 2006 there were ten paid-for dailies with an average circulation of 22,000, plus 31 non-dailies. For di People, the oldest independent newspaper, had the highest circulation in 2006 (5,000).

Tourism

Tourism is in the initial stages of development. In 2004 there were 44,000 foreign tourists, bringing revenue of US$58m.

DIPLOMATIC REPRESENTATIVES

Of Sierra Leone in the United Kingdom (41 Eagle St., Holborn, London, WC1R 4TL)
High Commissioner: Melvin Humpah Chalobah.

Of the United Kingdom in Sierra Leone (6 Spur Rd, Freetown)
High Commissioner: Ian Hughes.

Of Sierra Leone in the USA (1701 19th St., NW, Washington, D.C., 20009)
Ambassador: Bockari Kortu Stevens.

Of the USA in Sierra Leone (Corner Walpole and Siaka Stevens St., Freetown)
Ambassador: June C. Perry.

Of Sierra Leone to the United Nations
Ambassador: Shekou Touray.

Of Sierra Leone to the European Union
Ambassador: Christian Sheka Kargbo.

FURTHER READING

Abdullah, Ibrahim, (ed.) *Between Democracy and Terror: The Sierra Leone Civil War.* 2004

Conteh-Morgan, E. and Dixon-Fyle, M., *Sierra Leone at the End of the Twentieth Century: History, Politics, and Society.* 1999

Ferme, M., *The Underneath of Things: Violence, History, and the Everyday in Sierra Leone.* 2001

National Statistical Office: Statistics Sierra Leone, A. J. Momoh Street, Tower Hill, P.M.B. 595, Freetown.
Website: http://www.statistics.sl

SINGAPORE

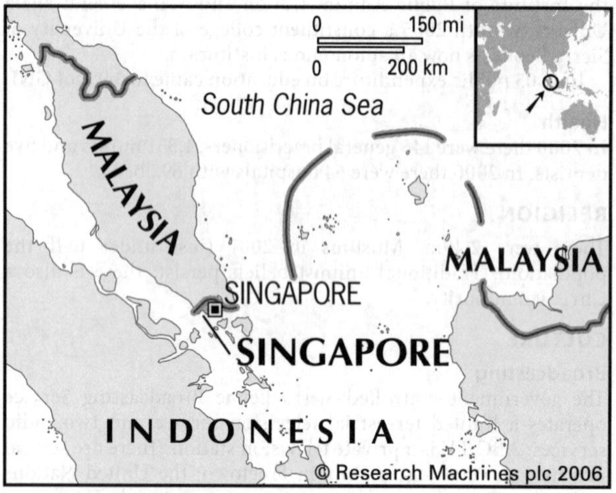

Republik Singapura
(Republic of Singapore)

Population estimate, 2010: 4·84m.
GDP per capita, 2007: (PPP$) 49,704
HDI/world rank: 0·944/23

KEY HISTORICAL EVENTS

The first known written account of the island of Singapore was by a Chinese explorer in the 3rd century AD. In a strategic location at the tip of the Malay peninsula, the island is likely to have been a port of call for sailors navigating the Melaka straits, although there is no evidence of settlement until the town of Temasek was described in the 13th century. Temasek was controlled by the Srivijaya Empire, centred on Palembang in Sumatra, during the 14th century, before falling to the Javanese Majapahit Empire. When Sultan Iksander Shah founded the Melaka Sultanate in the 1390s, he established a trading post on Singapore Island. After Portuguese forces sacked Melaka in 1511 the island came under the influence of the newly-created Johor Sultanate. In 1613 Singapore's main settlement was burnt down by Portuguese raiders and the island slipped into obscurity, with the ports of Melaka and Johor dominating the lucrative shipping routes that linked Europe and India with China and the East Indies.

In 1819 Sir Thomas Stamford Raffles, an administrator of the British East India Company based at the garrison of Bencoolen (Benkulu) in southwest Sumatra, established a trading settlement on Singapore Island to challenge Dutch supremacy of the region's ports. Raffles negotiated a deal with the ruling Sultan of Johor and left Col. William Farquhar in charge of the new settlement which was designated a free port. It grew rapidly, attracting Chinese, Malay, Bugis and Arab merchants who wanted to avoid the trade restrictions imposed at Dutch-controlled ports. In Aug. 1824 claims to Singapore by Britain and the East India Company were confirmed in treaties with the Dutch government and the Sultanate of Johor. Two years later Penang, Melaka and Singapore were combined as the Straits Settlements. With the opening of the Suez Canal in 1869 and the advent of ocean-going steamships, an era of prosperity began for Singapore. Growth was fuelled by the export of tin and rubber from the Malay peninsula, facilitated by the construction of a railway linking Singapore with Bangkok.

On 15 Feb. 1942, after capturing Malaya from the British in less than two months, Singapore was occupied by Japanese troops. Britain's return after Japan's surrender in 1945 was accompanied by growing nationalist sentiment. Britain formed the Federation of Malaya, administered by a high commissioner in Kuala Lumpur, and a separate Crown Colony of Singapore with a civil administration. Elections in both states in March 1948 were followed by outbreaks of anti-British violence, with the ethnic Chinese-dominated Malayan Communist Party demanding immediate independence and equality for all races. The British responded to 'the Emergency' by imposing hard-line restrictions on left-wing groups. Nevertheless, there was a gradual move towards self-government in Singapore in the 1950s and in June 1959, following the victory of the People's Action Party in the first legislative elections, Lee Kuan Yew became Singapore's first prime minister.

Singapore joined the Federation of Malaysia when it was formed in Sept. 1963 but tensions soon rose and in Aug. 1965 the Malaysian prime minister, Tunku Abdul Rahman, expelled Singapore from the Federation. It became an independent republic, which, under the authoritarian leadership of Lee Kuan Yew, saw rapid and sustained export-driven growth. Lee's resignation in Nov. 1990 saw Goh Chok Tong become prime minister. He served until Aug. 2004, when Lee Hsien Loong succeeded him.

TERRITORY AND POPULATION

The Republic of Singapore consists of Singapore Island and some 63 smaller islands. Singapore Island is situated off the southern extremity of the Malay peninsula, to which it is joined by a 1·1 km causeway carrying a road, railway and water pipeline across the Strait of Johor and by a 1·9 km bridge at Tuas, opened on 2 Jan. 1998. The Straits of Johor between the island and the mainland are 914 metres wide. The island is 682·3 sq. km in area, including the offshore islands.

Census of population (2000): Chinese residents 2,505,379 (76·8%), Malays 453,633 (13·9%), Indians 257,791 (7·9%) and others 46,406 (1·4%); resident population, 3,263,209. Total population in June 2008 was 4,839,400. The population is 100% urban. Population density, 7,093 per sq. km.

The UN gives an estimated resident population for 2010 of 4·84m.

Malay, Chinese (Mandarin), Tamil and English are the official languages; Malay is the national language and English is the language of administration.

SOCIAL STATISTICS

2008 births, 39,826; deaths, 17,222. Birth rate per 1,000 population, 2008, 10·2; death rate, 4·4. Annual population growth rate, 2000–05, 1·5%; infant mortality, 2005, 2 per 1,000 live births (one of the lowest in the world); life expectancy, 2007, 77·8 years for males and 82·6 years for females. Fertility rate, 2004, 1·3 births per woman. In 2003 the mean age of bridegrooms at first marriage was 30·2 years and of brides 27·2 years.

Source: Singapore Department of Statistics

CLIMATE

The climate is equatorial, with relatively uniform temperature, abundant rainfall and high humidity. Rain falls throughout the year but tends to be heaviest from Nov. to Jan. Average daily temperature is 26·8°C with a maximum daily average of 30·9°C and a minimum daily average of 23·9°C. Mean annual rainfall is 2,345 mm.

CONSTITUTION AND GOVERNMENT

Singapore is a republic with a parliamentary system of government. The organs of state—the executive, the legislature and the judiciary—are provided for by a written constitution. The Constitution is the supreme law of Singapore and any law enacted after the date of its commencement, which is inconsistent with its provisions, is void. The present constitution came into force on 3 June 1959 and was amended in 1965.

The Head of State is the *President*. The administration of the government is vested in the Cabinet headed by the *Prime Minister*. The Prime Minister and the other Cabinet Members are appointed by the President from among the Members of Parliament (MPs). The Cabinet is collectively responsible to Parliament.

Parliament is unicameral consisting of 84 elected members and one Non-Constituency MP (NCMP), elected by secret ballot from single-member and group representation constituencies as well as nine Nominated Members of Parliament (NMPs) who are appointed for a two-year term on the recommendation of a Special Select Committee of Parliament. With the customary exception of those serving criminal sentences, all citizens over 21 are eligible to vote. Voting in an election is compulsory. Group representation constituencies may return up to six Members of Parliament (four before 1996), one of whom must be from the Malay community, the Indian or other minority communities. To ensure representation of parties not in the government, provision is made for the appointment of three (or up to a maximum of six) NCMPs. The number of NCMPs is reduced by one for each opposition candidate returned. There is a common roll without communal electorates.

A Presidential Council to consider and report on minorities' rights was established in 1970. The particular function of this council is to draw attention to any Bill or to any subsidiary legislation which, in its opinion, discriminates against any racial or religious community.

Salaries for Singaporean politicians are the highest in the world. For 2009 the annual salary of the president was lowered to S$3,140,000 (US$2·2m.) and that of the prime minister to S$3,040,000 (US$2·1m.). Although this constitutes a 19% pay cut on the 2008 figure, Prime Minister Lee Hsien Loong's salary remains more than five times that of President Barack Obama.

National Anthem

'Majulah Singapura' ('Onward Singapore'); words and tune by Zubir Said.

GOVERNMENT CHRONOLOGY

Prime Ministers since 1959. (PAP = People's Action Party)

1959–90	PAP	Lee Kuan Yew
1990–2004	PAP	Goh Chok Tong
2004–	PAP	Lee Hsien Loong

RECENT ELECTIONS

In parliamentary elections held on 6 May 2006 the ruling People's Action Party (PAP) won 82 of 84 seats (with 66·6% of votes cast), including 37 seats won automatically before the election because the opposition did not contest them. The Workers' Party and the Singapore Democratic Alliance both took one seat each, with 16·3% and 13·0% of votes cast respectively.

Presidential elections were scheduled for 27 Aug. 2005. However, these were cancelled after the incumbent president S. R. Nathan emerged as the only candidate who satisfied the requirements of the certificate of eligibility. He thus gained the presidency unopposed.

CURRENT ADMINISTRATION

President: S. R. Nathan; b. 1924 (sworn in 1 Sept. 1999; re-elected unopposed in Aug. 2005).

In March 2010 the cabinet comprised:

Prime Minister: Lee Hsien Loong; b. 1952 (PAP; sworn in 12 Aug. 2004).

Senior Minister, Prime Minister's Office: Goh Chok Tong. *Senior Minister, Prime Minister's Office:* Prof. Shunmugam Jayakumar (*Co-ordinating Minister for National Security*). *Minister Mentor, Prime Minister's Office:* Lee Kuan Yew, GCMG, CH. *Deputy Prime Ministers:* Wong Kan Seng (*Minister for Home Affairs*); Teo Chee Hean (*Minister for Defence*).

Minister for Foreign Affairs: BG (NS) George Yong-Boon Yeo. *National Development:* Mah Bow Tan. *Trade and Industry:* Lim Hng Kiang. *Environment and Water Resources:* Dr Yaacob Ibrahim (also *in Charge of Muslim Affairs*). *Health:* Khaw Boon Wan. *Finance:* Tharman Shanmugaratnam. *Education:* Ng Eng Hen (also *Second Minister for Defence*). *Community Development, Youth and Sports:* Vivian Balakrishnan. *Transport:* Raymond Lim Siang Keat (also *Second Minister for Foreign Affairs*). *Law:* K. Shanmugam (also *Second Minister for Home Affairs*). *Manpower:* Gan Kim Yong. *Information, Communications and the Arts (acting):* Lui Tuck Yew. *Ministers in Prime Minister's Office:* Lim Boon Heng; Lim Swee Say; Lim Hwee Hua (also *Second Minister for Finance and Transport*).

Government Website: http://www.gov.sg

CURRENT LEADERS

Lee Hsien Loong

Position

Prime Minister

Introduction

When Lee Hsien Loong was sworn in as prime minister of Singapore on 12 Aug. 2004, it was only the second time the southeast Asian city-state had changed its leader since independence in the 1960s. His father, Lee Kuan Yew, was the country's charismatic leader for 31 years and oversaw a transformation from a third-world colony to a prosperous export-driven economy. Lee Hsien Loong, a former military strategist-turned-politician, pledged to sustain the vibrant economy while maintaining a cohesive society. In May 2006 his People's Action Party won parliamentary elections for the tenth successive time since independence.

Early Life

Lee Hsien Loong was born in Singapore on 10 Feb. 1952, the eldest son of a wealthy and well-connected Hakka-Chinese family. His father, Lee Kuan Yew, was Singapore's first prime minister, and led the former British colony as head of the People's Action Party (PAP) from its first period of self-governance in 1959, through independence in 1965, until 1990. Lee Hsien Loong attended state primary and secondary schools in Singapore, and was awarded a president's scholarship to study mathematics and computer science at Cambridge University in England. He graduated in 1974 with first class honours and returned to serve in the Singapore Armed Forces, rising through the ranks to become a Brig.-Gen. He gained a reputation for his analytical and problem-solving skills. He entered politics as an MP representing the PAP in the general election of Sept. 1984. The election was the first occasion since 1963 that two opposition parties—the Workers' Party and the Singapore Democratic Party—were able to win seats from the ruling PAP. Lee was elected to the Central Executive Committee of the PAP in 1986.

Lee Kuan Yew resigned in Nov. 1990 after 31 years in power and Goh Chok Tong became prime minister, appointing Lee Hsien Loong his deputy with responsibility for economic and civil service affairs. After three decades of authoritarian rule, Singapore underwent a cautious liberalization. Lee held his parliamentary seat in the 1991 and 1997 general elections, which were landslide victories for the PAP. In Jan. 1998 he was appointed chairman of the Monetary Authority of Singapore. When, in line with other southeast Asian economies, Singapore faced an economic downturn in 1998, the government responded by cutting wages, allowing its currency to adjust downward and positioning the country as a leading international financial centre. Despite continued economic pressures, the PAP won the 2001 general election by a large majority. Lee was re-elected, and was appointed minister of finance in Nov. 2001. He pursued a tax-cutting agenda and brought in pension reforms and policies to liberalize the financial sector.

Career in Office

On 12 Aug. 2004 Lee was sworn in as prime minister, handing the chairmanship of the Monetary Authority to Goh Chok Tong who became senior minister in the cabinet. Lee said his goal was to build a vibrant and competitive economy and he pledged to maintain the open, consultative style of the Goh Chok Tong era. He also signalled that social liberalization would continue, reflecting the demands of a highly-educated and increasingly less tractable population, as well as the government's realization that Singapore must move beyond manufacturing into 'knowledge-based' industries that depend more on individual creativity and entrepreneurship.

In April 2005 Lee announced his government's controversial decision to legalize gambling, paving the way for the building of two large casino resorts and perhaps hinting at a more permissive atmosphere within the country. Nevertheless, in 2007 parliament voted against a proposal to decriminalize sex between men, and international appeals for clemency failed to prevent the execution of two Nigerians for drug smuggling.

Singapore's usually fraught relations with neighbouring Malaysia improved in Jan. 2005 when the two countries settled a dispute over land reclamation work in their border waters.

In the first electoral test since his appointment in 2004, Lee's party won the May 2006 parliamentary elections overwhelmingly. In 2008 his government's budget included tax incentives to enhance business competition, but Singapore's export-led economy was one of the first in Asia to feel the impact of the global financial downturn. In Jan. 2009 the government announced a S$20·5bn. stimulus package to bolster the economy and by July the country was emerging from its deepest recession on record.

DEFENCE

Compulsory military service in peacetime for all male citizens and permanent residents was introduced in 1967. The period of service is 24 months. Reserve liability continues to age 50 for officers, 40 for other ranks. In 2006 the SAF (Singapore Armed Forces) comprised 312,500 Operationally Ready National Servicemen and an estimated 72,500 regulars and Full-Time National Servicemen.

An agreement with the USA in Nov. 1990 provided for an increase in US use of naval and air force facilities.

Singapore is a member of the Five Powers Defence Arrangement, with Australia, New Zealand, Malaysia and the UK.

In 2006 defence expenditure totalled US$6,321m. (US$1,407 per capita), representing 4·8% of GDP.

Army

Strength (2006) 50,000 (including 35,000 conscripts) plus 300,000 reserves. In addition there is a Civil Defence Force totalling 81,800 including 3,200 conscripts, 23,000 Operationally Ready National Servicemen and more than 54,000 civil defence volunteers.

Navy

The Republic of Singapore Navy comprises four commands: Fleet, Coastal Command (COSCOM), Naval Logistics Command and Training Command. The fleet includes four diesel submarines. The Navy numbers an estimated 9,000 personnel (1,800 conscripts, 2,200 regulars and 5,000 active reservists). There are two naval bases: Tuas Naval Base and Changi Naval Base, the first phase of which was completed in 2000 and replaces Brani Naval Base.

Air Force

The Republic of Singapore Air Force (RSAF) has fighter squadrons comprising the F16 Falcon and the F5S/F Tiger.

Personnel strength (2006) about 10,500 (3,000 conscripts). Equipment includes 111 combat capable aircraft and eight attack helicopters.

INTERNATIONAL RELATIONS

Singapore is a member of the UN, World Bank, IMF and several other UN specialized agencies, WTO, BIS, Commonwealth, Asian Development Bank, ASEAN and Colombo Plan.

ECONOMY

Services accounted for 72% of GDP in 2007 and industry 28%.

According to the anti-corruption organization *Transparency International*, Singapore ranked equal third in the world in a 2009 survey of the countries with the least corruption in business and government. It received 9·2 out of 10 in the annual index.

Overview

The Economist Intelligence Unit reports that Singapore has Asia's highest per capita GDP at purchasing power parity. It is credited with one of the least corrupt, most competitive and most open economies in the world. Manufacturing, particularly electronics, has been the country's main engine of growth. Industry is dominated by foreign multinationals and a few large domestic enterprises with government links. The economy's openness leaves it vulnerable to external demand shocks.

The government is seeking to shift the economy away from manufacturing, where other Asian countries are seen as rising competitors, into knowledge-driven industries. Singapore has become an important offshore banking centre. Liberal rules on stem cell research have helped attract foreign scientists in a bid to make the country a leading biomedical centre.

Economic growth averaged 8% between 2004 and 2007 but fell to 1·1% in 2008 as a result of the global financial crisis. After the economy contracted by 6·5% in the first half of 2009 the government announced a S$20·5bn. Resilience Package. Gains in the manufacturing sector, particularly the production of pharmaceutical ingredients, improved growth in the second half of 2009.

Currency

The unit of currency is the *Singapore dollar* (SGD) of 100 *cents*. It is managed against a basket of currencies of Singapore's main trading partners. In Aug. 2009 foreign exchange reserves totalled US$174,606m. and total money supply was S$89,258m.

Inflation rates (based on IMF statistics):

1999	*2000*	*2001*	*2002*	*2003*	*2004*	*2005*	*2006*	*2007*	*2008*
0·0%	1·3%	1·0%	–0·4%	0·5%	1·7%	0·5%	1·0%	2·1%	6·5%

Budget

The fiscal year begins on 1 April. In 2007 budgetary central government revenue totalled S$51,007m. (S$41,577m. in 2006) and expenditure S$33,875m. (S$31,446m. in 2006).

Principal sources of revenue in 2007 were: taxes on income, profits and capital gains, S$14,938m.; taxes on goods and services S$12,193m.; taxes on property, S$2,582m. Main items of expenditure by economic type in 2007: use of goods and services,

S$11,663m.; compensation of employees, S$8,575m.; social benefits, S$7,907m.

There is a Goods and Services Tax (GST) of 7%.

Performance

Real GDP growth rates (based on IMF statistics):

1999	2000	2001	2002	2003	2004	2005	2006	2007	2008
7·2%	10·1%	–2·4%	4·1%	3·8%	9·3%	7·3%	8·4%	7·8%	1·1%

Total GDP was US$181·9bn. in 2008. Singapore was ranked third in the Global Competitiveness Index in the World Economic Forum's *Global Competitiveness Report 2009–2010*.

Banking and Finance

The Monetary Authority of Singapore (*Chairman*, Goh Chok Tong) performs the functions of a central bank, except the issuing of currency which is the responsibility of the Board of the Commissioners of Currency.

The Development Bank of Singapore and the Post Office Savings Bank were merged in 1998 to become the largest bank in southeast Asia and one of the leading banks in Asia, with a customer base of more than 3·3m. and a total deposit base of about S$71bn. Together, their total asset value is approximately S$94·5bn.

In April 2004 there were 115 commercial banks in Singapore, of which five were local. There were 49 representative offices, 23 foreign banks with full licences, 37 with 'wholesale' licences and 50 with 'offshore' licences. The total assets/liabilities amounted to S$384,600m. in Dec. 2001. Total deposits of non-bank customers in Dec. 1999 amounted to S$174,454·1m. and advances including bills financing totalled S$147,185·5m. in 1999. There were 66 merchant banks as at 31 Dec. 1999.

The Singapore Exchange (SGX), a merger of the Stock Exchange of Singapore and the Singapore International Monetary Exchange, was officially launched on 1 Dec. 1999.

ENERGY AND NATURAL RESOURCES

Environment

Singapore's carbon dioxide emissions from the consumption and flaring of fossil fuels in 2008 were the equivalent of 34·6 tonnes per capita.

Electricity

In 1995 Singapore Power Pte. Ltd. took over from the Public Utilities Board the responsibility for the provision of electricity and gas. Electrical power is generated by five gas and oil-fired power stations, with a total generating capacity of 8,848m. kW (2003). Production (2004) 36,810m. kWh. Consumption per capita (2004) 8,682 kWh.

Oil and Gas

Replacing the Kallang Gasworks, the Senoko Gasworks started operations in Oct. 1996. It had a total gas production capacity of 1·6m. cu. metres per day. In Jan. 2001 a 640-km gas pipeline linking Indonesia's West Natuna field with Singapore came on stream. It is expected to provide Singapore with US$8bn. worth of natural gas over a 20-year period.

Water

Singapore uses an average of 1·25m. cu. metres of water per day. Singapore's water supply comes from local sources and sources in Johor, Malaysia. The total water supply system comprises 19 raw water reservoirs, nine treatment works, 15 storage or service reservoirs and 5,150 km of pipelines.

Agriculture

Only about 1·49% of the total area is used for farming. Local farms provide only about 35% of hen eggs, 1·6% of chickens and 2·4% of ducks. 18,928 tonnes of vegetables and fruits were produced for domestic consumption in 1999. In 2001 alone Singapore imported 44·1m. chickens, 7m. ducks, 722m. hen eggs, 210,077 tonnes of meat and meat products, 226,126 tonnes of fish and fish products, 352,919 tonnes of vegetables and 358,595 tonnes of fruits for local consumption.

Agro-technology parks house large-scale intensive farms to improve production of fresh food. As of the end of 2000, a total of 1,465 ha. of land in Murai, Sungei Tengah, Nee Soon, Loyang, Mandai and Lim Chu Kang had been developed into Agro-technology Parks. Through open tenders, auctions and direct allocations, 247 farms have been allocated 777 ha. of land for the production of livestock, eggs, milk, aquarium fish, food fish (fish for consumption), fruits, vegetables, orchids and ornamental and aquatic plants, as well as for the breeding of birds and dogs. When the Agro-technology Parks are fully developed, their output is expected to reach S$450m.

Forestry

In 2005 forests covered 2,000 ha., or 3·4% of the total land area.

Fisheries

The total catch in 2005 amounted to 1,920 tonnes. Singapore imported 528,000 tonnes of fish and fish products. There are 93 fish processing establishments supplying products for the domestic market, nine establishments for the EU export market and 88 licensed marine farms.

INDUSTRY

The leading companies by market capitalization in Singapore in March 2009 were: Singapore Telecommunications (US$26·5bn.); Wilmar International, the largest global palm oil processor and merchandiser (US$13·3bn.); and DBS Group Holdings, a banking group (US$12·7bn.).

The largest industrial area is at Jurong, with 35 modern industrial estates housing over 4,036 establishments (engaging ten people or more) in 1999, and 340,907 workers.

Production, 1999 (in S$1m.), totalled 134,533: including electronic products, 70,140·4; chemicals and chemical products, 13,684·1; petroleum, 13,621·6; fabricated metal products, 6,253·9; transport equipment, 5,772·8; food, beverages and tobacco, 3,407·2; publishing, printing and reproduction of recorded media, 2,997·0.

According to the World Bank's *Doing Business 2010* Singapore is the easiest country in which to do business.

Labour

In June 2004 Singapore's labour force comprised 2,183,300 people, of whom 2,066,900 were employed. The principal areas of employment in June 2004 were manufacturing (356,700 people), wholesale and retail trade (319,700), business services (254,000), transport, storage and communications (212,500) and hotels and restaurants (129,300). The unemployment rate averaged 3·4% throughout 2004 (4·0% in 2003). The average worker put in 46·3 hours a week in 2004; average monthly earnings in 2004 were S$3,329.

Legislation regulates the principal terms and conditions of employment such as hours of work, sick leave and other fringe benefits. Young people of 14–16 years may work in industrial establishments, and children of 12–14 years may be employed in approved apprenticeship schemes. A trade dispute may be referred to the Industrial Arbitration Court.

The Ministry of Manpower operates an employment service and provides clients with disabilities with specialized on-the-job training. The Central Provident Fund was established in 1955 to make provision for employees in their old age. At the end of 2004 there were 3,018,000 members with S$111,874m. standing to their credit in the fund. The legal retirement age is 62.

Source: Singapore Department of Statistics

Trade Unions

In 2001 there were 71 registered employee trade unions, three employer unions and one federation of trade unions—the National Trades Union Congress (NTUC). The total membership of the trade unions increased from 272,769 in 1998 to 338,311 in 2001. The vast majority (99%) of the total union membership belonged to the 69 NTUC-affiliated unions. The largest union, the United Workers of Electronic Industries (UWEEI), had 39,508 members in 2000.

INTERNATIONAL TRADE

Foreign investment of up to 40% of the equity of domestic banks is permitted.

Imports and Exports

Total imports were S$333,191m. in 2005; and total exports S$382,532m. in 2005. Exports in 2005 were worth 244% of GDP.

Imports and exports (in S$1m.), by country, 2005:

	Imports (c.i.f.)	*Exports (f.o.b.)*
Australia	4,850	14,045
China	34,170	32,909
Germany	9,915	10,504
Hong Kong	7,009	35,849
India	6,788	9,817
Indonesia	17,400	36,817
Japan	32,034	20,874
Korea, South	14,323	13,412
Malaysia	45,527	50,612
Saudi Arabia	14,894	708
Taiwan	19,720	14,938
Thailand	12,516	15,662
UK	6,554	10,525
USA	38,793	39,024

Main imports (2005, in S$1m.): machinery and equipment, 185,980; mineral fuels, 59,145; manufactured goods, 25,040; chemicals and chemical products, 20,744; food, 6,680; beverages and tobacco, 2,190; crude materials, 2,190; animal and vegetable oils, 479; miscellaneous manufactures, 26,526.

Main exports (2005, in S$1m.): machinery and transport equipment, 224,980; mineral fuels, 57,414; chemicals and chemical products, 43,611; manufactured goods, 17,498; food, 3,865; crude materials, 2,257; beverages and tobacco, 2,053; animal and vegetable oils, 422; miscellaneous manufactures, 26,049.

In May 2003 the USA and Singapore signed a free trade agreement removing tariffs on trade worth an estimated US$33bn. per annum.

Trade Fairs

Singapore ranked as the world's most important convention city in 2008 according to the Union des Associations Internationales (UAI). Singapore hosted 637 meetings recognized by UAI (5·8% of all meetings).

COMMUNICATIONS

Roads

In 2007 there were 3,297 km of public roads (100% asphalt-paved). Singapore has one of the densest road networks in the world. In 2007 there were 517,000 passenger cars, 14,500 buses and coaches, 151,000 vans and lorries, and 144,300 motorcycles and scooters.

Singapore was the top ranked nation for road infrastructure in the World Economic Forum's *Global Competitiveness Report 2009–2010*.

Rail

A 25·8-km main line runs through Singapore, connecting with the States of Malaysia and as far as Bangkok. Branch lines serve the port of Singapore and the industrial estates at Jurong. The total rail length of the Mass Rapid Transit (SMRT) metro is 89·4 km. The 20 km North-East Line (operated by SBS Transit), the world's first fully automated heavy metro, became operational in 2003. In late 1999 the Light Rapid Transit System (LRT) began operations, linking the Bukit Panjang Estate with Choa Chu Kang in the North West region.

Civil Aviation

As of Dec. 2001 Singapore Changi Airport was served by 61 airlines with more than 3,200 weekly flights to and from 138 cities in 50 countries. A total of 28,093,759 passengers were handled in 2001, and 1,507,062 tonnes of freight. The national airline is Singapore Airlines; its subsidiary, Silk Air, serves Asian destinations. In 2005 scheduled airline traffic of Singapore-based carriers flew 434·9m. km and carried 21,323,100 passengers.

In the World Economic Forum's *Global Competitiveness Report 2009–2010* Singapore ranked first for quality of air transport infrastructure.

Shipping

Singapore has a large container port, the world's busiest in terms of containers handled in 2006 and second only to Shanghai in terms of shipping tonnage. The economy is dependent on shipping and entrepôt trade. A total of 146,265 vessels of 960m. gross tonnes (GT) entered Singapore during 2001. In 2001, 3,353 vessels with a total of 23·2m. GT were registered in Singapore. The Singapore merchant fleet ranked 7th among the principal merchant fleets of the world in 2001. Total cargo handled in 2006 was 448·5m. freight tons, and total container throughput in 2006 was 24,792,000 TEUs (twenty-foot equivalent units).

Singapore was ranked first in the World Economic Forum's *Global Competitiveness Report 2009–2010* for the quality of its port facilities.

Telecommunications

In 2008 there were 1,857,000 main (fixed) telephone lines. In the same year mobile phone subscribers numbered 6,376,000 (1,381·5 per 1,000 persons). In 1997 Singapore Telecom, one of the largest companies in Asia, lost its monopoly with the entry of a new mobile phone operator. In 2007 Singapore had three mobile phone operators—SingTel Mobile (owned by Singapore Telecom), M1 and StarHub Mobile. In 2008 there were 3·4m. internet users. There were 19·9 broadband subscribers per 100 inhabitants in June 2007. The Telecommunication Authority of Singapore (TAS) is the national regulator and promoter of the telecommunication and postal industries.

Postal Services

In 1999 there were various postal outlets in operation, comprising 62 main branches and 90 smaller branches. Various services included stamp vendors, postage label vending machines and Self-Service Automated Machines (SAM). A total of 1,487m. postal articles were handled in 1999. During the late 1990s mail volume increased by about 30m. items per year.

SOCIAL INSTITUTIONS

Justice

There is a Supreme Court in Singapore which consists of the High Court and the Court of Appeal. The Supreme Court is composed of a Chief Justice and 11 Judges. The High Court has unlimited original jurisdiction in both civil and criminal cases. The Court of Appeal is the final appellate court. It hears appeals from any judgement or order of the High Court in any civil matter. The Subordinate Courts consist of a total of 47 District and Magistrates' Courts, the Civil, the Family and Crime Registries, the Primary Dispute Resolution Centre, and the Small Claims Tribunal. The right of appeal to the UK Privy Council was abolished in 1994.

Penalties for drug trafficking and abuse are severe, including a mandatory death penalty. In 1994 there were 76 executions, although since then the average annual number has generally been declining—there was just one confirmed execution in 2009.

The Technology Court was introduced in 1995 where documents were filed electronically. This process was implemented in Aug. 1998 in the Magistrates appeal and the Court of Appeal.

The average population in penal institutions in 2007 was 11,768 (267 per 100,000 of national population).

Education

The general literacy rate rose from 84% in 1980 to 92·5% in 2003 (male 96·6%; female 88·6%). Kindergartens are private and fee-paying. Compulsory primary state education starts at six years and culminates at 11 or 12 years with an examination which influences choice of secondary schooling. There are 17 autonomous and eight private fee-paying secondary schools. Tertiary education at 16 years is divided into three branches: junior colleges leading to university; four polytechnics; and ten technical institutes.

In 2007 there were 301,101 pupils with 14,743 teaching staff in primary schools, 232,100 pupils with 13,686 teaching staff in secondary schools and 183,627 students with 14,209 academic staff in tertiary education.

There are three universities: the National University of Singapore (established 1905) with 32,028 students in 2001–02, the Nanyang Technological University (established 1991) with 23,025 in 2001–02, and the Singapore Management University (established in 2000).

In 2001 public expenditure on education came to 3·1% of GNI and accounted for 23·6% of total government expenditure in 2000–01.

Health

There are 27 hospitals (five general hospitals, one community hospital, seven specialist hospitals/centres and 14 private), with 11,897 beds in 2001. In 2001 there were 5,747 doctors, 1,087 dentists, 17,398 registered nurses and midwives and 1,141 pharmacists.

The leading causes of death are cancer (4,238 deaths in 2000), heart disease (3,940) and pneumonia (1,794).

Welfare

The Central Provident Fund (CPF) was set up in 1955 to provide financial security for workers upon retirement or when they are no longer able to work. In 2001 there were 2,922,673 members with S$92,221m. standing to their credit in the Fund.

RELIGION

In 2001, 41·0% of the population were Buddhists and Taoists, 12·0% Muslims, 11·7% Christians and 3·2% Hindus; 0·5% belonged to other religions.

CULTURE

The National Arts Council (NAC) was established in 1991 to spearhead the development of the arts.

Broadcasting

The Media Development Authority of Singapore is the state broadcasting authority. MediaCorp (formerly the Television Corporation of Singapore), which is owned by a state investment company, is the dominant operator of television and radio stations, broadcasting in English, Chinese, Malay and Tamil. Colour is by PAL. Most householders also have access to cable TV services. Singapore is a regional pioneer of high-definition and mobile TV services. In 2006 there were 1·38m. TV sets and cable subscribers numbered 491,000.

Cinema

In 2008 there were 177 cinema screens. The total number of admissions was 15·6m. in 2006. Ten feature films were produced in 2006.

Press

In 2001 there were ten daily newspapers, in four languages, with a total daily circulation of about 1·59m. copies. In 2000 a new newspaper, *Project Eyeball*, and two free commuter tabloids, *Streats* and *Today*, were launched. *Project Eyeball* was suspended in June 2001.

Tourism

There were 10·3m. visitors in 2007. Most came from Indonesia, China, Australia, India, Malaysia, Japan, the UK and South Korea. The total tourism receipts for 2007 came to S$14·1bn. There were 98 gazetted hotels in 2007, providing 30,087 rooms.

Festivals

Every Jan. or Feb. the Lunar New Year is celebrated. Other Chinese festivals include Qing Ming (a time for the remembrance of ancestors), Yu Lan Jie (Feast of the Hungry Ghosts) and the Mid-Autumn Festival (Mooncake or Lantern festival).

Muslims in Singapore celebrate Hari Raya Puasa (to celebrate the end of a month-long fast) and Hari Raya Haji (a day of prayer and commemoration of the annual Mecca pilgrimage). There are also Muharram (a New Year celebration) and Maulud (Prophet Muhammad's birthday).

Hindus celebrate the Tamil New Year in mid-April. Thaipusam is a penitential Hindu festival popular with Tamils; and Diwali, the Festival of Lights, is celebrated by Hindus and Sikhs. Other festivals include Thimithi (a fire-walking ceremony) and Navarathiri (nine nights' prayer).

Buddhists observe Vesak Day, which commemorates the birth, enlightenment and Nirvana of the Buddha, and falls on the full moon day in May.

Christmas, Good Friday and Easter Sunday are also recognized.

Libraries

The National Library Board (NLB) was inaugurated on 3 July 1996, having become a statutory board in Sept. 1995. The Board's main aim is to implement the recommendations set down in the Library 2000 Report on how libraries can meet the needs of the 21st century.

In June 2003 the NLB had a national library, two regional libraries, 20 community libraries and 33 community children's libraries. In the 2002 financial year NLB's membership numbered 2,116,472; there were 32,105,184 loans; its collections included 4·30m. books (excluding serials) in English, 1·78m. in Chinese, 0·57m. in Malay and 0·22m. in Tamil.

Theatre and Opera

Some of the main theatre companies in Singapore, performing mainly in English, include TheatreWorks, The Necessary Stage and the Singapore Repertory Theatre. Other language companies include Teater Kami (Malay), The Theatre Practice (Chinese) and Ravindran Drama Group (Tamil).

Museums and Galleries

The National Heritage Board was formed on 1 Aug. 1993 through the amalgamation of the National Archives, the National Museum and the Oral History Department. The Board's National Museum arm comprises the Singapore History Museum, the Singapore Art Museum, the Asian Civilisations Museum and the Singapore Philatelic Museum.

DIPLOMATIC REPRESENTATIVES

Of Singapore in the United Kingdom (9 Wilton Cres., London, SW1X 8SP)
High Commissioner: Michael Eng Cheng Teo.

Of the United Kingdom in Singapore (100 Tanglin Rd, Singapore 247919)
High Commissioner: Paul Madden.

Of Singapore in the USA (3501 International Pl., NW, Washington, D.C., 20008)
Ambassador: Chan Heng Chee.

Of the USA in Singapore (27 Napier Rd, Singapore 258508)
Ambassador: Vacant.
Chargé d'Affaires a.i.: Daniel L. Shields III.

Of Singapore to the United Nations
Ambassador: Vanu Gopala Menon.

Of Singapore to the European Union
Ambassador: Anil Kumar Nayar.

FURTHER READING

Department of Statistics. *Monthly Digest of Statistics.—Yearbook of Statistics.*
The Constitution of Singapore. 1992
Information Division, Ministry of Information and the Arts. *Singapore [year]*: a Review of [*the previous year*].
Ministry of Trade and Industry, *Economic Survey of Singapore.* (Quarterly and Annual)

Chee-Kiong, T., *The Making of Singapore Sociology: State and Society.* 2002
Chew, E. C. T., *A History of Singapore.* 1992
Huff, W. G., *Economic Growth of Singapore: Trade and Development in the Twentieth Century.* 1994
Myint, S., *The Principles of Singapore Law.* 4th ed. 2001
Tan, C. H., *Financial Markets and Institutions in Singapore.* 11th ed. 2005
Vasil, R. K., *Governing Singapore.* 1992

National library: National Library, 91 Stamford Rd, Singapore 178896.
National Statistical Office: Department of Statistics, 100 High St. #05-01, The Treasury, Singapore 179434.
Website: http://www.singstat.gov.sg

SLOVAKIA

Slovenská Republika
(Slovak Republic)

Capital: Bratislava
Population estimate, 2010: 5·41m.
GDP per capita, 2007: (PPP$) 20,076
HDI/world rank: 0·880/42

KEY HISTORICAL EVENTS

There is evidence of human habitation from 270,000 BC. In the Bronze Age the region was a centre for copper manufacture and was ruled by Carpathian, Celtic and Germanic tribes. The date of the Slavic arrival is contested but there is evidence of their presence from the sixth century under the Roman Empire. Waves of invasion and migration followed Roman withdrawal and control fell variously to the Avars, Franks and Magyars.

The first brief period of Slavic rule was the Samo Empire (623–658) followed by the Moravian Empire from 833–907. The region subsequently became part of the Kingdom of Hungary. In 1241 the region was invaded by Mongols and was stricken with famine but grew in prosperity through the medieval period. From the 16th–19th centuries Slovakia was at the centre of Hungary under the Habsburg dynasty. After 1867 it became part of the Austro-Hungarian Empire and underwent 'Magyarization', a repressive attempt to impose Magyar culture. In response, a nationalist movement at home and among immigrants in America gained momentum in the First World War.

On 28 Oct. 1918, after the dissolution of Austria-Hungary, the Czechoslovak State was founded. Two days later the Slovak National Council voted to unite with the Czechs. The Treaty of St Germain-en-Laye (1919) recognized the Czechoslovak Republic, consisting of the Czech lands (Bohemia, Moravia, part of Silesia) and Slovakia. The new state was numerically dominated by Czechs, giving rise to some tensions and calls for Slovakian independence. In 1939 negotiations between European powers resulted in Germany incorporating the Czech lands into the Reich as the 'Protectorate of Bohemia and Moravia'. Meanwhile the German-sponsored Slovak government declared independence. A government-in-exile, headed by Dr Edvard Beneš, was set up in London during the war. In 1944 Slovak resistance fighters began an uprising; liberation was completed by Soviet and US forces in May 1945. Territories taken by Germans, Poles and Hungarians were restored to Czech sovereignty.

Elections in May 1946 returned a coalition government, under communist prime minister Klement Gottwald. On 20 Feb. 1948, 12 non-communist ministers resigned in protest at the infiltration of communists into the police. Gottwald formed a predominantly communist government and in May 1948, after the government won an 89% majority in rigged parliamentary elections, President Beneš resigned. During the next two decades the government banned other parties and followed Stalinist policies. On 14 May 1955 Czechoslovakia signed the Warsaw Pact, allying itself with the Soviet Union and other Eastern Bloc countries.

In 1968 pressure for liberalization culminated in the overthrow of the Stalinist leadership and under Alexander Dubček, new first secretary of the communist party, the 'Prague Spring' saw sweeping reforms including the abolition of censorship. Between May and Aug. 1968 the USSR put pressure on the government to abandon reforms. Finally, Warsaw Pact troops occupied Czechoslovakia on 21 Aug. The government was forced to reverse reforms and accept the stationing of Soviet troops. In April 1969, with Soviet support, Dubček was replaced by Gustáv Husák.

Demands for reform persisted and mass demonstrations began in Nov. 1989. When authorities used violence to break up a demonstration on 17 Nov., the communist leadership resigned. On 30 Nov. the federal assembly abolished the communists' sole right to govern. A new government was formed on 3 Dec. and another followed a week later as the protest movement grew. Gustáv Husák resigned as president and was replaced by Václav Havel by the unanimous vote of 323 members of the federal assembly on 29 Dec. This almost bloodless overthrow of communist rule became known as the 'Velvet Revolution'.

At the June 1992 elections the Movement for Democratic Slovakia, led by Vladimír Mečiar, campaigned for Slovak independence. On 17 July the Slovak National Council adopted a declaration of sovereignty by 113 to 24 votes, the 'Velvet Divorce'. Havel resigned as federal president on 20 July. A constitution ratified on 1 Sept. 1992 paved the way for independent Slovakia to come into being on 1 Jan. 1993. Economic property was divided between Slovakia and the Czech Republic, with government real estate remaining with the republic in which it was located. Other property was divided by special commissions in the proportion of two (Czech Republic) to one (Slovakia), on the basis of population size. Military equipment was also divided on the two-to-one principle and military personnel were invited to choose in which army to serve.

In the 1990s Slovakia resisted calls for economic reforms and closer ties with Western Europe. However, following the election of a coalition government under Mikuláš Dzurinda in Oct. 1998, the country implemented reforms and attracted foreign investment. It responded to criticism about its human rights record by improving conditions for its Romany and Hungarian minorities. Slovakia joined NATO in March 2004 and the European Union in May 2004. It elected a new coalition government under Prime Minister Robert Fico in June 2006.

TERRITORY AND POPULATION

Slovakia is bounded in the northwest by the Czech Republic, north by Poland, east by Ukraine, south by Hungary and southwest by Austria. Its area is 49,034 sq. km (18,932 sq. miles). Census population in 2001 was 5,379,455 (2,612,515 male; 2,766,940 female); density, 109·7 per sq. km. The estimated population on 31 Dec. 2008 was 5,412,254.

The UN gives an estimated population for 2010 of 5·41m.

In 2005, 56·2% of the population lived in urban areas. There are eight administrative regions *(Kraj)*, one of which is the capital, Bratislava. They have the same name as the main city of the region.

Region	Area in sq. km	2001 population
Banská Bystrica	9,455	662,121
Bratislava	2,053	599,015
Košice	6,753	766,012
Nitra	6,343	713,422
Prešov	8,993	789,968
Trenčín	4,501	605,582
Trnava	4,148	551,003
Žilina	6,788	692,332

The capital, Bratislava, had a population in 2001 of 428,700. The population of other principal towns (2001, in 1,000): Košice, 236; Prešov, 93; Nitra, 87; Žilina, 85; Banská Bystrica, 83; Trnava, 70; Martin, 60; Trenčín, 58.

The population is 85·8% Slovak, 9·7% Hungarian, 1·6% Roma and 0·8% Czech, with some Ruthenians, Ukrainians, Germans and Poles.

A law of Nov. 1995 makes Slovak the sole official language.

SOCIAL STATISTICS

Births, 2006, 53,904; deaths, 53,301; marriages, 25,939; divorces, 12,716. Rates (per 1,000 population), 2006: birth, 10·0; death, 9·9; marriage, 4·8; divorce, 2·4. Expectation of life, 2006, was 70·4 years for males and 78·2 for females. In 2006 the most popular age range for marrying was 25–29 for both males and females. Annual population growth rate, 1996–2006, 0·3%. Infant mortality, 2006 (per 1,000 live births), 6·6. Fertility rate, 2006, 1·2 births per woman (one of the lowest rates in the world).

CLIMATE

A humid continental climate, with warm summers and cold winters. Precipitation is generally greater in summer, with thunderstorms. Autumn, with dry, clear weather and spring, which is damp, are each of short duration. Bratislava, Jan. –0·7°C. June 19·1°C. Annual rainfall 649 mm.

CONSTITUTION AND GOVERNMENT

The constitution became effective on 1 Jan. 1993, creating a parliamentary democracy with universal suffrage from the age of 18. Parliament is the unicameral *National Council*. It has 150 members elected by proportional representation to serve four-year terms. The constitution was amended in Sept. 1998 to allow for the direct election of the *President*, who serves for a five-year term. The President may serve a maximum of two consecutive terms.

The Judicial Branch consists of a *Supreme Court*, whose judges are elected by the National Council, and a *Constitutional Court*, whose judges are appointed by the President from a group of nominees approved by the National Council.

Citizenship belongs to all citizens of the former federal Slovak Republic; other residents of five years standing may apply for citizenship. Slovakia grants dual citizenship.

National Anthem

'Nad Tatrou sa blýska' ('Storm over the Tatras'); words by J. Matúška, tune anonymous.

GOVERNMENT CHRONOLOGY

(DU = Democratic Union; HZD = Movement for Democracy; HZDS = Movement for a Democratic Slovakia; KDH = Christian Democratic Movement; SDK = Slovak Democratic Coalition; SDKÚ = Slovak Democratic and Christian Union; Smer = The Direction Party; SOP = Party of Civic Understanding; n/p = non-partisan)

Presidents since 1993.

1993–98	n/p	Michal Kováč
1999–2004	SOP, n/p	Rudolf Schuster
2004–	HZD, n/p	Ivan Gašparovič

Prime Ministers since 1993.

1993–94	HZDS	Vladimír Mečiar
1994	DU	Jozef Moravčík
1994–98	HZDS	Vladimír Mečiar
1998–2006	KDH/SDK, SDKÚ	Mikuláš Dzurinda
2006–	Smer	Robert Fico

RECENT ELECTIONS

Elections to the National Council were held on 17 June 2006. The Direction Party (Smer) won 50 seats with 29·1% of votes cast, ahead of Prime Minister Mikuláš Dzurinda's Slovak Democratic and Christian Union-Democratic Party 18·4% (31), the Slovak National Party (SNS) 11·7% (20), the Party of the Hungarian Coalition 11·7% (20), the People's Party-Movement for Democratic Slovakia (ĽS-HZDS) 8·8% (15) and the Christian Democratic Movement 8·3% (14). Turnout was 54·7%.

In the first round of presidential elections on 21 March 2009, incumbent president Ivan Gašparovič of the Movement for Democracy/HZD won 46·7% of the vote against 38·1% for Iveta Radičová (Slovak Democratic and Christian Union–Democratic Party/SDKÚ-DS). There were five other candidates. Turnout was 43·6%. In the run-off held on 4 April Gašparovič won 55·5% against 44·5% for Radičová. Turnout in the second round was 51·7%.

Parliamentary elections were scheduled to take place on 12 June 2010.

European Parliament

Slovakia has 13 (14 in 2004) representatives. At the June 2009 elections turnout was 19·6% (17·0% in 2004)—the lowest in the EU. Smer won 5 seats with 32·0% of votes cast (political affiliation in European Parliament: Progressive Alliance of Socialists and Democrats); SDKÚ-DS won 2 seats with 17·0% (European People's Party); the Party of the Hungarian Coalition, 2 with 11·3% (European People's Party); the Christian Democratic Movement, 2 with 10·9% (European People's Party); the ĽS-HZDS, 1 with 9·0% (Alliance of Liberals and Democrats for Europe); the SNS, 1 with 5·6% (Europe of Freedom and Democracy).

CURRENT ADMINISTRATION

President: Ivan Gašparovič; b. 1941 (ind.; sworn in 15 June 2004 and re-elected in April 2009).

A coalition government of Smer, the far-right SNS and ĽS-HZDS was formed following the elections of June 2006. In March 2010 the cabinet was composed as follows:

Prime Minister: Robert Fico; b. 1964 (Smer; sworn in 4 July 2006).

Deputy Prime Minister for a Knowledge-Based Society, European Affairs, and Human Rights and Minorities: Dušan Čaplovič (Smer). *Deputy Prime Minister and Minister of the Interior:* Robert Kaliňák (Smer). *Deputy Prime Minister and Minister of Justice:* Viera Petríková (ĽS-HZDS). *Deputy Prime Minister and Minister of Education:* Ján Mikolaj (SNS).

Minister of Agriculture: Vladimír Chovan (ĽS-HZDS). *Construction and Regional Development:* Igor Štefanov (SNS). *Culture:* Marek Maďarič (Smer). *Defence:* Jaroslav Baška (Smer). *Economy:* Ľubomír Jahnátek (Smer). *Environment:* Jozef Medveď (ind.). *Finance:* Ján Pociatek (Smer). *Foreign Affairs:* Miroslav Lajčák (Smer). *Health:* Richard Raši (Smer). *Labour, Social Affairs and the Family:* Viera Tomanová (Smer). *Transport, Post and Telecommunications:* Ľubomír Vážny (Smer).

The *Speaker* is Pavol Paška.

Government Website: http://www.government.gov.sk

CURRENT LEADERS

Ivan Gašparovič

Position

President

Introduction

Shortly before Slovakia became a member of the European Union on 1 May 2004, a respected lawyer, Ivan Gašparovič, was elected as the country's president. Instrumental in drawing up Slovakia's constitution prior to the dissolution of Czechoslovakia in 1993, he was also a close ally of the controversial nationalist former prime minister, Vladimír Mečiar, the man he beat in the second round of the presidential election. He was re-elected in April 2009.

Early Life

Ivan Gašparovič was born in Poltár, near Lučenec in southern Slovakia on 27 March 1941. His father, Vladimír Gašparovič, had migrated to the region from Rijeka, Croatia at the end of the First World War. The family moved to Bratislava, where Vladimír worked as a teacher in a secondary school. Having studied at the Law Faculty of the Komenský University in Bratislava from 1959–64, Ivan Gašparovič worked in the district prosecutor's office of Bratislava's Martin district (1965–66), and then became a prosecutor at the municipal prosecutor's office. In early 1968 he joined the Communist Party of Czechoslovakia and actively supported the reforms of Alexander Dubček, the party's Slovak first secretary. Under Dubček, in what became known as the Prague Spring, democratization went further than in any other Communist state—press censorship was reduced and Slovakia was granted political autonomy. However, opposition grew swiftly in the USSR and in other Warsaw Pact states which invaded Czechoslovakia on the night of 20 Aug. 1968. The following year Dubček was replaced by Gustáv Husák, who spearheaded a 'normalization' policy that turned Czechoslovakia into one of Central Europe's most repressive states.

Gašparovič left the Communist Party after the events of 1968 and began work as a teacher at the law faculty at the Komenský University. He remained there until 1990 when he became the vice chancellor in Feb. of that year, two months after the 'Velvet Revolution' had swept aside the Communists. Václav Havel, the playwright and former dissident who was elected federal president in Dec. 1989, nominated Gašparovič as prosecutor-general of Czechoslovakia. He moved to Prague and took up the post in July 1990, as the new government began to tackle the legacy of communism—a moribund economy, high unemployment and widespread social discontent. Under the 1968 constitution Czechoslovakia was a federal republic—each republic had a council and an assembly, but the federal government dealt with defence and foreign affairs. Arguments over the nature of the federation broke out and in 1991 Vladimír Mečiar formed the Movement for a Democratic Slovakia (HZDS). Gašparovič returned to Bratislava to teach at the Komenský University and joined the HZDS in 1992. Mečiar led the party to victory in the June 1992 elections, and Gašparovič became an HZDS member of the Slovak parliament. In late 1992 he was one of the authors of the constitution of Slovakia, which came into effect on 1 Jan. 1993 when the republic formally declared its independence.

Gašparovič was speaker of the Slovak parliament until Oct. 1998 and a close ally of Prime Minister Mečiar, whose controversial policies in the mid-1990s included stripping away the rights of the country's large Hungarian community and clamping down on the media. Slovakia became increasingly isolated from Western Europe until Mečiar's nationalist government was defeated in Sept. 1998 by an alliance of liberals, centrists, left-wingers and ethnic Hungarians. Mikuláš Dzurinda became prime minister and steered Slovakia through various reforms required for EU and NATO membership. From Oct. 1998–July 2002, when the HZDS was in opposition, Gašparovič was a member of the parliamentary committee for the supervision of the SIS (the Slovak equivalent of the US Central Intelligence Agency).

In July 2002 Gašparovič and others left the HZDS after being struck off the list of candidates for the parliamentary elections in Sept. The HZDS went on to poll only 3·3% of the vote, not enough to win any seats. Gašparovič returned to Komenský University, but also established a new political party called the Movement for Democracy (HZD). In April 2004 he ran for president against Mečiar, who was attempting to make a comeback after losing the 2002 legislative elections. Although Mečiar won more votes in the first round, he failed to win a majority. In the second round, Gašparovič secured nearly 60% of the vote with the support of the eliminated candidates.

Career in Office

Ivan Gašparovič succeeded Rudolf Schuster as president of the Slovak Republic on 15 June 2004 and began a five-year term of office. Following elections to the National Council in June 2006, Gašparovič asked Robert Fico, the leader of the social democratic Direction Party, to form a new coalition government in place of Mikuláš Dzurinda's SDKÚ-led administration. Gašparovič secured a second term as president in April 2009, winning 55·5% of the vote in a second round run-off.

Robert Fico

Position

Prime Minister

Introduction

Robert Fico was sworn in as prime minister on 4 July 2006 following inconclusive elections held in June. His social democratic Direction Party won nearly 30% of the vote but required support from the centre-left People's Party-Movement for a Democratic Slovakia and the right-wing Slovak National Party to form a workable government controlling 85 of the 150 seats in parliament.

Early Life

Robert Fico was born in Topoľčany, Czechoslovakia on 15 Sept. 1964. After studying law at Comenius University in Bratislava, he obtained a PhD in criminal law from the Slovak Academy of Sciences. On finishing military service in 1986 he worked for the law institute of the ministry of justice until 1995, holding the post of deputy director from 1992. From 1994–2000 he represented the Slovak Republic before the European Court of Human Rights and the European Commission of Human Rights.

A member of the Slovak parliament since 1992, he served on the parliamentary constitutional committee (1992–2002), as chairman of the prison commission (1995–2003) and on the parliamentary committee on human rights, national minorities and women's rights (2002–06). From 1999 he was chair of Smer and has served as its parliamentary leader since 2002.

Career in Office

Fico's government followed eight years of rule by a centre-right coalition led by Mikuláš Dzurinda, who won international praise for economic reforms but lacked domestic popularity. Fico said that he would aim to focus on social welfare, reversing some of the previous government's measures that saw unemployment rise to 15%, and to meet the strict public spending criteria set for Slovakia's target entry into the European single currency in 2009.

He removed Slovakian troops from Iraq and refused to allow forces to be deployed in southern Afghanistan. Scheduled visits to Libya and Venezuela in 2007 brought criticism that Fico was damaging Slovakia's international credibility, while the Alliance of European Socialists expelled his Direction Party in Oct. 2006 for forming a coalition with a far-right party.

In Nov. 2007 a scandal concerning land transfers led to the sacking of the agriculture minister, causing conflict within the coalition between Fico and the HZDS leader Vladimír Mečiar. However, Fico maintained his political authority when his budget, which was tied to a vote of confidence in his government, was approved by parliament the following month.

As planned, Slovakia became the 16th country to adopt the European single currency on 1 Jan. 2009. In Feb. the government adopted an anti-crisis economic package to combat the effects of the global economic downturn.

Simmering tensions between Slovakia and Hungary resurfaced in July 2009 when the Slovak parliament passed a new language law imposing fines for using minority languages in government buildings. Hungary condemned the law as discrimination against the Hungarian ethnic minority. However, in Sept., when the law took effect, both countries agreed to seek independent arbitration in the dispute.

DEFENCE

Since 1 Jan. 2006 Slovakia has had an all-volunteer professional army. In 2006 military expenditure totalled US$957m. (US$176 per capita), representing 1·7% of GDP.

Army

Personnel (2007), 7,324. In addition there is a national guard reserve force with an estimated strength of 20,000.

Air Force

There were 46 combat capable aircraft in 2007 (Su-22, MiG-21 and MiG-29 fighters) and 16 attack helicopters. Personnel (2007), 4,280.

INTERNATIONAL RELATIONS

Slovakia is a member of the UN, World Bank, IMF and several other UN specialized agencies, WTO, EU, Council of Europe, OSCE, CERN, CEI, Danube Commission, BIS, IOM, NATO, OECD and an associate partner of WEU. A referendum held on 16–17 May 2003 approved accession to the EU, with 92·5% of votes cast for membership and 7·5% against. Turnout was 52·2%. Slovakia became a member of NATO on 29 March 2004 and the EU on 1 May 2004.

In Dec. 2007 Slovakia acceded to the Schengen accord, which abolishes border controls between Slovakia, Austria, Belgium, Czech Republic, Denmark, Estonia, Finland, France, Germany, Greece, Hungary, Iceland, Italy, Latvia, Lithuania, Luxembourg, Malta, Netherlands, Norway, Poland, Portugal, Slovenia, Spain, Sweden and Switzerland.

Slovakia has had a long-standing dispute with Hungary over the Gabčíkovo-Nagymaros Project, involving the building of dam structures in both countries for the production of electric power, flood control and improvement of navigation on the Danube as agreed in a treaty signed in 1977 between Czechoslovakia and Hungary. In late 1998 Slovakia and Hungary signed a protocol easing tensions between the two nations and settling differences over the dam.

ECONOMY

Agriculture accounted for 4% of GDP in 2008, industry 41% and services 55%.

Overview

The economy has experienced rapid growth since 1998, driven by strong exports and foreign direct investment, particularly in the automotive industry. Real GDP has grown at approximately 4% per annum, private demand is strong and the export sector is expanding steadily. In 2007 there was real GDP growth of 10·4%, the result of strong domestic demand and buoyant exports. Unemployment fell to 11·2% but sharp regional differences remain. The fiscal deficit has been lowered since the early 2000s by structural reforms, including reduced expenditure on social benefits and health, and stood at 3·4% in 2006, down from 7·2% in 2002. Slovakia entered the ERM2 in 2005 and adopted the euro in Jan. 2009.

The economy has undergone constant restructuring since 1998 when policy shifted from state intervention towards pro-market reforms. In the first years after independence in 1993, economic policy was misdirected, with structural reforms postponed and expansionary fiscal policies supporting domestic consumption and employment. Following economic transition the heavy industry and agriculture sectors shrank while the service sector increased its share of GDP to 65% in 2004.

Currency

On 1 Jan. 2009 the euro (EUR) replaced the Slovak koruna (SKK) as the legal currency of Slovakia at the irrevocable conversion rate of 30·126 koruny to one euro. Foreign exchange reserves in Sept. 2009 were US$54m. (US$17,493m. in Sept. 2008) and gold reserves 1·02m. troy oz. Inflation rates (based on OECD statistics):

1999	*2000*	*2001*	*2002*	*2003*	*2004*	*2005*	*2006*	*2007*	*2008*
10·4%	12·2%	7·2%	3·5%	8·4%	7·5%	2·8%	4·3%	1·9%	3·9%

Total money supply in Dec. 2008 was €545,969m.

Budget

In 2005 budgetary central government revenue totalled 267·16bn. koruny (267·27bn. koruny in 2004) and expenditure 304·05bn. koruny (324·96bn. koruny in 2004).

VAT, personal and company income tax, real estate taxes and inheritance taxes came into force in Jan. 1993. VAT is 19% (reduced rate, 10%).

Performance

Real GDP growth rates (based on OECD statistics):

1999	*2000*	*2001*	*2002*	*2003*	*2004*	*2005*	*2006*	*2007*	*2008*
0·0%	1·4%	3·4%	4·8%	4·7%	5·2%	6·5%	8·5%	10·4%	6·4%

Slovakia's total GDP in 2008 was US$95·0bn.

Banking and Finance

The central bank and bank of issue is the Slovak National Bank, founded in 1993 (*Governor*, Jozef Makúch). It has an autonomous statute modelled on the German Bundesbank, with the duties of maintaining control over monetary policy and inflation, ensuring the stability of the currency, and supervising commercial banks. However, it is now proposed to amend the central bank law to allow the government to appoint half the members of the board and force the bank to increase its financing of the budget deficit.

In Oct. 1998 the Slovak National Bank abandoned its fixed exchange rate system, whereby the crown's value was fixed within a fluctuation band against a number of currencies, and chose to float the currency.

Decentralization of the banking system began in 1991, and private banks began to operate. The two largest Slovak banks were both privatized in 2001. The Austrian bank Erste Bank bought an 87·18% stake in Slovenská Sporiteľňa (Slovak Savings Bank) and the Italian bank IntesaBci bought a 94·47% stake in Všeobecná úverová banka (General Credit Bank). In 2006 Slovenská Sporiteľňa had assets of 298bn. koruny and Všeobecná úverová banka 241bn. koruny. In 2006 there were 24 commercial banks including three building savings banks.

Foreign direct investment in Slovakia in 2008 amounted to US$3,414m., more than a four-fold increase on the 1998 figure.

There is a stock exchange in Bratislava.

ENERGY AND NATURAL RESOURCES

Environment

Slovakia's carbon dioxide emissions from the consumption and flaring of fossil fuels in 2008 were the equivalent of 6·9 tonnes per capita.

Electricity

Installed capacity in 2004 was 8·6m. kW, of which 2·9m. kW is hydro-electric and 2·6m. kW nuclear. Production in 2004 was 30·57bn. kWh, with consumption per capita 5,335 kWh. There were five nuclear reactors in use in 2008. In 2004 about 56% of electricity was nuclear-generated.

Oil and Gas
In 2006 natural gas reserves were 14bn. cu. metres; oil reserves were 9m. bbls in 2007. Natural gas production in 2006 amounted to 123m. cu. metres. Slovakia relies on Russia for almost all of its oil and gas.

Minerals
In 2005, 2·51m. tonnes of lignite were produced. 6·61m. tonnes of limestone were extracted in 2006. There are also reserves of copper, lead, zinc, iron, dolomite, rock salt and others.

Agriculture
In 2006 there were 1·34m. ha. of arable land and 25,260 ha. of permanent crops. In 2006 agriculture employed 4·4% of the economically active population.

A federal law of May 1991 returned land seized by the Communist regime to its original owners, to a maximum of 150 ha. of arable to a single owner.

Production, 2006 (in 1,000 tonnes): sugar beets, 1,371; wheat, 1,343; maize, 838; barley, 642; potatoes, 263; rapeseed, 260; sunflower seeds, 229; grapes, 52; apples, 41, tomatoes, 36.

Livestock, 2006: pigs, 1·11m.; cattle, 508,000; sheep, 333,000; chickens, 13m. Livestock products (in 1,000 tonnes): meat (2006), 196; milk (2003), 1,166; cheese (2006), 72; eggs (2003), 68.

Forestry
The area under forests in 2005 was 1·93m. ha., or 40·1% of the total land area. In 2007 timber production was 8·87m. cu. metres.

Fisheries
In 2005 the total catch was 1,693 tonnes, exclusively freshwater fish.

INDUSTRY
The main industries in Slovakia are machine engineering, chemical products, electrical apparatus, textiles, clothing and footwear, metallurgy, food and beverages, paper, wood and woodworking. Output included (in 1m. tonnes): cement (2008), 6·4; crude steel (2007), 4·8; pig iron (2007), 4·0; distillate fuel oil (2004), 2·6; coke (2006), 1·9; petrol (2004), 1·7; residual fuel oil (2004), 0·6. Motor vehicle production (2008), 524,859 units. Slovakia has the highest per capita car production of any country.

Labour
Out of 2,216,200 people in employment in 2005, 591,900 were in manufacturing, 269,500 in wholesale and retail trade/repair of motor vehicles, motorcycles and personal and household goods, 209,800 in construction and 163,700 in education. The average monthly salary in 2007 was 21,658 koruny. In Oct. 2007 the monthly minimum wage was increased to 8,100 koruny. Unemployment stood at 19·4% in 2001, but then fell to 16·3% in 2005, 13·3% in 2006 and still further to 9·5% in 2008. However, it rose back up in the course of 2009 to reach 13·6% in Dec. Youth unemployment is particularly high—in Dec. 2009 it was in excess of 32%. In 2004 part-time work accounted for less than 3% of all employment in Slovakia—the lowest percentage in the EU.

INTERNATIONAL TRADE
Foreign debt was US$23,654m. in 2005.

Imports and Exports
In 2004 imports (f.o.b.) totalled US$29·26bn. (US$22·00bn. in 2003); exports (f.o.b.), US$27·78bn. (US$21·96bn. in 2003). Principal import sources in 2004 were: Germany, 23·8%; Czech Republic, 13·2%; Russia, 9·4%; Italy, 5·6%; Austria, 4·3%. The leading export markets in 2004 were: Germany, 28·6%; Czech Republic, 13·3%; Austria, 7·8%; Italy, 6·4%; Poland, 5·5%. In 2004 machinery and transport equipment accounted for 39·6% of Slovakia's imports and 45·9% of exports; chemicals, manufactured goods classified chiefly by material and miscellaneous manufactured articles 39·3% of imports and 41·4% of exports; mineral fuels, lubricants and related materials 12·5% of imports and 6·7% of exports; food, live animals, beverages and tobacco 4·7% of imports and 3·2% of exports; inedible crude materials, and animal and vegetable oil and fats 3·9% of imports and 2·8% of exports.

COMMUNICATIONS
Roads
In 2006 there were 43,770 km of roads, including 328 km of motorways. In 2007 there were 1,468,600 passenger cars in use, 244,800 vans and lorries, 10,300 buses and coaches and 61,200 motorcycles and mopeds. In 2006 there were 7,988 road accidents resulting in 608 fatalities.

Rail
In 2005 the length of railway routes was 3,661 km. Most of the network is 1,435 mm gauge with short sections on three other gauges. 51·3m. passengers were carried in 2003 and 47·7m. tonnes of freight in 2005. There are tram/light rail networks in Bratislava, Košice and Trenčianske Teplice.

Civil Aviation
The main international airport is at Bratislava (M. R. Stefánik), which handled 2,218,545 passengers in 2008 (77% of all passengers using Slovakian airports) and 6,961 tonnes of freight. There are also some international flights from Košice (590,919 passengers in 2008). Slovak Airlines (formerly the Slovak flag carrier) ceased operations in Feb. 2007, as did Air Slovakia in March 2010. SkyEurope (central Europe's first low-cost airline), which operated domestic services and also flew to a number of destinations in Europe, ceased operations in Sept. 2009. Danube Wings, launched in 2008, is now the only Slovakian carrier.

Shipping
In 2006 vessels registered by Slovak enterprises numbered 261. They carried 1·7m. tonnes of goods and 111,000 passengers using inland waterway transport.

Telecommunications
In 2008 there were 1,098,000 main (fixed) telephone lines. In 2007 mobile phone subscribers numbered 6,068,000 (112·5 per 100 persons). In 2000 Deutsche Telekom bought a 51% stake in the state-owned Slovakia Telecom. There were 2,320,000 PCs in use in 2006 and 3,556,500 internet users in 2008.

Postal Services
In 2003 there were 1,617 post offices.

SOCIAL INSTITUTIONS
Justice
The post-Communist judicial system was established by a federal law of July 1991. This provided for a unified system of four types of court: civil, criminal, commercial and administrative. Commercial courts arbitrate in disputes arising from business activities. Administrative courts examine the legality of the decisions of state institutions when appealed by citizens. In addition, there are military courts which operate under the jurisdiction of the Ministry of Defence. There is a Supreme Court, and a hierarchy of courts under the Ministry of Justice at republic, region and district level. District courts are courts of first instance. Cases are usually decided by senates comprising a judge and two associate judges, although occasionally by a single judge. (Associate judges are citizens in good standing over the age of 25 who are elected for four-year terms). Regional courts are courts of first instance in more serious cases and also courts of appeal for district courts. Cases are usually decided by a senate of two judges and three associate judges, although again occasionally by a single judge. The Supreme Court interprets law as a guide to other courts and functions also as a court of appeal. Decisions are made by senates of three judges. The judges of the Supreme Court

are nominated by the President; other judges are appointed by the National Council.

The population in penal institutions in Dec. 2007 was 7,986 (148 per 100,000 of national population).

Education

In 2006–07 there were 2,928 pre-school institutions with 140,014 children and 13,149 teachers, 2,283 primary schools with 508,130 pupils and 33,736 teachers, 246 grammar schools with 99,931 students and 7,602 teachers, and 249 vocational schools with 80,339 pupils and 7,728 teachers. There were 210 secondary vocational apprentice training centres with 60,621 pupils and 3,223 teachers, and 376 special schools with 31,390 children and 4,299 teachers. There were 30 universities or university-type institutions with 125,213 students.

In 2006 spending on education was 15·1% of total state budget expenditure.

The adult literacy rate in 2003 was 99·6% (99·7% among males and 99·6% among females).

Health

In 2008 there were 18,121 physicians, 2,745 dentists, 33,778 nurses and 2,777 pharmacists. There were 46,742 beds in health establishments in total in 2008, of which 33,912 were in hospitals. In 2007 Slovakia spent 7·7% of its GDP on health.

Welfare

The age of retirement is 62 for men and is set to rise from 53–57 to 62 for women by 2015. Pensions rose by 6·95% on 1 Jan. 2009. The average monthly old-age pension at Feb. 2009 was €335·50 with approximately 925,700 beneficiaries. Maternity benefit is paid for a total of 28 weeks or 37 weeks for a single mother and for multiple births. State unemployment benefit is 50% of previous earnings during the first three months, thereafter 45% of previous earnings.

RELIGION

A federal Czechoslovakian law of July 1991 provides the basis for church-state relations and guarantees the religious and civic rights of citizens and churches. Churches must register to become legal entities but operate independently of the state. A law of 1993 restored confiscated property to churches and religious communities unless it had passed into private hands, co-operative farms or trading companies. In 2001, 68·9% of the population were Roman Catholic, 6·9% members of the Evangelical Church of the Augsburg Confession, 4·1% Greek Catholic and 2·0% Calvinist. In Feb. 2010 there were two cardinals.

CULTURE

World Heritage Sites

There are seven UNESCO sites in Slovakia: Vlkolínec (inscribed on the list in 1993), a group of 45 traditional log houses; Banská Štiavnica (1993), a medieval mining town; Levoča, Spišský and the Associated Cultural Monuments (1993 and 2009)—13th century Spiš Castle is one of the largest castle complexes in central Europe; Bardejov Town Conservation Reserve (2000), a medieval fortified town; and Wooden Churches of the Slovak part of the Carpathian Mountain Area (2008).

Slovakia shares two UNESCO sites with other countries: the Caves of Aggtelek and Slovak Karst (1995, 2000 and 2008) with Hungary and the primeval beech forests of the Carpathians (2007) with Ukraine.

Broadcasting

Broadcasting is the responsibility of the government-controlled Council for Broadcasting and Retransmission (since 2000). The state-run Slovak Radio broadcasts on five networks and an external service, and there are over 20 private radio stations. Slovak Television is a public corporation operating two national networks (colour by PAL). There are several commercial stations (notably TV Markiza), and cable and satellite services are also available. In 2006 there were 2·24m. TV sets.

Cinema

In 2006 there were 217 cinemas; total admissions in 2007 were 2·8m.

Press

Slovakia had 13 daily newspapers in 2006 with a combined average daily circulation of 332,547. In 2006 a total of 9,638 book titles were published.

Tourism

In 2005, 1,515,000 non-resident tourists stayed in holiday accommodation; spending by tourists in 2005 totalled US$1,210m., excluding passenger transport.

Festivals

The Bratislava Rock Festival takes place in June and the Bratislava Music Festival and Interpodium is in Oct. The Myjava Folklore Festival is held each June, the Zvolen Castle Games in June–July, Theatrical Nitra is in Sept., and there is an annual Spring Music Festival in Košice.

DIPLOMATIC REPRESENTATIVES

Of Slovakia in the United Kingdom (25 Kensington Palace Gdns, London, W8 4QY)
Ambassador: Juraj Zervan.

Of the United Kingdom in Slovakia (Panska 16, 81101 Bratislava)
Ambassador: Michael Roberts.

Of Slovakia in the USA (3523 International Court, NW, Washington, D.C., 20008)
Ambassador: Peter Burian.

Of the USA in Slovakia (4 Hviezdoslavovo Namestie, 81102 Bratislava)
Ambassador: Vacant.
Chargé d'Affaires a.i.: Keith A. Eddins.

Of Slovakia to the United Nations
Ambassador: Miloš Koterec.

Of Slovakia to the European Union
Permanent Representative: Ivan Korčok.

FURTHER READING

Fisher, Sharon, *Political Change in Post-Communist Slovakia and Croatia: From Nationalist to Europeanist.* 2006

Kirschbaum, S. J., *A History of Slovakia: the Struggle for Survival.* 1995

National Statistical Office: Statistical Office of the Slovak Republic, Miletičova 3, 82467 Bratislava.
Website: http://portal.statistics.sk

SLOVENIA

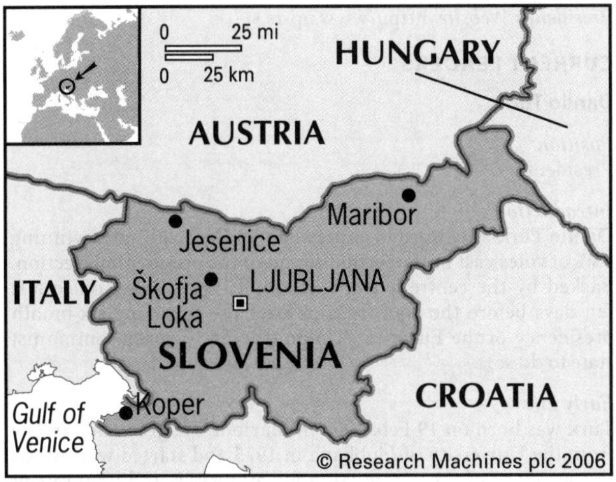

Republika Slovenija
(Republic of Slovenia)

Capital: Ljubljana
Population estimate, 2010: 2·03m.
GDP per capita, 2007: (PPP$) 26,753
HDI/world rank: 0·929/29

KEY HISTORICAL EVENTS

The region was settled by Celts and Illyrians in pre-Roman times and fell to Rome in the 1st century AD. In the 6th century Slavic tribes arrived and part of the territory came under the Slavic Duchy of Karantania in the 7th century. In 745 Karantania became part of the Frankish Empire as an independent country with its own laws and language. After passing under the rule of Bavarian dukes and the Republic of Venice, it joined its neighbouring Slovene-inhabited areas to become part of the Habsburg dynasty in the 14th century.

The Slovenes retained a strong national identity, aided by the printing of the first Slovenian books in 1550 and the translation of the Protestant Bible into Slovenian in 1584. A 12-day peasant revolt in 1573 was bloodily suppressed. In the 19th century a nationalist movement developed, demanding Slovenian autonomy within the Habsburg monarchy. Administrative autonomy was granted in the province of Carinthia while Slovenes in other areas gained some cultural rights. With the demise of the Habsburg monarchy, Slovenia became part of Austria-Hungary. Following Germany's defeat in the First World War, the Slovenes joined their Slav neighbours in the Kingdom of the Serbs, Croats and Slovenes on 1 Dec. 1918. The country was renamed Yugoslavia in 1929. During the Second World War Slovenian territory was divided and annexed by the Axis powers. In 1945 Slovenia became a constituent republic of the Socialist Federal Republic of Yugoslavia under Josep Tito.

In the 1980s nationalism grew stronger throughout Yugoslavia, spearheaded by the Serbs' call for Serbian unity. In Oct. 1989 the Slovene Assembly passed a constitutional amendment giving it the right to secede from Yugoslavia and in a referendum on 23 Dec. 1990, 88·5% voted for independence. Slovenia declared independence on 25 June 1991 but, at EU-sponsored peace talks, suspended the claim for three months. Fighting between Slovenia and federal troops ended with a federal withdrawal and on 8 Oct. 1991 Slovenia again declared its independence.

In 1992 Slovenia removed more than 18,000 non-Slovene residents from its records and cancelled their rights. Under pressure from the EU, which Slovenia joined in May 2004, partial restoration of citizenship was granted to about 12,000 people, though a 2004 referendum rejected proposals to restore full retrospective rights. Slovenia joined NATO in March 2004 and became the first former communist bloc country to adopt the euro in Jan. 2007.

TERRITORY AND POPULATION

Slovenia is bounded in the north by Austria, in the northeast by Hungary, in the southeast and south by Croatia and in the west by Italy. The length of coastline is 47 km. Its area is 20,273 sq. km. The capital is Ljubljana: Dec. 2008 population, 268,423. Maribor (population of 96,408 in 2008) is the other major city. In 2002 the census population was 1,964,036. Population (31 Dec. 2008), 2,032,362 (females, 1,028,417); density per sq. km, 100·2. In 2005, 51·0% of the population lived in urban areas.

The UN gives an estimated population for 2010 of 2·03m.

The official language is Slovene.

In April 2004 voters rejected plans to restore the civil rights of Slovenia's ethnic minorities, mainly nationals of other former Yugoslav republics, which were 'erased' in 1992.

SOCIAL STATISTICS

Statistics for calendar years:

	Live births	*Deaths*	*Growth rate per 1,000*	*Marriages*	*Divorces*
2004	17,961	18,523	–0·3	6,558	2,411
2005	18,157	18,825	–0·3	5,769	2,647
2006	18,932	18,180	0·4	6,368	2,334
2007	19,823	18,584	0·6	6,373	2,617
2008	21,817	18,308	1·7	6,703	2,246

Rates, 2008 (per 1,000 population): birth, 10·8; death, 9·1. Infant mortality, 2005: 3 (per 1,000 live births). There were 529 suicides in 2006 (22·8 per 100,000 population).

In 2005 the most popular age range for marrying was 25–29 years for both males and females. Expectation of life, 2007, was 74·4 years for males and 81·7 for females. Annual population growth rate, 2000–05, 0·1%. Fertility rate, 2004, 1·2 births per woman (one of the lowest rates in the world).

CLIMATE

Summers are warm, winters are cold with frequent snow. Ljubljana, Jan. –4°C, July 22°C. Annual rainfall 1,383 mm.

CONSTITUTION AND GOVERNMENT

The constitution became effective on 23 Dec. 1991. Slovenia is a parliamentary democratic republic with an executive that consists of a directly-elected president, aided by a council of ministers, and a prime minister. It has a bicameral parliament (*Skupšcina Slovenije*), consisting of a 90-member *National Assembly* (*Državni Zbor*), 88 members elected for four-year terms by proportional representation with a 4% threshold and two members elected by ethnic minorities; and a 40-member, advisory *State Council* (*Državni Svet*), elected for five-year terms by interest groups and regions. It has veto powers over the National Assembly. Administratively the country is divided into 136 municipalities and 11 urban municipalities.

The Judicial branch consists of a *Supreme Court*, whose judges are elected by the National Assembly, and a *Constitutional Court*, whose judges are elected for nine-year terms by the National Assembly and nominated by the president.

National Anthem

'Zdravljica' ('A Toast'); words by Dr France Prešeren, tune by Stanko Premrl.

GOVERNMENT CHRONOLOGY

(LDS = Liberal Democracy of Slovenia; NSi = New Slovenia Christian People's Party; SD = Social Democrats; SDS = Slovenian Democratic Party; SKD = Slovenian Christian Democrats; SLS+SKD = Slovenian People's Party; n/p = non-partisan)

Presidents since 1990.

1990–2002	n/p	Milan Kučan
2002–07	LDS	Janez Drnovšek
2007–	n/p	Danilo Türk

Prime Ministers since 1990.

1990–92	SKD	Lojze Peterle
1992–2000	LDS	Janez Drnovšek
2000	SLS+SKD, NSi	Andrej Bajuk
2000–02	LDS	Janez Drnovšek
2002–04	LDS	Anton (Tone) Rop
2004–08	SDS	Janez Janša
2008–	SD	Borut Pahor

RECENT ELECTIONS

Presidential elections were held on 21 Oct. and 11 Nov. 2007. The turnout in the first round was 57·6% and in the second round 58·4%. Lojze Peterle (ind.) won 28·7% of the vote in the first round, Danilo Türk (ind.) 24·5%, Mitja Gaspari (ind.) 24·1% and Zmago Jelinčič (Slovenian National Party) 19·2%. There were three other candidates. In the run-off held on 11 Nov. 2007 Danilo Türk received 68·0% of votes cast against 32·0% for Lojze Peterle.

Elections were held for the National Assembly on 21 Sept. 2008; turnout was 63·1%. The opposition Social Democrats (SD) won 29 seats with 30·5% of votes cast; the ruling centre-right Slovenian Democratic Party (SDS), 28 with 29·3%; Zares, 9 with 9·4%; Democratic Party of Pensioners of Slovenia (DeSUS), 7 with 7·5%; Slovenian National Party (SNS), 5 with 5·4%; Slovenian People's Party and Youth Party of Slovenia (SLS-SMS), 5 with 5·2%; Liberal Democracy of Slovenia (LDS), 5 with 5·2%.

European Parliament

Slovenia has seven representatives. At the June 2009 elections turnout was 28·3% (28·4% in 2004). The SDS won 2 seats with 26·9% of the vote (political affiliation in European Parliament: European People's Party); SD, 2 with 18·5% (Progressive Alliance of Socialists and Democrats); New Slovenia-Christian People's Party, 1 with 16·3% (European People's Party); LDS, 1 with 11·5% (Alliance of Liberals and Democrats for Europe); Zares, 1 with 9·8% (Alliance of Liberals and Democrats for Europe).

CURRENT ADMINISTRATION

President: Danilo Türk; b. 1952 (ind.; sworn in 22 Dec. 2007).

In March 2010 the coalition government of the Social Democrats (SD), Zares, Democratic Party of Pensioners of Slovenia (DeSUS) and Liberal Democracy of Slovenia (LDS) comprised:

Prime Minister: Borut Pahor; b. 1963 (SD; sworn in 21 Nov. 2008).

Minister of Culture: Majda Širca (Zares). *Defence:* Ljubica Jelušič (SD). *Economy:* Matej Lahovnik (Zares). *Education and Sport:* Igor Lukšič (SD). *Environment and Spatial Planning:* Dr Roko Žarnić (DeSUS). *Finance:* Franc Križanič (SD). *Foreign Affairs:* Samuel Žbogar (ind.). *Health:* Borut Miklavčič (ind.). *Higher Education, Science and Technology:* Gregor Golobič (Zares). *Interior:* Katarina Kresal (LDS). Justice: Aleš Zalar (LDS). *Labour, Family and Social Affairs:* Ivan Svetlik (ind.). *Public Administration:* Irma Pavlinič-Krebs (Zares). *Transport:* Patrick Vlačič (SD). *Minister without Portfolio Responsible for Local Self-Government and Regional Development, and Agriculture, Forestry and Food (acting):* Dr Henrik Gjerkeš (DeSUS). *Minister without Portfolio Responsible for Development and European Affairs:* Mitja Gaspari (ind.). *Minister without Portfolio Responsible for Slovenes Abroad:* Boštjan Žekš (ind.).

President's Website: http://www.up-rs.si

CURRENT LEADERS

Danilo Türk

Position

President

Introduction

Danilo Türk was sworn in as president in Dec. 2007 after winning 68% of votes cast in the second round of the presidential election. Backed by the centre-left opposition, Türk assumed office just ten days before the country took over the revolving six-month presidency of the European Union (the first former communist state to do so).

Early Life

Türk was born on 19 Feb. 1952 in Maribor. He graduated in law from the University of Ljubljana in 1975 and started working as the secretary of the commission for minorities and migrants of the Socialist Alliance of the Working People of Slovenia (SZDL). He also became involved with Amnesty International, acting as an advisor on human rights cases in the former Yugoslavia. In 1978 he obtained his masters degree in law from the University of Belgrade and returned to the University of Ljubljana as an academic assistant, teaching international law. Returning to his work for the SZDL, he served as its chairman until 1981. Türk was elected vice-chairman of the UN working group on the right to development in 1981 and held the post until 1984.

He obtained his law doctorate from the University of Ljubljana in 1982 and became assistant professor at the university's faculty of law in Dec. that year. From 1983–92 he headed the university's institute of international law and international relations. From 1984–92 he was a member of the UN sub-commission on prevention of discrimination and protection of minorities, becoming its chairman in 1991. In 1987 Türk helped establish the Human Rights Council in Slovenia, later becoming the vice-president. He was also promoted to the post of associate professor in 1987.

Following Slovenia's declaration of independence, Türk served in the Slovenian delegation at the Conference of Yugoslavia from July 1991–Aug. 1992. From 11 Sept. 1992 he represented Slovenia at the United Nations. During his ambassadorship Slovenia was elected to a non-permanent seat on the Security Council for the period of 1998–99 and held the presidency on two occasions (Aug. 1998 and Nov. 1999). He left his post as ambassador on 31 Jan. 2000 to become assistant secretary-general for political affairs at the United Nations. For the next five years Türk was closely involved in trying to solve crises in the Balkans, Afghanistan, Iraq and Haiti.

Türk returned to teaching international law at the University of Ljubljana in 2005 and in May 2006 was appointed vice-dean of the faculty of law. He formalized his candidacy for the presidency in June 2007 and was placed second in the first round of voting on 21 Oct. 2007, claiming 24·5% of the vote. In the run-off on 11 Nov. 2007 Türk beat his opponent, the centre-right candidate Lojze Peterle, in a landslide victory. He was sworn in on 22 Dec.

Career in Office

Although the role of the president is largely ceremonial, Türk has influence over defence and foreign policy. His long diplomatic experience assisted the smooth running of Slovenia's EU presidency from Jan.-June 2008. In domestic politics, he pledged 'constructive, co-ordinated and balanced co-operation with the government and parliament'.

Borut Pahor

Position
Prime Minister

Introduction
Borut Pahor became prime minister in Nov. 2008. He is the leader of the Social Democrats (SD) and the head of a centre-left coalition that defeated the conservative government of Janez Janša in parliamentary elections in Sept. 2008. Prior to winning the premiership, Pahor had never served in executive office. He was previously president of the National Assembly, the lower house of Slovenia's parliament.

Early Life
Pahor was born in 1963 in Postojna, southeast of Ljubljana. He studied political science at the University of Ljubljana, majoring in international relations. At the age of 26, Pahor became the youngest-ever member of the central committee of the Slovenian branch of the Communist Party, gaining a reputation as a leader of the party's reformist wing. In 1992, after the collapse of communism in eastern Europe and the fragmentation of Yugoslavia, he was elected a deputy in the National Assembly of the newly independent Slovenia.

A year later Pahor became deputy leader of the newly formed United List of Social Democrats (ZLSD). At the third ZLSD conference in March 1997 he was elected party leader on a centrist, 'third way' platform. At the 2000 elections, having led his party into a coalition with Janez Drnovšek's Liberal Democracy of Slovenia, Pahor won a third term in the National Assembly and became its president. In 2004 he was elected to the European Parliament, where he joined the Socialist Group. In the same year the centre-left coalition of which he was a member lost to the centre-right alliance led by the Slovenian Democratic Party. In 2005, on his initiative, the ZLSD was renamed the Social Democrats.

Parliamentary elections held on 21 Sept. 2008 saw the Social Democrats gain 29 of the 90 available seats to become the country's largest party. It formed a coalition government with Zares, Liberal Democracy of Slovenia and the Democratic Party of Pensioners of Slovenia. Pahor was sworn into office on 21 Nov. 2008.

Career in Office
Pahor promised to cut taxes, reform the national health and pension systems and increase investment incentives, but was forced to redraft the national budget for 2009 in the wake of the global financial crisis, allowing for a significant increase in the budget deficit.

In Dec. 2008, on the basis of an unresolved border dispute, Slovenia obstructed Croatia's accession to the European Union and, in March 2009, was the last member of NATO to ratify Croatia's accession to the alliance. However, Slovenia and Croatia subsequently agreed to allow international arbitrators to resolve the border issue and in Sept. 2009 Pahor said that the dispute would no longer prejudice Croatia's EU accession negotiations.

Following a gas dispute between Russia and Ukraine at the beginning of 2009, Pahor moved to diversify Slovenia's energy supply to reduce its dependence on Russia. To this end he established the Strategic Energy Council, a consultative body to advise the government. Pahor has also said that he is committed to the fight against climate change.

DEFENCE

Compulsory military service for seven months ended in Sept. 2003. The army is expected to become fully professional in the course of 2010 when the current compulsory reserve is replaced by a new system of voluntary reserve service.

In 2006 military expenditure totalled US$629m. (US$313 per capita), representing 1·7% of GDP.

Army
Personnel (2007), 5,973 and an army reserve of 20,000. There is a paramilitary police force of 4,500 with 5,000 reserves.

Navy
There is an Army Maritime element numbering 47 personnel in 2007.

Air Force
The Army Air element numbers 530 with eight combat capable helicopters.

INTERNATIONAL RELATIONS

Slovenia is a member of the UN, World Bank, IMF and several other UN specialized agencies, WTO, EU, Council of Europe, OSCE, CEI, BIS, IOM, NATO, Inter-American Development Bank and is an associate partner of WEU. Slovenia held a referendum on EU membership on 23 March 2003, in which 89·6% of votes cast were in favour of accession. It became a member of NATO on 29 March 2004 and the EU on 1 May 2004.

In Dec. 2007 Slovenia acceded to the Schengen accord, which abolishes border controls between Slovenia, Austria, Belgium, Czech Republic, Denmark, Estonia, Finland, France, Germany, Greece, Hungary, Iceland, Italy, Latvia, Lithuania, Luxembourg, Malta, Netherlands, Norway, Poland, Portugal, Slovakia, Spain, Sweden and Switzerland.

ECONOMY

Agriculture accounted for 2% of GDP in 2007, industry 34% and services 63%.

Overview
Slovenia was amongst the most developed of the ten countries that joined the EU in May 2004. In Jan. 2007 it was the first of the ten to adopt the euro. GDP per capita at purchasing power parity is 80% of the EU average, higher than that of Greece and Portugal. The economy benefits from a well-educated, productive workforce, excellent infrastructure and a strategic location between Western and Eastern Europe.

The economy enjoys sound macroeconomic policy, with tight monetary and fiscal policies contributing to small fiscal deficits and single-digit inflation. There is a heavy dependence on exports (roughly 50% for EU markets), leaving the country vulnerable to wider economic trends. Despite its success, Slovenia has been criticized for having an unfriendly, inefficient business environment. The pace of privatization has been slower than in most other Central and Eastern European countries, with enterprises in key sectors remaining under state ownership. It has consequently attracted less FDI than other 2004 EU accession countries, though this has helped to contain inflation and to maintain a favourable external financial position.

Unlike other accession countries Slovenia has not had a substantial current account deficit. However, it has one of the most generous welfare states in Europe and the European Commission warns of the heavy future cost of the pension system.

Currency
On 1 Jan. 2007 the euro (EUR) replaced the *tolar* (SLT) as the legal currency of Slovenia at the irrevocable conversion rate of 239·64 tolars to one euro. Inflation was 3·6% in 2007 and 5·7% in 2008. Foreign exchange reserves were US$7,944m. and gold reserves 243,000 troy oz in June 2005. Total money supply in July 2005 was 1,032·3bn. tolars.

Budget
In 2005 revenues totalled 2,739bn. tolars and expenditures 2,846bn. tolars. Tax revenue accounted for 51·7% of revenue and social security contributions 38·3%; social protection accounted for 40·8% of expenditure and health 14·6%.

VAT is 20·0% (reduced rate, 8·5%).

Performance

The GDP growth rate was 5·9% in 2006, 6·8% in 2007 and 3·5% in 2008. Of all the central and eastern European countries that joined the European Union in May 2004, Slovenia has the highest per capita GDP at 84% of the EU average (higher than in Portugal and only marginally lower than in Greece). Total GDP in 2008 was US$54·6bn.

Banking and Finance

The central bank and bank of issue, the Bank of Slovenia, was founded on 25 June 1991 upon independence. Its current *Governor* is Marko Kranjec, appointed on 3 July 2007 for a term of six years. In 2003 there were 20 commercial banks (five subsidiaries of foreign banks and one branch office of a foreign bank) and two savings banks. The largest bank is Nova Ljubljanska banka (NLB), which has a market share of around one third and had assets in 2003 of US$9·1bn. Other large banks are Nova Kreditna Banka Maribor (NKBM) and Abanka Vipa. In 2008 Slovenia received US$1,815m. of foreign direct investment, up from US$1,438m. in 2007.

There is a stock exchange in Ljubljana (LSE).

ENERGY AND NATURAL RESOURCES

Environment

Slovenia's carbon dioxide emissions from the consumption and flaring of fossil fuels were the equivalent of 8·3 tonnes per capita in 2008. An *Environmental Performance Index* compiled in 2008 ranked Slovenia 15th in the world, with 86·3%. The index examined various factors in six areas—air pollution, biodiversity and habitat, climate change, environmental health, productive natural resources and water resources.

Electricity

Installed capacity was estimated at 2·6m. kW in 2004. There was one nuclear power station in operation. The total amount of electricity produced in 2004 was 15,279m. kWh (5,718m. kWh thermal, 5,459m. kWh nuclear and 4,102m. kWh hydro-electric). Consumption per capita in 2004 was 7,262 kWh.

Minerals

Brown coal production was 617,000 tonnes in 2003.

Agriculture

Only around 1·4% of the population work in agriculture. Output (in 1,000 tonnes) in 2003: maize, 224; sugar beets, 202; wheat, 123; potatoes, 108; grapes, 104.

Livestock in 2003: pigs, 620,506; cattle, 450,226; sheep, 105,660; poultry, 4,533,674.. Livestock products, 2003: meat, 177,200 tonnes; milk, 64·24m. litres.

In 2003 there were 172,753 ha. of arable land and 28,608 ha. of permanent crops.

Forestry

In 2003 the area under forests was 1·16m. ha., or 57·2% of the total land area. Timber production in 2007 was 2·88m. cu. metres.

Fisheries

Total marine fish catch in 2005 was 1,223 tonnes. Freshwater farming produced 1,148 tonnes in 2003.

INDUSTRY

Industry contributed 19·8% of GDP in 2008. Traditional industries are metallurgy, furniture-making and textiles. The manufacture of electric goods and transport equipment is being developed.

Production in 2007 (in 1,000 tonnes): ready mixed concrete, 2,922; basic iron and steel and ferro alloys, 1,643; cement (2006), 1,269; paper and paperboard, 720; aluminium and aluminium products, 446; plastics in primary form, 291; passenger cars, 174,209 units.

Labour

Registered labour force was 874,921 in 2003. In 2003, 433,098 people worked in services, 308,059 in industry, and 36,092 in agriculture and forestry. In 2003 there were 97,674 registered unemployed; in 2003 the registered unemployment rate was 11·2%. In 2003 the average monthly gross wage per employee was 253,200 tolars.

INTERNATIONAL TRADE

Foreign debt amounted to US$8,799m. in 2002. In 1997 Slovenia accepted 18% of the US$4,400m. commercial bank debt of the former Yugoslavia.

Imports and Exports

Imports (f.o.b.) in 2006 were worth US$22,856m. and exports (f.o.b.) US$21,397m. Exports accounted for 56·5% of GDP in 2003.

Major imports are road vehicles, electrical machinery, industrial machinery, petroleum and petroleum products, and iron and steel. Major exports are electrical machinery, apparatus and appliances (11·6%), road vehicles and parts (11·4%), and furniture (6·9%).

Share of imports from principal markets in 2003: Germany, 19·3%; Italy, 18·3%; France, 10·1%; Austria, 8·6%; Croatia, 3·6%. Exports: Germany, 23·1%; Italy, 13·1%; Croatia, 8·9%; Austria, 7·3%; France, 5·7%. About 63% of trade is with EU countries.

COMMUNICATIONS

Roads

In 2007 there were 38,708 km of road including 606 km of motorways. There were in 2007: 1,020,100 passenger cars; 2,300 buses and coaches; 81,500 vans and lorries; and 71,500 motorcycles and mopeds. 817m. passenger-km were travelled by road in 2007. There were 11,414 traffic accidents in 2007 in which 293 persons were killed. With 14·5 deaths per 100,000 population in 2007, Slovenia has among the highest death rates in road accidents of any industrialized country.

Rail

In 2003 there were 1,229 km of 1,435 mm gauge, of which 504 km were electrified. In 2003, 15·1m. passengers and 17·3m. tonnes of freight were carried.

Civil Aviation

There is an international airport at Ljubljana (Brnik), which handled 927,440 passengers (all on international flights) and 6,239 tonnes of freight in 2003. The national carrier, Adria Airways, has flights to most major European cities and Tel Aviv. In 2003 scheduled airline traffic of Slovenia-based carriers flew 13m. km, carrying 758,000 passengers.

Shipping

The biggest port is at Koper. Sea-going shipping totalled 9,146 GRT in 2001. In 2002 vessels totalling 6,825,000 NRT entered ports and vessels totalling 4,430,000 NRT cleared.

Telecommunications

In 2007 Slovenia had 2,785,600 telephone subscribers (1,391·7 per 1,000 inhabitants), including 1,928,400 mobile phone subscribers. The leading telecommunications operator is the state-owned Telekom Slovenije. The number of internet users in 2007 was 1,060,800.

Postal Services

In 2003 there were 554 post offices.

SOCIAL INSTITUTIONS

Justice

There are 44 district courts, 11 regional courts, four higher courts, an administrative court and a supreme court. There are also four labour and social courts, and a higher labour and social court. The population in penal institutions in Sept. 2008 was 1,317 (65 per 100,000 of national population).

Education

Adult literacy rate in 2004 was 99·7%. In 2007 there were 95,173 pupils and 6,111 teaching staff in primary schools; and 165,467 pupils and 16,179 teaching staff in secondary schools. There were 115,944 students and 5,609 academic staff in tertiary education in 2007. There are three public universities—at Koper (University of Primorska), Ljubljana and Maribor—and one private university, the University of Nova Gorica.

In 2006 public expenditure on education came to 5·9% of GNI and 12·9% of total government spending.

Health

In 2001 there were 4,361 doctors and 28 hospitals with 10,286 beds. In 2001 there were 1,178 dentists, 14,245 nurses and 776 pharmacists.

Welfare

There were 551,258 people receiving pensions in 2008, of which 342,992 were old-age pensioners. In 2006 spending on social protection accounted for 22·8% of GDP.

RELIGION

57·8% of the population were Roman Catholic according to the 2002 census. In Feb. 2010 there was one cardinal.

CULTURE

World Heritage Sites

Slovenia has one site on the UNESCO World Heritage List: Škocjan Caves (inscribed on the list in 1986), consisting of limestone caves, passages and waterfalls more than 200 metres deep.

Broadcasting

The government-controlled RTV Slovenia broadcasts two national TV channels, two regional channels and channels for the Hungarian and Italian communities. Pop TV and Kanal A are the main private TV stations. About two-thirds of households can access cable or satellite services. RTV Slovenia operates three national radio stations, an external service and regional services. There are numerous commercial radio stations. There were 664,000 TV-equipped households in 2006.

Cinema

There were 54 cinemas in 2007 with a total admission of 2·4m. Five full-length and seven short films were made in 2007.

Press

In 2003 there were five national daily newspapers, 47 weeklies and four published twice a week. In 2003 a total of 3,965 book titles were published.

Tourism

In 2005, 1,555,000 non-resident tourists stayed in holiday accommodation; spending by tourists totalled US$1,894m.

Libraries

In 2002 there were one national library, 54 higher education libraries, 125 special libraries, 60 public libraries and 648 school libraries; they held a combined 26,820,000 volumes.

Museums and Galleries

Museums totalled 48 in 2007 and housed nearly 1·5m. items.

DIPLOMATIC REPRESENTATIVES

Of Slovenia in the United Kingdom (10 Little College St., London, SW1P 3SH)
Ambassador: Iztok Jarc.

Of the United Kingdom in Slovenia (4th Floor, 3 Trg Republike, 1000 Ljubljana)
Ambassador: Andrew Page.

Of Slovenia in the USA (1525 New Hampshire Ave., NW, Washington, D.C., 20036)
Ambassador: Roman Kirn.

Of the USA in Slovenia (Presernova 31, 1000 Ljubljana)
Ambassador: Vacant.
Chargé d'Affaires a.i.: Bradley Freden.

Of Slovenia to the United Nations
Ambassador: Sanja Štiglic.

Of Slovenia to the European Union
Permanent Representative: Igor Senčar.

FURTHER READING

Benderly, J. and Kraft, E. (eds.) *Independent Slovenia: Origins, Movements, Prospects.* 1995
Cox, John K., *Slovenia.* 2005
Fink-Hafner, Danica and Robbins, John R., (eds.) *Making a New Nation: Formation of Slovenia.* 1997

National Statistical Office: National Statistical Office, Vožarski Pot 12, 1000 Ljubljana.
Website: http://www.stat.si

SOLOMON ISLANDS

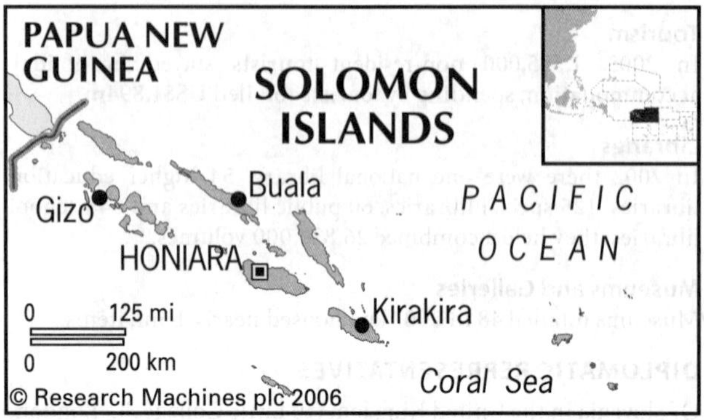

Capital: Honiara
Population estimate, 2010: 536,000
GDP per capita, 2007: (PPP$) 1,725
HDI/world rank: 0·610/135

KEY HISTORICAL EVENTS

The Solomon Islands were discovered by Europeans in 1568 but 200 years passed before contact was made again. The southern Solomon Islands were placed under British protection in 1893; the eastern and southern outliers were added in 1898 and 1899. Santa Isabel and the other islands to the north were ceded by Germany in 1900. Full internal self-government was achieved on 2 Jan. 1976 and independence on 7 July 1978.

In 1997 Bartholomew Ulufa'alu, a Malaitan, was elected prime minister. The following year, fighting broke out between the Isatubu Freedom Movement, which claimed to be representative of the native peoples of the island of Guadalcanal, and the Malaitan Eagle Force. In 2000 the Malaita Eagles led a coup which deposed Ulufa'alu, who was held at gunpoint for two days. After the failure of a 2001 peace accord, conflict between the Malaita Eagles and the Isatabu Freedom Movement escalated in 2003 and an Australian-led peacekeeping force landed to restore order. After some initial success the force was scaled back towards the end of the year.

In 2006 Manasseh Sogavare became prime minister, having previously held the office following the 2000 coup. His appointment was marked by rioting in Honiara and the destruction of the city's Chinatown as tensions rose over the political and business influence of the local Chinese population.

TERRITORY AND POPULATION

The Solomon Islands lie within the area 5° to 12° 30' S. lat. and 155° 30' to 169° 45' E. long. The group includes the main islands of Guadalcanal, Malaita, New Georgia, San Cristobal (now Makira), Santa Isabel and Choiseul; the smaller Florida and Russell groups; the Shortland, Mono (or Treasury), Vella La Vella, Kolombangara, Ranongga, Gizo and Rendova Islands; to the east, Santa Cruz, Tikopia, the Reef and Duff groups; Rennell and Bellona in the south; Ontong Java or Lord Howe to the north; and many smaller islands. The land area is estimated at 28,370 sq. km (10,954 sq. miles). The larger islands are mountainous and forest clad, with flood-prone rivers of considerable energy potential. Guadalcanal has the largest land area and the greatest amount of flat coastal plain. Population (1999 census), 409,042; density, 14·4 per sq. km. In 2005, 83·0% of the population lived in rural areas.

The UN gives an estimated population for 2010 of 536,000; density, 19 per sq. km.

The islands are administratively divided into nine provinces (plus a Capital Territory at the time of the 1999 census). Area and population:

Province	*Sq. km*	*Census 1999*	*Capital*
Capital Territory[1]	22	49,107	—
Central Islands	615	21,577	Tulagi
Choiseul	3,837	20,008	Taro
Guadalcanal[1]	5,336	60,275	Honiara
Isabel	4,136	20,421	Buala
Makira and Ulawa	3,188	31,006	Kirakira
Malaita	4,225	122,620	Auki
Rennell and Bellona	671	2,377	Tigoa
Temotu	895	18,912	Lata (Santa Cruz)
Western	5,475	62,739	Gizo

[1]Since 1999 Capital Territory has become part of the Guadalcanal province.

The capital, Honiara, on Guadalcanal, is the largest urban area, with an estimated population in 1999 of 68,000. 93% of the population are Melanesian; other ethnic groups include Polynesian, Micronesian, European and Chinese.

English is the official language, and is spoken by 1–2% of the population. In all 120 indigenous languages are spoken; Melanesian languages are spoken by 85% of the population.

SOCIAL STATISTICS

2002 estimates: births, 15,300; deaths, 2,100. Estimated birth rate in 2002 was 33·0 per 1,000 population; estimated death rate, 4·6. Life expectancy, 2007, 66·7 years for women and 64·9 for men. Annual population growth rate, 2000–05, 2·5%. Infant mortality, 2005, 24 per 1,000 live births; fertility rate, 2004, 4·2 births per woman.

CLIMATE

An equatorial climate with only small seasonal variations. Southeast winds cause cooler conditions from April to Nov., but northwest winds for the rest of the year bring higher temperatures and greater rainfall, with annual totals ranging between 80" (2,000 mm) and 120" (3,000 mm).

CONSTITUTION AND GOVERNMENT

The Solomon Islands are a constitutional monarchy with the British Sovereign (represented locally by a Governor-General, who must be a Solomon Island citizen) as Head of State. Legislative power is vested in the single-chamber *National Parliament* composed of 50 members, elected by universal adult suffrage for four years. Parliamentary democracy is based on a multi-party system. Executive authority is effectively held by the Cabinet, led by the Prime Minister.

The Governor-General is appointed for up to five years, on the advice of Parliament, and acts in almost all matters on the advice of the Cabinet. The Prime Minister is elected by and from members of Parliament. Other Ministers are appointed by the Governor-General on the Prime Minister's recommendation, from members of Parliament. The Cabinet is responsible to Parliament. Emphasis is laid on the devolution of power to provincial governments, and traditional chiefs and leaders have a special role within the arrangement.

National Anthem

'God save our Solomon Islands from shore to shore'; words and tune by P. Balekana.

RECENT ELECTIONS

National elections were held on 5 April 2006. The National Party won 4 seats, the Rural Advancement Party 4, the People's Alliance Party 3, the Democratic Party 3, ind. 30 and three other parties won 2 seats each.

On 13 Dec. 2007 the government of Prime Minister Manasseh Sogavare was defeated in a no confidence vote in parliament by 25 votes to 22. Derek Sikua was elected prime minister on 20 Dec., defeating Patteson Oti by 32 votes to 15 in the parliamentary vote.

Frank Kabui was elected governor-general by parliament on 15 June 2009. He defeated Edmund Andersen and the incumbent, Sir Nathaniel Waena.

CURRENT ADMINISTRATION

Governor-General: Frank Kabui (since 7 July 2009).

In March 2010 the government comprised:

Prime Minister: Derek Sikua; b. 1959 (sworn in 20 Dec. 2007).

Deputy Prime Minister and Rural Development and Indigenous Affairs: Fred Fono.

Minister of Agriculture and Livestock: Selwyn Riumana. *Development Planning and Aid Co-ordination:* Steve Abana. *Finance and the Treasury:* Snyder Rini. *Environment and Meteorology:* Gordon Darcy Lilo. *Police, National Security and Correctional Services:* James Tora. *Justice and Legal Affairs:* Laurie Chan. *Education and Human Resources Development:* Job Dudley Tausinga. *Health and Medical Services:* Martin Magga. *Foreign Affairs:* William Haomae. *Commerce and Employment:* Francis Billy Hilly. *Culture and Tourism:* Seth Gukuna. *Infrastructure:* Stanley Festus Sofu. *Communication and Civil Aviation:* Varian Lonamei. *Forests:* Sir Allan Kemakeza. *Fisheries and Marine Resources:* Nollen Leni. *Mines, Energy and Rural Electrification:* David Pacha. *Provincial Government and Institutional Strengthening:* Manasseh Maelanga. *Home Affairs:* Peter Tom. *National Reconciliation and Peace:* Sam S. Iduri. *Women, Youth and Children:* Johnson Koli. *Lands, Survey and Housing:* Samuel Manetoali. *Public Service:* Milner Tozaka.

Solomon Islands Parliament: http://www.parliament.gov.sb

CURRENT LEADERS

Derek Sikua

Position
Prime Minister

Introduction
Derek Sikua took office in Dec. 2007 to become the Solomon Islands' 13th prime minister since independence in 1978. He defeated the foreign minister, Patteson Oti, in the parliamentary poll.

Early Life
Derek Sikua was born on 10 Sept. 1959 in Ngalitavethi Village, East Tasiboko, Guadalcanal Province. He worked as a teacher and deputy principal from 1982–86 and graduated in education from the University of Southern Queensland (Australia) in 1985. He then took a masters degree in educational policy and administration at Monash University (Australia) and a PhD in educational decentralization at the University of Waikato (New Zealand).

Between 1993 and 1997 Sikua worked at the ministry of education and human resources development, devising and implementing educational policy in the Solomon Islands. From 1997–98 he was permanent secretary in the ministry of forests, environment and conservation. From 2003–05 he returned to the ministry of education and human resources development as permanent secretary, and from 2006 also served as chairman of the Solomon Islands national commission for UNESCO.

Career in Office
Sikua entered parliament on 5 April 2006, representing the North East Guadalcanal constituency in the government of Prime Minister Manasseh Sogavare. On 4 May 2006 he was appointed minister for education and human resources, a post he held until Nov. 2007. On 13 Dec. 2007 Sikua led a parliamentary motion of no confidence against Sogavare. Supported by seven other cabinet ministers and one backbencher, Sikua defected from the government.

The events leading to the no-confidence vote sparked the formation of the Coalition for National Unity and Rural Advancement under Sikua's leadership. On 20 Dec. he defeated Patteson Oti, the foreign affairs minister, by 32 votes to 15 to be elected prime minister. Sikua pledged to work towards economic reform (particularly rural development), to regulate the logging industry and to hold consultations on a new federal constitution. In Aug. 2008 he defeated a no-confidence motion brought by opposition members.

In April 2009 the government announced austerity measures as the effects of the global economic crisis depressed demand for commodity exports and reduced revenues.

DEFENCE

The marine wing of the Royal Solomon Islands Police operates three patrol boats and a number of fast crafts for surveillance of fisheries and maritime boundaries. There is also an RSI Police Field Force stationed at the border with Papua New Guinea.

In July 2003 an Australian-led peacekeeping force landed to restore stability after years of ethnic fighting and high-level corruption. The force included troops from the Fiji Islands, New Zealand, Papua New Guinea and Tonga.

INTERNATIONAL RELATIONS

The Solomon Islands are a member of the UN, World Bank, IMF and several other UN specialized agencies, WTO, Commonwealth, Asian Development Bank, Pacific Islands Forum, SPC and are an ACP member state of the ACP-EU relationship. The Solomon Islands are also a member of the World Trade Organization and other organizations for regional technical co-operation.

ECONOMY

Agriculture accounted for 35·1% of GDP in 2006, industry 9·0% and services 55·9%.

Overview
Since Australian intervention in 2003 to restore political stability after years of civil strife, economic performance has been robust with average annual growth of 7%. Real GDP growth increased to 10·7% in 2007, driven mainly by timber exports, emerging sectors including palm oil and growth in service industries. Inflation rose to over 10% by the end of 2007 and has continued to grow owing to higher world food and fuel prices, rapid private sector credit growth and an expansionary fiscal policy.

Declines in logging and aid present critical challenges to medium-term growth, highlighting the need for a broader revenue base. But there has been limited progress in stimulating other sources of growth. Gold mining operations were relaunched in March 2010; when production begins again this may help to alleviate pressure on balance of payments. Poor infrastructure, a shortage of skilled workers, land ownership issues and weak governance are further issues yet to be addressed. Per capita income remains below pre-conflict levels and the economy was ranked amongst the poorest of the Pacific Island countries in 2007.

Currency
The *Solomon Island dollar* (SBD) of 100 *cents* was introduced in 1977. It was devalued by 20% in Dec. 1997 and 25% in March 2002. Inflation was 7·7% in 2007, rising to 17·2% in 2008. In July

2005 foreign exchange reserves were US$83m. and total money supply was SI$447m.

Budget

In 2006 revenues totalled SI$946·2m. and expenditures SI$911·1m. Tax revenue accounted for 73·0% of revenues in 2006; current expenditure accounted for 90·5% of expenditures.

Performance

Real GDP growth was 10·7% in 2007 and 6·9% in 2008. Total GDP in 2008 was US$0·6bn.

Banking and Finance

The Central Bank of Solomon Islands is the bank of issue; its *Governor* is Denton Rarawa. There are three commercial banks and a development bank.

ENERGY AND NATURAL RESOURCES

Environment

Carbon dioxide emissions from the consumption and flaring of fossil fuels in 2008 were the equivalent of 0·4 tonnes per capita.

Electricity

Installed capacity in 2004 was approximately 12,000 kW. Production in 2004 was about 33m. kWh and consumption per capita an estimated 63 kWh.

Oil and Gas

The potential for oil, petroleum and gas production has yet to be tapped.

Minerals

In 1999 gold output from mining totalled 3,456 kg and silver output 2,138 kg. The only mine in the Solomon Islands closed in 2000 owing to the civil unrest. However, in March 2010 the mine was revived preparing the way for production to resume in early 2011. The value of gold exports in 1999 was SI$113·7m.

Agriculture

Land is held either as customary land (88% of holdings) or registered land. Customary land rights depend on clan membership or kinship. Only Solomon Islanders own customary land; only Islanders or government members may hold perpetual estates of registered land. Coconuts, cocoa, rice and other minor crops are grown. Production, 2003 estimates (in 1,000 tonnes): coconuts, 330; sweet potatoes, 83; taro, 38; palm oil, 34; yams, 28; copra, 30; palm kernels, 8. In 2007 there were an estimated 16,000 ha. of arable land and 60,000 ha. of permanent crops.

Livestock (2003 estimates): pigs, 68,000; cattle, 13,000.

Forestry

Forests covered 2·17m. ha. in 2005 (77·6% of the land area). In 2004 earnings from forestry and logging amounted to SI$280·7m. Timber production was 1·25m. cu. metres in 2007.

Fisheries

Solomon Islands' waters are among the richest in tuna. Catches have remained well below the maximum sustainable catch limits. Previously closed areas within its territorial waters have been opened to American fishing interests but sustainable harvest rates will not be at risk. The total catch in 2005 was an estimated 28,520 tonnes.

INDUSTRY

Industries include palm oil manufacture (35,000 tonnes in 2002), processed fish production (13,700 tonnes in 2000), rice milling, fish canning, fish freezing, saw milling, food, tobacco and soft drinks. Other products include wood and rattan furniture, fibreglass articles, boats, clothing and spices.

Labour

The Labour Division of the Ministry of Commerce, Employment and Tourism monitors and regulates the domestic labour market. The labour force in 1996 totalled 202,000 (54% males). Around 38% of the economically active population in 1993 were engaged in community, social and personal services and 27% in agriculture, fisheries and forestry.

Trade Unions

Trade Unions exist by virtue of the Trade Unions Act of 1976. The Solomon Islands Council of Trade Unions (SICTU) is the central body. Affiliated members of the SICTU are Solomon Islands National Union of Workers and the Solomon Islands Public Employees Union (SIPEU). SIPEU, which represents employees of the public sector, is the largest single trade union.

INTERNATIONAL TRADE

Total foreign debt in 2007 was US$178m.

Imports and Exports

Imports 2007, US$285·0m.; exports, US$158·5m. Main imports, 2007: machinery and transport equipment, 28·4%; mineral fuels and lubricants, 24·9%; food and live animals, 17·6%. Main exports, 2007: timber, 66·6%; fish products, 13·0%; palm oil, 8·8%. Principal import suppliers (2007): Australia, 31·5%; Singapore, 27·0%; Japan, 8·2%. Principal export markets (2007): China, 46·5%; Thailand, 7·2%; South Korea, 6·1%.

Trade Fairs

An annual National Trade and Cultural Show is held in July to coincide with the anniversary of independence.

COMMUNICATIONS

Roads

In 2002 there was estimated to be a total of 1,360 km of roads, of which 34 km were paved. The unpaved roads included 800 km of private plantation roads.

Civil Aviation

A new terminal has been opened at Henderson International Airport in Honiara. The national carrier is Solomon Airlines. In 2003 scheduled airline traffic of Solomon Islands-based carriers flew 2m. km, carrying 68,000 passengers (23,000 on international flights).

Shipping

There are international ports at Honiara, Yandina in the Russell Islands and Noro in New Georgia, Western Province. In 2002 the merchant marine totalled 8,000 GRT.

Telecommunications

Telecommunications are operated by Solomon Telekom, a joint venture between the government of Solomon Islands and Cable & Wireless (UK). Telecommunications between Honiara and provincial centres are facilitated by modern satellite communication systems. In 2008 there were 8,000 main (fixed) telephone lines; mobile phone subscribers numbered 30,000 (5·9 per 100 persons). There were 22,000 PCs in use in 2005 and an estimated 4,000 internet users.

Postal Services

The Solomon Islands Postal Corporation, a statutory company established in 1996, administers postal services. In 2003 there were 27 post offices.

SOCIAL INSTITUTIONS

Justice

Civil and criminal jurisdiction is exercised by the High Court of the Solomon Islands, constituted 1975. A Solomon Islands Court of Appeal was established in 1982. Jurisdiction is based on the principles of English law (as applying on 1 Jan. 1981). Magistrates' courts can try civil cases on claims not exceeding SI$2,000, and criminal cases with penalties not exceeding 14 years' imprisonment. Certain crimes, such as burglary and arson, where the maximum sentence is for life, may also be tried by magistrates. There are also local courts, which decide matters concerning customary titles to land; decisions may be put to the Customary Land Appeal Court. There is no capital punishment.

The population in penal institutions in 2004 was 275 (56 per 100,000 of national population).

Education

In 2005 there were 100,026 pupils at primary and 22,487 pupils at secondary level. The adult literacy rate in 1998 was 62·0%.

Training of teachers and trade and vocational training is carried out at the College of Higher Education. The University of the South Pacific Centre is at Honiara. Other rural training centres run by churches are also involved in vocational training.

In 2000–01 total expenditure on education came to 3·6% of GNP and in 1999–2000 accounted for 15·4% of total government spending.

Health

A free medical service is supplemented by the private sector. An international standard immunization programme is conducted in conjunction with the WHO for infants. Tuberculosis has been eradicated but malaria remains a problem. In 1997 there were 11 hospitals, 31 doctors and 464 registered nurses and 283 nursing aides.

RELIGION

92% of the population were Christians in 2001.

CULTURE

World Heritage Sites

The Solomon Islands has one site on the UNESCO World Heritage List: East Rennell (inscribed on the list in 1998), the largest raised coral atoll in the world.

Broadcasting

The Solomon Islands Broadcasting Corporation (SIBC) operates a public national radio service, an FM service for Honiara and two provincial stations. ZFM100 and Paoa FM are commercial stations. There are no television services based in the Solomon Islands, but foreign satellite TV stations can be received. There were 5,500 TV receivers in 2005.

Cinema

Private interests operate three cinemas in the capital. There are small cinemas in the provincial centres.

Press

There are three main newspapers in circulation. *The Solomon Star* (circulation: 5,000) is daily and the *Solomon Express* and *The Island Sun* are weekly. The Government Information Service publishes a monthly issue of the *Solomon Nius* which exclusively disseminates news of government activities. Non-government organizations such as the Solomon Islands Development Trust (SIDT) also publish monthly papers on environmental issues.

Tourism

Tourism in the Solomon Islands is still in a development stage. The emphasis is on establishing major hotels in the capital and provincial centres, to be supplemented by satellite eco-tourism projects in the rural areas. The Solomon Islands Visitors Bureau is the statutory institution for domestic co-ordination and international marketing. In 2007 there were 13,748 foreign tourists.

Festivals

Festivities and parades in the capital and provincial centres normally mark the National Day of Independence. The highlight is the annual National Trade and Cultural Show.

Libraries

There is a National Library operated by the government in Honiara. The other library facilities are those of the Solomon Islands College of Higher Education and the University of the South Pacific (SI) Centre.

Museums and Galleries

There is a National Museum which has a display of traditional artefacts. Early government and public records are kept at the National Archives and a National Art Gallery displays a number of fine arts and works by Solomon Islands artists.

DIPLOMATIC REPRESENTATIVES

Of the Solomon Islands in the United Kingdom
High Commissioner: Joseph Ma'ahanua (resides in Brussels).

Of the United Kingdom in the Solomon Islands (Telekom House, Mendana Ave., Honiara)
High Commissioner: Timothy Smart.

Of the Solomon Islands in the USA and to the United Nations (800 2nd Ave, Suite 400L, New York, NY 10017)
Ambassador: Collin Beck.

Of the USA in the Solomon Islands
Ambassador: Teddy B. Taylor (resides in Port Moresby, Papua New Guinea).

Of the Solomon Islands to the European Union
Ambassador: Joseph Ma'ahanua.

FURTHER READING

Bennett, J. A., *Wealth of the Solomons: A History of a Pacific Archipelago, 1800–1978*. 1987

Fraenkel, Jonathan, *Manipulation of Custom: From Uprising to Intervention in the Solomon Islands*. 2005

White, Geoffrey M., *Identity Through History: Living Stories in a Solomon Islands Society*. 2003

National Statistical Office: Solomon Islands National Statistical Office, PO Box G6, Department of Finance, Honiara.
Website: http://www.spc.int/prism/country/sb/stats

SOMALIA

Jamhuuriyada Demuqraadiga Soomaaliyeed
(Democratic Republic of Somalia)

Capital: Mogadishu
Population estimate, 2010: 9·36m.
GDP per capita: not available
GNI per capita, 2007: US$297

KEY HISTORICAL EVENTS

The origins of the Somali people can be traced back 2,000 years when they displaced an earlier Arabic people. They converted to Islam in the 10th century and were organized in loose Islamic states by the 19th century. The northern part of Somaliland was created a British protectorate in 1884. The southern part belonged to two local rulers who, in 1889, accepted Italian protection for their lands. The Italian invasion of Ethiopia in 1935 was launched from Somaliland and in 1936 Somaliland was incorporated with Eritrea and Ethiopia to become Italian East Africa. In 1940 Italian forces invaded British Somaliland but in 1941 the British, with South African and Indian troops, recaptured this territory as well as occupying Italian Somaliland. After the Second World War British Somaliland reverted to its colonial status and ex-Italian Somaliland became the UN Trust Territory of Somaliland, administered by Italy.

The independent Somali Republic came into being on 1 July 1960 as a result of the merger of the British Somaliland Protectorate, which first became independent on 26 June 1960, and the Italian Trusteeship Territory of Somaliland. On 21 Oct. 1969 Maj.-Gen. Mohammed Siyad Barre took power in a coup. Various insurgent forces combined to oppose the Barre regime in a bloody civil war. Barre fled on 27 Jan. 1991 but interfactional fighting continued. In Aug. 1992 a new coalition government agreed a UN military presence to back up relief efforts to help the estimated 1·5–2m. victims of famine. On 11 Dec. 1992 the leaders of the two most prominent of the warring factions, Ali Mahdi Muhammad and Muhammad Farah Aidid, agreed to a peace plan under the aegis of the UN and a pact was signed on 15 Jan. 1993. At the end of March, the warring factions agreed to disarm and form a 74-member National Transitional Council. On 4 Nov. 1994 the UN Security Council unanimously decided to withdraw UN forces; the last of these left on 2 March 1995.

The principal insurgent group in the north of the country, the Somali National Movement, declared the secession of an independent **'Somaliland Republic'** on 17 May 1991. The Somalian government rejected the secession and Muhammad Aidid's forces launched a campaign to reoccupy the 'Republic' in Jan. 1996. Muhammad Farah Aidid was assassinated in July 1996 and succeeded by his son Hussein Aidid. In July 1998 leaders in the northeast of Somalia proclaimed an 'autonomous state' named **Puntland.**

Peace efforts in neighbouring Djibouti culminated in July 2000 in the establishment of a power-sharing agreement and a national constitution to see Somalia through a three-year transitional period. The election of members of parliament and a civilian government followed in Aug. 2000, and in Oct. the new government moved from Djibouti back to Somalia. In April 2002 **'Southwestern Somalia'** broke away from Mogadishu, thereby creating a third autonomous Somali state.

In June 2006 after months of fighting an Islamic militia, the Islamic Courts Union, took control of the capital, Mogadishu, and a large part of southern Somalia. In Dec. 2006, following a sustained assault by government forces backed by Ethiopian troops, the Islamist militias withdrew from Mogadishu. The southern city of Kismayo, the Islamists' last stronghold, was recaptured in Jan. 2007.

TERRITORY AND POPULATION

Somalia is bounded north by the Gulf of Aden, east and south by the Indian ocean, and west by Kenya, Ethiopia and Djibouti. Total area 637,657 sq. km (246,201 sq. miles). At the last census, in 1987, the population was 7,114,431. Population counting is complicated owing to large numbers of nomads and refugee movements as a result of famine and clan warfare.

The UN gives an estimated population for 2010 of 9·36m.; density, 15 per sq. km.

In 2000 an estimated 66·7% of the population were rural.

The country is administratively divided into 18 regions (with chief cities): Awdal (Baki), Bakol (Xuddur), Bay (Baydhabo), Benadir (Mogadishu), Bari (Boosaso), Galgudug (Duusa Marreeb), Gedo (Garbahaarrey), Hiran (Beledweyne), Jubbada Dexe (Jilib), Jubbada Hoose (Kismayo), Mudug (Gaalkacyo), Nogal (Garowe), Woqooyi Galbeed (Hargeisa), Sanaag (Ceerigabo), Shabeellaha Dhexe (Jawhar), Shabeellaha Hoose (Marka), Sol (Las Anod), Togder (Burao). Somaliland comprises the regions of Awdal, Woqooyi Galbeed, Togder, Sanaag and Sol. Puntland consists of Bari, Nogal and northern Mudug. Southwestern Somalia consists of Bay, Bakol, Gedo, Jubbada Hoose and Shabeellaha Dhexe.

The capital is Mogadishu (1999 population, 1,162,000). Other large towns are (with 1990 estimates) Hargeisa (90,000), Kismayo (90,000), Berbera (70,000) and Marka (62,000).

The official language is Somali. Arabic, English and Italian are widely spoken.

SOCIAL STATISTICS

Births, 1997 estimate, 300,000; deaths, 121,000. Rates, 1997 estimate (per 1,000 population): birth, 45·5; death, 18·3. Infant mortality, 2005, 133 per 1,000 live births. Annual population growth rate, 1992–2002, 2·8%. Life expectancy at birth, 2007, was 48·3 years for men and 51·2 years for women. Fertility rate, 2004, 6·3 births per woman.

CLIMATE

Much of the country is arid, although rainfall is more adequate towards the south. Temperatures are very high on the northern coasts. Mogadishu, Jan. 79°F (26·1°C), July 78°F (25·6°C). Annual rainfall 17" (429 mm). Berbera, Jan. 76°F (24·4°C), July 97°F (36·1°C). Annual rainfall 2" (51 mm).

CONSTITUTION AND GOVERNMENT

The constitution of 1979 authorized a sole legal party, the Somali Revolutionary Socialist Party. There was an elected President and People's Assembly. The constitution was amended in 1984.

A conference of national reconciliation in July 1991 and again in March 1993 allowed for the setting up of a transitional government charged with reorganizing free elections, but inter-factional fighting and anarchy have replaced settled government.

In Aug. 2000 a transitional parliament with a three-year mandate was inaugurated, at the time in neighbouring Djibouti but subsequently in Mogadishu. There was a 245-member *Transitional National Assembly* appointed by clan chiefs.

Under an agreed charter the transitional assembly was to elect a president who in turn was to form a government. However, ongoing wrangling between Somalia's rival factions continues. In Nov. 2002 leaders of the Somali factions met in order to begin the process of drawing up a new federal constitution. In Jan. 2004 the country's leaders signed an agreement to form a new government based along clan lines. In Aug. 2004 a new 275-member Somali Transitional Federal Parliament (TFP) was inaugurated in Nairobi, Kenya. The newly-formed UN-backed government began the process of returning from Kenya to Somalia in June 2005. Amid concern over security in Mogadishu, parliament met for the first time in Feb. 2006 in Baidoa. However, when it fell to insurgents in Jan. 2009 the TFP met first in Djibouti and then in Mogadishu, before renewed fighting in the capital forced legislators to seek a new, temporary base. It was agreed in Jan. 2009 in Djibouti to double the number of members of parliament from 275 to 550.

Puntland. Puntland, in the northeast region of Somalia, declared itself an 'autonomous state' in July 1998 under the leadership of Abdullahi Yusuf. Since its creation, Puntland has been locked in dispute with Somaliland over control of the Sanaag and Sol areas.

Puntland covers 300,000 sq. km and had a population in 2000 of 2m. The capital is Garowe. Somali is the official language and the Somali shilling is the official currency. Puntland has not received international recognition.

Somaliland. An independent 'Somaliland Republic', based on the territory of the former British protectorate which ran from 1884 until Somali independence in 1960, was established on 17 May 1991 by the principal insurgent group in the north of the country, the Somali National Movement. The Somali government rejected the secession and an unsuccessful campaign to reoccupy Somaliland was launched in Jan. 1996. Somaliland is also engaged in a long-running dispute with Puntland over control of the Sanaag and Sol regions. The Republic has failed to secure international recognition although it has in effect seceded from Somalia.

Somaliland covers 137,600 sq. km. The capital is Hargeisa and there is a port at Berbera. There is a population of around 3·5m. Somali is the official language and Arabic and English are also widely used.

There is a bicameral government with a house of representatives and one of elected elders. Dahir Riyale Kahin became *President* in May 2002 and was re-elected in April 2004. The judiciary is independent. The official currency is the Somaliland shilling. The Bank of Somaliland, the central bank, was founded in 1994. The economy is reliant on livestock farming.

Southwestern Somalia. In April 2002 Southwestern Somalia broke away from Mogadishu and was declared an autonomous state by the Rahanwein Resistance Army. Hassan Muhammad Nur 'Shatigadud' was named president but fighting between Shatigadud and several of his deputies ensued, notably around the capital, Baydhabo.

National Anthem

'Somaliyaay toosoo' ('Somalia wake up'); words and tune anonymous.

RECENT ELECTIONS

Somalia's Transitional Federal Parliament elected Sheikh Sharif Sheikh Ahmed president on 31 Jan. 2009 in Djibouti. In the first round Sheikh Sharif Sheikh Ahmed won 215 votes, followed by Maslah Mohamed Siad with 60 and Prime Minister Col. Nur Hassan Hussein with 59. There were 11 other candidates. All candidates apart from Sheikh Sharif Sheikh Ahmed and Maslah Mohamed Siad withdrew after the first round. A subsequent run-off was held in which Ahmed won 293 votes against 126 for Siad.

CURRENT ADMINISTRATION

President: Sheikh Sharif Sheikh Ahmed (since 31 Jan. 2009).

In March 2010 the Transitional Federal Government comprised:

Prime Minister: Omar Abdirashid Ali Sharmarke; b. 1960 (since 14 Feb. 2009).

Deputy Prime Minister and Minister of Finance: Sharif Hassan Sheikh Adan. *Deputy Prime Minister and Minister of Fisheries and Marine Resources:* Abdirahman Haji Adan Ibbi. *Deputy Prime Minister and Minister of Energy and Fuel:* Abdiwahid Ilmi Gonjeh.

Minister of Agriculture: Mohamed Ibrahim Habsade. *Air and Land Transport:* Mohamed Abdi Gandhi. *Commerce:* Abdirashid Iro. *Constitution and Federal Affairs:* Madobe Nunow Muhammad. *Culture and Higher Education:* Ibrahim Hasan Adow. *Defence:* Abdalla Bos Ahmed. *Diaspora:* Abdullahi Ahmad Abdulle Azhari. *Education:* Ahmad Abdullahi Wayel. *Endowment and Religious Affairs:* Sheikh Nur Ali Adan. *Environment and Conservation of Trees:* Buri Hamza. *Foreign Affairs:* Ali Jama Ahmed Jengeli. *Health:* Qamar Adan Ali. *Humanitarian Assistance:* Dr Mahmud Abdi Ibrahim. *Industry:* Abdirahman Jama Abdalla. *Information:* Dahir Mohamud Gelle. *Interior:* Sheikh Abdulkadir Ali Omar. *Justice:* Abdirahman Mahmud Farah Janaqow. *Labour:* Muhammad Abdi Mareye. *Livestock Development:* Abukar Ali Usman. *Militia Disarmament:* Fahran Mohamud Ali. *National Heritage:* Muhammad Mursal. *National Planning and International Co-operation:* Abdirahman Abdishakur Warsame. *National Security:* Abdullahi Mohamed Ali. *Ports and Sea Transport:* Abdiaziz Hassan Mohamed. *Posts and Communications:* Abdirizak Usman Jurile. *Reconciliation:* Abdirashid Haji Deerow. *Reconstruction:* Husayn Elabe Fahiye. *Rehabilitation and the Disabled:* Muhammad Ali Ibrahim. *Research and Technology:* Muhammad Ali Haga. *Rural Development:* Khadija Muhammad Diriye. *Sports and Youth:* Saleban Olad Roble. *Tourism and Wildlife:* Muhammad Husayn Saeed. *Treasury:* Abdirahman Omar Osman. *Water and Mineral Resources:* Mohamed Abdullahi Omaar. *Women and Family Affairs:* Fowsiya Muhammad Sheikh. *Works and Housing:* Muhammad Abdi Yusuf.

Transitional Federal Government Website:
http://www.somaligov.net

CURRENT LEADERS

Sheikh Sharif Sheikh Ahmed

Position
President

Introduction
In Jan. 2009 Sheikh Sharif Sheikh Ahmed was elected president of Somalia at the head of a Transitional Federal Government (TFG).

Early Life
Ahmed was born in 1964 in the rural Mahaday district, northeast of Mogadishu. He comes from a section of the Abgaal clan of Hawiye, which dominates central-southern Somalia. He studied at a school attached to the local mosque before attending the Egyptian-run Sheikh Sufi Institute, associated with Cairo's Al Azhar University, in Mogadishu. In the 1990s Ahmed studied in Sudan and at the Open University in Libya, graduating in Islamic Sharia and Law in 1998 before returning to Somalia.

He became head of an Islamic court in Jowhar in 2002 but fled to Mogadishu in 2003 after forces led by the warlord Mohammed Dheere (a future mayor of Jowhar and a TFG ally) attacked the region. In Mogadishu Ahmed taught at Jubba Secondary School and became a central organizer of the Islamic Courts Union (ICU). In mid-2006 the ICU took control of the capital and Ahmed emerged as ICU chairman, working alongside Hassan Dahir Aweys. For six months the ICU controlled large swathes of southern and central Somalia, establishing varying degrees of Sharia law, reopening Mogadishu's sea- and airports and quelling piracy along the coast. In Dec. 2006, backed by Ethiopian forces, the TFG expelled the ICU and Ahmed fled to Kenya.

In Eritrea in 2007, Ahmed, Aweys and anti-TFG elements formed the Alliance for the Re-Liberation of Somalia (ARS). However, in 2008 Ahmed entered UN-brokered talks with the TFG in Djibouti and split from ARS hardliners including Aweys. Ahmed's supporters joined with the TFG to form a parliament that elected him president of Somalia in Jan. 2009. The election took place in Djibouti, with Ahmed securing a majority of votes from the 500 unelected lawmakers to defeat 14 rivals.

Career in Office
Throughout Ahmed's first year in office Somalia remained in turmoil from civil war, with thousands of civilians continuing to flee from the capital and with over 3m. people dependent on food aid. In June he declared a state of emergency as the Islamist insurgency intensified and appealed in vain for neighbouring Ethiopia and Kenya to send troops in support of the Somali government forces. In Sept. the Shahab Islamist group, controlling most of the south of the country, proclaimed its allegiance to Osama bin Laden, the leader of al-Qaeda, and the following month won control of the port city of Kismayo. Another major problem for the government has been the increasing incidence and range of piracy in the seas off Somalia. Many foreign navies have been deployed to patrol the area to deter Somali pirates but recorded hijackings continued to rise in 2009.

DEFENCE

With the breakdown of government following the 1991 revolution armed forces broke up into clan groupings, four of them in the north and six in the south.

Army

Following the 1991 revolution there are no national armed forces. In Northern Somalia the Somali National Movement controls an armed clan of 5–6,000 out of a total of 7,000 armed forces in the area. In the rest of the country several local groups control forces of which the Ali Mahdi Faction controls the largest, an armed clan of 10,000.

INTERNATIONAL RELATIONS

Somalia is a member of the UN, World Bank, IMF and several other UN specialized agencies, IOM, Islamic Development Bank, OIC, African Development Bank, African Union, Intergovernmental Authority on Development, the League of Arab States and is an ACP member state of the ACP-EU relationship.

ECONOMY

Agriculture accounts for approximately 59% of GDP, industry 10% and services 31%.

Somalia was rated the most corrupt country in the world in a 2009 survey of 180 countries carried out by the anti-corruption organization *Transparency International.*

Overview

Somalia has been entangled in civil conflict with no effective central government since 1991. A large private sector, trading locally and with neighbouring Asian economies, has compensated for a weak public sector. Remittances, amounting to around US$1bn. per year, have helped stimulate private investment in a number of commercial ventures, as well as partially offsetting a decline in per capita income. Social conditions have deteriorated since the onset of civil war, with an estimated 43% of the population living in extreme poverty. Economic growth is expected to remain minimal across most of the country until peace and stability return.

Currency

The unit of currency is the *Somali shilling* (SOS) of 100 *cents*.

Budget

Budget for 1991: revenue, Som.Sh. 151,453m.; expenditure, Som. Sh. 141,141m.

Performance

Real GDP growth was 3·5% in both 2002 and 2003. Total GDP in 2003 was US$1·5bn.

Banking and Finance

The bank of issue is the Central Bank of Somalia. The separatist Somaliland Republic has its own functioning central bank in Hargeisa, the Bank of Somaliland (*Governor*, Abdourahman Dualeh Mohamoud). Remittance companies (*hawala*) took the place of banks in the 1990s, channelling approximately US$800m. a year. Al-Barakaat, the largest *hawala*, was shut down in Nov. 2001. All national banks were bankrupted by 1990. The Universal Bank of Somalia, the first commercial bank in Mogadishu since 1990, opened with European backing in Jan. 2002.

ENERGY AND NATURAL RESOURCES

Environment

Carbon dioxide emissions from the consumption and flaring of fossil fuels in 2008 were the equivalent of 0·1 tonnes per capita.

Electricity

In 2004 installed capacity was estimated at 80,000 kW. Production (2004 estimate): 286m. kWh.

Oil and Gas

Proven natural gas reserves were 5·7bn. cu. metres in 2007.

Minerals

There are deposits of chromium, coal, copper, gold, gypsum, lead, limestone, manganese, nickel, sepiolite, silver, titanium, tungsten, uranium and zinc.

Agriculture

Somalia is essentially a pastoral country, and about 80% of the inhabitants depend on livestock-rearing. Half the population is nomadic. In 2002 there were about 1·05m. ha. of arable land and 26,000 ha. of permanent crops. Around 200,000 ha. were irrigated in 2002. There were about 1,700 tractors in 2002. Output, 2003 estimates (in 1,000 tonnes): sugarcane, 200; maize, 164; sorghum, 121; cassava, 85; bananas, 35. Livestock (2003 estimates): 13·1m. sheep; 12·7m. goats; 7·0m. camels; 5·1m. cattle. Somalia has the greatest number of camels of any country in the world.

Forestry
In 2005 the area under forests was 7·13m. ha., or 11·4% of the total land area. In 2007, 11·57m. cu. metres of roundwood were cut. Wood and charcoal are the main energy sources. Frankincense and myrrh are produced.

Fisheries
Approximately 30,000 tonnes of fish were caught in 2005, almost entirely from marine waters.

INDUSTRY

A few small industries exist including sugar refining (production was 20,000 tonnes in 2001), food processing and textiles.

Labour
The labour force totalled 4,291,000 in 1996 (57% males). Approximately 74% of the economically active population in 1995 were engaged in agriculture, fisheries and forestry.

INTERNATIONAL TRADE

Foreign debt was US$2,750m. in 2005.

Imports and Exports
Imports in 2003 were estimated at US$397m. and exports at US$95m.

Principal imports: manufactures, petroleum, foodstuffs. Main exports: livestock, hides and skins, bananas. Leading import suppliers, 2003: Djibouti, 32%; Kenya, 15%; Brazil, 11%; United Arab Emirates, 5%. Leading export markets, 2003: United Arab Emirates, 39%; Yemen, 24%; Oman, 11%; China, 6%.

COMMUNICATIONS

Roads
In 2002 there were an estimated 22,100 km of roads, of which 2,600 km were paved. Passenger cars numbered 12,700 in 2002, and there were 10,400 trucks and vans.

Civil Aviation
There are international airports at Mogadishu and Hargeisa. In 2003 there were flights to Addis Ababa, Dire Dawa, Djibouti, Jeddah and Nairobi in addition to internal services.

Shipping
There are deep-water harbours at Kismayo, Berbera, Marka and Mogadishu. The merchant fleet (2002) totalled 6,000 GRT.

Piracy off the coast of Somalia is intensifying, with 41 attacks in the waters off Somalia recorded in 2007, 111 in 2008 and 217 in 2009. There were 47 actual hijacks in 2009, up from 42 in 2008.

Telecommunications
Somalia had 100,000 main telephone lines in 2008 (11·2 per 1,000 persons); mobile phone subscribers numbered 627,000 (70·2 per 1,000 persons). In 2008 there were 102,000 internet users.

SOCIAL INSTITUTIONS

Justice
There are 84 district courts, each with a civil and a criminal section. There are eight regional courts and two Courts of Appeal (at Mogadishu and Hargeisa), each with a general section and an assize section. The Supreme Court is in Mogadishu. The death penalty is in force; there was one confirmed execution in 2008.

Education
The nomadic life of a large percentage of the population inhibits educational progress. In 1990 adult literacy was estimated at 24%. In 2004 there were an estimated 1,172 primary schools with over 285,500 children in attendance. In 2006, 23·5% of primary age children and 26·2% of secondary age children were attending school. The longest-established university was for many years the Somali National University in Mogadishu (founded 1954), but it was extensively damaged in the civil war and classes have been suspended indefinitely. A private university, Mogadishu University, was opened in 1997.

Health
In 1997 Somalia had 265 physicians, 13 dentists, 1,327 nurses and 70 pharmacists.

Somalia has among the highest percentages of undernourished people of any country—73% in 1996, up from fewer than 60% in the early 1980s.

RELIGION

The population is almost entirely Sunni Muslims.

CULTURE

Broadcasting
The state television station was destroyed in fighting in 1991 and there has since been no national domestic broadcaster. Radio is the dominant medium with an estimated 20 independent stations. These include Radio Mogadishu (operated by the transitional government), Radio Hargeisa (owned by the Somaliland government) and stations in Puntland, reflecting the regional divisions within the country. In 2003 there were 108,000 TV receivers (colour by PAL).

Press
The Somali press collapsed in 1991, with most of its facilities destroyed. Since 2000 several independent newspapers have emerged, including the daily Wartire in Hargeisa (Somaliland) and the weeklies Yamayska and Bulsho in Puntland. There were six daily newspapers in 2005. Average daily circulation of newspapers in 2005 totalled 20,000.

Tourism
In 1998 there were 10,000 foreign tourists.

DIPLOMATIC REPRESENTATIVES

The Embassy of Somalia in the United Kingdom closed on 2 Jan. 1992.

Of the United Kingdom in Somalia (Waddada Xasan Geedd Abtoow 7–8, Mogadishu)
Staff temporarily withdrawn.

The Embassy of Somalia in the USA closed on 8 May 1991. A liaison office opened in March 1994, and withdrew to Nairobi in Sept. 1994.

Of Somalia to the United Nations
Ambassador: Elmi Ahmed Duale.

Of Somalia to the European Union
Ambassador: Vacant.

FURTHER READING

Abdisalam, M. I.-S., *The Collapse of the Somali State.* 1995
Ghalib, J. M., *The Cost of Dictatorship: the Somali Experience.* 1995
Lewis, I. M., *Blood and Bone: the Call of Kinship in Somali Society.* 1995.—*Understanding Somalia: a Guide to Culture, History and Social Institutions.* 2nd ed. 1995.—*A Modern History of the Somali: Nation and State in the Horn of Africa.* 2002
Omar, M. O., *The Road to Zero: Somalia's Self-Destruction.* 1995
Samatar, A. I. (ed.) *The Somali Challenge: from Catastrophe to Renewal?* 1994
Woodward, Peter, *The Horn of Africa: Politics and International Relations.* 2002

National Statistical Office: Central Statistical Department, State Planning Commission, Mogadishu.

SOUTH AFRICA

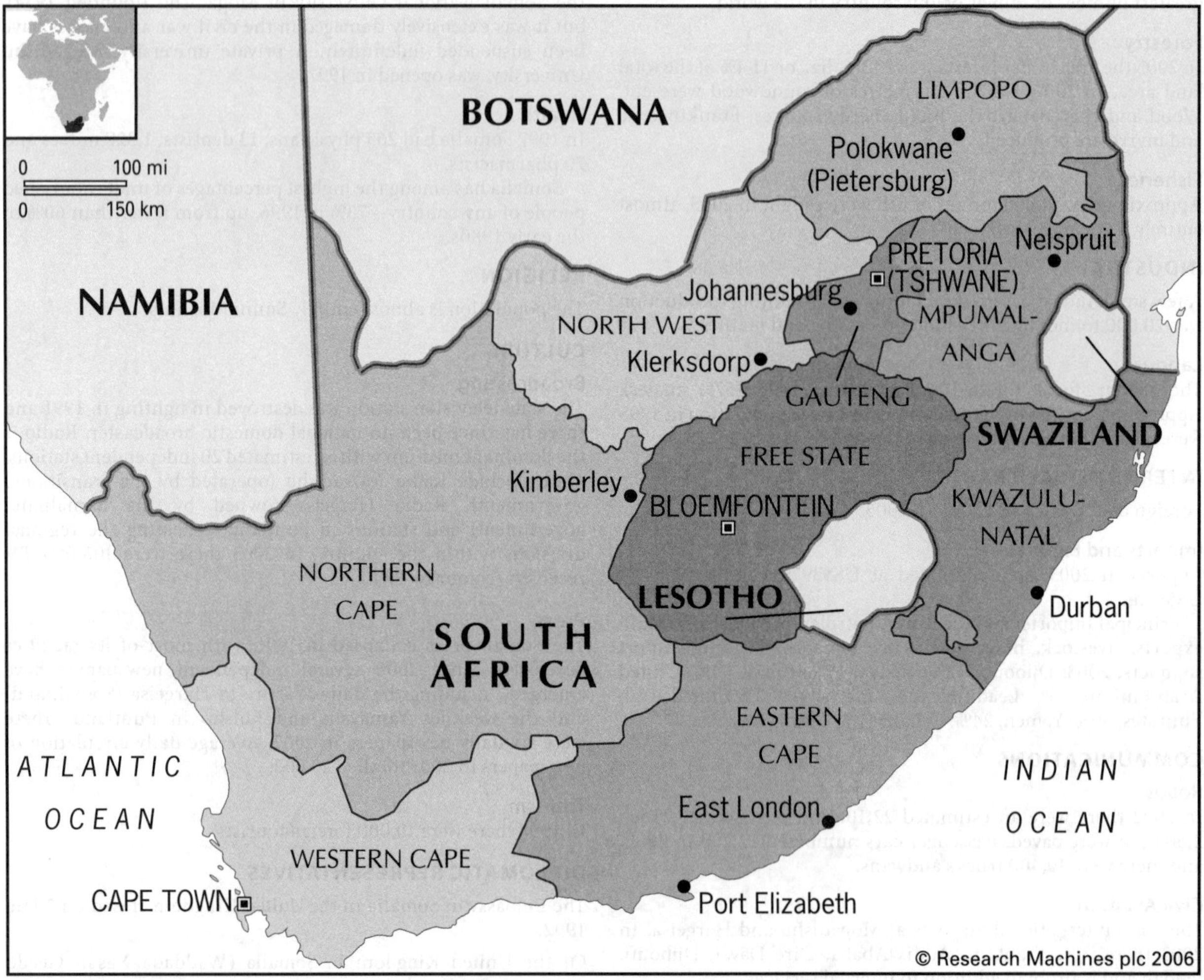

Republic of South Africa

Capital: Pretoria/Tshwane (Administrative), Cape Town (Legislative), Bloemfontein (Judicial)
Seat of Parliament: Cape Town
Seats of Government: Cape Town, Pretoria
Population estimate, 2010: 50·49m.
GDP per capita, 2007: (PPP$) 9,757
HDI/world rank: 0·683/129

KEY HISTORICAL EVENTS

The San and the Khoikhoi were the indigenous peoples of southern Africa. The San were nomadic hunter-gatherers who had lived from the land at the edge of the Kalahari desert for thousands of years. The Khoikhoi shared customs with the San and spoke related languages but also herded cattle and lived in more settled communities. The Khoikhoi settlements were most numerous in the Orange River valley and around the Cape. From the fourth century AD the eastern part of southern Africa was settled by Bantu-speaking groups, moving south from the continent's drier interior. They were mixed farmers: herding sheep and cattle, hunting game, cultivating sorghum and making tools and weapons from iron.

The hunting and herding communities of southern Africa came into contact with the wider world at the end of the fifteenth century. Portuguese mariners first rounded the Cape peninsula in 1487 and opened a trade route into the Indian Ocean. A century later the route was used by Spanish, English, Dutch and French seafarers. They landed occasionally on the Cape peninsula and bartered sheep and cattle with Khoikhoi pastoralists in return for iron and copper goods. In 1649 the Dutch East India Company, the world's most powerful trading corporation, established a trading post at the Cape. Three years later Jan van Riebeeck arrived with orders to establish a fort at Table Bay and supply passing ships with meat, fruit and vegetables. Within a decade slaves were brought in to work on building and maintaining the infrastructure, and settlers began to arrive from the Netherlands. Relations between the Dutch and the Khoikhoi soon deteriorated: quarrels over rights to graze cattle escalated into warfare as early as 1659.

Over the next century the population of the Cape Colony reached 10,000. It was a diverse community, where traders from Europe and Asia converged and exchanged goods and news.

Large farms, cultivating vines and grain, were established in the fertile valleys to the east of Cape Town. Devastated by smallpox in 1713, the Khoikhoi population was unable to prevent *trekboers* (Dutch pastoral farmers) from moving to the north and east of the Cape colony. By 1770 trekboers were grazing their cattle as far east as the Fish river, where they came into contact with Xhosa farmers. More numerous and powerful than the Khoikhoi, and with greater resistance to European diseases, the Xhosa fought the Dutch settlers in a series of 'Frontier Wars'.

By the late 18th century Dutch sea power was on the wane. Vying with France for control of the main trade routes to Asia and the Americas, the British first seized Cape Town in 1795. Following the peace treaties of 1814, which ended the Napoleonic Wars, British sovereignty over the colony was confirmed. For the British, the main purpose of their acquisition was to provide a stepping-stone to their increasingly important colonies in Asia.

In the first two decades of the 19th century the Zulu people of the northeastern region (Natal) strengthened their power-base under their leader, Shaka. In response to a prolonged drought the Zulus conquered lands from rival Nguni groups, which culminated in widespread havoc and destruction, known as the *Mfecane*. From the chaos new kingdoms emerged, notably Gaza and Swaziland, while the Sotho, under King Moshoshoe, formed the mountain territory now known as Lesotho.

The *Mfecane* led to the migration of thousands of Basotho and Batswana from the High Veld and Xhosa from the coastal plains into the Cape Colony. In the 1830s Boer settlers, increasingly dissatisfied with British rule and, realising that the *Mfecane* had caused the depopulation of land to the north and east, began to move there. In the 'Great Trek' that began in 1836, the Afrikaners were seeking a free and independent state which they achieved in the establishment of the Orange Free State and Transvaal in 1854.

Meanwhile, the British strengthened their hold over the Cape Colony and Natal by bringing in new settlers. Between 1860 and 1866, 6,000 Indians arrived in Natal from Madras and Calcutta to work as indentured labourers on the new sugar plantations. The population of the Cape Colony included many Afrikaners as well as the 'coloured' community (descendants of Khoikhoi, white settlers and Malay slaves). Most Coloureds spoke Afrikaans, an offshoot of Dutch.

Britain annexed the Transvaal in 1877, and in 1879 fought the Zulus. Under King Ketshwayo the Zulus were victorious at Isandhlwana but were then defeated at Ulundi. Britain restored independence to the Transvaal (the South African Republic) in 1884 and annexed Zululand in 1887. Both the British and the Boers fought African resistance for many years, the last major rising being in Natal in 1906. However, the British and Boers continued to be rivals, especially after the discovery of diamonds at Kimberley in 1867 and of gold in the Transvaal in 1884. This led to an economic boom. Cecil Rhodes, owner of the De Beers company and for a time prime minister of the Cape, was the dominant entrepreneurial figure.

Boer War

In the 1890s the British, under Rhodes, sought control over the Transvaal goldfields. Despite being thwarted in their attempts to spark off rebellion amongst the Afrikaners of the South African Republic, the British continued to press for control. The Afrikaners, led by Paul Kruger, decided they would have to fight to keep their independence and declared war on Britain in late 1899. The contest appeared unequal, with the might of the British army against only 35,000 Boer soldiers. The Boers suffered a heavy defeat at Paardeberg in 1900, but then switched to guerrilla warfare. The British army, led by Gen. Kitchener, responded by setting up concentration camps and destroying crops and farmsteads. The 'scorched earth' policy was strongly criticized in Europe, but had the desired effect—in 1902 the Boer republics signed the Treaty of Vereeniging and came under British rule. They were given self-government in 1907 and on 31 May 1910 the Cape Colony, Natal, the Transvaal and the Orange Free State combined to form the Union of South Africa, a self-governing dominion under the British Crown.

The first general election in 1910 demonstrated the power of the Afrikaners within the new union—the South African party won 67 seats compared with 39 seats for the mainly English-speaking Unionist Party. Louis Botha became prime minister and Jan Smuts was made Minister of the Interior, Mines and Defence. The Union's economy was based on gold and diamond mining, for which there was organized recruitment of migrant African labourers from Union territory and other parts of Africa. Pass Laws were in operation, controlling Africans' movements in the towns and industrial areas, where they were regarded officially as temporary residents and segregated in 'townships'. Following the Land Act of 1913, 87% of the land was reserved for white ownership while Africans farmed as tenants or squatters. White miners' annual earnings were 12 times those of their black counterparts in 1911. African protests at segregation and absence of political rights were led by the South African Native National Congress (SANNC), founded in 1912 and renamed the African National Congress (ANC) in 1923.

African rights were further suppressed after the coming to power in 1924 of the Afrikaner Nationalist Party, led by J. B. Hertzog. The government secured recognition of full independence for South Africa by the Statute of Westminster on 11 Dec. 1931. It also promoted the status of the Afrikaans language and introduced new segregation measures such as the Native Laws Amendment Act of 1937, which set limits on the numbers of blacks who could live in urban areas. Jan Smuts came to power in 1939 heading a coalition government broadly in favour of the war against Nazi Germany.

Apartheid

In 1948 Smuts' Unionist Party was sensationally defeated by the right-wing National Party which had campaigned for *apartheid*, a new policy for dealing with the 'racial problem'. After 1948 the term apartheid soon developed from a political slogan into a systematic programme of social engineering championed by Hendrik Verwoerd, who became prime minister in 1958. A plethora of new laws from the Group Areas Act to the Prohibition of Mixed Marriages Act strengthened existing segregation and increased racial inequality. Blacks were divided into one of ten tribal groups, and forced to move to so-called Homelands, which were intended to become self-sufficient, self-governing states. Chief Buthelezi was pivotal in the Inkatha movement which attempted, but ultimately failed, to unite Homeland leaders. The massacre by police of 69 protesters against the Pass Laws at Sharpeville on 21 March 1960 led to a major crisis from which, however, the government emerged even stronger. The ANC and the Pan African Congress were banned and the leaders, including Nelson Mandela, were jailed in 1964. After withdrawing from the British Commonwealth in 1961, South Africa became increasingly isolated. To the north, former European colonies were becoming independent, often socialist, republics.

On 16 June 1976 thousands of students demonstrated in Soweto, an African township outside Johannesburg, against mandatory schooling in Afrikaans. Many died when police broke up the demonstration and rioting spread throughout the country. When P. W. Botha became prime minister in 1978, elements of the apartheid system were modified. Africans were allowed to form legal trade unions and the acts banning marriage and sexual relations between people of different races were repealed.

A new constitution, approved in a referendum of white voters on 2 Nov. 1983 and in force from 3 Sept. 1984, created a three-part parliament, with a House of Assembly for the Whites, a House of

Representatives for the Coloureds and a House of Delegates for the Indians; Africans remained without representation. From late 1984 Blacks in the cities and industrial areas staged large-scale protests. In June 1986 a state of emergency was imposed. Foreign condemnation led to the first economic sanctions against South Africa, imposed by a number of countries including the USA and Britain.

By 1989 a start had been made on dismantling apartheid and the government, led by F. W. de Klerk, announced its willingness to consider the extension of black South Africans' political rights. In Feb. 1990 a 30-year ban on the ANC was lifted and Nelson Mandela was released from prison on 11 Feb. 1990. In the Whites-only referendum on 17 March 1992, on the granting of constitutional equality to all races, 1,924,186 (68·7%) votes were in favour; 875,619 against.

On 22 Dec. 1993 parliament approved (by 237 votes to 45) a transitional constitution paving the way for a new multi-racial parliament which was elected on 29 April 1994. There was a decisive victory for the ANC and on 9 May 1994 Nelson Mandela was elected president. The new government included six ministers from the National Party and three from the Inkatha Freedom Party.

In 1997 the Truth and Reconciliation Commission, chaired by Archbishop Desmond Tutu, began hearings on human rights violations between 1960 and 1993. The commission promised amnesty to those who confessed their crimes under the apartheid system. Nelson Mandela, whose term as president cemented his reputation as a world statesman, retired in 1999. His deputy, Thabo Mbeki, elected president in a landslide vote, had already assumed many of Mandela's governing responsibilities. Mbeki wrestled with a developing economy, continuing inequality and a high crime rate. The nation remains in the grip of an AIDS epidemic which Mbeki was slow to acknowledge. He stood down from the presidency in Sept. 2008 after the ruling ANC called on him to resign.

TERRITORY AND POPULATION

South Africa is bounded in the north by Namibia, Botswana and Zimbabwe, northeast by Mozambique and Swaziland, east by the Indian Ocean, and south and west by the South Atlantic, with Lesotho forming an enclave. Area: 1,219,090 sq. km. This area includes the uninhabited Prince Edward Island (41 sq. km) and Marion Island (388 sq. km), lying 1,900 km southeast of Cape Town. The islands were handed over to South Africa in Dec. 1947 to prevent their falling into hostile hands. In 1994 Walvis Bay was ceded to Namibia, and Transkei, Bophuthatswana, Venda and Ciskei were reintegrated into South Africa.

At the census of 2001 the population was 44,819,782 (23,385,739 females), consisting of: Black African, 35,416,167 (79·0% of total population); White, 4,293,641 (9·6%); Coloured, 3,994,506 (8·9%); Indian/Asian, 1,115,468 (2·5%). Estimated population at 30 June 2007 was 47,850,700 (24,288,100 female), consisting of: Black African, 38,079,900; White, 4,352,100; Coloured, 4,245,000; Indian/Asian, 1,173,700. The United Nations population estimate for 2007 was 49,173,000. The population has increased more than would have been expected since 2001 as huge numbers of migrants have entered South Africa from Zimbabwe, many of them undocumented.

The UN gives an estimated population for 2010 of 50·49m.

59·3% of the population was urban in 2005. In 2000 cities with the largest populations were (estimate in 1,000): Johannesburg (Gauteng), 2,732; Cape Town (Western Cape), 2,715; Durban (KwaZulu-Natal), 2,370; Pretoria/Tshwane (Gauteng), 1,084; Port Elizabeth (Eastern Cape), 958.

There were 10,714 immigrants in 2004 (10,578 in 2003) and 16,165 emigrants in 2003 (10,890 in 2002).

Population by province, according to the 2001 census:

Province	*Total (including unspecified)*	*African*	*White*	*Coloured*	*Indian/ Asian*
Eastern Cape	6,436,764	5,635,079	304,506	478,807	18,372
Free State	2,706,776	2,381,073	238,791	83,193	3,719
Gauteng	8,837,179	6,522,792	1,758,398	337,974	218,015
KwaZulu-Natal	9,426,017	8,002,407	483,448	141,887	798,275
Mpumalanga	3,122,991	2,886,345	203,244	22,158	11,244
Northern Cape	822,727	293,976	102,042	424,389	2,320
Northern Province (now Limpopo)	5,273,642	5,128,616	126,276	10,163	8,587
North-West	3,669,350	3,358,450	244,035	56,959	9,906
Western Cape	4,524,336	1,207,429	832,901	2,438,976	45,030

There are 11 official languages. Numbers of home speakers at the 2001 census: IsiZulu, 10,677,305 (23·8% of population); IsiXhosa, 7,907,153 (17·6%); Afrikaans, 5,983,426 (13·3%); Sesotho sa Leboa, 4,208,980 (9·4%); English, 3,673,203 (8·6%); Setswana, 3,677,016 (8·2%); Sesotho, 3,555,186 (8·2%); Xitsonga, 1,992,207 (4·4%); Siswati, 1,194,430 (2·75%); Tshivenda, 1,021,757 (2·3%); isINdebele, 711,821 (1·6%). The use of any of these languages is a constitutional right 'wherever practicable'. Each province may adopt any of these as its official language. English is the sole language of command and instruction in the armed forces.

SOCIAL STATISTICS

Births: total number of registered live births in 2006 was 1,346,119 (the lowest since 1998 and down from a high of 1,677,415 in 2003).

Officially recorded marriages: the following statistics reflect marriages contracted and divorces granted during 2003, as registered by the civil registration system. (From 1998, under a new bill, customary and traditional marriages are recognized in law.) The total number of marriages officially recorded in 2007 was 183,030 (176,521 in 2004). Western Cape had the highest marriage rate in 2005 (613·8 per 100,000), Northern Cape the second highest (515·7 per 100,000) followed by Gauteng (497·1 per 100,000). Limpopo had the lowest rate (186·9 per 100,000). Of the total marriages officially recorded in 2007, 93,828 (51·3%) were solemnized in religious ceremonies and 89,112 by civil rites. 90 were classed under 'unspecified'. In 2007 the most popular age for marrying was 31 years for men and 25 years for women. Divorces granted in 2007 totalled 29,639 (31,786 in 2004). Gauteng had the highest divorce rate in 2005 (943·5 per 100,000 married couples); Western Cape (763·8). Limpopo had the lowest rate (132·1 per 100,000). Same-sex marriage was legalized in Nov. 2006.

Deaths: the number of deaths increased from 318,287 in 1997 to 591,213 in 2005. A Statistics South Africa report published in Feb. 2005 concluded that the average number of deaths rose from 870 a day in 1997 to 1,370 a day in 2002, with AIDS as the factor underlying much of the increase in mortality. In 2007, 18·1% of all adults between 15 and 49 were infected with HIV. Estimated population growth rate, 2006–07, 1·0%. Fertility rate, 2004, 2·8 births per woman. Life expectancy at birth, 2007, was 49·8 years for males and 53·2 for females. Infant mortality, 2005, 51 per 1,000 live births.

CLIMATE

There is abundant sunshine and relatively low rainfall. The southwest has a Mediterranean climate, with rain mainly in winter, but most of the country has a summer maximum, although quantities show a decrease from east to west. Pretoria, Jan. 73·4°F (23·0°C), July 53·6°F (12·0°C). Annual rainfall 26·5" (674 mm). Bloemfontein, Jan. 73·4°F (23·0°C), July 45·9°F (7·7°C). Annual rainfall 22" (559 mm). Cape Town, Jan. 69·6°F (20·9°C), July 54·0°F (12·2°C). Annual rainfall 20·3" (515 mm). Johannesburg, Jan. 68·2°F (20·1°C), July 50·7°F (10·4°C). Annual rainfall 28·1" (713 mm).

CONSTITUTION AND GOVERNMENT

An Interim *Constitution* came into effect on 27 April 1994 and was in force until 3 Feb. 1997. Under it, the National Assembly and Senate formed a Constitutional Assembly, which had the task of drafting a definitive constitution. This was signed into law in Dec. 1996 and took effect on 4 Feb. 1997. The 1996 constitution defines the powers of the President, Parliament (consisting of the National Assembly and the National Council of Provinces—NCOP), the national executive, the judiciary, public administration, the security services and the relationship between the three spheres of government. It incorporates a Bill of Rights pertaining to, *inter alia*, education, housing, food and water supply, and security, in addition to political rights. All legislation must conform to the Constitution and the Bill of Rights. The Constitution was amended in 2001 to provide that Constitutional Court judges are appointed for a non-renewable 12-year term of office, or until they reach the age of 70 years, except where an Act of Parliament extends the term of office of a Constitutional Court judge. This Constitution Amendment Act also made the head of the Constitutional Court the Chief Justice. The head of the Supreme Court of Appeal is now the President of that Court.

A *Constitutional Court*, consisting of a president, a deputy president and nine other judges, was inaugurated in Feb. 1995. The Court's judges are appointed by the President of the Republic from a list provided by the Judicial Service Commission, after consulting the President of the Constitutional Court (now the Chief Justice) and the leaders of parties represented in the National Assembly.

Parliament is the legislative authority and has the power to make laws for the country in accordance with the Constitution. It consists of the National Assembly and the NCOP. Parliamentary sittings are open to the public.

The *National Assembly* consists of no fewer than 350 and no more than 400 members directly elected for five years, 200 from a national list and 200 from provincial lists in the following proportions: Eastern Cape, 28; Free State, 14; Gauteng, 44; KwaZulu-Natal, 42; Limpopo, 25; Mpumalanga, 11; Northern Cape, 4; North-West, 12; Western Cape, 20. In terms of the 1993 Constitution, which still regulated the 1999 elections, the nine provincial legislatures are elected at the same time and candidates may stand for both. If elected to both, they have to choose between sitting in the national or provincial assembly. In the former case, the runner-up is elected to the Provincial Assembly.

From 21 March 2003, for a period of two weeks, members of the National Assembly and provincial legislatures were allowed to defect to other political parties without losing their seats in both houses, in accordance with a constitutional amendment of 2003. The Act provided for three 'window' periods. The first one was a transitional arrangement consisting of a 15-day period starting on 21 March 2003. The second and third periods were to be for 15 days each, from 1 to 15 Sept. in the second and fourth years following the date of a national and provincial election.

The *National Council of Provinces* (NCOP) consists of 54 permanent members and 36 special delegates and aims to represent provincial interests in the national sphere of government. Delegations from each province consist of ten representatives. Bills (except finance bills) may be introduced in either house but must be passed by both. A finance bill may only be introduced in the National Assembly. If a bill is rejected by one house it is referred back to both after consideration by a joint National Assembly-NCOP committee called the Mediation Committee. Bills relating to the provinces must be passed by the NCOP. By Aug. 2003 more than 780 pieces of legislation had been passed since 1994.

The Constitution mandates the establishment of *Traditional Leaders* by means of either provincial or national legislation. The National House of Traditional Leaders was established in April 1997. Each provincial House of Traditional Leaders nominated three members to be represented in the National House. The National House advises national government on the role of traditional leaders and on customary law.

National Anthem

A combination of shortened forms of 'Die Stem van Suid-Afrika'/ 'The Call of South Africa' (words by C. J. Langenhoven; tune by M. L. de Villiers) and the ANC anthem 'Nkosi sikelel' iAfrika'/ 'God bless Africa' (words and tune by Enos Santonga).

GOVERNMENT CHRONOLOGY

Presidents from 1961. (ANC = African National Congress; NP = National Party; UP = United Party)

1961–67	NP	Charles Robberts Swart
1968–75	NP	Jacobus Johannes Fouché
1975–78	NP	Nicolaas Johannes Diederichs
1978–79	NP	Balthazar Johannes Vorster
1979–84	NP	Marais Viljoen
1984–89	NP	Pieter Willem Botha
1989–94	NP	Frederik Willem de Klerk
1994–99	ANC	Nelson Rolihlahla Mandela
1999–2008	ANC	Thabo Mvuyelwa Mbeki
2008–09	ANC	Kgalema Petrus Motlanthe
2009–	ANC	Jacob Gedleyihlekisa Zuma

Prime Ministers since 1939.

1939–48	military/UP	Jan Christiaan Smuts
1948–54	NP	Daniël François Malan
1954–58	NP	Johannes Gerhardus Strijdom
1958–66	NP	Hendrik Frensch Verwoerd
1966–78	NP	Balthazar Johannes Vorster
1978–84	NP	Pieter Willem Botha

RECENT ELECTIONS

Parliamentary elections were held on 22 April 2009. Turnout was 77·3%. The African National Congress (ANC) won 264 seats in Parliament's National Assembly with 65·9% of votes cast, Democratic Alliance (DA) 67 with 16·7%, Congress of the People (COPE) 30 with 7·4%, Inkatha Freedom Party (IFP) 18 with 4·6%, Independent Democrats (ID) 4 with 0·9%, United Democratic Movement (UDM) 4 with 0·9%, Freedom Front Plus (VF+) 4 with 0·8%, African Christian Democratic Party (ACDP) 3 with 0·8%, United Christian-Democratic Party (UCDP) 2 with 0·4%, Pan African Congress of Azania (PAC) 1 with 0·3%, Minority Front (MF) 1 with 0·3%, Azanian People's Organization (AZAPO) 1 with 0·2% and African People's Convention 1 with 0·2%.

CURRENT ADMINISTRATION

President: Jacob Zuma; b. 1942 (ANC; sworn in 9 May 2009).

Deputy President: Kgalema Motlanthe.

In March 2010 the government comprised:

Minister of Agriculture, Fisheries and Forestry: Tina Joemat-Pettersson. *Arts and Culture:* Lulu Xingwana. *Basic Education:* Angie Motshekga. *Communications:* Siphiwe Nyanda. *Co-operative Governance and Traditional Affairs:* Sicelo Shiceka. *Correctional Services:* Nosiviwe Mapisa-Nqakula. *Defence and Military Veterans:* Lindiwe Sisulu. *Economic Development:* Ebrahim Patel. *Energy:* Dipuo Peters. *Finance:* Pravin Gordhan. *Health:* Aaron Motsoaledi. *Higher Education and Training:* Blade Nzimande. *Home Affairs:* Nkosazana Dlamini-Zuma. *Human Settlements:* Tokyo Sexwale. *International Relations and Co-operation:* Maite Nkoana-Mashabane. *Justice and Constitutional Development:* Jeff Radebe. *Labour:* Membathisi Mdladlana. *Mining:* Susan Shabangu. *Policing:* Nathi Mthethwa. *Public*

Enterprises: Barbara Hogan. *Public Service and Administration:* Richard Baloyi. *Public Works:* Geoff Doidge. *Rural Development and Land Affairs:* Gugile Nkwinti. *Science and Technology:* Naledi Pandor. *Social Development:* Edna Molewa. *Sport and Recreation:* Makhenkesi Stofile. *State Security:* Siyabonga Cwele. *Tourism:* Marthinus van Schalkwyk. *Trade and Industry:* Rob Davies. *Transport:* Sbusiso Ndebele. *Water and Environmental Affairs:* Buyelwa Sonjica. *Women, Youth, Children and People with Disabilities:* Noluthando Mayende-Sibiya. *Minister in the Presidency Responsible for the National Planning Commission:* Trevor Manuel. *Minister in the Presidency Responsible for Performance, Monitoring and Evaluation, and Administration:* Collins Chabane.

Government Website: http://www.gov.za

CURRENT LEADERS

Jacob Gedleyihlekisa Zuma

Position
President

Introduction
Jacob Zuma became president of the ANC on 18 Dec. 2007 after defeating incumbent Thabo Mbeki in a leadership election. He was elected national president after the ANC won the general election of 22 April 2009.

Early Life
Zuma was born in what is now the KwaZulu-Natal Province on 12 April 1942. He had only five years of formal schooling and spent his early life travelling between Zululand and Durban. Zuma's father died in the Second World War and by the time he was 15, Zuma was taking odd jobs to supplement his mother's income. Influenced by his family's trade unionist background, he became involved in politics at the age of 17.

Zuma joined the ANC in 1959. With the party banned by the apartheid government the following year, by 1962 he was an active member of Umkhonto we Sizwe (the military wing of the ANC), which was subsequently classified as a terrorist organization. In 1963 Zuma was arrested and convicted of conspiring to overthrow the government. He was jailed for ten years, serving part of the sentence on Robben Island alongside Nelson Mandela.

After his release Zuma helped re-establish the ANC as an underground movement in Natal. In 1975 he left South Africa, living in Swaziland and then Mozambique where he dealt with thousands of exiles fleeing South Africa after the Soweto uprising. Zuma was appointed to the ANC national executive committee in 1977 and served as deputy chief representative of the ANC in Mozambique until the signing of the Nkomati Accord between South Africa and Mozambique in 1984, when he became chief representative of the ANC. Forced to leave Mozambique in 1987, Zuma was appointed head of underground structures and chief of the intelligence department, serving on the ANC's political and military council.

When the ban on the ANC was lifted in 1990 Zuma returned to South Africa and was elected ANC chairperson for the Southern Natal region. In 1991 he was elected the party's deputy secretary general, and at the 1994 general election he agreed to Thabo Mbeki running unopposed for the deputy presidency. Zuma was appointed to the executive committee of economic affairs and tourism for the ANC in the KwaZulu-Natal provincial government. In 1997 he became the ANC's deputy president and two years later was chosen as South Africa's executive deputy president.

In 2005, following the conviction of Zuma's financial adviser Schabir Shaik on charges of corruption and fraud, Zuma was dismissed as deputy president by Mbeki.

Career in Office
In Dec. 2007 Zuma was elected ANC party president against Mbeki. His rhetoric found favour with many disadvantaged South Africans who felt marginalized by Mbeki's business-friendly policies. Zuma was thus clear favourite to become the next president of South Africa.

On 28 Dec. 2007 the directorate of special operations (or Scorpions) indicted Zuma to stand trial on charges of racketeering, money laundering, corruption and fraud. The allegations were linked to a US$5bn. arms procurement deal made by the government in 1999. The trial was scheduled to start on 4 Aug. 2008 but was delayed when the charges were declared unlawful because Zuma had not had a chance to make representations pre-indictment. The national directorate of public prosecutions announced an appeal.

Mbeki resigned as president of South Africa on 21 Sept. 2008 after losing the support of the ANC over claims that he had interfered in the case against Zuma. The charges against Zuma were dropped, although prosecutors were given leave to appeal the following month. In April 2009 the National Prosecuting Authority dismissed all charges. The ANC triumphed at the general election on 22 April 2009 and Zuma was elected president by parliament. He was sworn into office on 9 May 2009, succeeding Kgalema Motlanthe, who stepped aside having replaced Mbeki.

Also in May, the South African economy officially went into recession following a sharp downturn in the manufacturing and mining sectors. Unemployment accelerated and strikes and violent protests in July–Aug. were roundly condemned by Zuma. In a speech to the ANC in Jan. 2010 he warned that recovery from the economic crisis would be slow and that there would be a lag in job creation.

DEFENCE

The South African National Defence Force (SANDF) comprises four services, namely the SA Army, the SA Air Force, the SA Navy and the SA Military Health Service (SAMHS). In 2007 the SANDF consisted of 62,334 active members (excluding 12,382 civilian employees). SAMHS personnel totalled 7,115 (including around 1,115 reservists) in 2007. South Africa ended conscription in 1994.

Defence expenditure totalled US$3,697m. in 2005 (equivalent to US$83 per capita), and represented 1·5% of GDP. Defence expenditure in 1985 was US$3,252m. (US$97 per capita and 3·8% of GDP). In 2008 South Africa was responsible for 15% of Africa's total defence expenditure. Only Algeria among African countries spent more on defence in 2008.

As at Oct. 2009, 2,152 personnel (1,970 troops, 154 police and 28 military observers) were deployed in UN peacekeeping operations.

Army
Army personnel totalled 41,350 in 2007. Regular army reserves numbered 38,545 in 2007. The army territorial reserve was disbanded in 2009.

Navy
Navy personnel in 2007 totalled 5,801, with 861 reserves. The fleet is based at the naval bases at Simon's Town on the west coast and Durban on the east and includes three submarines and four corvettes.

Air Force
Strength (2007) 9,183, with 831 reserves. In 2007 the Air Force had 29 combat capable aircraft (*Cheetah* Cs and *Cheetah* Ds) and 11 combat capable helicopters.

INTERNATIONAL RELATIONS

South Africa is a member of the UN, World Bank, IMF and several other UN specialized agencies, WTO, BIS, Commonwealth (except during 1961–94), IOM, African Development Bank, African Union, Southern African Development Community, Antarctic Treaty and is an ACP member state of the ACP-EU relationship.

ECONOMY

Agriculture accounted for 2·7% of GDP in 2006, industry 30·9% and services 66·4%.

Overview

South Africa is one of the few African countries to have reached the upper middle-income group. Its economy is the largest in the Sub-Saharan region and heavily influences trade and investment flows on the continent. However, the country suffers from massive inequality. Despite a rising black middle class, the World Bank estimates that only 13% of the population, mostly white, was living in 'first world' conditions in 2004, while just over half of the population lived in 'third world' conditions. The country has one of the highest HIV/AIDS infection rates, with 17% of those between the ages of 15 and 49 living with HIV in 2009. The unemployment rate, at 24·3% in the fourth quarter of 2009, is a further cause for concern.

Until recently the economy was dominated by agriculture and precious metals. South Africa is the world's second largest producer of gold and the world's largest producer of platinum. Mining remains an important source of foreign exchange while agriculture, which has become increasingly diversified away from maize, continues to be an important source of employment. However, manufacturing and financial services now account for a greater share of GDP. An advanced financial sector and growing tourism help make services the largest contributor to the country's total output. Manufacturing principally involves metals and engineering, especially steel-related products.

In the early 1990s the removal of international sanctions following the end of apartheid and the adoption of structural reforms opened the economy to international competition, leading to productivity gains and greater penetration of international markets. In the decade from 1994 the economy grew at an average annual rate of 2·9%, with less volatility than the previous decade when average annual growth was 1%.

Performance in the post-apartheid period was fostered by trade liberalization, increased private sector participation in the economy and sound macroeconomic management. Strong public finances sustained a competitive exchange rate and low interest rates while monetary policy contained inflationary pressures.

The economy grew by around 5% for three consecutive years up to 2007 on the back of strong household demand. However, there were increased inflationary pressures and a widening of the external current account deficit. In early 2008 an electricity crisis stemming from the state-owned supplier, Eskom, resulted in widespread blackouts and disruption to mining production. The crisis threatened to destroy investor confidence and derail growth targets.

Demand for South African exports fell sharply during the international financial crisis. An estimated 500,000 workers lost their jobs in 2009 and growth slowed after the second half of 2008.

Currency

The unit of currency is the *rand* (ZAR) of 100 *cents*. A single free-floating exchange rate replaced the former two-tier system on 13 March 1995. Inflation rates (based on IMF statistics):

1999	*2000*	*2001*	*2002*	*2003*	*2004*	*2005*	*2006*	*2007*	*2008*
5·2%	5·4%	5·7%	9·2%	5·8%	1·4%	3·4%	4·7%	7·1%	11·5%

Foreign exchange reserves were US$32,251m. in Sept. 2009 (US$4,171m. in 1998) and gold reserves 4·01m. troy oz. Total money supply was R419,506m. in Aug. 2009.

Budget

Consolidated national budget in R1bn.:

	2007–08	*2008–09*[1]	*2009–10*[1]	*2010–11*[1]
Revenue	580·4	650·0	720·1	789·0
Expenditure	560·1	631·5	704·1	768·5

[1]Budgeted figures.

Income tax is the Government's main source of income. As of 2001, South Africa's source-based income tax system was replaced with a residence-based system. With effect from the years of assessment commencing on or after 1 Jan. 2001, residents are (subject to certain exclusions) taxed on their worldwide income, irrespective of where their income is earned. Foreign taxes are credited against South African tax payable on foreign income. Foreign income and taxes are translated into the South African monetary unit, the Rand.

Value-added Tax (VAT) has remained at 14% since 1993. Corporate taxes were reduced to 28% in 2008. A tiered corporate tax was introduced in 2000 with taxes for small businesses reduced by half. R9·9bn. was returned to taxpayers in reduced personal income tax for all income groups but particularly for lower and middle income groups. The marginal tax rate for high-income earners was cut to 40% from 42% in 2001. A capital gains tax was introduced from 1 April 2001 and became effective on 1 Oct. 2001.

South Africa's fiscal year runs from 1 April to 31 March.

Performance

Real GDP growth rates (based on IMF statistics):

1999	*2000*	*2001*	*2002*	*2003*	*2004*	*2005*	*2006*	*2007*	*2008*
2·4%	4·2%	2·7%	3·7%	3·1%	4·9%	5·0%	5·3%	5·1%	3·1%

Total GDP in 2008 was US$276·8bn.

Banking and Finance

The central bank and bank of issue is the South African Reserve Bank (SARB; established 1920), which functions independently. Its *Governor* is Gill Marcus. The Banks Act, 1990 governs the operations and prudential requirements of banks.

At the end of Dec. 2008, 33 banks (excluding two mutual banks) were registered with the Office of the Registrar of Banks. Furthermore, 43 foreign banks had authorized representative offices in South Africa. The combined assets of the banking institutions amounted to R3,170bn. (31 Dec. 2008), total liabilities to R2,989bn. and total equity to R181bn. Total assets of the four largest commercial banks (Standard Bank, FirstRand, Absa and Nedbank) came to R2,676bn.

The stock exchange, the JSE Securities Exchange, is based in Johannesburg. Foreign nationals have been eligible for membership since Nov. 1995.

ENERGY AND NATURAL RESOURCES

Environment

In 1998 the Committee for Environmental Co-ordination was established to harmonize the work of government departments on environmental issues, and to co-ordinate environmental implementation and national management plans at provincial level.

South Africa's carbon dioxide emissions from the consumption and flaring of fossil fuels in 2008 were the equivalent of 9·2 tonnes per capita (compared to the average for Africa as a whole of 1·1 tonnes per capita).

Electricity

South African households use over 25% of the country's energy. Coal supplies 75% of primary energy requirements, followed by oil (21%), nuclear (3%) and natural gas (1%). There is one nuclear power station (Koeberg) with two reactors, two gas turbine generators, two conventional hydroelectric plants and two pumped storage stations. Nuclear energy is being investigated as a future potential energy source and alternative to coal. Eskom, a public utility, generates 95% of the country's electricity (as well as two-thirds of the electricity for the African continent) and owns and operates the national transmission system.

In 2008 Eskom electrified 168,538 homes against the government target of 160,321, bringing the total number of homes connected since the start of the electrification programme in 1991 to 3,638,188. The Government aims to achieve universal access to electricity by 2012. Capacity shortages from late 2007 forced Eskom into emergency reductions to protect the power system from potential failure and a national electricity crisis was declared in Jan. 2008. In 2005, 205,558 GWh of electricity were consumed.

The energy sector contributes about 15% to GDP and employs about 250,000 people. Because of South Africa's large coal deposits, the country is one of the cheapest electricity suppliers in the world.

The first wind-energy farm in Africa was opened at Klipheuwel in the Western Cape on 21 Feb. 2003.

Oil and Gas

South Africa has limited oil reserves and relies on coal for much of its oil production. It has a highly developed synthetic fuels industry. Sasol Oil and PetroSA are the two major players in the synthetic fuel market. Synfuels meet approximately 40% of local demand. Natural gas production in 2004 amounted to 2·0bn. cu. metres; however, the prospects for natural gas production have increased by the discovery of offshore reserves close to the Namibian border in 2000. The project is expected to be developed in four stages each lasting between three and five years, although work has yet to commence. Production will be channelled to regulate electricity production.

PetroSA is responsible for exploration of both offshore natural gas and onshore coal-bed methane. The EM gas-field complex off Mossel Bay in the Western Cape started production in 2000, and was to ensure sufficient feedstock to PetroSA to maintain current liquid fuel production levels at 36,000 bbls of petroleum products a day until 2009 although 2008 saw a decline in production levels. Planning is under way for the construction of a new refinery near Port Elizabeth that is expected to come online in 2015. The oilfield, Sable, situated about 150 km south off the coast of Mossel Bay, is expected to produce 17% of South Africa's oil needs. Coming into operation in Aug. 2003, it was initially projected to produce 30,000 to 40,000 bbls of crude oil a day. PetroSA's gas-to-liquid plant supplies about 7% of South Africa's liquid fuel needs.

South Africa is one of the major oil refining nations in Africa with a crude refining capacity of 543,000 bbls per day.

Minerals

Total sales of primary minerals increased to R223·9bn. in 2007; the value of exports of primary minerals increased to R161·8bn. Mining and quarrying contributed 8·2% of GDP in 2006, up from 6·9% in 1996 although down from 14·4% in 1986.

In 2007 employment in the mining sector rose by 8·6% from 456,337 in 2006 to 495,474. Over 50 different minerals were produced in 2007 from 1,414 mines and quarries.

Mineral production (in tonnes), 2005: coal, 244·9m.; iron ore (metal content), 24·9m.; limestone and dolomite, 24·8m.; chromium, 7·5m.; manganese, 4·6m.; aluminium, 846,000; copper (metal content), 97,000; nickel (metal content), 42,000; zinc (metal content), 32,000; platinum-group metals, 303; gold, 295; silver, 88. Diamond production, 2005: 15,776,000 carats. In 2007 gold production fell by 7·2% from 272 tonnes in 2006 to 253 tonnes (its lowest level in over 80 years) although sales revenue rose by 1·6% to R38bn. South Africa is the world's leading producer of platinum (and has the largest reserves of both platinum and gold). In 2007 South Africa lost its status as the world's largest gold producer to China.

Agriculture

South Africa has a dual agricultural economy, comprising a well-developed commercial sector and a predominantly subsistence-orientated sector. Much of the land suitable for mechanized farming has unreliable rainfall. Of the total farming area, natural pasture occupies 81% (69·6m. ha.) and planted pasture 2% (2m. ha.). About 12% of South Africa's surface area can be used for crop production. High potential arable land comprises only 22% of the total arable land. Annual crops and orchards are cultivated on 9·9m. ha. of dry land and 1·3m. ha. under irrigation. In 2007 there were 39,982 commercial farming units with a gross farming income of R79·6m. Agriculture, forestry, hunting and fishing contributed 2·9% of GDP in 2006, down from 4·2% in 1996. In 2007 there were 796,806 paid farm workers.

Production:

(*Field crops, 2006–07 unless otherwise indicated, in 1,000 tonnes*): sugarcane, 20,278; maize, 6,947 (2005–06); wheat, 1,913 (2007); lucerne hay, 1,232; sunflower seeds, 541 (2005–06); soybeans, 424 (2005–06); grain sorghum, 202; groundnuts, 66; seed cotton, 29; cotton seed, 18; tobacco, 14.

(*Horticulture, 2006–07, in 1,000 tonnes*): potatoes, 1,917 (2007); oranges, 1,336; apples, 646; tomatoes, 453; grapefruit, 415; onions, 405; bananas, 357; pears, 337. Wine production totalled 1,012m. litres in 2006, ranking South Africa eighth in the world.

(*Animal products, 2007–08*): 5,812,000 sheep and goats slaughtered; 2,989,000 cattle and calves slaughtered; 2,579,000 pigs slaughtered; 717m. broilers slaughtered (2006); fresh milk, 2,470m. litres (2007); wool, 48·4m. kg.

Gross value of field crops in 2007 (R1,000), 25,287,668; horticulture, 25,683,799; animal products, 48,967,173.

Agricultural exports contribute about 4% of total imports and 5% of total exports. In 2007 the estimated value of agricultural imports was R19·5bn. and exports R21·9bn. Fruit and vegetables accounted for 59% of agricultural exports in 2007.

Forestry

South Africa has developed one of the largest man-made forestry resources in the world with plantations covering an area of 1·3m. ha. Production from these plantations in 2007 amounted to 20·3m. cu. metres, valued at almost R5·2bn., the most important products by value being pulpwood (R3·6bn.) and sawlogs (R1·4bn.). In terms of volume, 13·2m. cu. metres and 5·4m. cu. metres of the aforementioned products were produced respectively. Collectively, the forestry sector employs about 170,000 people. An equivalent of about 107,000 full-time staff are employed in the primary sector (growing and harvesting), while the balance is employed in the processing industries (sawmilling, pulp and paper, mining timber and poles, and board products). In 2007 the forestry and forest products industry contributed 0·9% to South Africa's GDP.

In 2007 the area under all types of forests was 9·2m. ha. Of this, commercial plantations covered 1·3m. ha. and indigenous forests 534,000 ha. or 0·4% of the country's surface. The balance was 'woodland' forests. The private sector owned or controlled 1,051,223 ha. (83%) of the plantation area of 1,266,194 ha. as well as 174 of the 178 primary processing plants in the country. The remaining 17% (214,973 ha.) were owned by the state.

The industry was a net exporter to the value of R2·84bn. in 2007, almost 99% of which was in the form of converted value-added products. The forest-products industry contributed 2·5% of total exports and 1·7% of total imports in 2007. In that year paper exports were the most important (R5·51bn. or 45% of the total), followed by pulp (R3·52bn. or 29% of the total), solid wood products (R2·84bn. or 23% of the total) and other products (R0·32bn. or 3% of the total). Woodchip exports, mainly to Japan, accounted for 68% (R1·93bn.) of the total solid wood products exports.

Fisheries

The commercial marine fishing industry is valued at more than R3bn. annually and employs 28,000 people directly. It is an important employer because it pays a relatively high average wage (approximately R36,000) to its employees, of whom the majority are semi-skilled. In 2000 the commercial fishing fleet consisted of 4,477 vessels licensed by the department of environmental affairs and tourism.

The total number of fishing rights allocated stands at 2,200, 1,700 of which are small, medium and micro enterprises. The total catch in 2005 was 817,608 tonnes, over 99% of which came from marine fishing.

INDUSTRY

The leading companies by market capitalization in South Africa in March 2009 were: MTN Group, a mobile telecommunications company (US$20·6bn.); Sasol Ltd, a coal, oil and gas producer (US$18·4bn.); and Standard Bank Group (US$13·1bn.).

Actual value of sales of the principal groups of industries (in R1m.) in 2005: coke, petroleum, chemical products, rubber and plastic, 228·0; basic metals, fabricated metal products, machinery and equipment, and office, accounting and computing machinery, 190·1; food products and beverages, 158·7; transport equipment, 149·7; wood and wood products, paper, publishing and printing, 79·8; textiles, clothing, leather and footwear, 38·6. Total actual value including other groups, R953·9m. In 2003 industry accounted for 31·0% of GDP, with manufacturing contributing 18·9%.

Labour

The Employment Equity Act, 1998 signalled the beginning of the final phase of transformation in the job market, which began with the implementation of the Labour Relations Act. It aims to avoid all discrimination in employment. The Basic Conditions of Employment Act, 1997 applies to all workers except for the South African National Defence Force (SANDF), the South African Secret Service (SASS) and the National Intelligence Agency (NIA). The new provisions include a reduction in the maximum hours of work from 46 to 45 hours per week (however, the Act allows for the progressive reduction of working hours to 40 per week).

The labour force in South Africa numbered 17·1m. in the fourth quarter of 2009, of which 4·2m. were unemployed. In the fourth quarter of 2009 the unemployment rate was 24·3%, up from 21·9% in the fourth quarter of 2008.

The Unemployment Insurance Fund (UIF), providing benefits to unemployed workers, increased its income from R2·1bn. in 2001 to R3·8bn. in 2002–03. By June 2003 more than 530,000 employers had registered their employees with the UIF, while the number of employer declarations stood at 413,111, with a total of R8·2m. received in contributions. This translates to more than 67% of employers having registered.

Trade Unions

By mid-2003 there were 362 trade unions and 240 registered employer organizations operating in South Africa. In 2007 there were 3·1m. members of trade unions. The most important trade union groups or federations are Congress of South African Trade Unions (COSATU), Federation of Trade Unions of South Africa (FEDUSA) and National Council of Trade Unions (NACTU). The three largest trade unions are the National Union of Mineworkers (NUM), the National Union of Metalworkers of South Africa (NUMSA) and the National Education, Health and Allied Workers' Union (NEHAWU), all of which are COSATU affiliates.

INTERNATIONAL TRADE

South Africa's four main trading partners in 2006 were Germany, USA, Japan and China. Germany is South Africa's number one trading partner in terms of total trade (the sum of exports and imports) recorded in 2006. Exports to Germany rose in nominal terms from R21·1bn. in 2005 to R24·4bn. in 2006. Imports from Germany increased in nominal terms from R49·2bn. in 2005 to R53·9bn. in 2006.

In 2005 Europe accounted for 38·9% (R116·9bn.) of South Africa's total exports and 40·3% (R140·4bn.) of total imports. Seven of South Africa's top ten trading partners are European countries. A trade, co-operation and development agreement was provisionally implemented on 1 Jan. 2000, under the terms of which South Africa will grant duty-free access to 86% of EU imports over a period of 12 years, while the EU will liberalize 95% of South Africa's imports over a ten-year period. The Agreement provides for ongoing EU financial assistance in grants and loans for development co-operation, which amounts to some R900m. per annum.

In 2003 approximately 23% of South Africa's exports were destined for Africa while imports increased from only 4% of South Africa's total imports in 2003 to 40% in 2004. Within the Southern African Development Community (SADC), a smaller group of countries including South Africa, Botswana, Lesotho, Namibia and Swaziland have organized themselves into the Southern African Customs Union (SACU), sharing a common tariff regime without any internal barriers. Trade with SADC countries increased to R38bn. by 2004. Imports from within the region in 2004 totalled R6bn.

Japan is South Africa's largest trading partner in Asia. In 2006 total trade between the two countries amounted to R66·3bn.

Total foreign debt in 2005 was US$30,632m.

Imports and Exports

Trade in US$1m.:

	2001	*2002*	*2003*	*2004*
Imports (c.i.f.)	24,188·3	26,212·0	34,543·1	47,794·3
Exports (f.o.b.)	27,927·6	23,064·4	31,635·8	40,206·1

Main imports (in US$1m.):

	2002	*2003*	*2004*
Petroleum and petroleum products	3,134·7	3,934·5	6,647·6
Road vehicles	1,662·5	2,441·5	3,818·7
Telecommunications, sound recording and reproducing equipment	1,613·5	1,722·7	2,614·7
Other transport equipment	737·7	1,486·6	2,391·6
Office machines and automatic data processing machines	1,080·4	1,616·0	2,329·7

Main exports (in US$1m.):

	2002	*2003*	*2004*
Non-ferrous metals (including platinum)	1,099·1	4,423·5	6,927·8
Iron and steel	2,411·4	3,877·4	5,642·0
Road vehicles	2,396·7	3,114·5	3,540·6
Coal, coke and briquettes	1,839·1	1,804·8	2,432·6
Non-metallic mineral manufactures (including diamonds)	1,750·1	2,010·3	2,326·5

In Oct. 1998 a transshipment facility for containers opened at Kidatu, southwest of Dar es Salaam, Tanzania, providing a link between the 1,067 mm gauge railways of the southern part of Africa and the 1,000 mm gauge lines of the north. With the opening up of new markets for South Africa elsewhere in the continent, it has helped to boost trade and facilitate the shipment of cargo to countries to the north.

COMMUNICATIONS

The public company Transnet Limited was established on 1 April 1990. It handles 176m. tonnes of rail freight per year, 2·8m. tonnes of road freight and 194m. tonnes of freight through the harbours, while 13·8m. litres are pumped through its petrol pipelines annually. For the financial year ended 31 March 2007 Transnet reported a profit of R7,404m. (R4,930m. for 2006).

The company, through South African Airways (SAA), flies 6·1m. domestic, regional and international passengers per year. In total, Transnet is worth R72bn. in fixed assets and has a workforce of some 80,000 employees.

Transnet Limited consists of nine main divisions, a number of subsidiaries and related businesses—Transnet Freight Rail, the National Ports Authority (NPA), South African Port Operations (SAPO), Petronet, Freightdynamics, Propnet, Metrorail, Transtel and Transwerk.

Roads

In 2006 the South African road network comprised some 754,600 km of roads and streets. There is a primary roads network of 9,600 km, with plans to extend it to 20,000 km. Toll roads, which are serviced by 32 mainline toll plazas, cover about 2,400 km. The network includes 1,437 km of dual-carriage freeway, 440 km of single-carriage freeway and 56,967 km of single-carriage main road with unlimited access. South Africa has the longest road network in Africa.

As at 31 Dec. 2005 there were 7,971,187 registered motor vehicles. In 2007 a total of 14,920 people were killed in traffic accidents. With 31·2 deaths per 100,000 population in 2007, South Africa had the highest death rates in road accidents of any country.

Rail

The Passenger Rail Agency of South Africa (PRASA) was formed in March 2009 as an umbrella organization to oversee the day-to-day running of rail services in South Africa. PRASA operates Metrorail, offering commuter rail services in urban areas and transporting 1·7m. passengers on weekdays to 478 stations over 2,400 km of track; and Shosholoza Meyl, providing regional and long-distance rail transport.

Freight train services are provided by Transnet Freight Rail (formerly Spoornet), a public company owned solely by the South African government. Transnet transports 17% of the nation's freight annually and employs over 25,000 people.

Civil Aviation

Responsibility for civil aviation safety and security lies with the South African Civil Aviation Authority (SACAA). The Airports Company South Africa (ACSA) owns and operates South Africa's principal airports. The main international airports are: Johannesburg, Cape Town, Durban, Bloemfontein, Port Elizabeth, Pilanesberg, Lanseria and Upington. In April 2003 the Cabinet approved the status of the Kruger Mpumalanga Airport, near Nelspruit, as an international airport. ACSA also has a 35-year concession to operate Pilanesberg International Airport near Sun City in North-West Province.

South African Airways (SAA), Comair, SA Express and SA Airlink operate scheduled international air services. A further 18 independent operators provide internal flights and cargo services.

In 2007–08 O. R. Tambo International Airport (formerly Johannesburg International) handled 19,457,498 passengers (11,009,841 on domestic flights), Cape Town handled 8,426,618 passengers (6,950,061 on domestic flights) and Durban handled 4,792,553 passengers (4,747,202 on domestic flights). O. R. Tambo Airport is also the busiest airport for freight, handling 280,095 tonnes of cargo in 2005.

Shipping

The South African Maritime Safety Authority (SAMSA) was established on 1 April 1998 as the authority responsible for ensuring the safety of life at sea and the prevention of sea pollution from ships. Approximately 98% of South Africa's exports are conveyed by sea.

The National Ports Authority supervises South Africa's major ports. The largest ports include the deep water ports of Richards Bay, with its multi-product dry bulk handling facilities, multi-purpose terminal and the world's largest bulk coal terminal, and Saldanha featuring a bulk ore terminal adjacent to a bulk oil jetty with extensive storage facilities. Durban, Cape Town and Port Elizabeth provide large container terminals for deep-sea and coastal container traffic. The Port of Durban handles 1·0m. containers per annum. East London, the only river port, has a multi-purpose terminal and dry dock facilities. Mossel Bay is a specialized port serving the south coast fishing industry and offshore gas fields. Trade at the sea ports increased by 74% between 1994–2004, with container throughput more than doubling.

In 2002 the merchant fleet totalled 144,000 GRT, including oil tankers 3,000 GRT. During 2005–06 the major ports handled a total of 179,535,632 tonnes of cargo.

Telecommunications

In 2008 there were 4·4m. main (fixed) telephone lines. In the same year mobile phone subscribers numbered 45·0m. (906·0 per 1,000 persons). The largest mobile phone networks are Vodacom and MTN.

Between 1997 and 2002 Telkom SA, for many years the national operator, concentrated on replacing analogue lines with digital technology, under the terms of its final exclusive licence; the transmission network is now almost wholly digital. Under the Telecommunications Acts of 1996 and 2001, South Africa is beginning to liberalize its telecommunications industry. Telkom lost its monopoly on the fixed-line market in 2006 with the launch of Neotel, the country's second national operator. Telkom was offered on the Johannesburg Securities Exchange and the New York Stock Exchange in March 2003, realizing R3·9bn. on the first day.

There were 3,966,000 PCs in use in 2005, or 83·6 per 1,000 population, and internet users numbered 4,187,000 in 2008.

Postal Services

The South African Post Office handles an average of 6m. letters a day, 70% of which are prepaid mass-mailed letters sent by companies using franking machines. SAPO services over 40m. South Africans and numerous public and private institutions. It delivers mail items to over 7·5m. delivery points. SAPO has 2,760 postal outlets countrywide and 30 mail processing centres.

Public Internet Terminals (PiTs) offer government information and an email service, internet browsing, business sections and educational services. By March 2006, 672 installed terminals were operational.

SOCIAL INSTITUTIONS

Justice

All law must be consistent with the Constitution and its Bill of Rights. Judgments of courts declaring legislation, executive action, or conduct to be invalid are binding on all organs of state and all persons. The common law of the Republic is based on Roman-Dutch law—that is the uncodified law of Holland as it was at the date of the cession of the Cape to the United Kingdom in 1806. South African law has, however, developed its own unique characteristics.

Judges hold office until they attain the age of 70 or, if they have not served for 15 years, until they have completed 15 years of service or have reached the age of 75, when they are discharged from active service. A judge discharged from active service must be ready to perform service for an aggregate of three months a year until the age of 75. The Chief Justice of South Africa, the Deputy Chief Justice, the President of the Supreme Court of Appeal and the Deputy President of the Supreme Court of Appeal are appointed by the President after consulting the Judicial Service Commission. In the case of the Chief Justice and Deputy Chief Justice, the President must also consult the leaders of parties represented in the National Assembly. The President on the advice of the Judicial Service Commission (JSC) appoints all other judges. No judge may be removed from office unless the JSC finds that the judge suffers from incapacity, is grossly incompetent or is guilty of gross misconduct, and the National Assembly calls for that judge to be removed by a resolution supported by at least two thirds of its members.

The higher courts include: 1) *The Constitutional Court* (CC), which consists of the Chief Justice of South Africa, the Deputy Chief Justice of South Africa and nine other judges. It is the highest court in all matters in which the interpretation of the Constitution or its application to any law, including the common law, is relevant; 2) *The Supreme Court of Appeal*, consisting of a President, a Deputy President and the number of judges of appeal determined by an Act of Parliament. It is the highest court of appeal in all other matters; 3) *The High Courts*, which may decide constitutional matters other than those which are within the exclusive jurisdiction of the Constitutional Court, and any other matter other than one assigned by Parliament to a court of a status similar to that of a High Court. Each High Court is presided over by a Judge President who may divide the area under his jurisdiction into circuit districts. In each such district there shall be held at least twice in every year and at such times and places determined by the Judge President, a court which shall be presided over by a judge of the High Court. Such a court is known as the circuit court for the district in question; 4) *The Land Claims Court*, established under the Restitution of Land Rights Act of 1994 deals with claims for restitution of rights in land to persons or communities dispossessed of such rights after 1913 as a result of past racially discriminatory laws or practices. It has jurisdiction throughout the Republic and the power to determine such claims and related matters such as compensation and rights of occupation; 5) *The Labour Court*, established under the Labour Relations Act, 1995 deals with labour disputes. It is a superior court that has authority, inherent powers and standing in relation to matters under its jurisdiction, equal to that the High Court has in relation to matters under its jurisdiction. Appeals from decisions of the Labour Court lie to the Labour Appeal Court which has authority in labour matters equivalent to that of the Supreme Court of Appeal in other matters.

The lower courts are called Magistrates' Courts. Magisterial districts have been grouped into 13 clusters headed by chief magistrates. From the magistrates court there is an appeal to the High Court having jurisdiction in that area, and then to the Supreme Court of Appeal. In cases involving constitutional matters there is a further appeal to the Constitutional Court.

The death penalty was abolished in June 1995 and no executions have taken place since 1989. In 2005–06 there were 18,528 murders (down from a peak of 26,877 murders in 1995–96). Although steadily declining, South Africa's murder rate of 39 per 100,000 in 2005–06 is still one of the highest in the world. Budgeted spending on police, prisons and justice services for 2006–07 was R79·6bn. The population in penal institutions in Dec. 2006 was 189,748.

Education

The South African Schools Act, 1996 became effective on 1 Jan. 1997 and provides for: compulsory education for students between the ages of seven and 15 years of age, or students reaching the ninth grade, whichever occurs first. Pupils normally enrol for Grade 1 education at the beginning of the year in which they turn seven years of age although earlier entry at the age of six is allowed if the child meets specified criteria indicating that they have reached a stage of school readiness.

In 2003 the South African public education system accommodated 11·7m. school pupils, 448,868 university students, 216,499 technikon students and over 356,000 further education and training college students. There were 27,458 primary, secondary, combined and intermediate schools with 354,201 educators.

In the 2003–04 financial year R69,063m. was allocated to education. In 2007 public expenditure on education came to 5·4% of GDP and 17·4% of total government spending.

As a result of a major restructure of South African higher education during 2002–04, 36 universities and technikons were reduced by means of mergers and incorporations to 16 universities and seven universities of technology. The University of South Africa (UNISA) is the oldest and largest university in South Africa and one of the largest distance education institutions in the world. In 2007 UNISA had a total of 239,581 students and 4,064 teaching and research staff. In 2005 the Tshwane University of Technology had 60,400 students, University of Pretoria 46,400, University of Johannesburg 45,500, University of Kwazulu-Natal 40,700, North West University 38,600 and the Cape Peninsula University of Technology 29,000.

The adult literacy rate in 2007 was an estimated 88% (89% for males and 87% for females).

Health

Some 40% of South Africans live in poverty and 75% of these live in rural areas with limited access to health services. By April 2003 free public health services were provided at about 3,500 public health clinics nationwide. There is also a network of mobile clinics run by the government to provide primary and preventive health care.

33,220 doctors were registered with the Health Profession Council of South Africa (HPCSA) in April 2006. These include doctors working for the state, doctors in private practice and specialists. Doctors train at the medical schools of eight universities and the majority go on to practise privately. In April 2006, 4,799 dentists and 191,269 registered and enrolled nurses and enrolled nursing auxiliaries were registered with the HPCSA; and 955 oral hygienists and 433 dental therapists were registered. In Aug. 2006, 10,971 pharmacists were registered with the South African Pharmacy Council. Chris Hani Baragwanath Hospital, situated to the southwest of Johannesburg, with its 3,200 beds, is the largest hospital in the world.

In Oct. 1998 the first traditional hospital was opened in Mpumalanga—the Samuel Traditional Hospital. There are about 200,000 traditional healers in South Africa providing services to between 60% and 80% of their communities.

Approximately 5·5m. South Africans are HIV-infected, the highest number in the world (equivalent to nearly 12% of the population of South Africa). Government expenditure on HIV and AIDS increased substantially from R30m. in 1994 to R3bn. in 2005–06. In Aug. 2003 the government announced plans to roll out the provision of anti-retrovirals (ARVs) in the public health sector which would see 1·4m. people on treatment. It also envisaged that there would be at least one service point in every local municipality across the country by 2008. Although the latter has been achieved, it is clear that the number of people receiving ARVs is well behind the initial target.

In May 2007 the government endorsed a new five-year plan that aimed to cut the number of new HIV inflections by 50% and reduce the impact of HIV by expanding access to treatment and support to 80% of all people diagnosed by 2011. The plan also pledged to reduce the rates of mother-to-child transmission of HIV to less than 5% and to allocate 40% of the projected budget towards HIV treatment. Health facilities providing voluntary counselling and testing increased from 3,369 in 2004–05 to 4,930 in 2005–06.

Welfare

At Sept. 2003 the department of social development was disbursing grants through its provincial offices to 6·5m. beneficiaries at a monthly cost of R2·5bn. Recipients are means-tested to determine their eligibility. 3·8m. people received the child support grant (CSG) of R160 per month and 2m. (women aged 60 and above, men aged 65 and above) received old-age grants of R700 per month. The age of children eligible for the CSG will be progressively increased to include children up to the age of 14 years.

Other benefits paid are the disability, foster child, care dependency and war veterans' grants as well as institutional grants and grants in aid.

The total budget allocation for the payment of social assistance was R80·4bn. in 2009–10.

RELIGION

South Africa is a secular state and freedom of worship is guaranteed by the Constitution. Almost 80% of the population professes the Christian faith. Other major religious groups are Hindus, Muslims and Jews. A sizeable minority of the population subscribe to traditional African faiths. In 1992 the Anglican Church of Southern Africa voted by 79% of votes cast for the ordination of women. In Feb. 2010 there was one cardinal.

CULTURE

World Heritage Sites

UNESCO World Heritage sites under South African jurisdiction (with year entered on list) are: Greater St Lucia Wetland Park (1999), encompassing marine, wetland and savannah environments; Robben Island (1999), used since the 17th century as a prison, hospital and military base—it was the location for Nelson Mandela's incarceration; fossil hominid sites of Sterkfontein, Swartkrans, Kromdraai and environs (1999 and 2005), offering evidence of human evolution over 3·5m. years; uKhahlamba/Drakensberg Park (2000), including caves with 4,000-year old paintings; Mapungubwe Cultural Landscape (2003), a savannah landscape at the confluence of the Limpopo and Shashe rivers and the site of the largest kingdom in Africa in the 14th century; Cape Floral Region Protected Areas (2004); Vredefort Dome (2005), part of a meteorite impact structure; and Richtersveld cultural and botanical landscape (2007), covering 160,000 ha. of mountainous desert.

Broadcasting

Television and radio are regulated by an independent authority, ICASA. The South African Broadcasting Corporation (SABC), the country's public broadcaster, comprises three free-to-air channels as well as pay-TV services. M-Net, South Africa's first private subscription television service, has subscribers in about 50 countries across the African continent and Indian Ocean islands. The SABC's national radio network comprises 20 regional and national services, broadcasting in 11 languages. Between 1994 and 2006 more than 90 community radio broadcasting and ten commercial licences were awarded by ICASA. It is estimated that 88% of the rural population listens to the radio in a seven-day period, compared to 79% in 1994. About 50% of all programmes transmitted are produced in South Africa. There are more than 4m. licensed television households. Colour is by PAL.

Press

The major press groups are Independent Newspapers (Pty) Ltd, Media24 Ltd, CTP/Caxton Publishers and Printers Ltd, and Johnnic Publishing Ltd. Other important media players include Primedia, Nail (New Africa Investments Limited) and Kagiso Media. Nail has unbundled into a commercial company (New Africa Capital) and a media company (New Africa Media).

In 2006 there were nine paid-for dailies, 13 paid-for Sunday newspapers and 71 paid-for non-daily newspapers. Newspapers with the highest circulations (Jan.–March 2008): Sunday Times (504,193); Daily Sun (499,436); Rapport (301,827); Soccer-Laduma (292,701); Sunday World (203,460); Sunday Sun (202,524); City Press (201,790); Sowetan (145,173). Beeld is the largest Afrikaans daily (105,149) and Isolezwe the largest isiZulu daily (99,098).

Tourism

A record 9·59m. visitors travelled to the country in 2008, up from 9·09m. in 2007. Most visitors in 2008 came from Lesotho, Zimbabwe, Mozambique, Swaziland, Botswana, the UK, the USA and Germany. The number of people employed directly in tourism rose in 2007 to 411,900, with a further 534,400 employed indirectly. Gauteng and Western Cape were the most popular provinces visited in 2008 (with 32·3% and 26·9% of visitor nights respectively).

Festivals

Best-known arts festivals: the Klein Karoo Festival (Oudtshoorn, Western Cape), which has a strong Afrikaans component, is held in April; the Grahamstown Arts Festival in the Eastern Cape is held in June/July; the Mangaung African Cultural Festival (Macufe) is held in Sept. in Bloemfontein; and the Aardklop Arts Festival, in Potchefstroom in the North-West province, is held in Sept. The Encounters South African International Documentary Festival has been held since 1999.

DIPLOMATIC REPRESENTATIVES

Of South Africa in the United Kingdom (South Africa House, Trafalgar Square, London, WC2N 5DP)
High Commissioner: Dr Zola Sidney Themba Skweyiya.

Of the United Kingdom in South Africa (255 Hill St., Arcadia, Pretoria 0002)
High Commissioner: Dr Nicola Brewer.

Of South Africa in the USA (3051 Massachusetts Ave., NW, Washington, D.C., 20008)
Ambassador: Vacant.
Chargé d'Affaires a.i.: Johnny Moloto.

Of the USA in South Africa (877 Pretorius St., Arcadia, Pretoria 0083)
Ambassador: Donald H. Gips.

Of South Africa to the United Nations
Ambassador: Baso Sangqu.

Of South Africa to the European Union
Ambassador: Anil Sooklal.

FURTHER READING

Government Communication and Information System (GCIS), including extracts from the *South Africa Yearbook 2007/08*, compiled and published by GCIS.

Beinart, W., *Twentieth Century South Africa*. 1994
Brewer, J. (ed.) *Restructuring South Africa*. 1994
Butler, Anthony, *Contemporary South Africa*. 2nd ed. 2009
Davenport, T. R. H., *South Africa: a Modern History*. 5th ed. 2000
De Klerk, F. W., *The Last Trek—A New Beginning*. 1999
Fine, B and Rustomjee Z., *The Political Economy of South Africa*. 1996
Giliomee, Hermann, *The Afrikaners: Biography of a People*. 2003
Guelke, Adrian, *Rethinking the Rise of Apartheid*. 2004
Hough, M. and Du Plessis, A. (eds.) *Selected Documents and Commentaries on Negotiations and Constitutional Development in the RSA, 1989–1994*. 1994
Johnson, R. W. and Schlemmer, L. (eds.) *Launching Democracy in South Africa: the First Open Election, 1994*. 1996
Mandela, N., *Long Walk to Freedom: the Autobiography of Nelson Mandela*. 1994
Meredith, M., *South Africa's New Era: the 1994 Election*. 1994
Mostert, N., *Frontiers: the Epic of South Africa's Creation and the Tragedy of the Xhosa People*. 1992

Picard, Louis A., *The State of the State: Institutional Transformation, Capacity and Political Change in South Africa.* 2005
Sparks, Allister, *Beyond the Miracle: Inside the New South Africa.* 2006
Thompson, L., *A History of South Africa.* 2nd ed. 1996
The Truth and Reconciliation Commission of South Africa Report, 5 vols. 1999
Waldmeir, P., *Anatomy of a Miracle: the End of Apartheid and the Birth of the New South Africa.* 1997
Who's Who in South African Politics. Online only

National Statistical Office: Statistics South Africa, Private Bag X44, Pretoria 0001.
Website: http://www.statssa.gov.za

SOUTH AFRICAN PROVINCES

In 1994 the former provinces of the Cape of Good Hope, Natal, the Orange Free State and the Transvaal, together with the former 'homelands' or 'TBVC countries' of Transkei, Bophuthatswana, Venda and Ciskei, were replaced by nine new provinces. Transkei and Ciskei were integrated into Eastern Cape, Venda into Northern Province (now Limpopo), and Bophuthatswana into Free State, Mpumalanga and North-West.

The administrative powers of the provincial governments in relation to the central government are set out in the 1999 constitution after a revision of the original text, demanded by the Constitutional Court in 1996.

Eastern Cape

TERRITORY AND POPULATION

The area is 169,580 sq. km and the population at the 2001 census was 6,436,764, the third largest population in South Africa. Of that number: female, 3,461,251; African/Black, 5,635,079 (87% of the population); Coloured, 478,807 (7%); White, 304,506 (5%); Indian/Asian, 18,372 (0·3%). 38·6% of the population lived in urban areas in 2001. Density (2001), 38 per sq. km. Estimated population as at 30 June 2007, 6,906,200. Life expectancy at birth, 1996, was 60·4 years. At the 2001 census 83·2% spoke IsiXhosa as their home language, 9·3% Afrikaans, 3·6% English and 2·4% Sesotho.

Eastern Cape comprises 77 administrative districts (including Umzimkulu district, an enclave within KwaZulu-Natal).

SOCIAL STATISTICS

Registered live births in 2005 totalled 292,414; deaths, 92,915. Total number of marriages officially recorded in 2005 was 22,104 and divorces granted 1,928.

CONSTITUTION AND GOVERNMENT

The provincial capital is Bisho. There is a 63-seat provincial legislature.

RECENT ELECTIONS

At the provincial elections held on 22 April 2009, 44 seats were won by the African National Congress, nine by the Congress of the People, six by the Democratic Alliance, three by the United Democratic Movement and one by the African Independent Congress.

CURRENT ADMINISTRATION

In Feb. 2010 the ANC Executive Council comprised:

Premier: Noxolo Kiviet (took office on 6 May 2009).

Minister of Agriculture and Rural Development: Mbulelo Sogoni. *Education:* Mahlubandile Qwase. *Finance, Economic Development and Environmental Affairs:* Mcebisi Jonas. *Health:* Phumulo Masualle. *Housing:* Nombulelo Mabandla. *Local Government and Traditional Affairs:* Sicelo Gqobana. *Roads and Public Works:* Pemmy Majodina. *Social Development:* Nonkosi Mvana. *Sport, Recreation, Arts and Culture:* Xoliswa Tom. *Transport and Safety:* Ghishma Barry.

Speaker: Fikile Xasa. *Director-General:* Dr Sibongile Muthwa.

Government Website: http://www.ecprov.gov.za

ENERGY AND NATURAL RESOURCES

Electricity

In 2005, 7,713 GWh of electricity were consumed. Approximately 42% of households have electricity.

Oil and Gas

Planning has begun for a new oil refinery at Coega near Port Elizabeth. It is expected to be the biggest oil refinery in Africa when it comes online in 2015.

Minerals

In 2006, 964 people were employed in mining.

Agriculture

There are around 4,000 commercial farms with an average area of 1,500 ha. Of this area only 7% is arable land with 45% not farmed at present owing to land ownership disputes in the former homelands (Transkei and Ciskei). Livestock accounts for 77% of commercial agricultural production; 18% comprises horticulture. Gross farming income for 2007 was R5·4bn. Gross farming income of field crops (R1,000), 369,086; horticulture, 1,396,208; animal and animal products, 3,616,267. The total number of paid farm workers in 2007 was 64,818.

Fisheries

There is a relatively small sea-fishing industry based on squid, sardines, hake, kingklip and crayfish. Aquaculture produces abalone for export to the Far East.

INDUSTRY

Manufacturing is based mainly in Port Elizabeth and East London with motor manufacturing as the prime industry. Wool, mohair and hides are an important area of the province's agro-industry.

Labour

As at Sept. 2003 the economically active population numbered 1,636,000, of whom 520,000 were unemployed (31·8%), the highest unemployment rate of all the provinces. Eastern Cape is the centre of South Africa's motor manufacturing industry with the main production centres based at Port Elizabeth and East London.

COMMUNICATIONS

Roads

Total road network at Dec. 2000 was 38,000 km. Between Dec. 1999 and April 2000 the province's roads were severely damaged by floods. A R40m. reconstruction programme commenced in

Oct. 2000. There were 1,255 fatalities as a result of road traffic accidents in 2004.

Civil Aviation

The province has four airports (Port Elizabeth, East London, Umtata and Bulembu).

Shipping

There are three deep-water ports: Port Elizabeth, East London and Coega.

Telecommunications

According to a Statistics South Africa General Household Survey of 2004, 40·1% of households had access to a telephone or mobile phone, the lowest proportion of all the provinces.

SOCIAL INSTITUTIONS

Education

In 2004 there were 2,586,000 children enrolled in schools (including pre-schools) and a total of 63,370 teaching staff. Following a nationwide restructure of higher education, the Province has four universities: Walter Sisulu University for Technology and Science (formed by the merger of University of Transkei and two technikons), Rhodes University, the University of Fort Hare and Nelson Mandela Metropolitan University (formed by the merger of Port Elizabeth Technikon and the Port Elizabeth campus of Vista University). At the 2001 census more than 22·8% of people aged 20 years and above had no schooling at all, while 6·3% had completed higher education.

Health

In 2004 there were 1,008 health facilities (including clinics and community health care centres). In the 1997–98 financial year a total of R112m. was allocated to the Primary School Nutrition Programme.

CULTURE

Tourism

Overseas visitors to the province in 2008 totalled 403,000; domestic visitor trips, 5·4m.

Free State

TERRITORY AND POPULATION

The Free State lies in the centre of South Africa and is situated between the Vaal River in the north and the Orange River in the south. It borders on the Northern Cape, Eastern Cape, North-West, Mpumalanga, KwaZulu-Natal and Gauteng Province and shares a border with Lesotho. The area is 129,480 sq. km, 10·62% of South Africa's total surface area. The province is the third largest in South Africa but has the second smallest population and the second lowest population density. The population at the 2001 census was 2,706,776. Of that number: female, 1,409,171; African/Black, 2,381,073 (88% of the population); White, 238,791 (9%); Coloured, 83,193 (3%); Indian/Asian, 3,719 (0·1%). Estimated population as at 30 June 2007, 2,965,600. 63% of the population were between 15 and 64 and at least 69% of the population lived in urban areas in 1996 (in 1911, 80% lived in rural areas). Annual population growth rate: 1–2%. Density (2001), 21 per sq. km. Life expectancy at birth, 1996, was 52·8 years. At the 2001 census, 64·3% (1,742,939) of the population spoke Sesotho as their home language, 11·9% (323,082) Afrikaans, 9·1% (246,192) IsiXhosa, 6·8% (185,389) Setswana, 5·1% (138,091) IsiZulu and 1·2% (31,246) English.

Free State comprises 52 administrative districts. The provincial capital is Bloemfontein (meaning 'fountain of flowers'). Bloemfontein's indigenous name is Mangaung, which means 'place of the big cats'.

SOCIAL STATISTICS

Registered live births in 2005 totalled 68,487; deaths, 50,210. The total number of marriages officially recorded in 2005 was 14,475 and divorces granted 1,662.

CLIMATE

Temperatures are mild with averages ranging from 19·5°C in the west to 15°C in the east. Maximum temperatures in the west can reach 36°C in summer. Winter temperatures in the high-lying areas of the eastern Free State can drop as low as –15°C. The western and southern areas are semi-desert.

CONSTITUTION AND GOVERNMENT

There is a 30-seat provincial legislature. The Free State Executive Council, headed by the *Premier*, administers the province through ten Departments.

The Free State House of Traditional Leaders advises the Legislature on matters pertaining to traditional authorities and tribal matters.

RECENT ELECTIONS

At the provincial elections held on 22 April 2009 the African National Congress retained its majority and won 22 of the 30 seats; the Congress of the People four; the Democratic Alliance three; and Freedom Front Plus one.

CURRENT ADMINISTRATION

In Feb. 2010 the ANC Executive Council comprised:

Premier: Ace Magashule (took office on 6 May 2009).

Minister of Agriculture: Mamiki Qabathe. *Co-operative Governance, Traditional Leadership and Human Settlement:* Msebenzi Zwane. *Education:* Tate Makgoe. *Health:* Sisi Mabe. *Police, Roads and Transport:* Thabo Manyoni. *Public Works and Rural Development:* Fezi Ngumbentombi. *Social Development:* Sisi Ntombela. *Sports, Arts, Culture and Recreation:* Custa Khothule. *Tourism, Economic Development and Environmental Affairs:* Mxolisi Dukwana. *Treasury:* Seeiso Mohai.

Speaker: Pat Matosa. *Director-General:* Muzamani Charles Nwaila.

Government Website: http://www.fs.gov.za

ENERGY AND NATURAL RESOURCES

Electricity

In the Free State, Eskom distributes electricity through 3,000 km of distribution lines, 9,000 km of reticulation (network) lines; and has an installed capacity of 1,200,740 MVA. Mining (60% of sales) and local governments (30% of sales) are Eskom's biggest Free State's customers.

In 2005, 8,980 GWh of electricity were consumed.

Minerals

The province contributes about 16·5% of South Africa's total mineral output. Apart from rich gold and diamond deposits, the Free State is the source of numerous other minerals and is the founding home of South Africa's famous oil-from-coal industry centred on Sasolburg. Bentonite clays, gypsum, salt and phosphates are to be found while large concentrates of thorium-ilmenite-zircon also occur. In 2006, 46,067 people were employed in mining.

Agriculture

Good agricultural conditions allow for a wide variety of farming industries. Of the total 12·7m. ha., 90% (11·5m. ha.) is utilized as farmland. Of this, 63·9% is natural grazing; 2·1% is for nature conservation; and 1·1% is used for other purposes. Dryland cultivation is practised on 97% of the arable land, while the remaining 3% is under irrigation.

Free State has the highest number of commercial farming units of all the provinces: 7,515 in 2007 with a gross farming income of R11·9bn. Gross farming income of field crops in 2007 (R1,000), 4,226,749; horticulture, 984,203; animal and animal products, 6,718,152. Paid farm workers in the same year numbered 99,094. The eastern region is the major producer of small grains; the northern region, maize and beef; and the southern region, mutton and wool. The province produces about 40% of total maize and 50% of total wheat output in South Africa.

INDUSTRY

Labour

As at Sept. 2003 the economically active population numbered 1,046,000, of whom 300,000 were unemployed (28·6%).

COMMUNICATIONS

Roads

The Free State Department of Public Works, Roads and Transport is responsible for maintenance of a rural network, which consists of 20,452 km tertiary gravel roads, 21,470 km secondary gravel roads, 6,965 km primary paved roads, and 910 km national roads, of which 25 km are not tarred. There were 945 fatalities as a result of road traffic accidents in 2004.

Rail

Transnet Freight Rail is one of the biggest companies in the Free State with 4,217 employees. It transports most of the province's maize, wheat, gold ore, petroleum and fertilizer. The company's infrastructure consists of approximately 4,000 km of tracks, of which 1,300 km are electrified.

Telecommunications

According to a Statistics South Africa General Household Survey of 2004, 51·7% of households had access to a telephone or mobile phone.

Postal Services

In 2005 there were 105 post offices, 15 Postpoints (situated in locations such as chainstores, etc.) and 40 retail postal agencies.

SOCIAL INSTITUTIONS

Education

In 2004 there were 852,000 pupils (including pre-schools and farm schools) and 26,929 teachers. Following a nationwide restructure of higher education, the Province has two universities: the University of the Free State (established in 1904) and the Central University of Technology, Free State. According to the 2001 census, 16·0% of those aged 20 and over had no schooling; 30·7% had some secondary education.

Health

In 2003 there were 31 public hospitals with 4,649 beds and 20 private hospitals with 2,146 beds.

FURTHER READING

Free State: The Winning Province. 1997

Gauteng

TERRITORY AND POPULATION

Gauteng is the smallest province in South Africa, covering an area of 17,010 sq. km (approximately 1·4% of the total land surface of South Africa). The population at the 2001 census was 8,837,179. Of that number: female, 4,392,500; African/Black, 6,522,792 (74%); White, 1,758,398 (20%); Coloured, 337,974 (3·8%); Indian/Asian, 218,015 (2·5%). Estimated population as at 30 June 2007, 9,688,100. 97% of the population lived in urban areas in 1996. Density (2001), 470 per sq. km. Life expectancy at birth, 1996, was 59·6 years. At the 2001 census, 21·5% spoke IsiZulu as their home language, 14·3% Afrikaans, 13·1% Sesotho, 12·4% English, 10·7% Sesotho sa Leboa, 8·4% Setswana, 7·6% IsiXhosa, 5·7% Xitsonga, 1·9% IsiNdebele, 1·7% Tshivenda and 1·4% SiSwati.

The province of Gauteng, at first called Pretoria-Witwatersrand-Vereeniging (PWV), comprises 23 administrative districts. The provincial capital is Johannesburg. In the Sesotho language, Gauteng means 'Place of Gold'.

SOCIAL STATISTICS

Registered live births in 2005 totalled 210,817; deaths, 107,528. The total number of marriages officially recorded in 2005 was 44,831 and divorces granted 12,302.

CONSTITUTION AND GOVERNMENT

There is a 73-seat provincial legislature.

RECENT ELECTIONS

At the provincial elections held on 22 April 2009, 47 seats were won by the African National Congress, 16 by the Democratic Alliance, six by the Congress of the People and one each by the African Christian Democratic Party, the Independent Democrats, the Inkatha Freedom Party and Freedom Front Plus.

CURRENT ADMINISTRATION

In Feb. 2010 the ANC Executive Council comprised:

Premier: Nomvula Mokonyane; b. 1963 (took office on 6 May 2009).

Minister of Agriculture and Rural Development: Nomantu Nkomo-Ralehoko. *Community Safety:* Khabisi Mosunkutu. *Economic Development:* Firoz Cachali. *Education:* Barbara Creecy. *Finance:* Mandla Nkomfe. *Health and Social Development:* Qedani Dorothy Mahlangu. *Infrastructure Development:* Nonhlanhla Mazibuko. *Local Government and Housing:* Kgaogelo Lekgoro. *Roads and Transport:* Bheki Nkosi. *Sport, Arts, Recreation and Culture:* Neliswe Mthimkhulu-Mbatha.

Speaker: Richard Mdakane. *Acting Director-General:* Margaret-Ann Diedericks.

Government Website: http://www.gautengonline.gov.za

ENERGY AND NATURAL RESOURCES

Electricity

In 2005, 55,107 GWh of electricity were consumed.

Minerals

In 2006, 78,086 people were employed in mining.

Agriculture

There were 2,378 commercial farming units in 2007 with a gross farming income of R7·4bn. Gross farming income of field crops in 2007 (R1,000), 566,632; horticulture, 1,116,908; animal and animal products, 5,633,061. Paid farm workers in the same year numbered 34,936.

INDUSTRY

Labour

As at Sept. 2003 the economically active population numbered 4,499,000, of whom 1,269,000 were unemployed (28·2%). About 38,000 workers are employed by the motor manufacturing industry which contributes an estimated 4·3% of the province's GDP. The aluminium industry is worth about US$20m.

COMMUNICATIONS

Roads

There were 2,571 fatalities as a result of road traffic accidents in 2004.

Civil Aviation

O. R. Tambo International Airport is the main airport in the province.

Telecommunications

According to a Statistics South Africa General Household Survey of 2004, 69·6% of households had access to a telephone or mobile phone.

SOCIAL INSTITUTIONS

Education

In 2004 there were 2·1m. children enrolled in schools (including pre-schools) with a total of 45,558 teaching staff. The Province has six universities: University of South Africa, University of Johannesburg (formed in 2005 by the merger of Rand Afrikaans University and Technikon Witwatersrand), University of Pretoria, University of Witwatersrand, Tshwane University of Technology and Vaal University of Technology. According to the 2001 census, 8·4% of those aged 20 and over had no schooling; 34·3% had some secondary education.

Health

In 2004 there were 31 hospitals and 15,871 hospital beds.

CULTURE

Tourism

Overseas visitors to the province in 2008 totalled 4·5m. (the highest of any of the South African provinces); domestic visitor trips, 4·8m.

KwaZulu-Natal

TERRITORY AND POPULATION

The area is 92,100 sq. km and the population at the 2001 census was 9,426,017. Of that number: female, 5,016,926; African/Black, 8,002,407 (84·8% of the population); Indian/Asian, 798,275 (8·5%); White, 483,448 (5·1%); Coloured, 141,887 (1·5%). Estimated population as at 30 June 2007, 10,014,500. 43% lived in urban areas in 1996. Density (2001), 102 per sq. km. Life expectancy at birth, 1996, was 53·0 years. At the 2001 census, 80·8% spoke IsiZulu as their home language, 13·6% English, 2·3% IsiXhosa and 1·5% Afrikaans.

KwaZulu-Natal comprises 66 administrative districts. The provincial capital is Pietermaritzburg, chosen by referendum in 1995.

SOCIAL STATISTICS

Registered live births in 2005 totalled 304,206; deaths, 138,206. The total number of marriages officially recorded in 2005 was 28,461 and divorces granted 3,960.

CONSTITUTION AND GOVERNMENT

There is an 80-seat provincial legislature.

RECENT ELECTIONS

At the provincial elections held on 22 April 2009, 51 seats were won by the African National Congress, 18 by the Inkatha Freedom Party, seven by Democratic Alliance, two by the Minority Front, and one each by the African Christian Democratic Party and the Congress of the People.

CURRENT ADMINISTRATION

In Feb. 2010 the government comprised:

Premier: Dr Zweli Mkhize; b. 1956 (ANC; took office on 6 May 2009).

Minister of Agriculture, Environmental Affairs and Rural Development: Lydia Johnson. *Arts, Culture, Sport and Recreation:* Weziwe Thusi. *Economic Development and Tourism:* Mike Mabuyakhulu. *Education:* Senzo Mchunu. *Finance:* Ina Cronje. *Health:* Dr Maxwell Dlomo. *Human Settlement and Public Works:* Maggie Govender. *Local Government and Traditional Affairs:* Nomusa Dube. *Social Development:* Meshack Radebe. *Transport, Community Safety and Liaison:* Willies Mchunu.

Speaker: Peggy Nkonyeni. *Acting Director-General:* Roger Govender.

Government Website: http://www.kwazulunatal.gov.za

ENERGY AND NATURAL RESOURCES

Electricity

In 2005, 43,049 GWh of electricity were consumed.

Minerals

Coal is mined in the north of the province and titanium and zircon are produced at Richards Bay. In 2006, 9,198 people were employed in mining.

Agriculture

There were 3,560 commercial farming units in 2007 with a gross farming income of R10·1bn. Gross farming income of field crops in 2007 (R1,000), 2,867,839; horticulture, 1,086,975; animal and animal products, 5,794,379. Paid farm workers in the same year numbered 101,068. Sugarcane and maize are the principal crops.

INDUSTRY

Labour

As at Sept. 2003 the economically active population numbered 3,182,000, of whom 996,000 were unemployed (31·3%).

COMMUNICATIONS

Roads

In 2000 the road network totalled 42,000 km. There were 2,692 fatalities as a result of road traffic accidents in 2004.

Civil Aviation

Durban International Airport is the main airport in the province.

Shipping

Durban harbour is the busiest in South Africa and one of the ten largest harbours in the world. Coal is exported from Richards Bay.

Telecommunications

According to a Statistics South Africa General Household Survey of 2004, 45·7% of households had access to a telephone or mobile phone.

SOCIAL INSTITUTIONS

Education

Since 1995 education has been provided by a unified KwaZulu-Natal Education Department (KZNED). In 2004 there were 3,041,000 children enrolled in schools (including pre-schools) with (in 2002) a total of 82,725 teaching staff. Following a nationwide restructure of higher education, the Province has four universities: University of KwaZulu-Natal, University of Zululand, Durban University of Technology and Mangosuthu University of Technology. According to the 2001 census, 21·9% of the population aged 20 and above had no schooling; 28·8% had some secondary education.

Health

In 2001 there were 100 hospitals (including 41 private and semi-private hospitals) and 31,266 hospital beds.

CULTURE

Tourism
Overseas visitors to the province in 2008 totalled 1·2m.; domestic visitor trips, 10·4m.

Limpopo

TERRITORY AND POPULATION

The area is 123,910 sq. km and the population at the 2001 census was 5,273,642. Of that number: female, 2,878,858; African/ Black, 5,128,616 (97% of the population); White, 126,276 (2·4%); Coloured, 10,163 (0·2%); Indian/Asian, 8,587 (0·2%). Estimated population as at 30 June 2007, 5,402,900. 10·7% lived in urban areas in 2001. Density (2001), 43 per sq. km. Life expectancy at birth, 1996, was 60·1 years. At the 2001 census 52·0% spoke Sesotho sa Leboa as their home language, 22·3% Xitsonga, 15·9% Tshivenda, 2·3% Afrikaans and 1·5% IsiNdebele.

Limpopo (Northern Province until March 2003) comprises 32 administrative districts. The provincial capital is Polokwane (Pietersburg).

SOCIAL STATISTICS

Registered live births in 2005 totalled 159,924; deaths, 48,222. The total number of marriages officially recorded in 2005 was 10,529 and divorces granted 996.

CONSTITUTION AND GOVERNMENT

There is a 49-seat provincial legislature.

RECENT ELECTIONS

At the provincial elections held on 22 April 2009, 43 seats were won by the African National Congress, four by the Congress of the People and two by the Democratic Alliance.

CURRENT ADMINISTRATION

In Feb. 2010 the ANC Executive Council comprised:

Premier: Cassel Mathale (sworn in 6 May 2009).

Minister of Agriculture: Dipuo Letsatsi-Duba. *Economic Development, Environment and Tourism:* Pitsi Moloto. *Education:* Dickson Masemola. *Health and Social Development:* Mariam Sekgabutla. *Local Government and Housing:* Soviet Lekganyane. *Provincial Treasury:* Saad Cachalia. *Public Works:* George Phadagi. *Roads and Transport:* Pinky Kekana. *Safety, Security and Liaison:* Dikeledi Magadzi. *Sports, Arts and Culture:* Joyce Mashamba.

Speaker: Tshenwani Farasani. *Director-General:* Dr Nelly Manzini.

Government Website: http://www.limpopo.gov.za

ENERGY AND NATURAL RESOURCES

Electricity
In 2005, 10,281 GWh of electricity were consumed.

Minerals
Mining is an important industry in the province with, in 2006, 63,347 people employed.

Agriculture
There were 2,657 commercial farming units in 2007 with a gross farming income of R5·5bn. Gross farming income of field crops in 2007 (R1,000), 497,679; horticulture, 2,904,969; animal and animal products, 2,027,780. Paid farm workers in the same year numbered 67,561.

INDUSTRY

Labour
As at Sept. 2003 the economically active population numbered 1,139,000, of whom 349,000 were unemployed (30·6%).

COMMUNICATIONS

Roads
There were 1,068 fatalities as a result of road traffic accidents in 2004.

Telecommunications
According to a Statistics South Africa General Household Survey of 2004, 45·8% of households had access to a telephone or mobile phone.

SOCIAL INSTITUTIONS

Education
In 2004 there were 2,355,000 children enrolled in schools (including pre-schools) with a total of 40,917 teaching staff. Following a nationwide restructure of higher education, the Province has two universities: University of Limpopo and University of Venda. According to the 2001 census, 33·4% of those aged 20 and over had no schooling; 26·1% had some secondary education.

Health
In 2004 there were 43 public hospitals with 7,630 hospital beds.

Mpumalanga

TERRITORY AND POPULATION

The area is 78,490 sq. km and the population at the 2001 census was 3,122,991. Of that number: female, 1,625,658; African/Black, 2,886,345 (92·4% of the population); White, 203,244 (6·5%); Coloured, 22,158 (0·7%); Indian/Asian, 11,244 (0·4%). Estimated population as at 30 June 2007, 3,536,300. Around 41% lived in urban areas in 2001. Density (2001), 39 per sq. km. Life expectancy at birth, 1996, was 53·5 years. At the 2001 census, 30·8% spoke SiSwati as their home language, 26·3% IsiZulu, 12·1% IsiNdebele, 10·8% Sesotho sa Leboa, 6·1% Afrikaans, 3·8% Xitsonga, 3·7% Sesotho, 2·7% Setswana, 1·7% English and 1·5% IsiXhosa.

Mpumalanga comprises 28 administrative districts. The provincial capital is Nelspruit.

SOCIAL STATISTICS

Registered live births in 2005 totalled 99,772; deaths, 45,234. The total number of marriages officially recorded in 2005 was 9,397 and divorces granted 1,170.

CONSTITUTION AND GOVERNMENT

There is a 30-seat provincial legislature.

RECENT ELECTIONS

At the provincial elections held on 22 April 2009, 27 seats were won by the African National Congress, two by the Democratic Alliance and one by the Congress of the People.

CURRENT ADMINISTRATION

In Feb. 2010 the ANC government comprised:

Premier: David Mabuza (took office on 6 May 2009).

Minister of Agriculture and Land Administration: Meshack Malinga. *Community Safety, Security and Liaison:* Sibongile Manana. *Co-operative Governance and Traditional Affairs:* Norman Mokoena. *Culture, Sports and Recreation:* Vusi Shongwe. *Economic Development, Environment and Tourism:*

Jabu Mahlangu. *Education:* Regina Mhaule. *Finance:* Pinky Phosa. *Health and Social Development:* Dikeledi Mahlangu. *Human Settlement:* Madala Masuku. *Public Works, Roads and Transport:* Clifford Mukasi.

Speaker: Vacant. *Director-General:* Jacob Rabodila.

Government Website: http://www.mpumalanga.gov.za

ENERGY AND NATURAL RESOURCES

Electricity

In 2005, 29,469 GWh of electricity were consumed.

Minerals

In 2006, 73,608 people were employed in mining. The province is rich in coal reserves and produces about 80% of the country's supplies.

Agriculture

There were 3,376 commercial farming units in 2007 with a gross farming income of R9·2bn. Gross farming income of field crops in 2007 (R1,000), 2,608,493; horticulture, 1,748,584; animal and animal products, 4,689,232. Paid farm workers in the same year numbered 79,346.

INDUSTRY

Labour

As at Sept. 2003 the economically active population numbered 1,040,000, of whom 260,000 were unemployed (25·0%).

COMMUNICATIONS

Roads

There were 1,325 fatalities as a result of road traffic accidents in 2004.

Telecommunications

According to a Statistics South Africa General Household Survey of 2004, 58·6% of households had access to a telephone or mobile phone.

SOCIAL INSTITUTIONS

Education

In 2004 there were 961,834 children enrolled in schools (including pre-schools) with a total of 29,553 teaching staff. According to the 2001 census 27·5% of those aged 20 years and over had no schooling; 26·6% had some secondary education.

Health

In 2003 there were 26 public hospitals and (1999) 5,048 hospital beds. In Oct. 1998 the first traditional hospital was opened in Mpumalanga—the Samuel Traditional Hospital.

CULTURE

Tourism

Overseas visitors to the province in 2008 totalled 1·3m.; domestic visitor trips, 2·2m.

Northern Cape

TERRITORY AND POPULATION

The area is 361,830 sq. km and the population at the 2001 census was 822,727. Of that number: female, 421,559; Coloured, 424,389 (51·6% of the population); African/Black, 293,976 (35·7%); White, 102,042 (12·4%); Indian/Asian, 2,320 (0·3%). Estimated population as at 30 June 2007, 1,102,200. Around 83% lived in urban areas in 2001. Density (2001), 2 per sq. km. Life expectancy at birth, 1996, was 55·6 years. At the 2001 census, 68·0% spoke Afrikaans as their home language, 20·8% Setswana, 6·2% IsiXhosa and 2·5% English.

Northern Cape comprises six administrative districts: Diamond Fields with Kimberley as the provincial and economic capital; Kalahari, which is the second richest and densely populated area in the province and includes the magisterial districts of Kuruman and Postmasburg; Hantam (North-West) with the towns of Calvinia, Sutherland, Williston, Fraserburg and Carnavon; Benede-Orange with Upington as the agricultural, economic and cultural capital of the region; Bo-Karoo with De Aar as the capital of the area; and Namaqualand which is strong in mining.

SOCIAL STATISTICS

Registered live births in 2005 totalled 21,891; deaths, 12,058. The total number of marriages officially recorded in 2005 was 4,653 and divorces granted 520.

CONSTITUTION AND GOVERNMENT

There is a 30-seat provincial legislature.

RECENT ELECTIONS

At the provincial elections held on 22 April 2009, 19 seats were won by the African National Congress, five by the Congress of the People, four by the Democratic Alliance and two by the Independent Democrats.

CURRENT ADMINISTRATION

In Feb. 2010 the ANC Executive Council comprised:

Premier: Hazel Jenkins; b. 1960 (took office on 6 May 2009).

Minister of Agriculture and Land Reform: Norman Shushu. *Co-operative Governance, Human Settlement and Traditional Affairs:* Mosimanegape Mmoiemang. *Environmental Affairs and Nature Conservation:* Sylvia Lucas. *Education:* Grizelda Cjikela. *Finance, Economic Affairs and Tourism:* John Block. *Health:* Mxolisi Sokatsha. *Roads and Public Works:* Dawid Rooi. *Social Services and Population Development:* Alvin Botes. *Sport, Arts and Culture:* Pauline Williams. *Transport, Safety and Liaison:* Patrick Mabilo.

Speaker: Ghoolam Acharwaray. *Director-General (acting):* Moira Marais-Martin.

Government Website: http://www.northern-cape.gov.za

ENERGY AND NATURAL RESOURCES

Electricity

In 2005, 4,649 GWh of electricity were consumed.

Minerals

The province is well endowed with a variety of mineral deposits. Diamonds are found in shallow water at Port Nolloth, Hondeklipbaai and Lamberts Bay, and also mined inland along the entire coastal strip from the Orange river mouth in the north to Lamberts Bay in the south. Zircon is located along the west coast of Namaqualand. Limestone, asbestos and gypsum salt are also mined. Most of South Africa's reserves of zinc are found in the province in the Black Mountain, Broken Hill and Gamsberg. In 2006, 26,380 people were employed in mining.

Agriculture

Intensive irrigation takes place along the Orange River which supports vineyards and agribusiness. Stock farming predominates in the Bo-Karoo and Hantam areas. There were 5,226 commercial farming units in 2007 with a gross farming income of R4·8bn. Gross farming income of field crops in 2007 (R1,000), 1,148,288; horticulture, 1,243,491; animal and animal products, 2,371,143. Paid farm workers in the same year numbered 74,745.

INDUSTRY

Labour

As at Sept. 2003 the economically active population numbered 288,000, of whom 79,000 were unemployed (27·5%).

COMMUNICATIONS

Roads
Motor vehicles registered (2004) totalled 137,311, including 70,733 passenger cars, 45,605 light commercial vehicles, 3,206 minibuses and 4,186 motorcycles. There were 346 fatalities as a result of road traffic accidents in 2004.

Rail
The main rail link is between Cape Town and Johannesburg, via Kimberley. Other main lines link the Northern Cape with Port Elizabeth via De Aar while another links Upington with Namibia.

Civil Aviation
Five airports are used for scheduled flights—Kimberley, Upington, Aggeneys, Springbok and Alexander Bay.

Telecommunications
According to a Statistics South Africa General Household Survey of 2004, 48·2% of households had access to a telephone or mobile phone.

SOCIAL INSTITUTIONS

Education
In 2004 there were 209,000 children enrolled in schools (including pre-schools) with a total of 6,067 teaching staff. There is no university in the province but there are some technical colleges and a nursing college in Kimberley. According to the 2001 census 18·2% of those aged 20 years and over had no schooling; 29·9% had some secondary education.

Health
In 2000 there were 38 hospitals and 90 clinics (including some that are privately-run). In 2001 there were 176 doctors, 1,539 nurses and ten dentists.

CULTURE

Tourism
Parks are a major tourism asset with the total area under protection being 1,080,200 ha. Provincial nature reserves occupy 50,240 ha. Hunting is a growing activity in the province.

North-West

TERRITORY AND POPULATION
The area is 116,320 sq. km and the population at the 2001 census was 3,669,350. Of that number: female, 1,847,802; African/Black, 3,358,450 (91·3% of the total population); White, 244,035 (6·6%); Coloured, 56,959 (1·5%); Indian/Asian, 9,906 (0·3%). Estimated population as at 30 June 2007, 3,394,200. Density (2001), 32 per sq. km. Life expectancy at birth, 1996, was 53·3 years. At the 2001 census 65·2% spoke Setswana as their home language, 7·5% Afrikaans, 5·8% IsiXhosa, 5·7% Sesotho, 4·7% Xitsonga, 4·2% Sesotho sa Leboa, 2·5% IsiZulu, 1·3% IsiNdebele, 1·2% English and 0·6% SiSwati.

North-West Province comprises 32 administrative districts. The provincial capital is Mmabatho.

SOCIAL STATISTICS
Registered live births in 2005 totalled 98,961; deaths, 52,055. The total number of marriages officially recorded in 2005 was 13,312 and divorces granted 1,874.

CONSTITUTION AND GOVERNMENT
There is a 33-seat provincial legislature.

RECENT ELECTIONS
At the provincial elections held on 22 April 2009 the African National Congress won 25 seats, the Congress of the People and the Democratic Alliance three each, and the United Christian Democratic Party two.

CURRENT ADMINISTRATION
In Feb. 2010 the ANC Executive Council comprised:

Premier: Maureen Modiselle; b. 1941 (took office on 6 May 2009).

Minister of Agriculture, Conservation, Environment and Rural Development: Boitumelo Tshwene. *Economic Development and Tourism:* Wendy Matsemela. *Education:* Rev. Johannes Tselapedi. *Finance:* Louisa Mabe. *Health and Social Development:* Rebecca Kasienyane. *Housing:* Desbo Sefanyetso. *Local Government and Traditional Affairs:* Gordon Kegakilwe. *Public Safety:* Howard D. Yawa. *Public Works, Roads and Transport:* Mahlakeng Mahlakeng. *Sports, Arts and Culture:* Grace Pampiri.

Speaker: Nono Dumile Maloy. *Director-General:* Nana Magomola.

Government Website: http://www.nwpg.gov.za

ENERGY AND NATURAL RESOURCES

Electricity
In 2005, 24,865 GWh of electricity were consumed.

Minerals
In 2006, 157,565 people were employed in mining. Gold is mined at Klerksdorp, and diamonds at Lichtenburg, Koster, Christiana and Bloemhof.

Agriculture
There were 4,692 commercial farming units in 2007 with a gross farming income of R8·8bn. Gross farming income of field crops in 2007 (R1,000), 2,250,740; horticulture, 768,890; animal and animal products, 5,669,343. Paid farm workers in the same year numbered 85,749.

INDUSTRY

Labour
As at Sept. 2003 the economically active population numbered 1,184,000, of whom 348,000 were unemployed (29·4%). Manufacturing contributes 7% of the province's GDP and is mainly dependent on the production of fabricated metals (51%), non-metallic metals (21%) and the food sector (18%).

COMMUNICATIONS

Roads
There were 1,098 fatalities as a result of road traffic accidents in 2004.

Telecommunications
According to a Statistics South Africa General Household Survey of 2004, 51·4% of households had access to a telephone or mobile phone.

SOCIAL INSTITUTIONS

Education
In 2004 there were 1,167,000 children enrolled in schools (including pre-schools) with (in 2002) a total of 38,723 teaching staff. The Province has one university, the North-West University, formed by a merger with Potchefstroom University for Christian Education in 2004. According to the 2001 census, 19·9% of those aged 20 and over had no schooling; 29·0% had some secondary education.

Health
In 2004 there were 32 hospitals and 3,757 hospital beds.

CULTURE

Tourism

Overseas visitors to the province in 2008 totalled 643,000; domestic visitor trips, 1·2m.

Western Cape

TERRITORY AND POPULATION

The area is 129,370 sq. km. Population, 2001 census, 4,524,336. Of that number: females, 2,332,014; Coloured, 2,438,976 (53·9%); African/Black, 1,207,429 (26·7%); White, 832,901 (18·4%); Indian/Asian, 45,030 (1·0%). Density (2001), 35 per sq. km. Estimated population as at 30 June 2007, 4,839,800. Life expectancy at birth, 2003, was 61·5 years. At the 2001 census, 55·3% spoke Afrikaans as their home language, 23·7% IsiXhosa and 19·3% English. In 1996, 3·5m. (85% of total population) lived in urban areas.

There are 41 administrative districts. The capital is Cape Town.

SOCIAL STATISTICS

Registered live births in 2005 totalled 117,068; deaths, 44,396. The total number of marriages officially recorded in 2005 was 28,517 and divorces granted 5,381.

CONSTITUTION AND GOVERNMENT

There is a 42-seat provincial parliament.

RECENT ELECTIONS

At the provincial elections held on 22 April 2009, 22 seats were won by the Democratic Alliance (DA), 14 by the African National Congress, three by the Congress of the People, two by Independent Democrats and one by the African Christian Democratic Party.

CURRENT ADMINISTRATION

In Feb. 2010 the provincial cabinet comprised:

Premier: Helen Zille; b. 1951 (DA; took office on 6 May 2009).

Minister of Agriculture: Gerrit van Rensburg (DA). *Community Safety:* Lennit Max (DA). *Cultural Affairs and Sport:* Sakkie Jenner (ID). *Education:* Donald Grant (DA). *Finance, Economic Development and Tourism:* Alan Winde (DA). *Health:* Theuns Botha (DA). *Housing:* Bonginkosi Madikizela (DA). *Local Government, Environmental Affairs and Development Planning:* Anton Bredell (DA). *Social Development:* Dr Ivan Meyer (DA). *Transport and Public Works:* Robin Carlisle (DA).

Speaker: Shahid Esau (DA). *Director-General (acting):* Brent Gerber.

Government Website: http://www.capegateway.gov.za

ENERGY AND NATURAL RESOURCES

Electricity

In 2005, 21,445 GWh of electricity were consumed.

Minerals

In 2006, 3,385 people were employed in mining.

Agriculture

There were 6,682 commercial farming units in 2007 with a gross farming income of R16·6bn. Gross farming income of field crops in 2007 (R1,000), 1,466,533; horticulture, 7,764,317; animal and animal products, 7,219,245. Paid farm workers in the same year numbered 189,489. The province is one of the world's finest grape-growing regions as well as producing other fruits such as apples, peaches and oranges. The Klein Karoo region is the centre of the ostrich-farming industry in South Africa with leatherware, feathers and meat exported worldwide.

INDUSTRY

Labour

As at Sept. 2003 the economically active population numbered 2,179,000, of whom 448,000 were unemployed (20·6%), the lowest unemployment rate of all the provinces.

COMMUNICATIONS

Roads

Motor vehicles registered (2004) totalled 1,150,293, including 804,308 passenger cars, 210,997 light commercial vehicles, 35,026 minibuses and 35,368 motorcycles. There were 1,426 fatalities as a result of road traffic accidents in 2004.

Civil Aviation

Cape Town International Airport is the main airport in the province.

Telecommunications

According to a Statistics South Africa General Household Survey of 2004, 70·8% of households had access to a telephone or mobile phone, the highest proportion of all the provinces.

SOCIAL INSTITUTIONS

Education

In 2003 there were 1,006,892 children enrolled in schools with a total of 32,339 teaching staff. 323,504 persons aged 18 years or older had higher education in 2003. The Province has four universities: the University of the Western Cape, the University of Cape Town, Stellenbosch University and the Cape Peninsula University of Technology. The Western Cape has the highest adult-education level in South Africa with only 5·7% of the population aged 20 years and over with no schooling. According to the 2001 census, 36·5% had some secondary education—the highest rate in any of South Africa's provinces.

Health

In 2003 there were 55 public hospitals with (2002) 10,153 average useable beds. Of the nine provinces Western Cape has the lowest prevalence of HIV.

CULTURE

Tourism

Overseas visitors to the province in 2008 totalled 1·6m.; domestic visitor trips, 4·1m.

SPAIN

Reino de España
(Kingdom of Spain)

Capital: Madrid
Population estimate, 2010: 45·32m.
GDP per capita, 2007: (PPP$) 31,560
HDI/world rank: 0·955/15

KEY HISTORICAL EVENTS

A bridge between Europe and Africa, the Iberian peninsula has absorbed influences from both regions. The original inhabitants were Iberians, who spoke a non Indo-European language, and Celtic peoples, who were mainly to the north and west of the peninsula. From the 8th century BC the Phoenicians established trading colonies such as Gades (Cádiz), importing metalworking skills, music and literacy in the form of a semi-syllabic script. The Greeks established a trading settlement in Catalonia named Empirion (now Ampurias) around 575 BC, and there is evidence of other Greek and Phoenician settlements along the Mediterranean coast.

From 241 BC the Iberian peninsula came under the influence of Carthage in North Africa. The Carthaginians, led by Hamilcar Barca, landed at Cádiz and moved north and east. They eventually founded a new capital at Cartagena: the city grew rapidly and had a population of around 30,000 by 215 BC. A Roman presence began at this time, further north in Catalonia. The first legionnaires established their base at Tarragona, from where they waged war on the Carthaginians. Fighting between the two powers ebbed and flowed for years, until the Carthaginians were forced off the peninsula in 206 BC. Roman laws and customs were gradually adopted over the following six centuries, but there were frequent rebellions among the native peoples.

Roman rule was on the wane throughout Europe by AD 400, and Roman Hispania was no exception. In 409 Visigoths, Suevi and Vandals crossed the Pyrenees and began to establish themselves as the new rulers. By 470 most of the leading families were of Germanic origin. Toledo became the capital and seat of successive Visigothic monarchs until the early 700s. At this time, the Romans were defeated in North Africa by Muslim armies, who began to turn their attention to the Iberian peninsula. Toledo fell to Arab and Berber forces and the death of King Roderic in 711 marked the end of Visigothic hegemony.

The Muslim conquerors brought a new language, religion and culture, which dominated large parts of the Iberian peninsula for the next five hundred years, though there were sizeable Jewish communities in the southern and eastern towns and there were some Christian principalities in the north. The Umayyad dynasty used Córdoba as the administrative centre of al-Andalus ('Land of the Vandals') until 1031. New trade links were established, connecting Córdoba with Egypt and Persia and most of the Islamic world. People and ideas flooded in and the great cities of Córdoba and Seville became beacons of modernity and creativity in fields ranging from architecture to botany, medicine, poetry and techniques for irrigation.

While al-Andalus prospered, the Christian principalities to the north in places such as Asturia, the Basque territories and northern Catalonia remained relatively poor and agrarian. However, from about 900 there was a gradual expansion southwards towards al-Andalus, described as the start of the *Reconquista*, or reconquest of Spain by the Christians. By 1000 there was considerable contact between the Christian principalities and France: Norman knights fought in Catalonia and French settlers arrived in towns along the pilgrimage route to Santiago de Compostela, bringing with them new ideas and skills.

From the 1120s the Muslim governors of al-Andalus found themselves under threat from both northern Christian rulers and native Andalusi. Alfonso VII of Leon-Castile eventually conquered Córdoba in 1146 and the strategically important Almería, on the Mediterranean coast, in 1147. Following these victories, the three most powerful Christian kingdoms of Aragon, Castile and Portugal pushed south and east and by 1300 the last remaining Islamic dominion was the amirate of Granada. Muslim inhabitants were expelled from many towns and cities, though in rural areas the Islamic faith and the Arabic language survived for centuries. While Córdoba declined, Barcelona blossomed: it emerged as a great economic success story on a par with Genoa and Venice.

Castile and Aragon were the dominant kingdoms by the early 1300s, but they were both characterized by infighting and rebellion. King Pedro the Cruel of Castile was challenged by a coalition of nobles led by his half brother Enrique de Trastámara. The English supported Pedro (Peter) and his heirs and the French backed Enrique (Henry) and his supporters. Enrique eventually prevailed, and was crowned Enrique II in 1369.

The Modern State

The Spanish monarchy was founded in 1469 following the marriage of Isabel (Isabella), princess of Castile and Fernando (Ferdinand), heir to the throne of Aragon. Under their joint reign, they laid the foundations for a unified Spain. In 1478 they established the notorious Spanish Inquisition, expelling and executing tens of thousands of Jews and other non-Christians. Four years later the last Islamic territory of Granada was besieged. It surrendered in 1492, the year in which Christopher Columbus reached the New World.

When Fernando and Isabel's son Juan died in 1497, the succession to the Spanish crowns passed to his sister, Juana *la loca* (the Mad). Juana married Philip (Felipe) the Handsome, heir through his father, Emperor Maximilian I, to the Habsburg domains in Germany and Flanders. When Fernando died in 1516, Juana and Felipe's son, Charles of Ghent, inherited Spain, its colonies in the New World, Naples and, following the death of Maximilian I in 1519, the Habsburg territories. Shortly afterwards he was elected Holy Roman Emperor, a title he held as Charles V (Carlos I of Spain). In the space of only a few years, Charles commanded one of the most extensive empires since Rome.

Columbus paved the way for the Spanish colonies in the new world but for 30 years after his discoveries attention focused on the Caribbean. It was only in 1521 that Hernando Cortés overthrew the Aztecs, with help from native Indian allies. After 1540 gold and silver began pouring into Spanish coffers from mines in Peru and Mexico. Sugar plantations were established in the Caribbean and the indigenous populations were gradually wiped out. Maintaining control of the new empire was a serious challenge and Charles V relied heavily on co-operation from Italians, Flemings and Germans. The rise of Spain as a military power began in the 1560s in the reign of Felipe II. He built a powerful navy and annexed Portugal in 1580. The new fleet patrolled the American supply routes, fended off attacks from the English and set up new colonies in the Philippines and at Buenos Aires.

Spain's Golden Age began to lose its lustre in the late 16th century, following a popular uprising in the Netherlands under William of Orange. The Dutch were beginning to establish their own colonies in Asia and started making inroads in Brazil. Spain was weakened by the cost of defending its empire against France and England and in 1640 the unity of the Iberian peninsula itself came under threat by rebellions in Catalonia and Portugal. The crowning of Carlos II, a disabled child, in 1665 symbolized Spain's growing vulnerability and isolation from the rest of Europe.

Carlos II died without issue in 1700 and left the throne to Philippe, duke of Anjou and grandson of King Louis XIV of France. Felipe (Philippe) V was the first in a line of five Bourbon monarchs, who reigned in Spain until 1833. Under Felipe V, and his successor Fernando VI, Spain restored some of its influence in Europe, particularly in Italy, where Naples and Sicily were recovered from Austria in 1734. Educational reforms led to a period of Enlightenment in the 1760s, with many universities replacing conservative Jesuit doctrines with modern physics, astronomy and political theory. The 1780s, when Spain was ruled by Carlos III, were a period of stability and prosperity. Catalonia became a centre of the early industrial revolution with its booming textile trade and Madrid saw a flowering of artistic expression encapsulated by the work of Goya.

When Louis XVI was guillotined in 1793, the new French Republic turned its attention to neighbouring Spain and Britain. In 1794–95 French forces invaded Catalonia and the Basque provinces. Following these defeats, King Carlos IV of Spain formed an alliance with France under its new emperor, Napoleon. Hostilities with Britain were resumed, though defeat for the Franco-Spanish naval forces at the Battle of Trafalgar further undermined links with the Spanish colonies and damaged the economy.

In 1808 the weak and unpopular Carlos IV abdicated and the Spanish crown passed to Fernando VII, though his right to the throne was ceded to Napoleon later that year. However, Napoleon misjudged the mood of the Spanish public who rioted in Madrid and began a five-year war of independence. In 1813 the French forces were finally expelled but ideas from revolutionary France were beginning to take root. The medieval Cortes (parliament) was revived and a Liberal reformist group secured Spain's first constitution. The following year, Fernando VII was restored to the Spanish throne, a move generally welcomed by a war-ravaged public. But Fernando's first act was to abolish the constitution, and his 20 year reign was characterized by a return to the old regime: the Inquisition was re-established, the Liberals were persecuted, free speech was repressed and Spain entered a severe economic recession.

End of Empire

Queen Isabel II inherited the Spanish throne as a child in 1833. During her reign there were various attempts by the Liberals and progressives to reinstate a constitution. Her support for neo-catholic reactionaries in her governments of the 1860s fanned the flames of revolution. In 1868 Isabel was deposed and the Cortes approved a new constitution. Amadeo I of Savoy was chosen as monarch but he was unable to adapt to Spanish politics and abdicated in 1873. The Cortes immediately proclaimed a republic but in less than a year a coup restored the Bourbon monarchy, with Alfonso XII, the son of exiled Isabel II, as king.

The disastrous Spanish-American War of 1898 marked the end of the Spanish Empire. Spain was defeated by the USA in a series of one-sided naval battles, resulting in the loss of Cuba, Puerto Rico, Guam and the Philippines. Neutral in the First World War, Spain enjoyed a trade and industry boom. Barcelona's Hispano-Suiza factories produced aircraft engines for the French air force and luxury cars. However, prosperity did not filter through society and workers demonstrated against high food prices. In 1923 Gen. Miguel Primo de Rivera, marquis of Estella, led a coup, abolished the 1876 constitution and closed down the Cortes. Primo de Rivera was determined to clear out what he saw as corrupt, self-serving politicians. His alternative to the constitutional monarchy was the National Political Union but it attracted only opportunists and right-wing enthusiasts. There were improvements in the nation's infrastructure, but de Rivera's public works programmes were hit by financial difficulties in 1929, and the dictator resigned the following year.

1931 marked the beginning of a new genuinely democratic era for Spain. Municipal elections were held and won by a republican-socialist coalition. King Alfonso XIII went into exile and the Second Republic was declared. The 1936 elections saw the country split in two, with the Republican government and its supporters on one side (an uneasy alliance of communists, socialists and anarchists) and the Nationalists (the army, the Catholic church, monarchists and the fascist-style Falange Party) on the other.

Civil War

The assassination of the opposition leader José Calvo Sotelo by Republican police officers in July 1936 gave the army, led by Gen. Francisco Franco, an excuse to stage a coup. The failure of the military to overthrow the government led to a protracted civil war. The Nationalists received extensive military and financial support from fascist Germany and Italy, while the Republican government received support from the Soviet Union and, to a lesser degree, from the International Brigades, made up of foreign volunteers.

By 1939 the Nationalists, led by Franco, had prevailed. More than 350,000 Spaniards died in the fighting, but more bloodletting ensued. An estimated 100,000 Republicans were executed or died in prison after the civil war. Franco's cure for Spain's 'sick' economy was withdrawal from world markets and the establishment of a self-sufficient autarky which remained neutral in World War Two. But by the late 1940s inflation was rising steeply and Spain was losing ground to other European countries. Franco allowed a gradual liberalization of the economy, but despite this and the readmission of Spain to the UN in 1955 the economy remained in deep trouble. The desperate conditions endured by hundreds of thousands of workers led to nationwide strikes and growing opposition to the Franco regime among university students and intellectuals. In the 1960s the regime faced demands for independence in Catalonia and the Basque Country.

Franco died in 1975, having earlier named Juan Carlos, the grandson of Alfonso XIII, his successor. Under King Juan Carlos, Spain made the transition back to democracy. The first elections were held in 1977 and a new constitution was approved by referendum in 1978. In Feb. 1981 there was an attempted fascist coup, when for 18 hours the deputies of the lower house of parliament and the Cabinet were held hostage. The episode is now seen as the final, futile attempt to turn back the clock. The following year saw a spectacular victory for the socialist party which presided over a rapid expansion in the economy during its 14 years in power. In 1986 Spain joined the European Economic Community, cementing the nation's status as a popular location for foreign investors and tourists, though its international reputation has suffered from the ongoing violent campaign waged by ETA, the separatist terrorist group attempting to secure an independent Basque homeland.

In 1996 Spaniards voted in a conservative party under the leadership of José María Aznar. In March 2000 he was re-elected with an absolute majority; his success was attributed to the buoyant state of the Spanish economy, which averaged in excess of 4% annual growth during Aznar's first term of office.

Madrid suffered Spain's worst terrorist attack on 11 March 2004 when four commuter trains were bombed, killing 191 and injuring over 1,800 people. The government initially blamed ETA but suspicion quickly moved to al-Qaeda and North African operatives. On 14 March the Socialists, led by José Luis Rodríguez Zapatero, defeated the People's Party in general elections. The last Spanish troops left Iraq in May 2004. In March 2006 ETA announced a permanent ceasefire, but the truce ended in Dec. when the group carried out a car bomb attack at Madrid's Barajas airport.

TERRITORY AND POPULATION

Spain is bounded in the north by the Bay of Biscay, France and Andorra, east and south by the Mediterranean and the Straits of Gibraltar, southwest by the Atlantic and west by Portugal and the Atlantic. Continental Spain has an area of 492,592 sq. km, and including the Balearic and Canary Islands and the towns of Ceuta and Melilla on the northern coast of Africa, 506,030 sq. km (195,378 sq. miles). Population (census, 2001), 40,847,371 (20,825,521 females). In 2005, 76·7% of the population lived in urban areas; population density in 2001 was 83 per sq. km. The estimated population on 1 Jan. 2009 was 46,745,807. In 2005 foreigners resident in Spain numbered 3,730,610 (up from 923,789 in 2000), including 511,294 from Morocco, 497,799 from Ecuador, 317,366 from Romania, 271,239 from Colombia and 227,187 from the UK. Foreigners constituted 8·5% of the population in 2005 (2·3% in 2000). Only the USA had a larger annual net gain in migrants during the period 2000–05.

The UN gives an estimated population for 2010 of 45·32m.

The growth of the population has been as follows:

Census year	*Population*	*Rate of annual increase*	*Census year*	*Population*	*Rate of annual increase*
1860	15,655,467	0·34	1960	30,903,137	1·05
1910	19,927,150	0·72	1970	33,823,918	0·95
1920	21,303,162	0·69	1981	37,746,260	1·05
1930	23,563,867	1·06	1991	38,872,268	0·30
1940	25,877,971	0·98	2001	40,847,371	0·51
1950	27,976,755	0·81			

Area and population of the autonomous communities (in italics) and provinces at the 2001 census:

Autonomous community/ Province	*Area (sq. km)*	*Population*	*Per sq. km*
Andalusia	*87,595*	*7,357,558*	*84*
Almería	8,775	536,731	61
Cádiz	7,436	1,116,491	150
Córdoba	13,771	761,657	55
Granada	12,647	821,660	65
Huelva	10,128	462,579	45
Jaén	13,496	643,820	46
Málaga	7,306	1,287,017	176
Seville (Sevilla)	14,036	1,727,603	123
Aragón	*47,720*	*1,204,215*	*25*
Huesca	15,636	206,502	13
Teruel	14,810	135,858	9
Zaragoza (Saragossa)	17,274	861,855	50
Asturias	*10,604*	*1,062,998*	*100*
Baleares	*4,992*	*841,669*	*169*
Basque Country	*7,234*	*2,082,587*	*288*
Álava	3,037	286,387	94
Guipúzcoa	1,980	673,563	340
Vizcaya	2,217	1,122,637	506
Canary Islands	*7,492*	*1,694,477*	*226*
Palmas de Gran Canaria, Las	4,111	887,676	216
Santa Cruz de Tenerife	3,381	806,801	239
Cantabria	*5,321*	*535,131*	*101*
Castilla-La Mancha	*79,461*	*1,760,516*	*22*
Albacete	14,924	364,835	24
Ciudad Real	19,813	478,957	24
Cuenca	17,140	200,346	12
Guadalajara	12,214	174,999	14
Toledo	15,370	541,379	35
Castilla y León	*94,224*	*2,456,474*	*26*
Ávila	8,050	163,442	20
Burgos	14,292	348,934	24
León	15,581	488,751	31
Palencia	8,052	174,143	22
Salamanca	12,350	345,609	28
Segovia	6,921	147,694	21
Soria	10,306	90,717	9
Valladolid	8,111	498,094	61
Zamora	10,561	199,090	19
Catalonia	*32,113*	*6,343,110*	*198*
Barcelona	7,728	4,805,927	622
Girona	5,910	565,304	96
Lleida	12,172	362,206	30
Tarragona	6,303	609,673	97
Extremadura	*41,634*	*1,058,503*	*25*
Badajoz	21,766	654,882	30
Cáceres	19,868	403,621	20
Galicia	*29,575*	*2,695,880*	*91*
Coruña, La	7,951	1,096,027	138
Lugo	9,856	357,648	36
Ourense	7,273	338,446	47
Pontevedra	4,495	903,759	201
Madrid	*8,028*	*5,423,384*	*676*
Murcia	*11,314*	*1,197,646*	*106*
Navarra	*10,391*	*555,829*	*53*
Rioja, La	*5,045*	*276,702*	*55*
Valencian Community	*23,255*	*4,162,776*	*175*
Alicante	5,817	1,461,925	251
Castellón	6,632	484,566	73
Valencia	10,806	2,216,285	205
Ceuta[1]	*20*	*71,505*	*3,575*
Melilla[1]	*12*	*66,411*	*5,534*
Total	*506,030*	*40,847,371*	*81*

[1]Ceuta and Melilla gained limited autonomous status in 1994.

The capitals of the autonomous communities are: *Andalusia:* Seville (Sevilla); *Aragón:* Zaragoza (Saragossa); *Asturias:* Oviedo; *Baleares:* Palma de Mallorca; *Basque Country:* Vitoria-Gasteiz; *Canary Islands:* dual capitals, Las Palmas de Gran Canaria and Santa Cruz de Tenerife; *Cantabria:* Santander; *Castilla-La Mancha:* Toledo; *Castilla y León:* Valladolid; *Catalonia:* Barcelona; *Extremadura:* Mérida; *Galicia:* Santiago de Compostela; *Madrid:* Madrid; *Murcia:* Murcia (but regional parliament in Cartagena); *Navarra:* Pamplona; *La Rioja:* Logroño; *Valencian Community:* Valencia.

The capitals of the provinces are the towns from which they take the name, except in the cases of Álava (capital, Vitoria-Gasteiz), Guipúzcoa (San Sebastián) and Vizcaya (Bilbao).

The islands which form the Balearics include Majorca (Mallorca), Minorca (Menorca), Ibiza and Formentera. Those which form the Canary Archipelago are divided into two provinces, under the name of their respective capitals: Santa Cruz de Tenerife and Las Palmas de Gran Canaria. The province of Santa Cruz de Tenerife is constituted by the islands of Tenerife, La Palma, Gomera and Hierro; that of Las Palmas by Gran Canaria, Lanzarote and Fuerteventura, with the small barren islands of Alegranza, Roque del Este, Roque del Oeste, Graciosa, Montaña Clara and Lobos.

Places under Spanish sovereignty in Africa (Alhucemas, Ceuta, Chafarinas, Melilla and Peñón de Vélez) constitute the two provinces of Ceuta and Melilla.

Populations of principal towns in 2001:

Town	*Population*	*Town*	*Population*
Albacete	148,934	Madrid	2,938,723
Alcalá de Henares	176,434	Málaga	524,414
Alcobendas	92,090	Marbella	100,036
Alcorcón	153,100	Mataró	106,358
Algeciras	101,468	Móstoles	196,524
Alicante	284,580	Murcia	370,745
Almería	166,328	Ourense	107,510
Avilés	83,185	Oviedo	201,154
Badajoz	133,519	Palma de Mallorca	333,801
Badalona	205,836	Palmas de Gran Canaria, Las	354,863
Barakaldo	94,478	Pamplona (Iruña)	183,964
Barcelona	1,503,884	Reus	89,006
Bilbao	349,972	Sabadell	183,788
Burgos	166,187	Salamanca	156,368
Cáceres	82,716	San Cristóbal de La Laguna	128,822
Cádiz	133,363	San Fernando	88,073
Cartagena	184,686	San Sebastián (Donostia)	178,377
Castellón de la Plana	147,667	Santa Coloma de Gramenet	112,992
Córdoba	308,072	Santa Cruz de Tenerife	188,477
Coruña, La	236,379	Santander	180,717
Dos Hermanas	101,988	Santiago de Compostela	90,188
Elche (Elx)	194,767	Seville	684,633
Fuenlabrada	182,705	Tarragona	113,129
Getafe	151,479	Telde	87,949
Getxo	82,285	Terrassa	173,775
Gijón	266,419	Torrejón de Ardoz	97,887
Granada	240,661	Valencia	738,441
Huelva	142,284	Valladolid	316,580
Jaén	112,590	Vigo	280,186
Jerez de la Frontera	183,273	Vitoria-Gasteiz	216,852
Leganés	173,584	Zaragoza	614,905
León	130,916		
L'Hospitalet de Llobregat	239,019		
Lleida	112,199		
Logroño	133,058		
Lugo	88,414		

Languages

The Constitution states that 'Castilian is the Spanish official language of the State', but also that 'All other Spanish languages will also be official in the corresponding Autonomous Communities'. At the last linguistic census (2001) Catalan (an official EU language since 1990) was spoken in Catalonia by 74·5% of people and understood by 94·5%. It is also spoken in Baleares, Valencian Community (where it is frequently called Valencian), and in Aragón, a narrow strip close to the Catalonian and Valencian Community boundaries. Galician, a language very close to Portuguese, was understood in 1998 by 98·4% of people in Galicia and spoken by 89·2%; Basque by a significant and increasing minority in the Basque Country, and by a small minority in northwest Navarra. It is estimated that one-third of all Spaniards speaks one of the other three official languages as well as standard Castilian. In bilingual communities, both Castilian and the regional language are taught in schools and universities.

SOCIAL STATISTICS

Statistics for calendar years:

	Marriages	*Divorces*	*Births*	*Deaths*
2004	216,149	50,974	454,591	371,934
2005	208,146[1]	72,848	466,371	387,355
2006	203,453[1]	126,952	482,957	371,478
2007	201,579[1]	125,777	492,527	385,361
2008	193,064[1]	110,036	518,967	385,954

[1]Excluding same sex marriage, which was permitted from 3 July 2005.

Rate per 1,000 population, 2008: births, 11·7; deaths, 8·7; marriages, 4·3; divorces, 2·5. In 2005 the most popular age range for marrying was 25–29 for both males and females. Annual population growth rate, 2000–05, 1·5%. Suicide rate (per 100,000 population), 2005: 7·8. Expectation of life, 2007, was 77·5 years for males and 84·0 for females. Infant mortality, 2005, four per 1,000 live births; fertility rate, 2004, 1·3 births per woman. In 2005 Spain received 5,254 asylum applications, equivalent to 0·1 per 1,000 inhabitants.

A UNICEF report published in 2005 showed that 13·3% of children in Spain live in poverty (in households with income below 50% of the national median), compared to just 2·4% in Denmark.

In 2007–08, 19·6% of 15 to 34-year-olds used cannabis and 5·1% cocaine. A 2009 report found that use of cocaine in Spain was the highest in the European Union.

CLIMATE

Most of Spain has a form of Mediterranean climate with mild, moist winters and hot, dry summers, but the northern coastal region has a moist, equable climate, with rainfall well distributed throughout the year, mild winters and warm summers, and less sunshine than the rest of Spain. The south, in particular Andalusia, is dry and prone to drought.

Madrid, Jan. 41°F (5°C), July 77°F (25°C). Annual rainfall 16·8" (419 mm). Barcelona, Jan. 46°F (8°C), July 74°F (23·5°C). Annual rainfall 21" (525 mm). Cartagena, Jan. 51°F (10·5°C), July 75°F (24°C). Annual rainfall 14·9" (373 mm). La Coruña, Jan. 51°F (10·5°C), July 66°F (19°C). Annual rainfall 32" (800 mm). Seville, Jan. 51°F (10·5°C), July 85°F (29·5°C). Annual rainfall 19·5" (486 mm). Palma de Mallorca, Jan. 51°F (11°C), July 77°F (25°C). Annual rainfall 13·6" (347 mm). Santa Cruz de Tenerife, Jan. 64°F (17·9°C), July 76°F (24·4°C). Annual rainfall 7·72" (196 mm).

CONSTITUTION AND GOVERNMENT

Following the death of General Franco in 1975 and the transition to a democracy, the first democratic elections were held on 15 June 1977. A new constitution was approved by referendum on 6 Dec. 1978, and came into force 29 Dec. 1978. It established a parliamentary monarchy.

The reigning king is **Juan Carlos I** (Juan Carlos de Borbón), born 5 Jan. 1938. The eldest son of Don Juan, Conde de Barcelona, Juan Carlos was given precedence over his father as pretender to the Spanish throne in an agreement in 1954 between Don Juan and General Franco. Don Juan, who resigned his claims to the throne in May 1977, died on 1 April 1993. King (then Prince) Juan Carlos married, in 1962, Princess Sophia of Greece, daughter of the late King Paul of the Hellenes and Queen Frederika. *Offspring:* Elena, born 20 Dec. 1963, married 18 March 1995 Jaime de Marichalar, divorced 25 Nov. 2009 (*offspring:* Felipe, b. 17 July 1998; Victoria, b. 9 Sept. 2000); Cristina, born 13 June 1965, married 4 Oct. 1997 Iñaki Urdangarín (*offspring:* Juan, b. 29 Sept. 1999; Pablo, b. 6 Dec. 2000; Miguel, b. 30 April 2002; Irene, b. 5 June 2005); Felipe, Prince of Asturias, heir to the throne, born 30 Jan. 1968, married 22 May 2004 Letizia Ortiz Rocasolano (*offspring:* Leonor, b. 8 Nov. 2005; Sofia, b. 29 April 2007).

The King receives an allowance, part of which is taxable, approved by parliament each year. For 2010 this is €8·9m. There is no formal court; the (private) *Diputación de la Grandeza* represents the interests of the aristocracy.

Legislative power is vested in the *Cortes Generales*, a bicameral parliament composed of the Congress of Deputies (lower house) and the Senate (upper house). The *Congress of Deputies* has not less than 300 nor more than 400 members (350 in the general election of 2008) elected in a proportional system under which electors choose between party lists of candidates in multi-member constituencies.

The *Senate* has 264 members of whom 208 are elected by a majority system: the 47 mainland provinces elect four senators each, regardless of population; the larger islands (Gran Canaria, Majorca and Tenerife) elect three senators and each of the smaller islands or groups of islands (Ibiza-Formentera, Minorca, Fuerteventura, Gomera, Hierro, Lanzarote and La Palma) elect one senator. To these each self-governing community appoints one senator, and an additional senator for every million inhabitants in their respective territories. Currently 56 senators are appointed by the self-governing communities. Deputies and senators are elected by universal secret suffrage for four-year terms. The Prime Minister is elected by the Congress of Deputies.

The *Constitutional Court* is empowered to solve conflicts between the State and the Autonomous Communities; to determine if legislation passed by the Cortes is contrary to the Constitution; and to protect the constitutional rights of individuals violated by any authority. Its 12 members are appointed by the monarch. It has a nine-year term, with a third of the membership being renewed every three years.

National Anthem

'Marcha Real' ('Royal March'); no words, tune anonymous.

GOVERNMENT CHRONOLOGY

Heads of government since 1939. (PP = Popular Party; PSOE = Spanish Socialist Workers' Party; UCD = Central Democratic Union)

1939–73	military	Francisco Franco
1973	military	Luis Carrero
1973–76	civilian	Carlos Arias Navarro
1976	military	Fernando de Santiago
1976–81	UCD	Adolfo Suárez
1981–82	UCD	Leopoldo Calvo-Sotelo
1982–96	PSOE	Felipe González
1996–2004	PP	José María Aznar
2004–	PSOE	José Luis Rodríguez Zapatero

RECENT ELECTIONS

A general election took place on 9 March 2008. Turnout was 75·3%. In the *Congress of Deputies* the Spanish Socialist Workers' Party (PSOE) won 169 seats with 43·6% of votes cast; the Popular Party (PP), 153 with 40·1%; Convergence and Union (CiU; Catalan nationalists), 11 with 3·1%; Basque Nationalist Party (PNV), 6 with 1·2%; the Catalan separatist Republican Left of Catalunya (ERC), 3 with 1·2%; the Communist-led United Left Coalition (IU), 2 with 3·8%; Galician Nationalist Bloc (BNG), 2 with 0·8%; Canarian Coalition (CC), 2 with 0·6%; Union, Progress and Democracy (UPD), 1 with 1·2%; Navarra Yes, 1 with 0·2%. In the *Senate*, the PP won 101 seats; PSOE, 89; Entesa Catalana de Progrés, 12; CiU, 4; PNV, 2.

European Parliament

Spain has 50 (54 in 2004) representatives. At the June 2009 elections turnout was 44·9% (45·1% in 2004). The PP won 23 seats with 42·2% of votes cast (political affiliation in European Parliament: European People's Party); the PSOE, 21 with 38·5% (Progressive Alliance of Socialists and Democrats); the Coalition for Europe (a coalition of CiU, PNV, CC, the Andalusian Party, the Majorcan Union and the Valencian Nationalist Bloc), 2 with 5·1% (Alliance of Liberals and Democrats for Europe); the Left (a coalition of the IU, Initiative for Catalonia-Greens, United and Alternative Left, and the Bloc for Asturias) 2 with 3·7% (one with Greens/European Free Alliance and one with European United Left/Nordic Green Left); UPD, 1 with 2·9% (non-attached); Europe of the Peoples-Greens (a coalition of Eusko Alkartasuna, the Greens, Aralar, the Galician Nationalist Bloc, the Republican Left of Catalonia and the Chunta Aragonesista), 1 with 2·5% (Greens/European Free Alliance).

CURRENT ADMINISTRATION

In March 2010 the government comprised:

President of the Council and Prime Minister: José Luis Rodríguez Zapatero; b. 1960 (PSOE; sworn in 17 April 2004, re-elected 11 April 2008).

First Vice-President and Minister for the Presidency: María Teresa Fernandez de la Vega. *Second Vice-President and Minister for the Economy and Financial Affairs:* Elena Salgado. *Third Vice-President and Minister for Territorial Co-operation:* Manuel Chaves. *Foreign Affairs and Co-operation:* Miguel Ángel Moratinos. *Justice:* Francisco Caamaño. *Interior:* Alfredo Pérez Rubalcaba. *Defence:* Carme Chacón Piqueras. *Education and Universities:* Ángel Gabilondo. *Labour and Immigration:* Celestino Corbacho. *Health and Social Policy:* Trinidad Jiménez. *Rural, Marine and Natural Environment:* Elena Espinosa. *Development:* José Blanco. *Industry, Tourism and Commerce:* Miguel Sebastián Gascón. *Culture:* Ángeles González-Sinde. *Housing:* Beatriz Corredor. *Equality:* Bibiana Aído. *Science and Innovation:* Cristina Garmendia.

Government Website: http://www.la-moncloa.es

CURRENT LEADERS

José Luis Rodríguez Zapatero

Position

Prime Minister

Introduction

José Luis Rodríguez Zapatero, leader of the Spanish Socialist Workers' Party (PSOE; Partido Socialista Obrero Español), became prime minister in March 2004 when his party unexpectedly defeated the Popular Party (PP) in the aftermath of the terrorist attack that month on Madrid. After taking office, he announced the withdrawal of Spanish troops from Iraq and called for greater international co-operation against terrorism. However, his judgment has been called into question over his policy towards Basque separatism. Zapatero secured a second term after the PSOE won the March 2008 elections and he was re-elected in April.

Early Life

Rodríguez Zapatero (known as Zapatero) was born on 4 Aug. 1960 in Valladolid. He studied law at the Universidad de León before embarking on a career in politics. From a traditionally left-wing family, Zapatero was strongly inspired by his grandfather, a republican captain executed by nationalists in 1936 at the beginning of the Spanish Civil War. In 1977, before the first post-Franco democratic elections, Zapatero attended a socialist political rally in Gijón. He was inspired by former PSOE leader Felipe González Márquez and in 1978 he joined the PSOE as a youth member. Four years later he became the PSOE youth leader in his home region of León. In 1986 he was elected to parliament representing León, becoming the youngest member of the *Cortes* at that time. His party standing was further enhanced in 1988 when he became the regional leader of the León PSOE.

In 1996 the PSOE's 14-year domination ended with the election of José María Aznar. The following year González resigned as PSOE leader amid corruption charges and the revelation of his government's brutal treatment of captured Basque terrorists, for which two of his former ministers were imprisoned. During the following three years the party floundered under the leadership of Joaquín Almunia, who resigned in March 2000 following a humiliating election defeat. Zapatero then became one of four candidates for the party leadership, along with the better-known members José Bono, Matilde Fernández and Rosa Diez. At the 35th PSOE party conference, Zapatero won a surprise victory with 41·8%, narrowly defeating Bono's 40·8%.

On election Zapatero set out his plans for the rejuvenation of the flagging PSOE. He changed the party's executive committee, installing many young politicians in a bid to revitalize the party's image. Zapatero's ambition was to create an effective opposition to Aznar and present himself as a strong candidate for prime minister. His *Nueva Vía* (New Way) represented a shift from the traditions of socialism to more centrist politics, with echoes of Tony Blair's New Labour ideology in British politics. This move reduced the ideological distance between the ruling and opposition leaders, Aznar having abandoned traditional right-wing politics for a more moderate, centrist stance.

On 11 March 2004 Madrid's rail network was hit by terrorist bombings that killed 191 people. Aznar's government blamed ETA in the immediate aftermath, but evidence soon pointed to a link with North Africa. At the general election three days later, the PP suffered a backlash of voter hostility and were unexpectedly defeated by the PSOE. Zapatero was sworn in as prime minister on 17 April 2004.

Career in Office

Although lacking an absolute majority, Zapatero declined to form a coalition, saying that he would govern through consensus with other groups. Reiterating his opposition to the war in Iraq and criticizing the failure of US-led forces to install a workable post-war structure, he announced that Spanish troops would be withdrawn from Iraq by the end of May 2004. At the same time, he increased Spain's military commitment to the UN-led force in Afghanistan and called for increased international co-operation to counter terrorism. His domestic agenda included an expected increase in welfare spending and promised reform of the tax system. Observers believed he would be more sympathetic than his predecessor to regions with large nationalist movements.

In Feb. 2005 a car bomb exploded in Madrid, injuring about 40 people. Although ETA was thought to be responsible, the Zapatero government offered peace talks the following May if the organization would disarm. Also in Feb. the Spanish electorate endorsed the European Union's proposed new constitution treaty in a referendum. In June 2005 parliament defied the Roman Catholic Church by legalizing gay marriage and granting homosexual couples adoption and inheritance rights.

In March 2006 ETA declared a permanent ceasefire, marking a supposed end to four decades of separatist violence. However, Zapatero's willingness to negotiate with the organization was criticized severely when ETA broke the truce with a bomb attack on Madrid airport in Dec. which killed two people. In a subsequent parliamentary debate he apologized to the nation for having 'made a mistake' about ETA. Zapatero meanwhile gave his government's support to a new charter giving greater autonomy to Catalonia which was approved by 74% of voters in a referendum in the region in June 2006. Andalusia voted in favour of similar reforms in Feb. 2007.

After the ETA attack at Madrid airport Zapatero adopted a harder line against the group, suspending all peace moves. In response, ETA withdrew its ceasefire in June 2007. In Oct. several people were convicted and imprisoned for the Madrid train bombings in 2004.

In Nov. 2007 the Spanish parliament passed a bill formally denouncing the Franco dictatorship and ordering the removal of all related statues and symbols from streets and buildings.

The PSOE won the elections of March 2008, taking 169 of the 350 seats. Zapatero was subsequently re-elected prime minister by parliament in April 2008. His new cabinet for the first time included more women than men.

In response to sharply rising unemployment in the wake of the global financial crisis, Zapatero unveiled an €11bn. plan in Nov. 2008 to boost the economy through investment in public works and infrastructure. Spain nevertheless went into recession in Jan. 2009 and unemployment continued to rise through the year. In June the PSOE came second to the opposition Popular Party in the elections to the European Parliament.

Meanwhile, in July 2009, a Spanish government minister visited British Gibraltar for the first time in 300 years in a historic visit, but insisted that Spain would not relinquish its claim to the territory. In Jan. 2010 Spain took over the rotating six-month presidency of the European Union.

DEFENCE

Conscription was abolished in 2001. The government had begun the phased abolition of conscription in 1996. In 2002 the armed forces became fully professional. However, a shortfall in recruitment in Spain has meant that descendants of Spanish migrants, many of whom have never been to Europe, are now joining. Since 1989 women have been accepted in all sections of the armed forces.

In 2008 defence expenditure totalled US$19,196m. (US$430 per capita). In 2007 defence spending represented 1·2% of GDP.

As at Oct. 2009, 1,089 personnel (including 1,051 troops and 35 police) were deployed in UN peacekeeping operations.

Army

A Rapid Reaction Force is formed from the Spanish Legion and the airborne and air-portable brigades. There is also an Army Aviation Brigade consisting of 153 helicopters (28 attack).

Strength (2004) 95,600. There were 265,000 army reservists in 2004.

Guardia Civil

The paramilitary *Guardia Civil* numbers 72,600.

Navy

The principal ship of the Navy is the *Príncipe de Asturias*, a light vertical/short take-off and landing aircraft carrier. Her air group includes AV-8S Matador (Harrier) combat aircraft. There are also eight French-designed submarines and 16 frigates.

The Naval Air Service operates 17 combat aircraft and 37 armed helicopters. Personnel numbered 700 in 2004. There are 5,600 marines.

Main naval bases are at Ferrol, Rota, Cádiz, Cartagena, Palma de Mallorca, Mahón and Las Palmas de Gran Canaria (Canary Islands).

In 2004 personnel totalled 22,900 including the marines and naval air arm. There were 18,500 naval reservists in 2004.

Air Force

The Air Force is organized as an independent service, dating from 1939. It is administered through four operational commands. These are geographically oriented following a reorganization in 1991 and comprise Central Air Command, Strait Air Command, Eastern Air Command and Air Command of the Canaries.

There were 177 combat aircraft in 2004 including 91 EF/A-18s, 23 F-5Bs and 52 Mirage F-1s.

Strength (2004) 22,750. There were 45,000 air force reservists in 2004.

INTERNATIONAL RELATIONS

Spain is a member of the UN, World Bank, IMF and several other UN specialized agencies, WTO, EU, Council of Europe, WEU, OSCE, CERN, BIS, IOM, NATO, OECD, Inter-American Development Bank, Asian Development Bank and Antarctic Treaty, and is a signatory to the Schengen accord, which abolishes border controls between Spain, Austria, Belgium, Czech Republic, Denmark, Estonia, Finland, France, Germany, Greece, Hungary, Iceland, Italy, Latvia, Lithuania, Luxembourg, Malta, Netherlands, Norway, Poland, Portugal, Slovakia, Slovenia, Sweden and Switzerland.

Spain gave US$5·1bn. in international aid in 2007, equivalent to 0·37% of GNI (compared to the UN target of 0·7%).

ECONOMY

Agriculture accounted for 3% of GDP in 2007, industry 30% and services 67%.

Overview

Spain made significant economic strides in the 1980s when productivity growth was at its highest. After the Europe-wide recession of the early 1990s macroeconomic performance has been strong. Structural reforms and sound macroeconomic policies have encouraged growth and employment creation since the late 1990s. Fiscal policy saw annual budget deficits fall from 6%+ of GDP in the mid-1990s to near balance since 2001 and GDP growth was above 3% per year from 2003–07.

However, the global financial crisis starting in 2008 saw the housing construction bubble burst, resulting in slower growth, cuts in household consumption and rising unemployment. The economy contracted by 3·6% in 2009. The OECD predicted a further 0·25% decline in 2010 before a slow recovery in 2011. Unemployment stands close to 20%, double the average in the euro-area and second only to Latvia in the EU. The collapse of the housing boom accounted for the loss of 900,000 jobs, largely among unskilled construction workers. Public finances shifted from a budget surplus in 2007 to a deficit of over 10% of GDP in 2009. The European Commission forecasts debt to be 74% of GDP in 2011 if policies are unchanged. Average incomes in Spain remain below those of Western Europe but have converged significantly.

The services share of total GDP has grown at the expense of agriculture, forestry and fishing. Banking, retailing, telecommunications and tourism are the main components of the service sector. Strong demand for tourist-related buildings, foreign demand for property and high levels of investment in infrastructure combined to make the construction sector, as a share of GDP, twice as large as in other big European economies. Agriculture is concentrated on wine, olive oil, fruit and vegetables, with the southeast region a competitive supplier of fresh produce to European markets. The fishing industry is also highly developed, meeting significant domestic demand as well as serving international markets. Vehicle production for export is the most prominent manufacturing industry, accounting for 5% of GDP, with 80% of production going for export. Spanish banks are increasingly competitive on the international scene. A strong labour supply has done much to expand the domestic economy.

Research and development (R&D) activities are low by Western European standards. The OECD suggests fostering private R&D spending by improving framework conditions and sharpening incentives in the education system by giving schools greater autonomy, linking university financing to performance and raising university fees. Labour reforms together with product and service market reforms should help raise productivity and reduce costs, while the removal of wage indexation to inflation should support competitiveness.

Currency

On 1 Jan. 1999 the euro (EUR) became the legal currency in Spain at the irrevocable conversion rate of 166·386 pesetas to 1 euro. The euro, which consists of 100 cents, has been in circulation since 1 Jan. 2002. There are seven euro notes in different colours and sizes denominated in 500, 200, 100, 50, 20, 10 and 5 euros, and eight coins denominated in 2 and 1 euros, then 50, 20, 10, 5, 2 and 1 cents. On the introduction of the euro there was a 'dual circulation' period before the peseta ceased to be legal tender on 28 Feb. 2002. Euro banknotes in circulation on 1 Jan. 2002 had a total value of €68·6bn.

Foreign exchange reserves were US$12,657m. in Sept. 2009 (US$52,490m. in 1998) and gold reserves 9·05m. troy oz. Inflation rates (based on OECD statistics):

1999	*2000*	*2001*	*2002*	*2003*	*2004*	*2005*	*2006*	*2007*	*2008*
2·2%	3·5%	2·8%	3·6%	3·1%	3·1%	3·4%	3·6%	2·8%	4·1%

Total money supply was €506,714m. in Aug. 2009.

Budget

In 2004 central government revenues totalled €221,331m. and expenditures €219,015m. Principal sources of revenue in 2004: social security contributions, €101,255m.; taxes on income, profits and capital gains, €58,591m.; taxes on goods and services, €39,332m. Main items of expenditure by economic type in 2004: social benefits, €97·91bn.; grants, €50·54bn.; compensation of employees, €19·89bn.

VAT was 16% in 2009, with a rate of 7% on certain services (catering and hospitality) and 4% on basic foodstuffs.

Performance

Real GDP growth rates (based on OECD statistics):

1999	*2000*	*2001*	*2002*	*2003*	*2004*	*2005*	*2006*	*2007*	*2008*
4·7%	5·0%	3·6%	2·7%	3·1%	3·3%	3·6%	4·0%	3·6%	0·9%

The real GDP growth rate in 2009 according to Spain's National Statistics Institute was –3·6%. Total GDP (2008): US$1,604·2bn., making Spain the world's tenth largest economy.

Banking and Finance

The central bank is the Bank of Spain (*Governor*, Miguel Angel Fernández Ordóñez) which gained autonomy under an ordinance of 1994. Its Governor is appointed for a six-year term. The Banking Corporation of Spain, *Argentaria*, groups together the shares of all state-owned banks, and competes in the financial market with private banks. In 1993 the government sold 49·9% of the capital of Argentaria; the remainder in two flotations ending on 13 Feb. 1998.

Spanish banking is dominated by two main banks—Santander and BBVA (Banco Bilbao Vizcaya Argentaria). Santander had assets of €1,110·5bn. in Dec. 2009 and BBVA assets of €535·1bn.

There are stock exchanges in Madrid, Barcelona, Bilbao and Valencia.

ENERGY AND NATURAL RESOURCES

Environment

In 2008 Spain's carbon dioxide emissions from the consumption and flaring of fossil fuels were the equivalent of 8·9 tonnes per capita.

Electricity

Installed capacity was 76·4m. kW in 2004. The total electricity output in 2004 amounted to 280·01bn. kWh, of which 59·4% was thermal, 22·7% nuclear, 12·3% hydro-electric and 5·6% geothermal. Consumption per capita in 2004 was 6,412 kWh.

In Oct. 2000 Endesa SA and Iberdrola SA, the country's two largest electricity companies, announced merger plans. The new company would have been in charge of 80% of Spain's electricity output. However, in Feb. 2001 the two companies shelved the proposed merger. In 2003 there were nine nuclear reactors in operation.

Oil and Gas

Spain is heavily dependent on imported oil; Mexico is its largest supplier. Crude oil production (2004), 1·9m. bbls.

The government sold its remaining stake in the oil, gas and chemicals group Repsol in 1997. Natural gas production (2004) totalled 356m. cu. metres. Ever increasing consumption means that Spain has to import large quantities of natural gas, primarily from Algeria.

Wind

Spain is one of the world's largest wind-power producers, with an installed capacity of 10,028 MW in 2005.

Minerals

Coal production (2004), 8·91m. tonnes; other principal minerals (in 1,000 tonnes): gypsum and anhydrite (2004), 12,534; lignite (2004), 11,576; anthracite (2005), 8,553; salt (2005), 4,389; potash (2003), 594; aluminium (2005), 395; fluorspar (2005), 144; nickel (2005), 5. Gold production, 2005, 5,300 kg; silver production, 2005, 3,600 kg.

Agriculture

There were 1,287,000 farms in Spain in 2000. Agriculture employed about 5·9% of the workforce in 2002. It accounts for 15·8% of exports and 15·6% of imports.

There were 13·74m. ha. of arable land in 2002 and 4·98m. ha. of permanent crops. In 2002 there were 914,000 tractors, 52,000 harvester-threshers and 130,000 milking machines in use.

Principal crops	*Area (in 1,000 ha.)* 2000	2001	2002	*Yield (in 1,000 tonnes)* 2000	2001	2002
Barley	3,278	2,992	3,100	11,063	6,249	8,333
Sugar beets	125	107	115	7,930	6,755	8,040
Wheat	2,353	2,177	2,402	7,294	5,008	6,783
Maize	433	513	463	3,992	4,982	4,463
Potatoes	119	115	114	3,078	2,992	3,104
Oats	432	446	473	954	665	916
Rice	117	116	113	827	876	815
Sunflower seeds	839	858	754	919	871	757

Spain has more land dedicated to the grape than any other country in the world and is ranked third among wine producers (behind France and Italy). Production of wine (2006), 38,137,000 hectolitres (13·5% of the world total); of grapes (2003), 6,480,000 tonnes.

The area planted with tomatoes in 2002 was 60,000 ha., yielding 3,878,000 tonnes; with onions, 23,000 ha., yielding 992,000 tonnes; peppers, 23,000 ha., yielding 980,000 tonnes.

Fruit production (2002, in tonnes): oranges, 2,867,000; tangerines, 1,952,000; peaches, 1,247,000; lemons, 920,000; apples, 653,000; pears, 603,000.

Production of olives, 2001–02, 6,983,000 tonnes; olive oil, 1,422,000 tonnes. Spain is the world's leading producer both of olives and olive oil.

Livestock (2003): cattle, 6·48m.; sheep, 23·81m.; goats, 3·05m.; pigs, 23·52m.; chickens, 128·0m.; asses and mules, 0·26m.; horses, 0·24m. Livestock products (2003, in 1,000 tonnes): pork, bacon and ham, 3,322; beef and veal, 700; mutton and lamb, 237; poultry meat, 1,042; milk, 6,917; cheese, 198; eggs, 686.

Forestry

In 2005 the area under forests was 17·92m. ha., or 35·9% of the total land area. In 2007 timber production was 14·53m. cu. metres.

Fisheries

Spain is one of the leading fishing nations in the EU; it is also the EU's leading importer of fishery commodities. Fishing vessels had a total tonnage of 519,867 tonnes in 2002, the highest in the EU (596,441 GRT in 1994); fleets have been gradually reduced from 20,558 boats in 1991 to 14,887 in 2002. Total catch in 2005 amounted to 848,803 tonnes, almost exclusively sea fish.

INDUSTRY

The leading companies by market capitalization in Spain in March 2009 were: Telefónica SA (US$93·8bn.); Banco Santander Central Hispano (BSCH), US$56·2bn.; and Iberdrola SA, an electricity company (US$35·1bn.).

Industrial products, 2004 unless otherwise indicated (in tonnes): cement (2002), 42·4m.; distillate fuel oil, 21·6m.; crude steel (2003), 16·3m.; petrol, 10·4m.; residual fuel oil, 9·1m.; paper and paperboard (2002), 5·4m.; plastics (1999), 4·1m.; pig iron (2002), 4·0m.; sulphuric acid (1999), 3·3m.; jet fuel, 2·7m.; nitrogenous fertilizers (2000), 951,000; cigarettes (2001), 74·8bn. units.

The number of vehicles manufactured in 2005 was 2,752,000. 2·15m. refrigerators were manufactured in 2000, 2·7m. washing machines in 2002 and 4·2m. TV sets in 2002. In 2001, 4,730·5m. litres of soft drinks, 4,072·3m. litres of mineral water and 2,680·2m. litres of beer were produced.

Labour

Out of 18,973,200 people in employment in 2005, 3,113,000 worked in manufacturing; 2,886,800 in wholesale and retail trade/repair of motor vehicles, motorcycles and personal and household goods; 2,357,200 in construction; 1,678,400 in real estate, renting and business activities; 1,291,100 in hotels and restaurants; and 1,196,700 in public administration and defence/ compulsory social security. The monthly minimum wage for adults was €624·00 in 2009. The average working week in 2003 was 35·4 hours. The retirement age is 65 years. In 2004 part-time work accounted for less than 9% of all employment in Spain—the lowest percentage in western Europe.

Spain's unemployment rate reached a peak of nearly 25% in 1994 but then fell steadily, declining to 8·3% in 2007. However, as a result of the global economic crisis Spain's unemployment rate rose by more than seven percentage points in the space of 12 months from March 2008. In the period Jan.–March 2009 an average of 8,600 jobs were lost every day. In Feb. 2010 the rate stood at 19·0%, giving Spain the second highest unemployment rate in the EU after Latvia. Youth unemployment is particularly high, rising to 44·5% in Dec. 2009.

Between 1996 and 2005 strikes cost Spain an average of 186 days per 1,000 employees a year. Spain's figure was the highest in the EU.

Trade Unions

The Constitution guarantees the establishment and activities of trade unions provided they have a democratic structure. The most important trade unions are Comisiones Obreras (CO), with 790,000 members in 1997, and Unión General de Trabajadores (UGT), which had 775,000 members in 1997.

INTERNATIONAL TRADE

Imports and Exports

Trade in US$1m.:

	2000	2001	2002	2003	2004
Imports f.o.b.	152,856	152,039	161,794	203,203	249,984
Exports f.o.b.	115,769	117,522	127,161	158,047	184,154

In 2004 chemicals, manufactured goods classified chiefly by material and miscellaneous manufactured articles accounted for 41·7% of imports and 43·4% of exports; machinery and transport equipment 37·7% of imports and 40·3% of exports; food, live animals, beverages and tobacco 8·4% of imports and 12·2% of exports; mineral fuels, lubricants and related materials 8·8% of imports and 1·1% of exports; inedible crude materials, and animal and vegetable oil and fats 3·4% of imports and 3·0% of exports.

Leading import sources in 2004 were Germany (16·1%), France (15·2%), Italy (9·1%), United Kingdom (6·1%), Netherlands (4·1%); leading export markets in 2004 were: France (19·3%), Germany (11·7%), Portugal (9·4%), Italy (9·0%), United Kingdom (9·0%). In 2004 the EU accounted for 62·2% of Spain's imports and 70·0% of exports.

Trade Fairs

Barcelona ranks as the fifth most popular convention city in the world (behind Singapore, Paris, Brussels and Vienna) according to the Union des Associations Internationales (UAI), hosting 1·7% of all meetings held in 2008.

COMMUNICATIONS

Roads

In 2003 the total length of roads was 676,239 km; the network included 12,100 km of motorways, 23,367 km of highways/national roads and 139,672 km of secondary roads. 99% of all roads in Spain were paved in 2003. In 2003 road transport totalled 397,117m. passenger-km; freight transport totalled 132,868m. tonne-km in 2003. Number of passenger cars in use (2007), 21,760,200; lorries and vans, 5,140,600; buses and coaches, 61,000; motorcycles and mopeds, 2,311,300. In 2007, 3,823 persons were killed in road accidents (5,604 in 1997).

Rail

The total length of the state railways in 2005 was 12,808 km, mostly broad (1,668-mm) gauge (6,942 km electrified). The state railway system was divided in two in 2005; Administrador de Infraestructuras Ferroviarias (ADIF) now manages the infrastructure and Renfe Operadora runs train operations. There is an ever-expanding high-speed standard-gauge (1,435-mm) network. The first high-speed line, from Madrid to Seville, opened in 1992. It was extended northwards from Madrid initially to Lleida, with passenger services beginning in 2003, and further to Tarragona (2006) and Barcelona (2008). High-speed lines linking Madrid with Toledo and Valladolid were opened in 2005 and 2007 respectively. A high-speed link from Córdoba (on the Madrid to Seville line) to Málaga was also opened in 2007. Passenger-km travelled in 2005 came to 19·8bn. and freight tonne-km to 1·8bn. There are metros in Madrid (282 km), Valencia (152 km), Barcelona (105 km), Bilbao (38 km), Seville (18 km) and Palma de Mallorca (7 km).

In 2003 the construction of two 40 km-long rail tunnels under the Straits of Gibraltar was agreed with Morocco although there are ongoing talks as to the project's feasibility.

Civil Aviation

There are international airports at Madrid (Barajas), Barcelona (Prat del Llobregat), Alicante, Almería, Bilbao, Girona, Las Palmas de Gran Canaria, Ibiza, Lanzarote, Málaga, Palma de Mallorca, Santiago de Compostela, Seville, Tenerife (Los Rodeos and Reina Sofía), Valencia, Valladolid and Zaragoza. There are 43 airports open to civil traffic. A small airport in Seo de Urgel operates in Andorra. The former national carrier Iberia Airlines completed its privatization process in April 2001, when shares were listed for the first time on the stock exchange. Of other airlines, the largest are Air Europa and Spanair. Services are also provided by about 70 foreign airlines. In 2005 Iberia carried 27·4m. passengers (12·0m. on international flights); passenger-km totalled 49·0bn. Madrid was the busiest airport in 2001, handling 33,777,862 passengers (16,718,209 on domestic flights) and 294,692 tonnes of freight. Barcelona was the second busiest in 2001, with 20,545,680 (10,075,536 on domestic flights) and 76,966 tonnes of freight. Palma de Mallorca was the third busiest for passengers, with 19,122,832 (14,317,984 on international flights). Las Palmas was the third busiest for freight, with 40,615 tonnes in 2001.

Shipping

In 2000 the merchant fleet comprised 1,554 vessels (of 100 gross tons or more) totalling 2·03m. GRT (including oil tankers 600,000 GRT); shipyards launched 363,910 CGT in 2001. In 2001 vessels totalling 198,696,000 NRT entered ports and vessels totalling 59,267,000 NRT cleared. The leading ports are Algeciras-La Linea (51,251,000 tonnes of cargo in 2002), Barcelona, Bilbao, Ceuta, Las Palmas de Gran Canaria, Santa Cruz de Tenerife, Tarragona and Valencia.

Telecommunications

In 2008 there were 20,200,000 main (fixed) telephone lines. In the same year mobile phone subscribers numbered 49,678,000 (1,116·7 per 1,000 persons). The government disposed of its remaining 21% stake in Telefónica in Feb. 1997, bringing 1·4m. shareholders into the company's equity base. A second operator, Retevisión, accounts for 3% of the domestic market, which was wholly deregulated in 1998. The mobile phone business was deregulated in 1995; the market is shared by Movistar (with a 45% share of the market), Vodafone and Orange.

There were 16·0m. PCs in use in 2006 and 25·2m. internet users in 2008. The broadband penetration rate stood at 19·8 subscribers per 100 inhabitants in June 2008.

Postal Services

In 2003 there were 3,343 post offices; a total of 5,630m. pieces of mail were processed during the year, or 137 items per person.

SOCIAL INSTITUTIONS

Justice

Justice is administered by Tribunals and Courts, which jointly form the Judicial Power. Judges and magistrates cannot be removed, suspended or transferred except as set forth by law. The constitution of 1978 established the *General Council of the Judicial Power*, consisting of a President and 20 magistrates, judges, attorneys and lawyers, governing the Judicial Power in full independence from the state's legislative and executive organs. Its members are appointed by the *Cortes Generales*. Its President is that of the Supreme Court (*Tribunal Supremo*), who is appointed by the monarch on the proposal of the General Council of the Judicial.

The Judicature is composed of the Supreme Court; 17 Higher Courts of Justice, one for each autonomous community; 52 Provincial High Courts; Courts of First Instance; Courts of Judicial Proceedings, not passing sentences; and Penal Courts, passing sentences.

The Supreme Court consists of a President, and various judges distributed among seven chambers: one for civil matters, three for administrative purposes, one for criminal trials, one for social matters and one for military cases. The Supreme Court has disciplinary faculties; is court of appeal in all criminal trials; for administrative purposes decides in first and second instance disputes arising between private individuals and the State; and in social matters makes final decisions.

A new penal code came into force in May 1996, replacing the code of 1848. It provides for a maximum of 30 years imprisonment in specified exceptional cases, with a normal maximum of 20 years. Sanctions with a rehabilitative intent include fines adjusted to means, community service and weekend imprisonment. The death penalty was abolished by the 1978 constitution. The prison population in Nov. 2003 was 56,140 (138 per 100,000 of national population); 102,031 criminal sentences were passed in 2002. A jury system commenced operating in Nov. 1995 in criminal cases (first trials in May 1996). Juries consist of nine members.

A juvenile criminal law of 1995 lays emphasis on rehabilitation. It raised the age of responsibility from 12 to 14 years. Criminal conduct on the part of children under 14 is a matter for legal protection and custody. 14- and 15-year-olds are classified as 'minors'; 16- and 17-year-olds as 'young persons'; and the legal majority for criminal offences is set at 18 years. Persons up to the age of 21 may, at the courts' discretion, be dealt with as juveniles.

The *Audiencia Nacional* deals with terrorism, monetary offences and drug-trafficking where more than one province is involved. Its president is appointed by the General Council of the Judicial Power.

There is an Ombudsman (*Defensor del Pueblo*), who is elected for a five-year term (currently Enrique Múgica Herzog; b. 1932).

Education

In 1991 the General Regulation of the Educational System Act came into force. This Act gradually extends the school-leaving age to 16 years and determines the following levels of education: infants (3–5 years of age), primary (6–11), secondary (12–15) and baccalaureate or vocational and technical (16–17). Primary and secondary levels of education are now compulsory and free. Religious instruction is optional.

In Sept. 1997 a joint declaration with trade unions, parents' and schools' associations was signed in support of a new finance law guaranteeing that spending on education will reach 6% of GDP within five years, thus protecting it from changes in the political sphere. In 2006 public expenditure on education came to 4·4% of GNI and 11·1% of total government spending.

A new compulsory secondary education programme has replaced the Basic General Education programme which was in force since 1970. In addition, university entrance exams underwent reform in 1997, resulting in greater emphasis now being placed on the teaching of Humanities at secondary level.

In 2004–05 pre-primary education (under six years) was undertaken by 1,419,307 pupils; primary or basic education (6–14 years): 2,494,598 pupils. In 2004 there were 100,669 teaching staff in pre-primary and 179,271 teachers in primary schools. Secondary education (14–17 years), including high schools and technical schools, was conducted at 6,276 schools, with 3,054,263 pupils and 167,182 teachers in 2004–05.

In 2003 there were 71 universities: 50 public state universities and 21 private universities (including Catholic establishments). In 2004–05 there were 1,330,574 students at state universities; 132,197 at private universities.

The adult literacy rate is at least 99%.

Health

In 2003 there were 190,665 doctors, 56,501 pharmacists and 220,769 nurses (including 6,764 midwives). There were 17,538 dentists in 2000. Number of hospitals (2001), 767, with 146,367 beds. In 2007 Spain spent 8·5% of its GDP on health, with public spending accounting for 71·8% of total expenditure on health and private spending 28·2%.

Welfare

The social security budget was €82,425,871,000 in 2004, including €66·1bn. for pensions, €5·3bn. for temporary incapacity, €1·4bn. for health and €620m. for social services. The minimum pension in 2001 was the equivalent of just over €5,000 per year, made in 14 payments.

In 2003 the system of contributions to the social security and employment scheme was: for pensions, sickness, invalidity, maternity and children, a contribution of 28·3% of the basic wage (23·6% paid by the employer, 4·7% by the employee); for unemployment benefit, a contribution of 7·55% (6·0% paid by the employer, 1·55% by the employee). There are also minor contributions for a Fund of Guaranteed Salaries, working accidents and professional sicknesses, and for vocational training.

RELIGION

There is no official religion. Roman Catholicism is the religion of the majority. In Feb. 2010 there were ten cardinals. There are 11 metropolitan sees and 52 suffragan sees, the chief being Toledo, where the Primate resides. The archdioceses of Madrid-Alcalá and Barcelona depend directly from the Vatican. There are about 0·25m. other Christians, including several Protestant denominations, about 60,000 Jehovah's Witnesses and 29,000 Latter-day Saints (Mormons), and 0·45m. Muslims, including Spanish Muslims in Ceuta and Melilla. The first synagogue since the expulsion of the Jews in 1492 was opened in Madrid on 2 Oct. 1959. The number of people of Judaist faith is estimated at about 15,000.

CULTURE

World Heritage Sites

There are 41 sites under Spanish jurisdiction that appear on the UNESCO World Heritage List. They are (with year entered on list): the works of Antoni Gaudi in and around Barcelona (1984 and 2005), Burgos Cathedral (1984), Historic Centre of Córdoba (1984 and 1994), Alhambra, Generalife and Albayzin, Granada (1984 and 1994), Monastery and site of the Escurial, Madrid (1984), Altamira Cave (1985 and 2008), Old Town of Segovia and its Aqueduct (1985), Monuments of Oviedo and the Kingdom of the Asturias (1985 and 1998), Santiago de Compostela (Old Town) (1985), Old Town of Ávila, with its Extra-Muros churches (1985 and 2007), Mudéjar Architecture of Aragón (1986 and 2001), Historic City of Toledo (1986), Garajonay National Park (1986), Old Town of Cáceres (1986), Cathedral, Alcazar and Archivo de Indias in Seville (1987), Old City of Salamanca (1988), Poblet Monastery (1991), Archaeological Ensemble of Mérida (1993), Royal Monastery of Santa María de Guadalupe (1993), Route of Santiago de Compostela (1993), Doñana National Park (1994 and 2005), Historic Walled Town of Cuenca (1996), La Lonja de la Seda de Valencia (1996), Las Médulas (1997), the Palau de la Música Catalana and the Hospital de Sant Pau, Barcelona (1997 and 2008), San Millán Yuso and Suso Monasteries (1997), University and Historic Precinct of Alcalá de Henares (1998), Rock-Art of the Mediterranean Basin on the Iberian Peninsula (1998), Ibiza, Biodiversity and Culture (1999), San Cristóbal de La Laguna (1999), the Archaeological Ensemble of Tárraco (2000), the Palmeral of Elche (2000), the Roman Walls of Lugo (2000), Catalan Romanesque Churches of the Vall de Boí (2000), Archaeological Site of Atapuerca (2000), Aranjuez Cultural Landscape (2001), Renaissance monumental ensembles of Úbeda and Baeza (2003), Vizcaya Bridge (2006), Teide National Park, Tenerife (2007), the Tower of Hercules, La Coruña (2009); and shared by France and Spain: Pyrénées—Mount Perdu (1997).

Broadcasting

The state-owned Corporación de Radio y Televisión Española (RTVE), an autonomous organization which came into existence in 2007, controls the public radio and television service. The public Radio Nacional de España (RNE) broadcasts nationally and regionally and operates an international service. Large independent radio networks include Cadena SER (Sociedad Española de Radiodifusión), Cadena de Ondas Populares Españolas (owned by the Roman Catholic Church) and Onda Cero. Radio Exterior broadcasts abroad.

Televisión Española operates two public national networks and also an international channel. There are three nationwide commercial TV networks: Antena 3, Tele 5 and the pay-TV channel Cuatro (formerly Canal+). In addition, there are 13 regional TV stations backed by regional governments and numerous local stations. The number of cable and satellite TV channels is expanding. The transition to digital broadcasting was completed on 3 April 2010 when analogue transmissions were switched off. Colour transmissions are by PAL. Number of TV-equipped households (2006): 14·55m.

Cinema

There were 1,112 cinemas (4,348 screens) in 2004 with an audience of 141·5m. (18·8m. for Spanish films and 122·6m. for foreign films). In 2004 gross box office receipts came to €680m. In Nov. 1997 the Madrid School of Cinema was established.

Press

In 2003–04 there were 91 daily newspapers with a total daily circulation of 4·10m. copies. Eight publishing groups controlled around 80% of the daily press, with another 100 or so independents accounting for the other 20%. The main paid-for titles are: El País (average daily circulation 462,000), El Mundo (300,000) and ABC (276,000), along with the dedicated sports paper, Marca (386,000). The leading free papers, notably 20 Minutos, ADN and Que!, now have wider circulations than the paid-for dailies.

In 2003, 72,048 book titles were published of which 21,661 were categorized as literature, history and literary criticism.

Tourism

In 2006 Spain was behind only France in the number of foreign visitor arrivals, and behind only the USA for tourism receipts. In 2006, 58,190,000 tourists visited Spain; receipts for 2006 amounted to US$51,122m. Overnight stays in hotels in 2004 (provisional) totalled 235m. of which 48·8% were between June and Sept.; there were 1·1m. places available in hotels. Average occupancy rate was 53·6% in 2004.

Festivals

Religious Festivals: Epiphany (6 Jan.), the Feast of the Assumption (15 Aug.), All Saints Day (1 Nov.) and Immaculate Conception (8 Dec.) are all public holidays. Cultural Festivals: Day of Andalusia (28 Feb.), the Feast of San José in Valencia (19 March) is the culmination of a 13-day festival; the Festival of the Sardine in Murcia is an end of Easter parade in which a huge papier mâché sardine is burned; Feria de Abril is a major festival in Seville at the end of April which features flamenco dancing and bull-fighting; the San Fermines Festival, which takes place in mid-July, is most famous for the running of the bulls in the streets of Pamplona; La Tomatina, a battle of revellers armed with 50 tonnes of tomatoes, takes place on the last Wednesday in Aug. and is the highlight of the annual fiesta in Buñol, Valencia; National Day of Catalonia (11 Sept.); Spanish National Day (12 Oct.).

Libraries

In 2002 there were 3,832 public libraries, one national library, 1,762 specialized libraries, 410 for specific user groups, 355 higher education libraries and 11 central libraries of autonomous communities; they held a combined 117·6m. volumes. There were 153m. visits to libraries by more than 12·6m. users in 2002. 62·7% of libraries had internet access in 2002.

Museums and Galleries

Spain had 1,438 museums in 2000 with 3·7m. visitors. The Museu del Prado in Madrid received 1·8m. visitors in 2000.

DIPLOMATIC REPRESENTATIVES

Of Spain in the United Kingdom (39 Chesham Pl., London, SW1X 8SB)
Ambassador: Carles Casajuana i Palet.

Of the United Kingdom in Spain (Torre Espacio, Paseo de la Castellana 259D, 28046 Madrid)
Ambassador: Giles Paxman, LVO.

Of Spain in the USA (2375 Pennsylvania Ave., NW, Washington, D.C., 20037)
Ambassador: Jorge Dezcallar de Mazarredo.

Of the USA in Spain (Serrano 75, 28006 Madrid)
Ambassador: Alan D. Solomont.

Of Spain to the United Nations
Ambassador: Juan Antonio Yáñez-Barnuevo.

Of Spain to the European Union
Permanent Representative: Carlos Bastarreche Sagües.

FURTHER READING

Balfour, Sebastian, *The Politics of Contemporary Spain.* 2004
Barton, Simon, *A History of Spain.* 2004
Carr, Raymond, (ed.) *Spain: A History.* 2000
Closa, Carlos and Heywood, Paul, *Spain and the European Union.* 2004
Conversi, D., *The Basques, The Catalans and Spain.* 1997
Gunther, Richard, *Democracy in Modern Spain.* 2004
Harrison, Joseph and Corkhill, David, *Spain: A Modern European Economy.* 2004
Heywood, P., *The Government and Politics of Spain.* 1995
Hooper, John, *The New Spaniards.* 2nd ed. revised. 2006
Péréz-Díaz, V. M., *The Return of Civil Society: the Emergence of Democratic Spain.* 1993
Powell, C., *Juan Carlos of Spain: Self-Made Monarch.* 1996

National library: Biblioteca Nacional, Paseo de Recoletos, 20–22, 28071 Madrid.
National Statistical Office: Instituto Nacional de Estadística (INE), Paseo de la Castellana, 183, Madrid.
Website: http://www.ine.es

SRI LANKA

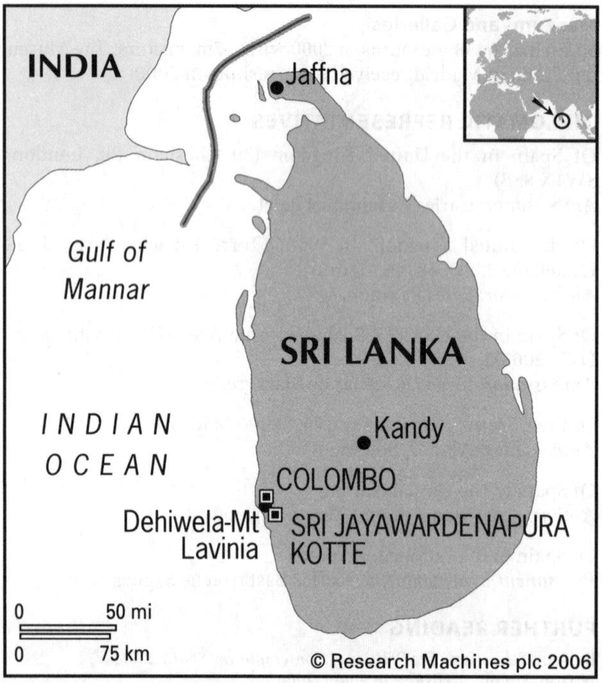

Sri Lanka Prajathanthrika Samajavadi Janarajaya (Democratic Socialist Republic of Sri Lanka)

Capital: Sri Jayewardenepura Kotte (Administrative and Legislative), Colombo (Commercial)
Population estimate, 2010: 20·41m.
GDP per capita, 2007: (PPP$) 4,243
HDI/world rank: 0·759/102

KEY HISTORICAL EVENTS

Archaeological evidence suggests Sri Lanka has been inhabited since at least the Mesolithic era 34,000 years ago, possibly by ancestors of the Vedda people, small numbers of whom live in the central highlands. The island's recorded history begins in 483 BC, when, according to the Sinhalese chronicle *Mahavamsa*, several hundred men led by Vijaya, a prince from Bengal, reached the island. Anuradhapura was founded in 377 BC, becoming the principal settlement. Introduced in 250 BC by the Indian Emperor, Ashoka, Buddhism was gradually adopted, becoming central to the developing Sinhalese culture even while its influence in India declined. Elaborate irrigation systems enabled rice cultivation and brought prosperity to the northern plain around Anuradhapura, which became a target for south Indian raiders. South Indian Chola kings controlled Anuradhapura in the second century BC until King Dutugemunu wrested control in 161 BC.

Invasions from south India continued while, at times, Sri Lankan kings seized control of parts of southern India. A spate of attacks in the 8th century AD prompted King Aggabodhi IV to move Sri Lanka's seat of government to Polonnaruwa. A Chola army under Rajarja I destroyed Anuradhapura in 993, although Sinhalese control was re-established in 1070. Trade with southeast Asia flourished in the 12th century under Parakramabahu I and Sinhalese civilization reached its height under Nissanka Mala (1187–96), the last Polonnaruwa king to rule the whole island. During the 13th century a Tamil kingdom was established in the northeast, centred on Jaffna. The seat of Sinhalese power gradually shifted to the southwest, where coastal provinces thrived on the spice trade with Arab merchants. King Alagakkonara established a fort at Kotte in 1369.

The arrival of Portuguese mariners in 1505 heralded a new era of European influence, initially centred on Kotte and the southwest. Many coastal provinces, including Jaffna, came under Portuguese rule from 1600, with missionaries promoting Roman Catholicism. A military expedition failed to take the province of Kandy in 1594 but Portuguese naval forces seized the Kandyan ports of Trincomalee and Batticaola in the 1620s. Dutch seafarers established a presence from the 1590s, gradually taking over Portuguese-run forts and controlling Sri Lanka's maritime regions from 1658. The trade in cinnamon was particularly lucrative. In 1670 the Dutch East Indian Company (VOC) declared a monopoly over exports including elephants and pearls and imports such as cotton. This prompted Kandyan attacks until a truce was signed with King Rajasingha II in 1775.

As Dutch power in Asia waned, its possessions came under attack from British and French forces. In 1796 Colombo, Trincomalee, Jaffna and Kalpitya surrendered to British rule, with control initially routed through Madras in India. In 1802 a separate colony (Ceylon) under the British Crown was constituted but an attempt to capture Kandy in 1803 failed. The Kandyan Convention of 1815 annexed Kandy to British Ceylon while recognizing most of the traditional rights of the chiefs. Disillusionment culminated in a Kandyan rebellion in 1818 that was harshly suppressed and the rights established by the Convention abolished.

Ceylon was then unified under a single administration for the first time in 400 years. Becoming aware of the island's economic potential, the British established plantations, initially based on coffee until an outbreak of *Hoemilia vastatrix* fungus in 1870 destroyed much of the crop. Large-scale cultivation of spices, cocoa and rice followed but tea and rubber became the main cash crops from the 1880s. When Kandyans refused plantation work, thousands of indentured labourers were brought in from south India.

As in other British colonies, the education system created an English-speaking elite. Ethnic and caste rivalries continued, notably between Kandyan villagers who were denied the welfare benefits given to Indian Tamil labourers on the plantations. Tensions between Sinhalese and Muslim merchants spilled into violent riots in 1915. A movement for self-government gained ground after the First World War through the Ceylon National Congress, in which Sinhalese and Ceylon Tamil groups peacefully negotiated with the British authorities.

Internal self-government under a directly elected State Council was granted in 1931. Ceylon's economy was hit hard in the 1930s, prompting demands for full independence. This followed on 4 Feb. 1948 with dominion status in the British Commonwealth. D. S. Senanayake, leader of the United National Party (UNP), became the first prime minister.

In 1956 Solomon Bandaranaike became prime minister at the head of the People's United Front, advocating neutrality and the promotion of Sinhalese national culture at home. Tamil demands for official recognition of their language and a separate state under a federal system caused riots in 1958, with considerable loss of life. Bandaranaike was assassinated in Sept. 1959. His widow, Sirimavo Bandaranaike, succeeded him the following year at the head of an increasingly left-wing government. In May 1972 Ceylon became a republic and adopted the name Sri Lanka.

In July 1977 the UNP (dominant until 1956) returned to power and in 1978 a new constitution set up a presidential system. The problem of communal unrest remained unsolved and Tamil separatists were active. In 1983 Tamil United Liberation Front members of parliament were asked to renounce their objective for a separate Tamil state in the north and the east of the country. They refused and withdrew from parliament. Militant Tamils then began armed action that developed into civil war.

A state of emergency ended on 11 Jan. 1989 but violence continued. President Ranasinghe Premadasa was assassinated on 1 May 1993. A ceasefire was signed on 3 Jan. 1995 but fighting broke out again in April. The Tamil stronghold of Jaffna in the far north of the country was captured by government forces in Dec. 1995 and by mid-1997 was under government control. In April 2000 the Tamil Tigers captured a military garrison at Elephant Pass, the isthmus that links Jaffna to the rest of Sri Lanka, threatening a recapture of the Jaffna peninsula. A month-long ceasefire in Dec. 2001 led to peace negotiations. On 22 Feb. 2002 the government and Tamil Tiger leaders agreed to an internationally-monitored ceasefire, paving the way to the first full-scale peace talks for seven years. An estimated 61,000 people had died during the previous 19 years of conflict.

In late 2002 the Tamil Tigers abandoned their ambitions for a separate state, settling instead for regional autonomy. However, in Nov. 2003 President Kumaratunga declared a state of emergency after dismissing three ministers, suspending parliament and sending troops on to the streets. She accused the government of making too many concessions to Tamil Tiger rebels.

On 26 Dec. 2004 Sri Lanka, along with a number of other south Asian countries, was hit by a devastating tsunami. The death toll in Sri Lanka was put at 35,000.

A series of incidents in early 2006 brought the country back to the brink of civil war. Fighting intensified throughout the year, with the government claiming success in the east of the country. After failed peace talks in Geneva in Oct. 2006, the government withdrew from the 2002 ceasefire agreement in Jan. 2008.

In early 2009 Sri Lankan military forces launched a major offensive on the Tamil Tigers, during which the Tigers' leader, Velupillai Prabhakaran, was killed. On 19 May 2009 President Mahinda Rajapaksa formally declared an end to the civil war, stating the country had been liberated from terrorism. The UN estimated that around 7,000 Tamil civilians were killed in the 2009 military action while some 135,000 displaced people remained in camps in northern Sri Lanka in late 2009.

TERRITORY AND POPULATION

Sri Lanka is an island in the Indian Ocean, south of the Indian peninsula from which it is separated by the Palk Strait. On 28 June 1974 the frontier between India and Sri Lanka in the Palk Strait was redefined, giving to Sri Lanka the island of Kachchativu.

Area (in sq. km) and population (2001 census):

District	*Area*	*Population*
Amparai	4,415	592,997
Anuradhapura	7,179	745,693
Badulla	2,861	779,983
Batticaloa	2,854	486,447[1]
Colombo	669	2,251,274
Galle	1,652	990,487
Gampaha	1,387	2,063,684
Hambantota	2,609	526,414
Jaffna	1,025	490,621[1]
Kalutara	1,598	1,066,239
Kandy	1,940	1,279,028
Kegalla	1,693	785,524
Kilinochchi	1,279	127,263[1]
Kurunegala	4,816	1,460,215
Mannar	1,996	151,577[1]
Matale	1,993	441,328
Matara	1,283	761,370
Moneragala	5,639	397,375
Mullaitivu	2,617	121,667[1]
Nuwara Eliya	1,741	703,610
Polonnaruwa	3,293	358,984
Puttalam	3,072	709,677
Ratnapura	3,275	1,015,807
Trincomalee	2,727	340,158[1]
Vavuniya	1,967	149,835[1]
Total	*65,610*	*18,797,257*

[1]Estimates.

Population (in 1,000) according to ethnic group and nationality at the 2001 census included: 13,815 Sinhalese, 1,351 Sri Lanka Moors, 856 Indian Tamils, 730 Sri Lanka Tamils, 48 Malays, 35 Burghers.

Population, 2001 (census), 18,797,257 (in some areas experiencing civil war estimates were used and combined with actual totals for other districts); density, 286 per sq. km. In 2005, 84·9% of the population lived in rural areas.

The UN gives an estimated population for 2010 of 20·41m.

Between the mid-1980s and the mid-1990s approximately 0·3m. Tamils left the country, one-third as refugees to India and two-thirds to seek political asylum in the West.

Colombo (the largest city) had 647,100 inhabitants in 2001. Other major towns and their populations (2001 census) are: Dehiwela-Mt Lavinia, 210,546; Moratuwa, 177,563; Jaffna, 145,600 (estimate); Negombo, 121,701; Sri Jayewardenepura Kotte (now the administrative and legislative capital), 116,366; Kandy, 109,343; Kalmunai, 94,579; Galle, 90,270.

Sinhala and Tamil are the official languages; English is in use.

SOCIAL STATISTICS

Statistics for 2008 (provisional): births, 379,912; deaths, 118,279. 2008 rates per 1,000 population (provisional): birth, 18·8; death, 5·8; infant mortality rate, 2005 (per 1,000 live births), 12. Life expectancy, 2007, 77·9 years for females and 70·3 for males. Annual population growth rate, 2000–05, 0·3%. Fertility rate, 2004, 1·9 births per woman. Sri Lanka has the third oldest population in Asia, after Japan and Singapore, thanks largely to relatively good health and a low fertility rate.

CLIMATE

Sri Lanka, which has an equatorial climate, is affected by the North-east Monsoon (Dec. to Feb.), the South-west Monsoon (May to July) and two inter-monsoons (March to April and Aug. to Nov.). Rainfall is heaviest in the southwest highlands while the northwest and southeast are relatively dry. Colombo, Jan. 79·9°F (26·6°C), July 81·7°F (27·6°C). Annual rainfall 95·4" (2,424 mm). Trincomalee, Jan. 78·8°F (26°C), July 86·2°F (30·1°C). Annual rainfall 62·2" (1,580 mm). Kandy, Jan. 73·9°F (23·3°C), July 76·1°F (24·5°C). Annual rainfall 72·4" (1,840 mm). Nuwara Eliya, Jan. 58·5°F (14·7°C), July 60·3°F (15·7°C). Annual rainfall 75" (1,905 mm).

On 26 Dec. 2004 an undersea earthquake centred off the Indonesian island of Sumatra caused a huge tsunami that flooded large areas along the southern and eastern coasts of Sri Lanka resulting in 35,000 deaths. In total there were more than 225,000 deaths in 14 countries.

CONSTITUTION AND GOVERNMENT

A new constitution for the Democratic Socialist Republic of Sri Lanka was promulgated on 7 Sept. 1978.

The Executive *President* is directly elected for a six-year term renewable once.

Parliament consists of one chamber, composed of 225 members (196 elected and 29 from the National List). Election is by proportional representation by universal suffrage at 18 years. The term of Parliament is six years. The Prime Minister and other Ministers, who must be members of Parliament, are appointed by the President.

National Anthem

'Sri Lanka Matha, Apa Sri Lanka' ('Mother Sri Lanka, thee Sri Lanka'); words and tune by A. Samarakone. There is a Tamil version, 'Sri Lanka thaaya, nam Sri Lanka'; words anonymous.

GOVERNMENT CHRONOLOGY

(UNP = United National Party; SLMP = Sri Lanka People's Party; SLFP = Sri Lanka Freedom Party; n/p = non-party)

Presidents since 1972.

1972–78	n/p	William Gopallawa
1978–89	UNP	Junius Richard Jayewardene
1989–93	UNP	Ranasinghe Premadasa
1993–94	UNP	Dingiri Banda Wijetunge
1994–2005	SLMP/SLFP	Chandrika Bandaranaike Kumaratunga
2005–	SLFP	Mahinda Rajapaksa

Prime Ministers since 1948.

1948–52	UNP	Don Stephen Senanayake
1952–53	UNP	Dudley Shelton Senanayake
1953–56	UNP	John Lionel Kotalawela
1956–59	SLFP	Solomon Ridgeway Dias Bandaranaike
1959–60	SLFP	Vijayananda Dahanayake
1960	UNP	Dudley Shelton Senanayake
1960–65	SLFP	Sirimavo Ratwatte Dias Bandaranaike
1965–70	UNP	Dudley Shelton Senanayake
1970–77	SLFP	Sirimavo Ratwatte Dias Bandaranaike
1977–78	UNP	Junius Richard Jayewardene
1978–89	UNP	Ranasinghe Premadasa
1989–93	UNP	Dingiri Banda Wijetunge
1993–94	UNP	Ranil Wickremasinghe
1994	SLMP/SLFP	Chandrika Bandaranaike Kumaratunga
1994–2000	SLFP	Sirimavo Ratwatte Dias Bandaranaike
2000–01	SLFP	Ratnasiri Wickremanayake
2001–04	UNP	Ranil Wickremesinghe
2004–05	SLFP	Mahinda Rajapaksa
2005–10	SLFP	Ratnasiri Wickremanayake
2010–	SLFP	Dissanayake Mudiyansalage Jayaratne

RECENT ELECTIONS

Presidential elections were held on 26 Jan. 2010. Incumbent President Mahinda Rajapaksa of the United People's Freedom Alliance (made up of several parties including the Sri Lanka Freedom Party) was re-elected with 57·9% of the vote, ahead of Sarath Fonseka, a former head of the army with 40·2%. There were 20 other candidates. Turnout was 74·5%.

At the parliamentary election of 8 and 20 April 2010 the United People's Freedom Alliance gained 144 seats with 60·3% of the vote; the United National Front (led by the Democratic People's Front) 60 with 29·3%; the Tamil National Alliance 14 with 2·9%; and the Democratic National Alliance 7 with 5·5%. Other parties received less than 1% of votes cast. Turnout was 61·3%.

CURRENT ADMINISTRATION

In April 2010 the cabinet comprised:

President and Minister of Defence, Finance and Planning, Ports and Aviation, and Highways: Mahinda Rajapaksa; b. 1945 (Sri Lanka Freedom Party; sworn in 19 Nov. 2005 and re-elected in Jan. 2010).

Prime Minister and Minister of Buddha Sasana and Religious Affairs: D. M. Jayaratne; b. 1931 (Sri Lanka Freedom Party; sworn in 21 April 2010).

Minister of Agriculture: Mahinda Yapa Abeywardena. *Child Development and Women's Affairs:* Tissa Karaliyadde. *Construction, Engineering Services, Housing and Common Amenities:* Wimal Weerawansa. *Co-operatives and Internal Trade:* Johnston Fernando. *Disaster Management:* A. H. M. Fowzie. *Economic Development:* Basil Rajapaksa. *Education:* Bandula Gunawardena. *Environment:* Anura Priyadarshana Yapa. *External Affairs:* G. L. Peiris. *Fisheries:* Rajitha Senaratne. *Health:* Maithripala Sirisena. *Indigenous Medicine:* Piyasena Gamage. *Industry and Commerce:* Rishad Bathiyutheen. *Irrigation and Water Resources Management:* Nimal Siripala de Silva. *Justice:* Athauda Seneviratne. *Labour Relations and Productivity Improvement:* Gamini Lokuge. *Land and Land Development:* Janaka Bandara Tennekoon. *Local Government and Provincial Councils:* A. L. M. Athaullah. *National Heritage and Cultural Affairs:* Pavithra Wanniarachchi. *National Languages and Social Integration:* S. B. Navinne. *Parliamentary Affairs:* Sumedha Jayasena. *Petroleum Industries:* Susil Premajayantha. *Plantations:* Mahinda Samarasinghe. *Post and Telecommunication:* Jeewan Kumaranatunga. *Power and Energy:* Champika Ranawaka. *Public Administration and Home Affairs:* John Seneviratne. *Public Management Reforms:* Ratnasiri Wickremanayake. *Rehabilitation and Prison Reforms:* D. E. W. Gunasekera. *Resettlement:* Milroy Fernando. *Social Services:* Felix Perera. *Sports:* C. B. Rathnayake. *State Resources and Enterprise Development:* P. Dayaratne. *Traditional Industries and Small Enterprise Development:* Douglas Devananda. *Transport:* Kumara Welgama. *Water Supply and Drainage:* Dinesh Gunawardena. *Youth Affairs:* Dullas Alahaperuma.

Government Website: http://www.priu.gov.lk

CURRENT LEADERS

Mahinda Rajapaksa

Position

President

Introduction

Mahinda Rajapaksa succeeded Chandrika Kumaratunga as the executive president of Sri Lanka in Nov. 2005. A human rights lawyer and former prime minister, he rejected outright the demands of the Liberation Tigers of Tamil Eelam (LTTE) for an ethnic homeland and sought to crush the Tamil rebellion through military force. He achieved this objective by May 2009 and was re-elected president in Jan. 2010.

Early Life

Mahinda Rajapaksa was born on 18 Nov. 1945 in Weeraketiya in the southern district of Hambantota. He was educated at Richmond College, Galle, followed by Nalanda and Thurston Colleges in Colombo. While studying law at Vidyodaya University he joined the centre-left Sri Lanka Freedom Party (SLFP) and in 1970 was elected as the party's parliamentary representative for Beliatta, Hambantota (a seat held by his father for the SLFP from 1948–65). Having graduated in 1974, Rajapaksa practised as a lawyer specializing in labour law and human rights and received plaudits for his work on behalf of the underprivileged.

Rajapaksa lost his parliamentary seat in the landslide defeat of the SLFP to the United National Party (UNP) in the general election of 1977. The UNP administration liberalized the economy and reduced unemployment but was unable to stem violence. The parliamentary elections in Feb. 1989 (in which Rajapaksa regained his seat) were preceded by terror campaigns by both the LTTE and the banned People's Liberation Front (JVP) in the south. Rajapaksa joined Mangala Samaraweera's 'Mother's Front', a group representing the mothers of those who 'disappeared' in the violence of 1988–89. He served on the central committee of the SLFP from the early 1990s and became an increasingly vocal critic of President Ranasinghe Premadasa's UNP government.

Following narrow victory for the SLFP (as part of the People's Alliance coalition) in the parliamentary elections of 1994, Rajapaksa was appointed minister for labour by President Chandrika Kumaratunga. His attempts to reform labour laws and introduce a workers' charter met with resistance. He was moved to the fisheries ministry, establishing a coastal guard service and a university of oceanography. Following defeat for the People's Alliance in elections in Dec. 2001, Rajapaksa became leader of the parliamentary opposition. He forged alliances including, controversially, the Sinhala-nationalist JVP to form the United People's Freedom Alliance (UPFA). The Alliance won the parliamentary elections that followed Kumaratunga's sacking of the UNP government in Feb. 2004. Kumaratunga then appointed Rajapaksa as prime minister and he was sworn in on 6 April 2004.

Career in Office

Without a commanding parliamentary majority, Rajapaksa's UPFA government struggled to implement its promises to halt privatization, increase wages and create 125,000 jobs within three months. It was also criticized for its handling of the aftermath of the Indian Ocean tsunami in Dec. 2004, which killed 31,000 Sri Lankans and displaced nearly half a million.

Rajapaksa was chosen as the SLFP's presidential candidate for the election of Nov. 2005 and narrowly defeated the UNP's Ranil Wickremesinghe. He vowed a tougher approach to dealings with the LTTE, arguing that the 2002 ceasefire agreement had not brought peace, and appointed Ratnasiri Wickremanayake as prime minister. The security situation deteriorated seriously in 2006, and Rajapaksa reiterated his determination to defeat rebel violence as he revived draconian anti-terrorism legislation that had been suspended in 2002. Further escalation in 2007 of LTTE attacks and retaliatory offensives by state forces on LTTE positions in the north and east culminated in the government's formal abrogation of the 2002 ceasefire in Jan. 2008.

Rajapaksa intensified the military campaign against strategic LTTE positions through 2008, making significant territorial advances. In Jan. 2009 government troops captured Kilinochchi, the rebels' administrative headquarters, and also Elephant Pass linking the Jaffna peninsula with the mainland. Despite international concern over the safety of Tamil civilians trapped in the remaining LTTE-controlled enclave, government forces maintained their offensive (reportedly entering the last rebel-held town in Feb.) until Rajapaksa delivered a victory speech to parliament in May.

Meanwhile, the global financial crisis had a significant negative impact on the economy and in July 2009 the IMF approved a stand-by arrangement equivalent to US$2·6bn. to support recovery and help rebuild after the civil war.

A bitter breakdown in the relationship between Rajapaksa and his army chief Sarath Fonseka led the latter to resign and challenge the president in the elections in Jan. 2010. Capitalizing on his post-war popularity among the Sinhalese majority population, Rajapaksa was re-elected with almost 58% of the vote, although the result was contested by Fonseka.

Dissanayake Mudiyanselage Jayaratne

Position

Prime Minister

Introduction

On 21 April 2010 D. M. Jayaratne was sworn in as prime minister, a largely ceremonial position. He also serves as minister for Buddha Sasana and religious affairs. One of the country's longest serving politicians, he has headed various government ministries and is the senior member of the Sri Lanka Freedom Party (SLFP).

Early Life

D. M. Jayaratne was born on 7 June 1931 in the Central Province hill town of Gampola. The fifth child of nine, he was schooled at Doluwa Maha Vidyalaya (Gampola), Zahira College (Kandy), and Mahatma Gandhi College (Kandy). In 1951 he became a teacher at Doluwa Maha Vidyalaya and from 1960–62 he was postmaster of Gampola.

By 1950 he was politically active, working in the grassroots community centre networks where he rose through the ranks, acting as secretary in the Kandy council and then chair of the island-wide network. In 1951 he joined the newly formed SLFP and in the 1970 general election he was elected to parliament as the representative for Gampola. In 1977 the SLFP suffered a landslide defeat and Jayaratne lost his seat. In 1989 he was elected MP for Kandy and appointed minister for agriculture, food and co-operatives.

Jayaratne was re-elected in 2000 and was reappointed to the agriculture, food and co-operatives portfolio. In 2004 he became minister of post and telecommunication and in 2007 took over at the ministry of plantation industries. He also served as chairman of the Asia-Pacific region of the Food and Agriculture Organization in 2001.

Career in Office

In April 2010 Jayaratne was appointed premier by President Mahinda Rajapaksa, heading up a seven-party United Popular Front coalition. With a coalition majority in parliament and backed by the popular president, Jayaratne began his tenure in a strong position. While his role is largely ceremonial, he is responsible for leading government business in parliament.

One of his key challenges is to oversee proposed constitutional reform, with Amnesty International waging a campaign for the government to lift 30 years of emergency powers and anti-terrorism laws. These, alongside reported human rights abuses and weak labour laws, have affected the country's international trading relations, particularly with the EU.

DEFENCE

Defence expenditure in 2006 totalled US$943m. (US$46 per capita), representing 3·4% of GDP. In 2008 Sri Lanka increased its military expenditure in real terms by 7·7%, the highest rate in South Asia.

As at Oct. 2009, 1,047 personnel (959 troops, 75 police and 13 military observers) were deployed in UN peacekeeping operations.

Army

Strength (2007), 117,900 (including 39,900 recalled reservists). In addition there were 1,100 reserves. Paramilitary forces consist of the Ministry of Defence Police (61,600, including 1,000 women and a 3,000-strong anti-guerrilla force), the Home Guard (13,000) and the National Guard (some 15,000).

Navy

The main naval base is at Trincomalee. Personnel in 2007 numbered 15,000, including a reserve of about 2,400.

Air Force

Main Air Force bases are at Katunayake, Minneriya, Ratmalana, Vavuniya and China Bay, Trincomalee. Total strength (2007) 18,000 with 22 combat capable aircraft and 13 attack helicopters. Main attack aircraft types included *Kfirs*, F-7s and MiG-27s.

INTERNATIONAL RELATIONS

Sri Lanka is a member of the UN, World Bank, IMF and several other UN specialized agencies, WTO, Commonwealth, IOM, Asian Development Bank, Colombo Plan and SAARC.

ECONOMY

Agriculture accounted for 11·3% of GDP in 2006, industry 30·6% and services 58·0%.

The conflict with the minority separatists, the Tamil Tigers, which lasted 26 years, is estimated to have cost the country between 1–1·5% in growth per year.

Overview

Three decades of civil war have disrupted inter-regional commerce, damaged infrastructure and weakened public finances. Yet the economy has grown on average by just under 5% per year since 1980, generating higher per capita income than in neighbouring India.

In 2001 the economy contracted for the first time since independence as a result of the global slowdown, power shortages, and security and budgetary problems. With the start of the peace process in Feb. 2002, the government embarked on reforms to revive the economy, including exchange rate and trade liberalization, privatization and the introduction of a VAT system. In May 2009 the quarter-century civil war ended, boosting economic prospects and providing renewed opportunity for reform.

The main sources of growth are domestic consumption, tourism and textile and garment exports. Growth has averaged 6·5% since 2002 and the poverty rate has fallen significantly, although the economy remains severely strained owing to the global slowdown and the costs of post-conflict relief and reconstruction. In July 2009 the IMF approved a US$2·6bn. loan to help the economy weather the effects of the financial crisis and to rebuild war-torn regions. The Asian Development Bank predicted economic activity would pick up in 2010, reaching 6% as the world economy recovered and international demand rebounded.

Currency

The unit of currency is the *Sri Lankan rupee* (LKR) of 100 *cents*. Foreign exchange reserves were US$2,236m. and gold reserves 167,000 troy oz in June 2005. Inflation was 10·0% in 2006, rising to 15·8% in 2007 and further still to 22·6% in 2008. Total money supply in March 2005 was Rs 208,095m.

Budget

In 2004 budgetary central government revenue was Rs 320,047m. (Rs 284,216m. in 2003) and expenditure Rs 433,036m. (Rs 373,202m. in 2003).

Principal sources of revenue in 2004 were: taxes on goods and services, Rs 191,525m.; taxes on international trade and transactions, Rs 48,655m.; taxes on income, profits and capital gains, Rs 41,372m. Main items of expenditure by economic type in 2004 were: interest, Rs 119,782m.; compensation of employees, Rs 106,187m.; social benefits, Rs 81,643m.

VAT is 12%.

Performance

Real GDP growth was 7·7% in 2006, 6·8% in 2007 and 6·0% in 2008. Total GDP in 2008 was US$40·7bn.

Banking and Finance

The Central Bank of Sri Lanka is the bank of issue (*Governor*, Ajith Nivard Cabraal). There are 23 commercial banks with a total asset base of Rs 1,774bn. This includes two state-owned banks, the Bank of Ceylon and People's Bank, which account for about 40% of assets, and 12 foreign banks. There are 14 specialized banks including the National Savings Bank, which in total have an asset base of Rs 356bn. In the period 2005–08 Sri Lanka attracted US$2,107m. in foreign direct investment, including a record US$752m. in 2008.

There is a stock exchange in Colombo.

ENERGY AND NATURAL RESOURCES

Environment

Carbon dioxide emissions from the consumption and flaring of fossil fuels in 2008 were the equivalent of 0·6 tonnes per capita.

Electricity

Installed capacity (2004), 3·1m. kW. Production, 2004, 8·1bn. kWh (36% hydro-electric). Consumption per capita in 2004 was 420 kWh.

Oil and Gas

In June 2007 construction began of a US$1bn. oil refinery as part of the Hambantota port development, with China financing 85% of the total cost.

Water

The Mahaweli Authority scheme, which began in 1978, had led to the irrigation of 354,000 ha. of land by 2001.

Minerals

Gems are among the chief minerals mined and exported (particularly sapphires). Output of principal products: sapphires (2003), 773,547 carats; phosphate rock (2003), 41,357 tonnes; quartzite (2004), 18,139 tonnes; ilmenite (2004), 8,115 tonnes. Salt extraction is the oldest industry; the method is the solar evaporation of sea-water. Production, 2003, 78,713 tonnes.

Agriculture

There were approximately 970,000 ha. of arable land and 950,000 ha. of permanent crops in 2007. In 2006, 32·2% of the economically active population were engaged in agriculture. Main crops in 2003 (in 1,000 tonnes): rice, 3,071; coconuts, 1,850; sugarcane, 956; bananas and plantains, 610; tea, 303; cassava, 228; pumpkins and squash, 170. Sri Lanka ranks third in the world for tea production, behind India and China.

Livestock in 2003: 1,139,000 cattle; 635,000 buffaloes; 490,000 goats; 10m. chickens.

Forestry

The area under forests in 2005 was 1·93m. ha., or 29·9% of the land area. In 2007, 6·13m. cu. metres of roundwood were cut.

Fisheries

Total catch in 2005 was 161,960 tonnes, of which 81% was from marine waters and 19% from inland waters.

INDUSTRY

The main industries are the processing of rubber, tea, coconuts and other agricultural commodities, tobacco, textiles, clothing and leather goods, chemicals, plastics, cement and petroleum refining. Industrial production rose by 8·1% in 2006.

Labour

The labour force in 2003 totalled 7,653,716 (67% males). In 2003 the economically active workforce numbered 7,012,755, of which 2,384,397 worked in agriculture, forestry and fishing, 1,156,682 in manufacturing and 867,131 in wholesale and retail trade, repair of motor vehicles and household goods. In 2003 the unemployment rate was 8·4%.

Trade Unions

In 2002 there were 1,513 functioning trade unions with 640,673 members.

INTERNATIONAL TRADE

Foreign debt in 2005 was US$11,444m.

Imports and Exports

Trade in US$1m.:

	2002	2003	2004	2005	2006
Imports f.o.b.	5,495	6,005	7,200	7,977	9,228
Exports f.o.b.	4,699	5,133	5,757	6,347	6,883

Principal imports in 2004: machinery and transport equipment, 20·4%; textile yarn, fabrics and finished articles,

19·5%; petroleum and petroleum products, 13·6%; food and livestock, 10·5%. Principal exports in 2004: clothing and apparel, 50·6%; tea, 13·4%; machinery and transport equipment, 6·2%; pearls and semi-precious stones, 4·0%.

In 2004 the leading import suppliers were India (17·3%), Singapore (9·3%), Hong Kong (7·9%), Iran (5·9%) and China (5·8%). The leading export markets in 2004 were the USA (34·0%), UK (14·2%), India (7·0%), Germany (5·0%) and Belgium (3·6%).

COMMUNICATIONS

Roads

In 2006 the road network totalled 91,907 km in length, including 11,716 km of national roads and 15,532 km of secondary roads. Number of motor vehicles, 2006, 2,269,575, comprising 338,608 passenger cars, 77,233 buses and coaches, 431,594 trucks and vans and 1,422,140 motorcycles and mopeds. There were 2,239 fatalities in road accidents in 2006.

Rail

In 2003 there were 1,449 km of railway (1,676 mm gauge). Passenger-km travelled in 2003 came to 4,258m. and freight tonne-km to 128m.

Civil Aviation

There is an international airport at Colombo (Bandaranaike). The national carrier is SriLankan Airlines, which has been part-owned and managed by Emirates since 1998. Mihin Lanka, a low-cost airline fully owned and funded by the government, was launched in 2007. In 2006 SriLankan Airlines carried 2,900,068 passengers (all on international flights). Colombo handled 4,740,187 passengers and 169,038 tonnes of freight in 2006.

Shipping

In 2002 the merchant marine totalled 81,000 GRT, including oil tankers 6,000 GRT. Colombo is a modern container port; Trincomalee and Galle are natural harbours. In 2003, 4,032 merchant vessels totalling 88m. GRT entered the ports: 19,959,000 tonnes of goods were unloaded and 10,541,000 tonnes loaded. In 2002 vessels totalling 39,336,000 NRT entered ports.

Telecommunications

In 2008 there were 3,446,400 main (fixed) telephone lines; mobile phone subscribers numbered 11,082,500 in 2008 (55·2 per 100 persons). There were 734,000 PCs in use in 2005 and 1,163,500 internet users in 2008.

Postal Services

In 2003 there were 4,680 post offices, or one for every 4,070 persons.

SOCIAL INSTITUTIONS

Justice

The systems of law which are valid are Roman-Dutch, English, Tesawalamai, Islamic and Kandyan.

Kandyan law applies in matters relating to inheritance, matrimonial rights and donations; Tesawalamai law applies in Jaffna as above and in sales of land. Islamic law is applied to all Muslims in respect of succession, donations, marriage, divorce and maintenance. These customary and religious laws have been modified by local enactments.

The courts of original jurisdiction are the High Court, Provincial Courts, District Courts, Magistrates' Courts and Primary Courts. District Courts have unlimited civil jurisdiction. The Magistrates' Courts exercise criminal jurisdiction. The Primary Courts exercise civil jurisdiction in petty disputes and criminal jurisdiction in respect of certain offences.

The Constitution of 1978 provided for the establishment of two superior courts, the Supreme Court and the Court of Appeal.

The Supreme Court is the highest and final superior court of record and exercises jurisdiction in respect of constitutional matters, jurisdiction for the protection of fundamental rights, final appellate jurisdiction in election petitions and jurisdiction in respect of any breach of the privileges of Parliament. The Court of Appeal has appellate jurisdiction to correct all errors in fact or law committed by any court, tribunal or institution.

The population in penal institutions in July 2007 was 25,537 (121 per 100,000 of national population). The death penalty, last used in 1976, was reactivated in Nov. 2004 after a 28-year moratorium.

Police

The strength of the police service in 2003 was 39,242.

Education

Education is free and is compulsory from age five to 14 years. The literacy rate in 2001 was 91·1% (male, 92·6%; female, 89·7%). Sri Lanka's rate compares very favourably with the rates of 58·0% in India and 44·0% in Pakistan.

In 2008 there were 9,335 schools with primary classes and 69,499 primary teachers for 1,626,285 pupils. The number of pupils in secondary classes in 2008 was 1,897,350, with 98,582 teachers. There were 401,666 students and 21,715 teachers in advanced level classes in 2008. There are 16 universities, including the Open University (distance) and the Buddhist and Pali University. In 2008, excluding at the two aforementioned universities, there were 66,675 undergraduates enrolled.

Health

In 2005 there were 609 hospitals and 413 central dispensaries. The hospitals had 60,237 beds. There were 9,290 physicians and 16,517 nurses in 2002; and 954 dentists, 907 pharmacists and 7,267 midwives in 2005. Total state budget expenditure on health, 2005, Rs 29,805m.

Welfare

To qualify for an old-age pension an individual must be above the age of 55 for men or 50 for women. However, a grant is payable at any age if the person is emigrating permanently. Old-age benefits are made up of a lump sum equal to total employee and employer contributions, plus interest.

The family allowances programme is being implemented in stages. Families earning below Rs1,000 a month are entitled to Rs500 a month benefit.

RELIGION

In 2001 the population was 71% Buddhist, 12% Hindu, 9% Muslim and 7% Roman Catholic.

CULTURE

World Heritage Sites

Sri Lanka has seven sites on the UNESCO World Heritage List: Sacred City of Anuradhapura (inscribed on the list in 1982); Ancient City of Polonnaruwa (1982); Ancient City of Sigiriya (1982); Sinharaja Forest Reserve (1988); Sacred City of Kandy (1988); Old Town of Galle and its Fortifications (1988); and the Golden Temple of Dambulla (1991).

Broadcasting

State-owned radio and television networks are provided by the Sri Lanka Broadcasting Corporation and Sri Lanka Rupavahini Corporation respectively. There are also a number of private radio and TV stations. In 2007 there were 14 television channels and 32 radio stations in total. There were 1·75m. TV-equipped households (colour by PAL) in 2005.

Press

In 2002 there were 13 daily newspapers with a combined circulation of 493,000, at a rate of 26 per 1,000 inhabitants.

Tourism

In 2004 there were 566,000 foreign tourists, bringing revenue of US$729m.

Festivals

Sri Lanka has an array of festivals principally centred on the Buddhist, Hindu, Muslim and Christian cultures. These include: Buddhist full moon celebrations (Poya Day), with the main festivals occurring in Jan., May, June, July/Aug. and Dec.; Deepavali (the Hindu Festival of Lights, held in Oct./Nov.); Milad-un-Nabi (Dec.); and Christmas. New Year is also widely celebrated by both the Sinhalese and Tamil ethnic groups.

DIPLOMATIC REPRESENTATIVES

Of Sri Lanka in the United Kingdom (13 Hyde Park Gdns, London, W2 2LU)
High Commissioner: Nihal Jayasinghe.

Of the United Kingdom in Sri Lanka (389 Bauddhaloka Mawatha, Colombo 7)
High Commissioner: Dr Peter Hayes.

Of Sri Lanka in the USA (2148 Wyoming Ave., NW, Washington, D.C., 20008)
Ambassador: Jaliya Wickramasuriya.

Of the USA in Sri Lanka (210 Galle Rd, Kollupitiya, Colombo 3)
Ambassador: Patricia A. Butenis.

Of Sri Lanka to the United Nations
Ambassador: Palitha Kohona.

Of Sri Lanka to the European Union
Ambassador: Ravinatha Pandukabhaya Aryasinha.

FURTHER READING

De Silva, C. R., *Sri Lanka: a History.* 1991

McGowan, W., *Only Man is Vile: the Tragedy of Sri Lanka.* 1992

Nira, Wickramasinghe, *Sri Lanka in the Modern Age: A History of Contested Identity.* 2005

Winslow, Deborah and Woost, Michael D., *Economy, Culture and Civil War in Sri Lanka.* 2004

National Statistical Office: Department of Census and Statistics, POB 563, Colombo 7.
Website: http://www.statistics.gov.lk

SUDAN

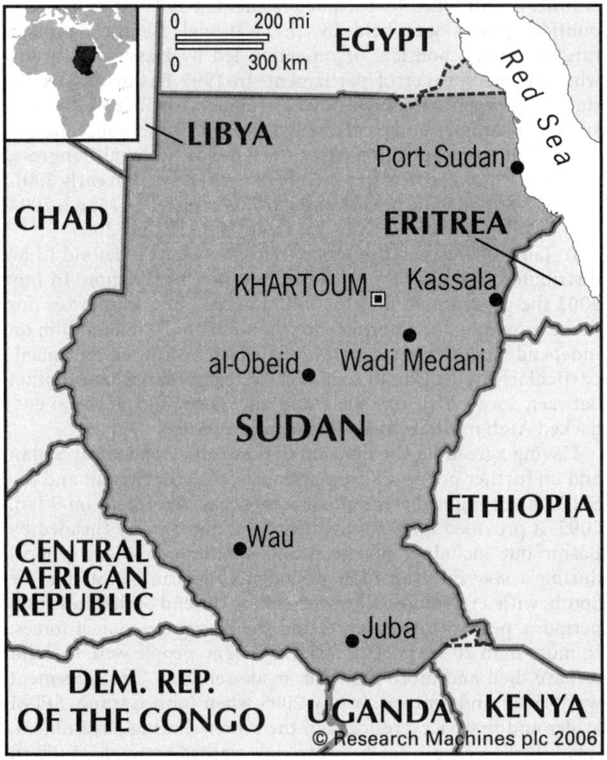

Jamhuryat es-Sudan
(The Republic of The Sudan)

Capital: Khartoum

Population estimate, 2010: 43·19m.

GDP per capita, 2007: (PPP$) 2,086

HDI/world rank: 0·531/150

KEY HISTORICAL EVENTS

The earliest inhabitants of Sudan were Mesolithic hunter-gatherers, who lived and travelled in the region around Khartoum from as early as 30,000 BC. They had domesticated animals by 4000 BC. Cultural influences from Egypt rippled through to Nubia in north-eastern Sudan from around 3000 BC as Egypt's first dynasty moved south along the river Nile in search of construction materials and slaves. By 2000 BC it had reached as far south as the river Nile's fourth cataract, more than 700 km beyond Aswan. Egyptian-controlled Nubia was divided into Wawat in the north—centred on Aswan—and Kush in the south—based at Nepata (modern Marawi). When Egypt's power waned in the 11th century BC (the end of the New Kingdom) Kush, with its Egyptian and African influences, mineral resources and its position on trade routes linking the Nile to the Red Sea, became a powerful kingdom. At its height, under King Piantkhi in 750 BC, the whole of Egypt was brought under Kushite control. However, the invasion of Egypt by Assyrian forces in 671 BC forced a retreat to Nepata. From there, the kingdom of Kush continued to exert control over the middle Nile for much of the next millennium, developing a distinctive culture and language. By AD 200 Kush was in decline and was finally overthrown in 350 by the king of Aksum from the Ethiopian highlands.

Sudan was brought back into contact with the Mediterranean world in the 6th century by the arrival of Coptic Christian missionaries. They travelled south along the Nile and established churches in the three middle-Nile kingdoms that had superseded Kush: Nobatia in the north and Maqurrah and 'Alwah in the south, near modern Khartoum. Egypt was invaded by Arabs in 639 and came under Muslim rule. Raiding parties moved up the Nile and absorbed Nobatia. The king of Maqurrah engineered a truce at Dunqulah with an Arab military expedition, commanded by 'Abd Allah ibn Sa'd, preserving the kingdom for a further six centuries.

In 1250 Egypt came under the control of Mamluk sultans, supported by a caste of warrior slaves. They pushed south into Nubia, bringing chaos and devastation to Maqurrah and opening it up to waves of Arab immigrants, particularly the Juhaynah people. They intermarried with the Nubians and introduced Arab Muslim culture. Alwah, to the south, retained its Christian traditions until 1500 when, weakened by Bedouin raids, it collapsed under an Arab confederation led by Abd Allah Jamma. The Arabs themselves came under attack in the region around modern Khartoum from warriors of the Funj dynasty, a kingdom that had its origins in the Blue Nile's upper reaches. The Funj established their supremacy in the Al Jazirah region by 1607 and expanded northwards under Badi II Abu Daqn later in the 17th century. It was a relatively peaceful and stable period and the teaching of Islam flourished in schools and mosques along the Nile. The Funj themselves adopted Islam but retained a number of traditional African customs and beliefs.

Egyptian Ascendancy

In 1820 Muhammad Ali, viceroy of Egypt under the Ottoman Turks, sent an army southward to conquer Sudan. The Funj kingdom collapsed and within a year Ali's forces had taken control of the Nile valley from Nubia to the Ethiopian foothills. There was initial resistance but the appointment of Ali Kurshid Agha as governor general in 1826 led to the establishment of Khartoum as the administrative capital, improvements to agriculture and the development of the trade in slaves and ivory. Ismail Pasha became viceroy of Egypt in 1863 and announced a grand scheme to modernize and control the entire Nile river system from the Mediterranean to the Great Lakes of East Africa. Ismail needed the financial help of the European powers who, in return, demanded an end to the slave trade. The British had a particular interest in Egyptian affairs following the opening of the Suez Canal in 1869. Ismail commissioned the Englishmen Samuel Baker and, later, Charles Gordon to establish Egyptian control in southern Sudan and Central Africa and to crush slavery. The controllers of the slave trade were powerful and proved hard to defeat, especially away from the Nile. In addition, there was unease among Muslims over the crusading style of the English anti-slavers. In 1879, amid rising discontent, Ismail's financial backing collapsed and his grand project was abandoned. Ismail was exiled and Gordon resigned.

Rise of the Mahdi

The power vacuum was filled by Muhammad Ahmad in 1881; he declared himself the Mahdi ('divinely guided one') and led a movement that sought an end to Egyptian (Ottoman) influence and a return to the simplicity of early Islam. By 1882 the Mahdi had garnered the support of a least 30,000 armed followers (the Ansar). They captured the town of Al Abayyid, which led to a British order for the evacuation of Egyptians and foreigners from Khartoum, where the military commander was Charles Gordon.

The campaign failed disastrously: Gordon was killed by Mahdists in early 1885. The Mahdi died in the same year, but his successor, the Khalifa Abdallahi, continued to build up the Mahdist state.

In the 1890s the European powers were vying for control of Africa and the British made plans for the control of the Nile valley and the reconquest of Sudan. In a series of attacks between 1896 and 1898, an Anglo-Egyptian force of 25,800 men under Herbert (later Lord) Kitchener destroyed the Mahdist state. Anglo-Egyptian agreements in 1899 established a joint (condominium) government of Sudan: in theory it was administered by a governor-general, appointed by Egypt with the consent of Great Britain. In practice the governor-general, Sir Reginald Wingate, controlled the condominium government from Khartoum. Sudanese resentment over colonial rule erupted in various Mahdist uprisings but with insufficient support to pose a threat to the government. In 1911 the Sudan Plantations syndicate launched a scheme to irrigate the Al Jazirah region and establish a large cotton plantation for Britain's textile industry. The cotton crop became the mainstay of the economy.

Sudanese nationalist sentiment grew in the early 1920s when 'Ali 'Abd al Latif, inspired by Egyptian nationalists, founded the White Flag League. When Governor-General Sir Lee Stack was assassinated in 1924 in Cairo (capital of newly-independent Egypt), the British ordered all Egyptian troops out of Sudan. British rule continued unchallenged until after the Second World War. The broad policy was to treat Sudan as two countries with the aim of integrating the southern provinces with their largely Christian and animist peoples with British East Africa. However, in 1948 a predominantly elective legislative assembly was convened for the whole territory. In the 1948 elections the Independence Front, which favoured the creation of an independent republic, gained a majority over the National Front, which aimed for union with Egypt.

Independence

Following the 1952 revolution in Egypt, Sudan became a parliamentary republic in 1956.

Sudan's democracy proved to be short-lived as the political parties became mired in internecine fighting. At the same time, a revolt raged in the south over Islamic domination. In 1958 Gen. Ibrahim Abboud led a military coup that ended the parliamentary system. In 1964, unable to improve Sudan's poor economic performance or to end the southern revolt, Abboud agreed to the re-establishment of civilian government. A coalition, headed by Muhammad Ahmad Mahjub, was weakened by factional disputes and little progress was made in solving the country's economic and social problems.

In 1969 Col. Muhammad Gaafur al-Nimeiry staged a successful coup. He banned all political parties and nationalized banks and numerous industries. The civil war was ended by an agreement between the government and the Southern Sudan Liberation Front signed in Addis Ababa in 1972. In the same year the Sudanese Socialist Union, the country's only political organization, elected a 'people's assembly' to draw up a new constitution, adopted in 1973. Nimeiry's regime was blamed for worsening economic conditions and came under Islamist attack for its support for Egypt's role in the Camp David Accords with Israel; in the late 1970s Nimeiry dismissed his cabinet and closed universities in an attempt to quell opposition.

Accelerating Violence

From the early 1980s political instability in southern Sudan worsened. Nimeiry responded by imposing Sharia law in 1983, inflaming a renewed civil war with the largely Christian and animist Sudan People's Liberation Movement (SPLM) led by John Garang. Having survived numerous earlier coup attempts, Nimeiry was overthrown in 1985. Following elections in 1986 a civilian government led by Sadiq al-Mahdi ruled until he was ousted three years later in a bloodless military coup. The new regime of Lieut.-Gen. Omar Ahmed al-Bashir strengthened ties with Libya, Iran, and Iraq, reinforced Islamic law, banned opposition parties and continued to pursue the war with the south against the backdrop of a stagnant economy and a catastrophic famine. Bashir officially became president in 1993 but significant political power was held by the National Islamic Front, a fundamentalist political organization led by Hassan al-Turabi, who became speaker of parliament. In 1999 Bashir declared a state of emergency during a power struggle with Turabi, who was eventually toppled and parliament dissolved. Turabi subsequently formed his own opposition party, the Popular National Congress, although he and other party members were arrested in early 2001. He was released in Oct. 2003, only to be rearrested in March 2004 over an alleged coup plot. He was freed again in June 2005.

In Jan. 2002 a ceasefire was declared to allow relief aid to be distributed in the drought-stricken south-central region. In July 2002 the government and the SPLM agreed to a framework for peace providing for autonomy for the south and a referendum on independence after six years. Nevertheless, hostilities continued, particularly in the Darfur region of western Sudan where conflict between local African rebels and the army and government-backed Arab militias intensified from early 2003.

Having agreed on the division of oil wealth in post-war Sudan and on further power-sharing protocols, the government and the SPLM finally signed a comprehensive peace agreement on 9 Jan. 2005. It provided for a government of national unity (headed by Bashir but including northern and southern political groups) during a six-year transition period; self-determination for the South, with a referendum on secession at the end of the transition period; a permanent ceasefire; and the disengagement of forces. In more than 20 years of civil war, over 2m. people were thought to have died and more than 4m. made refugees. The agreement was briefly undermined in July 2005 when John Garang, SPLM leader and first vice-president in the power-sharing government, was killed in an air crash, provoking clashes between southern Sudanese and northern Arabs in Khartoum. His SPLM deputy, Salva Kiir Mayardit, took over as first vice-president in Aug. The power-sharing government was formed officially in Sept. 2005 and a devolved government of southern Sudan was established in Oct.

Although the comprehensive peace agreement focused mainly on the north-south civil war, some of its provisions for power-sharing and decentralization are applicable to Darfur. However, despite ongoing peace talks and UN and other international intervention to stop the violence, the conflict has continued. The government and Arab militias have been accused of systematic abuses of human rights, crimes that the UN Security Council referred to the International Criminal Court in March 2005. The targeting of civilians in the conflict has resulted in up to 300,000 deaths and the displacement of some 2·7m. people since 2003.

TERRITORY AND POPULATION

Sudan is bounded in the north by Egypt, northeast by the Red Sea, east by Eritrea and Ethiopia, south by Kenya, Uganda and the Democratic Republic of the Congo, west by the Central African Republic and Chad, and northwest by Libya. Its area, including inland waters, is 2,505,810 sq. km, making it the largest country in Africa. In 1993 the census population was 25·6m. 2008 census population (provisional), 39,154,490, giving a density of 15·6 per sq. km. The United Nations population estimate for 2008 was 41,348,000. In 2005, 59·2% of the population were rural.

The UN gives an estimated population for 2010 of 43·19m.

The country is administratively divided into 25 states (with capitals): Al Qadarif (Al Qadarif), Blue Nile (Al Damazin), Central Equatoria (Juba), East Equatoria (Kapoita), Gezira (Wadi Medani), Jungoli (Bor), Kassala (Kassala), Khartoum (Khartoum), Lakes (Rumbek), North Bahr Al Ghazal (Awil), North Darfur (Al Fashir), North Kordufan (Al Obeid), Northern (Dongula), Red Sea (Port Sudan), River Nile (Al Damar), Sennar (Singa), South

Darfur (Nyala), South Kordufan (Kadugli), Unity (Bantio), Upper Nile (Malakal), Warap (Warap), West Bahr Al Ghazal (Wau), West Darfur (Geneina), West Equatoria (Yambio), White Nile (Rabak).

The capital, Khartoum, had a population of 2,628,000 in 1999. Other major cities, with 1993 populations, are Port Sudan (308,195), Kassala (234,622), Nyala (227,183), Al Obeid (229,425), Wadi Medani (211,362) and Al Qadarif (191,164).

The northern and central thirds of the country are populated by Arab and Nubian peoples, while the southern third is inhabited by Nilotic and Bantu peoples. Sudan has more internally displaced people (4m. in 2000) than any other country.

Arabic, one of two official languages, is spoken by 49% of inhabitants. English is also an official language.

SOCIAL STATISTICS

2004 estimates: births, 1,172,000; deaths, 391,000. Rates, 2004 estimates (per 1,000 population): birth, 33; death, 11. Infant mortality, 2005 (per 1,000 live births), 62. Expectation of life in 2007 was 59·4 years for females and 56·3 for males. Annual population growth rate, 2000–05, 2·6%. Fertility rate, 2004, 4·3 births per woman.

CLIMATE

Lying wholly within the tropics, the country has a continental climate and only the Red Sea coast experiences maritime influences. Temperatures are generally high for most of the year, with May and June the hottest months. Winters are virtually cloudless and night temperatures are consequently cool. Summer is the rainy season inland, with amounts increasing from north to south, but the northern areas are virtually a desert region. On the Red Sea coast, most rain falls in winter. Khartoum, Jan. 64°F (18·0°C), July 89°F (31·7°C). Annual rainfall 6" (157 mm). Juba, Jan. 83°F (28·3°C), July 78°F (25·6°C). Annual rainfall 39" (968 mm). Port Sudan, Jan. 74°F (23·3°C), July 94°F (34·4°C). Annual rainfall 4" (94 mm). Wadi Halfa, Jan. 50°F (10·0°C), July 90°F (32·2°C). Annual rainfall 0·1" (2·5 mm).

CONSTITUTION AND GOVERNMENT

The constitution was suspended after the 1989 coup and a 12-member Revolutionary Council then ruled. A 300-member Provisional National Assembly was appointed in Feb. 1992 as a transitional legislature pending elections. These were held in March 1996. On 26 May 1998 President Omar Hassan Ahmed al-Bashir approved a new constitution. Notably this lifted the ban on opposition political parties, although the government continued to monitor and control criticism until the constitution came legally into effect. The constitution was partially suspended in Dec. 1999.

In accordance with the peace deal agreed in Dec. 2004 to bring an end to the civil war and signed in Jan. 2005 there is a lower house, the 450-seat interim *National Assembly*, with members appointed by decree by the president, and an upper house, the *Council of States*, consisting of 50 members who are indirectly elected by state legislatures. The peace deal specified that 52% of National Assembly seats should go to the ruling National Congress Party, 28% to the former southern rebel Sudan People's Liberation Movement (the political wing of the Sudan People's Liberation Army), 14% to the northern opposition parties and 6% to their counterparts in the south. The agreement also allowed a referendum to be carried out in the south in 2011 to decide whether to become independent or maintain the unity of Sudan. A new interim power-sharing constitution was adopted on 6 July 2005 giving the south some autonomy and allowing former rebels to take up seats in the country's government.

National Anthem

'Nahnu Jundullah, Jundu Al-Watlan' ('We are the Army of God and of Our Land'); words by A. M. Salih, tune by A. Murjan.

GOVERNMENT CHRONOLOGY

(DUP = Democratic Unionist Party; NCP = National Congress party; NUP = National Unionist Party; SSU = Sudan Socialist Union; Umma = 'Community of the Believers' Party)

Heads of State since 1956.

Commission of Sovereignty
1956–58 Abd al-Fattah Mohammad al-Mughrabi; Mohammad Uthman ad-Dardiri; Ahmad Mohammad Yasin; Ahmad Mohammad Salih; Siricio Iro Wani

Chairman of the Supreme Council of the Armed Forces
1958–64 military Ibrahim Abboud

Commission of Sovereignty (I)
1964–65 Abd al-Halim Mohammad; Tijani al-Mahi; Mubarak Shaddad; Ibrahim Yusuf Sulayman; Luigi Adwok Bong Gicomeho

Commission of Sovereignty (II)
1965 Ismail al-Azhari; Abd Allah al-Fadil al-Mahdi, Luigi Adwok Bong Gicomeho; Abd al-Halim Mohammad; Khidr Hamad

Chairman of the Council of Sovereignty		
1965–69	NUP	Ismail al-Azhari
Chairmen of the Revolutionary Command Council		
1969–71	military, SSU	Gaafur Muhammad al-Nimeiry
1971	military, SSU	Abu Bakr an-Nur Uthman
1971	military, SSU	Gaafur Muhammad al-Nimeiry
President		
1971–85	military, SSU	Gaafur Muhammad al-Nimeiry
Chairman of the Transitional Military Council		
1985–86	military	Abd ar-Rahman Siwar ad-Dhahab
Chairman of the Council of Sovereignty		
1986–89	DUP	Ahmad Ali al-Mirghani
Chairman of the Revolutionary Command Council of National Salvation		
1989–93	military	Omar Hassan Ahmed al-Bashir
President		
1993–	military, NCP	Omar Hassan Ahmed al-Bashir

Heads of Government since 1952.

Chief Ministers		
1952–53	Umma	Abd ar-Rahman al-Mahdi
1954–56	NUP	Ismail al-Azhari
Prime Ministers		
1954–56	NUP	Ismail al-Azhari
1956–58	Umma	Abd Allah Khalil
1958–64	military (de facto)	Ibrahim Abboud
1964–65	n/p	Sirr al-Khatim al-Khalifah
1965–66	Umma	Muhammad Ahmad Mahgoub
1966–67	Umma	Sadiq al-Mahdi
1967–69	Umma	Muhammad Ahmad Mahgoub
1969	n/p	Babiker Awadalla
1969–76	military, SSU	Gaafur Muhammad al-Nimeiry
1976–77	SSU	Rashid Bakr
1977–85	military, SSU	Gaafur Muhammad al-Nimeiry
1985–86	n/p	al-Jazuli Dafallah
1986–89	Umma	Sadiq al-Mahdi

RECENT ELECTIONS

The first multi-party elections in 24 years were held from 11–15 April 2010 although they were boycotted by several of the main opposition parties. In presidential elections, incumbent Omar Hassan Ahmed al-Bashir was re-elected with 68·2% of votes cast. His nearest rival, Yasir Arman of the Sudan People's Liberation Movement (SPLM), gained 21·7% despite having withdrawn his candidature in late March owing to electoral irregularities and violence in Darfur. Abdullah Deng Nhial of the Popular Congress Party won 3·9% of the vote and Hatim Al-Sir of the Democratic Unionist Party 1·9%. There were eight other candidates who all gained less than 1% of the vote.

Results for the National Assembly elections held at the same time were not available at the time of going to press but preliminary results indicated that the ruling National Congress Party (NCP) took the majority of the 450 seats.

CURRENT ADMINISTRATION

President: Field Marshal Omar Hassan Ahmed al-Bashir; b. 1944 (NCP; appointed 1989, re-elected March 1996, Dec. 2000 and April 2010).

First Vice-President: Salva Kiir Mayardit. *Second Vice-President:* Ali Uthman Muhammad Taha.

In March 2010 the government comprised:

Minister of Agriculture and Forestry: Zubeir Beshir Taha. *Animal and Fish Resources:* Mohamed Ahmed al-Tahir Abu Kalabish. *Cabinet Affairs:* Kosti Manibe. *Culture, Youth and Sports:* Mohamed Yusif Abdella. *Defence:* Lieut.-Gen. Abdel Rahim Mohamed Hussein. *Education:* Hamid Mohamed Ibrahim. *Energy and Mining:* Al-Zobeir Ahmed Hassan. *Environment and Urban Development:* Dr Ahmed Babiker Nahar. *External Trade:* James Kock Rona. *Federal Government:* Abdalrahman Said. *Finance and National Economy:* Awad Ahmed al-Jaz. *Foreign Affairs:* Deng Alor Kuol. *Health:* Dr Tabitha Shokaya. *Higher Education and Scientific Research:* Peter Adock. *Humanitarian Affairs:* Harun Run Lual. *Industry:* Jalal Yousif el Degair. *Information and Communication:* Alzahawi Ibrahim Malik. *Interior:* Ibrahim Mahmoud Hamid. *International Co-operation:* Dr Altijani Salih Fidail. *Investment:* George Bioring Mayan. *Irrigation and Water Resources:* Kamal Ali Mohamed. *Justice:* Abdel Basit Salih Sebdarat. *Labour, Public Service and Development of Human Resources:* Alison Manani Magaya. *Parliamentary Affairs:* Joseph Okello. *Presidency:* Bakri Hassan Salih. *Religious Guidance and Awqaf:* Dr Azhari Altijani. *Science and Technology:* Ibrahim Ahmed Omar. *Tourism and Wildlife:* Joseph Malwal. *Transport, Roads and Bridges:* Philip Thon Leek. *Welfare, Women and Children's Affairs:* Samya Ahmed Mohamed.

Government Website: http://www.sudan.gov.sd

CURRENT LEADERS

Field Marshal Omar Hassan Ahmed al-Bashir

Position

President

Introduction

Omar al-Bashir is one of Africa's longest-serving presidents, having seized power in 1989. He has since been re-elected twice, in 1996 and 2000, although both polls were boycotted by the main opposition groups. His rule has been characterized by civil war and genocide, particularly in the western province of Darfur, although he signed a significant peace agreement in Jan. 2005 to end the long-running insurrection in southern Sudan.

Early Life

Bashir was born to a family of Sudanese peasants in 1944. He went to primary school in his home village before his family moved to Khartoum, where he completed secondary education. Having joined the Sudanese air force as a teenager, he soon made the grade as an officer and was sent to a military college in Egypt. He later served with a Sudanese unit that fought against Israel alongside Egyptian forces in the 1973 war. Promotions followed quickly and by the early 1980s he was a general. His political life began with the military coup of 1989 when, together with a group of middle-ranking officers, he overthrew the elected government of Sadiq al-Mahdi and installed a Revolutionary Command Council.

Career in Office

The National Islamic Front (later renamed the National Congress Party), led by Hassan al-Turabi, gave support to Bashir's new military regime. Influenced by Turabi, and by the long campaigns fought in southern Sudan against animist and Christian secessionist rebels, Bashir began the Islamization of Sudan and introduced Sharia law, policies that further alienated the South. He moved Sudan into the radical Arab camp, allying his country with Libya and Syria. Political and economic isolation followed, aggravating the distress caused by instability and civil war.

In 1993 Bashir declared himself president. Long-promised elections were held in March 1996, when Bashir was elected head of state against obscure candidates in a poll that was regarded internationally as deeply flawed. For a time Sudan provided a haven for radical Islamic refugees who had been forced to quit their own states. These fundamentalists included al-Qaeda's Osama bin Laden. In 1992 and 1994 Bashir stepped up the campaign against the southern rebel Sudan People's Liberation Movement (SPLM), but the latter regained most of their losses in 1995. By 1998 Sudan was regarded as a pariah state by the USA. In that year, US missiles destroyed a pharmaceutical factory in Khartoum that was suspected, wrongly as it turned out, of producing chemical weapons.

In 1999 Bashir declared a state of emergency during a power struggle with Turabi, then the speaker of the Sudanese parliament, who had moved to reduce the president's powers. Turabi, who had previously been regarded as Bashir's mentor, was toppled and parliament dissolved. In Dec. 2000 Bashir was re-elected as president, although the main opposition parties again boycotted the poll and disputed the result.

In the wake of the 11 Sept. 2001 attacks in the USA, Bashir made an effort to gain international acceptability. However, despite relaxations in the Sharia law, Sudan continued to be regarded by many in the West as a rogue state, crippled by poverty and conflict. Sudan was also cited by the UN for gross human rights violations, including forced labour, slavery and terrorism. Meanwhile, the civil war in the South continued, by this time having claimed over 2m. lives and displaced more than 4m. refugees.

On 9 Jan. 2005, after three years of talks, Bashir's government and the SPLM finally signed a comprehensive peace agreement. It provided for a government of national unity (headed by Bashir but also comprising members of the National Congress Party, the SPLM and other northern and southern political forces), self-determination for the South, a permanent ceasefire and the disengagement of forces. In July 2005 the agreement was briefly threatened when John Garang, the leader of the SPLM and first vice-president in the power-sharing government, was killed in a helicopter accident, provoking clashes between southern Sudanese and Arab northerners. Garang was replaced as first vice-president by his SPLM deputy, Salva Kiir Mayardit, in Aug. The formation of the national unity government was announced in Sept. 2005 and a devolved government of southern Sudan was established in Oct. In Oct. 2007 the SPLM suspended its participation in the national unity government, accusing the northern Sudanese of failing to honour the 2005 accord. There was no return to armed conflict on this occasion and, after dialogue, the SPLM rejoined the government in Dec. However, in May–June 2008 heavy fighting raged between northern and southern forces in the disputed town of Abyei (in an oil-rich area) before Bashir and the southern leader, Salva Kiir, agreed to seek international arbitration for a resolution.

In addition to the civil war in the South, Bashir's regime has also overseen fierce fighting in the western province of Darfur between government-backed Arab militias and local black rebel forces. Since 2003 the conflict has escalated despite international attempts to stop the violence, the targeting of civilians having led to a refugee crisis and a humanitarian catastrophe. In May 2006 the government and the largest insurgent faction in Darfur signed a power-sharing peace agreement following mediation by the African Union. However, two smaller rebel groups rejected the deal and fighting continued. Although prepared to tolerate a small African Union presence in the country, Bashir resisted calls for the deployment of a full United Nations peacekeeping force in Darfur, arguing that it would compromise Sudanese sovereignty. A report by UN investigators published in March 2007 accused the government of orchestrating 'gross and systematic' human rights abuses in Darfur and complained that the response of the international community had been 'inadequate and ineffective'. After months of negotiations Bashir finally agreed to the deployment of a hybrid UN-African peacekeeping force (UNAMID, under UN control) in Darfur to replace the African mission on 31 Dec. 2007. The transition came under immediate strain, however, when the government was forced to apologize after its troops opened fire on a UNAMID convoy in Jan. 2008. The Darfur conflict also undermined Sudan's already fractious relations with neighbouring Chad. Although Chad's President Déby and Bashir signed an accord in March 2008 to end mutual recriminations and hostilities between their two countries, alleged Chadian involvement in a Darfur rebel attack in May on Omdurman, near the Sudanese capital of Khartoum, prompted Bashir to sever diplomatic relations and Déby to close Chad's borders.

In July 2008 the International Criminal Court (ICC) indicted Bashir for alleged genocide and war crimes in Darfur. Although the Sudanese government rejected the accusation, violence across the region continued to generate further casualties and internal displacement. The announcement of a ceasefire by Bashir in Nov. 2008, widely viewed as an attempt to persuade the UN Security Council to suspend any ICC prosecution, was dismissed by the main rebel groups.

In 2009 sporadic violence in Darfur and southern Sudan continued, and the SPLM accused the Khartoum government of trying to destabilize the south. However, in Dec. it was reported that agreement had been reached on the terms of a referendum on independence for the south scheduled for Jan. 2011. In April 2010 Bashir won another term in the country's first multi-party poll in 24 years.

DEFENCE

There is conscription for two years. Defence expenditure totalled US$524m. in 2006 (US$13 per capita), representing 1·5% of GDP. According to *Deadly Arsenals*, published by the Carnegie Endowment for International Peace, Sudan has both biological and chemical weapons research programmes.

In Aug. 2007 the Sudanese government agreed to a joint African Union/United Nations peacekeeping force being deployed in Darfur. The mission, known as UNAMID or UN-AU Mission in Darfur, began operations on 31 Dec. 2007 and had 21,800 uniformed personnel in Feb. 2010.

Army

Strength (2007) 105,000 (around 20,000 conscripts). There is a paramilitary People's Defence Force of 17,500 and an additional 102,500 reservists.

Navy

The navy operates in the Red Sea and also on the River Nile. The flotilla suffers from lack of maintenance and spares. Personnel in 2007 numbered 1,300. Major bases are at Port Sudan (HQ), Flamingo Bay and Khartoum.

Air Force

Personnel totalled (2007) 3,000, with 51 combat capable aircraft, including A-5s (Chinese-built versions of MiG-19s), F-7s (Chinese-built versions of MiG-21s), MiG-23s and MiG-29s, and 23 attack helicopters.

INTERNATIONAL RELATIONS

Sudan is a member of the UN, World Bank, IMF and several other UN specialized agencies, IOM, Islamic Development Bank, OIC, African Development Bank, African Union, COMESA, Intergovernmental Authority on Development, League of Arab States and is an ACP member state of the ACP-EU relationship.

ECONOMY

Agriculture accounted for 30·1% of GDP, industry 29·2% and services 40·8% in 2006.

Sudan featured among the ten most corrupt countries in the world in a 2009 survey of 180 countries carried out by the anti-corruption organization *Transparency International*.

Overview

In the early and mid-1990s the economy suffered from macroeconomic instability and near financial collapse. 1997 saw the implementation of IMF-supported macroeconomic reforms that helped stabilize the economy.

Until the turn of the century the economy was almost entirely agrarian. In 1999 a pipeline from the Muglad Basin to a Red Sea export terminal was opened and Sudan began exporting crude oil, recording its first trade surplus. Oil production stood at 480,000 bbls per day in the first quarter of 2007. Most oil is produced for export, with four-fifths going to China. Oil production, infrastructure improvements, the development of export processing zones and increasing investment from Gulf states have helped transform the economy in recent years. But agriculture remains the country's most important sector, employing 80% of the population and accounting for one-third of the country's GDP. Sudan does not have a developed irrigation system and is vulnerable to droughts.

Despite high oil prices, demand for imports has remained strong, contributing to small current account deficits over the years. Sudan's external position remains vulnerable to fluctuations in oil prices and remittances sent home from expatriates working primarily in Gulf countries. The future value of oil production is also in question as the country's original, most reliable and most lucrative oilfields are maturing. Investment in Sudan is hindered by civil unrest and an unfavourable business climate.

Currency

The unit of currency is the *Sudanese pound* (SDG) of 100 *piastres*, introduced in Jan. 2007 to replace the *Sudanese dinar* (SDD) at a rate of 1 Sudanese pound = 100 Sudanese dinars. The dinar ceased to be legal tender on 30 June 2007. Inflation was 8·0% in 2007 and 14·3% in 2008. Foreign exchange reserves were US$2,107m. in July 2005 and total money supply was 705,505m. dinars.

Budget

In 2006 revenues totalled 1,507·5bn. dinars and expenditures 1,825·3bn. dinars.

VAT is 10%.

Performance

Real GDP growth exceeded 5% every year between 2000 and 2008—it was 10·2% in 2007 and 6·8% in 2008, driven by rising oil prices and increased demand from China. Sudan's total GDP in 2008 was US$58·4bn. Since oil production began in 1999 total GDP has more than trebled.

Banking and Finance

The Bank of Sudan (*Governor*, Sabir Mohammed Hassan) opened in Feb. 1960 with an authorized capital of £S1·5m. as the central bank and bank of issue. Banks were nationalized in 1970 but in 1974 foreign banks were allowed to open branches. The application of Islamic law from 1 Jan. 1991 put an end to the charging of interest in official banking transactions, and seven banks are run on Islamic principles. Mergers of seven local banks in 1993 resulted in the formation of the Khartoum Bank, the Industrial Development Bank and the Savings Bank.

A stock exchange opened in Khartoum in 1995.

ENERGY AND NATURAL RESOURCES

Environment

Sudan's carbon dioxide emissions from the consumption and flaring of fossil fuels in 2008 were the equivalent of 0·3 tonnes per capita.

Electricity

Installed capacity was an estimated 0·8m. kW in 2004. Production in 2004 was 3·88bn. kWh, with consumption per capita 116 kWh.

Oil and Gas

In 2008 oil reserves totalled 6·7bn. bbls. In June 1998 Sudan began exploiting its reserves and on 31 Aug. 1999 it officially became an oil producing country; production in 2008 totalled 23·7m. tonnes. An oil refinery at Al-Jayli, with a capacity of 2·5m. tonnes, opened in 2000. Natural gas reserves in 2007 were 85bn. cu. metres.

Minerals

Mineral deposits include graphite, sulphur, chromium, iron, manganese, copper, zinc, fluorspar, natron, gypsum and anhydrite, magnesite, asbestos, talc, halite, kaolin, white mica, coal, diatomite (kieselguhr), limestone and dolomite, pumice, lead, wollastonite, black sands and vermiculite pyrites. Chromite and gold are mined. Production of salt, 2003: 61,096 tonnes; chromite, 2005: 21,654 tonnes; gold, 2005: 3,625 kg.

Agriculture

80% of the population depends on agriculture. Land tenure is based on customary rights; land is ultimately owned by the government. There were about 19·32m. ha. of arable land in 2007 and 225,000 ha. of permanent crops. 1·15m. ha. were irrigated in 2007. There were ten tractors and one harvester-thresher per 10,000 ha. in 2006.

Production (2003 estimates) in 1,000 tonnes: sugarcane, 5,500; sorghum, 5,188; groundnuts, 1,200; millet, 784; tomatoes, 700; wheat, 363; dates, 330; seed cotton, 315; cottonseed, 200; mangoes, 195; melons and watermelons, 173.

Livestock (2003 estimates): sheep, 47·0m.; goats, 40·0m.; cattle, 38·3m.; camels, 3·2m.; chickens, 38m.

Livestock products (2003 estimates) in 1,000 tonnes: beef and veal, 325; lamb and mutton, 144; goat meat, 119; poultry meat, 30; cow's milk, 3,264; goat's milk, 1,295; sheep's milk, 463; cheese, 152; eggs, 47.

Forestry

Forests covered 67·55m. ha. in 2005, or 28·4% of the total land area. The annual loss of 589,000 ha. of forests between 2000 and 2005 was exceeded only in Brazil and Indonesia. In 2007, 20·28m. cu. metres of roundwood were cut.

Fisheries

In 2005 the total catch was 62,000 tonnes, of which approximately 91% were freshwater fish.

INDUSTRY

Production figures (in 1,000 tonnes): distillate fuel oil (2004), 1,400; sugar (2002), 744; wheat flour (1999), 532; residual fuel oil (2004), 361; cement (2001), 146; vegetable oils (2001), 32. In 2000 an industrial complex assembling 12,000 vehicles a year opened.

Labour

The total workforce in 1996 was 10,652,000 (71% males). 68% of the economically active population in 1995 were engaged in agriculture, fisheries and forestry.

INTERNATIONAL TRADE

Foreign debt was US$18,455m. in 2005.

Imports and Exports

In 2006 imports (f.o.b.) amounted to US$7,104·7m. (US$5,946·0m. in 2005); exports (f.o.b.) US$5,656·6m. (US$4,824·3m. in 2005). The main imports are petroleum products, machinery and equipment, foodstuffs, manufactured goods, medicines and chemicals. Main exports are oil (which accounts for about 87% of export revenues), cotton, gum arabic, oil seeds, sorghum, livestock, sesame, gold and sugar. The main import sources in 2006 were China (18·8%), Saudi Arabia (8·9%), Japan (8·1%), India (6·7%) and United Arab Emirates (5·6%). Principal export markets in 2006 were China (78·9%), Japan (5·5%), United Arab Emirates (5·1%), Saudi Arabia (2·8%) and Egypt (1·3%).

COMMUNICATIONS

Roads

In 2002 there were estimated to be 11,900 km of roads, of which 4,320 km were paved. There were an estimated 87,400 passenger cars and 57,400 trucks and vans in 2002.

Rail

Total length in 2005 was 4,578 km. In 2004 the railways carried 63,000 passengers and 1·3m. tonnes of freight.

Civil Aviation

There is an international airport at Khartoum. The national carrier is the government-owned Sudan Airways, which operates domestic and international services. In 2003 scheduled airline traffic of Sudan-based carriers flew 7m. km, carrying 420,000 passengers (264,000 on international flights).

Shipping

Supplementing the railways are regular steamer services of the Sudan Railways. Port Sudan is the major seaport; Suakin port opened in 1991. Sea-going shipping totalled 33,000 GRT in 2002, including oil tankers 1,000 GRT.

Telecommunications

In 2008 there were 366,200 main (fixed) telephone lines; mobile phone subscribers numbered 11,991,500 in 2008 (29·0 per 100 persons). There were 4·2m. PCs in use in 2006 and 4·2m. internet users in 2008.

Postal Services

In 2003 there were 218 post offices.

SOCIAL INSTITUTIONS

Justice

The judiciary is a separate independent department of state, directly and solely responsible to the President of the Republic. The general administrative supervision and control of the judiciary is vested in the High Judicial Council.

Civil Justice is administered by the courts constituted under the Civil Justice Ordinance, namely the High Court of Justice—consisting of the Court of Appeal and Judges of the High Court, sitting as courts of original jurisdiction—and Province Courts—consisting of the Courts of Province and District Judges. The law administered is 'justice, equity and good conscience' in all cases where there is no special enactment. Procedure is governed by the Civil Justice Ordinance.

Justice for the Muslim population is administered by the Islamic law courts, which form the Sharia Divisions of the Court of Appeal, High Courts and Kadis Courts; President of the Sharia Division is the Grand Kadi. In Dec. 1990 the government announced that Sharia would be applied in the non-Muslim southern parts of the country as well.

Criminal Justice is administered by the courts constituted under the Code of Criminal Procedure, namely major courts, minor courts and magistrates' courts. Serious crimes are tried by major courts, which are composed of a President and two members and have the power to pass the death sentence. In 2009 there were at least nine executions. Major Courts are, as a rule, presided over by a Judge of the High Court appointed to a Provincial Circuit or a Province Judge. There is a right of appeal to the Chief Justice against any decision or order of a Major Court, and all its findings and sentences are subject to confirmation by him.

Lesser crimes are tried by Minor Courts consisting of three Magistrates and presided over by a Second Class Magistrate, and by Magistrates' Courts.

The population in penal institutions in March 2003 was approximately 12,000 (36 per 100,000 of national population).

Education

In 2007 there were 28,185 teaching staff for 490,808 pupils at pre-primary schools; 107,933 teaching staff for 3·96m. pupils at primary schools; and 79,122 secondary school teaching staff for 1·46m. pupils. In 1996 there were 17 universities, two Islamic universities, one university of science and technology, and an institute of advanced banking. There were also 14 other higher education institutions. Adult literacy rate in 2001 was 58·8% (male, 70·0%; female, 47·7%).

Health

In 2000 there were 4,973 physicians, 218 dentists, 26,730 nurses and 311 pharmacists. Hospital bed provision in 2004 was 74 per 100,000 population.

RELIGION

Islam is the state religion. In 2001, 70% of the population were Sunni Muslims, concentrated in the north; Christians (17%) and traditional animists (12%) are concentrated in the south. In Feb. 2010 the Roman Catholic church had one cardinal.

CULTURE

World Heritage Sites

Sudan has one site on the UNESCO World Heritage List: Gebel Barkal and the Sites of the Napatan Region (inscribed on the list in 2003), a collection of tombs, pyramids and palaces of the Second Kingdom of Kush (900 BC to AD 350).

Broadcasting

Television and radio broadcasting is tightly state-controlled and reflects government policy. There are no privately-owned TV stations, with the exception of a cable network owned jointly by the government and private investors. Pan-Arab satellite stations can be received. 920,000 households were equipped with TV sets (colour by PAL) in 2005.

Press

In 2005 there were 28 daily newspapers with a combined circulation of 90,000. Opposition newspapers are permitted although they are vetted by an official censor.

Tourism

In 2005 there were 246,000 foreign tourists, spending a total of US$89m.

DIPLOMATIC REPRESENTATIVES

Of Sudan in the United Kingdom (3 Cleveland Row, London, SW1A 1DD)
Ambassador: Omar Mohammed Ahmed Siddig.

Of the United Kingdom in Sudan (off Sharia Al Baladia, Khartoum East)
Ambassador: Dr Rosalind M. Marsden, CMG.

Of Sudan in the USA (2210 Massachusetts Ave., NW, Washington, D.C., 20008)
Ambassador: Vacant.
Chargé d'Affaires a.i.: Akec Khoc Aciew Khoc.

Of the USA in Sudan (Sharia Ali Abdul Latif, POB 699, Khartoum)
Ambassador: Vacant.
Chargé d'Affaires a.i.: Robert E. Whitehead.

Of Sudan to the United Nations
Ambassador: Abdalmahmood Abdalhaleem Mohamad.

Of Sudan to the European Union
Ambassador: Najeib El Kheir Abdel Wahab.

FURTHER READING

Daly, M. W. and Sikainga, A. A. (eds.) *Civil War in the Sudan.* 1993
Deng, F. M., *War of Visions: Conflict of Identities in the Sudan.* 1995
Idris, Amir, *Conflict and Politics of Identity in Sudan.* 2006
Iyob, Ruth, *Sudan: The Elusive Quest for Peace.* 2006
Sidahmed, Alsir, *Sudan.* 2004
Woodward, Peter, *The Horn of Africa: Politics and International Relations.* 2002

SURINAME

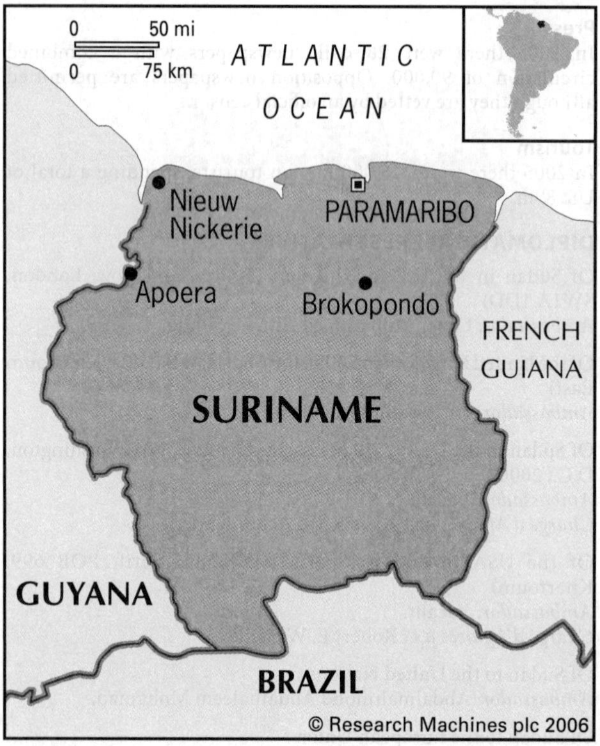

Republiek Suriname
(Republic of Suriname)

Capital: Paramaribo
Population estimate, 2010: 524,000
GDP per capita, 2007: (PPP$) 7,813
HDI/world rank: 0·769/97

KEY HISTORICAL EVENTS

The first Europeans to reach the area were the Spanish in 1499 but it was the British who established a colony in 1650. At the peace of Breda (1667), Suriname was assigned to the Netherlands in exchange for the colony of New Netherland in North America. Suriname was twice in British possession during the Napoleonic Wars, in 1799–1802 and 1804–16, when it was returned to the Netherlands.

On 25 Nov. 1975 Suriname gained full independence. On 25 Feb. 1980 the government was ousted in a coup and a National Military Council (NMC) established. A further coup on 13 Aug. replaced several members of the NMC and the State President. Other attempted coups took place in 1981 and 1982, with the NMC retaining control. In Oct. 1987 a new constitution was approved by referendum. Following elections in Nov. Suriname returned to democracy in Jan. 1988 but on 24 Dec. 1990 a further military coup deposed the government. There was a peace agreement with rebel groups in Aug. 1992 and elections were held in May 1996.

TERRITORY AND POPULATION

Suriname is located on the northern coast of South America between 2–6° North latitude and 54–59° West longitude. It is bounded in the north by the Atlantic Ocean, east by French Guiana, west by Guyana, and south by Brazil. Area, 163,820 sq. km. Census population, 2004, 492,829; density, 3·0 per sq. km.

The UN gives an estimated population for 2010 of 524,000.

The capital, Paramaribo, had (2004 census) 242,946 inhabitants.

Suriname is divided into ten districts. They are (with 2004 census population and chief town): Brokopondo, population 14,215 (Brokopondo); Commewijne, 24,649 (Nieuw Amsterdam); Coronie, 2,887 (Totness); Marowijne, 16,642 (Albina); Nickerie, 36,639 (Nieuw Nickerie); Para, 18,749 (Onverwacht); Paramaribo, 242,946—representing 49% of Suriname's total population (Paramaribo); Saramacca, 15,980 (Groningen); Sipaliwini, 34,136 (local authority in Paramaribo); Wanica, 85,986 (Lelydorp).

There is an ongoing unresolved dispute between Suriname and Guyana for the return of a triangle of uninhabited rainforest in Guyana between the New River and the Courantyne River, near the Brazilian border. In Sept. 2007 the UN settled a long-standing maritime boundary dispute between the two countries. The coastal area off both countries is believed to hold significant oil and gas deposits.

Major ethnic groups in percentages of the population in 2004: Indo-Pakistani, 26%; Creole, 18%; Javanese, 15%; Bushnegroes (Blacks), 15%; Amerindian, 4%. 73·9% of the population lived in urban areas in 2005.

The official language is Dutch. English is widely spoken next to Hindi, Javanese and Chinese as inter-group communication. A vernacular, called 'Sranan' or 'Surinamese', is used as a *lingua franca*. In 1976 it was decided that Spanish was to become the nation's principal working language.

SOCIAL STATISTICS

Births, 2003, 9,634; deaths, 3,154. 2003 rates per 1,000 population: birth rate, 20·0; death rate, 6·6. Expectation of life, 2007, was 65·3 years for males and 72·5 for females. Annual population growth rate, 2000–05, 1·5%. Infant mortality, 2005, 30 per 1,000 live births; fertility rate, 2004, 2·6 births per woman. Abortion is illegal.

CLIMATE

The climate is equatorial, with uniformly high temperatures and rainfall. The temperature is an average of 27°C throughout the year; there are two rainy seasons (May–July and Nov.–Jan.) and two dry seasons (Aug.–Oct. and Feb.–April). Paramaribo, Jan. 21°C, July 32·4°C. Average rainfall 182·3 mm.

CONSTITUTION AND GOVERNMENT

The current constitution was ratified on 30 Sept. 1987. Parliament is a 51-member *National Assembly*. The head of state is the *President*, elected for a five-year term by a two-thirds majority by the National Assembly, or, failing that, by an electoral college, the United People's Assembly, enlarged by the inclusion of regional and local councillors, by a simple majority.

National Anthem

'God zij met ons Suriname' ('God be with our Suriname'); words by C. A. Hoekstra, tune by J. C. de Puy. There is a Sranan version, 'Opo kondreman oen opo'; words by H. de Ziel.

RECENT ELECTIONS

Parliamentary elections were held on 25 May 2005. The New Front for Democracy (NF) won 23 of the available 51 seats (41·5% of the vote). The NF alliance comprises the National Party of Suriname (8 seats), the Progressive Reform Party (7), Pertjajah Luhur (6) and the Suriname Labour Party (2). The National Democratic

Party won 15 seats (22·8%), People's Alliance for Progress took 5 (14·6%), A-Com took 5 (7·0%) and Alternative-1 took 3 (6·3%).

On 3 Aug. 2005 Runaldo Ronald Venetiaan was re-elected *President* by the United People's Assembly, claiming 560 out of 879 votes, after no candidate had won the necessary two-thirds majority in two earlier elections in the National Assembly. Ram Sardjoe was elected *Vice-President* and *Prime Minister.*

Parliamentary elections were scheduled to take place on 25 May 2010.

CURRENT ADMINISTRATION

President: Runaldo Ronald Venetiaan; b. 1936 (National Party of Suriname; sworn in 12 Aug. 2000 for a second time, having previously held office from Sept. 1991 to Sept. 1996).

Vice-President and Prime Minister: Ram Sardjoe; b. 1935 (Progressive Reform Party; sworn in 12 Aug. 2005).

In March 2010 the government comprised:

Minister of Agriculture and Fisheries: Kermechend Raghoebarsingh. *Defence:* Ivan Fernald. *Education and Human Development:* Edwin Wolf. *Finance:* Humphrey Hildenberg. *Foreign Affairs:* Lygia Kraag-Keteldijk. *Health:* Celsius Waterberg. *Interior:* Maurits Hassankhan. *Justice and Police:* Chandrikapersad Santokhi. *Labour, Technological Development and Environment:* Joyce Amarello Williams. *Natural Resources:* Gregory Rusland. *Physical Planning, Land and Forestry Management:* Michael Jong Tjien Fa. *Planning and Development Co-operation:* Rick Van Ravenswaay. *Public Works:* Ganeshkoemar Kandhai. *Regional Development:* Michel Felisie. *Social Affairs:* Hendrik Setrowidjojo. *Trade and Industry:* Clifford Marica. *Transport, Communication and Tourism:* Richell Apensa.

National Assembly Website (Dutch only): http://www.dna.sr

CURRENT LEADERS

Runaldo Ronald Venetiaan

Position
President

Introduction
Runaldo Ronald Venetiaan has been president of Suriname since 2000, having previously held the office between 1991 and 1996. He was re-elected in 2005. Dedicated to free market principles, he has implemented a series of measures to bring the struggling economy that he inherited under control. His first term in office was also characterized by a programme of austerity measures.

Early Life
Venetiaan was born on 18 June 1936 in Paramaribo. He later moved to the Netherlands, where he studied mathematics and physics at Leiden University. Returning to Suriname, he undertook a teaching career before being appointed minister of education in 1973 in the government of Henck Arron, holding office until a military coup in 1980. After civilian government was re-established, Venetiaan resumed his role in the education ministry in 1988. In 1991 the New Front for Democracy won parliamentary elections and elected Venetiaan to the presidency.

Career in Office
In 1992 Venetiaan signed a peace accord with the rebel Surinamese Liberation Army, which had been operational since the mid-1980s. A primary aim of his first term was to secure economic stability after the years of coups and counter-coups. Despite stabilizing the currency and achieving a budget surplus, his austerity measures were widely unpopular and he lost the 1996 election to Jules Wijdenbosch, an ally of former military dictator Desi Bouterse, who instigated increased public spending.

With Wijdenbosch increasingly under attack for economic mismanagement, elections were called for May 2000 and Venetiaan led the New Front to victory. He again took over a faltering economy burdened by bureaucracy, high inflation, a devalued currency, overwhelming international debt and a collapsing healthcare system. In response, he cut public spending, replaced the guilder (in Jan. 2004) with the Suriname dollar and restructured the economically significant banana industry. Foreign relations were meanwhile dominated by a longstanding disagreement with Guyana over maritime boundaries. The UN established a tribunal to mediate in 2004 and in Sept. 2007 it awarded two-thirds of the disputed area to Guyana.

At the parliamentary elections of May 2005 Venetiaan's New Front for Democracy coalition returned the largest number of MPs, with the National Democratic Party of Bouterse second. However, the New Front failed to obtain the two-thirds majority required to elect the president. In Aug. 2005 Venetiaan won a second term of office when he polled 560 votes against 315 for his opponent, Rabin Parmessar, in a vote by the United People's Conference, consisting of MPs and elected local and district representatives.

DEFENCE

In 2006 defence expenditure totalled US$20m. (US$44 per capita), representing 1·3% of GDP.

Army
Total strength was 1,400 in 2007.

Navy
In 2007 personnel, based at Paramaribo, totalled around 240.

Air Force
Estimated personnel (2007): 200. There were four combat capable aircraft.

INTERNATIONAL RELATIONS

Suriname is a member of the UN, World Bank, IMF and several other UN specialized agencies, WTO, Islamic Development Bank, OIC, ACS, CARICOM, Inter-American Development Bank, SELA, OAS, UNASUR and is an ACP member state of the ACP-EU relationship.

ECONOMY

In 2006 agriculture contributed 5·2% of GDP, industry 35·7% and services 59·1%.

Overview
The economy is heavily dependent on the export of oil, gold and alumina, accounting for over 50% of GDP. Strong government policies and favourable terms of trade have allowed for positive economic performance in recent years. With monetary policy focused on reducing inflation and the central bank given greater independence, the exchange rate has remained stable since early 2004, with real GDP growth remaining above 4% each year since 2003. Government revenue has increased rapidly owing to high mineral-related receipts and a fall in the non-mineral deficit, while public debt fell to less than 30% of GDP in 2006.

Nonetheless, Suriname remains vulnerable to external commodity price shocks. The IMF recommends continued efforts to diversify the economy in order to maintain growth and reduce vulnerability, as well as to settle arrears with external creditors. It also recommends further steps to unify the two-tier exchange rate and to strengthen the management of state-owned banks.

Currency
The unit of currency is the *Suriname dollar* (SRD) of 100 *cents*, introduced on 1 Jan. 2004 to replace the *Suriname guilder* (SRG) at a rate of one Suriname dollar = 1,000 Suriname guilders. Foreign exchange reserves totalled US$140m. and gold reserves were 29,000 troy oz in July 2005. Total money supply in June 2005 was 777m. Suriname dollars. The rate of inflation, which had been 98·7% in 1999, was 6·4% in 2007 and 14·6% in 2008.

Budget
2004 revenue (in 1m. Suriname dollars) was 1,175·8 made up of: direct taxes, 368·4; indirect taxes, 431·1; bauxite levy and other revenues, 103·1; aid, 273·2.

Total expenditure in 2004 (in 1m. Suriname dollars) was 1,545·7, made up of: wages and salaries, 380·3; grants and contributions, 291·3; other current expenditures, 645·1; capital expenditure, 229·0.

VAT is 10% for goods and 8% for services.

Performance
After two years of recession in 1999 and 2000 the economy has enjoyed consistently strong growth. Real GDP growth was 5·4% in 2007 and 6·0% in 2008. In 2008 total GDP was US$2·9bn.

Banking and Finance
The Central Bank of Suriname (*Governor*, Andre Telting) is a bankers' bank and also the bank of issue. There are three commercial banks; the Suriname People's Credit Bank operates under the auspices of the government. There is a post office savings bank, a mortgage bank, an investment bank, a long-term investments agency, a National Development Bank and an Agrarian Bank.

ENERGY AND NATURAL RESOURCES

Environment
Suriname's carbon dioxide emissions from the consumption and flaring of fossil fuels in 2008 were the equivalent of 4·5 tonnes per capita.

Electricity
Installed capacity in 2003 was 0·2m. kW. Production (2004) 1·51bn. kWh; consumption per capita in 2004 was 3,437 kWh.

Oil and Gas
Crude oil production (2004), 4,098,463 bbls. Reserves in 2007 were 111m. bbls.

Minerals
Bauxite is the most important mineral. Suriname is the seventh largest bauxite producer in the world. Production (2004), 4,217,000 tonnes.

Agriculture
Agriculture is restricted to the alluvial coastal zone; in 2002 there were an estimated 57,000 ha. of arable land and 10,000 ha. of permanent crops. The staple food crop is rice: production, 163,000 tonnes in 2003. Other crops (2002 in 1,000 tonnes): sugarcane, 120; oranges, 11; plantains, 11; coconuts, 10; cassava, 4. Livestock in 2003 (estimates): cattle, 137,000; pigs, 24,000; sheep, 8,000; goats, 7,000; chickens, 4m.

Forestry
Forests covered 14·78m. ha. in 2005, or 94·7% of the land area. In terms of percentage coverage, Suriname was the world's most heavily forested country in 2005. Production of roundwood in 2007 was 214,000 cu. metres.

Fisheries
The catch in 2005 amounted to 39,949 tonnes, almost entirely from marine waters.

INDUSTRY
There is no longer any aluminium smelting, but there are food-processing and wood-using industries. Production: alumina (2007), 2,181,000 tonnes; residual fuel oil (2004), 335,000 tonnes; cement (2004), 65,000 tonnes; distillate fuel oil (2004), 39,000 tonnes; sawnwood (2007), 57,000 cu. metres.

Labour
Out of 156,705 people in employment in 2004, 27,995 were in public administration and defence; 25,012 in wholesale and retail trade; 14,031 in construction; 12,593 in agriculture, fishing, hunting and forestry; and 10,971 in manufacturing. In 2004 there were 16,425 unemployed persons, or 9·5% of the workforce.

INTERNATIONAL TRADE

Imports and Exports
In 2004 imports (f.o.b.) amounted to US$740·0m. (US$703·9m. in 2003); exports (f.o.b.) US$782·2m. (US$590·3m. in 2003).

Principal imports, 2004: nonelectrical machinery, 14·4%; food products, 11·9%; road vehicles, 9·5%. Principal exports, 2004: alumina, 40·8%; gold, 29·3%; crustaceans and molluscs, 3·6%.

In 2004 imports (in US$1m.) were mainly from the USA (165·2), Netherlands (147·8), Trinidad and Tobago (131·4), Japan (96·6) and the Netherlands Antilles (20·8); exports were mainly to Norway (173·0), USA (138·0), Canada (73·3), France (60·0) and the Netherlands (14·5).

COMMUNICATIONS

Roads
The road network covered 4,304 km in 2003, of which 26·2% were paved. In 2004 there were 76,466 passenger cars, 25,364 trucks and vans, 4,166 buses and coaches and 39,693 motorcycles and mopeds. There were 69 fatalities in road accidents in 2004.

Rail
There are two single-track railways.

Civil Aviation
There is an international airport at Paramaribo (Johan Adolf Pengel). The national carrier is Surinam Airways, which in 2003 had flights to Amsterdam, Belem, Cayenne, Curaçao, Georgetown, Haiti, Miami and Port of Spain. In 2003 scheduled airline traffic of Suriname-based carriers flew 5m. km, carrying 258,000 passengers (253,000 on international flights). In 2004 there were 149,589 passenger arrivals and 148,353 departures.

Shipping
The Royal Netherlands Steamship Co. operates services to the Netherlands, the USA, and regionally. The Suriname Navigation Co. maintains services from Paramaribo to Georgetown, Cayenne and the Caribbean area. Merchant shipping in 2002 totalled 5,000 GRT. In 2004 vessels totalling 1,518,000 NRT entered ports and vessels totalling 2,142,000 NRT cleared.

Telecommunications
Telephone subscribers numbered 401,500 in 2006, equivalent to 888·3 for every 1,000 persons. There were 320,000 mobile phone subscribers in 2006 and 38,000 internet users.

Postal Services
In 2002 there were 38 post offices.

SOCIAL INSTITUTIONS

Justice
Members of the court of justice are nominated by the President. There are three cantonal courts. Suriname was one of ten countries to sign an agreement in Feb. 2001 establishing a Caribbean Court of Justice to replace the British Privy Council as the highest civil and criminal court. In the meantime the number of signatories has risen to twelve. The court was inaugurated at Port-of-Spain, Trinidad on 16 April 2005.

The population in penal institutions in June 1999 was 1,933 (437 per 100,000 of national population).

Education
Adult literacy was 88·0% in 2003 (92·3% among males and 84·1% among females). In 2003–04, 298 primary schools out of a total of 312 had 3,096 teachers and 62,086 pupils; 124 secondary schools had 41,904 pupils. In 2000–01 the university had 2,745 students. There is a teacher training college with (2000–01) 1,942 students.

Health
In 2004 there were 1,611 general hospital beds. In 2003 there were 295 physicians.

RELIGION
At the 2004 census there were 200,744 Christians of varying denominations, 98,240 Hindus and 66,307 Muslims.

CULTURE
World Heritage Sites
Suriname has two sites on the UNESCO World Heritage List: Central Suriname Nature Reserve (inscribed on the list in 2000); and the Historic Inner City of Paramaribo (2002).

Broadcasting
The government controls the partly commercial Stichting Radio Omroep Suriname and Radio Suriname Internationaal, and the TV services Surinaamse Televisie Stichting and Algemene Televisie Verzorging. There were 62,000 TV-equipped households (colour by NTSC) in 2005. There were 27 radio and 16 television stations in 2005.

Cinema
There was one cinema in Paramaribo in 2007.

Press
There were four daily newspapers in 2005.

Tourism
In 2005 there were 160,000 non-resident tourist arrivals; tourist receipts totalled US$96m.

Festivals
The people of Suriname celebrate Chinese New Year (Jan.); Phagwa, a Hindu celebration (March–April); Id-Ul-Fitre, the sugar feast at the end of Ramadan (May); Avondvierdaagse, a carnival (during the Easter holidays); Suriflora, a celebration of plants and flowers (April–May); Keti koti, an Afro-Surinamese holiday to commemorate the abolition of slavery (1 July); Suripop, a popular music festival (July); Nationale Kunstbeurs, arts and crafts (Oct.–Nov.); Divali, the Hindu ceremony of light (Nov.); Djaran Kepang, a Javanese dance held on feast days; Winti-prey, a ceremony for the Winti gods.

Museums and Galleries
The main museums (1998) were: Surinaams Museum and Fort Zeelandia in Paramaribo; the Open Air Museum at Nieuw Amsterdam. Art Galleries include: Suriname Art 2000; the Academy for Higher Arts and Cultural Education; and the Ready Tex Art Boutique, all in Paramaribo; and Nola Hatterman Instituut at Fort Zeelandia.

DIPLOMATIC REPRESENTATIVES
Of Suriname in the United Kingdom
Ambassador: Urmila Joella-Sewnundun (resides in The Hague).

Of the United Kingdom in Suriname
Ambassador: Fraser Wheeler (resides in Georgetown, Guyana).

Of Suriname in the USA (4301 Connecticut Ave., NW, Washington, D.C., 20008)
Ambassador: Jacques Ruben Constantijn Kross.

Of the USA in Suriname (Dr Sophie Redmondstraat 129, Paramaribo)
Ambassador: John R. Nay.

Of Suriname to the United Nations
Ambassador: Henry Leonard Mac-Donald.

Of Suriname to the European Union
Ambassador: Gerhard Otmar Hiwat.

FURTHER READING
Dew, E. M., *Trouble in Suriname, 1975–1993.* 1995

National Statistical Office: Algemeen Bureau voor de Statistiek, POB 244, Paramaribo.
Website (limited English): http://www.statistics-suriname.org

SWAZILAND

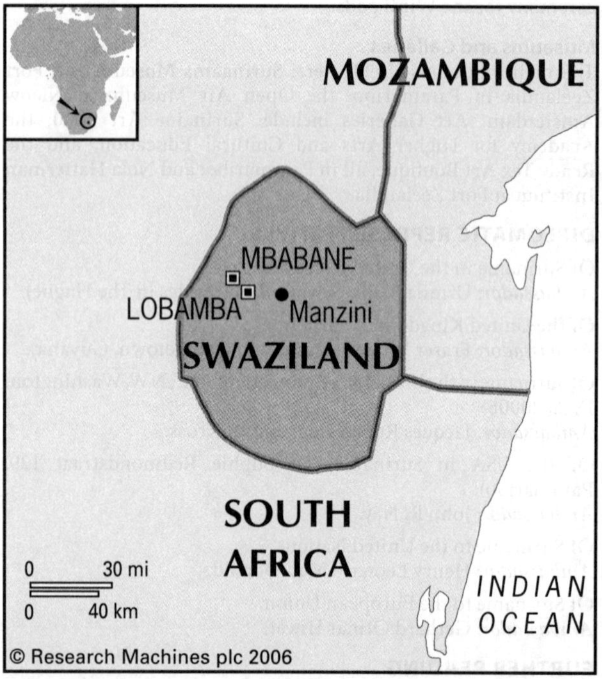

Umbuso weSwatini
(Kingdom of Swaziland)

Capital: Mbabane (Administrative), Lobamba (Legislative)
Population estimate, 2010: 1·20m.
GDP per capita, 2007: (PPP$) 4,789
HDI/world rank: 0·572/142

KEY HISTORICAL EVENTS

The Swazi migrated into the country to which they have given their name in the last half of the 18th century. The independence of the Swazis was guaranteed in the conventions of 1881 and 1884 between the British Government and the Government of the South African Republic. In 1894 the South African Republic was given powers of protection and administration. In 1902, after the conclusion of the Boer War, a special commissioner took charge, and under an order-in-council in 1903 the Governor of the Transvaal administered the territory. Swaziland became independent on 6 Sept. 1968. A state of emergency imposed in 1973 is still in force. On 25 April 1986 King Mswati III was installed as King of Swaziland.

TERRITORY AND POPULATION

Swaziland is bounded in the north, west and south by South Africa, and in the east by Mozambique. The area is 17,364 sq. km (6,704 sq. miles). *De jure* population (2007 provisional census), 953,524 (493,026 females); density, 54·9 per sq. km.

The UN gives an estimated population for 2010 of 1·20m.

In 2005, 75·9% of the population were rural. The country is divided into four districts: Hhohho, Lubombo, Manzini and Shiselweni.

Main urban areas: Mbabane, the administrative capital (73,000 inhabitants in 1999); Manzini; Big Bend; Mhlume; Nhlangano.

The population is 84% Swazi and 10% Zulu. The official languages are Swazi and English.

SOCIAL STATISTICS

2000 estimates: births, 35,000; deaths, 23,000. Estimated rates, 2000 (per 1,000 population): births, 33·4; deaths, 22·0. As a result of the impact of AIDS, expectation of life has been declining. It was 58 years in 1995, but by 2007 was down to 44·8 years for females and 45·7 years for males. In 2007, 26·1% of all adults between 15 and 49 were infected with HIV—the highest rate in any country. In Sept. 2001 King Mswati III told the teenage girls of the country to stop having sex for five years as part of the country's drive to reduce the spread of HIV. Annual population growth rate, 2000–05, 2·3%. Infant mortality, 2005, 104 per 1,000 live births; fertility rate, 2004, 3·8 births per woman.

CLIMATE

A temperate climate with two seasons. Nov. to March is the wet season, when temperatures range from mild to hot, with frequent thunderstorms. The cool, dry season from May to Sept. is characterized by clear, bright sunny days. Mbabane, Jan. 68°F (20°C), July 54°F (12·2°C). Annual rainfall 56" (1,402 mm).

CONSTITUTION AND GOVERNMENT

The reigning King is **Mswati III** (b. 1968; crowned 25 April 1986), who succeeded his father, King Sobhuza II (reigned 1921–82). The King rules in conjunction with the Queen Mother (his mother, or a senior wife). Critics of the King or his mother run the risk of arrest.

A new constitution was signed into law on 26 July 2005 and came into force in Jan. 2006. There is a *House of Assembly* of 65 members, 55 of whom are elected each from one constituency (*inkhundla*), and ten appointed by the King; and a *House of Senators* of 30 members, ten of whom are elected by the House of Assembly and 20 appointed by the King. Elections are held in two rounds, the second being a run-off between the five candidates who come first in each constituency.

There is also a traditional *Swazi National Council* headed by the King and Queen Mother at which all Swazi men are entitled to be heard.

National Anthem

'Nkulunkulu mnikati wetibusiso temaSwati' ('O Lord our God bestower of blessings upon the Swazi'); words by A. E. Simelane, tune by D. K. Rycroft.

RECENT ELECTIONS

At the elections of 19 Sept. 2008 only non-partisans were elected. Political parties are illegal and advocates of multi-party politics are considered to be troublemakers.

CURRENT ADMINISTRATION

In March 2010 the cabinet comprised:

Prime Minister: Barnabas Sibusiso Dlamini; b. 1942 (sworn in 23 Oct. 2008).

Deputy Prime Minister: Themba Masuku.

Minister for Agriculture: Clement Dlamini. *Commerce, Industry and Trade:* Jabulile Mashwama. *Economic Planning and Development:* Prince Hlangusemphi. *Education and Training:* Wilson Future Ntshangase. *Finance:* Majozi Sithole. *Foreign Affairs:* Lutfo Dlamini. *Health:* Bennedict Xaba. *Information, Communications and Technology:* Nelisiwe Shongwe. *Interior:* Mgwagwa Gamedze. *Justice and Constitutional Affairs:* Ndumiso Mamba. *Labour and Social Security:* Patrick Magwebetane

Mamba. *Local Government and Housing:* Pastor Lindiwe Gwebu. *Natural Resources and Energy:* Princess Tsandzile. *Public Service:* Mtiti Fakudze. *Public Works and Transport:* Ntuthuko Dlamini. *Sports, Culture and Youth:* Hlobsile Ndlovu. *Tourism and Environmental Affairs:* Macford Nsibandze.

Government Website: http://www.gov.sz

CURRENT LEADERS

Mswati III

Position
King

Introduction
Mswati came to the throne in 1986. Effectively an absolute monarchy, he has received domestic and international criticism for his suppression of political opposition. Among the greatest challenges of Mswati's reign has been the rapid increase in cases of HIV and AIDS in Swaziland.

Early Life
Mswati was born on 19 April 1968 in Manzini to one of the wives of King Sobhuza II and given the name Makhosetive (King of All Nations). Sobhuza's death in 1982 left a power vacuum that led to several years of infighting between various queens regent, crown princes and members of Liqoqo (the traditional advisory body which wielded significant power over the crown). In Oct. 1985 Makhosetive's mother dismissed several leading Liqoqo figures and recalled her son from his schooling in England. Makhosetive was crowned as Mswati III in April 1986.

Career in Office
Among Mswati's first acts as King was to dissolve the Liqoqo. Popular discontent grew at the prohibition on opposition political parties and Mswati's increasingly autocratic rule, leading to the establishment of the illegal People's United Democratic Movement (Pudemo). In 1990 Mswati agreed to open dialogue on the nation's political future. The national assembly was directly elected for the first time in 1993 and Mswati announced plans for a new constitution the following year.

With little progress having been made by 1996, Mswati established a constitutional commission. Pudemo continued to co-ordinate opposition, criticizing the King for filling the commission with his conservative supporters and boycotting the national assembly elections of Oct. 1998. In 2000 Pudemo leader Mario Masuku demanded an end to the state of emergency called 27 years earlier and was arrested for sedition. He was imprisoned pending his trial which collapsed in 2002. On his release he stated his belief that government could only be reformed when the monarchy was 'wiped out'. In 2001 the constitutional commission reported back, providing the framework for the writing of a new constitution but asserting that the majority of the population did not favour the formation of new parties. In Dec. 2002, amid declining relations with the judiciary, six court of appeal judges resigned in protest at the King's use of rule by decree. The judges claimed that Mswati's repeal of several court decisions was unconstitutional. The crisis gave renewed impetus to the opposition alliance who called for a series of mass strikes. A new draft constitution was presented to the King in 2003, introducing a bill of rights but maintaining the executive role of the monarchy and the ban on political parties. Having been adopted by parliament and signed by the King in 2005, the constitution came into force in Jan. 2006.

Swaziland has one of the highest AIDS rates in the world. In Oct. 2001 Mswati ordered that all virgins should abstain from sex for five years or face a fine. The following month Mswati made a gift of a cow in recompense for taking an 18 year-old bride, Zena Mahlangu. Mahlangu's mother accused aides of the King of kidnapping her daughter and undertook legal proceedings to secure her return. Although the case collapsed, it received international attention and highlighted the growing challenges to Mswati's autocratic style.

In 2007 trade unionists and political activists took part in demonstrations, including the blocking of border crossings with South Africa, demanding democratic reform.

Opposition groups boycotted the Sept. 2008 elections and were critical of the lavish celebrations of Mswati's 40th birthday, coupled with the 40th anniversary of Swaziland's independence.

Pudemo leader Masuku, who had again been detained under anti-terror laws in Nov. 2008, was released in Sept. 2009 vowing to continue campaigning for democracy.

DEFENCE

Army Air Wing
There are two Israeli-built Arava transports with weapon attachments for light attack duties.

INTERNATIONAL RELATIONS

Swaziland is a member of the UN, World Bank, IMF and several other UN specialized agencies, WTO, Commonwealth, African Development Bank, African Union, COMESA, SADC and is an ACP member state of the ACP-EU relationship.

ECONOMY

Agriculture accounted for 8·1% of GDP in 2006, industry 46·4% and services 45·5%.

At the core of Swazi society is Tibiyo Taka Ngwane. Created in 1968 by Royal Charter, Tibiyo is a national development fund which operates outside the government and falls directly under the King, who holds it in trust for the nation. Its money derives from its stake in virtually every sector of Swazi commerce and industry.

Overview
Despite strong ties with the South African economy, Swaziland's economic growth has lagged behind that of its neighbours. Real GDP growth has fallen from an average of 3·6% per year in the 1990s to just over 2% since 2000, around two percentage points lower than other members of the South African Customs Union (SACU). Contributing factors to sluggish growth include a worsening investment environment owing to the slow pace of economic reform, the loss of preferential trade agreements for exports of textiles and sugar, repeated droughts and declining competitiveness. Inflation has also picked up, reflecting rising world commodity prices. Years of low growth have resulted in high rates of unemployment and poverty, aggravated by high labour force absenteeism and low productivity.

Since 2006 the economy has enjoyed a high fiscal surplus owing to growth in SACU revenues, which account for around 60% of total government revenues. Given the level of revenues from the SACU, the IMF recommends accelerating reforms to address current macroeconomic, growth and poverty concerns.

Currency
The unit of currency is the *lilangeni* (plural *emalangeni*) (SZL) of 100 *cents* but Swaziland remains in the Common Monetary Area and the South African rand is legal tender. In 2008 inflation was 13·1%. In July 2005 foreign exchange reserves were US$291m. and total money supply was 1,229m. emalangeni.

Budget
The fiscal year begins on 1 April. Total revenue in 2003–04 came to 3,947m. emalangeni and total expenditure to 4,392m. emalangeni.

There is a sales tax of 14%.

Performance
Real GDP growth was 2·4% in 2008 (3·5% in 2007). Total GDP in 2008 was US$2·6bn.

Banking and Finance

The central bank and bank of issue is the Central Bank of Swaziland (*Governor*, Martin Dlamini), established in 1974. In 2004 there were four banking institutions, three foreign (South African-owned) private banks, Swazibank (state-owned) and a housing bank. In 2003 there were 178 credit and saving unions.

In 1990 Swaziland Stock Brokers was established to trade in stocks and shares for institutional and private clients.

ENERGY AND NATURAL RESOURCES

Environment

Swaziland's carbon dioxide emissions from the consumption and flaring of fossil fuels were the equivalent of 0·8 tonnes per capita in 2008.

Electricity

Installed capacity was 0·1m. kW in 2002. Production was about 348m. kWh in 2001; total consumption was an estimated 963m. kWh. Swaziland imports about two-thirds of its electricity needs from South Africa.

Minerals

Output (in tonnes) in 2004: coal, 488,000; quarry stone, 230,000 cu. metres. Swaziland's diamond mine closed down in 1996 (1996 production, 75,000 carats) and its asbestos mine in 2000 (2000 production, 12,690 tonnes).

The oldest known mine (iron ore) in the world, dating back to 41,000 BC, was located at the Lion Cavern Site on Ngwenya Mountain.

Agriculture

In 2007 the agricultural population was around 354,000, of which about 141,000 were economically active. There were approximately 178,000 ha. of arable land and 14,000 ha. of permanent cropland in 2007. Production of principal crops (2003 estimates, in 1,000 tonnes): sugarcane, 4,000; maize, 70; grapefruit and pomelos, 37; oranges, 36; pineapples, 32; potatoes, 6; seed cotton, 6; cottonseed, 4; groundnuts, 4.

Livestock (2003 estimates): cattle, 580,000; goats, 422,000; pigs, 30,000; sheep, 27,000; chickens, 3m.

Livestock products, 2003 estimates (in 1,000 tonnes): milk, 38; meat, 22.

Forestry

Forests covered 541,000 ha. in 2005, or 31·5% of the land area. In 2007 timber production was 1·34m. cu. metres.

Fisheries

Estimated total catch, 2005, approximately 70 tonnes, exclusively from inland waters.

INDUSTRY

Most industries are based on processing agricultural products and timber. Footwear and textiles are also manufactured, and some engineering products.

Labour

In 2002, 92,654 persons were in formal employment; 5,714 Swazis worked in gold mines in South Africa in 2002. Unemployment was about 40% in 2003.

Trade Unions

In 1998 there were 21 affiliated trade unions grouped in the Swaziland Federation of Trade Unions with a combined membership of 83,000, and four unions grouped in the Swaziland Federation of Labour.

INTERNATIONAL TRADE

Swaziland has a customs union with South Africa and receives a pro rata share of the dues collected. External debt was US$532m. in 2005.

Imports and Exports

Trade in US$1m.:

	2002	*2003*	*2004*	*2005*	*2006*
Imports f.o.b.	1,027·0	1,540·2	1,715·3	1,949·4	1,960·7
Exports f.o.b.	1,078·5	1,666·8	1,806·2	1,965·5	1,975·7

Main import products are motor vehicles, machinery, transport equipment, foodstuffs, petroleum products and chemicals; main export commodities are soft drink concentrates, sugar, wood pulp and cotton yarn. By far the most significant trading partner is South Africa. In 2005, 88·3% of imports came from South Africa; 74·6% of exports went to South Africa in 2005.

COMMUNICATIONS

Roads

The total length of roads in 2002 was 3,594 km, of which 1,465 km were main roads. There were 52,200 passenger cars in use in 2007 plus 41,800 lorries and vans and 8,100 buses and coaches. There were 235 fatalities in road accidents in 2007.

Rail

In 2005 the system comprised 301 km of route (1,067 mm gauge). In 2000–01, 4·3m. tonnes of freight were transported.

Civil Aviation

There is an international airport at Manzini (Matsapha). Swazi Express Airways had flights in 2003 to Durban and Maputo. In 1999 scheduled airline traffic of Swaziland-based carriers flew 0·6m. km, carrying 12,000 passengers (all on international flights).

Telecommunications

In 2008 there were 44,000 main (fixed) telephone lines; mobile phone subscribers numbered 531,600 in 2008 (45·5 per 100 persons). There were 42,000 PCs in use in 2006 and 80,000 internet users in 2008.

Postal Services

There were 58 post offices in 2003, or one for every 18,600 persons.

SOCIAL INSTITUTIONS

Justice

The constitutional courts practice Roman-Dutch law. The judiciary is headed by the Chief Justice. There is a High Court and various Magistrates and Courts. A Court of Appeal with a President and three Judges deals with appeals from the High Court. There are 16 courts of first instance. There are also traditional Swazi National Courts.

The population in penal institutions in June 2008 was 2,546 (231 per 100,000 of national population).

Education

In 2007 there were 232,572 primary school pupils with 7,169 teaching staff. The teacher/pupil ratio has decreased from 40/1 in the 1970s to 32/1. About half the children of secondary school age attend school. There are also private schools. In 2007 there were 83,049 pupils in secondary schools with 4,358 teaching staff. Many secondary and high schools teach agricultural activities.

There were 5,692 students in higher education in 2006 with 462 academic staff. The University of Swaziland (UNISWA), with its main campus at Kwaluseni, was founded in 1982 and has an enrolment of over 5,000 students.

Rural education centres offer formal education for children and adult education geared towards vocational training. The adult literacy rate in 2003 was 79·2% (80·4% among males and 78·1% among females).

In 2006 public expenditure on education came to 7·9% of GNI and 24·4% of total government spending.

Health

In 2005 there were 400 health institutions, of which nine were hospitals and 19 were health centres. There were 184 physicians, 3,345 nurses, 20 dentists and 46 pharmacists in 2000.

RELIGION

In 2001 there were 480,000 African Christians, 160,000 Protestants and the remainder of the population followed other religions (including traditional beliefs).

CULTURE

Broadcasting

The government-run Swaziland Broadcasting and Information Service and Swaziland Television Authority control broadcasting in Swaziland. There is also one Christian radio station. In 2005, 30,600 households were equipped with televisions (colour by PAL).

Press

In 2003 there were three daily newspapers: The Swazi Observer (English-language with a circulation of 3,000 in 1999), The Times of Swaziland (English, 15,000), founded in 1897, and Tikhatsi (siSwati, 7,500).

Tourism

There were 352,000 foreign tourists in 2004 (including 152,000 from other African countries and 111,000 from Europe), bringing revenue of US$26m.

Festivals

The annual Umhlanga (Reed Dance) takes place in Aug. or early Sept. in honour of the Queen Mother.

Libraries

There is a government-subsidized National Library Service, which comprises two libraries at Mbabane and Manzini with 11 branches throughout the country.

DIPLOMATIC REPRESENTATIVES

Of Swaziland in the United Kingdom (20 Buckingham Gate, London, SW1E 6LB)
Acting High Commissioner: Henry Zeeman.

Of the United Kingdom in Swaziland (High Commission in Mbabane closed in Aug. 2005)
High Commissioner: Dr Nicola Brewer (resides in Pretoria, South Africa).

Of Swaziland in the USA (1712 New Hampshire Ave., NW, Washington, D.C., 20009)
Ambassador: Ephraim M. Hlophe.

Of the USA in Swaziland (2350 Mbabane Place, Dulles, Mbabane)
Ambassador: Earl Irving.

Of Swaziland to the United Nations
Ambassador: Joel Musa Nhleko.

Of Swaziland to the European Union
Ambassador: Solomon Mnukwa Dlamini.

FURTHER READING

Gillis, D. Hugh, *The Kingdom of Swaziland: Studies in Political History.* 1999

Matsebula, J. S. M., *A History of Swaziland.* 3rd ed. 1992

National Statistical Office: Central Statistical Office, POB 456, Mbabane.
Website: http://www.gov.sz/home.asp?pid=75

SWEDEN

Konungariket Sverige
(Kingdom of Sweden)

Capital: Stockholm
Population estimate, 2010: 9·29m.
GDP per capita, 2007: (PPP$) 36,712
HDI/world rank: 0·963/7

KEY HISTORICAL EVENTS

Sweden was covered by a thick ice cap until 14,000 years ago, when the ice began to retreat. The first human traces, in southern Sweden, date from 10,000 BC. Between 8000 and 6000 BC the country was populated by hunters and fishermen, using simple stone tools. Artefacts found in graves show that the Bronze Age was marked by a relatively advanced culture. From 500 BC to AD 800 agriculture became the basis for society and the economy. The Viking Age (800–1050) took expansion eastwards. Swedish Vikings reached into today's Russia, where they set up trading stations and principalities, such as Novgorod and Rurik. The Vikings also travelled to the Black and Caspian Seas and developed trading links with the Byzantine Empire and the Arabs.

In 830 the Frankish monk Ansgar introduced Christianity to Sweden but made few converts. In the 11th century, English missionaries had greater success and by the end of the century the country was fully Christianized. Olof Skötkonung, who proclaimed himself ruler of Sweden, supported the new religion.

By 1200 Sweden had become a united kingdom with largely the same borders as it has today, except that Skåne, Halland and Blekinge in the south of Sweden formed part of Denmark, and Jämtland, Härjedalen and Bohuslän in the west belonged to Norway. There was a struggle for power between the Sverker and Erik families, who ruled alternately in 1160–1250. However, by the middle of the 13th century with the building of royal castles and introduction of provincial administration, the crown was able to assert the authority of the central government and impose laws valid for the whole kingdom. Among the most important figures of the 13th century was Birger Jarl, who promoted the newly founded city of Stockholm. At a time when Hanseatic merchants traded in Sweden, Stockholm contained a large German population while, on the southeast coast, Kalmar and Gotland were controlled by German immigrants. The Hanseatic trading posts to the east included Finland, which was brought into the Swedish kingdom. A new code of law, for the entire country, was introduced in 1350 by King Magnus Eriksson. In 1340 Valdemar Atterdag, King of Denmark, went to war with Sweden over the southern provinces of Skåne, Halland and Blekinge. He attacked Gotland in 1361 in one of the bloodiest battles in Nordic history, to secure a base for further assaults on Sweden and to overthrow the Hanseatic League.

In the 14th century trade increased and until the mid-16th century the Hanseatic League dominated Sweden's trade. In 1350 the Black Death decimated the population. Inheritance and marriage ties united the crowns of Denmark, Norway and Sweden in 1389, under the rule of Queen Margaret of Denmark. In 1397 the loose association known as the Union of Kalmar confirmed her five-year old nephew, Erik of Pomerania, as ruler of the three countries. The Swedish nationalist Sten Sture, who was made king of Sweden in 1470, defeated the Danes at the Battle of Brunkeberg in Stockholm. Following this success, Sten Sture promoted nationalistic sentiment by the public display of a great wood carving of St George slaying the dragon (now placed in Stockholm cathedral) and the setting up of the first Swedish university at Uppsala. The union period (1397–1521) was characterized by a struggle for power between the king, the nobility and the burghers and peasants. These conflicts culminated in the Stockholm Bloodbath in 1520, when eighty leading men in Sweden were executed on orders of the Danish king, Christian II. In 1521 Christian II was overthrown by Gustav Vasa, a Swedish nobleman, who was elected king in 1523.

Empire Building

Gustav Vasa (ruled 1523–60) laid the foundations of the Swedish national state. With the Reformation, Sweden was converted to Lutheranism and the church became a national institution. At the same time power was concentrated in the hands of the king and in 1544 a hereditary monarchy was established. By the 16th century Scandinavia was divided into two states, Sweden-Finland and Denmark-Norway. Since the dissolution of the union with Denmark and Norway, Swedish foreign policy focused on dominating the Baltic Sea, and this led to wars with Denmark from the 1560s.

In 1611 Gustavus Adolphus (Gustaf II Adolf) consolidated Sweden's position on the Russian side of the Baltic Sea. Sweden defeated Denmark in two wars (1643 and 1657) to take control of the previously Danish provinces of Skåne, Halland, Blekinge and Gotland and the Norwegian provinces of Bohuslän, Jämtland and Härjedalen. Gustavus Adolphus gave his support to the Protestant alliance in the Thirty Years War. This cost him his life but earned Sweden territory in the north of Germany. Finland and the present-day Baltic republics also belonged to Sweden making it a great power in northern Europe.

Following the death of King Karl XII in 1718 the Swedish Parliament (Riksdag) introduced a constitution that abolished royal absolutism. But royal authority was soon reasserted. After defeat in the Great Northern War (1700–21) against Denmark, Poland and Russia, Sweden lost most of its Baltic territories, including a part of Finland and all its north-German possessions except west Pomerania. During the Napoleonic Wars, Sweden lost Finland to Russia and withdrew from its remaining German provinces. In 1810 Napoleon's marshal Jean-Baptiste Bernadotte assumed power as Karl XIV Johan. He tried to win back Finland from Russia, but had to make do with a union of Sweden and Norway, confirmed by the treaty of Kiel in 1814.

The short war against Norway in 1814 was Sweden's last military adventure. Since then Sweden has favoured neutrality. For this reason, there was no early application to join the EEC (European Economic Community). But in line with a commitment to liberalize trade, Sweden was a founder member of EFTA (European Free Trade Agreement) in 1959. After the Cold War and the collapse of the Soviet Union, the policy of neutrality was seen by many as obsolete. Sweden became a member of the EU (European Union) in 1995.

Following constitutional reforms in 1974 the remaining powers of the king were reduced to purely ceremonial functions. Carl XVI Gustaf, who succeeded the throne in 1973, is the first Swedish king to be bound by the new constitution. In 1980 the order of succession was amended to allow for a female member of the royal family to inherit the crown. Consequently, Princess Victoria is the heir apparent rather than her younger brother Prince Carl Philip.

Modern Economy

After the Napoleonic Wars, Sweden suffered economic stagnation. The country was poor with 90% of the population living off the land. Out of a population of five million, over one million emigrated between 1866 and 1914, mostly to North America. Industry did not start to grow until the 1890s. However, it then developed rapidly and after the Second World War Sweden was transformed into one of the leading industrial nations in Europe. In the six years to 1951 the country's GNP rose by 20%. Economic success was partly thanks to the early utilization of hydro-electric power which supported the pulp and paper industries of the northern forests. Swedish inventors created the ball-bearing, the adjustable spanner, the primus stove and the cream separator, as well as the safety match and dynamite. By 1956 the economy was booming, poverty had almost disappeared and unemployment was at a minimum. Sweden was one of the richest countries in Europe.

Social democracy began as the political offshoot of the trade unions. The working class was supported by intellectuals, such as the scientist Hjalmar Branting, who was the first Scandinavian socialist prime minister. The first representative of social democracy entered the government in 1917. Universal suffrage was introduced for men in 1909 and for women in 1921. In the 1930s, when the Social Democrats had become the governing party, plans for the welfare society were laid. Reforms included restrictions on child and female labour, free elementary education and old-age pensions. A four-party coalition for the duration of the Second World War was succeeded by a Social Democrat government with Per Albin Hansson as prime minister. Following his death in 1946, Tage Erlander became prime minister and stayed in office until 1969. He was succeeded by Olof Palme who was prime minister between 1969 and 1976. Owing to the rise in oil prices in 1973, unemployment increased. From the mid-1970s, improvements in living standards slowed. Economic crisis drove the Social Democrats out of government and in 1976 a non-socialist coalition was formed under Centre Party chairman, Thorbjörn Fälldin. Conflicts over the expansion of nuclear power led to several government reshuffles. In 1982 the Social Democrats resumed office with Olof Palme as prime minister. The assassination of Palme in 1986 shook the country which had been spared political violence for nearly 200 years. Ingvar Carlsson took over as head of government. In the 1990s industrial production fell and unemployment rose, which led to a high budget deficit and increased national debt. Popular dissatisfaction showed in the 1991 election, when a non-socialist coalition government was formed with Carl Bildt as prime minister. Launching a programme of deregulation and privatization, Bildt did much to prepare the economy for closer involvement with Europe. Capital gains taxes were reduced, as too were social benefits. But the government failed to reduce unemployment, the budget deficit or the national debt. Hence, the 1994 election put the Social Democrats back in power, with Ingvar Carlsson again as prime minister. In 1996 he stepped down to be replaced by Göran Persson. Persson led a series of minority governments. His third term, which began in 2002, was marked by the murder of his foreign minister, Anna Lindh, in 2003 and the rejection by referendum of Sweden's entry into the single European currency. In Sept. 2006 the Social Democrats emerged from elections as the single biggest party but Fredrik Reinfeldt of the Moderate Party was able to form a centre-right 'Alliance for Sweden' coalition to end 12 years of Social Democratic government. Despite economic problems, the country still boasts one of the highest standards of living and one of the most advanced welfare systems.

TERRITORY AND POPULATION

Sweden is bounded in the west and northwest by Norway, east by Finland and the Gulf of Bothnia, southeast by the Baltic Sea and southwest by the Kattegat. The area is 450,295 sq. km, including water (96,000 lakes) totalling 39,960 sq. km. At the last census, in 1990, the population was 8,587,353. Parliament decided in 1995 to change to a register-based method of calculating the population. The recorded population at 31 Dec. 2008 was 9,256,347; density 23 per sq. km. In 2005, 84·2% of the population lived in urban areas.

The UN gives an estimated population for 2010 of 9·29m.

Area, population and population density of the counties (*län*):

	Land area (in sq. km)	*Population (1990 census)*	*Population (31 Dec. 2008)*	*Density per sq. km (31 Dec. 2008)*
Stockholm	6,519	1,640,389	1,981,263	304
Uppsala	8,208	268,503	327,188	40
Södermanland	6,103	255,546	267,524	44
Östergötland	10,605	402,849	423,169	40
Jönköping	10,495	308,294	335,246	32
Kronoberg	8,468	177,880	182,224	22
Kalmar	11,219	241,149	233,397	21
Gotland	3,151	57,132	57,004	18
Blekinge	2,947	150,615	152,259	52
Skåne	11,035	1,068,587	1,214,758	110
Halland	5,462	254,568	293,572	54
Västra Götaland	23,956	1,458,166	1,558,130	65
Värmland	17,591	283,148	273,374	16
Örebro	8,546	272,474	277,732	32
Västmanland	5,145	258,544	249,974	49
Dalarna	28,197	288,919	275,867	10
Gävleborg	18,200	289,346	275,908	15
Västernorrland	21,685	261,099	243,372	11
Jämtland	49,343	135,724	126,897	3
Västerbotten	55,190	251,846	257,812	5
Norrbotten	98,249	263,546	249,677	3

There are some 17,000 Sami (Lapps).

On 31 Dec. 2008 foreign-born persons in Sweden numbered 1,281,581. Of these, 269,681 were from Nordic countries; 459,139 from the rest of Europe; 90,733 from Africa; 28,750 from North America; 60,878 from South America; 361,333 from Asian countries; 6,437 from the former USSR; 3,957 from Oceania; and 673 country unknown. Of the total 175,113 were born in Finland. 13·8% of the population of Sweden is foreign-born, the highest proportion in any of the Nordic countries.

Immigration: 2006, 95,750; 2007, 99,485; 2008, 101,171. Emigration: 2006, 44,908; 2007, 45,418; 2008, 45,294.

Population of the 50 largest communities, 31 Dec. 2008:

Stockholm	810,120	Luleå	73,406
Gothenburg (Göteborg)	500,197	Kungsbacka	72,676
Malmö	286,535	Skellefteå	71,862
Uppsala	190,668	Solna	65,289
Linköping	141,863	Järfälla	64,355
Västerås	134,684	Karlskrona	62,804
Örebro	132,277	Täby	62,266
Norrköping	128,060	Sollentuna	62,097
Helsingborg	126,754	Kalmar	61,693
Jönköping	125,154	Mölndal	59,812
Umeå	112,728	Östersund	58,914
Lund	107,351	Gotland	57,004
Borås	101,487	Varberg	56,673
Sundsvall	94,955	Norrtälje	55,528
Eskilstuna	94,785	Örnsköldsvik	55,387
Huddinge	94,209	Falun	55,297
Gävle	93,509	Trollhättan	54,487
Halmstad	90,241	Uddevalla	51,186
Nacka	85,661	Nyköping	50,973
Södertälje	84,753	Skövde	50,610
Karlstad	83,994	Hässleholm	50,006
Växjö	81,074	Borlänge	48,185
Botkyrka	80,055	Lidingö	43,111
Kristianstad	77,977	Tyresö	42,332
Haninge	74,968	Motala	41,953

A 16-km long fixed link with Denmark was opened in July 2000 when the Öresund motorway and railway bridge between Malmö and Copenhagen was completed.

The *de facto* official language is Swedish.

SOCIAL STATISTICS

Statistics for calendar years:

	Total living births	*To mothers single, divorced or widowed*	*Stillborn*	*Marriages*	*Divorces*	*Deaths exclusive of still-born*
2004	100,928	55,991	318	43,088	20,106	90,532
2005	101,346	56,238	301	44,381	20,000	91,710
2006	105,913	58,820	319	45,551	20,295	91,177
2007	107,421	58,819	326	47,898	20,669	91,729
2008	109,301	59,832	396	50,332	21,377	91,449

Rates, 2008, per 1,000 population: births, 11·9; deaths, 9·9; marriages, 5·4; divorces, 2·3. Sweden has one of the highest rate of births outside marriage in Europe, at 55% in 2008. In 2008 the average age at first marriage was 35·1 years for males and 32·5 years for females. Expectation of life in 2007: males, 78·6 years; females, 83·0. Annual population growth rate, 2000–05, 0·4%. Infant mortality, 2006, 2·8 per 1,000 live births (one of the lowest rates in the world). Fertility rate, 2008, 1·9 births per woman. In 2008 Sweden received 24,353 asylum applications, equivalent to 2·6 per 1,000 inhabitants.

A UNICEF report published in 2005 showed that 4·2% of children in Sweden live in poverty (in households with income below 50% of the national median).

CLIMATE

The north has severe winters, with snow lying for 4–7 months. Summers are fine but cool, with long daylight hours. Further south, winters are less cold, summers are warm and rainfall well distributed throughout the year, although slightly higher in the summer. Stockholm, Jan. –2·8°C, July 17·2°C. Annual rainfall 385 mm.

CONSTITUTION AND GOVERNMENT

The reigning King is **Carl XVI Gustaf**, b. 30 April 1946, succeeded on the death of his grandfather Gustaf VI Adolf, 15 Sept. 1973, married 19 June 1976 to Silvia Renate Sommerlath, b. 23 Dec. 1943 (Queen of Sweden). *Daughter* and *Heir Apparent:* Crown Princess Victoria Ingrid Alice Désirée, Duchess of Västergötland, b. 14 July 1977; *son:* Prince Carl Philip Edmund Bertil, Duke of Värmland, b. 13 May 1979; *daughter:* Princess Madeleine Thérèse Amelie Josephine, Duchess of Hälsingland and Gästrikland, b. 10 June 1982. *Sisters of the King.* Princess Margaretha, b. 31 Oct. 1934, married 30 June 1964 to John Ambler, died 31 May 2008; Princess Birgitta (Princess of Sweden), b. 19 Jan. 1937, married 25 May 1961 (civil marriage) and 30 May 1961 (religious ceremony) to Johann Georg, Prince of Hohenzollern; Princess Désirée, b. 2 June 1938, married 5 June 1964 to Baron Niclas Silfverschiöld; Princess Christina, b. 3 Aug. 1943, married 15 June 1974 to Tord Magnuson. *Uncles of the King.* Count Sigvard Bernadotte of Wisborg, b. 7 June 1907, died 4 Feb. 2002; Count Carl Johan Bernadotte of Wisborg, b. 31 Oct. 1916.

Under the 1975 constitution Sweden is a representative and parliamentary democracy. The King is Head of State, but does not participate in government. Parliament is the single-chamber *Riksdag* of 349 members elected for a period of four years in direct, general elections.

The manner of election to the *Riksdag* is proportional. The country is divided into 29 constituencies. In these constituencies 310 members are elected. The remaining 39 seats constitute a nationwide pool intended to give absolute proportionality to parties that receive at least 4% of the votes. A party receiving less than 4% of the votes in the country is, however, entitled to participate in the distribution of seats in a constituency if it has obtained at least 12% of the votes cast there.

A parliament, the *Sameting*, was instituted for the Sami (Lapps) in 1993.

National Anthem

'Du gamla, du fria' ('Thou ancient, thou free'); words by R. Dybeck; folk-tune.

GOVERNMENT CHRONOLOGY

Prime Ministers since 1936. (C = Centre Party; FP = Liberal Party; M = Moderate Party/New Moderates; SAP = Swedish Social Democratic Labour Party)

1936–46	SAP	Per Albin Hansson
1946–69	SAP	Tage Fritiof Erlander
1969–76	SAP	Sven Olof Joachim Palme
1976–78	C	Thorbjörn Fälldin
1978–79	FP	Ola Ullsten
1979–82	C	Thorbjörn Fälldin
1982–86	SAP	Sven Olof Joachim Palme
1986–91	SAP	Ingvar Gösta Carlsson
1991–94	M	Carl Bildt
1994–96	SAP	Ingvar Gösta Carlsson
1996–2006	SAP	Göran Persson
2006–	M	John Fredrik Reinfeldt

RECENT ELECTIONS

In parliamentary elections held on 17 Sept. 2006 the ruling Swedish Social Democratic Labour Party (SAP) won 130 seats with 35·2% of votes cast (down from 144 with 39·8% in 2002), the New Moderates 97 with 26·1% (up from 55 with 15·2%), the Centre Party 29 with 7·9% (22 with 6·1%), the Liberal Party 28 with 7·5% (48 with 13·3%), the Christian Democratic Party 24 with 6·6% (33 with 9·1%), the Left Party 22 with 5·8% (30 with 8·3%) and the Green Party 19 with 5·2% (17 with 4·6%). Turnout was 82·0%. The centre-right 'Alliance for Sweden' coalition of the New Moderates, the Centre Party, the Christian Democratic Party and the Liberal Party won enough seats between them to remove the Social Democrats from power after 12 years in office. The election represented the worst result for the Social Democrats since 1914. Following the 2006 election, of the 349 Members of Parliament there were 185 men (53·0%) and 164 women (47·0%). Only Rwanda has a higher percentage of women in its parliament (although it has a quota system that guarantees a certain percentage of seats for women).

Parliamentary elections are scheduled to take place on 18 Sept. 2010.

European Parliament
Sweden has 18 (19 in 2004) representatives. At the June 2009 elections turnout was 45·5% (37·9% in 2004). The SAP won 5 seats with 24·4% of votes cast (political affiliation in European Parliament: Progressive Alliance of Socialists and Democrats); the New Moderates, 4 with 18·8% (European People's Party); the Liberal Party, 3 with 13·6% (Alliance of Liberals and Democrats for Europe); the Green Party, 2 with 11·0% (Greens/European Free Alliance); the Pirate Party, 1 with 7·1% (Greens/European Free Alliance); the Left Party, 1 with 5·7% (European United Left/Nordic Green Left); the Centre Party, 1 with 5·5% (Alliance of Liberals and Democrats for Europe); the Christian Democratic Party, 1 with 4·7% (European People's Party).

CURRENT ADMINISTRATION

Following parliamentary elections in Sept. 2006 a new centre-right coalition government was formed. In March 2010 the cabinet comprised:

Prime Minister: Fredrik Reinfeldt; b. 1965 (New Moderates; sworn in 6 Oct. 2006).

Deputy Prime Minister and Minister of Enterprise and Energy: Maud Olofsson.

Minister of Agriculture: Eskil Erlandsson. *Communications:* Åsa Torstensson. *Culture:* Lena Adelsohn Liljeroth. *Defence:* Sten Tolgfors. *Elderly Care and Public Health:* Maria Larsson. *Employment:* Sven Otto Littorin. *Environment:* Andreas Carlgren. *European Union Affairs:* Birgitta Ohlsson. *Finance:* Anders Borg. *Foreign Affairs:* Carl Bildt. *Health and Social Affairs:* Göran Hägglund. *Higher Education and Research:* Tobias Krantz. *Integration and Gender Equality:* Nyamko Sabuni. *International Development Co-operation:* Gunilla Carlsson. *Justice:* Beatrice Ask. *Local Government and Financial Markets:* Mats Odell. *Migration and Asylum Policy:* Tobias Billström. *Schools:* Jan Björklund. *Social Security:* Cristina Husmark Pehrsson. *Trade:* Ewa Björling.

The *Speaker* is Per Westerberg.

Government Website: http://www.sweden.gov.se

CURRENT LEADERS

Fredrik Reinfeldt

Position
Prime Minister

Introduction
Fredrik Reinfeldt led a centre-right alliance to victory in the Swedish legislative elections of Sept. 2006, ousting the Social Democrats after over a decade in power. After taking over the leadership of the crisis-hit Moderate Party in 2003, Reinfeldt rebranded it as a centrist party that would foster entrepreneurship and create jobs by reforming, rather than dismantling, Sweden's cherished welfare system. He pledged to reduce dependence on benefits and promised to tackle unemployment.

Early Life
John Fredrik Reinfeldt was born in Stockholm on 4 Aug. 1965 and brought up in Täby, a suburb northeast of the city. He joined the youth wing of the conservative Moderate Party in 1983. Having completed military service, in 1990 he graduated in business and economics from Stockholm University, where he was active in student politics. He immediately embarked on a political career, becoming chairman of the Moderate Youth League and standing in the legislative elections of Sept. 1991. He won a seat in parliament in a surprisingly strong performance by the Moderate Party, which emerged as the leading non-socialist party. The Social Democrats (SAP) remained the largest single party but failed to take an overall majority and Moderate leader Carl Bildt became the first Conservative prime minister since 1930, heading a four-party coalition. The government attempted to tackle the economic crisis that gripped Sweden in 1992 by introducing market reforms, imposing spending cuts and privatizing publicly-owned enterprises. It also entered negotiations for accession to the European Union.

In the Sept. 1994 elections Reinfeldt and his Moderate colleagues held on to the 80 seats they had won in 1991 but some of their centre-right coalition partners fared badly and the former Social Democrat prime minister, Ingvar Carlsson, was returned to power. Reinfeldt spent much of the mid- to late 1990s garnering support for his party at the grassroots level. He also served as a member of the parliamentary finance committee. After Bo Lundgren succeeded Bildt as leader of the Moderate Party in 1999, Reinfeldt was promoted to chairman of the parliamentary justice committee in 2001–02.

The Moderate Party's poor performance in the 2002 elections was compounded by a scandal in 2003 in which some representatives were accused of racism. Lundgren was forced to resign as leader in Oct. 2003 and Reinfeldt was elected unanimously to succeed him. Reinfeldt introduced sweeping changes, repackaging the party as the New Moderates and shifting the focus to the centre ground. Calls for tax cuts and major reforms to the welfare state were moderated and emphasis placed on the creation of jobs. In the run-up to the Sept. 2006 legislative elections, Reinfeldt formed the Alliance for Sweden, aiming to unite a four-party centre-right coalition (New Moderates plus the Centre Party, the Liberal Party and the Christian Democrats). Presenting a joint manifesto, the alliance narrowly beat the SAP on 17 Sept. 2006. The New Moderates took 26·1% of the vote, a record for the party, with the strongest support coming from the populous southern districts. Reinfeldt was nominated prime minister on 5 Oct. 2006.

Career in Office
The Alliance's victory and Reinfeldt's premiership were broadly welcomed after ten years of SAP rule. On taking office, he initiated a programme of reforms aimed at strengthening incentives to work, reducing welfare dependency and streamlining the state's role in the economy. However, in the wake of the global financial crisis, Sweden slipped into recession in the second quarter of 2008, and in Dec. Reinfeldt proposed a stimulus package in an attempt to boost the economy. The downturn nevertheless had a significant impact on Sweden's trade-oriented economy through 2009 as exports declined and job losses mounted.

Reinfeldt's own party is in favour of joining the single European currency and also, in principle, supports membership of NATO, although it accepts that this is not a view shared by all members of the Alliance for Sweden. In 2008 the Alliance, supported by the SAP, ratified the Lisbon Treaty (signed in Dec. 2007) on EU institutional and administrative reform. From July–Dec. 2009 Sweden held the rotating EU presidency and oversaw the treaty's eventual entry into force in Dec. The Swedish presidency also pressed the EU to take the lead in fighting climate change despite facing the worst recession since the 1930s. In Feb. 2009 Reinfeldt's government announced its intention to lift a 30-year-old ban on building new nuclear energy capacity.

DEFENCE

The Supreme Commander is, under the government, in command of the three services. The Supreme Commander is assisted by the Swedish Armed Forces HQ. There is also a Swedish Armed Forces Logistics Organization.

Conscripted military service has been phased out and was scheduled to end officially on 1 July 2010.

In 2006 military expenditure totalled US$5,780m. (US$641 per capita), representing 1·5% of GDP. Sweden's national security policy is currently undergoing a shift in emphasis. Beginning with the decommissioning of obsolete units and structures, the main thrust of policy is the creation of contingency forces adaptable to a variety of situations.

The government stressed that Sweden's membership of the EU (in 1995) did not imply any change in Sweden's traditional policy of non-participation in military alliances, with the option of staying neutral in the event of war in its vicinity.

Sweden has modern air raid shelters with capacity for some 7m. people. Since this falls short of providing protection for the whole population, evacuation and relocation operations would be necessary in the event of war.

The Swedish Civil Contingencies Agency is responsible for civil protection and emergency preparedness and has a mandate spanning the entire spectrum of threats and risks, including wartime defence.

Army

The Army consists of one division HQ and divisional units and three army brigade command and control elements. Army strength, 2007, 10,200 (4,300 conscripts). The Army can mobilize a reserve of 225,000. Voluntary auxiliary organizations numbered 42,000.

Navy

The Navy has two naval warfare flotillas and one submarine flotilla.

The personnel of the Navy in 2007 totalled 7,900 (active manpower, including 2,000 conscripts, 1,300 coastal defence and 320 naval aviation). Reserve strength, 20,000. In addition there is a paramilitary coast guard numbering 600.

Air Force

The Air Force consists of eight air-base battalions, four fighter squadrons, four air transport squadrons, one fighter control and air surveillance battalion, one anti-submarine warfare squadron, one signal intelligence squadron, one airborne early warning squadron and a training school.

Strength (2007) 5,900 (1,500 conscripts), plus 17,000 reserves. There were 130 combat capable aircraft in 2007 (JAS 39 *Gripens*).

In 1998 the helicopter units of the Swedish Army and Navy were merged with those of the Air Force to form a single helicopter wing, consisting of four squadrons and an independent unit, which since 2003 has fallen under the direct authority of the Air Force. Strength (2007), 1,050 (250 conscripts).

INTERNATIONAL RELATIONS

Sweden is a member of the UN, World Bank, IMF and several other UN specialized agencies, WTO, EU, Council of Europe, OSCE, CERN, Nordic Council, Council of the Baltic Sea States, BIS, IOM, NATO Partnership for Peace, OECD, Inter-American Development Bank, Asian Development Bank and Antarctic Treaty. Sweden is a signatory to the Schengen accord, which abolishes border controls between Sweden, Austria, Belgium, Czech Republic, Denmark, Estonia, Finland, France, Germany, Greece, Hungary, Iceland, Italy, Latvia, Lithuania, Luxembourg, Malta, Netherlands, Norway, Poland, Portugal, Slovakia, Slovenia, Spain and Switzerland.

Sweden gave US$4·3bn. in international aid in 2007, which at 0·93% of GNI made it the world's second most generous developed country as a percentage of its gross national income (after Norway).

In a referendum held on 14 Sept. 2003 Swedish voters rejected their country's entry into the common European currency, 56·1% opposing membership of the euro against 41·8% voting in favour. Turnout was 81·2%.

ECONOMY

Services accounted for 70% of GDP in 2007, industry 29% and agriculture 2%.

According to the anti-corruption organization *Transparency International*, Sweden ranked equal third in the world in a 2009 survey of the countries with the least corruption in business and government. It received 9·2 out of 10 in the annual index.

Overview

After the 2001 global technology crash damaged Ericsson, Sweden's largest exporter, the economy experienced an upswing until 2008, with strong recovery in the telecommunications and automobile sectors fuelling export growth from 2003–07. Growing exports combined with rising capacity utilization and low interest rates to prompt a revival in business investment. Growth was further buoyed by gains in consumer wealth.

However, the economy was hit hard by the global financial crisis in 2007, with exports significantly reduced and recession hitting in 2008. A rescue package for the banking sector was announced in early 2009.

Sweden combines an extensive welfare state with a market economy. Tax revenue as a percentage of GDP is among the highest in the world. Expenditure ceilings and a target for the cyclically adjusted budget surplus have governed fiscal policy since 1997 but the general government balance has been moving away from the 2% structural surplus target. Monetary policy has targeted a 2% inflation rate since 1993 and the IMF has praised the design and operation of the inflation-targeting framework implemented by the Riksbank. Until 2007 inflation was edging towards this target but increased to 3·4% in 2008. However, it was predicted to be below target again in 2009–10. In Sept. 2003 a referendum rejected adoption of the euro.

The employment rate is high by international standards but below the government target of 80%. Effective employment is lower than that portrayed by employment statistics because of large numbers of employees benefiting from sick leave, social assistance, labour market programmes and mid-life sabbaticals. So far Sweden's strong growth has failed to make an impact on unemployment. Increased employment has been offset by new entrants into the labour market. Over 20% of the labour force remains economically inactive and the unemployment rate remains stubbornly above 6%.

More than 28% of the total labour force was employed in the government sector in 2005. The share of the total labour force employed by government is the second highest in the OECD and more than double the OECD average. In 2004 total disability pensions increased by 12%, with almost 30% of the increase comprising pensioners below 40. The younger generation is also taking longer to complete tertiary education. Since 1987 the age at which a young person attains full-time employment has increased by five years. Raising productivity and enhancing effective labour supply is a key strategy in the management of demographic trends and in the maintenance of living standards.

The authorities have deregulated a number of sectors, including electricity, telecommunications and parts of transport. Sweden is facing further pressure from the EU to privatize its state monopolies in line with internal markets regulations, particularly in the pharmaceuticals, construction and alcoholic beverages sectors. A government target set in 2006 aims to reduce administrative costs for businesses by 25% by the end of 2010.

Currency

The unit of currency is the *krona* (SEK), of 100 *öre*. Inflation rates (based on OECD statistics):

1999	*2000*	*2001*	*2002*	*2003*	*2004*	*2005*	*2006*	*2007*	*2008*
0·5%	0·9%	2·4%	2·2%	1·9%	0·4%	0·5%	1·4%	2·2%	3·4%

Foreign exchange reserves were US$38,704m. and gold reserves 4·04m. troy oz in Sept. 2009. Total money supply was 1,486·7bn. kr. in Aug. 2009.

Budget

Revenue of 810·3bn. kr. and expenditure of 792·0bn. kr. was estimated for the total budget (Current and Capital) for financial year 2006.

Revenue and expenditure for 2005 (1m. kr.):

Revenue	
Tax revenues	682,268
—Taxes on income	85,257
—Social security contribution	271,415
—Taxes on property	37,780
—Taxes on goods and services	335,884
—Reallocation fee	-32,714
—Cash difference account	335
—Tax reductions	-15,689
From government activities	33,185
From sale of property	6,689
Loans repaid	2,303
Computed revenues	8,788
Contributions, etc., from the EU	12,592
Total revenue	745,825
Expenditure	
The Swedish political system	7,673
Economy and fiscal administration	10,972
Tax administration and collection	8,572
Justice	27,025
Foreign policy administration and international co-operation	1,365
Total defence	43,591
International development assistance	22,260
Immigrants and refugees	6,918
Health care, medical care, social services	38,473
Financial security in the event of illness and disability	127,049
Financial security in old age	46,120
Financial security for families and children	55,467
The labour market	69,568
Working life	1,153
Study support	19,779
Education and university research	43,695
Culture, the media, religious organizations and leisure	8,968
Community planning, housing supply and construction	8,737
Regional balance and development	3,286
General environment and conservation	4,254
Energy	1,396
Communications	31,833
Agriculture and forestry, fisheries, etc.	17,408
Business sector	3,775
General grants to municipalities	57,325
Interest on central government debt, etc.	32,657
Contribution to the European Community	25,635
Other expenditure	6,815
Total expenditure	731,771

VAT is 25% (reduced rates, 12% and 6%).

Performance

Real GDP growth rates (based on OECD statistics):

1999	*2000*	*2001*	*2002*	*2003*	*2004*	*2005*	*2006*	*2007*	*2008*
4·3%	4·5%	1·2%	2·4%	2·0%	3·5%	3·3%	4·5%	2·7%	−0·4%

The real GDP growth rate in 2009 according to Sweden's National Institute of Economic Research was negative, at –4·9%, the country's lowest rate since World War Two. Sweden's total GDP in 2008 was US$480·0bn.

Sweden was ranked fourth in the Global Competitiveness Index in the World Economic Forum's *Global Competitiveness Report 2009–2010*. The index analyses 12 areas of competitiveness for over 100 countries including macroeconomy, higher education and training, institutions, innovation and infrastructure.

In 2006 the state debt amounted to 1,270bn. kr.

Banking and Finance

The central bank and bank of issue is the Sveriges Riksbank. The bank has 11 trustees, elected by parliament, and is managed by a directorate, including the governor, appointed by the trustees. The *Governor* is Stefan Ingves, appointed for a six-year term. In 2004 there were 50 commercial banks. Their total deposits in 2000 amounted to 1,104,570m. kr.; advances to the public in 2000 amounted to 975,212m. kr. In April 2003 there were 77 savings banks and 20 branches of foreign banks. The largest banks are Nordea Bank AB (previously MeritaNorbanken, formed in 1997 when Nordbanken of Sweden merged with Merita of Finland), Svenska Handelsbanken, Skandinavska Enskilda Banken and FöreningsSparbanken. In April 2000 MeritaNordbanken acquired Denmark's Unidanmark, thereby becoming the Nordic region's biggest bank in terms of assets. It became Nordea Bank AB in Dec. 2001. By Oct. 2000 approximately 27% of the Swedish population were using e-banking.

There is a stock exchange in Stockholm.

ENERGY AND NATURAL RESOURCES

In 2003 Sweden obtained 34% of its energy from oil, down from 77% in 1970. It aims to end fossil fuel dependency completely by 2020.

Environment

Sweden's carbon dioxide emissions from the consumption and flaring of fossil fuels in 2008 were the equivalent of 6·2 tonnes per capita. An *Environmental Performance Index* compiled in 2008 ranked Sweden second in the world behind Switzerland, with 93·1%. The index examined various factors in six areas—air pollution, biodiversity and habitat, climate change, environmental health, productive natural resources and water resources.

Electricity

Sweden is rich in hydro-power resources. Installed capacity was 33,661 MW in 2005, of which 16,276 MW was in hydro-electric plants, 9,461 MW in nuclear plants and 7,426 MW in thermal plants. Electricity production in 2005 was 159,058m. kWh; consumption was 169,558 kWh. In 2004 consumption per capita was 16,670 kWh. A referendum of 1980 called for the phasing out of nuclear power by 2010. In Feb. 1997 the government began denuclearization by designating one of the 12 reactors for decommissioning. The state corporation Vattenfall was given the responsibility of financing and overseeing the transition to the use of non-fossil fuel alternatives. However, in Feb. 2009 the government announced an end to the 30-year ban on nuclear plant construction. In 2006 there were ten nuclear reactors in operation.

Minerals

Sweden is a leading producer of iron ore with around 2% of the world's total output. It is the largest iron ore exporter in Europe. There are also deposits of copper, gold, lead, zinc and alum shale containing oil and uranium. Iron ore produced, 2005, 23·3m. tonnes; zinc (mine output, zinc content), 214,600 tonnes; copper (mine output, copper content), 97,800 tonnes.

The mining industry accounts for 1·0% of the market value of Sweden's total industrial production and employs 0·5% of the total industrial labour force.

Agriculture

In 2005 agricultural land totalled 3,431,366 ha. There were 2,703,333 ha. of arable land in 2005 and 513,505 ha. of natural pasture on agricultural holdings of more than 2 ha. Of the land used for arable farming in 2005, 2–5 ha. holdings covered a total area of 50,637 ha.; 5·1–10 ha. holdings covered 102,723 ha.; 10·1–20 ha., 204,004; 20·1–30 ha., 186,590; 30·1–50 ha., 346,159; 50·1–100 ha., 671,052 and holdings larger than 100 ha. covered 1,141,892 ha. There were 75,808 agricultural enterprises in 2005 compared to 150,014 in 1971 and 282,187 in 1951. Around 37% of the enterprises were between 5 and 20 ha. In 2005 Sweden set aside 222,268 ha. (7·3% of its agricultural land—one of the highest proportions in the world) for the growth of organic crops.

Agriculture accounts for 5·8% of exports and 7·9% of imports. The agricultural sector employs 3% of the workforce.

	Area (1,000 ha.)			Production (1,000 tonnes)		
Chief crops	2004	2005	2006	2004	2005	2006
Ley	934·8	1,027·3	1,055·1	2,481·3	2,674·4	2,425·0
Sugarbeet	47·6	49·2	44·2	2,287·1	2,381·2	2,189·0
Wheat	403·4	354·8	360·9	2,412·3	2,246·8	1,967·4
Barley	397·3	378·6	315·1	1,691·9	1,592·9	1,110·6
Potatoes	31·7	30·5	28·2	979·1	947·3	777·8
Oats	229·7	200·1	206·1	925·3	746·3	624·4
Rye	24·4	21·4	23·5	133·4	112·3	115·4

Production (in 1,000 tonnes) in 2006: milk, 3,172; meat, 406; cheese, 119; butter, 42.

Livestock, 2006: pigs, 1,680,535; cattle, 1,590,406; sheep and lambs, 505,466; poultry, 6,170,320. There were 261,404 reindeer in Sami villages in 2005. Harvest of moose during open season 2006: 82,370.

Forestry

Forests form one of the country's greatest natural assets. The growing stock includes 42% spruce, 39% pine and 16% broad-leaved. In 2005 forests covered 27·53m. ha. (66·9% of the land area). Sweden's largest forest owner is Sveaskog, with holdings of 4·5m. ha. Since 2001 the company has been completely state-owned after taking over the part-privatized AssiDomän corporation. Public ownership (including the state) accounts for 19% of the forests, limited companies own 24% and the remaining 57% is in private hands. Of the 98·3m. cu. metres of wood felled in 2005, 56·6m. cu. metres were sawlogs, 35·3m. cu. metres pulpwood, 5·9m. cu. metres fuelwood and 0·5m. cu. metres other.

Fisheries

In 2004 the total catch was 262,272 tonnes, worth 870·7m. kr. In 2004 the fishing fleet comprised 1,602 vessels of 44,063 gross tonnes.

INDUSTRY

The leading companies by market capitalization in Sweden in March 2009 were: Hennes & Mauritz (H&M), a clothing company (US$27·3bn.); Ericsson, a technology hardware and equipment company (US$26·5bn.); and TeliaSonera, a mobile telecommunications company (US$21·5bn.).

Manufacturing is mainly based on metals and forest resources. Chemicals (especially petrochemicals), building materials and decorative glass and china are also important.

Industry groups	Sales value of production (gross) in 1m. kr. 2005
Manufacturing industry	*1,402,490*
Food products, beverages and tobacco	119,058
Textiles and textile products, leather and leather products	11,638
Wood and wood products	71,921
Pulp, paper and paper products, publishers and printers	170,664
Coke, refined petroleum products and nuclear fuel	10,287
Chemicals, chemical products and man-made fibres	112,757
Rubber and plastic products	35,602
Other non-metallic mineral products	25,514
Basic metals	116,856
Fabricated metal products, machinery and equipment	688,689
Other manufacturing industries	39,504
Mines and quarries	*22,206*

Labour

In 2006 there were 4,341,000 persons in the labour force, employed as follows: 810,000 in trade and communication; 701,000 in health and social work; 686,000 in manufacturing, mining, quarrying, electricity and water services; 633,000 in financial services and business activities; 534,000 in education, research and development; 361,000 in personal services and cultural activities, and sanitation; 271,000 in construction; 249,000 in public administration; 86,000 in agriculture, forestry and fishing. The unemployment rate in Dec. 2009 was 8·9%, but with youth unemployment of nearly 27%. In 2006, 76·8% of men and 72·1% of women were in employment. No other major industrialized nation has such a small gap between the employment rates of the sexes. The average monthly salary in 2006 was 25,000 kr. (27,100 kr. for men and 22,800 kr. for women).

In 2006 a total of 1,971 working days were lost through strikes, compared to 627,541 in 2003.

Trade Unions

At 31 Dec. 2006 the Swedish Trade Union Confederation (LO) had 15 member unions with a total membership of 1,803,800; the Central Government Organization of Salaried Employees (TCO) had 19, with 1,244,443; the Swedish Confederation of Professional Associations (SACO) had 25, with 586,110; the Central Organization of Swedish Workers (SAC) had 6,564 members. In the period March–June 2005, 79% of workers were unionized.

INTERNATIONAL TRADE

Imports and Exports

Imports and exports (in 1m. kr.):

	2002	2003	2004	2005	2006
Imports	656,664	679,329	739,203	832,640	935,675
Exports	805,696	825,850	904,532	970,815	1,085,287

Breakdown by Standard International Trade Classification (SITC, revision 3) categories (value in 1bn. kr.):

	Imports		Exports	
	2005	2006	2005	2006
0. Food and live animals	52·8	59·7	27·5	31·5
1. Beverages and tobacco	7·3	7·6	5·5	5·8
2. Crude materials	27·1	31·6	54·5	63·7
3. Fuels and lubricants	98·3	116·1	52·4	65·2
4. Animal and vegetable oils	2·2	3·3	1·6	1·5
5. Chemicals	88·6	97·9	109·0	124·8
6. Manufactured goods	126·1	143·2	198·5	218·3
7. Machinery and transport equipment	328·6	364·5	435·6	477·1
8. Miscellaneous manufactured items	101·4	111·4	83·5	94·2
9. Other	0·2	0·4	2·6	3·2

Principal imports in 2006 (in 1bn. kr.): road vehicles, 100·6; petroleum and petroleum products, 98·2; electrical machines, apparatus and appliances, 58·3; telecommunications, sound recording and similar appliances, 52·1; office machinery and computers, 39·4. Principal exports in 2006 (in 1bn. kr.): road vehicles, 146·3; telecommunications, sound recording and similar appliances, 91·3; paper, paperboard and manufactures thereof, 72·8; medical and pharmaceutical preparations, 64·4; iron and steel, 61·8. Machinery and transport equipment accounts for some 44% of Swedish exports. This includes the mobile phone sector, which is the largest product group in the Swedish export market. The telecommunications company Ericsson is now the leading export company, ahead of Volvo.

Imports and exports by countries (value in 1bn. kr.):

	Imports from		*Exports to*	
	2005	*2006*	*2005*	*2006*
Denmark	79·0	90·4	66·8	78·1
Finland	50·0	55·3	58·9	68·5
France	42·6	44·3	46·8	54·0
Germany	151·3	168·8	100·7	108·0
Netherlands	54·9	59·3	44·1	52·4
Norway	68·1	80·0	83·7	99·1
UK	57·7	58·6	75·6	78·7
USA	28·2	31·5	102·7	100·8

In 2006 other EU member countries accounted for 70·1% of imports and 60·1% of exports.

COMMUNICATIONS

Roads

In 2007 there were 214,926 km of roads open to the public of which 98,317 km were state-administered roads (main roads, 15,385 km; secondary roads, 82,932 km). There were also 1,744 km of motorway. 79% of all roads in 2005 were surfaced. Motor vehicles in 2006 included 4,202,000 passenger cars, 480,000 lorries, 14,000 buses and 446,000 motorcycles and mopeds. There were 1,015,997 Volvos, 434,757 Saabs, 343,060 Fords and 327,379 Volkswagens registered in 2006. Sweden has one of the lowest death rates in road accidents of any industrialized country, at 5·1 deaths per 100,000 people in 2007. 471 people were killed in traffic accidents in 2007.

Rail

Total length of railways at 31 Dec. 2005 was 11,017 km (7,737 km electrified). In 2005, 150m. passengers and 63m. tonnes of freight were carried. There is a metro in Stockholm (110 km), and tram/light rail networks in Stockholm (8 km), Gothenburg (118 km) and Norrköping (13 km).

Civil Aviation

The main international airports are at Stockholm (Arlanda), Gothenburg (Landvetter), Stockholm (Skavsta) and Malmö (Sturup). The principal carrier is Scandinavian Airlines System (SAS), which resulted from the 1950 merger of the three former Scandinavian airlines. SAS Sverige AB is the Swedish partner (SAS Denmark A/S and SAS Norge ASA being the other two). The Swedish government is the principal shareholder of SAS with a 21·4% share. The governments of Denmark and Norway each own 14·3%. Since 2001, 50% of SAS shares have been listed on the stock exchanges of Stockholm, Copenhagen and Oslo. SAS had a market capitalization in Oct. 2009 of 11,918m. kr. and an operating revenue in 2008 of 53,195m. kr.

Malmö Aviation and Skyways AB, both Sweden-based carriers, operate some international as well as domestic flights.

In 2008 Stockholm (Arlanda) handled 18,136,165 passengers (13,281,466 on international flights) and 187,000 tonnes of freight. Gothenburg (Landvetter) was the second busiest airport, handling 4,303,722 passengers (3,158,822 on international flights) and 100,000 tonnes of freight. Malmö handled 1,882,428 passengers in 2006 (1,181,970 on domestic flights).

Shipping

The mercantile marine consisted on 31 Dec. 2006 of 485 vessels of 4·48m. GRT. Cargo vessels entering Swedish ports in 2006 numbered 19,551 (119·92m. GRT) while there were 72,844 passenger ferries (995·04m. GRT). The number of cargo vessels leaving Swedish ports in 2006 totalled 19,448 (115·79m. GRT) and the number of passenger ferries leaving was 73,151 (958·58m. GRT).

The busiest port is Gothenburg. In 2006 a total of 39·91m. tonnes of goods were loaded and unloaded there (37·04m. tonnes unloaded from and loaded to foreign ports). Other major ports are Brofjorden, Trelleborg, Malmö and Karlshamn.

Telecommunications

In 2008 there were 5,323,000 main (fixed) telephone lines. In the same year mobile phone subscribers numbered 10,892,000 (1,183·3 per 1,000 persons). In June 2000 the state sold off a 30% stake in the Swedish telecommunications operator Telia. In Dec. 2002 Telia and the Finnish telecommunications operator Sonera merged to become TeliaSonera. The Swedish state owns 37·3% and the Finnish state 13·7%. There were 8·0m. PCs in 2006. Internet users numbered 8·1m. in 2008, or 87·8% of the total population (the second highest percentage in the world, after Iceland). In June 2008 the broadband penetration rate was 32·3 subscribers per 100 inhabitants.

Postal Services

The Swedish postal service, Posten AB, began to close down traditional post offices in 2001 and now local supermarkets, newsagents, petrol stations and similar shops act as postal service agents. In 2008 there were 2,400 postal service points for both handing in and collecting postal items, and 1,600 offices for handing in only.

In 2009 Posten AB and Post Danmark merged to form Posten Norden AB. In 2007 there were 33 licensed postal operators, although only CityMail, specialists in business bulk mail, offer serious competition to Posten Norden.

SOCIAL INSTITUTIONS

Justice

Sweden has two parallel types of courts—general courts that deal with criminal and civil cases and general administrative courts that deal with cases related to public administration. The general courts have three instances: district courts, courts of appeal and the Supreme Court. There are 60 district courts, of which 23 also serve as real estate courts and four courts of appeal. The administrative courts also have three instances: 23 county administrative courts, four administrative courts of appeal and the Supreme Administrative Court. In addition, a number of special courts and tribunals have been established to hear specific kinds of cases and matters.

Every district court, court of appeal, county administrative court and administrative court of appeal has a number of lay judges. These take part in the adjudication of both specific concrete issues and matters of law; each has the right to vote.

Criminal cases are normally tried by one judge and three lay judges. Civil disputes are normally heard by a single judge or three judges. In the courts of appeal, criminal cases are determined by three judges and two lay judges. Civil cases are tried by three or four judges. In the settlement of family cases, lay judges take part in the proceedings in both the district court and in the court of appeal. Proceedings in the general administrative courts are in writing; i.e. the court determines the case on the basis of correspondences between the parties. Nevertheless, it is also possible to hold a hearing. The cases are determined by a single judge or one judge and three lay judges. In the administrative court of appeal, cases are normally heard by three judges or three judges and two lay judges.

Those who lack the means to take advantage of their rights are entitled to legal aid. Everyone suspected of a serious crime or taken into custody has the right to a public counsel (advocate). The title advocate can only be used by accredited members of the Swedish Bar Association. Qualifying as an advocate requires extensive theoretical and practical training. All advocates in Sweden are employed in the private sector.

The control over the way in which public authorities fulfil their commitments is exercised by the Parliamentary Ombudsmen and the Chancellor of Justice. In 2005–06 the Ombudsmen received 6,008 cases altogether, of which 89 were instituted on their own initiative. Sweden has no constitutional court. However, in each particular case the courts do have a certain right to ascertain whether a statute meets the standards set out by superordinate provisions.

The population in penal institutions in April 2006 was 7,450 (82 per 100,000 of national population). There are 56 prisons spread throughout the country.

There were 209 reported murders in 2004 (121 in 1990 and 175 in 2000).

In June 2003 Sweden agreed to accommodate the prison term of Biljana Plavšić, the ex-president of the Republika Srpska in Bosnia and Herzegovina, who was sentenced to 11 years for crimes against humanity by the International War Crimes Tribunal at the Hague.

Education

In 2006–07 there were 962,349 pupils in 4,872 compulsory schools. In secondary education at the higher stage (the integrated upper secondary school) there were 376,087 pupils in Oct. 2006 (excluding pupils in the fourth year of the technical course regarded as third-level education). The folk high schools, 'people's colleges', had 26,098 pupils on courses of more than 15 weeks in the autumn of 2006.

In municipal adult education there were 227,682 students in 2005–06.

There are also special schools for pupils with visual and hearing impairments (548 pupils in 2006) and for those who are intellectually disabled (22,623 pupils).

In 2005–06 there were 389,089 students enrolled for undergraduate studies in integrated institutions for higher education. The number of students enrolled for postgraduate studies in 2006 was 17,987.

In 2006 public expenditure on education came to 7·0% of GDP (and accounted for 12·6% of total government expenditure). The adult literacy rate is at least 99%.

Health

In 2006 there were 28,300 doctors, 4,300 dentists, 86,100 nurses and midwives and 26,352 hospital beds. In 2007 Sweden spent 9·1% of its GDP on health.

In 2002–03, 17·5% of Swedes were smokers (males, 16%; females, 19%).

Welfare

Social insurance benefits are granted mainly according to uniform statutory principles. All persons resident in Sweden are covered, regardless of citizenship. All schemes are compulsory, except for unemployment insurance. Benefits are usually income-related. Most social security schemes are at present undergoing extensive discussion and changes.

Type of social insurance scheme	*Payments 2006 (in 1m. kr.)*
Old-age pension	197,727
Sickness insurance	107,306
Unemployment insurance	26,918
Parental insurance	25,627
Child allowance	23,611
Survivor's pension	16,840
Attendance allowance	16,084
Housing supplement	11,410
Work injury insurance	6,005

Under a Pension Reform Plan Sweden is one of the world's leaders in the shift to private pension systems. In the new system each worker's future pension will be based on the amount of money accumulated in two separate individual accounts. The bulk of retirement income will come from a notional account maintained by the government on behalf of the individual, but a significant portion of retirement income will come from a private individual account. There are two types of pension—the income pension and the premium pension. The income pension comes under a pay-as-you-go system, with the premium pension based on contributions invested in a fund chosen by the insured person.

There is also a guarantee pension for those aged 65 and resident in Sweden for the last three years but without an earnings-related pension. Its value in 2004 was 84,561 kr. for a single pensioner and 75,430 kr. for a married pensioner.

RELIGION

The Swedish Lutheran Church was disestablished in 2000. It is headed by Archbishop Anders Wejryd (b. 1948) and has its metropolitan see at Uppsala. In 2008 there were 13 bishoprics and 1,802 parishes. The clergy are chiefly supported from the parishes and the proceeds of the church lands. Around 73% of the population, equivalent to 6·8m. people, belong to the Church of Sweden. Other denominations, in 2001: Pentecostal Movement, 89,482 members; The Mission Covenant Church of Sweden, 65,299; InterAct, 28,955; Salvation Army, 19,745; Örebro Missionary Society (1996), 22,801; The Baptist Union of Sweden, 18,003; Swedish Evangelical Mission, 17,283; Swedish Alliance Missionary Society, 12,868; Holiness Mission (1996), 6,393. There were also 95,000 Roman Catholics (under a Bishop resident at Stockholm). The Orthodox and Oriental churches number around 98,500 members.

There were around 250,000 Muslims and 18,000 Jews in Sweden in 1998, making Islam Sweden's second largest religion.

CULTURE

World Heritage Sites

There are 14 sites under Swedish jurisdiction that appear on the UNESCO World Heritage List: the royal palace of Drottningholm (1991); the Viking settlements of Birka and Hovgården (1993); the Engelsberg ironworks (1993); the Bronze Age rock carvings in Tanum (1994); Skogskyrkogården cemetery (1994); the Hanseatic town of Visby (1995); the Lapponian area (home of the Sami people in the Arctic circle) (1996); the church town of Gammelstad in Luleå (1996); the naval port of Karlskrona (1998); the Kvarken Archipelago and High Coast (2000 and 2006), shared with Finland; the agricultural landscape of Southern Öland (2000); the Mining Area of the Great Copper Mountain in Falun (2001); the Varberg Radio Station (2004) at Grimeton in southern Sweden; and the Struve Geodetic Arc (2005). The Arc is a chain of survey triangulations spanning from Norway to the Black Sea that helped establish the exact shape and size of the earth and is shared with nine other countries.

Broadcasting

The Swedish Broadcasting Commission (SBC) is the national authority that oversees radio and television services. Sveriges Radio is a public broadcaster, operating four national stations, an external service and regional programming. There are around 100 private radio stations. Sveriges Television (SVT) is the public service television provider (colour by PAL); the main commercial terrestrial broadcaster is TV4. Most households also have access to satellite and cable TV. The switchover from analogue to digital television transmission was completed in Oct. 2007. There were 4·13m. households equipped with television sets in 2006 (94·0% of all households).

Cinema

In 2006 there were 1,171 cinemas. Total attendance was 15·3m. A total of 208 new foreign films and 44 new Swedish films were shown in 2006. In 2006 gross box office receipts came to 1,200m. kr.

Press

In 2006 there were 166 daily newspapers with an average weekday net circulation of 3·9m. The leading papers in terms of circulation in 2004 were the tabloid Social Democratic Aftonbladet, with average daily sales of 452,300; the independent Dagens Nyheter, with average daily sales of 368,200; the liberal tabloid Expressen, with average daily sales of 363,000; and the liberal Göteborgs-Posten, with average daily sales of 248,800. In 2006 a total of 21,765 book titles were published.

Tourism

In 2006 Swedes stayed 18,605,735 nights in hotels in Sweden and 4,693,379 in holiday villages and youth hostels; and foreign visitors stayed 5,606,018 nights in hotels and 1,257,618 in holiday villages and youth hostels. There were 2,925 accommodation establishments in 2006 with 285,783 beds. Of 12·5m. trips abroad with an overnight stay undertaken by Swedes in 2006, 2·5m. were for business purposes and 10·0m. were leisure trips.

Festivals

Important traditional festivals include Lucia, held in Dec, and Walpurgis Night, a spring celebration held in April. The eight-day Malmö Festival includes live music and other cultural events and is held annually in Aug.

Libraries

In 2006 there were 326 public libraries, 37 university libraries, 35 special libraries and one national library.

Theatre and Opera

State-subsidized theatres gave 13,730 performances for audiences totalling 2,956,249 in 2005. The National Theatre (Kungliga Dramatiska Teatern) and the National Opera (Operan) are both located in Stockholm.

Museums and Galleries

Sweden had 228 public museums and art galleries in 2006 with a combined total of 20,139,000 visits.

DIPLOMATIC REPRESENTATIVES

Of Sweden in the United Kingdom (11 Montagu Pl., London, W1H 2AL)
Ambassador: Staffan Carlsson.

Of the United Kingdom in Sweden (Skarpögatan 6–8, S-115 93 Stockholm)
Ambassador: Andrew Mitchell.

Of Sweden in the USA (1501 M St., NW, Suite 900, Washington, D.C., 20005-1702)
Ambassador: Jonas Hafström.

Of the USA in Sweden (Dag Hammarskjölds Väg 31, S-115 89 Stockholm)
Ambassador: Matthew W. Barzun.

Of Sweden to the United Nations
Ambassador: Anders Lidén.

Of Sweden to the European Union
Permanent Representative: Christian Danielsson.

FURTHER READING

Statistics Sweden. *Statistik Årsbok/Statistical Yearbook of Sweden.—Historisk statistik för Sverige* (Historical Statistics of Sweden). 1955 ff.—*Allmän månadsstatistik* (Monthly Digest of Swedish Statistics).—*Statistiska meddelanden* (Statistical Reports). From 1963

Henrekson, M., *An Economic Analysis of Swedish Government Expenditure.* 1992

Petersson, O., *Swedish Government and Politics.* 1994

Sveriges statskalender. Annual, from 1813

National library: Kungliga Biblioteket, PO Box 5039, SE-102 41 Stockholm.
National Statistical Office: Statistics Sweden, PO Box 24300, SE-104 51 Stockholm.
Website: http://www.scb.se
Swedish Institute Website: http://www.si.se

SWITZERLAND

Schweizerische Eidtgenossenschaft—
Confédération Suisse—
Confederazione Svizzera[1]
(Swiss Confederation)

Capital: Berne
Population estimate, 2010: 7·60m.
GDP per capita, 2007: (PPP$) 40,658
HDI/world rank: 0·960/9

KEY HISTORICAL EVENTS

Neolithic settlements from around 3,000 BC have been found. Celtic clans settled in fertile valleys in parts of present-day Switzerland from around 1,500 BC, with the Raetians in the east and the Helvetti to the west. A Bronze Age Celtic civilization reached its height around 100 BC. An attempt by the Helvetti to spread west into Gaul was quashed by Julius Caesar in 58 BC. As the Roman Empire expanded northward and westward, Switzerland came under its domain, centred on Aventicum (Avenches). The Romans constructed a road network from the strategically important Alpine passes but attempts to conquer Germanic tribes to the north and east of the Rhine were thwarted in 9 AD. Garrisons along the Rhine from Lake Constance to Basle were maintained until Roman forces withdrew in 401.

The Germanic Alemanni tribe became dominant in northern and central Switzerland as Rome's influence declined, while Latin-speaking Burgundians held sway in the Jura mountains. Celtic tribes were gradually subsumed over the following centuries. Frankish rulers established monasteries, enabling the spread of Christianity and feudalism throughout west-central Europe in the seventh and eighth centuries. Following the signing of the Treaty of Verdun in 840 western and southwest Switzerland came under the jurisdiction of the Burgundian king, Lothair I, and the north and east formed part of the domain of Louis the German. The Burgundian lands became part of the Holy Roman Empire in 1033, while various independent dukedoms emerged in the north and east, notably Swabia, Zahringen, Savoy and Kyberg. The Kyberg domains of central Switzerland passed to the Habsburgs in 1264. The expansion of this dynasty led to three mountain-based clans—the Uri, the Schwyz and the Unterwalden—forming a defensive league. Their agreement, renewed in 1291, is considered the founding document of the Swiss nation. The league defeated the Habsburgs at Mortgarten in 1315 and by 1353 the confederation had added the cantons of Glarus and Zug and the city states of Lucerne, Zürich and Berne, forming the 'Old Federation' of eight states within the Holy Roman Empire.

Defeat at the hands of French forces at Marignano in 1515 led the Swiss confederation to form a 'perpetual alliance' with France and marked the start of a neutral stance. Relations between the cantons deteriorated in the 16th century and during the Reformation, when the city-states of Zürich, Berne, Basle and St Gallen adopted Protestantism while Catholicism was retained in the four forest cantons. The 1531 Treaty of Kappel ended the civil war and preserved Catholicism in the rural south, though religious tensions continued in the late 16th century with the rural cantons and city states linked only by neutrality in the Thirty Years War. The War's end in 1648 and the subsequent Peace of Westphalia saw Switzerland declared independent of the Holy Roman Empire.

Geneva, Basle, Berne and Zürich grew prosperous in the 18th century, becoming Enlightenment centres of intellectual and cultural achievement. Power remained with the oligarchs until the arrival of French Revolutionary troops in their offensive against Austrian and Russian forces in 1798. Napoleon's Act of Mediation in 1803 partially restored political power to the cantons but it was not until 1815 that the Congress of Vienna re-established Switzerland's independence, its perpetual neutrality guaranteed by Austria, France, Great Britain, Portugal, Prussia, Spain and Sweden.

In 1848 a new constitution was approved following disputes between Protestant and Catholic cantons. The 22 cantons were linked by a federal government (consisting of a bicameral parliament that elected a seven-member governing council) and a federal tribunal to rule on intra-cantonal disputes. This constitution was revised in 1874 to allow for national and local referenda on a range of issues.

Switzerland maintained its status of armed neutrality in the First World War but was unable to avoid mass unemployment, leading to a national strike in 1918 and demands for social security. The 1919 Treaty of Versailles reaffirmed Switzerland's neutrality and a year later it joined the League of Nations (based in Geneva). The Federal Council issued a declaration of neutrality at the start of the Second World War and much effort went in to shoring up defences and remaining self-sufficient while surrounded by the Axis powers. The Swiss government subsequently expressed regrets about the country's behaviour in the Second World War following a report by an independent panel of historians on relations with the Nazis.

In 1959 Switzerland became a founding member of the European Free Trade Association but has remained outside the European Union. It joined the UN by a narrow majority in a referendum in 2002. In 2005 Switzerland signed up to the Schengen accord.

TERRITORY AND POPULATION

Switzerland is bounded in the west and northwest by France, north by Germany, east by Austria and Liechtenstein and south by Italy. Area and population by canton (with date of establishment):

[1]The Latin 'Confoederatio Helvetica' is also in use.

Canton	Area (sq. km) (1 Jan. 2008)	Census Population (1 Dec. 2000)	Population Estimate (31 Dec. 2008)
Uri (1291)	1,077	34,777	35,162
Schwyz (1291)	908	128,704	143,719
Obwalden (1291)	491	32,427	34,429
Nidwalden (1291)	276	37,235	40,737
Lucerne (1332)	1,493	350,504	368,742
Zürich (1351)	1,729	1,247,906	1,332,727
Glarus (Glaris) (1352)	685	38,183	38,370
Zug (1352)	239	100,052	110,384
Fribourg (Freiburg) (1481)	1,671	241,706	268,537
Solothurn (Soleure) (1481)	790	244,341	251,830
Basel-Town (Bâle-V.) (1501)	37	188,079	186,672
Basel-Country (Bâle-C.) (1501)	518	259,374	271,214
Schaffhausen (Schaffhouse) (1501)	298	73,392	75,303
Appenzell-Outer Rhoden (1513)	243	53,504	53,054
Appenzell-Inner Rhoden (1513)	173	14,618	15,549
Berne (Bern) (1553)	5,959	957,197	969,299
St Gallen (St Gall) (1803)	2,026	452,837	471,152
Graubünden (Grisons) (1803)	7,105	187,058	190,459
Aargau (Argovie) (1803)	1,404	547,493	591,632
Thurgau (Thurgovie) (1803)	991	228,875	241,811
Ticino (Tessin) (1803)	2,812	396,846	332,736
Vaud (Waadt) (1803)	3,212	640,657	688,245
Valais (Wallis) (1815)	5,224	272,399	303,241
Neuchâtel (Neuenburg) (1815)	803	167,949	170,924
Geneva (Genève) (1815)	282	413,673	446,106
Jura (1979)	839	68,224	69,822
Total	41,285	7,228,010	7,701,856

In 2006 there were 3,829,400 females and 1,554,500 resident foreign nationals. In 2006 foreign nationals made up 20·7% of the population, one of the highest proportions in western Europe. In 2006, 73·4% of the population lived in urban areas. Population density in 2006 was 187·7 per sq. km. The population at the 2000 census was 7,288,010.

The UN gives an estimated population for 2010 of 7·60m.

German, French, Italian and Romansch (spoken mostly in Graubünden) are the official languages. German is spoken by the majority of inhabitants in 19 of the 26 cantons, French in Fribourg, Vaud, Valais, Neuchâtel, Jura and Geneva, and Italian in Ticino. At the 2000 census 63·7% of the population gave German as their mother tongue, 20·4% French, 6·5% Italian, 0·5% Romansch and 9·0% other languages.

At the end of 2008 the five largest cities were Zürich (365,132); Geneva (183,287); Basle (164,937); Berne (122,925); Lausanne (122,284). In 2008 the population figures of conurbations were: Zürich, 1,154,500; Geneva, 513,200; Basle, 494,300; Berne, 348,700; Lausanne, 324,400; other towns, 2008 (and their conurbations), Winterthur, 98,238 (135,000); St Gallen, 72,040 (148,500); Lucerne, 59,241 (205,400); Lugano, 54,437 (133,400); Biel, 50,013 (92,300).

SOCIAL STATISTICS

Statistics for calendar years:

	Live births	Marriages	Divorces	Deaths
2004	73,082	39,460	17,949	60,180
2005	72,903	40,139	21,332	61,124
2006	73,371	39,817	20,981	60,283
2007	74,494	40,330	19,882	61,089
2008	76,691	41,534	19,613	61,233

Rates (2008, per 1,000 population): birth, 10·0; death, 8·0; marriage, 5·4; divorce, 2·6. In 2005 the most popular age range for marrying was 30–34 for males and 25–29 for females. Expectation of life, 2008: males, 79·7 years; females, 84·4. In 2007 the suicide rate per 100,000 population was 15·1 (males, 21·9; females, 9·1). Annual population growth rate, 2000–05, 0·7%. Infant mortality, 2008, four per 1,000 live births; fertility rate, 2008, 1·5 births per woman. In 2004 Switzerland received 14,217 asylum applications, equivalent to 1·9 per 1,000 inhabitants. The World Health Organization's *World Health Statistics 2009* put citizens of Switzerland in equal second place in a 'healthy life expectancy' list (level with San Marino and only behind Japan), with an expected 75 years of healthy life for babies born in 2007.

CLIMATE

The climate is largely dictated by relief and altitude, and includes continental and mountain types. Summers are generally warm, with quite considerable rainfall; winters are fine, with clear, cold air. Berne, Jan. 32°F (0°C), July, 65°F (18·5°C). Annual rainfall 39·4" (986 mm).

CONSTITUTION AND GOVERNMENT

A new constitution was accepted on 18 April 1999 in a popular vote and came into effect on 1 Jan. 2000, replacing the constitution dating from 1874. Switzerland is a republic. The highest authority is vested in the electorate, i.e. all Swiss citizens over 18. This electorate, besides electing its representatives to the Parliament, has the voting power on amendments to, or on the revision of, the Constitution as well as on Switzerland joining international organizations for collective security or supranational communities (mandatory referendum). It also takes decisions on laws and certain international treaties if requested by 50,000 voters or eight cantons (facultative referendum), and it has the right of initiating constitutional amendments, the support required for such demands being 100,000 voters (popular initiative). The Swiss vote in more referendums—three or four a year—than any other nation. A mandatory referendum and a constitutional amendment demanded by popular initiative require a double majority (a majority of the voters and a majority of the cantons voting in favour of the proposal) to be accepted while a facultative referendum is accepted if a majority of the voters vote in favour of the proposal. Between 1893 and the end of 2008, 169 initiatives were put to the vote but only 15 were adopted. The highest turnout for a popular initiative has been 80·5% and the lowest 32·1%.

The Federal government is responsible for legislating matters of foreign relations, defence (within the framework of its powers), professional education and technical universities, protection of the environment, water, public works, road traffic, nuclear energy, foreign trade, social security, residence and domicile of foreigners, civil law, banking and insurance, monetary policy and economic development. It is also responsible for formulating policy concerning statistics gathering, sport, forests, fishery and hunting, post and telecommunications, radio and television, private economic activity, competition policy, alcohol and gambling.

The legislative authority is vested in a parliament of two chambers: the Council of States (*Ständerat/Conseil des États*) and the National Council (*Nationalrat/Conseil National*). The Council of States is composed of 46 members, chosen and paid by the 23 cantons of the Confederation, two for each canton. The mode of their election and the term of membership depend on the canton. Three of the cantons are politically divided—Basle into Town and Country, Appenzell into Outer-Rhoden and Inner-Rhoden, and Unterwalden into Obwalden and Nidwalden. Each of these 'half-cantons' sends one member to the State Council. The Swiss parliament is a militia/semi-professional parliament.

The National Council has 200 members directly elected for four years, in proportion to the population of the cantons, with the proviso that each canton or half-canton is represented by at least one member. The members are paid from federal funds.

The parliament sits for at least four ordinary three-week sessions annually. Extraordinary sessions can be held if necessary and if demanded by the Federal Council, 25% of the National Council or five cantons.

The 200 seats are distributed among the cantons according to population size:

Zürich	34	Basel-Town (Bâle-V.)	5
Berne	26	Graubünden (Grisons)	5
Vaud (Waadt)	18	Neuchâtel (Neuenburg)	5
Aargau (Argovie)	15	Schwyz	4
St Gallen (St Gall)	12	Zug	3
Geneva	11	Jura	2
Lucerne	10	Schaffhausen (Schaffhouse)	2
Ticino (Tessin)	8	Appenzell Inner-Rhoden	1
Basel-Country (Bâle-C.)	7	Appenzell Outer-Rhoden	1
Fribourg (Freiburg)	7	Glarus	1
Solothurn (Soleure)	7	Nidwalden	1
Valais (Wallis)	7	Obwalden	1
Thurgau (Thurgovie)	6	Uri	1

A general election takes place by ballot every four years. Every citizen of the republic who has entered on his 18th year is entitled to a vote, and any voter may be elected a deputy. Laws passed by both chambers may be submitted to direct popular vote, when 50,000 citizens or eight cantons demand it; the vote can be only 'Yes' or 'No'. This principle, called the *referendum*, is frequently acted on.

The chief executive authority is deputed to the *Bundesrat*, or Federal Council, consisting of seven members, elected for four years by the *United Federal Assembly*, i.e. joint sessions of both chambers, such as to represent both the different geographical regions and language communities. The members of this council must not hold any other office in the Confederation or cantons, nor engage in any calling or business. In the Federal Parliament legislation may be introduced either by a member, or by either chamber, or by the Federal Council (but not by the people). Every citizen who has a vote for the National Council is eligible to become a member of the executive.

The *President* of the Federal Council (called President of the Confederation) and the Vice-President are the first magistrates of the Confederation. Both are elected by the United Federal Assembly for one calendar year from among the Federal Councillors, and are not immediately re-eligible to the same offices. The Vice-President, however, may be, and usually is, elected to succeed the outgoing President.

The seven members of the Federal Council act as ministers, or chiefs of the seven administrative departments of the republic. The city of Berne is the seat of the Federal Council and the central administrative authorities.

National Anthem

'Trittst im Morgenrot daher'/'Sur nos monts quand le soleil'/'Quando il ciel' di porpora' ('When the morning skies grow red'); German words by Leonard Widmer, French by C. Chatelanat, Italian by C. Valsangiacomo, tune by Alberik Zwyssig.

GOVERNMENT CHRONOLOGY

Presidents since 1945. (CVP/PDC = Christian Democratic People's Party; FDP/PRD = Free Democratic Party/Radical Democratic Party; SPS/PSD = Social Democratic Party of Switzerland; SVP/UDC = Swiss People's Party/Centre Democratic Union)

1945	SVP/UDC	Adolf Eduard von Steiger
1946	FDP/PRD	Karl Kobelt
1947	CVP/PDC	Philipp Etter
1948	CVP/PDC	Enrico Celio
1949	SPS/PSD	Ernst Nobs
1950	FDP/PRD	Max-Édouard Petitpierre
1951	SVP/UDC	Adolf Eduard von Steiger
1952	FDP/PRD	Karl Kobelt
1953	CVP/PDC	Philipp Etter
1954	FDP/PRD	Rodolphe Rubattel
1955	FDP/PRD	Max-Édouard Petitpierre
1956	SVP/UDC	Markus Feldmann
1957	FDP/PRD	Hans Streuli
1958	CVP/PDC	Thomas Emil Leo Holenstein
1959	FDP/PRD	Paul Chaudet
1960	FDP/PRD	Max-Édouard Petitpierre
1961	SVP/UDC	Friedrich Traugott Wahlen
1962	FDP/PRD	Paul Chaudet
1963	SPS/PSD	Willy Spühler
1964	CVP/PDC	Ludwig von Moos
1965	SPS/PSD	Hans-Peter Tschudi
1966	FDP/PRD	Hans Schaffner
1967	CVP/PDC	Roger Bonvin
1968	SPS/PSD	Willy Spühler
1969	CVP/PDC	Ludwig von Moos
1970	SPS/PSD	Hans-Peter Tschudi
1971	SVP/UDC	Rudolf Gnägi
1972	FDP/PRD	Nello Celio
1973	CVP/PDC	Roger Bonvin
1974	FDP/PRD	Ernst Brugger
1975	SPS/PSD	Pierre Graber
1976	SVP/UDC	Rudolf Gnägi
1977	CVP/PDC	Kurt Furgler
1978	SPS/PSD	Willi Ritschard
1979	CVP/PDC	Hans Hürlimann
1980	FDP/PRD	Georges-André Chevallaz
1981	CVP/PDC	Kurt Furgler
1982	FDP/PRD	Fritz Honegger
1983	SPS/PSD	Pierre Aubert
1984	SVP/UDC	Leon Schlumpf
1985	CVP/PDC	Kurt Furgler
1986	CVP/PDC	Alphons Egli
1987	SPS/PSD	Pierre Aubert
1988	SPS/PSD	Otto Stich
1989	FDP/PRD	Jean-Pascal Delamuraz
1990	CVP/PDC	Arnold Koller
1991	CVP/PDC	Flavio Cotti
1992	SPS/PSD	René Felber
1993	SVP/UDC	Adolf Ogi
1994	SPS/PSD	Otto Stich
1995	FDP/PRD	Kaspar Villiger
1996	FDP/PRD	Jean-Pascal Delamuraz
1997	CVP/PDC	Arnold Koller
1998	CVP/PDC	Flavio Cotti
1999	SPS/PSD	Ruth Dreifuss
2000	SVP/UDC	Adolf Ogi
2001	SPS/PSD	Moritz Leuenberger
2002	FDP/PRD	Kaspar Villiger
2003	FDP/PRD	Pascal Couchepin
2004	CVP/PDC	Joseph Deiss
2005	SVP/UDC	Samuel Schmid
2006	SPS/PSD	Moritz Leuenberger
2007	SPS/PSD	Micheline Calmy-Rey
2008	FDP/PRD	Pascal Couchepin
2009	FDP/PRD	Hans-Rudolf Merz
2010	CVP/PDC	Doris Leuthard

RECENT ELECTIONS

In elections to the *National Council* on 21 Oct. 2007 the Swiss People's Party/Centre Democratic Union (SVP) took 29·0% of the vote (62 seats), the Social Democratic Party of Switzerland (SPS) 19·5% (43), the Free Democratic Party/Radical Democratic Party (FDP) 15·6% (31), the Christian Democratic People's Party (CVP) 14·6% (31), the Green Party (GPS) 9·6% (20), the Evangelical People's Party (EVP) 2·4% (2), the Liberal Party (LPS) 1·8%

(4) and the Green Liberal Party (GLP) 1·4% (3). The following parties won one seat each: the Federal Democratic Union, the Swiss Labour Party, the Swiss Democrats and the League of Ticinesians. Turnout was 48·9%. By receiving 29·0% of the vote the SVP achieved the highest share of the vote of any party at a Swiss election since 1919.

In the Council of States the CVP hold 15 seats, the FDP 12, the SPS 9, the SVP 7, the GPS 2 and the GLP 1.

At an election held in the United Federal Assembly on 2 Dec. 2009 Doris Leuthard was elected president for 2010 and Moritz Leuenberger was elected vice-president.

CURRENT ADMINISTRATION

In March 2010 the Federal Council comprised:

President of the Confederation and Chief of the Department of Economic Affairs: Doris Leuthard; b. 1963 (CVP; sworn in 1 Jan. 2010).

Vice President and Chief of the Department of Transport, Communications and Energy: Moritz Leuenberger; b. 1946 (SPS; sworn in 1 Jan. 2010).

Minister of Defence, Civil Protection and Sports: Ueli Maurer (SVP). *Finance:* Hans-Rudolf Merz (FDP). *Foreign Affairs:* Micheline Calmy-Rey (SPS). *Home Affairs:* Didier Burkhalter (FDP). *Justice and Police:* Eveline Widmer-Schlumpf (SVP).

Federal Authorities Website: http://www.admin.ch

CURRENT LEADERS

Doris Leuthard

Position
President

Introduction
On 1 Dec. 2009 parliament elected Doris Leuthard to the presidency for the following calendar year. At 46 years old, the lawyer is the nation's youngest president since 1934. She faces a challengingly uncertain economic climate, ongoing concerns about immigration and international calls for further reforms to Switzerland's bank secrecy laws.

Early Life
Doris Leuthard was born in Merenschwand, Aargau canton, in northern Switzerland on 10 April 1963. She graduated in law from Zürich University and undertook further studies in Paris and Calgary during the late 1980s. While practising as a patent lawyer, Leuthard developed an interest in politics and was elected to Muri's local authority in 1993 and to Aargau canton's grand council four years later. In 1999 she was elected to represent Aargau on the Swiss National Council. A long-standing member of the centre-right Christian Democratic People's Party (CVP/PDC), Leuthard was elected as the party's vice-president at both cantonal and federal levels in 2000. Following the resignation of the CVP president, Philip Stähelin, Leuthard was elected party leader in Sept. 2004.

Leuthard participated in several committees on the Swiss National Council, including those concerning human rights and judicial and tax affairs. She was elected to the seven-member federal council (*Bundesrat*) on 1 Aug. 2006, succeeding Joseph Deiss as head of the department of economic affairs. There she established several bilateral free-trade agreements, including one with China. Responsible for delivering on jobs, training and innovation, she worked to create a more flexible labour market.

On 10 Dec. 2008 she was elected Switzerland's vice-president by the united federal assembly, alongside President Hans-Rudolf Merz of the Free Democratic Party. In March 2009 Switzerland agreed to conform to accepted standards of international tax evasion, a significant break with the country's tradition of banking secrecy. The action came in response to threats that Switzerland might be blacklisted as an uncooperative tax haven at the G20 summit in London in April 2009.

Leuthard expressed surprise when a motion to ban mosques from building new minarets won 57% support in a referendum in Nov. 2009, with majorities in 22 cantons. The poll had been demanded by the right-wing Swiss People's Party, the largest party in government, which also called for the abolition of the 'freedom of movement' agreement that allows EU citizens to live and work in Switzerland and vice versa. Leuthard suggested that the fallout from the global economic slowdown had precipitated a crisis of identity, adding that the nation's discussions on immigration should be transparent.

Career in Office
Leuthard was elected president on 1 Dec. 2009 by a broad majority of parliamentarians, winning 158 of 183 valid votes. Taking over from Hans-Rudolf Merz on 1 Jan. 2010, her priorities included steps to reform the federal council, boosting the economy and strengthening foreign relations. Her government adopted a conciliatory tone in early 2010 towards Germany's plan to use stolen Swiss bank data to investigate tax fraud.

DEFENCE

There are fortifications in all entrances to the Alps and on the important passes crossing the Alps and the Jura. Large-scale destruction of bridges, tunnels and defiles are prepared for an emergency.

Conscripts complete 18–21 weeks of basic training and then regular annual refresher training up to a set number of service days. In 2006 military expenditure totalled US$3,473m. (US$462 per capita), representing 0·9% of GDP.

Army

There are about 4,000 regular soldiers, but some 220,000 conscripts undergo training annually (18 or 21 weeks recruit training at 20; six or seven refresher courses of 19 days every year between 21 and 30). Proposals ('Army XXI') implemented in 2004 envisaged an Armed Forces based on the three areas of promoting peace, defence and general civil affairs support. Troop levels were cut to 220,000 (120,000 conscripts, 20,000 recruits, 80,000 reservists).

Since 2004 Switzerland has a Chief of the Armed Forces in the rank of a lieutenant-general. In peacetime the Army has no general; in time of war the Federal Assembly in joint session of both Houses appoints a general.

In 1999 for the first time a small Swiss contingent was deployed outside the country, in Kosovo.

Navy

There is no Navy in the Swiss Armed Forces but the Land Forces include a small Marine component with patrol boats.

Air Force

The Air Force has five air base commands. The fighter squadrons are equipped with Swiss-built F-5E Tiger IIs and F/A-18s. Personnel (2005), 19,000 on mobilization, with 85 combat aircraft.

INTERNATIONAL RELATIONS

Switzerland is a member of the UN, World Bank, IMF and several other UN specialized agencies, WTO, Council of Europe, OSCE, EFTA, CERN, BIS, IOM, International Organization of the Francophonie, NATO Partnership for Peace, OECD, Inter-American Development Bank, Asian Development Bank and Antarctic Treaty. In a referendum in 1986 the electorate voted against UN membership, but in a further referendum on 4 March 2002, 54·6% of votes cast were in favour of joining. Switzerland officially became a member at the UN's General Assembly in Sept. 2002. An official application for membership of the EU was made in May 1992, but in Dec. 1992 the electorate voted against joining the European Economic Area. At a referendum in March 2001, 76·7% of voters rejected membership talks with the EU, with just 23·3% in favour; turnout was 55·1%. The government still has plans to join the EU but as yet no entry talks are scheduled. In Dec. 2008 Switzerland became the most recent country to implement the Schengen accord, which abolishes border controls between Switzerland, Austria, Belgium, Czech Republic, Denmark, Estonia, Finland, France, Germany, Greece, Hungary, Iceland, Italy, Latvia, Lithuania, Luxembourg, Malta, Netherlands, Norway, Poland, Portugal, Slovakia, Slovenia, Spain and Sweden.

ECONOMY

Services accounted for 71·2% of GDP in 2006, industry 27·5% and agriculture 1·2%.

According to the anti-corruption organization *Transparency International*, Switzerland ranked fifth in the world in a 2009 survey of the countries with the least corruption in business and government. It received 9·0 out of 10 in the annual index.

Overview

Switzerland is a small economy with one of the highest living standards in the world. Owing to a lack of raw materials, prosperity is built on labour skills, a business-friendly environment and technological expertise. Major service sectors include tourism and banking. Switzerland experienced a downturn in growth during the global economic slowdown in 2001 but has witnessed moderate recovery since late 2003. The return to growth has not improved labour market conditions, with employment declining in manufacturing in 2004 and unemployment rising above 4%, although the opening of the labour market to EU workers has helped to reverse both these trends.

While remaining one of Europe's wealthiest countries, per capita GDP growth has been below that of the OECD average for several years. High labour costs and product market rigidities in the sheltered economy pose problems of competitiveness. In 2004 the authorities launched a reform agenda to open sheltered sectors, to reduce the role of the state, to encourage external economic relations and to improve the education system in a bid to boost competition and growth. Following these reforms growth has performed above trend and become broad-based, benefiting from buoyant global markets and supported by strong investment and private consumption.

The central government carries the responsibility for foreign policy, defence, pensions, postal services, telecommunications, railway services and currency. All other responsibilities are dealt with at the canton level, notably economic regulation, education, health care and the judiciary. This system has led to large income disparities across cantons, with tax revenue per capita differing by as much as a factor of two. In 2004 a referendum approved the New Financial Equalization System, which provided a clearer division between federal and local responsibilities.

In 2000 the National Bank introduced a monetary policy framework aimed at keeping inflation below 2%. Inflation has remained low for many years, contained primarily by strong retail competition and a flexible labour market. Tight expenditure controls and higher revenues have helped to reduce gross debt to around 48% of GDP, yet gross government financial liabilities had increased to 56% of GDP by 2006. Monetary independence has given Swiss companies a competitive advantage as it permits lower interest rates than those prevailing in the euro zone.

Pressures are building on the pension and health care systems, which generated a combined deficit of 5% of GDP in 2004. The projected 16% increase in the old-age dependency ratio by 2035 is likely to increase pressure on public finances. Switzerland is the world's second most expensive country for health care, which accounted for 10·8% of GDP in 2006. The health care system is mostly financed by the private sector and suffers a number of problems. Since there is little cost control in health care, the proportion of subsidized households is likely to grow rapidly. A lack of consensus on the solution to long-term fiscal challenges has led to the rejection by referendum of proposals to raise the retirement age and increase the VAT rate to finance social security.

Switzerland has suffered from the global economic turmoil that began in 2008. The dominant role of the financial sector leaves the economy exposed to risks. The government has promised to support the ailing banking sector (and particularly the country's largest bank, UBS) with a fund of US$60bn. to buy illiquid assets. The export sector has slowed owing to falling international demand and the consumer price index fell year-on-year by 0·7% in Dec. 2008.

Currency

The unit of currency is the *Swiss franc* (CHF) of 100 *centimes* or *Rappen*. Foreign exchange reserves were US$78,864m. in Sept. 2009 and gold reserves were 33·44m. troy oz (77·79m. troy oz in 2000). Inflation rates (based on OECD statistics):

1999	*2000*	*2001*	*2002*	*2003*	*2004*	*2005*	*2006*	*2007*	*2008*
0·8%	1·6%	1·0%	0·6%	0·6%	0·8%	1·2%	1·1%	0·7%	2·4%

Total money supply in July 2009 was 339,809m. Swiss francs.

Budget

Revenue and expenditure of the Confederation, in 1m. Swiss francs, for calendar years:

	2000	*2001*	*2002*	*2003*	*2004*
Revenue	51,683	48,908	47,405	47,161	48,629
Expenditure	47,131	50,215	50,722	49,962	50,285

VAT is 7·6%, with reduced rates of 3·6% and 2·4%.

Performance

Real GDP growth rates (based on OECD statistics):

1999	*2000*	*2001*	*2002*	*2003*	*2004*	*2005*	*2006*	*2007*	*2008*
1·3%	3·6%	1·2%	0·4%	–0·2%	2·5%	2·6%	3·6%	3·6%	1·8%

Total GDP was US$488·5bn. in 2008.

Switzerland was ranked first in the Global Competitiveness Index in the World Economic Forum's *Global Competitiveness Report 2009–2010*, up from second in the 2008–2009 report. The index analyses 12 areas of competitiveness for over 100 countries including macroeconomy, higher education and training, institutions, innovation and infrastructure.

Banking and Finance

The National Bank, with headquarters divided between Berne and Zürich, opened on 20 June 1907. It has the exclusive right to issue banknotes. The *Chairman* is Philipp Hildebrand.

On 31 Dec. 2004 there were 338 banks with total assets of 2,490,768m. Swiss francs. They included 24 cantonal banks, three big banks, 83 regional and saving banks, one Raiffeisen (consisting of around 420 member banks) and 277 other banks. The number of banks has come down from over 495 in 1990. In 2004 the largest banks in order of market capitalization were UBS (US$79·2bn.) and Crédit Suisse Groupe (US$37·2bn.). UBS ranks third in Europe by market capitalization. It is Europe's largest bank by assets, which totalled US$1,963,870m. in 2006. Banking, insurance and other finance activities is one of Switzerland's most successful industries, and contributes 14·5% of the country's GDP. Switzerland is the capital of the offshore private banking industry. It is reckoned that a third of the internationally invested private assets worldwide are managed by Swiss banks.

Money laundering was made a criminal offence in Aug. 1990. Complete secrecy about clients' accounts remains intact, but anonymity is lifted in cases of criminal offences such as money laundering, corruption and terrorism.

The stock exchange system has been reformed under federal legislation of 1990 on securities trading and capital market services. The four smaller exchanges have been closed and activity concentrated on the major exchanges of Zürich, Basle and Geneva, which harmonized their operations with the introduction of the Swiss Electronic Exchange (EBS) in Dec. 1995. Zürich is a major international insurance centre.

In Aug. 1998 Crédit Suisse and UBS AG agreed a deal to pay US$1·25bn. (£750m.) to Holocaust survivors over a three-year-period in an out-of-court settlement. The deal brought to an end the issue of money left in Holocaust victims' Swiss Bank accounts which were allowed to remain dormant after the war.

ENERGY AND NATURAL RESOURCES

Environment

In 2008 carbon dioxide emissions from the consumption and flaring of fossil fuels were the equivalent of 6·1 tonnes per capita. An *Environmental Performance Index* compiled in 2008 ranked Switzerland first in the world, with 95·5%. The index examined various factors in six areas—air pollution, biodiversity and habitat, climate change, environmental health, productive natural resources and water resources.

Switzerland is one of the world leaders in recycling. In 2005, 51% of all household waste was recycled, including 95% of glass and 90% of aluminium cans

Electricity

Installed capacity was 17·4m. kW in 2004. Domestic production was 63·5bn. kWh in 2004. 30·0% of energy produced in 2004 was hydro-electric from storage power stations, 40·0% nuclear, 25·3% hydro-electric from turbine power stations and 4·7% from conventional thermal. In 1990, 54% of citizens voted for a ten-year moratorium on the construction of new nuclear plants. A referendum was held in 2003 on proposals to write a commitment to phase out nuclear power altogether into the constitution. However, the proposal was rejected. There are currently five nuclear reactors in use. Consumption per capita in 2004 was 7,534 kWh.

Minerals

In 2007 approximately 5,000 people were employed in mining and quarrying. Production estimates in 2006 (in 1,000 tonnes): salt, 560; gypsum, 300; lime, 75.

Agriculture

The country is self-sufficient in milk. Agriculture is protected by subsidies and import controls. Farmers are guaranteed an income equal to industrial workers. In 2005 agriculture occupied 3·6% of the total workforce. There were 286,300 ha. of open arable land in 2005, 119,100 ha. of cultivated grassland and 625,100 ha. of natural grassland and pastures. In 2005 there were 12,900 ha. of vineyards. There were 63,300 farms in 2005 (41% in mountain or hill regions), of which 2,800 were under 1 ha., 19,900 over 20 ha. and 17,700 in part-time use. In 2005 there were 405,400 ha. of arable land and 22,900 ha. of permanent crops. Approximately 11·0% of all agricultural land is used for organic farming—one of the highest proportions in the world.

Area harvested, 2005 (in 1,000 ha.): cereals, 168; sugar beets, 18; potatoes, 13. Production, 2005 (in 1,000 tonnes): sugar beets, 1,409; wheat, 539; potatoes, 468; barley, 231; maize, 199; rapeseed, 56; carrots, 36. Fruit production (in 1,000 tonnes) in 2005 was: apples, 204; grapes, 127; pears, 65. Wine is produced in 25 of the cantons. In 2004 vineyards produced 109,000 tonnes of wine.

Livestock, 2005 (in 1,000): pigs, 1,609; cattle, 1,554; sheep, 446; goats, 74; horses, 55; chickens, 8,117. Livestock products, 2005 (in 1,000 tonnes): meat, 450; milk, 3,934; cheese, 168.

Forestry

The forest area was 1·20m. ha. in 2003 (30·3% of the land area). In 2007, 5·69m. cu. metres of roundwood were cut.

Fisheries

Total catch, 2005, 1,475 tonnes, exclusively freshwater fish.

INDUSTRY

The leading companies by market capitalization in Switzerland in March 2009 were: Nestlé SA, a world leader in food and beverages (US$129·6bn.); Roche AG, a health care company (US$119·4bn.); and Novartis AG, a pharmaceuticals company (US$100·2bn.).

The chief food producing industries, based on Swiss agriculture, are the manufacture of cheese, butter, sugar and meat. Among the other industries, the manufacture of textiles, clothing and footwear, chemicals and pharmaceutical products, the production of machinery (including electrical machinery and scientific and optical instruments) and watch and clock making are the most important. The leading industries in 2003 in terms of value added (in 1m. Swiss francs) were: construction, 23,914 (5·5% of GDP); chemicals and chemical products, 14,649 (3·3%); machinery, 11,655 (2·7%); medical and optical instruments and watches, 10,967 (2·5%); electricity and water production, transmission and supply, 10,253 (2·3%).

Labour

In the second quarter of 2005 the total working population was 3,974,000, of whom 645,000 people were in manufacturing, 565,000 in trade, 481,000 in health and social services, and 454,000 in property, renting and business activities. The unemployment rate for the quarter ending Sept. 2009 was 4·6%. In 2005, 83·9% of men and 70·4% of women between the ages of 15 and 64 were in employment. The percentage of men in employment is one of the highest among the major industrialized nations.

The foreign labour force was 829,000 in 2005 (335,000 women). Of these 167,000 were Italian, 162,000 from the West Balkan countries, 96,000 Portuguese, 93,000 German and 40,000 French. In 2005 approximately 522,000 EU citizens worked in Switzerland.

Trade Unions

The Swiss Federation of Trade Unions had about 540,000 members in 2005.

INTERNATIONAL TRADE

Legislation of 1991 increased the possibilities of foreign ownership of domestic companies.

Imports and Exports

Imports and exports, excluding gold (bullion and coins) and silver (coins), were (in 1m. Swiss francs):

	2000	*2001*	*2002*	*2003*	*2004*
Imports	139,402	141,889	130,193	129,743	138,778
Exports	136,015	138,492	136,523	135,405	147,388

In 2004 the EU accounted for 81·4% of imports (112·9bn. Swiss francs) and 61·9% of exports (91·3bn. Swiss francs). Main import suppliers in 2004 (share of total trade): Germany, 32·8%; Italy, 11·3%; France, 9·9%; Netherlands, 5·0%; USA, 4·7%. Main export markets: Germany, 20·2%; USA, 10·4%; France, 8·7%; Italy, 8·3%; UK, 5·1%.

Main imports in 2004 (in 1m. Swiss francs): consumer goods, 55,318; raw materials and semi-manufactures, 35,680; equipment goods, 34,946.

Main exports in 2004 (in 1m. Swiss francs): chemicals, 49,445; machinery and electronics, 33,479; precision instruments, clocks and watches and jewellery, 24,195.

COMMUNICATIONS

Roads

In 2007 there were 71,354 km of roads, comprising 1,765 km of motorways, 18,143 km of highways and national roads and 51,446 km of secondary and local roads. Motor vehicles in 2004 (in 1,000): passenger cars, 3,811; commercial vehicles, 298; buses, 17; motorcycles and mopeds, 745. Freight transported by road in

2007 totalled 361·2m. tonnes. Switzerland has one of the lowest death rates in road accidents of any industrialized country, at 5·5 deaths per 100,000 people in 2005. Road accidents injured 26,754 people in 2005 and killed 409 (down from 954 in 1990).

Switzerland was ranked fourth for its road infrastructure in the World Economic Forum's *Global Competitiveness Report 2009–2010*.

Rail

In 2002 the length of the general traffic railways was 5,021 km, of which the Swiss Federal Railways (SBB) 3,003 km. In 2002 the Federal Railway carried 319m. passengers and 59m. tonnes of freight. In 2000 work began on what is set to be the world's longest rail tunnel—the 58-km long tunnel under the Gotthard mountain range in the Alps linking Erstfeld and Bodio. The tunnel is scheduled to open in 2015. There are a number of tram/light rail networks, notably in Basle, Berne, Geneva, Lausanne, Neuchâtel and Zürich. There are many other lines, the most important of which are the Berne–Lötschberg–Simplon (114 km from Berne to Brig) and Rhaetian (397 km) networks.

Switzerland was ranked first for rail infrastructure in the World Economic Forum's *Global Competitiveness Report 2009–2010*.

Civil Aviation

Switzerland owns seven airports with international scheduled and charter traffic: Basle (the binational Euroairport, which also serves Mulhouse in France), Berne (Belp), Geneva (Cointrin), Lugano (Agno), Sion, St Gallen (Altenrhein) and Zürich (Kloten). In 2004 these airports handled almost 29m. passengers and around 326,000 tonnes of freight and mail. Swissair, the former national carrier, faced collapse and grounded flights in Oct. 2001. In April 2002 a successor airline, swiss, took over as the national carrier. Services were also provided in 2003 by over 80 foreign airlines. Zürich is the busiest airport, handling 20,814,000 passengers in 2001 (19,698,000 on international flights) and 352,600 tonnes of freight. Geneva handled 7,431,000 passengers and 29,000 tonnes of freight in 2001. Together these two airports accounted for over 90% of Swiss air traffic in 2004.

In the World Economic Forum's *Global Competitiveness Report 2009–2010* Switzerland ranked fifth for quality of air transport infrastructure.

Shipping

In 2005 there were 1,227 km of navigable waterways. 6,749,682 tonnes of freight were transported on the Rhine and Swiss lakes in 2006. A merchant marine was created in 1941, the place of registry of its vessels being Basle. In 2007 it totalled 581,683 GRT.

Telecommunications

In 2008 there were 4·8m. main (fixed) telephone lines. In the same year mobile phone subscribers numbered 8·9m. (1,179·7 per 1,000 persons). There were 6·6m. PCs in use in 2006 and 5·8m. internet users in 2008. The broadband penetration rate in June 2008 was 32·7 subscribers per 100 inhabitants.

Postal Services

In Jan. 2005 there were 2,585 post offices, or one for every 2,869 persons.

SOCIAL INSTITUTIONS

Justice

The Federal Court, which sits at Lausanne, consists of 30 judges and 30 supplementary judges, elected by the Federal Assembly for six years and eligible for re-election; the President and Vice-President serve for two years and re-election is not practised. The Tribunal has original and final jurisdiction in suits between the Confederation and cantons; between different cantons; between the Confederation or cantons and corporations or individuals; between parties who refer their case to it; or in suits which the constitution or legislation of cantons places within its authority. It is a court of appeal against decisions of other federal authorities, and of cantonal authorities applying federal laws. The Tribunal comprises two courts of public law, two civil courts, a chamber of bankruptcy, a chamber of prosecution, a court of criminal appeal, a court of extraordinary appeal and a Federal Criminal Court.

A Federal Insurance Court sits in Lucerne, and comprises 11 judges and 11 supplementary judges elected for six years by the Federal Assembly.

A federal penal code replaced cantonal codes in 1942. It abolished capital punishment except for offences in wartime; this latter proviso was abolished in 1992.

The population in penal institutions in 2008 was 5,780 (75 per 100,000 population), of which 69·7% were non-nationals.

Education

Education is administered by the confederation, cantons and communes and is free and compulsory for nine years. Compulsory education consists of four years (Basel-Town and Vaud), five years (Aargau, Basel-Country, Neuchâtel and Ticino) or six years (other cantons) of primary education, and the balance in Stage I secondary education. This is followed by three to five years of Stage II secondary education in general or vocational schools. Tertiary education is at universities, universities of applied science, higher vocational schools and advanced vocational training institutes.

In 2003 there were 153,780 children in pre-primary schools. There were 813,448 pupils in compulsory education (465,777 at primary, 297,240 at lower secondary and 50,431 at special schools), 91,796 in Stage II general secondary education and 218,846 in Stage II vocational education, and 160,165 students in higher education, including 111,100 students at universities and 43,525 at universities of applied sciences.

There are ten universities (date of foundation and students in 2004–05): Basle (1460, 9,222), Berne (1528, 13,274), Fribourg (1889, 9,913), Geneva (1559, 14,652), Lausanne (1537, 10,231), Lucerne (16th century, 1,500); Neuchâtel (1866, 3,296), St Gallen (1899, 4,556), Ticino (1996, 1,856), Zürich (1523, 23,395); and three institutions of equivalent status: St Gallen PHS (1867, 324), Federal Institute of Technology Lausanne (1853, 6,493), Federal Institute of Technology Zürich (1854, 12,388). The seven universities of applied sciences were founded in 1997. Enrolment figures for 2003 were: Espace Mittelland, 7,001; Western Switzerland, 4,689; Northwestern Switzerland, 5,547; Central Switzerland, 4,827; Ticino, 1,111; Eastern Switzerland, 2,496; Zürich, 17,854. About 17% of university students are foreign, a proportion exceeded only in Australia.

In 2006 public expenditure on education came to 5·1% of GNI and accounted for 16·3% of total government expenditure. The adult literacy rate is at least 99%.

Health

In 2006 there were 28,812 doctors, 3,847 dentists and 4,284 pharmacists. There were 334 hospitals with 41,196 beds in 2005. In 2007, 27·9% of the population were smokers. In 2006 Switzerland spent 10·8% of its GDP on health. Although active euthanasia is illegal in Switzerland, doctors may help patients die if they have given specific consent.

Welfare

The Federal Insurance Law against accident and illness, of 13 June 1911, entitled all citizens to insurance against illness; foreigners could also be admitted to the benefits. Major reform of the law was ratified in 1994 and came into effect in 1996, making it compulsory for all citizens. Subsidies are paid by the Confederation and the Cantons only for insured persons with low incomes. Also compulsory are the Old-Age and Survivors' Insurance (OASI, since 1948), Invalidity Insurance (II, since 1960) and Accident Insurance (1984/1996). Unemployment Insurance (1984) and Occupational benefit plans (Second Pillar, 1985) are compulsory for employees only.

The following amounts (in 1m. Swiss francs) were paid in social security benefits:

	2001	2002	2003
Old-age and survivors' insurance	28,624	28,710	29,695
Occupational pension plans	27,596	27,321	27,628
Sickness insurance	14,059	14,642	15,635
Disability insurance	8,751	9,287	10,014
Health system subsidies	6,442	7,255	7,669
Unemployment insurance	2,283	3,593	5,195
Accident insurance for employees	4,321	4,438	4,610
Family allowances	4,163	4,385	4,493
Wage continuation	3,761	4,063	3,460
Supplementary benefits (OASI/II)	2,351	2,528	2,671
Total (including other benefits)	108,194	112,345	117,663

RELIGION

There is liberty of conscience and of creed. At the 2000 census 41·8% of the population were Roman Catholic, 35·3% Protestant and 11·1% without religion. In 2000 the figures were estimated to be: Roman Catholics, 3,048,000; Protestants, 2,569,000; other, 1,671,000. In Feb. 2010 the Roman Catholic church had three cardinals with Swiss nationality.

CULTURE

World Heritage Sites

There are ten sites in Switzerland that appear on the UNESCO World Heritage List. They are (with the year entered on list): the Abbey-Cathedral of St Gallen (1983), the 9th-century Benedictine convent of St John at Müstair (1983), the Old City of Berne (1983), the three castles and city walls of Bellinzona (2000), the Jungfrau-Aletsch-Bietschhorn mountain region (2001 and 2007), Monte San Giorgio (2003), the Lavaux vineyard terraces (2007), the Swiss Tectonic Arena Sardona (2008) and La Chaux-de-Fonds/Le Locle watchmaking town-planning (2009). The Rhaetian Railway in the Albula/Bernina Landscapes (2008) is shared with Italy.

Broadcasting

Schweizerische Radio-und Fernsehgesellschaft/Société Suisse de Radiodiffusion et Télévision/Società Svizzera di Radiotelevisione (a non-profit-making company) operates seven television channels and 18 radio stations broadcasting in the national languages. There are six German-language stations, four French, three Italian and one Romansch. In addition there are three music stations from Swiss Satellite Radio and an English-language station, World Radio Switzerland. There are also private regional services (48 local radio and 19 local television stations in 2005) and cable and satellite TV stations from France, Germany and Italy are widely available. In 2006, 2·89m. radio licences and 2·86m. TV licences were issued. Colour is by PAL.

Cinema

There were 326 cinemas in 2004; total attendance for the year was 17·2m. 47 films were produced in 2004.

Press

There were 86 daily newspapers in 2004 and 134 non-daily papers; their combined circulation was 3,837,648 in 2004. Over 11,000 book titles were published in 2004; more than half of these were in German, 2,428 in French and 383 in Italian.

Tourism

Tourism is an important industry. In 2003 there were 11,400,000 foreign tourists staying in hotels and health establishments, bringing revenue of 5,178m. Swiss francs. In 1999 overnight stays by tourists totalled 67,772,000. 12·01m. Swiss citizens travelled abroad in 1999.

Festivals

The Lucerne Festival is one of Europe's leading cultural events and since 2001 has been split into three festivals: Ostern during Lent, Sommer in Aug.–Sept. and Piano in Nov. The 2008 summer festival was attended by 108,200 people. The Montreux Jazz Festival is held annually in July. The 2007 festival attracted 220,000 people.

Libraries

In 2003 there were three national libraries with a total of 4,048,693 volumes and at least 600 users; there were 14 university main libraries with 30,632,979 volumes and at least 238,000 users; 66 general public libraries with 11,036,983 volumes and at least 493,000 users. There were 28 specialist libraries with 3,891,626 volumes and at least 163,000 users.

Museums and Galleries

In 2003 there were 982 museums.

DIPLOMATIC REPRESENTATIVES

Of Switzerland in the United Kingdom (16–18 Montagu Pl., London, W1H 2BQ)
Ambassador: Alexis P. Lautenberg.

Of the United Kingdom in Switzerland (Thunstrasse 50, 3005 Berne)
Ambassador: Sarah Gillett, CMG, MVO.

Of Switzerland in the USA (2900 Cathedral Ave., NW, Washington, D.C., 20008)
Ambassador: Urs Ziswiler.

Of the USA in Switzerland (Sulgeneckstrasse 19, 3007 Berne)
Ambassador: Donald S. Beyer, Jr.

Of Switzerland to the United Nations
Ambassador: Peter Maurer.

Of Switzerland to the European Union
Ambassador: Jacques de Watteville.

FURTHER READING

Office Fédéral de la Statistique. *Annuaire Statistique de la Suisse.*

Butler, Michael, Pender, Malcolm and Charnley, Joy, *Making of Modern Switzerland, 1848–1998.* 2000

Church, Clive, *Politics and Government of Switzerland.* 2003

Kriesi, Hanspeter, Farago, Peter, Kohli, Martin and Zarin-Nejadan, Milad, *Contemporary Switzerland.* 2005

New, M., *Switzerland Unwrapped: Exposing the Myths.* 1997

National library: Bibliothèque Nationale Suisse, Hallwylstr. 15, 3003 Berne.

National Statistical Office: Office Fédéral de la Statistique, Espace de l'Europe 10, 2010 Neuchâtel.

SFSO Information Service email: *information@bfs.admin.ch*

Website: http://www.bfs.admin.ch

SYRIA

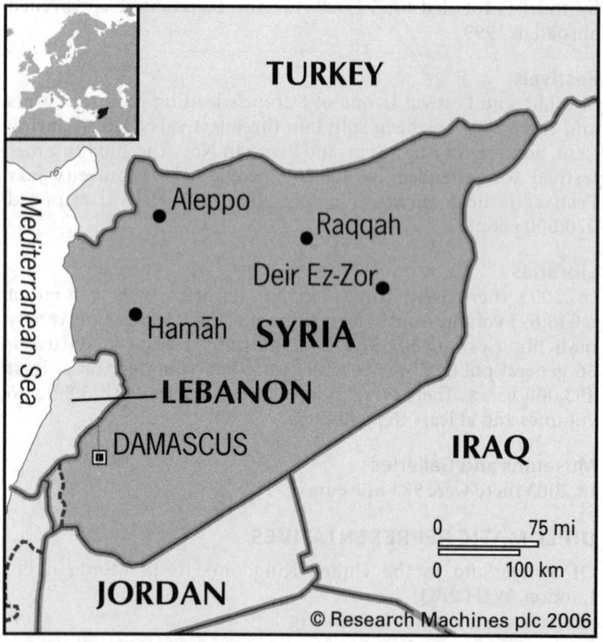

Jumhuriya al-Arabya as-Suriya
(Syrian Arab Republic)

Capital: Damascus
Population estimate, 2010: 22·51m.
GDP per capita, 2007: (PPP$) 4,511
HDI/world rank: 0·742/107

KEY HISTORICAL EVENTS

Ancient Syria, a region encompassing modern Israel, Palestine, Lebanon and Jordan, was home to some of the world's earliest civilizations. From the city of Ebla, founded around 3000 BC, the Semitic empire developed. This was succeeded around 2260 BC by the Akkadian empire, then by the Amorites whose cities fell to the Hittites in the mid-2nd millennium BC. During the next 500 years Canaanites, Phoenicians, Aryans, Aramaeans and Hebrews settled different parts of the region. From the 9th–7th centuries BC the Assyrian empire dominated until, weakened by Cimmerian and Scythian immigration, it gave way to Babylonian rule.

The Babylonian empire, which saw the enslavement of the Jews, was defeated in 539 BC by the Persian King Cyrus. In the 4th century BC Alexander the Great overthrew the Persians and Syria came under Greek rule until the expansion of Rome in the early 2nd century BC. Syria became a Roman province in 64 BC. The Greek cities of the interior (the Decapolis) were rebuilt, including Damascus. Palmyra, a key city on the trade routes to the Euphrates, rose against Rome under Queen Zenobia but was defeated in AD 272.

Syria became an important frontier zone under Diocletian, who established lines of defence (*limes*) against eastern invaders. Syrian cities such as Edessa had contained the earliest Christian communities, and Antioch, where St Peter preached, grew in significance when Emperor Constantine moved the seat of the Empire east to Byzantium in 303. In 451 it was made a patriarchate.

Syria prospered under Byzantium until the Persian invasions of the 6th century. In the 620s Emperor Heraclius briefly regained the region for Byzantium, before ceding it to Muslim Arab forces at the Battle of the Yarmuk River in 636. Syria was at the heart, geographically and politically, of the Ummayad empires for the next 100 years. From 661 Damascus was capital of the Ummayad Caliphate, though its influence declined after 750 when the Abbasid Caliphate moved the capital to Baghdad.

From 969 the resurgent Byzantine Empire challenged for control of the region, twice conquering its principal cities. In 1085 Syria was conquered by the Seljid Turks. With the beginning of the Crusades Muslim-held strongholds were repeatedly attacked by Christian invaders. Antioch and Edessa fell to the crusaders in 1098 and Jerusalem in 1099. In the 12th century Muslim tribes won back much land under the successive leaderships of Zengi of Mosul, Nur-ad Din and Salah ad-Din (Saladin). Salah ad-Din founded the Ayyubid dynasty and in 1187 his forces recaptured Jerusalem from the Christians.

In 1260 a series of Mongol invasions began from the east, destroying cities and agriculture before being repelled by the Egyptian Mamluks. The Mamluks also drove the last crusaders from the Holy Land in 1302. The area remained under Mamluk rule until it fell to the Ottoman Turks in 1516. In the 1830s Egyptian forces invaded Syria as part of a wider war against the Ottomans. European powers became involved, brokering several agreements and finally forcing Egypt to withdraw in 1840.

During the First World War, in which Turkey joined the Central Powers, the French and British drew up the Sykes–Picot agreement, which planned the division of the Middle East into areas of French and British control. After the end of the war, the Ottoman Empire was dissolved and Lebanon, Palestine and Transjordan were made separate territories, reducing Syria to its modern borders.

In March 1920 Faisal ibn Husayn of Mecca became king of Syria but was deposed by the French, who were awarded the Syrian mandate by the League of Nations later that year. A widespread revolt against French rule was suppressed in 1925, with French troops bombarding Damascus. An abortive attempt to negotiate independence in 1936 was followed by more fruitful discussions in 1941, when British and Free French forces occupied the country. Syria held elections in 1943, electing the nationalist Shukri al-Kuwatli as president. Syrian independence was recognized on 1 Jan. 1944 and European forces withdrew in 1946.

A series of military coups from 1949–54 interrupted civilian government. The 1948 Arab–Israeli War, in which Syria fought for the Palestinians, ushered in decades of mutual hostility with neighbouring Israel. In 1956 the Suez Crisis prompted a period of martial law. In the same year Syria signed a pact with the Soviet Union which ensured supplies of military equipment in return for Communist influence. Popular enthusiasm for the Pan-Arabist movement led Syria to unite with Egypt in 1958, creating the United Arab Republic. However, Syria seceded in Sept. 1961 and a series of military coups ensued, culminating in the Ba'ath Party taking power in 1963. After the Syrian Ba'athists split from the Iraqi Ba'athists in 1966, long-term tensions arose between the two countries and led to Syrian support for Iran.

The 1967 war with Israel resulted in the loss of the Golan Heights. In 1970 Hafez al-Assad (of the minority Alawite sect) seized power. He was elected president in 1971 and embarked on a 'corrective' movement to end corruption. Domestic opposition was suppressed and the Sunni fundamentalist Muslim Brotherhood was destroyed along with the city of Hamah in 1982.

Syrian forces invaded Lebanon in 1976 to prevent a Palestinian victory over the Maronite Christians, with whom Syria had political ties.

Assad joined the international coalition against the Iraqi occupation of Kuwait in 1991 and engaged in unsuccessful talks with Israel in the 1990s. His son, Bashar, took over on Assad's death in 2000. In 2003 Syria refused to back the US-led invasion of Iraq and relations with Washington were further strained over US accusations of Syrian support for terrorism. Though Syrian influence in Lebanon remained strong, it withdrew its last troops from the country in 2005, after being accused of involvement in the assassination of the former Lebanese prime minister, Rafiq al-Hariri. Following French-brokered talks, in Oct. 2008 Syria established diplomatic relations with Lebanon for the first time.

TERRITORY AND POPULATION

Syria is bounded by the Mediterranean and Lebanon in the west, by Israel and Jordan in the south, by Iraq in the east and by Turkey in the north. The frontier between Syria and Turkey was settled by the Franco-Turkish agreement of 22 June 1929. The area is 185,180 sq. km (71,498 sq. miles). The census of 2004 gave a population of 17,921,000; density, 97 per sq. km. Estimate, 2009, 20,367,000. In 2005, 50·6% of the population lived in urban areas.

The UN gives an estimated population for 2010 of 22·51m.

Area and population (2004 census, in 1,000) of the 14 districts *(mohafaza)*:

	Sq. km	*Population*
Aleppo (Halab)	18,500	4,045
Damascus City	105	1,552
Damascus District	18,032	2,273
Dará	3,730	843
Deir Ez-Zor	33,060	1,005
Hamah	8,883	1,385
Hasakah	23,334	1,275
Homs (Hims)	42,223	1,529
Idlib	6,097	1,258
Lattakia (Ladhiqiyah)	2,297	880
Qunaytirah	1,861	67
Raqqah	19,616	794
Suwaydá	5,550	313
Tartous	1,892	701

The capital is Damascus (Dimashq), with a 1999 population of 2,270,000. Other principal towns (population, 1994 in 1,000): Aleppo, 1,840 (1995); Homs, 558; Lattakia, 303; Hamah, 273; Al-Kamishli, 165; Raqqah, 138; Deir Ez-Zor, 133.

Over 1m. Iraqi refugees entered Syria between 2003 and 2007, although many started to return in late 2007. The government estimated that there were 1·5m. refugees in Syria in 2007, a figure exceeded only in Pakistan.

Arabic is the official language, spoken by 90% of the population, while 9% speak Kurdish (chiefly in Hasakah in the northeast of the country) and 1% other languages.

SOCIAL STATISTICS

2001 births, estimate, 524,000; deaths, 88,000. Rates, 2001 estimate (per 1,000 population): birth, 30·9; death, 5·2. Infant mortality, 2005 (per 1,000 live births), 14. Expectation of life, 2007, was 72·2 years for males and 76·0 for females. Annual population growth rate, 2000–05, 2·1%. Fertility rate, 2004, 3·3 births per woman.

CLIMATE

The climate is Mediterranean in type, with mild wet winters and dry, hot summers, though there are variations in temperatures and rainfall between the coastal regions and the interior, which even includes desert conditions. The more mountainous parts are subject to snowfall. Damascus, Jan. 38·1°F (3·4°C), July 77·4°F (25·2°C). Annual rainfall 8·8" (217 mm). Aleppo, Jan. 36·7°F (2·6°C), July 80·4°F (26·9°C). Annual rainfall 10·2" (258 mm). Homs, Jan. 38·7°F (3·7°C), July 82·4°F (28°C). Annual rainfall 3·4" (86·7 mm).

CONSTITUTION AND GOVERNMENT

A new constitution was approved by plebiscite on 12 March 1973 and promulgated on 14 March. It confirmed the Arab Socialist Renaissance *(Ba'ath)* Party, in power since 1963, as the 'leading party in the State and society'. Legislative power is held by a 250-member People's Assembly *(Majlis al-Sha'ab)*, renewed every four years in 15 multi-seat constituencies, in which 167 seats are guaranteed for the Al Jabha al Watniyah at Wahdwamiyah (JWW/National Progressive Front) alliance of parties (i.e. the Ba'ath party and partners). The government is formed by the Ba'ath.

The president is appointed by the Parliament and is confirmed for a seven-year term in a referendum. At a referendum on 27 May 2007 Bashar al-Assad (b. 1965) was confirmed as *President* for a second term, receiving 97·6% of the vote.

National Anthem

'Humata al Diyari al aykum salaam' ('Defenders of the Realm, on you be peace'); words by Khalil Mardam Bey, tune by M. S. and A. S. Flayfel.

GOVERNMENT CHRONOLOGY

Heads of State since 1943. (HS = People's Party; HSQ = Syrian National Party; KW = National Bloc)

President		
1943–49	KW	Shukri al-Kuwatli
Chairmen of Supreme Military Council		
1949	military	Husni al-Zaim
1949	military	Muhammad Sami Hilmi al-Hinnawi
President		
1949–51	KW	Hashim Bay Khalid al-Atassi
Chairman of Supreme Military Council		
1951	military	Adib ash-Shishakli
Presidents		
1951–53	military	Fawzi Silu
1953–54	military	Adib ash-Shishakli
1954–55	KW	Hashim Bay Khalid al-Atassi
1955–58	HSQ	Shukri al-Kuwatli
United Arab Republic		
1958–61		
President		
1961–63	HS	Nazim al-Qudsi
Chairmen of National Revolutionary Command Council		
1963	military/Ba'ath	Lu'ayy al-Atassi
1963–64	military/Ba'ath	Muhammad Amin al-Hafez
Chairman of Presidential Council		
1964–66	military/Ba'ath	Muhammad Amin al-Hafez
Heads of State		
1966–70	Ba'ath	Nur ad-Din Mustafa al-Atassi
1970–71	Ba'ath	Ahmad al-Hasan al-Khatib
1971	military/Ba'ath	Abu Sulayman Hafez al-Assad
Presidents		
1971–2000	Ba'ath	Abu Sulayman Hafez al-Assad
2000–	Ba'ath	Bashar al-Assad

RECENT ELECTIONS

Elections were held on 22 and 23 April 2007. The ruling National Progressive Front (led by the Ba'ath Party) won 172 of 250 seats and non-partisan candidates the remaining 78. Turnout was 56·1%.

CURRENT ADMINISTRATION

Following the death of Lieut.-Gen. Hafez al-Assad on 10 June 2000, a presidential referendum was held on 10 July 2000. The former president's son Bashar al-Assad won 97·3% of the vote.

President: Bashar al-Assad; b. 1965 (Ba'ath; sworn in 17 July 2000).

Vice-Presidents: Farouk al-Shara; Najah al-Attar.

In March 2010 the government comprised:

Prime Minister: Mohammed Naji al-Otari; b. 1944 (Ba'ath; sworn in 10 Sept. 2003).

Deputy Prime Minister for Economic Affairs: Abdullah Dardari.

Minister of Agriculture: Adel Safar. *Awqaf:* Mohammed Abdel-Sattar Sayyed. *Communications and Technology:* Imad Abd Al-Ghani Sabuni. *Culture:* Riyad Naasan Agha. *Defence:* Lieut.-Gen. Ali Habib Mahmud. *Economy and Trade:* Amer Hassan Loutfi. *Education:* Ali Saad. *Electricity:* Ahmad Qussay Kayyali. *Environment:* Kawkab al-Sabah Dayeh. *Expatriates:* Butheina Shaaban. *Finance:* Mohammed al-Hussein. *Foreign Affairs:* Walid Muallem. *Health:* Rida Saeed. *Higher Education:* Ghiath Barakat. *Housing and Building:* Omar Ibrahim Ghalawanji. *Industry:* Fouad Issa Jony. *Information:* Mohsen Bilal. *Interior:* Said Sammur. *Irrigation:* Nader al-Boni. *Justice:* Ahmad Yunis. *Local Affairs:* Tamer al-Hijeh. *Petroleum and Mineral Resources:* Sufian Allaw. *Presidential Affairs:* Mansur Azzam. *Social Affairs and Labour:* Diala Al-Hajj Aref. *Tourism:* Saadallah Agha al-Qalaa. *Transport:* Yarob Souleiman Badr.

Syrian Parliament (Arabic only): http://www.parliament.gov.sy

CURRENT LEADERS

Bashar al-Assad

Position
President

Introduction
Bashar al-Assad was confirmed as president in a national referendum in July 2000 following the death of his father the previous month. He had not been groomed for a political career, pursuing instead a medical education in England. However, on the death of his elder brother Basil—their father's chosen successor—in an accident in 1994, Assad was recalled to Damascus. Thereafter he rose through the senior ranks of the armed forces, consolidating his influence and authority within his father's regime to achieve the first-ever father-to-son succession to the highest office in an Arab republic.

Early Life
Assad was born in Damascus on 11 Sept. 1965. After attending high school in the capital, he went to London, England, to study ophthalmology. Having returned to Syria upon the death of his brother, he became commander of the Syrian army's armoured division. Assad reportedly used this position to install his own supporters and remove ageing senior figures and potential rivals from the army and security services. He was appointed to the rank of Colonel in 1999.

When President Hafez al-Assad died suddenly on 10 June 2000, Syria's political establishment was quick to demonstrate support for his son. The People's Assembly voted to change the constitution to lower the minimum age for a president from 40 to 34—Assad's age at that time. The Assembly and the dominant Ba'ath Party approved his nomination for the presidency (as the only candidate) and the party elected him as its secretary-general. He was also declared commander-in-chief of the armed forces, his military rank having been elevated to Lieutenant-General. In a national referendum held on 10 July 2000, Assad was endorsed as president with 97·3% of the votes cast.

Career in Office
In his inaugural address to the People's Assembly, Assad spoke of the need for economic reform. He called for the restructuring of the state-dominated economy and improved competitiveness, the dismantling of bureaucracy and the ending of corruption. Private investment has since been encouraged. However, initial signs of political liberalization—a partial lifting of censorship, the release of some political prisoners, tolerance of criticism of the government and party, and the limited introduction of the Internet—faded in 2001 as dissidents were again arrested and detained. On the international stage, peace with Israel remained a priority, although with the stipulation that the Israelis give up the whole of the Golan Heights seized in the Six-Day War of 1967. However, the renewed Palestinian *intifada* against Israeli occupation polarized the already volatile politics of the Middle East and a Syrian-Israeli accord became increasingly unlikely.

In 2002–03 Syria opposed US military threats against Iraq, fearing the consequences of another war in the Middle East. Syria claimed that UN Security Council Resolution 1441 did not support an invasion without further UN approval. US-led forces invaded Iraq in March 2003 and Saddam Hussein was toppled the following month. The USA subsequently threatened Assad with economic, diplomatic or other undefined sanctions, suggesting that Syria was harbouring members of Saddam Hussein's regime and had been involved in the development of chemical weapons.

In Jan. 2004 Assad visited Turkey, the first Syrian leader to do so, improving several decades of cool relations between the two countries. The following May the USA imposed economic sanctions on Syria for alleged support for terrorism and failure to stop militants entering Iraq. A UN Security Council resolution adopted in Sept. 2004 and the subsequent assassination of former Lebanese prime minister Rafiq al-Hariri in Beirut in Feb. 2005 (allegedly with Syrian involvement) increased the international pressure on Assad to remove Syria's forces from Lebanon completely. Although the withdrawal was completed in April, the UN continued through 2005 and 2006 to probe al-Hariri's murder, implicating senior Syrian officials and chiding Assad's government for its perceived lack of co-operation with UN investigators.

Syria's frosty diplomatic relationship with the USA was aggravated by Bashir's support for Hizbollah during the radical Lebanese militia's war against the Israeli military in July–Aug. 2006. Nevertheless, Syrian security forces joined US marines in defending the US embassy in Damascus against a terrorist car bomb in Sept.

Following the restoration of Iraqi-Syrian diplomatic ties in Nov. 2006, President Jalal Talabani became the first Iraqi head of state to visit Damascus for 30 years in Jan. 2007. In March the European Union reopened a dialogue with the Syrian government, and in May the US Secretary of State met the Syrian foreign minister in Egypt for the first high-level bilateral contact in two years. Relations with Israel, however, deteriorated further after an Israeli air strike against an undefined site in northern Syria in Sept. (which US intelligence sources claimed in April 2008 to have been a covert nuclear reactor plant).

Despite the ruling National Progressive Front's overwhelming victory in parliamentary elections in April 2007 and Assad's endorsement as president for a further term in a national referendum in May, a crackdown on dissent has remained in force. During that year several government critics and human rights campaigners were sentenced to terms of imprisonment, and in Jan. 2008 Syria's leading dissident, Riyad Seif, was detained by security services.

In Oct. 2008 Syria and Lebanon signed an accord establishing diplomatic relations for the first time in their turbulent post-independence history.

After several postponements, the Damascus stock exchange was launched in March 2009, marking a further step in the liberalization of Syria's state-controlled economy.

DEFENCE

Military service is compulsory for a period of 30 months. Defence expenditure in 2006 totalled US$1,739m. (US$92 per capita), representing 5·1% of GDP. Syria had 14,000 troops based in Lebanon in early 2005, but in March 2005 the two countries agreed that Syria would begin to redeploy the troops to the Bekaa Valley in the east of the country. They were subsequently all withdrawn from Lebanon.

In Sept. 2007 an Israeli air strike destroyed a suspected nuclear reactor in the Deir Ez-Zor region.

Army

Strength (2007) about 215,000 (including conscripts) with a further 280,000 available reservists. In addition there is a gendarmerie of 8,000 and a Workers Militia of approximately 100,000.

Navy

The Navy included two small frigates and 18 patrol and coastal combatants in 2007. A small naval aviation branch of the Air Force operates 13 attack helicopters. Personnel in 2007 numbered 7,600. The main base is at Tartous with additional bases located at Lattakia and Minet el-Baida.

Air Force

The Air Force, including Air Defence Command, had (2007) 30,000 personnel with an additional 10,000 reservists. Air Defence Command numbered 60,000 in 2007. There were 583 combat capable aircraft (including MiG-21, MiG-23, MiG-25 and MiG-29 supersonic interceptors and Su-22 and Su-24 fighter-bombers), and 71 attack helicopters.

INTERNATIONAL RELATIONS

Syria is a member of the UN, World Bank, IMF and several other UN specialized agencies, Islamic Development Bank, OIC and League of Arab States.

ECONOMY

In 2006 agriculture accounted for 18·3% of GDP, industry 32·2% and services 49·5%.

Overview

Syria's economy grew robustly throughout most of the 1990s. It was boosted by reform measures taken in the early 1990s and a major oil discovery. Syria is heavily dependent on the oil and agricultural sectors, which, combined, account for roughly half the country's GDP. Oil accounts for over two-thirds of export receipts and, together with worker remittances, is the main source of foreign earnings. However, the country's oil output is declining and the economy has already become a net oil importer.

Macroeconomic performance has continued to be strong, with growth averaging 4% per year since 2003. Non-oil growth has expanded at a rapid pace and government debt is low and declining. In the medium-term fiscal and current account deficits are expected to stabilize as a result of imminent fiscal reforms, including the proposed introduction of value added tax in 2011 and the resumption of strong growth in exports of goods and services. Syria's limited integration into the international financial system has limited downside risks to growth arising from the global downturn. Efforts to shift to a more market-based economy have improved growth prospects, with significant potential for tourism and raising foreign direct investment.

Currency

The monetary unit is the *Syrian pound* (SYP) of 100 *piastres*. Inflation was 4·7% in 2007 and 15·2% in 2008. Gold reserves were 833,000 troy oz in July 2004. Total money supply in March 2004 was £Syr.642,259m.

Budget

The fiscal year is the calendar year. In 2004 revenues were £Syr.342·5bn. and expenditures £Syr.405·1bn.

Performance

There was real GDP growth of 4·2% in 2007 and 5·2% in 2008; total GDP in 2008 was US$55·2bn.

Banking and Finance

The Central Bank is the bank of issue. Commercial banks were nationalized in 1963. The *Governor* of the Central Bank is Adib Mayaleh. In 2007 there were nine private banks.

In Aug. 2000 it was announced that private banks were to be established for the first time in nearly 40 years. Syria's first private banks since 1961 opened in 2004.

A stock exchange opened in Damascus in March 2009 with six listed companies.

Weights and Measures

The metric system is legal, although former weights and measures may still be in use: 1 *okiya* = 0·47 lb; 6 *okiyas* = 1 *oke* = 2·82 lb; 2 *okes* = 1 *rottol* = 5·64 lb; 200 *okes* = 1 *kantar*.

ENERGY AND NATURAL RESOURCES

Environment

Syria's carbon dioxide emissions from the consumption and flaring of fossil fuels in 2008 were the equivalent of 2·5 tonnes per capita.

Electricity

Installed capacity was 6·5m. kW in 2004. Production in 2004 was 32·08bn. kWh and consumption per capita 1,784 kWh.

Oil and Gas

Oil reserves in 2008 were 2·5bn. bbls; production, 19·8m. tonnes. Natural gas reserves (2008), 280bn. cu. metres; production, 5·5bn. cu. metres.

Minerals

Phosphate production, 2004, 2,883,000 tonnes; other minerals are gypsum (432,000 tonnes in 2004) and salt (141,000 tonnes in 2004). There are indications of lead, copper, antimony, nickel, chrome and other minerals widely distributed. Sodium chloride and bitumen deposits are being worked.

Agriculture

The arable area in 2001 was 4·64m. ha. and there were 815,000 ha. of permanent cropland. 1·27m. ha. were irrigated in 2001. In 2001 there were 100,347 tractors and 4,500 harvester-threshers in use. Production of principal crops, 2001 (in 1,000 tonnes): wheat, 4,745; sugar beets, 1,175; seed cotton, 1,010; olives, 866; tomatoes, 732; cottonseed, 656; potatoes, 480; oranges, 465. Livestock (2003 estimates, in 1,000): sheep, 13,500; goats, 1,000; cattle, 880; asses, 217; chickens, 30,000. Livestock products, 2003 (in 1,000 tonnes): milk, 1,768; meat, 368; eggs, 166; cheese, 91.

Forestry

In 2005 there were 461,000 ha. of forest (2·5% of the land area). Timber production in 2007 was 65,000 cu. metres.

Fisheries

The total catch in 2005 was 8,447 tonnes (56% freshwater fish).

INDUSTRY

Production (in tonnes): cement (2001), 5,428,000; residual fuel oil (2004), 4,536,000; distillate fuel oil (2004), 4,123,000; petrol

(2004), 1,338,000; fertilizers (2003), 304,000; vegetable oil (2001), 89,000; cotton yarn (2001), 83,000; refrigerators (2002), 113,000 units; washing machines (2002), 85,000 units; cigarettes (2001), 12·0bn. units; woollen carpets (2002), 2·2m. sq. metres.

Labour

In 2005 the labour force totalled 5,312,000. Unemployment was 11·5% in 2005.

Trade Unions

In 2001 there were 194 trade unions with 558,765 members.

INTERNATIONAL TRADE

Foreign debt was US$6,508m. in 2005.

Imports and Exports

Imports (c.i.f.) in 2004 totalled US$7,049m. (US$5,111m. in 2003) and exports (f.o.b.) US$5,383m. (US$5,731m. in 2003). Main imports, 2003, included: machinery and equipment, 18·3%; foodstuffs, 17·7%; chemicals and chemical products, 14·9%; base and fabricated metals, 14·6%. Main exports in 2003 included: crude petroleum, 62·5%; refined petroleum, 8·8%; live animals and meat, 4·2%; textiles, 4·2%. In 2003 imports came mainly from China (5·9%), Ukraine (5·8%), Turkey (5·7%) and USA (5·0%). Exports in 2003 went mainly to Italy (33·2%), France (14·4%), Turkey (7·5%) and Saudi Arabia (5·9%).

Trade Fairs

The annual Damascus International Fair is held in July and the Damascus Book Fair in Oct.

COMMUNICATIONS

Roads

In 2006 there were 40,032 km of roads, including 1,103 km of motorways, 5,971 km of main roads and 31,849 km of secondary roads. There were in 2007 a total of 446,100 passenger cars in use (22 per 1,000 inhabitants), 50,800 buses and coaches and 528,300 vans and lorries. In 2007 there were 13,465 road accidents involving injury resulting in 2,818 deaths.

Rail

In 2001 the network totalled 2,460 km of 1,435 mm gauge (Syrian Railways) and 338 km of 1,050 mm gauge (Hedjaz-Syrian Railway). Passenger-km travelled in 2001 came to 307m. and freight tonne-km to 1,492m.

Civil Aviation

The main international airport is at Damascus, with some international traffic at Aleppo and Lattakia. The national carrier is the state-owned Syrian Arab Airlines. In 2003 scheduled airline traffic of Syrian-based carriers flew 9m. km, carrying 940,000 passengers (908,000 on international flights). Damascus handled an estimated 1,747,000 passengers in 2000 (1,660,000 on international flights) and 25,000 tonnes of freight.

Shipping

In 2002 the merchant marine totalled 472,000 GRT. Vessels totalling 4,397,000 NRT entered ports in 2005 and vessels totalling 3,927,000 NRT cleared.

Telecommunications

In 2006 there were 3,243,000 main (fixed) telephone lines but 2,294,000 people were on the waiting list for a line. Mobile phone subscribers numbered 7,056,200 in 2008 (33·2 per 100 persons). There were 1·3m. PCs in use in 2006 and an estimated 3·6m. internet users in 2008.

Postal Services

There were 604 post offices in 2004, or one for every 30,800 persons.

SOCIAL INSTITUTIONS

Justice

Syrian law is based on both Islamic and French jurisprudence. There are two courts of first instance in each district, one for civil and one for criminal cases. There is also a Summary Court in each sub-district, under Justices of the Peace. There is a Court of Appeal in the capital of each governorate, with a Court of Cassation in Damascus. The death penalty is still in force; there were at least eight executions in 2009. Executions may be held in public.

The population in penal institutions in 2004 was 10,599 (57 per 100,000 of national population).

Education

In 2007 there were 145,781 pre-primary school children, 2,310,168 primary school pupils and 2,549,444 secondary school pupils. In 2001, 17 teacher colleges had 791 teachers and 8,204 students; 593 schools for technical education had 16,849 teachers and 139,551 students. Adult literacy in 2003 was 82·9% (male, 91·0%; female, 74·2%).

In 2001 there were four universities with 172,853 students and 6,913 academic staff. The establishment of private universities has been permitted since 2001.

In 2000–01 total expenditure on education came to 4·4% of GNP and accounted for 11·1% of total government expenditure.

Health

In 2001 there were 19,716 beds in 406 hospitals, and 1,046 health centres. There were 18,965 physicians, 9,611 dentists, 23,446 nurses, 7,536 pharmacists and 4,441 midwives in 2001.

RELIGION

In 2001 there were an estimated 14·39m. Muslims (namely Sunni with some Shias and Ismailis). There are also Druzes and Alawites. Christians (920,000 in 2001) include Greek Orthodox, Greek Catholics, Armenian Orthodox, Syrian Orthodox, Armenian Catholics, Protestants, Maronites, Syrian Catholics, Latins, Nestorians and Assyrians. There are also Jews and Yezides. In Feb. 2010 the Roman Catholic church had one cardinal.

CULTURE

World Heritage Sites

There are five UNESCO sites in Syria: the old city of Damascus, dating from the 3rd millennium BC and including the Umayyid Mosque (inscribed in 1979); the old city of Bosra, once the capital of the Roman province of Arabia and an important stopover on the ancient caravan routes (1980); Palmyra (Tadmur), a desert oasis northeast of Damascus, containing the ruins of a city that was one of the most prosperous centres of the ancient world (1980); the old city of Aleppo, located at the crossroads of various trade routes since the 2nd millennium BC (1986); and the two castles of Crac des Chevaliers and Qal'at Salah El-Din (2006).

Broadcasting

Broadcasting is government-controlled through the Syrian Radio and Television Organization. Programmes are transmitted in Arabic, English and French (colour by SECAM). Satellite reception is available. Al-Madina FM was launched in 2005 as the first private radio station, although commercial services may not transmit political content. In 2006 there were 3·75m. TV sets.

Press

In 2006 there were four national daily newspapers with a combined circulation of 130,000.

Tourism

In 2005 there were 3,368,000 non-resident tourists; receipts totalled US$2·28bn.

Festivals

Islamic religious festivals are observed throughout the year. Among the most colourful is Milad al-Nabi, held in April to commemorate the birth of Muhammad. The Silk Road Festival takes place in Sept./Oct., when all major cities hold celebrations and Damascus in particular is transformed back to the city that once served as a meeting place for the caravans travelling the Silk Road. Independence Day is widely observed on 17 April.

DIPLOMATIC REPRESENTATIVES

Of Syria in the United Kingdom (8 Belgrave Sq., London, SW1X 8PH)
Ambassador: Sami M. Khiyami.

Of the United Kingdom in Syria (Kotob Building, 11 Mohammad Kurd Ali St., Malki, Damascus POB 37)
Ambassador: Simon Collis.

Of Syria in the USA (2215 Wyoming Ave., NW, Washington, D.C., 20008)
Ambassador: Imad Moustapha.

Of the USA in Syria (Abu Rumaneh, Al Mansur St. No. 2, Damascus)
Ambassador: Vacant.
Chargé d'Affaires a.i.: Chuck Hunter.

Of Syria to the United Nations
Ambassador: Bashar Jaafari.

Of Syria to the European Union
Ambassador: Mohammad Ayman Jameel Soussan.

FURTHER READING

Choueiri, Y., *State and Society in Syria and Lebanon.* 1994
George, Alan, *Syria: Neither Bread nor Freedom.* 2003
Goodarzi, Jubin, *Syria and Iran: Diplomatic Alliance and Power Politics in the Middle East.* 2006
Hitti, Philip K., *History of Syria Including Lebanon and Palestine.* 2002
Kienle, Eberhard, *Contemporary Syria: Liberalization Between Cold War and Peace.* 1997
Moubayed, Sami, *Steel and Silk: Men and Women Who Shaped Syria 1900–2000.* 2005

National Statistical Office: Central Bureau of Statistics, Nizar Kabbani St., Abu Romanneh, Damascus.
Website: http://www.cbssyr.org

TAJIKISTAN

Jumkhurii Tojikiston
(Republic of Tajikistan)

Capital: Dushanbe
Population estimate, 2010: 7·08m.
GDP per capita, 2007: (PPP$) 1,753
HDI/world rank: 0·688/127

KEY HISTORICAL EVENTS

The Tajik Soviet Socialist Republic was formed from those regions of Bokhara and Turkestan where the population consisted mainly of Tajiks. It was admitted as a constituent republic of the Soviet Union on 5 Dec. 1929. In Aug. 1990 the Tajik Supreme Soviet adopted a declaration of republican sovereignty and in Sept. 1991 Tajikistan declared independence. In Dec. 1991 the republic became a member of the CIS. After demonstrations and fighting, the Communist government was replaced by a Revolutionary Coalition Council on 7 May 1992. Following further demonstrations, President Nabiev was ousted on 7 Sept. Civil war broke out, and the government resigned on 10 Nov. On 30 Nov. it was announced that a CIS peacekeeping force would be sent to Tajikistan. A state of emergency was imposed in Jan. 1993. On 23 Dec. 1996 a ceasefire was signed. A further agreement on 8 March 1997 provided for the disarmament of the Islamic-led insurgents, the United Tajik Opposition, and their eventual integration into the regular armed forces. A peace agreement brokered by Iran and Russia was signed in Moscow on 27 June 1997 stipulating that the opposition should have 30% of ministerial posts in a Commission of National Reconciliation. President Rakhmon (formerly Rakhmonov), first elected in 1994, won a second term in 1999. The country's first multi-party parliamentary election was held in Feb. 2000, although it was criticized by observers for failing to meet democratic standards.

Ethnic conflict and terrorist attacks continue to plague Tajikistan, with Russia offering military support. Fighting in the Fergana Valley, involving the Islamist Movement of Uzbekistan, is a cause for concern for all Central Asian governments.

TERRITORY AND POPULATION

Tajikistan is bordered in the north and west by Uzbekistan and Kyrgyzstan, in the east by China and in the south by Afghanistan. Area, 143,100 sq. km (55,240 sq. miles). It includes two regions (Sughd and Khatlon), one autonomous region (Gorno-Badakhshan Autonomous Region), the city of Dushanbe and regions of republican subordination. 2000 census population, 6,127,000 (3,082,000 males); density, 42·8 per sq. km. Estimate, Dec. 2007, 7,215,700. The United Nations population estimate for 2007 was 6,727,000. 80% of the population in 2000 were Tajiks, 15% Uzbeks and 1% Russians.

The UN gives an estimated population for 2010 of 7·08m.

In 2005, 75·3% of the population lived in rural areas, making it the most rural of the former Soviet republics.

The capital is Dushanbe (2000 population, 562,000). Other large towns are Khujand (formerly Leninabad), Kulyab (Kŭlob) and Kurgan-Tyube.

The official language is Tajik, written in Arabic script until 1930 and after 1992 (the Roman alphabet was used 1930–40; the Cyrillic, 1940–92).

SOCIAL STATISTICS

Estimates, 2003: births, 177,900; deaths, 33,200. Rates, 2003 estimate (per 1,000 population): births, 27·1; deaths, 5·0. Life expectancy, 2007, 63·7 years for men and 69·3 for women. Annual growth, 2000–05, 2·0%. Infant mortality, 2005, 59 per 1,000 live births; fertility rate, 2004, 3·7 births per woman.

CLIMATE

Considering its altitude, Tajikistan is a comparatively dry country. July to Sept. are particularly dry months. Winters are cold but spring comes earlier than farther north. Dushanbe, Jan. –10°C, July 25°C. Annual rainfall 375 mm.

CONSTITUTION AND GOVERNMENT

In Nov. 1994 a new constitution was approved by a 90% favourable vote by the electorate, which enhanced the President's powers. The head of state is the *President*, elected by universal suffrage. When the 1994 constitution took effect the term of office was five years. However, an amendment to the Constitution prior to the 1999 election extended the presidential term to seven years, although a president could only serve one term. A further referendum approved in June 2003 allowed President Rakhmonov (now Rakhmon) to serve two additional terms after the expiry of the one that he was serving at the time, in Nov. 2006, theoretically enabling him to remain in office until 2020. The Organization for Security and Co-operation in Europe and the USA expressed concerns at the result. Tajikistan has a bicameral legislature. The lower chamber is the 63-seat *Majlisi Namoyandagon* (*Assembly of Representatives*), with 41 members elected in single-seat constituencies and 22 by proportional representation for five-year terms. The upper chamber is the 34-seat *Majlisi Milliy* (*National Assembly*), with 25 members chosen for five-year terms by local deputies, eight appointed by the president and one seat reserved for the former president.

National Anthem

'Zinda bosh, ey Vatan, Tochikistoni ozodi man' ('Live long, O Nation, my free Tajikistan'); words by Gulnazar Keldi, tune by Suleiman Yudakov.

RECENT ELECTIONS

At presidential elections on 6 Nov. 2006 President Rakhmon was re-elected with 79·3% of votes cast. Opposition parties boycotted the poll.

In parliamentary elections held on 28 Feb. 2010 the People's Democratic Party of Tajikistan (PDPT) won 54 of 63 seats (71·0% of the vote), the Islamic Renaissance Party of Tajikistan (IRP) 2 (8·2%), the Communist Party (CP) 2 (7·0%), Agrarian Party 2 (5·1%) and the Party of Economic Reforms of Tajikistan 2 (5·1%). Turnout was 90·8%. The last seat went to the PDPT in a second round of voting held on 14 March bringing their total to 55. Elections to the National Assembly were held on 24 March 2005. 25 of the 33 seats were voted for by local majlisi deputies and 8 were appointed by the president.

CURRENT ADMINISTRATION

President: Emomalii Rakhmon; b. 1952 (PDPT; as Speaker elected by the former Supreme Soviet 19 Nov. 1992, re-elected 6 Nov. 1994, 6 Nov. 1999 and 6 Nov. 2006).

In March 2010 the government comprised:

Prime Minister: Akil Akilov; b. 1944 (PDPT; sworn in 20 Dec. 1999).

Deputy Prime Ministers: Asadullo Gulomov; Murodali Alimardon; Ruqiya Qurbonova.

Minister of Agriculture and Environmental Protection: Qosim Qosimov. *Culture:* Mirzoshorukh Asrori. *Defence:* Col.-Gen. Sherali Khairullaev. *Economic Development and Trade:* Farruh Hamraliev. *Education:* Abdujabbor Rahmonov. *Energy and Industry:* Sherali Gul. *Finance:* Safarali Najmuddinov. *Foreign Affairs:* Hamrokhon Zarifi. *Health:* Nusratullo Salimov. *Internal Affairs:* Abdurahim Qahorov. *Justice:* Bakhtiyor Khudoyorov. *Labour and Social Protection:* Shukurjon Zuhurov. *Land Reclamation and Water Resources:* Said Yoqubzod. *Transport and Communications:* Olimjon Boboev.

Office of the President: http://www.prezident.tj

CURRENT LEADERS

Emomalii Rakhmon

Position
President

Introduction
Emomalii Rakhmon (formerly Rakhmonov), a former cotton-farm administrator, became Tajikistan's head of state in Nov. 1992, after the country's first post-Soviet leader, Rahmon Nabiev, was forced to resign. Rakhmon has survived civil war and an assassination attempt, but reforming institutions and raising living standards in one of the region's poorest countries has proved a hard challenge. In March 2007 he announced that he was dropping the Russian suffix (-ov) from his surname.

Early Life
Emomalii Sharipovich Rakhmon was born on 5 Oct. 1952 in the Danghara district of the Kulob province of the Tajik Soviet Socialist Republic (SSR). He studied electronics and from 1969 worked at a vegetable-oil extraction factory in Qurghonteppa. After three years in the Soviet navy, Rakhmon became an administrator at Lenin *Kholkov* (collective farm) in Danghara, constructing a power base as chairman of the farm's trade union committee.

He studied economics by correspondence and in 1982 graduated from the Tajik State University. He was elected people's deputy of the supreme council of the Tajik SSR in 1990. Tajikistan declared independence in Sept. 1991 but hopes of an economically viable state were undermined by civil war. On 19 Nov. 1992, following Nabiev's forced resignation and the annulment of the office of president, Rakhmon was elected chairman of the supreme council and head of state. On 6 Nov. 1994, following inter-Tajik peace talks, he won presidential elections, claiming 58·3% of the vote.

Career in Office
Civil war continued through the early years of Rakhmon's presidency and by the time hostilities between the Islamist-led opposition and his Moscow-backed administration ended in June 1997, at least 50,000 people had died. In March 1998 he joined the centrist People's Democratic Party of Tajikistan (PDPT). He was re-elected president on 6 Nov. 1999 with 97% of the vote, and on 22 June 2003 won a referendum to allow him to run for two further seven-year terms. Rakhmon's grip on power was underlined in the general elections of Feb. 2005 when his PDPT won 52 of the 63 seats in the lower house of parliament. The opposition Islamic and communist parties alleged fraud and observers said the vote failed to meet international standards. He was again re-elected overwhelmingly to the presidency in Nov. 2006 as the opposition boycotted the vote. Earlier, in Aug., a former senior military commander was imprisoned for alleged terrorism and plotting to overthrow the government.

Tajikistan suffered a particularly severe winter in 2007–08 and also faced an energy crisis. Many industries were forced to shut down, some rural areas had no electricity and even the capital faced food shortages. In April 2008 the International Monetary Fund ordered the Tajik authorities to repay IMF disbursements that had been obtained on the basis of false data and misreporting. Rakhmon subsequently removed some senior National Bank officials from their positions.

In April 2009 the government finalized an agreement allowing the USA to transport non-military equipment to Afghanistan across Tajik territory.

DEFENCE

In 2007 the active armed forces had a strength of 8,800. Paramilitary forces totalled 7,500 including 3,800 interior troops and 2,500 emergencies ministry troops. 5,500 Russian Army personnel were stationed in the country in 2007.

Defence expenditure in 2006 totalled US$73m. (US$10 per capita), representing 2·7% of GDP.

Army
Personnel strength (2007) 7,300.

Air Force
Air Force/Air Defence strength (2007) 1,500.

INTERNATIONAL RELATIONS

Tajikistan is a member of the UN, World Bank, IMF and several other UN specialized agencies, OSCE, CIS, IOM, Islamic Development Bank, NATO Partnership for Peace, OIC and ECO.

ECONOMY

In 2006 agriculture accounted for 24·8% of GDP, industry 27·4% and services 47·8%.

Overview
The economy is mainly agrarian, with the sector employing two-thirds of the labour force and contributing 11% of export revenues—despite less than 10% of land being arable. Civil war and repeated changes of political leadership in the 1990s prevented the government from establishing a coherent economic policy to address the challenges of post-Soviet independence. As a result, the economy deteriorated more rapidly than in other ex-Soviet countries. In 1996 a reform programme began, supported by the IMF and the World Bank. Despite a slow start and the Russian financial crisis of 1998, the focus on economic reconstruction has enabled the economy to make significant progress in the transition towards a market economy.

Economic growth, which averaged 8% between 2000–06, has been heavily dependent on cotton and aluminium exports, as well as rising remittances of migrants since 2001. Sound macroeconomic management has enabled inflation to be effectively controlled, having reached levels of between 30–40% in the period 1998–2001. Since 2004 inflation has remained around 10% or lower, although lax monetary policy, failed harvests and higher fuel prices have recently led to accelerated inflation. Achievements include halving foreign debt, stabilizing the exchange rate and reducing poverty levels. However, social indicators remain poor and over half the population still live in poverty. Public services are deteriorating, governance and institutions are weak and unemployment is high.

Currency

The unit of currency is the *somoni* (TJS) of 100 *dirams*, which replaced the Tajik rouble on 30 Oct. 2000 at 1 somoni = 1,000 Tajik roubles. The introduction of the new currency was intended to strengthen the national banking system. The IMF voiced their support for the new currency, which it believed would contribute to macroeconomic stability and expedite the transition to a market economy. Inflation in 1993 was 2,195%, declining to 418% in 1996 and still further to 7·2% in 2004, the reduction being helped by a US$22m. IMF loan in 1996 and maintenance of a tighter monetary regime. However, by 2008 the rate had risen back up to 20·4%. Total money supply was 241m. somoni in Dec. 2004. Gold reserves stood at 47,000 troy oz in July 2005.

Budget

Budgetary central government revenue in 2004 totalled 761·5m. somoni (561·3m. somoni in 2003) and expenditure 744·9m. somoni (454·6m. somoni in 2003).

VAT is 20%.

Performance

Annual real GDP growth was negative for four consecutive years in the mid-1990s. Since then the economy has recovered—more recently there has been growth of 7·8% in 2007 and 7·9% in 2008. Total GDP in 2007 was US$3·7bn. Tajikistan ranks among the countries most reliant on remittances from abroad, which account for 36% of total GDP.

Banking and Finance

The central bank and bank of issue is the National Bank (*Chairman*, Sharif Rahimzoda). In 1998 there were 27 commercial and private banks but the number had fallen to 14 by 2002 after a process of consolidation.

ENERGY AND NATURAL RESOURCES

Environment

In 2008 Tajikistan's carbon dioxide emissions from the consumption and flaring of fossil fuels were the equivalent of 0·9 tonnes per capita.

Electricity

Estimated installed capacity in 2004 was 4·4m. kW. Production was 17·3bn. kWh in 2004 and consumption per capita 2,638 kWh.

Oil and Gas

Natural gas output in 2004 was 32m. cu. metres, with reserves of 5·7bn. cu. metres in 2007.

Minerals

There are deposits of brown coal, lead, zinc, iron ore, antimony, mercury, gold, silver, tungsten and uranium. Lignite production, 2004, 15,000 tonnes. Aluminium production, 2005, 380,000 tonnes.

Agriculture

In 2007 there were approximately 710,000 ha. of arable land and 101,000 ha. of permanent crops. Cotton is the major cash crop, with various fruits, sugarcane, jute, silk, rice and millet also being grown.

Output of main agricultural products (in 1,000 tonnes) in 2003: wheat, 660; seed cotton, 537; potatoes, 473; cottonseed, 215; tomatoes, 170; onions, 153. Livestock, 2003: 1·59m. sheep; 1·14m. cattle; 842,000 goats; 2m. chickens. Livestock products, 2003 (in 1,000 tonnes): meat, 30; milk, 412.

Forestry

Forests covered 410,000 ha. in 2005, or 2·9% of the land area. Timber production in 2007 was 90,000 cu. metres.

Fisheries

Total catch in 2004 was 184 tonnes, exclusively from inland waters.

INDUSTRY

Major industries: aluminium, electro-chemical plants, textile machinery, carpet weaving, silk mills, refrigerators, hydro-electric power. Output: cement (2001), 69,000 tonnes; mineral nitrogenous fertilizer (2000), 4,000 tonnes; cotton woven fabrics (2001), 14m. sq. metres; carpets and rugs (1999), 1m. sq. metres; silk fabrics (2001), 248,000 sq. metres; footwear (2001), 100,000 pairs.

Labour

The economically active force in 2005 totalled 2,154,000. The principal areas of activity were: agriculture, 1,424,000; education, 186,000; industry, 121,000. In 2005 the unemployment rate was 3·8%.

INTERNATIONAL TRADE

Total external debt was US$1,022m. in 2005.

Imports and Exports

In 2006 imports were valued at US$1,954·6m. (US$1,430·9m. in 2005) and exports at US$1,511·8m. (US$1,108·1m. in 2005). Main imports: petroleum products, grain, manufactured consumer goods; main exports: cotton and aluminium. Principal import suppliers, 2000: Uzbekistan, 28·8%; Russia, 16·1%; Ukraine, 13·1%; Kazakhstan, 12·8%. Principal export markets in 2000: Russia, 37·4%; Netherlands, 25·7%; Uzbekistan, 14·1%; Switzerland, 10·4%.

COMMUNICATIONS

Roads

In 2000 there were 27,767 km of roads. There were 193,000 passenger cars in use in 2007, 59,000 lorries and vans, 10,700 motorcycles and mopeds, and 5,400 buses and coaches. In 2007 there were 464 fatalities as a result of road accidents.

Rail

Length of railways, 2005, 617 km. Passenger-km travelled in 2002 came to 42m. and freight tonne-km to 1·09bn.

Civil Aviation

There are international airports at Dushanbe and Khujand. The national carrier is Tajik Air, which has flights to 12 international destinations as well as operating domestic services. In 2003 Tajik Air flew 10m. km, carrying 413,000 passengers.

Telecommunications

In 2008 there were 286,900 main (fixed) telephone lines in Tajikistan and mobile phone subscribers numbered 3,673,500 (53·7 per 100 persons). There were 84,600 PCs in use in 2005 and 600,000 internet users in 2008.

Postal Services

In 2003 there were 593 post offices.

SOCIAL INSTITUTIONS

Justice

In 1994, 14,279 crimes were reported, including 636 murders or attempted murders. The population in penal institutions in Sept. 2003 was approximately 10,000 (159 per 100,000 of national population). The death penalty is still in force.

Education
The adult literacy rate in 2003 was 99·5% (99·7% among males and 99·3% among females). In 2007 there were 680,308 pupils and 31,482 teaching staff at primary schools; 1,012,275 pupils and 61,186 teaching staff at secondary schools; and 147,294 students and 7,761 academic staff at higher education institutions. There were 32 higher education institutions in total in 2007.

In 2007 public expenditure on education came to 3·5% of GNI and 18·2% of total government spending.

Health
There were 449 hospitals in 1994. In 2001 there were 13,393 physicians, 1,051 dentists, 26,887 nurses, 680 pharmacists and 3,932 midwives.

Welfare
In Jan. 1994 there were 0·41m. old age pensioners and 0·2m. other pensioners.

RELIGION
The Tajiks are predominantly Sunni Muslims (80%); Shia Muslims, 5%.

CULTURE

Broadcasting
Tajik TV is the government-operated national television service. There are also public regional TV channels and private stations. State-run Tajik Radio operates two national networks, a Radio Moscow relay and a foreign service (in Dari, Farsi, Arabic and English). There are a few private radio stations. In 2005, 984,000 households were equipped with televisions.

Press
There were two daily newspapers in 1996 with a combined circulation of 120,000, equivalent to 21 per 1,000 inhabitants.

Tourism
In 2001, 4,000 foreign tourists visited Tajikistan.

DIPLOMATIC REPRESENTATIVES
Of Tajikistan in the United Kingdom (Grove House, 27 Hammersmith Grove, London, W6 0NE).
Ambassador: Erkin Kasymov.

Of the United Kingdom in Tajikistan (65 Mirzo Tursunzade St., Dushanbe)
Ambassador: Trevor Moore.

Of Tajikistan in the USA (1005 New Hampshire Ave., NW, Washington, D.C., 20037)
Ambassador: Abdujabbor Shirinov.

Of the USA in Tajikistan (109-A Ismoili Somoni Ave., Dushanbe)
Ambassador: Ken Gross.

Of Tajikistan to the United Nations
Ambassador: Sirodjidin Aslov.

Of Tajikistan to the European Union
Ambassador: Saymumin Yatimov.

FURTHER READING
Abdullaev, K. and Akbarzadeh, S., *Historical Dictionary of Tajikistan.* 2002
Akiner, S., *Tajikistan: Disintegration or Reconciliation?* 2001
Djalili, M. R. (ed.) *Tajikistan: The Trials of Independence.* 1998
Jonson, Lena, *Tajikistan in the New Central Asia: Geopolitics, Great Power Rivalry and Radical Islam.* 2006

Gorno-Badakhshan Autonomous Region

Comprising the Pamir massif along the borders of Afghanistan and China, the province was set up on 2 Jan. 1925, initially as the Special Pamir Province. Area, 63,700 sq. km (24,590 sq. miles). The population in 2007 was 218,000 (mainly Tajiks with a Kirghiz minority). Capital, Khorog (2007: 29,000). The inhabitants are predominantly Ismaili Muslims.

Mining industries are developed (gold, rock-crystal, mica, coal, salt). Wheat, fruit and fodder crops are grown, and cattle and sheep are bred in the western parts. Total area under cultivation, 16,236 ha. In 2004 the region was 69% self-sufficient in food; humanitarian aid had comprised 85% of all food consumed in 1993.

The area is the most impoverished in Tajikistan, with 84% of the population falling below the poverty line in 2003, compared to a national average of 64%. Around 20% of the population of working age is employed abroad, mainly in the Russian Federation. Unemployment is approximately 70%.

The Khorog State University was founded in 1992. One of the three campuses of the private University of Central Asia (the other two being in Tekeli, Kazakhstan and Naryn, Kyrgyzstan) in Khorog functions as a continuing and vocational centre in its temporary premises and hopes to accept its first undergraduate and graduate students by 2011. In 2004 there was one doctor per 476 inhabitants and 91 hospital beds per 10,000 inhabitants.

TANZANIA

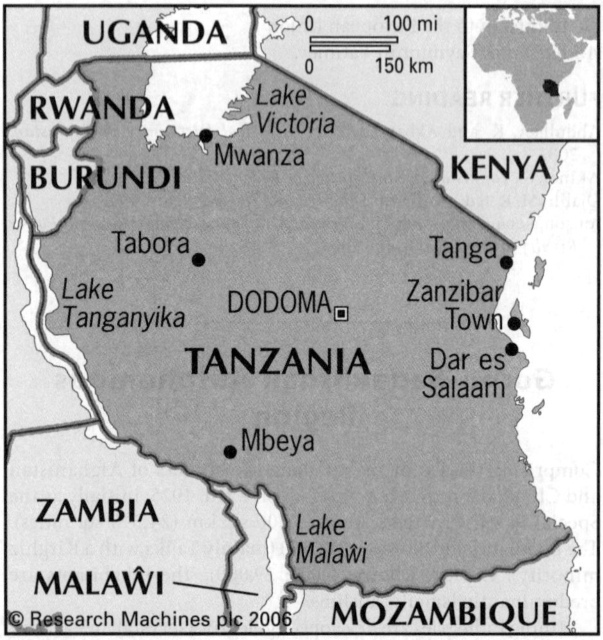

Jamhuri ya Muungano wa Tanzania
(United Republic of Tanzania)

Capital: Dodoma
Population estimate, 2010: 45·04m.
GDP per capita, 2007: (PPP$) 1,208
HDI/world rank: 0·530/151

KEY HISTORICAL EVENTS

Archaeological evidence suggests that present-day Tanzania was inhabited by Khoisan-speaking hunter-gatherers from at least 10,000 BC. The Sandawe and Hadze of north-central Tanzania are descendents of these groups. Cushitic-speaking cattle herders migrated south from Ethiopia and Sudan from around 1000 BC. Beginning in the first millennium AD, Tanzania was settled by Bantu-speaking iron-working farmers, whose origins are considered to be in the borderlands of present-day Nigeria and Cameroon.

Seafarers from Arabia established a trading settlement on the coast at Kilwa around AD 800, and Persian merchants settled on the islands of Zanzibar and Pemba. Nilotic-speaking pastoralists (including the Maasai and Luo) moved south into Tanzania between AD 900 and AD 1700. Sultan Hassan bin Sulaiman I established control of Kilwa around 1270. Islam spread and a thriving Afro-Arab 'Swahili' culture took hold in coastal areas.

Portuguese explorers arrived off Kilwa in 1500, heralding two centuries of Portuguese control over various East African trading ports. Zanzibar came under Omani control in the 1650s and prospered as a centre of the slave trade, extending its influence over the coastal hinterland and into the mainland interior. Britain attempted to end the slave trade by signing the Treaty of Moresby with the Sultan of Zanzibar in 1822. During the 1880s the German imperialist, Dr Carl Peters, founded German East Africa by signing agreements with local rulers. A series of agreements between Britain and Germany and the Sultan of Zanzibar saw Germany become the dominant influence over most of mainland Tanzania, while the Sultan of Zanzibar retained control of a strip of coastal territories and Britain ruled Zanzibar as a protectorate.

German East Africa was conquered by the Allies in the First World War and subsequently divided between the Belgians, the Portuguese and the British. The country was administered as a League of Nations mandate until 1946, and then as a UN trusteeship territory until 9 Dec. 1961. Tanganyika achieved responsible government in Sept. 1960 and full self-government on 1 May 1961. On 9 Dec. 1961 Tanganyika became a sovereign independent member state of the Commonwealth of Nations. On 9 Dec 1962 the country adopted a republican form of government (still within the British Commonwealth) and Dr Nyerere was elected as the first president.

Zanzibar gained internal self-government on 24 June 1963, followed by full independence on 9 Dec. 1963. On 12 Jan. 1964 the sultanate was overthrown by a revolt of the Afro-Shirazi Party leaders who established the People's Republic of Zanzibar. Also in Jan. 1964 there was an attempted coup against Nyerere who had to seek British military help. On 26 April 1964 Tanganyika, Zanzibar and Pemba combined to form the United Republic of Tanzania. The first multi-party elections were held in 1995.

TERRITORY AND POPULATION

Tanzania is bounded in the northeast by Kenya, north by Lake Victoria and Uganda, northwest by Rwanda and Burundi, west by Lake Tanganyika, southwest by Zambia and Malaŵi, and south by Mozambique. Total area 942,799 sq. km (364,881 sq. miles), including the offshore islands of Zanzibar (1,554 sq. km) and Pemba (906 sq. km) and inland water surfaces (59,050 sq. km). 2002 census population, 34,443,603 (17,613,742 females), giving a density of 36·5 per sq. km. The United Nations population estimate for 2002 was 35,958,000.

The UN gives an estimated population for 2010 of 45·04m.

In 2005, 75·8% of the population lived in rural areas. 0·5m. Hutu refugees were forcibly repatriated to Rwanda in Dec. 1996. In 2000 Tanzania hosted the highest number of refugees in Africa, with a population of over 680,000. By Nov. 2009 repatriation programmes had allowed the number of refugees to drop below 100,000 for the first time in 15 years.

The chief towns (2002 census populations) are Dar es Salaam, the chief port and former capital (2,339,910), Arusha (270,485), Mbeya (232,596) and Mwanza (209,806). Dodoma, the capital, had a population of 150,604 in 2002.

The United Republic is divided into 26 administrative regions of which 21 are in mainland Tanzania, three in Zanzibar and two in Pemba. Areas and 2002 populations of the regions:

Region	*Sq. km*	*Population*
Arusha	36,486	1,288,088
Dar es Salaam	1,393	2,487,288
Dodoma	41,311	1,692,025
Iringa	56,864	1,490,892
Kagera	28,388	2,028,157
Kigoma	37,037	1,674,047
Kilimanjaro	13,309	1,376,702
Lindi	66,046	787,624
Manyara	45,820	1,037,605
Mara	19,566	1,363,397
Mbeya	60,350	2,063,328
Morogoro	70,799	1,753,362
Mtwara	16,707	1,124,481
Mwanza	19,592	2,929,644
Pwani (Coast)	32,407	885,017
Rukwa	68,635	1,136,354

Region	Sq. km	Population
Ruvuma	63,498	1,113,715
Shinyanga	50,781	2,796,630
Singida	49,341	1,086,748
Tabora	76,151	1,710,465
Tanga	26,808	1,636,280
Zanzibar and Pemba	*2,460*	*981,754*
Pemba North	574	185,326
Pemba South	332	175,471
Zanzibar North	470	136,639
Zanzibar South	854	94,244
Zanzibar West	230	390,074

The official languages are Swahili (spoken as a mother tongue by only 8·8% of the population, but used as a *lingua franca* by 91%) and English.

SOCIAL STATISTICS

2000 estimates: births, 1,320,000; deaths, 460,000. Rates, 2000 estimates (per 1,000 population): births, 37·9; deaths, 13·1. Annual population growth rate, 1992–2002, 2·6%. Life expectancy in 2007 was 54·2 years for men and 55·8 for women. 45% of the population was below 15 years old in 2002. Infant mortality, 2005, 76 per 1,000 live births; fertility rate, 2004, 4·9 births per woman.

CLIMATE

The climate is very varied and is controlled largely by altitude and distance from the sea. There are three climatic zones: the hot and humid coast, the drier central plateau with seasonal variations of temperature, and the semi-temperate mountains. Dodoma, Jan. 75°F (23·9°C), July 67°F (19·4°C). Annual rainfall 23" (572 mm). Dar es Salaam, Jan. 82°F (27·8°C), July 74°F (23·3°C). Annual rainfall 43" (1,064 mm).

CONSTITUTION AND GOVERNMENT

The current constitution dates from 25 April 1977 but underwent major revisions in Oct. 1984. The *President* is head of state, chairman of the party and commander-in-chief of the armed forces. The *Prime Minister* is also the leader of government business in the National Assembly.

The 324-member *Bunge (National Assembly)* is composed of 232 constituency representatives, 75 appointed women, ten Union presidential nominees, five representatives of the Zanzibar House of Representatives and two *ex officio* members (one of whom is the Attorney General). In Dec. 1979 a separate constitution for Zanzibar was approved. Although at present under the same Constitution as Tanzania, Zanzibar has, in fact, been ruled by decree since 1964.

National Anthem

'God Bless Africa/Mungu ibariki Afrika'; words collective, tune by M. E. Sontonga and V. E. Webster.

GOVERNMENT CHRONOLOGY

Presidents since 1964. (TANU = Tanganyika African National Union; CCM = Chama Cha Mapinduzi (Revolutionary State Party))

1964–85	TANU/CCM	Julius Kambarage Nyerere
1985–95	CCM	Ali Hassan Mwinyi
1995–2005	CCM	Benjamin William Mkapa
2005–	CCM	Jakaya Mrisho Kikwete

RECENT ELECTIONS

Presidential and parliamentary elections were held on 14 Dec. 2005. Jakaya Kikwete of Chama Cha Mapinduzi (Revolutionary State Party) was elected president with 80·3% of votes cast against nine other candidates. Turnout was 72·4%. In the parliamentary elections Chama Cha Mapinduzi gained 206 of 232 seats, the Civic United Front 19, Chama Cha Democracia na Maendeleo (Party for Democracy and Progress) 5, the Tanzania Labour Party 1 and the United Democratic Party 1.

CURRENT ADMINISTRATION

President: Jakaya Kikwete; b. 1950 (Chama Cha Mapinduzi/CCM; sworn in 21 Dec. 2005).

Vice-President: Dr Ali Mohamed Sheni.

In March 2010 the government consisted of:

Prime Minister: Mizengo Kayanza Peter Pinda; b. 1948 (CCM; sworn in 9 Feb. 2008).

President of Zanzibar: Amani Abeid Karume.

Minister of Agriculture, Food Security and Co-operatives: Stephen Wassira. *Communication, Science and Technology:* Peter Mahmoud Msolla. *Community Development, Gender and Children:* Margareth Simwanza Sitta. *Defence and National Service:* Hussein Ali Mwinyi. *East African Co-operation:* Diodorus Buberwa Kamala. *Education and Vocational Training:* Jumanne Abdallah Maghembe. *Energy and Minerals:* William Ngeleje. *Finance and Economy:* Mustafa Mkuro. *Foreign Affairs and International Co-operation:* Bernard Membe. *Health and Social Welfare:* David Mwakyusa. *Home Affairs:* Lawrence Kego Masha. *Industry, Trade and Marketing:* Mary Michael Nagu. *Information, Culture and Sports:* George Mkuchika. *Infrastructure Development:* Shukuru Jumanne Kawambwa. *Justice and Constitutional Affairs:* Mathias Meinrad Chikawe. *Labour, Employment and Youth Development:* Juma Athumani Kapuya. *Lands, Housing and Human Settlements Development:* John Zefania Chiligati. *Livestock and Fisheries Development:* John Pombe Joseph Magufuli. *Natural Resources and Tourism:* Shamsa Mwangunga. *Water and Irrigation:* Mark James Mwandosya.

Government Website: http://www.tanzania.go.tz

CURRENT LEADERS

Jakaya Kikwete

Position
President

Introduction
Jakaya Kikwete became president of Tanzania on 14 Dec. 2005, winning an overwhelming majority in national elections that were generally considered free and fair. A Muslim from the coastal district of Bagamoyo, Kikwete was a military leader in the 1970s and 1980s and served as foreign minister for ten years from 1995.

Early Life
Jakaya Mrisho Kikwete was born on 7 Oct. 1950 in Msoga, Bagamoyo District on the coast of Tanganyika. He attended schools in Msoga and Kibaha, before studying economics at the University of Dar es Salaam. In 1975, while at university, Kikwete joined the ruling Tanganyika African National Union, which later became the Chama Cha Mapinduzi (CCM, Revolutionary State Party). Following his graduation in 1978, Kikwete joined the Tanzania People's Defence Force (TPDF), where he served as lieutenant from 1972–79 and subsequently as captain.

In 1984, having spent a year at the Monduli military officers college in Arusha, Kikwete became chief political instructor of the TPDF. In 1988 he was elected to represent Bagamoyo parliamentary constituency, a post he held for three consecutive terms. He was deputy minister of energy, water and minerals from 1988–90 before being promoted to minister and serving under President Ali Hassan Mwinyi for four years. Following constitutional reform that legalized opposition parties in 1992, Kikwete retired from the army.

In 1995, having served as finance minister for a year, Kikwete became one of fourteen challengers for the CCM leadership. He lost to Benjamin Mkapa, who led the party to victory in national elections in Oct. 1995 amid widespread allegations of voting irregularities. Kikwete was appointed foreign minister, a post he held until 2005, winning praise for his mediation work in war-torn Burundi and the Democratic Republic of the Congo. His department was credited with advancing regional integration within the East African Community and in the Southern African Development Community. Kikwete won the right to lead his party into the 2005 national elections and emerged victorious from the poll on 14 Dec. He received 80% of the vote and replaced Mkapa as president. The CCM retained its overwhelming majority in parliament, with 206 out of 232 seats.

Career in Office

In his inauguration speech, Kikwete vowed to continue the free-market policies of Mkapa and prioritized the improvement of relations with the semi-autonomous islands of Zanzibar. He inherited a country in which poverty is widespread but whose economy had been growing at a rate of 6% a year. He was expected to maintain political stability as the country benefited from rising gold production and donor-supported investment. In Aug. 2006, in recognition of the government's economic reform efforts, the African Development Bank cancelled US$645m. of Tanzanian debt and also agreed a loan of US$74m. for poverty reduction programmes.

In Feb. 2008 Prime Minister Edward Lowassa and two other ministers resigned in the wake of a corruption scandal involving an energy deal with a US-based electricity company, in response to which Kikwete dissolved the cabinet and appointed Mizengo Kayanza Peter Pinda as the new premier.

In 2008 Kikwete served as chairman of the African Union.

DEFENCE

Defence expenditure totalled US$143m. in 2006 (US$4 per capita), representing 1·2% of GDP.

Army

Strength (2007), 23,000. There is a paramilitary Police Field Force of 1,400.

Navy

Personnel in 2007 totalled about 1,000. The principal bases are at Dar es Salaam, Zanzibar and Mwanza.

Air Force

The Tanzanian People's Defence Force Air Wing was built up initially with the help of Canada, but combat equipment has been acquired from China. Air Defence Command personnel totalled 3,000 in 2007. Although there were a reported 19 combat capable aircraft in 2007 virtually no air defence assets were serviceable.

INTERNATIONAL RELATIONS

Tanzania is a member of the UN, World Bank, IMF and several other UN specialized agencies, WTO, Commonwealth, IOM, African Development Bank, African Union, COMESA, EAC, SADC and is an ACP member state of the ACP-EU relationship.

In Nov. 1999 a treaty was signed between Tanzania, Kenya and Uganda to create a new East African Community as a means of developing East African trade, tourism and industry and laying the foundations for a future common market and political federation.

ECONOMY

Agriculture accounted for 45·3% of GDP in 2006, industry 17·4% and services 37·3%.

Overview

Tanzania had per capita income of US$368 in 2007. An estimated 40% of the state budget is financed by aid. Agriculture employs over 80% of the workforce. From the late 1960s to the mid-1980s the economy stagnated under corrupt state control. From 1985 popular discontent encouraged the government of Ali Hassan Mwinyi to loosen control over prices and trade. Similar policies were pushed by President Benjamin Mkapa in the mid-1990s and there has been further liberalization of the financial sector and civil service as well as some privatization.

Tanzania is the fourth largest producer of gold in Africa and fourth largest producer of coffee in Eastern and Central Africa. Annual gold output increased from five to 50 tonnes between 1999–2007. Real GDP grew by an average 7% per year from 2001–05, driven mainly by mining and construction, the two fastest-growing sectors in the economy. Growth has also been boosted by the flourishing tourism industry and the successful implementation of economic reforms. After a blip in 2006 when drought damaged crops and cut hydro-power generation, growth returned to above 7% in 2007 and 2008.

Currency

The monetary unit is the *Tanzanian shilling* (TZS) of 100 *cents*. Foreign exchange reserves were US$3,533m. in Sept. 2009. Inflation, which had been 26·5% in 1995, was down to 4·1% in 2004, the lowest rate for more than 20 years. It has gone up since then and in 2008 was 10·3%. Total money supply in Aug. 2009 was Sh. 3,429·5bn.

Budget

The fiscal year ends 30 June. In 2006–07 revenues were Sh. 3,691·2bn. and expenditures Sh. 4,474·7bn. Tax revenue accounted for 68·5% of revenues in 2006–07 and current expenditure 70·1% of expenditures.

VAT is 18%.

Performance

Real GDP growth was 7·1% in 2007 and 7·4% in 2008. Total GDP in 2008 was US$20·5bn. (mainland Tanzania only).

Banking and Finance

The central bank is the Bank of Tanzania (*Governor*, Prof. Benno Ndulu).

On 6 Feb. 1967 all commercial banks with the exception of National Co-operative Banks were nationalized, and their interests vested in the National Bank of Commerce on the mainland and the Peoples' Bank in Zanzibar. However, in 1993 private-sector commercial banks were allowed to open. In 1997 the National Bank of Commerce, which controls 70% of the country's banking and has 34 branches, was split into a trade bank, a regional rural bank and a micro-finance bank. It was privatized in 2000, with the South African concern Absa Group Limited purchasing a 55% stake. The government retained 30% with the International Finance Corporation holding 15%. In 2000 there were 17 banks operating in Tanzania.

A stock exchange opened in Dar es Salaam in 1996.

ENERGY AND NATURAL RESOURCES

Environment

Tanzania's carbon dioxide emissions from the consumption and flaring of fossil fuels in 2008 were the equivalent of 0·1 tonnes per capita.

Electricity

Installed capacity was an estimated 0·4m. kW in 2004. Production in 2004 was 2·48bn. kWh, with consumption per capita 69 kWh. In 1998 only 10% of the population had access to electricity. By 2015 the government aims to have increased this to 40% under a new structure principally managed by the private sector.

Oil and Gas

A number of international companies are exploring for both gas and oil. In 2007 proven natural gas reserves were 6·5bn. cu. metres.

Minerals
Tanzania's mineral resources include gold, nickel, cobalt, silver and diamonds. International funds injected to improve Tanzania's economy have resulted in notable increases, particularly in gold production. The first commercial gold mine began operating in Mwanza in 1998. By 2005 the value of gold exports had reached US$642m., up from US$121m. in 2000. Gold production in 2005 totalled 52,236 kg. Large deposits of coal and tin exist but mining is on a small scale. Estimated diamond production in 2005 was 205,000 carats; exports totalled US$33·7m. in 2004.

Agriculture
About 80% of the workforce are engaged in agriculture, chiefly in subsistence farming. Agricultural produce contributes around 85% of exports. There were an estimated 4·0m. ha. of arable land in 2002 and 1·1m. ha. of permanent crops. Approximately 170,000 ha. were irrigated in 2002. There were about 7,600 tractors in 2002.

Production of main agricultural crops in 2002 (in 1,000 tonnes) was: cassava, 6,888; maize, 2,705; sugarcane, 1,600; sweet potatoes, 950; sorghum, 834; rice, 640; plantains, 602; coconuts, 370; millet, 300; dry beans, 270; potatoes, 240; seed cotton, 222. Zanzibar is a major producer of cloves.

Livestock (2003 estimates): 17·70m. cattle; 12·56m. goats; 3·52m. sheep; 30m. chickens.

Livestock products (2003 estimates, in 1,000 tonnes): beef and veal, 246; goat meat, 31; pork, bacon and ham, 13; lamb and mutton, 10; poultry meat, 45; goat's milk, 835; cow's milk, 100; eggs, 34; honey, 26.

Forestry
Forests covered 35·26m. ha. in 2005 (39·9% of the total land area). In 2007, 24·44m. cu. metres of roundwood were cut.

Fisheries
Catch (2004) 347,795 tonnes, of which 298,525 tonnes were from inland waters.

INDUSTRY

Industry is limited, and is mainly textiles, petroleum and chemical products, food processing, tobacco, brewing and paper manufacturing.

INTERNATIONAL TRADE

Foreign debt was US$7,763m. in 2005.

Imports and Exports
In 2006 imports (f.o.b.) amounted to US$3,864·1m. (US$2,997·6m. in 2005); exports (f.o.b.) US$1,723·0m. (US$1,675·8m. in 2005).

Principal imports, 2002: consumer goods, 31·0%; machinery and apparatus, 22·2%; transport equipment, 13·2%; crude and refined petroleum, 11·8%. Principal exports, 2002: minerals (notably gold), 42·4%; cashew nuts, 5·8%; tobacco, 5·6%; coffee, 4·0%; tea, 3·4%.

Main import suppliers, 2002: South Africa, 11·4%; Japan, 8·4%; India, 6·5%; Russia, 6·1%; UAE, 5·9%. Main export markets, 2002: UK, 18·5%; France, 17·4%; Japan, 11·0%; India, 7·3%; Netherlands, 6·2%.

COMMUNICATIONS

Roads
In 2003 there were 78,891 km of roads, of which 8·6% were paved. Passenger cars in use in 2007 numbered 80,900; there were also 369,900 lorries and vans, 23,100 buses and coaches, and 52,000 motorcycles and mopeds.

Rail
In 1977 the independent Tanzanian Railway Corporation was formed. The network totalled 2,707 km (metre-gauge) in 2005, excluding the joint Tanzania-Zambia (Tazara) railway's 961 km in Tanzania (1,067 mm gauge) operated by a separate administration. In 2004 the state railway carried 0·6m. passengers and 1·5m. tonnes of freight, and in 2003 the Tazara carried 1·4m. passengers and 0·6m. tonnes of freight.

In Oct. 1998 a transhipment facility for containers opened at Kidatu, southwest of Dar es Salaam, providing a link between the 1,067 mm gauge railways of the southern part of Africa and the 1,000 mm gauge lines of the north.

Civil Aviation
There are three international airports: Dar es Salaam, Zanzibar and Kilimanjaro (Moshi/Arusha). Air Tanzania, the national carrier, provides domestic services and in 2003 had flights to Abu Dhabi, Blantyre, Johannesburg, Lilongwe, Mombasa, Muscat and Nairobi. In 2003 scheduled airline traffic of Tanzanian-based carriers flew 4m. km, carrying 150,000 passengers (61,000 on international flights). Dar es Salaam is the busiest airport, handling 1,155,000 passengers in 2006 (659,000 on international flights), followed by Zanzibar with 486,000 (197,000 on international flights).

Shipping
In 2002 the merchant marine totalled 47,000 GRT, including oil tankers 8,000 GRT. The main seaports are Dar es Salaam, Mtwara, Tanga and Zanzibar. There are also ports on the lakes. In 1991, 1m. tonnes of freight were loaded, and 2·9m. unloaded.

Telecommunications
In 2008 there were 123,800 main (fixed) telephone lines; mobile phone subscribers numbered 13,006,800 in 2008 (30·6 per 100 persons). There were 356,000 PCs in use in 2005 and 520,000 internet users in 2008.

Postal Services
In 2003 there were 422 post offices.

SOCIAL INSTITUTIONS

Justice
The Judiciary is independent in both judicial and administrative matters and is composed of a four-tier system of Courts: Primary Courts; District and Resident Magistrates' Courts; the High Court and the Court of Appeal. The Chief Justice is head of the Court of Appeal and the Judiciary Department. The Court's main registry is at Dar es Salaam; its jurisdiction includes Zanzibar. The Principal Judge is head of the High Court, also headquartered at Dar es Salaam, which has resident judges at seven regional centres.

The population in penal institutions in Sept. 2006 was 43,911 (113 per 100,000 of national population).

Education
In 1999–2000 there were 11,409 primary schools with 103,731 teachers for 4·19m. pupils. At secondary level there were 247,579 pupils with 12,496 (1997) teachers in 826 schools, and at university level in 2000–01 there were 21,960 students with 2,192 academic staff. Primary school fees were abolished in Jan. 2002.

Technical and vocational education is provided at several secondary and technical schools, and at the Dar es Salaam Technical College. There are 53 teacher training colleges, including the college at Chang'ombe for secondary-school teachers.

There is one university, one university of agriculture and one open university. There are also nine other institutions of higher education.

Adult literacy rate in 2003 was 69·4% (male, 77·5%; female, 62·2%). In 1998–99 total expenditure on education came to 2·2% of GNP.

Health

In 2002 there were 822 physicians, 218 dentists (1995), 13,292 nurses, 13,953 midwives (1995) and 365 pharmacists. In 2005 there were 219 hospitals, 481 health centres and 4,679 dispensaries.

RELIGION

In 2001 there were 18·3m. Christians (including Roman Catholics, Anglicans and Lutherans) and 11·5m. Muslims. Muslims are concentrated in the coastal towns; Zanzibar is 99% Muslim. The remainder of the population follow traditional religions. In Feb. 2010 the Roman Catholic church had one cardinal.

CULTURE

World Heritage Sites

Tanzania has seven sites on the UNESCO World Heritage List: Ngorongoro Conservation Area (inscribed on the list in 1979); the Ruins of Kilwa Kisiwani and of Songo Mnara (1981); Serengeti National Park (1981); Selous Game Reserve (1982); Kilimanjaro National Park (1987); the Stone Town of Zanzibar (2000); and the Kondoa Rock-Art sites (2006).

Broadcasting

Mainland Tanzania and Zanzibar have separate broadcasting policies. Televisheni va Taifa (TVT) and TV Zanzibar are the respective government-operated television services (state-run TV was not introduced until 2001). Private TV stations (on the mainland only) include Independent Television (ITV), Dar es Salaam TV (DTV) and Coastal Television Network (CTN). A South African satellite TV channel (DSTV) is also available. State-run radio services include Radio Tanzania Dar es Salaam, Parapanda Radio Tanzania and Voice of Tanzania-Zanzibar. There are a number of private FM radio stations operating in mainland urban areas (though not in Zanzibar). 525,000 households were equipped with TV sets in 2006.

Press

In 2006 there were 14 dailies with a combined circulation of 115,000.

Tourism

There were 15 national parks in Tanzania in 2008. In 2004 there were 583,000 foreign tourists (excluding day-visitors), bringing revenue of US$610m. Tourism is the country's second largest foreign exchange earner after agriculture.

DIPLOMATIC REPRESENTATIVES

Of Tanzania in the United Kingdom (3 Stratford Pl., London, W1C 1AS)
High Commissioner: Mwanaidi Sinare Maajar.

Of the United Kingdom in Tanzania (Umoja House, Garden Ave., PO Box 9200 Dar es Salaam)
High Commissioner: Diane Louise Corner.

Of Tanzania in the USA (2139 R. St., NW, Washington, D.C., 20008)
Ambassador: Ombeni Yohana Sefue.

Of the USA in Tanzania (686 Old Bagamoyo Rd, Msasani, PO Box 9123, Dar es Salaam)
Ambassador: Alfonso E. Lenhardt.

Of Tanzania to the United Nations
Ambassador: Augustine Philip Mahiga.

Of Tanzania to the European Union
Ambassador: Simon Uforosia Ralph Mlay.

FURTHER READING

National Statistical Office: National Bureau of Statistics, Box 796, Dar es Salaam.
Website: http://www.tanzania.go.tz/statistics.html

THAILAND

Prathet Thai
(Kingdom of Thailand)

Capital: Bangkok
Population estimate, 2010: 68·14m.
GDP per capita, 2007: (PPP$) 8,135
HDI/world rank: 0·783/87

KEY HISTORICAL EVENTS

Excavations at Ban Chiang on the Khorat plateau in northeast Thailand suggest rice farming was under way by as early as 2500 BC. From around 300 BC the Indianized Funan kingdom held sway across much of southeast Asia, including eastern and central Thailand. Artifacts discovered at the Funan capital of Ba Phnom, in modern Cambodia, point to trading links with China and India and as far as the Middle East and Rome. At its height in the 6th century AD, Funan control included part of the Malay peninsula.

Mon, Tai and Khmer peoples first entered northern and eastern Thailand from southern China in the 5th century AD. Taking advantage of Funan's decline after the 6th century, the Mon began to establish independent kingdoms. Among them was Dvaravarti, which in the 10th century was absorbed by the Indian-influenced Khmer empire, centred on Angkor. Mongol incursions into Yunnan in southern China in the mid-13th century forced a new wave of Tai migration that culminated in the Sukhothai kingdom of north-central Thailand. Under Ramkhamhaeng (1279–98), its influence stretched southward to the Malay peninsula. Trade with India and China flourished and the Siamese language developed in written form.

The Tai kingdom of Lan Na emerged as the dominant power in northern Thailand in the 14th century while further south the declining Sukhothai came under the influence of Rama Tibodi, prince of U Tong, who, around 1350, established a Buddhist dynasty centered on Ayutthaya. Rice cultivation and trade brought prosperity and power to Siam over the next four centuries, though tempered by frequent warfare with the Khmer empire and the Lao state of Chiang Mai. Trade with Europe, the Middle East, China and Japan expanded considerably in the 16th and 17th centuries, notably under King Narai (1656–88). Relations with France developed in the 1680s but soured amid attempts to convert Narai to Christianity.

Ayutthaya suffered a series of attacks from Burma in the mid-1700s and fell in 1767 although Thai forces, led by Gen. Phya Tak (King Taksin), re-established control with the help of Chinese merchants within a decade. His successor, Chao Phraya Chakkri (Rama I), established Bangkok as his capital and restored the Buddhist religion during his reign (1782–1809). Subsequent Chakkri kings resumed relations with the West but, through skilful diplomacy, managed to preserve Siam's independence. The nation remained an absolute monarchy until 24 June 1932 when a group of rebels calling themselves the People's Party precipitated a bloodless coup. After King Prajadhipok tried to dissolve the newly appointed general assembly the army moved against him to become the dominant political force, a position it has held ever since. In 1939 Field Marshal Pibul Songgram became premier and embarked on a pro-Japanese policy that brought Thailand into the Second World War on Japan's side.

After 1945 periods of military rule were interspersed with attempts at democratic, civilian government. Democratic government was reintroduced for a short time after 1963 and again from 1969–71, until a military coup was staged aimed at checking crime and the communist insurgence. A moderately democratic constitution was introduced in 1978. On 23 Feb. 1991 a military junta seized power in Thailand's 17th coup since 1932. Following the appointment of Gen. Suchinda Kraprayoon as prime minister on 17 April 1992 there were violent anti-government demonstrations. Gen. Suchinda resigned and in May the legislative assembly voted that future prime ministers should be elected by its members rather than appointed by the military. The 1995 election was fought against a background of political and financial corruption. After the 1996 election a new constitution was drafted allowing for the separation of the executive, legislative and judicial branches of government.

On 26 Dec. 2004 Thailand, along with a number of other south Asian countries, was hit by a devastating tsunami. The death toll in Thailand was put at 8,000. The government of Thaksin Shinawatra was overthrown in a bloodless military coup on 19 Sept. 2006. Elections held in Dec. 2007 were won by the People's Power Party (PPP), the successor to Thaksin's banned Thai Rak Thai. Samak Sundaravej became prime minister in Feb. 2008, marking a return to civilian rule. When a Constitutional Court ruling removed him from office in Sept. 2008 he was replaced by Somchai Wongsawat. Wongsawat in turn had to step down in Dec. 2008 when the Constitutional Court disbanded the ruling PPP following accusations of electoral fraud. Opposition leader Abhisit Vejjajiva formed a parliamentary coalition and was elected to the premiership. In April 2009 anti-government protests by the pro-Thaksin United Front for Democracy against Dictatorship ('red-shirts') forced the government to declare a state of emergency and cancel the ASEAN Bangkok summit. In March and April 2010 renewed red-shirt protests calling for the government's resignation again disrupted Bangkok.

TERRITORY AND POPULATION

Thailand is bounded in the west by Myanmar, north and east by Laos and southeast by Cambodia. In the south it becomes a peninsula bounded in the west by the Indian Ocean, south by Malaysia and east by the Gulf of Thailand. The area is 513,115 sq. km (198,114 sq. miles).

At the 2000 census the population was 60,916,441 (30,901,208 females); density, 118·7 per sq. km. The United Nations population estimate for 2000 was 62,347,000. 20,825,262 lived in the Northeastern region, 11,433,061 in the Northern region, 14,215,503 in the Central region, 8,087,471 in the Southern region and 6,355,144 in Bangkok. In 2005, 67·7% of the population lived in rural areas.

The UN gives an estimated population for 2010 of 68·14m.

Thailand is divided into four regions, 75 provinces and Bangkok, the capital. Population of Bangkok (2000 census figure), 6,355,144. Other towns (2000 census figures): Samut Prakan (378,741), Nonthaburi (291,555), Udon Thani (222,425), Nakhon Ratchasima (204,641), Hat Yai (187,920).

Thai is the official language, spoken by 53% of the population as their mother tongue. 27% speak Lao (mainly in the northeast), 12% Chinese (mainly in urban areas), 3·7% Malay (mainly in the south) and 2·7% Khmer (along the Cambodian border).

SOCIAL STATISTICS

2005–06: births, 705,639; deaths, 440,024; marriages (2005), 345,234; divorces (2005), 90,688. Rates (per 1,000 population, 2005–06): birth, 10·9; death, 6·8; marriage (2005), 5·2; divorce (2005), 1·4. Annual population growth rate, 2000–05, 1·0%. Expectation of life (2007): 65·4 years for men; 72·1 years for women. Infant mortality, 2005, 18 per 1,000 live births; fertility rate, 2004, 1·9 births per woman.

CLIMATE

The climate is tropical, with high temperatures and humidity. Over most of the country, three seasons may be recognized. The rainy season is June to Oct., the cool season from Nov. to Feb. and the hot season is March to May. Rainfall is generally heaviest in the south and lightest in the northeast. Bangkok, Jan. 78°F (25·6°C), July 83°F (28·3°C). Annual rainfall 56" (1,400 mm).

On 26 Dec. 2004 an undersea earthquake centred off the Indonesian island of Sumatra caused a huge tsunami that flooded coastal areas in western Thailand resulting in 8,000 deaths. In total there were more than 225,000 deaths in 14 countries.

CONSTITUTION AND GOVERNMENT

The reigning King is **Bhumibol Adulyadej**, born 5 Dec. 1927. King Bhumibol married on 28 April 1950 Princess Sirikit, and was crowned 5 May 1950 (making him currently the world's longest-reigning monarch). *Offspring*: Princess Ubol Ratana (born 5 April 1951, married Aug. 1972 Peter Ladd Jensen); Crown Prince Vajiralongkorn (born 28 July 1952, married 3 Jan. 1977 Soamsawali Kitiyakra); Princess Maha Chakri Sirindhorn (born 2 April 1955); Princess Chulabhorn (born 4 July 1957, married 7 Jan. 1982 Virayudth Didyasarin).

Following the coup of Sept. 2006 an interim constitution was introduced on 1 Oct. 2006 to replace the 1997 constitution. In the country's first ever referendum, held on 19 Aug. 2007, 56·7% of votes cast were in favour of a new draft constitution (the 18th constitution since independence in 1932) that paved the way for elections before the end of the year, set a limit of two four-year terms for the prime minister and made it easier to impeach the prime minister. Turnout was low.

There is a 150-seat *Senate* (76 senators elected in the 76 provinces and 74 appointed by a selection panel) and a 480-seat *House of Representatives* (400 members elected by popular vote from constituencies and 80 selected on a proportional basis from party lists).

National Anthem

'Prathet Thai ruam nua chat chua Thai' ('Thailand, cradle of Thais wherever they may be'); words by Luang Saranuprapan, tune by Phrachen Duriyang.

GOVERNMENT CHRONOLOGY

Heads of Government since 1944. (PCT = Thai Nation Party; PKS = Social Action Party; PKWM = New Aspiration Party; PP = Democratic Party; PPP = People's Power Party; SP = United Thai People's Party; ST = Free Thai Movement; TRT = Thai Rak Thai; n/p = non-partisan)

Prime Ministers		
1944–45	military	Khuang Aphaiwong
1945	n/p	Tawee Boonyaket
1945–46	ST	Seni Pramoj
1946	military	Khuang Aphaiwong
1946	n/p	Pridi Phanomyong
1946–47	military	Thamrong Nawasawat
1948–57	military	Plaek Pibulsongkram
1957	n/p	Pote Sarasin
1958	military	Thanom Kittikachorn
1959–63	military	Sarit Thanarat
1963–73	military, SP	Thanom Kittikachorn
1973–75	n/p	Sanya Thammasak
1975	PP	Seni Pramoj
1975–76	PKS	Kukrit Pramoj
1976	PP	Seni Pramoj
Chairman of the National Administrative Reform Council		
1976–80	military (de facto ruler)	Sangad Chaloryu
Prime Ministers		
1976–77	n/p	Thanin Kraivichien
1977–80	military	Kriangsak Chomanan
1980–88	military	Prem Tinsulanonda
1988–91	PCT	Chatichai Choonhavan
Chairman of the National Peacekeeping Council		
1991	military	Sunthorn Kongsompong
Prime Ministers		
1991–92	n/p	Anand Panyarachun
1992	military	Suchinda Kraprayoon
1992	n/p	Anand Panyarachun
1992–95	PP	Chuan Leekpai
1995–96	PCT	Banharn Silpa-Archa
1996–97	PKWM	Chavalit Yongchaiyudh
1997–2001	PP	Chuan Leekpai
2001–06	TRT	Thaksin Shinawatra
2006	TRT	Chidchai Vanasatidya (acting for Thaksin Shinawatra)
Chairman of the Council for Democratic Reform under Constitutional Monarchy		
2006	military	Sonthi Boonyaratkalin
Prime Minister		
2006–08	n/p	Surayud Chulanont
2008	PPP	Samak Sundaravej
2008	PPP	Somchai Wongsawat
2008	PPP	Chaovarat Chanweerakul (acting)
2008–	PP	Abhisit Vejjajiva

RECENT ELECTIONS

At the elections to the House of Representatives of 23 Dec. 2007 the People's Power Party won 233 of 480 seats, the Democrat Party 165, Thai Nation Party 37, For the Motherland 24, Thais United National Development Party 9, Neutral Democratic Party 7 and Royalist People's Party 5. However, following allegations of vote rigging, the People's Power Party was disbanded in Dec. 2008 by the Constitutional Court, with party executives banned from political activity for five years.

There were elections to the 150-seat Senate on 2 March 2008. 76 members were elected, one for each of the country's provinces. The other 74 seats were appointed by a selection committee headed by a military-installed chief. Among the latter, 18 were former MPs or relatives of top politicians.

CURRENT ADMINISTRATION

Following a coup that removed former prime minister Somchai Wongsawat from power and led to the People's Power Party being dissolved, a new prime minister was elected by parliament. In March 2010 the coalition government comprised:

Prime Minister: Abhisit Vejjajiva; b. 1964 (PP; in office since 17 Dec. 2008).

Deputy Prime Ministers: Suthep Thaugsuban; Trairong Suwankiri; Sanan Kachornprasart. *Ministers in the Prime Minister's Office:* Satit Wongnongtaey; Virachai Virameteekul.

Minister of Agriculture: Theera Wongsamut. *Commerce:* Pornthiva Nakasai. *Culture:* Teera Slukpetch. *Defence:* Gen. Prawit Wongsuwan. *Education:* Chinnaworn Boonyakiat. *Energy:* Wannarat Channukul. *Finance:* Korn Chatikavanij. *Foreign Affairs:* Kasit Piromya. *Industry:* Charnchai Chairungrueng. *Information and Communications Technology:* Ranongruk Suwanchawee. *Interior:* Chaovarat Chanweerakul. *Justice:* Pirapan Salirathavibhaga. *Labour:* Phaithoon Kaeothong. *Natural Resources and Environment:* Suwit Khunkitti. *Public Health:* Jurin Laksanawisit. *Science and Technology:* Kalaya Sophonpanich. *Social Development and Human Security:* Issara Somchai. *Tourism and Sports:* Chumpol Silapa-Archa. *Transport:* Sophon Saram.

Government Website: http://www.thaigov.go.th

CURRENT LEADERS

Abhisit Vejjajiva

Position
Prime Minister

Introduction
Abhisit Vejjajiva was elected prime minister in Dec. 2008. His election, which took place two weeks after the constitutional court banned three parties from the previous coalition government, was marked by party defections and allegations of vote rigging. Abhisit has vowed to restore the economy and rebuild political confidence.

Early Life
Abhisit Vejjajiva was born in Newcastle-upon-Tyne, England to a family of wealthy Thai-Chinese physicians on 3 Aug. 1964. He attended Eton College before graduating from St John's College, Oxford with a degree in philosophy, politics and economics. After a brief teaching stint at Chulachomklao Royal Military Academy in Thailand, Abhisit returned to Oxford where he gained a master's degree in economics. Returning to Thailand, he taught economics at Thammasat University before graduating in law from Ramkhamhaeng University in 1990.

In 1992 Abhisit joined the Democrat Party and became the MP for Bangkok. Rising through the party ranks, he became deputy party leader in 1999 and leader in 2005. In 2006 he led a boycott against snap elections called by the incumbent prime minister, Thaksin Shinawatra, claiming they lacked legitimacy.

In April 2007 Abhisit campaigned for the premier's office with the slogan 'Putting People First' and an agenda filled with populist policies. Criticized over his muted condemnation of the Sept. 2006 military coup, Abhisit backed the junta's draft constitution as the 'lesser of two evils'. In 2007 and 2008 he lost two parliamentary votes for the premiership before finally winning on 15 Dec. 2008.

Career in Office
Lacking a popular mandate to lead, Abhisit came under intense pressure after taking office. He was accused of deal-brokering in cabinet appointments and faced allegations of corruption before defeating a vote of no confidence on 21 March 2009. Thaksin supporters continued to demand new elections and on 26 March stepped up their protests by surrounding Abhisit's office and calling for his resignation. Anti-government demonstrators also stormed the venue of an ASEAN summit meeting in Pattaya in April (Thailand having begun an 18-month term as chair of the organization in July 2008), forcing its abandonment. Abhisit declared a state of emergency in response and brought in troops in a crackdown on opposition.

In June 2009 parliament approved the government's US$23bn. fiscal stimulus plan to boost the economy in the wake of the global financial crisis.

In Nov. a diplomatic row broke out between Thailand and Cambodia over Thaksin's appointment as an economic adviser to the Cambodian government and the rejection of a Thai request for his extradition. In Feb. 2010 the Supreme Court stripped the Thaksin family of half its estimated US$1·4bn. fortune, claiming it was gained through corruption. Thaksin supporters responded the following month by surrounding the prime minister's office and again demanding his resignation. The demonstrations continued into April leading to violent clashes between protesters and the military.

DEFENCE

Conscription is for two years. In 2006 defence expenditure totalled US$2,275m. (US$35 per capita), representing 1·1% of GDP. Year-on-year expenditure rose in real terms by 25% in 2007 and 17% in 2008.

Army
Strength (2007) 190,000. In addition there were 45,000 National Security Volunteer Corps, around 20,000 *Thahan Phran* ('Hunter Soldiers', a volunteer irregular force), 41,000 Border Police and a 50,000 strong paramilitary provincial police force (including an estimated 500-strong special action force).

Navy
The Royal Thai Navy is, next to the Chinese, the most significant naval force in the South China Sea. The fleet includes a small Spanish-built vertical/short-take-off-and-land carrier *Chakrinaruebet,* which entered service in 1997 and operates nine ex-Spanish AV-8A Harrier aircraft (although their serviceability is in doubt) and helicopters, and ten frigates. Manpower was 70,600 (2007) including 25,849 conscripts and 1,940 naval aviation.

The main bases are at Bangkok, Sattahip, Songkla and Phang Nga, with the riverine forces based at Nakhon Phanom.

Air Force
The Royal Thai Air Force had a strength (2007) of 46,000 personnel and 165 combat capable aircraft, including F-16s and F-5Es. The RTAF is made up of four air divisions.

INTERNATIONAL RELATIONS

Thailand is a member of the UN, World Bank, IMF and several other UN specialized agencies, WTO, BIS, IOM, Asian Development Bank, APEC, Mekong Group, ASEAN and Colombo Plan.

ECONOMY

In 2006 agriculture accounted for 10·7% of GDP, industry 44·5% and services 44·8%.

Thailand's 'shadow' (black market) economy is estimated to constitute approximately 70% of the country's official GDP, one of the highest percentages of any country in the world.

Overview

Thailand has transformed into a diverse, industrialized economy in the last 30 years. An export-oriented, labour-intensive manufacturing sector has developed thanks largely to foreign investment.

The Asian financial crisis of the late 1990s saw GDP contracting by 10·5% in 1998 as high inflation, rising unemployment and poverty took grip. The economy recovered quickly and from 1999–2007 grew at over 4% every year except for 2001, when it grew by 2·2% against a global slowdown. Economic growth slowed in 2005 but remained healthy, overcoming several misfortunes (the tsunami, bird flu and drought) that damaged tourism. Robust export activity supported strong growth in 2006 in an uncertain political environment.

In late 2008 the global financial crisis and political turmoil reduced exports dramatically (the main source of growth) and undermined business confidence, resulting in one of the steepest contractions in southeast Asia. In response, the Bank of Thailand reduced interest rates by 1·25% between Dec. 2008 and April 2009, and the government initiated a US$3·4bn. fiscal stimulus in March 2009. A second package of public investment began in Oct. 2009, worth US$42bn. over three years. The fiscal and monetary stimulus coupled with improvement in the international economic climate was predicted to restore growth to the economy in 2010.

Currency

The unit of currency is the *baht* (THB) of 100 *satang*. After being pegged to the US dollar, the baht was devalued and allowed to float on 2 July 1997. It was the devaluation of the baht that sparked the financial turmoil that spread throughout the world over the next year. Foreign exchange reserves were US$127,165m. in Sept. 2009 (US$28,434m. in 1998) and gold reserves 2·70m. troy oz. Total money supply in Aug. 2009 was 1,022·2bn. baht. Inflation rates (based on IMF statistics):

1999	*2000*	*2001*	*2002*	*2003*	*2004*	*2005*	*2006*	*2007*	*2008*
0·3%	1·5%	1·6%	0·7%	1·8%	2·8%	4·5%	4·6%	2·2%	5·5%

Budget

The fiscal year runs from 1 Oct.–30 Sept. In 2002–03 budgetary central government revenue was 1,045·6bn. baht and expenditure 921·1bn. baht. Main sources of revenue in 2002–03: taxes on goods and services, 449·3bn. baht; taxes on income, profits and capital gains, 332·6bn. baht. Main items of expenditure by economic type in 2002–03: compensation of employees, 325·8bn. baht; use of goods and services, 213·3bn. baht.

Performance

Real GDP growth rates (based on IMF statistics):

1999	*2000*	*2001*	*2002*	*2003*	*2004*	*2005*	*2006*	*2007*	*2008*
4·4%	4·8%	2·2%	5·3%	7·1%	6·3%	4·6%	5·2%	4·9%	2·6%

Thailand's total GDP in 2008 was US$260·7bn.

Banking and Finance

The Bank of Thailand (founded in 1942) is the central bank and bank of issue, an independent body although its capital is government-owned. Its assets and liabilities in 2002 were 2,853,897m. baht. Its *Governor* is Tarisa Watanagase. In 2002 there were 30 commercial banks, 13 domestic banks and 21 foreign banks. In addition the Thai government controlled four banks in 2002: the Bank of Agriculture and Agricultural Co-operatives, the Government Housing Bank, the Government Savings Bank and the Export-Import Bank of Thailand. Total assets of commercial banks, 2002, 6,900,947m. baht. Deposits, 2001, 5,109,973m. baht.

There is a stock exchange (SET) in Bangkok.

Weights and Measures

The metric system is official but traditional units are still employed: one *catty* = 600 grams; one *picul* = 100 catty; one *wah* = 2 metres; one *sen* = 20 wah; one *rai* = 1 sq. sen.

ENERGY AND NATURAL RESOURCES

Environment

Thailand's carbon dioxide emissions from the consumption and flaring of fossil fuels were the equivalent of 3·9 tonnes per capita in 2008.

Electricity

Installed capacity, 2004, was 37·6m. kW. Output, 2004, 125·73bn. kWh, with consumption per capita 2,020 kWh.

Oil and Gas

Proven crude petroleum reserves in 2008 were 0·5bn. bbls. Production of oil (2008), 13·4m. tonnes. Thailand and Vietnam settled an offshore dispute in 1997 which stretched back to 1973. Demarcation allowed for petroleum exploration in the Gulf of Thailand, with each side required to give the other some revenue if an underground reservoir is discovered which straddles the border.

Production of natural gas (2008), 28·9bn. cu. metres. Reserves, 2008, 300bn. cu. metres. In April 1998 Thailand and Malaysia agreed to share equally the natural gas jointly produced in an offshore area (the Malaysian-Thailand Joint Development Area) which both countries claim as their own territory.

Minerals

The mineral resources include antimony, cassiterite (tin ore), copper, diatomite, dolomite, gold, gypsum, kaolin, lignite, limestone, manganese, marl, potash, rubies, sapphires, silica sand, silver and zinc. Production, 2005 unless otherwise indicated (in tonnes): limestone (2003), 112·94m.; lignite, 21·43m.; gypsum, 7·11m.; salt, 1·17m.; feldspar, 1·15m.; kaolin, 746,000; iron ore (metal content), 116,000 (estimate); zinc ore (metal content), 31,000 (estimate).

Agriculture

In 2002 there were an estimated 15·9m. ha. of arable land and 3·5m. ha. of permanent cropland. About 4·96m. ha. were irrigated in 2002. The chief produce is rice, a staple of the national diet. Output of the major crops in 2002 was (in 1,000 tonnes): sugarcane, 74,258; rice, 26,057; cassava, 16,868; maize, 4,230; natural rubber, 2,456; bananas, 1,800; pineapples, 1,739; mangoes, 1,750; coconuts, 1,418. Thailand is the world's leading producer of both natural rubber and pineapples. Livestock, 2003: pigs, 7,059,000; cattle, 5,048,000; buffaloes, 1,613,000; chickens, 177m.; ducks, 20m.

Forestry

Forests covered 14·52m. ha. in 2005, or 28·4% of the land area. Teak and other hardwoods grow in the deciduous forests of the north; elsewhere tropical evergreen forests are found, with the timber yang the main crop (a source of yang oil). In 2007, 28·32m. cu. metres of roundwood were cut.

Fisheries

In 2005 the total catch came to 2,599,387 tonnes with marine fishing accounting for 92% of all fish caught. Thailand is the third largest exporter of fishery commodities in the world, with exports in 2005 totalling US$4·47bn.

INDUSTRY

The leading companies by market capitalization in Thailand in Feb. 2009 were: PTT, a petroleum exploration and production company (US$12·2bn.); Advanced Info Service (AIS), a mobile phone provider (US$6·6bn.); and Bangkok Bank (US$3·9bn.).

Production (2002): 31·68m. tonnes of cement, 17·51m. tonnes of distillate fuel oil (2004), 6·67m. tonnes of petrol (2004), 6·34m. tonnes of residual fuel oil (2004), 5·95m. tonnes of sugar, 2·5m. tonnes of crude steel, 768,098 tonnes of synthetic fibre, 519,006 tonnes of galvanized iron sheets, 208,000 tonnes of tin plate (2001), 1,636·0m. litres of soft drinks (2001), 1,238·0m. litres of beer (2001), 30·8bn. cigarettes, 169,304 automobiles and 415,593 commercial vehicles, and 6,096,000 televisions.

Labour

In the period Sept.–Dec. 2003 the total labour force was 35·5m.; 14·2m. persons were employed in agriculture, hunting and forestry, 5·3m. in manufacturing, 5·2m. in wholesale and retail trade and 2·1m. in hotels and restaurants. The unemployment rate was 2·4% in June 2002. A minimum wage is set by the National Wages Committee. It varied between 140 baht and 184 baht per day in Jan. 2006.

INTERNATIONAL TRADE

Foreign debt was US$52,266m. in 2005.

Imports and Exports

In 2006 imports (f.o.b.) totalled US$113·4bn. (US$106·0bn. in 2005); exports (f.o.b.), US$128·2bn. (US$109·2bn. in 2005). Main imports in 2003: machinery and transport equipment, 43·5%; chemicals and related products, 11·2%; petroleum and petroleum products, 10·6%; iron and steel, 5·4%. Exports: machinery and transport equipment, 43·8%; chemicals and related products, 6·5%; fish and seafood, 4·9%; clothing and apparel, 4·5%. Main import sources in 2003: Japan (24·1%), USA (9·5%), China (8·0%), Malaysia (6·0%), South Korea (3·8%). Principal export destinations (2003): USA (17·0%), Japan (14·2%), Singapore (7·3%), China (7·1%), Hong Kong (5·4%).

COMMUNICATIONS

Roads

In 2006 there were 180,053 km of roads, of which 450 km were motorways. Vehicles in use in 2006 included: 3·80m. passenger cars, 4·99m. lorries and vans and 15·67m. motorcycles and mopeds.

Rail

The State Railway totalled 4,071 km in 2005. Passenger-km travelled in 2002 came to 8·9bn. and freight tonne-km to 2·4bn. A metro ('Skytrain'), or elevated transit system, was opened in Bangkok in 1999. A second (underground) mass transit system in Bangkok, the Bangkok Subway, was opened in 2004.

Civil Aviation

There are international airports at Bangkok (Suvarnabhumi), Chiangmai, Phuket and Hat Yai. The national carrier, Thai Airways International, is 51·03% state-owned. In 2005 scheduled airline traffic of Thai-based carriers flew 213·8m. km, carrying 21,507,900 passengers. Bangkok handled 28,808,422 passengers in 2001 (21,395,311 on international flights) and 840,033 tonnes of freight. Phuket is the second busiest airport for passenger traffic, with 3,557,319 passengers in 2001 (2,225,031 on domestic flights), and Chiangmai the second busiest for freight, with 23,786 tonnes in 2001. Suvarnabhumi, Bangkok's new international airport, opened in Sept. 2006 but has since experienced a number of safety issues that forced the government to reopen Don Muang, the old airport, for domestic flights in March 2007.

Shipping

In 2002 merchant shipping totalled 1,880,000 GRT, including oil tankers 209,000 GRT. Vessels totalling 68,079,000 NRT entered ports in 2000 and vessels totalling 33,154,000 NRT cleared.

Telecommunications

In 2008 there were 7·0m. main (fixed) telephone lines. In the same year mobile phone subscribers numbered 62·0m. (920·1 per 1,000 persons). 4·4m. PCs were in use in 2005 and there were 16·1m. internet users in 2008.

Postal Services

There were 4,453 post offices in 2003, or one for every 14,100 persons.

SOCIAL INSTITUTIONS

Justice

The judicial power is exercised in the name of the King, by *(a)* courts of first instance, *(b)* the court of appeal *(Uthorn)* and *(c)* the Supreme Court *(Dika)*. The King appoints, transfers and dismisses judges, who are independent in conducting trials and giving judgment in accordance with the law.

Courts of first instance are subdivided into 20 magistrates' courts *(Kwaeng)* with limited civil and minor criminal jurisdiction; 85 provincial courts *(Changwad)* with unlimited civil and criminal jurisdiction; the criminal and civil courts with exclusive jurisdiction in Bangkok; the central juvenile courts for persons under 18 years of age in Bangkok.

The court of appeal exercises appellate jurisdiction in civil and criminal cases from all courts of first instance. From it appeals lie to Dika Court on any point of law and, in certain cases, on questions of fact.

The Supreme Court is the supreme tribunal of the land. Besides its normal appellate jurisdiction in civil and criminal matters, it has semi-original jurisdiction over general election petitions. The decisions of Dika Court are final. Every person has the right to present a petition to the government who will deal with all matters of grievance.

The death penalty is still in force; there were two confirmed executions in 2009 (the first since 2003). The population in penal institutions in July 2005 was 164,443 (256 per 100,000 of national population).

Education

Education is compulsory for children for nine years and is free in local municipal schools. In 2007 there were 5,703,756 primary school pupils with 321,930 teaching staff. There were 4,789,339 secondary school pupils in 2007 with 227,929 teaching staff. There were 1,005,481 students in vocational education in 2005. In higher education there were 2,503,572 students in 2007 with 66,431 academic staff. In 2005 there were 78 public and 61 private institutions of higher education, 146 industry and community colleges, 110 technical colleges, 54 polytechnic colleges and 44 agricultural and technology colleges.

The adult literacy rate in 2003 was 92·6% (94·9% among males and 90·5% among females).

In 2007 public expenditure on education came to 4·0% of GNI and 20·9% of total government spending.

Health

In 2002 there were 3,658 hospitals, with a provision of 69 beds per 10,000 population. In 2000 there were 18,025 doctors, 4,141 dentists, 6,384 pharmacists, 70,978 nurses and (in 1997) 2,677 midwives. Thailand is considered to be the most successful country in the world in preventing the spread of HIV/AIDS. The number of annual new HIV cases has fallen to under 20,000 from a high of 140,000 in the mid 1990s.

RELIGION

At the 2000 census 94·6% of the population were Buddhists and 4·6% Muslims. In Feb. 2010 the Roman Catholic church had one cardinal.

CULTURE

World Heritage Sites

There are five UNESCO sites in Thailand. They are: the Thung Yai-Huai Kha Khaeng wildlife sanctuaries (inscribed in 1991); the palace, temples, Buddhas, etc. of the historic town of Sukhothai (1991); the 15th–18th century historic town of Ayutthaya (1991); the Bronze Age Ba Chiang archaeological site (1992); and the mountainous Dong Phayayen-Khao Yai forest complex (2005).

Broadcasting

Government agencies and the Thai military control most national terrestrial television networks and some radio stations, even after the end of military rule. A series of media reforms are currently under way, aimed at reducing military interest and influence in the media. Thai TV3, Modernine and National Broadcasting Services of Thailand (formerly Television of Thailand (TVT)), are run by government agencies; TV5 and BBTV are owned by the army. In Jan. 2008 the government finalized its takeover of Thai Independent Television (TITV)—the nation's only private station. Cable and satellite services are widely available. Radio Thailand (a national network and external service) and MCOT Radio Network are operated by state agencies. There are numerous private radio stations, particularly in the Bangkok area. In 2005, 17·4m. households had TV receivers (colour by PAL).

Press

In 2005 there were 45 daily newspapers, with a combined circulation of 7·3m. 9,068 book titles were published in 2002.

Tourism

In 2005, 11·57m. non-resident tourists visited Thailand. Tourist spending in 2005 was US$12·63bn.

Festivals

Songkran, celebrated on 13 April each year, is the traditional Thai New Year festival, although 1 Jan. was made the official New Year in 1940. Other notable festivals include: the colourful Bosang Umbrella Fair in Jan. and a Flower Carnival in Feb., both in Chiang Mai; a Candle Festival held in Ubon Ratchathani on Khao Phansa Day in July (the day after the full moon of the eighth lunar month, marking the start of Buddhist Lent); Buffalo Races, held during Oct. at Chonburi; and an annual Elephant Round-up in the third week of Nov. at Surin.

DIPLOMATIC REPRESENTATIVES

Of Thailand in the United Kingdom (29–30 Queen's Gate, London, SW7 5JB)
Ambassador: Kitti Wasinondh.

Of the United Kingdom in Thailand (14 Wireless Rd, Bangkok 10330)
Ambassador: Quinton Quayle.

Of Thailand in the USA (1024 Wisconsin Ave., NW, Washington, D.C., 20007)
Ambassador: Don Pramudwinai.

Of the USA in Thailand (120 Wireless Rd, Bangkok 10330)
Ambassador: Eric John.

Of Thailand to the United Nations
Ambassador: Norachit Sinhaseni.

Of Thailand to the European Union
Ambassador: Pisan Manawapat.

FURTHER READING

National Statistical Office *Thailand Statistical Yearbook.*

Krongkaew, M. (ed.) *Thailand's Industrialization and its Consequences.* 1995

Kulick, E. and Wilson, D., *Thailand's Turn: Profile of a New Dragon.* 1993 (NY, 1994)

National Statistical Office: National Statistical Office, Thanon Lan Luang, Bangkok 10100.
Website: http://web.nso.go.th

TIMOR-LESTE

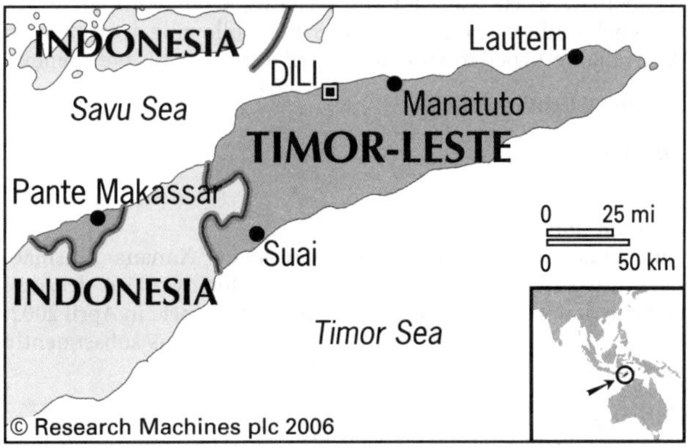

República Democrática de Timor-Leste
(Democratic Republic of East Timor)

Capital: Dili
Population estimate, 2010: 1·17m.
GDP per capita, 2007: (PPP$) 717
HDI/world rank: 0·489/162

KEY HISTORICAL EVENTS

Portugal abandoned its former colony, with its largely Roman Catholic population, in 1975, when it was occupied by Indonesia and claimed as the province of Timor Timur. The UN did not recognize Indonesian sovereignty over the territory. An independence movement, the Revolutionary Front for an Independent East Timor (FRETILIN), maintained a guerrilla resistance to the Indonesian government which resulted in large-scale casualties and alleged atrocities. On 24 July 1998 Indonesia announced a withdrawal of troops from Timor-Leste and an amnesty for some political prisoners, although no indication was given of how many of the estimated 12,000 troops and police would pull out. On 5 Aug. 1998 Indonesia and Portugal reached agreement on the outlines of an autonomy plan which would give the Timorese the right to self-government except in foreign affairs and defence.

In a referendum on the future of Timor-Leste held on 30 Aug. 1999 the electorate was some 450,000 and turnout was nearly 99%. 78·5% of voters opted for independence, but pro-Indonesian militia gangs wreaked havoc both before and after the referendum. The militias accused the UN of rigging the poll. There was widespread violence in and around Dili, the provincial capital, with heavy loss of life, and thousands of people were forced to take to the hills after intimidation. Timor-Leste's first democratic election took place on 30 Aug. 2001 in a ballot run by the UN, with FRETILIN winning 57% of the vote and 55 of the 88 seats in the new constituent assembly. Timor-Leste became an independent country on 20 May 2002 but unrest continues.

TERRITORY AND POPULATION

Timor-Leste (East Timor) has a total land area of 15,410 sq. km (5,950 sq. miles), consisting of the mainland (14,480 sq. km), the enclave of Oecussi-Ambeno in West Timor (815 sq. km), and the islands of Ataúro to the north (105 sq. km) and Jaco to the east (10 sq. km). The mainland area incorporates the eastern half of the island of Timor. Oecussi-Ambeno lies westwards, separated from the main portion of Timor-Leste by a distance of some 100 km. The island is bound to the south by the Timor Sea and lies approximately 500 km from the Australian coast.

The population according to the 2004 census was 923,198 (469,919 males); density, 60 per sq. km. The United Nations population estimate for 2004 was 951,000. The largest city is Dili, Timor-Leste's capital. In 2004 its population was 151,026. In 2005, 73·5% of the population was rural.

The UN gives an estimated population for 2010 of 1·17m.

The ethnic East Timorese form the majority of the population. Non-East Timorese, comprising Portuguese and West Timorese as well as persons from Sumatra, Java, Sulawesi and other parts of Indonesia, are estimated to constitute approximately 20% of the total population.

During Indonesian occupation the official language was Bahasa Indonesia. Timor-Leste's new constitution designates Portuguese and Tetum (the region's *lingua franca*) as the official languages, and English and Bahasa Indonesia as working languages.

SOCIAL STATISTICS

2002 estimates: births, 21,000; deaths, 11,000. Rates, 2002 estimates (per 1,000 population): births, 27·7; deaths, 14·0. Annual population growth rate in 1995–2000, 1·7%. Fertility rate, 2004, 7·8 children per woman (along with Niger the highest in the world). In 2007 life expectancy at birth was 59·8 years for males and 61·5 years for females.

From having the world's highest rate of infant mortality in the early 1980s, Timor-Leste's infant mortality rate has dropped to 52 per 1,000 live births in 2005, although the figure varies widely between urban and rural areas.

CLIMATE

In the north there is an average annual temperature of over 24°C (75°F), weak precipitation—below 1,500 mm (59") annually—and a dry period lasting five months. The mountainous zone, between the northern and southern parts of the island, has high precipitation—above 1,500 mm (59")—and a dry period of four months. The southern zone has precipitation reaching 2,000 mm (79") and is permanently humid. The monsoon season extends from Nov. to May.

CONSTITUTION AND GOVERNMENT

The constitution promulgated in 2002 created a unicameral system with a *National Parliament* with a minimum requirement of 52 directly-elected seats and a maximum of 65. For the first term after independence the parliament had 88 members but this was reduced after the June 2007 legislative elections.

The *President* is directly elected for a period of five years and may not serve more than two terms.

National Anthem

'Pátria, Pátria, Timor-Leste, nossa Nação' ('Fatherland, fatherland, East Timor our Nation'); words by F. Borja da Costa, tune by A. Araujo.

RECENT ELECTIONS

Presidential elections were held on 9 April and 8 May 2007. In the first round Francisco Guterres of the ruling FRETILIN party received 27·9% of votes cast against José Ramos-Horta (ind.) with 21·8%, Fernando de Araújo of the Democratic Party with 19·2%, Francisco Xavier do Amaral (ind.) with 14·4% and four other candidates. In the second round Ramos-Horta was elected president with 69·3% of the vote against 30·7% for Guterres.

Elections to the 65-member National Parliament took place on 30 June 2007. The Frente Revolucionária do Timor-Leste Independente (FRETILIN; Revolutionary Front for an Independent East Timor) won 29·0% of the vote and took

21 seats with 120,592 votes. The Congresso Nacional de Reconstrução de Timor-Leste (CNRT; National Congress for Timorese Reconstruction) won 24·1% of votes cast and 18 seats; the Coligação–Associação Social-Democrata Timorense/Partido Social Democrata (C–ASDT/PSD; Coalition–Timorese Social Democratic Association/Social Democratic Party) won 15·7% and 11 seats; the Partido Democrático (PD; Democratic Party) 11·3% and 8 seats; the Partido Unidade Nacional (PUN; National Unity Party) 4·6% and 3 seats. Two other parties won two seats each. Turnout was 80·5%.

CURRENT ADMINISTRATION

President: José Ramos-Horta; b. 1949 (ind.; since 20 May 2007).

In March 2010 the government was comprised as follows:

Prime Minister and Minister for Defence: Xanana Gusmão (National Congress for Timorese Reconstruction).

Deputy Prime Ministers: José Luís Guterres; Mario Viegas Carrascalão.

Minister for Agriculture and Fisheries: Mariano Sabino. *Economy and Development:* João Gonçalves. *Education, Culture, Youth and Sport:* João Câncio. *Foreign Affairs:* Zacarias da Costa. *Health:* Nélson Martins. *Infrastructure:* Pedro Lay da Silva. *Justice:* Lúcia Lobato. *Planning and Finance:* Emília Pires. *Social Solidarity:* Maria Domingas Fernandes Alves. *State Administration:* Arcângelo Leite. *Tourism, Commerce and Industry:* Gil Alves.

Office of the Prime Minister and Government Website: http://www.pm.gov.tp

CURRENT LEADERS

José Ramos-Horta

Position
President

Introduction
José Ramos-Horta was declared president after a landslide victory in the second round of presidential elections in May 2007. A key figure in Timor-Leste's struggle for independence for over 30 years, his election prompted hopes of increased stability. He survived an assassination attempt in Feb. 2008.

Early Life
Ramos-Horta was born on 26 Dec. 1949 in Dili to a Timorese mother and a Portuguese father who was a political exile in Timor-Leste. He was educated at a Catholic mission in Soibada. In 1969 he began his career as a journalist but was exiled to Mozambique for his political activities from 1970–71. As Portugal began to pull out of Timor-Leste in 1975, Ramos-Horta, a member of the Marxist Revolutionary Front for an Independent East Timor (FRETILIN), emerged as a key figure in the nationalist leadership. On 28 Nov. 1975 FRETILIN proclaimed independence and he was appointed foreign minister. Three days before Indonesia's invasion on 7 Dec. 1975 he travelled to New York to plead the Timorese case before the UN.

Stranded in exile, he acted as permanent representative of FRETILIN at the UN from 1977–85. Despite few funds and a smear campaign by the Indonesian government, Ramos-Horta kept Timor-Leste on the UN agenda. He also studied at The Hague Academy of International Law and trained at the International Institute of Human Rights in Strasbourg. He received his MA in peace studies from Antioch University in 1984. In Oct. 1996 Ramos-Horta and Carlos Filipe Ximines Belo jointly won the Nobel Peace Prize for their commitment to the East Timorese struggle for independence.

Following Indonesia's agreement to a referendum on Timor-Leste's status, Ramos-Horta returned home on 1 Dec. 1999. After independence in May 2002 he served as foreign minister (to July 2006) and then prime minister before winning the presidential election of May 2007.

Career in Office
The role of president is largely ceremonial, but Ramos-Horta pledged to work with the new government led by the National Congress for Timorese Reconstruction for reform and national reconciliation. He was shot and seriously wounded in an attack by rebel soldiers on 11 Feb. 2008 but, following treatment in Australia, returned to Dili on 17 April to resume his presidency.

Xanana Gusmão

Position
Prime Minister

Introduction
Independent Timor-Leste's first president, Xanana Gusmão, having led the independence movement for over two decades, came to power in a landslide victory in elections held in April 2002. He stood down as president in May 2007 but was subsequently appointed prime minister in Aug. that year.

Early Life
Xanana Gusmão was born José Alexandre Gusmão on 20 June 1946 in the town of Laleia, Manatuto. After studying at a Jesuit seminary in Soibada and then at Dare, he became a civil servant.

In 1974 he joined FRETILIN (the Revolutionary Front for an Independent East Timor), replacing Nicolau Lobato as its leader in 1978. In 1981 he was elected commander-in-chief of the organization's military wing. Leading the guerrilla movement, Gusmão worked to integrate the various groups fighting for independence.

On 20 Nov. 1992 he was captured by the Indonesian army and sentenced to life imprisonment on charges of subversion. Serving only six years, Gusmão remained the figurehead of the independence movement. Following an appeal from then UN Secretary-General Kofi Annan, Gusmão was released after the referendum of Sept. 1999 in which an overwhelming majority of East Timorese voted for independence.

Timor-Leste gained independence on 20 May 2002 and Gusmão was inaugurated as president, having won a landslide victory in elections the previous month.

Career in Office
Gusmão appealed for reconciliation and an end of violence against those who opposed independence. The authority of the state and its institutions, however, remained fragile. In April 2006, 600 striking soldiers who had been sacked by Prime Minister Alkatiri the previous month demonstrated in Dili. The protests turned into wider factional violence across the country and the government called in foreign troops led by Australia in May to restore law and order. At the same time, relations between president and prime minister broke down. In June Alkatiri stood down and was replaced by José Ramos-Horta. A UN peacekeeping mission was then set up in Aug. 2006.

Gusmão did not contest presidential elections held in April–May 2007, announcing his intention to run instead for prime minister as the leader of a new National Congress for Timorese Reconstruction, having become disillusioned with FRETILIN. His close ally José Ramos-Horta succeeded him as president. Despite FRETILIN winning the largest number of seats in parliamentary elections in June 2007, Gusmão was able to form a coalition government. He was sworn in as prime minister on 8 Aug. 2007, triggering violent protests from FRETILIN supporters.

Like President Ramos-Horta, Gusmão was also targeted by rebel soldiers on 11 Feb. 2008 in a separate attack, but was unhurt. He described the incident as a coup attempt and imposed a state of emergency.

In Oct. 2009 Gusmão's government survived an opposition vote of confidence in parliament over its controversial release of a pro-Indonesian militia leader accused of war crimes against Timorese citizens in 1999.

DEFENCE

The Timor-Leste Defence Force comprises an army and a small naval element. In 2005 there was a 1,250-strong army, but nearly half of the personnel were dismissed in early 2006 for going on strike. An Australian-led international force was sent to Timor-Leste in May 2006 following conflicts within the military that led to general violence throughout the country.

INTERNATIONAL RELATIONS

Timor-Leste is a member of the UN, World Bank, IMF and several other UN specialized agencies, and Asian Development Bank.

ECONOMY

Currency

The official currency is the US dollar. The Australian dollar and the Indonesian rupiah, both previously used, no longer serve as legal tender. Inflation was 7·6% in 2008.

Performance

Total GDP in 2008 was US$0·5bn. Real GDP growth was 12·8% in 2008 (the third highest in the world).

ENERGY AND NATURAL RESOURCES

Environment

Timor-Leste's carbon dioxide emissions from the consumption and flaring of fossil fuels were the equivalent of 0·3 tonnes per capita in 2008.

Electricity

Electricity produced in 2004 totalled an estimated 300m. kWh.

Oil and Gas

Although current production is small, the Timor Gap, an area of offshore territory between Timor-Leste and Australia, is one of the richest oilfields in the world outside the Middle East. Potential revenue from the area is estimated at US$11bn. The area is split into three zones with a central 'zone of occupation' (occupying 61,000 sq. km). Royalties on oil discovered within the central zone were split equally between Indonesia and Australia following the Timor Gap Treaty which came into force on 9 Feb. 1991. Questions over Timor-Leste's rights to oil revenue from the area have arisen following the 1999 independence referendum.

Minerals

Gold, iron sands, copper and chromium are present.

Agriculture

Although the presence of sandalwood was one of the principal reasons behind Portuguese colonization, its production has declined in recent years. In 2007 there were an estimated 170,000 ha. of arable land and 68,000 ha. of permanent crops. Coffee is grown extensively.

Forestry

Forests covered 798,000 ha. in 2005, representing 53·7% of the total land area.

Fisheries

The total fish catch in 2005 was approximately 350 tonnes.

INDUSTRY

Labour

In 2000 the unemployment rate exceeded 80% of the labour force.

INTERNATIONAL TRADE

Imports and Exports

All basic goods such as rice, sugar and flour are imported. Coffee and cattle are important exports.

COMMUNICATIONS

Civil Aviation

There is an international airport at Dili.

SOCIAL INSTITUTIONS

Justice

Timor-Leste's judiciary currently conforms to a UN-drafted legal system based on Indonesian law. This is scheduled to be replaced by a civil and penal judiciary system which will be based on Portuguese law. The Supreme Court of Justice is the highest court of law. There are four District Courts and a Court of Appeal.

Health

Plans for a medical system include 64 community health centres, 88 health posts, 117 mobile clinics and 21 doctors.

RELIGION

Over 90% of Timor-Leste's population are Roman Catholic, with Protestants, Muslims, Hindus and Buddhists accounting for the remainder.

CULTURE

Broadcasting

National public radio and television services, transmitted by Rádio Nacional de Timor-Leste (RTL) and Televisão de Timor-Leste (TVTL) were launched in May 2002. There are also a number of community radio stations.

Press

In 2004 there were two daily newspapers, the Timor Post and Suara Timor Lorosae.

DIPLOMATIC REPRESENTATIVES

Of the United Kingdom in Timor-Leste (embassy in Dili closed in Oct. 2006)
Ambassador: Martin Hatfull (resides in Jakarta, Indonesia).

Of Timor-Leste in the USA (3415 Massachusetts Ave., Washington, D.C., 20007)
Ambassador: Constancio C. Pinto.

Of the USA in Timor-Leste (Avenida de Portugal, Pantai Kelapa, Dili)
Ambassador: Hans G. Klemm.

Of Timor-Leste to the United Nations
Ambassador: Sofia Mesqíta Borges.

Of Timor-Leste to the European Union
Ambassador: José Antonio Amorim Dias.

FURTHER READING

Dunn, James, *East Timor: A Rough Passage to Independence.* 2003
Hainsworth, Paul and McCloskey, Stephen, (eds.) *The East Timor Question: The Struggle for Independence from Indonesia.* 2000
Kohen, Arnold S., *From the Place of the Dead: Bishop Belo and the Struggle for East Timor.* 2000
Kingsbury, Damien and Leach, Michael, (eds.) *East Timor: Beyond Independence.* 2007
Nevins, Joseph, *A Not-So-Distant Horror: Mass Violence in East Timor.* 2005
Tanter, Richard, Ball, Desmond and Van Klinken, Gerry, (eds.) *Masters of Terror: Indonesia's Military and Violence in East Timor.* 2006

National Statistical Office: Direcção Nacional de Estatística, Rua de Caicoli, P.O. Box 10, Dili.
Website: http://dne.mof.gov.tl

TOGO

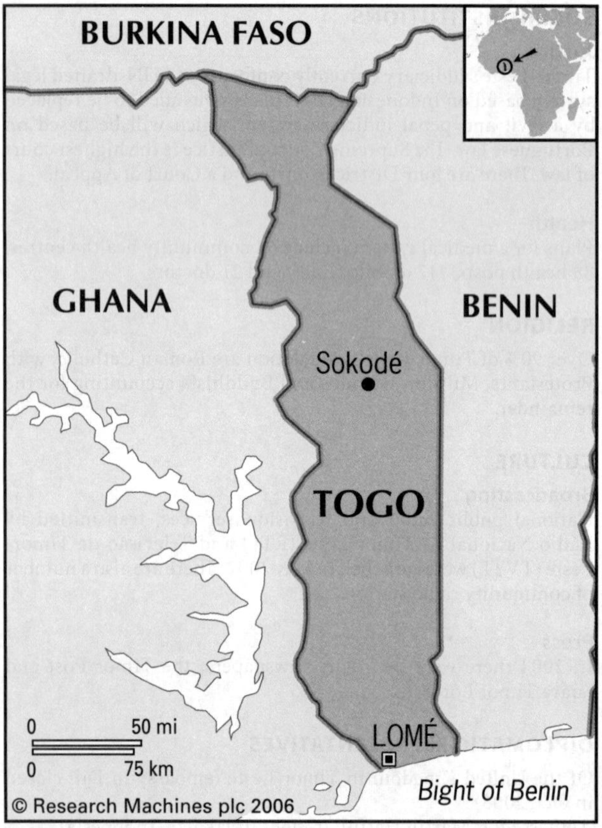

République Togolaise
(Togolese Republic)

Capital: Lomé
Population estimate, 2010: 6·78m.
GDP per capita, 2007: (PPP$) 788
HDI/world rank: 0·499/159

KEY HISTORICAL EVENTS

Eleventh century records relate Togo's settlement by a succession of tribes. The Kwa people from the Volta region were joined by the Ewe people from the Niger Valley, while later migrations included the Ana, Mina and Guin people from Ghana and the Ivory Coast, and the Nawdba from the east, who settled in northern Togo.

During 1471–72 Portuguese explorers and traders began trading along the coast in gold, silver and pepper. In the 16th century Britain, Denmark, Holland, France, Germany, Sweden and Portugal all shipped slaves from the region in co-operation with tribal leaders. The 18th century saw conflicts with the Akwamu Confederacy and the Ashanti Kingdom in the west, and the Kingdom of Dahomey in the east, as tribal rulers tried to consolidate their territory. Meanwhile, Britain, France and Germany became the dominant European powers in the region.

Following the abolition of slavery in the 19th century, British, French and German traders built up a flourishing palm oil export trade from Anecho, Agoue and Porto Seguro. As a result several Togolese families of partly Brazilian or Portuguese origin came to prominence, some retaining considerable influence to the present day.

Germany signed a treaty with chief Mlapa III on 5 July 1884 in the village of Togo (modern Togoville) to establish colonial rule on the coast. German control was then extended inland and, following agreement with Britain and France, the borders of German Togoland were defined. Using slave labour, the German administration developed the agricultural sector.

In 1914 the Allies overran German Togoland and in 1922 it was partitioned into a western British Mandated Territory and an eastern French Mandated Territory under the League of Nations. In 1946, following the Second World War, British Togoland and French Togoland became Trust territories under the United Nations. On 9 May 1956 a UN-sponsored referendum in British Togoland resulted in a majority vote for union with the neighbouring colony of Gold Coast. The territory soon merged with Gold Coast to become Ghana, despite objections from the southern Togolese, most of whom had voted for union with French Togo. In 1956 French Togo was granted partial self-government to become the Republic of Togo. It gained full independence on 27 April 1960.

Sylvanus Olympio was elected president in 1958. In 1961 a new constitution established a seven-year-term and broad executive powers for the presidency, alongside an elected national assembly. Olympio won the 1961 election and his party, Unité Togolaise (UT), took all 51 national assembly seats. In 1962 Olympio disbanded the main opposition parties, alleging they had plotted against his government. On 13 Jan. 1963 Olympio was assassinated by soldiers and the army voted in Nicolas Grunitsky as head of state. A military coup ousted Grunitsky in Jan. 1967 and on 14 April 1967 Gen. (then Col.) Etienne Gnassingbé Eyadéma took the presidency.

Eyadéma developed the country's investment banking sector and its phosphates exports, prompting economic growth until recession in the 1980s caused a price collapse. Eyadéma ruled as head of Togo's only officially recognized political party, the Rassemblement du Peuple Togolais (RPT), and survived several attempted coups. In Aug. 1991 a national conference of Togo's leading political movements led to a reduction in Eyadéma's executive powers. A transitional administration, the High Council of the Republic, was installed, led by Kokou Koffigoh.

In Nov. 1991 the new government banned the RPT and the army, which backed Eyadéma, attempted a coup. Eyadéma negotiated the return of some of his powers and won an election in Aug. 1992, though its validity was disputed and the main opposition parties boycotted it. In 1994 a coalition of the Comité d'Action pour le Renouveau and the Union Togolaise pour la Démocratie won a majority in the national assembly elections. The RPT returned to power in the election of June 1998 and Eyadéma retained the presidency throughout the entire period until his death in Feb. 2005.

On Eyadéma's death the military installed his son, Faure Gnassingbé, as president and the following day the constitution was amended to legalize his succession. Under domestic and international pressure he stepped down on 25 Feb. 2005 and parliament speaker Abbas Bonfoh became interim president. Faure Gnassingbé won the presidential election held in April 2005 but the opposition alleged vote rigging and 400–500 people died in riots. Gnassingbé was subsequently confirmed as president.

TERRITORY AND POPULATION

Togo is bounded in the west by Ghana, north by Burkina Faso, east by Benin and south by the Gulf of Guinea. The area is 56,785 sq. km. At the last census, in 1981, the population was 2,700,982.

The UN gives an estimated population for 2010 of 6·78m.; density, 119 per sq. km.

In 2005, 59·9% of the population lived in rural areas. In 2005, 43% were below the age of 15. The capital is Lomé (estimated population in 2005, 921,000), other towns being Sokodé (106,000), Kara (100,000), Atakpamé (73,000), Kpalimé (71,000), Dapaong (52,000), Tsévié (47,000) and Notsé (34,000).

Area, population and chief town of the five regions:

Region	*Area in sq. km*	*Population (2006 estimate)*	*Chief town*
Centrale	13,182	494,000	Sokodé
De La Kara	11,630	669,000	Kara
Des Plateaux	16,975	1,222,000	Atakpamé
Des Savanes	8,602	610,000	Dapaong
Maritime	6,396	2,342,000	Lomé

There are 37 ethnic groups. The south is largely populated by Ewe-speaking peoples (forming 23% of the population), Watyi (10%) and other related groups, while the north is mainly inhabited by Hamitic groups speaking Kabre (14%), Tem (6%) and Gurma (3%). The official language is French but Ewe and Kabre are also taught in schools.

SOCIAL STATISTICS

2000 estimates: births, 177,000; deaths, 60,000. Estimated rates, 2000 (per 1,000 population): births, 38·7; deaths, 13·2. Expectation of life (2007) was 60·4 years for males and 63·9 for females. Annual population growth rate, 2000–05, 2·8%. Infant mortality, 2005, 78 per 1,000 live births; fertility rate, 2004, 5·2 births per woman.

CLIMATE

The tropical climate produces wet seasons from March to July and from Oct. to Nov. in the south. The north has one wet season, from April to July. The heaviest rainfall occurs in the mountains of the west, southwest and centre. Lomé, Jan. 81°F (27·2°C), July 76°F (24·4°C). Annual rainfall 35" (875 mm).

CONSTITUTION AND GOVERNMENT

A referendum on 27 Sept. 1992 approved a new constitution by 98·11% of votes cast. Under this the *President* and the *National Assembly* were directly elected for five-year terms. Initially the president was allowed to be re-elected only once. However, on 30 Dec. 2002 parliament approved an amendment to the constitution lifting the restriction on the number of times that the president may be re-elected. The National Assembly has 81 seats and is elected for a five-year term.

National Anthem

'Terre de nos aïeux' ('Land of our forefathers').

RECENT ELECTIONS

In presidential elections held on 4 March 2010 Faure Gnassingbé was re-elected with 60·9% of the vote, ahead of Jean-Pierre Fabre of the Union of Forces for Change (Union des Forces de Changement) with 33·9% and Yawovi Agboyibo of the Action Committee for Renewal (Comité d'Action pour la Renouveau) with 3·0%. There were four other candidates. Turnout was 65·7%.

At the parliamentary elections on 14 Oct. 2007 the ruling RPT won 50 of 81 seats with 32·7% of votes cast, the Union of Forces for Change 27 with 30·8% and the Action Committee for Renewal 4 with 6·8%. Turnout was 94·8%.

CURRENT ADMINISTRATION

President: Faure Gnassingbé; b. 1966 (RPT; sworn in 4 May 2005 and re-elected 4 March 2010).

In March 2010 the government comprised:

Prime Minister: Gilbert Fossoun Houngbo; b. 1961 (ind.; sworn in 7 Sept. 2008).

Minister of State, Minister of Health: Komlan Mally. *Minister of State, Minister of Industry, Handicrafts and Technical Innovation:* Vacant. *Minister of State, Minister of Territorial Administration, Decentralization and Local Communities, and Spokesperson for the Government:* Pascal Bodjona. *Water, Sanitation and Village Water Resources:* Gen. Zakari Nandja.

Minister of Town Planning and Housing: Issifou Okoulou-Kantchati. *Economy and Finance:* Adji Ayassor. *Co-operation, Development and Territorial Administration:* Gilbert Bawara. *Justice and Keeper of the Seals:* Kokou Tozoun. *Foreign Affairs and Regional Integration:* Koffi Esaw. *Higher Education and Research:* Vacant. *Security and Civil Protection:* Atcha Titikpina. *Primary and Secondary Education:* Sambiani Sankardja Laré. *Post, Telecommunications and Technological Innovation:* Kokouvi Dogbé. *Social Affairs, Advancement of Women and the Protection of Children and the Aged:* Maïnounatou Ibrahima. *Agriculture, Animal Husbandry and Fisheries:* Kossi Messan Ewovor. *Mines, Energy and Water:* Noupoku Dammipi. *Labour and Social Security:* Octave Nicoué Broohm. *Environment and Forest Resources:* Kossivi Ayikoé. *Civil Service, Administrative Reform and Relations with Institutions:* Nissao Gnonfam. *Technical Education and Professional Training:* Henriette Kuévi Amédjogbé. *Tourism:* Batienne Kpabré Sylli. *Communication and Culture:* Ouligo Kéguéwa. *Civic Education, Human Rights and the Promotion of Democracy:* Yacoubou Amadou. *Public Works and Transport:* Komlan Kadjé. *Youth and Sports:* Padumhèkou Tchaou.

Government Website (French only):
http://www.republicoftogo.com

CURRENT LEADERS

Faure Gnassingbé

Position
President

Introduction
Faure Gnassingbé was installed as president after the death of his father, who had been one of Africa's longest-serving leaders. The appointment led to violent protests and international condemnation. Forced to step down, he contested a presidential election and emerged victorious in April 2005 with just over 60% of the vote. Faure then pursued a policy of political reconciliation, paving the way for peaceful parliamentary elections in Oct. 2007. He was re-elected to the presidency in March 2010.

Early Life
Faure Essozimna Gnassingbé was born in Afagnan, Togo on 6 June 1966. He is the son of Gnassingbé Eyadéma, a general from northern Togo who led a coup in 1963, declared himself president in April 1967 and remained head of state until his death on 5 Feb. 2005. Faure attended school in the capital, Lomé, followed by the Sorbonne University in Paris and the George Washington University in the USA, from which he graduated with an MBA. Returning to an unstable and economically crippled Togo in the mid-1990s, Faure began work as a civil servant.

He entered the political fray in 1998 when he was elected the representative of the ruling Togolese People's Assembly (RPT) for Blitta constituency in central Togo. Both the presidential and legislative elections were subject to allegations of vote-rigging and intimidation. Faure retained his seat in the June 2002 elections (which were boycotted by the opposition) and on 29 June 2003 he took office as minister of public works, mines and telecommunications.

On 6 Feb. 2005, the day after his father's death, Faure was proclaimed as his successor by the Togolese army, sparking widespread protest. Amid mounting international criticism and threats of sanctions, Faure announced that a presidential election would be held on 24 April 2005 and stepped down from office. Official results gave Faure over 60% of the vote at the subsequent elections and, despite violence erupting in Lomé amid claims of electoral fraud, he was sworn in as president on 4 May 2005.

Career in Office

Faure promised to push for economic growth, to reform institutions and to improve Togo's image abroad. Although most of the key government posts went to members of the ruling party, Edem Kodjo, the leader of a moderate opposition party, was named prime minister in June 2005. In Sept. 2006 Faure appointed another veteran opposition leader, Yawovi Madji Agboyibo of the Action Committee for Renewal, as prime minister with the task of forming a unity government. In Oct. 2007 the ruling RPT won parliamentary elections in which opposition parties took part for the first time in almost two decades and which were declared by international observers to be free and fair. Faure then appointed Komlan Mally prime minister and a new government was formed in Dec. When Mally resigned in Sept. 2008, Faure appointed Gilbert Houngbo, an independent, as the new premier. In April 2009 the government claimed that there had been a foiled coup plot against Faure involving his half-brother and former defence minister Kpatcha Gnassingbé. Faure was returned to office in presidential elections on 4 March 2010.

DEFENCE

There is selective conscription that lasts for two years. Defence expenditure totalled US$34m. in 2006 (US$6 per capita), representing 1·6% of GDP.

Army

Strength (2007) around 8,100, with a further 750 in a paramilitary gendarmerie.

Navy

In 2007 the Naval wing of the armed forces numbered about 200 and was based at Lomé.

Air Force

The Air Force—established with French assistance—numbered (2007) 250, with 16 combat aircraft although their serviceability is in doubt.

INTERNATIONAL RELATIONS

Togo is a member of the UN, World Bank, IMF and several other UN specialized agencies, WTO, IOM, International Organization of the Francophonie, Islamic Development Bank, OIC, African Development Bank, African Union, ECOWAS and is an ACP member state of the ACP-EU relationship.

ECONOMY

Agriculture contributed 44% of GDP in 2005, industry 24% and services 32%.

Overview

After civil and economic turmoil in the early 1990s, a structural redevelopment programme launched in 1994 resulted in positive growth. Following a downturn in 2005, the government instigated a series of political and economic reforms to restore fiscal discipline and strengthen governance. The promise of free parliamentary elections has further helped restore economic confidence.

Growth has been modest, with real GDP growth of 2·0% in 2006 as a result of easing political tensions and greater dynamism in trade-related services. Inflation remained low at 1·0% in 2007 but the economy continues to accumulate high public debt (currently 103% of GDP).

Social indicators are low, with the economy ranked 159th out of 182 countries on the Human Development Index. Further reforms toward strengthening fiscal governance are needed to improve revenue collection and allow for greater spending on health, education and infrastructure. Improved political conditions will encourage economic recovery and re-engagement with external donors.

Currency

The unit of currency is the *franc CFA* (XOF) with a parity of 655·957 francs CFA to one euro. Foreign exchange reserves were US$270m. in June 2005 and total money supply was 177,138m. francs CFA. Inflation in 2007 was 1·0%, rising to 8·4% in 2008.

Budget

In 2004 revenues were 170·7bn. francs CFA and expenditures 167·0bn. francs CFA. Tax revenue accounted for 85·1% of revenues in 2004; current expenditure accounted for 85·9% of expenditures.

VAT is 18%.

Performance

Real GDP growth was 1·9% in 2007 and 1·1% in 2008. Total GDP in 2008 was US$2·8bn.

Banking and Finance

The bank of issue is the Central Bank of West African States (BCEAO). The *Governor* is Philippe-Henri Dacoury-Tabley. In 2003 there were six commercial banks, three development banks, a savings bank and a credit institution.

ENERGY AND NATURAL RESOURCES

Environment

Togo's carbon dioxide emissions from the consumption and flaring of fossil fuels in 2008 were the equivalent of 0·5 tonnes per capita.

Electricity

Installed capacity in 2004 was an estimated 48,000 kW. In 2004 production totalled 262m. kWh. Additional electricity is imported from Ghana. Consumption per capita in 2004 was 102 kWh.

Minerals

Output of phosphate rock in 2002 was 1·3m. tonnes. Other minerals are limestone, iron ore and marble.

Agriculture

Agriculture supports about 80% of the population. Most food production comes from individual holdings under 3 ha. Inland, the country is hilly; dry plains alternate with arable land. There were an estimated 2·46m. ha. of arable land in 2007 and 0·17m. ha. of permanent crops. There are considerable plantations of oil and cocoa palms, coffee, cacao, kola, cassava and cotton. Production, 2003 (in 1,000 tonnes): cassava, 724; yams, 569; maize, 516; sorghum, 177; seed cotton, 159; cotton lint, 76; cottonseed, 75; rice, 68; millet, 50; dry beans, 44; groundnuts, 37.

Livestock (2003 estimates, in 1,000): sheep, 1,800; goats, 1,470; pigs, 310; cattle, 279; chickens, 8,000.

Forestry

Forests covered 386,000 ha. in 2005, or 7·1% of the land area. Teak plantations covered 8,600 ha. In 2007, 6·04m. cu. metres of roundwood were cut.

Fisheries

The catch in 2005 totalled 27,732 tonnes (82% from marine waters).

INDUSTRY

Industry is small-scale. Cement and textiles are produced and food processed. In 2001 industry accounted for 21·1% of GDP, with manufacturing contributing 9·7%.

Labour

In 1996 the workforce was 1,739,000 (60% males). Around 62% of the economically active population in 1995 were engaged in agriculture, fisheries and forestry. In 2002 the statutory minimum wage was 125·16 francs CFA per hour.

Trade Unions

With the abandonment of single-party politics, the former monolithic Togo National Workers Confederation (CNTT) has split into several federations and independent trade unions.

INTERNATIONAL TRADE

A free trade zone was established in 1990. Foreign debt was US$1,708m. in 2005.

Imports and Exports

In 2005 imports (c.i.f.) amounted to US$592·6m. (US$557·8m. in 2004); exports (f.o.b.) US$359·9m. (US$389·6m. in 2004). The main import suppliers in 2005 were France (17·6%), China (13·2%), Côte d'Ivoire (6·5%), Italy (4·5%) and Spain (4·2%). Principal export destinations in 2005 were Ghana (20·3%), Burkina Faso (18·4%), Benin (11·6%), Mali (7·4%) and India (5·9%). Leading imports are food, refined petroleum, and chemicals and chemical products; main exports are cement, phosphates and cotton.

COMMUNICATIONS

Roads

There were an estimated 7,520 km of roads in 2002, of which 2,380 km were paved. In 2007 there were 10,600 passenger cars in use, 2,200 lorries and vans and 34,200 motorcycles and mopeds.

Rail

There are four metre-gauge railways connecting Lomé, with Aného (continuing to Cotonou in Benin), Kpalimé, Tabligbo and (via Atakpamé) Blitta; total length in 2005, 532 km. In 2005 the railways carried 1·1m. tonnes of freight. There has been no passenger rail service since 1996.

Civil Aviation

In 2003 Trans African Airlines flew from Tokoin airport, near Lomé, to Abidjan, Bamako, Brazzaville, Cotonou, Dakar and Pointe-Noire. There were also international flights with other airlines to Addis Ababa, Brussels, Douala, Kinshasa, Lagos, Libreville, Ouagadougou and Paris. In 2001 Tokoin handled 151,000 passengers (all on international flights) and 5,100 tonnes of freight. In 2003 scheduled airline traffic of Togo-based carriers flew 1m. km, carrying 46,000 passengers (all on international flights).

Shipping

In 2002 merchant shipping totalled 13,000 GRT.

Telecommunications

In 2008 there were 140,900 main (fixed) telephone lines in Togo; mobile phone subscribers numbered 1,549,500 in 2008 (24·0 per 100 persons). There were 185,000 PCs in use in 2005 and 350,000 internet users in 2008.

Postal Services

In 2003 there were 54 post offices.

SOCIAL INSTITUTIONS

Justice

The Supreme Court and two Appeal Courts are in Lomé, one for criminal cases and one for civil and commercial cases. Each receives appeal from a series of local tribunals.

The death penalty was abolished in June 2009. The population in penal institutions in Aug. 2003 was 3,200 (65 per 100,000 of national population).

Education

The adult literacy rate in 2003 was 53·0% (68·5% among males and 38·3% among females). In 2007 there were 1,021,617 pupils and 26,103 teaching staff in primary schools, and 408,964 pupils in secondary schools with 11,518 teaching staff. In 2006 there were 32,502 students in higher education and 455 academic staff. In 2007 about 77% of children of primary school age were attending school. The University of Benin at Lomé (founded in 1970) is the leading institution of tertiary education.

In 2007 public expenditure on education came to 3·8% of GNI and accounted for 17·2% of total government expenditure.

Health

In 1990 hospital bed provision was 16 per 10,000 population. In 2001 there were 265 physicians, 25 dentists, 782 nurses, 346 midwives and 141 pharmacists. Government expenditure on health in 1995 was estimated at 5,900m. francs CFA.

RELIGION

In 2001, 38% of the population followed traditional animist religions; 35% were Christian and 19% Muslim.

CULTURE

World Heritage Sites

There is one UNESCO site in Togo: Koutammakou, the land of the Batammariba (inscribed on the list in 2004).

Broadcasting

Télévision Togolaise and Radio Togolaise are the state-run national TV and radio broadcasters. There are also a number of commercial and community radio services and a few private television stations. There were 165,000 TV receivers (colour by SECAM V) in 2006.

Press

There is one government-controlled daily newspaper, Togo-Presse (circulation of 5,000 in 2006).

Tourism

In 2004 there were 83,000 foreign tourists; spending by tourists totalled US$25m.

DIPLOMATIC REPRESENTATIVES

Of Togo in the United Kingdom
Ambassador: Tchao Sotou Bere (resides in Paris).

Of the United Kingdom in Togo
Ambassador: Dr Nicholas Westcott, CMG (resides in Accra, Ghana).

Of Togo in the USA (2208 Massachusetts Ave., NW, Washington, D.C., 20008)
Ambassador: Edawe Limbaye Kadangha Bariki.

Of the USA in Togo (Boulevard Eyadema, Lomé II, BP 852, Lomé)
Ambassador: Patricia M. Hawkins.

Of Togo to the United Nations
Ambassador: Kodjo Menan.

Of Togo to the European Union
Ambassador: Félix Kodjo Sagbo.

FURTHER READING

National Statistical Office: Direction Générale de la Statistique et de la Comptabilité Nationale, B.P. 118, Lomé.
Website (French only): http://www.stat-togo.org

TONGA

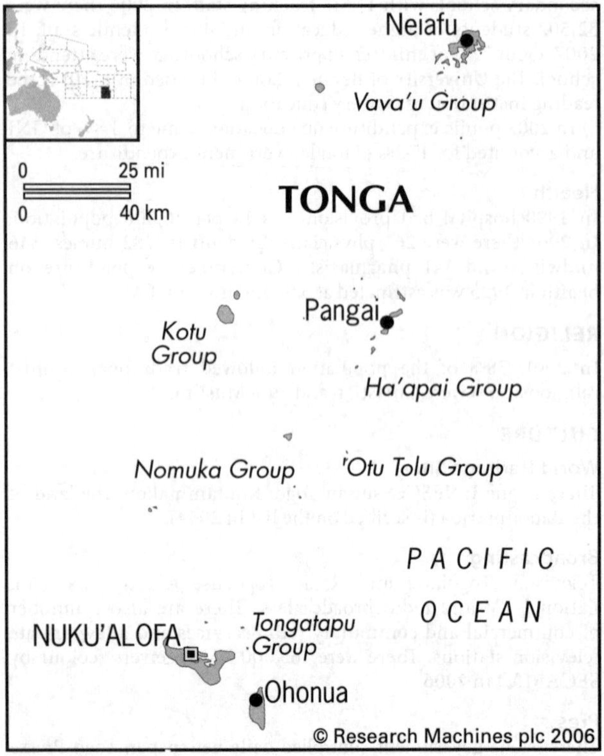

Pule'anga Fakatu'i 'o Tonga
(Kingdom of Tonga)

Capital: Nuku'alofa
Population estimate, 2010: 104,000
GDP per capita, 2007: (PPP$) 3,748
HDI/world rank: 0·768/99

KEY HISTORICAL EVENTS

The Tongatapu group of islands in the south western Pacific Ocean were discovered by Tasman in 1643. The Kingdom of Tonga attained unity under Taufa'ahau Tupou (George I) who became ruler of his native Ha'apai in 1820, of Vava'u in 1833 and of Tongatapu in 1845. By 1860 the kingdom had converted to Christianity. In 1862 the king granted freedom from arbitrary rule of minor chiefs and extended land rights. These institutional changes, together with the establishment of a parliament of chiefs, paved the way towards a democratic constitution. By the Anglo-German Agreement of 14 Nov. 1899, the Tonga Islands became a British protectorate. The protectorate was dissolved on 4 June 1970 when Tonga, the only ancient kingdom surviving from the pre-European period in Polynesia, achieved independence within the Commonwealth.

TERRITORY AND POPULATION

The Kingdom consists of some 169 islands and islets with a total area, including inland waters and uninhabited islands, of 748 sq. km (289 sq. miles), and lies between 15° and 23° 30' S. lat and 173° and 177° W. long, its western boundary being the eastern boundary of the Fiji Islands. The islands are split up into the following groups (reading from north to south): the Niuas, Vava'u, Ha'apai, Tongatapu and 'Eua. The three main groups, both from historical and administrative significance, are Tongatapu in the south, Ha'apai in the centre and Vava'u in the north. Census population (2006) 101,991 (51,772 males); density, 136 per sq. km. In 2005, 76·0% of the population lived in rural areas.

The UN gives an estimated population for 2010 of 104,000.

The capital is Nuku'alofa on Tongatapu; population (2006), 34,311 (urban population, 23,658).

There are five divisions comprising 23 districts:

Division	*Sq. km*	*Census 2006*	*Capital*
Niuas	72	1,665	Hihifo
Vava'u	119	15,505	Neiafu
Ha'apai	110	7,570	Pangai
Tongatapu	261	72,045	Nuku'alofa
'Eua	87	5,206	Ohonua

Both Tongan and English are recognized as official languages.

SOCIAL STATISTICS

Births, 2000, 2,471; deaths, 653; marriages, 747; divorces, 75. Expectation of life, 2007: males, 69·0 years; females, 74·6. Annual population growth rate, 1992–2002, 0·3%. Infant mortality, 2005, 20 per 1,000 live births. Fertility rate, 2004, 3·4 births per woman.

CLIMATE

Generally a healthy climate, although Jan. to March hot and humid, with temperatures of 90°F (32·2°C). Rainfall amounts are comparatively high, being greatest from Dec. to March. Nuku'alofa, Jan. 25·8°C, July 21·3°C. Annual rainfall 1,643 mm. Vava'u, Jan. 27·3°C, July 23·4°C. Annual rainfall 2,034 mm.

CONSTITUTION AND GOVERNMENT

The reigning King is **George Tupou V (Siaosi Tupou V)**, born 4 May 1948, succeeded on 11 Sept. 2006 on the death of his father, Taufa'ahau Tupou IV and crowned on 1 Aug. 2008.

The current Constitution is based on the one granted in 1875. It was last amended in 2003 to increase the constitutional powers of the King and restrict media freedom. There is a Privy Council, Cabinet, Legislative Assembly and Judiciary. The 33-member *Legislative Assembly*, which meets annually, is composed of nine nobles elected by their peers, nine elected representatives of the people, the prime minister and 14 other cabinet ministers.

National Anthem

'E 'Otua, Mafimafi, ko ho mau 'eiki Koe' ('Oh Almighty God above, thou art our Lord and sure defence'); words by Prince Uelingtoni Ngu Tupoumalohi, tune by K. G. Schmitt.

RECENT ELECTIONS

Elections were held on 23 and 24 April 2008 for the nine elected seats. Four seats were won by the Human Rights and Democracy Movement, three by independent candidates and two by the People's Democratic Party.

CURRENT ADMINISTRATION

In March 2010 the government comprised:

Prime Minister and Acting Minister of Defence and Foreign Affairs: Fred Sevele (in office since 11 Feb. 2006—acting until 30 March 2006).

Deputy Prime Minister and Minister of Health: Dr Viliami Tangi.

Minister of Agriculture, Food, Fisheries and Forests: Prince Tu'ipelehake. *Budget:* Sione Teisina Fuko. *Education, Women's*

Affairs and Culture: Tevita Hala Palefau. *Environment and Climate Change:* Ma'afu. *Finance, Planning and Public Enterprises:* Afu'alo Matoto. *Information and Communication:* 'Eseta Fusitu'a. *Justice:* Samiu Kuita Vaipulu. *Labour, Commerce and Industry:* Lisiate 'Akolo. *Lands, Land Surveys and Natural Resources, and Civil Aviation and Transport (acting):* Tuita. *Tourism:* Fineasi Funaki. *Training, Employment, Youth and Sports:* Tu'ivakano. *Works, and Natural Disaster Management:* Nuku. *Attorney General:* John Cauchi.

Government Website: http://www.pmo.gov.to

CURRENT LEADERS

Fred Sevele

Position
Prime Minister

Introduction
Fred Sevele was appointed Tonga's first 'citizen' prime minister in March 2006 by King Taufa'ahau Tupou IV. With a background in business, Sevele has aimed to boost the economy by developing the fishing and tourism sectors. Although an advocate of greater democracy, his early tenure was marked by civil disorder and the imposition of a state of emergency. His second term began in 2008 with plans to create a parliament with elected members and a cabinet drawn from the Legislative Assembly.

Early Life
Feleti 'Fred' Vaka'uta Sevele was born in 1945 in the Kingdom of Tonga and educated at Apifo'ou College, Tonga, followed by St John's College on Ovalau, Fiji Islands and the Marist Brothers High School on Suva, Fiji Islands. He later studied economic geography at the University of Canterbury, New Zealand, receiving his PhD in 1972. He went on to establish numerous businesses in Tonga, becoming one of the archipelago's most successful entrepreneurs. By the late 1990s he was a prominent supporter of the pro-democracy movement.

In March 1999 Sevele was elected as one of nine people's representatives to the Legislative Assembly, winning re-election in 2002 and 2005. In March 2005 King Taufa'ahau Tupou IV named Sevele as minister of labour, commerce and industries, in line with new guidelines requiring four cabinet ministers to be appointed from the elected members. Sevele won plaudits for negotiating Tonga's entry into the World Trade Organization.

When the prime minister, HRH Prince 'Ulukalala Lavaka Ata, unexpectedly resigned on 11 Feb. 2006 after six years in the post, the king appointed Sevele as acting prime minister. No official reason was given for 'Ulukalala's departure but it followed three years of political upheaval that saw the collapse of Royal Tongan Airlines, a strike by civil servants and budgetary shortfalls. On 30 March 2006 the king announced that Sevele had been appointed Tonga's first non-aristocratic prime minister.

Career in Office
Sevele stated his determination to make better use of local resources and rely less on overseas aid and assistance programmes. He was also expected to push for greater democracy, particularly in the wake of the death in Sept. 2006 of King Taufa'ahau Tupou IV and the succession of his eldest son as King Tupou V. However, impatience at the pace of reform led in Nov. 2006 to rioting in the capital, resulting in eight deaths, extensive commercial damage and the declaration of a state of emergency. In mid-2007 a tripartite committee of nobles, ministers and people's representatives was established to find a consensus on political reform and to make recommendations to parliament.

In polling for the nine elected seats in the 33-member Legislative Assembly in April 2008, pro-democracy candidates were returned in the majority of them, indicating growing popular support for faster political reform. The government proposed increasing the number of directly elected parliamentarians from 2010 and diluting the power of the monarchy, recommendations upheld by a constitutional review committee in Nov. 2009.

DEFENCE

Army
The Tonga Defence Services number around 450 troops.

Navy
A coastal naval force operating several small patrol boats is based at Touliki, Nuku'alofa.

Air Force
An Air Force was created in 1996. There is also a small naval aviation unit.

INTERNATIONAL RELATIONS

Tonga is a member of the UN, World Bank, IMF and several other UN specialized agencies, WTO, Commonwealth, Asian Development Bank, Pacific Islands Forum and SPC and is an ACP member state of the ACP-EU relationship.

ECONOMY

In 2006 agriculture accounted for 25·9% of GDP, industry 14·0% and services 60·1%.

Overview
Following riots in Nov. 2006 when much of the economy's business district was destroyed, Tonga is on the path to recovery. Strong remittances have underpinned growth, while donor-supported government reconstruction loans and the king's coronation in Aug. 2008 added further stimulus to the recovery. However, major increases in the price of imported food and fuel contributed to a sharp rise in inflation in 2008, while recession in the USA and New Zealand led to a reduction in remittances in the year to June 2009.

Tonga has underperformed relative to other Pacific Island countries. It relies heavily on imports, particularly food and fuel, making it vulnerable to external shocks. High labour costs, limited export diversification and lack of long-term investment to improve productivity and efficiency impede efforts for sustainable growth.

Currency
The unit of currency is the *pa'anga* (TOP) of 100 *seniti*. In 2008 there was inflation of 14·5%. In July 2005 foreign exchange reserves were US$49m. and total money supply was T$65m.

Budget
Revenues were T$172·4m. in 2005–06, with expenditures T$166·0m.

There is a sales tax of 5%.

Performance
In 2007 the economy shrank by 3·2% but there was a slight recovery in 2008 with growth of 1·2%. Total GDP in 2008 was US$0·3bn.

Banking and Finance
The National Reserve Bank of Tonga (*Governor*, Siosi Cocker Mafi) was established in 1989 as a bank of issue and to manage foreign reserves. The Bank of Tonga and the Tonga Development Bank are both situated in Nuku'alofa with branches in the main islands. Other commercial banks in Nuku'alofa are ANZ Banking Group Ltd, the MBF Bank Ltd, the National Reserve Bank of Tonga and the Westpac Banking Corp.

ENERGY AND NATURAL RESOURCES

Environment
Tonga's carbon dioxide emissions from the consumption and flaring of fossil fuels in 2008 were the equivalent of 1·7 tonnes per capita.

Electricity
Production (2004 estimate) 36m. kWh. Installed capacity (2004 estimate) 8,000 kW.

Agriculture
In 2007 there were approximately 15,000 ha. of arable land and 12,000 ha. of permanent crops. Production (2003 estimates, in 1,000 tonnes): coconuts, 58; pumpkins and squash, 20; cassava, 9; sweet potatoes, 6; taro, 4; yams, 4; plantains, 3.

Livestock (2003 estimates): pigs, 81,000; goats, 12,000; cattle, 11,000; horses, 11,000.

Fisheries
In 2004 the catch totalled 1,645 tonnes.

INDUSTRY
The main industries produce food and beverages, paper, chemicals, metals and textiles.

INTERNATIONAL TRADE
Foreign debt in 2007 amounted to US$91m.

Imports and Exports
In 2006 imports were valued at US$116·5m. and exports at US$9·6m. Main imports are food and live animals, basic manufactures, machinery and transport equipment, and mineral fuels and lubricants; main exports are coconut oil, vanilla beans, root crops, desiccated coconut and watermelons. The leading import suppliers in 2006 were New Zealand (33·1%), Fiji Islands (28·2%), Australia (12·5%) and the USA (9·8%); principal export markets were Japan (40·6%), USA (25·0%), Australia (14·6%) and South Korea (8·3%).

COMMUNICATIONS
Roads
In 2002 there were 680 km of roads (184 km paved). Vehicles in use in 2000 numbered approximately 8,400 passenger cars, 8,700 trucks and vans, and (1996) 40 buses and coaches.

Civil Aviation
There is an international airport at Nuku'alofa on Tongatapu. The national carrier was the state-owned Royal Tongan Airlines, but it ceased operations in May 2004 owing to financial difficulties. Two carriers, Peau Vava'u and Airlines Tonga, now provide inter-island services. In 1998 Nuku'alofa (Fua'Amotu International) handled 129,000 passengers (88,000 on international flights) and 1,100 tonnes of freight.

Shipping
In 2002 sea-going shipping totalled 291,000 GRT, including oil tankers 41,000 GRT. Two shipping lanes provide monthly services to American Samoa, Australia, the Fiji Islands, Kiribati, New Caledonia, New Zealand, Samoa and Tuvalu.

Telecommunications
The operation and development of the National Telecommunication Network and Services are the responsibilities of the Tonga Telecommunication Commission (TCC). In 2008 there were 25,500 main (fixed) telephone lines; mobile phone subscribers numbered 50,500 in 2008 (48·7 per 100 persons). There were 6,000 PCs in use in 2005 and 8,400 internet users in 2008. Ucall mobile GSM digital has been in operation in Tonga since Dec. 2001.

Postal Services
In 2001 there were eight post offices.

SOCIAL INSTITUTIONS
Justice
The judiciary is presided over by the Chief Justice. The enforcement of justice is the responsibility of the Attorney-General and the Minister of Police. In 1994 the UK ceased appointing Tongan judges and subsidizing their salaries.

The population in penal institutions in 2004 was 116 (105 per 100,000 of national population).

Education
In 2002 there were a total of 17,105 pupils with 773 teachers in primary schools and 14,567 pupils with 1,012 teachers in secondary schools. There is an extension centre of the University of the South Pacific at Nuku'alofa, a teacher training college and three technical institutes.

Adult literacy in 1996 was estimated at 98·5%. In 2004 public expenditure on education came to 5·0% of GDP.

Health
There were four hospitals in 1993 with a provision of 28 beds per 10,000 inhabitants. In 2001 there were 35 physicians, 33 dentists, 322 nurses, 19 midwives and 17 pharmacists.

RELIGION
In 2001 there were 44,000 adherents of the Free Wesleyan Church and 16,000 Roman Catholics, with the remainder of the population being followers of other religions (notably Latter-day Saints).

CULTURE
Broadcasting
State-owned Tonga Broadcasting Commission operates the free-to-air Television Tonga channel and three radio services (including a 24-hour Radio Australia relay). There are some private broadcasters, including OBN TV7, Tonfon TV, Radio Nuku'alofa and 93FM (a religious service). There were 5,000 television receivers in 2005.

Press
There are no daily newspapers. The government-owned weekly, *Tonga Chronicle*, had a circulation of 7,000 in 2002.

Tourism
There were 41,208 visitors in 2004. Receipts in 2004 totalled US$15m.

DIPLOMATIC REPRESENTATIVES
Of Tonga in the United Kingdom (36 Molyneux St., London, W1H 5BQ)

High Commissioner: Dr Sione Ngongo Kioa.

Of the United Kingdom in Tonga (High Commission in Nuku'alofa closed in March 2006)

High Commissioner: Mac McLachlan, MBE (resides in Suva, Fiji Islands).

Of Tonga in the USA (250 E. 51st St., New York, NY 10022)

Ambassador: Vacant.

Chargé d'Affaires a.i.: Viliami Malolo.

Of the USA in Tonga

Ambassador: C. Steven McGann (resides in Suva, Fiji Islands).

Of Tonga to the United Nations

Ambassador: Sonatane Tu'a Taumoepeau Tupou.

Of Tonga to the European Union

Ambassador: Sione Ngongo Kioa.

FURTHER READING
Campbell, I. C., *Island Kingdom: Tonga, Ancient and Modern.* 1994
Wood-Ellem, E., *Queen Salote of Tonga, The Story of an Era 1900–1965.* 2000

National Statistical Office: Tonga Statistics Department, P.O. Box 149, Nuku'alofa.

Website: http://www.spc.int/prism/Country/to/stats

TRINIDAD AND TOBAGO

Republic of Trinidad and Tobago

Capital: Port-of-Spain
Population estimate, 2010: 1·34m.
GDP per capita, 2007: (PPP$) 23,507
HDI/world rank: 0·837/64

KEY HISTORICAL EVENTS

When Columbus visited Trinidad in 1498 the island was inhabited by Arawak Indians. Tobago was occupied by the Caribs. Trinidad remained a neglected Spanish possession for almost 300 years until it was surrendered to a British naval expedition in 1797. The British first attempted to settle Tobago in 1721 but the French captured the island in 1781 and transformed it into a sugar-producing colony. In 1802 the British acquired Tobago and in 1899 it was administratively combined with Trinidad. When slavery was abolished in the late 1830s, the British subsidized immigration from India to replace plantation labourers. Sugar and cocoa declined towards the end of the 19th century. Oil and asphalt became the main sources of income. On 31 Aug. 1962 Trinidad and Tobago became an independent member of the Commonwealth. A Republican Constitution was adopted on 1 Aug. 1976.

TERRITORY AND POPULATION

The island of Trinidad is situated in the Caribbean Sea, about 12 km off the northeast coast of Venezuela; several islets, the largest being Chacachacare, Huevos, Monos and Gaspar Grande, lie in the Gulf of Paria which separates Trinidad from Venezuela. The smaller island of Tobago lies 30·7 km further to the northeast. Altogether, the islands cover 5,128 sq. km (1,980 sq. miles), of which Trinidad (including the islets) has 4,828 sq. km (1,864 sq. miles) and Tobago 300 sq. km (116 sq. miles). In 2000 the census population was 1,262,366 (Trinidad, 1,208,282; Tobago, 54,084); density, 246 per sq. km.

The UN gives an estimated population for 2010 of 1·34m.

In 2005, 87·8% of the population lived in rural areas. Capital, Port-of-Spain (2000 census, 49,031); other important towns, San Fernando (55,419), Arima (32,278) and Point Fortin (19,056). The main towns on Tobago are Scarborough and Plymouth. Those of African descent are (2000) 39·2% of the population; East Indians, 38·6%; mixed races, 16·3%; European, Chinese and others, 5·9%.

The official language is English.

SOCIAL STATISTICS

Births, 2002, 16,990; deaths, 9,797. 2002 birth rate (per 1,000 population), 13·3; death rate, 7·7. Expectation of life, 2007, was 65·6 years for males and 72·8 for females. Annual population growth rate, 1992–2002, 0·5%. Infant mortality, 2005, 17 per 1,000 live births; fertility rate, 2004, 1·6 births per woman.

CLIMATE

A tropical climate cooled by the northeast trade winds. The dry season runs from Jan. to June, with a wet season for the rest of the year. Temperatures are uniformly high the year round. Port-of-Spain, Jan. 76·3°F (24·6°C), July 79·2°F (26·2°C). Annual rainfall 1,870 mm.

CONSTITUTION AND GOVERNMENT

The 1976 constitution provides for a bicameral legislature of a *Senate* and a *House of Representatives*, who elect the *President*, who is head of state. The *Senate* consists of 31 members, 16 being appointed by the President on the advice of the Prime Minister, six on the advice of the Leader of the Opposition and nine at the discretion of the President.

The *House of Representatives* consists of 41 (39 for Trinidad and two for Tobago) elected members and a Speaker elected from within or outside the House.

Executive power is vested in the Prime Minister, who is appointed by the President, and the Cabinet.

National Anthem

'Forged from the love of liberty'; words and music by P. Castagne.

GOVERNMENT CHRONOLOGY

Presidents since 1976.

1976–87	Ellis Emmanuel Innocent Clarke
1987–97	Noor Mohammed Hassanali
1997–2003	Arthur Napoleon Raymond Robinson
2003–	George Maxwell Richards

Prime Ministers since independence. (PNM = People's National Movement; NAR = National Alliance for Reconstruction; UNC = United National Congress)

1962–81	PNM	Eric Eustace Williams
1981–86	PNM	George Michael Chambers
1986–91	NAR	Arthur Napoleon Raymond Robinson
1991–95	PNM	Patrick Augustus Mervyn Manning
1995–2001	UNC	Basdeo Panday
2001–	PNM	Patrick Augustus Mervyn Manning

RECENT ELECTIONS

In parliamentary elections held on 5 Nov. 2007 the ruling People's National Movement (PNM) won 26 out of 41 seats with 45·9% of votes cast, against 15 seats with 29·7% for the United National Congress (UNC). Congress of the People received 22·6% of the vote but did not win any seats. Turnout was 66·0%.

Parliamentary elections were scheduled to take place on 24 May 2010.

CURRENT ADMINISTRATION

President: Maxwell Richards; b. 1931 (PNM; sworn in 17 March 2003 and re-elected in Feb. 2008).

In March 2010 the cabinet comprised:

Prime Minister: Patrick Manning; b. 1946 (PNM; sworn in 24 Dec. 2001, having previously held office from Dec. 1991–Nov. 1995).

Minister of Finance: Karen Nunez-Tesheira. *Education:* Esther Le Gendre. *Science, Technology and Tertiary Education:* Christine Kangaloo. *Works and Transport:* Colm Imbert. *National Security:* Martin Joseph. *Legal Affairs:* Peter Taylor. *Public Administration:* Kennedy Swarathsingh. *Information:* Neil Parsanlal. *Public Utilities:* Mustapha Abdul-Hamid. *Sport and Youth Affairs:* Gary Hunt. *Tourism:* Joseph Ross. *Foreign Affairs:* Paula Gopee-Scoon. *Trade and Industry, and Minister in the Ministry of Finance:* Mariano Browne. *Agriculture, Land and Marine Resources:* Arnold Piggott. *Community Development, Culture and Gender Affairs:* Marlene McDonald. *Social Development:* Amery Browne. *Energy and Energy Industries:* Conrad Enil. *Planning, Housing and the Environment:* Emily Gaynor Dick-Forde. *Health:* Jerry Narace. *Labour, Small and Micro Enterprise Development:* Rennie Dumas. *Local Government:* Hazel Manning. *Attorney General:* Bridgid Annisette-George. *Minister in the Office of the Prime Minister:* Lenny Saith.

Government Website: http://www.gov.tt

CURRENT LEADERS

George Maxwell Richards

Position
President

Introduction
George Maxwell Richards became president of Trinidad and Tobago in March 2003. A chemical engineer by training, he is a non-partisan and it was hoped that his mixed-race background might defuse some of the ethnic tension in the country's political life. He was re-elected for a second term in Feb. 2008.

Early Life
Richards was born in San Fernando, Trinidad in 1931. He graduated from the Queen's Royal College in the capital, Port-of-Spain, in 1955 and took a masters degree in chemical engineering at Manchester University in the UK. In 1963 he obtained his PhD from Cambridge University.

Richards began his working life as a trainee with a Trinidadian oil company in 1950. From 1957–65 he worked for Shell Trinidad before taking a lectureship in chemical engineering at the University of the West Indies. Five years later he became professor of chemical engineering. In 1980 he was appointed deputy principal and pro-vice chancellor of the university and was promoted to principal in 1985, a post he held until late-1986. Richards was also active on the boards of several commercial companies and between 1977 and 2003 he chaired the government salaries review commission.

Following tied parliamentary elections in 2001, Arthur Robinson, then president, was forced to choose between Patrick Manning and Basdeo Panday for the premiership. When Robinson selected Manning he was accused of bias and the non-partisan nature of the presidency came under scrutiny. When Manning nominated Richards for the presidency, he cited Richards' lack of a party political background as a key reason.

Ganace Ramdial opposed Richards for the presidency, but in a secret ballot in Feb. 2003 parliament elected Richards by 43 votes to 25. He was sworn in on 17 March 2003.

Career in Office
The presidency is primarily a ceremonial role and, following the unavoidable politicizing of the position after the 2001 elections, Richards emphasized on assuming office that he was 'completely apolitical'. With his mixed race (including black, Chinese and white) roots, Richards has sought to diffuse some of the tensions resulting from Trinidad and Tobago's racially divided political structure. He has been outspoken in his criticism of the rising crime rate in the country. On 11 Feb. 2008 he was re-elected by parliament as the sole presidential candidate.

Patrick Manning

Position
Prime Minister

Introduction
Patrick Augustus Mervyn Manning became prime minister for the second time in Dec. 2001, having previously held the post from 1991–95. The elections of Dec. 2001 returned a hung parliament but Manning's People's National Movement (PNM) gained a majority at elections held in Oct. 2002. He then retained the premiership as a result of the PNM's re-election in Nov. 2007.

Early Life
Patrick Manning was born on 17 Aug. 1946 in San Fernando, Trinidad. He graduated from the town's Presentation College in 1965 and worked for a year as an oil refinery operator before studying geology at the University of the West Indies (Jamaica) from 1966–69. He was then employed as a geologist for the Texaco oil company until 1971.

In that year Manning joined parliament as the member for San Fernando East and was appointed parliamentary secretary at the ministry of petroleum and mines. Between 1973–78 he served as parliamentary secretary at the prime minister's office and at the ministries of planning and development, industry and commerce, and works, transport and communications. In 1978 he joined the finance ministry with responsibility for the maintenance portfolio and later the public service portfolio. He was then appointed minister of information in the prime minister's office. In 1981 he was named minister of information and minister of industry and commerce, and from 1981–86 served as minister of energy and natural resources.

In 1986 the PNM lost its first general election since independence in 1962. Manning succeeded George Chambers as party leader on an interim basis in Dec. 1986. He was confirmed in the job the following year and led the party to victory at the elections of Dec. 1991.

Career in Office
During his first tenure Manning set about making the economy more competitive. His government floated the Trinidad and Tobago dollar in a bid to encourage investment. In 1995 he attempted to dismiss the speaker of the House of Representatives, Occah Seapaul, over a scandal regarding testimony that Seapaul had given in a court trial. She refused to leave and suspended several government members. The PNM, already suffering a weakened majority after by-election losses the previous year, was thrown into crisis. Manning declared a state of emergency and put Seapaul under house arrest. He called early elections for Nov. 1995, hoping to take advantage of an improved economic outlook to bolster his government. However, the PNM lost to the United National Congress (UNC) and Manning was succeeded as prime minister by Basdeo Panday.

Panday won a second term in Dec. 2000 but at new elections 12 months later, following a split in the government, the UNC and PNM tied with 18 seats each. The two parties agreed a deal by which President Robinson would elect the prime minister. Panday withdrew from the pact when Manning was selected and demanded new elections. Without cross party co-operation

Manning was unable to form a workable government. Parliament was suspended in April 2002, and at elections held in Oct. the PNM won a majority, claiming 20 of the 36 available seats.

To reform the economy, Manning proposed reductions in income and corporation tax. He also aimed to exploit the country's tourism sector while continuing to develop the oil and gas industries. In foreign policy, he sought a more prominent role for Trinidad and Tobago within CARICOM. In April 2005 the Caribbean Court of Justice, a final court of appeal intended to replace the British Privy Council, was inaugurated in Trinidad. Manning has, however, been criticized for failing to bring the growing crime problem under control. In Oct. 2005 at least 10,000 people took part in a protest, named the Death March, against the level of violent crime, and in Jan. 2007 businesses and schools shut down in a mass demonstration against a spate of kidnappings. Also in Jan., the government announced that the country's long-established sugar industry could no longer be sustained because of cuts in European subsidies.

In Nov. 2007 Manning and the PNM retained power in elections, winning 26 of the 41 parliamentary seats.

DEFENCE

The Trinidad and Tobago Defence Force consists of the Trinidad and Tobago Regiment, the Coast Guard, the Air Guard and the Defence Force Reserves. Personnel in 2007 totalled around 2,700.

In 2006 defence expenditure totalled US$52m. (US$48 per capita), representing 0·3% of GDP.

Army

The Trinidad and Tobago Regiment (the Army) is part of the Trinidad and Tobago Defence Force. It has approximately 2,000 personnel organized into a Regiment Headquarters and four battalions.

Navy

In 2007 there was a Coast Guard of about 700.

Air Force

The Air Guard, formerly part of the Coast Guard, had 50 personnel and five aircraft in 2007.

INTERNATIONAL RELATIONS

Trinidad and Tobago is a member of the UN, World Bank, IMF and several other UN specialized agencies, WTO, Commonwealth, IOM, ACS, CARICOM, Caribbean Development Bank, Inter-American Development Bank, SELA, OAS and is an ACP member state of the ACP-EU relationship.

ECONOMY

Industry accounted for 59% of GDP in 2007 and services 41%.

Overview

Trinidad and Tobago has one of the highest per capita incomes in the Latin American and Caribbean region. From 1994–2006 the economy grew at an annual average of 6%, reaching 12% in 2006 thanks to rising oil and gas prices. The islands are rich in natural resources, with oil and gas making up 40% of GDP, 80% of exports and half of government revenues. However, the country is vulnerable to international markets. Few have benefited from the wealth created by oil and gas, which employs only 5% of the population. Social indicators are similar to other countries in the region despite outstanding economic performance. An estimated 17% of the population lives in poverty.

The global economic crisis has seen a sharp decline in the prices of major exports, including crude oil. Growth slowed to 2·3% in 2008 and there was negative growth of 0·9% in 2009. The country is a major financial centre in the Caribbean and a leader in regional economic integration, playing a key role in the CARICOM Single Market Economy since its establishment in 2006.

Currency

The unit of currency is the *Trinidad and Tobago dollar* (TTD) of 100 *cents*. Inflation was 7·9% in 2007 and 12·1% in 2008. In April 1994 the TT dollar was floated and managed by the Central Bank at TT$6·06 to US$1·00. Foreign exchange reserves in July 2005 were US$3,918m. and gold reserves 61,000 troy oz. Total money supply in May 2005 was TT$9,438m.

Budget

The fiscal year for the budget is 1 Oct. to 30 Sept. In 2003–04 total government revenue was TT$20,630m. and total expenditure was TT$19,120m. The petroleum sector accounted for 37·0% of revenues and individual income tax 15·9%; current expenditures accounted for 91·5% of total expenditure.

VAT is 15%.

Performance

Real GDP growth was 4·6% in 2007, 2·3% in 2008 and –0·9% in 2009. Total GDP in 2008 was US$23·9bn.

Banking and Finance

The Central Bank of Trinidad and Tobago began operations in 1964 (*Governor*, Ewart Williams). Its net reserves were US$1,281·1m. in Aug. 2000. There are seven commercial banks. Government savings banks are established in 69 offices, with a head office in Port-of-Spain. The stock exchange in Port-of-Spain participates in the regional Caribbean exchange.

ENERGY AND NATURAL RESOURCES

Environment

Carbon dioxide emissions from the consumption and flaring of fossil fuels were the equivalent of 41·0 tonnes per capita in 2008.

Electricity

In 2004 the estimated installed capacity was 1·40m. kW, electricity production was 6·43bn. kWh and consumption per capita 4,921 kWh.

Oil and Gas

Oil production is one of Trinidad's leading industries. Commercial production began in 1908; production of oil in 2008 was 6·9m. tonnes. Reserves in 2008 totalled 0·8bn. bbls. Crude oil is also imported for refining.

In 2008 production of natural gas was 39·3bn. cu. metres; proven reserves of natural gas were 480bn. cu. metres. A major discovery of approximately 50bn. cu. metres was made by BP in 2000, followed by a further discovery of approximately 30bn. cu. metres in 2002.

Agriculture

In 2007 the agricultural population was an estimated 94,000, of which some 49,000 were economically active. Production of main crops (2003 estimates, in 1,000 tonnes): sugarcane, 873; coconuts, 16; bananas, 7; pumpkins and squash, 6; oranges, 5; cucumbers and gherkins, 4; pineapples, 4; plantains, 4. There were around 25,000 ha. of arable land and 22,000 ha. of permanent cropland in 2007.

Livestock (2003 estimates): pigs, 76,000; goats, 23,000; cattle, 29,000; chickens, 28m.

Livestock products, 2003: meat, 60,000 tonnes (including poultry, 57,000 tonnes); milk, 9,000 tonnes.

Forestry

Forests covered 226,000 ha. in 2005, or 44·1% of the land area. Timber production for 2007 was 99,000 cu. metres.

Fisheries

The catch in 2005 totalled 13,414 tonnes.

INDUSTRY

Industrial production includes (in tonnes): ammonia and urea (1998), 3,946,700; iron and steel (2001), 3,550,800; residual fuel oil (2004), 2,971,000; methanol (1999), 2,149,800; distillate fuel oil (2004), 1,421,000; petrol (2004), 1,096,000; cement (2001), 697,000; sugar (2002), 104,000; rum (1998), 3,916,000 proof gallons; beer (2000), 62·5m. litres; cigarettes (2000), 2,050,000 units. Trinidad and Tobago ranks among the world's largest producers of ammonia and methanol.

Labour

The working population in the first quarter of 2003 was 588,300. The number of unemployed was 65,000. 77,300 people worked in construction (including electricity and water); 55,500 in manufacturing (including other mining and quarrying); 38,600 in transport storage and communication; 37,800 in agriculture; 17,500 in petroleum and gas; other services, 295,300. Total employment: 523,300. The unemployment rate in the fourth quarter of 2005 was a record low 6·7%.

Trade Unions

About 30% of the labour force belong to unions, which are grouped under the National Trade Union Centre.

INTERNATIONAL TRADE

The Foreign Investment Act of 1990 permits foreign investors to acquire land and shares in local companies, and to form companies. External debt was US$2,652m. in 2005.

Imports and Exports

In 2005 imports totalled US$5,725m. (US$4,894m. in 2004) and exports US$9,672m. (US$6,403m. in 2004). Crude petroleum accounts for 19% of imports, and refined petroleum 29% of exports. Trinidad and Tobago is the world's leading exporter of ammonia and methanol.

The principal import sources in 2005 were the USA (29·2%), Brazil (13·5%), Venezuela (6·0%), Colombia (5·6%) and Nigeria (5·1%). The main export markets in 2005 were the USA (58·6%), Jamaica (7·5%), France (4·4%), Barbados (4·3%) and Guyana (2·9%).

COMMUNICATIONS

Roads

In 2002 there were about 8,320 km of roads, of which 51·1% were paved. There were 177,900 passenger cars and 38,700 commercial vehicles in 2002.

Civil Aviation

There is an international airport at Port-of-Spain (Piarco) and in Tobago (Crown Point). In 2001 Piarco handled 1,725,111 passengers (1,317,811 on international flights) and 29,673 tonnes of freight. The national carrier is Caribbean Airlines, which has flights to 11 international destinations as well as operating domestic services. In 2003 scheduled airline traffic of Trinidad and Tobago-based carriers flew 31m. km, carrying 1,084,000 passengers (972,000 on international flights).

Shipping

Sea-going shipping totalled 27,000 GRT in 2002; 3,687,328 tonnes of cargo were handled at Port-of-Spain in 1999. There is a deep-water harbour at Scarborough (Tobago). The other main harbour is Point Lisas.

Telecommunications

International and domestic communications are provided by Telecommunications Services of Trinidad and Tobago (TSTT) by means of a satellite earth station and various high-quality radio circuits. The marine radio service is also maintained by TSTT. In 2008 there were 307,000 main (fixed) telephone lines; mobile phone subscribers numbered 1,505,000 in 2008 (112·9 per 100 persons). There were 228,000 PCs in use in 2006 and 227,000 internet users in 2008.

Postal Services

In 2003 there were 135 post offices.

SOCIAL INSTITUTIONS

Justice

The High Court consists of the Chief Justice and 11 puisne judges. In criminal cases a judge of the High Court sits with a jury of 12 in cases of treason and murder, and with nine jurors in other cases. The Court of Appeal consists of the Chief Justice and seven Justices of Appeal. In hearing appeals, the Court is comprised of three judges sitting together except when the appeal is from a Summary Court or from a decision of a High Court judge in chambers. In such cases two judges would comprise the Court. There is a limited right of appeal from it to the Privy Council. There are three High Courts and 12 magistrates' courts. There is an *Ombudsman*. Trinidad and Tobago was one of ten countries to sign an agreement in Feb. 2001 establishing a Caribbean Court of Justice to replace the British Privy Council as the highest civil and criminal court. In the meantime the number of signatories has risen to twelve. The court was inaugurated at Port-of-Spain on 16 April 2005.

The death penalty is authorized. There were ten executions in 1999, although none since.

The population in penal institutions in Oct. 2003 was 3,991 (307 per 100,000 of national population).

Education

In 2007 there were 130,242 pupils enrolled in primary schools with 8,171 teaching staff and 98,490 pupils in secondary schools with 7,041 teaching staff. There were 4,121 pupils enrolled in the three Technical and Vocational schools for the period 1998–99. In 2005 there were 16,920 students in higher education and 1,800 academic staff. The University of the West Indies campus in St Augustine (1999–2000) had 7,585 students and 477 academic staff. 1,307 of the students were from other countries.

Adult literacy was 98·4% in 2004.

In 2001 public spending on education came to 4·2% of GDP and accounted for 13·4% of total government expenditure.

Health

In 1999 there were 1,171 physicians, 189 dentists, 500 pharmacists and 71 hospitals and nursing homes with 4,384 beds. There were 1,936 nurses and midwives and 1,486 nursing assistants in government institutions.

RELIGION

In 2001, 29·9% of the population were Roman Catholics (under the Archbishop of Port-of-Spain), 24·2% Hindus, 19·2% Protestants, 11·2% Anglicans (under the Bishop of Trinidad and Tobago) and 6·0% Muslims.

CULTURE

Broadcasting

State-owned Caribbean New Media Group (CNMG) runs a television network and two radio stations. TV6 is the dominant private television service. Several private radio stations are operated by the Trinidad Broadcasting Company. 305,000 households had television receivers (colour by NTSC) in 2005.

Press

There were four daily newspapers in 2006 (*Trinidad Express*, *Trinidad Guardian*, *Newsday* and *The Wire*), with a total circulation of 160,000. Weekly newspapers include *Punch*, *The Catholic News*, *The Probe*, *The Bomb*, *Show Time*, *The Independent* and *The Chutney Star*. *The Mirror* is published three times a week.

Tourism
There were 457,387 tourist arrivals in 2006, plus a record 85,859 cruise ship visitors. Receipts from tourism in 2004 totalled US$568m.

Festivals
Religious festivals: the Feast of La Divina Pastora, or Sipari Mai, a Catholic and Hindu celebration of the Holy Mother Mary; Saint Peter's Day Celebration, the Patron Saint of Fishermen; Hosein, or Hosay, a Shia Muslim festival; Phagwah, a Hindu spring festival; Santa Rosa, a Caribbean Amerindian festival; Eid-ul-Fitr, the Muslim festival at the end of Ramadan; Divali, the Hindu festival of light; Christmas. Cultural festivals: Carnival (on 7 and 8 March in 2011); Spiritual Baptist Shouter Liberation Day, a recognition of the Baptist religion; Indian Arrival Day, commemorating the arrival of the first East Indian labourers; Sugar and Energy Festival; Pan Ramajay, a music festival of all types; Emancipation, a recognition of the period of slavery; Tobago Heritage Festival, celebrating Tobago's traditions and customs; Parang Festival, traditional folk music of Christmas; Pan Jazz Festival; Music Festival, predominantly classical music but Indian and Calypso are included.

When a public holiday falls on a Sunday, the holiday is celebrated on the Monday immediately following.

Libraries
The National Library and Information System Authority (NALIS), created in 1998, administers the public libraries. The new National Library building, in Port-of-Spain, was opened in March 2003. In 2004 there were 21 branch libraries, three mobile libraries and the San Fernando Carnegie Free Library.

Theatre and Opera
Trinidadian theatre was pioneered by the Trinidad Theatre Workshop, a company founded by Nobel Prize winner Derek Walcott in 1959. The Bagasse Company was founded in 1986.

DIPLOMATIC REPRESENTATIVES

Of Trinidad and Tobago in the United Kingdom (42 Belgrave Sq., London, SW1X 8NT)
Acting High Commissioner: Gail Guy.

Of the United Kingdom in Trinidad and Tobago (19 St Clair Ave., Port-of-Spain)
High Commissioner: Eric Jenkinson, OBE.

Of Trinidad and Tobago in the USA (1708 Massachusetts Ave., NW, Washington, D.C., 20036)
Ambassador: Glenda Morean-Phillip.

Of the USA in Trinidad and Tobago (15 Queen's Park West, Port-of-Spain)
Ambassador: Vacant.
Chargé d'Affaires a.i: Len Kusnitz.

Of Trinidad and Tobago to the United Nations
Ambassador: Marina Annette Valere.

Of Trinidad and Tobago to the European Union
Ambassador: Vacant.
Chargé d'Affaires a.i: Gerard Greene.

FURTHER READING

Meighoo, Kirk, *Politics in a Half-Made Society: Trinidad and Tobago, 1925–2001.* 2003

Williams, E., *History of the People of Trinidad and Tobago.* 1993

Central library: The Central Library of Trinidad and Tobago, Queen's Park East, Port-of-Spain.

National Statistical Office: Central Statistical Office, 80 Independence Square, Port-of-Spain.

Website: http://cso.gov.tt

TUNISIA

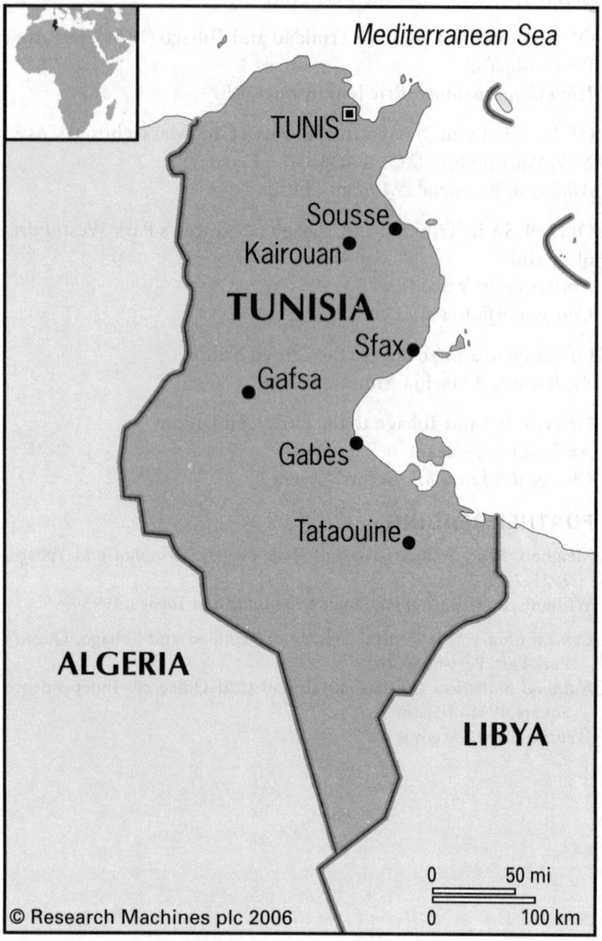

Jumhuriya at-Tunisiya
(Republic of Tunisia)

Capital: Tunis
Population estimate, 2010: 10·37m.
GDP per capita, 2007: (PPP$) 7,520
HDI/world rank: 0·769/98

KEY HISTORICAL EVENTS

Tunisia's earliest inhabitants included the semi-nomadic Berbers, whose descendants still live in North Africa's Atlas Mountains. Phoenician merchants established trading settlements throughout the central and western Mediterranean from the 10th century BC and founded the port of Carthage in 814 BC. By the 5th century Carthage had become the most powerful city in the western Mediterranean with an empire extending from present-day Morocco to Egypt and controlling Sardinia, the Balearic Islands, Malta and much of Sicily. A rival to the Roman Empire, the city was eventually destroyed in the Third Punic War. From 146 BC Tunisia was absorbed into the Roman Empire and its people sold into slavery.

Emperor Augustus supervised the reconstruction of Carthage in the 2nd century AD, although frequent revolts broke out as the Roman Empire waned. In 429 Tunisia was captured by the Vandals who ruled until ousted by the Byzantines in 534. Uqba ibn Nafa led an Arab Muslim army into Tunisia in 670 and founded the city of Kairouan. Most of the indigenous Berber population converted to Islam and the region, known as Ifriqiya, became part of the powerful caliphate centred on Baghdad where it reached its apotheosis under Harun al Rashid (786–809). Tunisia subsequently came under the control of the local Aghlabid dynasty and then under the Fatimids from 909. Bedouin Arabs from the Nile Valley (the Banu Hilal) entered the region around 1000 and from the 12th century Tunisia came under the orbit of the al-Muwahhid empire. The Berber general Abd al-Wahid ibn Abi Hafs wrested control in 1207, heralding three centuries of rule by the Hafsid dynasties. The port of Tunis was made capital and the term 'Tunisia' gradually replaced 'Ifriqiya'.

Ottoman troops advanced from the east in the early 16th century, forcing the Hafsids into an alliance with the Spanish Habsburgs in 1534. However, the Ottomans seized Tunis in 1574. Direct control from İstanbul was superseded by rule through local governors known as beys, such as the Muradid beys who made powerful alliances in the Tunisian hinterland and held sway from the 1640s to 1705. Al-Husayn ibn Ali (ruled 1705–40) founded the Husaynid dynasty and oversaw a period of prosperity through trade and piracy.

As the Ottoman Empire declined Tunisia became increasingly autonomous but attempts to establish a republic in the mid-19th century failed owing to a weak economy and political unrest. In 1869 Tunisia declared itself bankrupt and an international commission from France, Great Britain and Italy took over the country's finances. In 1881 Tunisia was invaded by France which alleged that Tunisian troops had been threatening the French colony of Algeria. Tunisia became a French protectorate despite Italian opposition.

Nationalist sentiment increased after the First World War and the Destour (Constitutional) Party was set up in 1920. Its more radical successor, the Neo-Destour Party, was established by Habib Bourguiba in 1934. Seen as a threat to colonial rule, Bourguiba was imprisoned in 1938. After the Second World War France offered increased autonomy. Nationalists, dismayed at the slow pace of reform, staged mass strikes and demonstrations in 1950. Violent protest increased until France granted internal self-government in 1955, with full independence on 20 March 1956. A constitutional assembly was established and Bourguiba became prime minister. The monarchy was abolished and a republic established the following year, with Bourguiba as president.

Taking a socialist secular line, Bourguiba promoted social and economic development. In 1975 the constitution was amended so that Bourguiba could be president-for-life. The late 1970s saw hardship and growing discontent. A general strike in Jan. 1978 erupted into riots and violence flared again in 1980 and 1984. Islamist groups became increasingly influential and Bourguiba was overthrown in a bloodless coup in 1987. His successor, Zine El Abidine Ben Ali, introduced democratic reforms, eased restrictive press laws and opened negotiations with Islamic groups, although he refused to recognize the prominent al-Nahda party. Ben Ali was re-elected president in 1994, 1999, 2004 and most recently in Oct. 2009.

TERRITORY AND POPULATION

Tunisia is bounded in the north and east by the Mediterranean Sea, west by Algeria and south by Libya. The area is 164,150 sq. km, including inland waters. In 2004 the census population was 9,910,872; density, 60 per sq. km. Estimate, 2008, 10,326,600. In 2005, 65·3% of the population were urban.

The UN gives an estimated population for 2010 of 10·37m.

The areas and populations (2004 census) of the 24 governorates:

	Land area in sq. km	Population
Aryanah (Ariana)	498	422,246
Bajah (Béja)	3,558	304,501
Banzart (Bizerta)	3,685	524,128
Bin Arus (Bin Arous)	761	505,773
Jundubah (Jendouba)	3,102	416,608
Kaf (Le Kef)	4,965	258,790
Madaniyin (Médénine)	8,588	432,503
Mahdiyah (Mahdia)	2,966	377,853
Manubah (Manouba)	1,060	335,912
Munastir (Monastir)	1,019	455,590
Nabul (Nabeul)	2,788	693,890
Qabis (Gabès)	7,175	342,630
Qafsah (Gafsa)	8,990	323,709
Qasrayn (Kassérine)	8,066	412,278
Qayrawan (Kairouan)	6,712	546,209
Qibili (Kebili)	22,084	143,218
Safaqis (Sfax)	7,545	855,256
Sidi Bu Zayd (Sidi Bouzid)	6,994	395,506
Silyanah (Siliana)	4,631	233,985
Susah (Sousse)	2,621	544,413
Tatawin (Tataouine)	38,889	143,524
Tawzar (Tozeur)	4,719	97,526
Tunis	346	983,861
Zaghwan (Zaghouan)	2,768	160,963

Tunis, the capital, had 728,500 inhabitants at the 2004 census. Other main cities (2004 census in 1,000): Sfax, 265·1; Ariana, 240·7; Sousse, 173·0; Ettadhamen, 118·5; Kairouan, a holy city of the Muslims, 117·9; Gabès, 116·3; Bizerta, 114·4.

The official language is Arabic but French is the main language in the media, commercial enterprise and government departments. Berber-speaking people form less than 1% of the population.

SOCIAL STATISTICS

2004 estimates: births, 167,000; deaths, 59,000; marriages (2005), 74,000. Rates (2004 estimates): birth, 16·8 per 1,000 population; death, 6·0. Annual population growth rate, 2000–05, 1·0%. In 2005 the most popular age range for marrying was 30–34 for males and 25–29 for females. Expectation of life, 2007, was 71·8 years for males and 76·0 for females. Infant mortality, 2005, 20 per 1,000 live births; fertility rate, 2004, 1·9 births per woman.

CLIMATE

The climate ranges from warm temperate in the north, where winters are mild and wet and the summers hot and dry, to desert in the south. Tunis, Jan. 48°F (8·9°C), July 78°F (25·6°C). Annual rainfall 16" (400 mm). Bizerta, Jan. 52°F (11·1°C), July 77°F (25°C). Annual rainfall 25" (622 mm). Sfax, Jan. 52°F (11·1°C), July 78°F (25·6°C). Annual rainfall 8" (196 mm).

CONSTITUTION AND GOVERNMENT

The Constitution was promulgated on 1 June 1959 and reformed in 1988. The office of President-for-life was abolished and Presidential elections were to be held every five years. On 26 May 2002 a referendum was held that abolished the three-term limit on the presidency with 99% of votes cast in favour of doing so and of raising the age limit for incumbent presidents from 70 to 75 years. The results were viewed with scepticism by human rights groups and opposition figures who saw the referendum as an attempt by President Zine El Abidine Ben Ali to retain power. Ben Ali was scheduled to retire in 2004 after his third presidential term but remains the president.

The 2002 referendum also replaced the unicameral *Majlis al-Nuwaab* (*National Assembly*) with a bicameral parliament consisting of the *Majlis al-Nuwaab* (*Chamber of Deputies*) and an upper house, the *Majlis al-Mustasharin* (*Chamber of Councillors*). The *President* and the *Chamber of Deputies* are elected simultaneously by direct universal suffrage for a period of five years while the *Chamber of Councillors* is appointed for six years with half of its members renewed every three years. The *Chamber of Deputies* has 214 seats, with 161 members elected in multi-member constituencies and the remainder through a closed-list proportional representation system. The *Chamber of Councillors* has 126 seats. Two-thirds of its members are elected by indirect suffrage and the remaining third is appointed by the president.

National Anthem

'Humata al Hima' ('Defenders of the Homeland'); words by Mustapha al Rafi and Abdoul Kacem Chabbi, tune by M. A. Wahab.

GOVERNMENT CHRONOLOGY

Presidents since 1957. (ND = Neo-Destour Party; PSD = Socialist Destourian Party; RCD = Constitutional Democratic Rally)

1957–87	ND, PSD	Habib Ali Bourguiba
1987–	PSD, RCD	Zine El Abidine Ben Ali

RECENT ELECTIONS

Presidential and parliamentary elections were held on 25 Oct. 2009; turnout was 89·4%. President Zine El Abidine Ben Ali (Constitutional Democratic Rally/RCD) was re-elected by 89·6% of votes cast against 5·0% for Mohamed Bouchiha (Popular Unity Party), 3·8% for Ahmed Inoubli (Unionist Democratic Union) and 1·6% for Ahmed Brahim (Ettajdid Movement). In the parliamentary elections the ruling RCD won 161 of 214 available National Assembly seats with 84·6% of votes cast, the Movement of Social Democrats 16 with 4·6%, the Popular Unity Party 12 with 3·4%, the Unionist Democratic Union 9 with 2·6%, the Social Liberal Party 8 with 2·2%, the Green Party for Progress 6 with 1·7% and the Ettajdid Movement 2 with 0·5%.

CURRENT ADMINISTRATION

President: Zine El Abidine Ben Ali; b. 1936 (RCD; sworn in 7 Nov. 1987, re-elected in March 1994, Oct. 1999, Oct. 2004 and Oct. 2009).

In March 2010 the cabinet comprised:

Prime Minister: Mohamed Ghannouchi; b. 1941 (RCD; sworn in 17 Nov. 1999).

Special Adviser to the President and Spokesman for the President: Abdelaziz Ben Dhia. *Minister of Agriculture, Water Resources and Fisheries:* Abdessalem Mansour. *Communication Technologies:* Mohamed Naceur Ammar. *Communications:* Oussama Romdhani. *Culture and Heritage Preservation:* Abderraouf El Basti. *Defence:* Ridha Grira. *Development and International Co-operation:* Mohamed Nouri Jouini. *Education:* Hatem Ben Salem. *Environment and Sustainable Development:* Nadhir Hamada. *Equipment, Housing and Land Development:* Slaheddine Malouche. *Finance:* Mohamed Ridha Chalghoum. *Foreign Affairs:* Kamel Morjane. *Higher Education, Scientific Research and Technology:* Bechir Tekkari. *Industry and Technology:* Afif Chelbi. *Interior and Local Development:* Rafik Belhaj Kacem. *Justice and Human Rights:* Lazhar Bououni. *Public Health:* Mondher Zenaidi. *Religious Affairs:* Boubaker El Akhzouri. *Social Affairs, Solidarity and Tunisians Abroad:* Naceur El Gharbi. *State Property and Land Affairs:* Zouheir M'dhaffar. *Tourism:* Slim Tlatli. *Trade and Handicrafts:* Ridha Ben Mosbah. *Transport:* Abderrahim Zouari. *Vocational Training and Employment:* Mohamed Agrebi. *Women's Affairs, Family, Children and Seniors:* Bibya Chihi. *Youth, Sport and Physical Education:* Samir Labidi. *Minister Director of the Presidential Office:* Ahmed Iyadh Ouederni.

Government Website: http://www.ministeres.tn

CURRENT LEADERS

Zine-Al Abidine Ben Ali

Position
President

Introduction
Appointed prime minister by Habib Bourguiba, Tunisia's leader from 1957, Zine El Abidine Ben Ali then became president after Bourguiba was deposed in 1987. Despite advocating moderate liberalization, his human rights record remains a source of international unease. He had been scheduled to retire in 2004, but secured support in a referendum for changes to the constitution allowing him a further two terms in office. He was re-elected in Oct. 2009.

Early Life
Ben Ali was born in Hammam Sousse on 3 Sept. 1936. As a teenager he became involved in the nationalist movement, which culminated in Tunisia's independence from France in 1956. He resumed his studies abroad, training at the military academy at Saint-Cyr and at the artillery school of Châlons-sur-Marne in France, and later studying in the USA where he obtained a degree in electronic engineering.

Returning to Tunisia, he was appointed head of military security from 1964–74 and became a military attaché to the Tunisian embassy in Morocco. Upon his return, he was made head of national security and later served as ambassador to Poland. In 1986 he was appointed minister of the interior.

Ben Ali was active in fighting militant fundamentalist groups. In Oct. 1987 he was appointed prime minister by President Habib Bourguiba. Bourguiba was dogged by rumours of intermittent senility and in Nov. was declared unfit to rule by a committee of doctors and deposed in a bloodless coup. Ben Ali replaced him as president.

Career in Office
As leader of the Constitutional Democratic Rally (RCD), Ben Ali has been overwhelmingly re-elected in March 1994, Oct. 1999, Oct. 2004 and Oct. 2009. The cancellation of the 1992 election at a point when the opposition seemed likely to win prompted international criticism. Scheduled to retire in 2004, he initiated changes to the constitution in 2002 to allow him to govern for another two terms. In the Oct. 2004 elections the main opposition group, the Progressive Democratic Party, withdrew its candidates two days before polling, arguing that the vote would be worthless.

Ben Ali inherited an economically stable country and has overseen a reduction in the poverty rate and improving literacy levels. He has expressed his commitment to furthering women's rights and has authorized the release of some political prisoners, but human rights groups remain critical of his regime. He has maintained tight control of the media and the treatment of journalists and political opponents critical of his rule has caused international concern.

Ben Ali was re-elected chairman of the RCD in July 2008 and president, with 90% of the vote, in Oct. 2009.

DEFENCE

Selective conscription is for one year. Defence expenditure in 2006 totalled US$435m. (US$43 per capita), representing 1·4% of GDP.

Army
Strength (2007) 27,000 (22,000 conscripts). There is also a National Guard numbering 12,000.

Navy
In 2007 naval personnel totalled around 4,800. Forces are based at Bizerta, Sfax and Kelibia.

Air Force
The Air Force operated 27 combat capable aircraft in 2007, including 12 F-5E/F Tiger II fighters and 12 Aero L-59s. Personnel (2007) 4,000.

INTERNATIONAL RELATIONS

Tunisia is a member of the UN, World Bank, IMF and several other UN specialized agencies, WTO, IOM, International Organization of the Francophonie, Islamic Development Bank, OIC, African Development Bank, African Union and League of Arab States.

ECONOMY

In 2006 agriculture accounted for 11·1% of GDP, industry 27·8% and services 61·1%.

Overview
Tunisia's economic record compares favourably with other developing countries, particularly those on the African continent. After a balance of payments crisis in the mid-1980s, the government introduced reforms to stabilize the economy. Steps were taken to improve macroeconomic policy, foster the non-public sector and liberalize prices and controls. The annual growth rate has been positive every year since 1987. In the 1990s the economy grew steadily at an average annual rate of 5%. Inflation and annual budget deficits have been brought down from previous high levels and poverty has been reduced.

In 1995 Tunisia signed an association agreement with the EU (the first by the EU with a Mediterranean neighbour), which was scheduled to phase out tariffs on both sides over 12 years. Tunisia's trade is highly oriented towards the EU, with France, Italy, Germany and Spain the country's most important trading partners in descending order. However, Tunisia's textile exporters lost EU market share to Asia as a result of the end of the Multi-Fibre Agreement quota system in Jan. 2005.

The economy is diversified relative to many of its non-European neighbours, with significant mining, tourism, energy, manufacturing and agricultural sectors. In the early 2000s growth was strong, except in 2002 when a drought hit the agricultural sector and growth slowed to 1·7%. Growth accelerated to 5·4% in 2006 from 4·0% in 2005, the result of a recovery in agricultural output, a strong services sector and the expansion of non-textile manufacturing. However, unemployment remains high at 14·2%. In 2007 the XIth Plan was approved with the aim of boosting annual growth to 6·1% over the period 2007–11 in order to create a high-value, knowledge-based economy.

Currency
The unit of currency is the *Tunisian dinar* (TND) of 1,000 *millimes*. The currency was made convertible on 6 Jan. 1993. Foreign exchange reserves were US$4,069m. and gold reserves 218,000 troy oz in July 2005. Inflation was 3·1% in 2007 and 5·0% in 2008. Total money supply was 8,339m. dinars in June 2005.

Budget
The fiscal year is the calendar year. Budgetary central government revenue totalled 7,611m. dinars in 2003 (7,342m. dinars in 2002) and expenditure 6,976m. dinars (6,624m. dinars in 2002). Taxes accounted for 87·1% of total revenues in 2003.

VAT is 18%.

Performance
Real GDP growth was 4·6% in 2008 (6·3% in 2007). Tunisia's total GDP in 2008 was US$40·2bn.

Banking and Finance
The Central Bank of Tunisia (*Governor*, Taoufik Baccar) is the bank of issue. In 2003 there were 12 commercial banks, six development banks, two merchant banks and five 'offshore' banks.

There is a small stock exchange (51 companies trading in 2007).

ENERGY AND NATURAL RESOURCES

Environment

Tunisia's carbon dioxide emissions from the consumption and flaring of fossil fuels in 2008 were the equivalent of 2·1 tonnes per capita.

Electricity

Installed capacity was 2·9m. kW in 2004. Production in 2004 was 13·07bn. kWh; consumption per capita was 1,313 kWh.

Oil and Gas

Oil production (2008) was 4·2m. tonnes with 0·6bn. bbls in proven reserves. Natural gas production (2004), 2·1bn. cu. metres; proven reserves were 65bn. cu metres in 2007.

Minerals

Mineral production (in 1,000 tonnes) in 2004: phosphate rock, 8,051; salt, 1,117; iron ore, 256; zinc ore (concentrated), 53; lead, 5.

Agriculture

There are five agricultural regions: the *north*, mountainous with large fertile valleys; the *northeast*, with the peninsula of Cap Bon, suited for the cultivation of oranges, lemons and tangerines; the *Sahel*, where olive trees abound; the *centre*, a region of high tablelands and pastures; and the *desert* of the south, where dates are grown.

In 2007 the economically active agricultural population was an estimated 787,000. Large estates predominate; smallholdings are tending to fragment, partly owing to inheritance laws. In 2006 356,000 ha. were irrigated. There were 2·76m. ha. of arable land in 2007 and 2·17m. ha. of permanent crops. There were 140 tractors and ten harvester-threshers per 10,000 ha. of arable land in 2006. The main crops are cereals, citrus fruits, tomatoes, melons, olives, dates, grapes and olive oil. Production, 2003 estimates (in 1,000 tonnes): wheat, 1,150; tomatoes, 800; melons and watermelons, 520; olives, 500; barley, 345; potatoes, 345; chillies and green peppers, 206; onions, 120; dates, 115; grapes, 115; oranges, 106; apples, 100; peaches and nectarines, 82; olive oil, 73; grapefruit and pomelos, 72; pears, 68.

Livestock, 2003 estimates (in 1,000): sheep, 6,850; goats, 1,400; cattle, 760; camels, 231; asses, 230; mules, 81; horses, 57. Livestock products, 2003 estimates (in 1,000 tonnes): meat, 250; milk, 989; eggs, 83.

Forestry

In 2005 there were 1·06m. ha. of forests (6·8% of the land area). Timber production in 2007 was 2·38m. cu. metres.

Fisheries

In 2005 the catch amounted to 109,117 tonnes, almost exclusively from marine waters.

INDUSTRY

Production (in 1,000 tonnes): cement (2003), 6,039; sulphuric acid (1999), 4,858; phosphoric acid (2003), 629; residual fuel oil (2004), 595; lime (2007), 394; distillate fuel oil (2004), 432; crude steel (2002), 220. Industry accounted for 28·8% of GDP in 2001, with manufacturing contributing 18·5%.

Labour

The economically active population totalled 3,593,200 in 2007. Out of 3,085,100 in employment, 48·6% were engaged in commerce and services, 32·1% in industry, mining, energy and construction, and 19·3% in agriculture and fisheries. Unemployment was 14·1% in 2007.

Trade Unions

The Union Générale des Travailleurs Tunisiens won 27 seats in the parliamentary elections of 1 Nov. 1981. There are also the Union Tunisienne de l'Industrie, du Commerce et de l'Artisanat (UTICA, the employers' union) and the Union National des Agriculteurs (UNA, farmers' union).

INTERNATIONAL TRADE

In Feb. 1989 Tunisia signed a treaty of economic co-operation with the other countries of Maghreb: Algeria, Libya, Mauritania and Morocco. Foreign debt was US$17,789m. in 2005.

Tunisia was the first country to sign a partnership agreement with the European Union, becoming fully integrated in its free trade zone in Jan. 2008.

Imports and Exports

Trade in US$1m.:

	2000	*2001*	*2002*	*2003*	*2004*
Imports f.o.b.	8,093	8,997	8,981	10,297	12,114
Exports f.o.b.	5,840	6,628	6,857	8,027	9,679

Main imports in 2004: textiles, 18·8%; electrical machinery, 11·9%; petroleum, 9·6%; motor vehicles, 7·3%; iron and steel, 6·0%. Main exports in 2004: textiles, 37·2%; electrical machinery, 13·9%; petroleum, 9·5%; olive oil, 5·9%; leather products, 5·2%.

The main import suppliers in 2004 were France (24·9%), Italy (18·9%), Germany (8·4%) and Spain (5·3%). Main export markets in 2004 were France (33·1%), Italy (25·3%), Germany (9·2%) and Spain (6·1%).

COMMUNICATIONS

Roads

The road network covered 19,232 km in 2004, including 262 km of motorways and 4,080 km of national roads. 65·8% of all roads in 2004 were paved. In 2007 there were 746,700 passenger cars, 300,500 lorries and vans, 10,100 buses and coaches, and 5,300 motorcycles and mopeds. There were 10,681 road accidents in 2007 resulting in 1,497 fatalities.

Rail

In 2007 there were 2,165 km of railways on metre and 1,435 mm gauge track. Passenger-km travelled in 2007 came to 1,487m. and freight tonne-km to 2,197m. There is a tramway in Tunis (32 km).

Civil Aviation

The national carrier, Tunisair, is 74·5% state-owned. Scheduled airline traffic of Tunisian-based carriers flew 43·2m. km and carried 2,098,300 passengers in 2005. There are six international airports. In 2001 Monastir (Habib Bourguiba) handled 3,894,000 passengers (3,885,000 on international flights) and 800 tonnes of freight. Tunis-Carthage handled 3,315,000 (3,061,000 on international flights) and 21,800 tonnes of freight. Djerba handled 2,161,000 passengers (1,945,000 on international flights) and 700 tonnes of freight.

Shipping

There are ports at Tunis, its outer port Tunis-Goulette, Sfax, Sousse and Bizerta, all of which are directly accessible to ocean-going vessels. The ports of La Skhirra and Gabès are used for the shipping of Algerian and Tunisian oil. In 2002 sea-going shipping totalled 186,000 GRT, including oil tankers 20,000 GRT. In 2005 vessels totalling 77,249,000 GRT entered ports and vessels totalling 77,255,000 GRT cleared.

Telecommunications

Tunisia had 1,273,300 fixed line telephone subscribers (126·5 per 1,000 persons) in 2007 and 7,842,600 mobile phone subscribers. There were 767,500 PCs in use in 2007 (75·0 per 1,000 persons) and 1,722,190 internet users.

Postal Services

In 2003 there were 1,221 post offices. A total of 123m. pieces of mail were processed in 2003.

SOCIAL INSTITUTIONS

Justice

There are 51 magistrates' courts, 13 courts of first instance, three courts of appeal (in Tunis, Sfax and Sousse) and the High Court in Tunis.

A Personal Status Code was promulgated on 13 Aug. 1956 and applied to Tunisians from 1 Jan. 1957. This raised the status of women, made divorce subject to a court decision, abolished polygamy and decreed a minimum marriage age.

The population in penal institutions in 2004 was approximately 26,000 (263 per 100,000 of national population).

Education

The adult literacy rate in 2003 was 74·3% (83·4% among males and 65·3% among females). All education is free from primary schools to university. Attendance at school is compulsory between the ages of six and 16. In 2007 there were 1,068,822 pupils in primary schools with 58,879 teaching staff and 1,268,219 pupils in secondary schools with 79,735 teaching staff.

In 2007 there were 13 public universities including the Virtual University of Tunis. There are a number of other public and private higher education institutions. There were 326,185 students in higher education in 2007 with 18,117 academic staff.

In 2005 public expenditure on education came to 7·2% of GDP and accounted for 20·8% of total government expenditure.

Health

There were 172 hospitals and 2,079 basic health centres in 2007 with a capacity of 17,998 beds. In 2006 there were 9,653 doctors, 1,858 dentists, 30,812 paramedical staff and 2,255 pharmacists.

RELIGION

The constitution recognizes Islam as the state religion. In 2001 there were 9·72m. Sunni Muslims. The remainder of the population follow other religions, including Roman Catholicism.

CULTURE

World Heritage Sites

Tunisia has eight sites on the UNESCO World Heritage List: the Amphitheatre of El Jem (inscribed on the list in 1979); the Site of Carthage (1979); the Medina of Tunis (1979); Ichkeul National Park (1980); the Punic Town of Kerkuane and its Necropolis (1985 and 1986); the Medina of Sousse (1988); Kairouan (1988); and Dougga/Thugga (1997).

Broadcasting

The state-run Établissement de la Radio et Télévision Tunisienne (ERTT) operates two national television services and several radio networks. A private satellite TV channel (Hannibal TV) started broadcasting in 2005. Egyptian and pan-Arab satellite TV stations can also be received. Colour is by SECAM V. The state monopoly on radio broadcasting ended in 2003; Radio Mosaïque FM became the first private station. Radio Tunisie Internationale is an external service. Number of TV sets (2006): 2·30m.

Press

In 2000 there were seven daily newspapers with a total average circulation of 179,963, giving a rate of 19 per 1,000 inhabitants. Press freedom is severely limited.

Tourism

In 2005 there were 6,378,000 foreign tourists, spending US$2·78bn.

DIPLOMATIC REPRESENTATIVES

Of Tunisia in the United Kingdom (29 Prince's Gate, London, SW7 1QG)
Ambassador: Hamida M'rabet Labidi.

Of the United Kingdom in Tunisia (Rue du Lac Windermere, Les Berges du Lac, 1053, Tunis)
Ambassador: Christopher O'Connor.

Of Tunisia in the USA (1515 Massachusetts Ave., NW, Washington, D.C., 20005)
Ambassador: Habib Mansour.

Of the USA in Tunisia (Les Berges du Lac, 1053 Tunis)
Ambassador: Gordon Gray.

Of Tunisia to the United Nations
Ambassador: Ghazi Jomaa.

Of Tunisia to the European Union
Ambassador: Abdessalem Hetira.

FURTHER READING

Hassan, Fareed M. A., *Tunisia: Understanding Successful Socioeconomic Development.* 2005

Murphy, Emma C., *Economic and Political Change in Tunisia: From Bourguiba to Ben Ali.* 2003

National Statistical Office: Institut National de la Statistique, 70 Rue Ech-cham, BP 265 CEDEX, Tunis.
Website: http://www.ins.nat.tn

TURKEY

Türkiye Cumhuriyeti
(Republic of Turkey)

Capital: Ankara
Population estimate, 2010: 75·71m.
GDP per capita, 2007: (PPP$) 12,955
HDI/world rank: 0·806/79

KEY HISTORICAL EVENTS

There is evidence of human habitation in Anatolia (Asia Minor) from around 7500 BC. Catal Huyuk (on the Konya Plain) flourished between 6500 and 5800 BC to become one of the world's largest and most important Neolithic sites. Between 1800 and 1200 BC much of Anatolia came under Hittite rule, initially centred on Cappadocia. The artistic work of the Hittites shows a high level of culture with Babylonian and Assyrian influence. Greek colonies were established around the Anatolian coast from around 700 BC including Byzantium, which was founded by Greeks from Megara in 667 BC. Anatolia was conquered by Persians in the 6th century BC.

Alexander the Great defeated the Persians around 330 BC. After his death there was a long civil war between the Seleucids and the Ptolemies, while the kingdoms of Galatia, Armenia, Pergamum, Cappadocia, Bithynia and Pontus all established footholds in the region. Rome gained dominance around the 2nd century BC and brought stability and prosperity. Turkey was home to some of the earliest centres of Christianity, such as Antioch (modern Antalya) and Ephesus. In AD 324 the Emperor Constantine began the construction of a new capital at Byzantium. Constantinople became the centre of the Byzantine (Eastern Roman) Empire, which peaked under Justinian in the mid-6th century.

Muslim Arab forces attacked Constantinople in the 670s and besieged the city again in 716 but were repelled, thwarting the expansion of the Umayyad Caliphate ruled by Umar II. Constantine V (741–75) led Christian Byzantine forces eastward to recover lands in Anatolia. The Seljuk Turks, whose origins were in central Asia, established dominance over much of Anatolia during the 11th century, led by Alp Arslan. They came under threat during the Crusades and were overrun by the Mongol hordes from 1243. The Ottoman principality was one of a number of small Turkish states that emerged in Anatolia amid the retreat of the Mongols and the waning of the Seljuk and Byzantine empires. Osman I led the early phase of Ottoman expansion, conquering Byzantine towns in northwest Anatolia in the early 14th century. Sultan Mehmed II seized Constantinople in 1453 and went on to establish Ottoman dominance in the Balkans and the Aegean. The empire expanded to its fullest extent under Suleiman the Magnificent (1494–1566), taking in North Africa, the Levant, Persia, Anatolia, the Balkans and the Caucasus.

From the early 17th century the Ottoman empire fell into a long decline, its power weakening rapidly in the 19th century. The Kingdom of Greece broke away from Ottoman rule in 1832, with Serbs, Romanians, Armenians, Albanians, Bulgarians and Arabs demanding independence soon afterwards. Attempts by Turkey to redefine itself were further hindered in the 20th century by the First World War, during which it sided with Germany. In fighting with Greece over disputed territory from 1920–22, the Turkish National Movement was led by Mustafa Kemal (Atatürk: 'Father of the Turks'), who wanted a republic based on a modern secular society. Turkey became a republic on 29 Oct. 1923, with Ankara its capital. Islam ceased to be the official state religion in 1928 and women were given the same rights to employment and education as men, although they were not able to vote in national elections until 1934. İsmet İnönü became president following Kemal's death in 1938 and steered a neutral course through the Second World War. The 1950s were marked by a policy of firm alignment with the West, and Turkey joined NATO in 1952.

On 27 May 1960 the Turkish army overthrew the government and party activities were suspended. A new constitution was approved in a referendum held on 9 July 1961. On 12 Sept. 1980 the Turkish armed forces again drove the government from office. A new constitution was enforced after a national referendum on 7 Nov. 1982. In the face of mounting Islamization of government policy, the Supreme National Security Council reaffirmed its commitment to the secular state. On 6 March 1997 Prime Minister Necmettin Erbakan, leader of the pro-Islamist Welfare Party, promised to combat Muslim fundamentalism but in June he was forced to resign by a campaign led by the army.

There are ongoing quarrels with Greece over the division of Cyprus, oil rights under the Aegean and ownership of uninhabited islands close to the Turkish coast. In Feb. 2000 the Kurdish Workers' Party (PKK) formally abandoned its 15-year rebellion and adopted the democratic programme urged by its imprisoned leader, Abdullah Öçalan. Despite being a long-term ally of the USA, the Turkish parliament voted against allowing US troops to attack Iraq from its southeastern border in 2003, with the incumbent Justice and Development Party (AKP) government harbouring concerns about the possibility of an independent Kurdish state arising from a divided Iraq.

An associate member of the EU since 1964, Turkey is in the process of accession pending the completion of negotiations. However, significant hurdles remain, including the status of Northern Cyprus, the issue of human rights in Turkey and lukewarm support for its accession in some EU states.

In Aug. 2007 Abdullah Gül became president, following several months of political wrangling over concerns that his Islamist background might compromise Turkey's constitutional secularism.

TERRITORY AND POPULATION

Turkey is bounded in the west by the Aegean Sea and Greece, north by Bulgaria and the Black Sea, east by Georgia, Armenia and Iran, and south by Iraq, Syria and the Mediterranean. The area (including lakes) is 780,580 sq. km (301,382 sq. miles). At the 1990 census the population was 56,473,035. The most recent census took place in Dec. 2007, by when the population had increased to 70,586,256. The United Nations population estimate for 2007 was 73,004,000. In 2005, 67·3% of the population lived in urban areas.

The UN gives an estimated population for 2010 of 75·71m.

Turkish is the official language. Kurdish and Arabic are also spoken.

Some 12m. Kurds live in Turkey. In Feb. 1991 limited use of the Kurdish language was sanctioned, and in Aug. 2002 parliament legalized Kurdish radio and television broadcasts.

Area and population of the 81 provinces at the 2007 census:

	Area in sq. km	*Population*		*Area in sq. km*	*Population*
Adana	12,788	2,006,650	Kahraman-maraş	14,327	1,004,414
Adıyaman	7,614	582,762	Karabük	4,074	218,463
Afyon[1]	14,230	701,572	Karaman	9,163	226,049
Ağri	11,376	530,879	Kars	9,442	312,205
Aksaray	7,626	366,109	Kastamonu	13,108	360,366
Amasya	5,520	328,674	Kayseri	16,917	1,165,088
Ankara	25,706	4,466,756	Kilis	1,338	118,457
Antalya	20,591	1,789,295	Kırıkkale	4,365	280,234
Ardahan	5,576	112,721	Kırklareli	6,550	333,256
Artvin	7,436	168,092	Kırşehir	6,570	223,170
Aydin	8,007	946,971	Kocaeli	3,626	1,437,926
Balıkesir	14,292	1,118,313	Konya	38,157	1,959,082
Bartın	2,140	182,131	Kütahya	11,875	583,910
Batman	4,694	472,487	Malatya	12,313	722,065
Bayburt	3,652	76,609	Manisa	13,810	1,319,920
Bilecik	4,307	203,777	Mardin	8,891	745,778
Bingöl	8,125	251,552	Mersin	15,853	1,595,938
Bitlis	6,707	327,886	Muğla	13,338	766,156
Bolu	10,037	270,417	Muş	8,196	405,509
Burdur	6,887	251,181	Nevşehir	5,467	280,058
Bursa	10,963	2,439,876	Niğde	7,312	331,677
Çanakkale	9,737	476,128	Ordu	6,001	715,409
Çankırı	7,388	174,012	Osmaniye	3,320	452,880
Çorum	12,820	549,828	Rize	3,920	316,252
Denizli	11,868	907,325	Sakarya	4,817	835,222
Diyarbakır	15,355	1,460,714	Samsun	9,579	1,228,959
Düzce	1,014	323,328	Şanliurfa	18,584	1,523,099
Edirne	6,276	396,462	Siirt	5,406	291,528
Elazığ	9,153	541,258	Sinop	5,862	198,412
Erzincan	11,903	213,538	Şırnak	7,172	416,001
Erzurum	25,066	784,941	Sivas	28,488	638,464
Eskişehir	13,652	724,849	Tekirdağ	6,218	728,396
Gaziantep	6,207	1,560,023	Tokat	9,958	620,722
Giresun	6,934	417,505	Trabzon	4,685	740,569
Gümüşhane	6,575	130,825	Tunceli	7,774	84,022
Hakkâri	7,121	246,469	Uşak	5,341	334,115
Hatay	5,403	1,386,224	Van	19,069	979,671
Iğdir	3,539	181,866	Yalova	674	181,758
Isparta	8,933	419,845	Yozgat	14,123	492,127
İstanbul	5,220	12,573,836	Zonguldak	3,481	615,890
İzmir	11,973	3,739,353			

[1]Since renamed Afyonkarahisar.

Population of cities of over 250,000 inhabitants in 2007:

İstanbul	10,757,327	Samsun	423,859
Ankara	3,763,591	Malatya	383,185
İzmir	2,606,294	Sakarya	377,683
Bursa	1,431,172	Kahramanmaraş	371,463
Adana	1,366,027	Erzurum	338,073
Gaziantep	1,175,042	Van	331,986
Konya	967,055	Denizli	323,151
Antalya	775,157	Elazığ	319,381
Kayseri	696,833	Gebze	310,815
Mersin	623,861	Sivas	294,402
Diyarbakır	592,557	Batman	293,024
Eskişehir	570,825	Manisa	281,890
Urfa	472,238	Sultanbeyli	272,758

SOCIAL STATISTICS

Births, 2001, 1,507,000; deaths, 463,000. 2001 birth rate per 1,000 population, 21·8; death rate, 6·7. 2001 marriages, 453,213 (rate of 6·5 per 1,000 population); divorces (2000), 34,862 (rate of 0·5 per 1,000 population). Annual population growth rate, 2000–05, 1·3%. Expectation of life, 2007, was 69·4 years for males and 74·2 for females. Infant mortality, 2005, 26 per 1,000 live births. Fertility rate, 2004, 2·4 births per woman. In 1999 the most popular age for marrying was 25–29 for males and 20–24 for females.

CLIMATE

Coastal regions have a Mediterranean climate, with mild, moist winters and hot, dry summers. The interior plateau has more extreme conditions, with low and irregular rainfall, cold and snowy winters, and hot, almost rainless summers. Ankara, Jan. 32·5°F (0·3°C), July 73°F (23°C). Annual rainfall 14·7" (367 mm). İstanbul, Jan. 41°F (5°C), July 73°F (23°C). Annual rainfall 28·9" (723 mm). İzmir, Jan. 46°F (8°C), July 81°F (27°C). Annual rainfall 28" (700 mm).

CONSTITUTION AND GOVERNMENT

On 7 Nov. 1982 a new constitution was adopted following its overwhelming endorsement in a referendum. The constitution was amended following a referendum on 21 Oct. 2007. The amendment states that in future the *President* of Turkey will be directly elected by the people, rather than by Parliament, as is currently the case. Furthermore, the President will be able to serve for up to two five-year terms, rather than being limited to a single seven-year term. This reform will come into force at the next presidential election (scheduled for Aug. 2014), and does not apply to the incumbent President. The Presidency is not an executive position; the President may not be linked to a political party but can veto laws and official appointments. There is a 550-member *Turkish Grand National Assembly*, elected by universal suffrage (at 18 years and over) for five-year terms (four after the next parliamentary election) by proportional representation. There is a *Constitutional Court* consisting of 15 regular and five alternating members.

National Anthem

'Korkma! Sönmez bu şafaklarda yüzen al sancak' ('Be not afraid! Our flag will never fade'); words by Mehmed Akif Ersoy, tune by Zeki Üngör.

GOVERNMENT CHRONOLOGY

(AKP = Justice and Development Party; ANAP = Motherland Party; AP = Justice Party; CGP = Republican Reliance Party; CHP = Republican People's Party; DP = Democrat Party; DSP = Democratic Left Party; DYP = True Path Party; RP = Welfare Party; n/p = non-partisan)

Heads of State since 1938.

Presidents of the Republic

1938–50	CHP	İsmet İnönü
1950–60	DP	Mahmut Celal Bayar

Chairman of the Committee of National Unity (MBK) and Head of State

1950–61	military	Cemal Gürsel

Presidents of the Republic

1961–66	n/p (ex-military)	Cemal Gürsel
1966–73	n/p (ex-military)	Cevdet Sunay
1973–80	n/p (ex-military)	Fahri Korutürk

Chairman of the National Security Council (MGK) and Head of State

1980–82	military	Kenan Evren

Presidents of the Republic

1982–89	n/p (ex-military)	Kenan Evren
1989–93	ANAP	Turgut Özal
1993–2000	DYP	Süleyman Demirel

2000–07	n/p	Ahmet Necdet Sezer
2007–	AKP	Abdullah Gül

Prime Ministers since 1921.

1921–22	military	Mustafa Fevzı Çakmak
1922–23	n/p	Hüseyin Rauf Bey
1923–23	CHP	Ali Fehti Okyar
1923–24	CHP	Mustafa İsmet İnönü
1924–25	CHP	Ali Fethi Okyar
1925–37	CHP	Mustafa İsmet İnönü
1937–39	CHP	Mahmut Celal Bayar
1939–42	CHP	Refık İbrahım Saydam
1942–46	CHP	Mehmet Şükrü Saraçoğlu
1946–47	CHP	Mehmet Recep Peker
1947–49	CHP	Hasan Saka
1949–50	CHP	Mehmet Şemsettin Günaltay
1950–60	DP	Adnan Menderes
1960–61	military	Cemal Gürsel
1961–65	CHP	Mustafa İsmet İnönü
1965	n/p	Suat Hayri Ürgüplü
1965–71	AP	Süleyman Demırel
1971–72	n/p	İsmaıl Nıhat Erım
1972–73	CGP	Ferit Melen
1973–74	n/p	Mehmet Naim Talu
1974–74	CHP	Mustafa Bülent Ecevıt
1975–77	AP	Süleyman Demırel
1977–77	CHP	Mustafa Bülent Ecevıt
1977–78	AP	Süleyman Demırel
1978–79	CHP	Mustafa Bülent Ecevıt
1979–80	AP	Süleyman Demırel
1980–83	n/p	Saim Bülent Ulusu
1983–89	ANAP	Turgut Özal
1989–91	ANAP	Yıldırım Akbulut
1991	ANAP	Ahmet Mesut Yılmaz
1991–93	DYP	Süleyman Demırel
1993–96	DYP	Tansu Çıller
1996	ANAP	Ahmet Mesut Yılmaz
1996–97	RP	Necmettin Erbakan
1997–99	ANAP	Ahmet Mesut Yılmaz
1999–2002	DSP	Mustafa Bülent Ecevıt
2002–03	AKP	Abdullah Gül
2003–	AKP	Recep Tayyip Erdoğan

RECENT ELECTIONS

Parliamentary elections were held on 22 July 2007. The ruling Justice and Development Party (AKP)—former Islamists—won 341 of the 550 seats with 46·7% of votes cast, against 112 seats and 20·8% for the Republican People's Party (CHP) and 71 seats and 14·3% for the Nationalist Movement Party. The remaining seats went to independents. There were 11 parties that failed to secure the 10% of votes needed to gain parliamentary representation. Turnout was 84·4%.

In the presidential elections held on 27 April and 6 May 2007, the AKP nominee Abdullah Gül failed to gain the backing of enough members of the assembly. Amid concerns that Gül's Islamist background would compromise the country's secular status, the presidential vote was postponed until after early parliamentary elections that were brought forward to July. In the second presidential elections of 2007 the first round was held on 20 Aug. Abdullah Gül received 347 votes, Sabahattin Çakmakoğlu (Nationalist Movement Party) 70 and Tayfun İçli (Democratic Left Party) 13, with 23 votes blank and one invalid. As 367 votes (a two-thirds majority) were required to be elected in either the first or second round a second round was held on 24 Aug., with Gül receiving 337 votes, Çakmakoğlu 71 and İçli 14; 24 votes were blank. A third round was therefore held on 28 Aug. at which only a simple majority was required. Gül received 339 votes, Çakmakoğlu 70 and Içli 13.

CURRENT ADMINISTRATION

President: Abdullah Gül; b. 1950 (sworn in 28 Aug. 2007).

In March 2010 the government comprised:

Prime Minister: Recep Tayyip Erdoğan; b. 1954 (AKP; sworn in 14 March 2003).

Deputy Prime Ministers: Bülent Arınç (also *Minister of State*); Ali Babacan (also *Minister of State in Charge of the Economy*); Cemil Çiçek (also *Minister of State*).

Minister of Agriculture and Rural Affairs: Mehmet Mehdi Eker. *Culture and Tourism:* Ertuğrul Günay. *Defence:* Vecdi Gönül. *Education:* Nimet Çubukçu. *Energy and Natural Resources:* Taner Yıldız. *Environment and Forestry:* Veysel Eroğlu. *Finance:* Mehmet Şimşek. *Foreign Affairs:* Ahmet Davutoğlu. *Health:* Recep Akdağ. *Industry and Trade:* Nihat Ergün. *Interior:* Beşir Atalay. *Justice:* Sadullah Ergin. *Labour and Social Security:* Ömer Dinçer. *Public Works and Housing:* Mustafa Demir. *Transport:* Binali Yıldırım. *Ministers of State:* Mehmet Aydın; Egemen Bağış; Mehmet Zafer Çağlayan; Faruk Çelik; Selma Aliye Kavaf; Faruk Nafiz Özak; Hayati Yazıcı; Cevdet Yilmaz.

The *Speaker* is Mehmet Ali Şahin.

Office of the Prime Minister (Turkish only):
http://www.basbakanlik.gov.tr

CURRENT LEADERS

Abdullah Gül

Position

President

Introduction

Abdullah Gül was elected president on 28 Aug. 2007. His background in Islamist politics and membership of political parties banned under the country's secular constitution stoked widespread concern when he was nominated as a presidential candidate. A former prime minister and close ally of the incumbent premier, Recep Tayyip Erdoğan, Gül has taken a moderate line since 2001, advocating a pro-Western agenda and eventual EU membership.

Early Life

Abdullah Gül was born on 29 Oct. 1950 in Kayseri, central Turkey. He graduated in economics from İstanbul University in 1971 and began an academic career there. From 1980–83 he taught economics at the Sakarya School of Engineering and Architecture. As a devout Muslim, and having received a PhD in 1983, he joined the Islamic Development Bank (in Jeddah, Saudi Arabia) as an economist, a position he held for eight years.

Returning to Turkey in 1991, Gül entered politics. Campaigning for the Islamist Welfare Party, he was elected representative for Kayseri. He rose through the party ranks to become state minister and speaker for the Erbakan government in 1996. He was initially critical of Turkey's overtures towards the West and opposed EU membership. His ambitions were curtailed in 1997 by a military-backed campaign to oust the government. The following year a ban was imposed on the Welfare Party which was said to threaten the secular constitution. Gül, along with around 100 Welfare Party members, joined the Virtue Party, contesting its leadership in 2000. This party was banned in June 2001.

In Aug. 2001 Gül and other ex-party members joined Recep Tayyip Erdoğan's newly formed Justice and Development Party (AKP), which presented itself as pro-Western and democratic. In the 2002 parliamentary elections Erdoğan led a high profile campaign, but was barred from standing because he had a criminal conviction for reading an Islamic poem at a political rally. The AKP found popularity with voters dissatisfied with the ruling government and won an outright victory to replace the three-party coalition. Two weeks after the election the party nominated Gül for the premiership.

Career in Office

As prime minister, Gül wanted to prove that Turkey could operate as both a Muslim and democratic state. The AKP campaigned on a pro-Western agenda and was committed to steering Turkey towards EU membership. Gül announced plans to reform the laws on the freedom of expression and human rights that had been partly responsible for Turkey's omission from the EU expansion plans in 2002. He supported further privatization and sought to achieve a modernized and efficient administration, reducing his cabinet from 36 to 26 places. In Dec. 2002 President Ahmet Necdet Sezer agreed to constitutional changes that would allow Erdoğan to stand for a parliamentary seat and thus become eligible for the premiership.

In the run-up to the US-led invasion of Iraq in March 2003, parliament refused to allow the USA to deploy troops on Turkish territory, though permission was given to use its airspace. Erdoğan returned to parliament in a by-election the same month and was appointed prime minister. Gül became foreign minister, working to achieve an EU accession date, although this was thwarted by the continued impasse over the status of Cyprus.

Prime Minister Erdoğan announced in April 2007 that Gül would be the AKP candidate in the 2007 presidential election. This sparked Turkey's most serious political crisis in a decade, with mass protests in the big cities in support of secularism. The military also warned that it would defend secularism. The AKP was forced to call early elections for 22 July, which it won decisively. Gül was re-nominated as the AKP candidate and on 28 Aug. he was elected president in the third round of voting. The chief of the general staff absented himself from the swearing-in ceremony.

In his inauguration speech, Gül sought to dispel secularist fears of an AKP Islamist agenda. However, parliament's vote to remove the ban on women wearing headscarves at universities in Feb. 2008 was seized on by secularists as evidence that Gül was attempting to introduce Islamic rule. In June the Constitutional Court rejected the move in a ruling that was viewed as a setback for the AKP government.

In July 2009 Gül approved controversial government legislation allowing civilian courts to prosecute military personnel for offences against the state.

Recep Tayyip Erdoğan

Position

Prime Minister

Introduction

Recep Tayyip Erdoğan became prime minister in March 2003. He led the Justice and Development Party (AKP) to victory at the general elections of Nov. 2002 but, because of a previous criminal conviction, was banned from standing for a parliamentary seat thus making him ineligible for the premiership. A constitutional amendment allowed him to stand for election in early 2003 and he subsequently replaced his party deputy, Abdullah Gül, as prime minister. For many years a prominent Islamist spokesman, Erdoğan has remoulded himself as a pro-European moderate conservative, although he continues to cause unease among many of Turkey's secularists. He identified Turkey's admission to the European Union as his government's top priority and introduced reforms that paved the way for the opening of membership talks from Oct. 2005. However, the EU negotiations have since been hampered by Turkey's continuing refusal to recognize the government of Greek Cyprus. In July 2007 Erdoğan was returned for a second term as premier as the AKP won parliamentary elections with almost 47% of the vote.

Early Life

Erdoğan was born in 1954 in Rize and his family later moved to İstanbul. He attended a Koranic college before graduating in economics in 1981 from Marmara University in İstanbul where he met Necmettin Erbakan, who would become Turkey's first Islamist premier. From the mid-1980s Erdoğan became active in the pro-Islamist Welfare Party. In 1994 he was made mayor of İstanbul and was noted for running an effective administration free of corruption.

The Welfare Party was outlawed in 1998 for contravening Turkey's secularist constitution. In the same year Erdoğan was imprisoned for inciting racial hatred when he read a pro-Islamist poem at a political rally. He served four months of a ten-month sentence. Following the banning of the Virtue Party (the successor party to Welfare) in June 2001, Erdoğan established the AKP, espousing pro-Western and democratic policies, and the party won an outright victory at the general elections of Nov. 2002. Erdoğan remained the AKP's figurehead while Abdullah Gül, his deputy and a former foreign minister, was named prime minister.

Following constitutional changes in Dec. 2002, Erdoğan was able to successfully contest a by-election in Feb. 2003. Gül stood down to be replaced by Erdoğan the following month.

Career in Office

Despite the AKP's Islamic roots, Erdoğan believes that Turkey can operate as both a Muslim and democratic state within Europe. He has voiced his commitment to democratization—including liberalizing laws on freedom of expression and human rights that were partly responsible for Turkey's omission from the EU expansion plans advanced in 2002—and confirmed his support for further privatization.

Erdoğan's early tenure was dominated by the US-led invasion of neighbouring Iraq from March 2003. Mirroring Turkish popular opinion, the government refused to allow the deployment of US ground troops on its territory, endangering aid and loans from the USA and IMF until the Turkish parliament agreed to the use of its airspace by the US air force. Turkey's deployment of troops in Kurdish-held northern Iraq to block any attempts to establish a Kurdish separatist state meanwhile caused international concern.

Turkey's wish for early entry into the EU was undermined by the failure in 2003 of the leaders of the Greek and Turkish sectors of Cyprus to agree on UN proposals for the island's reunification. A revised UN reunification plan was put to both sides in twin referenda in April 2004, which was endorsed by Turkish Cypriots but rejected by Greek Cypriots. Because both sides had to approve the proposals, the island remained divided as it joined the EU the following month. To fulfil the political criteria for EU membership, Erdoğan had pushed through parliament a series of reform packages in 2003 to bring Turkey into line with EU legislation. Human rights were addressed with guarantees of freedom of speech for the Kurdish minority, and the influence of the military in the political system—seen as unacceptable by EU countries—was curbed. In 2004 a protocol abolishing the death penalty was signed and penal reforms introduced tougher measures to prevent torture and violence against women. Once Erdoğan's government had introduced the necessary legislative and constitutional reforms, and made a deal accepting Cyprus as an EU member, the European Council agreed in Dec. 2004 to open accession negotiations with Turkey which began in Oct. 2005.

Bomb attacks in Turkey in 2006 were attributed to Islamist extremists and Kurdish separatists. In Sept. Erdoğan rejected a ceasefire by the Kurdish Workers' Party (PKK), denouncing the group as a terrorist organization. Later in the year, the EU partially suspended Turkey's membership negotiations because of the government's failure to open its ports and airports to Cypriot traffic. Erdoğan emphasized that the accession process would nevertheless continue, but also said that he expected the EU to take steps to end the Turkish Cypriot community's economic isolation.

In early 2007 Erdoğan decided not to stand for election to the state presidency in view of strong secular opposition, and instead put forward foreign minister Abdullah Gül as the AKP candidate. Gül was equally unpalatable to secular and particularly military opinion, leading to a political stand-off in the National Assembly. However, Erdoğan consequently called an early general election for July, which returned the AKP to power, and in Aug. the new parliament endorsed Gül as president,.

Turkey's diplomatic relations with the USA again came under strain in Oct. 2007 after a US congressional committee recognized the mass killing of Armenians in 1915 during Ottoman rule as genocide. Meanwhile, Erdoğan's government adopted a harder line towards Kurdish separatist insurgents based in northern Iraq, leading to cross-border Turkish air and artillery assaults towards the end of the year and in early 2008.

Secular concerns over the AKP's Islamist intentions resurfaced in Feb. 2008 when parliament voted to remove the ban on women wearing headscarves at universities. The Constitutional Court overturned the proposed law in June and then only narrowly ruled in July against a petition by state prosecutors to ban the AKP for alleged anti-secular activities, which could have led to a political crisis and Erdoğan's disqualification from politics.

In Oct. 2008 the controversial trial began of suspected members of a shadowy nationalist group accused of attempting to provoke a military coup against the government. By the end of Jan. 2009 around 200 people had been arrested for their alleged involvement in the conspiracy, including military figures, journalists, academics and politicians.

In an effort to revive Turkey's EU membership ambitions, Erdoğan visited Brussels in Jan. 2009 for the first time in four years. At the end of the month he clashed publicly with the president of Israel at the World Economic Forum in Davos over Israeli military action against the Palestinian Gaza Strip.

In March 2009 the AKP did unexpectedly badly in local elections, taking a sharply reduced share of the vote compared to the 2007 general election.

In a new initiative to end the conflict with Kurdish separatists, and despite nationalist opposition, Erdoğan's government put forward measures in parliament in Dec. 2009 to extend Kurdish linguistic and cultural rights and to limit the military presence in the mainly Kurdish southeast of the country.

Despite Turkey's rejection of charges of genocide in Armenia in 1915, in Oct. 2009 the two governments agreed on a framework to normalize relations, subject to parliamentary ratification by both sides.

DEFENCE

The President of the Republic is C.-in-C. of the armed forces. The *National Security Council*, chaired by the Prime Minister and comprising military leaders and the ministers of defence and the economy, also functions as a *de facto* constitutional watchdog. Reforms passed in July 2003 in preparation for EU membership aimed to reduce the influence of the military in the political system. In Oct. 2003 the Turkish parliament voted to send 10,000 troops to Iraq, which would have made it the third largest force in the country after the USA and the UK, but the Iraqi Governing Council rejected the plan.

Conscription is 15 months for privates, 12 months for reserve officers and six months for privates who have completed a university degree.

In 2006 defence expenditure totalled US$11,630m., with spending per capita US$165. The 2006 expenditure represented 2·9% of GDP.

Army

Strength (2007) 660,700 (including 325,000 conscripts and 258,700 reservists). There is also a paramilitary gendarmerie-cum-national guard of 150,000. In addition around 36,000 Turkish troops are stationed in Northern Cyprus.

Navy

The fleet includes 13 diesel submarines and 24 frigates. The main naval base is at Gölcük in the Gulf of İzmit. Other bases are located at Aksaz-Karaağaç, Antalya, Bartın, Çanakkale, Erdek, Eregli, Foça, İskenderun, İstanbul, İzmir and Mersin. There are three naval shipyards: Gölcük, İzmir and Taşkizak.

The naval air component operates 11 combat capable helicopters. There is a 3,100-strong Marine Regiment. The Coast Guard numbers 3,250 (including 1,400 conscripts).

Personnel in 2007 totalled 48,600 (34,500 conscripts) including marines and coast guard.

Air Force

The Air Force is organized as two tactical air forces, with headquarters at Eskişehir and Diyarbakır. There were 435 combat capable aircraft in operation in 2007 including F-5A/Bs, F-4E Phantoms and F-16C/Ds.

Personnel strength (2007), 60,000.

INTERNATIONAL RELATIONS

Relations between Turkey and Iraq have long been strained over activity in the borderlands of northern Iraq by Kurdish separatist movements including the PKK. In Dec. 2007 Turkey launched air strikes on Iraqi territory against the PKK and in Feb. 2008 Turkish troops made a week-long incursion into northern Iraq to fight rebels.

Turkey is a member of the UN, World Bank, IMF and several other UN specialized agencies, WTO, Council of Europe, OSCE, BSEC, BIS, IOM, Islamic Development Bank, NATO, OECD, OIC, Asian Development Bank, ECO and an associate member of WEU, and has applied to join the European Union. At the EU's Helsinki Summit in Dec. 1999 Turkey was awarded candidate status. Talks on membership began in Oct. 2005 but Turkey is unlikely to join the EU before 2015 at the earliest.

ECONOMY

Agriculture accounted for 9·5% of GDP in 2006, industry 28·7% and services 61·8%.

Overview

Long-term macroeconomic mismanagement has left the country vulnerable to financial crises. In recent years strong growth has been interrupted by sharp recessions in 1994, 1999, 2001 and 2008. In 2000 Turkey committed to a programme of wide-ranging structural reforms, strong fiscal adjustment and a pre-announced exchange rate crawl. However, the financial and currency crisis in 2001 caused the collapse of the three-year exchange rate-based stabilization programme and brought the country to the brink of debt default. A strengthened programme was introduced in May 2001 with additional IMF support. Key structural reforms emphasized public sector standards, liberalizing markets and building a strong banking sector. The crisis led to Turkey's central bank becoming independent. Tight fiscal policies, IMF-inspired reforms and central bank independence have brought Turkey improved macroeconomic health.

Debt ratios have been reduced significantly, interest rates slashed and inflation brought under control in spite of high crude oil prices. Inflation fell to 8·2% in 2005, its lowest level in 30 years, but increased to over 10% in 2008 as problems in world markets caused sharp depreciations of the lira. External debt has fallen, from 77·8% in 2001 to 53·4% in 2004 and 34·0% in 2007.

In 2003–07 annual GDP growth averaged nearly 7% but the global economic slowdown in 2007 hit Turkey hard. Oil and food import prices surged and unemployment reached 13·6% in mid-2009, higher than during the 2001 crisis. GDP growth dropped to 0·9% in 2008, with domestic political tensions adding to the country's vulnerability.

Agriculture accounts for roughly a third of total employment. The largest industrial sector is textiles and clothing, while the auto, autoparts and electronics industries have grown strongly. In 2005 the Baku–Tblisi–Ceyhan oil pipeline opened, bringing up to 1m. bbls per day from the Caspian to the Ceyhan Marine Terminal in Turkey. The country also has one of the most successful tourism sectors in the region. In 1996 a customs union was established with the EU and in 2005 Turkey began the EU accession process, providing further incentive to maintain macroeconomic and structural reforms.

Currency

The unit of currency is the Turkish *lira* (TRY) of 100 *kuruş*. It was introduced on 1 Jan. 2005 as the new Turkish lira—officially abbreviated as YTL—replacing the Turkish lira (TRL) at 1 new Turkish lira = 1m. Turkish lira. On 1 Jan. 2009 the 'new' was removed and its official name is again just 'Turkish lira'. Gold reserves were 3·73m. troy oz in Sept. 2009 and foreign exchange reserves US$69,387m. Inflation rates (based on OECD statistics):

1999	*2000*	*2001*	*2002*	*2003*	*2004*	*2005*	*2006*	*2007*	*2008*
64·9%	54·9%	54·4%	45·0%	21·6%	8·6%	8·2%	9·6%	8·8%	10·4%

Total money supply in July 2009 was YTL88,267m.

Budget

The fiscal year is the calendar year. Budgetary central government revenue totalled YTL218,858m. in 2007 (YTL189,578m. in 2006) and expenditure YTL206,695m. (YTL167,990m. in 2006). Tax revenues were YTL157,913m. in 2007. VAT is 18%, with reduced rates of 8% and 1%.

Performance

Real GDP growth rates (based on OECD statistics):

1999	*2000*	*2001*	*2002*	*2003*	*2004*	*2005*	*2006*	*2007*	*2008*
–3·4%	6·8%	–5·7%	6·2%	5·3%	9·4%	8·4%	6·9%	4·7%	0·9%

GDP contracted by 4·7% in 2009 according to TurkStat, the national statistics institute. Total GDP was US$794·2bn. in 2008.

Banking and Finance

The Central Bank (Merkez Bankası; *Governor*, Durmuş Yılmaz) is the bank of issue. In 2003 there were 36 commercial banks (three state-owned, two under the Deposit Insurance Fund, 18 private, 13 foreign), and 14 development and investment banks. The Central Bank's assets were US$51·66bn. in 2003. The assets and liabilities of deposit money banks were US$25·8bn. Turkey's two state-owned banks, Ziraat Bankası (the Agricultural Bank, with a public mission to lend to farmers) and Halk Bankası (with a public mission to lend to small and medium sized enterprises), together accounted for 27% of total assets in the Turkish banking sector in Dec. 2002. Ziraat Bankası is Turkey's largest bank, with 18·1% of total assets as of March 2003. The second largest bank (and the largest private bank) is Türkiye İş Bankası. A comprehensive restructuring plan for Ziraat has been developed with the assistance of international consultants and the IMF in preparation for privatization. In May 2007 the government sold off 25% of its shares in Halk Bankası although initial plans to fully privatize the bank were cancelled.

Foreign direct investment in 2008 was US$18,198m., down from US$22,046m. in 2007. In Sept. 2000 a Banking Regulation and Supervision Board was established to serve as an independent banking regulator. In Dec. 2000 the IMF gave Turkey an emergency loan of US$7·5bn. as the country experienced a financial crisis after ten banks were placed in receivership. The economic crisis continued as the lira was floated on the international market and lost 30% of its value against the US dollar in the space of 12 hours in Feb. 2001. Within a week the lira had been devalued by approximately 40%. In April 2001 Turkey secured a further US$10bn. loan from the IMF and the World Bank. This was followed in Feb. 2002 with a three-year US$16bn. loan from the IMF, taking total loans paid or pledged to USS$31bn.

There is a stock exchange in İstanbul (ISE).

ENERGY AND NATURAL RESOURCES

Environment

In 2008 Turkey's carbon dioxide emissions from the consumption and flaring of fossil fuels were the equivalent of 3·6 tonnes per capita.

Electricity

In 2004 installed capacity was 36·82m. kW (12·65m. kW hydro-electric); gross production in 2004 was 150·7bn. kWh and consumption per capita 2,112 kWh. Demand for electricity was forecast to exceed supply by 2009 and a deal to import electricity from Armenia was brokered in Sept. 2008. However, demand fell in the early 2009 as a result of a reduction in industrial activity and falling domestic consumption.

Oil and Gas

Crude oil production (2004) was 2,251,000 tonnes. Reserves in 2005 were 296m. bbls. Refinery distillation output in 2004 amounted to 26·0m. tonnes. In 2004, 23,918,000 tonnes of crude petroleum were imported. Natural gas output was 708m. cu. metres in 2004.

Accords for the construction of an oil pipeline from Azerbaijan through Georgia to the Mediterranean port of Ceyhan in southern Turkey (the BTC pipeline) were signed in Nov. 1999. Work on the pipeline began in Sept. 2002 and it was officially opened in May 2005.

A gas pipeline from Baku in Azerbaijan (the South Caucasus pipeline) through Georgia to Erzurum was commissioned in June 2006.

Minerals

Turkey is rich in minerals, and is a major producer of chrome.

Production of principal minerals (in 1,000 tonnes, in 2002 unless otherwise indicated) was: lignite (2004), 44,431; iron, 3,433; magnesite, 3,044; copper (gross weight), 2,940; boron, 2,214; salt, 2,197; coal (2004), 1,946; chrome, 327.

Agriculture

In 2002 there were 6,745,000 households engaged in farming, of which 148,190 were engaged purely in animal farming. Holdings are increasingly fragmented by the custom of dividing land equally amongst sons. Agriculture accounts for 45% of the workforce but only 11·5% of GDP. In 2002 Turkey had 25·94m. ha. of arable land and 2·59m. ha. of permanent crops. 5·2m. ha. were irrigated in 2002. Vineyards, orchards and olive groves occupied 2,776,000 ha. in 2005.

Production (2005, in 1,000 tonnes) of principal crops: wheat, 21,500; sugar beets, 15,181; tomatoes, 10,050; barley, 9,500; melons and watermelons, 5,795; maize, 4,200; potatoes, 4,090; grapes, 3,850; apples, 2,570; dry onions, 2,070; peppers, 1,829; cucumbers, 1,745; cottonseed (2004), 1,426; oranges, 1,202; sunflower seeds, 975; cotton lint (2004), 936; aubergines, 930; apricots, 860; olives, 800; cabbage, 675; chick-peas, 600; lemons, 600; hazelnuts, 530; mandarins, 526. Turkey is the largest producer of apricots and hazelnuts.

Livestock, 2002 (in 1,000): sheep, 26,972; cattle, 10,548; goats, 7,022; asses, 462; horses, 271; buffaloes, 138; mules, 97; chickens, 218,000. Livestock products, 2002 (in 1,000 tonnes): milk, 8,409; meat, 1,376; eggs, 543; cheese, 113; honey, 75.

Forestry

There were 10·18m. ha. of forests in 2005, or 13·2% of the total land area. Timber production was 17·66m. cu. metres in 2007.

Fisheries

The catch in 2005 totalled 426,496 tonnes (380,381 tonnes from marine waters). Aquaculture production, 2002, 61,165 tonnes (mainly trout).

INDUSTRY

The leading companies by market capitalization in March 2009 were: Turkcell, a telecommunications company (US$10·7bn.); Akbank (US$8·8bn.); and Türk Telekom (US$8·1bn.).

Production in 2005 (in 1,000 tonnes unless otherwise stated): cement, 41,100; crude steel, 20,965; iron and steel bars, 11,854; residual fuel oil (2004), 7,845; distillate fuel oil, 6,389; petrol (2004), 3,479; coke (2002), 2,598; sugar, 1,928; nitrogenous fertilizers, 1,525; paper and paperboard, 1,005; cotton yarn, 459; olive oil, 301; polyethylene, 274; pig iron, 178; sulphuric acid, 165; PVC, 133; cotton woven fabrics, 609m. metres; woollen woven fabrics, 32m. metres; carpets, 58,034,681 sq. metres; TV sets, 20,790,123 units; refrigerators, 5,098,866 units; cars, 635,137 units; lorries, 39,324 assembled units; tractors, 38,800 units; cigarettes, 104,170 tonnes.

Labour

Out of 22,047,000 people in employment in 2005 (16,346,000 men), 6,493,000 were engaged in agriculture, hunting, forestry and fisheries, 4,083,000 in manufacturing, 3,610,000 in wholesale and retail trade/repair of motor vehicles, motorcycles and personal and household goods and 1,246,000 in public administration and defence/compulsory social security. The unemployment rate for the quarter ending Sept. 2009 was 13·1%. The gross monthly minimum wage was YTL666 in Jan. 2009.

Trade Unions

There are four national confederations (including Türk-İş and Disk) and six federations. There are 35 unions affiliated to Türk-İş and 17 employers' federations affiliated to Disk, whose activities were banned on 12 Sept. 1980. In 2001 labour unions totalled 104 and employers' unions 49. Some 2·75m. workers belonged to unions in 2003. Membership is forbidden to civil servants (including schoolteachers). There were 52 strikes in 2000 involving 18,705 workers, with 368,475 working days lost.

INTERNATIONAL TRADE

Total foreign debt in June 2005 was US$171,059m. A customs union with the EU came into force on 1 Jan. 1996.

Imports and Exports

Imports (c.i.f.) in 2006 totalled US$138,581m. (US$116,774m. in 2005) and exports (f.o.b.) US$85,526m. (US$73,476m. in 2005). Chief imports (2005) in US$1m.: machinery and transport equipment, 37,809; manufactured goods, 19,990; chemicals and related products, 16,167; petroleum and petroleum products, 12,413; crude materials excluding fuels, 7,661. Chief exports: machinery and transport equipment, 21,509; apparel and clothing accessories, 11,833; textile yarn, fabrics and finished articles, 7,076; food and live animals, 6,512; iron and steel, 5,827.

The main import suppliers in 2006 (in US$1m.) were: Russia, 17,645; Germany, 14,653; China, 9,601; Italy, 8,597; France, 7,212; USA, 6,221. Main export markets, 2006: Germany, 9,684; UK, 6,813; Italy, 6,753; USA, 5,061; France, 4,604; Spain, 3,721. The EU accounted for 40·7% of imports and 54·3% of exports in 2006.

COMMUNICATIONS

Roads

In 2006 there were 427,099 km of roads, including 1,987 km of motorway. In 2007 road vehicles in use included 6,472,200 passenger cars, 2,619,700 lorries and vans, 561,700 buses and coaches and 2,003,500 motorcycles and mopeds. There were 5,002 fatalities from road accidents in 2007.

Rail

Total length of railway lines in 2005 was 8,697 km (1,435 mm gauge), of which 2,336 km were electrified. Passenger-km travelled in 2005 came to 5·04bn. and freight tonne-km to 9·15bn. There are metro systems operating in Adana, Ankara, Bursa, İstanbul and İzmir.

Civil Aviation

There are international airports at İstanbul (Atatürk), Dalaman (Muğla), Ankara (Esenboga), İzmir (Adnan Menderes), Adana and Antalya. The national carrier is Turkish Airlines, which is 49·1% state-owned. In 2006 it flew 207·2m. km and carried 16,946,000 passengers (8,041,000 on international flights). In 2001 İstanbul handled 12,601,431 passengers (8,827,732 on international flights) and 161,359 tonnes of freight. Antalya was the second busiest airport for passenger traffic, with 9,170,469 passengers (8,638,634 on international flights) and Ankara third with 3,159,315 passengers (2,107,013 on domestic flights).

Shipping

In 2000 the merchant shipping fleet consisted of 1,153 vessels totalling 5,833,000 GRT, including oil tankers 625,000 GRT. The main ports are: İskenderun, İstanbul, İzmir, Mersin, Samsun and Trabzon.

In 2001 vessels totalling 125,997,000 GRT entered ports and vessels totalling 96,867,000 GRT cleared.

Telecommunications

In 2008 there were 17,502,000 main (fixed) telephone lines. In the same year mobile phone subscribers numbered 65,824,000 (890·5 per 1,000 persons). In Nov. 2005 the government sold a 55% stake in Türk Telecom to a consortium led by Saudi Arabia's Oger Telecom and Telecom Italia. There were 4·4m. PCs in use in 2006 and 25·4m. internet users in 2008.

Postal Services

In 2003 there were 4,421 post offices. A total of 990m. pieces of mail were processed in 2003.

SOCIAL INSTITUTIONS

Justice

The unified legal system consists of: (1) justices of the peace (single judges with limited but summary penal and civil jurisdiction); (2) courts of first instance (single judges, dealing with cases outside the jurisdiction of (3) and (4)); (3) central criminal courts (a president and two judges, dealing with cases where the crime is punishable by imprisonment over five years); (4) commercial courts (three judges); (5) state security courts, to prosecute offences against the integrity of the state (a president and two judges).

The civil and military High Courts of Appeal sit at Ankara. The Council of State is the highest administrative tribunal; it consists of five chambers. Its 31 judges are nominated from among high-ranking personalities in politics, economy, law, the army, etc. The Military Administrative Court deals with the judicial control of administrative acts and deeds concerning military personnel. The Court of Jurisdictional Disputes is empowered to resolve disputes between civil, administrative and military courts. The Supreme Council of Judges and Public Prosecutors appoints judges and prosecutors to the profession and has disciplinary powers.

The Civil Code and the Code of Obligations have been adapted from the corresponding Swiss codes. The Penal Code is largely based upon the Italian Penal Code, and the Code of Civil Procedure closely resembles that of the Canton of Neuchâtel. The Commercial Code is based on the German.

The population in penal institutions in Sept. 2003 was 64,051 (92 per 100,000 of national population).

The death penalty, not used since 1984, was abolished in peacetime in Aug. 2002. The government signed a European Convention protocol abolishing the death penalty entirely in Jan. 2004.

Education

Adult literacy in 2003 was 88·3% (male, 95·7%; female, 81·1%). The Basic Education Law of 1997 extended the duration of compulsory schooling from five to eight years. Primary education is compulsory and co-educational from the age of six to 14 and, in state schools, free. There are plans to raise the duration of compulsory schooling to 12 years. Religious instruction (Sunni Muslim) in state schools is now compulsory. In Aug. 2002 parliament legalized education in Kurdish. In 1991 there were 5,197 religious secondary schools with 0·29m. pupils up to 14 years.

Statistics for 2005–06	*Number*	*Teachers*	*Students*
Pre-school institutions	18,539	20,910	550,146
Primary schools	34,990	389,859	10,673,935
High schools	3,406	102,581	2,075,617
Vocational and technical high schools	4,029	82,736	1,182,637

In 2003 there were 76 universities. In 2002–03 a total of 1,894,000 students enrolled at 1,379 establishments of higher education (including the universities); teaching staff numbered 74,134. In 2001, 41,867 students were studying abroad.

In 2004 public expenditure on education came to 4·1% of GNI.

Health

In 2003 there were 97,763 physicians, 18,073 dentists, 82,246 nurses, 23,757 pharmacists and 41,273 midwives. There were 1,217 hospitals with 187,788 beds in 2004 and 114 health centres.

Welfare

In 2000, 1,349,151 beneficiaries received TRL2,273,278,239m. from the Government Employees Retirement Fund. Of these, 820,167 persons were retired and 376,131 were widows, widowers or orphans of retired persons. There were 3,339,327 beneficiaries from the Social Insurance Institution in 2000 (3,216,445 through disability, old age and death insurance).

RELIGION

Islam ceased to be the official religion in 1928. The Constitution guarantees freedom of religion but forbids its political exploitation or any impairment of the secular character of the republic.

In 2001 there were 64·36m. Muslims, two-thirds Sunni and one-third Shia (Alevis). The Greek Orthodox, Gregorian Armenian, Armenian Apostolic and Roman Catholic Churches are represented in İstanbul, and there are small Uniate, Protestant and Jewish communities.

CULTURE

İstanbul is one of three European Capitals of Culture for 2010. The title attracts large European Union grants.

World Heritage Sites

UNESCO World Heritage sites under Turkish jurisdiction (with year entered on list) are: Historic Areas of İstanbul (1985), including the ancient Hippodrome of Constantine, the 6th-century Hagia Sophia and the 16th-century Suleymaniye Mosque; Göreme National Park and the Rock Sites of Cappadocia (1985); Great Mosque and Hospital of Divriği (1985), founded in the early 13th century; Hattusha (1986), the former capital of the Hittite Empire; Nemrut Dağ (1987), including the 1st century BC mausoleum of Antiochus I; Xanthos-Letoon (1988), the capital of Lycia; Hierapolis-Pamukkale (1988), including mineral forests, petrified waterfalls and the ruins of ancient baths, temples and other Greek monuments; City of Safranbolu (1994), a caravan station from the 13th century; Archaeological Site of Troy (1998).

Broadcasting

Broadcasting is regulated by the Radio and Television Supreme Council. The government monopoly of broadcasting was abolished in 1994 and by 2002 there were 36 national, 108 regional and 1,054 local radio stations; and 15 national, 16 regional and 229 local TV stations (colour by PAL). The Turkish Radio and Television Corporation (TRT) is the public broadcaster, operating four national TV networks, four national radio channels, a radio channel for foreign tourists and the Voice of Turkey international service. A public Kurdish-language TV station, TRT 6, was launched in Jan. 2009. Number of households with televisions: (2006), 17·6m.

Press

In 2006 there were 81 daily newspapers with a combined average daily circulation of 5·1m. The best-selling newspapers are Posta and Zaman, with average daily circulations of 635,000 and 565,000 respectively. In 2003, 15,976 book titles were published.

Tourism

In 2005 there were 20,273,000 non-resident tourists. Receipts totalled US$18·15bn. in 2005 (excluding passenger transport).

DIPLOMATIC REPRESENTATIVES

Of Turkey in the United Kingdom (43 Belgrave Sq., London, SW1X 8PA)
Ambassador: Mehmet Yiğit Alpogan.

Of the United Kingdom in Turkey (Sehit Ersan Caddesi 46/A, Cankaya, Ankara)
Ambassador: David Reddaway, CMG, MBE.

Of Turkey in the USA (2525 Massachusetts Ave., NW, Washington, D.C., 20008)
Ambassador: Vacant.
Chargé d'Affaires a.i: Ali Murat Ersoy.

Of the USA in Turkey (110 Atatürk Blvd, Ankara)
Ambassador: James F. Jeffrey.

Of Turkey to the United Nations
Ambassador: Ertuğrul Apakan.

Of Turkey to the European Union
Ambassador: Volkan Bozkır.

FURTHER READING

State Institute of Statistics. *Türkiye İstatistik Yilliği/Statistical Yearbook of Turkey.—Diş Ticaret İstatistikleri/Foreign Trade Statistics* (Annual).—*Aylik İstatistik Bülten* (Monthly).

Abramowitz, Morton, (ed.) *Turkey's Transformation and American Policy.* 2000

Howe, Marvin, *Turkey Today: A Nation Divided over Islam's Revival.* 2000

İnalcık, H., Faroqhi, S., McGowan, B., Quataert, D. and Pamuk, Ş., *An Economic and Social History of the Ottoman Empire.* 1994

Jenkins, Gareth, *Political Islam in Turkey: Running West, Heading East.* 2008

Joseph, Joseph S., *Turkey and the European Union: Internal Dynamics and External Challenges.* 2006

Kalaycioğlu, Ersin, *Turkish Dynamics: Bridge Across Troubled Lands.* 2006.—*Turkish Democracy Today.* 2006

LaGro, Esra and Jørgensen, Knud Erik, *Turkey and the European Union: Prospects for a Difficult Encounter.* 2007

National Statistical Office: Turkstat, Necatibey Caddesi no. 114, 06100 Ankara.
Website: http://www.tuik.gov.tr

TURKMENISTAN

Türkmenistan
Capital: Ashgabat
Population estimate, 2010: 5·18m.
GDP per capita: not available
GNI per capita, 2007: US$1,552
HDI/world rank: 0·739/109

KEY HISTORICAL EVENTS

Until 1917 Russian Central Asia was divided politically into the Khanate of Khiva, the Emirate of Bokhara and the Governor-Generalship of Turkestan. The Khan of Khiva was deposed in Feb. 1920 and a People's Soviet Republic was set up. In Aug. 1920 the Amir of Bokhara suffered the same fate. The former Governor-Generalship of Turkestan was constituted an Autonomous Soviet Socialist Republic within the RSFSR on 11 April 1921. In the autumn of 1924 the Soviets of the Turkestan, Bokhara and Khiva Republics decided to redistribute their territories on a nationality basis. The redistribution was completed in May 1925 when the new states of Uzbekistan, Turkmenistan and Tadzhikistan were accepted into the USSR as Union Republics. Following the break-up of the Soviet Union, Turkmenistan declared independence in Oct. 1991. Saparmurad Niyazov was elected president and founded the Democratic Party of Turkmenistan, the country's only legal party. Also prime minister and supreme commander of the armed forces, parliament proclaimed Niyazov head of state for life in Dec. 1999. He held the official title of 'Turkmenbashi', leader of all Turkmen. In July 2000 President Niyazov introduced a law requiring all officials to speak Turkmen. He died of a heart attack in Dec. 2006.

TERRITORY AND POPULATION

Turkmenistan is bounded in the north by Kazakhstan, in the north and northeast by Uzbekistan, in the southeast by Afghanistan, in the southwest by Iran and in the west by the Caspian Sea. Area, 448,100 sq. km (186,400 sq. miles). The 1995 census population was 4,483,251; density 10·0 per sq. km. In 1999, 85% of the population were Turkmen, 7% Russian, 5% Uzbek and 3% other. Since then the Russian population has declined dramatically as the rights of Russians living in Turkmenistan deteriorated considerably. A dual-citizenship treaty between Turkmenistan and Russia has been rescinded. In 2005, 53·8% of the population lived in rural areas.

The UN gives an estimated population for 2010 of 5·18m.; density 12 per sq. km.

There are five administrative regions (*velayaty*): Ahal, Balkan, Dashoguz, Lebap and Mary, comprising 42 rural districts, 15 towns and 74 urban settlements. The capital is Ashgabat (formerly Ashkhabad; 1999 population, 525,000); other large towns are Turkmenabat (formerly Chardzhou), Mary (Merv), Balkanabad (Nebit-Dag) and Dashoguz.

The official language is Turkmen, spoken by 77% of the population; Uzbek is spoken by 9% and Russian by 7%.

SOCIAL STATISTICS

2002 estimates: births, 105,000; deaths, 31,000. Estimated rates, 2002 (per 1,000 population): births, 22·0; deaths, 6·4. Annual population growth rate, 1992–2002, 2·1%. Life expectancy, 2007: 60·6 years for males and 68·8 for females. Infant mortality, 2005, 81 per 1,000 live births; fertility rate, 2004, 2·7 births per woman.

CLIMATE

The summers are warm to hot but the humidity is relatively low. The winters are cold but generally dry and sunny over most of the country. Ashgabat, Jan. –1°C, July 25°C. Annual rainfall 375 mm.

CONSTITUTION AND GOVERNMENT

A new constitution was adopted on 26 Sept. 2008. It provided for a head of state who is elected by popular vote for a five-year term and abolished the 2,500-member *Khalk Maslakhaty* (People's Council), formerly the highest representative body. The *Majlis* (Assembly), which now serves as the sole legislative body, was increased from 65 to 125 members. The constitution also allows for a multiparty system.

At a referendum on 16 Jan. 1994, 99·99% of votes cast were in favour of prolonging President Niyazov's term of office to 2002. In 1999 the *Khalk Maslakhaty* declared him president for life.

National Anthem

'Turkmenbasyn guran beyik binasy' ('The country which Turkmenbashi has built'); composed by Veli Muhatov.

RECENT ELECTIONS

The presidential election of 11 Feb. 2007 was won by the acting president, Gurbanguly Berdymukhammedov, with 89·2% of the vote, ahead of Amanyaz Atajykov with 3·2%, Ishanguly Nuriyev (2·4%), Muhammetnazar Gurbanov (2·4%), Orazmyrat Garajayev (1·5%) and Ashyrniyaz Pomanov (1·3%). Turnout was 98·7%.

Majlis elections were held on 14 Dec. 2008. Most of the candidates were from the Democratic Party (DP; former Communists). 123 of 125 seats were filled on 14 Dec. 2008 and results in the remaining two constituencies were decided by run-offs held on 28 Dec. 2008 and 8 Feb. 2009. The official turnout figure of 93·9% was disputed by human rights groups.

CURRENT ADMINISTRATION

President and Prime Minister: Gurbanguly Berdymukhammedov; b. 1957 (DP; in office since 21 Dec. 2006—acting until 14 Feb. 2007).

In March 2010 the government comprised:

Deputy Prime Ministers: Myratgeldy Akmammedov; Tuvakmammed Japarov; Rashid Meredov (also *Minister of Foreign Affairs*); Hojamuhammet Muhammedov; Deryageldi Orazov; Hydyr Saparliyev; Nazarguly Shagulyev; Baymyrat Hodzhamuhammedov; Maisa Yazmukhammedova.

Minister of Agriculture: Esenmyrat Orazgeldiev. *Communications:* Ovliyaguly Jumaguliyev. *Construction:* Dzhumageldi Bayramov. *Construction Materials Industry:* Yazmyrat Hommadov. *Culture and Broadcasting:* Gulmyrat Meredov. *Defence:* Yaylim Berdiyev. *Economic Policy and Development:* Byashimmyrat Khojamammedov. *Education:* Goulshat Mammedova. *Energy and Industry:* Yazmuhamed Orazguliyev. *Environmental Protection:* Babageldi Annabayramov. *Finance:* Annamuhammet Gochiyev. *Health and Pharmaceutical Industries:* Ata Serdarov. *Internal Affairs:* Isgender Mulikov. *Justice:* Murad Karryev. *Motor Transport:* Gurbanmyrat Hanguliyev. *National Security:* Charymyrat Amanov. *Oil and Gas, and Mineral Resources:* Bairamgeldy Nedirov. *Railways:* Rozymyrat Seyitkuliev. *Social Security:* Bekmyrat Shamyradov. *Textile Industry:* Aynabat Babayeva. *Trade and Foreign Economic Relations:* Bayar Abayev. *Water Resources and Irrigation:* Annageldi Yazmyradov.

Chairman, Supreme Council (Majlis): Akja Nurberdiyeva.

Government Website: http://www.turkmenistan.gov.tm

CURRENT LEADERS

Gurbanguly Berdymukhammedov

Position

President

Introduction

Gurganbuly Berdymukhammedov came to power in 2006 following the death of President Saparmurad Niyazov, known as Turkmenbashi. Berdymukhammedov had served as minister of health in Niyazov's government since 1997, implementing the closure of rural hospitals. Though not initially regarded as a frontrunner for the presidency, he became acting president when Niyazov's constitutional successor, Ovezgeldi Atayev, was charged with criminal offences. Having won the Feb. 2007 presidential election, Berdymukhammedov began to strengthen ties with the outside world. He has also introduced some constitutional reforms, although critics have questioned their democratic validity.

Early Life

Berdymukhammedov was born in Babaarap village in the region of Ashgabat in 1957. He graduated in dentistry from the Turkmen state medical institute in 1979 and later completed a PhD in medical sciences in Moscow. In 1995 he was appointed head of the dentistry centre of the ministry of health and became associate professor and dean of the dentistry faculty of the state medical institute. He was Niyazov's personal dentist and in 1997 entered political life as the minister for health and the medical industry.

In April 2001 Berdymukhammedov was appointed deputy chairman of the council of ministers. Under Niyazov's autocratic regime the health service suffered acute financial problems. In April 2004 Niyazov announced that since state healthcare workers were not being paid, Berdymukhammedov would also forfeit his pay for three months. In the same year Berdymukhammedov implemented drastic cuts, closing all rural hospitals and sacking 15,000 healthcare workers, replacing them with untrained army conscripts.

When Niyazov died of a heart attack on 21 Dec. 2006, the Turkmen constitution provided for Ovezgeldi Atayev, chairman of the *Khalk Maslakhaty* (People's Council), to become acting president. However, Berdymukhammedov assumed the role and announced that Atayev was the subject of criminal investigation. On 26 Dec. an extraordinary session of the *Khalk Maslakhaty* amended the constitution to allow the acting president to stand in presidential elections. It also blocked the candidacy of leading opposition figures based abroad.

Berdymukhammedov was said to have the backing of Akmurad Rejepo, head of the presidential security service, and although five other candidates stood in the elections, his victory was widely predicted. During his campaign Berdymukhammedov promised to reform the agricultural sector and to improve living conditions. He pledged that the government would continue to provide free natural gas, electricity, salt and water, and that salaries and pensions would be increased regularly.

Career in Office

On 11 Feb. 2007 Berdymukhammedov was elected president with nearly 90% of the vote. While making no decisive break with Niyazov's isolationist policies, there were early indications of a more outward-looking stance. Representatives of many foreign governments attended his inauguration and he subsequently received delegations from China, Russia and the USA. He confirmed that Turkmenistan would honour its gas contracts with Russia and moved towards stronger relations with neighbouring Afghanistan by writing off US$4m. of debt. The government also announced that it was reinforcing commercial ties with Iran.

Berdymukhammedov extended the period of formal schooling, reintroduced foreign languages to the curriculum and lifted restrictions on travel within Turkmenistan. He raised the prospect of reopening rural hospitals and promised to widen Internet access (available to 1% of the population when he came to power). However, these reforms would be dependent on an economic upturn. A new constitution was adopted in Sept. 2008 that increased the number of parliamentary seats to 125 and increased the influence of the *Majlis*. Nevertheless, Berdymukhammedov's hold on power was reinforced as parliamentary elections in Dec. returned an overwhelming number of candidates from his dominant Democratic Party.

The cult of personality around the presidency has lessened under Berdymukhammedov but the government retains tight control over political organizations and continues to attract criticism for human rights violations and the opaqueness of the electoral system.

The government has sought to diversify its gas markets and break free of Russian dominance of the export routes. An export pipeline to China was inaugurated in Dec. 2009 and in Jan. 2010 a second pipeline to Iran opened.

DEFENCE

Defence expenditure in 2006 totalled US$184m. (US$36 per capita), representing 1·8% of GDP.

Army

In 2007 the Army was 18,500-strong.

Navy

A Navy/Coast Guard is in the process of being formed and is expected to be completed in 2015. In 2007 it numbered 500 and operated from a minor base at Turkmenbashi with six patrol and coastal combatants. The Caspian Sea Flotilla is operating as a joint Russian, Kazakhstani and Turkmenistani flotilla under Russian command. It is based at Astrakhan.

Air Force

The Air Force, with 3,000 personnel (including Air Defence), had 94 combat capable aircraft in 2007 including Su-17s and MiG-29s.

INTERNATIONAL RELATIONS

Turkmenistan is a member of the UN, World Bank, IMF and several other UN specialized agencies, OSCE, CIS, Islamic Development Bank, NATO Partnership for Peace, OIC, Asian Development Bank and ECO.

ECONOMY

In 2002 agriculture accounted for 21·3% of GDP, industry 41·0% and services 37·7%. In 1999 an estimated 25% of economic output was being produced by the private sector.

Overview

Turkmenistan is home to the fifth largest oil and gas reserves in the world. Hydrocarbons comprise 80% of exports and are the chief factor in the country's recent economic upturn. Other major exports include textiles and raw cotton. Despite a privatization programme launched in 1994, most businesses remain state-run and foreign investment levels are low.

When Turkmenistan gained independence from the Soviet Union in 1991 the economy suffered from the break in traditional economic ties, poor harvests and mismanagement of state-run industries. The situation worsened in 1997 when natural gas exports were halted as a result of non-payment by Commonwealth of Independent States (CIS) countries but improved the following year with the resumption of gas exports to Ukraine and Russia.

Government sources report growth of 17% annually since 1999 but research by international organizations suggest a lower figure. Nevertheless, growth in the past has been impressive, driven by state investment (around 30% of GDP) in oil refineries, food processing, transportation and textiles.

Turkmenistan reached agreement with Russia in 2003 and China in 2005 to supply natural gas, guaranteeing income in the medium term. However, gas exports are hindered by reliance on Russian pipelines while government expenditures have focused on infrastructure and national prestige projects that bring little revenue.

Currency

The unit of currency is the *new manat* (TMT) of 100 *tenge*, introduced on 1 Jan. 2009 to replace the *manat* (TMM) at a rate of 1 TMT = 5,000 TMM. Foreign exchange reserves were US$300m. in 1993. Inflation was 6·3% in 2007 and 14·5% in 2008.

Budget

Revenues were 3,693bn. manat in 1999 and expenditures 3,894bn. manat.

VAT is 20%.

Performance

Total GDP in 2008 was US$18·3bn. Annual real GDP growth averaged –10·6% between 1994 and 1997. However, a spectacular revival led to average annual economic growth of 15·9% between 1999 and 2006. Real GDP growth was 11·6% in 2007 and 10·5% in 2008. The rapid growth of recent years is largely down to large-scale gas exports to Russia.

Banking and Finance

There are two types of bank in Turkmenistan—state commercial banks and joint stock open-end commercial banks. The central bank is the State Central Bank of Turkmenistan (*Chairman*, Guvanchmyrat Goklenov). A government-led restructuring of the banking sector in 1999 saw the total number of banks reduced from 67 to 12 by 2002.

ENERGY AND NATURAL RESOURCES

Environment

Carbon dioxide emissions from the consumption and flaring of fossil fuels in 2008 were the equivalent of 11·8 tonnes per capita.

Electricity

Installed capacity in 2004 was an estimated 3·9m. kW. Production was 11·47bn. kWh in 2004, with consumption per capita 2,060 kWh.

Oil and Gas

Turkmenistan possesses the world's fourth largest reserves of natural gas and substantial oil resources, but disputes with Russia have held up development. Oil production in 2008 was 10·2m. tonnes.

In 2008 natural gas reserves were estimated at 7,940bn. cu. metres and oil reserves at 0·6bn. bbls. In 2008 natural gas production was 66·1bn. cu. metres.

Minerals

There are reserves of coal, sulphur, magnesium, potassium, lead, barite, viterite, bromine, iodine and salt.

Agriculture

Cotton and wheat account for two-thirds of agricultural production. Barley, maize, corn, rice, wool, silk and fruit are also produced. Production of main crops (2003, in 1,000 tonnes): wheat, 2,534; seed cotton, 714; cottonseed, 480; sugar beets, 255; watermelons, 230; tomatoes, 150; cotton lint, 140; grapes, 130; rice, 110. There were approximately 1·85m. ha. of arable land in 2007 and 63,000 ha. of permanent crops.

Livestock, 2003 estimates: sheep, 6·0m.; cattle, 860,000; goats, 370,000; pigs, 45,000; chickens, 5m.

Forestry

There were 4·13m. ha. of forests (8·8% of the land area) in 2005.

Fisheries

There are fisheries in the Caspian Sea. The total catch in 2004 was 14,992 tonnes, exclusively freshwater fish.

INDUSTRY

Main industries: oil refining, gas extraction, chemicals, manufacture of machinery, fertilizers, textiles and clothing. Output, 2004 (in tonnes): distillate fuel oil, 2,511,000; residual fuel oil, 1,745,000; petrol, 1,265,000; cement (2001), 448,000; cotton woven fabrics (2001), 61·0m. sq. metres; footwear (2001), 375,000 pairs.

Labour

The labour force in 1996 totalled 1,750,000 (55% males). Of the total workforce, 44% were engaged in agriculture, 21% in services and 10% in mining, manufacturing and public utilities. Average monthly wage in 1994 was 1,000 manat.

INTERNATIONAL TRADE

External debt was US$1,092m. in 2005.

Imports and Exports

Imports, 2000, US$1,785m.; exports, US$2,506m. Main imports: light manufactured goods, processed food, metalwork, machinery and parts. Main exports: gas, oil and cotton. The main import suppliers in 1998 were Ukraine (16·1%), Turkey (13·1%), Russia (11·6%), Germany (6·9%) and the USA (6·4%). The leading export markets were Iran (24·1%), Turkey (18·3%), Azerbaijan (6·9%), UK (4·9%) and Russia (4·7%).

COMMUNICATIONS

Roads

Length of roads in 2002, 58,592 km (of which 81·2% were paved). In 2006 there were 650 fatalities as a result of road accidents.

Rail

Length of railways in 2005, 2,313 km of 1,520 mm gauge. A rail link to Iran was opened in May 1996, and there are plans to build a further 2,000 km of rail network. In 2001, 3·1m. passengers and 17·2m. tonnes of freight were carried.

Civil Aviation

In 2003 Avia Company Turkmenistan operated flights from Ashgabat to Abu Dhabi, Almaty, Amritsar, Bangkok, Birmingham, Delhi, Dubai, Frankfurt, İstanbul, Kyiv, London, Moscow and Tashkent. In 2005 scheduled airline traffic of Turkmenistan-based carriers flew 9·5m. km, carrying 1,899,800 passengers.

Shipping
In 2002 sea-going shipping totalled 46,000 GRT (including oil tankers, 6,000 GRT). The main port is Turkmenbashi, on the Caspian Sea. In 1993, 1·1m. tonnes of freight were carried by inland waterways.

Telecommunications
Telephone subscribers numbered 805,500 in 2007 (162·2 per 1,000 population), including 347,600 mobile phone subscribers. There were 70,000 internet users in 2007. The internet was banned under the former president, Saparmurad Niyazov, and has only been available since Feb. 2007.

Postal Services
There were 195 post offices in 2003.

SOCIAL INSTITUTIONS

Justice
In 1994, 14,824 crimes were reported, including 308 murders and attempted murders. The death penalty was abolished in 1999 (there were over 100 executions in 1996). The population in penal institutions in Oct. 2000 was approximately 22,000 (489 per 100,000 of national population).

Education
There is compulsory education from age seven to 15 years of age. In 1994–95 there were 1,900 primary and secondary schools with 940,600 pupils; and in 1993–94 there were 11 higher educational institutions with 38,900 students, 41 technical colleges with 29,000 students, and 11 music and art schools. Since June 2004 degrees obtained abroad have ceased to be recognized as valid.

In Jan. 1994, 0·2m. children (29·5% of those eligible) were attending pre-school institutions. In 1999 adult literacy was over 98%.

Health
There were 270 hospitals in 2002 with 32,000 beds. In 1997 there were 14,022 physicians, 1,010 dentists, 21,436 nurses, 1,566 pharmacists and 3,664 midwives.

Welfare
In Jan. 1994 there were 0·3m. old-age, and 0·16m. other, pensioners.

RELIGION

Around 87% of the population in 2001 were Muslims (mostly Sunni).

CULTURE

World Heritage Sites
Turkmenistan has three sites on the UNESCO World Heritage List: the State Historical and Cultural Park 'Ancient Merv' (inscribed on the list in 1999), the oldest and best-preserved Central Asian Silk Route city, dominated by Seljuk architecture; Kunya-Urgench (2005), the ancient capital of the Khorezem region; and the Parthian Fortresses of Nisa (2007), the site of one of the earliest and most important cities of the Parthian Empire.

Broadcasting
Broadcasting is controlled by the government. Turkmen TV transmits on four channels and Turkmen Radio operates two national stations. Voice of Turkmen is a foreign radio service. In 2003 there were 855,000 television sets.

Press
In 2005 there were two daily newspapers with a combined average circulation of 56,000. Approval is required from the president's office before publication.

Tourism
In 2005 there were 12,000 non-resident tourists.

Calendar
In Aug. 2002 President Saparmurad Niyazov renamed the days of the week and the months, for example with Jan. becoming 'Turkmenbashi' after the president's official name, meaning 'head of all the Turkmen'. April was renamed in honour of the president's mother. Tuesday was renamed 'Young Day' and Saturday 'Spiritual Day'. However, in April 2008 President Gurbanguly Berdymukhammedov reversed his predecessor's decisions.

DIPLOMATIC REPRESENTATIVES

Of Turkmenistan in the United Kingdom (2nd Floor, St George's House, 14–17 Wells St., London, W1T 3PD)
Ambassador: Yazmurad N. Seryaev.

Of the United Kingdom in Turkmenistan (301–308 Office Building, Ak Atin Plaza Hotel, Ashgabat)
Ambassador: Keith Allan.

Of Turkmenistan in the USA (2207 Massachusetts Ave., NW, Washington, D.C., 20008)
Ambassador: Meret Bairamovich Orazov.

Of the USA in Turkmenistan (9 Puskin St., Ashgabat)
Ambassador: Vacant.
Chargé d'Affaires a.i.: Sylvia Curran.

Of Turkmenistan to the United Nations
Ambassador: Aksoltan T. Ataeva.

Of Turkmenistan to the European Union
Ambassador: Karadjan Mommadov.

FURTHER READING

Abazov, Rafis, *Historical Dictionary of Turkmenistan.* 2005

TUVALU

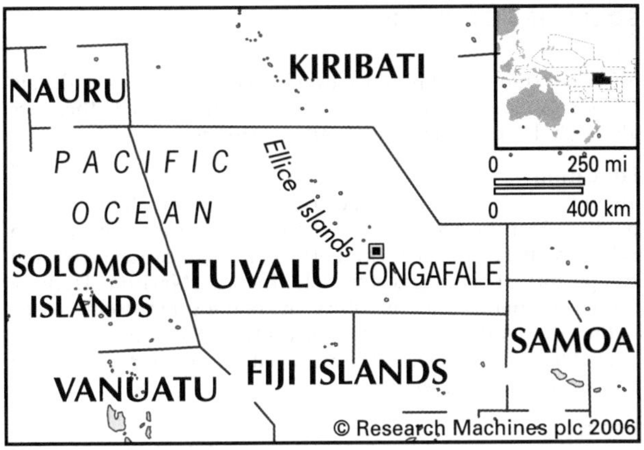

Capital: Fongafale
Population, 2002: 10,000
GDP per capita: not available
GNI per capita, 2007: US$3,050

KEY HISTORICAL EVENTS

Formerly known as the Ellice Islands, Tuvalu is a group of nine islands in the western central Pacific. Joining the British controlled Gilbert Islands Protectorate in 1916, they became the Gilbert and Ellice Islands colony.

After the Japanese occupied the Gilbert Islands in 1942, US forces occupied the Ellice Islands. A referendum held in 1974 produced a large majority in favour of separation from the Ellice Islands. Independence was achieved on 1 Oct. 1978. Early in 1979 the USA signed a treaty of friendship with Tuvalu and relinquished its claim to the four southern islands in return for the right to veto any other nation's request to use any of Tuvalu's islands for military purposes.

TERRITORY AND POPULATION

Tuvalu lies between 5° 30' and 11° S. lat. and 176° and 180° E. long. and comprises Nanumea, Nanumaga, Niutao, Nui, Vaitupu, Nukufetau, Funafuti (administrative centre; 2002 estimated population, 4,492), Nukulaelae and Niulakita. Population (census 2002) 9,561, excluding an estimated 1,500 who were working abroad, mainly in Nauru and Kiribati. Area approximately 26 sq. km (10 sq. miles). Density, 2002, 373 per sq. km.

In 2002 an estimated 52·9% of the population lived in rural areas. The population is of a Polynesian race.

The official languages are Tuvaluan and English.

SOCIAL STATISTICS

2002 births, 156; deaths, 87. Rates (per 1,000 population), 2002: births, 16; deaths, 9; infant mortality (per 1,000 live births, 2005), 31. Expectation of life, 2002: males, 61·7 years; females, 65·1. Annual population growth rate, 1992–2002, 1·4%; fertility rate, 2004, 3·7 births per woman.

CLIMATE

A pleasant but monotonous climate with temperatures averaging 86°F (30°C), though trade winds from the east moderate conditions for much of the year. Rainfall ranges from 120" (3,000 mm) to over 160" (4,000 mm). Funafuti, Jan. 84°F (28·9°C), July 81°F (27·2°C). Annual rainfall 160" (4,003 mm). Although the islands are north of the recognized hurricane belt they were badly hit by hurricanes in the 1990s, raising fears for the long-term future of Tuvalu as the sea level continues to rise.

CONSTITUTION AND GOVERNMENT

The Head of State is the British sovereign, represented by an appointed Governor-General. The Constitution provides for a Prime Minister and the cabinet ministers to be elected from among the 15 members of the *Fale I Fono* (*Parliament*).

National Anthem

'Tuvalu mote Atua' ('Tuvalu for the Almighty'); words and tune by A. Manoa.

RECENT ELECTIONS

Elections were held on 3 Aug. 2006. Only non-partisans were elected as there are no political parties. Apisai Ielemia was elected prime minister by parliament on 14 Aug. 2006.

CURRENT ADMINISTRATION

Governor-General: Filoimea Telito (sworn in 15 April 2005).

In March 2010 the cabinet comprised:

Prime Minister and Minister of Foreign Affairs and Labour: Apisai Ielemia (sworn in 14 Aug. 2006).

Deputy Prime Minister and Minister of Natural Resources: Tavau Teii. *Communication, Transport, Works and Energy:* Taukelina Finikaso. *Finance, Economic Planning and Industries:* Lotoala Metia. *Health, Education and Sport:* Iakoba Italeli. *Home Affairs, Rural and Urban Development:* Willy Telavi.

Speaker: Kamuta Latasi.

CURRENT LEADERS

Apisai Ielemia

Position
Prime Minister

Introduction
Apisai Ielemia took office in Aug. 2006, succeeding Maatia Toafa. He declared Tuvalu in immediate danger from rising sea levels and has requested international assistance with evacuating and resettling residents. His other top priority has been to address Tuvalu's economic difficulties.

Early Life
Born in Tuvalu on 19 Aug. 1955, Ielemia attended Hiram Bingham high school in Kiribati. In 1973 he entered the civil service and became island executive officer, based in Funafuti. From 1978–94 he was executive officer for the Tuvalu high commission and from 1994–98 was its first secretary.

From 1985–94 Ielemia was clerk to the Tuvalu parliament. In 1993 he graduated in management and political science from the University of the South Pacific in Suva in the Fiji Islands. In 1994 he became assistant secretary at the ministries of health and education and of foreign affairs and in 1998 was named permanent secretary at the ministry of tourism, trade and commerce.

In 2004 Ielemia became leader of the opposition. When parliamentary elections ousted most of the existing cabinet in Aug. 2006, he was appointed prime minister by a majority of one. He promised to lift restrictions on the media and improve economic administration, and also took responsibility for foreign affairs.

Career in office
To combat rising sea levels Ielemia has requested help from Australia, New Zealand and the wider international community

to evacuate and rehouse islanders. To date almost a quarter of the population has been evacuated; the largest exile community is in Auckland, New Zealand. In Dec. 2006 Ielemia visited Taiwan and secured increased financial aid and agreement on joint shipping and fishing ventures. He has also taken some controversial measures to improve the economy, such as restricting MPs' spending allowances. In Jan. 2009 Tuvalu applied for membership of the International Monetary Fund.

INTERNATIONAL RELATIONS

Tuvalu is a member of the UN, Commonwealth, Asian Development Bank, Pacific Islands Forum and SPC, and is an ACP member state of the ACP-EU relationship.

ECONOMY

Currency

The unit of currency is the Australian *dollar* although Tuvaluan coins up to $A1 are in local circulation.

Budget

In 2005 revenues totalled $A25·5m. and expenditures $A22·3m.

Performance

Real GDP growth was 4·0% in 2003 (5·5% in 2002).

Banking and Finance

The Tuvalu National Bank was established at Funafuti in 1980, and is a joint venture between the Tuvalu government and Westpac International. There is also a development bank.

ENERGY AND NATURAL RESOURCES

Electricity

Installed capacity was 2·6 MW in 2002; production was 4,355 MWh.

Agriculture

Coconut palms are the main crop. Production of coconuts (2003 estimate), 2,000 tonnes. Fruit and vegetables are grown for local consumption. Livestock, 2003 estimate: pigs, 13,000.

Fisheries

Total catch, 2005, 2,560 tonnes. A seamount was discovered in Tuvaluan waters in 1991 and is a good location for deep-sea fish. The sale of fishing licences to American and Japanese fleets provides a significant source of income.

INDUSTRY

Small amounts of copra, handicrafts and garments are produced.

INTERNATIONAL TRADE

Imports and Exports

Main sources of income are copra, stamps, handicrafts and remittances from Tuvaluans abroad. 2004 imports, $A15·5m.; 2004 exports, $A0·2m. The leading import suppliers are Australia, the Fiji Islands, New Zealand and Japan. The main export destination is Australia.

COMMUNICATIONS

Roads

In 2002 there were 20 km of roads.

Civil Aviation

In 2002 Air Kiribati operated four flights a week from Funafuti International to Suva.

Shipping

Funafuti is the only port and a deep-water wharf was opened in 1980. In 2002 merchant shipping totalled 49,000 GRT.

Telecommunications

In 2008 there were approximately 1,500 main telephone lines in operation. There were some 2,000 mobile phone subscribers and 4,200 internet users in 2008.

SOCIAL INSTITUTIONS

Justice

There is a High Court presided over by the Chief Justice of the Fiji Islands. A Court of Appeal is constituted if required. There are also eight Island Courts with limited jurisdiction.

Education

There were 1,798 pupils at nine primary schools in 2001, and 558 pupils at Motufoua Secondary School in 2001. The Fetuvalu High School reopened in 2002 with Form 3 only. Education is free and compulsory from the ages of six to 15. There is a Maritime Training School at Funafuti, and the University of the South Pacific, based in the Fiji Islands, has an extension centre at Funafuti.

In 1999–2000 total expenditure on education came to 16·8% of total government expenditure.

Health

In 2002 there was one central hospital situated at Funafuti and clinics on each of the other eight islands; there were seven doctors and 34 nurses.

RELIGION

The majority of the population are Christians, mainly Protestant, but with small groups of Roman Catholics, Seventh Day Adventists, Jehovah's Witnesses and Bahais. There are some Muslims and Latter-day Saints (Mormons).

CULTURE

Broadcasting

The state-owned Tuvalu Media Corporation operates the Radio Tuvalu service. Foreign television stations can be accessed via satellite.

Press

The Government Broadcasting and Information Division produces Tuvalu Echoes, a fortnightly publication, and Te Lama, a monthly religious publication.

Tourism

There were 1,130 visitor arrivals in 2007.

DIPLOMATIC REPRESENTATIVES

Of Tuvalu in the United Kingdom (Tuvalu House, 230 Worple Rd, London, SW20 8RH)
Honorary Consul: Dr Iftikhar A. Ayaz.

Of the United Kingdom in Tuvalu
High Commissioner: Mac McLachlan, MBE (resides in Suva, Fiji Islands).

Of Tuvalu in the USA
Ambassador: Vacant.

Of the USA in Tuvalu
Ambassador: C. Steven McGann (resides in Suva, Fiji Islands).

Of Tuvalu to the United Nations
Ambassador: Afelee F. Pita.

Of Tuvalu to the European Union
Ambassador: Panapasi Nelesone.

FURTHER READING

Bennetts, P. and Wheeler, T., *Time and Tide: The Islands of Tuvalu.* 2001

National Statistical Office: Ministry of Finance, Economic Planning and Industries, Private Bag, Vaiaku, Funafuti.
Website: http://www.spc.int/prism/country/tv/stats

UGANDA

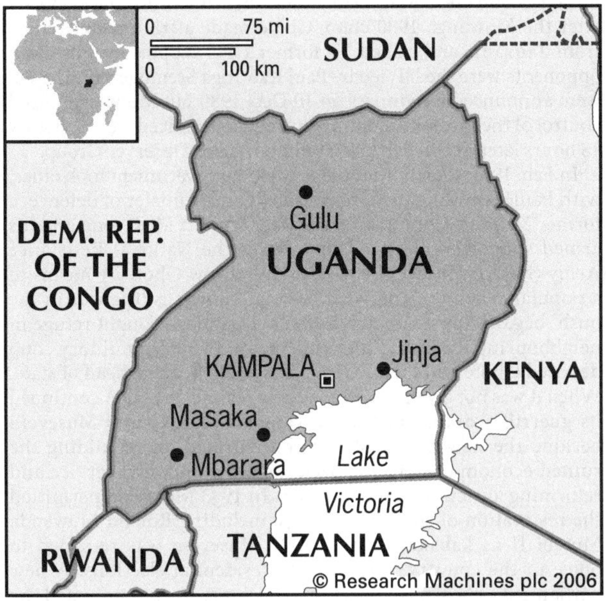

Republic of Uganda

Capital: Kampala
Population estimate, 2010: 33·80m.
GDP per capita, 2007: (PPP$) 1,059
HDI/world rank: 0·514/157

KEY HISTORICAL EVENTS

Bantu-speaking mixed farmers first migrated into southwest Uganda from the west around 500 BC. There is evidence that they smelted iron for tools and weapons. In the following centuries Nilotic-speaking pastoralists entered northern Uganda from the upper Nile valley (now southern Sudan). By AD 1300 several kingdoms (the Chwezi states) had been established in southern Uganda. In 1500 Nilotic-speaking Luo people invaded the Chwezi states and established the kingdoms of Buganda, Bunyoro and Ankole. At this time, northern Uganda became home to the Alur and Acholi ethnic groups. During the 17th century Bunyoro was southern Uganda's most powerful state, controlling an area that stretched into present-day Rwanda and Tanzania. From about 1700 the kingdom of Buganda expanded (largely at the expense of Bunyoro), and a century later it dominated a large territory bordering Lake Victoria from the Victoria Nile to the Kagera River. The *kabaka* (king) maintained a large court and a powerful army and traded in cattle, ivory and slaves.

Arab traders from Zanzibar on Africa's east coast reached Lake Victoria by 1844. A prominent trader, Ahmad bin Ibrahim, introduced the kabaka to foreign trade; imported cloth and firearms were exchanged for ivory and slaves. Ibrahim also introduced Islam to the region. In 1862 John Speke, a British explorer who was attempting to find the source of the Nile, became the first European to visit Buganda, by then a highly developed state supported by an army of more than 150,000 and a navy.

He met with Kabaka Mutesa I; as did Henry Stanley, who reached Buganda in 1875. Mutesa, fearful of attacks from Egypt, agreed to Stanley's proposal to allow Christian missionaries to enter his realm. Members of the British Protestant Church Missionary Society arrived in 1877 and were followed two years later by representatives of the French Roman Catholic White Fathers. Both were successful in attracting converts but by the 1880s they were in fierce competition. Trade with the Indian Ocean ports continued, bringing with it greater Islamic influence.

Mutesa was succeeded by Mwanga in 1884. He was wary of the new foreign ideologies and attempted to halt their spread but was deposed by Christian and Muslim converts in 1888. He was later reinstated but with considerably reduced power and influence. In 1889 Mwanga was visited by Carl Peters, a German doctor, and the kabaka subsequently signed a treaty of friendship with Germany. Britain was concerned by the growth of German influence and the potential threat to its position on the Nile. In 1890 the two European powers signed a treaty giving Britain rights to what was to become Uganda and giving Germany control over land to the southeast (now Tanzania). Frederick Lugard, acting as an agent of the Imperial British East Africa Company (IBEA), arrived in Buganda with a detachment of troops and in 1892 he backed Protestant converts in an attack on the French Catholic mission.

British Rule

In 1894 Britain made Uganda a protectorate. Allying with the Protestant Baganda chiefs, the British set about conquering the rest of the country, assisted by Nubian mercenary troops, formerly in the service of the khedive of Egypt. The British deposed Mwanga and replaced him with his infant son Daudi Chwa. Bunyoro had been spared the religious civil wars of Buganda and was firmly united by its king, Kabarega. Following five years of conflict, the British occupied Bunyoro and conquered Acholi and the northern region. Other African chiefdoms, such as Ankole in the southwest, signed treaties with the British, as did the chiefdoms of Busoga. In 1900 an agreement was signed between the British administration under Sir Harry Johnston and Buganda, giving the kingdom considerable autonomy and transforming it into a constitutional monarchy controlled largely by Protestant chiefs. Half of Bunyoro's conquered territory was also awarded to Buganda, including the historic heartland of the kingdom containing several royal tombs. Buganda doubled in size from ten to twenty counties (*sazas*), but the 'lost counties' of Bunyoro remained a grievance.

Economic Development

In 1901 a railway from Mombasa on the Indian Ocean reached Kisumu, on Lake Victoria, connected by boat with Uganda. The railway was later extended to Kampala. The railway had cost far more than was anticipated and the British, anxious for a return on their investment, turned to cotton to provide raw materials for British mills. Buganda, with its strategic location on the north shore of Lake Victoria, reaped the benefits of cotton growing; it soon became the major export crop and made the Buganda kingdom relatively prosperous. Coffee and sugar production accelerated in the 1920s. The country attracted few permanent European settlers and the cash crops were mostly produced by African smallholders, rather than the plantation system used in other colonies. Many South Asians were encouraged to settle in Uganda, where they played a leading role in the country's commerce. In 1921 a legislative council for the protectorate was established (although its first African member was admitted only in 1945).

The colonial government regulated the buying and processing of cash crops, setting prices and reserving the role of intermediary for Asians, who were thought to be more efficient. The British and Asians repelled African attempts to break into cotton ginning, leading to resentment among the Baganda. In addition, on the

Asian-owned sugar plantations established in the 1920s, labour for sugarcane and other cash crops was increasingly provided by migrants from the fringes of Uganda and beyond. In 1949 discontented Baganda rioted and burned down the houses of pro-government chiefs in Kampala. The rioters had three demands: the right to bypass government price controls on the sales of cotton, the removal of the Asian monopoly over cotton ginning, and the right to have their own representatives in local government. They were also critical of the young kabaka, Frederick Walugembe Mutesa II. The British governor, Sir John Hall, regarded the riots as the work of communist-inspired agitators such as the Uganda African Farmers Union (UAFU), founded by I. K. Musazi in 1947. The UAFU was banned and none of the requested reforms were implemented. Musazi's Uganda National Congress replaced the UAFU in 1952 but remained a discussion group rather than an organized political party.

Meanwhile, the British began to prepare for an independent Uganda. Britain's post-war withdrawal from India, nationalism in West Africa and a more liberal philosophy in the Colonial Office all had an effect. Sir Andrew Cohen was installed as governor in 1952 and pursued economic and political reforms: removing obstacles to African cotton ginning, encouraging co-operatives, establishing the Uganda Development Corporation and reorganizing the Legislative Council to include Africans elected from districts across the country for the first time. There was also talk of a future federation of east African territories (Kenya, Uganda and Tanganyika). However, there was resistance among the Baganda, who feared the erosion of their power-base. Mutesa II refused to co-operate with Cohen's plan for an integrated Buganda. Cohen deported him to exile in London, setting off a storm of protest. Two year later Mutesa II was reinstated, officially as a constitutional monarch, but in reality having considerable political clout. In 1960 a political organizer from Lango, Milton Obote, formed a new party, the Uganda People's Congress (UPC), as a coalition of all those who opposed Buganda dominance (apart from the Catholic-dominated Democratic Party (DP)).

Independence

On 9 Oct. 1962 Uganda became independent, with Obote as prime minister and the kabaka as head of state. Buganda was given considerable autonomy. In 1963 Uganda became a republic and Mutesa II was elected president. The first years of independence were dominated by a struggle between the central government and Buganda. In 1966 Obote introduced a new constitution that ended Buganda's autonomy and restored the 'lost counties' to the Bunyoro. Obote then captured the kabaka's palace at Mengo and forced the kabaka to flee the country. In 1967 a new constitution was introduced giving the central government—especially the president—greater power and dividing Buganda into four districts. The traditional kingships were also abolished (in the case of Buganda retroactive to 1966). The 1960s saw a steady build-up of military power in Uganda, under Major Gen. Idi Amin Dada.

In Jan. 1971 Obote was deposed in a coup by Idi Amin. Amin was faced with opposition within the army by officers and troops loyal to Obote but by the end of 1971 he was in firm control. In 1972 he ordered Asians who were not citizens of Uganda to leave the country and within three months all 60,000 had left, most of them for Britain. Their expulsion hit the Ugandan economy hard. Amin's rule became increasingly dictatorial and brutal; it is estimated that over 300,000 Ugandans were killed during the 1970s. His corrupt administration led to divisions in the military and a number of coup attempts. Israel conducted a successful raid on the Entebbe airport in 1976 to rescue passengers on a plane hijacked by Palestinian terrorists. Amin's expulsion of Israeli technicians won him the support of Arab nations such as Libya.

In 1976 Amin declared himself president for life and two years later he invaded Tanzania in an attempt to annex the Kagera region. The following year Tanzania launched a successful counter-invasion, unifying anti-Amin forces under the Uganda National Liberation Front (UNLF). Amin's forces were driven out and he fled to exile in Saudi Arabia. Tanzania left an occupation force in Uganda. Yusufu Lule was installed as president but was quickly replaced by Godfrey Binaisa, who was then overthrown in a military coup on 10 May 1980, headed by Paulo Muwanga. Shortly after the Muwanga 1980 coup, Obote made a triumphant return from Tanzania and rallied his former UPC supporters. His main opponents were the DP, led by Paul Kawanga Ssemogerere. The DP were announced as winners on 10 Dec. 1980 but Muwanga seized control of the Electoral Commission and announced a UPC victory 18 hours later, verified by the Commonwealth Observer Group.

In Feb. 1981, shortly after the new Obote government took office, with Paulo Muwanga as vice-president and minister of defence, a former Military Commission member, Yoweri Museveni, and his armed supporters declared themselves the National Resistance Army (NRA). Museveni vowed to overthrow Obote by means of a popular rebellion, and what became known as 'the war in the bush' began. Approximately 200,000 Ugandans sought refuge in neighbouring Rwanda, Zaïre and Sudan. In 1985 a military coup deposed Obote and Lieut.-Gen. Tito Okello became head of state. When it was not given a role in the new regime, the NRA continued its guerrilla campaign. It took Kampala in 1986 and Museveni became the new president. He concentrated on rebuilding the ruined economy by cutting back the army and civil service and reforming agriculture and industry. In 1993 Museveni permitted the restoration of traditional kings, including Ronald Muwenda Mutebi II as kabaka. In May 1996 Museveni was returned to office in the country's first direct presidential elections. A new parliament, chosen in elections in June, was dominated by Museveni supporters.

Museveni was re-elected in March 2001, following a period of relative stability and economic growth. However, his popularity was diminished by discontent with Uganda's intervention in the Democratic Republic of the Congo's (formerly Zaïre) civil war and signs of corruption in the government. Uganda's forces were largely withdrawn from the Democratic Republic of the Congo by the end of 2002. In 2005 the International Court in The Hague ordered Uganda to pay compensation to the DRC for its activities there between 1998 and 2003.

In Feb. 2006 Museveni won a new presidential term. In July 2006 peace talks commenced between the government and the Lord's Resistance Army (LRA), a fanatically religious group led by Joseph Kony that has terrorized northern Uganda for many years. A ceasefire was declared in Aug. 2006 but subsequent talks have been marred by disputes and walkouts.

TERRITORY AND POPULATION

Uganda is bounded in the north by Sudan, in the east by Kenya, in the south by Tanzania and Rwanda, and the west by the Democratic Republic of the Congo. Total area 241,548 sq. km, including inland waters.

The 2002 census population was 24,442,084 (11,929,803 males, 12,512,281 females); density, 101 per sq. km. The United Nations population estimate for 2002 was 26,035,000. The largest city is Kampala, the capital (population of 1,189,142 in 2002). Other major towns are Gulu, Lira, Jinja, Mbale, Mbarara, Masaka and Entebbe. In 2005, 87·4% of the population lived in rural areas.

The estimated population for 2010 is 33·80m.

The country is administratively divided into 77 districts, which are grouped in four geographical regions (which do not have administrative status). Area and population of the regions in 2002:

Region	*Area in sq. km*	*Population in 1,000*
Central Region	61,510	6,575·4
Eastern Region	39,953	6,204·9
Northern Region	84,658	5,363·7
Western Region	54,917	6,298·1

The official languages are English and (since 2005) Kiswahili. About 70% of the population speak Bantu languages; Nilotic languages are spoken in the north and east.

Uganda is host to around 500,000 refugees from a number of neighbouring countries, and internally displaced people. Probably in excess of 100,000 southern Sudanese fled to Uganda during 1996.

SOCIAL STATISTICS

2000 estimates: births, 1,188,000; deaths, 404,000. Rates, 2000 estimates (per 1,000 population): births, 50·6; deaths, 17·2. Uganda has one of the youngest populations of any country, with half of the population under the age of 15. Uganda's life expectancy at birth in 2007 was 51·4 years for males and 52·4 years for females. Life expectancy declined dramatically until the late 1990s, largely owing to the huge number of people in the country with HIV. However, for both males and females expectation of life is now starting to rise again. Annual population growth rate, 1992–2002, 3·0%. Infant mortality, 2005, 79 per 1,000 live births; fertility rate, 2004, 7·1 births per woman.

CLIMATE

Although in equatorial latitudes, the climate is more tropical because of its elevation, and is characterized by two distinct rainy seasons, March–May and Sept.–Nov. In comparison, June–Aug. and Dec.–Feb. are relatively dry. Temperatures vary little over the year. Kampala, Jan. 74°F (23·3°C), July 70°F (21·1°C). Annual rainfall 46·5" (1,180 mm). Entebbe, Jan. 72°F (22·2°C), July 69°F (20·6°C). Annual rainfall 63·9" (1,624 mm).

CONSTITUTION AND GOVERNMENT

The *President* is head of state and head of government, and is elected for a five-year term by adult suffrage. In Aug. 2005 Parliament amended the constitution to allow an incumbent to hold office for more than two terms, thus enabling President Museveni to serve another term in office. Having lapsed in 1966, the kabakaship was revived as a ceremonial office in 1993. Ronald Muwenda Mutebi (b. 13 April 1955) was crowned Mutebi II, 36th Kabaka, on 31 July 1993.

Until 1994 the national legislature was the 278-member National Resistance Council, but this was replaced by a 284-member *Constituent Assembly* in March 1994. A new constitution was adopted on 8 Oct. 1995 and the Constituent Assembly dissolved. Uganda's parliament is now the 332-member *National Assembly* (215 members elected by popular vote, 104 indirectly elected from special interest groups, including women and the army, and 13 *ex officio* seats filled by cabinet ministers). A referendum on the return of multi-party democracy was held on 29 June 2000, but 88% of voters supported President Museveni's 'no-party' Movement system of government. Turnout was 51%. In Feb. 2003 President Museveni pledged to lift the ban on political parties. In a referendum held on 28 July 2005, 92·4% of voters backed the restoration of a multi-party political system, although the opposition called for a boycott.

National Anthem

'Oh, Uganda, may God uphold thee'; words and tune by G. W. Kakoma.

RECENT ELECTIONS

Presidential elections were held on 23 Feb. 2006. President Museveni was re-elected by 59·3% of votes cast, with his main rival, Kizza Besigye, receiving 37·4% of the vote. Turnout was 68·6%.

Parliamentary elections were held on 23 Feb. 2006. Of the 215 directly elected seats, 142 went to the National Resistance Movement, 27 to Forum for Democratic Change, 9 to the Uganda People's Congress, 8 to the Democratic Party and one each to the Conservative Party and the Justice Forum, with 26 going to independents and one vacant. Turnout was 72%.

CURRENT ADMINISTRATION

President: Yoweri K. Museveni; b. 1945 (sworn in 27 Jan. 1986; re-elected 1996, 2001 and 2006).

In March 2010 the government comprised:

Vice-President: Prof. Gilbert Bukenya (sworn in 6 June 2003).

Prime Minister: Apollo Nsibambi; b. 1938 (sworn in 5 April 1999).

First Deputy Prime Minister and Minister of East African Affairs: Eriya Kategaya. *Second Deputy Prime Minister and Minister of Public Service:* Henry Muganwa Kajura. *Third Deputy Prime Minister and Minister of Internal Affairs:* Kirunda Kivejinja.

Minister of Agriculture, Animal Industry and Fisheries: Hope Mwesigye. *Communication and Information Communication Technology:* Aggrey Awori. *Defence:* Crispus Kiyonga. *Education and Sports:* Namirembe Bitamazire. *Energy and Mineral Development:* Hillary Onek. *Finance, Planning and Economic Development:* Syda Bbumba. *Foreign Affairs:* Sam Kutesa. *Gender, Labour and Social Development:* Gabriel Opio. *Health:* Dr Stephen Mallinga. *Information and National Guidance:* Kabakumba Matsiko. *Justice, Constitutional Affairs and Attorney General:* Kiddu Makubuya. *Lands, Housing and Urban Development:* Omara Atubo. *Local Government:* Adolf Mwesigye. *Presidency:* Beatrice Wabudeya. *Relief and Disaster Preparedness:* Tarsis Kabwegyere. *Security:* Amama Mbabazi. *Trade and Industry:* Kahinda Otafiire. *Transport and Works:* John Nasasira. *Water and Environment:* Maria Mutagamba. *Minister without Portfolio:* Dorothy Hyuha. *Office of the Prime Minister (Minister of General Duties):* Janat Mukwaya.

Speaker of Parliament: Edward Ssekandi.

Ugandan Parliament: http://www.parliament.go.ug

CURRENT LEADERS

Yoweri Museveni

Position

President

Introduction

Yoweri Museveni became president of Uganda in 1986 and has been largely credited with transforming the country's economy after the years of misrule by Idi Amin Dada and Milton Obote. He won the first direct presidential elections in 1996 and was re-elected in 2001. In July 2005 a national referendum approved the lifting of restrictions on multi-party politics (in force since Museveni came to power) and the National Assembly abolished a constitutional limit on presidential terms. He won a further term in Feb. 2006. His government has been in faltering talks with the Lord's Resistance Army (LRA) since 2006 in an attempt to end the conflict with the rebel group that has simmered for more than two decades.

Early Life

Yoweri Kaguta Museveni was born in 1944 in Ankole, western Uganda, where he attended Mbarara High School and Ntare School. He studied economics and political science at the University of Dar es Salaam, Tanzania, graduating in 1970. While at university Museveni was politically active and became the chairman of a leftist student group linked to African liberation movements. In 1971 Idi Amin Dada came to power in Uganda and Museveni went back to Tanzania. He was a founder of the Front for National Salvation, one of the rebel groups that overthrew Amin in 1979. Museveni held various ministerial posts before running for president in 1980. Defeated by Milton Obote, he formed the National Resistance Army, which took power on 26 Jan. 1986 when Museveni declared himself president and minister of defence. His movement was supported by Col. Qadhafi of Libya.

Career in Office

For much of his presidency, Museveni has been favoured by Western nations and foreign aid donors for opening up the Ugandan economy and reducing poverty. Primary school education increased markedly and, thanks to anti-AIDS campaigns, he succeeded in reducing HIV levels. But Museveni's image was tarnished internationally when Ugandan troops invaded eastern Democratic Republic of the Congo in 1998 in support of rebel forces. In Sept. 2002 a peace agreement was signed, committing Uganda to withdraw its troops.

After coming to power, Museveni claimed that political parties divided poor countries like Uganda into ethnic, religious and tribal groups. His preferred system therefore had individuals competing for political office on individual merit. However, after 2001 calls for a return to multi-party democracy in Uganda became more persistent, and this was approved in a national referendum in July 2005, although the turnout was low. Museveni's government nevertheless supported the restoration. Parliament meanwhile voted to lift the constitutional two-term limit on the office of president. Museveni stood for re-election in Feb. 2006 and won a further term with almost 60% of the vote.

In Oct. 2005 Kizza Besigye—Museveni's main opposition rival in the 2001 presidential poll which had been tainted by violence—returned to Uganda from exile in South Africa to contest the 2006 elections. His subsequent arrest for treason provoked violent street protests before his release on bail in Jan. 2006. Meanwhile, concern over alleged human rights abuses by Museveni's government led the UK and other European countries to suspend direct development aid in Dec. 2005. Britain later agreed to resume aid in Nov. 2007 at the biennial Commonwealth Heads of Government conference hosted by Museveni in Kampala.

In July 2006 the government opened peace talks with the rebel LRA, which has conducted an insurgency in northern Uganda since the 1980s involving atrocities against the local population. A truce was signed in Aug., but subsequent political progress was limited amid reported divisions within the LRA itself. In early 2008 the LRA announced that its leader, Joseph Kony, was ready to sign a peace agreement. Optimism proved unfounded, however, leading to a new offensive in Dec. against the rebels by troops from Uganda, southern Sudan and the Democratic Republic of the Congo. In Jan. 2009 the LRA called for a new ceasefire and in March Ugandan troops ended their offensive. Museveni's government claimed that the campaign had seriously hampered LRA capabilities and also rescued many kidnap victims.

Following the announcement in Jan. 2009 of a significant oil discovery in Uganda by a British exploration company, Museveni said that the income from the oil, if well invested, could transform the country's economy and development.

In Sept. 2009 there were riots in Kampala by supporters of Ronald Mutebi, the king of Buganda (one of five ancient kingdoms that had been restored by Museveni) and leader of Uganda's largest ethnic group. Tensions between Museveni's government and Buganda grew when parliament passed new land legislation that the king had opposed because it eroded his ownership rights.

In Dec. 2009 the National Resistance Movement endorsed Museveni as its candidate for the next presidential election in 2011.

DEFENCE

Defence expenditure in 2006 totalled US$192m. (US$7 per capita), representing 1·9% of GDP.

Army

The Uganda People's Defence Forces had a strength estimated at 45,000 in 2007. There is a Border Defence Unit about 600-strong and local defence units estimated at 10,000.

Navy

There is a Marine unit of the police (about 400-strong in 2007).

Air Force

In 2007 the Army's aviation wing operated 14 combat capable aircraft (although the serviceability of some was in doubt) and one attack helicopter. There was also a police air wing around 800-strong.

INTERNATIONAL RELATIONS

Uganda is a member of the UN, World Bank, IMF and several other UN specialized agencies, WTO, Commonwealth, IOM, Islamic Development Bank, OIC, African Development Bank, African Union, COMESA, EAC, Intergovernmental Authority on Development and is an ACP member state of the ACP-EU relationship.

In Nov. 1999 Uganda, Tanzania and Kenya created a new East African Community to develop East African trade, tourism and industry and to lay the foundations for a future common market and political federation.

ECONOMY

In 2006 agriculture accounted for 31·1% of GDP, industry 18·1% and services 50·7%.

Overview

Despite some growth during the 1990s and early 2000s, Uganda remains one of the poorest nations. In the early 1990s GDP growth was robust and inflation fell to under 10%. Growth was around 6% per year between 1998–2003, while average underlying inflation stayed around 5%. Since 2003 growth rates have declined slightly, owing to prolonged droughts, energy shortages, falling industrial production and high oil prices (Uganda being a net oil importer).

A Poverty Eradication Action Plan (PEAP) was launched in 1997 with the aim of reducing the number of people living in poverty to less than 10% of the population by 2017. While the long term growth rate has fallen short of achieving this target, the poverty rate fell from 44% of the population in 1997 to 31·5% in 2006. However, poverty levels remain high in the north and east of the country. Fiscal and external stability indicators have declined in recent years, prompting the government to set out a plan for fiscal consolidation that includes increasing revenue collection and decreasing public administration expenditure. The government is heavily dependent on foreign aid.

The main export commodities are coffee, fish and fish products, cotton, corn, beans and sesame. The economy is highly vulnerable to external shocks, though recent trends show a shift from agriculture to industry and services. Agriculture as a share of GDP had fallen by 20% since 1985 to 31% in 2002, while industry's share doubled in the same period and services also expanded.

Currency

The monetary unit is the *Uganda shilling* (UGX) notionally divided into 100 *cents*. In 1987 the currency was devalued by 77% and a new 'heavy' shilling was introduced worth 100 old shillings. Inflation was 6·8% in 2007 and 7·3% in 2008. Foreign exchange reserves in June 2005 were US$1,326m. Total money supply in July 2005 was Shs 1,513·0bn.

Budget

The financial year runs from 1 July–30 June. Revenues for 2003–04 were Shs 2,939bn and expenditures Shs 3,170bn. Tax revenue accounted for 52·7% of revenues in 2003–04; current expenditure accounted for 58·8% of expenditures.

VAT is 18%.

Performance

Real GDP growth was 8·4% in 2007 and 9·0% in 2008. In recent times Uganda has consistently been among Africa's best performers. In spite of growth rates which averaged 6·4% over ten years to 1998, per capita income is only just around the level of 1971, when Gen. Idi Amin came to power. Uganda's total GDP in 2008 was US$14·5bn.

Banking and Finance

The Bank of Uganda (*Governor*, Emmanuel Tumusiime Mutebile) was established in 1966 and is the central bank and bank of issue. In addition there are five foreign, six commercial and two development banks. There is also the state-owned Uganda Development Bank, which is scheduled for eventual privatization.

In 2008 foreign direct investment totalled US$787m.

ENERGY AND NATURAL RESOURCES

Environment

Uganda's carbon dioxide emissions from the consumption and flaring of fossil fuels were the equivalent of 0·1 tonnes per capita in 2008.

Electricity

Installed capacity in 2004 was approximately 0·3m. kW, about 95% of which was provided by the Owen Falls Extension Project (a hydro-electric scheme). Production (2004 estimate) 1·9bn. kWh. Per capita consumption (2004 estimate) 63 kWh. Only 5% of the population has access to electricity, and less than 1% of the rural population. About a quarter of the country's daily electricity demand cannot be met.

Oil and Gas

Oil was first discovered in Uganda in 2006. There was a further major find in 2009, which may represent the largest onshore discovery in sub-Saharan Africa. Reserves have been estimated at 2bn. bbls. It is hoped that production will begin in 2011.

Minerals

In Nov. 1997 extraction started on the first of an estimated US$400m. worth of cobalt from pyrites. Tungsten and tin concentrates are also mined. There are also significant quantities of clay and gypsum.

Agriculture

80% of the workforce is involved with agriculture. In 2007 the agricultural area included an estimated 5·5m. ha. of arable land and about 2·2m. ha. of permanent crops. Agriculture is one of the priority areas for increased production, with many projects funded both locally and externally. It contributes 90% of exports. Production (2003 estimates) in 1,000 tonnes: cassava, 13,500; plantains, 10,000; sweet potatoes, 2,600; sugarcane, 1,600; maize, 1,200; bananas, 615; millet, 584; potatoes, 546; dry beans, 535; sorghum, 395; coffee, 186. Coffee is the mainstay of the economy, accounting for more than 50% of the annual commodity export revenue. Uganda is the world's leading producer of plantains.

Livestock (2003 estimates): goats, 6·9m.; cattle, 6·1m.; pigs, 1·7m.; sheep, 1·2m.; chickens, 33m. Livestock products, 2003 estimates (in 1,000 tonnes): milk, 700; meat, 293.

Forestry

In 2005 the area under forests was 3·63m. ha., or 18·4% of the total land area. Exploitable forests consist almost entirely of hardwoods. Timber production in 2007 totalled 41·08m. cu. metres. Uganda has great potential for timber-processing for export, manufacture of high-quality furniture and wood products, and various packaging materials.

Fisheries

In 2005 fish landings totalled 416,758 tonnes, entirely from inland waters. Fish farming (especially carp and tilapia) is a growing industry. Uganda's fish-processing industry has greatly expanded in recent years, and fisheries exports, valued at US$87m. in 2002, now rival coffee and tourism as the major foreign currency earners.

INDUSTRY

Production (in 1,000 tonnes): cement (2001), 416; sugar (2002), 160; soap (2002), 92; beer (2002), 98·9m. litres. In 2001 industry accounted for 20·9% of GDP, with manufacturing contributing 9·8%. Industrial production grew by 5·4% in 2001.

Labour

The labour force in 2002–03 totalled 9,772,600 (47% males). In 2002–03 the unemployment rate was 3·2%.

INTERNATIONAL TRADE

Foreign debt was US$4,463m. in 2005.

Imports and Exports

In 2006 imports (f.o.b.) amounted to US$2,239·1m. (US$1,780·4m. in 2005); exports (f.o.b.) US$1,003·9m. (US$864·2m. in 2005). Coffee, fish, gold, tobacco and tea are the principal exports. Major imports are machinery and transport equipment, and food, beverages and tobacco products. The main import suppliers in 2006 were Kenya (15·7%), UAE (12·7%) and India (8·2%). In 2006 the main export markets were UAE (19·4%), Sudan (9·5%) and Kenya (9·1%).

COMMUNICATIONS

Roads

In 2003 there were 70,746 km of roads, of which 23% were paved. There were 81,300 passenger cars in use in 2007, 79,300 lorries and vans, 40,500 buses and coaches, and 176,500 motorcycles and mopeds. In 2007 there were 17,428 road accidents resulting in 2,779 deaths.

In 2007 the government established the Uganda Road Fund, a body responsible for financing road maintenance. The estimated budget in 2007–08 totalled US$111·35m.

Rail

In 2005 the Uganda Railways network totalled 1,241 km (metre gauge). In 1996 passenger services were suspended and have not been reinstated in the meantime. Freight tonne-km in 2003 came to 218m.

A US$20m. project is under way to establish a direct rail link between Kampala and Johannesburg, South Africa.

Civil Aviation

There is an international airport at Entebbe, 40 km from Kampala. The main Ugandan carrier is East African Airlines, which in 2003 flew to Bujumbura, Johannesburg and Nairobi. In 2003 scheduled airline traffic of Uganda-based carriers flew 2m. km, carrying 40,000 passengers (all on international flights). In 2001 Entebbe handled 370,063 passengers (343,722 on international flights) and 37,195 tonnes of freight.

Telecommunications

In 2008 there were 168,500 main (fixed) telephone lines; mobile phone subscribers numbered 8,554,900 in 2008 (27·0 per 100 persons). There were 500,000 PCs in use in 2006 and 2·5m. internet users in 2008.

Postal Services

In 2005 there were 303 post offices.

SOCIAL INSTITUTIONS

Justice

The Supreme Court of Uganda, presided over by the Chief Justice, is the highest court. There is a Court of Appeal and a High Court below that. Subordinate courts, presided over by Chief Magistrates and Magistrates of the first, second and third grade, are established in all areas: jurisdiction varies with the grade of Magistrate. Chief and first-grade Magistrates are professionally qualified; second- and third-grade Magistrates are trained to diploma level at the Law Development Centre, Kampala. Chief Magistrates exercise supervision over and hear appeals from second- and third-grade courts, and village courts.

The population in penal institutions in April 2007 was 26,273 (88 per 100,000 of national population). The death penalty is still in force. In 2006 there were two executions.

Education

In 2007 there were 7,537,971 pupils and 132,325 teaching staff at primary schools. In 1995, 93·9% of primary schools were government-aided and 6·1% private. There were 1,000,580 students and 54,267 teaching staff at secondary schools in 2007. In 1995 there were 13,174 students in 94 primary teacher training colleges; 13,360 students in 24 technical institutes and colleges; 22,703 students in 10 national teachers' colleges; 1,628 students in 5 colleges of commerce; 504 students in the Uganda Polytechnic, Kyambogo; 800 students in the National College of Business Studies, Nakawa. In 1995–96 there was one university and one university of science and technology in the public sector, and one Christian, one Roman Catholic and one Islamic university in the private sector. In 2004 there were 88,360 students in tertiary education and 4,168 academic staff. The adult literacy rate was 68·9% in 2002 (78·8% among males and 59·2% among females).

School attendance has trebled since Yoweri Museveni became president in 1986. In 1997 free primary education was introduced, initially for four children in every family but from 2003 for all children. In 2004 public expenditure on education came to 5·3% of GNI and 18·3% of total government spending.

Health

In 2001 there were 946 health centres (189 private) and 104 hospitals (49 private). In 2002 there were 1,175 physicians, 75 dentists, 1,350 nurses and 850 midwives. Uganda has been one of the most successful African countries in the fight against AIDS. A climate of free debate, with President Museveni recognizing the threat as early as 1986 and making every government department take the problem seriously, resulted in HIV prevalence among adults declining from approximately 30% in 1992 to 11% in 2000.

RELIGION

In 2001 there were 10·05m. Roman Catholics, 9·45m. Anglicans and 1·25m. Muslims. In Feb. 2010 there was one Roman Catholic cardinal. Traditional beliefs are also widespread.

CULTURE

World Heritage Sites

Uganda has three sites on the UNESCO World Heritage List: Bwindi Impenetrable National Park (inscribed on the list in 1994); Rwenzori Mountains National Park (1994); and the Tombs of the Buganda Kings at Kasubi (2001).

Broadcasting

Public television and radio broadcasting is the responsibility of the Uganda Broadcasting Corporation (UBC), which was inaugurated in 2005 following legislation to merge Uganda Television and Radio Uganda. UBC Radio operates five networks in English and vernacular languages. There are around 100 commercial TV and radio services. There were 650,000 television sets in 2006. Colour is by PAL.

Press

There were five daily newspapers in 2004 with a combined average daily circulation of 89,000, plus 93 non-dailies.

Tourism

In 2005 there were 468,000 non-resident tourists; spending by tourists totalled US$357m.

Festivals

The main festivals are for Islamic holidays (March and June), Martyrs' Day (3 June), Heroes' Day (9 June) and Independence Day (9 Oct.).

Theatre and Opera

There is a National Theatre at Kampala.

Museums and Galleries

The Nommo Gallery houses famous works of art, and is involved in educational and other cultural programmes.

DIPLOMATIC REPRESENTATIVES

Of Uganda in the United Kingdom (Uganda House, 58/59 Trafalgar Square, London, WC2N 5DX)
High Commissioner: Joan Kakima Nyakatuura Rwabyomere.

Of the United Kingdom in Uganda (4 Windsor Loop, PO Box 7070, Kampala)
High Commissioner: Martin Shearman.

Of Uganda in the USA (5911 16th St., NW, Washington, D.C., 20011)
Ambassador: Perezi Kamunanwire.

Of the USA in Uganda (1577 Ggaba Rd, Kampala)
Ambassador: Jerry P. Lanier.

Of Uganda to the United Nations
Ambassador: Ruhakana Rugunda.

Of Uganda to the European Union
Ambassador: Stephen T. Kapimpina Katenta-Apuli.

FURTHER READING

Museveni, Y., *What is Africa's Problem?* 1993.—*The Mustard Seed.* 1997
Mutibwa, P., *Uganda since Independence: a Story of Unfulfilled Hopes.* 1992
Ofcansky, Thomas P., *Uganda: Tarnished Pearl of Africa.* 1999

National Statistical Office: Uganda Bureau of Statistics, P. O. Box 7186, Kampala.
Website: http://www.ubos.org

UKRAINE

Ukraina

Capital: Kyiv (formerly Kiev)
Population estimate, 2010: 45·43m.
GDP per capita, 2007: (PPP$) 6,914
HDI/world rank: 0·796/85

KEY HISTORICAL EVENTS

Kyiv (formerly Kiev) was the centre of the Rus principality in the 11th and 12th centuries and is still known as the Mother of Russian cities. The western Ukraine principality of Galicia was annexed by Poland in the 14th century. At about the same time, Kyiv and the Ukrainian principality of Volhynia were conquered by Lithuania before being absorbed by Poland. Poland, however, could not subjugate the Ukrainian cossacks, who allied themselves with Russia. Ukraine, except for Galicia (part of the Austrian Empire, 1772–1919), was incorporated into the Russian Empire after the second partition of Poland in 1793.

In 1917, following the Bolshevik revolution, the Ukrainians in Russia established an independent republic. Austrian Ukraine proclaimed itself a republic in 1918 and was federated with its Russian counterpart. The Allies ignored Ukrainian claims to Galicia, however, and in 1918 awarded that area to Poland. From 1922 to 1932, drastic efforts were made by the USSR to suppress Ukrainian nationalism. Ukraine suffered from the forced collectivization of agriculture and the expropriation of foodstuffs; the result was the famine of 1932–33 when more than 7m. people died. Following the Soviet seizure of eastern Poland in Sept. 1939, Polish Galicia was incorporated into the Ukrainian SSR. When the Germans invaded Ukraine in 1941 hopes that an autonomous or independent Ukrainian republic would be set up under German protection were disappointed. Ukraine was retaken by the USSR in 1944. The Crimean region was joined to Ukraine in 1954.

On 5 Dec. 1991 the Supreme Soviet declared Ukraine's independence. Ukraine was one of the founder members of the Commonwealth of Independent States in Dec. 1991. After independence Crimea, which was part of Russia until 1954, became a source of contention between Moscow and Kyiv. The Russian Supreme Soviet laid claim to the Crimean port city of Sevastopol, the home port of the 350-ship Black Sea Fleet, despite an agreement to divide the fleet. There was also conflict between Ukraine and Russia over possession and transfer of nuclear weapons, delivery of Russian fuel to Ukraine and military and political integration within the CIS. Leonid Kuchma was elected president in 1994 and re-elected in 1999. Support for him fell after public demonstrations against maladministration including the accusation that he was responsible for the murder of a radical journalist. Conflicts between the presidential administration and government led to the sacking of reform-minded prime minister Viktor Yushchenko in April 2001, who was replaced by Kuchma loyalist Anatolii Kinakh at the end of May.

The Pope's historic visit to Ukraine in June 2001 was accompanied by disturbances, particularly in the capital. Presidential elections in Oct. and Nov. 2004 were won by Kuchma's chosen successor, Viktor Yanukovych, who defeated Viktor Yushchenko in the second round run-off. But observers claimed the election failed to meet democratic standards and in Kyiv widespread protests came to be known as the 'Orange Revolution'. After the poll was declared invalid Yushchenko was elected president in a repeat of the run-off. However, infighting between the leaders of the revolution led to growing popular discontent. In Feb. 2010 Yanukovych was elected president, defeating Yuliya Tymoshenko, a figurehead of the 2004 protests.

TERRITORY AND POPULATION

Ukraine is bounded in the east by the Russian Federation, north by Belarus, west by Poland, Slovakia, Hungary, Romania and Moldova, and south by the Black Sea and Sea of Azov. Area, 603,700 sq. km (233,090 sq. miles). In 2001 the census population was 48,457,102, of whom 26,015,758 were female; density, 80 per sq. km. 78% of the population were Ukrainians, 17% Russians and 5% others—Belarusians, Moldovans, Hungarians, Bulgarians, Poles and Crimean Tatars (most of the Tatars were forcibly transported to Central Asia in 1944 for anti-Soviet activities during the Second World War). Ukraine's population is projected to drop to 41·62m. by 2025, a reduction of 8% in 15 years. In 2005, 67·8% of the population lived in urban areas.

The UN gives an estimated population for 2010 of 45·43m.

Ukraine is divided into 24 provinces, two municipalities (Kyiv and Simferopol) and the Autonomous Republic of Crimea. Area and populations (2001 census):

	Area (sq. km)	*Population*
Cherkaska	20,900	1,402,969
Chernihivska	31,900	1,245,260
Chernivetska	8,100	922,817
Crimea	26,100	2,033,736
Dnipropetrovska	31,900	3,567,567
Donetska	26,500	4,841,074
Ivano-Frankivska	13,900	1,409,760
Kharkivska	31,400	2,914,212
Khersonska	28,500	1,175,122
Khmelnitska	20,600	1,430,775
Kirovohradska	24,600	1,133,052
Kyiv	800	2,611,327
Kyivska	28,100	1,827,894
Luhanska	26,700	2,546,178
Lvivska	21,800	2,626,543
Mykolaïvska	24,600	1,264,743
Odeska	33,300	2,469,057

	Area (sq. km)	Population
Poltavska	28,800	1,630,092
Rivnenska	20,100	1,173,304
Sevastopol	900	379,492
Sumska	23,800	1,299,746
Ternopilska	13,800	1,142,416
Vinnytska	26,500	1,772,371
Volynska	20,200	1,060,694
Zakarpatska	12,800	1,258,264
Zaporizhska	27,200	1,929,171
Zhytomyrska	29,900	1,389,466

The capital is Kyiv (population 2,611,327 in 2001). Other towns with 2001 populations over 0·2m. are:

	Population		Population
Kharkiv	1,470,902	Chernihiv	304,994
Dnipropetrovsk	1,065,008	Cherkasy	295,414
Odesa	1,029,049	Sumy	293,141
Donetsk	1,016,194	Horlivka	292,250
Zaporizhzhya	815,256	Zhytomyr	284,236
Lviv	732,818	Dniprodzerzhynsk	255,841
Kryvy Rih	668,980	Kirovohrad	254,103
Mykolaïv	514,136	Khmelnitsky	253,994
Mariupol	492,176	Rivne	248,813
Luhansk	463,097	Chernivtsi	240,621
Makiïvka	389,589	Kremenchuk	234,073
Vinnytsya	356,665	Ternopil	227,755
Simferopol	343,644	Ivano-Frankivsk	218,359
Sevastopol	342,451	Lutsk	208,816
Kherson	328,360	Bila Tserkva	200,131
Poltava	317,998		

The 1996 constitution made Ukrainian the sole official language. Russian (the language of 33% of the population), Romanian, Polish and Hungarian are also spoken. Additionally, the 1996 constitution abolished dual citizenship, previously available if there was a treaty with the other country (there was no such treaty with Russia). Anyone resident in Ukraine since 1991 may be naturalized.

SOCIAL STATISTICS

2005 births, 426,085; deaths, 781,964; marriages, 332,138; divorces, 183,455. Rates (per 1,000 population), 2005: births, 9·0; deaths, 16·6. Annual population growth rate, 2000–05, –0·9%. Life expectancy, 2007: males, 62·7 years, females, 73·8. In 2003 the most popular age range for marrying was 20–24 for both males and females. Infant mortality, 2005, 13 per 1,000 live births; fertility rate, 2004, 1·1 births per woman (the lowest rate of any country).

CLIMATE

Temperate continental with a subtropical Mediterranean climate prevalent on the southern portions of the Crimean Peninsula. The average monthly temperature in winter ranges from 17·6°F to 35·6°F (–8°C to 2°C), while summer temperatures average 62·6°F to 77°F (17°C to 25°C). The Black Sea coast is subject to freezing, and no Ukrainian port is permanently ice-free. Precipitation generally decreases from north to south; it is greatest in the Carpathians where it exceeds more than 58·5" (1,500 mm) per year, and least in the coastal lowlands of the Black Sea where it averages less than 11·7" (300 mm) per year.

CONSTITUTION AND GOVERNMENT

In a referendum on 1 Dec. 1991, 90·3% of votes cast were in favour of independence. Turnout was 83·7%.

A new constitution was adopted on 28 June 1996. It defines Ukraine as a sovereign, democratic, unitary state governed by the rule of law and guaranteeing civil rights. The head of state is the *President*, elected directly by the people for a five-year term. An amendment to the constitution that came into effect on 1 Jan. 2006 gives increased powers to parliament, including the right to appoint and dismiss the prime minister. However, after parliament dismissed the prime minister and the cabinet on 10 Jan. 2006 President Yushchenko stated that only the new parliament that was to be elected in March 2006 would have such powers.

Parliament is the 450-member unicameral *Verkhovna Rada* (*Supreme Council*), elected for four-year terms. Prior to the March 2006 election half of the members were chosen from party lists by proportional vote and half from individual constituencies, but in accordance with a constitutional amendment for the 2006 election all 450 members were chosen from party lists.

There is an 18-member *Constitutional Court*, six members being appointed by the President, six by parliament and six by a panel of judges. Constitutional amendments may be initiated at the President's request to parliament, or by at least one third of parliamentary deputies. The Communist Party was officially banned in the country in 1991, but was renamed the Socialist Party of Ukraine. Hard-line Communists protested against the ban, which was rescinded by the Supreme Council in May 1993.

National Anthem

'Shche ne vmerla, Ukraïny i slava, i volya' ('Ukraine's freedom and glory has not yet perished'); words by P. Chubynsky, tune by M. Verbytsky.

GOVERNMENT CHRONOLOGY

Presidents since 1991.

1991–94	Leonid Makarovich Kravchuk
1994–2005	Leonid Danylovich Kuchma
2005–10	Viktor Andriyovich Yushchenko
2010–	Viktor Fedorovych Yanukovych

Prime Ministers since 1990.

1990–92	Vitold Pavlovich Fokin
1992	Valentyn Kostyantynovich Symonenko
1992–93	Leonid Danylovich Kuchma
1994–95	Vitaliy Anriyovich Masol
1995–96	Yevhen Kyrylovich Marchuk
1996–97	Pavlo Ivanovich Lazarenko
1997–99	Valeriy Pavlovich Pustovoytenko
1999–01	Viktor Andriyovich Yushchenko
2001–02	Anatolii Kyrylovich Kinakh
2002–05	Viktor Fedorovych Yanukovych
2005	Yuliya Volodymyrivna Tymoshenko
2005–06	Yuriy Ivanovich Yekhanurov
2006–07	Viktor Fedorovych Yanukovych
2007–10	Yuliya Volodymyrivna Tymoshenko
2010–	Mykola Yanovych Azarov

RECENT ELECTIONS

Presidential elections were held in two rounds on 17 Jan. and 7 Feb. 2010. In the first round Viktor Yanukovych won 35·3% of the vote against 25·1% for prime minister Yuliya Tymoshenko, 13·1% for Sergei Tigipko, 7·0% for Arseniy Yatsenyuk and 5·5% for incumbent President Viktor Yushchenko. There were 13 other candidates. Turnout was 66·8%. Yanukovych won the second round with 49·0% against 45·5% for Tymoshenko. However, the results were suspended after Tymoshenko accused Yanukovych of electoral fraud prompting an inquiry. She withdrew her appeal on 20 Feb. but did not attend Yanukovych's inauguration on 25 Feb. and refused to recognize his position. On 3 March, Tymoshenko's government lost a parliamentary vote of confidence and she was ousted as prime minister.

In parliamentary elections held on 30 Sept. 2007 the Party of Regions won 175 seats with 34·4% of the vote, the Yuliya Tymoshenko Bloc 156 (30·7%), the Our Ukraine–People's Self Defence Bloc 72 (14·2%), the Communist Party of Ukraine 27 (5·4%) and the Lytvyn Bloc 20 (4·0%). Turnout was 62·0%.

CURRENT ADMINISTRATION

President: Viktor Yanukovych; b. 1950 (ind.; sworn in 25 Feb. 2010).

In March 2010 the 'Stability and Reform' coalition of the Party of Regions, Lytvyn Bloc and the Communist Party of Ukraine formed a new government comprising:

Prime Minister: Mykola Azarov; b. 1947 (Party of Regions; sworn in 11 March 2010).

First Deputy Prime Minister: Andrii Kliuyev. *Deputy Prime Ministers:* Borys Kolesnikov; Volodymyr Semynozhenko; Volodymyr Sivkovych; Viktor Slauta; Sergei Tigipko; Viktor Tikhonov.

Minister of Agrarian Policy: Mykola Prysiazhniuk. *Coal Industry:* Yurii Yashchenko. *Culture and Tourism:* Mykhailo Kulyniak. *Defence:* Mykhailo Ezhel. *Economics:* Vasyl Tsushko. *Education and Science:* Dmytro Tabachnyk. *Emergency Situations:* Nestor Shufrych. *Environmental Protection:* Viktor Boiko. *Family, Youth Affairs and Sports:* Ravil Safiullin. *Finance:* Fedir Yaroshenko. *Foreign Affairs:* Kostyantyn Hryshchenko. *Fuel and Energy:* Yurii Boiko. *Health:* Zynovii Mytnik. *Housing and Communal Services:* Oleksandr Popov. *Industrial Policy:* Dmytro Kolyesnikov. *Interior:* Anatoliy Mohylyov. *Justice:* Oleksandr Lavrynovych. *Labour and Social Policy:* Vasyl Nadraha. *Regional Development and Construction:* Volodymyr Yatsuba. *Transport and Communications:* Kostiantyn Yefymenko. *Minister of the Cabinet:* Anatolii Tolstoukhov.

Government Website: http://www.kmu.gov.ua

CURRENT LEADERS

Viktor Yanukovych

Position
President

Introduction
Having served as prime minister under President Kuchma from 2002–05, Viktor Yanukovych was briefly declared president after the bitterly contested 2004 election. When the result was annulled he lost the re-run and resigned as prime minister. In March 2006 his Party of the Regions won the largest number of seats in parliament and in Aug. 2006 he became prime minister in a coalition government. His power base is in eastern Ukraine, where he has strong links with industrialists, and he favours close ties between Ukraine and Russia. On 18 Dec. 2007 Yanukovych was formally dismissed by parliament. In 2010 he fought a bitterly contested presidential election against Yuliya Tymoshenko, narrowly defeating her in the second round of voting. Tymoshenko contested the results accusing Yanukovych of electoral misconduct. Nonetheless he was sworn in as president on 25 Feb.

Early Life
Viktor Yanukovych was born on 9 July 1950 in Yenakiyeve, Donetsk Oblast, in Russian-speaking eastern Ukraine. His mother, an ethnic Ukrainian nurse, died when he was two, and his father, an ethnic Belarusian train driver, died when he was in his teens, leaving him in the care of his grandmother. He served a prison sentence in 1967 for robbery and another in 1970 for bodily injury, although he claims to have been later cleared of both crimes. In 1972 he began working in the transport department for the Donetsk coal industry and completed his education, graduating in mechanical engineering from Donetsk Polytechnic Institute in 1980. He joined the Communist Party and rose rapidly as a manager in Donetsk regional transport.

He entered politics in Aug. 1996 as deputy head of Donetsk Oblast administration and was appointed head of administration in May 1997. From May 1999–May 2001 he was head of the Donetsk Oblast regional council and became closely associated with a group of business and political figures known as the 'Clan of Donetsk', led by the coal and steel oligarch Rinat Akhmetov. His lobbying for them brought him strong political and financial support but also fuelled rumours of links to organized crime. In Nov. 2002 he was appointed prime minister by President Leonid Kuchma.

Yanukovych oversaw the continuing liberalization of the economy, cutting higher rates of income tax and encouraging land privatization. He often favoured the interests of Ukrainian industrialists over international investors, helping power the domestic economy but leading to allegations of corruption. He maintained strong links with Russia and spoke against Ukraine joining the EU and NATO. In 2003 his government signed an agreement to take Ukraine into a free trade zone and customs alliance with Russia, Belarus and Kazakhstan, although negotiations subsequently stalled. Kuchma chose not to fight the 2004 presidential election and Yanukovych stood as his successor, openly supported by Russia's President Putin.

Yanukovych lost the first round to Viktor Yushchenko of the pro-west, liberal Our Ukraine party but won the second round on 21 Nov. 2004. The result was challenged and Yushchenko's supporters staged huge street protests dubbed the 'Orange Revolution'. The supreme court annulled the result and a re-run of the second round saw Yushchenko triumph. Following a parliamentary vote of no confidence in his government Yanukovych resigned as prime minister in Jan. 2005.

Yanukovych spent 2005 building on his grassroots support in eastern Ukraine. He profited from disillusionment with Yushchenko's government, which was divided and indecisive. Yanukovych's Party of the Regions won the March 2006 parliamentary elections with 186 seats out of 450, ahead of the Tymoshenko Bloc and Our Ukraine. Under new rules the cabinet was to appoint the prime minister and with no party having an overall majority, months of wrangling ensued. In Aug. 2006 Yanukovych agreed a coalition deal with Yushchenko's party, centred round a pact of national unity that preserved certain Yushchenko policies. These included Ukraine remaining a unitary state with Ukrainian as the state language, and talks on EU and WTO membership. The pact also promised a referendum on NATO membership and further constitutional reform.

The working relationship between the two parties was uneasy from the outset. Yanukovych took a strong interest in foreign affairs, visiting Russia and promising to work towards a resolution over Russian gas prices. In Dec. 2006 he visited the USA in a demonstration of east-west balance but distanced himself from the idea of a referendum on NATO membership and warned that moves towards EU membership could harm Ukraine's standing with Russia.

Yanukovych was formally dismissed on 18 Dec. 2007 by parliament after Yuliya Tymoshenko was elected prime minister, although the close result of the election left the shadow cabinet, headed by Yanukovych, in a strong position. The cabinet aimed to control the work of the Tymoshenko government and to draft state policy proposals. In particular, Yanukovych sought to influence the government's budget plans in 2008 and 2009, which maintained his high public profile ahead of presidential polls in early 2010.

Career in Office
Yanukovych regained the presidency on 25 Feb. 2010 after comprehensively defeating Viktor Yushchenko in the first round of presidential elections. He then saw off his main opponent, prime minister Yuliya Tymoshenko, in the second winning by a 3·5% margin. Tymoshenko accused him of widescale vote-rigging and challenged the results, which were suspended on 17 Feb. pending a full electoral inquiry. However, Tymoshenko dropped her appeal on 20 Feb. stating that she would not receive a fair hearing. She and her party refused to recognize Yanukovych's election and boycotted the inauguration ceremony.

Mykola Azarov

Position
Prime Minister

Introduction
Mykola Azarov was appointed prime minister on 11 March 2010. A close ally of President Viktor Yanukovych, his predecessor as leader of the Party of Regions, Azarov is regarded as a technocrat. Ethnically Russian, he is a veteran of the country's turbulent political system, having previously served as deputy prime minister, foreign minister and, on two occasions, acting prime minister.

Early Life
Mykola Azarov was born on 17 Dec. 1947 in the town of Kaluga, in what is now Russia. He studied geology at Moscow State University before working at a coal mine in the Russian city of Tula. In 1984 he moved to Donetsk to serve first as deputy director and later as director of the Ukrainian State Geological Institute. He became a member of Ukraine's parliament in 1994 and two years later was appointed head of the state tax authority.

During his six years there Azarov had a reputation for authoritarianism and controversy. It was alleged that he promoted electoral fraud and the intimidation of journalists to secure the re-election of President Leonid Kuchma in 1999. Azarov staunchly denied the accusations, citing a plot against him by rivals.

In 2002 the European Choice parliamentary group, of which he was chairman, nominated Azarov for prime minister. He declined and stood aside for Yanukovych, who assumed both the leadership of the Party of Regions and the premiership. Yanukovych appointed Azarov as deputy prime minister and finance minister in his first cabinet, with Azarov serving until 2005 and then again in 2006–07. His most notable reform was to bring the variable tax rate on personal income down to a uniform flat rate.

During the political upheaval that accompanied the Orange Revolution over the winter of 2004–05, Azarov twice served briefly as acting prime minister. After masterminding Yanukovych's victorious presidential election campaign in 2010, he assumed the leadership of the Party of Regions and was confirmed as prime minister by parliament on 11 March 2010.

Career in Office
Azarov declared that his primary task was to restore the struggling economy. Admitting that 'the coffers are empty', he pledged to push through a programme of budgetary restraints to encourage the IMF to resume funding suspended in 2009. Criticized by opponents for his poor grasp of the Ukrainian language, Azarov has promised that government affairs will be conducted in Ukrainian. Along with President Yanukovych, he has sought to repair strained relations with Moscow.

DEFENCE

The 1996 constitution bans the stationing of foreign troops on Ukrainian soil, but permits Russia to retain naval bases. Ukraine hosts Russia's Black Sea Fleet at Sevastopol in Crimea under a lease that is scheduled to end in 2042 (having been extended by 25 years in April 2010). Conscription is for 12 months. The government has announced its intention to end conscription and move towards a professional military; this will be a gradual process that is scheduled to start in 2011. On 31 May 1997 the presidents of Ukraine and Russia signed a Treaty of Friendship and Co-operation which provided *inter alia* for the division of the former Soviet Black Sea Fleet and shore installations. There were around 1m. armed forces reserves in 2007.

Military expenditure in 2006 totalled US$1,723m. (US$37 per capita), representing 1·6% of GDP.

Army

In 2007 ground forces numbered 70,753. Equipment included 2,984 main battle tanks (T-55s, T-64s, T-72s, T-80s and T-84s) and 139 attack helicopters.

In addition there were around 39,900 Ministry of Internal Affairs troops, 45,000 Border Guards and some 9,500 civil defence troops.

Navy

In 2007 the Navy numbered 13,932, including some 2,500 Naval Aviation and 3,000 naval infantry. The main base is located at Sevastopol. The operational forces include one frigate.

The aviation forces of the former Soviet Black Sea Fleet under Ukrainian command operate ten combat capable aircraft and 77 helicopters.

Air Force

There are three air commands—West, South and Central—plus a Task Force 'Crimea'.

Equipment includes 211 combat capable aircraft (MiG-29s, Su-24s, Su-25s and Su-27s).

Personnel, 2007, 45,240.

INTERNATIONAL RELATIONS

Ukraine is a member of the UN, World Bank, IMF and several other UN specialized agencies, Council of Europe, WTO, OSCE, CEI, BSEC, Danube Commission, CIS, IOM and NATO Partnership for Peace.

ECONOMY

In 2006 agriculture accounted for 8·6% of GDP, industry 34·1% and services 57·3%.

Overview

The economy experienced a sharp slowdown in 2005 following the political upheaval of the 2004 presidential elections but has since rebounded. Economic growth, led by improved industrial production, averaged 8·4% from 2000–04, peaking at 12·1% in 2004, the highest rate in Europe. The 2005 slowdown was the result of a slowing global economy, an appreciating exchange rate, loose monetary policy and increased taxes. Nominal public wages were increased by more than 50%, fuelling inflation. Growth rebounded after a recovery in export prices for steel, together with robust consumption and buoyant investment (particularly foreign direct investment).

While the economy has proved resilient in the face of domestic political uncertainties and rising energy prices, global financial turmoil has seen a withdrawal of funds from investors in Ukraine and a collapse in steel export prices. In Oct. 2008 the IMF approved a US$16·4bn. loan to restore financial and macroeconomic stability, amid forecasts of an imminent recession. However, the economic downturn has been more pronounced in the region than expected and the State Statistics Committee reported a real GDP contraction of 15·1% in 2009.

Currency

The unit of currency is the *hryvnia* (UAH) of 100 *kopiykas*, which replaced karbovanets on 2 Sept. 1996 at 100,000 karbovanets = 1 hryvnia. 2000 saw the introduction of a floating exchange rate for the hryvnia.

Inflation rates (based on IMF statistics):

2000	*2001*	*2002*	*2003*	*2004*	*2005*	*2006*	*2007*	*2008*
28·2%	11·9%	0·7%	5·2%	9·0%	13·5%	9·1%	12·8%	25·2%

Inflation had been 4,735% in 1993. Foreign exchange reserves in Sept. 2009 were US$25,189m., gold reserves were 864,000 troy oz and total money supply was 221,530m. hryvnias.

Budget
In 2006 revenues were 133,464m. hryvnias and expenditures 137,063m. hryvnias. Tax revenue accounted for 71·0% of revenues in 2006; social security accounted for 22·1% of expenditures in 2006, education and health 12·8% and transportation and communications 4·9%.

VAT is 20%.

Performance
Real GDP growth rates (based on IMF statistics):

2000	2001	2002	2003	2004	2005	2006	2007	2008
5·9%	9·2%	5·2%	9·6%	12·1%	2·7%	7·3%	7·9%	2·1%

Between 1994 and 1998 average annual real GDP growth was –10·0%, and it was still negative in 1999, at –0·2%. In 2000, however, the economy expanded considerably and this resurgence continued in the following years with per capita income more than tripling in the period 2000–06. Ukraine's economy did, however, experience a downturn again in the global financial crisis that started in 2008. In 2009 the State Statistics Committee reported negative GDP growth of 15·1%. Ukraine's total GDP in 2008 was US$180·4bn.

Banking and Finance
A National Bank was founded in March 1991. It operates under government control, its Governor being appointed by the President with the approval of parliament. The *Governor* is Volodymyr Stelmakh. There were 176 banks in all in 2003, with assets totalling 85,232m. hryvnias. The largest banks are PrivatBank, Bank Aval and PromInvestBank. In Aug. 2005 Raiffeisen International, an Austrian bank, bought a 93·5% stake in Bank Aval.

There is a stock exchange in Kyiv.

ENERGY AND NATURAL RESOURCES

Environment
Carbon dioxide emissions from the consumption and flaring of fossil fuels in 2008 were the equivalent of 7·6 tonnes per capita.

Electricity
Installed capacity was an estimated 52·8m. kW in 2004. In 2005 production was 186·06bn. kWh; consumption per capita in 2004 was 3,727 kWh. A Soviet programme to greatly expand nuclear power-generating capacity in the country was abandoned in the wake of the 1986 accident at Chernobyl. Chernobyl was closed down on 15 Dec. 2000. In 2007 there were 15 nuclear reactors in use supplying 47·5% of output.

Oil and Gas
In 2004 output of crude petroleum was 22m. bbls; in 2008 production of natural gas was 18·7bn. cu. metres, with 920bn. cu. metres of proven natural gas reserves.

Water
In 2004 water consumption totalled 9,973m. cu. metres.

Minerals
Ukraine's industrial economy, accounting for more than a quarter of total employment, is based largely on the republic's vast mineral resources. The Donetsk Basin contains huge reserves of coal, and the nearby iron-ore reserves of Kryvy Rih are equally rich. Among Ukraine's other mineral resources are manganese, bauxite, nickel, titanium and salt. Iron ore production, 2004, 65·5m. tonnes; coal production, 2004, 59·2m. tonnes; manganese ore production, 2004, 2·4m. tonnes; salt production, 2004, 2·3m. tonnes.

Agriculture
Ukraine has extremely fertile black-earth soils in the central and southern portions, totalling nearly two-thirds of the territory. In 2002 there were 32·54m. ha. of arable land and 0·91m. ha. of permanent crops. Output (in 1,000 tonnes) in 2002: wheat, 20,556; potatoes, 16,620; sugar beets, 14,452; barley, 10,364; maize, 4,180; sunflower seeds, 3,270; rye, 1,509; cabbage, 1,229; tomatoes, 1,038. Livestock, 2003: 9,203,000 pigs, 9,108,000 cattle, 1,034,000 goats, 950,000 sheep, 148m. chickens, 20m. ducks. Livestock products, 2003 (in 1,000 tonnes): milk, 13,660; meat, 1,649; eggs, 656.

Forestry
The area under forests in Ukraine in 2005 was 9·58m. ha. (16·5% of the total land area). In 2007, 16·88m. cu. metres of timber were produced.

Fisheries
In 2005 the catch totalled 244,943 tonnes, of which 238,916 tonnes were from sea fishing. The total catch in 1988 had been 1,048,157 tonnes.

INDUSTRY
In 2007 industry accounted for 28·2% of GDP, with manufacturing contributing 20·5%. Industrial production grew by 10·2% in 2007. Output, 2007 (in tonnes unless otherwise stated): pig iron, 35·6m.; crude steel, 29·0m.; rolled ferrous metals, 24·5m.; cement, 15·0m.; petrol, 4·2m.; distillate fuel oil, 4·1m.; residual fuel oil, 3·4m.; mineral fertilizer, 2·8m.; bread and bakery products, 2·0m.; sugar, 1·9m.; sulphuric acid, 1·6m.; fabrics, 114m. sq. metres; footwear, 22·5m. pairs; refrigerators, 824,000 units; television sets, 507,000 units; passenger cars, 380,000 units; washing machines, 173,000 units; cigarettes, 129bn. units.

Labour
In 2000 a total of 18,063,000 persons were in employment. The principal areas of activity were (in 1,000): agriculture, hunting, forestry and fishing, 4,977; manufacturing, 2,914; wholesale and retail trade, and restaurants and hotels, 1,406; transport, storage and communication, 1,228. In April 2001 there were 1,149,200 unemployed and the registered level of unemployment was 4·2%.

Trade Unions
Trade unions are grouped in a Federation of Ukrainian Trade Unions (*President*, Vasyl Khara).

INTERNATIONAL TRADE
In 2005 total foreign debt was US$33,297m.

Imports and Exports
In 2004 imports (f.o.b.) amounted to US$29,691m. (US$23,221m. in 2003); exports (f.o.b.) US$33,432m. (US$23,739m. in 2003). Main import suppliers in 2004: Russia, 40·7%; Germany, 9·4%; Turkmenistan, 6·7%; Poland, 3·3%; Italy, 2·8%. Main exports markets in 2004: Russia, 18·0%; Germany, 5·8%; Turkey, 5·7%; Italy, 5·0%; USA, 4·6%. Main imports, 2004: crude petroleum, 16·7%; machinery, 16·3%; chemicals and chemical products, 12·6%; natural gas, 12·4%. Main exports: ferrous and nonferrous metals, 39·9%; food and raw materials, 10·6%; chemicals and chemical products, 9·9%; machinery, 9·3%.

COMMUNICATIONS

Roads
In 2007 there were 169,422 km of roads, including 20,497 km of national roads. There were 5,939,600 passenger cars in use in 2007 and 714,300 motorcycles and mopeds. There were 63,554 road accidents involving injury in 2007 (9,574 fatalities).

Rail
Total length was 21,951 km in 2004, of which 9,170 km were electrified. Passenger-km travelled in 2004 came to 51·7bn. and freight tonne-km to 234·0bn. There are metros in Kyiv, Kharkiv, Kryvy Rih and Dnipropetrovsk.

Civil Aviation
The main international airport is Kyiv (Boryspil), and there are international flights from seven other airports. There are

two major Ukrainian carriers. Ukraine International Airlines operated international flights in 2005 to Amsterdam, Barcelona, Berlin, Brussels, Dubai, Düsseldorf, Helsinki, Kuwait, Lisbon, London, Madrid, Paris, Rome, Vienna and Zürich. Aerosvit had international flights in 2005 to Ashgabat, Athens, Baku, Bangkok, Beijing, Belgrade, Birmingham, Budapest, Cairo, Delhi, Dubai, Hamburg, İstanbul, Lanarca, Moscow, New York, Prague, St Petersburg, Sofia, Stockholm, Tel Aviv, Toronto and Warsaw.

In 2001 Kyiv handled 1,517,130 passengers (1,458,524 on international flights) and 11,875 tonnes of freight. Simferopol was the second busiest airport for passenger traffic, with 325,323 passengers (248,574 on international flights), and Odesa the second busiest for freight, with 3,588 tonnes.

Shipping

In 2007, 2m. passengers and 15m. tonnes of freight were carried by inland waterways. In Jan. 2003 the merchant marine comprised 253 vessels of 300 GRT and over (including 32 oil tankers) totalling 926,000 DWT. The main seaports are Illichivsk, Izmail, Mariupol, Mykolaïv, Odesa and Yuzhny. Odesa is the leading port, and takes 31m. tonnes of cargo annually. In 2004 vessels totalling 11,675,000 NRT entered ports and vessels totalling 65,436,000 NRT cleared.

Telecommunications

In 2008 there were 13,177,000 main (fixed) telephone lines. In the same year mobile phone subscribers numbered 55,695,000 (1,210·9 per 1,000 persons). Ukraine had 6·4m. internet subscribers in 2007, of which 0·8m. were broadband subscribers.

Postal Services

In 2003 there were 15,252 post offices. In 2003, 340m. pieces of mail were processed.

SOCIAL INSTITUTIONS

Justice

A new civil code was voted into law in June 1997. Justice is administered by the Constitutional Court of Ukraine and by courts of general jurisdiction. The Supreme Court of Ukraine is the highest judicial organ of general jurisdiction. The death penalty was abolished in 1999. Over the period 1991–95, 642 death sentences were awarded and 442 carried out; there were 169 executions in 1996. In March 1997 death penalties were still being awarded but not carried out. 553,994 crimes were reported in 2000.

The population in penal institutions in April 2003 was 198,858 (415 per 100,000 of national population).

Education

In 2003–04 the number of pupils in 21,900 primary and secondary schools was 5·9m.; 339 further education establishments had 1,843,800 students, and 670 technical colleges had 592,900 students; 977,000 children were attending pre-school institutions.

In 2005–06 there were 16 universities including an international university of information systems, management and business.

Adult literacy rate in 2003 was 99·4% (male, 99·7%; female, 99·2%).

In 2006 public expenditure on education came to 6·2% of GDP and 19·3% of total government spending.

Health

In 2007 there were 223,294 physicians, 25,450 dentists, 340,986 nurses, 23,645 midwives and 21,745 pharmacists. There were 439,549 beds in 2,843 hospitals in 2007.

Welfare

There were 10·3m. old-age pensioners in 2002 and 3·5m. other pensioners. The total included 821,000 Chernobyl victims. In 2002 social insurance and pension security programmes totalled 27·4bn. hryvnias, representing 12·4% of GDP.

RELIGION

The majority faith is the Orthodox Church, which is split into three factions. The largest is the Ukrainian Orthodox Church, Moscow Patriarchate (the former exarchate of the Russian Orthodox Church), headed by Metropolitan Volodymyr (Sabodan), Metropolitan of Kyiv and All Ukraine, which recognizes Kirill I (Vladimir Mikhailovich Gundyayev) as Patriarch of Moscow and All Russia and insists that all Ukrainian churches should be under Moscow's jurisdiction. There were 9·5m. adherents in 2001. The second largest is the Ukrainian Orthodox Church, Kyivan Patriarchate, headed by Metropolitan Filaret (Denysenko), Patriarch of Kyiv and All Rus-Ukraine, which was created in June 1992. It had 4·8m. adherents in 2001. Metropolitan Filaret was excommunicated by the Ukrainian Orthodox Church, Moscow Patriarchate in Feb. 1997. The third faction is the Ukrainian Autocephalous Orthodox Church, headed by Metropolitan Mefodiy (Kudryakov) of Ternopil, which favours the unification of the three bodies. Only the Ukrainian Orthodox Church, Moscow Patriarchate is in communion with world Orthodoxy.

The hierarchy of the Roman Catholic Church (*Primate*, Cardinal Mieczysław Mokrzycki, Archbishop Metropolitan of Lviv) was restored by the Pope's confirmation of ten bishops in Jan. 1991. In Feb. 2010 there were two cardinals. The Ukrainian Greek Catholic Church (*Head*, Cardinal Lubomyr Husar, Major Archbishop, Metropolitan of Lviv and Galicia) is a Church of the Byzantine rite, which is in full communion with the Roman Church. Catholicism is strong in the western half of the country.

CULTURE

World Heritage Sites

Ukraine has four sites on the UNESCO World Heritage List: Kyiv—Saint Sophia Cathedral and Related Monastic Buildings, Kyiv—Pechersk Lavra (inscribed on the list in 1990 and 2005); Lviv—the Ensemble of the Historic Centre (1998 and 2008); the Struve Geodetic Arc (2005), a chain of survey triangulations spanning from Norway to the Black Sea that helped establish the exact shape and size of the earth, which is shared with nine other countries; and the primeval beech forests of the Carpathians (2007), shared with Slovakia.

Broadcasting

Broadcasting is administered by the National Council for Television and Radio Broadcasting. The state-run National TV Company operates three television channels. There are also several commercial networks, in particular InterTV and Studio 1+1. The state-run National Radio Company broadcasts on three networks and an external service (Radio Ukraine International), and there are dozens of private FM radio channels. 18·9m. households were equipped with television receivers in 2005 (colour by SECAM H).

Press

In 2006 there were 41 daily newspapers with an average combined circulation of 3,511,000. In 2003 a total of 13,805 book titles were published.

Tourism

There were 15,629,000 non-resident tourists in 2004; total receipts were US$2,931m.

DIPLOMATIC REPRESENTATIVES

Of Ukraine in the United Kingdom (60 Holland Park, London, W11 3SJ)
Ambassador: Ihor Kharchenko.

Of the United Kingdom in Ukraine (9 Desyatinna St., 01025 Kyiv)
Ambassador: Leigh Turner.

Of Ukraine in the USA (3350 M St., NW, Washington, D.C., 20007)
Ambassador: Oleh Shamshur.

Of the USA in Ukraine (4 Hlybochtska, Kyiv)
Ambassador: John F. Tefft.

Of Ukraine to the United Nations
Ambassador: Yuriy Serheyev.

Of Ukraine to the European Union
Ambassador: Andriy Veselovskyi.

FURTHER READING

Encyclopedia of Ukraine, 5 vols. 1984–93

Aslund, Anders, *Revolution in Orange: The Origins of Ukraine's Democratic Breakthrough*. 2006

D'Anieri, Paul, *Economic Interdependence in Ukrainian–Russian Relations*. 2000.—*Understanding Ukrainian Politics: Power, Politics and Institutional Design*. 2006

Kuzio, Taras, Kravchuk, Robert and D'Anieri, Paul, *State and Institution Building in Ukraine*. 2000

Kuzio, T. and Wilson, A., *Ukraine: Perestroika to Independence*. 1994

Lieven, Anatol, *Ukraine and Russia: A Fraternal Rivalry*. 2000

Magocsi, P. R., *A History of Ukraine*. 1997

Motyl, A. J., *Dilemmas of Independence: Ukraine after Totalitarianism*. 1993

Nahaylo, B., *Ukrainian Resurgence*. 2nd ed. 2000

Wilson, Andrew, *The Ukrainians: Unexpected Nation*. 2000.—*Ukraine's Orange Revolution*. 2006

National Statistical Office: State Committee of Statistics of Ukraine, 3 Shota Rustavely St., Kyiv 01023.
Website: http://www.ukrstat.gov.ua

Crimea

The Crimea is a peninsula extending southwards into the Black Sea with an area of 26,100 sq. km. Population (Oct. 2005), 1,990,000 (ethnic groups, 2001 census: Russians, 58·3%; Ukrainians, 24·3%; Tatars, 12·0%). The capital is Simferopol (2001 census, 363,000).

It was occupied by Tatars in 1239, conquered by Ottoman Turks in 1475 and retaken by Russia in 1783. In 1921 after the Communist revolution it became an autonomous republic, but was transformed into a province (*oblast*) of the Russian Federation in 1945, after the deportation of the Tatar population in 1944 for alleged collaboration with the German invaders in the Second World War. 46% of the total Tatar population perished during the deportation. Crimea was transferred to Ukraine in 1954 and became an autonomous republic in 1991. About half the surviving Tatar population of 0·5m. had returned from exile by 2000. The Tatar population is disproportionately disadvantaged within Crimea, with an unemployment rate of over 60% in 2000.

At elections held in two rounds on 16 and 30 Jan. 1994 Yuri Meshkov was elected *President*. The post of president was abolished by Ukraine in March 1995 after calls for a referendum on Crimean independence. Parliamentary elections were held on 26 March 2006. The Bloc For Yanukovych! (Party of Regions and the Russian Bloc) obtained 44 seats, Soiuz 10, Kunitsyn's Electoral Bloc 10, the Communist Party of Ukraine 9, the People's Movement of Ukraine 8, the Yuliya Tymoshenko Electoral Bloc 8, the People's Opposition Bloc of Natalia Vitrenko 7 and the Opposition Bloc Ne Tak 4. The *Prime Minister* is Vasyl Dzharty and the *Chairman of Parliament* Volodymyr Konstantynov.

On 2 Nov. 1995 parliament adopted a new constitution which defines the Crimea as 'an autonomous republic forming an integral part of Ukraine'. The status of 'autonomous republic' was confirmed by the 1996 Ukrainian Constitution, which provides for Crimea to have its own constitution as approved by its parliament. The Prime Minister is appointed by the Crimean parliament with the approval of the Ukrainian parliament.

The Tatar National Kurultay (Parliament) elects an executive board (*Mejlis*). The *Chairman* is Mustafa Jemilev. A power-sharing agreement of 12 May 2005 guarantees the Crimean Tatars two ministry portfolios and the post of deputy prime minister in the Crimean local government.

In 2004 there were 624 pre-school institutions with 38,000 pupils and 638 primary and secondary schools with 241,000 students and 20,396 teachers. There were 68,000 students studying at 35 institutes of higher education in 2004.

UNITED ARAB EMIRATES

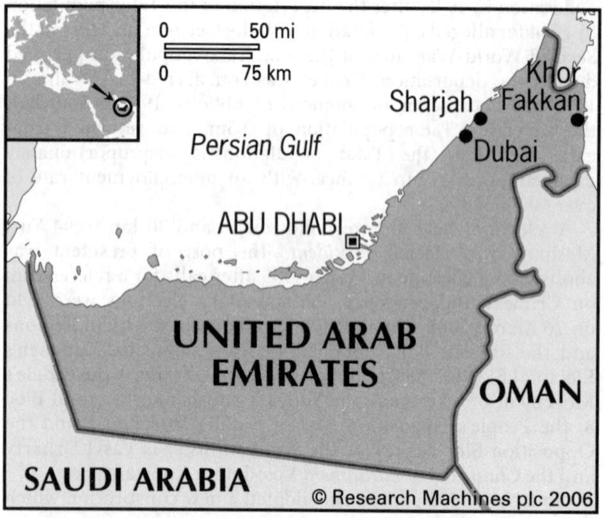

Imarat al-Arabiya al-Muttahida

Capital: Abu Dhabi

Population estimate, 2010: 4·71m.

GDP per capita, 2005: (PPP$) 25,514

HDI/world rank: 0·903/35

KEY HISTORICAL EVENTS

Archaeological evidence indicates that in the 3rd millennium BC a culture known as Umm al-Nar developed in modern-day Abu Dhabi, its influence spreading inland and along the coast of Oman to the south. There was trade with both the Mesopotamian civilization and the Indus culture, particularly the export of copper (then the most valuable natural resource) from the Hajar mountains. Later settlements, with Hellenistic features and dating from between the 3rd century BC and the 3rd century AD, have been discovered at Meleiha, near the Sharjah coast, and at Al-Dur in the emirate of Umm al Qaiwain. There are indications that the coastal areas of the United Arab Emirates (UAE) and Oman came under Sassanian (Persian) influence from the 4th century AD until the early 7th century when the Islamic era began. After the death of the Prophet Muhammad, tribes in the Dibba region along the eastern coast rebelled before Islamic forces won a decisive battle in AD 632.

In the Middle Ages much of the region was part of the Persian Kingdom of Hormuz (from 1300), which controlled the approach to the Gulf and most of the trade. European intervention in the Gulf began in the early 16th century when the Portuguese established a commercial monopoly, building a number of forts including Julfar (in modern-day Ras al-Khaimah), a major medieval trading centre. Portuguese ascendancy was later challenged by the Dutch and then by the British, who exercised their naval power in the Gulf in the 18th century to protect trade with India.

By that time two major tribal confederations had grown powerful along the coast of the lower Gulf. The largest tribal grouping, the Bani Yas, was established on the coast by the late 16th century. A large Bani Yas settlement was founded in Abu Dhabi in the 1760s, following the discovery of water on Abu Dhabi island, and in 1793 it became the seat of government of the al-Nahyan branch of the tribal confederation. There is further evidence of elements of the Bani Yas population extending from Qatar in the west to Dubai in the east and inland to the Liwa oasis belt. The Qawasim, a branch of the Huwalah tribe, were a maritime people (largely operating from Ras al-Khaimah) who emerged as an important group once the Omani empire of the late 17th and early 18th centuries was destroyed at the end of the Omani-Persian war in 1720. They established control over other strands of the Huwalah between Sharjah and Musandam and with a large fleet, posed a serious challenge to British shipping.

Piracy was rife until the early 19th century when the British sent several naval expeditions to the Gulf ports to suppress the raiders. In 1820 Britain signed the General Treaty of Peace against piracy and the slave trade with the principal Arab sheikhdoms. From this and later agreements the area became known as the Trucial Coast from the 1850s (the term Trucial referring to the fact that the component sheikhdoms were bound by the truces concluded with Britain). Britain assumed responsibility for the defence of the territory under the maritime treaty of 1853 and, under the exclusive treaties of 1892, for external relations of each of the Trucial sheikhdoms. The sheikhdoms were otherwise autonomous and followed the traditional form of Arab monarchy, with each ruler having virtually absolute power over his subjects.

The collapse of the pearl market, which was believed to have originated in the Gulf in the late Stone Age, and the world economic depression of the early 20th century undermined the economies of the Trucial States. Their subsequent transformation began with the discovery of oil off the coast of Abu Dhabi. Sheikh Shakhbut bin Sultan al-Nahyan, the ruler of Abu Dhabi from 1928–66, granted the first of several oil exploration concessions to foreign companies in 1939. However, the Second World War delayed exploration. The first commercial discovery was made in the late 1950s and the first exports began in 1962.

Sheikh Shakhbut, who was seen as an obstacle to the development of the oil industry, was deposed in 1966 in favour of his younger brother Sheikh Zayed bin Sultan al-Nahyan. The president of the UAE for more than 30 years until his death in 2004, he was re-elected by the rulers of the other emirates at five-year intervals. In the late 1960s oil was discovered in Dubai and in Sharjah, and then in Ras al-Khaimah in the 1980s.

In Jan. 1968 Britain announced the withdrawal of its military forces from the area by 1971. In March the Trucial States joined Bahrain and Qatar (which were also under British protection) in what was named the Federation of Arab Emirates. It was intended that the Federation should become fully independent but the interests of Bahrain and Qatar proved to be incompatible with those of the other sheikhdoms and both seceded from the Federation in 1971 to become separate independent entities. Six of the Trucial States (Abu Dhabi, Dubai, Sharjah, Umm al Qaiwain, Ajman and Fujairah) had agreed a federal constitution for achieving independence as the United Arab Emirates. The British accordingly terminated its special treaty relationship, and the UAE became independent on 2 Dec. 1971. The remaining sheikhdom, Ras al-Khaimah, joined the UAE in Feb. 1972. At independence Sheikh Zayed of Abu Dhabi took office as the first President of the loose federation. Sheikh Rashid bin Said al-Maktoum, the ruler of Dubai for over 30 years from 1958, became Vice-President. The al-Maktoum family, like the al-Nahyan rulers of Abu Dhabi, are a dynastic line of the Bani Yas tribe. The UAE instituted the Federal National Council, a 40-member consultative body appointed by the seven rulers. After the oil price increases of 1973–74—the UAE having given support to the Arab cause in the 1973 war with Israel—the economy and wealth of the new federation developed rapidly.

An attempted coup took place in Sharjah in 1987. Sheikh Sultan Bin Mohammad al-Qassimi abdicated in favour of his brother after admitting mismanagement of the emirate's economy but was restored to power by the Supreme Council of Rulers. In 1991 the UAE became involved in a major international financial scandal when the Bank of Credit and Commerce International (BCCI), in which the Abu Dhabi ruling family held a controlling 77% interest, collapsed. Abu Dhabi sued BCCI for damages in 1993 and several executives were convicted of fraud, given prison sentences and ordered to pay compensation.

Sheikh Rashid bin Said al-Maktoum died in 1990 and was succeeded by his son Sheikh Maktoum bin Rashid al-Maktoum as ruler of Dubai and UAE vice-president. In June 1996 the Federal National Council approved a permanent constitution replacing the provisional document that had been renewed every five years since 1971. At the same time, Abu Dhabi City was designated as the UAE's permanent capital.

In foreign relations the UAE has adopted a largely pro-Western and anti-Iranian stance. Following the fall of the Shah of Iran in 1979 and the outbreak of the Iran–Iraq war in 1980, the stability of the entire region was threatened. Partly in response to Iranian threats to close the Strait of Hormuz to shipping carrying oil exports from Gulf countries, the UAE joined with five other states to form the Gulf Co-operation Council (GCC) in 1981 to work towards political and economic integration. There has been further tension with Iran relating to territorial claims over the island of Abu Musa and the Greater and Lesser Tunb islands, strategically located in the Strait of Hormuz. Iran claimed sovereignty over the islands in the early 1990s and rejected a proposal by the GCC for the claim to be resolved by the International Court of Justice. In 1996 Iran opened an airport on Abu Musa and a power station on Greater Tunb, further damaging relations. Following UAE criticism of a rapprochement between Saudi Arabia and Iran, the GCC reiterated its support for the Emirates in the dispute in 2001. Iran rejected what it claimed was a biased decision. An agreement on the demarcation of the border between the UAE and Oman was ratified in 2003.

UAE forces joined the US-led international coalition against Iraq after the invasion of Kuwait in 1990. Following the Sept. 2001 attacks in the USA, the UAE's banking sector was subject to international scrutiny, and the government consequently ordered financial institutions to freeze the assets of 62 organizations and individuals suspected of funding terrorist movements. The USA stationed forces in the UAE during the invasion of Iraq in March 2003.

TERRITORY AND POPULATION

The Emirates are bounded in the north by the Persian Gulf, northeast by Oman, east by the Gulf of Oman and Oman, south and west by Saudi Arabia. Their area is approximately 83,600 sq. km (32,300 sq. miles), excluding over 100 offshore islands. The total population at the 2005 census was 4,106,427 (68·3% male); density, 49 per sq. km. Estimate, 1 July 2008, 4,765,000. The United Nations population estimate for 2008 was 4,485,000. About one-tenth are nomads. In 2005, 76·7% of the population lived in urban areas. Approximately 80% of the population are foreigners, the highest percentage of any country.

The UN gives an estimated population for 2010 of 4·71m.

Populations of the seven Emirates, 2005 census (in 1,000): Abu Dhabi, 1,399; Ajman, 207; Dubai, 1,321; Fujairah, 126; Ras al-Khaimah, 210; Sharjah, 794; Umm al Qaiwain, 49. The chief cities are Dubai (2005 census population of 1,305,060), Abu Dhabi, the federal capital (959,692 in 2005), Sharjah and Al-'Ayn. In addition to being the most populous Emirate, Abu Dhabi is also the wealthiest, ahead of Dubai.

The official language is Arabic; English is widely spoken.

SOCIAL STATISTICS

2002 births, 58,070; deaths, 5,994. 2002 birth rate (per 1,000 population), 19·8; death rate, 2·0; infant mortality rate (per 1,000 live births), 8 (2005). The UAE's 2002 death rate was the second lowest in the world (only Kuwait's was lower). Life expectancy, 2007, 76·6 years for men and 78·7 years for women. Annual population growth rate, 1992–2002, 2·8%; fertility rate, 2004, 2·5 births per woman.

CLIMATE

The country experiences desert conditions, with rainfall both limited and erratic. The period May to Sept. is generally rainless. Abu Dhabi, Jan. 65°F (18·3°C), July 95°F (35·0°C). Annual rainfall 3·5" (89 mm). Dubai, Jan. 66°F (18·9°C), July 94°F (34·4°C). Annual rainfall 3·7" (94 mm).

CONSTITUTION AND GOVERNMENT

The Emirates is a federation, headed by a *Supreme Council of Rulers* which is composed of the seven rulers which elects from among its members a *President* and *Vice-President* for five-year terms, and appoints a *Council of Ministers*. The Council of Ministers drafts legislation and a federal budget; its proposals are submitted to a *Federal National Council* of 40 appointed members which may propose amendments but has no executive power. It was announced in Dec. 2005 that 20 of the 40 members would in future be elected through councils for each of the seven Emirates. There is a *National Consultative Council* made up of citizens.

The current constitution came into force on 2 Dec. 1971 and was made permanent in 1996.

National Anthem

'Ishy Biladi' (Long live my Homeland); words by Abdullah Al Hassan, tune by Mohamed Abdel Wahab.

GOVERNMENT CHRONOLOGY

Presidents since 1971.

1971–2004	Sheikh Zayed bin Sultan al-Nahyan
2004–	Sheikh Khalifa bin Zayed al-Nahyan

CURRENT ADMINISTRATION

President: HH Sheikh Khalifa bin Zayed al-Nahyan, Ruler of Abu Dhabi (b. 1948; appointed 3 Nov. 2004).

Members of the Supreme Council of Rulers:

President: HH Sheikh Khalifa bin Zayed al-Nahyan.

Vice-President and Prime Minister: HH Sheikh Muhammad bin Rashid al-Maktoum, Ruler of Dubai (b. 1949).

HH Dr Sheikh Sultan bin Mohammed al-Qassimi, Ruler of Sharjah.

HH Sheikh Saqr bin Mohammed al-Qassimi, Ruler of Ras al-Khaimah.

HH Sheikh Hamad bin Mohammed al-Sharqi, Ruler of Fujairah.

HH Sheikh Humaid bin Rashid al-Nuaimi, Ruler of Ajman.

HH Sheikh Saud bin Rashid al-Mualla, Ruler of Umm al Qaiwain.

In March 2010 the cabinet comprised:

Prime Minister and Minister of Defence: HH Sheikh Muhammad bin Rashid al-Maktoum; b. 1949 (sworn in 5 Jan. 2006).

Deputy Prime Ministers: HH Maj.-Gen. Sheikh Saif bin Zayed al-Nahyan (also *Minister of the Interior*); HH Sheikh Mansour bin Zayed al-Nahyan (also *Minister of Presidential Affairs*).

Minister of Finance and Industry: HH Sheikh Hamdan bin Rashid al-Maktoum. *Economy:* Sultan bin Said al-Mansouri. *Culture, Youth and Community Development:* Abdul Rahman Mohammed al-Owais. *Education:* Humaid Mohammed Obeid al-Qattami. *Higher Education and Scientific Research:* Sheikh Nahyan bin Mubarak al-Nahyan. *Energy:* Mohammed bin Dhaen al-Hamili. *Labour:* Saqr Ghobash Said Ghobash. *Justice:* Hadef bin Juaan al-Dhaheri. *Foreign Affairs:* Sheikh Abdullah bin Zayed al-Nahyan. *Foreign Trade:* Lubna Bint Khalid al-Qasimi. *Health:* Hanif Hassan Ali. *Public Works and Housing:* Sheikh Hamdan bin Mubarak al-Nahyan. *Social Affairs:* Mohammed Khalfan al-Roumi. *Environment and Water:* Rashid Ahmed bin Fahad. *Cabinet Affairs:* Mohammed al-Gergawi.

Government Website: http://www.uae.gov.ae

CURRENT LEADERS

Sheikh Khalifa bin Zayed al-Nahyan

Position
President

Introduction
Sheikh Khalifa bin Zayed al-Nahyan was appointed president on 3 Nov. 2004, the day after the death of his father, Sheikh Zayed, who helped establish the country in 1971 and presided over it for 33 years. Sheikh Khalifa has continued his father's policies of co-operation with neighbouring Arab countries and with the USA, and reducing the UAE's economy's dependence on oil and gas extraction.

Early Life
Sheikh Khalifa bin Zayed al-Nahyan, the eldest son of his father, was born in 1948 in the oasis-town of Al-'Ayn in the east of the emirate of Abu Dhabi. In 1966, following his father's promotion to the post of Ruler of Abu Dhabi, he was appointed as Ruler's Representative in the Emirate's eastern province. Three years later Sheikh Khalifa was nominated as Crown Prince and head of Abu Dhabi's new Department of Defence.

When, in July 1971, Sheikh Zayed took the initiative to bring together the rulers of the Trucial States to form the United Arab Emirates (becoming the federation's president later in 1971), he appointed Sheikh Khalifa as prime minister of Abu Dhabi. Following the dissolution of Abu Dhabi's cabinet in late 1973 (it became the Abu Dhabi Executive Council) as part of the strengthening of the UAE's new institutions, Sheikh Khalifa assumed two posts—deputy prime minister in the UAE's federal cabinet and chairman of the Abu Dhabi Executive Council. He oversaw the implementation of a massive development programme in Abu Dhabi, funded by revenue from the Emirate's vast oil reserves, which included the construction of housing, water mains, roads and general infrastructure. In May 1976, following the unification of the armed forces of the seven Emirates, Sheikh Khalifa was nominated as Deputy Supreme Commander of the UAE Armed Forces. He went on to establish numerous military training institutions and was responsible for the procurement of equipment and weapons.

To advance the development of Abu Dhabi and ensure that citizens benefited from the country's growing wealth, Sheikh Khalifa established the Abu Dhabi Department of Social Services and Commercial Buildings in 1981 to offer low-interest loans for house building. The scheme was extended in 1991 and 2000, in line with the rapid increase in the country's population. From the late 1980s, Sheikh Khalifa was Chairman of the Supreme Petroleum Council, where he worked to develop the UAE's petrochemicals and industrial complex at Ruwais in an attempt to diversify the economy. He also served as chairman of the Abu Dhabi Fund for Development (responsible for the country's overseas aid programme), chairman of the Abu Dhabi Investment Authority and head of the Environmental Research and Wildlife Development Agency. In late 1991 and early 1992 Sheikh Khalifa and his father were mired in the scandal surrounding the collapse of the BCCI bank, 77% of which was owned by the Abu Dhabi government. This followed a fraud in which its founder, Agha Hassan Abedi, and other officers stole billions of dollars. Sheikh Khalifa's scheme to compensate creditors resulted in a payout of US$1·8bn.

When Sheikh Zayed's health began to decline in the late 1990s, Sheikh Khalifa became the public face of the UAE, along with Sheikh Maktoum, Ruler of Dubai. On 3 Nov. 2004, the day after the death of Sheikh Zayed, Sheikh Khalifa was appointed president of the UAE.

Career in Office
Speaking after the swearing-in ceremony for new cabinet ministers on 21 Nov. 2004, Sheikh Khalifa said his key objective as president was to continue on the path laid down by his father. A strong supporter of the six-member Gulf Co-operation Council, Sheikh Khalifa was expected to follow his father's example of promoting solidarity between Arab states, supporting the Palestinian people and helping to restore stability in Iraq. In Dec. 2005 he announced plans for the UAE's first elections, in which half of the members of the consultative Federal National Council would be elected by a limited number of citizens. The non-party elections were held in Dec. 2006, and the government said that they marked the start of a wider process to extend political participation.

In May 2009 the UAE withdrew from plans for Gulf monetary union, undermining prospects for further economic integration in the region. This move followed the decision to locate the headquarters of the Gulf Co-operation Council Monetary Council in Saudi Arabia. Meanwhile, the UAE and particularly Dubai were adversely affected by the global financial crisis, as banks were overexposed to a serious reversal in the property market. In Feb. 2009, and again in Dec., the Abu Dhabi government intervened to support the banking sector, to prevent a debt default by Dubai and to reassure the financial markets. Sheikh Khalifa also issued a statement saying the UAE economy as a whole was in good condition.

In Jan. 2010 the world's tallest building, the Burj Khalifa tower (named after Sheikh Khalifa), was inaugurated in Dubai.

DEFENCE

In 2006 defence expenditure totalled US$9,482m. (US$3,643 per capita), representing 6·7% of GDP. The expenditure per capita in 2006 was the highest in the world.

In the period 2004–08 the UAE's spending on major conventional weapons, at US$7·1bn., was the third highest behind China and India.

Army
The strength was (2007) 44,000 (including Dubai independent forces).

Navy
The combined naval flotilla of the Emirates includes two frigates and two corvettes. Personnel in 2007 numbered around 2,500. The main base is at Abu Dhabi, with minor bases in the other Emirates.

Air Force
Personnel (2007) 4,500, with 184 combat capable aircraft (including F-16s, Mirage 2000s and *Hawks*), and some 40 attack helicopters.

INTERNATIONAL RELATIONS

The UAE is a member of the UN, World Bank, IMF and several other UN specialized agencies, WTO, Islamic Development Bank, OIC, Gulf Co-operation Council, League of Arab States and OPEC.

ECONOMY

In 2005 agriculture accounted for 2% of GDP, industry 57% and services 40%.

Overview
The UAE has a strong record of market-oriented economic reform and prudent macroeconomic management. The economy has been

liberalized and the private sector has grown in importance. The UAE is the sixth largest oil exporter in the world, with the oil and gas sector accounting for one third of GDP. There has also been diversification into manufacturing, tourism, media, shipping, and financial and commercial services.

Growth has been consistently strong, reaching 9·4% in 2006, buoyed by persistently high oil prices and the rapid expansion of construction, financial services and trade services. The economy has been running significant current account surpluses (US$36bn. in 2006), primarily from oil although non-oil exports in manufacturing, agriculture and services have also grown. Domestic demand has been strong as a result of favourable economic conditions and population growth driven by the influx of expatriate workers.

Demand strength has raised inflation, particularly in real estate and some services. An anticipated reduction in capacity constraints, particularly within housing, is expected to ease inflationary pressures in the medium-term. Abu Dhabi remains the UAE's dominant economy but Dubai's growth makes it increasingly important. However, the economy has been adversely affected by the global financial crisis, causing a slowdown in real estate and construction, weakening tourism, trade and financial services and lowering oil prices. In Nov. 2009 Dubai World, one of three government-backed conglomerates, requested a standstill on repayments of US$26bn. of debt, panicking global markets. By mid-Dec. Abu Dhabi provided US$10bn. to Dubai's government to help repay some of its debt but the crisis has caused uncertainty in the economy's medium-term outlook.

Currency

The unit of currency is the *dirham* (AED) of 100 *fils*. Gold reserves are negligible. In March 2009 foreign exchange reserves were US$34,040m. and total money supply was DH 211,314m. Inflation rates (based on IMF statistics):

1999	*2000*	*2001*	*2002*	*2003*	*2004*	*2005*	*2006*	*2007*	*2008*
2·1%	1·4%	2·7%	2·9%	3·2%	5·0%	6·2%	9·3%	11·1%	12·3%

In 2001 the six Gulf Arab states—the United Arab Emirates, along with Bahrain, Kuwait, Oman, Qatar and Saudi Arabia—signed an agreement to establish a single currency by 2010. In June 2009 it was agreed to postpone the implementation of the new currency, the *khaleeji*, until 2013. Both Oman and the United Arab Emirates have now withdrawn from the scheme, in 2007 and 2009 respectively.

Budget

The fiscal year is the calendar year. Revenue in 2006 totalled DH 200,704m. and expenditure DH 128,238m.

Revenue is principally derived from oil-concession payments. Defence, education, and public order and safety are the main items of expenditure.

Performance

Real GDP growth rates (based on IMF statistics):

1999	*2000*	*2001*	*2002*	*2003*	*2004*	*2005*	*2006*	*2007*	*2008*
3·1%	12·4%	1·7%	2·6%	11·9%	9·7%	8·2%	9·4%	6·3%	7·4%

In 2006 total GDP was US$163·3bn.

Banking and Finance

The UAE Central Bank was established in 1980 (*Governor*, Sultan bin Nasser Al-Suwaidi). The largest bank is the Emirates National Bank of Dubai, with assets of nearly DH 200bn., created in July 2007 through the merger of the National Bank of Dubai and Emirates Bank International. Foreign banks are restricted to eight branches each.

There are stock exchanges in Abu Dhabi and Dubai.

ENERGY AND NATURAL RESOURCES

Environment

In 2008 carbon dioxide emissions from the consumption and flaring of fossil fuels were the equivalent of 43·1 tonnes per capita, among the highest in the world.

Electricity

Installed capacity was 5·9m. kW in 2003. Production in 2004 was 52·42bn. kWh, with consumption per capita 12,000 kWh. Construction of the first of four nuclear plants to meet energy demand is expected to begin in 2012, with all four scheduled for completion by 2020.

Oil and Gas

Oil and gas provided about 33·7% of GDP in 2002. Oil production, 2008, 139·5m. tonnes. The UAE had reserves in 2008 amounting to 97·8bn. bbls. Oil production in Abu Dhabi is 85% of the UAE's total.

Abu Dhabi has reserves of natural gas, nationalized in 1976. There is a gas liquefaction plant on Das Island. Proven natural gas reserves (2008) were 6,430bn. cu. metres. Natural gas production, 2008, 50·2bn. cu. metres.

Minerals

Sulphur, gypsum, chromite and lime are mined.

Agriculture

The fertile Buraimi Oasis, known as Al Ain, is largely in Abu Dhabi territory. A lack of water and good soil means few natural opportunities for agriculture but there is a programme of fostering agriculture by desalination, dam-building and tree-planting; strawberries, flowers and dates are now cultivated for export. In 2002 there were 75,000 ha. of arable land and 191,000 ha. of permanent cropland. Output, 2002 (in 1,000 tonnes): dates, 758; tomatoes, 231; cabbage, 30; cucumbers and gherkins, 26; pumpkins and squash, 21; melons and watermelons, 19; aubergines, 18; lemons and limes, 15. Livestock products, 2003 estimates (in 1,000 tonnes): meat, 74; milk, 56; eggs, 18.

Livestock (2002): goats, 1·4m.; sheep, 554,000; camels, 246,000; cattle, 107,000; chickens, 12m.

Forestry

312,000 ha. were under forests in 2005 (3·7% of the total land area).

Fisheries

Estimated catch, 2005, 90,000 tonnes (exclusively marine fish).

INDUSTRY

The largest company in the United Arab Emirates by market capitalization in March 2009 was Etisalat, a telecommunications company (US$21·6bn.).

In 2001 industry accounted for 52·4% of GDP, with manufacturing contributing 13·8%. Products include aluminium, cable, cement, chemicals, fertilizers (Abu Dhabi), rolled steel and plastics (Dubai, Sharjah), and tools and clothing (Dubai). The diamond business is becoming increasingly important in Dubai.

Labour

Males constituted 85% of the economically active labour force in 2005 (one of the highest percentages of any country in the world). Foreign workers make up over 90% of the workforce in the private sector. A total of 2,660,000 persons were in employment in 2005, with the leading areas of activity as follows: community, social and personal services, 587,900; construction, 502,700; wholesale and retail trade, restaurants and hotels, 460,200; manufacturing, 292,600. In 2005 the unemployment rate was 1·9%.

INTERNATIONAL TRADE

There are free trade zones at Jebel Ali (administered by Dubai), Sharjah and Fujairah. Foreign companies may set up wholly owned subsidiaries. In 1994 there were 650 companies in the Jebel Ali zone.

The United Arab Emirates, along with Bahrain, Kuwait, Oman, Qatar and Saudi Arabia entered into a customs union in Jan. 2003.

Imports and Exports

Imports in 2001 totalled DH 120·6bn.; exports DH 176·9bn. Principal imports: machinery and transport equipment, food and textiles. Crude petroleum and natural gas are the main exports.

Main import suppliers, 2001: Japan (10·2%), USA (9·6%), UK (8·8%), China (8·6%). Main export markets: Japan (36·4%), India (7·5%), South Korea (7·1%), Singapore (6·3%).

COMMUNICATIONS

Roads

In 2004 there were 4,030 km of roads. There were 1,279,100 passenger cars (293 per 1,000 inhabitants), 48,200 buses and coaches and 39,400 lorries and vans in 2007.

Rail

A rail network linking the seven Emirates is in the planning stage and is expected to become operational in 2016.

A metro system opened in Dubai in Sept. 2009.

Civil Aviation

There are international airports at Abu Dhabi, Al Ain, Dubai, Fujairah, Ras al-Khaimah and Sharjah. Dubai is the busiest airport, handling 12,401,000 passengers and 611,900 tonnes of freight in 2001. Dubai set up its own airline, Emirates, in 1985. It now operates internationally, and in 2006–07 flew to 89 destinations worldwide and carried 17,544,140 passengers. Etihad Airways, the national airline of the United Arab Emirates, began operations in Nov. 2003. Air Arabia is a low-cost airline based in Sharjah, flying to 35 destinations (mainly in Asia). Abu Dhabi withdrew from the Gulf Air partnership with Bahrain and Oman in 2006.

In the World Economic Forum's *Global Competitiveness Report 2009–2010* the UAE ranked third for quality of air transport infrastructure.

Shipping

There are 15 commercial seaports, of which five major ports are on the Persian Gulf (Zayed in Abu Dhabi, Rashid and Jebel Ali in Dubai, Khalid in Sharjah, and Saqr in Ras al-Khaimah) and two on the Gulf of Oman: Fujairah and Khor Fakkan. Rashid and Fujairah are important container terminals. In 2002 the merchant marine totalled 703,000 GRT, including oil tankers 221,000 GRT.

Telecommunications

In 2008 there were 1,508,000 main (fixed) telephone lines. In the same year active mobile phone subscribers numbered 9·4m. (2,086·5 per 1,000 persons—the highest rate of any country). There were 1·4m. PCs in use in 2006 and 2·9m. internet users in 2008.

Postal Services

In 2003 there were 279 post offices.

SOCIAL INSTITUTIONS

Justice

The basic principles of the law are Islamic. Legislation seeks to promote the harmonious functioning of society's multi-national components while protecting the interests of the indigenous population. Each Emirate has its own penal code. A federal code takes precedence and ensures compatibility. There are federal courts with appellate powers, which function under federal laws. Emirates have the option to merge their courts with the federal judiciary.

The death penalty is in force; there was one confirmed execution in 2008 (although none in 2009).

Education

In 2007 there were 100,269 pre-primary pupils with 4,823 teaching staff, 284,034 primary pupils with 16,523 teaching staff, and 310,999 secondary pupils with 24,152 teaching staff. In 2002–03 there were 16,128 students at the Emirates University and 14,265 students in higher colleges. There were 2,245 students at the four faculties of Zayed University in 2002–03. The adult literacy rate in 2004 was 88·7%. In 2004 public expenditure on education came to 1·6% of GNI and 25·0% of total government spending.

Health

In 2003 there were 38 government hospitals with 5,722 beds. In 2003 there were 27 private hospitals, 131 government health centres and 1,281 private clinics. There were 5,825 physicians in 2001 and 954 dentists, 12,045 nurses and 1,086 pharmacists.

RELIGION

Most inhabitants are Sunni Muslims, with a small Shia minority.

CULTURE

Broadcasting

Television service providers include Dubai Media Incorporated (DMI), Abu Dhabi TV, Ajman TV, Sharjah TV and Dubai-based MBC. Radio stations (the majority based in Abu Dhabi and Dubai) transmit in Arabic or English, Hindi and Urdu. The major satellite news channels are Al-Arabiya, based in Dubai, and Abu Dhabi TV. Both came to prominence at the time of the war in Iraq in March–April 2003. There were 843,000 TV sets (colour by PAL) in 2004.

Press

In 2006 there were 14 daily newspapers with a combined circulation of 901,000.

Tourism

In 2005, 7,126,000 tourists stayed in hotels and similar accommodation; spending by tourists in 2005 totalled US$3,218m.

DIPLOMATIC REPRESENTATIVES

Of the UAE in the United Kingdom (30 Prince's Gate, London, SW7 1PT)
Ambassador: Abdul Rahman Ghanim Al Mutaiwee.

Of the United Kingdom in the UAE (POB 248, Abu Dhabi)
Ambassador: Edward Oakden, CMG.

Of the UAE in the USA (3522 International Court, NW, Washington, D.C., 20008)
Ambassador: Yousef Al Otaiba.

Of the USA in the UAE (POB 4009, Abu Dhabi)
Ambassador: Richard Olson.

Of the UAE to the United Nations
Ambassador: Ahmad Abdul Rahman Al Jarman.

Of the UAE to the European Union
Ambassador: Mohammed Salem Alsuweidi.

FURTHER READING

Davidson, Christopher M., *The United Arab Emirates: A Study in Survival.* 2005

Vine, P. and Al Abed, I., *United Arab Emirates: A New Perspective.* 2001

National Statistical Office: Ministry of Economy, P.O. Box 901–904, Abu Dhabi.

Website: http://www.economy.ae/English/EconomicAndStatisticReports/Pages/default.aspx

UNITED KINGDOM OF GREAT BRITAIN AND NORTHERN IRELAND

Capital: London
Population estimate, 2010: 61·90m.
GDP per capita, 2007: (PPP$) 35,130
HDI/world rank: 0·947/21

KEY HISTORICAL EVENTS

Remains of Stone Age settlements of hunters and fishermen suggest that the first inhabitants crossed from the low countries of Continental Europe on one or more wide causeways. By the time their successors had turned to subsistence farming, the land links to the continent had disappeared under the sea. These offshore islands created at the ending of the Ice Age shared, with nearside Europe, a slowly evolving agricultural economy using bronze and iron tools. The Ancient Britons were Celts, whose ancestors had migrated from the valleys of the Rhine, the Rhône and the Danube. Having asserted their command of northern Italy and France (Gaul), the Celts established a bridgehead to Ireland and thence to Britain. By 600 BC they were the undisputed dominant force of Western Europe and were to remain so until challenged by the Romans.

The Romans were dominant from AD 78. From the 3rd century they were increasingly harried by tribes of Celts from Scotland and Ireland and by Angles and Saxons from northern Germany. Celtic tradition, presided over by druids (religious leaders) and bards (storytellers), survived most successfully in Ireland and Wales where Roman influence was barely visible. Scotland resisted the Roman legions; Hadrian's Wall was built as a northern frontier between the Tyne and Solway Firth in the early 2nd century AD. Roman authority was challenged, notably by Boudicca, queen of the Iceni tribe of East Anglia. The rebellion and the brutal repression that followed led to a long period of peaceful settlement, during which the Romans established a road network linking new towns such as Londinium (London) and Eboracum (York). But by the 5th century Roman Britain had disintegrated into a collection of warring kingdoms. The English and Welsh economies thrived on the export of silver, lead, gold, iron and other minerals. With the spread of Christianity, chiefly by Irish missionaries, came the beginnings of an education and legal system.

After the withdrawal of the Roman legions in the early 5th century, the Romano-British were pushed back to higher land in the west by waves of invading Saxons, Angles and Jutes. Danish invasions in 865 established the Danelaw in northern England. Alfred the Great of Wessex resisted Danish expansion, strengthening Anglo-Saxon unity.

Norman Conquest

William, duke of Normandy, led the Norman Conquest and was crowned king in 1066. When William died in 1087 he left Normandy to his eldest son Robert, thus separating it from England. The French dialect known as Anglo-Norman was spoken by the ruling class in England for two centuries after the Conquest. The Norman heritage was preserved also in the overlap between French and English feudal lords. Henry II, the founder of the Plantagenet dynasty, was feudatory lord of half of France. But most of the French possessions were lost by Henry's son John. Thereafter, the Norman baronage came to regard themselves as English. The ambitions of Edward III began and those of Henry V renewed the Hundred Years War (1338–1453) with France, which ended with the loss of all the remaining French possessions except Calais.

The dynastic struggle between the rival houses of York and Lancaster was concluded by the invasion of Henry (VII) Tudor in 1485. His son, Henry VIII, asserted royal authority over the church and rejected papal authority. Tudor power reached its zenith with Elizabeth I, under whom Protestantism became firmly established in England. The Spanish Armada—an attempt by Catholic Spain to return England to the papal fold—was repelled in 1588.

The accession of James VI of Scotland to the English throne in 1603 brought the two countries into dynastic union. A struggle for supremacy between Crown and Parliament culminated in the Civil War, begun in 1642. Charles I was executed by Parliament in 1649, beginning the rule of Protector Oliver Cromwell. The Stuart monarchy was restored in 1660, on terms which conceded financial authority and thus decision-making power to Parliament. The attempt of James II, a Catholic, to restore the royal prerogative led to the intervention of William of Orange. James fled the country and the crown was taken by William (III) and his wife Mary as queen regnant. The accession of William involved England in a protracted war against France.

The parliaments of England and Scotland were united in 1707 under Queen Anne, the first British monarch. With the accession of the Hanoverian George I in 1714, the system of Parliamentary party government took hold. By the mid-18th century London had taken over from Amsterdam as the leading financial centre. With easy access to capital, entrepreneurs were able to invest in new, improved methods of production. With the harnessing of steam power made possible by the engineering genius of Thomas Newcomen and James Watt, economic enterprise shifted away from the southeast to the north of England, Scotland and South Wales where there were large reserves of coal. The demand for raw materials and the pursuit of markets for finished goods opened up trade throughout the civilized world and extended British influence.

American Colonies

Britain's first successful colonies in North America were established in the reign of James I of England (1603–25) and, soon afterwards, Bermuda, St Kitts, Barbados and Nevis were colonized. By the mid-17th century, Britain controlled the American east coast and had strong bases in India and in the West Indies, where the sugar economy was dependent on slave labour imported from West Africa. Critical to imperial expansion was Britain's rivalry with France. Britain emerged much strengthened from the War of the League of Augsburg (1689–97) and the War of Spanish Succession (1702–13) while French ambitions in Europe and beyond were severely curtailed. But it was the Seven Years' War (1756–63), in which France and Prussia were the chief contenders, that deprived France of her remaining territorial claims in North America and India and confirmed Britain as the world's leading maritime power.

Relations between Parliament and Crown went through an unsettled period in the reign of George III, who was blamed for the loss of the American colonies. The War of Independence ended with Britain's recognition of American right to self-government in 1783. In 1793 revolutionary France declared war and was not finally defeated until 1815. The demands of war further stimulated the new, steam-powered industries. Despite Britain finding itself the pre-eminent world power, after 1815 there was frequent unrest as an increasingly urban and industrial society found its interests poorly represented by a parliament composed chiefly of landowners. The Reform Act of 1832 extended representation in Parliament and further acts (1867, 1884, 1918 and 1928) led gradually to universal adult suffrage.

Ireland was brought under direct rule from Westminster in 1801, creating the United Kingdom of Great Britain and Ireland. The accession of Victoria in 1837 was the beginning of an era of unprecedented material progress. Early industrial development produced great national wealth but its distribution was uneven and the condition of the poor improved slowly. Whereas early Victorian reforms were responses to obvious distress, governments after 1868 were more inclined towards preventive state action.

The Victorian empire included India, Canada, Australasia and vast territories in Africa and Eastern Asia. There was war with Russia in the Crimea (1854–56); most wars, however, were fought to conquer or pacify colonies. After 1870 the Suez Canal enabled Britain to control the empire more efficiently; Britain became a 40% shareholder in 1875 and the controlling power in Egypt in 1882. The most serious imperial wars were the Boer Wars of 1881 and 1899–1902 against the Dutch settlers in South Africa. After a less than glorious victory, Britain negotiated a Union of South Africa, by which South Africa enjoyed the same autonomy agreed for Canada (1867), Australia (1901) and later New Zealand (1907). The 'dominion status' of these countries was clarified by the Statute of Westminster (1931).

With the spread of trade unionism and the emergence of the Labour Party, the gap between right- and left-wing politics widened after 1900. Labour had to wait until 1924 to form its first government but the Liberal landslide of 1906 carried forward the programme of social reform. David Lloyd George's People's Budget led to the abolition of the House of Lords' right to override the House of Commons while a contributory insurance scheme to cover basic health care, a modest benefit for the unemployed, free school meals and non-contributory old age pensions were all introduced.

On 3 Aug. 1914 Germany invaded Belgium. Britain was obliged by treaty to retaliate by declaring war. Four years of bloody trench warfare ensued in northern France and Belgium, with American intervention in 1917 helping to break the stalemate. The United Kingdom alone lost 715,000 soldiers and another 200,000 from the empire. Rebellions broke out in Ireland, born of the failure of successive attempts to agree a formula for Irish Home Rule. The issue was complicated by factional disagreement in southern Ireland and the wish of northern Ireland (Ulster) to remain in the United Kingdom. In 1920, after four years' conflict, the Government of Ireland Act partitioned the country. The northern six counties remained British, a parliament was created and a Unionist government took office. The southern 26 counties moved by stages to complete independence as the Irish Free State in 1922.

Second World War

A post-war boom was followed by a lengthy recession and heavy unemployment, exacerbated by the reluctance of politicians to adopt Keynesian economics. Germany revived as a military power in the 1930s, unchecked by reluctant neighbours after the punitive Treaty of Versailles. British Prime Minister Neville Chamberlain agreed to the German acquisition of parts of Czechoslovakia at the Munich Agreement in 1938. His policy of appeasement was much criticized, though it is arguable that Britain was in no position to go to war in 1938. Germany invaded Poland on 1 Sept. 1939. Britain, bound once more by treaty, declared war. In May 1940 Chamberlain was replaced as prime minister by Winston Churchill, who formed a national unity government. Although British military casualties were less than in the 1914–18 war, the civilian population was hit much worse during the Second World War; over 90,000 died, many as a result of German bombing in the Battle of Britain in 1940.

The war ended with German and Japanese defeat in 1945, by which stage the United Kingdom was virtually bankrupt. In 1939 the country had had assets of around £3,000m. By the end of the war, it owed about the same amount. A pre-war balance of payments deficit averaging £43m. a year had jumped to £750m. It was a time of great social upheaval. In the 1945 election a Labour government under Clement Attlee was returned with a large majority and a socialist programme, which emphasized wealth distribution above wealth creation, was implemented. It undertook to establish a free National Health Service, an ambitious housing programme and the state control of major industries. Subsequent governments modified but generally accepted the changes.

With Britain bankrupted, the United States stepped into the breach as the now undisputed free world leader. Fearing a European breakdown and a Communist takeover, the Marshall Plan was implemented by the USA, providing massive investment to rebuild Europe. An essential condition of the Marshall Plan was a joint effort of the participating nations to put their economies in order. But when continental leaders made the first tentative moves towards European unity, the UK was unwilling to be closely involved. With the independence of India (and Pakistan), the centrepiece of the British Empire, in 1947, decolonization took root, reaching its climax in the 1960s. Rather than to Europe, Britain now looked instead to a Commonwealth of freely associated states, recognizing the British monarch as symbolic Commonwealth head (some states chose to retain the monarch as head of state), and to the 'special relationship' with the United States.

In March 1957 France, Germany, Italy, Belgium, the Netherlands and Luxembourg signed the Treaty of Rome, which laid down terms for the European Economic Community. Two years later seven of the European countries outside the Common Market—Austria, Denmark, Norway, Portugal, Sweden, Switzerland and the UK—formed the European Free Trade Association. When the United Kingdom moved to join the EEC in 1962, five of the six members of the Community were willing to support the application but France vetoed it. A second application, in 1967, also failed but admission was achieved in 1973 under the Conservative government of Edward Heath. Membership of the Community was endorsed by referendum in 1975.

On the wider international scene, the limits of independent military action were made clear by the Suez crisis of 1956 when the UK, in collusion with France and Israel, used force to stop President Nasser of Egypt nationalizing the Suez Canal. Assumed American support was not forthcoming and the enterprise collapsed when the UK was left alone to cope with a potentially disastrous run on sterling. In the 1960s and 1970s the UK began to come to terms with advanced technology. Old-established industries such as textiles, shipbuilding, iron and steel and coal mining, the leaders of the first industrial revolution, gave way to manufacturing that relied on the microchip. Service industries, particularly in the financial sector, occupied an increasing share of the economy and trade restrictions were dismantled throughout the world.

In 1979 a Conservative government led by Margaret Thatcher came to power, committed to a free market economy. State industry was returned to private enterprise, the trade unions (blamed for the crippling 1978–79 Winter of Discontent) lost much of their power to direct government policy, and high earners were to benefit from lower taxation. A period of readjustment climaxed with a coal miners' strike during 1984–85 that turned into a trial of strength between the government and organized labour. The Labour Party and allied unions, themselves in the process of modernization, distanced themselves from the socialist rhetoric of the miners' leaders and the strike collapsed.

Despite rising living standards, there was concern about the quality of essential services such as education and health and disillusionment with a Conservative administration unable to construct a coherent European policy. In 1997 a Labour government, led by Tony Blair, was returned with a large Commons majority. Like Thatcher, he believed in the free market. In addition he introduced reforms in the system of government including the abolition of voting rights of hereditary peers in the House of Lords and the setting up of directly elected assemblies for Scotland, Wales and Northern Ireland. Blair showed greater enthusiasm for involvement in Europe while the war in Iraq went some way to recementing the 'special' relationship with the USA. Fears of terrorist reprisals for British involvement in the Iraq war were realised on 7 July 2005 when bombs planted on three London underground trains and a bus killed 52 people. Gordon Brown, the chancellor during Blair's premiership, succeeded him as prime minister in June 2007. He was replaced by Conservative leader David Cameron, who took office in May 2010 in a coalition with the Liberal Democrats to end 13 years of Labour rule.

TERRITORY AND POPULATION

Area (in sq. km) and population at the census taken on 29 April 2001:

Divisions	*Area*	*Population*
England	130,281	49,138,831
Wales	20,732	2,903,085
Scotland	77,925	5,062,011
Northern Ireland	14,135	1,685,267
	243,073	58,789,194

The next census will take place on 27 March 2011.

Population of the United Kingdom (present on census night) at the four previous decennial censuses:

Divisions	*1961*	*1971*	*1981*	*1991*
England[1]	43,460,525	46,018,371	46,226,100[2]	46,382,050
Wales	2,644,023	2,731,204	2,790,500[2]	2,811,865
Scotland	5,179,344	5,228,963	5,130,700	4,998,567
Northern Ireland	1,425,042	1,536,065	1,532,196[3]	1,577,836
United Kingdom	52,708,934	55,514,603	55,679,496[2]	55,770,318

[1]Areas now included in Wales formed the English county of Monmouthshire until 1974.

[2]The final counts for England and Wales are believed to be over-stated as a result of an error in processing. The preliminary counts presented here rounded to the nearest hundred are thought to be more accurate.

[3]There was a high level of non-enumeration in Northern Ireland during the 1981 census mainly as a result of protests in Catholic areas about the Republican hunger strikes.

UK population estimate, mid-2008, 61,383,200 (31,231,800 females and 30,151,300 males); density, 252 per sq. km. London had a population of 7,619,800 in 2008. In 2005, 89·7% of the population lived in urban areas.

The UN gives an estimated population for 2010 of 61·90m.

Population of the United Kingdom by sex at census day 2001:

Divisions	*Males*	*Females*
England	23,923,390	25,215,441
Wales	1,403,900	1,499,185
Scotland	2,432,494	2,629,517
Northern Ireland	821,449	863,818
United Kingdom	28,581,233	30,207,961

Households in the United Kingdom at the 2001 census: England, 21,262,000; Wales, 1,276,000; Scotland, 2,192,000; Northern Ireland, 627,000.

The age distribution in the United Kingdom at census day in 2001 was as follows (in 1,000):

Age-group	*England and Wales*	*Scotland*	*Northern Ireland*	*United Kingdom*
Under 5	3,094	277	115	3,486
5 and under 10	3,308	307	123	3,738
10 " 15	3,425	323	133	3,881
15 " 20	3,217	317	129	3,663
20 " 25	3,122	314	109	3,545
25 " 35	7,419	699	242	8,360
35 " 45	7,749	781	247	8,777
45 " 55	6,887	689	199	7,775
55 " 65	5,507	550	162	6,219
65 " 70	2,292	239	65	2,596
70 " 75	2,074	207	58	2,339
75 " 85	2,933	271	77	3,281
85 and upwards	1,012	88	23	1,123

In 2001, 18·85% of the population of the UK were under the age of 15, 60·35% between 15 and 59, 13·29% between 60 and 74, and 7·51% aged 75 and over. In 1951 only 3·54% of the population had been 75 and over.

England and Wales. The census population (present on census night) of England and Wales 1801 to 2001:

Date of enumeration	*Population*	*Pop. per sq. mile*[1]	*Date of enumeration*	*Population*	*Pop. per sq. mile*[1]
1801	8,892,536	152	1901	32,527,843	558
1811	10,164,256	174	1911	36,070,492	618
1821	12,000,236	206	1921	37,886,699	649
1831	13,896,797	238	1931	39,952,377	685
1841	15,914,148	273	1951	43,757,888	750
1851	17,927,609	307	1961	46,104,548	791
1861	20,066,224	344	1971	48,749,575	323
1871	22,712,266	389	1981	49,016,600	325
1881	25,974,439	445	1991	49,193,915	330
1891	29,002,525	497	2001	52,041,916	345

[1]Per sq. km from 1971.

Estimated population of England and Wales, mid-2008, 54,535,000 (27,720,000 females and 26,815,000 males).

The birthplaces of the population of Great Britain at census day 2001 were: England, 43,967,372; Wales, 2,815,088; Scotland, 5,229,366; Northern Ireland, 256,503; Ireland, 494,154; other European Union countries, 763,171; elsewhere, 3,578,273.

Ethnic Groups. The 1991 census was the first to include a question on ethnic status.

Percentage figures from the 2001 census relating to ethnicity in England and Wales:

	England and Wales (%)	*England (%)*	*Wales (%)*
White			
British	87·5	87·0	96·0
Irish	1·2	1·3	0·6
Other	2·6	2·7	1·3
Mixed			
White and Black Caribbean	0·5	0·5	0·2
White and Black African	0·2	0·2	0·1
White and Asian	0·4	0·4	0·2
Other Mixed	0·3	0·3	0·1
Asian or Asian British			
Indian	2·0	2·1	0·3
Pakistani	1·4	1·4	0·3
Bangladeshi	0·5	0·6	0·2
Other Asian	0·5	0·5	0·1
Black or Black British			
Caribbean	1·1	1·1	0·1
African	0·9	1·0	0·1
Other Black	0·2	0·2	0·0
Chinese	0·4	0·4	0·2
Other ethnic groups	0·4	0·4	0·2

In Scotland about 2% of the population in 2001 were from a minority (non-White) ethnic group, compared with 1·3% in 1991. Pakistanis formed the largest such group, constituting 0·3%.

The following table shows the distribution of the urban and rural population of England and Wales (persons present) in 1951, 1961, 1971 and 1981:

	Population			*Percentage*	
	England and Wales	*Urban districts*[1]	*Rural districts*[1]	*Urban*	*Rural*
1951	43,757,888	35,335,721	8,422,167	80·8	19·2
1961	46,071,604	36,838,442	9,233,162	80·0	20·0
1971	48,755,000	38,151,000	10,598,000	78·2	21·5
1981	49,011,417	37,686,863	11,324,554	76·9	23·1

[1]As existing at each census.

Urban and rural areas were re-defined for the 1981 and 1991 censuses on a land use basis. In Scotland 'localities' correspond to urban areas. The 1981 census gave the usually resident population of England and Wales as 48,521,596, of which 43,599,431 were in urban areas; and of Scotland as 5,035,315, of which 4,486,140 were in localities.

British Citizenship. Under the British Nationality Act 1981 there are three main forms of citizenship: citizenship for persons closely connected with the UK; British Dependent Territories citizenship; British Overseas citizenship. British citizenship is acquired automatically at birth by a child born in the UK if his or her mother or father is a British citizen or is settled in the UK. A child born abroad to a British citizen is a British citizen by descent. British citizenship may be acquired by registration for stateless persons, and for children not automatically acquiring such citizenship or born abroad to parents who are citizens by descent; and, for other adults, by naturalization. Requirements for the latter include five years' residence (three years for applicants married to a British citizen). The Hong Kong (British Nationality) Order 1986 created the status of British National (Overseas) for citizens connected with Hong Kong before 1997, and the British Nationality (Hong Kong) Act 1990 made provision for up to 50,000 selected persons to register as British citizens.

Emigration and Immigration. Immigration is mainly governed by the Immigration Act 1970 and Immigration Rules made under it. British and Commonwealth citizens with the right of abode before 1983 are not subject to immigration control, nor are citizens of European Economic Area countries. Other persons seeking to work or settle in the UK must obtain a visa or entry clearance.

Total international migration estimates for recent years are as follows.

Inflows (in 1,000):

	Total	*British*	*Non-British*
2004	586	88	498
2005	563	96	466
2006	591	81	510
2007	577	75	502

Outflows (in 1,000):

	Total	*British*	*Non-British*
2004	342	195	147
2005	359	185	174
2006	400	207	194
2007	340	171	169

The number of immigrants into the UK in 2006, at 591,000, was the highest on record for a calendar year. The number of emigrants from the UK in 2006, at 400,000, was also the highest on record for a calendar year. The number of emigrants in 2007 was the lowest since 2001.

In 2007 (provisional) there were 124,855 grants of settlement in the UK (134,445 in 2006 and 179,120 in 2005), including from Asia, 67,955; and Africa, 34,050. Main individual countries were: India, 14,865; Pakistan, 10,825; Philippines, 8,485; Iraq, 7,020; South Africa, 5,805; Zimbabwe, 4,280.

Asylum. In 2008 there were 25,670 applications for asylum, up from 23,430 in 2007 (the lowest total since 1993), although down from a record 84,130 in 2002. The main countries of origin in 2008 were Afghanistan, Zimbabwe, Eritrea, Iran, Iraq and Sri Lanka. Applications, including dependants, were 28,300 in 2007. While respecting its obligations to political refugees under the UN Convention and Protocol relating to the status of Refugees, the government has powers under the Asylum and Immigration Act 1996 to weed out applicants seeking entry for non-political reasons and to designate certain countries as not giving risk of persecution. In the period 2003–07 the UK received 156,115 applications for asylum and granted asylum to 14,695 persons (compared to 46,455 in 1999–2003). The number of applicants granted asylum in 2007 was 3,800, the highest total since 2003.

Coleman, D. and Salt, J., *The British Population: Patterns, Trends and Processes*. 1992

See also ENGLAND, SCOTLAND, WALES *and* NORTHERN IRELAND: Territory and Population.

Language. Although there is no legally defined official language in the United Kingdom, English is the *de facto* official language.

SOCIAL STATISTICS

UK statistics, 2007: births, 772,245 (343,000 outside marriage); deaths, 574,687; marriages, 273,923; divorces, 143,955. The number of births in the UK in 2007 was the highest since 1994; the number of deaths in 2006 (572,224) was the lowest since the early 1930s. Provisional statistics, 2008: births, 794,400; deaths, 579,700. Great Britain statistics, 2007: births, 747,794; deaths, 560,038; marriages, 265,236; divorces, 141,042; abortions, a record 219,336. The number of births in the UK went up in 2007 for the sixth consecutive year. In 1976, for the only time in the 20th century, deaths in the UK (680,800) exceeded births

(675,500). In 2007 cancer caused 159,000 deaths (28% of all deaths in the UK, making it the biggest killer, ahead of coronary heart disease, at 91,000 (16%) and respiratory diseases, at 78,000 (14%)). UK life expectancy, 2005–07: males, 77·2 years; females, 81·5. The World Health Organization's *World Health Statistics 2009* put the UK in joint 21st place in a 'healthy life expectancy' list, with an expected 72 years of healthy life for babies born in 2007. Annual population growth rate, 2001–04, 0·4%. In 2008 there were 5,735 suicides (4,347 of whom were men), giving a suicide rate of nine per 100,000 population. Infant mortality, 2007, 4·8 per 1,000 live births. Fertility rate, 2007, 1·9 births per woman. Of the 772,245 live births in the UK in 2007, 44·4% were to unmarried women, up from 6% in 1961 and 20% in 1986. The rate of births to teenagers in England and Wales was 26·0 per 1,000 women in 2007. In 1999 for the first time there were more births to women in the 30–34 age group in the UK than in the 25–29 bracket. UK rates (per 1,000 population), 2007: birth, 12·7; death, 9·4; marriage, 4·5; divorce, 2·4. The average age of first marriage in England and Wales in 2007 was 32 years for men and 30 years for women, up from 25 years for men and 23 years for women in 1971. 66% of marriages in England and Wales in 2007 were civil and 34% religious, compared to 51% religious and 49% civil in 1991. The marriage rate in England and Wales has fallen to its lowest level since 1862. Same-sex civil partnerships were legalized in Dec. 2005.

In 2007, 16·0% of the total population was over 65, up from 11·7% in 1960. By 2008 the number of centenarians had reached an estimated 9,600 in England and Wales.

In 2009 the average household in Great Britain consisted of 2·4 people, down from 3·1 in 1961. 63% of dependent children lived in married couple families in the UK in 2008 and 23% in single-parent families.

England and Wales statistics (in 1,000), 2007 (and 2006): births, 690 (670); deaths, 504 (503); marriages, 235 (237); divorces, 129 (133). In 2003 there was a rise in the number of births for the first time since 1996, a trend which continued in 2004, 2005, 2006 and 2007.

Britain has one of the highest rates of drug usage in Europe. Figures released in 2005 showed that 38% of schoolchildren in England and Wales aged 15 and 16 have used cannabis. In 2007–08, 15·4% of 16 to 30-year-olds had used cannabis and 5·0% cocaine. A 2009 report found that use of ecstasy and amphetamines in England and Wales was the highest in the European Union and cocaine use the second highest after Spain. There were 2,640 recorded drug-related deaths in England and Wales in 2007, up from 2,570 in 2006 (although down from a peak of 3,110 in 1999).

A UNICEF report published in 2005 showed that 15·4% of children in Great Britain live in poverty (in households with income below 50% of the national median), compared to just 2·4% in Denmark.

See also NORTHERN IRELAND: Social Statistics.

CLIMATE

The climate is cool temperate oceanic, with mild conditions and rainfall evenly distributed over the year, though the weather is very changeable because of cyclonic influences. In general, temperatures are higher in the west and lower in the east in winter and rather the reverse in summer. Rainfall amounts are greatest in the west, where most of the high ground occurs.

London, Jan. 39°F (3·9°C), July 64°F (17·8°C). Annual rainfall 25" (635 mm). Aberdeen, Jan. 38°F (3·3°C), July 57°F (13·9°C). Annual rainfall 32" (813 mm). Belfast, Jan. 40°F (4·5°C), July 59°F (15·0°C). Annual rainfall 37·4" (950 mm). Birmingham, Jan. 38°F (3·3°C), July 61°F (16·1°C). Annual rainfall 30" (749 mm). Cardiff, Jan. 40°F (4·4°C), July 61°F (16·1°C). Annual rainfall 42·6" (1,065 mm). Edinburgh, Jan. 38°F (3·3°C), July 58°F (14·5°C). Annual rainfall 27" (686 mm). Glasgow, Jan. 39°F (3·9°C), July 59°F (15·0°C). Annual rainfall 38" (965 mm). Manchester, Jan. 39°F (3·9°C), July 61°F (16·1°C). Annual rainfall 34·5" (876 mm).

CONSTITUTION AND GOVERNMENT

The reigning Queen, Head of the Commonwealth, is **Elizabeth II** Alexandra Mary, b. 21 April 1926, daughter of King George VI and Queen Elizabeth; married on 20 Nov. 1947 Lieut. Philip Mountbatten (formerly Prince Philip of Greece), created Duke of Edinburgh, Earl of Merioneth and Baron Greenwich on the same day and created Prince Philip, Duke of Edinburgh, 22 Feb. 1957; succeeded to the crown on the death of her father, on 6 Feb. 1952.

Offspring. Prince Charles Philip Arthur George, Prince of Wales (Heir Apparent), b. 14 Nov. 1948; married Lady Diana Frances Spencer on 29 July 1981; after divorce, 28 Aug. 1996, Diana, Princess of Wales. She died in Paris in a road accident on 31 Aug. 1997; married Camilla Parker Bowles on 9 April 2005. *Offspring of first marriage:* William Arthur Philip Louis, b. 21 June 1982; Henry Charles Albert David, b. 15 Sept. 1984. Princess Anne Elizabeth Alice Louise, the Princess Royal, b. 15 Aug. 1950; married Mark Anthony Peter Phillips on 14 Nov. 1973; divorced, 1992; married Cdr Timothy Laurence on 12 Dec. 1992. *Offspring of first marriage:* Peter Mark Andrew, b. 15 Nov. 1977; married Autumn Patricia Kelly on 17 May 2008; Zara Anne Elizabeth, b. 15 May 1981. Prince Andrew Albert Christian Edward, created Duke of York, 23 July 1986, b. 19 Feb. 1960; married Sarah Margaret Ferguson on 23 July 1986; after divorce, 30 May 1996, Sarah, Duchess of York. *Offspring:* Princess Beatrice Mary, b. 8 Aug. 1988; Princess Eugenie Victoria Helena, b. 23 March 1990. Prince Edward Antony Richard Louis, created Earl of Wessex and Viscount Severn, 19 June 1999, b. 10 March 1964; married Sophie Rhys-Jones, Countess of Wessex, on 19 June 1999. *Offspring:* Louise Alice Elizabeth Mary, Lady Louise Windsor, b. 8 Nov. 2003; James Alexander Philip Theo, Viscount Severn, b. 17 Dec. 2007.

Sister of the Queen. Princess Margaret Rose, Countess of Snowdon, b. 21 Aug. 1930; married Antony Armstrong-Jones (created Earl of Snowdon, 3 Oct. 1961) on 6 May 1960; divorced, 1978; died 9 Feb. 2002. *Offspring:* David Albert Charles (Viscount Linley), b. 3 Nov. 1961, married Serena Alleyne Stanhope on 8 Oct. 1993. *Offspring:* Charles Patrick Inigo Armstrong-Jones, b. 1 July 1999; Margarita Elizabeth Rose Alleyne Armstrong-Jones, b. 14 May 2002. Lady Sarah Frances Elizabeth Chatto, b. 1 May 1964; married Daniel Chatto on 14 July 1994. *Offspring:* Samuel David Benedict Chatto, b. 28 July 1996; Arthur Robert Nathaniel Chatto, b. 5 Feb. 1999.

The Queen's legal title rests on the statute of 12 and 13 Will. III, ch. 3, by which the succession to the Crown of Great Britain and Ireland was settled on the Princess Sophia of Hanover and the 'heirs of her body being Protestants'. By proclamation of 17 July 1917 the royal family became known as the House and Family of Windsor. On 8 Feb. 1960 the Queen issued a declaration varying her confirmatory declaration of 9 April 1952 to the effect that while the Queen and her children should continue to be known as the House of Windsor, her descendants, other than descendants entitled to the style of Royal Highness and the title of Prince or Princess, and female descendants who marry and their descendants should bear the name of Mountbatten-Windsor.

Lineage to the throne. 1) Prince of Wales. 2) Prince William of Wales. 3) Prince Henry of Wales. 4) Duke of York. 5) Princess Beatrice of York. 6) Princess Eugenie of York.

By letters patent of 30 Nov. 1917 the titles of Royal Highness and Prince or Princess are restricted to the Sovereign's children, the children of the Sovereign's sons and the eldest living son of the eldest son of the Prince of Wales.

Provision is made for the support of the royal household, after the surrender of hereditary revenues, by the settlement of the Civil List soon after the beginning of each reign. The Civil List Act of 1 Jan. 1972 provided for a decennial, and the Civil List (Increase of Financial Provision) Order 1975 for an annual review of the List, but in July 1990 it was again fixed for one decade.

The Civil List of 2001–10 provides for an annuity of £7,900,000 to the Queen annually; and £359,000 to Prince Philip. These amounts are the same as for the period 1991–2000. The income of the Prince of Wales derives from the Duchy of Cornwall. The Civil List was exempted from taxation in 1910. The Queen has paid income tax on her private income since April 1993.

The supreme legislative power is vested in Parliament, which consists of the Crown, the House of Lords and the House of Commons, and dates in its present form from the middle of the 14th century. A Bill which is passed by both Houses and receives Royal Assent becomes an Act of Parliament and part of statute law.

Parliament is summoned, and a General Election is called, by the sovereign on the advice of the Prime Minister. A Parliament may last up to five years, normally divided into annual sessions. A session is ended by prorogation, and most Public Bills which have not been passed by both Houses then lapse, unless they are subject to a carry over motion. A Parliament ends by dissolution, either by will of the sovereign or by lapse of the five-year period.

Under the Parliament Act 1911 all Money Bills (so certified by the Speaker of the House of Commons), if not passed by the Lords without amendment, may become law without their concurrence within one month of introduction in the Lords. Under the Parliament Acts 1911 and 1949 Public Bills, other than Money Bills or a Bill extending the maximum duration of Parliament, if passed by the Commons in two successive sessions and rejected each time by the Lords, may become law without being passed by the Lords provided that one year has elapsed between Commons second reading in the first session and passing of the bill by the Commons in the second session, and that the Bill reaches the Lords at least one month before the end of the second session. The Parliament Acts have been used four times since 1949: in 1991 for the War Crimes Act, in 1999 for the European Parliamentary Elections Act, in 2000 for the Sexual Offences (Amendment) Act and for the Hunting Act in 2004.

Peerages are created by the sovereign, on the advice of the Prime Minister, with no limits on their number. The following are the main categories of membership (composition at 1 Dec. 2009, excluding 12 members who were on leave of absence, 16 disqualified as senior members of the judiciary and one disqualified as an MEP):

Party	*Life Peers*	*Hereditary: Elected by Party*	*Hereditary: Elected Office Holders*	*Hereditary: Royal Office Holders*	*Bishops*	*Total*
Conservative	141	39	9	...	...	189
Labour	207	2	2	...	...	211
Liberal Democrat	67	3	2	...	...	72
Crossbench	150	29	2	2	...	183
Archbishops and Bishops	...	...	...	...	26	26
Other	23	2	...	...	...	25
Total	588	75	15	2[1]	26	706

[1]The Duke of Norfolk, Earl Marshal and the Marquess of Cholmondeley, Lord Great Chamberlain.

Composition by type:

Archbishops and bishops	26
Life Peers under the Appellate Jurisdiction Act 1876	23 (1 woman)
Life Peers under the Life Peerages Act 1958	594 (144 women)
Peers under the House of Lords Act 1999	92 (2 women)
Total	735

The House of Commons consists of Members (of both sexes) representing constituencies determined by the Boundary Commissions. Persons under 18 years of age (since July 2006—formerly 21 years), Clergy of the Church of England and of the Scottish Episcopal Church, Ministers of the Church of Scotland, Roman Catholic clergymen, civil servants, members of the regular armed forces, policemen, most judicial officers and other office-holders named in the House of Commons (Disqualification) Act are disqualified from sitting in the House of Commons. In general hereditary peers are no longer disqualified from membership of the Commons, following the passage of the House of Lords Act 1999. However, the 92 hereditary peers who still sit in the Lords remain disqualified, as do the few hereditary peers who were given life peerages after the passing of the 1999 Act. Life peers are disqualified from membership of the House of Commons.

The Representation of the People Act 1948 abolished the business premises and university franchises, thus ending the practice of plural voting previously afforded certain graduates and business-owners. Only registered persons can vote at Parliamentary elections. No person may vote in more than one constituency at a general election. All persons may apply to vote by post if they are unable to vote in person, or if they fulfil certain legal requirements they may also be entitled to vote by proxy. Elections are held on the first-past-the-post system, in which the candidate who receives the most votes is elected.

All persons over 18 years old and not subject to any legal incapacity to vote and who are either British subjects or citizens of Ireland are entitled to be included in the register of electors for the constituency containing the address at which they were residing on the qualifying date for the register, and are entitled to vote at elections held during the period for which the register remains in force.

Members of the armed forces, Crown servants employed abroad and the wives accompanying their husbands, are entitled, if otherwise qualified, to be registered as 'service voters' provided they make a 'service declaration'. To be effective for a particular register, the declaration must be made on or before the qualifying date for that register. In certain circumstances, British subjects living abroad may also vote.

The Parliamentary Constituencies Act 1986, as amended by the Boundary Commissions Act 1992, provided for the setting up of Boundary Commissions for England, Wales, Scotland and Northern Ireland. The Commissions' last reports were made in Feb. 2007, and future reports will be due at intervals of not less than eight and not more than 12 years; and may be submitted from time to time with respect to the area comprised in any particular constituency or constituencies where some change appears necessary. Any changes giving effect to reports of the Commissions are to be made by Orders in Council laid before Parliament for approval by resolution of each House. The Parliamentary electorate of the United Kingdom and Northern Ireland in the register in Dec. 2009 numbered 45,420,808 (38,129,082 in England, 2,261,269 in Wales, 3,869,700 in Scotland and 1,160,757 in Northern Ireland).

At the UK general election held on 6 May 2010, 649 out of 650 members were returned, 532 from England, 59 from Scotland, 40 from Wales and 18 from Northern Ireland. Every constituency returns a single member. Voting was postponed in Thirsk and Malton owing to the death of a candidate shortly before the election.

One of the main aspects of the former Labour government's programme of constitutional reform was Scottish and Welsh devolution. In the referendum on Scottish devolution on 11 Sept. 1997, 1,775,045 votes (74·3%) were cast in favour of a Scottish parliament and 614,400 against (25·7%). The turnout was 60·4%, so around 44·8% of the total electorate voted in favour. For the second question, on the Parliament's tax-raising powers, 1,512,889 votes were cast in favour (63·5%) and 870,263 against (36·5%). This represented 38·4% of the total electorate.

On 18 Sept. 1997 in Wales there were 559,419 votes cast in favour of a Welsh assembly (50·3%) and 552,698 against (49·7%). The turnout was 51·3%.

For MPs' salaries *see below*. Members of the House of Lords are unsalaried but may recover expenses incurred in attending sittings of the House within maxima for each day's attendance of £86·50 for day subsistence, £174 for night subsistence and £75 for secretarial and research assistance and office expenses. Additionally, Members of the House who are disabled may recover the extra cost of attending the House incurred by reason of their disablement. In connection with attendance at the House and parliamentary duties within the UK, Lords may also recover the cost of travelling to and from home.

The executive government is vested nominally in the Crown, but practically in a committee of Ministers, called the Cabinet, which is dependent on the support of a majority in the House of Commons. The head of the Cabinet is the *Prime Minister*, a position first constitutionally recognized in 1905. The Prime Minister's colleagues in the Cabinet are appointed on his recommendation.

Salaries. Members of Parliament received an annual salary of £64,766 in 2009–10. Ministers who are MPs also receive a ministerial salary. Total salaries accepted for 2009–10 (including parliamentary salaries where applicable): Prime Minister, £197,689 (£132,923 ministerial salary); Cabinet Ministers, £144,520 (in the House of Lords, £108,253); Ministers of State, £106,136 (in the Lords £84,524); Parliamentary Under-Secretaries, £96,167 (in the Lords, £73,617); Government Chief Whip, £144,520 (in the Lords, £84,524); Leader of the Opposition, £138,383 (in the Lords, £73,617); Speaker, £144,520; Attorney General, £113,248; Solicitor General, £134,257; Advocate General for Scotland, £98,307. Cabinet Ministers in the Commons (but not the Lords) receive the parliamentary salary. Following a scandal over MPs' abuse of expenses, the Parliamentary Standards Act 2009 was passed in July 2009 creating the Independent Parliamentary Standards Authority (IPSA). Reforms to the expenses system were introduced by the IPSA in May 2010.

The Privy Council. Before the development of the Cabinet System, the Privy Council was the chief source of executive power, but now its functions are largely formal. It advises the monarch to approve Orders in Council and on the issue of royal proclamations, and has some independent powers such as the supervision of the registration of the medical profession. It consists of all Cabinet members, the Archbishops of Canterbury and York, the Speaker of the House of Commons and senior British and Commonwealth statesmen. There are a number of advisory Privy Council committees. The Judicial Committee is the final court of appeal from courts of the UK dependencies, the Channel Islands and the Isle of Man, and some Commonwealth countries.

Freedom of Information Act. The Freedom of Information Act 2000 was implemented gradually between Nov. 2002 and Jan. 2005 when the General Right of Access to all information became law. Not to be confused with the Data Protection Act of 1998, the FOIA allows individuals to gain access to information held by public authorities in England, Wales and Northern Ireland. A separate Act applies in Scotland. Some information is exempted from release, for example security-related documents. An independent Commissioner for Information oversees the process.

Bogdanor, V., *Devolution in the United Kingdom*. 1999
Bruce, A., *et al. The House of Lords: 1,000 Years of British Tradition*. 1994
Butler, David and Butler, Gareth, *British Political Facts Since 1979*. 2005
Dod's Parliamentary Companion. Published after elections
Harrison, B., *The Transformation of British Politics, 1860–1995*. 1996
Kavanagh, Dennis and Butler, David, *The British General Election of 2005*. 2005
Norris, P., *Electoral Change in Britain since 1945*. 1996
Rush, Michael and Giddings, Philip, *Palgrave Review of British Politics 2006*. 2007
The Times Guide to the House of Commons. Published after elections
Waller, R. and Criddle, B., *The Almanac of British Politics*. 8th ed. 2007

See also NORTHERN IRELAND: Constitution and Government

Local Government

Administration is carried out by four types of bodies: (i) local branches of some central ministries, such as the Departments of Health and Social Security; (ii) local sub-managements of nationalized industries; (iii) specialist authorities such as the National Rivers Authority; and (iv) the system of local government described below. The phrase 'local government' has come to mean that part of the local administration conducted by elected councils. There are separate systems for England, Wales and Scotland.

The Local Government Act 1992 provided for the establishment of new unitary councils (authorities) in England, responsible for all services in their areas, though the two-tier structure of district and county councils remained for much of the country. In 1996 all of Wales and Scotland was given unitary local government systems. In April 2009 a further nine single-tier unitary authorities were created in a bid to simplify the system.

Local authorities have statutory powers and claims on public funds. Relations with central government are maintained through the Department for Communities and Local Government in England, and through the Welsh and Scottish Executives. In England the Home Office is concerned with some local government functions. (These are performed by departments within the Welsh and Scottish Offices.) Ministers have powers of intervention to protect individuals' rights and safeguard public health, and the government has the power to cap (i.e. limit) local authority budgets.

The chair of the council (known as the Mayor in boroughs and cities) is traditionally one of the councillors elected by the rest. However, the Mayor of London has been directly elected since 1999 and following the Local Government Act 2000, 12 councils in England have also introduced direct mayoral elections. Mayors of cities may have the title of Lord Mayor conferred on them. 53 towns in England and Wales and five in Scotland have the status of city. Brighton and Hove, Wolverhampton and Inverness were awarded city status in 2000. In 2002 Preston, Newport, Stirling, Lisburn and Newry were given city status to mark Queen Elizabeth II's golden jubilee. This status is granted by the personal command of the monarch and confers no special privileges or powers. In Scotland, the chair of city councils is deemed Lord Provost, and is elsewhere known as Convenor or Provost. In Wales, the chair is called Chairman in counties and Mayor in county boroughs. Any parish or community council can by simple resolution adopt the style 'town council' and the status of town for the parish or community.

Functions. Legislation in the 1980s initiated a trend for local authorities to provide services by, or in collaboration with, commercial or voluntary bodies rather than provide them directly. Savings are encouraged by compulsory competitive tendering. In England, county councils are responsible for strategic planning, transport planning, non-trunk roads and regulation of traffic, personal social services, consumer protection, disposal of waste, the fire and library services and, partially, for education. District councils are responsible for environmental health, housing, local planning applications (in the first instance) and refuse collection. Unitary authorities combine the functions of both levels.

Finance. Revenue is derived from the Council Tax, which supports about one-fifth of current expenditure, the remainder being funded by central government grants and by the redistribution of revenue from the national non-domestic rate (property tax). Capital expenditure is financed by borrowing within government-set limits and sales of real estate.

Elections. England: The 36 metropolitan districts are divided into wards, each represented by three councillors. One-third of the councillors are elected each year for three years out of four. All metropolitan districts had an election on 6 May 2010. The 201 district councils and the 56 English unitary authorities are divided into wards. Each chooses either to follow the metropolitan district system, or to have all seats contested once every four years, or to elect by halves every two years. All 231 district councils (since reduced to 201) had an election on 3 May 2007. The 27 county councils have one councillor for each electoral division, elected every four years, with elections next scheduled for 2013.

In London there are 33 councils (including the City of London), the whole of which are elected every four years. London borough elections took place on 6 May 2010. The Greater London Authority has a 25-member Assembly, elected using AMS (Additional Member System), and a directly elected mayor, elected by the SV (Supplementary Vote) system. For the election of London Assembly members London is divided into 14 constituencies. Each constituency elects one member, in addition to which there are 11 'London Member' seats. Boris Johnson (Con.) was elected mayor on 1 May 2008.

Wales: The 22 unitary authorities are split between single and multi-member wards, elected every four years. Elections were last held on 1 May 2008.

Scotland: The 32 unitary authorities hold elections every four years. The last elections were held on 3 May 2007.

Resident citizens of the UK, Ireland, a Commonwealth country or an EU country may vote and stand for election at age 18. The minimum age for standing was lowered from 21 to 18 for the 2007 local elections.

Election Results. English local government elections for 36 metropolitan district councils, 32 London boroughs, 20 unitary authorities and 76 shire district councils were held on 6 May 2010. The Conservatives emerged with control of 65 councils (a net loss of 8), Labour 37 (net gain 15), Liberal Democrats 13 (net loss 4), with no overall control in 45. The Conservatives lost 123 seats (bringing their total to 3,367), Labour gained 420 (total 2,892), the Liberal Democrats lost 144 (total 1,640), Residents' Association gained 2 (total 51), the Greens lost 4 (total 34) and others lost 147 (total 328).

The elections to provide London with a Mayor and a 25-member London Assembly took place on 1 May 2008. Boris Johnson (Con.) won with 53·18% of the vote after counting second preferences. He gained 1,168,738 votes (1,043,761 as first votes) against 1,028,966 votes (893,877 as first votes) for incumbent Ken Livingstone (Lab.).

National Anthem

'God Save the Queen' (King) (words and tune anonymous; earliest known printed source, 1744).

GOVERNMENT CHRONOLOGY

Governments and Prime Ministers since the Second World War (Con = Conservative Party; Lab = Labour Party):

1945–51	Lab	Clement Attlee
1951–55	Con	Winston Churchill
1955–57	Con	Sir Anthony Eden
1957–63	Con	Harold Macmillan
1963–64	Con	Sir Alec Douglas-Home
1964–70	Lab	Harold Wilson
1970–74	Con	Edward Heath
1974–76	Lab	Harold Wilson
1976–79	Lab	James Callaghan
1979–90	Con	Margaret Thatcher
1990–97	Con	John Major
1997–2007	Lab	Tony Blair
2007–10	Lab	Gordon Brown
2010–	Con	David Cameron

RECENT ELECTIONS

At the general election of 6 May 2010, 29,653,638 votes were cast. The Conservative Party won 306 seats with 36·1% of votes cast (197 with 32·3% in 2005); the Labour Party 258 with 29·0% (356 seats with 35·2%); the Liberal Democrats 57 with 23·0% (62 with 22·1%); Green 1 (others 3). Regional parties (Scotland): the Scottish National Party won 6 seats (6 in 2005); (Wales): Plaid Cymru 3 (3); (Northern Ireland): the Democratic Unionist Party 8 (9); Sinn Féin 5 (5); the Social and Democratic Labour Party 3 (3); the Alliance Party 1 (0). There was one seat outstanding following the death of a candidate. The Conservatives gained 100 seats and lost 3; Labour gained 3 seats and lost 94; the Liberal Democrats gained 8 seats and lost 13. Turnout was 65·1% (61·3% in 2005).

Barry Turner, editor of The Statesman's Yearbook, writes:

After five days of hard bargaining between the main parties, a Conservative led coalition with the Liberal Democrats put David Cameron into Downing Street. Can he succeed? The precedents are not encouraging. Short of dire emergency, the British political system has not so far lent itself to lasting co-operation across party lines. Churchill's grand coalition held together throughout the Second World War but quickly fell apart once peace was declared. When neither Labour nor Conservatives won a clear mandate in the first of the 1974 elections, a coalition with the then Liberal Party was discounted in favour of a Labour minority government. It lasted eight months before securing a narrow majority in a second appeal to the electorate. Three years on, a weak Labour government was kept alive, albeit briefly, by a loose alliance with the Liberals. Frustrated by the absence of firm leadership, the electorate turned to Margaret Thatcher, awarding her a clear parliamentary majority, a victory that was so decisive as to suspend any talk of coalitions for twenty years. In the run-up to the 1997 election, talk of Labour and the Liberal Democrats making common cause turned to serious negotiation but the hope of a radical coalition faded on Tony Blair's landslide victory.

So what, if anything, is different now? The change that gives this coalition a better than even chance of success is in the collapse of the old class loyalties. It used to be that Labour and Conservative could each rely on the knee jerk support of up to 40 percent of the electorate. In the latest election, the Conservatives won just 36 percent of the vote with Labour down to a mere 29 percent. Put another way, one third of the electorate shopped around, backing the Liberal Democrats, nationalists or one of the fringe parties. Add to this a growing public distrust of all politicians and the stage is set for a radical realignment which puts political reform at the top of the agenda.

But there is a downside—David Cameron as prime minister and Nick Clegg, leader of the Liberal Democrats, as deputy prime minister, have pledged to restore trust in parliamentary democracy while coming up with proposals to plug the ever widening hole in the national finances. To achieve both, a return to public confidence in government along with tax increases and/or savage cuts in state expenditure, will be a hard trick to pull.

May 2010

European Parliament

The United Kingdom has 72 (78 in 2004) representatives. At the June 2009 elections turnout was 34·7% (38·5% in 2004). The Conservative Party won 25 seats with 27·0% of votes cast (political affiliation in European Parliament: 24 with European Conservatives and Reformists and one non-attached); UK Independence Party, 13 with 16·1% (Europe of Freedom and Democracy); the Labour Party, 13 with 15·3% (Progressive Alliance of Socialists and Democrats); the Liberal Democrats, 11 with 13·4% (Alliance of Liberals and Democrats for Europe); the

Green Party, 2 with 8·4% (Greens/European Free Alliance); the British National Party, 2 with 6·0% (non-attached); the Scottish National Party, 2 with 2·1% (Greens/European Free Alliance); Plaid Cymru, 1 with 0·8% (Greens/European Free Alliance). Voting for these parties was on a proportional system. Voting in Northern Ireland was by the transferable vote system: Sinn Féin (European United Left/Nordic Green Left), the Democratic Unionist Party (non-attached) and the Ulster Unionist Party (European Conservatives and Reformists) gained 1 seat each.

CURRENT ADMINISTRATION

In May 2010 the coalition government comprising the Conservative Party (Con.) and the Liberal Democrats (LD) consisted of the following:

(a) 23 MEMBERS OF THE CABINET

Prime Minister and First Lord of the Treasury: David Cameron (Con.), b. 1966.

Deputy Prime Minister: Nick Clegg (LD), b. 1967.

Secretary of State for Business, Innovation and Skills: Vince Cable (LD), b. 1943.

Chancellor of the Exchequer: George Osborne (Con.), b. 1971.

Secretary of State for Foreign and Commonwealth Affairs: William Hague (Con.), b. 1961.

Secretary of State for Justice and Lord Chancellor: Ken Clarke (Con.), b. 1940.

Secretary of State for the Home Department: Theresa May (Con.), 1956.

Secretary of State for Environment, Food and Rural Affairs: Caroline Spelman (Con.), b. 1958.

Secretary of State for International Development: Andrew Mitchell (Con.), b. 1956.

Secretary of State for Communities and Local Government: Eric Pickles (Con.), b. 1952.

Secretary of State for Education: Michael Gove (Con.), b. 1967.

Secretary of State for Energy and Climate Change: Chris Huhne (LD), b. 1954.

Secretary of State for Health: Andrew Lansley (Con.), b. 1956.

Secretary of State for Northern Ireland: Owen Paterson (Con.), b. 1956.

Leader of the House of Lords and Chancellor of the Duchy of Lancaster: Lord Strathclyde (Con.), b. 1960.

Secretary of State for Scotland: Danny Alexander (LD), b. 1972.

Secretary of State for Work and Pensions: Iain Duncan Smith (Con.), b. 1954.

Chief Secretary to the Treasury: David Laws (LD), b. 1965.

Secretary of State for Wales: Cheryl Gillan (Con.), b. 1952.

Secretary of State for Defence: Liam Fox (Con.), b. 1961.

Secretary of State for Transport: Philip Hammond (Con.), b. 1955.

Secretary of State for Culture, Olympics, Media and Sport: Jeremy Hunt (Con.), b. 1966.

Minister without Portfolio: Baroness Warsi (Con.), b. 1971.

(Non-cabinet members but attend cabinet meetings): Patrick McLoughlin (Con.), b. 1957, *Parliamentary Secretary to the Treasury and Chief Whip;* Francis Maude (Con.), b. 1953, *Minister for the Cabinet Office and Paymaster General;* Oliver Letwin (Con.), b. 1956, *Minister of State for the Cabinet Office;* David Willetts (Con.), b. 1956, *Minister of State for Universities and Science;* Sir George Young (Con.), b. 1941, *Leader of the House of Commons.*

(b) LAW OFFICERS

Attorney General: Dominic Grieve, QC (Con.), b. 1956 *(invited to attend Cabinet when required).*

Solicitor General: Edward Garnier, QC (Con.), b. 1952.

Advocate General for Scotland: Jim Wallace, Baron Wallace of Tankerness, QC (LD), b. 1954.

Attorney General for Northern Ireland: John Larkin, QC (ind.), b. 1964.

The *Speaker* of the House of Commons is John Bercow (Con.), elected on 22 June 2009.

Government Website: http://www.direct.gov.uk

CURRENT LEADERS

David Cameron

Position
Prime Minister

Introduction
David Cameron became prime minister on 11 May 2010, five days after the general election, in a coalition government with the Liberal Democrats. In so doing he returned the Conservatives to power after 13 years of Labour rule. After winning the Conservative leadership in 2005, Cameron aligned his party with the centre ground of politics, declaring his allegiance to good public services. In opposition, Cameron argued that sections of British society were 'broken' and identified himself as a force for change. In foreign policy he has embraced broadly the same approach as the previous government, aligning Britain with the USA and supporting British military involvement in Iraq and Afghanistan. He takes a more sceptical stance on Europe and has promised to hold public referenda on any future proposals to transfer sovereign powers to the EU. He came to power promising to reduce the national debt while protecting public services. He supports a move towards lower taxes but has signalled that he will take a cautious approach given the UK's weak economy.

Early Life
David William Duncan Cameron was born on 9 Oct. 1966 in London, the son of a stockbroker and a baronet's daughter. He grew up in Peasemore, Berkshire and was educated at Heatherdown Preparatory School and Eton College. From 1985–88 he studied politics, philosophy and economics at Brasenose College, Oxford, after which he worked for the research department of the ruling Conservative party. He rose to lead the department's political section and in 1992 headed the economic section of the Conservatives' general election campaign team. Following their victory, he was appointed special adviser. He was working for the chancellor of the exchequer, Norman Lamont, when the government was forced to withdraw sterling from the European Exchange Rate Mechanism on 'Black Wednesday', 16 Sept. 1992. In May 1993 he was appointed adviser to the home office where, under home secretary Michael Howard, he helped introduce the Criminal Justice Bill and promoted initiatives for private companies to build and run prisons. Cameron left politics in 1994 to work in corporate affairs at media company Carlton Communications, where for seven years he worked closely with chairman Michael Green, handling public relations and communications. At the 1997 general election he unsuccessfully contested Stafford for the Conservatives. During this campaign he broke with official Conservative party policy to oppose joining the single European currency. In the June 2001 election, he was elected MP for Witney in Oxfordshire, increasing the Conservative share of the vote. In the subsequent Conservative leadership contest he initially supported modernizer Michael Portillo, before finally voting for Iain Duncan Smith, who was seen as an outsider candidate and a eurosceptic.

Cameron was appointed to the Home Affairs Select Committee, where he argued for a review of legislation on illegal drugs. He supported British participation in the 2003 Iraq war, in line with Conservative party policy, despite expressing doubts in the press. In June 2003 he was appointed shadow minister in the Privy Council office and in Nov. that year became deputy chairman of the Conservative party under newly elected leader Michael Howard. Cameron was named spokesman on local government finance in March 2004 and in June 2004, following poor local election results for the Conservatives, he was given responsibility for party policy co-ordination.

He played a key role in developing the party's 2005 general election manifesto, which promised to cut taxes, increase numbers of police and prisons, and oppose the introduction of a European constitution. In May 2005 the Conservatives gained votes but failed to prevent a third successive Labour victory. Cameron was subsequently appointed shadow education secretary and when Howard resigned in Sept. 2005, Cameron entered the contest for the party leadership. He positioned himself as a modernizer, able to appeal to a wide range of voters, while also winning the support of eurosceptics with a pledge to withdraw Conservative MEPs from the European People's Party (the EU's main centre-right grouping) on the grounds that it was too federalist. After initially trailing his main rival, right-winger David Davis, he won support with a strong speech at the party conference in Oct. 2005. In the final ballot on 6 Dec. 2005 he defeated Davis with 67% of the vote. In his acceptance speech he promised to address the under-representation of women among Conservative MPs, to reformulate the party's approach to the inner cities and to end 'Punch and Judy politics' by supporting government initiatives where they were in line with Conservative thinking. In July 2006 Cameron fulfilled his campaign promise and withdrew Conservative MEPs from the EPP, forming a new alliance with Czech and Polish MEPs, a move criticised by some as taking the party too far to the right. He supported the 2006 education bill that diluted local council control over schools. Identifying himself as a liberal conservative on social matters, he spoke in support of civil partnerships for gay couples at the 2006 party conference. During the same year he introduced the 'A-list' initiative, which required constituency parties to choose their parliamentary candidate from a centrally approved list. Intended to improve representation of women and ethnic minority candidates, this met resistance at local level. In March 2007 Cameron launched a review into the quality of childhood in Britain and promised to promote marriage through taxation reforms. He repeatedly depicted Britain as a society in moral and economic decline, an interpretation summed up in his phrase 'broken Britain', and declared his support for economic liberalism combined with the promotion of voluntary and charity work.

During 2007 he said that a Conservative government would aim for lower taxes, with priority given to reducing inheritance tax liability. These proposals were widely credited with prompting government reforms to inheritance tax thresholds in Oct. 2007. Cameron also announced his intention to diversify provision of public services, in particular in education and the health service, proposing that funds could be diverted from state agencies to private enterprise or the voluntary sector. Though widely welcomed by Conservative voters, some were disappointed by his refusal to consider creating more grammar schools.

In foreign policy Cameron continued to support British troop deployment in Iraq and Afghanistan. On domestic security issues, in June 2008 he opposed increasing the maximum period of detention without charge from 28 to 42 days, arguing that it threatened civil liberties. He advocated a new border protection service that would include armed police officers. In Feb. 2009 he pledged to repeal the human rights act and replace it with a British bill of rights, in response to public anxieties that the act could be used to protect criminals. Cameron advocated increased prioritization of environmental policies and developed an approach similar to the government's, including proposals to expand nuclear energy. He opposed government plans to build a third runway at Heathrow airport. During the international financial crisis in autumn 2008, Cameron supported the government's rescue package, though he strongly criticized its record of financial management, particularly the high level of national debt. The subsequent financial downturn forced him to reassess his party's policies. In 2009 he announced that tax cuts would be contingent on economic improvement and confirmed that this meant postponing further inheritance tax reforms. In Dec. 2009 ratification of the Lisbon Treaty on the European constitution obviated his previous pledge to hold a referendum on the issue. Instead he issued a promise to introduce a sovereignty bill that would prevent any further transfer of power to the EU without a referendum. Cameron fought the 2010 general election on a platform of reduced government spending (with the exception of the NHS and overseas aid), fewer business regulations and increased choice in health and education services.

Career in Office

Cameron became prime minister on 11 May 2010. Although the Conservatives failed to secure an absolute majority in the election of 6 May they did win 306 seats compared to 258 for Labour and succeeded in forming a coalition (the UK's first since the Second World War) with the Liberal Democrats, who had won 57 seats. Cameron's key challenges are to address the weakness of the economy, the growing gap between rich and poor, and the fragility of the power-sharing government in Northern Ireland. Security remains a pressing issue as the UK continues to face the threat of terrorism, both imported and home-grown. Internationally, he must oversee continued British engagement in Afghanistan.

DEFENCE

The Defence Council was established on 1 April 1964 under the chairmanship of the Secretary of State for Defence, who is responsible to the Sovereign and Parliament for the defence of the realm. Vested in the Defence Council are the functions of commanding and administering the Armed Forces. The Secretary of State heads the Department of Defence.

Total full-time trained strength in 2008 numbered 174,000, untrained regulars 18,400 and (2005) reserve personnel 235,600. In 2007 UK armed forces abroad included 21,400 personnel based in Germany, 7,400 in Afghanistan (in most cases serving as part of ISAF), 6,400 in Iraq and 3,000 in Cyprus. Deaths in the UK regular armed forces totalled 205 in 2009, up from 137 in 2008. The last British troops left Iraq in July 2009. By Dec. 2009 the number of British troops in Afghanistan had increased to 9,500. British troop deaths in Iraq between 2003 and July 2009 totalled 179; deaths in Afghanistan between 2001 and April 2010 totalled 281.

The ban on homosexuals serving in the armed forces, which had been upheld by a House of Commons vote in May 1996, was suspended in Sept. 1999 after the European Court of Human Rights ruled that the current ban was unlawful.

Defence Budget. It was announced in July 2007 that the defence budget would rise by £4·3bn. (US$8·9bn.) over three years, the largest sustained increase in planned defence spending in over 20 years. The defence budget for 2007–08 was £32,579m. (US$67,191m.), rising to £34,057m. (US$70,239m.) for 2008–09, £35,365m. (US$72,936m.) for 2009–10 and £36,890m. (US$76,082m.) for 2010–11. Defence spending in 2006 represented 2·3% of GDP (the lowest level since the 1930s), down from 5·2% in 1985. Per capita defence expenditure in 2008 totalled £638 (US$1,070).

Nuclear Weapons. Having carried out its first test in 1952, there have been 45 tests in all (the last in 1991). The nuclear arsenal consisted of approximately 160 Trident submarine-launched ballistic missile warheads in Jan. 2009 according to the Stockholm International Peace Research Institute.

Arms Trade. The UK is a net exporter of arms and in 2006 was the world's third largest exporter after the USA and Russia (with sales worth US$3·3bn., or 12·2% of the world total).

In 2007 BAE Systems was the UK's largest arms producing company and the 2nd largest in the OECD. It accounted for US$29·9bn. of arms sales. Rolls Royce, QinetiQ and VT Group are other significant UK arms-producing companies.

The UK was the 19th largest recipient of major conventional weapons in the world during the period 2004–08, spending US$1,915m. over the five-year period.

Army

The British Army's operations fall into three categories: permanent tasks (e.g. Cyprus and the Falkland Islands); contingent tasks to meet a challenge to national interests and/or in support of international peace and stability (as in Afghanistan or Bosnia); and tasks in circumstances that are unlikely to arise without a significant period of preparation (e.g. general war). If not committed, units are also available to support the civil authorities.

The Chief of the General Staff (CGS) is the head of the Army and is responsible for implementing departmental decisions within the Army. He gives advice to ministers on managerial and operational issues and sets the strategic direction of the Army. CGS is accountable to the Defence Board for the fighting effectiveness and efficiency of the Army and the delivery of military capability.

Commander-in-Chief (C-in-C) Land Forces is responsible to CGS for the delivery of appropriately manned, equipped, trained and sustained force elements. The Army's Headquarters, Headquarters Land Forces (HQLF) is located at Wilton, near Salisbury, but is scheduled to move to Andover, Hants in the course of 2010 as part of a wider restructuring termed Project Hyperion. HQLF was formed on 1 April 2008 through the merger of the Land Command and Adjutant General. There are three subordinate commands to the C-in-C: Personnel and Support Command (PSC), commanded by the Adjutant General; Force Development and Training Command (FDT Comd), commanded by Commander Force Development and Training; and the Field Army, commanded by Commander Field Army.

On operations command rests with the Ministry of Defence (MOD) via the tri-service Permanent Joint Headquarters (PJHQ) at Northwood, north London.

The established strength of the Regular Army as at 1 April 2009 was 112,030 (including soldiers under training and Ghurkhas). The established strength of Ghurkhas was 3,580 as at 1 April 2009. 23,704 Army officers and soldiers were liable for recall as at 1 April 2009. Women serve throughout the Army although they do not currently serve in the infantry or armoured roles.

The Territorial Army (TA) acts as a general Reserve for the Regular Army by reinforcing it with formed units of individual reinforcements for operations, and by providing the framework and basis for regeneration and reconstruction to cater for the unforeseen in times of national emergency. The TA also provides a nationwide link between the military and civil communities. Strength, 1 April 2009, 35,350.

British Army equipment includes the tracked range of Challenger 2 main battle tanks, Warrior Infantry Armoured Fighting vehicles and the Combat Vehicle Reconnaissance (Tracked) series. The wheeled range includes the Mastiff and Ridgeback and Jackal Protective Patrol Vehicles. Additionally the British Army has a fleet of AH-64D Apache and Merlin helicopters.

Marquess of Anglesey, *A History of the British Cavalry 1816–1919*. 8 vols. 2007

Navy

Control of the Royal Navy is vested in the Defence Council and is exercised through the Admiralty Board, chaired by the Secretary of State for Defence.

The First Sea Lord and Chief of Naval Staff is the professional head of the Royal Navy and is responsible to the Secretary of State for Defence for the fighting effectiveness, efficiency and morale of the Naval Service. Subordinate to the First Sea Lord, the C.-in-C. Fleet, headquartered at Northwood, is responsible for operations, while the Second Sea Lord at Portsmouth is responsible for naval personnel. Main naval bases are at Devonport, Portsmouth and Faslane, with a minor base overseas at Gibraltar.

The roles of the Royal Navy are to deploy the national strategic nuclear deterrent, to provide maritime defence of the UK and its dependent territories, to contribute to the maritime elements of NATO's force structure and to meet national maritime objectives outside the NATO area.

The strength of the fleet's major units in the respective years:

	2004	*2005*	*2006*	*2007*	*2008*	*2009*
Strategic Submarines	4	4	4	4	4	4
Nuclear Submarines	11	9	9	9	9	8
Aircraft Carriers	2[1]	2[1]	2[1]	2[1]	2[1]	2[1]
Destroyers	11	8	8	8	7	6
Frigates	21	17	17	17	17	17
Landing Platform Docks	2	2	2	2	2	2
Landing Platform Helicopters	1	1	1	1	1	1

[1]Following government policy, of the three Carriers held, only two are kept in operational status.

The strategic deterrent is borne by four Trident submarines—*Vanguard, Victorious, Vigilant* and *Vengeance*. They are each capable of deploying 16 US-built Trident II D5 missiles. The principal surface ships are the Light vertical/short take-off and landing Aircraft Carriers of the Invincible class (*Invincible, Illustrious* and *Ark Royal*) completed 1980–85. Two of these ships are maintained in the operational fleet, with the third (currently *Invincible*) in extended readiness. These ships are to be replaced with a new class of two large aircraft carriers due in service in 2016 (HMS *Queen Elizabeth*) and 2018 (HMS *Prince of Wales*). A Helicopter Carrier, specifically designed for amphibious operations, HMS *Ocean*, entered service in 1998 and was joined by two amphibious Landing Platform Docks (LPD), HMS *Albion* and HMS *Bulwark*, in 2003 and 2004 respectively.

The Fleet Air Arm (5,250-strong in 2009) had 159 aircraft in 2009; the Royal Navy contributes a further 34 helicopters to the Joint Helicopter Command. Additionally, the Naval Strike Wing operates 16 Harrier aircraft as part of Joint Force Harrier (to be replaced by the Joint Strike Fighter in 2018, currently being built in collaboration with the USA).

The Royal Naval Reserve (RNR) and the Royal Marines Reserve (RMR) are volunteer forces that together numbered 3,000 in Dec. 2009. The RNR provides trained personnel in war to supplement regular forces.

The Royal Marines Command, 6,960-strong in 2009, provides a commando brigade comprising three commando groups. The Special Boat Squadron and specialist defence units complete the operational strength.

The total number of trained naval service personnel was 35,000 in Dec. 2009 (down from 45,600 in April 1996).

Air Force

The Royal Air Force was formed on 1 April 1918 through the merger of the Royal Flying Corps and the Royal Naval Air Service. Since 2007 operational and support functions have been vested in Headquarters Air Command at High Wycombe. Ten home stations and 27 squadrons make up Number 1 Group with bases such as Coningsby (Lincs), Cottesmore (Leics), Leuchars (Fife), Lossiemouth (Moray) and Marham (Norfolk) home to combat aircraft, support helicopters and Hawk trainers for advanced instruction.

The operational fleet comprised 853 aircraft in March 2008. The Typhoon is in the process of replacing Tornados in both air defence and ground attack roles and will be capable of carrying the new Paveway IV 'smart' bombs and Stormshadow missiles for long-range attack. Harriers, being upgraded for service until 2020, will gradually be replaced from around 2015 by the F-35 Lightning II otherwise known as the Joint Strike Fighter, which will also be flown from the two new Royal Navy aircraft carriers. Attack versions of Tornado have been upgraded and fitted with

RAPTOR (Reconnaissance Airborne Pod for Tornado). Options for the expanded use of unmanned air vehicles (UAVs) are also being researched.

There are three main pillars within Number 2 Group: Air Transport (AT) and Air-to-Air Refuelling (AAR); Intelligence, Surveillance, Target Acquisition and Reconnaissance (ISTAR); and Force Protection. AT/AAR provides rapid strategic and tactical reach, including airborne delivery of men and equipment. Force protection comprises the Regiment, Police and the Joint Chemical, Biological, Radiological and Nuclear Regiment. Operational Support Squadrons of the Royal Auxiliary Air Force are also included in Number 2 Group, as are Regiment Auxiliaries and the Mountain Rescue Service.

Mainstays of the AT and AAR force are Hercules, VC10s, TriStars and C-17 Globemasters based at Lyneham (Wilts) and Brize Norton (Oxon). The Airbus A400M will replace the oldest half of the Hercules fleet and another Airbus, the A330, will supplant VC10 and TriStar AAR aircraft as part of the Future Strategic Tanker Aircraft programme.

ISTAR aircraft, at Waddington (Lincs), are the E-3D Sentry Airborne Warning and Control System aircraft, Sentinel Airborne Stand-Off Radar ground surveillance radar platform and Nimrod R1 electronic intelligence-gatherer. The Nimrod MR2 flies from Kinloss (Moray).

The UK Air Surveillance and Control Systems organization has a deployable radar capability provided through No. 1 Air Control Centre. Another key element is the space surveillance and missile warning radar at Fylingdales (N. Yorks).

Number 22 Group recruits and provides trained specialist personnel. With an annual 55,000 trainees, it also manages the Air Cadet Organisation and the University Air Squadrons. Best-known of Number 22 Group aircraft are the Red Arrows but the Group also operates basic trainers, helicopters, fast-jet and multi-engine aircraft.

RAF personnel, 1 April 2007, 45,370 (including 5,810 women); total trained personnel, 43,200. Since Dec. 1991 women have been eligible to fly combat aircraft. There were 9,200 Air Force regular reserves in 2006 including 1,400 volunteers. There were also 26,600 ex-RAF personnel with a recall liability, having left the RAF with a service pension.

INTERNATIONAL RELATIONS

The UK is a member of the UN (and a permanent member of its Security Council), World Bank, IMF and several other UN specialized agencies, WTO, EU, Council of Europe, WEU, OSCE, CERN, BIS, Commonwealth, IOM, NATO, OECD, Inter-American Development Bank, Asian Development Bank and Antarctic Treaty.

In 2007 the UK gave US$9·8bn. in international aid, representing 0·35% of its GNI. In actual terms this made the UK the fourth most generous country in the world, but as a percentage of GNI only the 14th most generous. In 2006 it had given US$12·5bn., representing 0·51%.

ECONOMY

In 2003 services accounted for 72·4% of GDP, industry 26·6% and agriculture 1·0%.

According to the anti-corruption organization *Transparency International*, in 2009 the United Kingdom ranked equal 17th in the world in a survey of the countries with the least corruption in business and government. It received 7·7 out of 10 in the annual index.

Overview

The UK ranks among the world's five largest economies. From 1993–2004 the UK enjoyed sustained non-inflationary growth, the longest period of expansion in 30 years.

Private consumption accounts for nearly 70% of GDP. Despite almost closing the GDP per capita gap with other European countries, the disparity with the most successful OECD countries (Canada, USA and Australia) remains, partly because of weaker productivity levels in the UK. In addition, low levels of gross fixed investment (approximately 17% of GDP) have constrained productivity growth.

The service sector accounts for nearly three-quarters of GDP. The financial services sector represents 20% of GDP thanks to the strength of the City of London and the rapid growth in business services catering to an international market. The strong growth performance over the decade to 2007 was partly attributable to the high share of value added produced in high growth sectors, especially knowledge intensive services.

High technology industries, such as pharmaceuticals, aircraft, information communications technology equipment and precision instruments, accounted for almost 35% of manufacturing exports in 2005. Knowledge intensive services, such as telecommunications, insurance, finance and business services, accounted for 23% of value added in 2005.

From 1979–97 the Conservative government introduced reforms making the UK one of Europe's freest economies. The subsequent Labour government continued with privatization, deregulation and competition reforms. In 2005 the OECD declared the UK to be among the leading countries in terms of liberal product market regulation and of labour market flexibility. Low product market regulation, low barriers to foreign investment and labour market flexibility have prompted higher levels of foreign direct investment than in most other EU countries. The UK has exceptionally high numbers of non-EU businesses when compared with its European neighbours.

While strong performance has been driven by the services sector and buoyant domestic demand, weaknesses in the manufacturing sector and erratic export performance remain hindrances. In 2007 the manufacturing sector accounted for 12·4% of gross value added, making it the fourth largest sector in the UK. However, it has declined in terms of employment share more than in other industrialized countries, in part as a result of the strong currency and low productivity.

Monetary policy has been conducted by the Bank of England since 1997. Between 1997–2004 average RPIX inflation was stable at around the 2·5% target, despite housing appreciation. Rising commodity and services prices resulted in inflation being above target in March 2007, prompting the first open explanatory letter from the governor to the chancellor since the Bank assumed responsibility for monetary policy. Consumer price index (CPI) inflation continued to exceed the 2 per cent target by more than one percentage point, resulting in further open explanatory letters from the governor to the chancellor in May, Aug. and Nov. 2008. Following the return of VAT to 17·5% in Jan. 2010 after a period at 15%, CPI inflation was above the 2% target but is expected to fall below that level by the end of the year.

British bank Northern Rock was taken into 'temporary' public ownership in Feb. 2008 as a result of credit market problems caused by the subprime crisis in the USA in the summer of 2007. Following major turbulence in global financial markets UK mortgage lender Bradford & Bingley became the second bank to be nationalized. In Oct. 2008 continued instability in the financial markets prompted a government injection of £37bn. into three of the UK's biggest banks, Royal Bank of Scotland, Lloyds TSB and Halifax Bank of Scotland. The Bank of England reduced interest rates six times from Oct. 2008 to a record low of 0·5% in March 2009 in an attempt to stave off a deep and prolonged recession. By Feb. 2010 the Bank of England had injected a total of £200bn. into the economy as part of an asset-purchase programme labelled 'quantitative easing'.

The economy officially fell into recession following contractions in the second and third quarters of 2008. It continued to shrink up to Sept. 2009 but exited from recession in the fourth quarter with GDP expanding by 0·4%. The Office of National Statistics announced a 4·9% contraction of the economy over the full year. Preliminary OECD figures suggest growth of around 1·2% in 2010 rising to 2·2% in 2011, supported by improving financial conditions, expansionary monetary policy and a strong international bounce-back.

The Code for Fiscal Stability, introduced in 1998, stipulated that the government may borrow only to invest and not to support current spending. The 'sustainable investment' or 'golden' rule looked to maintain the public sector net debt below 40% of GDP over the economic cycle. In April 2009 Chancellor Alistair Darling confirmed in his Budget report that borrowing would be taken to record levels to help the government manage the escalating economic crisis. By Sept. 2009 overall government debt stood at 57·5% of GDP, its highest level since 1974. In the March 2010 Budget, Darling announced that net borrowing for the financial year would total £167bn., with total government debt scheduled to reach 75% of GDP by 2014–15. Subsequent governments are likely to face severe fiscal constraints, requiring a prolonged period of higher taxes and limits to public spending.

Spending on health care and education are low compared to other OECD and EU countries and public services are overstretched. Nonetheless, public expenditure on health, education and infrastructure as a share of GDP rose by nearly 5% in the period 2000–05 to nearly 45%. The IMF suggests that implementing structural reforms to limit the rise in age-related costs will help improve long-term fiscal sustainability. As an increasing number of companies close final pension schemes the government has encouraged individuals to take more responsibility for their retirement.

Currency

The unit of currency is the *pound sterling* (£; GBP) of 100 *pence* (p.). Before decimalization on 15 Feb. 1971 £1 = 20 shillings (*s*) of 12 pence (*d*). A gold standard was adopted in 1816, the sovereign, a £1, or twenty-shilling gold coin, weighing 7·98805 grams. It is eleven-twelfths pure gold and one-twelfth alloy. Currency notes for £1 and 10*s*. were first issued by the Treasury in 1914, replacing the circulation of sovereigns. The issue of £1 and 10*s*. notes was taken over by the Bank of England in 1928. 10*s*. notes ceased to be legal tender in 1970 and £1 notes (in England and Wales) in 1988. Sterling was a member of the exchange rate mechanism of the European Monetary System from 8 Oct. 1990 until 16 Sept. 1992 ('Black Wednesday').

Inflation. Consumer Price Index (CPI) inflation rates (based on OECD statistics):

1999	*2000*	*2001*	*2002*	*2003*	*2004*	*2005*	*2006*	*2007*	*2008*
1·3%	0·8%	1·2%	1·3%	1·4%	1·3%	2·0%	2·3%	2·3%	3·6%

The inflation rate in 2009 according to the Office of National Statistics was 2·2%.

Coinage. Estimated number of coins in circulation at 31 March 2007: £2, 298m.; £1, 1,468m.; 50p, 806m.; 20p, 2,263m.; 10p, 1,615m.; 5p, 3,723m.; 2p, 6,543m.; 1p, 10,765m.

Banknotes. The Bank of England issues notes in denominations of £5, £10, £20 and £50 up to the amount of the fiduciary issue. Under the provisions of the Currency Act 1983 the amount of the fiduciary issue is limited, but can be altered by direction of HM Treasury on the advice of the Bank of England. Since Oct. 2004 the limit has been £53,500m.

All current series Bank of England notes are legal tender in England and Wales. Some banks in Scotland (Bank of Scotland, Clydesdale Bank and the Royal Bank of Scotland) and Northern Ireland (Bank of Ireland, First Trust Bank, Northern Bank and Ulster Bank) have note-issuing powers.

The total amount of Bank of England notes in circulation at 28 Feb. 2007 was £38,449m.

Foreign exchange reserves were US$39,736m. and gold reserves 9·98m. troy oz in Sept. 2009 (22·98m. troy oz in April 1999, before the Treasury's announcement of its intention to sell nearly 60% of UK gold reserves over the medium term).

Budget

The fiscal year runs from 6 April to 5 April. The March 2010 budget estimated public sector borrowing for 2009–10 at £167bn. (against £178bn. predicted in the 2009 budget), with a forecast of £163bn. in 2010–11, then £131bn. in 2011–12, £110bn. in 2012–13, £89bn. in 2013–14 and £74bn. in 2014–15. Public sector net debt as a proportion of GDP is put at 54% for 2009–10, rising to 75% by 2014–15. As a share of GDP, this will see borrowing fall from 11·1% in 2010–11 to 4·0% by 2014–15.

Current spending for 2009–10 is set at £563·7bn., increasing to £725bn. by 2014–15. Net investment is to fall from £50·0bn. in 2009–10 to £23bn. by 2014–15.

The Chancellor forecast that the economy would grow by 1–1·25% in 2010, increasing to 3–3·5% in 2011. Among the budget's provisions was a stamp duty moratorium on properties worth up to £250,000 to be financed by a 5% stamp duty (up from 4%) on properties over £1m. The inheritance tax threshold is to be frozen until 2014 and personal tax allowance thresholds are also kept at existing levels.

Royal Bank of Scotland and Lloyds Bank, in large part owned by the state, were instructed to provide £94bn. in loans to new business, with half earmarked for small- and medium-sized businesses. A credit adjudication service is to be established to handle complaints from SMEs that believe they have been unfairly denied credit. A further 1m. people are to be brought into the banking system within five years, leaving only 750,000 adults without a bank account. A 'green investment bank' is also to be set up, using £1bn. of public money and the same amount from private funds.

The previously announced 2·5 pence increase in fuel duty is to be introduced in three stages up to Jan. 2011. Public sector pay rises will be held at 1% for two years from 2011 and 15,000 civil service posts will be moved out of London within five years. A one-off £2·5bn. jobs and training package is to be funded in part by the previous budget's one-off tax on bank bonuses. A programme to be introduced over two years will ensure any under-24 year-old unemployed for six months will be offered either work or training. A £270m. fund has been set aside to create 20,000 new university places in specific subjects, including engineering, maths and science. Pensioners had the higher winter fuel payment (£250 for those under 80, and £400 of the over 80s) guaranteed for a further year and an additional £4bn.+ was set aside for ongoing operations in Afghanistan.

'Mr Darling has a good story to tell on state activity through the crisis and the downturn … But the state of public finances remains dire… The chancellor's pitch is that while the recovery takes root, government will continue to be on the side of families and businesses – just as it has been through the worst of the crisis and its aftermath. This is a powerful message to people still worried about their jobs and the UK's prospects. It sounds like a more difficult case to make when post-election cuts in spending must surely reduce the role of the state.' (*Financial Times*, 24 March 2010).

Current Budget (in £1bn.)	*2008–09 Outturn*	*2009–10 Estimate*	*2010–11 Projection*
Current Receipts	533·5	507·5	541·0
Current Expenditure	563·7	604·6	644·0
Surplus on Current Budget (in £1bn.)	*2008–09 Outturn*	*2009–10 Estimate*	*2010–11 Projection*
	−48·9	−116·6	−124·0
Current Receipts (in £1bn.)	*2008–09 Outturn*	*2009–10 Estimate*	*2010–11 Projection*
Total HM Revenue and Customs	439·1	406·5	431·8

Current Receipts (in £1bn.)	*2008–09 Outturn*	*2009–10 Estimate*	*2010–11 Projection*
Taxes and National Insurance Contributions	507·9	476·4	507·0
Current Receipts	533·5	507·5	540·8

Departmental Expenditure Limits (Resource Budget, in £1bn.)	*2008–09 Outturn*	*2009–10 Estimate*	*2010–11 Planned*
Children, Schools and Families	46·8	49·6	51·5
Health	92·3	99·6	104·1
of which: NHS England	90·7	98·0	102·1
Transport	5·7	6·9	7·0
CLG Communities	4·2	4·5	4·4
CLG Local Government	24·7	25·5	26·3
Business, Innovation and Skills	18·0	19·5	19·6
Home Office	9·2	9·5	9·8
Justice	9·1	9·9	9·4
Law Officers' Departments	0·7	0·7	0·7
Defence	36·7	39·1	40·4
Foreign and Commonwealth Office	2·1	2·3	2·2
International Development	4·8	5·4	6·2
Energy and Climate Change	0·4	1·2	1·2
Environment, Food and Rural Affairs	2·6	2·7	2·7
Culture, Media and Sport	1·5	1·7	1·7
Work and Pensions	8·0	9·1	9·3
Scotland[1]	24·6	25·6	26·2
Wales[1]	12·9	14·0	14·0
Northern Ireland Executive[1]	8·0	9·0	8·7
Northern Ireland Office	1·3	1·2	1·2
Chancellor's Departments	4·5	4·5	4·3
Cabinet Office	2·1	2·2	2·4

[1]For Scotland, Wales and Northern Ireland, the split between current and capital budgets is indicative and reflects the consequentials of the application of the Barnett formula to planned changes in UK departments' spending.

VAT, introduced on 1 April 1973, was reduced from 17·5% to 15% for the period 1 Dec. 2008 to 31 Dec. 2009. The standard rate reverted back to 17·5% on 1 Jan. 2010. The reduced rate is 5·0%. In 2009–10 tax revenues were estimated at 33·9% of GDP (35·4% in 2008–09).

Rates of Income Tax for 2010–11	
Income between	*%*[1]
£0–£37,400 (basic rate)	20
Over £37,401–£150,000	40
Over £150,000	50

[1]The rate of tax applicable to savings income is 10% for income up to £2,440, then 20% up to the basic rate limit, 40% to the higher rate limit and thereafter 50%. The rates applicable to dividends are 10% for income up to the basic rate limit, 32·5% to the higher rate limit and 42·5% above that.

Performance

In 2008 total GDP was US$2,645·6bn. (£1,576·0bn.), the sixth highest in the world.

Real GDP growth rates (based on OECD statistics):

1999	*2000*	*2001*	*2002*	*2003*	*2004*	*2005*	*2006*	*2007*	*2008*
3·5%	3·9%	2·5%	2·1%	2·8%	3·0%	2·2%	2·9%	2·6%	0·5%

The real GDP growth rate in 2009 according to the Office of National Statistics was –4·9%, the worst since records began in 1948. With the economy contracting in both the second and third quarters of 2008 the UK went into recession for the first time since 1991. There were six consecutive quarters of negative growth before the economy expanded by 0·4% in the fourth quarter of 2009.

In the 2010 budget the estimated growth rate for the year was put at 1–1·25%. Growth for 2011 is forecast to be 3–3·5%.

The UK was ranked 13th in the Global Competitiveness Index in the World Economic Forum's *Global Competitiveness Report 2009–2010*. The index analyses 12 areas of competitiveness for over 100 countries including macroeconomy, higher education and training, institutions, innovation and infrastructure.

Banking and Finance

The Bank of England is the government's banker and the 'banker's bank'. It has the sole right of note issue in England and Wales. It was founded by Royal Charter in 1694 and nationalized in 1946. The capital stock has, since 1 March 1946, been held by HM Treasury. The *Governor* (appointed for five-year terms) is Mervyn King (b. 1948; took office 2003, reappointed in Jan. 2008).

The statutory Bank Return is published weekly. End-Dec. figures are as follows (in £1):

	Notes in circulation	*Reserve balances*	*Other liabilities*
2006	42,202,859,930	20,132,207,781	23,257,885,477
2007	45,021,539,520	25,767,671,241	31,452,007,954
2008	46,885,821,070	48,628,063,155	142,976,600,357

Major British Banking Groups' statistics at end Sept. 2008: total deposits (sterling and currency), £3,177,375m.; sterling market loans, £238,412m.; market loans (sterling and currency), £568,245m.; advances (sterling and currency), £2,223,818m.; sterling investments, £252,771m.

In April 2010 Britain's largest bank by market capitalization was HSBC (US$183,197m.) and by assets Royal Bank of Scotland (US$2,728bn.).

Between 2000 and 2007 the number of adults banking online increased by 505%. In 2007, 35% of the population were using e-banking.

In May 1997 the power to set base interest rates was transferred from the Treasury to the Bank of England. The government continues to set the inflation target but the Bank has responsibility for setting interest rates to meet the target. Base rates are now set by a nine-member Monetary Policy Committee at the Bank; members include the Governor. Membership of the Court (the governing body) was widened. The 1998 Act provides for Court to consist of the Governor, two Deputy Governors and 16 Directors. The Act also established the MPC as a Committee of the Bank and sets a framework for its operations. Responsibility for supervising banks was transferred from the Bank to the Financial Services Authority (FSA). The bank rate was lowered from 1·0% to 0·5% on 5 March 2009 (the lowest since the Bank of England was founded in 1694).

National Savings Bank. Statistics for 2006–07 and 2007–08:

	Ordinary accounts		*Investment accounts*		*Premium bonds*	
	2006–07 in £1,000	*2007–08 in £1,000*	*2006–07 in £1,000*	*2007–08 in £1,000*	*2006–07 in £1,000*	*2007–08 in £1,000*
Amounts—						
Received	760	1,598	555,032	541,871	8,422,391	6,637,597
Interest credited	3,571	5,665	202,644	223,766	—	—
Paid	(20,069)	(12,965)	(1,181,818)	(974,945)	(5,346,953)	(6,341,256)
Due to depositors at 31 March	312,994	307,292	5,643,572	5,434,264	35,249,099	36,923,456

The London Stock Exchange (called International Stock Exchange until May 1991) originated over 300 years ago, although a regulated stock exchange did not come into existence until 1801. In July 1991 the 91 shareholders voted unanimously for a new memorandum and articles of association which devolves power to a wider range of participants in the securities industry, and replaces the Stock Exchange Council with a 14-member board. The Financial Times Stock Exchange 100 (FTSE 100) ended 2009 at 5,412·9, up from 4,434·2 at the end of 2008 (rising 22·1% during the year).

The UK received US$96·94bn. worth of foreign direct investment in 2008, down from US$183·39bn. in 2007. In the period 1999–2008 the UK attracted foreign direct investment totalling US$968·65bn.

Roberts, R. and Kynaston, D. (eds.) *The Bank of England: Money, Power and Influence, 1694–1994.* 1995

Weights and Measures

Conversion to the metric system, which replaced the imperial system, became obligatory on 1 Oct. 1995. The use of the pint for milk deliveries and bar sales, and use of miles and yards in road signs, is exempt indefinitely, and the use of the pound (weight) in selling greengrocery was exempt until 1999.

ENERGY AND NATURAL RESOURCES

Environment

The UK's carbon dioxide emissions from the consumption and flaring of fossil fuels in 2008 were the equivalent of 9·4 tonnes per capita. The UK's total emission of greenhouse gases is estimated to have fallen from 809m. tonnes in 1990 to 707m. tonnes by 2007. An *Environmental Performance Index* compiled in 2008 ranked the UK 14th in the world, with 86·3%. The index examined various factors in six areas—air pollution, biodiversity and habitat, climate change, environmental health, productive natural resources and water resources.

Electricity

The Electricity Act of 1989 implemented the restructuring and privatization of the electricity industry. In 1999 the domestic electricity market (peak load below 100 kW) was opened to competition.

(England and Wales)

Generators. Under the 1989 Act, National Power and Powergen took over the fossil fuel and hydro-electric power stations previously owned by the Central Electricity Generating Board, and were privatized in 1991. A succession of takeovers and mergers saw the rapid diversification of the UK generation market, with 30 major power producers operating in 2007 compared to seven in 1990. There were a total of 19 nuclear reactors in use in the UK at ten nuclear power stations in Nov. 2007. However, two of these, Oldbury and Wylfa, both owned by BNFL Magnox, are scheduled to cease generation by the end of 2010. The remaining eight stations are operated by British Energy, which was acquired by EDF Energy in Jan. 2009. EDF Energy plans to build several new nuclear power stations in the UK. A variety of companies are planning investment in new generation capacity in order to meet rising demand and replace ageing power stations.

Transmission. Since 2005 the electricity systems of England, Wales and Scotland have been integrated and operate under the British Electricity Trading and Transmission Arrangements (BETTA). National Grid became the operator of the UK transmission networks under the new arrangements.

Distribution and Supply. The 12 Area Boards were replaced under the 1989 Act by regional electricity companies (RECs), which were privatized in 1990; 14 public electricity suppliers then came into operation which, under the terms of the Utilities Act of 2000, needed separate licences for their supply businesses and distribution networks. Subsequent market liberalization has seen a sharp increase in the number of electricity suppliers in operation, among the largest of which are British Gas, EDF Energy, E.ON, RWE npower, Scottish & Southern Energy and ScottishPower.

See also SCOTLAND.

Electricity Associations. The Electricity Association, formerly the trade association of the UK electricity companies, was replaced in Oct. 2003 by three industry bodies. The Energy Networks Association represents the transmission and distribution companies for both gas and electricity. The Association of Electricity Producers represents companies that generate electricity using coal, gas and nuclear power as well as renewable sources such as wind, biomass and water. The Energy Retail Association represents Britain's domestic electricity and gas suppliers in the internal market.

Regulation. The Office of Electricity Regulation ('Offer') was set up under the 1989 Act to protect consumer interests following privatization. In 1999 it was merged with the Office of Gas Supply ('Ofgas') to form the Office of Gas and Electricity Markets ('Ofgem'), reflecting the opening up of all markets for electricity and gas supply to full competition from May that year, with many suppliers now offering both gas and electricity to customers.

Statistics. The electricity industry contributed about 1·05% of the UK's Gross Domestic Product in 2007. The installed capacity of all UK power stations in 2007 was 82,951 MW. In 2007 the fuel generation mix was: gas 41·9%, coal 34·8%, nuclear 16·1%, hydro and renewables 5·3%, oil 1·2% and other 0·7%. Final consumption totalled 341,945 GWh, of which domestic users took 33·6%, industrial users 34·4% and commercial and other users the remaining 32·0%. Consumption per capita in 2004 was 6,756 kWh.

Electrica Services. *Electricity Industry Review.* Annual
Surrey, J. (ed.) *The British Electricity Experience: Privatization—the Record, the Issues, the Lessons.* 1996

Oil and Gas

Production in 1,000 tonnes, in 2007: throughput of crude and process oils, 81,117; refinery use, 4,307. Refinery output: gas/diesel oil, 26,391; motor spirit, 21,231; fuel oil, 10,690; aviation turbine fuel, 6,176; burning oil, 2,968; butane, propane and other petroleum gases, 2,776; naphtha, 2,561; bitumen, 1,628. Total output of refined products, 76,903. Total indigenous oil production (2008), 72·2m. tonnes. The UK had proven oil reserves of 3·4bn. bbls in 2008. The UK became a net importer of oil in 2005, having been a net exporter since 1980.

In 2007 the total income from sales of oil and gas produced was £30·1bn. (oil, £20·7bn.). The UK ranks 8th among the world's largest gas producers and 18th among the largest oil producers.

The first significant offshore gas discovery was made in 1965 in the North Sea, followed in 1969 by the first commercial oil offshore. Offshore production of gas began in 1967 and oil in 1975.

Oil and gas have played an important part in providing the UK's energy needs. In 2007, either through direct use or as a source of energy to produce electricity, oil and gas accounted for some 74% (41% gas and 33% oil) of total UK energy consumption, with UK-based production supplying some 93% of all the oil and gas consumed. However, oil production peaked in 1999 as did natural gas production in 2000, and annual production of both has gradually been declining in the years since then.

Oil products also provide important contributions to other industries, such as feedstocks for the petrochemical industry and lubricants for various uses. While the importance of oil as a source of energy for electrical generation and use by industry and commercial operations has declined with the increasing use of gas, oil still makes up around 14% of total industrial uses of energy. Its prime importance is in the transport sector, where it provides 99% of the total energy used.

The United Kingdom usually exports around two-thirds of the oil it produces, with the key export markets being the USA and other EU countries.

The reform of the old nationalized gas industry began with the Gas Act of 1986, which paved the way for the privatization later that year of the British Gas Corporation, and established the Director General of Gas Supply (DGSS) as the independent regulator. This had a limited effect on competition, as British Gas retained a monopoly on tariff (domestic) supply. Competition progressively developed in the industrial and commercial (non-tariff) market.

The Gas Act 1995 amended the 1986 Act to prepare the way for full competition, including the domestic market. It created three separate licences—for Public Gas Transporters who operate pipelines, for Shippers (wholesalers) who contract for gas to be transported through the pipelines, and for Suppliers (retailers) who then market gas to consumers. It also placed the DGSS under a statutory duty to secure effective competition.

The domestic market was progressively opened to full competition from 1996 until May 1998.

In 1997 British Gas took a commercial decision to de-merge its trading business. Centrica plc (a new company) was formed to handle the gas sales, gas trading, services and retail businesses of BG, together with the gas production businesses of the North and South Morecambe Field. The remaining parts of the business, including transportation and storage and the international downstream activities, were contained in BG plc. As a result of subsequent changes, National Grid Gas plc now owns and operates the UK's national gas transmission system.

The Department of Energy and Climate Change (DECC) was created on 3 Oct. 2008 to oversee the UK oil and gas industry. The regulator for Britain's gas and electricity industries is *Ofgem* (Office of the Gas and Electricity Markets), created in 1999 through the merger of *Ofgas* (Office of Gas Supply) and *Offer* (Office of Electricity Regulation). Its role is to protect and advance the interests of consumers by promoting competition where possible.

A second European Directive was published in June 2003 with rules for the internal market in natural gas. Member states were allowed one year to execute its provisions; the UK implemented the directive in July 2004.

The UK became a net importer of gas in 2004. To help ensure a secure gas supply as the UK becomes more dependent on imported gas, several gas infrastructure projects have been developed. These supply the UK with gas from a number of sources, including Norway and the Netherlands. There is already a pipeline (the Interconnector) linking the UK and European gas grids via Belgium. This link to Continental Europe opened in Oct. 1998 and has an export capacity of 20·0bn. cu. metres a year and an import capacity of 25·5bn. cu. metres a year.

Proven natural gas reserves in 2008 were 340bn. cu. metres. Production was 69·6bn. cu. metres in 2008. The UK's natural gas output has declined every year since 2000, when it totalled 108·4bn. cu. metres. In 2007, 33·0% of the UK's total gas supply was used by domestic users and 33·4% by electricity generators.

Wind

In 2007 there were 164 wind farms and 1,941 turbines with a capacity of 2,388·4 MW for electricity generation.

Minerals

Legislation to privatize the coal industry was introduced in 1994 and established the Coal Authority to take over from British Coal Corporation. The Coal Authority is the owner of almost all the UK's coal reserves; it licenses private coal-mining and disposes of property not required for operational purposes. The Coal Authority also deals with the historic legacy of coal mining including handling subsidence claims in former mining areas, treating mine water discharges and dealing with surface hazards. In 2007 there were seven former British Coal collieries, eleven additional deep mines and 33 opencast mines, employing some 5,397 mineworkers.

Total production from deep mines was 8·1m. tonnes for the year ended 31 March 2007 (83·8m. tonnes in 1988). Output from opencast sites for the year ended 31 March 2007 was 8·4m. tonnes (1988, 17·9m. tonnes). In 2007 inland coal consumption was 62·9m. tonnes (113·3m. tonnes in 1988).

Output of non-fuel minerals in Great Britain, 2007 (in 1,000 tonnes): limestone, 83,482; sand and gravel, 80,501; igneous rock, 50,684; sandstone, 11,978; clay and shale, 10,104; dolomite, 7,622; chalk, 7,565; salt, 5,320; industrial sand, 4,909; china clay, 1,821.

Steel and metals

Steel production in recent years (in 1m. tonnes):

2004	13·8
2005	13·2
2006	13·9
2007	14·3
2008	13·5

Deliveries of finished steel products from UK mills in 2008 were worth £8·5bn. in product sales and comprised 6·2m. tonnes to the UK domestic market and 7·3m. tonnes for export. About 70% of UK steel exports went to other EU countries. UK steel imports in 2008 were about 6·9m. tonnes. The UK steel industry's main markets are construction (29%), engineering (25%), automotive (15%) and metal goods (8%). Corus Group (part of the TATA Steel Group) is the UK's largest steel producer and in 2008 made around 80% of UK crude steel.

Agriculture

Land use in 2007: agriculture, 73%; forests, 12%; other, 15%. In 2007 agricultural land in the UK totalled (in 1,000 ha.) 18,602, comprising agricultural holdings, 17,363; and common grazing, 1,238. Land use of the former in 2007 (in 1,000 ha.): all grasses, 7,141; crops, 4,350; rough grazing, 4,313; bare fallow, 165; other, 1,394. Area sown to crops in 2008 (in 1,000 ha.): cereals, 3,274; other arable crops (including potatoes), 1,296; horticultural crops (including fruit), 170.

In 2005 there were 5·73m. ha. of arable land and 47,000 ha. of permanent crops.

In Jan. 2007 the area of fully organic farmland in the UK was 498,646 ha. Including land in conversion, 3·6% of the agricultural land was managed organically in Jan. 2007. Organic food sales for the UK in 2008 totalled £2·1bn., up from £1·1bn. in 2003–04.

Farmers receiving financial support under the EU's Common Agricultural Policy are obliged to 'set-aside' land in order to control production. In 2007 such set-aside totalled 440,000 ha.

There were 820 tractors and 77 harvester-threshers per 1,000 ha. of arable land in 2006.

The number of workers employed in agriculture was, in June 2008, 172,800 (47,100 female) of whom 61,700 were seasonal or casual workers. Of the 111,100 regular workers, 45,100 were part-time. In 1990 the number of workers employed in agriculture had been 273,800. There were some 315,900 farm holdings in 2006. Average size of holdings, 56·3 ha.

Total farm incomes dropped from £5·3bn. to £1·7bn. between 1995 and 2000, before rising to £2·3bn. in 2006. Food and live animals accounted for 3·4% of exports and 7·5% of imports in 2008, down from 4·5% of exports and 8·6% of imports in 1991.

Area given over to principal crops in the UK:

	Wheat	*Sugar beets*	*Potatoes*	*Barley*	*Oilseed rape*	*Oats*
	Area (1,000 ha.)					
2004	1,990	154	148	1,007	498	108
2005	1,867	148	137	938	519	90
2006	1,836	130	140	881	568	121
2007	1,830	125	140	898	674	129
2008	2,080	120	144	1,032	598	135

Production of principal crops in the UK:

	Wheat	Sugar beets	Potatoes	Barley	Oilseed rape	Oats
			Total product (1,000 tonnes)			
2003	14,282	9,168	5,918	6,360	1,771	749
2004	15,468	8,850	6,316	5,799	1,608	626
2005	14,863	8,687	5,979	5,495	1,901	532
2006	14,735	7,400	5,727	5,239	1,870	728
2007	13,221	7,525	5,564	5,079	—	712

Horticultural crops. 2008–09 output (in 1,000 tonnes): carrots, 732; onions, 349; apples, 243; cabbage, 234; peas, 159; cauliflowers, 119; lettuce, 117; turnips and swedes, 105.

Livestock in the UK as at June in each year (in 1,000):

	2004	2005	2006	2007	2008
Sheep	35,817	35,416	34,722	33,946	33,131
Cattle	10,588	10,440	10,324	10,304	10,107
(dairy)	(2,129)	(2,063)	(2,066)	(1,954)	(1,909)
(beef)	(1,736)	(1,762)	(1,733)	(1,698)	(1,670)
Pigs	5,159	4,862	4,933	4,834	4,714
Poultry	181,759	173,909	173,081	167,667	166,200

Livestock products, 2007 (1,000 tonnes): beef and veal, 888; pork, bacon and ham, 707; lamb and mutton, 328; poultry meat, 1,459; cheese, 378; hens' eggs, 8,640m. (units). Milk production in 2007 totalled 13,442m. litres.

In March 1996 the government acknowledged the possibility that bovine spongiform encephalopathy (BSE) might be transmitted to humans as a form of Creutzfeldt-Jakob disease via the food chain. Confirmed cases of BSE in cattle in the UK: 1988, 2,188; 1989, 7,166; 1990, 14,294; 1991, 25,202; 1992, 37,056; 1993, 34,829; 1994, 24,290; 1995, 14,475; 1996, 8,090; 1997, 4,336; 1998, 3,198; 1999, 2,283; 2000, 1,430; 2001, 1,187; 2002, 1,137; 2003, 611; 2004, 343; 2005, 225; 2006, 114; 2007, 67; 2008, 37; 2009, 12. Confirmed deaths attributed to nvCJD (new variant Creutzfeldt-Jakob Disease, the form of the disease thought to be linked to BSE): 1995, 3; 1996, 10; 1997, 10; 1998, 18; 1999, 15; 2000, 28; 2001, 20; 2002, 17; 2003, 18; 2004, 9; 2005, 5; 2006, 5; 2007, 5; 2008, 1; 2009, 3.

British beef was widely banned overseas and in March 1996 the European Commission introduced a ban on the export of bovine animals, semen and embryos, beef and beef products and mammalian meat and bonemeal from the UK. The government introduced a number of preventive measures including bans on sales of older meat and the use of meat in animal feed and fertilizer, and compensation schemes. Following inspections, the European Commission allowed for the export of deboned beef and beef products beginning 1 Aug. 1999. In March 2006 the ban was also lifted on exporting live animals born after 1 Aug. 1996 and exporting beef and beef products made from cattle slaughtered after 15 June 2005.

In Feb. 2001 the UK was hit by a major foot-and-mouth disease epidemic for the first time since 1967–68, with 2,030 confirmed cases and 4,050,000 animals being slaughtered during the months which followed. In the 1967–68 epidemic there had been 2,364 cases with approximately 434,000 animals slaughtered.

Forestry

In March 2009 the area of woodland in Britain was 2,841,000 ha., of which the Forestry Commission managed 814,000 ha. In the year to March 2009, 5,900 ha. of new woodland was created (900 ha., Forestry Commission; 5,000 ha., private woodlands) and 15,900 ha. restocked after harvesting. UK production of roundwood in 2008 was 8·4m. cu. metres underbark.

In 2008 imports of wood products (wood, panels, pulp and paper) were equivalent to 45·7m. cu. metres underbark; exports 5·4m. cu. metres underbark.

Forestry Commission (*Website:* http://www.forestry.gov.uk/statistics).
Forestry Facts and Figures. Annual

Fisheries

Quantity (in 1,000 tonnes) and value (in £1m.) of all fish landings into the UK and UK vessels' landings abroad (excluding salmon and sea-trout):

Quantity	2004	2005	2006	2007	2008
Wet fish	335·4	367·2	283·2	299·6	266·6
Shell fish	126·1	124·5	133·4	140·3	142·8
	461·5	491·7	416·5	439·8	409·4
Value					
Wet fish	232·5	272·3	256·6	264·1	260·4
Shell fish	173·1	183·8	237·1	270·9	257·4
	405·6	456·1	493·8	535·0	517·8

In Dec. 2008 the fishing fleet comprised 5,936 registered vessels excluding Channel Islands and the Isle of Man (11,108 in 1993). Major fishing ports: (England) Plymouth, Brixham, Leigh-on-Sea, Newlyn; (Scotland) Peterhead, Lerwick, Fraserburgh, Aberdeen, Scrabster. Peterhead is the UK's leading port, with 113,300 tonnes of fish landed by UK vessels in 2008 (with a value of £99·1m.).

In the period 2001–03 the average person in the UK consumed 20 kg of fish and fishery products a year, compared to the European Union average of 26 kg.

INDUSTRY

The UK's largest company by market capitalization on 9 April 2010 was BP, at £120,384m. (US$183,261m.), compared to £85,719m. (US$125,037m.) in April 2009; HSBC was the second largest at £120,342m. (US$183,197m.), compared to £52,768m. (US$76,953m.) in April 2009.

In 2008 there were 162,785 manufacturing firms, of which 600 employed 500 or over persons, and 94,570 employed four or fewer.

Chemicals and chemical products. Manufacturers' sales, (in £1m.) in 2007: primary plastics and other plastic products (excluding plastic packing goods), 15,815; pharmaceutical preparations and basic pharmaceutical products, 11,757; organic basic chemicals, 7,101; paints, etc., 2,822; rubber products (2006), 2,105; perfumes and toilet products, 1,888; soap, polish and detergents, 1,753; inorganic basic chemicals, 1,211; dyes, 1,047; fertilizers, etc., 945.

Construction. Total value (in £1m.) of constructional work in Great Britain in 2008 was 123,584, including new work, 67,829 (of which housing, 20,235). Cement production, 2007, 11,892,000 tonnes; building brick production, 2008, 1,932m. units.

Electrical Goods. Manufacturers' sales (in £1m.) for 2007: electric motors, generators and transformers, 2,756; electricity distribution and control apparatus, 2,682; electronic valves and tubes and other electronic components, 2,304; television and radio receivers, sound or video recording, 2,092; electric domestic appliances, 1,741; radio and electronic capital goods, 1,730.

Engineering, machinery and instruments. Manufacturers' sales (in £1m.) for 2007: motor vehicles, 25,543; aircraft and spacecraft, 10,667; parts and accessories for motor vehicles and engines, 9,428; appliances for measuring, checking and testing, 5,731; non-domestic cooling and ventilation equipment, 3,275; lifting and handling equipment, 3,261; medical and surgical equipment and orthopaedic appliances, 2,771. Car production, 2008, 1,446,619 units (down 5·7% from 2007).

Foodstuffs, etc. Manufacturers' sales (in £1m.) for 2007: operation of dairies, 6,110; bread, fresh pastry goods and cakes, 4,596; meat production and preservation, 4,320; cocoa, chocolate and sugar confectionery, 3,609; beer, 3,578; mineral water and soft drinks, 3,273; biscuits, rusks, preserved pastry goods and cakes (2006),

3,089; grain mill products, 2,911; prepared feeds for farm animals, 2,685; fruit and vegetable processing and preservation, 2,637; poultry production and preservation, 2,432; distilled alcoholic beverages (2004), 2,216; fish and fish products processing and preservation, 1,805; tobacco products, 1,626. Alcoholic beverage production, 2008: beer, 4,946·9m. litres (5,955·2m. litres in 1991); wine, 1,348·3m. litres (658·3m. litres in 1991); spirits, 694·9m. litres (447·6m. litres in 1991).

Metals. Manufacturers' sales (in £1m.) for 2007: metal structures and parts of structures, 7,328; general mechanical engineering, 3,732; aluminium production, 2,339; forging, pressing, stamping and roll forming of metal, 2,135; steel tubes, 1,690; treatment and coating of metals, 1,335; builders' carpentry and joinery of metal, 1,259.

Textiles and clothing. Manufacturers' sales (in £1m.) in 2007: women's outerwear and underwear(2006), 990; carpets and rugs, 773; household textiles, 686; soft furnishings, 646; textile weaving, 578; finishing of textiles, 468; preparation and spinning of textile fibres, 386; men's outerwear and underwear, 230.

Wood products, furniture, paper and printing. Manufacturers' sales (in £1m.) in 2007: furniture of whatever construction, 7,318; journals and periodicals, 7,304; wood products except furniture, 6,774; newspapers, 4,120; publishing of books, 3,458; cartons, boxes and cases, 3,050; paper and paperboard, 2,759.

Labour

In 2008 the UK's total economically active population (i.e. all persons in employment plus the claimant unemployed) was (in 1,000) 31,190 (14,626 females), of whom 29,443 (13,549 females) were in employment, including 25,407 (12,396 females) as employees and 3,826 (1,047 females) as self-employed. In 1998 only 26,795,000 people had been in employment, representing an increase of 2,648,000 in ten years. UK employees by form of employment in 2008 (in 1,000): real estate renting and business activities, 4,766; wholesale and retail trade, repair of motor vehicles, motorcycles and household goods, 4,583; health and social work, 3,421; retail trade except motor vehicles/motorcycles and repair of household goods, 2,871; manufacturing industry, 2,869; education, 2,420; hotels and restaurants, 1,835; transport, storage and communications, 1,596; public administration and defence, compulsory social security, 1,474; construction, 1,319; wholesale trade and commission trade except motor vehicles, 1,151; financial intermediation, 1,049; agriculture, hunting, forestry and fishing, 269. Between 2004 and 2008 employment in service industries increased by 1,044,000 while employment in manufacturing declined by 376,000 over the same period.

Registered unemployed in UK in April–June (in 1,000; figures seasonally adjusted): 2003, 1,468 (5·0%); 2004, 1,439 (4·8%); 2005, 1,438 (4·8%); 2006, 1,687 (5·5%); 2007, 1,662 (5·4%); 2008, 1,685 (5·4%). In the three-month period June–Aug. 2004 the rate fell to 4·7%, the lowest since 1975, although it has risen steadily in the meantime. Of the 1,685,000 unemployed people in the period April–June 2008, 990,000 were men and 695,000 women. The number of jobless people was 2,457,000 in the period Oct.–Dec. 2009 (down slightly from 2,482,000 in the period Aug.–Oct. 2009, which was the highest since 1995). The number of unemployed people on benefits (the 'claimant count') was 1·64m. in Jan. 2010—the highest total since April 1997—giving a rate of 5·0%, up from 3·9% in Jan. 2009 and 2·5% in Jan. 2008. The unemployment rate on the International Labour Organization (ILO) definition, which includes all those who are looking for work whether or not claiming unemployment benefits, was 7·8% in the period Oct.–Dec. 2009 (compared to 6·4% in the fourth quarter of 2008 and 5·2% in the fourth quarter of 2007). Youth unemployment (aged 18–24) was 17·6% in the period Oct.–Dec. 2009 (down from a high of 18·2% in the three-month period Aug.–Oct. 2009 although up from 14·7% in the fourth quarter of 2008 and 12·0% in the fourth quarter of 2007).

Of 4·9m. businesses in the UK in early 2008, 2·2m. were registered for VAT and/or PAYE; 2·7m. businesses were registered at Companies House in March 2008. Approximately 98·1% of UK businesses have fewer than 50 employees. There were an estimated 471,500 business start-ups in 2007, with business closures numbering 498,900.

Workers (in 1,000) involved in industrial stoppages (and working days lost): 2003, 151 (0·50m.); 2004, 293 (0·90m.); 2005, 93 (0·16m.); 2006, 713 (0·76m.); 2007, 745 (1·04m.). In 1975, 6m. working days had been lost through stoppages. Between 2001 and 2007 strikes cost Britain an average of 28 working days per 1,000 employees a year.

The Wages Councils set up in 1909 to establish minimum rates of pay (in 1992 of 2·5m. workers) were abolished in 1993. The Labour government that came to power in May 1997 was committed to the introduction of a National Minimum Wage and established a Low Pay Commission to advise on its implementation. It is currently £5·80 an hour for adults and £4·83 for 18–21 year olds. In April 2009 the median gross salary for full-time employees was £25,800 (£28,300 for men and £22,200 for women). Median hourly pay for full-time employees excluding overtime in April 2009 in the UK was £10·99 (£12·42 for males and £9·68 for females). Median weekly earnings in April 2009 were highest in London, at £627·40, and lowest in the North East, at £435·90.

Britons in full-time employment worked an average of 40·9 hours a week in the period July–Sept. 2008, compared to the EU average of 40·4 hours. In 2008, 3·28m. Britons (2·55m. men and 730,000 women) worked more than an average of 48 hours a week.

Trade Unions

In 2007 there were 59 unions affiliated to the Trades Union Congress (TUC) with a total membership of 6·4m. (2·8m. of them women), down from a peak of 12·2m. in 1980. The unions affiliated to the TUC in 2007 ranged in size from Unite (created in May 2007 through the merger of Amicus and the Transport and General Workers' Union) with 1·9m. members covering workers in virtually every sector of the economy to small specialist organizations with fewer than 5,000 members each. The three largest unions account for well over half the total TUC membership. In 2007, 59% of public-sector employees and 16% of private-sector employees were unionized.

The TUC's executive body, the General Council, is elected at the annual Congress. Congress consists of representatives of all unions according to the size of the organization, and is the principal policy-making body.

The General Secretary (Brendan Barber, b. 1951) is elected from nominations submitted by the unions and heads a staff of 300 in London and at regional offices. The TUC draws up policies and promotes and publicizes them. It makes representations to government, employers and international bodies. The TUC also carries out research and campaigns, and provides a range of services to unions including courses for union representatives.

The TUC is affiliated to the International Trade Union Confederation, the Trade Union Advisory Committee of OECD and the European Trade Union Confederation. The TUC provides a service of trade union education. It provides members to serve, with representatives of employers, on the managing boards of such bodies as the Health and Safety Commission and the Advisory, Conciliation and Arbitration Service.

Clegg, H. A., *A History of British Trade Unions since 1889* [until 1951]. 3 vols. 1994
Pelling, H., *A History of British Trade Unionism*. 5th ed. 1992.
Taylor, R., *The TUC From the General Strike to New Unionism*. 2000
Willman, P. *et al.*, *Union Business: Trade Union Organization and Financial Reform in the Thatcher Years*. 1993

INTERNATIONAL TRADE

Imports and Exports

Value of the imports and exports of goods (in £1m.):

	Total imports	*Total exports*
2007	310,612	220,858
2008	343,979	251,102

In 2008 the UK's goods imports from other EU member countries totalled £180,363m. and from non-EU member countries £163,616m., compared to £169,799m. and £140,813m. respectively in 2007. Goods exports to other EU member countries in 2008 totalled £141,119m. and to non-EU member countries £109,983m., compared to £127,813m. and £93,045m. respectively in 2007.

In 2008 other EU members accounted for 54·0% of the UK's foreign trade in goods (52·4% of imports and 56·2% of exports). The USA accounted for 10·3% of foreign trade and the rest of the world 35·7%.

Figures for trade in goods by country and groups of countries (in £1m.):

	Imports from		*Exports to*	
EU-27 countries	*2007*	*2008*	*2007*	*2008*
EU total	169,799	180,363	127,813	141,119
Austria	2,488	2,329	1,376	1,464
Belgium	15,127	16,441	11,851	13,353
Bulgaria	239	206	202	253
Cyprus	193	157	415	527
Czech Republic	2,983	3,561	1,401	1,536
Denmark	3,444	3,912	2,182	2,579
Estonia	226	144	228	220
Finland	2,619	2,764	1,958	1,900
France	21,896	23,046	18,103	18,057
Germany	44,565	44,521	24,699	27,899
Greece	640	664	1,350	1,651
Hungary	2,377	2,521	863	1,008
Ireland	11,338	12,252	17,801	19,011
Italy	13,316	14,099	9,189	9,332
Latvia	605	374	145	167
Lithuania	299	348	311	281
Luxembourg	693	825	271	202
Malta	179	138	362	441
Netherlands	23,079	25,829	15,115	19,812
Poland	3,695	4,295	2,372	2,993
Portugal	1,506	1,736	1,481	1,635
Romania	938	758	668	752
Slovakia	1,273	1,623	382	455
Slovenia	318	314	205	222
Spain	10,489	10,717	9,979	10,182
Sweden	5,274	6,789	4,904	5,187
Other foreign countries				
Europe—				
Belarus	584	106	72	95
Croatia	75	91	159	217
Iceland	415	457	198	187
Norway	14,316	21,599	2,697	2,847
Russia	5,248	6,907	2,893	4,264
Switzerland	4,746	5,253	3,808	4,654
Turkey	4,632	4,874	2,283	2,560
Ukraine	129	150	449	611
Other in Europe	435	457	419	715
Africa—				
Egypt	538	638	686	942
Morocco	435	436	294	516
South Africa	3,060	4,725	2,244	2,654
Other in Africa	5,431	6,535	2,810	4,748
Asia—				
China	18,734	23,107	3,860	5,072
Hong Kong	6,939	8,057	2,726	3,668
India	3,809	4,478	2,968	4,125
Indonesia	925	1,183	289	384
Iran	63	70	392	438
Israel	1,045	1,153	1,257	1,337

	Imports from		*Exports to*	
Asia—	*2007*	*2008*	*2007*	*2008*
Japan	7,885	8,512	3,866	3,897
Korea (South)	3,073	3,498	1,914	2,543
Malaysia	1,684	1,869	975	1,130
Pakistan	512	628	423	472
Philippines	717	626	251	245
Saudi Arabia	821	672	1,857	2,189
Singapore	4,247	3,995	2,467	2,813
Taiwan	2,418	2,591	957	888
Thailand	2,012	2,419	613	756
Other in Asia	5,161	5,944	6,771	7,879
Oceania—				
Australia	2,245	2,380	2,630	3,092
New Zealand	667	744	364	385
Other in Oceania	100	165	56	103
Americas—				
Brazil	2,061	2,611	1,108	1,689
Canada	5,793	5,786	3,291	3,251
Chile	502	580	191	264
Colombia	354	686	142	163
Mexico	582	787	801	902
USA	26,095	25,848	32,274	35,351
Venezuela	493	600	259	282
Other in America	1,418	1,838	1,097	1,338
Total, foreign countries	310,612	343,979	220,858	251,102

In 2008 machinery and transport equipment accounted for 35·0% of the UK's imports and 35·7% of exports; manufactured goods and articles 27·6% of imports and 24·5% of exports; chemicals and related products 11·3% of imports and 17·6% of exports; and mineral fuels, lubricants and related products 13·1% of imports and 13·4% of exports.

The UK's trade deficit in goods in 2008 totalled a record £92,877m., up from £89,754m. in 2007 and £12,342m. in 1997. The trade surplus in services in 2008 was a record £54,479m., giving a trade deficit in goods and services combined of £38,398m. (compared to the record deficit of £44,947m. in 2007).

COMMUNICATIONS

Roads

Responsibility for the construction and maintenance of trunk roads belongs to central government. Roads not classified as trunk roads are the responsibility of county or unitary councils.

In 2007 there were 394,879 km of public roads in Great Britain, classified as: motorways, 3,559 km; trunk roads, 8,683 km; other major roads, 38,060 km; minor roads, 344,577 km.

In 2007 journeys by car, vans and taxis totalled 689bn. passenger km (less than 60bn. in the early 1950s). Even in the early 1950s passenger km in cars, vans and taxis exceeded the annual total at the end of the 20th century by rail. Licensed motor vehicles in 2008 included 27,021,000 passenger cars, 1,160,000 mopeds, scooters and motorcycles, 111,000 public transport vehicles and 3,303,000 other private and light goods vehicles. In 2006, 76% of households had regular use of a car with 32% of households having use of two or more cars. New vehicle registrations in 2008, 2,672,200. Driving tests, 2008–09 (in 1,000): applications, 1,796; tests held, 1,717; tests passed, 777; pass rate, 45% (49% among males and 42% among females). The driving test was extended in July 1996 to include a written examination.

Road casualties in Great Britain in 2008, 230,905 including 2,538 killed (the lowest total since records began in 1926). Britain has one of the lowest death rates in road accidents of any industrialized country, at 4·2 deaths per 100,000 people in 2008.

Inter- and intra-urban bus and coach journeys average 50bn. passenger-km annually. Passenger journeys by local bus services,

2007–08, 5,164m. For London buses *see* Transport for London *under* Rail, *below.*

Rail

In 1994 the nationalized railway network was restructured to allow for privatization. Ownership of the track, stations and infrastructure was vested in a government-owned company, Railtrack, which was privatized in May 1996.

Passenger operations were reorganized into 25 train-operating companies, which were transferred to the private sector by Feb. 1997. By March 1997 all freight operations were also privatized. On 3 Oct. 2002 a new private sector not-for-dividend company limited by guarantee, Network Rail, took over from Railtrack plc as network owner and operator. The train-operating companies pay Network Rail for access to the rail network, and lease the rolling stock from three private-sector companies.

The rail network comprises 15,814 route km (around a third electrified). Annual passenger-km were 50·7bn. in 2008–09. There were 1·27bn. passenger journeys in 2008–09 on franchised operated services (1·23bn. in 2007–08). The amount of freight moved declined gradually over many years to 13·0bn. tonne-km in 1994–95 but has since risen and totalled 20·6bn. tonne-km in 2008–09. In 2007 a total of 27 people (excluding suicides and trespassers) were fatally injured on the railways and 12 people on level crossings (compared to 2,946 deaths in road accidents in 2007).

Eurotunnel PLC holds a concession from the government to operate the Channel Tunnel (49·4 km), through which vehicle-carrying and Eurostar passenger trains are run in conjunction with French and Belgian railways. Since Nov. 2007 a new dedicated high-speed line connects the Channel Tunnel to London St Pancras. Domestic trains began using the line on regular services in Dec. 2009.

Transport *for* London (T*f*L) is accountable to the Mayor of London and is responsible for implementing his Transport Strategy as well as planning and delivering a range of transport facilities. T*f*L's remit covers London Underground (since July 2003), London Buses, the Docklands Light Railway and Croydon Tramlink. It is also responsible for London River Services, Victoria Coach Station and London's Transport Museum, and provides transport for users with reduced mobility via Dial-a-Ride. As well as running the central London congestion charging scheme, T*f*L manages a 580 km network of London's main roads, all 4,600 traffic lights and the private hire trade. It also provides grants to London Boroughs to fund local transport improvements.

Every weekday in Greater London, 5·4m. journeys are made on London's buses, 3m. on the underground, 7m. on foot, 0·3m. by bicycle, 0·2m. by taxi, 160,000 on the Docklands Light Railway and 60,000 on Croydon Tramlink.

The privately franchised Docklands Light Railway is operated in east inner London.

There are metros in Glasgow and Newcastle, and light rail systems in Birmingham/Wolverhampton, Blackpool, Manchester, Nottingham and Sheffield.

Civil Aviation

All UK airports handled a total of 236·1m. passengers in 2008 (240·9m. in 2007). London area airports (Heathrow, Gatwick, London City, Luton, Southend and Stansted) handled 137·1m. passengers in 2008.

Busiest airports in 2008:

	Passengers	*International*		*Freight (tonnes)*
Heathrow	67,054,745	61,344,438	Heathrow	1,397,054
Gatwick	34,205,887	30,431,051	East Midlands International	261,507
Stansted	22,360,364	19,996,947	Stansted	197,738
Manchester	21,219,195	18,119,230	Manchester	141,781
Luton	10,180,734	8,853,224	Gatwick	107,702

Heathrow was the world's third busiest airport for passenger traffic in 2008 and Europe's busiest, ahead of Paris Charles de Gaulle, Frankfurt, Madrid, Amsterdam, Rome, Munich and Gatwick (the eighth busiest in 2008). More international passengers use Heathrow than any other airport in the world.

Following the Civil Aviation Act 1971, the Civil Aviation Authority (CAA) was established as an independent public body responsible for the economic and safety regulation of British civil aviation. A CAA wholly owned subsidiary, National Air Traffic Services, operates air traffic control. Highlands and Islands Airports Ltd is owned by the Scottish Government and operates ten airports.

There were 19,890 civil aircraft registered in the UK at 1 Jan. 2008.

British Airways is the largest UK airline in terms of numbers of aircraft and distance flown, with a total of 235 aircraft in service at 31 Dec. 2008. It operates long- and short-haul international services, as well as an extensive domestic network. British Airways also has franchise agreements with two other operators: Comair and Sun-Air of Scandinavia. Other major airlines in 2008 (with numbers of aircraft): BMI Group (70); easyJet (153); Flybe (76); Thomas Cook Airlines (42); Thomson Airways (76 following merger in June 2008 of Thomsonfly with First Choice Airways); Virgin Atlantic (38). According to CAA airline statistics, in 2008 easyJet overtook British Airways in terms of passengers carried to become the largest airline as measured by passenger numbers—easyJet carried 37,569,379 passengers in 2008 (31,956,979 on international flights) and flew 335·7m. km while British Airways carried 31,620,390 passengers in 2008 (27,628,502 on international flights), although it flew 624·1m. km. In April 2003 British Airways announced that Concorde, the world's first supersonic jet which began commercial service in 1976, would be permanently grounded from Oct. 2003. In recent years low-cost airlines such as Ryanair and easyJet have become increasingly popular. Serving mostly domestic and European destinations, they recovered quickly from the slump of the airline business following the attacks on New York and Washington on 11 Sept. 2001.

The most frequently flown route into and out of the UK in 2008 was Heathrow–New York John F. Kennedy and vice-versa (2,802,870 passengers), followed by Heathrow–Dublin and vice-versa (1,812,028) and Heathrow–Amsterdam Schiphol and vice-versa (1,709,135).

Shipping

The UK-owned merchant fleet (trading vessels over 100 GT) in Dec. 2008 totalled 754 ships of 21·3m. DWT and 18·8m. GT. The UK-owned and registered fleet totalled 400 ships of 6·6m. DWT. The average age (DWT) of the UK-owned trading vessels was 16·8 years.

Total gross international revenue in 2008 was £13,176m. The net direct contribution to the UK balance of payments was £5,293m.; there were import savings of £1,764m., giving a total contribution of £7,057m.

The ports handling the most domestic and international passengers on short sea routes are (with 1m. passengers handled in 2008, excluding inter-island traffic): Dover (13·8), Portsmouth (2·1), Holyhead (2·0), Belfast (1·3), Stranraer (1·1). Domestic sea passengers totalled 3·7m. in 2008. The principal ports in terms of freight are (with 1m. tonnes of cargo handled in 2008): Grimsby and Immingham (65·3), London (53·0), Tees and Hartlepool (45·4), Southampton (41·0), Forth, including Grangemouth, Leith and Rosyth (39·1). Total traffic in 2008 was 562·2m. tonnes.

Inland Waterways

There are approximately 3,500 miles (5,630 km) of navigable canals and river navigations in Great Britain. Of these, the publicly-owned British Waterways (BW) is responsible for some 385 miles (620 km) of commercial waterways (maintained for freight traffic) and some 1,160 miles (1,868 km) of cruising waterways (maintained for pleasure cruising, fishing and amenity). BW is also responsible for a further 450 miles (732 km) of canals, some of which are not navigable. BW's trading income for the year to 31 March 2006 was £99·9m. Third party-funding principally for restoration schemes contributed £14·5m. Additionally, British Waterways was in receipt of Government grants of £76·1m.

River navigations and canals managed by other authorities include the Thames, Great Ouse and Nene, Norfolk Broads and Manchester Ship Canal.

The Association of Inland Navigation Authorities (AINA) represents some 30 navigation authorities providing an almost complete UK coverage.

Telecommunications

In 2009 there were around 120 operators offering fixed telecommunication services and five mobile networks. Fixed telephony services were offered by BSkyB, BT, Cable & Wireless, Carphone Warehouse, Kingston Communications (Hull) and Virgin Media among others. BT (then British Telecom) was established in 1981 to take over the management of telecommunications from the Post Office. In 1984 it was privatized as British Telecommunications plc, changing its trading name from British Telecom to BT in 1991.

By 1998 all of the BT system was served by digital exchanges. In 2007 there were 105,675,000 telephone subscribers in total (equivalent to 1,739·0 per 1,000 population). 85% of UK households had a fixed telephone in 2009, a fall from a peak of 94% in 2000 as increasingly UK consumers use mobile telephones and other forms of communications such as email and instant messaging. In June 2009, 71% of fixed lines were residential and 29% business. There were 62,000 public payphones in 2008 (146,000 in 2002). BT handles a daily average of 103m. telephone calls a day and 22m. calls to emergency fire, police or ambulance services a year. Total estimated UK retail telecommunications expenditure in the year to June 2009 was £31·4bn., a decrease of 1% from the previous year.

Electronic services include email and a complete corporate global messaging network. BT telephone, television and business services are carried by 15–20 satellites. In 2008 BT employed 111,800 persons worldwide.

In 2008 there were 77,361,000 mobile telephone subscribers in the UK (1,263·4 per 1,000 persons), up from 2,268,000 in 1993. The leading operators are Vodafone (with an estimated 25·4% share of the market); O2, including Tesco Mobile (25·2%); T-Mobile, including Virgin Mobile (23·4%); Orange (21·6%); and 3 (4·5%). 3 was launched by Hutchison on 3 March 2003 and is the UK's first mainland third generation mobile network. The broadband penetration rate in June 2008 was 27·6 subscribers per 100 inhabitants.

Telecommunications services are regulated by the Office of Communications (*'Ofcom'*) in the interests of consumers.

Internet

In 2008 there were 46·7m. internet users in the UK (the second highest total in Europe after Germany), just over 76% of the total population. According to a report published in March 2006, 48% of children aged 8–11 and 65% of children aged 12–15 used the internet at home. In 2006, 67% of households had a home computer; in the same year there were a total of 48·6m. PCs in use. In 2005, 55% of households had internet access. By the end of 2004 around 30% of fixed lines were either ISDN or broadband enabled and there were over 6m. UK broadband subscribers (38% of all internet connections).

Postal Services

Royal Mail Group plc operates three distinct businesses: Royal Mail (letter delivery), Parcelforce Worldwide (parcel delivery) and Post Office Ltd (retailing and agency services). Royal Mail collects and delivers 84m. letters a day to the 27m. UK addresses. Other services include Special Delivery (tracked and traced, guaranteed to arrive the following day) plus a same day courier service and international deliveries.

There were 14,300 post offices in 2006 including 490 crown offices, owned and operated by the business. The remainder are franchised. There are some 120,000 posting points apart from post offices. 193,000 people worked for Royal Mail Group in 2006. The UK's postal service market was fully liberalized on 1 Jan. 2006, since when any licensed operator has been able to deliver mail.

SOCIAL INSTITUTIONS

Justice

England and Wales. The legal system of England and Wales, divided into civil and criminal courts, has at the head of the superior courts, as the ultimate court of appeal, the Supreme Court of the United Kingdom, which hears appeals for all civil law cases in the UK and for all criminal cases in England, Wales and Northern Ireland (Scotland's highest court for criminal cases is the High Court of Justiciary). The Supreme Court was created as a result of the Constitutional Reform Act 2005 and came into being on 1 Oct. 2009, replacing the Appellate Committee of the House of Lords. In order that civil cases may go from the Court of Appeal (or Court of Session in Scotland) to the Supreme Court, it is necessary to obtain the leave of either the respective lower court, although in certain limited cases an appeal may lie direct to the Supreme Court from the decisions of the High Courts. Appeals may be brought to the Supreme Court provided that the lower Court is satisfied that a point of law 'of general public importance' is involved, and that it is in the public interest that a further appeal should be brought. As a judicial body, the Supreme Court consists of 12 Justices drawn from the different jurisdictions of the United Kingdom, and is led by the President of the Supreme Court, the Rt Hon. the Lord Phillips of Worth Matravers. The final court of appeal for certain of the Commonwealth countries, the UK overseas territories and the British Crown dependencies is the Judicial Committee of the Privy Council which includes Justices of the Supreme Court, other Lords of Appeal and Privy Councillors who hold or have held high judicial office in the UK or Privy Councillors who are or have been Chief Justices or Judges of certain Superior Courts of Commonwealth countries.

Civil Law. The main courts of original civil jurisdiction are the High Court and county courts.

The High Court has exclusive jurisdiction to deal with specialist classes of case, e.g. judicial review. It has concurrent jurisdiction with county courts in cases involving contract and tort although it will only hear those cases where the issues are complex or important. The High Court also has appellate jurisdiction to hear appeals from lower tribunals.

The judges of the High Court are attached to one of its three divisions: Chancery, Queen's Bench and Family; each with its separate field of jurisdiction. The Heads of the three divisions are the Lord Chief Justice (Queen's Bench), the Vice-Chancellor (Chancery) and the President of the Family Division. In addition there are 107 High Court judges (100 men and seven women). For the hearing of cases at first instance, High Court judges sit singly. Appellate jurisdiction is usually exercised by Divisional Courts consisting of two (sometimes three) judges, though in certain circumstances a judge sitting alone may hear the appeal. High Court business is dealt with in the Royal Courts of Justice and by over 130 District Registries outside London.

County courts can deal with all contract and tort cases, and recovery of land actions, regardless of value. They have upper financial limits to deal with specialist classes of business such as equity and Admiralty cases. Certain county courts have been designated to deal with family, bankruptcy, patents and discrimination cases.

There are about 220 county courts located throughout the country, each with its own district. A case may be heard by a circuit judge or by a district judge. Defended claims are allocated to one of three tracks—the small claims track, the fast track and the multi-track. The small claims track provides a simple and informal procedure for resolving disputes, mainly in claims for debt, where the value of the claim is no more than £5,000. Parties should be able to do this without the need for a solicitor. Other claims valued between £5,000 and £15,000 will generally be allocated to the fast track, and higher valued claims which could not be dealt with justly in the fast track may be allocated to the multi-track.

Specialist courts include the Patents Court, which deals only with matters concerning patents, registered designs and appeals against the decision of the Comptroller General of Patents. Cases suitable to be heard by a county court are dealt with at Central London County Court.

The Court of Appeal (Civil Division) hears appeals in civil actions from the High Court and county courts, and tribunals. Its President is the Master of the Rolls, aided by up to 38 Lords Justices of Appeal (as at July 2008) sitting in six or seven divisions of two or three judges each.

Civil proceedings are instituted by the aggrieved person, but as they are a private matter, they are frequently settled by the parties through their lawyers before the matter comes to trial. In very limited classes of dispute (e.g. libel and slander), a party may request a jury to sit to decide questions of fact and the award of damages.

Criminal Law. At the base of the system of criminal courts in England and Wales are the magistrates' courts which deal with over 96% of criminal cases. In general, in exercising their summary jurisdiction, they have power to pass a sentence of up to six months imprisonment and to impose a fine of up to £5,000 on any one offence. They also deal with the preliminary hearing of cases triable at the Crown Court. In addition to dealing summarily with over 2·0m. cases, which include thefts, assaults, drug abuse, etc., they also have a limited civil and family jurisdiction.

Magistrates' courts normally sit with a bench of three lay justices. Although unpaid they are entitled to loss of earnings and travel and subsistence allowance. They undergo training after appointment and they are advised by a professional legal adviser. In central London and in some provincial areas full-time District Judges (formerly known as stipendiary magistrates) have been appointed. Generally they possess the same powers as the lay bench, but they sit alone. On 1 April 2007 the total strength of the lay magistracy was 29,816 including 14,809 women. Justices are appointed on behalf of the Queen by the Lord Chancellor.

Justices are selected and trained specially to sit in Youth and Family Proceedings Courts. Youth Courts deal with cases involving children and young persons up to and including the age of 17 charged with criminal offences (other than homicide and other grave offences). These courts normally sit with three justices, including at least one man and one woman, and are accommodated separately from other courts.

Family Proceedings Courts deal with matrimonial applications and Children Act matters, including care, residence and contact and adoption. These courts normally sit with three justices including at least one man and one woman.

Above the magistrates' courts is the Crown Court. This was set up by the Courts Act 1971 to replace quarter sessions and assizes. Unlike quarter sessions and assizes, which were individual courts, the Crown Court is a single court which is capable of sitting anywhere in England and Wales. It has power to deal with all trials on indictment and has inherited the jurisdiction of quarter sessions to hear appeals, proceedings on committal of persons from the magistrates' courts for sentence, and certain original proceedings on civil matters under individual statutes.

The jurisdiction of the Crown Court is exercisable by a High Court judge, a Circuit judge or a Recorder or Assistant Recorder (part-time judges) sitting alone, or, in specified circumstances, with justices of the peace. The Lord Chief Justice has given directions as to the types of case to be allocated to High Court judges (the more serious cases) and to Circuit judges or Recorders respectively.

Appeals from magistrates' courts go either to a Divisional Court of the High Court (when a point of law alone is involved) or to the Crown Court where there is a complete rehearing on appeals against conviction and/or sentence. Appeals from the Crown Court in cases tried on indictment lie to the Court of Appeal (Criminal Division). Appeals on questions of law go by right, and appeals on other matters by leave. The Lord Chief Justice or a Lord Justice sits with judges of the High Court to constitute this court. Thereafter, appeals in England and Wales can be made to the House of Lords.

There remains as a last resort the invocation of the royal prerogative exercised on the advice of the Home Secretary. In 1965 the death penalty was abolished for murder and in 1998 abolished for all crimes.

All contested criminal trials, except those which come before the magistrates' courts, are tried by a judge and a jury consisting of 12 members. The prosecution or defence may challenge any potential juror for cause. The jury decides whether the accused is guilty or not. The judge is responsible for summing up on the facts and directing the jury on the relevant law. He sentences offenders who have been convicted by the jury (or who have pleaded guilty). If, after at least two hours and ten minutes of deliberation, a jury is unable to reach a unanimous verdict it may, on the judge's direction, provided that in a full jury of 12 at least ten of its members are agreed, bring in a majority verdict. The failure of a jury to agree on a unanimous verdict or to bring in a majority verdict may involve the retrial of the case before a new jury.

The Employment Appeal Tribunal. The Employment Appeal Tribunal, which is a superior Court of Record with the like powers, rights, privileges and authority of the High Court, was set up in 1976 to hear appeals on questions of law against decisions of employment tribunals and of the Certification Officer. The appeals are heard by a judge sitting alone or with two members (in exceptional cases four) appointed for their special knowledge or experience of industrial relations either on the employer or the trade union side, with always an equal number on each side. The great bulk of their work is concerned with the problems which can arise between employees and their employers.

Military Courts. Under the Armed Forces Act 2006, criminal offences and disciplinary offences alleged against service personnel subject to service law (or civilians overseas who are subject to service discipline) may be tried in the Court Martial. Lower-level offences by service personnel may be dealt with at a summary hearing by their commanding officer, subject to appeal to the Summary Appeal Court.

The Personnel of the Law. All judicial officers are independent of Parliament and the Executive. They are appointed by the Crown on the advice of the Prime Minister or the Lord Chancellor, or directly by the Lord Chancellor himself, and hold office until retiring age. Under the Judicial Pensions and Retirement Act 1993 judges normally retire by age 70 years.

The legal profession is divided; barristers, who advise on legal problems and can conduct cases before all courts, usually act for the public only through solicitors, who deal directly with the legal business brought to them by the public and have rights to present cases before certain courts. The distinction between the two branches of the profession has been weakened since the passing of the Courts and Legal Services Act 1990, which has enabled solicitors to obtain the right to appear as advocates before all courts. Long-standing members of both professions are eligible for appointment to most judicial offices.

For all judicial appointments up to and including the level of Circuit Judge, it is necessary to apply in writing to be considered for appointment. Vacancies are advertised. A panel consisting of a judge, an official and a lay member decide whom to invite for interview and also interview the shortlisted applicants. They make recommendations to the Lord Chancellor, who retains the right of final recommendation to the Sovereign or appointment, as appropriate.

Legal Services. The system of legal aid in England and Wales was established after the Second World War under the Legal Aid and Advice Act 1949. The Legal Aid Board was then set up under the Legal Aid Act 1988, and took over the administration of legal aid from the Law Society in 1989. The Legal Services Commission (LSC) was set up under the Access to Justice Act 1999 and replaced the Legal Aid Board on 1 April 2000. The LSC is an executive non-departmental public body. It comprises a Chair and 11 Commissioners, all appointed by the Lord Chancellor. It is responsible for the development and administration of two schemes in England and Wales: the *Community Legal Service*, which from 1 April 2000 replaced the old civil scheme of legal aid, bringing together networks of funders and suppliers into partnerships to provide the widest possible access to information and advice; and the *Criminal Defence Service*, which from 2 April 2001 replaced the old system of criminal legal aid and provides criminal services to people accused of crimes. Only organizations with a contract with the LSC are able to provide advice or representation funded by the LSC.

Under the Community Legal Service, which improves access to justice for those most in need, the LSC directly funds legal services for eligible clients. Some solicitors are prepared to give a free or low-cost initial interview whether or not the client qualifies for funding. The different levels of service in civil matters are *Legal Help, Help at Court, Family Mediation, Family Help* and *Legal Representation. Family Help* can be either *Family Help (Lower)* or *Family Help (Higher)*; *Legal Representation* is available in two forms (*Investigative Help* and *Full Representation*).

The purpose of the Criminal Defence Service is to ensure that people suspected or accused of a crime have access to advice, assistance and representation, as the interests of justice require. The different levels of service are: *Police Station Advice and Assistance* (covers support for individuals questioned by police about an offence, whether or not they have been arrested); *Advice and Assistance* (covers help from a solicitor with general advice, writing letters, negotiating, obtaining a barrister's opinion and preparing a written case); *Advocacy Assistance* (covers the cost of a solicitor to prepare a client's case and initial representation in certain proceedings in both the magistrates' and the crown court); *Representation* (covers the cost of a solicitor to prepare a client's defence before a court appearance and to represent the client there, plus dealing with issues such as bail).

In 2008–09 the Commission received funding of £2·2bn. with which to fund the provision of services and spent £124·4m. on administration costs. A total of 2,869,000 acts of assistance were carried out in 2008–09, of which 1,556,000 were provided by Criminal Defence Services. The operating expenditure in 2008–09 was £914·7m. for Community Legal Services and £1,176·3m. for Criminal Defence Services, giving a net Legal Services Commission operating expenditure of £2·09bn.

See also SCOTLAND.

CIVIL JUDICIAL STATISTICS

ENGLAND AND WALES

	Number of cases 2007
Appellate Courts	
Judicial Committee of the Privy Council	71
House of Lords	51
Court of Appeal	1,114
High Court of Justice (appeals and special cases from inferior courts)	6,690
Courts of First Instance (excluding Magistrates' Courts and Tribunals)	
High Court of Justice:	
Chancery Division	45,541
Queen's Bench Division	18,505
County courts: Matrimonial suits	137,465[1]
County courts: Non-family work	2,014,962

[1]Includes dissolutions of civil partnerships.

CRIMINAL STATISTICS

ENGLAND AND WALES

	Total number of offenders (in 1,000)		*Indictable offences[1] (in 1,000)*	
	2007	*2008*	*2007*	*2008*
Aged 10 and over				
Proceeded against in magistrates' courts	1,733	1,640	405	397
Found guilty at all courts	1,416	1,363	313	317
Cautioned	363	327	205	180
Aged 10 and under 18				
Proceeded against in magistrates' courts	126	111	67	59
Found guilty at all courts	98	88	51	46
Cautioned[2]	127	98	75	58

[1]On the principal offence basis. [2]From 1 June 2000 the Crime and Disorder Act 1998 came into force nationally and removed the use of cautions for persons under 18 and replaced them with reprimands and final warnings.

British Crime Survey (BCS) interviews in 2006–07 estimate that there were approximately 11·3m. crimes against adults living in private households in England and Wales. This represents an increase of 3% compared with the estimate based on interviews for 2005–06. In the year to March 2007 crimes recorded by the police in England and Wales totalled 5·4m., a fall of 2% compared with 2005–06. 73% of all recorded crimes were against property.

In June 2008 the prison population in England and Wales was 83,194 (79,734 in June 2007). In 2008 the incarceration rate of 153 people per 100,000 inhabitants was the second highest in western Europe after Spain. The annual average prison population rose 26% between 1998 and 2008, from 65,298 to 82,572. During this time the annual average female prison population rose by 42%, from 3,105 to 4,414; the annual average male population rose by 26% from 62,194 to 78,158. These figures do not include prisoners held in police cells.

See also SCOTLAND *and* NORTHERN IRELAND.

Police

In England and Wales there are 43 police forces, each maintained by a police authority typically comprising nine local councillors, three magistrates and five independent members. London is policed by the Metropolitan Police Service (responsible to the 23-member Metropolitan Police Authority, 11 of whom are members of the Greater London Assembly, plus the Mayor) and the City of London Police (whose police authority is the City of London Corporation). A similar tripartite arrangement (Cabinet Secretary, Chief Constable and Joint Police Board/Police Authority) exists for the accountability of the police service in Scotland.

Figures show that the total strength of the police service in England and Wales at 31 March 2008 was 140,230 (including

32,931 women). Police officers are supported by police staff and at the end of March 2008 there were 77,350 police staff (approximately 47,000 female), including 1,903 designated officers (investigation officers, detention officers and escort officers). In addition there were 15,805 police community support officers on 31 March 2008 (including approximately 6,800 women). There were 14,547 special constables in March 2008 (including 3,828 women). The Police Service in England and Wales has benefited from a significant increase in resources over a sustained period. On a like-for-like basis government grant for the police will have increased by more than 60% or over £3·7bn. between 1997–98 and 2010–11.

Education

Adult Literacy and Numeracy. The government published the *Skills for Life Strategy* in 2001 in response to the recommendations in the 1999 Moser report (*A Fresh Start. Improving Literacy and Numeracy).* The strategy covers adults aged 16 and above at skills levels of pre-entry up to and including Level 2. The results of the 2003 *Skills for Life Needs and Impact Survey* showed that in England 5·2m. adults aged 16–65 have literacy levels below Level 1 (equivalent to the level expected of an average 11-year-old) and 15m. have numeracy skills below Level 1. From April 2001 to May 2006, 1,416,000 learners achieved at least one qualification in literacy, numeracy or language. In terms of participation in literacy-, language- or numeracy-learning a total of 4·5m. learners took up 9·7m. learning opportunities between April 2001 and May 2006.

The Publicly Maintained System of Education. Compulsory schooling begins at the age of five (four in Northern Ireland). The minimum leaving age for all pupils was 16 but as a result of the Education and Skills Act of Nov. 2008 this will be raised in stages to 18. From 2015, all young people will remain in education or training to 18. No tuition fees are payable in any publicly maintained school (but parents can choose to pay for their children to attend independent schools run by individuals, companies or charitable institutions). The post-school or tertiary stage, which is voluntary, includes universities, further education establishments and other higher education establishments, as well as adult education and youth services. Financial assistance (grants and loans) is generally available to students in higher education and to some students on other courses in further education.

National Curriculum. The National Curriculum was introduced in 1988 and has undergone a number of revisions—the latest taking place in 2008. It determines the content of what will be taught, sets attainment targets for learning and determines how performance will be assessed and reported.

The National Curriculum comprises the core subjects of English, mathematics and science; and foundation subjects of information communication technology, design and technology, history, geography, modern foreign languages, art and design, music, physical education and citizenship.

At key stage 4 (ages 14–16) schools must provide access for each pupil to a minimum of one course in the arts (art and design, music, dance, drama and media arts); one course in the humanities (history and geography); at least one modern foreign language; and design and technology. However, since Sept. 2004 these subject areas are no longer compulsory for key stage 4 pupils.

In addition, pupils must be taught religious education during all four key stages, although parents have the right to withdraw their children from this provision. Careers and sex education are compulsory at Key Stages 3 and 4, and work-related learning is compulsory at Key Stage 4. The subject of personal, social and health education is not statutory but should be taught across all four key stages. Every school must also provide a form of daily collective worship, but with the right to withdraw.

In Sept. 2008 the Early Years Foundation Stage (EYFS) replaced the Foundation Stage curriculum which was a distinct phase of education for children aged three to the end of the reception year of primary school. The EYFS is a national play-based framework for supporting the learning, development and safety of children from birth to the age of five. The EYFS does not form part of the National Curriculum. All state and independent schools and 'registered' early years providers are required to meet the learning and development requirements of the EYFS.

Early Learning. All three- and four-year-olds are entitled to 12·5 hours per week of free early learning for 38 weeks per year until they reach compulsory school age. The entitlement will be extended to 15 hours per week from Sept. 2010. Free early-learning places can be delivered by state nursery schools; nursery classes in primary schools and reception classes; and private, voluntary and independent providers and registered childminders who are part of a quality assured network. There are around 38,900 sites currently involved in delivering free early-learning. Local authorities have a duty to ensure that there are sufficient free early learning places for all three- and four-year-olds.

Primary Schools. These provide compulsory education for pupils from the age of five up to the age of 11 (12 in Scotland). Most public sector primary schools take boys and girls in mixed classes. Some pre-compulsory age pupils attend nursery classes within primary schools, however, and in England some middle schools cater for pupils at either side of the secondary education transition age. There are 21,768 public sector mainstream primary schools in the United Kingdom, with an average of 21 pupils per teacher.

Middle Schools. A number of local authorities operate a middle school system. These provide for pupils from the age of 8, 9 or 10 up to the age of 12, 13 or 14, and are deemed either primary or secondary according to the age range of the pupils.

Secondary Schools. There are 4,209 state-funded secondary schools in the United Kingdom providing for pupils from the age of 11 upwards. Some local authorities have retained a selective admissions policy at age 11 (mainly for entry to grammar schools), and some 233 state-funded secondary schools in the United Kingdom operate a selective admissions policy. There are 172 secondary modern schools in England providing a general education up to the minimum school leaving age of 16, although some pupils stay on beyond that age. In state-funded secondary schools in the United Kingdom there are an average 16 pupils per teacher.

Almost all local authorities operate a system of comprehensive schools to which pupils are admitted without reference to ability or aptitude. There are 3,304 such schools in Great Britain with over 3·3m. pupils. With the development of comprehensive education, various patterns of secondary schools have come into operation. Principally these are: 1) All-through schools with pupils aged 11 to 18 or 11 to 16; pupils over 16 being able to transfer to an 11 to 18 school or a sixth form college providing for pupils aged 16 to 19. (Since 1 April 1993, sixth form colleges have been part of the further education sector—there are 95 sixth form colleges). 2) Local authorities operating a three-tier system involving middle schools where transfer to secondary school is at ages 12, 13 or 14. These correspond to 12 to 18, 13 to 18 and 14 to 18 comprehensive schools respectively. 3) In areas where there are no middle schools a two-tier system of junior and senior comprehensive schools for pupils aged 11 to 18, with optional transfer to these schools at age 13 or 14.

Specialist Schools. The Specialist Schools Programme began with specialist Technology Colleges in 1994; by Oct. 2008 over 2,900 had specialized in a diverse range of subject areas. Specialist Schools have access to additional funding and support that allows them to focus on a particular part of the curriculum both in their own school and with other schools whilst continuing to cover the full National Curriculum.

Academies. Academies (only in England) are independent state schools open to all abilities. They are usually in disadvantaged areas and are established by sponsors from business, faith, or voluntary groups. In July 2006 the endowment model of sponsorship was announced. Sponsors now establish an endowment fund with the Academy Trust using the revenue generated from the endowment to support the objectives of the Academy. The Department for Children, Schools and Families (DCSF) provide the capital and running costs. In Sept. 2008 there were 130 Academies.

City Technology Colleges. CTCs are independent all-ability secondary schools established in partnership between government and business sponsors under the Education Reform Act 1988. They teach the full National Curriculum but give special emphasis to technology, science and mathematics. The government meets all recurrent costs. Although there were originally 14 CTCs, there are now only two remaining as 12 have been converted to Academies.

Music and Dance Scheme (formerly the Music and Ballet Scheme). The 'Aided Pupil Scheme' for boys and girls with outstanding talent in music or dance (principally ballet) helps parents with the fees and boarding costs at eight specialist private schools in England. Since 2004 the scheme has been developed to include 20 new centres for advanced training and a national grants scheme for out-of-school-hours training.

Special Education. It is estimated that, nationally, 20% of the school population will have special educational needs at some time during their school career. For some 2·8% of pupils the local authority will need to make a statutory assessment of special educational needs under the Education Act 1996 and draw up a legal document, the statement, which sets out the extra provision a child needs. (In Scotland pupils are assessed for a Coordinated Support Plan.)

Maintained schools must use their best endeavours to make provision for such pupils. The Special Educational Needs Code of Practice, a revised version of which came into force on 1 Jan. 2002, gives practical guidance.

Further Education (Non-University). The English Further Education (FE) system provides a wide range of education and training opportunities for individuals and employers. Learning opportunities are provided, from age 14 upwards, at all levels from basic skills to higher education. The FE system's primary purpose is to help people gain the skills they need to improve their employability.

The Learning and Skills Council (LSC) is primarily responsible for funding full- and part-time education and training provision for people aged 16 to 19 in FE colleges, sixth form colleges and school sixth forms, work-based and local authority maintained institutions. It also makes provision for adult and community learning for those aged 19 and over.

Further education is the largest sector providing educational opportunities for the over 16s. There are 386 FE colleges in England, with around 6m. learners in the sector as a whole; 4·2m. learners in FE colleges and institutions. Of the students on LSC funded provision, 17% were under 19 and 74% were adults aged 19 to 59.

Youth Work. The priority age group for agencies and services providing youth work is 13–19 year-olds, but the target age group may extend to 11–25 year-olds. Provision is usually in the form of positive activities delivered in youth clubs and centres, or through 'detached' or outreach work aimed at young people at risk from alcohol or drug misuse, or of drifting into crime. There is an increasing emphasis on youth workers working with disaffected, and socially excluded, young people and providing services at times and in places where young people want them. Youth work can be delivered by local authority youth services, the voluntary and community sector, and other specialist youth agencies.

Independent/State School Partnerships Grant Scheme. The aim is to promote collaborative working between the independent and state school sectors to raise standards in education. A total of 24 projects are receiving more than £4m. of funding over the period 2008–11. In excess of 330 projects received funding totalling £10m. in the first nine years of the scheme (1998–2007).

Higher Education (HE) Student Support. All students are expected to make a contribution towards their tuition fees. The maximum that a student who started their course after 1 Sept. 2010 is expected to pay towards their tuition is £3,290 (students who started their course before 1 Sept. 2006 will continue to make a contribution of up to £1,200). However, no eligible student (new or existing) has to pay their fees either before or during their course, as a Student Loan for Tuition Fees is available. Students in the fifth or later years of medical or dental courses and on NHS-funded courses in professions allied to medicine may be eligible for a means-tested grant from the NHS Bursary system. Postgraduate trainee teachers may be eligible for tax-free bursaries; these range from £4,000 to £9,000 depending on the teaching subject. Non-repayable Maintenance Grants of up to £2,906 are also available, targeted at students from lower income backgrounds.

Universities and colleges wishing to charge maximum fees must also make bursaries available to students who are in receipt of the full Maintenance Grant—for a student paying £3,290 fees this bursary is a minimum of £329.

A Student Loan for Maintenance is available to help with students' living costs. All students are entitled to 72% of the maximum loan, with the balance subject to income assessment. The maximum loans available from 2009–10 are: £6,928 (living away from home and studying in London); £4,950 (living away from home and studying outside London); and £3,838 (living at home). Neither the Student Loan for Tuition Fees nor the Student Loan for Maintenance has to be repaid until the student has left university or college and is earning over £15,000 a year.

Applications for student finance are made through Local Authorities or, under a pilot scheme operating in some areas, direct to the Student Loans Company. The Student Loans Company manages loan accounts and the payment of the student finance package.

Postgraduate studentships and research grants are available from the Arts and Humanities Research Council (AHRC) or similar councils. There are six other grant-awarding Research Councils which each report to the Department of Business, Innovation and Skills. They offer awards to students studying within the broad spectrum of economics, engineering, astronomy and medical, biological and physical sciences.

Each year the AHRC provides approximately £102m. from the government to support research and postgraduate study in the arts and humanities, from languages and law, archaeology and English literature to design and creative and performing arts. In any one year the AHRC makes approximately 700 research awards and around 1,350 postgraduate awards. Awards are made after a rigorous peer review process, to ensure that only applications of the highest quality are funded.

Career Development Loans (CDLs). Introduced in 1988, CDLs are specifically designed to help individuals acquire and improve vocational skills, and are aimed at those who would otherwise not have reasonable or adequate access to the funds. Loans of between £300 and £8,000 can be applied for to support up to two years of education or learning (plus up to one year's practical work experience where it forms part of the course). The Learning and Skills Council (LSC) operates the programme in partnership with three high street banks (Barclays, The Co-operative and the Royal Bank of Scotland). The LSC pays the interest on the loan for the period of supported learning and for up to one month afterwards. The individual then repays the loan to the bank in accordance with their loan agreement. Subject to certain conditions it may be possible for individuals to defer their loan repayments for up to 17 months.

By Oct. 2004 over £750m. had been advanced to over 208,000 applicants.

Teachers. Qualified teacher status (QTS) is obtained through either an undergraduate or postgraduate course of initial teacher training. Training courses are either college-based or employment-based, the latter allowing trainees to teach as unqualified teachers and also study for QTS at the same time. As well as meeting common professional standards, trainees must also pass computerized skills tests in information and communication technology, numeracy and literacy in order to be awarded QTS. Newly qualified teachers are then required to complete an induction programme during their first year of teaching.

Those who are recognized as qualified teachers in Scotland or Northern Ireland are also entitled to apply to the General Teaching Council for England or the General Teaching Council for Wales for QTS without undertaking further training. Nationals of European Economic Area (EEA) countries who are recognized as schoolteachers in an EEA member state can apply to the GTCE for QTS without undertaking further training.

Teachers who qualified as teachers in countries outside of the EEA are allowed to teach for four years in state maintained and non-maintained special schools in England. This is subject to satisfying Home Office rules on employing overseas workers. They are only allowed to teach beyond four years if they have been awarded QTS which can be obtained through undertaking an employment-based training programme.

In 2007–08, 31,300 trainees began college-based initial teacher training courses and a further 7,120 trainees were expected to enter employment-based initial teacher training.

In 2007–08, 477,100 full-time equivalent teachers were employed in maintained nursery, primary and secondary schools in the United Kingdom.

Finance. Total education expenditure by central and local government in the United Kingdom for 2006–07 was £70·7bn. representing 5·3% of GDP, compared with £44·4bn. and 4·6% of GDP in 2000–01.

Independent Schools. Independent schools which belong to an association affiliated to the Independent Schools Council (accounting for 80% of pupils) are subject to an inspection regime agreed between the government and the ISC. The Schools Inspection Service inspects schools affiliated to the Focus Learning Trust, and the Bridge Schools Inspectorate inspects schools affiliated to the Christian Schools Trust and the Association of Muslim Schools, also under arrangements agreed with the government. Non-association schools are inspected by Ofsted on a regular cycle.

The earliest of the independent schools were founded by medieval churches. Many were founded as 'grammar' (classical) schools in the 16th century, receiving charters from the reigning sovereign. Reformed mainly in the middle of the 19th century, among the best-known are Eton College, founded in 1440 by Henry VI; Winchester College (1394), founded by William of Wykeham, Bishop of Winchester; Harrow School, founded in 1560 as a grammar school by John Lyon, a yeoman; and Charterhouse (1611). Among the earliest foundations are King's School, Canterbury, founded 600; King's School, Rochester (604) and St Peter's, York (627).

Higher Education. In 2008–09 there were almost 2·4m. students in the UK at 166 higher education institutions, of which 116 were universities. The higher education student population was 57·1% female in 2007–08. 37% of the UK population between the ages of 25 and 34 have attained a tertiary qualification (OECD average, 34%), compared to only 25% of those aged between 55 and 64.

Total funding for higher education institutions in the UK was around £23·4bn. in 2007–08. Of this £8·5bn. came from funding council grants; £6·3bn. from tuition fees and education grants and contracts; £3·7bn. from research grants and contracts; £0·5bn. from endowment and investment income; and £4·4bn. from other income. Higher education institutions are funded by four UK bodies, one each for England, Scotland, Wales and Northern Ireland. Their roles include: allocating funds for teaching and research; promoting high-quality education and research; advising government on the needs of higher education; informing students about the quality of higher education available; and ensuring the proper use of public funds.

Open University. The Open University received its Royal Charter on 1 June 1969 and is an independent, self-governing institution, awarding its own degrees at undergraduate and postgraduate level. It is financed by the government through the Higher Education Funding Council for England for all its students in England, Wales and Northern Ireland and through the Scottish Funding Council for the teaching of its students in Scotland, and by the receipt of students' fees. At the heart of most courses is a series of specially produced textbooks or 'course units' (which are also widely used in the rest of the HE sector). They are closely integrated with a varying mix of set books, recommended reading, audio and video materials, home experiment kits, computer-based learning programmes, multimedia resources and network services. There are also 339 local tutorial centres where face-to-face tutorials may be offered. No formal qualifications are required for entry to the majority of undergraduate courses. Residents from most countries of Western Europe may apply (though some courses are not available outside the UK). There are over 250 undergraduate courses; many are available on a one-off basis. In 2004–05 there were over 154,000 undergraduates and over 20,000 postgraduate level students. The university has 4,300 full-time staff working at Milton Keynes and in 13 Regional Centres throughout the country. There are almost 7,500 part-time associate lecturers.

The only university independent of the state system is the *University of Buckingham*, which opened in 1976 and received a Royal Charter in 1983. It offers two-year honours degrees, the academic year commencing in Jan., July or Oct., and consisting of four ten-week terms. There are four areas of study: Business; Humanities; Law; and Sciences. In 2006 there were 525 full-time and 46 part-time undergraduate students and 148 postgraduate students. There were 66 teachers (seven part-time).

All universities charge fees, but financial help is available to students from several sources, and the majority of students receive some form of financial assistance.

See also ENGLAND, SCOTLAND *and* NORTHERN IRELAND.

British Council

The purpose of the British Council is to build mutually beneficial relationships between people in the UK and other countries, and to increase appreciation of the UK's creative ideas and achievements. Established in 1934 and incorporated by Royal Charter in 1940, it is the UK's international organization for educational and cultural relations. Its headquarters are in London and Manchester, with further centres in Belfast, Cardiff and Edinburgh. Independent and non-political, it is represented in 110 countries, running a mix of offices, libraries, information centres, Knowledge and Learning Centres and English-teaching operations. Its main areas of activity are in education and training, examination administration, English language teaching, learning and capacity building, the arts and sciences, sport, governance and civil society. The British Council's total income in 2006–07 was £551m. This was made up of government grants (£195m.), revenues from English-language teaching and client-funded education services (£232m.) and development programmes, principally in education and training, which are managed on behalf of the British government and other clients (£122m.).

Chair: Vernon Ellis.

Director-General: Martin Davidson, CMG.

Headquarters: 10 Spring Gdns, London, SW1A 2BN.

Website: http://www.britishcouncil.org

Health

The National Health Service (NHS) in England and Wales started on 5 July 1948. There is a separate Act for Scotland.

The NHS is a charge on the national income in the same way, for example, as the armed forces. Every person normally resident in the UK is entitled to use any part of the service, and no insurance qualification is necessary.

Since its inception, the NHS has been funded from general taxation and National Insurance (NI) contributions, and the present government has maintained the original principle that the NHS should be a service provided to all those who need it, regardless of their ability to pay or where they live. In 2008–09 the NHS in England was funded 17·5% by NI contributions, 71·9% by general taxation with the remainder coming from charges and receipts, including land sales and proceeds from income generation schemes. Health authorities may raise funds from voluntary sources; hospitals may take private, paying patients.

Health is the second largest government spending sector after social protection. In 2008–09 estimated NHS expenditure on health was £110·5bn. When combined with private expenditure on health care, the estimated overall percentage of UK GDP spent on health was 8·9%.

Organization. The National Health Service and Community Care Act, 1990, provided for a major restructuring of the NHS. From 1 April 1991 health authorities became the purchasers of health care, concentrating on their responsibilities to plan and obtain services for their local residents by the placement of health service contracts with the appropriate units. Day-to-day management tasks became the responsibility of hospitals and other units, with whom the contracts are placed, in their capacity as providers of care.

The 28 Strategic Health Authorities (SHAs), created in 2002, control local health care and are the key link between the Department of Health and the NHS. They monitor performance and standards of local NHS organizations (apart from NHS Foundation Trusts).

Primary Care Trusts (PCTs), introduced in 2000, control local health care and are financed directly by the Department of Health (around 80% of the NHS budget). They hold to account provider organizations (including NHS Foundation Trusts) for delivery of services that they have commissioned. At 1 Oct. 2006 there were 156 PCTs. The 2006–07 and 2007–08 PCT revenue allocations represented £135bn. of investment in the NHS in England, with over £64bn. in 2006–07 and over £70bn. in 2007–08. These allocations cover Hospital and Community Health Services (HCHS), prescription of drugs, HIV/AIDS and GP infrastructure (staff, premises and IT).

Services. The NHS broadly consists of hospital and specialist services, general medical, dental and ophthalmic services, pharmaceutical services, community health services and school health services. In general these services are free of charge; the main exceptions are prescriptions, spectacles, dental and optical examination, dentures and dental treatment, amenity beds in hospitals, and some community services, for which contributory charges are made with certain exemptions.

As at 30 Sept. 2008 there were 34,010 general medical practitioners in England excluding registrars and retainers (an increase of 1·9% since Sept. 2007), with an average of 1,586 patients per doctor; there were 1,940 in Wales, with an average of 1,605; and 4,260 in Scotland. There were 20,887 NHS dentists in England as at 31 Dec. 2006. At 31 March 2007 there were 2,009 general dental practitioners in Scotland; there were 1,141 in Wales. In England in 2008 there were 408,160 qualified nursing and midwifery staff, including GP practice nurses. As at 30 Sept. 2008 there were 34,910 consultants in England (24,401 in 2000) and 3,203 GP registrars. In 2008–09 provision of beds in England was 31 per 10,000 population. There were 159,386 hospital beds in England in 2008–09 (282,918 in 1988–89).

Private. In recent years increasing numbers of people have turned to private medical insurance. This covers the costs of private medical treatment (PMI) for curable short-term medical conditions. PMI includes the costs of surgery, specialists, nursing and accommodation at a private hospital or in a private ward of an NHS hospital. Approximately 13% of the UK population have private medical insurance. The leading companies are BUPA Healthcare, AXA PPP Healthcare and Standard Life Healthcare.

In 2007, 21% of the population of the UK aged 16 and over smoked. In 1974 the percentage had been 45%, with 51% of males and 41% of females smoking. Over the years the difference between the percentage of men and of women who smoke has been declining—in 2007 the rates were 22% for men and 20% for women. Among 11- to 15-year-olds in England 10% of girls but only 7% of boys smoked in 2004. The overall percentage of the UK population who are smokers is similar to the average for the EU as a whole, but among men the percentage of smokers in the UK is lower than in the EU as a whole whereas among women it is higher. Alcohol consumption has increased in recent years. Whereas in 1961 the average Briton consumed the equivalent of 4·5 litres of pure alcohol a year, by 2006 this figure had risen to 8·9 litres (although down from a peak of 9·4 litres in 2004).

There were an estimated 77,400 people living with HIV in the UK in 2007 (0·1% of the population).

See also NORTHERN IRELAND.

Personal Social Services

Under the Local Authority Social Services Act, 1970, and in Scotland the Social Work (Scotland) Act, 1968, the welfare and social work services provided by local authorities were made the responsibility of a new local authority department—the Social Services Department in England and Wales, and Social Work Departments in Scotland headed by a Director of Social Work, responsibility in Scotland passing in 1975 to the local authorities. The social services thus administered include: the fostering, care and adoption of children, welfare services and social workers for people with learning difficulties and the mentally ill, the disabled and the aged, and accommodation for those needing residential care services. Legislation of 1996 permits local authorities to make cash payments as an alternative to community care. In Scotland the Social Work Departments' functions also include the supervision of persons on probation, of adult offenders and of persons released from penal institutions or subject to fine supervision orders.

Personal Social Services staff numbered 256,100 in England at 30 Sept. 2008 and 27,287 in Wales at 31 March 2009. Scottish Social Work Services staff numbered around 56,900 in Oct. 2008. The total expenditure (2007–08) for PSS was £18,500m. in England and £1,303m. in Wales. Scotland's expenditure on social work (2007–08) was £2,368m. Expenditure is reviewed by the Social Services Inspectorate and the Audit Commission (in Scotland by the Social Work Services Inspectorate and the Accounts Commission).

Welfare

The National Insurance Act 1965 now operates under the Social Security Contributions and Benefits Act 1992 and the Social Security Administration Act 1992.

Since 1975 Class 1 contributions have been related to the employee's earnings and are collected with PAYE income tax. Class 2 and Class 3 contributions remain flat-rate, but, in addition to Class 2 contributions, those who are self-employed may be liable to pay Class 4 contributions, which for the year 2010–11 are at the rate of 8% on profits or gains between £5,715 and £43,875 (with a further 1% contribution on any profit exceeding the upper limit), which are assessable for income tax under Schedule D. The non-employed and others whose contribution record is not sufficient to give entitlement to benefits are able to pay a Class 3 contribution of £12·05 per week in 2010–11 voluntarily, to qualify for a limited range of benefits. Class 2 weekly contributions for 2010–11 for men and women are £2·40. Class 1A contributions are paid by employers who provide employees with a car and fuel for their private use.

The Social Security Pensions Act 1975 introduced earnings-related retirement, invalidity and widows' pensions. Members of occupational pension schemes may be contracted out of the earnings-related part of the state scheme relating to retirement and widows' benefits. Employee's national insurance contribution liability depends on whether he/she is in contracted-out or not contracted-out employment.

Full-rate contributions for non-contracted-out employment in 2010–11:

Weekly Earnings (in £1)	*Employee pays*	*Employer pays*
Below 97 (Lower Earnings Limit)	Nil	Nil
97–110 (Primary Threshold/Secondary Threshold)	Nil	Nil
110–844 (Upper Earnings Limit)	11%	12·8%
Over 844 (Upper Earnings Limit)	See footnote[1]	12·8%

[1]£80·74 plus 1% on earnings over £844 per week.

For contracted-out employment, the contracted-out rebate for primary contributions (employee's contribution) is 1·6% of earnings between the lower earnings limit and the upper earnings limit for all forms of contracting-out; the contracted-out rebate for secondary contributions (employer's contributions) is 3·7% of earnings between the lower earnings limit and the upper earnings limit.

Contributions together with interest on investments form the income of the *National Insurance Fund* from which benefits are paid. 28,330,000 persons (12,780,000 women) paid contributions in 2006–07, including 25,170,000 employees at standard rate.

Receipts, 2007–08 (in £1m.), 121,464, including: contributions, 77,224; investment income, 2,452; compensation for Statutory Sick Pay/Statutory Maternity Pay, 1,919. Disbursements (in £1m.), 72,158, including: retirement pensions, 58,921; Incapacity, 6,945; Personal Pensions, 2,557; administration, 1,430; Bereavement Benefits, 760; transfers to Northern Ireland, 452; Jobseeker's Allowance (Contributory), 435; maternity, 250; redundancy payments, 215; pensioners' lump sum payments, 131.

Statutory Sick Pay (SSP). Employers are responsible for paying Statutory Sick Pay (SSP) to their employees who are absent from work through illness or injury for up to 28 weeks in any three-year period. All employees aged between 16 and 65 (60 for women) with earnings above the Lower Earnings Limit are covered by the scheme whenever they are sick for four or more days consecutively. The weekly rate is £79·15. For most employees SSP completely replaces their entitlement to state incapacity benefit which is not payable as long as any employer's responsibility for SSP remains.

Contributory benefits. Qualification for these depends upon fulfilment of the appropriate contribution conditions, except that persons who are incapable of work as the result of an industrial accident may receive incapacity benefit followed by invalidity benefit without having to satisfy the contributions conditions.

Jobseeker's Allowance. Unemployed persons claiming the allowance must sign a 'Jobseeker's Agreement' setting out a plan of action to find work. The allowance is not payable to persons who left their job voluntarily or through misconduct. Claimants with sufficient National Insurance contributions are entitled to the allowance for six months regardless of their means; otherwise, recipients qualify through a means test and the allowance is fixed according to family circumstances, at a rate corresponding to Income Support for an indefinite period. In May 2008 there were 788,000 people receiving the Jobseeker's Allowance (576,700 males). Payments start at £51·85 per week.

Incapacity benefit. Entitlement begins when entitlement to SSP (if any) ends. There are three rates: a lower rate for the first 28 weeks; a higher rate between the 29th and 52nd week; and a long-term rate from the 53rd week of incapacity. It also comprises certain age additions and increases for adult and child dependants. A more objective medical test of incapacity for work was introduced for incapacity benefit as well as for other social security benefits paid on the basis of incapacity for work. This test applies after 28 weeks' incapacity for work and assesses ability to perform a range of work-related activities rather than the ability to perform a specific job. Benefit is taxable after 28 weeks. Some 2,382,000 claims were being made in May 2008.

Statutory Maternity Pay. Pregnant working women may be eligible to receive Statutory Maternity Pay directly from their employer for a maximum of 39 weeks if average gross earnings are £97 a week or more (2010–11). There are two rates: a higher rate (90% of average earnings for the first six weeks), and a lower rate of £124·88 or 90% of earnings (whichever is less) for up to 33 weeks. For women who do not qualify for Statutory Maternity Pay, including self-employed women, there is a Maternity Allowance.

A payment of £500 from the Social Fund (Sure Start Maternity Grant) may be available if the mother or her partner are receiving Income Support, income-based Jobseeker's Allowance, Pension Credit, Child Tax Credit (at a rate higher than the family element) or Working Tax Credit (in cases of disability). It is also available if a parent adopts a baby, is granted a parental order on a surrogate birth or is granted a residence order on a child (subject to certain conditions).

Statutory Paternity Pay. Since 6 April 2003 working fathers have had the right to two weeks paid paternity leave providing average gross earnings are £97 a week or more (2010–11). This will be paid at the same rate as the lower rate of Statutory Maternity Pay (£124·88 a week or 90% of average weekly earnings if this is less than £124·88).

Statutory Adoption Pay. Paid adoption leave is for up to 39 weeks at the same rate as Statutory Paternity Pay. It is available to employed people adopting a child on their own, or for one member of a couple adopting together. Parents adopting from overseas are also eligible, although conditions may differ.

Bereavement Benefits. Available to both men and women, Bereavement Benefits were introduced from 9 April 2001 to replace the former Widows' Benefit scheme. There are three main types of Bereavement Benefits available to men and women widowed on or after 9 April 2001: bereavement payment, widowed parent's allowance and bereavement allowance. *Bereavement Payment* is a single tax-free lump sum of £2,000 payable immediately on bereavement. A widower/widow may be able to get this benefit if their late spouse has paid enough National Insurance Contributions (NIC) and was under 60 at death; or was not getting a Category A State Retirement Pension at death. *Widowed Parent's Allowance* is a weekly benefit payable when the widower/widow is receiving Child Benefit. The amount of Widowed Parent's Allowance is based on the late spouse's NIC record. He/she may also get benefit for the eldest dependent child and further higher benefit for each subsequent child; also an additional pension based on their late spouse's earnings. If the late spouse was a member of a contracted-out occupational scheme or a personal pension scheme, that scheme is responsible for paying the whole or part of the additional pensions. Widowed Parent's Allowance is taxable. *Bereavement Allowance* is a weekly benefit payable to widows and widowers without dependent children and is payable between age 45 and State Pension age. The amount of Bereavement Allowance payable to a widower/widow between 45 and 54 is related to their age at the date of entitlement. Their weekly rate is reduced by 7% for each year they are aged under 55 so that they get 93% rate at age 54, falling to 30% at age 45. Those aged 55 or over at the date of entitlement will get the full rate of Bereavement Allowance. The amount of Bereavement Allowance is based on the late spouse's NIC record and is payable for a maximum of 52 weeks from the date of bereavement. A widower/widow cannot get a Bereavement Allowance at the same time as a Widowed Parent's Allowance. Women widowed before 9 April 2001 continue to receive their Widows' Benefit entitlement on the arrangements that existed before that date so long as they continue to satisfy the qualifying conditions. There were 77,900 recipients of Widows' Benefits and 59,850 recipients of Bereavement Benefits in May 2008.

Retirement Pension. The state retirement ('old-age') pension scheme has two components: a basic pension and an earnings-related pension (State Earnings Related Pension—SERPS). The amount of the first is subject to National Insurance contributions made; SERPS is 1·25% of average earnings between the lower weekly earnings limit for Class I contribution liability and the upper earnings limit for each year of such earnings, building up to 25% in 20 years. For individuals reaching pensionable age after 6 April 1999, changes in the way pensions are calculated will be phased in over ten years to include a lifetime's earnings with an accrual rate of 20%. Pensions are payable to women at 60 years of age and men at 65, but the age differential is being progressively phased out as from April 2010. There are standard rates for single persons and for married couples, the latter being 159% of two single-person rates. Proportionately reduced pensions are payable where contribution records are deficient. Proposals were announced in Nov. 2005 for the state-pension age to be increased to 66 by 2030, 67 by 2040 and 68 by 2050.

Employees in an occupational scheme may contract out of SERPS provided that the occupational scheme provides a pension not less than the 'guaranteed minimum pension'. Self-employed persons, and also employees, may substitute personal pension schemes for SERPS.

Self- and non-employed persons may contribute voluntarily for retirement pension.

Persons who defer claiming their pension during the five years following retirement age are paid an increased amount, as do men and women who had paid graduated contributions. 12,050,000 persons were receiving National Insurance retirement pensions in May 2008 (7,529,400 women and 4,520,600 men). The full basic state pension in 2010–11 is £97·65 per week for a single person and £156·15 per week for a married couple. Since 1 Oct. 1989 the pension for which a person has qualified may be paid in full whether a person continues in work or not irrespective of the amount of earnings. Although for males the official retirement age is 65, in 2004 the average actual retirement age among males was 63·8 years.

At the age of 80 a small age addition is payable. In addition non-contributory pensions are now payable, subject to residence conditions, to persons aged 80 and over who do not qualify for a retirement pension or qualify for one at a low rate.

Pensioners whose pension is insufficient to live on may qualify for Income Support.

Non-Contributory Benefits

Child Benefit. Child Benefit is a tax-free cash allowance normally paid to the mother. The weekly rates are highest for the eldest qualifying child (£20·30 weekly in 2010–11) and less for each other child (£13·40 weekly in 2010–11). Child Benefit is payable for children under 16, for 16- and 17-year-olds registered for work or training, and for those under 19 receiving full-time non-advanced education. Some 7,530,000 families received benefit in Aug. 2007.

Child Support Agency. The Child Support Agency is responsible for calculating, collecting and enforcing child maintenance payments. The non-resident parent pays 15% of their net income if they have one child, 20% for two and 30% for three or more children. The agency currently deals with around 1·5m. child support cases. In Dec. 2006 the Child Maintenance White Paper announced the establishment of a new and radically different organization called the Child Maintenance and Enforcement Commission. It assumed responsibility for the Child Support Agency in Nov. 2008, and will introduce a tougher enforcement regime that encourages parents to take greater responsibility for the financial support of their children. A single system of child maintenance is expected to be in place by 2013–14.

Working Tax Credit. This tackles poor work incentives and persistent poverty among working people. For families with children, credit is available for those with low incomes. It also extends support to low-income working people without children aged 25 or over working 30 hours or more a week. The Working Tax Credit is not just restricted to those with children; the amount of the award varies considerably depending on the prevailing circumstances. Both single persons and couples may be eligible.

Child Tax Credit. The Child Tax Credit aims at creating a single system of support for families with children, payable irrespective of the work status of the adults in the household. This means that the Child Tax Credit forms a stable and secure income bridge as families move off welfare and into work. It also provides a common framework of assessment, so that all families are part of the same inclusive system. The Child Tax Credit provides a family element of up to £545 per year and a child element of up to £2,300 per child per year in addition to Child Benefit. The amount paid varies depending on the number of children and the gross annual joint income.

Guardian's Allowance. A person responsible for an orphan child may be entitled to a Guardian's Allowance in addition to Child Benefit. Normally, both the child's parents must be dead but when they never married or were divorced, or one is missing or serving a long sentence of imprisonment, the allowance may be paid on the death of one parent only. Some 3,300 families received benefit in Aug. 2007.

Attendance Allowance. This is a tax-free Social Security benefit for disabled people over 65 who need help with personal care. The rates are increased for the terminally ill. There were 1,546,680 recipients in May 2008.

Carers' Allowance. This is a taxable benefit paid to those who care for a disabled person for at least 35 hours per week. The carer must be at least 16, not in full-time education of 21 hours or more per week, and not earn more than £100 per week after certain deductions have been made—such as income tax. This is a weekly rate (£53·90 in 2010–11), with increases for dependants. In May 2008 there were 480,730 recipients.

Disability Living Allowance. This is a non-taxable benefit available to people disabled before the age of 65, who need help with getting around or with personal care for at least three months. The mobility component has two weekly rates, the care component has three. There were 2,973,540 recipients in May 2008.

Industrial Injuries Disablement and Death Benefits. The scheme provides a system of insurance against 'personal injury by accident arising out of and in the course of employment' and against certain prescribed diseases and injuries owing to the nature of the employment. There are no contribution conditions for the payment of benefit. There were 261,990 recipients in March 2008. Two types of benefit are provided:

—*Disablement Benefit.* This is payable where, as the result of an industrial accident or prescribed disease, there is a loss of physical or mental faculty. The loss of faculty will be assessed as a percentage by comparison with a person of the same age and sex whose condition is normal. If the assessment is between 14–100% benefit will be paid as weekly pension. The rates vary from 20% disabled to 100% disablement. Assessments of less than 14% do not normally attract basic benefit except for certain progressive chest diseases. Pensions for persons under 18 are at a reduced rate. When injury benefit was abolished for industrial accidents occurring and prescribed diseases commencing on or after 6 April 1983, a common start date was introduced for the payment of Disablement Benefit 90 days (excluding Sundays) after the date of the relevant accident or onset of the disease.

—*Death Benefit.* This is payable to the widow, widower or children of a person who died before 11 April 1988 as the result of an industrial accident or a prescribed disease. For deaths which occurred on or after 11 April 1988, standard Bereavement Benefits apply (and, until 2001, Widows' Benefits). Allowances may be paid to people who are suffering from pneumoconiosis or byssinosis or certain other slowly developing diseases due to employment before 5 July 1948. They must not at any time have been entitled to benefit under the Industrial Injuries provision of the Social Security Act, or compensation under Workmen's Compensation Acts, or have received damages through the courts.

War Pensions. Pensions are payable for disablement or death as a result of service in the armed forces. Similar schemes exist for other groups such as merchant seamen injured as a result of war or for civilians injured by enemy action in the Second World War. The amount depends on the degree of disablement. There were 201,270 recipients in March 2008.

Housing Benefit. The Housing Benefit scheme assists persons who need help to pay their rent, using general assessment rules and benefit levels similar to those for the income support scheme. The scheme sets a limit of £16,000 on the amount of capital a person may have and still remain entitled. Restrictions on the granting of benefit to persons under 25 were introduced in 1995. In May 2007 there were 4,031,810 beneficiaries.

Income Support. Income Support is a non-contributory benefit for people aged 16 or over, not working 16 hours or more a week or with a partner not working more than 24 hours or more per week, and not required to be available for employment. These include single parents, long-term sick or disabled persons, and those caring for them who qualify for Invalid Care Allowance. Income Support is not payable if the claimant (or claimant and partner together) has capital assets that total more than £16,000. These include savings, investments or property other than their home. Savings/capital assets worth under £6,000 are ignored. Savings between £6,000 and £16,000 are treated as if each £250 or part of £250 brings in an income of £1 per week. Income Support claimants whose partners are of pensionable age may have up to £12,000 and still be entitled to Income Support. Claimants in residential care and nursing homes are allowed to have up to £16,000 and still be entitled to Income Support. From 6 Oct. 2003 a new Pension Credit replaced Minimum Income Guarantee (Income Support for people aged 60 and over). In May 2008 there were 2,091,520 Income Support claimants and 2,719,140 Pension Credit claimants. The average weekly award was £82·35 in May 2008.

Council Tax Benefit. Subject to rules broadly similar to those governing the provision of income support and housing benefit, people may receive rebates of up to 100% of their council tax. In May 2007, 5,076,900 households received such help. A person who is liable for the council tax may also claim benefit (called 'second adult rebate') for a second adult who is not liable to pay the council tax and who is living in the home on a non-commercial basis.

The Social Fund. This comprises: *Sure Start Maternity Grant* (a payment of up to £500 for each baby expected, born or adopted, payable to persons receiving Income Support, Income-based Jobseeker's Allowance, Child Tax Credit, Working Tax Credit or Pension Credit); *Funeral Payments* (a payment of fees levied by the burial authorities and crematoria, plus up to £700 for other funeral expenses, to persons receiving Income Support, Income-based Jobseeker's Allowance, Housing Benefit, Child Tax Credit, Working Tax Credit or Pension Credit); *Cold Weather Payments* (a payment of £25 for any consecutive seven days when the temperature is below freezing to persons receiving income support who are pensioners, disabled or have a child under five); *Winter Fuel Payments* (a payment of £250 to every household with a person aged 60 or over providing they do not live permanently in a hospital, residential care or nursing home, or £400 if the household has someone aged 80 years old or over). The Discretionary Social Fund comprises: *Community Care Grants* (payments to help persons receiving income support to move into the community or avoid institutional care); *Budgeting Loans* (interest-free loans to persons receiving income support for expenses difficult to budget for); *Crisis Loans* (interest-free loans to anyone without resources in an emergency where there is no other means of preventing serious risk to health or safety). Savings over £500 (£1,000 for persons aged 60 or over) are taken into account before payments are made.

Hill, M., *The Welfare State in Britain: a Political History since 1945.* 1993
Timmins, N., *The Five Giants: a Biography of the Welfare State.* 1995

RELIGION

The Anglican Communion originated from the Church of England and parallels in its fellowship of autonomous churches the evolution of British influence beyond the seas from colonies to dominions and independent nations. The Archbishop of Canterbury presides as *primus inter pares* at the decennial meetings of the bishops of the Anglican Communion at the Lambeth Conference and at the biennial meetings of the Primates and the Anglican Consultative Council. The 2008 Conference was held in Canterbury and was attended by 670 bishops. Average attendance at Sunday worship in 2004 numbered 1·0m., compared to 3·5m. in 1950. There were 1,543,000 Anglicans on the electoral roll in 2005.

The Anglican Communion (Anglican Episcopal family) consists of an estimated 80m. Christians who are members of 44 different Churches (including six Extra-Provincial Dioceses). These are: The Anglican Church in Aotearoa, New Zealand and Polynesia; The Anglican Church of Australia; The Church of Bangladesh; The Anglican Church of Bermuda (Extra-Provincial to the Archbishop of Canterbury); The Episcopal Anglican Church of Brazil; The Anglican Church of Burundi; The Anglican Church of Canada; The Church of the Province of Central Africa; The Anglican Church of the Central America Region; The Church of Ceylon (Sri Lanka) (Extra-Provincial to the Archbishop of Canterbury); The Province of the Anglican Church of the Congo; The Episcopal Church of Cuba (under a Metropolitan Council); The Church of England; The Parish of the Falkland Islands (Extra-Provincial to the Archbishop of Canterbury); Hong Kong Sheng Kung Hui; The Church of the Province of the Indian Ocean; The Church of Ireland; The Nippon Sei Ko Kai; The Episcopal Church in Jerusalem and the Middle East; The Anglican Church of Kenya; The Anglican Church of Korea; The Lusitanian Church (Portugal) (Extra-Provincial to the Archbishop of Canterbury); The Church of the Province of Melanesia; The Anglican Church of Mexico; The Church of the Province of Myanmar (Burma); The Church of Nigeria (Anglican Communion); The Church of North India; The Church of Pakistan; The Anglican Church of Papua New Guinea; The Episcopal Church in the Philippines; The Episcopal Church of Rwanda; The Scottish Episcopal Church; The Church of the Province of South East Asia; The Church of South India; The Anglican Church of Southern Africa; The Anglican Church of the Southern Cone of America; The Reformed Episcopal Church of Spain (Extra-Provincial to the Archbishop of Canterbury); The Episcopal Church of the Sudan; The Anglican Church of Tanzania; The Church of the Province of Uganda; The Episcopal Church in the United States of America; The Church in Wales; The Church of the Province of West Africa; and The Church in the Province of the West Indies. New provinces are also currently in formation. Churches in Communion include the Mar Thoma Syrian Church, the Philippine Independent Church, and some Lutheran and Old Catholic Churches in Europe. The Church in China is known as a 'post-denominational' Church whose formation included Anglicans in the Holy Catholic Church in China.

England and Wales. The established Church of England, which baptizes about 13% of infants born in England (i.e. excluding Wales but including the Isle of Man and the Channel Islands), is Anglican. Civil disabilities on account of religion do not attach to any class of British subject. Under the Welsh Church Acts, 1914 and 1919, the Church in Wales and Monmouthshire was disestablished as from 1 April 1920, and Wales was formed into a separate Province.

The Queen is, under God, the supreme governor of the Church of England, with the right, regulated by statute, to nominate to the vacant archbishoprics and bishoprics. The Queen, on the advice of the First Lord of the Treasury, also appoints to such deaneries, prebendaries and canonries as are in the gift of the Crown, while a large number of livings and also some canonries are in the gift of the Lord Chancellor.

There are two archbishops (at the head of the two Provinces of Canterbury and York), and 44 diocesan sees including the diocese in Europe, which is part of the Province of Canterbury. Dr Rowan Williams was enthroned as *Archbishop of Canterbury* in Feb. 2003. Each archbishop also has his own particular diocese, wherein he exercises episcopal, as in his Province he exercises metropolitan, jurisdiction. In Dec. 2008 there were 42 serving bishops, 64 suffragan and assistant bishops, 42 deans and provosts of cathedrals and 110 archdeacons. The *General Synod*, which replaced the Church Assembly in 1970 in England, consists of a House of Bishops, a House of Clergy and a House of Laity, and has power to frame legislation regarding Church matters. The first two Houses consist of the members of the Convocations of Canterbury and York, each of which consists of the diocesan bishops and elected representatives of the suffragan bishops, five for Canterbury province and three for York (forming an Upper House); deans and archdeacons, and a certain number of proctors elected as the representatives of the priests and deacons in each diocese, together with, in the case of Canterbury Convocation, four representatives of the Universities of Oxford, Cambridge, London and the Southern Universities, and in the case of York two representatives of the Universities of Durham and Newcastle and the other Northern Universities, and three archdeacons to the Armed Forces, the Chaplain General of Prisons and two representatives of the Religious Communities (forming the Lower House). The House of Laity is elected by the lay members of the Deanery Synods but also includes two representatives of the Religious Communities. The Houses of Clergy and Laity also include a small number of *ex officio* members. Every Measure passed by the General Synod must be submitted to the Ecclesiastical Committee, consisting of 15 members of the House of Lords nominated by the Lord Chancellor and 15 members of the House of Commons nominated by the Speaker. This committee reports on each Measure to Parliament, and the Measure receives the Royal Assent and becomes law if each House of Parliament resolves that the Measure be presented to the Queen.

Parochial affairs are managed by annual parochial church meetings and parochial church councils. In 2008 there were 12,702 ecclesiastical parishes, inclusive of the Isle of Man and the Channel Islands. These parishes do not, in many cases, coincide with civil parishes. Although most parishes have their own churches, not every parish nowadays can have its own incumbent or priest. About 3,290 non-stipendiary clergy hold a bishop's licence to officiate at services.

In 2008 there were 4,431 incumbents excluding dignitaries, 1,913 other clergy of incumbent status and 1,301 assistant curates working in the parishes.

Women have been admitted to Holy Orders (but not the Episcopate) as deacons since 1987 and as priests since 1994. At 31 Dec. 2008 there were 1,596 full-time stipendiary women clergy, 1,497 of whom were in the parochial ministry. Between 1993 and 2002, 495 clergymen resigned because they disagreed with the ordination of women. 67 clergymen subsequently re-entered the Church of England ministry and of the 495 who resigned, 258 are known to have joined the Roman Catholic Church and 29 the Orthodox Church.

Private persons possess the right of presentation to over 2,000 benefices; the patronage of the others belongs mainly to the Queen, the bishops and cathedrals, the Lord Chancellor, the colleges of the Universities of Oxford and Cambridge and other patronage trusts. More than 750 benefices include patronage trusts among their patrons. In addition to the dignitaries and parochial clergy already identified there were, in 2008, 143 cathedral and 342 full-time non-parochial clergy working within the diocesan framework, giving a total of 8,346 full-time stipendiary clergy working within the diocesan framework as at Dec. 2008. In addition there were 311 part-time stipendiary clergy. Although these figures account for the majority of active clergy in England, there are many others serving in institutions and elsewhere who cannot be quantified with any certainty. They include 1,609 chaplains in hospitals, the forces, prisons, schools and colleges, and those in mission agencies and religious communities.

Of the 40,474 buildings registered for the solemnization of marriages at 30 June 2005 (statistics from the Office of National Statistics), 16,426 belonged to the Church of England and the Church in Wales, and 24,048 to other religious denominations (Methodist, 6,463; Roman Catholic, 3,323; Baptist, 3,079; United Reformed, 1,615; Congregationalist, 1,250; Calvinistic Methodist, 1,067, Jehovah's Witnesses, 831; Brethren, 740; Salvation Army, 729; Unitarians, 164; other Christian, 4,247; Sikhs, 154; Muslims, 146; other non-Christian, 240). Of the 247,805 marriages celebrated in 2005 (331,150 in 1990), 61,155 were in the Established Church and the Church in Wales (115,328 in 1990), 24,481 in other denominations (43,837 in 1990) and 162,169 were civil marriages in Register Offices (156,875 in 1990).

The Roman Catholic population in England and Wales (the number of adherents) was estimated at 4,106,000 in 2004; 1,682,000 regularly attended Mass in the UK in 2005. There are 22 dioceses in five provinces and one Bishopric of the Forces (also covers Scotland). Vincent Nichols was installed as *Archbishop of Westminster* on 21 May 2009. In Feb. 2010 there were two Roman Catholic cardinals, one of whom is in Scotland. There are five archbishops, 17 other diocesan bishops and seven auxiliary or assistant bishops. There are 5,128 priests in active ministry and 2,799 parish churches. There are 1,250 convents of female religious, who number 8,450.

Membership of other denominations in the UK in 2005 (and 1975): Presbyterians, 876,970 (1·65m.); Methodists, 303,973 (0·61m.); Baptists, 199,171 (0·27m.); other Protestants, 298,744; independent churches, 171,993; Orthodox, 271,158 (0·2m.); Pentecostals (including Afro-Caribbean churches), 288,183;

Latter-day Saints (Mormons), 175,000; Jehovah's Witnesses, 128,333; Spiritualists, 30,000; Muslims, 893,700 active members (0·4m.); Sikhs, 184,000 active members (0·12m.); Hindus, 305,000 active members (0·1m.); Jews (2001), 267,373 (0·11m.).

In 2001 for the first time the census asked an optional question about religion. In England and Wales 37·3m. people described themselves as Christian. In England, 3·1% of the population stated their religion as Muslim, 1·1% Hindu, 0·7% Sikh, 0·5% Jewish and 0·3% Buddhist. In Wales, 0·7% of the population stated their religion as Muslim, 0·2% Buddhist, 0·2% Hindu, 0·1% Jewish and 0·1% Sikh. In England and Wales 7·7m. people said they had no religion (14·6% in England and 18·5% in Wales). Just over 4m. people chose not to answer the religion question.

In Scotland the 2001 census asked two questions on religion—religion of upbringing and current religion. For religion of upbringing, the largest groups were Church of Scotland (47%), no religion (18%) and Roman Catholic (17%). The equivalent percentages for current religion were 42%, 28% and 16%.

Across all denominations, adult church attendance in Great Britain was 6·5% of the population in 2005.

The Salvation Army is an international Christian church working in 109 countries. In 2004 in the UK it had 821 local church centres and 92 social service centres with 4,545 employees and 1,507 active Salvation Army officers (ministers).

There is a 400-member Board of Deputies of British Jews.

In 2005 there were approximately 1·05m. visits to Canterbury Cathedral, 1·03m. to Westminster Abbey, London, 803,000 visits to York Minster and 729,000 to St Paul's Cathedral, London.

See also SCOTLAND *and* NORTHERN IRELAND.

Bradley, I., *Marching to the Promised Land: Has the Church a Future?* 1992
De La Noy, M., *The Church of England: a Portrait.* 1993

CULTURE

World Heritage Sites

Sites under UK jurisdiction which appear on UNESCO's World Heritage List are (with year entered on list): Giant's Causeway and Causeway Coast (1986), rock formations on the Antrim Plateau in Northern Ireland; Durham Castle and Cathedral (1986 and 2008), the largest example of a Norman cathedral; Ironbridge Gorge (1986), built in the 18th century and considered the emblem of the industrial revolution; Studley Royal Park, including the Ruins of Fountains Abbey (1986), developed from the 18th century on the site of a former Cistercian abbey in Yorkshire; Stonehenge, Avebury and Associated Sites (1986 and 2008), among the world's most famous pre-historic monoliths; Castles and Town Walls of King Edward in Gwynedd (1986), a testament to the early period of English colonization in the late 13th century; St Kilda (1986, 2004 and 2005), a volcanic archipelago on the coast of the Hebrides; Blenheim Palace (1987), seat of the Dukes of Marlborough near Oxford and birthplace of Sir Winston Churchill; City of Bath (1987), with remains from its time as a Roman spa town, and home to many examples of neo-classical Georgian architecture; Westminster Palace, Westminster Abbey and Saint Margaret's Church (1987 and 2008)—the palace is the medieval seat of parliament rebuilt in the 19th century, the abbey the site of all coronations since the 11th century and Saint Margaret's is a small medieval gothic church; Henderson Island (1988), a South Pacific atoll; Tower of London (1988), a Norman fortress built to guard London; Canterbury Cathedral, St Augustine's Abbey and St Martin's Church (1988), the spiritual seat of the Church of England; Old and New Towns of Edinburgh (1995), the Scottish capital; Gough and Inaccessible Islands (1995 and 2004), two of the least disturbed islands and marine eco-systems in the South Atlantic; Maritime Greenwich (1997), including Britain's first Palladian building, designed by Inigo Jones, Christopher Wren's Royal Naval College and the Royal Observatory; Heart of Neolithic Orkney (1999), comprising several important neolithic monuments; Historic Town of St George's and Related Fortifications, Bermuda (2000), an example of early English New World colonialism; Blaenavon Industrial Landscape (2000), a symbol of South Wales' role as a coal and iron provider in the 19th century; Dorset and East Devon Coast (2001), which demonstrate rock formations and fossil remains from the Mesozoic Era; Derwent Valley Mills (2001), 18th-century cotton mills at the forefront of the Industrial Revolution; New Lanark (2001), Robert Owen's model industrial community and cotton mills of the early 19th century; Saltaire (2001), a mid-19th century planned industrial community for the textile industry; Royal Botanical Gardens, Kew (2003), containing important botanical collections in a historic landscape; Liverpool—Maritime Mercantile City (2004); the Cornwall and West Devon mining landscape (2006); and the Pontcysyllte Aqueduct and Canal near Wrexham (2009), a feat of civil engineering by Thomas Telford during the Industrial Revolution.

The UK also shares the Frontiers of the Roman Empire sites (1987, 2005 and 2008) with Germany, containing the border line of the Roman Empire at its greatest extent in the 2nd century AD (specifically Hadrian's Wall).

Broadcasting

Radio and television services are provided by the British Broadcasting Corporation (BBC), by licensees of the Office of Communications (Ofcom) and by the Welsh-language Sianel Pedwar Cymru (S4C, Channel 4 Wales). The BBC, constituted by Royal Charter, has responsibility for providing domestic and external broadcast services, the former financed from the television licence revenue, the latter by government grant. The domestic services provided by the BBC include eight national television services, ten national radio network services and a network of local radio stations. Government proposals for the future of the BBC after 2006 were published in March 2005.

Ofcom is responsible for licensing and regulating all non-BBC TV services (except S4C), provided in and from the UK whether analogue or digital. These include ITV1 (regional and breakfast-time licensees), Channel 4, Channel 5, cable and satellite and additional services, such as teletext. Ofcom is also responsible for licensing and regulating independent and national, local and community radio services. S4C is transmitted in Wales, and is funded by the government. The Welsh Authority is the regulator and board of management of S4C.

The BBC's domestic radio services are available on Long Wave, Medium Wave and VHF/FM; those licensed by Ofcom on Medium Wave and VHF/FM. Television services other than those only on cable and satellite are broadcast at UHF in 625-line definition and in colour (by PAL). The BBC World Service, which started life in 1932 as the Empire Service, broadcasts in English and 31 other languages to over 180m. listeners. As the self-financed BBC Worldwide TV, the BBC is also involved in commercial joint ventures to provide international television services.

The broadcasting authorities are independent of government and are publicly accountable to Parliament for the discharge of their responsibilities. Their duties and powers are laid down in the BBC Royal Charter and the Communications Act 2003.

All independent (non-BBC) radio and television services other than S4C are financed by the sale of broadcasting advertising time, commercial sponsorship, subscription (in the case of cable and satellite services) and ancillary services, such as sales of goods and products, interactive services and pay-per-view revenues.

Ofcom became the new communications sector regulator at the end of 2003, taking over from the Broadcasting Standards Commission (BSC), the Independent Television Commission (ITC), Oftel, the Radio Authority and the Radiocommunications Agency. The aims of Ofcom are: to balance the promotion of choice and competition with the duty to foster plurality, informed citizenship, protect viewers, listeners and customers and promote cultural diversity; serve the interests of the citizen-consumer as the communications industry enters the digital age; support the need for innovators, creators and investors to flourish within markets driven by full and fair competition between all providers; and to encourage the evolution of electronic media and communications networks to the greater benefit of all who live in the UK.

The number of television receiving licences in force on 31 March 2008 was 24,740,000, of which 24,706,000 were for colour and 34,000 for black and white only. NTL and Telewest, the two largest cable TV companies, merged in 2005 to form NTL Telewest (subsequently rebranded as Virgin Media in 2007). There were 10·6m. pay-TV digital subscribers in 2006 (7·7m. with Sky and 2·8m. with NTL Telewest). Freeview, a free-to-view digital TV service, was launched in 2002 and by 2006 had 6·4m. subscribers. The government has announced that analogue television broadcasting will end in 2012. In 2008, 80% of households received digital TV.

Cinema

In 2008 there were 726 cinemas in the UK (727 in 2007) with 3,610 screens (3,514 in 2007) including 310 digital screens. Admissions were 164·2m. in 2008. Admissions reached a high of 1·6bn. in 1946, but had fallen as low as 54m. in 1984. Gross box office takings in 2008 amounted to £850m. (£821m. in 2007). In 2008, 527 films were released in the UK and Ireland and 111 films were produced in the UK (including USA/UK films and UK co-productions).

Press

In Feb. 2010 there were ten national dailies with a combined average daily circulation of 9,844,247, and ten national Sunday newspapers (9,728,689). In Dec. 2008 there were also 124 morning, evening and Sunday regional newspapers and 1,145 weeklies (624 of these for free distribution). In 2006 there were about 6,500 other commercial periodicals and 5,142 professional and business journals. In 2005 the number of daily national newspapers sold per annum was 3·8bn., down more than 20% from 5bn. in 1962. The most widely read daily is the tabloid *The Sun*, with an average daily circulation of 2,972,763 in Feb. 2010. The most widely read Sunday paper is the tabloid *News of the World*, which had an average circulation of 2,993,709 in Feb. 2010.

In Jan. 1991 the Press Complaints Commission replaced the former Press Council. It has 15 members and a chair (Baroness Buscombe), including five editors. It is funded by the newspaper industry.

In 2008 a total of 120,947 book titles were published in the UK (115,420 in 2007).

Tourism

In 2008 UK residents made 117·7m. trips within the UK, passing 378·4m. nights in accommodation and spending £21,107m. Of these, 75·4m. were holidaymakers spending £14,100m. Visits from foreign tourists to the UK totalled 32·0m. in 2008 (down from a record 32·8m. in 2007). Spending was £16·4bn. in 2008. In 2007 the UK ranked sixth in the international tourism earnings league behind the USA, Spain, France, Italy and China. The main countries of origin for foreign visitors in 2008 were: France (3·6m.), Ireland (3·1m.), USA (3·0m.), Germany (2·9m.) and Spain (2·0m.).

The leading free admission attraction in 2005 was Blackpool Pleasure Beach, Lancs, with an estimated 6·0m. visits. The leading tourist attractions charging admission in 2005 were: the British Airways London Eye, with 3·2m. visits; Xscape Castleford, a sport and leisure activity centre, with an estimated 3·2m.; the Tower of London, with 1·9m.; Flamingo Land Theme Park in Malton, N. Yorks, with an estimated 1·4m.; and Pleasure Beach in Great Yarmouth, with an estimated 1·4m.

In June 2008 there were 1·5m. (not seasonally adjusted) people working in tourism-related industries.

UK residents made 68·8m. trips abroad in 2008 (39·6m. in 1994). Spain is the most popular destination for Britons travelling abroad for leisure (26·6% of holidays taken abroad by UK residents in 2008), followed by France (16·7%), the USA (5·4%) and Italy (5·2%).

Festivals

Among the most famous music festivals are the Promenade Concerts or 'Proms', which take place at the Royal Albert Hall in London every year from July to Sept; the Glyndebourne season in Sussex (May to Aug.); the Aldeburgh Festival in Suffolk (June); the Glastonbury Festival in Somerset (June); and the Buxton Festival in Derbyshire (July). The annual London Film Festival takes place in Oct. Literary festivals include the Oxford Literary Festival in March, the Hay Festival at Hay-on-Wye in Powys (late May/early June) and the Cheltenham Festival of Literature in Gloucestershire (Oct.). The Edinburgh Festival and the Fringe Festival both take place in Aug./early Sept. and are major international festivals of culture. The Brighton Festival in May is England's largest arts festival. The multicultural Notting Hill Carnival in London takes place at the end of Aug. Other major events in the annual calendar are the New Year's Day Parade in London, the Crufts Dog Show at the Birmingham National Exhibition Centre (March), the Ideal Home Exhibition in London (March–April), the London Marathon (April), the Chelsea Flower Show (May), Royal Ascot (horse racing, in June), Wimbledon (tennis, in June–July), Henley Royal Regatta (July), Cowes (yachting, in Aug.) and the Lord Mayor's Show in London (Nov.).

Libraries

In 2007–08 there were 4,540 public libraries, six national libraries and 941 academic libraries (2006–07); in 2006–07 the public and academic libraries held a combined 219,800,000 volumes. There were 328,485,000 visits to public libraries in 2007–08.

Museums and Galleries

The museums with the highest number of visitors are all in London. In 2006 there were 4,915,376 visits to the Tate Modern, 4,837,878 to the British Museum, 4,562,471 to the National Gallery, 3,754,496 to the Natural History Museum and 2,440,253 to the Science Museum.

DIPLOMATIC REPRESENTATIVES

Of the USA in Great Britain (24/31 Grosvenor Sq., London, W1A 1AE)
Ambassador: Louis B. Susman.

Of Great Britain in the USA (3100 Massachusetts Ave., NW, Washington, D.C., 20008)
Ambassador: Sir Nigel Sheinwald, KCMG.

Of Great Britain to the United Nations
Ambassador: Sir Mark Lyall Grant.

Of Great Britain to the European Union
Permanent Representative: Kim Darroch, CMG.

FURTHER READING

Office for National Statistics titles are published by Palgrave Macmillan, Basingstoke. The Stationery Office (TSO) publishes most other government publications.

Annual Abstract of Statistics.—Monthly Digest of Statistics.—Social Trends.—Regional Trends.

Central Office of Information. *The Monarchy.* 1992

Directory of British Associations. Annual

Bache, Ian and Jordan, Andrew, *The Europeanization of British Politics.* 2006

Beech, Matt and Lee, Simon, (eds.) *Ten Years of New Labour.* 2008

Black, Jeremy, *A History of the British Isles.* 2nd ed. 2002

Bogdanor, Vernon, *Devolution in the United Kingdom.* 1999.—*The New British Constitution.* 2009

Bourke, Richard, *Peace in Ireland: The War of Ideas.* 2003

Cairncross, A., *The British Economy Since 1945: Economic Policy and Performance, 1945–1995.* 2nd ed. 1995
Casey, Terence, (ed.) *The Blair Legacy: Politics, Policy, Governance, and Foreign Affairs.* 2009
Davies, Norman, *The Isles: A History.* 1999
Dunleavy, Patrick, Cowley, Philip, Heffernan, Richard and Hay, Colin (eds.) *Developments in British Politics 8.* 2006
Gascoigne, B. (ed.) *Encyclopedia of Britain.* 1994
Harbury, C. D. and Lipsey, R. G., *Introduction to the UK Economy.* 4th ed. 1993
Irwin, J. L., *Modern Britain: an Introduction.* 3rd ed. 1994
Kellner, Peter, *Democracy: 1,000 Years in Pursuit of British Liberty.* 2009
Leese, Peter, *Britain Since 1945.* 2006
Leventhal, F. M. (ed.) *20th-Century Britain: an Encyclopedia.* 1995
Marquand, David, *Britain Since 1918: The Strange Career of British Democracy.* 2008
Marr, A., *Ruling Britannia: the Failure and Future of British Democracy.* 1995
McCormick, John, *Contemporary Britain.* 2nd ed. 2007
Neumann, Peter R., *Britain's Long War: British Strategy in the Northern Ireland Conflict, 1969–98.* 2003
Oakland, John, *British Civilization: an Introduction.* 6th ed. 2003
Oxford History of the British Empire. 2 vols. 1999
Palmer, A. and Palmer, V., *The Chronology of British History.* 1995
Penguin History of Britain. 9 vols. 1996
Robbins, Keith, *A Bibliography of British History 1914–1989.* 1996
Sked, A. and Cook, C., *Post-War Britain: a Political History.* 4th ed. 1993
Speck, W. A., *A Concise History of Britain, 1707–1975.* 1993
Wall, Stephen, *A Stranger in Europe: Britain and the EU from Thatcher to Blair.* 2008

Other more specialized titles are listed under TERRITORY AND POPULATION; CONSTITUTION AND GOVERNMENT; ARMY; NAVY; BANKING AND FINANCE; ELECTRICITY; TRADE UNIONS; RELIGION; *and* WELFARE, *above. See also Further Reading in Scotland, Wales and Northern Ireland.*

National Statistical Office: UK Statistics Authority, Statistics House, Tredegar Park, Newport, Gwent, NP10 8XG. *National Statistician:* Jil Matheson.

Website: http://www.statistics.gov.uk

ENGLAND

KEY HISTORICAL EVENTS

Emperor Claudius' invasion in AD 43 established Roman rule in southern England. After the failed rebellions in AD 60 of Queen Boudicca of the Iceni and the suppression of Wales by AD 78, there was a long period of peaceful settlement, during which the Romans established new towns such as Londinium (London) and Eboracum (York). After the withdrawal of the Roman legions in the early 5th century, Pictish and Saxon raiders harassed the British towns. Defensive Saxon settlements were at first encouraged by the authorities but their rebellion soon threatened the Roman way of life. The Romano-British were pushed back to higher land in the west by waves of invading Saxons, Angles and Jutes. After a period of Mercian supremacy under Offa in the 8th century, the West Saxons (Wessex) dominated southern England. Danish invasions in 865 established the Danelaw in northern England. Alfred the Great of Wessex and his son Edward resisted Danish expansion, strengthening Anglo-Saxon unity under Alfred's successors—Athelstan became the first king of all England in 927.

Danish rule over England was reasserted by Sweyn in 994 and his son, Canute. The Anglo-Saxon restoration was short-lived; William, duke of Normandy led the Norman Conquest in 1066, defeating Harold II at the Battle of Hastings. When William died in 1087, he left Normandy to his eldest son Robert, thus separating it from England. Henry II, the founder of the Plantagenet dynasty, was feudatory lord of half of France but Henry's son John lost most of the French possessions. The barons forced John to sign the Magna Carta in 1215, later interpreted as the source of English civil liberties. Thereafter, the Norman baronage came to regard themselves as English.

The Hundred Years War (1338–1453) with France ended with the loss of all remaining French possessions except Calais. In 1387 and in later outbreaks, the Black Death reduced the population by over a third. A dynastic struggle between the rival houses of York and Lancaster was concluded by the invasion of Henry Tudor in 1485. His son, Henry VIII, asserted royal authority over the church, breaking with Rome. Tudor power reached its zenith with Elizabeth I. Philip II's Spanish Armada, destroyed in 1588, was sent to turn back the Protestant tide in England and to counter English ambitions in the New World.

The accession of James VI of Scotland to the English throne in 1603 brought the two countries into personal union. Charles I's defeat in the Civil War resulted in a republican Commonwealth but the Stuart monarchy was restored in 1660. England and Scotland were united in 1707 under Anne, queen of Great Britain.

TERRITORY AND POPULATION

At the census taken on 29 April 2001 the area of England was 130,281 sq. km and the population 49,138,831, giving a density of 377 per sq. km. England covers 53·7% of the total area of the United Kingdom. Households at the 2001 census: 21,262,000. Estimated population of England, mid-2008, 51,446,200 (26,127,500 females and 25,318,800 males).

Population (present on census night) at the four previous decennial censuses:

1961	*1971*	*1981*	*1991*
43,460,525[1]	46,018,371[1]	46,226,100[2]	46,382,050

[1]Area now included in Wales formed the English county of Monmouthshire until 1974. [2]The final count is believed to be over-stated as a result of an error in processing. The preliminary counts presented here rounded to the nearest hundred are thought to be more accurate.

Population at census day 2001:

Males	*Females*	*Total*
23,923,390	25,215,441	49,138,831

For further statistical information, *see under* Territory and Population, United Kingdom.

The population on census day in 2001 in the nine English Government Office regions (created in 1994) was as follows: East, 5,388,154; East Midlands, 4,172,179; London, 7,172,036; North East, 2,515,479; North West, 6,730,800; South East, 8,000,550; South West, 4,928,458; West Midlands, 5,267,337; Yorkshire and the Humber, 4,965,838.

Following the local government reorganization in the mid-1990s, there is a mixed pattern to local government in England. Apart from Greater London, England is divided into 27 counties with two tiers of administration; a county council and district councils. There are six metropolitan county areas containing 36 single-tier metropolitan districts.

In addition, there are 56 single-tier unitary authorities which, with the exception of the Isle of Wight, were formerly district councils in the shire counties of England. The Isle of Wight is a unitary county council. The Isles of Scilly have a unitary council but are considered a district of 'Cornwall and the Isles of Scilly'.

As a consequence of the establishment of the 56 unitary authorities, a number of county areas were abolished. These were Avon, Cleveland and Humberside. Berkshire County Council was also abolished but the county itself is retained for ceremonial purposes. Greater London comprises 32 boroughs and the City of London.

Area in sq. km of English counties and unitary authorities, and population at census day 2001:

	Area (sq. km)	*Population*
Metropolitan counties		
Greater Manchester	1,276	2,482,352
Merseyside	645	1,362,034
South Yorkshire	1,552	1,266,337
Tyne and Wear	540	1,075,979
West Midlands	902	2,555,596
West Yorkshire	2,029	2,079,217
Non-metropolitan counties		
Bedfordshire (Beds)[1]	1,192	381,571
Buckinghamshire (Bucks)	1,565	479,028
Cambridgeshire (Camb)	3,046	552,655
Cheshire[2]	2,083	673,777
Cornwall and Isles of Scilly[3]	3,563	501,267
Cumbria	6,768	487,607
Derbyshire	2,547	734,581
Devon	6,564	704,499
Dorset	2,542	390,986
Durham[4]	2,226	493,470
East Sussex	1,709	492,324
Essex	3,465	1,310,922
Gloucestershire (Gloucs)	2,653	564,559
Hampshire (Hants)	3,679	1,240,032
Hertfordshire (Herts)	1,643	1,033,977
Kent	3,544	1,329,653
Lancashire (Lancs)	2,903	1,134,976
Leicestershire (Leics)	2,083	609,579
Lincolnshire (Lincs)	5,921	646,646
Norfolk	5,371	796,733
Northamptonshire (Northants)	2,364	629,676
Northumberland[5]	5,013	307,186
North Yorkshire (N. Yorks)	8,038	569,660
Nottinghamshire (Notts)	2,085	748,503
Oxfordshire (Oxon)	2,605	605,492
Shropshire (Salop)[6]	3,197	283,240
Somerset (Som)	3,451	498,093
Staffordshire (Staffs)	2,620	806,737
Suffolk	3,801	668,548
Surrey	1,663	1,059,015
Warwickshire	1,975	505,885
West Sussex	1,991	753,612
Wiltshire (Wilts)[7]	3,255	432,973
Worcestershire	1,741	542,107

	Area (sq. km)	*Population*
Unitary Authorities		
Bath and North East Somerset	346	169,045
Blackburn with Darwen	137	137,471
Blackpool	35	142,284
Bournemouth	46	163,441
Bracknell Forest	109	109,606
Brighton and Hove	83	247,820
Bristol, City of	110	380,615
Darlington	197	97,822
Derby	78	221,716
East Riding of Yorkshire	2,408	314,076
Halton	79	118,215
Hartlepool	94	88,629
Herefordshire, County of	2,180	174,844
Isle of Wight	380	132,719
Kingston upon Hull, City of	71	243,595
Leicester	73	279,923
Luton	43	184,390
Medway	192	249,502
Middlesbrough	54	134,847
Milton Keynes	309	207,063
North East Lincolnshire	192	157,983
North Lincolnshire	846	152,839
North Somerset	374	188,556
Nottingham	75	266,995
Peterborough	343	156,060
Plymouth	80	240,718
Poole	65	138,299
Portsmouth	40	186,704
Reading	40	143,214
Redcar and Cleveland	245	139,141
Rutland	382	34,560
Slough	33	119,070
South Gloucestershire	497	245,644
Southampton	50	217,478
Southend-on-Sea	42	160,256
Stockton-on-Tees	204	178,405
Stoke-on-Trent	93	240,643
Swindon	230	180,061
Telford and Wrekin	290	158,285
Thurrock	163	143,042
Torbay	63	129,702
Warrington	181	191,084
West Berkshire	704	144,445
Windsor and Maidenhead	197	133,606
Wokingham	179	150,257
York	272	181,131

[1]Status since changed with creation of two unitary authorities—Bedford Borough and Central Bedfordshire—in April 2009. [2]Status since changed with creation of two unitary authorities—Cheshire East, and Cheshire West & Chester—in April 2009. [3]Status of Cornwall and the Isles of Scilly since changed with creation of a unitary authority—Cornwall Council—in April 2009. The Isles of Scilly already had a unitary authority. [4]Status of County Durham since changed with creation of a unitary authority in April 2009. [5]Status of Northumberland since changed with creation of a unitary authority in April 2009. [6]Status of Shropshire since changed with creation of a unitary authority in April 2009. [7]Status of Wiltshire since changed with creation of a unitary authority in April 2009.

Source: Office of National Statistics

In 2008 London had a population of 7,619,800. Populations of next largest cities in 2008 were: Birmingham, 1,016,800; Leeds, 770,800; Sheffield, 534,500; Bradford, 501,700; Manchester, 464,200; Liverpool, 434,900; Bristol, 421,300.

Greater London Boroughs. Total area 1,572 sq. km. Population at census day 2001: 7,172,036 (inner London, 2,765,975). Population by borough (census day 2001):

Barking and Dagenham	163,944	Islington[1]	175,787
Barnet	314,561	Kensington and Chelsea[1]	158,922
Bexley	218,307	Kingston upon Thames	147,295
Brent	263,463	Lambeth[1]	266,170
Bromley	295,530	Lewisham[1]	248,924
Camden[1]	198,027	Merton	187,908
Croydon	330,688	Newham[1]	243,737
Ealing	300,947	Redbridge	238,628
Enfield	273,563	Richmond upon Thames	172,327
Greenwich	214,540	Southwark[1]	244,867
Hackney[1]	202,819	Sutton	179,667
Hammersmith and Fulham[1]	165,243	Tower Hamlets[1]	196,121
Haringey[1]	216,510	Waltham Forest	218,277
Harrow	207,389	Wandsworth[1]	260,383
Havering	224,248	Westminster, City of[1]	181,279
Hillingdon	242,435		
Hounslow	212,344		

[1]Inner London borough.

Source: Office of National Statistics

The City of London (677 acres) is administered by its Corporation which retains some independent powers. Population at census day 2001: 7,186.

CLIMATE

For more detailed information, *see under* Climate, United Kingdom.

London, Jan. 39°F (3·9°C), July 64°F (17·8°C). Annual rainfall 25" (635 mm). Birmingham, Jan. 38°F (3·3°C), July 61°F (16·1°C). Annual rainfall 30" (749 mm). Manchester, Jan. 39°F (3·9°C), July 61°F (16·1°C). Annual rainfall 34·5" (876 mm).

CONSTITUTION AND GOVERNMENT

The Parliamentary electorate of England in the register in Dec. 2009 numbered 38,129,082.

RECENT ELECTIONS

At the UK general election held in May 2010, 532 members were returned from England. Voting in Thirsk and Malton was postponed owing to the death of a candidate. A by-election was subsequently scheduled for 27 May 2010.

See also Constitution and Government, Recent Elections *and* Current Administration in United Kingdom.

DEFENCE

For information on defence, *see* United Kingdom.

ECONOMY

For information on the economy, *see* United Kingdom.

ENERGY AND NATURAL RESOURCES

For information on energy and natural resources, *see* United Kingdom.

Environment

35·5% of household waste was recycled in 2007–08.

Water

The Water Act of Sept. 1989 privatized the nine water and sewerage authorities in England: Anglian; North West (now United Utilities Water plc); Northumbrian; Severn Trent; South West; Southern; Thames; Wessex; Yorkshire. There are also 16 water only companies in England and Wales. The Act also inaugurated the National Rivers Authority, with environmental and resource management responsibilities, and the 'regulator' *Office of Water Services (Ofwat)*, charged with protecting consumer interests.

INDUSTRY

Labour

The unemployment rate in the spring of 2006 was 5·3%, compared to 5·2% for the UK as a whole. Unemployment was lowest in the southwest (3·6%) and highest in London (7·7%).

INTERNATIONAL TRADE

For information on international trade, *see* United Kingdom.

COMMUNICATIONS

For information on communications, *see* United Kingdom.

Shipping

Total cargo handled in 2004 was 379·2m. tonnes.

SOCIAL INSTITUTIONS

Education

For details on the nature and types of school, *see under* Education, United Kingdom.

In 2006–07 education expenditure by central and local government in England was just under £58bn.

In Jan. 2008 there were 445 public sector and two direct grant nursery schools in England with provision for children under five. In 2008 there were 37,380 pupils under five attending public sector nursery schools. Some of these children were attending part-time.

In Jan. 2008 there were 4,087,790 pupils at 17,205 primary schools in England. Nearly all primary schools take both boys and girls. Almost 15% of primary schools had 100 full-time pupils or fewer.

In Jan. 2008 there were 320 middle schools deemed either primary or secondary according to the age range of the school concerned.

In Jan. 2008 there were 3,383 state-funded secondary schools in England (including City Technology Colleges and Academies). Some local authorities continue to operate a selective admissions policy at age 11, as do 164 state-funded secondary schools in England. There were 172 secondary modern schools in 2006, providing a general education up to the minimum school leaving age of 16, although some pupils stay on beyond that age.

Almost all local education authorities operate a system of comprehensive schools to which pupils are admitted without reference to ability or aptitude. In Jan. 2008 there were 2,704 such schools in England with almost 2·8m. pupils. With the development of comprehensive education, various patterns of secondary schools have come into operation. Principally these are: 1) All-through schools with pupils aged 11 to 18 or 11 to 16; pupils over 16 being able to transfer to an 11 to 18 school or a sixth form college providing for pupils aged 16 to 19—there are currently 98 sixth form colleges in England; 2) Local authorities operating a three-tier system involving middle schools where transfer to secondary school is at ages 12, 13 or 14. These correspond to 12 to 18, 13 to 18 and 14 to 18 comprehensive schools respectively; or 3) In areas where there are no middle schools a two-tier system of junior and senior comprehensive schools for pupils aged 11 to 18 with optional transfer to these schools at age 13 or 14.

Under the Education Act 1996 children have special educational needs if they have a learning difficulty which calls for special educational provision to be made for them. In some cases the local authority will need to make a statutory assessment of special educational needs under the Education Act 1996, which may ultimately lead to a 'statement'. In England the total number of pupils with statements in 2008 was 223,600. In 2008 there were 993 maintained special schools and 72 non-maintained special schools.

Outside the state system of education there were 2,327 independent schools (excluding direct grant nursery schools) in England in Jan. 2008, ranging from large prestigious schools to small local ones. Some provide boarding facilities but the majority include non-resident day pupils. There are about 582,330 pupils in these schools, which represent about 7% of the total pupil population in England.

Further Education (Non-University). In 2006–07, 4·2m. students were enrolled at FE colleges in England and around 6m. in the sector as a whole. Total funding for the FE sector in 2006–07 was £4·8bn.

Higher Education. As of Aug. 2008 there were 132 higher education institutions in England, of which 91 were universities. The main funding body is the Higher Education Funding Council for England (HEFCE), which distributes public money for teaching and research to universities and colleges. It works in partnership with the higher education sector and advises government on higher education policy. In 2008–09 HEFCE distributed a total of £7·48bn., including £4·63bn. for teaching and £1·46bn. for research.

a) *Universities*

Name (Location)	*No. of students (2007–08)*	*No. of academic staff (2005–06)*
Anglia Ruskin University (Chelmsford)	19,005	1,150
Aston University (Birmingham)	9,570	470
University of Bath	12,965	1,420
Bath Spa University	7,470	330
University of Bedfordshire	14,195	370
University of Birmingham	28,240	2,465
Birmingham City University	23,765	1,750
University of Bolton	8,590	270
Bournemouth University (Poole)	17,875	740
University of Bradford	12,375	870
University of Brighton	21,220	1,320
University of Bristol	21,740	2,320
Brunel University (Uxbridge)	14,265	1,185
Buckinghamshire New University	9,380	570
University of Cambridge[1]	22,745	3,945
Canterbury Christ Church University	15,545	535
University of Central Lancashire (Preston)	31,245	1,170
University of Chester	13,515	490
University of Chichester	4,805	345
City University (London)	21,410	1,660
Coventry University	20,505	1,090
University for the Creative Arts (Canterbury, Epsom, Farnham, Maidstone and Rochester)	7,755	240

Name (Location)	No. of students (2007–08)	No. of academic staff (2005–06)
University of Cumbria (Carlisle)	12,045	530[2]
De Montfort University (Leicester)	21,215	1,430
University of Derby	22,865	1,005
University of Durham	16,275	1,205
University of East Anglia (Norwich)	15,695	1,475
University of East London	19,430	650
Edge Hill University (Ormskirk)	20,140	735
University of Essex (Colchester)	11,510	980
University of Exeter	14,705	1,045
University of Gloucestershire (Cheltenham)	8,920	625
University of Greenwich (London)	24,505	1,010
University of Hertfordshire (Hatfield)	23,005	1,515
University of Huddersfield	20,430	1,305
University of Hull	21,005	950
Imperial College London	13,845	3,175
Keele University (Newcastle-under-Lyme)	11,415	705
University of Kent (Canterbury)	17,805	1,240
Kingston University (Kingston upon Thames)	24,135	1,510
University of Lancaster	13,720	1,395
University of Leeds	32,250	2,675
Leeds Metropolitan University	41,245	1,495
University of Leicester	15,355	1,260
University of Lincoln	16,115	670
University of Liverpool	19,380	1,950
Liverpool Hope University	7,110	285
Liverpool John Moores University	24,445	1,235
University of London[1]	123,080	16,965[3]
London Metropolitan University	28,525	1,050
London South Bank University	23,225	800
Loughborough University	17,650	1,530
University of Manchester	37,360	3,960
Manchester Metropolitan University	33,155	2,015
Middlesex University (London)	21,625	845
University of Newcastle upon Tyne	19,050	2,295
University of Northampton	11,585	480
University of Northumbria at Newcastle	30,470	1,080
University of Nottingham	31,830	2,745
Nottingham Trent University	23,845	1,460
Open University[4]	181,695	7,645
University of Oxford[1]	23,985	4,190
Oxford Brookes University	18,385	1,240
University of Plymouth	29,375	1,110
University of Portsmouth	19,805	1,240
University of Reading	14,470	1,210
Roehampton University	8,235	595
University of Salford	19,180	1,465
University of Sheffield	24,560	2,595
Sheffield Hallam University	31,090	1,750
University of Southampton	23,765	2,300
Southampton Solent University	18,170	645
Staffordshire University (Stoke-on-Trent)	15,735	745
University of Sunderland	17,820	880
University of Surrey (Guildford)	15,070	1,100
University of Sussex (Brighton)	12,450	1,455
University of Teesside (Middlesbrough)	26,210	655
Thames Valley University (London)	18,135	1,170
University of Warwick (Coventry)	28,445	1,815
University of the West of England, Bristol	31,700	1.630
University of Westminster (London)	23,225	1,650
University of Winchester	5,235	360
University of Wolverhampton	21,305	1,020
University of Worcester	7,765	335
University of York	13,185	1,305
York St John University	6,205	235

[1]See listing of colleges below. [2]Excluding staff of the former Carlisle and Penrith campuses of the University of Central Lancashire. [3]Excluding Imperial College London, which became independent of the University of London in July 2007. [4]Entirely distance learning—see page 1298.

b) *University of Cambridge; University of London; University of Oxford*

University of Cambridge Colleges:
Christ's College; Churchill College; Clare College; Clare Hall; Corpus Christi College; Darwin College; Downing College; Emmanuel College; Fitzwilliam College; Girton College; Gonville and Caius College; Homerton College; Hughes Hall; Jesus College; King's College; Lucy Cavendish; Magdalene College; New Hall; Newnham College; Pembroke College; Peterhouse; Queen's College; Robinson College; St Catharine's College; St Edmund's College; St John's College; Selwyn College; Sidney Sussex College; Trinity College; Trinity Hall; Wolfson College.

University of London Colleges (no. of full-time equivalent students/ academic staff 2005–06):
Birkbeck (17,225/578); Central School of Speech and Drama (880/ NA); Courtauld Institute of Art (440/33); Goldsmiths College (7,605/435); Heythrop College (745/40); Institute of Cancer Research (300/511); Institute of Education (7,385/308); King's College London (21,110/2,537); London Business School (1,555/113); London School of Economics and Political Science (9,105/828); London School of Hygiene and Tropical Medicine (1,100/398); Queen Mary, University of London (13,610/1,348); Royal Academy of Music (730/86); Royal Holloway, University of London (8,385/1,065); Royal Veterinary College (1,795/187); St George's Hospital Medical School (4,160/448); School of Oriental and African Studies (4,730/411); School of Pharmacy (1,230/110); University College London (20,990/3,898). In 2005–06 the University of London had 36,000 external programme students.

University of Oxford Colleges:
All Souls College; Balliol College; Brasenose College; Christ Church; Corpus Christi College; Exeter College; Green Templeton College; Harris Manchester College; Hertford College; Jesus College; Keble College; Kellogg College; Lady Margaret Hall; Linacre College; Lincoln College; Magdalen College; Mansfield College; Merton College; New College; Nuffield College; Oriel College; Pembroke College; The Queen's College; St Anne's College; St Antony's College; St Catherine's College; St Cross College; St Edmund Hall; St Hilda's College; St Hugh's College; St John's College; St Peter's College; Somerville College; Trinity College; University College; Wadham College; Wolfson College; Worcester College. *Permanent Private Halls:* Blackfriars; Campion Hall; Greyfriars; Regent's Park College; St Benet's Hall; St Stephen's House; Wycliffe Hall.

c) *Colleges of Art, Dance, Drama and Music*
2007–08: Arts Institute at Bournemouth; Conservatoire for Dance and Drama (London)[1]; Guildhall School of Music and Drama (London); Leeds College of Music; Liverpool Institute for Performing Arts; University of the Arts, London; Norwich University College of the Arts; Ravensbourne College of Design and Communication (Bromley); Rose Bruford College of Theatre & Performance (Sidcup); Royal College of Art (London); Royal College of Music (London); Royal Northern College of Music (Manchester); Trinity Laban (London).

[1]Affiliate schools: Bristol Old Vic Theatre School; Central School of Ballet; The Circus Space; London Academy of Music and Dramatic Art; London Contemporary Dance School; Northern School of Contemporary Dance; Rambert School of Ballet and Contemporary Dance; The Royal Academy of Dramatic Art.

d) *Other Institutions*
2007–08: University College Birmingham; Bishop Grosseteste College Lincoln; Cranfield University[1]; University College Falmouth Incorporating Dartington College of Arts; Harper Adams University College (Newport); Leeds Trinity and All Saints; University of London (Institutes and Activities); Newman University College (Birmingham); University College Plymouth St Mark and St John; Royal Agricultural College (Cirencester); St Mary's University College, Twickenham; University Campus Suffolk; Writtle College (Chelmsford).

[1]Postgraduate only.

Health

As at 30 Sept. 2004 there were around 1·3m. employees in the National Health Service including 117,036 doctors, 397,515 qualified nursing, midwifery and health visiting staff (including practice nurses) and 17,272 qualified ambulance staff.

In 2007, 24% of men and 24% of women were obese (having a body mass index over 30), up from 17% and 20% in 1997 respectively.

CULTURE

Tourism

The leading free admission attraction in 2005 was Blackpool Pleasure Beach, Lancs, with an estimated 6·0m. visits. The leading tourist attractions charging admission in 2005 were: the British Airways London Eye, with 3·2m. visits; Xscape Castleford, with an estimated 3·2m.; the Tower of London, with 1·9m.; Flamingo Land Theme Park in Malton, N. Yorks, with an estimated 1·4m.; and Pleasure Beach in Great Yarmouth, with an estimated 1·4m.

FURTHER READING

See Further Reading in United Kingdom.

SCOTLAND

KEY HISTORICAL EVENTS

Earliest evidence of human settlement in Scotland dates from the Middle Stone Age. Hunters and fishermen on the west coast were succeeded by farming communities as far north as Shetland. The Romans, who were active in the first century AD, built Hadrian's Wall between the Tyne and Solway Firth as their northern frontier. At this time, the Picts formed two kingdoms north of the Firth of Clyde. From the 6th century, the Celtic Scots from Dalriada, northern Ireland, fought with Angles and Britons for control of southern Scotland.

In 843 Kenneth MacAlpine united the Scots and the Picts to found the kingdom of Scotland. A legal and administrative uniformity was established by David I (reigned 1124–53). William the Lion abandoned claims to Northumbria in 1209 but began the alliance with France. In 1286 Edward I of England asserted his claim as overlord of Scotland and appointed his son to succeed to the crown. Resistance to English rule was led by William Wallace and later by Robert Bruce, who defeated the English at Bannockburn in 1314. His grandson, Robert II, became the first Stewart (Stuart) king in 1371.

Royal minorities undermined the authority of the crown in the 15th century until the accession of James IV in 1488. Relations with England improved after his marriage to Margaret Tudor in 1503 but when Henry VIII invaded France, James attacked England and was killed at the Battle of Flodden in 1513. The young James V was assailed by conflicting pressures from pro-French and pro-English factions but having secured his personal rule, he entered into two successive French marriages. His daughter, Mary Queen of Scots, married the French Dauphin in 1558. Protestant opposition to French influence was bolstered by Elizabeth I of England, who sent troops. Mary was in France when the Scottish parliament renounced papal authority, bolstering the reformist movement, led by John Knox. Returning to Scotland after her husband's death in 1561, Mary was forced to take refuge in England. Her son, James VI, survived the animosity between his own and his mother's followers to make an alliance with England. Deemed a threat because of her claim to the English throne, Mary was executed on Elizabeth's orders in 1587.

Elizabeth died without issue in 1603 and was succeeded by James. Although he styled himself 'king of Great Britain', England and Scotland remained independent. Charles I alienated much of the Scottish nobility and was defeated in the Bishops' Wars by the Covenanters, who rejected English interference in the Scottish church. Scottish armies fought for both sides in the English Civil War, which led to the execution of Charles I in 1649. However, the Scots soon united to accept Charles II as their king. Having established dominance in England, Cromwell moved against Scotland forcing Charles II into exile. His restoration in 1660 was welcomed in both kingdoms. His successor, James VII (James II of England), was less astute in managing religious and political differences. The collapse of his regime in 1688 and the arrival of William of Orange confirmed the Protestant ascendancy in Scotland and England.

The union of parliament in 1707 brought Scotland more directly under English authority. However, Scotland retained its own legal and ecclesiastical systems. The remaining supporters of James VII, the Jacobites, led two abortive risings on behalf of James' son and grandson (the old and young Pretenders) but were defeated decisively at Culloden in 1746.

TERRITORY AND POPULATION

The total area of Scotland is 77,925 sq. km (2001), including its islands, 186 in number, and inland water 1,580 sq. km. Scotland covers 32·1% of the total area of the United Kingdom.

Population (including military in the barracks and seamen on board vessels in the harbours) at the dates of each census:

Date of enumeration	*Population*	*Pop. per sq. mile*[1]
1801	1,608,420	53
1811	1,805,864	60
1821	2,091,521	70
1831	2,364,386	79
1841	2,620,184	88
1851	2,888,742	97
1861	3,062,294	100
1871	3,360,018	113
1881	3,735,573	125
1891	4,025,647	135
1901	4,472,103	150
1911	4,760,904	160
1921	4,882,497	164
1931	4,842,980	163
1951	5,096,415	171
1961	5,179,344	174
1971	5,228,963	67
1981	5,130,735	66
1991	4,998,567	60
2001	5,062,011	65

[1]Per sq. km from 1971.

Population at census day 2001:

Males	*Females*	*Total*
2,432,494	2,629,517	5,062,011

In 2001, 58,652 people aged three and over spoke Gaelic (65,978 in 1991). Households at the 2001 census: 2,192,000.

The age distribution in Scotland at census day on 2001 was as follows (in 1,000):

Age-group	
Under 5	277
5 and under 10	307
10 » 15	323
15 » 20	317
20 » 25	314
25 » 35	699
35 » 45	781
45 » 55	689
55 » 65	550

Age-group			
65	»	70	239
70	»	75	207
75	»	85	271
85 and upwards			88

Land area and population by administrative area (30 June 2008):

Council Area	*Area (sq. km)*	*Population*
Aberdeen City	186	206,880
Aberdeenshire	6,313	236,260
Angus	2,182	109,320
Argyll and Bute	6,909	91,390
Clackmannanshire	159	48,900
Dumfries and Galloway	6,426	148,030
Dundee City	60	142,170
East Ayrshire	1,262	119,290
East Dunbartonshire	175	105,460
East Lothian	679	92,830
East Renfrewshire	174	89,290
Edinburgh, City of	264	463,510
Eilean Siar[1]	3,071	26,350
Falkirk	297	149,680
Fife	1,325	358,930
Glasgow City	175	580,690
Highland	25,659	215,310
Inverclyde	160	81,540
Midlothian	354	79,290
Moray	2,238	86,750
North Ayrshire	885	135,490
North Lanarkshire	470	323,780
Orkney Islands	990	19,770
Perth and Kinross	5,286	140,190
Renfrewshire	261	169,590
Scottish Borders	4,732	110,240
Shetland Islands	1,466	21,880
South Ayrshire	1,222	111,670
South Lanarkshire	1,772	307,670
Stirling	2,187	87,810
West Dunbartonshire	159	91,240
West Lothian	427	165,700
Total	77,925	5,116,900

[1]Formerly Western Isles.

Estimated population of Scotland, mid-2008, 5,168,500 (2,668,300 females and 2,500,200 males), giving a density of 66 per sq. km.

Glasgow is Scotland's largest city, with an estimated population of 584,240 in 2008, followed by Edinburgh, the capital (estimated 2008 population, 471,650), and Aberdeen, with 210,400.

The birthplaces of the 2001 census day population in Scotland were: Scotland, 4,410,400; England, 408,948; Northern Ireland, 33,528; Ireland 21,774; Wales, 16,623; other European Union countries, 44,432; elsewhere, 126,306.

SOCIAL STATISTICS

	Estimated resident population at 30 June[1]	*Total births*	*Live births outside marriage*	*Deaths*	*Marriages*	*Divorces, annulments and dissolutions*
2003	5,057,400	52,432	23,864	58,472	30,757	10,928
2004	5,078,400	53,957	25,202	56,187	32,154	11,227
2005	5,094,800	54,386	25,617	55,747	30,881	10,940
2006	5,116,900	55,690	26,584	55,093	29,898	13,014
2007	5,144,200	57,781	28,377	55,986	29,866	12,773
2008	5,168,500	60,041	30,055	55,700	28,903	11,474

[1]Includes merchant navy at home and forces stationed in Scotland.

Birth rate, 2008, per 1,000 population, 11·6; death rate, 10·8; marriage, 5·6; infant mortality per 1,000 live births, 4·2; sex ratio, 1,037 male births to 1,000 female. Average age of marriage in 2008: males, 37·0, females, 34·5. Expectation of life, 2006–08: males, 75·0 years, females, 79·9.

CLIMATE

For more detailed information, *see under* Climate, United Kingdom.

Aberdeen, Jan. 38°F (3·3°C), July 57°F (13·9°C). Annual rainfall 32" (813 mm). Edinburgh, Jan. 38°F (3·3°C), July 58°F (14·5°C). Annual rainfall 27" (686 mm). Glasgow, Jan. 39°F (3·9°C), July 59°F (15°C). Annual rainfall 38" (965 mm).

CONSTITUTION AND GOVERNMENT

In a referendum on devolution on 11 Sept. 1997, Scotland's voters opted for devolved government, calling for the reinstatement of a separate parliament in Scotland, the first since union with England in 1707. 1,775,045 votes (74·3%) were cast in favour of a Scottish parliament and 614,400 against (25·7%). On a turnout of 60·4%, around 44·8% of the total electorate voted in favour. For the second question, on the Parliament's tax-raising powers, 1,512,889 votes were cast in favour (63·5%) and 870,263 against (36·5%). This represented 38·4% of the total electorate. The Parliamentary electorate of Scotland in the register in Dec. 2009 numbered 3,869,700.

The Scottish Parliament is made up of 129 members and managed a budget of £27·4bn. in 2005–06. The parliament may pass laws and has limited tax raising powers; it is also responsible for devolved issues, including health, education, police and fire services; however, 'reserved issues' (foreign policy, constitutional matters, and many domestic areas including social security, trade and industry, and employment legislation) remain the responsibility of the British Parliament in Westminster.

RECENT ELECTIONS

At the UK general election held in May 2010, 59 members were returned from Scotland. Labour won 41 seats; the Liberal Democrats, 11; the Scottish National Party, 6; Conservative, 1. At the June 2009 European Parliament elections Labour won 2 seats, the Scottish National Party 2, the Conservatives 1 and Liberal Democrats 1.

In elections to the Scottish Parliament on 3 May 2007, the Scottish National Party (SNP) won 47 seats (26 by regional list), against 46 (9 by regional list) for Labour, 17 (13 by regional list) for the Conservatives, 16 (5 by regional list) for the Liberal Democrats, 2 (both by regional list) for the Greens, and 1 ind. Of the 129 seats, 73 were won on a first-past-the-post basis and 56 through proportional representation (regional list). Turnout was 51·8% but an investigation was launched after almost 140,000 ballot papers were spoilt. SNP leader Alex Salmond was elected *First Minister* on 16 May 2007, defeating previous incumbent Jack McConnell (Labour). Despite forming a pact with the Greens, the SNP were unable to form a coalition that would give them a parliamentary majority, choosing instead to rule as a minority government.

See also Constitution and Government, Recent Elections *and* Current Administration in United Kingdom.

CURRENT ADMINISTRATION

First Minister: Alex Salmond; b. 1954 (Scottish National Party).
Presiding Officer: Alex Fergusson.

Scottish Executive: http://www.scotland.gov.uk

DEFENCE

For information on defence, *see* United Kingdom.

ECONOMY

Currency

The Bank of Scotland, Clydesdale Bank and the Royal Bank of Scotland have note-issuing powers.

Budget
Government expenditure in Scotland came to £49·9bn. in 2006–07 (including social protection £16·2bn., health £9·1bn. and education £6·9bn.). Revenues totalled £42·4bn. (including income tax £10·3bn., national insurance contributions £7·5bn. and VAT £7·4bn.).

Performance
The real GDP growth rate in 2006 was 2·6%.

ENERGY AND NATURAL RESOURCES

Environment
35% of household waste was recycled in 2008–09.

Electricity
The Electricity Act 1989 led to the privatization of the industry in Scotland and the creation of three new companies: ScottishPower, Scottish Hydro-Electric and Scottish Nuclear. After a series of acquisitions and mergers, in Dec. 1998 Scottish Hydro-Electric became part of the newly-formed Scottish and Southern Energy, a vertically integrated company that covers generation, transmission, distribution and supply in northern Scotland. ScottishPower runs distribution in central and southern Scotland and in 2007 became a subsidiary of the Spanish company Iberdrola. Scottish Nuclear, responsible for operating the two Scottish nuclear power stations, merged with British Energy in 1996, which in turn became a subsidiary of EDF in Jan. 2009.

Water
Water supply is the responsibility of the Regional and Island local authorities. Seven river purification boards are responsible for environmental management.

Agriculture
In 2005 total agricultural area was 5,516,693 ha., of which 3,342,315 ha. were used for rough grazing and 1,855,756 ha. for crops and grass.

Selected crop production, 2005 (1,000 tonnes): barley, 1,738; potatoes, 1,083; wheat, 822; oats, 113.

Livestock, 2005 (in 1,000): sheep, 7,998; cattle, 1,980; pigs, 471; poultry, 14,723.

Forestry
Total forest area in March 2009 was 1,341,000 ha., of which 447,000 ha. was owned by the Forestry Commission.

Fisheries
The major fishing ports in terms of value of fish landed are Peterhead, Lerwick, Fraserburgh and Aberdeen. At 31 Dec. 2005 there were 2,376 fishing vessels that landed 483,000 tonnes of fish worth £349m.

INDUSTRY

Labour
In 2007 the economically active population numbered 2,670,000 (1,262,000 females), of whom 135,000 (60,000 females) were unemployed. This equates to an unemployment rate of 5·1% (5·3% for men and 4·8% for women). In March 2007 employment in Scotland was at its highest in over 40 years. In Sept. 2009, 37·1% of employee jobs were in public and other services, 22·0% in retail, wholesale and hotels, 18·7% in finance and business, and 8·7% in manufacturing.

COMMUNICATIONS

Roads
Responsibility for the construction and maintenance of trunk roads belongs to the Scottish Office. Roads not classified as trunk roads are the responsibility of county or unitary councils. In 2006 there were 54,900 km of public roads, of which 559 km were motorways. There were 2·59m. licensed private and light goods vehicles.

Rail
Total railway length in 2006–07 was 2,736 km. In 2006–07 a total of 79·5m. passengers travelled by rail and 13·0m. tonnes of freight were carried. There is a metro in Glasgow.

Civil Aviation
There are major airports at Aberdeen, Edinburgh, Glasgow and Prestwick. In 2006 Glasgow was the seventh busiest for passenger traffic in the UK, with 8,848,755 passengers (4,603,417 on domestic flights). Edinburgh was the seventh busiest UK airport for freight in 2006, handling 36,389 tonnes. In 2006, 24,522,555 passengers and 77,885 tonnes of freight were carried by Scottish airports.

Shipping
The principal Scottish port is Forth (including Grangemouth, Leith and Rosyth), which handled 39·1m. tonnes of cargo in 2008.

SOCIAL INSTITUTIONS

Justice
The High Court of Justiciary is the supreme criminal court in Scotland and has jurisdiction in all cases of crime committed in any part of Scotland, unless expressly excluded by statute. It consists of the Lord Justice General, the Lord Justice Clerk and 30 other Judges, who are the same Judges who preside in the Court of Session, the Scottish Supreme Civil Court. One Judge is seconded to the Scottish Law Commission. The Court is presided over by the Lord Justice General, whom failing, by the Lord Justice Clerk, and exercises an appellate jurisdiction as well as being a court of first instance. The home of the High Court is Edinburgh, but the court visits other towns and cities in Scotland on circuit and indeed the busiest High Court sitting is in Glasgow. The court sits in Edinburgh both as a Court of Appeal (the *quorum* being two judges if the appeal is against sentence or other disposals, and three in all other cases) and on circuit as a court of first instance. Although the decisions of the High Court are not subject to review by the Supreme Court of the United Kingdom, with the Scotland Act 1998 coming into force on 20 May 1999, there is a limited right of appeal against the termination of a devolution issue to the Supreme Court of the United Kingdom. One Judge sitting with a Jury of 15 persons can, and usually does, try cases, but two or more Judges (with a Jury) may do so in important or complex cases. The court has a privative jurisdiction over cases of treason, murder, rape, breach of duty by Magistrates and certain statutory offences under the Official Secrets Act 1911 and the Geneva Conventions Act 1957. It also tries the most serious crimes against person or property and those cases in which a sentence greater than imprisonment for three years is likely to be imposed.

The appellate jurisdiction of the High Court of Justiciary extends to all cases tried on indictment, whether in the High Court or the Sheriff Court, and persons so convicted may appeal to the court against conviction or sentence, or both, except where the sentence is fixed by law. In such an appeal, a person may bring under review any alleged miscarriage of justice including an alleged miscarriage of justice based on the existence and significance of evidence not heard at the original proceedings provided there is reasonable explanation of why it was not heard and an alleged miscarriage of justice where the Jury returned a verdict which no reasonable Jury, properly directed, could have returned. It is also a court of review from courts of summary jurisdiction, and on the final termination of any summary prosecution the convicted person may appeal to the court by way of stated case on questions of law, but not on questions of fact, except in relation to a miscarriage of justice alleged by the person accused on the basis of the existence and significance of additional evidence not heard at the original proceedings provided that there is a reasonable explanation of why it was not heard. Before cases proceed to a full hearing, leave of appeal must first be granted. Grounds of appeal and any relevant reports are sifted by a Judge sitting alone in chambers, who will decide if there are arguable grounds of appeal. Should leave of appeal be refused, this decision may be appealed to the High Court within 14 days, when the matter will be reviewed by three Judges. The Lord Advocate is entitled to appeal to the High Court against any sentence passed on indictment on the ground that it is unduly lenient, or on a point of law. Both the prosecution and defence, at any time in solemn and summary proceedings, may appeal by way of Bill of Advocation in order to correct irregularities in the preliminary stages of a case. In summary proceedings the accused may appeal by Bill of Suspension, where he desires to bring under review a warrant, conviction or judgement issued by an inferior Judge. In summary proceedings the accused can also appeal against sentence alone by way of Stated Case. In summary proceedings the Crown can appeal against a sentence on the grounds that it is unduly lenient. The court also hears appeals under the Courts-Martial (Appeals) Act 1951.

The Sheriff Court has an inherent universal criminal jurisdiction (as well as an extensive civil one), limited in general to crimes and offences committed within a sheriffdom (a specifically defined region), which has, however, been curtailed by statute or practice under which the High Court of Justiciary has exclusive jurisdiction in relation to the crimes mentioned above. The Sheriff Court is presided over by a Sheriff Principal or a Sheriff, who when trying cases on indictment sits with a Jury of 15 people. His powers of awarding punishment involving imprisonment are restricted to a maximum of three years, but he may under certain statutory powers remit the prisoner to the High Court for sentence if this is felt to be insufficient. The Sheriff also exercises a wide summary criminal jurisdiction and when doing so sits without a Jury; and he has concurrent jurisdiction with every other court within his Sheriff Court district in regard to all offences competent for trial in summary courts. The great majority of offences which come before courts are of a more minor nature and as such are disposed of in the Sheriff Summary Courts or in the District Courts (*see* below). Where a case is to be tried on indictment either in the High Court of Justiciary or in the Sheriff Court, the Judge may, before the trial, hold a preliminary or first diet to decide questions of a preliminary nature, whether relating to the competency or relevancy of proceedings or otherwise. Any decision at a preliminary diet (other than a decision to adjourn the first or preliminary diet or discharge trial diet) can be the subject of an appeal to the High Court of Justiciary prior to the trial. The High Court also has the exclusive power to provide a remedy for all extraordinary occurrences in the course of criminal business where there is no other mode of appeal available. This is known as the Nobile Officium powers of the High Court and all petitions to the High Court as the Nobile Officium must be heard before at least three judges.

In cases to be tried on indictment in the Sheriff Court a first diet is mandatory before the trial diet to decide questions of a preliminary nature and to identify cases which are unlikely to go to trial on the date programmed. Likewise in summary proceedings, an intermediate diet is again mandatory before trial. In High Court cases such matters may be dealt with at a preliminary diet.

District Courts have jurisdiction in more minor offences occurring within a district which before recent local government reorganization corresponded to district council boundaries. These courts are presided over by Lay Magistrates, known as Justices, who have limited powers for fine and imprisonment. In Glasgow District there are also Stipendiary Magistrates, who are legally qualified, and who have the same sentencing powers as Sheriffs.

The Court of Session, presided over by the Lord President (the Lord Justice General in criminal cases), is divided into an inner-house comprising two divisions of five judges each with a mainly appellate function, and an outer-house comprising 22 single Judges sitting individually at first instance; it exercises the highest civil jurisdiction in Scotland, with the Supreme Court of the United Kingdom as the final Court of Appeal.

CIVIL JUDICIAL STATISTICS

	2007[1]
House of Lords (Appeals from Court of Session)	10
Court of Session—	
General Department	3,689
Petition Department	3,196
Sheriff Courts—Ordinary Cause	59,459
Sheriff Courts—Summary Cause	34,253
Small Claims	24,997

[1]Provisional. The Scottish Court Service, the main provider of the data concerned, is working with the Justice Analytical Services to improve the accuracy and level of detail of the civil judicial statistics it collects.

CRIMINAL STATISTICS
(Persons proceeded against in Scottish courts)

	2002–03	2003–04	2004–05
Persons proceeded against:			
All crimes[1]	418,281	414,214	438,121
Non-sexual crimes of violence	16,074	15,187	14,728
All offences[1]	517,545	607,621	632,982
Persons with a charge proved:			
All crimes and offences	128,867	134,931	131,366
Crimes	43,498	43,604	42,492
Persons aged 8–15[2]	136	113	127
Average prison population	6,475	6,621	6,779

[1]Scottish criminal law generally uses the term 'crime' for more serious criminal acts, and 'offence' for less serious ones. 'Seriousness' is generally related to the maximum sentence that can be imposed. The distinction is only made for working purposes. [2]Except for serious offences which qualify for solemn proceedings, children aged 8–15 are not proceeded against in Scottish courts. Children within this age group that commit crime are generally referred to the reporter of the children's panel or are given a police warning.

Police

In Scotland, the unitary councils have the role of police authorities. Establishment levels were abolished in Scotland on 1 April 1996. The actual strength at 30 Sept. 2006 was 12,805 men and 3,456 women. There were 1,332 special constables. The total police net expenditure in Scotland for 2006–07 was £1,045m.

Education

In Sept. 2007 there were 2,729 publicly funded (local authority, grant-aided and self-governing) primary, secondary and special schools. All teachers employed in these schools are required to be qualified.

Pre-school Education. In Jan. 2007 there were 2,823 pre-school centres that were in partnership with their local authority and 106,060 pupils enrolled in these centres.

Primary Education. In Sept. 2007 there were 2,168 publicly funded primary schools with 375,946 pupils and 23,508 full-time equivalent teachers.

Secondary Education. In Sept. 2007 there were 378 publicly funded secondary schools with 309,560 pupils and 26,365 full-time equivalent teachers. All but 21 schools provided a full range of Scottish Certificate of Education courses and non-certificate courses. Pupils who start their secondary education in schools which do not cater for a full range of courses may be transferred at the end of their second or fourth year to schools where a full range of courses is provided.

Independent schools. There were 157 independent schools in Sept. 2007, with a total of 30,981 pupils and 3,396 full-time equivalent teachers. A small number of the Scottish independent schools are of the 'public school' type, but they are not known as 'public schools' since in Scotland this term is used to denote education authority (i.e. state) schools.

Special Education. In Sept. 2007 there were 183 publicly funded special schools with 6,709 pupils.

Further Education. Under the Further and Higher Education (Scotland) Act 1992 funding of the Further Education colleges was transferred to central government in 1993. Scotland's FE colleges are funded by the Scottish Funding Council (SFC), which replaced the Scottish Further Education Funding Council and the Scottish Higher Education Funding Council in Oct. 2005.

There are 43 incorporated FE colleges as well as the FE colleges in Orkney and Shetland, which are run by the local education authorities, and two privately managed colleges, Sabhal Mor Ostaig and Newbattle Abbey College. The colleges offer training in a wide range of vocational areas and co-operate with the Scottish Qualifications Authority, the Enterprise, Energy and Lifelong Learning Directorate and the Education Directorate of the Scottish Executive in the development of new courses. The qualifications offered by colleges aim to improve the skills of the nation's workforce and increase the country's competitiveness. The colleges benefit from co-operation with industry, through involvement with Industry Lead Bodies and National Training Organizations whose responsibility it is to identify education, training and skills needs at sectoral level. Industry is also represented on college boards of management. Colleges and schools in Scotland are directly involved in providing the new national qualifications introduced in 1999 as a result of the Higher Still development programme.

In 2005–06 there were 359,530 students and a total of 446,619 enrolments on courses at Scotland's 43 further education institutions; the full-time equivalent staff number in the colleges was 12,338.

Full-time students resident in Scotland (and EU students) undertaking non-advanced (further education) courses are mainly supported through discretionary further education bursaries which are administered locally by further education colleges within National Policy Guidelines issued by the SFC. The Colleges have delegated discretionary powers for some aspects of the bursary support award.

In May 2000 the Scottish Executive announced the abolition of tuition fees for all eligible Scottish (and EU) full-time further education students from autumn 2000. The Executive also made a commitment to take steps to align, from autumn 2001, the levels of support available on a weekly basis for FE students with those that will apply for HE students and to begin to align the systems of assessment of parental/family contributions.

Higher Education. In Scotland in 2006 there were 21 institutions of higher education funded by the Scottish Higher Education Funding Council (now incorporated into the SFC), with the exception of the Scottish Agricultural College which is funded by the Scottish Executive Rural Affairs Department. Included in this total is the Open University. The Scottish Higher Education Funding Council (SHEFC) took over the responsibility for funding the Open University in Scotland at the start of the 2000–01 academic session. University education in Scotland has a long history. Four universities—St Andrews, Glasgow, Aberdeen and Edinburgh, known collectively as the 'ancient Scottish universities'—were founded in the 15th and 16th centuries. Four further universities—Strathclyde, Heriot-Watt, Stirling and Dundee—were formally established as independent universities between 1964 and 1967, and four others—Napier, Paisley (now the University of the West of Scotland), Robert Gordon and Glasgow Caledonian—were granted the title of university in 1992, with a fifth, the University of Abertay, Dundee, being added in 1994.

Of the remaining higher education institutions, which all offer courses at degree level (although not themselves universities), five were formerly Central Institutions: Edinburgh College of Art, Glasgow School of Art, Queen Margaret University College (Edinburgh), Royal Scottish Academy of Music and Drama (Glasgow) and Scottish Agricultural College (Perth).

Two additional higher education institutions were established in 2001. UHI Millennium Institute was designated as a higher education institution on 1 April when it took over from the local colleges of further education and other non-SHEFC funded institutions responsibility for all HE provision and all students on courses of HE in the Academic Partner institutions. Bell College of Technology became a higher education institution on 1 Aug. when its transfer from the further to the higher education sector was completed. On 1 Aug. 2007 Bell College merged with the University of Paisley. The merged institution operated under the name University of Paisley until the Privy Council approved the new name—University of the West of Scotland—on 30 Nov. 2007.

Further education colleges may also provide higher education courses.

University and HE student and staff figures:

Name (and Location)	*Students (2005–06)*	*Staff (2006–07)*
Aberdeen Univ.	15,225	1,435
Abertay Dundee Univ.	4,100	215
Bell College (Hamilton)[1]	4,860	190
Dundee Univ.	19,230	1,395
Edinburgh College of Art	1,680	140
Edinburgh Univ.	24,370	2,890
Glasgow School of Art	1,535	155
Glasgow Caledonian Univ.	17,180	895
Glasgow Univ.	23,145	2,580
Heriot-Watt Univ. (Edinburgh)	24,205	665
Napier Univ. (Edinburgh)	15,785	865
Paisley Univ.[1]	13,400	410
Queen Margaret University College (Edinburgh)	5,400	200
Robert Gordon Univ. (Aberdeen)	12,530	735
Royal Scottish Academy of Music and Drama (Glasgow)	680	60
St Andrews Univ.	8,365	890
Scottish Agricultural College (Perth)	750	195
Stirling Univ.	8,875	990
Strathclyde Univ. (Glasgow)	25,700	1,440
UHI Millennium Institute (Inverness)	7,205	10

[1]Merged in Aug. 2007 to form the University of the West of Scotland.

All the higher education institutions are independent and self-governing. In addition to funding through the higher education funding councils, they receive tuition fees from the Students Awards Agency for Scotland for students domiciled in Scotland, and through local education authorities for students domiciled in England and Wales. Institutions which carry out research may also receive funding through the five Research Councils administered by the Office of Science and Technology.

Health

As at 30 Sept. 2006 there were 4,130 general medical practitioners excluding registrars and retainers, and 2,434 general dental practitioners and assistants.

In 2003, 22% of men and 26% of women were obese (having a body mass index over 30), up from 16% and 17% in 1995 respectively.

Welfare

In Feb. 2004 there were 941,800 retirement pensioners, 290,000 beneficiaries of incapacity benefit, 285,800 recipients of disability living allowance, 239,400 claimants of income support, 235,200 of pension credit, 134,600 recipients of attendance allowance and 106,900 claimants of Jobseeker's Allowance. A total of 438,200 households were receiving housing benefit in Feb. 2004 and 528,200 council tax benefit. There were 0·5m. families with child tax credit or working tax credit awards, or with children and receiving out-of-work benefits in Jan. 2004.

RELIGION

The Church of Scotland, which was reformed in 1560, subsequently developed a presbyterian system of church government which was established in 1690 and has continued to the present day.

The supreme court is the General Assembly, which now consists of some 800 voting members, ministers and elders in equal numbers, together with some members of the diaconate, all commissioned by presbyteries. It meets annually in May, under the presidency of a Moderator appointed by the Assembly. The Queen is normally represented by a Lord High Commissioner, but has occasionally attended in person. The royal presence in a special throne gallery in the hall but outside the Assembly symbolizes the independence from state control of what is nevertheless recognized as the national Church in Scotland.

There are also 43 presbyteries in Scotland, providing governance and supervision at regional level, together with the presbyteries of England, Europe and Jerusalem. At the base of this conciliar structure of Church courts are the Kirk Sessions, of which there were 1,523 on 31 Dec. 2005. The total communicant membership of the Church on 31 Dec. 2006 was 504,363.

The Episcopal Church of Scotland is a province of the Anglican Church and is one of the historic Scottish churches. It consists of seven dioceses. As at 31 Dec. 2005 it had 303 churches and missions, 487 clergy and 42,571 members, of whom 28,695 were communicants.

There are in Scotland some small outstanding Presbyterian bodies and also Baptists, Congregationalists, Methodists and Unitarians.

The Roman Catholic Church which celebrated the centenary of the restoration of the Hierarchy in 1978, had in Scotland (2005) one cardinal archbishop, one archbishop, six bishops, two bishops emeriti, 29 permanent deacons, 822 clergy, 472 parishes and 750,000 adherents.

The proportion of marriages in Scotland according to the rites of the various Churches in 2006 was: Church of Scotland, 26·8%; Roman Catholic, 6·7%; Baptist Union of Scotland, 1·3%; United Free Church of Scotland, 0·6%; others 13·8%; civic; 50·8%.

CULTURE

Press

Average daily circulation in Feb. 2010 for the daily *Scotsman* was 45,695 and the *Daily Record* 328,183; and for *Scotland on Sunday* 58,278 and the *Sunday Mail* 397,458.

Tourism

There were 2·39m. overseas visitors to Scotland in 2005, spending £1·2bn. Overall tourism receipts totalled £4·2bn. The tourist attraction receiving the most visitors is Edinburgh Castle, with 1,187,342 visits in 2005. In 2005 around 9% of the workforce was employed in the tourism industry.

Festivals

The Edinburgh Festival and the Fringe Festival both take place in Aug./early Sept. and are major international festivals of culture.

Museums and Galleries

The most visited museum in 2005 was the Royal Museum and Museum of Scotland in Edinburgh with 828,367 visits.

FURTHER READING

Scottish Executive. Scottish Economic Report. Twice yearly—*Scottish Abstract of Statistics.* Annual

Brown, A., *et al., Politics and Society in Scotland.* 1996
Bruce, D., *The Mark of the Scots.* 1997
Dennistoun, R. and Linklater, M. (eds.) *Anatomy of Scotland.* 1992
Devine, T. M. and Finlay, R. J. (eds.) *Scotland in the 20th Century.* 1996
Harvie, C., *Scotland and Nationalism: Scottish Society and Politics, 1707–1994.* 2nd ed. 1994
Hunter, J., *A Dance Called America: The Scottish Highlands, the United States and Canada.* 1997
Keay, J. and J., *Collins Encyclopedia of Scotland: The Story of a Nation.* 2000
Macleod, J., *Highlanders: A History of the Gaels.* 1997
Magnusson, M., *Scotland: The Story of a Nation.* 2000
McCaffrey, J. F., *Scotland in the Nineteenth Century.* 1998
McGarvey, Neil and Cairney, Paul, (eds.) *Scottish Politics: An Introduction.* 2008
Mitchell, James, *Governing Scotland.* 2003

Statistical office: Room 1N.04, St Andrew's House, Regent Road, Edinburgh, EH1 3DG.
Website: http://www.scotland.gov.uk/Topics/Statistics

WALES

KEY HISTORICAL EVENTS

After the Roman evacuation, Wales divided into tribal kingdoms. Cunedda Wledig, a prince from southern Scotland, founded a dynasty in the northwest region of Gwynedd—to become the focus for Welsh unity—while the Irish exerted an influence in the kingdom of Dyfed. Offa's Dyke, a defensive earthwork, was the dividing line between England and Wales. In the late 9th century the kings of southern Wales swore fealty to Alfred of Wessex, a relationship assumed by the English crown. Gruffydd ap Llywelyn of Gwynedd briefly united Wales from 1055–63. His death was followed by Norman expansion into southern Wales, where the Marcher lordships were created.

With the accession of Llywelyn the Great (1194–1240), the house of Gwynedd overcame rival claims from Powys and Deheubarth to forge a stable political state under English suzerainty. His grandson, Llywelyn ap Gruffydd (1246–82), was recognized as prince of Wales by Henry III but Llywelyn intrigued against Edward I, who reduced Gwynedd's hegemony. Wales was annexed and subdued by a network of castles. Edward's infant son, born at Caernarfon, was made prince of Wales.

Loyalty to Henry VIII, who was of Welsh descent, was rewarded with political influence. The Act of Union in 1536 made English law general, admitted Welsh representatives to Parliament and established the Council of Wales and the Marches.

TERRITORY AND POPULATION

At the census taken on 29 April 2001 the population was 2,903,085. The area of Wales is 20,732 sq. km. Population density, 2001 census: 140 per sq. km. Wales covers 8·5% of the total area of the United Kingdom.

Population at census day 2001:

Males	*Females*	*Total*
1,403,900	1,499,185	2,903,085

Population (present on census night) at the four previous decennial censuses:

1961	1971	1981	1991
2,644,023[1]	2,731,204[1]	2,790,500[2]	2,811,865

[1]Areas now recognized as Monmouthshire and small sections of various other counties formed the county of Monmouthshire in England until 1974. [2]The final count is believed to be over-stated as a result of an error in processing. The preliminary counts presented here rounded to the nearest hundred are thought to be more accurate.

Estimated population, mid-2008, 2,993,400 (1,531,900 females and 1,461,500 males). Cardiff, the capital and largest city, had a population in 2001 of 305,340; Swansea, the second largest city, had a population of 223,293 in 2001.

In 2001, 457,950 people aged three and over were able to speak, read and write Welsh. Households at the 2001 census: 1,276,000.

For further statistical information, *see under* Territory and Population, United Kingdom.

Wales is divided into 22 unitary authorities (cities and counties, counties and county boroughs).

Designations, areas and populations of the unitary authority areas at census day 2001:

Unitary Authority	*Designation*	*Area (sq. km)*	*Population*
Blaenau Gwent	County Borough	109	70,058
Bridgend	County Borough	251	128,650
Caerphilly	County Borough	278	169,521
Cardiff	City and County	139	305,340
Carmarthenshire	County	2,394	173,635
Ceredigion	County	1,792	75,384
Conwy	County Borough	1,126	109,597
Denbighshire	County	837	93,092
Flintshire	County	438	148,565
Gwynedd	County	2,535	116,838
Isle of Anglesey	County	711	66,828
Merthyr Tydfil	County Borough	111	55,983
Monmouthshire	County	849	84,879
Neath and Port Talbot	County Borough	441	134,471
Newport	County Borough	190	137,017
Pembrokeshire	County	1,589	112,901
Powys	County	5,181	126,344
Rhondda Cynon Taff	County Borough	424	231,952
Swansea	City and County	378	223,293
The Vale of Glamorgan	County Borough	331	119,500
Torfaen	County Borough	126	90,967
Wrexham	County Borough	504	128,477

SOCIAL STATISTICS

2006: births, 33,628 (11·3 per 1,000 population); deaths, 31,086 (10·5 per 1,000 population); infant deaths, 139 (4·1 per 1,000 live births); marriages (2004, provisional), 14,826; divorces (2005), 7,191.

CLIMATE

For more detailed information, *see under* Climate, United Kingdom.

Cardiff, Jan. 40°F (4·4°C), July 61°F (16·1°C). Annual rainfall 42·6" (1,065 mm).

CONSTITUTION AND GOVERNMENT

One of the main aspects of the British Labour government's programme of constitutional reform is devolution. On 18 Sept. 1997 in the referendum there were 559,419 votes cast in favour of a Welsh assembly (50·3%) and 552,698 against (49·7%). The turnout was 51·3%.

The Parliamentary electorate of Wales in the register in Dec. 2009 numbered 2,261,269.

RECENT ELECTIONS

At the UK general election in May 2010, 40 members were returned from Wales. Labour won 26 seats (29 in 2005), Conservatives 8 seats (3), Liberal Democrats 3 (4), Plaid Cymru 3 seats (3).

At the 2009 European Parliamentary elections the Conservatives, Labour, Plaid Cymru and UKIP won one seat each.

In the elections to the Welsh Assembly on 3 May 2007, Labour won 26 seats (2 by regional list), followed by Plaid Cymru with 15 (8 by regional list), the Conservatives with 12 (7 by regional list), the Liberal Democrats with 6 (3 by regional list) and 1 independent constituency. Of the 60 seats, 40 seats were won on a first-past-the-post basis and 20 through proportional representation (regional list). 28 seats were won by women. Turnout was 43·7%. In July 2007 Labour agreed to form a coalition government with Plaid Cymru.

See also Constitution and Government, Recent Elections *and* Current Administration in United Kingdom.

CURRENT ADMINISTRATION

First Secretary: Carwyn Jones; b. 1967 (Labour).

Presiding Officer: Lord Elis-Thomas.

National Assembly for Wales: http://wales.gov.uk

DEFENCE

For information on defence, *see* United Kingdom.

ECONOMY

For information on the economy, *see* United Kingdom.

ENERGY AND NATURAL RESOURCES

For information on energy and natural resources, *see* United Kingdom.

Environment

41% of municipal waste was recycled in April–June 2009.

Water

The Water Act of Sept. 1989 privatized Welsh Water (Dŵr Cymru Cyfyngedig), along with the nine water authorities in England.

Agriculture

In 2005 there were 36,968 agricultural holdings. Of these, 12,485 were under 5 ha., 8,288 were between 5 and 20 ha., 7,221 were between 20 and 50 ha. and 8,974 were over 50 ha. The average size of a holding in Wales in 2005 was 39 ha.

The area of tillage in 2005 was 65,738 ha. (64,988 ha. for crops and 750 ha. bare fallow). Major crops, 2004 (1,000 tonnes): barley, 126; wheat, 116; potatoes, 70; oats, 17.

Livestock, 2005: sheep and lambs, 9,510,400; cattle and calves, 1,240,800; pigs, 28,400; poultry, 7,191,800.

Forestry

In March 2009 there were 105,000 ha. of Forestry Commission woodland and 179,000 ha. of non-Forestry Commission woodland.

Fisheries

The major fishing port is Milford Haven. In 2006, in all ports in Wales, 17,450 tonnes of fish and shellfish worth £23,577,270 were landed. There were 506 fishing vessels registered in Wales in 2006.

INDUSTRY

Main industrial production (gross value added), 2004 (£1m.): basic metals and fabricated metal products, 1,044; electrical and optical equipment, 986; transport equipment, 956; food products, beverages and tobacco, 921; chemicals, chemical products and man-made fibres, 819.

Labour

In the period May–July 2007 there were 1,358,000 people in employment. The number of claimant count unemployed in Aug. 2007 was 40,200. A total of 203,000 people were self-employed in June 2007. The largest employment sectors in 2005 were: public administration, education and health, 391,000; retail, wholesale, hotels and restaurants, 304,000; finance and business activities, 174,000; manufacturing, 171,000. As a proportion of total employment, 76·9% of the active workforce in 2005 were in service industries. The ILO unemployment rate in May–July 2007 was 5·5%, compared to 5·4% for the UK as a whole. In 2006, 62,000 working days were lost as a result of industrial disputes.

INTERNATIONAL TRADE

For information on international trade, *see* United Kingdom.

COMMUNICATIONS

Roads

Responsibility for the construction and maintenance of trunk roads belongs to the Welsh Assembly Government. Roads not classified as trunk roads are the responsibility of county or unitary councils. In 2006 there were 133 km of motorway, 1,578 km of trunk roads and 2,736 km of principal roads. 1,663,800 vehicles were licensed in 2005, including 1,429,000 private and light goods vehicles. In 2006 there were 8,701 reported accidents which led to 12,692 casualties, including 163 deaths.

Civil Aviation

Cardiff Airport handled 1,764,753 passengers in 2005 (1,454,016 on international flights) and 2,564 tonnes of freight.

Shipping

The principal ports are (with 1m. tonnes of cargo handled in 2004): Milford Haven (38·5) and Port Talbot (8·6).

Postal Services

Royal Mail employs 6,500 people in Wales and delivers 25m. letters to 1·52m. addresses each week.

SOCIAL INSTITUTIONS

Justice

As at 31 March 2007 police strength amounted to 7,627. During the financial year 2007–08 there were 243,623 notable offences, including 49,376 violent and 2,574 sexual offences. The clear-up rate was 31·0%. 14,959 people were found guilty of indictable offences in Magistrates' Courts in 2005 and 3,068 in Crown Courts.

Education

In April 2006 ACCAC (the qualification, curriculum and assessment authority), Dysg (the Welsh operation of the Learning and Skills Development Agency), ELWa (the National Council for Education and Training Wales) and the Wales Youth Agency merged with the Welsh Assembly Government's Department for Training and Education to form a new department, the Department for Children, Education, Lifelong Learning and Skills (DCELLS) in the Welsh Assembly Government.

There were 31 maintained nursery schools in Jan. 2007, and 62,735 pupils under five years provided for in nursery schools and in nursery or infants classes in primary schools.

In Jan. 2007 there were 263,261 pupils at 1,527 primary schools. Of these, 466 primary schools use Welsh as the sole or main medium of instruction. Such schools are to be found in all parts of Wales but are mainly concentrated in the predominantly Welsh-speaking areas of west and northwest Wales. Generally, children transfer from primary to secondary schools at 11 years of age.

In Jan. 2007 there were 224 secondary schools. All maintained secondary schools are classified as comprehensive; there are no middle schools in Wales. In 2006–07, 54 of the secondary schools were classed as Welsh-speaking as defined in section 354(b) of the Education Act 1996.

Since Sept. 1999, in accordance with the Schools Standards and Framework Act 1998, all maintained schools, including grant maintained schools, in Wales had to change category to one of the following: Community, Community Special, Foundation, Voluntary Controlled, Voluntary Aided. These categories continued with the introduction of the Education Act 2002.

Under the Education Act 1996, children have special educational needs if they have a learning difficulty which calls for special educational provision to be made for them. In a minority of cases the local education authority will need to make a statutory assessment of special educational needs under the Education Act 1996, which may ultimately lead to a 'statement of Special Educational Needs'. The total number of pupils with statements in Jan. 2007 was 15,579. Since April 2002 Special Educational Needs (SEN) guidance for Wales has been set out in the SEN Code of Practice for Wales.

In Jan. 2007, 9,452 full-time pupils and 247 part-time pupils attended 66 independent schools.

Post-16 Learning. The responsibilities of DCELLS (*see* above) include the planning and promoting of further, adult and continuing education, work-based training and school sixth forms. The consolidated financial statements of the National Council for Education and Training Wales identified funding amounting to £504·1m. in 2004–05 for further education, training and development, including £445·0m. learner provision purchasing at FE institutions, school sixth forms, work-based learning providers and LEA community learning providers. In 2004–05, 41,835 full-time students and 208,830 students studying part-time in the further education sector (excluding work-based learning) were supported at 25 further education institutions and 11 higher education institutions. The proportion of 16- to 18-year-olds with no qualifications fell from 12% in 2001 to 11% in 2005. The proportion of working age adults with no qualifications fell from 21% in 2001 to 16% in 2005; and 45% of working age adults had an NVQ Level 3 or equivalent in 2005, compared to 40% in 2001.

Higher Education. In 2005–06 there were 12 higher education institutions in Wales with a total income of £922m., of which 41·6% came from the Higher Education Funding Council for Wales (HEFCW) grant. There were 135,420 students in the higher education sector in 2005–06, including those registered with the Open University in Wales, of which 74,990 were full-time and 60,435 part-time students, excluding those enrolled on higher education provision at further education colleges.

Higher Education Institutes (HEIs)	*Full-time/sandwich HE students at HEIs (2005–06)*	*No. of academic staff (2005–06)*
Univ. of Glamorgan (Pontypridd)	9,715	1,040
Univ. of Wales, Aberystwyth[1]	6,355	780
Univ. of Wales, Bangor[2]	5,820	695
Cardiff University	16,305	2,865
Univ. of Wales, Lampeter	1,100	135
Univ. of Wales, Newport	3,010	430
Univ. of Wales, Swansea[3]	8,580	725
Univ. of Wales Institute, Cardiff	6,380	565
North East Wales Institute of Higher Education (Wrexham)[4]	2,640	255
Royal Welsh College of Music and Drama[5]	520	210
Swansea Institute of Higher Education[6]	3,100	300
Trinity College Carmarthen	1,250	125

[1]Since renamed Aberystwyth University. [2]Since renamed Bangor University. [3]Since renamed Swansea University. [4]Since renamed Glyndŵr University. [5]Since merged with the University of Glamorgan. [6]Since renamed Swansea Metropolitan University.

Health

In 2005–06 there were 1,952 GPs, 1,031 general dental practitioners and 28,152 whole-time equivalent nursing, midwifery and health visiting staff. The average daily number of hospital beds available in 2005–06 was 13,808, of which 11,444 were occupied. 501,894 in-patient cases were reported, with stays lasting an average 8·3 days. At 30 Nov. 2006, 65,416 people were waiting for treatment on an in-patient or day case basis and 183,251 people waiting for a first out-patient consultation.

The 2008 Welsh Health Survey found that 21% of adults were obese (having a body mass index over 30).

Welfare

In Feb. 2008, 609,000 people received state retirement pensions; 284,000 people received some form of income support including 162,000 who received pension credit; and in Aug. 2007, 361,000 families received child benefit.

RELIGION

Under the Welsh Church Acts, 1914 and 1919, the Church in Wales and Monmouthshire was disestablished as from 1 April 1920, and Wales was formed into a separate Province.

CULTURE

Broadcasting

Radio and television services are provided by the Welsh-language Sianel Pedwar Cymru (S4C, Channel 4 Wales). S4C is funded by the government. It acts as both broadcaster and regulator. In 2000–01 there were 1,150,100 television licenses, of which 1,143,500 were colour.

Tourism

In 2004 there were some 9m. domestic trips (from elsewhere in the UK) into Wales. Visitors stayed 31·5m. nights and spent £1·5bn.

Festivals

Every year there are local and national *eisteddfods* (festivals for musical competitions, etc.). The National Eisteddfod of Wales takes place every Aug. alternating between north and south Wales. In 2011 it will be held in Wrexham.

Libraries

In 2007–08 there were 368 public libraries with 6,262,000 books. The National Library is in Aberystwyth.

Theatre and Opera

There is a Welsh National Opera and the BBC National Orchestra of Wales.

Museums and Galleries

The leading museum is the National History Museum, St Fagans, Cardiff, which received 631,731 visits in 2004.

FURTHER READING

National Assembly. Digest of Welsh Statistics. National Statistics. Great Britain (annual)

Andrews, Leighton, *Wales Says Yes. The Inside Story of the Yes for Wales Referendum Campaign.* 1999

Davies, J., *History of Wales.* 1993

History of Wales. vols. 3, 4 (1415–1780). 2nd ed. 1993

Jenkins, G. H., *The Foundations of Modern Wales 1642–1780.* 1988.—*The Welsh Language and its Social Domains 1801–1911: A Social History of the Welsh Language.* 2000

Jones, G. E., *Modern Wales: a Concise History.* 2nd ed. 1994

May, J. (ed.) *Reference Wales.* 1994

Morgan, K. and Mungham, G., *Redesigning Democracy. The Making of the Welsh Assembly.* 2000

Statistical office: Statistical Directorate, Welsh Assembly Government, Cathays Park, Cardiff CF10 3NQ.

Website: http://www.statswales.wales.gov.uk

NORTHERN IRELAND

KEY HISTORICAL EVENTS

The Government of Ireland Act 1920 granted Northern Ireland its own bicameral parliament (Stormont). The rejection of home rule by the rest of Ireland (which pursued independence) forced a separation along primarily religious lines, with a large Catholic minority in the six northern counties. Between 1921–72 Stormont had full responsibility for local affairs except for taxation and customs; Northern Ireland was on the whole neglected by Westminster, allowing the virtual exclusion of Catholics from political office. The (predominantly Protestant) Unionist government ignored demands from London and the Catholic community to end communal discrimination.

In the late 1960s a Civil Rights campaign and reactions to it escalated into serious rioting and sectarian violence involving the Irish Republican Army (IRA, a terrorist organization aiming to unify Northern Ireland with the Republic of Ireland) and loyalist paramilitary organizations, such as the Ulster Defence Association. The British Army was deployed to protect civilians and was at first welcomed by the Catholic community. However, British soldiers shot dead 13 Catholic civil rights protesters in (London)Derry on 30 Jan. 1972—'Bloody Sunday'—prompting the Republic of Ireland's foreign minister to demand United Nations intervention. 467 people died in 1972, on account of 'the Troubles', and nearly 1,800 between 1971–77. The Northern Ireland government resigned and direct rule from Westminster was imposed.

Attempts have been made by successive governments to find a means of restoring greater power to Northern Ireland's political representatives on a widely acceptable basis, including a Constitutional Convention (1975–76), a Constitutional Conference (1979–80) and 78-member Northern Ireland Assembly elected by proportional representation in 1982. This was dissolved in 1986, partly in response to Unionist reaction to the Anglo-Irish Agreement signed on 15 Nov. 1985, which established an Intergovernmental Conference of British and Irish ministers to monitor issues of concern to the nationalist community. The Provisional IRA bombing of a Remembrance Day service in Enniskillen in 1987 killed 11. Universally condemned, it galvanized the anti-violence campaign.

On 15 Dec. 1993 the British and Irish prime ministers, John Major and Albert Reynolds, issued a joint declaration as a basis for all-party talks to achieve a political settlement. They invited Sinn Féin, the political wing of the IRA, to join the talks in an All-Ireland Forum after the cessation of terrorist violence. The IRA announced 'a complete cessation of military operations' on 31 Aug. 1994. On 13 Oct. 1994 the anti-IRA Combined Loyalist Military Command also announced a ceasefire 'dependent upon the continued cessation of all nationalist republican violence'.

Elections were held on 30 May 1996 to constitute a 110-member forum to take part in talks with the British and Irish governments. The Ulster Unionist Party won 30 seats, the Democratic Unionist Party 24 seats, the Social Democratic and Labour Party 21 seats and Sinn Féin 17 seats. Opening plenary talks, excluding Sinn Féin, began under the chairmanship of US Senator George Mitchell on 12 June 1996. A marathon negotiating struggle on 9–10 April 1998 led to agreement on a framework for sharing power designed to satisfy Protestant demands for a reaffirmation of their national identity as British, Catholic desires for a closer relationship with the Republic of Ireland and Britain's wish to return to Northern Ireland the powers London assumed in 1972.

Under the Good Friday Agreement, there was to be a democratically elected legislature in Belfast, a ministerial council giving the governments of Northern Ireland and Ireland joint responsibilities in areas like tourism, transportation and the environment, and a consultative council meeting twice a year to bring together ministers from the British and Irish parliaments, and the three assemblies being created in Northern Ireland and in Scotland and Wales. The Irish government eliminated from its constitution its territorial claim on Northern Ireland.

In the referendum on 22 May 1998, 71·1% of votes in Northern Ireland were cast in favour of the Good Friday peace agreement and 94·4% in the Republic of Ireland. As a consequence, in June, Northern Ireland's 1·2m. voters elected the first power-sharing administration since the collapse of the Sunningdale Agreement in 1974.

On 15 Aug. 1998 a 200 kg bomb exploded in the centre of Omagh. The dissident republican group the 'Real IRA' claimed responsibility. 29 people died and over 200 were injured, making it the single bloodiest incident of the Troubles—about 3,500 deaths had been recorded since the Troubles began by the end of 2001.

In Nov. 1999 the Mitchell talks finally produced an agreement between the Ulster Unionists and Sinn Féin, paving the way for devolved government. The new Northern Ireland Assembly met on 29 Nov. 1999 and on 2 Dec. legislative powers were fully devolved from London to Belfast. However, on 11 Feb. 2000 the Assembly was suspended following a breakdown in negotiations on the decommissioning of IRA weapons. Direct rule from London was restored. Devolved government resumed on 30 May after the IRA agreed to open their arms dumps to independent inspection. First Minister David Trimble resigned on 30 June 2001 to pressure republicans over decommissioning but on 22 Oct. Sinn Féin president Gerry Adams announced that he had recommended a 'ground-breaking' step on the arms issue. The IRA made a start on decommissioning arms, ammunition and explosives. David Trimble was re-elected first minister on 6 Nov. 2001.

On 15 Oct. 2002 the Assembly executive was again suspended over allegations of IRA spying at the Northern Ireland Office, although all charges were dropped in Jan. 2006. Direct rule from London was reimposed and on 30 Oct. the IRA cut off its links with the weapons decommissioning body. The Ulster Volunteer Force followed suit on 17 Jan. 2003. Elections for the Northern Ireland Assembly took place on 26 Nov. 2003. The theft of £26·5m. from the Northern Bank in Belfast in Dec. 2004 suggested closer than acknowledged associations between Sinn Féin and the IRA. Controversy surrounding the raid put the peace process on hold. In July 2005 the IRA formally announced an end to its armed campaign. In Sept. 2005 it claimed to have destroyed its arsenal of weapons.

The Stormont assembly met in May 2006 for the first time in more than three years, charged with restoring devolution by 24 Nov. On that date a transitional assembly was established and in Jan. 2007 Sinn Féin voted to support policing policies in Northern Ireland, a key requirement for a workable power-sharing agreement. The transitional assembly was dissolved at the end of that month ahead of assembly elections in March 2007, in which the DUP and Sinn Féin made strong gains. Both parties came under pressure to compromise and on 26 March reached an historic agreement to share power from 8 May with a devolved Northern Ireland government replacing direct rule from London.

TERRITORY AND POPULATION

Area (revised by Ordnance Survey of Northern Ireland) and population were as follows:

District	*Mid-year population estimates 2004*	*Area in ha. (including inland water)*
Antrim	49,833	57,686
Ards	74,648	37,619
Armagh	54,876	67,060
Ballymena	60,026	63,202
Ballymoney	28,260	41,820
Banbridge	43,774	45,263
Belfast	268,978	11,488
Carrickfergus	38,715	8,184
Castlereagh	65,795	8,514
Coleraine	56,530	48,551
Cookstown	33,660	62,244
Craigavon	83,168	37,842
Derry (Londonderry)	106,889	38,731
Down	66,759	64,670
Dungannon	49,307	78,360
Fermanagh	59,279	187,582
Larne	30,908	33,567
Limavady	34,010	58,558
Lisburn	110,247	44,684
Magherafelt	41,296	57,280
Moyle	16,424	47,976
Newry and Mourne	90,290	90,243
Newtownabbey	80,279	15,056
North Down	77,624	8,149
Omagh	50,082	113,045
Strabane	38,665	86,165
Northern Ireland	*1,710,322*	*1,413,540*

Northern Ireland's area of 14,135 sq. km represents 5·8% of the total area of the United Kingdom. Chief town (mid-year estimate, 2004): Belfast, 268,978.

Population by gender at the 2004 mid-year estimate was: females, 51·09%; males, 48·91%. Mid-year population estimate, 2008: 1,775,000 (904,100 females and 870,900 males).

SOCIAL STATISTICS

In 2006 there were 23,272 births, 14,532 deaths, 8,259 marriages and 2,565 divorces.

CLIMATE

For more detailed information, *see under* Climate, United Kingdom.

Belfast, Jan. 40°F (4·5°C), July 59°F (15·0°C). Annual rainfall 37·4" (950 mm).

CONSTITUTION AND GOVERNMENT

Under the Northern Ireland Act 1998 power that was previously exercised by the NI Departments was devolved to the Northern Ireland Assembly and its Executive Committee of Ministers. In April 2010 a new justice department came into existence to take responsibility for policing and judicial matters, which had previously been under the jurisdiction of the Secretary of State. Constitutional and national security issues along with firearms and explosives licensing and legislation remain the domain of the Secretary of State, who is also involved in public inquiries and some policy-making decisions.

The Parliamentary electorate of Northern Ireland in the register in Dec. 2009 numbered 1,160,757.

Secretary of State for Northern Ireland. Owen Paterson.

RECENT ELECTIONS

At the general election of 6 May 2010, 18 members were returned from Northern Ireland. The Democratic Unionist Party won 8 seats (9 in 2005); Sinn Féin 5 (5); the Social and Democratic Labour Party 3 (3); the Alliance Party 1 (0); others 1 (1).

In the Northern Ireland Assembly elections on 7 March 2007 the Democratic Unionist Party won 36 of the 108 seats (30·1% of the vote), Sinn Féin 28 (26·2%), the Ulster Unionist Party 18 (14·9%), the Social Democratic and Labour Party 16 (15·2%), Alliance Party of Northern Ireland 7 (5·2%), Green Party 1 (1·7%), Progressive Unionist Party 1 (0·6%). One other candidate was elected. Turnout was 63·5%.

At the June 2009 European Parliament elections, voting was by the single transferable vote system: Sinn Féin (26·0%), the Democratic Unionist Party (18·2%) and the Ulster Conservatives and Unionists–New Force (17·1%) gained 1 seat each. Turnout was 42·8%.

CURRENT ADMINISTRATION

Peter Robinson (Democratic Unionist Party) was sworn in as first minister of the Northern Ireland Assembly on 5 June 2008. Martin McGuinness (Sinn Féin) was initially sworn in as deputy first minister on 8 May 2007 and reappointed on 5 June 2008. They are joint leaders of the administration. On 11 Jan. 2010 Peter Robinson temporarily stood down as first minister after he was accused of political misconduct concerning illegal financial dealings carried out by his wife. Enterprise minister Arlene Foster (also Democratic Unionist Party) became acting first minister for a six-week period. The Assembly was restored on 8 May 2007 for the first time since its suspension on 14 Oct. 2002.

Northern Ireland Executive: http://www.northernireland.gov.uk

ECONOMY

Overview

The Northern Ireland government Department of Enterprise, Trade and Investment (DETI) is responsible for economic development policy, economic and financial infrastructure in support of economic development, energy, social economy, companies registry, insolvency service, consumer affairs, European Union support for economic development, mineral exploitation and development, InterTradeIreland, Tourism Ireland Ltd, air access, Giant's Causeway, Geological Survey of Northern Ireland, economic research and economic statistics and company law. DETI also has four agencies: Invest Northern Ireland (Invest NI), the Northern Ireland Tourist Board (NITB), the Health and Safety Executive for Northern Ireland (HSENI) and the General Consumer Council for Northern Ireland (GCCNI).

Currency

Banknotes are issued by Allied Irish Banks, Bank of Ireland, First Trust Bank, Northern Bank and Ulster Bank.

Banking and Finance

The Department of Finance and Personnel is responsible for control of the expenditure of Northern Ireland departments, involving liaison with HM Treasury, the European Commission and the Northern Ireland Office on financial matters, economic and social research and analysis; to review and develop rating policy and legislation; procurement for the Northern Ireland public sector; formulation of policy for central personnel management, and legal services, including law reform. The Department's Agencies are: Land Registers NI; Northern Ireland Statistics and Research Agency; and Land and Property Services Agency.

Public income of Northern Ireland (in £1,000 sterling):

	2003–04	*2004–05*	*2005–06*
Block grant	8,505,000	8,950,000	9,030,000
Regional and district rates	650,852	717,010	784,684
Interest on loans made from the Consolidated Fund	126,322	123,690	123,183
Miscellaneous receipts EU	314,947	111,660	217,523
Other	96,700	382,305	380,671
Total public income	9,693,821	10,284,665	10,536,061

ENERGY AND NATURAL RESOURCES

Environment

29% of municipal waste was recycled in 2007–08.

Electricity

There are three power stations with an installed capacity of some 2,100 MW.

In addition, electricity is also supplied through a 500 MW interconnector linking the Northern Ireland Electricity (NIE) and Scottish Power networks and a number of interconnectors linking the NIE network with the Electricity Supply Board (ESB) network in the Republic of Ireland.

Oil and Gas

In Sept. 2001 the Northern Ireland executive approved grant support for the development of the gas network outside the Greater Belfast area, to the North/North West region and for the construction of a South/North pipeline. The North West gas pipeline was completed in late 2004 and supplies gas for the Combined Cycle Turbine power station at Coolkeeragh outside Londonderry, which opened in June 2005. The South/North pipeline was commissioned in Oct. 2006, connecting the grids of Northern Ireland and the Republic of Ireland for the first time. The Northern Ireland Authority for Energy Regulation has granted a license to supply gas to the major towns along the route of both these.

Minerals

Output of minerals (in 1,000 tonnes), 2004: sandstone, 6,915; basalt and igneous rock (other than granite), 6,844; limestone, 5,634; sand and gravel, 5,084; other minerals (rock salt, fireclay, diatomite, granite, chalk, clay and shale), 1,266. There are lignite deposits of 1,000m. tonnes which have not yet been developed.

Agriculture

Provisional gross output in 2005:

	Quantity	*Value (£1m.)*
Cattle and calves	406,170	240·1
Sheep and lambs	956,180	42·3
Pigs	898,940	66·8
Poultry (1,000 tonnes)	228·6	137·3
Eggs (m. dozen)	61·7	22·9
Milk (1m. litres)	1,868·0	342·5
Other livestock products	—	8·7
Cereals (1,000 tonnes)	204·2	15·9
Potatoes (1,000 tonnes)	181·4	13·2
Fruit (1,000 tonnes)	49·1	5·8
Vegetables (1,000 tonnes)	52·7	15·2
Mushrooms (1,000 tonnes)	19·4	24·2
Other crops	—	7·5
Flowers, ornamentals and nurserystock	—	14·3
Capital formation	—	48·6
Contract work	—	44·4
Other items	—	24·0
Gross output	—	1,073·8

Area (in 1,000 ha.) on farms:

	2003	*2004*	*2005*
Cereals	38	38	36
Potatoes	6	6	5
Horticulture	3	3	3
Other crops	6	7	7
Grass	848	838	811
Rough grazing	153	151	149
Other land	20	20	19
Total area	1,074	1,063	1,030

Livestock (in 1,000 heads) on farms at June census:

	2003	2004	2005
Dairy cows	209	288	291
Beef cows	295	296	297
Other cattle	1,100	1,094	1,078
Ewes	1,106	1,101	1,027
Sows	43	38	37
Laying hens	2,203	2,266	2,319
Broilers	12,811	15,007	12,526

INDUSTRY

Labour

The main sources of employment statistics are the Census of Employment, conducted every two years, and the Quarterly Employment Survey. In June 2007 there were 716,760 employees, of whom 350,010 were males. Employment in services amounted to 567,050 (79% of all employees in employment) and in manufacturing and construction to 132,480 (18%). There were 88,410 people working in manufacturing and 44,070 in construction. The unemployment rate in the period May–July 2007, at 3·4%, was the lowest ever recorded in Northern Ireland.

COMMUNICATIONS

Roads

In April 2005 the total length of public roads was 24,968 km, graded for administrative purposes as follows: motorway, 133 km (including 19 km slip roads); Class '1' dual carriageway, 157 km; Class '1' single carriageway, 2,115 km; Class '2', 2,880 km; Class '3', 4,703 km; unclassified, 14,980 km.

The Northern Ireland Transport Holding Company (NITHC) oversees the provision of public transport services in Northern Ireland. Its subsidiary companies, Ulsterbus, Citybus and Northern Ireland Railways, are responsible for the delivery of most bus and rail services under the brand name of Translink.

At 31 March 2007 there were 2,379 professional hauliers and 6,609 vehicles licensed to engage in road haulage.

The number of motor vehicles licensed at 31 Dec. 2006 was 958,677, including private light goods, 800,969; heavy goods vehicles, 24,806; motorcycles, scooters and mopeds, 27,083.

Rail

Northern Ireland Railways, a subsidiary of the Northern Ireland Transport Holding Company, provides rail services within Northern Ireland and cross-border services to Dublin, jointly with Irish Rail. The number of track km operated is 340. In 2004–05 railways carried 7·4m. passengers, generating passenger receipts of £17·2m.

Civil Aviation

There are scheduled air services to three airports in Northern Ireland: Belfast International, George Best (Belfast City) and City of Derry. Scheduled services are provided by easyJet, bmibaby (British Midland), British Airways, British Northwest, Aer Arann, Aer Lingus, British European (Flybe), BMI, Jet2.com, Continental and Ryanair. In 2004–05 the airports collectively handled approximately 6·5m. passengers. Belfast International, the busiest airport, is Northern Ireland's main charter airport with holiday flights operated direct to European destinations by a wide range of local and UK tour operators. In 2005, it launched a direct service to New York with Continental Airlines. Belfast International handled 4·5m. passengers in 2004.

Belfast City Airport offers commuter services to 18 regional airports in Great Britain and the Republic of Ireland including services to London Heathrow. The City of Derry Airport provides services from the northwest of Ireland to Dublin and to four United Kingdom destinations including London Stansted. There are two other licensed airfields at St Angelo and Newtownards. They are used principally by flying clubs, private owners and air taxi businesses.

Shipping

There are five commercial ports in Northern Ireland. Belfast is the largest port, competing with Larne for the majority of the passenger and Roll-on Roll-off services that operate to and from Northern Ireland. Passenger services are currently available to Liverpool, Stranraer, Cairnryan and Troon. In addition, Belfast, Londonderry and Warrenpoint ports offer bulk cargo services mostly for British and European markets. They also occasionally service other international destinations direct.

Total tonnage of goods through the principal ports in Northern Ireland in 2004 was 23·4m. tonnes. Belfast handled 13·6m. tonnes of cargo in 2004.

SOCIAL INSTITUTIONS

Justice

The Lord Chief Justice of Northern Ireland is President of the Courts of Northern Ireland and Head of the Judiciary and as such is responsible for assigning the judiciary to the courts. The Lord Chief Justice is also Chairman of the Judicial Appointments Commission which is responsible for selecting and recommending to the Lord Chancellor candidates for judicial appointment in Northern Ireland. The court structure in Northern Ireland has three tiers: the Court of Judicature of Northern Ireland (comprising the Court of Appeal, the High Court and the Crown Court), the County Courts and the Magistrates' Courts. There are 21 Petty Sessions districts which when grouped together for administration purposes form seven County Court Divisions and four Crown Court Circuits.

The County Court has general civil jurisdiction subject to an upper monetary limit. Appeals from the Magistrates' Courts lie to the County Court, or to the Court of Appeal on a point of law, while appeals from the County Court lie to the High Court or, on a point of law, to the Court of Appeal.

Police

Following legislation introduced in the House of Commons in May 2000, the name of the Royal Ulster Constabulary was changed to the Police Service of Northern Ireland (PSNI). The Police Authority for Northern Ireland has been replaced by the Northern Ireland Policing Board. The Police Service continues to undergo significant changes arising from the recommendations of the Commission into the future of policing in Northern Ireland published in 1999. In Dec. 2005 the PSNI comprised 7,503 regular officers including those student officers undergoing training, 1,060 full-time reserve officers and 854 part-time reserves. The proportion of Catholic regular officers, which was around 8% in Sept. 1999, had increased to 19·1% by Jan. 2006.

The population in penal institutions in Nov. 2003 was 1,220 (70 per 100,000 population).

Education

Public education, other than university education, is presently administered by the Department of Education, the Department of Employment and Learning, and locally by five Education and Library Boards. The Department of Education is concerned with the range of education from nursery education through to secondary, youth services and for the development of community relations within and between schools. The Department of Employment and Learning is responsible for higher education, further education, student support, postgraduate awards, and the funding of teacher training.

Each Education and Library Board is the local education and library authority for its area. Boards are statutory bodies which perform a wide range of functions in the funding and delivery of local education, youth and library services. Boards were first appointed in 1973 and are normally reappointed every four years following the District Council elections. The members of each Board are all Ministerial appointees and consist of district councillors, representatives of transferors of schools, representatives of trustees of maintained schools and other persons who are interested in the service for which the Board is responsible. The aim of each Board is to provide or secure the provision of high quality education, library and youth services, by making the best possible use of the resources made available to it in a way which ensures equality of opportunity for all.

Boards have a duty, amongst other things, to ensure that there are sufficient schools of all kinds to meet the needs of their areas. Boards are also directly responsible for the Local Management of Schools under the Common Funding Scheme. Boards are responsible under legislation for securing the provision in their areas of the following services: Primary and Secondary Education; Educational Services for Children with Special Needs; The Library Service; The Youth Service; Adult Education; School Meals; and Other services ancillary to education such as the Education Welfare Service, the Psychology Service and the Curriculum Advisory Service. Boards also have responsibilities in relation to: Student Support; Allocation of teaching posts in controlled schools; Transport for eligible pupils to and from school; School Boarding, maintenance and clothing allowances; and Other Miscellaneous Education Services. Boards are financed almost entirely by central government funds. Boards are accountable to the general public for their stewardship of public funds and to the Minister for Education for the performance of their functions.

The Boards are responsible for costs associated with capital works at controlled schools. Voluntary schools, including maintained and voluntary grammar schools, can receive grant-aid from the Department of Education toward capital works of up to 85%, or 100% if they have opted to change their management structures so that no single interest group has a majority of nominees. Most voluntary grammar schools can receive the same rate of grant on the purchase of equipment. Integrated schools receive 100% funding for recurrent costs from the Department of Education, and, where long-term viability has been established, for capital works.

The Education Reform (NI) Order 1989 made provision for the setting up of a Council for Catholic Maintained Schools with effect from April 1990. The Council has responsibility for all maintained schools under Roman Catholic Management which are under the auspices of the diocesan authorities and of religious orders. The main objective of the Council is to promote high standards of education in the schools for which it is responsible. Its functions include providing advice on matters relating to its schools, the employment of teaching staff and administration of appointment procedures, the promotion of effective management, and the promotion and co-ordination of effective planning and rationalization of school provision in the Catholic Maintained sector. The membership of the Council consists of trustee representatives appointed by the Northern Roman Catholic Bishops, parents, teachers, and persons appointed by the Head of the Department of Education in consultation with the Bishops.

There is a Council for the Curriculum, Examinations and Assessment which conducts public examinations and oversees the selection procedure and arrangements for pupil assessment. There is also the Northern Ireland Council for Integrated Education, both of which are grant-aided by the Department of Education.

Integrated Schools. The Department of Education has a statutory duty to encourage and facilitate the development of integrated education. It does not seek to impose integration but responds to parental demand for new integrated schools where this does not involve unreasonable public expenditure. The emphasis for future development of the integrated sector has increasingly been on the transformation of existing schools to integrated status. In Dec. 2005 there were 56 grant-aided integrated schools, with a total enrolment of 17,134 pupils, over 5% of all pupils.

Irish Medium Education. Following a commitment in the Belfast Agreement, the 1998 Education Order placed a statutory duty on the Department to encourage and facilitate the development of Irish-medium education. It also provided for the funding of an Irish-medium promotional body, and funding of Irish-medium schools on the same basis as integrated schools. In Dec. 2005 there were 19 Irish-medium primary schools, one post-primary and twelve units, two of which are post-primary catering for 2,935 pupils.

Pre-school Education is provided in nursery schools or nursery classes in primary schools, reception classes and in funded places in voluntary and private settings. There were 100 nursery schools in 2005–06 with 6,175 pupils, and 8,049 nursery pupils in primary schools. A further 754 reception pupils were enrolled in primary schools. In addition there were 5,952 children in funded places in voluntary and private pre-school education centres in 2004–05.

Primary Education is from four to 11 years. In 2005–06 there were 886 primary schools with 158,665 pupils. There were also 17 preparatory departments of grammar schools with 2,478 pupils. In 2004–05 there were 8,353 FTE primary school teachers and 149 FTE preparatory department teachers.

Secondary Education is compulsory from 11 to 16 years. In 2005–06 there were 69 grammar schools with 62,419 pupils and 161 secondary schools with 89,421 pupils. In 2004–05 there were 6,527 FTE secondary school teachers and 4,171 FTE grammar school teachers.

Further Education. There are 16 institutions of further education. In 2003–04 there were 1,703 full-time and 3,068 part-time teachers, approximately 31,000 full-time enrolments and approximately 110,000 part-time assembled enrolments. There were about 72,000 students on non-vocational (mostly evening) courses.

Special Education. The Education and Library Boards provide for children with special educational needs up to the age of 19. This provision may be made in ordinary classes in primary or secondary schools or in special units attached to those schools, or in special schools. In 2005–06 there were 48 special schools with 4,895 pupils. This includes three hospital schools.

Universities. There are two universities: the Queen's University of Belfast (founded in 1849 as a college of the Queen's University of Ireland and reconstituted as a separate university in 1908), which had 23,675 students, 1,368 full-time and 81 part-time academic staff in 2003–04; and the University of Ulster, formed on 1 Oct. 1984, which has campuses in Belfast, Coleraine, Jordanstown and Londonderry. In 2003–04 it had 26,202 students, 1,112 full-time and 360 part-time academic staff.

Full-Time Initial Teacher Education takes place at both universities and at two university colleges of education—Stranmillis and St Mary's—the latter mainly for the primary school sector, in respect of which four-year (Hons) BEd courses are available. The training of teachers for secondary schools is provided, in the main, in the education departments of the two universities, but four-year (Hons) BEd courses are also available in the colleges for intending secondary teachers of religious education, business studies and craft, design and technology. There were a total of 2,015 students (1,642 women) in training at the two university colleges and the two universities during 2003–04.

Health

The Department of Health, Social Services and Public Safety has three main business responsibilities: Health and Personal Social Services (HPSS), which includes policy and legislation for hospitals, family practitioner services, and community health and personal social services; Public Health, which covers policy, legislation and administrative action to promote and protect the health and well-being of the population; and Public Safety, which covers policy and legislation for fire, rescue and ambulance services.

The four Health and Social Services Boards commission health and personal social services for their resident populations from providers including HSS Trusts, and voluntary and private sector bodies. The 19 Health and Social Services Trusts, established under the Health and Personal Social Services (NI) Order 1991, are managerially independent but accountable to the Minister. They are the main providers of health and personal social services as commissioned by the HSS Boards and are responsible for the management of staff and services of hospitals and other health and personal social services establishments. Seven provide hospital services only, five provide community and personal social services only and six provide both. In 2007 there were 1,127 doctors (principals) with an average of 1,626 patients each.

The Northern Ireland Health and Social Welfare Survey 2005/06 found that around 24% of adults were obese (having a body mass index over 30).

Welfare

The Social Security Agency's remit is now part of the Department for Social Development, and social security schemes are similar to those in Great Britain.

National Insurance. During the year ended 31 March 2005 the expenditure of the National Insurance Fund at £1,671m. exceeded contributions by £33m. Total benefit expenditure was £1,671m. Jobseeker's Allowance contributions amounted to £13·4m. Retirement Pensions amounted to £1,192·3m. and Widow's Benefit to £34·2m. Incapacity Benefits totalled £313·0m. Maternity Allowance of £4·5m. was paid and employers were reimbursed £35·8m. in respect of Statutory Maternity Pay. £66·4m. was given to personal pension plan providers.

Child Benefit. In the year ended 31 March 2006 a total of £321m. was paid. In 2004–05, 142,000 families benefited from Child and Working Tax Credits.

RELIGION

According to the 2001 census there were: Roman Catholics, 678,462; Presbyterians, 348,742; Church of Ireland, 257,788; Methodists, 59,173; other Christian, 102,221; other religions and philosophies, 5,028. There were also 233,853 persons with no religion or religion was not stated.

CULTURE

Tourism

There were 2·11m. visits to Northern Ireland in 2007, contributing £376m. to the economy. Domestic holiday makers contributed a further £134m. The Northern Ireland Tourist Board is responsible for providing strategic direction, development of the tourism industry and marketing of tourism in Northern Ireland and the Republic of Ireland. Nine Areas of Outstanding Natural Beauty and 47 National Nature Reserves have been declared, and there are many country and regional parks.

FURTHER READING

Adshead, Maura and Tonge, Jonathan, *Politics in Ireland: Convergence and Divergence in a Two-Polity Island.* 2009
Aughey, A. and Morrow, D. (eds.) *Northern Ireland Politics.* 1996
Bardon, Jonathan, *A History of Ulster.* 1992
Bloomfield, D., *Peacemaking Strategies in Northern Ireland.* 1998
Bourke, Richard, *Peace in Ireland: The War of Ideas.* 2003
Bow, P. and Gillespie, G., *Northern Ireland: a Chronology of the Troubles, 1968–1993.* 1993
Dixon, Paul, *Northern Ireland: The Politics of War and Peace.* 2nd ed. 2008
Fay, Marie-Thérèse, Morrisey, Mike and Smyth, Marie, *Northern Ireland's Troubles.* 1999
Fletcher, Martin, *Silver Linings: Travels Around Northern Ireland.* 2000
Hennessey, T., *A History of Northern Ireland 1920–96.* 1998
Kennedy-Pipe, C., *The Origins of the Present Troubles in Northern Ireland.* 1997
Keogh, D. and Haltzel, M. (eds.) *Northern Ireland and the Politics of Reconciliation.* 1994
Loughlin, James, *The Ulster Question Since 1945.* 1998
McGarry, J. and O'Leary, B. (eds.) *Explaining Northern Ireland: Broken Images.* 1995
Neumann, Peter R., *Britain's Long War: British Strategy in the Northern Ireland Conflict, 1969–98.* 2003
Patterson, Henry, *Ireland Since 1939: The Persistence of Conflict.* 2006
Rose, Peter, *How the Troubles Came to Northern Ireland.* 1999
Ruane, J. and Todd, J., *The Dynamics of Conflict in Northern Ireland: Power, Conflict and Emancipation.* 1997
Tonge, Jonathan, *The New Northern Irish Politics?* 2004

Statistical office: Northern Ireland Statistics and Research Agency (NISRA), McAuley House, 2–14 Castle St., Belfast BT1 1SA.
Website: http://www.nisra.gov.uk

ISLE OF MAN

KEY HISTORICAL EVENTS

The Isle of Man was first inhabited 10,000 years ago. Part of Norway in the 9th century, in 1266 it was ceded to Scotland but came under English control in 1333.

The Isle of Man has been a British Crown dependency since 1765, with the British government responsible for its defence and foreign policy. Otherwise it has extensive right of self-government.

A special relationship exists between the Isle of Man and the European Union providing for free trade, and adoption by the Isle of Man of the EU's external trade policies with third countries. The island remains free to levy its own taxes.

TERRITORY AND POPULATION

Area, 572 sq. km (221 sq. miles); resident population census April 2006, 80,058, giving a density of 140 per sq. km. In 2006 an estimated 76% of the population lived in urban areas. The principal towns are Douglas (population, 26,218), Onchan (adjoining Douglas; 9,172), Ramsey (7,309), Peel (4,280) and Castletown (3,109). The island is divided into six sheadings—Ayre, Garff, Glenfaba, Michael, Middle and Rushen. Garff is further subdivided into two parishes and the others each have three parishes. Just over half the population at the 2006 census was born outside of the island.

SOCIAL STATISTICS

2006: births, 905; deaths, 768; marriages (2004), 399. Annual growth rate, 2001–06, 1·0%.

CLIMATE

Lying in the Irish Sea, the island's climate is temperate and lacking in extremes. Thunderstorms, snow and frost are infrequent, although the island tends to be windy. July and Aug. are the warmest months with an average daily maximum temperature of around 17·6°C (63°F).

CONSTITUTION AND GOVERNMENT

As a result of Revestment in 1765, the Isle of Man became a dependency of the British Crown. The UK government is responsible for the external relations of the island, including its defence and international affairs, and the island makes a financial contribution to the cost of these services. The Isle of Man has a special relationship with the European Union. It neither contributes funds to, nor receives money from, the EU. The Isle of Man is not represented in either the UK or European Parliaments.

The island is administered in accordance with its own laws by the High Court of *Tynwald*, consisting of the President of Tynwald, the *Legislative Council* and the *House of Keys*. The Legislative Council is composed of the Lord Bishop of Sodor and Man, eight members selected by the House of Keys and the Attorney General, who has no vote. The House of Keys is an assembly of 24 members chosen by adult suffrage. The minimum age for voting was lowered to 16 in 2006. The President of Tynwald is chosen by the Legislative Council and the House of Keys, sitting together as Tynwald. An open-air Tynwald ceremony is held in early July each year at St Johns. Until 1990 the Lieut.-Governor, appointed by the UK government, presided over Tynwald.

A Council of Ministers was instituted in 1990, replacing the Executive Council which had acted as an advisory body to the Lieut.-Governor. The Council of Ministers consists of the Chief Minister (elected for a five-year term) and the ministers of the nine major departments, being the Treasury; Agriculture, Fisheries and Forestry; Education; Health and Social Security; Home Affairs; Local Government and the Environment; Tourism and Leisure; Trade and Industry; and Transport.

RECENT ELECTIONS

Elections to the House of Keys were held on 23 Nov. 2006. Independents took 21 of the 24 seats, the Liberal Vannin Party 2 and the Manx Labour Party 1. Turnout was 61·2%.

CURRENT ADMINISTRATION

Lieut.-Governor: Sir Paul Haddacks.

President: Noel Cringle (elected April 2000).

In March 2010 the *Chief Minister* was Tony Brown. *Treasury Minister:* Allan Bell.

Website: http://www.gov.im

ECONOMY

Currency

The Isle of Man government issues its own notes and coins on a par with £ sterling. Various commemorative coins have been minted. Inflation was 3·0% in 2006.

Budget

The Isle of Man is statutorily required to budget for a surplus of revenue over expenditure. Revenue is raised from income tax, taxes on expenditure, health and social security contributions, and fees and charges for services.

The standard rate of tax is 10% for personal income, and there is a higher rate of 18%. Banking and land property businesses are liable at 10% on their first £100m. of taxable income and 18% on the balance.

There is a Customs and Excise Agreement with the UK, and rates of tax on expenditure are the same as those in the UK with very few exceptions. In addition, there is a reciprocal agreement on social security with the UK, and the rates of most health and social security (National Insurance) contributions are the same as in the UK.

In 2007–08 the Isle of Man government budgeted for expenditure of £809m. and revenue of £845m.

Performance

In 2005–06 GNP was £1,700m. and GDP was £1,634m. Real GDP growth in 2005–06 was 5·7%. Just over 80% of national income is generated from services with the finance sector being the single largest contributor (36%).

Banking and Finance

The banking sector is regulated by the Financial Supervision Commission which is responsible for the licensing and supervision of banks, deposit-takers and financial intermediaries giving financial advice, and receiving client monies for investment and management. A compensation fund to protect investors was set up in 1991 under the Commission.

In Dec. 2006 the deposit base was £43bn., and there were 42 licensed banks, 65 investment businesses and three building societies with Isle of Man licences.

The insurance industry is regulated by the Insurance and Pensions Authority. In June 2006 there were 178 insurance companies.

ENERGY AND NATURAL RESOURCES

Electricity

The Manx Electricity Authority generates most of the island's electricity by oil-fired power stations although there is a small hydro-electric plant. A cable link with the UK power grid came into operation in Nov. 2000. In 2006, 379m. kWh were sold.

Oil and Gas

All oil and gas needs are met from imports, with gas being imported via a link to the Scotland–Eire gas pipeline. The island's gas suppliers and distributors are in the private sector.

Minerals

Although lead and tin mining industries were major employers in the past, they have long since shut down and the only mining activity in the island is now for aggregates. The Lady Isabella, built in 1854 to drain the mines above Laxey, is one of the largest waterwheels in Europe.

Agriculture

The area farmed is about 104,000 acres, being 74% of a total land area of around 141,500 acres. 65,000 acres are grassland with a further 27,000 acres for rough grazing. There are approximately 137,000 sheep, 30,000 cattle, 20,000 poultry and 600 pigs on the island's 658 farms. Agriculture now contributes less than 2% of the island's GDP.

Forestry

The Department of Agriculture, Fisheries and Forestry has a forestry estate of some 6,800 acres. Commercial forestry is directed towards softwood production. The Manx National Glens and other amenity areas are maintained for public use by the Department, which owns some 18,000 acres of the island's hills and uplands open for public use.

Fisheries

The Isle of Man is noted for the Manx kipper, a gutted smoked herring. Scallops and the related queen scallops (queenies) are the economic mainstay of the Manx fishing fleet. In 2006 the total catch was about 2,000 tonnes.

INDUSTRY

Labour

The economically active population in 2006 was 41,793, of whom 6,381 were self-employed and 1,010 were unemployed. Employment by sector: finance, 23%; professional services, 20%; distributive services, 11%; construction, 8%; manufacturing, 5%.

At the end of 2006 there were 577 persons on the unemployment register, giving an unemployment rate of 1·4%.

Trade Unions

There were 42 registered trade unions in 2007.

INTERNATIONAL TRADE

The Isle of Man forms part of the customs union of the European Union, although the island is not part of the EU itself. The relationship with the EU provides for free trade and the adoption of the EU's external trade policies and tariffs with non-EU countries.

Imports and Exports

The Isle of Man is in customs and excise union with the United Kingdom, which is also its main trading partner.

COMMUNICATIONS

Roads

There are 800 km of good roads. At the end of March 2003 there were 63,233 licensed vehicles, with 50,596 of these being private cars. Omnibus services operate to all parts of the island. The TT (Tourist Trophy) motorcycle races take place annually on the 60·75-km Mountain Circuit.

Rail

Several novel transport systems operate on the island during the summer season from May to Sept. Horse-drawn trams run along Douglas promenade, and the Manx Electric Railway links Douglas, Laxey, Ramsey and Snaefell Mountain (621 metres) in the north. The Isle of Man Steam Railway also operates between Douglas and Port Erin in the south.

Civil Aviation

Ronaldsway Airport in the south handles scheduled services linking the island with Belfast, Birmingham, Blackpool, Bristol, Brussels, Dublin, East Midlands, Edinburgh, Glasgow, Jersey, Leeds, Liverpool, London, Manchester, Prestwick and Southampton. Air taxi services also operate.

Shipping

Car ferries run between Douglas and the UK and the Irish Republic. In 2006 there were 316 merchant vessels on the island's shipping register.

Telecommunications

Manx Telecom Limited, a wholly owned subsidiary of O2, holds the telecommunications licence issued by the Communications Commission for the Isle of Man.

Postal Services

The Isle of Man Post Office Authority operates the island's mail system and issues various commemorative stamps.

SOCIAL INSTITUTIONS

Justice

The First Deemster is the head of the Isle of Man's judiciary. The Isle of Man Constabulary numbered 236 all ranks in 2007.

The average size of the prison population during 2006 was 72·8, equivalent to 91 per 100,000 of national population. A further four persons are serving their sentences in the United Kingdom.

Education

Education is compulsory between the ages of five and 16. In 2006 there were 6,610 pupils in the 35 infant and junior schools and 5,667 pupils in the five secondary schools operated by the Department of Education. The Department also runs a college of further education and a special school. Government expenditure on education was budgeted to be £100m. in 2007–08. The island has a private primary school, a private secondary school and an international business school.

Health

The island has had its own National Health Service since 1948, providing medical, dental and ophthalmic services. In 2007–08 government expenditure on the NHS was budgeted to be £129m. There are two hospitals, one of which opened in 2003. In 2006 there were 120 full-time equivalent physicians, 41 full-time and seven part-time general practitioners, 42 full-time and two part-time dentists, and 24 pharmacies.

Welfare

Numbers receiving certain benefits at July 2007: Retirement Pension, 16,713; Child Benefit, 9,781; Sick and Disablement Benefits, 5,518; Income Support, 3,008; Jobseekers' Allowance, 163. Total government expenditure on the social security system in 2007–08 was budgeted to be £201m.

RELIGION

The island has a rich heritage of Christian associations, and the Diocese of Sodor and Man, one of the oldest in the British Isles, has existed since 476.

CULTURE

Broadcasting

Manx Radio is a commercial broadcaster operated by the government from Douglas.

Press

In 2007 there were three weekly newspapers and one quarterly newspaper. There are also various magazines concentrating on Manx issues.

Tourism

During the late 19th century through to the middle of the 20th century, tourism was one of the island's main sources of income and employment. Tourism now contributes around 5% of the island's GDP. There were 219,000 visitors during 2006.

FURTHER READING

Additional information is available from: Economic Affairs Division, Illiam Dhone House, 2 Circular Rd, Douglas, Isle of Man, IM1 1PQ. *Email:* economics@gov.im

Isle of Man Digest of Economic and Social Statistics. Annual

Belchem, J. (ed.) *A New History of the Isle of Man, Volume V—The Modern Period 1830–1999.* 2000

Kermode, D. G., *Offshore Island Politics: The Constitutional and Political Development of the Isle of Man in the Twentieth Century.* 2001

Moore, A. W., *A History of the Isle of Man.* 1900; reprinted 1992

Solly, M., *Government and Law in the Isle of Man.* 1994

Manx National Heritage publishes a series of booklets including *Early Maps of the Isle of Man, The Art of the Manx Crosses, The Ancient & Historic Monuments of the Isle of Man, Pre-historic Sites of the Isle of Man.*

CHANNEL ISLANDS

KEY HISTORICAL EVENTS

The Channel Islands consist of Jersey, Guernsey and the following dependencies of Guernsey: Alderney, Brechou, Great Sark, Little Sark, Herm, Jethou and Lihou. They were an integral part of the Duchy of Normandy at the time of the Norman Conquest of England in 1066. Since then they have belonged to the British Crown and are not part of the UK. The islands have created their own self-government, with the British government at Westminster being responsible for defence and foreign policy. The Lieut.-Governors of Jersey and Guernsey, appointed by the Crown, are the personal representatives of the Sovereign as well as being the commanders of the armed forces. The legislature of Jersey is 'The States of Jersey', and that of Guernsey is 'The States of Deliberation'.

Left undefended from 1940 to 1945 the islands were the only British territory to fall to Germany.

TERRITORY AND POPULATION

The Channel Islands cover a total of 194 sq. km (75 sq. miles), and in 2008 had a population of approximately 150,000.

The official languages are French and English, but English is now the main language.

CLIMATE

The climate is mild, with an average temperature for the year of 11·5°C. Average yearly rainfall totals: Jersey, 862·9 mm; Guernsey, 858·9 mm. The wettest months are in the winter. Highest temperatures recorded: Jersey (St Helier), 36·0°C; Guernsey (airport), 33·7°C. Maximum temperatures usually occur in July and Aug. (daily maximum 20·8°C in Jersey, slightly lower in Guernsey). Lowest temperatures recorded: Jersey, –10·3°C; Guernsey, –7·4°C. Jan. and Feb. are the coldest months (mean temperature approximately 6°C).

CONSTITUTION AND GOVERNMENT

The Lieut.-Governors and Cs.-in-C. of Jersey and Guernsey are the personal representatives of the Sovereign, the Commanders of the Armed Forces of the Crown, and the channel of communication between the Crown and the insular governments. They are appointed by the Crown and have a voice but no vote in the islands' legislatures. The Secretaries to the Lieut.-Governors are their staff officers.

ENERGY AND NATURAL RESOURCES

Fisheries

Total catch in 2005 was 3,505 tonnes, exclusively from sea fishing.

EXTERNAL ECONOMIC RELATIONS

The Channel Islands are not members of the European Union but under a special relationship accept a number of European laws, including certain EU customs regulations. Trade with the UK is classed as domestic.

COMMUNICATIONS

Civil Aviation

Scheduled air services are maintained by Aer Lingus, Aurigny Air Services, bmibaby, British Airways, British Midland, Cathay Pacific Airways, Flybe British European, Scot Airways and VLM Airlines.

Shipping

Passenger and cargo services between Jersey, Guernsey, England (Poole, Portsmouth and Weymouth) and France (St Malo) are maintained by Condor Ferries. Local companies run between Guernsey, Alderney and England, and between Guernsey and Sark. In 2003 the merchant marine totalled 1,000 GRT.

SOCIAL INSTITUTIONS

Justice

Justice is administered by the Royal Courts of Jersey and Guernsey, each of which consists of the Bailiff and 12 Jurats (magistrates), the latter being elected by an electoral college. There is an appeal from the Royal Courts to the Courts of Appeal of Jersey and of Guernsey. A final appeal lies to the Privy Council in certain cases. A stipendiary magistrate in each, Jersey and Guernsey, deals with minor civil and criminal cases.

RELIGION

Jersey and Guernsey each constitutes a deanery under the jurisdiction of the Bishop of Winchester. The rectories (12 in Jersey; 10 in Guernsey) are in the gift of the Crown. The Roman Catholic and various Nonconformist Churches are represented.

FURTHER READING

Lemprière, R., *History of the Channel Islands.* Rev. ed. 1980

Jersey

TERRITORY AND POPULATION

The area is 116·2 sq. km (44·9 sq. miles). Resident population (2001 census), 87,186 (44,701 females); density, 750 per sq. km. The chief town is St Helier on the south coast. It had a population of 28,310 in 2001. The official language is English (French until 1960). The island has its own language, known as Jersey French, or Jérriaise. French, Portuguese and Polish are also spoken.

SOCIAL STATISTICS

In 2007 there were 1,030 births and 707 deaths. Infant mortality rate, 2004 (per 1,000 live births), 3·0. In 2007 there were 586 marriages. Life expectancy, 2000–04: males, 72 years; females, 79 years.

CONSTITUTION AND GOVERNMENT

The island parliament is the *States of Jersey*. The States comprises the Bailiff, the Lieut.-Governor, the Dean of Jersey, the Attorney-General and the Solicitor-General, and 53 members elected by universal suffrage: 12 Senators (elected for six years, six retiring every third year), the Constables of the 12 parishes (every third year) and 29 Deputies (every third year). They all have the right to speak in the Assembly, but only the 53 elected members have the right to vote; the Bailiff has a casting vote. Except in specific instances, enactments passed by the States require the sanction of The Queen-in-Council. The Lieut.-Governor has the power of veto on certain forms of legislation.

A new post of Chief Minister was inaugurated in 2005. The chief minister, who is elected by the States, presides over a nine-member Council of Ministers responsible for government policy.

RECENT ELECTIONS

On 8 Dec. 2008 parliament elected Terry Le Sueur Chief Minister by 36 votes to 17.

CURRENT ADMINISTRATION

Lieut.-Governor and C.-in-C. of Jersey: Lieut.-Gen. Andrew Ridgway, CB, CBE, QCVS.

Secretary and Aide-de-Camp to the Lieut.-Governor: Lieut. Col. C. Woodrow, OBE, MC, QGM.

Bailiff of Jersey and President of the States: Michael Birt.

Chief Minister: Terry Le Sueur.

Government Website: http://www.gov.je

ECONOMY

Currency

The States issue banknotes in denominations of £50, £20, £10, £5 and £1. Coinage from 1p to 50p is struck in the same denominations as the UK. There were £75·6m. worth of States of Jersey banknotes and £6·7m. worth of coinage in circulation in 2007. Inflation in Sept. 2007 was 3·9%.

Budget

2004 general funds income, £441m.; expenditure, £412m. Income from taxation was forecast to be £363m.

Parochial rates are payable by owners and occupiers.

Performance

In 2005 total GDP was £2·8bn.

Banking and Finance

In 2007 there were 48 banks; combined deposits were £219·5bn. There were 4,050 registered companies in 2007.

A 0% rate of company tax was introduced on 1 Jan. 2009.

ENERGY AND NATURAL RESOURCES

Agriculture

2003 total agricultural exports, £28,010,729. Jersey Royal New Potatoes account for 60% of Jersey's agricultural exports to the UK. 48·9% of the island's land area was farmed commercially in 2003. There were 294 commercial farms. In 2003 there were 5,708 cattle (3,615 milch cows).

Fisheries

There were 184 fishing vessels in 2005. The total catch in 2006 was 1,720 tonnes, plus 771 farmed oysters and mussels. The value of the fishing industry in 2006 was £6m.

INDUSTRY

Principal activities: light industry, mainly electrical goods, textiles and clothing.

Labour

In June 2005, 52,910 persons were economically active; in July 2005, 355 persons were registered unemployed. Financial and legal services was the largest employment sector, followed by wholesale and retail trades and the public sector.

EXTERNAL ECONOMIC RELATIONS

Imports and Exports

Since 1980 the Customs have ceased recording imports and exports. Principal imports: machinery and transport equipment, manufactured goods, food, mineral fuels, and chemicals. Principal exports: machinery and transport equipment, food, and manufactured goods.

COMMUNICATIONS

Roads

In 2002 there were 74,007 private cars, 3,599 hire cars, 7,899 vans, 4,211 lorries, 847 buses and coaches, and 8,505 motorcycles and scooters.

Civil Aviation

Jersey airport is situated at St Peter. It covers approximately 375 acres. In 2005 the airport handled 1,483,000 passengers.

Shipping

All vessels arriving in Jersey from outside Jersey waters report at St Helier or Gorey on first arrival. There is a harbour of minor importance at St Aubin. Number of commercial vessels entering St Helier in 2002, 3,346; number of visiting yachts, 6,741. There were 459,594 passenger arrivals and 459,348 passenger departures in 2002.

Telecommunications

Postal, and overseas telephone and telegraph services, are maintained by the Postal Administration of Jersey. The local telephone service is maintained by the Insular Authority. In 2008 main telephone lines numbered 74,000. There were 83,900 mobile phone subscribers in 2004.

Postal Services

In 2003 there were 21 post offices; a total of 72·5m. letters were processed.

SOCIAL INSTITUTIONS

Justice

Justice is administered by the Royal Court, consisting of the Bailiff and 12 Jurats (magistrates). There is a final appeal in certain cases to the Sovereign in Council. There is also a Court of Appeal, consisting of the Bailiff and two judges. Minor civil and criminal cases are dealt with by a stipendiary magistrate.

In 2002 there were 15,201 telephone calls requiring operational response; there were 5,427 crime offences, 1,134 disorder offences and 716 road traffic accidents. In 2005 the daily average prison population was 172.

Education

In 2007 there were six States secondary schools (two fee-paying), one high school and four special needs secondary schools. There were 24 States primary schools (two fee-paying). 4,196 pupils attended secondary schools and 5,675 attended primary schools, and there were 288 pupils with special needs. There were five private primary schools with 1,330 pupils and three private secondary schools with 1,078 pupils. Public expenditure on education amounted to 2·8% of GNI in 2006.

Health

Expenditure on health and social services in 2005 was £127,493,000. In 2007 there was one general hospital with about 175 beds. In 2007 there were 97 doctors (general practitioners).

Welfare

A contributory Health Insurance Scheme is administered by the Social Security Department. In 2002 state expenditure for supplementation on the Social Security Fund was £48,136,000. £4,925,000 was paid out in Family Allowance, £5,823,000 on Disability Transport Allowance, £2,910,000 on Non-native Welfare, £3,094,000 on Attendance Allowance and £1,151,000 on the administration of community benefits.

CULTURE

Tourism

In 2005 there were 752,270 visitors to the island, spending £220m.

FURTHER READING

Balleine, G. R., *A History of the Island of Jersey.* Rev. ed. 1981

States of Jersey Library: Halkett Place, St Helier.
Statistical Office: Statistics Unit, P.O. Box 140, Cyril Le Marquand House, The Parade, St Helier, Jersey, JE4 8QT.
Website: http://www.gov.je/ChiefMinister/Statistics

Guernsey

TERRITORY AND POPULATION

The area is 63·4 sq. km. Census population (2001) 59,807; 2007 population estimate, 61,811. The main town is St Peter Port (2001 population of 16,488).

English is the most widely spoken language. A Norman-French dialect (called Guernsey French or Guernesiais) is spoken by a small number of (mainly older) people. It is now being reintroduced into some school curriculums.

SOCIAL STATISTICS

Births during 2007 were 645; deaths, 513.

CONSTITUTION AND GOVERNMENT

The States of Deliberation, the Parliament of Guernsey, is composed of the following members: the Bailiff, who is President *ex officio*; H.M. Procureur and H.M. Comptroller (Law Officers of the Crown), who have a voice but no vote; 45 People's Deputies elected by popular franchise; ten Douzaine Representatives elected by their Parochial Douzaines; two representatives of the States of Alderney. Since May 2004 there has been a slimmed-down States of Deliberation, and an executive form of government has been introduced. For the first time a Chief Minister has been appointed. There are also ministers, a deputy chief minister, members of departmental committees, chairmen and members of committees.

The States of Election, an electoral college, elects the Jurats (magistrates). It is composed of the following members: the Bailiff (President *ex officio*); the 12 Jurats or 'Jurés-Justiciers'; H.M. Procureur and H.M. Comptroller; the 45 People's Deputies and 34 representatives from the 10 Parochial Douzaines.

Since Jan. 1949 all legislative powers and functions (with minor exceptions) formerly exercised by the Royal Court have been vested in the States of Deliberation. Projets de Loi (Bills) require the sanction of The Queen-in-Council.

RECENT ELECTIONS

Elections for People's Deputies were held on 23 April 2008.

CURRENT ADMINISTRATION

Lieut.-Governor and C.-in-C. of Guernsey and its Dependencies: Vice Adm. Sir Fabian Malbon, KBE.

Secretary and Aide-de-Camp to the Lieut.-Governor: Colonel R. H. Graham, MBE.

Bailiff of Guernsey and President of the States: Geoffrey Rowland.

Chief Minister: Lyndon Trott.

Government Website: http://www.gov.gg

ECONOMY

Budget

Year ended 31 Dec. 2007: revenue £365,000,000; expenditure, £294,000,000. The standard rate of income tax is 20p in the pound. States and parochial rates are very moderate. No super-tax or death duties are levied.

Banking and Finance

In March 2008 there were 346 employers in the finance and legal sector, employing a total of 7,893 people. Financial services accounts for approximately 35% of Guernsey's GDP.

The general rate of income tax payable by Guernsey companies, formerly 20%, has been 0% since 1 Jan. 2008.

INDUSTRY

Trade Unions

There is a Transport & General Workers' Union.

EXTERNAL ECONOMIC RELATIONS

Imports and Exports

In 2007, 125,538,000 litres of oil were imported. Horticulture exports (2006) in £1m.: plants, 34·95; postal flowers, 6·62; food, 3·26; cut flowers, 2·08.

COMMUNICATIONS

Civil Aviation

The airport is situated at La Villiaze. There were direct flights in 2008 to Alderney, Birmingham, Bristol, Dinard, East Midlands, Exeter, Geneva, Grenoble, Isle of Man, Jersey, London (Gatwick and Stansted), Manchester, Plymouth, Rotterdam, Southampton and Zürich. In 2008 passenger movements totalled 918,978.

Shipping

The principal port is St Peter Port. There is also a harbour at St Sampson's (mainly for commercial shipping). In 2008 sea passenger movements totalled 333,865. There were 277 fishing vessels registered in 2008 and more than 5,000 other craft.

Telecommunications

There were 45,100 main telephone lines in 2004, or 809 per 1,000 population. Mobile phone subscribers numbered 43,800 in 2004. Guernsey Telecom was sold to Cable and Wireless in May 2002 and now trades as C & W Guernsey.

SOCIAL INSTITUTIONS

Justice

The population in penal institutions in Nov. 2003 was 83 (equivalent to 128 per 100,000 population).

Education

There are two public schools, one grammar school, a number of modern secondary and primary schools, and a College of Further Education. The total number of schoolchildren in Jan. 2008 was 9,033. Facilities are available for the study of art, domestic science and many other subjects of a technical nature.

Health

Guernsey is not covered by the UK National Health Service. Public health is overseen by the States of Guernsey Insurance Authority and Department of Health. A private medical insurance scheme to provide specialist cover for all residents was implemented by the States on 1 Jan. 1996. In 2005 there was one hospital and 112 general practitioners and consultants.

CULTURE

Broadcasting

Guernsey is served by BBC Radio Guernsey, Island FM and Channel Television.

Press

The *Guernsey Evening Press* is published daily except Sundays.

Tourism

There were 316,000 visitors to Guernsey in 2006 (332,000 in 2005). In 2006 there were 220,000 holidaymakers (218,000 in 2005), 54,000 people visiting friends and relatives (70,000 in 2005) and 36,000 business visitors (41,000 in 2005).

FURTHER READING

Marr, L. J., *A History of Guernsey.* 1982
Statistical office: Policy and Research Unit, P. O. Box 43, Sir Charles Frossard House, La Charroterie, St. Peter Port, GY4 6EF.
Website: http://www.gov.gg/ccm/navigation/government/facts---figures

Alderney

GENERAL DETAILS

Population (2001 estimate), 2,400. The main town is St Anne's. The island has an airport.

The Constitution of the island (reformed 1987) provides for its own popularly elected President and States (10 members), and its own Court. Elections were held for the five members of the States in Dec. 2008. Alderney levies its taxes at Guernsey rates and passes the revenue to Guernsey, which charges for the services it provides.

President of the States. Sir Norman Browse.
Chief Executive. David Jeremiah, OBE, QC.
Greffier. Sarah Kelly.

FURTHER READING

Coysh, V., *Alderney.* 1974

Sark

GENERAL DETAILS

2001 population estimate, 580. In order to comply with European human rights legislation, the constitution was amended in Jan. 2008 to make the Chief Pleas (parliament) democratically electable. Previously 40 out of 52 seats were reserved for land-owners. Elections took place in Dec. 2008 for a fully-elected 28-seat chamber that held its first session on 21 Jan. 2009. In addition, the powers of the Seigneur (who is head of the island) have been restricted. These changes are a decisive move away from the previously feudal system. Sark has no income tax. Motor vehicles, except tractors, are not allowed.

Seigneur. J. M. Beaumont.
Seneschal. R. J. Guille.

FURTHER READING

Hathaway, S., *Dame of Sark: An Autobiography.* 1961

UNITED KINGDOM OVERSEAS TERRITORIES

There are 14 British Overseas Territories: Anguilla; Bermuda; British Antarctic Territory; British Indian Ocean Territory; British Virgin Islands; Cayman Islands; Falkland Islands; Gibraltar; Montserrat; Pitcairn Islands; St Helena, Ascension and Tristan da Cunha; South Georgia and the South Sandwich Islands; the Sovereign Base Areas of Akrotiri and Dhekelia in Cyprus; and the Turks and Caicos Islands. Three (British Antarctic Territory, British Indian Ocean Territory and South Georgia and the South Sandwich Islands) have no resident populations and are administered by a commissioner instead of a governor.

Gibraltar is a peninsula bordering the south coast of Spain; the Sovereign Base Areas are in Cyprus and the remainder are islands in the Caribbean, Pacific, Indian Ocean and South Atlantic. Gibraltar and the Falkland Islands are the subjects of territorial claims by Spain and Argentina respectively.

The Overseas Territories are constitutionally not part of the United Kingdom. They have separate constitutions, and most of them have elected governments with varying degrees of responsibilities for domestic matters. The Governor, who is appointed by, and represents, HM the Queen, retains responsibility for external affairs, internal security, defence, and in most cases the public service.

At the launch of the White Paper 'Partnership for Progress and Prosperity', in March 1999, the UK Foreign Secretary at the time, Robin Cook, outlined four underlying principles for the relationship between Britain and the Overseas Territories: self-determination for the Territories; mutual obligations and responsibilities; freedom for the Territories to run their own affairs to the greatest degree possible; and Britain's firm commitment to help the territories develop economically and to assist them in emergencies. He also offered British citizenship, with the right of abode in the UK, to those citizens of the Overseas Territories who did not already enjoy it. The Overseas Territories Consultative Council was established in 1999. The Council, which meets annually, is a forum for discussion of key policy issues between British government ministers and heads of territory governments. On 21 May 2002 the citizenship provisions of the British Overseas Territories Act came into force. It granted British citizenship to the citizens of all Britain's Overseas Territories (except those who derived their British nationality by virtue only of a connection with the Sovereign Base Areas of Akrotiri and Dhekelia in Cyprus).

Anguilla

KEY HISTORICAL EVENTS

Anguilla was probably given its name by the Spaniards or the French because of its eel-like shape. It was inhabited by Arawaks for several centuries before the arrival of Europeans. Anguilla was colonized in 1650 by English settlers from neighbouring St Kitts. In 1688 the island was attacked by a party of Irishmen who then settled. Anguilla was subsequently administered as part of the Leeward Islands and from 1825 became even more closely associated with St Kitts. In 1875 a petition sent to London requesting separate status and direct rule from Britain met with a negative response. Again, in 1958, the islanders petitioned the Governor requesting a dissolution of the political and administrative association with St Kitts, but this too failed. From 1958 to 1962 Anguilla was part of the Federation of the West Indies.

Opposition to rule from St Kitts erupted on 30 May 1967 when St Kitts policemen were evicted from the island and Anguilla refused to recognize the authority of the State government any longer. During 1968–69 the British government maintained a 'Senior British Official' to advise the local Anguilla Council and devise a solution to the problem. In March 1969, following the ejection from the island of a high-ranking British civil servant, British security forces occupied Anguilla. A Commissioner was installed, and in 1969 Anguilla became *de facto* a separate dependency of Britain, a situation rendered *de jure* on 19 Dec. 1980 under the Anguilla Act 1980 when Anguilla formally separated from the territory of St Kitts-Nevis-Anguilla. A new constitution came into effect in 1982 providing for a large measure of autonomy under the Crown.

TERRITORY AND POPULATION

Anguilla is the most northerly of the Leeward Islands, some 112 km (70 miles) to the northwest of St Kitts and 8 km (5 miles) to the north of St Martin/Sint Maarten. The territory also comprises the island of Sombrero and several other off-shore islets or cays. The total area of the territory is about 155 sq. km (60 sq. miles). *De jure* census population (2001) was 11,561; density of 74·6 per sq. km. Average annual population increase between 1992 and 2001 was 3·2%. People of African descent make up 90% of the population, mixed origins 5% and white 4%. The capital is The Valley.

The official language is English.

SOCIAL STATISTICS

Births, 2001, 183; deaths, 66. In 2001 life expectancy at birth for females was 78·0 years and for males 77·9 years. Households numbered 3,788 in 2001.

CLIMATE

Tropical oceanic climate with rain throughout the year, particularly between May and Dec. Tropical storms and hurricanes may occur between July and Nov. Generally summers are hotter than winters although there is little variation in temperatures.

CONSTITUTION AND GOVERNMENT

A set of amendments to the constitution came into effect in 1990, providing for a Deputy Governor, a Parliamentary Secretary and an Opposition Leader. The *House of Assembly* consists of a Speaker, Deputy Speaker, seven directly elected members for five-year terms, two nominated members and two *ex officio* members: the Deputy Governor and the Attorney-General. The Governor discharges his executive powers on the advice of an Executive Council comprising a Chief Minister, three Ministers and two *ex officio* members: the Deputy Governor, Attorney-General and the Secretary to the Executive Council.

RECENT ELECTIONS

In parliamentary elections held on 15 Feb. 2010 the Anguilla United Movement won four of seven seats, the United Front (Anguilla National Alliance and Anguilla Democratic Party) two and the Anguilla Progressive Party one. Turnout was 82·1%.

CURRENT ADMINISTRATION

Governor: Alistair Harrison (took office on 21 April 2009).

Chief Minister: Hubert Hughes; b. 1933 (Anguilla United Movement; sworn in 16 Feb. 2010).

Government Website: http://www.gov.ai

ECONOMY

Currency

The *East Caribbean dollar* (*see* ANTIGUA AND BARBUDA: Currency).

Budget
In 1998 government revenue was EC$72·3m. and expenditure EC$71·0m. The main sources of revenue are custom duties, tourism and bank licence fees. There is little taxation.

Performance
2002 saw a recession, with the economy shrinking by 3·7%. There was then a recovery in 2003, with growth of 3·8%.

Banking and Finance
The East Caribbean Central Bank based in St Kitts-Nevis functions as a central bank. The *Governor* is Sir Dwight Venner. There is a small offshore banking sector. In 1996 there were two domestic and two foreign commercial banks.

ENERGY AND NATURAL RESOURCES

Electricity
Production (2004) 62m. kWh.

Agriculture
Because of low rainfall, agriculture potential is limited. About 1,200 ha. are cultivable. Main crops are pigeon peas, maize and sweet potatoes. Livestock consists of sheep, goats, pigs and poultry. The island relies on imports for food.

Fisheries
Fishing is a thriving industry (mainly lobster). The total catch in 2005 was 250 tonnes.

INDUSTRY

Labour
The unemployment rate was 7·8% in July 2002.

EXTERNAL ECONOMIC RELATIONS

Imports and Exports
Imports in 2005 (and 2004) totalled US$114·3m. (US$90·2m.); exports in 2005 (and 2004) totalled US$15·0m. (US$6·0m.).

COMMUNICATIONS

Roads
There are about 63 km of main roads and 112 km of secondary roads. In 2004 there were 6,681 vehicles in use, including 4,193 passenger cars and 219 vans and lorries.

Civil Aviation
Wallblake is the airport for The Valley. Anguilla is linked to neighbouring islands by services operated by American Airlines, Caribbean Star Airlines, Coastal Air Transport, LIAT and WINAIR.

Shipping
The main seaports are Sandy Ground and Blowing Point, the latter serving passenger and cargo traffic to and from St Martin. In 2002 merchant shipping totalled 1,000 GRT.

Telecommunications
There is a modern internal telephone service with (2008) 5,800 main lines in operation; and fax and internet services. In 2008 there were 13,100 mobile phone subscribers.

SOCIAL INSTITUTIONS

Justice
Justice is based on UK common law as exercised by the Eastern Caribbean Supreme Court on St Lucia. Final appeal lies to the UK Privy Council.

Education
Adult literacy was 80% in 1995. Education is free and compulsory between the ages of five and 17 years. There are six government primary schools with (1996) 1,540 pupils and one comprehensive school with (1996) 1,060 pupils. Higher education is provided at regional universities and similar institutions.

In 1998–99 expenditure on education came to 14·4% of total expenditure.

Health
In 2003 there was one hospital with a total of 36 beds; there were also four health centres and a government dental clinic. There were nine government-employed and five private doctors, two dentists and 32 nurses in 2003.

RELIGION
There were in 2001 Anglicans (29%), Methodists (24%), plus Seventh Day Adventists, Pentecostalists, Church of God, Baptists and Roman Catholics as significant minorities.

CULTURE

Broadcasting
There is one government (Radio Anguilla) and two other radio broadcasters. TV is privately owned; there are two channels and a cable system. In 1997 there were 1,000 television receivers.

Press
In 2006 there were two weeklies, *The Anguillan* and *The Light*.

Tourism
Tourism accounts for 50% of GDP. In 2003 there were 47,000 visitor arrivals, with revenue totalling US$60m.

FURTHER READING

Petty, C. L., *Anguilla: Where there's a Will, there's a Way.* 1984.—*A Handbook History of Anguilla.* 1991.

Statistical office: Anguilla Statistics Department, PO Box 60, The Valley, Anguilla.
Website: http://www.gov.ai/statistics

Bermuda

KEY HISTORICAL EVENTS
The islands were discovered by Juan Bermúdez, probably in 1503, but were uninhabited until British colonists were wrecked there in 1609. A plantation company was formed; in 1684 the Crown took over the government. A referendum in Aug. 1995 rejected independence from the UK.

TERRITORY AND POPULATION
Bermuda consists of a group of 138 islands and islets (about 20 inhabited), situated in the western Atlantic (32° 18' N. lat., 64° 46' W. long.); the nearest point of the mainland, 940 km distant, is Cape Hatteras (North Carolina). The area is 53·3 sq. km (20·6 sq. miles). In June 1995 the USA surrendered its lease on land used since 1941 for naval and air force bases. At the 2000 census the population numbered 62,059; density, 1,164 per sq. km. Capital, Hamilton; population, 2000, 969. Population of St George's, 2000, 1,752. 2005 estimate: 63,600.

Ethnic composition, 2000: Black, 54·8%; White, 34·0%.

The official language is English.

SOCIAL STATISTICS
In 2006 there were 798 live births, 876 marriages and 461 deaths. Average annual growth rate, 2000–05, 0·2%. Life expectancy at birth, 2001: 70 years (male); 78 years (female).

CLIMATE
A pleasantly warm and humid climate, with up to 60" (1,500 mm) of rain spread evenly throughout the year. Hamilton, Jan. 63°F (17·2°C), July 79°F (26·1°C). Annual rainfall 58" (1,463 mm).

CONSTITUTION AND GOVERNMENT

Under the 1968 constitution the *Governor*, appointed by the Crown, is normally bound to accept the advice of the Cabinet in matters other than external affairs, defence, internal security and the police, for which he retains special responsibility. The legislature consists of a Senate of 11 members, five appointed by the Governor on the recommendation of the Premier, three by the Governor on the recommendation of the Opposition Leader and three by the Governor in his own discretion. The members of the *House of Assembly* are elected, one from each of 36 constituencies (as of 2003) by universal suffrage.

At a referendum on 17 Aug. 1995, 16,369 votes were cast against the option of independence, and 5,714 were in favour. The electorate was 38,000; turnout was 58%.

RECENT ELECTIONS

A general election was held on 18 Dec. 2007. Turnout was 75·6%. The ruling Progressive Labour Party (PLP) won 22 of the 36 seats in parliament, with 52·5% of votes cast. The United Bermuda Party (UBP) won 14 seats, with 47·3%. The PLP is largely representative of the black population, while the UBP membership is mostly white.

CURRENT ADMINISTRATION

Governor: Sir Richard Gozney; b. 1951 (took office on 12 Dec. 2007).

Premier: Ewart Brown; b. 1946 (took office on 30 Oct. 2006).

Government Website: http://www.gov.bm

DEFENCE

The Bermuda Regiment numbers 600 personnel, mostly part-time. There are 29 professional staff. Bermuda, unlike the rest of the UK, retains conscription.

ECONOMY

Bermuda is the world's third largest insurance market after London and New York. Reserves of insurance companies total BD$39bn. Bermuda has one of the highest per capita incomes of any country thanks to the ever-increasing role of the offshore banking sector.

Currency

The unit of currency is the *Bermuda dollar* (BMD) of 100 *cents* at parity with the US dollar. Inflation was 3·1% in both 2005 and 2006.

Budget

The fiscal year ends on 31 March. The 2002–03 budget envisaged revenue of BD$609m. and current expenditure of BD$571m. Estimated chief sources of revenue (in BD$1m.) in 2002–03: customs duties, 177; companies fees, 48; land tax, 37; passenger tax, 22; vehicle licences, 22.

Performance

GDP was BD$5·86bn. in 2007; GDP per capita was BD$91,477. Real GDP growth was 5·4% in 2006.

Banking and Finance

Bermuda is an offshore financial centre with tax exemption facilities. In 2002 there were 13,318 international companies registered in Bermuda, with insurers the most important category. There are three commercial banks, with total assets of BD$17,974m. in 2001. HSBC bought the Bank of Bermuda in 2003 for US$1·3bn. Bermuda is now the world's third largest insurance market after London and New York. The Bermuda Monetary Authority (*Chairman,* Alan Richardson) acts as a central bank. There is a stock exchange, the BSX.

Weights and Measures

Metric, except that US and Imperial (British) measures are used in certain fields.

ENERGY AND NATURAL RESOURCES

Environment

Bermuda's carbon dioxide emissions from the consumption and flaring of fossil fuels in 2008 were the equivalent of 10·2 tonnes per capita

Electricity

Installed capacity was 0·2m. kW in 2003. Production in 2003 was 664m. kWh, with consumption per capita 10,710 kWh.

Minerals

Bermuda is rich in limestone.

Agriculture

The chief products are fresh vegetables, bananas and citrus fruit. In 2005 there were an estimated 800 acres of land being used for arable purposes. The gross value added of agricultural products was BD$6,575,255 in 2005. In 2001, 613 persons were employed in agriculture. Livestock, 2002: 1,000 cattle, 1,000 horses, 1,000 pigs.

Forestry

Approximately 20% of land is woodland.

Fisheries

In 2003 there were 361 registered commercial fishing vessels and 381 registered fishermen. The total catch in 2005 was 406 tonnes. Fishing is centred on reef-dwelling species such as groupers and lobsters.

INDUSTRY

Bermuda's leading industry is tourism, with annual revenue in excess of US$350m.

Labour

The labour force numbered 37,597 in 2001.

EXTERNAL ECONOMIC RELATIONS

Foreign firms conducting business overseas only are not subject to a 60% Bermuda ownership requirement. In 2002, 10,328 international companies had a physical presence in Bermuda.

Imports and Exports

The visible adverse balance of trade is more than compensated for by invisible exports, including tourism and off-shore insurance business.

Merchandise imports totalled BD$964m. in 2005 and exports BD$25m. In 2005 the USA accounted for 74·5% of imports, Canada 4·4% and the UK 4·2%.

Principal imports are food, beverages and tobacco, machinery, chemicals, clothing, fuels and transport equipment. The bulk of exports comprise sales of fuel to aircraft and ships, and re-exports of pharmaceuticals.

COMMUNICATIONS

Roads

There are 225 km of public highway and 222 km of private roads. In 2001 there were a total of 45,342 vehicles including: 20,334 private cars; 856 buses, taxis and limousines; 3,676 trucks; 7,724 auxiliary cycles; and 11,918 motorcycles and scooters. There are heavy fines for breaking the speed limit of 35 km/h (22 mph). Bermuda limits cars to one per household and bans hire vehicles.

Civil Aviation

The Bermuda International Airport is 19 km from Hamilton. It handled 833,511 passengers and 5,771 tonnes of freight in 2001. Air Canada, American Airlines, British Airways, Continental

Airlines, Delta Airlines and US Airways serve Bermuda with regular scheduled services.

Shipping

There are three ports: Hamilton, St George's and Dockyard. There is an open shipping registry. In 2002 ships registered totalled 4·80m. GRT, including oil tankers 898,000 GRT. In 2001, 1,566 overseas ships called in Bermuda.

Telecommunications

In 2008 there were 57,600 main (fixed) telephone lines; mobile phone subscribers numbered 79,000 in 2008 (122·1 per 100 persons). There were 51,000 internet users in 2008. In 2006 Bermuda had the highest broadband penetration rate in the world, at 36·7 subscribers per 100 inhabitants.

Postal Services

There were 15 post offices in 2001.

SOCIAL INSTITUTIONS

Justice

There are four magistrates' courts, three Supreme Courts and a Court of Appeal. The police had a strength of about 433 men and women in 2003.

Bermuda is the only country in the world where McDonald's restaurants are banned by law.

Education

Education is compulsory between the ages of five and 16, and government assistance is given by the payment of grants and, where necessary, school fees. In 2005 there were 5,863 pupils in government schools and 3,470 in private schools. There were 789 full-time students attending the Bermuda College in 2005.

In 2002 the adult literacy rate was 98%. In 2004–05 total expenditure on education came to 16·5% of total government spending.

Health

In 2001 there were two hospitals, 120 physicians and surgeons, 62 dentists and hygienists, eight optometrists, 36 pharmacists, 14 dieticians and 528 nurses.

RELIGION

Many religions are represented, but the larger number of worshippers are attracted to the Anglican, Methodist, Roman Catholic, Seventh Day Adventist, African Methodist Episcopal and Baptist faiths.

CULTURE

Broadcasting

Radio and television broadcasting are commercial; there are four broadcasting companies which offer a choice of five AM and five FM radio stations, and three TV channels. Two cable TV services also offer some 80 channels each (colour by NTSC). There were 52,422 colour TVs in households in 2004 (846 TVs per 1,000 inhabitants).

Press

In 2003 there was one daily newspaper with a circulation of about 17,000 and two weeklies with a combined circulation of about 15,000.

Tourism

In 2007 there were a record 659,572 visitors to Bermuda, including 354,024 cruise ship visitors. Tourist expenditure in 2005 was US$393m.

FURTHER READING

Government Department of Statistics. *Bermuda Facts and Figures.* Annual.
Ministry of Finance. *Economic Review.* Annual.
Zuill, W. S., *The Story of Bermuda and Her People.* 2nd ed. 1992

National library: The Bermuda National Library, Hamilton.
Statistical office: Government Department of Statistics, Hamilton.

British Antarctic Teritory

KEY HISTORICAL EVENTS

The British Antarctic Territory was established on 3 March 1962, as a consequence of the entry into force of the Antarctic Treaty, to separate those areas of the then Falkland Islands Dependencies which lay within the Treaty area from those which did not (i.e. South Georgia and the South Sandwich Islands).

TERRITORY AND POPULATION

The territory encompasses the lands and islands within the area south of 60°S latitude lying between 20°W and 80°W longitude (approximately due south of the Falkland Islands and the Dependencies). It covers an area of some 1,700,000 sq. km, and its principal components are the South Orkney and South Shetland Islands, the Antarctic Peninsula (Palmer Land and Graham Land), the Filchner and Ronne Ice Shelves and Coats Land.

There is no indigenous or permanently resident population. There is, however, an itinerant population of scientists and logistics staff of about 300, manning a number of research stations.

CURRENT ADMINISTRATION

Commissioner: Colin Roberts (non-resident).
Administrator: Rob Bowman.

British Indian Ocean Territory

KEY HISTORICAL EVENTS

This territory was established to meet UK and US defence requirements by an Order in Council on 8 Nov. 1965, consisting then of the Chagos Archipelago (formerly administered from Mauritius) and the islands of Aldabra, Desroches and Farquhar (all formerly administered from Seychelles). The latter islands became part of Seychelles when that country achieved independence on 29 June 1976. In Nov. 2000 the High Court ruled that the 2,000 Ilois people (native to the archipelago) deported between 1967 and 1973 to accommodate a US military base on Diego Garcia had been removed unlawfully. Chagos islanders subsequently lost a UK High Court case for compensation and the right to return in 2003. However, further High Court rulings in 2006 and 2007 went against the UK government. Nonetheless, return by the Ilois to the archipelago (excepting Diego Garcia) is unlikely until all appeal processes have been exhausted.

TERRITORY AND POPULATION

The group, with a total land area of 60 sq. km (23 sq. miles), comprises five coral atolls (Diego Garcia, Peros Banhos, Salomon, Eagle and Egmont), of which the largest and southernmost, Diego Garcia, covers 44 sq. km (17 sq. miles) and lies 725 km (450 miles) south of the Maldives. A US Navy support facility has been established on Diego Garcia. There is no permanent population.

CURRENT ADMINISTRATION

Commissioner: Colin Roberts (non-resident).
Administrator: Joanne Yeadon.

British Virgin Islands

KEY HISTORICAL EVENTS

Discovered by Columbus on his second voyage in 1493, British Virgin Islands were first settled by the Dutch in 1648 and taken over in 1666 by a group of English planters. The islands were annexed to the British Crown in 1672. Constitutional government was granted in 1773, but was later surrendered in 1867. A Legislative Council formed in that year was abolished in 1902. In 1950 a partly nominated and partly elected Legislative Council was restored. A ministerial system of government was introduced in 1967.

TERRITORY AND POPULATION

The Islands form the eastern extremity of the Greater Antilles and number 60, of which 16 are inhabited. The largest, with census populations (2001), are Tortola, 19,282; Virgin Gorda, 3,203; Anegada, 250; and Jost Van Dyke, 244. Other islands had a total population (2001 census) of 182 (including marine population). Total area 151 sq. km (58 sq. miles); total population (2001 census), 23,161. In 2000, 61·1% of the population were urban. The capital, Road Town, on the southeast of Tortola, is a port of entry; population (estimate 2000), 7,974.

The official language is English. Spanish and Creole are also spoken.

SOCIAL STATISTICS

Birth rate, 2001, was 15·4 per 1,000 population; death rate, 4·9 per 1,000. Life expectancy in 2001 was an estimated 75·5 years. Annual growth rate, 1·96% in 2000.

CLIMATE

A pleasant healthy sub-tropical climate with summer temperatures lowered by sea breezes and cool nights. Road Town (1999), Jan. 21°C, July 27°C; rainfall (1998), 1471 mm.

CONSTITUTION AND GOVERNMENT

The constitution became effective on 15 June 2007. It granted the British Virgin Islands greater autonomy and self-determination. There is a *Premier* (formerly *Chief Minister*) and a *House of Assembly* (formerly *Legislative Council*). The Premier is appointed by the *Governor*. The House of Assembly consists of thirteen members elected for a four-year term (five directly elected members from constituencies and four members from 'at large' seats covering the territory as a whole), a Speaker and the Attorney General *ex officio*. The Cabinet consists of the Premier, four other Ministers and the Attorney General *ex officio*.

RECENT ELECTIONS

In parliamentary elections on 20 June 2007 the opposition Virgin Islands Party (VIP) won ten of the 13 available seats, ahead of the National Democratic Party (NDP) with two; an independent took one seat. The remaining two seats are held by a Speaker and the Attorney General. Turnout was 62·3%.

CURRENT ADMINISTRATION

Governor: David Pearey.

Premier: Ralph O'Neal (VIP; sworn in 23 Aug. 2007).

INTERNATIONAL RELATIONS

The Islands are an associate member of UNESCO, CARICOM and OECS.

ECONOMY

The economy is based on tourism and international financial services.

Currency

The official unit of currency is the US dollar.

Budget

In 2000 revenue was US$183·1m. and expenditure US$134·6m. Outstanding debt, in 2000, US$37·1m.

Performance

Real GDP growth was 8·7% in 2001 following growth of 4·4% in 2000. Total GDP was US$943m. in 2004; GDP per capita amounted to US$43,366.

Banking and Finance

In 2003 there were 13 banks. As of Sept. 2001 total deposits were US$1,143·8m. Financial services have surpassed the performance of the tourism industry to become the largest contributor to the GDP. As of 30 June 2001, 448,767 International Business Companies were registered in the British Virgin Islands.

ENERGY AND NATURAL RESOURCES

Environment

Carbon dioxide emissions from the consumption and flaring of fossil fuels in 2008 were the equivalent of 4·9 tonnes per capita.

Electricity

Production, 2004 estimate, 45m. kWh. In 2004 installed capacity was 10,000 kW.

Agriculture

Agricultural production is limited, with the chief products being livestock (including poultry), fish, fruit and vegetables.

Livestock (2002): cattle, 2,000; pigs, 2,000; sheep, 6,000; goats, 10,000.

Forestry

The area under forests in 2005 was 4,000 ha., or 24·4% of the total land area.

Fisheries

The total catch was 1,262 tonnes in 2004.

INDUSTRY

The construction industry is a significant employer. There are ice-making plants, cottage industries producing tourist items and a rum distillery.

Labour

In 2005 there were 16,232 employed persons (51% males). 5,142 persons were employed in government services, 2,573 in hotels and restaurants and 1,624 in wholesale and retail trade.

EXTERNAL ECONOMIC RELATIONS

Imports and Exports

In 2000 imports were US$237·6m. and exports US$26·6m.

COMMUNICATIONS

Roads

In 2000 there were 362·09 km of paved roads and 10,631 registered vehicles.

Civil Aviation

Beef Island Airport, about 16 km from Road Town, is capable of receiving 80-seat short-take-off-and-landing jet aircraft. Several airlines serve the British Virgin Islands, notably LIAT and Caribbean Star Airlines. There are scheduled flights to Puerto Rico and a number of islands in the Eastern Caribbean.

Shipping

There are two deep-water harbours: Port Purcell and Road Town. There are services to the Netherlands, UK, USA and other Caribbean islands. Merchant shipping totalled 23,000 GRT in 2002.

Telecommunications

In 2008 there were 18,900 main telephone lines and 23,000 mobile phone subscribers (100·9 per 100 persons).

SOCIAL INSTITUTIONS

Justice

Law is based on UK common law. There are courts of first instance. The appeal court is in the UK.

Education

In 1997 adult literacy was 98·2%. Primary education is provided in 15 government schools, three secondary divisions, 16 private schools and one school for children with special needs. Total number of pupils in primary schools (1997) 2,633.

Secondary education to GCSE level and Caribbean Examination Council level is provided by the BVI High School, and the secondary divisions of the schools on Virgin Gorda and Anegada. Total number of secondary level pupils (1997), 1,424. In 1996 the total number of classroom teachers in all government schools was 116.

In 1986 a branch of the Hull University (England) School of Education was established.

Health

As of 31 Dec. 2000 there were 19 doctors, 74 nurses, 44 public hospital beds and one private hospital with ten beds. Expenditure, 2000 (estimate) was US$7·6m.

RELIGION

There are Anglican, Methodist, Seventh-Day Adventist, Roman Catholic, Baptist, Pentecostal and other Christian churches in the Territory. There are also Jehovah's Witness and Hindu congregations.

CULTURE

Broadcasting

Radio ZBVI transmits 10,000 watts; and British Virgin Islands Cable TV operates a cable system of 43 television channels and one pay-per-view channel (colour by NTSC). In 2000 there were 6,200 TV receivers.

Press

In 2006 there were three weekly newspapers.

Tourism

Tourism is one of the mainstays of the economy, along with financial services. There were 356,271 overnight visitors and 473,987 cruise passenger arrivals in 2006. Total tourist expenditure for 2005 was US$437m.

FURTHER READING

Statistical Office: The Development Planning Unit, Central Administration Complex, Road Town, Tortola.
Website: http://www.dpu.gov.vg

Cayman Islands

KEY HISTORICAL EVENTS

The islands were discovered by Columbus on 10 May 1503 and (with Jamaica) were recognized as British possessions by the Treaty of Madrid in 1670. Grand Cayman was settled in 1734 and the other islands in 1833. They were administered by Jamaica from 1863, but remained under British sovereignty when Jamaica became independent on 6 Aug. 1962.

TERRITORY AND POPULATION

The Islands consist of Grand Cayman, Cayman Brac and Little Cayman. They are located in the Caribbean Sea, about 305 km (190 miles) northwest of Jamaica; area, 259 sq. km (100 sq. miles). Census population of 1999, 39,410 (52·5% Caymanians by birth). Estimated population in 2008, 57,009, giving a density of 220 per sq. km. The official language is English. The chief town is George Town with a population of 20,626 (1999).

The areas and populations of the islands are:

	Sq. km	*1989*	*1999*
Grand Cayman	197	23,881	37,473
Cayman Brac	36	1,441	1,822
Little Cayman	26	33	115

SOCIAL STATISTICS

2005: births, 699; deaths, 170. 2005: resident marriages, 810. Population growth rate, 2000–05, 3·7%.

CLIMATE

The climate is tropical maritime, with a cool season from Nov. to March. The average yearly temperature is 27°C, and rainfall averages 57" (1,400 mm) a year at George Town. Hurricanes may be experienced between July and Nov.

CONSTITUTION AND GOVERNMENT

The Cayman Islands are a self-governing overseas territory of the United Kingdom. A new draft constitution granting the Islands more political autonomy was approved at a national referendum on 20 May 2009, with 63·1% of votes cast in favour. It took effect on 6 Nov. 2009, creating the office of premier and enlarging the Legislative Assembly to 18 members. The premier is limited to serving two consecutive four-year terms of office.

RECENT ELECTIONS

At the Legislative Assembly elections on 20 May 2009 the United Democratic Party won 9 of the 15 available seats, the People's Progressive Movement 5 and ind. 1. Turnout was 80·6%.

CURRENT ADMINISTRATION

Governor: Duncan Taylor.

Premier: W. McKeeva Bush.

ECONOMY

Currency

The unit of currency is the *Cayman Island dollar* (KYD), usually written as CI$, of 100 *cents*.

Budget

In 2007 revenues totalled CI$513·0m. and expenditures CI$552·0m.

Performance

Real GDP growth in 2002 was an estimated 1·9%; in 2000 growth slowed to an estimated 3·2%, down from a five-year average of 5%.

Banking and Finance

Financial services, the Islands' chief industry, are monitored by the Cayman Islands Monetary Authority (*Chairman*, Carlyle McLaughlin). At June 2008, 416 banks and trust companies held licenses that permit the holders to offer services to the public, 19 domestically. Most of the world's leading banks have branches or subsidiaries in the Cayman Islands. In 2007, 87,109 companies, almost all offshore, were registered as well as 10,037 mutual funds and 800 insurance companies. Net domestic assets of Cayman-registered banks totalled CI$2,409·0m.

ENERGY AND NATURAL RESOURCES

Environment
Carbon dioxide emissions from the consumption and flaring of fossil fuels in 2008 were the equivalent of 10·3 tonnes per capita.

Electricity
Installed capacity on Grand Cayman was 136·6 MW in 2007. Production in 2003 was 414m. kWh; consumption per capita was 9,857 kWh.

Agriculture
Mangoes, bananas, citrus fruits, yams, cassava, breadfruit, tomatoes, honey, beef, pork and goat meat are produced for local consumption.

Fisheries
In 2005 the total catch was 125 tonnes.

INDUSTRY

Labour
Unemployment rate: 7·5% of workforce in Oct. 2002 (10% Oct. 2001).

EXTERNAL ECONOMIC RELATIONS

Imports and Exports
2005: imports, US$1·19bn.; exports, US$1·56m.

COMMUNICATIONS

Roads
In 2007 there were about 304 miles of paved roads on the Cayman Islands and 34,031 licensed motor vehicles.

Civil Aviation
George Town (Owen Roberts) on Grand Cayman and Cayman Brac (Gerrard Smith) have international airports. George Town handled 909,500 passengers and 3,650 tonnes of freight in 2007. Cayman Airways provides a regular inter-island service and also flies to Chicago, Miami, New York, Tampa, Washington D.C., Cuba and Jamaica. Eight additional international airlines provide services to London, Toronto, the Bahamas, Honduras, Jamaica and the USA.

Shipping
Motor vessels ply regularly between the Cayman Islands, Cuba, Jamaica and Florida. In 2007, 329,133 tonnes of cargo were offloaded at George Town.

Telecommunications
At the end of 2007 there were 130,622 fixed and mobile telephone lines.

SOCIAL INSTITUTIONS

Justice
There is a Grand Court, sitting six times a year for criminal sessions at George Town under a Chief Justice and two puisne judges. There are three Magistrates presiding over the Summary Court.

The population in penal institutions in Nov. 2003 was 210 (equivalent to 501 per 100,000 population, one of the highest rates in the world).

Education
In 2007 there were 17 government schools with 4,637 pupils and 2,692 students were enrolled in ten private schools. There are two government facilities for special educational needs: a school for children and a training centre for adults. Four institutions—a private four-year college, a private medical and veterinary college, the government community college and a law school—provide tertiary education.

Health
The government's health services complex in George Town includes a 101-bed hospital, a dental clinic and an eye clinic. On Grand Cayman there are four district health centres. There is a hospital on Cayman Brac (18 beds) and a health centre on Little Cayman. In 2007 there were 46 doctors in government service (including five on Cayman Brac) and 44 in private practice.

RELIGION
The residents are primarily Christian (85%) and over 12 denominations meet regularly; Church of God, Presbyterian/United, Roman Catholic, Baptist and Seventh-Day Adventists are the largest. Other religions, including Ba'hai, Buddhism, Hinduism, Islam and Judaism, have representation in the community.

CULTURE

Broadcasting
There are seven radio stations (one Christian), four broadcast television channels (two Christian) and a 38-channel microwave relay cable system.

Press
In 2005 there was one daily newspaper, the *Caymanian Compass*, with a circulation of 10,000.

Tourism
Tourism is the chief industry after financial services, and in 2007 there were 2,197 rooms in hotels and 287 rooms in apartments, guest houses and cottages. In 2007 there were 291,503 tourist arrivals by air and 1,715,666 cruise passenger arrivals. Tourism receipts in 2007 totalled CI$399·1m.

FURTHER READING

Compendium of Statistics of the Cayman Islands, 2007. 2008
Cayman Islands Annual Report 2004–2005. 2005

Statistical Office: The Information Centre, Economics & Statistics Office, Government Administration Building, Grand Cayman, KY1-9000.
Website: http://www.eso.ky

Falkland Islands

KEY HISTORICAL EVENTS
France established a settlement in 1764 and Britain a second settlement in 1765. In 1770 Spain bought out the French and drove off the British. This action on the part of Spain brought that country and Britain to the verge of war. The Spanish restored the settlement to the British in 1771, but the settlement was withdrawn on economic grounds in 1774. In 1806 Spanish rule was overthrown in Argentina, and the Argentine claimed to succeed Spain in the French and British settlements in 1820. The British objected and reclaimed their settlement in 1832 as a Crown Colony.

On 2 April 1982 Argentine forces occupied the Falkland Islands. On 3 April the UN Security Council called, by 10 votes to one, for Argentina's withdrawal. After a military campaign, but without a formal declaration of war, the UK regained possession on 14–15 June when Argentina surrendered. In April 1990 Argentina's Congress declared the Falkland and other British-held South Atlantic islands part of the new Argentine province of Tierra del Fuego though the threat of hostilities has been lifted.

TERRITORY AND POPULATION
The Territory comprises numerous islands situated in the South Atlantic Ocean about 480 miles northeast of Cape Horn covering

12,200 sq. km. The main East Falkland Island, 6,760 sq. km; the West Falkland, 5,410 sq. km, including the adjacent small islands. The population at the census of 2001 was 2,379. The only town is Stanley, in East Falkland, with a 2001 population of 1,989. The population is nearly all of British descent, with 1,326 born in the Islands (2001 census figures) and 925 in the UK. In 2000, 78·8% lived in urban areas. There is a British garrison of about 500 servicemen, stationed in East Falkland.

The official language is English.

SOCIAL STATISTICS

In 2008 there were 29 births and 22 deaths on the islands.

CLIMATE

A cool temperate climate, much affected by strong winds, particularly in spring. Stanley, Jan. 49°F (9·4°C), July 35°F (1·7°C). Annual rainfall 24" (625 mm).

CONSTITUTION AND GOVERNMENT

A new constitution came into force in 1997, updating the previous constitution of 1985 which incorporated a chapter protecting fundamental human rights, and in the preamble recalled the provisions on the right of self-determination contained in international covenants.

Executive power is vested in the Governor who must consult the Executive Council except on urgent or trivial matters. He must consult the Commander British Forces on matters relating to defence and internal security (except police).

There is a *Legislative Council* consisting of eight members (five from Stanley and three from Camp, elected every four years) and two *ex officio* members, the Chief Executive and Financial Secretary. Only elected members have a vote.

British citizenship was withdrawn by the British Nationality Act 1981, but restored after the Argentine invasion of 1982.

RECENT ELECTIONS

Elections to the Legislative Assembly were held on 17 Nov. 2005. Only non-partisans were elected.

CURRENT ADMINISTRATION

Governor: Alan Huckle.

Chief Executive: Tim Thorogood.

Government Website: http://www.falklands.gov.fk

DEFENCE

Since 1982 the Islands have been defended by a 2,000-strong garrison of British servicemen. In addition there is a local volunteer defence force.

ECONOMY

The economy of the Islands grew considerably in the second half of the 1980s as a result of the expansion of the fishing industry. In 2007 the GDP was estimated at £104m., up from £5m. in 1980.

Currency

The unit of currency is the *Falkland Islands pound* (FKP) of 100 *pence*, at parity with £1 sterling.

Budget

Revenue and expenditure (in £ sterling) for fiscal year ending 30 June 2000 was: revenue, 52·3m.; expenditure, 40·4m.

Banking and Finance

The only bank is Standard Chartered Bank, which had assets of £31m. in 1997.

ENERGY AND NATURAL RESOURCES

Electricity

Electricity production in 2004 totalled about 16m. kWh. Installed capacity in 2004 was estimated at 9,000 kW.

Oil and Gas

In 1996 the Falkland Islands government awarded production licences to Shell, Amerada Hess, Desire Petroleum and International Petroleum Corporation (Sodra), allowing them to begin oil exploration. The licensed areas are situated 150 km north of the Islands over the North Falkland Basin. Six exploration wells were drilled in 1998 and analysis of the findings suggested that in excess of 60bn. bbls of oil have been generated in the basin.

In Feb. 2010 a British-contracted rig began a new round of oil exploration in waters north of the islands. With the potential for significant oil riches, Buenos Aries appealed to the UN to bring the UK into renewed talks over the sovereignty of the territory.

Agriculture

The economy was formerly based solely on agriculture, principally sheep farming. Following a programme of sub-division, much of the land is divided into family-size units. There were 100 farms in 1997, averaging 33,600 acres and 8,200 sheep. Wool is the principal product; 1,870,000 tonnes worth £2,292,000 was exported to the UK in 1998.

Livestock: in April 2000 there were over 700,000 sheep. 2002 estimates: cattle, 4,000; horses, 1,000.

Fisheries

The total catch in 2005 was 84,546 tonnes, up from 27,190 tonnes in 1995.

INDUSTRY

Labour

In 2001 there were 2,025 people employed full-time, including 358 in construction and 326 in agriculture, hunting and fishing. The growth of the fishing industry has ensured practically zero unemployment.

EXTERNAL ECONOMIC RELATIONS

Around 85% of trade is with the UK, the rest with Latin America, mainly Chile. In 2007 imports totalled £35m.; exports (mainly fish), £134m.

COMMUNICATIONS

Roads

There are over 50 km of surfaced roads and another 400 km of unsurfaced road. This includes the 80 km between Stanley and Mount Pleasant Airport. Other settlements outside Stanley are linked by tracks. There were about 1,100 private cars in 1996.

Civil Aviation

Air communication is currently via Ascension Island. An airport, completed in 1986, is sited at Mount Pleasant on East Falkland. RAF Tristar aircraft operate a twice-weekly service between the Falklands and the UK. A Chilean airline, LAN Airlines, runs a weekly service to Puerto Montt, Punta Arenas, Rio Gallegos and Santiago.

Shipping

A charter vessel calls four or five times a year to and from the UK. Vessels of the Royal Fleet Auxiliary run regularly to South Georgia. Sea links with Chile and Uruguay began in 1989. In 2002 merchant shipping totalled 54,000 GRT.

Telecommunications

Number of telephone main lines in 2008 was 2,000. International direct dialling is available, as are international fax links. In 2008 there were 2,800 internet users.

Postal Services
In 2003 there were two post offices. Airmail is generally received and dispatched twice weekly and surface post is airlifted out about once every two weeks. Surface mail is received approximately once every three weeks.

SOCIAL INSTITUTIONS

Justice
There is a Supreme Court, and a Court of Appeal sits in the UK; appeals may go from that court to the judicial committee of the Privy Council. The senior resident judicial officer is the Senior Magistrate. There is an Attorney General and a Senior Crown Counsel.

Education
Education is compulsory between the ages of five and 16 years. In Stanley in 2002 there were 30 pre-school pupils, 190 primary pupils (18 teachers) and 160 pupils in the 11–16 age range (18 teachers). In rural areas students attend small settlement schools or are visited by one of seven travelling teachers. Lessons may also be carried out over the radio or telephone.

Health
The Government Medical Department is responsible for all medical services to civilians. Primary and secondary health care facilities are based at the King Edward VII Memorial Hospital, the only hospital on the islands. It has 28 beds. It is staffed by five doctors, six sisters (including four midwives), eight staff nurses, a health visitor, counsellor, physiotherapist, social worker and an auxiliary nursing staff. The Royal Army Medical Corps staff the surgical facilities. There are two dentists on the island.

Welfare
In 1998 total amount spent on old age pension payments was £504,075. Total amount spent on family allowance payments was £336,365.

CULTURE

Broadcasting
The Falkland Islands Broadcasting Station (FIBS), in conjunction with British Forces Broadcasting Service (BFBS), broadcasts 24 hours a day on FM and MW. Some BBC World Service programmes are also available.

BFBS also provides a single channel TV service (UKPAL) to Stanley, Mount Pleasant and most outlying camp settlements and a cable TV service is also in operation. In 1997 there were 1,000 TV sets.

Press
In 2006 there was one weekly newspaper, the *Penguin News*.

Tourism
In the 2008–09 season there were a record 62,488 cruise ship visitors. There are a variety of lodges around the Islands. Stanley has one major hotel and some guest houses.

FURTHER READING

Gough, B., *The Falkland Islands/Malvinas: the Contest for Empire in the South Atlantic*. 1992

Gibraltar

KEY HISTORICAL EVENTS
The Rock of Gibraltar was settled by Moors in 711. In 1462 it was taken by the Spaniards, from Granada. It was captured by Admiral Sir George Rooke on 24 July 1704, and ceded to Great Britain by the Treaty of Utrecht, 1713. The cession was confirmed by the treaties of Paris (1763) and Versailles (1783). In 1830 Gibraltar became a British crown colony.

On 10 Sept. 1967 a UN resolution on the decolonization of Gibraltar led to a referendum to ascertain whether the people of Gibraltar wished to retain their link with the UK. Out of an electorate of 12,762, an overwhelming majority voted to retain the British connection.

The border was closed by Spain in 1969, opened to pedestrians in 1982 and fully opened in 1985. In 1973 Gibraltar joined the European Community as a dependent territory of the United Kingdom. In 2001 talks were held between Britain and Spain over the colony's sovereignty. In a joint statement, the British and Spanish foreign ministers said they would work towards a comprehensive agreement by the summer of 2002. Gibraltar's government held an unofficial referendum on sharing sovereignty with Spain on 7 Nov. 2002 in which 98·97% of votes cast were against joint sovereignty. While Britain sees the principle of shared sovereignty as the definitive solution, Spain maintains its historic claim to outright control. An agreement reached in Sept. 2006 eased border controls and opened up Gibraltar to flights from Spain and other European countries.

TERRITORY AND POPULATION
Gibraltar is situated in latitude 36°07' N and longitude 05°21' W. Area, 6·5 sq. km (2½ sq. miles) including port and harbour. Total population (2007), 29,257 (of whom 23,616 were British Gibraltarian, 3,223 Other British and 2,418 Non-British); density, 4,501 per sq. km. The population is mostly of Genoese, Portuguese, Maltese and Spanish descent.

The official language is English; Spanish is also spoken.

SOCIAL STATISTICS
Statistics (2007): births, 401; deaths, 202; marriages, 929. Rates per 1,000 population, 2006: birth, 12·6; death, 8·0.

CLIMATE
The climate is warm temperate, with westerly winds in winter bringing rain. Summers are pleasantly warm and rainfall is low. Mean maximum temperatures: Jan. 16°C, July 28°C. Annual rainfall 722 mm.

CONSTITUTION AND GOVERNMENT
A new constitution was approved in a referendum on 30 Nov. 2006 and came into effect on 2 Jan. 2007, giving Gibraltar full internal self-government. The *Gibraltar House of Assembly* (itself an amalgamation of the former Legislative and City Councils) was renamed the *Gibraltar Parliament*. The legislature of Gibraltar consists of the Queen as head of state and the Gibraltar Parliament. The Governor remains Commander-in-Chief but only retains direct constitutional responsibility for matters relating to defence, external affairs and some aspects of internal security. There is a Council of Ministers presided over by the Chief Minister who is appointed by the Governor. The constitution also abolished the former Gibraltar Council.

The Gibraltar Parliament consists of a Speaker appointed by the parliament and at least 17 elected members. A Mayor of Gibraltar is elected by the members of parliament (excluding the Speaker).

Gibraltarians have full UK citizenship.

RECENT ELECTIONS
At the elections of 11 Oct. 2007 turnout was 81·4%. The ruling Gibraltar Social Democratic Party (GSD) gained 10 seats with 49·3% of votes cast. The opposition alliance of the Gibraltar Socialist Labour Party and the Liberal Party took 45·5% of the vote, gaining four and three seats respectively.

CURRENT ADMINISTRATION
Governor and C.-in-C: Vice Adm. Sir Adrian Johns, KCB, CBE, ADC (sworn in 26 Oct. 2009).

Chief Minister: Peter Caruana; b. 1956 (GSD; elected in 1996, re-elected in 2000 and 2003).

Deputy Chief Minister and Minister for Enterprise, Development and Technology: Joe Holliday. *Education and Training:* Clive Beltran. *Health and Civil Protection:* Yvette del Agua. *Housing:* Fabian Vinet. *Justice:* Daniel Feetham. *Family, Youth and Community Affairs:* Jaime Netto. *Environment, Traffic and Transport:* Lieut. Col. Ernest Britto. *Culture, Heritage, Sport and Leisure:* Edwin Reyes. *Employment, Labour and Industrial Relations:* Luis Montiel.

The *Speaker* is Haresh Budhrani, QC.

Government Website: http://www.gibraltar.gov.gi

DEFENCE

The Ministry of Defence presence consists of a tri-service garrison numbering approximately 900 uniformed personnel. Supporting the garrison are approximately 1,100 locally-employed civilian personnel. The garrison supports a NATO Headquarters.

ECONOMY

Overview

The economy is primarily dependent on service industries and port facilities, with income derived from tourism, transhipment and, perhaps most importantly in terms of growth, the provision of financial services.

Currency

The legal tender currency is UK sterling. Also legal tender are Government of Gibraltar Currency notes and coins. The *Gibraltar pound* (GIP) of 100 *pence* is at parity with the UK £1 sterling. The total of Government of Gibraltar notes in circulation at 31 March 2008 was £18·7m. The annual rate of inflation was 2·6% in Jan. 2008.

Budget

Departmental revenue credited to the consolidated fund for the year ending 31 March 2007 totalled £212m. whilst expenditure amounted to £171m. The main sources of consolidated fund revenues were income tax (£97m.), import duties (£35m.) and company taxes (£24m.). Main items of consolidation fund expenditure: health and civil contingency (£26m.), education (£22m.) and social and civic affairs (£19m.).

Performance

In 2006–07 Gibraltar's GDP was £660m., equivalent to £22,900 per head.

Banking and Finance

At March 2007 there were 18 authorized banks. The majority of these are either subsidiaries or branches of major UK or other European Economic Area (EEA) banks. Ten of these banks are incorporated in Gibraltar and are licensed by the Financial Services Commission. The banking sector provides services to both local and non-resident customers. Many of these banks specialize in providing private banking to high net worth individuals who are not resident in Gibraltar.

ENERGY AND NATURAL RESOURCES

Environment

Gibraltar's carbon dioxide emissions from the consumption and flaring of fossil fuels in 2008 were the equivalent of 161·6 tonnes per capita, the highest in the world.

Electricity

Production in 2007 amounted to 154·8m. kWh.

Oil and Gas

Gibraltar is dependent on imported petroleum for its energy supplies.

Agriculture

Gibraltar lacks agricultural land and natural resources; the territory is dependent on imports of foodstuffs and fuels.

INDUSTRY

The industrial sector (including manufacturing, construction and power) employed around 16% of the working population in 2007.

Labour

The total number of employee jobs at Oct. 2007 was 19,696. Principal areas of employment (Oct. 2007): community, social and personal services, 4,042; trade, restaurants and hotels, 3,887; construction, 2,486; manufacturing, 411; other, 8,870. (Figures cover only non-agricultural activities, excluding mining and quarrying). 3·3% of the labour force were unemployed in 2005.

EXTERNAL ECONOMIC RELATIONS

Gibraltar has a special status within the EU which exempts it from the latter's fiscal policy.

Imports and Exports

Imports in 2007 totalled £425·7m. and exports £151·8m. (excluding petroleum products).

Britain provided 27% of imports in 2007 and is the largest source. Other major trade partners include Spain, the Netherlands and Denmark. Foodstuffs accounted for 6% of total imports in 2007. Mineral fuels comprised about 68% of the value of total imports in 2007. Exports are mainly re-exports of petroleum and petroleum products supplied to shipping, and include manufactured goods, wines, spirits, malt and tobacco. Gibraltar depends largely on tourism, offshore banking and other financial sector activity, the entrepôt trade and the provision of supplies to visiting ships. Exports of domestic produce are negligible. In 2007 Gibraltar recorded a visible trade deficit of £316·9m.

COMMUNICATIONS

Roads

There are 56 km of roads including 6·8 km of pedestrian way. In 2006 there were 14,637 private vehicles, 7,024 motorcycles, 1,391 goods vehicles, 112 taxis and 99 buses.

Civil Aviation

There is an international airport, Gibraltar North Front. Scheduled flights were operated in 2007 by British Airways to London (Gatwick), by Monarch Airlines to London (Luton) and, following an agreement signed by the Spanish and British governments in Sept. 2006, by Iberia to Madrid. In 2007, 179,267 passengers arrived by air and 180,563 departed; 62 tonnes of freight were loaded and 333 tonnes were unloaded (figures exclude military freight).

Shipping

The Strait of Gibraltar is a principal ocean route between the Mediterranean and Black Sea areas and the rest of the world. A total of 9,618 merchant ships of 282·1m. GRT entered port during 2007, including 6,889 deep-sea ships of 191·2m. GRT. In 2007, 3,459 calls were made by yachts of 462,525 GRT. 227 cruise liners called during 2007 involving 279,885 passengers.

Telecommunications

Gibtelecom, jointly owned by Telekom Slovenije and the Government of Gibraltar, is the main provider of fixed, wireless and internet services to residential and business customers.

As at 1 Jan. 2008 the Group's fixed exchange lines stood at 24,035. At the end of 2006 there were 8,000 internet accounts in Gibraltar.

Postal Services

Airmail is dispatched to London, and via London to destinations worldwide, six times a week in direct flights. Surface letter mail and parcel mail to and from the United Kingdom is dispatched and received via the land frontier five times a week.

SOCIAL INSTITUTIONS

Justice

The judicial system is based on the English system. There is a Court of Appeal, a Supreme Court, presided over by the Chief Justice, a Court of First Instance and a Magistrates' Court.

The population in penal institutions in Nov. 2003 was 31 (equivalent to 112 per 100,000 population).

Education

Free compulsory education is provided between the ages of four and 15 years. The medium of instruction is English. The comprehensive system was introduced in Sept. 1972 and all schools currently follow a locally adapted version of the National Curriculum for England and Wales. In the 2007–08 academic year there were 11 primary and two secondary schools. Primary schools are divided into first schools for children aged 4–8 years and middle schools for children aged 8–12 years. All primary schools are mixed though secondary schools are single-sex.

Vocational education and training is available at the Gibraltar College (a post-15 institution), the Construction Training Centre and the Cammell Laird Training Centre; the former two are managed by the Gibraltar government and the latter by Cammell Laird, a shipbuilding company (and part-funded by the Government). In Sept. 2007 there were 2,937 pupils at government primary schools, 271 at private primary schools and 180 at the Services school. 1,025 pupils were enrolled at the boys' comprehensive school and 1,066 at the girls' comprehensive. There were 370 students in the Gibraltar College. Government expenditure on education in the year ended 31 March 2008 was £23·8m.

Health

The Gibraltar Health Authority is the organization responsible for providing health care in Gibraltar. The Authority operates a Group Practice Medical Scheme which is a contributory scheme and enables registered persons to access free medical treatment. In 2002 there were two hospitals with 226 beds. Total expenditure on medical and health services during year ended 31 March 2007 was £60·3m.

Welfare

The social security system consists of: the Social Security (Employment Injuries Insurance) Scheme which only applies to employed persons; the Social Security (Short-Term Benefits) Scheme which provides for payments of maternity grants. maternity allowance, death grants and unemployment benefit; and the Social Security (Open Long-Term Benefits) Scheme which provides for pensions and widows' allowances.

RELIGION

According to the 2001 census 78·1% of the population were Roman Catholic, 7·0% Church of England, 4·0% Muslim, 2·1% Jewish and 1·8% Hindu. In 2004 there were seven Roman Catholic and three Anglican churches (including one Catholic and one Anglican cathedral), one Presbyterian and one Methodist church, four synagogues and two mosques.

CULTURE

Broadcasting

Radio Gibraltar broadcasts for 24 hours daily, 22 hours in English and two hours in Spanish; and GBC Television operates for 24 hours daily in English (colour by PAL). At 31 Dec. 2003 there were 7,500 TV licences.

Press

In 2007 there were two daily and two weekly newspapers.

Tourism

In 2007 nearly 9·5m. tourists visited Gibraltar (including day-visitors) bringing in revenue of £230·6m. Tourism accounts for an estimated 35% of GDP.

FURTHER READING

Gibraltar Year Book. Annual

Morris, D. S. and Haigh, R. H., *Britain, Spain and Gibraltar, 1940–90: the Eternal Triangle*. 1992

Statistical Office: Statistics Office, 99 Harbours Walk, The New Harbours, Gibraltar.

Montserrat

KEY HISTORICAL EVENTS

Montserrat was discovered by Columbus in 1493 and colonized by Britain in 1632, who brought Irish settlers to the island. Montserrat formed part of the federal colony of the Leeward Islands from 1871 until 1958, when it became a separate colony following the dissolution of the Federation.

On 18 July 1995 the Soufriere Hills volcano erupted for the first time in recorded history, which led to over half the inhabitants being evacuated to the north of the island, and the relocation of the chief town, Plymouth. Another major eruption on 25 June 1997 caused a number of deaths and led to further evacuation.

TERRITORY AND POPULATION

Montserrat is situated in the Caribbean Sea, 43 km southwest of Antigua. The area is 102·3 sq. km (39·5 sq. miles). Census population, 2001, 4,482. What was previously the capital, Plymouth, is now deserted as a result of the continuing activity of the Soufriere Hills volcano. The safe area is in the north of the island.

The official language is English.

CLIMATE

A tropical climate with an average annual rainfall of 60" (1,500 mm) the wettest months being Sept.–Dec., with a hurricane season June–Nov. Plymouth, Jan. 76°F (24·4°C), July 81°F (27·2°C).

CONSTITUTION AND GOVERNMENT

Montserrat is a British Overseas Territory. The Constitution dates from the 1989 Montserrat Constitutional Order. The head of state is Queen Elizabeth II, represented by a *Governor* who heads an Executive Council, comprising also the Chief Minister, the Financial Secretary, the Attorney-General and three other ministers. The *Legislative Council* consists of nine elected members and two *ex officio* members (the Attorney-General and Financial Secretary); it sits for five-year terms.

RECENT ELECTIONS

In elections to the Legislative Council on 8 Sept. 2009 the Movement for Change and Prosperity won six of nine seats with ind. winning the other three.

CURRENT ADMINISTRATION

Governor: Peter Waterworth; b. 1957 (since 27 July 2007).

Chief Minister: Reuben Meade; b. 1952 (since 10 Sept. 2009).

INTERNATIONAL RELATIONS

Montserrat is a member of CARICOM and OECS.

ECONOMY

Currency

Montserrat's currency is the *East Caribbean dollar* (*see* ANTIGUA AND BARBUDA: Currency).

Budget

In 1998 the estimated expenditure was EC$60·6m. compared with actual expenditure of EC$63·5m. in 1997, a reduction of 5%.

Performance

Real GDP growth was 7·6% in 2002, but there was then a recession with the economy contracting by 4·7% in 2003.

Banking and Finance

The East Caribbean Central Bank based in St Kitts and Nevis functions as a central bank. The *Governor* is Sir Dwight Venner. In 2003 there were four commercial banks and in 1996 there were 21 offshore banks. Responsibility for overseeing offshore banking rests with the Governor.

ENERGY AND NATURAL RESOURCES

Environment

Carbon dioxide emissions from the consumption and flaring of fossil fuels in 2008 were the equivalent of 18·2 tonnes per capita.

Electricity

Production (2004) 21m. kWh. Installed capacity (2004): 10,000 kW.

Agriculture

The volcanic eruptions in 1997 dramatically reduced the area of land under cultivation. Agriculture, now concentrated in the north, is showing signs of recovering. In 2002 there were 2,000 ha. of arable and permanent crop land. The main products have traditionally been potatoes, tomatoes, onions, mangoes and limes. Meat production began in 1994 and the island soon became self-sufficient in chicken, mutton and beef.

Livestock (2002); cattle, 10,000; pigs, 1,000; sheep, 5,000; goats, 7,000.

Forestry

The area under forests in 2005 was 4,000 ha., or 35·0% of the total land area.

Fisheries

The total catch in 2005 was estimated at 50 tonnes.

INDUSTRY

Manufacturing has in recent years contributed about 6% to GDP and accounted for 10% of employment, but has been responsible for about 80% of exports. It has been limited to rice milling and the production of light consumer goods such as electronic components, light fittings, plastic bags and leather goods. The volcanic activity has put a halt to the milling of rice in the exclusion zone and curtailed the production of light consumer goods.

Trade Unions

There is one trade union, the Montserrat Allied Workers Union (MAWU).

EXTERNAL ECONOMIC RELATIONS

Imports and Exports

Imports in 2005 totalled US$26·2m.; exports, US$1·8m. The USA is the main trading partner.

COMMUNICATIONS

Roads

In 1995 there were 205 km of paved roads, 25 km of unsurfaced roads and 50 km of tracks. In 1995 there were 2,700 cars and 400 commercial vehicles registered. These figures changed as a result of the volcanic eruptions of 1995 and 1997 but since then the government, through the Ministry of Communications and Works, has been focusing its road developments in the north of the island, and a number of road work projects are under way.

Civil Aviation

At the W. H. Bramble airport LIAT used to provide services to Antigua with onward connections to the rest of the eastern Caribbean, but it was closed in June 1997 as volcanic activity increased. A new airport opened in Feb. 2005.

Shipping

Plymouth is the port of entry, but alternative anchorage was provided at Old Bay Road during the volcanic crisis.

Telecommunications

In 2008 there were 2,800 main (fixed) telephone lines; mobile phone subscribers numbered 3,000 in 2008 (50·8 per 100 persons). There were 1,200 internet users in 2008.

SOCIAL INSTITUTIONS

Justice

Law is based on UK common law as exercised by the Eastern Caribbean Supreme Court. Final appeal lies to the UK Privy Council. Law is administered by the West Indies Associated States Court, a Court of Summary Jurisdiction and Magistrate's Courts.

Education

In 1996–97 there were 11 primary schools (only four open), a comprehensive secondary school with three campuses, and a technical college. Schools are run by the government, the churches and the private sector. There is a medical school, the American University of the Caribbean.

In 2000–01 total expenditure on education came to 7·9% of total government spending.

Health

In 1996 there were four medical officers, one surgeon, one dentist and one hospital with 69 beds.

RELIGION

In 1997, 25% of the population were Anglican, 20% Methodist, 15% Pentecostal, 10% Adventist and 10% Roman Catholic.

CULTURE

Broadcasting

There is a government-owned radio station (ZJB) and two commercial stations (Radio Antilles and GEM Radio). There is a commercial cable TV company (colour by NTSC).

Press

In 2006 there were two weekly newspapers.

Tourism

Tourism at one time contributed about 30% of GDP. There were 36,077 visitors including 11,636 cruise ship arrivals in 1994. However, after the volcanic eruptions the tourist industry declined dramatically; over half the island is closed. There were 7,991 visitors in 2006.

FURTHER READING

Fergus, H. A., *Montserrat: History of a Caribbean Colony.* 1994

Pitcairn Island

KEY HISTORICAL EVENTS

Pitcairn was discovered by Carteret in 1767, but remained uninhabited until 1790, when it was occupied by nine mutineers of HMS *Bounty*, with 12 women and six men from Tahiti. Nothing was known of their existence until the island was visited in 1808.

TERRITORY AND POPULATION

Pitcairn Island (4·6 sq. km; 1·75 sq. miles) is situated in the Pacific Ocean, nearly equidistant from New Zealand and Panama (25° 04' S. lat., 130° 06' W. long.). Adamstown is the only settlement. The population in 2003 was 48. The uninhabited islands of Henderson (31 sq. km), Ducie (3·9 sq. km) and Oeno (5·2 sq. km) were annexed in 1902. Henderson is a World Heritage Site. English is the official language but Pitkern is also spoken.

CLIMATE

An equable climate, with average annual rainfall of 80" (2,000 mm) spread evenly throughout the year. Mean monthly temperatures range from 75°F (24°C) in Jan. to 66°F (19°C) in July.

CONSTITUTION AND GOVERNMENT

The Local Government Ordinance of 1964 constitutes a *Council* of ten members; four councillors and the chairman of the internal committee are elected annually, one is nominated by the Council and two—including the island secretary—are appointed by the Governor. It is presided over by the island mayor. There is also a commissioner liaising between the Governor and the Council. No political parties exist. The Island Magistrate, who is elected triennially, presides over the Council; other members hold office for only one year. Liaison between Governor and Council is through a Commissioner in the Auckland, New Zealand, office of the British Consulate-General.

CURRENT ADMINISTRATION

Governor: George Fergusson.

Mayor: Mike Warren.

Government Website: http://www.government.pn

ECONOMY

Currency

New Zealand currency is used.

Budget

For the year to 31 March 1997 revenue was NZ$604,234 and expenditure NZ$601,665.

ENERGY AND NATURAL RESOURCES

Fisheries

The catch in 2005 was approximately three tonnes.

COMMUNICATIONS

Roads

There were (1997) 6 km of roads. In 1997 there were 29 motorcycles.

SOCIAL INSTITUTIONS

Justice

The Island Court consists of the Island Magistrate and two assessors.

Education

In 2004 there was one teacher and nine pupils.

FURTHER READING

Murray, S., *Pitcairn Island: the First 200 Years*. 1992

St Helena, Ascension and Tristan da Cunha

KEY HISTORICAL EVENTS

The island of St Helena was uninhabited when discovered by the Portuguese in 1502. It was administered by the East India Company from 1659 and became a British colony in 1834. Napoleon died there in exile in 1821. In 2009 a new constitution saw the territory renamed from St Helena and Dependencies to St Helena, Ascension and Tristan da Cunha.

TERRITORY AND POPULATION

St Helena, of volcanic origin, is 3,100 km from the west coast of Africa. Area, 122 sq. km (47 sq. miles), with a cultivable area of 243 ha. The population of St Helena at the 2008 census (provisional) was 5,661 (including the then dependencies of Ascension and Tristan da Cunha) of which St Helena itself had a population of 4,255. In 2003, 64·5% of the population were rural. The capital and port is Jamestown, population (2008 provisional) 714.

The official language is English.

Ascension is a small island of volcanic origin, of 88 sq. km (34 sq. miles), 700 miles northwest of St Helena. There are 120 ha. providing fresh meat, vegetables and fruit. The population in 2008 was 1,122.

The island is the resort of sea turtles, rabbits, the sooty tern or 'wideawake', and feral donkeys.

A cable station connects the island with St Helena, Sierra Leone, St Vincent, Rio de Janeiro and Buenos Aires. There is an airstrip (Miracle Mile) near the settlement of Georgetown; the Royal Air Force maintains an air link with the Falkland Islands.

Administrator: Ross Denny.

Tristan da Cunha is the largest of a small group of islands in the South Atlantic, lying 2,124 km (1,320 miles) southwest of St Helena, of which they became dependencies on 12 Jan. 1938. Tristan da Cunha has an area of 98 sq. km and a population (2008) of 284, all living in the settlement of Edinburgh. Inaccessible Island (10 sq. km) lies 20 miles west, and the three Nightingale Islands (2 sq. km) lie 20 miles south of Tristan da Cunha; they are uninhabited. Gough Island (90 sq. km) is 220 miles south of Tristan and has a meteorological station.

Tristan consists of a volcano rising to a height of 2,060 metres, with a circumference at its base of 34 km. The volcano, believed to be extinct, erupted unexpectedly early in Oct. 1961. The whole population was evacuated without loss and settled temporarily in the UK; in 1963 they returned to Tristan. Potatoes remain the chief crop. Cattle, sheep and pigs are now reared, and fish are plentiful.

The original inhabitants were shipwrecked sailors and soldiers who remained behind when the garrison from St Helena was withdrawn in 1817.

At the end of April 1942 Tristan da Cunha was commissioned as HMS *Atlantic Isle*, and became an important meteorological and radio station. In Jan. 1949 a South African company commenced crawfishing operations. An Administrator was appointed at the end of 1948 and a body of basic law brought into operation. The Island Council, which was set up in 1932, consists of a Chief Islander, three nominated and eight elected members (including one woman), under the chairmanship of the Administrator.

Administrator: David Morley.

SOCIAL STATISTICS

2001 figures for St Helena: births, 36; deaths, 41; marriages, 20; divorces (2000), 9. Annual growth rate, 1990–95, 0·6%.

CLIMATE

A mild climate, with little variation. Temperatures range from 75–85°F (24–29°C) in summer to 65–75°F (18–24°C) in winter. Rainfall varies between 13" (325 mm) and 37" (925 mm) according to altitude and situation.

CONSTITUTION AND GOVERNMENT

A new constitution came into force on 1 Sept. 2009, replacing its 20-year old predecessor. Under the terms of the new constitution, the territory changed its official name from St Helena and Dependencies to St Helena, Ascension and Tristan da Cunha. It included a bill of rights, allowing citizens to appeal to local courts on human rights issues rather than address the European Court of Human Rights in Strasbourg as they had done previously. Constraints were placed on the powers of the Governor (who no longer holds the title of 'Commander-in-Chief') and the independence of the judiciary and public service were constitutionally enshrined.

The territory's *Legislative Council* consists of twelve elected members, three non-voting *ex officio* members (the Chief Secretary, the Financial Secretary and the Attorney General) and the Speaker and Deputy Speaker. The Governor is advised by an *Executive Council* comprising three non-voting *ex officio* members (the Chief Secretary, the Financial Secretary and the Attorney General) and five elected members from the Legislative Council. The Governor must, except in certain prescribed circumstances, act in accordance with the advice of the Executive Council.

RECENT ELECTIONS

The last Legislative Council elections were on 31 Aug. 2005. Only non-partisans were elected.

CURRENT ADMINISTRATION

Governor: Andrew Gurr.

ENERGY AND NATURAL RESOURCES

Environment

Carbon dioxide emissions from the consumption and flaring of fossil fuels in 2008 were the equivalent of 1·9 tonnes per capita.

Electricity

Production in 2004 totalled 8m. kWh. Installed capacity in 2004 was 4,000 kW.

Agriculture

In 2007 there were about 4,000 ha. of arable land.

Fisheries

The total catch in 2005 was 1,130 tonnes.

INDUSTRY

Labour

In 2000 there were 270 registered unemployed persons.

COMMUNICATIONS

Roads

There were (2003) 94 km of all-weather motor roads. There were 1,931 vehicles in 2002.

Shipping

There is a service from Cardiff (UK) six times a year, and links with South Africa and neighbouring islands. In 1995 vessels entered totalling 55,000 net registered tons.

Telecommunications

In 2006 there were 2,200 main telephone lines in operation. There were 800 internet users in 2008.

SOCIAL INSTITUTIONS

Justice

Police force, 32; cases are dealt with by a police magistrate.

Education

In 2002–03 there were eight schools with, in 1999–2000, 87 teachers and 860 pupils. The Prince Andrew School (opened in 1989) offers vocational courses leading to British qualifications.

Health

There were four doctors, one dentist and one hospital in 2001.

RELIGION

There are ten Anglican churches, four Baptist chapels, three Salvation Army halls, one Seventh Day Adventist church and one Roman Catholic church.

CULTURE

Broadcasting

The Cable & Wireless Ltd cable connects St Helena with Cape Town and Ascension Island. The government-run Radio St Helena broadcasts daily and relays BBC programmes. Television reception was introduced in 1996 from the BBC World Service, South African M-Net and a US Satellite channel. There were some 2,000 TV receivers in 1997.

South Georgia and the South Sandwich Islands

KEY HISTORICAL EVENTS

The first landing and exploration was undertaken by Capt. James Cook, who formally took possession in the name of George III on 17 Jan. 1775. British sealers arrived in 1788 and American sealers in 1791. Sealing reached its peak in 1800. A German team was the first to carry out scientific studies there in 1882–83. Whaling began in 1904 and ceased in 1966, and the civil administration was withdrawn. Argentine forces invaded South Georgia on 3 April 1982. A British naval task force recovered the Island on 25 April 1982.

TERRITORY AND POPULATION

South Georgia lies 1,300 km southeast of the Falkland Islands and has an area of 3,760 sq. km. The South Sandwich Islands are 760 km southeast of South Georgia and have an area of 340 sq. km. In 1993 crown sovereignty and jurisdiction were extended from 19 km (12 miles) to 322 km (200 miles) around the islands. There is no permanent population. The British Antarctic Survey operate a fisheries science facility at King Edward Point and a biological station on Bird Island. The South Sandwich Islands are uninhabited.

CLIMATE

The climate is wet and cold, with strong winds and little seasonal variation. 15°C is occasionally reached on a windless day. Temperatures below –15°C at sea level are unusual.

CONSTITUTION AND GOVERNMENT

Under the new Constitution which came into force on 3 Oct. 1985 the Territories ceased to be dependencies of the Falkland Islands. The Government of South Georgia and the South Sandwich Islands (GSGSSI) administers the islands. The local administration is the responsibility of the Government Officer based at King Edward Point. Executive power is vested in a Commissioner, who is also the Governor of the Falkland Islands. On matters relating to defence, the Commissioner consults the officer commanding Her Majesty's British Forces in the South Atlantic. The Commissioner, whenever practicable, consults the Executive Council of the Falkland Islands on the exercise of functions that in his opinion might affect the Falkland Islands. There is no Legislative Council. Laws are made by the Commissioner (Alan Huckle, resident in the Falkland Islands).

ECONOMY

Budget

The total projected revenue of the Territories (2006) was £4,037,700, of which 85% from fishing licenses, 8% landing fees, 3% philatelic sales and 2% harbour dues. Expenditure (projected), £4,265,900, includes 50% fisheries research and protection, 12% King Edward Point running costs, 11% observer fees and 6% Grytviken remediation and maintenance projects.

COMMUNICATIONS

The bases at King Edward Point and Bird Island have modern satellite communication systems. King Edward Point is regularly visited by the GSGSSI Fishery Patrol Vessel. Other visiting vessels include cruise ships, BAS research ships, warships and auxiliaries, fishing vessels and yachts.

SOCIAL INSTITUTIONS

Justice

There is a Supreme Court for the Territories and a Court of Appeal in the United Kingdom. Appeals may go from that court to the Judicial Committee of the Privy Council. The British Antarctic Survey base commander at King Edward Point is usually appointed a magistrate.

CULTURE

Tourism

In the region of 4,000 tourists visit the island annually.

FURTHER READING

Headland, R.K., *The Island of South Georgia.* 1984

Sovereign Base Areas of Akrotiri and Dhekelia in Cyprus

KEY HISTORICAL EVENTS

The Sovereign Base Areas (SBAs) are those parts of the island of Cyprus that stayed under British jurisdiction and remained British sovereign territory when the 1960 Treaty of Establishment created the independent Republic of Cyprus. The Akrotiri facility formed a strategic part of the West's nuclear capacity during the Cold War. The SBAs were used for the deployment of troops in the Gulf War in 1991. Military intelligence is now the key role of the SBAs. The construction of massive antennae at the RAF communications base at Akrotiri sparked violent riots in 2001 and 2002, led by a Greek Cypriot MP. In Feb. 2003 the British Government offered to surrender approximately half the area of the SBAs as an incentive for a settlement between the Greek and Turkish administrations in Cyprus.

TERRITORY AND POPULATION

The Sovereign Base Areas (SBAs), with a total land area of 254 sq. km (98 sq. miles), comprise the Western SBA (123 sq. km), including Episkopi Garrison and RAF Akrotiri (opened 1956), and the Eastern SBA (131 sq. km), including Dhekelia Garrison. The SBAs cover 3% of the land area of the island of Cyprus. There are approximately 3,000 military personnel and approximately 5,000 civilians. The British Government has declared that it will not develop the SBAs other than for military purposes. Citizens and residents of the Republic of Cyprus are guaranteed freedom of access and communications to and through the SBAs.

The SBAs are administered as military bases reporting to the Ministry of Defence in London. The Administrator is the Commander, British Forces Cyprus. The joint force headquarters are at Episkopi. Greek and English are spoken.

CURRENT ADMINISTRATION

Commander British Forces Cyprus: Maj.-Gen. Jamie Gordon (appointed Oct. 2008).

The Turks and Caicos Islands

KEY HISTORICAL EVENTS

After a long period of rival French and Spanish claims the islands were secured to the British Crown in 1766, and became a separate colony in 1973 after association with the colonies of the Bahamas and Jamaica. In 2009 the British government imposed direct rule after allegations of widespread corruption among the islands' ruling class.

TERRITORY AND POPULATION

The Islands are situated between 21° and 22°N. lat. and 71° and 72°W. long., about 80 km east of the Bahamas, of which they are geographically an extension. There are over 40 islands, covering an estimated area of 500 sq. km (193 sq. miles). Only seven are inhabited: Grand Caicos, the largest, is 48 km long by 3 to 5 km broad; Grand Turk, the capital and main political and administrative centre, is 11 km long by 2 km broad. Population, 2001 census, 19,886; Grand Turk, 3,976; Middle Caicos, 301; North Caicos, 1,347; Parrot Cay, 58; Providenciales, 13,021; Salt Cay, 120; South Caicos, 1,063. The estimated population for 2006 was 33,202. 54·8% of the population were rural in 2000.

The official language is English.

SOCIAL STATISTICS

2004: births, 300; deaths, 218. Population growth rate, 2004, 9·4%.

CLIMATE

An equable and healthy climate as a result of regular trade winds, though hurricanes are sometimes experienced. Grand Turk, Jan. 76°F (24·4°C), July 83°F (28·3°C). Annual rainfall 21".

CONSTITUTION AND GOVERNMENT

A new constitution entered force on 9 Aug. 2006. It granted the Turks and Caicos Islands further self-government, while at the same time incorporating provisions enabling the Government to fulfil their responsibilities for the territory. It made provision for the establishment of an Advisory National Security Council, and changed the title of Chief Minister and Deputy Chief Minister to Premier and Deputy Premier. Following the resignation of premier Michael Misick in March 2009 on corruption charges, the UK government dissolved the cabinet and the House of Assembly in Aug. 2009 and placed the island under direct rule. The Cabinet (formerly Executive Council) comprised the Governor, the Premier, six other Ministers and the Attorney General. Previously the House of Assembly (formerly Legislative Council) consisted of a Speaker, one official member (the Attorney General), 15 elected members and four appointed members.

RECENT ELECTIONS

At general elections held on 9 Feb. 2007 for the 15 elective seats in the House of Assembly, the Progressive National Party won 13 seats with 59·7% of the vote and the People's Democratic Movement two with 40·3%.

CURRENT ADMINISTRATION

Governor: Gordon Wetherell; b. 1948 (took office on 5 Aug. 2008).

The UK suspended self-government on 14 Aug. 2009, with Governor Wetherell put in direct control of the islands.

INTERNATIONAL RELATIONS

The Islands are a member of CARICOM.

ECONOMY

Overview

The economy is based on free-market private sector-led development. The focus is on the service sector, with tourism and finance still the dominant industries.

Currency

The US dollar is the official currency. Inflation was 2·9% in 2007 (3·7% in 2006).

Budget

In 2004–05 current revenues were US$118m. and current expenditures US$122m.

Performance

Real GDP growth was 12·7% in 2005 (11·6% in 2004).

Banking and Finance

There were six commercial banks in 2004. Offshore finance is a major industry.

Weights and Measures

The Imperial system is generally in use.

ENERGY AND NATURAL RESOURCES

Environment

Carbon dioxide emissions from the consumption and flaring of fossil fuels in 2008 were the equivalent of 0·7 tonnes per capita.

Electricity

Electrical services are provided to all of the inhabited islands. Total electricity production for 2004 was 10m. kWh. Installed capacity in 2004 was an estimated 4,000 kW. Total electrical power consumption in 2003 was 102m. kWh.

Agriculture

Farming is done on a small scale mainly for subsistence.

Fisheries

In 2005 the total catch was 5,491 tonnes.

INDUSTRY

Labour

In 2001, out of a total population of 13,436 aged 15 or over, 10,181 were working, 1,094 unemployed and 2,161 economically inactive.

EXTERNAL ECONOMIC RELATIONS

Imports and Exports

Imports, 2004, US$220·6m.; exports, US$12·2m. The main export is dried, frozen and processed fish.

COMMUNICATIONS

Civil Aviation

The international airports are on Grand Turk and Providenciales. International services are provided by Air Canada, Air Jamaica, American Airlines, Bahamasair, British Airways, Delta Airlines, TCI Skyking, Tropical Airways d'Haiti and US Airways. An internal air service provides regular daily flights between the inhabited islands.

Shipping

The main ports are at Grand Turk, Cockburn Harbour and Providenciales. There is a service to Miami. In 2002 the merchant fleet totalled 1,000 GRT.

Telecommunications

There are internal and international cable, telephone, telegraph and fax services.

Postal Services

Postal services are provided on all of the inhabited islands by the government. Postal agencies such as UPS, DHL and Federal Express also exist. There were six post offices in 2003.

SOCIAL INSTITUTIONS

Justice

Laws are a mixture of Statute and Common Law. There is a Magistrates Court and a Supreme Court. Appeals lie from the Supreme Court to the Court of Appeal which sits in Nassau, Bahamas. There is a further appeal in certain cases to the Privy Council in London.

Education

The adult literacy rate is 98%. Education is free between the ages of five and 14 in the ten government primary schools; there are also four private primary schools. Total school enrolment in 2004–05 was 1,931 in government primary schools and 1,282 in government secondary schools. There were 1,670 pupils enrolled in the private schools.

In 2005 public expenditure on education came to 11·8% of total government spending.

Health

In 2004 there were 17 doctors, two dentists and 43 hospital beds.

RELIGION

There are Anglican, Catholic, Methodist, Baptist and Evangelist groups.

CULTURE

Broadcasting

The government operates the semi-commercial Radio Turks and Caicos. There are also two commercial stations and one religious. There is cable and satellite TV.

Press

In 2006 there were two weekly newspapers.

Tourism

Number of visitors, 2004, 171,500. Tourism receipts totalled US$292m. in 2002. In 2002 tourism accounted for 33·9% of GDP.

FURTHER READING

Statistical Office: Department of Economic Planning and Statistics, Ministry of Finance, South Base, Grand Turk.
Website: http://www.depstc.org

UNITED STATES OF AMERICA

Capital: Washington, D.C.
Population estimate, 2010: 317·64m.
GDP per capita, 2007: (PPP$) 45,592
HDI/world rank: 0·956/13

KEY HISTORICAL EVENTS

The earliest inhabitants of the north American continent can be traced back to Palaeolithic times. The Pueblo culture in modern-day Colorado and New Mexico flourished from the 11th to the 14th century AD. In the 12th century permanent settlements appeared in the east where cultivation and fishing supported major fortified towns. The first Europeans to make their presence felt were the Spanish, who based themselves in Florida before venturing north and west. Santa Fe in New Mexico was founded in 1610. But by the mid-17th century there was competition centred on Quebec from the French who colonized the banks of the St Lawrence River.

Elizabethan adventurers were eager to exploit the New World but it was not until 1607 that an English colony was established. This was at Jamestown in what is now southern Virginia. After a perilous start when disease and malnutrition carried off most of the settlers, Virginia's population grew rapidly to meet the European demand for tobacco. Maryland, originally a refuge for persecuted Catholics, also thrived on the tobacco trade. To make up for the shortage of labour, slaves were imported from Africa.

In 1620 a hundred pilgrims landed at Plymouth Rock to found a Puritan enclave, which became the colony of Massachusetts. Other settlements soon followed, accommodating a broad range of Christian radicals fleeing persecution. Not all were tolerant of beliefs that differed from their own. Pennsylvania, the colony named after the Quaker William Penn, was exceptional in offering freedom of worship to 'all persons who confess and acknowledge the one almighty and eternal God'. In 1664 the British took control of neighbouring Dutch colonies. New Amsterdam became New York. Almost all of the eastern seaboard was now claimed by British settlers who were also venturing inland.

Their main European rivals were the French who claimed a vast area around and to the southwest of the Great Lakes. With American Indian tribes allied to both sides, there was heavy fighting in 1744 and 1748. But within a decade British forces had captured most of the French strongholds. After the Treaty of Paris in 1763, Britain commanded the whole of North America east of the Mississippi while Spain, having surrendered Florida, gained Louisiana from France. For a brief period colonization was restricted to the area east of the Appalachians, the rest of the territory being reserved for Indian tribes. This soon became a point of issue between the settlers who were intent on expansion and the government in London, which wanted a settled, self-supporting community benefiting British trade. Having disposed of the French threat, the colonists felt confident enough to defy orders that ignored their interests. In particular, they objected to the Navigation Acts which required goods to be carried in British vessels and to various taxes imposed without consultation. 'No taxation without representation' became a rallying cry for disaffected colonists. The centre of opposition was Boston, scene of the infamous 'tea party' when, in 1773, militants destroyed a cargo of East India tea. In 1775 the arrest of rebel ringleaders served only to provoke the 13 colonies to co-operate in further acts of rebellion, including the setting up of a *de facto* government which appointed George Washington commander of American forces.

Independence

The War of Independence was by no means a clear-cut affair. British forces, never more than 50,000 strong, were supported by a powerful body of colonists who remained loyal to the Crown. The war lasted for seven years from 1776 with both sides often getting close to a conclusive victory. The decisive moment came at last with the surrender of Gen. Burgoyne and his 8,000 troops in upper New York state in Oct. 1777, a defeat that persuaded a cautious France to enter the war. Under the peace terms secured in 1783 Britain kept Canada leaving the new United States with territory stretching from the Atlantic to the Mississippi. A constitution based on democratic principles buttressed by inalienable rights including the ownership of property came into force in 1789. It allowed for a federal government headed by a president and executive, a legislature with a House of Representatives and a Senate, and a judiciary with ultimate authority on constitutional matters exercised by a Supreme Court. The first president was George Washington, who was elected in 1789. In 1800 Washington, D.C. was declared the national capital.

Hostilities with Britain resumed in 1812 amidst accusations that Britain was using the excuse of the Napoleonic wars to harass American shipping and to encourage Indian resistance to expansion into the Midwest. Most of the fighting took place on the Canadian border where an attempted invasion was decisively repulsed. But Louisiana, having reverted to French rule and subsequently sold to the USA, was secured for the Union. With the exception of Louisiana, other American territories that had once been part of the Spanish empire fell to Mexico. But not for long. In 1836 Texas broke away from Mexico, surviving as an independent republic until 1845 when it was annexed by the USA. This provoked war with Mexico which ended in 1848 with the USA taking over what are now the states of California, Arizona, Colorado, Utah, Nevada and New Mexico. Any temptation there might have been for European involvement in the struggle was removed by the Monroe Doctrine, a declaration by President Monroe that interference from the Old World in matters concerning the western hemisphere would not be tolerated. It was a measure of the growing military and economic self confidence of the USA that such a warning, delivered in 1823, was taken seriously.

The westward expansion began soon after independence but accelerated with the destruction of Indian power and the removal of the native population to designated reservations. In 1846 a long-running dispute with Britain confirming US title to Oregon acted as a spur to migration as did the Californian gold rush of 1848. By the 1850s the railway network was bringing people and economic prosperity to the mid-west. Population quadrupled between 1815 to 1860, from 8m. to almost 31m. In 1862 the Homestead Act allocated 160 acres to anyone who was ready to farm it. By 1890 the west was won.

Civil War

The transition from a rural society to an industrial power of world importance created tensions, not least between the slave-owning southern states and the rest of the Union which favoured the abolition of slavery. Economic as well as humanitarian factors were in play since the North resented the advantage cheap labour gave to the South. The opposing view held that the South, by now the world's largest cotton producer, depended on slavery for its commercial survival. Mutual antagonism came to a head with the secession of the southern states from the Union in 1860–61 and their formation as a Confederacy. Despite sporadic outbreaks of violence, civil war was not in prospect until Confederate troops fired on the US flag at Fort Sumter. President Abraham Lincoln ordered a blockade of the South. The recruitment of rival armies followed within weeks. The war turned out to be much bloodier than anyone had expected. More American lives were lost in the Civil War than in the two world wars combined. The military balance was maintained until 1863 when the North secured a crushing victory at the Battle of Gettysburg. However, the war continued until April 1865 when Robert E. Lee surrendered to Ulysses S. Grant at Appomattox Courthouse in Virginia. A few days later Lincoln was assassinated, a loss that the southern states had subsequent cause to regret. Contrary to Lincoln's hopes, a generous settlement was now out of the question. Instead of a gradual transition to a new society, the South was rushed into a social revolution. This in turn led to terrorist violence and acts of vengeance against freed slaves. From this carnage emerged the notorious Ku Klux Klan as the standard bearer of lynch law. While the 13th amendment prohibited slavery, political freedom was denied to the black community by state-imposed literacy tests and discriminatory property taxes.

That America had interests beyond its own borders was made evident by the Spanish war of 1898 which resulted in the USA becoming the dominant power in the Caribbean though the effort to take over in the Philippines came up against Filipino resistance and led to a heavy death toll.

By 1900 the USA rivalled Britain and Germany as the world's dominant power. With vast natural resources and a manufacturing capacity that secured 11% of world trade, it was clear that Europe was soon to lose its grip on world affairs. Ironically, though, it was Europe as the chief supplier of labour that gave the USA the impetus it needed to fulfil its promise. Between 1881 and 1920, 23m. immigrants entered the USA, the largest population movement ever recorded.

Given the heterogeneous background of the American population in the early 20th century it is scarcely surprising that popular opinion was against involvement in the First World War. But events, including German U-boat harassment of American shipping, soon proved that isolationism was not an option. It was not until 1917 that America joined the hostilities but the resurgence of energy created by the arrival of the American Expeditionary Force was critical to the Allied breakthrough.

Post-war America, relatively unscathed by the European conflict, was unquestionably the most powerful nation and as such was able to dictate terms at the Versailles peace conference. But President Wilson's 'fourteen points' which set out a plan for collective security policed by a League of Nations failed to win support in the one country that was critical to its success. The Treaty was rejected by the Senate in 1920 and America retreated once again into isolationism.

A resumption of economic growth was accompanied by a struggle to impose a common set of values, chiefly white and

Protestant, on a diverse population. To outsiders the most extraordinary experiment in social engineering was Prohibition, a federal imposed attempt to outlaw all alcoholic drinks. Whatever gain there was to the health of the nation, the chief beneficiaries were the bosses of organized crime.

New Deal

Dreams of everlasting prosperity were shattered by the 1929 Stock Market Crash. A succession of bank failures was followed by widespread bankruptcies and mass unemployment which sent the economy into a further downward spin. The beginning of the end to the agony came with the election to the presidency of Franklin D. Roosevelt, who pushed through Congress a series of radical measures known collectively as the New Deal, aimed at revitalizing the nation. With the abandonment of the gold standard, cheap loans to restart factories and farms and huge investment in public works proved to be the key to recovery though unemployment remained high until production was boosted by the demands of another world war. In 1935 Roosevelt's social security act provided the bare bones of an American welfare state.

Roosevelt was well aware of the dangers to the USA if the fascist dictators were allowed to triumph, but as in 1914, there was formidable opposition to direct involvement. Roosevelt compromised by supplying Britain with much needed armaments on favourable terms. But it was events in Asia rather than in Europe that eventually persuaded America of the need for direct action. Opposition to Japanese expansion into China and southeast Asia, including an oil embargo and a freezing of Japanese assets in the USA, brought a savage retaliation at Pearl Harbor, when much of the US fleet was destroyed. America declared war on Japan while Germany declared war on America. The US military effort focused initially on the Pacific but after 1942 American forces were also committed to the campaign in north Africa and Europe. With the D-Day landings in June 1944, US troops led the attack on Germany and in May 1945, within a month of Roosevelt's death, Germany surrendered. By then Vice President Harry Truman had been confirmed as Roosevelt's successor and forced a Japanese surrender by sacrificing Hiroshima and Nagasaki to the atomic bomb.

This time, in the aftermath of war, the USA needed no encouragement to assume the leadership of the free world. The threat of a Soviet takeover in Europe was countered by the formation of NATO in 1949 and the provision of dollar aid under the 1947 Marshall Plan to kick-start European economic recovery. In addition, the Truman doctrine provided a $400m. aid package for the Turkish and Greek governments. The risk of a return to isolationism receded still further when China fell to communism. In 1950 American troops went to the aid of South Korea when it was invaded by the communist North. Though technically under the aegis of the UN, the campaign was an almost entirely American affair led by General Douglas MacArthur. When Chinese forces became involved, MacArthur spoke openly of extending the war to the Chinese mainland, a threat countered strongly by President Truman who forced MacArthur's resignation to establish undisputed political control over the military.

A ceasefire was negotiated after Dwight Eisenhower was elected president in 1953. The USA took the lead in setting up the South East Asia Treaty Organization on the same lines as NATO. Eisenhower had a decisive influence on the Suez crisis in 1956 when he refused to support the invasion of Egypt by British, French and Israeli forces. Domestically he made little headway against a powerful Democratic opposition in both Houses of Congress. His attempts to thaw the Cold War also met with frustration. He handed over the Republican presidential candidacy to his vice-president Richard Nixon, who lost the 1960 election by a slim margin to John F. Kennedy.

Civil Rights

In the early 1960s civil rights were high on the political agenda. The thuggish tactics of Senator Joe McCarthy and the House Committee on Un-American Activities during the previous decade brought into focus basic democratic freedoms guaranteed by the Constitution while growing protests against racial discrimination led to legislation to enforce equality of opportunity in education and employment. The civil rights movement peaked in the early 1960s when the imposition of federal law in the South led to acts of violence against liberal protesters. Foremost among the campaigners for racial equality was Martin Luther King, Jr. who was awarded the Nobel Peace Prize in 1964 and who was assassinated four years later.

Social tensions were exacerbated by the Cold War confrontation. In his first year of office Kennedy was embarrassed by the failed Bay of Pigs invasion when anti-Castro Cubans, trained and supported by the CIA, attempted to overthrow the country's communist regime. The building of the Berlin Wall in Aug. 1961 symbolized a hardening of the Cold War. In 1962 Kennedy had to confront the prospect of the Soviets placing missiles in Cuba. The prospect of world war was only too real until an agreement between the two nations allowed for a withdrawal of the missiles on the condition of a US promise not to invade Cuba. The incident prompted a thawing in East–West relations and in 1963 the USA, UK and USSR signed the Limited Test Ban Treaty which, for the first time, put a brake on the spread of nuclear weapons. Less hopeful was the acceleration of the conflict in Vietnam. Kennedy increased the American military presence in South Vietnam from 700 at the beginning of his term in office to 15,000 to counter the threat of communist domination by the North. Domestically, Kennedy's government pledged $1·2bn. for social and housing programmes.

Kennedy was assassinated in Dallas in Nov. 1963 and his vice president, Lyndon Johnson, was inaugurated as his successor. Johnson oversaw the implementation of civil rights legislation initiated by the Kennedy administration, epitomized by the Voting Rights Act, and also introduced Medicare (health insurance for the elderly). By 1966 over 350,000 American troops were in Vietnam and by the following year almost 80,000 Americans had been killed or wounded. The public turned against involvement in southeast Asia, not least because increased military expenditure led to a delay in domestic reforms.

Watergate

Johnson decided not to contest the 1968 presidential election. His likely successor for the Democrat nomination was John Kennedy's brother, Bobby, but he was assassinated in June of that year. The Republican nominee, Richard Nixon, won the presidency. With falling support for US involvement in Vietnam, he reduced the number of troops stationed there from 550,000 in 1969 to 30,000 three years later but authorized military operations in North Vietnam, Laos and Cambodia in the hope of forcing North Vietnam to the negotiating table. Elsewhere, he signed the Strategic Arms Limitation Treaty (SALT) with Moscow in 1972 and relaxed trade restrictions against China.

Nixon was re-elected as president in 1973 and shortly afterwards agreed a ceasefire with North Vietnam. However, his second term of office was cut short by the Watergate scandal. The charges against him centred on White House-released taped transcripts of discussions in which Nixon authorized a cover-up of a break-in at the Democratic party headquarters in the Watergate complex, Washington, D.C. in 1972. Threatened with Congressional impeachment, Nixon announced his resignation in Aug. 1974.

Gerald Ford, who replaced Nixon, granted his predecessor a controversial 'full, free and absolute pardon'. Ford lost the 1976 presidential election to Democrat Jimmy Carter. Perceived as a Washington outsider, Carter's often strained relations with Congress and the Senate obstructed his domestic agenda. The economy suffered and by 1980 inflation and unemployment were both running high. Internationally, he secured the neutrality of the Panama Canal and brokered the influential Camp David talks between Egypt and Israel. He also re-established diplomatic ties with China. Henry Kissinger, who was secretary of state for part of Nixon's and all of Carter's years in office, oversaw America's withdrawal from southeast Asia, winning the Nobel Peace Prize jointly with his North Vietnamese counterpart Le Duc Tho in 1974. Attempts at further improving US–Soviet relations were scuppered when the signing of the Strategic Arms Limitation Treaty (SALT II) was postponed because of the Soviet invasion of Afghanistan in 1979. The incursion also led to a US boycott of the 1980 Moscow Olympics. Radical Iranian students stormed the US embassy in Tehran in late 1979 and seized over 50 US hostages. After a year of negotiations, a secret US military rescue mission failed and contributed to Republican Ronald Reagan's landslide victory at the 1980 presidential polls.

Reagan's economic policies, known as 'Reaganomics', redefined American society in the 1980s. In his first year of office he introduced a 25% tax cut for individuals and corporations. He slashed welfare but increased military expenditure. In terms of governmental structure, he was intent on delegating many federal programmes to state and local levels. A recession in 1982 prompted tax increases and set the pattern of boom and bust that characterized his tenure. In 1986 he reduced the number of tax rates, abolishing tax altogether for many low-income earners. In Oct. 1987 the stock market collapsed, losing a third of its value over two months, and by the end of his presidency, Reagan had seen the national debt more than triple to $2·5trn.

End to the Cold War

Relations between the USA and USSR deteriorated in the early 1980s. The shooting down of a South Korean airliner carrying American citizens in 1983 led to a further deployment of US missiles in Western Europe while US proposals for the Strategic Defense Initiative (known as 'Star Wars') added to tensions. In 1983 the USA invaded Grenada, scene of a coup, in a bid to curb Soviet–Cuban influence in the Caribbean. However, relations between the two superpowers improved in the mid-eighties after successful negotiations on nuclear arms limitations. Reagan met Soviet leader Mikhail Gorbachev in 1985 and in 1987 the two leaders signed a treaty in Washington, D.C. agreeing to destroy a range of intermediate-range nuclear weapons.

Reagan's foreign policy elsewhere was unstinting in its protection of US interests. In 1986 he bombed Tripoli after Libya was accused of involvement in the bombing of a nightclub in West Berlin which killed two American servicemen. The following year he became embroiled in the Iran-Contra affair. The CIA was found to have sold arms to Iran to fund anti-communist guerrillas in Nicaragua. Reagan and his deputy, George Bush, were cleared of direct involvement but Reagan was censured for allowing the affair to develop.

Bush took over the presidency in 1989 and continued an active foreign policy. At the end of 1989 he authorized the invasion of Panama to remove Gen. Manuel Antonio Noriega from power. The collapse of the Soviet empire in 1990 extended US economic aid to Eastern Europe and Bush signed a non-aggression pact with Soviet leader Mikhail Gorbachev which effectively ended the Cold War. In 1990–91 Bush led a coalition of European and Arab states to counter the Iraqi invasion of Kuwait. Around 500,000 US troops were stationed in the Persian Gulf and when trade embargoes and diplomacy failed to persuade Iraq to withdraw, Bush authorized a military offensive in Jan. 1991. By the end of Feb. Kuwaiti independence had been restored. Domestically, Bush was badly damaged when he was forced to raise taxes despite his election promise of 'no new taxes'.

The Democrats regained control of the White House with the election of Bill Clinton in 1992. Clinton combined economic recovery at home with an active foreign policy which underlined America's role as the only superpower. He secured the passage of the North American Free Trade Agreement, which created a free-trade zone between the United States, Canada and Mexico, cut the United States budget deficit by 50% in his first term and in his second term authorized America's first tax cut since 1981. Unemployment reached its lowest levels since the late-1960s and in 1998 there was a federal budget surplus for the first time in almost 30 years. His social legislation included anti-crime provisions, the Family and Medical Leave Act, a welfare reform bill and an increase in the minimum wage. He also appointed Madeleine Albright as the first-ever female secretary of state.

On the international scene Clinton brokered talks between the Palestinian leader Yasser Arafat and Israeli Prime Minister Yitzhak Rabin which resulted in limited Palestinian self-rule. He sent peacekeeping troops both to Bosnia and Herzegovina and to Haiti. In 1995 he was instrumental in securing the Dayton accords that offered peace between Yugoslavia, Croatia and Bosnia and Herzegovina. Relations with Vietnam were normalized and diplomatic and trade links with China much improved. He was also an important figure in the formulation of the 1998 Good Friday agreement which sought to reach a peace settlement in Northern Ireland.

Clinton retained a hard-line stance against Iraq, sending forces against Saddam Hussein in 1994, 1996 and 1998. Sudan and Afghanistan were attacked in 1998 having been linked with the al-Qaeda terrorist network held responsible for the bombing of US embassies in Tanzania and Kenya. In 1999 there was a Clinton-led NATO campaign of air strikes against Yugoslavia when the country's leaders refused to end a campaign of violence against ethnic Albanians in Kosovo. Yugoslav president Slobodan Milošević was forced to withdraw his troops and allow an international peacekeeping force in Kosovo.

However, Clinton's second term of office was dominated by scandal. He reached an out-of-court agreement with Paula Jones, a state government employee who had accused him of sexual harassment. Clinton and his wife, Hillary, were also accused of criminal wrongdoing over a land deal in Arkansas, known as Whitewater, though they were both eventually cleared of the charges. Most damagingly, Clinton had an affair with Monica Lewinsky, a White House intern. Having denied the sexual nature of the affair under oath, Clinton was impeached for perjury and obstruction of justice although the senate trial ended when neither motion gained a simple majority.

In 2000 Clinton's vice president, Al Gore, lost the presidential election to George W. Bush, son of the earlier President George Bush. Gore was defeated despite winning the popular vote. In 2001 Bush's first budget included a $1·25trn. tax cut. He attracted international criticism in his early months in office for refusing to ratify the Kyoto Agreement on global warming and climate change and for his bid to replace the 1972 Anti-Ballistic Missile Treaty with a new accord allowing for a missile defence system in the United States. Following talks with Russian President Vladimir Putin in June 2001 the two leaders signed an anti-nuclear deal to reduce their respective strategic nuclear warheads by two-thirds over the next ten years.

War on Terrorism

On 11 Sept. 2001 the heart of New York City was devastated after hijackers flew two jet airliners into the World Trade Center. A plane also crashed into the Pentagon, in Washington, D.C., and a fourth hijacked plane crashed near the town of Shanksville, Pennsylvania. The death toll, initially put at 6,700, was eventually lowered to 2,752, with 67 countries reporting dead or missing citizens. Osama bin Laden, the Saudi dissident leader of the al-Qaeda terrorist network and believed to be living in Afghanistan at the invitation of the ruling Taliban, immediately became the chief suspect and military action against Afghanistan followed, with air strikes beginning on 7 Oct. 2001. Despite the UN establishing a fragile multi-party government in Afghanistan, the USA continues to carry out special missions against Taliban and al-Qaeda targets.

In early 2002 Bush declared North Korea, Iran and Iraq 'an axis of evil' and by Sept. 2002 was pressing the UN to act against Iraq. Bush's foreign policy was played out against a background of domestic recession. On 20 March 2003 US forces, supported by the UK, launched attacks on Iraq, and initiated a war aimed at 'liberating Iraq'. On 9 April 2003 American forces took control of central Baghdad, effectively bringing an end to Saddam Hussein's rule. In Nov. 2004 Bush won a second term as president, which was dominated by continuing military engagement in Iraq and Afghanistan and by the collapse in 2007 of the US sub-prime mortgage sector. He was succeeded by the Democrat Barack Obama, who won the presidential election of 2008. Obama took office with the global financial system in turmoil.

TERRITORY AND POPULATION

The United States is bounded in the north by Canada, east by the North Atlantic, south by the Gulf of Mexico and Mexico, and west by the North Pacific Ocean. The area of the USA is 3,794,083 sq. miles (9,826,629 sq. km), of which 3,537,439 sq. miles (9,161,924 sq. km) are land and 256,644 sq. miles (664,705 sq. km) are water (comprising Great Lakes, inland and coastal water).

Population at each census from 1790 to 2000 (including Alaska and Hawaii from 1960). Figures do not include Puerto Rico, Guam, American Samoa or other Pacific islands, or the US population abroad. Residents of Indian reservations not included before 1890.

	White	*Black*	*Other races*	*Total*
1790	3,172,464	757,208	—	3,929,672
1800	4,306,446	1,002,037	—	5,308,483
1810	5,862,073	1,377,808	—	7,239,881
1820	7,866,797	1,771,562	—	9,638,359
1830	10,537,378	2,328,642	—	12,866,020
1840	14,195,805	2,873,648	—	17,069,453
1850	19,553,068	3,638,808	—	23,191,876
1860	26,922,537	4,441,830	78,954	31,443,321
1870	34,337,292	5,392,172	88,985	39,818,449
1880	43,402,970	6,580,793	172,020	50,155,783
1890	55,101,258	7,488,676	357,780	62,947,714
1900	66,868,508	8,834,395	509,265	76,212,168
1910	81,812,405	9,828,667	587,459	92,228,531
1920	94,903,540	10,463,607	654,421	106,021,568
1930	110,395,753	11,891,842	915,065	123,202,660
1940	118,357,831	12,865,914	941,384	132,165,129
1950	135,149,629	15,044,937	1,131,232	151,325,798
1960	158,831,732	18,871,831	1,619,612	179,323,175
1970	177,748,975	22,580,289	2,882,662	203,211,926
1980	188,371,622	26,495,025	11,679,158	226,545,805
1990	199,686,070	29,986,060	19,037,743	248,709,873
2000[1]	211,460,626	34,658,190	35,303,090	281,421,906

[1]'White' refers to the White-alone population, 'Black' to the Black-alone population and 'Other races' to the population in all the remaining race groups, including those reporting two or more races.

The mid-year population estimate for 2009 was 307,006,550, although the United Nations estimate was higher, at 314,659,000.

The UN gives an estimated population for 2010 of 317·64m.

2000 density, 30·7 per sq. km (79·6 per sq. mile). Urban population (persons living in places with at least 2,500 inhabitants) at the 2000 census was 222,360,539 (79·0%); rural, 59,061,367. In 1990 it was 75·2%; in 1980, 73·7%; in 1970, 73·6%.

Sex distribution by race of the population at the 2000 census:

	Males	*Females*
White	103,773,194	107,687,432
Black or African American	16,465,185	18,193,005
American Indian and Alaska Native	1,233,982	1,241,974
Asian	4,948,741	5,294,257
Native Hawaiian and Other Pacific Islander	202,629	196,206
Other Race	8,009,214	7,349,859
Two or More Races	3,420,618	3,405,610
Total	138,053,563	143,368,343

Alongside these racial groups, and applicable to all of them, a category of 'Hispanic origin' comprised 35,305,818 persons (including 20,640,711 of Mexican ancestry), up 12,951,759 from 22,354,059 in 1990. Hispanics are now the largest ethnic minority in the USA.

Among ten-year age groups the 35–44 age group contained most people according to the 2000 census, with a total of 45,148,527 (16·0% of the population).

At the 2000 census there were 105,480,101 households, up from 91,947,410 in 1990.

At the 2000 census there were 50,454 people aged 100 or over, compared to 37,306 in 1990. Of the 50,454 centenarians in 2000, 40,397 were female, and of the 37,306 in 1990, 29,405 were female.

There is no official language, though English has been provided with official status in 30 states. The 2000 census showed that 47·0m. persons five years and over spoke a language other than English in the home, including Spanish or Spanish Creole by 28·1m.; French or French Creole by 2·1m.; Chinese by 2·0m.; German by 1·4m.; Tagalog by 1·2m.; Italian by 1·0m.; Vietnamese by 1·0m.

The following table includes population statistics, the year in which each of the original 13 states (Connecticut, Delaware, Georgia, Maryland, Massachusetts, New Hampshire, New Jersey, New York, North Carolina, Pennsylvania, Rhode Island, South Carolina, Virginia) ratified the constitution, and the year when each of the other states was admitted into the Union. Traditional abbreviations for the names of the states are shown in brackets with postal codes for use in addresses.

The USA is divided into four geographic regions comprised of nine divisions. These are, with their 2000 census populations: Northeast (comprised of the New England and Middle Atlantic divisions), 53,594,378; Midwest (East North Central, West North Central), 64,392,776; South (South Atlantic, East South Central, West South Central), 100,236,820; West (Mountain, Pacific), 63,197,932.

Geographic divisions and states		*Land area: sq. miles, 2000*	*Census population 1 April 2000*	*Pop. per sq. mile, 2000*
United States		3,537,439	281,421,906	79·6
New England		62,810	13,922,517	221·7
Connecticut (1788)	*(Conn./CT)*	4,845	3,405,565	702·9
Maine (1820)	*(Me./ME)*	30,862	1,274,923	41·3
Massachusetts (1788)	*(Mass./MA)*	7,840	6,349,097	809·8
New Hampshire (1788)	*(N.H./NH)*	8,968	1,235,786	137·8
Rhode Island (1790)	*(R.I./RI)*	1,045	1,048,319	1,003·2
Vermont (1791)	*(Vt./VT)*	9,250	608,827	65·8
Middle Atlantic		99,448	39,671,861	398·9
New Jersey (1787)	*(N.J./NJ)*	7,417	8,414,350	1,134·4
New York (1788)	*(N.Y./NY)*	47,214	18,976,457	401·9
Pennsylvania (1787)	*(Pa./PA)*	44,817	12,281,054	274·0
East North Central		243,513	45,155,037	185·4
Illinois (1818)	*(Ill./IL)*	55,584	12,419,293	223·4
Indiana (1816)	*(Ind./IN)*	35,867	6,080,485	169·5

Geographic divisions and states		*Land area: sq. miles, 2000*	*Census population 1 April 2000*	*Pop. per sq. mile, 2000*
Michigan (1837)	*(Mich./MI)*	56,804	9,938,444	175·0
Ohio (1803)	*(Oh./OH)*	40,948	11,353,140	277·3
Wisconsin (1848)	*(Wis./WI)*	54,310	5,363,675	98·8
West North Central		507,913	19,237,739	37·9
Iowa (1846)	*(Ia./IA)*	55,869	2,926,324	52·4
Kansas (1861)	*(Kans./KS)*	81,815	2,688,418	32·9
Minnesota (1858)	*(Minn./MN)*	79,610	4,919,479	61·8
Missouri (1821)	*(Mo./MO)*	68,886	5,595,211	81·2
Nebraska (1867)	*(Nebr./NE)*	76,872	1,711,263	22·3
North Dakota (1889)	*(N.D./ND)*	68,976	642,200	9·3
South Dakota (1889)	*(S.D./SD)*	75,885	754,844	9·9
South Atlantic		266,115	51,769,160	194·5
Delaware (1787)	*(Del./DE)*	1,954	783,600	401·0
Dist. of Columbia (1791)[1]	*(D.C./DC)*	61	572,059	9,378·0
Florida (1845)	*(Fla./FL)*	53,927	15,982,378	296·4
Georgia (1788)	*(Ga./GA)*	57,906	8,186,453	141·4
Maryland (1788)	*(Md./MD)*	9,774	5,296,486	541·9
North Carolina (1789)	*(N.C./NC)*	48,711	8,049,313	165·2
South Carolina (1788)	*(S.C./SC)*	30,110	4,012,012	133·2
Virginia (1788)	*(Va./VA)*	39,594	7,078,515	178·8
West Virginia (1863)	*(W. Va./WV)*	24,078	1,808,344	75·1
East South Central		178,596	17,022,810	95·3
Alabama (1819)	*(Al./AL)*	50,744	4,447,100	87·6
Kentucky (1792)	*(Ky./KY)*	39,728	4,041,769	101·7
Mississippi (1817)	*(Miss./MS)*	46,907	2,844,658	60·6
Tennessee (1796)	*(Tenn./TN)*	41,217	5,689,283	138·0
West South Central		426,094	31,444,850	73·8
Arkansas (1836)	*(Ark./AR)*	52,068	2,673,400	51·3
Louisiana (1812)	*(La./LA)*	43,562	4,468,976	102·6
Oklahoma (1907)	*(Okla./OK)*	68,667	3,450,654	50·3
Texas (1845)	*(Tex./TX)*	261,797	20,851,820	79·6
Mountain		856,078	18,172,295	21·2
Arizona (1912)	*(Ariz./AZ)*	113,635	5,130,632	45·2
Colorado (1876)	*(Colo./CO)*	103,718	4,301,261	41·5
Idaho (1890)	*(Id./ID)*	82,747	1,293,953	15·6
Montana (1889)	*(Mont./MT)*	145,552	902,195	6·2
Nevada (1864)	*(Nev./NV)*	109,826	1,998,257	18·2
New Mexico (1912)	*(N. Mex./NM)*	121,356	1,819,046	15·0
Utah (1896)	*(Ut./UT)*	82,144	2,233,169	27·2
Wyoming (1890)	*(Wyo./WY)*	97,100	493,782	5·1
Pacific		896,874	45,025,637	50·2
Alaska (1959)	*(Ak./AK)*	571,951	626,932	1·1
California (1850)	*(Calif./CA)*	155,959	33,871,648	217·2
Hawaii (1960)	*(Hi./HI)*	6,423	1,211,537	188·6
Oregon (1859)	*(Oreg./OR)*	95,997	3,421,399	35·6
Washington (1889)	*(Wash./WA)*	66,544	5,894,121	88·6
Outlying Territories, total		4,031	4,198,855	1,041·6
American Samoa		77	57,291	744·0
Guam		210	154,805	737·2
Johnston Atoll		1	315	315·0
Midway Islands		2	0	0
Northern Marianas		179	69,221	386·7
Puerto Rico		3,425	3,808,610	1,112·0
Virgin Islands		134	108,612	810·5
Wake Island		3	1	0·3

[1]District of Columbia selected as site of national government in 1791.

The 2000 census showed 31,107,889 foreign-born persons. The ten countries contributing the largest numbers who were foreign-born were: Mexico, 9,177,487; Philippines, 1,369,070; India, 1,022,552; China, 988,857; Vietnam, 988,174; Cuba, 872,716; Korea, 864,125; Canada, 820,771; El Salvador, 817,336; Germany, 706,704; Dominican Republic, 687,677. In fiscal year 2000 a total of 841,002 persons obtained legal permanent resident status (1,535,872 in fiscal year 1990). In 2007 the estimate for the foreign-born population reached an all-time high of 38·1m., representing 12·6% of the population.

Population of cities with over 100,000 inhabitants at the censuses of 1990 and 2000:

Cities	*Census 1990*	*Census 2000*	*Cities*	*Census 1990*	*Census 2000*
New York, NY	7,322,564	8,008,278	Colorado Springs, CO	281,140	360,890
Los Angeles, CA	3,485,398	3,694,820	St Louis, MO	396,685	348,189
Chicago, IL	2,783,726	2,896,016	Wichita, KS	304,011	344,284
Houston, TX	1,630,553	1,953,631	Santa Ana, CA	293,742	337,977
Philadelphia, PA	1,585,577	1,517,550	Pittsburgh, PA	369,879	334,563
Phoenix, AZ	983,403	1,321,045	Arlington, TX	261,721	332,969
San Diego, CA	1,110,549	1,223,400	Cincinnati, OH	364,040	331,285
Dallas, TX	1,006,877	1,188,580	Anaheim, CA	266,406	328,014
San Antonio, TX	935,933	1,144,646	Toledo, OH	332,943	313,619
Detroit, MI	1,027,974	951,270	Tampa, FL	280,015	303,447
San Jose, CA	782,248	894,943	Buffalo, NY	328,123	292,648
Indianapolis, IN	741,952	791,926	St Paul, MN	272,235	287,151
San Francisco, CA	723,959	776,733	Corpus Christi, TX	257,453	277,454
Jacksonville, FL	635,230	735,617	Aurora, CO	222,103	276,393
Columbus, OH	632,910	711,470	Raleigh, NC	207,951	276,093
Austin, TX	465,622	656,562	Newark, NJ	275,221	273,546
Baltimore, MD	736,014	651,154	Lexington-Fayette, KY	225,366	260,512
Memphis, TN	610,337	650,100	Anchorage, AK	226,338	260,283
Milwaukee, WI	628,088	596,974	Louisville, KY	269,063	256,231
Boston, MA	574,283	589,141	Riverside, CA	226,505	255,166
Washington, DC	606,900	572,059	St Petersburg, FL	238,629	248,232
Nashville-Davidson, TN	510,784	569,891	Bakersfield, CA	174,280	247,057
El Paso, TX	515,342	563,662	Stockton, CA	210,943	243,771
Seattle, WA	516,259	563,374	Birmingham, AL	265,968	242,820
Denver, CO	467,610	554,636	Jersey City, NJ	228,537	240,055
Charlotte, NC	395,934	540,828	Norfolk, VA	261,229	234,403
Fort Worth, TX	447,619	534,694	Baton Rouge, LA	219,531	227,818
Portland, OR	437,319	529,121	Hialeah, FL	188,004	226,419
Oklahoma City, OK	444,719	506,132	Lincoln, NE	191,972	225,581
Tucson, AZ	405,390	486,699	Greensboro, NC	183,521	223,891
New Orleans, LA	496,938	484,674	Plano, TX	128,713	222,030
Las Vegas, NV	258,295	478,434	Rochester, NY	231,636	219,773
Cleveland, OH	505,616	478,403	Glendale, AZ	148,134	218,812
Long Beach, CA	429,433	461,522	Garland, TX	180,650	215,768
Albuquerque, NM	384,736	448,607	Madison, WI	191,262	208,054
Kansas City, MO	435,146	441,545	Fort Wayne, IN	173,072	205,727
Fresno, CA	354,202	427,652	Fremont, CA	173,339	203,413
Virginia Beach, VA	393,069	425,257	Scottsdale, AZ	130,069	202,705
Atlanta, GA	394,017	416,474	Montgomery, AL	187,106	201,568
Sacramento, CA	369,365	407,018	Shreveport, LA	198,525	200,145
Oakland, CA	372,242	399,484	Augusta-Richmond County, GA[2]	44,639	199,775
Mesa, AZ	288,091	396,375	Lubbock, TX	186,206	199,564
Tulsa, OK	367,302	393,049	Chesapeake, VA	151,976	199,184
Omaha, NE	335,795	390,007	Mobile, AL	196,278	198,915
Minneapolis, MN	368,383	382,618	Des Moines, IA	193,187	198,682
Honolulu, HI[1]	365,272	371,657	Grand Rapids, MI	189,126	197,800
Miami, FL	358,548	362,470	Richmond, VA	203,056	197,790
			Yonkers, NY	188,082	196,086
			Spokane, WA	177,196	195,629
			Glendale, CA	180,038	194,973

Cities	Census 1990	Census 2000	Cities	Census 1990	Census 2000
Tacoma, WA	176,664	193,556	Sunnyvale, CA	117,229	131,760
Irving, TX	155,037	191,615	Savannah, GA	137,560	131,510
Huntington Beach, CA	181,519	189,594	Fontana, CA	87,535	128,929
Arlington, VA[3]	170,897	189,453	Orange, CA	110,658	128,821
Modesto, CA	164,730	188,856	Naperville, IL	85,351	128,358
Durham, NC	136,611	187,035	Alexandria, VA	111,183	128,283
Columbus, GA	179,278	186,291	Rancho Cucamonga, CA	101,409	127,743
Orlando, FL	164,693	185,951	Grand Prairie, TX	99,616	127,427
Boise City, ID	125,738	185,787	Fullerton, CA	114,144	126,003
Winston-Salem, NC	143,485	185,776	Corona, CA	76,095	124,966
San Bernardino, CA	164,164	185,401	Flint, MI	140,761	124,943
Jackson, MS	196,637	184,256	Mesquite, TX	101,484	124,523
Little Rock, AR	175,795	183,133	Sterling Heights, MI	117,810	124,471
Salt Lake City, UT	159,936	181,743	Sioux Falls, SD	100,814	123,975
Reno, NV	133,850	180,480	New Haven, CT	130,474	123,626
Newport News, VA	170,045	180,150	Topeka, KS	119,883	122,377
Chandler, AZ	90,533	176,581	Concord, CA	111,348	121,780
Laredo, TX	122,899	176,576	Evansville, IN	126,272	121,582
Henderson, NV	64,942	175,381	Hartford, CT	139,739	121,578
Knoxville, TN	165,121	173,890	Fayetteville, NC	75,695	121,015
Amarillo, TX	157,615	173,627	Cedar Rapids, IA	108,751	120,758
Providence, RI	160,728	173,618	Elizabeth, NJ	110,002	120,568
Chula Vista, CA	135,163	173,556	Lansing, MI	127,321	119,128
Worcester, MA	169,759	172,648	Lancaster, CA	97,291	118,718
Oxnard, CA	142,216	170,358	Fort Collins, CO	87,758	118,652
Dayton, OH	182,044	166,179	Coral Springs, FL	79,443	117,549
Garden Grove, CA	143,050	165,196	Stamford, CT	108,056	117,083
Oceanside, CA	128,398	161,029	Thousand Oaks, CA	104,352	117,005
Tempe, AZ	141,865	158,625	Vallejo, CA	109,199	116,760
Huntsville, AL	159,789	158,216	Palmdale, CA	68,842	116,670
Ontario, CA	133,179	158,007	Columbia, SC	98,052	116,278
Chattanooga, TN	152,466	155,554	El Monte, CA	106,209	115,965
Fort Lauderdale, FL	149,377	152,397	Abilene, TX	106,654	115,930
Springfield, MA	156,983	152,082	North Las Vegas, NV	47,707	115,488
Springfield, MO	140,494	151,580	Beaumont, TX	114,323	113,866
Santa Clarita, CA	110,642	151,088	Waco, TX	103,590	113,726
Salinas, CA	108,777	151,060	Independence, MO	112,301	113,288
Tallahassee, FL	124,773	150,624	Peoria, IL	113,504	112,936
Rockford, IL	139,426	150,115	Inglewood, CA	109,602	112,580
Pomona, CA	131,723	149,473	Springfield, IL	105,227	111,454
Paterson, NJ	140,891	149,222	Simi Valley, CA	100,217	111,351
Overland Park, KS	111,790	149,080	Lafayette, LA	94,440	110,257
Santa Rosa, CA	113,313	147,595	Gilbert, AZ	29,188	109,697
Syracuse, NY	163,860	147,306	Carrollton, TX	82,169	109,576
Kansas City, KS	149,767	146,866	Bellevue, WA	86,874	109,569
Hampton, VA	133,793	146,437	West Valley City, UT	86,976	108,896
Lakewood, CO	126,481	144,126	Clearwater, FL	98,784	108,787
Vancouver, WA	46,380	143,560	Costa Mesa, CA	96,357	108,724
Irvine, CA	110,330	143,072	Peoria, AZ	50,618	108,364
Aurora, IL	99,581	142,990	South Bend, IN	105,511	107,789
Moreno Valley, CA	118,779	142,381	Downey, CA	91,444	107,323
Pasadena, TX	119,363	141,674	Waterbury, CT	108,961	107,271
Hayward, CA	111,498	140,030	Manchester, NH	99,567	107,006
Brownsville, TX	98,962	139,722	Allentown, PA	105,090	106,632
Bridgeport, CT	141,686	139,529	McAllen, TX	84,021	106,414
Hollywood, FL	121,697	139,357	Joliet, IL	76,836	106,221
Warren, MI	144,864	138,247	Lowell, MA	103,439	105,167
Torrance, CA	133,107	137,946	Provo, UT	86,835	105,166
Eugene, OR	112,669	137,893	West Covina, CA	96,086	105,080
Pembroke Pines, FL	65,452	137,427	Wichita Falls, TX	96,259	104,197
Salem, OR	107,786	136,924	Erie, PA	108,718	103,717
Pasadena, CA	131,591	133,936	Daly City, CA	92,311	103,621
Escondido, CA	108,635	133,559	Clarksville, TN	75,494	103,445
			Norwalk, CA	94,279	103,298
			Gary, IN	116,646	102,746

Cities	Census 1990	Census 2000	Cities	Census 1990	Census 2000
Berkeley, CA	102,724	102,743	Westminster, CO	74,625	100,940
Santa Clara, CA	93,613	102,361	San Buenaventura (Ventura), CA	92,575	100,916
Green Bay, WI	96,466	102,313	Portsmouth, VA	103,907	100,565
Cape Coral, FL	74,991	102,286	Livonia, MI	100,850	100,545
Arvada, CO	89,235	102,153	Burbank, CA	93,643	100,316
Pueblo, CO	98,640	102,121			
Athens-Clarke County, GA	45,734	101,489			
Cambridge, MA	95,802	101,355			

[1]Honolulu CDP (census designated place) is not incorporated as a city. [2]Augusta City only in 1990 (Augusta-Richmond County created in 1996). [3]Arlington, VA CDP (census designated place) is not incorporated as a city.

Immigration and naturalization. The Immigration and Nationality Act, as amended, provides for the numerical limitation of most immigration. The Immigration Act of 1990 established major revisions in the numerical limits and preference system regulating legal immigration. The numerical limits are imposed on visas issued and not admissions. The maximum number of visas allowed to be issued under the preference categories in fiscal year 2008 was 388,704: 226,000 for family-sponsored immigrants and 162,704 for employment-based immigrants. Within the overall limitations the per-country limit for independent countries is set to 7% of the total family and employment limits, while dependent areas are limited to 2% of the total. Immigrants not subject to any numerical limitation are spouses, children, and parents of US citizens who are 21 years of age or older; certain former US citizens; ministers of religion; certain long-term US government employees; refugees and asylum-seekers adjusting to immigrant status; and certain other groups of immigrants.

Immigrant aliens admitted to the USA for permanent residence, by country or region of birth, for fiscal years:

Country or region of birth	Immigrants admitted 2005	2006	2007	2008
All countries	1,122,257	1,266,129	1,052,415	1,107,126
Europe	176,516	164,244	120,821	119,138
Germany	9,264	8,436	7,582	7,091
Poland	15,351	17,051	10,355	8,354
Russia	18,055	13,159	9,426	11,695
Ukraine	22,745	17,140	11,001	10,813
UK	19,800	17,207	14,545	14,348
Other Europe	91,301	91,251	67,912	66,837
Asia	400,098	422,284	383,508	383,608
Bangladesh	11,487	14,644	12,074	11,753
China (mainland)	69,933	87,307	76,655	80,271
India	84,680	61,369	65,353	63,352
Iran	13,887	13,947	10,460	13,852
Japan	8,768	8,265	6,748	6,821
Korea (North and South)	26,562	24,386	22,405	26,666
Pakistan	14,926	17,418	13,492	19,719
Philippines	60,746	74,606	72,596	54,030
Taiwan	9,196	8,086	8,990	9,073
Thailand	5,505	11,749	8,751	6,637
Uzbekistan	2,887	4,015	4,665	6,375
Vietnam	32,784	30,691	28,691	31,497
Other Asia	58,737	65,801	52,628	53,562
North and Central America	345,561	414,075	339,355	393,253
Canada	21,878	18,207	15,495	15,109
Cuba	36,261	45,614	29,104	49,500
Dominican Republic	27,503	38,068	28,024	31,879
El Salvador	21,359	31,782	21,127	19,659
Guatemala	16,818	24,133	17,908	16,182
Haiti	14,524	22,226	30,405	26,007

Country or region of birth	Immigrants admitted 2005	2006	2007	2008
Honduras	7,012	8,177	7,646	6,540
Jamaica	18,345	24,976	19,375	18,477
Mexico	161,445	173,749	148,640	189,989
Other North America	183	333	171	216
Other Central America	20,233	26,810	21,460	19,695
South America	103,135	137,986	106,525	98,555
Brazil	16,662	17,903	14,295	12,195
Colombia	25,566	43,144	33,187	30,213
Ecuador	11,608	17,489	12,248	11,663
Guyana	9,317	9,552	5,726	6,823
Peru	15,676	21,718	17,699	15,184
Venezuela	10,645	11,341	10,692	10,514
Other South America	13,661	16,839	12,678	11,963
Africa	85,098	117,422	94,711	105,915
Egypt	7,905	10,500	9,267	8,712
Ethiopia	10,571	16,152	12,786	12,917
Ghana	6,491	9,367	7,610	8,195
Kenya	5,347	8,779	7,030	6,998
Liberia	4,880	6,887	4,102	7,193
Nigeria	10,597	13,459	12,448	12,475
Somalia	5,829	9,462	6,251	10,745
Other Africa	33,478	42,816	35,217	38,680
Other countries	11,849	10,118	7,495	6,657

The total number of immigrants admitted from 1820 to 2008 was 74,225,904; this included 7,476,092 from Mexico, 7,275,320 from Germany and 5,455,888 from Italy.

The number of immigrants admitted for legal permanent residence in the United States in fiscal year 2008 was 1,107,126. Included in this total were 466,558 aliens previously living abroad who obtained immigrant visas through the US Department of State and became legal permanent residents upon entry into the United States. The remaining 640,568 legal immigrants, including former undocumented immigrants, refugees and asylees, had adjusted status through the Citizenship and Immigration Services (USCIS). The USA has by far the largest annual net gain in migrants of any country.

A record 1,046,539 persons were naturalized in fiscal year 2008 (including 231,815 persons born in Mexico, the highest total since 1996).

The refugee admissions ceiling for fiscal year 2009 was fixed at 80,000.

SOCIAL STATISTICS

Figures only include Alaska and Hawaii from 1960 onwards.

	Live births	Deaths	Marriages	Divorces	Deaths under 1 year
1900	—	343,217	709,000	56,000	—
1910	2,777,000	696,856	948,000	83,000	—
1920	2,950,000	1,118,070	1,274,476	170,505	170,911
1930	2,618,000	1,327,240	1,126,856	195,961	143,201
1940	2,559,000	1,417,269	1,595,879	264,000	110,984
1950	3,632,000	1,452,454	1,667,231	385,144	103,825
1960	4,257,850	1,711,982	1,523,000	393,000	110,873
1970	3,731,386	1,921,031	2,158,802	708,000	74,667
1980	3,612,258	1,989,841	2,390,252	1,189,000	45,526
1990	4,158,212	2,148,463	2,443,489	1,182,000	38,351
2000	4,058,814	2,403,351	2,315,000	—	28,035
2001	4,025,933	2,416,425	2,326,000	—	27,568
2002	4,021,726	2,443,387	2,290,000	—	28,034
2003	4,089,950	2,448,288	2,245,000	—	28,025
2004	4,112,052	2,397,615	2,279,000	—	27,936
2005	4,138,349	2,448,017	2,249,000	—	28,440
2006	4,265,555	2,426,264	2,193,000[1]	—	28,527
2007[2]	4,317,119	2,423,995	2,197,000	—	29,241

[1]Excluding Louisiana. [2]Provisional.

Rates (per 1,000 population):

	Birth	Death	Marriage	Divorce
2000	14·4	8·5	8·2	—
2001	14·1	8·5	8·2	—
2002	13·9	8·5	7·9	—
2003	14·1	8·4	7·7	—
2004	14·0	8·2	7·8	—
2005	14·0	8·3	7·6	—
2006	14·2	8·1	7·4[1]	—

[1]Excluding Louisiana.

Although divorce figures are not available since 1997 as not all states maintain complete statistics, it is estimated that the rate fell from 4·3 per 1,000 population in 1997 to 3·6 per 1,000 in 2007. Rate of natural increase per 1,000 population: 5·7 in 2005; 6·1 in 2006. Population growth rate, 2007, 1·0%.

Even though the marriage rate shows a gradual decline, it remains much higher than in most other industrial countries. The most popular age range for marrying is 25–29 for males and 20–24 for females. The number of births to unmarried women in 2006 was 1,641,946 (38·5% of all births), compared to 666,000 in 1980 and 1,527,034 in 2005. The rate of births to teenagers was 42·5 per 1,000 women in 2007. Between 1970 and 2006 the annual number of births rose by 14·3%. The number of births within marriage declined by 19·8% between 1970 and 2005 whereas the number outside of marriage rose by 283·0%. Whereas in 1970 as many as 83·4% of children lived with both biological parents, by 2004 only 59·9% were living with married biological parents and 2·5% with unmarried biological parents.

Infant mortality rates, per 1,000 live births: 29·2 in 1950; 12·9 in 1980; 6·7 in 2006. Fertility rate, 2005, 2·1 births per woman (3·6 in 1960).

There were a reported 846,181 abortions in 2006 (giving an abortion rate of 16 per 1,000 women aged 15–44 years), down from a peak in 1990 of 1,429,247 reported abortions.

Expectation of life, 1970: males, 67·1 years; females, 74·7 years. 2007: males, 76·7 years; females, 81·3 years.

Numbers of deaths by principal causes, 2006 (and as a percentage of all deaths): heart disease, 631,636 (26·0%); cancer, 559,888 (23·1%); stroke, 137,119 (5·7%); chronic lower respiratory disease, 124,583 (5·1%); accidents, 121,599 (5·0%); diabetes mellitus, 72,449 (3·0%); Alzheimer's disease, 72,432 (3·0%); pneumonia and influenza, 56,326 (2·3%); kidney diseases, 45,344 (1·9%); septicemia, 34,234 (1·4%); suicide, 33,300 (1·4%); liver diseases, 27,555 (1·1%).

The number of Americans living in poverty in 2008 was 39·8m. or 13·2% of the total population, down from 15·1% in 1993 but up 0·7% on 2007.

A UNICEF report published in 2005 showed that 21·9% of children in the USA live in poverty (in households with income below 50% of the national median), compared to just 2·4% in Denmark.

CLIMATE

For temperature and rainfall figures, *see* entries on individual states as indicated by regions, below, of mainland USA.

Pacific Coast. The climate varies with latitude, distance from the sea and the effect of relief, ranging from polar conditions in North Alaska through cool to warm temperate climates further south. The extreme south is temperate desert. Rainfall everywhere is moderate. *See* Alaska, California, Oregon, Washington.

Mountain States. Very varied, with relief exerting the main control; very cold in the north in winter, with considerable snowfall. In the south, much higher temperatures and aridity produce desert conditions. Rainfall everywhere is very variable as a result of rain-shadow influences. *See* Arizona, Colorado, Idaho, Montana, Nevada, New Mexico, Utah, Wyoming.

High Plains. A continental climate with a large annual range of temperature and moderate rainfall, mainly in summer, although unreliable. Dust storms are common in summer and blizzards in winter. *See* Nebraska, North Dakota, South Dakota.

Central Plains. A temperate continental climate, with hot summers and cold winters, except in the extreme south. Rainfall is plentiful and comes at all seasons, but there is a summer maximum in western parts. *See* Mississippi, Missouri, Oklahoma, Texas.

Mid-West. Continental, with hot summers and cold winters. Rainfall is moderate, with a summer maximum in most parts. *See* Indiana, Iowa, Kansas.

Great Lakes. Continental, resembling that of the Central Plains, with hot summers but very cold winters because of the freezing of the lakes. Rainfall is moderate with a slight summer maximum. *See* Illinois, Michigan, Minnesota, Ohio, Wisconsin.

Appalachian Mountains. The north is cool temperate with cold winters, the south warm temperate with milder winters. Precipitation is heavy, increasing to the south but evenly distributed over the year. *See* Kentucky, Pennsylvania, Tennessee, West Virginia.

Gulf Coast. Conditions vary from warm temperate to sub-tropical, with plentiful rainfall, decreasing towards the west but evenly distributed over the year. *See* Alabama, Arkansas, Florida, Louisiana.

Atlantic Coast. Temperate maritime climate but with great differences in temperature according to latitude. Rainfall is ample at all seasons; snowfall in the north can be heavy. *See* Delaware, District of Columbia, Georgia, Maryland, New Jersey, New York State, North Carolina, South Carolina, Virginia.

New England. Cool temperate, with severe winters and warm summers. Precipitation is well distributed with a slight winter maximum. Snowfall is heavy in winter. *See* Connecticut, Maine, Massachusetts, New Hampshire, Rhode Island, Vermont. *See* also Hawaii and Outlying Territories.

CONSTITUTION AND GOVERNMENT

The form of government of the USA is based on the constitution adopted on 17 Sept. 1787 and effective from 4 March 1789.

By the constitution the government of the nation is composed of three co-ordinate branches, the executive, the legislative and the judicial.

The Federal government has authority in matters of general taxation, treaties and other dealings with foreign countries, foreign and inter-state commerce, bankruptcy, postal service, coinage, weights and measures, patents and copyright, the armed forces (including, to a certain extent, the militia), and crimes against the USA; it has sole legislative authority over the District of Columbia and the possessions of the USA.

The 5th article of the constitution provides that Congress may, on a two-thirds vote of both houses, propose amendments to the constitution, or, on the application of the legislatures of two-thirds of all the states, call a convention for proposing amendments, which in either case shall be valid as part of the constitution when ratified by the legislatures of three-fourths of the several states, or by conventions in three-fourths thereof, whichever mode of ratification may be proposed by Congress. Ten amendments (called collectively 'the Bill of Rights') to the constitution were added 15 Dec. 1791; two in 1795 and 1804; a 13th amendment, 6 Dec. 1865, abolishing slavery; a 14th in 1868, including the important 'due process' clause; a 15th, 3 Feb. 1870, establishing equal voting rights for white and black; a 16th, 3 Feb. 1913, authorizing the income tax; a 17th, 8 April 1913, providing for popular election of Senators; an 18th, 16 Jan. 1919, prohibiting alcoholic liquors; a 19th, 18 Aug. 1920, establishing woman suffrage; a 20th, 23 Jan. 1933, advancing the date of the President's and Vice-President's inauguration and abolishing the 'lameduck' sessions of Congress; a 21st, 5 Dec. 1933, repealing the 18th amendment; a 22nd, 27 Feb. 1951, limiting a President's tenure of office to two terms, or two full terms in the case of a Vice-President who has succeeded to the office of President and has served two years or less of another President's term, or one full term in the case of a Vice-President who has succeeded to the office of President and has served more than two years of another President's term; a 23rd, 30 March 1961, granting citizens of the District of Columbia the right to vote in national elections; a 24th, 4 Feb. 1964, banning the use of the poll-tax in federal elections; a 25th, 10 Feb. 1967, dealing with Presidential disability and succession; a 26th, 22 June 1970, establishing the right of citizens who are 18 years of age and older to vote; a 27th, 7 May 1992, providing that no law varying the compensation of Senators or Representatives shall take effect until an election has taken place.

National motto. 'In God we trust'; formally adopted by Congress 30 July 1956.

Presidency

The executive power is vested in a president, who holds office for four years, and is elected, together with a vice-president chosen for the same term, by electors from each state, equal to the whole number of Senators and Representatives to which the state may be entitled in the Congress. The President must be a natural-born citizen, resident in the country for 14 years, and at least 35 years old.

The presidential election is held every fourth (leap) year on the Tuesday after the first Monday in Nov. Technically, this is an election of presidential electors, not of a president directly; the electors thus chosen meet and give their votes (for the candidate to whom they are pledged, in some states by law, but in most states by custom and prudent politics) at their respective state capitals on the first Monday after the second Wednesday in Dec. next following their election; and the votes of the electors of all the states are opened and counted in the presence of both Houses of Congress on the sixth day of Jan. The total electorate vote is one for each Senator and Representative. Electors may not be a member of Congress or hold federal office. If no candidate secures the minimum 270 college votes needed for outright victory, the 12th Amendment to the Constitution applies, and the House of Representatives chooses a president from among the first three finishers in the electoral college. (This last happened in 1824).

If the successful candidate for President dies before taking office the Vice-President-elect becomes President; if no candidate has a majority or if the successful candidate fails to qualify, then, by the 20th amendment, the Vice-President acts as President until a president qualifies. The duties of the Presidency, in absence of the President and Vice-President by reason of death, resignation, removal, inability or failure to qualify, devolve upon the Speaker of the House under legislation enacted on 18 July 1947. In case of absence of a Speaker for like reason, the presidential duties devolve upon the President *pro tem.* of the Senate and successively upon those members of the cabinet in order of precedence, who have the constitutional qualifications for President.

The presidential term, by the 20th amendment to the constitution, begins at noon on 20 Jan. of the inaugural year. This amendment also installs the newly elected Congress in office on 3 Jan. instead of—as formerly—in the following Dec. The President's salary is $400,000 per year (taxable), with an additional $50,000 to assist in defraying expenses resulting from official duties. Also he may spend up to $100,000 non-taxable for travel and $19,000 for official entertainment. In 1999 the presidential salary was increased for the president taking office in Jan. 2001, having remained at $200,000 a year since 1969. The office of Vice-President carries a salary of $230,700 and $20,000 allowance for expenses, all taxable. The Vice-President is *ex officio* President of the Senate, and in the case of 'the removal of the President, or of his death, resignation, or inability to discharge the powers and duties of his office', he becomes the President for the remainder of the term.

Cabinet. The administrative business of the nation has been traditionally vested in several executive departments, the heads of which, unofficially and *ex officio*, formed the President's cabinet. Beginning with the Interstate Commerce Commission in 1887, however, an increasing amount of executive business has been entrusted to some 60 so-called independent agencies, such as the Housing and Home Finance Agency, Tariff Commission, etc.

All heads of departments and of the 60 or more administrative agencies are appointed by the President, but must be confirmed by the Senate.

Congress. The legislative power is vested by the Constitution in a Congress, consisting of a Senate and House of Representatives.

Electorate. By amendments of the constitution, disqualification of voters on the ground of race, colour or sex is forbidden. The electorate consists of all citizens over 18 years of age. Literacy tests have been banned since 1970. In 1972 durational residency requirements were held to violate the constitution. In 1973 US citizens abroad were enfranchised.

With limitations imposed by the constitution, it is the states which determine voter eligibility. In general states exclude from voting: persons who have not established residency in the jurisdiction in which they wish to vote; persons who have been convicted of felonies whose civil rights have not been restored; persons declared mentally incompetent by a court.

Illiterate voters are entitled to receive assistance in marking their ballots. Minority-language voters in jurisdictions with statutorily prescribed minority concentrations are entitled to have elections conducted in the minority language as well as English. Disabled voters are entitled to accessible polling places. Voters absent on election days or unable to go to the polls are generally entitled under state law to vote by absentee ballot.

The Constitution guarantees citizens that their votes will be of equal value under the 'one person, one vote' rule.

Senate. The Senate consists of two members from each state (but not from the District of Columbia), chosen by popular vote for six years, approximately one-third retiring or seeking re-election every two years. Senators must be no less than 30 years of age; must have been citizens of the USA for nine years, and be residents in the states for which they are chosen. The Senate has complete freedom to initiate legislation, except revenue bills (which must originate in the House of Representatives); it may, however, amend or reject any legislation originating in the lower house. The Senate is also entrusted with the power of giving or withholding its 'advice and consent' to the ratification of all treaties initiated by the President with foreign powers, a two-thirds majority of Senators present being required for approval. (However, it has no control over 'international executive agreements' made by the President with foreign governments; such 'agreements' cover a wide range and are more numerous than formal treaties.)

The Senate has 21 Standing Committees to which all bills are referred for study, revision or rejection. The House of Representatives has 20 such committees. In both Houses each Standing Committee has a chairman and a majority representing the majority party of the whole House; each has numerous sub-committees. The jurisdictions of these Committees correspond largely to those of the appropriate executive departments and agencies. Both Houses also have a few select or special Committees with limited duration.

House of Representatives. The House of Representatives consists of 435 members elected every second year. The number of each state's Representatives is determined by the decennial census, in the absence of specific Congressional legislation affecting the basis. The number of Representatives for each state in the 111th congress, which began in Jan. 2009 (based on the 2000 census), is given below:

Alabama	7	Louisiana	7	Ohio	18
Alaska	1	Maine	2	Oklahoma	5
Arizona	8	Maryland	8	Oregon	5
Arkansas	4	Massachusetts	10	Pennsylvania	19
California	53	Michigan	15	Rhode Island	2
Colorado	7	Minnesota	8	South Carolina	6
Connecticut	5	Mississippi	4	South Dakota	1
Delaware	1	Missouri	9	Tennessee	9
Florida	25	Montana	1	Texas	32
Georgia	13	Nebraska	3	Utah	3
Hawaii	2	Nevada	3	Vermont	1
Idaho	2	New Hampshire	2	Virginia	11
Illinois	19	New Jersey	13	Washington	9
Indiana	9	New Mexico	3	West Virginia	3
Iowa	5	New York	29	Wisconsin	8
Kansas	4	North Carolina	13	Wyoming	1
Kentucky	6	North Dakota	1		

The constitution requires congressional districts within each state to be substantially equal in population. Final decisions on congressional district boundaries are taken by the state legislatures and governors. By custom the Representative lives in the district from which he is elected. Representatives must be not less than 25 years of age, citizens of the USA for seven years and residents in the state from which they are chosen.

In addition, five delegates (one each from the District of Columbia, American Samoa, Guam, the US Virgin Islands and Puerto Rico) are also members of Congress. They have a voice but no vote, except in committees. The delegate from Puerto Rico is the resident commissioner. Puerto Ricans vote at primaries, but not at national elections. Each of the two Houses of Congress is sole 'judge of the elections, returns and qualifications of its own members'; and each of the Houses may, with the concurrence of two-thirds, expel a member. The period usually termed 'a Congress' in legislative language continues for two years, terminating at noon on 3 Jan.

The salary of a Senator is $174,000 per annum, with tax-free expense allowance and allowances for travelling expenses and for clerical hire. The salary of the Speaker of the House of Representatives is $223,500 per annum, with a taxable allowance. The salary of a Member of the House is $174,000 ($193,400 for the Majority Leader and Minority Leader).

No Senator or Representative can, during the time for which he is elected, be appointed to any *civil* office under authority of the USA which shall have been created or the emoluments of which shall have been increased during such time; and no person holding *any* office under the USA can be a member of either House during his continuance in office. No religious text may be required as a qualification to any office or public trust under the USA or in any state.

Indians. By an Act passed on 2 June 1924 full citizenship was granted to all Indians born in the USA, though those remaining in tribal units were still under special federal jurisdiction. The Indian Reorganization Act of 1934 gave the tribal Indians, at their own option, substantial opportunities of self-government and the establishment of self-controlled corporate enterprises empowered to borrow money and buy land, machinery and equipment; these corporations are controlled by democratically elected tribal councils. Recently a trend towards releasing Indians from federal supervision has resulted in legislation terminating supervision over specific tribes. In 1988 the federal government recognized that it had a special relationship with, and a trust responsibility for, federally recognized Indian entities in continental USA and tribal entities in Alaska. In 2003 the

Bureau of Indian Affairs listed 562 'Indian Entities Recognized and Eligible to Receive Services'. American Indian lands covered 112,637 sq. miles in 2000. Indian lands are held free of taxes. Total Indian population at the 2000 census was 2,475,956, of which California (333,346), Oklahoma (273,230), Arizona (255,879) and New Mexico (173,483) accounted for more than 40%.

The **District of Columbia,** ceded by the State of Maryland for the purposes of government in 1791, is the seat of the US government. It includes the city of Washington, and embraces a land area of 61 sq. miles. The Reorganization Plan No. 3 of 1967 instituted a Mayor Council form of government with appointed officers. In 1973 an elected Mayor and elected councillors were introduced; in 1974 they received power to legislate in local matters. Congress retains power to enact legislation and to veto or supersede the Council's acts. Since 1961 citizens have had the right to vote in national elections. On 23 Aug. 1978 the Senate approved a constitutional amendment giving the District full voting representation in Congress. This has still to be ratified.

The Commonwealth of the Northern Mariana Islands, the Commonwealth of the Puerto Rico, American Samoa, Guam and the Virgin Islands each have a local legislature, whose acts may be modified or annulled by Congress, though in practice this has seldom been done. Puerto Rico, since its attainment of commonwealth status on 25 July 1952, enjoys practically complete self-government, including the election of its governor and other officials. The conduct of foreign relations, however, is still a federal function and federal bureaux and agencies still operate in the island.

General supervision of territorial administration is exercised by the Office of Territories in the Department of Interior.

Local Government

The Union comprises 13 original states, seven states which were admitted without having been previously organized as territories, and 30 states which had been territories—50 states in all. Each state has its own constitution (which the USA guarantees shall be republican in form), deriving its authority, not from Congress, but from the people of the state. Admission of states into the Union has been granted by special Acts of Congress, either (1) in the form of 'enabling Acts' providing for the drafting and ratification of a state constitution by the people, in which case the territory becomes a state as soon as the conditions are fulfilled, or (2) accepting a constitution already framed, and at once granting admission.

Each state is provided with a legislature of two Houses (except Nebraska, which since 1937 has had a single-chamber legislature), a governor and other executive officials, and a judicial system. Both Houses of the legislature are elective, but the senators (having larger electoral districts usually covering two or three counties compared with the single county or, in some states, the town, which sends one representative to the Lower House) are less numerous than the representatives, while in 38 states their terms are four years; in 12 states the term is two years. Of the four-year senates, Illinois, Montana and New Jersey provide for two four-year terms and one two-year term in each decade. Terms of the lower houses are usually shorter; in 45 states, two years. The trend is towards annual sessions of state legislatures; most meet annually now whereas in 1939 only four did.

The Governor is elected by direct vote of the people over the whole state for a term of office ranging in the various states from two to four years, and with a salary ranging from $70,000 (Maine) to $179,000 (New York State). His duty is to see to the faithful administration of the law, and he has command of the military forces of the state. He may recommend measures but does not present bills to the legislature. In some states he presents estimates. In all but one of the states (North Carolina) the Governor has a veto upon legislation, which may, however, be overridden by the two Houses, in some states by a simple majority, in others by a three-fifths or two-thirds majority. In some states the Governor, on his death or resignation, is succeeded by a Lieut.-Governor who was elected at the same time and has been presiding over the state Senate. In several states the Speaker of the Lower House succeeds the Governor.

National Anthem

The Star-spangled Banner, 'Oh say, can you see by the dawn's early light'; words by F. S. Key, 1814, tune by J. S. Smith; formally adopted by Congress 3 March 1931.

GOVERNMENT CHRONOLOGY

PRESIDENTS OF THE USA

Name	*Party*[1]	*From state*	*Term of service*	*Born*	*Died*
George Washington	(F.)	Virginia	1789–97	1732	1799
John Adams	(F.)	Massachusetts	1797–1801	1735	1826
Thomas Jefferson	(D.)	Virginia	1801–09	1743	1826
James Madison	(D.)	Virginia	1809–17	1751	1836
James Monroe	(D.)	Virginia	1817–25	1759	1831
John Quincy Adams	(n.p.)	Massachusetts	1825–29	1767	1848
Andrew Jackson	(D.)	Tennessee	1829–37	1767	1845
Martin Van Buren	(D.)	New York	1837–41	1782	1862
William H. Harrison	(W.)	Ohio	Mar.–Apr. 1841	1773	1841
John Tyler	(W.)	Virginia	1841–45	1790	1862
James K. Polk	(D.)	Tennessee	1845–49	1795	1849
Zachary Taylor	(W.)	Louisiana	1849–July 1850	1784	1850
Millard Fillmore	(W.)	New York	1850–53	1800	1874
Franklin Pierce	(D.)	New Hampshire	1853–57	1804	1869
James Buchanan	(D.)	Pennsylvania	1857–61	1791	1868
Abraham Lincoln	(R.)	Illinois	1861–Apr. 1865	1809	1865
Andrew Johnson	(D.)	Tennessee	1865–69	1808	1875
Ulysses S. Grant	(R.)	Illinois	1869–77	1822	1885
Rutherford B. Hayes	(R.)	Ohio	1877–81	1822	1893
James A. Garfield	(R.)	Ohio	Mar.–Sept. 1881	1831	1881
Chester A. Arthur	(R.)	New York	1881–85	1830	1886
Grover Cleveland	(D.)	New York	1885–89	1837	1908
Benjamin Harrison	(R.)	Indiana	1889–93	1833	1901
Grover Cleveland	(D.)	New York	1893–97	1837	1908
William McKinley	(R.)	Ohio	1897–Sept. 1901	1843	1901
Theodore Roosevelt	(R.)	New York	1901–09	1858	1919
William H. Taft	(R.)	Ohio	1909–13	1857	1930
Woodrow Wilson	(D.)	New Jersey	1913–21	1856	1924
Warren Gamaliel Harding	(R.)	Ohio	1921–Aug. 1923	1865	1923
Calvin Coolidge	(R.)	Massachusetts	1923–29	1872	1933
Herbert C. Hoover	(R.)	California	1929–33	1874	1964
Franklin D. Roosevelt	(D.)	New York	1933–Apr. 1945	1882	1945
Harry S Truman	(D.)	Missouri	1945–53	1884	1972
Dwight D. Eisenhower	(R.)	New York	1953–61	1890	1969
John F. Kennedy	(D.)	Massachusetts	1961–Nov. 1963	1917	1963
Lyndon B. Johnson	(D.)	Texas	1963–69	1908	1973
Richard M. Nixon	(R.)	California	1969–74	1913	1994
Gerald R. Ford	(R.)	Michigan	1974–77	1913	2006
James Earl Carter	(D.)	Georgia	1977–81	1924	—
Ronald W. Reagan	(R.)	California	1981–89	1911	2004
George H. Bush	(R.)	Texas	1989–93	1924	—
Bill (William J.) Clinton	(D.)	Arkansas	1993–2001	1946	—
George W. Bush	(R.)	Texas	2001–09	1946	—
Barack H. Obama	(D.)	Illinois	2009–	1961	—

[1]F. = Federalist; D. = Democrat; n.p. = no party; W. = Whig; R. = Republican.

VICE-PRESIDENTS OF THE USA

Name	*Party*[1]	*From state*	*Term of service*	*Born*	*Died*
John Adams	(F.)	Massachusetts	1789–97	1735	1826
Thomas Jefferson	(R.)	Virginia	1797–1801	1743	1826
Aaron Burr	(R.)	New York	1801–05	1756	1836
George Clinton	(R.)	New York	1805–12[2]	1739	1812

Name	Party[1]	From state	Term of service	Born	Died
Elbridge Gerry	(R.)	Massachusetts	1813–14[2]	1744	1814
Daniel D. Tompkins	(R.)	New York	1817–25	1774	1825
John C. Calhoun	(NR./D.)	South Carolina	1825–32[2]	1782	1850
Martin Van Buren	(D.)	New York	1833–37	1782	1862
Richard M. Johnson	(D.)	Kentucky	1837–41	1780	1850
John Tyler	(D.)	Virginia	Mar.–Apr.1841[2]	1790	1862
George M. Dallas	(D.)	Pennsylvania	1845–49	1792	1864
Millard Fillmore	(W.)	New York	1849–50[2]	1800	1874
William R. King	(D.)	Alabama	Mar.–Apr. 1853[2]	1786	1853
John C. Breckinridge	(D.)	Kentucky	1857–61	1821	1875
Hannibal Hamlin	(R.)	Maine	1861–65	1809	1891
Andrew Johnson	(D.)	Tennessee	Mar.–Apr. 1865[2]	1808	1875
Schuyler Colfax	(R.)	Indiana	1869–73	1823	1885
Henry Wilson	(R.)	Massachusetts	1873–75[2]	1812	1875
William A. Wheeler	(R.)	New York	1877–81	1819	1887
Chester A. Arthur	(R.)	New York	Mar.–Sept. 1881[2]	1830	1886
Thomas A. Hendricks	(D.)	Indiana	Mar.–Nov. 1885[2]	1819	1885
Levi P. Morton	(R.)	New York	1889–93	1824	1920
Adlai Stevenson	(D.)	Illinois	1893–97	1835	1914
Garret A. Hobart	(R.)	New Jersey	1897–99[2]	1844	1899
Theodore Roosevelt	(R.)	New York	Mar.–Sept. 1901[2]	1858	1919
Charles W. Fairbanks	(R.)	Indiana	1905–09	1855	1920
James S. Sherman	(R.)	New York	1909–12[2]	1855	1912
Thomas R. Marshall	(D.)	Indiana	1913–21	1854	1925
Calvin Coolidge	(R.)	Massachusetts	1921–Aug. 1923[2]	1872	1933
Charles G. Dawes	(R.)	Illinois	1925–29	1865	1951
Charles Curtis	(R.)	Kansas	1929–33	1860	1935
John N. Garner	(D.)	Texas	1933–41	1868	1967
Henry A. Wallace	(D.)	Iowa	1941–45	1888	1965
Harry S. Truman	(D.)	Missouri	1945–Apr. 1945[2]	1884	1972
Alben W. Barkley	(D.)	Kentucky	1949–53	1877	1956
Richard M. Nixon	(R.)	California	1953–61	1913	1994
Lyndon B. Johnson	(D.)	Texas	1961–Nov. 1963[2]	1908	1973
Hubert H. Humphrey	(D.)	Minnesota	1965–69	1911	1978
Spiro T. Agnew	(R.)	Maryland	1969–73	1918	1996
Gerald R. Ford	(R.)	Michigan	1973–74	1913	2006
Nelson Rockefeller	(R.)	New York	1974–77	1908	1979
Walter Mondale	(D.)	Minnesota	1977–81	1928	—
George H. Bush	(R.)	Texas	1981–89	1924	—
Danforth Quayle	(R.)	Indiana	1989–93	1947	—
Albert Gore	(D.)	Tennessee	1993–2001	1948	—
Richard B. Cheney	(R.)	Wyoming	2001–09	1941	—
Joseph R. Biden	(D.)	Delaware	2009–	1942	—

[1]F. = Federalist; R. = Republican; NR. = National Republican; D. = Democrat; W. = Whig. [2]Position vacant thereafter until commencement of the next presidential term.

RECENT ELECTIONS

At the presidential election on 4 Nov. 2008 Barack Obama (Democrat) was elected president with 365 electoral college votes (and 52·9% of the popular vote) against 173 (and 45·7%) for John McCain (Republican).

Electoral college votes by state in 2008:

a) Won by Obama

State	Electoral college votes	State	Electoral college votes
California	55	Maryland	10
Colorado[1]	9	Massachusetts	12
Connecticut	7	Michigan	17
Delaware	3	Minnesota	10
D.C.	3	Nebraska[2]	1
Florida[1]	27	Nevada[1]	5
Hawaii	4	New Hampshire	4
Illinois	21	New Jersey	15
Indiana[1]	11	New Mexico[1]	5
Iowa[1]	7	New York	31
Maine	4	North Carolina[1]	15
Ohio[1]	20	Vermont	3
Oregon	7	Virginia[1]	13
Pennsylvania	21	Washington	11
Rhode Island	4	Wisconsin	10

[1]Won by Bush in 2004.
[2]McCain won Nebraska but Obama won in one of the congressional districts—Nebraska (along with Maine) splits its electoral votes into districts.

b) Won by McCain

State	Electoral college votes	State	Electoral college votes
Alabama	9	Montana	3
Alaska	3	Nebraska[1]	4
Arizona	10	North Dakota	3
Arkansas	6	Oklahoma	7
Georgia	15	South Carolina	8
Idaho	4	South Dakota	3
Kansas	6	Tennessee	11
Kentucky	8	Texas	34
Louisiana	9	Utah	5
Mississippi	6	West Virginia	5
Missouri	11	Wyoming	3

[1]McCain won Nebraska but Obama won in one of the congressional districts—Nebraska (along with Maine) splits its electoral votes into districts.

In Feb. 2010 the 111th Congress (2009–11) was constituted as follows: Senate—57 Democrats, 41 Republicans and 2 ind. who both caucus with the Democrats (49 Republicans, 49 Democrats and 2 ind. for the 110th Congress); House of Representatives—256 Democrats, 178 Republicans and 1 vacancy (233 Democrats and 202 Republicans for the 110th Congress). 17 of the 100 Senators and 73 of the 435 Representatives are women.

CURRENT ADMINISTRATION

President of the United States: Barack Obama, of Hawaii; b. 1961. Majored in Political Science at Columbia (1983); MA at Harvard Law (1991); Fellow of University of Chicago Law School teaching constitutional law (1992–2004); Senator for the 13th District of Illinois (1996–2004); US Senator (2004–08).

Vice President: Joe Biden, b. Pennsylvania, 1942. First elected to the Senate in 1972; Chair of the Senate Judiciary Committee (1987–95); Adjunct Professor at Widener University School of Law since 1991.

In March 2010 the cabinet consisted of the following:

1. *Secretary of State* (created 1789). Hillary Clinton, b. Illinois, 1947. Counsel on House Judiciary Committee (1974); wife of former US president Bill Clinton; elected to US senate in 2000; unsuccessful candidate for Democratic nomination for president (2008).

2. *Secretary of the Treasury* (1789). Timothy F. Geithner, b. New York, 1961. Under Secretary of the Treasury for International Affairs (1999–2001); Senior Fellow on the Council on Foreign Relations (2001); Director of the Policy Development and Review Department at the International Monetary Fund (2001–03); President and CEO of the Federal Reserve Bank of New York (2003–09).

3. *Secretary of Defense* (1947). Dr Robert M. Gates, b. Kansas, 1943. Joined CIA in 1966 and moved to National Security Council Staff in 1974; rejoined CIA in 1979; Assistant to the President and Deputy for National Security Affairs (1989–91); Director of Central Intelligence (1991–93); President of Texas A&M University (2002–06). Secretary of Defense since 2006.

4. *Attorney General* (Department of Justice, 1870). Eric Holder, b. New York, 1951. Judge of the Superior Court of the District of Columbia (1988–93); Attorney for the District of Columbia

(1993–97); Deputy Attorney General (1997–2001); Acting Attorney General (2001).

5. *Secretary of the Interior* (1849). Ken Salazar, b. Colorado, 1955. Chief legal counsel in Colorado Governor Roy Romer's cabinet (1987–90); Executive Director of Colorado Department of Natural Resources (1990–94); founding member and Chairman of Great Outdoors Colorado (1992); Attorney General for Colorado (1999–2005); member of US Senate (2005–09).

6. *Secretary of Agriculture* (1889). Tom Vilsack, b. Pennsylvania, 1950. Mayor of Mount Pleasant (1987–92); elected to the Iowa State Senate in 1992; Governor of Iowa (1999–2007); unsuccessfully ran for the Democratic nomination for president (2008).

7. *Secretary of Commerce* (1903). Gary Locke, b. Washington, 1950. Member of the Washington State House of Representatives (1982–93); Chief Executive of King County (1994–97); Governor of Washington (1997–2005).

8. *Secretary of Labor* (1913). Hilda Solis, b. California, 1957. California State Senator (1994–2000); first elected to US House of Representatives in 2000; member of the Congressional Hispanic Caucus; received the John F. Kennedy Profile in Courage Award for her work on environmental justice issues in California (2000).

9. *Secretary of Health and Human Services* (1953). Kathleen Sebelius, b. Ohio, 1948. Member of the Kansas House of Representatives (1987–94); Insurance Commissioner (1995–2003); Governor of Kansas (2003–09).

10. *Secretary of Housing and Urban Development* (1966). Shaun Donovan, b. New York, 1966. Deputy Assistant Secretary for Multifamily Housing at Department of Housing and Urban Development (2000–01); Acting Federal Housing Association Commissioner (2001); Commissioner of New York City Department of Housing Preservation and Development (2004–09).

11. *Secretary of Transportation* (1967). Ray LaHood, b. Illinois, 1945. Teacher; Director of Rock Island County Youth Services Bureau (1972–74); member of the Illinois State House of Representatives (1982–83); Republican member of US Congress (1995–2009).

12. *Secretary of Energy* (1977). Steven Chu, b. Missouri, 1948. Head of Quantum Electronic Department at AT&T Bell Laboratories (1983–87); Nobel Prize winner for Physics (1997); Professor of Physics at Stanford (1987–2009), chair of department (1990–93 and 1999–2001); Director of Lawrence Berkeley National Laboratory (2004–09).

13. *Secretary of Education* (1979). Arne Duncan, b. Illinois, 1964. Professional basketball player (1987–91); Director of Ariel Education Initiative (1992–98); joined Chicago Public Schools in 1998, appointed Deputy Chief of Staff in 1999 and CEO in 2001.

14. *Secretary of Veterans' Affairs* (1989). Retd Gen. Eric Shinseki, b. Hawaii, 1942. Graduated from US Military Academy at West Point (1965); two combat tours of Vietnam (1966 and 1970) receiving two Purple Hearts for injuries sustained; Commander of NATO Stabilization Force in Bosnia and Herzegovina (1996); US Army Vice Chief of Staff (1998); US Army Chief of Staff (1999–2003); retired from the Army in 2003.

15. *Secretary of Homeland Security* (2002). Janet Napolitano, b. New York, 1957. US Attorney for the District of Arizona (1993–98); Attorney General of Arizona (1999–2002); Governor of Arizona (2003–09).

Each of the above cabinet officers receives an annual salary of $193,400 and holds office during the pleasure of the President.

The following also have cabinet status:

Chair of the Council of Economic Advisers: Christina Romer; Environmental Protection Agency Administrator: Lisa Jackson; Director of the Office of Management and Budget: Peter Orszag; US Trade Representative: Ron Kirk; US Ambassador to the United Nations: Susan Rice; White House Chief of Staff: Rahm Emanuel.

Office of the President: http://www.whitehouse.gov

CURRENT LEADERS

Barack Obama

Position
President

Introduction
Barack Obama became the 44th president of the USA in Jan. 2009 and the first African American to hold the office. Having secured the Democratic candidacy with a hard-fought victory over Hillary Clinton, Obama contested the presidential election in Nov. 2008 against a background of deepening economic crisis. Viewed as on the centre-liberal wing of his party, Obama's principal electoral pledges included the introduction of a national health insurance plan and a scaling-down of the American troop presence in Iraq. In response to the economic turmoil, he supported President Bush's $700bn. emergency rescue package. His rapid recognition of the scale of economic problems contrasted with the more cautious response of his Republican opponent, John McCain, and found favour with the public. Since taking office, Obama has countered the economic crisis with a stimulus plan worth $787bn. His Republican opponents advocate a curb on spending. On foreign policy, Obama has signalled a willingness to talk to Syria and Iran subject to their compliance with international laws on terrorism and nuclear development.

Early Life
Barack Hussein Obama was born on 4 Aug. 1961 in Honolulu, Hawaii, to a Kenyan father and white American mother. His parents divorced and, following his mother's remarriage in 1967, the family moved to Indonesia, where Obama was educated until the age of ten. He attended Punahou School in Honolulu and Occidental College, Los Angeles, before graduating from Columbia University, New York, in 1983 with a BA in political science. From 1983–85 he worked at Business International Corporation and at the New York Public Interest Research Group, then moved to Chicago to become director of the church-based Developing Communities Project (DCP). From 1985–88 he led the DCP, expanding its staff and budget and establishing new projects. He attended Harvard Law School from 1988–91 and was elected president of the *Harvard Law Review* in 1990.

Following his graduation Obama took up a fellowship with the University of Chicago Law School, where he taught constitutional law from 1992–2004. In 1992 he directed 'Illinois Project Vote!', a campaign to register African Americans to vote, and from 1992–2002 he served on the boards of various community organizations and foundations, including the Joyce Foundation and Public Allies. In 1993 he joined law firm Davis, Miner, Barnhill & Galland, practising first as an associate then as a counsel. In 1995 he published a memoir, *Dreams from My Father: A Story of Race and Inheritance*.

In 1996 Obama was elected senator for the 13th District of Illinois, subsequently winning re-election in 1998 and 2002. As senator he supported health care and welfare reforms, sponsored a law to increase tax credits for low paid workers, and promoted tighter regulation of the mortgage industry. In 2003, in co-operation with Republican senators, he led legislation to monitor police procedures in the state of Illinois, requiring police to profile the ethnicity of motorists they stopped and making it compulsory to videotape interrogations of homicide suspects.

After an unsuccessful run for the House of Representatives in 2000, Obama mounted a campaign for the 2004 US Senate elections. He attracted national attention at that year's National Democratic Convention when he gave a keynote speech, 'The Audacity of Hope', in which he spoke of the shared aspirations and efforts of American citizens and set out government's obligations towards them. In Nov. 2004 Obama was elected to the US Senate with 70% of the vote, the largest winning margin in Illinois state history. In office he supported legislation to reduce carbon emissions, voted for robust border controls and immigration reform, and campaigned for controls on political financing, in particular gifts and funding provided by lobbyists.

Having opposed military action against Iraq in 2003, he continued to criticize the conduct of the war. As a member of the Senate's foreign relations committee, he explored ways of reducing the threat from conventional weapons and, with Republican Senator Richard G. Lugar, co-authored a law extending US co-operation in identifying and disposing of stockpiled weapons. He supported successive bills calling for international intervention in Sudan and in 2006 voted for a no-fly zone over Darfur. Obama also served on the health, education, labour and pensions committees, the committee on veterans' affairs and the committee on homeland security and governmental affairs. In these areas, he supported moves to expand early years schooling, to increase financial help for low-income high school and college students and to provide funding for veterans to attend college.

In Feb. 2007 Obama announced his candidacy for the Democratic presidential nomination. Campaigning on the themes of change and unity, he promised to address the key issues of Iraq, health care and the USA's dependence on oil. Obama fought a vigorous contest with main rival Hillary Clinton throughout 2007 and early 2008, gaining praise for his oratory while defending himself against charges of inexperience. In May 2007 he pledged a national health insurance plan open to all. Criticized by environmentalists for supporting liquefied coal, he subsequently modified his position. On the Iraq War, he argued for the phased redeployment of US forces and the withdrawal of combat troops, as proposed in his Iraq War De-Escalation Act of 2007.

By June 2008 Obama had secured the support of a majority of Democratic Party delegates and was confirmed at the Democratic National Convention of Aug. 2008. He selected Joe Biden, the long-serving senator of Delaware, as his running mate.

Some commentators claimed that during the campaign Obama softened his line on troop withdrawal from Iraq and on gun control. His decision to use private donations for his presidential campaign reversed an earlier pledge to work within federal public funding limits. He accused his opponents of 'gaming this broken system' when turning his back on $84m. that would have been available to him and, in doing so, becoming the first presidential candidate in over three decades to bypass the federal system in favour of raising unlimited private finance. During the early weeks of campaigning, polls showed a close contest between Obama and Republican candidate John McCain, with Obama being seen as inexperienced in foreign affairs. However, the failure of key US financial institutions in late 2008 focused attention on the economy, prompting a spike in Obama's support. He called for regulatory reforms and a bipartisan approach to tackling the crisis and voted in favour of President Bush's $700bn. package to buy up mortgage-related securities. Obama won the election on 4 Nov. 2008 with 53% of the vote to McCain's 46% and by 365 electoral college votes to 173.

In the transition between his election and inauguration, Obama appointed Rahm Emanuel as chief of staff and former rival, Hillary Clinton, as secretary of state. Both appointments were seen as an indication that he would tap the experience of long-serving politicians and officials and retain much of the previous administration's foreign policy. He also gathered an economic team and began preparing a stimulus plan to aid economic recovery through investment.

Career in Office

Obama was inaugurated on 20 Jan. 2009. Because of a minor misreading of the oath of office on the part of Chief Justice John Roberts, which caused Obama to make a similar error, he took the oath for a second time on 21 Jan. 2009. Among his first presidential acts was the fulfilment of an election pledge that the administration would run down and eventually close the detention facility for terrorist suspects at the US naval base in Guantanamo Bay (although he later acknowledged in Nov. 2009 that the deadline of Jan. 2010 could not be achieved). Other early measures included tighter restrictions on lobbyists joining the administration, introducing stricter curbs on fuel emissions, enacting equal pay legislation and expanding children's health care.

Obama sought bipartisan support for a $825bn. stimulus package, which aimed to boost economic recovery through sustained investment programmes. However, most Republicans opposed the package, arguing for less direct government spending and tax reductions. After Republicans forced substantial amendments, the American Recovery and Reinvestment Act was passed on 13 Feb. 2009, relying almost exclusively on Democrat support. Worth a slightly reduced $787bn., it detailed plans for unprecedented levels of investment in education, health care, infrastructure, the environment, employment and tax reduction. In addition, Obama developed plans for a $3·6trn. budget, though it faced opposition from critics who predicted that it would create an unmanageable national debt. Obama also faced public anger about the use of taxpayers' money to provide bonuses for executives at American International Group and other loss-making financial institutions.

On foreign policy, Obama's early months saw a move away from the hawkish tone of the previous administration. In Feb. 2009 he announced that most US troops would be withdrawn from Iraq by 31 Aug. 2010, with residual troops leaving by the end of 2011. He also signalled a change of approach on Afghanistan, indicating that though troop numbers would initially be increased, in an echo of the 'surge' tactics employed in Iraq, he was reviewing strategy and did not believe the region could be stabilized by military means alone. Obama also changed the tone of the USA's dealings with the Middle East, sending envoys to Syria in March 2009 and expressing a willingness to talk to Iran's leaders, subject to their compliance with UN directives on nuclear development. In the meantime, policy was to remain unchanged and in March 2009 he renewed US sanctions against Iran.

He was similarly cautious on the Israeli–Palestinian conflict, sending envoy George Mitchell and Secretary of State Hillary Clinton to Israel and the Palestinian Territories in early 2009 but without setting out new proposals. Clinton reaffirmed the USA's commitment to pursuing a two-state solution but maintained the previous administration's stance of refusing to talk to the militant Hamas leadership of Gaza. Obama gave moderate encouragement to the idea of closer dialogue between the USA and China and opened up the possibility of negotiations between the USA and Russia on cutting nuclear stockpiles and on curbing the development of new weapons.

One year on from his inauguration Obama had yet to secure any major policy objectives and his personal approval rating among voters had slipped markedly according to opinion polls. Despite the significant injections of borrowed money to stimulate demand and boost the economy, job creation proved slow and unemployment rose to 10% in 2009, although official figures indicated a return to growth in the third quarter of the year. Economic weakness in turn further undermined the country's fiscal position, heralding a projected increase in the already large budget deficit in 2010. In Feb. 2010 Obama proposed a record $3·8trn. budget plan for the fiscal year starting in Oct., including a new tax on banks, more spending on jobs and the cancellation of manned space missions to the Moon.

Obama's radical health care reform plan to extend insurance cover to all Americans proved particularly contentious and, as of end-Feb. 2010, remained the subject of fierce public and congressional division. The House of Representatives and the Senate each passed their own bills on health care reform in late 2009. In Jan. 2010 the loss of the Democrats' critical 60-40 majority in the Senate upset plans to reconcile the two bills.

Nonetheless, the health care reform was passed in March 2010, by 56–43 votes in the Senate and by 220–207 in the House of Representatives. It was hoped that under its terms coverage would extend to a further 32m. Americans.

Obama's early pressure on the new Israeli government to stop settlement building on Palestinian land in the Middle East was largely resisted by Prime Minister Netanyahu. Relations between the two countries were further strained in March 2010 when Israeli plans to build new homes in East Jerusalem brought criticism from Washington and ended hopes of indirect, US-brokered talks between the Israeli and Palestinian authorities. US moves to curb the nuclear ambitions of both Iran and North Korea were also proving ineffective, but there was some progress in relations with Syria and a US ambassador was appointed in Feb. 2010 after a five-year gap. Meanwhile, Obama escalated the war in Afghanistan, announcing in Dec. 2009 the deployment of a further 30,000 troops over six months to fight the Taliban insurgency, while at the same time setting a tentative date of mid-2011 for starting a withdrawal of forces.

In Sept. 2009 Obama eased friction with Russia as he announced the abandonment of a controversial missile defence deployment in the Czech Republic and Poland. In March 2010 the two countries agreed a treaty to replace the START Treaty on nuclear arms reduction. Under the terms of the new deal, both sides were limited to 1,550 warheads, a 30% drop on previous levels. Relations with China, however, deteriorated over trade, US weapons sales to Taiwan and, in Feb. 2010, the president's meeting in Washington with the Dalai Lama of Tibet. More positively, Obama was awarded the Nobel Peace Prize in Oct. 2009 for his efforts to strengthen diplomacy and create a new international atmosphere.

DEFENCE

The President is C.-in-C. of the Army, Navy and Air Force.

The National Security Act of 1947 provides for the unification of the Army, Navy and Air Forces under a single Secretary of Defense with cabinet rank. The President is also advised by a National Security Council and the Office of Civil and Defense Mobilization.

Defence expenditure in 2008 totalled US$607,263m. (US$1,697 per capita). Defence spending in 2007 represented 4·0% of GDP (down from 6·1% of GDP in 1985 although up from 3·0% in 2000). The USA spent more on defence in 2008 than the next 15 biggest spenders combined. US expenditure was 41·5% of the world total, although its population is less than 5% of the world total. In 1997 the Quadrennial Defense Review (QDR) was implemented—a plan to transform US defence strategy and military forces.

Conscription was first introduced during the American Civil War in 1862 and operated during all subsequent major periods of conflict including World Wars I and II, the Korean War and the Vietnam War. A limited draft was also employed in peacetime in the Cold War and early 1960s. The final draft ended in 1973 when the USA converted to an all-volunteer military. Although conscription is not currently in force the Military Selective Service Act requires all males between the ages of 18 and 26 to register for compulsory military service should the need arise.

Total active strength in Nov. 2007 numbered 1,498,200, plus 10,100 civilians and 1,082,700 reserve personnel. Women account for 14% of active personnel (14% in the Army, 20% in the Air Force, 15% in the Navy and 6% in the Marine Corps). In March 2008 US armed forces abroad numbered 290,200, including 195,000 in Iraq and 31,100 in Afghanistan. Active duty military deaths in the US armed forces totalled 1,441 in 2008, down from 1,953 in 2007. As of March 2010 there were 96,000 troops stationed in Iraq. It was anticipated that all combat troops would be withdrawn by 1 Sept. 2010. By March 2010 the number of US military personnel in Afghanistan had reached 78,000, with plans for an additional 20,000 troops to be in place before the end of 2010. US troop deaths in Iraq between 2003 and April 2010 totalled 4,390; deaths in Afghanistan between 2001 and April 2010 totalled 1,040.

The USA is the world's largest exporter of arms, with sales in 2006 worth $14·0bn., or 51·9% of the world total. In 2007 Boeing and Lockheed Martin were the two largest arms producing companies in the USA, accounting for $30·5bn. and $29·4bn. worth of sales respectively.

The USA's last nuclear test was in 1993. In accordance with START I—the treaty signed by the US and USSR in 1991 to reduce strategic offensive nuclear capability—the number of strategic nuclear warheads (intercontinental ballistic missiles, submarine-launched ballistic missiles and bombers) in Jan. 2009 was 2,202. There were also 500 non-strategic warheads in Jan. 2009, making a total of 2,702 deployed warheads. There are a further 2,500 warheads held in reserve and another 4,200 scheduled to be dismantled. In 1990 the number of warheads had been 12,718. Strategic nuclear delivery vehicles were made up as follows:

Intercontinental ballistic missiles: 450 Minuteman III.
Submarine-launched ballistic missiles: 228 Trident II.
Bombers: 93 B-52H; 20 B-2.

START I expired in Dec. 2009. In July 2007 the Bush administration decided not to extend the treaty beyond the original expiry date. In May 2001 President Bush called for the development of an anti-missile shield to move beyond the constraints of the Anti-Ballistic Missile Treaty. In Dec. 2001 he announced that the USA was unilaterally abandoning the Treaty. On 24 May 2002 the USA and Russia signed an arms control treaty (the Strategic Offensive Reductions Treaty or Moscow Treaty) to reduce the number of US and Russian warheads, from between 6,000 and 7,000 each to between 1,700 and 2,200 each, over the next ten years. A replacement agreement to START I, called the Measures to Further Reduction and Limitation of Strategic Offensive Arms, was signed in April 2010. It laid out terms for the number of warheads on each side to be limited to 1,550 by 2017, a 30% drop on previous levels.

Estimates of the number of small arms in the country are around 270m., equivalent to 90 firearms for every 100 people, making the USA the world's most heavily armed country.

Army

Secretary of the Army. John McHugh.

The Secretary of the Army is the head of the Department of the Army. Subject to the authority of the President as C.-in-C. and of the Secretary of Defense, he is responsible for all affairs of the Department.

The Army consists of the Active Army, the Army National Guard of the US, the Army Reserve and civilian workforce; and all persons appointed to or enlisted into the Army without component; and all persons serving under call or conscription, including members of the National Guard of the States, etc., when in the service of the US. The strength of the Active Army was (2006) 489,000 (plus 107,000 reservists).

The Army budget for fiscal years 2008–10 was as follows: 2008, $250,603m.; 2009, $235,752m.; 2010, $216,601m.

The US Army Forces Command, with headquarters at Fort McPherson, Georgia, commands the Third US Army; four continental US Armies, and all assigned Active Army and US Army Reserve troop units in the continental US, the Commonwealth of Puerto Rico, and the Virgin Islands of the USA. The headquarters of the continental US Armies are: First US Army, Fort George G. Meade, Maryland; Second US Army, Fort Gillem, Georgia; Fifth US Army, Fort Sam Houston, Texas; Sixth US Army, Presidio of San Francisco, California. The US Army Space Command, with headquarters in Colorado Springs (CO), is the Army component to the US Space Command.

Approximately 32% of the Active Army is deployed outside the continental USA. Several divisions, which are located in the USA, keep equipment in Germany and can be flown there in 48–72 hours. Headquarters of US Seventh and Eighth Armies are in Europe and Korea respectively.

Combat vehicles of the US Army are the tank, armoured personnel carrier, infantry fighting vehicle, and the armoured command vehicle. The first-line tanks are the M1A1 Abrams tank, and the M1 Abrams. The standard armoured infantry personnel carrier is the M2 Bradley Fighting Vehicle (BFV), which is replacing the older M113.

The Army has nearly 4,900 aircraft, all but about 300 of them helicopters, including AH-1 Cobra and AH-64 Apache attack helicopters.

Over 95% of recruits enlisting in the Army have a high-school education and over 50% of the Army is married. Women serve in both combat support and combat service support units.

The National Guard is a reserve military component with both a state and a federal role. Enlistment is voluntary. The members are recruited by each state, but are equipped and paid by the federal government (except when performing state missions). As the organized militia of the several states, the District of Columbia, Puerto Rico and the Territories of the Virgin Islands and Guam, the Guard may be called into service for local emergencies by the chief executives in those jurisdictions; and may be called into federal service by the President to thwart invasion or rebellion or to enforce federal law. In its role as a reserve component of the Army, the Guard is subject to the order of the President in the event of national emergency. In 2006 it numbered 458,030 (Army, 351,350; Air Force, 106,680).

The Army Reserve is designed to supply qualified and experienced units and individuals in an emergency. Members of units are assigned to the Ready Reserve, which is subject to call by the President in case of national emergency without declaration of war by Congress. The Standby Reserve and the Retired Reserve may be called only after declaration of war or national emergency by Congress. In 2006 the Army Reserve numbered 324,100.

Navy

Secretary of the Navy. Ray Mabus.

The Navy's Operating Forces include the Atlantic Fleet, divided between the 2nd fleet (home waters) and 6th fleet (Mediterranean) and the Pacific Fleet, similarly divided between the 3rd fleet (home waters), the 7th fleet (West Pacific) and the 5th fleet (Indian Ocean), which was formally activated in 1995 and maintained by units from both Pacific and Atlantic.

The authorized budget for the Department of the Navy (which includes funding both for the Navy and Marine Corps) for fiscal years 2008–10 was as follows: 2008, $164,893m.; 2009, $166,765m.; 2010, $170,072m.

Personnel and fleet strength declined during the mid-1990s but are now stabilizing. The Navy personnel total in 2006 was 376,750.

The operational strength of the Navy in the year indicated:

Category	*1992*	*1997*	*2005*	*2006*
Strategic Submarines	23	18	16	14
Nuclear Attack Submarines	87	67	56	58
Aircraft Carriers	12	11[1]	12[1]	12[1]
Amphibious Carriers	13	11	11	11
Cruisers	46	30	27	25
Destroyers	51	56	49	47
Frigates	90	31	30	30

[1]Includes the USS *John F. Kennedy* as 'operational and training reserve carrier' in the Naval Reserve Force.

Ships in the inactive reserve are not included in the table, but those serving as Naval Reserve Force training ships are.

Submarine Forces. A principal part of the US naval task is to deploy the seaborne strategic deterrent from nuclear-powered ballistic missile-carrying submarines (SSBN), of which there were 14 in 2006, all of the Ohio class. The listed total of 58 nuclear-powered attack submarines comprises 50 of the Los Angeles class, four converted submarines of the Ohio class, three of the Seawolf class and one of the new Virginia class.

Surface Combatant Forces. The surface combatant forces are comprised of modern cruisers, destroyers and frigates. These ships provide multi-mission capabilities to achieve maritime dominance in the crowded and complex littoral warfare environment.

The cruiser force consists of 25 Ticonderoga class ships. There are 47 guided-missile Arleigh Burke Aegis class destroyers and 30 (22 active and eight in the reserve force) Oliver Hazard Perry class guided missile frigates.

Aircraft carriers. There are ten nuclear-powered Nimitz class carriers, the first of which, USS *Nimitz*, was commissioned on 3 May 1975 and the tenth and last of which, USS *George H. W. Bush*, was commissioned on 10 Jan. 2009. USS *Enterprise*, completed in 1961, was the prototype nuclear-powered carrier. USS *Kitty Hawk*, the only ship of the Kitty Hawk class and the last oil-fired carrier, was decommissioned on 12 May 2009. All carriers deploy an air group which comprises on average two squadrons each of F-14 Tomcat fighters and three squadrons each of F/A-18 Hornet fighter/ground attack aircraft.

Naval Aviation. The principal function of the naval aviation organization (strength in 2006 of 98,588) is to train and provide combat ready aviation forces. The main carrier-borne combat aircraft in the current inventory are 587 F/A-18 Hornet dual-purpose fighter/attack aircraft out of a total of 982 combat aircraft.

The Marine Corps

While administratively part of the Department of the Navy, the Corps ranks as a separate armed service, with the Commandant serving in his own right as a member of the Joint Chiefs of Staff, and responsible directly to the Secretary of the Navy. Its strength had stabilized at 175,350 by 2006.

The role of the Marine Corps is to provide specially trained and equipped amphibious expeditionary forces. The Corps includes an autonomous aviation element numbering 34,700 in 2006.

The US Coast Guard

The Coast Guard operates under the Department of Homeland Security in time of peace and as part of the Navy in time of war or when directed by the President. The act of establishment stated the Coast Guard 'shall be a military service and branch of the armed forces of the United States at all times'.

The Coast Guard is the country's oldest continuous sea-going service and its missions include maintenance of aids to navigation, icebreaking, environmental response (oil spills), maritime law enforcement, marine licensing, port security, search and rescue and waterways management.

The workforce in 2008 was made up of approximately 41,948 military personnel augmented by 7,654 civilians. On an average Coast Guard day, the service saves 14 lives, boards 193 ships and boats, seizes US$12·9m. worth of illegal drugs, conducts 74 search and rescue cases, processes 375 seaman's documents, investigates 24 marine casualty accidents, inspects 18 commercial fishing vessels, assists 98 people in distress, services 135 aids to navigation and interdicts 17 illegal immigrants.

Air Force

Secretary of the Air Force. Michael B. Donley.

The Department of the Air Force was activated within the Department of Defense on 18 Sept. 1947, under the terms of the National Security Act of 1947.

The USAF has the mission to defend the USA through control and exploitation of air, space and cyberspace. For operational purposes the service is divided into nine major commands, 35 field operating agencies and four direct-reporting units. In addition there are two reserve components: the Air Force Reserve and the Air National Guard.

Major commands accomplish designated phases of USAF worldwide activities. They also organize, administer, equip and train their subordinate elements. In descending order, elements of major commands include numbered air forces, wings, groups, squadrons and flights. The basic unit for generating and employing combat capability is the wing, considered to be the Air Force's prime war-fighting instrument. The bulk of the combat forces are grouped under the Air Combat Command, which controls strategic bombing, tactical strike, air defence and reconnaissance assets in the USA.

Air Force bombers include the B-1B Lancer, the B-2A and the B-52G/H Stratofortress, which has been the primary manned strategic bomber for 50 years. In the fighter category are the F-22A, F-15 Eagle and the F-16 Fighting Falcon.

The Air Force budget for fiscal years 2008–10 was as follows: 2008, $159,729m.; 2009, $163,138m.; 2010, $159,936m.

In 2006 the Air Force had approximately 347,400 military personnel. Since 1991 women have been authorized to fly combat aircraft, but not until 1993 were they allowed to fly fighters.

INTERNATIONAL RELATIONS

The USA is a member of the UN (and a permanent member of its Security Council), World Bank, IMF and several other UN specialized agencies, WTO, OSCE, BIS, IOM, NATO, OECD, Inter-American Development Bank, OAS, Asian Development Bank, Colombo Plan, SPC, Antarctic Treaty and North American Free Trade Agreement.

In 2007 the USA gave US$21·8bn. in international aid, the highest figure of any country. In terms of a percentage of GNI, however, the USA was one of the least generous major industrialized countries, giving just 0·16% (compared to more than 0·6% in the early 1960s).

ECONOMY

Services accounted for approximately 72% of GDP in 2003, industry 26% and agriculture 2%.

According to the anti-corruption organization *Transparency International*, in 2009 the USA ranked 19th in the world in a survey of the countries with the least corruption in business and government. It received 7·5 out of 10 in the annual index.

Per capita income in 2008 was $40,208, up from $19,477 in 1990.

Overview

The USA is the world's largest single-country economy. At purchasing power parity it is roughly three times the size of that of Japan and its volume of trade is the largest in the world, although the value of the external sector as a percentage of GDP is relatively low. However, in 2007 the EU replaced the USA as the world's largest economic area. The USA is self-sufficient in most raw materials, with the notable exception of oil. Core industries include motor vehicles, steel, aerospace, chemicals, telecommunications, electronics and computers. Since 1992 the economy has grown at higher average rates than the OECD and G7 in most years and per capita GDP is higher than in other G7 countries.

In 1995 labour productivity in advanced European countries had reached US levels but since then US labour and total factor productivity growth has outpaced that of Europe and Japan. The principal sectors in which the USA outperforms its rivals are retail, wholesale and finance. It has also been able to extract greater efficiency gains from IT-related investments. US firms enjoy greater flexibility than their counterparts in Western Europe and Japan in laying off workers and in introducing labour-saving equipment. However, income inequality is higher than in other advanced economies and the gap between skilled and unskilled labour incomes has been growing over the last three decades. Most income gains have accrued to the richest 20% of Americans.

The attacks of 11 Sept. 2001 posed serious challenges to the dollar payment system and the stock market. Business fixed investment relative to GDP plummeted in 2001–02 after reaching record highs in 2000–01. Confidence in the corporate market declined after the collapse of energy giant Enron in Dec. 2002 was followed by other accounting scandals. With investor confidence low, the dollar fell to near parity with the euro for the first time since the introduction of the euro in Jan. 2002. In the third quarter of 2003 the economy recorded an annualized growth rate of 6·9%, fuelled by tax cuts, low interest rates and increased consumer and business spending. Interest rates began rising from historic lows in 2003 with the federal funds rate reaching 5·25% by the end of 2006. Growth remained strong through 2006 despite the impact of Hurricane Katrina and high oil prices. The domestic economy was buoyed by strong consumer demand, which in turn increased personal debt.

The sub-prime mortgage crisis of 2007 damaged the wider economy. A sharp rise in defaults and foreclosures as a result of the rapid decline in house market prices began in 2006, spreading panic through the banking sector. A stimulus package enacted in early 2008 (consisting of targeted tax rebates and investment incentives) together with interest rate cuts amounting to 3·75% by Oct. 2008 were aimed at raising confidence in the financial markets. However, nervousness increased with tougher lending criteria and declining asset prices. In Sept. 2008 Lehman Brothers became the first major bank to collapse since the start of the credit crisis. The US government announced rescue packages for mortgage giants Fannie Mae and Freddie Mac—between them responsible for half of the outstanding mortgages in the economy—along with AIG, the country's biggest insurance company.

In Oct. 2008 the House of Representatives passed a $700bn. government plan aimed at purchasing bad debts of failing institutions. However, continued market turmoil resulted in a further $250bn. investment plan that gave the government stakes in a range of banks. Interest rates reached their lowest recorded level at between 0–0·25% in Dec. 2008. In Feb. 2009 Congress approved President Obama's $787bn. economic stimulus package, comprising tax breaks and money for social programmes, a move that substantially increased the fiscal deficit.

The government reported growth of 2·2% in the third quarter of 2009, the first quarterly increase since the second quarter of 2008, indicating that the recession had ended. Recovery was underpinned by strong government stimulus, a rebound in world trade (with increasing demand from large emerging-market economies) and house market stabilization. The economy contracted by 2·4% in 2009 as a whole, although growth of 2·5% is expected for 2010. Unemployment was predicted to peak in the first half of 2010.

Further fiscal pressures have emerged with the retirement of the baby-boom generation from 2008 and the rise in life expectancy, increasing the strain on entitlement programmes. In March 2010 the US House of Representatives approved a health care reform bill that was expected to extend health insurance to an additional 32m. Americans, impose new taxes on the wealthy and outlaw restrictive insurance practices. According to the Congressional Budget Office, the health care bill will cut the federal deficit by US$138bn. over ten years.

Having peaked in 2006, the current account deficit declined owing to a weakening dollar and strong foreign activity. Federal fiscal deficits rose in the short term as a result of the growth slowdown and stimulus packages but were expected to narrow to 2·5% of GDP in 2010 as a result of lower commodity prices.

Currency

The unit of currency is the *dollar* (USD) of 100 *cents*. Notes are issued by the 12 Federal Reserve Banks, which are denoted by a branch letter (A = Boston, MA; B = New York, NY; C = Philadelphia, PA; D = Cleveland, OH; E = Richmond, VA; F = Atlanta, GA; G = Chicago, IL; H = St Louis, MO; I = Minneapolis, MN; J = Kansas City, MO; K = Dallas, TX; L = San Francisco, CA).

Inflation rates (based on OECD statistics):

1999	*2000*	*2001*	*2002*	*2003*	*2004*	*2005*	*2006*	*2007*	*2008*
2·2%	3·4%	2·8%	1·6%	2·3%	2·7%	3·4%	3·2%	2·9%	3·8%

The inflation rate in 2009 according to the Bureau of Labour Statistics was –0·4% (the lowest rate since 1955). Foreign exchange reserves in Sept. 2009 were US$51,840m. and gold reserves were 261·50m. troy oz. The USA has the most gold reserves of any country, and more than the combined reserves of the next two (Germany and Italy). Total money supply in June 2009 was $1,497·4bn.

Budget

The budget covers virtually all the programmes of federal government, including those financed through trust funds, such as for social security, Medicare and highway construction. Receipts of the government include all income from its sovereign or compulsory powers; income from business-type or market-orientated activities of the government is offset against outlays. The fiscal year ends on 30 Sept. (before 1977 on 30 June). Budget receipts and outlays, including off-budget receipts and outlays (in $1m.):

Fiscal year ending in	*Receipts*	*Outlays*	*Surplus (+) or deficit (–)*
1950	39,443	42,562	–3,119
1960	92,492	92,191	+301
1970	192,807	195,649	–2,842
1980	517,112	590,941	–73,829
1990	1,031,972	1,253,007	–221,036
2000	2,025,198	1,788,957	+236,241
2005	2,153,625	2,471,971	–318,346
2006	2,406,876	2,655,057	–248,181
2007	2,568,001	2,728,702	–160,701
2008	2,523,999	2,982,554	–458,555
2009	2,104,995	3,517,681	–1,412,686
2010[1]	2,165,119	3,720,701	–1,555,582
2011[1]	2,567,181	3,833,861	–1,266,680

[1]Estimates.

President Barack Obama unveiled his second budget proposals in Feb. 2010, outlining plans to reduce the government deficit from 10·6% of GDP in 2010 (equating to US$1,556bn.) to below 4·0% (equating to US$706bn.) by 2014. Revenue raising strategies include the non-renewal of Bush-era tax cuts for those earning over US$250,000 (raising a projected US$678bn.), a three-year freeze on non-security discretionary spending (US$250bn.) and a proposed levy on banks bailed out with public money (US$90bn.) An additional US$192bn. has been earmarked for supplementary financing of the military in Iraq and Afghanistan.

Budget and off-budget receipts, by source, for fiscal years (in $1m.):

Source	*2009*	*2010*[1]	*2011*[1]
Individual income taxes	915,308	935,771	1,121,296
Corporation income taxes	138,229	156,741	296,902
Social insurance and retirement receipts	890,917	875,756	935,116
Excise taxes	62,483	73,204	74,288
Other	98,058	123,647	139,579
Total	2,104,995	2,165,119	2,567,181

[1]Estimates.

Budget and off-budget outlays, by function, for fiscal years (in $1m.):

Function	*2009*	*2010*[1]	*2011*[1]
National defence	661,049	719,179	749,748
Education, training, employment and social service	79,746	142,521	126,399
Health	334,327	372,336	400,661
Medicare	430,093	457,159	497,341
Income security	533,224	685,870	595,005
Social security	682,963	721,496	736,284
Veterans' benefits and services	95,429	124,655	124,539
Energy	4,749	18,952	24,863
Natural resources and environment	35,574	47,039	42,537
Commerce and housing credit	291,535	–25,319	22,127
Transportation	84,289	106,458	104,189
Community and regional development	27,650	28,469	31,973
Net interest	186,902	187,772	250,709
International affairs	37,529	51,138	54,192
General science, space and technology	29,449	33,032	31,554
Agriculture	22,237	26,610	25,590
Administration of justice	51,549	55,025	57,280
General government	22,026	29,290	27,670
Allowances	—	18,750	21,676
Undistributed offsetting receipts	–92,639	–79,731	–90,476
Total	3,517,681	3,720,701	3,833,861

[1]Estimates.

Budget and off-budget outlays, by agency, for fiscal years (in $1m.):

Agency	*2009*	*2010*[1]	*2011*[1]
Legislative Branch	4,702	5,423	5,579
The Judiciary	6,645	7,159	7,512
Agriculture	114,440	142,016	145,748
Commerce	10,718	16,714	11,500
Defence—Military	636,775	692,031	721,285
Education	53,389	106,944	94,261
Energy	23,683	38,278	44,390
Health and Human Services	796,267	868,762	934,426
Homeland Security	51,725	52,903	54,723
Housing and Urban Development	61,019	62,518	53,082
Interior	11,775	12,042	14,045
Justice	27,711	30,333	31,924
Labor	138,157	209,265	116,902
State	21,427	25,726	28,745
Transportation	73,004	90,944	86,665
Treasury	701,775	502,980	593,550
Veterans' Affairs	95,457	124,565	124,215
Corps of Engineers	6,842	10,536	6,929
Defence—Civil	57,276	54,317	55,719
Environmental Protection Agency	8,070	11,301	11,177
Executive Office of the President	743	715	501
General Services Administration	319	1,782	2,279
International Assistance Programmes	14,797	23,899	24,343
National Aeronautics and Space Administration	19,168	19,123	17,863
National Science Foundation	5,958	7,819	7,647
Office of Personnel Management	72,302	71,603	73,463
Small Business Administration	2,246	5,978	1,388
Social Security Administration	727,549	768,975	789,553
Other independent agencies	47,939	8,427	36,058
Allowances	–4	18,750	21,676
Undistributed Offsetting Receipts	–274,193	–271,127	–283,287
Total	3,517,681	3,720,701	3,833,861

[1]Estimates.

National Debt. Federal debt held by the public (in $1m.), and per capita debt (in $1) on 30 June to 1976 and on 30 Sept. since then:

	Public debt	*Per capita*
1920	24,299	229
1930	16,185	132
1940	42,772	324
1950	219,023	1,447
1960	236,840	1,321
1970	283,198	1,394
1980	711,923	3,143
1990	2,411,558	9,696
2000	3,409,804	12,084
2005	4,592,212	15,527
2006	4,828,972	16,172
2007	5,035,129	16,696
2008	5,803,050	19,065
2009	7,544,707	24,575

National Income

The Bureau of Economic Analysis of the Department of Commerce prepares detailed estimates on the national income and product. In Dec. 2003 the Bureau revised these accounts back to 1929. The principal tables are published monthly in *Survey of Current Business;* the complete set of national income and product tables are published in the *Survey* normally each Aug., showing data for recent years.

Gross Domestic Product

(in $1,000m.)

	2004	*2005*	*2006*	*2007*	*2008*
Gross Domestic Product	11,867·8	12,638·4	13,398·9	14,077·6	14,441·4
Personal consumption expenditures	8,285·1	8,819·0	9,322·7	9,826·4	10,129·9
Goods	2,892·3	3,073·9	3,221·7	3,365·0	3,403·2
Durable goods	1,061·6	1,105·5	1,133·0	1,160·5	1,095·2
Nondurable goods	1,830·7	1,968·4	2,088·7	2,204·5	2,308·0
Services	5,392·8	5,745·1	6,100·9	6,461·4	6,726·8
Gross private domestic investment	1,968·6	2,172·2	2,327·2	2,288·5	2,136·1
Fixed investment	1,903·6	2,122·3	2,267·2	2,269·1	2,170·8
Nonresidential	1,223·0	1,347·3	1,505·3	1,640·2	1,693·6
Structures	306·7	351·8	433·7	535·4	609·5
Equipment and software	916·4	995·6	1,071·7	1,104·8	1,084·1
Residential	680·6	775·0	761·9	629·0	477·2
Change in private inventories	64·9	50·0	60·0	19·4	–34·8
Net exports of goods and services	–618·7	–722·7	–769·3	–713·8	–707·8
Exports	1,180·2	1,305·1	1,471·0	1,655·9	1,831·1
Goods	817·0	906·1	1,024·4	1,139·4	1,266·9
Services	363·2	399·0	446·6	516·5	564·2
Imports	1,798·9	2,027·8	2,240·3	2,369·7	2,538·9
Goods	1,501·7	1,708·0	1,884·9	1,987·7	2,126·4
Services	297·3	319·8	355·4	382·1	412·4
Government consumption expenditures and gross investment	2,232·8	2,369·9	2,518·4	2,676·5	2,883·2
Federal	824·6	876·3	931·7	976·7	1,082·6
National defence	550·8	589·0	624·9	662·1	737·9
Nondefence	273·9	287·3	306·8	314·5	344·7
State and local	1,408·2	1,493·6	1,586·7	1,699·8	1,800·6

Relation of Gross Domestic Product, Gross National Product, Net National Product, National Income and Personal Income

(in $1,000m.)

	2004	*2005*	*2006*	*2007*	*2008*
Gross domestic product	11,867·8	12,638·4	13,398·9	14,077·6	14,441·4
Plus: Income receipts from the rest of the world	448·6	573·0	721·1	861·8	809·2
Less: Income payments to the rest of the world	357·4	475·9	648·6	746·0	667·3
Equals: Gross national product	11,959·0	12,735·5	13,471·3	14,193·3	14,583·3
Less: Consumption of fixed capital	1,432·8	1,541·4	1,660·7	1,760·0	1,847·1
Private	1,200·9	1,290·8	1,391·4	1,469·6	1,536·2
Domestic business	978·7	1,045·7	1,123·3	1,188·5	1,252·3
Capital consumption allowances	1,138·8	965·6	1,027·7	1,089·7	1,340·2
Less: Capital consumption adjustment	160·1	–80·1	–95·6	–98·8	87·8
Households and institutions	222·2	245·1	268·1	281·1	283·9
Government	231·9	250·6	269·3	290·4	310·9
General government	193·4	208·7	224·7	242·4	259·5
Government enterprises	38·5	41·9	44·6	48·1	51·4
Equals: Net national product	10,526·2	11,194·2	11,810·7	12,433·3	12,736·2
Less: Statistical discrepancy	–7·8	–79·7	–220·6	–14·8	101·0
Equals: National income	10,534·0	11,273·8	12,031·2	12,448·2	12,635·2
Less: Corporate profits with inventory valuation and capital consumption adjustments	1,246·9	1,456·1	1,608·3	1,541·7	1,360·4
Taxes on production and imports less subsidies	817·0	869·3	935·5	974·0	993·8
Contributions for government social insurance (domestic)	827·3	872·7	921·8	959·3	990·6
Net interest and miscellaneous payment on assets	461·6	543·0	652·2	739·2	815·1
Business current transfer payments (net)	81·7	95·9	83·0	102·2	118·8
Current surplus of government enterprises	1·2	–3·5	–4·2	–6·6	–6·9
Wage accruals less disbursements	–15·0	5·0	1·3	–6·3	–5·0

Relation of Gross Domestic Product, Gross National Product, Net National Product, National Income and Personal Income

(in $1,000m.)

	2004	2005	2006	2007	2008
Plus: Personal income receipts on assets	1,408·5	1,542·0	1,829·7	2,031·5	1,994·4
Personal current transfer receipts	1,415·5	1,508·6	1,605·0	1,718·0	1,875·9
Equals: Personal income	9,937·2	10,485·9	11,268·1	11,894·1	12,238·8
Addenda:					
Gross domestic income	11,875·6	12,718·0	13,619·5	14,092·5	14,340·4
Gross national income	11,966·8	12,815·2	13,691·9	14,208·2	14,482·3
Gross national factor income	11,066·9	11,853·5	12,677·7	13,138·6	13,376·7
Net domestic product	10,435·0	11,097·0	11,738·2	12,317·6	12,594·3
Net domestic income	10,442·8	11,176·7	11,958·8	12,332·4	12,493·3
Net national factor income	9,634·1	10,312·2	11,017·0	11,378·6	11,529·6

National Income by Type of Income

(in $1,000m.)

	2004	2005	2006	2007	2008
National income	10,534·0	11,273·8	12,031·2	12,448·2	12,635·2
Compensation of employees	6,693·4	7,065·0	7,477·0	7,856·5	8,037·4
Wage and salary accruals	5,410·7	5,706·0	6,070·1	6,402·6	6,540·8
Government	952·8	991·5	1,035·2	1,089·1	1,141·3
Other	4,547·9	4,714·5	5,035·0	5,313·5	5,399·6
Supplements to wages and salaries	1,282·7	1,359·1	1,406·9	1,453·8	1,496·6
Employer contributions for employee pension and insurance funds	874·6	931·6	960·1	993·0	1,023·9
Employer contributions for government social insurance	408·1	427·5	446·7	460·8	472·7
Proprietors' income with inventory valuation and capital consumption adjustments	1,033·8	1,069·8	1,133·0	1,096·4	1,106·3
Farm	49·7	43·9	29·3	39·4	48·7
Nonfarm	984·1	1,025·9	1,103·6	1,056·9	1,057·5
Rental income of persons with capital consumption adjustment	198·4	178·2	146·5	144·9	210·4
Corporate profits with inventory valuation and capital consumption adjustments	1,246·9	1,456·1	1,608·3	1,541·7	1,360·4
Taxes on corporate income	306·1	412·4	473·3	451·5	292·2
Profits after tax with inventory valuation and capital consumption adjustments	940·8	1,043·7	1,135·0	1,090·2	1,068·2
Net dividends	550·3	557·3	704·8	767·8	689·9
Undistributed profits with inventory valuation and capital consumption adjustments	390·5	486·4	430·3	322·4	378·3
Net interest and miscellaneous payments	461·6	543·0	652·2	739·2	815·1
Taxes on production and imports	863·4	930·2	986·8	1,028·7	1,047·3
Less: Subsidies	46·4	60·9	51·4	54·8	53·5
Business current transfer payments (net)	81·7	95·9	83·0	102·2	118·8
To persons (net)	16·9	25·8	21·4	30·2	32·6
To government (net)	52·5	55·2	59·6	65·4	78·8
To the rest of the world (net)	12·2	14·8	2·0	6·6	7·3
Current surplus of government enterprises	1·2	–3·5	–4·2	–6·6	–6·9
Addenda for corporate cash flow:					
Net cash flow with inventory valuation adjustments	1,190·1	1,337·0	1,356·1	1,303·4	1,478·4
Undistributed profits with inventory valuation and capital consumption adjustments	390·5	486·4	430·3	322·4	378·3
Consumption of fixed capital	809·2	862·9	925·9	981·0	1,036·8
Less: Capital transfers paid (net)	9·5	12·2	0·0	0·0	–63·3
Addenda:					
Proprietors' income with inventory valuation and capital consumption adjustments	1,033·8	1,069·8	1,133·0	1,096·4	1,106·3
Farm	49·7	43·9	29·3	39·4	48·7
Proprietors' income with inventory valuation adjustment	54·5	49·4	35·4	45·8	55·6
Capital consumption adjustment	–4·9	–5·5	–6·0	–6·4	–6·8
Nonfarm	984·1	1,025·9	1,103·6	1,056·9	1,057·5
Proprietors' income (without inventory valuation and capital consumption adjustments)	861·7	936·3	1,004·3	950·4	888·0
Inventory valuation adjustment	–4·2	–4·1	–3·6	–6·2	–5·1
Capital consumption adjustment	126·6	93·6	103·0	112·8	174·6
Rental income of persons with capital consumption adjustment	198·4	178·2	146·5	144·9	210·4
Rental income of persons (without capital consumption adjustment)	211·8	193·0	162·8	161·5	226·2
Capital consumption adjustment	–13·4	–14·8	–16·2	–16·6	–15·8
Corporate profits with inventory valuation and capital consumption adjustments	1,246·9	1,456·1	1,608·3	1,541·7	1,360·4

National Income by Type of Income

	(in $1,000m.)				
	2004	*2005*	*2006*	*2007*	*2008*
Corporate profits with inventory valuation adjustment	1,195·1	1,609·5	1,784·7	1,730·4	1,424·5
Profits before tax (without inventory valuation and capital consumption adjustments)	1,229·4	1,640·2	1,822·7	1,774·4	1,462·7
Taxes on corporate income	306·1	412·4	473·3	451·5	292·2
Profits after tax (without inventory valuation and capital consumption adjustments)	923·3	1,227·8	1,349·5	1,332·8	1,170·6
Net dividends	550·3	557·3	704·8	767·8	689·9
Undistributed profits (without inventory valuation and capital consumption adjustments)	373·0	670·5	644·7	555·1	480·7
Inventory valuation adjustment	–34·3	–30·7	–38·0	–44·0	–38·2
Capital consumption adjustment	51·8	–153·4	–176·4	–188·7	–64·1

Real Gross Domestic Product

	(in 1,000m. chained [2005] dollars[1])				
	2004	*2005*	*2006*	*2007*	*2008*
Gross domestic product	12,263·8	12,638·4	12,976·2	13,254·1	13,312·2
Personal consumption expenditures	8,532·7	8,819·0	9,073·5	9,313·9	9,290·9
Goods	2,955·3	3,073·9	3,173·9	3,273·7	3,206·0
Durable goods	1,051·0	1,105·5	1,150·4	1,199·9	1,146·3
Nondurable goods	1,904·6	1,968·4	2,023·6	2,074·8	2,057·3
Services	5,577·6	5,745·1	5,899·7	6,040·8	6,083·1
Gross private domestic investment	2,058·2	2,172·2	2,230·4	2,146·2	1,989·4
Fixed investment	1,992·5	2,122·3	2,171·3	2,126·3	2,018·4
Nonresidential	1,263·0	1,347·3	1,453·9	1,544·3	1,569·7
Structures	346·7	351·8	384·0	441·4	486·8
Equipment and software	917·3	995·6	1,069·6	1,097·0	1,068·6
Residential	729·5	775·0	718·2	585·0	451·1
Change in private inventories	66·3	50·0	59·4	19·5	–25·9
Net exports of goods and services	–688·0	–722·7	–729·2	–647·7	–494·3
Exports	1,222·8	1,305·1	1,422·0	1,546·1	1,629·3
Goods	842·9	906·1	991·4	1,064·8	1,127·5
Services	380·0	399·0	430·6	481·3	501·7
Imports	1,910·8	2,027·8	2,151·2	2,193·8	2,123·5
Goods	1,599·7	1,708·0	1,808·8	1,839·6	1,767·3
Services	311·0	319·8	342·4	354·2	356·5
Government consumption expenditures and gross investment	2,362·0	2,369·9	2,402·1	2,443·1	2,518·1
Federal	865·0	876·3	894·9	906·4	975·9
National defence	580·4	589·0	598·4	611·5	659·4
Nondefence	284·6	287·3	296·6	294·9	316·4
State and local	1,497·1	1,493·6	1,507·2	1,536·7	1,543·7
Residual	–3·5	–0·2	–1·7	0·3	20·0

[1]In 1996 the chain-weighted method of estimating GDP replaced that of constant base-year prices. In chain-weighting the weights used to value different sectors of the economy are continually updated to reflect changes in relative prices.

Performance

Total GDP in 2008 was US$14,204·3bn. (nearly three times larger than Japan, the second largest economy), representing 23% of the world's total GDP. Real GDP growth rates (based on OECD statistics):

1999	*2000*	*2001*	*2002*	*2003*	*2004*	*2005*	*2006*	*2007*	*2008*
4·8%	4·1%	1·1%	1·8%	2·5%	3·6%	3·1%	2·7%	2·1%	0·4%

The real GDP growth rate in 2009 according to the Bureau of Economic Analysis was –2·4%. The USA's economy shrank by 2·7% in the third quarter of 2008, by 5·4% in the fourth quarter and by 6·4% in the first quarter of 2009 (the steepest quarterly fall since 1982). There was also negative growth in the second quarter of 2009, of 0·7%. The recession ended with growth of 2·2% in the third quarter of 2009.

The USA was ranked second behind Switzerland in the Global Competitiveness Index in the World Economic Forum's *Global Competitiveness Report 2009–2010*, down from first in the 2008–2009 report. In the 2009 *World Competitiveness Yearbook*, compiled by the International Institute for Management Development, the USA came top in the world ranking.

Banking and Finance

The Federal Reserve System, established under The Federal Reserve Act of 1913, comprises the Board of seven Governors, the 12 regional Federal Reserve Banks with their 25 branches, and the Federal Open Market Committee. The seven members of the Board of Governors are appointed by the President with the consent of the Senate. Each Governor is appointed to a full term of 14 years or an unexpired portion of a term, one term expiring every two years. The Board exercises broad supervisory authority over the operations of the 12 Federal Reserve Banks, including approval of their budgets and of the appointments of their presidents and first vice presidents; it designates three of the nine directors of each Reserve Bank including the Chairman and Deputy Chairman. The Chairman of the Federal Reserve Board is appointed by the President for four-year terms. The *Chairman* is Ben Bernanke. The Board has supervisory and regulatory responsibilities over banks that are members of the Federal Reserve System, bank holding companies, bank mergers, Edge Act and agreement corporations, foreign activities of member banks, international banking facilities in the USA, and activities of the US branches and agencies of foreign banks. Legislation of 1991 requires foreign banks to prove that they are subject to comprehensive consolidated supervision by a regulator at home, and have the Board's approval to establish branches, agencies and representative offices. The Board also assures the smooth functioning and continued development of the nation's vast payments system. Another area of the Board's responsibilities involves the implementation by regulation of major federal laws governing consumer credit.

From 1968 the Congress passed a number of consumer financial protection acts, the first of which was the Truth in Lending Act, for which it has directed the Board to write implementing regulations and assume partial enforcement responsibility. Others include the Equal Credit Opportunity Act, Home Mortgage Disclosure Act, Consumer Leasing Act, Fair Credit Billing Act, Truth in Savings Act and Electronic Fund Transfer Act. To manage these responsibilities the Board has established a Division of Consumer and Community Affairs. To assist it, the Board consults with a Consumer Advisory Council, established by the Congress in 1976 as a statutory part of the Federal Reserve System.

Another statutory body, the Federal Advisory Council, consists of 12 members (one from each district); it meets in Washington four times a year to advise the Board of Governors on economic and banking developments. Following the passage of the Monetary Control Act of 1980, the Board of Governors established the Thrift Institutions Advisory Council to provide information and views on the special needs and problems of thrift institutions. The group is comprised of representatives of mutual savings banks, savings and loan associations, and credit unions.

All depository institutions (commercial and savings banks, savings and loan associations, credit unions, US agencies and branches of foreign banks, and Edge Act and agreement corporations) must meet reserve requirements set by the Federal Reserve and hold the reserves in the form of vault cash or deposits at Federal Reserve Banks.

All depository institutions (commercial and savings banks, savings and loan associations, credit unions, US agencies and branches of foreign banks, and Edge Act and agreement corporations) must meet reserve requirements set by the Federal Reserve and hold the reserves in the form of vault cash or deposits at Federal Reserve Banks.

Banks which participate in the federal deposit insurance fund have their deposits insured against loss up to $100,000 for each account. The fund is administered by the Federal Deposit Insurance Corporation established in 1933; it obtains resources through annual assessments on participating banks. All members of the Federal Reserve System are required to insure their deposits through the Corporation, and non-member banks may apply and qualify for insurance.

The Federal Deposit Insurance Corporation Improvement Act of 1992 originated with bank reform initiatives. It imposed new capital rules on banks, new reporting requirements and a code of 'safety and soundness' standards. The main aim of the Act is to reduce risk through rigorous enforcement of capital requirements. Regulators are required to take action where banks fail to observe these standards.

In 2009 the largest banks in the USA in terms of market value were: J. P. Morgan Chase ($85·9bn.); Wells Fargo ($51·3bn.); Bank of New York Mellon ($25·5bn.).

The key stock exchanges are the New York Stock Exchange (NYSE) and the Nasdaq Stock Exchange (NASDAQ). There are several other stock exchanges, in Philadelphia, Boston, San Francisco (Pacific Stock Exchange) and Chicago, although trading is very limited in them.

The USA received $271·18bn. worth of foreign direct investment in 2007 and $316·11bn. in 2008. By the end of 2008 the total stock of foreign direct investment was $2,278·9bn.

By Dec. 2005 approximately 21% of the population were using e-banking.

Weights and Measures

The US Customary System derives from the British Imperial System. It differs in respect of the *gallon* (= 0·83268 Imperial gallon); *bushel* (= 0·969 Imperial bushel); *hundredweight* (= 100 lb); and the *short* or *net ton* (= 2,000 lb).

ENERGY AND NATURAL RESOURCES

Environment

The USA's carbon dioxide emissions from the consumption and flaring of fossil fuels in 2008 accounted for 19·2% of the world total (the second highest after China) and were equivalent to 19·2 tonnes per capita (down from 20·4 tonnes per capita in 2004). The population of the USA is only 4·6% of the world total. An *Environmental Performance Index* compiled in 2008 ranked the USA 39th in the world, with 81·0%. The index examined various factors in six areas—air pollution, biodiversity and habitat, climate change, environmental health, productive natural resources and water resources.

In March 2001 then President Bush rejected the 1997 Kyoto Protocol, which aims to combat the rise in the earth's temperature through the reduction of industrialized nations' carbon dioxide emissions from the consumption and flaring of fossil fuels by an average 5·2% below 1990 levels by 2012. In Feb. 2002 he unveiled an alternative climate-change plan to the Kyoto Protocol, calling for voluntary measures to reduce the rate of increase of US carbon dioxide emissions from the consumption and flaring of fossil fuels.

The USA recycled 33·2% of its municipal solid waste in 2008.

Electricity

Net summer capacity in 2008 was 1,008·6m. kW. Fossil fuel accounts for approximately 71% of electricity generation. In 2008, 20% of electricity was produced by nuclear reactors. (The last one to begin commercial operation was in 1996.) The USA has more nuclear reactors in use than any other country in the world. In 2007 the USA had a nuclear generating capacity of 100,266 MW, with 104 nuclear reactors. Electricity production in 2008 was the highest in the world, at 4,110,259m. kWh. Consumption per capita in 2004 was 14,240 kWh.

Oil and Gas

Crude oil production (2007), 1,848m. bbls. Production has been gradually declining since the mid-1980s, when annual production was 3,274m. bbls. Only Saudi Arabia and Russia produce more crude oil. Proven reserves were 21·3bn. bbls in 2007, but they are expected to be exhausted by 2020. Output (2007) was valued at $122·96bn. Offshore oil accounts for about 33% of total production, but this is likely to increase in the future. Crude oil imports began to exceed production in 1993 and in 2007 totalled 3,656m. bbls, with Canada supplying nearly a fifth of US oil imports. In Oct. 2002 the USA took its first delivery of Russian oil for its Strategic Petroleum Reserve as a consequence of an energy dialogue declared by then Presidents George W. Bush and Vladimir Putin at their summit in May 2002. The USA is by far the largest single consumer of oil (943·8m. tonnes in 2006).

The USA is by some distance the greatest single consumer of natural gas, and the second largest producer after Russia. Natural gas production, 2008, was 21·46trn. cu. ft. Proven natural gas reserves in 2008 totalled 238trn. cu. ft.

Wind

The USA is one of the largest producers of wind-power. In 2007 total installed capacity amounted to 16,596 MW.

Ethanol

The USA is the largest producer of ethanol (from maize). Production totalled 6,499m. gallons in 2007 (4,855m. gallons in 2006 and 3,904m. gallons in 2005).

Water

The total area covered by water is 256,645 sq. miles. Americans' average annual water usage is nearly 67,000 cu. ft per person—more than twice the average for an industrialized nation.

Non-Fuel Minerals

The USA is wholly dependent upon imports for columbium, bauxite, mica sheet, manganese, strontium and graphite, and imports over 80% of its requirements of industrial diamonds, fluorspar, platinum, tantalum, tungsten, chromium and tin.

Total value of non-fuel minerals produced in 2006 was $65,500m. ($33,445m. in 1990). Details of some of the main minerals produced are given in the following tables.

Production of metals:

	Unit	*Quantity 2006*
Copper	1,000 tonnes	1,200
Gold	tonnes	252
Iron ore	1m. tonnes	53
Lead	1,000 tonnes	419
Silver	tonnes	1,140
Zinc	1,000 tonnes	727

In 2007 the value of metal mine production was $25·3bn.

Precious metals are mined mainly in California and Utah (gold); and Nevada, Arizona and Idaho (silver).

Production of non-metals:

	Unit	*Quantity 2006*
Barite	1,000 tonnes	589
Boron	1,000 tonnes	1,150[1]
Bromine	1,000 tonnes	243
Cement	1m. short tons	98
Clays	1,000 tonnes	41,200
Diatomite	1,000 tonnes	799
Feldspar (including aplite)	1,000 tonnes	760
Garnet (industrial)	1,000 tonnes	34
Gypsum	1m. tonnes	21
Lime	1m. tonnes	21
Phosphate rock	1m. tonnes	30
Pumice	1,000 tonnes	1,540
Salt	1m. tonnes	44
Sand and gravel	1m. tonnes	1,352
Stone (crushed/broken)	1m. tonnes	1,720

[1]2005.

In 2007 the value of non-metal mineral production was $44·2bn.

Aluminium production for 2006, 2·28m. tonnes; uranium production for 2007, 1,654 tonnes. The USA is the world's leading producer of salt.

Coal

Proven recoverable coal reserves were 263,781m. short tons in 2005, more than a quarter of the world total. Output in 2006 (in 1m. short tons): 1,162·7 including bituminous coal, 561·6; sub-bituminous coal, 515·3; lignite, 84·2; anthracite, 1·5. 2006 output from opencast workings, 803·7m. short tons; underground mines, 359·0m. short tons. Value of total output, 2006, $29·25bn.

Agriculture

Agriculture in the USA is characterized by its ability to adapt to widely varying conditions, and still produce an abundance and variety of agricultural products. From colonial times to about 1920 the major increases in farm production were brought about by adding to the number of farms and the amount of land under cultivation. During this period nearly 320m. acres of virgin forest were converted to crop land or pasture, and extensive areas of grasslands were ploughed. Improvident use of soil and water resources was evident in many areas.

During the next 20 years the number of farms reached a plateau of about 6·5m., and the acreage planted to crops held relatively stable around 330m. acres. The major source of increase in farm output arose from the substitution of power-driven machines for horses and mules. Greater emphasis was placed on development and improvement of land, and the need for conservation of basic agricultural resources was recognized. A successful conservation programme, highly co-ordinated and on a national scale—to prevent further erosion, to restore the native fertility of damaged land and to adjust land uses to production capabilities and needs—has been in operation since early in the 1930s.

Since the Second World War the uptrend in farm output has been greatly accelerated by increased production per acre and per farm animal. These increases are associated with a higher degree of mechanization; greater use of lime and fertilizer; improved varieties, including hybrid maize and grain sorghums; more effective control of insects and disease; improved strains of livestock and poultry; and wider use of good husbandry practices, such as nutritionally balanced feeds, use of superior sites and better housing. During this period land included in farms decreased slowly, crop land harvested declined somewhat more rapidly, but the number of farms declined sharply.

All land in farms totalled less than 500m. acres in 1870, rose to a peak of over 1,200m. acres in the 1950s and declined to 931m. acres in 2007, even with the addition of the new States of Alaska and Hawaii in 1960. The number of farms declined from 6·35m. in 1940 to 2·08m. in 2007, as the average size of farms doubled. The average size of farms in 2007 was 449 acres, but ranged from a few acres to many thousand acres. In 2007 the total value of land and buildings was $1,744,295m. The average value of land and buildings per acre in 2007 was $1,892.

At the 2000 census 59,063,597 persons (21·0% of the population) were rural, of whom 2,987,531 (just over 1% of the total population) lived on farms. In 2007 there were 1,906,335 farms managed by families or individuals (86·5% of all farms); 1,522,033 farms (69·0% of all farms) were managed by full owners (farmers who own all the land they operate). Hired farmworkers numbered 2,636,509 in 2007. There were 4·4m. tractors in 2007 and an estimated 411,000 harvester-threshers. In 2007 there were an estimated 170·43m. ha. of arable land and 2·73m. ha. of permanent crops. 22·9m. ha. were irrigated in 2007.

Cash receipts from farm marketings and government payments (in $1bn.):

	Crops	*Livestock and livestock products*	*Total*
2006	122·6	118·2	240·8
2007	149·9	138·6	288·5
2008	183·1	141·1	324·2

Net farm income was $87·1bn. in 2008 ($70·9bn. in 2007).

The harvest area and production of the principal crops for 2006 and 2007 were:

	2006			*2007*		
	Harvested 1m. acres	*Produc-tion 1m.*	*Yield per acre*	*Harvested 1m. acres*	*Produc-tion 1m.*	*Yield per acre*
Corn for grain (bu.)	70·6	10,535	149	86·5	13,074	151
Soybeans (bu.)	74·6	3,188	42·7	62·8	2,585	41·0
Wheat (bu.)	46·8	1,812	38·7	51·0	2,067	40·5
Cotton (bales)[1]	12·7	21·6	814	10·5	19·0	871
Potatoes (cwt.)	1·1	441	393	1·1	449	398
Hay (sh. tons)	60·9	142	2·34	61·6	150	2·44

[1]Yield in lb.

The USA is the world's leading producer of maize, soybeans, sorghum and tree nuts and the second largest producer of tomatoes and apples.

Fruit. Utilized production, in 1,000 tons:

	2005	*2006*	*2007*
Apples	4,801	4,878	4,650
Grapefruit	1,018	1,232	1,577
Grapes	7,811	6,366	6,729
Oranges	9,252	9,021	7,589
Peaches	1,145	987	1,101
Strawberries	1,161	1,202	1,250

The farm value of the above crops in 2007 was: apples, $2,398m.; grapefruit, $283m.; grapes, $3,381m.; oranges, $2,111m.; peaches, $499m.; strawberries, $1,746m.

In 2005 there were 1,723,271 acres of organic crops. Certified organic producers numbered 10,159 in 2007. Organic food sales for the USA in 2005 totalled $13·8bn. (the highest in the world).

Dairy produce. In 2007 production of milk was 185,600m. lb; cheese, 9,700m. lb; butter, 1,533m. lb; ice cream, 951m. gallons; non-fat dry milk, 1,298m. lb; yoghurt, 3,478m. lb. The USA is the world's largest producer of both cheese and milk.

Livestock. In 2007 there were 8,898m. broilers and 272m. turkeys. Eggs produced, 2007, 90·6bn.

Value of production (in $1m.) was:

	2005	*2006*	*2007*
Cattle and calves	36,629	35,555	36,067
Hogs and pigs	13,607	12,702	13,468
Broilers	20,878	17,739	21,460
Turkeys	3,183	3,574	3,711
Eggs	4,049	4,432	6,678

Livestock numbered, in 2008 (1m.): cattle and calves (including milch cows), 96·7; hogs and pigs, 65·1; sheep and lambs, 6·1. Approximate value of livestock (in $1bn.), 2008: cattle, 95·4; hogs and pigs, 4·7; sheep and lambs (in $1m.), 836.

Forestry

Forests covered a total area of 751m. acres (303m. ha.) in 2007, or 33% of the land area. The national forests had an area of 147,181,000 acres in 2007. In 2007 there were 514m. acres of timberland (99m. acres national forest, 59m. acres state, county or municipality owned, 356m. acres private). Timber production was 15,680m. cu. ft in 2007. The USA is the world's largest producer of roundwood (12·4% of the world total in 2007). It is also the highest consumer of roundwood; timber consumption in 2007 totalled 15·41bn. cu. ft.

In 2008 there were 704 designated wilderness areas throughout the USA, covering a total of 107·4m. acres (43·5m. ha.). More than half of the areas are in Alaska (53·5%), followed by California (13·3%), Arizona, Washington and Idaho.

Fisheries

In 2006 the domestic catch was 9,489·0m. lb, valued at $3,993·4m. (including 1,108·0m. lb of shellfish valued at $2,042·9m.). Main species landed in terms of value ($1m.): crabs, 428·8; shrimp, 419·3; American lobsters, 394·7; sea scallops, 386·0; Alaska pollock, 329·9. Disposition of the domestic catch in 2006 (1m. lb): fresh or frozen, 7,752; tinned, 463; cured, 108; reduced to meal or oil, 1,166. The USA's imports of fishery commodities in 2005 ($11·98bn.) were exceeded only by those of Japan.

In the period 2003–05 the average American citizen consumed 53·4 lb (24·2 kg) of fish and fishery products a year, compared to an average 36·2 lb (16·4 kg) for the world as a whole.

Tennessee Valley Authority

Established by Act of Congress, 1933, the TVA is a multiple-purpose federal agency which carries out its duties in an area embracing some 41,000 sq. miles in the seven Tennessee River Valley states: Tennessee, Kentucky, Mississippi, Alabama, North Carolina, Georgia and Virginia. In addition, 76 counties outside the Valley are served by TVA power distributors. It is the largest public power company in the USA. Its three directors are appointed by the President, with the consent of the Senate; headquarters are in Knoxville (TN).

INDUSTRY

The largest companies in the USA by market capitalization in April 2010 were: The Exxon Mobil Corporation ($320·4bn.), the world's largest integrated oil company; The Microsoft Corporation ($262·4bn.), the world's leading software company; and Wal-Mart Stores ($208·2bn.), the world's largest retailer. According to a survey published by the New York-based Interbrand in July 2009, Coca-Cola is the world's most valuable brand, worth $68·73bn.

The following table presents industry statistics of manufactures as reported at various censuses from 1909 to 1980 and from the Annual Survey of Manufactures for years in which no census was taken.

The annual Surveys of Manufactures carry forward the key measures of manufacturing activity which are covered in detail by the Census of Manufactures. The large plants in the surveys account for approximately two-thirds of the total employment in operating manufacturing establishments in the USA.

	Production workers (average for year)	*Production workers' wages total ($1,000)*	*Value added by manufacture ($1,000)*
1909	3,261,736	3,205,213	8,160,075
1919	9,464,916	9,664,009	23,841,624
1929	8,369,705	10,884,919	30,591,435
1933	5,787,611	4,940,146	14,007,540
1939	7,808,205	8,997,515	24,487,304
1950	11,778,803	34,600,025	89,749,765
1960	12,209,514	55,555,452	163,998,531
1970	13,528,000	91,609,000	300,227,600
1980	13,900,100	198,164,000	773,831,300
1990	12,232,700	275,208,400	1,346,970,100
2000	11,943,646	363,380,819	1,973,622,421
2001	11,212,063	342,268,242	1,850,709,351
2002	10,319,528	336,540,063	1,889,290,940
2003	9,796,581	330,480,113	1,923,414,910
2004	9,365,130	332,873,474	2,041,433,991
2005	9,235,635	337,980,878	2,210,349,247
2006	9,175,328	344,192,729	2,285,928,967

The total number of employees in the manufacturing industry in 2006 was approximately 12,985,000; there were 331,062 manufacturing establishments in 2006. Manufacturing employment has declined every year since 1998. Much of the decline reflects the recession that began in 2001 and the relatively weak recovery in demand that followed. In 2007 manufacturing contributed 11·7% of GDP, down from 14·5% of GDP in 2000. The leading industries in 2006 in terms of value added by manufacture (in $1m.) were: chemicals, 350,786; transportation equipment, 260,380; food, 233,741; computer and electronic products, 230,262; fabricated metal products, 169,381. In 2008 a total of 8,673,000 motor vehicles were made in the USA, the lowest annual total since the 1980s.

In 2007 principal commodities produced (by value of shipments, in $1m.) were: transportation equipment, 693,036; chemicals, 664,057; food, 573,563; petroleum and coal products, 564,114; computer and electronic products, 386,897.

Net profits (2007) for manufacturing corporations were $610bn. before tax ($445bn. after tax). Hourly earnings of production workers in Dec. 2008 were $18·06 in manufacturing and $22·52 in construction.

The USA is the second largest beer producer after China, with 6,151m. gallons in 2007; and second after China for cigarette production, with 484bn. units in 2006.

Iron and Steel. Output of the iron and steel industries (in 1m. net tons of 2,000 lb) in recent years was:

			Steel by method of production[1]	
	Pig iron	Raw steel	Electric	Basic Oxygen
2003	40·6	93·7	47·8	45·9
2004	42·3	99·7	51·9	47·8
2005	37·2	94·9	52·2	42·7
2006	37·9	98·2	42·1	56·1
2007	36·3	98·1	41·0	57·1

[1]The sum of these two items should equal the total in the preceding column; any difference is due to rounding.

In 2006 iron and steel mills and ferroalloy manufacturing employed 101,606 persons (an average 81,900 production workers). The total payroll in 2006 amounted to $7,011·1m.

According to the World Bank's *Doing Business 2010* the USA is the third easiest country in which to do business, after Singapore and New Zealand, and the sixth easiest country in which to start a business.

Labour

The Bureau of Labor Statistics estimated that in 2008 the civilian labour force was 154,287,000 (66·0% of those 16 years and over), of whom 145,362,000 were employed and 8,924,000 (5·8%) were unemployed. The unemployment rate was 9·7% in March 2010, up from 5·8% in 2008 as a whole. Payroll employment fell by 779,000 in Jan. 2009, the largest monthly fall since 1945. In 2009 as a whole 4·8m. jobs were lost—the highest number since records began in 1939. Employment by industry in 2008:

Industry Group	Male	Female	Total	Percentage distribution
Employed (1,000 persons):	77,486	67,876	145,362	100·0
Agriculture, forestry, fisheries, and hunting	1,650	518	2,168	1·5
Mining	714	105	819	0·6
Construction	9,905	1,069	10,974	7·5
Manufacturing: Durable goods	7,649	2,624	10,273	7·1
Manufacturing: Non-durable	3,601	2,030	5,631	3·9
Wholesale and retail trade	11,327	9,257	20,585	14·2
Transportation and utilities	5,940	1,786	7,727	5·3
Information	2,032	1,449	3,481	2·4
Financial activities	4,623	5,605	10,228	7·0
Professional and business services	8,957	6,584	15,540	10·7
Education and health services	7,799	23,603	31,402	21·6
Leisure and hospitality	6,192	6,575	12,767	8·8
Other services	3,390	3,615	7,005	4·8
Public administration	3,707	3,056	6,763	4·7

A total of 21 strikes and lockouts of 1,000 workers or more occurred in 2007, involving 189,000 workers and 1,265,000 idle days.

On 24 July 2007 the federal hourly minimum wage was raised from $5·15 to $5·85 an hour. It had been $5·15 for nearly ten years, having previously been increased from $4·75 an hour on 1 Sept. 1997. It was raised again on 24 July 2008, to $6·55 an hour, and on 24 July 2009, to $7·25. Americans worked an average 1,703 hours per person in 2008. Median weekly earnings were $722 in 2008 ($798 among men and $638 among women).

Labour relations are legally regulated by the National Labor Relations Act, amended by the Labor–Management Relations (Taft–Hartley) Act, 1947 as amended by the Labor–Management Reporting and Disclosure Act, 1959, again amended in 1974, and the Railway Labor Act of 1926, as amended in 1934 and 1936.

Trade Unions

The labour movement comprises national and international labour organizations plus a large number of small independent local or single-firm labour organizations. The American Federation of Labor and the Congress of Industrial Organizations merged into one organization, the AFL–CIO, in 1955, with 56 unions and 11m. members in 2008. Its president is Richard L. Trumka, elected 2009. Seven unions, comprising 6m. members, split from the AFL–CIO to form the Change to Win Federation in 2005. However, in early 2009 both organizations came under pressure from the Obama administration to reunite. There were 15,670,000 union members in total in 2007.

Unaffiliated or independent labour organizations, inter-state in scope, had an estimated total membership excluding all foreign members (1993) of about 3m.

Labour organizations represented 13·3% (17·2m.) of wage and salary workers in 2007. 12·1% of wage and salary workers were actual members of unions in 2007, down from 20·1% in 1983. 35·9% of employees in the public sector, and 7·5% in the private sector, were members of unions in 2007. Whereas union membership among workers in the public sector has risen slightly over the past 30 years, the rate among private sector workers has more than halved. Strongholds of organized labour are, industry-wise, iron and steel, railways, coal mining and car building; region-wise, East coast cities and the mid-West industrial belt.

INTERNATIONAL TRADE

The North American Free Trade Agreement (NAFTA) between the USA, Canada and Mexico was signed on 7 Oct. 1992 and came into effect on 1 Jan. 1994. The Central America-Dominican Republic-United States Free Trade Agreement (CAFTA-DR) between the USA, Costa Rica, the Dominican Republic, El Salvador, Guatemala, Honduras and Nicaragua entered into force for the USA on 1 March 2006. The UK has had 'most-favoured-nation' status since 1815.

Imports and Exports

Total value of imports and exports of goods (in $1bn.):

	Imports	Exports	Trade Balance
2004	1,469·7	814·9	–654·8
2005	1,673·5	901·1	–772·4
2006	1,853·9	1,026·0	–828·0
2007	1,957·0	1,148·2	–808·8
2008	2,201·2	1,287·4	–913·7

In 2007 the USA's merchandise trade deficit fell after six consecutive years in which it had risen, before reaching a record $913·7bn. in 2008. Its deficit with China went up from US$103·1bn. in 2002 to US$256·2bn. in 2007. Its largest surplus is with the Netherlands (US$14·6bn. in 2007). The USA is both the world's leading importer and the leading trading nation, although only the third largest exporter after China and Germany. In 2008 its trade accounted for 13·2% of the world's imports and 8·1% of exports.

Principal imports and exports (in $1m.), 2007:

	Imports	Exports
Agricultural commodities		
Animal feeds	1,008	5,506
Cereal flour	3,774	2,839
Corn	257	10,095
Cotton, raw and linters	14	4,589
Meat and preparations	5,355	9,131
Soybeans	97	10,002
Vegetables and fruits	17,671	12,125
Wheat	501	8,328
Manufactured goods		
Airplane parts	8,434	21,666
Airplanes	13,286	51,854
Alcoholic beverages, distilled	5,521	984
Aluminium	13,947	5,806
Artwork/antiques	8,740	4,335

	Imports	Exports
Basketware, etc.	10,810	6,995
Chemicals – cosmetics	8,872	10,120
Chemicals – dyeing	3,115	5,807
Chemicals – fertilizers	4,981	3,339
Chemicals – inorganic	13,349	10,807
Chemicals – medicinal	53,798	32,755
Chemicals – organic	42,178	33,869
Chemicals – plastics	18,248	37,129
Chemicals – misc.	10,851	20,730
Clothing	81,176	3,209
Computer and telecommunications equipment, etc.	101,602	29,914
Copper	11,532	3,489
Cork, wood, lumber	8,282	4,412
Crude fertilizers	1,854	2,009
Electrical machinery	113,613	81,452
Fish and preparations	13,519	4,044
Footwear	19,408	578
Furniture and bedding	33,853	5,123
Gem diamonds	18,937	5,305
General industrial machinery	63,940	48,641
Glass	2,885	3,350
Gold, non-monetary	4,670	13,344
Iron and steel mill products	30,890	14,018
Jewellery	11,193	4,538
Lighting, plumbing	8,111	2,090
Metal manufactures, misc.	29,929	17,315
Metal ores; scrap	7,549	22,999
Metalworking machinery	7,723	5,351
Nickel	4,903	1,379
Optical goods	4,698	3,210
Paper and paperboard	17,913	13,480
Photographic equipment	2,760	3,612
Plastic articles, misc.	15,348	9,427
Platinum	7,716	1,615
Power generating machinery	50,191	49,933
Printed materials	5,548	6,190
Pulp and waste paper	3,734	6,906
Records/magnetic media	7,382	5,088
Rubber articles, misc.	3,212	1,953
Rubber tyres and tubes	9,380	3,517
Scientific instruments	35,604	42,315
Ships/boats	1,921	3,062
Specialized industrial machinery	35,761	48,357
Televisions, etc.	129,796	24,735
Textile yarn, fabric	22,759	11,861
Toys/games/sporting goods	31,807	5,039
Travel goods	7,625	436
Vehicles	210,431	95,187
Watches/clocks/parts	4,454	392
Wood manufactures	10,390	2,125
Mineral fuel		
Coal	2,451	4,288
Crude oil	245,771	1,015
Liquefied propane/butane	4,024	1,048
Mineral fuel, misc.	3,717	4,708
Natural gas	31,938	3,130
Petroleum preparations	74,108	26,522

Imports and exports by selected countries for the calendar years 2006 and 2007 (in $1m.):

	General imports		*Exports incl. re-exports*	
Country	*2006*	*2007*	*2006*	*2007*
Algeria	15,456	17,816	1,102	1,652
Australia	8,204	8,615	17,779	19,212
Belgium	14,405	15,281	21,340	25,290
Brazil	26,367	25,644	19,231	24,626
Canada	302,438	317,057	230,656	248,888
China	287,774	321,443	55,186	65,236
Colombia	9,266	9,434	6,709	8,558
France	37,040	41,553	24,217	27,413
Germany	89,082	94,164	41,319	49,651
Hong Kong	7,947	7,026	17,776	20,118
India	21,831	24,073	10,056	17,589
Indonesia	13,425	14,301	3,079	4,235
Ireland	28,526	30,445	8,516	9,009
Israel	19,167	20,794	10,965	13,019
Italy	32,655	35,028	12,546	14,150
Japan	148,181	145,463	59,613	62,704
South Korea	45,804	47,562	32,442	34,645
Malaysia	36,533	32,629	12,544	11,680
Mexico	198,253	210,714	133,979	136,092
Netherlands	17,342	18,403	31,129	32,963
Nigeria	27,863	32,770	2,234	2,778
Russia	19,828	19,314	4,701	7,365
Saudi Arabia	31,689	35,626	7,640	10,396
Singapore	17,768	18,394	24,684	26,284
Spain	9,778	10,498	7,426	9,862
Switzerland	14,230	14,760	14,375	17,039
Taiwan	38,212	38,278	23,047	26,309
Thailand	22,466	22,755	8,147	8,455
UK	53,513	56,858	45,410	50,229
Venezuela	37,174	39,910	9,002	10,201

COMMUNICATIONS

Roads

On 31 Dec. 2006 the total public road mileage was 4,016,741 miles (urban, 1,029,366; rural, 2,987,375). Of the urban roads, 14% were state controlled and 85% under local control. 21% of rural roads were controlled by the states, 75% of rural roads were under local control and the remainder were federal park and forest roads. State highway funds were $117,048m. in 2006.

Motor vehicles registered in 2007: 247,265,000, of which 135,933,000 automobiles, 110,497,000 trucks and 834,000 buses. There were 202,810,000 licensed drivers in 2006 and 6,643,000 motorcycle registrations. The average distance travelled by a passenger car in the year 2006 was 12,400 miles. There were 41,259 fatalities in road accidents in 2007, the lowest annual total since 1994, and 37,261 in 2008 (provisional), which would be the lowest annual total since 1961.

Rail

Freight service is provided by 12 major independent railroad companies and several hundred smaller operators. Long-distance passenger trains are run by the National Railroad Passenger Corporation (Amtrak), which is federally assisted. Amtrak was set up in 1971 to maintain a basic network of long-distance passenger trains, and is responsible for almost all non-commuter services. In 2007 the operational Amtrak rail system measured 21,708 miles. Outside the major conurbations, there are almost no regular passenger services other than those of Amtrak, which carried nearly 28·7m. passengers in fiscal year 2008. Passenger revenue for Amtrak in fiscal year 2008 was $1,955m.; revenue passenger miles, 6,160m.

Civil Aviation

The busiest airport in 2008 was Atlanta (Hartsfield International), which handled 90,039,280 passengers. The second busiest was Chicago (O'Hare) with 69,353,876 passengers, followed by Los Angeles International, with 59,497,539 passenger enplanements. As well as being the three busiest airports in the USA for passenger traffic in 2008, they are also three of the six busiest in the world. The six busiest in the world in 2008 were Atlanta, Chicago O'Hare, London Heathrow, Tokyo Haneda, Paris Charles de Gaulle and Los Angeles. New York (John F. Kennedy) was the busiest airport in the USA for international passengers in 2007, with 21,443,000, ahead of Los Angeles International with 16,869,000.

There were 22 airports with more than 10m. enplanements in 2006. These were, in descending order: Atlanta (Hartsfield); Chicago (O'Hare); Dallas/Fort Worth; Los Angeles; Denver; Las

Vegas (McCarran); Phoenix; Houston (George Bush); Detroit (Metropolitan-Wayne County); Minneapolis/St Paul; New York (Newark); Orlando International; Philadelphia; New York (John F. Kennedy); Seattle; Charlotte; San Francisco; Miami; Boston; New York (LaGuardia); Salt Lake City; Baltimore.

The leading airports in 2006 on the basis of aircraft departures completed were Atlanta, Hartsfield International (467,101); Chicago, O'Hare (441,231); Dallas/Fort Worth (334,254).

In 2008 the low-cost carrier Southwest Airlines carried the most scheduled passengers of any airline in the world with 101,921,000 (all on domestic flights), ahead of American Airlines, with 92,772,000 (around 77% on domestic flights), and Delta Air Lines, with 71,843,000 (around 83% on domestic flights). American Airlines carried the most international passengers of any US carrier, with 21,154,000 in 2008 (ranking it eighth in the world for international passengers carried). Delta Air Lines filed for bankruptcy in Sept. 2005, but emerged from bankruptcy protection in April 2007. Delta Air Lines bought Northwest Airlines in Oct. 2008, in the process creating the world's largest airline.

In 2007 US flag carriers in scheduled service enplaned 769·2m. revenue passengers.

Shipping

At the end of 2007 the cargo-carrying US-owned fleet comprised 40,250 vessels, of which 39,695 were US-flag vessels. There were 38,936 US-flag tugs and barges for domestic coastwise, Great Lakes and inland waterway trade, 523 US-flag offshore supply vessels (which service offshore oil exploration and production) and 236 US-flag ocean and Great Lakes self-propelled vessels (10,000 DWT or greater) for US coastwise and international trade (of which 55 tankers, 76 containerships, 37 roll-on/roll-off carriers, 61 dry bulk carriers and seven general cargo carriers). Of the ocean-going fleet, 146 have coastwise trading privileges (Jones Act), which means that they were built or reconstructed in the USA or foreign-built but seized for violation of US law and registered under the US flag.

In 2004 vessels totalling 538,513,000 NRT entered, and 347,086,000 NRT cleared, all US ports. The busiest port is South Louisiana, which handled 225,489,000 tons of cargo in 2006. Other major ports are Houston, New York-New Jersey, Long Beach, Beaumont and Corpus Christi.

Telecommunications

Regional private companies formed from the American Telephone and Telegraph Co. after its dissolution in 1995 ('Baby Bells') operate the telephone and electronic transmission services system at the national and local levels. Telegram services are still available through iTelegram and Globegram. In 2008 there were 154·65m. main telephone lines in operation (49·62 per 100 inhabitants), down from 182·93m. in 2003. There were 270·5m. cellphone subscribers in 2008 (867·9 per 1,000 persons), up from 160·6m. in 2003. In addition the proportion of households that only have cellphones has rapidly increased, to such an extent that by Dec. 2008 the number of cellphone-only households had surpassed landline-only households, with 20% of households being cellphone-only. The leading cellphone operators are Verizon Wireless (with more than 91m. subscribers), AT&T Mobility, Sprint Nextel and T-Mobile. In 2006 there were 240·5m. PCs (805·4 for every 1,000 persons). Internet users numbered 230·6m. in 2008, or 74·0% of the population. Internet commerce, or e-commerce, amounted to $3,333bn. in 2007, the highest in the world. The broadband penetration rate in June 2008 was 25·0 subscribers per 100 inhabitants.

Postal Services

The US Postal Service superseded the Post Office Department on 1 July 1971.

Postal business for the years ended in Sept. included the following items:

	2005	2006	2007
Number of post offices, stations and branches	37,142	36,826	36,721
Operating revenue ($1m.)	69,993	72,817	74,973
Operating expenditures ($1m.)	68,283	71,681	80,105

SOCIAL INSTITUTIONS

Justice

Legal controversies may be decided in two systems of courts: the federal courts, with jurisdiction confined to certain matters enumerated in Article III of the Constitution, and the state courts, with jurisdiction in all other proceedings. The federal courts have jurisdiction exclusive of the state courts in criminal prosecutions for the violation of federal statutes, in civil cases involving the government, in bankruptcy cases and in admiralty proceedings, and have jurisdiction concurrent with the state courts over suits between parties from different states, and certain suits involving questions of federal law.

The highest court is the Supreme Court of the US, which reviews cases from the lower federal courts and certain cases originating in state courts involving questions of federal law. It is the final arbiter of all questions involving federal statutes and the Constitution; and it has the power to invalidate any federal or state law or executive action which it finds repugnant to the Constitution. This court, consisting of nine justices appointed by the President who receive salaries of $213,900 a year (the Chief Justice, $223,500), meets from Oct. until June every year. For the term beginning Oct. 2006 it disposed of 8,923 cases, deciding 78 on their merits. In the remainder of cases it either summarily affirms lower court decisions or declines to review. A few suits, usually brought by state governments, originate in the Supreme Court, but issues of fact are mostly referred to a master.

The US courts of appeals number 13 (in 11 circuits composed of three or more states and one circuit for the District of Columbia and one Court of Appeals for the Federal Circuit); the 179 circuit judges receive salaries of $184,500 a year. Any party to a suit in a lower federal court usually has a right of appeal to one of these courts. In addition, there are direct appeals to these courts from many federal administrative agencies. In the year ending 30 Sept. 2007, 58,410 appeals were filed in the courts of appeals, in addition to 1,406 in the US Court of Appeals for the Federal Circuit.

The trial courts in the federal system are the US district courts, of which there are 94 in the 50 states, one in the District of Columbia and one each in the Commonwealth of Puerto Rico and the Territories of the Virgin Islands, Guam and the Northern Marianas. Each state has at least one US district court, and three states have four apiece. Each district court has from one to 28 judgeships. There are 674 US district judges ($174,000 a year), who received 257,507 civil cases in 2006–07.

In addition to these courts of general jurisdiction, there are special federal courts of limited jurisdiction. The US Court of Federal Claims (16 judges at $174,000 a year) decides claims for money damages against the federal government in a wide variety of matters; the Court of International Trade (13 judges at $174,000) determines controversies concerning the classification and valuation of imported merchandise.

The judges of all these courts are appointed by the President with the approval of the Senate; to assure their independence, they hold office during good behaviour and cannot have their salaries reduced. This does not apply to judges in the Territories, who hold their offices for a term of ten years or to judges of the US Court of Federal Claims. The judges may retire with full pay at the age of 70 years if they have served a period of ten years, or at 65 if they have 15 years of service, but they are subject to call for such judicial duties as they are willing to undertake.

In 2006–07, of the 257,507 civil cases filed in the district courts, 159,916 arose under various federal statutes (such as labour, social security, tax, patent, securities, antitrust and civil rights laws); 61,359 involved personal injury or property damage claims; 33,939 dealt with contracts; and 5,180 were actions concerning real property. In the year ending Sept. 2007, 801,269 cases were filed in the US Bankruptcy Courts (down from 1,112,542 in 2006 and the lowest since 1990), 775,344 of which involved individuals or non-businesses.

In 2000 the number of lawyers in the USA passed the 1m. mark, the equivalent to 363 per 100,000 people, reaching 1·2m. by 2008.

There were 68,413 criminal cases filed for the year ending Sept. 2007 of which 17,046 involved drugs. Among the 74,782 offenders convicted in 2004 in the district courts, 24,472 persons were charged with alleged infractions of drug laws, 14,819 with immigration offences, 12,202 with property offences, 8,082 with weapon offences, 4,398 with public order offences and 2,569 with violent offences. All other people convicted were charged with miscellaneous general offences.

Persons convicted of federal crimes may be fined, released on probation under the supervision of the probation officers of the federal courts, confined in prison, or confined in prison with a period of supervised release to follow, also under the supervision of probation officers of the federal courts. Federal prisoners are confined in 87 institutions incorporating various security levels that are operated by the Bureau of Prisons. On 30 June 2008 the total number of prisoners under the jurisdiction of Federal or State adult correctional authorities was 1,525,428. A record 2,310,984 inmates were held in Federal or State prisons or local jails in June 2008, giving a rate of 762 per 100,000 population (the highest of any country). Although the USA has less than 5% of the world's population it has around 24% of the world's prisoners.

The state courts have jurisdiction over all civil and criminal cases arising under state laws, but decisions of the state courts of last resort as to the validity of treaties or of laws of the USA, or on other questions arising under the Constitution, are subject to review by the Supreme Court of the US. The state court systems are generally similar to the federal system, to the extent that they generally have a number of trial courts and intermediate appellate courts, and a single court of last resort. The highest court in each state is usually called the Supreme Court or Court of Appeals with a Chief Justice and Associate Justices, usually elected but sometimes appointed by the Governor with the advice and consent of the State Senate or other advisory body; they usually hold office for a term of years, but in some instances for life or during good behaviour. The lowest tribunals are usually those of Justices of the Peace; many towns and cities have municipal and police courts, with power to commit for trial in criminal matters and to determine misdemeanours for violation of the municipal ordinances.

There were no executions from 1968 to 1976. The US Supreme Court had held the death penalty, as applied in general criminal statutes, to contravene the eighth and fourteenth amendments of the US constitution, as a cruel and unusual punishment when used so irregularly and rarely as to destroy its deterrent value. The death penalty was reinstated by the Supreme Court in 1976, but has not been authorized in Alaska, the District of Columbia, Hawaii, Iowa, Kansas, Maine, Massachusetts, Michigan, Minnesota, New Jersey, New York, North Dakota, Rhode Island, Vermont, West Virginia and Wisconsin. At 1 July 2009 there were 3,279 (including 60 women) prisoners under sentence of death. 106 people were sentenced to death in 2009, the lowest number since 1976. In 2009 there were 52 executions (a fall from 98 in 1999, though there were only 14 in 1991). From 1977–2009 there were 1,188 executions of which 447 were in Texas and 105 in Virginia. The death penalty for offenders under the age of 18 was abolished in March 2005. For the first time since 1963, there were two executions under federal jurisdiction in 2001. In Sept. 2003 the federal Court of Appeals in San Francisco overturned over 100 death sentences in Arizona, Idaho and Montana on the grounds that judges, not juries, had passed sentence, contravening a Supreme Court ruling of 2002.

There were 16,272 murders in 2008, the lowest total since 2004. The murder rate in 2008 was 5·4 per 100,000 persons, the lowest since 1965 (5·1 per 100,000) and down from 10·5 per 100,000 in 1980. 68% of all murders in 2005 were carried out with firearms.

Education

The adult literacy rate is at least 99%.

Elementary and secondary education is mainly a state responsibility. Each state and the District of Columbia has a system of free public schools, established by law, with courses covering 12 years plus kindergarten. There are three structural patterns in common use; the K8-4 plan, meaning kindergarten plus eight elementary grades followed by four high school grades; the K6-3-3 plan, or kindergarten plus six elementary grades followed by a three-year junior high school and a three-year senior high school; and the K5-3-4 plan, kindergarten plus five elementary grades followed by a three-year middle school and a four-year high school. All plans lead to high-school graduation, usually at age 17 or 18. Vocational education is an integral part of secondary education. Many states also have two-year colleges in which education is provided at a nominal cost. Each state has delegated a large degree of control of the educational programme to local school districts (numbering 14,165 in school year 2005–06), each with a board of education (usually three to nine members) selected locally and serving mostly without pay. The school policies of the local school districts must be in accord with the laws and the regulations of their state Departments of Education. While regulations differ from one jurisdiction to another, in general it may be said that school attendance is compulsory from age seven to 16.

'Charter schools' are legal entities outside the school boards administration. They retain the basics of public school education, but may offer unconventional curricula and hours of attendance. Founders may be parents, teachers, public bodies or commercial firms. Organization and conditions depend upon individual states' legislation. The first charter schools were set up in Minnesota in 1991. By Oct. 2005, 3,780 charter schools were operating in 40 states and Washington, D.C.

Since 1940 data have been tabulated using a definition of 'functionally illiterate', comprising those who had completed fewer than five years of elementary schooling; for persons 25 years of age or over this percentage was 1·5 in March 2007 (for the Black population as a whole it was 1·2%); it was 0·2% for both Whites and Blacks and 3·9% for Hispanics in the 25–29-year-old group. It was reported in March 2007 that 85·7% of all persons 25 years old and over had completed four years of high school or more, and that 28·7% had completed a bachelor's degree or more. In the age group 25 to 29, 87·0% had completed four years of high school or more, and 29·6% had completed a bachelor's degree or more. However, according to a study conducted in 2007 about a third of American fourth graders (aged 9–10) are unable to read at a basic level.

In the fall of 2005, 17,487,475 students (10,797,011 full-time and 10,031,550 women) were enrolled in 4,276 colleges and universities; 2,657,338 were first-time students. It is projected that in 2016 the student population will number 20,442,000.

In 2005–06 expenditure for public elementary and secondary education totalled $521·7bn., comprising $443·4bn. for current operating expenses, $53·0bn. for capital outlay, $15·8bn. for interest on school debt and $9·5bn. for other expenses. The current expenditure per pupil in average daily attendance was $9,100.

In 2006–07 total expenditure on education came to 7·4% of GDP, of which 2·8% (about two-thirds private funding and a third public) was on tertiary education. Spending as a proportion of GDP on tertiary education is the highest in the world, although spending on non-tertiary education is only around the average for an industrialized country.

Estimated total expenditures for private elementary and secondary schools in 2006–07 were about \$46·0bn. In 2006–07 college and university spending totalled about \$373·0bn., of which about \$239·0bn. was spent by institutions under public control. In 2004–05 the federal government contributed about 15% of total revenue for public institutions; state governments, 29%; student tuition and fees, 16%; and all other sources, 40%. Federal support for vocational education in fiscal year 2006 amounted to about \$2·0bn.

Summary of statistics of regular schools (public and private), teachers and pupils for 2005–06 (compiled by the US National Center for Education Statistics):

Schools by level	*Number of schools*	*Teachers (in 1,000)*	*Enrolment (in 1,000)*
Elementary and secondary schools:			
Public	97,382	3,143	49,113
Private	34,681[1]	450	6,111
Higher education:			
Public	1,693	841	13,022
Private	2,583	449	4,466
Total	136,339	4,883	72,712

[1]Data from 2003–04.

In the fall of 2005 there were 15·7 pupils per teacher in public schools in the USA and 13·5 pupils per teacher in private schools.

Most of the private elementary and secondary schools are affiliated with religious denominations. In 2005–06 there were 7,634 Catholic schools with 2,246,000 pupils and 149,000 teachers, and 14,445 schools of other religious affiliations with 1,885,000 pupils and 175,000 teachers.

During the school year 2005–06 high-school graduates numbered about 3,191,000 (of whom about 2,882,000 were from public schools). Institutions of higher education conferred about 1,485,000 bachelor's degrees during the year 2005–06; 713,000 associate's degrees; 594,000 master's degrees; 56,000 doctorates; and 88,000 first professional degrees. In the fiscal year 2006 the US Department of Education provided \$88·2bn. in grants, loans, work-study programmes and other financial assistance to post-secondary students.

During the academic year 2005–06, 564,766 foreign students were enrolled in American colleges and universities. The countries with the largest numbers of students in American colleges were: India, 76,503; China, 62,582; South Korea, 59,022; Japan, 38,712; Canada, 28,202; Taiwan, 27,876.

In 2005, 38,672 US students were enrolled in degree programmes in colleges and universities outside of the USA. The country attracting the most students from the USA was the United Kingdom, with 14,385. In addition to these students, well over 150,000 US college students attend short programmes in other countries every year.

School enrolment, Oct. 2005, embraced 95·4% of the children who were 5 and 6 years old; 98·6% of the children aged 7–13 years; 96·5% of those aged 14–17; 67·6% of those aged 18–19; and 36·1% of those aged 20–24.

The US National Center for Education Statistics estimates the total enrolment in the fall of 2007 at all of the country's elementary, secondary and higher educational institutions (public and private) at 73·7m. (68·7m. in the fall of 2000).

The number of teachers in public and private elementary and secondary schools in 2007 increased slightly to about 3,679,000. The estimated average annual salary of public school teachers was \$49,109 in 2005–06.

Health

Admission to the practice of medicine (for both doctors of medicine and doctors of osteopathic medicine) is controlled in each state by examining boards directly representing the profession and acting with authority conferred by state law. Although there are a number of variations, the usual time now required to complete training is eight years beyond the secondary school with up to three or more years of additional graduate training. Certification as a specialist may require between three and five more years of graduate training plus experience in practice. In Dec. 2006 the estimated number of physicians (MD and DO—in all forms of practice) in the USA, Puerto Rico and outlying US areas was 921,900 (615,400 in 1990 and 467,700 in 1980).

Dental employment in 2006 numbered around 161,000.

Number of hospitals listed by the American Hospital Association in 2006 was 5,747, with 947,000 beds (equivalent to 3·2 beds per 1,000 population). Of the total, 221 hospitals with 46,000 beds were operated by the federal government; 1,119 with 128,000 beds by state and local government; 2,919 with 559,000 beds by non-profit organizations (including church groups); 889 with 115,000 beds were investor-owned. The categories of non-federal hospitals were (2006): 4,927 short-term general and special hospitals with 802,000 beds; 127 non-federal long-term general and special hospitals with 16,000 beds; 462 psychiatric hospitals with 84,000 beds; two tuberculosis hospitals with fewer than 500 beds.

Patient admissions to community hospitals (2006) was 35,377,000; average daily census was 538,400. There were 599·5m. outpatient visits.

Personal health care costs in 2006 totalled \$1,762,037m., distributed as follows: hospital care, \$648,225m.; physicians and clinical services, \$447,571m.; prescription drugs, \$216,705m.; nursing-home care, \$124,911m.; dental services, \$91,498m.; home health care, \$52,705m.; medical durables, \$23,709m.; other personal health care, \$156,714m. Total national health expenditure in 2006 amounted to \$2,105·5bn. In 2007 the USA spent 16·0% of its GDP on health—5% more than any other leading industrialized nation. Public spending on health amounted to 45·4% of total health spending in 2007 (the lowest percentage of any major industrialized nation). In March 2010 President Obama secured the passage of a health care reform package that was expected to increase insurance coverage to a further 32m. citizens. The US Census Bureau had estimated in 2008 that 46·3m. people in America were uninsured.

In 2006, 20·2% of Americans (22·2% of males and 18·5% of females) were smokers, down from a peak of over 40% in 1964. In 2005–06, 34·3% of the adult population were considered obese (having a body mass index over 30), compared to 14·6% in the early 1970s.

Welfare

Social welfare legislation was chiefly the province of the various states until the adoption of the Social Security Act of 14 Aug. 1935. This as amended provides for a federal system of old-age, survivors and disability insurance; health insurance for the aged and disabled; supplemental security income for the aged, blind and disabled; federal state unemployment insurance; and federal grants to states for public assistance (medical assistance for the aged and aid to families with dependent children generally and for maternal and child health and child welfare services).

Legislation of Aug. 1996 began the transfer of aid administration back to the states, restricted the provision of aid to a maximum period of five years, and abolished benefits to immigrants (both legal and illegal) for the first five years of their residence in the USA. The Social Security Administration (formerly part of the Department of Health and Human Services but an independent agency since March 1995) has responsibility for a number of programmes covering retirement, disability,

Medicare, Supplemental Security Income and survivors. The Administration for Children and Families (ACF), an agency of the Department of Health and Human Services, is responsible for federal programmes which promote the economic and social wellbeing of families, children, individuals and communities. ACF has federal responsibility for the following programmes: Temporary Assistance for Needy Families; low income energy assistance; Head Start; child care; child protective services; and a community services block grant. The ACF also has federal responsibility for social service programmes for children, youth, native Americans and persons with developmental disabilities.

The Administration on Aging (AoA), an agency in the US Department of Health and Human Services, is one of the nation's largest providers of home- and community-based care for older persons and their caregivers. Created in 1965 with the passage of the Older Americans Act (OAA), AoA is part of a federal, state, tribal and local partnership called the National Network on Aging. It serves about 9m. older persons and their caregivers, and consists of 56 State Units on Aging, 655 Area Agencies on Aging, 236 Tribal and Native organizations, two organizations that serve Native Hawaiians, 29,000 service providers and thousands of volunteers. These organizations provide assistance and services to older individuals and their families in urban, suburban, and rural areas throughout the USA.

The Centers for Medicare and Medicaid Services (formerly the Health Care Financing Administration), an agency of the Health and Human Services Department, has federal responsibility for health insurance for the aged and disabled. Unemployment insurance is the responsibility of the Department of Labor.

In 2006 an average of 1,807,000 families (4,230,000 recipients) were receiving payments under Temporary Assistance for Needy Families. Total payments under Temporary Assistance for Needy Families were $25,594m. in 2006. The role of Child Support Enforcement is to ensure that children are supported by their parents. Money collected is for children who live with only one parent because of divorce, separation or birth outside marriage. In 2006, $23,933m. was collected on behalf of these children.

The Social Security Act provides for protection against the cost of medical care through Medicare, a two-part programme of health insurance for people age 65 and over, people of any age with permanent kidney failure, and for certain disabled people under age 65 who receive Social Security disability benefits. In 2007 payments totalling $210,502m. were made under the hospital portion of Medicare. During the same period, $224,199m. was paid under the voluntary medical insurance portion of Medicare. Medicare enrolment in July 2007 totalled 44·2m.

In 2009 about 52m. beneficiaries were on the rolls. Full retirement benefits are now payable at age 66, with reduced benefits available as early as age 62. Pensions may also be deferred up to age 70. The age for full retirement benefits is gradually increasing until it reaches 67 in 2027. Claimants must have at least 40 credits of insurance coverage. This equates to ten years of work. In 2008 the average actual retirement age for both males and females was 63·6 years. The maximum monthly payment for claimants retiring at the full retirement age in 2009 was $2,323. The minimum social security benefit was eliminated in Jan. 1982 for all workers becoming eligible for retirement or disability insurance benefits after Dec. 1981. A means-tested supplemental income benefit is available to over-65s and disabled and blind individuals with limited income and limited resources.

Medicaid is a jointly-funded, Federal-State health insurance programme for certain low-income and vulnerable people. It covered 57·6m. individuals in 2005 including children, the aged, blind, and/or disabled, and people who are eligible to receive federally-assisted income maintenance payments.

In Dec. 2006, 7·24m. persons were receiving Supplementary Security Income payments. 1,212,000 old-age persons received $5,116m. in benefits; 73,000 blind people received $409m.; and 5,951,000 disabled people received $33,364m. Payments, including supplemental amounts from various states, totalled $38,889m. in 2006.

In 2007 the food stamp programme helped 26,469,000 persons at a cost of $30,373m.; and 30·5m. persons received help from the national school lunch programme at a cost of $7,706m.

RELIGION

The Yearbook of American and Canadian Churches, published by the National Council of the Churches of Christ in the USA, New York, gave the following figures available from official statisticians of church bodies: the principal religions (numerically or historically) or groups of religious bodies (in 2006 unless otherwise stated) are shown below:

	No. of churches	*Membership (in 1,000)*
Baptist bodies		
Southern Baptist Convention	44,223	16,306
National Baptist Convention, USA, Inc. (2004)	9,000	5,000
National Baptist Convention of America, Inc. (2000)	2,500[1]	3,500
National Missionary Baptist Convention of America (1992)	—	2,500
Progressive National Baptist Convention, Inc. (1995)	2,000	2,500
Churches of Christ	13,000	1,639
American Baptist Churches in the USA	5,659	1,371
Baptist Bible Fellowship International (1997)	4,500	1,200
Christian Churches and Churches of Christ (1988)	5,579	1,072
Christian Church (Disciples of Christ) (2003)	3,717	771
Church of the Nazarene (2000)	5,070	637
Baptist Missionary Association of America (2000)	1,322	295
American Baptist Association (1998)	1,760	275
Conservative Baptist Association of America (2000)	1,191	224
The Episcopal Church	7,095	2,155
Jehovah's Witnesses	12,487	1,070
Latter-day Saints		
Church of Jesus Christ of Latter-day Saints (Mormons)	13,010	5,779
Reorganized Church of Jesus Christ of Latter-day Saints (1999)	1,236	137
Lutheran bodies		
Evangelical Lutheran Church in America	10,470	4,774
The Lutheran Church–Missouri Synod	6,155	2,418
Wisconsin Evangelical Lutheran Synod (2000)	1,241	722
Mennonite churches		
Mennonite Church (2000)	1,063	120
Old Order Amish Church (2000)	1,290	97
Methodist bodies		
United Methodist Church (2005)	34,397	7,995
African Methodist Episcopal Church (1999)	4,174	2,500
African Methodist Episcopal Zion Church	3,310	1,443
Christian Methodist Episcopal Church	3,500	850
Wesleyan Church (USA) (2000)	1,602	123
Pentecostal bodies		
The Church of God in Christ (1991)	15,300	5,500
Assemblies of God	12,311	2,836
Pentecostal Assemblies of the World, Inc.	1,750	1,500
Church of God (Cleveland, Tenn.)	6,569	1,033
Presbyterian bodies		
Presbyterian Church (USA)	11,903	3,026
Presbyterian Church in America (2000)	1,458	306
Reformed Churches		
United Church of Christ	5,452	1,219
The Salvation Army (2000)	1,332	415
Reformed Church in America (2000)	898	289
Christian Reformed Church in North America (1999)	739	197
Seventh-day Adventist Church	4,820	981
Roman Catholic Church[2]	19,044	67,515

	No. of churches	Membership (in 1,000)
Orthodox Churches		
Greek Orthodox Archdiocese of America	560	1,500
Orthodox Church in America (2004)	737	1,064
Oriental Orthodox Churches		
Armenian Apostolic Church, Diocese of America (1991)	72	414
Armenian Apostolic Church of America (2000)	36	360
Coptic Orthodox Church (2000)	100	300
Non-Christian Religions		
Judaism (2001)	—	2,831
Islam (2001)	—	1,104
Buddhism (2001)	—	1,082
Hinduism (2001)	—	766

[1]1987. [2]In Feb. 2010 there were 16 cardinals.

CULTURE

World Heritage Sites

There are 20 sites under American jurisdiction that appear on the UNESCO World Heritage List. They are (with year entered on list): Mesa Verde National Park, Colorado (1978); Yellowstone National Park, Wyoming/Idaho/Montana (1978); Everglades National Park, Florida (1979); Grand Canyon National Park, Arizona (1979); Independence Hall, Pennsylvania (1979); Redwood National and State Parks, California (1980); Mammoth Cave National Park, Kentucky (1981); Olympic National Park, Washington State (1981); Cahokia Mounds State Historic Site, Illinois (1982); Great Smoky Mountains National Park, North Carolina/Tennessee (1983); San Juan National Historic Site and La Fortaleza, Puerto Rico (1983); the Statue of Liberty, New York (1984); Yosemite National Park, California (1984); Monticello and the University of Virginia, Charlottesville, Virginia (1987); Chaco Culture National Historic Park, New Mexico (1987); Hawaii Volcanoes National Park, including Mauna Loa, Hawaii (1987); Pueblo de Taos, New Mexico (1992); Carlsbad Caverns National Park, New Mexico (1995).

Two UNESCO World Heritage sites fall under joint US and Canadian jurisdiction: Kluane/Wrangell-St Elias/Glacier Bay/Tatshenshini-Alsek (1979, 1992 and 1994), parks in Alaska, the Yukon Territory and British Columbia; Waterton Glacier International Peace Park (1995), in Montana and Alberta.

Broadcasting

The licensing agency for broadcasting stations is the Federal Communications Commission, an independent federal body composed of five Commissioners appointed by the President. Its regulatory activities comprise: allocation of spectrum space; consideration of applications to operate individual stations; and regulation of their operations. In 2007 there were 11,066 commercial radio stations, 1,379 commercial TV stations, 380 non-commercial TV stations and 6,101 cable TV systems. There are five national TV networks (three commercial; colour by NTSC) with 46 national cable networks. All major cities have network affiliates and additional commercial stations.

Legislation deregulated the media and telecommunications from 1999 while preserving safeguards against over-concentration of individual ownership: a single company may not control a network reaching more than 35% of TV viewers, or produce a newspaper and a television service in the same market. Local companies are permitted to operate long-distance telephone services and also cable TV services.

Broadcasting to countries abroad is conducted by The Voice of America, which functions under a seven-member council nominated by the President and reviewed by Congress. Voice of America has an annual audience of 94m. and broadcasts in over 50 languages.

In 2006, 110·2m. households were equipped with TVs (94·7% of all households). In 2005 there were 65·4m. cable TV subscribers.

Cinema

In 2008 there were 40,194 screens, including 718 drive-ins. Attendance in 2008 totalled 1·36bn.; gross box office receipts came to $9·79bn. 610 new films were released in 2008.

Press

In 2007 there were 1,422 daily newspapers with a combined daily circulation of 50·7m., the fourth highest in the world behind China, India and Japan. There were 867 morning papers and 565 evening papers, plus 907 Sunday papers (circulation, 51·2m.). Unlike China and India, where circulation is rising, in the USA it has fallen since 1985, when daily circulation was 62·8m. The most widely read newspapers are *USA Today* (average daily circulation in the period April–Sept. 2008 of 2·3m.), followed by the *Wall Street Journal* (2·0m.) and the *New York Times* (1·0m.). According to research carried out by the Pew Research Centre, in 2008 for the first time more Americans obtained national and international news from the internet than from newspapers.

Total book sales in 2007 reached a record high of 407,646, largely as a result of print on demand and short run book sales which totalled 123,276 (up from 21,936 in 2006). Of the 284,370 traditional print books published, 53,590 were fiction, 31,009 juvenile, 24,546 sociology and economics and 19,540 religion. However, US book sales in 2008 fell by 2·8% from 2007 to $24,255m.

Tourism

In 2007 the USA received 55,986,000 foreign visitors (51,063,000 in 2006), of whom 17,761,000 were from Canada and 14,333,000 from Mexico. 20% of all tourists were from Europe. Only France and Spain received more tourists than the USA in 2007.

In 2006 visitors to the USA spent approximately $85·72bn. In 2006 the USA had the highest annual revenue from tourists of any country (Spain, which received the second most, had US$51bn.). Expenditure by US travellers in foreign countries for 2006 was an estimated $72,104m.

Festivals

There are major opera festivals at Cooperstown (Glimmerglass), New York State (July–Aug.); Santa Fe, New Mexico (June–Aug.); and Seattle, Washington (Aug.). Among the many famous film festivals are the Sundance Film Festival in Jan. and the New York Film Festival in late Sept./early Oct.

Museums and Galleries

Among the most famous museums are the National Gallery in Washington, D.C., the Museum of Fine Arts in Boston, the Metropolitan Museum, the Guggenheim Museum, and the Museum of Modern Art, all in New York, and the Museum of Art in Philadelphia. In 2007, 12·2% of US adults visited a museum at least once and 3·9% an art gallery or exhibition.

DIPLOMATIC REPRESENTATIVES

Of the USA in the United Kingdom (24 Grosvenor Sq., London, W1A 1AE)
Ambassador: Louis B. Susman.

Of the United Kingdom in the USA (3100 Massachusetts Ave., NW, Washington, D.C., 20008)
Ambassador: Sir Nigel Sheinwald, KCMG.

Of the United States to the United Nations
Ambassador: Susan Rice.

Of the United States to the European Union
Ambassador: Kristen L. Silverberg.

FURTHER READING

OFFICIAL STATISTICAL INFORMATION

The Office of Management and Budget, Washington, D.C., 20503 is part of the Executive Office of the President; it is responsible for co-ordinating all the statistical work of the different Federal government agencies. The Office does not collect or publish data itself. The main statistical agencies are as follows:

(1) Data User Services Division, Bureau of the Census, Department of Commerce, Washington, D.C., 20233. Responsible for decennial censuses of population and housing, quinquennial census of agriculture, manufactures and business; current statistics on population and the labour force, manufacturing activity and commodity production, trade and services, foreign trade, state and local government finances and operations. (*Statistical Abstract of the United States*, annual, and others).

(2) Bureau of Labor Statistics, Department of Labor, 441 G Street NW, Washington, D.C., 20212. (*Monthly Labor Review* and others).

(3) Information Division, Economic Research Service, Department of Agriculture, Washington, D.C., 20250. (*Agricultural Statistics*, annual, and others).

(4) National Center for Health Statistics, Department of Health and Human Services, 3700 East-West Highway, Hyattsville, MD 20782. (*Vital Statistics of the United States*, monthly and annual, and others).

(5) Bureau of Mines Office of Technical Information, Department of the Interior, Washington, D.C., 20241. (*Minerals Yearbook*, annual, and others).

(6) Office of Energy Information Services, Energy Information Administration, Department of Energy, Washington, D.C., 20461.

(7) Statistical Publications, Department of Commerce, Room 5062 Main Commerce, 14th St and Constitution Avenue NW, Washington, D.C., 20230; the Department's Bureau of Economic Analysis and its Office of Industry and Trade Information are the main collectors of data.

(8) Center for Education Statistics, Department of Education, 555 New Jersey Avenue NW, Washington, D.C., 20208.

(9) Public Correspondence Division, Office of the Assistant Secretary of Defense (Public Affairs P.C.), The Pentagon, Washington, D.C., 20301-1400.

(10) Bureau of Justice Statistics, Department of Justice, 633 Indiana Avenue NW, Washington, D.C., 20531.

(11) Public Inquiry, APA 200, Federal Aviation Administration, Department of Transportation, 800 Independence Avenue SW, Washington, D.C., 20591.

(12) Office of Public Affairs, Federal Highway Administration, Department of Transportation, 400 7th St. SW, Washington, D.C., 20590.

(13) Statistics Division, Internal Revenue Service, Department of the Treasury, 1201 E St. NW, Washington, D.C., 20224.

Statistics on the economy are also published by the Division of Research and Statistics, Federal Reserve Board, Washington, D.C., 20551; the Congressional Joint Committee on the Economy, Capitol; the Office of the Secretary, Department of the Treasury, 1500 Pennsylvania Avenue NW, Washington, D.C., 20220.

OTHER OFFICIAL PUBLICATIONS

Economic Report of the President. Annual. Bureau of the Census. *Statistical Abstract of the United States*. Annual. *Historical Statistics of the United States, Colonial Times to 1970*.

United States Government Manual. Annual.

The official publications of the USA are issued by the US Government Printing Office and are distributed by the Superintendent of Documents, who issued in 1940 a cumulative *Catalogue of Public Documents of the Congress and of All Departments of the Government of the United States*. This *Catalog* is kept up to date by *United States Government Publications, Monthly Catalog* with annual index and supplemented by *Price Lists*. Each *Price List* is devoted to a special subject or type of material.

Treaties and other International Acts of the United States of America (Edited by Hunter Miller), 8 vols. 1929–48. This edition stops in 1863. It may be supplemented by *Treaties, Conventions, International Acts, Protocols and Agreements Between the US and Other Powers, 1776–1937* (Edited by William M. Malloy and others). 4 vols. 1909–38. A new Treaty Series, *US Treaties and Other International Agreements*, was started in 1950.

Writings on American History. Washington, annual from 1902 (except 1904–5 and 1941–47).

NON-OFFICIAL PUBLICATIONS

The Cambridge Economic History of the United States. vol. 1. 1996; vol. 2. 2000; vol. 3. 2000

Bacevich, Andrew J., *American Empire: The Realities and Consequences of US Diplomacy*. 2002

Brogan, H., *The Longman History of the United States of America*. 2nd ed. 1999

Daalder, Ivo H. and Lindsay, James M., *America Unbound: the Bush Revolution in Foreign Policy*. 2003

Duncan, Russell and Goddard, Joe, *Contemporary America*. 3rd ed. 2009

Fawcett, E. and Thomas, T., *America and the Americans*. 1983

Foner, E. and Garraty, J. A. (eds.) *The Reader's Companion to American History*. 1992

Haass, Richard, *The Reluctant Sheriff: The United States After the Cold War*. 1998

Heilemann, John and Halperin, Mark, *Game Change: Obama and the Clintons, McCain and Palin, and the Race of a Lifetime*. 2010

Jenkins, Philip, *A History of the United States*. 3rd ed. 2007

Jennings, F., *The Creation of America*. 2000

Jentleson, B. W. and Paterson, T. G. (eds.) *Encyclopedia of US Foreign Relations*. 4 vols. 1997

Little, Douglas, *American Orientalism: The United States and the Middle East since 1945*. 2002

Lord, C. L. and E. H., *Historical Atlas of the US*. Rev. ed. 1969

Merriam, L. A. and Oberly, J. (eds.) *United States History: an Annotated Bibliography*. 1995

Morison, S. E. with Commager, H. S., *The Growth of the American Republic*. 2 vols. 5th ed. 1962–63

Norton, M. B., *People and Nation: the History of the United States*. 4th ed. 2 vols. 1994

Peele, Gillian, Bailey, Christopher, J., Cain, Bruce and Peters, B. Guy (eds.) *Developments in American Politics 5*. 2006

Pfucha, F. P., *Handbook for Research in American History: a Guide to Bibliographies and Other Reference Works*. 2nd ed. 1994

Prestowitz, Clyde, *Rogue Nation: American Unilateralism and the Failure of Good Intentions*. 2003

Who's Who in America. Annual

Zunz, Oliver, *Why the American Century?* 1999

National library: The Library of Congress, Independence Ave. SE, Washington, D.C., 20540. *Librarian*: James H. Billington.

National statistical office: Bureau of the Census, Washington, D.C., 20233. *Director*: Robert Groves.

Website: http://www.census.gov

STATES AND TERRITORIES

GENERAL DETAILS

Against the names of the Governors, Lieut.-Governors and the Secretaries of State, (D.) stands for Democrat and (R.) for Republican.

See also Local Government on page 1355.

FURTHER READING

Official publications of the various states and insular possessions are listed in the *Monthly Check-List of State Publications*, issued by the Library of Congress since 1910.

The Book of the States. Biennial. 1953 ff.

State Government Finances. Annual. 1966 ff.

Bureau of the Census. *State and Metropolitan Area Data Book*. Irregular.—*County and City Data Book*. Irregular.

Hill, K. Q., *Democracy in the 50 States*. 1995

Alabama

KEY HISTORICAL EVENTS

The early European explorers were Spanish, but the first permanent European settlement was French, as part of French Louisiana after 1699. During the 17th and 18th centuries the British, Spanish and French all fought for control of the territory; it passed to Britain in 1763 and thence to the USA in 1783, except for a Spanish enclave on Mobile Bay, which lasted until 1813. Alabama was organized as a Territory in 1817 and was admitted to the Union as a state on 14 Dec. 1819.

The economy was then based on cotton, grown in white-owned plantations by black slave labour imported since 1719.

Alabama seceded from the Union at the beginning of the Civil War (1861) and joined the Confederate States of America; its capital Montgomery became the Confederate capital. After the defeat of the Confederacy the state was readmitted to the Union in 1878. Attempts made during the reconstruction period to find a role for the newly freed black slaves—who made up about 50% of the population—largely failed, and when whites regained political control in the 1870s a strict policy of segregation came into force. At the same time Birmingham began to develop as an important centre of iron- and steel-making. Most of the state was still rural. In 1915 a boll-weevil epidemic attacked the cotton and forced diversification into other farm produce. More industries developed from the power schemes of the Tennessee Valley Authority in the 1930s. The black population remained mainly rural, poor and without political power, until the 1960s when confrontations on the issue of civil rights produced reforms.

TERRITORY AND POPULATION

Alabama is bounded in the north by Tennessee, east by Georgia, south by Florida and the Gulf of Mexico and west by Mississippi. Land area, 50,744 sq. miles (131,426 sq. km). Census population, 1 April 2000, 4,447,100 (55·4% urban), an increase of 10·1% since 1990; July 2009 estimate, 4,708,708.

Population in five census years was:

	White	*Black*	*Indian*	*Asiatic*	*Total*	*Per sq. mile*
1930	1,700,844	944,834	465	105	2,646,248	51·3
			All others			
1970	2,533,831	903,467	6,867		3,444,165	66·7
1980	2,872,621	996,335	24,932		3,893,888	74·9
1990	2,975,797	1,020,705	44,085		4,040,587	79·6
2000	3,162,808	1,155,930	128,362		4,447,100	87·6

Of the total population in 2000, 2,300,596 were female, 3,323,678 were 18 years old or older and 2,462,673 were urban. In 2000 the Hispanic population was 75,830, up from 24,629 in 1990 (an increase of 207·9%).

The large cities (2000 census) were: Birmingham, 242,820 (metropolitan area, 921,106); Montgomery (the capital), 201,568 (333,055); Mobile, 198,905 (540,258); Huntsville, 158,216 (342,376); Tuscaloosa, 77,906 (164,875).

SOCIAL STATISTICS

Births, 2007 (provisional), 65,219 (14·1 per 1,000 population); deaths, 2006, 46,977 (10·2). Infant deaths, 2006, 9·0 per 1,000 live births. 2006: marriages, 39,600 (8·6 per 1,000 population); divorces and annulments, 22,100 (4·8).

CLIMATE

Birmingham, Jan. 46°F (7·8°C), July 80°F (26·7°C). Annual rainfall 54" (1,372 mm). Mobile, Jan. 52°F (11·1°C), July 82°F (27·8°C). Annual rainfall 62" (1,575 mm). Montgomery, Jan. 49°F (9·4°C), July 81°F (27·2°C). Annual rainfall 52" (1,321 mm). The growing season ranges from 190 days (north) to 270 days (south). Alabama belongs to the Gulf Coast climate zone (*see* UNITED STATES: Climate).

CONSTITUTION AND GOVERNMENT

The current constitution dates from 1901; it has had 742 amendments (as at April 2005). The legislature consists of a Senate of 35 members and a House of Representatives of 105 members, all elected for four years. The Governor and Lieut.-Governor are elected for four years.

For the 111th Congress, which convened in Jan. 2009, Alabama sends seven members to the House of Representatives. It is represented in the Senate by Richard Shelby (D. 1987–94; R. 1994–2011) and Jeff Sessions (R. 1997–2015).

Applicants for registration must take an oath of allegiance to the United States and fill out an application showing evidence that they meet State voter registration requirements.

Montgomery is the capital.

RECENT ELECTIONS

In the 2008 presidential elections John McCain won Alabama with 60·3% of the vote (George W. Bush won in 2004).

CURRENT ADMINISTRATION

Governor: Bob Riley (R.), 2007–11 (salary: $112,895).

Lieut.-Governor: Jim Folsom, Jr (D.), 2007–11 ($69,030).

Secretary of State: Beth Chapman (R.), 2007–11 ($79,580).

Government Website: http://www.alabama.gov

ECONOMY

Per capita personal income (2008) was $33,768.

Budget

In 2008 total state revenue was $18,354m. Total expenditure was $24,893m. (education, $10,658m.; public welfare, $4,582m.; hospitals, $1,808m.; highways, $1,373m.; health, $699m.) Outstanding debt in 2008, $8,472m.

Performance

Gross Domestic Product by state was $170,014m. in 2008 (provisional), ranking Alabama 25th in the United States.

ENERGY AND NATURAL RESOURCES

Oil and Gas

In 2005 Alabama produced 7·9m. bbls of crude petroleum and 297bn. cu. ft of natural gas.

Water

The total area covered by water is approximately 1,675 sq. miles.

Minerals

Principal minerals, 2005–06 (in net 1,000 tons): limestone, 51,127; coal, 19,270; sand and gravel, 12,925. Value of non-fuel mineral production in 2006 was $1,360m.

Agriculture

The number of farms in 2002 was 47,000, covering 8·9m. acres; the average farm had 189 acres and was valued at $1,698 per acre.

Cash receipts from farm marketings, 2006: crops, $696m.; livestock and poultry products, $3,043m.; total, $3,739m. The net farm income in 2006 was $1,580m. Principal sources: broilers, cattle and calves, eggs, hogs, dairy products, greenhouses and nursery products, peanuts, soybeans, cotton and vegetables. In 2002 broilers accounted for the largest percentage of cash receipts from farm marketings; cattle and calves were second, eggs third, cotton fourth.

Forestry

Alabama had 22·69m. acres of forested land in 2007 of which 746,000 acres were national forest. Harvest volumes in 2004, 334·15m. cu. ft pine saw timber, 86·81m. cu. ft hardwood saw timber, 839·11m. cu. ft pulp wood and 8·83m. cu. ft poles. Total harvest, 2004, was 1,268·90m. cu. ft. Georgia is the only state with a larger annual harvest. The estimated delivered timber value of forest products in 2004 was $1·6bn.

INDUSTRY

In 2005 the state's 4,953 manufacturing establishments had 282,000 employees, earning $10,526m. Total value added by manufacturing in 2006 was $40,334m. Alabama is both an industrial and service-oriented state. The chief industries are lumber and wood products, food and kindred products, textiles and apparel, non-electrical machinery, transportation equipment and primary metals.

Labour

In 2007, 2,006,000 were employed in non-agricultural sectors, of whom 396,000 were in trade, transportation and utilities; 376,000 in government; 297,000 in manufacturing; 221,000 in professional and business services; 209,000 in education and health services. In 2007 the unemployment rate was 4·0%.

COMMUNICATIONS

Roads

Total road length in 2007 was 97,323 miles, comprising 75,299 miles of rural road and 22,024 miles of urban road. Registered motor vehicles numbered 4,677,771.

Rail

In 2001 the railroads had a length of 4,728 miles including side and yard tracks.

Civil Aviation

In 2005 there were 97 public-use airports. There were 2,795,014 passenger enplanements in 2007.

Shipping

There are 1,600 miles of navigable inland water and 50 miles of Gulf Coast. The only deep-water port is Mobile, with a large ocean-going trade; total tonnage (2003), 50·2m. tons. The Alabama State Docks also operates a system of ten inland docks; there are several privately run inland docks.

SOCIAL INSTITUTIONS

Justice

In Dec. 2008 the prison population totalled 30,508. Following the reinstatement of the death penalty by the US Supreme Court in 1976 death sentences have been awarded since 1983. There were six executions in 2009 (none in 2008).

In 41 counties the sale of alcoholic beverages is permitted, and in 26 counties it is prohibited; but it is permitted in eight cities within those 26 counties. Draught beverages are permitted in 22 counties.

Education

In 2004–05 there were 1,554 public elementary and high schools with 51,594 teachers and 730,140 students enrolled in grades K–12. Average public school teacher salary in 2003–04 was $38,325. Spending per student in 2002–03 was $6,300.

As of fall 2005 there were 66 degree-granting institutions (39 public and 27 private) with 256,389 enrolled students. Enrolment for four-year courses at Auburn University totalled 23,333, the University of Alabama at Tuscaloosa 21,793, University of Alabama at Birmingham 16,572 and Troy University 14,957.

Health

In 2006 there were 109 community hospitals with 15,600 beds. A total of 683,000 patients were admitted during the year.

Welfare

Medicare enrolment in July 2004 totalled 733,090. In fiscal year 2006 a total of 844,988 people in Alabama received Medicaid. In Dec. 2008 there were 952,511 Old-Age, Survivors, and Disability Insurance (OASDI) beneficiaries. A total of 43,347 people were receiving payments under Temporary Assistance for Needy Families (TANF) in Dec. 2008.

RELIGION

Membership in selected religious bodies (in 2000): Southern Baptist Convention (1,380,121), United Methodist Church (327,734), Roman Catholic (150,647), Churches of Christ (119,049), Church of God (68,766), Assemblies of God (59,970). There are also large numbers of Black Baptists and members of the African Methodist Episcopal Zion Church.

CULTURE

Tourism

In 2004, 61,000 overseas visitors (excluding those from Mexico and Canada) visited Alabama.

FURTHER READING

Alabama Official and Statistical Register. Quadrennial
Alabama County Data Book. Annual
Directory of Health Care Facilities.
Economic Abstract of Alabama. 2000

Alaska

KEY HISTORICAL EVENTS

Discovered in 1741 by Vitus Bering, Alaska's first settlement, on Kodiak Island, was in 1784. The area known as Russian America with its capital (1806) at Sitka was ruled by a Russo-American fur company and vaguely claimed as a Russian colony. Alaska was purchased by the United States from Russia under the treaty of 30 March 1867 for $7·2m. Settlement was boosted by gold workers in the 1880s. In 1884 Alaska became a 'district' governed by the code of the state of Oregon. By Act of Congress approved 24 Aug. 1912 Alaska became an incorporated Territory; its first legislature in 1913 granted votes to women, seven years in advance of the Constitutional Amendment.

During the Second World War the Federal government acquired large areas for defence purposes and for the construction of the strategic Alaska Highway. In the 1950s oil was found. Alaska became the 49th state of the Union on 3 Jan. 1959. In the 1970s new oilfields were discovered and the Trans-Alaska pipeline was opened in 1977. The state obtained most of its income from petroleum by 1985.

Questions of land-use predominate; there are large areas with valuable mineral resources, other large areas held for the native peoples and some still held by the Federal government. The population increased by over 400% between 1940 and 1980.

TERRITORY AND POPULATION

Alaska is bounded north by the Beaufort Sea, west and south by the Pacific and east by Canada. The total area is 663,267 sq. miles (1,717,854 sq. km), making it the largest state of the USA; 571,951 sq. miles (1,481,346 sq. km) are land and 91,316 sq. miles (236,507 sq. km) are water. It is also the least densely populated state. Census population, 1 April 2000, was 626,932, an increase of 14·0% over 1990; July 2009 estimate, 698,473.

Population in five census years was:

	White	*Black*	*All Others*	*Total*	*Per sq. mile*
1950	92,808	—	35,835	128,643	0·23
1970	236,767	8,911	54,704	300,382	0·53
1980	309,728	13,643	78,480	401,851	1·00
1990	415,492	22,451	112,100	550,043	1·00
2000	434,534	21,787	170,611	626,932	1·10

Of the total population in 2000, 324,112 were male, 436,215 were 18 years old or older and 411,257 were urban. Alaska's Hispanic population was 24,795 in 2000, up from 17,803 in 1990. As of July 2003, 19% of Alaska's population was identified as Alaska Native or American Indian.

The largest county equivalent and city is in the borough of Anchorage, which had a 2000 census population of 260,283.

Census populations of the other 14 county equivalents, 2000: Fairbanks North Star, 82,840; Matanuska-Susitna, 59,322; Kenai Peninsula, 49,691; Juneau, 30,711; Bethel, 16,006; Ketchikan Gateway, 14,070; Kodiak Island, 13,913; Valdez-Cordova, 10,195; Nome, 9,196; Sitka, 8,835; North Slope, 7,385; Northwest Arctic, 7,208; Wade Hampton, 7,028; Wrangell-Petersburg, 6,684. Largest incorporated places in 2000 were: Anchorage, 260,683; Juneau, 30,711; Fairbanks, 30,224; Sitka, 8,335; Ketchikan, 7,922; Kenai, 6,942; Kodiak, 6,334; Bethel, 5,471; Wasilla, 5,469; Barrow, 4,581.

SOCIAL STATISTICS

Births, 2007 (provisional), 11,060 (16·2 per 1,000 population); deaths, 2006, 3,354 (5·0—the lowest rate in any US state). Infant mortality, 2006, 6·9 per 1,000 live births. 2006: marriages, 5,300 (7·8 per 1,000 population); divorces and annulments, 3,000 (4·4).

CLIMATE

Anchorage, Jan. 12°F (–11·1°C), July 57°F (13·9°C). Annual rainfall 15" (371 mm). Fairbanks, Jan. –11°F (–23·9°C), July 60°F (15·6°C). Annual rainfall 12" (300 mm). Sitka, Jan. 33°F (0·6°C), July 55°F (12·8°C). Annual rainfall 87" (2,175 mm). Alaska belongs to the Pacific Coast climate zone (*see* UNITED STATES: Climate).

CONSTITUTION AND GOVERNMENT

The state has the right to select 103·55m. acres of vacant and unappropriated public lands in order to establish 'a tax basis'; it can open these lands to prospectors for minerals, and the state is to derive the principal advantage in all gains resulting from the discovery of minerals. In addition, certain federally administered lands reserved for conservation of fisheries and wild life have been transferred to the state. Special provision is made for federal control of land for defence in areas of high strategic importance.

The constitution of Alaska was adopted by public vote, 24 April 1956. The state legislature consists of a Senate of 20 members (elected for four years) and a House of Representatives of 40 members (elected for two years).

For the 111th Congress, which convened in Jan. 2009, Alaska sends one member to the House of Representatives. It is represented in the Senate by Lisa Murkowski (R. 2002–11) and Mark Begich (D. 2009–15). The franchise may be exercised by all citizens over 18.

The capital is Juneau.

RECENT ELECTIONS

In the 2008 presidential elections John McCain won Alaska with 59·4% of the vote (George W. Bush won in 2004).

CURRENT ADMINISTRATION

Governor: Sean R. Parnell (R.), July 2009–Dec. 2010 (salary: $125,000).

Lieut.-Governor: Craig E. Campbell (R.), July 2009–Dec. 2010 ($100,000).

Government Website: http://www.alaska.gov

ECONOMY

Per capita personal income (2008) was $44,039.

Budget

In 2008 total state revenue was $16,028m. Total expenditure was $10,116m. (education, $2,165m.; public welfare, $1,477m.; highways, $1,316m.; government administration, $575m.; natural resources, $285m.) Outstanding debt in 2008, $6,492m.

Performance

2008 Gross Domestic Product by state was $47,912m. (provisional), ranking Alaska 44th in the United States.

ENERGY AND NATURAL RESOURCES

Oil and Gas

Alaska ranks second behind Texas among the leading oil producers in the USA, with 15% of the national total. Commercial production of crude petroleum began in 1959 and by 1961 had become the most important mineral by value. Production in 2006 totalled 270m. bbls (value, $15,380m.). Proven reserves in 2006 were 3,879m. bbls. Alaska's crude petroleum production in 2006 was the second largest of any state, after that of California. Oil comes mainly from Prudhoe Bay, the Kuparuk River field and several Cook Inlet fields. Oil from the Prudhoe Bay Arctic field is now carried by the Trans-Alaska pipeline to Prince William Sound on the south coast, where a tanker terminal has been built at Valdez.

Natural gas marketed production, 2006, 445bn. cu. ft, with reserves of 10,245bn. cu. ft.

Water

The total area covered by water is approximately 91,316 sq. miles.

Minerals

Estimated value of production, 2003, in $1,000: zinc, 486,916; gold, 191,986; industrial minerals (including sand, gravel and building stone), 100,000; silver, 90,773; lead, 70,094; coal, 37,975; peat, 175. Total 2003 value, $980·3m. Value of non-fuel mineral production in 2006 was $3,010m.

Agriculture

In some parts of the state the climate during the brief spring and summer (about 100 days in major areas and 152 days in the southeastern coastal area) is suitable for agricultural operations, thanks to the long hours of sunlight, but Alaska is a food-importing area. In 2002 there were 590 farms covering a total of 920,000 acres. The average farm had 1,559 acres in 2002 and was valued at $367 per acre.

Farm income, 2006: crops, $25m.; livestock and products, $39m. The net farm income in 2006 was $20m. Principal sources: greenhouse products, hay, dairy products and potatoes.

In 2002 there were 12,609 cattle and calves, 530 sheep and lambs, 1,200 hogs and pigs, and 2,900 poultry. There were about 15,000 reindeer in Alaska in 2002. Sales of reindeer meat and by-products in 2002 were valued at $453,000.

Forestry

Of the 126·87m. forested acres of Alaska (the highest acreage of any state), 10·46m. acres are national forest land. The interior forest covers 115m. acres; more than 13m. acres are considered commercial forest, of which 3·4m. acres are in designated parks or wilderness and unavailable for harvest. The coastal rain forests provide the bulk of commercial timber volume; of their 13·6m. acres, 7·6m. acres support commercial stands, of which 1·9m. acres are in parks or wilderness and unavailable for harvest. In 2006 timber removals were 66m. cu. ft (59m. cu. ft softwoods and 7m. cu. ft hardwoods).

In 2008 there were 704 designated wilderness areas throughout the USA, covering a total of 107·4m. acres (43·5m. ha.). More than 53% of the system is in Alaska (57·4m. acres or 23·2m. ha.).

Fisheries

In 2002 commercial fishing landed 5,066m. lb of fish and shellfish at a value of $811·5m. The most important species are salmon, crab, herring, halibut and pollock.

INDUSTRY

In 2005 the state's 514 manufacturing establishments had 10,000 employees, earning $403m. Total value added by manufacturing in 2006 was $1,659m. The largest manufacturing sectors are wood processing, seafood products and printing and publishing.

Labour

Total non-agricultural employment, 2007: 318,000. Employees by branch, 2007: government, 82,000; trade, transportation and utilities, 64,000; education and health services, 37,000; leisure and hospitality, 32,000; professional and business services, 25,000. The unemployment rate in 2007 was 6·2%.

COMMUNICATIONS

Roads

Alaska's highway and road system, 2007, totalled 14,438 miles comprising 2,357 miles of urban road and 12,081 miles of rural road. Registered motor vehicles numbered 680,141.

The Alaska Highway extends 1,523 miles from Dawson Creek, British Columbia, to Fairbanks, Alaska. It was built by the US Army in 1942, at a cost of $138m. The greater portion of it, because it lies in Canada, is maintained by Canada.

Rail

There is a railroad from Skagway to the town of Whitehorse, the White Pass and Yukon route, in the Canadian Yukon region (this service operates seasonally, although only the section between Skagway and Carcross is in service). The government-owned Alaska Railroad runs from Seward to Fairbanks. This is a freight service with only occasional passenger use. In 2003 there were 466 miles of main line and 59 miles of branch line.

Civil Aviation

Alaska's largest international airports are Anchorage and Fairbanks. In 2008 Alaska Airlines carried 16·8m. passengers and flew to 59 destinations. There were 4,560,483 passenger enplanements statewide in 2007. General aviation aircraft in the state per 1,000 population is about ten times the US average.

Shipping

Regular shipping services to and from the USA are furnished by two steamship and several barge lines operating out of Seattle and other Pacific coast ports. A Canadian company also furnishes a regular service from Vancouver, BC. Anchorage is the main port.

A 1,435 nautical-mile ferry system for motor cars and passengers (the 'Alaska Marine Highway') operates from Bellingham, Washington and Prince Rupert (British Columbia) to Juneau, Haines (for access to the Alaska Highway) and Skagway. A second system extends throughout the south-central region of Alaska linking the Cook Inlet area with Kodiak Island and Prince William Sound.

SOCIAL INSTITUTIONS

Justice

The death penalty was abolished in Alaska in 1957. In Dec. 2008 the jail and prison population totalled 5,014.

Education

In 2004–05 there were 520 elementary and secondary schools with 132,970 pupils and 7,756 teachers; total expenditure on public schools in 2003–04 was $1,621m. Average teacher salary in 2003–04 was $51,736.

There are eight higher education institutions (five public and three private). The University of Alaska (founded in 1922) had 16,412 students at fall 2005 and comprised eight teaching units at the main campus in Anchorage.

Health

In 2006 there were 22 community hospitals with 1,500 beds. A total of 52,000 patients were admitted during the year.

Welfare

Medicare enrolment in July 2004 totalled 49,967. In fiscal year 2006 a total of 120,508 people in Alaska received Medicaid. In Dec. 2008 there were 71,145 Old-Age, Survivors, and Disability Insurance (OASDI) beneficiaries. A total of 7,546 people were receiving payments under Temporary Assistance for Needy Families (TANF) in Dec. 2008.

RELIGION

Many religions are represented, including Roman Catholic, Southern Baptist, Mormon, Lutheran and other denominations.

CULTURE

Tourism

About 2·7m. people visited the state in 2003–04.

FURTHER READING

Statistical Information: Department of Commerce and Economic Development, Economic Analysis Section, POB 110804, Juneau 99811. Publishes *The Alaska Economy Performance Report.*
Alaska Industry–Occupation Outlook to 1995. 1992
Annual Financial Report.

Naske, C.-M. and Slotnick, H. E., *Alaska: a History of the 49th State.* 2nd ed. 1995
State library: POB 110571, Juneau, Alaska 99811-0571.

Arizona

KEY HISTORICAL EVENTS

Spaniards looking for sources of gold or silver entered Arizona in the 16th century finding there American natives, including Tohono O'odham, Navajo, Hopi and Apache. The first Spanish Catholic mission was founded in the early 1690s by Father Eusebio Kino. Settlements were made in 1752 and a Spanish army headquarters was set up at Tucson in 1776. The area was governed by Mexico after the collapse of Spanish colonial power. Mexico ceded it to the USA in the Treaty of Guadalupe Hidalgo after the Mexican-American war (1848). Arizona was then part of New Mexico; the Gadsen Purchase (of land south of the Gila River) was added to it in 1853. The whole was organized as the Arizona Territory on 24 Feb. 1863.

Miners and ranchers began settling in the 1850s. Conflicts between Indian and immigrant populations intensified when troops were withdrawn to serve in the Civil War. The Navajo surrendered in 1865, but the Apache continued to fight, under Geronimo and other leaders, until 1886. Arizona was admitted to the Union as the 48th state in 1912.

Large areas of the state have been retained as Indian reservations and as parks to protect the exceptional desert and mountain landscape. In recent years this landscape and the Indian traditions have been used to attract tourists.

TERRITORY AND POPULATION

Arizona is bounded north by Utah, east by New Mexico, south by Mexico, west by California and Nevada. Land area, 113,634 sq. miles (294,313 sq. km). Of the total area in 2001, 27% was Indian Reservation, 17% was in individual or corporate ownership, 20% was held by the US Bureau of Land Management, 16% by the US Forest Service, 13% by the State and 7% by others. Census population on 1 April 2000 was 5,130,632, an increase of 40·0% over 1990. July 2009 estimate, 6,595,778. The rate of Arizona's population increase during the 1990s was the second fastest in the USA, at 40%.

Population in six census years:

	White	*Black*	*American Indian*	*Chinese*	*Japanese*	*Total*	*Per sq. mile*
1910	171,468	2,009	29,201	1,305	371	204,354	1·8
1930	378,551	10,749	43,726	1,110	879	435,573	3·8
1960	1,169,517	43,403	83,387	2,937	1,501	1,302,161	11·3

	White	Black	American Indian	All others	Total	Per sq. mile
1980	2,260,288	74,159	162,854	383,768	2,718,215	23·9
1990	2,963,186	110,524	203,527	387,991	3,665,228	32·3
2000	3,873,611	158,873	255,879	842,269	5,130,632	45·2

Of the total population in 2000, 2,561,057 were female, 3,763,685 were 18 years old or older and 4,523,535 were urban. Arizona's Hispanic population was 1,295,617 in 2000 (25·3%) up from 739,861 in 1990 (an increase of 88·2%).

In 2004 the estimated population of Phoenix was 1,416,055; Tucson, 521,605; Mesa, 447,130; Glendale, 233,330; Scottsdale, 221,130; Chandler, 220,705; Tempe, 160,820; Gilbert, 164,685; Peoria, 132,300; Yuma, 86,070. The Phoenix–Mesa metropolitan area had a 2000 census population of 3,251,876.

SOCIAL STATISTICS

Births, 2007 (provisional), 103,646 (16·4 per 1,000 population); deaths, 2006, 46,365 (7·5). Infant mortality, 2006, 6·4 per 1,000 live births. 2006 marriages, 39,000 (6·3); divorces and annulments, 24,300 (3·9).

CLIMATE

Phoenix, Jan. 53·6°F (12°C), July 93·5°F (34°C). Annual rainfall 7·66" (194 mm). Yuma, Jan. 56·5°F (13·6°C), July 93·7°F (34·3°C). Annual rainfall 3·17" (80 mm). Flagstaff, Jan. 28·7°F (–1·8°C), July 66·3°F (19·1°C). Annual rainfall 22·8" (579 mm). Arizona belongs to the Mountain States climate zone (*see* UNITED STATES: Climate).

CONSTITUTION AND GOVERNMENT

The state constitution (1911, with 129 amendments) placed the government under direct control of the people through the initiative, referendum and the recall provisions. The state Senate consists of 30 members, and the House of Representatives consists of 60, all elected for two years.

For the 111th Congress, which convened in Jan. 2009, Arizona sends eight members to the House of Representatives. It is represented in the Senate by John McCain (R. 1987–2011) and Jon Kyl (R. 1995–2013).

The state capital is Phoenix. The state is divided into 15 counties.

RECENT ELECTIONS

In the 2008 presidential elections John McCain won Arizona with 53·6% of the vote (George W. Bush won in 2004).

CURRENT ADMINISTRATION

Governor: Janice K. Brewer (R.), 2009–11 (salary: $95,000).

Secretary of State: Ken Bennett (R.), 2009–11 ($70,000).

Government Website: http://az.gov

ECONOMY

Per capita personal income (2008) was $34,335.

Budget

In 2008 total state revenue was $27,698m. Total expenditure was $30,779m. (education, $9,409m.; public welfare, $7,927m.; highways, $2,367m.; health, $1,621m.; correction, $1,024m.) Outstanding debt in 2008, $10,519m.

Performance

Gross Domestic Product by state was $248,888m. in 2008 (provisional), ranking Arizona 19th in the United States.

ENERGY AND NATURAL RESOURCES

Primary energy sources are coal (35·2%), nuclear (24·5%), gas (19·5%) and hydroelectric (18·9%).

Electricity

Electricity production in 2005 totalled 101·5bn. kWh.

Oil and Gas

In 2004 oil production totalled 51,972 bbls from 18 producing wells. Gas totalled 331m. cu. ft from nine producing wells.

Water

The total area covered by water is approximately 364 sq. miles.

Minerals

The mining industry historically has been and continues to be a significant part of the economy. By value the most important mineral produced is copper. Production in 2003 was 834,426 short tons. Most of the state's silver and gold are recovered from copper ore. Other minerals include sand and gravel, molybdenum, coal and gemstones. Value of non-fuel mineral production in 2006 was $6,740m.

Agriculture

Arizona, despite its dry climate, is well suited for agriculture along the water-courses and where irrigation is practised on a large scale from great reservoirs constructed by the USA as well as by the state government and private interests. Irrigated area in 2002 was 931,735 acres. The wide pasture lands are favourable for the rearing of cattle and sheep, but numbers are either stationary or declining compared with 1920.

In 2002 Arizona contained 7,300 farms and ranches and the total farm and pastoral area was 26·5m. acres; in 2002 there were 1,261,894 acres of crop land. In 2002 the average farm was 3,645 acres (the second largest average size in the USA after Wyoming) and was valued at $398 per acre. Farming is highly commercialized and mechanized and concentrated largely on cotton picked by machines.

Area under cotton in 2004: upland cotton, 240,000 acres (723,000 bales harvested); American Pima cotton, 3,000 acres (5,600 bales harvested).

In 2006 the cash income from crops was $1,558m., and from livestock and products $1,321m. The net farm income in 2006 was $774m. Most important cereals are wheat, corn and barley; most important crops include lettuce, cotton, citrus fruit, broccoli, spinach, cauliflower, melons, onions, potatoes and carrots. In 2004 there were 860,000 cattle, 114,000 sheep, 127,000 hogs and 30,000 goats.

Forestry

The state had a forested area of 18,671,000 acres in 2007, of which 7,663,000 acres were national forest.

INDUSTRY

In 2005 the state's 4,858 manufacturing establishments had 168,000 employees, earning $7,828m. Total value added by manufacturing in 2006 was $27,172m.

Labour

In 2007 total non-agricultural employment was 2,666,000. Employees by branch, 2007 (in 1,000): trade, transportation and utilities, 525; government, 423; professional and business services, 402; education and health services, 304; leisure and hospitality, 273. The unemployment rate in 2007 was 3·9%.

COMMUNICATIONS

Roads

In 2007 there were 60,593 miles of roads comprising 22,918 miles of urban road and 37,675 miles of rural road. There were 4,372,035 registered vehicles.

Civil Aviation

In 2005 there were 6,487 registered aircraft and 323 landing facilities of which 217 were airports (including 81 for public use) and 106 were heliports. There were 23,330,939 passenger enplanements statewide in 2007.

SOCIAL INSTITUTIONS

Justice

A 'right-to-work' amendment to the constitution, adopted 5 Nov. 1946, makes illegal any concessions to trade-union demands for a 'closed shop'.

In Dec. 2008 the prison population totalled 39,589. Chain gangs were reintroduced into prisons in 1995. The death penalty is authorized. There was one execution in 2007 (the first since 2000) but none in 2008 or 2009.

Education

School attendance is compulsory between the ages of six and 16. In 2003–04, K-12 enrolment numbered 1,012,068 students. There are 234 school districts containing 1,199 elementary schools, 305 high schools and 72 combined schools. Charter schools first opened their doors in 1995. There are 694 charter schools providing parents and students with expanded educational choices. In 2003–04 the total funds appropriated by the state legislature for all education, including the Board of Regents and community colleges, was $4,181,833,300. The state maintains three universities: the University of Arizona (Tucson) with an enrolment of 33,070 in 2004; Arizona State University (three campuses) with 49,495; Northern Arizona University (Flagstaff) with 17,221.

Health

In 2006 the state had 66 community hospitals with 11,900 beds. A total of 664,000 patients were admitted during the year. In 2005 there were more than 17,000 licensed physicians, 4,005 dentists and 46,681 registered nurses.

Welfare

Medicare enrolment in July 2004 totalled 753,934. In fiscal year 2006 a total of 1,018,666 people in Arizona received Medicaid. Old-age assistance (maximum depending on the programme) is given to needy citizens 65 years of age or older through the federal supplemental security income (SSI) programme. In Dec. 2008 SSI payments went to 13,807 aged, and 89,436 disabled and blind (average of $487·57 each). In Dec. 2008 there were 986,539 Old-Age, Survivors, and Disability Insurance (OASDI) beneficiaries. A total of 82,639 people were receiving payments under Temporary Assistance for Needy Families (TANF) in Dec. 2008.

RELIGION

The leading religious bodies are Roman Catholics and Latter-day Saints (Mormons); others include United Methodists, Presbyterians, Baptists, Lutherans, Episcopalians, Eastern Orthodox, Jews and Muslims.

CULTURE

Tourism

In 2004 Arizona had 28·4m. visitors (27·8m. domestic visitors and 0·6m. overseas visitors) and 434,635 tourism-related jobs. In 2004 domestic visitors spent $13·07bn.

FURTHER READING

Statistical information: College of Business and Public Administration, Univ. of Arizona, Tucson 85721. Publishes *Arizona Statistical Abstract.*

Alexander, David V., *Arizona Frontier Military Place Names: 1846–1912.* 1998

Arizona Commission of Indian Affairs. *2007–2008 Tribal-State Resource Directory.* 2007

Arizona Department of Commerce. *Community Profiles.* Online only

Arizona Department of Health Services, Center for Health Statistics. *Arizona Health Status and Vital Statistics, 2006.* Online only

Arizona Historical Society. *1999/2000 Official Directory, Arizona Historical Museums and Related Support Organizations.* 1999

August, Jack L., *Vision in the Desert: Carl Hayden and the Hydropolitics in the American Southwest.* 1999

Leavengood, Betty, *Lives Shaped by Landscape: Grand Canyon Women.* 1999

Office of the Secretary of State. *Arizona Blue Book, 2007–08.* 2008

Shillingberg, William B., *Tombstone, A. T.: A History of Early Mining, Milling and Mayhem.* 1999

State Government Website: http://www.az.gov/webapp/portal

Arizona State Library, Archives and Public Records (ASLAPR): 1700 West Washington, Suite 200, Phoenix. *Website:* http://www.lib.az.us

---

Arkansas

KEY HISTORICAL EVENTS

In the 16th and 17th centuries French and Spanish explorers encountered tribes of Chaddo, Osage and Quapaw. The first European settlement was French, at Arkansas Post in 1686, and the area became part of French Louisiana. The USA bought Arkansas from France as part of the Louisiana Purchase in 1803; it was organized as a Territory in 1819 and entered the Union on 15 June 1836 as the 25th state.

The eastern plains by the Mississippi were settled by white plantation-owners who grew cotton with black slave labour. The rest of the state attracted a scattered population of small farmers. The plantations were the centre of political power. Arkansas seceded from the Union in 1861 and joined the Confederate States of America. At that time the slave population was about 25% of the total.

In 1868 the state was readmitted to the Union. Attempts to integrate the black population into state life achieved little, and a policy of segregation was rigidly adhered to until the 1950s. In 1957 federal authorities ordered that high school segregation must end. The state governor called on the state militia to prevent desegregation; there was rioting, and federal troops entered Little Rock, the capital, to restore order. It was another ten years before school segregation finally ended.

The main industrial development followed the discovery of large reserves of bauxite.

TERRITORY AND POPULATION

Arkansas is bounded north by Missouri, east by Tennessee and Mississippi, south by Louisiana, southwest by Texas and west by Oklahoma. Land area, 52,068 sq. miles (134,855 sq. km). Census population on 1 April 2000 was 2,673,400, an increase of 13·7% from that of 1990. July 2009 estimate, 2,889,450.

Population in five census years was:

	White	*Black*	*Indian*	*Asiatic*	*Total*	*Per sq. mile*
1910	1,131,026	442,891	460	472	1,574,449	30·0
1960	1,395,703	388,787	580	1,202	1,786,272	34·0
			All others			
1980	1,890,332	373,768	22,335		2,286,435	43·9
1990	1,944,744	373,912	32,069		2,350,725	45·1
2000	2,138,598	418,950	115,852		2,673,400	51·3

Of the total population in 2000, 1,368,707 were female, 1,993,031 were 18 years old or older and 1,404,179 were urban. In 2000 the Hispanic population of Arkansas was 86,866, up from 19,876 in 1990. The increase of 337% was the second largest increase in the USA over the same period.

Little Rock (capital) had a population of 183,183 in 2000; Fort Smith, 80,268; North Little Rock, 60,433; Fayetteville, 58,047; Jonesboro, 55,515; Pine Bluff, 55,085; Springdale, 45,798; Conway, 43,167. The population of the largest metropolitan statistical areas in 2000 was: Little Rock–North Little Rock, 583,845; Fayetteville–Springdale–Rogers, 311,121; Fort Smith, 207,290; Texarkana, 129,749; Pine Bluff, 84,278.

SOCIAL STATISTICS

Births, 2007 (provisional), were 40,939 (14·4 per 1,000 population); deaths, 2006, 27,901 (9·9). Infant mortality, 2006, 8·5 per 1,000 live births. 2006: marriages, 34,300 (12·2 per 1,000 population); divorces and annulments, 16,200 (5·7).

CLIMATE

Little Rock, Jan. 39·9°F, July 84°F. Annual rainfall 52·4". Arkansas belongs to the Gulf Coast climate zone (*see* UNITED STATES: Climate).

CONSTITUTION AND GOVERNMENT

The General Assembly consists of a Senate of 35 members elected for four years, partially renewed every two years, and a House of Representatives of 100 members elected for two years. The sessions are biennial and usually limited to 60 days. The Governor and Lieut.-Governor are elected for four years.

For the 111th Congress, which convened in Jan. 2009, Arkansas sends four members to the House of Representatives. It is represented in the Senate by Blanche Lincoln (D. 1999–2011) and Mark Pryor (D. 2003–15).

The state is divided into 75 counties; the capital is Little Rock.

RECENT ELECTIONS

In the 2008 presidential elections John McCain won Arkansas with 58·7% of the vote (George W. Bush won in 2004).

CURRENT ADMINISTRATION

Governor: Mike Beebe (D.), 2007–11 (salary: $87,352).
Lieut.-Governor: Bill Halter (D.), 2007–11 ($42,219).
Secretary of State: Charlie Daniels (D.), 2007–11 ($54,594).

Government Website: http://www.ar.gov

ECONOMY

Per capita personal income (2008) was $32,397.

Budget

In 2008 total revenue was $15,107m. Total expenditure was $15,656m. (education, $6,312m.; public welfare, $3,772m.; highways, $916m.; hospitals, $811m.; government administration, $591m.) Outstanding debt in 2008, $4,283m.

Performance

2008 Gross Domestic Product by state was $98,331m. (provisional), ranking Arkansas 34th in the United States.

Banking and Finance

At 30 June 2006 total bank deposits were $44,220m.

ENERGY AND NATURAL RESOURCES

Oil and Gas

2007 production of crude oil was 6m. bbls; natural gas, 270bn. cu. ft.

Water

The total area covered by water is approximately 1,110 sq. miles.

Minerals

Employment in mining, quarrying, and oil and gas extraction totalled 6,364 in March 2007. Crushed stone was the leading mineral commodity produced, in terms of value, followed by bromine. Value of domestic non-fuel mineral production in 2006 was $789m.

Agriculture

In 2007, 49,346 farms had a total area of 13·9m. acres; average farm was 281 acres and was valued at $2,343 per acre. 7·37m. acres were harvested cropland. Arkansas ranked first in the acreage and production of rice in 2007 (48·4% of US total production), second in the production of broilers (1,172m. birds) and third in turkeys (29·2m. birds).

Farm income, 2006: crops, $2,397m.; livestock and products, $3,767m. The net farm income in 2006 was $1,951m.

Forestry

In 2007 the state had a forested area of 18,830,000 acres, of which 2,546,000 acres were national forest.

INDUSTRY

In 2005 the state's 3,105 manufacturing establishments had 198,000 employees, earning $6,577m. Total value added by manufacturing in 2006 was $27,574m.

Labour

Total non-agricultural employment, 2007: 1,204,000. Employees by branch, 2007 (in 1,000): trade, transportation and utilities, 250; government, 210; manufacturing, 189; education and health services, 154; professional and business services, 117. The unemployment rate in 2007 was 5·6%.

COMMUNICATIONS

Roads

Total road mileage (2007), 99,558 miles—urban, 11,966; rural, 87,592. There were 2,010,301 registered motor vehicles.

Rail

In 2003 there were 2,750 miles of commercial railroad in Arkansas. In 2002 rail service was provided by three Class I (1,893 miles) and 23 short-line (Class III) railroads (857 miles).

Civil Aviation

In 2005 there were 241 airports (100 public-use and 141 private). There were 1,965,835 passenger enplanements statewide in 2007.

Shipping

There are about 1,000 miles of navigable rivers, including the Mississippi, Arkansas, Red, White and Ouachita Rivers. The Arkansas River/Kerr-McClellan Channel flows diagonally eastward across the state and gives access to the sea via the Mississippi River.

SOCIAL INSTITUTIONS

Justice

In Dec. 2008 there were 14,716 federal and state prisoners. There was one execution in 2004 and one in 2005, but the death penalty was suspended in 2006.

Education

In 2004–05 there were 1,158 public elementary and secondary schools with 463,115 enrolled pupils and 31,234 teachers. Total expenditure on public elementary and secondary education in 2003–04 was $3,543m. and average teacher salary was $39,314. Spending per student in 2002–03 was $6,482.

In fall 2005 there were 33 public and 15 private higher education institutions. Total student enrolment in 2005 was 140,700 (127,949 public and 12,751 private). Arkansas State University (founded in 1909) includes the Jonesboro, Beebe, Mountain Home, Newport, Heber Springs, Marked Tree and Searcy campuses; total student enrolment was 16,937 in fall 2005.

Health

In 2006 there were 84 community hospitals with 9,300 beds. A total of 373,000 patients were admitted during the year.

Welfare

Medicare enrolment in July 2004 totalled 460,312. In fiscal year 2006 a total of 753,166 people in Arkansas received Medicaid. In

Dec. 2008 there were 602,017 Old-Age, Survivors, and Disability Insurance (OASDI) beneficiaries. A total of 19,791 people were receiving payments under Temporary Assistance for Needy Families (TANF) in Dec. 2008.

RELIGION

There were (2000) 665,307 Southern Baptists, 179,383 United Methodists, 115,967 Roman Catholics, 87,244 Baptist Missionary Association members and 86,342 adherents of the Church of Christ.

FURTHER READING

Statistical information: Arkansas Institute for Economic Advancement, Univ. of Arkansas at Little Rock, Little Rock 72204. Publishes *Arkansas State and County Economic Data.*
Agricultural Statistics for Arkansas. Annual
Current Employment Developments. Monthly
Statistical Summary for the Public Schools of Arkansas. Annual

California

KEY HISTORICAL EVENTS

There were many small Indian tribes, but no central power, when the area was discovered in 1542 by the Spanish navigator Juan Cabrillo. The Spaniards did not begin to establish missions until the 18th century, when the Franciscan friar Junipero Serra settled at San Diego in 1769. The missions became farming and ranching villages with large Indian populations. When the Spanish empire collapsed in 1821, the area was governed from newly independent Mexico.

The first wagon-train of American settlers arrived from Missouri in 1841. In 1846, during the war between Mexico and the USA, Americans in California proclaimed it to be part of the USA. The territory was ceded by Mexico on 2 Feb. 1848 and became the 31st state of the Union on 9 Sept. 1850.

Gold was discovered in 1848–49 and there was an immediate influx of population. The state remained isolated, however, until the development of railways in the 1860s. From then on the population doubled on average every 20 years. The sunny climate attracted fruit-growers, market-gardeners and wine producers. In the early 20th century the bright lights and cheap labour attracted film-makers to Hollywood, Los Angeles.

Southern California remained mainly agricultural with an Indian or Spanish-speaking labour force until after the Second World War. Now more than 90% of the population is urban, with the manufacturing emphasis on hi-technology equipment, much of it for the aerospace, computer and office equipment industries.

TERRITORY AND POPULATION

Land area, 155,959 sq. miles (403,932 sq. km). Census population, 1 April 2000, 33,871,648, an increase of 4,111,627, or 13·8%, over 1990. July 2009 estimate, 36,961,664. The growth rate reflects continued high though somewhat reduced natural increase (excess of births over deaths) as well as substantial net immigration.

Population in five census years was:

	White	Black	Japanese	Chinese	Total (incl. all others)	Per sq. mile
1910	2,259,672	21,645	41,356	36,248	2,377,549	15·2
1930	5,408,260	81,048	97,456	37,361	5,677,251	36·4
1960	14,455,230	883,861	157,317	95,600	15,717,204	100·8

	White	Black	Asian/other	Hispanic	Total	Per sq. mile
1990	20,524,327	2,208,801	7,026,893	7,687,938	29,760,021	190·8
2000	20,170,059	2,263,882	11,437,707	10,966,556	33,871,648	217·2

Of the total population in 2000, 16,996,756 (50·2%) were female, 24,621,819 were 18 years old or older and 31,989,663 were urban (94·44%, the highest of the states).

In addition to having the highest population of any state in the USA, California has the largest Hispanic population of any state in terms of numbers and the second largest in terms of percentage of population. In 2000 there were 10,966,556 Hispanics living in California (32·4% of the overall population), representing a rise of 3,278,618 since 1990, the largest numeric rise of any state over the same period. By 2020 Hispanics are projected to form a majority.

The 50 largest cities with 2008 population estimates are:

Los Angeles	4,045,873	Rancho Cucamonga	174,308
San Diego	1,336,865	Ontario	173,690
San Jose	989,496	Garden Grove	173,067
San Francisco	824,525	Pomona	163,405
Long Beach	492,642	Santa Rosa	159,981
Fresno	486,171	Salinas	150,898
Sacramento	475,743	Hayward	149,205
Oakland	420,183	Torrance	148,965
Santa Ana	353,184	Pasadena	148,126
Anaheim	346,823	Palmdale	147,897
Bakersfield	328,692	Corona	147,428
Riverside	296,842	Lancaster	145,243
Stockton	289,927	Escondido	143,389
Chula Vista	231,305	Orange	140,849
Fremont	213,512	Elk Grove	139,542
Modesto	209,936	Sunnyvale	137,538
Irvine	209,806	Fullerton	137,437
Glendale	207,157	Thousand Oaks	128,650
San Bernardino	205,493	El Monte	126,053
Huntington Beach	201,993	Simi Valley	125,657
Oxnard	194,905	Concord	123,776
Fontana	188,498	Vallejo	121,097
Moreno Valley	183,860	Visalia	120,958
Oceanside	178,806	Inglewood	118,878
Santa Clarita	177,045	Santa Clara	115,503

Metropolitan areas (2000 census): Los Angeles–Riverside–Orange County, 16,373,645; San Francisco–Oakland–San Jose, 7,039,362; San Diego, 2,813,833; Sacramento–Yolo, 1,796,857; Fresno, 922,516.

SOCIAL STATISTICS

Births, 2007 (provisional), 566,388 (15·5 per 1,000 population); deaths, 2006, 237,126 (6·5). Marriages, 2006, 225,341. Infant deaths, 2006, 5·0 per 1,000 live births. California was the second state after Massachusetts to allow same-sex marriage when it became legal in June 2008, but the ruling was nullified when 52·5% of votes cast in a referendum held on 4 Nov. 2008 were in favour of a ban.

CLIMATE

Los Angeles, Jan. 58°F (14·4°C), July 74°F (23·3°C). Annual rainfall 15" (381 mm). Sacramento, Jan. 45°F (7·2°C), July 76°F (24·4°C). Annual rainfall 18" (457 mm). San Diego, Jan. 57°F (13·9°C), July 71°F (21·7°C). Annual rainfall 10" (259 mm). San Francisco, Jan. 51°F (10·6°C), July 59°F (15°C). Annual rainfall 20" (508 mm). Death Valley, Jan. 52°F (11°C), July 100°F (38°C). Annual rainfall 1·6" (40 mm). California belongs to the Pacific Coast climate zone (*see* UNITED STATES: Climate).

CONSTITUTION AND GOVERNMENT

The present constitution became effective from 4 July 1879; it has had numerous amendments since 1962. The Senate is composed of 40 members elected for four years—half being elected every two years—and the Assembly, of 80 members, elected for two years. Two-year regular sessions convene in Dec. of each even numbered year. The Governor and Lieut.-Governor are elected for four years.

For the 111th Congress, which convened in Jan. 2009, California sends 53 members to the House of Representatives. It is represented in the Senate by Dianne Feinstein (D. 1993–2013) and Barbara Boxer (D. 1993–2011).

The capital is Sacramento. The state is divided into 58 counties.

RECENT ELECTIONS

In the 2008 presidential elections Barack Obama won California with 61·0% of the vote (John Kerry won in 2004).

CURRENT ADMINISTRATION

Governor: Arnold Schwarzenegger (R.), 2007–11 (salary: $173,987).

Lieut.-Governor: Abel Maldonado (R.), 2010–11 ($130,490).

Secretary of State: Debra Bowen (D.), 2007–11 ($130,490).

Attorney General: Jerry Brown (D.), 2007–11 ($151,127).

Government Website: http://www.ca.gov

ECONOMY

Per capita personal income (2008) was $43,641.

Budget

For the year ending 30 June 2009, total state revenues were $106·3bn. Total expenditures were $114·8bn. (education, $45·0bn.; health and human services, $35·0bn.; corrections and rehabilitation, $9·7bn.) Debt outstanding (2009) $73·5bn.

Performance

California's economy, the largest among the 50 states and one of the largest in the world, has major components in high technology, trade, entertainment, agriculture, manufacturing, tourism, construction and services. California is home to leading innovators and entrepreneurs and to firms like Apple, Cisco and Intel in technology; eBay, Facebook, Google and Yahoo in pioneering the use of the Internet; Amgen and Genentech in biotech; and DreamWorks and Pixar in combining technology and entertainment. California experienced an economic recession in 2001 and a sluggish recovery in 2002, with greatest impacts in the high technology sector. The economic recovery broadened and strengthened in 2003 and improved considerably through 2005. A housing downturn that began in the fall of 2005 and worsened in 2006 and 2007 was instrumental in slowing average monthly job growth from 27,400 in 2005 to 3,400 in 2007—a downward trend that continued with average job losses of 21,500 per month in 2008. Falling house prices, worsening credit availability, shrinking equity values and growing job losses delivered a crushing blow to the California economy in 2008.

If California were a country in its own right it would be the world's eighth largest economy, after the USA, Japan, China, Germany, France, the United Kingdom and Italy. 2008 Gross Domestic Product by state was $1,846,757m. (provisional), the highest in the United States and representing more than 13% of the USA's total GDP. Taxable sales in 2007 totalled $561,050m.

Banking and Finance

In 2002 there were 9,510 establishments of depository institutions which included 5,807 commercial banks, 2,225 savings institutions and 1,378 credit unions.

In 2007 savings and loan associations had deposits of $46,507m. Total mortgage loans in 2007 were $54,118m. On 31 Dec. 2007 all insured commercial banks had demand deposits of $23,030m. and time and savings deposits of $221,565m. Total loans reached $270,619m., of which real-estate loans were $190,656m. Credit unions had assets totalling $120,607m. and total loans outstanding were $86,562m.

ENERGY AND NATURAL RESOURCES

Electricity

Californians spent $33bn. on electricity in 2006. Total consumption amounted to 262,959m. kWh. 82% of electricity is derived from in-state resources. In 2000 and 2001 California suffered an energy crisis characterized by electricity price instability and four major blackouts affecting millions of customers.

Oil and Gas

California is the nation's third largest oil producing state. Total onshore and offshore production was 243m. bbls in 2007. California ranks tenth out of US states for the production of natural gas. Net natural gas production in 2007 was 277bn. cu. ft.

Water

The total area covered by water is approximately 7,736 sq. miles. Water quality is judged to be good along 83% of the 960 miles of assessed coastal shoreline.

Minerals

Gold output was 19,400 troy oz in 2007. Asbestos, boron minerals, diatomite, sand and gravel, lime, salt, magnesium compounds, clays, cement, silver, gypsum and iron ore are also produced.

In 2007 California ranked third among the states in non-fuel mineral production, accounting for more than 6% of the US total. The market value of non-fuel minerals produced was $4·3bn. (the second highest behind Arizona); the mining industry employed around 26,000 persons in 2007 (compared to 48,000 in the early 1980s).

Agriculture

California is the most diversified agricultural economy in the world, producing more than 350 agricultural commodities. It is by far the largest agricultural producer and exporter in the United States. The state grows more than half of the nation's total of fruits, nuts and vegetables. Many of these commodities are specialty crops and almost solely produced in California. There were, in 2006, 76,000 farms, comprising 26·1m. acres; average farm, 346 acres. The average California farm operation produced $413,000 in commodity sales in 2006. The net farm income in 2007 was $12,665m. (the largest of any state). In 2007 income from marketings reached $36·57bn. Fruit and nut cash receipts, at $10·54bn., were 3% above the previous year and comprised 29% of the total. Vegetable receipts were up 8% from the previous year at $7·97bn., comprising 22% of total sales. Livestock and poultry receipts rose 42% from 2006 at $10·73bn. and comprised 29% of total sales. California's three leading commodities in cash receipts are milk and cream with $7·33bn., grapes with $3·08bn. and lettuce with $2·18bn.

Production of cotton lint in 2007 was 346,300 short tons; other field and seed crops included (in 1m. short tons): hay and alfalfa, 9; rice, 2; sugar beets, 1; wheat, 1. Principal fruit, nut and vegetable crops in 2007 (in 1,000 short tons): tomatoes, 12,697; grapes, 6,211; lettuce, 4,524; oranges, 1,725; onions, 1,510; carrots, 1,128; strawberries, 1,077; celery, 967; peaches, 949; broccoli, 945; lemons, 703; almonds, 695.

In 2007 there were 1·8m. milch cows; 5·5m. all cattle and calves; 610,000 sheep and lambs; and 155,000 hogs and pigs.

Forestry

In 2007 California had 32·82m. acres of forested land, of which 14,906,000 acres were national forest. There are about 16·6m. acres of productive forest land, from which about 2,900m. bd ft are harvested annually. Total value of timber harvest, 2007, $474m. Lumber production, 2007, 1,626m. bd ft.

Fisheries

The catch in 2007 was 384m. lb; leading species in landings were sardine, squid, anchovy, mackerel, crab, urchin, sole, whiting, sablefish and tuna.

INDUSTRY

California's economy is highly diversified. In terms of jobs, the largest sectors in California are trade, transportation and utilities, government, and professional and business services. In terms of output the largest sector is finance, followed by trade, transportation and utilities. Construction was the fastest-growing sector in California until 2007 when the housing downturn and financial crisis worsened.

Farm production in California has risen despite declines in acreage. Farm-related sales have more than quadrupled over the past three decades. Largest production categories are fruits and nuts, livestock and poultry, vegetables and melons.

Labour

In 2007 the civilian labour force was 18·2m., of whom 17·2m. were employed. A total of 114,100 jobs were created during 2007, led by education and health services, state and local government, leisure and hospitality, trade, transportation and utilities, and professional and business services. The unemployment rate was 5·4% in 2007.

INTERNATIONAL TRADE

Imports and Exports

Estimated foreign trade through Californian ports totalled $516bn. in 2007. Exports of made-in-California goods totalled $134·2bn., an increase of 5% on 2006. Of the total $43·7bn. was computers and electronics, $14·5bn. non-electrical machinery, $13·7bn. transportation equipment and $10·4bn. chemicals.

Total agricultural exports for 2006 were $9·8bn. California's top markets are the European Union, Canada, Japan, China, Hong Kong, Mexico, South Korea, Taiwan, India, Australia and the United Arab Emirates.

COMMUNICATIONS

Roads

In 2007 California had 73,570 miles of roads inside cities and 97,584 miles outside. There were 33,935,386 registered motor vehicles (including 20,037,727 automobiles). Motor vehicle collision fatalities in 2007 were 3,967.

Rail

In addition to Amtrak's long-distance trains, local and medium-distance passenger trains run in the San Francisco Bay area sponsored by the California Department of Transportation, and a network of commuter trains around Los Angeles opened in 1992. There are metro and light rail systems in San Francisco and Los Angeles, and light rail lines in Sacramento, San Diego and San Jose.

Civil Aviation

In 2003 there were a total of 939 public and private airports, heliports, stolports and seaplane bases.

A total of 59,815,646 passengers (16,684,782 international; 43,130,864 domestic) embarked/disembarked at Los Angeles airport in 2008. It handled approximately 1,796,543 tonnes of freight (996,504 international; 800,039 domestic). At San Francisco airport, in 2008, 37,066,729 passengers (8,964,202 international; 28,102,527 domestic) embarked/disembarked, and 431,110 tonnes of freight (254,506 tonnes international; 176,604 tonnes domestic) were handled. There were a total of 48,459,259 passenger enplanements at Los Angeles and San Francisco in 2008.

Shipping

The chief ports are San Francisco and Los Angeles.

SOCIAL INSTITUTIONS

Justice

A 'three strikes law', making 25-years-to-life sentences mandatory for third felony offences, was adopted in 1994 after an initiative (i.e. referendum) was 72% in favour. However, the state's Supreme Court ruled in June 1996 that judges may disregard previous convictions in awarding sentences. In Jan. 2009 there were 33 adult prisons. State prisons, 30 Jan. 2009, had 152,530 male and 11,213 female inmates. On 30 Dec. 2008 there were 1,734 juveniles in custody. As of Dec. 2008 there were 8,409 adults serving 'three strikes' sentences. The death penalty has been authorized following its reinstatement by the US Supreme Court in 1976. Death sentences have been passed since 1980. The first execution since 2002 was carried out in Jan. 2005. There was one execution in total in 2006. A moratorium on death sentences was ordered in Dec. 2006. The California Department of Corrections and Rehabilitation has not indicated when it expects to successfully overcome legal challenges related to executions although a new execution chamber has been completed at San Quentin State Prison.

Education

Full-time attendance at school is compulsory for children from six to 18 years of age for a minimum of 175 days per annum. In fall 2006 there were 6·9m. pupils enrolled in both public and private elementary and secondary schools. Total state expenditure on public education, 2006–07, was $51·3bn.

Community colleges had 1,637,767 students in fall 2006.

California has two publicly-supported higher education systems: the University of California (1868) and the California State University and Colleges. In fall 2006 the University of California, with campuses for resident instruction and research at Berkeley, Los Angeles (UCLA), San Francisco and seven other centres, had 214,298 students. California State University and Colleges with campuses at Sacramento, Long Beach, Los Angeles, San Francisco and 18 other cities had 417,156 students. In addition to the 32 publicly-supported institutions for higher education there are 117 private colleges and universities which had a total estimated enrolment of 486,323 in the fall of 2005.

Health

In 2008 there were 6,906 state licensed facilities; capacity, 260,036 beds. On 30 June 2008 state hospitals for the mentally disabled had 6,080 patients.

Welfare

Medicare enrolment in July 2005 totalled 4,158,000. In fiscal year 2006 a total of 10,427,093 people in California received Medicaid.

On 1 Jan. 1974 the federal government (Social Security Administration) assumed responsibility for the Supplemental Security Income/State Supplemental Program which replaced the State Old-Age Security. The SSI/SSP provides financial assistance for needy aged (65 years or older), blind or disabled persons. An individual recipient may own assets up to $2,000; a couple up to $3,000, subject to specific exclusions. In 2007–08 fiscal year an average of 99,996 cases per month were receiving an average of $223 in assistance in the general relief programme. On average 465,959 families and 917,126 children were receiving payments under Temporary Assistance for Needy Families (TANF) in 2007–08.

RELIGION

There is a strong Roman Catholic presence. There were an estimated 994,000 Jews and 529,575 Latter-day Saints (Mormons) in 2000.

CULTURE

Tourism

The travel and tourism industry provides 2·5% of the state's $1·8trn. economy. Visitors in 2007 spent $96·7bn. generating $5·8bn. in state and local tax revenues. Tourist spending has increased at an average annual rate of 5·5% since 2003. California was the state most visited by overseas travellers in 2007, when international tourists spent $16·7bn. (more than 17% of all tourist spending).

FURTHER READING

California Government and Politics. Hoeber, T. R., *et al*., (eds.) Annual
California Statistical Abstract. Annual; online only
Economic Report of the Governor. Annual

Bean, W. and Rawls, J. J., *California: an Interpretive History*. 9th ed. 2006
Gerston, L. N. and Christensen, T., *California Politics and Government: a Practical Approach*. 10th ed. 2008

State library: The California State Library, Library-Courts Bldg, Sacramento 95814.

Colorado

KEY HISTORICAL EVENTS

Spanish explorers claimed the area for Spain in 1706; it was then the territory of the Arapaho, Cheyenne, Ute and other Plains and Great Basin Indians. Eastern Colorado, the hot, dry plains, passed to France in 1802 and then to the USA as part of the Louisiana Purchase in 1803. The rest remained Spanish, becoming Mexican when Spanish power in the Americas ended. In 1848, after war between Mexico and the USA, Mexican Colorado was ceded to the USA. A gold rush in 1859 brought a great influx of population, and in 1861 Colorado was organized as a Territory. The Territory officially supported the Union in the Civil War of 1861–65, but its settlers were divided and served on both sides.

Colorado became a state in 1876. Mining and ranching were the mainstays of the economy. In the 1920s the first large projects were undertaken to exploit the Colorado River. The Colorado River Compact was agreed in 1922, and the Boulder Dam (now Hoover Dam) was authorized in 1928. Since then irrigated agriculture has overtaken mining as an industry and is as important as ranching. In 1945 the Colorado-Big Thompson project diverted water by tunnel beneath the Rocky Mountains to irrigate 700,000 acres (284,000 ha.) of northern Colorado. Now more than 80% of the population is urban, with the majority engaged in telecommunications, aerospace and computer technology.

TERRITORY AND POPULATION

Colorado is bounded north by Wyoming, northeast by Nebraska, east by Kansas, southeast by Oklahoma, south by New Mexico and west by Utah. Land area, 103,718 sq. miles (268,628 sq. km).

Census population, 1 April 2000, 4,301,261, an increase of 30·6% over 1990. July 2009 estimate, 5,024,748.

Population in five census years was:

	White	Black	Indian	Asiatic	Total	Per sq. mile
1910	783,415	11,453	1,482	2,674	799,024	7·7
1950	1,296,653	20,177	1,567	5,870	1,325,089	12·7
			All others			
1980	2,571,498	101,703	216,763		2,889,964	27·9
1990	2,905,474	133,146	255,774		3,294,394	31·8
2000	3,560,005	165,063	576,193		4,301,261	41·5

Of the total population in 2000, 2,165,983 were male, 3,200,466 were 18 years old or older and 3,633,185 were urban. The Hispanic population in 2000 was 735,601, up from 424,302 in 1990 (an increase of 73·4%). Large cities, with 2008 populations: Denver City, 566,974; Colorado Springs, 372,437; Aurora, 305,582; Lakewood, 140,024; Fort Collins, 129,467; Westminster, 105,753; Arvada, 104,830; Pueblo, 103,730.

Main metropolitan areas (2008): Denver–Aurora, 2,506,626; Colorado Springs, 617,714; Boulder, 293,161; Fort Collins–Loveland, 292,825; Greeley, 249,715; Pueblo, 156,737; Grand Junction, 143,171.

SOCIAL STATISTICS

Births, 2007 (provisional), were 70,992 (14·6 per 1,000 population); deaths, 2006, 29,521 (6·2). Infant mortality, 2006, 5·7 per 1,000 live births. 2006: marriages, 36,100 (7·6 per 1,000 population); divorces and annulments, 21,100 (4·4).

CLIMATE

Denver, Jan. 31°F (–0·6°C), July 73°F (22·8°C). Annual rainfall 14" (358 mm). Pueblo, Jan. 30°F (–1·1°C), July 83°F (28·3°C). Annual rainfall 12" (312 mm). Colorado belongs to the Mountain States climate zone (*see* UNITED STATES: Climate).

CONSTITUTION AND GOVERNMENT

The constitution adopted in 1876 is still in effect with (2006) 153 amendments. The General Assembly consists of a Senate of 35 members elected for four years, one-half retiring every two years, and of a House of Representatives of 65 members elected for two years. Sessions are annual, beginning 1951. Qualified as electors are all citizens, male and female (except convicted, incarcerated criminals), 18 years of age, who have resided in the state and the precinct for 32 days immediately preceding the election. There is a seven-member State Supreme Court.

For the 111th Congress, which convened in Jan. 2009, Colorado sends seven members to the House of Representatives. It is represented in the Senate by Michael Bennet (D. 2009–11) and Mark Udall (D. 2009–15).

The capital is Denver. There are 64 counties.

RECENT ELECTIONS

In the 2008 presidential elections Barack Obama won Colorado with 53·7% of the vote (George W. Bush won in 2004).

CURRENT ADMINISTRATION

Governor: Bill Ritter, Jr (D.), 2007–11 (salary: $90,000).
Lieut.-Governor: Barbara O'Brien (D.), 2007–11 ($68,500).
Secretary of State: Bernie Buescher (D.), 2009–11 ($68,500).

Government Website: http://www.colorado.gov

ECONOMY

Per capita personal income (2008) was $42,985.

Budget

In 2008 total revenue was $26,522m. and total expenditure $22,857m. Major areas of expenditure were: education, $7,986m.; public welfare, $4,557m.; highways, $1,282m.; correction, $996m.; government administration, $870m. Debt outstanding, in 2008, was $15,879m.

Performance

2008 Gross Domestic Product by state was $248,603m. (provisional), ranking Colorado 20th in the United States.

Banking and Finance

There are 180 commercial banks insured with the Federal Deposit Insurance Corporation, with $47,631m. in total assets.

ENERGY AND NATURAL RESOURCES

Oil and Gas

In 2008 Colorado produced 1,250bn. cu. ft of natural gas and 23m. bbls of crude oil. It ranked fifth in the USA for daily gas production, and eleventh in crude oil production. Total production value of all hydrocarbons was $9·8bn.

Water
The Rocky Mountains of Colorado form the headwaters for four major American rivers: the Colorado, Rio Grande, Arkansas and Platte. The total area covered by water is approximately 376 sq. miles.

Minerals
Coal (2008): 34·5m. short tons were produced. In 2008 there were 29,900 people employed in mining, including 7,882 in extracting oil and natural gas. Value of domestic non-fuel mineral production in 2008 was $1,746m.

Agriculture
In 2002 farms and ranches numbered 30,000, with a total of 31·3m. acres of agricultural land. 5,748,610 acres were harvested crop land; average farm, 1,043 acres. Average value of farmland and buildings per acre in 2002 was $756. Farm income 2006: from crops, $1,553m.; from livestock and products, $4,062m. The net farm income in 2006 was $734m.

Production of principal crops in 2001: corn for grain, 149·8m. bu.; wheat for grain, 69·2m. bu.; barley for grain, 8·6m. bu.; hay, 4,780,000 tons; dry beans, 1,785,000 cwt; oats and sorghum, 11·4m. bu.; sugar beets, 824,000 tons; potatoes, 23,274,000 cwt; vegetables, 9,523 tons; fruits, 21,900 tons.

In 2001 the number of farm animals was: 3,050,000 cattle, 91,000 milch cows, 780,000 swine and 370,000 sheep.

Forestry
The state had a forested area of 22,612,000 acres in 2007, of which 11,259,000 acres were national forest.

INDUSTRY
In 2005 the state's 5,189 manufacturing establishments had 136,000 employees, earning $6,279m. Total value added by manufacturing in 2006 was $20,825m.

Labour
Total non-agricultural employment, 2007: 2,330,000. Employees by branch, 2007 (in 1,000): trade, transportation and utilities, 430; government, 375; professional and business services, 348; leisure and hospitality, 270; education and health services, 240. The unemployment rate in 2007 was 3·7%.

Trade Unions
In 2006 there were 165,000 union members in Colorado (7·7% of workers).

INTERNATIONAL TRADE

Imports and Exports
In 2008 Colorado exported $7·7bn. in goods. The largest trading partners were Canada, China (including Hong Kong), Mexico, Malaysia and Japan. Largest export categories are industrial machinery (including computers), electrical machinery, and optic, photographic and medical/surgical instruments.

Trade Fairs
The National Western Stock Show and Rodeo is the largest event of its kind in the USA, drawing over 600,000 visitors.

COMMUNICATIONS

Roads
In 2007 there were 88,163 miles of road, of which 19,229 miles were urban roads and 68,934 miles rural roads. There were 1,707,139 motor vehicle registrations.

Rail
There were 2,747 miles of railroad in 2002.

Civil Aviation
In 2007 there were 74 airports open to the public; 14 with commercial service, 60 public non-commercial (general aviation) and 14 private non-commercial. Denver International Airport, the largest airport in the state and tenth busiest in the world, handled 51,245,334 passengers in 2008.

SOCIAL INSTITUTIONS

Justice
In Dec. 2008 there were 23,274 federal and state prisoners. The death penalty is authorized but has not been used since 1997.

Education
In 2004–05 there were 1,693 public elementary and secondary schools with 765,976 pupils and 45,165 teachers. In 2003–04 teachers' salaries averaged $43,319.

Enrolments in four-year state universities and colleges in fall 2005 were: University of Colorado at Boulder, 31,589 students; University of Colorado at Denver and Health Sciences Center, 19,766; University of Colorado at Colorado Springs, 9,333; Colorado State University (Fort Collins), 27,780; University of Northern Colorado (Greeley), 13,622; Colorado School of Mines (Golden), 4,318; Metropolitan State College of Denver, 21,010; Colorado State University-Pueblo (was University of Southern Colorado), 5,870; Mesa State College (Grand Junction), 6,062; Fort Lewis College (Durango), 3,946; Adams State College (Alamosa), 9,157; Western State College of Colorado (Gunnison), 2,253.

Total enrolment in private degree-granting universities and colleges in fall 2004 was 61,606.

Health
In 2006 there were 73 community hospitals with 9,500 beds. A total of 420,000 patients were admitted during the year.

Welfare
Medicare enrolment in July 2004 totalled 505,618. In fiscal year 2006 a total of 624,889 people in Colorado received Medicaid. In Dec. 2008 there were 635,816 Old-Age, Survivors, and Disability Insurance (OASDI) beneficiaries. A total of 20,640 people were receiving payments under Temporary Assistance for Needy Families (TANF) in Dec. 2008.

RELIGION
The leading religious denominations (2000) in the state are: 752,505 Roman Catholics; 92,326 Latter-day Saints (Mormons); 85,083 Southern Baptists; 77,286 United Methodists; 72,000 Jews.

CULTURE

Broadcasting
There are 97 commercial and public radio stations, broadcasting on both AM and FM frequencies. There are also 14 commercial and four public television stations.

Press
There are 27 daily newspapers. In addition there are 41 weekly newspapers including seven regional business journals.

Tourism
Skiing is a major tourist attraction. Colorado is particularly renowned for the Rocky Mountain National Park and the Mesa Verde National Park, a World Heritage Site.

FURTHER READING
Statistical information: Business Research Division, Univ. of Colorado, Boulder 80309. Publishes *Statistical Abstract of Colorado.*

Griffiths, M. and Rubright, L., *Colorado: a Geography.* 1983

State library: Colorado State Library, 201 E. Colfax, Rm. 314, Denver 80203.

Connecticut

KEY HISTORICAL EVENTS

Formerly territory of Algonquian-speaking Indians, Connecticut was first colonized by Europeans during the 1630s, when English Puritans moved there from Massachusetts Bay. Settlements were founded in the Connecticut River Valley at Hartford, Saybrook, Wethersfield and Windsor in 1635. They formed an organized commonwealth in 1637. A further settlement was made at New Haven in 1638 and was united to the commonwealth under a royal charter in 1662. The charter confirmed the commonwealth constitution, drawn up by mutual agreement in 1639 and called the Fundamental Orders of Connecticut.

The area was agricultural and its population of largely English descent until the early 19th century. After the War of Independence, Connecticut was one of the original 13 states of the Union. Its state constitution came into force in 1818 and lasted with amendments until 1965 when a new one was adopted.

In the early 1800s a textile industry thrived on water power. By 1850 the state had more employment in industry than in agriculture, and immigration from Europe (and especially from southern and eastern Europe) grew rapidly throughout the 19th century. Some immigrants worked in whaling and iron-mining, but most sought industrial employment. Settlement was spread over a large number of small towns, with no single dominant culture.

Yale University was founded at New Haven in 1701. The US Coastguard Academy was founded in 1876 at New London, a former whaling port.

TERRITORY AND POPULATION

Connecticut is bounded in the north by Massachusetts, east by Rhode Island, south by the Atlantic and west by New York. Land area, 4,845 sq. miles (12,548 sq. km).

Census population, 1 April 2000, 3,405,565, an increase of 3·6% since 1990. July 2009 estimate, 3,518,288.

Population in five census years was:

	White	*Black*	*Indian*	*Asian*	*Total*	*Per sq. mile*
1910	1,098,897	15,174	152	533	1,114,756	231·3
1930	1,576,700	29,354	162	687	1,606,903	333·4
1980	2,799,420	217,433	4,533	18,970	3,107,576	634·3

	White	*Black*	*Indian*	*Asian*	*Others*	*Total*	*Per sq. mile*
1990	2,859,353	274,269	6,654	50,078	96,762	3,287,116	678·6
2000	2,780,355	309,843	9,639	82,313	148,567	3,405,565	702·9

Of the total population in 2000, there were 320,323 persons of Hispanic origin, up from 213,116 in 1990 (an increase of 50·3%). Of the total population in 2000, 1,756,246 were female, 2,563,877 were 18 years old or older and 2,988,057 were urban. There were 183 residents in five Indian Reservations.

The chief cities and towns are (2000 census populations):

Bridgeport	139,529	Danbury	74,848
New Haven	123,626	New Britain	71,538
Hartford	121,578	West Hartford	63,589
Stamford	117,083	Greenwich	61,101
Waterbury	107,271	Bristol	60,062
Norwalk	82,951	Meriden	58,244

SOCIAL STATISTICS

Births, 2007 (provisional), 41,684 (11·9 per 1,000 population); deaths, 2006, 29,260 (8·3). Infant mortality rate, 2006, 6·2 per 1,000 live births. 2006: marriages, 17,400 (5·0 per 1,000 population); divorces and annulments, 9,800 (2·8). Connecticut became the third state after Massachusetts and California to allow same-sex marriage when it became legal in Oct. 2008 (although it was subsequently banned in California).

CLIMATE

New Haven: Jan. 25°F (–3·8°C), July 74°F (23·4°C). Annual rainfall 45" (1,143 mm). Connecticut belongs to the New England climate zone (*see* UNITED STATES: Climate).

CONSTITUTION AND GOVERNMENT

The 1818 constitution was revised in 1955. On 30 Dec. 1965 a new constitution went into effect, having been framed by a constitutional convention in the summer of 1965 and approved by the voters in Dec. 1965.

The General Assembly consists of a Senate of 36 members and a House of Representatives of 151 members. Members of each House are elected for the term of two years. Legislative sessions are annual.

For the 111th Congress, which convened in Jan. 2009, Connecticut sends five members to the House of Representatives. It is represented in the Senate by Christopher Dodd (Democrat, 1981–2011) and Joseph Lieberman (Democrat, 1989–2006; Independent Democrat, 2007–13).

There are eight counties. The state capital is Hartford.

RECENT ELECTIONS

In the 2008 presidential elections Barack Obama won Connecticut with 60·6% of the vote (John Kerry won in 2004).

CURRENT ADMINISTRATION

Governor: M. Jodi Rell (R.), 2007–11 (salary: $150,000).

Lieut.-Governor: Michael Fedele (R.), 2007–11 ($110,000).

Secretary of State: Susan Bysiewicz (D.), 2007–11 ($110,000).

Government Website: http://www.ct.gov

ECONOMY

Per capita personal income (2008) was $56,272, the second highest in the country (after the District of Columbia).

Budget

In 2008 total state revenue was $20,930m. Total expenditure was $23,529m. (education, $5,850m.; public welfare, $5,621m.; hospitals, $1,396m.; government administration, $1,116m.; health, $901m.) Outstanding debt in 2008, $27,554m.

Performance

Gross Domestic Product by state in 2008 was $216,174m. (provisional), ranking Connecticut 24th in the United States.

ENERGY AND NATURAL RESOURCES

Water

The total area covered by water is approximately 699 sq. miles.

Minerals

The state has some mineral resources: crushed stone, sand, gravel, clay, dimension stone, feldspar and quartz. Total non-fuel mineral production in 2006 was valued at $168m.

Agriculture

In 2007 the state had 4,916 farms with a total area of 405,616 acres; the average farm size was 83 acres, valued at $12,667 per acre in 2007. Farm income 2006: crops $372m., and livestock and products $151m. The net farm income in 2006 was $183m. Principal crops are greenhouse and nursery products, grains, hay, tobacco, vegetables, maize, melons, fruit, nuts and berries.

In 2007 there were 50,213 all cattle (value $81·7m.), 5,767 sheep and 3,645 swine.

Forestry

Total forested area was 1,859,000 acres in 2008.

INDUSTRY

In 2005 the state's 5,037 manufacturing establishments had 185,000 employees, earning $9,767m. Total value added by manufacturing in 2006 was $32,159m.

Labour

Total non-agricultural employment, 2007, 1,698,000. Employees by branch, 2007 (in 1,000): trade, transportation and utilities, 311; education and health services, 288; government, 249; professional and business services, 206; manufacturing, 191. The unemployment rate in 2007 was 4·5%.

COMMUNICATIONS

Roads

The total length of highways in 2007 was 21,295 miles comprising 15,108 miles of urban road and 6,187 miles of rural road. Motor vehicles registered in 2007 numbered 3,047,330.

Rail

In 2003 there were 597 miles of railroad route.

Civil Aviation

In 2005 there were 54 airports (44 private), 92 heliports and six seaplane bases. There were 3,268,469 passenger enplanements statewide in 2007.

SOCIAL INSTITUTIONS

Justice

In Dec. 2008 the jail and prison population totalled 20,661. The death penalty for murder is authorized, and was used in May 2005 for the first time since 1960.

Education

Instruction is free for all children and young people between the ages of four and 21 years, and compulsory for all children between the ages of five and 18 years. In 2004–05 there were 663 public elementary schools, 172 middle/junior high schools, 168 high schools, 17 technical high schools, 48 pre-kindergarten schools, 14 charter schools, 40 full-time magnet schools and 383 non-public schools. In 2004–05 there were 577,390 public school pupils and 38,808 teachers. In 2003–04 total expenditure on public elementary and secondary education was $7,549m. and average teacher salary was $57,337 (the highest in the United States). In 2002–03 spending per pupil was $11,057.

In 2002 Connecticut had 46 colleges, of which one state university, one external degree college, four state colleges, 12 community-technical colleges and a US Coast Guard Academy were state-funded. The state colleges had 35,448 students in 2003. The University of Connecticut at Storrs (founded in 1881), had 26,629 students in 2003. In 2005 Yale University, New Haven (founded in 1701) had 11,483 students; Wesleyan University, Middletown (1831), 3,205 students; Trinity College, Hartford (1823), 2,470 students; Connecticut College, New London (1915), 1,898 students; and the University of Hartford (1877), 7,260 students. The US Coast Guard Academy had 1,005 students in 2005. There were 20 independent (four-year course) colleges and three independent (two-year course) colleges as well as two seminaries and the International College of Hospitality Management.

Health

In 2006 there were 35 community hospitals with 7,900 beds. A total of 406,000 patients were admitted during the year.

Welfare

Medicare enrolment in July 2004 totalled 524,614. In fiscal year 2006 a total of 517,529 people in Connecticut received Medicaid. In Dec. 2008 there were 599,533 Old-Age, Survivors, and Disability Insurance (OASDI) beneficiaries. A total of 32,959 people were receiving payments under Temporary Assistance for Needy Families (TANF) in Dec. 2008.

RELIGION

The leading religious denominations (2000) in the state are Roman Catholic (1,372,562 members), United Churches of Christ (124,770), Jewish (108,280), Protestant Episcopal (73,550) and United Methodist (51,183). There are also large numbers of Black Baptists.

CULTURE

Broadcasting

In 2003 there were 71 broadcasting stations and 12 television stations.

Press

In 2008 there were 18 daily, 14 Sunday and 74 weekly newspapers.

Tourism

In 2005, 260,000 overseas visitors (excluding those from Mexico and Canada) visited Connecticut.

FURTHER READING

State Register and Manual. Annual

Halliburton, W. J., *The People of Connecticut.* 1985

State library: Connecticut State Library, 231 Capitol Avenue, Hartford (CT) 06105.

State Book Store: Dept. of Environmental Protection, 79 Elm St., Hartford (CT) 06106.

Business Incentives: Connecticut Economic Resource Center, 805 Brook St., Rocky Hill (CT) 06067.

Connecticut Tourism: Dept. of Economic and Community Development, 865 Brook St., Rocky Hill (CT) 06067.

Delaware

KEY HISTORICAL EVENTS

Delaware was the territory of Algonquian-speaking Indians who were displaced by European settlement in the 17th century. The first settlers were Swedes who came in 1638 to build Fort Christina (now Wilmington), and colonize what they called New Sweden. In 1655 their colony was taken by the Dutch, who were based in New Amsterdam. In 1664 the British took the whole New Amsterdam colony, including Delaware, and called it New York.

In 1682 Delaware was granted to William Penn, who wanted access to the coast for his Pennsylvania colony. Union of the two colonies was unpopular, and Delaware gained its own government in 1704, although it continued to share a royal governor with Pennsylvania until the War of Independence. Delaware then became one of the 13 original states of the Union and the first to ratify the federal constitution (on 7 Dec. 1787).

The population was of Swedish, Finnish, British and Irish extraction. The land was low-lying and fertile, and the use of slave labour was legal. There was a significant number of black slaves, but Delaware was a border state during the Civil War (1861–65) and did not leave the Union.

19th-century immigrants were mostly European Jews, Poles, Germans and Italians. The north became industrial and densely populated, more so after the Second World War with the rise of the petrochemical industry. Industry in general profited from the opening of the Chesapeake and Delaware Canal in 1829; it was converted to a toll-free deep channel for ocean-going ships in 1919.

TERRITORY AND POPULATION

Delaware is bounded in the north by Pennsylvania, northeast by New Jersey, east by Delaware Bay, south and west by Maryland. Land area 1,954 sq. miles (5,061 sq. km). Census population, 1 April 2000, was 783,600, an increase of 17·6% since 1990. July 2009 estimate, 885,122.

Population in five census years was:

	White	*Black*	*Indian*	*Asiatic*	*Total*	*Per sq. mile*
1910	171,102	31,181	5	34	202,322	103·0
1960	384,327	60,688	597	410	446,292	224·0
			All others			
1980	488,002	96,157	10,179		594,338	290·8
1990	535,094	112,460	18,614		666,168	325·9
2000	584,773	150,666	48,161		783,600	401·0

Of the total population in 2000, 403,059 were female, 589,013 were 18 years old or older and 627,758 were urban. The Hispanic population in 2000 was 37,277, up from 15,824 in 1990 (an increase of 135·6%).

The 2000 census figures show Wilmington with a population of 72,664; Dover, 32,135; Newark, 28,547; Milford City, 6,732; Seaford City, 6,699; Middletown, 6,161.

SOCIAL STATISTICS

Births, 2007 (provisional), 11,774 (13·6 per 1,000 population); deaths, 2006, 7,204 (8·4). 2006 infant mortality, 8·3 per 1,000 live births. 2006: marriages, 5,200 (6·0 per 1,000 population); divorces and annulments, 3,800 (4·5).

CLIMATE

Wilmington, Jan. 31°F (–0·6°C), July 76°F (24·4°C). Annual rainfall 43" (1,076 mm). Delaware belongs to the Atlantic Coast climate zone (*see* UNITED STATES: Climate).

CONSTITUTION AND GOVERNMENT

The present constitution (the fourth) dates from 1897, and has had 51 amendments; it was not ratified by the electorate but promulgated by the Constitutional Convention. The General Assembly consists of a Senate of 21 members elected for four years and a House of Representatives of 41 members elected for two years.

For the 111th Congress, which convened in Jan. 2009, Delaware sends one member to the House of Representatives. It is represented in the Senate by Thomas Carper (D. 2001–13) and Ted Kaufman (D. 2009–15).

The state capital is Dover. Delaware is divided into three counties.

RECENT ELECTIONS

In the 2008 presidential elections Barack Obama won Delaware with 61·9% of the vote (John Kerry won in 2004).

CURRENT ADMINISTRATION

Governor: Jack Markell (D.), 2009–13 (salary: $171,000).

Lieut.-Governor: Matt Denn (D.), 2009–13 ($74,345).

Secretary of State: Jeffrey W. Bullock (D.), appointed Jan. 2009 ($120,755).

Government Website: http://www.delaware.gov

ECONOMY

Per capita personal income (2008) was $40,519.

Budget

In 2008 total revenue was $6,658m. Total expenditure was $7,152m. (education, $2,263m.; public welfare, $1,451m.; highways, $496m.; government administration, $484m.; health, $393m.) Debt outstanding in 2008, $5,723m.

Performance

2008 Gross Domestic Product by state was $61,828m. (provisional), ranking Delaware 39th in the United States.

Banking and Finance

Delaware National Bank has branches statewide. Also based in Delaware, MBNA is the world's largest independent credit card issuer, with managed loans of $97·5bn.

ENERGY AND NATURAL RESOURCES

Electricity

Net generation of electric energy, 2005, 8·1bn. kWh.

Water

The total area covered by water is approximately 536 sq. miles.

Minerals

The mineral resources of Delaware are not extensive, consisting chiefly of clay products, stone, sand and gravel and magnesium compounds. Total non-fuel mineral production in 2006 was valued at $22m.

Agriculture

Delaware is mainly an industrial state, with agriculture as its principal industry. There were 560,000 acres in 2,400 farms in 2002. The average farm was 233 acres and was valued (land and buildings) at $4,054 per acre in 2002. Farm income 2006: crops $183m., and livestock and products $786m. The net farm income in 2006 was $388m. The major product is broilers, accounting for $494·2m. in cash receipts in 2002, out of total farm cash receipts of $727·7m.

The chief crops are corn for feed, greenhouse products and soybeans.

Forestry

Total forested area was 383,000 acres in 2007.

INDUSTRY

In 2005 the state's 652 manufacturing establishments had 36,000 employees, earning $1,661m. Total value added by manufacturing in 2006 was $8,862m. Main manufactures are chemicals, transport equipment and food.

Labour

Total non-agricultural employment, 2007, 437,000. Employees by branch, 2007 (in 1,000): trade, transportation and utilities, 83; government, 61; professional and business services, 60; education and health services, 58; financial activities, 45. The unemployment rate in 2007 was 3·5%.

COMMUNICATIONS

Roads

In 2007 there were 6,242 miles of roads comprising 2,963 miles of urban road and 3,279 miles of rural road. In 2007 total vehicles registered numbered 851,223.

Rail

In 1999 the state had 271 miles of active rail line, 23 miles of which is part of Amtrak's high-speed Northeast corridor. In 1999 there were 710,245 passenger trips beginning or ending in Delaware—645,808 of which were commuter trips. An important component of Delaware's freight infrastructure is the rail access to the Port of Wilmington.

Civil Aviation

In 2005 Delaware had 15 public-use airports and one helistop. There were 12,143 passenger enplanements statewide in 2007.

SOCIAL INSTITUTIONS

Justice

In Dec. 2008 the jail and prison population totalled 7,075. The death penalty was suspended in July 2006. There were two executions in 2001, none in 2002, 2003 or 2004, and one in 2005.

Education

The state has free public schools and compulsory school attendance to age 16. In 2004–05 the 222 elementary and secondary public schools had 119,091 enrolled pupils and 7,856 classroom teachers. Another 25,576 children were enrolled in private and parochial schools in 2003–04. Total expenditure for public elementary and secondary education in 2003–04 was $1,379m. and average teacher salary was $49,366. Expenditure per pupil was $9,693 in 2002–03.

The state supports the University of Delaware at Newark (founded in 1834) which had 1,077 full-time faculty members and 20,982 students in 2005; Delaware State University, Dover (1891), with 170 full-time faculty members in 2004 and 3,722 students in 2005; and the campuses of Delaware Technical and Community College at Newark with 7,473 students in 2005, Dover with 2,569 students and Georgetown with 3,936 students.

Health

In 2006 there were six community hospitals with 2,100 beds. A total of 105,000 patients were admitted during the year.

Welfare

Medicare enrolment in July 2004 totalled 122,843. In fiscal year 2006 a total of 170,659 people in Delaware received Medicaid. In Dec. 2008 there were 161,314 Old-Age, Survivors, and Disability Insurance (OASDI) beneficiaries. A total of 12,831 people were receiving payments under Temporary Assistance for Needy Families (TANF) in Dec. 2008.

RELIGION

The leading religious denominations are Roman Catholics, Methodists, Episcopalians and Lutherans.

FURTHER READING

Statistical information: Delaware Economic Development Office, Dover, DE 19901. Publishes *Delaware Statistical Overview.*

State Manual, Containing Official List of Officers, Commissions and County Officers. Annual

Smeal, L., *Delaware Historical and Biographical Index.* 1984

District of Columbia

KEY HISTORICAL EVENTS

The District of Columbia, organized in 1790, is the seat of the government of the USA, for which the land was ceded by the states of Maryland and Virginia to the USA as a site for the national capital. It was established under Acts of Congress in 1790 and 1791. Congress first met in it in 1800 and federal authority over it became vested in 1801. In 1846 the land ceded by Virginia (about 33 sq. miles) was given back.

TERRITORY AND POPULATION

The District forms an enclave on the Potomac River, where the river forms the southwest boundary of Maryland. The land area of the District of Columbia is 61 sq. miles (159 sq. km).

Census population, 1 April 2000, was 572,059 (100% urban), a decrease of 5·72% from that of 1990. July 2009 estimate, 599,657. Metropolitan area of Washington, D.C.–Baltimore (2000), 7,608,070. The Hispanic population in 2000 was 44,953, up from 32,710 in 1990 (an increase of 37·4%). Of the total population in 2000, 302,693 were female and 457,067 were 18 years old or older.

Population in five census years was:

	White	*Black*	*Indian*	*Chinese and Japanese*	*Total*	*Per sq. mile*
1910	236,128	94,446	68	427	331,069	5,517·8
1960	345,263	411,737	587	3,532	763,956	12,523·9
			All others			
1980	171,768	448,906	17,659		638,333	10,464·4
1990	179,667	339,604	87,629		606,900	9,949·2
2000	176,101	343,312	52,646		572,059	9,378·0

Blacks constituted 60·0% of the population at the 2000 census—the highest proportion in the USA.

SOCIAL STATISTICS

Births, 2007 (provisional), 7,628 (13·0 per 1,000 population); deaths, 2006, 5,344 (9·2). Infant mortality rate, 2006, 11·3 per 1,000 live births. 2006: marriages, 2,300 (3·9 per 1,000 population); divorces and annulments, 1,300 (2·1). The abortion rate, at 39 for every 1,000 women in 2002, is the highest in the USA.

CLIMATE

Washington, Jan. 34°F (1·1°C), July 77°F (25°C). Annual rainfall 43" (1,064 mm). The District of Columbia belongs to the Atlantic Coast climate zone (*see* UNITED STATES: Climate).

CONSTITUTION AND GOVERNMENT

Local government, from 1 July 1878 until Aug. 1967, was that of a municipal corporation administered by a board of three commissioners, of whom two were appointed from civil life by the President, and confirmed by the Senate, for a term of three years each. The other commissioner was detailed by the President from the Engineer Corps of the Army. The Commission form of government was abolished in 1967 and a new Mayor Council instituted with officers appointed by the President with the advice and consent of the Senate. On 24 Dec. 1973 the appointed officers were replaced by an elected Mayor and councillors, with full legislative powers in local matters as from 1974. Congress retains the right to legislate, to veto or supersede the Council's acts. The 23rd amendment to the federal constitution (1961) conferred the right to vote in national elections. The District has one delegate and one shadow delegate to the House of Representatives and two shadow senators. The Congressman may participate but not vote on the House floor.

RECENT ELECTIONS

In the 2008 presidential elections Barack Obama won the District of Columbia with 92·5% of the vote (John Kerry won in 2004).

CURRENT ADMINISTRATION

Mayor: Adrian Fenty (D.), 2007–11 (salary: $200,000).

Secretary of the District: Stephanie Scott (D.), appointed Jan. 2007 (salary: $120,000).

Government Website: http://www.dc.gov

ECONOMY

Per capita personal income (2008) was $66,119, the highest in the country.

Budget

The District's revenues are derived from a tax on real and personal property, sales taxes, taxes on corporations and companies, licences for conducting various businesses and from federal payments. The District of Columbia has no bonded debt not covered by its accumulated sinking fund.

Performance
Gross Domestic Product by state in 2008 was $97,235m. (provisional).

ENERGY AND NATURAL RESOURCES
Water
The total area covered by water is approximately 7 sq. miles.

INDUSTRY
In 2005 there were 142 manufacturing establishments with 2,000 employees, earning $75m. Total value added by manufacturing in 2006 was $172m. The main industries are communications, finance, government service, insurance, real estate, services, transport, utilities, and wholesale and retail trade.

Labour
Total non-agricultural employment, 2007, 695,000. Employees by branch, 2007 (in 1,000): government, 232; professional and business services, 154; education and health services, 98; leisure and hospitality, 55; financial activities, 29. In 2007 the unemployment rate was 5·5%.

COMMUNICATIONS
Roads
In 2007 there were 1,505 miles of roads. There were 217,521 registered vehicles in 2007.

Rail
There is a metro in Washington extending to 130 km, and two commuter rail networks.

Civil Aviation
The District is served by three general airports; across the Potomac River in Arlington, Va., is National Airport; in Chantilly, Va., is Dulles International Airport; and in Maryland is Baltimore–Washington International Airport.

SOCIAL INSTITUTIONS
Justice
The death penalty was declared unconstitutional in the District of Columbia on 14 Nov. 1973.

The District's Court system is the Judicial Branch of the District of Columbia. It is the only completely unified court system in the United States, possibly because of the District's unique city-state jurisdiction. Until the District of Columbia Court Reform and Criminal Procedure Act of 1970, the judicial system was almost entirely in the hands of Federal government. Since that time, the system has been similar in most respects to the autonomous systems of the states.

Education
In 2004–05 there were 76,714 pupils enrolled at 216 elementary and secondary public schools with 5,387 teachers. Average expenditure per pupil in 2002–03 was $11,847.

Higher education is given through the Consortium of Universities of the Metropolitan Washington Area, which consists of six universities and three colleges: Georgetown University, founded in 1795 by the Jesuit Order; George Washington University, non-sectarian founded in 1821; Howard University, founded in 1867; Catholic University of America, founded in 1887; American University (Methodist), founded in 1893; University of District of Columbia, founded 1976; Gallaudet College, founded 1864; Trinity College in Washington, D.C. (women's college), founded 1897. There are 18 institutes of higher education altogether.

Health
In 2006 there were 11 community hospitals with 3,600 beds. A total of 139,000 patients were admitted during the year.

Welfare
Medicare enrolment in July 2004 totalled 73,632 (down 0·2% on the July 2003 total). In fiscal year 2006 a total of 159,335 people in the District of Columbia received Medicaid. In Dec. 2008 there were 71,468 Old-Age, Survivors, and Disability Insurance (OASDI) beneficiaries. A total of 12,510 people were receiving payments under Temporary Assistance for Needy Families (TANF) in Dec. 2008.

RELIGION
The largest churches are the Protestant and Roman Catholic Christian churches; there are also Jewish, Eastern Orthodox and Islamic congregations.

CULTURE
Tourism
About 20m. visitors stay in the District every year and spend about $1,000m.

FURTHER READING
Statistical Information: The Metropolitan Washington Board of Trade publications.
Reports of the Commissioners of the District of Columbia. Annual.
Bowling, K. R., *The Creation of Washington D.C.: the Idea and the Location of the American Capital.* 1991

Florida

KEY HISTORICAL EVENTS
Of the French and Spanish settlements in Florida in the 16th century, the Spanish, at St Augustine from 1565, survived. Florida was claimed by Spain until 1763 when it passed to Britain. Although regained by Spain in 1783, the British used it as a base for attacks on American forces during the war of 1812. Gen. Andrew Jackson captured Pensacola for the USA in 1818. In 1819 a treaty was signed which ceded Florida to the USA with effect from 1821 and it became a Territory of the USA in 1822.

Florida had been the home of the Apalachee and Timucua Indians. After 1770 groups of Creek Indians began to arrive as refugees from the European-Indian wars. These 'Seminoles' or runaways attracted other refugees including slaves, the recapture of whom was the motive for the first Seminole War of 1817–18. A second war followed in 1835–42, when the Seminoles retreated to the Everglades swamps. After a third war in 1855–58 most Seminoles were forced or persuaded to move to reserves in Oklahoma.

Florida became a state in 1845. About half of the population were black slaves. At the outbreak of Civil War in 1861 the state seceded from the Union.

During the 20th century Florida continued to grow fruit and vegetables, but real-estate development (often for retirement) and the growth of tourism and the aerospace industry set it apart from other ex-plantation states.

TERRITORY AND POPULATION
Florida is a peninsula bounded in the west by the Gulf of Mexico, south by the Straits of Florida, east by the Atlantic, north by Georgia and northwest by Alabama. Land area, 53,927 sq. miles (139,670 sq. km). Census population, 1 April 2000, 15,982,378, an increase of 23·5% since 1990. July 2009 estimate, 18,537,969.

Population in five federal census years was:

	White	*Black*	*All Others*	*Total*	*Per sq. mile*
1950	2,166,051	603,101	2,153	2,771,305	51·1
1970	5,719,343	1,041,651	28,449	6,789,443	125·6
1980	8,319,448	1,342,478	84,398	9,746,324	180·1
1990	10,749,285	1,759,534	429,107	12,937,926	238·9
2000	12,465,029	2,335,505	1,181,844	15,982,378	296·4

Of the total population in 2000, 8,184,663 were female, 12,336,038 were 18 years old or older and 14,270,020 were urban. The Hispanic population in 2000 was 2,682,715, up from 1,574,143 in 1990 (a rise of 70·4%, the third largest numeric increase of any state in the USA).

The largest cities in the state, 2000 census (and 1990) are: Jacksonville, 735,617 (635,230); Miami, 362,470 (358,548); Tampa, 303,447 (280,015); St Petersburg, 248,232 (238,629); Hialeah, 226,419 (188,004); Orlando, 185,951 (164,693); Fort Lauderdale, 152,397 (149,377); Tallahassee, 150,624 (124,773); Hollywood, 139,357 (121,697); Pembroke Pines, 137,427 (65,452); Coral Springs, 117,549 (79,443); Clearwater, 108,787 (98,784); Cape Coral, 102,286 (74,991); Gainesville, 95,447 (84,770); Port St Lucie, 88,769 (55,759); Miami Beach, 87,933 (92,639); Sunrise, 85,779 (65,683); Plantation, 82,934 (66,814); West Palm Beach, 82,103 (67,764); Palm Bay, 79,413 (62,543); Lakeland, 78,452 (70,576); Pompano Beach, 78,191 (72,411).

Population of the largest metropolitan areas (2000): Miami–Fort Lauderdale, 3,876,380; Tampa-St Petersburg-Clearwater, 2,395,997; Orlando, 1,644,561.

SOCIAL STATISTICS

Births, 2007 (provisional), 239,273 (13·1 per 1,000 population); deaths, 2006, 170,066 (9·4). Infant mortality, 2006, 7·3 per 1,000 live births. 2006: marriages, 155,500 (8·6 per 1,000 population); divorces and annulments, 87,800 (4·9).

CLIMATE

Jacksonville, Jan. 55°F (12·8°C), July 81°F (27·2°C). Annual rainfall 54" (1,353 mm). Key West, Jan. 70°F (21·1°C), July 83°F (28·3°C). Annual rainfall 39" (968 mm). Miami, Jan. 67°F (19·4°C), July 82°F (27·8°C). Annual rainfall 60" (1,516 mm). Tampa, Jan. 61°F (16·1°C), July 81°F (27·2°C). Annual rainfall 51" (1,285 mm). Florida belongs to the Gulf Coast climate zone (*see* UNITED STATES: Climate).

CONSTITUTION AND GOVERNMENT

The 1968 Legislature revised the constitution of 1885. The state legislature comprises the Senate and House of Representatives. The Senate has 40 members elected for four years. Half of the membership is elected every two years. The House has 120 members, all of whom are elected every two years during elections held in even-numbered years. Sessions of the legislature are held annually, and are limited to 60 days. Senate and House districts are based on population, with each senator and member representing approximately the same number of residents. The Senate and House are reapportioned every ten years when the federal census is released. In addition to the Governor and Lieut.-Governor (who are elected for four years), the constitution provides for a cabinet composed of an attorney general, a chief financial officer and a commissioner of agriculture.

For the 111th Congress, which convened in Jan. 2009, Florida sends 25 members to the House of Representatives. It is represented in the Senate by Bill Nelson (D. 2001–13) and George LeMieux (R. 2009–11).

The state capital is Tallahassee. The state is divided into 67 counties.

RECENT ELECTIONS

In the 2008 presidential elections Barack Obama won Florida with 51·0% of the vote (George W. Bush won in 2004).

CURRENT ADMINISTRATION

Governor: Charlie Crist (R.), 2007–11 (salary: $130,273).

Lieut.-Governor: Jeff Kottkamp (R.), 2007–11 ($124,851).

Secretary of State: Kurt S. Browning (R.), appointed Dec. 2006 ($120,000).

Government Website: http://www.myflorida.com

ECONOMY

Per capita personal income (2008) was $39,267.

Budget

In 2008 total state revenue was $69,229m. Total expenditure was $76,973m. (including: education, $23,192m.; public welfare, $18,063m.; highways, $7,164m.; health, $3,601m.; government administration, $2,983m.) Outstanding debt in 2008, $42,321m.

Performance

2008 Gross Domestic Product by state was $744,120m. (provisional), ranking Florida 4th in the United States.

Banking and Finance

In 2002 there were 301 financial institutions in Florida insured by the US Federal Deposit Insurance Corporation, with assets worth $99,900m. They had 4,626 offices with total deposits of $242,800m.

ENERGY AND NATURAL RESOURCES

Electricity

Electricity production in 2005 totalled 220·3bn. kWh.

Water

The total area covered by water is approximately 11,828 sq. miles.

Minerals

The chief mineral is phosphate rock, of which marketable production in 2002 was 27m. tonnes. This was approximately 75% of US and 25% of the world supply of phosphate in 2002. Other important non-fuel minerals include crushed stone, cement, and sand and gravel. Total non-fuel mineral production for 2006 was valued at $3,220m.

Agriculture

In 2002 there were 10·2m. acres of farmland; 44,000 farms with an average of 232 acres per farm. The total value of land and buildings was $29,330m. in 2002; average value (2002) of land and buildings per acre, $2,836.

Farm income from crops and livestock (2006) was $6,974m., of which crops provided $5,669m. and livestock $1,305m. Major crop contributors are greenhouse products, oranges, sugarcane, tomatoes, grapefruit, peppers, other winter vegetables and indoor and landscaping plants. The net farm income in 2006 was $2,340m. In 2003 poultry farms produced 106m. chickens, 2,804m. eggs and 511m. lb of broilers. In 2002 the state had 1·74m. cattle, including 144,800 milch cows, and 33,500 swine.

Forestry

In 2007 Florida had 16·15m. acres of forested land (11·43m. acres privately-owned), including 1·07m. acres of national forests.

Fisheries

Florida has extensive fisheries with shrimp the highest value fish commodity. Other important catches are spiny lobster, snapper, crabs, hard clams, swordfish and tuna. Commercial catch (2002) totalled 115·6m. lb of fish at a value of $184·6m.

INDUSTRY

In 2005 the state's 14,286 manufacturing establishments had 371,000 employees, earning $14,907m. Total value added by manufacturing in 2006 was $50,945m. Main industries include: printing and publishing, machinery and computer equipment, apparel and finished products, fabricated metal products, and lumber and wood products.

Labour

Total non-agricultural employment, 2007, 8,041,000. Employees by branch, 2007 (in 1,000): trade, transportation and utilities, 1,611; professional and business services, 1,329; government,

1,124; education and health services, 1,007; leisure and hospitality, 929. In 2007 the unemployment rate was 4·1%.

INTERNATIONAL TRADE

Imports and Exports

Export sales of merchandise in 2000 totalled $24·2bn. Florida exported to 213 foreign markets in 2000: Canada was the biggest (10·3% of exports), followed by Brazil (8·4%) and Mexico (8·1%). Other important markets include Japan, Venezuela, Dominican Republic, UK, Colombia, Germany, Argentina and China. The leading export category is computers and electronic products (accounting for 33% of total exports in 2000). Other manufactured exports include transportation equipment, machinery, chemicals, electrical equipment, appliances and parts, and miscellaneous manufactures. The state also exports significant quantities of farm products and other non-manufactured commodities. Total agricultural exports were worth $1·2bn. in 2001.

COMMUNICATIONS

Roads

The state (2007) had 121,526 miles of highways, roads and streets (81,270 miles being urban roads and 40,256 rural). In 2007 there were 16,473,908 vehicle registrations and 3,214 traffic accident fatalities.

Rail

In 2002 there were 2,871 miles of railroad and 13 rail companies. There is a metro of 22 miles, a peoplemover and a commuter rail route in Miami.

Civil Aviation

In 2002 Florida had 475 public and private airports (12 international and 20 scheduled commercial service airports), 280 heliports, 13 stolports and 45 seaplane bases. Annual economic activity at Florida airports is responsible for more than 4·7% of Gross State Product. More than 50% of tourists arrive in the state by air each year. There were 69,752,006 passenger enplanements at Florida airports in 2007: the busiest were Orlando International (17,614,745), Miami International (16,194,277), Fort Lauderdale/Hollywood International (11,079,402) and Tampa International (9,306,354).

Shipping

There are 14 deepwater ports: those on the Gulf coast handle mainly domestic trade and those on the Atlantic coast primarily international trade and cruise ship traffic. In 2002–03 the tonnage of total waterborne trade by port was 118·2m. tons (including Tampa: 48·5m. tons; Everglades: 23·3m. tons; Jacksonville: 18·7m. tons; Miami: 9·0m. tons; and Manatee: 7·0m. tons). Almost 14m. cruise passengers embarked and disembarked from Florida ports in 2002–03, principally from Canaveral (4·1m.), Miami (4·0m.) and Everglades (3·4m.). There were 1,540 miles of inland waterways in 2000.

SOCIAL INSTITUTIONS

Justice

The state resumed the use of the death penalty in 1979. There have been 68 executions since 1976, including two in both 2008 and 2009. In Dec. 2008 there were 102,388 federal and state prisoners, up 4·2% from 98,219 in Dec. 2007. Chain gangs were introduced in 1995.

Education

Attendance at school is compulsory between six and 16. In 2004–05 there were 3,700 public elementary and secondary schools with 2,639,336 enrolled pupils and 154,864 teachers. According to the National Center for Education Statistics, Florida's public schools have the highest average enrolment in the country: in the 2001–02 school year there were 674 pupils per elementary school (compared to a national average of 441), 1,069 pupils per middle school (national average 612) and 1,565 pupils per high school (more than twice the national average of 753). Total expenditure on public elementary and secondary education in 2003–04 was $21,374m. and the average teacher salary was $40,604. Spending per pupil in 2002–03 was $6,439.

In fall 2005 there were 169 higher education institutions (40 public and 129 private) with 872,662 enrolled students. There are 11 state universities with a total of 258,874 students in 2002: the University of Florida at Gainesville (founded 1853) with 46,850 students; the Florida State University at Tallahassee (founded in 1857) with 36,651; the University of South Florida at Tampa (founded 1960) with 37,764; Florida A. & M. (Agricultural and Mechanical) University at Tallahassee (founded 1887) with 12,467; Florida Atlantic University (founded 1964) at Boca Raton with 23,996; the University of West Florida at Pensacola with 9,206; the University of Central Florida at Orlando with 38,795; the University of North Florida at Jacksonville with 13,460; Florida International University at Miami with 33,799; Florida Gulf Coast University (founded 1997) at Fort Myers with 5,236; and New College of Florida (founded 2001) at Sarasota with 650. There are 28 private colleges and universities belonging to the Independent Colleges and Universities of Florida (ICUF) association. Their enrolments vary from fewer than 100 to more than 22,000 students.

Health

In 2006 there were 203 community hospitals with 51,400 beds. A total of 2,373,000 patients were admitted during the year.

Welfare

Medicare enrolment in July 2004 totalled 2,980,279. In fiscal year 2006 a total of 3,123,301 people in Florida received Medicaid. In Dec. 2008 there were 3,547,492 Old-Age, Survivors, and Disability Insurance (OASDI) beneficiaries. A total of 94,824 people were receiving payments under Temporary Assistance for Needy Families (TANF) in Dec. 2008.

RELIGION

The main religious denominations are Roman Catholic, Baptist, Jewish, Methodist, Presbyterian and Episcopalian.

CULTURE

Tourism

In 2002, 73·9m. tourists visited Florida (67·9m. domestic visitors, 4·4m. overseas visitors and 1·6m. from Canada). They generated $48·7bn. in taxable sales and $2·9bn. in state sales tax revenues, making tourism the state's biggest industry.

There are 156 state parks, three national parks, three national forests, 31 state forests, and five national monuments and memorials. In 2002 there were 17·7m. visitors to state parks, raising $31·9m. in revenue.

FURTHER READING

Statistical information: Bureau of Economic and Business Research, Univ. of Florida, Gainesville 32611. Publishes *Florida Statistical Abstract.*

Benton, J. E. (ed.) *Government and Politics in Florida.* 3rd ed. 2008
Morris, A., *The Florida Handbook.* Biennial
Wilson, P. A. (ed.) *2008 Florida Statistical Abstract.* 2009

State library: 500 S Bronough Street, Tallahassee 32399.

Georgia

KEY HISTORICAL EVENTS

Originally the territory of Creek and Cherokee tribes, Georgia was first settled by Europeans in the 18th century. James Oglethorpe founded Savannah in 1733, intending it as a colony offering a new start to debtors, convicts and the poor. Settlement was slow until 1783, when growth began in the cotton-growing areas west of Augusta. The Indian population was cleared off the rich cotton land and moved beyond the Mississippi. Georgia became one of the original 13 states of the Union.

A plantation economy developed rapidly, using slave labour. In 1861 Georgia seceded from the Union and became an important source of supplies for the Confederate cause, although some northern areas never accepted secession and continued in sympathy with the Union during the Civil War. At the beginning of the war 56% of the population were white, descendants of British, Austrian and New England immigrants; the remaining 44% were black slaves.

The city of Atlanta, which grew as a railway junction, was destroyed during the war but revived to become the centre of southern reconstruction in the post-war period. It was confirmed as the state capital in 1877. Successive movements for black freedom in social, economic and political life have developed in the city, notably the Southern Christian Leadership Conference, led by Martin Luther King, who was assassinated in 1968.

TERRITORY AND POPULATION

Georgia is bounded north by Tennessee and North Carolina, northeast by South Carolina, east by the Atlantic, south by Florida and west by Alabama. Land area, 57,906 sq. miles (149,976 sq. km). Census population, 1 April 2000, was 8,186,453, an increase of 26·4% since 1990. July 2009 estimate, 9,829,211.

Population in five census years was:

	White	*Black*	*Indian*	*Asiatic*	*Total*	*Per sq. mile*
1910	1,431,802	1,176,987	95	237	2,609,121	44·4
1930	1,837,021	1,071,125	43	317	2,908,506	49·7
			All others			
1980	3,948,007	1,465,457	50,801		5,464,265	92·7
1990	4,600,148	1,746,565	131,503		6,478,216	110·0
2000	5,327,281	2,349,542	509,630		8,186,453	141·4

Of the total population in 2000, 4,159,340 were female, 6,017,219 were 18 years old or older and 5,864,163 were urban. The estimated Hispanic population was 435,277 in 2000, up from 108,933 in 1990 (an increase of 299·6%).

The largest cities are: Atlanta (capital), with a population (2000 census) of 416,474; Augusta-Richmond County, 199,775; Columbus, 186,291; Savannah, 131,510; Athens-Clarke County, 101,489. The Atlanta metropolitan area had a 2000 census population of 4,112,198.

SOCIAL STATISTICS

Births, 2007 (provisional), 147,294 (15·4 per 1,000 population); deaths, 2006, 67,808 (7·2). Infant mortality, 2006, 8·1 per 1,000 live births. Marriages, 2006, 66,500 (7·1 per 1,000 population).

CLIMATE

Atlanta, Jan. 43°F (6·1°C), July 78°F (25·6°C). Annual rainfall 49" (1,234 mm). Georgia belongs to the Atlantic Coast climate zone (*see* UNITED STATES: Climate).

CONSTITUTION AND GOVERNMENT

A new constitution was ratified in the general election of 2 Nov. 1976, proclaimed on 22 Dec. 1976 and became effective on 1 Jan. 1977. The General Assembly consists of a Senate of 56 members and a House of Representatives of 180 members, both elected for two years. Legislative sessions are annual, beginning the 2nd Monday in Jan. and lasting for 40 days.

Georgia was the first state to extend the franchise to all citizens 18 years old and above.

For the 111th Congress, which convened in Jan. 2009, Georgia sends 13 members to the House of Representatives. It is represented in the Senate by Saxby Chambliss (R. 2003–15) and Johnny Isakson (R. 2005–11).

The state capital is Atlanta. Georgia is divided into 159 counties.

RECENT ELECTIONS

In the 2008 presidential elections John McCain won Georgia with 52·2% of the vote (George W. Bush won in 2004).

CURRENT ADMINISTRATION

Governor: Sonny Perdue (R.), 2007–11 (salary: $139,339·44).
Lieut.-Governor: Casey Cagle (R.), 2007–11 ($91,609·44).
Secretary of State: Brian Kemp (R.), 2010–11 ($130,690·80).

Government Website: http://www.georgia.gov

ECONOMY

Per capita personal income (2008) was $34,893.

Budget

In 2008 total state revenue was $41,267m. Total expenditure was $41,165m. (education, $16,180m.; public welfare, $9,645m.; highways, $2,287m.; correction, $1,572m.; health, $1,259m.) Outstanding debt in 2008, $13,072m.

Performance

Gross Domestic Product by state was $397,756m. in 2008 (provisional), ranking Georgia 10th in the United States.

ENERGY AND NATURAL RESOURCES

Water

The total area covered by water is approximately 1,519 sq. miles.

Minerals

Georgia is the leading producer of kaolin. The state ranks first in production of crushed and dimensional granite, and second in production of fuller's earth and marble (crushed and dimensional). Total value of non-fuel mineral production for 2006 was $2,080m.

Agriculture

In 2002, 50,000 farms covered 11m. acres; the average farm was of 220 acres. In 2002 the average value of farmland and buildings was $2,112 per acre. For 2002 cotton output was 1·6m. bales (of 480 lb). Other major crops include tobacco, corn, wheat, soybeans, peanuts and pecans. Cash receipts from farm marketings, 2006: crops, $2,240m.; livestock and products, $3,765m.; total, $6,005m. The net farm income in 2006 was $2,388m.

In 2002 farm animals included 1·27m. cattle, 347,816 swine and (2003) 2,546m. poultry.

Forestry

The forested area in 2007 was 24·78m. acres with 736,000 acres of national forest. Annual timber removals are the highest of any state, at 1,341m. cu. ft in 2006 (1,044m. cu. ft softwoods and 297m. cu. ft hardwoods).

INDUSTRY

In 2005 the state's 8,623 manufacturing establishments had 428,000 employees, earning $16,219m. Total value added by manufacturing in 2006 was $61,916m.

Labour

Total non-agricultural employment, 2007, 4,147,000. Employees by branch, 2007 (in 1,000): trade, transportation and utilities, 888; government, 676; professional and business services, 560;

education and health services, 456; manufacturing, 431. Georgia's unemployment rate in 2007 was 4·3%.

COMMUNICATIONS

Roads

In 2007 there were 118,779 miles of roads comprising 37,683 miles of urban road and 81,096 miles of rural road. There were 8,512,511 motor vehicles registered.

Rail

In 2002 there were 4,820 miles of freight railroad, including 3,516 miles of Class I railroads. There is a metro in Atlanta.

Civil Aviation

In June 2004 there were 335 airports (106 public, 219 private) and 104 heliports. There were 44,432,464 passenger enplanements statewide in 2007. Hartsfield–Jackson Atlanta International Airport handled 43,082,000 passenger enplanements in 2008—the highest number of any airport in the world.

Shipping

There are deepwater ports at Savannah, the principal port, and Brunswick.

SOCIAL INSTITUTIONS

Justice

In Dec. 2008 there were 52,719 federal and state prisoners. The death penalty is authorized for capital offences. There were three executions in 2009.

Under a Local Option Act, the sale of alcoholic beverages is prohibited in some counties.

Education

Since 1945 education has been compulsory; tuition is free until the age of 18 and school attendance is compulsory for pupils between the ages of six and 16 years. In 2002–03 there were 2,236 public elementary and secondary schools with 1·49m. pupils and 96,044 teachers; total expenditure on public schools was $12,571m. Teachers' salaries averaged $45,533 in 2003.

The University of Georgia (Athens) was founded in 1785 and was the first chartered State University in the USA (33,878 students in 2003). Other institutions of higher learning include Georgia Institute of Technology, Atlanta (16,643); Emory University, Atlanta (11,654); Georgia State University, Atlanta (28,042); Georgia Southern University, Statesboro (15,704). The Atlanta University Center, devoted primarily to Black education, includes co-educational Clark Atlanta University (4,915); Morehouse College (2,859), a liberal arts college for men; Interdenominational Theological Center (406), a co-educational school; and Spelman College (2,063), the first liberal arts college for Black women in the USA. Wesleyan College (745), near Macon, is the oldest chartered women's college in the world.

Health

In 2006 there were 147 community hospitals with 24,700 beds. A total of 956,000 patients were admitted during the year.

Welfare

Medicare enrolment in July 2004 totalled 994,569. In fiscal year 2006 a total of 1,817,822 people in Georgia received Medicaid. In Dec. 2008 there were 1,347,932 Old-Age, Survivors, and Disability Insurance (OASDI) beneficiaries. A total of 39,222 people were receiving payments under Temporary Assistance for Needy Families (TANF) in Dec. 2008.

RELIGION

In 2000 there were 1,719,484 Southern Baptist adherents, 570,674 United Methodists, 374,185 Roman Catholics, 138,123 Church of God members and 105,774 Presbyterian Church (USA) members.

CULTURE

Tourism

In 2003 there were 48m. visitors to and through Georgia; tourism expenditures totalled $25bn., supporting 209,500 tourist-related jobs. Tourism provided $708·5m. in state tax revenue. There were 12·4m. visitors to the 48 state parks.

FURTHER READING

Statistical information: Selig Center for Economic Growth, Univ. of Georgia, Athens 30602. Publishes *Georgia Statistical Abstract.*

Rowland, A. R., *A Bibliography of the Writings on Georgia History.* 1978

State Law Library: Judicial Building, Capital Sq., Atlanta.

Hawaii

KEY HISTORICAL EVENTS

The islands of Hawaii were settled by Polynesian immigrants, probably from the Marquesas Islands, about AD 400. A second major immigration, from Tahiti, occurred around 800–900. In the late 18th century all the islands were united into one kingdom by Kamehameha I. Western exploration began in 1778, and Christian missions were established after 1820. Europeans called Hawaii the Sandwich Islands. The USA, Britain and France all claimed an interest. Kamehameha III placed Hawaii under US protection in 1851. US sugar-growing companies became dominant and in 1887 the USA obtained a naval base at Pearl Harbor. A struggle developed between forces for and against annexation by the USA. In 1893 the monarchy was overthrown. The republican government agreed to be annexed to the USA in 1898, and Hawaii became a US Territory in 1900.

The islands and the naval base were of great strategic importance during the Second World War, when the Japanese attack on Pearl Harbor brought the USA into the war.

Hawaii became the 50th state of the Union in 1959. The 19th-century plantation economy encouraged the immigration of workers, especially from China and Japan. Hawaiian laws, religions and culture were gradually adapted to the needs of the immigrant community.

TERRITORY AND POPULATION

The Hawaiian Islands lie in the North Pacific Ocean, between 18° 54' and 28° 15' N. lat. and 154° 40' and 178° 25' W. long., about 2,090 nautical miles southwest of San Francisco. There are 137 named islands and islets in the group, of which seven major and five minor islands are inhabited. Land area, 6,423 sq. miles (16,636 sq. km). Census population, 1 April 2000, 1,211,537, an increase of 9·3% since 1990; density was 188·6 per sq. mile in 2000. July 2009 population estimate, 1,295,178. Of the total population in 2000, 608,671 were male, 915,770 were 18 years old or older, and 1,108,225 were urban (91·47%, the fourth most urban state).

The principal islands are Hawaii, 4,028 sq. miles, population 2000, 148,677; Maui, 727 sq. miles, population 117,644; Oahu, 600 sq. miles, population 876,151; Kauai, 552 sq. miles, population 58,303; Molokai, 260 sq. miles, population 7,404; Lanai, 141 sq. miles, population 3,193; Niihau, 70 sq. miles, population 160; Kahoolawe, 45 sq. miles (uninhabited). The capital Honolulu—on the island of Oahu—had a population in 2000 of 371,657, and Hilo—on the island of Hawaii—40,759.

Figures for main racial groups, 2000, were (excluding persons in institutions or military barracks): 294,102 White; 201,764 Japanese; 170,635 Filipino; 80,137 Native Hawaiian; 56,600 Chinese (including Taiwanese); 25,537 Korean; 22,003 Black or African American; 16,166 Samoan; 7,867 Vietnamese.

SOCIAL STATISTICS

Births, 2007 (provisional), 19,110 (14·9 per 1,000 population); deaths, 2006, 9,432 (7·3). Infant deaths, 2006, were at a rate of 5·6 per 1,000 live births. Marriages, 2006, 28,700 (22·4 per 1,000 population). Inter-marriage between the races is common. In 2002, 56·0% of marriages were inter-racial. 65·4% were non-resident marriages.

CLIMATE

All the islands have a tropical climate, with an abrupt change in conditions between windward and leeward sides, most marked in rainfall. Temperatures vary little. Average temperatures in Honolulu: Jan. 73·0°F, July 80·8°F. Average annual rainfall in Honolulu: 18·29".

CONSTITUTION AND GOVERNMENT

Hawaii was officially admitted into the United States on 21 Aug. 1959. However, the constitution of the State of Hawaii was created by the 1950 Constitutional Convention, ratified by the voters of the Territory on 7 Nov. 1950, and amended on 27 June 1959. The Legislature consists of a Senate of 25 members elected for four years and a House of Representatives of 51 members elected for two years. There have been two constitutional conventions since 1950, in 1968 and 1978. In addition to amendments proposed by these conventions the Legislature is able to propose amendments to voters during the general election. This has resulted in numerous amendments.

For the 111th Congress, which convened in Jan. 2009, Hawaii sends two members to the House of Representatives. It is represented in the Senate by Daniel Inouye (D. 1963–2011) and Daniel Akaka (D. 1990–2013).

The state capital is Honolulu. There are five counties.

RECENT ELECTIONS

In the 2008 presidential elections Barack Obama won Hawaii with 71·8% of the vote (John Kerry won in 2004).

CURRENT ADMINISTRATION

Governor: Linda Lingle (R.), Dec. 2006–Dec. 2010 (salary: $117,306).

Lieut.-Governor: James R. 'Duke' Aiona, Jr (R.), Dec. 2006–Dec. 2010 ($114,422).

Government Website: http://www.ehawaii.gov

ECONOMY

Per capita personal income (2008) was $42,055.

Budget

Revenue is derived mainly from taxation of sales and gross receipts, real property, corporate and personal income, and inheritance taxes, licences, public land sales and leases.

In 2008 total state revenue was $9,299m. Total expenditure was $10,534m. (education, $3,394m.; public welfare, $1,564m.; health, $678m.; hospitals, $531m.; government administration, $487m.) Outstanding debt in 2008, $6,028m.

Performance

2008 Gross Domestic Product by state was $63,847m. (provisional), ranking Hawaii 38th in the United States.

Banking and Finance

In 2005 there were four state-chartered banks (assets of $27,715m.) and one federal bank.

ENERGY AND NATURAL RESOURCES

Electricity

Installed capacity in 2003 was 1,669,000 kW; total power consumed was 10,206m. kWh.

Oil and Gas

In 2005, $84·5m. was generated by gas sales.

Water

The total area covered by water is approximately 4,508 sq. miles, of which 38 sq. miles are inland. Water consumption in 2005 amounted to 77,171m. gallons.

Minerals

Production in 2004: crushed stone, 5·2m. tonnes; construction sand and gravel, 1·3m. tonnes. Total value of non-fuel mineral production in 2006 was $145m.

Agriculture

Farming is highly commercialized and highly mechanized. In 2002 there were about 5,300 farms covering an area of 1·44m. acres; average number of acres per farm, 272, valued at $3,507 per acre. Paid workforce totalled 11,600 in 2002.

Greenhouse products, pineapples, sugarcane and macadamia nuts are the staple crops. Farm income, 2006, from crop sales was $467m., and from livestock $88m. The net farm income in 2006 was $106m.

Forestry

Hawaii had 1·75m. acres of forested land in 2007. In 2003 conservation district forest land amounted to 971,876 acres (of which 328,742 acres were privately owned); there were 46,191 acres of planted forest; and 109,164 acres of natural area.

Fisheries

In 2002 the commercial fish catch was 23·84m. lb with a value of $52·1m. There were 3,081 commercial fishermen in 2002.

INDUSTRY

In 2005 the state's 946 manufacturing establishments had 15,000 employees, earning $479m. Total value added by manufacturing in 2006 was $2,049m.

Labour

Total non-agricultural employment amounted to 624,000 in 2007. Employees by branch, 2007 (in 1,000): government, 122; trade, transportation and utilities, 121; leisure and hospitality, 110; professional and business services, 76; education and health services, 73. The unemployment rate in 2007 was 2·9%.

Trade Unions

In 2003 there were 113 trade unions with a combined membership of 167,000.

COMMUNICATIONS

Roads

In 2007 there were 4,341 miles of roads comprising 2,300 miles of urban road and 2,041 miles of rural road. There were 993,117 registered motor vehicles.

Civil Aviation

There were 11 commercial airports in 2004. In 2001 passengers arriving from overseas numbered 7·27m., and there were 9·17m. passengers between the islands. In 1999 Hawaiian Airlines flew 34·8m. km, carrying 5,409,700 passengers (19,100 on international flights). There were 17,430,169 passenger enplanements in 2007.

Shipping

Several lines of steamers connect the islands with the mainland USA, Canada, Australia, the Philippines, China and Japan. In 2002, 1,270 overseas and 2,663 inter-island vessels entered the port of Honolulu carrying a total of 130,792 overseas and 19,952 inter-island passengers as well as 6,425,288 tonnes of overseas and 1,796,910 tonnes inter-island cargo.

SOCIAL INSTITUTIONS

Justice

There is no capital punishment in Hawaii. In Dec. 2008 the jail and prison population totalled 5,955.

Education

Education is free and compulsory between the ages of six and 18. The language in the schools is English. In 2004–05 there were 285 public schools with 183,185 pupils and 11,146 teachers. In 2003–04 there were 133 private schools with 37,228 pupils and 3,070 full time teachers. In 2003–04, $1,735m. was spent on public elementary and secondary education and average teacher salary was $45,479. In fall 2005 the number of students enrolled in higher education institutions was 67,083.

Health

In 2006 there were 24 community hospitals with 2,900 beds. A total of 111,000 patients were admitted during the year.

Welfare

Medicare enrolment in July 2004 totalled 177,690. In fiscal year 2006 a total of 227,043 people in Hawaii received Medicaid. In Dec. 2008 there were 212,890 Old-Age, Survivors, and Disability Insurance (OASDI) beneficiaries. A total of 14,331 people were receiving payments under Temporary Assistance for Needy Families (TANF) in Dec. 2008.

RELIGION

2000 membership of leading religious denominations: Roman Catholic Church, 240,813; Buddhism (1999), 100,000; Church of Jesus Christ of Latter-day Saints, 42,758; United Church of Christ, 22,856; Assembly of God, 21,754; Southern Baptist, 20,901; International Church of the Foursquare Gospel, 15,076; Episcopal Church, 11,084.

CULTURE

Broadcasting

In 2002 there were 76 commercial radio and 23 commercial television stations (excluding cable television companies). Colour is by NTSC.

Tourism

Tourism is outstanding in Hawaii's economy. Tourist arrivals numbered only 687,000 in 1965, but were 6·9m. in 2004. Tourist expenditure ($380m. in 1967) contributed $10,861·8m. to the state's economy in 2004.

FURTHER READING

Statistical information: Hawaii State Department of Business, POB 2359, Honolulu 96804. Publishes *The State of Hawaii Data Book.*

Atlas of Hawaii. 3rd ed. 1998

Oliver, Anthony M., *Hawaii Facts and Reference Book: Recent Historical Facts and Events in the Fiftieth State.* 1995

Idaho

KEY HISTORICAL EVENTS

Kutenai, Kalispel, Nez Percé and other tribes lived on the Pacific watershed of the northern Rocky Mountains. European exploration began in 1805, and after 1809 there were trading posts and small settlements, with fur-trapping as the primary activity. The area was disputed between Britain and the USA until 1846 when British claims were dropped. In 1860 the discovery of gold and silver brought a rush of immigrant prospectors. An area including present-day Montana was created a Territory in March 1863. Montana was separated from it in 1864. Population growth was stimulated by refugees from the Confederate states after the Civil War and by settlements of Mormons from Utah.

Fur-trapping and mining gave way to arable farming. Idaho became a state in 1890, with its capital at Boise. The population of the Territory capital, Idaho City, a gold-mining boom town in the 1860s (about 40,000 at its height), was the largest in the Pacific Northwest. By 1869 the population was down to 1,000.

In the 20th century the Indian population shrank to 1%. The Mormon community has grown to include much of southeastern Idaho and more than half the church-going population of the state.

The Snake River of southern Idaho has supported hydro-electricity and irrigation. Food processing, minerals and timber are important. So too are the high technology companies in Idaho's metropolitan areas. Much of the state, however, remains sparsely populated and rural.

TERRITORY AND POPULATION

Idaho is within the Rocky Mountains and bounded north by Canada, east by Montana and Wyoming, south by Nevada and Utah, west by Oregon and Washington. Land area, 82,747 sq. miles (214,314 sq. km). Census population, 1 April 2000, 1,293,953, an increase of 28·5% since 1990. July 2009 estimate, 1,545,801.

Population in five census years was:

	White	*Black*	*Indian*	*Asiatic*	*Total*	*Per sq. mile*
1910	319,221	651	3,488	2,234	325,594	3·9
1930	438,840	668	3,638	1,886	445,032	5·4
1980	901,641	2,716	10,521	5,948	943,935	11·3
1990	950,451	3,370	13,780	9,365	1,006,749	12·2
2000	1,177,304	5,456	17,645	13,197	1,293,953	15·6

Of the total population in 2000, 648,660 were male, 924,923 were 18 years old or older and 859,497 were urban. In 2000 Idaho's Hispanic population was 101,690, up from 52,927 in 1990 (an increase of 92·1%).

The largest cities are: Boise City, with a 2003 population of 190,117; Nampa, 64,269; Idaho Falls, 51,507; Pocatello, 51,009; Meridian, 41,127; Coeur d'Alene, 37,262; Twin Falls, 36,742; Caldwell, 31,041; Lewiston, 30,937.

SOCIAL STATISTICS

Births, 2007 (provisional), 25,053 (16·7 per 1,000 population); deaths, 2006, 10,613 (7·2). Infant mortality rate, 2006, 6·8 per 1,000 live births. 2006: marriages, 14,800 (10·1 per 1,000 population); divorces and annulments, 7,500 (5·1).

CLIMATE

Boise City, Jan. 29°F (–1·7°C), July 74°F (23·3°C). Annual rainfall 12" (303 mm). Idaho belongs to the Mountain States climate zone (*see* UNITED STATES: Climate).

CONSTITUTION AND GOVERNMENT

The constitution adopted in 1890 is still in force; it has had 105 amendments. The Legislature consists of a Senate of 35 members and a House of Representatives of 70 members, all the legislators being elected for two years. It meets annually.

For the 111th Congress, which convened in Jan. 2009, Idaho sends two members to the House of Representatives. It is represented in the Senate by Michael Crapo (R. 1999–2011) and James Risch (R. 2009–15).

The state is divided into 44 counties. The capital is Boise City.

RECENT ELECTIONS

In the 2008 presidential elections John McCain won Idaho with 61·5% of the vote (George W. Bush won in 2004).

CURRENT ADMINISTRATION

Governor: C. L. 'Butch' Otter (R.), 2007–11 (salary: $115,349).
Lieut.-Governor: Brad Little (R.), 2009–11 ($30,400).
Secretary of State: Ben Ysursa (R.), 2007–11 ($93,756).

Government Website: http://www.idaho.gov

ECONOMY

Per capita personal income (2008) was $33,074.

Budget

In 2008 total state revenue was $7,107m. Total expenditure was $7,675m. (education, $2,775m.; public welfare, $1,615m.; highways, $696m.; government administration, $360m.; correction, $245m.) Outstanding debt in 2008, $3,379m.

Performance

Gross Domestic Product by state in 2008 was $52,747m. (provisional), ranking Idaho 42nd in the United States.

ENERGY AND NATURAL RESOURCES

Electricity

Idaho's rivers provide dependable and low-cost electrical power. Almost two-thirds of Idaho's electrical needs come from this resource, resulting in electricity rates much lower than those found in the East and Midwest.

Water

The total area covered by water is approximately 823 sq. miles. Idaho is second only to California in the amount of water used for irrigating crops. Much of Idaho's surface water flows out of the high mountains and is generally of excellent quality. High quality groundwater is pumped for agricultural, industrial and residential use.

Minerals

Principal non-fuel minerals are processed phosphate rock, silver, gold, molybdenum and sand and gravel. Value of non-fuel mineral output for 2006 was $797m.

Agriculture

Agriculture is the second largest industry, despite a great part of the state being naturally arid. Extensive irrigation works have been carried out, bringing an estimated 3·5m. acres under irrigation, and there are over 50 soil conservation districts.

In 2003 there were 25,000 farms with a total area of 11·8m. acres; average value per acre (2002), $1,270. In 2003 the average farm was 472 acres.

Farm income 2006: from crops, $2,000m.; from livestock and products, $2,416m. The most important crops are potatoes and wheat. Other crops are sugar beets, hay, barley, field peas and beans, onions and apples. The net farm income in 2006 was $758m. In 2003 there were 2·0m. cattle, 260,000 sheep, 26,000 hogs and 1·2m. poultry. There were 34m. food-sized trout produced on fish farms. The dairy industry is the fastest-growing sector in Idaho agriculture.

Forestry

In 2007 there was a total of 21·43m. acres of forest, of which 16·38m. acres were national forest (the highest acreage of any state).

Fisheries

74% of the commercial trout processed in the USA was produced in Idaho in 2002. Idaho ranked first in state trout production by producing fish to a value of $30·5m.

INDUSTRY

In 2005 Idaho's 1,849 manufacturing establishments had approximately 61,000 employees, with a payroll of $2,393m. Total value added by manufacturing in 2006 was $7,045m.

Labour

Total non-agricultural employment 2007, 656,000. Employees by branch, 2007 (in 1,000): trade, transportation and utilities, 132; government, 118; professional and business services, 83; education and health services, 74; manufacturing, 66. State unemployment averaged 3·0% in 2007.

Trade Unions

Idaho has a right-to-work law. In 2005, 31,000 people were union members.

COMMUNICATIONS

Roads

In 2007 there were 48,416 miles of public roads (42,810 miles rural, 5,606 urban). There were 1,281,899 registered motor vehicles in 2007.

Rail

The state had (2001) approximately 1,700 miles of railroads (including one Amtrak route).

Civil Aviation

There were 68 municipally-owned airports in 2003. There were 2,056,775 passenger enplanements statewide in 2007.

Shipping

Water transport is provided from the Pacific to the port of Lewiston, by way of the Columbia and Snake rivers, a distance of 464 miles.

Postal Services

Idaho is served by the United States Postal Service. Major private carriers, including UPS, Federal Express, and DHL Worldwide Express, provide Idaho residents with global shipping access. There are numerous local mailing and shipping services available in Idaho's larger cities.

SOCIAL INSTITUTIONS

Justice

The death penalty may be imposed for first degree murder or aggravated kidnapping, but the judge must consider mitigating circumstances before imposing a sentence of death. The only execution since 1976 was in 1994. In Dec. 2008 there were 7,290 prisoners in federal and state prisons.

Education

In 2003–04 public elementary schools (grades K to 6) had 135,216 pupils and 8,048 teachers; secondary schools had 116,821 pupils and 7,387 classroom teachers. Average salary (2003–04) of teachers was $40,301 (elementary) and $41,422 (secondary).

The University of Idaho, founded at Moscow in 1889, had 559 full-time instructional faculty in 2003, and a total enrolment of 12,895. Boise State University had 278 full-time instructional faculty in 2003 and a total enrolment of 18,332. Idaho State University had 401 full-time instructional faculty in 2003 and a total enrolment of 13,621. There were seven other higher education institutions, three of them public institutions. College and university enrolment in the fall of 2003 was 73,275.

Health

In 2006 there were 38 community hospitals with 3,300 beds. A total of 141,000 patients were admitted during the year.

Welfare

Medicare enrolment in July 2004 totalled 183,508. In fiscal year 2006 a total of 216,958 people in Idaho received Medicaid. Old-age, Survivors, and Disability Insurance (OASDI) is granted to persons if they paid sufficiently into the system or meet other qualifications; in Dec. 2008 there were 247,847 beneficiaries. A total of 2,396 people were receiving payments under Temporary Assistance for Needy Families (TANF) in Dec. 2008.

RELIGION

The leading religious denominations are the Church of Jesus Christ of Latter-day Saints (Mormons; 311,425 adherents in 2000), Roman Catholics, Methodists, Presbyterians, Episcopalians and Lutherans.

CULTURE

Broadcasting

In 2003 there were 112 radio stations and 23 television stations.

Press

Idaho has 15 daily newspapers and 52 weekly papers.

FURTHER READING

Statistical information: Idaho Commerce and Labor, 700 West State St., Boise 83720. Publishes *County Profiles of Idaho, Community Profiles of Idaho* and *Profile of Rural Idaho* on the Internet.

Schwantes, C. A., *In Mountain Shadows: a History of Idaho.* 1996

Website: http://labor.idaho.gov

Illinois

KEY HISTORICAL EVENTS

Home to Algonquian-speaking tribes, Illinois was explored first by the French in 1673. France claimed the area until 1763 when, after the French and Indian War, it was ceded to Britain along with all the French land east of the Mississippi. In 1783 Britain recognized US claims to Illinois, which became part of the North West Territory of the USA in 1787, and of Indiana Territory in 1800. Illinois became a Territory in its own right in 1809, and a state in 1818.

Immigration increased greatly with the opening in 1825 of the Erie Canal from New York, along which farmer settlers could move west and their produce back east for sale. Chicago was incorporated as a city in 1837 and quickly became the transport, trading and distribution centre of the mid west. Industrial growth brought a further wave of immigration in the 1840s, mainly of European refugees. This movement continued with varying force until the 1920s, when it was largely replaced by immigration of black work-seekers from the southern states.

In the 20th century the population was urbanized and heavy industry was established along a network of rail and waterway routes. Chicago recovered from a destructive fire in 1871 to become the hub of this network and at one time the second largest American city.

TERRITORY AND POPULATION

Illinois is bounded north by Wisconsin, northeast by Lake Michigan, east by Indiana, southeast by the Ohio River (forming the boundary with Kentucky), and west by the Mississippi River (forming the boundary with Missouri and Iowa). Land area in 2000: 55,584 sq. miles (143,962 sq. km). Census population, 2000, 12,419,293, an increase of 8·6% since 1990. July 2009 estimate, 12,910,409.

Population in five census years was:

	White	*Black*	*Indian*	*All others*	*Total*	*Per sq. mile*
1910	5,526,962	109,049	188	2,392	5,638,591	100·6
1930	7,266,361	328,972	469	35,321	7,630,654	136·4
			All others			
1980	9,233,327	1,675,398	517,793		11,426,518	203·0

	White	*Black*	*American Indian or Alaska Native*	*Asian or Pacific Islander*	*Other*	*Total*	*Per sq. mile*
1990	8,957,923	1,690,855	24,077	284,944	472,803	11,430,602	205·6
2000	9,125,471	1,876,875	31,006	428,213	957,728	12,419,293	223·4

Of the total population in 2000, 6,338,957 were female, 9,173,842 were 18 years old or older and 10,909,520 were urban. In 2000 the Hispanic population was 1,527,573 (904,449 in 1990).

The most populous cities (2006) are: Chicago, 2,833,321; Aurora, 170,617; Rockford, 155,138; Naperville, 142,901; Joliet, 142,702; Springfield, 116,482; Peoria, 113,107; Elgin, 101,903; Waukegan, 92,066.

Metropolitan area populations, 2000 census: Chicago–Gary–Kenosha, 9,157,540; Rockford, 371,236; Peoria–Pekin, 347,387; Springfield, 201,437; Champaign–Urbana, 179,669.

SOCIAL STATISTICS

Births, 2007 (provisional), 182,135 (14·2 per 1,000 population); deaths, 2006, 102,171 (8·0). Infant mortality rate, 2006, 7·3 per 1,000 live births. 2006: marriages, 78,000 (6·1 per 1,000 population); divorces and annulments, 32,200 (2·5).

CLIMATE

Chicago, Jan. 25·3°F (–3·7°C), July 75·4°F (24·1°C). Annual rainfall 38·0". Illinois belongs to the Great Lakes climate zone (*see* UNITED STATES: Climate).

CONSTITUTION AND GOVERNMENT

The present constitution became effective on 1 July 1971. The General Assembly consists of a House of Representatives of 118 members elected for two years, and a Senate of 59 members who are divided into three groups; in one, they are elected for terms of four years, four years, and two years; in the next, for terms of four years, two years, and four years; and in the last, for terms of two years, four years, and four years. Sessions are annual. The state is divided into legislative districts, in each of which one senator is chosen; each district is divided into two representative districts, in each of which one representative is chosen.

For the 111th Congress, which convened in Jan. 2009, Illinois sends 19 members to the House of Representatives. It is represented in the Senate by Richard Durbin (D. 1997–2015) and Roland Burris (D. 2009–11).

The capital is Springfield.

RECENT ELECTIONS

In the 2008 presidential elections Barack Obama won Illinois with 61·9% of the vote (John Kerry won in 2004).

CURRENT ADMINISTRATION

Governor: Patrick Quinn (D.), 2009–11 (salary: $177,500).
Lieut.-Governor: Vacant until Nov. 2010 election ($135,700).
Secretary of State: Jesse White (D.), 2007–11 ($156,600).

Government Website: http://www.illinois.gov

ECONOMY

Per capita personal income (2008) was $42,347.

Budget

In 2008 total state revenues amounted to $58,524m. Total expenditure was $63,368m. (public welfare, $17,167m.; education, $16,343m.; highways, $4,510m.; health, $2,337m.; correction, $1,244m.) Debt outstanding, in 2008, $58,437m.

Performance

Gross Domestic Product by state in 2008 was $633,697m. (provisional), ranking Illinois 5th in the United States.

Banking and Finance
In 2003 there were 502 state-chartered banks, 17 foreign banks and 211 corporate fiduciaries. The assets of state-chartered banks in Illinois totalled $152bn. in 2003.

ENERGY AND NATURAL RESOURCES

Electricity
Electricity production 2005, 194·1bn. kWh. In 2005 there were six nuclear plants, with net production of 93·3bn. kWh.

Oil and Gas
In 2005 Illinois produced 10·2m. bbls of crude petroleum.

Water
The total area covered by water is approximately 2,331 sq. miles. In 2006 there were more than 26,400 miles of rivers and streams.

Minerals
The chief mineral product is coal. In 2004 there were 18 operative mines; output was 32,279,112 tons. Mineral production also includes sand, gravel and limestone. Value of non-fuel mineral production in 2006 was $1,220m.

Agriculture
In 2006 there were 72,400 farms in Illinois that contained 27·3m. acres of land. The average size of farms was 377 acres and, in 2002, was valued at $2,425 per acre. In 2006 cash receipts from farm marketings in Illinois totalled $8·64bn. In 2002 cash receipts for corn totalled $2·9bn.; for soybeans, $2·1bn.; for livestock and products, $1·8bn.; for hogs, $920m.; for cattle, $528m.; for dairy products, $301m.; for wheat, $111m. The net farm income in 2006 was $1,511m. In 2006 Illinois was the second largest producer among US states of corn and soybeans, producing 1·82bn. bu. and 482m. bu. respectively. In 2004 there were 3·85m. hogs and pigs, 1·31m. cattle including 416,000 beef cows and 69,300 milch cows, and 63,000 sheep and lambs. Wool production in 2003 totalled 395,000 lb.

Forestry
In 2004 there were seven state forests and 25 conservation areas. In 2007 there was a total of 4·53m. acres of forest, of which 290,000 acres were national forest.

Fisheries
In 2001, four hatcheries in Illinois had 75m. fish.

INDUSTRY
Important industries include financial services, manufacturing, retail and transportation. In 2005 the state's 16,073 manufacturing establishments had 676,000 employees, earning $30,078m. Total value added by manufacturing in 2006 was $107,548m.

Labour
Total non-agricultural employment, 2007, 5,981,000. Employees by branch, 2007 (in 1,000): trade, transportation and utilities, 1,212; professional and business services, 869; government, 851; education and health services, 779; manufacturing, 676. In 2007 the unemployment rate was 5·1%.

Trade Unions
Labour union membership in 2005 was 927,000. Approximately 16·9% of workers in Illinois were members of unions in 2005.

INTERNATIONAL TRADE

Imports and Exports
In 2005 exports from Illinois totalled approximately $35·8bn. Exports included computer equipment, industrial machinery, chemicals and agricultural products.

COMMUNICATIONS

Roads
In 2007 there were 139,157 miles of roads comprising 40,952 miles of urban road and 98,205 miles of rural road. There were 9,757,004 registered motor vehicles in 2007.

Rail
Union Station, Chicago is the home of Amtrak's national hub. Amtrak trains provide service to cities in Illinois to many destinations in the USA. Illinois is also served by a metro (CTA) system, and by seven groups of commuter railroads controlled by METRA, which has many stations and serves several Illinois counties. Total passengers using Amtrak stations in 2000 were 3,583,707. State system mileage, Dec. 2002: Federal aid interstate non-toll, 1,890 miles; other marked non-toll, 11,420 miles; state supplementary non-toll, 2,590 miles; total length, 15,900 miles. There is also a metro system in Chicago (108 miles).

Civil Aviation
In 2005 there were 114 public airports and 275 heliports; in 2001 there were 496 restricted landing areas. There were 46,991,136 passenger enplanements statewide in 2007.

Shipping
In 2005 total cargo handled at the port of Chicago was 25,820,513 tons.

Postal Services
In 2004 there were approximately 1,200 postal stations.

SOCIAL INSTITUTIONS

Justice
There were 45,474 federal and state prisoners in Dec. 2008.

Executions began in 1990 following the US Supreme Court's reinstatement of capital punishment in 1976, with the most recent execution being on 17 March 1999. However, on 31 Jan. 2000 the death penalty was suspended.

A Civil Rights Act (1941), as amended, bans all forms of discrimination by places of public accommodation, including inns, restaurants, retail stores, railroads, aeroplanes, buses, etc., against persons on account of 'race, religion, colour, national ancestry or physical or mental handicap'; another section similarly mentions 'race or colour'.

The Fair Employment Practices Act of 1961, as amended, prohibits discrimination in employment based on race, colour, sex, religion, national origin or ancestry, by employers, employment agencies, labour organizations and others. These principles are embodied in the 1971 constitution.

The Illinois Human Rights Act (1979) prevents unlawful discrimination in employment, real property transactions, access to financial credit and public accommodations, by authorizing the creation of a Department of Human Rights to enforce, and a Human Rights Commission to adjudicate, allegations of unlawful discrimination.

Education
Education is free and compulsory for children between seven and 17 years of age. In 2005–06 there were 4,280 public schools (elementary, junior high, secondary, special education and others) and 1,220 non-public schools; pre kindergarten-grade 8 enrolment (public) was 1,480,508; pre kindergarten-grade 8 (non-public), 200,022; grades 9–12 enrolment (public), 631,198; grades 9–12 (non-public), 57,172. In 2004–05 pre kindergarten teachers (public) totalled 1,313; pre kindergarten teachers (non-public), 1,757; kindergarten teachers (public), 4,212; kindergarten teachers (non-public), 1,327. The total number of elementary teachers (public) was 77,467; elementary teachers (non-public), 9,376; secondary teachers (public), 33,279; secondary teachers (non-public), 4,133. In 2004–05 the median salary for all classroom

(pre kindergarten-grade 12) teachers was $51,830. In fall 2005 higher education institutions had a total enrolment of 835,031 at 172 higher education colleges and universities (60 public, 84 not-for-profit independent and 28 for-profit independent). Total expenditure on education in 2004–05 was US$20,937m.

Major colleges and universities (fall 2005):

Founded	Name	Place	Control	Enrolment
1851	Northwestern University	Evanston	Independent	18,065
1857	Illinois State University	Normal	Public	20,653
1867	University of Illinois	Urbana/ Champaign	Public	41,938
		Springfield (1969)		4,517
		Chicago (1946)		24,812
1867	Chicago State University	Chicago	Public	7,131
1869	Southern Illinois University	Carbondale	Public	21,441
		Edwardsville (1957)		13,460
1890	Loyola University of Chicago	Chicago	Roman Catholic	14,764
1891	University of Chicago	Chicago	Independent	14,150
1895	Eastern Illinois University	Charleston	Public	12,129
1895	Northern Illinois University	DeKalb	Public	25,208
1897	Bradley University	Peoria	Independent	6,154
1899	Western Illinois University	Macomb	Public	13,404
1940	Illinois Institute of Technology	Chicago	Independent	6,472
1945	Roosevelt University	Chicago	Independent	7,234
1961	Northeastern Illinois University	Chicago	Public	12,227
1969	Governors State University	University Park	Public	5,405

Health

In 2006 there were 190 community hospitals, with 34,100 beds. A total of 1,583,000 patients were admitted during the year.

Welfare

Medicare enrolment in July 2004 totalled 1,677,224. In fiscal year 2006 a total of 2,194,730 people in Illinois received Medicaid. In Dec. 2008 there were 1,948,578 Old-Age, Survivors, and Disability Insurance (OASDI) beneficiaries. A total of 52,083 people were receiving payments under Temporary Assistance for Needy Families (TANF) in Dec. 2008.

RELIGION

In 2000 there were 6,457,000 Christians and (2002) 270,000 Jews in Illinois. Among the larger Christian denominations are: Roman Catholic (3·6m.), United Methodist (505,000), Lutheran Church Missouri Synod (325,000), Southern Baptist (265,000), Lutheran Church in America (200,000), Presbyterian Church, USA (200,000), United Church of Christ (192,000), American Baptist (105,000), Disciples of Christ (75,000), Assembly of God (63,000) and Church of Nazarene (50,000). At the end of 2006 the number of churches in Illinois totalled 15,694.

CULTURE

Broadcasting

In 2002 there were 210 radio stations, 18 radio networks and 64 television broadcasting stations.

FURTHER READING

Statistical information: Department of Commerce and Community Affairs, 620 Adams St., Springfield 62701. Publishes *Illinois State and Regional Economic Data Book*. Bureau of Economic and Business Research, Univ. of Illinois, 1206 South 6th St., Champaign 61820. Publishes *Illinois Statistical Abstract*.

Blue Book of the State of Illinois. Edited by Secretary of State. Biennial

Miller, D. L., *City of the Century: The Epic of Chicago and the Making of America*. 1996

The Illinois State Library: Springfield, IL 62756.

Indiana

KEY HISTORICAL EVENTS

The area was inhabited by Algonquian-speaking tribes when the first European explorers (French) laid claim to it in the 17th century. They established fortified trading posts but there was little settlement. In 1763 the area passed to Britain, with other French-claimed territory east of the Mississippi. In 1783 Indiana became part of the North West Territory of the USA; it became a separate territory in 1800 and a state in 1816. Until 1811 there was continuing conflict with the Indian inhabitants, who were then defeated at Tippecanoe.

Early farming settlement was by families of British and German descent, including Amish and Mennonite communities. Later industrial development offered an incentive for more immigration from Europe, and, subsequently, from the southern states. In 1906 the town of Gary was laid out by the United States Steel Corporation and named after its chairman, Elbert H. Gary. The industry benefited from navigable water to supplies of iron ore and of coal. Indiana Port on Lake Michigan was a thriving trade centre, especially after the opening of the St Lawrence Seaway in 1959. The Ohio River also carried freight.

Indianapolis was built after 1821 and became the state capital in 1825. Natural gas was discovered in the neighbourhood in the late 19th century. This stimulated the growth of a motor industry, celebrated by the Indianapolis 500 race, held annually since 1911.

TERRITORY AND POPULATION

Indiana is bounded west by Illinois, north by Michigan and Lake Michigan, east by Ohio and south by Kentucky across the Ohio River. Land area, 35,867 sq. miles (92,895 sq. km). Census population, 1 April 2000, was 6,080,485, an increase of 9·7% since 1990. July 2009 estimate, 6,423,113.

Population in five census years was:

	White	Black	Indian	Asiatic	Other	Total	Per sq. mile
1930	3,125,778	111,982	285	458	—	3,238,503	89·4
1960	4,388,554	269,275	948	2,447	—	4,662,498	128·9
1980	5,004,394	414,785	7,836	20,557	42,652	5,490,224	152·8
1990	5,020,700	432,092	12,720	37,617	41,030	5,544,159	154·6
2000	5,320,022	510,034	15,815	61,131	173,483	6,080,485	169·5

Of the total population in 2000, 3,098,011 were female, 4,506,089 were 18 years old or older and 4,304,011 were urban. Indiana's Hispanic population was 214,536 in 2000, a 117·2% increase on the 1990 total of 98,789.

The largest cities with census population, 2000, are: Indianapolis (capital), 761,296; Fort Wayne, 205,727; Evansville, 121,582; South Bend, 107,789; Gary, 102,746; Hammond, 83,048; Bloomington, 69,291; Muncie, 67,430; Anderson, 59,734; Terre Haute, 59,614.

SOCIAL STATISTICS

Births, 2007 (provisional), 89,916 (14·2 per 1,000 population); deaths, 2006, 55,622 (8·8). Infant mortality rate, 2006, 8·0 per 1,000 live births. 2006: marriages, 50,900 (8·1 per 1,000 population).

CLIMATE

Indianapolis, Jan. 29°F (–1·7°C), July 76°F (24·4°C). Annual rainfall 41" (1,034 mm). Indiana belongs to the Mid-West climate zone (*see* UNITED STATES: Climate).

CONSTITUTION AND GOVERNMENT

The present constitution (the second) dates from 1851. The General Assembly consists of a Senate of 50 members elected for four years, and a House of Representatives of 100 members elected for two years. It meets annually.

For the 111th Congress, which convened in Jan. 2009, Indiana sends nine members to the House of Representatives. It is represented in the Senate by Richard Lugar (R. 1977–2013) and Evan Bayh (D. 1999–2011).

The state capital is Indianapolis. The state is divided into 92 counties and 1,008 townships.

RECENT ELECTIONS

In the 2008 presidential elections Barack Obama won Indiana with 49·9% of the vote (George W. Bush won in 2004).

CURRENT ADMINISTRATION

Governor: Mitch Daniels (R.), 2009–13 (salary: $95,000).

Lieut.-Governor: Becky Skillman (R.), 2009–13 ($76,000).

Secretary of State: Todd Rokita (R.), 2007–11 ($66,000).

Government Website: http://www.in.gov

ECONOMY

Per capita personal income (2008) was $34,605.

Budget

In 2008 total state revenue was $29,115m. Total expenditure was $30,783m. (including: education, $10,617m.; public welfare, $8,034m.; highways, $1,997m.; correction, $677m.; government administration, $639m.) Outstanding debt in 2008, $19,916m.

Performance

In 2008 Gross Domestic Product by state was $254,861m. (provisional), ranking Indiana 17th in the United States.

ENERGY AND NATURAL RESOURCES

Water

The total area covered by water is approximately 551 sq. miles.

Minerals

The state produced 53,500,000 tonnes of crushed stone and 257m. tonnes of dimension stone in 2003. Production of coal (2003) was 35·4bn. short tons. Value of domestic non-fuel mineral production in 2006 was $982m.

Agriculture

Indiana is largely agricultural, about 75% of its total area being in farms. In 2003, 59,500 farms had 15·0m. acres (average, 253 acres). The average value of land and buildings per acre was $2,750 in 2003. Acreage harvested in 2003 was 12·0m., with a market value of $3,462m. for the top two crops (corn and soybeans).

Farm income 2006: crops, $3,919m.; livestock and products, $2,054m.; total, $5,973m. The net farm income in 2006 was $1,545m. The four most important products were corn, soybeans, hogs and dairy products. The livestock on 1 Jan. 2004 included 830,000 all cattle, 153,000 milch cows, 45,000 sheep and lambs, 3·1m. hogs and pigs, 22·7m. chickens and 13·1m. turkeys. In 2003 the wool clip yielded 270,000 lb of wool from 40,000 sheep and lambs.

Forestry

In 2007 there were 4·66m. acres of forest including 189,000 acres of national forest.

INDUSTRY

In 2005 Indiana's 8,970 manufacturing establishments had 554,000 employees, earning $24,192m. Total value added by manufacturing in 2006 was $90,192m. The steel industry is the largest in the country.

Labour

Total non-agricultural employment, 2007, 2,988,000. Employees by branch, 2007 (in 1,000): trade, transportation and utilities, 588; manufacturing, 550; government, 432; education and health services, 396; professional and business services, 290. The unemployment rate in 2007 was 4·6%.

INTERNATIONAL TRADE

Imports and Exports

Exports valued $16·4bn. in 2003.

COMMUNICATIONS

Roads

In 2007 there were 95,469 miles of public roads (73,320 miles rural). There were 4,955,539 registered motor vehicles.

Rail

In 2002 there were 4,255 miles of mainline railroad of which 3,872 miles were Class I.

Civil Aviation

Of airports in 2003, 115 were for public use and 581 were for private use. There were 5,019,406 passenger enplanements statewide in 2007.

SOCIAL INSTITUTIONS

Justice

Following the US Supreme Court's reinstatement of the death penalty in 1976, death sentences have been given since 1980. There were two executions in 2007, none in 2008 and one in 2009. In Dec. 2008, 28,322 prisoners were under the jurisdiction of state and federal correctional authorities.

The Civil Rights Act of 1885 forbids places of public accommodation to bar any persons on grounds not applicable to all citizens alike; no citizen may be disqualified for jury service 'on account of race or colour'. An Act of 1947 makes it an offence to spread religious or racial hatred.

A 1961 Act provided 'all of its citizens equal opportunity for education, employment and access to public conveniences and accommodations' and created a Civil Rights Commission.

Education

School attendance is compulsory from seven to 18 years. In 2003–04 there were an estimated 551,398 pupils attending elementary schools and 459,290 at secondary schools. The average expenditure per pupil was $8,582. Teachers' salaries averaged $45,791 (2003–04). Total expenditure for public schools, 2001–02, $7,988m.

Some leading institutions for higher education were (2003):

Founded	*Institution*	*Control*	*Students (full-time)*
1801	Vincennes University	State	8,185[1]
1824	Indiana University, Bloomington	State	29,768
1832	Wabash College, Crawfordsville	Independent	858
1837	De Pauw University, Greencastle	Methodist	2,319
1842	University of Notre Dame	R.C.	8,303
1847	Earlham College, Richmond	Quaker	1,125
1850	Butler University, Indianapolis	Independent	4,424
1859	Valparaiso University, Valparaiso	Evangelical Lutheran Church	3,003
1870	Indiana State University, Terre Haute	State	9,394
1874	Purdue University, Lafayette	State	30,424
1898	Ball State University, Muncie	State	17,411
1902	University of Indianapolis, Indianapolis	Methodist	2,916
1963	Ivy Tech State College, Indianapolis	State	9,054

Founded	Institution	Control	Students (full-time)
1969	Indiana University-Purdue University, Indianapolis	State	21,015
1985	University of Southern Indiana, Evansville	State	8,813

[1]2001.

Health

In 2006 there were 114 community hospitals with 18,000 beds. A total of 726,000 patients were admitted during the year.

Welfare

Medicare enrolment in July 2004 totalled 889,315. In fiscal year 2006 a total of 999,079 people in Indiana received Medicaid. In Dec. 2008 there were 1,121,662 Old-Age, Survivors, and Disability Insurance (OASDI) beneficiaries. A total of 105,995 people were receiving payments under Temporary Assistance for Needy Families (TANF) in Dec. 2008.

RELIGION

Religious denominations include Methodists, Roman Catholics, Disciples of Christ, Baptists, Lutherans, Presbyterian churches, Society of Friends and Episcopalians.

CULTURE

Broadcasting

In 2004 there were 81 television stations and 301 radio stations.

Press

There were 332 newspapers in circulation in 2004.

Tourism

In 2005, 152,000 overseas visitors (excluding those from Mexico and Canada) visited Indiana.

FURTHER READING

Statistical information: Indiana Business Research Center, Indiana Univ., Indianapolis 46202. Publishes *Indiana Factbook.*

Gray, R. D. (ed.) *Indiana History: a Book of Readings.* 1994
Martin, J. B., *Indiana: an Interpretation.* 1992

State library: Indiana State Library, 140 North Senate, Indianapolis 46204.

Iowa

KEY HISTORICAL EVENTS

Originally the territory of the Iowa Indians, the area was explored by the Frenchmen Marquette and Joliet in 1673. French trading posts were set up, but there were few other settlements. In 1803 the French sold their claim to Iowa to the USA as part of the Louisiana Purchase. The land was still occupied by Indians but, in the 1830s, the tribes sold their land to the US government and migrated to reservations. Iowa became a US Territory in 1838 and a state in 1846.

The state was settled by immigrants drawn mainly from neighbouring states to the east. Later there was more immigration from Protestant states of northern Europe. The land was extremely fertile and most immigrants came to farm. Not all the Indian population had accepted the cession and there were some violent confrontations, notably the murder of settlers at Spirit Lake in 1857. The capital, Des Moines, was founded in 1843 as a fort to protect Indian rights. It expanded rapidly along with coal mining after 1910.

TERRITORY AND POPULATION

Iowa is bounded east by the Mississippi River (forming the boundary with Wisconsin and Illinois), south by Missouri, west by the Missouri River (forming the boundary with Nebraska), northwest by the Big Sioux River (forming the boundary with South Dakota) and north by Minnesota. Land area, 55,869 sq. miles (144,700 sq. km). Census population, 1 April 2000, 2,926,324, an increase of 5·4% since 1990. July 2009 estimate, 3,007,856.

Population in five census years was:

	White	Black	Indian	Asiatic	Total	Per sq. mile
1870	1,188,207	5,762	48	3	1,194,020	21·5
1930	2,452,677	17,380	660	222	2,470,939	44·1
			All others			
1980	2,839,225	41,700	32,882		2,913,808	51·7
1990	2,683,090	48,090	45,575		2,776,755	49·7
2000	2,748,640	61,853	115,831		2,926,324	52·4

Of the total population in 2000, 1,490,809 were female, 2,192,686 were 18 years old or older and 1,787,432 were urban. In 2000 the Hispanic population was 82,473, up from 32,647 in 1990 (an increase of 152·6%).

The largest cities in the state, with their population in 2003, are: Des Moines (capital), 196,093; Cedar Rapids, 122,542; Davenport, 97,512; Sioux City, 83,876; Waterloo, 67,054; Iowa City, 63,807; Council Bluffs, 58,656; Dubuque, 57,204; Ames, 53,284; West Des Moines, 51,699; Cedar Falls, 36,429; Urbandale, 31,868; Bettendorf, 31,456; Ankeny, 31,144; Marion, 28,756.

SOCIAL STATISTICS

Births, 2007 (provisional), 40,778 (13·6 per 1,000 population); deaths, 2006, 27,362 (9·2). Infant mortality, 2006, 5·1 per 1,000 live births. 2006: marriages, 20,000 (6·7 per 1,000 population); divorces and annulments, 8,000 (2·7). Same-sex marriage became legal in April 2009.

CLIMATE

Cedar Rapids, Jan. 17·6°F, July 74·2°F. Annual rainfall 34". Des Moines, Jan. 19·4°F, July 76·6°F. Annual rainfall 33". Iowa belongs to the Mid-West climate zone (*see* UNITED STATES: Climate).

CONSTITUTION AND GOVERNMENT

The constitution of 1857 still exists; it has had 46 amendments. The General Assembly comprises a Senate of 50 and a House of Representatives of 100 members, meeting annually for an unlimited session. Senators are elected for four years, half retiring every second year: Representatives for two years. The Governor and Lieut.-Governor are elected for four years.

For the 111th Congress, which convened in Jan. 2009, Iowa sends five members to the House of Representatives. It is represented in the Senate by Chuck Grassley (R. 1981–2011) and Tom Harkin (D. 1985–2015).

Iowa is divided into 99 counties; the capital is Des Moines.

RECENT ELECTIONS

In the 2008 presidential elections Barack Obama won Iowa with 53·7% of the vote (George W. Bush won in 2004).

CURRENT ADMINISTRATION

Governor: Chet Culver (D.), 2007–11 (salary: $130,000).
Lieut.-Governor: Patty Judge (D.), 2007–11 ($103,212).
Secretary of State: Michael A. Mauro (D.), 2007–11 ($103,212).

Government Website: http://www.iowa.gov

ECONOMY

Per capita personal income (2008) was $37,402.

Budget
In 2008 total state revenue amounted to $15,940m. Total state expenditure was $16,523m. (education, $5,791m.; public welfare, $3,905m.; highways, $1,382m.; hospitals, $1,093m.; government administration, $555m.) Outstanding debt in 2008, $7,236m.

Performance
Gross Domestic Product by state was $135,702m. in 2008 (provisional), ranking Iowa 30th in the United States.

ENERGY AND NATURAL RESOURCES

Water
The total area covered by water is approximately 402 sq. miles.

Minerals
Production in 2003: crushed stone, 34·7m. tonnes; sand and gravel, 14·0m. tonnes. The value of domestic non-fuel mineral products in 2006 was $696m.

Agriculture
Iowa is the wealthiest of the agricultural states, partly because nearly the whole area (92%) is arable and included in farms. The total farm area, 2003, is 31·7m. acres. The average farm in 2002 was 352 acres. The average value of buildings and land per acre was, in 2002, $2,005. The number of farms declined in the latter years of the 20th century, from 174,000 in 1960 to 90,000 in 2003.

Farm income 2006: crops, $7,229m.; livestock and products, $7,879m.; total, $15,108m. The net farm income in 2006 was $3,275m. In 2002 production of corn was 1,963m. bu.[1], value $4,359m.; and soybeans, 499m. bu.[1], value $2,766m. In 2003 livestock included: swine, 15·8m.[1]; milch cows, 201,000; all cattle, 3·30m.; sheep and lambs, 255,000. The wool clip yielded 1·36m. lb.

[1]More than any other state.

Forestry
Total forested area was 2·88m. acres in 2007.

INDUSTRY
In 2005 Iowa's 3,800 manufacturing establishments had 226,000 employees, earning $9,026m. Total value added by manufacturing in 2006 was $41,011m.

Labour
Total non-agricultural employment, 2007, 1,517,000. Employees by branch, 2007 (in 1,000): trade, transport and utilities, 309; government, 250; manufacturing, 230; education and health services, 203; leisure and hospitality, 137. Iowa had an unemployment rate of 3·7% in 2007.

COMMUNICATIONS

Roads
In 2007 there were 114,193 miles of streets and highways, of which 102,905 miles were rural and 11,288 urban. There were 3,360,196 motor vehicle registrations.

Rail
In 2004 the state had 4,163 miles of track, three Class I, four Class II and 12 Class III railroads.

Civil Aviation
Airports numbered 226 in 2004, consisting of 103 publicly owned, 115 privately owned and eight commercial facilities. There were 3,803 registered aircraft in 2003 and 1,630,755 passenger enplanements in 2007.

SOCIAL INSTITUTIONS

Justice
The death penalty was abolished in Iowa in 1965. There were 8,766 federal and state prisoners in Dec. 2008.

Education
School attendance is compulsory for 24 consecutive weeks annually during school age (6–16). In 2003–04, 485,011 pupils were attending primary and secondary schools; 37,243 pupils attending non-public schools; classroom teachers numbered 33,688 for public schools with an average salary of $39,432. In 2004 the state spent an average of $6,372 on each elementary and secondary school student.

Leading institutions for higher education enrolment figures (fall 2004) were:

Founded	*Institution*	*Control*	*Professors*	*Full-time students*
1843	Clarke College, Dubuque	Independent	83	1,180
1846	Grinnell College, Grinnell	Independent	142	1,485
1847	University of Iowa, Iowa City	State	1,713	29,745
1851	Coe College, Cedar Rapids	Independent	73	1,218
1852	Wartburg College, Waverly	Evangelical Lutheran	104	1,804
1853	Cornell College, Mount Vernon	Independent	85	1,154
1854	Upper Iowa University, Fayette	Independent	36	2,758
1858	Iowa State University, Ames	State	1,369	23,783
1859	Luther College, Decorah	Evangelical Lutheran	197	2,497
1876	Univ. of Northern Iowa, Cedar Falls	State	561	11,424
1881	Drake University, Des Moines	Independent	245	2,954
1882	St Ambrose University, Davenport	Roman Catholic	160	2,413
1891	Buena Vista University, Storm Lake	Presbyterian	82	2,775
1894	Morningside College, Sioux City	Methodist	65	806

Health
In 2006 the state had 117 community hospitals with 10,500 beds. A total of 363,000 patients were admitted during the year.

Welfare
Iowa has a Civil Rights Act (1939) which makes it a misdemeanour for any place of public accommodation to deprive any person of 'full and equal enjoyment' of the facilities it offers the public.

Medicare enrolment in July 2004 totalled 485,630. In fiscal year 2006 a total of 431,184 people in Iowa received Medicaid. In Dec. 2008 there were 563,610 Old-Age, Survivors, and Disability Insurance (OASDI) beneficiaries.

Supplemental Security Income (SSI) assistance is available for the aged (65 or older), the blind and the disabled. As of June 2004, 3,748 elderly persons were drawing an average of $198·86 per month, 738 blind persons $335·79 per month and 36,152 disabled persons $372·26 per month. In 2008 Temporary Assistance to Needy Families (TANF) was received by on average 39,071 recipients monthly.

RELIGION
Chief religious bodies in 2004: Roman Catholics, 529,776 members; Evangelical Lutherans in America, 260,832 baptized members; United Methodists, 195,877; USA Presbyterians, 49,389; United Church of Christ, 38,945.

CULTURE
There were a total of 80 venues for live performances (2003).

Broadcasting
In 2004 there were 256 radio stations and 24 television stations.

Press

In 2004 there were a total of 326 newspapers.

Tourism

In 2003 there were 16·6m. visitors; value of industry, $4·6bn.

FURTHER READING

Annual Survey of Manufactures.
Government Finance.
Official Register. Secretary of State. Biennial
State Government Website: http://www.iowa.gov

State Library of Iowa: Des Moines 50319.

Kansas

KEY HISTORICAL EVENTS

The area was explored from Mexico in the 16th century, when Spanish travellers encountered Kansas, Wichita, Osage and Pawnee tribes. The French claimed Kansas in 1682, establishing a valuable fur trade with local tribes in the 18th century. In 1803 the area passed to the USA as part of the Louisiana Purchase and became a base for pioneering trails further west. After 1830 it was 'Indian Territory' and a number of tribes displaced from eastern states were settled there. In 1854 the Kansas Territory was created and opened for white settlement. The early settlers were farmers from Europe or New England, but the Territory's position also brought it into contact with southern culture. Slavery was prohibited by the Missouri Compromise of 1820 but the 1854 Kansas-Nebraska Act affirmed the principle of 'popular sovereignty' to settle the issue, which was then fought out by opposing factions throughout 'Bleeding Kansas'.

Kansas entered the Union (as a non-slave state) in 1861, minus the territory that is now in Colorado.

The economy was based on cattle-ranching and railways. Herds were driven to the railheads and shipped from vast stockyards, or slaughtered and processed in railhead meat-packing plants. Wheat and sorghum also became important once the plains could be ploughed on a large scale.

TERRITORY AND POPULATION

Kansas is bounded north by Nebraska, east by Missouri, with the Missouri River as boundary in the northeast, south by Oklahoma and west by Colorado. Land area, 81,815 sq. miles (211,900 sq. km). Census population, 1 April 2000, 2,688,418, an increase of 8·5% since 1990. July 2009 estimate, 2,818,747.

Population in five federal census years was:

	White	*Black*	*Indian*	*Asiatic*	*Total*	*Per sq. mile*
1870	346,377	17,108	914	—	364,399	4·5
1930	1,811,997	66,344	2,454	204	1,880,999	22·9
			All others			
1980	2,168,221	126,127	69,888		2,364,236	28·8
1990	2,231,986	143,076	102,512		2,477,574	30·3
2000	2,313,944	154,198	220,276		2,688,418	32·9

Of the total population in 2000, 1,359,944 were female, 1,975,425 were 18 years old or older and 1,920,669 were urban. In 2000 the estimated Hispanic population was 188,252, up from 93,670 in 1990 (an increase of 101·0%).

Cities, with 2000 census population: Wichita, 344,284; Overland Park, 149,080; Kansas City, 146,866; Topeka (capital), 122,377; Olathe, 92,962; Lawrence, 80,098.

SOCIAL STATISTICS

Births, 2007 (provisional), 42,268 (15·2 per 1,000 population); deaths, 2006, 24,553 (8·9). Infant mortality, 2006, 7·1 per 1,000 live births. 2006: marriages, 18,900 (6·8 per 1,000 population); divorces and annulments, 9,200 (3·3 per 1,000 population).

CLIMATE

Dodge City, Jan. 29°F (–1·7°C), July 78°F (25·6°C). Annual rainfall 21" (518 mm). Kansas City, Jan. 30°F (–1·1°C), July 79°F (26·1°C). Annual rainfall 38" (947 mm). Topeka, Jan. 28°F (–2·2°C), July 78°F (25·6°C). Annual rainfall 35" (875 mm). Wichita, Jan. 31°F (–0·6°C), July 81°F (27·2°C). Annual rainfall 31" (777 mm). Kansas belongs to the Mid-West climate zone (*see* UNITED STATES: Climate).

CONSTITUTION AND GOVERNMENT

The year 1861 saw the adoption of the present constitution; it has had 89 amendments. The Legislature includes a Senate of 40 members, elected for four years, and a House of Representatives of 125 members, elected for two years. Sessions are annual.

For the 111th Congress, which convened in Jan. 2009, Kansas sends four members to the House of Representatives. It is represented in the Senate by Pat Roberts (R. 1997–2015) and Sam Brownback (R. 1997–2011).

The capital is Topeka. The state is divided into 105 counties.

RECENT ELECTIONS

In the 2008 presidential elections John McCain won Kansas with 56·6% of the vote (George W. Bush won in 2004).

CURRENT ADMINISTRATION

Governor: Mark Parkinson (D.), 2009–11 (salary: $110,707).
Lieut.-Governor: Troy Findley (D.), 2009–11 ($31,313).
Secretary of State: Ron Thornburgh (R.), 2007–11 ($86,003).

Government Website: http://www.kansas.gov

ECONOMY

Per capita income (2008) was $38,820.

Budget

In 2008 total state revenue was $13,542m. Total expenditure was $14,969m. (including: education, $5,750m.; public welfare, $3,168m.; highways, $1,214m.; hospitals, $973m.; government administration, $459m.) Outstanding debt in 2008, $5,837m.

Performance

Gross Domestic Product by state in 2008 was $122,731m. (provisional), ranking Kansas 32nd in the United States.

ENERGY AND NATURAL RESOURCES

Oil and Gas

In 2006 Kansas produced 371bn. cu. ft of natural gas and 36m. bbls of crude oil.

Water

The total area covered by water is approximately 462 sq. miles.

Minerals

Important fuel minerals are coal, petroleum and natural gas. Non-fuel minerals, mainly cement, salt and crushed stone, were worth $973m. in 2006.

Agriculture

Kansas is pre-eminently agricultural, but sometimes suffers from lack of rainfall in the west. In 2002 there were 63,000 farms with a total acreage of 47·4m. Average number of acres per farm was 752. Average value of farmland and buildings per acre, in 2002, was

$687. Farm income 2006: from crops, $3,365m.; and from livestock and products, $6,971m. Chief crops: wheat, corn and soybeans. The net farm income in 2006 was $1,614m. Wheat production was 262·98m. bu. in 2002. There is an extensive livestock industry, comprising, in 2000, 6·55m. cattle (only Texas had more), 100,000 sheep, 1·46m. pigs and 1·75m. poultry.

Forestry

The state had a forested area of 2·11m. acres in 2007.

INDUSTRY

In 2005 the state's 3,128 manufacturing establishments had 177,000 employees, earning $7,222m. Total value added by manufacturing in 2006 was $25,332m.

Labour

Total non-agricultural employment, 2007, 1,379,000. Employees by branch, 2007 (in 1,000): trade, transportation and utilities, 264; government, 258; manufacturing, 186; education and health services, 171; professional and business services, 144. In 2007 the state unemployment rate was 4·1%.

COMMUNICATIONS

Roads

In 2007 there were 140,271 miles of roads (127,612 miles rural). There were 2,429,064 registered motor vehicles.

Rail

There were 5,084 miles of railroad as of 31 Dec. 2003.

Civil Aviation

There is an international airport at Wichita. There were 829,534 passenger enplanements statewide in 2007.

SOCIAL INSTITUTIONS

Justice

In Dec. 2008 there were 8,539 federal and state prisoners. The death penalty was declared unconstitutional in Kansas in 2004. The last execution was in 1965.

Education

In 2004–05 there were 469,136 public elementary and secondary pupils enrolled in 1,400 schools with 32,932 teachers. Total expenditure on public elementary and secondary education in 2003–04 was $3,937m. and average teacher salary was $38,623. Spending per pupil in 2002–03 was $7,454.

The Kansas Board of Regents governs six state universities: Kansas State University, Manhattan (founded in 1863); University of Kansas, Lawrence (1864); Emporia State University, Emporia; Pittsburg State University, Pittsburg; Fort Hays State University, Hays; and Wichita State University, Wichita. It also supervises and co-ordinates 19 community colleges, five technical colleges, six technical schools and a municipal university.

Health

In 2006 there were 129 community hospitals with 10,000 beds. A total of 332,000 patients were admitted during the year.

Welfare

Medicare enrolment in July 2004 totalled 397,231. In fiscal year 2006 a total of 343,498 people in Kansas received Medicaid. In Dec. 2008 there were 464,699 Old-Age, Survivors, and Disability Insurance (OASDI) beneficiaries. A total of 30,874 people were receiving payments under Temporary Assistance for Needy Families (TANF) in Dec. 2008.

RELIGION

The most numerous religious bodies are Roman Catholics, Methodists and Disciples of Christ.

FURTHER READING

Statistical information: Institute for Public Policy and Business Research, Univ. of Kansas, 607 Blake Hall, Lawrence 66045. Publishes *Kansas Statistical Abstract.*
Annual Economic Report of the Governor.

Drury, J. W., *The Government of Kansas.* 1970

State library: Kansas State Library, Topeka.

Kentucky

KEY HISTORICAL EVENTS

Lying west of the Appalachians and south of the Ohio River, the area was the meeting place and battleground for the eastern Iroquois and the southern Cherokees. Northern Shawnees were also present. The first successful white settlement took place in 1769 when Daniel Boone reached the Bluegrass plains from the eastern, trans-Appalachian, colonies. After 1783 immigration from the east was rapid, settlers travelling by river or crossing the mountains by the Cumberland Gap. The area was originally attached to Virginia but became a separate state in 1792.

Large plantations dependent on slave labour were established, as were small farms worked by white owners. The state became divided on the issue of slavery, although plantation interests (mainly producing tobacco) dominated state government. In the event the state did not secede in 1861, and the majority of citizens supported the Union. Public opinion was more favourable to the south in the hard times of the reconstruction period.

The eastern mountains became an important coal-mining area, tobacco-growing continued and the Bluegrass plains produced livestock, including especially fine thoroughbred horses.

TERRITORY AND POPULATION

Kentucky is bounded in the north by the Ohio River (forming the boundary with Illinois, Indiana and Ohio), northeast by the Big Sandy River (forming the boundary with West Virginia), east by Virginia, south by Tennessee and west by the Mississippi River (forming the boundary with Missouri). Land area, 39,728 sq. miles (102,895 sq. km). Census population, 2000, 4,041,769, an increase of 9·7% since 1990. July 2009 estimate, 4,314,113.

Population in five census years was:

	White	*Black*	*All Others*	*Total*	*Per sq. mile*
1930	2,388,364	226,040	185	2,614,589	65·1
1960	2,820,083	215,949	2,124	3,038,156	76·2
1980	3,379,006	259,477	22,294	3,660,777	92·3
1990	3,391,832	262,907	30,557	3,685,296	92·8
2000	3,640,889	295,994	104,886	4,041,769	101·7

Of the total population in 2000, 2,066,401 were female, 3,046,951 were 18 years old or older and 2,253,800 were urban. Kentucky's Hispanic population was estimated to be 59,939, up 172·4% on the 1990 census figure of 22,005.

The principal cities with census population in 2000 are: Lexington-Fayette, 260,512; Louisville, 256,321; Owensboro, 54,067; Bowling Green, 49,296; Covington, 43,370; Hopkinsville, 30,089; Frankfort (capital), 27,741; Henderson, 27,373; Richmond, 27,152; Jeffersontown, 26,633.

SOCIAL STATISTICS

Births, 2007 (provisional), 59,127 (13·9 per 1,000 population); deaths, 2006, 40,102 (9·5). Infant mortality, 2006, 7·5 per 1,000 live births. 2006: marriages, 36,900 (8·8 per 1,000 population); divorces and annulments, 21,500 (5·1).

CLIMATE

Kentucky is in the Appalachian Mountains climatic zone (*see* UNITED STATES: Climate). It has a temperate climate. Temperatures are moderate during both winter and summer, precipitation is ample without a pronounced dry season, and winter snowfall amounts are variable. Mean annual temperatures range from 52°F in the northeast to 58°F in the southwest. Annual rainfall averages at about 45". Snowfall ranges from 5 to 10" in the southwest of the state, to 25" in the northeast, and 40" at higher altitudes in the southeast.

CONSTITUTION AND GOVERNMENT

The constitution dates from 1891; there had been three preceding it. The 1891 constitution was promulgated by convention and provides that amendments be submitted to the electorate for ratification. The General Assembly consists of a Senate of 38 members elected for four years, one half retiring every two years, and a House of Representatives of 100 members elected for two years. It has annual sessions. All citizens of 18 or over are qualified as electors.

For the 111th Congress, which convened in Jan. 2009, Kentucky sends six members to the House of Representatives. It is represented in the Senate by Mitch McConnell (R. 1985–2015) and Jim Bunning (R. 1999–2011).

The capital is Frankfort. The state is divided into 120 counties.

RECENT ELECTIONS

In the 2008 presidential elections John McCain won Kentucky with 57·4% of the vote (George W. Bush won in 2004).

CURRENT ADMINISTRATION

Governor: Steve Beshear (D.), Dec. 2007–Dec. 2011 (salary: $115,096·68).

Lieut.-Governor: Daniel Mongardo (D.), Dec. 2007–Dec. 2011 ($97,848·22).

Secretary of State: Trey Grayson (R.), Dec. 2007–Dec. 2011 ($108,720·24).

Government Website: http://kentucky.gov

ECONOMY

Per capita personal income (2008) was $32,076.

Budget

In 2008 total state revenue was $20,582m. Total expenditure was $25,422m. (including: education, $8,719m.; public welfare, $6,199m.; highways, $2,241m.; hospitals, $1,101m.; government administration, $840m.) Debt outstanding in 2008, $12,210m.

Performance

Gross Domestic Product by state in 2008 was $156,436m. (provisional), ranking Kentucky 27th in the United States.

ENERGY AND NATURAL RESOURCES

Electricity

In 2004 production was 94,530m. kWh, of which 86,121m. kWh was from coal.

Oil and Gas

Production of crude oil in 2006 was 2m. bbls; natural gas, 95bn. cu. ft.

Water

The total area covered by water is approximately 681 sq. miles. Kentucky has 12 major river basins that contain nearly 90,000 miles of streams. Virtually all of these streams form part of the larger Ohio River basin. The state's surface water includes more than 2,700 natural and artificial impoundments, of which roughly one-third are larger than ten acres in size. Wetlands comprise approximately 300,000 acres in the state. Kentucky has two major ground water regions—the alluvial valley along the Ohio River and beach and gravel deposits located west of Kentucky Lake.

Minerals

The principal mineral is coal: 119m. short tons were mined in 2004–05, value $3·25bn. In 2004, 55·6m. tonnes of crushed stone were mined, value $347m.; 10·3m. tonnes of sand and gravel, value $49·7m.; 1·0m. tonnes of clay, value $4·5m. Other minerals include fluorspar, ball clay, gemstones, dolomite, cement and lime. Total value of non-fuel mineral production for 2006 was $806m.

Agriculture

In 2002, 89,000 farms covered an area of 13·6m. acres. The average farm was 153 acres. In 2002 the average value of farmland and buildings per acre was $1,824.

Farm income, 2006: from crops, $1,299m.; and from livestock, $2,708m. The net farm income in 2006 was $1,742m. The chief crop is tobacco: production, in 2001, 254·6m. lb. Other principal crops include corn (156·2m. bu.), soybeans, wheat, hay, fruit and vegetables, sorghum grain and barley.

Stock-raising is important in Kentucky, which has long been famous for its horses. The livestock in 2001 included 128,000 milch cows, 2·3m. cattle and calves, 21,000 sheep, 5·6m. chickens and 0·45m. swine.

Forestry

In 2007 Kentucky had 11·97m. acres forested land, of which 744,000 acres were national forest.

Fisheries

Cash receipts from aquaculture totalled $1·1m. in 2001.

INDUSTRY

In 2005 Kentucky's 4,152 manufacturing establishments had 254,000 employees, earning $10,626m. The value added by manufacture in 2006 was $43,009m.

Labour

Total non-agricultural employment, 2007, 1,869,000. Employees by branch, 2007 (in 1,000): trade, transportation and utilities, 387; government 325; manufacturing, 256; education and health services, 241; professional and business services, 182. The unemployment rate in 2007 was 5·4%.

Trade Unions

In 2006 there were 172,100 union members in Kentucky (9·8% of workers).

INTERNATIONAL TRADE

Imports and Exports

Exports in 2001 totalled $9·04bn. with manufactured goods accounting for 95% of total exports. Transportation equipment, industrial machinery and chemicals were important manufactured exports. Livestock and coal were major non-manufactured goods exported.

COMMUNICATIONS

Roads

In 2007 there were 78,587 miles of roads comprising 12,479 miles of urban road and 66,108 miles of rural road. There were 3,546,620 registered motor vehicles.

Rail

In 2004 there were 2,760 miles of railroad of which 2,299 miles were Class I.

Civil Aviation

There were (2005) 62 publicly used airports. Commercial airports providing scheduled airline services in Kentucky are located in

Erlanger (Covington/Cincinnati area), Louisville, Lexington, Owensboro and Paducah. There were 10,184,752 passenger enplanements statewide in 2007.

Shipping

There is barge traffic on the 1,100 miles of navigable rivers. There are six public river ports, over 30 contract terminal facilities and 150 private terminal operations. Kentucky's waterways have access to the junction of the upper and lower Mississippi, Ohio and Tennessee-Tombigbee navigation corridors.

SOCIAL INSTITUTIONS

Justice

There are 12 adult prisons within the Department of Corrections Adult Institutions and three privately run adult institutions. In Dec. 2008 there were 21,706 prison inmates. The death penalty is authorized for murder and kidnapping. As of Oct. 2004 there were 35 persons (including one female) under sentence of death. There was one execution in 2008 but none in 2009.

Education

Attendance at school between the ages of six and 16 years (inclusive) is compulsory, the normal term being 175 days. In 2001–02, 40,789 teachers were employed in public elementary and secondary schools. There were 630,436 pupils in public elementary and secondary schools. Public school classroom teachers' salaries (2001–02) averaged $36,688. The average total expenditure per pupil was $6,720.

There were also 4,207 teachers working in private elementary and secondary schools with some 71,812 students in 2001–02.

The state has 28 universities and senior colleges, one junior college and 28 community and technical colleges, with a total enrolment of 187,270 students (fall 2001). Of these universities and colleges, 36 are state-supported and the remainder are supported privately. The largest of the institutions of higher learning are (fall 2001): University of Kentucky, with 24,791 students; University of Louisville, 20,394; Western Kentucky University, 16,579; Eastern Kentucky University, 14,697; Northern Kentucky University, 12,548; Murray State University, 9,648; Morehead State University, 9,027; Kentucky State University, 2,314. Five of the several privately endowed colleges of standing are Berea College, Berea; Centre College, Danville; Transylvania University, Lexington; Georgetown College, Georgetown; and Bellarmine College, Louisville.

Health

In 2006 there were 104 community hospitals with 14,500 beds. A total of 612,000 patients were admitted during the year.

Welfare

Medicare enrolment in July 2004 totalled 660,213. In fiscal year 2006 a total of 899,616 people in Kentucky received Medicaid. In Dec. 2008 there were 844,573 Old-Age, Survivors, and Disability Insurance (OASDI) beneficiaries. A total of 60,627 people were receiving payments under Temporary Assistance for Needy Families (TANF) in Dec. 2008.

RELIGION

The chief religious denominations in 2000 were: Southern Baptists, with 979,994 members, Roman Catholics (406,021), United Methodists (208,720), Christian Churches and Church of Christ (106,638) and Christian (Disciples of Christ) (67,611).

CULTURE

The Kentucky Center for the Arts hosts productions by the Kentucky Opera Association, the Louisville Ballet, the Louisville Orchestra and Broadway touring productions.

Tourism

In 2005 tourist expenditure was $9·4bn., producing over $952m. in tax revenues and supporting 176,200 jobs. The state had (2005) 52 state parks.

FURTHER READING

Kentucky Deskbook of Economic Statistics, Lackey, Brent, (ed.) Kentucky Cabinet for Economic Development, Frankfort

Miller, P. M., *Kentucky Politics and Government: Do We Stand United?* 1994

Ulack, R. (ed.) *Atlas of Kentucky*. 1998

Louisiana

KEY HISTORICAL EVENTS

Originally the territory of Choctaw and Caddo tribes, the area was claimed for France in 1682. In 1718 the French founded New Orleans which became the centre of a crown colony in 1731. France ceded the area west of the Mississippi (most of the present state) to Spain in 1762 and the eastern area, north of New Orleans, to Britain in 1763. The British section passed to the USA in 1783 but France bought back the rest from Spain in 1800, including New Orleans and the mouth of the Mississippi. The USA, fearing exclusion from a strategically important and commercially promising shipping area, persuaded France to sell Louisiana in 1803. The present states of Missouri, Arkansas, Iowa, North Dakota, South Dakota, Nebraska and Oklahoma were included in the purchase.

The area became the Territory of New Orleans in 1804 and was admitted to the Union as a state in 1812. The economy initially depended on cotton and sugarcane plantations. The population was of French, Spanish and black descent, with a growing number of American settlers. Plantation interests succeeded in achieving secession in 1861 but New Orleans was occupied by the Union in 1862. Planter influence was reasserted in the late 19th century, imposing rigid segregation and denying black rights.

The state has become mainly urban industrial, with the Mississippi ports growing rapidly. There is petroleum and natural gas, and a strong tourist industry based on the French culture and Caribbean atmosphere of New Orleans.

Louisiana, and New Orleans in particular, suffered widespread damage and loss of life after Hurricane Katrina struck the Gulf Coast on 31 Aug. 2005.

TERRITORY AND POPULATION

Louisiana is bounded north by Arkansas, east by Mississippi, south by the Gulf of Mexico and west by Texas. Land area, 43,562 sq. miles (112,825 sq. km). Census population, 1 April 2000, 4,468,976, an increase of 5·9% since 1990. July 2009 estimate, 4,492,076.

Population in five census years was:

	White	*Black*	*Indian*	*Asiatic*	*Total*	*Per sq. mile*
1930	1,322,712	776,326	1,536	1,019	2,101,593	46·5
1960	2,211,715	1,039,207	3,587	2,004	3,257,022	72·2
			All others			
1980	2,911,243	1,237,263	55,466		4,205,900	93·5
1990	2,839,138	1,299,281	81,554		4,219,973	96·9
2000	2,856,161	1,451,944	160,871		4,468,976	102·6

Of the total population in 2000, 2,306,073 were female, 3,249,177 were 18 years old or older and 3,245,665 were urban. The Hispanic population was 107,738 in 2000, an increase of 14,671 (15·8%) on the 1990 census figure of 93,067.

The largest cities with their 2000 census population are: New Orleans, 484,674; Baton Rouge, 227,818; Shreveport, 200,145; Lafayette, 100,257; Lake Charles, 71,757; Kenner, 70,517; Bossier City, 56,461; Monroe, 53,107. In Jan. 2006 the population of New Orleans was estimated at 144,000 in the wake of Hurricane Katrina, making Baton Rouge temporarily the most populous city in Louisiana. By 1 Jan. 2007 population estimates for New Orleans had increased to 255,000.

SOCIAL STATISTICS

Births, 2007 (provisional), 65,219 (15·2 per 1,000 population); deaths, 2006, 40,045 (9·3). Infant deaths, 2006, 9·9 per 1,000 live births. Marriages, 2005, 36,600 (8·1 per 1,000 population).

CLIMATE

New Orleans, Jan. 54°F (12·2°C), July 83°F (28·3°C). Annual rainfall 58" (1,458 mm). Louisiana belongs to the Gulf Coast climate zone (*see* UNITED STATES: Climate).

CONSTITUTION AND GOVERNMENT

The present constitution dates from 1974. The Legislature consists of a Senate of 39 members and a House of Representatives of 105 members, both chosen for four years. Sessions are annual; a fiscal session is held in even years.

For the 111th Congress, which convened in Jan. 2009, Louisiana sends seven members to the House of Representatives. It is represented in the Senate by Mary Landrieu (D. 1997–2015) and David Vitter (R. 2005–11).

Louisiana is divided into 64 parishes (corresponding to the counties of other states). The capital is Baton Rouge.

RECENT ELECTIONS

In the 2008 presidential elections John McCain won Louisiana with 58·6% of the vote (George W. Bush won in 2004).

CURRENT ADMINISTRATION

Governor: Bobby Jindal (R.), 2008–12 (salary: $130,000).
Lieut.-Governor: Mitch Landrieu (D.), 2008–12 ($115,000).
Secretary of State: Jay Dardenne (R.), 2008–12 ($115,000).

Government Website: http://www.louisiana.gov

ECONOMY

Per capita personal income (2008) was $36,424.

Budget

In 2008 total revenue was $30,308m. Total expenditure in 2008 was $33,004m. (education, $9,083m.; public welfare, $5,829m.; highways, $2,132m.; hospitals, $1,021m.; government administration, $930m.) Debt outstanding, in 2008, $16,388m.

Performance

Gross Domestic Product by state in 2008 was $222,218m. (provisional), ranking Louisiana 23rd in the United States.

ENERGY AND NATURAL RESOURCES

Electricity

Electricity production 2006, 90·9bn. kWh.

Oil and Gas

Louisiana ranks fourth among states of the USA for oil production and fifth for natural gas production. Production in 2006 of crude oil was 74m. bbls; and of natural gas, 1,361bn. cu. ft.

Water

The area covered by water was approximately 8,278 sq. miles in 2000.

Minerals

Principal non-fuel minerals are salt and sand, gravel, and lime. Total non-fuel mineral production in 2006 was $481m.

Agriculture

The state is divided into two parts, the uplands and the alluvial and swamp regions of the coast. A delta occupies about one-third of the total area. Manufacturing is the leading industry, but agriculture is important. The number of farms in 2003 was 27,200 covering 7·85m. acres; the average farm had 289 acres. Average value of farmland per acre, in 2002, was $1,534.

Farm income, 2006: from crops, $1,322m.; and from livestock, $864m. The net farm income in 2006 was $766m. Principal crops, 2003 production, were: soybeans, 25·16m. bu.; sugarcane, 12·84m. tons; rice, 26·40m. cwt; corn, 67·00m. bu.; cotton, 1·03m. bales; sweet potatoes, 3·15m. cwt; sorghum, 14·03m. bu.

Forestry

In 2007 the state had 14·22m. acres forested land, of which 695,000 acres were national forest. Production 2003: sawtimber, 1,266·18m. bd ft; cordwood, 6·74m. standard cords. The economic impact of forestry and forest products industries in Louisiana was $3·7bn. in 2003.

Fisheries

In 2003 Louisiana's commercial fisheries catch for all species totalled 1,189·7m. lb (539,635 tonnes), valued at $294·1m.

INDUSTRY

Louisiana's leading manufacturing activity is the production of chemicals, followed, in order of importance, by the processing of petroleum and coal products, the production of transportation equipment and production of paper products. In 2005 the state's 3,377 manufacturing establishments had 145,000 employees, earning $7,074m. Total value added by manufacturing in 2006 was $77,850m.

Labour

Total non-agricultural employment, 2007, 1,921,000. Employees by branch, 2007 (in 1,000): trade, transportation and utilities, 383; government, 359; education and health services, 247; professional and business services, 201; leisure and hospitality, 194. The unemployment rate was 4·3% in 2007.

INTERNATIONAL TRADE

In 2004 foreign investment amounted to $33·1bn.

Imports and Exports

In 2003 exports were valued at $18,390·13m.

COMMUNICATIONS

Roads

In 2007 there were 61,008 miles of road (44,731 miles rural). Registered motor vehicles numbered 3,926,741.

Rail

In 2003 there were approximately 2,748 miles of main-line track in the state. There is a tramway in New Orleans.

Civil Aviation

In 2004 there were 71 public airports. There were 5,071,477 passenger enplanements statewide in 2007.

Shipping

There are ports at New Orleans, Baton Rouge, St Bernard, Plaquemines and Lake Charles. The Mississippi and other waterways provide 7,500 miles of navigable water.

SOCIAL INSTITUTIONS

Justice

In Dec. 2008 there were 38,381 federal and state prisoners. There was an execution in Jan. 2010, the first since 2002.

Education

School attendance is compulsory between the ages of seven and 18. In 2003 there were 1,505 public schools with 723,252 registered pupils, and 49,371 teachers paid an average salary of $36,433. There are 16 public colleges and universities and ten non-public institutions of higher learning. There are 42 state trade and vocational technical schools, three law schools, three medical schools and a biomedical research centre affiliated with Louisiana's universities.

In 2003–04 there were 210,484 students enrolled at public two- and four-year colleges and universities. Enrolment, 2003–04, in the University of Louisiana System was 83,303 (Lafayette, 16,208; Southeastern, 15,662; Louisiana Tech., 11,960; Northwestern, 10,505; Monroe, 8,592; McNeese, 8,447; Nicholls, 7,260; Grambling, 4,669); Louisiana State University, 62,841 (with campuses at Alexandria, Baton Rouge, Eunice, New Orleans and Shreveport); Southern University System, 15,044. Major private institutions: Tulane University, 9,920; Loyola University, 5,900; Xavier University, 3,994; Dillard University, 1,953.

Health

In 2006 there were 132 community hospitals with 15,800 beds. A total of 623,000 patients were admitted during the year.

Welfare

Medicare enrolment in July 2004 totalled 628,401. In fiscal year 2006 a total of 1,148,972 people in Louisiana received Medicaid. In Dec. 2008 there were 748,171 Old-Age, Survivors, and Disability Insurance (OASDI) beneficiaries. In fiscal year 2003–04 Family Independence Temporary Assistance Program (FITAP) payments to 434,707 recipients totalled $40,056,233. In the fiscal year 2003–04 Food Stamp benefits totalling $735,959,328 were paid to 7,972,477 recipients.

RELIGION

The Roman Catholic Church is the largest denomination in Louisiana. The leading Protestant Churches are Southern Baptist and Methodist.

CULTURE

Broadcasting

In 2004 there were 215 radio stations (77 AM; 138 FM) and 48 television stations.

Press

In 2004 there were 309 newspapers in circulation.

Tourism

Tourism is the second most important industry for state income. In 2003 there were over 25m. visitors to the state. Tourism was a $9·4bn. industry in 2003; it provided more than 119,900 jobs and generated in excess of $1·2bn. in tax revenue for federal, state and local governments.

FURTHER READING

Louisiana State Census Data Center. Online only

Calhoun, Milburn, (ed.) *Louisiana Almanac 2008–2009 Edition.* 2008

Wall, Bennett H., *et al.*, (eds.) *Louisiana: a History, Fifth Edition.* 2008

Wilds, J., *et al.*, (eds.) *Louisiana Yesterday and Today: a Historical Guide to the State.* 1996

State library: The State Library of Louisiana, 701 North 4th St., Baton Rouge.

Maine

KEY HISTORICAL EVENTS

Originally occupied by Algonquian-speaking tribes, the Territory was disputed between groups of British settlers, and between the British and French, throughout the 17th and most of the 18th centuries. After 1652 Maine was governed as part of Massachusetts, and French claims finally failed in 1763. Most of the early settlers were English and Protestant Irish, with many Quebec French.

The Massachusetts settlers gained control when the first colonist, Sir Ferdinando Gorges, supported the losing royalist side in the English civil war. During the English-American war of 1812, Maine residents claimed that the Massachusetts government did not protect them against British raids. Maine was separated from Massachusetts and entered the Union as a state in 1820.

Maine is a mountainous state and even the coastline is rugged, but the coastal belt is where most settlement has developed. In the 19th century there were manufacturing towns making use of cheap water-power and the rocky shore supported a shell-fish industry. The latter still flourishes, together with intensive horticulture, producing potatoes and fruit. The other main economic activity is forestry for timber, pulp and paper.

The capital is Augusta, a river trading post which was fortified against Indian attacks in 1754, incorporated as a town in 1797 and chosen as capital in 1832.

TERRITORY AND POPULATION

Maine is bounded west, north and east by Canada, southeast by the Atlantic, south and southwest by New Hampshire. Land area, 30,862 sq. miles (79,932 sq. km). Census population, 1 April 2000, 1,274,923, an increase of 3·8% since 1990. July 2009 estimate, 1,318,301. Maine was one of three states where the population fell between July 2008 and July 2009 (the others being Michigan and Rhode Island).

Population for five census years was:

	White	*Black*	*Indian*	*Asiatic*	*Total*	*Per sq. mile*
1910	739,995	1,363	992	121	742,371	24·8
1950	910,846	1,221	1,522	185	913,774	29·4
			All others			
1980	1,109,850	3,128	12,049		1,125,027	36·3
1990	1,208,360	5,138	14,430		1,227,928	39·8
2000	1,236,014	6,760	32,149		1,274,923	41·3

Of the total population in 2000, 654,614 were female, 973,685 were 18 years old or older and 762,045 were rural (59·8%). Only Vermont has a more rural population. In 2000 the Hispanic population was 9,360, an increase of 37·1% on the 1990 census figure of 6,829. Only North Dakota and Vermont have fewer persons of Hispanic origin in the USA.

The largest city in the state is Portland, with a census population of 64,249 in 2000. Other cities (with population in 2000) are: Lewiston, 35,690; Bangor, 31,473; South Portland, 23,324; Auburn, 23,203; Augusta (capital), 21,819; Brunswick, 21,172; Biddeford, 20,942; Sanford, 20,806.

SOCIAL STATISTICS

Births, 2007 (provisional), 14,177 (10·8 per 1,000 population); deaths, 2006, 12,294 (9·3). Infant mortality rate, 2006, 6·3 per 1,000 live births. 2006: marriages, 9,700 (7·4 per 1,000 population); divorces and annulments, 4,800 (3·6).

CLIMATE

Average maximum temperatures range from 56·3°F in Waterville to 48·3°F in Caribou, but record high (since *c.* 1950) is 103°F.

Average minimum ranges from 36·9°F in Rockland to 28·3°F in Greenville, but record low (also in Greenville) is –42°F. Average annual rainfall ranges from 48·85" in Machias to 36·09" in Houlton. Average annual snowfall ranges from 118·7" in Greenville to 59·7" in Rockland. Maine belongs to the New England climate zone (*see* UNITED STATES: Climate).

CONSTITUTION AND GOVERNMENT

The constitution of 1820 is still in force, but it has been amended 170 times. In 1951, 1967, 1973, 1983, 1993 and 2003 the Legislature approved recodifications of the constitution as arranged by the Chief Justice under special authority.

The Legislature consists of the Senate with 35 members and the House of Representatives with 151 members, both Houses being elected simultaneously for two years. Sessions are annual.

For the 111th Congress, which convened in Jan. 2009, Maine sends two members to the House of Representatives. It is represented in the Senate by Olympia Snowe (R. 1995–2013) and Susan Collins (R. 1997–2015).

The capital is Augusta. The state is divided into 16 counties.

RECENT ELECTIONS

In the 2008 presidential elections Barack Obama won Maine with 57·7% of the vote (John Kerry won in 2004).

CURRENT ADMINISTRATION

Governor: John Baldacci (D.), 2007–11 (salary: $70,000).
Senate President: Elizabeth Mitchell (D.). 2008–10 ($14,811).
Secretary of State: Matthew Dunlap (D.), 2009–11 ($83,970).

Government Website: http://www.maine.gov

ECONOMY

Per capita income (2008) was $36,457.

Budget

In 2008 total state revenue was $7,552m. Total expenditure was $8,175m. (public welfare, $2,493m.; education, $2,019m.; health, $491m.; highways, $480m.; government administration, $326m.) Outstanding debt in 2008, $5,296m.

Performance

Gross Domestic Product by state was $49,709m. in 2008 (provisional), ranking Maine 43rd in the United States.

ENERGY AND NATURAL RESOURCES

Water

The total area covered by water is approximately 4,523 sq. miles.

Minerals

Minerals include sand and gravel, stone, lead, clay, copper, peat, silver and zinc. Total value of non-fuel mineral production for 2006 was $158m.

Agriculture

In 2004, 7,200 farms occupied 1·37m. acres; the average farm was 190 acres. Average value of farmland and buildings per acre in 2004 was $1,850. Farm income, 2006: from crops, $303m.; and from livestock and products, $289m. The net farm income in 2006 was $217m. Principal commodities are potatoes, dairy products, blueberries and chicken eggs.

Forestry

There were 17·67m. acres of forested land in 2007, of which 53,000 acres were national forests. Commercial forest includes pine, spruce and fir. Wood products industries are of great economic importance.

Fisheries

In 2004 the commercial catch was 304·0m. lb, valued at $404·7m.

INDUSTRY

In 2005 the state's 1,850 manufacturing establishments had 61,000 employees, earning $2,497m. Total value added by manufacturing in 2006 was $7,795m.

Labour

Total non-agricultural employment, 2007, 617,000. Employees by branch, 2007 (in 1,000): trade, transportation and utilities, 126; education and health services, 116; government, 104; leisure and hospitality, 60; manufacturing, 59. The unemployment rate in 2007 was 4·7%.

COMMUNICATIONS

Roads

In 2007 there were 22,792 miles of road (19,805 miles rural). There were 1,079,843 registered motor vehicles.

Rail

In 2002 there were 1,195 miles of mainline railroad tracks.

Civil Aviation

There are international airports at Portland and Bangor. There were 1,058,062 passenger enplanements statewide in 2007.

SOCIAL INSTITUTIONS

Justice

In Dec. 2008 there were 2,195 federal and state prisoners. Capital punishment was abolished in 1887.

Education

Education is free for pupils from five to 21 years of age, and compulsory from seven to 17. In 2002 there were 204,337 pupils and 16,837 teachers in public elementary and secondary schools. Education expenditure by state and local government in 2002, $1,844m.

The University of Maine System, created by Maine's state legislature in 1965, consists of seven universities: the University of Maine (founded in 1865); the University of Maine at Augusta, at Farmington, at Fort Kent (1878), at Machias (1909), at Presque Isle (1903); and the University of Southern Maine (1878, campuses at Portland, Gorham and Lewiston-Auburn).

There are several independent universities, including: Bowdoin College, founded in 1794 at Brunswick; Bates College at Lewiston; Colby College at Waterville; Husson College at Bangor; Westbrook College at Westbrook; Unity College at Unity; and the University of New England (formerly St Francis College) at Biddeford.

Health

In 2006 there were 37 community hospitals with 3,400 beds. A total of 150,000 patients were admitted during the year.

Welfare

Medicare enrolment in July 2004 totalled 231,070. In fiscal year 2004 a total of 293,966 people in Maine received Medicaid. In Dec. 2008 there were 286,123 Old-Age, Survivors, and Disability Insurance (OASDI) beneficiaries. A total of 24,470 people were receiving payments under Temporary Assistance for Needy Families (TANF) in Dec. 2008.

RELIGION

The largest religious bodies are Roman Catholics, Baptists and Congregationalists.

FURTHER READING

Statistical information: Maine Department of Economic and Community Development, State House Station 59, Augusta 04333. Publishes *Maine: a Statistical Summary.*

Palmer, K. T., *et al.*, *Maine Politics and Government.* 1993

Maryland

KEY HISTORICAL EVENTS

The first European visitors found Algonquian-speaking tribes, often under attack by Iroquois from further north. The first white settlement was made by the Calvert family, British Roman Catholics, in 1634. The settlers received some legislative rights in 1638. In 1649 their assembly passed the Act of Toleration, granting freedom of worship to all Christians. A peace treaty was signed with the Iroquois in 1652, after which it was possible for farming settlements to expand north and west. The capital (formerly at St Mary's City) was moved to Annapolis in 1694. Baltimore, which became the state's main city, was founded in 1729.

The first industry was tobacco-growing, which was based on slave-worked plantations. There were also many immigrant British small farmers, tradesmen and indentured servants.

At the close of the War of Independence, the treaty of Paris was ratified in Annapolis. Maryland became a state of the Union in 1788. In 1791 the state ceded land for the new federal capital, Washington, and its economy has depended on the capital's proximity ever since. Baltimore also grew as a port and industrial city, attracting European immigration in the 19th century. Although in sympathy with the south, Maryland remained in the Union in the Civil War albeit under the imposition of martial law.

TERRITORY AND POPULATION

Maryland is bounded north by Pennsylvania, east by Delaware and the Atlantic, south by Virginia and West Virginia, with the Potomac River forming most of the boundary, and west by West Virginia. Chesapeake Bay almost cuts off the eastern end of the state from the rest. Land area, 9,774 sq. miles (25,315 sq. km). Census population, 1 April 2000, 5,296,486, an increase since 1990 of 10·8%. July 2009 estimate, 5,699,478.

Population for five federal censuses was:

	White	*Black*	*Indian*	*Asiatic*	*Total*	*Per sq. mile*
1920	1,204,737	244,479	32	400	1,449,661	145·8
1930	1,354,226	276,379	50	857	1,631,526	165·0
1960	2,573,919	518,410	1,538	5,700	3,100,689	314·0
			All others			
1990	3,393,964	1,189,899	197,605		4,781,468	489·2
2000	3,391,308	1,477,411	427,767		5,296,486	541·9

Of the total population in 2000, 2,738,692 were female, 3,940,314 were 18 years old or older and 4,558,668 were urban. In 2000 Maryland's Hispanic population was 227,916, up from 125,102 in 1990 (an increase of 82·2%).

The largest city in the state (containing 12·3% of the population) is Baltimore, with 651,154 (2000 census); Washington, D.C.–Baltimore metropolitan area, 7,608,070 (2000). Maryland residents in the Washington, D.C., metropolitan area total more than 1·8m. Other main population centres (2000 census) are Columbia (88,254); Silver Spring (76,540); Dundalk (62,306); Wheaton-Glenmont (57,694); Ellicott City (56,397); Germantown (55,419); Bethesda (55,277). Incorporated places, 2000: Frederick, 52,767; Gaithersburg, 52,613; Bowie, 50,269; Rockville, 47,388; Hagerstown, 36,687; Annapolis, 35,838; College Park, 24,657; Salisbury, 23,743; Cumberland, 21,518; Greenbelt, 21,456.

SOCIAL STATISTICS

Births, 2007 (provisional), 79,476 (14·1 per 1,000 population); deaths, 2006, 43,582 (7·8). Infant mortality, 2006, 8·0 per 1,000 live births. 2006: marriages, 36,500 (6·5 per 1,000 population); divorces and annulments, 17,000 (3·0).

CLIMATE

Baltimore, Jan. 36°F (2·2°C), July 79°F (26·1°C). Annual rainfall 42" (1,066 mm). Maryland belongs to the Atlantic Coast climate zone (*see* UNITED STATES: Climate).

CONSTITUTION AND GOVERNMENT

The present constitution dates from 1867; it has had 125 amendments. Amendments are proposed and considered annually by the General Assembly and must be ratified by the electorate. The General Assembly consists of a Senate of 47, and a House of Delegates of 141 members, both elected for four years, as are the Governor and Lieut.-Governor. Voters are citizens who have the usual residential qualifications.

For the 111th Congress, which convened in Jan. 2009, Maryland sends eight members to the House of Representatives. It is represented in the Senate by Barbara Mikulski (D. 1987–2011) and Benjamin Cardin (D. 2007–13).

The state capital is Annapolis. The state is divided into 23 counties and Baltimore City.

RECENT ELECTIONS

In the 2008 presidential elections Barack Obama won Maryland with 61·9% of the vote (John Kerry won in 2004).

CURRENT ADMINISTRATION

Governor: Martin O'Malley (D.), 2007–11 (salary: $150,000).

Lieut.-Governor: Anthony Brown (D.), 2007–11 ($125,000).

Secretary of State: John P. McDonough, appointed July 2008 ($87,500).

Government Website: http://www.maryland.gov

ECONOMY

Per capita income (2008) was $48,378. Maryland had the highest average household income in 2008, at $70,545.

Budget

In 2008 total state revenue was $28,423m. Total expenditure was $34,030m. (education, $10,991m.; public welfare, $7,119m.; highways, $2,510m.; health, $1,958m.; correction, $1,366m.) Outstanding debt in 2008, $23,070m.

Performance

Gross Domestic Product by state in 2008 was $273,333m. (provisional), ranking Maryland 15th in the United States.

ENERGY AND NATURAL RESOURCES

Electricity

The territory is served by four investor-owned utilities, five municipal systems and four rural co-operatives. 75% of electricity comes from fossil fuels and 25% from nuclear power.

Oil and Gas

Natural gas is produced (34m. cu. ft in 2004) from one field in Garrett County. A second gas field is used for natural gas storage. No oil is produced and there are no major reserves located in Maryland.

Water

The total area covered by water is approximately 2,633 sq. miles. Abundant fresh water resources allow water withdrawals for neighbouring states and the District of Columbia. The state straddles the upper portions of the world's largest freshwater estuary, Chesapeake Bay.

Minerals

Value of non-fuel mineral production in 2006 was $653m. The leading mineral commodities by weight are crushed stone (29·9m.

tonnes in 2004) and sand and gravel (12·7m. tonnes in 2004). Stone is the leading mineral commodity by value followed by Portland cement, coal, and sand and gravel. In 2004 output of crushed stone was valued at $185m. and Portland cement at $175m. Coal output was 5·22m. short tons in 2004.

Agriculture

In 2002 there were 12,200 farms with an area of 2·1m. acres. The average number of acres per farm was 172. The average value per acre in 2002 was $4,084. In 2003, 1·27m. people were employed in agriculture.

Farm animals, 2002 were: milch cows, 72,800; all cattle, 241,000; swine (2001), 52,000; and sheep, 22,700. As of 2002, chickens (not broilers), 3·17m. Farm income cash receipts, 2006: crops, $726m.; livestock and products, $872m.; total, $1,598m. The net farm income in 2006 was $595m. Milk (2002 value $169·5m.) and broilers ($440·5m.) are important products.

Forestry

Total forested area was 2·57m. acres in 2007.

Fisheries

In 2002, 53·2m. lb of seafood was landed at a dockside value of $49m. The total estimated value of the seafood industry was $700m.

INDUSTRY

In 2005 the state's 3,742 manufacturing establishments had 135,000 employees, earning $6,717m. Total value added by manufacturing in 2006 was $22,812m.

Labour

In 2006, 24·9% of the workforce were professional and technical workers. The workforce is well educated with one-third of the population over age 25 holding a bachelor's or higher degree (2006); 15·2% held a graduate or professional degree in 2006. Total non-agricultural employment, 2007, 2,610,000. Employees by branch, 2007 (in 1,000): government, 479; trade, transportation and utilities, 477; professional and business services, 397; education and health services, 374; leisure and hospitality, 235. The unemployment rate in 2007 was 3·6%.

COMMUNICATIONS

Roads

In 2007 there were 31,300 miles of road comprising 17,276 miles of urban road and 14,024 miles of rural road. There were 4,510,464 registered vehicles in 2007.

Rail

Maryland is served by CSX Transportation, Norfolk Southern Railroad as well as by six short-line railroads. Metro lines also serve Maryland in suburban Washington, D.C. Amtrak provides passenger service linking Baltimore and BWI Airport to major cities on the Atlantic Coast. MARC commuter rail serves the Baltimore–Washington metropolitan area.

Civil Aviation

There were (2005) 35 public-use airports, and 27 commercial airlines at Baltimore/Washington International Airport (BWI). The airport served 20·7m. passengers in 2006. Air cargo throughput has grown rapidly to over 350m. tons per annum, with increases planned. There were 10,509,826 passenger enplanements in 2007.

Shipping

In 2003 Baltimore was the 13th largest US seaport in value of imports, and 20th largest in value of exports; it ranked 18th in terms of total tonnage handled. It is located about 200 miles further inland than any other Atlantic seaport.

SOCIAL INSTITUTIONS

Justice

Prisons in Dec. 2008 held 23,324 inmates. Maryland's prison system has conducted a work-release programme for selected prisoners since 1963. All institutions have academic and vocational training programmes. There was one execution in 2004, the first since 1998, and one in 2005, but the death penalty was suspended in 2006.

Education

Education is compulsory from five to 16 years of age. In 2004–05 there were 1,421 public schools with 865,561 pupils and 55,101 teachers. Average teacher salary in 2003–04 was $50,261. Total expenditure on public elementary and secondary education in 2003–04 was $8,818m. Per pupil spending in 2002–03 was $9,153.

In 2005 there were 59 institutions of higher learning (30 public and 29 private). The largest is the University System of Maryland (created in 1988), with 128,425 students (fall 2005), consisting of 11 campuses, two major research institutions, two regional higher education centres and a system office. The USM colleges and universities are: Bowie State University; Coppin State College; Frostburg State University; Salisbury University; Towson University; the University of Baltimore; and the five campuses of the University of Maryland (Baltimore, Baltimore County, College Park, Eastern Shore and University College).

Health

In 2006 there were 50 community hospitals with 11,400 beds. A total of 690,000 patients were admitted during the year.

Welfare

Medicare enrolment in July 2004 totalled 685,055. In fiscal year 2006 a total of 759,002 people in Maryland received Medicaid. In Dec. 2008 there were 802,066 Old-Age, Survivors, and Disability Insurance (OASDI) beneficiaries. A total of 53,866 people were receiving payments under Temporary Assistance for Needy Families (TANF) in Dec. 2008.

RELIGION

Maryland was the first US state to give religious freedom to all who came within its borders. Chief religious bodies (2000) are Catholics, with 952,389 members, United Methodists (297,729), Jews (216,000), Southern Baptists (142,401) and Evangelical Lutherans (103,644).

CULTURE

Cultural venues include: Frostburg Performing Arts Center, Strathmore Hall Arts Center and Center Stage. Performing arts institutions include the Baltimore Opera Company, Peabody Music Conservatory and Arena Players.

Broadcasting

There are 15 TV stations, 22 cable television stations, 48 FM radio and 31 AM radio stations.

FURTHER READING

Statistical Information: Maryland Department of Economic and Employment Development, 217 East Redwood St., Baltimore 21202.

DiLisio, J. E., *Maryland.* 1982
Rollo, V. F., *Maryland's Constitution and Government.* 1982

State library: Maryland State Library, Annapolis.

Massachusetts

KEY HISTORICAL EVENTS

The first European settlement was at Plymouth, where the *Mayflower* landed its English religious separatists in 1620. In 1626–30 more colonists arrived, the main body being English Puritans who founded a Puritan commonwealth. This commonwealth, of about 1,000 colonists led by John Winthrop, became the Massachusetts Bay Colony and was founded under a company charter. Following disagreement between the English government and the colony, the charter was withdrawn in 1684, but in 1691 a new charter united a number of settlements under the name of Massachusetts Bay. The colony's government was rigidly theocratic.

Shipbuilding, iron-working and manufacturing were more important than farming, the land being poor. The colony was Protestant and of English descent until the War of Independence. The former colony adopted its present constitution in 1780. In the struggle which ended in the separation of the American colonies from the mother country, Massachusetts took the foremost part, and on 6 Feb. 1788 became the 6th state to ratify the US constitution. The state acquired its present boundaries (having previously included Maine) in 1820.

During the 19th century, industrialization and immigration from Europe increased while Catholic Irish and Italian immigrants began to change the population's character. The main inland industry was textile manufacture, the main coastal occupation, whaling; both have now gone. Boston has remained the most important city of New England, attracting a large black population since 1950.

TERRITORY AND POPULATION

Massachusetts is bounded north by Vermont and New Hampshire, east by the Atlantic, south by Connecticut and Rhode Island and west by New York. Land area, 7,840 sq. miles (20,306 sq. km). Census population, 1 April 2000, 6,349,097, an increase of 5·5% since 1990. July 2009 estimate, 6,593,587.

Population at five federal census years was:

	White	*Black*	*All Others*	*Total*	*Per sq. mile*
1950	4,611,503	73,171	5,840	4,690,514	598·4
1970	5,477,624	175,817	35,729	5,689,170	725·8
1980	5,362,836	221,279	152,922	5,737,037	732·0
1990	5,405,374	300,130	310,921	6,016,425	767·6
2000	5,367,286	343,454	638,357	6,349,097	809·8

Of the total population in 2000, 3,290,281 were female, 4,849,003 were 18 years old or older and 5,801,367 were urban (91·37%). In 2000 the Hispanic population was 428,729, up from 287,549 in 1990 (an increase of 49·1%).

Population of the largest cities at the 2000 census: Boston, 589,141; Worcester, 172,648; Springfield, 152,082; Lowell, 105,167; Cambridge, 101,355; Brockton, 94,304; New Bedford, 93,768; Fall River, 91,938; Lynn, 89,050; Quincy, 88,025; Newton, 83,829. The Boston–Worcester–Lawrence metropolitan area had a 2000 census population of 5,819,100.

SOCIAL STATISTICS

Births, 2007 (provisional), 77,731 (12·1 per 1,000 population); deaths, 2006, 53,450 (8·3). Infant mortality, 2006, 4·8 per 1,000 live births. 2006: marriages, 38,500 (6·0 per 1,000 population); divorces and annulments, 14,600 (2·3). Massachusetts was the first state to allow same-sex marriage.

CLIMATE

Boston, Jan. 28°F (–2·2°C), July 71°F (21·7°C). Annual rainfall 41" (1,036 mm). Massachusetts belongs to the New England climate zone (*see* UNITED STATES: Climate).

CONSTITUTION AND GOVERNMENT

The constitution dates from 1780 and has had 117 amendments. The legislative body, styled the General Court of the Commonwealth of Massachusetts, meets annually, and consists of the Senate with 40 members and the House of Representatives of 160 members, both elected for two years.

For the 111th Congress, which convened in Jan. 2009, Massachusetts sends ten members to the House of Representatives. It is represented in the Senate by John Kerry (D. 1985–2015) and Scott Brown (R. 2010–13).

The capital is Boston. The state has 14 counties.

RECENT ELECTIONS

In the 2008 presidential elections Barack Obama won Massachusetts with 61·8% of the vote (John Kerry won in 2004).

CURRENT ADMINISTRATION

Governor: Deval Patrick (D.), 2007–11 (salary: $140,535).

Lieut.-Governor: Timothy P. Murray (D.), 2007–11 ($130,916).

Secretary of the Commonwealth: William F. Galvin (D.), 2007–11 ($130,916).

Government Website: http://www.mass.gov

ECONOMY

Per capita income (2008) was $51,254, the fourth highest in the country.

Budget

In 2008 total state revenue was $51,760m. Total expenditure was $45,635m. (public welfare, $12,683m.; education, $10,714m.; highways, $2,246m.; government administration, $1,667m.; correction, $1,333m.) Outstanding debt in 2008, $71,892m.

Performance

Gross State Product by state in 2008 was $364,988m. (provisional), ranking Massachusetts 13th in the United States.

ENERGY AND NATURAL RESOURCES

Water

The total area covered by water is approximately 2,715 sq. miles.

Minerals

Total domestic non-fuel mineral output in 2006 was valued at $294m., most of which came from sand, gravel, crushed stone and lime.

Agriculture

In 2002 there were approximately 6,000 farms with an average area of 93 acres and a total area of 560,000 acres. Average value per acre in 2002 was $9,234. Farm income 2006: from crops, $344m.; and from livestock and products, $89m. Principal commodities are greenhouse products, cranberries, dairy products and sweetcorn. The net farm income in 2006 was $115m.

Forestry

About 62% of the state is forest. In 2007 state forests covered about 603,000 acres, with total forest land covering 3·17m. acres. Commercially important hardwoods are sugar maple, northern red oak and white ash; softwoods are white pine and hemlock.

Fisheries

In 2002 commercial fishing produced 243·8m. lb of fish with a value of $297·3m.

INDUSTRY

In 2005 the state's 7,915 manufacturing establishments had 286,000 employees, earning $15,570m. Total value added by manufacturing in 2006 was $48,519m.

Labour
Total non-agricultural employment, 2007, 3,277,000. Employees by branch, 2007 (in 1,000): education and health services, 624; trade, transportation and utilities, 571; professional and business services, 482; government, 433; leisure and hospitality, 302. The state unemployment rate was 4·6% in 2007.

COMMUNICATIONS

Roads
In 2007 there were 36,008 miles of public road (28,041 miles urban, 7,967 rural). There were 5,366,708 registered motor vehicles.

Rail
In 2002 there were 1,251 miles of freight railroad, including 436 miles of Class I railroads. There are metro, light rail, tramway and commuter networks in and around Boston.

Civil Aviation
As at June 2004 there were 77 airports and 139 heliports. There is an international airport at Boston. In 2007 there were 14,138,992 passenger enplanements statewide.

Shipping
The state has three deep-water harbours, the largest of which is Boston. Other ports are Fall River and New Bedford.

SOCIAL INSTITUTIONS

Justice
There were 11,408 federal and state prisoners in Dec. 2008. The death penalty was abolished in 1984.

Education
School attendance is compulsory for ages six to 16. In 2002–03 there were 1,904 public elementary and secondary schools with 982,989 pupils and 74,214 teachers; total expenditure on public schools was $10,293m. Teachers' average salaries were $50,819m. in 2003.

Some leading higher education institutions are:

Year opened	*Name and location of universities and colleges*	*Students 2003*
1636	Harvard University, Cambridge	24,851
1839	Framingham State College	6,153
1839	Westfield State College	4,937
1840	Bridgewater State College	9,626
1852	Tufts University, Medford[1]	9,509
1854	Salem State College	9,120
1861	Mass. Institute of Technology, Cambridge	10,340
1863	University of Massachusetts, Amherst	24,310
1863	Boston College (RC), Chestnut Hill	13,728
1865	Worcester Polytechnic Institute, Worcester	3,843
1869	Boston University, Boston	29,049
1874	Worcester State College	5,471
1894	Fitchburg State College	4,917
1894	University of Massachusetts, Lowell	11,706
1895	University of Massachusetts, Dartmouth	8,284
1898	Northeastern University, Boston[2]	22,944
1899	Simmons College, Boston[3]	4,121
1905	Wentworth Institute of Technology	3,453
1906	Suffolk University	7,822
1917	Bentley College	5,678
1919	Western New England College	4,448
1919	Babson College	3,342
1947	Merrimack College	2,407
1948	Brandeis University, Waltham	4,985
1964	University of Massachusetts, Boston	12,394

[1]Includes Jackson College for women.
[2]Includes Forsyth Dental Center School. [3]For women only.

Health
In 2006 there were 80 community hospitals with 16,300 beds. A total of 834,000 patients were admitted during the year.

Welfare
Medicare enrolment in July 2004 totalled 968,796. In fiscal year 2006 a total of 1,166,759 people in Massachusetts received Medicaid. In Dec. 2008 there were 1,094,012 Old-Age, Survivors, and Disability Insurance (OASDI) beneficiaries. A total of 92,961 people were receiving payments under Temporary Assistance for Needy Families (TANF) in Dec. 2008.

RELIGION
The principal religious bodies are the Roman Catholics, Jewish Congregations, Methodists, Episcopalians and Unitarians.

CULTURE

Tourism
In 2005, 867,000 overseas visitors (excluding those from Mexico and Canada) visited Massachusetts.

FURTHER READING
Levitan, D. with Mariner, E. C., *Your Massachusetts Government.* 1984

Michigan

KEY HISTORICAL EVENTS
The French were the first European settlers, establishing a fur trade with the local Algonquian Indians in the late 17th century. They founded Sault Ste Marie in 1668 and Detroit in 1701. In 1763 Michigan passed to Britain, along with other French territory east of the Mississippi, and from Britain it passed to the USA in 1783. Britain, however, kept a force at Detroit until 1796, and recaptured Detroit in 1812. Regular American settlement did not begin until later. The Territory of Michigan (1805) had its boundaries extended after 1818 and 1834. It was admitted to the Union as a state (with its present boundaries) in 1837.

During the 19th century there was rapid industrial growth, especially in mining and metalworking. The largest groups of immigrants were British, German, Irish and Dutch. Other groups came from Scandinavia, Poland and Italy. Many settled as miners, farmers and industrial workers. The motor industry became dominant, especially in Detroit. Lake Michigan ports shipped bulk cargo of iron ore and grain.

Detroit was the capital until 1847, when that function passed to Lansing. Detroit remained, however, an important centre of flour-milling and shipping and, after the First World War, of the motor industry.

TERRITORY AND POPULATION
Michigan is divided into two by Lake Michigan. The northern part is bounded south by the lake and by Wisconsin, west and north by Lake Superior, east by the North Channel of Lake Huron; between the two latter lakes the Canadian border runs through straits at Sault Ste Marie. The southern part is bounded in the west and north by Lake Michigan, east by Lake Huron, Ontario and Lake Erie, south by Ohio and Indiana. Total area is 96,716 sq. miles (250,493 sq. km) of which 56,804 sq. miles (147,122 sq. km) are land and 39,912 sq. miles (103,372 sq. km) water. Census population, 1 April 2000, 9,938,444, an increase of 6·9% since 1990. July 2009 estimate, 9,969,727. Michigan was one of three states where the population fell between July 2008 and July 2009 (the others being Maine and Rhode Island).

Population of five federal census years was:

	White	*Black*	*Indian*	*Asiatic*	*Total*	*Per sq. mile*
1910	2,785,247	17,115	7,519	292	2,810,173	48·9
1930	4,663,507	69,453	7,080	2,285	4,842,325	84·9

	White	Black	All others	Total	Per sq. mile
1980	7,872,241	1,199,023	190,814	9,262,078	162·6
1990	7,756,086	1,291,706	247,505	9,295,297	160·0
2000	7,966,053	1,412,742	559,649	9,938,444	175·0

Of the total population in 2000, 5,065,349 were female, 7,342,677 were 18 years old or older and 7,419,457 were urban. In 2000 the Hispanic population was 323,877, up from 201,596 in 1990 (an increase of 60·7%).

Populations of the chief cities in 2000 were: Detroit, 951,270; Grand Rapids, 197,800; Warren, 138,247; Flint, 124,943; Sterling Heights, 124,471; Lansing, 119,128; Ann Arbor, 114,024; Livonia, 100,545. The Detroit–Ann Arbor–Flint metropolitan area had a 2000 census population of 5,456,428.

SOCIAL STATISTICS

Births, 2007 (provisional), 125,880 (12·5 per 1,000 population); deaths, 2006, 86,042 (8·5). Infant mortality, 2006, 7·4 per 1,000 live births. 2006: marriages, 59,200 (5·9 per 1,000 population); divorces and annulments, 35,600 (3·5).

CLIMATE

Detroit, Jan. 23·5°F (–5·0°C), July 72°F (22·5°C). Annual rainfall 32" (810 mm). Grand Rapids, Jan. 22°F (–5·5°C), July 71·5°F (22·0°C). Annual rainfall 34" (860 mm). Lansing, Jan. 22°F (–5·5°C), July 70·5°F (21·5°C). Annual rainfall 29" (740 mm). Michigan belongs to the Great Lakes climate zone (*see* UNITED STATES: Climate).

CONSTITUTION AND GOVERNMENT

The present constitution became effective on 1 Jan. 1964. The Senate consists of 38 members, elected for four years, and the House of Representatives of 110 members, elected for two years. Sessions are biennial.

For the 111th Congress, which convened in Jan. 2009, Michigan sends 15 members to the House of Representatives. It is represented in the Senate by Carl Levin (D. 1979–2015) and Debbie Stabenow (D. 2001–13).

The capital is Lansing. The state is organized in 83 counties.

RECENT ELECTIONS

In the 2008 presidential elections Barack Obama won Michigan with 57·4% of the vote (John Kerry won in 2004).

CURRENT ADMINISTRATION

Governor: Jennifer Granholm (D.), 2007–11 (salary: $177,000).
Lieut.-Governor: John D. Cherry, Jr (D.), 2007–11 ($123,900).
Secretary of State: Terri Lynn Land (R.), 2007–11 ($124,900).

Government Website: http://www.michigan.gov

ECONOMY

Per capita income (2008) was $34,949.

Budget

In 2008 total state revenue was $42,259m. Total expenditure was $56,869m. (education, $21,963m.; public welfare, $13,431m.; highways, $2,764m.; hospitals, $2,299m.; correction, $1,863m.) Outstanding debt in 2008, $29,065m.

Performance

Gross Domestic Product by state in 2008 was $382,544m. (provisional), ranking Michigan 12th in the United States.

ENERGY AND NATURAL RESOURCES

Electricity

Electricity sales for 2005 were 110·4bn. kWh.

Oil and Gas

Natural gas production in 2006 was 365bn. cu. ft; production of crude oil was 5m. bbls.

Water

The total area covered by water is approximately 39,912 sq. miles.

Minerals

Domestic non-fuel mineral output in 2006 was valued at $1,910m. according to the US Geological Survey. Output was mainly iron ore, cement, crushed stone, sand and gravel.

Agriculture

The state, formerly agricultural, is now chiefly industrial. It contained 52,000 farms in 2002, with a total area of 10·4m. acres; the average farm was 200 acres. In 2000, 6,898,000 acres were harvested. Average value per acre in 2002 was $2,667. Principal crops are soybeans, corn, wheat, oats, sugar beets, hay and dry beans. Principal fruit crops include apples, cherries (tart and sweet), plums and peaches. In 2002 there were 297,000 milch cows, 73,000 beef cows, 3·66m. chickens and 960,000 pigs. Output in 2002 included 77,000 lb of blueberries, 20,160 pots of geraniums and 335,000 cwt of black beans. Farm income in 2006: total $4,488m.; crops, $2,833m.; livestock and products, $1,654m. The net farm income in 2006 was $1,321m.

Forestry

Forests covered 19·55m. acres in 2007, with 2·64m. acres of national forest. In 2003 about 18·7m. acres was timberland acreage. Three-quarters of the timber volume was hardwoods, principally hard and soft maples, aspen, oak and birch. Christmas trees are another important forest crop. Net annual growth of growing stock and saw timber was 923m. cu. ft and 3·3bn. bd ft respectively in 2004.

Fisheries

In 2005 recreational fishing licences were purchased by 982,544 residents and 270,800 non-residents. Recreational fishing revenue (2001) was approximately $839m.

INDUSTRY

Manufacturing is important; among principal products are motor vehicles and trucks, machinery, fabricated metals, primary metals, cement, chemicals, furniture, paper, foodstuffs, rubber, plastics and pharmaceuticals. In 2005 Michigan's 14,033 manufacturing establishments had 635,000 employees, earning $31,631m. Total value added by manufacturing in 2006 was $89,022m.

Labour

Total non-agricultural labour force in 2007 was 4,262,000. Employees by branch, 2007 (in 1,000): trade, transportation and utilities, 788; government, 657; manufacturing, 617; education and health services, 595; professional and business services, 573. The unemployment rate in 2007 was 7·1%, the highest of all the states.

COMMUNICATIONS

Roads

In 2007 there were 121,593 miles of road (85,837 miles of rural road and 35,756 miles of urban road). Vehicle registrations in 2007 numbered 8,191,748.

Rail

In 2000 there were 3,950 miles of railroad in Michigan and a 3-mile light rail peoplemover in Detroit.

Civil Aviation

There are international airports at Detroit, Flint, Grand Rapids, Kalamazoo, Port Huron, Saginaw and Sault Ste Marie. There were 20,064,544 passenger enplanements statewide in 2007.

Shipping

There are over 100 commercial and recreational ports spanning the state's 3,200 miles of shoreline. In 2000, 39 of these ports served commercial cargoes. The 20 ferry services carried 848,998 passengers and 529,809 vehicles in 68,571 crossings in 2000. Stone, sand, iron ore and coal accounted for 87% of approximately 94·2m. tonnes of traffic in 2004.

SOCIAL INSTITUTIONS

Justice

A Civil Rights Commission was established, and its powers and duties were implemented by legislation in the extra session of 1963. Statutory enactments guaranteeing civil rights in specific areas date from 1885. The legislature has a unique one-person grand jury system. The Michigan Supreme Court consists of seven non-partisan elected justices. In Dec. 2008 there were 48,738 prisoners in state or federal correctional institutions. Capital punishment was officially abolished in 1964 but there has never been an execution in Michigan.

Education

Education is compulsory for children from six to 16 years of age. In 2004–05 there were 1,750,919 pupils and 100,634 teachers in 4,067 public schools. Total expenditure on public elementary and secondary education in 2003–04 was $18,569m. and average teacher salary was $54,412. Spending per pupil in 2002–03 was $8,781.

In fall 2005 there were 104 institutes of higher education (45 public and 59 private) with 626,751 students.

Universities and students (fall 2002):

Founded	*Name*	*Students*
1817	University of Michigan, Ann Arbor	38,972
(1956	University of Michigan, Flint	6,524)
(1959	University of Michigan, Dearborn	10,379)
1849	Eastern Michigan University	23,710
1855	Michigan State University	41,114
1868	Wayne State University	28,161
1884	Ferris State University	11,074
1885	Michigan Technological University	6,625
1892	Central Michigan University	19,380
1899	Northern Michigan University	8,577
1903	Western Michigan University	28,931
1946	Lake Superior State University	3,077
1957	Oakland University	16,059
1960	Grand Valley State University	19,762
1963	Saginaw Valley State University	8,938

Health

In 2006 there were 142 community hospitals with 25,900 beds. A total of 1,205,000 patients were admitted during the year.

Welfare

Medicare enrolment in July 2004 totalled 1,465,155. In fiscal year 2006 a total of 1,872,398 people in Michigan received Medicaid. In Dec. 2008 there were 1,840,547 Old-Age, Survivors, and Disability Insurance (OASDI) beneficiaries. A total of 158,943 people were receiving payments under Temporary Assistance for Needy Families (TANF) in Dec. 2008.

RELIGION

Roman Catholics make up the largest body and the largest Protestant denominations are: Lutherans, United Methodists, United Presbyterians and Episcopalians.

CULTURE

Tourism

In 2005, 325,000 overseas visitors (excluding those from Mexico and Canada) visited Michigan.

FURTHER READING

Michigan Manual. Biennial
Michigan Economic Development Corporation. *Economic Profiler.* Online only

Browne, W. P. and Verburg, K., *Michigan Politics and Government: Facing Change in a Complex State.* 1995
Dunbar, W. F. and May, G. S., *Michigan: A History of the Wolverine State.* 3rd ed. 1995

State Library Services: Library of Michigan, Lansing 48909.

Minnesota

KEY HISTORICAL EVENTS

Minnesota remained an Indian territory until the middle of the 19th century, the main groups being Chippewa and Sioux. In the 17th century there had been some French exploration, but no permanent settlement. After passing under the nominal control of France, Britain and Spain, the area became part of the Louisiana Purchase and was sold to the USA in 1803.

Fort Snelling was founded in 1819. Early settlers came from other states, especially New England, to exploit the great forests. Lumbering gave way to homesteading, and the American settlers were joined by Germans, Scandinavians and Poles. Agriculture, mining and forest industries became the mainstays of the economy. Minneapolis, founded as a village in 1856, grew first as a lumber centre, processing the logs floated down the Minnesota River, and then as a centre of flour-milling and grain marketing. St Paul, its twin city across the river, became Territorial capital in 1849 and state capital in 1858. St Paul also stands at the head of navigation on the Mississippi which rises in Minnesota.

The Territory (1849) included parts of North and South Dakota, but at its admission to the Union in 1858, the state of Minnesota had its present boundaries.

TERRITORY AND POPULATION

Minnesota is bounded north by Canada, east by Lake Superior and Wisconsin, with the Mississippi River forming the boundary in the southeast, south by Iowa, west by South and North Dakota, with the Red River forming the boundary in the northwest. Land area, 79,610 sq. miles (206,189 sq. km). Census population, 1 April 2000, 4,919,479, an increase of 12·4% since 1990. July 2009 estimate, 5,266,214.

Population in five census years was:

	White	*Black*	*Indian*	*Asiatic*	*Total*	*Per sq. mile*
1910	2,059,227	7,084	9,053	344	2,075,708	25·7
1930	2,542,599	9,445	11,077	832	2,563,953	32·0
			All others			
1980	3,935,770	53,344	86,856		4,075,970	51·4
1990	4,130,395	94,944	149,760		4,375,099	55·0
2000	4,400,282	171,731	347,466		4,919,479	61·8

Of the total population in 2000, 2,483,848 were female, 3,632,585 were 18 years old or older and 3,490,059 were urban. In 2000 the Hispanic population was 143,382, up from 53,888 in 1990 (an increase of 116·1%).

The largest cities (with 2000 census population) are Minneapolis (362,618), St Paul (287,151), Duluth (86,918), Rochester (85,806) and Bloomington (85,172). The Minneapolis–St Paul metropolitan area had a 2000 census population of 2,968,806.

SOCIAL STATISTICS

Births, 2007 (provisional), 73,599 (14·2 per 1,000 population); deaths, 2006, 37,028 (7·2). Infant mortality, 2006, 5·2 per 1,000 live births. 2006: marriages, 30,900 (6·0 per 1,000 population); divorces (2004), 14,200 (2·8).

CLIMATE

Duluth, Jan. 8°F (–13·3°C), July 63°F (17·2°C). Annual rainfall 29" (719 mm). Minneapolis-St. Paul, Jan. 12°F (–11·1°C), July 71°F (21·7°C). Annual rainfall 26" (656 mm). Minnesota belongs to the Great Lakes climate zone (*see* UNITED STATES: Climate).

CONSTITUTION AND GOVERNMENT

The original constitution dated from 1857; it was extensively amended and given a new structure in 1974. The Legislature consists of a Senate of 67 members, elected for four years, and a House of Representatives of 134 members, elected for two years. It meets for 120 days within each two years.

For the 111th Congress, which convened in Jan. 2009, Minnesota sends eight members to the House of Representatives. It is represented in the Senate by Amy Klobuchar (D. 2007–13) and Al Franken (D. 2009–15).

The capital is St Paul. There are 87 counties.

RECENT ELECTIONS

In the 2008 presidential elections Barack Obama won Minnesota with 54·1% of the vote (John Kerry won in 2004).

CURRENT ADMINISTRATION

Governor: Tim Pawlenty (R.), 2007–11 (salary: $120,303).

Lieut.-Governor: Carol L. Molnau (R.), 2007–11 ($78,197).

Secretary of State: Mark Ritchie (Democratic-Farmer-Labor), 2007–11 ($90,227).

Government Website: http://www.state.mn.us

ECONOMY

Per capita income (2008) was $43,037.

Budget

In 2008 total state revenue was $29,707m. Total expenditure was $34,284m. (education, $12,425m.; public welfare, $9,046m.; highways, $2,137m.; government administration, $857m.; health, $654m.) Outstanding debt in 2008, $9,539m.

Performance

In 2008 Gross Domestic Product by state was $262,847m. (provisional), ranking Minnesota 16th in the United States.

ENERGY AND NATURAL RESOURCES

Water

The total area covered by water is approximately 7,329 sq. miles.

Minerals

The iron ore and taconite industry is the most important in the USA. Production of usable iron ore in 2003 was 34·8m. tons, value $969m. Other important minerals are sand and gravel, crushed and dimension stone, clays and peat. Total value of non-fuel mineral production in 2006 was $2,540m.

Agriculture

In 2002 there were 80,839 farms with a total area of 27·5m. acres; the average farm was of 340 acres. Average value of land and buildings per acre, 2002, $1,513. Farm income, 2006: from crops, $5,128m.; and from livestock and products, $4,642m. The net farm income in 2006 was $2,494m. Important products: corn, soybeans, sugar beets, spring wheat, processing sweet corn, oats, dry milk, cheese, mink, turkeys, wild rice, butter, eggs, flaxseed, milch cows, barley, swine, cattle for market, honey, potatoes, rye, chickens, sunflower seed and dry edible beans. In 2002 there were 2·3m. cattle (0·5m. milch cows) and 6·4m. hogs and pigs. In 2002 the wool clip amounted to 986,437 lb of wool from 154,900 sheep.

Forestry

In 2007 Minnesota had 16,391,000 acres of forested land, including 2,459,000 acres of national forest.

INDUSTRY

In 2005 the state's 7,957 manufacturing establishments had 336,000 employees, earning $15,435m. Total value added by manufacturing in 2006 was $49,430m.

Labour

Total non-agricultural employment, 2007, 2,771,000. Employees by branch, 2007 (in 1,000): trade, transportation and utilities, 530; education and health services, 428; government, 415; manufacturing, 341; professional and business services, 329. In 2007 the unemployment rate was 4·6%.

COMMUNICATIONS

Roads

In 2007 there were 137,693 miles of public roads (119,310 miles rural). There were 4,755,753 registered motor vehicles in 2007.

Rail

There are three Class I and 16 Class II and smaller railroads operating, with total mileage of 4,526.

Civil Aviation

In 2004 there were 143 airports for public use and 17 public seaplane bases. There were 17,380,618 passenger enplanements statewide in 2007.

SOCIAL INSTITUTIONS

Justice

In Dec. 2008 there were 9,406 federal and state prisoners. There is no death penalty.

Education

In 2003–04 there were 842,915 students and 55,501 teachers in public elementary and secondary schools. In 2003–04 there were 1,863 public schools and 113 charter schools. There were 86,513 students enrolled in 495 private schools.

The Minnesota State Colleges and Universities System (created in 1995) is composed of 37 state colleges and universities. In 2003 enrolled students at state colleges numbered 78,300. There are seven universities in the system: St Cloud State University, with 14,217 students in 2003; Minnesota, Mankato, 13,157; Winona, 7,583; Minnesota, Moorhead, 6,993; Metropolitan State University (in Minneapolis and St Paul), 4,516; Bemidji State University, 4,362; Southwest Minnesota State University (in Marshall), 3,458. Minnesota State University's Akita campus in Japan closed in 2003.

The University of Minnesota (founded in 1851) has four campuses at Crookston, Duluth, Morris and Twin Cities.

Health

In 2006 there were 131 community hospitals with 15,800 beds. A total of 633,000 patients were admitted during the year.

Welfare

Medicare enrolment in July 2004 totalled 686,522. In fiscal year 2006 a total of 717,738 people in Minnesota received Medicaid. In Dec. 2008 there were 831,763 Old-Age, Survivors, and Disability Insurance (OASDI) beneficiaries. A total of 45,300 people were receiving payments under Temporary Assistance for Needy Families (TANF) in Dec. 2008.

RELIGION

In 2000 the chief religious bodies were: Roman Catholic with 1,261,000 members; Mainline Protestant, 1,135,000; Evangelical, 510,000; Orthodox, 7,100; other faiths, 67,100. Total membership of all denominations, 2,979,300.

CULTURE

Tourism

In 2003 travel and tourism accounted for $9·2bn. gross receipts and sales. The industry employed about 117,000.

FURTHER READING

Statistical Information: Department of Trade and Economic Development, 500 Metro Square, St Paul 55101. Publishes *Compare Minnesota: an Economic and Statistical Factbook.—Economic Report to the Governor.*
Legislative Manual. Biennial
Minnesota Agriculture Statistics. Annual

Mississippi

KEY HISTORICAL EVENTS

Mississippi was one of the territories claimed by France and ceded to Britain in 1763. The indigenous people were Choctaw and Natchez. French settlers at first traded amicably, but in the course of three wars (1716, 1723 and 1729) the French allied with the Choctaw to drive the Natchez out. The Natchez massacred the settlers of Fort Rosalie, which the French had founded in 1716 and which was later renamed Natchez.

In 1783 the area became part of the USA except for Natchez which was under Spanish control until 1798. The United States then made it the capital of the Territory of Mississippi. The boundaries of the Territory were extended in 1804 and again in 1812. In 1817 it was divided into two territories, with the western part becoming the state of Mississippi. (The eastern part became the state of Alabama in 1819.) The city of Jackson was laid out in 1822 as the new state capital.

A cotton plantation economy developed, based on black slave labour and by 1860 the majority of the population was black. Mississippi joined the Confederacy during the Civil War. After defeat and reconstruction there was a return to rigid segregation and denial of black rights. This situation lasted until the 1960s. There was a black majority until the Second World War, when out-migration began to change the pattern. By 1990 about 35% of the population was black, and manufacture (especially clothing and textiles) had become the largest single employer of labour.

Mississippi suffered widespread damage and loss of life after Hurricane Katrina struck the Gulf Coast on 31 Aug. 2005.

TERRITORY AND POPULATION

Mississippi is bounded in the north by Tennessee, east by Alabama, south by the Gulf of Mexico and Louisiana, and west by the Mississippi River forming the boundary with Louisiana and Arkansas. Land area, 46,907 sq. miles (121,489 sq. km). Census population, 1 April 2000, 2,844,658, an increase of 10·5% since 1990. July 2009 estimate, 2,951,996.

Population of five federal census years was:

	White	*Black*	*Indian*	*Asiatic*	*Total*	*Per sq. mile*
1910	786,111	1,009,487	1,253	263	1,797,114	38·8
1930	998,077	1,009,718	1,458	568	2,009,821	42·4
				All others		
1980	1,615,190	887,206		18,242	2,520,638	53·0
1990	1,633,461	915,057		24,698	2,573,216	54·8
2000	1,746,099	1,033,809		63,372	2,844,658	60·6

Of the total population in 2000, 1,373,554 were male, 2,069,471 were 18 years old or older and 1,457,307 were rural (51·2% of the population). In 2000 Mississippi's Hispanic population was estimated to be 39,569, up from 15,998 in 1990 (an increase of 147%).

The largest city (2000 census) is Jackson, 184,256. Others (2000 census) are: Gulfport, 71,127; Biloxi, 50,644; Hattiesburg, 44,779; Greenville, 41,633; Meridian, 39,968; Tupelo, 34,211; Southaven, 28,977; Vicksburg, 26,407; Pascagoula, 26,200; Columbus, 25,944.

SOCIAL STATISTICS

2007: births, 46,455 (15·9 per 1,000 population); deaths, 27,994 (9·6 per 1,000 population). Infant mortality, 2007, 10·1 per 1,000 live births. 2007: marriages, 15,827; divorces, 13,060.

Mississippi has the highest proportion of people living in poverty of any state, at 20·6% in 2006.

CLIMATE

Jackson, Jan. 47°F (8·3°C), July 82°F (27·8°C). Annual rainfall 49" (1,221 mm). Vicksburg, Jan. 48°F (8·9°C), July 81°F (27·2°C). Annual rainfall 52" (1,311 mm). Mississippi belongs to the Central Plains climate zone (*see* UNITED STATES: Climate).

CONSTITUTION AND GOVERNMENT

The present constitution was adopted in 1890 without ratification by the electorate; there were 123 amendments by 2008.

The Legislature consists of a Senate (52 members) and a House of Representatives (122 members), both elected for four years. Electors are all citizens who have resided in the state, in the county and in the election district for 30 days prior to the election and have been registered according to law.

For the 111th Congress, which convened in Jan. 2009, Mississippi sends four members to the House of Representatives. It is represented in the Senate by Thad Cochran (R. 1977–2015) and Roger Wicker (R. 2007–13).

The capital is Jackson; there are 82 counties.

RECENT ELECTIONS

In the 2008 presidential elections John McCain won Mississippi with 56·2% of the vote (George W. Bush won in 2004).

CURRENT ADMINISTRATION

Governor: Haley Barbour (R.), 2008–12 (salary: $122,160).
Lieut.-Governor: Phil Bryant (R.), 2008–12 ($60,000).
Secretary of State: Delbert Hosemann (R.), 2008–12 ($90,000).

Government Website: http://www.mississippi.gov

ECONOMY

Per capita income (2008) was $30,399, the lowest in the country. Mississippi also had the lowest average household income in 2008, at $37,790.

Budget

For the fiscal year ending 30 June 2008 general revenue was $17,238m. General expenditures were $16,854m. (education, $4,197m.; public welfare, including public health and health care, $1,447m.; highways, $1,202m.; police protection, $151m.) Long-term debt outstanding, on 30 June 2008, $4,524m.

Performance

Gross Domestic Product by state in 2008 was $91,782m. (provisional), ranking Mississippi 35th in the United States.

ENERGY AND NATURAL RESOURCES

Oil and Gas

Petroleum and natural gas account for about 90% (by value) of mineral production. Output of petroleum, 2007, was 20,394,840 bbls and of natural gas 278,525,561,000 cu. ft. There are four oil refineries.

Water

The total area covered by water is approximately 1,523 sq. miles.

Minerals

The value of domestic non-fuel mineral production in 2006 was $270m.

Agriculture

Agriculture is the leading industry of the state because of the semi-tropical climate and a rich productive soil. In 2007 farms numbered 41,700 with an area of 11·0m. acres. Average size of farm was 264 acres. This compares with an average farm size of 176 acres in 1967. Average value of farm land and farm buildings per acre in 2008 was $2,230.

Cash income from all crops and livestock in 2007 was $4,342m. Cash income from crops was $1,588m., and from livestock and products $2,754m. The net farm income in 2006 was $1,230m. The chief product is cotton, cash income (2007) $454m. from 655,000 acres producing 1,318,000 bales of 480 lb. Soybeans, rice, corn, hay, wheat, oats, sorghum, peanuts, pecans, sweet potatoes, peaches, blueberries, other vegetables, nursery and forest products continue to contribute.

On 1 Jan. 2008 there were 990,000 head of cattle and calves on Mississippi farms. In Jan. 2008 milch cows totalled 21,000; beef cows, 519,000; hogs and pigs (Dec. 2008), 375,000. Of cash income from livestock and products, 2007, $194,778,000 was credited to cattle and calves. Cash income from poultry and eggs, 2007, totalled $2,160·2m.; swine, $71·3m.; dairy products, $65·7m.

Forestry

In 2007 income from forestry amounted to $1·1bn.; output of pine logs was 1·32bn. bd ft; of hardwood lumber, 335m. bd ft; pulpwood, 5·78m. cords. There were 19·62m. acres of forest in 2007, with 1·33m. acres of national forest area.

Fisheries

Commercial catch, in 2007, totalled 228m. lb of fish with a value of $39·9m. Mississippi has the largest aquaculture industry of any state; value in 2005 was $250m. (of which catfish sales accounted for $243m.)

INDUSTRY

In 2007 the 2,670 manufacturing establishments had average monthly employment of 169,657 workers, earning $6,328,752,348. The average annual wage was $37,303. Total value added by manufacturing in 2006 was $20,690m.

Labour

In 2007 total non-agricultural employment was 1,152,100. Employees by branch, 2007 (in 1,000): services, 258; government, 244; wholesale and retail trade, 179; manufacturing, 170. The unemployment rate in 2007 was 6·4%.

COMMUNICATIONS

Roads

The state as of 1 July 2007 maintained 14,354 miles of highways, of which 14,347 miles were paved. In fiscal year 2008, 2·6m. passenger vehicles and pick-ups were registered.

Rail

In 2008 the state had 3,065 main-line and short-line miles of railroad.

Civil Aviation

There were 79 public airports in 2008, 72 of them general aviation airports. There were 1,227,433 passenger enplanements statewide in 2008.

SOCIAL INSTITUTIONS

Justice

The death penalty is authorized; there were two executions in 2008 but none in 2009. As of 1 Jan. 2009 the state prison system had 26,234 inmates.

Education

Attendance at school is compulsory as laid down in the Education Reform Act of 1982. The public elementary and secondary schools in 2007–08 had 493,302 pupils and 34,390 classroom teachers.

In 2007–08 teachers' average salary was $40,982. The expenditure per pupil in average daily attendance, 2006–07, was $8,298.

There are 20 universities and senior colleges, of which eight are state-supported. In fall 2008 the University of Mississippi, Oxford had 1,703 faculty and 21,381 students; Mississippi State University, Starkville, 1,053 faculty and 17,824 students; Mississippi University for Women, Columbus, 194 faculty and 2,365 students; University of Southern Mississippi, Hattiesburg, 929 faculty and 14,793 students; Jackson State University, Jackson, 535 faculty and 8,376 students; Delta State University, Cleveland, 258 faculty and 4,064 students; Alcorn State University, Lorman, 226 faculty and 3,100 students; Mississippi Valley State University, Itta Bena, 179 faculty and 2,929 students. State support for the universities (2007–08) was $443,145,614.

Community and junior colleges had (2007–08) 87,134 full-time equivalent students and 4,345 full-time instructors. The state appropriation for junior colleges, 2007–08, was $229,948,182.

Health

In 2007 the state had 106 acute general hospitals (11,594 beds) listed by the State Department of Health; 20 hospitals with facilities for the care of the mentally ill had 805 licensed beds. In addition, 15 rehabilitation hospitals had 380 beds.

Welfare

Medicare enrolment in July 2006 totalled 458,556. The Division of Medicaid paid (fiscal year 2007) $2,915,222,378 for medical services, including $765,434,000 for hospital services, $635,193,695 for skilled nursing home care and $274,757,341 for drugs. There were 187,026 persons eligible for Aged Medicaid benefits as of 30 June 2007 and 70,451 persons eligible for Disabled Medicaid benefits. In 2008, 11,161 families with 17,605 dependent children received $1,528,572 in the Temporary Assistance to Needy Families programme. The average monthly payment was $137·42 per family or $67·11 per recipient.

RELIGION

In 2007: Southern Baptists in Mississippi, 696,719 members; United Methodists, 184,453. In 2008: Roman Catholics in Jackson Diocese, 49,794; in 2007 Roman Catholics in Biloxi Diocese, 58,548.

CULTURE

Tourism

Total receipts in 2008 amounted to $6·0bn.; an estimated 10·1m. overnight tourists visited the state.

FURTHER READING

College of Business and Industry, Mississippi State Univ., Mississippi State 39762. Publishes *Mississippi Statistical Abstract*.

Secretary of State. *Mississippi Official and Statistical Register*. Quadrennial

Mississippi Library Commission: 3881 Eastwood Drive, Jackson, MS 39211.

Missouri

KEY HISTORICAL EVENTS

Territory of several Indian groups, including the Missouri, the area was not settled by European immigrants until the 18th century. The French founded Ste Genevieve in 1735, partly as a lead-mining community. St Louis was founded as a fur-trading base in 1764. The area was nominally under Spanish rule from 1770 until 1800 when it passed back to France. In 1803 the USA bought it as part of the Louisiana Purchase.

St Louis was made the capital of the whole Louisiana Territory in 1805, and of a new Missouri Territory in 1812. In that year American immigration increased markedly. The Territory became a state in 1821. Bitter disputes between slave-owning and anti-slavery factions led to the former obtaining statehood without the prohibition of slavery required of all other new states north of latitude 36° 30'. This was achieved by the Missouri Compromise of 1820. The Compromise was repealed in 1854 and declared unconstitutional in 1857. During the Civil War the state held to the Union side, although St Louis was placed under martial law.

With the development of steamboat traffic on the Missouri and Mississippi rivers, and the expansion of railways, the state became the transport hub of all western movement. Lead and other mining remained important, as did livestock farming. European settlers came from Germany, Britain and Ireland.

TERRITORY AND POPULATION

Missouri is bounded north by Iowa, east by the Mississippi River forming the boundary with Illinois and Kentucky, south by Arkansas, southeast by Tennessee, southwest by Oklahoma, west by Kansas and Nebraska, with the Missouri River forming the boundary in the northwest. Land area, 68,886 sq. miles (178,414 sq. km).

Census population, 1 April 2000, 5,595,211, an increase since 1990 of 9·3%. July 2009 estimate, 5,987,580.

Population of five federal census years was:

	White	Black	Indian	Asiatic	Total	Per sq. mile
1930	3,403,876	223,840	578	1,073	3,629,367	52·4
1960	3,922,967	390,853	1,723	3,146	4,319,813	62·5
			All others			
1980	4,345,521	514,276	56,889		4,916,686	71·3
1990	4,486,228	548,208	82,637		5,117,073	74·3
2000	4,748,083	629,391	217,737		5,595,211	81·2

Of the total population in 2000, 2,875,034 were female, 4,167,519 were 18 years old or older and 3,883,442 were urban. In 2000 Missouri's Hispanic population was 118,592, up from 61,702 in 1990 (an increase of 92·2%).

The principal cities at the 2000 census were:

Kansas City	441,545	St Joseph	73,990
St Louis	348,189	Lee's Summit	70,700
Springfield	151,580	St Charles	60,321
Independence	113,288	St Peters	51,381
Columbia	84,531	Florissant	50,497

Metropolitan areas, 2000: St Louis, 2,603,607; Kansas City, 1,776,062.

SOCIAL STATISTICS

Births, 2007 (provisional), 81,827 (13·9 per 1,000 population); deaths, 2006, 54,681 (9·4). Infant mortality, 2006, 7·4 per 1,000 live births. 2006: marriages, 40,700 (7·0 per 1,000 population); divorces and annulments, 22,900 (3·9).

CLIMATE

Kansas City, Jan. 30°F (–1·1°C), July 79°F (26·1°C). Annual rainfall 38" (947 mm). St Louis, Jan. 32°F (0°C), July 79°F (26·1°C). Annual rainfall 40" (1,004 mm). Missouri belongs to the Central Plains climate zone (*see* UNITED STATES: Climate).

CONSTITUTION AND GOVERNMENT

A new constitution, the fourth, was adopted on 27 Feb. 1945; it has had 108 amendments in the meantime. The General Assembly consists of a Senate of 34 members elected for four years (half for re-election every two years), and a House of Representatives of 163 members elected for two years. The Governor and Lieut.-Governor are elected for four years.

For the 111th Congress, which convened in Jan. 2009, Missouri sends nine members to the House of Representatives. It is represented in the Senate by Christopher Bond (R. 1987–2011) and Claire McCaskill (D. 2007–13).

Jefferson City is the state capital. The state is divided into 114 counties and the city of St Louis.

RECENT ELECTIONS

In the 2008 presidential elections John McCain won Missouri with 49·4% of the vote (George W. Bush won in 2004).

CURRENT ADMINISTRATION

Governor: Jay Nixon (D.), 2009–13 (salary: $133,821).

Lieut.-Governor: Peter Kinder (R.), 2009–13 (salary: $86,484).

Secretary of State: Robin Carnahan (D.), 2009–13 (salary: $107,746).

Government Website: http://www.mo.gov

ECONOMY

Per capita income (2008) was $36,631.

Budget

In 2008 total state revenue was $25,243m. Total expenditure was $26,789m. (education, $8,605m.; public welfare, $6,232m.; highways, $2,034m.; hospitals, $1,322m.; health, $1,163m.) Outstanding debt in 2008, $19,709m.

Performance

In 2008 Gross Domestic Product by state was $237,797m. (provisional), ranking Missouri 22nd in the United States.

ENERGY AND NATURAL RESOURCES

Water

The total area covered by water is approximately 818 sq. miles.

Minerals

The three leading mineral commodities are lead, portland cement and crushed stone. Value of domestic non-fuel mineral production was $2,070m. in 2006.

Agriculture

In 2002 there were 107,000 farms in Missouri producing crops and livestock on 29·8m. acres; the average farm had 279 acres and was valued at $1,508 per acre. Production of principal crops, 2002: corn, 268·2m. bu.; soybeans, 165·05m. bu.; wheat, 34·9m. bu.; sorghum grain, 16·6m. bu.; oats, 1·29m. bu.; rice, 9·96m.

cwt; cotton, 608,280 bales (of 480 lb). Farm income 2006: crops, $2,628m.; livestock and products, $2,994m.; total, $5,621m. The net farm income in 2006 was $1,697m.

Forestry

The state had a forested area of 15,078,000 acres in 2007, of which 1,493,000 acres were national forest.

INDUSTRY

In 2005 the state's 6,935 manufacturing establishments had 298,000 employees, earning $11,640m. Total value added by manufacturing in 2006 was $45,141m.

Labour

Total non-agricultural employment, 2007, 2,796,000. Employees by branch, 2007 (in 1,000): trade, transportation and utilities, 549; government, 440; education and health services, 384; professional and business services, 338; manufacturing, 300. The unemployment rate was 5·0% in 2007.

COMMUNICATIONS

Roads

In 2007 there were 129,122 miles of road (106,412 miles rural) and 4,916,993 registered motor vehicles.

Rail

The state has five Class I railroads; approximate total mileage, 4,159. There are four Class II and Class III railroads (switching, terminal or short-line); total mileage 590 in 2002. There is a light rail line in St Louis.

Civil Aviation

In 2005 there were 127 public airports and 279 private airports. There were 13,426,357 passenger enplanements statewide in 2007.

Shipping

Two major barge lines (1993) operated on about 1,050 miles of navigable waterways including the Missouri and Mississippi Rivers. Boat shipping seasons: Missouri River, April–end Nov.; Mississippi River, all seasons.

SOCIAL INSTITUTIONS

Justice

In Dec. 2008 there were 30,186 federal and state prisoners. The death penalty was reinstated in 1978. Executions were suspended between June 2006 and June 2007. There was one execution in 2009, the first since 2005. The Missouri Law Enforcement Assistance Council was created in 1969 for law reform. With reorganization of state government in 1974 the duties of the Council were delegated to the Department of Public Safety. The Department of Corrections was organized as a separate department of State by an Act of the Legislature in 1981.

Education

School attendance is compulsory for children from seven to 16 years. In 2004–05 there were 2,363 public schools (kindergarten through grade 12) with 905,449 pupils and 65,481 teachers. Total expenditure on public elementary and secondary education in 2003–04 was $7,726m.; teacher salaries averaged $38,006. Spending per pupil in 2002–03 was $7,495.

Institutions for higher education include the University of Missouri, founded in 1839, with campuses at Columbia (with 27,930 enrolled students in fall 2005), Kansas City (14,310), Rolla (5,600 students) and St Louis (15,548). Washington University at St Louis, an independent college founded in 1857, had 13,383 students in fall 2005; St Louis University, an independent Roman Catholic college founded in 1818, had 14,966 students. There were 374,445 students in higher education in fall 2005.

Health

In 2006 there were 119 community hospitals with 18,800 beds. A total of 830,000 patients were admitted during the year.

Welfare

Medicare enrolment in July 2004 totalled 896,152. In fiscal year 2006 a total of 1,136,495 people in Missouri received Medicaid. In Dec. 2008 there were 1,106,923 Old-Age, Survivors, and Disability Insurance (OASDI) beneficiaries. A total of 84,962 people were receiving payments under Temporary Assistance for Needy Families (TANF) in Dec. 2008.

RELIGION

Chief religious bodies (2000) are Catholics, with 856,964 members, Southern Baptists (797,732), United Methodists (226,578), Christian Churches (183,818) and Lutherans (140,315). Total membership, all denominations, 2·8m. in 2000.

CULTURE

Broadcasting

In 2004 there were 117 AM and 254 FM radio stations. 50 TV stations broadcast in Missouri in 2007.

Press

There were 51 daily and 220 weekly newspapers in 2004.

FURTHER READING

Statistical information: Business and Public Administration Research Center, Univ. of Missouri, Columbia 65211. Publishes *Statistical Abstract for Missouri.*
Missouri Area Labor Trends. Monthly
Missouri Farm Facts. Annual
Report of the Public Schools of Missouri. Annual

Montana

KEY HISTORICAL EVENTS

Originally the territory of many Indian hunters including the Sioux, Cheyenne and Chippewa, Montana was not settled by American colonists until the 19th century. The area passed to the USA with the Louisiana Purchase of 1803, but the area west of the Rockies was disputed with Britain until 1846. Trappers and fur-traders were the first immigrants, and the fortified trading post at Fort Benton (1846) became the first permanent settlement. Colonization increased when gold was found in 1862. Montana was created a separate Territory (out of Idaho and Dakota Territories) in 1864. In 1866 large-scale grazing of sheep and cattle provoked violent confrontation with the indigenous people whose hunting lands were invaded. Indian wars led to the defeat of federal forces at Little Bighorn in 1876 and at Big Hole Basin in 1877, but by 1880 the Indians had been moved to reservations. Montana became a state in 1889.

Helena, the capital, was founded as a mining town in the 1860s. In the early 20th century there were many European immigrants who settled as farmers or as copper-miners, especially at Butte.

TERRITORY AND POPULATION

Montana is bounded north by Canada, east by North and South Dakota, south by Wyoming and west by Idaho and the Bitterroot Range of the Rocky Mountains. Land area, 145,552 sq. miles (336,978 sq. km). In 2000 American Indian lands covered 13,358 sq. miles (13,094 sq. miles in reservations and 264 sq. miles in off-reservation trust land). Census population, 1 April 2000, 902,195, an increase of 12·9% since 1990. July 2009 estimate, 974,989.

Population in five census years was:

	White	Black	American Indian	Asiatic	Total	Per sq. mile
1910	360,580	1,834	10,745	2,870	376,053	2·6
1930	519,898	1,256	14,798	1,239	537,606	3·7
1980	740,148	1,786	37,270	2,503	786,690	5·3
1990	741,111	2,381	47,679	4,259	799,065	5·4
2000	817,229	2,692	56,068	5,161	902,195	6·2

Of the total population in 2000, 452,715 were female, 672,133 were 18 years old or older and 487,878 were urban. Median age, 33·8 years. Households, 306,163. In 2000 Montana's Hispanic population was estimated to be 18,081, up from 12,174 in 1990 (an increase of 48·5%).

The largest cities, 2000, are Billings, 89,847; Missoula, 57,053; Great Falls, 56,690. Others: Butte-Silver Bow, 34,606; Bozeman, 27,509; Helena (capital), 25,780; Kalispell, 14,223; Havre, 9,621; Anaconda-Deer Lodge County, 9,417.

SOCIAL STATISTICS

Births, 2007 (provisional), 12,407 (13·0 per 1,000 population); deaths, 2006, 8,472 (9·0). Infant mortality rate, 2006, 5·8 per 1,000 live births. 2006: marriages, 6,800 (7·1 per 1,000 population); divorces and annulments, 3,400 (3·6).

CLIMATE

Helena, Jan. 18°F (–7·8°C), July 69°F (20·6°C). Annual rainfall 13" (325 mm). Montana belongs to the Mountain States climate zone (*see* UNITED STATES: Climate).

CONSTITUTION AND GOVERNMENT

A new constitution came into force on 1 July 1973. The Senate consists of 50 senators, elected for four years, one half at each biennial election. The 100 members of the House of Representatives are elected for two years.

For the 111th Congress, which convened in Jan. 2009, Montana sends one member to the House of Representatives. It is represented in the Senate by Max Baucus (D. 1978–2015) and Jon Tester (D. 2007–13).

The capital is Helena. The state is divided into 56 counties.

RECENT ELECTIONS

In the 2008 presidential elections John McCain won Montana with 49·5% of the vote (George W. Bush won in 2004).

CURRENT ADMINISTRATION

Governor: Brian Schweitzer (D.), 2009–13 (salary: $100,120).
Lieut.-Governor: John Bohlinger (R.), 2009–13 ($79,007).
Secretary of State: Linda McCulloch (D.), 2009–13 ($79,129).

Government Website: http://www.mt.gov

ECONOMY

Per capita income (2008) was $34,644.

Budget

In 2008 total state revenue was $6,403m. Total expenditure was $6,138m. (education, $1,840m.; public welfare, $889m.; highways, $617m.; government administration, $363m.; health, $330m.) Outstanding debt in 2008, $4,924m.

Performance

Gross Domestic Product by state in 2008 was $35,891m. (provisional), ranking Montana 47th in the United States.

ENERGY AND NATURAL RESOURCES

Oil and Gas

Montana has vast technically recoverable oil reserves in the northeast of the state in an area known as the Bakken Formation.

Water

The total area covered by water is approximately 1,490 sq. miles.

Minerals

The total value of non-fuel mineral production for 2006 was $1,070m. Principal minerals include copper, gold, platinum-group metals, molybdenum and silver.

Agriculture

In 2002 there were 27,870 farms and ranches with an area of 59·6m. acres. Large-scale farming predominates; in 2002 the average size per farm was 2,139 acres. The average value per acre in 2002 was $386. In 2005 a total of 9·5m. acres were harvested, including 5·2m. acres of wheat.

The chief crops are wheat, hay, barley, oats, sugar beets, potatoes, corn, dry beans and cherries. Farm income, 2006: from crops, $1,070m.; and from livestock and products, $1,279m. In 2002 there were 2·4m. cattle and calves; value, $1,015m. The net farm income in 2006 was $257m.

Forestry

In 2007 there were 25·01m. acres of forested land with 15·00m. acres in 11 national forests.

INDUSTRY

In 2005 the state's 1,283 manufacturing establishments had 19,000 employees, earning $740m. Total value added by manufacturing in 2006 was $3,476m.

Labour

Total non-agricultural employment, 2007, 443,000. Employees by branch, 2007 (in 1,000): trade, transportation and utilities, 92; government, 85; education and health services, 59; leisure and hospitality, 58; professional and business services, 41. In 2007 the unemployment rate was 3·6%.

COMMUNICATIONS

Roads

In 2007 there were a total of 73,203 miles of road comprising 2,983 miles of urban road and 70,220 miles of rural road. There were 948,528 registered motor vehicles.

Rail

In 2005 there were 3,280 miles of freight railroad, including 2,091 miles of Class I railroads.

Civil Aviation

In 2005 there were 119 public-use airports. There were 1,515,635 passenger enplanements statewide in 2007.

SOCIAL INSTITUTIONS

Justice

In Dec. 2008 there were 3,607 prison inmates. The death penalty is authorized; there was one execution in 2006, the first since 1998.

Education

In 2004–05 the 854 public elementary and secondary schools had 146,705 pupils and 10,224 teachers. Total expenditure on public school education in 2003–04 was $1,223m. and average teacher salary was $37,184. Spending per pupil in 2002–03 was $7,496.

In fall 2005 there were 47,850 students enrolled at 23 higher education institutions. The Montana State University System (created in 1994) consists of the Montana State University at Bozeman (2005 enrolment: 12,143 students), founded 1893; Montana State University-Billings (3,832); Montana State University-Northern at Havre (1,347); and Montana State University-Great Falls (1,875). The University of Montana System comprises the University of Montana at Missoula, founded in 1893 (2005 enrolment: 13,569); Montana Tech at Butte (1,813); and the University of Montana-Western at Dillon (1,159). The private University of Great Falls (founded in 1932) had 778 students in fall 2005.

Health

In 2006 there were 52 community hospitals with 4,000 beds. A total of 106,000 patients were admitted during the year.

Welfare

Medicare enrolment in July 2004 totalled 144,995. In fiscal year 2006 a total of 115,278 people in Montana received Medicaid. In Dec. 2008 there were 180,802 Old-Age, Survivors, and Disability Insurance (OASDI) beneficiaries. A total of 8,766 people were receiving payments under Temporary Assistance for Needy Families (TANF) in Dec. 2008.

RELIGION

The leading religious bodies are Roman Catholic, followed by Lutheran and Methodist.

FURTHER READING

Statistical information. Census and Economic Information Center, Montana Department of Commerce, 1425 9th Ave., Helena 59620.

Lang, W. L. and Myers, R. C., *Montana, Our Land and People.* 1979

Nebraska

KEY HISTORICAL EVENTS

The Nebraska region was first reached by Europeans from Mexico under the Spanish general Coronado in 1541. It was ceded by France to Spain in 1763, returned to France in 1801, and sold by Napoleon to the USA as part of the Louisiana Purchase in 1803. During the 1840s the Platte River valley was the trail for thousands of pioneers' wagons heading for Oregon and California. The need to serve and protect the trail led to the creation of Nebraska as a Territory in 1854. In 1862 the Homestead Act opened the area for settlement, but colonization was slow until the Union Pacific Railroad was completed in 1869. Omaha, developed as the starting point of the Union Pacific, became one of the largest railway towns in the country.

Nebraska became a state in 1867, with approximately its present boundaries except that it later received small areas from the Dakotas. Many early settlers were from Europe, brought in by railway-company schemes, but from the late 1880s eastern Nebraska suffered catastrophic drought. Crop and stock farming recovered but crop growing was only established in the west by means of irrigation.

TERRITORY AND POPULATION

Nebraska is bounded in the north by South Dakota, with the Missouri River forming the boundary in the northeast and the boundary with Iowa and Missouri to the east, south by Kansas, southwest by Colorado and west by Wyoming. Land area, 76,872 sq. miles (199,098 sq. km). Census population, 1 April 2000, 1,711,263, an increase of 8·4% since 1990. July 2009 estimate, 1,796,619.

Population in five census years was:

	White	*Black*	*Indian*	*Asiatic*	*Total*	*Per sq. mile*
1910	1,180,293	7,689	3,502	730	1,192,214	15·5
1960	1,374,764	29,262	5,545	1,195	1,411,330	18·3
			All others			
1980	1,490,381	48,390	31,054		1,569,825	20·5
1990	1,480,558	57,404	40,423		1,578,385	20·5
2000	1,533,261	68,541	109,461		1,711,263	22·3

Of the total population in 2000, 867,912 were female, 1,261,021 were 18 years old or older and 1,193,725 were urban. In 2000 the estimated Hispanic population of Nebraska was 94,425, up from 36,969 in 1990 (a rise of 155·4%). The largest cities in the state are: Omaha, with a census population, 2000, of 390,007; Lincoln, 225,581; Bellevue, 44,382; Grand Island, 42,940; Kearney, 27,431; Fremont, 25,174; Hastings, 24,064; North Platte, 23,878; Norfolk, 23,516.

In 2006 the Bureau of Indian Affairs administered 64,932 acres, of which 21,742 acres were allotted to tribal control.

SOCIAL STATISTICS

Births, 2007 (provisional), 26,967 (15·2 per 1,000 population); deaths, 2006, 14,899 (8·4). Infant mortality rate, 2006, 5·6 per 1,000 live births. 2006: marriages, 12,000 (6·8 per 1,000 population); divorces and annulments, 6,200 (3·5).

CLIMATE

Omaha, Jan. 22°F (–5·6°C), July 77°F (25°C). Annual rainfall 29" (721 mm). Nebraska belongs to the High Plains climate zone (*see* UNITED STATES: Climate).

CONSTITUTION AND GOVERNMENT

The present constitution was adopted in 1875; it had been amended 186 times by 2004. By an amendment of 1934 Nebraska has a single-chambered legislature (elected for four years) of 49 members elected on a non-party ballot and classed as senators—the only state in the USA to have one. It meets annually.

For the 111th Congress, which convened in Jan. 2009, Nebraska sends three members to the House of Representatives. It is represented in the Senate by Ben Nelson (D. 2001–13) and Mike Johanns (R. 2009–15).

The capital is Lincoln. The state has 93 counties.

RECENT ELECTIONS

In the 2008 presidential elections John McCain won Nebraska—although Barack Obama won in one of the congressional districts—with 56·5% of the vote (George W. Bush won in 2004).

CURRENT ADMINISTRATION

Governor: David Heineman (R.), 2007–11 (salary: $105,000).
Lieut.-Governor: Rick Sheehy (R.), 2007–11 ($75,000).
Secretary of State: John Gale (R.), 2007–11 ($85,000).

Government Website: http://www.nebraska.gov

ECONOMY

Per capita income (2008) was $39,150.

Budget

In 2008 total state revenue was $8,388m. Total expenditure was $8,443m. (education, $2,910m.; public welfare, $2,099m.; highways, $631m.; health, $415m.; hospitals, $239m.) Outstanding debt in 2008, $2,719m.

Performance
Gross Domestic Product by state was $83,273m. in 2008 (provisional), ranking Nebraska 36th in the United States.

ENERGY AND NATURAL RESOURCES

Water
The total area covered by water is approximately 481 sq. miles.

Minerals
Output of non-fuel minerals, 2004 (in 1,000 tonnes): sand and gravel for construction, 15,100; stone, 6,900; clays, 133. Other minerals include limestone, potash, pumice, slate and shale. Total value of non-fuel mineral output in 2006 was $129m.

Agriculture
Nebraska is one of the most important agricultural states. In 2002 it contained approximately 52,000 farms, with a total area of 46·4m. acres. The average farm was 892 acres and was valued in 2002 at $776 per acre. In 2002 the total acreage harvested was 17·34m. acres.

In 2006 net farm income was $2,297m. Farm income 2006: from crops, $4,359m.; and from livestock and products, $7,683m. Principal crops were corn, soybeans, hay, barley, sorghum for grain and wheat. Livestock, 2001: cattle, 6·6m.; 2002: pigs, 2·93m.; sheep, 97,400; chickens, 13·7m.; turkeys, 3·5m.

Forestry
The state had a forested area of 1,245,000 acres in 2007, of which 48,000 acres were national forest.

INDUSTRY
In 2005 the state's 1,985 manufacturing establishments had 102,000 employees, earning $3,663m. Total value added by manufacturing in 2006 was $15,641m.

Labour
Total non-agricultural employment, 2007, 963,000. Employees by branch in 2007 (in 1,000): trade, transportation and utilities, 205; government, 164; education and health services, 132; professional and business services, 104; manufacturing, 101. In 2007 the unemployment rate was 3·1%.

COMMUNICATIONS

Roads
In 2007 there were 93,398 miles of road (87,176 miles rural). Registered motor vehicles in 2007 numbered 1,739,072.

Rail
In 2002 there were 3,537 miles of railroad. There were two Class I operators (2,706 miles), three Class II operators (326 miles) and three Class III operators (505 miles).

Civil Aviation
Publicly owned airports in 2005 numbered 86. There were 2,382,088 passenger enplanements statewide in 2007.

SOCIAL INSTITUTIONS

Justice
A 'Civil Rights Act' revised in 1969 provides that all people are entitled to a full and equal enjoyment of public facilities. In Dec. 2008 there were 4,520 prison inmates. The last execution was in 1997.

Education
School attendance is compulsory for children from six to 18 years of age. There were 1,256 public elementary and secondary schools in 2004–05 with 285,761 pupils and 21,077 teachers. In 2003–04 there were 39,454 pupils in private schools. Total enrolment in institutions of higher education, fall 2005, was 121,236. In fall 2004 there were 27,858 students in independent institutions.

Founded	*Institution*	*Students (fall 2005)*
1867	Peru State College	1,959
	University of Nebraska (State)	38,621
1869	Lincoln	19,513
1902	Medical Center	2,735
1905	Kearney	5,542
1908	Omaha	10,831
1965	College of Technical Agriculture, Curtis	262
1872	Doane College, Crete (United Church of Christ)	2,394
1878	Creighton University, Omaha (Roman Catholic)	6,791
1882	Hastings College (Presbyterian)	1,189
1883	Midland Lutheran College, Fremont (Lutheran Church of America)	926
	Nebraska Methodist College of Nursing and Allied Health, Omaha (Private)	565
1884	Dana College, Blair (American Lutheran)	673
1887	Nebraska Wesleyan University (Private)	2,016
1888	Clarkson College, Omaha (Private)	711
1890	York College[1] (Private)	450
1891	Union College, Lincoln (Seventh Day Adventist)	930
1894	Concordia University Nebraska, Seward (Lutheran)	1,330
1910	Wayne State College	3,322
1911	Chadron State College	2,472
1923	College of St Mary (Roman Catholic)	955
1943	Grace University, Omaha (Mennonite)	440
1945	Nebraska Christian College (Church of Christ)	143
1966	Bellevue University (Private)	5,929
1971	Nebraska Community Colleges (Local government)	39,851
	Central Area	6,564
	Metropolitan Area	13,237
	Mid Plains Area	2,607
	Northeast Area	5,101
	Southeast Area	10,059
	Western Area	2,283
1972	Nebraska Indian Community College	107

[1]Two-year college.

Health
In 2006 there were 85 community hospitals with 7,300 beds. A total of 215,000 patients were admitted during the year.

Welfare
Medicare enrolment in July 2004 totalled 258,844. In fiscal year 2006 a total of 247,503 people in Nebraska received Medicaid. In Dec. 2008 there were 297,811 Old-Age, Survivors, and Disability Insurance (OASDI) beneficiaries. A total of 17,909 people were receiving payments under Temporary Assistance for Needy Families (TANF) in Dec. 2008.

RELIGION
The Roman Catholics had 372,791 members in 2000; Evangelical Lutheran Church, 128,570; Lutheran Church-Missouri Synod, 117,419; United Methodists, 117,277; Presbyterian Church (USA), 39,420.

CULTURE

Tourism
In 2004 there were an estimated 19·6m. visits. Travellers and tourists spent over $2·9bn.

FURTHER READING

Statistical information: Department of Economic Development, Box 94666, Lincoln 68509.
Nebraska Blue Book. Biennial

Olson, J. C., *History of Nebraska.* 3rd ed. 1997

State library: Nebraska State Library, PO Box 98931, State Capitol Bldg, Lincoln.

Nevada

KEY HISTORICAL EVENTS

The area was part of Spanish America until 1821 when it became part of the newly independent state of Mexico. Following a war between Mexico and the USA, Nevada was ceded to the USA as part of California in 1848. Settlement began in 1849 and the area was separated from California and joined with Utah Territory in 1850. In 1859 a rich deposit of silver was found in the Comstock Lode. Virginia City was founded as a mining town and immigration increased rapidly. Nevada Territory was formed in 1861. During the Civil War the Federal government, allegedly in order to obtain the wealth of silver for the Union cause, agreed to admit Nevada to the Union as the 36th state. This was in 1864. Areas of Arizona and Utah Territories were added in 1866–67.

The mining boom lasted until 1882, by which time cattle ranching in the valleys, where the climate is less arid, had become equally important. Carson City, the capital, developed in association with the nearby mining industry. The largest cities, Las Vegas and Reno, grew in the 20th century with the building of the Hoover dam, the introduction of legal gambling and of easy divorce.

After 1950 much of the desert area was adopted by the Federal government for weapons testing and other military purposes.

TERRITORY AND POPULATION

Nevada is bounded north by Oregon and Idaho, east by Utah, southeast by Arizona, with the Colorado River forming most of the boundary, south and west by California. Land area, 109,889 sq. miles (284,613 sq. km). In 2003 the federal government owned 91·9% of the land area.

Census population on 1 April 2000, 1,998,257, an increase of 66·3% since 1990. July 2009 estimate, 2,643,085.

Population in five census years was:

	White	*Black*	*American Indian*	*Others*	*Total*	*Per sq. mile*
1910	74,276	513	5,240	1,846	81,875	0·7
1930	84,515	516	4,871	1,156	91,058	0·8
1980	700,360	50,999	13,308	35,841	800,508	7·2
1990	1,012,695	78,771	19,637	90,730	1,201,833	10·9
2000	1,501,886	135,477	26,420	334,474	1,998,257	18·2

Of the total population in 2000, 1,018,051 were male, 1,486,458 were 18 years old or older and 1,828,646 were urban (91·51%, the third highest of the states). In 2000 the Hispanic population was 393,970, up from 124,419 in 1990 (an increase of 216·6%). Nevada's recent overall population rate increase made it the fastest-growing state in the USA every year between 1986 and 2005. In the year 1 July 2005–30 June 2006 it was surpassed by Arizona and although it was the fastest again in 2006–07 it fell to eighth fastest in 2007–08.

The largest cities in 2000 were: Las Vegas, 478,434; Reno, 180,480; Henderson, 175,381; North Las Vegas, 115,448; Sparks, 66,346; Carson City (the capital), 52,457.

SOCIAL STATISTICS

Births, 2007 (provisional), were 41,041 (16·0 per 1,000 population); deaths, 2006, 18,872 (7·6). Infant mortality rate, 2006, 6·4 per 1,000 live births. 2006: marriages, 131,800 (52·9 per 1,000 population); divorces and annulments, 16,700 (6·7).

CLIMATE

Las Vegas, Jan. 57°F (14°C), July 104°F (40°C). Annual rainfall 4·13" (105 mm). Reno, Jan. 45°F (7°C), July 91°F (33°C). Annual rainfall 7·53" (191 mm). Nevada belongs to the Mountain States climate zone (*see* UNITED STATES: Climate).

CONSTITUTION AND GOVERNMENT

The constitution adopted in 1864 is still in force, with 146 amendments as of 2004. The Legislature meets biennially (and in special sessions) and consists of a Senate of 21 members elected for four years, with half their number elected every two years, and an Assembly of 42 members elected for two years. The Governor may be elected for two consecutive four-year terms.

For the 111th Congress, which convened in Jan. 2009, Nevada sends three members to the House of Representatives. It is represented in the Senate by Harry Reid (D. 1987–2011) and John Ensign (R. 2001–13).

The state capital is Carson City. There are 16 counties, 18 incorporated cities and 49 unincorporated communities and one city-county (the Capitol District of Carson City).

RECENT ELECTIONS

In the 2008 presidential elections Barack Obama won Nevada with 55·1% of the vote (George W. Bush won in 2004).

CURRENT ADMINISTRATION

Governor: Jim Gibbons (R.), 2007–11 (salary: $141,000).
Lieut.-Governor: Brian Krolicki (R.), 2007–11 ($60,000).
Secretary of State: Ross Miller (D.), 2007–11 ($97,000).

Government Website: http://www.nv.gov

ECONOMY

Per capita personal income (2008) was $41,182.

Budget

In 2008 total state revenue was $10,439m. Total expenditure was $10,845m. (including: education, $4,069m.; public welfare, $1,580m.; highways, $609m.; government administration, $367m.; correction, $301m.) Outstanding debt in 2008, $4,249m.

Performance

Gross Domestic Product by state in 2008 was $131,233m. (provisional), ranking Nevada 31st in the United States.

ENERGY AND NATURAL RESOURCES

Electricity

In 2006 there were 15 geothermal electric plants in ten locations. Total electricity capacity in 2004 was 8·7m. kW. In 2004 total net electrical production was 37·7bn. kWh.

Water

The total area covered by water is approximately 735 sq. miles.

Minerals

Nevada led the nation in precious metal production in 2004, producing 84% of gold and 24% of silver. Nevada has been first in silver production since 1987 and first in gold since 1981. In 2000 Nevada produced 267,000 kg of gold and 722,000 kg of silver. Nevada was the only state in 2000 to produce magnesite, lithium minerals, brucite and mercury. Nevada also produces other minerals such as aggregates, clays, copper, diatomite, dolomite, geothermal energy, gypsum, lapidary, lime and limestone. The total value of Nevada's non-fuel mineral production in 2006 was $5,140m.

Agriculture

In 2002 there were an estimated 3,000 farms. Farms averaged 2,267 acres; farms and ranches totalled 6·8m. acres. Average value per acre in 2002 was $446.

In 2001, 45·3% of farm income came from cattle and calves, 14·7% from dairy products, 0·6% from sheep and lambs, and 3·3% from other livestock. Hay production was 22% of all farm income, potatoes 2·4%, vegetables 4·6%, wheat 0·4% and other crops 6·7%. In 2006 farm income from crops totalled $166m., and from livestock and products $280m. The net farm income in 2006 was $85m.

In 2002 there were 500,000 cattle and 100,000 sheep.

Forestry

Nevada had, in 2007, 11·09m. acres of forested land with 3·36m. acres of national forest.

INDUSTRY

The main industry is the service industry, especially tourism and legalized gambling. Gaming industry gross revenue for 2001 was $9,220m. In 2006 there were 423 non-restricted licensed casinos and 2,924 licences in force. Nevada receives 41% of its tax revenue from the gaming industry.

In 2005 Nevada's 1,863 manufacturing establishments had 45,000 employees, earning $1,897m. Total value added by manufacturing in 2006 was $7,462m.

Labour

Total non-agricultural employment in 2007 was 1,292,000. Employees by branch in 2007 (in 1,000): leisure and hospitality, 339; trade, transportation and utilities, 232; professional and business services, 158; government, 157; construction, 134. The unemployment rate in 2007 was 4·6%.

COMMUNICATIONS

Roads

In 2007 there were 33,872 miles of road, of which 26,794 miles were rural roads and 7,078 urban. Vehicle registrations in 2007 numbered 1,424,322.

Rail

In 2003 there were 1,449 miles of main-line railroad. Nevada is served by the Southern Pacific, Union Pacific and Burlington Northern BPH Nevada Railroad railroads, and Amtrak passenger service for Las Vegas, Elko, Reno, Caliente, Lovelock, Stateline, Winnemucca and Sparks. Las Vegas has a 4-mile monorail metro system.

Civil Aviation

There were 104 airports and 32 heliports in 2005. During 2007 there were 24,980,175 enplanements statewide. There are international airports at Las Vegas (McCarran) and Reno-Tahoe.

SOCIAL INSTITUTIONS

Justice

Capital punishment was reintroduced in 1978, and executions began in 1979. There was one execution in 2006 but none in 2007, 2008 or 2009. In Dec. 2008 there were 12,743 prison inmates in state or federal correctional institutions.

Education

School attendance is compulsory for children from seven to 18 years of age. Numbers of pupils in public schools, 2001–02: pre-kindergarten, 2,147; kindergarten, 26,877; elementary, 177,342; secondary grades 7–9, 87,538; secondary grades 10–12, 60,470; special education, 40,196. Numbers of teachers in public schools, 2001: elementary, 9,870; secondary, 6,070; special education, 2,646; occupational, 198. Numbers of pupils in private schools, 2001–02: kindergarten, 3,109; elementary, 8,281; secondary grades 7–9, 2,892; secondary grades 10–12, 2,056. Number of private school teachers, 2003–04, 1,327. By 2004–05 there were 572 public schools with 400,083 pupils and 20,950 teachers.

The University of Nevada System comprises the University of Nevada, Las Vegas and Reno, the Nevada State College (at Henderson), the Community College of Southern Nevada (at Las Vegas and Henderson), Great Basin College (at Elko), Truckee Meadows Community College (at Reno) and Western Nevada Community College (at Carson City, Minden and Fallon). In fall 2002 there were 54,832 students (50,527 in 2001).

Health

In 2006 there were 33 community hospitals with 4,800 beds. A total of 245,000 patients were admitted during the year.

Welfare

Medicare enrolment in July 2004 totalled 286,713. In fiscal year 2005 a total of 256,812 people in Nevada received Medicaid. In Dec. 2008 there were 374,289 Old-Age, Survivors, and Disability Insurance (OASDI) beneficiaries. A total of 20,021 people were receiving payments under Temporary Assistance for Needy Families (TANF) in Dec. 2008.

RELIGION

Many faiths are represented in Nevada, including Church of Jesus Christ of Latter Day Saints (Mormons), Protestantism, Roman Catholicism, Judaism and Buddhism.

CULTURE

Tourism

In 2005, 1,821,000 overseas visitors (excluding those from Mexico and Canada) visited Nevada.

FURTHER READING

Statistical information: Budget and Planning Division, Department of Administration, Capitol Complex, Carson City, Nevada 89710. Publishes *Nevada Statistical Abstract* (Biennial).

Bowers, Michael W., *The Stagebrush State: Nevada's History, Government, and Politics.* 1996

Hulse, J. W., *The Nevada Adventure: a History.* 6th ed. 1990.—*The Silver State: Nevada's Heritage Reinterpreted.* 1998

State Government Website: http://www.nv.gov

Nevada State Library: Nevada State Library and Archives, Carson City.

New Hampshire

KEY HISTORICAL EVENTS

The area was part of a grant by the English crown to John Mason and fellow-colonists and was first settled in 1623. In 1629 an area between the Merrimack and Piscatagua rivers was called New Hampshire. More settlements followed, and in 1641 they were taken under the jurisdiction of the governor of Massachusetts. New Hampshire became a separate colony in 1679.

After the War of Independence New Hampshire was one of the 13 original states of the Union, ratifying the US constitution in 1788. The state constitution, which dates from 1776, was almost totally rewritten in 1784 and amended again in 1792.

The settlers were Protestants from Britain and Northern Ireland. They developed manufacturing industries, especially shoe-making, textiles and clothing, to which large numbers of French Canadians were attracted after the Civil War.

Portsmouth, originally a fishing settlement, was the colonial capital and is the only seaport. In 1808 the state capital was moved to Concord (having had no permanent home since 1775); Concord produced the Concord Coach which was widely used on the stagecoach routes of the West until 1900.

TERRITORY AND POPULATION

New Hampshire is bounded in the north by Canada, east by Maine and the Atlantic, south by Massachusetts and west by Vermont. Land area, 8,968 sq. miles (23,227 sq. km). Census population, 1 April 2000, 1,235,786, an increase of 11·4% since 1990. July 2009 estimate, 1,324,575.

Population at five federal censuses was:

	White	*Black*	*Indian*	*Asiatic*	*Total*	*Per sq. mile*
1910	429,906	564	34	68	430,572	47·7
1960	604,334	1,903	135	549	606,921	65·2
			All others			
1980	910,099	3,990	6,521		920,610	101·9
1990	1,087,433	7,198	14,621		1,109,252	123·7
2000	1,186,851	9,035	39,900		1,235,786	137·8

Of the total population in 2000, 628,099 were female, 926,224 were 18 years old or older and 732,335 were urban. In 2000 the Hispanic population was estimated to be 20,489, up from 11,333 in 1990 (an increase of 80·8%). The largest city in the state is Manchester, with a 2000 census population of 107,006. The capital is Concord, with 40,687. Other main cities and towns (with 2000 populations) are: Nashua, 86,605; Derry, 34,021; Rochester, 28,461; Salem, 28,112; Dover, 26,884; Merrimack, 25,119; Londonderry, 23,236; Hudson, 22,928; Keene, 22,563; Portsmouth, 20,784.

SOCIAL STATISTICS

Births, 2007 (provisional), 14,397 (10·9 per 1,000 population); deaths, 2006, 10,060 (7·7). Infant mortality rate, 2006, 6·1 per 1,000 live births. 2006: marriages, 9,300 (7·1 per 1,000 population); divorces and annulments, 5,300 (4·0). Same-sex marriage became legal in Jan. 2010.

CLIMATE

New Hampshire is in the New England climate zone (*see* UNITED STATES: Climate). Manchester, Jan. 22°F (–5·6°C), July 70°F (21·1°C). Annual rainfall 40" (1,003 mm).

CONSTITUTION AND GOVERNMENT

While the present constitution dates from 1784, it was extensively revised in 1792 when the state joined the Union. Since 1775 there have been 16 state conventions with 49 amendments adopted to change the constitution.

The Legislature (called the General Court) consists of a Senate of 24 members, elected for two years, and a House of Representatives, of 400 members, elected for two years. It meets annually. The Governor and five administrative officers called 'Councillors' are also elected for two years.

For the 111th Congress, which convened in Jan. 2009, New Hampshire sends two members to the House of Representatives. It is represented in the Senate by Judd Gregg (R. 1993–2011) and Jeanne Shaheen (D. 2009–15).

The capital is Concord. The state is divided into ten counties.

RECENT ELECTIONS

In the 2008 presidential elections Barack Obama won New Hampshire with 54·4% of the vote (John Kerry won in 2004).

CURRENT ADMINISTRATION

Governor: John Lynch (D.), 2009–11 (salary: $113,537·88).

Senate President: Sylvia Larsen (D.), 2009–11 ($250 per term)

Secretary of State: William M. Gardner (D.), first elected by legislature in 1976 ($100,165·92).

Government Website: http://www.nh.gov

ECONOMY

Per capita income (2008) was $43,623.

Budget

New Hampshire has no general sales tax or state income tax but does have local property taxes. Other government revenues come from rooms and meals tax, business profits tax, motor vehicle licences, fuel taxes, fishing and hunting licences, state-controlled sales of alcoholic beverages, and cigarette and tobacco taxes.

In 2008 total state revenue was $6,292m. Total expenditure was $6,602m. (education, $2,020m.; public welfare, $1,545m.; highways, $440m.; government administration, $238m.; health, $159m.) Outstanding debt in 2008, $7,909m.

Performance

Gross Domestic Product by state in 2008 was $60,005m. (provisional), ranking New Hampshire 41st in the United States.

ENERGY AND NATURAL RESOURCES

Water

The total area covered by water is approximately 382 sq. miles.

Minerals

Minerals are little worked; they consist mainly of sand and gravel, stone, and clay for building and highway construction. Value of domestic non-fuel mineral production in 2006 was $112m.

Agriculture

In 2002 there were 3,100 farms covering around 410,000 acres; average farm was 132 acres. Average value per acre in 2002, $3,131. Farm income 2006: from crops, $98m.; from livestock and products, $64m. The net farm income in 2006 was $43m.

The chief field crops are hay and vegetables; the chief fruit crop is apples. Livestock, 2005: cattle, 40,000; sheep, 7,423 (2002); pigs, 3,600; chickens (including broilers), 204,129 (2002).

Forestry

In 2007 the state had a forested area of 4,850,000 acres, of which 719,000 acres were national forest.

Fisheries

2003 commercial fishing landings amounted to 27·4m. lb worth $15·1m.

INDUSTRY

Principal manufactures: electrical and electronic goods, machinery and metal products. In 2005 the state's 2,155 manufacturing establishments had 76,000 employees, earning $3,550m. Total value added by manufacturing in 2006 was $9,203m.

Labour

Total non-agricultural employment, 2007, 649,000. Employees by branch, 2007 (in 1,000): trade, transportation and utilities, 142; education and health services, 103; government, 94; manufacturing, 78; professional and business services, 66. In 2007 the unemployment rate was 3·6%.

COMMUNICATIONS

Roads

In 2007 there were 15,839 miles of road (11,017 miles rural). There were 1,184,842 registered motor vehicles.

Rail

In 2005 there were 421 miles of freight railroad.

Civil Aviation

In 2005 there were 25 airports and two heliports. There were 1,988,312 passenger enplanements statewide in 2007.

SOCIAL INSTITUTIONS

Justice

There were 2,904 prison inmates in Dec. 2008. The death penalty was abolished in May 2000—the last execution had been in 1939.

Education

School attendance is compulsory for children from six to 18 years of age (since 1 July 2009—previously school attendance had only been compulsory to 16). Employed illiterate minors between 16 and 21 years of age must attend evening or special classes, if provided by the district.

In 2002 the public elementary and secondary schools had 207,000 pupils and 15,000 teachers. Public school salaries, 2003, averaged $41,900. An average of $8,683 was spent on education per pupil.

Of the 4-year colleges, the University of New Hampshire (founded in 1866) had 13,349 students in 2005; Dartmouth College (1769), 5,529; Keene State College (1909), 4,463; Plymouth State University (1871), 4,453; Southern New Hampshire University (1932, was New Hampshire College), 3,744. Total enrolment, 2005–06, in the 26 institutions of higher education was 69,893.

Health

In 2006 there were 28 community hospitals with 2,800 beds. A total of 118,000 patients were admitted during the year.

Welfare

Medicare enrolment in July 2004 totalled 186,651. In fiscal year 2006 a total of 126,458 people in New Hampshire received Medicaid. In Dec. 2008 there were 237,498 Old-Age, Survivors, and Disability Insurance (OASDI) beneficiaries. A total of 11,818 people were receiving payments under Temporary Assistance for Needy Families (TANF) in Dec. 2008.

RELIGION

The Roman Catholic Church is the largest single body. The largest Protestant churches are Congregational, Episcopal, Methodist and United Baptist Convention of N.H.

CULTURE

Press

In 2003 there were 11 daily and eight Sunday newspapers in circulation.

FURTHER READING

Delorme, D. (ed.) *New Hampshire Atlas and Gazetteer.* 1983

New Jersey

KEY HISTORICAL EVENTS

Originally the territory of Delaware Indians, the area was settled by immigrant colonists in the early 17th century, when Dutch and Swedish traders established fortified posts on the Hudson and Delaware Rivers. The Dutch gave way to the English in 1664. In 1676 the English divided the area; the eastern portion was assigned to Sir George Carteret and the western granted to Quaker settlers. This lasted until 1702 when New Jersey was united as a colony of the Crown and placed under the jurisdiction of the governor of New York. It became a separate colony in 1738.

During the War of Independence crucial battles were fought at Trenton, Princeton and Monmouth. New Jersey became the 3rd state of the Union in 1787. Trenton, the state capital since 1790, began as a Quaker settlement and became an iron-working town. Industrial development grew rapidly, there and elsewhere in the state, after the opening of canals and railways in the 1830s. Princeton, also a Quaker settlement, became an important post on the New York road; the college of New Jersey (Princeton University) was transferred there from Newark in 1756.

The need for supplies in the Civil War stimulated industry and New Jersey became a manufacturing state. The growth of New York and Philadelphia, however, encouraged commuting to employment in both centres. By 1980 about 60% of the state's population lived within 30 miles of New York.

TERRITORY AND POPULATION

New Jersey is bounded north by New York, east by the Atlantic with Long Island and New York City to the northeast, south by Delaware Bay and west by Pennsylvania. Land area, 7,417 sq. miles (19,209 sq. km). Census population, 1 April 2000, 8,414,350, an increase of 8·9% since 1990. July 2009 estimate, 8,707,739.

Population at five federal censuses was:

	White	*Black*	*Asiatic*	*Others*	*Total*	*Per sq. mile*
1910	2,445,894	89,760	1,345	168	2,537,167	337·7
1930	3,829,663	208,828	2,630	213	4,041,334	537·3
1980	6,127,467	925,066	103,848	208,442	7,364,823	986·2
1990	6,130,465	1,036,825	272,521	290,377	7,730,188	1,042·0
2000	6,104,705	1,141,821	483,605	684,219	8,414,350	1,134·4

Of the total population in 2000, 4,331,537 were female, 6,326,792 were 18 years old or older and 7,939,087 were urban (94·35%, marginally less than California, the highest). In 2000 the Hispanic population was 1,117,191, up from 739,861 in 1990 (an increase of 51·0%).

Census populations of the largest cities and towns in 2000 were:

Newark	273,546	Union City	67,088
Jersey City	240,055	Middletown	66,327
Paterson	149,222	Gloucester	64,350
Elizabeth	120,568	Bayonne	61,842
Edison	97,687	Irvington	60,695
Woodbridge	97,203	Old Bridge	60,456
Dover	89,706	Lakewood	60,352
Hamilton	87,109	North Bergen	58,092
Trenton (capital)	85,403	Vineland	56,271
Camden	79,904	Union Township	54,405
Clifton	78,672	Wayne	54,069
Brick	76,119	Franklin	50,903
Cherry Hill	69,965	Parsippany-Troy Hills	50,649
East Orange	69,824	Piscataway	50,482
Passaic	67,861		

Largest metropolitan areas (2000) are: Newark, 2,032,989; Bergen–Passaic, 1,373,167; Middlesex–Somerset–Hunterdon, 1,169,641; Monmouth–Ocean, 1,126,217; Jersey City, 608,975.

SOCIAL STATISTICS

Births, 2007 (provisional), 115,294 (13·3 per 1,000 population); deaths, 2006, 70,356 (8·1). Infant mortality, 2006, 5·5 per 1,000 live births. 2006: marriages, 42,400 (4·9 per 1,000 population); divorces and annulments, 25,800 (3·0).

CLIMATE

Jersey City, Jan. 31°F (–0·6°C), July 75°F (23·9°C). Annual rainfall 41" (1,025 mm). Trenton, Jan. 32°F (0°C), July 76°F (24·4°C). Annual rainfall 40" (1,003 mm). New Jersey belongs to the Atlantic Coast climate zone (*see* UNITED STATES: Climate).

CONSTITUTION AND GOVERNMENT

The present constitution, ratified by the registered voters on 4 Nov. 1947, has been amended 45 times. There is a 40-member Senate and an 80-member General Assembly. Assembly members serve two years, senators four years, except those elected at the election following each census, who serve for two years. Sessions are held throughout the year.

For the 111th Congress, which convened in Jan. 2009, New Jersey sends 13 members to the House of Representatives. It is represented in the Senate by Frank Lautenberg (D. 1982–2001, 2003–15) and Robert Menendez (D. 2007–13).

The capital is Trenton. The state is divided into 21 counties, which are subdivided into 566 municipalities—cities, towns, boroughs, villages and townships.

RECENT ELECTIONS

In the 2008 presidential elections Barack Obama won New Jersey with 57·3% of the vote (John Kerry won in 2004).

CURRENT ADMINISTRATION

Governor: Chris Christie (R.), 2010–14 (salary: $175,000).

Lieut.-Governor and Secretary of State: Kim Guadagno (R.), 2010–14 ($141,000).

Government Website: http://www.nj.gov

ECONOMY

Per capita income (2008) was $51,358, the third highest in the country.

Budget

In 2008 total state revenue was $55,046m. Total expenditure was $58,539m. (including: education, $15,432m.; public welfare, $12,421m.; highways, $2,736m.; hospitals, $2,062m.; government administration, $1,861m.) Outstanding debt in 2008, $52,785m.

Performance

Gross Domestic Product by state in 2008 was $474,936m. (provisional), ranking New Jersey 7th in the United States.

ENERGY AND NATURAL RESOURCES

Water

The total area covered by water is approximately 1,304 sq. miles.

Minerals

In 2002 the chief minerals were stone (22·6m. tons, value $127m.) and sand and gravel (17·6m. tons, value $96m.); others are clays, peat and gemstones. New Jersey is a leading producer of greensand marl, magnesium compounds and peat. Total value of domestic non-fuel mineral products for 2006 was $547m.

Agriculture

Livestock raising, market-gardening, fruit-growing, horticulture and forestry are pursued. In 2003 there were 9,900 farms covering a total of 820,000 acres with an average farm size of 83 acres. Average value per acre in 2002 was $9,245—making it the second most valuable land per acre in the USA, after Connecticut.

Cash receipts from farm marketings, 2006: crops, $763m.; livestock and products, $161m. The net farm income in 2006 was $305m.

Leading crops (2003) are blueberries (value, $45·7m.), tomatoes ($28·0m.), peppers ($25·6m.), peaches ($24·2m.), soybeans ($16·1m.), cranberries ($15·1m.), sweet corn ($12·1m.), corn for grain ($7·1m.). Livestock, 2003: 12,000 milch cows, 46,000 all cattle, 15,300 sheep and lambs and 12,000 swine.

Forestry

Total forested area was 2,132,000 acres in 2007.

Fisheries

2002 commercial fishing landings amounted to 162·2m. lb worth $112·7m.

INDUSTRY

In 2005 the state's 9,575 manufacturing establishments had 305,000 employees, earning $15,353m. Total value added by manufacturing in 2006 was $51,693m.

Labour

Total non-agricultural employment, 2007, 4,074,000. Employees by branch, 2007 (in 1,000): trade, transportation and utilities, 876; government, 648; professional and business services 608; education and health services, 580; leisure and hospitality, 340. The unemployment rate in 2007 was 4·2%.

COMMUNICATIONS

Roads

In 2007 there were 38,752 miles of road, of which 31,455 miles were urban. There were 6,247,130 registered vehicles in 2007.

Rail

NJ Transit, the USA's third largest provider of bus, rail and light rail transit, has a fleet of 2,027 buses, 711 trains and 45 light rail vehicles, which serve approximately 725,550 passengers daily on 11 rail lines (848·3 track miles) and 236 bus routes. The state is also served by 13 shortline freight railroads, three Class I rail carriers (Norfolk Southern, CSX and CP Rail) and two statewide terminal railroads (Conrail Shared Assets Carrier and NYS & W Ry) which deliver freight on behalf of Class I rail carriers.

There is a metro link to New York (22 km), a light rail line (7 km) and extensive commuter railroads around Newark.

Civil Aviation

There is an international airport at Newark. In June 2004 there were 119 airports and 251 heliports. In total there are an estimated 72,000 jobs in New Jersey that are linked to the general aviation airport system. The annual payroll associated with these jobs is estimated at $2·4bn. The annual value of goods and services purchased by airport tenants, visitors and general aviation-dependent businesses exceeds $4·6bn. There were 18,759,303 passenger enplanements statewide in 2007.

Shipping

In 2004 the maritime industry contributed more than $50bn. to the state economy. The two largest ports are the Port of

Newark-Elizabeth and the Port of Camden. The Port of Newark-Elizabeth, the premier port on the Eastern seaboard, employed 229,000 people in 2003.

SOCIAL INSTITUTIONS

Justice

In Dec. 2008 there were 25,953 prison inmates. The death penalty was abolished on 17 Dec. 2007, after its initial suspension in Jan. 2006. The death penalty was last used in 1963.

Education

Elementary instruction is compulsory for all from six to 16 years of age and free to all from five to 20 years of age. 128 school districts with high concentrations of disadvantaged children must offer free pre-school education to three- and four-year olds. In 2002–03 there were 2,454 public elementary and secondary schools with 1,367,438 pupils and 107,004 teachers; total expenditure on public schools was $17,303m. Teachers' salaries averaged $54,158 in 2003.

There are 57 universities and colleges in New Jersey. In fall 2002 public institutions had 289,275 students, including 138,924 in community colleges. Enrolment in fall 2002: Rutgers, the State University (founded as Queen's College in 1766), had 51,480 students at campuses in Camden, Newark and New Brunswick; The College of New Jersey (1855; formerly Trenton State College), 6,948; Kean University, at Union City (1855), 12,779; Montclair State University (1908), 134,673; Rowan University, at Glassboro (1923), 9,685; William Paterson University, at Wayne (1855), 10,924.

Independent institutions had 72,482 students. Princeton University (founded in 1746) had 6,646 students; Fairleigh Dickinson University, at Teaneck (1941), 10,368; Seton Hall University, at South Orange (1856), 9,596.

Health

In 2006 there were 79 community hospitals with 22,000 beds. A total of 1,111,000 patients were admitted during the year.

Welfare

Medicare enrolment in July 2004 totalled 1,226,016. In fiscal year 2006 a total of 1,004,370 people in New Jersey received Medicaid. In Dec. 2008 there were 1,407,621 Old-Age, Survivors, and Disability Insurance (OASDI) beneficiaries. A total of 79,134 people were receiving payments under Temporary Assistance for Needy Families (TANF) in Dec. 2008.

RELIGION

In 2000 the Roman Catholic population of New Jersey was 3·4m., and there were 468,000 Jews. Among Protestant sects were United Methodists, 140,133; Presbyterian Church (USA) members, 119,735; Episcopalians, 91,964; American Baptists, 88,521; Lutherans, 79,264.

CULTURE

Tourism

In 2005, 997,000 overseas visitors (excluding those from Mexico and Canada) visited New Jersey.

FURTHER READING

Statistical information: New Jersey State Data Center, Department of Labor, CN 388, Trenton 08625. Publishes *New Jersey Statistical Factbook.*

Legislative District Data Book. Annual

Manual of the Legislature of New Jersey. Annual

Cunningham, J. T., *New Jersey: America's Main Road.* Rev. ed. 1976

State library: 185 W. State Street, Trenton, CN 520, NJ 08625.

New Mexico

KEY HISTORICAL EVENTS

The first European settlement was established in 1598. Until 1771 New Mexico was the Spanish 'Kingdom of New Mexico'. In 1771 it was annexed to the northern province of New Spain. When New Spain won its independence in 1821, it took the name of Republic of Mexico and established New Mexico as its northernmost department. Ceded to the USA in 1848 after war between the USA and Mexico, the area was recognized as a Territory in 1850, by which time its population was Spanish and Indian. There were frequent conflicts between new settlers and raiding parties of Navajo and Apaches. The Indian war lasted from 1861–66, and from 1864–68 about 8,000 Navajo were imprisoned at Bosque Redondo.

The boundaries were altered several times when land was taken into Texas, Utah, Colorado and lastly (1863) Arizona. New Mexico became a state in 1912.

Settlement proceeded by means of irrigated crop-growing and Mexican-style ranching. During the Second World War the desert areas were used as testing zones for atomic weapons. Mineral related industries developed after the discovery of uranium and petroleum.

TERRITORY AND POPULATION

New Mexico is bounded north by Colorado, northeast by Oklahoma, east by Texas, south by Texas and Mexico and west by Arizona. Land area, 121,356 sq. miles (316,901 sq. km). In 2003 the federal government owned 26,518,360 acres, or 34·1% of the land area.

Census population, 1 April 2000, 1,819,046, an increase of 20·1% since 1990. Of the total population in 2000, 924,729 were female, 1,310,472 were 18 years old or older and 1,363,501 were urban. July 2009 estimate, 2,009,671.

The population in five census years was:

	White	*Black*	*American Indian*	*Asian and Pacific Island*	*Other*	*Total*	*Per sq. mile*
1910	304,594	1,628	20,573	506	—	327,301	2·7
1940	492,312	4,672	34,510	324	—	531,818	4·4
1980	977,587	24,020	106,119	6,825	188,343	1,302,894	10·7
1990	1,146,028	30,210	134,355	14,124	190,352	1,515,069	12·5
2000	1,214,253	34,343	173,483	20,758	376,209	1,819,046	15·0

Before 1930 New Mexico was largely a Spanish-speaking state, but after 1945 an influx of population from other states considerably reduced the percentage of persons of Spanish origin or descent. However, in recent years the percentage of the Hispanic population has begun to rise again. In 2000 the Hispanic population was 765,386, up from 579,224 in 1990 (an increase of 32·1%). At 42·1%, New Mexico has the largest percentage of persons of Hispanic origin of any state in the USA.

The largest cities are Albuquerque, with 2000 census population of 448,607; Las Cruces, 74,267; Santa Fe, 62,203; Rio Rancho, 51,765; Roswell, 45,293.

SOCIAL STATISTICS

Births, 2007 (provisional), 30,392 (15·4 per 1,000 population); deaths, 2006, 15,296 (7·8). Infant mortality, 2006, 5·8 per 1,000 live births. 2006: marriages, 13,400 (6·9 per 1,000 population); divorces and annulments, 8,400 (4·3).

CLIMATE

Santa Fe, Jan. 26·4°F (–3·1°C), July 68·4°F (20°C). Annual rainfall 15·2" (386 mm). New Mexico belongs to the Mountain States climate zone (*see* UNITED STATES: Climate).

CONSTITUTION AND GOVERNMENT

The constitution of 1912 is still in force with 152 amendments. The state Legislature, which meets annually, consists of 42 members of the Senate, elected for four years, and 70 members of the House of Representatives, elected for two years.

For the 111th Congress, which convened in Jan. 2009, New Mexico sends three members to the House of Representatives. It is represented in the Senate by Jeff Bingaman (D. 1983–2013) and Tom Udall (D. 2009–15).

The state capital is Santa Fe. The state is divided into 33 counties.

RECENT ELECTIONS

In the 2008 presidential elections Barack Obama won New Mexico with 56·9% of the vote (George W. Bush won in 2004).

CURRENT ADMINISTRATION

Governor: Bill Richardson (D.), 2007–11 (salary: $110,000).

Lieut.-Governor: Diane D. Denish (D.), 2007–11 ($85,000).

Secretary of State: Mary Herrera (D.), 2007–11 ($85,000).

Government Website: http://www.newmexico.gov

ECONOMY

Per capita income (2008) was $33,430.

Budget

In 2008 total state revenue was $12,893m. Total expenditure was $15,793m. (including: education, $5,025m.; public welfare, $3,559m.; highways, $896m.; hospitals, $750m.; government administration, $528m.) Outstanding debt in 2008, $7,764m.

Performance

Gross Domestic Product by state in 2008 was $79,901m. (provisional), ranking New Mexico 37th in the United States.

ENERGY AND NATURAL RESOURCES

Oil and Gas

2006 production: petroleum, 60m. bbls; natural gas, 1,609bn. cu. ft. New Mexico ranks third in the USA behind Texas and Oklahoma for natural gas production and also has natural gas reserves third only to Texas and Wyoming.

Water

The total area covered by water is approximately 234 sq. miles.

Minerals

New Mexico is one of the largest energy producing states in the USA. Production in 2001: potash, 1,086,410 short tons; copper, 154,580 short tons; coal, 30,525,401 short tons. New Mexico is the country's leading potash producer, accounting for approximately 70% of all potash mined in the USA, and ranked third for copper production in 2001. The value of coal output in 2001 was $584·9m.; total non-fuel mineral output had a value of $1,470m. in 2006.

Agriculture

New Mexico produces grains, vegetables, hay, livestock, milk, cotton and pecans. In 2002 there were 15,000 farms covering 44·0m. acres; average farm size 2,933 acres. In 2002 average value of farmland and buildings per acre was $234.

2006 cash receipts from crops, $602m.; and from livestock products, $1,861m. The net farm income in 2006 was $423m. Principal crops are hay (1·6m. tons from 0·38m. acres), cotton (65m. lb from 0·70m. acres) and chilli (162m. lb from 0·18m. acres). Farm animals in 2001 included 290,000 milch cows, 1·6m. all cattle, 230,000 sheep and 3,000 swine.

Forestry

The state had a forested area of 16,682,000 acres in 2007, of which 8,092,000 acres were national forest.

INDUSTRY

In 2005 the state's 1,531 manufacturing establishments had 35,000 employees, earning $1,392m. Total value added by manufacturing in 2006 was $9,070m.

Labour

Total non-agricultural employment, 2007, 843,000. Employees by branch, 2007 (in 1,000): government, 195; trade, transportation and utilities, 144; education and health services, 111; professional and business services, 109; leisure and hospitality, 88. The unemployment rate in 2007 was 3·7%.

COMMUNICATIONS

Roads

In 2007 there were 68,339 miles of road (60,351 miles rural). There were 1,599,333 registered motor vehicles.

Rail

In 2005 there were 1,993 miles of freight railroad, including 1,589 miles of Class I railroads.

Civil Aviation

There were 61 public-use airports in 2005. There were 3,299,608 passenger enplanements statewide in 2007.

SOCIAL INSTITUTIONS

Justice

In Dec. 2008 there were 6,402 prison inmates in state or federal correctional institutions. The death penalty was abolished with effect from 1 July 2009 for crimes committed after that date, although two prisoners remained on death row. It was most recently used in 2001 (one execution) for the first time since 1960.

Since 1949 the denial of employment by reason of race, colour, religion, national origin or ancestry has been forbidden. A law of 1955 prohibits discrimination in public places because of race or colour. An 'equal rights' amendment was added to the constitution in 1972.

Education

Elementary education is free, and compulsory between five and 18 years. In 2004–05 the 89 school districts had an enrolment of 326,102 students in 842 public elementary and secondary schools and 21,730 teachers; average teacher salary in 2003–04 was $38,067. Total expenditure on public school education in 2003–04 was $2,912m. Spending per pupil in 2002–03 was $7,125.

In fall 2002 there were 51,648 students attending public universities and 62,002 students attending community colleges. The state-supported four-year institutes of higher education are (fall 2002 enrolment):

	Students
University of New Mexico, Albuquerque	24,645
New Mexico State University, Las Cruces	15,621
Eastern New Mexico University, Portales	3,756
New Mexico Highlands University, Las Vegas	3,024
Western New Mexico University, Silver City	2,551
New Mexico Institute of Mining and Technology, Socorro	1,747

Health

In 2006 there were 36 community hospitals with 3,500 beds. A total of 160,000 patients were admitted during the year.

Welfare

Medicare enrolment in July 2004 totalled 256,744. In fiscal year 2006 a total of 515,658 people in New Mexico received Medicaid. In Dec. 2008 there were 335,471 Old-Age, Survivors, and Disability Insurance (OASDI) beneficiaries. A total of 39,813 people were receiving payments under Temporary Assistance for Needy Families (TANF) in Dec. 2008.

RELIGION

Chief religious bodies (2000) were Catholics, with 670,511 members; Southern Baptists, 132,675; Latter-day Saints (Mormons), 42,261; United Methodists, 41,597; Assemblies of God, 22,070.

CULTURE

Tourism

In 2004, 81,000 overseas visitors (excluding those from Mexico and Canada) visited New Mexico.

FURTHER READING

Bureau of Business and Economic Research, Univ. of New Mexico—*Census in New Mexico* (Continuing series. Vols. 1-5, 1992-).—*Economic Census: New Mexico* (Continuing series. Vols. 1-3).—*New Mexico Business.* Monthly; annual review in Jan.-Feb. issue.

Etulain, R., *Contemporary New Mexico, 1940–1990.* 1994

New York State

KEY HISTORICAL EVENTS

The first European immigrants came in the 17th century, when there were two powerful Indian groups in rivalry: the Iroquois confederacy (Mohawk, Oneida, Onondaga, Cayuga and Seneca) and the Algonquian-speaking Mohegan and Munsee. The Dutch made settlements at Fort Orange (now Albany) in 1624 and at New Amsterdam in 1625, trading with the Indians for furs. In the 1660s there was conflict between the Dutch and the British in the Caribbean; as part of the concluding treaty the British, in 1664, received Dutch possessions in the Americas, including New Amsterdam, which they renamed New York.

In 1763 the Treaty of Paris ended war between the British and the French in North America (in which the Iroquois had allied themselves with the British). Settlers of British descent in New England then felt confident enough to expand westward. The climate of northern New York being severe, most settled in the Hudson river valley. After the War of Independence New York became the 11th state of the Union (1778), having first declared itself independent of Britain in 1777.

The economy depended on manufacturing, shipping and other means of distribution and trade. During the 19th century New York became the most important city in the USA. Its industries, especially clothing, attracted thousands of European immigrants. Industrial development spread along the Hudson-Mohawk valley, which was made the route of the Erie Canal (1825) linking New York with Buffalo on Lake Erie and thus with the developing farmlands of the middle west.

On 11 Sept. 2001 New York City was attacked by hijackers when two commercial airliners were flown into the World Trade Center. The building was destroyed and 2,749 people died.

TERRITORY AND POPULATION

New York is bounded west and north by Canada with Lake Erie, Lake Ontario and the St Lawrence River forming the boundary; east by Vermont, Massachusetts and Connecticut, southeast by the Atlantic, south by New Jersey and Pennsylvania. Land area, 47,214 sq. miles (122,284 sq. km). Census population, 1 April 2000, 18,976,457, an increase of 5·5% since 1990. July 2009 estimate, 19,541,453.

Population in five census years was:

	White	*Black*	*Indian*	*Asiatic*	*Total*	*Per sq. mile*
1910	8,966,845	134,191	6,046	6,532	9,113,614	191·2
1930	12,143,191	412,814	6,973	15,088	12,588,066	262·6
			All others			
1980	13,961,106	2,401,842	1,194,340		17,557,288	367·0
1990	13,385,255	2,859,055	1,746,145		17,990,455	381·0
2000	12,893,689	3,014,385	3,068,383		18,976,457	401·9

Of the total population in 2000, 9,829,709 were female, 14,286,350 were 18 years old or older and 16,602,582 were urban. In 2000 the Hispanic population was 2,867,583, up from 2,214,026 in 1990 (an increase of 29·5%). California and Texas are the only states with a higher Hispanic population.

The population of New York City, by boroughs, census of 1 April 2000 was: Manhattan, 1,537,195; Bronx, 1,332,650; Brooklyn, 2,465,326; Queens, 2,229,379; Staten Island, 443,728; total, 8,008,278. The New York–Northern New Jersey–Long Island metropolitan area had, in 2000, a population of 21,199,865.

Population of other large cities and incorporated places at the 2000 census was:

Buffalo	292,648	Valley Stream	36,368
Rochester	219,773	Long Beach	35,462
Yonkers	196,086	Rome	34,950
Syracuse	147,306	North Tonawanda	33,262
Albany (capital)	95,658	Jamestown	31,730
New Rochelle	72,182	Elmira	30,940
Mount Vernon	68,381	Poughkeepsie	29,871
Schenectady	61,821	Ithaca	29,287
Utica	60,651	Auburn	28,574
Hempstead	56,554	Newburgh	28,259
Niagara Falls	55,593	Lindenhurst	27,819
White Plains	53,077	Watertown	26,705
Troy	49,170	Glen Cove	26,622
Binghampton	47,380	Saratoga Springs	26,186
Freeport	43,783		

Other large urbanized areas, census 2000; Buffalo–Niagara Falls, 1,170,111; Rochester, 1,098,201; Albany–Schenectady–Troy, 875,583.

SOCIAL STATISTICS

Births, 2007 (provisional), 258,249 (13·4 per 1,000 population); deaths, 2006, 148,806 (7·7). Infant mortality rate, 2006, 5·6 per 1,000 live births. 2006: marriages, 127,400 (6·6 per 1,000 population); divorces and annulments, 55,600 (2·9).

CLIMATE

Albany, Jan. 24°F (–4·4°C), July 73°F (22·8°C). Annual rainfall 34" (855 mm). Buffalo, Jan. 24°F (–4·4°C), July 70°F (21·1°C). Annual rainfall 36" (905 mm). New York, Jan. 30°F (–1·1°C), July 74°F (23·3°C). Annual rainfall 43" (1,087 mm). New York belongs to the Atlantic Coast climate zone (*see* UNITED STATES: Climate).

CONSTITUTION AND GOVERNMENT

New York State has had five constitutions, adopted in 1777, 1821, 1846, 1894 and 1938. The constitution produced by the 1938 convention (which was substantially a modification of the 1894 one), forms the fundamental law of the state (as modified by subsequent amendments). A proposed new constitution in 1967 was rejected by the electorate. In 1997 voters rejected a proposal to hold a new constitutional convention.

The Legislature comprises the Senate, with 62 members, and the Assembly, with 150. All members are elected in even-numbered years for two-year terms. The Legislature meets every year, typically for several days a week from Jan.–June and, if recalled by leaders of the Legislature, at other times during the year. The Governor can also call the Legislature into extraordinary session. The state capital is Albany. For local government the state is divided into 62 counties, five of which constitute the city of New York.

Each of the state's 62 cities is incorporated by charter, under special legislation. The government of New York City is vested in the mayor (Michael Bloomberg), elected for four years, and a city council, whose president and members are elected for four years. The council has a President and 51 members, each elected from a district wholly within the city. The mayor appoints all the heads of departments, except the comptroller (the chief financial officer), who is elected. Each of the five city boroughs (Manhattan, Bronx, Brooklyn, Queens and Staten Island) has a president, elected for four years. Each borough is also a county, although Manhattan borough, as a county, is called New York, Brooklyn is called Kings, and Staten Island is called Richmond.

For the 111th Congress, which convened in Jan. 2009, New York State sends 29 members to the House of Representatives. It is represented in the Senate by Charles Schumer (D. 1999–2011) and Kirsten Gillibrand (D.), who succeeded Hillary Clinton (D. 2001–09) following the latter's appointment as Secretary of State. Gillibrand is scheduled to contest a special election in Nov. 2010 to take on the remainder of Clinton's term, which was set to end in 2013.

RECENT ELECTIONS

In the 2008 presidential elections Barack Obama won New York State with 62·8% of the vote (John Kerry won in 2004).

CURRENT ADMINISTRATION

Governor: David A. Paterson (D.), 2008–11 (salary: $179,000).

Lieut.-Governor: Richard Ravitch (D.), 2009–11 ($151,500).

Secretary of State: Lorraine Cortes-Vazquez, appointed Dec. 2006 ($120,800).

Government Website: http://www.ny.gov

ECONOMY

Per capita income (2008) was $48,753.

Budget

In 2008 total state revenue was $147,340m. Total expenditure was $157,398m. (public welfare, $44,763m.; education, $39,764m.; health, $7,088m.; government administration, $5,876m.; hospitals, $4,896m.) Outstanding debt in 2008 was $114,240m.

Performance

Gross Domestic Product by state was $1,144,481m. in 2008 (provisional), ranking New York third after California and Texas.

Banking and Finance

In 2002 there were 211 financial institutions in New York State insured by the US Federal Deposit Insurance Corporation, with assets worth $1,620bn. They had 4,526 offices with total deposits of $516bn.

ENERGY AND NATURAL RESOURCES

Water

The total area covered by water is approximately 7,342 sq. miles.

Minerals

Principal minerals are: sand and gravel, salt, titanium concentrate, talc, abrasive garnet, wollastonite and emery. Quarry products include trap rock, slate, marble, limestone and sandstone. Value of domestic non-fuel mineral output in 2006 was $1,330m.

Agriculture

New York has large agricultural interests. In 2002 it had 37,000 farms, with a total area of 7·6m. acres; average farm was 205 acres. Average value per acre in 2002 was $1,708.

Farm income, 2006: from crops, $1,527m.; and from livestock, $1,982m. The net farm income in 2006 was $869m. Dairying is an important type of farming. Field crops comprise maize, winter wheat, oats and hay. New York ranks second in the USA in the production of apples and maple syrup. Other products are grapes, tart cherries, peaches, pears, plums, strawberries, raspberries, cabbage, onions, potatoes and maple sugar. Estimated farm animals, 2003, included 1,450,000 all cattle, 680,000 milch cows, 65,000 sheep and lambs, 73,000 swine and 4·9m. chickens.

Forestry

Total forested area was 18,669,000 acres in 2007, of which 11,000 acres were national forest. There were state parks and recreation areas covering 300,000 acres in 2003.

INDUSTRY

Leading industries are clothing, non-electrical machinery, printing and publishing, electrical equipment, instruments, food and allied products and fabricated metals. In 2005 the state's 19,349 manufacturing establishments had 572,000 employees, earning $24,908m. Total value added by manufacturing in 2006 was $93,103m.

Labour

Total non-agricultural employment, 2007, 8,738,000. Employees by branch, 2007 (in 1,000): education and health services, 1,602; trade, transportation and utilities, 1,526; government, 1,504; professional and business services, 1,137; financial activities, 731. In 2007 the unemployment rate was 4·6%.

COMMUNICATIONS

Roads

In 2007 there were 113,740 miles of road (65,874 miles rural). The New York State Thruway extends 559 miles from New York City to Buffalo. The Northway, a 176-mile toll-free highway, is a connecting road from the Thruway at Albany to the Canadian border at Champlain, Quebec.

There were 11,494,513 motor vehicle registrations in 2007 and 1,333 traffic accident fatalities.

Rail

There were, in 2000, 2,258 miles of Class I railroads. In addition the State had 534 miles of regional railroad and 1,068 miles of local railroad. New York City has NYCTA and PATH metro systems, and commuter railroads run by Metro-North, New Jersey Transit and Long Island Rail Road. Buffalo has a 7-mile metro line.

Civil Aviation

At Jan. 2003 there were 542 aviation facilities in New York State. Of these, 160 were public-use airports, 382 were private-use airports; two were private-use glider ports, six public-use heliports, 144 private-use heliports, nine public-use seaplane bases and ten private-use seaplane bases. There were 45,434,709 passenger enplanements statewide in 2007. The busiest airports are New York City's John F. Kennedy International (which handled 31,732,371 passengers in 2003) and LaGuardia (22,482,770 passengers in 2003).

Shipping

The canals of the state, combined in 1918 in what is called the Improved Canal System, have a length of 524 miles, of which the Erie or Barge canal has 340 miles.

SOCIAL INSTITUTIONS

Justice

The State Human Rights Law was approved on 12 March 1945, effective on 1 July 1945. The State Division of Human Rights is charged with the responsibility of enforcing this law. The division may request and utilize the services of all governmental departments and agencies; adopt and promulgate suitable rules and regulations; test, investigate and pass judgment upon complaints alleging discrimination in employment, in places of public accommodation, resort or amusement, education, and in housing, land and commercial space; hold hearings, subpoena witnesses and require the production for examination of papers relating to matters under investigation; grant compensatory damages and require repayment of profits in certain housing cases among other provisions; apply for court injunctions to prevent frustration of orders of the Commissioner.

In Dec. 2008 there were 60,347 federal and state prisoners, down 3·6% from 62,620 in Dec. 2007—the largest fall in any state over the same period.

The death penalty was declared unconstitutional in New York in 2004. The last execution was in 1963.

Education

Education is compulsory between the ages of six and 16. In 2001–02 the public elementary and secondary schools had 2,826,620 pupils and 217,210 teachers. There were 493,913 pupils at non-public schools.

The state's educational system, including public and private schools and secondary institutions, universities, colleges, libraries, museums, etc., constitutes (by legislative act) the 'University of the State of New York', which is governed by a Board of Regents consisting of 15 members appointed by the Legislature. Within the framework of this 'University' was established in 1948 a 'State University' (SUNY), which controls 64 colleges and educational centres, 30 of which are locally operated community colleges. The 'State University' is governed by a board of 16 Trustees, appointed by the Governor with the consent and advice of the Senate.

Higher education in the state is conducted in 322 institutions. 1,097,015 students enrolled in fall 2002. There were 46,399 full-time faculty staff (13,898 at SUNY) in 2001.

Student enrolment (fall 2002) in higher education in the state included:

Founded	*Name and place*	*Students*
1754	Columbia University, New York City	22,393
1795	Union College, Schenectady and Albany	2,512
1824	Rensselaer Polytechnic Institute, Troy	7,670
1829	Rochester Institute of Technology, Rochester	13,720
1831	New York University, New York City	38,096
1836	Alfred University, Alfred	1,604
1841	Manhattanville College, New York City	2,564
1846	Colgate University, Hamilton	2,837
1846	Fordham University, New York City	14,318
1847	The City University of New York (CUNY), New York City	208,862
1848	University of Rochester, Rochester	8,516
1854	Polytechnic University, New York City	3,032
1856	St Lawrence University, Canton	2,293
1859	Cooper Union for the Advancement of Science and Art, NYC	947
1861	Vassar College, Poughkeepsie	2,472
1863	Manhattan College, New York City	3,207
1865	Cornell University, Ithaca	12,566
1870	Syracuse University, Syracuse	19,301
1870	St John's University, New York City	19,288
1892	Ithaca College, Ithaca	6,431
1906	Pace University, New York City and Westchester	14,095
1926	Long Island University	21,470
1929	Marist College, Poughkeepsie	5,866
1935	Hofstra University, Hempstead	13,412
1948	State University of New York (SUNY)	402,945

Health

In 2006 there were 203 community hospitals with 63,500 beds. A total of 2,571,000 patients were admitted during the year.

Welfare

Medicare enrolment in July 2004 totalled 2,778,892. In fiscal year 2006 a total of 5,194,373 people in New York State received Medicaid. In Dec. 2008 there were 3,143,642 Old-Age, Survivors, and Disability Insurance (OASDI) beneficiaries. A total of 257,205 people were receiving payments under Temporary Assistance for Needy Families (TANF) in Dec. 2008.

RELIGION

The main religious denominations are Roman Catholics, Jews and Protestant Episcopalians.

CULTURE

Tourism

In 2003 there were a record 37·8m. visitors to New York City (33·0m. domestic and 4·8m. overseas), up from 35·3m. in 2002. Visitor spending in 2002 was $14,100m.

FURTHER READING

Statistical information: Nelson Rockefeller Institute of Government, 411 State St., Albany 12203. Publishes *New York State Statistical Yearbook.*
New York Red Book. Biennial.
Legislative Manual. Biennial.
The Modern New York State Legislature: Redressing the Balance. 1991
State library: The New York State Library, Albany 12230.

North Carolina

KEY HISTORICAL EVENTS

The early inhabitants were Cherokees. European settlement was attempted in 1585–87, following an exploratory visit by Sir Walter Raleigh, but this failed. Settlers from Virginia came to the shores of Albemarle Sound after 1650 and in 1663 Charles II chartered a private colony of Carolina. In 1691 the north was put under a deputy governor who ruled from Charleston in the south. The colony was formally separated into North and South Carolina in 1712. In 1729 control was taken from the private proprietors and vested in the Crown, whereupon settlement grew, and the boundary between north and south was finally fixed (1735).

After the War of Independence, North Carolina became one of the original 13 states of the Union. The city of Raleigh was laid out as the new capital. Having been a plantation colony North Carolina continued to develop as a plantation state, growing tobacco with black slave labour. It was also an important source of gold before the western gold-rushes of 1848.

In 1861 at the outset of the Civil War, North Carolina seceded from the Union, but General Sherman occupied the capital unopposed. A military governor was admitted in 1862, and civilian government restored with readmission to the Union in 1868.

TERRITORY AND POPULATION

North Carolina is bounded north by Virginia, east by the Atlantic, south by South Carolina, southwest by Georgia and west by Tennessee. Land area, 48,711 sq. miles (126,161 sq. km). Census population, 1 April 2000, 8,049,313, an increase of 21·4% since 1990. July 2009 estimate, 9,380,884.

Population in five census years was:

	White	*Black*	*Indian*	*Asiatic*	*Total*	*Per sq. mile*
1910	1,500,511	697,843	7,851	82	2,206,287	45·3
1930	2,234,958	918,647	16,579	92	3,170,276	64·5
			All others			
1980	4,453,010	1,316,050	105,369		5,874,429	111·5
1990	5,008,491	1,456,323	163,823		6,628,637	136·1
2000	5,804,656	1,737,545	507,112		8,049,313	165·2

Of the total population in 2000, 4,106,618 were female, 6,085,266 were 18 years old or older and 4,849,482 were urban. In 2000 North Carolina's Hispanic population was 378,963, up from 76,726 in 1990. This represented a rise of 393·9%, the largest increase of any state in the USA over the same period.

The principal cities (with census population in 2000) are: Charlotte, 540,828; Raleigh, 276,093; Greensboro, 223,891; Durham, 187,035; Winston-Salem, 185,776; Fayetteville, 121,015; Cary, 94,536; High Point, 85,839; Wilmington, 75,838.

SOCIAL STATISTICS

Births, 2007 (provisional), 131,314 (14·5 per 1,000 population); deaths, 2006, 74,716 (8·4). Infant mortality rate, 2006, 8·1 per 1,000 live births. 2006: marriages, 55,300 (6·2 per 1,000 population); divorces and annulments, 36,400 (4·1).

CLIMATE

Climate varies sharply with altitude; the warmest area is in the southeast near Southport and Wilmington; the coldest is Mount Mitchell (6,684 ft). Raleigh, Jan. 42°F (5·6°C), July 79°F (26·1°C). Annual rainfall 46" (1,158 mm). North Carolina belongs to the Atlantic Coast climate zone (*see* UNITED STATES: Climate).

CONSTITUTION AND GOVERNMENT

The present constitution dates from 1971 (previous constitutions, 1776 and 1868); it has had 30 amendments. The General Assembly consists of a Senate of 50 members and a House of Representatives of 120 members; all are elected by districts for two years. It meets in odd-numbered years in Jan.

The Governor and Lieut.-Governor are elected for four years; they can be elected to only one additional consecutive term. There are also 19 executive departments—eight have elected heads (for four-year terms) and ten have heads appointed by the Governor; the other department is the North Carolina Community College System, under a president.

For the 111th Congress, which convened in Jan. 2009, North Carolina sends 13 members to the House of Representatives. It is represented in the Senate by Richard Burr (R. 2005–11) and Kay Hagan (D. 2009–15).

The capital is Raleigh. There are 100 counties.

RECENT ELECTIONS

In the 2008 presidential elections Barack Obama won North Carolina with 49·7% of the vote (George W. Bush won in 2004).

CURRENT ADMINISTRATION

Governor: Beverly Perdue (D.), 2009–13 (salary: $97,600).

Lieut.-Governor: Walter Dalton (D.), 2009–13 ($87,000).

Secretary of State: Elaine F. Marshall (D.), 2009–13 ($87,000).

Government Website: http://www.nc.gov

ECONOMY

Per capita income (2008) was $35,344.

Budget

In 2008 total state revenue was $51,421m. Total expenditure was $46,995m. (education, $17,438m.; public welfare, $11,653m.; highways, $3,254m.; health, $1,654m.; hospitals, $1,461m.) Outstanding debt in 2008, $19,605m.

Performance

Gross Domestic Product by state in 2008 was $400,192m. (provisional), ranking North Carolina 9th in the United States.

ENERGY AND NATURAL RESOURCES

Water

The total area covered by water is approximately 5,108 sq. miles.

Minerals

Principal minerals are stone, sand and gravel, phosphate rock, feldspar, lithium minerals, olivine, kaolin and talc. North Carolina is a leading producer of bricks, making more than 1bn. bricks a year. Value of domestic non-fuel mineral production in 2006 was $1,020m.

Agriculture

In 2002 there were 56,000 farms covering 9·1m. acres; average size of farms was 163 acres and average value per acre in 2002 was $1,661.

Farm income, 2006: from crops, $2,925m.; and from livestock and products, $5,274m. The net farm income in 2006 was $3,702m. Main crop production: greenhouse products, flue-cured tobacco, maize, soybeans, peanuts, wheat, sweet potatoes and apples.

Livestock, 2002: cattle, 848,000; pigs, 9·9m.; chickens, 17·04m.

Forestry

Forests covered 18·45m. acres in 2007, with 1·17m. acres of national forest. In 2006 timber removals were 1,075m. cu. ft (636m. cu. ft softwoods and 439m. cu. ft hardwoods). Main products are hardwood veneer and hardwood plywood, furniture woods, pulp, paper and lumber.

Fisheries

Commercial fish catch, 2002, had a value of approximately $98·7m. and produced 159·6m. lb. The catch is mainly of blue crab, menhaden, Atlantic croaker, flounder, shark, sea trout, mullet, blue fish and shrimp.

INDUSTRY

The leading industries by employment are textiles, clothing, furniture, electrical machinery and equipment, non-electrical machinery and food processing. In 2005 the state's 10,138 manufacturing establishments had 554,000 employees, earning $20,682m. Total value added by manufacturing in 2006 was $106,988m.

Labour
Total non-agricultural employment, 2007, 4,146,000. Employees by branch, 2007 (in 1,000): trade, transport and utilities, 778; government, 695; manufacturing, 539; education and health services, 514; professional and business services, 500. The unemployment rate in 2007 was 4·5%.

COMMUNICATIONS

Roads
In 2007 there were 104,412 miles of road (71,306 miles rural). There were 6,317,148 registered motor vehicles.

Rail
In 2002 there were 3,345 miles of freight railroad in operation, including 2,580 miles of Class I railroads.

Civil Aviation
In June 2004 there were 305 airports and 74 heliports. There were 23,808,445 passenger enplanements statewide in 2007.

Shipping
There are two ocean ports, Wilmington and Morehead City.

SOCIAL INSTITUTIONS

Justice
There were five executions in 2005 and four in 2006, but the death penalty was suspended in Jan. 2007. In Dec. 2008 there were 39,482 federal and state prisoners.

Education
School attendance is compulsory between seven and 16. In fall 2002 there were 1,332,140 pupils and 85,557 teachers at public and charter schools; there were 92,890 pupils at 661 independent and religious schools. Total expenditure on public schools was $9,821m. in 2002–03; teachers' salaries in 2003 averaged $43,076.

The 16 senior universities are all part of the University of North Carolina system (176,967 students enrolled in fall 2002). The largest institution is the North Carolina State University (founded 1887), at Raleigh, with 29,637 students in fall 2002. The University of North Carolina at Chapel Hill (founded in 1789; the first state university to open in America in 1795) had 26,028 students in 2002; East Carolina University (founded in 1907), at Greenville, had 20,577. There were 78,028 students at 37 independent universities and colleges in fall 2002.

Health
In 2006 there were 114 community hospitals with 23,400 beds. A total of 1,015,000 patients were admitted during the year.

Welfare
Medicare enrolment in July 2004 totalled 1,233,919. In fiscal year 2006 a total of 1,631,243 people in North Carolina received Medicaid. In Dec. 2008 there were 1,631,266 Old-Age, Survivors, and Disability Insurance (OASDI) beneficiaries. A total of 49,256 people were receiving payments under Temporary Assistance for Needy Families (TANF) in Dec. 2008.

RELIGION
Leading denominations are the Baptists (41·4% of church membership), Methodists (17·5%), Roman Catholics (8·6%), Presbyterians (5·6%) and Lutherans (2·4%). Total estimate of all denominations in 2000 was 3·7m.

CULTURE

Tourism
There were about 49m. visitors in 2004, spending $13·25bn. across the state and supporting almost 183,000 jobs; tourism spending generated $710m. in state sales tax receipts and $437m. in local tax revenue.

FURTHER READING

Statistical information: Office of State Planning, 116 West Jones St., Raleigh 27603. Publishes *Statistical Abstract of North Carolina Counties.*
North Carolina Manual. Biennial

Fleer, J. D., *North Carolina: Government and Population.* 1995

North Dakota

KEY HISTORICAL EVENTS
The original inhabitants were Plains Indians. French explorers and traders were active in the 18th century, often operating from French possessions in Canada. France claimed the area until 1803, when it passed to the USA as part of the Louisiana Purchase, except for the northeastern part which was held by the British until 1818.

Trading with the Indians, mainly for furs, continued until the 1860s, with American traders succeeding the French. In 1861 the Dakota Territory (North and South) was established. In 1862 the Homestead Act was passed (allowing 160 acres of public land free to any family who had worked and lived on it for five years) and this greatly stimulated settlement. Farming settlers came to the wheat lands in great numbers, many of them from Canada, Norway and Germany.

Bismarck, the capital, began as a crossing-point on the Missouri and was fortified in 1872 to protect workers building the Northern Pacific Railway. There followed a gold-rush nearby and the town became a service centre for prospectors. In 1889 North and South Dakota were admitted to the Union as separate states with Bismarck as the Northern capital. The largest city, Fargo, was also a railway town, named after William George Fargo, the express-company founder.

The population grew rapidly until 1890 and steadily until 1930 by which time it was about one-third European in origin. Between 1930 and 1970 there was a steady population drain, increasing whenever farming was affected by the extremes of the continental climate.

TERRITORY AND POPULATION
North Dakota is bounded north by Canada, east by the Red River (forming a boundary with Minnesota), south by South Dakota and west by Montana. Land area, 68,976 sq. miles (178,647 sq. km). In 2000 American Indian lands covered 3,542 sq. miles (3,467 sq. miles in reservations and 75 sq. miles in off-reservation trust land). Census population, 1 April 2000, 642,200, an increase of 0·5% since 1990. July 2009 estimate, 646,844.

Population at five census years was:

	White	*Black*	*Indian*	*Asiatic*	*Total*	*Per sq. mile*
1910	569,855	617	6,486	98	577,056	8·2
1930	671,851	377	8,617	194	680,845	9·7
			All others			
1980	625,557	2,568	24,692		652,717	9·5
1990	604,142	3,524	31,134		638,800	9·3
2000	593,182	3,916	45,102		642,200	9·3

Of the total population in 2000, 321,676 were female, 481,351 were 18 years old or older and 358,958 were urban. Estimated outward migration, 2000–05, 23 per 1,000 population. Only Vermont has fewer persons of Hispanic origin than North Dakota. In 2000 the Hispanic population was 7,786, up from 4,665 in 1990 (an increase of 66·9%).

The largest cities are Fargo with a population, census 2000, of 90,599; Bismarck (capital), 55,532; Grand Forks, 49,321; and Minot, 36,567.

SOCIAL STATISTICS

Births, 2007 (provisional), 8,837 (13·8 per 1,000 population); deaths, 2006, 5,868 (9·2). Infant mortality rate, 2006, 5·8 per 1,000 live births. 2006: marriages, 4,300 (6·8 per 1,000 population); divorces and annulments, 1,700 (2·6).

CLIMATE

Bismarck, Jan. 8°F (–13·3°C), July 71°F (21·1°C). Annual rainfall 16" (402 mm). Fargo, Jan. 6°F (–14·4°C), July 71°F (21·1°C). Annual rainfall 20" (503 mm). North Dakota belongs to the High Plains climate zone (*see* UNITED STATES: Climate).

CONSTITUTION AND GOVERNMENT

The present constitution dates from 1889; it has had 133 amendments as of 2005. The Legislative Assembly consists of a Senate of 47 members elected for four years, and a House of Representatives of 94 members elected for four years. The Governor and Lieut.-Governor are elected for four years.

For the 111th Congress, which convened in Jan. 2009, North Dakota sends one member to the House of Representatives. It is represented in the Senate by Kent Conrad (D. 1987–2013) and Byron Dorgan (D. 1992–2011).

The capital is Bismarck. The state has 53 organized counties.

RECENT ELECTIONS

In the 2008 presidential elections John McCain won North Dakota with 53·3% of the vote (George W. Bush won in 2004).

CURRENT ADMINISTRATION

Governor: John Hoeven (R.), Dec. 2008–Dec. 2012 (salary: $105,034).

Lieut.-Governor: Jack Dalrymple (R.), Dec. 2008–Dec. 2012 ($81,538).

Secretary of State: Alvin A. Jaeger (R.), Jan. 2007–Dec. 2010 ($83,550).

Government Website: http://www.nd.gov

ECONOMY

Per capita income (2008) was $39,870.

Budget

In 2008 total state revenue was $5,019m. Total expenditure was $4,126m. (education, $1,325m.; public welfare, $773m.; highways, $459m.; natural resources, $166m.; government administration, $123m.) Outstanding debt in 2008, $1,952m.

Performance

Gross Domestic Product by state in 2008 was $31,208m. (provisional), ranking North Dakota 49th in the United States.

ENERGY AND NATURAL RESOURCES

Oil and Gas

The mineral resources of North Dakota consist chiefly of oil, which was discovered in 1951. Production in 2006 of crude petroleum was 40m. bbls; of natural gas, 55bn. cu. ft.

Water

The total area covered by water is approximately 1,724 sq. miles.

Minerals

Output of lignite coal in 2003 was 30·8m. tons. Total value of domestic non-fuel mineral production in 2006 was $44m.

Agriculture

In 2002 there were 30,000 farms (61,963 in 1954) in an area of 39·4m. acres and with an average farm acreage of 1,313. In 2002 the average value of farmland and buildings per acre was $404.

Farm income, 2006: from crops, $3,088m.; and from livestock, $892m. The net farm income in 2006 was $606m. Production, 2002: barley, 56·8m. bu.; wheat (durum), 48·9m. bu.; honey, 24m. lb; oats, 12·5m. bu.; flaxseed, 12·2m. bu.; dry edible beans, 10·1m. cwt; sunflower (all), 1,710m. lb. Other important products are all beans, all wheat and rye.

The state has also an active livestock industry, chiefly cattle raising. Livestock, 2002: cattle, 1·87m.; pigs, 138,800; sheep, 114,000; poultry, 200,400.

Forestry

Forest area, 2007, was 724,000 acres, of which 72,000 acres were national forest.

INDUSTRY

Though the state is still mainly agricultural it is diversifying into high tech and information technology industries. In 2005 the state's 748 manufacturing establishments had 25,000 employees, earning $827m. Total value added by manufacturing in 2006 was $3,877m.

Labour

Total non-agricultural employment, 2007, 358,000. Employees by branch, 2007 (in 1,000): government, 76; trade, transportation and utilities, 76; education and health services, 51; leisure and hospitality, 33; professional and business services, 30. The unemployment rate in 2007 was 3·2%.

COMMUNICATIONS

Roads

In 2007 there were 86,842 miles of road (84,945 miles rural). There were 710,537 registered motor vehicles.

Rail

In 2002 there were 3,707 miles of railroad.

Civil Aviation

In 2005 there were 90 public airports and 204 private airports. There were 657,416 passenger enplanements statewide in 2007.

SOCIAL INSTITUTIONS

Justice

In Dec. 2008 there were 1,452 federal and state prisoners. The Missouri River Correctional Center is a minimum custody institution. There is no death penalty.

Education

School attendance is compulsory between the ages of seven and 16. In 2004–05 the 551 public schools had 100,513 pupils with 8,070 teachers. According to the National Center for Education Statistics, North Dakota has the smallest average high school enrolment in the country with 210 pupils in the 2001–02 school year. State expenditure per pupil in elementary and secondary schools in 2002–03 was $6,870. Average teacher salary was $35,441 in 2003–04.

The University of North Dakota in Grand Forks, founded in 1883, had 12,954 students in fall 2005; North Dakota State

University in Fargo, 12,099 students. Total enrolment in the 22 institutions of higher education (14 public and eight private) in fall 2005 was 49,389.

Health

In 2006 there were 41 community hospitals with 3,500 beds. A total of 88,000 patients were admitted during the year.

Welfare

Medicare enrolment in July 2004 totalled 103,549. In fiscal year 2006 a total of 74,076 people in North Dakota received Medicaid. In Dec. 2008 there were 117,130 Old-Age, Survivors, and Disability Insurance (OASDI) beneficiaries. A total of 5,855 people were receiving payments under Temporary Assistance for Needy Families (TANF) in Dec. 2008.

RELIGION

Church membership totalled 467,925 in 2000. The leading religious denominations were: Roman Catholics, 179,349 members; Evangelical Lutherans, 174,554; Lutheran Church-Missouri Synod, 23,720; Methodists, 20,159; Assemblies of God, 9,994.

FURTHER READING

Statistical information: Bureau of Business and Economic Research, Univ. of North Dakota, Grand Forks 58202. Publishes *Statistical Abstract of North Dakota.*
North Dakota Blue Book.

Jelliff, T. B., *North Dakota: A Living Legacy.* 1983

Ohio

KEY HISTORICAL EVENTS

The land was inhabited by Delaware, Miami, Shawnee and Wyandot Indians. It was explored by French and British traders in the 18th century and confirmed as part of British North America in 1763. After the War of Independence it became part of the Northwest Territory of the new United States. Former independence fighters came in from New England in 1788 to make the first permanent white settlement at Marietta, at the confluence of the Ohio and Muskingum rivers. In 1803 Ohio was separated from the rest of the Territory and admitted to the Union as the 17th state.

In the early 19th century there was steady immigration from Europe, mainly of Germans, Swiss, Irish and Welsh. Industrial growth began with the processing of farm, forest and mining products; it increased rapidly with the need to supply the Union armies in the Civil War of 1861–65.

As the industrial cities grew, so immigration began again, with many whites from eastern Europe and the Balkans and blacks from the southern states looking for work in Ohio.

Cleveland, which developed rapidly as a Lake Erie port after the opening of commercial waterways to the interior and the Atlantic coast (1825, 1830 and 1855), became an iron-and-steel town during the Civil War.

TERRITORY AND POPULATION

Ohio is bounded north by Michigan and Lake Erie, east by Pennsylvania, southeast and south by the Ohio River (forming a boundary with West Virginia and Kentucky) and west by Indiana. Land area, 40,948 sq. miles (106,055 sq. km). Census population, 1 April 2000, 11,353,140, an increase of 4·7% since 1990. July 2009 estimate, 11,542,645.

Population at five census years was:

	White	*Black*	*Indian*	*Asiatic*	*Total*	*Per sq. mile*
1910	4,654,897	111,452	127	645	4,767,121	117·0
1930	6,335,173	309,304	435	1,785	6,646,697	161·6
			All others			
1980	9,597,458	1,076,748	123,424		10,797,630	263·2
1990	9,521,756	1,154,826	170,533		10,847,115	264·5
2000	9,645,453	1,301,307	406,380		11,353,140	277·3

Of the total population in 2000, 5,840,878 were female, 8,464,801 were 18 years old or older and 8,782,329 were urban. In 2000 the Hispanic population was 217,123, up from 139,696 in 1990 (an increase of 55·4%).

Census population of chief cities on 1 April 2000 was:

Columbus	711,470	Springfield	65,358	Cuyahoga Falls	49,374
Cleveland	478,403	Hamilton	60,690	Mansfield	49,346
Cincinnati	331,285	Kettering	57,502	Warren	46,832
Toledo	313,619	Lakewood	56,646	Newark	46,279
Akron	217,074	Elyria	55,953	Strongsville	43,858
Dayton	166,179	Euclid	52,717	Fairfield	42,097
Parma	85,655	Middletown	51,605	Lima	40,081
Youngstown	82,026	Mentor	50,278		
Canton	80,806	Cleveland Heights	49,458		
Lorain	68,652				

Metropolitan areas, 2000 census: Cleveland–Akron, 2,945,831; Cincinnati–Hamilton, 1,979,202; Columbus (the capital), 1,540,157; Dayton–Springfield, 950,558; Toledo, 618,203; Youngstown–Warren, 594,746; Canton–Massillon, 404,934.

SOCIAL STATISTICS

Births, 2007 (provisional), 150,892 (13·2 per 1,000 population); deaths, 2006, 106,825 (9·3). Infant mortality, 2006, 7·8 per 1,000 live births. 2006: marriages, 73,833 (6·4 per 1,000 population); divorces, 40,314 (3·5).

CLIMATE

Cincinnati, Jan. 30·6°F, July 76·8°F, annual rainfall 39·6"; Cleveland, Jan. 25·7°F, July 71·9°F, annual rainfall 38·7"; Columbus, Jan. 28·3°F, July 74·7°F, annual rainfall 40·0". Ohio belongs to the Great Lakes climate zone (*see* UNITED STATES: Climate).

CONSTITUTION AND GOVERNMENT

The question of a general revision of the constitution drafted by an elected convention is submitted to the people every 20 years. The constitution dates from 1851, since when there have been 161 amendments adopted to change the constitution.

The Senate consists of 33 members and the House of Representatives of 99 members. The Senate is elected for four years, half every two years; the House is elected for two years; the Governor, Lieut.-Governor and Secretary of State for four years. Qualified as electors are (with necessary exceptions) all citizens 18 years of age who have the usual residential qualifications.

For the 111th Congress, which convened in Jan. 2009, Ohio sends 18 members to the House of Representatives. It is represented in the Senate by George Voinovich (R. 1999–2011) and Sherrod Brown (D. 2007–13).

The capital (since 1816) is Columbus. Ohio is divided into 88 counties.

RECENT ELECTIONS

In the 2008 presidential elections Barack Obama won Ohio with 51·5% of the vote (George W. Bush won in 2004).

CURRENT ADMINISTRATION

Governor: Ted Strickland (D.), 2007–11 (salary: $141,708·02).
Lieut.-Governor: Lee Fisher (D.), 2007–11 ($85,075·52).
Secretary of State: Jennifer L. Brunner (D.), 2007–11 ($108,183·85).

Government Website: http://ohio.gov

ECONOMY

Per capita income (2008) was $36,021.

Budget

In 2008 total state revenue was $65,860m. Total expenditure was $67,789m. (education, $20,120m.; public welfare, $16,114m.; highways, $3,216m.; health, $2,471m.; hospitals, $2,090m.) Outstanding debt in 2008, $26,885m.

Performance

In 2008 Gross Domestic Product by state was $471,508m. (provisional), ranking Ohio 8th in the United States.

ENERGY AND NATURAL RESOURCES

Oil and Gas

In 2005, 5·65m. bbls of crude oil and 84,135m. cu. ft of gas were produced. In 2005 the value of oil and gas production was $1·06bn.

Water

Lake Erie supplies northern Ohio with its water. The total area covered by water is approximately 3,877 sq. miles, of which Lake Erie covers 3,499 sq. miles.

Minerals

Ohio has extensive mineral resources, of which coal is the most important by value: production (2004), 23,460,615 short tons. Coal production in 2004 was valued at $533,659,428. Production of other minerals totalled 145,023,268 short tons. Limestone, dolomite, sand and gravel accounted for 97% of the total production; the remainder was comprised of various amounts of salt, sandstone, clay, shale, gypsum and peat. The combined value of all non-fuel industrial minerals sold in 2006 was $1,270m.

Agriculture

Ohio is extensively devoted to agriculture. In 2006, 76,200 farms covered 14·3m. acres; average farm value per acre, $3,480. The average size of a farm in 2006 was 188 acres.

Farm income 2006: from crops, $3,448m.; from livestock, $2,031m.; total, $5,480m. The net farm income in 2006 was $1,614m. Production (2006): corn for grain (470·6m. bu.), soybeans (217·1m. bu.), wheat (65·3m. bu.), oats (4·13m. bu.). In 2006 there were 1·56m. pigs, 1·28m. cattle and 141,000 sheep.

Forestry

Forest area, 2007, 7,894,000 acres. State forest lands area, 2007, 191,142 acres. In 2008 there were 74 state parks covering 323,215 acres.

INDUSTRY

In 2005, 16,617 manufacturing establishments employed 792,783 persons, earning $35,677m. Total value added by manufacturing in 2006 was $124,949m. The largest industries were manufacturing of transport equipment, fabricated metal products and machinery.

Labour

In Aug. 2006, 5,609,100 people were in employment out of a labour force of 5,934,000. Employees by branch, 2007 (in 1,000): trade, transportation and utilities, 1,051; government, 798; education and health services, 790; manufacturing, 773; professional and business services, 666. In 2007 the unemployment rate was 5·6%.

INTERNATIONAL TRADE

Imports and Exports

Ohio exports had a total value of $37·8bn. in 2006 (an increase of 8·7% from 2005), making it the eighth largest exporting state in the USA.

COMMUNICATIONS

Roads

In 2007 there were 125,160 miles of road; there were 10,848,476 registered motor vehicles in the same year.

Rail

Ohio has about 5,800 miles of railroad track. Cleveland has a 19-mile metro system.

Civil Aviation

In 2003 there were more than 800 airports of varying sizes in the state. There are 165 public-use airports and 23 public-use heliports. There were 11,690,451 passenger enplanements in 2007.

Shipping

Ohio has more than 700 miles of navigable waterways, with Lake Erie having a 265-mile shoreline. There are nine deep-draft ports in the state. The busiest port is Cleveland, which handles 18m. tons of cargo annually.

SOCIAL INSTITUTIONS

Justice

In June 2006 there were 46,839 inmates (43,560 males) in the 32 adult correctional institutions. There were 187 death-row inmates (185 male) in Nov. 2007: 97 were African Americans; 82 Caucasians (two females); four Hispanics; two Native Americans; and two Arab Americans. There were five executions in 2009.

Education

School attendance during full term is compulsory for children from six to 18 years of age. In 2005–06 public schools had 1,842,943 enrolled pupils. Teachers' salaries (2005–06) averaged $50,654. Estimated expenditure on elementary and secondary schools for 2006 was $8,349m., 39·0% of the total state budget. In 2003–04 total expenditure for the co-ordination of higher education in Ohio (controlled by the Board of Regents) was $5·54bn.

Public colleges and universities had a total enrolment (2006–07) of 457,322 students. Independent colleges and universities enrolled 132,139 students. Average annual charge (for undergraduates in 2006–07): $8,553 (state); $19,111 (private) (2005–06).

Main campuses, fall 2006:

Founded	*Institutions*	*Enrolments*
1804	Ohio University, Athens (State)	20,408
1809	Miami University, Oxford (State)	15,726
1819	University of Cincinnati (State)	28,327
1826	Case Western Reserve University, Cleveland	9,592
1850	University of Dayton (R.C.)	10,502
1870	University of Akron (State)	21,882
1870	Ohio State University, Columbus (State)	51,818
1872	University of Toledo (State)	19,374
1908	Youngstown University (State)	13,183
1910	Bowling Green State University (State)	19,108
1910	Kent State University (State)	22,317
1964	Cleveland State University (State)	15,471

Founded	Institutions	Enrolments
1964	Wright State University, Dayton (State)	16,093
1986	Shawnee State University, Portsmouth (State)	3,889

Health

In 2006 the state had 171 registered community hospitals with 32,822 beds. A total of 1,542,000 patients were admitted during the year. State facilities for the severely mentally retarded had ten developmental centres serving 1,597 residents.

Welfare

Public assistance is administered through the Ohio Works First programme (OWF). In 2006–07 OWF-Combined assistance groups had 169,218 recipients and money payments totalled $308,786,133. OWF-Regular assistance groups had 156,124 recipients with $292,020,311 paid out in 2006–07. OWF-Unemployed had 13,094 recipients and money payments were $16,765,822 in 2006–07. Disability Assistance had 13,991 recipients in 2006–07; and food stamps, 1,069,561 recipients.

In 2006–07 Disability Assistance totalled $22,847,689; food stamps in 2006–07 totalled $1,287,406,968; and foster care totalled $175,540,449. Optional State Supplement is paid to aged, blind or disabled adults. Free social services available to those eligible by income or circumstances.

RELIGION

Many religious faiths are represented, including (but not limited to) the Baptist, Jewish, Lutheran, Methodist, Muslim, Orthodox, Presbyterian and Roman Catholic.

FURTHER READING

Official Roster: Federal, State, County Officers and Department Information. Biennial

Shkurti, W. J. and Bartle, J. (eds.) *Benchmark Ohio.* 1991

Oklahoma

KEY HISTORICAL EVENTS

Francisco Coronado led a Spanish expedition in 1541, claiming the land for Spain. There were several Indian groups but no strong political unit. In 1714 Juchereau de Saint Denis made the first French contact. During the 18th century French fur-traders were active. A French and Spanish struggle for control was resolved by the French withdrawal in 1763. France returned briefly in 1800–03, and the territory then passed to the USA as part of the Louisiana Purchase.

In 1828 the Federal government set aside the area of the present state as Indian Territory (a reservation and sanctuary for Indian tribes who had been driven off their lands elsewhere by white settlement). About 70 tribes came, among whom were Creeks, Choctaws and Cherokees from the southeastern states, and Plains Indians.

In 1889 the government took back about 2·5m. acres of the Territory and opened it to white settlement. About 10,000 homesteaders gathered at the site of Oklahoma City on the Santa Fe Railway in the rush to stake their land claims. The settlers' area, and others subsequently opened to settlement, were organized as the Oklahoma Territory in 1890. In 1907 the Oklahoma and Indian Territories were combined and admitted to the Union as a state. Indian reservations were established within the state.

The economy first depended on ranching and farming, with packing stations on the railways. A mining industry grew in the 1870s attracting foreign immigration, mainly from Europe. In 1901 oil was found near Tulsa.

TERRITORY AND POPULATION

Oklahoma is bounded north by Kansas, northeast by Missouri, east by Arkansas, south by Texas (the Red River forming part of the boundary) and, at the western extremity of the 'panhandle', by New Mexico and Colorado. Land area, 68,667 sq. miles (177,847 sq. km). Census population, 1 April 2000, 3,450,654, an increase of 9·7% since 1990. July 2009 estimate, 3,687,050.

The population at five federal censuses was:

	White	Black	American Indian	Other	Total	Per sq. mile
1930	2,130,778	172,198	92,725	339	2,396,040	34·6
1960	2,107,900	153,084	68,689	1,414	2,328,284	33·8
1980	2,597,783	204,658	169,292	53,557	3,025,486	43·2
1990	2,583,512	233,801	252,420	119,723	3,189,456	44·5
2000	2,628,434	260,968	273,230	288,022	3,450,654	50·3

Of the total population in 2000, 1,754,759 were female, 2,558,294 were 18 years old or older and 2,254,563 were urban. Oklahoma is home to 39 recognized Indian tribes. In 2000 Oklahoma's Hispanic population was 179,304, up from 86,160 in 1990 (an increase of 108·1%).

The most important cities with population, 2000, are Oklahoma City (capital), 506,132; Tulsa, 393,049; Norman, 95,694; Lawton, 92,757; Broken Arrow, 74,859; Edmond, 68,315; Midwest City, 54,088; Enid, 47,045; Moore, 41,138; Stillwater, 39,065; Muskogee, 38,310; Bartlesville, 34,748.

SOCIAL STATISTICS

Births, 2007 (provisional), 55,372 (15·3 per 1,000 population); deaths, 2006, 35,427 (9·9). Infant mortality rate, 2006, 8·0 per 1,000 live births. 2006: marriages, 26,300 (7·3 per 1,000 population); divorces and annulments, 19,000 (5·3).

CLIMATE

Oklahoma City, Jan. 34°F (1°C), July 81°F (27°C). Annual rainfall 31·9" (8,113 mm). Tulsa, Jan. 34°F (1°C), July 82°F (28°C). Annual rainfall 33·2" (8,438 mm). Oklahoma belongs to the Central Plains climate zone (*see* UNITED STATES: Climate).

CONSTITUTION AND GOVERNMENT

The constitution, dating from 1907, provides for amendment by initiative petition and legislative referendum; it has had 200 amendments (as of Sept. 2005).

The Legislature consists of a Senate of 48 members, who are elected for four years, and a House of Representatives elected for two years and consisting of 101 members. The Governor and Lieut.-Governor are elected for four-year terms; the Governor can only be elected for two terms in succession. Electors are (with necessary exceptions) all citizens 18 years or older, with the usual qualifications.

For the 111th Congress, which convened in Jan. 2009, Oklahoma sends five members to the House of Representatives. It is represented in the Senate by James Inhofe (R. 1994–2015) and Tom Coburn (R. 2005–11).

The capital is Oklahoma City. The state has 77 counties.

RECENT ELECTIONS

In the 2008 presidential elections John McCain won Oklahoma with 65·6% of the vote (George W. Bush won in 2004).

CURRENT ADMINISTRATION

Governor: Brad Henry (D.), 2007–11 (salary: $147,000).

Lieut.-Governor: Jari Askins (D.), 2007–11 ($114,713).

Secretary of State: M. Susan Savage (D.), appointed Jan. 2003 ($94,500).

Government Website: http://www.ok.gov

ECONOMY

Per capita income (2008) was $35,985.

Budget

In 2008 total state revenue was $18,810m. Total expenditure was $19,518m. (education, $7,047m.; public welfare, $4,821m.; highways, $1,472m.; health, $781m.; correction, $617m.) Outstanding debt in 2008, $9,130m.

Performance

Gross Domestic Product by state in 2008 was $146,448m. (provisional), ranking Oklahoma 29th in the United States.

ENERGY AND NATURAL RESOURCES

Oil and Gas

Production of crude oil (2006), 63m. bbls; natural gas (2006), 1,689bn. cu. ft. Oklahoma ranks third in the USA for natural gas production behind Texas and Wyoming. In 2005 there were 9,407 persons employed in crude petroleum and natural gas extraction.

Water

The total area covered by water is approximately 1,231 sq. miles.

Minerals

Coal production (2003), 1,565,000 tons. Principal minerals are: crushed stone, cement, sand and gravel, iodine, glass sand, gypsum. Other minerals are helium, clay and sand, zinc, lead, granite, tripoli, bentonite, lime and volcanic ash. Total value of domestic non-fuel minerals produced in 2006 was $684m.

Agriculture

In 2002 the state had 87,000 farms and ranches with a total area of 34m. acres; average size was 391 acres and average value per acre was $699. Area harvested, 2002, 7,705,860 acres. Livestock, 2002: cattle, 5·2m.; sheep and lambs, 80,100; hogs and pigs, 2·25m.

Farm income 2006: from crops, $974m.; from livestock and products, $4,120m. The net farm income in 2006 was $877m. The major cash grain is winter wheat (value, 2002, $340m.): 102m. bu. of wheat for grain were harvested in 2002. Other crops include barley, oats, rye, grain, corn, soybeans, grain sorghum, cotton, peanuts and peaches. Value of cattle and calves produced, 2002, $2,448m.

The Oklahoma Conservation Commission works with 91 conservation districts, universities, state and federal government agencies. The early work of the conservation districts, beginning in 1937, was limited to flood and erosion control: since 1970, they also include urban areas.

Irrigated production has increased in the Oklahoma 'panhandle'. The Ogalala aquifer is the primary source of irrigation water there and in western Oklahoma, a finite source because of its isolation from major sources of recharge. Declining groundwater levels necessitate the most effective irrigation practices.

Forestry

There were 7,665,000 acres of forested land in 2007, with 245,000 acres of national forest. The forest products industry is concentrated in the 118 eastern counties. There are three forest regions: Ozark (oak, hickory); Ouachita highlands (pine, oak); Cross-Timbers (post oak, black jack oak). Southern pine is the chief commercial species, at almost 80% of saw-timber harvested annually. Replanting is essential.

INDUSTRY

In 2005 Oklahoma's 3,865 manufacturing establishments had 140,000 employees, earning $5,557m. Total value added by manufacturing in 2006 was $24,025m.

Labour

Total non-agricultural employment in 2007 was 1,566,000. Employees by branch, 2007 (in 1,000): government, 321; trade, transportation and utilities, 288; education and health services, 193; professional and business services, 181; manufacturing, 150. Oklahoma's unemployment rate was 4·4% in 2007.

COMMUNICATIONS

Roads

In 2007 there were 112,922 miles of road comprising 15,633 miles of urban road and 97,289 miles of rural road. There were 3,224,653 registered motor vehicles.

Rail

In 2005 there were 3,237 miles of freight railroad, including 2,019 miles of Class I railroads.

Civil Aviation

Airports in 2005 numbered 351, of which 142 were publicly owned. There were 3,513,358 passenger enplanements statewide in 2007.

Shipping

The McClellan-Kerr Arkansas Navigation System provides access from east central Oklahoma to New Orleans through the Verdigris, Arkansas and Mississippi rivers. In 2004, 12·9m. tons were shipped inbound and outbound on the Oklahoma Segment. Commodities shipped are mainly chemical fertilizer, farm produce, petroleum products, iron and steel, coal, sand and gravel.

SOCIAL INSTITUTIONS

Justice

There were 25,864 federal and state prisoners in Dec. 2008. In 2006 there were 17 state correctional facilities, 15 community work centres and seven community correctional centres. The death penalty was suspended in 1966 and reimposed in 1976. There were three executions in 2009. Oklahoma's total of 92 executions between 1977 and 2009 is the third highest in the USA behind Texas and Virginia.

Education

In 2003–04 there were 619,200 pupils and 34,700 teachers at public elementary and secondary school. The average teacher salary per annum was $34,779. In 2003 total expenditure on the 1,769 schools was $4·1bn. There were 234,900 students enrolled at the 42 higher education establishments in 2004.

Institutions of higher education include:

Founded	*Name*	*Place*	*2004 enrolment*
1890	University of Oklahoma	Norman	31,529
1890	Oklahoma State University	Stillwater	27,419
1890	University of Central Oklahoma	Edmond	18,107
1894	The University of Tulsa	Tulsa	4,629
1897	Langston University	Langston	3,827

Founded	Name	Place	2004 enrolment
1897	Northeastern State University	Tahlequah	11,217
1897	Northwestern Oklahoma State University	Alva	2,731
1897	Southwestern Oklahoma State University	Weatherford	6,352
1908	Cameron University	Lawton	7,917
1909	East Central University	Ada	5,606
1909	Oklahoma Panhandle State University	Goodwell	1,425
1909	Southeastern Oklahoma State University	Durant	5,150
1909	Rogers State College	Claremore	4,896
1950	Oklahoma Christian University of Science and Arts	Oklahoma City	1,725
1969	Rose State College	Midwest City	13,804
1970	Tulsa Community College	Tulsa	26,838
1972	Oklahoma City Community College	Oklahoma City	19,700

Health

In 2006 there were 112 community hospitals with 10,700 beds. A total of 454,000 patients were admitted during the year.

Welfare

Medicare enrolment in July 2004 totalled 529,148. In fiscal year 2006 a total of 725,736 people in Oklahoma received Medicaid. In Dec. 2008 there were 669,673 Old-Age, Survivors, and Disability Insurance (OASDI) beneficiaries. A total of 18,948 people were receiving payments under Temporary Assistance for Needy Families (TANF) in Dec. 2008.

RELIGION

The chief religious bodies are Baptists, followed by United Methodists, Roman Catholics, Churches of Christ, Assembly of God, Disciples of Christ, Presbyterian, Lutheran, Nazarene and Episcopal.

CULTURE

Broadcasting

In 2005 there were 107 radio and 20 television broadcasting stations, and 100 cable-TV companies.

Press

There were 47 daily newspapers in 2005 and 171 weeklies.

FURTHER READING

Center for Economic and Management Research, Univ. of Oklahoma, 307 West Brooks St., Norman 73019. *Statistical Abstract of Oklahoma.*
Oklahoma Department of Libraries. *Oklahoma Almanac.* Biennial

Goins, Charles Robert and Goble, Danney, *Historical Atlas of Oklahoma.* 4th ed. 2006

State library: Oklahoma Department of Libraries, 200 Northeast 18th Street, Oklahoma City 73105.

Oregon

KEY HISTORICAL EVENTS

The area was divided between many Indian tribes including the Chinook, Tillamook, Cayuse and Modoc. In the 18th century English and Spanish visitors tried to establish claims, based on explorations of the 16th century. The USA also laid claim by right of discovery when an expedition entered the mouth of the Columbia River in 1792.

Oregon was disputed between Britain and the USA. An American fur trading settlement established at Astoria in 1811 was taken by the British in 1812. The Hudson Bay Company was the most active force in Oregon until the 1830s when American pioneers began to migrate westwards along the Oregon Trail. The dispute between Britain and the USA was resolved in 1846 with the boundary fixed at 49°N. lat. Oregon was organized as a Territory in 1848 but with wider boundaries; it became a state with its present boundaries in 1859.

Early settlers were mainly American. They came to farm in the Willamette Valley and to exploit the western forests. Portland developed as a port for ocean-going traffic, although it was 100 miles inland at the confluence of the Willamette and Columbia rivers. Industries followed when the railways came and the rivers were exploited for hydro-electricity. The capital of the Territory from 1851 was Salem, a mission for Indians on the Willamette river; it was confirmed as state capital in 1864. Salem became the processing centre for the farming and market-gardening of the Willamette Valley.

TERRITORY AND POPULATION

Oregon is bounded in the north by Washington, with the Columbia River forming most of the boundary, east by Idaho, with the Snake River forming most of the boundary, south by Nevada and California and west by the Pacific. Land area, 95,997 sq. miles (248,631 sq. km). The federal government owned (2003) 30,638,949 acres (49·7% of the state area). Census population, 1 April 2000, 3,421,399, an increase of 20·4% since 1990. July 2009 estimate, 3,825,657.

Population at five federal censuses was:

	White	Black	American Indian	Asiatic	Total	Per sq. mile
1930	938,598	2,234	4,776	8,179	953,786	9·9
1960	1,732,037	18,133	8,026	9,120	1,768,687	18·4
1980	2,490,610	37,060	27,314	34,775	2,633,105	27·3
	White	Black	American Indian	All others	Total	Per sq. mile
1990	2,636,787	46,178	38,496	120,860	2,842,321	29·6
2000	2,961,623	55,662	45,211	358,903	3,421,399	35·6

Of the total population in 2000, 1,724,849 were female, 2,574,843 were 18 years old or older and 2,694,144 were urban. In 2000 the Hispanic population was 275,314, up from 112,707 in 1990 (an increase of 144·3%).

In 2000 American Indian lands covered 1,377 sq. miles (1,342 sq. miles in reservations and 35 sq. miles in off-reservation trust land).

The largest cities (2000 census figures) are: Portland, 529,121; Eugene, 137,893; Salem (the capital), 136,924; Gresham, 90,205; Beaverton, 76,129; Hillsboro, 70,186; Medford, 63,154; Springfield, 52,864; Bend, 52,029. Primary statistical (metropolitan) areas: Portland–Salem, 2,265,223; Eugene-Springfield, 322,959.

SOCIAL STATISTICS

Births, 2007 (provisional), 48,957 (13·1 per 1,000 population); deaths, 2006, 31,380 (8·5). Infant mortality rate, 2006, 5·5 per 1,000 live births. 2006: marriages, 26,900 (7·3 per 1,000 population); divorces and annulments, 14,200 (3·9).

CLIMATE

Jan. 32°F (0°C), July 66°F (19°C). Annual rainfall 28" (710 mm). Oregon belongs to the Pacific coast climate zone (*see* UNITED STATES: Climate).

CONSTITUTION AND GOVERNMENT

The present constitution dates from 1859; some 250 items in it have been amended. The Legislative Assembly consists of a Senate of 30 members, elected for four years (half their number retiring every two years), and a House of 60 representatives, elected for two years. The Governor is elected for four years. The constitution reserves to the voters the rights of initiative and referendum and recall.

For the 111th Congress, which convened in Jan. 2009, Oregon sends five members to the House of Representatives. It is represented in the Senate by Ron Wyden (D. 1996–2011) and Jeff Merkley (D. 2009–15).

The capital is Salem. There are 36 counties in the state.

RECENT ELECTIONS

In the 2008 presidential elections Barack Obama won Oregon with 56·7% of the vote (John Kerry won in 2004).

CURRENT ADMINISTRATION

Governor: Ted Kulongoski (D.), 2007–11 (salary: $93,600).
Secretary of State: Kate Brown (D.), 2009–13 ($72,000).

Government Website: http://www.oregon.gov

ECONOMY

Per capita income (2008) was $36,297.

Budget

In 2008 total state revenue was $17,138m. Total expenditure was $22,387m. (including: education, $6,768m.; public welfare, $4,311m.; highways, $1,529m.; hospitals, $1,154m.; government administration, $889m.) Outstanding debt in 2008, $11,647m.

Performance

Gross Domestic Product by state was $161,573m. in 2008 (provisional), ranking Oregon 26th in the United States.

ENERGY AND NATURAL RESOURCES

Water

The total area covered by water is approximately 2,384 sq. miles.

Minerals

Mineral resources include gold, silver, lead, mercury, chromite, sand and gravel, stone, clays, lime, silica, diatomite, expansible shale, scoria, pumice and uranium. There is geothermal potential. The total value of non-fuel mineral production in 2006 was $509m.

Agriculture

Oregon, which has an area of 61,557,184 acres, is divided by the Cascade Range into two distinct climate zones. West of the Cascade Range there is a good rainfall and almost every variety of crop common to the temperate zone is grown; east of the Range stock-raising and wheat-growing are the principal industries and irrigation is needed for row crops and fruits.

There were, in 2008, 38,600 farms with an acreage of 16·4m. and an average farm size of 425 acres; most are family-owned corporate farms. Average value per acre (2007), $1,890.

Farm income in 2006: from crops, $2,961m.; from livestock and products, $1,030m. The net farm income in 2006 was $876m. Principal crops in 2008: greenhouse and nursery products (estimate, $880·1m.), hay ($613·3m.), grass seed (estimate, $510·3m.), wheat ($340·2m.), potatoes ($211·0m.), Christmas trees (estimate, $122·8m.), onions ($97·5m.), pears ($92·5m.).

Livestock, 2009: cattle and calves, 1·24m. (including 115,000 milch cows); sheep and lambs, 220,000; goats, 38,000; hogs, 20,000 (2008).

Forestry

Oregon had 30,169,000 acres of forest in 2007, with 14,012,000 acres of national forest. In 2006 ownership was as follows (acres): US Forestry Service, 12·5m.; US Bureau of Land Management, 2·4m.; other federal, 338,000; State of Oregon, 969,000; tribal, 622,000; local government, 287,000; industrial private, 5·3m.; non-industrial private, 5·0m. Oregon's commercial forest lands provided an estimated 2007 harvest of 3·8bn. bd ft of logs, as well as the benefits of recreation, water, grazing, wildlife and fish. Trees vary from the coastal forest of hemlock and spruce to the state's primary species, Douglas-fir, throughout much of western Oregon. In eastern Oregon, ponderosa pine, lodgepole pine and true firs are found. Here, forestry is often combined with livestock grazing to provide an economic operation. Along the Cascade summit and in the mountains of northeast Oregon, alpine species are found.

Total covered payroll in the forestry and logging industry in 2008 was $515·2m.

Fisheries

Commercial fish and shellfish landings in 2008 was 260·3m. lb and amounted to a value of $126·5m. The most important are: ground fish, crab, shrimp, tuna, whiting and salmon.

INDUSTRY

Forest products manufacturing is Oregon's leading industry, followed by high technology. In 2005 the state's 5,559 manufacturing establishments had 185,000 employees, earning $7,988m. Total value added by manufacturing in 2006 was $39,502m.

Labour

Total non-agricultural employment, 2007, 1,732,000. Employees by branch, 2007 (in 1,000): trade, transportation and utilities, 340; government, 290; education and health services, 212; manufacturing, 204; professional and business services, 198. The unemployment rate was 5·2% in 2007.

COMMUNICATIONS

Roads

In 2007 there were 59,758 miles of road (46,975 miles rural). There were 3,088,313 registered vehicles in 2007.

Rail

In 2008 there were 2,388 total miles of active track and 22 federally franchised freight railroads. There is a light rail network in Portland.

Civil Aviation

In 2005 there were one public-use and 103 personal-use heliports; 251 personal-use and 95 public-use airports; and three sea-plane bases, two public-use and one personal-use. There were 8,294,811 passenger enplanements statewide in 2007.

Shipping

Portland is a major seaport for large ocean-going vessels and is 101 miles inland from the mouth of the Columbia River. In 2005 Portland handled 28,126,716 tons of cargo; Coos Bay, the second busiest port, handled 2,244,032 tons of cargo in 2005. Portland was the 29th busiest US port overall in 2005 but the eighth busiest for exports.

SOCIAL INSTITUTIONS

Justice

There are 14 correctional institutions in Oregon. In Dec. 2008 there were 14,167 federal and state prisoners. The sterilization law, originally passed in 1917, was amended in 1967 and abolished in 1993. Some categories of euthanasia were legalized in Dec. 1994.

The death penalty is authorized but there have been no executions since 2001.

Education

School attendance is compulsory from seven to 18 years of age if the twelfth year of school has not been completed; those between the ages of 16 and 18 years, if legally employed, may attend part-time or evening schools. Others may be excused under certain circumstances. In 2004–05 the 1,289 public elementary and secondary schools had 552,322 students and 27,431 teachers; average salary for teachers (2003–04), $49,169. Total expenditure on elementary and secondary education (2003–04) was $4,706m.

Leading state-supported institutions of higher education (fall 2005) included:

	Students
University of Oregon, Eugene	20,347
Oregon Health and Science University, Portland	2,511
Oregon State University, Corvallis	19,224
Portland State University, Portland	23,929
Western Oregon State College, Monmouth	4,872
Southern Oregon State College, Ashland	4,986
Eastern Oregon State College, La Grande	3,533
Oregon Institute of Technology, Klamath Falls	3,347

Total enrolment in the 26 public and 34 private colleges and universities, in fall 2005, was 200,033 students. Largest of the privately endowed universities are Lewis and Clark College, Portland, with 3,433 students; University of Portland, 3,415 students; Willamette University, Salem, 2,642 students; Reed College, Portland, 1,340 students; Linfield College, McMinnville, 1,750 students; Marylhurst College, 1,268 students; and George Fox College, Newberg, 3,267 students.

Health

In 2006 there were 58 community hospitals with 6,600 beds. A total of 341,000 patients were admitted during the year.

Welfare

Medicare enrolment in July 2004 totalled 524,336. In fiscal year 2006 a total of 516,067 people in Oregon received Medicaid. In Dec. 2008 there were 659,719 Old-Age, Survivors, and Disability Insurance (OASDI) beneficiaries. A total of 46,376 people were receiving payments under Temporary Assistance for Needy Families (TANF) in Dec. 2008.

RELIGION

The chief religious bodies are Catholic, Baptist, Lutheran, Methodist, Presbyterian and Latter-day Saints (Mormons).

CULTURE

Press

In 2009 there were 19 daily newspapers with a circulation of more than 610,000 and 74 non-daily newspapers.

Tourism

In 2005, 173,000 overseas visitors (excluding those from Mexico and Canada) visited Oregon.

FURTHER READING

Oregon Blue Book. Biennial

Conway, F. D. L., *Timber in Oregon: History and Projected Trends.* 1993
Friedman, R., *The Other Side of Oregon.* 1993
McArthur, L. A., *Oregon Geographic Names.* 7th ed. 2003
Orr, E. L., *et al.*, *Geology of Oregon.* 1992

State library: The Oregon State Library, 250 Winter St. NE, Salem 97301–3950.

Pennsylvania

KEY HISTORICAL EVENTS

Pennsylvania was occupied by four powerful tribes in the 17th century: Delaware, Susquehannock, Shawnee and Iroquois. The first white settlers were Swedish, arriving in 1643. The British became dominant in 1664 and in 1681 William Penn, an English Quaker, was given a charter to colonize the area as a sanctuary for his fellow Quakers. Penn's ideal was peaceful co-operation with the Indians and religious toleration within the colony. Several religious groups were attracted to Pennsylvania, including Protestant sects from Germany and France. In the 18th century, co-operation with the Indians failed as the settlers extended their territory.

The Declaration of Independence was signed in Philadelphia while Pennsylvania became one of the original 13 states of the Union. In 1812 the state capital was moved to its current location in Harrisburg, originally a trading post and ferry point on the Susquehanna River in the south-central part of the state. The Mason-Dixon line, the state's southern boundary, was the dividing line between free and slave states in the build-up to the Civil War. Gettysburg and other crucial battles were fought in the state. Industrial growth was rapid after the war. Pittsburgh, founded as a British fort in 1761 during war with the French, had become an iron-making town by 1800 and grew rapidly when canal and railway links opened in the 1830s. The American Federation of Labor was founded in Pittsburgh in 1881, by which time the city was of national importance producing coal, iron, steel and glass.

At the beginning of the 20th century, industry attracted immigration from Italy and eastern Europe. In farming areas the early sect communities survive, notably Amish and Mennonites. (The Pennsylvania 'Dutch' are of German extraction.)

TERRITORY AND POPULATION

Pennsylvania is bounded north by New York, east by New Jersey, south by Delaware and Maryland, southwest by West Virginia, west by Ohio and northwest by Lake Erie. Land area, 44,817 sq. miles (116,075 sq. km). Census population, 1 April 2000, 12,281,054, an increase of 3·4% since 1990. July 2009 estimate, 12,604,767.

Population at five census years was:

	White	*Black*	*Indian*	*All others*	*Total*	*Per sq. mile*
1910	7,467,713	193,919	1,503	1,976	7,665,111	171·0
1930	9,196,007	431,257	523	3,563	9,631,350	214·8
			All others			
1980	10,652,320	1,046,810	164,765		11,863,895	264·7
1990	10,520,201	1,089,795	271,647		11,881,643	265·1
2000	10,484,203	1,224,612	572,239		12,281,054	274·0

Of the total population in 2000, 6,351,391 were female, 9,358,833 were 18 years old or older and 9,464,101 were urban. In 2000 Pennsylvania's Hispanic population was 394,088, up from 232,262 in 1990 (a rise of 69·7%).

The population of the largest cities and townships, 2000 census, was:

Philadelphia	1,517,550	Reading	81,207
Pittsburgh	334,563	Scranton	76,415
Allentown	106,632	Bethlehem	71,329
Erie	103,717	Lower Merion	59,850
Upper Darby	81,821	Bensalem	58,434

The Philadelphia–Wilmington–Atlantic City metropolitan area had a 2000 census population of 6,188,463.

SOCIAL STATISTICS

Births, 2007 (provisional), 149,970 (12·1 per 1,000 population); deaths, 2006, 125,539 (10·1). Infant mortality, 2006, 7·6 per 1,000 live births. 2006: marriages, 68,600 (5·5 per 1,000 population); divorces and annulments, 27,400 (2·2).

CLIMATE

Philadelphia, Jan. 32°F (0°C), July 77°F (25°C). Annual rainfall 40" (1,006 mm). Pittsburgh, Jan. 31°F (–0·6°C), July 74°F (23·3°C). Annual rainfall 37" (914 mm). Pennsylvania belongs to the Appalachian Mountains climate zone (*see* UNITED STATES: Climate).

CONSTITUTION AND GOVERNMENT

The present constitution dates from 1968. The General Assembly consists of a Senate of 50 members chosen for four years, one-half being elected biennially, and a House of Representatives of 203 members chosen for two years. The Governor and Lieut.-Governor are elected for four years. Every citizen 18 years of age, with the usual residential qualifications, may vote. Registered voters in Nov. 2004, 8,366,663.

For the 111th Congress, which convened in Jan. 2009, Pennsylvania sends 19 members to the House of Representatives. It is represented in the Senate by Arlen Specter (D. 1981–2011) and Robert Casey, Jr (D. 2007–13). In April 2009 Specter, then a Republican, announced that he was changing parties and that he would be running as a Democrat candidate in the Senate election of Nov. 2010.

The state capital is Harrisburg. The state is organized in counties (numbering 67), cities, boroughs, townships and school districts.

RECENT ELECTIONS

In the 2008 presidential elections Barack Obama won Pennsylvania with 54·3% of the vote (John Kerry won in 2004).

CURRENT ADMINISTRATION

Governor: Edward G. Rendell (D.), 2007–11 (salary: $174,914).

Lieut.-Governor: Joseph B. Scarnati (R.), 2008–11 ($146,926).

Secretary of the Commonwealth: Pedro A. Cortés (D.), appointed 2003 ($125,939).

Government Website: http://www.pa.gov

ECONOMY

Per capita income (2008) was $40,140.

Budget

In 2008 total state revenue was $71,492m. Total expenditure was $71,940m. (including: education, $19,199m.; public welfare, $19,033m.; highways, $6,570m.; hospitals, $2,821m.; government administration, $2,508m.) Outstanding debt in 2008, $40,672m.

Performance

Gross Domestic Product by state in 2008 was $553,301m. (provisional), ranking Pennsylvania 6th in the United States.

ENERGY AND NATURAL RESOURCES

Oil and Gas

2006 production: crude petroleum, 4m. bbls; natural gas, 158bn. cu. ft.

Water

The total area covered by water is approximately 1,239 sq. miles.

Minerals

Pennsylvania is almost the sole producer of anthracite coal. Production, 2002: industrial minerals (shale, limestone, sandstone, clay, dolomite, sand and gravel), 139,072,832 tons; bituminous coal, 70,044,685 tons; anthracite coal, 4,262,856 tons. Non-fuel mineral production was worth $1,710m. in 2006.

Agriculture

Agriculture, market-gardening, fruit-growing, horticulture and forestry are pursued within the state. In 2002 there were 59,000 farms with a total farm area of 7·7m. acres. Average number of acres per farm in 2002 was 131 and the average value per acre was $3,419. Cash receipts, 2006: from crops, $1,723m.; and from livestock and products, $2,968m. The net farm income in 2006 was $1,516m.

In 2002 Pennsylvania ranked first in the production of mushrooms (459·6m. lb, value $390·3m.). Other production figures include (2001): corn for grain (97m. bu., value $223·2m.); sweet corn (701,000 cwt, value $18·58m.) and tomatoes (537,000 cwt, value $19·65m.). Pennsylvania is also a major fruit producing state. In 2002 apples totalled 370m. lb (value $37·2m.); peaches, 60m. lb (value $19·8m.); and grapes, 53·2m. tons (value $14·9m.). Pennsylvania ranked fourth in milk production in 2002 with 10,780m. lb (6·3% of US milk production). Egg production totalled 6,520m., value $279·3m.; chicken production (excluding broilers) was 29·3m., value $52·7m.; and production of broilers was 133·2m., value $225·9m. Other products included turkey (9·9m. poults, value $91·1m.) and cheese (374m. lb).

In 2002 there were on farms: 1·63m. cattle and calves, 102,890 sheep, and 1·23m. hogs and swine.

Forestry

In 2007 the total forested area was 16,577,000 acres, of which 497,000 acres were national forest. In 2009 state forest land totalled 2,145,804 acres; state park land, 274,105 acres; state game land, 1,400,000 acres.

INDUSTRY

In 2005 the state's 15,624 manufacturing establishments had 664,000 employees, earning $28,644m. Total value added by manufacturing in 2006 was $112,486m.

Labour

Total non-agricultural employment, 2007, 5,796,000. Employees by branch, 2007 (in 1,000): trade, transportation and utilities, 1,135; education and health services, 1,074; government, 744; professional and business services, 704; manufacturing, 658. The unemployment rate in 2007 was 4·3%.

COMMUNICATIONS

Roads

In 2007 highways and roads in the state (federal, local and state combined) totalled 121,581 miles (76,451 miles rural). Registered motor vehicles numbered 9,937,941.

Rail

In 2002 there were 6,967 miles of freight railroad in operation, including 3,649 miles of Class I railroads. There are metro, light rail and tramway networks in Philadelphia and Pittsburgh, and commuter networks around Philadelphia.

Civil Aviation

In June 2004 there were 467 public and private airports and 317 heliports in operation. There were 22,179,686 passenger enplanements statewide in 2007.

Shipping

The major ports are Pittsburgh, Philadelphia, Marcus Hook, Penn Manor, Chester and Erie. In 2001 waterborne imports totalled 46,590,000 short tons of cargo (including 33,920,000 short tons by tanker), and exports 718,700 short tons.

SOCIAL INSTITUTIONS

Justice

The death penalty is authorized. The last execution was in 1999. There were 50,147 prisoners in state correctional institutions in Dec. 2008, up 9·1% from 45,969 in Dec. 2007—the largest rise in any state over the same period.

Education

School attendance is compulsory for children eight to 17 years of age. In 2002–03 there were 3,264 public elementary and secondary schools with 1,816,747 pupils and 118,256 teachers; total expenditure on public schools was $17,888m. Teachers' salaries averaged $51,428 in 2003.

Leading senior academic institutions include:

Founded	*Institutions*	*Faculty*[1] *(fall 2003)*	*Students*[2] *(fall 2004)*
1740	University of Pennsylvania (non-sect.)	8,416	23,305
1787	University of Pittsburgh (all campuses)	7,402	33,796
1832	Lafayette College, Easton (Presbyterian)	240	2,303
1833	Haverford College	132	1,172
1842	Villanova University (R.C.)	1,158	10,610
1846	Bucknell University (Baptist)	319	3,609
1851	St Joseph's University, Philadelphia (R.C.)	565	7,730
1852	California University of Pennsylvania	491	6,640
1855	Pennsylvania State University (all campuses)	11,405	74,667
1855	Millersville University of Pennsylvania	457	7,998
1863	LaSalle University, Philadelphia (R.C.)	468	6,194
1864	Swarthmore College	230	1,474
1866	Lehigh University, Bethlehem (non-sect.)	1,089	6,641
1871	West Chester University of Pennsylvania	844	12,822
1875	Indiana University of Pennsylvania	1,097	13,998
1878	Duquesne University, Pittsburgh (R.C.)	1,321	9,722
1884	Temple University, Philadelphia	3,703	33,551
1885	Bryn Mawr College	285	1,772
1888	University of Scranton (R.C.)	478	4,795
1891	Drexel University, Philadelphia	2,262	17,656
1900	Carnegie-Mellon University, Pittsburgh	2,884	9,803

[1]Includes full-time and part-time.
[2]Includes undergraduate, graduate and first professional students.

Health

In 2006 there were 188 community hospitals with 39,500 beds. A total of 1,866,000 patients were admitted during the year.

Welfare

Medicare enrolment in July 2004 totalled 2,119,566. In fiscal year 2006 a total of 2,064,061 people in Pennsylvania received Medicaid. In Dec. 2008 there were 2,481,695 Old-Age, Survivors, and Disability Insurance (OASDI) beneficiaries. A total of 112,592 people were receiving payments under Temporary Assistance for Needy Families (TANF) in Dec. 2008.

RELIGION

The principal religious bodies in 2000 were the Roman Catholics (3,802,524 members), Protestants (2,890,130) and Jews (283,000). The five largest Protestant denominations by adherents were the United Methodist Church (659,350), the Evangelical Lutheran Church in America (611,913), the Presbyterian Church (USA) (324,714), the United Church of Christ (241,844) and the American Baptist Church (132,858).

CULTURE

Tourism

In 2005, 629,000 overseas visitors (excluding those from Mexico and Canada) visited Pennsylvania.

FURTHER READING

Statistical information: Pennsylvania State Data Center, 777 West Harrisburg Pike, Middletown 17057. Publishes *Pennsylvania Statistical Abstract.*

Downey, D. B. and Bremer, F. (eds.) *Guide to the History of Pennsylvania.* 1994

Rhode Island

KEY HISTORICAL EVENTS

The earliest white settlement was founded by Roger Williams, an English Puritan who was expelled from Massachusetts because of his dissident religious views and his insistence on the land-rights of the Indians. At Providence he bought land from the Narragansetts and founded a colony there in 1636. A charter was granted in 1663. Religious toleration attracted Jewish and nonconformist settlers; later there was French Canadian settlement.

Shipping and fishing developed strongly, especially at Newport and Providence. These two cities were twin capitals until 1900, when the capital was fixed at Providence.

Significant actions took place in Rhode Island during the War of Independence. In 1790 the state accepted the federal constitution and was admitted to the Union.

Early farming development was most successful in dairying and poultry. Early industrialization from the 1790s was mainly in textiles. Thriving on abundant water power, the industry began to decline after the First World War. British, Irish, Polish, Italian and Portuguese workers settled in the state, working in the mills or in the shipbuilding, shipping, fishing and naval ports. The growth of the cities led to the abolition of the property qualification for the franchise in 1888.

TERRITORY AND POPULATION

Rhode Island is bounded north and east by Massachusetts, south by the Atlantic and west by Connecticut. Land area, 1,045 sq. miles (2,707 sq. km). Census population, 1 April 2000, 1,048,319, an increase of 4·5% since 1990. July 2009 estimate, 1,053,209. Rhode Island was one of three states where the population fell between July 2008 and July 2009 (the others being Maine and Michigan).

Population of five census years was:

	White	*Black*	*Indian*	*Asiatic*	*Total*	*Per sq. mile*
1910	532,492	9,529	284	305	542,610	508·5
1930	677,026	9,913	318	240	687,497	649·3
			All others			
1980	896,692	27,584	22,878		947,154	903·0
1990	917,375	38,861	4,071	18,325	1,003,164	960·3
2000	891,191	46,908	5,121	24,232	1,048,319	1,003·2

Of the total population in 2000, 554,684 were female, 800,497 were 18 years old or older and 953,146 were urban (90·92%). In 2000 the Hispanic population was 90,820, up from 45,752 in 1990 (an increase of 98·5%).

The chief cities and their population (census, 2000) are Providence, 173,618; Warwick, 85,808; Cranston, 79,269; Pawtucket, 72,958; East Providence, 48,688.

SOCIAL STATISTICS

Births, 2007 (provisional), 12,503 (11·8 per 1,000 population); deaths, 2006, 9,690 (9·1). Infant mortality rate, 2006, 6·1 per 1,000 live births. 2006: marriages, 6,900 (6·5 per 1,000 population); divorces and annulments, 3,100 (2·9).

CLIMATE

Providence, Jan. 28°F (–2·2°C), July 72°F (22·2°C). Annual rainfall 43" (1,079 mm). Rhode Island belongs to the New England climate zone (*see* UNITED STATES: Climate).

CONSTITUTION AND GOVERNMENT

The present constitution dates from 1843; it has had 62 amendments. The General Assembly consists of a Senate of 38 members and a House of Representatives of 75 members, both elected for two years. The Governor and Lieut.-Governor are now elected for four years. Every citizen, 18 years of age, who has resided in the state for 30 days, and is duly registered, is qualified to vote.

For the 111th Congress, which convened in Jan. 2009, Rhode Island sends two members to the House of Representatives. It is represented in the Senate by Jack Reed (D. 1997–2015) and Sheldon Whitehouse (D. 2007–13).

The capital is Providence. The state has five counties but no county governments. There are 39 municipalities, each having its own form of local government.

RECENT ELECTIONS

In the 2008 presidential elections Barack Obama won Rhode Island with 63·1% of the vote (John Kerry won in 2004).

CURRENT ADMINISTRATION

Governor: Donald L. Carcieri (R.), 2007–11 (salary: $117,817).

Lieut.-Governor: Elizabeth H. Roberts (D.), 2007–11 ($102,584).

Secretary of State: A. Ralph Mollis (D.), 2007–11 ($105,167).

Government Website: http://www.ri.gov

ECONOMY

Per capita income (2008) was $41,368.

Budget

In 2008 total state revenue was $6,691m. Total expenditure was $7,496m. (including: public welfare, $2,231m.; education, $1,703m.; government administration, $362m.; highways, $202m.; correction, $199m.) Outstanding debt in 2008, $8,912m.

Performance

Gross Domestic Product in 2008 was $47,364m. (provisional), ranking Rhode Island 45th in the United States.

ENERGY AND NATURAL RESOURCES

Water

The total area covered by water is approximately 500 sq. miles.

Minerals

The small non-fuel mineral output—mostly stone, sand and gravel—was valued at $44m. in 2006.

Agriculture

In 2002 there were 700 farms with an area of 60,000 acres. The average size of a farm was 86 acres. In 2002 the average value of land and buildings per acre was $9,225. Farm income 2006: from crops, $56m.; livestock and products, $10m. The net farm income in 2006 was $26m. Principal commodities are greenhouse products, dairy products, sweetcorn and aquaculture.

Forestry

Total forested area was 356,000 acres in 2007.

Fisheries

In 2002 the commercial catch was 103·7m. lb (mainly lobster and quahog) valued at $64·3m.

INDUSTRY

Manufacturing is the chief source of income and the largest employer. Principal industries are jewellery and silverware, electrical machinery, electronics, plastics, metal products, instruments, chemicals and boat building. In 2005 the state's 1,956 manufacturing establishments had 59,000 employees, earning $2,367m. Total value added by manufacturing in 2006 was $7,824m.

Labour

In 2007 total non-agricultural employment was 493,000. Employees by branch, 2007 (in 1,000): education and health services, 99; trade, transportation and utilities, 80; government, 65; professional and business services, 56; leisure and hospitality, 51; manufacturing, 51. The unemployment rate in 2007 was 4·9%.

COMMUNICATIONS

Roads

In 2007 there were 6,510 miles of roads (5,240 miles urban). There were 796,683 registered motor vehicles.

Rail

Amtrak's New York-Boston route runs through the state, serving Providence.

Civil Aviation

In 2004 there were six state-owned airports. Theodore Francis Green airport at Warwick, near Providence, is served by 13 airlines, and handled 5·5m. passengers in 2004. There were 2,518,749 passenger enplanements statewide in 2007.

Shipping

Waterborne freight through the port of Providence (2003) totalled 9·2m. short tons.

SOCIAL INSTITUTIONS

Justice

In Dec. 2008 the jail and prison population totalled 4,045. The death penalty was abolished in 1852, except that it is mandatory in the case of murder committed by a prisoner serving a life sentence.

Education

In 2004–05 there were 156,498 pupils attending 342 public elementary and secondary schools with 11,898 teachers. In 2003–04, 28,119 pupils were enrolled in 139 private schools which had 2,563 teachers. Total expenditure on elementary and secondary education in 2003–04 was $1,838m. Spending per pupil (2002–03) was $10,349.

There were 14 institutions of higher education (three public and 11 private) in fall 2005. The state maintained Rhode Island College, Providence, with 8,871 students; the University of Rhode Island, Kingston, with 15,095; and the Community College of Rhode Island, Warwick, with 16,042. Among the private institutions, Brown University at Providence, founded in 1764, had 8,261 students; Providence College at Providence, founded in 1917, by the Dominican Order of Preachers, had 5,457 students; Bryant University at Smithfield had 3,642 students; Rhode Island School of Design in Providence had 2,258 students; and Johnson and Wales University in Providence had 10,171 students.

Health
In 2006 there were 11 community hospitals with 2,300 beds. A total of 127,000 patients were admitted during the year.

Welfare
Medicare enrolment in July 2004 totalled 172,897. In fiscal year 2006 a total of 212,491 people in Rhode Island received Medicaid. In Dec. 2008 there were 196,161 Old-Age, Survivors, and Disability Insurance (OASDI) beneficiaries. A total of 18,488 people were receiving payments under Temporary Assistance for Needy Families (TANF) in Dec. 2008.

RELIGION
Chief religious bodies are Roman Catholic, Protestant Episcopal (baptized persons), Jewish, Baptist, Congregational and Methodist.

FURTHER READING
Statistical information: Rhode Island Economic Development Corporation, 1 West Exchange Street, Providence, RI 02903. Publishes *Rhode Island Basic Economic Statistics.*
Rhode Island Manual.

Wright, M. I. and Sullivan, R. J., *Rhode Island Atlas.* 1983

State library: Rhode Island State Library, State House, Providence 02908.

South Carolina

KEY HISTORICAL EVENTS
Originally the territory of Yamasee Indians, the area attracted French and Spanish explorers in the 16th century. There were attempts at settlement on the coast, none of which lasted. Charles I of England made a land grant in 1629 but the first permanent white settlement began at Charles Town in 1670, moving to Charleston in 1680. This was a proprietorial colony including North Carolina until 1712; both passed to the Crown in 1729.

The coastlands developed as plantations worked by slave labour. In the hills there were small farming settlements and many trading posts, dealing with Indian suppliers.

After active campaigns during the War of Independence, South Carolina became one of the original states of the Union in 1788.

In 1793 the cotton gin was invented, enabling the speedy mechanical separation of seed and fibre. This made it possible to grow huge areas of cotton and meet the rapidly-growing needs of new textile industries. Plantation farming spread widely and South Carolina became hostile to the anti-slavery campaign which was strong in northern states. The state first attempted to secede from the Union in 1847, but was not supported by other southern states until 1860, when secession led to civil war.

At that time the population was about 703,000, of whom 413,000 were black. During the reconstruction periods there was some political power for black citizens but control was back in white hands by 1876. The constitution was amended in 1895 to disenfranchise most black voters and they remained with hardly any voice in government until the Civil Rights movement of the 1960s. Columbia became the capital in 1786.

TERRITORY AND POPULATION
South Carolina is bounded in the north by North Carolina, east and southeast by the Atlantic, southwest and west by Georgia. Land area, 30,110 sq. miles (77,982 sq. km). Census population, 1 April 2000, 4,012,012, an increase of 15·1% since 1990. July 2009 estimate, 4,561,242.

The population in five census years was:

	White	*Black*	*Indian*	*Asiatic*	*Total*	*Per sq. mile*
1910	679,161	835,843	331	65	1,515,400	49·7
1930	944,049	793,681	959	76	1,738,765	56·8
			All others			
1980	2,150,507	948,623	22,703		3,121,833	100·3
1990	2,406,974	1,039,884	39,845		3,486,703	115·8
2000	2,695,560	1,185,216	131,236		4,012,012	133·2

Of the total population in 2000, 2,063,083 were female, 3,002,371 were 18 years old or older and 2,427,124 were urban. In 2000 the Hispanic population of South Carolina was 95,076, up from 30,551 in 1990 (an increase of 211·2%).

Population estimate of large towns in 2005: Columbia (capital), 117,088; Charleston, 106,712; North Charleston, 86,313; Rock Hill, 59,554; Mount Pleasant, 57,932; Greenville, 56,676.

SOCIAL STATISTICS
Births, 2007 (provisional), 62,851 (14·3 per 1,000 population); deaths, 2006, 38,761 (9·0). Infant deaths, 2006, 8·4 per 1,000 live births. 2006: marriages, 32,800 (7·6 per 1,000 population); divorces and annulments, 12,800 (3·0).

CLIMATE
Columbia, Jan. 44·7°F (7°C), Aug. 80·2°F (26·9°C). Annual rainfall 49·12" (1,247·6 mm). South Carolina belongs to the Atlantic Coast climate zone (*see* UNITED STATES: Climate).

CONSTITUTION AND GOVERNMENT
The present constitution dates from 1895, when it went into force without ratification by the electorate. The General Assembly consists of a Senate of 46 members, elected for four years, and a House of Representatives of 124 members, elected for two years. It meets annually. The Governor and Lieut.-Governor are elected for four years.

For the 111th Congress, which convened in Jan. 2009, South Carolina sends six members to the House of Representatives. It is represented in the Senate by Lindsey Graham (R. 2003–15) and Jim DeMint (R. 2005–11).

The capital is Columbia. There are 46 counties.

RECENT ELECTIONS
In the 2008 presidential elections John McCain won South Carolina with 53·9% of the vote (George W. Bush won in 2004).

CURRENT ADMINISTRATION
Governor: Mark Sanford, Jr (R.), 2007–11 (salary: $106,078).
Lieut.-Governor: André Bauer (R.), 2007–11 ($46,545).
Secretary of State: Mark Hammond (R.), 2007–11 ($92,007).

Government Website: http://www.sc.gov

ECONOMY
Per capita income (2008) was $32,666.

Budget
In 2008 total state revenue was $23,595m. Total expenditure was $27,594m. (including: education, $8,151m.; public welfare, $5,478m.; hospitals, $1,685m.; government administration, $1,095m.; highways, $1,065m.) Outstanding debt in 2008, $15,213m.

Performance
Gross Domestic Product by state was $156,384m. in 2008 (provisional), ranking South Carolina 28th in the United States.

ENERGY AND NATURAL RESOURCES

Water
The total area covered by water is approximately 1,911 sq. miles.

Minerals
Gold is found, though non-metallic minerals are of chief importance: value of non-fuel mineral output in 2006 was $735m., chiefly from cement (Portland), stone and gold. Production of kaolin, vermiculite and scrap mica is also important.

Agriculture
In 2002 there were 24,500 farms covering a farm area of 4·8m. acres. The average farm was of 196 acres. The average value of farmland and buildings per acre was $2,067 in 2002.

Farm income, 2006: from crops, $788m.; from livestock and products, $1,103m. The net farm income in 2006 was $722m. Chief crops are tobacco, soybeans, wheat, cotton, peanuts and corn. Production, 2002: cotton, 131,000 bales; peanuts, 19·14m. lb; soybeans, 7·1m. bu.; tobacco, 55·5m. lb; corn, 11·96m. bu.; wheat, 7·03m. bu. Livestock on farms, 2002: 432,300 all cattle, 291,700 swine.

Forestry
The forest industry is important; total forest land (2007), 12·75m. acres. National forests amounted to 641,000 acres.

INDUSTRY
In 2005 the state's 4,289 manufacturing establishments had 271,000 employees, earning $10,959m. Total value added by manufacturing in 2006 was $37,953m.

Labour
Total non-agricultural employment, 2007, 1,950,000. Employees by branch, 2007 (in 1,000): trade, transportation and utilities, 377; government, 338; manufacturing, 250; professional and business services, 227; leisure and hospitality, 218. The unemployment rate in 2007 was 5·6%.

COMMUNICATIONS

Roads
In 2007 there were 66,248 miles of road comprising 16,422 miles of urban road and 49,826 miles of rural road. There were 3,521,026 registered motor vehicles.

Rail
In 2005 there were 2,283 miles of freight railroad, including 1,959 miles of Class I railroads.

Civil Aviation
In 2005 there were 68 public-use airports and 30 heliports. There were 3,471,352 passenger enplanements statewide in 2007.

Shipping
The state has three deep-water ports.

SOCIAL INSTITUTIONS

Justice
In Dec. 2008 there were 24,326 federal and state prisoners. The death penalty is authorized. There were two executions in 2009.

Education
In 2004–05 there were 703,736 pupils and 46,914 teachers in 1,172 public schools. Total expenditure on public elementary and secondary education in 2003–04 was $5,916m. and average teaching salary was $41,162. Spending per pupil in 2002–03 was $7,040. In 2003–04 there were 345 private schools with total enrolment of 58,005 pupils and 5,339 teachers.

For higher education the state operates the University of South Carolina (USC), founded at Columbia in 1801, with (fall 2005) 27,065 enrolled students; USC Aiken, with 3,303 students; USC Spartanburg, with 4,484 students; Clemson University, founded in 1889, with 17,165 students; Citadel Military College at Charleston with 3,386 students; Winthrop University, Rock Hill, with 6,480 students; Medical University of South Carolina, at Charleston, with 2,499 students; South Carolina State University, at Orangeburg, with 4,446 students; Francis Marion University, at Florence, with 4,008 students; the College of Charleston with 11,332 students; and Lander University, at Greenwood, with 2,703 students.

Health
In 2006 there were 66 community hospitals with 11,700 beds. A total of 521,000 patients were admitted during the year.

Welfare
Medicare enrolment in July 2004 totalled 623,547. In fiscal year 2006 a total of 861,838 people in South Carolina received Medicaid. In Dec. 2008 there were 850,368 Old-Age, Survivors, and Disability Insurance (OASDI) beneficiaries. A total of 39,081 people were receiving payments under Temporary Assistance for Needy Families (TANF) in Dec. 2008.

RELIGION
Chief religious bodies (2000) were Southern Baptists, with 928,341 members, United Methodists (302,528), Roman Catholics (136,719), Presbyterian Church (USA) (103,883) and the Evangelical Lutheran Church in America (61,380).

FURTHER READING
Statistical information: Budget and Control Board, R. C. Dennis Bldg, Columbia 29201. Publishes *South Carolina Statistical Abstract.*

South Carolina Legislative Manual. Annual

Edgar, W. B., *South Carolina in the Modern Age.* 1992

Graham, C. B. and Moore, W. V., *South Carolina Politics and Government.* 1995

State library: South Carolina State Library, Columbia.

South Dakota

KEY HISTORICAL EVENTS
The area was part of the hunting grounds of nomadic Dakota (Sioux) Indians. French explorers visited the site of Fort Pierre in 1742–43 and claimed the area for France. In 1763 the claim, together with French claims to all land west of the Mississippi, passed to Spain. Spain held the Dakotas until defeated by France in the Napoleonic Wars when France regained the area and sold it to the USA as part of the Louisiana Purchase in 1803.

Fur-traders were active but there was no settlement until Fort Randall was founded on the Missouri river in 1856. In 1861 North and South Dakota were united as the Dakota Territory. The Homestead Act of 1862 stimulated settlement, mainly in the southeast until there was a gold-rush in the Black Hills of the west in 1875–76. Colonization was by farming communities in the east with miners and ranchers in the west. Livestock farming predominated, attracting European settlers from Scandinavia, Germany and Russia.

In 1889 the North and South were separated and admitted to the Union as states. Pierre, founded as a railhead in 1880, was confirmed as the capital in 1904. It faces Fort Pierre, the former centre of the fur trade, across the Missouri river. During the 20th century there have been schemes to exploit the Missouri for power and irrigation.

TERRITORY AND POPULATION

South Dakota is bounded in the north by North Dakota, east by Minnesota, southeast by the Big Sioux River (forming the boundary with Iowa), south by Nebraska (with the Missouri River forming part of the boundary) and west by Wyoming and Montana. Land area, 75,885 sq. miles (196,541 sq. km). In 2000 American Indian lands covered 14,966 sq. miles (14,061 sq. miles in reservations and 905 sq. miles in off-reservation trust land). The federal government, 2003, owned 2,314,006 acres.

Census population, 1 April 2000, 754,844, an increase of 8·5% since 1990. July 2009 estimate, 812,383.

Population in five federal censuses was:

	White	*Black*	*American Indian*	*Asiatic*	*Total*	*Per sq. mile*
1910	563,771	817	19,137	163	583,888	7·6
1930	669,453	646	21,833	101	692,849	9·0
			All others			
1980	638,955	2,144	49,079		690,178	9·0
				Asian/ other		
1990	637,515	3,258	50,575	4,656	696,004	9·2
2000	669,404	4,685	62,283	18,472	754,844	9·9

Of the total population in 2000, 380,286 were female, 552,195 were 18 years old or older and 391,427 were urban. In 2000 the Hispanic population was 10,903, up from 5,252 in 1990 (an increase of 107·6%).

Population of the chief cities (census of 2000) was: Sioux Falls, 123,975; Rapid City, 59,607; Aberdeen, 24,658; Watertown, 20,237; Brookings, 18,507; Mitchell, 14,558; Pierre, 13,876; Yankton, 13,528; Huron, 11,893; Vermillion, 9,765; Spearfish, 8,606; Madison, 6,540; Sturgis, 6,442.

SOCIAL STATISTICS

Births, 2007 (provisional), 12,344 (15·5 per 1,000 population); deaths, 2006, 7,084 (9·1). Infant mortality, 2006, 6·9 per 1,000 live births. 2006: marriages, 6,300 (8·0 per 1,000 population); divorces and annulments, 2,500 (3·2).

CLIMATE

Rapid City, Jan. 25°F (–3·9°C), July 73°F (22·8°C). Annual rainfall 19" (474 mm). Sioux Falls, Jan. 14°F (–10°C), July 73°F (22·8°C). Annual rainfall 25" (625 mm). South Dakota belongs to the High Plains climate zone (*see* UNITED STATES: Climate).

CONSTITUTION AND GOVERNMENT

Voters are all citizens 18 years of age or older. The people reserve the right of the initiative and referendum. The Senate has 35 members, and the House of Representatives 70 members, all elected for two years; the Governor and Lieut.-Governor are elected for four years.

For the 111th Congress, which convened in Jan. 2009, South Dakota sends one member to the House of Representatives. It is represented in the Senate by Tim Johnson (D. 1997–2015) and John Thune (R. 2005–11).

The capital is Pierre. The state is divided into 66 organized counties.

RECENT ELECTIONS

In the 2008 presidential elections John McCain won South Dakota with 53·2% of the vote (George W. Bush won in 2004).

CURRENT ADMINISTRATION

Governor: Michael Rounds (R.), 2007–11 (salary: $115,331).

Lieut.-Governor: Dennis Daugaard (R.), 2007–11 ($17,699; part-time).

Secretary of State: Chris Nelson (R.), 2007–11 ($78,363).

Government Website: http://www.sd.gov

ECONOMY

Per capita income (2008) was $38,661.

Budget

In 2008 total state revenue was $2,910m. Total expenditure was $3,698m. (education, $1,104m.; public welfare, $812m.; highways, $430m.; government administration, $169m.; health, $126m.) Outstanding debt in 2008, $3,408m.

Performance

Gross Domestic Product by state in 2008 was $36,959m. (provisional), ranking South Dakota 46th in the United States.

ENERGY AND NATURAL RESOURCES

Water

The total area covered by water is approximately 1,232 sq. miles.

Minerals

Following the national trend, gold production has continued to decline, falling from 389,875 oz in 1998 to 78,805 oz by 2003. Gross value has fallen in the same period from $115m. to $29m. In 2004 sand and gravel was the major non-metallic industrial mineral commodity with 14·0m. tonnes produced. Other major minerals were: Sioux quartzite (3·2m. tonnes); limestone (2·0m.); clays (188,000). Value of non-fuel mineral production in 2006 was $223m.

Agriculture

In 2002 there were 32,500 farms with an acreage of 44m. and an average farm size of 1,354 acres. Average value of farmland and buildings per acre in 2002 was $442. Farm income, 2006: from crops, $2,065m.; from livestock and products, $2,652m. The net farm income in 2006 was $742m.

In 2002 South Dakota was a major producer of oats (5·7m. bu.), rye (672,000 bu.) and sunflower oil (303·2m. lb). The other important crops were corn for grain (295·2m. bu.), soybeans (126·6m. bu.), spring wheat (23·5m. bu.), winter wheat (18·8m. bu.), sorghum for grain (2·4m. bu.), barley (1·1m. bu.) and durum wheat (127,822 bu.). Total planted area of cropland was 20·3m. acres with 13·5m. being harvested.

The farm livestock in 2002 included 3·9m. cattle; 376,500 sheep and lambs; and 1·4m. hogs. In 2002, 11·5m. lb of honey were produced.

Forestry

South Dakota had 1,682,000 acres of forested land in 2007, of which 1,039,000 acres were national forest.

INDUSTRY

In 2005 the state's 964 manufacturing establishments had 39,000 employees, earning $1,314m. Total value added by manufacturing in 2006 was $5,381m.

Labour

Total non-agricultural employment, 2007, 406,000. Employees by branch, 2007 (in 1,000): trade, transportation and utilities, 82; government, 76; education and health services, 60; leisure and hospitality, 43; manufacturing, 42. The state unemployment rate in 2007 was 2·9%.

COMMUNICATIONS

Roads

In 2007 there were 83,744 miles of road comprising 2,878 miles of urban road and 80,866 miles of rural road. There were 864,838 registered vehicles.

Rail

In 2003 there were 1,839·5 miles of track.

Civil Aviation

In 2005 there were 75 public-use airports and 33 heliports. There were 682,039 passenger enplanements statewide in 2007.

SOCIAL INSTITUTIONS

Justice

In Dec. 2008 there were 3,342 adults in state prisons. The death penalty is authorized and was used in 2007 for the first time in 60 years, although it has not been used again since.

Education

School attendance is compulsory between the ages of six and 18 (since 1 July 2009—previously school attendance had only been compulsory to 16). In 2004–05 there were 122,798 pupils at 722 public schools with 9,064 teachers. In 2003–04 the 95 private schools had 10,817 pupils and 922 teachers. Public school teacher salaries in 2003–04 averaged $33,236. Total expenditure on public elementary and secondary education in 2003–04 was $996m. Spending per pupil (2002–03) was $6,547.

Higher (public) education in fall 2005: the School of Mines at Rapid City, established 1885, had 2,313 students; South Dakota State University at Brookings, 10,938; the University of South Dakota, founded at Vermillion in 1882, 8,641; Northern State University, Aberdeen, 2,631; Black Hills State University at Spearfish, 3,919; and Dakota State University at Madison, 2,319. There were 11,110 students at 12 private colleges in fall 2004.

Health

In 2006 there were 52 community hospitals with 4,300 beds. A total of 96,000 patients were admitted during the year.

Welfare

Medicare enrolment in July 2004 totalled 122,991. In fiscal year 2006 a total of 130,509 people in South Dakota received Medicaid. In Dec. 2008 there were 146,991 Old-Age, Survivors, and Disability Insurance (OASDI) beneficiaries. A total of 6,129 people were receiving payments under Temporary Assistance for Needy Families (TANF) in Dec. 2008.

RELIGION

The chief religious bodies are: Lutherans, Roman Catholics, Methodists, United Church of Christ, Presbyterians, Baptists and Episcopalians.

FURTHER READING

Statistical information: State Data Center, Univ. of South Dakota, Vermillion 57069.

Governor's Budget Report. South Dakota Bureau of Finance and Management. Annual

South Dakota Historical Collections. 1902–82

South Dakota Legislative Manual. Biennial

Berg, F. M., *South Dakota: Land of Shining Gold.* 1982

State library: South Dakota State Library, 800 Governor's Drive, Pierre, S.D. 57501–2294.

Tennessee

KEY HISTORICAL EVENTS

Bordered on the west by the Mississippi, Tennessee was part of an area inhabited by Cherokee. French, Spanish and British explorers navigated the Mississippi to trade with the Cherokee in the late 16th and 17th centuries. French claims were abandoned in 1763. Colonists from the British colonies of Virginia and Carolina then began to cross the Appalachians westwards, but there was no organized Territory until after the War of Independence. In 1784 there was a short-lived, independent state called Franklin. In 1790 the South West Territory (including Tennessee) was formed and Tennessee entered the Union as a state in 1796.

The state was active in the war against Britain in 1812. After the American victory, colonization increased and pressure for land mounted. The Cherokee were forcibly removed during the 1830s and taken to Oklahoma, a journey on which many died.

Tennessee was a slave state and seceded from the Union in 1861, although eastern Tennessee was against secession. There were important battles at Shiloh, Chattanooga, Stone River and Nashville. In 1866 Tennessee was readmitted to the Union.

Nashville, the capital since 1843, Memphis, Knoxville, and Chattanooga all developed as river towns, Memphis becoming an important cotton and timber port. Growth was greatly accelerated by the creation of the Tennessee Valley Authority in the 1930s, producing power for industry. With an expanding economy, by 1970, the southern pattern of emigration and population loss had been reversed.

TERRITORY AND POPULATION

Tennessee is bounded north by Kentucky and Virginia, east by North Carolina, south by Georgia, Alabama and Mississippi and west by the Mississippi River (forming the boundary with Arkansas and Missouri). Land area, 41,217 sq. miles (106,752 sq. km). Census population, 1 April 2000, 5,689,283, an increase of 16·7% since 1990. July 2009 estimate, 6,296,254.

Population in five census years was:

	White	Black	Indian	Asiatic	Total	Per sq. mile
1910	1,711,432	473,088	216	53	2,184,789	52·4
1930	2,138,644	477,646	161	105	2,616,556	62·4
			All others			
1980	3,835,452	725,942	29,726		4,591,120	111·6
1990	4,048,068	778,035	51,082		4,877,185	115·7
2000	4,563,310	932,809	193,164		5,689,283	138·0

Of the total population in 2000, 2,919,008 were female, 4,290,762 were 18 years old or older and 3,620,018 were urban. In 2000 the Hispanic population of Tennessee was 123,828, up from 32,741 in 1990 (an increase of 278·2%).

The cities, with population (2000) are Memphis, 650,100; Nashville (capital), 569,891; Knoxville, 167,535; Chattanooga, 150,425; Clarksville, 94,879; Johnson City, 55,542; Murfreesboro, 53,996; Jackson, 50,406; Kingsport, 41,335; Oak Ridge, 27,742. Metropolitan Statistical Areas, with 2000 populations: Nashville, 1,231,311; Memphis, 1,135,614; Knoxville, 687,249; Johnson City–Kingsport–Bristol, 480,091; Chattanooga, 465,161; Clarksville–Hopkinsville, 207,033; Jackson, 107,377.

SOCIAL STATISTICS

Births, 2007 (provisional), 85,894 (14·0 per 1,000 population); deaths, 2006, 56,838 (9·4). Infant mortality, 2006, 8·7 per 1,000 live births. 2006: marriages, 64,000 (10·5 per 1,000 population); divorces and annulments, 25,900 (4·3).

CLIMATE

Memphis, Jan. 41°F (5°C), July 82°F (27·8°C). Annual rainfall 49" (1,221 mm). Nashville, Jan. 39°F (3·9°C), July 79°F (26·1°C). Annual rainfall 48" (1,196 mm). Tennessee belongs to the Appalachian Mountains climate zone (*see* UNITED STATES: Climate).

CONSTITUTION AND GOVERNMENT

The state has operated under three constitutions, the last of which was adopted in 1870 and has been since amended 30 times (first in 1953). Voters at an election may authorize the calling of a convention limited to altering or abolishing one or more specified sections of the constitution. The General Assembly consists of a Senate of 33 members and a House of Representatives of 99 members, senators elected for four years and representatives for two years. Qualified as electors are all citizens (usual residential and age (18) qualifications).

For the 111th Congress, which convened in Jan. 2009, Tennessee sends nine members to the House of Representatives. It is represented in the Senate by Lamar Alexander (R. 2003–15) and Bob Corker (R. 2007–13).

The capital is Nashville. The state is divided into 95 counties.

RECENT ELECTIONS

In the 2008 presidential elections John McCain won Tennessee with 56·9% of the vote (George W. Bush won in 2004).

CURRENT ADMINISTRATION

Governor: Phil Bredesen (D.), 2007–11 (salary: $164,292, but not presently taken).

Lieut.-Governor (Senate President): Ron Ramsey (R.), 2009–11 ($75,289).

Secretary of State: Tre Hargett (R.), 2009–13 ($180,000).

Government Website: http://www.tennessee.gov

ECONOMY

Per capita personal income (2008) was $34,976.

Budget

In 2008 total state revenue was $25,699m. Total expenditure was $26,403m. (public welfare, $8,664m.; education, $8,480m.; highways, $1,669m.; health, $1,282m.; government administration, $789m.) Outstanding debt in 2008, $4,366m.

Performance

Gross Domestic Product by state in 2008 was $252,127m. (provisional), ranking Tennessee 18th in the United States.

ENERGY AND NATURAL RESOURCES

Water

The total area covered by water is approximately 926 sq. miles.

Minerals

Domestic non-fuel mineral production was worth $856m. in 2006.

Agriculture

In 2002, 90,000 farms covered 11·7m. acres. The average farm was of 130 acres. In 2002 the average value of farmland and buildings per acre was $2,405.

Farm income 2006: from crops $1,373m.; from livestock, $1,192m. The net farm income in 2006 was $722m. Main crops were cotton and greenhouse products.

In 2002 the domestic animals included 84,000 milch cows, 2·2m. all cattle, 23,300 sheep and 230,500 swine.

Forestry

Forests occupied 14·48m. acres in 2007. The forest industry and industries dependent on it employ about 0·04m. workers. Wood products are valued at over $500m. per year. National forest system land (2007) 741,000 acres.

INDUSTRY

The manufacturing industries include iron and steel working, but the most important products are chemicals, including synthetic fibres and allied products, electrical equipment and food. In 2005 the state's 6,671 manufacturing establishments had 396,000 employees, earning $15,565m. Total value added by manufacturing in 2006 was $62,045m.

Labour

In 2007 total non-agricultural employment was 2,797,000. Employees by branch, 2007 (in 1,000): trade, transportation and utilities, 611; government, 421; manufacturing, 381; education and health services, 350; professional and business services, 322. The unemployment rate in 2007 was 4·6%.

COMMUNICATIONS

Roads

In 2007 there were 91,058 miles of roads (69,345 miles rural). There were 5,339,946 registered motor vehicles.

Rail

The state had (2002) 3,150 miles of track. There is a tramway in Memphis.

Civil Aviation

In 2005 Tennessee had 81 public airports; there were also 101 heliports. There were 11,836,090 passenger enplanements state-wide in 2007. Memphis International handled 3,598,500 tonnes of freight in 2005—the most of any airport in the world.

SOCIAL INSTITUTIONS

Justice

There were two executions in 2007, none in 2008 and two in 2009. Prior to 2006 there had been only one execution since 1976. In Dec. 2008 there were 27,228 prison inmates.

Education

School attendance has been compulsory since 1925 and the employment of children under 16 years of age in workshops, factories or mines is illegal.

In 2004–05 there were 1,710 public schools with 941,091 pupils and 60,022 teachers. Total expenditure on public elementary and secondary education was $6,656m. in 2003–04 and average teacher salary was $40,318. Spending per pupil (2002–03) was $6,118.

Tennessee has 22 public colleges and universities (nine four-year and 13 two-year institutions). In fall 2005 the universities included the University of Tennessee, Knoxville (founded 1794), with 28,512 students; Vanderbilt University, Nashville (1873) with 11,479; Tennessee State University (1912) with 8,880; the University of Tennessee at Chattanooga (1886) with 8,656; University of Memphis (1912) with 20,465; and Fisk University (1866) with 920.

Health

In 2006 there were 130 community hospitals with 20,300 beds. A total of 853,000 patients were admitted during the year.

Welfare
Medicare enrolment in July 2004 totalled 890,685. In fiscal year 2006 a total of 1,590,807 people in Tennessee received Medicaid. In Dec. 2008 there were 1,168,699 Old-Age, Survivors, and Disability Insurance (OASDI) beneficiaries. A total of 147,865 people were receiving payments under Temporary Assistance for Needy Families (TANF) in Dec. 2008.

RELIGION
In 2000 there were 1,414,199 Southern Baptists, 393,994 United Methodists, 216,648 members of the Church of Christ, 183,161 Catholics, and followers of various other religions.

CULTURE

Tourism
In 2004, 43m. tourists spent $11,400m.

FURTHER READING
Statistical information: Center for Business and Economic Research, Univ. of Tennessee, Knoxville 37996. Publishes *Tennessee Statistical Abstract*

Tennessee Blue Book.

Dykeman, W., *Tennessee.* Rev. ed. 1984

State library: State Library and Archives, 403 7th Avenue North, Nashville.

Texas

KEY HISTORICAL EVENTS
A number of Indian tribes occupied the area before French and Spanish explorers arrived in the 16th century. In 1685 La Salle established a colony at Fort St Louis, but Texas was confirmed as Spanish in 1713. Spanish missions increased during the 18th century with San Antonio (1718) as their headquarters.

In 1820 a Virginian colonist, Moses Austin, obtained permission to begin a settlement in Texas. In 1821 the Spanish empire in the Americas came to an end and Texas, together with Coahuila, formed a state of the newly independent Mexico. The Mexicans agreed to the Austin venture and settlers of British and American descent came in.

Discontented with Mexican government, the settlers declared independence in 1836. Warfare, including the siege of the Alamo fort, ended with the foundation of the independent Republic of Texas which lasted until 1845. During this period the Texas Rangers were organized as a police force and border patrol. Texas was annexed to the Union in Dec. 1845, as the Federal government feared its vulnerability to Mexican occupation. This led to war between Mexico and the USA from 1845 to 1848. In 1861 Texas left the Union and joined the southern states in the Civil War, being readmitted in 1869. Ranching and cotton-growing were the main activities before the discovery of oil in 1901.

TERRITORY AND POPULATION
Texas is bounded north by Oklahoma, northeast by Arkansas, east by Louisiana, southeast by the Gulf of Mexico, south by Mexico and west by New Mexico. Land area, 261,797 sq. miles (678,051 sq. km). Census population, 1 April 2000, 20,851,820, an increase of 22·8% since 1990. July 2009 estimate, 24,782,302.

Population for five census years was:

	White	Black	American Indian	Asian	Total	Per sq. mile
1910	3,204,848	690,049	702	943	3,896,542	14·8
1930	4,967,172	854,964	1,001	1,578	5,824,715	22·1
			All others			
1980	11,197,663	1,710,250	1,320,470		14,228,383	54·2
				Asian/ other		
1990	12,774,762	2,021,632	65,877	2,124,239	16,986,510	64·9
2000	14,799,505	2,404,566	118,362	3,529,387	20,851,820	79·7

Of the total population in 2000, 10,498,910 were female, 14,965,061 were 18 years old or older, and 17,204,281 were urban. In 2000 the Hispanic population was 6,669,666, up from 4,339,905 in 1990 (an increase of 53·7%). The numerical increase was the second largest in the Hispanic population of any state in the USA, after California. Only New Mexico and California have a greater percentage of Hispanics in the state population.

The largest cities, with census population in 2000, are:

Houston	1,700,672	Pasadena	127,843
Dallas	1,036,309	Beaumont	118,289
San Antonio	991,861	Brownsville	117,326
El Paso	554,496	Mesquite	108,960
Austin (capital)	501,637	Waco	107,191
Fort Worth	459,085	Grand Prairie	103,913
Arlington	277,939	Abilene	100,661
Corpus Christi	266,958	Wichita Falls	98,356
Lubbock	193,194	Midland	95,003
Garland	187,439	Odessa	92,257
Irving	166,523	McAllen	91,184
Amarillo	163,569	Carrollton	90,934
Plano	153,624	San Angelo	87,980
Laredo	140,688		

Metropolitan statistical areas, 2000: Dallas–Fort Worth, 5,221,801; Houston–Galveston–Brazoria, 4,669,571; San Antonio, 1,592,383; Austin–San Marcos, 1,249,763.

SOCIAL STATISTICS
Births, 2007 (provisional), 405,376 (17·0 per 1,000 population); deaths, 2006, 157,150 (6·7). Infant mortality, 2006, 6·2 per 1,000 live births. 2006: marriages, 175,000 (7·5 per 1,000 population); divorces and annulments, 78,100 (3·3).

CLIMATE
Dallas, Jan. 45°F (7·2°C), July 84°F (28·9°C). Annual rainfall 38" (945 mm). El Paso, Jan. 44°F (6·7°C), July 81°F (27·2°C). Annual rainfall 9" (221 mm). Galveston, Jan. 54°F (12·2°C), July 84°F (28·9°C). Annual rainfall 46" (1,159 mm). Houston, Jan. 52°F (11·1°C), July 83°F (28·3°C). Annual rainfall 48" (1,200 mm). Texas belongs to the Central Plains climate zone (*see* UNITED STATES: Climate).

CONSTITUTION AND GOVERNMENT
The present constitution dates from 1876; it has been amended 432 times since. The state legislature consists of the Senate and House of Representatives. The Senate has 31 members elected for four-year terms. Half of the membership is elected every two years. The House has 150 members, elected for two-year terms during polling held in even-numbered years. The legislature meets in regular session for about five months every other year. The session begins in Jan. of odd-numbered years and lasts no more than 140 days (although special sessions can be called by the Governor). The Governor and Lieut.-Governor are elected for four years.

For the 111th Congress, which convened in Jan. 2009, Texas sends 32 members to the House of Representatives. It is represented in the Senate by Kay Hutchison (R. 1993–2013) and John Cornyn (R. 2002–15).

The capital is Austin. The state has 254 counties.

RECENT ELECTIONS

In the 2008 presidential elections John McCain won Texas with 55·5% of the vote (George W. Bush won in 2004).

CURRENT ADMINISTRATION

Governor: Rick Perry (R.), 2007–11 (salary: $150,000).

Lieut.-Governor: David Dewhurst (R.), 2007–11 ($7,200 plus legislature session salary).

Secretary of State: Esperanza 'Hope' Andrade (R.), appointed July 2008 ($125,880).

Government Website: http://www.tx.gov

ECONOMY

Per capita personal income (2008) was $37,774.

Budget

In 2008 total state revenue was $119,141m. Total expenditure was $100,939m. (education, $40,672m.; public welfare, $23,049m.; highways, $7,916m.; hospitals, $3,571m.; correction, $3,565m.) Outstanding debt in 2008, $33,299m.

Performance

In 2008 Gross Domestic Product by state was $1,223,511m. (provisional), ranking Texas second after California. If Texas were a country in its own right it would be the world's 12th largest economy.

Banking and Finance

In 2002 there were 751 financial institutions in Texas insured by the US Federal Deposit Insurance Corporation, with assets worth $216,900m. They had 4,980 offices with total deposits of $256,600m.

As at Dec. 2003 there were 351 state-chartered banks operating in Texas, with total assets of $121,970m. The largest banks were International Bank of Commerce, Laredo (with assets of $5,294·2m.), Texas State Bank, McAllen ($4,215·6m.), Sterling Bank, Houston ($3,110·1m.), Prosperity Bank, El Campo ($2,395·0m.) and PlainsCapital Bank, Lubbock ($2,061·8m.).

ENERGY AND NATURAL RESOURCES

Electricity

In 2005 total net electrical production was 396·7bn. kWh.

Oil and Gas

Texas is the leading producer in the USA of both oil and natural gas. In 2006 it produced 21% of the country's oil and 28% of its natural gas. Production, 2006: crude petroleum, 397m. bbls (value, $24,354m.); natural gas, 5,513bn. cu. ft (value, $36,365m.). Natural gasoline, butane and propane gases are also produced.

Water

The total area covered by water is approximately 6,784 sq. miles.

Minerals

Minerals include helium, crude gypsum, granite and sandstone, salt and cement. Total value of domestic non-fuel mineral products in 2006 was $2,980m.

Agriculture

Texas is one of the most important agricultural states. In 2002 it had 230,000 farms covering 131m. acres; average farm was of 570 acres. Both the number of farms and the total area covered are the highest in the USA. In 2002 land and buildings were valued at $768 per acre. Large-scale commercial farms, highly mechanized, dominate in Texas; farms of 1,000 acres or more in number far exceed that of any other state, but small-scale farming persists. Soil erosion is a serious problem in some parts.

Production: corn, barley, beans, cotton, hay, oats, peanuts, rye, sorghum, soybeans, sunflowers, wheat, oranges, grapefruit, peaches, sweet potatoes. Farm income, 2006: from crops $5,703m.; from livestock and products, $10,324m. The net farm income in 2006 was $4,866m.

The state has an important livestock industry, leading in the number of all cattle (13·98m.) and sheep (1·03m.); it also had 0·31m. milch cows and 0·95m. swine in 2002.

Forestry

There were 17,273,000 acres of forested land in 2007, with 682,000 acres of national forest.

INDUSTRY

In 2005 the state's 20,552 manufacturing establishments had 816,000 employees, earning $38,225m. Total value added by manufacturing in 2006 was $196,580m.

Labour

Total non-agricultural employment, 2007, 10,359,000. Employees by branch, 2007 (in 1,000): trade, transportation and utilities, 2,104; government, 1,728; professional and business services, 1,291; education and health services, 1,255; leisure and hospitality, 980. The unemployment rate in 2007 was 4·3%.

INTERNATIONAL TRADE

Imports and Exports

Exports in 2003 totalled $98·8bn. (an increase of 3·6% from 2002), ranking Texas as the leading US state by export revenue for the second consecutive year. The main export category is computer and electronic products, which accounted for 29% of total exports in 2003. Other major exports are chemicals, non-electrical machinery, transportation equipment, and petroleum and coal products. The leading destinations for exports in 2003 were Mexico (42%), Canada (11%) and China (3%). Asian and Pacific Rim countries accounted for 35% of exports and the European Union (principally the UK) for 2%. Texas is a major producer of agricultural products with exports valued at $2·6bn. in 2003.

COMMUNICATIONS

Roads

In 2007 there were 305,855 miles of road comprising 84,194 miles of urban road and 221,661 miles of rural road. There were 18,072,148 registered motor vehicles and 3,363 traffic accident fatalities.

Rail

In 2005 there were 10,386 miles of freight railroad (the most in any US state), including 8,270 miles of Class I railroads.

Civil Aviation

There were 70,940,435 passenger enplanements in 2007. In 2002 Texas had 295 public and 1,073 private airports, 429 heliports and 8 stolports. In 2003 a total of 52,465,427 passengers (48,036,422 domestic and 4,429,005 international) embarked and disembarked at Dallas/Fort Worth International airport. It handled 736,023 tons of freight in 2003. The Houston Airport System (HAS) recorded a total of 42,034,978 passengers arriving and departing that year; of these, George Bush Intercontinental airport served 34,151,342 (28,530,960 domestic and 5,620,382 international). HAS cargo shipments in 2003 reached 335,753 tons in 2003.

Shipping

The port of Houston, connected by the Houston Ship Channel (50 miles long) with the Gulf of Mexico, is a large cotton market. Total cargo handled by all ports in 2002 was 442,251,000 tons. There were 1,021 miles of inland waterways (271 miles of deep-draft channels and 750 miles of shallow-draft channels) in 2007.

SOCIAL INSTITUTIONS

Justice

In Dec. 2008 there were 172,506 prison inmates. Between 1977 and 2009 Texas was responsible for 447 of the USA's 1,188 executions (more than four times as many as any other state), although it was not until 1982 that Texas reintroduced the death penalty. In 2009, 24 people were executed in Texas; in 2000, 40 people had been executed, the highest number in a year in any state since the authorities began keeping records in 1930.

Education

School attendance is compulsory from six to 18 years of age.

In the 2001–02 school year there were 7,646 public elementary and secondary schools with 4,163,447 enrolled pupils; there were 282,583 teachers. Total expenditure on public schools in 2000–01 was $26,547m.

In 2003 there were 142 higher education institutions (35 public universities, 38 independent colleges and universities, 50 public community college districts, four campuses of the Texas State Technical College System, three public Lamar state colleges, nine public health-related institutions, one independent medical school and two independent junior colleges). The headcount enrolment in higher education in 2002 was 1,102,504 students, including 455,719 at public universities, 114,082 at independent universities and colleges and 505,212 at public community and state colleges. Enrolment in fall 2003 was an estimated 1·14m.

Public universities and student enrolment, 2002:

Institutions	*Students*
University of Texas System	153,404
Texas A&M University System	96,729
Texas State University System	57,016
University of Houston System	54,910
Texas Technical University System	36,272
University of North Texas System	30,183
Stephen F. Austin State University, Nacogdoches	11,312
Texas Southern University, Houston	9,739
Midwestern State University, Wichita Falls	6,157

Independent colleges and universities with the largest student enrolments, 2002:

Institutions	*Students*
Baylor University, Waco	14,159
Southern Methodist University, Dallas	10,955
Texas Christian University, Fort Worth	8,074
Wayland Baptist University, Plainview	5,773
University of St Thomas, Houston	5,116
William Marsh Rice University, Houston	4,784
Abilene Christian University, Abilene	4,668
Dallas Baptist University, Dallas	4,417

Health

In 2006 there were 417 community hospitals with 58,900 beds. A total of 2,528,000 patients were admitted during the year.

Welfare

Medicare enrolment in July 2004 totalled 2,449,965. In fiscal year 2006 a total of 3,910,487 people in Texas received Medicaid. In Dec. 2008 there were 3,192,227 Old-Age, Survivors, and Disability Insurance (OASDI) beneficiaries. A total of 112,929 people were receiving payments under Temporary Assistance for Needy Families (TANF) in Dec. 2008.

RELIGION

Religious bodies represented include Roman Catholics, Baptists, Methodists, Churches of Christ, Lutherans, Presbyterians and Episcopalians.

CULTURE

Tourism

In 2005, 7·8m. overseas visitors visited Texas (6·5m. from Mexico). In 2002 there were 17,090,000 visitors to state parks and recreation areas.

FURTHER READING

Texas Almanac. Biennial

Kingston, M., *Texas Almanac's Political History of Texas.* 1992

Kraemer, R., Newell, C. and Prindle, D., *Essentials of Texas Politics.* 10th ed. 2007

Legislative Reference Library: Box 12488, Capitol Station, Austin, Texas 78711-2488.

Utah

KEY HISTORICAL EVENTS

Spanish Franciscan missionaries explored the area in 1776, finding Shoshoni Indians. Spain laid claim to Utah and designated it part of Spanish Mexico. As such it passed into the hands of the Mexican Republic when Mexico rebelled against Spain and gained independence in 1821.

In 1848, at the conclusion of war between the USA and Mexico, the USA received Utah along with other southwestern territory. Settlers had already arrived in 1847 when the Mormons (the Church of Jesus Christ of Latter-day Saints) arrived, having been driven on by hostility in Ohio, Missouri and Illinois. Led by Brigham Young, they entered the Great Salt Valley and colonized it. In 1849 they applied for statehood but were refused. In 1850 Utah and Nevada were joined as one Territory. The Mormon community continued to ask for statehood but this was only granted in 1896, after they had renounced polygamy and disbanded their People's Party.

Mining, especially of copper, and livestock farming were the basis of the economy. Settlement had to adapt to desert conditions and the main centres of population were in the narrow belt between the Wasatch Mountains and the Great Salt Lake. Salt Lake City, the capital, was founded in 1847 and laid out according to Joseph Smith's plan for the city of Zion. It was the centre of the Mormons' provisional 'State of Deseret' and Territorial capital from 1856 until 1896, except briefly in 1858 when federal forces occupied it during conflict between territorial and Union governments.

TERRITORY AND POPULATION

Utah is bounded north by Idaho and Wyoming, east by Colorado, south by Arizona and west by Nevada. Land area, 82,144 sq. miles (212,752 sq. km). In 2000 American Indian lands covered 8,937 sq. miles (8,910 sq. miles in reservations and 27 sq. miles in off-reservation trust land).

Census population, 1 April 2000, 2,233,169, an increase of 29·6% since 1990. July 2009 estimate, 2,784,572.

Population at five federal censuses was:

	White	Black	American Indian	Asiatic	Total	Per sq. mile
1910	366,583	1,144	3,123	2,501	373,851	4·5
1930	499,967	1,108	2,869	3,903	507,847	6·2
1980	1,382,550	9,225	19,256	15,076	1,461,037	17·7
1990	1,615,845	11,576	24,283	25,696	1,722,850	21·0
2000	1,992,975	17,657	29,684	37,108	2,233,169	27·2

Of the total population in 2000, 1,119,031 were male, 1,514,471 were 18 years old or older and 1,970,344 were urban. In 2000 the Hispanic population was 201,559, up from 84,597 in 1990 (an increase of 138·3%). In the year 1 July 2008–30 June 2009 Utah's population showed the second largest percentage growth of any state, after Wyoming.

The largest cities are Salt Lake City, with a population (census, 2000) of 181,743; West Valley City, 108,896; Provo, 105,166; Sandy City, 88,418; Orem, 84,324; Ogden, 77,226.

SOCIAL STATISTICS

Births, 2007 (provisional), 55,002 (20·8 per 1,000 population—the highest rate in any US state); deaths, 2006, 13,764 (5·4). Infant mortality rate, 2006, 5·1 per 1,000 live births. 2006: marriages, 23,700 (9·2 per 1,000 population); divorces and annulments, 9,900 (3·8). Fertility rate, 2003, 2·6 births per woman (the highest of any American state).

CLIMATE

Salt Lake City, Jan. 29°F (–1·7°C), July 77°F (25°C). Annual rainfall 16" (401 mm). Utah belongs to the Mountain States climate region (*see* UNITED STATES: Climate).

CONSTITUTION AND GOVERNMENT

Utah adopted its present constitution in 1896; it has had numerous amendments since then. The Legislature consists of a Senate (in part renewed every two years) of 29 members, elected for four years, and of a House of Representatives of 75 members elected for two years. It sits annually in Jan. The Governor is elected for four years. The constitution provides for the initiative and referendum.

For the 111th Congress, which convened in Jan. 2009, Utah sends three members to the House of Representatives. It is represented in the Senate by Orrin Hatch (R. 1977–2013) and Robert Bennett (R. 1993–2011).

The capital is Salt Lake City. There are 29 counties in the state.

RECENT ELECTIONS

In the 2008 presidential elections John McCain won Utah with 62·6% of the vote (George W. Bush won in 2004).

CURRENT ADMINISTRATION

Governor: Gary R. Herbert (R.), 2009–13 (salary: $109,900).
Lieut.-Governor: Gregory S. Bell (R.), 2009–13 ($104,400).

Government Website: http://www.utah.gov

ECONOMY

Per capita income (2008) was $31,944.

Budget

In 2008 total state revenue was $15,243m. Total expenditure was $14,294m. (education, $6,036m.; public welfare, $2,203m.; highways, $1,061m.; hospitals, $823m.; government administration, $713m.) Outstanding debt in 2008, $5,907m.

Performance

Gross Domestic Product by state in 2008 was $109,777m. (provisional), ranking Utah 33rd in the United States.

ENERGY AND NATURAL RESOURCES

Oil and Gas

In 2006 Utah produced 348bn. cu. ft of natural gas and 18m. bbls of crude oil.

Water

The total area covered by water is approximately 2,755 sq. miles.

Minerals

The principal minerals are: copper, gold, magnesium, petroleum, lead, silver and zinc. The state also has natural gas, clays, tungsten, molybdenum, uranium and phosphate rock. The value of domestic non-fuel mineral production in 2006 was $3,960m.

Agriculture

In 2002 Utah had 15,000 farms covering 11·6m. acres. In 2002 about 2·1m. acres were crop land, about 602,300 acres pasture and about 1·1m. acres had irrigation. In 2002 the average farm was of 773 acres and the average value per acre was $756.

Farm income, 2006: from crops, $313m.; and from livestock and products, $931m. The net farm income in 2006 was $264m. The principal crops are: barley, wheat (spring and winter), oats, potatoes, hay (alfalfa, sweet clover and lespedeza) and maize. Livestock, 2002: cattle, 877,000; pigs, 670,000; sheep, 311,000; poultry, 3·4m.

Forestry

Forest area, 2007, was 17,962,000 acres and included 6,259,000 acres of national forest.

INDUSTRY

Leading manufactures by value added are primary metals, ordinances and transport, food, fabricated metals and machinery, and petroleum products. In 2005 Utah's 3,165 manufacturing establishments had 116,000 employees, earning $4,624m. Total value added by manufacturing in 2006 was $16,801m.

Labour

Total non-agricultural employment, 2007, 1,252,000. Employees by branch, 2007 (in 1,000): trade, transportation and utilities, 246; government, 207; professional and business services, 161; education and health services, 140; manufacturing, 128. The unemployment rate in 2007 was 2·6%, the lowest of all the states.

COMMUNICATIONS

Roads

In 2007 there were 44,221 miles of road (32,672 miles rural). There were 2,320,171 registered motor vehicles.

Rail

In 2004 Utah had approximately 1,400 miles of freight railroad track. There was no dedicated passenger rail trackage, although the Utah Transit Authority is preparing a commuter rail service.

Civil Aviation

There is an international airport at Salt Lake City. There were 10,673,984 passenger enplanements statewide in 2007.

SOCIAL INSTITUTIONS

Justice

In Dec. 2008 there were 6,546 prison inmates. The death penalty is authorized; the last execution took place in 1999.

Education

School attendance is compulsory for children from six to 18 years of age. There are 40 school districts. Teachers' salaries, 2003–04, averaged $38,976. In 2004–05 there were 503,607 pupils and 22,287 teachers in 930 public elementary and secondary schools.

In 2003–04 total expenditure on elementary and secondary education was $3,036m. Spending per pupil (2002–03) was $4,838.

In fall 2005 there were 200,691 students enrolled in 13 public and 18 private colleges and universities. Among the public institutions, the University of Utah (founded in 1850) in Salt Lake City had 30,558 students; Utah State University (1890) in Logan, 14,458; Weber State University in Ogden, 18,142; Southern Utah University in Cedar City, 6,859; College of Eastern Utah in Price, 2,178; Snow College in Ephraim, 3,333; Dixie State College in St George, 8,945; Utah Valley State College in Orem, 24,180; and Salt Lake Community College in Salt Lake City, 24,111. The Mormon Church maintains the private Brigham Young University at Provo (1875) with 30,067 students in fall 2005.

Health

In 2006 there were 43 community hospitals with 4,500 beds. A total of 220,000 patients were admitted during the year.

Welfare

Medicare enrolment in July 2004 totalled 226,495. In fiscal year 2006 a total of 288,149 people in Utah received Medicaid. In Dec. 2008 there were 299,088 Old-Age, Survivors, and Disability Insurance (OASDI) beneficiaries. A total of 13,821 people were receiving payments under Temporary Assistance for Needy Families (TANF) in Dec. 2008.

RELIGION

Latter-day Saints (Mormons) numbered 1,483,858 in 2000. World membership was 12,276,000 in 2004. The President of the Mormon Church is Thomas S. Monson (born 1927). The Roman Catholic church and most Protestant denominations are represented.

FURTHER READING

Statistical information: Bureau of Economic and Business Research, Univ. of Utah, 401 Kendall D. Garff Bldg., Salt Lake City 84112. Publishes *Statistical Abstract of Utah.*

Utah Foundation. *Statistical Review of Government in Utah.* 1991

Vermont

KEY HISTORICAL EVENTS

The original Indian hunting grounds of the Green Mountains and lakes was explored by the Frenchman, Samuel de Champlain, in 1609. He reached Lake Champlain on the northwest border. The first attempt at permanent settlement was also French, on Isle la Motte in 1666. In 1763 the British gained the area by the Treaty of Paris. The Treaty, which also brought peace with the Indian allies of the French, opened the way for settlement, but in a mountain area transport was slow and difficult. Montpelier, the state capital from 1805, was chartered as a township site in 1781 to command the main pass through the Green Mountains.

In the War of Independence Vermont declared itself an independent state to avoid being taken over by New Hampshire and New York. In 1791 it became the 14th state of the Union.

Most early settlers were New Englanders of British and Protestant descent. After 1812 a granite-quarrying industry grew around the town of Barre, attracting immigrant workers from Italy and Scandinavia. French Canadians settled in Winooski. Textile and engineering industries developed in the 19th century attracted more European workers.

Vermont saw the only Civil War action north of Pennsylvania when a Confederate raiding party attacked from Canada in 1864.

During the 20th century the textile and engineering industries have declined but paper and lumber industries flourish. Settlement is still mainly rural or in small towns.

TERRITORY AND POPULATION

Vermont is bounded in the north by Canada, east by New Hampshire, south by Massachusetts and west by New York. Land area, 9,250 sq. miles (23,957 sq. km). Census population, 1 April 2000, 608,827, an increase of 8·2% since 1990. July 2009 estimate, 621,760.

Population at five census years was:

	White	*Black*	*Indian*	*Asiatic*	*Total*	*Per sq. mile*
1910	354,298	1,621	26	11	355,956	39·0
1930	358,966	568	36	41	359,611	38·8
1980	506,736	1,135	984	1,355	511,456	55·1
1990	555,088	1,951	1,696	3,215[1]	562,758	60·8
2000	589,208	3,063	2,420	5,358[1]	608,827	65·8

[1]Includes Pacific Islander.

Of the total population in 2000, 310,490 were female, 461,304 were 18 years old or older and 376,379 (61·8%) were rural (67·8% in 1990). Vermont has the highest rural population percentage of any state in the USA. In 2000 the Hispanic population was 5,504, the lowest total of any state. However, this figure represents a rise of 50·3% compared to the 1990 census figure of 3,661. The largest cities are Burlington, with an estimated population (2002) of 38,885; Essex, 18,863; Rutland City, 17,309; Colchester, 17,245.

SOCIAL STATISTICS

Births, 2007 (provisional), 6,492 (10·4 per 1,000 population—the lowest rate in any US state); deaths, 2006, 5,048 (8·1). Infant deaths, 2006, 5·5 per 1,000 live births. 2006: marriages, 5,400 (8·7 per 1,000 population); divorces and annulments, 2,200 (3·5). Same-sex marriage became legal in Sept. 2009.

CLIMATE

Burlington, Jan. 17°F (–8·3°C), July 70°F (21·1°C). Annual rainfall 33" (820 mm). Vermont belongs to the New England climate zone (*see* UNITED STATES: Climate).

CONSTITUTION AND GOVERNMENT

The constitution was adopted in 1793 and has since been amended. Amendments are proposed by two-thirds vote of the Senate every four years, and must be accepted by two sessions of the legislature; they are then submitted to popular vote. The state Legislature, consisting of a Senate of 30 members and a House of Representatives of 150 members (both elected for two years), meets in Jan. every year. The Governor and Lieut.-Governor are elected for two years. Electors are all citizens who possess certain residential qualifications and have taken the freeman's oath set forth in the constitution.

For the 111th Congress, which convened in Jan. 2009, Vermont sends one member to the House of Representatives. It is represented in the Senate by Patrick Leahy (Democrat, 1975–2011) and Bernard Sanders (Independent Democrat, 2007–13).

The capital is Montpelier (estimated population of 8,028 in 2002). There are 14 counties and 251 cities, towns and other administrative divisions.

RECENT ELECTIONS

In the 2008 presidential elections Barack Obama won Vermont with 67·5% of the vote (John Kerry won in 2004).

CURRENT ADMINISTRATION

Governor: James Douglas (R.), 2009–11 (salary: $142,564).

Lieut.-Governor: Brian E. Dubie (R.), 2009–11 ($63,701).

Secretary of State: Deborah L. Markowitz (D.), 2009–11 ($90,398).

Government Website: http://vermont.gov

ECONOMY

Per capita income (2008) was $38,686.

Budget

In 2008 total state revenue was $5,149m. Total expenditure was $5,070m. (education, $2,063m.; public welfare, $1,254m.; highways, $325m.; health, $167m.; government administration, $156m.) Outstanding debt in 2008, $3,372m.

Performance

Gross Domestic Product by state was $25,442m. in 2008 (provisional), ranking Vermont 50th in the United States.

Banking and Finance

In 2003 there were 19 banking institutions domiciled in Vermont, and 16 out-of-state banks operating.

ENERGY AND NATURAL RESOURCES

Water

The total area covered by water is approximately 365 sq. miles. There are 46 utility-owned hydro-sites and 35 independently owned sites providing about 10% of Vermont's energy.

Minerals

Stone, chiefly granite, marble and slate, is the leading mineral produced in Vermont, contributing about 60% of the total value of mineral products. Other products include asbestos, talc, sand and gravel. Value of domestic non-fuel mineral products in 2006 was $84m.

Agriculture

Agriculture is the most important industry. In 2002 the state had 6,600 farms covering 1·34m. acres; the average farm was of 203 acres and the average value per acre of land and buildings was $2,051. In 2006 farm income from crops totalled $86m.; from livestock and products, $415m. The net farm income in 2006 was $103m. The 1,415 dairy farms produced about 2·6bn. lb of milk in 2002. The chief agricultural crops are greenhouse products, maple products, hay, apples and silage. In 2002 Vermont had 255,000 cattle and calves and 2,000 hogs and pigs.

Forestry

The state is 78% forest, with 17% in public ownership. In 2007 Vermont had 4,618,000 acres of forested land with 337,000 acres of national forest. State-owned forests, parks, fish and game areas (2007), 475,655 acres. In 2006 timber removals were 44m. cu. ft (27m. cu. ft hardwoods and 17m. cu. ft softwoods).

INDUSTRY

In 2005 the state's 1,126 manufacturing establishments had 37,000 employees, earning $1,655m. Total value added by manufacturing in 2006 was $5,089m.

Labour

Total non-agricultural employment, 2007, 308,000. Employees by branch, 2007 (in 1,000): trade, transportation and utilities, 59; education and health services, 57; government, 54; manufacturing, 36; leisure and hospitality, 33. The unemployment rate in 2007 was 4·0%.

COMMUNICATIONS

Roads

In 2007 there were 14,400 miles of road comprising 1,421 miles of urban road and 12,979 miles of rural road. Motor vehicle registrations totalled 564,967.

Rail

There were, in 2001, 747 miles of railroad, 391 miles of which are state owned.

Civil Aviation

There were 17 airports in 2003, of which ten were state operated, two municipally owned and five private. Some are only open in summer. There were 704,823 passenger enplanements statewide in 2007.

SOCIAL INSTITUTIONS

Justice

In Dec. 2008 the jail and prison population totalled 2,116. The death penalty was officially abolished in 1987 but effectively in 1964.

Education

School attendance during the full school term is compulsory for children from six to 16 years of age, unless they have completed the 10th grade or undergo approved home instruction. In 2003–04 the public elementary and secondary schools had 99,104 pupils and 9,004 teachers. Average teacher's salary was $43,009. State and local government expenditure on public schools in 2003–04 totalled $944m.

In 2003–04 the University of Vermont (1791), in Burlington, had 10,940 students; Norwich University (1834, founded as the American Literary, Scientific and Military Academy in 1819), had 2,183; St Michael's College (1904), 1,945 (full time undergraduates only); there are four other state colleges and 15 other private schools of higher education.

Health

In 2006 there were 14 community hospitals with 1,300 beds. A total of 50,000 patients were admitted during the year.

Welfare

In 2003 Social Services provided approximately $2·4m. to 500 families and 12,600 individuals. Medicare enrolment in July 2004 totalled 94,357. In fiscal year 2006 a total of 149,808 people in Vermont received Medicaid. In Dec. 2008 there were 120,249 Old-Age, Survivors, and Disability Insurance (OASDI) beneficiaries. A total of 6,445 people were receiving payments under Temporary Assistance for Needy Families (TANF) in Dec. 2008.

RELIGION

The principal denominations are Roman Catholic, United Church of Christ, United Methodist, Protestant Episcopal, Baptist and Unitarian–Universalist.

CULTURE

Broadcasting

In 2004 there were 56 radio stations, 11 television stations and 27 cable TV systems.

Press

There were ten dailies and 44 weekly newspapers in 2004.

FURTHER READING

Statistical information: Office of Policy Research and Coordination, Montpelier 05602

Legislative Directory. Biennial
Vermont Annual Financial Report. Annual
Vermont Atlas and Gazetteer. 11th ed. 2008
Vermont Year-Book, formerly *Walton's Register.* Annual
State library: Vermont Dept. of Libraries, 109 State St., Montpelier.

Virginia

KEY HISTORICAL EVENTS

In 1607 a British colony was founded at Jamestown, on a peninsula in the James River, to grow tobacco. The area was marshy and unhealthy but the colony survived and in 1619 introduced a form of representative government. The tobacco plantations expanded and African slaves were imported. Jamestown was later abandoned but tobacco-growing continued and spread through the eastern part of the territory.

In 1624 control of the colony passed from the Virginia Company of London to the Crown. Growth was rapid during the 17th and 18th centuries. The movement for American independence was strong in Virginia; George Washington and Thomas Jefferson were both Virginians, and crucial battles of the War of Independence were fought there.

When the Union was formed, Virginia became one of the original states, but with reservations because of its attachment to slave-owning. In 1831 there was a slave rebellion. The tobacco plantations began to decline, and plantation owners turned to the breeding of slaves. While the eastern plantation lands seceded from the Union in 1861, the small farmers and miners of the western hills refused to secede and remained in the Union as West Virginia.

Richmond, the capital, became the capital of the Confederacy. Much of the Civil War took place in Virginia, with considerable damage to the economy. After the war the position of the black population was little improved. Blacks remained without political or civil rights until the 1960s.

TERRITORY AND POPULATION

Virginia is bounded northwest by West Virginia, northeast by Maryland and the District of Columbia, east by the Atlantic, south by North Carolina and Tennessee and west by Kentucky. Land area, 39,594 sq. miles (102,548 sq. km). Census population, 1 April 2000, 7,078,515, an increase of 14·4% since 1990. July 2009 estimate, 7,882,590.

Population for five federal census years was:

	White	Black	Indian	Asian/other	Total	Per sq. mile
1910	1,389,809	671,096	539	168	2,061,612	51·2
1930	1,770,441	650,165	779	466	2,421,851	60·7
			All others			
1980	4,230,000	1,008,311	108,517		5,346,818	134·7
1990	4,791,739	1,162,994	15,282	217,343	6,187,358	155·9
2000	5,120,110	1,390,293	21,172	546,940	7,078,515	178·8

Of the total population in 2000, 3,606,620 were female, 5,340,253 were 18 years old or older and 5,169,955 were urban. In 2000 the Hispanic population was 329,540, up from 160,288 in 1990 (an increase of 105·6%).

The population (2003 estimates) of the principal cities was: Virginia Beach, 439,467; Norfolk, 241,727; Chesapeake, 210,834; Richmond, 194,729; Arlington CDP, 187,873; Newport News, 181,647; Hampton, 146,878; Alexandria, 128,923.

SOCIAL STATISTICS

Births, 2007 (provisional), 109,615 (14·2 per 1,000 population); deaths, 2006, 57,690 (7·5). Infant mortality, 2006, 7·1 per 1,000 live births. 2006: marriages, 60,800 (8·0 per 1,000 population); divorces and annulments, 31,100 (4·1).

CLIMATE

Average temperatures in Jan. are 41°F (5°C) in the Tidewater coastal area and 32°F (0°C) in the Blue Ridge mountains; July averages, 78°F (25·5°C)and 68°F (20°C) respectively. Precipitation averages 36" (914 mm) in the Shenandoah valley and 44" (1,118 mm) in the south. Snowfall is 5–10" (125–250 mm) in the Tidewater and 25–30" (625–750 mm) in the western mountains. Norfolk, Jan. 41°F (5°C), July 79°F (26°C). Annual rainfall 46" (1,145 mm). Virginia belongs to the Atlantic Coast climate zone (*see* UNITED STATES: Climate).

CONSTITUTION AND GOVERNMENT

The present constitution became effective in 1971. The General Assembly consists of a Senate of 40 members, elected for four years, and a House of Delegates of 100 members, elected for two years. It sits annually in Jan. The Governor and Lieut.-Governor are elected for four years.

For the 111th Congress, which convened in Jan. 2009, Virginia sends 11 members to the House of Representatives. It is represented in the Senate by Jim Webb (D. 2007–13) and Mark Warner (D. 2009–15).

The state capital is Richmond; the state contains 95 counties and 40 independent cities.

RECENT ELECTIONS

In the 2008 presidential elections Barack Obama won Virginia with 52·6% of the vote (George W. Bush won in 2004).

CURRENT ADMINISTRATION

Governor: Bob McDonnell (R.), 2010–14 (salary: $175,000).

Lieut.-Governor: William T. Bolling (R.), 2010–14 ($36,321).

Secretary of the Commonwealth: Janet Polarek (R.), appointed Dec. 2009 ($152,793).

Government Website: http://www.virginia.gov

ECONOMY

Per capita personal income (2008) was $44,224.

Budget

In 2008 total state revenue was $36,233m. Total expenditure was $39,880m. (education, $14,053m.; public welfare, $7,355m.; highways, $3,147m.; hospitals, $2,850m.; correction, $1,548m.) Outstanding debt in 2008, $21,875m.

Performance

Gross Domestic Product by state in 2008 was $397,025m. (provisional), ranking Virginia 11th in the United States.

ENERGY AND NATURAL RESOURCES

Water

The total area covered by water is approximately 3,180 sq. miles.

Minerals

Coal is the most important mineral, with output (2003) of 31,596,000 short tons. Lead and zinc ores, stone, sand and gravel, lime and titanium ore are also produced. Total domestic non-fuel mineral output was valued at $1,270m. in 2006.

Agriculture

In 2003 there were 47,500 farms with an area of 8·6m. acres; the average farm had 181 acres, and the average value per acre was $2,700. Farm income, 2006: from crops, $834m.; and from livestock and products, $1,855m. The net farm income in 2006 was $678m. The chief crops are tobacco, soybeans, peanuts, winter wheat, maize, tomatoes, apples, potatoes and sweet potatoes. Livestock, 2002: cattle and calves, 1·62m.; milch cows, 115,000; sheep and lambs, 72,000; hogs and pigs, 409,300; turkeys, 20m.; broilers, 266·1m.

Forestry

Forests covered 15,766,000 acres in 2007, including 1,692,000 acres of national forest.

Fisheries

Commercial catch (2002) totalled 442·5m. lb of fish, worth $123·3m.

INDUSTRY

The manufacture of cigars and cigarettes, of rayon and allied products, and the building of ships lead in value of products. In 2005 the state's 5,798 manufacturing establishments had 290,000 employees, earning $11,987m. Total value added by manufacturing in 2006 was $50,506m.

Labour

Total non-agricultural employment, 2007, 3,761,000. Employees by branch, 2007 (in 1,000): government, 686; trade, transportation and utilities, 668; professional and business services, 644; education and health services, 417; leisure and hospitality, 346. The unemployment rate in 2007 was 3·1%.

COMMUNICATIONS

Roads

In 2007 there were 72,662 miles of roads (50,350 miles rural). There were 6,613,781 registered motor vehicles.

Rail

In 2003 there were 3,399 miles of track including commuter services to Washington, D.C.

Civil Aviation

There are international airports at Norfolk, Dulles, Richmond, Arlington and Newport News. There were 25,607,060 passenger enplanements statewide in 2007.

SOCIAL INSTITUTIONS

Justice

In Dec. 2008 there were 38,276 prison inmates. The death penalty is authorized. Between 1977 and 2009 there were 105 executions in Virginia, after Texas the most of any state. There were three executions in 2009 (four in 2008).

Education

Elementary and secondary instruction is free, and for ages 5–18 attendance is compulsory.

There are 134 school districts. In 2005–06 there were 1,214,472 pupils in 2,094 elementary and secondary schools, with 96,158 teachers. Average annual salary in 2004–05 for public elementary and secondary teachers was $44,763. Total expenditure on education, 2004–05, was $11,955m.

In fall 2006 there were 110 degree-granting education institutions (39 public and 71 private) including:

Founded	*Name and place of college*	*Students 2006–07*
1693	College of William and Mary, Williamsburg (State)	7,709
1749	Washington and Lee University, Lexington	2,149
1776	Hampden-Sydney College, Hampden-Sydney (Presbyterian)	1,108
1819	University of Virginia, Charlottesville (State)	24,068
1832	Randolph-Macon College, Ashland (Methodist)	1,146
1832	University of Richmond, Richmond (Baptist)	4,496
1838	Virginia Commonwealth University, Richmond	30,189
1839	Virginia Military Institute Lexington (State)	1,397
1865	Virginia Union University, Richmond	1,599
1868	Hampton University	6,152
1872	Virginia Polytechnic Institute and State University, Blacksburg	28,470
1882	Virginia State University, Petersburg	4,872
1908	James Madison University, Harrisonburg	17,393
1910	Radford University (State)	9,220
1930	Old Dominion University, Norfolk	16,490
1935	Norfolk State University (State)	6,238
1957	George Mason University (State), Fairfax	29,889

Health

In 2006 there were 88 community hospitals with 17,200 beds. A total of 778,000 patients were admitted during the year.

Welfare

Medicare enrolment in July 2004 totalled 966,275. In fiscal year 2006 a total of 820,625 people in Virginia received Medicaid. In Dec. 2008 there were 1,207,101 Old-Age, Survivors, and Disability Insurance (OASDI) beneficiaries. A total of 69,563 people were receiving payments under Temporary Assistance for Needy Families (TANF) in Dec. 2008.

RELIGION

The principal churches are the Baptist, Methodist, Protestant Episcopal, Roman Catholic and Presbyterian.

FURTHER READING

Statistical information: Cooper Center for Public Service, Univ. of Virginia, 918 Emmet St. N., Suite 300, Charlottesville 22903-4832. Publishes *Virginia Statistical Abstract.—Population Estimates of Virginia Cities and Counties.*

Rubin, L. D. Jr., *Virginia: a Bicentennial History.* 1977
Salmon, E. J. and Campbell Jr., E. D. C., *The Hornbook of Virginia History: A Ready-Reference Guide the Old Dominion's People, Places, and Past.* 1994

State library: Library of Virginia, Richmond 23219.

Washington State

KEY HISTORICAL EVENTS

The strongest Indian tribes in the 18th century were Chinook, Nez Percé, Salish and Yakima. The area was designated by European colonizers as part of the Oregon Country. Between 1775 and 1800 it was claimed by Spain, Britain and the USA; the dispute between the two latter nations was not settled until 1846.

The first small white settlements were Indian missions and fur-trading posts. In the 1840s American settlers began to push westwards along the Oregon Trail, making a settlement with

Britain a matter of urgency. When this was achieved the whole area was organized as the Oregon Territory in 1848. Washington was made a separate Territory in 1853.

Apart from trapping and fishing, the chief industry was supplying timber for the new settlements of California. After 1870 the westward extension of railways encouraged settlement. Statehood was granted in 1889. Settlers were mostly Americans from neighbouring states to the east and Canadians. Scandinavian immigrants followed. Seattle, laid out in 1853 as a saw-milling town, was named after the Indian chief who had ceded the land and befriended the settlers. It grew as a port during the Alaskan and Yukon gold-rushes of the 1890s. The economy thrived on exploiting the Columbia River for hydro-electric power.

TERRITORY AND POPULATION

Washington is bounded north by Canada, east by Idaho, south by Oregon with the Columbia River forming most of the boundary, and west by the Pacific. Land area, 66,544 sq. miles (172,348 sq. km). Lands owned by the federal government, 2003, were 13,246,559 acres or 31·0% of the total area. Census population, 1 April 2000, 5,894,121, an increase of 21·1% since 1990. July 2009 estimate, 6,664,195.

Population in five federal census years was:

	White	*Black*	*American Indian*	*Asian/ other*	*Total*	*Per sq. mile*
1910	1,109,111	6,058	10,997	15,824	1,141,990	17·1
1930	1,521,661	6,840	11,253	23,642	1,563,396	23·3
1980	3,779,170	105,574	60,804	186,608	4,132,156	62·1
1990	4,308,937	149,801	81,483	326,471	4,866,692	73·1
2000	4,821,823	190,267	93,301	788,730	5,894,121	88·6

Of the total population in 2000, 2,959,821 were female, 4,380,278 were 18 years old or older and 4,831,106 were urban. In 2000 the Hispanic population was 441,509, up from 214,570 in 1990 (a rise of 105·8%).

There were 26 Indian reservations in 2000. American Indian lands covered 5,963 sq. miles (5,157 sq. miles in reservations).

Leading cities are Seattle, with a population in 2000 of 563,374; Spokane, 195,629; Tacoma, 193,556; Vancouver, 143,560; Bellevue, 109,569. Others: Everett, 91,488; Federal Way, 83,259; Kent, 79,524; Yakima, 71,845; Bellingham, 67,171; Lakewood, 58,211; Kennewick, 54,693; Shoreline, 53,025; Renton, 50,052. The Seattle–Tacoma–Bremerton metropolitan area had a 2000 census population of 3,554,760.

SOCIAL STATISTICS

Births, 2007 (provisional), 89,387 (13·8 per 1,000 population); deaths, 2006, 46,120 (7·2). Infant mortality rate, 2006, 4·7 per 1,000 live births. 2006: marriages, 41,000 (6·4 per 1,000 population); divorces and annulments, 24,000 (3·8).

CLIMATE

Seattle, Jan. 40°F (4·4°C), July 63°F (17·2°C). Annual rainfall 34" (848 mm). Spokane, Jan. 27°F (–2·8°C), July 70°F (21·1°C). Annual rainfall 14" (350 mm). Washington belongs to the Pacific Coast climate zone (*see* UNITED STATES: Climate).

CONSTITUTION AND GOVERNMENT

The constitution, adopted in 1889, has had 96 amendments. The Legislature consists of a Senate of 49 members elected for four years, half their number retiring every two years, and a House of Representatives of 98 members, elected for two years. The Governor and Lieut.-Governor are elected for four years.

For the 111th Congress, which convened in Jan. 2009, Washington sends nine members to the House of Representatives. It is represented in the Senate by Patty Murray (D. 1993–2011) and Maria Cantwell (D. 2001–13).

The capital is Olympia. The state contains 39 counties.

RECENT ELECTIONS

In the 2008 presidential elections Barack Obama won Washington State with 57·7% of the vote (John Kerry won in 2004).

CURRENT ADMINISTRATION

Governor: Christine Gregoire (D.), 2009–13 (salary: $166,891).
Lieut.-Governor: Brad Owen (D.), 2009–13 ($93,948).
Secretary of State: Sam Reed (R.), 2009–13 ($116,950).

Government Website: http://access.wa.gov

ECONOMY

Per capita personal income (2008) was $42,857.

Budget

In 2008 total state revenue was $36,645m. Total expenditure was $39,690m. (education, $14,109m.; public welfare, $7,613m.; highways, $2,924m.; hospitals, $1,744m.; health, $1,606m.) Outstanding debt in 2008, $23,524m.

Performance

In 2008 Gross Domestic Product by state was $322,778m. (provisional), ranking Washington 14th in the United States.

ENERGY AND NATURAL RESOURCES

Water

The total area covered by water is approximately 4,756 sq. miles.

Minerals

Mining and quarrying are not as important as forestry, agriculture or manufacturing. Total value of non-fuel mineral production in 2006 was $718m.

Agriculture

Agriculture is constantly growing in value because of more intensive and diversified farming, and because of the 1m.-acre Columbia Basin Irrigation Project.

In 2002 there were 39,000 farms with an acreage of 15·7m.; the average farm was 403 acres. Average value of farmland and buildings per acre in 2002 was $1,486. Apples, milk, wheat, cattle and calves and potatoes are the top five commodities. In 2002 livestock included 248,700 beef cows, 246,800 milch cows, and 58,500 sheep and lambs. Hogs and pigs as of 2002 totalled 31,000 head.

Farm income, 2006: from crops, $4,524m.; from livestock and products, $1,615m. The net farm income in 2006 was $958m.

Forestry

Forests covered 22·28m. acres in 2007, of which 8·2m. acres were national forest. In 2006 timber harvested totalled 3,484m. bd ft. Production of wood and bark residues, 2004, was 5,956,000 tons.

Fisheries

Salmon and shellfish are important; total commercial catch, 2002, was 362·0m. lb, and was worth an estimated $142·5m.

INDUSTRY

Principal manufactures are aircraft, pulp and paper, lumber and plywood, aluminium, processed fruit and vegetables. In 2005 the state's 7,404 manufacturing establishments had

257,000 employees, earning $12,548m. Total value added by manufacturing in 2006 was $48,877m.

Labour

In 2007 total non-agricultural employment was 2,932,000. Employees by branch, 2007 (in 1,000): trade, transportation and utilities, 553; government, 533; education and health services, 348; professional and business services, 345; manufacturing, 293. The unemployment rate in 2007 was 4·6%.

COMMUNICATIONS

Roads

In 2007 there were 83,431 miles of road comprising 22,551 miles of urban road and 60,880 miles of rural road. There were 5,757,943 registered motor vehicles.

Rail

In 2005 there were 3,166 miles of freight railroad, including 1,798 miles of Class I railroads.

Civil Aviation

There are international airports at Seattle/Tacoma, Spokane and Boeing Field. There were 17,892,317 passenger enplanements statewide in 2007.

SOCIAL INSTITUTIONS

Justice

In Dec. 2008 there were 17,926 prison inmates. There was one execution in 2001 but none since then.

Education

Education is given free to all children between the ages of five and 21 years, and is compulsory for children from eight to 18 years of age. In Oct. 2003 there were 1,014,142 pupils in public elementary and secondary schools; and 76,845 pupils in private schools. In Oct. 2002 there were 52,888 classroom teachers; average salary, $47,642.

The University of Washington, founded 1861, at Seattle, had, fall 2002, 39,215 students; and Washington State University at Pullman, founded 1890, for science and agriculture, had 22,184 students. Eastern Washington University had 9,178; Central Washington University, 8,768; The Evergreen State College, 4,318; Western Washington University, 12,493. All counts are state-funded enrolment students. Community colleges had (2002) a total of 191,554 state-funded and excess enrolment students.

Health

In 2006 there were 88 community hospitals with 10,900 beds. A total of 556,000 patients were admitted during the year.

Welfare

Medicare enrolment in July 2004 totalled 794,979. In fiscal year 2006 a total of 1,127,976 people in Washington received Medicaid. In Dec. 2008 there were 1,008,804 Old-Age, Survivors, and Disability Insurance (OASDI) beneficiaries. A total of 132,476 people were receiving payments under Temporary Assistance for Needy Families (TANF) in Dec. 2008.

RELIGION

Religious faiths represented include the Roman Catholic (716,133 adherents in 2000), United Methodist, Lutheran, Presbyterian and Episcopalian. There were 178,000 Latter-day Saints (Mormons) in 2000.

FURTHER READING

Statistical information: State Office of Financial Management, POB 43113, Olympia 98504-3113. Publishes *Washington State Data Book*

Dodds, G. B., *American North-West: a History of Oregon and Washington.* 1986

West Virginia

KEY HISTORICAL EVENTS

In 1861 the slave-owning state of Virginia seceded from the Union. The 40 western counties, mostly hilly country and settled by miners and small farmers who were not slave-owners, were declared a new state. On 20 June 1863 West Virginia became the 35th state of the Union.

The capital, Charleston, was an 18th-century fortified post on the early westward migration routes across the Appalachians. In 1795 local brine wells were tapped and the city grew as a salt town. Coal, oil, natural gas and a variety of salt brines were all found in due course. Huntington, the next largest town, served the same industrial area as a railway terminus and port on the Ohio river. Wheeling, the original state capital, located on the major transportation routes of the Ohio River, Baltimore and Ohio Railroad and the National Road, was a well established, cosmopolitan city when it hosted the statehood meetings in 1861.

Three-quarters of the state is forest. Settlement has been concentrated in the mineral-bearing Kanawha valley, along the Ohio river and in the industrial Monongahela valley of the north. More than half of the population is still classified as rural. However, the majority commute to industrial employment.

TERRITORY AND POPULATION

West Virginia is bounded in the north by Pennsylvania and Maryland, east and south by Virginia, southwest by the Big Sandy River (forming the boundary with Kentucky) and west by the Ohio River (forming the boundary with Ohio). Land area, 24,077 sq. miles (62,359 sq. km). Census population, 1 April 2000, 1,808,344, an increase of 0·8% since 1990. July 2009 estimate, 1,819,777.

Population in five federal census years was:

	White	*Black*	*American Indian*	*Asiatic*	*Total*	*Per sq. mile*
1910	1,156,817	64,173	36	93	1,221,119	50·8
1960	1,770,133	89,378	181	419	1,860,421	77·3
1980	1,874,751	65,051	1,610	5,194	1,949,644	80·3
1990	1,725,523	56,295	2,458	7,459	1,793,477	74·0
2000	1,718,777	57,232	3,606	9,834	1,808,344	75·1

Of the total population in 2000, 929,174 were female, 1,405,951 were 18 years old or older and 975,564 (53·9%) were rural. In 2000 the Hispanic population was 12,279, up from 8,489 in 1990 (an increase of 44·6%).

The 2000 census population of the principal cities was: Charleston, 53,421; Huntington, 51,475. Others: Parkersburg, 33,099; Wheeling, 31,419; Morgantown, 26,809; Weirton, 20,411; Fairmont, 19,097; Beckley, 17,254; Clarksburg, 16,743.

SOCIAL STATISTICS

Births, 2007 (provisional), 21,432 (11·8 per 1,000 population); deaths, 2006, 20,672 (11·4—the highest rate in any US state). Infant mortality, 2006, 7·4 per 1,000 live births. 2006: marriages, 13,100 (7·3 per 1,000 population); divorces and annulments, 8,500 (4·7).

CLIMATE

Charleston, Jan. 34°F (1·1°C), July 76°F (24·4°C). Annual rainfall 40" (1,010 mm). West Virginia belongs to the Appalachian Mountains climate zone (*see* UNITED STATES: Climate).

CONSTITUTION AND GOVERNMENT

The present constitution was adopted in 1872; it has had 17 amendments. The Legislature consists of the Senate of 34 members elected for a term of four years, one-half being elected biennially, and the House of Delegates of 100 members, elected biennially. The Governor is elected for four years and may serve one successive term.

For the 111th Congress, which convened in Jan. 2009, West Virginia sends three members to the House of Representatives. It is represented in the Senate by Robert Byrd (D. 1959–2013) and Jay Rockefeller IV (D. 1985–2015). Byrd is not only the longest-serving current senator but also the longest-serving in the Senate's history.

The state capital is Charleston. There are 55 counties.

RECENT ELECTIONS

In the 2008 presidential elections John McCain won West Virginia with 55·7% of the vote (George W. Bush won in 2004).

CURRENT ADMINISTRATION

Governor: Joe Manchin, III (D.), 2009–13 (salary: $150,000).

Senate President: Earl Ray Tomblin (D.), 2009–11.

Secretary of State: Natalie Tennant (D.), 2009–13 ($95,000).

Government Website: http://www.wv.gov

ECONOMY

Per capita personal income (2008) was $31,641.

Budget

Total revenues in 2008 were $10,854m. Total expenditures were $10,140m. (education, $3,677m.; public welfare, $2,565m.; highways, $1,016m.; government administration, $412m.; health, $357m.) Outstanding debt in 2008, $6,366m.

Performance

Gross Domestic Product by state in 2008 was $61,652m. (provisional), ranking West Virginia 40th in the United States.

Banking and Finance

There were 50 state banks and 14 national banks with a total of $15,170m. in deposits in 2005. There were also seven saving institutions, with total deposits in June 2006 of $805m.

ENERGY AND NATURAL RESOURCES

Oil and Gas

Petroleum output (2006), 2m. bbls; natural gas production (2006), 226bn. cu. ft.

Water

The total area covered by water is approximately 152 sq. miles.

Minerals

38% of the state is underlain with mineable coal; 139·7m. short tons of coal were produced in 2003. Salt, sand and gravel, sandstone and limestone are also produced. The total value of non-fuel mineral production in 2006 was $230m.

Agriculture

In 2002 the state had 20,500 farms with an area of 3·6m. acres; average size of farm was 176 acres, valued at $1,315 per acre. Livestock farming predominates.

Cash income, 2006: from crops was $80m.; from livestock and products, $370m. The net farm income in 2006 was $50m. Main crops harvested: hay (1·31m. tons); all corn (1·3m. bu.); tobacco (1·8m. lb). Area of main crops: hay, 0·61m. acres; corn, 55,000 acres. Apples (90m. lb) and peaches (1m. lb) are important fruit crops.

Livestock on farms, 2000, included 400,000 cattle, of which 17,000 were milch cows; sheep, 35,000; hogs, 10,000; chickens, 1·86m. excluding broilers. Production included 91·3m. broilers; 20·75m. dozen eggs; 4·1m. turkeys.

Forestry

Forests covered 12,007,000 acres in 2007, with 1,073,000 acres of national forest. 78·5% of the state is woodland.

Fisheries

In 2000, nine state fish hatcheries and one federal fish hatchery sold 363,000 lb of trout and stocked 815,000 lb of trout, in addition to 2·4m. fry, 507,162 fingerlings and 5,000 adults of other types of fish.

INDUSTRY

In 2005 the state's 1,406 manufacturing establishments had 63,000 employees, earning $2,574m. Total value added by manufacturing in 2006 was $10,476m.

Labour

Total non-agricultural employment, 2007, 757,000. Employees by branch, 2007 (in 1,000): government, 145; trade, transportation and utilities, 143; education and health services, 114; leisure and hospitality, 71; professional and business services, 61. The state unemployment rate in 2007 was 4·6%.

INTERNATIONAL TRADE

Imports and Exports

The state's major export markets are the EU and Canada, with coal being a major export commodity. West Virginia staffs trade offices in Nagoya, Japan; Taipei, Taiwan; and Munich, Germany.

COMMUNICATIONS

Roads

In 2007 there were 38,274 miles of road (32,995 miles rural). There were 1,413,467 registered motor vehicles.

Rail

In 2001 the state had 2,659 miles of railroad.

Civil Aviation

There were 37 public airports in 2001. There were 361,779 passenger enplanements statewide in 2007.

Shipping

There are some 420·5 miles of navigable rivers.

Postal Services

In 2001 there were 1,012 postal facilities.

SOCIAL INSTITUTIONS

Justice

The state court system consists of a Supreme Court, 31 circuit courts, and magistrate courts in each county. The Supreme Court of Appeals, exercising original and appellate jurisdiction, has five members elected by the people for 12-year terms. Each circuit court has from one to seven judges (as determined by the Legislature on the basis of population and case-load) chosen by the voters within each circuit for eight-year terms.

In Dec. 2008, 6,059 prisoners were under the jurisdiction of state and federal correctional authorities. Capital punishment was abolished in 1965. The last execution was in 1959.

Education

School attendance is compulsory for all between the ages of six and 16. In 2004–05, 791 public elementary and secondary schools had 280,129 pupils and 19,958 teachers. Total expenditure on public elementary and secondary education in 2003–04 was $2,643m. and average teacher salary was $38,461. Spending per pupil in 2002–03 was $8,318.

In fall 2005 there were 23 public and 21 private degree-granting institutions; leading public institutions of higher education included:

Founded		*Students*
1837	Marshall University, Huntington	13,988[1]
1837	West Liberty State College, West Liberty	2,248
1867	Fairmont State University, Fairmont	4,740
1868	West Virginia University, Morgantown	26,051
1872	Concord College, Athens	2,826
1872	Glenville State College, Glenville	1,392
1872	Shepherd University, Shepherdstown	3,901
1891	West Virginia State University, Institute	3,491
1895	West Virginia Univ. Inst. of Technology, Montgomery	1,551
1895	Bluefield State College, Bluefield	1,708
1901	Potomac State College of West Virginia Univ., Keyser	1,279
1961	West Virginia Univ. at Parkersburg, Parkersburg	3,772
1976	School of Osteopathic Medicine, Lewisburg	394

[1]Includes Marshall Univ. Graduate College, South Charleston, founded in 1972.

Health

In 2006 there were 56 community hospitals with 7,100 beds. A total of 281,000 patients were admitted during the year.

Welfare

The Department of Health Human Resources, originating in the 1930s as the Department of Public Assistance, is both state and federally financed. Medicare enrolment in July 2004 totalled 350,914. In fiscal year 2006 a total of 373,296 people in West Virginia received Medicaid. In Dec. 2008 there were 429,613 Old-Age, Survivors, and Disability Insurance (OASDI) beneficiaries. A total of 20,743 people were receiving payments under Temporary Assistance for Needy Families (TANF) in Dec. 2008.

RELIGION

Chief denominations in 2001 were: United Methodists (115,062 members), Roman Catholics (97,232), Baptists American (94,000) and Southern (33,000).

CULTURE

Broadcasting

In 2001 there were 156 commercial, 14 college and 14 public radio stations. Television stations numbered 14 commercial and three public.

Tourism

There are 35 state parks, nine state forests, 58 wildlife management areas and two state trails. Visitors are attracted to the area by whitewater rafting, hiking, skiing and biking and the winter outdoor light display at Oglebay Park in Wheeling.

FURTHER READING

West Virginia Blue Book. Annual, since 1916

Statistical Handbook, 2001. 2001

Lewis, R. L. and Hennen, J. C., *West Virginia History: Critical Essays on the Literature.* 1993

Rice, O. K., *West Virginia: A History.* 2nd ed. 1994

State library: Archives and History, Division of Culture and History, Charleston.

Wisconsin

KEY HISTORICAL EVENTS

The French were the first European explorers of the territory; Jean Nicolet landed at Green Bay in 1634, a mission was founded in 1671 and a permanent settlement at Green Bay followed. In 1763 French claims were surrendered to Britain. In 1783 Britain ceded the area to the USA which designated the Northwest Territory, of which Wisconsin was part. In 1836 a separate Territory of Wisconsin included the present Iowa, Minnesota and parts of the Dakotas.

In 1836 James Duane Doty founded Madison and, even before it was inhabited, successfully pressed its claim to be the capital of the Territory. In 1848 Wisconsin became a state, with its present boundaries.

The city of Milwaukee was founded on Lake Michigan when Indian tribes gave up their claims to the land in 1831–33. It grew rapidly as a port and industrial town, attracting German settlers in the 1840s and Poles and Italians 50 years later. The Lake Michigan shore was developed as an industrial area; the rest of the south proved suitable for dairy farming; the north, mainly forests and lakes, has remained sparsely settled except for tourist bases.

There are 11 Indian reservations where more than 15,500 of Wisconsin's 47,000 Indians live. Since the Second World War there has been black immigration from the southern states to the industrial lake-shore cities.

TERRITORY AND POPULATION

Wisconsin is bounded north by Lake Superior and the Upper Peninsula of Michigan, east by Lake Michigan, south by Illinois, and west by Iowa and Minnesota, with the Mississippi River forming most of the boundary. Land area, 54,310 sq. miles (140,662 sq. km). Census population, 1 April 2000, 5,363,675, an increase of 9·6% since 1990. July 2009 estimate, 5,654,774.

Population in five census years was:

	White	*Black*	*All Others*	*Total*	*Per sq. mile*
1910	2,320,555	2,900	10,405	2,333,860	42·2
1930	2,916,255	10,739	12,012	2,939,006	53·7
1980	4,443,035	182,592	80,015	4,705,642	86·4
1990	4,512,523	244,539	134,707	4,891,769	90·1
2000	4,769,857	304,460	289,358	5,363,675	98·8

Of the total population in 2000, 2,714,634 were female, 3,994,919 were 18 years old or older and 3,663,643 were urban. In 2000 Wisconsin's Hispanic population was 192,921, up from 93,194 in 1990 (an increase of 107·0%).

Population of the large cities, 2000 census, was as follows:

Milwaukee	596,974	Oshkosh	62,916
Madison	208,054	Eau Claire	61,704
Green Bay	102,313	West Allis	61,254
Kenosha	90,352	Janesville	59,498
Racine	81,855	La Crosse	51,818
Appleton	70,087	Sheboygan	50,792
Waukesha	64,825	Wauwatosa	47,271

Fond du Lac	42,203	New Berlin	38,220
Brookfield	38,649	Beloit	35,775
Wausau	38,426	Greenfield	35,476

Population of largest metropolitan areas, 2000 census: Milwaukee–Racine, 1,689,572; Madison, 426,526; Appleton–Oshkosh–Neenah, 358,365; Duluth–Superior (Minn.–Wis.), 243,815; Green Bay, 226,778.

SOCIAL STATISTICS

Births, 2007 (provisional), 72,932 (13·0 per 1,000 population); deaths, 2006, 46,153 (8·3). Infant deaths, 2006, 6·4 per 1,000 live births. 2006: marriages, 32,600 (5·8 per 1,000 population); divorces and annulments, 16,000 (2·9).

CLIMATE

Milwaukee, Jan. 19°F (–7·2°C), July 70°F (21·1°C). Annual rainfall 29" (727 mm). Wisconsin belongs to the Great Lakes climate zone (*see* UNITED STATES: Climate).

CONSTITUTION AND GOVERNMENT

The constitution, which dates from 1848, has 141 amendments. The legislative power is vested in a Senate of 33 members elected for four years, one-half elected alternately, and an Assembly of 99 members all elected simultaneously for two years. The Governor and Lieut.-Governor are elected for four years.

For the 111th Congress, which convened in Jan. 2009, Wisconsin sends eight members to the House of Representatives. It is represented in the Senate by Herbert Kohl (D. 1989–2013) and Russell Feingold (D. 1993–2011).

The capital is Madison. The state has 72 counties.

RECENT ELECTIONS

In the 2008 presidential elections Barack Obama won Wisconsin with 56·2% of the vote (John Kerry won in 2004).

CURRENT ADMINISTRATION

Governor: Jim Doyle (D.), 2007–11 (salary: $144,423).

Lieut.-Governor: Barbara Lawton (D.), 2007–11 ($76,261).

Secretary of State: Douglas LaFollette (D.), 2007–11 ($68,556).

Government Website: http://www.wisconsin.gov

ECONOMY

Per capita personal income (2008) was $37,767.

Budget

Total state revenues in 2008 were $25,644m.; total expenditure, $32,649m. (including: education, $10,330m.; public welfare, $6,524m.; highways, $1,901m.; hospitals, $1,106m.; correction, $1,084m.) Outstanding debt in 2008, $22,107m.

Performance

Gross Domestic Product by state in 2008 was $240,429m. (provisional), ranking Wisconsin 21st in the United States.

Banking and Finance

On 30 Sept. 2004 there were 232 state chartered banks with assets of $68·5bn., and 45 federally chartered banks with $23·7bn. in assets. On 30 Sept. 2004, 19 state chartered savings institutions had $4·2bn. in assets and 20 federally chartered savings institutions had $18·8bn. in assets. As of 30 June 2004 there were 293 state chartered credit unions with $13·5bn. in assets.

ENERGY AND NATURAL RESOURCES

Electricity

57,241m. kWh of electricity were produced in 2003; and 10,766m. kWh were imported. Fossil fuel plants accounted for 72·3% of state production, nuclear 21·7% and hydropower 3·0%. Coal accounted for 62% of utility energy use in 2003; nuclear fuel, 17%; natural gas, 3%; renewable sources, 2%; and electricity imports, 16%.

Oil and Gas

Petroleum accounted for 29% of the total energy consumed in 2003 and natural gas 22%. Transportation accounted for 83% of petroleum consumption. Natural gas accounted for 51% of residential end use and petroleum 14%. There are no known petroleum or natural gas reserves in Wisconsin.

Water

The total area covered by water is approximately 11,188 sq. miles.

Minerals

Construction sand and gravel, crushed stone, industrial or specialty sand and lime are the chief mineral products. Mineral production in 2006 was valued at $566m.

Agriculture

On 1 Jan. 2004 there were 76,500 farms (16,096 dairy herds) with a total acreage of 15·6m. acres and an average size of 204 acres, compared with 142,000 farms with a total acreage of 22·4m. acres and an average of 158 acres in 1959. In 2003 the average value per acre was $2,350. Farm income, 2006: from crops $2,135m.; from livestock and products, $4,656m. The net farm income in 2006 was $1,091m.

Dairy farming is important, with 1·25m. milch cows in 2003. Production of cheese accounted for 27% of the USA's total in 2003. Production of the principal field crops in 2003 included: corn for grain, 368m. bu.; corn for silage, 14·1m. tons; oats, 15·4m. bu.; all hay, 4·4m. tons. Other crops of importance: 46·8m. bu. of soybeans, 32·8m. cwt of potatoes, 3·6m. bbls of cranberries, 96,000 tons of carrots and the processing crops of 687,400 tons of sweet corn, 84,300 tons of green peas, 270,800 tons of snap beans, 36,100 tons of cucumbers for pickles, 13·8m. lb of tart cherries and 989,000 cwt of cabbage.

Wisconsin is also a major producer of mink pelts.

Forestry

Wisconsin had (2007) 16,275,000 acres of forested land, with 1,407,000 acres of national forest. In 2006 timber removals were 454m. cu. ft (349m. cu. ft hardwoods and 105m. cu. ft softwoods).

INDUSTRY

Wisconsin has much heavy industry, particularly in the Milwaukee area. Three-fifths of manufacturing employees work on durable goods. Industrial machinery is the major industrial group (17% of all manufacturing employment) followed by fabricated metals, food and kindred products, printing and publishing, paper and allied products, electrical equipment and transportation equipment. In 2005 the state's 9,754 manufacturing establishments had 494,000 employees, earning $21,148m. Total value added by manufacturing in 2006 was $72,015m.

Labour

Total non-agricultural employment, 2007, 2,882,000. Employees by branch, 2007 (in 1,000): trade, transportation and utilities, 547; manufacturing, 501; government, 416; education and health services, 399; professional and business services, 277. Average annual pay per worker (2005) was $35,471. Average unemployment was 5·0% in 2007.

Trade Unions
Labour union membership numbered 414,000 in 2003 and represented 15·9% of the workforce. Union membership was 19·9% of workers in the manufacturing sector in 2002.

COMMUNICATIONS
Roads
In 2007 the state had 114,705 miles of road of which 92,557 miles were rural roads. There were 5,017,895 registered motor vehicles.

Rail
On 31 Dec. 2002 the state had 5,095 track-miles of railroad and 12 railroads that hauled 158m. tons of freight.

Civil Aviation
There were, in 2002, 134 public access airports. There were 5,606,008 passenger enplanements statewide in 2007.

Shipping
Lake Superior and Lake Michigan ports handled 47·8m. tons of freight in 2002; 87% of it at Superior, one of the world's biggest grain ports, and much of the rest at Milwaukee and Green Bay.

SOCIAL INSTITUTIONS
Justice
In Dec. 2008 there were 23,380 prison inmates. The death penalty was abolished in 1853.

Education
All children between the ages of six and 18 are required to attend school full-time to the end of the school term in which they become 18 years of age. In 2003–04 the public school grades kindergarten-12 had 853,363 pupils. There were 61,394 (full-time equivalent) teachers in 2002–03. Private schools enrolled 124,248 students grades kindergarten-12. Public pre-schools enrolled 26,668 children, and private 13,604. Average public school teacher salary in 2003–04 was $42,882 and the total expenditure for public elementary and secondary education was $8,713m. Spending per pupil in 2002–03 was $9,004.

In 2002–03 technical colleges had an enrolment of 429,355 and 4,902 (full-time equivalent) teachers, and two Indian tribe community colleges enrolled 1,060 (2003–04). There is a school for the visually handicapped and a school for the deaf.

The University of Wisconsin, established in 1848, was joined by law in 1971 with the Wisconsin State Universities System to become the University of Wisconsin System with 13 degree granting campuses, 13 two-year campuses in the Center System and the University Extension. The system had, in 2002–03, 6,718 full-time professors and instructors. In fall 2003, 160,703 students enrolled (10,599 at Eau Claire, 5,448 at Green Bay, 8,746 at La Crosse, 40,769 at Madison, 24,875 at Milwaukee, 11,013 at Oshkosh, 5,072 at Parkside, 6,134 at Platteville, 5,799 at River Falls, 8,750 at Stevens Point, 7,708 at Stout, 2,832 at Superior, 10,548 at Whitewater and 12,410 at the Center System freshman-sophomore centres).

UW-Extension enrolled 176,793 students in its continuing education programmes in 2001–02. There are also several independent institutions of higher education: Marquette University (Jesuit), in Milwaukee (11,000 in 2002–03); Cardinal Strich University (Franciscan), with campuses in Milwaukee, Madison and Edina, Minnesota (6,588 in 2002–03); Concordia University Wisconsin (Lutheran), in Mequon (4,541 in 2002–03); and Lawrence University, Appleton (1,325 in 2002–03). There were also 16 higher education colleges, four technical and professional schools and four theological seminaries in 2003. The state's educational and broadcasting service is licensed through the UW Board of Regents.

The total expenditure, 2001–02, for all public education (except capital outlay and debt service) was $12,170·8m. ($2,253 per capita).

Health
In 2006 there were 124 community hospitals with 14,100 beds. A total of 609,000 patients were admitted during the year.

Welfare
In Nov. 2004 there were 136,488 Supplemental Security Income (SSI) recipients in the state; set monthly payments (2005) are $663 for a single individual, $709 for an eligible individual with an ineligible spouse and $1,001 for an eligible couple. A special payment level of $759 for an individual and $1,346 for a couple may be paid with special approval for SSI recipients who are developmentally disabled or chronically mentally ill, living in a non-medical living arrangement not his or her own home. There is a monthly cash benefit for each child living with an SSI parent of $250 for the first child and $150 for each additional child. All SSI recipients receive state medical assistance coverage and may qualify for food stamps.

Wisconsin completed its conversion to the W-2 (Wisconsin Works) programme on 31 March 1998, ending the 62-year-old Aid to Families with Dependent Children (AFDC) programme. W-2 clients (Nov. 2004) totalled 15,374 with 11,148 receiving cash assistance. W-2 clients must be working, seeking employment or be enrolled in job-training programmes. Recipients are limited to 60 months of financial assistance (consecutive or non-consecutive). Participants are eligible for child care assistance, a state subsidized health plan, job and transportation assistance and food stamps. In Aug. 2004 there were 322,405 (132,313 households) food stamp recipients. In fiscal year 2006 a total of 973,369 people in Wisconsin received Medicaid. An additional 94,257 (Aug. 2004) are provided for under BadgerCare, a state-funded medical insurance programme for certain low-income families.

RELIGION
Wisconsin church affiliation, as a percentage of the 2004 population, was estimated at 31% Catholic, 25% Protestant Mainline, 22% Evangelical and 14% unaffiliated.

CULTURE
There are two professional opera companies in Wisconsin: the Madison Opera, and the Florentine Opera in Milwaukee.

Broadcasting
In 2003 there were 32 commercial TV stations; eight educational TV stations; 265 commercial radio stations; and 51 non-commercial.

Press
There were 36 daily newspapers in 2003.

Tourism
The tourist-vacation industry ranks among the first three in economic importance in Wisconsin with an estimated $11,710m. spent in 2003. The Department of Tourism budgeted $13,665,400 to promote tourism in 2004–05.

FURTHER READING
Wisconsin Blue Book. Biennial

State Historical Society of Wisconsin: *The History of Wisconsin.* Vol. IV [J. Buenker]. 1999

State Information Agency: Legislative Reference Bureau, One East Main St., Suite 200, Madison, WI 53703-2037.
Website: http://www.legis.state.wi.us

Wyoming

KEY HISTORICAL EVENTS

The territory was inhabited by Plains Indians (Arapahoes, Sioux and Cheyenne) in the early 19th century. There was some trading with white Americans, but very little white settlement. In the 1840s the great western migration routes, the Oregon and the Overland Trails, ran through the territory with Wyoming offering mountain passes accessible to wagons. Once migration became a steady flow forts were built to protect the route from Indian attack.

In 1867 coal was discovered. In 1868 Wyoming was organized as a separate Territory and in 1869 the Sioux and Arapaho were confined to reservations. At the same time the route of the Union Pacific Railway brought railway towns to southern Wyoming. Settlement of the north was delayed until after the final defeat of hostile Indians in 1876.

The economy was based on ranching. Cheyenne, made Territorial capital in 1869, also functioned as a railway town moving cattle. Casper, on the site of a fort on the Pony Express route, was also a railway town on the Chicago and North Western. Laramie started as a Union Pacific construction workers' shanty town in 1868. In 1890 oil was discovered at Casper, and Wyoming became a state the same year. Subsequently, mineral extraction became the leading industry, as natural gas, uranium, bentonite and trona were exploited as well as oil and coal.

TERRITORY AND POPULATION

Wyoming is bounded north by Montana, east by South Dakota and Nebraska, south by Colorado, southwest by Utah and west by Idaho. Land area, 97,100 sq. miles (251,488 sq. km). The Yellowstone National Park occupies about 2·22m. acres; the Grand Teton National Park has 307,000 acres. The federal government in 2003 owned 49,268 sq. miles (50·6% of the total area of the state). The Federal Bureau of Land Management administers 17·4m. acres.

Census population, 1 April 2000, 493,782, an increase of 8·9% since 1990; July 2009 estimate, 544,270. Wyoming has the smallest population of any of the states of the USA, but in the year 1 July 2008–30 June 2009 the state's population showed the largest percentage growth of any in the USA.

Population in five census years was:

	White	Black	American Indian	Asiatic		Total	Per sq. mile
1910	140,318	2,235	1,486	1,926		145,965	1·5
1930	221,241	1,250	1,845	1,229		225,565	2·3
			All others				
1980	446,488	3,364	19,705			469,557	4·8
	White	Black	American Indian	Asian/Pacific Islands	Other	Total	Per sq. mile
1990	427,061	3,606	9,479	2,806	10,636	453,588	4·7
2000	454,670	3,722	11,133	3,073	21,184	493,782	5·1

Of the total population in 2000, 248,374 were male, 364,909 were 18 years old or older and 321,344 were urban. At the 2000 census the Hispanic population of Wyoming was 31,669, up from 25,751 in 1990 (an increase of 23%).

The largest towns (with 2000 census population) are Cheyenne, 53,011; Casper, 49,644; Laramie, 27,204; Gillette, 19,646; Rock Springs, 18,708; Sheridan, 15,804; Green River, 11,808.

SOCIAL STATISTICS

Births, 2007 (provisional), 7,858 (15·0 per 1,000 population); deaths, 2006, 4,311 (8·4). Infant mortality rate, 2006, 7·0 per 1,000 live births. 2006: marriages, 5,000 (9·8 per 1,000 population); divorces and annulments, 2,700 (5·4). The abortion rate, at less than 1 for every 1,000 women in 2002, is the lowest of any US state.

CLIMATE

Cheyenne, Jan. 25°F (–3·9°C), July 66°F (18·9°C). Annual rainfall 15" (376 mm). Yellowstone Park, Jan. 18°F (–7·8°C), July 61°F (16·1°C). Annual rainfall 18" (444 mm). Wyoming belongs to the Mountain States climate region (*see* UNITED STATES: Climate).

CONSTITUTION AND GOVERNMENT

The constitution, drafted in 1890, has since had 76 amendments. The Legislature consists of a Senate of 30 members elected for staggered four-year terms, and a House of Representatives of 60 members elected for two years. It sits annually in Jan. or Feb. The Governor is elected for four years.

For the 111th Congress, which convened in Jan. 2009, Wyoming sends one member to the House of Representatives. It is represented in the Senate by Michael Enzi (R. 1997–2015) and John Barrasso (R. 2007–13).

The capital is Cheyenne. The state contains 23 counties.

RECENT ELECTIONS

In the 2008 presidential elections John McCain won Wyoming with 64·4% of the vote (George W. Bush won in 2004).

CURRENT ADMINISTRATION

Governor: David D. Freudenthal (D.), 2007–11 (salary: $105,000).

Secretary of State: Max Maxfield (R.), 2007–11 ($92,000).

Government Website: http://wyoming.gov

ECONOMY

Per capita personal income (2008) was $48,608.

Budget

In 2008 total state revenue was $6,481m. Total expenditure was $5,082m. (education, $1,538m.; public welfare, $656m.; highways, $521m.; natural resources, $310m.; health, $281m.) Outstanding debt in 2008, $1,343m.

Performance

Gross Domestic Product by state was $35,310m. in 2008 (provisional), ranking Wyoming 48th in the United States.

Banking and Finance

In 2005 there were 17 national and 26 state banks with a total of $8,563m. deposits.

ENERGY AND NATURAL RESOURCES

Oil and Gas

Wyoming produces significant quantities of oil and natural gas. In 2006 the output of oil was 53m. bbls; natural gas, 1,816bn. cu. ft (the second highest total after Texas).

Water

The total area covered by water is approximately 713 sq. miles.

Minerals

In 2004 the output of coal was 395·5m. short tons; trona (2004), 18·7m. short tons; uranium (2003), 1·2m. lb. Wyoming is the USA's leading coal producer, accounting for 35% of the country's coal output in 2004. It also has 14% of the country's coal reserves. Total value of non-fuel mineral production in 2006 was $1,590m.

Agriculture

Wyoming is semi-arid, and agriculture is carried on by irrigation and dry farming. In 2004 there were 9,200 farms and ranches; total farm area was 34·4m. acres; average size of farm in 2004 was 3,743 acres (the largest of any state). In 2004 the average value of farmland was $315 per acre.

Total value, 2006, of crops produced, $162m.; of livestock and products, $859m. The net farm income in 2006 was $65m. Crop production in 2004 (1,000 bu.): barley, 6,900; corn for grain, 6,681; wheat, 3,510; oats, 795; sugar beets, 812,000 tons. Animals on farms included 1·35m. cattle, 450,000 sheep and 114,000 hogs and pigs. Total egg production in 2004 was 3·6m.

Forestry
The state had a forested area of 11,445,000 acres in 2007, of which 6,028,000 acres were national forest.

INDUSTRY
In 2005 the state's 543 manufacturing establishments had 10,000 employees, earning $463m. Total value added by manufacturing in 2006 was $3,418m. In 2003 there were 760 mining establishments. A large portion of the manufacturing in the state is based on natural resources, mainly oil and farm products. Leading industries are food, wood products (except furniture) and machinery (except electrical).

Labour
Total non-agricultural employment, 2007, 288,000. Employees by branch, 2007 (in 1,000): government, 67; trade, transportation and utilities, 55; leisure and hospitality, 34; construction, 26; education and health services, 23. The unemployment rate was 2·9% in 2007.

Trade Unions
There were 18,000 working members in trade unions (6·6% of total employment) in 2004.

INTERNATIONAL TRADE
Imports and Exports
In 2004 total export from Wyoming was $680·2m.

COMMUNICATIONS
Roads
In 2007 there were 2,642 miles of urban roads and 25,410 miles of rural roads. There were 652,102 motor vehicle registrations in 2007.

Rail
In 2002, 1,886 miles of railroad were operated.

Civil Aviation
In 2005 there were 41 public-use airports and 23 heliports. There were 499,423 passenger enplanements statewide in 2007.

SOCIAL INSTITUTIONS
Justice
In Dec. 2008 there were 2,084 prison inmates. Capital punishment is authorized but has been used only once, in 1992, since the US Supreme Court reinstated the death penalty in 1976.

Education
In 2004–05, 378 public elementary and secondary schools had 84,733 pupils and 6,657 teachers. In 2003–04 pupils in private elementary and secondary schools numbered 2,079. The average expenditure per pupil for 2004 was $10,206. State and local government expenditure in 2003–04 was $991m.

The University of Wyoming, founded at Laramie in 1887 had, in the academic year 2004–05, 13,207 students. There were seven community colleges in 2004–05 with 14,774 students.

Health
In 2005 the state had 26 general hospitals with 1,378 beds, and 39 registered nursing homes with 3,032 beds.

Welfare
In 2004, $25m. was distributed in food stamps. In fiscal year 2006 a total of 69,461 people in Wyoming received Medicaid, with total payments of $412m. Medicare enrolment in July 2004 totalled 69,712. In Dec. 2008 there were 85,755 Old-Age, Survivors, and Disability Insurance (OASDI) beneficiaries. A total of 555 people were receiving payments under Temporary Assistance for Needy Families (TANF) in Dec. 2008. In 2004–05, $814,034 was distributed under the TANF programme.

RELIGION
Chief religious bodies in 2000 were Protestants (with 101,468 members), Roman Catholics (80,421) and Latter-day Saints (Mormons) (47,129).

CULTURE
Broadcasting
In 2004 there were 32 AM, 57 FM radio stations and 16 television stations.

Press
In 2004 there were 43 newspapers, two of which were published daily.

Tourism
There are over 7m. tourists annually, mainly outdoor enthusiasts. The state has large elk and pronghorn antelope herds, ten fish hatcheries and numerous wild game. In 2004, 2·5m. people visited state parks and historic sites. In 2004, 715,000 fishing, gaming and bird licences were sold. In 2005 there were ten operational ski areas.

FURTHER READING

Equality State Almanac 2008. Wyoming Department of Administration and Information. Division of Economic Analysis. Cheyenne, WY 82002

Wyoming Official Directory. Secretary of State. Annual

Treadway, T., *Wyoming.* 1982

Statistics Website: http://eadiv.state.wy.us

OUTLYING TERRITORIES

The outlying territories of the USA comprise the two Commonwealths of the Northern Mariana Islands and Puerto Rico, the incorporated territory of Palmyra Atoll, a number of unincorporated territories (including American Samoa, Guam and the US Virgin Islands) in the Pacific Ocean and one unincorporated territory in the Caribbean Sea.

Commonwealth of the Northern Mariana Islands

KEY HISTORICAL EVENTS

In 1889 Spain ceded Guam (largest and southernmost of the Marianas Islands) to the USA and sold the rest to Germany. Occupied by Japan in 1914, the islands were administered by Japan under a League of Nations mandate until occupied by US forces in Aug. 1944. In 1947 they became part of the US-administered Trust Territory of the Pacific Islands. On 17 June 1975 the electorate voted for a Commonwealth in association with the USA; this was approved by the US government in April 1976 and came into force on 1 Jan. 1978. In Nov. 1986 the islanders were granted US citizenship. The UN terminated the Trusteeship status on 22 Dec. 1990.

TERRITORY AND POPULATION

The Northern Marianas form a single chain of 16 mountainous islands extending north of Guam for about 560 km, with a total area of 5,050 sq. km (1,950 sq. miles) of which 464 sq. km (179 sq. miles) are dry land, and with a population (2000 census) of 69,221 (female, 37,237).

The areas and populations of the islands are as follows:

Island(s)	*Sq. km*	*1995 Census*	*2000 Census*
Northern Group[1]	171	8	6
Saipan	122	52,698	62,392
Tinian (with Aguijan)	101[2]	2,631	3,540
Rota	83	3,509	3,283

[1]Pagan, Agrihan, Alamagan and nine uninhabited islands.
[2]Including uninhabited Aguijan.

In 2003, 23% spoke Chinese, 22% Chamorro and 24% Filipino languages. English remains an official language along with Carolinian and Chamorro. The largest town is Chalan Kanoa on Saipan.

SOCIAL STATISTICS

Births, 2006, 1,422 (17·2 per 1,000 population); deaths, 170 (2·1). Infant mortality, 2002, 6 per 1,000 live births.

CONSTITUTION AND GOVERNMENT

The Constitution was approved by a referendum on 6 March 1977 and came into force on 9 Jan. 1978. The legislature comprises a nine-member *Senate*, with three Senators elected from each of the main three islands for a term of four years, and an 20-member *House of Representatives*, elected for a term of two years.

The Commonwealth is administered by a Governor and Lieut.-Governor, elected for four years.

As from Jan. 2009 the Commonwealth sends one delegate to the US House of Representatives. The Congressman may participate but not vote on the House floor.

RECENT ELECTIONS

At the elections of 3 Nov. 2007 the Republican Party won 12 seats in the House of Representatives, the Covenant Party 4 and the Democratic Party 1. Three independents were elected.

In the gubernatorial elections of 7 Nov. 2009 Heinz S. Hofschneider received 36·3% of votes cast, incumbent Benigno R. Fitial 36·2%, Juan Guerrero 19·3% and Ramon Guerrero 8·0%. In a run-off on 23 Nov. between Fitial and Hofschneider, Fitial retained power after winning 51·4% of the vote to Hofschneider's 48·6%.

CURRENT ADMINISTRATION

Governor: Benigno R. Fitial (Covenant Party), 2010–15 (salary: $70,000).

Lieut.-Governor: Eloy S. Inos (Covenant Party), 2010–15 ($60,000).

Legislature Website: http://www.cnmileg.gov.mp

ENERGY AND NATURAL RESOURCES

Water

The total area covered by water is approximately 10 sq. miles.

Fisheries

In 2005 total catch was 432,000 lb (196 tonnes), entirely from marine waters.

INDUSTRY

Labour

In 1990 there were 7,476 workers from the indigenous population and 21,188 were foreign workers; 2,699 were unemployed.

INTERNATIONAL TRADE

Imports and Exports

In 1997 imports totalled $836·2m.; in 1999 exports totalled $1,049·0m. Most imports came from other US Pacific territories, Hong Kong and Japan.

COMMUNICATIONS

Roads

There are about 381 km of roads.

Civil Aviation

There are six airports in all. Saipan handled 677,000 passengers (595,000 on international flights) and 9,500 tonnes of freight in 2001.

Telecommunications

There were 24,700 main telephone lines in 2008, equivalent to 289·3 per 1,000 inhabitants, and 20,500 mobile phone subscribers in 2004.

SOCIAL INSTITUTIONS

Education

In 2000 there were 679 pupils enrolled in nursery school and pre-school, 946 in kindergarten, 7,884 in elementary school (grades 1–8), 2,750 in high school (grades 9–12) and 1,130 in college or graduate school.

Health

In 1999 there were 31 doctors, three dentists, 123 nursing personnel, four pharmacists and 14 midwives. In 2001 there was one hospital with 86 beds.

RELIGION

The population is predominantly Roman Catholic.

CULTURE

Broadcasting

There were six radio stations, one television station and two cable TV stations on Saipan in 1998. In 1999 there were 4,100 television receivers.

Tourism

In 2004 there were 525,000 tourists (excluding day-visitors).

Commonwealth of Puerto Rico

KEY HISTORICAL EVENTS

A Spanish dependency since the 16th century, Puerto Rico was ceded to the USA in 1898 after the Spanish defeat in the Spanish-American war. In 1917 US citizenship was conferred and in 1932 there was a name change from Porto Rico to Puerto Rico. In 1952 Puerto Rico was proclaimed a commonwealth with a representative government and a directly elected governor.

TERRITORY AND POPULATION

Puerto Rico is the easternmost of the Greater Antilles and lies between the Dominican Republic and the US Virgin Islands. The total area is 13,791 sq. km (5,325 sq. miles), of which 8,871 sq. km (3,425 sq. miles) are dry land; the population, according to the census of 2000, was 3,808,610, an increase of 8·1% over 1990. The urban population was 3,595,521 in 2000, representing 94·4% (73·3% in 1995) of the total population. Population density was 1,112 per sq. mile in 2000. Of the total population in 2000, 1,975,033 were female. Population estimate in July 2009 was 3,967,288. The UN gives an estimated population for 2010 of 4·00m.

Chief towns, 2005 estimates, are: San Juan (the capital), 432,692; Bayamón, 226,789; Carolina, 191,214; Ponce, 185,276; Caguas, 143,844.

The Puerto Rican island of Vieques, 10 miles to the east, has an area of 51·7 sq. miles and 9,259 (2005) inhabitants. The island of Culebra, between Puerto Rico and St Thomas, has an area of 10 sq. miles and 1,960 (2005) inhabitants. Both islands have good harbours.

Spanish and English are the joint official languages.

SOCIAL STATISTICS

Births, 2007 (provisional), 46,551 (11·8 per 1,000 population); deaths, 2006, 28,206 (7·2). Marriages, 2004, 23,650; infant mortality rate, 2005, 9·2 per 1,000 live births. Annual growth rate, 2000–05, 0·5%. In 2003 the most popular age range for marrying was 20–24 for both males and females. Fertility rate, 2003, 1·8 births per woman.

CLIMATE

Warm, sunny winters with hot summers. The north coast experiences more rainfall than the south coast and generally does not have a dry season as rainfall is evenly spread throughout the year. San Juan, Jan. 25°C, July 28°C. Annual rainfall 1,246 mm.

CONSTITUTION AND GOVERNMENT

Puerto Rico is a self-governing commonwealth (*Estado Libre Asociado*) in association with the United States. The chief of state is the President of the United States of America. The head of government is an elected Governor. There are two legislative chambers: the 51-member House of Representatives and the 27-member Senate. Both houses meet annually in Jan. The executive power is exercised by the Governor, elected every four years, who leads a cabinet of 15 ministers.

Puerto Rico has authority over its internal affairs, but the USA controls areas generally regulated by the federal government. Puerto Ricans are US citizens and possess most of the rights and obligations of citizens from the 50 states, such as paying Social Security and receiving federal welfare. The main differences are Puerto Rico's local taxation system and exemption from Internal Revenue Code, its lack of voting representation in either house of the US Congress (they have one non-voting representative) and the ineligibility of Puerto Ricans to vote in presidential elections. Puerto Rican men are subject to subscription in the US Armed Forces, but the commonwealth sends independent teams to the Olympics.

A new constitution was drafted by a Puerto Rican Constituent Assembly and approved by the electorate at a referendum on 3 March 1952. It was then submitted to Congress, which struck out Section 20 of Article 11 covering the 'right to work' and the 'right to an adequate standard of living'; the remainder was passed and proclaimed by the Governor on 25 July 1952.

RECENT ELECTIONS

At the gubernatorial election on 4 Nov. 2008 Luis Guillermo Fortuño (New Progressive Party /PNP) won with 52·8% of the vote, ahead of incumbent Aníbal Acevedo Vilá (Popular Democratic Party/PPD) with 41·3%, Rogelio Figueroa (Puerto Ricans for Puerto Rico/PPR) with 2·8% and Edwin Irizarry Mora (Puerto Rican Independence Party/PIP) with 2·0%.

In elections to the Chamber of Representatives on 4 Nov. 2008 the New Progressive Party (PNP) polled 74·5% of the vote and claimed 38 of the 51 seats and the Popular Democratic Party (PPD) 25·5% and 13 seats. In the Senate elections of the same day PNP took 22 seats and PPD took 5.

At a plebiscite on 14 Nov. 1993 on Puerto Rico's future status, 48·6% of votes cast were for Commonwealth (status quo), 46·3% for Statehood (51st State of the USA) and 4·4% for full independence. In a further plebiscite in Dec. 1998, some 52·2% of voters backed the opposition's call for no change, while 46·5% supported statehood. Independence was supported by 2·5%, while free association received 0·3%.

CURRENT ADMINISTRATION

Governor: Luis Guillermo Fortuño (PNP), 2009–13 (salary: $63,000).

Secretary of State: Kenneth McClintock (PNP), appointed Jan. 2009 ($81,000).

Government Website (Spanish only): http://www.gobierno.pr

ECONOMY

Budget

Revenues in 2005 totalled $12,444·0m. and expenditures were $25,205·0m. Tax revenues accounted for 60·8% of revenue. Main items of expenditure were social development (52%), economic development (20%), debt service (13%) and protection and security (7%).

Per capita personal income (2005) was $12,502.

Performance

Real GDP growth was 0·3% in 2005. Total GDP in 2005 was $82,032m.

Banking and Finance

Banks on 30 June 2005 had total deposits of $53,440·9m. Bank loans were $54,128·9m. This includes 13 commercial banks and two government banks.

ENERGY AND NATURAL RESOURCES

Environment

Puerto Rico's carbon dioxide emissions from the consumption and flaring of fossil fuels in 2008 were the equivalent of 8·0 tonnes per capita.

Electricity

Installed capacity was 5·4m. kW in 2004. Production in 2005 was 24·5bn. kWh. Consumption per capita in 2004 was 6,195 kWh.

Water

The total area covered by water is approximately 81 sq. miles.

Agriculture

Gross agricultural income in 2005 was $803·1m. In 2002, 2·0% of the economically active population was employed in agriculture. Production estimates in 2002 (in 1,000 tonnes): sugarcane, 320; plantains, 82; bananas, 50; oranges, 26; mangoes, 17; pineapples, 15; coffee, 13; pumpkins and squash, 11; tomatoes, 5. Livestock (2002): cattle, 390,000; pigs, 118,000; poultry, 12m.

Forestry

In 2005 the area under forests was 408,284 ha., or 46·3% of the total land area.

Fisheries

The total catch in 2005 was 3,791,000 lb (1,720 tonnes), mainly from sea fishing.

INDUSTRY

Manufacturing contributed $33,132m. to total GDP in 2005. There is some production of cement (1·58m. tonnes in 2004).

Labour

There were 1,238,000 people in employment in 2005, including 274,000 people in public administration, 261,000 in wholesale and retail trade and 138,000 in manufacturing. There were 147,000 unemployed persons in 2005 (rate of 10·6%).

INTERNATIONAL TRADE

Imports and Exports

In 2005 imports amounted to $38,905·2m., of which $19,133·7m. came from the USA; exports were valued at $56,543·2m., of which $46,703·0m. went to the USA.

Main imports in 2005 were (in $1m.): chemicals, 17,086·8; petroleum and coal products, 2,924·5; computers and electronic products, 2,833·8. Main exports in 2005 were (in $1m.): chemical products, 38,618·9; computer and electronic products, 7,452·1; medical equipment and supplies, 4,993·8.

Puerto Rico is not permitted to levy taxes on imports.

COMMUNICATIONS

Roads

In 2007 there were 16,397 miles of roads and 2,531,199 registered motor vehicles.

Rail

There are 96 km of railroad, although no passenger service. There is a 17·2-km urban train system in use.

Civil Aviation

San Juan's Luis Muñoz Marin airport handled 10,677,671 passengers and 275,908 tonnes of freight in 2005.

Shipping

In 2005, 4,721 vessels of 55,119,179 gross tons entered and cleared Puerto Rico.

Telecommunications

In 2005 there were 1,217,702 telephone lines, excluding mobile phones. Mobile phone subscribers numbered 1,993,150 in 2005. There were 925,000 internet users in 2005.

SOCIAL INSTITUTIONS

Justice

The Judicial power of the commonwealth is vested in a unified judicial system with regard to jurisdiction, operation and administration. It consists of the Supreme Court, the Court of Appeals and the Court of First Instance, which jointly constitute the General Court of Justice. The Supreme Court is the court of last instance, and is composed of seven members (a chief justice and six associate justices) named by the Governor with the consent of the Senate.

The Court of First Instance is a court of original general jurisdiction consisting of a Superior Court (253 judges) and municipal courts (85 judges). There are 13 judicial regions in the First Instance Court. Final judgments made by the Court of First Instance must be appealed at the Court of Appeals.

The population in penal institutions in Dec. 2005 was 14,412 (368 per 100,000 population).

Education

Education was made compulsory in 1899. The percentage of literacy in 2002 was 94·1% of those 15 years of age or older. Total enrolment in public day schools, 2004–05, was 575,993. All private schools had a total enrolment of 138,560 pupils in 2004–05. Puerto Rico has 20 specialized schools in music, arts, theatre, science and mathematics, and communication in radio and television.

In 2004–05 the University of Puerto Rico had eleven units with a total of 66,389 students. Other institutions of higher education in the public sector had a total of 4,655 students in 2004–05: San Juan Technology College, 936 students; Corporation of Music of Puerto Rico, 298 students; School of Plastic Arts, 461 students; Technology Institute of Puerto Rico of the Department of Education, 2,960 students. Private sector higher education institutions in 2004–05 (with enrolment): the American University, 3,403 students; Caribbean University, 5,078; Columbia College, 1,086; Electronic Data Processing College of Puerto Rico, 2,017; Huertas Junior College, 1,459; Commercial Institute of Puerto Rico Junior College, 1,300; National University College, 4,460; Pontifical Catholic University of Puerto Rico, 10,124; Fundación Ana G. Méndez, 34,217; Sacred Heart University, 5,206; Inter-American University of Puerto Rico, 43,937. Other private universities and colleges had 24,274 students.

Health

There were 66 hospitals in 2004, with a hospital bed provision of 33 per 10,000 population. In 2002 there were 9,511 non-federal physicians.

RELIGION

In 2001 about 65% of the population were Roman Catholic. In Feb. 2010 there was one cardinal.

CULTURE

Broadcasting

In 2005 there were 75 radio and 32 television stations (including relay stations). Colour is by NTSC. There were 530,000 TV receivers in 2001.

Press

In 2005 there were three main newspapers: El Nuevo Día had an estimated daily circulation of 210,571; El Vocero, 140,944; San Juan Star, 104,000.

Tourism

There were 5,072,800 non-resident visitors in 2005, with spending from such visitors totalling $3,238·6m.

FURTHER READING

Statistical Information: The Program of Economic Research and Social Planning of the Puerto Rico Planning Board publishes: *(a) Economic Report to the Governor* (annual); *(b) External Trade Statistics* (annual); *(c) Reports on national income and balance of payments; and other socioeconomic statistics* (since 1940). There is a weekly economic summary (in Spanish) at http://www.jp.gobierno.pr

Office of Economic Studies and Analysis: Government Development Bank for Puerto Rico, PO Box 42001, San Juan 00940-2001.

Website: http://www.gdb-pur.com
Commonwealth Library: Univ. of Puerto Rico Library, Rio Piedras.

American Samoa

KEY HISTORICAL EVENTS

The first recorded visit by Europeans was in 1722. On 14 July 1889 a treaty between the USA, Germany and Great Britain proclaimed the Samoan Islands neutral territory, under a four-power government consisting of the three treaty powers and the local native government. By the Tripartite Treaty of 7 Nov. 1899, ratified 19 Feb. 1900, Great Britain and Germany renounced, in favour of the USA, all rights over the islands of the Samoan group east of 171° long. west of Greenwich. The islands to the west of that meridian, now the independent state of Samoa, were assigned to Germany. The islands of Tutuila and Aunu'u were ceded to the USA by their High Chiefs on 17 April 1900, and the islands of the Manu'a group on 16 July 1904. Congress accepted the islands under a Joint Resolution approved 20 Feb. 1929. Swain's Island, 210 miles north of the Samoan Islands, was annexed in 1925 and is administered as an integral part of American Samoa.

TERRITORY AND POPULATION

The islands (Tutuila, Aunu'u, Ta'u, Olosega, Ofu and Rose) are approximately 650 miles east-northeast of the Fiji Islands. The total area is 1,511 sq. km (583 sq. miles), of which 200 sq. km (77 sq. miles) are dry land; population (2000 census), 57,291 (29,264 males), nearly all Polynesians or part-Polynesians. Population density was 286 per sq. km in 2000.

In 2000, 88·8% of the population lived in urban areas. The capital is Pago Pago, which had a population of 14,000 in 1999. The island's three Districts are Eastern (population, 2000, 23,441), Western (32,435) and Manu'a (1,378). There is also Swain's Island, with an area of 1·9 sq. miles and 37 inhabitants (2000), which lies 210 miles to the northwest. Rose Island (uninhabited) is 0·4 sq. mile in area. In 1990 some 85,000 American Samoans lived in the USA.

The official languages are Samoan and English.

SOCIAL STATISTICS

Births, 2006, 1,442 (25·0 per 1,000 population); deaths, 266 (4·6). Infant mortality, 2003, 12·4 per 1,000 live births.

CLIMATE

A tropical maritime climate with a small annual range of temperature and plentiful rainfall. Pago Pago, Jan. 83°F (28·3°C), July 80°F (26·7°C). Annual rainfall 194" (4,850 mm).

CONSTITUTION AND GOVERNMENT

American Samoa is constitutionally an unorganized, unincorporated territory of the USA administered under the Department of the Interior. Its indigenous inhabitants are US nationals and are classified locally as citizens of American Samoa with certain privileges under local laws not granted to non-indigenous persons. Polynesian customs (not inconsistent with US laws) are respected.

Fagatogo is the seat of the government.

The islands are organized in 15 counties grouped in three districts; these counties and districts correspond to the traditional political units. On 25 Feb. 1948 a bicameral legislature was established, at the request of the Samoans, to have advisory legislative functions. With the adoption of the constitution of 22 April 1960, and the revised Constitution of 1967, the legislature was vested with limited law-making authority. The lower house, or House of Representatives, is composed of 20 members elected by universal adult suffrage and one non-voting member for Swain's Island. The upper house, or Senate, is comprised of 18 members elected, in the traditional Samoan manner, in meetings of the chiefs. The Governor and Lieut.-Governor have been popularly elected since 1978. American Samoa also sends one delegate to the US House of Representatives. The Congressman may participate but not vote on the House floor.

RECENT ELECTIONS

At elections to the Senate and House of Representatives on 4 Nov. 2008, only non-partisans were elected.

At gubernatorial elections on the same day incumbent Togiola Tulafono (Democrat) received 41·3% of votes cast, Utu Abe Malae (ind.) 31·4% and Afoa Moega Lutu (ind.) 26·8%. In the run-off held on 18 Nov. 2008 Togiola Tulafono won with 56·5% of the vote against Utu Abe Malae with 43·5%.

CURRENT ADMINISTRATION

Governor: Togiola Tulafono (D.), Jan. 2009–Jan. 2013 (salary: $85,000).

Lieut.-Governor: Faoa A. Sunia (D.), Jan. 2009–Jan. 2013 ($75,000).

Government Website: http://www.government.as

ECONOMY

Overview

The Economic Development and Planning Office promotes economic expansion and outside investment.

Budget

The chief sources of revenue are annual federal grants from the USA, local revenues from taxes, duties, receipts from commercial operations (enterprise and special revenue funds), utilities, rents and leases, and liquor sales. In 2001–02 revenues were $211·5m. and expenditures $180·5m.

Banking and Finance

The American Samoa branch of the Bank of Hawaii and the American Samoa Bank offer all commercial banking services. The Development Bank of American Samoa, government-owned, is concerned primarily through loans and guarantees with the economic advancement of the Territory.

ENERGY AND NATURAL RESOURCES

Environment

American Samoa's carbon dioxide emissions from the consumption and flaring of fossil fuels in 2008 were the equivalent of 9·2 tonnes per capita.

Electricity

Installed capacity was estimated at 58,000 kW in 2004. Production in 2004 was about 138m. kWh. Per capita consumption in 2004 was an estimated 2,226 kWh. All the Manu'a islands have electricity.

Water

The total area covered by water is approximately 13 sq. miles.

Agriculture

Of the 48,640 acres of land area, 11,000 acres are suitable for tropical crops; most commercial farms are in the Tafuna plains and west Tutuila. Principal crops are coconuts, taro, bread-fruit, yams and bananas.

Livestock (2002): pigs, 11,000.

Fisheries

Total catch in 2005 was 8,693,000 lb (3,943 tonnes).

INDUSTRY

Fish canning is important, employing the second largest number of people (after government). Attempts are being made to provide a variety of light industries. Tuna fishing and local inshore fishing are both expanding.

Labour

In 2000 the civilian labour force numbered 17,627, of whom 16,718 were employed. The unemployment rate in 2000 was 5·2%.

INTERNATIONAL TRADE

Imports and Exports

Imports in 2006 totalled $579m. and exports $439m.

Chief imports are fish for canning, building materials, fuel oil, food, jewellery, machines and parts, alcoholic beverages and cigarettes. Chief exports are canned tuna, watches, pet foods and handicrafts.

COMMUNICATIONS

Roads

There are about 150 km of paved roads and 200 km of unpaved roads in all. Motor vehicles in use, 1995, 5,900 (5,300 passenger cars and 600 commercial vehicles).

Civil Aviation

Polynesian Airlines operate daily services between American Samoa (Pago Pago) and Samoa (Apia). Hawaiian Airlines also operates between Pago Pago and Honolulu. Manu'a Air Transport runs local services. There are three airports. There were 24,331 passenger enplanements in 2000.

Shipping

The harbour at Pago Pago, which nearly bisects the island of Tutuila, is the only good harbour for large vessels in American Samoa. By sea there is a twice-monthly service between the Fiji Islands, New Zealand and Australia and regular services between the USA, South Pacific ports, Honolulu and Japan. In 2002–03 vessels entering totalled 191,000 net registered tons.

Telecommunications

A commercial radiogram service is available to all parts of the world and commercial phone services are operated to all parts of the world. There were 10,400 main telephone lines in operation in 2004 and 2,300 mobile phone subscribers.

SOCIAL INSTITUTIONS

Justice

Judicial power is vested firstly in a High Court. The trial division has original jurisdiction of all criminal and civil cases. The probate division has jurisdiction of estates, guardianships, trusts and other matters. The land and title division decides cases relating to disputes involving communal land and Matai title court rules on questions and controversy over family titles. The appellate division hears appeals from trial, land and title, and probate divisions as well as having original jurisdiction in selected matters. The appellate court is the court of last resort. Two American judges sit with five Samoan judges permanently. In addition there are temporary judges or assessors who sit occasionally on cases involving Samoan customs. There is also a District Court with limited jurisdiction and there are 69 village courts.

The population in penal institutions in Dec. 2007 was 236 (equivalent to 410 per 100,000 population).

Education

Education is compulsory between the ages of six and 18. In 2000 there were 1,557 pupils enrolled in nursery school and pre-school, 1,736 in kindergarten, 11,418 in elementary school (grades 1–8), 4,645 in high school (grades 9–12) and 1,474 in college or graduate school.

Welfare

In Dec. 2001 there were 5,320 beneficiaries including 1,470 survivors, 1,370 retired workers and 1,240 disabled workers. Total payments came to $2m. with average monthly benefits of $442.

RELIGION

In 2001 about 41% of the population belonged to the Congregational Church and 19% were Roman Catholics. Methodists and Latter-day Saints (Mormons) are also represented.

CULTURE

Broadcasting

In 2000 there were 13,200 TV sets (colour by NTSC).

Tourism

In 2005 there were 24,000 tourist arrivals.

Guam

Guahan

KEY HISTORICAL EVENTS

Magellan is said to have discovered the island in 1521; it was ceded by Spain to the USA by the Treaty of Paris (10 Dec. 1898). The island was captured by the Japanese on 10 Dec. 1941 and retaken by American forces following the Battle of Guam (21 July–8 Aug. 1944). Guam is of strategic importance; substantial numbers of naval and air force personnel occupy about one-third of the usable land.

TERRITORY AND POPULATION

Guam is the largest and most southern island of the Marianas Archipelago, in 13° 26' N. lat., 144° 45' E. long. Total area, 212 sq. miles (549 sq. km). Hagåtña (previously Agaña), the seat of government, is about eight miles from the anchorage in Apra Harbor. The census in 2000 showed a population of 154,805 (79,181 males), of whom 80,737 were born in Guam; density, 282·0 per sq. km. In 2004 an estimated 59·0% of the population lived in rural areas. The UN gives an estimated population for 2010 of 180,000. The Malay strain is predominant. Chamorro, the native language, and English are the official languages.

SOCIAL STATISTICS

Births, 2006, 3,391 (19·8 per 1,000 population); deaths, 679 (4·0). Infant mortality rate, 2005, 10·7 per 1,000 live births. Life expectancy, 2004, was 75·1 years for males and 81·3 years for females. Fertility rate, 2003, 2·7 births per woman.

CLIMATE

Tropical maritime, with little difference in temperatures over the year. Rainfall is copious at all seasons, but is greatest from July to Oct. Hagåtña, Jan. 81°F (27·2°C), July 81°F (27·2°C). Annual rainfall 93" (2,325 mm).

CONSTITUTION AND GOVERNMENT

Guam's constitutional status is that of an 'unincorporated territory' of the USA. In Aug. 1950 the President transferred the administration of the island from the Navy Department to the Interior Department. The transfer conferred full citizenship on the Guamanians, who had previously been 'nationals' of the USA. There was a referendum on status on 30 Jan. 1982. 38% of eligible voters voted; 48·5% of those favoured Commonwealth status.

The Governor and Lieut.-Governor are elected for four-year terms. The legislature is a 15-member elected Senate; its powers are similar to those of an American state legislature. Guam sends one non-voting delegate (Madeleine Bordallo, D., 2009–11) to the US House of Representatives.

RECENT ELECTIONS

At the election of 7 Nov. 2006 for the Guam Legislature the Republicans won eight seats and the Democrats won seven. In gubernatorial elections held on the same day, incumbent governor Felix Camacho (Republican) won 48·8% of the vote against 46·7% for Robert Underwood (Democrat). Camacho was sworn in for a second term in Jan. 2007. Underwood announced his intention to challenge the election result in the Supreme Court but the request was rejected.

CURRENT ADMINISTRATION

Governor: Felix Perez Camacho (R.), 2007–11 (salary: $90,000).

Lieut.-Governor: Michael W. Cruz (R.), 2007–11 ($85,000).

ECONOMY

Budget

Total revenue (2003) $426m.; expenditure $343m.

Banking and Finance

Banking law makes it possible for foreign banks to operate in Guam. In 2003 there were 12 commercial banks.

ENERGY AND NATURAL RESOURCES

Environment

Guam's carbon dioxide emissions from the consumption and flaring of fossil fuels in 2008 were the equivalent of 9·9 tonnes per capita.

Electricity

Installed capacity was an estimated 0·4m. kW in 2004. Production was 1,589m. kWh in 2004. Consumption per capita in 2004 was 9,567 kWh.

Water

The total area covered by water is approximately 7 sq. miles. Supplies are from springs, reservoirs and groundwater; 65% comes from water-bearing limestone in the north. The Navy and Air Force conserve water in reservoirs. The Water Resources Research Centre is at Guam University.

Agriculture

The major products of the island are sweet potatoes, cucumbers, watermelons and beans. In 2002 there were approximately 5,000 acres of arable land and 9,000 acres of permanent cropland. Production (2002 estimates, in 1,000 tonnes): coconuts, 52; copra, 2; watermelons, 2. Livestock (2002) included 1,000 goats and 5,000 pigs. There is an agricultural experimental station at Inarajan.

Fisheries

In 2005 total catch was 357,000 lb (162 tonnes), exclusively from sea fishing.

INDUSTRY

Guam Economic Development Authority controls three industrial estates: Cabras Island (32 acres); Calvo estate at Tamuning (26 acres); Harmon estate (16 acres). Industries include textile manufacture, cement and petroleum distribution, warehousing, printing, plastics and ship-repair. Other main sources of income are construction and tourism.

Labour

In 2000 there were 105,014 persons of employable age, of whom 68,894 were in the workforce (64,452 civilian). 7,399 were unemployed.

INTERNATIONAL TRADE

Guam is the only American territory which has complete 'free trade'; excise duties are levied only upon imports of tobacco, liquid fuel and liquor.

Imports and Exports

In 2002 imports were valued at $389m. and exports at $37m. Main export destinations in 2001 were Japan, 50·0%; Palau, 9·4%; Micronesia, 9·1%.

COMMUNICATIONS

Roads

There are 674 km of all-weather roads. In 2002 there were 59,700 passenger cars and 20,100 commercial vehicles in use.

Civil Aviation

There is an international airport at Tamuning. Seven commercial airlines serve Guam. There were 1,004,354 passenger enplanements in 2000.

Shipping

There is a port at Apra Harbor.

Telecommunications

Overseas telephone and radio dispatch facilities are available. Telephone subscribers numbered 145,300 in 2003 (887·3 per 1,000 inhabitants). Mobile phone subscribers numbered 98,000 in 2004 and internet users 60,000.

SOCIAL INSTITUTIONS

Justice

The Organic Act established a District Court with jurisdiction in matters arising under both federal and territorial law; the judge is appointed by the President subject to Senate approval. There is also a Supreme Court and a Superior Court; all judges are locally appointed except the Federal District judge. Misdemeanours are under the jurisdiction of the police court. The Spanish law was superseded in 1933 by five civil codes based upon California law.

The population in penal institutions in July 2008 was 559 (318 per 100,000 population).

Education

Education is compulsory from five to 16. Bilingual teaching programmes integrate the Chamorro language and culture into public school courses. Public school enrolment in 2002–03: 2,806 pupils in Head Start and kindergarten, 12,361 in 27 elementary schools (grades 1–5); 7,554 in seven middle schools (grades 6–8); and 9,081 in four high schools (grades 9–12). In 2003 there were about 25 private schools (nine Catholic). The University of Guam is in Mangilao and Guam Community College is in Barrigada.

Health

There is a hospital, eight nutrition centres, a school health programme and an extensive immunization programme. Emphasis is on disease prevention, health education and nutrition.

Welfare

In 2000, $38·9m. was paid in public assistance to individuals, including $19·1m. temporary aid to needy families, $11·5m. Medicaid and $1·5m. old-age assistance.

RELIGION

About 75% of the Guamanians are Roman Catholics; the other 25% are Baptists, Episcopalians, Bahais, Lutherans, Latter-day Saints (Mormons), Presbyterians, Jehovah's Witnesses and members of the Church of Christ and Seventh Day Adventists.

CULTURE

Broadcasting

There are four commercial stations, a commercial television station, a public broadcasting station and a cable television station with 24 channels. In 1997 there were 106,000 TV sets (colour by NTSC).

Press

In 2006 there was one daily newspaper, as well as two weekly publications aimed at military personnel.

Tourism

There were 1,228,000 tourist arrivals in 2005.

FURTHER READING

Report (Annual) of the Governor of Guam to the US Department of Interior
Guam Annual Economic Review.

Rogers, R. F., *Destiny's Landfall: a History of Guam.* 1995
Wuerch, W. L. and Ballendorf, D. A., *Historical Dictionary of Guam and Micronesia.* 1995

Statistical Office: P.O. Box 2950, Hagåtña, Guam 96932.
Website: http://bsp.guam.gov

Virgin Islands of the United States

KEY HISTORICAL EVENTS

The Virgin Islands of the United States, formerly known as the Danish West Indies, were named and claimed for Spain by Columbus in 1493. They were later settled by Dutch and English planters, invaded by France in the mid-17th century and abandoned by the French *c.* 1700, by which time Danish influence had been established. St Croix was held by the Knights of Malta between two periods of French rule.

The Virgin Islands were purchased from Denmark by the United States for $25m. on 31 March 1917. Their value was wholly strategic, inasmuch as they commanded the Anegada Passage from the Atlantic Ocean to the Caribbean Sea and the approach to the Panama Canal. Although the inhabitants were made US citizens in 1927, the islands are constitutionally an 'unincorporated territory'.

TERRITORY AND POPULATION

The Virgin Islands group, lying about 40 miles due east of Puerto Rico, comprises the islands of St Thomas (31 sq. miles), St Croix (83 sq. miles), St John (20 sq. miles) and 65 small islets or cays, mostly uninhabited. The total area is 1,910 sq. km (738 sq. miles), of which 346 sq. km (134 sq. miles) are dry land.

The population according to the 2000 census was 108,612 (females, 56,748); density 811 per sq. mile. 92·6% of the population were urban in 2000.

Population (2000 census) of St Croix, 53,234; St Thomas, 51,181; St John, 4,197. In 2000, 69·8% of the population were native born.

The UN gives an estimated population for 2010 of 109,000.

The capital and only city, Charlotte Amalie, on St Thomas, had a population (2000 census) of 11,044. There are two towns on St Croix with 2000 census populations of: Christiansted, 2,637; Frederiksted, 732. The official language is English. Spanish is also spoken.

SOCIAL STATISTICS

Births, 2006, 1,687 (15·5 per 1,000 population); deaths, 624 (5·7). Infant mortality, 1997, 13·0 per 1,000 live births.

CLIMATE

Average temperatures vary from 77°F to 82°F throughout the year; humidity is low. Average annual rainfall, about 45". The islands lie in the hurricane belt; tropical storms with heavy rainfall can occur in late summer.

CONSTITUTION AND GOVERNMENT

The Organic Act of 22 July 1954 gives the US Department of the Interior full jurisdiction; some limited legislative powers are given to a single-chambered legislature, composed of 15 senators elected for two years representing the two legislative districts of St Croix and St Thomas-St John.

The Governor is elected by the residents. Since 1954 there have been four attempts to redraft the Constitution, to provide for greater autonomy. Each has been rejected by the electorate. The latest was defeated in a referendum in Nov. 1981, with 50% of the electorate participating.

For administration, there are 14 executive departments, 13 of which are under commissioners and the other, the Department of Justice, under an Attorney-General. The US Department of the Interior appoints a Federal Comptroller of government revenue and expenditure.

The franchise is vested in residents who are citizens of the United States, 18 years of age or over. They do not participate in the US presidential election but they have a non-voting representative in Congress.

The capital is Charlotte Amalie, on St Thomas Island.

RECENT ELECTIONS

In elections for governor held on 7 Nov. 2006 John deJongh, Jr (Democrat) won 49·3% of the votes, against 27·1% for Kenneth Mapp (ind.) and 23·5% for Adlah Donastorg, Jr (ind.). A run-off was held on 21 Nov. 2006 in which John deJongh, Jr won 57·3% and Kenneth Mapp 42·7%. In Senate elections held on 4 Nov. 2008 the Democratic Party of the Virgin Islands won 10 out of 15 seats.

CURRENT ADMINISTRATION

Governor: John P. deJongh, Jr (D.), 2007–11 (salary: $150,000).
Lieut.-Governor: Gregory R. Francis (D.), 2007–11 ($125,000).

US Virgin Islands Government: http://ltg.gov.vi

ECONOMY

Currency

United States currency became legal tender on 1 July 1934.

Budget

Under the 1954 Organic Act finances are provided partly from local revenues—customs, federal income tax, real and personal property tax, trade tax, excise tax, pilotage fees, etc.—and partly from Federal Matching Funds, being the excise taxes collected by the federal government on such Virgin Islands products transported to the mainland as are liable.

Per capita income, 2000, $13,139.

Revenues in 2004 totalled US$557·9m.; expenditures were US$592·0m.

Banking and Finance

Banks include the Chase Manhattan Bank; the Bank of Nova Scotia; the First Federal Savings and Loan Association of Puerto Rico; the Banco Popular of the Virgin Islands; First Bank of Puerto Rico; the Virgin Islands Community Bank; the Bank of St Croix; Barclays Bank International; Citibank; Banco Popular de Puerto Rico; and FirstBank Virgin Islands.

ENERGY AND NATURAL RESOURCES

Environment

Carbon dioxide emissions from the consumption and flaring of fossil fuels in 2008 were the equivalent of 126·5 tonnes per capita, the second highest in the world.

Electricity

The Virgin Islands Water and Power Authority provides electric power from generating plants on St Croix and St Thomas; St John is served by power cable and emergency generator. Production in 2004 was about 1·05bn. kWh. Per capita consumption in 2004 was an estimated 9,633 kWh. Installed capacity in 2003 was 323,000 kW.

Water

There are six desalinization plants with maximum daily capacity of 8·7m. gallons of fresh water. Rainwater remains the most reliable source. Every building must have a cistern to provide rainwater for drinking, even in areas served by mains (10 gallons capacity per sq. ft of roof for a single-storey house).

The total area covered by water is approximately 604 sq. miles, of which 16 sq. miles are inland.

Agriculture

Land for fruit, vegetables and animal feed is available on St Croix, and there are tax incentives for development.

Livestock (2002): cattle, 8,000; goats, 4,000; pigs, 3,000; sheep, 3,000.

Fisheries

There is a fishermen's co-operative with a market at Christiansted. There is a shellfish-farming project at Rust-op-Twist, St Croix. The total catch in 2005 was approximately 2,798,000 lb (1,269 tonnes).

INDUSTRY

The main occupations on St Thomas are tourism and government service; on St Croix manufacturing is more important. Manufactures include rum (the most valuable product), watches, pharmaceuticals and fragrances. Industries in order of revenue: tourism, refining oil, watch assembly, rum distilling, construction.

Labour

In 2000 the total labour force was 51,042, of whom 7,351 were employed in the arts, entertainment, recreation, accommodation and food services, 6,742 were employed in educational, health and social services, 6,476 in retail trade, 4,931 in public administration and 4,900 in construction. In 2000 there were 4,368 registered unemployed persons, or 5·6% of the workforce.

INTERNATIONAL TRADE

Imports and Exports

Imports, 2005, totalled $10,243m. and exports $10,476m. The main import is crude petroleum, while the principal exports are petroleum products.

COMMUNICATIONS

Roads

In 1996 the Virgin Islands had 856 km of roads.

Civil Aviation

There is a daily cargo and passenger service between St Thomas and St Croix. Alexander Hamilton Airport on St Croix can take all types of aircraft. Cyril E. King Airport on St Thomas takes 727-class aircraft. There are air connections to mainland USA and other Caribbean islands. There were 658,905 passenger enplanements in 2000.

Shipping

The whole territory has free port status. There is an hourly boat service between St Thomas and St John and a 75-minute catamaran service between St Croix and St Thomas two to three times a day.

Telecommunications

All three Virgin Islands have a dial telephone system. Telephone subscribers numbered 152,000 in 2005 (1,359·4 per 1,000 population). Direct dialling to Puerto Rico and the mainland, and internationally, is now possible. In 2005 there were 80,300 mobile phone subscribers. Internet users numbered 30,000 in 2007.

Postal Services

In 2004 there were 12 post offices.

SOCIAL INSTITUTIONS

Justice

The population in penal institutions in Dec. 2007 was 555 (512 per 100,000 population).

Education

In 2000 there were 32,119 people enrolled in schools, of which 2,484 in nursery and pre-school, 2,230 in kindergarten, 16,858 in elementary school, 7,440 in high school and 3,107 in college or graduate school. In 2003 there were 746 elementary teachers and 734 secondary teachers. In fall 2005 the University of the Virgin Islands (St Thomas and St Croix campuses, with an ecological research station on St John) had 2,392 students (1,263 full-time and 1,129 part-time) and 107 full-time instructional staff; 77% of the students were female.

Health

In 2004 there were 208 active physicians and 45 licensed dentists. The Roy Lester Schneider Hospital on St Thomas had 169 beds in 2008. The Governor Juan F. Luis Hospital, Christiansted, serves St Croix, with 188 beds in 2008.

Welfare

In 2001 federal direct payments for individuals totalled $233·4m., including: retirement insurance, $72·0m.; housing assistance, $53·4m.; survivors insurance, $20·2m.; disability insurance, $18·0m.; food stamps, $17·6m.

RELIGION

At the 2000 census 42% of the population were Baptists, 34% were Roman Catholics and 17% were Episcopalians.

There are places of worship of the Protestant, Roman Catholic and Jewish faiths in St Thomas and St Croix, and Protestant and Roman Catholic churches in St John.

CULTURE

Broadcasting

In 2002 there were 16 radio stations and one public and one commercial TV station. In 2000 there were 64,700 TV receivers (colour by NTSC).

Press

In 2006 there was one daily with a circulation of 17,000.

Tourism

Tourism accounts for some 70% of GDP. In 2006 there were 671,362 staying visitors and 1,903,533 cruise passenger arrivals, down from 697,033 and 1,912,548 respectively in 2005. Receipts from tourism amounted to $1,493m. in 2005.

Other Unincorporated Territories

Baker Island

A small Pacific island 2,600 km southwest of Hawaii. Administered under the US Department of the Interior. Area 1 sq. mile; population (2000), nil. The islands are considered part of the United States Pacific Island Wildlife Refuges.

Howland Island

A small Pacific island 2,600 km southwest of Hawaii. Administered under the US Department of the Interior. Area 1 sq. mile; population (2000), nil. The islands are considered part of the United States Pacific Island Wildlife Refuges.

Jarvis Island

A small Pacific island 2,100 km south of Hawaii. Administered under the US Department of the Interior. Area 2 sq. miles; population (2000), nil. The islands are considered part of the United States Pacific Island Wildlife Refuges.

Johnston Atoll

Two small Pacific islands 1,100 km southwest of Hawaii, administered by the US Air Force. Area, under 1 sq. mile; population (2000) numbered 315. The islands are considered part of the United States Pacific Island Wildlife Refuges.

Kingman Reef

Small Pacific reef 1,500 km southwest of Hawaii, administered by the US Navy. Area one tenth of a sq. mile; population (2000), nil. The islands are considered part of the United States Pacific Island Wildlife Refuges.

Midway Islands

Two small Pacific islands at the western end of the Hawaiian chain, administered by the US Navy. Area, 2 sq. miles; population (2000), nil. The islands are considered part of the United States Pacific Island Wildlife Refuges.

Navassa Island

Small Caribbean island 48 km west of Haiti, administered by US Coast Guards. Area 2 sq. miles; population (2000), nil.

Wake Island

Three small Pacific islands 3,700 km west of Hawaii, administered by the US Air Force. Area, 3 sq. miles; population (2000) numbered 1.

Incorporated Territories

Palmyra Atoll

Small atoll 1,500 km southwest of Hawaii, administered by the US Department of the Interior. It is part federally-owned and part privately-owned. Area 5 sq. miles; population (2000), nil.

URUGUAY

República Oriental del Uruguay
(Oriental Republic of Uruguay)

Capital: Montevideo
Population estimate, 2010: 3·37m.
GDP per capita, 2007: (PPP$) 11,216
HDI/world rank: 0·865/50

KEY HISTORICAL EVENTS

From around 4000 BC Uruguay was populated principally by Charrúa and Guaraní Indians. The Charrúa migrated seasonally between coastal and inland areas, while the Guaraní settled in the eastern forests and in the north. Smaller groups also settled the region and lands were fought over vigorously. In 1516 the first Europeans to enter the territory, Spanish navigator Juan Díaz de Solis and his party, were killed. Other Spanish and Portuguese expeditions followed and in the late 16th century the Spanish laid claim to the Río de la Plata. In 1603 Spanish governor Hernando Arias de Saavedra is said to have shipped cattle and horses from the Paraguay region into Río de la Plata, and Spanish, Portuguese and English settlers began livestock farming. The native peoples resisted the European colonizers but were killed in large numbers in warfare and by European disease.

In 1680 the Portuguese established the settlement of Colonia do Sacramento on the Río de la Plata. In 1726 the Spanish founded San Felipe de Montevideo as a fortified port and settled its hinterland. For the next 50 years the two powers fought over the coastal region and in 1776 the Spanish established the viceroyalty of the Río de la Plata, with Buenos Aires as its capital. While the Napoleonic wars were weakening Spain, an autonomous junta was established in Montevideo and in 1810 *criollos* (ethnic Spanish born in South America) seized power from the Spanish in Buenos Aires. A federalist movement originating in the inland region of the Banda Oriental challenged both Montevideo and Buenos Aires. In the ensuing conflict Portuguese Brazil annexed the Banda Oriental from 1820–25, until Uruguayan federalists led a successful uprising and regained control. Banda Oriental declared its independence and its incorporation into the United Provinces of Río de la Plata on 25 Aug. 1825. Fighting continued until 1828 when negotiations began with Brazil and Argentina. On 18 July 1830 the constitution of the Oriental Republic of Uruguay was approved.

Conflict between the two main political parties, the *colorados* and *blancos*, dominated the next 90 years, factionalizing the nation and leading to the economically damaging War of the Triple Alliance (1864–70), fought between Paraguay and the unified forces of Uruguay, Argentina and Brazil. In 1905 the first democratic elections took place, returning the *colorados* to government under President José Batlle y Ordónez. In the early 20th century ranching brought prosperity and an influx of immigrants, and a welfare state was developed. In 1919 a new constitution aimed to protect against dictatorship by providing for a plural executive known as a *colegiado*. However, economic depression led to instability and in 1933 presidential government and quadrennial elections were introduced.

Collective leadership returned from 1951–56 but a series of strikes and riots in the 1960s led to the extension of army influence. The military took repressive measures and the presidency was restored in 1967. Marxist urban guerrillas, the Tupamaro, fought a violent campaign against the regime but were finally defeated in 1972. The military took over the government in 1973. A period of harsh repression followed during which thousands were arrested and human rights abuses were rife. Economic difficulties in the 1980s weakened the military government and the country returned to civilian rule in 1985. Economic growth in the 1990s was followed by a downturn from 1999–2002. In 2005 Uruguay elected its first left-wing leader, Tabaré Vázquez of the Progressive Encounter-Broad Front-New Majority coalition.

TERRITORY AND POPULATION

Uruguay is bounded on the northeast by Brazil, on the southeast by the Atlantic, on the south by the Río de la Plata and on the west by Argentina. The area, including inland waters, is 176,215 sq. km (68,037 sq. miles). The following table shows the area and the population of the 19 departments at census 2004:

Departments	*Sq. km*	*Census 2004*	*Capital*
Artigas	11,928	78,019	Artigas
Canelones	4,536	485,240	Canelones
Cerro-Largo	13,648	86,564	Melo
Colonia	6,106	119,266	Colonia
Durazno	11,643	58,859	Durazno
Flores	5,144	25,104	Trinidad
Florida	10,417	68,181	Florida
Lavalleja	10,016	60,925	Minas
Maldonado	4,793	140,192	Maldonado
Montevideo	530	1,325,968	Montevideo
Paysandú	13,922	113,244	Paysandú
Río Negro	9,282	53,989	Fray Bentos
Rivera	9,370	104,921	Rivera
Rocha	10,551	69,937	Rocha
Salto	14,163	123,120	Salto
San José	4,992	103,104	San José
Soriano	9,008	84,563	Mercedes
Tacuarembó	15,438	90,489	Tacuarembó
Treinta y Tres	9,529	49,318	Treinta y Tres

Total population, census (2004) 3,241,003; population density, 18·4 per sq. km. The United Nations population estimate for 2004 was 3,324,000.

The UN gives an estimated population for 2010 of 3·37m.

In 2004 Montevideo (the capital) accounted for 39·2% of the total population. It had a population in 2004 of 1,269,600. Other major cities are Salto (population of 99,072 in 2004) and Paysandú (73,272 in 2004). In 2005, 92·0% of the population lived in urban areas.

13% of the population are over 65; 24% are under 15; 63% are between 15 and 64.

The official language is Spanish.

SOCIAL STATISTICS

2004: births, 50,052; deaths, 32,222. Rates (per 1,000 population), 2004: birth, 15·4; death, 9·9. Annual population growth rate, 2000–05, 0·0%. Infant mortality, 2005 (per 1,000 live births), 13. Life expectancy in 2007 was 72·6 years among males and 79·8 years among females. Fertility rate, 2004, 2·3 births per woman.

CLIMATE

A warm temperate climate, with mild winters and warm summers. The wettest months are March to June, but there is really no dry season. Montevideo, Jan. 72°F (22·2°C), July 50°F (10°C). Annual rainfall 38" (950 mm).

CONSTITUTION AND GOVERNMENT

The Constitution was adopted on 27 Nov. 1966 and became effective in Feb. 1967; it has been amended in 1989, 1994, 1996 and 2004.

Congress consists of a *Senate* of 31 members and a *Chamber of Deputies* of 99 members, both elected by proportional representation for five-year terms although in the case of the Senate only 30 members are elected with one seat reserved for the Vice-President. The electoral system provides that the successful presidential candidate be a member of the party which gains a parliamentary majority. Electors vote for deputies on a first-past-the-post system, and simultaneously vote for a presidential candidate of the same party. The winners of the second vote are credited with the number of votes obtained by their party in the parliamentary elections. Referendums may be called at the instigation of 10,000 signatories. Voting is compulsory.

National Anthem

'Orientales, la patria o la tumba' ('Easterners, the fatherland or the tomb'); words by F. Acuña de Figueroa, tune by F. J. Deballi.

GOVERNMENT CHRONOLOGY

Heads of State since 1943. (FA = Broad Front; PC = Colorado Party; PN = National Party (Blancos); PS = Socialist Party of Uruguay)

Presidents of the Republic

1943–47	PC	Juan José Amézaga Landaraso
1947	PC	Tomás Berreta Gandolfo
1947–51	PC	Luis Conrado Batlle Berres
1951–52	PC	Andrés Martínez Trueba

Chairman of the 1st National Council of Government

1952–55	PC	Andrés Martínez Trueba

Chairmen of the 2nd National Council of Government

1955–56	PC	Luis Conrado Batlle Berres
1956–57	PC	Alberto Fermín Zubiría Urtiague
1957–58	PC	Arturo Lezama Bagez
1958–59	PC	Carlos Lorenzo Fischer Brusoni

Chairmen of the 3rd National Council of Government

1959–60	PN	Martín Recaredo Echegoyen Machicote
1960–61	PN	Benito Nardone Cetrulo
1961–62	PN	Eduardo Víctor Haedo
1962–63	PN	Faustino Harrison Usoz

Chairmen of the 4th National Council of Government

1963–64	PN	Daniel Fernández Crespo
1964–65	PN	Luis Giannattasio Finocchietti
1965–66	PN	Washington Beltrán Mullin
1966–67	PN	Alberto Heber Usher

Presidents of the Republic

1967	PC	Óscar Diego Gestido Pose
1967–72	PC	Jorge Pacheco Areco
1972–76	PC[1]	Juan María Bordaberry Arocena
1976–81	PN[2]	Aparicio Méndez Manfredini
1981–85	military	Gregorio Conrado Álvarez Armellino
1985–90	PC	Julio María Sanguinetti Coirolo
1990–95	PN	Luis Alberto Lacalle de Herrera
1995–2000	PC	Julio María Sanguinetti Coirolo
2000–05	PC	Jorge Luis Batlle Ibáñez
2005–10	PS, FA	Tabaré Ramón Vázquez Rosas
2010–	FA	José Alberto Mujica

[1]Civilian president under military rule 1973–76.
[2]Civilian president under military rule.

RECENT ELECTIONS

Elections for the General Assembly were held on 25 Oct. 2009. In elections to the Chamber of Deputies, the Broad Front (FA) won 50 seats, the National Party (PN) 30, the Colorado Party (PC) 17 and the Independent Party 2. In the Senate election FA won 16 seats, PN 9 and PC 5.

In the presidential election, also held on 25 Oct. 2009, José Alberto Mujica Cordano (FA) received 48·0% of the vote, Luis Alberto Lacalle de Herrera (PN) 29·1%, Pedro Bordaberry Herrán (Colorado Party) 17·0% and Pablo Mieres (Independent Party) 2·5%. Three other candidates received less than 1% of the vote each. Mujica won the 29 Nov. run-off with 54·8% of the vote to Lacalle's 45·2%. Turnout was 89·9% in the first round and 89·1% in the run-off.

CURRENT ADMINISTRATION

President: José Alberto Mujica; b. 1935 (FA; sworn in 1 March 2010).

Vice-President: Danilo Astori.

In March 2010 the government comprised:

Minister of Agriculture, Livestock and Fisheries: Tabaré Aguerre. *Defence:* Luis Rosadilla. *Economy and Finance:* Fernando Lorenzo. *Education and Culture:* Ricardo Ehrlich. *Foreign Affairs:* Luis Almagro. *Housing, Land Management and Environment:* Graciela Muslera. *Industry, Energy and Mining:* Roberto Kreimerman. *Interior:* Eduardo Bonomi. *Public Health:* Daniel Olesker. *Social Development:* Ana Vignoli. *Tourism and Sports:* Héctor Lescano. *Transport and Public Works:* Enrique Pintado. *Work and Social Security:* Eduardo Brenta.

Presidency Website (Spanish only):
http://www.presidencia.gub.uy

CURRENT LEADERS

José Mujica

Position
President

Introduction
José Mujica took office on 1 March 2010 after winning a presidential run-off in Nov. 2009. A former leftist guerrilla, Mujica received 55% of the vote after campaigning on a platform of continued economic growth and policies to tackle crime and poverty.

Early Life
Mujica was born in Montevideo on 20 May 1935. He was a member of the centre-right Partido Nacional (National Party) in his youth before joining the newly-formed Movimiento de Liberación Nacional (popularly known as the Tupamaros) in the 1960s, an armed guerrilla movement inspired by the Cuban revolution.

He took part in the takeover of Pando, a town outside Montevideo, in 1969 and in 1971 was convicted by a military tribunal under the government of Jorge Pacheco Areco of killing a police officer. He escaped from Punta Carretas prison but was re-arrested in 1972. Following the 1973 military coup Mujica was transferred to a military prison where he was subjected to torture and solitary confinement. When the military dictatorship ended in 1985 he was freed under a general amnesty covering political crimes since 1962.

On his release and the restoration of democracy, Mujica steered the Tupamaros away from its guerrilla past and remodelled it into the Movimiento de Participación Popular (Movement of Popular Participation), a legitimate political party that later joined the left-wing Frente Amplio (Broad Front) coalition. He was elected to the chamber of deputies in 1994 and in 1999 won a seat in the senate, gaining re-election five years later.

On 1 March 2005 he resigned from the senate when he was appointed minister of livestock, agriculture and fisheries by then president, Tabaré Vázquez. During his tenure Mujica intervened to keep down the price of beef, a staple of the Uruguayan people, winning popular acclaim for his stance as the affair becoming known as 'Pepe's barbeque' (a reference to his nickname). In 2008 he returned to the senate after losing his cabinet post in a reshuffle.

On 28 June 2009 Mujica became Frente Amplio's presidential candidate after winning the coalition's primary election. He pledged to maintain the policies of outgoing President Vázquez, whose term of office had seen prolonged economic growth and strong social interventions by the government. In the first round of elections held in Oct. 2009 Mujica received 48% of the vote and on 30 Nov. 2009 he was declared winner of a run-off against Luis Alberto Lacalle of the National Party, with 55% of the vote.

Career in Office
Keen to maintain his predecessor's legacy, Mujica left the vice-president, Danilo Astori, in charge of economic policy. Mujica is expected to improve Uruguay's often strained relations with its neighbours and he has expressed his support for MERCOSUR, the regional economic bloc. His other priorities include the improvement of educational standards and the maintenance of energy supplies.

DEFENCE

Defence expenditure totalled US$227m. in 2006 (US$66 per capita), representing 1·2% of GDP.

Army

The Army consists of volunteers who enlist for one to two years service. There are four military regions with divisional headquarters. Strength (2007), 17,000. In addition there are government paramilitary forces numbering 920.

Navy

The Navy includes two frigates. A 280-strong naval aviation service operates one combat capable aircraft. Personnel in 2007 totalled 5,000 including 450 naval infantry and 1,600 coast guards. The main base is at Montevideo.

Air Force

Organized with US aid, the Air Force had (2007) 3,000 personnel and 19 combat capable aircraft.

INTERNATIONAL RELATIONS

Uruguay is a member of the UN, World Bank, IMF and several other UN specialized agencies, WTO, IOM, Inter-American Development Bank, SELA, LAIA, OAS, MERCOSUR, UNASUR and Antarctic Treaty.

ECONOMY

In 2006 agriculture contributed 9·2% of GDP, industry 32·4% and services 58·4%.

Overview

The economy benefits from a favourable climate for agriculture and tourism and substantial hydropower potential. Economic links with its larger neighbours, Brazil and Argentina, are a mixed blessing. The creation of the Southern Common Market (MERCOSUR) in the 1990s cemented links and increased exports to these markets.

From 1990–98 the economy grew 3·9% per annum, above the country's long-term trend of 2% from 1960–2000. In 1999 the economy shrank by 2·8% after the devaluation of the Brazilian *real* and a serious drought. Weak banking and strong links with Argentina left Uruguay exposed to Argentina's economic collapse in 2002. This led to a run on Uruguay's banks, the forced flotation of the *peso* in June 2002 and a deep recession from 2002–03. The events of 1999–2003 highlighted macroeconomic and structural weaknesses that leave the economy vulnerable to a weak banking system and high trade dependence on the MERCOSUR region.

However, unlike Argentina, Uruguay did not default on its debt and the country has relatively effective public institutions. Since the crisis, farming, tourism and finance, the traditional pillars of the economy, have performed well. In 2006 the economy grew briskly on the back of strong fixed investment and private consumption growth on the demand side and a solid performance from agriculture, manufacturing and construction on the supply side. The country's trade position has deteriorated in recent years and there is a need to diversify export markets. In Jan. 2007 Uruguay signed a framework agreement on trade with the USA, a first step towards a free trade agreement.

Currency

The unit of currency is the *Uruguayan peso* (UYU), of 100 *centésimos*, which replaced the nuevo peso in March 1993 at 1 Uruguayan peso = 1,000 nuevos pesos. In June 2002 Uruguay allowed the peso to float freely. Inflation, which had been over 100% in 1990, was 7·9% in 2008. In July 2005 total money supply was 22,794m. pesos, foreign exchange reserves were US$2,578m. and gold reserves were 8,000 troy oz (1·8m. troy oz in Nov. 1999).

Budget

In 2005 revenues totalled 82,343m. pesos and expenditures 89,947m. pesos.

Standard rate of VAT is 22% (reduced rate, 10%).

Performance

Uruguay depends heavily on its two large neighbours, Brazil and Argentina. Uruguay suffered four successive years of negative growth between 1999 and 2002, culminating in the economy shrinking by 7·1% in 2002, as the general downturn in the world economy was exacerbated by Argentina's crisis. However, the economy has since recovered to achieve GDP growth rates of 7·6% in 2007 and 8·9% in 2008. Total GDP in 2008 was US$32·2bn.

Banking and Finance

The Central Bank (*President*, Mario Bergara) was inaugurated on 16 May 1967. It is the bank of issue and supreme regulatory authority. In 2003 there were three other state banks, three principal commercial banks, ten foreign banks and two major credit co-operatives. Savings banks deposits were 1,993,029m. pesos in 1995.

There is a stock exchange in Montevideo.

ENERGY AND NATURAL RESOURCES

Environment

Uruguay's carbon dioxide emissions from the consumption and flaring of fossil fuels in 2008 were the equivalent of 2·2 tonnes per capita.

Electricity

Installed capacity was 1·8m. kW in 2003. Production in 2004 was 5·94bn. kWh, with consumption per capita 2,408 kWh.

Agriculture

Rising investment has helped agriculture, which has given a major boost to the country's economy. Some 41m. acres are devoted to farming, of which 90% to livestock and 10% to crops. Some large *estancias* have been divided up into family farms; the average farm is about 250 acres. In 2007 there were approximately 1·35m. ha. of arable land and 33,000 ha. of permanent crops. 169,000 ha. were irrigated in 2006.

Main crops (in 1,000 tonnes), 2003: rice, 1,250; wheat, 326; barley, 324; sunflower seeds, 234; soybeans, 183; maize, 178; sugarcane, 165; potatoes, 151; oranges, 122; grapes, 103; tangerines and mandarins, 75; apples, 72; wine, 72; sweet potatoes, 65; sorghum, 60; lemons and limes, 40; oats, 40. The country has some 6m. fruit trees, principally peaches, oranges, tangerines and pears.

Livestock, 2003: cattle, 11·69m.; sheep, 9·78m.; horses, 380,000; pigs, 240,000; chickens, 13m.

Livestock products, 2003 (in 1,000 tonnes): beef and veal, 424; lamb and mutton, 42; pork, bacon and ham, 17; poultry meat, 54; milk 1,495; greasy wool, 43; eggs, 42.

Forestry

In 2005 the area under forests was 1·51m. ha. (mainly eucalyptus and pine), representing 8·6% of the total land area. In 2007, 7·17m. cu. metres of roundwood were cut.

Fisheries

The total catch in 2005 was 125,906 tonnes, almost entirely marine fish.

INDUSTRY

In 2001 industry accounted for 26·6% of GDP, with manufacturing contributing 16·6%. Industries include meat packing, oil refining, cement manufacture, foodstuffs, beverages, leather and textile manufacture, chemicals, light engineering and transport equipment. Output in 1,000 tonnes (2004 unless otherwise indicated): distillate fuel oil, 772; cement (2001), 674; petrol, 520; residual fuel oil, 519; meat-packing (1991), 1,132,000 head; 9·6bn. cigarettes (2001).

Labour

In 1996 the retirement age was raised from 55 to 60 for women; it remains 60 for men. The labour force in 2005 totalled 1,269,300 (54% males). In 2001, 22·4% of the urban workforce was engaged in wholesale and retail trade/repair of motor vehicles, motorcycles and personal and household goods/hotels and restaurants; 15·5% in manufacturing/electricity, gas and water supply; 9·2% in private households with employed persons; and 9·1% in financial intermediation and real estate, renting and business activities. In 2001 the unemployment rate in urban areas was 15·3%.

INTERNATIONAL TRADE

External debt was US$14,551m. in 2005.

Imports and Exports

Trade in US$1m.:

	2000	2001	2002	2003	2004
Imports f.o.b.	3,311·1	2,914·7	1,873·8	2,097·8	2,990·2
Exports f.o.b.	2,383·8	2,139·4	1,922·1	2,281·1	3,021·3

Main imports in 2004: petroleum, 24·1%; chemicals and chemical products, 16·0%; machinery and appliances, 14·1%; food, beverages and tobacco, 8·5%; plastic products, 6·2%. Main exports in 2004: beef, 20·6%; hides and leather goods, 9·5%; textiles, 8·1%; dairy products, 7·0%; rice, 6·2%.

In 2004 the main import suppliers were Argentina (22·2%), Brazil (21·7%), Russia (11·0%), USA (7·1%) and China (5·5%). Leading export destinations in 2004 were the USA (19·8%), Brazil (16·5%), Argentina (7·6%), Germany (5·2%) and Mexico (4·0%).

COMMUNICATIONS

Roads

In 2002 there were 8,984 km of roads, including 2,612 km of national roads and 5,246 km of regional roads. Passenger cars in 2007 numbered 553,200 (151 per 1,000 inhabitants in 2005). There were 150 fatalities as a result of road accidents in 2005.

Rail

The total railway system open for traffic in 2005 was 1,508 km of 1,435 mm gauge. Passenger services, which had been abandoned in 1988, were resumed on a limited basis in 1993. In 2004 the railways carried 450,000 passengers and 1·2m. tonnes of freight.

Civil Aviation

There is an international airport at Montevideo (Carrasco). The national carrier is Pluna. In 2003 it operated domestic services and maintained routes to Asunción, Buenos Aires, Madrid, Porto Alegre, Rio de Janeiro, Santiago and São Paulo. There were 60 airports in 1996, 45 with paved runways and 15 with unpaved runways. In 1999 Montevideo handled an estimated 1,423,000 passengers (1,115,000 on international flights) and 25,500 tonnes of freight. In 2003 scheduled airline traffic of Uruguay-based carriers flew 8m. km, carrying 464,000 passengers (all on international flights).

Shipping

In 2002 sea-going shipping totalled 75,000 GRT, including oil tankers 6,000 GRT. In 2004 vessels totalling 5,067,000 NRT entered ports and vessels totalling 22,262,000 NRT cleared. Navigable inland waterways total 1,600 km.

Telecommunications

The telephone system in Montevideo is controlled by the State; small companies operate in the interior. Uruguay had 3,969,500 telephone subscribers in 2007 (1,188·6 for every 1,000 persons). There were 3,004,300 mobile phone subscribers in 2007. Internet users numbered 968,000 in 2007 (including 165,000 broadband subscribers).

Postal Services

In 2003 there were 1,269 post offices.

SOCIAL INSTITUTIONS

Justice

The Supreme Court is elected by Congress; it appoints all other judges. There are six courts of appeal, each with three judges. There are civil and criminal courts. Montevideo has ten courts of first instance, Paysandú and Salto have two each and the other departments have one each. There are approximately 300 lower courts.

The population in penal institutions in Sept. 2003 was 7,100 (209 per 100,000 of national population).

Education

Adult literacy in 2002 was 97·7% (male, 97·3%; female, 98·1%). The female literacy rate is the second highest in South America, behind Guyana. Primary education is obligatory; both primary and secondary education are free. In 2007 there were 122,089 pupils in pre-primary schools with 5,220 teaching staff, 359,439 primary school pupils with 23,175 teaching staff and at secondary level there were 294,852 pupils and 21,369 teaching staff.

There is one state university, one independent Roman Catholic university and one private institute of technology. In 2007 there were 158,841 students and 15,789 academic staff in tertiary education.

In 2006 public expenditure on education came to 3·0% of GNI and represented 11·6% of total government expenditure.

Health
In 2003 there were 13,071 physicians, 4,154 dentists, 3,118 nurses, 1,323 pharmacists and 572 midwives. There were 107 hospitals with 6,661 beds.

Welfare
The welfare state dates from the beginning of the 1900s. In 2002 there were 0·5m. recipients of pensions and benefits. A private pension scheme inaugurated in 1996 had 315,000 members at 31 Dec. 1996. State spending on social security has been capped at 15% of GDP.

RELIGION

State and Church are separate, and there is complete religious liberty. In 2001 there were 2·6m. Roman Catholics and 710,000 persons with other beliefs.

CULTURE

World Heritage Sites
Uruguay has one site on the UNESCO World Heritage List: the Historic Quarter of the City of Colonia del Sacramento (inscribed on the list in 1995), founded in 1680 by the Portuguese.

Broadcasting
In 2005 television receivers numbered 1·32m. (colour by PAL). Cable TV is widely available. State-run TV and radio services are operated by the Servicio Oficial de Difusión, Radiotelevisión y Espectáculos (SODRE).

Press
In 2006 there were 12 paid-for dailies with an average circulation of 135,000. The newspaper with the highest circulation is El País, which sold a daily average of 46,000 copies in 2005.

Tourism
There were 1·81m. non-resident tourists in 2005, mainly from Argentina. Receipts totalled US$690m.

DIPLOMATIC REPRESENTATIVES

Of Uruguay in the United Kingdom (1st Floor, 125 Kensington High St., London, W8 5SF)
Ambassador: Julio Moreira Móran.

Of the United Kingdom in Uruguay (Calle Marco Bruto 1073, 11300 Montevideo)
Ambassador: Patrick Mullee.

Of Uruguay in the USA (1913 I St., NW, Washington, D.C., 20006)
Ambassador: Carlos Gianelli.

Of the USA in Uruguay (Lauro Muller 1776, Montevideo)
Ambassador: David D. Nelson.

Of Uruguay to the United Nations
Ambassador: José Luis Cancela.

Of Uruguay to the European Union
Ambassador: Luis Sica Bergara.

FURTHER READING

González, L. E., *Political Structures and Democracy in Uruguay.* 1992
Sosnowski, S. (ed.) *Repression, Exile and Democracy: Uruguayan Culture.* 1993

National library: Biblioteca Nacional del Uruguay, 18 de julio de 1790, Montevideo.
National Statistical Office: Instituto Nacional de Estadística (INE), Rio Negro 1520, Montevideo.
Website (Spanish only): http://www.ine.gub.uy

UZBEKISTAN

Uzbekiston Respublikasy
(Republic of Uzbekistan)

Capital: Tashkent
Population estimate, 2010: 27·79m.
GDP per capita, 2007: (PPP$) 2,425
HDI/world rank: 0·710/119

KEY HISTORICAL EVENTS

Evidence of human settlement from at least 2200 BC is believed to be that of the Oxus civilization which extended across central Asia from Turkmenistan to Tajikistan. The region came under the influence of the first Persian Empire, centred on Persepolis, from around 550 BC when it was known as Sogdiana. Alexander the Great conquered Sogdiana and the ancient Greek kingdom of Bactria in 327 BC, marrying Roxane, daughter of a Sogdian chieftain.

Turkic nomads entered the area from the 5th century AD and control subsequently passed to Arabs, who introduced Islam to Transoxiana in the 8th century. The Persian Samanid dynasty, centred on the cities of Bukhara, Samarkand and Heart, held sway from around 875 AD for over a century, before falling to the Khara-Khanid Khanate.

Much of present-day Uzbekistan came under the control of Seljuk Turks from the 11th century. Led by Alp Arslan, they went on to conquer Georgia, Armenia, Syria and most of Anatolia. Khwarazm in northwest Uzbekistan gained independence from the Seljuks in the late 12th century, expanding westward as far as the Caspian Sea. Ghenghis Khan's Mongol Hordes overran Central Asia from 1221 and retained power until the rise of Timur, who made his native Samarkand the capital of an empire that by 1405 stretched from western India to the Black Sea. The subsequent Timurid dynasty was ruled by Shahrukh and, from 1447, by Ulugh-beg. Located on the trade routes between Europe, Persia, India and China, the oasis cities of Samarkand, Bukhara and Tashkent became prosperous centres of culture and learning.

The Uzbeks were Turkic-speaking tribes who moved into the region from the steppes to the north of the Aral Sea from the early 16th century. They established separate principalities, notably the Emirate of Bukhara and the Khanates of Khiva and Kokand. The fall of the Timurid Empire presaged the gradual decline of the Central Asian trade routes, partly as a result of the opening of shipping lines between Western Europe and India and East Asia.

During the 1850s the Russian empire began to expand into central Asia. In 1865 Russian forces seized the city of Tashkent and a year later the Khanate of Kokand was dissolved and incorporated into the Governor-Generalship of Turkestan. The Khanate of Khiva and the Emirate of Bukhara became protectorates. Russian colonists, settling throughout Central Asia, developed the region's infrastructure while exploiting the abundant minerals and promoting the growth of cash crops such as cotton. There were periodic revolts against Russian rule, notably the Andijan Uprising of 1898. The chaos surrounding the Bolshevik Revolution of 1917 precipitated the growth of an Uzbek guerrilla army, 'the Basmachi', although their efforts to establish a democratic republic were unsuccessful. In 1924 the Khorezm and Bukhara People's Republics were incorporated into the Uzbekistan Soviet Socialist Republic (SSR), which also included Tajikistan until it became a separate SSR in 1929. The Soviet period brought collectivization and rapid industrialization, particularly around the capital, Tashkent, leading to an influx of Russian migrant workers. Uzbekistan SSR became the primary cotton-producing region of the Soviet Union, although the large-scale diversion of rivers for irrigation had disastrous consequences for the Aral Sea, which lost two-thirds of its volume.

On 20 June 1990 the Supreme Soviet adopted a declaration of sovereignty, although the Communist Party, led by Islam Karimov, remained the only official political party. Following the collapse of the Soviet Union, Uzbekistan was declared an independent republic on 31 Aug. 1991. In Dec. 1991 Uzbekistan became a member of the Commonwealth of Independent States and Karimov was elected president by popular vote. He subsequently cracked down on political opponents, notably the Birlik party and the Islamic Renaissance Party, citing the need for 'stability'.

Bomb blasts in Tashkent, one of which almost killed the president in Feb. 1999, were blamed on extremists from the Islamist Movement of Uzbekistan (IMU), which operates largely in the Ferghana valley and aims to create a pan-Central Asian Islamic state. The IMU leader, Juma Namangoniy, was reportedly killed in Aug. 2002. Nearly 50 people died in a series of bombings and shootings in March 2004, allegedly perpetrated by Islamic militants. Suicide bombers targeted the US and Israeli embassies in Tashkent in July 2004.

On 13 May 2005 several hundred demonstrators were killed in Andijan after troops fired into a crowd protesting against the imprisonment of local businessmen. The USA joined calls for an international inquiry into the shootings. In Nov. 2005 the USA closed its military air base at Karshi-Khanabad which had been used for operations in Afghanistan.

TERRITORY AND POPULATION

Uzbekistan is bordered in the north by Kazakhstan, in the east by Kyrgyzstan and Tajikistan, in the south by Afghanistan and in the west by Turkmenistan. Area, 447,400 sq. km (172,741 sq. miles). At the last census, in 1989, the population was 19,810,077. In 1998, 75·8% of the population was Uzbek, 6·0% Russian, 4·8% Tajik, 4·1% Kazakh, 1·6% Tatar and 7·7% other. In 2005, 63·3% of the population lived in rural areas.

The UN gives an estimated population for 2010 of 27·79m.; density, 62 per sq. km.

The areas and populations of the 12 regions, the Karakalpak Autonomous Republic (Karakalpakstan) and the city of Tashkent are as follows (Uzbek spellings in brackets):

Region	Area (in sq. km)	Population (2008 estimate)	Capital	Population (1999 estimate)
Andizhan (Andijon)	4,200	2,477,900	Andizhan	323,900
Bukhara (Bukhoro)	39,400	1,576,800	Bukhara	237,900
Dzhizak (Jizzakh)	20,500	1,090,900	Dzhizak	126,400
Ferghana (Farghona)	7,100	2,997,400	Ferghana	182,800
Khorezm (Khorazm)	6,300	1,517,600	Urgench (Urganch)	139,100
Kashkadar (Qashqadaryo)	28,400	2,537,600	Karshi (Qarshi)	197,600
Karakalpak Autonomous Republic (Qoraqalpoghiston)	164,900	1,612,300	Nukus (Nuqus)	199,000
Namangan	7,900	2,196,200	Namangan	376,600
Navoi (Nawoiy)	110,800	834,100	Nawoiy	117,600
Samarkand (Samarqand)	16,400	3,032,000	Samarkand	362,300
Syr-Darya (Sirdaryo)	5,100	698,100	Gulistan (Guliston)	56,900[1]
Surkhan-Darya (Surkhondaryo)	20,800	2,012,600	Termez (Termiz)	111,500
Tashkent (Toshkent)	15,600	4,730,200	Tashkent	2,142,700

[1]1991.

Regions are further subdivided into 227 districts and cities.

The capital is Tashkent (1999 population estimate, 2,142,700); other large towns are Namangan, Samarkand, Andizhan, Bukhara, Nukus, Karshi, Kokand, Ferghana, Chirchik, Margilan and Urgench. There are 124 towns, 97 urban settlements and 155 rural districts.

The Roman alphabet (in use 1929–40) was reintroduced in 1994. Arabic script was in use prior to 1929, and Cyrillic from 1940–94.

The official language is Uzbek. Russian and Tajik are also spoken.

SOCIAL STATISTICS

2001 births, 512,950; deaths, 132,542; marriages, 170,101; divorces, 15,646. Rates, 2001: birth (per 1,000 population), 20·5; death, 5·3; marriage, 6·8; divorce, 0·6. Life expectancy, 2007, 64·5 years for men and 70·9 for women. Annual population growth rate, 1992–2002, 1·8%. In 2000 the most popular age range for marrying was 20–24 for both males and females. Infant mortality, 2005, 57 per 1,000 live births; fertility rate, 2004, 2·7 births per woman.

CLIMATE

The summers are warm to hot but the heat is made more bearable by the low humidity. The winters are cold but generally dry and sunny. Tashkent, Jan. –1°C, July 25°C. Annual rainfall 14·76" (375 mm).

CONSTITUTION AND GOVERNMENT

A new constitution was adopted on 8 Dec. 1992 stating that Uzbekistan is a pluralist democracy. The constitution restricts the president to standing for two five-year terms. In Jan. 2002 a referendum was held at which 91% of the electorate voted in favour of extending the presidential term from five to seven years. Voters were also in favour of changing from a single-chamber legislature to a bicameral parliament. Based on the constitution President Karimov's term of office that started in Jan. 2000 ended in Jan. 2007, but according to election law a vote must be held in Dec. of the year in which the president's term expires. Pro-Karimov legislators maintained that he was eligible to stand again in the Dec. 2007 elections as he had only served one seven-year term despite having been president since 1990.

Uzbekistan switched to a bicameral legislature in Jan. 2005 with the establishment of the 100-member *Senate* (with 16 members appointed by the president and 84 elected from the ranks of regional, district and city legislative councils). The lower house is the 150-member *Oliy Majlis* (Supreme Assembly). 135 seats are elected by popular vote for five-year terms and 15 are reserved for the Ecological Movement.

National Anthem

'Serquyosh, hur o'lkam, elga baxt najot' ('Stand tall, my free country, good fortune and salvation to you'); words by Abdulla Aripov, tune by Mutal Burhanov.

GOVERNMENT CHRONOLOGY

President since 1990. (n/p = non-partisan)

1990–	n/p	Islam Abduganiyevich Karimov

RECENT ELECTIONS

Presidential elections were held on 23 Dec. 2007. Incumbent Islam Karimov was elected against three opponents with 90·8% of the vote, although the elections were condemned by the OSCE. Turnout was 90·6%.

In parliamentary elections held in two rounds on 27 Dec. 2009 and 10 Jan. 2010, the Liberal-Democratic Party won 53 of the 150 seats, followed by the People's Democratic Party with 32, the National Revival Democratic Party with 31 and the Justice Social Democratic Party with 19. A further 15 seats were reserved for the Ecological Movement of Uzbekistan. All parties taking part in the election were loyal to President Islam Karimov—opposition parties were barred from participating.

CURRENT ADMINISTRATION

President: Islam Karimov; b. 1938 (sworn in 24 March 1990).

In March 2010 the government comprised:

Prime Minister: Shavkat Mirziyayev; b. 1957 (People's Democratic Party; in office since 11 Dec. 2003).

First Deputy Prime Minister: Rustam Azimov (also *Minister of Finance*). *Deputy Prime Ministers:* Farida Akbarova; Abdulla Aripov; Elyor Ganiyev (also *Minister of Foreign Economic Relations, Investments and Trade)*; Botir Khodjaev; Ulugbek Rozukulov; Ergash Shaismatov.

Minister of Agriculture and Water Resources: Zafar Ruziev. *Culture and Sports:* Anvar Jabborov. *Defence:* Kobil Berdiev. *Economy:* Sunatilla Bekenov. *Emergency Situations:* Kasimali Akhmedov. *Foreign Affairs:* Vladimir Norov. *Health:* Adkham Ikramov. *Higher and Secondary Specialized Education:* Bakhodir Khodiev. *Internal Affairs:* Bakhodir Matlyubov. *Justice:* Ravshan Mukhitdinov. *Labour and Social Protection (acting):* Aktam Haitov. *National Education:* Avazjon Marahimov.

Chairman, Oliy Majlis: Dilorom Tashmuhamedova.

Office of the President: http://www.gov.uz

CURRENT LEADERS

Islam Abduganievich Karimov

Position

President

Introduction

Islam Karimov, a former Soviet official, has been president since Uzbekistan declared independence in 1990. His regime has been characterized by the suppression of domestic political and religious opposition, and his electoral victories have been questioned for their irregularities. Karimov has sought to build ties with the West, and won US favour for co-operation in the war against terrorism in the aftermath of the 11 Sept. 2001 attacks. However, reports of torture and other human rights violations, culminating in an alleged massacre of Uzbek civilians in Andizhan in May 2005, have provoked increasing international criticism of his regime. In Dec. 2007 he retained the presidency, claiming a landslide victory in an election widely condemned as undemocratic and constitutionally illegal.

Early Life

Karimov was born on 30 Jan. 1938 in Samarkand. He qualified as a mechanical engineer at the Central Asian Polytechnical Institute and graduated in economics from the Tashkent Institute of National Economy. He then worked in Tashkent at farm machinery and aircraft plants. In 1966 he moved to the state planning committee of Uzbekistan, attaining the rank of vice-chairman.

In 1983 Karimov was appointed finance minister for Uzbekistan and three years later became deputy head of government, as well as chairman of the state planning committee. In 1989 he was named head of the Uzbek Communist Party. The following year Uzbekistan claimed sovereignty from the USSR and Karimov was chosen as president. Following the attempted coup against Mikhail Gorbachev in Moscow in 1991, Karimov declared full independence.

Career in Office

Against little organized opposition, Karimov dominated presidential elections and led Uzbekistan into the Commonwealth of Independent States. In 1992 he continued his campaign against domestic opposition, banning two leading parties—Birlik (Unity) and Erk (Freedom)—and imprisoning many members. In 1994 he agreed an economic integration treaty with Russia and signed a co-operation pact with Kazakhstan and Kyrgyzstan which was developed into a single economic community in 1996. In 1995 Karimov won a further five years in office by plebiscite.

In 1999 Tashkent was the scene of several car bombings which Karimov blamed on the Islamic Movement of Uzbekistan (IMU). Government and IMU forces clashed several times, the culmination of growing tensions between the two sides since the mid-1990s. In the same year Karimov withdrew Uzbekistan from the CIS agreement on collective security, increasing the nation's isolation among Central Asian nations predominantly loyal to Moscow.

Karimov was re-elected to the presidency in 2000 with over 90% of the vote, although the electoral process was severely criticized by the international community, notably the opposition candidate's assertion that he himself would vote for Karimov. Following the 11 Sept. terrorist attacks in New York and Washington, Karimov permitted the USA to use Uzbek air bases for the war in Afghanistan. In the same year he signed up to the Shanghai Co-operation Society (with China, Russia, Kazakhstan, Kyrgyzstan and Tajikistan), established to promote regional economic co-operation and fight religious and ethnic militancy.

In Jan. 2002 Karimov secured a constitutional change, accepted by referendum, extending the presidential term from five to seven years. His assistance in the US campaign in Afghanistan was meanwhile rewarded by US$160m. worth of aid from Washington. Also in 2002 a long-running border feud with Kazakhstan was settled.

In March 2004 a series of shootings and explosions in the Tashkent and Bukhara regions left dozens of people dead. Further bombings near the US and Israeli embassies and in the Prosecutor General's Office in Tashkent occurred in July. Karimov's government blamed Islamic militants. Then in May 2005 several hundred civilians, protesting against the trial of local businessmen accused of Islamic extremism, were reportedly killed by security forces in Andizhan. Unrest also spread to the towns of Paktabad and Kara Suu before troops reasserted government control. At the end of July, in a punitive response to international criticism of the massacre, Karimov gave the USA six months to close its military airbase in Uzbekistan. His relations with the European Union also became increasingly strained in the wake of the events in Andizhan and the subsequent convictions of those accused of instigating unrest. The EU imposed an arms embargo and a visa ban, and these sanctions were extended in 2006. Uzbekistan meanwhile sought to strengthen its military and economic co-operation with Russia.

In Dec. 2007 Karimov's re-election as president failed to meet democratic standards, according to international observers, and was condemned by opposition activists as a sham.

In late 2008 and early 2009 there was some improvement in relations with the West as Karimov allowed the USA and NATO to transport non-lethal supplies through Uzbekistan to their armed forces in Afghanistan and the EU eased sanctions despite continuing concerns about human rights. The EU's decision followed the release of some political prisoners and the abolition of the death penalty.

In mid-2009 two terrorist incidents in Andizhan and Khanabad were attributed to increasing Islamist militancy.

DEFENCE

Conscription is for 12 months. Defence expenditure in 2006 totalled US$85m. (US$3 per capita), representing 0·5% of GDP.

Army

Personnel, 2007, 50,000. There are, in addition, paramilitary forces totalling up to 20,000.

Air Force

Personnel, 2007, 17,000. There were 135 combat capable aircraft in operation (including Su-17s, Su-24s, Su-25s, Su-27s and MiG-29s) and 29 attack helicopters.

INTERNATIONAL RELATIONS

Uzbekistan is a member of the UN, World Bank, IMF and several other UN specialized agencies, OSCE, CIS, Islamic Development Bank, NATO Partnership for Peace, OIC, Asian Development Bank and ECO.

ECONOMY

Agriculture accounted for 26·1% of GDP in 2006, industry 27·4% and services 46·5%.

Uzbekistan featured among the ten most corrupt countries in the world in a 2009 survey of 180 countries carried out by the anti-corruption organization *Transparency International*.

Overview

Since the collapse of the Soviet Union, Uzbekistan has embarked on a cautious transition of its economy. There is a heavy dependence on state controls and planning, foreign exchange and trade restrictions and large public investments aimed at achieving import-substitution industrialization and self-sufficiency in food and energy.

The business climate is unfavourable to private enterprise. Heavily populated river valleys are intensely cultivated and irrigated. The land is rich in natural resources and primary commodities (cotton, gold, copper, energy resources and precious stones) account for the majority of exports. Uzbekistan is the world's second-largest cotton exporter behind the USA and relies on the crop as a source of export earnings. In recent years strong cotton and gold prices, with growing exports of natural gas and manufactured products, have strengthened the economy and its external financial position.

The country receives significant remittances from citizens who work abroad, primarily in Russia and Kazakhstan. Uzbekistan has increasingly looked towards Russia, China and other central Asian countries to build economic links. Neighbouring countries are keen to develop Uzbekistan's oil and gas industry.

Currency

A coupon for a new unit of currency, the *soum* (UZS), was introduced alongside the rouble on 15 Nov. 1993. This was replaced by the *soum* proper at 1 soum = 1,000 coupons on 1 July

1994. In 1994 inflation was 1,568% but has since declined, and was 12·7% in 2008.

Budget
In 1999 revenues amounted to 611,897m. soums and expenditures to 654,259m. soums.

Performance
Real GDP growth was 7·3% in 2006, 9·5% in 2007 and 9·0% in 2008; total GDP in 2008 was US$27·9bn.

Banking and Finance
The Central Bank is the bank of issue (*Chairman*, Faizulla Mullajanov). In 2001 there were 38 commercial banks, of which 16 were privately owned.

ENERGY AND NATURAL RESOURCES

Environment
Irrigation of arid areas has caused the drying up of the Aral Sea. Uzbekistan's carbon dioxide emissions from the consumption and flaring of fossil fuels in 2008 were the equivalent of 4·6 tonnes per capita.

Electricity
Installed capacity was an estimated 11·7m. kW in 2004. Production was 51·0bn. kWh in 2004 and consumption per capita 1,944 kWh.

Oil and Gas
Oil production was 4·8m. tonnes in 2008; natural gas output was 62·2bn. cu. metres. In 2008 there were proven oil reserves of 0·6bn. bbls and natural gas reserves of 1,580bn. cu. metres.

Minerals
Lignite production in 2004 was 2·70m. tonnes. In 2005, 84 tonnes of gold and an estimated 60 tonnes of silver were produced. There are also large reserves of uranium, copper, lead, zinc and tungsten; all uranium mined (2,629 tonnes in 2005) is exported.

Agriculture
Farming is intensive and based on irrigation. In 2002 there were 4·48m. ha. of arable land and 0·34m. ha. of permanent cropland. Approximately 4·28m. ha. were irrigated in 2002.

Output of main agricultural products (2003, in 1,000 tonnes): wheat, 5,331; seed cotton, 2,856; cottonseed, 1,720; tomatoes, 1,100; cotton lint, 946; cabbage, 900; potatoes, 760; grapes, 510; apples, 503; watermelons, 460; rice, 311; cucumbers and gherkins, 300. Livestock, 2003 estimates: 8·2m. sheep; 5·4m. cattle; 820,000 goats; 14m. chickens. Livestock products, 2003 estimates (in 1,000 tonnes): meat, 508; milk, 3,790; eggs, 83.

Forestry
In 2005 the area under forests was 3·30m. ha., accounting for 8·0% of the total land area. In 2007, 31,000 cu. metres of timber were produced.

Fisheries
The total catch in 2004 was 1,230 tonnes, exclusively freshwater fish.

INDUSTRY
Industrial production grew by 3·4% in 2002. Major industries include fertilizers, agricultural and textile machinery, aircraft, metallurgy and chemicals. Output (in tonnes): cement (2001), 3,700,000; distillate fuel oil (2004), 1,879,000; residual fuel oil (2004), 1,814,000; petrol (2004), 1,736,000; sulphuric acid (2000), 823,000; mineral fertilizer (2000), 800,000; cotton woven fabrics (2000), 360m. sq. metres; 1,000 tractors (2000); 26,000 TV sets (2000).

Labour
In 1999 a total of 8,885,000 persons were in employment, including: 3,421,000 engaged in agriculture, hunting, forestry and fishing; 1,968,000 in community, social and personal services; 1,142,000 in manufacturing, mining and quarrying, electricity, gas and water; and 734,000 in wholesale and retail trade, restaurants and hotels. In 2000 the unemployment rate was 0·6%. Average monthly salary in 1999 was 8,823 soums. A minimum wage of 6,530 soums a month was imposed on 1 Aug. 2004.

INTERNATIONAL TRADE
External debt was US$4,226m. in 2005.

Imports and Exports
In 2002 imports were valued at US$2,712m. and exports at US$2,988m. Principal imports, 2002, were machinery and equipment, 41·4%; chemicals and chemical products, 15·1%; foodstuffs, 12·5%; ferro and non-ferro metals, 8·0%.

The main import sources in 2002 were Russia (20·5%), South Korea (17·4%), Germany (8·9%) and Kazakhstan (7·5%). Principal export markets in 2002 were Russia (17·3%), Ukraine (10·2%), Italy (8·3%) and Tajikistan (7·8%).

COMMUNICATIONS

Roads
Length of roads, 2000, was 86,496 km (87·3% paved).

Rail
The total length of railway in 2005 was 3,986 km of 1,520 mm gauge (619 km electrified). In 2001, 15m. passengers and 41·5m. tonnes of freight were carried. There is a metro in Tashkent.

Civil Aviation
The main international airport is in Tashkent (Vostochny). Andizhan, Namangan and Samarkand also have airports. The national carrier is the state-owned Uzbekistan Airways, which in 2003 operated domestic services and flew to Almaty, Amritsar, Ashgabat, Athens, Baku, Bangkok, Beijing, Birmingham, Bishkek, Chelyabinsk, Delhi, Dhaka, Ekaterinburg, Frankfurt, İstanbul, Kazan, Khabarovsk, Krasnodar, Krasnoyarsk, Kuala Lumpur, Kyiv, London, Mineralnye Vody, Moscow, New York, Novosibirsk, Omsk, Osaka, Paris, Rome, Rostov, St Petersburg, Samara, Seoul, Sharjah, Simferopol, Tel Aviv, Tokyo, Tyumen and Ufa. In 2003 scheduled airline traffic of Uzbekistan-based carriers flew 40m. km, carrying 1,466,000 passengers (1,048,000 on international flights). In 2001 Tashkent handled 1,387,000 passengers (884,000 on international flights) and 36,200 tonnes of freight.

Shipping
The total length of inland waterways in 1990 was 1,100 km.

Telecommunications
In 2008 there were 1,849,600 main (fixed) telephone lines; mobile phone subscribers numbered 12,733,700 in 2008 (46·8 per 100 persons). There were 830,000 PCs in use in 2006 and 2,469,000 internet users in 2008.

Postal Services
In 2003 there were 3,211 post offices.

SOCIAL INSTITUTIONS

Justice
In 1994, 73,561 crimes were reported, including 1,219 murders and attempted murders. The death penalty was abolished in Jan. 2008. The population in penal institutions in Aug. 2003 was 48,000 (184 per 100,000 of national population).

Education
In 2007 there were 562,000 pre-primary pupils with 60,642 teaching staff, 2·16m. primary pupils with 118,676 teaching staff and 4·60m. secondary pupils with 352,001 teaching staff. There

were 288,550 students and 23,354 academic staff in tertiary education in 2007. There are universities and medical schools in Tashkent and Samarkand. Adult literacy rate in 2002 was 99·3% (99·6% among males and 98·9% among females).

Health

In 1995 there were 192 hospitals, with a provision of 84 beds per 10,000 population. There were 73,041 physicians, 5,283 dentists, 252,430 nurses, 673 pharmacists and 20,684 midwives in 2001.

Welfare

In Jan. 1994 there were 1,726,000 old-age pensioners and 1,007,000 other pensioners.

RELIGION

The Uzbeks are predominantly Sunni Muslims.

CULTURE

World Heritage Sites

Uzbekistan has four sites on the UNESCO World Heritage List: Itchan Kala (inscribed on the list in 1990); the Historic Centre of Bukhara (1993); the Historic Centre of Shakhrisyabz (2000); and Samarkand—Crossroads of Cultures (2001).

Broadcasting

There are private as well as public television and radio stations, but the government maintains a tight grip over broadcasting content. The state-run National Television and Radio Company transmits national and regional radio programmes and operates two TV networks. Private regional television services include MTRK, Bekabad TV and Samarkand TV. Foreign channels are available via cable TV. Oriat FM, Radio Grand and Uzbegim Taronasi are among the private radio stations. There were 6·1m. television receivers in 2006. Colour transmission is by SECAM.

Press

In 2006 there were four daily newspapers with a combined circulation of 30,000.

Tourism

There were 262,000 non-resident tourists in 2004. Receipts totalled US$57m.

DIPLOMATIC REPRESENTATIVES

Of Uzbekistan in the United Kingdom (41 Holland Park, London, W11 3RP)
Ambassador: Otabek Akbarov.

Of the United Kingdom in Uzbekistan (Ul. Gulyamova 67, 700000 Tashkent)
Ambassador: Rupert Joy.

Of Uzbekistan in the USA (1746 Massachusetts Ave., NW, Washington, D.C., 20036)
Ambassador: Ilkhom Nematov.

Of the USA in Uzbekistan (3 Moyqorghon St., 5th Block, Yunusobod District, 100093 Tashkent)
Ambassador: Richard B. Norland.

Of Uzbekistan to the United Nations
Ambassador: Murad Askarov.

Of Uzbekistan to the European Union
Ambassador: Ison Mustafoev.

FURTHER READING

Bohr, A. (ed.) *Uzbekistan: Politics and Foreign Policy.* 1998
Kalter, J. and Pavaloi, M., *Uzbekistan: Heir to the Silk Road.* 1997
Melvin, N. J., *Uzbekistan: Transition to Authoritarianism on the Silk Road.* 2000
Yalcin, Resul, *The Rebirth of Uzbekistan: Politics, Economy and Society in the Post-Soviet Era.* 2002

National Statistical Office: State Committee of the Republic of Uzbekistan on Statistics, Mustakillik Avenue 63, Tashkent 100077.
Website: http://www.stat.uz

Karakalpak Autonomous Republic (Karakalpakstan)

Area, 166,600 sq. km (64,320 sq. miles); population (2008 estimate), 1,612,300. Capital, Nukus (1999 estimate, 199,000). The Qoraqalpoghs came under Russian rule in the second half of the 19th century. On 11 May 1925 the territory was constituted within the then Kazakh Autonomous Republic (of the Russian Federation) as an Autonomous Region. On 20 March 1932 it became an Autonomous Republic within the Russian Federation, and on 5 Dec. 1936 it became part of the Uzbek SSR. The main ethnic groups are Qoraqalpoghs, Uzbeks and Kazakhs.

Its manufactures are in the field of light industry—bricks, leather goods, furniture, canning and wine. The principal crops are rice and cotton.

The shrinking of the Aral Sea has had a detrimental effect on agriculture and public health in the region. In 2002 the incidence of poverty was 36·4%, compared to 9·2% in Tashkent, the Uzbek capital. Estimates place unemployment at around the 70% mark.

In 2004–05 there were 6,800 students at Karakalpak State University. There is a branch of the Uzbek Academy of Sciences.

Total spending on health care in 2002 was US$10m., or US$6·50 per capita.

VANUATU

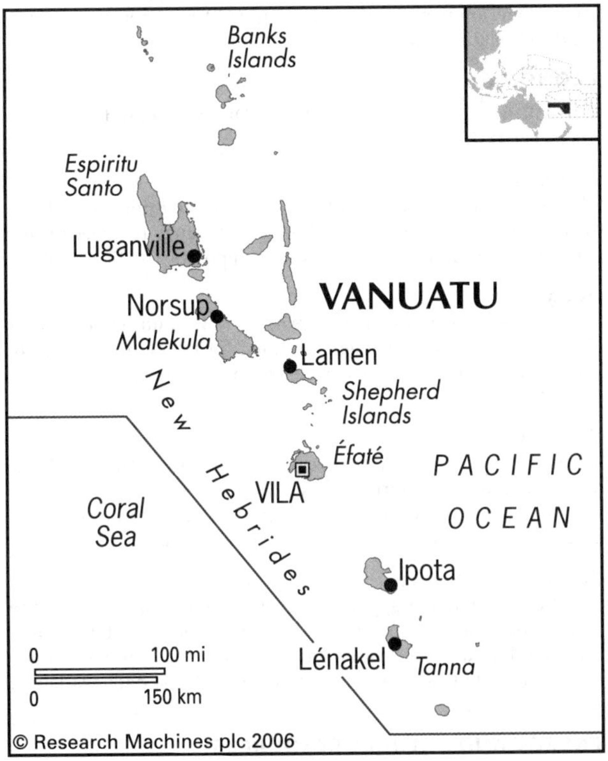

Ripablik blong Vanuatu
(Republic of Vanuatu)

Capital: Vila
Population estimate, 2010: 246,000
GDP per capita, 2007: (PPP$) 3,666
HDI/world rank: 0·693/126

KEY HISTORICAL EVENTS

Vanuatu occupies the group of islands formerly known as the New Hebrides, in the southwestern Pacific Ocean. Capt. Bligh and his companions, cast adrift by the *Bounty* mutineers, sailed through part of the island group in 1789. Sandalwood merchants and European missionaries came to the islands in the mid-19th century and were then followed by cotton planters—mostly French and British—in 1868. In response to Australian calls to annexe the islands, Britain and France agreed on joint supervision. Joint sovereignty was held over the indigenous Melanesian people but each nation retained responsibility for its own nationals according to a protocol of 1914. The island group escaped Japanese invasion during the Second World War and became an Allied base. On 30 July 1980 New Hebrides became an independent nation under the name of Vanuatu, meaning 'Our Land Forever'.

TERRITORY AND POPULATION

Vanuatu comprises 80 islands, which lie roughly 800 km west of the Fiji Islands and 400 km northeast of New Caledonia. The estimated land area is 12,190 sq. km (4,706 sq. miles). The larger islands of the group are: (Espiritu) Santo, Malekula, Epi, Pentecost, Aoba, Maewo, Paama, Ambrym, Efate, Erromanga, Tanna and Aneityum. They also claim Matthew and Hunter islands. 67 islands were inhabited in 1990. Population at the 1999 census, 186,678, giving a density of 15·3 per sq. km.

The UN gives an estimated population for 2010 of 246,000; density, 20 per sq. km.

In 2005, 76·5% of the population lived in rural areas. Vila (the capital) has a population of 26,000 (1999 estimate), and Luganville 10,000.

40% of the population is under 15 years of age, 57% between the ages of 15 and 64 and 3% 65 or over.

The national language is Bislama (spoken by 57% of the population): English and French are also official languages; about 30,000 speak French.

SOCIAL STATISTICS

2002 estimates: births, 6,500; deaths, 1,100. Rates, 2002 estimates (per 1,000 population): births, 31·6; deaths, 5·5. Annual population growth rate, 1992–2002, 2·7%. Life expectancy, 2007, was 68·1 years for males and 72·0 years for females. Infant mortality, 2005, 31 per 1,000 live births; fertility rate, 2004, 4·0 births per woman.

CLIMATE

The climate is tropical, but moderated by oceanic influences and by trade winds from May to Oct. High humidity occasionally occurs and cyclones are possible. Rainfall ranges from 90" (2,250 mm) in the south to 155" (3,875 mm) in the north. Vila, Jan. 80°F (26·7°C), July 72°F (22·2°C). Annual rainfall 84" (2,103 mm).

CONSTITUTION AND GOVERNMENT

Legislative power resides in a 52-member unicameral Parliament elected for a term of four years. The *President* is elected for a five-year term by an electoral college comprising Parliament and the presidents of the 11 regional councils. Executive power is vested in a Council of Ministers, responsible to Parliament, and appointed and led by a Prime Minister who is elected from and by Parliament.

There is also a *Council of Chiefs*, comprising traditional tribal leaders, to advise on matters of custom.

National Anthem

'Yumi, yumi, yumi i glat blong talem se, yumi, yumi, yumi i man blong Vanuatu' ('We, we, we are glad to tell, we, we, we are the people of Vanuatu'); words and tune by F. Vincent Ayssav.

RECENT ELECTIONS

Parliamentary elections were held on 2 Sept. 2008. The Party of Our Land (VP) won 11 of 52 seats, the National United Party (NUP) 8, the Union of Moderate Parties (UMP) 7, the Vanuatu Republican Party (VRP) 7, ind. 4, the People's Progressive Party 4, the Green Confederation 2 and nine other parties one each. On 22 Sept. 2008 parliament elected Edward Natapei (VP) prime minister, with 27 votes, against 25 for Maxime Carlot Korman (VRP).

Iolu Abil was elected president on 2 Sept. 2009 by an electoral college after a series of votes in the third round of voting, receiving 41 votes against 16 for outgoing president Kalkot Mataskelekele.

CURRENT ADMINISTRATION

President: Iolu Abil; b. 1942 (ind; since 2 Sept. 2009).

Prime Minister and Minister of Public Service: Edward Natapei, b. 1954 (VP; since 22 Sept. 2008). He put together a multi-party coalition which in March 2010 comprised:

Deputy Prime Minister, Minister for External Trade: Sato Kilman.

Minister for Foreign Affairs and Telecommunications: Joe Natuman. *Infrastructure and Public Utilities:* Serge Vohor. *Agriculture, Forestry and Fisheries:* Steven Kalsakau. *Finance and Economic Management:* Sela Molisa. *Ni-Vanuatu Business:* Dunstun Hilton. *Health:* Moses Kahu. *Internal Affairs:* Moana Carcasses Kalosil. *Justice:* Pakoa Kaltonga. *Youth and Sports:* Raphael Worwor. *Education:* Charlot Salwai. *Lands, Geology and Mines, and Natural Resources:* Paul Telukluk. *Trade, Industry and Commerce:* James Bulé.

Speaker: George Wells.

Government Website: http://www.governmentofvanuatu.gov.vu

CURRENT LEADERS

Edward Natapei

Position

Prime Minister

Introduction

Edward Natapei was appointed prime minister on 22 Sept. 2008, having previously served in the post from 2001–04. First elected to parliament in 1983, Natapei is a veteran of Vanuatu's volatile political system and has also served as deputy prime minister and, in 1999, as acting president. He is the leader of the Vanua'aku Pati (Party of Our Land), the country's oldest political party. An active member of the Presbyterian Church and longstanding critic of parliamentary corruption, Natapei came to power promising to continue the liberal reforms of his predecessor, Ham Lini.

Early Life

Natapei was born on Futuna, an island in the Tafea province of Vanuatu, in 1954. Before joining the Vanua'aku Pati in 1982 he studied business in Fiji and worked for the Co-operatives Federation in Vanuatu. Elected to government in 1983 as the representative for Tafea, Natapei won re-election in 1987 and 1991. Since 1995 he has held the seat of the Porta Vila constituency.

Having served for three years as speaker of parliament, Natapei became leader of Vanua'aku Pati in 1999, the year he narrowly lost a parliamentary vote for the premiership to Barack Sopé. Two years later Natapei succeeded Sopé following a vote of no-confidence against the prime minister. Natapei retained the post after the general election of May 2002 but was ousted after the poor performance of his party in the 2004 election. In 2007 Natapei became deputy prime minister in the government of Ham Lini.

Career in Office

Natapei was elected prime minister by parliament following the general election of Sept. 2008. He gained 27 votes against 25 for Maxime Carlot Korman, leader of the Francophone Parti Républicain de Vanuatu (Vanuatu Republican Party). Within days Natapei faced a vote of no-confidence after the defection of three government members to the opposition, a motion which was defeated on 3 Oct. On 25 Nov. he survived another vote of no-confidence by 26 votes to 24. A further vote of no-confidence tabled by the opposition was ruled invalid by the speaker in Nov. 2008 and a fourth motion was withdrawn by the opposition on 9 Dec. 2008 after it became apparent that it had insufficient support. Natapei survived a fifth no-confidence vote in June 2009 but was then stripped of his office and his parliamentary seat in Nov., apparently because of an administrative oversight in explaining his absence from parliamentary sittings to the speaker while abroad attending a Commonwealth summit. However, he challenged the legality of the speaker's decision and the chief justice ruled in his favour, after which he comfortably survived a further no-confidence motion in parliament in Dec.

DEFENCE

Vanuatu does not have an army but there is a Vanuatu Police Force and a paramilitary Vanuatu Mobile Force.

INTERNATIONAL RELATIONS

Vanuatu is a member of the UN, World Bank, IMF and several other UN specialized agencies, Commonwealth, International Organization of the Francophonie, Pacific Islands Forum, SPC, Asian Development Bank and is an ACP member state of the ACP-EU relationship.

ECONOMY

Agriculture accounted for 14·7% of GDP in 2006, industry 8·6% and services 76·7%.

Currency

The unit of currency is the *vatu* (VUV) with no minor unit. There was inflation in 2008 of 4·8%. Foreign exchange reserves in July 2005 were US$60m. and total money supply was 14,373m. vatu.

Budget

In 2005 revenues totalled 8,795·8m. vatu and expenditures 7,964·2m. vatu. Tax revenue accounted for 83·5% of revenues in 2005; wages and salaries accounted for 53·0% of expenditures.

VAT is 12·5%.

Performance

Vanuatu experienced a two-year recession in 2001 and 2002, when the economy contracted by 2·5% and 7·4% respectively. The economy has since recovered to achieve GDP growth rates of 6·8% in 2007 and 6·6% in 2008. Total GDP in 2008 was US$0·6bn.

Banking and Finance

The Reserve Bank blong Vanuatu (*Governor*, Odo Tevi) is the central bank and bank of issue. There is also the state-owned National Bank, two development banks and three foreign banks. Commercial banks' assets at 31 Dec. 1988 (latest data available), 20,900m. vatu.

ENERGY AND NATURAL RESOURCES

Environment

Vanuatu's carbon dioxide emissions from the consumption and flaring of fossil fuels in 2008 were the equivalent of 0·5 tonnes per capita.

Electricity

Electrical capacity in 2004 was an estimated 12,000 kW. Production in 2004 was about 44m. kWh and consumption per capita an estimated 206 kWh.

Agriculture

About 65% of the labour force are employed in agriculture. In 2007 there were approximately 20,000 ha. of arable land and 85,000 ha. of permanent crops. The main commercial crops are copra, coconuts, cocoa and coffee. Production (2003 estimates, in 1,000 tonnes): coconuts, 206; copra, 23; bananas, 14; groundnuts, 2. 80% of the population are engaged in subsistence agriculture; yams, taro, cassava, sweet potatoes and bananas are grown for local consumption. A large number of cattle are reared on plantations, and a beef industry is developing.

Livestock (2003 estimates): cattle, 130,000; pigs, 62,000; goats, 12,000; horses, 3,000.

Forestry

There were 440,000 ha. of forest in 2005 (36·1% of the land area). In 2007, 119,000 cu. metres of roundwood were cut.

Fisheries

The principal catch is tuna, mainly exported to the USA. The total catch in 2005 was 151,079 tonnes.

INDUSTRY

Principal industries include copra processing, meat canning and fish freezing, a saw-mill, soft drinks factories and a print works.

Building materials, furniture, aluminium and cement are also produced.

In 2006 industry accounted for 8·6% of GDP, with manufacturing contributing 3·2%.

INTERNATIONAL TRADE

Foreign debt in 2007 amounted to US$94m.

Imports and Exports

In 2007 imports (f.o.b.) amounted to US$201·7m. (US$159·1m. in 2006); exports (f.o.b.) US$29·9m. (US$36·7m. in 2006). In 2007 the main import suppliers were Australia, New Zealand, Singapore, the Fiji Islands and China. The main export destinations were the Philippines, New Caledonia, the Fiji Islands, Japan and Singapore.

The main exports are copra, beef, timber and cocoa.

COMMUNICATIONS

Roads

In 2002 there were 1,070 km of roads, about 260 km paved, mostly on Efate Island and Espiritu Santo. There were estimated to be 8,200 passenger cars and 2,100 commercial vehicles in use in 2002.

Civil Aviation

There is an international airport at Bauerfield Port Vila. In 2003 the state-owned Air Vanuatu flew to Auckland, Brisbane, Honiara, Nadi, Nouméa and Sydney. Domestic services were provided by Vanair, a subsidiary of Air Vanuatu. In 2003 scheduled airline traffic of Vanuatu-based carriers flew 3m. km, carrying 83,000 passengers (all on international flights).

Shipping

Sea-going shipping totalled 1·38m. GRT in 2002, including oil tankers 55,000 GRT. Several international shipping lines serve Vanuatu, linking the country with Australia, New Zealand, other Pacific territories, China (Hong Kong), Japan, North America and Europe. The chief ports are Vila and Santo. Small vessels provide frequent inter-island services.

Telecommunications

In 2008 there were 10,400 main (fixed) telephone lines; mobile phone subscribers numbered 36,000 in 2008 (15·4 per 100 persons). There were 3,000 PCs in use in 2005 and 17,000 internet users in 2008.

Postal Services

In 2003 there were 33 post offices.

SOCIAL INSTITUTIONS

Justice

The legal system is based on British common law and French civil law. There is a Supreme Court with a Chief Justice and a Magistrates Court.

The death penalty was abolished in 1980. The population in penal institutions in June 2007 was 117 (53 per 100,000 of national population).

Education

In 2006 there were 1,316 pupils with 111 teaching staff in pre-primary schools. There were 37,518 pupils in primary schools in 2007 with (2004) 1,947 teaching staff, and 13,837 pupils in secondary schools in 2004. Tertiary education is provided at the Vanuatu Technical Institute and the Teachers College, while other technical and commercial training is through regional institutions in the Solomon Islands, the Fiji Islands and Papua New Guinea. There were 955 students in tertiary education in 2004. The adult literacy rate in 1998 stood at 64%, up from 53% in 1979. In 2003 public expenditure on education came to 10·0% of GNI.

Health

There were 21 physicians in 1997 and three dentists, 259 nurses, six pharmacists and 33 midwives in 1995. There were 90 hospitals in 1995, with a provision of 32 beds per 10,000 population.

RELIGION

About two-thirds of the population are Christians, but animist beliefs are still prevalent.

CULTURE

World Heritage Sites

Vanuatu has one site on the UNESCO World Heritage List: Chief Roi Mata's Domain (inscribed on the list in 2008), three sites on the islands of Efate, Lelepa and Artok that contain the chief's residence and burial chamber.

Broadcasting

The government-owned Vanuatu Broadcasting and Television Corporation operates the national Radio Vanuatu network and the single television service. In 2005 there were 2,700 television sets.

Press

In 2005 there was one daily newspaper with a circulation of 3,000.

Tourism

In 2005 there were 62,000 non-resident tourists to Vanuatu. Receipts totalled US$93m.

DIPLOMATIC REPRESENTATIVES

Of Vanuatu in the United Kingdom
High Commissioner: Vacant.

Of the United Kingdom in Vanuatu (High Commission in Port Vila closed in Oct. 2005)
High Commissioner: Mac McLachlan, MBE (resides in Suva, Fiji Islands).

Of Vanuatu in the USA
Ambassador: Vacant.

Of the USA in Vanuatu
Ambassador: Teddy B. Taylor (resides in Port Moresby, Papua New Guinea).

Of Vanuatu to the United Nations
Ambassador: Donald Kalpokas.

Of Vanuatu to the European Union
Ambassador: Roy Mickey Joy.

FURTHER READING

Miles, W. F. S., *Bridging Mental Boundaries in a Postcolonial Microcosm: Identity and Development in Vanuatu.* 1998

National Statistical Office: Vanuatu Statistics Office, Private Mail Bag 019, Port Vila.
Website: http://www.spc.int/prism/country/vu/stats

VATICAN CITY STATE

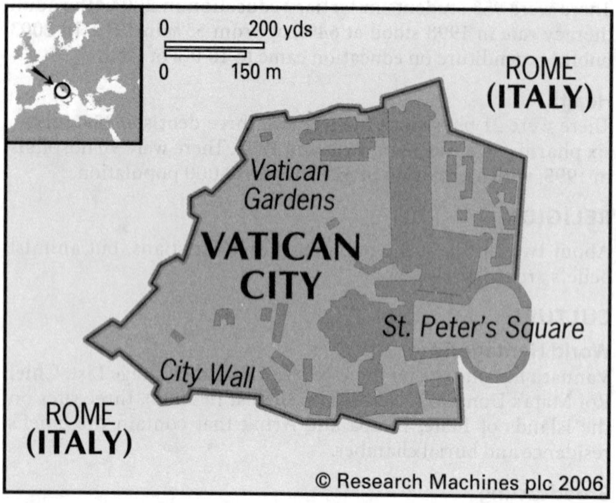

Stato della Città del Vaticano

Population estimate, 2000: 800

KEY HISTORICAL EVENTS

The history of the Vatican as a papal residence in Rome dates from the 5th century, following the construction of St Peter's Basilica by Emperor Constantine I. For many centuries the Popes bore temporal sway over much of the Italian peninsula. In 1860, following prolonged civil unrest, Victor Emmanuel's army seized the Papal States, leaving only Rome and surrounding coastal regions under papal control. When Rome was captured in 1871 and declared the capital of the Kingdom of Italy, papal temporal power was brought to an end. On 11 Feb. 1929 a treaty between the Italian Government and the Vatican recognized the sovereignty of the Holy See in the city of the Vatican.

TERRITORY AND POPULATION

The area of Vatican City is 44 ha. (108·7 acres). It includes the Piazza di San Pietro (St Peter's Square), which is to remain normally open to the public and subject to the powers of the Italian police. It has its own railway station (for freight only), postal facilities, coins and radio. Twelve buildings in and outside Rome enjoy extra-territorial rights, including the Basilicas of St John Lateran, St Mary Major and St Paul without the Walls, the Pope's summer villa at Castel Gandolfo and a further Vatican radio station on Italian soil. *Radio Vaticana* broadcasts an extensive service in 40 languages from the transmitters in Vatican City and in Italy. The Holy See and the Vatican are not synonymous—the Holy See, referring to the primacy of the Pope, is located in Vatican City. The *de facto* official language is Latin.

Vatican City has about 800 inhabitants.

CONSTITUTION AND GOVERNMENT

Vatican City State is governed by a Commission appointed by the Pope. The reason for its existence is to provide an extra-territorial, independent base for the Holy See, the government of the Roman Catholic Church. The Pope exercises sovereignty and has absolute legislative, executive and judicial powers. The judicial power is delegated to a tribunal in the first instance, to the Sacred Roman Rota in appeal and to the Supreme Tribunal of the Signature in final appeal.

A new Fundamental Law was promulgated by Pope John Paul II on 26 Nov. 2000 and became effective on 22 Feb. 2001; this replaced the first Fundamental Law of 1929. The Pope is elected by the College of Cardinals, meeting in secret conclave. The election is by scrutiny and requires a two-thirds majority.

National Anthem

'Inno e Marcia Pontificale' ('Hymn and Pontifical March'); words by Raffaello Lavagna, tune by Charles-François Gounod.

GOVERNMENT CHRONOLOGY

Popes since 1939.

1939–58	Pius XII (Eugenio Maria Pacelli)	Italian
1958–63	John XXIII (Angelo Giuseppe Roncalli)	Italian
1963–78	Paul VI (Giovanni Battista Montini)	Italian
1978	John Paul I (Albino Luciani)	Italian
1978–2005	John Paul II (Karol Józef Wojtyła)	Polish
2005–	Benedict XVI (Joseph Alois Ratzinger)	German

CURRENT ADMINISTRATION

Supreme Pontiff: **Benedict XVI** (Joseph Ratzinger), born at Marktl am Inn, in Bavaria, Germany, 16 April 1927. Archbishop of Munich and Freising 1977–82, created Cardinal in 1977; elected Pope 19 April 2005, inaugurated 24 April 2005. Pope Benedict XVI is the eighth German to be elected Pope and the first since the 11th century.

Secretary of State: Tarcisio Cardinal Bertone.

Secretary for Relations with Other States: Archbishop Dominique Mamberti.

Office of the Sovereign of the Vatican City: http://www.vatican.va

CURRENT LEADERS

Benedict XVI

Position

Pope

Introduction

Joseph Ratzinger was elected head of the Roman Catholic Church on 19 April 2005, becoming Pope Benedict XVI. His appointment followed the death of the popular and charismatic Pope John Paul II. A highly intellectual theologian from southern Germany, Benedict XVI has served in the Vatican as head of the department that defends Catholic orthodoxy since 1981. He was expected to reinforce the broadly conservative policies of John Paul II, his friend and close ally, and to tackle secularism and relativism, which he has described as 'letting oneself be tossed and swept by every wind of teaching'.

Early Life

Joseph Ratzinger was born in Marktl am Inn, southeastern Bavaria, Germany, on 16 April 1927, the third and youngest child of a police officer and his wife. In 1929 his father was posted to the town of Tittmoning on the Austrian border, where the family remained for three years, before moving to Aschau am Inn and then to Hufschlag, near Traunstein, when his father retired in 1937. Ratzinger attended the high school in Traunstein, and later opted to train for the priesthood, entering the town's seminary in 1939. At 14 years of age he joined the Hitler Youth—a legal requirement as part of the Nazis' efforts to convert the German population to the 'National Socialist spirit'. Two years later Ratzinger was drafted into the anti-aircraft artillery corps. His unit guarded facilities including an aircraft-engine plant near Munich. In late 1944 Ratzinger was drafted into the German army and served in and around Munich. Reportedly a reluctant soldier, he deserted weeks before Germany's surrender in 1945, and rejoined the seminary in Traunstein. After two years he took up a place at the Herzogliches Georgianum, a theological institute linked to the University of Munich. On 29 June 1951 he was ordained to the priesthood in the cathedral at Freising, near Munich.

Ratzinger continued with his study of theology at the University of Munich—his doctoral thesis focused on St Augustine and his view of Christianity in the fifth century. Having gained his doctorate in July 1953, he began post-doctoral research about St Bonaventure, a Franciscan theologian of the 13th century. In 1959 Ratzinger moved to Bonn to take up a professorship in fundamental theology at the city's university. He taught at the University of Münster for three years from 1963, before joining the University of Tübingen, near Stuttgart. When the wave of student uprisings swept across Europe in 1968, it brought Marxism to the Tübingen campus. Ratzinger was horrified by what he saw as a 'tyrannical, brutal and cruel' ideology that was undermining the Church. He accepted an offer of a teaching position at the new University of Regensburg a year later, and remained in the Bavarian city for the next seven years. He began to take a more conservative approach to theology, and rose to become the dean and then vice-president of the university.

On 24 March 1977 Ratzinger was elected archbishop of Munich and Freising by Pope Paul VI. He was ordained to the episcopal order in May 1977 and a month later was elevated to cardinal priest. However, his work as an archbishop was to prove relatively short-lived. In Nov. 1981 he was called to Rome by Pope John Paul II (who had been elected in 1978) to take over the Congregation for the Doctrine of the Faith, the department in the Vatican responsible for defending and reinforcing Catholic orthodoxy (once known as the Inquisition). At the same time, he became president of the International Theological Commission and the Pontifical Biblical Commission. The Congregation for the Doctrine of the Faith courted controversy after publishing 'Dominus Jesus', which described other Christian faiths and world religions as 'deficient or not quite real churches'.

Ratzinger was elevated to the position of cardinal bishop of the diocese of Velletri-Signi on 5 April 1993, and was elected vice-dean of the College of Cardinals in 1998. When he was appointed dean of the College in late 2002 (and cardinal bishop of the diocese of Ostia), Ratzinger had become one of the Vatican's most powerful and influential figures. He presided over the funeral of Pope John Paul II in St Peter's Basilica on 8 April 2005, and subsequently inaugurated the conclave for the election of the successor to St Peter in the Sistine chapel. On 19 April, after the fourth ballot of the conclave, the proto-deacon of the College of Cardinals, Jorge Estévez, announced to a crowd of tens of thousands in St Peter's Square: 'Dear brothers and sisters, we have a Pope. The most eminent and most reverend Lord, Lord Joseph, Cardinal of Holy Roman Church, Ratzinger, who has taken the name Benedict XVI.'

Career in Office

Pope Benedict XVI swiftly reappointed all former officers who had served under John Paul II. A hint of future Vatican policy came with the appointment of the US non-Cardinal William Joseph Levada to the post of prefect of the Congregation for the Doctrine of the Faith on 13 May 2005. The elevation of this deeply conservative prelate archbishop of the Archdiocese of San Francisco to one of the church's most powerful positions raised fears among reform-minded Catholics.

Controversy from another direction erupted in Sept. 2006 after the Pope delivered a lecture in Germany including a reference to a medieval text perceived as hostile to Islam. This provoked almost worldwide Muslim protest, forcing the Vatican to apologize for any unintentional offence. The incident threatened to derail a planned papal visit in Nov. to Turkey, a predominantly Muslim country, but the trip went ahead successfully, with Benedict advocating 'authentic dialogue' based on mutual respect between Christians and Muslims.

In 2007 the Pope met Russian president Vladimir Putin for the first time, and also King Abdullah of Saudi Arabia. It was the first such meeting between the head of the Roman Catholic Church and a Saudi monarch. In March 2009 he toured Africa and in May visited the Middle East where he appealed for peace and religious coexistence.

In Dec. 2008 Benedict again courted social controversy with a perceived attack on homosexuality that angered gay rights groups and activists. Then, in Jan. 2009, his controversial decision to readmit to the Church an ultraconservative bishop who had denied the Holocaust angered Jews and many Catholics. Moreover, his assertion in Feb. 2010 that the effect of some equality legislation in Britain had been to impose unjust limitations on the freedom of religious communities to act in accordance with their beliefs was condemned by human rights campaigners.

In Oct. 2009 Benedict made an unprecedented offer to disaffected Anglicans to join the Catholic Church while still maintaining many of their own spiritual traditions. In early 2010 he was the subject of allegations that he failed to take timely action against paedophile priests, this while prefect of the Congregation for the Doctrine of the Faith (1981–2005), where he had responsibility for dealing with clerical abuse. The Vatican denied any wrongdoing.

ECONOMY

Overview

The economy is supported by donations from Roman Catholics across the world, the sale of postage stamps and tourist souvenirs, admission fees to museums and publication sales. The global economic turmoil reduced donations from US$79·8m. in 2007 to US$75·8m. in 2008. The cost of restoring the Vatican's cultural treasures and ensuring security contributed to a deficit of around €15m. by the end of 2008, compared to a surplus of nearly €7m. in 2007.

Currency

Since 1 Jan. 2002 the Vatican City has been using the euro (EUR). Italy has agreed that the Vatican City may mint a small part of the total Italian euro coin contingent with their own motifs.

Budget

Revenues in 2006 were €227·8m. and expenditures €225·4m.

Performance

Real GDP growth was 1·7% in 2001.

COMMUNICATIONS

Civil Aviation

The Vatican launched a charter airline, Mistral Air, in Aug. 2007 to fly pilgrims to holy sites across the world.

SOCIAL INSTITUTIONS

Justice

In 2002 the Vatican City's legal system hosted 397 civil cases and 608 criminal cases. Most of the offences are committed by outsiders, principally at St Peter's Basilica and the museums.

ROMAN CATHOLIC CHURCH

As the Vicar of Christ and the Successor of St Peter, the Pope is held to be by divine right the centre of all Catholic unity and exercises universal governance over the Church. He is also the sovereign ruler of Vatican City State. He has for advisers the Sacred College of Cardinals, consisting in Feb. 2010 of 182 cardinals from 64 countries (four created by Pope Paul VI, 142 created by Pope John Paul II and 36 created by Pope Benedict XVI), of whom 111 are cardinal electors—those under the age of 80 who may enter into conclave to elect a new Pope. Cardinals, addressed by the title of

'Eminence', are appointed by the Pope from senior ecclesiastics who are either the bishops of important Sees or the heads of departments at the Roman Curia. In addition to the College of Cardinals, there is a Synod of Bishops, created by Pope Paul VI and formally instituted on 15 Sept. 1965. This consists of the Patriarchs and certain Metropolitans of the Catholic Church of Oriental Rite, of elected representatives of the national episcopal conferences and religious orders of the world, of the cardinals in charge of the Roman Congregations and of other persons nominated by the Pope. The Synod meets in both general (global) and special (regional) assemblies. General Synods normally take place every three years.

The central administration of the Roman Catholic Church is carried out by permanent organisms called Congregations, Council, Commissions and Offices. The Congregations are composed of cardinals and diocesan bishops (both appointed for five-year periods), with Consultors and Officials. There are nine Congregations, viz.: Doctrine, Oriental Churches, Bishops, the Sacraments and Divine Worship, Clergy, Religious, Catholic Education, Evangelization of the Peoples and Causes of the Saints. Pontifical Councils have replaced some of the previously designated Secretariats and Prefectures and now represent the Laity, Christian Unity, the Family, Justice and Peace, Cor Unum, Migrants, Health Care Workers, Interpretation of Legislative Texts, Inter-Religious Dialogue, Culture, Preserving the Patrimony of Art and History, and a Commission for Latin America. There are three academies: the Pontifical Academy for Sciences, the Pontifical Academy for Life and the Pontifical Academy for Social Sciences, the latter two instituted by Pope John Paul II.

CULTURE

World Heritage Sites

The Holy See has two sites on the UNESCO World Heritage List: Vatican City (inscribed on the list in 1984)—the centre of the Roman Catholic Church, it contains some of the greatest pieces of European art and architecture, including St Peter's Basilica.

The Historic Centre of Rome, the properties of the Holy See in that city enjoying extraterritorial rights (inscribed on the list in 1980 and 1990), is shared with Italy.

Broadcasting

Vatican Radio was inaugurated in 1931 and broadcasts religious news globally in over 40 languages.

Press

In 2006 there was one daily evening paper, L'Osservatore Romano.

DIPLOMATIC REPRESENTATIVES

In its diplomatic relations with foreign countries the Holy See is represented by the Secretariat of State and the Second Section (Relations with States) of the Council for Public Affairs of the Church. It maintains permanent observers to the UN.

Of the Holy See in the United Kingdom (54 Parkside, London, SW19 5NE)
Apostolic Nuncio: Archbishop Faustino Sainz Muñoz.

Of the United Kingdom at the Holy See (Osborne House, Via XX Septembre 80A, 00187 Rome)
Ambassador: Francis Campbell.

Of the Holy See in the USA (3339 Massachusetts Ave., NW, Washington, D.C., 20008)
Apostolic Nuncio: Pietro Sambi.

Of the USA at the Holy See (Villa Domiziana, Via Delle Terme Deciane 26, 00153 Rome)
Ambassador: Dr Miguel Humberto Diaz.

Of the Holy See to the European Union
Apostolic Nuncio: Archbishop André Dupuy.

FURTHER READING

Reese, T., *Inside the Vatican.* 1997

Permanent Observer Mission to the UN: http://www.holyseemission.org

VENEZUELA

República Bolivariana de Venezuela
(Bolivarian Republic of Venezuela)

Capital: Caracas
Population estimate, 2010: 29·04m.
GDP per capita, 2007: (PPP$) 12,156
HDI/world rank: 0·844/58

KEY HISTORICAL EVENTS

Present-day Venezuela was inhabited by hunter-gatherers from at least 3000 BC. The Arawaks and Carib lived mainly in the north and around the Orinoco river system. Christopher Columbus landed at Macuro with three Spanish ships on 5 Aug. 1498. A year later the area was explored by Alonso de Ojeda and Amerigo Vespucci. They named it Venezuela (Little Venice) after the indigenous villages built on stilts over water. Spanish settlements were established on the Caribbean coast from the early 16th century and ruled from Santo Domingo (Dominican Republic). Santiago de León de Caracas, founded in 1567, became the seat of the government of the province of Venezuela in 1578. Cocoa plantations developed slowly and much of the forested interior remained unexplored.

In 1717 Venezuela came under the Spanish Viceroyalty of New Granada, centred on Bogotá. In May 1795 rumblings of discontent over Spanish rule erupted into a revolt, led by José Leonardo Chirino who was inspired by the French Revolution. Francisco de Miranda and Simón Bolívar led further rebellions from 1805 and, following Napoleon's defeat of Spain, independence was declared in 1811. Spanish control was restored but the colonial power's defeat in the battle of Carabobo in June 1821 ensured that Venezuela became part of the federal republic of Greater Colombia. Gen. José Páez opposed the Colombian leadership and led revolts, culminating in a congress in 1830 that created a constitution for a new Republic of Venezuela and elected Páez the first president.

Páez was succeeded by José Tadeo Monagas and then by his brother, José Gregorio Monagas, who governed Venezuela until he was overthrown in 1858. Gen. Antonio Guzmán Blanco came to power in the April Revolution of 1870 and dominated politics for the next 18 years. He improved education, modernized the country's infrastructure and forced the separation of church and state. Blanco's autocratic rule was followed by the dictatorships of Joaquín Crespo (1892–98) and Cipriano Castro (1899–1908). Castro's corrupt and inefficient administration led to civil strife and, in 1902, to a major international incident known as the Venezuela Claims when Great Britain, Germany and Italy dispatched a joint naval force to Venezuela to seek redress for unpaid loans.

The brutal dictatorship of Juan Vicente Gómez began in Dec. 1908 when he seized power from the ailing Castro. Gómez's tyrannical regime, which endured until his death in 1935 did, however, develop the nation's oil industry. The election of Isaías Medina Angarita as president on 28 April 1941 led to the re-establishment of political parties, including *Acción Democrática* (AD), founded in Sept. 1941. In 1945 a three-day revolt against the government of Gen. Isaías Medina led to constitutional and economic reforms. In 1947 the writer Rómulo Gallegos was elected president but it was to be a short-lived democratic spell as the government was overthrown in a military coup in Nov. 1948 and the subsequent dictatorship of Marcos Jiménez lasted until 1958.

In 1961 a new constitution provided for a presidential election every five years, a national congress, and state and municipal legislative assemblies. Twenty political parties participated in the 1983 elections, with the economy in crisis and corruption linked to drug trafficking widespread. In Feb. 1992 there were two abortive coups and a state of emergency was declared. In Dec. 1993 Dr Rafael Caldera Rodríguez's election as president reflected disenchantment with the established political parties. He took office in the early stages of a banking crisis that cost 15% of GDP to resolve. Fiscal tightening backed by the IMF brought rapid recovery. Hugo Chávez Frías, who became president in Feb. 1999, continued with economic reforms and amended the constitution to increase presidential powers. The country was given a new name—the Bolivarian Republic of Venezuela. In Dec. 1999 the north coast of Venezuela was hit by devastating floods and mudslides which resulted in 30,000 deaths.

President Chávez was deposed and arrested on 12 April 2002 in a coup following a general strike but was back in the presidential palace within 48 hours. Opposition pressure intensified in 2002 and 2003 with more protests, a prolonged general strike and an attempt to petition for a referendum on the president's rule. Chávez faced a referendum on 15 Aug. 2004 and emerged victorious. His 'socialist revolution' and opposition to US policies has won him support but his long term impact has still to be assessed.

TERRITORY AND POPULATION

Venezuela is bounded to the north by the Caribbean with a 2,813 km coastline, east by the Atlantic and Guyana, south by Brazil, and southwest and west by Colombia. The area is 916,445 sq. km (353,839 sq. miles) including 72 islands in the Caribbean. Population at the 2001 census was 23,054,210 (11,651,341 females); density, 25·1 per sq. km. The United Nations population estimate in 2001 was 24,871,000. Venezuela has the highest percentage of urban population in South America, with 93·4% living in urban areas in 2005.

The UN gives an estimated population for 2010 of 29·04m.

The official language is Spanish. English is taught as a mandatory second language in high schools.

Area, population and capitals of the 23 states (*estados*), one federal dependency (*dependencias federales*) and one capital district (*distrito capital*):

State	*Area (sq. km)*	*2001 census population*	*Capital*	*Density; inhabitants per sq. km*
Distrito Capital	433	1,836,286	Caracas	4,240·8
Amazonas	180,145	70,464	Puerto Ayacucho	0·4
Anzoátegui	43,300	1,222,225	Barcelona	28·2
Apure	76,500	377,756	San Fernando	4·9
Aragua	7,014	1,449,616	Maracay	206·7
Barinas	35,200	624,508	Barinas	17·7
Bolívar	238,000	1,214,846	Ciudad Bolívar	5·1
Carabobo	4,650	1,932,168	Valencia	415·5
Cojedes	14,800	253,105	San Carlos	17·1
Delta Amacuro	40,200	97,987	Tucupita	2·4
Falcón	24,800	763,188	Coro	30·8
Guárico	64,986	627,086	San Juan de los Morros	9·7
Lara	19,800	1,556,415	Barquisimeto	78·6
Mérida	11,300	715,268	Mérida	63·3
Miranda	7,950	2,330,872	Los Teques	293·2
Monagas	28,900	712,626	Maturín	24·7
Nueva Esparta	1,150	373,851	La Asunción	325·1
Portuguesa	15,200	725,740	Guanare	47·8
Sucre	11,800	786,483	Cumaná	66·7
Táchira	11,100	992,669	San Cristóbal	89·4
Trujillo	7,400	608,563	Trujillo	82·2
Vargas	1,497	298,109	La Guaira	199·1
Yaracuy	7,100	499,049	San Felipe	70·3
Zulia	63,100	2,983,679	Maracaibo	47·3
Dependencias Federales	120	1,651		

37·3% of all Venezuelans are under 15 years of age, 58·7% are between the ages of 15 and 64, and 4·0% are over the age of 65.

Caracas, Venezuela's largest city, is the political, financial, commercial, communications and cultural centre of the country. Metropolitan Caracas had a 2003 population estimate of 3,226,000. Maracaibo, the nation's second largest city (estimated 2001 population of 1·6m.), is located near Venezuela's most important petroleum fields and richest agricultural areas. Other major cities are Valencia, Barquisimeto and Ciudad Guayana.

SOCIAL STATISTICS

2002 births, 492,678; deaths, 105,388. 2002 birth rate per 1,000 population, 19·5; death rate, 4·2. Annual population growth rate, 2000–05, 1·8%. Life expectancy, 2007, was 70·7 years for males and 76·7 years for females. Infant mortality, 2005, 18 per 1,000 live births; fertility rate, 2004, 2·7 births per woman. In 2002 the most popular age for marrying was 20–24 for both men and women.

CLIMATE

The climate ranges from warm temperate to tropical. Temperatures vary little throughout the year and rainfall is plentiful. The dry season is from Dec. to April. The hottest months are July and Aug. Caracas, Jan. 65°F (18·3°C), July 69°F (20·6°C). Annual rainfall 32" (833 mm). Ciudad Bolívar, Jan. 79°F (26·1°C), July 81°F (27·2°C). Annual rainfall 41" (1,016 mm). Maracaibo, Jan. 81°F (27·2°C), July 85°F (29·4°C). Annual rainfall 23" (577 mm).

CONSTITUTION AND GOVERNMENT

The present constitution was approved in a referendum held on 15 Dec. 1999. Venezuela is a federal republic, comprising 34 federal dependencies, 23 states and one federal district. Executive power is vested in the *President*. The ministers, who together constitute the Council of Ministers, are appointed by the President and head various executive departments. There are 17 ministries and seven officials who also have the rank of Minister of State.

92% of votes cast in a referendum (the first in Venezuela's history) on 25 April 1999 were in favour of the plan to rewrite the constitution proposed by President Chávez. As a result, on 25 July the public was to elect a constitutional assembly to write a new constitution, which was subsequently to be voted on in a national referendum. In Aug. 1999 the constitutional assembly declared a national state of emergency. It subsequently suspended the Supreme Court, turned the elected Congress into little more than a sub-committee, stripping it of all its powers, and assumed many of the responsibilities of government. In Dec. 1999 the President's plan to redraft the constitution was approved by over 70% of voters in a referendum. As a result presidents were able to serve two consecutive six-year-terms instead of terms of five years which could not be consecutive, the senate was abolished and greater powers were given to the state and the armed forces. President Chávez has effectively taken over both the executive and the judiciary. The constitution provides for procedures by which the president may reject bills passed by Congress, as well as provisions by which Congress may override such presidential veto acts. In Aug. 2007 President Chávez presented a set of constitutional reforms, including an end to presidential term limits. The proposals were rejected in a national referendum held on 2 Dec. 2007, with 49% of votes cast in favour of the amendments to the constitution and 51% against. However, a referendum on 15 Feb. 2009 to abolish presidential term limits (and those of various other elected officials including National Assembly deputies) was approved with 54% of votes cast in favour and 46% against.

Since the senate was dissolved under the constitution adopted in Dec. 1999 Venezuela has become a unicameral legislature, the 167-seat *National Assembly*, with members being elected for five-year terms.

National Anthem

'Gloria al bravo pueblo' ('Glory to the brave people'); words by Vicente Salias, tune by Juan Landaeta.

GOVERNMENT CHRONOLOGY

Heads of State since 1941. (AD = Democratic Action; CD = Democratic Convergence; COPEI = Social Christian Party; MVR = Movement for the Fifth Republic; n/p = non-partisan)

President of the Republic
1941–45 military Isaías Medina Angarita

Revolutionary Junta of Government
1945–48 Rómulo E. Betancourt Bello (AD) (chair); Luis Beltrán Prieto Figueroa (AD); Carlos Román Delgado Chalbaud (military); Raúl Leoni Otero (AD); Gonzalo Barrios Bustillos (AD); Mario Ricardo Vargas Cárdenas (military); Edmundo Fernández (n/p)

President of the Republic
1948 AD Rómulo Ángel Gallegos Freire

Junta of Government
1948–52 Carlos Román Delgado Chalbaud (military); Germán Suárez Flamerich (n/p); Marcos Evangelista Pérez Jiménez (military); Luis Felipe Llovera Páez (military)

President of the Republic
1952–58 military Marcos Evangelista Pérez Jiménez

Junta of Government (I)
1958 Wolfgang Enrique Larrazábal Ugueto (military) (chair); Pedro José Quevedo (military); Roberto Casanova (military); Carlos Luis Araque (military); Abel

		Romero Villate (military); Eugenio Mendoza Goiticoa (n/p); Blas Lamberti Cano (n/p); Arturo Sosa Fernández (n/p); Edgar Sanabria Arcia (n/p)

Junta of Government (II)

1958–59	Edgard Sanabria Arcia (n/p) (chair); Arturo Sosa Fernández (n/p); Miguel J. Rodríguez Olivares (military); Carlos Luis Araque (military); Pedro José Quevedo (military)

Presidents of the Republic

1959–64	AD	Rómulo Ernesto Betancourt Bello
1964–69	AD	Raúl Leoni Otero
1969–74	COPEI	Rafael Caldera Rodríguez
1974–79	AD	Carlos Andrés Pérez Rodríguez
1979–84	COPEI	Luis Antonio Herrera Campins
1984–89	AD	Jaime Lusinchi
1989–93	AD	Carlos Andrés Pérez Rodríguez
1994–99	CD	Rafael Caldera Rodríguez
1999–	MVR	Hugo Rafael Chávez Frías

RECENT ELECTIONS

Presidential elections were held on 3 Dec. 2006. Incumbent Hugo Chávez Frías (Movement for the Fifth Republic/MVR) was re-elected president with 62·9% of the vote, ahead of Manuel Rosales (A New Time/UNT) with 36·9%. There were 12 other candidates. Turnout was 74·9%.

In elections to the Congress, held on 4 Dec. 2005, 167 seats were contested. Movimiento V República (Movement for the Fifth Republic/MVR) won 114 seats with the remaining seats going to its allies. Opposition parties boycotted the elections.

Parliamentary elections are scheduled to take place on 26 Sept. 2010.

CURRENT ADMINISTRATION

President: Hugo Chávez Frías; b. 1954 (MVR; sworn in 2 Feb. 1999 and re-elected in July 2000 and Dec. 2006).

Executive Vice President and Minister of Agriculture and Lands: Elías Jaua.

In March 2010 the government comprised:

Minister of the Interior and Justice: Tarek El Aissami. *Foreign Affairs:* Nicolás Maduro. *Economy and Finance, and Planning and Development:* Jorge Giordani. *Defence:* Carlos Mata. *Commerce:* Richard Cannan. *Basic Industry and Mines:* Rodolfo Sanz. *Tourism:* Alejandro Fleming. *Higher Education:* Edgardo Ramírez. *Education:* Héctor Navarro. *Health and Social Protection:* Luis Reyes Reyes. *Labour and Social Security:* María Cristina Iglesias. *Public Works and Housing:* Diosdado Cabello. *Energy and Petroleum:* Rafael Ramírez. *Environment:* Alejandro Hitcher. *Science, Technology and Intermediary Industries:* Ricardo Menéndez. *Communications and Information:* Blanca Eekhout. *Communes:* Érika Farías. *Food Affairs:* Félix Osorio Guzmán. *Culture:* Francisco Sesto. *Sports:* Victoria Mata. *Indigenous Peoples:* Nicia Maldonado. *Electricity:* Alí Rodríguez Araque. *Presidential Secretariat:* Isis Ochoa Cañizales.

Government Website (Spanish only): http://www.gobiernoenlinea.ve

CURRENT LEADERS

Hugo Chávez

Position

President

Introduction

Hugo Rafael Chávez Frías of the Movimiento V República (Movement for the Fifth Republic/MVR—which he founded in 1997) was elected president in Dec. 1998 as the candidate for the left-wing 'Patriotic Pole' coalition. Although re-elected in 2000, he was subsequently challenged by anti-government protests and a failed coup. He was nevertheless re-elected again at the end of 2006, and in Jan. 2007 was granted the power by parliament to rule by decree for 18 months. In Dec. 2007 he suffered his first defeat in a popular vote when proposals to extend his powers and accelerate his socialist revolution were rejected in a referendum.

Early Life

The son of teachers, Chávez was born on 28 July 1954 in Sabaneta, Barinas state in the Andean west of Venezuela. Embarking on a military career, he completed his higher education at the Academia Militar de Venezuela, graduating in 1975 with a degree in military science. After further military training, he took a masters degree in social science at the Universidad Simón Bolívar.

In 1982 Chávez co-founded the MBR-200, based on the ideals of the independence hero, Simón Bolívar. In Feb. 1992 Chávez led an abortive military coup attempting to overthrow the government of Carlos Andrés Pérez. He was captured and imprisoned until 1994 when he was pardoned by President Rafael Caldera. Having reformed the MBR-200 as the Movement for the Fifth Republic/MVR, he promised to fight social inequality in Venezuela, a country rich in natural resources but where the wealth benefited the minority elite. By 1998 over 90% of Venezuelans lived below the poverty line, social services had deteriorated to pre-1950s levels and inflation was high.

In Nov. 1998 Chávez's Patriotic Pole coalition won 34% of seats in legislative elections. The following month he ran for the presidency against the Proyecto Venezuela candidate, Henrique Salas Romer. With the highest majority for 40 years, Chávez won 56·5% of votes to 39·5%. His win ended the 40-year domination of Acción Democrática (Democratic Action) and the Partido Social Cristiano (Social Christian Party).

Career in Office

On election, Chávez pledged to modernize the government, root out corruption, implement radical reforms and revive the economy. In April 1999 he called a referendum in which 92% of voters called for a new constitution. In July elections to the constitutional assembly, Chávez supporters won 121 seats against ten for the opposition. A second referendum was called for Dec. in which 72% approved a new constitution, modelled on France's Fifth Republic. The two-tiered congress was combined into one National Assembly, the presidential term was extended from five to six years, presidential power over legislation and the budget was increased, and a second consecutive presidential term was permitted. Further changes included a reformed judiciary, an extension of universal economic and social rights, increased rights for indigenous Venezuelans, and more military involvement in policy implementation. Despite Chávez's popular support, members of the business community and the middle classes were wary of the power granted the president and US$4bn. was transferred out of the country. Nonetheless, a rise in oil prices compensated for this financial loss and inflation fell, although the country suffered a recession following the 1998 economic crisis. Disastrous mudslides in Dec. 1999 in which tens of thousands of people died brought further financial strain for the government.

In the July 2000 presidential elections Chávez beat his former ally from the 1992 coup Lt.-Col. Francisco Arias Cárdenas with 59·8% of votes to 37·5%. His MVR party was equally successful in regional elections. Opposition candidates claimed the votes had been rigged and the military was called in to disperse protestors. On re-election Chávez pledged to fight unemployment with public spending, introduce a land rights bill to ease rural poverty, offer tax breaks for businesses, build new schools and encourage foreign investment. Though lacking a MVR majority in the assembly, Chávez was able to secure wide legislative powers. One of his first moves was to seek a union with the oil-producing Arab states which would reject Western pressure for increased output (and thus lower prices). In Sept. he made his international position clear by criticizing US involvement in Colombian military efforts to combat left-wing rebels (the Fuerzas Armadas Revolucionarias de Colombia or FARC), and by praising Cuban leader Fidel Castro's defiant rejection of US domination, as well as his economic and social policies. During a visit by Castro, Chávez agreed to sell oil to Cuba at a discounted price. In April 2001 Chávez hosted talks with Mexico and Colombia to pursue the implementation of a free trade zone, and to work towards extending free trade throughout the Americas. Despite international fears of a Castro reincarnate, he also visited the USA and Europe on numerous occasions.

As his 'Bolivarian Revolution' failed to produce the promised social and economic improvements, the country became increasingly divided between Chávez's supporters and opponents. In April 2002 anti-government protesters descended on the capital demanding his resignation. Taking advantage of the instability, a military coup was mounted with businessman Pedro Carmona Estanga at its head. Chávez was forced to resign and Carmona assumed the presidency. Western and Latin American governments (but not the USA) condemned the coup, refusing to acknowledge the new government, and protests by Chávez supporters quickly led to his reinstatement.

Nevertheless, Venezuelans remained polarized and more protests were staged in June and July. In Dec. 2002 a national strike was called by the opposition following a decision by the Supreme Court to overrule a referendum on Chávez's presidency called for Feb. 2003 by the Electoral Council. Protests focused on the state-owned petrol company Petróleos de Venezuela (PDVSA), the provider of around 40% of the country's revenues. Oil production plummeted and world prices increased, causing OPEC to increase production. The strike continued into 2003, threatening to destabilize the country's economy, but Chávez remained defiant. The strike abated in Feb. 2003, although workers at PDVSA continued to protest and the opposition petitioned for early elections.

In Aug. 2004 Chávez survived a national referendum on whether he should be allowed to serve the remainder of his term of office until 2006. Although credited with about 59% of the vote, opposition parties denounced the victory as electoral fraud. Then, in parliamentary elections in Dec. 2005 boycotted by the opposition, his MVR party won 114 of 167 National Assembly seats, with the remaining seats being won by his allies.

In Dec. 2006 Chávez won a third presidential term, defeating the main opposition candidate Manuel Rosales with 63% of the vote in the election. Pledging to maintain his socialist revolution, including widespread nationalization, he was granted sweeping powers by parliament at the end of Jan. 2007 to legislate by decree for an 18-month period. In the same month he announced that key energy and telecommunications utilities would be nationalized and in May the government took control of oil projects in the Orinoco Delta. Nationalizations continued into 2008, including in the banking, cement, steel and fuel sectors.

Popular discontent meanwhile surfaced over the closure in May 2007 of Radio Caracas Televisión (RCTV), the country's most popular—but anti-Chávez—television channel, which provoked large domestic demonstrations as well as international condemnation. Then in Dec. the president's proposal to reform the constitution and allow him to run for continuous re-election and to reinforce his socialist agenda was unexpectedly rejected by voters in a national referendum. Some disaffection with Chávez was also reflected in opposition gains in regional and mayoral elections in Nov. 2008. However, in a further constitutional referendum in Feb. 2009, there was a 54% majority in favour of abolishing presidential limits, clearing the way for Chávez to run for re-election in 2012.

In 2007 Colombia's president Uribe invited Chávez to try and broker a peace deal with the FARC. However, Uribe subsequently ended Chávez's involvement after a series of apparent diplomatic breaches. Relations between the two countries then deteriorated sharply in March 2008 after Colombian armed forces raided a FARC base in Ecuador, a Venezuelan ally. Chávez mobilized troops along Venezuelan–Colombian border and briefly threatened war before the crisis was defused diplomatically. Tensions again escalated in the second half of 2009 as US–Colombian plans for closer military ties in a drive against drug trafficking culminated in an agreement allowing US forces the use of Colombian bases. In response, Chávez ordered troops to the border, citing increased violence by the Colombian military.

As an oil-producing economy Venezuela suffered from the fall in the international price of oil that accompanied the global economic downturn from 2008. In Jan. 2010 Chávez devalued the currency against the US dollar (by up to 50% under a dual exchange rate) to boost revenue from oil exports. To counter the likelihood of higher inflation, he also threatened to close businesses that increased prices.

Increasing signs of popular discontent with Chávez's rule have been reflected in recent opinion polls and in Jan. 2010 the resignation of the vice president and defence minister, Ramón Carrizález, prompted speculation about tensions within the regime.

DEFENCE

There is selective conscription for 30 months. Defence expenditure totalled US$2,588m. in 2006 (US$101 per capita), representing 1·4% of GDP.

Army

The Army has six divisions (four infantry, one armoured and one cavalry), one combat engineer corps, one aviation command and one logistics command. Equipment includes 81 main battle tanks. Strength (2007) around 63,000. There were an additional 8,000 reserves.

A 23,000-strong volunteer National Guard is responsible for internal security.

Navy

Strength (2007) around 17,500 (3,200 conscripts). The combatant fleet comprises two submarines and six frigates. Naval Aviation, 500 strong, operates ten combat capable aircraft. Main bases are at Caracas, Puerto Cabello and Punto Fijo.

Air Force

The Air Force was 11,500 strong in 2007 and had 94 combat capable aircraft. Main aircraft types include CF-5s, Mirage 50s, F-16A/Bs and Su-30s.

INTERNATIONAL RELATIONS

Venezuela is a member of the UN, World Bank, IMF and several other UN specialized agencies, WTO, IOM, ACS, Inter-American Development Bank, SELA, LAIA, OAS, MERCOSUR, UNASUR and OPEC.

In March 2008 Venezuela sent large numbers of troops to the border with Colombia. The action was in sympathy with Ecuador, whose border was violated when Colombian troops crossed it to attack forces of the rebel FARC movement. Within seven days of the mobilization, a diplomatic solution saw the troops stand down.

ECONOMY

In 2005 industry accounted for 58% of GDP, services 38% and agriculture 4%.

Overview

In the 1970s per capita GDP grew by over 300% but about two-thirds of these gains were lost in the following decade. When oil prices fell from their 1970s peak, debt spiralled out of control to leave the country in depression. By the late 1990s per capita GDP had returned to 1970s levels but poverty had also increased. According to the World Bank, the percentage of the population living in poverty rose from 32·2% in 1991 to 48·5% in 2000 and the inequality gap continued to widen.

Venezuela's mineral and oil deposits are among the largest in the world. The country supplied roughly 13·5% of US crude oil imports in 2002 and the oil industry currently accounts for over 90% of export revenues, over 25% of GDP and over 50% of government revenues. In Dec. 2002 a two-month national strike paralysed the oil industry, causing world oil prices to reach two-year highs in Feb. 2003. In 2004, following two years of sharp recession, annual GDP growth recovered to 18·3%.

The global financial turmoil that began in 2008 coupled with the fall in oil prices (from US$126 per bbl. in mid-2008 to US$30 per bbl. in Dec. 2008) saw GDP growth slow to 4·6% in 2008. Inflation rose to 30·4% in 2008, its highest level in five years. President Chávez had used previous strong oil revenue growth to spend heavily on social welfare programmes and his government intends to maintain social spending in anticipation of a recovery in the oil price. In the interim private banks and the central bank will be expected to finance the deficit. Meanwhile, Petróleos de Venezuela, the state oil company, is looking to partnerships with foreign oil companies to mitigate against falling revenues.

Currency

The unit of currency is the *bolívar fuerte* (VEF) of 100 *céntimos*. It was introduced on 1 Jan. 2008, replacing the *bolívar* (VEB) at a rate of one bolívar fuerte = 1,000 bolívares. In Aug. 2009 foreign exchange reserves were US$18,559m., gold reserves were 11·46m. troy oz and total money supply was 186,679m. Bs.F. Exchange controls were abolished in April 1996. The bolívar was devalued by 12·6% in 1998, and in Feb. 2002 it was floated, ending a regime that permitted the bolívar to trade only within a fixed band. However, in Feb. 2003 it was pegged to the dollar at Bs2·15 = US$1 (and after the introduction of the *bolívar fuerte* in Jan. 2008 officially at 2·15 Bs.F = US$1). In Jan. 2010 the bolívar was devalued by 17% to 2·6 Bs.F = US$1 and a second rate, known as the 'oil bolívar' for its aim of boosting revenue from oil exports, was introduced at 4·3 Bs.F = US$1. Inflation rates (based on IMF statistics):

1999	*2000*	*2001*	*2002*	*2003*	*2004*	*2005*	*2006*	*2007*	*2008*
23·6%	16·2%	12·5%	22·4%	31·1%	21·7%	16·0%	13·7%	18·7%	30·4%

The inflation rate in 2001 of 12·5% was the lowest in more than 15 years.

Budget

The fiscal year is the calendar year. Revenues and expenditures in Bs 1m.:

	1997	*1998*	*1999*	*2000*	*2001*
Revenue	10,240,962	9,157,084	11,251,838	16,873,493	19,326,543
Expenditure	8,894,305	11,014,036	12,169,972	17,860,230	22,883,815

VAT is 12% (reduced rate, 11%).

Performance

Real GDP growth rates (based on IMF statistics):

1999	*2000*	*2001*	*2002*	*2003*	*2004*	*2005*	*2006*	*2007*	*2008*
–6·0%	3·7%	3·4%	–8·9%	–7·8%	18·3%	10·3%	10·3%	8·4%	4·8%

Total GDP in 2008 was US$313·8bn.

Banking and Finance

A law of Dec. 1992 provided for greater autonomy for the Central Bank. Its *President*, currently Nelson Merentes, is appointed by the President for five-year terms. Since 1993 foreign banks have been allowed a controlling interest in domestic banks. In 2003 there were 24 commercial banks and three foreign banks.

Foreign direct investment was US$1,716m. in 2008, up from US$646m. in 2007. The total stock of FDI at the end of 2008 was US$41·38bn.

There is a stock exchange in Caracas.

ENERGY AND NATURAL RESOURCES

Environment

Carbon dioxide emissions from the consumption and flaring of fossil fuels in 2008 were the equivalent of 7·0 tonnes per capita.

Electricity

Installed capacity in 2004 was 22·1m. kW; production was 98·48bn. kWh in 2004 and consumption per capita 3,770 kWh.

Oil and Gas

Proven reserves of oil were 99·4bn. bbls in 2008. Venezuela has the highest reserves of oil of any country outside the Middle East. The oil sector was nationalized in 1976. Private and foreign investment were permitted after 1992, before President Chávez instigated a 'renationalization' following strikes in Dec. 2002–Feb. 2003. In Feb. 2007 Chávez announced that the last foreign-controlled oil production sites would be brought under government control. Oil production in 2008 was 131·6m. tonnes. Oil provides about 50% of Venezuela's revenues. Natural gas production in 2008 was 31·5bn. cu. metres. Natural gas reserves in 2008 were 4,840bn. cu. metres, the largest in Latin America.

Minerals

Output (in 1,000 tonnes) in 2004: iron ore, 19,196; limestone (2002), 13,434; coal, 6,748; bauxite, 5,842; alumina (2003), 1,882; gold, 9,690 kg. Estimated diamond production in 2005 was 115,000 carats.

Agriculture

Coffee, cocoa, sugarcane, maize, rice, wheat, tobacco, cotton, beans and sisal are grown. 50% of farmers are engaged in subsistence agriculture. There were approximately 2·44m. ha. of arable land in 2002 and 0·81m. ha. of permanent crops. About 575,000 ha. were irrigated in 2002.

Production in 2003 in 1,000 tonnes: sugarcane, 6,825; maize, 1,505; plantains, 760; rice, 701; bananas, 639; sorghum, 600; cassava, 490; pineapples, 384; oranges, 316; melons and watermelons, 308; potatoes, 298; onions, 237.

Livestock (2003): cattle, 16·07m.; pigs, 2·92m.; goats, 2·70m.; sheep, 820,000; horses, 500,000; chickens, 110m.

Forestry

In 2005 the area under forests was 47·71m. ha., or 54·1% of the total land area. Timber production in 2007 was 6·06m. cu. metres.

Fisheries

In 2005 the total catch was estimated at 470,000 tonnes (mostly from marine waters).

INDUSTRY

Production (2004, in tonnes): petrol, 15·5m.; distillate fuel oil, 14·7m.; residual fuel oil, 14·5m.; cement (2001), 8·7m.; crude steel (2002), 4·2m.; sugar (2001), 585,000.

Labour

Out of 9,698,900 people in employment in 2002, 2,932,700 were in community, social and personal services, 2,585,300 in wholesale and retail trade, restaurants and hotels, 1,150,300 in manufacturing and 949,000 in agriculture, hunting, fishing and forestry. In Sept. 2005, 11·5% of the workforce was unemployed, down from 14·5% a year earlier.

In late 2002 and early 2003 a two-month long general strike intended to oust President Chávez ended in failure, instead crippling an already depressed economy.

Trade Unions

The most powerful confederation of trade unions is the CTV (Confederación de Trabajadores de Venezuela, formed 1947).

INTERNATIONAL TRADE

Foreign debt was US$44,201m. in 2005.

Imports and Exports

Trade in US$1m.:

	2002	2003	2004	2005	2006
Imports f.o.b.	13,360	10,483	17,021	23,693	32,226
Exports f.o.b.	26,781	27,230	39,668	55,473	65,210

Exports of oil in 2001 were valued at US$19bn., the third highest export revenues after Saudi Arabia and Iran. Oil revenues account for 93% of all export revenues.

The main import sources in 2000 were the USA (37·8%), Colombia (7·4%), Brazil (5·0%) and Italy (4·4%). The main markets for exports in 2000 were the USA (59·6%), Netherlands Antilles (5·6%), Brazil (3·6%) and Colombia (2·8%).

COMMUNICATIONS

Roads

In 2002 there were 96,155 km of roads, of which 33·6% were paved. There were 2,952,100 passenger cars in use in 2007 (107 per 1,000 inhabitants) plus 84,000 lorries and vans. There were 2,900 fatalities as a result of road accidents in 1996.

Rail

The railway network comprises 630 km of 1,435 gauge track. Passenger-km travelled came to 12m. in 1995 and freight tonne-km to 59m. in 2000.

There are metros in Caracas, Los Teques, Maracaibo and Valencia.

Civil Aviation

The main international airport is at Caracas (Simon Bolívar), with some international flights from Maracaibo. Aeropostal Alas de Venezuela is the leading Venezuelan carrier. In 2005 scheduled airline traffic of Venezuela-based carriers flew 31·0m. km, carrying 3,240,200 passengers.

Shipping

Ocean-going shipping totalled 865,000 GRT in 2002, including oil tankers 376,000 GRT. La Guaira, Maracaibo, Puerto Cabello, Puerto Ordaz and Guanta are the chief ports. In 1995 vessels totalling 21,009,000 NRT entered ports and vessels totalling 8,461,000 NRT cleared. The principal navigable rivers are the Orinoco and its tributaries the Apure and Arauca.

Telecommunications

In 2008 there were 6,304,000 main (fixed) telephone lines. There were 23,820,000 mobile phone subscribers in 2007 (861·3 per 1,000 persons). CANTV, the national telephone company, lost its 50-year monopoly on fixed-line telephony in 2000. In 2005, 2,475,000 PCs were in use and in 2007 the number of internet users was 5,720,000.

Postal Services

In 2003 there were 381 post offices, or one for every 67,500 persons.

SOCIAL INSTITUTIONS

Justice

A new penal code was implemented on 1 July 1999. The new, US-style system features public trials, verbal arguments, prosecutors, citizen juries and the presumption of innocence, instead of an inquisitorial system inherited from Spain which included secretive trials and long exchanges of written arguments.

In Aug. 1999 the new constitutional assembly declared a judicial emergency, granting itself sweeping new powers to dismiss judges and overhaul the court system. The assembly excluded the Supreme Court and the national Judicial Council from a commission charged with reorganizing the judiciary. President Chávez declared the assembly the supreme power in Venezuela.

The court system is plagued by chronic corruption and a huge case backlog. Only about 40% of the country's prisoners in 1999 had actually been convicted. In Oct. 1999 over 100 judges accused of corruption were suspended. The population in penal institutions in 2003 was 19,554 (76 per 100,000 population).

Venezuela's murder rate, at 45 per 100,000 population in 2006, is among the highest in the world.

Education

In 2007 there were 3,521,139 primary school pupils (184,409 teaching staff in 2005) and 2,174,619 secondary school pupils (187,737 teaching staff in 2005).

The leading institute of higher education is the Central University of Venezuela (Universidad Central de Venezuela), founded in 1721 in Caracas. The Bolivarian University of Venezuela (Universidad Bolivariana de Venezuela) was founded in 2003 by President Chávez in order to give lower-income students the opportunity to study free of charge regardless of academic qualifications or prior education. More than 75% of students are from poor backgrounds. There were 1,381,126 students in tertiary education in 2006 with 108,594 academic staff.

Adult literacy was 93·0% in 2003 (male, 93·3%; female, 92·7%).

Public expenditure on education came to 3·7% of GNI in 2007.

Health

In 2002 there were 567 hospitals with 19 beds per 10,000 inhabitants. There were 48,000 physicians and 13,680 dentists in 2001; and 46,305 nurses and 8,751 pharmacists in 1997.

Welfare

The official retirement age is 60 years (men) or 55 years (women). However, the pensionable age is lower for those in arduous or unhealthy employment. The old-age pension is 296,525 bolivares a month, plus 30% of average earnings during the previous five years or the average of the best five years in the previous ten (whichever is higher), plus an increment of 1% of earnings for every 50-week period of contributions beyond 750 weeks. The minimum pension is 40% of earnings.

Unemployment benefit is 60% of the insured person's average weekly wage during the previous 50 weeks. The benefit is paid for up to 18 weeks but may be extended to 26 weeks.

RELIGION

In 2001 there were 22·05m. Roman Catholics. There are four archbishops, one at Caracas, who is Primate of Venezuela, two at Mérida and one at Ciudad Bolívar. There are 19 bishops. There was one cardinal in Feb. 2010. The remainder of the population follow other religions, notably Protestantism.

CULTURE

World Heritage Sites

Venezuela has three sites on the UNESCO World Heritage List: Coro and its Port (inscribed on the list in 1993); Canaima National Park (1994); and La Ciudad Universitaria de Caracas (2000).

Broadcasting

Venezuela has a multiplicity of private broadcasters operating alongside state television and radio networks. The government runs Venezolana de Televisión and is a shareholder in Telesur, a pan-American TV channel based in Caracas and supported by four South American states. RCTV (Radio Caracas Televisión), the country's oldest private network, went off the air in May 2007 when the government terminated its licence. State broadcaster Radio Nacional de Venezuela operates 15 radio stations. In 2006 TV receivers numbered 5·7m. (colour by NTSC).

Cinema
There were 284 cinemas in 1998 and 14·2m. admissions.

Press
In 2004 there were 92 daily newspapers with a circulation of almost 2·5m.

Tourism
In 2005 there were 706,000 non-resident tourists; spending by tourists totalled US$713m.

Festivals
Among the country's most celebrated festivals is the Procession of the Holy Shepherdess (Jan.), which has run annually since 1856. Its centrepiece is a grand procession taking a statue of the divine shepherdess from Santa Rosa to the city of Barquisimeto, before the return trip is made at Easter. Celebrations to mark the initial declaration of independence from Spain in 1810 fall on 19 April, which is also designated as Day of the Indian. Independence Day is observed on 5 July while the birthday of Simón Bolívar is celebrated on 24 July.

Libraries
The Public Libraries National System comprises 727 libraries. The National Library of Venezuela was founded in 1833 and is located in Caracas. It holds over 7m. volumes in its collection.

Museums and Galleries
Venezuela had 148 museums in 2009 of which 44 are art museums, 78 social science and humanities museums and 18 science and technology museums.

DIPLOMATIC REPRESENTATIVES

Of Venezuela in the United Kingdom (1 Cromwell Rd, London, SW7 2HW)
Ambassador: Samuel Moncada.

Of the United Kingdom in Venezuela (Torre La Castellana, Piso 11, Avenida Principal de La Castellana, Caracas 1061)
Ambassador: Catherine Royle.

Of Venezuela in the USA (1099 30th St., NW, Washington, D.C., 20007)
Ambassador: Bernardo Alvarez Herrera.

Of the USA in Venezuela (Calle Suapure, con calle F. Colinas de Valle Arriba, Caracas)
Ambassador: Patrick Duddy.

Of Venezuela to the United Nations
Ambassador: Jorge Valero Briceño.

Of Venezuela to the European Union
Ambassador: Alejandro Antonio Fleming Cabrera.

FURTHER READING

Dirección General de Estadística, Ministerio de Fomento, Boletín Mensual de Estadística.—Anuario Estadístico de Venezuela. Annual

Canache, D., *Venezuela: Public Opinion and Protest in a Fragile Democracy.* 2002

Rudolph, D. K. and Rudolph, G. A., *Historical Dictionary of Venezuela.* 2nd ed. 1995

Wilpert, Greg, *Changing Venezuela by Taking Power: the History and Policies of the Chavez Government.* 2006

National Statistical Office: Instituto Nacional de Estadística, Avenida Boyacá Edificio Fundación La Salle, Piso 4, Maripérez, Caracas.
Website (Spanish only): http://www.ine.gov.ve

VIETNAM

Công Hòa Xã Hôi Chu Nghĩa Viêt Nam
(Socialist Republic of Vietnam)

Capital: Hanoi
Population estimate, 2010: 89·03m.
GDP per capita, 2007: (PPP$) 2,600
HDI/world rank: 0·725/116

KEY HISTORICAL EVENTS

By the end of the 15th century, the Vietnamese had conquered most of the Kingdom of Champa (now Vietnam's central area) and by the end of the 18th century they had acquired Cochin-China (now its southern area). At the end of the 18th century, France helped to establish the Emperor Gia-Long as ruler of a unified Vietnam. Cambodia became a French protectorate in 1863 and in 1899, after the extension of French protection to Laos in 1893, the Indo Chinese Union was created.

In 1940 Vietnam was occupied by the Japanese. In Aug. 1945 they allowed the Viet Minh movement to seize power, dethrone the Emperor and establish a republic known as Vietnam. On 6 March 1946 France recognized 'the Democratic Republic of Vietnam' as a 'Free State within the Indo-Chinese Federation'. On 19 Dec. Viet Minh forces made a surprise attack on Hanoi, the signal for nearly eight years of hostilities. An agreement on the cessation of hostilities was reached on 20 July 1954. The French withdrew and by the Paris Agreement of 29 Dec. 1954 completed the transfer of sovereignty to Vietnam which was divided along the 17th parallel into Communist North Vietnam and the non-Communist South. From 1959 the North promoted insurgency in the south, provoking retaliation from the USA. A full scale guerrilla war developed.

In Paris on 27 Jan. 1973 an agreement was signed ending the war in Vietnam. However, hostilities continued between the North and the South until the latter's defeat in 1975. Between 150,000 and 200,000 South Vietnamese fled the country. The unification of North and South Vietnam into the Socialist Republic of Vietnam took place on 2 July 1976. Vietnam invaded Cambodia in Dec. 1978 and China attacked Vietnam in consequence. In 1986 Vietnam implemented economic reforms, gradually shifting to a multi-sectoral market economy under state regulation. On 11 July 1995 Vietnam and the USA normalized relations. On 28 July 1995 Vietnam became a member of the Association of South East Asian Nations (ASEAN) and in the same month signed a trade agreement with the European Union.

TERRITORY AND POPULATION

Vietnam is bounded in the west by Cambodia and Laos, north by China and east and south by the South China Sea. It has a total area of 331,212 sq. km and is divided into eight regions, 58 provinces and five municipalities (Can Tho, Da Nang, Hai Phong, Hanoi and Thanh Pho Ho Chi Minh). The areas and 2009 census populations (provisional) were as follows:

Region/Province	*Area (sq. km)*	*Census population, 2009 (provisional)*	*Capital*
Dac Lac	13,139	1,728,380	Buon Me Thuot
Dac Nong	6,517	489,442	Gia Nghia
Gia Lai	15,537	1,272,792	Play Cu
Kon Tum	9,691	430,037	Kon Tum
Lam Dong	9,776	1,186,786	Da Lat
Central Highlands	54,660	5,107,437	
An Giang	3,537	2,144,772	Long Xuyen
Bac Lieu	2,584	856,250	Bac Lieu
Ben Tre	2,360	1,254,589	Ben Tre
Ca Mau	5,332	1,205,108	Ca Mau
Can Tho	1,402	1,187,089	Can Tho
Dong Thap	3,376	1,665,420	Sa Dec
Hau Giang	1,601	756,625	Vi Thanh
Kien Giang	6,348	1,683,149	Rach Gia
Long An	4,494	1,436,914	Tan An
Soc Trang	3,312	1,289,441	Soc Trang
Tien Giang	2,484	1,670,216	My Tho
Tra Vinh	2,295	1,000,933	Tra Vinh
Vinh Long	1,479	1,028,365	Vinh Long
Mekong River Delta	40,605	17,178,871	
Ha Tinh	6,027	1,227,554	Ha Tinh
Nghe An	16,499	2,913,055	Vinh
Quang Binh	8,065	846,924	Dong Hoi
Quang Tri	4,760	597,985	Dong Ha
Thanh Hoa	11,136	3,400,239	Thanh Hoa
Thua Thien-Hue	5,065	1,087,579	Hue
North Central Coast	51,552	10,073,336	
Bac Can	4,868	294,660	Bac Can
Bac Giang	3,827	1,555,720	Bac Giang
Cao Bang	6,725	510,884	Cao Bang
Ha Giang	7,946	724,353	Ha Giang
Lang Son	8,331	731,887	Lang Son

Region/Province	Area (sq. km)	Census population, 2009 (provisional)	Capital
Lao Cai	6,384	613,075	Lao Cai
Phu Tho	3,528	1,313,926	Phu Tho
Quang Ninh	6,099	1,144,381	Ha Long
Thai Nguyen	3,547	1,124,786	Thai Nguyen
Tuyen Quang	5,870	725,467	Tuyen Quang
Yen Bai	6,900	740,905	Yen Bai
North East	64,025	9,480,044	
Dien Bien	9,563	491,046	Dien Bien Phu
Hoa Binh	4,684	786,964	Hoa Binh
Lai Chau	9,112	370,135	Lai Chau
Son La	14,174	1,080,641	Son La
North West	37,534	2,728,786	
Bac Ninh	823	1,024,151	Bac Ninh
Ha Nam	860	785,057	Phu Ly
Hai Duong	1,653	1,703,492	Hai Duong
Hai Phong	1,521	1,837,302	Hai Phong
Hanoi[1]	3,120	6,448,837	Hanoi
Hung Yen	924	1,128,702	Hung Yen
Nam Dinh	1,651	1,825,771	Nam Dinh
Ninh Binh	1,392	898,459	Ninh Binh
Thai Binh	1,547	1,780,954	Thai Binh
Vinh Phuc	1,373	1,000,838	Vinh Yen
Red River Delta	14,863	18,433,563	
Binh Dinh	6,040	1,485,943	Quy Nhon
Da Nang	1,257	887,069	Da Nang
Khanh Hoa	5,218	1,156,903	Nha Trang
Phu Yen	5,061	861,993	Tuy Hoa
Quang Nam	10,438	1,419,503	Tam Ky
Quang Ngai	5,153	1,217,159	Quang Ngai
South Central Coast	33,166	7,028,570	
Ba Ria (Vung Tau)	1,990	994,837	Vung Tau
Binh Duong	2,696	1,482,636	Thu Dau Mot
Binh Phuoc	6,884	874,961	Dong Xoai
Binh Thuan	7,837	1,169,450	Phan Thiet
Dong Nai	5,904	2,483,211	Bien Hoa
Ninh Thuan	3,363	564,129	Phan Rang
Tay Ninh	4,036	1,066,402	Tay Ninh
Thanh Pho Ho Chi Minh	2,099	7,123,340	Ho Chi
South East[2]	34,808	15,758,966	

[1]Includes former province of Ha Tay. [2]Formerly North East South.

At the 2009 census the provisional population was 85,789,573; density, 259 per sq. km. The United Nations population estimate for 2009 was 88,069,000. 73·6% of the population live in rural areas (2005).

The UN gives an estimated population for 2010 of 89·03m.

Major cities: Ho Chi Minh City (2009 provisional population: 5,929,479), Hanoi (2009 provisional population: 2,632,087), Hai Phong (2009 provisional population: 847,058), Da Nang (2009 provisional population: 770,499), Buon Me Thuot (2002: 282,095), Nha Trang (2002: 221,331), Hue (2002: 219,149), Can Tho (2002: 215,587).

85% of the population are Vietnamese (Kinh). There are also 53 minority groups thinly spread in the extensive mountainous regions. The largest minorities are: Tay, Khmer, Thai, Muong, Nung, Meo, Dao.

The official language is Vietnamese. Chinese, French and Khmer are also spoken.

SOCIAL STATISTICS

2002 estimates: births, 1,598,000; deaths, 522,000. Estimated birth rate in 2002 was 19·9 per 1,000 population; estimated death rate, 6·5. Life expectancy, 2007, was 72·3 years for males and 76·1 years for females. Annual population growth rate, 2000–05, 1·4%. Infant mortality, 2005, 16 per 1,000 live births; fertility rate, 2004, 2·3 births per woman. Vietnam has had one of the largest reductions in its fertility rate of any country in the world in recent years, having had a rate of 5·8 births per woman in 1975. Sanctions are imposed on couples with more than two children. The rate at which Vietnam has reduced poverty, from 58% of the population in 1993 to 20% in 2004, is among the most dramatic of any country in the world. Vietnam has a young population; 59% were born after 1975.

CLIMATE

The humid monsoon climate gives tropical conditions in the south, with a rainy season from May to Oct., and sub-tropical conditions in the north, though real winter conditions can affect the north when polar air blows south over Asia. In general, there is little variation in temperatures over the year. Hanoi, Jan. 62°F (16·7°C), July 84°F (28·9°C). Annual rainfall 72" (1,830 mm).

CONSTITUTION AND GOVERNMENT

The National Assembly unanimously approved a new constitution on 15 April 1992. Under this the Communist Party retains a monopoly of power and the responsibility for guiding the state according to the tenets of Marxism-Leninism and Ho Chi Minh, but with certain curbs on its administrative functions. The powers of the National Assembly are increased. The 493-member *National Assembly* is elected for five-year terms. Candidates may be proposed by the Communist Party or the Fatherland Front (which groups various social organizations), or they may propose themselves as individual Independents. The Assembly convenes three times a year and appoints a prime minister and cabinet. It elects the *President*, the head of state. The latter heads a *State Council* which issues decrees when the National Assembly is not in session.

The ultimate source of political power is the Communist Party of Vietnam, founded in 1930; it had 2·2m. members in 1996.

National Anthem

'Doàn quân Viêt Nam di chung lòng cúú quóc' ('Soldiers of Vietnam, we are advancing'); words and tune by Van Cao.

GOVERNMENT CHRONOLOGY

General Secretaries of the Communist Party since 1976.

1976–86	Le Duan
1986	Truong Chinh
1986–91	Nguyen Van Linh
1991–97	Do Muoi
1997–2001	Le Kha Phieu
2001–	Nong Duc Manh

Heads of State since 1976.

Presidents

1976–80	Ton Duc Thang
1980–81	Nguyen Huu Tho

Chairmen of the State Council

1981–87	Truong Chinh
1987–92	Vo Chi Cong

Presidents

1992–97	Le Duc Anh
1997–2006	Tran Duc Luong
2006–	Nguyen Minh Triet

Prime Ministers since 1976.

1976–87	Pham Van Dong
1987–88	Pham Hung
1988	Vo Van Kiet
1988–91	Do Muoi
1991–97	Vo Van Kiet
1997–2006	Phan Van Khai
2006–	Nguyen Tan Dung

RECENT ELECTIONS

In parliamentary elections held on 20 May 2007 Communist Party members won 450 of 493 seats, with 43 seats going to non-party candidates. All but one of the elected candidates were members of the Vietnamese Fatherland Front, a political coalition organization led by the Communist Party. Turnout was more than 99%.

CURRENT ADMINISTRATION

President (titular head of state): Nguyen Minh Triet; b. 1942 (in office since 27 June 2006).

Vice-President: Nguyen Thi Doan.

Full members of the Politburo of the Communist Party of Vietnam: Nong Duc Manh (b. 1940; *Secretary General*); Le Hong Anh; Nguyen Tan Dung; Nguyen Minh Triet; Truong Tan Sang; Nguyen Phu Trong; Pham Gia Khiem; Phung Quang Thanh; Truong Vinh Trong; Le Thanh Hai; Nguyen Sinh Hung; Pham Quang Nghi; Ho Duc Viet; Nguyen Van Chi; To Huy Rua.

In March 2010 the government comprised:

Prime Minister: Nguyen Tan Dung; b. 1949 (in office since 27 June 2006).

Deputy Prime Ministers: Nguyen Sinh Hung; Truong Vinh Trong; Pham Gia Khiem (also *Minister of Foreign Affairs*); Hoang Trung Hai; Nguyen Thien Nhan (also *Minister of Education and Training*).

Minister of National Defence: Phung Quang Thanh. *Public Security:* Le Hong Anh. *Justice:* Ha Hung Cuong. *Planning and Investment:* Vo Hong Phuc. *Finance:* Vu Van Ninh. *Industry and Trade:* Vu Huy Hoang. *Interior:* Tran Van Tuan. *Agriculture and Rural Development:* Cao Duc Phat. *Transport:* Ho Nghia Dung. *Construction:* Nguyen Hong Quan. *Labour, War Invalids and Social Affairs:* Nguyen Thi Kim Ngan. *Science and Technology:* Hoang Van Phong. *Culture, Sports and Tourism:* Hoang Tuan Anh. *Health:* Nguyen Quoc Trieu. *Natural Resources, Environment and Sea:* Pham Khoi Nguyen. *Information and Communications:* Le Doan Hop.

Chairman of the National Assembly: Nguyen Phu Trong.

Vietnamese Parliament: http://www.na.gov.vn

CURRENT LEADERS

Nong Duc Manh

Position

Secretary General of the Communist Party

Introduction

Nong Duc Manh was elected secretary general of the ruling Communist Party in 2001 and so became Vietnam's effective centre of power. Regarded as a modernizer, he set out to accelerate industrialization and encourage foreign investment, which enabled Vietnam to join the World Trade Organization as its 150th member in Jan. 2007.

Early Life

Nong Duc Manh was born on 11 Sept. 1940 into the Tay ethnic group in Hung Cuong commune, Na Ri district in the then-province of Bach Thai. From 1958–65 he worked as an engineer with the provincial forestry service and during this period joined the Communist Party. In 1966 he was appointed to the board of the forestry service. From the mid-1970s he ascended the party structure, sitting as a member of the Bach Thai executive committee. In 1986 he was made an alternate member of the Communist central committee and was elected to full membership three years later. In the same year he became deputy chairman of the National Assembly. He was chosen as chairman in Sept. 1992 and re-elected to the post in 1997. He was elected secretary general of the Communist Party in April 2001.

Career in Office

Manh set out his plans to modernize Vietnam's political and legal systems, reducing corruption and streamlining bureaucracy. However, Vietnam has remained a one-party state with tight Communist control over the media, and critics suggest political suppression is widespread. He has continued the economic liberalization that began in the 1980s and growth rates have been strong as foreign investment and aid have increased. Nevertheless, there remains a large gap in wealth between the richer urban and struggling rural populations. Manh's crackdown on organized crime was exemplified by the trial in 2003 of over 150 gangsters, particularly Nam Cam (a Ho Chi Minh City criminal), who was executed in 2004.

On the international stage, Manh has pursued closer relations with the USA. Trade relations were normalized in Dec. 2001 and the USA has become Vietnam's chief export destination. Commercial flights from the USA resumed in 2004 for the first time since the end of the Vietnam war. In June 2005 the then prime minister, Phan Van Khai, travelled to the USA for a meeting with President George W. Bush, the first post-war meeting between leaders from the two countries. In May 2002 Russia relinquished control of the Cam Ranh Bay naval base, previously the biggest Soviet-operated base outside of the Warsaw Pact countries.

Manh was reappointed for a further five-year term in April 2006, although two months later the prime minister, president and National Assembly chairman were replaced by younger political leaders. In 2007 there were several high-profile arrests and trials of political activists. This refocused international attention on Vietnam's human rights record, particularly in June during President Nguyen Minh Triet's first visit by a Vietnamese head of state to the USA since the end of the Vietnam War.

Despite a broad amnesty in Jan. 2009 in which more than 15,000 prisoners were granted early release, there has been no easing of policy towards political dissent, particularly with regard to the media and the internet. In Jan. 2009 two pro-reform newspaper editors were convicted for their reporting of a high-level corruption trial, in Sept. the government restricted the right to conduct research on the Communist Party, in Dec. another dissident was jailed for allegedly posting pro-democracy articles on the internet and in Jan. 2010 four activists, including a human rights lawyer and an internet entrepreneur, were jailed for advocating multi-party democracy.

Nguyen Tan Dung

Position

Prime Minister

Introduction

Nguyen Tan Dung was appointed prime minister in June 2006. Part of the new generation aspiring to leadership of Vietnam's single-party government, he is a proponent of economic reform and liberalization.

Early Life

Nguyen Tan Dung was born in Ca Mau in the south of Vietnam on 17 Nov. 1949. While serving in the army he joined the Communist Party in 1967, and then enrolled in the elite Nguyen Ai Quoc Party School in 1981 to study political theory.

Dung advanced rapidly within the party, serving on influential committees and supporting Vietnam's 'doi moi' programme of economic reform to move the country towards a market economy. In Jan. 1995 he became deputy minister for home affairs and in May the following year he became the youngest person ever to be appointed to the politburo. Tipped as a future party leader, he was appointed deputy prime minister and also director of the central committee's economic commission in charge of the party's finances in 1997. The following year he took over as governor of the state bank.

From 1998–2006 Dung was groomed for leadership by the then prime minister Phan Van Khai, a fellow modernizer. Appointed to a range of key party posts during that time, he oversaw the continuing liberalization of Vietnam's economy. Dung expanded foreign trade relations and prepared Vietnam's accession to the World Trade Organization (WTO). He was also given responsibility for tackling domestic corruption and organized crime. When Khai resigned the premiership, Dung was confirmed as prime minister by the National Assembly on 27 June 2006.

Career in Office

Dung reiterated his intention to proceed with economic and social reform. His first action was to replace several government figures who had been implicated in corruption. He has sought to strengthen commercial links internationally, notably with the European Union. In Nov. 2006 Vietnam was approved for membership of the WTO and also hosted the annual Asia-Pacific Economic Co-operation meeting, which was attended by US President George W. Bush. Reappointed as prime minister in July 2007, Dung signalled a willingness to implement further reforms.

In Nov. 2009 the government devalued the Vietnamese currency (for the third time since June 2008) by about 5% against the US dollar, at the same time increasing interest rates in a bid to dampen rising inflation. While Vietnam experienced a sharp decline in exports in 2009 because of the global economic slowdown, there was positive growth of 5·3% for the year as a whole (although this was the lowest annual rate since 1999). In Dec. the World Bank approved a loan for the first time to Vietnam worth US$500m.

During an official visit to Moscow in Dec. 2009, Dung announced multi-billion dollar contracts to buy submarines, fighter jets and other military hardware from Russia, as well as agreements on co-operation relating to oil and gas, mining and financial services.

DEFENCE

Conscription is for two years (army) or three years (air force and navy). For specialists it is also three years.

In 2006 defence expenditure totalled US$3,439m. (US$41 per capita), representing 5·6% of GDP.

Army

There are nine military regions (including the capital). Strength (2007) was estimated to be 412,000. Paramilitary Local Defence forces number around 5m. and include the Peoples' Self-Defence Force (urban) and the People's Militia (rural). There is also a paramilitary Border Defence Corps numbering some 40,000.

Navy

The fleet includes two diesel submarines (although their serviceability is in doubt) and five frigates. In 2007 personnel was estimated at 13,000 plus an additional Naval Infantry force of about 27,000.

Air Force

In 2007 the People's Air Force had 30,000 personnel, with 219 combat capable aircraft (Su-22s, Su-27s, Su-30s and MiG-21s) and 26 attack helicopters.

INTERNATIONAL RELATIONS

Vietnam is a member of the UN, World Bank, IMF and several other UN specialized agencies, WTO, IOM, International Organization of the Francophonie, Asian Development Bank, APEC, ASEAN, Mekong Group and Colombo Plan.

ECONOMY

Agriculture accounted for 20·4% of GDP in 2006, industry 41·6% and services 38·1%.

Overview

Vietnam has experienced strong growth for over a decade, leading to a reduction in poverty from over 50% in the mid-1990s to 16% in 2006. Efforts on the part of the Vietnamese government, including accession negotiations with the WTO that culminated in membership in Jan. 2007, have led to a significant increase in international integration.

Vietnam signed bilateral trade agreements with the USA in 2000 and with the EU in 2004. Imports have been liberalized and the export sector grew 21% in value terms between 1990–2002, when the export to GDP ratio rose from 22% to 50%. Since 2000, output has grown by over 6% a year, strongly aided by the USA–Vietnam bilateral trade agreement and rises in oil prices. The oil sector plays an important role in the economy, with exports of crude oil accounting for 20% of total exports.

Despite strong exports, the trade deficit has been rising since 2000 because of high levels of foreign direct investment (FDI) and imports of capital goods. Core inflation remains high and more entrenched than in neighbouring economies.

Currency

The unit of currency is the *dong* (VND). In March 1989 the dong was brought into line with free market rates. The direct use of foreign currency was made illegal in Oct. 1994. Foreign exchange reserves were US$8,268m. in May 2005 and total money supply was 192,281bn. dong. Inflation was 23·1% in 2008.

Budget

In 2003 revenues were 123,700bn. dong and expenditures 148,400bn. dong. Tax revenue accounted for 77·9% of revenues in 2003, non-tax revenue 20·5% and grants 1·6%; current expenditure accounted for 64·6% of expenditures and capital expenditure 35·4%.

VAT is 10% (reduced rate, 5%).

Performance

Real GDP growth rates have been consistently strong since 1994, and averaged 7·6% between 2001 and 2006. This robust performance continued into 2007 and 2008, with growth rates of 8·5% and 6·2% respectively. GDP per head, which was US$98 in 1990, had risen to US$815 by 2007. Vietnam's total GDP in 2008 was US$90·7bn.

Banking and Finance

The central bank and bank of issue is the State Bank of Vietnam (founded in 1951; *Governor*, Nguyen Van Giau). In 2003 there were four state-owned commercial banks, 37 joint-stock private banks, four joint venture banks, and 50 representative offices and 26 branches of foreign banks. Vietcombank is the foreign trade bank. Foreign direct investment in Vietnam was US$8·1bn. in 2008, up from US$2·0bn. in 2005.

There are stock exchanges in Ho Chi Minh City, which opened in July 2000, and Hanoi, which opened in March 2005.

ENERGY AND NATURAL RESOURCES

Environment

Vietnam's carbon dioxide emissions from the consumption and flaring of fossil fuels were the equivalent of 1·1 tonnes per capita in 2008.

Electricity

Total installed capacity of power generation in 2004 was an estimated 6·8m. kW. In 2004, 46·03bn. kWh of electricity were produced; consumption per capita was 560 kWh. A hydro-electric power station with a capacity of 2m. kW was opened at Hoa-Binh in 1994. The proportion of households with electricity has doubled in the past 20 years, to 94% by 2007.

Oil and Gas

Oil reserves in 2008 totalled 4·7bn. bbls. In Aug. 2001 an offshore oil mine containing more than 400m. bbls of petroleum was discovered. Oil production in 2008, 15·4m. tonnes. Natural gas reserves in 2008 were 560bn. cu. metres; production was 7·9bn. cu. metres.

Minerals
Vietnam is endowed with an abundance of mineral resources such as coal (3·5bn. tonnes), bauxite (3bn. tonnes), apatite (1bn. tonnes), iron ore (700m. tonnes), chromate (10m. tonnes), copper (600,000 tonnes) and tin (70,000 tonnes); coal production was 34·1m. tonnes in 2005. There are also deposits of manganese, titanium, a little gold and marble. 2005 output (in 1,000 tonnes): sand and gravel, 146,400; lime, 1,718; salt, 925.

Agriculture
Agriculture employs 70% of the workforce. Ownership of land is vested in the state, but since 1992 farmers may inherit and sell plots allocated on 20-year leases. There were an estimated 6·35m. ha. of arable land in 2007 and 3·08m. ha. of permanent crops.

Production in 1,000 tonnes in 2003: rice, 34,519; sugarcane, 16,525; cassava, 5,228; maize, 2,934; sweet potatoes, 1,592; bananas, 1,221; coconuts, 920; coffee, 771; cabbage, 606; oranges, 500. Vietnam is the second largest coffee producer in the world after Brazil, and the second largest exporter of rice behind Thailand.

Livestock, 2003: pigs, 24·89m.; cattle, 4·39m.; buffaloes, 2·84m.; goats, 780,000; chickens, 185m.; ducks, 69m.

Livestock products (2003): meat, 2,487,000 tonnes; eggs, 234,000 tonnes; milk, 158,000 tonnes.

There were 257 tractors and 365 harvester-threshers per 10,000 ha. of arable land in 2006.

Forestry
In 2005 forests covered 12·93m. ha., or 39·7% of the land area. Timber exports were prohibited in 1992. Timber production was 34·17m. cu. metres in 2007, nearly all of it for fuel.

Fisheries
Total catch, 2005, 1,929,900 tonnes (93% from sea fishing).

INDUSTRY
Estimated total industrial output in 2002 was 260,202·0bn. dong. In 2002 estimated production (in 1,000 tonnes) was: processed sea produce, 288,701; cement, 19,482; steel, 2,429; fertilizers, 1,176; sugar, 1,074; paper (2003), 800; detergents, 381; beer (2003), 1,049·8m. litres; clothes, 47·6m. items.

Labour
In 2004 a total of 41·6m. persons were in employment. Agriculture and forestry accounted for 23·0m. people; industry, 5·3m.; trade, 4·8m.; construction, 1·9m.; culture, health and education, 1·7m. A liberal Enterprise Law was adopted in 2000, leading to the creation of over 50,000 new private businesses and more than 1·5m. new jobs during the next three years. Official statistics put unemployment at 7·4% of the workforce in early 2000.

Trade Unions
There are 53 trade union associations.

INTERNATIONAL TRADE
In Feb. 1994 the USA lifted the trade embargo it had imposed in 1975, and in Nov. 2001 a trade agreement with the USA was ratified. The agreement allows Vietnam's exports access to the US market on the same terms as those enjoyed by most other countries. The 1992 constitution regulates joint ventures with western firms; full repatriation of profits and non-nationalization of investments are guaranteed.

Foreign debt was US$19,287m. in 2005.

Imports and Exports
Trade is conducted through the state import-export agencies. Imports in 2005, US$33,280m. (US$17,760m. in 2002); exports, US$32,442m. (US$16,706m. in 2002). In 2002 the main imports (by value) were: machinery (19%), petroleum (10%), textiles and garments (9%) and steel (7%). Other significant imports were plastics, vehicles, fertilizers and chemicals. Main exports: crude oil (20%), textiles and garments (16%), sea produce (12%), footwear (11%) and rice (4%). Other significant exports were electronics, coffee, latex, cashew nuts, pepper and coal.

The main import suppliers in 2000 were Singapore (15·1%), Japan (14·0%), South Korea (11·9%) and China (10·9%). Principal export markets in 2000 were Japan (18·6%), Australia (9·7%), Germany (7·7%) and China (6·6%).

COMMUNICATIONS
Roads
There were 160,089 km of roads in 2007, of which 47·6% were paved. In 2007 there were 1,146,300 passenger cars in use and around 21·78m. motorcycles and mopeds. There were 13,200 fatalities in road accidents in 2007.

Rail
There were 2,402 km of railways in 2005, mostly metre gauge. Rail links with China were reopened in Feb. 1996. In 2003, 11·6m. passengers and 8·3m. tonnes of freight were carried.

Civil Aviation
There are international airports at Hanoi (Noi Bai) and Ho Chi Minh City (Tan Son Nhat) and 13 domestic airports. The national carrier is Vietnam Airlines, which provides domestic services and in 2003 had international flights to Bangkok, Beijing, Dubai, Guangzhou, Hong Kong, Kaohsiung, Kuala Lumpur, Kunming, Manila, Melbourne, Moscow, Osaka, Paris, Phnom Penh, Seoul, Siem Reap, Singapore, Sydney, Taipei, Tokyo and Vientiane. In 2005 scheduled airline traffic of Vietnam-based carriers flew 43·7m. km, carrying 3,762,200 passengers. The busiest airport is Ho Chi Minh City, which in 2001 handled 4,306,143 passengers and 96,560 tonnes of freight. Hanoi handled 2,207,052 passengers and 40,668 tonnes of freight in 2001.

Shipping
In 2002 sea-going vessels totalled 1,131,000 GRT, including oil tankers 162,000 GRT. The major ports are Hai Phong, which can handle ships of 10,000 tons, Ho Chi Minh City and Da Nang. There are regular services to Hong Kong, Singapore, Thailand, Cambodia and Japan. There are some 19,500 km of navigable waterways.

Telecommunications
Vietnam Posts and Telecommunications and the military operate telephone systems with the assistance of foreign companies. In 2008 there were 29·6m. main (fixed) telephone lines; mobile phone subscribers numbered 70m. in 2008 (80·4 per 100 persons). There were 8·1m. PCs in use in 2006 and 20·8m. internet users in 2008.

Postal Services
In 2003 there were 12,505 post offices, or one for every 6,500 persons.

SOCIAL INSTITUTIONS
Justice
A new penal code came into force on 1 Jan. 1986 'to complete the work of the 1980 constitution'. Penalties (including death) are prescribed for opposition to the people's power and for economic crimes. The judicial system comprises the Supreme People's Court, provincial courts and district courts. The president of the Supreme Court is responsible to the National Assembly, as is the Procurator-General, who heads the Supreme People's Office of Supervision and Control.

The death penalty is still in force; there were at least nine executions in 2009.

The population in penal institutions in 2005 was 88,000 (105 per 100,000 of national population).

Education
Adult literacy rate in 2001 was 92·7% (94·5% among males and 90·9% among females). Primary education consists of a ten-year course divided into three levels of four, three and three years respectively. In 2007 there were 7,041,312 pupils and 344,547 teaching staff in primary schools, and 9,845,407 pupils and 451,165 teaching staff at secondary schools. About 75% of children of secondary school age were in school by 2003, up from around a third in 1990. In 1995–96 there were seven universities, two open (distance) universities and nine specialized universities (agriculture, three; economics, two; technology, three; water resources, one). In 2007 there were 1,587,609 students in higher education with 53,518 academic staff.

Health
In 2001 there were 42,327 physicians, 44,539 nurses, 14,662 midwives and 5,977 pharmacists. There were 842 hospitals in 2003 with a provision of 24 beds per 10,000 population.

RELIGION
Taoism is the traditional religion but Buddhism is widespread. At a Conference for Buddhist Reunification in Nov. 1981, nine sects adopted a charter for a new Buddhist church under the Council of Sangha. The Hoa Hao sect, associated with Buddhism, claimed 1·7m. adherents in 2001. Caodaism, a synthesis of Christianity, Buddhism and Confucianism founded in 1926, has some 2·8m. followers. In 2001 there were 53·3m. Buddhists and 6·2m. Roman Catholics. In Feb. 2010 there was one cardinal. There is an Archbishopric of Hanoi and 13 bishops. There were six seminaries in 2003.

CULTURE

World Heritage Sites
Vietnam has five sites on the UNESCO World Heritage List: the Complex of Hue Monuments (inscribed on the list in 1993); Ha Long Bay (1994 and 2000); Hoi An Ancient Town (1999); My Son Sanctuary (1999); and Phong Nha-Ke Bang National Park (2003).

Broadcasting
Broadcasting is under the control of the Communist government. Voice of Vietnam operates two national radio networks, various local stations and an external service. Vietnam Television is the national broadcaster and there are provincial TV stations. There were 17·0m. TV receivers in 2003 (colour by PAL).

Press
In 2004 there were 28 national newspapers with a combined circulation of 2·6m. There were two English-language dailies, *The Vietnam News* and *Saigon Times Daily*. The Communist Party controls all print media but some criticism of government policy is allowed. In 2002, 9,018 book titles were published.

Tourism
There were 3,468,000 foreign tourists in 2005 (2,928,000 in 2004); spending by tourists in 2005 totalled US$1,880m.

DIPLOMATIC REPRESENTATIVES
Of Vietnam in the United Kingdom (12–14 Victoria Rd, London, W8 5RD)
Ambassador: Tran Quang Hoan.

Of the United Kingdom in Vietnam (Central Building, 31 Hai Ba Trung, Hanoi)
Ambassador: Mark Kent.

Of Vietnam in the USA (1233 20th St., NW, Suite 400, Washington, D.C., 20036)
Ambassador: Le Cong Phung.

Of the USA in Vietnam (7 Lang Ha, Ba Dinh District, Hanoi)
Ambassador: Michael W. Michalak.

Of Vietnam to the United Nations
Ambassador: Le Luong Minh.

Of Vietnam to the European Union
Ambassador: Nguyen Manh Dung.

FURTHER READING
Trade and Tourism Information Centre with the General Statistical Office. *Economy and Trade of Vietnam* [various 5-year periods]

Gilbert, Marc Jason, (ed.) *Why the North Won the Vietnam War.* 2002
Harvie, C. and Tran Van Hoa V., *Reforms and Economic Growth.* 1997
Karnow, S., *Vietnam: a History.* 2nd ed. 1992
Morley, J. W. and Nishihara M., *Vietnam Joins the World.* 1997
Norlund, I. (ed.) *Vietnam in a Changing World.* 1994

National Statistical Office: General Statistical Office, No. 2 Hoang Van Thu St., Ba Dinh District, Hanoi.
Website: http://www.gso.gov.vn

YEMEN

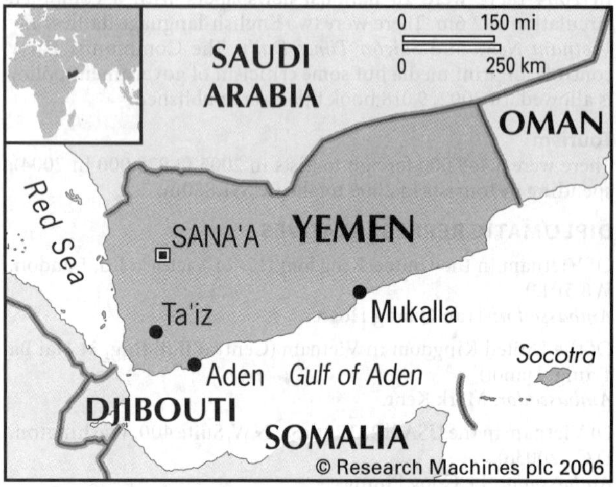

Jamhuriya al Yamaniya
(Republic of Yemen)

Capitals: Sana'a (Legislative and Administrative), Aden (Commercial)
Population estimate, 2010: 24·26m.
GDP per capita, 2007: (PPP$) 2,335
HDI/world rank: 0·575/140

KEY HISTORICAL EVENTS

One of the earliest recorded pre-Islamic Arab civilizations was the Sabaean culture, which flourished in what is now Yemen and southwestern Saudi Arabia during the 1st millennium BC. The wealth of the kingdom of Saba (or Sheba) was based on the incense and spice trade and on agriculture. Beginning in about 115 BC, the Himyarites gradually absorbed Saba and Hadhramaut (to the east) to claim control of all of the southwest Arabian peninsula by the 4th century AD. Himyarite dominance came to an end in the 6th century as Abyssinian (Ethiopian) forces invaded in AD 525. Abyssinian rule was overthrown in 575 by Persian military intervention, and Persian control then endured until the advent of Islam in 628.

Yemen became a province of the Muslim caliphate. Thereafter its fortunes reflected the fluctuating power of the imams (kings and spiritual leaders) of the Zaidi sect—who built the theocratic political structure of Yemen that endured from the 9th century until 1962—and of rival dynasties and conquerors. These included the Fatimid caliphs of Egypt, who occupied most of Yemen from about 1000 until 1175 and, subsequently, the Ayyubids, who ruled until about 1250. The Rasulids, who had served as governors of Yemen under the Ayyubid dynasty, then exercised a measure of sovereignty. However, central authority had fragmented by the time the Ottoman Turks, fearful of Christian Portuguese influence in southern Arabia, intervened in Yemen in the first half of the 16th century. They held nominal but tenuous sovereignty until the end of the First World War (when Yemen became independent), and conflict with the Zaidi imams was frequent.

The southern Yemeni port of Aden was a coveted commercial location on the trading routes to the wider East from ancient times. By the end of the 18th century its strategic importance had increased as Britain sought to contain the French threat to colonial communications with British India following Napoleon's conquest of Egypt. With the coming of the steamship, Britain's need for a military and refuelling base in the region became more pressing. In 1839 the British captured Aden, attaching it administratively to India. In the 1850s the Perim, Kamaran and Kuria Muria islands were made part of Aden which became a free port. Britain also purchased areas on the mainland from local rulers and entered into protectionist agreements with them. The opening of the Suez Canal in 1869 further enhanced both Aden's strategic significance and British colonial consolidation.

In the early 1870s, tribal and religious warfare led the Ottoman Turks to reassert authority over northern Yemen, an occupation that lasted until the armistice of 1918. After the Ottoman evacuation, Imam Yahya, who had supported the Turks during the First World War despite leading an earlier revolt against them in 1911, sought to expand Yemeni territory. However, in 1934, after brief hostilities with Saudi Arabia (by then under the rule of Ibn Saud) and skirmishes with British forces from Aden, a trilateral treaty to fix Yemen's boundaries was agreed. The treaty heralded a period of generally peaceful coexistence, which lasted for the rest of Imam Yahya's reign. Aden, meanwhile, was formally made a British crown colony in 1937 and the surrounding region became known as the Aden protectorate.

Opposition to the theocratic and despotic rule of Imam Yahya led to his assassination in Feb. 1948. His son, Crown Prince Ahmad, succeeded him and put down the insurgents. Ahmad's reign was marked by further repression, renewed friction over the British presence in southern Yemen and growing pressure in the 1950s to support the Arab nationalist objectives of the new Nasser regime in Egypt. Following Ahmad's death his son, Muhammad al-Badr, was deposed a week after his accession in Sept. 1962 by revolutionary forces aided by Egypt. The rebels took control of the capital, Sana'a, and proclaimed the Yemen Arab Republic (YAR). Saudi Arabia and Jordan supported al-Badr's royalist forces against the new republic and conflict continued periodically until 1970. Despite its instability, the YAR regime retained power and secured international recognition.

In 1963 the Aden colony was merged into the Federation of South Arabia. A power struggle between rival nationalist groups after the British withdrawal in 1967 led to an independent Marxist state with Aden as the capital. This was renamed the People's Democratic Republic of Yemen (PDRY) in 1970. Mistrust and frequent border clashes between the YAR and the PDRY characterized the next decade, despite an accord in 1972 to merge the two entities.

A coup in the YAR brought Lieut.-Col. Ibrahim al-Hamadi to power in 1974. However, he was assassinated in Oct. 1977, as was his successor, Lieut.-Col. Ahmad al-Ghashmi, in June 1978. The following month Lieut.-Col. Ali Abdullah Saleh, the commander of the Ta'iz military area, was elected president by the Constitutional Assembly. Saleh's first months in power were turbulent. In early 1979 sporadic fighting erupted into full-scale war between North and South Yemen. Arab League mediation brought the hostilities to an end and both sides acknowledged the need to effect permanent Yemeni union. Saleh was meanwhile re-elected as YAR President by the Constituent Assembly in May 1983 and again in July 1988 by a new Consultative Council.

In the PDRY the chairman of the Presidential Council, Salem Rubayyi Ali, was overthrown in June 1978. Prime Minister Ali Nasser Muhammad briefly assumed the chairmanship before Abdul Fattah Ismail, a hard-line orthodox Marxist, was elected as head of state by the new Presidium of the People's Supreme Assembly in Dec. 1978. Ismail resigned unexpectedly in April 1980 and went to the Soviet Union, to be replaced by Ali Nasser Muhammad. While maintaining South Yemen's close relations with the Soviet Union, Muhammad favoured reconciliation with moderate Arab states. In particular, he viewed improved relations with Saudi Arabia as necessary to further the proposed merger with the YAR. In Feb. 1985 Muhammad resigned as prime minister but remained head of state and secretary-general of the dominant Yemeni Socialist Party (YSP). The rest of that year was marked by the re-emergence of political rivalries, aggravated by the return of Ismail from the Soviet Union, which triggered a brief civil war in Jan. 1986. Ismail was killed and Muhammad fled into exile, after which a new government was formed.

In May 1988 the YAR and PDRY governments reached an agreement on renewing unification discussions and demilitarizing their borders. Their respective leaders, Ali Abdullah Saleh and Ali Salem Albidh, agreed in late 1989 a draft unity constitution (originally drawn up in 1981) and on 22 May 1990 the Republic of Yemen was declared. A five-member Presidential Council assumed power and Saleh was appointed as president for a transitional period. By 1993 relations between the North and South had again deteriorated, Vice-President Albidh having withdrawn to Aden to demand political reforms. Sporadic military clashes escalated into full civil war in May 1994 between disaffected southern forces and Yemen's northern-based government. Southern officials announced their secession from Yemen on 21 May 1994, but northern forces quickly prevailed and Aden was captured on 7 July 1994. The former vice-president and other southern leaders went into exile.

Confirmed in office by parliament in Oct. 1994 for a five-year term, President Saleh's political position was further consolidated when he was re-elected by popular vote in Sept. 1999 (though the turnout was low, particularly in the south). An extension of his term of office from five to seven years was approved in a referendum in Feb. 2001. In April 2003 Saleh's ruling General People's Congress retained power in parliamentary elections with over two-thirds of the seats in the 301-member Assembly of Representatives. However, the main opposition parties claimed that polling was tainted by ballot rigging and intimidation.

In foreign affairs Yemen suffered diplomatic isolation and economic sanctions in the early 1990s for its equivocal response to Iraq's invasion of Kuwait. Its stance incurred US resentment and exacerbated longstanding tensions with neighbouring Saudi Arabia although a border dispute was brought to a close by an agreement signed in June 2000. More recent attacks on Western targets in Yemeni territory—most notably the suicide bombing of the US naval vessel *USS Cole* in Oct. 2000 and an apparent bomb attack on a French supertanker, the *Limburg*, off the Yemeni coast in Oct. 2002—fuelled concerns that Yemen might have become a haven for Islamic extremists. Nevertheless, President Saleh pledged full support for the USA's global campaign against terrorism in the wake of the events of 11 Sept. 2001.

In 1995 Yemen clashed with Eritrea over control of the Hanish Islands in the Red Sea. Following arbitration by an international panel, Yemen assumed control of the main islands in 1998.

TERRITORY AND POPULATION

Yemen is bounded in the north by Saudi Arabia, east by Oman, south by the Gulf of Aden and west by the Red Sea. The territory includes 112 islands including Kamaran (181 sq. km) and Perim (300 sq. km) in the Red Sea and Socotra (3,500 sq. km) in the Gulf of Aden. The islands of Greater and Lesser Hanish are claimed by both Yemen and Eritrea. On 15 Dec. 1995 Eritrean troops occupied them, and Yemen retaliated with aerial bombardments. A ceasefire was agreed at presidential level on 17 Dec. On 20 Dec. the UN resolved to send a good offices mission to the area. In an agreement of 21 May 1996 brokered by France, Yemen and Eritrea renounced the use of force to settle the dispute and agreed to submit it to arbitration. Following a ruling issued by the Permanent Court of Arbitration in the Hague, Yemen assumed control of the main islands in 1998. The area is 555,000 sq. km excluding the desert Empty Quarter (Rub Al-Khahi).

A dispute with Saudi Arabia broke out in Dec. 1994 over some 1,500–2,000 km of undemarcated desert boundary. A memorandum of understanding signed on 26 Feb. 1995 reaffirmed the border agreement reached at Taif in 1934, and on 12 June 2000 a 'final and permanent' border treaty between the two countries was signed. An agreement of June 1995 completed the demarcation of the border with Oman.

Census population, 2004: 19,685,161; density, 35 persons per sq. km. In 2005, 72·7% of the population lived in rural areas.

The UN gives an estimated population for 2010 of 24·26m.

In 2004 there were 20 governorates plus the capital city, Sana'a:

	2004 census population		*2004 census population*
Abyan	433,819	Lahej	722,694
Aden	589,419	Mahrah	88,594
Amran	877,786	Mahwit	494,557
Bayd	577,369	Marib	238,522
Dhala	470,564	Raymah	394,448
Dhamar	1,330,108	Sa'adah	695,033
Hadhramout	1,028,556	Sana'a (city)	1,747,834
Hajjah	1,479,568	Sana'a	919,215
Hodeida	2,157,552	Shabwah	470,440
Ibb	2,131,861	Ta'iz	2,393,425
Jawf	443,797		

The population of the capital, Sana'a, was 1,707,586 in 2004. The commercial capital is the port of Aden, with a population of (2004) 589,419. Other important towns are Ta'iz, the port of Hodeida, Mukalla, Ibb and Abyan. Sana'a is currently the fastest-growing city in the world, with a population increase of 832·6% in the period 1975–2000 and a projected increase of 128·2% between 2000–15, by when it is expected to have 3·03m. inhabitants.

The official language is Arabic.

SOCIAL STATISTICS

2004 estimates: births, 789,000; deaths, 158,000. Rates, 2004 estimates (per 1,000 population): birth, 40; death, 8. Yemen has a young population, with 45% of the population under the age of 15. Life expectancy, 2007, was 60·9 years for males and 64·1 years for females. Infant mortality, 2005, 76 per 1,000 live births. Annual population growth rate, 1992–2002, 3·9%; fertility rate, 2004, 6·0 births per woman.

CLIMATE

A desert climate, modified by relief. Sana'a, Jan. 57°F (13·9°C), July 71°F (21·7°C). Aden, Jan. 75°F (24°C), July 90°F (32°C). Annual rainfall 20" (508 mm) in the north, but very low in coastal areas: 1·8" (46 mm).

CONSTITUTION AND GOVERNMENT

Parliament consists of a 301-member *Assembly of Representatives* (*Majlis al-Nuwaab*), elected for a six-year term in single-seat constituencies and, since 2001, a 111-member *Shura Council* (*Majlis al-Shura*), appointed by the president.

The constitution was adopted in May 1991 but was drastically amended in 1994 following the civil war. On 28 Sept. 1994 the Assembly of Representatives unanimously adopted the amended constitution founded on Islamic law. It abolished the former five-member Presidential Council and installed a *President* elected by parliament for a five-year term, subsequently amended to a seven-year term through a referendum held on 20 Feb. 2001. As a result of the same referendum the term for MPs was extended from four to six years. Although President Saleh had stated in 2005 that he would not run for a further term at the 2006 presidential elections, he subsequently reversed his decision following 'an appeal from the popular masses'.

National Anthem

'Raddidi Ayyatuha ad Dunya nashidi' ('Repeat, O World, my song'); words by A. Noman, tune by Ayub Tarish.

GOVERNMENT CHRONOLOGY

Presidents since 1990. (MSA = General People's Congress)

1990– MSA Ali Abdullah Saleh

RECENT ELECTIONS

The *President*, Ali Abdullah Saleh, was elected for his first term in 1990. At the election of 20 Sept. 2006 he was voted in for a fourth term, winning 77·2% of the vote, against 21·8% for his nearest rival, Faisal Bin Shamlan. There were three other candidates. Turnout was 65·2%.

Parliamentary elections were held on 27 April 2003, in which the General People's Congress (MSA) gained 238 seats (58·0% of the vote), Yemeni Congregation for Reform (Islah) 46 seats (22·6%), Yemeni Socialist Party 8 seats (3·8%), Nasserite Unionist People's Organization (TWSN) 3 seats (1·9%), the Arab Socialist Rebirth Party (Baath) 2 seats (0·7%) and ind. 4 seats. Turnout was 76·0%.

CURRENT ADMINISTRATION

President: Ali Abdullah Saleh; b. 1942 (MSA; in office since 1990, reappointed in 1994 and re-elected in 1999 and 2006).

In March 2010 the government comprised:

Prime Minister: Ali Mohammed Mujawar; b. 1953 (MSA; in office since 7 April 2007).

Deputy Prime Minister for Security, Defence and Local Administration: Rashad Al-Alimi. *Deputy Prime Minister for Economic Affairs:* Abdul Kareem Al-Arhabi. *Deputy Prime Minister in Charge of Local Authority Affairs:* Sadiq Amin Abu Ras.

Minister of Finance: Noman Taha Al-Souhaybi. *Defence:* Muhammad Nasser Ali. *Foreign Affairs:* Abubakr Al-Qirbi. *Interior:* Mutahar Rashid Al-Masri. *Oil and Mineral Resources:* Amir Al-Aydarus. *Legal Affairs:* Rashad Al-Rassas. *Justice:* Ghazi Shaif Al-Agbari. *Higher Education and Scientific Research:* Saleh Ali Ba-Surah. *Labour and Social Affairs:* Amat Al-Razaq Ali Hamad. *Communications and Information Technology:* Kamal Hussein Al-Jabri. *Fisheries:* Muhammad Saleh Shamlan. *Transport:* Khaled Ibrahim Al-Wazir. *Information:* Hassan Al-Lawzi. *Human Rights:* Houda Ali Abdellatif Al-Ban. *Youth and Sports:* Hamoud Ubad. *Electricity:* Awad Al-Swqatri. *Agriculture and Irrigation:* Mansour Ahmed Al-Hawchabi. *Trade and Industry:* Yahia Al-Mutawakel. *Culture:* Mohammed Abu Bakr Al-Maflahi. *Technical and Vocational Training:* Ibrahim Omar Hajri. *Public Health and Population:* Abdul Kareem Rasei. *Education:* Abdulsalam Al-Jufi. *Awqaf:* Hamoud Abdulhamid Al-Hitar. *Water and Environment:* Abdul Al-Eryani. *Civil Service and Social Security:* Yahya Al-Shuibi. *Tourism:* Nabil Al-Faqih. *Parliament and Shura Council:* Khalid al-Sharif. *Public Works and Roads:* Omar Al-Qurshumi. *Expatriate Affairs:* Ahmad Musaed Husayn.

Speaker: Yahya al-Ra'ei.

Office of the President: http://www.presidentsaleh.gov.ye

CURRENT LEADERS

Ali Abdullah Saleh

Position

President

Introduction

Ali Abdullah Saleh came to power at the age of 36 in July 1978 as president and commander-in-chief of the armed forces of the Yemen Arab Republic (YAR). He retained these offices throughout the 1980s. On the YAR's unification with the People's Democratic Republic (South Yemen) in May 1990, he assumed the presidency of the new Republic of Yemen. In 1994 his regime crushed an attempted secession by southern forces in a brief civil war. Secure in power, Saleh was re-elected president in 1999 and 2006. His government has co-operated in international efforts to combat terrorism despite internal political dissension and tensions between the north and the south of the country.

Early Life

Saleh was born in 1942 in Bait Al Ahmar in Sana'a governorate and joined the armed forces at the age of 16. In Sept. 1962 Imam Muhammad al-Badr (king and spiritual leader) was deposed a week after his accession (following the death of his father) in a military revolution. An eight-year civil war ensued, in which Saleh fought for the new Yemen Arab Republic government, aided by Egypt, against the royalist forces supported by Saudi Arabia. The YAR regime retained power and secured international recognition, but remained unstable throughout the 1970s, partly owing to tensions with the Marxist regime in southern Yemen. Saleh meanwhile gained military promotions, and reportedly played a role in a coup that brought Ibrahim al-Hamadi to power in 1974. When President Ahmad al-Ghashmi (in power from Oct. 1977) was assassinated in June 1978, Saleh was military commander of Ta'iz governorate. After the assassination (blamed on the regime in Aden), the Constituent Assembly formed a provisional Presidential Council, including Saleh. On 17 July the Assembly elected him president of the YAR.

Career in Office

Saleh's early months in power were turbulent. In Sept.–Oct. 1978 he survived an assassination attempt and a subsequent coup plot, both thought to have external backing. In Feb.–March 1979 further sporadic conflict with South Yemen escalated into full-scale war. Arab League mediation brought the fighting to an end and both sides acknowledged the need to effect permanent Yemeni union. Protracted negotiations resulted in reunification as the Republic of Yemen on 22 May 1990. Saleh had previously been re-elected as YAR president by the Constituent Assembly in May 1983 and again in July 1988 by a new Consultative Council. On unification and political liberalization in May 1990, a five-member Presidential Council assumed power and Saleh was chosen as president of the new republic for a transitional period. He was re-elected as president of the Presidential Council in Oct. 1993. A rebellion by disaffected southern forces was suppressed in 1994. In Oct. of that year he was elected president of the republic by parliament. Saleh's position was further reinforced in Sept. 1999 when he was directly elected by the people as president for the first time (albeit on a low turnout, particularly in the south of the country). An extension of his presidential term of office from five to seven years was approved in a referendum in Feb. 2001 and he continues to head the General People's Congress, which won decisively the most recent parliamentary elections in April 2003. In Sept. 2006 Saleh was re-elected for a further presidential term with 77% of the popular vote, defeating Faisal Bin Shamlan representing a broad coalition of opposition parties.

Saleh imposed a crackdown against Islamic terrorism following al-Qaeda attacks on a US warship in Aden in Oct. 2000 and on a French supertanker off the Yemeni coast in Oct. 2002. However, the country has remained vulnerable to anti-Western terrorist violence, with a series of bomb attacks on official, diplomatic, business and tourist targets in March 2008 and a suicide bombing strike against the US embassy in Sana'a in Sept. that year. In Jan. 2010 the US, UK and French embassies in Yemen were closed temporarily owing to fears of imminent terrorist attack and government forces stepped up their campaign to counter the growing and destabilizing al-Qaeda presence in Yemen.

Since 2004 there has been frequent fighting in north Yemen between government forces and rebellious tribesmen, known as Houthis, demanding regional autonomy. The most violent clashes to date, which began in Aug. 2009 and were still in progress in

Feb. 2010, also provoked military confrontation with Saudi Arabia along the two countries' common border.

DEFENCE

Conscription is for two years. Defence expenditure in 2006 totalled US$824m. (US$38 per capita), representing 4·2% of GDP (down from 7·1% in 2003).

Estimates of the number of small arms in the country are around 12m., equivalent to 61 firearms for every 100 people, making Yemen second only behind the USA as the world's most heavily armed country.

Army

Strength (2007), 60,000 (including conscripts). There are paramilitary tribal levies numbering at least 20,000 and a Ministry of Security force of 50,000.

Navy

Navy forces are based at Aden and Hodeida, with other facilities at Mukalla, Perim and Socotra. Personnel in 2007 numbered 1,700.

Air Force

The unified Air Forces of the former Arab Republic and People's Democratic Republic are now under one command, although this unity was broken by the attempted secession of the south in 1994 which resulted in heavy fighting between the air forces of Sana'a and Aden. Personnel (2007), 3,000. There were 79 combat capable aircraft in 2007 including Su-17/20/22s, MiG-21s and MiG-29s.

INTERNATIONAL RELATIONS

Yemen is a member of the UN, World Bank, IMF and several other UN specialized agencies, IOM, Islamic Development Bank, OIC and League of Arab States.

ECONOMY

Crude petroleum and natural gas accounted for 28% of GDP in 2007; trade, restaurants and hotels 16%; transport and communication 12%; and finance and real estate 11%.

Overview

Yemen is the poorest country in the Middle East and its outlook is unpromising. It has limited resources, including declining oil reserves, little arable land and scarce water supplies. Oil dominates the economy, accounting for 70% of government revenue and more than 90% of export earnings. With one of the highest population growth rates in the world, over 40% of the population lives in poverty, mostly in rural areas. The problem was aggravated by a 60% increase in food prices in 2007–08. The economy has also been hampered by long-running political and social unrest, including a civil war from 1990–94.

In 2006 Yemen agreed to work with the World Bank on a country assistance strategy with the aim of diversifying the economy, improving human development indicators and promoting fiscal and resource sustainability. Despite a relatively insulated financial sector, Yemen suffered during the global economic crisis with declining FDI and remittances, sharp decreases in oil revenues and reduced public expenditure.

Currency

The unit of currency is the *riyal* (YER) of 100 *fils*. During the transitional period to north-south unification the northern *riyal* of 100 *fils* and the southern *dinar* of 1,000 *fils* co-existed. There were three foreign exchange rates operating: an internal clearing rate, an official rate and a commercial rate. In 1996 the official rate was abolished. Total money supply in June 2005 was 372,105m. riyals, gold reserves totalled 50,000 troy oz and foreign exchange reserves were US$5,253m. Inflation was 19·0% in 2008.

Budget

The fiscal year is the calendar year. Total revenues in 2004 were 804,200m. riyals and expenditures 626,300m. riyals. Tax revenue accounted for 94·0% of total revenues in 2004. The main items of expenditure in 2004 were transfers and subsidies (36·0%), wages and salaries (25·5%) and defence (16·8%).

Performance

Real GDP growth was 3·6% in 2008; total GDP in 2008 was US$26·6bn.

Banking and Finance

The *Governor* of the Central Bank of Yemen is Ahmed Abdul Rahman Al-Samawi. Total reserves of the Central Bank were 81,089m. riyals in 2002 and there were 446,287m. riyals in deposits.

ENERGY AND NATURAL RESOURCES

Environment

Yemen's carbon dioxide emissions from the consumption and flaring of fossil fuels were the equivalent of 0·9 tonnes per capita in 2008. An *Environmental Performance Index* compiled in 2008 ranked Yemen 141st in the world out of 149 countries analysed, with 49·7%. The index examined various factors in six areas—air pollution, biodiversity and habitat, climate change, environmental health, productive natural resources and water resources.

Electricity

Installed capacity was an estimated 0·8m. kW in 2004. Production in 2004 was 4·34bn. kWh; consumption per capita was 208 kWh.

Oil and Gas

In 2008 there were oil reserves of 2·7bn. bbls; mostly near the former north-south border. Oil production (2008): 14·4m. tonnes. Natural gas reserves in 2008 were 490bn. cu. metres.

Minerals

In 2003, 116,000 tonnes of salt were produced. In 2003, 42,000 tonnes of gypsum were extracted and 2·33m. cu. metres of stone.

Agriculture

In 2007 there were around 1·38m. ha. of arable land and 250,000 ha. of permanent cropland. 772,000 ha. were irrigated in 2006. In the south, agriculture is largely of a subsistence nature, sorghum, sesame and millet being the chief crops, and wheat and barley being widely grown at the higher elevations. Cash crops include cotton. Fruit is plentiful in the north. Estimated production (2003, in 1,000 tonnes): tomatoes, 273; sorghum, 260; alfalfa, 242; potatoes, 213; oranges, 191; grapes, 169. Livestock in 2003 (estimates): goats, 7·3m.; sheep, 6·5m.; cattle, 1·4m.; chickens, 35m. Livestock products, 2003 estimates (in 1,000 tonnes): milk, 237; meat, 215.

Forestry

There were 549,000 ha. of forest in 2005 (1·0% of the total land area). Timber production in 2007 was 395,000 cu. metres.

Fisheries

Fishing is a major industry. Total catch in 2005 was 263,000 tonnes, exclusively marine fish.

INDUSTRY

Output (2004 unless otherwise indicated, in 1,000 tonnes): cement (2001), 1,493; petrol, 1,138; distillate fuel oil, 883; wheat flour (2003), 667; jet fuel, 317; residual fuel oil, 268; kerosene, 109. In 2001 industry accounted for 49·2% of GDP, with manufacturing contributing 6·7%.

Labour

Of 3,621,700 persons in employment in 2002, 1,927,700 were engaged in agriculture, hunting and forestry; 394,200 in wholesale and retail trade/repair of motor vehicles, motorcycles and personal and household goods; 358,000 in public administration and defence/compulsory social security; and 238,200 in construction. Unemployment was 18% in 2004.

INTERNATIONAL TRADE

Foreign debt was US$5,363m. in 2005.

Imports and Exports

Trade in US$1m.:

	2000	2001	2002	2003	2004
Imports f.o.b.	2,484·4	2,600·4	2,932·0	3,557·4	3,858·6
Exports f.o.b.	3,797·2	3,366·9	3,620·7	3,934·3	4,675·7

Main import suppliers, 2004: United Arab Emirates, 16·7%; Saudi Arabia, 8·8%; China, 6·4%; Kuwait, 6·2%. Main export markets, 2004: Thailand, 29·0%; China, 28·7%; India, 13·2%; Singapore, 4·7%.

Oil, cotton and fish are major exports, the largest imports being food and live animals. Oil accounts for more than 80% of exports. A large transhipment and entrepôt trade is centred on Aden, which was made a free trade zone in May 1991.

COMMUNICATIONS

Roads

There were 71,300 km of roads in 2005 (8·7% paved). In 2007 there were 777,700 vehicles in use.

Civil Aviation

There are international airports at Sana'a and Aden. In 2001 Sana'a handled 881,000 passengers (707,000 on international flights) and 15,900 tonnes of freight. The national carrier is Yemenia, which operates internal services and in 2003 had international flights to Abu Dhabi, Addis Ababa, Amman, Asmara, Bahrain, Beirut, Cairo, Damascus, Dar es Salaam, Djibouti, Doha, Dubai, Frankfurt, Jakarta, Jeddah, Khartoum, Kuala Lumpur, London, Marseille, Milan, Moroni, Mumbai, Paris, Riyadh and Rome. In 2003 Yemenia flew 18m. km, carrying 844,000 passengers (622,000 on international flights).

Shipping

In 2002 sea-going shipping totalled 78,000 GRT, including oil tankers 51,000 GRT. There are ports at Aden, Mokha, Hodeida, Mukalla and Nashtoon. In 2003 vessels totalling 16,182,000 NRT entered ports and vessels totalling 10,794,000 NRT cleared.

Telecommunications

In 2008 there were 1·1m. main (fixed) telephone lines in Yemen; mobile phone subscribers numbered 3·7m. in 2008 (16·1 per 100 persons). There were 600,000 PCs in use in 2006 and 370,000 internet users in 2008.

Postal Services

In 2003 there were 243 post offices.

SOCIAL INSTITUTIONS

Justice

A civil code based on Islamic law was introduced in 1992. Amnesty International reported that there were at least 30 executions in 2009.

Education

In 2005 there were 17,993 children in pre-primary schools, 3·21m. pupils in primary schools and 1·46m. pupils in secondary schools. In 2006 there were 209,386 students in higher education. The adult literacy rate in 2002 was 49·0% (69·5% among males but only 28·5% among females, the biggest difference in literacy rates between the sexes of any country).

In 2000–01 total expenditure on education came to 10·6% of GNP and accounted for 32·8% of total government expenditure.

Health

In 2003 there were 68 hospitals with 8,871 beds. There were 4,078 physicians, 222 dentists, 8,342 nurses and 750 pharmacists in 2001; and 385 midwives in 1994.

RELIGION

In 2001 there were some 18·05m. Muslims (mostly Sunnis) and approximately 20,000 followers of other religions.

CULTURE

World Heritage Sites

There are four sites under Yemeni jurisdiction that appear in the UNESCO World Heritage List. They are (with year entered on the list): the old walled city of Shibam (1982); the old city of Sana'a (1986); the historic town of Zabid (1993); and the Socotra Archipelago (2008).

Broadcasting

Broadcasting is state-controlled through the Yemen Radio and Television Corporation, operating two television and two radio networks. Programmes are transmitted from Sana'a and Aden. In 2005 there were 1·26m. households equipped with TV receivers (colour by PAL).

Press

In 2006 there were three daily newspapers with a combined average daily circulation of 40,000.

Tourism

There were 336,000 foreign tourists in 2005, bringing revenue of US$262m.

DIPLOMATIC REPRESENTATIVES

Of Yemen in the United Kingdom (57 Cromwell Rd, London, SW7 2ED)
Ambassador: Mohamed Taha Mustafa.

Of the United Kingdom in Yemen (POB 1287, 938 Thayer Himiyar St., East Ring Rd, Sana'a)
Ambassador: Tim Torlot.

Of Yemen in the USA (2319 Wyoming Ave., NW, Washington, D.C., 20008)
Ambassador: Abdulwahab Al-Hajjri.

Of the USA in Yemen (Sa'awan St., Himyar Zone, Sana'a)
Ambassador: Stephen A. Seche.

Of Yemen to the United Nations
Ambassador: Abdullah Al-Saidi.

Of Yemen to the European Union
Ambassador: Abdulwahab Mohammed Alshawkani.

FURTHER READING

Central Statistical Organization. *Statistical Year Book*

Al-Rasheed, Madawi and Vitalis, Robert (eds.) *Counter-Narratives: History, Contemporary Society, and Politics in Saudi Arabia and Yemen*. 2004

Bruck, Gabriele vom, *Islam, Memory and Morality in Yemen: Ruling Families in Transition*. 2005

Dresch, Paul, *A History of Modern Yemen*. 2001

Mackintosh-Smith, T., *Yemen—Travels in Dictionary Land*. 1997

Manea, Elham, *Regional Politics in the Gulf: Saudi Arabia, Oman and Yemen*. 2005

National Statistical Office: Central Statistical Organization, Ministry of Planning and Development.

Website: http://www.cso-yemen.org

ZAMBIA

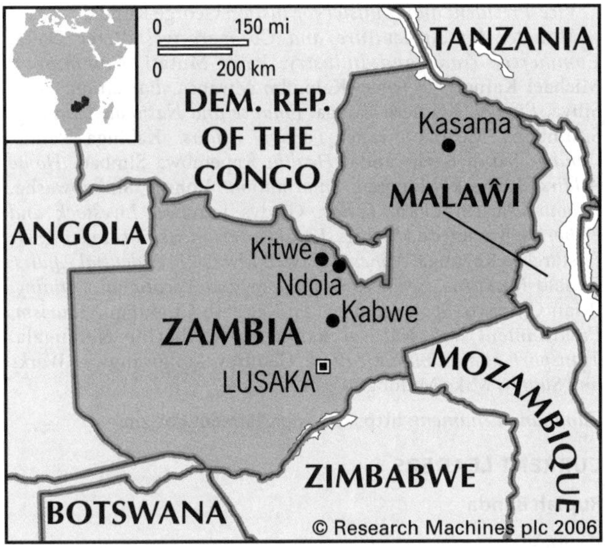

Republic of Zambia

Capital: Lusaka
Population estimate, 2010: 13·26m.
GDP per capita, 2007: (PPP$) 1,358
HDI/world rank: 0·481/164

KEY HISTORICAL EVENTS

The earliest known inhabitants were nomadic bushmen. From the 4th century AD, Bantu tribes farmed the region and established villages. Copper was mined for weapons and tools and from the 11th century, trade developed with neighbouring regions in copper and textiles. From 1500–1900 the region was divided into four tribal kingdoms: the Kazembe-Lunda in the north, the Bemba in the northeast, the Chewa in the east and the Barotse, later known as the Lozi, in the west. An inland region, it was not penetrated by non-Africans until the late 18th century, when Portuguese traders arrived near Lake Mweru. The Scottish explorer David Livingstone followed in the mid-19th century, and in the 1880s the British colonialist and mining magnate, Cecil Rhodes, arrived.

As part of his expansion north from the Transvaal, Rhodes persuaded the British government to secure Bechuanaland in 1885, and in 1888 he obtained mining rights in the territory of the Ndebele, which reached to the Zambezi river. In 1890 the chief of the Lozi, Lewanika, granted Rhodes mining rights in Lozi territory (known as Barotseland) in return for British protection. In 1891 the British government granted Rhodes' British South Africa Company a charter to administer the area from the Zambezi river to Lake Tanganyika.

From 1900 the territory was administered as two separate protectorates, Northwestern and Northeastern Rhodesia. Lead, zinc and copper were discovered, attracting more European prospectors. In 1911 the two protectorates were merged to become Northern Rhodesia and in 1924 the British Crown took over direct administration, while the British South Africa Company retained mineral rights. The territory was governed through a legislative council whose members were elected by the European population. The detection of rich copper seams—known as the Copper Belt—led to a huge increase in mining activity. The European population grow tenfold to 40,000 over the next three decades. Meanwhile, the African majority (98% of the country) was increasingly voicing its opposition to European rule. In 1948 some African members were added to the legislative council. In the same year the country's first African political party, the Northern Rhodesian Congress, was established by members of welfare societies from mining and rural communities. Connected to the African National Congress (ANC), in 1951 it renamed itself the Northern Rhodesian African National Congress.

In 1953 the British government imposed a federation consisting of Northern Rhodesia, its southern self-governing neighbour Rhodesia and Nyasaland. The Federation was welcomed by most Europeans in the territories as a means of consolidating their economic and political control but was opposed by most Africans for the same reason. Political dissent grew, with each region pressing its own claims for independence. In 1958 Kenneth Kaunda led a breakaway group from the Northern Rhodesian ANC to found the more radical Zambian African National Congress. After he was jailed for leading a civil disobedience campaign, the United National Independence Party (UNIP) was formed and elected Kaunda its leader on his release in Jan. 1960. Membership grew rapidly, convincing the British to accept it as a negotiating partner. At a London conference in Dec. 1960, Kaunda and other UNIP members secured a timetable for independence.

Elections in 1962 resulted in a UNIP–ANC coalition. The Federation was dissolved on 31 Dec. 1963 and in general elections held that year, with universal adult suffrage, UNIP won a clear victory. On 24 Oct. 1964 the country declared independence as the Republic of Zambia, named after the Zambezi river. The government took over mineral rights and oversaw a period of prosperity until copper prices collapsed in the 1970s. Further difficulties were caused by UN-imposed sanctions on Rhodesia—a key trading partner for Zambia—and rising oil prices, so that by the late 1970s Zambia was greatly indebted to the IMF.

In response to domestic dissent, Kaunda brought in a series of centralizing and authoritarian measures, including a new constitution making Zambia a one-party state. Living standards fell as copper production, Zambia's biggest foreign exchange earner, almost halved. Food riots and widespread unrest resulted in the 1991 electoral victory of the Movement for Multi-Party Democracy (MMD). However, allegations of corruption dogged the MMD government throughout successive terms, while the economy remained weak. Privatization of the copper mines in 2000 and other market-orientated reforms in the early 2000s reduced inflation but food security remained a serious issue. Failed harvests in 2001 resulted in the country receiving food aid.

TERRITORY AND POPULATION

Zambia is bounded by the Democratic Republic of the Congo in the north, Tanzania in the northeast, Malaŵi in the east, Mozambique in the southeast, Zimbabwe and Namibia in the south, and by Angola in the west. The area is 752,612 sq. km (290,584 sq. miles). Population (2000 census), 9,885,591; population density, 13·1 per sq. km. In 2005, 65·0% of the population were rural.

The UN gives an estimated population for 2010 of 13·26m.

The republic is divided into nine provinces. Area, population at the 2000 census and chief towns:

Province	Area (in sq. km)	Population	Chief Town
Central	94,394	1,012,257	Kabwe
Copperbelt	31,328	1,581,221	Ndola
Eastern	69,106	1,306,173	Chipata
Luapula	50,567	775,353	Mansa
Lusaka	21,896	1,391,329	Lusaka
Northern	147,826	1,258,696	Kasama
North-Western	125,827	583,350	Solwezi
Southern	85,283	1,212,124	Livingstone
Western	126,386	765,088	Mongu

The capital is Lusaka, which had a census population in 2000 of 1,084,703. Other major towns (with 2000 census population in 1,000) are: Ndola, 375; Kitwe, 364; Kabwe, 177; Chingola, 147; Mufulira, 122; Luanshya, 116.

The population consists of over 70 Bantu-speaking ethnic groups, with the main groups being the Bemba (18%), Tonga (10%), Nyanja (8%) and Lozi (6%). The official language is English.

SOCIAL STATISTICS

Estimates, 2000: births, 421,000; deaths, 191,000. Estimated birth rate in 2000 was 41·5 per 1,000 population; estimated death rate, 18·8. Zambia's life expectancy at birth in 2007 was 44·0 years for males and 45·0 for females. Life expectancy has declined over the last 15 years, largely owing to the huge number of people in the country with HIV. In 2007, 15·2% of all adults between 15 and 49 were infected with HIV. Annual population growth rate, 1992–2002, 2·1%. Infant mortality, 2005, 104 per 1,000 live births; fertility rate, 2004, 5·5 births per woman.

CLIMATE

The climate is tropical, but has three seasons. The cool, dry one is from May to Aug., a hot dry one follows until Nov., when the wet season commences. Frosts may occur in some areas in the cool season. Lusaka, Jan. 70°F (21·1°C), July 61°F (16·1°C). Annual rainfall 33" (836 mm). Livingstone, Jan. 75°F (23·9°C), July 61°F (16·1°C). Annual rainfall 27" (673 mm). Ndola, Jan. 70°F (21·1°C), July 59°F (15°C). Annual rainfall 52" (1,293 mm).

CONSTITUTION AND GOVERNMENT

Zambia has a unicameral legislature, the 159-seat *National Assembly*, with 150 members elected for a five-year term in single-member constituencies, eight appointed members and the Speaker. Candidates for election as president must have both parents born in Zambia (this excludes ex-president Kaunda). The constitution was adopted on 24 Aug. 1991 and was amended in 1996, shortly before the parliamentary and presidential elections. The amendment restricts the president from serving more than two terms of office.

National Anthem

'Lumbanyeni Zambia' ('Stand and Sing of Zambia'); words collective, tune by M. E. Sontonga.

RECENT ELECTIONS

Presidential elections took place on 30 Oct. 2008. Acting president Rupiah Banda (Movement for Multi-Party Democracy) won 40·1% of the vote, Michael Sata (Patriotic Front) 38·1%, Hakainde Hichilema (United Party for National Development) 19·7% and Godfrey Miyanda (Heritage Party) 0·8%. Turnout was 45·4%. Sata's supporters subsequently staged protests over alleged vote fraud but the result stood.

In the parliamentary elections held on 28 Sept. 2006, Levy Patrick Mwanawasa's party, the Movement for Multi-Party Democracy (MMD), gained 72 of the 150 elected seats in the National Assembly; the Patriotic Front gained 44; the United Democratic Alliance 27. Turnout was 70·8%.

CURRENT ADMINISTRATION

President: Rupiah Banda; b. 1937 (MMD; since 19 Aug. 2008—acting until 2 Nov. 2008).

In March 2010 the government comprised:

Vice-President and Minister for Justice: George Kunda.

Minister for Agriculture and Co-operatives: Peter Daka. *Commerce, Trade and Industry:* Felix Mutati. *Community:* Michael Kaingu. *Defence:* Kalombo Mwansa. *Education:* Dora Siliya. *Energy:* Kenneth Konga. *Finance and National Planning:* Situmbeko Musokotowane. *Foreign Affairs:* Kabinga Pande. *Gender:* Sarah Sayifwanda. *Health:* Kapembwa Simbao. *Home Affairs:* Lameck Mangani. *Information:* Ronnie Shikapwasha. *Labour:* Austin Liato. *Lands:* Gladys Lundwe. *Livestock and Fisheries:* Brandford Machila. *Local Government and Housing:* Dr Eustarckio Kazonga. *Mines:* Maxwell Mwale. *Presidential Affairs:* Ronald Mukuma. *Science, Technology and Vocational Training:* Brian Chituwo. *Sports and Youth:* Kenneth Chipungu. *Tourism, Environment and Natural Resources:* Catherine Namugala. *Transport and Communication:* Geoffrey Lungwangwa. *Works and Supply:* Mike Mulongoti.

Zambian Parliament: http://www.parliament.gov.zm

CURRENT LEADERS

Rupiah Banda

Position

President

Introduction

Rupiah Banda became president on 2 Nov. 2008 after winning the general election following the death of the incumbent Levy Mwanawasa. A career diplomat, the centrist Banda was a leading figure in Kenneth Kaunda's Marxist regime before joining the ruling Movement for Multi-Party Democracy in 2002.

Early Life

Rupiah Banda was born on 19 Feb. 1937 in Gwanda, then in British-ruled Southern Rhodesia, to parents originally from Northern Rhodesia. He was educated at Munali Secondary School in Lusaka from 1954–58, where he joined the youth wing of the United National Independence Party (UNIP), headed by Kenneth Kaunda. Banda studied economics at the University of Ethiopia in Addis Ababa and then at Sweden's Lund University from 1960. While there, he served as UNIP's representative in northern Europe, organising scholarships for several other Africans who would later play a role in their countries' independence movements. Returning to Lusaka in newly independent Zambia in 1964, Banda enrolled at the National Institute for Public Affairs, which presaged a diplomatic career. Postings to Egypt (1965–67) and the USA (1967–69) followed.

Banda was a manager at the Rural Development Corporation and National Agricultural Marketing Board in the early 1970s. He also developed business interests, taking stakes in engineering firms linked to the copper mines that formed the backbone of the steadily growing economy. Returning to the international stage, Banda became Zambia's permanent representative to the United Nations in New York in 1974. He was chairman on the UN Council for Namibia, set up to steer South West Africa towards liberation from South Africa. The following year he was appointed the minister of foreign affairs in Kaunda's UNIP government (UNIP being the only legal party after Kaunda signed a constitutional amendment in Dec. 1972). Much of his work involved attempts to bring peace to Angola and to improve relations between the 'frontline states' (Angola, Botswana, Lesotho, Mozambique, Swaziland, Tanzania and Zambia) and South Africa.

Elected as an MP for the Munali constituency south of Lusaka in Dec. 1978, Banda's early parliamentary careers coincided with a collapse in copper prices that brought serious economic decline and growing opposition to Kaunda's regime. Banda lost his seat in the 1983 election and subsequently worked as a civil servant in Lusaka's civic authority, before being appointed minister of state for mines. Banda recaptured his parliamentary seat in 1988 but his party was beset by deteriorating economic conditions, corruption scandals and mismanagement. When multi-party democracy returned to Zambia following a referendum in Aug. 1991, the Movement for Multi-Party Democracy (MMD) brought an end to the Kaunda era. Having lost his seat to an MMD candidate, Ronald Penza, in the Oct. 1991 general election, Banda resumed his business interests.

He left the UNIP in 2000 and two years later joined the MMD, whose leader, Dr Mwanawasa, displayed an openness towards former opposition MPs. Banda helped galvanize support for the MMD in the east of the country and was rewarded with the position of vice president after the MMD victory at the Sept. 2006 general election. Following President Mwanawasa's death in Aug. 2008, Banda became acting president and stood as the MMD's candidate in the presidential election of 30 Oct. Initial results showed Banda's main challenger, Michael Sata of the Patriotic Front (PF), in the lead but as votes from rural areas were counted, Banda closed the gap. Final results on 2 Nov. 2008 showed Banda with 40% of the vote against 38% for Sata. The PF alleged vote rigging and refused to recognize Banda's victory, with Sata's supporters rioting in Lusaka and Kitwe.

Career in Office

Banda pledged to continue his predecessor's pro-business policies and anti-corruption efforts, as well as address the country's widespread poverty. He urged the opposition to set aside divisions after the closely fought election. He faced growing unrest in 2009 as the global economic downturn brought down the price of Zambia's main export commodities and led to job cuts.

DEFENCE

In 2006 defence expenditure totalled US$245m. (US$22 per capita), representing 2·4% of GDP.

Army

Strength (2007) 13,500. There are also two paramilitary police units totalling 1,400.

Air Force

In 2007 the Air Force had 29 combat capable aircraft including F-6 (Chinese-built MiG-19s) and MiG-21s. Serviceability of most types is reported to be low. Personnel (2007) 1,600.

INTERNATIONAL RELATIONS

Zambia is a member of the UN, World Bank, IMF and several other UN specialized agencies, WTO, Commonwealth, IOM, African Development Bank, African Union, COMESA, SADC and is an ACP member state of the ACP-EU relationship.

During the 1990s Zambia received foreign aid equivalent to approximately US$900 a head, but according to the *World Bank* GNP per head declined from US$390 in 1991 to US$330 in 1999.

ECONOMY

In 2006 agriculture accounted for 20·9% of GDP, industry 32·9% and services 46·2%.

Overview

The economy is primarily agrarian, employing 85% of the population. The main industries are copper mining and processing, accounting for more than 80% of foreign currency intake. Having experienced negative growth of nearly 5% per year between 1974–90, a change of political power in 1990 prompted an upswing in the economy.

Copper mines were privatized in 2000 and monetary and fiscal policies were tightened. Since 2002 GDP has grown at over 5% per year, helped by expansion in the mining sector and a recovery in agricultural production. Inflation has been at its lowest level for 30 years, while record high copper prices and a rise in copper exports have boosted Zambia's external position. Nonetheless, social indicators remain poor and HIV/AIDS-related issues put a continual strain on government resources.

Currency

The unit of currency is the *kwacha* (ZMK) of 100 *ngwee*. Foreign exchange reserves were US$477m. in July 2005. In Dec. 1992 the official and free market exchange rates were merged and the kwacha devalued 29%. Inflation, which was 183·3% in 1993, was down to 9·0% in 2006. Rates have since risen slightly to 10·7% in 2007 and 12·4% in 2008. Total money supply in June 2005 was 2,140·3bn. kwacha.

Budget

The fiscal year is the calendar year. Revenues in 2006 totalled 16,635bn. kwacha and expenditures 9,248bn. kwacha. Grants accounted for 60·2% of total revenue in 2006; current expenditures accounted for 77·1% of total expenditure.

VAT is 17·5%.

Performance

Real GDP growth was 6·3% in 2007 and 5·8% in 2008. Total GDP in 2008 was US$14·3bn.

Banking and Finance

The central bank is the Bank of Zambia (*Governor*, Dr Caleb Fundanga). In 2003 there were five commercial banks, six foreign banks and four development banks. The Bank of Zambia monitors and supervises the operations of financial institutions. Banks and building societies are governed by the Banking and Financial Services Act 1994.

There is a stock exchange in Lusaka. Its market capitalization was US$301m. in 1998, a 58% fall from 1997's figure of US$705m.

ENERGY AND NATURAL RESOURCES

Environment

Zambia's carbon dioxide emissions from the consumption and flaring of fossil fuels in 2008 were the equivalent of 0·3 tonnes per capita.

Electricity

Installed capacity in 2004 was an estimated 2·3m. kW. Production in 2004 was 8·51bn. kWh, almost exclusively hydro-electric; consumption per capita was 721 kWh.

Oil and Gas

Oil and gas were both discovered in the northwest of Zambia in 2006. Exploration companies have yet to determine the size of the identified reserves.

Minerals

Minerals produced (in 1,000 tonnes): copper (2004), 427; cobalt (2003), 6·6; silver (2005 estimate), 2,000 kg; gold (2005 estimate), 440 kg. Zambia is well-endowed with gemstones, especially emeralds, amethysts, aquamarine, tourmaline and garnets. Zambia Consolidated Copper Mines, privatized in 2000, is the country's largest employer. In 1990 the government freed the gemstones trade from restrictions. In 2004, 233,000 tonnes of coal were produced.

Agriculture

70% of the population is dependent on agriculture. There were an estimated 5·26m. ha. of arable land in 2007 and 29,000 ha. of permanent crops. Principal agricultural products (2003 estimates, in 1,000 tonnes): sugarcane, 1,800; maize, 1,161; wheat, 100; seed cotton, 62; sweet potatoes, 53; groundnuts, 42.

Livestock (2003 estimates): cattle, 2·6m.; goats, 1·3m.; pigs, 340,000; sheep, 150,000; chickens, 30m.

Forestry

Forests covered 42·45m. ha. in 2005, or 57·1% of the total land area. Timber production in 2007 was 10·03m. cu. metres, most of it for fuel.

Fisheries

Total catch, 2005, approximately 65,000 tonnes (exclusively from inland waters).

INDUSTRY

In 2006 industry accounted for 32·9% of GDP, with manufacturing contributing 10·8%. Industrial production grew by 9·1% in 2006. Zambia's economy is totally dependent upon its mining sector. Other industries include construction, foodstuffs, beverages, chemicals and textiles.

Labour

The labour force totalled 3,165,200 in 2000 (59% males). 71·6% of the economically active population in 2000 were engaged in agriculture, 7·5% in community services and 6·8% in trade.

Trade Unions

There is a Zambia Congress of Trade Unions.

INTERNATIONAL TRADE

In 2005 foreign debt was US$5,668m.

Imports and Exports

In 2007 imports were valued at US$3,971·1m. and exports at US$4,618·6m.

Imports declined every year from 1997 to 1999 before increasing by 12% in 2000, and exports declined every year from 1997 to 2000, However, between 2003 and 2007 there was a 150% increase in imports and exports increased by 370%. In 2007 copper provided 71% of all exports (by value). Since 1990 non-copper exports have increased in value from US$50m. to US$1·1bn.

The main import sources in 2007 were South Africa (47·4%), United Arab Emirates (6·4%), China (5·9%) and India (4·1%). Principal export markets were Switzerland (41·8%), South Africa (12·0%), Thailand (5·9%) and the Democratic Republic of the Congo (5·3%).

COMMUNICATIONS

Roads

There were, in 2001, 91,440 km of roads, including 4,222 km of highway. 93,400 passenger cars were in use in 2002 (9·3 per 1,000 inhabitants) and there were 68,000 trucks and vans.

Rail

In 2005 there were 1,271 km of the state-owned Zambia Railways (ZR) and 891 km of the Tanzania-Zambia (Tazara) Railway, both on 1,067 mm gauge. ZR carried 0·8m. passengers and 1·7m. tonnes of freight in 2000.

Civil Aviation

The main carrier, Zambian Airways, operates internal flights and in 2007 flew to Dar es Salaam, Harare and Johannesburg as well as operating domestic services. Lusaka is the principal international airport. In 2001 Lusaka International handled 410,000 passengers (359,000 on international flights) and 24,800 tonnes of freight. In 2003 scheduled airline traffic of Zambian-based carriers flew 2m. km, carrying 45,000 passengers (17,000 on international flights).

Telecommunications

In 2008 there were 90,600 main (fixed) telephone lines; mobile phone subscribers numbered 3,539,000 in 2008 (28·0 per 100 persons). Telecel (2) Ltd. has been licensed to run a mobile telecommunications service in addition to the Zambia Telecommunications Company (ZAMTEL) since 1996. Internet services are provided by Zambia Communications Systems (ZAMNET), a private company of ZAMTEL. There were 131,000 PCs in use in 2005 and some 700,000 internet users in 2008.

Postal Services

In 2003 Zambia Postal Services Corporation (ZAMPOST) operated 235 permanent post offices.

SOCIAL INSTITUTIONS

Justice

The Judiciary consists of the Supreme Court, the High Court and four classes of magistrates' courts; all have civil and criminal jurisdiction.

The Supreme Court hears and determines appeals from the High Court. Its seat is at Lusaka. The High Court exercises the powers vested in the High Court in England, subject to the High Court ordinance of Zambia. Its sessions are held where occasion requires, mostly at Lusaka and Ndola. All criminal cases tried by subordinate courts are subject to revision by the High Court.

The death penalty is authorized, the last execution having taken place in 1997. The population in penal institutions in Dec. 2005 was 14,347 (122 per 100,000 of national population).

Education

Schooling is for nine years. In April 2002 President Mwanawasa announced the reintroduction of universal free primary education, abolished under former President Chiluba. In 2007 there were 2,790,312 pupils in primary schools with 56,557 teaching staff and 607,296 pupils in secondary schools with 14,246 teaching staff.

There are two universities, three teachers' colleges and one Christian college. In 1998 there were 4,797 university students. The University of Zambia, at Lusaka, was founded in 1965; Copperbelt University, at Kitwe, in 1987. In addition the government sponsored 150 students to be trained abroad.

The adult literacy rate in 2001 was 79·0% (85·8% among males and 72·7% among females).

In 2004 public expenditure on education came to 3·0% of GNI and accounted for 14·8% of total government expenditure.

Health

In 2004 there were 1,264 physicians, 19,014 nurses, 2,996 midwives, 491 dentists and 1,039 pharmacists. There were 88 public hospitals in 2004, with a total of 22,800 beds (207 per 100,000 population).

RELIGION

In 1993 the president declared Zambia to be a Christian nation, but freedom of worship is a constitutional right. In 2001 there were 3·89m. Christians. Traditional beliefs are also widespread.

CULTURE

World Heritage Sites

Zambia shares one site with Zimbabwe on the UNESCO World Heritage List: the Victoria Falls/Mosi-oa-Tunya (inscribed on the list in 1989), waterfalls on the Zambezi River.

Broadcasting

The Zambia National Broadcasting Corporation is a statutory body which oversees the single-channel public television service and three radio networks (one multilingual and two in English). Privately-owned radio stations are mainly non-political and include Radio Phoenix, QFM, Radio Christian Voice and (Catholic) Yatsani Radio; pay-TV services are available. There were 726,000 TV receivers in 2003 (colour by PAL).

Press

In 2004 there were two state-owned daily papers, *The Times of Zambia* and the *Zambia Daily Mail*, both with Sunday editions.

Privately owned papers include *The Post* (daily), *The National Mirror*, *The Monitor*, *Today*, *The Star* and *Business and Leisure Times*.

Tourism

In 2005, 668,862 foreign tourists visited Zambia. Most visitors in 2005 were from Zimbabwe (148,436), followed by South Africa (110,272), Tanzania (65,881) and the UK (44,369). Spending by tourists in 2005 totalled US$98m.

Festivals

The N'cwala ceremony is held in Feb. by the Ngoni people to commemorate their arrival in Zambia in 1835 and the first produce of the year. The Kuomboka, in Feb. or March, is the canoe procession of the Lozi chief and his family from the palace at Leaului down the Zambezi to Limulunga for the rainy season. The National Fishing Competition is held at Lake Tanganyika in March. Likumbi Lya Mize, held at Mize in July, celebrates the Luvale tribe's cultural heritage. The Livingstone Cultural and Arts Festival, held annually in Sept. since 1994, brings together many of Zambia's tribes and their traditional rulers. Independence Day is celebrated on 24 Oct.

DIPLOMATIC REPRESENTATIVES

Of Zambia in the United Kingdom (2 Palace Gate, London, W8 5NG)
High Commissioner: Prof. Royson Mukwena.

Of the United Kingdom in Zambia (5210 Independence Ave., 15101 Ridgeway, Lusaka)
High Commissioners: Carolyn Davidson and Thomas Carter.

Of Zambia in the USA (2419 Massachusetts Ave., NW, Washington, D.C., 20008)
Ambassador: Inonge Mbikusita-Lewanika.

Of the USA in Zambia (Corner of Independence and United Nations Road, PO Box 31617, Lusaka)
Ambassador: Donald E. Booth.

Of Zambia to the United Nations
Ambassador: Lazarous Kapambwe.

Of Zambia to the European Union
Ambassador: Irene Mumba Kamanga.

FURTHER READING

Chiluba, F., *Democracy: the Challenge of Change.* 1995
Sardanis, Andrew, *Africa: Another Side of the Coin: Northern Rhodesia's Final Years and Zambia's Nationhood.* 2003
Simon, David J., Pletcher, James R. and Siegel, Brian V., *Historical Dictionary of Zambia.* 2008

Central Statistical Office. *Monthly Digest of Statistics.*
National Statistical Office: Central Statistical Office, PO Box 31908, Lusaka.
Website: http://www.zamstats.gov.zm

ZIMBABWE

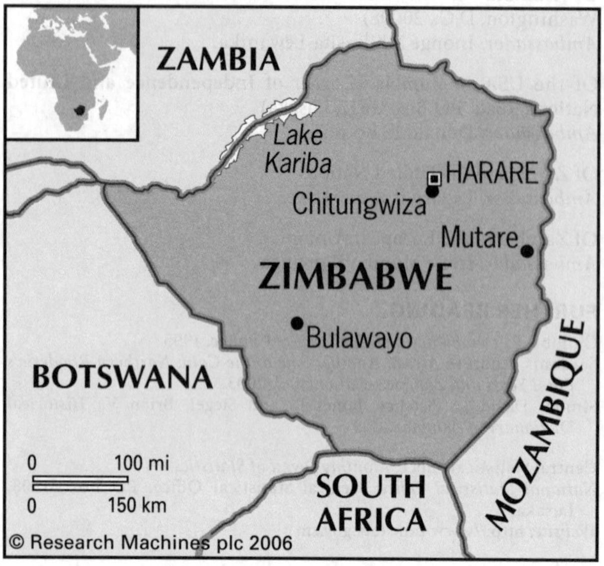

Republic of Zimbabwe

Capital: Harare
Population estimate, 2010: 12·64m.
GDP per capita, 2005: (PPP$) 2,038

KEY HISTORICAL EVENTS

Archaeological evidence shows human settlement dating back several thousand years. The Khoisan people were early inhabitants of the region, followed from around AD 500 by the Bantu-speaking Gokomere. Trading civilizations flourished from the 9th century, culminating in the Mwene Mutapa Empire (Empire of Great Zimbabwe) from the 15th century. Its stronghold was a fortified stone town known as Great Zimbabwe ('houses of stone'), which was founded around 1000 and had a population of up to 18,000 at its peak. During the 16th and 17th centuries the area came under partial control by the Portuguese until the Shona people defeated them in 1693 and established the Rozwi Empire. This fell to the migrating Ndebele (Matabele) in 1834.

King Lobengula of Matabeleland signed the Rudd Concession on 13 Oct. 1888, giving the British mining rights. The British South Africa Company, under Cecil Rhodes, colonized the territory from 1890. European immigration increased after white settlers won the first Matabele war in 1893–94. Following unsuccessful Ndebele and Shona uprisings in 1896 and 1897, indigenous people were increasingly displaced from their land. In 1911 the region was divided into Southern and Northern Rhodesia (*see* ZAMBIA: Key Historical Events) and in 1923 became a self-governing colony. In 1953 Southern and Northern Rhodesia joined with Nyasaland to form the Federation of Rhodesia and Nyasaland, a move opposed by African nationalists who feared it would entrench white minority rule. The South Rhodesian African National Congress was founded in 1957 and campaigned for self-rule by the African majority until it was banned in 1960. After unrest mounted in Nyasaland and neighbouring states, the federation was dissolved on 31 Dec. 1963 and Southern Rhodesia reverted to self-governing colony status within the British Commonwealth under the name of Rhodesia.

On 11 Nov. 1965 Rhodesia's white-dominated government issued a unilateral declaration of independence (UDI) to forestall any British attempt to grant black majority rule. The British governor dismissed the prime minister, Ian Smith, and his cabinet, and the British government reasserted its formal responsibility for Rhodesia although the Smith cabinet was effectively left to run the country. Britain imposed economic sanctions, as did the UN in 1968. On 2 March 1970 the Smith government declared Rhodesia a republic and adopted a new constitution. From 1966–79 the Zimbabwe African People's Union (ZAPU) and its off-shoot, the Zimbabwe African National Union (ZANU)—both of which were banned—led a sporadic guerrilla campaign. On 3 March 1978 Smith signed a constitutional agreement with the internationally-backed nationalist leaders. A draft constitution was published in Jan. 1979 and accepted by the white electorate in a referendum. Following the Commonwealth Conference in Lusaka in Aug. 1979, elections in March 1980 resulted in victory for ZANU. Southern Rhodesia became the Republic of Zimbabwe on 18 April 1980.

Political conflict between ZANU and ZAPU supporters in Matabeleland led to allegations of atrocities by government forces in 1983–84. Land reform—the redistribution of good farming land from the minority white population to the African population—became a pressing issue. President Mugabe's government bought 3·5m. ha. of land from white farmers, with the UK funding the £44m. bill. However, only 70,000 families benefited amid allegations of government profiteering. In early 2000 a policy of land occupation began, with black settlers taking over white-owned farms by force. President Mugabe ignored international pressure to restore the rule of law and violence escalated. During campaigning for the 2002 presidential election, which failed to meet international democratic standards, the opposition leader, Morgan Tsvangirai, was charged with treason. Zimbabwe was suspended from the Commonwealth in March 2002 over the conduct of the election and when the suspension was extended in 2003 it pulled out altogether.

In the early 2000s agricultural production fell drastically, the result of drought and of the continuing land seizures. In Sept. 2005 President Mugabe nationalized all land and ended the right of landowners to challenge government expropriations in the courts. In May 2005 the government began the mass demolition of urban slums, claiming it would improve law and order. Around 700,000 people were left homeless. The conduct of parliamentary and senate elections in 2005, which resulted in victory for President Mugabe's party, was criticized by the international community and in March 2007 evidence that Morgan Tsvangirai had been tortured by police caused an international outcry. In 2006 and 2007 the population experienced mass hunger, with UNICEF estimating that 4m. needed aid. The country's AIDS pandemic continued to worsen in 2007, with 24% of children under 17 orphaned by the disease.

In 2008 elections held against a backdrop of hyperinflation, Mugabe's ZANU-PF lost their parliamentary majority—to the MDC—for the first time since independence. Mugabe retained the presidency when Morgan Tsvangirai, leader of the MDC, pulled out of a run-off, claiming his supporters had suffered intimidation at the hands of Mugabe's supporters. An international outcry forced Mugabe into talks with Tsvangirai that resulted in a power-sharing agreement in Sept. 2008. The agreement faltered over the allocation of ministries until the composition of the new cabinet was finalized in Feb. 2009. By the end of 2008 millions of civilians relied on food relief, while a cholera outbreak had claimed over 2,000 lives by Jan. 2009, with 1,500 new cases a day being reported.

TERRITORY AND POPULATION

Zimbabwe is bounded in the north by Zambia, east by Mozambique, south by South Africa and west by Botswana and the Caprivi Strip of Namibia. The area is 390,757 sq. km (150,871 sq. miles). The 1992 census population was 10,401,767 (51·2% female). 2002 census population, 11,631,657; density, 29·8 per sq. km. The United Nations population estimate for 2002 was 12,518,000. In 2005, 64·1% of the population were rural. Although the population is still rising, it is doing so at a lower rate than had been previously expected, partly owing to the large number of AIDS-related deaths and partly as a result of over 3m. Zimbabweans having left the country as President Mugabe's grip on power strengthened, with the vast majority choosing to live in South Africa.

The UN gives an estimated population for 2010 of 12·64m.

There are eight provinces and two cities, Harare and Bulawayo, with provincial status. Area and population (2002 census):

	Area (sq. km)	*Population*
Bulawayo	479	676,650
Harare	872	1,896,134
Manicaland	36,459	1,568,930
Mashonaland Central	28,347	995,427
Mashonaland East	32,230	1,127,413
Mashonaland West	57,441	1,224,670
Masvingo	56,566	1,320,438
Matabeleland North	75,025	704,948
Matebeleland South	54,172	653,054
Midlands	49,166	1,463,993

Harare, the capital, had a population in 2002 of 1,444,534. Other main cities (with 2002 census populations) were Bulawayo (676,787), Chitungwiza (321,782), Mutare (170,106) and Gweru (141,260). The population is approximately 98% African, 1% mixed and Asian and there are around 70,000 whites. The main ethno-linguistic groups are the Shona (71%), Ndebele (16%), Ndau (3%) and Nyanja (3%). Other smaller ones include Kalanga, Manyika, Tonga and Lozi.

The official language is English.

SOCIAL STATISTICS

2000 estimates: births, 425,000; deaths, 215,000. Rates (2000 estimates, per 1,000 population); birth, 35·1; death, 17·8. Annual population growth rate, 1992–2002, 1·5%. Zimbabwe's expectation of life at birth in 2007 was 43·6 years for females and 42·6 for males, down from an average of 54 years in 1993. The sharp decline is largely attributed to the huge number of people in the country with HIV. In 2007, 15·3% of all adults between 15 and 49 were infected with HIV. Zimbabwe had both the lowest overall life expectancy of any country in 2007 and the lowest for males, although Afghanistan's life expectancy for females was lower. Infant mortality, 2005, 60 per 1,000 live births; fertility rate, 2004, 3·4 births per woman.

CLIMATE

Though situated in the tropics, conditions are remarkably temperate throughout the year because of altitude, and an inland position keeps humidity low. The warmest weather occurs in the three months before the main rainy season, which starts in Nov. and lasts until March. The cool season is from mid-May to mid-Aug. and, though days are mild and sunny, nights are chilly. Harare, Jan. 69°F (20·6°C), July 57°F (13·9°C). Annual rainfall 33" (828 mm). Bulawayo, Jan. 71°F (21·7°C), July 57°F (13·9°C). Annual rainfall 24" (594 mm). Victoria Falls, Jan. 78°F (25·6°C), July 61°F (16·1°C). Annual rainfall 28" (710 mm).

CONSTITUTION AND GOVERNMENT

The 1979 Constitution, with 18 amendments, provides for a single-chamber 150-member Parliament (*House of Assembly*), universal suffrage for citizens over the age of 18, an *Executive President*, an independent judiciary enjoying security of tenure and a Declaration of Rights, derogation from certain of the provisions being permitted, within specified limits, during a state of emergency. The House of Assembly is elected for five-year terms: up to and including the 2005 elections 120 members were elected by universal suffrage, ten were chiefs elected by all the country's tribal chiefs, 12 were appointed by the President and eight were provincial governors. A constitutional amendment of Aug. 2005 allowed for the reintroduction of a 66-member *Senate*, which had been abolished in 1987. It also enables the government to expropriate land without being challenged in court and to remove the right to a passport if it is deemed in the national interest. The constitution can be amended by a two-thirds parliamentary majority. A further amendment of Oct. 2007 provided for simultaneous parliamentary and presidential elections, reduced the presidential term from six to five years and enabled parliament to choose a successor to President Mugabe. Additionally, the number of seats in the House of Assembly was increased to 210 (all directly elected for five-year terms) and in the Senate to 93 (60 directly elected members, ten provincial governors, the president and deputy president of the Chiefs' Council, 16 chiefs and five senators appointed by the President).

In a referendum on 12–13 Feb. 2000 on the adoption of a new constitution 697,754 (54·6%) voted against and only 578,210 in favour. Under the new constitution Zimbabwe would have had an Executive President and an Executive Prime Minister sharing power, but many people felt that this would have strengthened President Mugabe's control over the country.

National Anthem

'Kalibusiswe Ilizwe leZimbabwe' ('Blessed be the Land of Zimbabwe'); words by Dr Solomon M. Mutswairo; tune by Fred Changundega.

GOVERNMENT CHRONOLOGY

Presidents since 1980. (ZANU = Zimbabwe African National Union; ZANU-PF = Zimbabwe African National Union-Patriotic Front)

1980–87	ZANU	Canaan Sodindo Banana
1987–	ZANU-PF	Robert Gabriel Mugabe

Prime Ministers since 1980. (MDC-T = Movement for Democratic Change-Tsvangirai; ZANU = Zimbabwe African National Union)

1980–87	ZANU	Robert Gabriel Mugabe
2009–	MDC-T	Morgan Richard Tsvangirai

RECENT ELECTIONS

Parliamentary and presidential elections took place on 29 March 2008. Of the 207 seats contested in the House of Assembly the Movement for Democratic Change-Tsvangirai (MDC-T) won 99 seats, against 97 for the Zimbabwe African National Union-Patriotic Front (ZANU-PF). This was the first time that ZANU-PF, the party of incumbent president Robert Mugabe, had lost its legislative majority since the country gained independence in 1980. Of the remaining seats, ten were claimed by the Movement for Democratic Change-Mutambara (MDC-M), a splinter faction of the MDC, and one by an independent candidate. In the Senate elections, the 60 available seats were divided equally between the ZANU-PF (30 seats) and the combined opposition of the MDC-T (24) and the MDC-M (6).

The results of the presidential election were contested. On 13 April the Zimbabwe Electoral Commission announced a full recount of both parliamentary and presidential votes in 23 constituencies. Following the recount it was confirmed that Morgan Tsvangirai, leader of the MDC-T, had won the highest proportion of the votes, but had not gained the absolute majority necessary to avoid a second round run-off against incumbent president Robert Mugabe. On 22 June Tsvangirai withdrew from the second round citing a campaign of violence against the MDC's supporters. Mugabe won the second round on 27 June with 85·5% of votes cast, against 9·3% for Tsvangirai (as his name was still on the ballot). Under international pressure, Mugabe entered into talks with Tsvangirai, resulting in a power-sharing deal in Sept. 2008 that saw Mugabe remain president while Tsvangirai eventually became prime minister in Feb. 2009.

CURRENT ADMINISTRATION

Executive President: Robert G. Mugabe; b. 1924 (ZANU-PF; sworn in 30 Dec. 1987, having previously been prime minister from 1980 to 1987; re-elected April 1990, March 1996, March 2002 and June 2008).

Vice-Presidents: Joyce Mujuru (ZANU-PF); John Landa Nkomo (ZANU-PF).

In Feb. 2009 a coalition government was formed that in March 2010 comprised:

Prime Minister: Morgan Tsvangirai; b. 1952 (MDC-T; sworn in 11 Feb. 2009).

Deputy Prime Ministers: Arthur Mutambara (MDC-M); Thokozani Khuphe (MDC-T).

Minister for Agriculture: Joseph Mtakwese Made (ZANU-PF). *Constitutional and Parliamentary Affairs:* Eric Matinenga (MDC-T). *Defence:* Emmerson Mnangagwa (ZANU-PF). *Economic Planning and Investment Promotion:* Elton Mangoma (MDC-T). *Education, Sport and Culture:* David Coltart (MDC-M). *Energy and Power Development:* Elias Mudzuri (MDC-T). *Environment:* Francis Nhema (ZANU-PF). *Finance:* Tendai Biti (MDC-T). *Foreign Affairs:* Simbarashe Mumbengegwi (ZANU-PF). *Health and Child Welfare:* Dr Henry Madzorera (MDC-T). *Higher and Tertiary Education:* Stanislaus Mudenge (ZANU-PF). *Home Affairs:* Giles Mutsekwa (MDC-T); Kembo Mohadi (ZANU-PF). *Industry and Commerce:* Welshman Ncube (MDC-M). *Information and Publicity:* Webster Shamu (ZANU-PF). *Information Communication Technology:* Nelson Chamisa (MDC-T). *Justice:* Patrick Chinamasa (ZANU-PF). *Labour and Social Welfare:* Paurina Mpariwa (MDC-T). *Lands and Land Resettlement:* Herbert Murerwa (ZANU-PF). *Local Government and Urban Development:* Ignatius Chombo (ZANU-PF). *Mines and Mining Development:* Obert Mpofu (ZANU-PF). *National Housing and Social Amenities:* Fidelis Mhashu (MDC-T). *Public Service:* Elphas Mukonoweshuro (MDC-T). *Public Works:* Theresa Makoni (MDC-T). *Regional Integration and International Co-operation:* Priscilla Misihairabwi-Mushonga (MDC-M). *Science and Technology Development:* Henry Dzinotyiwei (MDC-T). *State Enterprise and Parastatals:* Joel Gabuza (MDC-T). *Tourism:* Walter Mzembi (ZANU-PF). *Transport:* Nicholas Goche (ZANU-PF). *Water Resources Development and Management:* Samuel Nkomo (MDC-T). *Women's Affairs, Gender and Community Development:* Olivia Muchena (ZANU-PF). *Youth Development, Indigenization and Empowerment:* Savior Kasukuwere (ZANU-PF).

Speaker: Lovemore Moyo (MDC-T).

Government Website: http://www.gta.gov.zw

CURRENT LEADERS

Robert Mugabe

Position

President

Introduction

Robert Mugabe came to power as newly-independent Zimbabwe's (formerly Rhodesia) first prime minister in 1980, becoming president in 1987. Although initially hailed as a democratic reformer, his economic mismanagement of the country, violent electoral campaigns and controversial programme of land seizures have tarnished his image at home and abroad. He has defended his land reform programme as the conclusion of the process of decolonization, but his policies have been widely perceived as short-term political expediency for the maintenance of personal power. In the wake of the disputed presidential elections in 2008, Mugabe conceded to power-sharing with the opposition Movement for Democratic Change (MDC) after protracted negotiations, but doubts remained over his willingness to relax his autocratic grip on the country.

Early Life

The son of a carpenter, Robert Gabriel Mugabe was born 21 Feb. 1924 at Kutama mission, northwest of Harare. After an early education at a Roman Catholic mission school, he studied at the University College of Fort Hare, South Africa, marking the beginning of an academic career boasting seven university degrees, three of which he completed during imprisonment. He worked as a primary school teacher in Ghana from 1956–60 when he returned to Rhodesia and joined Joshua Nkomo's Zimbabwe African People's Union (ZAPU). In 1963 he became a founding member of the breakaway Zimbabwe African National Union (ZANU) with Rev. Ndabaningi Sithole. A year later Mugabe was arrested for subversion and imprisoned, without trial, for ten years. Despite imprisonment, he remained politically active and was able to orchestrate, in 1974, a coup against Sithole to become party leader. In 1975, freed from prison, Mugabe joined Nkomo as joint leader of the Patriotic Front of Zimbabwe which waged a guerrilla war against Ian Smith's white Rhodesian Front government. In 1980 independence was achieved and parliamentary elections took place in which Mugabe, at the head of ZANU, won a landslide victory to become prime minister.

Career in Office

In office Mugabe appeared set to usher in a bright new era for the country. Having built a coalition government with ZAPU, he adopted a conciliatory stance towards the white, landowning minority. He introduced higher wages, credit programmes and food subsidies for poor farmers, a better infrastructure and equal land rights for women. Reform in the education system saw primary school enrolment trebled and secondary school enrolment increased five-fold during the first ten years of his rule (with Zimbabwe laying claim to the highest literacy rate of any African nation).

Troubles began in 1982 when ethnic turmoil between the Shona majority (represented by ZANU) and the Ndebele minority (represented by ZAPU) broke out after Mugabe dismissed Nkomo and ZAPU from government. The ensuing violence prompted much of the white population to emigrate, in turn creating an economic downturn. Centred in Matabeleland, the conflict drew international attention after the discovery of mass graves and alleged atrocities.

In 1987 Mugabe won the presidential elections and set about bringing ZAPU back into government. A unity agreement was signed and Nkomo became senior minister in a newly-formed Zimbabwe African National Union-Patriotic Front (ZANU-PF) government. Mugabe was again re-elected in 1990 (in polling marred by violence) and 1996, but throughout the 1990s he adopted a series of unpopular policies. His military support for President Kabila's beleaguered government in the Democratic Republic of the Congo led to strikes within his own country. An announcement of pay increases for himself and his party officials in 1998 prompted rioting, coming as it did amidst a growing economic crisis. Plans to raise food and fuel prices and to introduce a tax to support war veterans from the 1970s were blocked by trades unions and further diminished his popularity.

In Feb. 2000 Mugabe lost a referendum in which he sought to increase his presidential powers. Blaming the white minority for the defeat, he then targeted the issue of land ownership. A programme of violent land seizure followed, with black settlers taking over white-owned farms. A court order to halt the seizures was ignored and Mugabe subsequently replaced high court judges with political allies. In June 2000 parliamentary elections were held. Mugabe won the elections, but only by a narrow margin and after a campaign of intimidation which led to more than 30 deaths.

Mugabe was re-elected president in March 2002. Final results gave him 56·2% of the vote against 42·0% for opposition rival, Morgan Tsvangirai, the leader of the MDC. However, the elections failed to meet international democratic standards. They were preceded by violence against opposition supporters, the passing of a law limiting press freedom, the withdrawal of the EU monitoring team and the arrest of Mugabe's main political rival on charges of treason. As a result, Zimbabwe was suspended from the Commonwealth and a range of targeted sanctions from the UK, the USA and the European Union (EU) were placed on Mugabe and his cabinet. In March 2003 the USA froze Zimbabwean assets and forbade US citizens from undertaking economic dealings with Mugabe and his government colleagues.

The state of political uncertainty and violence following the 2000 referendum damaged investor confidence, causing export prices to decline and unemployment and food shortages to rise. Coupled with this, severe drought in early 2002 raised the threat of mass starvation. In April 2002 Mugabe declared a state of disaster, allowing him the temporary use of 'extraordinary measures' to cope with the situation. Although little was done in practical terms to relieve the threat of famine, Mugabe pushed ahead with the land redistribution programme. In June 2002 he ordered almost 3,000 white farmers to leave their land within 45 days, or face imprisonment. In Sept. 2002 new legislation was passed allowing farmers only a week's notice after receiving an eviction order. In March 2003 Amnesty International reported that up to 500 people had been arrested following a general strike, with members of the MDC especially targeted. In the same month the Commonwealth extended Zimbabwe's suspension until at least Dec. 2003. In June 2003 police detained Tsvangirai, who had called for mass popular protests against Mugabe's government, and in Jan. 2004 he went on trial for treason. Although he was acquitted in Oct. 2004 of charges relating to an assassination plot against Mugabe, he still faced a separate treason charge. Meanwhile, relations with the international community worsened. In Dec. 2003 the Commonwealth (despite South African disapproval) again extended Zimbabwe's suspension, prompting Mugabe's withdrawal from the organization.

At the parliamentary elections in March 2005, ZANU-PF took 78 of 150 seats. The MDC claimed that there had been widespread vote rigging and intimidation. Then, in May, Mugabe's government launched a demolition of urban slum dwellings and illegal settlements, including business premises, around the country without compensation. The policy drew international condemnation as an estimated 700,000 people (according to the UN) lost their homes, or source of livelihood, or both. In Aug. 2005 parliament approved amendments to the constitution, including the reintroduction of the Senate, which had been abolished in 1990. Other changes provided for the government to confiscate passports of those deemed to pose a threat to national security and to strengthen control over land redistribution with no right of appeal. Also in Aug., the authorities dropped the remaining treason charge against Tsvangirai. ZANU-PF won the Nov. 2005 elections to the new Senate, securing an overwhelming majority of 66 seats amid low voter turnout and opposition calls for a boycott.

Repression of the MDC and wider opposition intensified from 2006, particularly in March 2007 when Tsvangirai was beaten by security forces and hospitalized after his arrest at a political rally. A meeting of regional leaders subsequently invited South Africa's president, Thabo Mbeki, to mediate in Zimbabwe's political and economic crisis. In Dec. 2007 Mugabe's presence at the EU–Africa summit in Lisbon provoked criticism of his regime's abuse of human rights.

Mugabe was endorsed as the ZANU-PF candidate for the March 2008 presidential (and parliamentary) elections. After a relatively peaceful campaign the MDC made a strong showing and ZANU-PF lost its legislative majority. Tsvangirai also claimed outright victory in the presidential race but Mugabe challenged the results. Despite international pressure, the electoral commission delayed the publication of results and a second round run-off was scheduled. There followed an orchestrated campaign of brutality against supporters of the opposition, which led to the withdrawal of Tsvangirai from the race in June. The international community was united in its condemnation of Mugabe's actions. The electoral crisis took place against a backdrop of economic meltdown, with inflation at over 100,000% (up from 1,600% in Jan. 2007).

Under international pressure, talks between Mugabe and Tsvangirai were brokered in Aug. 2008, which resulted in a deal the following month that saw Mugabe remain as president while Tsvangirai was to become executive prime minister. However, implementation of the agreement then stalled for several months over the allocation of cabinet posts between ZANU-PF and the MDC. The political deadlock was further exacerbated by the collapse of the economy and of basic services, which contributed to a serious outbreak of the disease cholera in Nov. 2008. In Jan. 2009, after months of acrimony and pressure from neighbouring states, Mugabe agreed to put power-sharing into effect and on 11 Feb. Tsvangirai was sworn in as prime minister. However, the failure of Mugabe's military and security service chiefs to attend the inauguration ceremony and the controversial detention of an MDC ministerial nominee did not represent an auspicious start for the new unity government.

In Sept. 2009 the EU sent its first high-level delegation to Zimbabwe for several years but refused to lift targeted sanctions. Donors were also cautious about releasing aid money to the government, fearing that it could be misused. In Oct. Mugabe called for improved relations with the West but added that the lifting of sanctions, which he blamed for ruining the country's economy, was an essential prerequisite. Mugabe's supporters had meanwhile continued to harass MDC activists, leading in Oct. to a stand-off between Mugabe and Tsvangirai in which the latter led an MDC boycott of cabinet meetings. The boycott was called off, however, after the intervention of the Southern African Development Community, which insisted that all 'outstanding issues' in the power-sharing pact be finally settled (although no conclusion had been reached by early Feb. 2010).

In Dec. 2009 Mugabe was re-elected as ZANU-PF leader for a further five years at a party congress in Harare.

Morgan Tsvangirai

Position

Prime Minister

Introduction

Morgan Tsvangirai is leader of the Movement for Democratic Change (MDC), the only significant opposition to President Robert Mugabe's regime since independence was established in 1980. Tsvangirai became an increasingly credible alternative to Mugabe as dissatisfaction with the ever more authoritarian regime and its vast mishandling of the national economy grew. This electoral viability made Tsvangirai and his supporters a target for violence and intimidation, culminating in the nationwide bloodshed that followed the disputed 2008 presidential elections. Subsequently, however, the implementation of a power-sharing agreement brokered with Mugabe under international pressure led to Tsvangirai's inauguration as executive prime minister of a unity government in Feb. 2009. Despite some progress in Zimbabwe's economic fortunes, political instability has nevertheless persisted.

Early Life
Tsvangirai was born in 1952 in Buhera, then part of Southern Rhodesia. He left school at 16 and took a job in a textile factory and then at a nickel mine in Bindura, eventually becoming general foreman and branch chairman of the Associated Mineworkers' Union (AMU). A strong supporter of Mugabe's ZANU-PF, Tsvangirai was brought into the first post-independence government. However, Tsvangirai's lack of direct involvement in the guerrilla war that led to the end of minority white rule in 1980 has been used against him by Mugabe's supporters.

In 1985 Tsvangirai left to become vice president of the AMU, having been voted onto the national executive two years earlier. In 1987 he was named secretary-general of the Southern Africa Miners' Federation. After a period studying in the UK, Tsvangirai was named general secretary of the Zimbabwe Congress of Trade Unions (ZCTU) in 1988. Six years later he became secretary general of the Southern African Trade Union co-ordinating council.

Under his leadership the ZCTU began to dissent from the ZANU-PF line. In the late-1980s and early-1990s Tsvangirai and Mugabe repeatedly clashed, notably over a programme of structural reform adopted by Mugabe. Though in line with IMF demands, Tsvangirai condemned the programme as an attack on workers' rights. He led several mass protests against the proposals, which forced Mugabe to back down. Tsvangirai was later jailed on unproven charges of being a South African spy.

Over the course of the 1990s the ZCTU became the focus of opposition to Mugabe's government. In Sept. 1999 Tsvangirai formed the MDC to formally challenge the dominance of ZANU-PF. In Feb. 2000 the MDC co-ordinated the defeat in a referendum of a government-championed constitutional amendment that would have extended Mugabe's personal power. It represented Mugabe's first significant defeat in a public vote since taking office. In Sept. 2000 Tsvangirai was charged with treason for comments made against Mugabe but the charges were later judged to be unconstitutional.

At the parliamentary elections of June 2000 the MDC won 57 of 150 seats, only five behind ZANU-PF. Mugabe's pre-election campaign received widespread international condemnation as white-owned farms were illegally seized and opposition supporters intimidated. Tsvangirai was defeated at the presidential elections of March 2002, winning 42·1% against Mugabe's 56·1%. However, observers claimed the elections failed to meet international standards and it was widely believed that Tsvangirai would have triumphed in a free vote.

Shortly before the election a video tape was exhibited allegedly showing Tsvangirai discussing an assassination attempt against Mugabe. Tsvangirai was charged with treason, carrying a possible death sentence, and his trial began in Feb. 2003. In June 2003 he called for mass action against Mugabe via a general strike and anti-government rallies. The MDC was targeted by government forces in the preceding weeks and Tsvangirai was arrested and subjected to new treason charges. He was acquitted of all charges in 2004.

Mugabe's regime met with international condemnation in March 2007 when Tsvangirai suffered serious head injuries whilst in police custody. More than 50 opposition leaders were arrested during a prayer meeting although no-one was charged. In June Tsvangirai toured Western Europe with rival opposition leader Arthur Mutambara, calling on European politicians to support their struggle for democracy.

In the general election of 29 March 2008 the MDC gained a majority in the House of Assembly, removing ZANU-PF from overall parliamentary control for the first time since Zimbabwe gained independence. Tsvangirai claimed the largest number of votes in the presidential election of the same date, winning 47·9% of the ballot against 43·2% for President Mugabe (according to the Zimbabwe Electoral Commission). However, the margin of victory was disputed, with the MDC claiming that Tsvangirai had gained the absolute majority required to avoid a second round run-off against the incumbent. These claims were rejected by the government and a run-off was scheduled for 27 June. There followed a sustained campaign of intimidation and violence against supporters of Tsvangirai. The MDC reported the death of 85 and the displacement of 200,000 of its followers over the following weeks. Five days before the ballot, having been forced to take refuge in the Dutch embassy, Tsvangirai withdrew from the race, professing that he could no longer force the Zimbabwean people to 'suffer this torture'. Over the following days he appealed to the international community, contending that 'the words of indignation from global leaders [must] be backed by the moral rectitude of military force'. Nevertheless, he subsequently entered into talks with Mugabe in Aug. 2008, which resulted in a deal the following month that provided for Mugabe to remain as president with Tsvangirai taking the premiership.

Career in Office
Implementation of the power-sharing deal was hampered by disagreements over the allocation of ministerial portfolios in a unity government until the end of Jan. 2009 when Tsvangirai accepted an arrangement giving the Movement for Democratic Change-Tsvangirai/MDC-T and the Movement for Democratic Change-Mutambara/MDC-M 16 and four posts respectively in a 35-member cabinet. On 11 Feb. Tsvangirai was sworn in as prime minister. However, there remained deep-seated domestic and international reservations about the viability of the new government, given the animosity between prime minister and president, Mugabe's autocratic track record and the conspicuous absence of the pro-Mugabe leaders of the security forces from Tsvangirai's inauguration ceremony.

With the finance portfolio under MDC control, the use of foreign currency was authorized, effectively replacing the worthless Zimbabwean dollar by the US dollar and South African rand and helping to bring about an end to years of hyperinflation. During a tour of the USA and Europe in June 2009, Tsvangirai successfully lobbied Western donors and the IMF to restore aid for essential services, although they refused to lift sanctions or release more substantive aid until the new administration had undertaken political and other reforms. However, progress towards a new constitution was hindered by further political wrangling and in Oct. Tsvangirai temporarily boycotted meetings of the cabinet in protest at Mugabe's failure to honour agreements (the resolution of which still remained elusive by early Feb. 2010). The MDC meanwhile continued to face violence and intimidation from ZANU-PF supporters. In Jan 2010 Tsvangirai again urged the easing of targeted international sanctions in recognition of the unity government's economic record.

On 6 March 2009 Tsvangirai survived a road accident in which his wife, Susan, died.

DEFENCE
In 2006 military expenditure totalled US$156m. (US$13 per capita), representing 2·8% of GDP.

Army
Strength in 2007 was estimated at 25,000. There were a further 21,800 paramilitary police including a police support unit of 2,300.

Air Force
The Air Force (ZAF) had a strength in 2007 of about 4,000 personnel. The headquarters of the ZAF and the main ZAF stations are in Harare; the second main base is at Gweru, with many secondary airfields throughout the country. There were 45 combat capable aircraft (including *Hunters* and F-7s (MiG-21)) in 2007 although the serviceability of some aircraft was in doubt, and six attack helicopters.

INTERNATIONAL RELATIONS

Zimbabwe is a member of the UN, World Bank, IMF and several other UN specialized agencies, WTO, IOM, African Development Bank, African Union, COMESA, SADC and is an ACP member state of the ACP-EU relationship. Following the controversial presidential election of March 2002 Zimbabwe was suspended from the Commonwealth's councils for a year, extended for nine months in March 2003. It withdrew from the Commonwealth in Dec. 2003.

ECONOMY

Agriculture accounted for 19% of GDP in 2007, industry 24% and services 57%.

Since Robert Mugabe came to power in 1980 the economy has collapsed with the country experiencing sustained periods of roaring inflation and heavy unemployment. Shortages of food and other necessities culminated in the authorities making an international appeal for food in July 2001. In Feb. 2000 the country ran out of gasoline because it could not pay the import bills.

Overview

The Zimbabwean economy is in chaos. At the time of independence Zimbabwe was the second largest economy in Africa but the macroeconomic situation has deteriorated sharply since 1998. Real GDP has contracted by nearly 35% since 1999. According to the IMF, the economic crisis is attributable to loose fiscal and monetary policies, an overvalued fixed exchange rate, excessive administrative controls and regulations, and chronic shortages of goods and foreign exchange. The effect of these policies has been magnified by collapsing health and education systems, the HIV pandemic, the fast track land reform programme and recurring droughts.

There is currently hyperinflation as a result of excessive money creation. An extremely large public sector, insufficient external financing, the collapse of agricultural and mining exports and an unsustainable external debt burden have fuelled this rapid monetary expansion. Most Western donors have reduced or withdrawn operations, with financial support confined to humanitarian aid. While China remains a major donor of both finance and food, it made some aid cuts in 2007 under pressure from Western governments. Unemployment and poverty rates are near 80% and there are severe shortages of food. Despite boasting several major attractions, tourism has declined since 2000 as a result of the internal crises, with numerous airlines suspending flights to the country.

Currency

The unit of currency is the *Zimbabwe fourth dollar* (ZWL), introduced on 2 Feb. 2009, with 12 zeros being removed to make 1trn. dollars (ZWR) equal to one new dollar. However, both companies and individuals are increasingly using the US dollar and the South African rand to transact domestic business. The *Zimbabwe third dollar* (ZWR) had replaced the *Zimbabwe second dollar* (ZWD) on 1 Aug. 2008, with a conversion rate of 1 revalued dollar = 10bn. old dollars (ZWD). The currency was devalued 17% in Jan. 1994 and made fully convertible. Its value dropped by 65% in 1998. It was devalued again in Aug. 2000 by 24%, in May 2005 by 45% and in July 2005 by 94%. It was further devalued by 60% in July 2006 and the following day the *Zimbabwean new (second) dollar* became the new currency. Inflation, which was 18·9% in 1997, rose to 133·2% in 2002 and 6,723·7% in 2007. The last official annual rate calculated in Zimbabwe dollars was 231,150,888·9% in July 2008, although the Central Statistical Office released monthly inflation rates calculated in US dollars for Oct. and Nov. 2009 of 0·8% and –0·1% respectively. Total money supply was Z$425,445·0bn. in Dec. 2007, up from Z$0·4bn. in Dec. 2002 and Z$44·7bn. in Dec. 2005.

Budget

Revenues in 2004 totalled Z$8,071·7bn. and expenditures Z$9,630·9bn. Tax revenues accounted for 96·2% of total revenue in 2004; current expenditures accounted for 87·3% of total expenditure. VAT was reduced from 17·5% to 15% in Jan. 2006.

Performance

Since Zimbabwe's economy began to collapse in 1998 real GDP growth has been negative every year from 1999 through to 2008. The economy contracted by 7·3% in 2000, 2·7% in 2001, 4·4% in 2002, 10·4% in 2003, 3·6% in 2004, 4·0% in 2005, 6·3% in 2006, 6·9% in 2007 and 14·1% in 2008—in 2006, 2007 and 2008 Zimbabwe was the world's worst performing economy. Total GDP in 2005 was US$3·4bn.

Banking and Finance

The Reserve Bank of Zimbabwe is the central bank (established 1965; *Governor*, Dr Gideon Gono). It acts as banker to the government and to the commercial banks, is the note-issuing authority and co-ordinates the application of the government's monetary policy. The Zimbabwe Development Bank, established in 1983 as a development finance institution, is 30·6% government-owned. In 2003 there were seven commercial and four merchant banks. In 1997 there were five registered finance houses, three of which are subsidiaries of commercial banks.

In Aug. 2003 Zimbabwe's banks ran out of banknotes as inflation reached 360%.

There is a stock exchange in Harare.

Weights and Measures

The metric system is in use but the US short ton is also used.

ENERGY AND NATURAL RESOURCES

Environment

Carbon dioxide emissions from the consumption and flaring of fossil fuels were the equivalent of 1·0 tonnes per capita in 2008.

Electricity

Installed capacity was an estimated 2·0m. kW in 2004. Production in 2004 was 9·91bn. kWh. Consumption per capita in 2004 was 924 kWh.

Minerals

The total value of all minerals produced in 2001 was US$39,701·4m. 2004 production: coal, 2·48m. tonnes; asbestos, 104,000 tonnes; nickel, 9,776 tonnes; gold, 21·3 tonnes. Diamond production in 2004 totalled 44,454 carats. Production at Zimbabwe's only commercial mine, Murowa, averaged 21,000 carats per month in 2005.

Agriculture

Agriculture is the largest employer, providing jobs for 25% of the workforce. In 2002 there were an estimated 3·22m. ha. of arable land and 0·13m. ha. of permanent crops. Approximately 117,000 ha. were irrigated in 2002. There were about 24,000 tractors in 2002 and 800 harvester-threshers.

A constitutional amendment providing for the compulsory purchase of land for peasant resettlement came into force in March 1992. A provision to seize white-owned farmland for peasant resettlement was part of the government's new draft constitution that was rejected in the referendum of Feb. 2000. Various deadlines were given for white farmers to abandon their property during Aug. and Sept. 2002. The government claims that 300,000 landless black Zimbabweans have been resettled on seized land.

The staple food crop is maize, but 2003 production (at 803,000 tonnes) was less than a half of the 2000 figure. Tobacco is the most important cash crop, although production fell from 237,000 tonnes in 2000 to 68,000 tonnes in 2004. Production of other leading crops, 2002, in 1,000 tonnes: sugarcane, 4,100; seed cotton,

200; cassava, 175; wheat, 150; cottonseed, 127; groundnuts, 110; oranges, 93; bananas, 85; soybeans, 83; sorghum, 80; cotton lint, 72.

Livestock (2003 estimates): cattle, 5·75m.; goats, 2·97m.; sheep, 610,000; pigs, 605,000; chickens, 22m. Livestock products (2003 estimates, in 1,000 tonnes): milk, 280; meat, 206.

Forestry

In 2005 forests covered 17·54m. ha., or 45·3% of the total land area. Timber production in 2007 was 9·23m. cu. metres.

Fisheries

Trout, prawns and bream are farmed to supplement supplies of fish caught in dams and lakes. The catch in 2005 was approximately 13,000 tonnes (all from inland waters).

INDUSTRY

Metal products account for over 20% of industrial output. Important agro-industries include food processing, textiles, furniture and other wood products.

Labour

The labour force in 1996 totalled 5,281,000 (56% males). Unemployment in March 2007 was around 80%.

Trade Unions

There is a Zimbabwe Congress of Trade Unions which has 26 affiliated unions, representing more than 400,000 workers in 1998.

INTERNATIONAL TRADE

Foreign debt was US$4,257m. in 2005.

Imports and Exports

In 2005 imports totalled US$2,072m.; exports, US$1,394m.

Main imports in 2004 (in US$1m.): machinery and transport equipment, 581·7; manufactured goods, 370·3; food and livestock, 282·2; petroleum and petroleum products, 278·1; chemicals and related products, 270·6. Main exports in 2004: tobacco and tobacco manufactures, 443·3; textile fibres, 243·4; metalliferous ore and scrap metal, 212·9; iron and steel 211·5.

Main import suppliers, 2005: Zambia, 40·9%; South Africa, 15·0%; Mozambique, 9·9%; Botswana, 5·0%; Kuwait, 4·0%. Main export destinations, 2005: South Africa, 41·5%; USA, 6·9%; Switzerland, 6·4%; Zambia, 5·6%; UK, 5·3%.

COMMUNICATIONS

Roads

The road network covers some 97,000 km but much of it is in poor condition. Number of vehicles in use, 2007: passenger cars, 1,214,100; lorries and vans, 186,800; buses and coaches, 15,600; motorcycles and mopeds, 109,000. There were 1,037 road accident fatalities in 2006.

Rail

In 2005 the National Railways of Zimbabwe had 2,759 km (1,067 mm gauge) of route ways (483 km electrified). In 2005 the railways carried 3m. passengers and 6·1m. tonnes of freight (including the Beitbridge-Bulawayo Railway).

Civil Aviation

There are three international airports: Harare (the main airport), Bulawayo and Victoria Falls. Air Zimbabwe, the state-owned national carrier, operates domestic services and in 2003 flew to Blantyre, Johannesburg, Lilongwe, London, Lusaka, Mauritius and Nairobi. In 2003 scheduled airline traffic of Zimbabwe-based carriers flew 6m. km, carrying 201,000 passengers (102,000 on international flights). In 1999 Harare handled an estimated 1,276,000 passengers (995,000 on international flights).

Shipping

Zimbabwe's outlets to the sea are Maputo and Beira in Mozambique, Dar es Salaam, Tanzania and the South African ports.

Telecommunications

In 2008 there were 348,000 main (fixed) telephone lines; mobile phone subscribers numbered 1,654,700 in 2008 (13·3 per 100 persons). There were 865,000 PCs in use in 2006 and 1,421,000 internet users in 2008.

Postal Services

In 2003 there were 324 post offices, or one for every 39,800 persons. A total of 87m. pieces of mail were handled in 2003.

SOCIAL INSTITUTIONS

Justice

The general common law of Zimbabwe is the Roman Dutch law as it applied in the Colony of the Cape of Good Hope on 10 June 1891, as subsequently modified by statute. Provision is made by statute for the application of African customary law by all courts in appropriate cases.

The death penalty is authorized. In 2003 there were four executions.

The Supreme Court consists of the Chief Justice and at least two Supreme Court judges. It is the final court of appeal. It exercises appellate jurisdiction in appeals from the High Court and other courts and tribunals; its only original jurisdiction is that conferred on it by the Constitution to enforce the protective provisions of the Declaration of Rights. The Court's permanent seat is in Harare but it also sits regularly in Bulawayo.

The High Court is also headed by the Chief Justice, supported by the Judge President and an appropriate number of High Court judges. It has full original jurisdiction, in both Civil and Criminal cases, over all persons and all matters in Zimbabwe. The Judge President is in charge of the Court, subject to the directions of the Chief Justice. The Court has permanent seats in both Harare and Bulawayo and sittings are held three times a year in three other principal towns.

Regional courts, established in Harare and Bulawayo but also holding sittings in other centres, exercise a solely criminal jurisdiction which is intermediate between that of the High Court and the Magistrates' courts. Magistrates' courts, established in 20 centres throughout the country, and staffed by full-time professional magistrates, exercise both civil and criminal jurisdiction.

Primary courts consist of village courts and community courts. Village courts are presided over by officers selected for the purpose from the local population, sitting with two assessors. They deal with specific classes of civil cases and have jurisdiction only where African customary law is applicable. Community courts are presided over by officers in full-time public service, who may also be assisted by assessors. They have jurisdiction in all civil cases determinable by African customary law and also deal with appeals from village courts. They also have limited criminal jurisdiction in respect of petty offences.

The population in penal institutions in June 2007 was 17,967 (136 per 100,000 of national population).

Education

Education is compulsory. 'Manageable' school fees were introduced in 1991; primary education had hitherto been free to all. All instruction is given in English. In 2006 there were 2,445,520 pupils at primary schools (64,001 teaching staff) and 831,488 pupils at secondary schools (33,964 teaching staff in 2003). In May 2004 the 45 private schools were closed down for increasing fees without state approval although they have for the most part since reopened. Private school fees are out of reach of the majority of families. Tens of thousands of teachers have left

Zimbabwe and thousands more have left the profession. In 2004 the adult literacy rate was 89·4%. Both the overall rate and the rate for males are the highest in Africa. As the crisis in Zimbabwe worsens, so primary school attendance has been declining, from 95% among boys and 90% among girls in 2000 to 67% among boys and 63% among girls in 2003.

There are 12 universities, the oldest and largest of which is the University of Zimbabwe, founded in 1952. Although formerly very successful, the university has experienced a series of problems ranging from staff shortages to electricity supply issues and remained closed during much of 2008.

In 2003 there were 55,689 students in tertiary education.

Health

There were 1,378 government hospitals in 1993. All mission health institutions get 100% government grants-in-aid for recurrent expenditure. In 2002 there were 736 physicians, 15 dentists, 6,951 nurses, 3,078 midwives (1995) and 12 pharmacists. It is estimated that one in three adults are HIV infected.

Welfare

It is a statutory responsibility of the government in many areas to provide: processing and administration of war pensions and old age pensions; protection of children; administration of remand, probation and correctional institutions; registration and supervision of welfare organizations.

RELIGION

In 2001, 4·58m. persons were African Christians, 1·40m. Protestants, 1·09m. Roman Catholics and 870,000 followers of other religions. There were also 3·43m. followers of animist beliefs in 2001.

CULTURE

World Heritage Sites

Zimbabwe has five sites on the UNESCO World Heritage List: Mana Pools National Park, Sapi and Chewore Safari Areas (inscribed on the list in 1984); the Great Zimbabwe National Monument (1986); the Khambi Ruins National Monument (1986); and Matobo Hills (2003).

Zimbabwe shares with Zambia the Victoria Falls/Mosi-oa-Tunya (1989), waterfalls on the Zambezi River.

Broadcasting

All radio and television services are state-controlled through the Zimbabwe Broadcasting Corporation (ZBC). ZBC operates four radio networks, broadcasting in English, Shona and Ndebele, and the sole public television channel (colour by PAL). Foreign radio stations critical of the government have been jammed. In 2006 TV sets numbered 930,000.

Press

In 2005 there were three daily newspapers, all controlled by the government, with a combined circulation of 125,000. In Jan. 2002 parliament passed an Access to Information Bill restricting press freedom, making it an offence to report from Zimbabwe unless registered by a state-appointed commission. In Sept. 2003 the independent *Daily News* was shut down for contraventions of the new press law. Zimbabwe's High Court ordered the government to allow its reopening but the order was ignored.

Tourism

There were 1,559,000 foreign tourists in 2005 (down from 1,854,000 in 2004); spending by tourists totalled US$99m.

Festivals

Of particular importance are the Harare International Festival of the Arts (April) and the Bulawayo Music Festival (May). The Zimbabwe International Film Festival is held in Harare in Aug./Sept.

DIPLOMATIC REPRESENTATIVES

Of Zimbabwe in the United Kingdom (Zimbabwe House, 429 Strand, London, WC2R 0JR)
High Commissioner: Gabriel Mharadze Machinga.

Of the United Kingdom in Zimbabwe (3 Norfolk Rd, Mount Pleasant, Harare, P.O. Box 4490)
High Commissioner: Mark Canning, CMG.

Of Zimbabwe in the USA (1608 New Hampshire Ave., NW, Washington, D.C., 20009)
Ambassador: Dr Machivenyika Mapuranga.

Of the USA in Zimbabwe (172 Herbert Chitepo Ave., Harare)
Ambassador: Charles A. Ray.

Of Zimbabwe to the United Nations
Ambassador: Boniface Guwa Chidyausiku.

Of Zimbabwe to the European Union
Ambassador: Gift Punungwe.

FURTHER READING

Central Statistical Office. *Monthly Digest of Statistics.*

Hatchard, J., *Individual Freedoms and State Security in the African Context: the Case of Zimbabwe.* 1993
Hill, Geoff, *What Happens After Mugabe? Can Zimbabwe Rise From the Ashes?* 2005
Meredith, Martin, *Mugabe: Power and Plunder in Zimbabwe.* 2002
Skålnes, T., *The Politics of Economic Reform in Zimbabwe: Continuity and Change in Development.* 1995
Weiss, R., *Zimbabwe and the New Elite.* 1994

National Statistical Office: Central Statistical Office, POB 8063, Causeway, Harare.

STATESMAN'S YEARBOOK SOURCES

The Statesman's Yearbook references the following sources to maintain accuracy and currency of information contained in our database:

- United Nations Statistical Yearbook
- Euromonitor International Marketing Data and Statistics
- United Nations Development Programme Human Development Report
- United Nations World Population Prospects
- United Nations World Urbanization Prospects
- United Nations Demographic Yearbook
- Stockholm International Peace Research Institute Yearbook
- International Institute of Strategic Studies Military Balance
- International Monetary Fund World Economic Outlook
- Selected International Monetary Fund Reports
- Selected European Union Reports
- Selected Organization for Economic Co-operation and Development Reports
- Selected World Bank Reports
- Selected World Trade Organization Reports
- International Monetary Fund Government Finance Statistics Yearbook
- United Nations Energy Statistics Yearbook
- Food and Agricultural Organization Production Yearbook
- Food and Agricultural Organization Forest Products Yearbook
- Food and Agricultural Organization Fishery Statistics – Capture Production
- United Nations Industrial Commodity Statistics Yearbook
- International Labour Organization Yearbook of Labour Statistics
- International Monetary Fund Balance of Payments Statistics Yearbook
- United Nations International Trade Statistics Yearbook
- International Road Federation World Road Statistics
- Railway Directory
- International Civil Aviation Organization Civil Aviation Statistics of the World
- International Civil Aviation Organization Airport Traffic
- International Telecommunication Union Yearbook of Statistics
- United Nations Educational, Scientific and Cultural Organization Statistical Yearbook
- Religious Trends No 7
- World Association of Newspapers World Press Trends
- Statistical offices, government departments, embassies and international organizations throughout the world
- Selected print and online national and international news media

ABBREVIATIONS

ACP	African Caribbean Pacific
Adm.	Admiral
Adv.	Advocate
a.i.	ad interim
b.	born
bbls	barrels
bd	board
bn.	billion (one thousand million)
Brig.	Brigadier
bu.	bushel
Capt.	Captain
Cdr	Commander
CFA	Communauté Financière Africaine
CFP	Comptoirs Français du Pacifique
CGT	compensated gross tonnes
c.i.f.	cost, insurance, freight
C.-in-C.	Commander-in-Chief
CIS	Commonwealth of Independent States
cm	centimetre(s)
Cres.	Crescent
cu.	cubic
CUP	Cambridge University Press
cwt	hundredweight
D.	Democratic Party
DWT	dead weight tonnes
ECOWAS	Economic Community of West African States
EEA	European Economic Area
EEZ	Exclusive Economic Zone
EMS	European Monetary System
EMU	European Monetary Union
ERM	Exchange Rate Mechanism
est.	estimate
f.o.b.	free on board
FDI	foreign direct investment
ft	foot/feet
FTE	full-time equivalent
G8 Group	Canada, France, Germany, Italy, Japan, UK, USA, Russia
GDP	gross domestic product
Gdns	Gardens
Gen.	General
GNI	gross national income
GNP	gross national product
GRT	gross registered tonnes
GW	gigawatt
GWh	gigawatt hours
ha.	hectare(s)
HDI	Human Development Index
ind.	independent(s)
ICT	information and communication technology
ISO	International Organization for Standardization (domain names)
K	kindergarten
kg	kilogramme(s)
kl	kilolitre(s)
km	kilometre(s)
kW	kilowatt
kWh	kilowatt hours
lat.	latitude
lb	pound(s) (weight)
Lieut.	Lieutenant
long.	longitude
m.	million
Maj.	Major
MW	megawatt
MWh	megawatt hours
NA	not available
n.e.c.	not elsewhere classified
NRT	net registered tonnes
NTSC	National Television System Committee (525 lines 60 fields)
OUP	Oxford University Press
oz	ounce(s)
PAL	Phased Alternate Line (625 lines 50 fields 4·43 MHz sub-carrier)
PAL M	Phased Alternate Line (525 lines 60 PAL 3·58 MHz sub-carrier)
PAL N	Phased Alternate Line (625 lines 50 PAL 3·58 MHz sub-carrier)
PAYE	Pay-As-You-Earn
PPP	Purchasing Power Parity
R.	Republican Party
Rd	Road
retd	retired
Rt Hon.	Right Honourable
SADC	Southern African Development Community
SDR	Special Drawing Rights
SECAM H	Sequential Couleur avec Memoire (625 lines 50 fields Horizontal)
SECAM V	Sequential Couleur avec Memoire (625 lines 50 fields Vertical)
sq.	square
St.	Street
SSI	Supplemental Security Income
TAFE	technical and further education
TEU	twenty-foot equivalent units
trn.	trillion (one million million)
TV	television
Univ.	University
VAT	value-added tax
v.f.d.	value for duty

CURRENT LEADERS INDEX

An * denotes a further reference in 'As we go to press', page xxx

PLACE AND INTERNATIONAL ORGANIZATIONS INDEX

Italicized page numbers refer to extended entries
An * denotes a further reference in 'As we go to press', page xxx

B

C

E

G

H

J

K

L

P

Q

R

U

V

W

X

Y

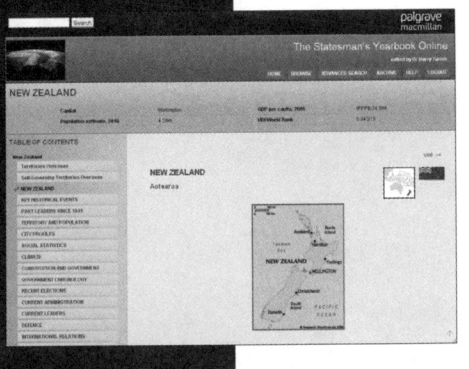

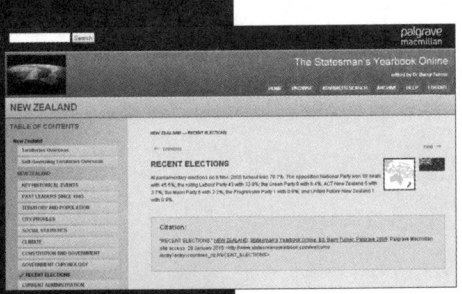